Labels used in the dictionary

The following labels are used with words that express a particular attitude or are appropriate in a particular situation.

approving expressions show that you feel approval or admiration, for example *feisty*, *petite*.

disapproving expressions show that you feel disapproval or contempt, for example *blinkered*, *newfangled*.

figurative language is used in a non-literal or metaphorical way, as in *He didn't want to cast a shadow on* (= spoil) *their happiness*.

formal expressions are usually only used in serious or official language and would not be appropriate in normal everyday conversation. Examples are *admonish*, *besmirch*.

humorous expressions are intended to be funny, for example *ankle-biter*, *lurgy*.

informal expressions are used between friends or in a relaxed or unofficial situation. They are not appropriate for formal situations. Examples are *bonkers*, *dodgy*.

ironic language uses words to mean the opposite of the meaning that they seem to have, as in *You're a great help, I must say!* (= no help at all).

literary language is used mainly in literature and imaginative writing, for example *aflame*, *halcyon*.

offensive expressions are used by some people to address or refer to people in a way that is very insulting, especially in connection with their race, religion, sex or disabilities, for example *half-caste*, *slut*. You should not use these words.

slang is very informal language, sometimes restricted to a particular group of people, for example people of the same age or those who have the same interests or do the same job. Examples are *dingbat*, *dosh*.

taboo expressions are likely to be thought by many people to be obscene or shocking. You should not use them. Examples are *bloody*, *shit*.

technical language is used by people who specialize in particular subject areas, for example *accretion*, *adipose*.

The following labels show other restrictions on the use of words.

dialect describes expressions that are mainly used in particular regions of the British Isles, not including Ireland, Scotland or Wales, for example *beck*, *nowt*.

old-fashioned expressions are passing out of current use, for example *balderdash*, *beanfeast*.

old use describes expressions that are no longer in current use, for example *ere*, *perchance*.

saying describes a well-known fixed or traditional phrase, such as a proverb, that is used to make a comment, give advice, etc, for example *actions speak louder than words*.

TM shows a trademark of a manufacturing company, for example *Band-Aid*, *Frisbee*.

and muscle; (of meat) containing no fat. ❷ not productive; of poor quality, as *a lean harvest; lean years* (i. e. years during which not much is produced). —*n.* [U] meat without fat. **lean-ness** [líːnnis] *n.*

²lean [liːn] *vi. & t.* (pret. & p.p. **leaned** [liːnd] or **leant** [lent]) ❶ (P 21, 23) slope or incline; be out of the perpendicular, as *the Leaning Tower of Pisa; trees that lean over in the wind.* ❷ (P 23, 24) rest on or against something in order to get support, as *to lean on a table; to lean upon one's elbows* (i. e. bend the upper part of the body and support oneself on the elbows). *Lean on my arm.* ❸ (P 23, 24) bend the body, as *to lean forward [back]; to lean over a fence; to lean out of a window.* ❹ (P 24) (fig.) rely or depend, as *to lean on a friend's advice; to lean on others for support.* ❺ (P 24) tend to or be inclined to. *Do all oriental philosophies lean towards fatalism?* ❻ (P 18) cause to rest against; put into a leaning position, as *to lean a ladder against a wall; to lean one's elbows on the table.* —*n.* a slope, as *a tower with a slight lean.* **lean-ing** [líːniŋ] *n.* [C] a tendency or liking, as *to have a leaning towards pacifism.*

The Leaning Tower of Pisa

leant [lent] pret. & p. p. of *lean.*

lean=to [líːntúː] *n.* a building or shelter (usu. small) that has a roof that slopes only in one way and which rests against the wall of another building (or a wall of rock); (used attrib.) *a lean-to roof [shelter].*

leap [liːp] *vi. & t.* (pret. & p.p. **leapt** [lept] or **leaped** [liːpt]) ❶ (P 21, 23, 24) jump. *He leapt on his enemy with a knife in his hand. Look before you leap. He leapt at the opportunity* (fig., i. e. seized it eagerly). ❷ (P 1) jump or spring over, as *to leap a wall;* cause to jump over, as *to leap a horse over a hedge.* —*n.* a jump or spring; a sudden forward or upward movement. **a leap in the dark,** an attempt to do something, the result of which must be very doubtful. **by leaps and bounds,** with very rapid progress. **leap=frog,** *n.* a game in which one player jumps over others standing with bent backs. **leap year,** *n.* a year in which February has 29 days.

Playing leap-frog

leapt [lept] pret. & p.p. of *leap.*

learn [ləːn] *vt. & i.* (pret. & p.p. **learned** [ləːnd] or **learnt** [ləːnt]) (P 1, 2, 10, 11, 13, 15, 21) gain as knowledge; become familiar with by studying, by being taught, by practice, etc.; become aware; be informed of. *How long have you been learning English? He is learning to swim. You should learn (how) to ride a horse. Has he learnt his lessons? I was sorry to learn the sad news of his death [to learn that he died]. We have not yet learned* (i. e. been informed) *whether he arrived safely. Some boys learn slowly.* **learn-er** [lə́ːnə] *n.* one who is learning; a beginner.

learn-ed [lə́ːnid] *part. adj.* having or showing much knowledge; scholarly, as *a learned man [book]; to look learned.* **learn-ed-ly,** *adv.*

learn-ing [lə́ːniŋ] *n.* [U] knowledge gained by study, as *a man of great learning.*

learnt [ləːnt] pret. & p. p. of *learn.*

lease [liːs] *n.* [C] a contract or agreement by which one person (the *lessor*) agrees to allow another (the *lessee*) to use land or a building for a certain period of time, usu. in return for a money payment (called *rent*); the rights given under such a contract, as *to take a house [farm, etc.] on a lease of several years; to take a lease of a piece of land; to put out land on lease. When does the lease expire* (i. e. how long does it last)? *We hold the land by [on] lease.* **a new lease of life,** a new chance of living or of being active, due to recovery of health, the removal of anxiety, etc. —*vt.* (P 1) give or take possession of (land, a

Oxford Advanced Learner's Dictionary *of Current English*

A S Hornby

Eighth edition

Managing Editor **Joanna Turnbull**

Principal Editor Diana Lea

Senior Editor Dilys Parkinson

Editors Patrick Phillips
Ben Francis
Suzanne Webb
Victoria Bull

Phonetics Editor Michael Ashby

UNIVERSITY PRESS

OXFORD
UNIVERSITY PRESS

Great Clarendon Street, Oxford OX2 6DP

Oxford University Press is a department of the University of Oxford.

It furthers the University's objective of excellence in research, scholarship, and education by publishing worldwide in

Oxford New York

Auckland Cape Town Dar es Salaam Hong Kong Karachi
Kuala Lumpur Madrid Melbourne Mexico City Nairobi
New Delhi Shanghai Taipei Toronto

With offices in

Argentina Austria Brazil Chile Czech Republic France Greece
Guatemala Hungary Italy Japan Poland Portugal Singapore
South Korea Switzerland Thailand Turkey Ukraine Vietnam

First published 1948 (12 impressions)
Second edition 1963 (19 impressions)
Third edition 1974 (28 impressions)
Fourth edition 1989 (50 impressions)
Fifth edition 1995 (65 impressions)
Sixth edition 2000 (117 impressions)
Seventh edition 2005 (105 impressions)
Eighth edition 2010
2015 2014 2013 2012 2011
9 8 7 6 5 4 3 2 1

This dictionary includes some words which have or are asserted to have proprietary status as trademarks or otherwise. Their inclusion does not imply that they have acquired for legal purposes a non-proprietary or general significance nor any other judgement concerning their legal status. In cases where the editorial staff have some evidence that a word has proprietary status this is indicated in the entry for that word but no judgement concerning the legal status of such words is made or implied thereby

Any websites referred to in this publication are in the public domain and their addresses are provided by Oxford University Press for information only. Oxford University Press disclaims any responsibility for the content

The British National Corpus is a collaborative project involving Oxford University Press, Longman, Chambers, the Universities of Oxford and Lancaster and the British Library

ISBN: 978-0-19-4799003 (paperback)
ISBN: 978-0-19-4799027 (paperback/CD pack)
ISBN: 978-0-19-4799041 (hardback/CD pack)

Contents

inside front cover Abbreviations, symbols and labels used in the dictionary
vii Foreword
ix Key to dictionary entries
xii Numbers

1–1796 **The Dictionary**

WT1–32 Oxford Writing Tutor

V1–64 Visual Vocabulary Builder

R1–48 Reference Section

Advisers

Advisory Board

Dr Keith Brown
Prof Guy Cook
Dr Alan Cruse
Ruth Gairns
Moira Runcie
Prof Gabriele Stein
Dr Norman Whitney
Prof Henry Widdowson

Consultants

Prof Choong Bae Kim
Prof Paul Gunashekar
Prof Hirosada Iwasaki
Prof Masanori Toyota

American English

Jamie Greene
Stephanie Hirschman
Karen Stern

Advisers on World English

Dr Modupe M Alimi (*West African*)
Tony Deverson (*New Zealand*)
Heather Fitzgerald (*Canadian*)
Prof Paul Gunashekar (*Indian*)
Megan Hall (*South African*)
Leah Kariuki (*East African*)
Dr Bruce Moore (*Australian*)
John Muitung'u (*East African*)
Joseph Noble (*South African*)

Advisers on scientific words

Dr James Mendelssohn
Dr Geoffrey Neuss

Foreword

Michael Swan

When A S Hornby began the work that was ultimately to lead to this 8th edition of the *Oxford Advanced Learner's Dictionary*, language teaching was in a transitional phase. The old bias towards teaching the written language, with heavy use of translation, was being replaced in many quarters by a focus on teaching speech without recourse to the mother tongue – a movement in which Hornby was heavily involved. However, the emphasis was still largely on presenting and practising forms rather than on training learners to deploy them in natural communication. Our profession was, at that time, decidedly better at teaching languages than at teaching people to use them.

In the intervening seventy years there have been profound changes, whose nature and scale Hornby could hardly have foreseen. The communicative language teaching movement and its offshoots have encouraged us to analyse and teach 'language in use'. We have become skilled at bridging the gap between the classroom and the world outside, and at producing learners who are able to use the languages they have studied for 'real life' purposes. The danger is that, as we concentrate on teaching learners to do things with language, we may lose our focus on the actual language that is needed to do these things. Discourse skills, negotiation for meaning, communication strategies, task performance, pragmatic competence and our various other current concerns may well be important, but the fundamental priorities have not changed. Language teaching is, ultimately, teaching language. Grammar, lexis and phonology remain central, and an adequate command of these is as necessary as it has ever been for efficient and effective communication. Today's learners of English, just like Hornby's students, need well-planned teaching and reference material to underpin their study.

Hornby's mission was to provide such material. He was by no means only a lexicographer. He wrote a widely-used three-level course, the *Oxford Progressive English Course*. His *Guide to Patterns and Usage in English*, which provided information about the structures into which individual nouns, verbs and adjectives enter, explored the interface between lexis and grammar long before electronic corpora made this an easy task. But Hornby was well aware that, of all the knowledge and skills which a language learner must master, the most important element, and the one involving the heaviest learning load, is an adequate working vocabulary. In this connection he saw clearly that, along with a good learner's grammar, a student of English can benefit enormously from a well-produced, pedagogically-oriented monolingual dictionary. Such a work has the space to provide detailed practical information about the most important words of the language: pronunciations, key meanings, collocations, grammatical patterning, synonym comparisons, constraints on usage and so on. Hornby was that rare combination, a scholar-pedagogue who was equally at home analysing language and teaching a class, and he was the ideal person to produce a dictionary of this very special kind. It was perhaps inevitable that this gifted lexicographer should ultimately find himself in partnership with the world's most experienced dictionary publisher. The rest is history.

Hornby would have had no difficulty in recognizing this 8th edition as a continuation of his work. It has all the features that he regarded as essential: accurate simple definitions, realistic examples, information on pronunciation, guidance on the grammatical and collocational patterns that words enter into, and notes on synonym distinctions and other aspects of usage. At the same time, it contains a wealth of additional features that Hornby might not have foreseen, but would certainly have welcomed. The clarity of definitions is rigorously controlled with the help of a list of 3000 keyword families. There are various useful appendices, including pictorial vocabulary-building materials. There is even a 32-page 'Writing Tutor', with language banks for different genres and further interactive guidance on the CD-ROM. The electronic version of the dictionary also provides additional examples, etymologies, and thesaurus-type information. Hornby would, I believe, have been surprised and delighted at the character of his braingrandchild (if I may be allowed to infiltrate a new word into this lexicographical heartland).

This new edition of a classic dictionary brings together, once again, the work of a distinguished pedagogic lexicographer and an outstanding reference publisher, and in doing so makes an invaluable contribution to the central business of language teaching – teaching the language.

The Hornby Trust

The A S Hornby Educational Trust was set up by A S Hornby in 1961 and he generously gave a large part of his income to it. Today, a royalty from every copy of the *OALD* sold still goes to the Trust. Thanks to the Trust, in conjunction with the British Council, hundreds of teachers have had the opportunity to take part in regional ELT workshops around the world. Each year a number of Hornby scholarships are offered by the British Council, allowing teachers and teacher trainers from countries around the world to spend a year studying linguistics and ELT at British universities. Dr Amol Padwad was a Hornby scholar from 1999 to 2000.

Being a Hornby Scholar

The Hornby scholarship and the year of study at the University of Leeds are perhaps the most significant turning points in my personal and professional life. Personally, living in a different country and culture enriched my understanding and broadened my perspectives. Professionally, I gained a deeper understanding of my profession, saw my own context in a different light, and developed a greater sense of purpose and commitment. It was amazing and extremely helpful to join the global ELT community, and the fabulous Hornby Alumni family, with networking and contacts all over the world. I am still reaping the rich benefits of this membership.

Upon returning home to India, the contribution I could make to the ELT community in my area was more satisfying than the personal gains of prestige, recognition and career advancement. If asked for specific instances, I would like to list three: raising the awareness of the teachers of English in my area about ELT; promoting networking opportunities and the professional association for teachers; and launching some innovative initiatives in teacher development.

While trying to organize the first-ever ELT conference in 2003 in my district, I had to first explain what ELT meant, as it was an unknown term in that area a few years ago. The subsequent annual ELT conferences and other events over the years have changed the situation remarkably. Most teachers are now aware of ELT- our annual conferences attract a wide range of teachers and a variety of presentations related to ELT.

The national association ELTAI (English Language Teachers' Association of India) too was unheard of in my region, nor was there any awareness about joining professional associations for one's development. I was able to set up an ELTAI chapter in the region, now one of the most vibrant ones in India, which organizes ELT conferences and other events and promotes research in ELT.

Perhaps the most direct relation between my being a Hornby scholar and my contributions to the local ELT community is the ongoing 'English Teachers' Clubs (ETCs)' experiment. Taking my cue from a small voluntary group of young teachers from my town, who frequently met to tackle some of their urgent crises, I encouraged them to form an ETC as a long-term and sustainable professional development enterprise. It was the Hornby Trust which supported the ETC idea at the pilot stage and later as a larger project. Thanks to this project several ETCs in different parts of India are promoting the professional development of the member teachers, as well as strengthening ELT activities in the region. An informal online group of teachers from over 25 countries is at present trying out the experiment in their own contexts. Two masters-level studies (at the University of Exeter and the Institute of Education, London) have studied this experiment.

Six former Hornby Scholars from India, including me, were supported by the Hornby Trust in a unique nationwide project on the adaptation of prescribed course material for effective teaching, with Prof. N S Prabhu as the consultant. This project trained over 400 teachers in adapting prescribed materials to their diverse contexts, and also involved compiling a handbook for teachers based on the insights from the project.

It is difficult to fully convey the tremendous value a Hornby scholarship adds to a person and a community. I salute the great A S Hornby for his vision and his endowment. One way of repaying the great debt we owe to him is to continue working for the empowerment of teachers of English and to take the Hornby legacy further.

Dr. Amol Padwad
Head, Department of English, J M Patel College, Bhandara, India.
Hornby Scholar 1999-2000

Key to dictionary entries

Finding the word

Information in the dictionary is given in **entries**, arranged in alphabetical order of **headwords. Compound words** are in separate entries, also arranged alphabetically.

headwords

book·bind·er /ˈbʊkbaɪndə(r)/ *noun* a person whose job is fastening the pages of books together and putting covers on them ▶ **book·bind·ing** *noun* [U]

book·case /ˈbʊkkeɪs/ *noun* a piece of furniture with shelves for keeping books on ➲ VISUAL VOCAB page V18

ˈbook club *noun* **1** an organization that sells books cheaply to its members **2** = BOOK GROUP

entry

Some headwords can have more than one part of speech.

blind·fold /ˈblaɪndfəʊld; *NAmE* -foʊld/ *noun, verb, adj., adv.*

headword and all possible parts of speech

Squares show where the information on each part of speech begins.

■ ***noun*** something that is put over sb's eyes so they cannot see

■ ***verb*** **~ sb** to cover sb's eyes with a piece of cloth or other covering so that they cannot see: *The hostages were tied up and blindfolded.*

■ ***adj., adv.*** (*BrE*) (also **blind·fold·ed** *BrE, NAmE*) with the eyes covered: *The reporter was taken blindfold to a secret location.* ◇ *I knew the way home blindfold* (= because it was

There are some words in English that have the same spelling as each other but different pronunciations.

The small **homonym number** shows that this is the first of two headwords spelled *gill*.

gill[1] /ɡɪl/ *noun* [usually pl.] one of the openings on the side of a fish's head that it breathes through ➲ VISUAL VOCAB page V10

IDM **to the ˈgills** (*informal*) completely full: *I was stuffed to the gills with chocolate cake.*

Different pronunciation is given at each headword.

gill[2] /dʒɪl/ *noun* a unit for measuring liquids. There are four gills in a pint.

There are also some words in English that have more than one possible spelling, and both spellings are acceptable. Information about these words is given at the most frequent spelling.

The variant spelling is given in brackets.

ban·is·ter (also **ban·nis·ter**) /ˈbænɪstə(r)/ *noun* (*BrE* also **ban·is·ters** [pl.]) the posts and rail which you can hold for support when going up or down stairs: *to hold on to the banister/banisters* ➲ picture at STAIRCASE

At the entry for the less frequent spelling a cross-reference directs you to the main entry.

ban·nis·ter = BANISTER

Irregular forms of verbs are treated in the same way.

Some words that are **derivatives** of other words do not have their own entry in the dictionary because they can be easily understood from the meaning of the word from which they are derived (the root word). They are given in the same entry as the root word, in a specially marked section.

be·lated /bɪˈleɪtɪd/ *adj.* coming or happening late: *a belated birthday present* ▶ **be·lated·ly** *adv.*

The blue triangle shows where the derivative section starts.

You can find **idioms** and **phrasal verbs** in separate sections, marked with special symbols.

fetch 0-т /fetʃ/ *verb*
1 0-т (*especially BrE*) to go to where sb/sth is and bring them/it back: **~ sb/sth** *to fetch help/a doctor* ◇ *She's gone to fetch the kids from school.* ◇ **~ sb sth** *Could you fetch me my bag?* **2 ~ sth** to be sold for a particular price **SYN** **sell for**: *The painting is expected to fetch $10 000 at auction.*
IDM **fetch and 'carry (for sb)** to do a lot of little jobs for sb as if you were their servant
PHR V **,fetch 'up** (*informal, especially BrE*) to arrive somewhere without planning to

phrasal verbs section with symbol PHR V (see pages R9–10)

idioms section with symbol IDM (see page R14)

Finding the meaning

Some words have very long entries. It is not usually necessary to read the whole entry from the beginning, if you already know something about the general meaning that you are looking for.

spin 0-т /spɪn/ *verb, noun*
▪ ***verb*** (**spin·ning, spun, spun** /spʌn/)
▸ TURN ROUND QUICKLY **1** 0-т [I, T] to turn round and round quickly; to make sth do this: **(+ adv./prep.)** *The plane was spinning out of control.* ◇ **~ (round/around)** *The dancers spun round and round.* ◇ **~ sth (round/around)** *to spin a ball/coin/wheel* **2** 0-т [I, T] **~ (sb) round/around** | **+ adv./prep.** to turn round quickly once; to make sb do this: *He spun around to face her.*
▸ MAKE THREAD **3** [I, T] to make thread from wool, cotton, silk, etc. by twisting it: *She sat by the window spinning.*

Short cuts show the context or general meaning.

Meanings that are closely related share the same short cut.

Understanding and using the word

aban·doned 0-т **AW** /ə'bændənd/ *adj.*
1 0-т left and no longer wanted, used or needed: *an abandoned car/house* ◇ *The child was found abandoned but unharmed.* **2** (of people or their behaviour) wild; not following accepted standards

Words printed in larger type and with a 0-т symbol are part of the **Oxford 3000** list of important words (see page **R43**). Small keys indicate which parts of the entry are most important.

Words from the Academic Word List are marked with **AW** (see page **R44**).

aard·vark /'ɑːdvɑːk; *NAmE* 'ɑːrdvɑːrk/ *noun* an animal from southern Africa that has a long nose and tongue and that eats insects

pronunciation, with American pronunciation where it is different (see pages **R45–6**)

,baby 'grand *noun* a small GRAND PIANO

Stress marks show stress on compounds.

cling /klɪŋ/ *verb* (**clung, clung** /klʌŋ/) **1** [I] to hold on tightly to sb/sth: **~ to sb/sth** *survivors clinging to a raft* ◇ **~ on to sb/sth** *She clung on to her baby.* ◇ **~ on** *Cling on tight!* ◇ **~ together** *They clung together, shivering with cold.* ➲ SYNONYMS at HOLD **2** [I] to stick to sth: *a dress that clings* (= fits closely and shows the shape of your body) ◇ **~ to sth** *The wet shirt clung to his chest.* **3** [I] **~ (to sb)** (usually *disapproving*) to stay close to sb, especially because you need them emotionally

Irregular forms of verbs, with their pronunciations. Irregular plurals of nouns are also shown.

prepositions, adverbs and structures that can be used with this word

examples of use in *italic type*

label giving information about usage (see inside front cover)

hearty /'hɑːti; *NAmE* 'hɑːrti/ *adj., noun*
▪ ***adj.*** (**heart·ier, hearti·est**) **1** [usually before noun] showing friendly feelings for sb: *a hearty welcome* **2** (sometimes *disapproving*) loud, cheerful and full of energy: *a hearty and boisterous fellow* ◇ *a hearty voice* **3** [only before noun] (of a

comparatives and superlatives of adjectives

information on use of adjectives (see page **R12**)

dock /dɒk; *NAmE* dɑːk/ *noun, verb*
■ ***noun*** **1** [C] a part of a port where ships are repaired, or where goods are put onto or taken off them: *dock workers* ◇ *The ship was* ***in dock.*** ➲ see also DRY DOCK **2** **docks** [pl.] a group of docks in a port and the buildings around them that are used for repairing ships, storing goods, etc. **3** [C] (*NAmE*) = JETTY **4** [C] (*NAmE*) a raised platform for loading vehicles or trains **5** [C] the part of a court where the person who has been accused of a crime stands or sits during a trial: *He's been* ***in the dock*** (= on trial for a crime) *several times already.* ➲ COLLOCATIONS at JUSTICE **6** [U] a wild plant of northern Europe with large thick leaves that can be rubbed on skin that has been stung by NETTLES to make it less painful: *dock leaves*
■ ***verb*** **1** [I, T] **~ (sth)** if a ship **docks** or you **dock** a ship, it sails into a HARBOUR and stays there: *The ferry is expected to dock at 6.* **2** [I, T] **~ (sth)** if two SPACECRAFT **dock**, or **are docked**, they are joined together in space

fixed form of noun

information on different types of noun (see pages **R11–12**)

common phrase in **bold type** in example (see page **R13**)

word used in definition that is not in the **Oxford 3000**

verb codes and frames (see pages **R5–8**)

Build your vocabulary

The dictionary also contains a lot of information that will help you increase your vocabulary and use the language productively.

stable O‑‑ AW /ˈsteɪbl/ *adj., noun, verb*
■ ***adj.*** **1** O‑‑ firmly fixed; not likely to move, change or fail SYN **steady**: *stable prices* ◇ *a stable relationship* ◇ *This ladder doesn't seem very stable.* ◇ *The patient's condition is stable* (= it is not getting worse). **2** O‑‑ (of a person) calm and reasonable; not easily upset SYN **balanced**: *Mentally, she is not very stable.* **3** (*technical*) (of a substance) staying in the same chemical or ATOMIC state: *chemically stable* OPP **unstable** ▸ **sta·bly** /ˈsteɪbli/ *adv.*

WORD FAMILY
stable *adj.* (≠ unstable)
stability *noun* (≠ instability)
stabilize *verb*

Special symbols show synonyms and opposites.

Word families show words related to the headword.

Notes help you choose the right word, and also help with difficult grammar points. They are all listed on pages **R15–19**.

Synonyms

valuable

precious • priceless • irreplaceable

These words all describe sth that is worth a lot of money or very important to sb.

valuable worth a lot of money: *The thieves took three pieces of valuable jewellery.*

precious rare and worth a lot of money; loved or valued very much: *a precious Chinese vase, valued at half a million pounds* ◇ *precious memories of our time together*

priceless extremely valuable; loved or valued very much: *a priceless collection of antiques*

irreplaceable too valuable or special to be replaced

PATTERNS
■ valuable/precious/priceless/irreplaceable **possessions**
■ valuable/precious/priceless **antiques/jewels/jewellery**

words listed in order of how frequent they are

Cross-references refer you to information in other parts of the dictionary.

bear O‑‑ /beə(r); *NAmE* ber/ *verb, noun*
■ ***noun*** **1** a heavy wild animal with thick fur and sharp CLAWS (= pointed parts on the ends of its feet). There are many types of bear: *a black bear* ➲ see also GRIZZLY BEAR, POLAR BEAR, TEDDY BEAR **2** (*finance*) a person who sells shares in a company, etc., hoping to buy them back later at a lower price ➲ compare BULL ➲ see also BEARISH
IDM **like a bear with a sore ˈhead** (*informal*) bad-tempered or in a bad-tempered way

See also refers you to a word with a similar or related meaning.

Compare refers you to a word with a contrasting meaning.

Numbers

10000-foot view /ˌten ˈθaʊznd ˈfʊt ˈvjuː/ *noun* (*business*) a broad general view or description of a problem SYN HELICOPTER VIEW, OVERVIEW: *Let me give you the 10000-foot view.*

1040 form /ˌten ˈfɔːti fɔːm; *NAmE* ˈfɔːrti fɔːrm/ *noun* (in the US) an official document in which you give details of the amount of money that you have earned so that the government can calculate how much tax you have to pay

12 /twelv/ *noun* (in Britain) a label that is given to a film/movie to show that it can be watched legally only by people who are at least twelve years old; a film/movie that has this label: *I can take the kids too – it's a 12.*

1471 /ˈwʌn fɔː sevn wʌn; *NAmE* fɔːr/ (in Britain) the telephone number you can use to find out the telephone number of the person who called you most recently, and the time the call was made

15 /ˌfɪfˈtiːn/ *noun* (in Britain) a label that is given to a film/movie to show that it can be watched legally only by people who are at least fifteen years old; a film/movie that has this label

18 /ˌeɪˈtiːn/ *noun* (in Britain) a label that is given to a film/movie to show that it can be watched legally only by people who are at least eighteen years old; a film/movie that has this label

18-wheeler /ˌeɪtiːn ˈwiːlə(r)/ *noun* (*NAmE*) a very large truck with nine wheels on each side

20/20 vision /ˌtwenti twenti ˈvɪʒn/ *noun* the ability to see perfectly without using glasses or CONTACT LENSES

2.1 /ˌtuː ˈwʌn/ *noun* the upper level of the second highest standard of degree given by a British or an Australian university: *I got a 2.1*

2.2 /ˌtuː ˈtuː/ *noun* the lower level of the second highest standard of degree given by a British or an Australian university

24-hour clock /ˌtwenti fɔːr aʊə ˈklɒk; *NAmE* aʊər ˈklɑːk/ *noun* the system of using twenty four numbers to talk about the hours of the day, instead of dividing it into two units of twelve hours

24/7 /ˌtwenti fɔː ˈsevən: *NAmE* fɔːr/ *adv.* (*informal*) twenty-four hours a day, seven days a week (used to mean 'all the time'): *She's with me all the time—24/7.*

3-D (also **three-D**) /ˌθriː ˈdiː/ *noun* [U] the quality of having, or appearing to have, length, width and depth: *These glasses allow you to see the film in 3-D.*

3G /ˌθriː ˈdʒiː/ *abbr.* third generation (used to describe a level of performance for MOBILE/CELL PHONES that makes it possible to move data to and from the Internet): *3G technology*

35mm /ˌθɜːtifaɪv ˈmɪlimiːtə(r); *NAmE* ˌθɜːrti-/ *noun* the size of film that is usually used in cameras for taking photographs and making films/movies

360-degree feedback /ˈθriː hʌndrəd ən sɪksti dɪˈgriː ˈfiːdbæk/ (also **360-degree appraisal**) noun [U] (*business*) information provided by all the people that an employee deals with, used as a way of deciding how well the employee does their job: *360-degree feedback assessments*

4×4 /ˌfɔː baɪ ˈfɔː; *NAmE* ˌfɔːr baɪ ˈfɔːr/ *noun* a vehicle with a system in which power is applied to all four wheels, making it easier to control

411 /ˌfɔː wʌn ˈwʌn: *NAmE* ˌfɔːr/ *noun* **1** [U] the telephone number of the service that you use in the US to find out a person's telephone number: *Call 411.* **2 the 411** [sing.] (*NAmE, informal*) the true facts about a situation or the information you need: *He'll give us the 411 on what to expect.*

7/7 /ˌsevn ˈsevn/ *noun* (*BrE*) the abbreviation for the date 7 July, 2005, when several bomb attacks took place in London

the $64,000 question /ˌsɪksti fɔː ˌθaʊznd ˌdɒlə ˈkwestʃən; *NAmE* fɔːr, ˌdɑːlər/ *noun* (*informal*) the thing that people most want to know, or that is most important: *It's a clever plan, but the sixty-four thousand dollar question is: will it work?*

9/11 /ˌnaɪn ɪˈlevn/ *noun* the abbreviation for the date September 11, 2001, when TERRORISTS flew planes into the World Trade Center in New York, the Pentagon in Washington, D.C., and a field in Pennsylvania, killing thousands of people

911 /ˌnaɪn wʌn ˈwʌn/ the telephone number used in the US to call the police, fire or ambulance services in an emergency: (*NAmE*) *Call 911.*

99 /ˌnaɪntiˈnaɪn/ *noun* (*BrE*) an ice cream in a CONE with a stick of chocolate in the top

999 /ˌnaɪn naɪn ˈnaɪn/ the telephone number used in Britain to call the police, fire or ambulance services in an emergency: (*BrE*) *Dial 999.*

Aa

A /eɪ/ *noun, symbol, abbr.*
■ ***noun*** (also **a**) (*pl.* **As, A's, a's** /eɪz/) **1** [C, U] the first letter of the English alphabet: *'Apple' begins with (an) A/'A'.* **2 A** [C, U] (*music*) the 6th note in the SCALE of C MAJOR **3** [C, U] the highest mark/grade that a student can get for a piece of work or course of study: *She got (an)* ***A in/for*** *Biology.* ◇ *He had* ***straight A's*** (= nothing but A's) *all through high school.* **4 A** [U] used to represent the first of two or more possibilities: *Shall we go for plan A or plan B?* **5 A** [U] used to represent a person, for example in an imagined situation or to hide their identity: *Assume A knows B is guilty.* ➲ see also A-FRAME, A LEVEL, A-ROAD
IDM **from A to B** from one place to another: *For me a car is just a means of getting from A to B.* **from A to Z** including everything there is to know about sth: *He knew his subject from A to Z.*
■ ***symbol*** **1** used in Britain before a number to refer to a particular important road: *the A34 to Newbury* **2** used (but not in the US) before numbers which show standard METRIC sizes of paper: *a sheet of* ***A4*** *paper* (= 297 × 210mm) ◇ ***A3*** (= 420 × 297mm) ◇ ***A5*** (= 210 × 148mm)
■ ***abbr.*** (in writing) AMP(S)

a 0-π /ə; *strong form* eɪ/ (also **an** /ən; *strong form* æn/) *indefinite article*
HELP The form **a** is used before consonant sounds and the form **an** before vowel sounds. When saying abbreviations like 'FM' or 'UN', use **a** or **an** according to how the first letter is said. For example, **F** is a consonant, but begins with the sound /e/ and so you say: *an FM radio.* **U** is a vowel but begins with /j/ and so you say: *a UN declaration.* **1** 0-π used before countable or singular nouns referring to people or things that have not already been mentioned: *a man/horse/unit* ◇ *an aunt/egg/hour/x-ray* ◇ *I can only carry two at a time.* ◇ *There's a visitor for you.* ◇ *She's a friend of my father's* (= one of my father's friends). **2** 0-π used before uncountable nouns when these have an adjective in front of them, or phrase following them: *a good knowledge of French* ◇ *a sadness that won't go away* **3** 0-π any; every: *A lion is a dangerous animal.* **4** 0-π used to show that sb/sth is a member of a group or profession: *Their new car's a BMW.* ◇ *She's a Buddhist.* ◇ *He's a teacher.* ◇ *Is that a Monet* (= a painting by Monet)? **5** used in front of two nouns that are seen as a single unit: *a knife and fork* **6** used instead of *one* before some numbers: *A thousand people were there.* **7** used when talking about prices, quantities and rates SYN **per**: *They cost 50p a kilo.* ◇ *I can type 50 words a minute.* ◇ *He was driving at 50 miles an hour.* **8** a person like sb: *She's a little Hitler.* **9** used before sb's name to show that the speaker does not know the person: *There's a Mrs Green to see you.* **10** used before the names of days of the week to talk about one particular day: *She died on a Tuesday.*

a- /eɪ/ *prefix* (in nouns, adjectives and adverbs) not; without: *atheist* ◇ *atypical* ◇ *asexually*

A1 /ˌeɪ ˈwʌn/ *adj.* (*informal*) very good: *The car was in A1 condition.*

A2 (level) /ˌeɪ ˈtuː levl/ *noun* [C, U] a British exam usually taken in Year 13 of school or college (= the final year) when students are aged 18. Students must first have studied a subject at AS level before they can take an A2 exam. Together AS and A2 level exams form the A-level qualification, which is needed for entrance to universities: *A2 exams* ◇ *Students will normally take three A2 subjects.* ◇ *He's* ***doing an A2 (level)*** *in History.* ◇ *More than 20 subjects are on offer* ***at A2 level*** *at our college.*

AA /ˌeɪ ˈeɪ/ *abbr.* **1** (usually **the AA**) Automobile Association (a British organization which provides services for car owners) **2** ALCOHOLICS ANONYMOUS

AAA /ˌeɪ eɪ ˈeɪ/ *abbr.* **1** American Automobile Association (an American organization which provides services for car owners) **2** (in the UK) Amateur Athletic Association

A & E /ˌeɪ ənd ˈiː/ *abbr.* ACCIDENT AND EMERGENCY

A & R /ˌeɪ ənd ˈɑː(r)/ *abbr.* artists and repertoire (the department in a record company that is responsible for finding new singers and bands and getting them to sign a contract with the company)

aard·vark /ˈɑːdvɑːk; *NAmE* ˈɑːrdvɑːrk/ *noun* an animal from southern Africa that has a long nose and tongue and that eats insects

aargh /ɑː; *NAmE* ɑːr/ *exclamation* used to express fear, anger, or some other strong emotion: *Aargh—get that cat off the table!*

aback /əˈbæk/ *adv.*
IDM **be taken aˈback (by sb/sth)** to be shocked or surprised by sb/sth: *She was completely taken aback by his anger.* ➲ see also TAKE SB ABACK ➲ SYNONYMS at SURPRISE

aba·cus /ˈæbəkəs/ *noun* (*pl.* **aba·cuses** /-kəsɪz/) a frame with small balls which slide along wires. It is used as a tool or toy for counting.

aba·lone /ˌæbəˈləʊni; *NAmE* -ˈloʊ-/ *noun* [C, U] a SHELLFISH that can be eaten and whose shell contains MOTHER-OF-PEARL

aban·don 0-π AW /əˈbændən/ *verb, noun*
■ ***verb*** **1** 0-π to leave sb, especially sb you are responsible for, with no intention of returning: **~ sb** *The baby had been abandoned by its mother.* ◇ **~ sb to sth** *The study showed a deep fear among the elderly of being abandoned to the care of strangers.* **2** 0-π to leave a thing or place, especially because it is impossible or dangerous to stay SYN **leave**: **~ sth** *Snow forced many drivers to abandon their vehicles.* ◇ *He gave the order to* ***abandon ship*** (= to leave the ship because it was sinking). ◇ **~ sth to sb/sth** *They had to abandon their lands to the invading forces.* **3** 0-π **~ sth** to stop doing sth, especially before it is finished; to stop having sth: *They abandoned the match because of rain.* ◇ *She abandoned hope of any reconciliation.* **4** to stop supporting or helping sb; to stop believing in sth: **~ sb** *The country abandoned its political leaders after the war.* ◇ **~ sth** *By 1930 he had abandoned his Marxist principles.* **5 ~ yourself to sth** (*literary*) to feel an emotion so strongly that you can feel nothing else: *He abandoned himself to despair.*
■ ***noun*** [U] (*formal*) an uncontrolled way of behaving that shows that sb does not care what other people think: *He signed cheques with careless abandon.* IDM see GAY *adj.*

aban·doned 0-π AW /əˈbændənd/ *adj.*
1 0-π left and no longer wanted, used or needed: *an abandoned car/house* ◇ *The child was found abandoned but unharmed.* **2** (of people or their behaviour) wild; not following accepted standards

aban·don·ment AW /əˈbændənmənt/ *noun* [U] (*formal*) **1** the act of leaving a person, thing or place with no intention of returning **2** the act of giving up an idea or stopping an activity with no intention of returning to it: *the government's abandonment of its new economic policy*

abase /əˈbeɪs/ *verb* **~ yourself** (*formal*) to act in a way that shows that you accept sb's power over you ▶ **abase·ment** *noun* [U]

abashed /əˈbæʃt/ *adj.* [not before noun] embarrassed and ashamed because of sth that you have done OPP **unabashed**

abate /əˈbeɪt/ *verb* [I, T] (*formal*) to become less strong; to make sth less strong: *The storm showed no signs of abating.* ◇ **~ sth** *Steps are to be taken to abate pollution.* ▶ **abate·ment** *noun* [U]

ab·at·toir /ˈæbətwɑː(r)/ *noun* (*BrE*) = SLAUGHTERHOUSE

abaya /əˈbeɪə; *NAmE* əˈbaɪjə/ *noun* a full-length piece of clothing worn over other clothes by Arab men or women

abba /ˈʌbə/ (also **appa**) *noun* (*IndE*) (especially as a form of address) a father

ab·bess /ˈæbes/ *noun* a woman who is the head of a CONVENT

A

abbey /ˈæbi/ *noun* a large church together with a group of buildings in which MONKS or NUNS live or lived in the past: *Westminster Abbey* ◇ *a ruined abbey*

abbot /ˈæbət/ *noun* a man who is the head of a MONASTERY or an ABBEY

ab·bre·vi·ate /əˈbriːvieɪt/ *verb* [usually passive] **~ sth (to sth)** to make a word, phrase or name shorter by leaving out letters or using only the first letter of each word **SYN shorten**: *the Jet Propulsion Laboratory (usually abbreviated to JPL)* ▸ **ab·bre·vi·ated** *adj.*: *Where appropriate, abbreviated forms are used.*

ab·bre·vi·ation /əˌbriːviˈeɪʃn/ *noun* **1** [C] **~ (of/for sth)** a short form of a word, etc: *What's the abbreviation for 'Saint'?* **2** [U] the process of abbreviating sth

ABC /ˌeɪ biː ˈsiː/ *noun, abbr.*
■ ***noun*** [sing.] (*BrE*) (*NAmE* **ABCs** [pl.]) **1** all the letters of the alphabet, especially as they are learnt by children: *Do you know your ABC?* **2** the basic facts about a subject: *the ABC of gardening* **IDM** see EASY
■ ***abbr.*** **1** American Broadcasting Company (a large national American television company) **2** Australian Broadcasting Corporation (the Australian national public broadcasting company)

ABD /ˌeɪ biː ˈdiː/ *abbr.* (*NAmE*) all but dissertation (having completed all the work for a higher degree except the DISSERTATION): *ABD students may apply.*

ab·di·cate /ˈæbdɪkeɪt/ *verb* **1** [I, T] to give up the position of being king or queen: *He abdicated in favour of his son.* ◇ **~ sth** *She was forced to abdicate the throne of Spain.* **2** [T] **~ responsibility/your responsibilities** to fail or refuse to perform a duty ▸ **ab·di·ca·tion** /ˌæbdɪˈkeɪʃn/ *noun* [U, C]

ab·do·men /ˈæbdəmən/ *noun* **1** the part of the body below the chest that contains the stomach, BOWELS, etc. **2** the end part of an insect's body that is attached to its THORAX ➲ **VISUAL VOCAB** page V11

ab·dom·inal /æbˈdɒmɪnl; *NAmE* -ˈdɑːm-/ *adj., noun*
■ ***adj.*** [only before noun] (*anatomy*) relating to or connected with the abdomen: *abdominal pains*
■ ***noun* abdominals** (also *informal* **abs**) [pl.] the muscles of the abdomen

ab·duct /æbˈdʌkt/ *verb* **~ sb** to take sb away illegally, especially using force **SYN kidnap** ▸ **ab·duc·tion** /æbˈdʌkʃn/ *noun* [U, C]

ab·duct·ee /ˌæbdʌkˈtiː/ *noun* a person who has been abducted

ab·duct·or /æbˈdʌktə(r)/ *noun* **1** a person who abducts sb **2** (also **abˈductor muscle**) (*anatomy*) a muscle that moves a body part away from the middle of the body or from another part ➲ compare ADDUCTOR

abed /əˈbed/ *adv.* (*old use*) in bed

Aber·do·nian /ˌæbəˈdəʊniən; *NAmE* ˌæbərˈdoʊ-/ *noun* a person from Aberdeen in Scotland ▸ **Aber·do·nian** *adj.*

ab·er·rant /æˈberənt/ *adj.* (*formal*) not usual or not socially acceptable: *aberrant behaviour*

ab·er·ra·tion /ˌæbəˈreɪʃn/ *noun* [C, U] (*formal*) a fact, an action or a way of behaving that is not usual, and that may be unacceptable

abet /əˈbet/ *verb* (-tt-) **~ sb** to help or encourage sb to do sth wrong: *He was abetted in the deception by his wife.* **IDM** see AID *v.*

abey·ance /əˈbeɪəns/ *noun* [U]
IDM in abeyance (*formal*) not being used, or being stopped for a period of time

ABH /ˌeɪ biː ˈeɪtʃ/ *abbr.* (*BrE, law*) ACTUAL BODILY HARM

abhor /əbˈhɔː(r)/ *verb* (-rr-) (not used in the progressive tenses) **~ sth** (*formal*) to hate sth, for example a way of behaving or thinking, especially for moral reasons **SYN detest, loathe**

ab·hor·rence /əbˈhɒrəns; *NAmE* -ˈhɔːr-; -ˈhɑːr-/ *noun* [U, sing.] (*formal*) a feeling of strong hatred, especially for moral reasons

ab·hor·rent /əbˈhɒrənt; *NAmE* -ˈhɔːr-; -ˈhɑːr-/ *adj.* **~ (to sb)** (*formal*) causing hatred, especially for moral reasons **SYN repugnant**: *Racism is abhorrent to a civilized society.*

abide /əˈbaɪd/ *verb* (**abided, abided**) **HELP** In sense 2 **abode** is also used for the past tense and past participle. **1** [T] **can't/couldn't abide sb/sth** to dislike sb/sth so much that you hate having to be with or deal with them **SYN bear, stand**: *I can't abide people with no sense of humour.* ◇ *He couldn't abide the thought of being cooped up in an office.* **2** [I] **+ adv./prep.** (*old use* or *formal*) to stay or live in a place: *May joy and peace abide in us all.*
PHR V aˈbide by sth (*formal*) to accept and act according to a law, an agreement, etc: *You'll have to abide by the rules of the club.* ◇ *We will abide by their decision.*

abid·ing /əˈbaɪdɪŋ/ *adj.* (*formal*) (of a feeling or belief) lasting for a long time and not changing

abil·ity 🔑 /əˈbɪləti/ *noun* (*pl.* -ies)
1 🔑 [sing.] **~ to do sth** the fact that sb/sth is able to do sth: *The system has the ability to run more than one program at the same time.* ◇ *Everyone has the right to good medical care regardless of their ability to pay.* ◇ *A gentle form of exercise will increase your ability to relax.* **OPP inability** **2** 🔑 [C, U] a level of skill or intelligence: *Almost everyone has some musical ability.* ◇ *He was a man of extraordinary abilities.* ◇ *students of mixed abilities* ◇ *A woman of her ability will easily find a job.* ◇ *I try to do my job* ***to the best of my ability*** (= as well as I can).

-ability, -ibility ➲ -ABLE

abi·ot·ic /ˌeɪbaɪˈɒtɪk; *NAmE* -ˈɑːtɪk/ *adj.* (*technical*) not involving biology or living things: *abiotic processes*

ab·ject /ˈæbdʒekt/ *adj.* [usually before noun] (*formal*) **1** terrible and without hope: ***abject poverty/misery/failure*** **2** without any pride or respect for yourself: *an abject apology* ▸ **ab·ject·ly** *adv.*

ab·jure /əbˈdʒʊə(r); *NAmE* əbˈdʒʊr/ *verb* **~ sth** (*formal*) to promise publicly that you will give up or reject a belief or a way of behaving **SYN renounce**

ab·la·tion /əˈbleɪʃn/ *noun* [U] (*geology*) the loss of material from a large mass of ice, snow or rock as a result of the action of the sun, wind or rain

ab·la·tive /ˈæblətɪv/ *noun* (*grammar*) (in some languages) the form that a noun, a pronoun or an adjective can take to show, for example, who or what sth is done by or where sth comes from ➲ compare ACCUSATIVE, DATIVE, GENITIVE, NOMINATIVE, VOCATIVE ▸ **ab·la·tive** *adj.*

ablaze /əˈbleɪz/ *adj.* [not before noun] **1** burning quickly and strongly: *The whole building was soon ablaze.* ◇ *Cars and buses were* ***set ablaze*** *during the riot.* **2** full of bright light or colours: *There were lights still ablaze as they drove up to the house.* ◇ **~ with sth** *The trees were ablaze with the colours of autumn.* **3 ~ (with sth)** full of strong emotion or excitement: *He turned to her, his eyes ablaze with anger.*

able 🔑 /ˈeɪbl/ *adj.*
1 🔑 **~ to do sth** (used as a modal verb) to have the skill, intelligence, opportunity, etc. needed to do sth: *You must be able to speak French for this job.* ◇ *A viral illness left her barely able to walk.* ◇ *I didn't feel able to disagree with him.* ◇ *Will you be able to come?* **OPP unable** ➲ note at CAN[1] **2** (**abler** /ˈeɪblə(r)/, **ablest** /ˈeɪblɪst/) intelligent; good at sth: *the ablest student in the class* ◇ *We aim to help the less able in society to lead an independent life.* ➲ see also ABLY

> **WORD FAMILY**
> **able** *adj.* (≠ unable)
> **ably** *adv.*
> **ability** *noun* (≠ inability)
> **disabled** *adj.*
> **disability** *noun*

-able, -ible *suffix* (in adjectives) **1** that can or must be: *calculable* ◇ *taxable* **2** having the quality of: *fashionable* ◇ *comfortable* ◇ *changeable* ▸ **-ability, -ibility** (in nouns): *capability* ◇ *responsibility* **-ably, -ibly** (in adverbs): *noticeably* ◇ *incredibly*

ˌable-ˈbodied *adj.* physically healthy, fit and strong in contrast to sb who is weak or disabled

ˌable ˈseaman *noun* a sailor of lower rank in the British navy

ab·lu·tions /əˈbluːʃnz/ *noun* [pl.] (*formal* or *humorous*) the act of washing yourself

ably /ˈeɪbli/ *adv.* skilfully and well: *We were ably assisted by a team of volunteers.* ➲ see also ABLE (2)

ABM /ˌeɪ biː ˈem/ *noun* (*CanE*) the abbreviation for 'automated banking machine' ➲ CASH MACHINE

ab·neg·ation /ˌæbnɪˈɡeɪʃn/ *noun* [U] (*formal*) the act of not allowing yourself to have sth that you want; the act of rejecting sth ▶ **ab·neg·ate** /ˈæbnɪɡeɪt/ *verb* **~ sth**

ab·nor·mal AW /æbˈnɔːml; *NAmE* -ˈnɔːrml/ *adj.* different from what is usual or expected, especially in a way that is worrying, harmful or not wanted: *abnormal levels of sugar in the blood* ◇ *They thought his behaviour was abnormal.* OPP **normal** ▶ **ab·nor·mal·ly** AW /æbˈnɔːməli; *NAmE* -ˈnɔːrm-/ *adv.*: *abnormally high blood pressure*

ab·nor·mal·ity /ˌæbnɔːˈmæləti; *NAmE* -nɔːrˈm-/ *noun* (*pl.* -ies) [C, U] a feature or characteristic in a person's body or behaviour that is not usual and may be harmful, worrying or cause illness: *abnormalities of the heart* ◇ ***congenital/foetal abnormality***

Abo /ˈæbəʊ; *NAmE* ˈæboʊ/ *noun* (*pl.* -os) (*AustralE, taboo, informal*) an extremely offensive word for an Aborigine

aboard /əˈbɔːd; *NAmE* əˈbɔːrd/ *adv., prep.* on or onto a ship, plane, bus or train SYN **on board**: *We went aboard.* ◇ *He was already aboard the plane.* ◇ *The plane crashed, killing all 157 passengers aboard.* ◇ ***All aboard!*** (= the bus, boat, etc. is leaving soon) ◇ ***Welcome aboard!*** (= used to welcome passengers or a person joining a new organization, etc.)

abode /əˈbəʊd; *NAmE* əˈboʊd/ *noun* [usually sing.] (*formal* or *humorous*) the place where sb lives: *homeless people **of no fixed abode*** (= with no permanent home) ◇ *You are most welcome to my humble abode.* ➲ see also ABIDE *v.*, RIGHT OF ABODE

abol·ish /əˈbɒlɪʃ; *NAmE* əˈbɑːl-/ *verb* **~ sth** to officially end a law, a system or an institution: *This tax should be abolished.*

abo·li·tion /ˌæbəˈlɪʃn/ *noun* [U] the ending of a law, a system or an institution: *the abolition of slavery*

abo·li·tion·ist /ˌæbəˈlɪʃənɪst/ *noun* a person who is in favour of the abolition of sth

ˈA-bomb *noun* = ATOM BOMB

abom·in·able /əˈbɒmɪnəbl; *NAmE* əˈbɑːm-/ *adj.* extremely unpleasant and causing disgust SYN **appalling, disgusting**: *The judge described the attack as an abominable crime.* ◇ *We were served the most abominable coffee.* ▶ **abom·in·ably** /əˈbɒmɪnəbli; *NAmE* əˈbɑːm-/ *adv.*: *She treated him abominably.*

Aˌbominable ˈSnowman *noun* = YETI

abom·in·ate /əˈbɒmɪneɪt; *NAmE* əˈbɑːm-/ *verb* (not used in the progressive tenses) **~ sth/sb** (*formal*) to feel hatred or disgust for sth/sb

abom·in·ation /əˌbɒmɪˈneɪʃn; *NAmE* əˌbɑːm-/ *noun* (*formal*) a thing that causes disgust and hatred, or is considered extremely offensive

abo·ri·ginal /ˌæbəˈrɪdʒənl/ *adj., noun*

■ ***adj.* 1** (usually **Aboriginal**) relating to the original people living in Australia: *the issue of Aboriginal land rights* **2** relating to the original people, animals, etc. of a place and to a period of time before Europeans arrived: *the aboriginal peoples of Canada* ◇ *aboriginal art/culture*

■ ***noun*** (usually **Aboriginal**) a member of a race of people who were the original people living in a country, especially Australia ➲ see also KOORI

abo·ri·gine /ˌæbəˈrɪdʒəni/ *noun* **1** a member of a race of people who were the original people living in a country **2 Aborigine** a member of the race of people who were the original people of Australia ➲ see also KOORI

abort /əˈbɔːt; *NAmE* əˈbɔːrt/ *verb* **1** [T] **~ sth** to end a PREGNANCY early in order to prevent a baby from developing and being born alive: *to **abort a child/pregnancy/foetus*** **2** [I] (*technical*) to give birth to a child or young animal too early for it to survive: *The virus can cause pregnant animals to abort.* ➲ see also MISCARRY **3** [I, T, often passive] to end or cause sth to end before it has been completed, especially because it is likely to fail: (*computing*) *If the wrong password is given the program aborts.* ◇ **~ sth** *We had no option but to abort the mission.* ◇ *The plan was aborted at the last minute.*

abor·tion /əˈbɔːʃn; *NAmE* əˈbɔːrʃn/ *noun* **1** [U] the deliberate ending of a PREGNANCY at an early stage: *to **support/oppose abortion*** ◇ *a woman's right to abortion* ◇ *abortion laws* ◇ *I've always been anti-abortion.* **2** [C] a medical operation to end a PREGNANCY at an early stage: *She decided to **have an abortion**.* SYN **termination** ➲ compare MISCARRIAGE

abor·tion·ist /əˈbɔːʃənɪst; *NAmE* əˈbɔːrʃ-/ *noun* a person who performs abortions, especially illegally

abort·ive /əˈbɔːtɪv; *NAmE* əˈbɔːrtɪv/ *adj.* (*formal*) (of an action) not successful; failed SYN **unsuccessful**: *an abortive military coup* ◇ *abortive attempts to divert the course of the river*

abound /əˈbaʊnd/ *verb* [I] to exist in great numbers or quantities: *Stories about his travels abound.*

PHR V **aˈbound with/in sth** to have sth in great numbers or quantities: *The lakes abound with fish.* ➲ see also ABUNDANCE, ABUNDANT

about 0-w /əˈbaʊt/ *adv., prep., adj.*

■ ***adv.* 1** 0-w a little more or less than; a little before or after SYN **approximately**: *It costs about $10.* ◇ *They waited (for) about an hour.* ◇ *He arrived (at) about ten.* **2** 0-w nearly; very close to: *I'm just about ready.* ◇ *This is about the best we can hope for.* **3** 0-w (*especially BrE*) in many directions; here and there: *The children were rushing about in the garden.* **4** 0-w (*especially BrE*) in no particular order; in various places: *Her books were lying about on the floor.* **5** (*especially BrE*) doing nothing in particular: *People were standing about in the road.* **6** (*especially BrE*) able to be found in a place: *There was nobody about.* ◇ *There's a lot of flu about.* **7** (*technical* or *formal*) facing the opposite direction: *He brought the ship about.* ➲ note at AROUND

IDM **that's about ˈall | that's about ˈit** used to say that you have finished telling sb about sth and there is nothing to add: *'Anything else?' 'No, that's about it for now.'* ➲ more at JUST *adv.*, OUT *adv.*

■ ***prep.* 1** 0-w on the subject of sb/sth; in connection with sb/sth: *a book about flowers* ◇ *Tell me **all about** it.* ◇ *What's she so angry about?* ◇ *There's something strange about him.* ◇ *I don't know what you're **on about*** (= talking about). ◇ *There's nothing you can do about it now.* **2** 0-w used to describe the purpose or an aspect of sth: *Movies are **all about** making money these days.* ◇ ***What was all that about?*** (= what was the reason for what has just happened?) **3** 0-w busy with sth; doing sth: *Everywhere people were going about their daily business.* ◇ *And **while you're about it** ...* (= while you're doing that) **4** (*especially BrE*) in many directions in a place; here and there: *We wandered about the town for an hour or so.* ◇ *He looked about the room.* **5** (*especially BrE*) in various parts of a place; here and there: *The papers were strewn about the room.* **6** (*especially BrE*) next to a place or person; in the area mentioned: *She's somewhere about the office.* **7** (*literary*) surrounding sb/sth: *She wore a shawl about her shoulders.*

IDM **how/what about...? 1** 0-w used when asking for information about sb/sth: *How about Ruth? Have you heard from her?* ◇ *I'm having fish. What about you?* **2** 0-w used to make a suggestion: *How about going for a walk?* ◇ (*especially NAmE*) *How about we go for a walk?* ◇ *What about a break?*

■ ***adj.***

IDM **be about to do sth** 0-w to be close to doing sth; to be going to do sth very soon: *I was just about to ask you the same thing.* **not be about to do sth** to not be willing to do sth; to not intend to do sth: *I've never done any cooking and I'm not about to start now.*

aˌbout-ˈturn (*BrE*) (also **aˌbout-ˈface** *NAmE, BrE*) *noun* [sing.] a complete change of opinion, plan or behaviour: *The government did an about-turn over nuclear energy.*

A

Language Bank

about

Saying what a text is about

- The book **is about** homeless people in the cities.
- The report **deals with** the issue of homelessness in London.
- The writer **discusses** the problems faced by homeless people.
- The article **presents an overview of** the issues surrounding homelessness.
- The novel **explores** the theme of friendship among homeless people.
- The first chapter **examines** the relationship between homelessness and drug addiction.
- The paper **considers** the question of why so many young people become homeless.

above 0-ᴛ /ə'bʌv/ *prep., adv., adj.*

■ ***prep.* 1** 0-ᴛ at or to a higher place or position than sth/sb: *The water came above our knees.* ◇ *We were flying above the clouds.* ◇ *the people in the apartment above mine* ◇ *A captain in the navy ranks above a captain in the army.* ◇ *They finished the year six places above their local rivals.* **2** 0-ᴛ more than sth; greater in number, level or age than sb/sth: *Inflation is above 6%.* ◇ *Temperatures have been above average.* ◇ *We cannot accept children above the age of 10.* **3** of greater importance or of higher quality than sb/sth: *I rate her above most other players of her age.* **4** too good or too honest to do sth: *She's not above lying when it suits her.* ◇ *He's above suspicion* (= he is completely trusted). **5** (of a sound) louder or clearer than another sound: *I couldn't hear her above the noise of the traffic.*

IDM **above 'all** 0-ᴛ most important of all; especially: *Above all, keep in touch.* ➲ LANGUAGE BANK at EMPHASIS **a'bove yourself** (*disapproving*) having too high an opinion of yourself ➲ more at OVER *prep.*

■ ***adv.* 1** 0-ᴛ at or to a higher place: *Put it on the shelf above.* ◇ *Seen from above the cars looked tiny.* ◇ *They were acting on instructions from above* (= from sb in a higher position of authority). **2** 0-ᴛ greater in number, level or age: *increases of 5% and above* ◇ *A score of 70 or above will get you an 'A'.* ◇ *children aged 12 and above* **3** earlier in sth written or printed: *As was stated above...* ◇ *See above, page 97.*

■ ***adj.*** [only before noun] mentioned or printed previously in a letter, book, etc: *Please write to us at the above address.* ▶ **the above** *noun* [sing.+ sing./pl. v.]: *Please notify us if the above is not correct.* ◇ *All the above* (= people mentioned above) *have passed the exam.*

Which Word?

above / over

- **Above** and **over** can both be used to describe a position higher than something: *They built a new room above/over the garage.* When you are talking about movement from one side of something to the other, you can only use **over**: *They jumped over the stream.* **Over** can also mean 'covering': *He put a blanket over the sleeping child.*
- **Above** and **over** can also mean 'more than'. **Above** is used in relation to a minimum level or a fixed point: *2 000 feet above sea level* ◇ *Temperatures will not rise above zero tonight.* **Over** is used with numbers, ages, money and time: *He's over 50.* ◇ *It costs over £100.* ◇ *We waited over 2 hours.*

a,bove 'board *adj., adv.* legal and honest; in a legal and honest way: *Don't worry; the deal was completely above board.* ORIGIN If card players keep their hands above the table (the board), other players can see what they are doing.

a,bove-'mentioned *adj.* [only before noun] mentioned or named earlier in the same letter, book, etc.

a,bove-the-'fold *adj.* in a position where it is seen first, for example on the top half of the front page of a newspaper or in the part of a web page that you see first when you open it: *above-the-fold images* ◇ *The company logo must be placed in an above-the-fold position.* ➲ compare BELOW-THE-FOLD IDM see FOLD *n.*

abra·ca·dabra /,æbrəkə'dæbrə/ *exclamation* a word that people say when they do a magic trick, in order to make it successful

ab·rade /ə'breɪd/ *verb* ~ **sth** (*technical*) to rub the surface of sth, such as rock or skin, and damage it or make it rough

ab·ra·sion /ə'breɪʒn/ *noun* (*technical*) **1** [C] a damaged area of the skin where it has been rubbed against sth hard and rough: *He suffered cuts and abrasions to the face.* **2** [U] damage to a surface caused by rubbing sth very hard against it: *Diamonds have extreme resistance to abrasion.*

abra·sive /ə'breɪsɪv/ *adj., noun*

■ ***adj.* 1** an **abrasive** substance is rough and can be used to clean a surface or to make it smooth: *abrasive kitchen cleaners* **2** (of a person or their manner) rude and unkind; acting in a way that may hurt other people's feelings ▶ **abra·sive·ly** *adv.* **abra·sive·ness** *noun* [U]

■ ***noun*** a substance used for cleaning surfaces or for making them smooth

abreast /ə'brest/ *adv.* next to sb/sth and facing the same way: *cycling two abreast* ◇ **~ of sb/sth** *A police car* ***drew abreast*** *of us and signalled us to stop.*

IDM **keep abreast of sth** to make sure that you know all the most recent facts about a subject: *It is almost impossible to keep abreast of all the latest developments in computing.*

abridge /ə'brɪdʒ/ *verb* ~ **sth** to make a book, play, etc. shorter by leaving parts out ▶ **abridged** *adj.*: *an* ***abridged edition/version*** OPP **unabridged** **abridge·ment** (also **abridg·ment**) *noun* [U, C]

abroad 0-ᴛ /ə'brɔːd/ *adv.* (*especially BrE*)

1 0-ᴛ in or to a foreign country: *to* ***be/go/travel/live abroad*** ◇ *She worked abroad for a year.* ◇ *imports of cheap food from abroad* ◇ *He was famous, both* ***at home and abroad*** (= in his own country and in other countries). **2** (*formal*) being talked about or felt by many people: *There was news abroad that a change was coming.* **3** (*old use*) outside; outdoors

ab·ro·gate /'æbrəgeɪt/ *verb* ~ **sth** (*technical*) to officially end a law, an agreement, etc. SYN **repeal** ▶ **ab·ro·ga·tion** /,æbrə'geɪʃn/ *noun* [U]

ab·rupt /ə'brʌpt/ *adj.* **1** sudden and unexpected, often in an unpleasant way: *an* ***abrupt change/halt/departure*** **2** speaking or acting in a way that seems unfriendly and rude; not taking time to say more than is necessary SYN **brusque, curt**: *an abrupt manner* ◇ *She was very abrupt with me in our meeting.* ▶ **ab·rupt·ly** *adv.* **ab·rupt·ness** *noun* [U]

ABS /,eɪ biː 'es/ *abbr.* anti-lock braking system ➲ see also ANTI-LOCK

abs /æbz/ *noun* [pl.] (*informal*) = ABDOMINALS

ab·scess /'æbses/ *noun* a swollen and infected area on your skin or in your body, full of a thick yellowish liquid (called PUS)

ab·scissa /æb'sɪsə/ (*pl.* **ab·scissae** /-siː/ or **ab·scissas**) *noun* (*mathematics*) the COORDINATE that gives the distance along the horizontal AXIS ➲ compare ORDINATE

ab·scond /əb'skɒnd; *NAmE* əb'skɑːnd/ *verb* [I] **1** ~ **(from sth)** to escape from a place that you are not allowed to leave without permission **2** ~ **(with sth)** to leave secretly and take with you sth, especially money, that does not belong to you: *He absconded with the company funds.*

ab·seil /'æbseɪl/ (*BrE*) (*NAmE* **rap·pel**) *verb* [I] ~ **(down, off, etc. sth)** to go down a steep CLIFF or rock while attached to a rope, pushing against the slope or rock with your feet ➲ VISUAL VOCAB page V40 ▸ **ab·seil** (*BrE*) (*NAmE* **rap·pel**) *noun*

ab·sence 0-w /ˈæbsəns/ *noun*
1 0-w [U, C] the fact of sb being away from a place where they are usually expected to be; the occasion or period of time when sb is away: *The decision was made* ***in my absence*** (= while I was not there). ◇ *We did not receive any news during his long absence.* ◇ **~ from ...** *absence from work* ◇ *repeated absences from school* ➲ see also LEAVE **2** 0-w [U] the fact of sb/sth not existing or not being available; a lack of sth: *The case was dismissed* ***in the absence of*** *any definite proof.* ◇ *the absence of any women on the board of directors* **OPP** **presence**
IDM ˌ**absence makes the heart grow ˈfonder** (*saying*) used to say that when you are away from sb that you love, you love them even more ➲ more at CONSPICUOUS

ab·sent 0-w *adj., verb*
■ ***adj.*** /ˈæbsənt/ **1** 0-w **~ (from ...)** not in a place because of illness, etc: *to be absent from work* **OPP** **present** **2** 0-w **~ (from sth)** not present in sth: *Love was totally absent from his childhood.* **OPP** **present** **3** showing that you are not really looking at or thinking about what is happening around you: *an absent expression* ➲ see also ABSENTLY
■ ***verb*** /æbˈsent/ **~ yourself (from sth)** (*formal*) to not go to or be in a place where you are expected to be: *He had absented himself from the office for the day.*

ab·sen·tee /ˌæbsənˈtiː/ *noun* a person who is not at a place where they were expected to be

ˌ**absentee ˈballot** (*NAmE*) (*BrE* ˈ**postal vote**) *noun* a vote in an election that you can send when you cannot be present

ab·sen·tee·ism /ˌæbsənˈtiːɪzəm/ *noun* [U] the fact of being frequently away from work or school, especially without good reasons

ˌ**absentee ˈlandlord** *noun* a person who rents their property to sb, but does not live in it and rarely visits it

ab·sen·tia ➲ IN ABSENTIA

ab·sent·ly /ˈæbsəntli/ *adv.* in a way that shows you are not looking at or thinking about what is happening around you: *He nodded absently, his attention absorbed by the screen.*

ˌ**absent-ˈminded** *adj.* tending to forget things, perhaps because you are not thinking about what is around you, but about sth else **SYN** **forgetful** ▸ ˌ**absent-ˈminded·ly** *adv.* ˌ**absent-ˈminded·ness** *noun* [U]

ab·sinthe /ˈæbsɪnθ/ *noun* [U] a very strong green alcoholic drink that tastes of ANISEED

ab·so·lute 0-w /ˈæbsəluːt/ *adj., noun*
■ ***adj.*** **1** 0-w total and complete: *a class for absolute beginners* ◇ *absolute confidence/trust/silence/truth* ◇ *'You're wrong,' she said with absolute certainty.* **2** 0-w [only before noun] used, especially in spoken English, to give emphasis to what you are saying: *There's absolute rubbish on television tonight.* ◇ *He must earn an absolute fortune.* **3** definite and without any doubt or confusion: *There was no absolute proof.* ◇ *He taught us that the laws of physics were absolute.* ◇ *The divorce became absolute last week.* ➲ see also DECREE ABSOLUTE **4** not limited or restricted: ***absolute power/authority*** ◇ *an* ***absolute ruler/monarchy*** (= one with no limit to their power) **5** existing or measured independently and not in relation to sth else: *Although prices are falling* ***in absolute terms****, energy is still expensive.* ◇ *Beauty cannot be measured by any absolute standard.* ➲ compare RELATIVE
■ ***noun*** an idea or a principle that is believed to be true or valid in any circumstances: *Right and wrong are, for her, moral absolutes.*

ab·so·lute·ly 0-w /ˈæbsəluːtli/ *adv.*
1 0-w used to emphasize that sth is completely true: *You're absolutely right.* ◇ *He made it absolutely clear.* **2** 0-w **absolutely no..., absolutely nothing** used to emphasize sth negative: *She did absolutely no work.* ◇ *There's absolutely nothing more the doctors can do.* **3** 0-w used with adjectives or verbs that express strong feelings or extreme qualities to mean 'extremely': *I was absolutely furious with him.* ◇ *She absolutely adores you.* ◇ *He's an absolutely brilliant cook.* **4** 0-w /ˌæbsəˈluːtli/ used to emphasize that you agree with sb, or to give sb permission to do sth: *'They could have told us, couldn't they?' 'Absolutely!'* ◇ *'Can we leave a little early?' 'Absolutely!'* **5** 0-w **absolutely not** used to emphasize that you strongly disagree with sb, or to refuse permission: *'Was it any good?' 'No, absolutely not.'*

ˌ**absolute maˈjority** *noun* more than half of the total number of votes or winning candidates

ˌ**absolute ˈtemperature** *noun* [U, C] temperature measured from absolute zero in degrees KELVIN

ˌ**absolute ˈzero** *noun* [U] the lowest temperature that is thought to be possible

ab·so·lu·tion /ˌæbsəˈluːʃn/ *noun* [U] (especially in the Christian Church) a formal statement that a person is forgiven for what he or she has done wrong

ab·so·lut·ism /ˈæbsəluːtɪzəm/ *noun* [U] **1** a political system in which a ruler or government has total power at all times **2** belief in a political, religious or moral principle which is thought to be true in all circumstances ▸ **ab·so·lut·ist** *noun, adj.*

ab·solve /əbˈzɒlv; *NAmE* əbˈzɑːlv/ *verb* (*formal*) **1 ~ sb (of/from sth)** to state formally that sb is not guilty or responsible for sth: *The court absolved him of all responsibility for the accident.* **2 ~ sb (from/of sth)** to give ABSOLUTION to sb: *I absolve you from all your sins.*

ab·sorb 0-w /əbˈsɔːb; -ˈzɔːb; *NAmE* -ˈsɔːrb; -ˈzɔːrb/ *verb*
▸ LIQUID/GAS **1** 0-w to take in a liquid, gas or other substance from the surface or space around: **~ sth** *Plants absorb oxygen.* ◇ **~ sth into sth** *The cream is easily absorbed into the skin.*
▸ MAKE PART OF STH LARGER **2** [often passive] to make sth smaller become part of sth larger: **~ sth** *The country simply cannot absorb this influx of refugees.* ◇ **~ sth into sth** *The surrounding small towns have been absorbed into the city.*
▸ INFORMATION **3** 0-w **~ sth** to take sth into the mind and learn or understand it **SYN** **take in**: *It's a lot of information to absorb all at once.*
▸ INTEREST SB **4 ~ sb** to interest sb very much so that they pay no attention to anything else **SYN** **engross**: *This work had absorbed him for several years.*
▸ HEAT/LIGHT/ENERGY **5 ~ sth** to take in and keep heat, light, energy, etc. instead of reflecting it: *Black walls absorb a lot of heat during the day.*
▸ SHOCK/IMPACT **6 ~ sth** to reduce the effect of a blow, hit, etc: *This tennis racket absorbs shock on impact.* ➲ see also SHOCK ABSORBER
▸ MONEY/TIME/CHANGES **7 ~ sth** to use up a large supply of sth, especially money or time: *The new proposals would absorb $80 billion of the federal budget.* **8 ~ sth** to deal with changes, effects, costs, etc: *The company is unable to absorb such huge losses.*

ab·sorb·able /əbˈsɔːbəbl; -ˈzɔːb-; *NAmE* -ˈsɔːrb-; -ˈzɔːrb-/ *adj.* able to be absorbed, especially into the body: *absorbable gases*

ab·sor·bance /əbˈsɔːbəns; -ˈzɔːb-; *NAmE* -ˈsɔːrb-; -ˈzɔːrb-/ *noun* (*physics*) the ability of a substance to absorb light

ab·sorbed /əbˈsɔːbd; -ˈzɔːbd; *NAmE* -ˈsɔːrbd; -ˈzɔːrbd/ *adj.* [not usually before noun] **~ in sth/sb** very interested in sth/sb so that you are not paying attention to anything else: *She seemed totally absorbed in her book.*

ab·sorb·ent /əbˈsɔːbənt; -ˈzɔːb-; *NAmE* -ˈsɔːrb-; -ˈzɔːrb-/ *adj.* able to take in sth easily, especially liquid: ***absorbent paper/materials*** ▸ **ab·sorb·ency** /-ənsi/ *noun* [U]

ab·sorb·ing /əbˈsɔːbɪŋ; -ˈzɔːb-; *NAmE* -ˈsɔːrb-; -ˈzɔːrb-/ *adj.* interesting and enjoyable and holding your attention completely: *an absorbing book/game* ➲ SYNONYMS at INTERESTING

ab·sorp·tion /əbˈsɔːpʃn; -ˈzɔːp-; *NAmE* -ˈsɔːrp-; -ˈzɔːrp-/ *noun* [U] **1** the process of a liquid, gas or other substance being taken in: *Vitamin D is necessary to aid the absorption of calcium from food.* **2** the process of a smaller group, country, etc. becoming part of a larger group or country:

the absorption of immigrants into the host country **3 ~ (in sth)** the fact of sb being very interested in sth so that it takes all their attention: *His work suffered because of his total absorption in sport.*

ab·stain /əb'steɪn/ *verb* [I] **1 ~ (from sth)** to choose not to use a vote, either in favour of or against sth: *Ten people voted in favour, five against and two abstained.* **2 ~ (from sth)** to decide not to do or have sth, especially sth you like or enjoy, because it is bad for your health or considered morally wrong: *to abstain from alcohol/sex/drugs* **3 ~ (from sth)** (*IndE*) to stay away from sth: *The workers who abstained from work yesterday have been suspended.* ➲ see also ABSTENTION, ABSTINENCE

ab·stain·er /əb'steɪnə(r)/ *noun* **1** a person who chooses not to vote either in favour of or against sth **2** a person who never drinks alcohol

ab·ste·mi·ous /əb'sti:miəs/ *adj.* (*formal*) not allowing yourself to have much food or alcohol, or to do things that are enjoyable

ab·sten·tion /əb'stenʃn/ *noun* **1** [C, U] **~ (from sth)** an act of choosing not to use a vote either in favour of or against sth: *The voting was 15 in favour, 3 against and 2 abstentions.* **2** [U] (*formal*) the act of not allowing yourself to have or do sth enjoyable or sth that is considered bad ➲ see also ABSTAIN

ab·stin·ence /'æbstɪnəns/ *noun* [U] **~ (from sth)** (*formal*) the practice of not allowing yourself sth, especially food, alcoholic drinks or sex, for moral, religious or health reasons: *total abstinence from strong drink* ➲ see also ABSTAIN

ab·stin·ent /'æbstɪnənt/ *adj.* not allowing yourself sth, especially alcoholic drinks, for moral, religious or health reasons

ab·stract AW *adj., noun, verb*

■ ***adj.*** /'æbstrækt/ **1** based on general ideas and not on any particular real person, thing or situation: ***abstract knowledge/principles*** ◇ *The research shows that pre-school children are capable of thinking in abstract terms.* ➲ compare CONCRETE *adj.* (2) **2** existing in thought or as an idea but not having a physical reality: *We may talk of beautiful things but beauty itself is abstract.* **3** (of art) not representing people or things in a realistic way, but expressing the artist's ideas about them ➲ compare FIGURATIVE (2), REPRESENTATIONAL ▶ **ab·stract·ly** AW *adv.*

■ ***noun*** /'æbstrækt/ **1** an abstract work of art **2** a short piece of writing containing the main ideas in a document SYN **summary**

IDM **in the 'abstract** in a general way, without referring to a particular real person, thing or situation

■ ***verb*** /æb'strækt/ **1 ~ sth (from sth)** to remove sth from somewhere: *She abstracted the main points from the argument.* ◇ *a plan to abstract 8 million gallons of water from the river* **2 ~ sth** (*technical*) to make a written summary of a book, etc.

ab·stract·ed /æb'stræktɪd/ *adj.* (*formal*) thinking deeply about sth and not paying attention to what is around you ▶ **ab·stract·ed·ly** *adv.*

ˌabstract ex'pressionism *noun* [U] a style and movement in abstract art that developed in New York in the middle of the 20th century and tries to express the feelings of the artist rather than showing a physical object ▶ **ˌabstract ex'pressionist** *noun*: *abstract expressionists like Jackson Pollock* **ˌabstract ex'pressionist** *adj.* [usually before noun]: *abstract expressionist art*

ab·strac·tion AW /æb'strækʃn/ *noun* **1** [C, U] (*formal*) a general idea not based on any particular real person, thing or situation; the quality of being abstract **2** [U] (*formal*) the state of thinking deeply about sth and not paying attention to what is around you **3** [U, C] (*technical*) the action of removing sth from sth else; the process of being removed from sth else: *water abstraction from rivers*

ab·strac·tion·ism /æb'strækʃnɪzəm/ *noun* [U] **1** (*technical*) the principles and practices of ABSTRACT art **2** the expression of ideas in an abstract way ▶ **ab·strac·tion·ist** *noun, adj.* [usually before noun]

ˌabstract 'noun *noun* (*grammar*) a noun, for example *goodness* or *freedom*, that refers to an idea or a general quality, not to a physical object ➲ compare COMMON NOUN, PROPER NOUN

ab·struse /əb'stru:s; æb-/ *adj.* (*formal*, often *disapproving*) difficult to understand: *an abstruse argument*

ab·surd /əb'sɜ:d; *NAmE* əb'sɜ:rd/ *adj.* **1** completely ridiculous; not logical and sensible SYN **ridiculous**: *That uniform makes the guards look absurd.* ◇ *Of course it's not true, what an absurd idea.* **2 the absurd** *noun* [sing.] things that are or that seem to be absurd: *He has a good sense of the absurd.* ▶ **ab·surd·ity** *noun* [U, C] (*pl.* **-ies**): *It was only later that she could see the absurdity of the situation.* **ab·surd·ly** *adv.* SYN **ridiculously**: *The paintings were sold for absurdly high prices.*

ab·surd·ism /əb'sɜ:dɪzəm; *NAmE* -'sɜ:rd-/ *noun* [U] the belief that humans exist in a world with no purpose or order ▶ **ab·surd·ist** *noun* **ab·surd·ist** *adj.* [usually before noun]: *absurdist literature*

ABTA /'æbtə/ *abbr.* Association of British Travel Agents (an organization in Britain that protects customers, for example by giving them back the money for their tickets if a travel agent goes BANKRUPT)

abun·dance /ə'bʌndəns/ *noun* [sing., U] **~ (of sth)** (*formal*) a large quantity that is more than enough

IDM **in abundance** in large quantities: *Fruit and vegetables grew in abundance on the island.*

abun·dant /ə'bʌndənt/ *adj.* (*formal*) existing in large quantities; more than enough SYN **plentiful**: *Fish are abundant in the lake.* ◇ *We have abundant evidence to prove his guilt.*

abun·dant·ly /ə'bʌndəntli/ *adv.* **1 ~ clear** very clear: *She made her wishes abundantly clear.* **2** in large quantities: *Calcium is found most abundantly in milk.*

abuse 🔑 *noun, verb*

■ ***noun*** /ə'bju:s/ **1** 🔑 [U, sing.] the use of sth in a way that is wrong or harmful SYN **misuse**: ***alcohol/drug/solvent abuse*** ◇ *The system of paying cash bonuses is* ***open to abuse*** (= might be used in the wrong way). ◇ **~ of sth** *He was arrested on charges of corruption and* ***abuse of power.*** ◇ *What she did was an abuse of her position as manager.* **2** 🔑 [U, pl.] unfair, cruel or violent treatment of sb: *child abuse* ◇ *sexual abuse* ◇ *reported abuses by the secret police* ◇ *She suffered years of physical abuse.* **3** 🔑 [U] rude and offensive remarks, usually made when sb is very angry SYN **insults**: *to* ***scream/hurl/shout abuse*** ◇ *a* ***stream/torrent of abuse***

■ ***verb*** /ə'bju:z/ **1** 🔑 **~ sth** to make bad use of sth, or to use so much of sth that it harms your health: *to* ***abuse alcohol/drugs*** ◇ *He systematically abused his body with heroin and cocaine.* **2** 🔑 **~ sth** to use power or knowledge unfairly or wrongly: *She abused her position as principal by giving jobs to her friends.* ◇ *He felt they had abused his trust by talking about him to the press* (= tricked him, although he had trusted them). **3** 🔑 **~ sb/sth** to treat a person or an animal in a cruel or violent way, especially sexually: *All the children had been physically and emotionally abused.* ◇ *He had abused his own daughter* (= had sex with her). ◇ *The boy had been sexually abused.* **4 ~ sb** to make rude or offensive remarks to or about sb SYN **insult**: *The referee had been threatened and abused.* ▶ **ab·user** *noun*: *a drug abuser* ◇ *a child abuser*

abu·sive /ə'bju:sɪv/ *adj.* **1** (of speech or of a person) rude and offensive; criticizing rudely and unfairly: ***abusive language/remarks*** ◇ *He became abusive when he was drunk.* **2** (of behaviour) involving violence: *an abusive relationship* ▶ **abu·sive·ly** *adv.*

abut /ə'bʌt/ *verb* (**-tt-**) [I, T] **~ (on/onto) sth** (*formal*) (of land or a building) to be next to sth or to have one side touching the side of sth: *His land abuts onto a road.*

abys·mal /ə'bɪzməl/ *adj.* extremely bad or of a very low standard SYN **terrible** ▶ **abys·mal·ly** *adv.*

abyss /ə'bɪs/ *noun* [usually sing.] (*formal* or *literary*) a very deep wide space or hole that seems to have no bottom: *Ahead of them was a gaping abyss.* ◇ (*figurative*) *an* ***abyss of ignorance/despair/loneliness*** ◇ (*figurative*) *The country is stepping back from the edge of an abyss.*

AC /ˌeɪ 'siː/ *abbr.* **1** (also **ac, a/c**) (*especially NAmE*) AIR CONDITIONING **2** ALTERNATING CURRENT ➲ compare DIRECT CURRENT

a/c (in writing) *abbr.* **1** ACCOUNT **2** AIR CONDITIONING

aca·cia /ə'keɪʃə/ (also **a'cacia tree**) *noun* a tree with yellow or white flowers. There are several types of acacia tree, some of which produce a sticky liquid used in making glue.

aca·demia AW /ˌækə'diːmiə/ (also *formal* or *humorous* **aca·deme** /'ækədiːm/) *noun* [U] the world of learning, teaching, research, etc. at universities, and the people involved in it

aca·dem·ic 🔑 AW /ˌækə'demɪk/ *adj., noun*

■ ***adj.*** **1** 🔑 [usually before noun] connected with education, especially studying in schools and universities: *The students return in October for the start of the new academic year.* ◇ *high/low academic standards* ◇ *an academic career* **2** 🔑 [usually before noun] involving a lot of reading and studying rather than practical or technical skills: ***academic subjects/qualifications*** **3** 🔑 good at subjects involving a lot of reading and studying: *She wasn't very academic and hated school.* **4** not connected to a real or practical situation and therefore not important: *It is a purely academic question.* ◇ *The whole thing's academic now—we can't win anyway.* ▸ **aca·dem·ic·al·ly** AW /-kli/ *adv.*: *You have to do well academically to get into medical school.*

■ ***noun*** a person who teaches and/or does research at a university or college

acad·em·ician /əˌkædə'mɪʃn; *NAmE* ˌækədə'mɪʃn/ *noun* a member of an academy (2)

ˌacademic 'year *noun* the period of the year during which students go to school or university

acad·emy AW /ə'kædəmi/ *noun* (*pl.* **-ies**) **1** a school or college for special training: *the Royal Academy of Music* ◇ *a* ***police/military academy*** **2** (usually **Academy**) a type of official organization which aims to encourage and develop art, literature, science, etc: *the Royal Academy of Arts* **3** a SECONDARY SCHOOL in Scotland **4** a private school in the US **5** a SECONDARY SCHOOL in England which receives some of its money from a private business or person instead of from the government

Aˌcademy A'ward™ (also **Oscar™**) *noun* one of the awards given every year by the US Academy of Motion Picture Arts and Sciences for achievement in the making of films/movies

Aca·dian /ə'keɪdiən/ *noun* **1** a French-speaking Canadian from New Brunswick, and parts of Quebec near it, Nova Scotia or Prince Edward Island **2** (in the US) a person from Louisiana whose family originally came from the French COLONY of Acadia in what is now Nova Scotia

a cap·pella /ˌæ kə'pelə; ˌɑː/ *adj.* (of music) for singing voices alone, without musical instruments ▸ **a cap·pella** *adv.*

ACAS /'eɪkæs/ *abbr.* (in Britain) Advisory, Conciliation and Arbitration Service (the organization that helps employers and employees settle disagreements)

ac·cede /ək'siːd/ *verb* [I] (*formal*) **1** ~ **(to sth)** to agree to a request, proposal, etc: *He acceded to demands for his resignation.* **2** ~ **(to sth)** to achieve a high position, especially to become king or queen: *Queen Victoria acceded to the throne in 1837.* ➲ see also ACCESSION

ac·cel·er·ate /ək'seləreɪt/ *verb* **1** [I, T] to happen or to make sth happen faster or earlier than expected: *Inflation continues to accelerate.* ◇ **~ sth** *Exposure to the sun can accelerate the ageing process.* **2** [I] (of a vehicle or person) to start to go faster: *The runners accelerated smoothly around the bend.* ◇ *The car accelerated to overtake me.* OPP **decelerate**

ac·cel·er·ation /əkˌselə'reɪʃn/ *noun* **1** [U, sing.] **~ (in sth)** an increase in how fast sth happens: *an acceleration in the rate of economic growth* **2** [U] the rate at which a vehicle increases speed: *a car with good acceleration* **3** [U] (*physics*) the rate at which the VELOCITY (= speed in a particular direction) of an object changes

ac·cel·er·ator /ək'seləreɪtə(r)/ *noun* **1** (*BrE*) (also **'gas pedal** *NAmE, BrE*) the PEDAL in a car or other vehicle that you press with your foot to control the speed of the engine ➲ COLLOCATIONS at DRIVING ➲ VISUAL VOCAB page V42 **2** (*physics*) a machine for making ELEMENTARY PARTICLES move at high speeds

ac'celerator board (also **ac'celerator card**) *noun* (*computing*) a CIRCUIT BOARD that can be put into a small computer to increase the speed at which it processes information

ac·cel·er·om·eter /əkˌselə'rɒmɪtə(r); *NAmE* -'rɑːm-/ *noun* (*physics*) an instrument for measuring ACCELERATION

ac·cent 🔑 *noun, verb*

■ ***noun*** /'æksent; -sənt/ **1** 🔑 a way of pronouncing the words of a language that shows which country, area or social class a person comes from: *a northern/Dublin/Indian/Scottish accent* ◇ *a* ***strong/broad accent*** (= one that is very noticeable) ◇ *She spoke English* ***with an accent.*** ➲ compare DIALECT **2** 🔑 the emphasis that you should give to part of a word when saying it SYN **stress**: *In 'today' the accent is on the second syllable.* **3** 🔑 a mark on a letter to show that it should be pronounced in a particular way: *Canapé has an accent on the 'e'.* **4** [sing.] a special importance that is given to sth SYN **emphasis**: *In all our products* ***the accent is on*** *quality.*

■ ***verb*** /æk'sent/ **~ sth** to emphasize a part of sth

ac·cent·ed /'æksentɪd/ *adj.* **1** spoken with a foreign accent: *He spoke heavily accented English.* **2** (*technical*) spoken with particular emphasis: ***accented vowels/syllables*** **3** (*technical*) (of a letter of the alphabet) written or printed with a special mark on it to show it should be pronounced in a particular way: ***accented characters***

ac·cen·tu·ate /ək'sentʃueɪt/ *verb* **~ sth** to emphasize sth or make it more noticeable ▸ **ac·cen·tu·ation** /əkˌsentʃu'eɪʃn/ *noun* [U]

ac·cept 🔑 /ək'sept/ *verb*

▸ OFFER/INVITATION **1** 🔑 [I, T] to take willingly sth that is offered; to say 'yes' to an offer, invitation, etc: *He asked me to marry him and I accepted.* ◇ **~ sth** *Please accept our sincere apologies.* ◇ *It was pouring with rain so I accepted his offer of a lift.* ◇ *She's decided not to accept the job.* ◇ **~ sth from sb** *He is charged with accepting bribes from a firm of suppliers.* ◇ **~ sth for sth** *She said she'd accept $15 for it.* OPP **refuse**

▸ RECEIVE AS SUITABLE **2** 🔑 [T] to receive sth as suitable or good enough: **~ sth** *This machine only accepts coins.* ◇ *Will you accept a cheque?* ◇ **~ sth for sth** *My article has been accepted for publication.*

▸ AGREE **3** 🔑 [T] to agree to or approve of sth: **~ sth** *They accepted the court's decision.* ◇ *He accepted all the changes we proposed.* ◇ **~ sth from sb** *She won't accept advice from anyone.* OPP **reject** ➲ SYNONYMS at AGREE

▸ RESPONSIBILITY **4** 🔑 [T] **~ sth** to admit that you are responsible or to blame for sth: *He accepts full responsibility for what happened.* ◇ *You have to accept the consequences of your actions.*

▸ BELIEVE **5** 🔑 [T] to believe that sth is true: **~ sth** *I don't accept his version of events.* ◇ **~ sth as sth** *Can we accept his account as the true version?* ◇ **~ that...** *I accept that this will not be popular.* ◇ **it is accepted that...** *It is generally accepted that people are motivated by success.* ◇ **it is accepted to be, have, etc. sth** *The workforce is generally accepted to have the best conditions in Europe.*

▸ DIFFICULT SITUATION **6** 🔑 [T] to continue in a difficult situation without complaining, because you realize that you cannot change it: **~ sth** *You just have to* ***accept the fact that*** *we're never going to be rich.* ◇ *Nothing will change as long as the workers continue to accept these appalling conditions.* ◇ **~ sth as sth** *They accept the risks as part of the job.* ◇

A

~ that... *He just refused to accept that his father was no longer there.*

▸ WELCOME **7** 🔑 [T] to make sb feel welcome and part of a group: **~ sb** *It may take years to be completely accepted by the local community.* ◇ **~ sb into sth** *She had never been accepted into what was essentially a man's world.* ◇ **~ sb as sth** *He never really accepted her as his own child.* OPP **reject**

▸ ALLOW SB TO JOIN **8** 🔑 [T] to allow sb to join an organization, attend an institution, use a service, etc: **~ sb** *The college he applied to has accepted him.* ◇ **~ sb into sth** *She was disappointed not to be accepted into the club.* ◇ **~ sb as sth** *The landlord was willing to accept us as tenants.* ◇ **~ sb to do sth** *She was accepted to study music.* OPP **reject**

ac·cept·able 🔑 /ək'septəbl/ *adj.* **1** 🔑 agreed or approved of by most people in a society: *Children must learn socially acceptable behaviour.* **2** 🔑 that sb agrees is of a good enough standard or allowed: *For this course a pass in English at grade B is acceptable.* ◇ *Air pollution in the city had reached four times the acceptable levels.* ◇ **~ to sb** *We want a political solution that is acceptable to all parties.* **3** 🔑 not very good but good enough: *The food was acceptable, but no more.* OPP **unacceptable** ▸ **ac·cept·abil·ity** /əkˌseptə'bɪləti/ *noun* [U] **ac·cept·ably** /-bli/ *adv.*

ac·cept·ance /ək'septəns/ *noun* **1** [U, C] the act of accepting a gift, an invitation, an offer, etc: *Please confirm your acceptance of this offer in writing.* ◇ *He made a short* ***acceptance speech/speech*** *of acceptance.* **2** [U] the act of agreeing with sth and approving of it: *The new laws have* ***gained widespread acceptance.*** **3** [U] the process of allowing sb to join sth or be a member of a group: *Your acceptance into the insurance plan is guaranteed.* ◇ *Social acceptance is important for most young people.* **4** [U] willingness to accept an unpleasant or difficult situation: *acceptance of death/suffering*

ac·cess 🔑 AW /'ækses/ *noun, verb*

■ ***noun*** [U] **1** 🔑 a way of entering or reaching a place: *The police* ***gained access*** *through a broken window.* ◇ **~ to sth** *The only access to the farmhouse is across the fields.* ◇ *Disabled visitors are welcome; there is good wheelchair access to most facilities.* ➲ compare EGRESS **2** 🔑 **~** (**to sth**) the opportunity or right to use sth or to see sb/sth: *Students must* ***have access*** *to good resources.* ◇ *You need a password to* ***get access*** *to the computer system.* ◇ *access to confidential information* ◇ *Journalists were* ***denied access*** *to the President.* ◇ *Many divorced fathers only have access to their children at weekends* (= they are allowed by law to see them only at weekends). ➲ compare VISITATION

■ ***verb*** **1 ~ sth** (*computing*) to open a computer file in order to get or add information **2 ~ sth** (*formal*) to reach, enter or use sth: *The loft can be accessed by a ladder.*

'access course *noun* (*BrE*) a course of education that prepares students without the usual qualifications, in order that they can study at university or college

ac·cess·ible AW /ək'sesəbl/ *adj.* **1** that can be reached, entered, used, seen, etc: *The remote desert area is accessible only by helicopter.* ◇ **~ to sb** *These documents are not accessible to the public.* **2** easy to understand: *Her poetry is always very accessible.* ◇ **~ to sb** *a programme making science more accessible to young people* **3** (of a person) easy to talk to and to get to know OPP **inaccessible** ▸ **ac·ces·si·bil·ity** AW /əkˌsesə'bɪləti/ *noun* [U]

ac·ces·sion /æk'seʃn/ *noun* **1** [U] **~** (**to sth**) the act of becoming a ruler of a country: *the accession of Queen Victoria to the throne* ➲ see also ACCEDE **2** [U] **~** (**to sth**) the act of becoming part of an international organization: *the accession of new member states to the EU in 2004* ◇ *the new* ***accession states*** *of the EU* **3** [C] (*technical*) a thing that is added to a collection of objects, paintings, etc. in a library or museum

ac·ces·sor·ize (*BrE* also **-ise**) /ək'sesəraɪz/ *verb* **~ sth** to add fashionable items or extra decorations to sth, especially to your clothes

ac·ces·sory /ək'sesəri/ *noun, adj.*

■ ***noun*** (*pl.* -ies) **1** [usually pl.] an extra piece of equipment that is useful but not essential or that can be added to sth else as a decoration: *bicycle accessories* ◇ *a range of furnishings and accessories for the home* **2** [usually pl.] a thing that you can wear or carry that matches your clothes, for example a belt or a bag ➲ VISUAL VOCAB pages V52, V53 **3** (*law*) a person who helps sb to commit a crime or who knows about it and protects the person from the police: *an* ***accessory before/after the fact*** (= before/after the crime was committed) ◇ **~ to sth** *He was charged with being an accessory to murder.*

■ ***adj.*** (*technical*) not the most important when compared to others: *the accessory muscles of respiration*

'access road *noun* a road used for driving into or out of a particular place ➲ compare SLIP ROAD

'access time *noun* [U, C] (*computing*) the time taken to obtain data stored on a computer

ac·ci·dent 🔑 /'æksɪdənt/ *noun* **1** 🔑 [C] an unpleasant event, especially in a vehicle, that happens unexpectedly and causes injury or damage: *a* ***car/road/traffic accident*** ◇ *He was killed* ***in an accident.*** ◇ *One in seven accidents is caused by sleepy drivers.* ◇ *The accident happened at 3 p.m.* ◇ *to* ***have an accident*** ◇ *a* ***serious/minor accident*** ◇ *a* ***fatal accident*** (= in which sb is killed) ◇ *accidents in the home* ◇ *a* ***climbing/riding accident*** ◇ *Take out* ***accident insurance*** *before you go on your trip.* ◇ *I didn't mean to break it—****it was an accident.*** **2** [C, U] something that happens unexpectedly and is not planned in advance: *Their early arrival was just an accident.* ◇ *It is* ***no accident*** *that men fill most of the top jobs in nursing.* ◇ *an* ***accident of birth/fate/history*** (= describing facts and events that are due to chance or circumstances) ➲ SYNONYMS at LUCK

IDM **ˌaccidents will 'happen** people say **accidents will happen** to tell sb who has had an accident, for example breaking sth, that it does not matter and they should not worry **by accident** 🔑 in a way that is not planned or organized: *We met by accident at the airport.* ◇ *Helen got into acting purely by accident.* OPP **deliberately, on purpose** ➲ more at CHAPTER, WAIT *v.*

ac·ci·den·tal 🔑 /ˌæksɪ'dentl/ *adj.* happening by chance; not planned: *a verdict of accidental death* ◇ *I didn't think our meeting was accidental—he must have known I would be there.* ▸ **ac·ci·den·tal·ly** 🔑 /-təli/ *adv.*: *As I turned around, I accidentally hit him in the face.* ◇ *The damage couldn't have been caused accidentally.*

ˌaccident and e'mergency (*abbr.* A & E) (*BrE*) *noun* [U] (*NAmE* **e'mergency room**) the part of a hospital where people who need urgent treatment are taken: *the hospital accident and emergency department* ➲ see also CASUALTY

'accident-prone *adj.* more likely to have accidents than other people

ac·claim /ə'kleɪm/ *verb, noun*

■ ***verb*** [usually passive] to praise or welcome sb/sth publicly: **~ sb/sth** *a* ***highly/widely acclaimed*** *performance* ◇ **~ sb/sth as sth** *The work was acclaimed as a masterpiece.*

■ ***noun*** [U] praise and approval for sb/sth, especially an artistic achievement: ***international/popular/critical acclaim***

ac·clam·ation /ˌæklə'meɪʃn/ *noun* [U] **1** (*formal*) loud and enthusiastic approval or welcome **2** (*technical*) the act of electing sb using a spoken not written vote: *The decision was taken* ***by acclamation.***

ac·cli·mate /'ækləmeɪt/ *verb* (*NAmE*) = ACCLIMATIZE ▸ **ac·cli·ma·tion** /ˌæklə'meɪʃn/ *noun* [U]

ac·cli·ma·tize (*BrE* also **-ise**) /ə'klaɪmətaɪz/ (*NAmE* also **ac·cli·mate**) *verb* [I, T] to get used to a new place, situation or climate: **~** (**to sth**) *Arrive two days early in order to acclimatize.* ◇ **~ yourself** (**to sth**) *She was fine once she had acclimatized herself to the cold.* ▸ **ac·cli·ma·tiza·tion, -isa·tion** /əˌklaɪmətaɪ'zeɪʃn; *NAmE* -tə'z-/ *noun* [U]

ac·col·ade /'ækəleɪd; ˌækə'leɪd/ *noun* (*formal*) praise or an award for an achievement that people admire

ac·com·mo·date AW /ə'kɒmədeɪt; *NAmE* ə'kɑːm-/ *verb* **1** [T] **~ sb** to provide sb with a room or place to sleep, live or sit: *The hotel can accommodate up to 500 guests.* **2** [T]

A

~ sb/sth to provide enough space for sb/sth: *Over 70 minutes of music can be accommodated on one CD.* **3** [T] **~ sth** (*formal*) to consider sth, such as sb's opinion or a fact, and be influenced by it when you are deciding what to do or explaining sth: *Our proposal tries to accommodate the special needs of minority groups.* **4** [T] **~ sb (with sth)** (*formal*) to help sb by doing what they want SYN **oblige**: *I have accommodated the press a great deal, giving numerous interviews.* **5** [I, T] **~ (sth/yourself) to sth** (*formal*) to change your behaviour so that you can deal with a new situation better: *I needed to accommodate to the new schedule.*

ac·com·mo·dat·ing /ə'kɒmədeɪtɪŋ; *NAmE* ə'kɑːm-/ *adj.* (*formal*) willing to help and do things for other people SYN **obliging**

ac·com·mo·da·tion 🔑 AW /əˌkɒmə'deɪʃn; *NAmE* əˌkɑːm-/ *noun*
1 🔑 [U] (*BrE*) a place to live, work or stay in: ***rented/temporary/furnished accommodation*** ◇ *Hotel accommodation is included in the price of your holiday.* ◇ *The building plans include much needed new office accommodation.* ◇ *First-class accommodation is available on all flights.* **2 accommodations** [pl.] (*NAmE*) somewhere to live or stay, often also providing food or other services: *More and more travelers are looking for bed and breakfast accommodations in private homes.* **3** [C, U] (*formal*) an agreement or arrangement between people or groups with different opinions which is acceptable to everyone; the process of reaching this agreement: *They were forced to reach an accommodation with the rebels.*

ac·com·pani·ment AW /ə'kʌmpənimənt/ *noun*
1 [C, U] **~ (to sth)** music that is played to support singing or another instrument: *traditional songs with piano accompaniment* **2** [C] **~ (to sth)** something that you eat, drink or use together with sth else: *The wine makes a good accompaniment to fish dishes.* **3** [C] **~ (to sth)** (*formal*) something that happens at the same time as another thing: *High blood pressure is a common accompaniment to this disease.*
IDM **to the accompaniment of sth 1** while a musical instrument is being played: *They performed to the accompaniment of guitars.* **2** while sth else is happening: *She made her speech to the accompaniment of loud laughter.*

ac·com·pan·ist /ə'kʌmpənɪst/ *noun* a person who plays a musical instrument, especially a piano, while sb else plays or sings the main part of the music

ac·com·pany 🔑 AW /ə'kʌmpəni/ *verb* (**ac·com·pan·ies, ac·com·pany·ing, ac·com·pan·ied, ac·com·pan·ied**)
1 🔑 **~ sb** (*formal*) to travel or go somewhere with sb: *His wife accompanied him on the trip.* **2** 🔑 **~ sth** to happen or appear with sth else: *strong winds accompanied by heavy rain* ◇ *Each pack contains a book and accompanying CD.* **3 ~ sb (at/on sth)** to play a musical instrument, especially a piano, while sb else sings or plays the main tune: *The singer was accompanied on the piano by her sister.*

ac·com·plice /ə'kʌmplɪs; *NAmE* ə'kɑːm-/ *noun* a person who helps another to commit a crime or to do sth wrong

ac·com·plish /ə'kʌmplɪʃ; *NAmE* ə'kɑːm-/ *verb* **~ sth** to succeed in doing or completing sth SYN **achieve**: *The first part of the plan has been safely accomplished.* ◇ *I don't feel I've accomplished very much today.* ◇ *That's it.* ***Mission accomplished*** (= we have done what we aimed to do).

ac·com·plished /ə'kʌmplɪʃt; *NAmE* ə'kɑːm-/ *adj.* very good at a particular thing; having a lot of skills: *an accomplished artist/actor/chef* ◇ *She was an elegant and accomplished woman.*

ac·com·plish·ment /ə'kʌmplɪʃmənt; *NAmE* ə'kɑːm-/ *noun* **1** [C] an impressive thing that is done or achieved after a lot of work SYN **achievement**: *It was one of the President's greatest accomplishments.* **2** [C, U] a skill or special ability: *Drawing and singing were among her many accomplishments.* ◇ *a poet of rare accomplishment* **3** [U] (*formal*) the successful completing of sth: *Money will be crucial to the accomplishment of our objectives.*

ac·cord /ə'kɔːd; *NAmE* ə'kɔːrd/ *noun, verb*
▪ ***noun*** a formal agreement between two organizations, countries, etc: *The two sides signed a* ***peace accord*** *last July.*
IDM **in accord (with sth/sb)** (*formal*) in agreement with: *This action would not be in accord with our policy.* **of your own ac'cord** without being asked, forced or helped: *He came back of his own accord.* ◇ *The symptoms will clear up of their own accord.* **with ˌone ac'cord** (*BrE, formal*) if people do sth **with one accord**, they do it at the same time, because they agree with each other
▪ ***verb*** (*formal*) **1** [T] to give sb/sth authority, status or a particular type of treatment: **~ sth to sb/sth** *Our society accords great importance to the family.* ◇ **~ sb/sth sth** *Our society accords the family great importance.* **2** [I] **~ (with sth)** to agree with or match sth: *These results accord closely with our predictions.*

ac·cord·ance /ə'kɔːdns; *NAmE* ə'kɔːrdns/ *noun*
IDM **in accordance with sth** (*formal*) according to a rule or the way that sb says that sth should be done: *in accordance with legal requirements*

ac·cord·ing·ly /ə'kɔːdɪŋli; *NAmE* ə'kɔːrd-/ *adv.* **1** in a way that is appropriate to what has been done or said in a particular situation: *We have to discover his plans and act accordingly.* **2** (used especially at the beginning of a sentence) for that reason SYN **therefore**: *The cost of materials rose sharply last year. Accordingly, we were forced to increase our prices.*

ac·cord·ing to 🔑 /ə'kɔːdɪŋ tə; *NAmE* ə'kɔːrdɪŋ/ *prep.*
1 🔑 as stated or reported by sb/sth: *According to Mick, it's a great movie.* ◇ *You've been absent six times according to our records.* ➲ LANGUAGE BANK at ILLUSTRATE **2** 🔑 following, agreeing with or depending on sth: *The work was done according to her instructions.* ◇ *Everything* ***went according to plan.*** ◇ *The salary will be fixed according to qualifications and experience.* IDM see COAT *n.*

Language Bank

according to

Reporting someone's opinion

- Photography is, **according to** Vidal, the art form of untalented people.
- **For** Vidal, photography is the art form of untalented people.
- His **view is that** photography is not art but merely the mechanical reproduction of images.
- Smith **takes the view that** photography is both an art and a science.
- **In** Brown's **view**, photography should be treated as a legitimate art in its own right.
- James **is of the opinion that** a good painter can always be a good photographer if he or she so decides.
- Emerson **believed that** a photograph should only reflect what the human eye can see.

➲ Language Banks at ARGUE, OPINION

ac·cor·dion /ə'kɔːdiən; *NAmE* ə'kɔːrd-/ *noun* a musical instrument that you hold in both hands to produce sounds. You press the two ends together and pull them apart and press buttons and/or keys to produce the different notes. ➲ see also PIANO ACCORDION

accordion

concertina

ac·cost /ə'kɒst; *NAmE* ə'kɔːst; ə'kɑːst/ *verb* **~ sb** (*formal*) to go up to sb and speak to them, especially in a way that is rude or threatening: *She was accosted in the street by a complete stranger.*

ac·count 0‐ /əˈkaʊnt/ *noun, verb*

■ ***noun***

▸ AT BANK **1** 0‐ (*abbr.* a/c) an arrangement that sb has with a bank, etc. to keep money there, take some out, etc: *I don't have a bank account.* ◇ *to have an* ***account at/with*** *a bank* ◇ *to* ***open/close an account*** ◇ *What's your account number please?* ◇ *I paid the cheque into my savings account.* ◇ *a joint account* (= one in the name of more than one person) ➲ COLLOCATIONS at FINANCE ➲ see also BUDGET ACCOUNT, CHECKING ACCOUNT, CURRENT ACCOUNT, DEPOSIT ACCOUNT

▸ BUSINESS RECORDS **2** 0‐ [usually pl.] a written record of money that is owed to a business and of money that has been paid by it: *to do the accounts* ◇ *the accounts department* ➲ see also EXPENSE ACCOUNT, PROFIT AND LOSS ACCOUNT

▸ WITH SHOP/STORE **3** (*BrE* also ˈ**credit account**) (*NAmE* also ˈ**charge account**) an arrangement with a shop/store or business to pay bills for goods or services at a later time, for example in regular amounts every month: *Put it on my account please.* ◇ *We have accounts with most of our suppliers.* ➲ SYNONYMS at BILL

▸ REGULAR CUSTOMER **4** (*business*) a regular customer: *The agency has lost several of its most important accounts.*

▸ COMPUTING **5** an arrangement that sb has with a company that allows them to use the Internet, send and receive messages by email, etc: *an* ***Internet/email account***

▸ DESCRIPTION **6** a written or spoken description of sth that has happened: *She gave the police a full account of the incident.* ➲ SYNONYMS at REPORT **7** an explanation or a description of an idea, a theory or a process: *the Biblical account of the creation of the world*

IDM **by/from all accounts** according to what other people say: *I've never been there, but it's a lovely place, by all accounts.* **by your own account** according to what you say yourself: *By his own account he had an unhappy childhood.* **give a good/poor acˈcount of yourself** (*BrE*) to do sth or perform well or badly, especially in a contest: *The team gave a good account of themselves in the match.* **of no/little acˈcount** (*formal*) not important **on account** if you buy sth or pay **on account**, you pay nothing or only a small amount immediately and the rest later **on sb's account** because of what you think sb wants: *Please don't change your plans on my account.* **on account of sb/sth** 0‐ because of sb/sth: *She retired early on account of ill health.* ➲ LANGUAGE BANK at BECAUSE OF **on no account** | **not on any account** (used to emphasize sth) not for any reason: *On no account should the house be left unlocked.* **on your own acˈcount 1** for yourself: *In 2006 Smith set up in business on his own account.* **2** because you want to and you have decided, not sb else: *No one sent me, I am here on my own account.* **on this/that account** (*formal*) because of the particular thing that has been mentioned: *Weather conditions were poor, but he did not delay his departure on that account.* **put/turn sth to good acˈcount** (*formal*) to use sth in a good or helpful way **take account of sth** | **take sth into account** to consider particular facts, circumstances, etc. when making a decision about sth: *The company takes account of environmental issues wherever possible.* ◇ *Coursework is taken into account as well as exam results.* ◇ *The defendant asked for a number of other offences to be taken into account.* ➲ more at BLOW *n.*, CALL *v.*, SETTLE *v.*

■ ***verb*** [usually passive] (*formal*) to have the opinion that sb/sth is a particular thing: **~ sb/sth + adj.** *In English law a person is accounted innocent until they are proved guilty.* ◇ **~ sb/sth + noun** *The event was accounted a success.*

IDM **there's no accounting for ˈtaste** (*saying*) used to say how difficult it is to understand why sb likes sb/sth that you do not like at all: *She thinks he's wonderful—oh well, there's no accounting for taste.*

PHR V **acˈcount for sth 1** 0‐ to be the explanation or cause of sth SYN **explain**: *The poor weather may have accounted for the small crowd.* ◇ *Oh well, that accounts for it* (= I understand now why it happened). **2** 0‐ to give an explanation of sth SYN **explain**: *How do you account for the show's success?* **3** 0‐ to be a particular amount or part of sth: *The Japanese market accounts for 35% of the company's revenue.* ➲ LANGUAGE BANK at PROPORTION **acˈcount for sb/sth 1** to know where sb/sth is or what has happened to them, especially after an accident: *All passengers have now been accounted for.* **2** (*informal*) to defeat or destroy sb/sth: *Our anti-aircraft guns accounted for five enemy bombers.* **acˈcount for sth (to sb)** to give a record of how the money in your care has been spent: *We have to account for every penny we spend on business trips.*

ac·count·able /əˈkaʊntəbl/ *adj.* [not usually before noun] responsible for your decisions or actions and expected to explain them when you are asked: **~ to sb** *Politicians are ultimately accountable to the voters.* ◇ **~ for sth** *Someone must be* ***held accountable*** *for the killings.* ▸ **ac·count·abil·ity** /əˌkaʊntəˈbɪləti/ *noun* [U]: (*formal*) *the accountability of a company's directors to the shareholders*

ac·count·ancy /əˈkaʊntənsi/ *noun* [U] the work or profession of an accountant

ac·count·ant /əˈkaʊntənt/ *noun* a person whose job is to keep or check financial accounts

acˈcount executive *noun* a business person, especially one working in advertising, who is responsible for dealing with one of the company's regular customers

ac·count·ing /əˈkaʊntɪŋ/ *noun* [U] the process or work of keeping financial accounts: *a career in accounting* ◇ *accounting methods*

acˌcounts ˈpayable *noun* [pl.] (*business*) money that is owed by a company

acˌcounts reˈceivable *noun* [pl.] (*business*) money that is owed to a company

ac·coutre·ments /əˈkuːtrəmənts/ (*US* also **ac·cou·ter·ments** /əˈkuːtərmənts/) *noun* [pl.] (*formal* or *humorous*) pieces of equipment that you need for a particular activity

ac·credit /əˈkredɪt/ *verb* **1** [usually passive] (*formal*) to believe that sb is responsible for doing or saying sth: **~ sth to sb** *The discovery of distillation is usually accredited to the Arabs of the 11th century.* ◇ **~ sb with sth** *The Arabs are usually accredited with the discovery of distillation.* **2** [usually passive] **~ sb to ...** (*technical*) to choose sb for an official position, especially as an AMBASSADOR: *He was accredited to Madrid.* **3 ~ sth/sb** to officially approve sth/sb as being of an accepted quality or standard: *Institutions that do not meet the standards will not be accredited for teacher training.*

ac·credit·ation /əˌkredɪˈteɪʃn/ *noun* [U] official approval given by an organization stating that sb/sth has achieved a required standard: *a letter of accreditation*

ac·credit·ed /əˈkredɪtɪd/ *adj.* [usually before noun] **1** (of a person) officially recognized as sth; with official permission to be sth: *our accredited representative* ◇ *Only accredited journalists were allowed entry.* **2** officially approved as being of an accepted quality or standard: *a fully* ***accredited school/university/course***

ac·cre·tion /əˈkriːʃn/ *noun* (*technical* or *formal*) **1** [C] a layer of a substance that is slowly added to sth **2** [U] the process of new layers being slowly added to sth

ac·crue /əˈkruː/ *verb* (*formal*) **1** [I] to increase over a period of time: *Interest will accrue if you keep your money in a savings account.* ◇ **~ (to sb) (from sth)** *economic benefits accruing to the country from tourism* **2** [T] **~ sth** to allow a sum of money or debts to grow over a period of time SYN **accumulate**: *The firm had accrued debts of over $6m.* ▸ **ac·crual** /əˈkruːəl/ *noun* [U, C]: *the accrual of interest*

ac·cul·tur·ate /əˈkʌltʃəreɪt/ *verb* [I, T] **~ (sb) (to sth)** (*formal*) to learn to live successfully in a different culture; to help sb to do this ▸ **ac·cul·tur·ation** /əˌkʌltʃəˈreɪʃn/ *noun* [U]

ac·cu·mu·late AW /əˈkjuːmjəleɪt/ *verb* **1** [T] **~ sth** to gradually get more and more of sth over a period of time

SYN **amass**: *I seem to have accumulated a lot of books.* ◇ *By investing wisely she accumulated a fortune.* ➲ SYNONYMS at COLLECT **2** [I] to gradually increase in number or quantity over a period of time **SYN** **build up**: *Debts began to accumulate.* ➲ SYNONYMS at COLLECT ▸ **ac·cu·mu·la·tion** **AW** /əˌkjuːmjəˈleɪʃn/ *noun* [U, C]: *the accumulation of wealth* ◇ *an accumulation of toxic chemicals*

ac·cu·mu·la·tive /əˈkjuːmjələtɪv/ *adj.* (*formal*) growing by increasing gradually: *the accumulative effects of pollution*

ac·cu·mu·la·tor /əˈkjuːmjəleɪtə(r)/ *noun* **1** (*computing*) a section of a computer that is used for storing the results of what has been calculated **2** (*BrE*) (*NAmE* **ˈstorage battery**) a large battery that you can fill with electrical power (= that you can RECHARGE) **3** (*BrE*) a bet on a series of races or other events, where the money won or originally bet is placed on the next race, etc.

ac·cur·acy **AW** /ˈækjərəsi/ *noun* [U] the state of being exact or correct; the ability to do sth skilfully without making mistakes: *They questioned the accuracy of the information in the file.* ◇ *She hits the ball with great accuracy.* **OPP** **inaccuracy**

ac·cur·ate 🔑 **AW** /ˈækjərət/ *adj.*
1 🔑 correct and true in every detail: *an accurate description/account/calculation* ◇ *accurate information/data* ◇ *Accurate records must be kept.* **2** 🔑 able to give completely correct information or to do sth in an exact way: *a highly accurate electronic compass* ◇ *accurate to within 3 mm* ◇ *My watch is not very accurate.* **3** 🔑 an **accurate** throw, shot, weapon, etc. hits or reaches the thing that it was aimed at **OPP** **inaccurate** ▸ **ac·cur·ate·ly** 🔑 **AW** *adv.*: *The article accurately reflects public opinion.* ◇ *You need to hit the ball accurately.*

ac·cur·sed /əˈkɜːsɪd; *NAmE* -ˈkɜːrs-/ *adj.* (*old-fashioned*) having a CURSE (= a bad magic SPELL) on it

ac·cus·ation /ˌækjuˈzeɪʃn/ *noun* [C, U] a statement saying that you think a person is guilty of doing sth wrong, especially of committing a crime; the fact of accusing sb: *I don't want to* ***make an accusation*** *until I have some proof.* ◇ *There was a hint of accusation in her voice.* ◇ **~ of sth** *accusations of corruption/cruelty/racism* ◇ **~ against sb** *No one believed her wild accusations against her husband.* ◇ **~ that...** *He denied the accusation that he had ignored the problems.*

ac·cusa·tive /əˈkjuːzətɪv/ *noun* (*grammar*) (in some languages) the form of a noun, a pronoun or an adjective when it is the DIRECT OBJECT of a verb, or connected with the DIRECT OBJECT: *In the sentence, 'I saw him today', the word 'him' is* ***in the accusative***. ➲ compare ABLATIVE, DATIVE, GENITIVE, NOMINATIVE, VOCATIVE ▸ **ac·cusa·tive** *adj.*

ac·cusa·tory /əˈkjuːzətəri; ˌækjuˈzeɪtəri; *NAmE* -tɔːri/ *adj.* (*formal*) suggesting that you think sb has done sth wrong

ac·cuse 🔑 /əˈkjuːz/ *verb* **~ sb (of sth)** to say that sb has done sth wrong or is guilty of sth: *to accuse sb of murder/theft* ◇ *She accused him of lying.* ◇ *The government was accused of incompetence.* ◇ (*formal*) *They* ***stand accused*** *of crimes against humanity.* ▸ **ac·cuser** *noun*

> **WORD FAMILY**
> accuse *verb*
> accusation *noun*
> accusing *adj.*
> accusatory *adj.*
> accused *noun*

the ac·cused /əˈkjuːzd/ *noun* (*pl.* **the ac·cused**) a person who is on trial for committing a crime: *The accused was found innocent.* ◇ *All the accused have pleaded guilty.* ➲ compare DEFENDANT

ac·cus·ing /əˈkjuːzɪŋ/ *adj.* showing that you think sb has done sth wrong: *an* ***accusing look/finger/tone*** ◇ *Her accusing eyes were fixed on him.* ▸ **ac·cus·ing·ly** *adv.*

ac·cus·tom /əˈkʌstəm/ *verb*
PHR V **acˈcustom yourself/sb to sth** to make yourself/sb familiar with sth or become used to it: *It took him a while to accustom himself to the idea.*

ac·cus·tomed /əˈkʌstəmd/ *adj.* **1** (rather *formal*) familiar with sth and accepting it as normal or usual **SYN** **used to**: **~ to sth** *to* ***become/get accustomed*** *to sth* ◇ *My eyes slowly* ***grew accustomed*** *to the dark.* ◇ **~ to doing sth** *She was a person accustomed to having eight hours' sleep a night.* **2** [usually before noun] (*formal*) usual **SYN** **habitual**: *He took his accustomed seat by the fire.* **OPP** **unaccustomed**

AC/DC /eɪ siː ˈdiː siː/ *adj.* (*slang*) = BISEXUAL

ace /eɪs/ *noun, adj., verb*
■ ***noun*** **1** a PLAYING CARD with a large single symbol on it, which has either the highest or the lowest value in a particular card game: *the* ***ace of spades/hearts/diamonds/clubs*** ➲ VISUAL VOCAB page V32 **2** (*informal*) a person who is very good at doing sth: *a soccer/flying ace* ◇ *an ace marksman* **3** (in TENNIS) a SERVE (= the first hit) that is so good that your opponent cannot reach the ball: *He served 20 aces in the match.*
IDM **an ace up your ˈsleeve** (*BrE*) (*NAmE* **an ace in the ˈhole**) (*informal*) a secret advantage, for example a piece of information or a skill, that you are ready to use if you need to **hold all the aces** to have all the advantages in a situation **play your ˈace** to use your best argument, etc. in order to get an advantage in a situation **within an ace of sth/of doing sth** (*BrE*) very close to sth: *We came within an ace of victory.*
■ ***adj.*** (*informal*) very good: *We had an ace time.*
■ ***verb*** **~ sth** (*informal, especially NAmE*) to be successful in sth: *He aced all his tests.*

acel·lu·lar /ˌeɪˈseljələ(r)/ *adj.* (*biology*) not consisting of or divided into cells

acer /ˈeɪsə(r)/ *noun* [C, U] a tree or plant that is often grown for its attractive leaves and bright autumn/fall colours

acerb·ic /əˈsɜːbɪk; *NAmE* əˈsɜːrb-/ *adj.* (*formal*) (of a person or what they say) critical in a direct and rather cruel way: *The letter was written in her usual acerbic style.* ▸ **acerb·ity** /əˈsɜːbəti; *NAmE* əˈsɜːrb-/ *noun* [U]

acet·amino·phen /əˌsiːtəˈmɪnəfen/ (*NAmE*) (*BrE* **para·ceta·mol**) *noun* [U, C] a drug used to reduce pain and fever

acet·ate /ˈæsɪteɪt/ *noun* **1** [U] a chemical made from acetic acid, used in making plastics, etc. **2** [U] a chemical used to make FIBRES which are used to make clothes, etc. **3** [C] a transparent plastic sheet that you can write or print sth on and show on a screen using an OVERHEAD PROJECTOR

acet·ic acid /əˌsiːtɪk ˈæsɪd/ *noun* [U] the acid in VINEGAR that gives it its taste and smell

acet·one /ˈæsɪtəʊn; *NAmE* -toʊn/ *noun* [U] a clear liquid with a strong smell used for cleaning things, making paint thinner and producing various chemicals

acetyl·ene /əˈsetəliːn/ (also **eth·yne**) *noun* [U] (*symb.* C_2H_2) a gas that burns with a very hot bright flame, used for cutting or joining metal

ach /ɑːx/ *exclamation* (*ScotE*) used to express the fact that you are surprised, sorry, etc.

ach·cha /ʌˈtʃɑː/ *exclamation* (*IndE, informal*) **1** used to show that the speaker agrees with, accepts, understands, etc. sth: *Achcha! We'll meet at eight.* **2** used to express surprise, happiness, etc.

ache /eɪk/ *verb, noun*
■ ***verb*** **1** [I] to feel a continuous dull pain **SYN** **hurt**: *I'm aching all over.* ◇ **~ from sth** *Her eyes ached from lack of sleep.* ◇ (*figurative*) *It makes my heart ache* (= it makes me sad) *to see her suffer.* ➲ SYNONYMS at HURT **2** [I, T] (*formal*) to have a strong desire for sb/sth or to do sth **SYN** **long**: **~ for sb/sth** *I was aching for home.* ◇ **~ to do sth** *He ached to see her.*
■ ***noun*** (often in compounds) a continuous feeling of pain in a part of the body: *Mummy, I've got a tummy ache.* ◇ *Muscular* ***aches and pains*** *can be soothed by a relaxing massage.* ◇ (*figurative*) *an ache in my heart* (= a continuous sad feeling) ➲ see also ACHY, BELLYACHE, HEARTACHE

A

achieve 0‑ AW /əˈtʃiːv/ *verb* **1** 0‑ [T] **~ sth** to succeed in reaching a particular goal, status or standard, especially by making an effort for a long time SYN **attain**: *He had finally achieved success.* ◇ *They could not achieve their target of less than 3% inflation.* **2** [T] **~ sth** to succeed in doing sth or causing sth to happen SYN **accomplish**: *I haven't achieved very much today.* ◇ *All you've achieved is to upset my parents.* **3** [I] to be successful: *Their background gives them little chance of achieving at school.* ▸ **achiev·able** AW *adj.*: *Profits of $20m look achievable.* ◇ *achievable goals* OPP **unachievable**

achieve·ment 0‑ AW /əˈtʃiːvmənt/ *noun* **1** 0‑ [C] a thing that sb has done successfully, especially using their own effort and skill: *the greatest scientific achievement of the decade* ◇ *It was a remarkable achievement for such a young player.* ◇ *They were proud of their children's achievements.* **2** 0‑ [U] the act or process of achieving sth: *the need to raise standards of achievement in education* ◇ *Even a small success gives you **a sense of achievement*** (= a feeling of pride).

achiever /əˈtʃiːvə(r)/ *noun* **1** a person who achieves a high level of success, especially in their career **2** (after an adjective) a person who achieves the particular level of success that is stated: *a low achiever*

Achil·les heel /əˌkɪliːz ˈhiːl/ *noun* [sing.] a weak point or fault in sb's character, which can be attacked by other people ORIGIN Named after the Greek hero **Achilles**. When he was a small child, his mother held him below the surface of the river Styx to protect him against any injury. She held him by his heel, which therefore was not touched by the water. Achilles died after being wounded by an arrow in the heel.

AˌchiI·les ˈten·don (also **Achil·les**) *noun* the TENDON that connects the muscles at the back of the lower part of the leg to the heel

ach·ing·ly /ˈeɪkɪŋli/ *adv.* (of qualities or feelings) very great and affecting you deeply: *an achingly beautiful song*

ach·kan /ˈʌʃkən/ *noun* a piece of men's clothing that reaches to the knees, with buttons down the front, worn in S Asia

achy /ˈeɪki/ *adj.* (*informal*) suffering from a continuous slight pain: *I feel all achy.* ◇ *an achy back*

acid 0‑ /ˈæsɪd/ *noun, adj.*
■ ***noun*** **1** 0‑ [U, C] (*chemistry*) a chemical, usually a liquid, that contains HYDROGEN and has a pH of less than seven. The HYDROGEN can be replaced by a metal to form a salt. Acids are usually sour and can often burn holes in or damage things they touch. ➲ compare ALKALI ➲ see also ACETIC ACID, AMINO ACID, ASCORBIC ACID, CITRIC ACID, HYDROCHLORIC ACID, LACTIC ACID, NITRIC ACID, NUCLEIC ACID, SULPHURIC ACID **2** [U] (*slang*) = LSD
■ ***adj.*** **1** (*technical*) that contains acid or has the essential characteristics of an acid; that has a pH of less than seven: *Rye is tolerant of poor, acid soils.* ➲ compare ALKALINE **2** that has a bitter sharp taste SYN **sour**: *acid fruit* ➲ SYNONYMS at BITTER **3** (of a person's remarks) critical and unkind SYN **sarcastic, cutting**: *an acid wit*

ˈacid house *noun* [U] a type of electronic music with a strong steady beat, often played at parties where some people take harmful drugs

acid·ic /əˈsɪdɪk/ *adj.* **1** very sour: *Some fruit juices are very acidic.* **2** containing acid: *acidic soil*

acid·ify /əˈsɪdɪfaɪ/ *verb* (**acid·ifies, acid·ify·ing, acid·ified, acid·ified**) [I, T] **~ (sth)** (*technical*) to become or make sth become an acid

acid·ity /əˈsɪdəti/ *noun* [U] the state of having a sour taste or of containing acid

ˌacid ˈjazz *noun* [U] a type of dance music that combines JAZZ, FUNK, SOUL, and HIP HOP

acid·ly /ˈæsɪdli/ *adv.* in an unpleasant or critical way: *'Thanks for nothing,' she said acidly.*

ˌacid ˈrain *noun* [U] rain that contains harmful chemicals from factory gases and that damages trees, crops and buildings ➲ VISUAL VOCAB page V6

ˌacid ˈtest (also **ˈlitmus test** especially in *NAmE*) *noun* [sing.] a way of deciding whether sth is successful or true: *The acid test of a good driver is whether he or she remains calm in an emergency.*

ackee (also **akee**) /ˈæki/ *noun* **1** [C] a type of tree that produces bright red fruit, originally from W Africa **2** [U] the fruit from this tree, which is poisonous to eat unless it is completely RIPE

ac·know·ledge 0‑ AW /əkˈnɒlɪdʒ; *NAmE* əkˈnɑːl-/ *verb*
▸ ADMIT **1** 0‑ to accept that sth is true: **~ sth** *She refuses to acknowledge the need for reform.* ◇ *a generally acknowledged fact* ◇ **~ that...** *I did not acknowledge that he had done anything wrong.* ◇ **~ sth to be, have, etc. sth** *It is generally acknowledged to be true.* ➲ SYNONYMS at ADMIT
▸ ACCEPT STATUS **2** 0‑ to accept that sb/sth has a particular authority or status SYN **recognize**: **~ sb/sth** *The country acknowledged his claim to the throne.* ◇ **~ sb/sth as sth** *He is widely acknowledged as the best player in the world.* ◇ **~ sb/sth to be, have, etc. sth** *He is widely acknowledged to be the best player in the world.*
▸ REPLY TO LETTER **3** **~ sth** to tell sb that you have received sth that they sent to you: *All applications will be acknowledged.* ◇ *Please acknowledge receipt of this letter.*
▸ SMILE/WAVE **4** **~ sb/sth** to show that you have noticed sb/sth by smiling, waving, etc: *I was standing right next to her, but she didn't even acknowledge me.*
▸ EXPRESS THANKS **5** **~ sth** to publicly express thanks for help you have been given: *I gratefully acknowledge financial support from several local businesses.*

ac·know·ledge·ment AW (also **ac·know·ledg·ment**) /əkˈnɒlɪdʒmənt; *NAmE* əkˈnɑːl-/ *noun* **1** [sing., U] an act of accepting that sth exists or is true, or that sth is there: *This report is an acknowledgement of the size of the problem.* ◇ *She gave me a smile of acknowledgement* (= showed that she had seen and recognized me). **2** [C, U] an act or a statement expressing thanks to sb; something that is given to sb as thanks: *The flowers were a small acknowledgement of your kindness.* ◇ *I was sent a free copy **in acknowledgement of** my contribution.* **3** [C] a letter saying that sth has been received: *I didn't receive an acknowledgement of my application.* **4** [C, usually pl.] a statement, especially at the beginning of a book, in which the writer expresses thanks to the people who have helped

acme /ˈækmi/ *noun* [usually sing.] (*formal*) the highest stage of development or the most excellent example of sth SYN **height**

acne /ˈækni/ *noun* [U] a skin condition, common among young people, that produces many PIMPLES (= spots), especially on the face and neck: *to **suffer from/have acne***

aco·lyte /ˈækəlaɪt/ *noun* **1** (*formal*) a person who follows and helps a leader **2** (*technical*) a person who helps a priest in some church ceremonies

acorn /ˈeɪkɔːn; *NAmE* -kɔːrn/ *noun* the small brown nut of the OAK tree, that grows in a base shaped like a cup IDM see OAK ➲ VISUAL VOCAB page V8

acous·tic /əˈkuːstɪk/ *adj.* (*NAmE* also **acous·tic·al** /əˈkuːstɪkl/) **1** related to sound or to the sense of hearing **2** [usually before noun] (of a musical instrument or performance) designed to make natural sound, not sound produced by electrical equipment ➲ VISUAL VOCAB page V31 ▸ **acous·tic·al·ly** /-kli/ *adv.*

acous·tics /əˈkuːstɪks/ *noun* **1** [pl.] (also **acoustic** [sing.]) the shape, design, etc. of a room or theatre that make it good or bad for carrying sound: *The acoustics of the new concert hall are excellent.* **2** [U] the scientific study of sound

ac·quaint /əˈkweɪnt/ *verb* **~ sb/yourself with sth** (*formal*) to make sb/yourself familiar with or aware of sth: *Please acquaint me with the facts of the case.* ◇ *You will first need to acquaint yourself with the filing system.*

ac·quaint·ance /əˈkweɪntəns/ *noun* **1** [C] a person that you know but who is not a close friend: *Claire has a wide circle of **friends and acquaintances**.* ◇ *He's just a business*

A

acquaintance. **2** [U, C] **~ (with sb)** (*formal*) slight friendship: *He hoped their acquaintance would develop further.* **3** [U, C] **~ with sth** (*formal*) knowledge of sth: *I had little acquaintance with modern poetry.*

IDM **make sb's acquaintance | make the acquaintance of sb** (*formal*) to meet sb for the first time: *I am delighted to make your acquaintance, Mrs Baker.* ◇ *I made the acquaintance of several musicians around that time.* **of your ac'quaintance** (*formal*) that you know: *No one else of my acquaintance was as rich or successful.* **on first ac'quaintance** (*formal*) when you first meet sb: *Even on first acquaintance it was clear that he was not 'the right type'.* ⇨ more at NOD *v.*

ac'quaintance rape *noun* [U, C] (*especially NAmE*) the crime of RAPING sb, committed by a person he or she knows

ac·quaint·ance·ship /ə'kweɪntənsʃɪp/ *noun* [U, C, usually sing.] (*formal*) a slight friendship with sb or knowledge of sth: *It was unfair to judge her on such a brief acquaintanceship.*

ac·quaint·ed /ə'kweɪntɪd/ *adj.* [not before noun] **1 ~ with sth** (*formal*) familiar with sth, having read, seen or experienced it: *The students are already acquainted with the work of Shakespeare.* ◇ *Employees should be fully acquainted with emergency procedures.* **2** not close friends with sb, but having met a few times before: *We got acquainted at the conference* (= met and started to get to know each other). ◇ **~ with sb** *I am well acquainted with her family.*

ac·qui·esce /ˌækwi'es/ *verb* [I] **~ (in/to sth)** (*formal*) to accept sth without arguing, even if you do not really agree with it: *Senior government figures must have acquiesced in the cover-up.*

ac·qui·es·cence /ˌækwi'esns/ *noun* [U] (*formal*) the fact of being willing to do what sb wants and to accept their opinions, even if you are not sure that they are right: *There was general acquiescence in the UN sanctions.* ▶ **ac·qui·es·cent** /-'esnt/ *adj.*

ac·quire 0‑ AW /ə'kwaɪə(r)/ *verb* (*formal*)
1 0‑ **~ sth** to gain sth by your own efforts, ability or behaviour: *She has acquired a good knowledge of English.* ◇ *He has acquired a reputation for dishonesty.* ◇ *I have recently* ***acquired a taste*** *for olives.* **2** 0‑ **~ sth** to obtain sth by buying or being given it: *The company has just acquired new premises.* ◇ *I've suddenly acquired a stepbrother.*

IDM **an acquired 'taste** a thing that you do not like much at first but gradually learn to like: *Abstract art is an acquired taste.*

ac·qui·si·tion AW /ˌækwɪ'zɪʃn/ *noun* **1** [U] the act of getting sth, especially knowledge, a skill, etc: *theories of child language acquisition* **2** [C] something that sb buys to add to what they already own, usually sth valuable: *His latest acquisition is a racehorse.* **3** [C, U] (*business*) a company, piece of land, etc. bought by sb, especially another company; the act of buying it: *They have made acquisitions in several EU countries.* ◇ *the acquisition of shares by employees*

ac·quisi·tive /ə'kwɪzətɪv/ *adj.* (*formal, disapproving*) wanting very much to buy or get new possessions ▶ **ac·quisi·tive·ness** *noun* [U]

ac·quit /ə'kwɪt/ *verb* (-tt-) **1 ~ sb (of sth)** to decide and state officially in court that sb is not guilty of a crime: *The jury acquitted him of murder.* OPP **convict** **2 ~ yourself well, badly, etc.** (*formal*) to perform or behave well, badly, etc: *He acquitted himself brilliantly in the exams.*

ac·quit·tal /ə'kwɪtl/ *noun* [C, U] an official decision in court that a person is not guilty of a crime: *The case resulted in an acquittal.* ◇ *The jury voted for acquittal.* OPP **conviction** ⇨ COLLOCATIONS at JUSTICE

acre /'eɪkə(r)/ *noun* a unit for measuring an area of land; 4 840 square yards or about 4 050 square metres: *3 000 acres of parkland* ◇ *a three-acre wood* ◇ (*informal*) *Each house has acres of space around it* (= a lot of space).

acre·age /'eɪkərɪdʒ/ *noun* [U, C] an area of land measured in acres

acrid /'ækrɪd/ *adj.* having a strong, bitter smell or taste that is unpleasant SYN **pungent**: *acrid smoke from burning tyres* ⇨ SYNONYMS at BITTER

acri·mo·ni·ous /ˌækrɪ'məʊniəs; *NAmE* -'moʊ-/ *adj.* (*formal*) (of an argument, etc.) angry and full of strong bitter feelings and words SYN **bitter**: *His parents went through an acrimonious divorce.* ▶ **acri·mo·ni·ous·ly** *adv.*

acri·mony /'ækrɪməni; *NAmE* -moʊni/ *noun* [U] (*formal*) angry bitter feelings or words: *The dispute was settled without acrimony.*

acro·bat /'ækrəbæt/ *noun* an entertainer who performs difficult acts such as balancing on high ropes, especially at a CIRCUS

acro·bat·ic /ˌækrə'bætɪk/ *adj.* involving or performing difficult acts or movements with the body: *acrobatic feats* ◇ *an acrobatic dancer* ▶ **acro·bat·ic·al·ly** /-kli/ *adv.*

acro·bat·ics /ˌækrə'bætɪks/ *noun* [pl.] acrobatic acts and movements: *acrobatics on the high wire* ◇ (*figurative*) *vocal acrobatics* (= performing skilfully with the voice when singing)

acro·nym /'ækrənɪm/ *noun* a word formed from the first letters of the words that make up the name of sth, for example 'AIDS' is an acronym for 'acquired immune deficiency syndrome'

acrop·olis /ə'krɒpəlɪs; *NAmE* ə'krɑːp-/ *noun* (in an ancient Greek city) a castle, or an area that is designed to resist attack, especially one on top of a hill

across 0‑ /ə'krɒs; *NAmE* ə'krɔːs; ə'krɑːs/ *adv., prep.*
■ ***adv.*** HELP For the special uses of **across** in phrasal verbs, look at the entries for the verbs. For example **come across** is in the phrasal verb section at **come.** **1** 0‑ from one side to the other side: *It's too wide. We can't swim across.* ◇ *The yard measures about 50 feet across.* **2** 0‑ in a particular direction towards or at sb/sth: *When my name was called, he looked across at me.* **3** 0‑ **across from** opposite: *There's a school just across from our house.* **4** (of an answer in a CROSSWORD) written from side to side: *I can't do 3 across.*
■ ***prep.*** **1** 0‑ from one side to the other side of sth: *He walked across the field.* ◇ *I drew a line across the page.* ◇ *A grin spread across her face.* ◇ *Where's the nearest bridge across the river?* **2** 0‑ on the other side of sth: *There's a bank right across the street.* **3** on or over a part of the body: *He hit him across the face.* ◇ *It's too tight across the back.* **4** in every part of a place, group of people, etc. SYN **throughout**: *Her family is scattered across the country.* ◇ *This view is common across all sections of the community.*

ac·ros·tic /ə'krɒstɪk; *NAmE* -'krɔːs-; -'krɑːs-/ *noun* a poem or other piece of writing in which particular letters in each line, usually the first letters, can be read downwards to form a word or words

acryla·mide /ə'krɪləmaɪd/ *noun* [U, C] a substance used in various industrial processes. Acrylamide is also found in food that has been cooked at high temperatures, and may be a cause of cancer.

acryl·ic /ə'krɪlɪk/ *adj., noun*
■ ***adj.*** made of a substance produced by chemical processes from a type of acid: ***acrylic paints/fibres*** ◇ *an acrylic sweater*
■ ***noun*** **1** [U] a type of FIBRE produced by chemical processes, used to make clothes, etc. **2** [C, usually pl.] a type of paint used by artists

ACT /ˌeɪ siː 'tiː/ *abbr.* American College Test (an exam that some HIGH SCHOOL students take before they go to college)

act 0‑ /ækt/ *noun, verb*
■ ***noun***
▸ STH THAT SB DOES **1** 0‑ [C] a particular thing that sb does: *a criminal act* ◇ **~ of sth** *an act of kindness* ◇ *acts of terrorism* ◇ **~ of sb** *The murder was the act of a psychopath.* ⇨ SYNONYMS at ACTION
▸ LAW **2** 0‑ [C] a law that has been passed by a parliament: *an Act of Congress* ◇ *the Banking Act 2009*
▸ PRETENDING **3** 0‑ [sing.] a way of behaving that is not sin-

A

cere but is intended to have a particular effect on others: *Don't take her seriously—it's all an act.* ◇ *You could tell she was just* **putting on an act**.

▸ IN PLAY/ENTERTAINMENT **4** [C] one of the main divisions of a play, an OPERA, etc: *a play in five acts* ◇ *The hero dies in Act 5, Scene 3.* **5** [C] one of several short pieces of entertainment in a show: *a* **circus/comedy/magic act** **6** [C] a performer or group of musicians: *They were one of rock's most impressive live acts.*

IDM ˌ**act of ˈGod** (*law*) an event caused by natural forces beyond human control, such as a storm, a flood or an EARTHQUAKE **be/get in on the act** (*informal*) to be/become involved in an activity that sb else has started, especially to get sth for yourself **do, perform, stage a disapˈpearing/ˈvanishing act** (*informal*) to go away or be impossible to find when people need or want you **get your ˈact together** (*informal*) to organize yourself and your activities in a more effective way in order to achieve sth: *He needs to get his act together if he's going to pass.* **a ˌhard/ˌtough act to ˈfollow** a person who is so good or successful at sth that it will be difficult for anyone else coming after them to be as good or successful **in the act (of doing sth)** while you are doing sth: *He was* **caught in the act** *of stealing a car.* ➲ more at CLEAN *v.*, READ *v.*

■ *verb*

▸ DO STH **1** 🔑 [I] to do sth for a particular purpose or in order to deal with a situation: *It is vital that we act to stop the destruction of the rainforests.* ◇ *The girl's life was saved because the doctors acted so promptly.* ◇ *He claims he acted in self-defence.*

▸ BEHAVE **2** 🔑 [I] to behave in a particular way: **+ adv.** *John's been acting very strangely lately.* ◇ **~ like sb/sth** *Stop acting like spoilt children!* ◇ **~ as if/though...** *She was acting as if she'd seen a ghost.* HELP In spoken English people often use **like** instead of **as if** or **as though** in this meaning, especially in *NAmE*: *She was acting like she'd seen a ghost.* This is not considered correct in written *BrE*.

▸ PRETEND **3** 🔑 [I] to pretend by your behaviour to be a particular type of person: **+ noun** *He's been acting the devoted husband all day.* ◇ **+ adj.** *I decided to act dumb.*

▸ PERFORM IN PLAY/MOVIE **4** 🔑 [I, T] to perform a part in a play or film/movie: *Have you ever acted?* ◇ *Most of the cast act well.* ◇ **~ sth** *Who's acting (the part of) Hamlet?* ◇ *The play was well acted.*

▸ PERFORM FUNCTION **5** [I] to perform a particular role or function: **~ as sth** *Can you act as interpreter?* ◇ **~ like sth** *hormones in the brain that act like natural painkillers*

▸ HAVE EFFECT **6** [I] **~ (on sth)** to have an effect on sth: *Alcohol acts quickly on the brain.* IDM see AGE *n.*, FOOL *n.*, OWN *v.*

PHR V ˈ**act for/on behalf of sb** to be employed to deal with sb's affairs for them, for example by representing them in court ˈ**act on/upon sth** to take action as a result of advice, information, etc: *Acting on information from a member of the public, the police raided the club.* ◇ *Why didn't you act on her suggestion?* ˌ**act sth↔ˈout 1** to perform a ceremony or show how sth happened, as if performing a play: *The ritual of the party conference is acted out in the same way every year.* ◇ *The children started to act out the whole incident.* **2** to act a part in a real situation: *She acted out the role of the wronged lover.* ˌ**act ˈup** (*informal*) **1** to behave badly: *The kids started acting up.* **2** to not work as it should: *How long has your ankle been acting up?*

act·ing /ˈæktɪŋ/ *noun, adj.*

■ *noun* [U] the activity or profession of performing in plays, films/movies, etc.

■ *adj.* [only before noun] doing the work of another person for a short time SYN **temporary**: *the acting manager*

ac·tin·ium /ækˈtɪniəm/ *noun* [U] (*symb.* Ac) a chemical element. Actinium is a RADIOACTIVE metal.

ac·tion 🔑 /ˈækʃn/ *noun, verb*

■ *noun*

▸ WHAT SB DOES **1** 🔑 [U] the process of doing sth in order to make sth happen or to deal with a situation: *The time has come for action if these beautiful animals are to survive.* ◇ *Firefighters* **took action** *immediately to stop the blaze spreading.* ◇ *What is the best* **course of action** *in the circumstances?* ◇ *She began to explain her* **plan of action** *to the group.* ➲ see also DIRECT ACTION, INDUSTRIAL ACTION **2** 🔑 [C] a thing that sb does: *Her quick action saved the child's life.* ◇ *Each of us must take responsibility for our own actions.*

▸ LEGAL PROCESS **3** 🔑 [C, U] a legal process to stop a person or company from doing sth, or to make them pay for a mistake, etc: *A libel action is being brought against the magazine that published the article.* ◇ *He is considering taking legal action against the hospital.*

▸ IN WAR **4** 🔑 [U] fighting in a battle or war: *military action* ◇ *soldiers killed* **in action**

▸ IN STORY/PLAY **5** [U] the events in a story, play, etc: *The action takes place in France.*

▸ EXCITING EVENTS **6** 🔑 [U] exciting events: *I like films with plenty of action.* ◇ *New York is* **where the action is**.

▸ EFFECT **7** [U] **~ of sth (on sth)** the effect that one substance or chemical has on another: *the action of sunlight on the skin*

▸ OF PART OF THE BODY **8** [U, C] (*technical*) the way a part of the body moves or functions: *a study of the action of the liver*

▸ OF MACHINE **9** [sing.] the MECHANICAL parts of a piano, gun, clock, etc. or the way the parts move ➲ see also PUMP-ACTION

Synonyms

action

measure • step • act • move

These are all words for a thing that sb does.

action a thing that sb does: *Her quick action saved the child's life.*

measure an official action that is done in order to achieve a particular aim: *Tougher measures against racism are needed.*

step one of a series of things that you do in order to achieve sth: *This was a first step towards a united Europe.*

act a thing that sb does: *an act of kindness*

ACTION OR ACT?

These two words have the same meaning but are used in different patterns. An **act** is usually followed by *of* and/or used with an adjective. **Action** is not usually used with *of* but is often used with *his, her, etc.*: *a heroic act of bravery* ◇ ~~*a heroic action of bravery*~~ ◇ *his heroic actions/acts during the war.* **Action** often combines with *take* but **act** does not: ~~*We shall take whatever acts are necessary.*~~

move (used especially in journalism) an action that you do or need to do to achieve sth: *They are waiting for the results of the opinion polls before deciding their next move.*

PATTERNS

- to **take** action/measures/steps
- to **make** a step/move
- a **heroic/brave/daring** action/step/act/move

IDM **actions speak louder than ˈwords** (*saying*) what a person actually does means more than what they say they will do **in ˈaction** 🔑 if sb/sth is **in action**, they are doing the activity or work that is typical for them: *Just press the button to see your favourite character in action.* ◇ *I've yet to see all the players in action.* **into ˈaction** 🔑 if you put an idea or a plan **into action**, you start making it happen or work: *The new plan for traffic control is being put into action on an experimental basis.* **out of ˈaction** not able to work or be used because of injury or damage: *Jon will be out of action for weeks with a broken leg.* ◇ *The photocopier is out of action today.* **a piece/slice of the ˈaction** (*informal*) a share or role in an interesting or exciting activity, especially in order to make money: *Foreign firms will all* *want a piece of the action if the new airport goes ahead.* ➲ more at EVASIVE, SPRING *v.*, SWING *v.*

■ ***verb* ~ sth** to make sure that sth is done or dealt with: *Your request will be actioned.*

ac·tion·able /'ækʃənəbl/ *adj.* giving sb a valid reason to bring a case to court

ac·tion·er /'ækʃənə(r)/ *noun* (*NAmE, informal*) = ACTION MOVIE

'action figure *noun* a DOLL representing a soldier or a character from a film/movie, TV show, etc.

'action film *noun* (*BrE*) = ACTION MOVIE

'action group *noun* (often as part of a name) a group that is formed to work for social or political change: *the Child Poverty Action Group*

'Action Man™ *noun* **1** a toy in the form of a soldier **2** an active and aggressive man: *The illness damaged his Action Man image.*

'action movie (*BrE* also **'action film**) (also *NAmE informal* **ac·tion·er**) *noun* a film/movie that has a lot of exciting action and adventure

'action-packed *adj.* full of exciting events and activity: *an action-packed weekend*

'action point *noun* a suggestion for action that must be taken, especially one that is made in a meeting

,action 'replay *noun* (*BrE*) **1** (*NAmE* **,instant 'replay**) part of sth, for example a sports game on television, that is immediately repeated, often more slowly, so that you can see a goal or another exciting or important moment again **2** an event or a situation that repeats sth that has happened before: *It was an action replay of the problems of his first marriage.*

'action research *noun* [U] studies done to improve the working methods of people who do a particular job or activity, especially in education

'action stations *noun* [pl.] the positions to which soldiers go to be ready for fighting

ac·ti·vate /'æktɪveɪt/ *verb* **~ sth** to make sth such as a device or chemical process start working: *The burglar alarm is activated by movement.* ◇ *The gene is activated by a specific protein.* ▶ **ac·ti·vation** /,æktɪ'veɪʃn/ *noun* [U]

ac·tive 🔑 /'æktɪv/ *adj., noun*

■ ***adj.***

▸ BUSY **1** 🔑 always busy doing things, especially physical activities: *Although he's nearly 80, he is still very active.* **OPP** **inactive**

▸ TAKING PART **2** 🔑 involved in sth; making a determined effort and not leaving sth to happen by itself: *They were both politically active.* ◇ ***active involvement/participation/support/resistance*** ◇ *She takes an **active part** in school life.* ◇ *The parents were active in campaigning against cuts to the education budget.* ◇ *They took active steps to prevent the spread of the disease.*

▸ DOING AN ACTIVITY **3** 🔑 doing sth regularly; functioning: *sexually active teenagers* ◇ *animals that are active only at night* ◇ *The virus is still active in the blood.* ◇ *an active volcano* (= likely to ERUPT) **OPP** **inactive** ➲ compare DORMANT

▸ LIVELY **4** lively and full of ideas: *That child has a very active imagination.*

▸ CHEMICAL **5** having or causing a chemical effect: *What is the active ingredient in aspirin?* **OPP** **inactive**

▸ GRAMMAR **6** connected with a verb whose subject is the person or thing that performs the action: *In 'He was driving the car', the verb is active.* ➲ compare PASSIVE

▶ **ac·tive·ly** 🔑 *adv.*: *Your proposal is being actively considered.* ◇ *She was actively looking for a job.*

■ ***noun*** (also **'active voice**) [sing.] the form of a verb in which the subject is the person or thing that performs the action ➲ compare PASSIVE

'active list *noun* **1** a list of people that an organization may contact at any time, offering a service, providing information, or asking them to do sth: *Please email us to be removed from our active list of blood donors.* **2** a list of officers or former officers connected to one of the armed forces who can be called for duty

,active 'service (*NAmE* also **,active 'duty**) *noun* [U] the work of a member of the armed forces, especially during a war: *troops on active service*

ac·tiv·ist /'æktɪvɪst/ *noun* a person who works to achieve political or social change, especially as a member of an organization with particular aims: *gay activists* ▶ **ac·tiv·ism** /'æktɪvɪzəm/ *noun* [U]

ac·tiv·ity 🔑 /æk'tɪvəti/ *noun* (*pl.* -ies)

1 🔑 [U] a situation in which sth is happening or a lot of things are being done: *economic activity* ◇ *The streets were noisy and full of activity.* ◇ *Muscles contract and relax during physical activity.* ➲ compare INACTIVITY **2** 🔑 [C, usually pl.] a thing that you do for interest or pleasure, or in order to achieve a particular aim: ***leisure/outdoor/classroom activities*** ◇ *The club provides a wide variety of activities including tennis, swimming and squash.* ◇ ***illegal/criminal activities***

actor 🔑 /'æktə(r)/ *noun*

a person who performs on the stage, on television or in films/movies, especially as a profession

,actor-'manager *noun* an actor who is in charge of a theatre company and acts in the plays that they perform

ac·tress 🔑 /'æktrəs/ *noun*

a woman who performs on the stage, on television or in films/movies, especially as a profession **HELP** Many women now prefer to be called **actors**, although when the context is not clear, **an actor** is usually understood to refer to a man. ➲ note at GENDER

ac·tual 🔑 /'æktʃuəl/ *adj.* [only before noun]

1 🔑 used to emphasize sth that is real or exists in fact: *What were his actual words?* ◇ *The actual cost was higher than we expected.* ◇ *James looks younger than his wife but **in actual fact*** (= really) *he is five years older.* **2** 🔑 used to emphasize the most important part of sth: *The wedding preparations take weeks but the actual ceremony takes less than an hour.*

Which Word?

actual / current / present

■ **Actual** does not mean **current** or **present**. It means 'real' or 'exact', and is often used in contrast with something that is not seen as real or exact: *I need the actual figures, not an estimate.*

■ **Present** means 'existing or happening now': *How long have you been in your present job?*

■ **Current** also means 'existing or happening now', but can suggest that the situation is temporary: *The factory cannot continue its current level of production.*

■ **Actually** does not mean 'at the present time'. Use **currently, at present** or **at the moment** instead.

➲ note at PRESENTLY

,actual ,bodily 'harm *noun* [U] (*abbr.* ABH) (*BrE, law*) the crime of causing sb physical injury ➲ compare GRIEVOUS BODILY HARM

ac·tu·al·ity /,æktʃu'æləti/ *noun* (*pl.* -ies) (*formal*) **1** [U] the state of sth existing in reality: *The building looked as impressive **in actuality** as it did in photographs.* **2** [C, usually pl.] things that exist **SYN** **facts, realities**: *the grim actualities of prison life*

ac·tu·al·ize (*BrE* also **-ise**) /'æktʃuəlaɪz/ *verb* **~ sth** to make sth real; to make sth happen: *He finally actualized his dream.*

ac·tu·al·ly 🔑 /'æktʃuəli/ *adv.*

1 🔑 used in speaking to emphasize a fact or a comment, or that sth is really true: *What did she actually say?* ◇ *It's not actually raining now.* ◇ *That's the only reason I'm actually going.* ◇ *There are lots of people there who can actually help you.* ◇ *I didn't want to say anything without actually reading the letter first.* **2** 🔑 used to show a contrast between what is true and what sb believes, and to show surprise about

A

this contrast: *It was actually quite fun after all.* ◇ *The food was not actually all that expensive.* ◇ *Our turnover actually increased last year.* **3** used to correct sb in a polite way: *We're not American, actually. We're Canadian.* ◇ *Actually, it would be much more sensible to do it later.* ◇ *They're not married, actually.* **4** used to get sb's attention, to introduce a new topic or to say sth that sb may not like, in a polite way: *Actually, I'll be a bit late home.* ◇ *Actually, I'm busy at the moment—can I call you back?* ➲ note at ACTUAL

ac·tu·ary /'æktʃuəri; *NAmE* -eri/ *noun* (*pl.* -ies) a person whose job involves calculating insurance risks and payments for insurance companies by studying how frequently accidents, fires, deaths, etc. happen ▸ **ac·tu·ar·ial** /ˌæktʃu'eəriəl; *NAmE* -'eriəl/ *adj.*

ac·tu·ate /'æktʃueɪt/ *verb* (*formal*) **1 ~ sth** to make a machine or device start to work SYN **activate** **2** [usually passive] **~ sb** to make sb behave in a particular way SYN **motivate**: *He was actuated entirely by malice.*

acu·ity /ə'kju:əti/ *noun* [U] (*formal*) the ability to think, see or hear clearly

acu·men /'ækjəmən; ə'kju:mən/ *noun* [U] the ability to understand and decide things quickly and well: ***business/commercial/financial acumen***

acu·pres·sure /'ækjupreʃə(r)/ (also **shi·atsu**) *noun* [U] a form of medical treatment, originally from Japan, in which pressure is applied to particular parts of the body using the fingers

acu·punc·ture /'ækjupʌŋktʃə(r)/ *noun* [U] a Chinese method of treating pain and illness using special thin needles which are pushed into the skin in particular parts of the body

acu·punc·tur·ist /'ækjupʌŋktʃərɪst/ *noun* a person who is trained to perform acupuncture

acute /ə'kju:t/ *adj.* **1** very serious or severe: *There is an acute shortage of water.* ◇ *acute pain* ◇ *the world's acute environmental problems* ◇ *Competition for jobs is acute.* **2** an acute illness is one that has quickly become severe and dangerous: *acute appendicitis* OPP **chronic** **3** (of the senses) very sensitive and well developed SYN **keen**: *Dogs have an acute sense of smell.* **4** intelligent and quick to notice and understand things: *He is an acute observer of the social scene.* ◇ *Her judgement is acute.* **5** (*geometry*) (of an angle) less than 90° ▸ **acute·ness** *noun* [U]

aˌcute 'accent *noun* the mark placed over a vowel to show how it should be pronounced, as over the *e* in *fiancé* ➲ compare CIRCUMFLEX, GRAVE[2], TILDE, UMLAUT

aˌcute 'angle *noun* an angle of less than 90° ➲ VISUAL VOCAB page V58 ➲ compare OBTUSE ANGLE, REFLEX ANGLE, RIGHT ANGLE

acute·ly /ə'kju:tli/ *adv.* **1 ~ aware/conscious** noticing or feeling sth very strongly: *I am acutely aware of the difficulties we face.* **2** (describing unpleasant feelings) very; very strongly: *acutely embarrassed*

-acy ➲ -CY

acyc·lic /ˌeɪ'saɪklɪk/ *adj.* **1** (*technical*) not occurring in cycles **2** (*chemistry*) (of a COMPOUND or MOLECULE) containing no rings of atoms

AD (*BrE*) (*NAmE* **A.D.**) /ˌeɪ 'di:/ *abbr.* used in the Christian CALENDAR to show a particular number of years since the year when Christ was believed to have been born (from Latin 'Anno Domini'): *in (the year) AD 55* ◇ *in 55 AD* ◇ *in the fifth century AD* ➲ compare AH, BC, BCE, CE

ad /æd/ *noun* (*informal*) = ADVERTISEMENT: *We put an ad in the local paper.* ◇ *an ad for a new chocolate bar* ➲ SYNONYMS at ADVERTISEMENT ➲ see also BANNER AD

adage /'ædɪdʒ/ *noun* a well-known phrase expressing a general truth about people or the world SYN **saying**

ada·gio /ə'dɑ:dʒiəʊ; *NAmE* -dʒioʊ/ *noun* (*pl.* -os) (*music*) a piece of music to be played slowly ▸ **ada·gio** *adj., adv.*

Adam /'ædəm/ *noun* IDM see KNOW *v.*

ad·am·ant /'ædəmənt/ *adj.* determined not to change your mind or to be persuaded about sth: *Eva was adamant that she would not come.* ▸ **ad·am·ant·ly** *adv.*: *His family were adamantly opposed to the marriage.*

ad·am·ant·ine /ˌædə'mæntaɪn/ *adj.* (*literary*) very strong and impossible to break

ˌAdam's 'apple *noun* the lump at the front of the throat that sticks out, particularly in men, and moves up and down when you swallow

adapt AW /ə'dæpt/ *verb* **1** [T] to change sth in order to make it suitable for a new use or situation SYN **modify**: **~ sth** *These styles can be adapted to suit individual tastes.* ◇ **~ sth for sth** *Most of these tools have been specially adapted for use by disabled people.* **2** [I, T] to change your behaviour in order to deal more successfully with a new situation SYN **adjust**: *It's amazing how soon you adapt.* ◇ *The organisms were forced to adapt in order to survive.* ◇ **~ to sth** *We have had to adapt quickly to the new system.* ◇ *A large organization can be slow to adapt to change.* ◇ **~ yourself to sth** *It took him a while to adapt himself to his new surroundings.* **3** [T] **~ sth (for sth) (from sth)** to change a book or play so that it can be made into a play, film/movie, television programme, etc: *Three of her novels have been adapted for television.*

adapt·able AW /ə'dæptəbl/ *adj.* (*approving*) able to change or be changed in order to deal successfully with new situations: *Older workers can be as adaptable and quick to learn as anyone else.* ◇ *Successful businesses are highly adaptable to economic change.* ▸ **adapt·abil·ity** AW /əˌdæptə'bɪləti/ *noun* [U]

adap·ta·tion AW /ˌædæp'teɪʃn/ (also *less frequent* **adap·tion** /ə'dæpʃn/) *noun* **1** [C] a film/movie, book or play that is based on a particular piece of work but that has been changed for a new situation: *a screen adaptation of Shakespeare's 'Macbeth'* **2** [U] the process of changing sth, for example your behaviour, to suit a new situation: *the adaptation of desert species to the hot conditions*

adap·tive AW /ə'dæptɪv/ *adj.* (*technical*) concerned with changing; able to change when necessary in order to deal with different situations

adap·tor (also **adap·ter**) /ə'dæptə(r)/ *noun* **1** a device for connecting pieces of electrical equipment that were not designed to fit together **2** (*BrE*) a device for connecting more than one piece of equipment to the same SOCKET (= a place in the wall where equipment is connected to the electricity supply)

ADC /ˌeɪ di: 'si:/ *abbr.* AIDE-DE-CAMP

add /æd/ *verb* **1** [T] to put sth together with sth else so as to increase the size, number, amount, etc: **~ sth** *Next add the flour.* ◇ *The juice contains no added sugar.* ◇ *The plan has the added (= extra) advantage of bringing employment to rural areas.* ◇ **~ sth to sth** *A new wing was added to the building.* ◇ *Shall I add your name to the list?* **2** [I, T] to put numbers or amounts together to get a total: **~ A to B** *Add 9 to the total.* ◇ **~ A and B together** *If you add all these amounts together you get a huge figure.* OPP **subtract** **3** [T] to say sth more; to make a further remark: **+ speech** *'And don't be late,' she added.* ◇ **~ sth (to sth)** *I have nothing to add to my earlier statement.* ◇ **~ that...** *He added that they would return a week later.* **4** [T] **~ sth (to sth)** to give a particular quality to an event, a situation, etc: *The suite will add a touch of class to your bedroom.*

IDM **add ˌinsult to 'injury** to make a bad relationship with sb worse by offending them even more **'added to this...** | **'add to this...** used to introduce another fact that helps to emphasize a point you have already made: *Add to this the excellent service and you can see why it's the most popular hotel on the island.*

PHR V **ˌadd sth↔'in** to include sth with sth else: *Remember to add in the cost of drinks.* **ˌadd sth↔'on (to sth)** to include or attach sth extra: *A service charge of 15% was added on to the bill.* ➲ related noun ADD-ON **'add to sth** to increase sth in size, number, amount, etc: *The bad weather only added to our difficulties.* ◇ *The house has been added to (= new rooms, etc. have been built on to it) from time to time.* **ˌadd 'up** (*informal*) **1** (especially in negative sentences) to seem reasonable; to make sense: *His story just doesn't add up.* **2** (not used in the progressive tenses) to increase by small amounts until there is a large total: *When you're feeding a family of six the bills soon add up.* **ˌadd ˈup | ˌadd sth↔ˈup** 🔑 to calculate the total of two or more numbers or amounts: *The waiter can't add up.* ◇ *Add up all the money I owe you.* **ˌadd ˈup to sth 1** 🔑 to make a total amount of sth: *The numbers add up to exactly 100.* **2** to lead to a particular result; to show sth **SYN amount to sth**: *These clues don't really add up to very much* (= give us very little information).

ADD /ˌeɪ diː ˈdiː/ *abbr.* ATTENTION DEFICIT DISORDER

ad·den·dum /əˈdendəm/ *noun* (*pl.* **ad·denda** /-də/) (*formal*) a section of extra information that is added to sth, especially to a book

adder /ˈædə(r)/ *noun* a small poisonous snake, often with diamond-shaped marks on its back. Adders are the only poisonous snakes in Britain.

ad·dict /ˈædɪkt/ *noun* **1** a person who is unable to stop taking harmful drugs: *a* ***heroin/drug/nicotine addict*** **2** a person who is very interested in sth and spends a lot of their free time on it: *a video game addict*

ad·dict·ed /əˈdɪktɪd/ *adj.* [not before noun] **1 ~ (to sth)** unable to stop taking harmful drugs, or using or doing sth as a habit: *to become addicted to drugs/gambling* **2 ~ (to sth)** spending all your free time doing sth because you are so interested in it: *He's addicted to computer games.*

ad·dic·tion /əˈdɪkʃn/ *noun* [U, C] the condition of being addicted to sth: *cocaine addiction* ◇ **~ to sth** *He is now fighting his addiction to alcohol.* ➲ COLLOCATIONS at ILL

ad·dict·ive /əˈdɪktɪv/ *adj.* **1** if a drug is **addictive**, it makes people unable to stop taking it: *Heroin is highly addictive.* **2** if an activity or type of behaviour is **addictive**, people need to do it as often as possible because they enjoy it: *I find jogging very addictive.*

ˈadd-in *noun* (*computing*) **1** a computer program that can be added to a larger program to allow it do more things **2** = EXPANSION CARD ▶ **ˈadd-in** *adj.* [only before noun]: *add-in software*

Language Bank

addition

Adding another item

- Bilingual children do better in IQ tests than children who speak only one language. **In addition/What is more**, they seem to find it easier to learn third or even fourth languages.
- Learning another language **not only** improves children's job prospects in later life, **but also** boosts their self-esteem.
- Teaching children a second language improves their job prospects in later life. **Other** benefits **include** increased self-esteem and greater tolerance of other cultures.
- **Another/One further/One additional** reason for encouraging bilingual education is that it boosts children's self-esteem.
- Studies suggest that bilingual children find it easier to learn additional languages. There is, **moreover**, increasing evidence that bilingual children perform better across a range of school subjects, not just foreign languages.
- His claim that children find bilingual education confusing is based on very little evidence. **Moreover**, the evidence he does provide is seriously flawed.
- Research has shown that first-language development is not impeded by exposure to a second language. **Furthermore**, there is no evidence to support the claim that children find bilingual education confusing.

add·ition 🔑 /əˈdɪʃn/ *noun*
1 🔑 [U] the process of adding two or more numbers together to find their total: *children learning addition and subtraction* **OPP subtraction 2** 🔑 [C] **~ (to sth)** a thing that is added to sth else: *the latest addition to our range of cars* ◇ *an addition to the family* (= another child) **3** 🔑 [U] **~ (of sth)** the act of adding sth to sth else: *Pasta's basic ingredients are flour and water, sometimes* ***with the addition of*** *eggs or oil.* **4** (*NAmE*) (*BrE* **extension**) [C] **~ (to sth)** a new part that is added to a building: *architects who specialize in home additions*

IDM in addition (to sb/sth) 🔑 used when you want to mention another person or thing after sth else: *In addition to these arrangements, extra ambulances will be on duty until midnight.* ◇ *There is, in addition, one further point to make.*

add·ition·al 🔑 /əˈdɪʃənl/ *adj.*
more than was first mentioned or is usual **SYN extra**: *additional resources/funds/security* ◇ *The government provided an additional £25 million to expand the service.* ▶ **add·ition·al·ly** /-ʃənəli/ *adv.* **SYN in addition**: *Additionally, the bus service will run on Sundays, every two hours.*

addi·tive /ˈædətɪv/ *noun* a substance that is added in small amounts to sth, especially food, in order to improve it, give it colour, make it last longer, etc: *food additives* ◇ *additive-free orange juice* ◇ *chemical additives in petrol* ➲ COLLOCATIONS at DIET

addle /ˈædl/ *verb* **~ sth** to make sb unable to think clearly; to confuse sb: *Being in love must have addled your brain.*

ad·dled /ˈædld/ *adj.* **1** (*old-fashioned*) confused; unable to think clearly: *his addled brain* **2** (*BrE*) (of an egg) not fresh; bad to eat

ˈadd-on *noun* a thing that is added to sth else: *The company offers scuba-diving as an add-on to the basic holiday price.* ◇ *add-on software* (= added to a computer)

ad·dress 🔑 *noun, verb*
▪ **noun** /əˈdres; *NAmE* əˈdres; ˈædres/ **1** 🔑 [C] details of where sb lives or works and where letters, etc. can be sent: *What's your* ***name and address***? ◇ *I'll give you my address and phone number.* ◇ *Is that your* ***home address***? ◇ *Please note my* ***change of address***. ◇ *Police found him at an address* (= a house or flat/apartment) *in West London.* ◇ *people* ***of no fixed address*** (= with no permanent home) ➲ see also FORWARDING ADDRESS **2** 🔑 [C] (*computing*) a series of words and symbols that tells you where you can find sth using a computer, for example on the Internet: *What's your* ***email address***? ◇ *The project has a new* ***website address***. **3** [C] a formal speech that is made in front of an audience: *tonight's televised presidential address* ➲ SYNONYMS at SPEECH ➲ COLLOCATIONS at VOTE **4** [U] **form/mode of ~** the correct title, etc. to use when you talk to sb
▪ **verb** /əˈdres/ **1** 🔑 [usually passive] to write on an envelope, etc. the name and address of the person, company, etc. that you are sending it to by mail: **~ sth** *The letter was correctly addressed, but delivered to the wrong house.* ◇ **~ sth to sb/sth** *Address your application to the Personnel Manager.* ➲ compare READDRESS ➲ see also SAE, SASE **2** to make a formal speech to a group of people: *to address a meeting* **3** (*formal*) to say sth directly to sb: **~ sb** *I was surprised when he addressed me in English.* ◇ **~ sth to sb** *Any questions should be addressed to your teacher.* **4 ~ sb (as sth)** to use a particular name or title for sb when you speak or write to them: *The judge should be addressed as 'Your Honour'.* **5** (*formal*) to think about a problem or a situation and decide how you are going to deal with it: **~ sth** *Your essay does not address the real issues.* ◇ **~ yourself to sth** *We must address ourselves to the problem of traffic pollution.*

ad·dress·able /əˈdresəbl/ *adj.* **1** (of a problem or situation) that can be addressed: *Let's start with the more easily addressable issues.* **2** (*computing*) (of a part of a computer system) that is identified using its own address

adˈdress bar *noun* a line near the top of a page on an Internet BROWSER where you can type in the address of a website or where the website address is displayed

A

ad'dress book *noun* **1** a book in which you keep addresses, phone numbers, etc. **2** a computer file where you store email and Internet addresses

ad·dress·ee /ˌædreˈsiː/ *noun* a person that a letter, etc. is addressed to

ad·duce /əˈdjuːs; *NAmE* əˈduːs/ *verb* [often passive] **~ sth** (*formal*) to provide evidence, reasons, facts, etc. in order to explain sth or to show that sth is true SYN **cite**: *Several factors have been adduced to explain the fall in the birth rate.*

ad·duct·or /əˈdʌktə(r)/ (also **ad'ductor muscle**) *noun* (*anatomy*) a muscle that moves a body part towards the middle of the body or towards another part ➲ compare ABDUCTOR

ad·en·oids /ˈædənɔɪdz/ *noun* [pl.] pieces of soft TISSUE at the back of the nose and throat, that are part of the body's IMMUNE SYSTEM and that can swell up and cause breathing difficulties, especially in children ▸ **ad·en·oid·al** /ˌædəˈnɔɪdl/ *adj.*

adept /əˈdept/ *adj.* **~ (at/in sth)** | **~ (at/in doing sth)** good at doing sth that is quite difficult SYN **skilful** ▸ **adept** /ˈædept/ *noun* **adept·ly** *adv.*

ad·equate 0-w AW /ˈædɪkwət/ *adj.* enough in quantity, or good enough in quality, for a particular purpose or need: *an adequate supply of hot water* ◇ *The room was small but adequate.* ◇ *There is a lack of adequate provision for disabled students.* ◇ *He didn't give an adequate answer to the question.* ◇ **~ for sth** *The space available is not adequate for our needs.* ◇ **~ to do sth** *training that is adequate to meet the future needs of industry* OPP **inadequate** ▸ **ad·equacy** AW /ˈædɪkwəsi/ *noun* [U]: *The adequacy of the security arrangements has been questioned.* OPP **inadequacy** **ad·equate·ly** 0-w AW *adv.*: *Are you adequately insured?* OPP **inadequately**

ADHD /ˌeɪ diː eɪtʃ ˈdiː/ *abbr.* ATTENTION DEFICIT HYPERACTIVITY DISORDER

ad·here /ədˈhɪə(r); *NAmE* ədˈhɪr/ *verb* [I] **~ (to sth)** (*formal*) to stick firmly to sth: *Once in the bloodstream, the bacteria adhere to the surface of the red cells.*

PHR V **ad'here to sth** (*formal*) to behave according to a particular law, rule, set of instructions, etc; to follow a particular set of beliefs or a fixed way of doing sth: *For ten months he adhered to a strict no-fat low-salt diet.* ◇ *She adheres to teaching methods she learned over 30 years ago.*

ad·her·ence /ədˈhɪərəns; *NAmE* ədˈhɪr-/ *noun* [U] the fact of behaving according to a particular rule, etc, or of following a particular set of beliefs, or a fixed way of doing sth: *strict adherence to the rules*

ad·her·ent /ədˈhɪərənt; *NAmE* ədˈhɪr-/ *noun* (*formal*) a person who supports a political party or set of ideas SYN **supporter**

ad·he·sion /ədˈhiːʒn/ *noun* [U] (*technical*) the ability to stick or become attached to sth

ad·he·sive /ədˈhiːsɪv; -ˈhiːz-/ *noun, adj.*
- *noun* [C, U] a substance that you use to make things stick together
- *adj.* that can stick to sth SYN **sticky**: *adhesive tape* ➲ see also SELF-ADHESIVE

ad hoc /ˌæd ˈhɒk; *NAmE* ˈhɑːk/ *adj.* (from *Latin*) arranged or happening when necessary and not planned in advance: *an ad hoc meeting to deal with the problem* ◇ *The meetings will be held* **on an ad hoc basis.** ▸ **ad hoc** *adv.*

ad hom·in·em /ˌæd ˈhɒmɪnem; *NAmE* ˈhɑːm-/ *adj., adv.* (*formal*) directed against a person's character rather than their argument: *an ad hominem attack*

adieu /əˈdjuː; *NAmE* əˈduː/ *exclamation* (*old use* or *literary*) goodbye: *I bid you adieu.*

ad in·fin·itum /ˌæd ˌɪnfɪˈnaɪtəm/ *adv.* (from *Latin*) without ever coming to an end; again and again: *You cannot stay here ad infinitum without paying rent.* ◇ *The problem would be repeated ad infinitum.*

adi·pose /ˈædɪpəʊs; -z; *NAmE* -poʊ-/ *adj.* (*technical*) (of body TISSUE) used for storing fat

ad·ja·cent AW /əˈdʒeɪsnt/ *adj.* (of an area, a building, a room, etc.) next to or near sth: *The planes landed on adjacent runways.* ◇ **~ to sth** *Our farm land was adjacent to the river.*

aˌdjacent 'angle *noun* (*geometry*) one of the two angles formed on the same side of a straight line when another line meets it

ad·jec·tive /ˈædʒɪktɪv/ *noun* (*grammar*) a word that describes a person or thing, for example *big, red* and *clever* in *a big house, red wine* and *a clever idea* ▸ **ad·jec·tival** /ˌædʒekˈtaɪvl/ *adj.*: *an adjectival phrase* **ad·jec·tival·ly** /-ˈtaɪvəli/ *adv.*: *In 'bread knife', the word 'bread' is used adjectivally.*

ad·join /əˈdʒɔɪn/ *verb* [T, I] **~ (sth)** (*formal*) to be next to or joined to sth: *A barn adjoins the farmhouse.* ▸ **ad·join·ing** *adj.* [usually before noun]: *They stayed in adjoining rooms.* ◇ *We'll have more space if we knock down the adjoining wall* (= the wall between two rooms).

ad·journ /əˈdʒɜːn; *NAmE* əˈdʒɜːrn/ *verb* [I, T, often passive] (*formal*) to stop a meeting or an official process, especially a trial, for a period of time: *The court adjourned for lunch.* ◇ **~ sth** *The trial has been adjourned until next week.* ▸ **ad·journ·ment** *noun* [C, U]: *The judge granted us a short adjournment.*

PHR V **ad'journ to...** (*formal* or *humorous*) to go to another place, especially in order to relax

ad·judge /əˈdʒʌdʒ/ *verb* [usually passive] (*formal*) to make a decision about sb/sth based on the facts that are available: **~ sth + adj.** *The company was adjudged bankrupt.* ◇ **~ sth + noun** *The tour was adjudged a success.* ◇ **sth is adjudged to be, have, etc. sth** *The reforms were generally adjudged to have failed.*

ad·ju·di·cate /əˈdʒuːdɪkeɪt/ *verb* **1** [I, T] to make an official decision about who is right in a disagreement between two groups or organizations: **~ (on/upon/in sth)** *A special subcommittee adjudicates on planning applications.* ◇ **~ (sth) (between A and B)** *Their purpose is to adjudicate disputes between employers and employees.* **2** [I] to be a judge in a competition: *Who is adjudicating at this year's contest?* ▸ **ad·ju·di·ca·tion** /əˌdʒuːdɪˈkeɪʃn/ *noun* [U, C]: *The case was referred to a higher court for adjudication.* **ad·ju·di·ca·tor** *noun*: *You may refer your complaint to an independent adjudicator.*

ad·junct /ˈædʒʌŋkt/ *noun* **1** (*grammar*) an adverb or a phrase that adds meaning to the verb in a sentence or part of a sentence: *In 'She went home yesterday' and 'He ran away in a panic', 'yesterday' and 'in a panic' are adjuncts.* **2** (*formal*) a thing that is added or attached to sth larger or more important: *The memory expansion cards are useful adjuncts to the computer.*

ad·jure /əˈdʒʊə(r); *NAmE* əˈdʒʊr/ *verb* **~ sb to do sth** (*formal*) to ask or to order sb to do sth: *He adjured them to tell the truth.*

ad·just 0-w AW /əˈdʒʌst/ *verb*
1 0-w [T] to change sth slightly to make it more suitable for a new set of conditions or to make it work better: **~ sth** *Watch out for sharp bends and adjust your speed accordingly.* ◇ *This button is for adjusting the volume.* ◇ **~ sth to sth** *Adjust your language to the age of your audience.* **2** 0-w [I, T] to get used to a new situation by changing the way you behave and/or think SYN **adapt**: *They'll be fine—they just need time to adjust.* ◇ **~ to sth** *After a while his eyes adjusted to the dark.* ◇ **~ to doing sth** *It took her a while to adjust to living alone.* ◇ **~ yourself to sth** *You'll quickly adjust yourself to student life.* **3** [T] **~ sth** to move sth slightly so that it looks neater or feels more comfortable: *He smoothed his hair and adjusted his tie.* ➲ see also WELL ADJUSTED

ad·just·able /əˈdʒʌstəbl/ *adj.* that can be moved to different positions or changed in shape or size: *adjustable seat belts* ◇ *The height of the bicycle seat is adjustable.*

ˌadjustable 'spanner (*BrE*) (also **'monkey wrench** *NAmE, BrE*) *noun* a tool that can be adjusted to hold and turn things of different widths ➲ VISUAL VOCAB page V17 ➲ compare SPANNER, WRENCH

ad·just·ment AW /əˈdʒʌstmənt/ *noun* [C, U] **1** a small change made to sth in order to correct or improve it: *I've made a few adjustments to the design.* ◇ *Some adjustment of the lens may be necessary.* **2** a change in the way a person behaves or thinks: *She went through a period of emotional adjustment after her marriage broke up.*

ad·ju·tant /ˈædʒʊtənt/ *noun* an army officer who does office work and helps other officers

ˌAdjutant ˈGeneral *noun* (*pl.* ˌAdjutants ˈGeneral) **1** an officer of very high rank in the British army who is responsible for organization **2** the officer of very high rank in the US army who is in charge of organization

ad-lib /ˌæd ˈlɪb/ *verb* (-bb-) [I, T] to say sth in a speech or a performance that you have not prepared or practised SYN **improvise**: *She abandoned her script and began ad-libbing.* ◇ **~ sth** *I lost my notes and had to ad-lib the whole speech.* ▶ **ad lib** *noun*: *The speech was full of ad libs.* **ad lib** *adj.*: *an ad lib speech* **ad lib** *adv.*: *She delivered her lines ad lib.*

adman /ˈædmæn/ *noun* (*pl.* -men /-men/) (*informal*) a person who works in advertising

admin /ˈædmɪn/ *noun* [U] (*BrE, informal*) = ADMINISTRATION: *a few admin problems* ◇ *She works in admin.*

ad·min·is·ter /ədˈmɪnɪstə(r)/ *verb* **1** [often passive] **~ sth** to manage and organize the affairs of a company, an organization, a country, etc. SYN **manage**: *to administer a charity/fund/school* ◇ *The pension funds are administered by commercial banks.* **2 ~ sth** to make sure that sth is done fairly and in the correct way: *to* ***administer justice/the law*** ◇ *The questionnaire was administered by trained interviewers.* **3 ~ sth (to sb)** (*formal*) to give or to provide sth, especially in a formal way: *The teacher has the authority to administer punishment.* **4** [often passive] (*formal*) to give drugs, medicine, etc. to sb: **~ sth** *Police believe his wife could not have administered the poison.* ◇ **~ sth to sb** *The dose was administered to the child intravenously.* **5 ~ a kick, a punch, etc. (to sb/sth)** (*formal*) to kick or to hit sb/sth: *He administered a severe blow to his opponent's head.*

ad·min·is·tra·tion AW /ədˌmɪnɪˈstreɪʃn/ *noun* **1** (also *BrE informal* **admin**) [U] the activities that are done in order to plan, organize and run a business, school or other institution: *Administration costs are passed on to the customer.* ◇ *the day-to-day administration of a company* ◇ *I work in the Sales Administration department.* **2** [U] the process or act of organizing the way that sth is done: *the administration of justice* **3** [C] the people who plan, organize and run a business, an institution, etc: *university administrations* **4** (often **Administration**) [C] the government of a country, especially the US: *the Obama administration* ◇ *Successive administrations have failed to solve the country's economic problems.* **5** [U] (*formal*) the act of giving a drug to sb: *the administration of antibiotics* **6** [U] (*BrE, AustralE, law*) a situation in which the financial affairs of a business that cannot pay its debts are managed by an independent administrator: *If it cannot find extra funds, the company will* ***go into administration.*** ➲ compare CHAPTER 11

ad·min·is·tra·tive AW /ədˈmɪnɪstrətɪv; *NAmE* -streɪtɪv/ *adj.* connected with organizing the work of a business or an institution: *an* ***administrative job/assistant/error*** ▶ **ad·min·is·tra·tive·ly** AW *adv.*

ad·min·is·tra·tor AW /ədˈmɪnɪstreɪtə(r)/ *noun* a person whose job is to manage and organize the public or business affairs of a company or an institution: *a hospital administrator*

ad·mir·able /ˈædmərəbl/ *adj.* (*formal*) having qualities that you admire and respect SYN **commendable**: *Her dedication to her work was admirable.* ◇ *He made his points with admirable clarity.* ▶ **ad·mir·ably** /-əbli/ *adv.*: *Joe coped admirably with a difficult situation.*

ad·miral /ˈædmərəl/ *noun* an officer of very high rank in the navy: *The admiral visited the ships under his command.* ◇ *Admiral Lord Nelson* ➲ see also REAR ADMIRAL, RED ADMIRAL

ˌAdmiral of the ˈFleet (*BrE*) (*US* ˈ**Fleet Admiral**) *noun* an admiral of the highest rank in the navy

the Ad·mir·alty /ˈædmərəlti/ *noun* [sing.+ sing./pl. v.] (in Britain in the past) the government department controlling the navy

ad·mir·ation 0‑w /ˌædməˈreɪʃn/ *noun* [U] a feeling of respect and liking for sb/sth: *to* ***watch/gaze in admiration*** ◇ **~ for sb/sth** *I have great admiration for her as a writer.*

ad·mire 0‑w /ədˈmaɪə(r)/ *verb*
1 0‑w to respect sb for what they are or for what they have done: **~ sb/sth** *I really admire your enthusiasm.* ◇ *You have to* ***admire the way*** *he handled the situation.* ◇ **~ sb/sth for sth** *The school is widely admired for its excellent teaching.* ◇ **~ sb for doing sth** *I don't agree with her, but I admire her for sticking to her principles.* **2** 0‑w **~ sth** to look at sth and think that it is attractive and/or impressive: *He stood back to admire his handiwork.* ▶ **ad·mir·ing** *adj.*: *She was used to receiving admiring glances from men.* **ad·mir·ing·ly** *adv.*

ad·mirer /ədˈmaɪərə(r)/ *noun* **1 ~ of sb/sth** a person who admires sb/sth, especially a well-known person or thing: *He is a great admirer of Picasso's early paintings.* **2** a man who is attracted to a woman and admires her: *She never married but had many admirers.*

ad·mis·sible /ədˈmɪsəbl/ *adj.* that can be allowed or accepted, especially in court OPP **inadmissible** ▶ **ad·mis·si·bil·ity** /ədˌmɪsəˈbɪləti/ *noun* [U]

ad·mis·sion /ədˈmɪʃn/ *noun* **1** [U, C] the act of accepting sb into an institution, organization, etc; the right to enter a place or to join an institution or organization: *Hospital admission is not necessary in most cases.* ◇ *Hospital admissions for asthma attacks have doubled.* ◇ *the university* ***admissions policy/office*** ◇ *They tried to get into the club but were refused admission.* ◇ *She failed to* ***gain admission*** *to the university of her choice.* ◇ **~ to sth** *countries applying for admission to the European Union* ◇ *Last admissions to the park are at 4 p.m.* **2** [C] a statement in which sb admits that sth is true, especially sth wrong or bad that they have done: *He is a thief* ***by his own admission*** (= he has admitted it). ◇ **~ of sth** *an* ***admission of guilt/failure/defeat*** ◇ **~ that ...** *The minister's resignation was an admission that she had lied.* **3** [U] the amount of money that you pay to go into a building or to an event: ***admission charges/prices*** ◇ *£5 admission* ◇ *What's the admission?*

admit 0‑w /ədˈmɪt/ *verb* (-tt-)

▸ ACCEPT TRUTH **1** 0‑w [I, T] **~ (to sb) (that...)** to agree, often unwillingly, that sth is true SYN **confess**: *It was a stupid thing to do, I admit.* ◇ **+ speech** *'I'm very nervous,' she admitted reluctantly.* ◇ **~ to sth** *Don't be afraid to admit to your mistakes.* ◇ **~ to doing sth** *She admits to being strict with her children.* ◇ **~ sth** *He admitted all his mistakes.* ◇ *She stubbornly refuses to admit the truth.* ◇ *Why don't you just* ***admit defeat*** (= recognize that you cannot do sth) *and let someone else try?* ◇ *Admit it! You were terrified!* ◇ **~ (that)...** *They freely admit (that) they still have a lot to learn.* ◇ ***You must admit that*** *it all sounds very strange.* ◇ **~ to sb that...** *I couldn't admit to my parents that I was finding the course difficult.* ◇ **be admitted that...** *It was generally admitted that the government had acted too quickly.* ◇ **be admitted to be, have, etc. sth** *The appointment is now generally admitted to have been a mistake.*

▸ ACCEPT BLAME **2** 0‑w [I, T] to say that you have done sth wrong or illegal SYN **confess to**: **~ to sth** *He refused to admit to the other charges.* ◇ **~ to doing sth** *She admitted to having stolen the car.* ◇ **~ sth** *She admitted theft.* ◇ *He refused to admit his guilt.* ◇ **~ doing sth** *She admitted having driven the car without insurance.*

▸ ALLOW TO ENTER/JOIN **3** 0‑w [T] (*formal*) to allow sb/sth to enter a place: **~ sb/sth** *Each ticket admits one adult.* ◇ **~ sb/sth to/into sth** *You will not be admitted to the theatre after the performance has started.* ◇ *The narrow windows admit little light into the room.* **4** [T] (*formal*) to allow sb to become a member of a club, a school or an organization: **~ sb** *The society admits all US citizens over 21.* ◇ **~ sb to/into sth** *Women were only admitted into the club last year.*

▸ TO HOSPITAL **5** [T, often passive] **~ sb to/into a hospital, an**

A

institution, etc. (*formal*) to take sb to a hospital, or other institution where they can receive special care: *Two crash victims were admitted to the local hospital.*
PHR V **ad'mit of sth** (*formal*) to show that sth is possible or probable as a solution, an explanation, etc.

Synonyms

admit

acknowledge • recognize • concede • confess

These words all mean to agree, often unwillingly, that sth is true.

admit to agree, often unwillingly, that sth is true: *It was a stupid thing to do, I admit.*

acknowledge (*rather formal*) to accept that sth exists, is true or has happened: *She refuses to acknowledge the need for reform.*

recognize to admit or be aware that sth exists or is true: *They recognized the need to take the problem seriously.*

concede (*rather formal*) to admit, often unwillingly, that sth is true or logical: *He was forced to concede (that) there might be difficulties.*

ADMIT OR CONCEDE?

When sb **admits** sth, they are usually agreeing that sth which is generally considered bad or wrong is true or has happened, especially when it relates to their own actions. When sb **concedes** sth, they are usually accepting, unwillingly, that a particular fact or statement is true or logical.

confess (*rather formal*) to admit sth that you feel ashamed or embarrassed about: *She was reluctant to confess her ignorance.*

PATTERNS

- to admit/acknowledge/recognize/concede/confess that...
- to admit/confess **to sth**
- to admit/concede/confess sth **to sb**
- to admit/acknowledge/recognize **the truth**
- to admit/confess your **mistakes/ignorance**

ad·mit·tance /əd'mɪtns/ *noun* [U] (*formal*) the right to enter or the act of entering a building, an institution, etc: *Hundreds of people were unable to* ***gain admittance*** *to the hall.*

ad·mit·ted·ly /əd'mɪtɪdli/ *adv.* used, especially at the beginning of a sentence, when you are accepting that sth is true: *Admittedly, it is rather expensive but you don't need to use much.*

ad·mix·ture /əd'mɪkstʃə(r)/ *noun* (*formal*) **1** a mixture: *an admixture of aggression and creativity* **2** something, especially a small amount of sth, that is mixed with sth else: *a French-speaking region with an admixture of German speakers*

ad·mon·ish /əd'mɒnɪʃ; *NAmE* -'mɑːn-/ *verb* (*formal*) **1 ~ sb (for sth/for doing sth)** | **+ speech** to tell sb firmly that you do not approve of sth that they have done SYN **reprove**: *She was admonished for chewing gum in class.* **2 ~ sb (to do sth)** to strongly advise sb to do sth: *A warning voice admonished him not to let this happen.*

ad·mon·ition /ˌædmə'nɪʃn/ (also *less frequent* **ad·mon·ish·ment** /əd'mɒnɪʃmənt; *NAmE* -'mɑːn-/) *noun* [C, U] (*formal*) a warning to sb about their behaviour ▸ **ad·moni·tory** /əd'mɒnɪtri; *NAmE* -'mɑːn-/ *adj.*

ad nau·seam /ˌæd 'nɔːziæm/ *adv.* (from *Latin*) if a person says or does sth **ad nauseam**, they say or do it again and again so that it becomes boring or annoying: *Sports commentators repeat the same phrases ad nauseam.*

ado /ə'duː/ *noun*
IDM **without further/more ado** (*old-fashioned*) without delaying; immediately

adobe /ə'dəʊbi; *NAmE* ə'doʊbi/ *noun* [U] mud that is dried in the sun, mixed with STRAW and used as a building material

ado·les·cence /ˌædə'lesns/ *noun* [U] the time in a person's life when he or she develops from a child into an adult SYN **puberty** ➲ COLLOCATIONS at AGE

ado·les·cent /ˌædə'lesnt/ *noun* a young person who is developing from a child into an adult: *adolescents between the ages of 13 and 18 and the problems they face* ▸ **ado·les·cent** *adj.*: ***adolescent boys/girls/experiences***

Ado·nis /ə'dəʊnɪs; *NAmE* ə'doʊ-/ *noun* an extremely attractive young man ORIGIN From the name of the beautiful young man in ancient Greek myths, who was loved by both Aphrodite and Persephone. He was killed by a wild boar but Zeus ordered that he should spend the winter months in the underworld with Persephone and the summer months with Aphrodite.

adopt 🔑 /ə'dɒpt; *NAmE* ə'dɑːpt/ *verb*
▸ CHILD **1** 🔑 [I, T] to take sb else's child into your family and become its legal parent(s): *a campaign to encourage childless couples to adopt* ◇ **~ sb** *to adopt a child* ◇ *She was forced to have her baby adopted.* ➲ COLLOCATIONS at CHILD ➲ compare FOSTER
▸ METHOD **2** 🔑 [T] **~ sth** to start to use a particular method or to show a particular attitude towards sb/sth: *All three teams adopted different approaches to the problem.*
▸ SUGGESTION **3** 🔑 [T] **~ sth** to formally accept a suggestion or policy by voting: *to adopt a resolution* ◇ *The council is expected to adopt the new policy at its next meeting.*
▸ NEW NAME/COUNTRY **4** [T] **~ sth** to choose a new name, a country, a custom, etc. and begin to use it as your own: *to* ***adopt a name/title/language*** ◇ *Early Christians in Europe adopted many of the practices of the older, pagan religions.*
▸ WAY OF BEHAVING **5** [T] **~ sth** (*formal*) to use a particular manner, way of speaking, expression, etc: *He adopted an air of indifference.*
▸ CANDIDATE **6** [T] **~ sb (as sth)** (*BrE, politics*) to choose sb as a candidate in an election or as a representative: *She was adopted as parliamentary candidate for Wood Green.*

adopt·ed /ə'dɒptɪd; *NAmE* ə'dɑːp-/ *adj.* **1** an **adopted** child has legally become part of a family which is not the one in which he or she was born: *Danny is their adopted son.* **2** an **adopted** country is one in which sb chooses to live although it is not the one they were born in

adop·ter /ə'dɒptə(r); *NAmE* ə'dɑːp-/ *noun* **1** a person who adopts a child **2** a person who starts using a new technology: ***early/late adopters*** *of DVD players*

adop·tion /ə'dɒpʃn; *NAmE* ə'dɑːpʃn/ *noun* **1** [U, C] the act of adopting a child: *She put the baby up for adoption.* ➲ COLLOCATIONS at CHILD **2** [U] the decision to start using sth such as an idea, a plan or a name: *the adoption of new technology* **3** [U, C] (*BrE, politics*) the act of choosing sb as a candidate for an election: *his adoption as the Labour candidate*

adop·tive /ə'dɒptɪv; *NAmE* ə'dɑːp-/ *adj.* [usually before noun] an **adoptive** parent or family is one that has legally adopted a child

ador·able /ə'dɔːrəbl/ *adj.* very attractive and easy to feel love for: *What an adorable child!* ▸ **ador·ably** /-əbli/ *adv.*

ad·or·ation /ˌædə'reɪʃn/ *noun* [U] a feeling of great love or worship: *He gazed at her with pure adoration.* ◇ *The painting is called 'Adoration of the Infant Christ'.*

adore /ə'dɔː(r)/ *verb* (not used in the progressive tenses) **1 ~ sb** to love sb very much: *It's obvious that she adores him.* ➲ SYNONYMS at LOVE **2** (*informal*) to like sth very much: **~ sth** *I simply adore his music!* ◇ **~ doing sth** *She adores working with children.* ➲ SYNONYMS at LIKE

ador·ing /ə'dɔːrɪŋ/ *adj.* [usually before noun] showing much love and admiration ▸ **ador·ing·ly** *adv.*

adorn /ə'dɔːn; *NAmE* ə'dɔːrn/ *verb* [often passive] (*formal*) to make sth/sb look more attractive by decorating it or them with sth: **~ sth/sb** *Gold rings adorned his fingers.* ◇ (*ironic*) *Graffiti adorned the walls.* ◇ **~ sth/sb/yourself with**

A

sth *The walls were adorned with paintings.* ◇ *The children adorned themselves with flowers.* ▸ **adorn·ment** *noun* [U, C] : *A plain necklace was her only adornment.*

ad·renal gland /əˈdriːnl glænd/ *noun* either of the two small organs above the KIDNEYS that produce adrenaline and other HORMONES

adrena·line /əˈdrenəlɪn/ (also **adrena·lin**) *noun* [U] a substance produced in the body when you are excited, afraid or angry. It makes the heart beat faster and increases your energy and ability to move quickly: *The excitement at the start of a race can really* ***get the adrenaline flowing****.*

adrift /əˈdrɪft/ *adj.* [not before noun] **1** if a boat or a person in a boat is **adrift**, the boat is not tied to anything or is floating without being controlled by anyone: *The survivors were adrift in a lifeboat for six days.* **2** (*BrE*) (of a person) feeling alone and without a direction or an aim in life: *young people adrift in the big city* **3** no longer attached or fixed in the right position: *I nearly suffocated when the pipe on my breathing apparatus* ***came adrift****.* ◇ (*figurative*) *She had been* ***cut adrift*** *from everything she had known.* ◇ (*figurative*) *Our plans had gone badly adrift.* **4 ~ (of sb/sth)** (*BrE*) (in sport) behind the score or position of your opponents: *The team are now just six points adrift of the leaders.*

IDM **cast/set sb adrift** [usually passive] to leave sb to be carried away on a boat that is not being controlled by anyone: (*figurative*) *Without language human beings are cast adrift.*

adroit /əˈdrɔɪt/ *adj.* (*formal*) skilful and clever, especially in dealing with people SYN **skilful**: *an adroit negotiator* ▸ **adroit·ly** *adv.* **adroit·ness** *noun* [U]

ADSL /ˌeɪ diː es ˈel/ *abbr.* asymmetric digital subscriber line (a system for connecting a computer to the Internet using a telephone line)

ad·sorb /ədˈsɔːb; -ˈzɔːb; *NAmE* -ˈzɔːrb; -ˈsɔːrb/ *verb* **~ sth** (*technical*) if sth **adsorbs** a liquid, gas or other substance, it holds it on its surface: *The dye is adsorbed onto the fibre.*

ADT /ˌeɪ diː ˈtiː/ *abbr.* ATLANTIC DAYLIGHT TIME

aduki /əˈduːki/ *noun* = ADZUKI

adu·la·tion /ˌædjuˈleɪʃn; *NAmE* ˌædʒəˈl-/ *noun* [U] (*formal*) admiration and praise, especially when this is greater than is necessary ▸ **adu·la·tory** /ˌædjuˈleɪtəri; *NAmE* ˈædʒələtɔːri/ *adj.*

adult 0- AW /ˈædʌlt; əˈdʌlt/ *noun, adj.*

■ ***noun*** **1** 0- a fully grown person who is legally responsible for their actions SYN **grown-up**: *Children must be accompanied by an adult.* ◇ *Why can't you two act like civilized adults?* **2** 0- a fully grown animal: *The fish return to the river as adults in order to breed.*

■ ***adj.*** **1** 0- fully grown or developed: *preparing young people for adult life* ◇ *the adult population* ◇ *adult monkeys* **2** behaving in an intelligent and responsible way; typical of what is expected of an adult SYN **grown-up**: *When my parents split up, it was all very adult and open.* **3** [only before noun] intended for adults only, because it is about sex or contains violence: *an adult movie* ➲ see also ADULTHOOD

ˌadult eduˈcation (also **conˌtinuing eduˈcation**) *noun* [U] education for adults that is available outside the formal education system, for example at evening classes

adul·ter·ate /əˈdʌltəreɪt/ *verb* [often passive] **~ sth (with sth)** to make food or drink less pure by adding another substance to it SYN **contaminate** ➲ see also UNADULTERATED ▸ **adul·ter·ation** /əˌdʌltəˈreɪʃn/ *noun* [U]

adul·ter·er /əˈdʌltərə(r)/ *noun* (*formal*) a person who commits adultery

adul·ter·ess /əˈdʌltərəs/ *noun* (*formal*) a woman who commits adultery

adul·tery /əˈdʌltəri/ *noun* [U] sex between a married person and sb who is not their husband or wife: *He was accused of* ***committing adultery****.* ▸ **adul·ter·ous** /əˈdʌltərəs/ *adj.*: *an adulterous relationship*

adult·hood AW /ˈædʌlthʊd; əˈdʌlt-/ *noun* [U] the state of being an adult: *a child reaching adulthood*

ad·um·brate /ˈædəmbreɪt; *NAmE* also əˈdem-/ *verb* **~ sth** (*formal*) to give a general idea or description of sth without details SYN **outline**

ad·vance 0- /ədˈvɑːns; *NAmE* -ˈvæns/ *noun, verb, adj.*

■ ***noun***

▸ FORWARD MOVEMENT **1** 0- [C] the forward movement of a group of people, especially armed forces: *We feared that an advance on the capital would soon follow.* ➲ COLLOCATIONS at WAR

▸ DEVELOPMENT **2** 0- [C, U] **~ (in sth)** progress or a development in a particular activity or area of understanding: *recent advances in medical science* ◇ *We live in an age of rapid technological advance.*

▸ MONEY **3** [C, usually sing.] money paid for work before it has been done or money paid earlier than expected: *They offered an advance of £5 000 after the signing of the contract.* ◇ *She asked for an advance on her salary.*

▸ SEXUAL **4 advances** [pl.] attempts to start a sexual relationship with sb: *He had* ***made advances*** *to one of his students.*

▸ PRICE INCREASE **5** [C] **~ (on sth)** (*business*) an increase in the price or value of sth: *Share prices showed significant advances.*

IDM **in advance (of sth)** **1** 0- before the time that is expected; before sth happens: *a week/month/year in advance* ◇ *It's cheaper if you book the tickets in advance.* ◇ *People were evacuated from the coastal regions in advance of the hurricane.* **2** more developed than sb/sth else: *Galileo's ideas were well in advance of the age in which he lived.*

■ ***verb***

▸ MOVE FORWARD **1** 0- [I] to move forward towards sb/sth, often in order to attack or threaten them or it: *The troops were finally given the order to advance.* ◇ *They had advanced 20 miles by nightfall.* ◇ *the advancing Allied troops* ◇ **~ on/towards sb/sth** *The mob advanced on us, shouting angrily.* ➲ compare RETREAT

▸ DEVELOP **2** 0- [I, T] if knowledge, technology, etc. **advances**, it develops and improves: *Our knowledge of the disease has advanced considerably over recent years.* ◇ **~ sth** *This research has done much to advance our understanding of language learning.*

▸ HELP TO SUCCEED **3** [T] to help sth to succeed SYN **further**: *Studying for new qualifications is one way of advancing your career.* ◇ *They worked together to advance the cause of democracy.*

▸ MONEY **4** [T] to give sb money before the time it would usually be paid: **~ sth to sb** *We are willing to advance the money to you.* ◇ **~ sb sth** *We will advance you the money.*

▸ SUGGEST **5** [T] **~ sth** (*formal*) to suggest an idea, a theory, or a plan for other people to discuss SYN **put forward**: *The article advances a new theory to explain changes in the climate.*

▸ MAKE EARLIER **6** [T] **~ sth** (*formal*) to change the time or date of an event so that it takes place earlier SYN **bring forward**: *The date of the trial has been advanced by one week.* OPP **postpone**

▸ MOVE FORWARD **7** [I, T] (*formal*) to move forward to a later part of sth; to move sth forward to a later part: *Users advance through the program by answering a series of questions.* ◇ **~ sth** *This button advances the tape to the beginning of the next track.*

▸ INCREASE **8** [I] (*business*) (of prices, costs, etc.) to increase in price or amount: *Oil shares advanced amid economic recovery hopes.*

■ ***adj.*** [only before noun] **1** done or given before sth is going to happen: *Please give us* ***advance warning*** *of any changes.* ◇ *We need* ***advance notice*** *of the numbers involved.* ◇ *No* ***advance booking*** *is necessary on most departures.* **2 ~ party/team** a group of people who go somewhere first, before the main group

ad·vanced 0- /ədˈvɑːnst; *NAmE* -ˈvænst/ *adj.* **1** 0- having the most modern and recently developed ideas, methods, etc: *advanced technology* ◇ *advanced industrial societies* **2** 0- (of a course of study) at a high or difficult level: *There were only three of us on the advanced course.* ◇ *an advanced student of English* **3** at a late stage of development: *the advanced stages of the disease*

IDM **of advanced ˈyears** | **sb's advanced ˈage** used in

polite expressions to describe sb as 'very old': *He was a man of advanced years.* ◇ *(humorous) Even at my advanced age I still know how to enjoy myself!*

Ad,vanced 'Higher *noun* (in Scotland) an exam in a particular subject at a higher level than HIGHER, taken by some school students at the age of around 18

ad'vanced level *noun* = A LEVEL: *For this course, you need two GCE Advanced Level passes.*

ad,vanced 'placement *noun* [U] (*abbr.* AP) an advanced course for high school students in the US by which students can gain college CREDITS before they actually go to college

ad'vance guard (also **ad'vanced guard**) *noun* [C+sing./pl. v.] a group of soldiers who go somewhere to make preparations before other soldiers arrive

ad·vance·ment /əd'vɑːnsmənt; *NAmE* -'væns-/ *noun* (*formal*) **1** [U, C] the process of helping sth to make progress or succeed; the progress that is made: *the* ***advancement of knowledge/education/science*** **2** [U] progress in a job, social class, etc: *There are good opportunities for advancement if you have the right skills.*

ad·van·cing /əd'vɑːnsɪŋ; *NAmE* -'væns-/ *adj.* **~ years/age** used as a polite way of referring to the fact of time passing and of sb growing older: *She is still very active, in spite of her advancing years.*

ad·van·tage 0‑ /əd'vɑːntɪdʒ; *NAmE* -'væn-/ *noun*, *verb*

■ ***noun*** [C, U] **1** 0‑ a thing that helps you to be better or more successful than other people: *a* ***big/great/definite advantage*** ◇ *an unfair advantage* (= sth that benefits you, but not your opponents) ◇ *She* ***had the advantage of*** *a good education.* ◇ *You will* ***be at an advantage*** (= have an advantage) *in the interview if you have thought about the questions in advance.* ◇ **~ over sb** *Being tall gave him an advantage over the other players.* OPP **disadvantage** **2** 0‑ a quality of sth that makes it better or more useful: *A small car* ***has the*** *added* ***advantage of*** *being cheaper to run.* ◇ *One advantage of/One of the advantages of living in the country is the fresh air.* ◇ *Each of these systems has its advantages and disadvantages.* OPP **disadvantage** **3** (in TENNIS) the first point scored after a score of 40–40: *Advantage Federer.*

IDM **be/work to your ad'vantage** to give you an advantage; to change a situation in a way that gives you an advantage: *It would be to your advantage to attend this meeting.* ◇ *Eventually, the new regulations will work to our advantage.* **take ad'vantage of sth/sb** **1** 0‑ to make use of sth well; to make use of an opportunity: *She took advantage of the children's absence to tidy their rooms.* ◇ *We* ***took full advantage of*** *the hotel facilities.* **2** 0‑ to make use of sb/sth in a way that is unfair or dishonest SYN **exploit**: *He took advantage of my generosity* (= for example, by taking more than I had intended to give). **to (good/best) ad'vantage** in a way that shows the best of sth: *The photograph showed him to advantage.* **turn sth to your ad'vantage** to use or change a bad situation so that it helps you

■ ***verb*** **~ sb** (*formal*) to put sb in a better position than other people or than they were in before

ad·van·taged /əd'vɑːntɪdʒd; *NAmE* -'væn-/ *adj.* being in a good social or financial situation: *We aim to improve opportunities for the less advantaged in society.* OPP **disadvantaged**

ad·van·ta·geous /,ædvən'teɪdʒəs/ *adj.* **~ (to sb)** good or useful in a particular situation SYN **beneficial**: *A free trade agreement would be advantageous to both countries.* OPP **disadvantageous** ▸ **ad·van·ta·geous·ly** *adv.*

ad·vent /'ædvent/ *noun* **1** [sing.] **the ~ of sth/sb** the coming of an important event, person, invention, etc: *the advent of new technology* **2 Advent** [U] (in the Christian religion) the period of approximately four weeks before Christmas

'Advent calendar *noun* a piece of stiff paper with a picture and 24 small doors with numbers on. Children open a door each day during Advent and find a picture or a piece of chocolate behind each one.

ad·ven·ti·tious /,ædven'tɪʃəs/ *adj.* (*formal*) happening by accident; not planned

ad·ven·ture 0‑ /əd'ventʃə(r)/ *noun*
1 0‑ [C] an unusual, exciting or dangerous experience, journey or series of events: *her adventures travelling in Africa* ◇ *When you're a child, life is one big adventure.* ◇ *adventure stories* **2** 0‑ [U] excitement and the willingness to take risks, try new ideas, etc: *a* ***sense/spirit of adventure***

ad'venture game *noun* a type of computer game in which you play a part in an adventure

ad,venture 'playground *noun* (*BrE*) an area where children can play, with large structures, ropes, etc. for climbing on

ad·ven·turer /əd'ventʃərə(r)/ *noun* **1** (*old-fashioned*) a person who enjoys exciting new experiences, especially going to unusual places **2** (often *disapproving*) a person who is willing to take risks or act in a dishonest way in order to gain money or power

ad·ven·ture·some /əd'ventʃəsəm; *NAmE* -tʃərs-/ *adj.* (*NAmE*) = ADVENTUROUS

ad·ven·tur·ess /əd'ventʃəres/ *noun* **1** (*old-fashioned*) a woman who enjoys exciting new experiences, especially going to unusual places **2** (often *disapproving*) a woman who is willing to take risks or act in a dishonest way in order to gain money or power

ad·ven·tur·ism /əd'ventʃərɪzəm/ *noun* [U] (*disapproving*) a willingness to take risks in business or politics in order to gain sth for yourself

ad·ven·tur·ous /əd'ventʃərəs/ *adj.* **1** (*NAmE* also **adven·ture·some**) (of a person) willing to take risks and try new ideas; enjoying being in new, exciting situations: *For the more adventurous tourists, there are trips into the mountains with a local guide.* ◇ *Many teachers would like to be more adventurous and creative.* **2** including new and interesting things, methods and ideas: *The menu contained traditional favourites as well as more adventurous dishes.* **3** full of new, exciting or dangerous experiences: *an* ***adventurous trip/lifestyle*** OPP **unadventurous** ▸ **ad·ven·tur·ous·ly** *adv.*

ad·verb /'ædvɜːb; *NAmE* -vɜːrb/ *noun* (*grammar*) a word that adds more information about place, time, manner, cause or degree to a verb, an adjective, a phrase or another adverb: *In 'speak kindly', 'incredibly deep', 'just in time' and 'too quickly', 'kindly', 'incredibly', 'just' and 'too' are all adverbs.* ➲ see also SENTENCE ADVERB ▸ **ad·ver·bial** /æd'vɜːbiəl; *NAmE* -'vɜːrb-/ *adj.*: *'Very quickly indeed' is an adverbial phrase.*

ad,verbial 'particle *noun* (*grammar*) an adverb used especially after a verb to show position, direction of movement, etc: *In 'come back', 'break down' and 'fall off', 'back', 'down' and 'off' are all adverbial particles.*

ad·ver·sar·ial /,ædvə'seəriəl; *NAmE* -vər'seriəl/ *adj.* (*formal* or *technical*) (especially of political or legal systems) involving people who are in opposition and who make attacks on each other: *the adversarial nature of the two-party system* ◇ *an adversarial system of justice*

ad·ver·sary /'ædvəsəri; *NAmE* -vərseri/ *noun* (*pl.* **-ies**) (*formal*) a person that sb is opposed to and competing with in an argument or a battle SYN **opponent**

ad·verse /'ædvɜːs; əd'vɜːs; *NAmE* -vɜːrs/ *adj.* [usually before noun] negative and unpleasant; not likely to produce a good result: ***adverse change/circumstances/weather conditions*** ◇ *Lack of money will have an* ***adverse effect*** *on our research programme.* ◇ *They have attracted strong adverse criticism.* ◇ *This drug is known to have adverse side effects.* ▸ **ad·verse·ly** *adv.*: *Her health was* ***adversely affected*** *by the climate.*

ad·ver·sity /əd'vɜːsəti; *NAmE* -'vɜːrs-/ *noun* [U, C] (*pl.* **-ies**) (*formal*) a difficult or unpleasant situation: *courage* ***in the face of adversity*** ◇ *He overcame many personal adversities.*

ad·vert 0‑ /'ædvɜːt; *NAmE* -vɜːrt/ *noun* (*BrE*) (*informal*) = ADVERTISEMENT: *the adverts on television* ◇

When the adverts came on I got up to put the kettle on. ➲ SYNONYMS at ADVERTISEMENT

ad·ver·tise 🔑 /ˈædvətaɪz; *NAmE* -vərt-/ *verb* **1** 🔑 [I, T] to tell the public about a product or a service in order to encourage people to buy or to use it: *If you want to attract more customers, try advertising in the local paper.* ◇ **~ sth (as sth)** *The cruise was advertised as the 'journey of a lifetime'.* **2** 🔑 [I, T] to let people know that sth is going to happen, or that a job is available by giving details about it in a newspaper, on a notice in a public place, on the Internet, etc: **~ (for sb/sth)** *We are currently advertising for a new sales manager.* ◇ **~ sth** *We advertised the concert quite widely.* **3** [T] **~ sth** to show or tell sth about yourself to other people SYN **publicize**: *I wouldn't advertise the fact that you don't have a work permit.*

ad·ver·tise·ment 🔑 /ədˈvɜːtɪsmənt; *NAmE* ˌædvərˈtaɪz-/ *noun* **1** 🔑 [C] (also *informal* **ad**) (*BrE* also *informal* **ad·vert**) **~ (for sth)** a notice, picture or film telling people about a product, job or service: *Put an advertisement in the local paper to sell your car.* ➲ VISUAL VOCAB page V2 ➲ see also CLASSIFIED ADVERTISEMENTS **2** [C] (*BrE* also **ad·vert**) **~ for sth** an example of sth that shows its good qualities: *Dirty streets and homelessness are no advertisement for a prosperous society.* **3** [U] the act of advertising sth and making it public

Synonyms

advertisement

publicity • ad • commercial • promotion • trailer

These are all words for a notice, picture or film/movie telling people about a product, job or service.

advertisement a notice, picture or film/movie telling people about a product, job or service; an example of sth that shows its good qualities; the act of advertising sth and making it public: *Put an advertisement in the local paper to sell your car.* ◇ *Dirty streets are no advertisement for a prosperous society.*

publicity [U] the business of attracting the attention of the public to sb/sth such as a company, book, film/movie, film/movie star or product; the things that are done to attract attention: *She works in publicity.* ◇ *There has been a lot of advance publicity for her new film.*

ad (*informal*) a notice, picture or film/movie telling people about a product, job or service: *We put an ad in the local paper.* ◇ *an ad for a new chocolate bar*

commercial an advertisement on television or on the radio.

promotion a set of advertisements for a particular product or service; activities done in order to increase the sales of a product or service: *a special promotion of local products* ◇ *She works in sales and promotion.*

trailer (*especially BrE*) a series of short scenes from a film/movie or television programme, shown in advance to advertise it.

PATTERNS

- (a/an) advertisement/publicity/ad/commercial/promotion/trailer **for** sth
- a **TV/television/radio/cinema** advertisement/ad/commercial/promotion
- to **run/show** a(n) advertisement/ad/commercial/trailer

ad·ver·tiser /ˈædvətaɪzə(r); *NAmE* -vərt-/ *noun* a person or company that advertises

ad·ver·tis·ing 🔑 /ˈædvətaɪzɪŋ; *NAmE* -vərt-/ *noun* [U] the activity and industry of advertising things to people on television, in newspapers, on the Internet, etc: *A good **advertising campaign** will increase our sales.* ◇ *Cigarette advertising has been banned.* ◇ ***radio/TV advertising*** ◇ *Val works for an **advertising agency*** (= a company that designs advertisements). ◇ *a career in advertising*

ad·ver·tor·ial /ˌædvəˈtɔːriəl; *NAmE* -vərˈt-/ *noun* an advertisement that is designed to look like an article in the newspaper or magazine in which it appears

ad·vice 🔑 /ədˈvaɪs/ *noun* [U] **~ (on sth)** an opinion or a suggestion about what sb should do in a particular situation: *advice on road safety* ◇ *They **give advice** to people with HIV and AIDS.* ◇ ***Ask** your teacher's **advice/Ask** your teacher **for advice** on how to prepare for the exam.* ◇ *We were advised to **seek legal advice**.* ◇ *Let me give you **a piece of advice**.* ◇ *A **word of advice**. Don't wear that dress.* ◇ ***Take my advice**. Don't do it.* ◇ *I chose it **on his advice**.*

adˈvice column (*NAmE*) (*BrE* **ˈagony column**) *noun* part of a newspaper or magazine in which sb gives advice to readers who have sent letters about their personal problems

adˈvice columnist (*NAmE*) (*BrE* **ˈagony aunt/uncle**) *noun* a person who writes in a newspaper or magazine giving advice in reply to people's letters about their personal problems

ad·vis·able /ədˈvaɪzəbl/ *adj.* [not usually before noun] sensible and a good idea in order to achieve sth: *Early booking is advisable.* ◇ **~ to do sth** *It is advisable to book early.* OPP **inadvisable** ▸ **ad·vis·abil·ity** /ədˌvaɪzəˈbɪləti/ *noun* [U]

ad·vise 🔑 /ədˈvaɪz/ *verb* **1** 🔑 [I, T] to tell sb what you think they should do in a particular situation: **~ (sb) against sth/against doing sth** *I would **strongly advise** against going out on your own.* ◇ **~ sb** *Her mother was away and couldn't advise her.* ◇ **~ sth** *I'd advise extreme caution.* ◇ **+ speech** *'Get there early,' she advised (them).* ◇ **~ sb to do sth** *Police are advising people to stay at home.* ◇ *I'd advise you not to tell him.* ◇ **~ that…** *They advise that a passport be carried with you at all times.* ◇ (*BrE* also) *They advise that a passport should be carried with you at all times.* ◇ **it is advised that…** *It is strongly advised that you take out insurance.* ◇ **~ doing sth** *I'd advise buying your tickets well in advance if you want to travel in August.* ➲ see also ILL-ADVISED, WELL ADVISED ➲ SYNONYMS at RECOMMEND **2** 🔑 [I, T] to give sb help and information on a subject that you know a lot about: **~ (sb) on/about sth/about doing sth** *We employ an expert to advise on new technology.* ◇ *She advises the government on environmental issues.* ◇ **~ (sb) what, which, whether, etc…** *The pharmacist will advise which medicines are safe to take.* ◇ *Your lawyer can advise you whether to take any action.* **3** [T] (*formal*) to officially tell sb sth SYN **inform**: **~ sb of sth** *Please advise us of any change of address.* ◇ **~ sb when, where, how, etc …** *I will contact you later to advise you when to come.* ◇ **~ sb that…** *I regret to advise you that the course is now full.*

ad·vised·ly /ədˈvaɪzədli/ *adv.* (*formal*) if you say that you are using a word **advisedly**, you mean that you have thought carefully before choosing it

ad·vise·ment /ədˈvaɪzmənt/ *noun* [U] (*NAmE*, *formal*) advice: *the University Advisement Center*
IDM **take sth under adˈvisement** to think carefully about sth before making a decision about it: *The judge has taken the matter under advisement.*

ad·viser (also **ad·visor**) /ədˈvaɪzə(r)/ *noun* a person who gives advice, especially sb who knows a lot about a particular subject: *a financial adviser* ◇ **~ (to sb) (on sth)** *a special adviser to the President on education*

ad·vis·ory /ədˈvaɪzəri/ *adj.*, *noun*
■ ***adj.*** having the role of giving professional advice: *an **advisory committee/body/service*** ◇ *He acted in an advisory capacity only.*
■ ***noun*** (*pl.* -ies) (*NAmE*) an official warning that sth bad is going to happen: *a tornado advisory*

ad·vo·cacy AW /ˈædvəkəsi/ *noun* [U] **1 ~ (of sth)** (*formal*) the giving of public support to an idea, a course of action or a belief **2** (*technical*) the work of lawyers who speak about cases in court

A

'advocacy group *noun* (*NAmE*) a group of people who work together to achieve sth, especially by putting pressure on the government, etc, usually on behalf of people who are unable to speak for themselves: *an advocacy group for the rights of the mentally ill* ➲ compare INTEREST GROUP, PRESSURE GROUP

ad·vo·cate AW *verb, noun*

▪ **verb** /'ædvəkeɪt/ (*formal*) to support sth publicly: **~ sth** *The group does not advocate the use of violence.* ◇ **~ (sb) doing sth** *Many experts advocate rewarding your child for good behaviour.* ◇ **~ that...** *The report advocated that all buildings be fitted with smoke detectors.* ◇ (*BrE* also) *The report advocated that all buildings should be fitted with smoke detectors.* ➲ SYNONYMS at RECOMMEND

▪ **noun** /'ædvəkət/ **1** a person who supports or speaks in favour of sb or of a public plan or action: **~ (for sth/sb)** *an advocate for hospital workers* ◇ **~ (of sth/sb)** *a staunch advocate of free speech* ➲ see also DEVIL'S ADVOCATE **2** a person who defends sb in court **3** (in Scotland) a lawyer who has the right to argue cases in higher courts ➲ note at LAWYER

adze (*BrE*) (*US* **adz**) /ædz/ *noun* a heavy tool with a curved blade at RIGHT ANGLES to the handle, used for cutting or shaping large pieces of wood

ad·zuki /əd'zu:ki/ (also **ad'zuki bean**, **aduki**) *noun* a type of small round dark red BEAN that you can eat

aegis /'i:dʒɪs/ *noun*

IDM **under the aegis of sb/sth** (*formal*) with the protection or support of a particular organization or person

ae·olian (*especially US* **eo·lian**) /i:'əʊliən; *NAmE* i:'oʊ-/ *adj.* (*technical*) connected with or caused by the action of the wind

aeon (*BrE*) (also **eon** *NAmE, BrE*) /'i:ən/ *noun* **1** (*formal*) an extremely long period of time; thousands of years **2** (*geology*) a major division of time, divided into ERAS: *aeons of geological history*

aer·ate /'eəreɪt; *NAmE* 'er-/ *verb* **1 ~ sth** to make it possible for air to become mixed with soil, water, etc: *Earthworms do the important job of aerating the soil.* **2 ~ sth** to add a gas, especially CARBON DIOXIDE, to a liquid under pressure: *aerated water* ▸ **aer·ation** /eə'reɪʃn; *NAmE* e'reɪ-/ *noun* [U]

aer·ial /'eəriəl; *NAmE* 'er-/ *noun, adj.*

▪ **noun** (*BrE*) (also **an·tenna** *NAmE, BrE*) a piece of equipment made of wire or long straight pieces of metal for receiving or sending radio and television signals ➲ VISUAL VOCAB pages V15, V42

▪ **adj. 1** from a plane: ***aerial attacks/bombardment/photography*** ◇ *an aerial view of Palm Island* **2** in the air; existing above the ground: *The banyan tree has aerial roots.*

aerie (*NAmE*) = EYRIE

aero- /'eərəʊ; *NAmE* 'eroʊ/ *combining form* (in nouns, adjectives and adverbs) connected with air or aircraft: *aerodynamic* ◇ *aerospace*

aero·bat·ics /ˌeərə'bætɪks; *NAmE* ˌerə-/ *noun* [U+sing./pl. v.] exciting and skilful movements performed in an aircraft, such as flying upside down, especially in front of an audience ▸ **aero·batic** *adj.*: *an aerobatic display* ➲ VISUAL VOCAB page V43

aer·obic /eə'rəʊbɪk; *NAmE* e'roʊ-/ *adj.* **1** (*biology*) needing OXYGEN: *aerobic bacteria* **2** (of physical exercise) especially designed to improve the function of the heart and lungs OPP **anaerobic**

aer·obics /eə'rəʊbɪks; *NAmE* e'roʊ-/ *noun* [U] physical exercises intended to make the heart and lungs stronger, often done in classes, with music: *to do aerobics*

aero·drome /'eərədrəʊm; *NAmE* 'erədroʊm/ (*BrE*) (*US* **air·drome**) *noun* (*old-fashioned*) a small airport

aero·dy·nam·ics /ˌeərəʊdaɪ'næmɪks; *NAmE* ˌeroʊ-/ *noun* **1** [pl.] the qualities of an object that affect the way it moves through the air: *Research has focused on improving the car's aerodynamics.* **2** [U] the science that deals with how objects move through air ▸ **aero·dy·nam·ic** /-mɪk/ *adj.*: *the car's aerodynamic shape* (= making it able to move faster) **aero·dy·nam·ic·al·ly** /-kli/ *adv.*

aero·foil /'eərəfɔɪl; *NAmE* 'er-/ (*BrE*) (*NAmE* **air·foil**) *noun* the basic curved structure of an aircraft's wing that helps to lift it into the air

aero·gramme (*BrE*) (*NAmE* **aero·gram**) /'eərəgræm; *NAmE* 'erə-/ (also **'air letter** *NAmE, BrE*) *noun* a sheet of light paper that can be folded and sent by air as a letter

aero·naut /'eərənɔ:t; *NAmE* 'erə-/ *noun* a traveller in a HOT-AIR BALLOON or AIRSHIP

aero·naut·ics /ˌeərə'nɔ:tɪks; *NAmE* ˌerə-/ *noun* [U] the science or practice of building and flying aircraft ▸ **aero·naut·ic·al** /-'nɔ:tɪkl/ *adj.*: *an aeronautical engineer*

aero·plane /'eərəpleɪn; *NAmE* 'erə-/ (*BrE*) (also **air·plane** especially in *NAmE*) (also **plane** *BrE, NAmE*) *noun* a flying vehicle with wings and one or more engines ➲ VISUAL VOCAB page V43

aero·sol /'eərəsɒl; *NAmE* 'erəsɔ:l; 'erəsɑ:l/ *noun* a metal container in which a liquid such as paint or HAIRSPRAY is kept under pressure and released as a spray: *ozone-friendly aerosols* ◇ *an* ***aerosol can/spray*** ➲ VISUAL VOCAB page V29

aero·space /'eərəʊspeɪs; *NAmE* 'eroʊ-/ *noun* [U] the industry of building aircraft, vehicles and equipment to be sent into space: *jobs in aerospace and defence* ◇ *the aerospace industry*

aero·stat /'eərəstæt; *NAmE* 'erə-/ *noun* (*technical*) an aircraft filled with hot air, such as an AIRSHIP or HOT-AIR BALLOON

aes·thete (*NAmE* also **es·thete**) /'i:sθi:t; 'es-; *NAmE* 'es-/ *noun* (*formal*, sometimes *disapproving*) a person who has a love and understanding of art and beautiful things

aes·thet·ic (*NAmE* also **es·thet·ic**) /i:s'θetɪk; es-; *NAmE* es-/ *adj., noun*

▪ **adj. 1** concerned with beauty and art and the understanding of beautiful things: *an aesthetic appreciation of the landscape* ◇ *The benefits of conservation are both financial and aesthetic.* **2** made in an artistic way and beautiful to look at: *Their furniture was more aesthetic than functional.* ▸ **aes·thet·ic·al·ly** (*NAmE* also **es-**) /-kli/ *adv.*: *aesthetically pleasing colour combinations*

▪ **noun 1** [C] the aesthetic qualities and ideas of sth: *The students debated the aesthetic of the poems.* **2 aesthetics** [U] the branch of philosophy that studies the principles of beauty, especially in art ▸ **aes·theti·cism** (*NAmE* also **es-**) /i:s'θetɪsɪzəm; es-; *NAmE* es-/ *noun* [U]

aeti·ology (*BrE*) (*NAmE* **eti·ology**) /ˌi:ti'ɒlədʒi; *NAmE* -'ɑ:l-/ *noun* [U] (*medical*) the scientific study of the causes of disease

afar /ə'fɑ:(r)/ *adv.*

IDM **from a'far** (*literary*) from a long distance away: *He loved her from afar* (= did not tell her he loved her).

afara /ə'fɑ:rə/ (also **limba**) *noun* **1** [C] a tall tree that grows in W Africa **2** [U] the wood from this tree, often used for making furniture **3** [C] (*WAfrE*) a bridge, usually made of wood

AFC /ˌeɪ ef 'si:/ *abbr.* **1** (*BrE*) Association Football Club: *Leeds United AFC* **2** (*NAmE*) American Football Conference (one of the two groups of teams in the NFL) **3** (*BrE*) Air Force Cross (an award given to members of the AIR FORCE, for being brave when flying rather than when fighting the enemy) **4** automatic frequency control (a system which allows radios and televisions to continue to receive the same signal)

af·fable /'æfəbl/ *adj.* pleasant, friendly and easy to talk to SYN **genial** ▸ **af·fa·bil·ity** /ˌæfə'bɪləti/ *noun* [U] **af·fably** *adv.*

af·fair O‑‑ /ə'feə(r); *NAmE* ə'fer/ *noun*

▸ PUBLIC/POLITICAL ACTIVITIES **1** O‑‑ **affairs** [pl.] events that are of public interest or political importance: ***world/international/business affairs*** ◇ *an expert on foreign affairs* (= political events in other countries) ◇ *affairs of state* ➲ see also CURRENT AFFAIRS

▸ EVENT **2** O‑‑ [C, usually sing.] an event that people are talking about or describing in a particular way: *The newspapers* *exaggerated the whole affair wildly.* ◇ *The debate was a pretty disappointing affair.* ◇ *She wanted the celebration to be a simple* ***family affair****.*

▸ RELATIONSHIP **3** [C] a sexual relationship between two people, usually when one or both of them is married to sb else: *She* ***is having an affair*** *with her boss.* ➲ see also LOVE AFFAIR

▸ PRIVATE BUSINESS **4** **affairs** [pl.] matters connected with a person's private business and financial situation: *I looked after my father's financial affairs.* ◇ *She wanted to* ***put her affairs in order*** *before she died.* **5** [sing.] a thing that sb is responsible for (and that other people should not be concerned with) SYN **business**: *How I spend my money is my affair.*

▸ OBJECT **6** [C] (*old-fashioned*) (with an adjective) an object that is unusual or difficult to describe: *Her hat was an amazing affair with feathers and a huge brim.* IDM see STATE *n.*

af·faire /ə'feə(r); *NAmE* ə'fer/ *noun* (from *French, literary*) a love affair

af·fect AW /ə'fekt/ *verb*
1 [often passive] **~ sb/sth** to produce a change in sb/sth: *How will these changes affect us?* ◇ *Your opinion will not affect my decision.* ◇ *The south of the country was worst affected by the drought.* **2** [often passive] **~ sb/sth** (of a disease) to attack sb or a part of the body; to make sb become ill/sick: *The condition affects one in five women.* ◇ *Rub the cream into the affected areas.* **3 ~ sb** [often passive] to make sb have strong feelings of sadness, pity, etc: *They were deeply affected by the news of her death.* **4 ~ (to do) sth** (*formal*) to pretend to be feeling or thinking sth: *She affected a calmness she did not feel.* **5 ~ sth** (*formal, disapproving*) to use or wear sth that is intended to impress other people SYN **put on**: *I wish he wouldn't affect that ridiculous accent.*

Which Word?

affect / effect

- **affect** *verb* = 'to have an influence on sb/sth': *Does television affect children's behaviour?* It is not a noun.
- **effect** *noun* = 'result, influence': *Does television have an effect on children's behaviour?*
- **effect** *verb* is quite rare and formal and means 'to achieve or produce'. *They hope to effect a reconciliation.*

af·fect·ation /ˌæfek'teɪʃn/ *noun* [C, U] behaviour or an action that is not natural or sincere and that is often intended to impress other people: *His little affectations irritated her.* ◇ *Kay has no affectation at all.* ◇ *He raised his eyebrows with an affectation of surprise* (= pretending to be surprised).

af·fect·ed /ə'fektɪd/ *adj.* (of a person or their behaviour) not natural or sincere: *an* ***affected laugh/smile*** OPP **unaffected** ▸ **af·fect·ed·ly** *adv.*

af·fect·ing /ə'fektɪŋ/ *adj.* (*formal*) producing strong feelings of sadness and sympathy

af·fec·tion /ə'fekʃn/ *noun*
1 [U, sing.] the feeling of liking or loving sb/sth very much and caring about them: *Children need lots of love and affection.* ◇ *He didn't* ***show*** *his wife any* ***affection****.* ◇ *She was held in deep affection by all her students.* ◇ **~ for sb/sth** *Mr Darcy's affection for his sister* ◇ *I have a great affection for New York.* ➲ COLLOCATIONS at MARRIAGE **2 affections** [pl.] (*formal* or *literary*) a person's feelings of love: *Anne had two men trying to win her affections.*

af·fec·tion·ate /ə'fekʃənət/ *adj.* showing caring feelings and love for sb SYN **loving**: *He is very affectionate towards his children.* ◇ *an affectionate kiss* ▸ **af·fec·tion·ate·ly** *adv.*: *William was affectionately known as Billy.*

af·fect·ive AW /ə'fektɪv/ *adj.* (*technical*) connected with emotions and attitudes: *affective disorders* ▸ **af·fect·ive·ly** AW *adv.*

af·fi·da·vit /ˌæfə'deɪvɪt/ *noun* (*law*) a written statement that you swear is true, and that can be used as evidence in court

af·fili·ate *verb, noun*
■ ***verb*** /ə'fɪlieɪt/ **1** [T, usually passive] **~ sb/sth (with/to sb/sth)** to link a group, a company or an organization very closely with another, larger one: *The hospital is affiliated with the local university.* ◇ *The group is not affiliated to any political party.* **2** [T, I] **~ (yourself) (with sb/sth)** to join, to be connected with, or to work for an organization: *The majority of people questioned affiliated themselves with a religious group.*
■ ***noun*** /ə'fɪliət/ a company, an organization, etc. that is connected with or controlled by another, larger one

af·fili·ated /ə'fɪlieɪtɪd/ *adj.* [only before noun] closely connected to or controlled by a group or an organization: *All affiliated members can vote.* ◇ *a government-affiliated institute* OPP **unaffiliated**

af·fili·ation /əˌfɪli'eɪʃn/ *noun* [U, C] (*formal*) **1** a person's connection with a political party, religion, etc: *He was arrested because of his political affiliation.* **2** one group or organization's official connection with another

af·fin·ity /ə'fɪnəti/ *noun* (*pl.* -ies) (*formal*) **1** [sing.] **~ (for/with sb/sth)** | **~ (between A and B)** a strong feeling that you understand sb/sth and like them or it SYN **rapport**: *Sam was born in the country and had a deep affinity with nature.* **2** [U, C] **~ (with sb/sth)** | **~ (between A and B)** a close relationship between two people or things that have similar qualities, structures or features: *There is a close affinity between Italian and Spanish.*

af'finity card *noun* a CREDIT CARD printed with the name of an organization, for example a charity, which receives a small amount of money each time the card is used

af'finity group *noun* (*especially NAmE*) a group of people who share the same interest or purpose

af·firm /ə'fɜːm; *NAmE* ə'fɜːrm/ *verb* (*formal*) to state firmly or publicly that sth is true or that you support sth strongly SYN **confirm**: **~ sth** *Both sides affirmed their commitment to the ceasefire.* ◇ **~ that...** *I can affirm that no one will lose their job.* ▸ **af·firm·ation** /ˌæfə'meɪʃn; *NAmE* ˌæfər'm-/ *noun* [U, C]: *She nodded in affirmation.*

af·firma·tive /ə'fɜːmətɪv; *NAmE* ə'fɜːrm-/ *adj., noun*
■ ***adj.*** (*formal*) an **affirmative** word or reply means 'yes' or expresses agreement OPP **negative** ▸ **af·firma·tive·ly** *adv.*: *90% voted affirmatively.*
■ ***noun*** (*formal*) a word or statement that means 'yes'; an agreement or a CONFIRMATION: *She answered* ***in the affirmative*** (= said 'yes'). OPP **negative**

afˌfirmative 'action (*especially NAmE*) (*BrE* usually ˌ**positive disˌcrimin'ation**) *noun* [U] the practice or policy of making sure that a particular number of jobs, etc. are given to people from groups that are often treated unfairly because of their race, sex, etc. ➲ compare REVERSE DISCRIMINATION

affix *verb, noun*
■ ***verb*** /ə'fɪks/ [often passive] **~ sth (to sth)** (*formal*) to stick or attach sth to sth else: *The label should be firmly affixed to the package.*
■ ***noun*** /'æfɪks/ (*grammar*) a letter or group of letters added to the beginning or end of a word to change its meaning. The PREFIX *un-* in *unhappy* and the SUFFIX *-less* in *careless* are both affixes.

af·flict /ə'flɪkt/ *verb* [often passive] (*formal*) to affect sb/sth in an unpleasant or harmful way: **~ sb/sth** *Aid will be sent to the afflicted areas.* ◇ **be afflicted with sth** *About 40% of the country's population is afflicted with the disease.*

af·flic·tion /ə'flɪkʃn/ *noun* [U, C] (*formal*) pain and suffering or sth that causes it

af·flu·ent /'æfluənt/ *adj.* (*formal*) having a lot of money and a good standard of living SYN **prosperous, wealthy**: *affluent Western countries* ◇ *a very affluent neighbourhood* ➲ SYNONYMS at RICH ▸ **af·flu·ence** /'æfluəns/ *noun* [U] SYN **prosperity**

A

af·ford 0‑w /əˈfɔːd; *NAmE* əˈfɔːrd/ *verb* **1** 0‑w [no passive] (usually used with *can*, *could* or *be able to*, especially in negative sentences or questions) to have enough money or time to be able to buy or to do sth: **~ sth** *Can we afford a new car?* ◇ *None of them could afford £50 for a ticket.* ◇ *She felt she couldn't afford any more time off work.* ◇ **~ to do sth** *We can't afford to go abroad this summer.* ◇ *She never took a taxi, even though she could afford to.* ◇ **~ sth to do sth** *He couldn't afford the money to go on the trip.* **2** 0‑w [no passive] (usually used with *can* or *could*, especially in negative sentences and questions) if you say that you **can't afford** to do sth, you mean that you should not do it because it will cause problems for you if you do: **~ to do sth** *We cannot afford to ignore this warning.* ◇ (*formal*) *They could* ***ill afford*** *to lose any more staff.* ◇ **~ sth** *We cannot afford any more delays.* **3** (*formal*) to provide sb with sth: **~ sth** *The tree affords some shelter from the sun.* ◇ **~ sb sth** *The programme affords young people the chance to gain work experience.* ▸ **af·ford·abil·ity** /əˌfɔːdəˈbɪləti; *NAmE* əˌfɔːrd-/ *noun* [U] **af·ford·able** /əˈfɔːdəbl; *NAmE* əˈfɔːrd-/ *adj.*: *affordable prices/housing* OPP **unaffordable** ➲ SYNONYMS at CHEAP **af·ford·ably**: *affordably priced apartments*

af·for·est·ation /əˌfɒrɪˈsteɪʃn; *NAmE* əˌfɔːr-; əˌfɑːr-/ *noun* [U] (*technical*) the process of planting areas of land with trees in order to form a forest ➲ compare DEFORESTATION ▸ **af·for·est** /əˈfɒrɪst; *NAmE* əˈfɔːr-; əˈfɑːr-/ *verb* [usually passive] **~ sth**

af·fray /əˈfreɪ/ *noun* [C, usually sing., U] (*law*) a fight or violent behaviour in a public place

af·fri·cate /ˈæfrɪkət/ *noun* (*phonetics*) a speech sound that is made up of a PLOSIVE followed immediately by a FRICATIVE, for example /tʃ/ and /dʒ/ in *chair* and *jar*

af·front /əˈfrʌnt/ *noun, verb*

■ ***noun*** [usually sing.] **~ (to sb/sth)** a remark or an action that insults or offends sb/sth

■ ***verb*** [usually passive] **~ sb/sth** (*formal*) to insult or offend sb: *He hoped they would not feel affronted if they were not invited.* ◇ *an affronted expression*

Afghan hound /ˌæfgæn ˈhaʊnd/ *noun* a tall dog with long soft hair and a pointed nose

afi·cion·ado /əˌfɪʃəˈnɑːdəʊ; *NAmE* -doʊ/ *noun* (*pl.* -os) a person who likes a particular sport, activity or subject very much and knows a lot about it

afield /əˈfiːld/ *adv.*

IDM **far/farther/further aˈfield** far away from home; to or in places that are not near: *You can hire a car if you want to explore further afield.* ◇ *Journalists came* ***from as far afield as*** *China.*

aflame /əˈfleɪm/ *adj.* [not before noun] (*literary*) **1** burning; on fire SYN **ablaze**: *The whole building was soon aflame.* **2** full of bright colours and lights SYN **ablaze**: *The woods were aflame with autumn colours.* **3** showing excitement or embarrassment: ***eyes/cheeks aflame***

AFL-CIO /ˌeɪ ef el siː aɪ ˈəʊ; *NAmE* ˈoʊ/ *abbr.* American Federation of Labor and Congress of Industrial Organizations (an organization of TRADE/LABOR UNIONS)

afloat /əˈfləʊt; *NAmE* əˈfloʊt/ *adj.* [not before noun] **1** floating on water: *Somehow we kept the boat afloat.* **2** (of a business, etc.) having enough money to pay debts; able to survive: *They will have to borrow £10 million next year, just to* ***stay afloat***.

afoot /əˈfʊt/ *adj.* [not before noun] being planned; happening: *There are plans afoot to increase taxation.* ◇ *Changes were afoot.*

afore·men·tioned /əˌfɔːˈmenʃənd; *NAmE* əˌfɔːrˈm-/ (also **afore·said** /əˈfɔːsed; *NAmE* əˈfɔːrsed/) (also **said**) *adj.* [only before noun] (*formal* or *law*) mentioned before, in an earlier sentence: *The aforementioned person was seen acting suspiciously.*

afore·thought /əˈfɔːθɔːt; *NAmE* əˈfɔːrθ-/ *adj.* IDM see MALICE

a for·ti·ori /ˌeɪ ˌfɔːtiˈɔːraɪ; *NAmE* ˌfɔːrt-/ *adv.* (*formal* or *law*) (from *Latin*) for or with an even stronger reason

afoul /əˈfaʊl/ *adv.* (*NAmE*)

IDM **run aˈfoul of sth** to do sth that is not allowed by a law or rule, or to do sth that people in authority disapprove of: *to run afoul of the law*

afraid 0‑w /əˈfreɪd/ *adj.* [not before noun] **1** 0‑w feeling fear; frightened because you think that you might be hurt or suffer: *Don't be afraid.* ◇ **~ of sb/sth** *It's all over. There's nothing to be afraid of now.* ◇ *Are you afraid of spiders?* ◇ **~ of doing sth** *I started to feel afraid of going out alone at night.* ◇ **~ to do sth** *She was afraid to open the door.* **2** 0‑w worried about what might happen: **~ of doing sth** *She was afraid of upsetting her parents.* ◇ **~ to do sth** *Don't be afraid to ask if you don't understand.* ◇ **~ (that...)** *We were afraid (that) we were going to capsize the boat.* **3 ~ for sb/sth** worried or frightened that sth unpleasant, dangerous, etc. will happen to a particular person or thing: *I'm not afraid for me, but for the baby.* ◇ *They had already fired three people and he was afraid for his job.*

IDM **I'm afraid** 0‑w used as a polite way of telling sb sth that is unpleasant or disappointing, or that you are sorry about: *I can't help you, I'm afraid.* ◇ *I'm afraid we can't come.* ◇ *I'm afraid that it's not finished yet.* ◇ *He's no better,* ***I'm afraid to say.*** ◇ *'Is there any left?'* ***'I'm afraid not.'*** ◇ *'Will it hurt?'* ***'I'm afraid so.'***

Synonyms

afraid

frightened • scared • terrified • alarmed • paranoid

These words all describe feeling or showing fear.

afraid [not before noun] feeling fear; worried that sth bad might happen: *There's nothing to be afraid of.* ◇ *Aren't you afraid (that) you'll fall?*

frightened feeling fear; worried that sth bad might happen: *a frightened child* ◇ *She was frightened that the glass would break.*

scared (*rather informal*) feeling fear; worried that sth bad might happen: *The thieves got scared and ran away.*

AFRAID, FRIGHTENED OR SCARED?

Scared is more informal, more common in speech, and often describes small fears. **Afraid** cannot come before a noun. It can only take the preposition *of*, not *about*. If you are **afraid/frightened/scared of** sb/sth/doing sth or **afraid/frightened/scared to** do sth, you think you are in danger of being hurt or suffering in some way. If you are **frightened/scared about** sth/doing sth, it is less a fear for your personal safety and more a worry that sth unpleasant might happen.

terrified very frightened: *I was terrified (that) she wouldn't come.* ◇ *She looked at him with wide, terrified eyes.*

alarmed afraid that sth dangerous or unpleasant might happen: *She was alarmed at the prospect of travelling alone.*

paranoid (*rather informal*) afraid or suspicious of other people and believing that they are trying to harm you, in a way that is not reasonable: *You're just being paranoid.*

PATTERNS

- afraid/frightened/scared **of** spiders, etc.
- frightened/scared/paranoid **about** ...
- afraid/frightened/scared/terrified **that** ...
- afraid/frightened/scared **to** open the door, etc.
- **Don't be** afraid/frightened/scared/alarmed.

ˈA-frame (also **ˌA-frame ˈhouse**) *noun* (*especially NAmE*) a house with very steep sides that meet at the top in the shape of the letter A

ˈA-frame tent *noun* = RIDGE TENT

afresh /ə'freʃ/ *adv.* (*formal*) again, especially from the beginning or with new ideas: *It was a chance to **start afresh**.*

Af·ri·can /'æfrɪkən/ *adj., noun*
- ***adj.*** of or connected with Africa
- ***noun*** a person from Africa, especially a black person

ˌAfrican A'merican *noun* a person from America who is a member of a race of people who have dark skin, originally from Africa ▸ **ˌAfrican A'merican** *adj.*

ˌAfrican Ca'nadian *noun* a Canadian citizen whose family was originally from Africa ▸ **African Canadian** *adj.*

ˌAfrican re'naissance *noun* [sing.] a period of time when Africa will experience great development in its economy and culture. Some people believe that this started at the end of the 20th century.

Af·ri·kaans /ˌæfrɪ'kɑːns/ *noun* [U] a language that has developed from Dutch, spoken in South Africa

Af·ri·kaner /ˌæfrɪ'kɑːnə(r)/ *noun* a person from South Africa, usually of Dutch origin, whose first language is Afrikaans

Afro /'æfrəʊ; *NAmE* 'æfroʊ/ *noun* (*pl.* -os) a HAIRSTYLE sometimes worn by black people and popular in the 1970s, in which the hair forms a round mass of tight curls

Afro- /'-frəʊ; *NAmE* 'æfroʊ/ *combining form* (in nouns and adjectives) African: *Afro-Asian*

Afro·beat /'æfrəʊbiːt; *NAmE* 'æfroʊ/ *noun* [U] a type of music that combines traditional Nigerian rhythms and singing styles with JAZZ and FUNK

ˌAfro-Carib'bean *noun* a person who comes, or whose family comes, from the Caribbean and who is a member of a group of people with dark skin who originally came from Africa ▸ **ˌAfro-Carib'bean** *adj.*

aft /ɑːft; *NAmE* æft/ *adv.* (*technical*) in, near or towards the back of a ship or an aircraft ▸ **aft** *adj.* ⊃ compare FORE

after 🔑 /'ɑːftə(r); *NAmE* 'æf-/ *prep., conj., adv., adj.*
- ***prep.*** **1** 🔑 later than sth; following sth in time: *We'll leave after lunch.* ◇ *They arrived **shortly after** 5.* ◇ ***Not long after that** he resigned.* ◇ *Let's meet **the day after tomorrow/the week after next**.* ◇ *After winning the prize she became famous overnight.* ◇ *After an hour I went home* (= when an hour had passed). ◇ (*NAmE*) *It's ten after seven in the morning* (= 7.10 a.m.) **2** 🔑 **... after...** used to show that sth happens many times or continuously: *day after day of hot weather* ◇ *I've told you time after time not to do that.* ⊃ see also ONE AFTER ANOTHER at ONE **3** 🔑 behind sb when they have left; following sb: *Shut the door after you.* ◇ *I'm always having to clean up after the children* (= clean the place after they have left it dirty and untidy). ◇ *He ran after her with the book.* ◇ *She was left staring after him.* **4** 🔑 next to and following sb/sth in order or importance: *Your name comes after mine in the list.* ◇ *He's the tallest, after Richard.* ◇ ***After you*** (= Please go first). ◇ ***After you with** the paper* (= Can I have it next?). **5** 🔑 in contrast to sth: *It was pleasantly cool in the house after the sticky heat outside.* **6** 🔑 as a result of or because of sth that has happened: *I'll never forgive him after what he said.* **7** despite sth; although sth has happened: *I can't believe she'd do that, not after all I've done for her.* **8** trying to find or catch sb/sth: *The police are after him.* ◇ *He's after a job at our place.* **9** about sb/sth: *She asked after you* (= how you were). **10** in the style of sb/sth; following the example of sb/sth: *a painting after Goya* ◇ *We named the baby 'Ena' after her grandmother.* **11 after-** (in adjectives) happening or done later than the time or event mentioned: *after-hours drinking* (= after closing time) ◇ *an after-school club* ◇ *after-dinner mints*

IDM **ˌafter 'all 1** 🔑 despite what has been said or expected: *So you made it after all!* **2** 🔑 used when you are explaining sth, or giving a reason: *He should have paid. He suggested it, after all.* **be after doing sth** (*IrishE*) **1** to be going to do sth soon; to be intending to do sth soon **2** to have just done sth
- ***conj.*** 🔑 at a time later than sth; when sth has finished: *I'll call you after I've spoken to them.* ◇ *Several years after they'd split up they met again by chance in Paris.*
- ***adv.*** 🔑 later in time; afterwards: *That was in 1996. **Soon after**, I heard that he'd died.* ◇ *I could come next week, or the week after.* ◇ *And they all **lived happily ever after**.*
- ***adj.*** [only before noun] (*old use*) following; later: *in after years*

after·birth /'ɑːftəbɜːθ; *NAmE* 'æftərbɜːrθ/ *noun* (usually **the afterbirth**) [sing.] the material that comes out of a woman or female animal's body after a baby has been born, and which was necessary to feed and protect the baby SYN **placenta**

after·burn·er /'ɑːftəbɜːnə(r); *NAmE* 'æftərbɜːrnər/ *noun* (*technical*) a device for increasing the power of a JET ENGINE

after·care /'ɑːftəkeə(r); *NAmE* 'æftərker/ *noun* [U] **1** care or treatment given to a person who has just left hospital, prison, etc: *aftercare services* **2** (*BrE*) service and advice that is offered by some companies to customers who have bought a car, WASHING MACHINE, etc.

'after-effect *noun* [usually pl.] the **after-effects** of a drug, an illness or an unpleasant event are the feelings that you experience later as a result of it

after·glow /'ɑːftəgləʊ; *NAmE* 'æftərgloʊ/ *noun* [usually sing.] (*literary*) **1** the light that is left in the sky after the sun has set **2** a pleasant feeling after a good experience

after·life /'ɑːftəlaɪf; *NAmE* 'æftərl-/ *noun* [sing.] a life that some people believe exists after death

after·math /'ɑːftəmæθ; -mɑːθ; *NAmE* 'æftərmæθ/ *noun* [usually sing.] the situation that exists as a result of an important (and usually unpleasant) event, especially a war, an accident, etc: *A lot of rebuilding took place **in the aftermath of** the war.* ◇ *the assassination of the Prime Minister and its immediate aftermath*

after·noon 🔑 /ˌɑːftə'nuːn; *NAmE* ˌæftər'n-/ *noun* [U, C]
the part of the day from 12 midday until about 6 o'clock: ***this/yesterday/tomorrow afternoon*** ◇ ***In the afternoon** they went shopping.* ◇ *She studies art two afternoons a week.* ◇ *Are you ready for this afternoon's meeting?* ◇ *The baby always has an afternoon nap.* ◇ *Come over on Sunday afternoon.* ◇ *Where were you **on the afternoon of** May 21?* ⊃ see also GOOD AFTERNOON

after·noons /ˌɑːftə'nuːnz; *NAmE* ˌæftər'n-/ *adv.* during the afternoon every day: *Afternoons he works at home.*

af·ters /'ɑːftəz; *NAmE* 'æftərz/ *noun* [U] (*BrE, informal*) a sweet dish that you eat at the end of a meal: *fruit salad for afters* ⊃ see also DESSERT, PUDDING, SWEET *n.*

ˌafter-ˌsales 'service *noun* [U] the fact of providing help to customers after they have bought a product, usually involving doing repairs that are needed or giving advice on how to use the product

after·shave /'ɑːftəʃeɪv; *NAmE* 'æftərʃ-/ *noun* [U, C] a liquid with a pleasant smell that men sometimes put on their faces after they shave

after·shock /'ɑːftəʃɒk; *NAmE* 'æftərʃɑːk/ *noun* a small EARTHQUAKE that happens after a bigger one

after·taste /'ɑːftəteɪst; *NAmE* 'æftərt-/ *noun* [sing.] a taste (usually an unpleasant one) that stays in your mouth after you have eaten or drunk sth

after·thought /'ɑːftəθɔːt; *NAmE* 'æftərθ-/ *noun* [usually sing.] a thing that is thought of, said or added later, and is often not carefully planned: *They only invited Jack and Sarah **as an afterthought**.*

after·wards 🔑 /'ɑːftəwədz; *NAmE* 'æftərwərdz/ (*especially BrE*) (*NAmE* usually **after·ward**) *adv.*
at a later time; after an event that has already been mentioned: *Afterwards she was sorry for what she'd said.* ◇ *Let's go out now and eat afterwards.* ◇ *Shortly afterwards he met her again.*

after·word /'ɑːftəwɜːd; *NAmE* 'æftərwɜːrd/ *noun* a section at the end of a book that says sth about the main text, and may be written by a different author ⊃ compare FOREWORD

A

ag /æx; ʌx/ *exclamation* (*SAfrE*) used when you are reacting to sth that has been said, or when you are angry or irritated by sth: *Ag, don't worry about it.* ◇ *Ag, no man!*

Aga™ /ˈɑːgə/ *noun* (*BrE*) a type of British cooker/stove made of solid iron that is also used for heating. 'Aga saga' is a humorous name for a novel about the lives of British middle-class women, because Agas are very popular with this group.

again 🔑 /əˈgen; əˈgeɪn/ *adv.* **1** 🔑 one more time; on another occasion: *Could you say it again, please?* ◇ *When will I see you again?* ◇ *This must never happen again.* ◇ ***Once again*** (= as had happened several times before), *the train was late.* ◇ *I've told you **again and again*** (= many times) *not to do that.* ◇ *I'll have to write it **all over again*** (= again from the beginning). **2** 🔑 showing that sb/sth is in the same place or state that they were in originally: *He was glad to be home again.* ◇ *She spends two hours a day getting to work and **back again**.* ◇ *You'll soon feel well again.* **3** added to an amount that is already there: *The cost is about **half as much again** as it was two years ago.* ◇ *I'd like **the same again*** (= the same amount or the same thing). **4** used to show that a comment or fact is connected with what you have just said: *And again, we must think of the cost.* **5 then/there ~** used to introduce a fact or an opinion that contrasts with what you have just said: *We might buy it but then again we might not.* **6** used when you ask sb to tell you sth or repeat sth that you think they have told you already: *What was the name again?* IDM see NOW *adv.*, SAME *pron.*, TIME *n.*

against 🔑 /əˈgenst; əˈgeɪnst/ *prep.* HELP For the special uses of **against** in phrasal verbs, look at the entries for the verbs. For example **count against sb** is in the phrasal verb section at **count**. **1** 🔑 opposing or disagreeing with sb/sth: *the fight against terrorism* ◇ *We're playing against the league champions next week.* ◇ *We were rowing against the current.* ◇ *That's against the law.* ◇ *She was forced to marry against her will.* ◇ *Are you for or against the death penalty?* ◇ *She is against seeing* (= does not want to see) *him.* ◇ *I'd advise you against doing that.* **2** 🔑 not to the advantage or favour of sb/sth: *The evidence is against him.* ◇ *Her age is against her.* ➲ compare FOR *prep.* (7) **3** close to, touching or hitting sb/sth: *Put the piano there, against the wall.* ◇ *The rain beat against the windows.* **4** in order to prevent sth from happening or to reduce the damage caused by sth: *an injection against rabies* ◇ *They took precautions against fire.* ◇ *Are we insured against theft?* **5** with sth in the background, as a contrast: *His red clothes stood out clearly against the snow.* ◇ (*figurative*) *The love story unfolds against a background of civil war.* **6** used when you are comparing two things: *You must weigh the benefits against the cost.* ◇ *Check your receipts against the statement.* ◇ *What's the rate of exchange against the dollar?* IDM see AS *conj.*, STACKED

agape[1] /əˈgeɪp/ *adj.* [not before noun] (*formal*) if a person's mouth is **agape**, it is wide open, especially because they are surprised or shocked

agar /ˈeɪgɑː(r)/ (also ˌ**agar-ˈagar**) *noun* [U] a substance like jelly, used by scientists for growing CULTURES

agate /ˈægət/ *noun* [U, C] a hard stone with bands or areas of colour, used in jewellery

agave /əˈgeɪvi; -ˈgɑːv-; *NAmE* əˈgɑːvi/ *noun* a plant that grows in hot dry areas of N and S America, with sharp points on the leaves and tall groups of flowers

ag·bada /ægˈbɑːdə/ *noun* a long ROBE (= long piece of clothing) worn by men in some parts of W Africa

age 🔑 /eɪdʒ/ *noun, verb*
■ ***noun*** **1** 🔑 [C, U] the number of years that a person has lived or a thing has existed: *He left school **at the age of** 18.* ◇ *She needs more friends of her own age.* ◇ *children from 5–10 **years of age*** ◇ *Young people of all ages go there to meet.* ◇ *When I was your age I was already married.* ◇ *He started playing the piano **at an early age**.* ◇ *All ages admitted.* ◇ *Children **over the age of** 12 must pay full fare.* ◇ *She was beginning to **feel her age*** (= feel that she was getting old). ◇ *He was tall **for his age*** (= taller than you would expect, considering his age). ◇ *There's a big **age gap** between them* (= a big difference in their ages). ◇ *ways of calculating the age of the earth* **2** 🔑 [U, C] a particular period of a person's life: *middle age* ◇ *15 is an awkward age.* ◇ *He died of old age.* ➲ see also THE THIRD AGE **3** 🔑 [C] a particular period of history: *the nuclear age* ◇ *the age of the computer* ➲ see also BRONZE AGE, IRON AGE, NEW AGE, STONE AGE **4** 🔑 [U] the state of being old: *Wine improves **with age**.* ◇ *The jacket was showing signs of age.* ◇ *the wisdom that comes with age* **5** 🔑 **ages** [pl.] (also **an age** [sing.]) (*informal, especially BrE*) a very long time: *I waited **for ages**.* ◇ *It'll probably **take ages** to find a parking space.* ◇ *Carlos left **ages ago**.* ◇ *It's been an age since we've seen them.* **6** [C] (*geology*) a length of time which is a division of an EPOCH

Collocations

The ages of life

Childhood/youth

- **be born and raised/bred** in Oxford; into a wealthy/middle-class family
- **have** a happy/an unhappy/a tough childhood
- **grow up** in a musical family/an orphanage; on a farm
- **be/grow up** an only child (= with no brothers or sisters)
- **reach/hit/enter/go through** adolescence/puberty
- **be in** your teens/early twenties/mid-twenties/late twenties
- **undergo/experience** physical/psychological changes
- **give in to/succumb to/resist** peer pressure
- **assert** your independence/individuality

Adulthood

- **leave** school/university/home
- **go out to** work (at sixteen)
- **get/find** a job/partner
- **be/get** engaged/married
- **have/get** a wife/husband/mortgage/steady job
- **settle down and have** kids/children/a family
- **begin/start/launch/build** a career (in politics/science/the music industry)
- **prove (to be)/represent/mark/reach** a (major) turning point for sb/in your life/career
- **reach/be well into/settle into** middle age
- **have/suffer/go through** a midlife crisis
- **take/consider** early retirement
- **approach/announce/enjoy** your retirement

Old age

- **have/see/spend time with** your grandchildren
- **take up/pursue/develop** a hobby
- **get/receive/draw/collect/live on** a pension
- **approach/save for/die from** old age
- **live to** a ripe old age
- **reach** the grand old age of 102/23 (*often ironic*)
- **be/become/be getting/be going** senile (*often ironic*)
- **die (peacefully)/pass away** in your sleep/after a brief illness

IDM ˌ**be/**ˌ**act your** ˈ**age** to behave in a way that is suitable for sb of your age and not as though you were much younger ˌ**come of** ˈ**age 1** when a person **comes of age**, they reach the age when they have an adult's legal rights and responsibilities ➲ see also COMING OF AGE **2** if sth **comes of age**, it reaches the stage of development at which people accept and value it ˌ**look your** ˈ**age** to seem as old as you really are and not younger or older ˌ**under** ˈ**age** not legally old enough to do a particular thing: *It is illegal to sell cigarettes to children who are under age.* ➲ see also UNDERAGE ➲ more at ADVANCED, CERTAIN, DAY, FEEL *v.*, GRAND *adj.*, RIPE

■ ***verb*** (**ag·ing, aged, aged**) HELP In *BrE* the present participle can also be spelled **age·ing**. **1** [I] to become older: *As he aged, his memory got worse.* ◇ *The population is aging* (= more people are living longer). **2** [T] to make sb/sth look, feel or seem older: **~ sb** *The shock has aged her.* ◇ **~ sth** *Exposure to the sun ages the skin.* **3** [I, T] to develop in flavour over a period of time; to allow sth to do this SYN **mature**: *The cheese is left to age for at least a year.* ◇ **~ sth** *The wine is aged in oak casks.*

-age *suffix* (in nouns) **1** the action or result of: *breakage* **2** a state or condition of: *bondage* **3** a set or group of: *baggage* **4** an amount of: *mileage* **5** the cost of: *postage* **6** a place where: *anchorage*

aged 🔑 *adj.*
1 🔑 /eɪdʒd/ [not before noun] of the age of: *They have two children aged six and nine.* ◇ *volunteers aged between 25 and 40* **2** /ˈeɪdʒɪd/ (*formal*) very old: *my aged aunt* ➲ SYNONYMS at OLD **3 the aged** /ˈeɪdʒɪd/ *noun* [pl.] very old people: *services for the sick and the aged*

ˈage group (also *less frequent* **ˈage bracket**) *noun* people of a similar age or within a particular range of ages: *men in the older age group* ◇ *education for the 16–18 age group* ◇ *Which age bracket are you? (Please tick the box).*

age·ing (*BrE*) (also **aging** *NAmE, BrE*) /ˈeɪdʒɪŋ/ *noun, adj.*
■ ***noun*** [U] the process of growing old: *signs of ageing*
■ ***adj.*** [usually before noun] becoming older and usually less useful, safe, healthy, etc: *ageing equipment* ◇ *an ageing rock star*

age·ism (*NAmE* also **agism**) /ˈeɪdʒɪzəm/ *noun* [U] unfair treatment of people because they are considered too old ▸ **age·ist** *adj.* **age·ist** *noun*

age·less /ˈeɪdʒləs/ *adj.* (*literary*) **1** never looking old or never seeming to grow old SYN **timeless**: *Her beauty appeared ageless.* **2** existing for ever; impossible to give an age to SYN **timeless**: *the ageless mystery of the universe*

ˈage limit *noun* the oldest or youngest age at which you are allowed to do sth: *the* ***upper/lower age limit***

agency 🔑 /ˈeɪdʒənsi/ *noun* (*pl.* -ies)
1 🔑 a business or an organization that provides a particular service especially on behalf of other businesses or organizations: *an* ***advertising/employment agency*** ◇ *You can book at your local* ***travel agency***. ◇ *international* ***aid agencies*** *caring for refugees* ➲ see also DATING AGENCY, NEWS AGENCY, PRESS AGENCY **2** 🔑 (*especially NAmE*) a government department that provides a particular service: *the Central Intelligence Agency (CIA)*
IDM **through the agency of** (*formal*) as a result of the action of sb/sth

agenda /əˈdʒendə/ *noun* a list of items to be discussed at a meeting: *The next item* ***on the agenda*** *is the publicity budget.* ◇ *For the government, education is now* ***at the top of the agenda*** (= most important). ◇ *In our company, quality is* ***high on the agenda***. ◇ *Newspapers have been accused of trying to* ***set the agenda*** *for the government* (= decide what is important). ➲ see also HIDDEN AGENDA

Which Word?

agenda / diary / schedule / timetable

- A book with a space for each day where you write down things that you have to do in the future is called a **diary** or a **datebook** (*NAmE*) (not an *agenda*). You may also have a **calendar** on your desk or hanging up in your room, where you write down your appointments. A **diary** or a **journal** is also the record that some people keep of what has happened during the day: *the Diary of Anne Frank*.
- In *BrE* your **schedule** is a plan that lists all the work that you have to do and when you must do each thing and a **timetable** is a list showing the fixed times at which events will happen: *a bus/train timetable*. In *NAmE* these are both called a **schedule**.

agent 🔑 /ˈeɪdʒənt/ *noun*
1 🔑 a person whose job is to act for, or manage the affairs of, other people in business, politics, etc: *an insurance agent* ◇ *Our agent in New York deals with all US sales.* ➲ see also ESTATE AGENT, LAND AGENT, TRAVEL AGENT **2** 🔑 a person whose job is to arrange work for an actor, musician, sports player, etc. or to find sb who will publish a writer's work: *a* ***theatrical/literary agent*** ➲ see also PRESS AGENT **3** = SECRET AGENT: *an enemy agent* ➲ see also DOUBLE AGENT, SPECIAL AGENT **4** (*formal*) a person or thing that has an important effect on a situation: *The charity has been an agent for social change.* **5** (*technical*) a chemical or a substance that produces an effect or a change or is used for a particular purpose: ***cleaning/oxidizing agents*** **6** (*grammar*) the person or thing that does an action (expressed as the subject of an active verb, or in a 'by' phrase with a passive verb) ➲ compare PATIENT ➲ see also FREE AGENT

ˌAgent ˈGeneral *noun* (*pl.* **ˌAgents ˈGeneral**) the representative of an Australian state or Canadian PROVINCE in a foreign country

agent pro·voca·teur /ˌæʒɒ̃ prəˌvɒkəˈtɜː(r); *NAmE* ˌɑːʒɑ̃ː proʊˌvɑːkəˈtɜːr/ (also **pro·voca·teur**) *noun* (*pl.* **agents pro·voca·teurs** /ˌæʒɒ̃ prəˌvɒkəˈtɜː(r); *NAmE* ˌɑːʒɑ̃ː proʊˌvɑːkəˈtɜːr/) (from *French*) a person who is employed by a government to encourage people in political groups to do sth illegal so that they can be arrested

ˌage of conˈsent *noun* [sing.] the age at which sb is legally old enough to agree to have a sexual relationship

ˌage-ˈold *adj.* [usually before noun] having existed for a very long time: *an* ***age-old custom/problem***

ˈage-set *noun* (*EAfrE*) a group of boys or men of a similar age

ag·glom·er·ate *verb, noun, adj.* (*formal*)
■ ***verb*** /əˈɡlɒməreɪt; *NAmE* əˈɡlɑːm-/ [I, T] to form into a mass or group; to collect things and form them into a mass or group: *These small particles agglomerate together to form larger clusters.* ◇ **~ sth** *They agglomerated many small pieces of research into a single large study.*
■ ***noun*** /əˈɡlɒmərət; *NAmE* əˈɡlɑːm-/ a mass or collection of things: *a multimedia agglomerate* (= group of companies)
■ ***adj.*** /əˈɡlɒmərət; *NAmE* əˈɡlɑːm-/ formed into a mass or group

ag·glom·er·ation /əˌɡlɒməˈreɪʃn; *NAmE* əˌɡlɑːm-/ *noun* [C, U] (*formal*) a group of things put together in no particular order or arrangement

ag·glu·tin·ative /əˈɡluːtɪnətɪv/ *adj.* (*linguistics*) = SYNTHETIC

ag·grand·ize·ment (*BrE* also **-ise·ment**) /əˈɡrændɪzmənt/ *noun* [U] (*formal, disapproving*) an increase in the power or importance of a person or country: *Her sole aim is personal aggrandizement.*

ag·gra·vate /ˈæɡrəveɪt/ *verb* **1 ~ sth** to make an illness or a bad or unpleasant situation worse SYN **worsen**: *Pollution can aggravate asthma.* ◇ *Military intervention will only aggravate the conflict even further.* **2 ~ sb** (*informal*) to annoy sb, especially deliberately SYN **irritate** ▸ **ag·gra·vat·ing** *adj.* **ag·gra·va·tion** /ˌæɡrəˈveɪʃn/ *noun* [U, C]: *I don't need all this aggravation at work.* ◇ *The drug may cause an aggravation of the condition.*

ag·gra·vat·ed /ˈæɡrəveɪtɪd/ *adj.* [only before noun] (*law*) an **aggravated** crime involves further unnecessary violence or unpleasant behaviour

ag·gre·gate AW *noun, adj., verb*
■ ***noun*** /ˈæɡrɪɡət/ **1** [C] a total number or amount made up of smaller amounts that are collected together **2** [U, C] (*technical*) sand or broken stone that is used to make concrete or for building roads, etc.
IDM **in (the) ˈaggregate** (*formal*) added together as a total or single amount **on ˈaggregate** (*BrE, sport*) when the scores of a number of games are added together: *They won 4–2 on aggregate.*
■ ***adj.*** /ˈæɡrɪɡət/ [only before noun] (*economics* or *sport*) made up of several amounts that are added together to form a

total number: ***aggregate demand/investment/turnover*** ◇ *(BrE) an aggregate win over their rivals*
■ ***verb*** /ˈæɡrɪɡeɪt/ [usually passive] **~ sth (with sth)** (*formal* or *technical*) to put together different items, amounts, etc. into a single group or total: *The scores were aggregated with the first round totals to decide the winner.* ▶ **ag·gre·ga·tion** AW /ˌæɡrɪˈɡeɪʃn/ *noun* [U, C]: *the aggregation of data*

ag·gre·ga·tor /ˈæɡrɪɡeɪtə(r)/ *noun* (*computing*) an Internet company that collects information about other companies' products and services and puts it on a single website: *a news aggregator*

ag·gres·sion /əˈɡreʃn/ *noun* [U] **1** feelings of anger and hatred that may result in threatening or violent behaviour: *The research shows that computer games may cause aggression.* **2** a violent attack or threats by one person against another person or by one country against another country: *unprovoked military aggression*

ag·gres·sive 0- /əˈɡresɪv/ *adj.*
1 0- angry, and behaving in a threatening way; ready to attack: *He gets aggressive when he's drunk.* ◇ *a dangerous aggressive dog* **2** 0- acting with force and determination in order to succeed: *an aggressive advertising campaign* ◇ *A good salesperson has to be aggressive in today's competitive market.* ▶ **ag·gres·sive·ly** *adv.*: *'What do you want?' he demanded aggressively.* ◇ *aggressively marketed products* **ag·gres·sive·ness** *noun* [U]

ag·gres·sor /əˈɡresə(r)/ *noun* a person, country, etc. that attacks first

ag·grieved /əˈɡriːvd/ *adj.* **1 ~ (at/by sth)** feeling that you have been treated unfairly **2** (*law*) suffering unfair or illegal treatment and making a complaint: *the aggrieved party* (= person) in the case

aggro /ˈæɡrəʊ; NAmE ˈæɡroʊ/ *noun* [U] (*BrE, informal*) **1** violent aggressive behaviour: *Don't give me any aggro or I'll call the police.* **2** problems and difficulties that are annoying: *I had a lot of aggro at the bank.*

aghast /əˈɡɑːst; NAmE əˈɡæst/ *adj.* [not before noun] filled with horror and surprise when you see or hear sth SYN **horrified**: *Erica looked at him aghast.* ◇ **~ at sth** *He stood aghast at the sight of so much blood.*

agile /ˈædʒaɪl; NAmE ˈædʒl/ *adj.* **1** able to move quickly and easily SYN **nimble 2** able to think quickly and in an intelligent way: *an **agile mind/brain*** ▶ **agil·ity** /əˈdʒɪləti/ *noun* [U]: *He had the agility of a man half his age.*

aging, agism = AGEING, AGEISM

agi·tate /ˈædʒɪteɪt/ *verb* **1** [I, T] to argue strongly for sth you want, especially for changes in a law, in social conditions, etc. SYN **campaign**: **~ (for/against sth)** *political groups agitating for social change* ◇ **~ to do sth** *Her family are agitating to have her transferred to a prison in the UK.* **2** [T] **~ sb** to make sb feel angry, anxious or nervous **3** [T] **~ sth** (*technical*) to make sth, especially a liquid, move around by stirring or shaking it

agi·tated /ˈædʒɪteɪtɪd/ *adj.* showing in your behaviour that you are anxious and nervous: *Calm down! Don't get so agitated.*

agi·ta·tion /ˌædʒɪˈteɪʃn/ *noun* **1** [U] worry and anxiety that you show by behaving in a nervous way: *Dot arrived in a state of great agitation.* **2** [U, C] **~ (for/against sth)** public protest in order to achieve political change: *widespread agitation for social reform* **3** [U] (*technical*) the act of stirring or shaking a liquid

agi·ta·tor /ˈædʒɪteɪtə(r)/ *noun* (*disapproving*) a person who tries to persuade people to take part in political protest

agit·prop /ˈædʒɪtprɒp; NAmE -prɑːp/ *noun* [U] the use of art, films/movies, music, etc. to spread LEFT-WING political ideas

aglow /əˈɡləʊ; NAmE əˈɡloʊ/ *adj.* [not before noun] (*literary*) shining with warmth and colour or happiness

AGM /ˌeɪ dʒiː ˈem/ *abbr.* (*BrE*) annual general meeting (an important meeting which the members of an organization hold once a year in order to elect officers, discuss past and future activities and examine the accounts)

ag·nos·ia /æɡˈnəʊsiə; -ziə; NAmE æɡˈnoʊʒə/ *noun* [U] (*medical*) the lack of the ability to recognize things and people

ag·nos·tic /æɡˈnɒstɪk; NAmE -ˈnɑːs-/ *noun* a person who believes that it is not possible to know whether God exists or not ➲ compare ATHEIST ▶ **ag·nos·tic** *adj.* **ag·nos·ti·cism** /æɡˈnɒstɪsɪzəm; NAmE -ˈnɑːs-/ *noun* [U]

ago 0- /əˈɡəʊ; NAmE əˈɡoʊ/ *adv.*
used in expressions of time with the simple past tense to show how far in the past sth happened: *two weeks/months/years ago* ◇ *The letter came a few days ago.* ◇ *She was here just a minute ago.* ◇ *a short/long time ago* ◇ *How long ago did you buy it?* ◇ *It was on TV not (so) long ago.* ◇ *He stopped working some time ago* (= quite a long time ago). ◇ *They're getting married? It's not that long ago* (= it's only a short time ago) *that they met!*

agog /əˈɡɒɡ; NAmE əˈɡɑːɡ/ *adj.* [not before noun] excited and very interested to find out sth

ag·on·ize (*BrE* also **-ise**) /ˈæɡənaɪz/ *verb* [I] **~ (over/about sth)** to spend a long time thinking and worrying about a difficult situation or problem: *I spent days agonizing over whether to take the job or not.*

ag·on·ized (*BrE* also **-ised**) /ˈæɡənaɪzd/ *adj.* suffering or expressing severe pain or anxiety: *agonized cries*

ag·on·iz·ing (*BrE* also **-is·ing**) /ˈæɡənaɪzɪŋ/ *adj.* causing great pain, anxiety or difficulty: *his father's agonizing death* ◇ *It was the most agonizing decision of her life.*

ag·on·iz·ing·ly (*BrE* also **-is·ing·ly**) /ˈæɡənaɪzɪŋli/ *adv.* used meaning 'extremely' to emphasize sth negative: *an agonizingly slow process*

agony /ˈæɡəni/ *noun* (*pl.* -ies) [U, C] extreme physical or mental pain: *Jack collapsed **in agony** on the floor.* ◇ *It was agony not knowing where the children were.* ◇ *She waited in an agony of suspense.* ◇ *The worst agonies of the war were now beginning.* ◇ *Tell me now! Don't **prolong the agony*** (= make it last longer). IDM see PILE *v.*

ˈagony aunt (*BrE*) (*NAmE* **adˈvice columnist**) *noun* a person who writes in a newspaper or magazine giving advice in reply to people's letters about their personal problems ➲ compare AGONY UNCLE

ˈagony column (*BrE*) (*NAmE* **adˈvice column**) *noun* part of a newspaper or magazine in which sb gives advice to readers who have sent letters about their personal problems

ˈagony uncle *noun* (*BrE*) (*NAmE* **adˈvice columnist**) a man who writes in a newspaper or magazine giving advice in reply to people's letters about their personal problems ➲ compare AGONY AUNT

agora /ˈæɡɒrə; NAmE ˈæɡərə/ *noun* (*pl.* **agorae** /-riː/ or **agoras**) in ancient Greece, an open space used for markets and public meetings

agora·pho·bia /ˌæɡərəˈfəʊbiə; NAmE -ˈfoʊ-/ *noun* [U] (*technical*) a fear of being in public places where there are many other people ➲ compare CLAUSTROPHOBIA

agora·pho·bic /ˌæɡərəˈfəʊbɪk; NAmE -ˈfoʊ-/ *noun* a person who suffers from agoraphobia ▶ **agora·pho·bic** *adj.*

agrar·ian /əˈɡreəriən; NAmE əˈɡrer-/ *adj.* [usually before noun] (*technical*) connected with farming and the use of land for farming

aˌgrarian revoˈlution *noun* [sing.] (often **the Agrarian Revolution**) a period when farming in a country changes completely as a result of new methods or a change in who owns the land

agree 0- /əˈɡriː/ *verb*
▸ SHARE OPINION **1** 0- [I, T] to have the same opinion as sb; to say that you have the same opinion: *When he said that, I had to agree.* ◇ **+ speech** *'That's true', she agreed.* ◇ **~ (with sb) (about/on sth)** *He agreed with them about the need for change.* ◇ **~ with sth** *I agree with her analysis of the situation.* ◇ **~ (that)...** *We agreed (that) the proposal was a good*

one. ◇ *'It's terrible.' 'I couldn't agree more!'* (= I completely agree) OPP **disagree** **2** [T] if people **are agreed** or sth **is agreed**, everyone has the same opinion about sth: **be agreed (on/about sth)** *Are we all agreed on this?* ◇ **be agreed (that...)** *It was agreed (that) we should hold another meeting.*
▸ SAY YES **3** [I, T] to say 'yes'; to say that you will do what sb wants or that you will allow sth to happen: *I asked for a pay rise and she agreed.* ◇ **~ to sth** *Do you think he'll agree to their proposal?* ◇ **~ (that)...** *She agreed (that) I could go early.* ◇ **~ to do sth** *She agreed to let me go early.*
▸ DECIDE **4** [I, T] to decide with sb else to do sth or to have sth: **~ on sth** *Can we agree on a date?* ◇ **~ sth** *They met at the agreed time.* ◇ *Can we agree a price?* ◇ *They left at ten, **as agreed**.* ◇ **~ to do sth** *We agreed to meet on Thursday.* ◇ **~ what, where, etc...** *We couldn't agree what to do.*
▸ ACCEPT **5** [T] **~ sth** to officially accept a plan, request, etc. SYN **approve**: *Next year's budget has been agreed.*
▸ BE THE SAME **6** [I] to be the same as sth SYN **tally**: *The figures do not agree.* ◇ **~ with sth** *Your account of the accident does not agree with hers.* OPP **disagree**
▸ GRAMMAR **7** [I] **~ (with sth)** to match a word or phrase in NUMBER, GENDER or PERSON: *In 'Tom likes jazz', the singular verb 'likes' agrees with the subject 'Tom'.*
IDM **a,gree to 'differ** if two people **agree to differ**, they accept that they have different opinions about sth, but they decide not to discuss it any longer
PHR V **not a'gree with sb** (of food) to make you feel ill/sick: *I love strawberries, but they don't agree with me.*

Synonyms

agree

accept • approve • go along with sb/sth • consent

These words all mean to say that you will do what sb wants or that you will allow sth to happen.

agree to say that you will do what sb wants or that you will allow sth to happen: *He agreed to let me go early.*

accept to be satisfied with sth that has been done, decided or suggested: *They accepted the court's decision.*

approve to officially agree to a plan, suggestion or request: *The committee unanimously approved the plan.*

go along with sb/sth (*rather informal*) to agree to sth that sb else has decided; to agree with sb else's ideas: *She just goes along with everything he suggests.*

consent (*rather formal*) to agree to sth or give your permission for sth: *She finally consented to answer our questions.*

PATTERNS

- to agree/consent **to** sth
- to agree/consent **to do sth**
- to agree to/accept/approve/go along with/consent to a **plan/proposal**
- to agree to/accept/approve a **request**

agree·able /ə'griːəbl/ *adj.* (*formal*) **1** pleasant and easy to like: *We spent a most agreeable day together.* ◇ *He seemed extremely agreeable.* OPP **disagreeable** **2** [not before noun] **~ (to sth)** willing to do sth or allow sth: *Do you think they will be agreeable to our proposal?* **3** **~ (to sb)** able to be accepted by sb: *The deal must be agreeable to both sides.*

agree·ably /ə'griːəbli/ *adv.* (*formal*) in a pleasant, nice way: *an agreeably warm day* ◇ *They were agreeably surprised by the quality of the food.*

agree·ment /ə'griːmənt/ *noun*
1 [C] an arrangement, a promise or a contract made with sb: *an international peace agreement* ◇ *The agreement* (= the document recording the agreement) *was signed during a meeting at the UN.* ◇ **~ with sb** *They have a free trade agreement with Australia.* ◇ **~ between A and B** *An agreement was finally **reached** between management and employees.* ◇ **~ to do sth** *They had made a verbal agreement to sell.* ◇ *They had an agreement never to talk about work at home.* ➲ see also GENTLEMAN'S AGREEMENT, PRENUPTIAL AGREEMENT **2** [U] the state of sharing the same opinion or feeling: *The two sides failed to **reach agreement**.* ◇ **in ~** *Are we in agreement about the price?* OPP **disagreement** **3** [U] the fact of sb approving of sth and allowing it to happen: *You'll have to get your parents' agreement if you want to go on the trip.* **4** [U] **~ (with sth)** (*grammar*) (of words in a phrase) the state of having the same NUMBER, GENDER or PERSON SYN **concord**: *In the sentence 'They live in the country', the plural form of the verb 'live' is in agreement with the plural subject 'they'.*

agri- ➲ AGRO-

agri·busi·ness /'ægrɪbɪznəs/ *noun* [U, C] (*technical*) an industry concerned with the production and sale of farm products, especially involving large companies

agri·cul·tur·al·ist /,ægrɪ'kʌltʃərəlɪst/ *noun* an expert in agriculture who gives advice to farmers

agri·cul·ture /'ægrɪkʌltʃə(r)/ *noun* [U] the science or practice of farming: *The number of people employed in agriculture has fallen in the last decade.* ➲ COLLOCATIONS at TOWN ▸ **agri·cul·tural** /,ægrɪ'kʌltʃərəl/ *adj.*: *agricultural policy/land/production/development*

agri·tour·ism /'ægrɪtʊərɪzəm; -tɔːr-; *NAmE* -tʊr-/ *noun* [U] holidays/vacations in which tourists visiting a country stay with local people who live in the countryside

agro- /'ægrəʊ-; *NAmE* 'ægroʊ-/ (also **agri-**) *combining form* (in nouns, adjectives and adverbs) connected with farming: *agro-industry* ◇ *agriculture*

agro·chem·ical /,ægrəʊ'kemɪkl; *NAmE* ,ægroʊ-/ *noun* any chemical used in farming, especially for killing insects or for making plants grow better

,agro-'industry *noun* [U] industry connected with farming ▸ **,agro-in'dustrial** *adj.*

agrono·mist /ə'grɒnəmɪst; *NAmE* ə'grɑːn-/ *noun* a scientist who studies the relationship between crops and the environment ▸ **agron·omy** *noun* [U]

aground /ə'graʊnd/ *adv.* if a ship **runs/goes aground**, it touches the ground in shallow water and cannot move ▸ **aground** *adj.* [not before noun]

ague /'eɪgjuː/ *noun* [U] (*old-fashioned*) a disease such as MALARIA that causes fever and SHIVERING (= shaking of the body)

AH (*BrE*) (*US* **A.H.**) /,eɪ 'eɪtʃ/ *abbr.* used in the Muslim CALENDAR to show a particular number of years since the year when Muhammad left Mecca in AD 622 (from Latin 'Anno Hegirae'): *a Koran dated 556 AH* ➲ compare AD, BC, BCE, CE

ah /ɑː/ *exclamation* used to express surprise, pleasure, admiration or sympathy, or when you disagree with sb: *Ah, there you are!* ◇ *Ah, this coffee is good.* ◇ *Ah well, better luck next time.* ◇ *Ah, but that may not be true.*

aha /ɑː'hɑː/ *exclamation* used when you are expressing pleasure that you have understood sth or found sth out: *Aha! So that's where I left it!*

ahchoo /ɑː'tʃuː; ə'tʃuː/ *exclamation* = ATISHOO

ahead /ə'hed/ *adv.*
HELP For the special uses of **ahead** in phrasal verbs, look at the entries for the verbs. For example **press ahead (with sth)** is in the phrasal verb section at **press**.
1 further forward in space or time; in front: *I'll run ahead and warn them.* ◇ *The road ahead was blocked.* ◇ *We've got a lot of hard work ahead.* ◇ *This will create problems in the months ahead.* ◇ *He was looking straight ahead* (= straight forward, in front of him). **2** earlier SYN **in advance**: *The party was planned weeks ahead.* **3** winning; further advanced: *Our team was ahead by six points.* ◇ *You need to work hard to keep ahead.*

a'head of *prep.* **1** further forward in space or time than sb/sth; in front of sb/sth: *Two boys were ahead of us.* ◇ *Ahead of us lay ten days of intensive training.* **2** earlier than sb/sth: *I finished several days ahead of the deadline.* **3** further advanced than sb/sth; in front of sb, for example in a race or competition: *She was always* **well ahead** *of the rest of the class.* ◇ *His ideas were way* **ahead of their time** (= very new and so not widely understood or accepted).

ahem /ə'hem; ə'həm/ *exclamation* used in writing to show the sound of a short cough made by sb who is trying to get attention or to say sth that is difficult or embarrassing: *Ahem, can I make a suggestion?*

ahis·tor·ic·al /ˌeɪhɪ'stɒrɪkl; *NAmE* -'stɔːr-; -'stɑːr-/ *adj.* (*formal*) not showing any knowledge of history or of what has happened before

-aholic /ə'hɒlɪk; *NAmE* ə'hɔːl-; ə'hɑːl-/ *suffix* (in nouns) liking sth very much and unable to stop doing or using it: *a shopaholic* ◇ *a chocaholic*

ahoy /ə'hɔɪ/ *exclamation* used by people in boats to attract attention: *Ahoy there!* ◇ *Ship ahoy!* (= there is a ship in sight)

AI /ˌeɪ 'aɪ/ *abbr.* **1** ARTIFICIAL INSEMINATION: *AID or artificial insemination by a donor* **2** ARTIFICIAL INTELLIGENCE

aid 🔑 AW /eɪd/ *noun, verb*

■ ***noun*** **1** 🔑 [U] money, food, etc. that is sent to help countries in difficult situations: ***economic/humanitarian/emergency aid*** ◇ *An extra £10 million in* ***foreign aid*** *has been promised.* ◇ ***aid agencies*** (= organizations that provide help) ◇ *medical aid programmes* ➲ COLLOCATIONS at INTERNATIONAL ➲ see also FINANCIAL AID, LEGAL AID **2** 🔑 [U] help that you need to perform a particular task: *He was breathing only* **with the aid of** *a ventilator.* ◇ *This job would be impossible* **without the aid of** *a computer.* **3** [U] (*formal*) help that is given to a person: *One of the staff saw he was in difficulty and* **came to his aid** (= helped him). ➲ see also FIRST AID **4** [C] an object, a machine, etc. that you use to help you do sth: *a hearing aid* ◇ *Photos make useful teaching aids.*

IDM **in aid of sth/sb** 🔑 (*BrE*) in order to help sb/sth: *collecting money in aid of charity* **what's... in aid of?** (*BrE*) used to ask why sth is happening: *What's all this crying in aid of?*

■ ***verb*** 🔑 [I, T] (*formal*) to help sb/sth to do sth, especially by making it easier SYN **assist**: **~ (sb/sth) in sth/in doing sth** *The new test should aid in the early detection of the disease.* ◇ **~ sb (to do sth)** *This feature is designed to aid inexperienced users.* ◇ **~ sth** *Aided by heat and strong winds, the fire quickly spread.* ◇ *They were accused of aiding his escape.* ◇ **~ sb/sth in sth/in doing sth** *They were accused of aiding him in his escape.* ◇ **~ sb (with sth)** *Words will be displayed around the room to aid students with spelling.*

IDM **ˌaid and a'bet** (*law*) to help sb to do sth illegal or wrong: *She stands accused of aiding and abetting the crime.*

aide /eɪd/ *noun* a person who helps another person, especially a politician, in their job: *White House aides*

aide-de-camp /ˌeɪd də 'kɒ̃; *NAmE* 'kæmp/ *noun* (*pl.* **aides-de-camp** /ˌeɪd də 'kɒ̃; *NAmE* 'kæmp/) (*abbr.* ADC) an officer in the army or navy who helps a more senior officer

aide-memoire /ˌeɪd mem'wɑː(r)/ *noun* (from *French*) (*pl.* **aides-memoire, aides-memoires** /ˌeɪd mem'wɑː(r)/) a thing, especially a book or document, that helps you to remember sth

AIDS (*BrE* usually **Aids**) /eɪdz/ *noun* [U] the abbreviation for 'Acquired Immune Deficiency Syndrome' (an illness which attacks the body's ability to resist infection and which usually causes death): ***AIDS research/education/victims*** ◇ *He developed* ***full-blown AIDS*** *five years after contracting HIV.*

ai·kido /aɪ'kiːdəʊ; *NAmE* -doʊ/ *noun* [U] (from *Japanese*) a Japanese system of fighting in which you hold and throw your opponent

ail /eɪl/ *verb* **1 ~ sth** (*formal*) to cause problems for sb/sth: *They discussed the problems ailing the steel industry.* **2 ~ sb** (*old use*) to make sb ill/sick: *What is ailing you?*

ail·eron /'eɪlərɒn; *NAmE* -rɑːn/ *noun* (*technical*) a part of the wing of a plane that moves up and down to control the plane's balance ➲ VISUAL VOCAB page V43

ail·ing /'eɪlɪŋ/ *adj.* (*formal*) **1** ill/sick and not improving: *She looked after her ailing father.* **2** (of a business, government, etc.) having problems and getting weaker: *measures to help the ailing economy*

ail·ment /'eɪlmənt/ *noun* an illness that is not very serious: ***childhood/common/minor ailments*** ➲ SYNONYMS at DISEASE

aim 🔑 /eɪm/ *noun, verb*

■ ***noun*** **1** 🔑 [C] the purpose of doing sth; what sb is trying to achieve: *the aims of the lesson* ◇ *She went to London* ***with the aim of*** *finding a job.* ◇ *Our main aim is to increase sales in Europe.* ◇ *Bob's one aim in life is to earn a lot of money.* ◇ *Teamwork is required in order to* ***achieve these aims.*** ◇ *She set out the company's* ***aims and objectives*** *in her speech.* ➲ SYNONYMS at PURPOSE **2** [U] the action or skill of pointing a weapon at sb/sth: *Her aim was good and she hit the lion with her first shot.* ◇ *The gunman* ***took aim*** (= pointed his weapon) *and fired.*

IDM **take 'aim at sb/sth** (*NAmE*) to direct your criticism at sb/sth

■ ***verb*** **1** 🔑 [I, T] to try or plan to achieve sth: *He has always* ***aimed high*** (= tried to achieve a lot). ◇ **~ for sth** *We should aim for a bigger share of the market.* ◇ **~ at sth** *The government is aiming at a 50% reduction in unemployment.* ◇ **~ to do sth** *They are aiming to reduce unemployment by 50%.* ◇ *We aim to be there around six.* ◇ **~ at doing sth** *They're aiming at training everybody by the end of the year.* **2** 🔑 [T] **be aimed at sth/at doing sth** to have sth as an aim: *These measures are aimed at preventing violent crime.* **3** 🔑 [I, T] to point or direct a weapon, a shot, a kick, etc. at sb/sth: **~ at sb/sth** *I was aiming at the tree but hit the car by mistake.* ◇ **~ for sb/sth** *Aim for the middle of the target.* ◇ **~ sth (at sb/sth)** *The gun was aimed at her head.* **4** 🔑 [T, usually passive] **~ sth at sb** to say or do sth that is intended to influence or affect a particular person or group: *The book is aimed at very young children.* ◇ *My criticism wasn't aimed at you.*

aim·less /'eɪmləs/ *adj.* having no direction or plan: *My life seemed aimless.* ▸ **aim·less·ly** *adv.*: *He drifted aimlessly from one job to another.* **aim·less·ness** *noun* [U]

ain't /eɪnt/ *short form* (*non-standard* or *humorous*) **1** am not/is not/are not: *Things ain't what they used to be.* **2** has not/have not: *I ain't got no money.* ◇ *You ain't seen nothing yet.*

IDM **if it ain't ˌbroke, don't 'fix it** (*informal*) used to say that if sth works well enough, it should not be changed

aioli /aɪ'əʊli; *NAmE* aɪ'oʊli/ *noun* [U] (from *French*) a thick cold sauce made of MAYONNAISE and GARLIC

air 🔑 /eə(r); *NAmE* er/ *noun, verb*

■ ***noun***

▸ GAS **1** 🔑 [U] the mixture of gases that surrounds the earth and that we breathe: *air pollution* ◇ *Let's go out for some* ***fresh air.*** ◇ *I need to put some air in my tyres.* ◇ *currents of warm air*

▸ SPACE **2** 🔑 [U] (usually **the air**) the space above the ground or that is around things: *I kicked the ball high* ***in/into the air.*** ◇ *Spicy smells wafted* ***through the air.*** ◇ *Music filled the night air.* ➲ see also OPEN AIR

▸ FOR PLANES **3** 🔑 [U] the space above the earth where planes fly: *It only takes three hours* ***by air*** (= in a plane). ◇ ***air travel/traffic*** ◇ *The temple was clearly visible from the air.* ◇ *A surprise air attack* (= from aircraft) *was launched at night.*

▸ IMPRESSION **4** [sing.] the particular feeling or impression that is given by sb/sth; the way sb does sth: *The room had an air of luxury.* ◇ *She looked at him with a defiant air.*

▸ TUNE **5** [C] (*old-fashioned*) (often used in the title of a piece of music) a tune: *Bach's Air on a G string*

▸ BEHAVIOUR **6 airs** [pl.] (*disapproving*) a way of behaving that shows that sb thinks that they are more important, etc. than they really are: *I hate the way she* ***puts on airs.***

IDM **ˌairs and 'graces** (*BrE, disapproving*) a way of behaving that shows that sb thinks that they are more important, etc. than they really are SYN **airs** **float/walk on 'air** to feel very happy **in the 'air** felt by a number of people to exist or to be happening: *There's romance in the air.* **ˌon/ˌoff (the) 'air** broadcasting or not broadcasting on television or radio: *We will be back on air tomorrow morning at 7.*

◇ *The programme was taken off the air over the summer.* **up in the 'air** not yet decided: *Our travel plans are still up in the air.* ➲ more at BREATH, CASTLE, CLEAR *v.*, NOSE *n.*, PLUCK *v.*, THIN *adj.*

■ ***verb***

▸ CLOTHES **1** [T, I] **~ (sth)** (*especially BrE*) to put clothing, etc. in a place that is warm or has plenty of air so that it dries completely and smells fresh; to be left to dry somewhere: *Air the sheets well.* ◇ *Leave the towels out to air.*

▸ A ROOM **2** [T, I] **~ (sth)** (*BrE*) (*NAmE* **ˌair (sth) ˈout**) to allow fresh air into a room or a building; to be filled with fresh air: *The rooms had all been cleaned and aired.*

▸ OPINIONS **3** [T] **~ sth** to express your opinions publicly SYN **voice**: *The weekly meeting enables employees to* ***air their grievances.***

▸ RADIO/TV PROGRAMME **4** [T, I] **~ (sth)** (*especially NAmE*) to broadcast a programme on the radio or on television; to be broadcast: *The show will be aired next Tuesday night.* ◇ *The program aired last week.*

PHR V **ˌair ˈout** | **ˌair sth↔ˈout** (*NAmE*) = AIR (2)

ˌair ˈambulance *noun* (*especially BrE*) an aircraft, especially a HELICOPTER, with special equipment, used for taking sick or injured people to a hospital, especially in cases where a road vehicle cannot get through or cannot make the journey quickly enough ➲ compare MEDEVAC

air·bag /ˈeəbæg; *NAmE* ˈer-/ *noun* a safety device in a car that fills with air if there is an accident, to protect the people in the car

air·base /ˈeəbeɪs; *NAmE* ˈerb-/ *noun* a place where military aircraft fly from and are kept, and where some staff live

air·bed /ˈeəbed; *NAmE* ˈer-/ (*BrE*) (also **ˈair mattress** *NAmE, BrE*) *noun* a large plastic or rubber bag that can be filled with air and used as a bed ➲ VISUAL VOCAB page V20

air·borne /ˈeəbɔːn; *NAmE* ˈerbɔːrn/ *adj.* **1** [not before noun] (of a plane or passengers) in the air: *Do not leave your seat until the plane is airborne.* **2** [only before noun] carried through the air: ***airborne seeds/viruses*** ➲ compare WATERBORNE **3** [only before noun] (of soldiers) trained to jump out of aircraft onto enemy land in order to fight: *an airborne division*

ˈair brake *noun* a BRAKE in a vehicle that is worked by air pressure

ˈair bridge (*BrE*) (*NAmE* **Jet·way™**) *noun* a bridge that can be moved and put against the door of an aircraft, so people can get on and off

air·brush /ˈeəbrʌʃ; *NAmE* ˈerb-/ *noun, verb*

■ ***noun*** an artist's tool for spraying paint onto a surface, that works by air pressure

■ ***verb*** to paint sth with an airbrush; to change a detail in a photograph with an airbrush: **~ sth** *an airbrushed photograph of a model* ◇ **~ sth out** *Somebody had been airbrushed out of the picture.*

Air·bus™ /ˈeəbʌs; *NAmE* ˈerbʌs/ *noun* a large plane that carries passengers over short and medium distances

ˌair chief ˈmarshal *noun* an officer of very high rank in the British AIR FORCE: *Air Chief Marshal Sir Robin Hall*

ˌair ˈcommodore *noun* an officer of high rank in the British AIR FORCE: *Air Commodore Peter Shaw*

ˈair conditioner *noun* a machine that cools and dries air

ˈair conditioning (also **ˈair con**) *noun* [U] (*abbr.* AC, a/c) a system that cools and dries the air in a building or car ▸ **ˈair-conditioned** *adj.*: *air-conditioned offices*

ˈair-cooled *adj.* made cool by a current of air

ˈair corridor *noun* an area in the sky that aircraft must stay inside when they fly over a country

ˈair cover *noun* [U] protection which aircraft give to soldiers and military vehicles on the land or sea

air·craft 🔑 /ˈeəkrɑːft; *NAmE* ˈerkræft/ *noun* (*pl.* aircraft)
any vehicle that can fly and carry goods or passengers: ***fighter/transport/military aircraft*** ➲ VISUAL VOCAB page V43 ➲ see also LIGHT AIRCRAFT

ˈaircraft carrier *noun* a large ship that carries aircraft which use it as a base to land on and take off from

air·craft·man /ˈeəkrɑːftmən; *NAmE* ˈerkræft-/, **air·craft·woman** /ˈeəkrɑːftwʊmən; *NAmE* ˈerkræft-/ *noun* (*pl.* **-men** /-mən/, **-women** /-wɪmɪn/) the lowest rank in the British AIR FORCE: *Aircraftman John Green*

air·crew /ˈeəkruː; *NAmE* ˈerk-/ *noun* [C+sing./pl. v.] the pilot and other people who fly a plane, especially in the air force

ˈair-dash *verb* [I] **+ adv./prep.** (*IndE, informal*) (especially of officials) to go somewhere by plane suddenly and/or quickly: *The minister air-dashed to Delhi because of the parliamentary crisis.*

air·drome /ˈeədrəʊm; *NAmE* ˈerdroʊm/ (*US*) (*BrE* **aero·drome**) *noun* (*old-fashioned*) a small airport

air·drop /ˈeədrɒp; *NAmE* ˈerdrɑːp/ *noun* the act of dropping supplies, soldiers, etc. from an aircraft by PARACHUTE: *The UN has begun making airdrops of food to refugees.* ▸ **air·drop** *verb* (**-pp-**) **~ sth**

air·fare /ˈeəfeə(r); *NAmE* ˈerfer/ *noun* the money that you pay to travel by plane: *Take advantage of low-season airfares.*

air·field /ˈeəfiːld; *NAmE* ˈerf-/ *noun* an area of flat ground where military or private planes can take off and land

air·flow /ˈeəfləʊ; *NAmE* ˈerfloʊ/ *noun* [U] the flow of air around a moving aircraft or vehicle

air·foil /ˈeəfɔɪl; *NAmE* ˈerf-/ (*NAmE*) (*BrE* **aero·foil**) *noun* the basic curved structure of an aircraft's wing that helps to lift it into the air

ˈair force *noun* [C+sing./pl. v.] the part of a country's armed forces that fights using aircraft: *the US Air Force* ◇ *air-force officers* ➲ COLLOCATIONS at WAR

ˌAir Force ˈOne *noun* the name given to a special aircraft in the US AIR FORCE when the US President is using it

air·freight /ˈeəfreɪt; *NAmE* ˈerf-/ *noun* [U] goods that are transported by aircraft; the system of transporting goods by aircraft ▸ **air·freight** *verb* **~ sth**

ˈair freshener *noun* [C, U] a substance or device for making a place smell more pleasant

ˈair guitar *noun* [C, U] used to describe a person playing an imaginary electric GUITAR, especially while listening to rock music

ˈair·gun /ˈeəgʌn; *NAmE* ˈer-/ (also **ˈair rifle**) *noun* a gun that uses air pressure to fire small metal balls (called PELLETS)

air·head /ˈeəhed; *NAmE* ˈerh-/ *noun* (*informal, disapproving*) a stupid person: *She's a total airhead!*

ˈair hostess *noun* (*BrE, old-fashioned*) a female FLIGHT ATTENDANT

air·ily /ˈeərəli; *NAmE* ˈer-/ *adv.* (*formal*) in a way that shows that you are not worried or that you are not treating sth as serious

air·ing /ˈeərɪŋ; *NAmE* ˈerɪŋ/ *noun* [sing.] **1** the expression or discussion of opinions in front of a group of people: *an opportunity to give your views an airing* ◇ *The subject got a thorough airing in the British press.* **2** the act of allowing warm air to make clothes, beds, etc. fresh and dry

ˈairing cupboard *noun* (*BrE*) a warm cupboard in which clean sheets, clothes, etc. are put to make sure they are completely dry

ˈair kiss *noun* a way of saying hello or goodbye to sb by kissing them near the side of their face but not actually touching them ▸ **ˈair-kiss** *verb* [T, I] **~ (sb/sth)**

air·less /ˈeələs; *NAmE* ˈerl-/ *adj.* not having any fresh or moving air or wind, and therefore unpleasant: *a stuffy, airless room* ◇ *The night was hot and airless.*

ˈair letter *noun* = AEROGRAMME

air·lift /ˈeəlɪft; *NAmE* ˈerl-/ *noun, verb*

■ ***noun*** an operation to take people, soldiers, food, etc. to or

A

from an area by aircraft, especially in an emergency or when roads are closed or dangerous
▪ *verb* **~ sb/sth** to take sb/sth to or from an area by aircraft, especially in an emergency or when roads are closed or dangerous: *Two casualties* ***were airlifted*** *to* ***safety.*** ➲ compare SEALIFT

air·line /ˈeəlaɪn; *NAmE* ˈerl-/ *noun* [C+sing./pl. v.] a company that provides regular flights to take passengers and goods to different places: *international airlines* ◇ *an airline pilot* ➲ COLLOCATIONS at TRAVEL

air·liner /ˈeəlaɪnə(r); *NAmE* ˈerl-/ *noun* a large plane that carries passengers

air·lock /ˈeəlɒk; *NAmE* ˈerlɑːk/ *noun* **1** a small room with a tightly closed door at each end, which you go through to reach another area at a different air pressure, for example on a SPACECRAFT or SUBMARINE **2** a bubble of air that blocks the flow of liquid in a PUMP or pipe

air·mail /ˈeəmeɪl; *NAmE* ˈerm-/ *noun* [U] the system of sending letters, etc. by air: *Send it airmail/by airmail.*

air·man /ˈeəmən; *NAmE* ˈerm-/, **air·woman** /ˈeəwʊmən; *NAmE* ˈerw-/ *noun* (*pl.* **-men** /-mən/, **-women** /-wɪmɪn/) **1** a member of the British AIR FORCE, especially one below the rank of an officer **2** a member of one of the lowest ranks in the US AIR FORCE: *Airman Brines*

ˈair marshal *noun* **1** an officer of very high rank in the British AIR FORCE: *Air Marshal Gordon Black* **2** (also ˈ**sky marshal**) an armed guard, especially a government official, who travels on a plane with the passengers in order to protect the plane from TERRORISTS

ˈair mattress (*especially NAmE*) (*BrE* also **air·bed**) *noun* a large plastic or rubber bag that can be filled with air and used as a bed ➲ VISUAL VOCAB page V20

ˈAir Miles™ *noun* [pl.] points that you collect by buying plane tickets and other products, which you can then use to pay for air travel

air·miss /ˈeəmɪs; *NAmE* ˈerm-/ *noun* (*BrE*) an occasion when two or more aircraft fly too close to one another and a crash nearly happens

ˈair pistol *noun* a small gun that uses air pressure to fire small metal balls (called PELLETS)

air·plane /ˈeəpleɪn; *NAmE* ˈerp-/ *noun* (*especially NAmE*) = PLANE: *They arrived in Belgium* ***by airplane.*** ◇ *an* ***airplane crash/flight*** ◇ *a* ***commercial/jet/military airplane***

air·play /ˈeəpleɪ; *NAmE* ˈerp-/ *noun* [U] time that is spent broadcasting a particular record, performer, or type of music on the radio: *The band is starting to get a lot of airplay.*

ˈair pocket *noun* **1** a closed area that becomes filled with air **2** an area of low air pressure that makes a plane suddenly drop while flying

air·port 0→ /ˈeəpɔːt; *NAmE* ˈerpɔːrt/ *noun* a place where planes land and take off and that has buildings for passengers to wait in: *Gatwick Airport* ◇ *waiting in the airport lounge*

ˌairport ˈfiction *noun* [U] novels that are popular and easy to read, often bought by people at airports

ˈair power *noun* [U] military forces involving aircraft

ˈair pump *noun* a piece of equipment for sending air into or out of sth

ˈair quality *noun* [U] the degree to which the air is clean and free from pollution

ˈair quotes *noun* [pl.] imaginary quotation marks made in the air with your fingers when you are speaking, to show that you are using a word or phrase in an unusual way

ˈair raid *noun* an attack by a number of aircraft dropping many bombs on a place: *The family was killed in an air raid.* ◇ *an* ***air-raid shelter/warning***

ˈair rifle *noun* = AIR GUN

ˌair-sea ˈrescue *noun* [C, U] (*especially BrE*) the process of rescuing people from the sea using aircraft

air·ship /ˈeəʃɪp; *NAmE* ˈerʃɪp/ *noun* a large aircraft without wings, filled with a gas which is lighter than air, and driven by engines ➲ VISUAL VOCAB page V43

ˈair show *noun* a show at which people can watch aircraft flying

air·sick /ˈeəsɪk; *NAmE* ˈersɪk/ *adj.* [not usually before noun] feeling ill/sick when you are travelling on an aircraft ▸ **air·sick·ness** *noun* [U]

air·space /ˈeəspeɪs; *NAmE* ˈers-/ *noun* [U] the part of the sky where planes fly, usually the part above a particular country that is legally controlled by that country: *The jet entered Chinese airspace without permission.*

air·speed /ˈeəspiːd; *NAmE* ˈer-/ *noun* the speed of an aircraft relative to the air through which it is moving ➲ compare GROUND SPEED

air·stream /ˈeəstriːm; *NAmE* ˈerstriːm/ *noun* a movement of air, especially a strong one

ˈair strike *noun* an attack made by aircraft

air·strip /ˈeəstrɪp; *NAmE* ˈers-/ (also ˈ**landing strip**) *noun* a narrow piece of cleared land that an aircraft can land on

ˈair support *noun* [U] help which aircraft give to soldiers and military vehicles on the land or sea

ˈair terminal *noun* **1** a building at an airport that provides services for passengers travelling by plane **2** (*BrE*) an office in a city from which passengers can catch buses to the airport

air·tight /ˈeətaɪt; *NAmE* ˈert-/ *adj.* not allowing air to get in or out: *Store the cake in an airtight container.* ◇ (*figurative*) *an airtight alibi* (= one that cannot be proved to be false)

air·time /ˈeətaɪm; *NAmE* ˈert-/ *noun* [U] **1** the amount of time that is given to a particular subject on radio or television **2** the amount of time that is paid for when you are using a mobile/cell phone

ˌair-to-ˈair *adj.* [usually before noun] from one aircraft to another while they are both flying: *an air-to-air missile*

ˌair-to-ˈground *adj.* [usually before noun] directed or operating from an aircraft to the surface of the land: *air-to-ground weapons*

ˌair-to-ˈsurface *adj.* [usually before noun] moving or passing from a flying aircraft to the surface of the sea or land: *air-to-surface missiles*

ˌair traffic conˈtrol *noun* [U] **1** the activity of giving instructions by radio to pilots of aircraft so that they know when and where to take off or land **2** the group of people or the organization that provides an air traffic control service: *The pilot was given clearance to land by air traffic control.*

ˌair traffic conˈtroller *noun* a person whose job is to give instructions by radio to pilots of aircraft so that they know when and where to take off or land

ˌair vice-ˈmarshal *noun* an officer of very high rank in the British AIR FORCE: *Air Vice-Marshal Andrew Burns*

air·waves /ˈeəweɪvz; *NAmE* ˈerw-/ *noun* [pl.] radio waves that are used in broadcasting radio and television: *More and more TV and radio stations are crowding the airwaves.* ◇ *A well-known voice came* ***over the airwaves.***

air·way /ˈeəweɪ; *NAmE* ˈerweɪ/ *noun* **1** (*medical*) the passage from the nose and throat to the lungs, through which you breathe **2** (often used in names of AIRLINES) a route regularly used by planes: *British Airways*

air·worthy /ˈeəwɜːði; *NAmE* ˈerwɜːrði/ *adj.* (of aircraft) safe to fly ▸ **air·worthi·ness** *noun* [U]

airy /ˈeəri; *NAmE* ˈeri/ *adj.* (**air·ier, airi·est**) **1** with plenty of fresh air because there is a lot of space: *The office was light and airy.* **2** (*formal*) acting or done in a way that shows that you are not worried or that you are not treating sth as serious: *He dismissed her with an airy wave.* ➲ see also AIRILY **3** (*formal, disapproving*) not serious or practical: ***airy promises/speculation***

ˌairy-ˈfairy *adj.* (*BrE, informal, disapproving*) not clear or practical

aisle /aɪl/ *noun* a passage between rows of seats in a church, theatre, train, etc, or between rows of shelves in a supermarket: *an aisle seat* (= in a plane) ◇ *Coffee and tea are in the next aisle.* ➲ compare GANGWAY

IDM **go/walk down the 'aisle** (*informal*) to get married ➲ more at ROLL *v.*

aitch /eɪtʃ/ *noun* the letter H written as a word: *He spoke with a cockney accent and* **dropped his aitches** (= did not pronounce the letter H at the start of words).

ajar /ə'dʒɑː(r)/ *adj.* [not before noun] (of a door) slightly open: *I'll leave the door ajar.*

aka /ˌeɪ keɪ 'eɪ/ *abbr.* also known as: *Antonio Fratelli, aka 'Big Tony'*

akimbo /ə'kɪmbəʊ; *NAmE* -boʊ/ *adv.*

IDM **(with) arms a'kimbo** with your hands on your hips and your elbows pointing away from your body

akin /ə'kɪn/ *adj.* **~ to sth** (*formal*) similar to: *What he felt was more akin to pity than love.*

-al *suffix* **1** (in adjectives) connected with: *magical* ◇ *verbal* ➲ see also -ALLY **2** (in nouns) a process or state of: *survival*

à la /'ɑː lɑː/ *prep.* (from *French*) in the same style as sb/sth else: *a new band that sings à la Beatles*

ala·bas·ter /'æləbɑːstə(r); *NAmE* -bæs-/ *noun* [U] a type of white stone that is often used to make statues and decorative objects: *an alabaster tomb* ◇ (*literary*) *her pale, alabaster* (= white and smooth) *skin*

à la carte /ˌɑː lɑː 'kɑːt; *NAmE* 'kɑːrt/ *adj., adv.* (from *French*) if food in a restaurant is **à la carte**, or if you eat **à la carte**, you choose from a list of dishes that have separate prices, rather than having a complete meal at a fixed price

alack /ə'læk/ *exclamation* (*old use* or *humorous*) used to show you are sad or sorry: ***Alas and alack****, we had missed our bus.*

alac·rity /ə'lækrəti/ *noun* [U] (*formal*) great willingness or enthusiasm: *They accepted the offer with alacrity.*

Aˌladdin's 'cave *noun* a place where there are many wonderful objects

à la mode /ˌɑː lɑː 'məʊd; *NAmE* 'moʊd/ *adj., adv.* (from *French*) **1** [not before noun] (*old-fashioned*) fashionable; in the latest fashion **2** [after noun] (*NAmE*) served with ice cream: *apple pie à la mode*

alarm 🔑 /ə'lɑːm; *NAmE* ə'lɑːrm/ *noun, verb*

■ ***noun*** **1** 🔑 [U] fear and anxiety that sb feels when sth dangerous or unpleasant might happen: *'What have you done?' Ellie cried* ***in alarm****.* ◇ *I felt a growing sense of alarm when he did not return that night.* ◇ *The doctor said there was no* ***cause for alarm****.* ➲ SYNONYMS at FEAR **2** 🔑 [C, usually sing.] a loud noise or a signal that warns people of danger or of a problem: *She decided to* ***sound the alarm*** (= warn people that the situation was dangerous). ◇ *I hammered on all the doors to* ***raise the alarm****.* ➲ see also FALSE ALARM **3** 🔑 [C] a device that warns people of a particular danger: *a* ***burglar/fire/smoke alarm*** ◇ *The cat* ***set off the alarm*** (= made it start ringing). ◇ *A car* ***alarm went off*** *in the middle of the night* (= started ringing). **4** = ALARM CLOCK: *The* ***alarm went off*** *at 7 o'clock.*

IDM **a'larm bells ring/start ringing** if you say that **alarm bells are ringing**, you mean that people are starting to feel worried and suspicious

■ ***verb*** **1** 🔑 **~ sb** to make sb anxious or afraid SYN **worry**: *The captain knew there was an engine fault but didn't want to alarm the passengers.* ➲ SYNONYMS at FRIGHTEN **2 ~ sth** to fit sth such as a door with a device that warns people when sb is trying to enter illegally

a'larm call *noun* **1** a telephone call which is intended to wake you up: *Could I have an alarm call at 5.30 tomorrow, please?* **2** a cry of warning made by a bird or animal

a'larm clock (also **alarm**) *noun* a clock that you can set to ring a bell, etc. at a particular time and wake you up: *I set the alarm clock for 7 o'clock.* ➲ picture at CLOCK

alarmed 🔑 /ə'lɑːmd; *NAmE* ə'lɑːrmd/ *adj.*

1 🔑 **~ (at/by sth)** anxious or afraid that sth dangerous or unpleasant might happen: *She was alarmed at the prospect of travelling alone.* ➲ SYNONYMS at AFRAID **2** [not before noun] protected by an alarm: *This door is alarmed.*

alarm·ing 🔑 /ə'lɑːmɪŋ; *NAmE* ə'lɑːrm-/ *adj.* causing worry and fear: *an alarming increase in crime* ◇ *The rainforests are disappearing* ***at an alarming rate****.* ▸ **alarm·ing·ly** *adv.*: *Prices have risen alarmingly.*

alarm·ist /ə'lɑːmɪst; *NAmE* ə'lɑːrm-/ *adj.* (*disapproving*) causing unnecessary fear and anxiety: *A spokesperson for the food industry said the TV programme was alarmist.* ▸ **alarm·ist** *noun*

alas /ə'læs/ *exclamation* (*old use* or *literary*) used to show you are sad or sorry: *For many people, alas, hunger is part of everyday life.*

al·ba·tross /'ælbətrɒs; *NAmE* -trɔːs; -trɑːs/ *noun* **1** a very large white bird with long wings that lives in the Pacific and Southern Oceans ➲ VISUAL VOCAB page V10 **2** [usually sing.] (*formal*) a thing that causes problems or prevents you from doing sth

al·beit AW /ˌɔːl'biːɪt/ *conj.* (*formal*) although: *He finally agreed, albeit reluctantly, to help us.*

al·bin·ism /'ælbɪnɪzəm/ *noun* [U] (*technical*) the condition of being an albino

al·bino /æl'biːnəʊ; *NAmE* -'baɪnoʊ/ *noun* (*pl.* **-os**) a person or an animal that is born with no colour (=PIGMENT) in the hair or skin, which are white, or in the eyes, which are pink ▸ **al·bino** *adj.* [only before noun]

Al·bion /'ælbiən/ *noun* [U] (*literary*) an ancient name for Britain or England

album /'ælbəm/ *noun* **1** a book in which you keep photographs, stamps, etc: *a photo album* ◇ *an online album* (= a website where you can store and view photographs) ➲ VISUAL VOCAB page V35 **2** a collection of pieces of music released as a single item, usually on a CD, CASSETTE, or on the Internet: *the band's latest album* ◇ *an online album* (= an album that you can listen to on the Internet) ➲ COLLOCATIONS at MUSIC ➲ compare SINGLE

al·bu·men /'ælbjumɪn; *NAmE* æl'bjuːmən/ *noun* [U] (*technical*) the clear inside part of an egg that is white when cooked SYN **white** ➲ compare YOLK

Al·ca·traz /'ælkətræz/ *noun* a small US island near San Francisco where there is a former prison: *The clinic felt like Alcatraz. There was no escape.*

al·chem·ist /'ælkəmɪst/ *noun* a person who studied alchemy

al·chemy /'ælkəmi/ *noun* [U] **1** a form of chemistry studied in the Middle Ages which involved trying to discover how to change ordinary metals into gold **2** (*literary*) a mysterious power or magic that can change things

al·cher·inga /ˌæltʃə'rɪŋgə/ (also **Dream·time**) *noun* [U] according to some Australian Aboriginals, the time when the first people were created

al·co·hol 🔑 /'ælkəhɒl; *NAmE* -hɔːl; -hɑːl/ *noun* [U] **1** 🔑 drinks such as beer, wine, etc. that can make people drunk: *He never drinks alcohol.* ◇ *alcohol abuse* ➲ COLLOCATIONS at DIET **2** 🔑 the clear liquid that is found in drinks such as beer, wine, etc. and is used in medicines, cleaning products, etc: *Wine contains about 10% alcohol.* ◇ *levels of alcohol in the blood* ◇ *He pleaded guilty to driving with excess alcohol.* ◇ ***low-alcohol*** *beer* ◇ ***alcohol-free*** *beer* ➲ see also ABSOLUTE ALCOHOL

al·co·hol·ic 🔑 /ˌælkə'hɒlɪk; *NAmE* -'hɔːl-; -'hɑːl-/ *adj., noun*

■ ***adj.*** **1** 🔑 connected with or containing alcohol: *alcoholic drinks* OPP **non-alcoholic** ➲ see also SOFT DRINK **2** caused by drinking alcohol: *The guests left in an alcoholic haze.*

■ ***noun*** 🔑 a person who regularly drinks too much alcohol and cannot easily stop drinking, so that it has become an illness ➲ see also LUSH

Alcoˌholics A'nonymous *noun* [U] (*abbr.* AA) an international organization, begun in Chicago in 1935, for people who are trying to stop drinking alcohol. They have meetings to help each other.

al·co·hol·ism /ˈælkəhɒlɪzəm; *NAmE* -hɔːl-; -hɑːl-/ *noun* [U] the medical condition caused by drinking too much alcohol regularly

al·co·pop /ˈælkəʊpɒp; *NAmE* -koʊpɑːp/ *noun* (*BrE*) a sweet FIZZY (= with bubbles) drink that contains alcohol

al·cove /ˈælkəʊv; *NAmE* -koʊv/ *noun* an area in a room that is formed by part of a wall being built farther back than the rest of the wall: *The bookcase fits neatly into the alcove.*

al dente /ˌæl ˈdenteɪ; -ti/ *adj.* (from *Italian*) (of cooked food, especially PASTA) firm, but not hard, when bitten ▸ **al dente** *adv.*

alder /ˈɔːldə(r)/ *noun* a tree like a BIRCH that grows in northern countries, usually in wet ground

al·der·man /ˈɔːldəmən; *NAmE* -dərm-/ *noun* (*pl.* **-men** /-mən/) **1** (in England and Wales in the past) a senior member of a town, BOROUGH or county council, below the rank of a MAYOR, chosen by other members of the council **2** (*feminine* **al·der·woman**, *pl.* **-women** /-wɪmɪn/) (in the US, Canada and Australia) an elected member of a town or city council: *Alderman Tim Evans*

ale /eɪl/ *noun* **1** [U, C] a type of beer, usually sold in bottles or cans. There are several kinds of ale: ***brown/pale ale*** **2** [C] a glass, bottle or can of ale: *Two light ales please.* **3** [U] (*old-fashioned*) beer generally ➲ see also BROWN ALE, GINGER ALE, REAL ALE

alec, aleck ➲ SMART ALEC

ale·house /ˈeɪlhaʊs/ *noun* (*old-fashioned, BrE*) a place where people used to drink beer

alert /əˈlɜːt; *NAmE* əˈlɜːrt/ *adj., verb, noun*

■ ***adj.*** **1** able to think quickly; quick to notice things: *Suddenly he found himself awake and fully alert.* ◇ *Two alert scientists spotted the mistake.* **2 ~ to sth** aware of sth, especially a problem or danger: *We must be alert to the possibility of danger.* ▸ **alert·ly** *adj.* **alert·ness** *noun* [U]

■ ***verb*** [often passive] **1 ~ sb (to do sth) | ~ sb (that)...** to warn sb about a dangerous or urgent situation: *Neighbours quickly alerted the emergency services.* ◇ *Alerted by a noise downstairs, he sat up and turned on the light.* **2 ~ sb to sth** to make sb aware of sth: *They had been alerted to the possibility of further price rises.*

■ ***noun*** **1** [sing., U] a situation in which people are watching for danger and ready to deal with it: *Police are warning the public to* ***be on the alert for*** *suspicious packages.* ◇ *More than 5 000 troops have been placed* ***on*** (***full***) ***alert***. **2** [C] a warning of danger or of a problem: *a* ***bomb/fire alert*** ➲ see also RED ALERT

A level /ˈeɪ levl/ (*also* **ad'vanced level**) *noun* [C, U] a British exam taken in a particular subject, usually in the final year of school at the age of 18: *You need three A levels to get onto this university course.* ◇ *What A levels are you doing?* ◇ *I'm doing maths A level.* ◇ *two A level passes/two passes at A level* ➲ compare A2, AS, GCE, GCSE, NVQ

Alexander technique /ˌælɪgˈzɑːndə tekniːk; *NAmE* -ˈzændər/ *noun* [sing., U] a method of improving sb's health by teaching them how to stand, sit and move correctly

alex·an·drine /ˌælɪgˈzɑːndrɪn; -aɪn; *NAmE* -ˈzæn-/ *adj.* (*technical*) (of lines of poetry) containing six IAMBIC FEET ▸ **alex·an·drine** *noun*

al·fal·fa /ælˈfælfə/ *noun* [U] a plant with small divided leaves and purple flowers, grown as food for farm animals and as a salad vegetable

al fresco /æl ˈfreskəʊ; *NAmE* -koʊ/ *adj.* outdoors: *an al fresco lunch party* ▸ **al·fresco** *adv.*: *eating al fresco*

algae /ˈældʒiː; ˈælgiː/ *noun* [U, pl.] (*sing.* **alga** /ˈælgə/) (*technical*) very simple plants, such as SEAWEED, that have no real leaves, STEMS or roots, and that grow in or near water ▸ **algal** /ˈælgəl/ *adj.* [only before noun]: ***algal blooms/growth***

al·ge·bra /ˈældʒɪbrə/ *noun* [U] a type of mathematics in which letters and symbols are used to represent quantities ▸ **al·ge·bra·ic** /ˌældʒɪˈbreɪɪk/ *adj.*

al·go·rithm /ˈælgərɪðəm/ *noun* (*computing*) a set of rules that must be followed when solving a particular problem

al·haja /ælˈhædʒə/ *noun* (*WAfrE*) a woman who is a Muslim and has completed a religious journey to Mecca (often used as a title) ➲ compare ALHAJI

al·haji /ælˈhædʒi/ *noun* (*WAfrE*) a man who is a Muslim and has completed a religious journey to Mecca (often used as a title) ➲ compare ALHAJA

-alia /-eɪliə/ *suffix* (in plural nouns) items connected with the particular area of activity or interest mentioned: *kitchenalia*

alias /ˈeɪliəs/ *adv., noun*

■ ***adv.*** used when a person, especially a criminal or an actor, is known by two names: *Mick Clark, alias Sid Brown* ◇ *Hercule Poirot, alias David Suchet* (= David Suchet plays the part of Hercule Poirot) ◇ *David Suchet, alias Hercule Poirot of the famous TV series*

■ ***noun*** **1** a false or different name, especially one that is used by a criminal: *He checked into the hotel under an alias.* **2** (*computing*) a name that can be used instead of the actual name for a file, Internet address, etc.

alibi /ˈæləbaɪ/ *noun* **1** evidence that proves that a person was in another place at the time of a crime and so could not have committed it: *The suspects all had alibis for the day of the robbery.* **2** an excuse for sth that you have done wrong

Alice band /ˈælɪs bænd/ *noun* (*BrE*) a band which holds your hair back away from your face, but lets it hang freely at the back

ˌAlice in ˈWonder·land *noun* [U] used to describe a situation that is very strange, in which things happen that do not make any sense and are the opposite of what you would expect: *The country's economic system is pure Alice in Wonderland.* ▸ **Alice-in-Wonderland** *adj.* [only before noun]: *I felt I was in an Alice-in-Wonderland world.* ORIGIN From the title of a children's story by Lewis Carroll

alien /ˈeɪliən/ *adj., noun*

■ ***adj.*** **1 ~ (to sb/sth)** strange and frightening; different from what you are used to SYN **hostile**: *an alien environment* ◇ *In a world that had suddenly become alien and dangerous, he was her only security.* **2** (*often disapproving*) from another country or society; foreign: *an alien culture* **3** (*disapproving*) not usual or acceptable: **~ to sb/sth** *The idea is alien to our religion.* ◇ *Cruelty was quite alien to him.* **4** connected with creatures from another world: *alien beings from outer space*

■ ***noun*** **1** (*NAmE* also **ˌnon-ˈcitizen**) (*law* or *technical*) a person who is not a citizen of the country in which they live or work: *an illegal alien* ➲ compare RESIDENT ALIEN **2** a creature from another world: *aliens from outer space*

alien·ate /ˈeɪliəneɪt/ *verb* **1 ~ sb** to make sb less friendly or sympathetic towards you: *His comments have alienated a lot of young voters.* **2 ~ sb (from sth/sb)** to make sb feel that they do not belong in a particular group: *Very talented children may feel alienated from the others in their class.* ▸ **alien·ation** /ˌeɪliəˈneɪʃn/ *noun* [U]: *The new policy resulted in the alienation of many voters.* ◇ *Many immigrants suffer from a sense of alienation.*

alight /əˈlaɪt/ *adj., verb*

■ ***adj.*** [not before noun] **1** on fire: *A cigarette* ***set*** *the dry grass* ***alight***. ◇ *Her dress* ***caught alight*** *in the fire.* **2** (*formal*) (of faces or eyes) showing a feeling of happiness or excitement IDM see WORLD

■ ***verb*** (*formal* or *literary*) **1** [I] **~ (in/on/upon sth)** (of a bird or an insect) to land in or on sth after flying to it SYN **land** **2** [I] **~ (from sth)** to get out of a bus, a train or other vehicle SYN **get off**: *Do not alight from a moving bus.*

PHR V **aˈlight on/upon sth** to think of, find or notice sth, especially by chance: *Eventually, we alighted on the idea of seeking sponsorship.* ◇ *Her eyes suddenly alighted on the bundle of documents.*

align /əˈlaɪn/ *verb* **1** [I, T] **~ (sth) (with sth)** to arrange sth in the correct position, or to be in the correct position, in relation to sth else, especially in a straight line: *Make sure the shelf is aligned with the top of the cupboard.* ◇ *The top and bottom line of each column on the page should align.* **2** [T] **~ sth** (**with/to sth**) to change sth slightly so that it is in the correct relationship to sth else: *Domestic prices have been aligned with those in world markets.*

PHR V **a'lign yourself with sb/sth** to publicly support an organization, a set of opinions or a person that you agree with

align·ment /ə'laɪnmənt/ *noun* [U, C] **1** arrangement in a straight line: *A bone in my spine was* ***out of alignment.*** **2** political support given to one country or group by another: *Japan's alignment with the West*

alike /ə'laɪk/ *adj., adv.*

■***adj.*** [not before noun] very similar: *My sister and I do not look alike.* ➲ compare UNLIKE

■***adv.*** **1** in a very similar way: *They tried to treat all their children alike.* **2** used after you have referred to two people or groups, to mean 'both' or 'equally': *Good management benefits employers and employees alike.* IDM see GREAT *adj.*, SHARE *v.*

ali·men·tary canal /ˌælɪmentəri kə'næl/ *noun* the passage in the body that carries food from the mouth to the ANUS

ali·mony /'ælɪməni; *NAmE* -moʊni/ *noun* [U] (*especially NAmE*) the money that a court orders sb to pay regularly to their former wife or husband when the marriage is ended ➲ compare MAINTENANCE, PALIMONY

'A-line *adj.* (of a skirt or dress) wider at the bottom than at the top

ali·quot /'ælɪkwɒt; *NAmE* -kwɑːt/ *noun* **1** (*technical*) a small amount of sth that is taken from a larger amount, especially when it is taken in order to do chemical tests on it **2** (*mathematics*) a quantity which can be exactly divided into another

'A-list *adj.* [usually before noun] used to describe the group of people who are considered to be the most famous, successful or important: *He only invited* ***A-list celebrities*** *to his parties.* ➲ compare B-LIST

alive 0-w /ə'laɪv/ *adj.* [not before noun]

1 0-w living; not dead: *We don't know whether he's alive or dead.* ◇ *Is your mother* ***still alive?*** ◇ *Doctors* ***kept*** *the baby* ***alive*** *for six weeks.* ◇ *I was glad to hear you're* ***alive and well.*** ◇ *She had to steal food just to* ***stay alive.*** ◇ *He was* ***buried alive*** *in the earthquake.* **2 ~** (**with sth**) full of emotion, excitement, activity, etc: *Ed was alive with happiness.* **3** continuing to exist: *to* ***keep*** *a tradition* ***alive*** **4 ~ with sth** full of living or moving things: *The pool was alive with goldfish.* **5 ~ to sth** aware of sth; knowing sth exists and is important: *to be alive to the dangers/facts/possibilities*

IDM **aˌlive and 'kicking** very active, healthy or popular **bring sth a'live** to make sth interesting: *The pictures bring the book alive.* **come a'live 1** (of a subject or an event) to become interesting and exciting SYN **come to life**: *The game came alive in the second half.* **2** (of a place) to become busy and full of activity SYN **come to life**: *The city starts to come alive after dark.* **3** (of a person) to show interest in sth and become excited about it: *She came alive as she talked about her job.* ➲ more at EAT

al·kali /'ælkəlaɪ/ *noun* [C, U] (*chemistry*) a chemical substance that reacts with acids to form a salt and gives a SOLUTION with a pH of more than seven when it is dissolved in water ➲ compare ACID

al·ka·line /'ælkəlaɪn/ *adj.* **1** (*chemistry*) having the nature of an alkali **2** (*technical*) containing alkali: *alkaline soil* ➲ compare ACID

al·ka·lin·ity /ˌælkə'lɪnəti/ *noun* [U] the state of being or containing an ALKALI

al·kal·oid /'ælkəlɔɪd/ *noun* (*biology* or *medical*) a poisonous substance found in some plants. There are many different alkaloids and some are used as the basis for drugs.

al·kane /'ælkeɪn/ *noun* (*chemistry*) any of a series of COMPOUNDS that contain CARBON and HYDROGEN: *Methane and propane are alkanes.*

Alka-Seltzer™ /ˌælkə 'seltsə(r)/ *noun* [C, U] a medicine that you mix with water to make a drink that helps with INDIGESTION

al·kene /'ælkiːn/ *noun* (*chemistry*) any of a series of gases that contain HYDROGEN and CARBON and that have a double BOND (= force of attraction) between two of the CARBON atoms

all 0-w /ɔːl/ *det., pron., adv.*

■***det.*** **1** 0-w (used with plural nouns. The noun may have *the, this, that, my, her, his*, etc. in front of it, or a number.) the whole number of: *All horses are animals, but not all animals are horses.* ◇ *Cars were coming from all directions* (= every direction). ◇ *All the people you invited are coming.* ◇ *All my plants have died.* ◇ *All five men are hard workers.* **2** 0-w (used with uncountable nouns. The noun may have *the, this, that, my, her, his*, etc. in front of it.) the whole amount of: *All wood tends to shrink.* ◇ *You've had all the fun and I've had all the hard work.* ◇ *All this mail must be answered.* ◇ *He has lost all his money.* **3** 0-w used with singular nouns showing sth has been happening for a whole period of time: *He's worked hard all year.* ◇ *She was unemployed for all that time.* **4** the greatest possible: *In all honesty* (= being as honest as I can), *I can't agree.* **5** consisting or appearing to consist of one thing only: *The magazine was all advertisements.* ◇ *She was* ***all smiles*** (= smiling a lot). **6** any whatever: *He denied all knowledge of the crime.*

IDM **and all 'that** (**jazz, rubbish, etc.**) (*informal*) and other similar things: *I'm bored by history—dates and battles and all that stuff.* **not all that good, well, etc.** not particularly good, well, etc: *He doesn't sing all that well.* **not as bad(ly), etc. as all 'that** not as much as has been suggested: *They're not as rich as all that.* **of 'all people, things, etc.** (*informal*) used to express surprise because sb/sth seems the least likely person, example, etc.: *I didn't think you, of all people, would become a vegetarian.* **of 'all the...** (*informal*) used to express anger: *I've locked myself out. Of all the stupid things to do!* ➲ more at FOR *prep.*

■***pron.*** **1** 0-w the whole number or amount: *All of the food has gone.* ◇ *They've eaten all of it.* ◇ *They've eaten it all.* ◇ *I invited some of my colleagues but not all.* ◇ *Not all of them were invited.* ◇ *All of them enjoyed the party.* ◇ *They all enjoyed it.* ◇ *His last movie was best of all.* **2** 0-w (followed by a relative clause, often without *that*) the only thing; everything: *All I want is peace and quiet.* ◇ *It was all that I had.* ➲ note at ALTOGETHER

IDM **all in 'all** when everything is considered: *All in all it had been a great success.* **all in 'one** having two or more uses, functions, etc: *It's a corkscrew and bottle-opener all in one.* **and 'all 1** also; included; in addition: *She jumped into the river, clothes and all* (= with her clothes on). **2** (*informal*) as well; too: *'I'm freezing.' 'Yeah, me and all.'* (**not**) **at all** 0-w in any way; to any degree: *I didn't enjoy it at all.* **in all** as a total SYN **altogether**: *There were twelve of us in all for dinner.* ◇ *That's £25.40 in all.* **ˌnot at 'all** 0-w used as a polite reply to an expression of thanks: *'Thanks very much for your help.' 'Not at all, it was a pleasure.'* **your 'all** everything you have: *They gave their all* (= fought and died) *in the war.* ➲ more at ABOVE *prep.*, AFTER *prep.*, END *v.*, END *n.*, FOR *prep.*, SIDE *n.*

■***adv.*** **1** 0-w completely: *She was dressed all in white.* ◇ *He lives all alone.* ◇ *The coffee went all over my skirt.* **2** (*informal*) very: *She was all excited.* ◇ *Now don't get all upset about it.* **3 ~ too...** used to show that sth is more than you would like: *I'm all too aware of the problems.* ◇ *The end of the trip came all too soon.* **4** (in sports and games) to each side: *The score was four all.*

IDM **all a'long** all the time; from the beginning: *I realized it was in my pocket all along.* **all a'round** ➲ ALL ROUND **all the better, harder, etc.** so much better, harder, etc: *We'll have to work all the harder with two people off sick.* **all but 1** almost: *The party was all but over when we arrived.* ◇ *It was all but impossible to read his writing.* **2** everything or everyone except sth/sb: *All but one of the plates were damaged.* **all 'in 1** physically tired SYN **exhausted**: *At the end of the race he felt all in.* **2** (*BrE*) including everything: *The* *holiday cost £250 all in.* ➲ see also ALL-IN **all of sth** (often *ironic*) used to emphasize an amount, a size, etc. usually when it is very small: *It must be all of 100 metres to the car!* **all ˈover 1** everywhere: *We looked all over for the ring.* **2** (*informal*) what you would expect of the person mentioned: *That sounds like my sister all over.* **all ˈround** (*BrE*) (*NAmE* **all aˈround**) **1** in every way; in all respects: *a good performance all round* **2** for each person: *She bought drinks all round.* **ˌall ˈthere** (*informal*) having a healthy mind; thinking clearly: *He behaves very oddly at times—I don't think he's quite all there.* **be all about sb/sth** used to say what the most important aspect of sth is: *It's all about money these days.* **be all for sth/for doing sth** (*informal*) to believe strongly that sth should be done: *They're all for saving money where they can.* **be all ˈover sb** (*informal*) to show a lot of affection for or enthusiasm about sb: *He was all over her at the party.* **be all ˈthat** (*US, informal*) to be very attractive or impressive: *He thinks he's all that.* **be all up (with sb)** (*old-fashioned, informal*) to be the end for sb: *It looks as though it's all up with us now* (= we are ruined, have no further chances, etc.).

all- /ɔːl/ *combining form* (in adjectives and adverbs) **1** completely: *an all-British cast* ◇ *an all-inclusive price* **2** in the highest degree: *all-important* ◇ *all-powerful*

ˌall-ˈaction *adj.* [only before noun] having a lot of exciting events: *an all-action movie*

Allah /ˈælə/ *noun* the name of God among Muslims

ˌall-Aˈmerican *adj.* **1** having good qualities that people think are typically American: *a clean-cut all-American boy* **2** (of a sports player) chosen as one of the best players in the US

ˌall-aˈround (*NAmE*) (*BrE* **ˌall-ˈround**) *adj.* [only before noun] **1** including many different subjects, skills, etc. **2** (of a person) with a wide range of skills or abilities

allay /əˈleɪ/ *verb* **~ sth** (*formal*) to make sth, especially a feeling, less strong: *to **allay fears/concern/suspicion***

the ˈAll Blacks *noun* [pl.] the RUGBY team of New Zealand

ˌall-Caˈnadian *adj.* **1** chosen as one of the best in, or representing the whole of, Canada, for example in sports **2** having qualities that people think are typically Canadian

the ˌall-ˈclear *noun* [sing.] **1** a signal (often a sound) which shows that a place or situation is no longer dangerous **2** if a doctor gives sb **the all-clear**, they tell the person that he/she does not have any health problems **3** permission to do sth: *The ship was given the all-clear to sail.*

ˌall-ˈcomers *noun* [pl.] anyone who wants to take part in an activity or a competition

ˌall-conˈsum·ing *adj.* (of an interest) taking up all of your time or energy: *an all-consuming love of jazz*

ˈall-day *adj.* [only before noun] continuing for the whole day: *an all-day meeting*

al·le·ga·tion /ˌæləˈɡeɪʃn/ *noun* a public statement that is made without giving proof, accusing sb of doing sth that is wrong or illegal SYN **accusation**: *to **investigate/deny/withdraw an allegation*** ◇ **~ of sth** *Several newspapers **made allegations** of corruption in the city's police department.* ◇ **~ (of sth) against sb** *allegations of dishonesty against him* ◇ **~ about sb/sth** *The committee has made serious allegations about interference in its work.* ◇ **~ that...** *an allegation that he had been dishonest* ➲ SYNONYMS at CLAIM

al·lege /əˈledʒ/ *verb* [often passive] (*formal*) to state sth as a fact but without giving proof: **~ (that)...** *The prosecution alleges (that) she was driving carelessly.* ◇ **it is alleged (that)** ... *It is alleged that he mistreated the prisoners.* ◇ **be alleged to be, have, etc. sth** *He is alleged to have mistreated the prisoners.* ◇ **~ sth** *This procedure should be followed in cases where dishonesty has been alleged.* ▶ **al·leged** *adj.* [only before noun]: (*formal*) *the **alleged attacker/victim/killer*** (= that sb says is one) ◇ *the **alleged attack/offence/incident*** (= that sb says has happened) **al·leged·ly** /əˈledʒɪdli/ *adv.*: *crimes allegedly committed during the war*

al·le·giance /əˈliːdʒəns/ *noun* [U, C] a person's continued support for a political party, religion, ruler, etc: *to **switch/transfer/change allegiance*** ◇ ***an oath/a vow/a statement of allegiance*** ◇ *People of various party allegiances joined the campaign.* ◇ **~ (to sb/sth)** *to **pledge/swear allegiance*** ◇ *He affirmed his allegiance to the president.*

al·le·gory /ˈæləɡəri; *NAmE* -ɡɔːri/ *noun* [C, U] (*pl.* **-ies**) a story, play, picture, etc. in which each character or event is a symbol representing an idea or a quality, such as truth, evil, death, etc; the use of such symbols: *a political allegory* ◇ *the poet's use of allegory* ➲ see also FABLE ▶ **al·le·gor·ic·al** /ˌæləˈɡɒrɪkl; *NAmE* -ˈɡɔːr-/ *adj.*: *an **allegorical figure/novel*** **al·le·gor·ic·al·ly** *adv.*

al·legro /əˈleɡrəʊ; *NAmE* -ɡroʊ/ *noun* (*pl.* **-os**) (*music*) a piece of music to be played in a fast and lively manner ▶ **al·legro** *adj., adv.*

al·lele /əˈliːl/ *noun* (*biology*) one of two or more possible forms of a GENE that are found at the same place on a CHROMOSOME

al·le·luia /ˌælɪˈluːjə/ *noun, exclamation* = HALLELUJAH

ˌall-emˈbracing *adj.* (*formal*) including everything

ˌall-enˈcompass·ing *adj.* (*formal*) including everything

Allen key™ /ˈælən kiː/ (*BrE*) (*NAmE* **ˈAllen wrench™**) *noun* a small tool used for turning an Allen screw ➲ picture at KEY

ˈAllen screw™ *noun* a screw with a hole that has six sides

al·ler·gen /ˈælədʒən; *NAmE* ˈælərdʒən/ *noun* a substance that causes an allergy

al·ler·gic /əˈlɜːdʒɪk; *NAmE* əˈlɜːrdʒɪk/ *adj.* **1 ~ (to sth)** having an allergy to sth: *I like cats but unfortunately I'm allergic to them.* **2** caused by an allergy: *an **allergic reaction/rash*** **3** [not before noun] **~ to sth** (*informal, humorous*) having a strong dislike of sth/sb: *You could see he was allergic to housework.*

al·lergy /ˈælədʒi; *NAmE* ˈælərdʒi/ *noun* (*pl.* **-ies**) **~ (to sth)** a medical condition that causes you to react badly or feel ill/sick when you eat or touch a particular substance: *I have an allergy to animal hair.*

al·le·vi·ate /əˈliːvieɪt/ *verb* **~ sth** to make sth less severe SYN **ease**: *to alleviate suffering* ◇ *A number of measures were taken to alleviate the problem.* ▶ **al·le·vi·ation** /əˌliːviˈeɪʃn/ *noun* [U]

alley /ˈæli/ *noun* **1** (also **al·ley·way** /ˈæliweɪ/) a narrow passage behind or between buildings: *a **narrow/dark alley*** ➲ VISUAL VOCAB page V3 ➲ see also BLIND ALLEY, BOWLING ALLEY **2** (*NAmE*) (*BrE* **tram·lines**) (*informal*) the pair of parallel lines on a TENNIS or BADMINTON COURT that mark the extra area that is used when four people are playing

IDM **(right) up your ˈalley** (*NAmE*) = (RIGHT) UP YOUR STREET at STREET

ˈalley cat *noun* a cat that lives on the streets

al·li·ance /əˈlaɪəns/ *noun* **1** an agreement between countries, political parties, etc. to work together in order to achieve sth that they all want: *to **form/make an alliance*** ◇ **~ with sb/sth** *The Social Democrats are now **in alliance with** the Greens.* ◇ **~ between A and B** *an alliance between education and business to develop the use of technology in schools* **2** a group of people, political parties, etc. who work together in order to achieve sth that they all want

al·lied 0‑w *adj.*
1 0‑w /ˈælaɪd/ (often **Allied**) [only before noun] connected with countries that unite to fight a war together, especially the countries that fought together against Germany in the First and Second World Wars: *Italy joined the war on the Allied side in 1915.* ◇ ***allied forces/troops*** **2** /əˈlaɪd; ˈælaɪd/ (*formal*) (of two or more things) similar or existing together; connected with sth: *medicine, nursing, physiotherapy and other allied professions* ◇ **~ to/with sth** *In this job you will need social skills allied with technical knowledge.* ➲ see also ALLY

al·li·ga·tor /ˈælɪɡeɪtə(r)/ *noun* a large REPTILE similar to a CROCODILE, with a long tail, hard skin and very big

JAWS, that lives in rivers and lakes in N and S America and China

ˈalligator clip *noun* (*especially NAmE*) = CROCODILE CLIP

ˌall-imˈport·ant *adj.* extremely important

ˌall-ˈin *adj.* [only before noun] (*BrE*) including the cost of all parts of sth SYN **inclusive**: *an all-in price of £500 with no extras to pay*

ˌall-inˈclusive *adj.* including everything or everyone: *Our trips are all-inclusive—there are no hidden costs.*

ˌall-in-ˈone *adj.* [only before noun] (*BrE*) able to do the work of two or more things that are usually separate: *an all-in-one shampoo and conditioner* ▶ **ˌall-in-ˈone** *noun*: *We sell printers and scanners, and all-in-ones that combine the two.*

al·lit·er·ation /əˌlɪtəˈreɪʃn/ *noun* [U] (*technical*) the use of the same letter or sound at the beginning of words that are close together, as in *sing a song of sixpence* ▶ **al·lit·era·tive** /əˈlɪtrətɪv; *NAmE* əˈlɪtəreɪtɪv/ *adj.*

al·lium /ˈæliəm/ *noun* (*technical*) any plant that belongs to the same group as onions and GARLIC

ˌall-ˈnight *adj.* [only before noun] **1** (of a place) open through the night: *an all-night cafe* **2** (of an activity) continuing through the night: *an all-night party*

ˌall-ˈnighter *noun* (*NAmE, informal*) a time when you stay awake all night studying

al·lo·cate AW /ˈæləkeɪt/ *verb* to give sth officially to sb/sth for a particular purpose: **~ sth (for sth)** *A large sum has been allocated for buying new books for the library.* ◇ **~ sth (to sb/sth)** *They intend to allocate more places to mature students this year.* ◇ *More resources are being allocated to the project.* ◇ **~ sb/sth sth** *The project is being allocated more resources.*

al·lo·ca·tion AW /ˌæləˈkeɪʃn/ *noun* **1** [C] an amount of money, space, etc. that is given to sb for a particular purpose **2** [U] the act of giving sth to sb for a particular purpose: *the allocation of food to those who need it most*

allo·morph /ˈæləmɔːf; *NAmE* -mɔːrf/ *noun* (*linguistics*) one possible form of a particular MORPHEME. The forms /s/, /z/ and /ɪz/ in *cats*, *dogs* and *horses* are allomorphs of the plural ending *s*.

allo·phone /ˈæləfəʊn; *NAmE* -foʊn/ *noun* **1** (*phonetics*) a sound that is slightly different from another sound, although both sounds belong to the same PHONEME and the difference does not affect meaning. For example, the /l/ at the beginning of *little* is different from the /l/ at the end. **2** (*CanE*) a person who comes to live in Canada, especially Quebec, from another country, whose first language is neither French nor English ▶ **allo·phone** *adj.*: *Within French-speaking Quebec, anglophone, allophone and Aboriginal minorities also exist.*

ˌall-or-ˈnothing *adj.* used to describe two extreme situations which are the only possible ones: *an all-or-nothing decision* (= one which could either be very good or very bad)

allo·saurus /ˌæləˈsɔːrəs/ *noun* a type of large DINOSAUR

allot /əˈlɒt; *NAmE* əˈlɑːt/ *verb* (**-tt-**) to give time, money, tasks, etc. to sb/sth as a share of what is available: **~ sth** *I completed the test within the **time allotted**.* ◇ **~ sth to sb/sth** *How much money has been allotted to us?* ◇ **~ sb/sth sth** *How much money have we been allotted?*

al·lot·ment /əˈlɒtmənt; *NAmE* əˈlɑːt-/ *noun* **1** [C] (*BrE*) a small area of land in a town which a person can rent in order to grow vegetables on it **2** [C, U] (*formal*) an amount of sth that sb is given or allowed to have; the process of giving sth to sb: *Water allotments to farmers were cut back in the drought.* ◇ *the allotment of shares to company employees*

allo·trope /ˈælətrəʊp; *NAmE* -troʊp/ *noun* (*chemistry*) one of the different forms in which a chemical element exists. For example, diamond and GRAPHITE are allotropes of CARBON.

ˌall-ˈout *adj.* [only before noun] using or involving every possible effort and done in a very determined way: *all-out war* ◇ *an all-out attack on the opposition* ▶ **ˌall ˈout** *adv.*: *We're going all out to win.*

ˈall-over *adj.* [only before noun] covering the whole of sth: *an all-over tan*

allow 🔑 /əˈlaʊ/ *verb*

▸ LET SB/STH DO STH **1** 🔑 to let sb/sth do sth; to let sth happen or be done: **~ sb to do sth** *His parents won't allow him to stay out late.* ◇ *He **is not allowed to** stay out late.* ◇ *They shouldn't be allowed to get away with it.* ◇ **~ sth to do sth** *He allowed his mind to wander.* ◇ **~ yourself to do sth** *She won't allow herself to be dictated to.* ◇ **~ sth** *Smoking is not allowed in the hall.* **2** 🔑 **~ sb/yourself sth** to let sb have sth: *You're allowed an hour to complete the test.* ◇ *I'm not allowed visitors.* **3** 🔑 [usually passive] to let sb/sth go into, through, out of, etc. a place: **~ sth** *No dogs allowed* (= you cannot bring them in). ◇ **~ sb/sth + adv./prep.** *The prisoners are **allowed out** of their cells for two hours a day.* ◇ *The crowd parted to **allow her through**.* ◇ *You won't be **allowed up*** (= out of bed) *for several days.*

▸ MAKE POSSIBLE **4** 🔑 **~ sth** to make sth possible: *A ramp allows easy access for wheelchairs.* ➲ LANGUAGE BANK at PROCESS

▸ TIME/MONEY/FOOD, ETC. **5** 🔑 **~ sth (for sb/sth)** to make sure that you have enough of sth for a particular purpose: *You need to allow three metres of fabric for the dress.*

▸ ACCEPT/ADMIT **6** (*formal*) to accept or admit sth; to agree that sth is true or correct: **~ sth** *The judge allowed my claim.* ◇ (in a court of law) *'Objection!' 'I'll allow it.'* ◇ **~ that ...** *He refuses to allow that such a situation could arise.* ◇ **~ sb sth** *She was very helpful when my mother was ill—I'll allow you that.* ➲ compare DISALLOW

IDM **allow ˈme** used to offer help politely ➲ more at REIN *n.*

PHR V **alˈlow for sb/sth** 🔑 to consider or include sb/sth when calculating sth: *It will take about an hour to get there, allowing for traffic delays.* ◇ *All these factors must be allowed for.* **alˈlow of sth** (*formal*) to make sth possible: *The facts allow of only one explanation.*

al·low·able /əˈlaʊəbl/ *adj.* **1** that is allowed, especially by law or by a set of rules **2** (*BrE*) **allowable** amounts of money are amounts that you do not have to pay tax on

al·low·ance /əˈlaʊəns/ *noun* **1** an amount of money that is given to sb regularly or for a particular purpose: *an allowance of $20 a day* ◇ *a **clothing/living/travel allowance*** ◇ *Do you get an allowance for clothing?* ➲ see also ATTENDANCE ALLOWANCE **2** the amount of sth that is allowed in a particular situation: *a baggage allowance of 20 kilos* **3** (*BrE*) an amount of money that can be earned or received before you start paying tax: *personal tax allowances* **4** (*especially NAmE*) = POCKET MONEY

IDM **make allowance(s) for sth** to consider sth, for example when you are making a decision or planning sth: *The budget made allowance for inflation.* ◇ *The plan makes no allowance for people working at different rates.* **make allowances (for sb)** to allow sb to behave in a way that you would not usually accept, because of a problem or because there is a special reason

alloy *noun, verb*

▪ ***noun*** /ˈælɔɪ/ [C, U] a metal that is formed by mixing two types of metal together, or by mixing metal with another substance: *Brass is an alloy of copper and zinc.*

▪ ***verb*** /əˈlɔɪ/ **~ sth (with sth)** (*technical*) to mix one metal with another, especially one of lower value

ˌall-ˈparty *adj.* [usually before noun] involving all political parties: *all-party support*

ˌall-points ˈbulletin *noun* (*abbr.* **APB**) (*US*) a radio message sent to every officer of a police force, giving details of people who are suspected of a crime, of stolen vehicles, etc.

ˌall-ˈpowerful *adj.* having complete power: *the all-powerful secret police*

ˌall-ˈpurpose *adj.* [only before noun] having many different uses; able to be used in many situations

ˌall-purpose ˈflour (*NAmE*) (*BrE* **ˌplain ˈflour**) *noun* [U] flour that does not contain BAKING POWDER ➲ compare SELF-RISING FLOUR

A

all 'right (also *non-standard* or *informal* **al·right**) *adj., adv., exclamation*
■ *adj., adv.* **1** acceptable; in an acceptable manner SYN **OK**: *Is the coffee all right?* ◇ *Are you getting along all right in your new job?* ◇ *'They're off to Spain next week.' 'It's all right for some, isn't it?'* (= some people are lucky) **2** safe and well SYN **OK**: *I hope the children are all right.* ◇ *Do you feel all right?* ➲ SYNONYMS at WELL **3** only just good enough SYN **OK**: *Your work is all right but I'm sure you could do better.* **4** that can be allowed SYN **OK**: *Are you sure it's all right for me to leave early?* **5** (*informal*) used to emphasize that there is no doubt about sth: *'Are you sure it's her?' 'Oh, it's her all right.'*
IDM **I'm all 'right, Jack** (*BrE, informal*) used by or about sb who is happy with their own life and does not care about other people's problems **it'll be all ˌright on the 'night** (*saying*) used to say that a performance, an event, etc. will be successful even if the preparations for it have not gone well ➲ more at BIT
■ *exclamation* **1** used to check that sb agrees or understands SYN **OK**: *We've got to get up early, all right?* **2** used to say that you agree SYN **OK**: *'Can you do it?' 'Oh, all right.'* **3** used when accepting thanks for help or a favour, or when sb says they are sorry SYN **OK**: *'I'm really sorry.' 'That's all right, don't worry.'* **4** used to get sb's attention SYN **OK**: *All right class, turn to page 20.* **5** (*BrE, informal*) used to say hello: *'All right, Bill.' 'All right.'* **6 you're all right** (*BrE, slang*) used to refuse an offer or invitation, especially one that you think is unreasonable or not very good: *'Could I interest you in our special offer?' 'No, you're all right, mate.'*

ˌall-'round (*BrE*) (*NAmE* **ˌall-a'round**) *adj.* [only before noun] **1** including many different subjects, skills, etc: *an all-round education* **2** (of a person) with a wide range of skills or abilities: *She's a good all-round player.*

all-'rounder *noun* (*BrE*) a person who has many different skills and abilities

ˌAll 'Saints' Day *noun* a Christian festival in honour of the SAINTS, held on 1 November

ˌall-'singing, ˌall-'dancing *adj.* [only before noun] (*BrE, informal*) (of a machine or system) having a lot of advanced technical features and therefore able to perform many different functions

ˌAll 'Souls' Day *noun* a Christian festival in honour of the dead, held on 2 November

all·spice /ˈɔːlspaɪs/ *noun* [U] the dried BERRIES of a tree from the West Indies, used in cooking as a spice

'all-star *adj.* [only before noun] including many famous actors, players, etc: *an all-star cast*

ˌall-terrain 'board *noun* = MOUNTAINBOARD

ˌall-terrain 'vehicle *noun* = ATV

ˌall-'ticket *adj.* [usually before noun] for which tickets need to be obtained in advance: *an all-ticket match*

'all-time *adj.* [only before noun] (used when you are comparing things or saying how good or bad sth is) of any time: *one of the all-time great players* ◇ *my all-time favourite song* ◇ *Unemployment reached an all-time record of 3 million.* ◇ *Profits are at an* ***all-time high/low.***

al·lude /əˈluːd/ *verb*
PHR V **al'lude to sb/sth** (*formal*) to mention sth in an indirect way ➲ see also ALLUSION

al·lure /əˈlʊə(r); *NAmE* əˈlʊr/ *noun* [U] (*formal*) the quality of being attractive and exciting: *sexual allure* ◇ *the allure of the big city*

al·lur·ing /əˈlʊərɪŋ; *NAmE* əˈlʊrɪŋ/ *adj.* attractive and exciting in a mysterious way: *an alluring smile*
▸ **al·lur·ing·ly** *adv.*

al·lu·sion /əˈluːʒn/ *noun* [C, U] **~ (to sb/sth)** (*formal*) something that is said or written that refers to or mentions another person or subject in an indirect way (= ALLUDES to it): *His statement was seen as an allusion to the recent drug-related killings.* ◇ *Her poetry is full of obscure literary allusion.*

al·lu·sive /əˈluːsɪv/ *adj.* (*formal*) containing allusions: *an allusive style of writing*

al·lu·vial /əˈluːviəl/ *adj.* [usually before noun] (*geology*) made of sand and earth that is left by rivers or floods

al·lu·vium /əˈluːviəm/ *noun* [U] (*geology*) sand and earth that is left by rivers or floods

ˌall-'weather *adj.* [usually before noun] suitable for all types of weather: *an all-weather football pitch*

ˌall-wheel 'drive *noun* (*especially NAmE*) = FOUR-WHEEL DRIVE

ally *noun, verb*

> **WORD FAMILY**
> **ally** *verb, noun*
> **allied** *adj.*
> **alliance** *noun*

■ *noun* /ˈælaɪ/ (*pl.* **-ies**) **1** [C] a country that has agreed to help and support another country, especially in case of a war **2** [C] a person who helps and supports sb who is in a difficult situation, especially a politician: *a close ally and friend of the prime minister* **3 the Allies** [pl.] the group of countries including Britain and the US that fought together in the First and Second World Wars
■ *verb* /əˈlaɪ/ (**al·lies, ally·ing, al·lied, al·lied**) [T, I] **~ (yourself) with sb/sth** to give your support to another group or country: *The prince allied himself with the Scots.*

-ally *suffix* (makes adverbs from adjectives that end in *-al*): *magically* ◇ *sensationally*

Alma Mater /ˌælmə ˈmɑːtə(r); ˈmeɪtə(r)/ (also **alma mater**) *noun* [sing.] (*especially NAmE*) the school, college or university that sb went to

al·manac (also *less frequent* **al·man·ack**) /ˈɔːlmənæk; ˈæl-/ *noun* **1** a book that is published every year giving information for that year about a particular subject or activity **2** a book that gives information about the sun, moon, times of the TIDES (= the rise and fall of the sea level), etc. for each day of the year

> **Synonyms**
>
> **almost / nearly / practically**
>
> These three words have similar meanings and are used frequently with the following words:
>
> | almost ~ | nearly ~ | practically ~ |
> |---|---|---|
> | certainly | (numbers) | all |
> | all | all | every |
> | every | always | no |
> | entirely | every | nothing |
> | impossible | finished | impossible |
> | empty | died | anything |
>
> ■ They are used in positive sentences: *She almost/nearly/practically missed her train.* They can be used before words like *all, every* and *everybody*: *Nearly all the students have bikes.* ◇ *I've got practically every CD they've made.* **Practically** is used more in spoken than in written English. **Nearly** is the most common with numbers: *There were nearly 200 people at the meeting.* They can also be used in negative sentences but it is more common to make a positive sentence with **only just**: *We only just got there in time.* (or: *We almost/nearly didn't get there in time.*)
>
> ■ **Almost** and **practically** can be used before words like *any, anybody, anything*, etc: *I'll eat almost anything.* You can also use them before *no, nobody, never*, etc. but it is much more common to use **hardly** or **scarcely** with *any, anybody, ever*, etc: *She's hardly ever in* (or: *She's almost never in*).
>
> ■ **Almost** can be used when you are saying that one thing is similar to another: *The boat looked almost like a toy.*
>
> ■ In *BrE* you can use *very* and *so* before **nearly**: *He was very nearly caught.*
>
> ➲ note at HARDLY

al·mighty /ɔːlˈmaɪti/ *adj.* **1** (in prayers) having complete power: *Almighty God, have mercy on us.* **2** [only before noun] (*informal*) very great or severe: *an* ***almighty bang/crash/roar*** **3** (*taboo, offensive*) used in the expressions shown in the example, to express surprise or anger: *Christ/God Almighty! What the hell do you think you are doing?* **4 the Almighty** *noun* [sing.] God

al·mond /ˈɑːmənd/ *noun* the flat pale sweet nut of the **almond tree** used in cooking and to make almond oil: *ground almonds* ◇ ***blanched almonds*** (= with their skins removed) ◇ *almond paste* ◇ *almond eyes* (= eyes shaped like almonds) ➲ VISUAL VOCAB page V28

al·most 🔑 /ˈɔːlməʊst; *NAmE* -moʊst/ *adv.* not quite SYN **nearly**: *I like almost all of them.* ◇ *It's a mistake they almost always make.* ◇ *The story is almost certainly false.* ◇ *It's almost time to go.* ◇ *Dinner's almost ready.* ◇ *He slipped and almost fell.* ◇ *Their house is almost opposite ours.* ◇ *They'll eat almost anything.* ◇ *Almost no one* (= hardly anyone) *believed him.*

alms /ɑːmz/ *noun* [pl.] (*old-fashioned*) money, clothes and food that are given to poor people

alms·house /ˈɑːmzhaʊs/ *noun* (in the past in Britain) a house owned by a charity where poor people (usually the old) lived without paying rent

aloe /ˈæləʊ; *NAmE* ˈæloʊ/ *noun* a tropical plant with thick leaves with sharp points that contain a lot of water. The juice of some types of aloe is used in medicine and COSMETICS.

aloe vera /ˌæləʊ ˈvɪərə; *NAmE* ˌæloʊ ˈvɪrə/ *noun* **1** [U] a substance that comes from a type of aloe, used in products such as skin creams **2** [C] the aloe that this substance comes from

aloft /əˈlɒft; *NAmE* əˈlɔːft/ *adv.* (*formal*) high in the air

aloha /əˈləʊhə; *NAmE* əˈloʊhə/ *exclamation* a Hawaiian word meaning 'love', used to say hello or gooodbye

a'loha shirt *noun* = HAWAIIAN SHIRT

alone 🔑 /əˈləʊn; *NAmE* əˈloʊn/ *adj.* [not before noun], *adv.*

1 🔑 without any other people: *I don't like going out alone at night.* ◇ *He lives alone.* ◇ *Finally the two of us were* ***alone together.*** ◇ *She was sitting* ***all alone*** *in the hall.* ◇ *Tom is* ***not alone in*** *finding Rick hard to work with.* **2** 🔑 without the help of other people or things: *It's hard bringing up children alone.* ◇ *The assassin said he had acted alone.* **3** 🔑 lonely and unhappy or without any friends: *Carol felt all alone in the world.* ◇ *I've been so alone since you went away.* **4** used after a noun or pronoun to show that the person or thing mentioned is the only one: *You can't blame anyone else; you alone made the decision.* **5** used after a noun or pronoun to emphasize one particular thing: *The shoes alone cost £200.*

IDM **go it a'lone** to do sth without help from anyone: *Andrew decided to go it alone and start his own business.* **leave/let sb alone** 🔑 to stop annoying sb or trying to get their attention: *She's asked to be left alone but the press photographers follow her everywhere.* **leave/let sth alone** 🔑 to stop touching, changing, or moving sth: *I've told you before—leave my things alone!* **let alone** used after a statement to emphasize that because the first thing is not true or possible, the next thing cannot be true or possible either: *There isn't enough room for us, let alone any guests.* **stand a'lone 1** to be independent or not connected with other people, organizations or ideas: *These islands are too small to stand alone as independent states.* **2** to be not near other objects or buildings: *The arch once stood alone at the entrance to the castle.* ➲ more at TIME *n.*

along 🔑 /əˈlɒŋ; *NAmE* əˈlɔːŋ; əˈlɑːŋ/ *prep., adv.*

■ ***prep.*** **1** 🔑 from one end to or towards the other end of sth: *They walked slowly along the road.* ◇ *I looked along the shelves for the book I needed.* **2** 🔑 in a line that follows the side of sth long: *Houses had been built along both sides of the river.* **3** 🔑 at a particular point on or beside sth long: *You'll find his office just along the corridor.*

■ ***adv.*** HELP For the special uses of **along** in phrasal verbs, look at the entries for the verbs. For example **get along with sb** is in the phrasal verb section at **get. 1** 🔑 forward: *I was just walking along singing to myself.* ◇ *He pointed out various landmarks as we drove along.* **2** 🔑 with sb: *We're going for a swim. Why don't you come along?* ◇ *I'll be along* (= I'll join you) *in a few minutes.* **3** 🔑 towards a better state or position: *The book's coming along nicely.*

IDM **along with sb/sth** 🔑 in addition to sb/sth; in the same way as sb/sth: *She lost her job when the factory closed, along with hundreds of others.*

> **Which Word?**
>
> **alone / lonely / lone**
>
> ■ **Alone**, and **on your own/by yourself** (which are less formal and are the normal phrases used in spoken English), describe a person or thing that is separate from others. They do not mean that the person is unhappy: *I like being alone in the house.* ◇ *I'm going to London by myself next week.* ◇ *I want to finish this on my own* (= without anyone's help).
>
> ■ **Lone/solitary/single** mean that there is only one person or thing there; **lone** and **solitary** may sometimes suggest that the speaker thinks the person involved is lonely: *a lone jogger in the park* ◇ *long, solitary walks*
>
> ■ **Lonely** (*NAmE* also **lonesome**) means that you are alone and sad: *a lonely child* ◇ *Sam was very lonely when he first moved to New York.* It can also describe places or activities that make you feel lonely: *a lonely house*

along·side 🔑 /əˌlɒŋˈsaɪd; *NAmE* əˌlɔːŋ-; əˌlɑːŋ-/ *prep.* **1** 🔑 next to or at the side of sth: *A police car pulled up alongside us.* **2** 🔑 together with or at the same time as sth/sb: *Traditional beliefs still flourish alongside a modern urban lifestyle.* ▸ **along·side** 🔑 *adv.*: *Nick caught up with me and rode alongside.*

aloo (also **alu**) /ˈæluː/ *noun* [U] (*IndE*) potatoes

aloof /əˈluːf/ *adj.* [not usually before noun] not friendly or interested in other people SYN **distant, remote** ▸ **aloof·ness** *noun* [U]

IDM **keep/hold (yourself) aloof | remain/stand aloof** to not become involved in sth; to show no interest in people: *The Emperor kept himself aloof from the people.*

alo·pe·cia /ˌæləˈpiːʃə/ *noun* [U] (*medical*) loss of hair from the head and body, often caused by illness

aloud 🔑 /əˈlaʊd/ *adv.*

1 🔑 in a voice that other people can hear: *The teacher listened to the children* ***reading aloud.*** ◇ *He read the letter aloud to us.* ◇ *'What am I going to do?' she wondered aloud.* ➲ note at LOUD **2** in a loud voice: *She cried aloud in protest.* IDM see THINK *v.*

al·paca /ælˈpækə/ *noun* **1** [C] a S American animal that is related to the LLAMA and has long hair **2** [U] a type of soft wool or cloth made from the hair of the alpaca, used especially for making expensive clothes: *an alpaca coat*

alpha /ˈælfə/ *noun* the first letter of the Greek alphabet (Α, α)

al·pha·bet 🔑 /ˈælfəbet/ *noun* a set of letters or symbols in a fixed order used for writing a language ORIGIN From *alpha* and *beta*, the first two letters of the Greek alphabet

al·pha·bet·ic /ˌælfəˈbetɪk/ (also **al·pha·bet·ic·al**) *adj.* (of a written or printed character) being one of the letters of the alphabet, rather than a number or other symbol ➲ compare NON-ALPHABETIC

al·pha·bet·ic·al 🔑 /ˌælfəˈbetɪkl/ *adj.* **1** 🔑 according to the correct order of the letters of the alphabet: *The names on the list are* ***in alphabetical order.*** **2** = ALPHABETIC ▸ **al·pha·bet·ic·al·ly** 🔑 /-kli/ *adv.*: ***arranged/listed/stored alphabetically***

A

al·pha·bet·ize (*BrE* also **-ise**) /ˈælfəbətaɪz/ *verb* **~ sth** to arrange a list of words in alphabetical order

ˌalphabet ˈsoup *noun* [U] **1** (*informal*) language that is extremely difficult to understand, especially because it contains many symbols or abbreviations **2** soup that contains PASTA in the shape of letters

ˌalpha ˈmale *noun* [usually sing.] the man or male animal in a particular group who has the most power

alpha·numer·ic /ˌælfənjuːˈmerɪk; *NAmE* -nuːˈm-/ (also **alpha·numer·ic·al** /-ɪkl/) *adj.* containing both letters and numbers: *an alphanumeric code*

ˈalpha particle *noun* (*technical*) the NUCLEUS of a HELIUM atom; a PARTICLE with a positive electrical charge passing through it, that is produced in a nuclear reaction

ˈalpha test *noun* (*technical*) a test done by a company on a new product that they are developing ➲ compare BETA TEST ▸ **ˈalpha-test** *verb* **~ sth**

al·pine /ˈælpaɪn/ *adj., noun*

■ ***adj.*** existing in or connected with high mountains, especially the Alps in Central Europe

■ ***noun*** any plant that grows best on mountains

al·pi·nist /ˈælpɪnɪst/ *noun* a person who climbs high mountains as a sport, especially in the Alps ▸ **al·pi·nism** /ˈælpɪnɪzəm/ *noun* [U]

al·ready 🔑 /ɔːlˈredi/ *adv.*

1 🔑 before now or before a particular time in the past: *'Lunch?' 'No thanks, I've already eaten.'* ◇ *We got there early but Mike had already left.* **2** 🔑 used to express surprise that sth has happened so soon or so early: *Is it 10 o'clock already?* ◇ *You're not leaving already, are you?* **3** 🔑 used to emphasize that a situation or problem exists: *I'm already late.* ◇ *There are far too many people already. We can't take any more.* IDM see ENOUGH *det.*

British / American

already / just / yet

- **Already** and **yet** are usually used with the present perfect tense, but in *NAmE* they can also be used with the simple past tense: *I already did it.* ◇ *Did you eat yet?*
- However, this is much more common in spoken than in written English and some Americans do not consider it acceptable, even in speech. The present perfect is more common in *NAmE* and almost always used in *BrE*: *I've already done it.* ◇ *Have you eaten yet?*
- **Just** is mostly used with the perfect tenses in *BrE* and with the simple past in *NAmE*: *I've just had some bad news.* (*BrE*) ◇ *I just got some bad news.* (*NAmE*)

al·right /ɔːlˈraɪt/ *adv.* (*informal*) = ALL RIGHT HELP Some people consider that this form should not be used in formal writing.

Al·sa·tian /ælˈseɪʃn/ (*BrE*) (also ˌ**German** ˈ**shepherd** *NAmE, BrE*) *noun* a large dog, often trained to help the police, to guard buildings or (especially in the US) to help blind people find their way

also 🔑 /ˈɔːlsəʊ; *NAmE* ˈɔːlsoʊ/ *adv.*

(not used with negative verbs) in addition; too: *She's fluent in French and German. She also speaks a little Italian.* ◇ *rubella, **also known as** German measles* ◇ *I didn't like it that much. Also, it was much too expensive.* ◇ *Jake's father had also been a doctor* (= both Jake and his father were doctors). ◇ *She was **not only** intelligent **but also** very musical.* ➲ LANGUAGE BANK at ADDITION

Which Word?

also / as well / too

- **Also** is more formal than **as well** and **too**, and it usually comes before the main verb or after *be*: *I went to New York last year, and I also spent some time in Washington.* In *BrE* it is not usually used at the end of a sentence. **Too** is much more common in spoken and informal English. It is usually used at the end of a sentence: *'I'm going home now.' 'I'll come too.'*. In *BrE* **as well** is used like **too**, but in *NAmE* it sounds formal or old-fashioned.
- When you want to add a second negative point in a negative sentence, use **not...either**: *She hasn't phoned and she hasn't written either.* If you are adding a negative point to a positive one, you can use **not...as well/too**: *You can have a burger, but you can't have fries as well.*

ˈalso-ran *noun* a person who is not successful, especially in a competition or an election

altar /ˈɔːltə(r)/ *noun* a holy table in a church or TEMPLE: *the high altar* (= the most important one in a particular church)

IDM **at/on the altar of sth** (*formal*) because of sth that you think is worth suffering for: *He was willing to sacrifice his happiness on the altar of fame.*

ˈaltar boy *noun* a boy who helps the priest in church services, especially in the Roman Catholic church

al·tar·piece /ˈɔːltəpiːs; *NAmE* -tərp-/ *noun* a painting or other piece of art, located near the ALTAR in a church

alter 🔑 AW /ˈɔːltə(r)/ *verb*

1 🔑 [I, T] to become different; to make sb/sth different: *Prices did not alter significantly during 2007.* ◇ *He had altered so much I scarcely recognized him.* ◇ **~ sb/sth** *It doesn't alter the way I feel.* ◇ *Nothing can **alter the fact that** we are to blame.* ◇ *The landscape has been radically altered, severely damaging wildlife.* **2** 🔑 [T] **~ sth** to make changes to a piece of clothing so that it will fit you better ▸ **al·ter·able** AW *adj.* (*formal*) OPP **unalterable**

al·ter·ation AW /ˌɔːltəˈreɪʃn/ *noun* **1** [C] a change to sth that makes it different: ***major/minor alterations*** ◇ *They are **making** some **alterations to** the house.* ◇ *an **alteration in** the baby's heartbeat* **2** [U] the act of making a change to sth: *The dress will not need much alteration.*

al·ter·ca·tion /ˌɔːltəˈkeɪʃn; *NAmE* -tərˈk-/ *noun* [C, U] (*formal*) a noisy argument or disagreement

alter ego /ˌæltər ˈiːgəʊ; ˌɔːl-; *NAmE* ˈiːgoʊ/ *noun* (*pl.* **alter egos**) (from *Latin*) **1** a person whose personality is different from your own but who shows or acts as another side of your personality: *Superman's alter ego was Clark Kent.* **2** a close friend who is very like yourself

al·ter·nate AW *adj., verb, noun*

■ ***adj.*** /ɔːlˈtɜːnət; *NAmE* ˈɔːltərnət/ [usually before noun] **1** (of two things) happening or following one after the other regularly: *alternate layers of fruit and cream* **2** if sth happens on **alternate** days, nights, etc. it happens on one day, etc. but not on the next: *John has to work on alternate Sundays.* **3** (*especially NAmE*) = ALTERNATIVE ▸ **al·ter·nate·ly** *adv.*: *He felt alternately hot and cold.*

■ ***verb*** /ˈɔːltəneɪt; *NAmE* -tərn-/ **1** [T] to make things or people follow one after the other in a repeated pattern: **~ A and B** *Alternate cubes of meat and slices of red pepper.* ◇ **~ A with B** *Alternate cubes of meat with slices of red pepper.* **2** [I] (of things or people) to follow one after the other in a repeated pattern: *alternating dark and pale stripes* ◇ **~ with sth** *Dark stripes alternate with pale ones.* **3** [I] **~ between A and B** to keep changing from one thing to another and back again: *Her mood alternated between happiness and despair.* ▸ **al·ter·na·tion** /ˌɔːltəˈneɪʃn; *NAmE* -tərˈn-/ *noun* [U, C]: *the alternation of day and night*

■ ***noun*** /ˈɔːltɜːnət; *NAmE* -tərn-/ (*NAmE*) a person who does a job for sb who is away

alˌternate ˈangles (also **ˈZ angles**) *noun* [pl.] (*geometry*) equal angles formed on opposite sides of a line that crosses two parallel lines, in the position of the inner angles of a Z ➲ VISUAL VOCAB page V58 ➲ compare CORRESPONDING ANGLES

ˌalternating ˈcurrent *noun* [U, C] (*abbr.* AC) an electric current that changes its direction at regular intervals many times a second ➲ compare DIRECT CURRENT

A

al·ter·na·tive 🔑 AW /ɔːlˈtɜːnətɪv; *NAmE* -ˈtɜːrn-/ *noun, adj.*
■ ***noun*** 🔑 a thing that you can choose to do or have out of two or more possibilities: *You can be paid in cash weekly or by cheque monthly; those are the two alternatives.* ◇ *We had* ***no alternative but to*** *fire Gibson.* ◇ *There is a vegetarian alternative on the menu every day.* ➲ SYNONYMS at OPTION
■ ***adj.*** [only before noun] **1** 🔑 (also **al·ter·nate** especially in *NAmE*) that can be used instead of sth else: *an alternative method of doing sth* ◇ *Do you have an alternative solution?* **2** 🔑 different from the usual or traditional way in which sth is done: ***alternative comedy/lifestyles/values*** ◇ ***alternative energy*** (= electricity or power that is produced using the energy from the sun, wind, water, etc.)

alˌternative ˈfuel *noun* [C, U] fuel that can be used instead of FOSSIL FUELS such as coal and oil, and instead of nuclear fuel

al·ter·na·tive·ly 🔑 AW /ɔːlˈtɜːnətɪvli; *NAmE* -ˈtɜːrn-/ *adv.*
used to introduce a suggestion that is a second choice or possibility: *The agency will make travel arrangements for you. Alternatively, you can organize your own transport.*

alˌternative ˈmedicine *noun* [C, U] any type of treatment that does not use the usual scientific methods of Western medicine, for example one using plants instead of artificial drugs

al·ter·na·tor /ˈɔːltəneɪtə(r); *NAmE* -tərn-/ *noun* a device, used especially in a car, that produces an ALTERNATING CURRENT

al·though 🔑 (also *US informal* **altho**) /ɔːlˈðəʊ; *NAmE* ɔːlˈðoʊ/ *conj.*
1 🔑 used for introducing a statement that makes the main statement in a sentence seem surprising SYN **though**: *Although the sun was shining, it wasn't very warm.* ◇ *Although small, the kitchen is well designed.* ➲ LANGUAGE BANK at HOWEVER **2** 🔑 used to mean 'but' or 'however' when you are commenting on a statement: *I felt he was wrong, although I didn't say so at the time.*

Which Word?

although / even though / though

- You can use these words to show contrast between two clauses or two sentences. **Though** is used more in spoken than in written English. You can use **although**, **even though** and **though** at the beginning of a sentence or clause that has a verb. Notice where the commas go: *Although/Even though/Though everyone played well, we lost the game.* ◇ *We lost the game, although/even though/though everyone played well.*
- You cannot use **even** on its own at the beginning of a sentence or clause instead of **although**, **even though** or **though**: ~~*Even everyone played well, we lost the game.*~~

al·tim·eter /ˈæltɪmiːtə(r); *NAmE* ælˈtɪmətər/ *noun* an instrument for showing height above sea level, used especially in an aircraft

al·ti·tude /ˈæltɪtjuːd; *NAmE* -tuːd/ *noun* **1** [C, usually sing.] the height above sea level: *We are flying* ***at an altitude of*** *6 000 metres.* ◇ *The plane made a dive to a lower altitude.* **2** [C, usually pl., U] a place that is high above sea level: *Snow leopards live* ***at high altitudes.*** ◇ *The athletes trained* ***at altitude*** *in Mexico City.*

ˈaltitude sickness *noun* [U] illness caused by a lack of OXYGEN, because of being very high above sea level, for example on a mountain

Alt key /ˈɔːlt kiː/ (also **ALT key**) *noun* a key on a computer keyboard which you press while pressing other keys, in order to change their function

alto /ˈæltəʊ; *NAmE* ˈæltoʊ/ *noun, adj.*
■ ***noun*** (*pl.* **-os**) **1** (also **con·tralto**) [C] a singing voice with a lower range than that of a SOPRANO; a person with an alto voice **2** [sing.] a musical part that is written for an alto voice ➲ compare BARITONE, BASS, COUNTERTENOR, TENOR
■ ***adj.*** [only before noun] (of a musical instrument) with the second highest range of notes in its group: *an alto saxophone* ➲ compare SOPRANO, TENOR

al·together 🔑 /ˌɔːltəˈgeðə(r)/ *adv., noun*
■ ***adv.*** **1** 🔑 (used to emphasize sth) completely; in every way: *The train went slower and slower until it stopped altogether.* ◇ *I don't altogether agree with you.* ◇ *I am* ***not altogether*** *happy* (= I am very unhappy) *about the decision.* ◇ *It was an altogether different situation.* **2** 🔑 used to give a total number or amount: *You owe me £68 altogether.* **3** 🔑 used to introduce a summary when you have mentioned a number of different things: *The food was good and we loved the music. Altogether it was a great evening.*
■ ***noun***
IDM **in the altoˈgether** (*old-fashioned, informal*) without any clothes on

Which Word?

altogether / all together

- **Altogether** and **all together** do not mean the same thing. **Altogether** means 'in total' or (in *BrE*) 'completely': *We have invited fifty people altogether.* ◇ *I am not altogether convinced by this argument.*
- **All together** means 'all in one place' or 'all at once': *Can you put your books all together in this box?* ◇ *Let's sing 'Happy Birthday'. All together now!*

al·tru·ism /ˈæltruɪzəm/ *noun* [U] (*formal*) the fact of caring about the needs and happiness of other people more than your own ▶ **al·tru·is·tic** /ˌæltruˈɪstɪk/ *adj.*: *altruistic behaviour*

alu = ALOO

alum /ˈæləm/ *noun* [U] a substance formed from ALUMINIUM/ALUMINUM and another metal, used, for example, to prepare leather and to change the colour of things

alu·mina /əˈluːmɪnə/ *noun* [U] (*technical*) a white substance found in many types of rock, especially CLAY

alu·min·ium /ˌæljəˈmɪniəm; ˌælə-/ (*BrE*) (*NAmE* **alu·mi·num** /əˈluːmɪnəm/) *noun* [U] (*symb.* **Al**) a chemical element. Aluminium is a light, silver-grey metal used for making pans, etc: *aluminium saucepans/window frames* ◇ ***aluminium foil*** (= for example, for wrapping food in)

alumna /əˈlʌmnə/ *noun* (*pl.* **alum·nae** /-niː/) (*formal, especially NAmE*) a former woman student of a school, college or university

alumni /əˈlʌmnaɪ/ *noun* [pl.] (*especially NAmE*) the former male and female students of a school, college or university: *Harvard Alumni Association*

alum·nus /əˈlʌmnəs/ *noun* (*pl.* **alumni** /-naɪ/) (*formal, especially NAmE*) a former male student of a school, college or university

al·veo·lar /ælˈviːələ(r); *BrE* also ˌælviˈəʊlə(r)/ *noun* (*phonetics*) a speech sound made with the tongue touching the part of the mouth behind the upper front teeth, for example /t/ and /d/ in *tie* and *die* ▶ **al·veo·lar** *adj.*

al·veo·lus /ælˈviːələs; *BrE* also ˌælviˈəʊləs/ *noun* (*pl.* **al·veoli** /ælˈviːəlaɪ; -liː; *BrE* also ˌælviˈəʊlaɪ; -liː/) (*anatomy*) one of the many small spaces in each lung where gases can pass into or out of the blood

al·ways 🔑 /ˈɔːlweɪz/ *adv.*
1 🔑 at all times; on every occasion: *There's always somebody at home in the evenings.* ◇ *Always lock your car.* ◇ *She always arrives at 7.30.* ◇ *The children always seem to be hungry.* ◇ *We're not always this busy!* **2** 🔑 for a long time; since you can remember: *Pat has always loved gardening.* ◇ *This is the way we've always done it.* ◇ *This painting is very good—Ellie always was very good at art* (= so it is not very surprising). ◇ *Did you always want to be an actor?* **3** 🔑 for all future time: *I'll always love you.* **4** 🔑 if you say a person is **always doing** sth, or sth is **always happening**, you mean

A

that they do it, or it happens, very often, and that this is annoying: *She's always criticizing me.* ◇ *That phone's always ringing.* **5 can/could always..., there's always ...** used to suggest a possible course of action: *If it doesn't fit, you can always take it back.* ◇ *If he can't help, there's always John.*

IDM **as 'always** as usually happens or is expected SYN **as usual**: *As always, Polly was late for school.* ➲ more at ONCE *adv.*

Alz·heim·er's dis·ease /'æltshaɪməz dɪzi:z; *NAmE* -ərz/ (also **Alz·heim·er's**) *noun* [U] a serious disease, especially affecting older people, that prevents the brain from functioning normally and causes loss of memory, loss of ability to speak clearly, etc. SYN **senile dementia**

AM /ˌeɪ 'em/ *abbr.* **1** amplitude modulation (one of the main methods of broadcasting sound by radio) **2** Assembly Member (a person who has been elected to represent an area of Wales in the Welsh Assembly, the parliament for Wales): *Peter Black AM* ◇ *Labour AMs*

am /əm; *strong form* æm/ ➲ BE

a.m. (*NAmE* also **A.M.**) /ˌeɪ 'em/ *abbr.* between midnight and midday (from Latin 'ante meridiem'): *It starts at 10 a.m.* ➲ compare P.M.

amah /'ɑ:mə/ *noun* (in S or E Asia) a woman employed by a family to clean, care for children, etc.

amal·gam /ə'mælgəm/ *noun* **1** [C, usually sing.] **~ (of sth)** (*formal*) a mixture or combination of things: *The film script is an amalgam of all three books.* **2** [U] (*technical*) a mixture of MERCURY and another metal, used especially to fill holes in teeth

amal·gam·ate /ə'mælgəmeɪt/ *verb* **~ (sth) (with/into sth) 1** [I, T] if two organizations **amalgamate** or **are amalgamated**, they join together to form one large organization SYN **merge**: *A number of colleges have amalgamated to form the new university.* ◇ **~ with/into sth** *The company has now amalgamated with another local firm.* ◇ **~ sth** *They decided to amalgamate the two schools.* ◇ **~ sth with/into sth** *The two companies were amalgamated into one.* **2** [T] **~ sth (into/with sth)** to put two or more things together so that they form one SYN **merge**: *This information will be amalgamated with information obtained earlier.* ▸ **amal·gam·ation** /əˌmælgə'meɪʃn/ *noun* [U, C]: *the amalgamation of small farms into larger units*

amanu·en·sis /əˌmænju'ensɪs/ *noun* (*pl.* **amanu·en·ses** /-si:z/) (*formal*) **1** a person who writes down your words when you cannot write, for example if you are injured and have an exam **2** an assistant, especially one who writes or types for sb

amar·yl·lis /ˌæmə'rɪlɪs/ *noun* [C, U] a tall white, pink or red flower shaped like a TRUMPET

amasi /ə'mɑ:si/ (also **maas**) *noun* [U] (*SAfrE*) sour milk

amass /ə'mæs/ *verb* **~ sth** to collect sth, especially in large quantities SYN **accumulate**: *He amassed a fortune from silver mining.* ➲ SYNONYMS at COLLECT

ama·teur /'æmətə(r); -tʃə(r)/ *noun, adj.*

▪ *noun* **1** a person who takes part in a sport or other activity for enjoyment, not as a job: *The tournament is open to both amateurs and professionals.* **2** (usually *disapproving*) a person who is not skilled: *This work was done by a bunch of amateurs!* OPP **professional** ▸ **ama·teur·ism** /'æmətərɪzəm; -tʃə-/ *noun* [U]: *New rules on amateurism allow payment for promotional work.*

▪ *adj.* **1** [usually before noun] doing sth for enjoyment or interest, not as a job: *an amateur photographer* **2** [usually before noun] done for enjoyment, not as a job: *amateur athletics* **3** (usually *disapproving*) = AMATEURISH OPP **professional**

ˌamateur dra'matics *noun* [U] (*BrE*) the activity of producing and acting in plays for the theatre, by people who do it for enjoyment, not as a job

ama·teur·ish /'æmətərɪʃ; -tʃə-/ (also **ama·teur**) *adj.* (usually *disapproving*) not done or made well or with skill: *Detectives described the burglary as 'crude and amateurish'.* OPP **professional**

ama·tory /'æmətəri; *NAmE* -tɔ:ri/ *adj.* [only before noun] (*formal* or *humorous*) relating to or connected with sexual desire or activity: *his amatory exploits*

amaze /ə'meɪz/ *verb* to surprise sb very much: **~ sb** *Just the size of the place amazed her.* ◇ **~ sb what, how, etc... It never ceases to amaze me** *what some people will do for money.* ◇ ***What amazes me is*** *how long she managed to hide it from us.* ◇ **it amazes sb that.../to see, find, learn, etc.** *It amazed her that he could be so calm at such a time.* ➲ SYNONYMS at SURPRISE

amazed /ə'meɪzd/ *adj.* very surprised: *an amazed silence* ◇ **~ at sb/sth** *I was amazed at her knowledge of French literature.* ◇ **~ by sb/sth** *We were amazed by his generosity.* ◇ **~ (that)...** *I was banging so loudly I'm amazed (that) they didn't hear me.* ◇ **~ how...** *She was amazed how little he had changed.* ◇ **~ to see, find, learn, etc.** *We were amazed to find that no one was hurt.*

amaze·ment /ə'meɪzmənt/ *noun* [U] a feeling of great surprise: ***To my amazement,*** *he remembered me.* ◇ *She looked at him* ***in amazement.***

amaz·ing /ə'meɪzɪŋ/ *adj.* very surprising, especially in a way that makes you feel pleasure or admiration SYN **astounding, incredible**: *an amazing achievement/discovery/success/performance* ◇ *That's amazing, isn't it?* ◇ ***It's amazing how*** *quickly people adapt.* ▸ **amaz·ing·ly** *adv.*: *Amazingly, no one noticed.* ◇ *The meal was amazingly cheap.*

Amazon /'æməzən; *NAmE* also -zɑ:n/ *noun* **1** (in ancient Greek stories) a woman from a group of female WARRIORS (= soldiers) **2 amazon** (*literary*) a tall strong woman

am·bas·sador /æm'bæsədə(r)/ *noun* an official who lives in a foreign country as the senior representative there of his or her own country: *the British Ambassador to Italy/in Rome* ◇ *a former ambassador to the UN* ◇ (*figurative*) *The best ambassadors for the sport are the players.* ▸ **am·bas·sador·ial** /æmˌbæsə'dɔ:riəl/ *adj.*

amber /'æmbə(r)/ *noun* [U] **1** a hard clear yellowish-brown substance, used in making decorative objects or jewellery: *amber beads* **2** a yellowish-brown colour: *The traffic lights were on amber.* ▸ **amber** *adj.*

ˌamber 'fluid (also **ˌamber 'liquid**) *noun* [U] (*AustralE, informal*) beer

am·ber·gris /'æmbəgri:s; -grɪs; *NAmE* 'æmbər-/ *noun* [U] a substance that is used in making some PERFUMES. It is produced naturally by a type of WHALE.

ambi- /'æmbi/ *prefix* (in nouns, adjectives and adverbs) referring to both of two: *ambidextrous* ◇ *ambivalent*

ambi·dex·trous /ˌæmbi'dekstrəs/ *adj.* able to use the left hand or the right hand equally well

am·bi·ence (also **am·bi·ance**) /'æmbiəns/ *noun* [sing.] the character and atmosphere of a place: *the relaxed ambience of the city*

am·bi·ent /'æmbiənt/ *adj.* **1** [only before noun] (*technical*) relating to the surrounding area; on all sides: ***ambient temperature/light/conditions*** **2** (especially of music) creating a relaxed atmosphere: *a compilation of ambient electronic music* ◇ *soft, ambient lighting*

am·bi·gu·ity AW /ˌæmbɪ'gju:əti/ *noun* (*pl.* **-ies**) **1** [U] the state of having more than one possible meaning: *Write clear definitions in order to avoid ambiguity.* **2** [C] a word or statement that can be understood in more than one way: *There were several inconsistencies and ambiguities in her speech.* **3** [U, C] the state of being difficult to understand or explain because of involving many different aspects: *You must understand the ambiguity of my position.*

am·bigu·ous AW /æm'bɪgjuəs/ *adj.* **1** that can be understood in more than one way; having different meanings: *an* ***ambiguous word/term/statement*** ◇ *Her account was deliberately ambiguous.* **2** not clearly stated or defined: *His role has always been ambiguous.*

OPP **unambiguous** ▸ **am·bigu·ous·ly** *adv.*: *an ambiguously worded agreement*

ambit /ˈæmbɪt/ *noun* [sing.] (*formal*) the range of the authority or influence of sth: *This case falls clearly* ***within the ambit of*** *the 2001 act.*

am·bi·tion 0‑ /æmˈbɪʃn/ *noun*
1 0‑ [C] something that you want to do or achieve very much: *It had been her* ***lifelong ambition.*** ◇ ***political/literary/sporting ambitions*** ◇ **~ of being/doing sth** *She never* ***achieved her ambition*** *of becoming a famous writer.* ◇ **~ to be/do sth** *His burning ambition was to study medicine.* **2** 0‑ [U] the desire or determination to be successful, rich, powerful, etc: *motivated by personal ambition* ◇ *She was intelligent but suffered from a lack of ambition.*

am·bi·tious /æmˈbɪʃəs/ *adj.* **1** determined to be successful, rich, powerful, etc: *a fiercely ambitious young manager* ◇ *They were very ambitious for their children* (= they wanted them to be successful). **2** needing a lot of effort, money or time to succeed: *the government's ambitious plans for social reform* **OPP** **unambitious** ▸ **am·bi·tious·ly** *adv.*

am·biva·lent /æmˈbɪvələnt/ *adj.* **~ (about/towards sb/sth)** having or showing both good and bad feelings about sb/sth: *She seems to feel ambivalent about her new job.* ◇ *He has an ambivalent attitude towards her.* ▸ **am·biva·lence** *noun* [U, sing.]: **~ (about/towards sb/sth)** *Many people feel some ambivalence towards television and its effect on our lives.* **am·biva·lent·ly** *adv.*

amble /ˈæmbl/ *verb* [I] **+ adv./prep.** to walk at a slow relaxed speed **SYN** **stroll**: *We ambled down to the beach.*

am·bro·sia /æmˈbrəʊziə; *NAmE* -ˈbroʊ-/ *noun* [U] **1** (in ancient Greek and Roman stories) the food of the gods **2** (*literary*) something that is very pleasant to eat

am·bu·lance 0‑ /ˈæmbjələns/ *noun*
a vehicle with special equipment, used for taking sick or injured people to a hospital: *the ambulance service* ◇ *ambulance staff* ◇ *Call an ambulance!*

ˈambulance chaser *noun* (*informal, disapproving, especially NAmE*) a lawyer who earns money by encouraging people who have been in an accident to make claims in court

am·bu·la·tory /ˈæmbjələtəri; *NAmE* -tɔːri/ *adj.* **1** (*formal*) related to or adapted for walking: *an ambulatory corridor* **2** (*formal*) that is not fixed in one place and can move around easily **SYN** **mobile**: *an ambulatory care service* **3** (*medical*) = AMBULANT

am·bush /ˈæmbʊʃ/ *noun, verb*
■ ***noun*** [C, U] the act of hiding and waiting for sb and then making a surprise attack on them: *Two soldiers were killed in a terrorist ambush.* ◇ *They were* ***lying in ambush,*** *waiting for the aid convoy.*
■ ***verb*** **~ sb/sth** to make a surprise attack on sb/sth from a hidden position: *The guerrillas ambushed them near the bridge.* ◇ (*figurative*) *She was ambushed by reporters.*

ameba, ameb·ic (*US*) = AMOEBA, AMOEBIC

ameli·or·ate /əˈmiːliəreɪt/ *verb* **~ sth** (*formal*) to make sth better: *Steps have been taken to ameliorate the situation.* ▸ **ameli·or·ation** /əˌmiːliəˈreɪʃn/ *noun* [U]

amen /ɑːˈmen; eɪˈmen/ (also **Amen**) *exclamation, noun* a word used at the end of prayers and HYMNS, meaning 'may it be so': *We ask this through our Lord, Amen.* ◇ *Amen to that* (= I certainly agree with that).

amen·able /əˈmiːnəbl/ *adj.* **1** (of people) easy to control; willing to be influenced by sb/sth: *They had three very amenable children.* ◇ **~ to sth** *He seemed most amenable to my idea.* **2 ~ to sth** (*formal*) that you can treat in a particular way: *'Hamlet' is the least amenable of all Shakespeare's plays to being summarized.*

amend **AW** /əˈmend/ *verb* **~ sth** to change a law, document, statement, etc. slightly in order to correct a mistake or to improve it: *He asked to see the amended version.*

amend·ment **AW** /əˈmendmənt/ *noun* **1** [C, U] a small change or improvement that is made to a law or a document; the process of changing a law or a document: *to* ***introduce/propose/table an amendment*** (= to suggest it) ◇ *Parliament passed the bill without further amendment.* ◇ **~ to sth** *She made several minor amendments to her essay.* **2 Amendment** [C] a statement of a change to the CONSTITUTION of the US: *The 19th Amendment gave women the right to vote.*

amends /əˈmendz/ *noun* [pl.]
IDM **make amends (to sb) (for sth/for doing sth)** to do sth for sb in order to show that you are sorry for sth wrong or unfair that you have done **SYN** **make up for sth**

amen·ity /əˈmiːnəti; *NAmE* əˈmenəti/ *noun* [usually pl.] (*pl.* **-ies**) a feature that makes a place pleasant, comfortable or easy to live in: *The campsite is close to all* ***local amenities.*** ◇ *Many of the houses lacked even* ***basic amenities*** (= baths, showers, hot water, etc.).

amen·or·rhoea (*BrE*) (*NAmE* **amen·or·rhea**) /əˌmenəˈriːə; *NAmE* eɪˌmen-/ *noun* [U] (*medical*) a condition in which an adult woman does not MENSTRUATE (= there is no flow of blood from her WOMB every month)

Amer·asian /ˌæməˈreɪʃn; -ˈreɪʒn/ *noun* a person with one Asian parent and one parent from the US ▸ **Amer·asian** *adj.*

Ameri·can /əˈmerɪkən/ *noun, adj.*
■ ***noun*** **1** a person from America, especially the US ➲ see also AFRICAN AMERICAN, NATIVE AMERICAN **2** (also **Aˈmerican English**) the English language as spoken in the US
■ ***adj.*** of or connected with N or S America, especially the US: *I'm American.* ◇ *American culture/tourists*
IDM **as Aˌmerican as apple ˈpie** used to say that sth is typical of America

More About

America

- The continent of **America** is divided into **North America** and **South America**. The narrow region joining North and South America is **Central America**.
- **North America**, which is a geographical term, consists of the **United States of America**, **Canada** and **Mexico**. **Latin America**, a cultural term, refers to the non-English speaking countries of Central and South America, where mainly Portuguese and Spanish are spoken. Mexico is part of Latin America.
- The **United States of America** is usually shortened to the **USA**, the **US**, the **States** or simply **America**: *the US President* ◇ *Have you ever been to the States?* ◇ *She emigrated to America in 1995.* Many people from other parts of the continent dislike this use of **America** to mean just the US, but it is very common.
- **American** is usually used to talk about somebody or something from the United States of America: *Do you have an American passport?* ◇ *American football* ◇ *I'm not American, I'm Canadian.* **Latin American** and **South American** are used to refer to other parts of the continent: *Latin American dance music* ◇ *Quite a lot of South Americans study here.*

Ameri·cana /əˌmerɪˈkɑːnə/ *noun* [pl.] things connected with the US that are thought to be typical of it

Aˌmerican ˈbreakfast *noun* a large breakfast which can include CEREAL and cooked food, such as eggs with HAM ➲ see also ENGLISH BREAKFAST, CONTINENTAL BREAKFAST

Aˌmerican ˈcheese *noun* [U] (*US*) a kind of orange cheese that is usually sold in thin slices wrapped in plastic

the Aˌmerican ˈdream *noun* [sing.] the values and social standards that people traditionally try to achieve in the US, such as DEMOCRACY, equal rights and wealth

the Aˌmerican ˈeagle *noun* a bird with a white head and white tail feathers that is the national symbol of the US

A

A,merican 'football (*BrE*) (*NAmE* **foot·ball**) *noun* [U] a game played by two teams of 11 players, using an OVAL ball which players kick, throw, or carry. Teams try to put the ball over the other team's line. ➲ VISUAL VOCAB page V36

A,merican 'Indian *noun* = NATIVE AMERICAN

Ameri·can·ism /ə'merɪkənɪzəm/ *noun* **1** [C] a word, phrase or spelling that is typical of American English, used in another variety of English **2** [U] the essential quality of being American

Ameri·can·ize (*BrE* also **-ise**) /ə'merɪkənaɪz/ *verb* **~ sb/sth** to make sb/sth American in character ▸ **Ameri·can·iza·tion, -isa·tion** /ə,merəkənaɪ'zeɪʃn; *NAmE* -nə'z-/ *noun* [U]

the A'merican League *noun* (in the US) one of the two organizations for professional BASEBALL ➲ see also NATIONAL LEAGUE

A,merican 'plan *noun* [U] = FULL BOARD

ameri·cium /,æmə'rɪsiəm; -'rɪʃi-/ *noun* [U] (*symb.* Am) a chemical element. Americium is a RADIOACTIVE metal.

Amer·in·dian /,æmə'rɪndiən/ *noun* (*old-fashioned*) = NATIVE AMERICAN

ameth·yst /'æməθɪst/ *noun* [C, U] a purple SEMI-PRECIOUS STONE, used in making jewellery: *an amethyst ring*

ami·able /'eɪmiəbl/ *adj.* pleasant; friendly and easy to like SYN **agreeable**: *an amiable tone of voice* ◇ *Her parents seemed very amiable.* ▸ **ami·abil·ity** /,eɪmiə'bɪləti/ *noun* [U] **ami·ably** *adv.*: *'That's fine,' he replied amiably.*

am·ic·able /'æmɪkəbl/ *adj.* done or achieved in a polite or friendly way and without arguing: *an amicable relationship* ◇ *An amicable settlement was reached.* ▸ **am·ic·ably** *adv.*

amid /ə'mɪd/ (also **mid, amidst** /ə'mɪdst/) *prep.* (*formal*) **1** in the middle of or during sth, especially sth that causes excitement or fear: *He finished his speech amid tremendous applause.* ◇ *The firm collapsed amid allegations of fraud.* **2** surrounded by sth: *The hotel was in a beautiful position amid lemon groves.*

amid·ships /ə'mɪdʃɪps/ *adv.* (*technical*) in or near the middle part of a ship

amino acid /ə,mi:nəʊ 'æsɪd; *NAmE* -noʊ/ *noun* (*chemistry*) any of the substances that combine to form the basic structure of PROTEINS

amir = EMIR

the Amish /'ɑ:mɪʃ; *BrE* also 'æmɪʃ/ *noun* [pl.] the members of a strict religious group in N America. The Amish live a simple farming life and reject some forms of modern technology. ▸ **Amish** *adj.*

amiss /ə'mɪs/ *adj., adv.*

■ ***adj.*** [not before noun] wrong; not as it should be: *She sensed something was amiss and called the police.*

■ ***adv.***

IDM **not come/go a'miss** (*BrE*) to be useful or pleasant in a particular situation: *A little luck wouldn't go amiss right now!* **take sth a'miss** (*BrE*) to feel offended by sth, perhaps because you have understood it in the wrong way: *Would she take it amiss if I offered to help?*

amity /'æməti/ *noun* [U] (*formal*) a friendly relationship between people or countries

amma /'ʌmɑ:/ *noun* (*IndE*) (especially as a form of address) a mother

am·meter /'æmi:tə(r)/ *noun* an instrument for measuring the strength of an electric current

ammo /'æməʊ; *NAmE* 'æmoʊ/ *noun* [U] (*old-fashioned, informal*) = AMMUNITION

am·mo·nia /ə'məʊniə; *NAmE* ə'moʊ-/ *noun* [U] (*symb.* NH_3) a gas with a strong smell; a clear liquid containing ammonia, used as a cleaning substance

am·mon·ite /'æmənaɪt/ *noun* a FOSSIL of a simple sea creature which no longer exists, and which was related to SNAILS

ammonite

am·mo·nium /ə'məʊniəm; *NAmE* ə'moʊ-/ *noun* [U] (*chemistry*) a salt made from AMMONIA containing NITROGEN and HYDROGEN together with another element

am·mu·ni·tion /,æmju'nɪʃn/ *noun* [U] **1** a supply of bullets, etc. to be fired from guns **2** information that can be used against another person in an argument: *The letter gave her all the ammunition she needed.*

am·nesia /æm'ni:ziə; *NAmE* -'ni:ʒə/ *noun* [U] a medical condition in which sb partly or completely loses their memory ▸ **am·nesiac** /æm'ni:ziæk; *NAmE* -'ni:ʒ-/ *noun*: *This new discovery helps amnesiacs keep their memory.*

am·nesty /'æmnəsti/ *noun* (*pl.* -ies) **1** [C, usually sing., U] an official statement that allows people who have been put in prison for crimes against the state to go free: *The president granted a general amnesty for all political prisoners.* **2** [C, usually sing.] a period of time during which people can admit to a crime or give up weapons without being punished: *2 000 knives have been handed in during the month-long amnesty.*

,Amnesty Inter'national *noun* an international human rights organization that works to help people who have been put in prison for their beliefs or race and not because they have committed a crime. It also works to prevent TORTURE and punishment by death.

am·nio·cen·tesis /,æmniəʊsen'ti:sɪs; *NAmE* -nioʊ-/ *noun* [U, sing.] a medical test that involves taking some liquid from a pregnant woman's WOMB in order to find out if the baby has particular illnesses or health problems

am·ni·ot·ic fluid /,æmniɒtɪk 'flu:ɪd; *NAmE* -ɑ:tɪk/ *noun* [U] the liquid that surrounds a baby inside the mother's WOMB

amn't /'æmənt/ *short form* (*ScotE, IrishE, non-standard*) am not

amoeba (*US* also **ameba**) /ə'mi:bə/ *noun* (*pl.* **amoe·bas** or **amoe·bae** /-bi:/) a very small living creature that consists of only one cell

amoeb·ic (*US* also **ameb·ic**) /ə'mi:bɪk/ *adj.* related to or similar to an amoeba

a,moebic 'dysentery (*US* also **a,mebic 'dysentery**) *noun* [U] an infection of the INTESTINE caused by an amoeba

amok /ə'mɒk; *NAmE* ə'mɑ:k/ *adv.*

IDM **run amok** to suddenly become very angry or excited and start behaving violently, especially in a public place

among 0-w /ə'mʌŋ/ (also **amongst** /ə'mʌŋst/) *prep.* **1** 0-w surrounded by sb/sth; in the middle of sb/sth: *a house among the trees* ◇ *They strolled among the crowds.* ◇ *I found the letter amongst his papers.* ◇ *It's OK, you're among friends now.* **2** 0-w being included or happening in groups of things or people: *A British woman was among the survivors.* ◇ *He was among the last to leave.* ◇ *This attitude is common among the under-25s.* ◇ *'What was wrong with the job?' 'Well, the pay wasn't good,* ***among other things.'*** ◇ *Discuss it* ***among yourselves*** (= with each other) *first.* **3** 0-w used when you are dividing or choosing sth, and three or more people or things are involved: *They divided the money up among their three children.*

amoral /,eɪ'mɒrəl; *NAmE* -'mɔ:r-/ *adj.* not following any moral rules and not caring about right and wrong ➲ compare IMMORAL, MORAL ▸ **amor·al·ity** /,eɪmə'ræləti/ *noun* [U]

am·or·ous /'æmərəs/ *adj.* showing sexual desire and love towards sb: *Mary rejected Tony's amorous advances.* ▸ **am·or·ous·ly** *adv.*

amorph·ous /ə'mɔ:fəs; *NAmE* -'mɔ:rf-/ *adj.* [usually before noun] (*formal*) having no definite shape, form or structure SYN **shapeless**: *an amorphous mass of cells with no identity at all*

amort·ize (*BrE* also **-ise**) /ə'mɔːtaɪz; *NAmE* 'æmərtaɪz/ *verb* ~ **sth** (*business*) to pay back a debt by making small regular payments over a period of time ▶ **amort·iza·tion, -isa·tion** /əˌmɔːtaɪ'zeɪʃn; *NAmE* ˌæmərtə'z-/ *noun* [U, C]

amount O→ /ə'maʊnt/ *noun, verb*

■ **noun** [C, U] **1** O→ a sum of money: *The insurance company will refund any amount due to you.* ◇ *You will receive a bill for the full amount.* **2** O→ ~ (**of sth**) (used especially with uncountable nouns) a quantity of sth: *an amount of time/money/information* ◇ *We've had an enormous amount of help from people.* ◇ *The server is designed to store huge amounts of data.*

IDM **any amount of sth** a large quantity of sth: *There's been any amount of research into the subject.* **no amount of sth** used for saying that sth will have no effect: *No amount of encouragement would make him jump into the pool.*

■ ***verb***

PHR V **a'mount to sth 1** O→ to add up to sth; to make sth as a total: *His earnings are said to amount to £300 000 per annum.* ◇ *They gave me some help in the beginning but it* ***did not amount to much*** (= they did not give me much help). **2** to be equal to or the same as sth: *Her answer amounted to a complete refusal.* ◇ *Their actions amount to a breach of contract.* ◇ *It'll cost a lot—well, take a lot of time, but it* ***amounts to the same thing***.

amour /ə'mʊə(r); *NAmE* ə'mʊr/ *noun* (*old-fashioned*, from *French*) a love affair, especially a secret one

amour propre /ˌæmʊə 'prɒprə; *NAmE* ˌɑːmʊr 'prɔːprə/ *noun* [U] (*formal*, from *French*) a feeling of pride in your own character and abilities

amp /æmp/ *noun* **1** (also **am·pere** /'æmpeə(r); *NAmE* 'æmpɪr; -per/) (*abbr.* A) the unit for measuring electric current: *a 13 amp fuse/plug* **2** (*informal*) = AMPLIFIER

amped /æmpt/ (also ˌ**amped 'up**) *adj.* (*NAmE, informal*) excited, especially because of an event: *an amped audience of hardcore fans* ◇ *I get pretty amped up before I compete.*

am·per·age /'æmpərɪdʒ/ *noun* [U] the strength of an electric current, measured in AMPS

am·per·sand /'æmpəsænd; *NAmE* -pərs-/ *noun* the symbol &, used to mean 'and': *She works for Bond & Green.*

am·phet·amine /æm'fetəmiːn/ *noun* [C, U] a drug that makes you feel excited and full of energy. Amphetamines are sometimes taken illegally.

am·phib·ian /æm'fɪbiən/ *noun* any animal that can live both on land and in water. Amphibians have cold blood and skin without SCALES. FROGS, TOADS and NEWTS are all amphibians. ➲ COLLOCATIONS at LIFE ➲ VISUAL VOCAB page V11 ➲ compare REPTILE

am·phibi·ous /æm'fɪbiəs/ *adj.* **1** able to live both on land and in water **2** (of military operations) involving soldiers landing at a place from the sea **3** suitable for use on land or water: *amphibious vehicles*

amphi·theatre (*especially US* **-ter**) /'æmfɪθɪətə(r); *NAmE* -θiːətər/ *noun* **1** a round building without a roof and with rows of seats that rise in steps around an open space. Amphitheatres were used especially in ancient Greece and Rome for public entertainments. ➲ VISUAL VOCAB page V13 **2** a room, hall or theatre with rows of seats that rise in steps **3** (*technical*) an open space that is surrounded by high sloping land

am·phora /'æmfərə; *NAmE* also æm'fɔːrə/ *noun* (*pl.* **am·phorae** /'æmfəriː; *NAmE* also æm'fɔːriː/ or **am·phoras**) a tall ancient Greek or Roman container with two handles and a narrow neck

ampi·cil·lin /ˌæmpɪ'sɪlɪn/ *noun* [U] a form of PENICILLIN that is used to treat certain infections

ample /'æmpl/ *adj.* **1** enough or more than enough SYN **plenty of**: *ample opportunity/evidence/space/proof* ◇ *There was ample time to get to the airport.* ◇ *Ample free parking is available.* **2** (of a person's figure) large, often in an attractive way: *an ample bosom* ▶ **amply** /'æmpli/ *adv.*: *His efforts were amply rewarded.*

amp·li·fier /'æmplɪfaɪə(r)/ (also *informal* **amp**) *noun* an electrical device or piece of equipment that makes sounds or radio signals louder: *a 25 watt amplifier* ➲ VISUAL VOCAB page V31

amp·lify /'æmplɪfaɪ/ *verb* (**amp·li·fies**, **amp·li·fy·ing**, **amp·li·fied**, **amp·li·fied**) **1** [T] ~ **sth** to increase sth in strength, especially sound: *to* ***amplify a guitar/an electric current/a signal*** **2** [I, T] (*formal*) to add details to a story, statement, etc: *She refused to amplify further.* ◇ ~ **sth** *You may need to amplify this point.* ▶ **amp·li·fi·ca·tion** /ˌæmplɪfɪ'keɪʃn/ *noun* [U]: *electronic amplification* ◇ *That comment needs some amplification.*

amp·li·tude /'æmplɪtjuːd; *NAmE* -tuːd/ *noun* [U, C] (*physics*) the greatest distance that a wave, especially a sound or radio wave, VIBRATES (= moves up and down) ➲ picture at WAVELENGTH

amply *adv.* ➲ AMPLE

am·poule (*US* also **am·pule**) /'æmpuːl; *NAmE* also -'pjuːl/ *noun* a small container, usually made of glass, containing a drug that will be used for an INJECTION

am·pu·tate /'æmpjuteɪt/ *verb* [T, I] ~ (**sth**) to cut off sb's arm, leg, finger or toe in a medical operation: *He had to have both legs amputated.* ◇ *They may have to amputate.* ➲ COLLOCATIONS at INJURY ▶ **am·pu·ta·tion** /ˌæmpju'teɪʃn/ *noun* [U, C]

am·pu·tee /ˌæmpju'tiː/ *noun* a person who has had an arm or a leg amputated

amu·let /'æmjʊlət/ *noun* a piece of jewellery that some people wear because they think it protects them from bad luck, illness, etc.

amuse O→ /ə'mjuːz/ *verb*

1 O→ to make sb laugh or smile: ~ **sb** *My funny drawings amused the kids.* ◇ *This will amuse you.* ◇ **it amuses sb to do sth** *It amused him to think that they were probably talking about him at that very moment.* **2** O→ to make time pass pleasantly for sb/yourself SYN **entertain**: ~ **sb** *She suggested several ideas to help Laura amuse the twins.* ◇ ~ **yourself** *I'm sure I'll be able to amuse myself for a few hours.*

amused O→ /ə'mjuːzd/ *adj.*

thinking that sb/sth is funny, so that you smile or laugh: *There was an amused look on the President's face.* ◇ *Janet was* ***not amused*** (= she was annoyed or angry). ◇ ~ **at/by sth** *We were all amused at his stories.* ◇ ~ **to see, find, learn, etc.** *He was amused to see how seriously she took the game.*

IDM **keep sb a'mused** to give sb interesting things to do, or to entertain them so that they do not become bored: *Playing with water can keep children amused for hours.*

amuse·ment /ə'mjuːzmənt/ *noun* **1** [U] the feeling that you have when sth is funny or amusing, or it entertains you: *She could not hide her amusement at the way he was dancing.* ◇ ***To my amusement*** *he couldn't get the door open.* ◇ *Her eyes twinkled* ***with amusement***. **2** [C, usually pl.] a game, an activity, etc. that provides entertainment and pleasure: *traditional seaside amusements including boats, go-karts and a funfair*

a'musement arcade (*BrE*) (also **ar·cade** *NAmE, BrE*) *noun* a place where you can play games on machines which you use coins to operate

a'musement park *noun* a large park which has a lot of things that you can ride and play on and many different activities to enjoy

amus·ing O→ /ə'mjuːzɪŋ/ *adj.*

funny and enjoyable: *an amusing story/game/incident* ◇ *I didn't find the joke at all amusing.* ➲ SYNONYMS at FUNNY ▶ **amus·ing·ly** *adv.*

amyg·dala /ə'mɪɡdələ/ *noun* (*pl.* **amyg·da·lae** /ə'mɪɡdəliː/) (*anatomy*) either of two areas in the brain that are linked to memory, the emotions and the sense of smell

amy·lase /'æmɪleɪz; *NAmE* 'æməleɪs/ *noun* [U] (*chemistry*) an ENZYME (= a substance that helps a chemical change to take place) that allows the body to change some substances into simple sugars

A

an *indefinite article* ➲ A

-an, -ana ➲ -IAN, -IANA

ana·bol·ic ster·oid /ˌænəbɒlɪk ˈsterɔɪd; ˈstɪə-; *NAmE* ˌænəbɑːlɪk ˈster-; ˈstɪr-/ *noun* an artificial HORMONE (= a chemical substance) that increases the size of the muscles. It is sometimes taken illegally by people who play sports. ➲ see also STEROID

an·achron·ism /əˈnækrənɪzəm/ *noun* **1** a person, a custom or an idea that seems old-fashioned and does not belong to the present: *The monarchy is seen by many people as an anachronism in the modern world.* **2** something that is placed, for example in a book or play, in the wrong period of history ▸ **ana·chron·is·tic** /əˌnækrəˈnɪstɪk/ *adj.*

ana·conda /ˌænəˈkɒndə; *NAmE* -ˈkɑːn-/ *noun* a large S American snake of the BOA family, that crushes other animals to death before eating them

an·aemia (*BrE*) (*NAmE* **an·e·mia**) /əˈniːmiə/ *noun* [U] a medical condition in which sb has too few red cells in their blood, making them look pale and feel weak

an·aemic (*BrE*) (*NAmE* **an·emic**) /əˈniːmɪk/ *adj.* **1** suffering from anaemia: *She looks anaemic.* **2** weak and not having much effect SYN **feeble**: *an anaemic performance*

an·aer·obic /ˌæneəˈrəʊbɪk; *NAmE* ˌæneˈroʊ-/ *adj.* **1** (*biology*) not needing OXYGEN: *anaerobic bacteria* **2** (of physical exercise) not especially designed to improve the function of the heart and lungs OPP **aerobic**

an·aes·the·sia /ˌænəsˈθiːziə/ (*especially US* **an·es·the·sia** /-ˈθiːʒə/) *noun* [U] **1** the use of anaesthetic during medical operations **2** (*technical*) the state of being unable to feel anything, especially pain

an·aes·thet·ic (*especially US* **an·es·thet·ic**) /ˌænəsˈθetɪk/ *noun, adj.*

■ ***noun*** [U, C] a drug that makes a person or an animal unable to feel anything, especially pain, either in the whole body or in a part of the body: *How long will I* ***be under anaesthetic****?* ◊ *They gave him a* ***general anaesthetic*** (= one that makes you become unconscious). ◊ *(a)* ***local anaesthetic*** (= one that affects only a part of the body)

■ ***adj.*** [only before noun] containing a substance that makes a person or an animal unable to feel pain in all or part of the body: *an* ***anaesthetic drug/spray***

an·aes·the·tist (*especially US* **an·es·the·tist**) /əˈniːsθətɪst/ *noun* a person who is trained to give anaesthetics to patients

an·aes·the·tize (*BrE* also **-ise**) (*especially US* **an·es·the·tize**) /əˈniːsθətaɪz/ *verb* **~ sb** to make a person unable to feel pain, etc, especially by giving them an anaesthetic before a medical operation

ana·gram /ˈænəɡræm/ *noun* a word or phrase that is made by arranging the letters of another word or phrase in a different order: *An anagram of 'Elvis' is 'lives'.*

anal /ˈeɪnl/ *adj.* **1** connected with the ANUS: *the anal region* **2** (also ˌ**anal-reˈtentive**) (*disapproving*) caring too much about small details and about how things are organized ▸ **anal·ly** /-nəli/ *adv.*

an·al·gesia /ˌænəlˈdʒiːziə; *NAmE* -ʒə/ *noun* [U] (*medical*) the loss of the ability to feel pain while still conscious

an·al·gesic /ˌænəlˈdʒiːzɪk/ *noun* (*medical*) a substance that reduces pain SYN **painkiller**: *Aspirin is a mild analgesic.* ▸ **an·al·gesic** *adj.*: ***analgesic drugs/effects***

analo·gous AW /əˈnæləɡəs/ *adj.* (*formal*) **~ (to/with sth)** similar in some way to another thing or situation and therefore able to be compared with it: *Sleep has often been thought of as being in some way analogous to death.*

ana·logue (*BrE*) (*NAmE* **ana·log**) /ˈænəlɒɡ; *NAmE* -lɔːɡ; -lɑːɡ/ *adj., noun*

■ ***adj.*** (*technical*) **1** (of an electronic process) using a continuously changing range of physical quantities to measure or store data: *an* ***analogue circuit/computer/signal*** **2** (*BrE* also **ana·log**) (of a clock or watch) showing the time using hands on a DIAL and not with a display of numbers ➲ compare DIGITAL

■ ***noun*** (*formal* or *technical*) a thing that is similar to another thing: *Scientists are attempting to compare features of extinct animals with living analogues.*

ana·logy AW /əˈnælədʒi/ *noun* (*pl.* -ies) **1** [C] a comparison of one thing with another thing that has similar features; a feature that is similar: **~ (between A and B)** *The teacher* ***drew an analogy*** *between the human heart and a pump.* ◊ **~ (with sth)** *There are no analogies with any previous legal cases.* **2** [U] the process of comparing one thing with another thing that has similar features in order to explain it: *learning* ***by analogy***

an·al·pha·bet·ic /ˌænælfəˈbetɪk/ *adj.* **1** (*technical*) completely unable to read or write **2** = NON-ALPHABETIC **3** (*linguistics*) representing sounds with signs made of several parts rather than by single letters or symbols

ˌ**anal-reˈtentive** *adj.* (*disapproving*) = ANAL

ana·lyse O‑w AW (*BrE*) (*NAmE* **ana·lyze**) /ˈænəlaɪz/ *verb*

1 O‑w to examine the nature or structure of sth, especially by separating it into its parts, in order to understand or explain it: **~ sth** *The job involves gathering and analysing data.* ◊ *He tried to analyse his feelings.* ◊ **~ what, how, etc...** *We need to analyse what went wrong.* ➲ SYNONYMS at EXAMINE **2 ~ sb** = PSYCHOANALYSE

an·aly·sis O‑w AW /əˈnæləsɪs/ *noun* (*pl.* an·aly·ses /-siːz/)

1 O‑w [U, C] the detailed study or examination of sth in order to understand more about it; the result of the study: *statistical analysis* ◊ *The book is an analysis of poverty and its causes.* **2** O‑w [U, C] a careful examination of a substance in order to find out what it consists of: *The blood samples are sent to the laboratory* ***for analysis****.* ◊ *You can ask for a chemical analysis of your tap water.* **3** [U] = PSYCHOANALYSIS: *In analysis the individual resolves difficult emotional conflicts.*

IDM **in the ˌfinal/ˌlast aˈnalysis** used to say what is most important after everything has been discussed, or considered: *In the final analysis, it's a matter of personal choice.*

ana·lyst AW /ˈænəlɪst/ *noun* **1** a person whose job involves examining facts or materials in order to give an opinion on them: *a political/food analyst* ◊ *City analysts forecast huge profits this year.* ➲ see also SYSTEMS ANALYST **2** = PSYCHOANALYST

ana·lyt·ic AW /ˌænəˈlɪtɪk/ *adj.* **1** (also **isol·at·ing**) (*linguistics*) (of languages) using word order rather than word endings to show the functions of words in a sentence ➲ compare SYNTHETIC **2** = ANALYTICAL

ana·lyt·ic·al AW /ˌænəˈlɪtɪkl/ (also **ana·lyt·ic**) *adj.* **1** using a logical method of thinking about sth in order to understand it, especially by looking at all the parts separately: *She has a clear analytical mind.* ◊ *an analytic approach to the problem* **2** using scientific analysis in order to find out about sth: *analytical methods of research* ▸ **ana·lyt·ic·al·ly** AW /-kli/ *adv.*

ana·lyze AW (*NAmE*) = ANALYSE

ana·paest /ˈænəpiːst; -pest/ (*BrE*) (*NAmE* **ana·pest** /ˈænəpest/) *noun* (*technical*) a unit of sound in poetry consisting of two weak or short syllables followed by one strong or long syllable ▸ **ana·paes·tic, ana·pes·tic** /ˌænəˈpiːstɪk; -ˈpestɪk; *NAmE* ˌænəˈpestɪk/ *adj.*

anaphor /ˈænəfə(r); -fɔː(r)/ *noun* (*grammar*) a word or phrase that refers back to an earlier word or phrase. For example, in the phrase 'My mother said she was leaving', 'she' is used as an anaphor for 'my mother'

anaph·ora /əˈnæfərə/ *noun* [U] the use of a word that refers to or replaces another word used earlier in a sentence, for example the use of 'does' in the sentence 'I disagree and so does John' ▸ **ana·phor·ic** /ˌænəˈfɒrɪk; *NAmE* -ˈfɔːr-; -ˈfɑːr-/ *adj.*

ana·phyl·axis /ˌænəfɪˈlæksɪs/ *noun* [U, C] (*pl.* **ana·phyl·axes** /ˌænəfɪˈlæksiːz/) (*medical*) an extreme ALLERGIC reaction to sth that you eat or touch ▸ **ana·phyl·ac·tic** /ˌænəfɪˈlæktɪk/ *adj.*: *anaphylactic shock*

an·arch·ism /ˈænəkɪzəm; *NAmE* ˈænərk-/ *noun* [U] the political belief that laws and governments are not necessary

an·arch·ist /ˈænəkɪst; *NAmE* ˈænərk-/ *noun* a person who believes that laws and governments are not necessary ▸ **an·arch·is·tic** /ˌænəˈkɪstɪk; *NAmE* ˌænərˈk-/ *adj.*

an·archy /ˈænəki; *NAmE* ˈænərki/ *noun* [U] a situation in a country, an organization, etc. in which there is no government, order or control: *The overthrow of the military regime was followed by a period of anarchy.* ◇ *There was complete anarchy in the classroom when their usual teacher was away.* ▸ **an·arch·ic** /əˈnɑːkɪk; *NAmE* əˈnɑːrkɪk/ (also *less frequent* **an·arch·ic·al** /-kl/) *adj.*

anath·ema /əˈnæθəmə/ *noun* [U, C, usually sing.] (*formal*) a thing or an idea which you hate because it is the opposite of what you believe: *Racial prejudice is (an) anathema to me.*

anato·mist /əˈnætəmɪst/ *noun* a scientist who studies anatomy

anat·omy /əˈnætəmi/ *noun* (*pl.* -ies) **1** [U] the scientific study of the structure of human or animal bodies **2** [C, U] the structure of an animal or a plant: *the anatomy of the horse* ◇ *human anatomy* **3** [C] (*humorous*) a person's body: *Various parts of his anatomy were clearly visible.* **4** [C] (*formal*) an examination of what sth is like or why it happens: *an anatomy of the current recession* ▸ **ana·tom·ical** /ˌænəˈtɒmɪkl; *NAmE* -ˈtɑːm-/ *adj.*: *anatomical diagrams* **ana·tom·ic·al·ly** /-kli/ *adv.*

ANC /ˌeɪ en ˈsiː/ *abbr.* African National Congress (= a political party in South Africa)

-ance, -ence *suffix* (in nouns) the action or state of: *assistance* ◇ *confidence*

an·ces·tor /ˈænsestə(r)/ *noun* **1** a person in your family who lived a long time ago SYN **forebear**: *His ancestors had come to America from Ireland.* **2** an animal that lived in the past which a modern animal has developed from: *a reptile that was the common ancestor of lizards and turtles* **3** an early form of a machine which later became more developed SYN **forerunner**: *The ancestor of the modern bicycle was called a penny-farthing.* ➲ compare DESCENDANT ▸ **an·ces·tral** /ænˈsestrəl/ *adj.*: *her ancestral home* (= that had belonged to her ANCESTORS)

an·ces·try /ˈænsestri/ *noun* [C, usually sing., U] (*pl.* -ies) the family or the race of people that you come from: *to have Scottish ancestry* ◇ *He was able to trace his ancestry back over 1 000 years.*

an·chor /ˈæŋkə(r)/ *noun, verb*

■ *noun* **1** [C, U] a heavy metal object that is attached to a rope or chain and dropped over the side of a ship or boat to keep it in one place: *to* ***drop anchor*** ◇ *The ship lay* ***at anchor*** *two miles off the rocky coast.* ◇ *We* ***weighed anchor*** (= pulled it out of the water). **2** [C] a person or thing that gives sb a feeling of safety: *the anchor of the family* **3** [C] (*especially NAmE*) = ANCHORMAN, ANCHORWOMAN

anchor

■ *verb* **1** [I, T] **~ (sth)** to let an anchor down from a boat or ship in order to prevent it from moving away: *We anchored off the coast of Spain.* **2** [T] **~ sth** to fix sth firmly in position so that it cannot move: *Make sure the table is securely anchored.* **3** [T, usually passive] **~ sb/sth (in/to sth)** to firmly base sth on sth else: *Her novels are anchored in everyday experience.* **4** [I, T] **~ (sth)** (*NAmE*) to be the person who introduces reports or reads the news on television or radio: *She anchored the evening news for seven years.*

an·chor·age /ˈæŋkərɪdʒ/ *noun* [C, U] **1** a place where ships or boats can anchor **2** a place where sth can be fastened to sth else: *anchorage points for a baby's car seat*

an·chor·man /ˈæŋkəmæn; *NAmE* -kərm-/, **an·chor·woman** /ˈæŋkəwʊmən; *NAmE* -kərw-/ *noun* (*pl.* **-men** /-men/, **-women** /-wɪmɪn/) (also **an·chor** especially in *NAmE*) a man or woman who presents a live radio or television programme and introduces reports by other people

an·chovy /ˈæntʃəvi; *NAmE* -tʃoʊvi/ *noun* [C, U] (*pl.* -ies) a small fish with a strong salty flavour: *a pizza topped with cheese and anchovies*

an·cient 0→ /ˈeɪnʃənt/ *adj.*
1 0→ belonging to a period of history that is thousands of years in the past OPP **modern**: ***ancient history/civilization*** ◇ *ancient Greece* **2** 0→ very old; having existed for a very long time: *an ancient oak tree* ◇ *ancient monuments* ◇ (*humorous*) *He's ancient—he must be at least fifty!* **3 the ancients** *noun* [pl.] the people who lived in ancient times, especially the Egyptians, Greeks and Romans ▸ **an·cient·ly** *adv.*: *the area where the market was anciently held* (= in ancient times)

an·cil·lary /ænˈsɪləri; *NAmE* ˈænsəleri/ *adj.* **~ (to sth)** **1** providing necessary support to the main work or activities of an organization SYN **auxiliary**: ***ancillary staff/services/equipment*** ◇ ***ancillary workers*** *in the health service such as cooks and cleaners* **2** in addition to sth else but not as important: *ancillary rights*

-ancy, -ency *suffix* (in nouns) the state or quality of: *expectancy* ◇ *complacency*

and 0→ /ənd; ən; *also* n; *especially after* /t/ ; /d/ ; *strong form* ænd/ *conj.*
(used to connect words or parts of sentences) **1** 0→ also; in addition to: *bread and butter* ◇ *a table, two chairs and a desk* ◇ *Sue and I left early.* ◇ *Do it slowly and carefully.* ◇ *Can he read and write?* ◇ *I cooked lunch. And I made a cake.* (= you are emphasizing how much you have done) HELP When **and** is used in common phrases connecting two things or people that are closely linked, the determiner is not usually repeated before the second: *a knife and fork* ◇ *my father and mother*, but: *a knife and a spoon* ◇ *my father and my uncle.* **2** 0→ added to SYN **plus**: *5 and 5 makes 10.* ◇ *What's 47 and 16?* HELP When numbers (but not dates) are spoken, **and** is used between the hundreds and the figures that follow: *2 264—two thousand, two hundred* ***and*** *sixty-four*, but: *1964—nineteen sixty-four.* **3** 0→ then; following this: *She came in and took her coat off.* **4** 0→ **go, come, try, stay, etc. ~** used before a verb instead of *to*, to show purpose: *Go and get me a pen please.* ◇ *I'll come and see you soon.* ◇ *We stopped and bought some bread.* HELP In this structure **try** can only be used in the infinitive or to tell somebody what to do. **5** 0→ used to introduce a comment or a question: *'We talked for hours.' 'And what did you decide?'* **6** 0→ as a result: *Miss another class and you'll fail.* **7** 0→ used between repeated words to show that sth is repeated or continuing: *He tried and tried but without success.* ◇ *The pain got worse and worse.* **8** used between repeated words to show that there are important differences between things or people of the same kind.: *I like city life but there are cities and cities.* ➲ see also AND/OR

an·dante /ænˈdænteɪ/ *noun* (*music*) a piece of music to be played fairly slowly ▸ **an·dante** *adv., adj.*

and/or *conj.* (*informal*) used when you say that two situations exist together, or as an alternative to each other: *There is no help for those with lots of luggage and/or small children.*

an·dro·gen /ˈændrədʒən/ *noun* (*biology*) a male sex HORMONE, for example TESTOSTERONE

an·drogy·nous /ænˈdrɒdʒənəs; *NAmE* -ˈdrɑːdʒ-/ *adj.* having both male and female characteristics; looking neither strongly male nor strongly female

an·droid /ˈændrɔɪd/ (also **droid**) *noun* a ROBOT that looks like a real person

an·ec·dotal /ˌænɪkˈdəʊtl; *NAmE* -ˈdoʊtl/ *adj.* based on anecdotes and possibly not true or accurate: *anecdotal evidence* ▸ **an·ec·dot·al·ly** /-təli/ *adv.*: *This reaction has been reported anecdotally by a number of patients.*

an·ec·dote /ˈænɪkdəʊt; *NAmE* -doʊt/ *noun* [C, U] **1** a short, interesting or amusing story about a real person or event: *amusing anecdotes about his brief career as an actor*

A

2 a personal account of an event: *This research is based on anecdote, not fact.*

an·emia, an·emic (*NAmE*) = ANAEMIA, ANAEMIC

an·emom·eter /ˌænɪˈmɒmɪtə(r); *NAmE* -ˈmɑːm-/ (also ˈ**wind gauge**) *noun* an instrument for measuring the speed of the wind or of a current of gas

anem·one /əˈneməni/ *noun* a small plant with white, red, blue or purple flowers that are shaped like cups and have dark centres ➲ see also SEA ANEMONE

an·es·the·sia, an·es·thet·ic, an·es·the·tist, an·es·the·tize (*NAmE*) = ANAESTHESIA, ANAESTHETIC, ANAESTHETIST, ANAESTHETIZE

an·es·the·sio·logist /ˌænəsˌθiːziˈɒlədʒɪst; *NAmE* -ˈɑːlə-/ *noun* (*NAmE*) a doctor who studies the use of anaesthetics

an·eur·ysm /ˈænjərɪzəm/ *noun* (*medical*) an area of extreme swelling on the wall of an ARTERY

anew /əˈnjuː; *NAmE* əˈnuː/ *adv.* (*formal*) if sb does sth **anew**, they do it again from the beginning or do it in a different way: *They started life anew in Canada.*

angel /ˈeɪndʒl/ *noun* **1** a spirit who is believed to be a servant of God, and is sent by God to deliver a message or perform a task. Angels are often shown dressed in white, with wings. ➲ see also GUARDIAN ANGEL **2** a person who is very good and kind; a child who behaves well: *John* ***is no angel****, believe me* (= he does not behave well). **3** (*informal*) used when you are talking to sb and you are grateful to them: *Thanks Dad,* ***you're an angel****.* ◇ ***Be an angel*** *and make me a cup of coffee.* IDM see FOOL *n.*

Angel·eno (also **Angel·ino**) /ˌændʒəˈliːnəʊ; *NAmE* -ˈliːnoʊ/ *noun* (*pl.* -os) (*informal*) a person who lives in Los Angeles

angel·fish /ˈeɪndʒlfɪʃ/ *noun* (*pl.* **angel·fish** or **angel·fishes**) a type of brightly coloured FRESHWATER or SALTWATER fish with a thin deep body and long FINS

ˈ**angel food cake** *noun* [U, C] (*NAmE*) a light cake made with the white part of eggs and without fat, often baked in a ring shape

an·gel·ic /ænˈdʒelɪk/ *adj.* good, kind or beautiful; like an angel: *an angelic smile* ▸ **an·gel·ic·al·ly** *adv.* /-kli/

an·gel·ica /ænˈdʒelɪkə/ *noun* [U] pieces of a plant with a sweet smell, that have been boiled in sugar and are used to decorate cakes

an·gelus /ˈændʒələs/ (also **the Angelus**) *noun* [sing.] (in the Roman Catholic Church) prayers said in the morning, at midday and in the evening; a bell rung when it is time for these prayers

anger 🔑 /ˈæŋɡə(r)/ *noun, verb*

■ ***noun*** 🔑 [U] the strong feeling that you have when sth has happened that you think is bad and unfair: *Jan slammed her fist on the desk* ***in anger****.* ◇ *the growing anger and frustration of young unemployed people* ◇ **~ at sb/sth** *He was filled with anger at the way he had been treated.*

■ ***verb*** [often passive] **~ sb** to make sb angry: *The question clearly angered him.*

an·gina /ænˈdʒaɪnə/ (also *technical* **an·gina pec·toris** /ænˌdʒaɪnə ˈpektərɪs/) *noun* [U] (*medical*) severe pain in the chest caused by a low supply of blood to the heart during exercise because the ARTERIES are partly blocked

angio·plasty /ˈændʒiəʊplæsti; *NAmE* ˈændʒioʊ-/ *noun* [C, U] (*pl.* -ies) (*medical*) a medical operation to repair or open a blocked BLOOD VESSEL, especially either of the two ARTERIES that supply blood to the heart

angle 🔑 /ˈæŋɡl/ *noun, verb*

■ ***noun*** **1** 🔑 the space between two lines or surfaces that join, measured in degrees: *a 45° angle* ➲ VISUAL VOCAB page V58 ➲ see also ACUTE ANGLE, ADJACENT ANGLE, CORRESPONDING ANGLES, OBTUSE ANGLE, RIGHT ANGLE, WIDE-ANGLE LENS **2** 🔑 the direction that sth is leaning or pointing in when it is not in a vertical or horizontal line: *The tower of Pisa leans* ***at an angle****.* ◇ *The plane was coming in at a steep angle.* ◇ *His hair was sticking up at all angles.* **3** 🔑 a position from which you look at sth: *The photo was taken from an unusual angle.* **4** 🔑 a particular way of presenting or thinking about a situation, problem, etc: *We need a new angle for our next advertising campaign.* ◇ *You can look at the issue from many different angles.* ◇ *The article concentrates on the human angle* (= the part that concerns people's emotions) *of the story.*

■ ***verb*** **1** [T] **~ sth** to move or place sth so that it is not straight or not directly facing sb/sth: *He angled his chair so that he could sit and watch her.* **2** [T] **~ sth** to present information, a report, etc. based on a particular way of thinking or for a particular audience: *The programme is angled towards younger viewers.* **3** (usually **go angling**) [I] to catch fish with a line and a hook

PHR V ˈ**angle for sth** to try to get a particular reaction or response from sb, without directly asking for what you want: *She was angling for sympathy.*

ˈ**angle bracket** *noun* [usually pl.] one of a pair of marks, < >, used around words or figures to separate them from the surrounding text

ang·ler /ˈæŋɡlə(r)/ *noun* a person who catches fish (= goes angling) as a hobby ➲ compare FISHERMAN

An·gli·can /ˈæŋɡlɪkən/ *noun* a member of the Church of England or of a Church connected with it in another country ▸ **An·gli·can** *adj.*: *the Anglican Church*

An·gli·cism /ˈæŋɡlɪsɪzəm/ *noun* a word or phrase from the English language that is used in another language: *Many French people try to avoid Anglicisms such as 'weekend' and 'shopping'.*

an·gli·cize (*BrE* also **-ise**) /ˈæŋɡlɪsaɪz/ *verb* **~ sb/sth** to make sb/sth English in character: *Gutmann anglicized his name to Goodman.*

an·gling /ˈæŋɡlɪŋ/ *noun* [U] (*BrE*) the art or sport of catching fish with a FISHING ROD, usually in rivers and lakes rather than in the sea

Anglo /ˈæŋɡləʊ; *NAmE* ˈæŋɡloʊ/ *noun* (*pl.* -os) **1** (*especially US*) a white person of European origin **2** (*CanE, informal*) = ANGLOPHONE

Anglo- /ˈæŋɡləʊ; *NAmE* ˈæŋɡloʊ/ *combining form* (in nouns and adjectives) English or British: *Anglo-American* ◇ *Anglophile* ◇ *Anglo-Indian*

ˌ**Anglo-ˈCatholic** *noun* a member of the part of the Church of England that is most similar to the Roman Catholic Church in its beliefs and practices

anglo·mania /ˌæŋɡləʊˈmeɪniə; *NAmE* ˌæŋɡloʊ-/ *noun* [U] an extremely strong admiration for England or English customs

ˌ**Anglo-ˈNorman** *noun* [U] a form of Norman French spoken in England in the MIDDLE AGES

Anglo·phile /ˈæŋɡləʊfaɪl; *NAmE* ˈæŋɡloʊ-/ *noun* a person who is not British but who likes Britain or British things very much

Anglo·pho·bia /ˌæŋɡləʊˈfəʊbiə; *NAmE* ˌæŋɡloʊˈfoʊbiə/ *noun* [U] hatred or fear of England or Britain ▸ **Anglo·phobe** /ˈæŋɡləʊfəʊb; *NAmE* ˈæŋɡloʊfoʊb/ *noun*: *Her father was an Anglophobe.* **Anglo·phobic** /ˌæŋɡləʊˈfəʊbɪk; *NAmE* ˌæŋɡloʊˈfoʊbɪk/ *adj.*

anglo·phone /ˈæŋɡləʊfəʊn; *NAmE* -oʊfoʊn/ *noun* a person who speaks English, especially in countries where English is not the only language that is spoken ▸ **anglo·phone** *adj.*: *anglophone communities*

ˌ**Anglo-ˈSaxon** *noun* **1** [C] a person whose ANCESTORS were English **2** [C] an English person of the period before the Norman Conquest **3** [U] the Old English language ▸ ˌ**Anglo-ˈSaxon** *adj.*: *Anglo-Saxon kings*

the Anglo·sphere /ˈæŋɡləʊsfɪə(r); *NAmE* ˈæŋɡloʊsfɪr/ *noun* [sing.] the group of countries where English is the main language

an·gora /æŋˈɡɔːrə/ *noun* **1** [C] a breed of cat, GOAT or RABBIT that has long smooth hair **2** [U] a type of soft wool or cloth made from the hair of the angora GOAT or RABBIT: *an angora sweater*

An·gos·tura™ /ˌæŋɡəˈstjʊərə; *NAmE* -ˈstʊrə/ (also ˌ**Angostura ˈbitters**) *noun* [U] a bitter liquid, flavoured with the BARK of a tropical tree, that is used to give flavour to alcoholic drinks

angrez /ʌŋˈreɪz/ *noun* (*pl.* **angrez**) (*IndE, informal*) an English person

angry 🗝 /ˈæŋɡri/ *adj.* (**an·grier, an·gri·est**)
HELP You can also use **more angry** and **most angry**.
1 🗝 having strong feelings about sth that you dislike very much or about an unfair situation: *Her behaviour really* ***made me angry.*** ◇ *Thousands of angry demonstrators filled the square.* ◇ *The comments provoked an angry response from union leaders.* ◇ **~ with/at sb** *Please don't* ***be angry*** *with me. It wasn't my fault.* ◇ **~ with/at sb about/for sth** *I was very angry with myself for making such a stupid mistake.* ◇ **~ at/about/over sth** *He felt angry at the injustice of the situation.* ◇ *The passengers grew angry about the delay.* **2** (of a wound) red and infected **3** (*literary*) (of the sea or the sky) dark and STORMY ▸ **an·grily** 🗝 /-əli/ *adv.*: *Some senators reacted angrily to the President's remarks.* ◇ *He swore angrily.*

Synonyms

angry

mad • indignant • cross • irate

These words all describe people feeling and/or showing anger.

angry feeling or showing anger: *Please don't be angry with me.* ◇ *Thousands of angry demonstrators filled the square.*

mad [not before noun] (*informal, especially NAmE*) angry: *He* ***got mad*** *and walked out.* ◇ *She's* ***mad at me*** *for being late.* NOTE **Mad** is the usual word for 'angry' in informal American English. In British English, the phrase 'go mad' means 'very angry': *Dad'll go mad when he sees what you've done.* 'Go mad' can also mean 'go crazy' or 'get very excited'.

indignant feeling or showing anger and surprise because you think that you or sb else has been treated unfairly: *She was very indignant at the way she had been treated.*

cross (*especially BrE, rather informal*) rather angry or annoyed: *I was quite cross with him for being late.* NOTE This word is often used by or to children.

irate very angry: *irate customers* ◇ *an irate letter* NOTE **Irate** is not usually followed by a preposition: ~~*She was irate with me/about it.*~~

PATTERNS

- angry/mad/indignant/cross **about/at** sth
- angry/cross **with** sb (for doing sth)
- angry/mad/indignant/cross **that** ...
- to **get** angry/mad/cross
- to **make sb** angry/mad/cross

angst /æŋst/ *noun* [U] (from *German*) a feeling of anxiety and worry about a situation, or about your life: *songs full of teenage angst*

ˈ**angst-ridden** *adj.* having feelings of angst: *a generation of angst-ridden adolescents*

ang·strom /ˈæŋstrəm/ *noun* (*chemistry, physics*) a very small unit of length, equal to $1x10^{-10}$ metre, used for measuring WAVELENGTHS and the distance between atoms

angsty /æŋsti/ *adj.* having or showing feelings of angst: *Stefan plays the role of a rebellious, angsty outsider who joins a terrorist cell.* ◇ *angsty poetry/drama/lyrics*

an·guish /ˈæŋɡwɪʃ/ *noun* [U] (*formal*) severe pain, mental suffering or unhappiness: *He groaned in anguish.* ◇ *Tears of anguish filled her eyes.* ▸ **an·guished** *adj.*: *anguished cries* ◇ *an anguished letter from her prison cell*

an·gu·lar /ˈæŋɡjələ(r)/ *adj.* **1** (of a person) thin and without much flesh so that the bones are noticeable: *an angular face* ◇ *a tall angular woman* **2** having angles or sharp corners: *a design of large angular shapes*

ani·mal 🗝 /ˈænɪml/ *noun, adj.*
■ ***noun*** **1** 🗝 a creature that is not a bird, a fish, a REPTILE, an insect or a human: *the animals and birds of South America* ◇ *a small furry animal* ◇ *Fish oils are less saturated than animal fats.* ◇ *domestic animals such as dogs and cats* **2** 🗝 any living thing that is not a plant or a human: *the animal kingdom* ◇ *This product has not been tested on animals.* ➲ VISUAL VOCAB pages V10, V11 **3** 🗝 any living creature, including humans: *Humans are the only animals to have developed speech.* ➲ COLLOCATIONS at LIFE ➲ compare VEGETABLE **4** a person who behaves in a cruel or unpleasant way, or who is very dirty: *The person who did this is an animal, a brute.* **5** a particular type of person, thing, organization, etc: *She's not a political animal.* ◇ *The government that followed the election was a very different animal.* ➲ see also DUMB ANIMAL, HIGHER ANIMALS
■ ***adj.*** [only before noun] relating to the physical needs and basic feelings of people: ***animal desires/passion/instincts*** ◇ ***animal magnetism*** (= a quality in sb that other people find attractive, usually in a sexual way)

ˌ**animal conˈtrol officer** *noun* (*NAmE, formal*) a person whose job is to catch animals that are walking freely in the streets and do not seem to have a home ➲ compare DOGCATCHER

ˌ**animal ˈhusbandry** *noun* [U] (*technical*) farming that involves keeping animals to produce food

ˌ**animal ˈrights** *noun* [pl.] the rights of animals to be treated well, for example by not being hunted or used for medical research: *His research work was attacked by* ***animal rights activists.***

an·im·ate *verb, adj.*
■ ***verb*** /ˈænɪmeɪt/ **1 ~ sth** to make sth more lively or full of energy: *A smile suddenly animated her face.* **2** [usually passive] **~ sth** to make models, toys, etc. seem to move in a film/movie by rapidly showing slightly different pictures of them in a series, one after another
■ ***adj.*** /ˈænɪmət/ (*formal*) living; having life: *animate beings* OPP **inanimate**

ani·mated /ˈænɪmeɪtɪd/ *adj.* **1** full of interest and energy SYN **lively**: *an* ***animated discussion/conversation*** ◇ *Her face suddenly became animated.* **2** (of pictures, drawings, etc. in a film/movie) made to look as if they are moving: ***animated cartoons/graphics/models*** ▸ **ani·mated·ly** *adv.*: *People were talking animatedly.*

an·ima·teur /ˌænɪməˈtɜː(r)/ *noun* (from *French*) a person whose job is to organize or encourage artistic or social projects and activities

ani·ma·tion /ˌænɪˈmeɪʃn/ *noun* **1** [U] energy and enthusiasm in the way you look, behave or speak: *His face was drained of all colour and animation.* ➲ see also SUSPENDED ANIMATION **2** [U] the process of making films/movies, videos and computer games in which drawings or models of people and animals seem to move: ***computer/cartoon animation*** **3** [C] a film/movie in which drawings of people and animals seem to move: *The electronic dictionary included some animations.*

ani·ma·tor /ˈænɪmeɪtə(r)/ *noun* a person who makes animated films

anima·tron·ics /ˌænɪməˈtrɒnɪks; *NAmE* -ˈtrɑːn-/ *noun* [U] the process of making and operating ROBOTS that look like real people or animals, used in films/movies and other types of entertainment ▸ **anima·tron·ic** *adj.*

anime /ˈænɪmeɪ; ˈænɪmə/ *noun* [U] Japanese film/movie and television ANIMATION, often with a SCIENCE FICTION subject

ani·mism /ˈænɪmɪzəm/ *noun* [U] **1** the belief that plants, objects and natural things such as the weather have a living soul **2** belief in a power that organizes and controls the universe ▸ **ani·mist** /ˈænɪmɪst/ *noun* **ani·mis·tic** /ˌænɪˈmɪstɪk/ *adj.*

ani·mos·ity /ˌænɪˈmɒsəti; *NAmE* -ˈmɑːs-/ *noun* [U, C] (*pl.* -ies) a strong feeling of opposition, anger or hatred SYN **hostility**: **~ (toward(s) sb/sth)** *He felt no animosity to-*

A

wards his critics. ◇ ~ (**between A and B**) *personal animosities between members of the two groups*

ani·mus /ˈænɪməs/ *noun* [U, sing.] ~ (**against sb/sth**) (*formal*) a strong feeling of opposition, anger or hatred

anion /ˈænaɪən/ *noun* (*chemistry, physics*) an ION with a negative electrical CHARGE ➲ compare CATION

anise /ˈænɪs/ *noun* [U] a plant with seeds that smell sweet

ani·seed /ˈænəsiːd/ *noun* [U] the dried seeds of the anise plant, used to give flavour to alcoholic drinks and sweets/candy

ankh /æŋk/ *noun* an object or design like a cross but with a LOOP instead of the top arm, sometimes worn as jewellery. The ankh was used in ancient Egypt as the symbol of life.

ankh

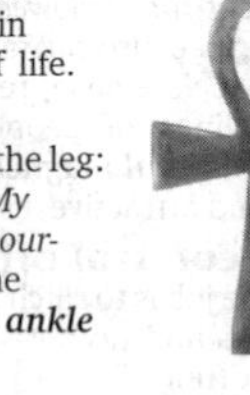

ankle 🗝 /ˈæŋkl/ *noun* the joint connecting the foot to the leg: *to* ***sprain/break your ankle*** ◇ *My ankles have swollen.* ◇ *We found ourselves* ***ankle-deep*** *in water* (= the water came up to our ankles). ◇ ***ankle boots*** (= that cover the ankle) ➲ VISUAL VOCAB page V48

ˈ**ankle sock** (*BrE*) (*US* **ank·let**) *noun* a type of very short sock: *a girl in a blue dress and ankle socks*

ank·let /ˈæŋklət/ *noun* **1** a piece of jewellery worn around the ankle **2** (*US*) (*BrE* ˈ**ankle sock**) a type of very short sock

an·ky·lo·saur /ˈæŋkɪləsɔː(r)/ *noun* a type of plant-eating DINOSAUR covered with hard plates made of bone for protection

anna /ˈʌnə/ *noun* (*IndE*) **1** an older brother **2** the leader of a group of young people who go around together and sometimes cause trouble

annals /ˈænlz/ *noun* [pl.] **1** an official record of events or activities year by year; historical records: *His deeds went down* ***in the annals of*** *British history.* **2** used in the title of academic JOURNALS: *Annals of Science, vol. viii*

an·neal /əˈniːl/ *verb* ~ **sth** (*technical*) to heat metal or glass and allow it to cool slowly, in order to make it stronger or softer

annex /əˈneks/ *verb* ~ **sth** (*formal*) to take control of a country, region, etc, especially by force SYN **occupy**: *Germany annexed Austria in 1938.* ▶ **an·nex·ation** /ˌænekˈseɪʃn/ *noun* [U, C]

an·nexe (*BrE*) (also **annex** *NAmE, BrE*) /ˈæneks/ *noun* **1** a building that is added to, or is near, a larger one and that provides extra living or work space: *Our rooms were in the annexe.* **2** (*formal*) an extra section of a document SYN **appendix**

an·ni·hi·late /əˈnaɪəleɪt/ *verb* **1** ~ **sb/sth/yourself** to destroy sb/sth completely: *The human race has enough weapons to annihilate itself.* **2** ~ **sb/sth** to defeat sb/sth completely: *She annihilated her opponent, who failed to win a single game.* ▶ **an·ni·hi·la·tion** /əˌnaɪəˈleɪʃn/ *noun* [U]: *the annihilation of the whole human race*

an·ni·ver·sary 🗝 /ˌænɪˈvɜːsəri; *NAmE* -ˈvɜːrs-/ *noun* (*pl.* **-ies**) a date that is an exact number of years after the date of an important or special event: *on the anniversary of his wife's death* ◇ *to celebrate your* ***wedding anniversary*** ◇ *the theatre's 25th anniversary celebrations* ➲ COLLOCATIONS at MARRIAGE

an·no·tate /ˈænəteɪt/ *verb* ~ **sth** to add notes to a book or text, giving explanations or comments ▶ **an·no·ta·tion** /ˌænəˈteɪʃn/ *noun* [C, U]: *It will be published with annotations and an index.* **an·no·tated** *adj.*: *an annotated edition*

an·nounce 🗝 /əˈnaʊns/ *verb* **1** 🗝 to tell people sth officially, especially about a decision, plans, etc: ~ **sth** *They haven't formally announced their engagement yet.* ◇ (*figurative*) *A ring at the doorbell announced Jack's arrival.* ◇ ~ **sth to sb** *The government yesterday announced to the media plans to create a million new jobs.* HELP You cannot 'announce somebody something': ~~*They announced us their decision.*~~: ~ **that...** *We are pleased to announce that all five candidates were successful.* ◇ **it is announced that...** *It was announced that new speed restrictions would be introduced.* ➲ SYNONYMS at DECLARE **2** 🗝 to give information about sth in a public place, especially through a LOUDSPEAKER: ~ **sth** *Has our flight been announced yet?* ◇ + **speech** *'Now boarding flight 897, destination Seattle,' the loudspeaker announced.* ◇ ~ **that...** *They announced that the flight would be delayed.* **3** 🗝 to say sth in a loud and/or serious way: + **speech** *'I've given up smoking,' she announced.* ◇ ~ **that...** *She announced that she'd given up smoking.* ➲ SYNONYMS at DECLARE **4** ~ **yourself/sb** to tell sb your name or sb else's name when you or they arrive at a place: *Would you announce the guests as they arrive?* (= call out their names, for example at a formal party) **5** ~ **sth** to introduce, or to give information about, a programme on the radio or television

an·nounce·ment /əˈnaʊnsmənt/ *noun* **1** [C] a spoken or written statement that informs people about sth: *to* ***make an announcement*** ◇ *Today's announcement of a peace agreement came after weeks of discussion.* ◇ *Announcements of births, marriages and deaths appear in some newspapers.* ➲ SYNONYMS at STATEMENT **2** [U] the act of publicly informing people about sth: *Announcement of the verdict was accompanied by shouts and cheers.*

an·noun·cer /əˈnaʊnsə(r)/ *noun* **1** a person who introduces, or gives information about, programmes on the radio or television ➲ see also HOST, PRESENTER **2** a person who gives information about sth in a station, an airport, etc, especially through a LOUDSPEAKER

annoy 🗝 /əˈnɔɪ/ *verb* **1** 🗝 to make sb slightly angry SYN **irritate**: ~ **sb** *His constant joking was beginning to annoy her.* ◇ **it annoys sb when...** *It really annoys me when people forget to say thank you.* ◇ ~ **sb to do sth** ***It annoys me to*** *see him getting ahead of me.* **2** 🗝 ~ **sb** to make sb uncomfortable or unable to relax SYN **bother**: *He swatted a fly that was annoying him.*

an·noy·ance /əˈnɔɪəns/ *noun* **1** [U] the feeling of being slightly angry SYN **irritation**: *He could not conceal his annoyance at being interrupted.* ◇ *Much* ***to our annoyance****, they decided not to come after all.* ◇ *She stamped her foot* ***in annoyance.*** **2** [C] something that makes you slightly angry

annoy·ed 🗝 /əˈnɔɪd/ *adj.* [not usually before noun] slightly angry SYN **irritated**: ~ (**with sb**) (**at/about sth**) *He was beginning to get very annoyed with me about my carelessness.* ◇ *I was* ***annoyed with myself*** *for giving in so easily.* ◇ *I bet she was annoyed at having to write it out again.* ◇ ~ **that...** *I was annoyed that they hadn't turned up.* ◇ ~ **to find, see, etc.** *He was annoyed to find himself going red.*

annoy·ing 🗝 /əˈnɔɪɪŋ/ *adj.* making sb feel slightly angry SYN **irritating**: *This interruption is very annoying.* ◇ *Her most annoying habit was eating with her mouth open.* ▶ **an·noy·ing·ly** *adv.*

an·nual 🗝 AW /ˈænjuəl/ *adj., noun*

■ ***adj.*** [usually before noun] **1** 🗝 happening or done once every year: *an* ***annual meeting/event/report*** **2** 🗝 relating to a period of one year: *an* ***annual income/subscription/budget*** ◇ *an average annual growth rate of 8%* ◇ *annual rainfall* ➲ compare BIANNUAL

■ ***noun*** **1** a book, especially one for children, that is published once a year, with the same title each time, but different contents **2** any plant that grows and dies within one year or season ➲ compare BIENNIAL *n.*, PERENNIAL *n.*

an·nu·al·ized (*BrE* also **-ised**) /ˈænjuəlaɪzd/ *adj.* (*technical*) calculated for a period of a year but based on the amounts for a shorter period

an·nu·al·ly 🗝 AW /ˈænjuəli/ *adv.* once a year: *The exhibition is held annually.*

an·nu·ity /əˈnjuːəti; *NAmE* -ˈnuː-/ *noun* (*pl.* **-ies**) **1** a fixed amount of money paid to sb each year, usually for the rest of their life **2** a type of insurance that pays a fixed amount of money to sb each year

annul /ə'nʌl/ *verb* (-ll-) **~ sth** to state officially that sth is no longer legally valid: *Their marriage was annulled after just six months.* ▸ **an·nul·ment** *noun* [C, U]

an·nu·lar /'ænjələ(r)/ *adj.* (*technical*) shaped like a ring

an·nun·ci·ation /ə,nʌnsi'eɪʃn/ *noun* [sing.] **the Annunciation** (in the Christian religion) the occasion when Mary was told that she was to be the mother of Christ, celebrated on 25 March

anode /'ænəʊd; *NAmE* 'ænoʊd/ *noun* (*technical*) the ELECTRODE in an electrical device where OXIDATION occurs; the positive electrode in an ELECTROLYTIC cell and the negative electrode in a battery ➲ compare CATHODE

ano·dize (*BrE* also **-ise**) /'ænədaɪz/ *verb* **~ sth** to cover a metal, especially ALUMINIUM/ALUMINUM, with a layer of OXIDE in order to protect it

ano·dyne /'ænədaɪn/ *adj.* (*formal*) unlikely to cause disagreement or offend anyone; not expressing strong opinions SYN **bland**

anoint /ə'nɔɪnt/ *verb* **~ sb/sth** (**with sth**) to put oil or water on sb's head as part of a religious ceremony: *The priest anointed her with oil.*

anom·al·ous /ə'nɒmələs; *NAmE* -'nɑːm-/ *adj.* (*formal*) different from what is normal or expected ▸ **anom·al·ous·ly** *adv.*

anom·aly /ə'nɒməli; *NAmE* ə'nɑːm-/ *noun* (*pl.* -ies) **~ (in sth)** a thing, situation, etc. that is different from what is normal or expected: *the many anomalies in the tax system* ◇ *the apparent anomaly that those who produced the wealth, the workers, were the poorest*

an·omie (also **anomy**) /'ænəmi/ *noun* [U] (*formal*) a lack of social or moral standards

anon /ə'nɒn; *NAmE* ə'nɑːn/ *adv.* (*old-fashioned* or *literary*) soon: *See you anon.*

anon. /ə'nɒn; *NAmE* ə'nɑːn/ *abbr.* ANONYMOUS

ano·nym·ity /,ænə'nɪməti/ *noun* [U] **1** the state of remaining unknown to most other people: *Names of people in the book were changed to preserve anonymity.* ◇ *the anonymity of the city* (= where people do not know each other) ◇ (*especially NAmE*) *He agreed to give an interview* ***on condition of anonymity*** (= if his name was not mentioned). **2** the state of not having any unusual or interesting features: *the anonymity of the hotel decor*

ano·nym·ize (*BrE* also **-ise**) /ə'nɒnɪmaɪz; *NAmE* ə'nɑːn-/ *verb* **1 ~ sth** (*technical*) if you **anonymize** a test result, especially a medical test result, you remove any information that shows who it belongs to **2 ~ sth** (*computing*) if you **anonymize** data that is sent or received over the Internet, you remove any information that identifies which particular computer that data originally came from

an·onym·ous /ə'nɒnɪməs; *NAmE* ə'nɑːn-/ *adj.* **1** (of a person) with a name that is not known or that is not made public: *an anonymous donor* ◇ *The money was donated by a local businessman who wishes to* ***remain anonymous***. **2** (*abbr.* **anon.**) written, given, made, etc. by sb who does not want their name to be known or made public: *an anonymous letter* **3** without any unusual or interesting features: *long stretches of dull and anonymous countryside* ▸ **an·onym·ous·ly** *adv.*

a,nonymous FT'P *noun* [U] (*computing*) a system that allows anybody to DOWNLOAD files from the Internet without having to give their name

ano·rak /'ænəræk/ *noun* **1** (*especially BrE*) a short coat with a HOOD that is worn as protection against rain, wind and cold ➲ VISUAL VOCAB page V50 **2** (*BrE*, *informal*) a person who spends a lot of time learning facts or collecting things that most other people think are boring

an·or·exia /,ænə'reksiə/ (also **an·or·exia ner·vosa** /,ænə,reksiə nɜː'vəʊsə; *NAmE* nɜːr'voʊsə/) *noun* [U] an emotional DISORDER, especially affecting young women, in which there is an ABNORMAL fear of being fat, causing the person to stop eating, leading to dangerous weight loss ➲ COLLOCATIONS at DIET ➲ compare BULIMIA

an·or·exic /,ænə'reksɪk/ *noun* a person who is suffering from anorexia ▸ **an·or·exic** *adj.*: *She's anorexic.*

an·other 0‑w /ə'nʌðə(r)/ *det.*, *pron.* **1** 0‑w one more; an extra thing or person: *Would you like another drink?* ◇ *'Finished?' 'No, I've got another three questions to do.'* ◇ *We've still got another* (= a further) *forty miles to go.* ◇ *'It's a bill.' 'Oh no, not another!'* ◇ *I got another of those calls yesterday.* HELP **Another** can be followed by a singular noun, by **of** and a plural noun, or by a number and a plural noun. ➲ compare OTHER ➲ LANGUAGE BANK at ADDITION **2** 0‑w different; a different person or thing: *Let's do it another time.* ◇ *We need another computer* (= a new one). ◇ *We can try that—but whether it'll work is* ***another matter***. ◇ *The room's too small. Let's see if they've got* ***another one***. ◇ *I don't like this room. I'm going to ask for another.* **3** a person or thing of a very similar type: *She's going to be another Madonna* (= as famous as her). ◇ *There'll never be another like him.* ➲ see also ONE ANOTHER
IDM **of one kind, sort, etc. or a'nother** used when you are referring to various types of a thing, without saying exactly what you mean: *We've all got problems of one kind or another.* ➲ more at ONE

A. N. Other /,eɪ en 'ʌðə(r)/ *noun* [sing.] a person whose name is not known or not yet decided, for example in a list of players in a team

an·swer 0‑w /'ɑːnsə(r); *NAmE* 'æn-/ *noun*, *verb*
■ ***noun*** **1** 0‑w something that you say, write or do to react to a question or situation: *I rang the bell, but there was no answer.* ◇ **~ to sth** *I can't easily* ***give an answer*** *to your question.* ◇ *Have you had an answer to your letter?* ◇ *As if* ***in answer to*** *our prayers, she offered to lend us £10 000.* ◇ *She had no answer to the accusations.* **2** 0‑w something that you write or say in reply to a question in a test, an exam, an exercise, etc; the correct reply to a question in a test, etc: *Write your answers on the sheet provided.* ◇ *Do you know the answer* (= the right one) *to question 12?* **3** 0‑w a solution to a problem: *There is no easy answer.* ◇ *This could be the answer to all our problems.* ◇ *The obvious answer would be to cancel the party.* **4** a person or thing from one place that may be thought to be as good as a famous person or thing from another place: *The new theme park will be Britain's answer to Disneyland.*
IDM **have/know all the 'answers** (*informal*, often *disapproving*) to be confident that you know sth, especially when you actually do not: *He thinks he knows all the answers.* ➲ more at NO *exclam.*
■ ***verb*** **1** 0‑w [I, T] to say, write or do sth as a reaction to a question or situation SYN **reply**: *I repeated the question, but she didn't answer.* ◇ **~ sth** *You haven't* ***answered my question***. ◇ *to* ***answer a letter/an advertisement*** ◇ *to* ***answer the phone*** (= to pick up the phone when it rings) ◇ *to* ***answer the door*** (= to open the door when sb knocks/rings) ◇ *My* ***prayers have been answered*** (= I have got what I wanted). ◇ *He refused to answer the charges against him.* ◇ **~ (sb)** *Come on, answer me! Where were you?* ◇ *He answered me with a smile.* ◇ **+ speech** *'I'd prefer to walk,' she answered.* ◇ **~ sb + speech** *'I'd prefer to walk,' she answered him.* ◇ **~ (sb) that...** *She answered that she would prefer to walk.* ◇ **~ sb sth** *Answer me this: how did they know we were here?* **2** [T] **~ sth** (*formal*) to be suitable for sth; to match sth: *Does this answer your requirements?*
IDM **answer to the name of sth** (especially of a pet animal) to be called sth ➲ more at DESCRIPTION
PHR V **,answer 'back** to defend yourself against criticism: *He was given the chance to answer back in a radio interview.* **,answer 'back** | **,answer sb 'back** to speak rudely to sb in authority, especially when they are criticizing you or telling you to do sth: *Don't answer back!* ◇ *Stop answering your mother back!* **'answer for sth 1** to accept responsibility or blame for sth: *You will have to answer for your behaviour one day.* ◇ *This government* ***has a lot to answer for*** (= is responsible for a lot of bad things). **2** to promise that sb has a particular quality or can be relied on to do sth: *I can answer for her honesty.* **'answer for sb** (usually in negative sentences) to say that sb else will do sth or have a particular opinion: *I agree, but I can't answer for my colleagues.* **'answer to sb** (**for sth**) to have to explain your actions or decisions to sb: *All sales clerks answer to the store manager.*

A

Which Word?

answer / reply

Verbs

- **Answer** and **reply** are the most common verbs used for speaking or writing as a reaction to a question, letter, etc.
- Note that you **answer** a person, question or letter, not *answer to* them, but you **reply to** somebody or something: *I'm writing to answer your questions* ◇ *I'm writing to reply to your questions.* ◇ ~~*I'm writing to answer to your questions.*~~
- **Answer** can be used with or without an object: *I haven't answered her email yet.* ◇ *I knocked on the door but nobody answered.* **Reply** is often used with the actual words spoken: *'I won't let you down,' he replied.*
- **Respond** is less common and more formal: *The directors were unwilling to* ***respond to*** *questions.*
- You can only **answer** a door or a phone.

➲ see also REJOIN, RETORT, GET BACK TO SB

Nouns

- Note the phrases **in answer to** and **in reply to**: *I'm writing in answer to your letter.*

➲ see also RESPONSE, REJOINDER, RETORT

an·swer·able /'ɑːnsərəbl; *NAmE* 'æn-/ *adj.* **1** [not before noun] **~ to sb** (**for sth**) having to explain your actions to sb in authority over you: *She was a free agent, answerable to no one for her behaviour.* **2** [not before noun] **~** (**for sth**) responsible for sth and ready to accept punishment or criticism for it: *Ministers must be made answerable for their decisions.* **3** (of a question) that can be answered

'answering machine (*BrE* also **an·swer·phone**) *noun* a machine that you connect to your telephone to answer your calls and record any message left by the person calling: *I called several times, but only got the answering machine.*

an·swer·phone /'ɑːnsəfəʊn; *NAmE* 'ænsərfoʊn/ *noun* (*BrE*) = ANSWERING MACHINE: *She left her name and number on his answerphone.*

ant /ænt/ *noun* a small insect that lives in highly organized groups. There are many types of ant: *an ants' nest* ◇ *an ant colony* ➲ VISUAL VOCAB page V11 ➲ see also ANTHILL
IDM **have 'ants in your pants** (*informal*) to be very excited or impatient about sth and unable to stay still

-ant, -ent *suffix* **1** (in adjectives) that is or does sth: *significant* ◇ *different* **2** (in nouns) a person or thing that: *inhabitant* ◇ *deterrent*

ant·acid /ænt'æsɪd/ *noun* a medicine that prevents or corrects ACIDITY, especially in the stomach

an·tag·on·ism /æn'tæɡənɪzəm/ *noun* [U, pl.] **~** (**to/toward(s) sb/sth**) | **~** (**between A and B**) feelings of hatred and opposition SYN **hostility**: *The antagonism he felt towards his old enemy was still very strong.* ◇ *the racial antagonisms in society*

an·tag·on·ist /æn'tæɡənɪst/ *noun* (*formal*) a person who strongly opposes sb/sth SYN **opponent**

an·tag·on·is·tic /æn,tæɡə'nɪstɪk/ *adj.* **~** (**to/toward(s) sb/sth**) (*formal*) showing or feeling opposition SYN **hostile** ▸ **an·tag·on·is·tic·al·ly** /-kli/ *adv.*

an·tag·on·ize (*BrE* also **-ise**) /æn'tæɡənaɪz/ *verb* **~ sb** to do sth to make sb angry with you: *Not wishing to antagonize her further, he said no more.*

the Ant·arc·tic /æn'tɑːktɪk; *NAmE* -'tɑːrk-/ *noun* [sing.] the regions of the world around the South Pole ▸ **Ant·arc·tic** *adj.* [only before noun]: *Antarctic explorers* ➲ compare ARCTIC

the An,tarctic 'Circle *noun* [sing.] the line of LATITUDE 66° 33′ South ➲ compare ARCTIC

ante /'ænti/ *noun* [sing.]
IDM **raise/up the 'ante** to increase the level of sth, especially demands or sums of money

ante- /'ænti/ *prefix* (in nouns, adjectives and verbs) before; in front of: *ante-room* ◇ *antenatal* ◇ *antedate* ➲ compare POST-, PRE-

ant·eat·er /'æntiːtə(r)/ *noun* an animal with a long nose and tongue that eats ANTS

ante·bellum /,ænti'beləm/ *adj.* [only before noun] (*formal*) connected with the years before a war, especially the American Civil War: *the laws of the antebellum American South*

ante·ce·dent /,æntɪ'siːdnt/ *noun, adj.*
■ ***noun*** **1** [C] (*formal*) a thing or an event that exists or comes before another, and may have influenced it **2 antecedents** [pl.] (*formal*) the people in sb's family who lived a long time ago SYN **ancestors, forebears 3** [C] (*grammar*) a word or phrase to which the following word, especially a pronoun, refers: *In 'He grabbed the ball and threw it in the air', 'ball' is the antecedent of 'it'.*
■ ***adj.*** (*formal*) previous: *antecedent events*

ante·cham·ber /'æntitʃeɪmbə(r)/ *noun* (*formal*) = ANTEROOM

ante·date /,ænti'deɪt/ *verb* **~ sth** = PREDATE

ante·di·lu·vian /,æntidɪ'luːviən/ *adj.* (*formal* or *humorous*) very old-fashioned

ante·lope /'æntɪləʊp; *NAmE* -loʊp/ *noun* (*pl.* **ante·lope** or **ante·lopes**) an African or Asian animal like a DEER, that runs very fast. There are many types of antelope.

ante·natal /,ænti'neɪtl/ (*BrE*) (also **pre·natal** *NAmE, BrE*) *adj.* [only before noun] relating to the medical care given to pregnant women: ***antenatal care/classes/screening*** ◇ *an* ***antenatal clinic*** ➲ compare POST-NATAL

an·tenna /æn'tenə/ *noun* **1** (*pl.* **an·ten·nae** /-niː/) either of the two long thin parts on the heads of some insects and some animals that live in shells, used to feel and touch things with SYN **feeler**: (*figurative*) *The minister was praised for his acute political antennae* (= ability to understand complicated political situations). ➲ VISUAL VOCAB page V11 **2** (*pl.* **an·ten·nas** or **an·ten·nae**) (*especially NAmE*) (*BrE* also **aer·ial**) a piece of equipment made of wire or long straight pieces of metal for receiving or sending radio and television signals: *radio antennas* ➲ VISUAL VOCAB pages V15, V42

an·ter·ior /æn'tɪəriə(r); *NAmE* -'tɪr-/ *adj.* [only before noun] (*technical*) (of a part of the body) at or near the front OPP **posterior**

ante·room /'æntiruːm; -rʊm/ (also *formal* **ante·cham·ber**) *noun* a room where people can wait before entering a larger room, especially in an important public building

an·them /'ænθəm/ *noun* **1** a song that has a special importance for a country, an organization or a particular group of people, and is sung on special occasions: *The European anthem was played at the opening and closing ceremonies.* ➲ see also NATIONAL ANTHEM **2** a short religious song for a CHOIR (= a group of singers), often with an organ

an·them·ic /æn'θiːmɪk/ *adj.* (*formal*) (of a piece of music) that makes you feel happy and enthusiastic

an·ther /'ænθə(r)/ *noun* (*biology*) the part of a flower at the top of a STAMEN that produces POLLEN ➲ VISUAL VOCAB page V9

ant·hill /'ænthɪl/ *noun* a pile of earth formed by ANTS over their nests

an·tholo·gize (*BrE* also **-ise**) /æn'θɒlədʒaɪz; *NAmE* -'θɑːl-/ *verb* **~ sb/sth** to include a writer or piece of writing in an anthology

an·thol·ogy /æn'θɒlədʒi; *NAmE* -'θɑːl-/ *noun* (*pl.* **-ies**) a collection of poems, stories, etc. that have been written by different people and published together in a book

A

an·thra·cite /ˈænθrəsaɪt/ *noun* [U] a very hard type of coal that burns slowly without producing a lot of smoke or flames

an·thrax /ˈænθræks/ *noun* [U] a serious disease that affects sheep and cows and sometimes people, and can cause death

an·thro·po- /ˈænθrəpəʊ; *NAmE* -poʊ/ *combining form* (in nouns, adjectives and adverbs) connected with humans: *anthropology*

an·thro·po·cen·tric /ˌænθrəpəˈsentrɪk/ *adj.* believing that humans are more important than anything else ▸ **an·thro·po·cen·trism** /ˌænθrəpəˈsentrɪzəm/ *noun* [U]

an·thro·poid /ˈænθrəpɔɪd/ *adj., noun* (*technical*)
▪ ***adj.*** (of an APE) looking like a human
▪ ***noun*** any type of APE that is similar to a human

an·thro·polo·gist /ˌænθrəˈpɒlədʒɪst; *NAmE* -ˈpɑːl-/ *noun* a person who studies anthropology

an·thro·pol·ogy /ˌænθrəˈpɒlədʒi; *NAmE* -ˈpɑːl-/ *noun* [U] the study of the human race, especially of its origins, development, customs and beliefs ▸ **an·thro·po·logic·al** /ˌænθrəpəˈlɒdʒɪkl; *NAmE* -ˈlɑːdʒ-/ *adj.*

an·thro·po·morph·ic /ˌænθrəpəˈmɔːfɪk; *NAmE* -ˈmɔːrf-/ *adj.* (of beliefs or ideas) treating gods, animals or objects as if they had human qualities ▸ **an·thro·po·morph·ism** /ˌænθrəpəˈmɔːfɪzəm; *NAmE* -ˈmɔːrf-/ *noun* [U]

anti /ˈænti/ *prep.* (*informal*) if sb is **anti** sb/sth, they do not like or agree with that person or thing ➲ compare PRO

anti- 0‑ᵥ /ˈænti/ *prefix* (in nouns and adjectives)
1 0‑ᵥ opposed to; against: *anti-tank weapons* ◇ *antisocial* ➲ compare PRO- **2** 0‑ᵥ the opposite of: *anti-hero* ◇ *anticlimax* **3** 0‑ᵥ preventing: *antifreeze*

ˌ**anti-ˈaircraft** *adj.* [only before noun] designed to destroy enemy aircraft: ***anti-aircraft fire/guns/missiles***

anti·bac·ter·ial /ˌæntibækˈtɪəriəl; *NAmE* -ˈtɪriəl/ *adj.* that kills bacteria: *antibacterial treatments*

anti·bi·ot·ic /ˌæntibaɪˈɒtɪk; *NAmE* -ˈɑːtɪk/ *noun* [usually pl.] a substance, for example PENICILLIN, that can destroy or prevent the growth of bacteria and cure infections: *The doctor put her on antibiotics* (= told her to take them). ▸ **anti·bi·ot·ic** *adj.*: *an antibiotic drug* ◇ *effective antibiotic treatment*

anti·body /ˈæntibɒdi; *NAmE* -bɑːdi/ *noun* (*pl.* **-ies**) a substance that the body produces in the blood to fight disease, or as a reaction when certain substances are put into the body

ˌ**anti-ˈchoice** *adj.* (*NAmE, disapproving*) against giving women the right to have an ABORTION ➲ compare PRO-CHOICE

Anti·christ /ˈæntikraɪst/ (usually **the Antichrist**) *noun* [sing.] (in Christianity) the DEVIL; Christ's greatest enemy

an·tici·pate 0‑ᵥ AW /ænˈtɪsɪpeɪt/ *verb*
1 0‑ᵥ to expect sth: **~ sth** *We don't anticipate any major problems.* ◇ *Our anticipated arrival time is 8.30.* ◇ *The eagerly anticipated movie will be released next month.* ◇ **~ doing sth** *They anticipate moving to bigger premises by the end of the year.* ◇ **~ sth doing sth** *I don't anticipate it being a problem.* ◇ **~ that...** *We anticipate that sales will rise next year.* ◇ **it is anticipated that...** *It is anticipated that inflation will stabilize at 3%.* ➲ compare UNANTICIPATED **2** 0‑ᵥ to see what might happen in the future and take action to prepare for it: **~ sth** *We need someone who can anticipate and respond to changes in the fashion industry.* ◇ **~ what, how, that, etc...** *Try and anticipate what the interviewers will ask.* **3 ~ (doing) sth** | **~ (sth doing) sth** to think with pleasure and excitement about sth that is going to happen: *We eagerly anticipated the day we would leave school.* ◇ *The more I anticipated arriving somewhere, the more disappointed I was.* **4 ~ sb (doing sth)** (*formal*) to do sth before it can be done by sb else SYN **forestall**: *When Scott reached the South Pole he found that Amundsen had anticipated him.* ▸ **an·tici·pa·tory** /ænˌtɪsɪˈpeɪtəri; *NAmE* ænˈtɪsəpətɔːri/ *adj.*: (*formal*) *a fast anticipatory movement by the goalkeeper*

an·tici·pa·tion AW /ænˌtɪsɪˈpeɪʃn/ *noun* [U] **1** the fact of seeing that sth might happen in the future and perhaps doing sth about it now: *He bought extra food* ***in anticipation of*** *more people coming than he'd invited.* **2** a feeling of excitement about sth (usually sth good) that is going to happen: ***happy/eager/excited anticipation*** ◇ *The courtroom was filled with anticipation.*

anti·cler·ic·al /ˌæntiˈklerɪkl/ *adj.* opposed to priests and their influence in political life: *anticlerical movements in the seventeenth century* ▸ **anti·cler·ic·al·ism** /-ɪzəm/ *noun* [U]

anti·cli·max /ˌæntiˈklaɪmæks/ *noun* [C, U] a situation that is disappointing because it happens at the end of sth that was much more exciting, or because it is not as exciting as you expected: *Travelling in Europe was something of an anticlimax after the years he'd spent in Africa.* ◇ *a* ***sense/feeling of anticlimax*** ➲ compare CLIMAX ▸ **anti·cli·mac·tic** /ˌæntiklaɪˈmæktɪk/ *adj.*

anti·cline /ˈæntiklaɪn/ *noun* (*geology*) an area of ground where layers of rock in the earth's surface have been folded into a curve that is higher in the middle than at the ends ➲ compare SYNCLINE

anti·clock·wise /ˌæntiˈklɒkwaɪz; *NAmE* -ˈklɑːk-/ (*BrE*) (*NAmE* **coun·ter·clock·wise**) *adv., adj.* in the opposite direction to the movement of the hands of a clock: *Turn the key anticlockwise/in an anticlockwise direction.* OPP **clockwise**

anti·coagu·lant /ˌæntikəʊˈægjələnt; *NAmE* -koʊ-/ *noun* (*medical*) a substance that stops the blood from becoming thick and forming CLOTS

anti·con·vul·sant /ˌæntikənˈvʌlsənt/ *noun* a drug used to prevent EPILEPTIC FITS or similar illnesses ▸ **anti·con·vul·sant** *adj.*

antics /ˈæntɪks/ *noun* [pl.] **1** behaviour which is silly and funny in a way that people usually like: *The bank staff got up to all sorts of antics to raise money for charity.* **2** behaviour which is ridiculous or dangerous

anti·cyc·lone /ˌæntiˈsaɪkləʊn; *NAmE* -kloʊn/ *noun* an area of high air pressure that produces calm weather conditions with clear skies ➲ compare DEPRESSION

anti·depres·sant /ˌæntidɪˈpresnt/ *noun* a drug used to treat DEPRESSION ▸ **anti·depres·sant** *adj.* [only before noun]: *antidepressant drugs*

anti·dote /ˈæntidəʊt; *NAmE* -doʊt/ *noun* **1 ~ (to sth)** a substance that controls the effects of a poison or disease: *There is no known antidote to the poison.* **2 ~ (to sth)** anything that takes away the effects of sth unpleasant: *A Mediterranean cruise was the perfect antidote to a long cold winter.*

anti·freeze /ˈæntifriːz/ *noun* [U] a chemical that is added to the water in the RADIATOR of cars and other vehicles to stop it from freezing

anti·gen /ˈæntɪdʒən/ *noun* (*medical*) a substance that enters the body and starts a process that can cause disease. The body then usually produces ANTIBODIES to fight the antigens.

anti·glob·al·iza·tion (*BrE* also **-isa·tion**) /ˌæntiˌɡləʊbəlaɪˈzeɪʃn; *NAmE* -ˌɡloʊbələˈz-/ *noun* [U] opposition to the increase in the power of large international companies and institutions because of the bad effects on the economies of individual countries, especially poorer ones: *antiglobalization protests at the G8 summit* ◇ *the antiglobalization movement*

anti·grav·ity /ˌæntiˈɡrævɪti/ *noun* [U] (*physics*) an imaginary force that works against GRAVITY

ˈ**anti-hero** *noun* the main character in a story, but one who does not have the qualities of a typical hero, and is either more like an ordinary person or is morally bad

anti·his·ta·mine /ˌæntiˈhɪstəmiːn/ *noun* [C, U] a drug used to treat ALLERGIES, especially HAY FEVER: ***antihistamine cream/injections/shots***

A

ˌanti-inˈflam·ma·tory *adj.* (of a drug) used to reduce INFLAMMATION ▶ **anti-inflam·ma·tory** *noun* (*pl.* -ies)

ˈanti-lock *adj.* [only before noun] **anti-lock** BRAKES stop the wheels of a vehicle locking if you have to stop suddenly, and so make the vehicle easier to control: *an anti-lock braking system or ABS*

anti·mat·ter /ˈæntimætə(r)/ *noun* [U] (*physics*) matter that is made up of antiparticles

an·tim·ony /ˈæntɪməni; *NAmE* -moʊni/ *noun* [U] (*symb.* Sb) a chemical element. Antimony is a silver-white metal that breaks easily, used especially in making ALLOYS.

anti·oxi·dant /ˌæntiˈɒksɪdənt; *NAmE* -ˈɑːks-/ *noun* **1** (*biology*) a substance such as VITAMIN C or E that removes dangerous MOLECULES, etc, such as FREE RADICALS from the body **2** (*chemistry*) a substance that helps prevent OXIDATION, especially one used to help prevent stored food products from going bad

anti·par·ticle /ˈæntipɑːtɪkl; *NAmE* -pɑːrt-/ *noun* (*physics*) a very small part of an atom that has the same mass as a normal PARTICLE but the opposite electrical CHARGE

anti·pasto /ˌæntiˈpæstəʊ; *NAmE* -oʊ/ *noun* (*pl.* **anti·pasti** /-ti/) (in Italian cooking) a small amount of food that you eat before the main part of a meal SYN **appetizer, starter**

an·tip·athy /ænˈtɪpəθi/ *noun* [U, C, usually sing.] (*pl.* -ies) ~ (**between A and B**) | ~ (**to/toward(s) sb/sth**) (*formal*) a strong feeling of dislike SYN **hostility**: ***personal/mutual antipathy*** ◇ *a **growing antipathy** towards the idea* ▶ **anti·path·et·ic** /ˌæntɪpəˈθetɪk/ *adj.*: ~ (**to sb/sth**) *antipathetic to change*

ˌanti-personˈnel *adj.* [only before noun] (of weapons) designed to kill or injure people, not to destroy buildings or vehicles, etc.

anti·per·spir·ant /ˌæntiˈpɜːspərənt; *NAmE* -ˈpɜːrs-/ *noun* [U, C] a substance that people use, especially under their arms, to prevent or reduce sweat ➲ see also DEODORANT

the An·tipo·des /ænˈtɪpədiːz/ *noun* [pl.] (*BrE*) a way of referring to Australia and New Zealand, often used in a humorous way ▶ **An·tipo·dean** /ˌæntɪpəˈdiːən/ *adj.*

anti·pro·ton /ˈæntiprəʊtɒn; *NAmE* -proʊtɑːn/ *noun* (*physics*) a PARTICLE that has the same mass as a PROTON, but a negative electrical CHARGE

anti·quar·ian /ˌæntɪˈkweəriən; *NAmE* -ˈkwer-/ *adj.*, *noun*
- ***adj.*** [usually before noun] connected with the study, collection or sale of valuable old objects, especially books
- ***noun*** (also *less frequent* **anti·quary** /ˈæntɪkwəri; *NAmE* -kweri/) a person who studies, collects or sells old and valuable objects

anti·quark /ˈæntikwɑːk; *NAmE* -kwɑːrk/ *noun* (*physics*) the ANTIPARTICLE of a QUARK

anti·quated /ˈæntɪkweɪtɪd/ *adj.* (usually *disapproving*) (of things or ideas) old-fashioned and no longer suitable for modern conditions SYN **outdated**

an·tique /ænˈtiːk/ *adj.*, *noun*
- ***adj.*** [usually before noun] (of furniture, jewellery, etc.) old and often valuable: *an antique mahogany desk*
- ***noun*** an object such as a piece of furniture that is old and often valuable: *Priceless antiques were destroyed in the fire.* ◇ *an antique shop* (= one that sells antiques) ◇ *an antique dealer / antiques dealer* (= a person who sells antiques)

an·tiquity /ænˈtɪkwəti/ *noun* (*pl.* -ies) **1** [U] the ancient past, especially the times of the Greeks and Romans: *The statue was brought to Rome **in antiquity**.* **2** [U] the state of being very old or ancient: *A number of the monuments are of considerable antiquity.* **3** [C, usually pl.] an object from ancient times: *Egyptian/Roman antiquities*

anti·retro·viral /ˌæntiˌretrəʊˈvaɪrəl; *NAmE* -troʊ-/ *adj.* designed to stop viruses such as HIV damaging the body: *antiretroviral drugs*

ˌanti-ˈroll bar *noun* a metal bar that is part of a car's SUSPENSION, which stops the car from leaning too much when it goes around corners

anti-Semitism /ˌænti ˈsemətɪzəm/ *noun* [U] hatred of Jews; unfair treatment of Jews ➲ COLLOCATIONS at RACE ▶ **anti-Semitic** /ˌænti səˈmɪtɪk/ *adj.*: *anti-Semitic propaganda* **anti-Semite** /ˌænti ˈsiːmaɪt/ *noun*: *He was a notorious anti-Semite.*

anti·sep·tic /ˌæntiˈseptɪk/ *noun, adj.*
- ***noun*** [C, U] a substance that helps to prevent infection in wounds by killing bacteria SYN **disinfectant**
- ***adj.*** **1** able to prevent infection: ***antiseptic cream/lotion/wipes*** **2** very clean and free from bacteria SYN **sterile**: *Cover the burn with an antiseptic dressing.*

anti·social /ˌæntiˈsəʊʃl; *NAmE* -ˈsoʊʃl/ *adj.* **1** harmful or annoying to other people, or to society in general: *anti-social behaviour* **2** not wanting to spend time with other people: *They'll think you're being antisocial if you don't go.* ➲ compare SOCIABLE

ˌanti-ˈtank *adj.* [only before noun] (of weapons) for use against enemy tanks: *anti-tank missiles/mines*

an·tith·esis /ænˈtɪθəsɪs/ *noun* [usually sing.] (*pl.* **an·tith·eses** /ænˈtɪθəsiːz/) (*formal*) **1** the opposite of sth: *Love is the antithesis of selfishness.* ◇ *Students finishing their education at 16 is the **very antithesis** of what society needs.* **2** a contrast between two things: *There is an antithesis between the needs of the state and the needs of the people.* ▶ **an·ti·thet·ic·al** /ˌæntɪˈθetɪkl/ *adj.* ~ (**to sth**)

anti·trust /ˌæntiˈtrʌst/ *adj.* [only before noun] (of laws) preventing companies or groups of companies from controlling prices unfairly

anti·viral /ˌæntiˈvaɪrəl/ *adj.* (of a drug) used to treat infectious diseases caused by a virus

anti·virus /ˈæntivaɪrəs/ *adj.* (*computing*) designed to find and destroy computer viruses: *antivirus software*

ant·ler /ˈæntlə(r)/ *noun* [usually pl.] one of the two horns that grow on the head of male DEER ➲ VISUAL VOCAB page V10

ant·onym /ˈæntənɪm/ *noun* (*technical*) a word that means the opposite of another word SYN **opposite**: *'Old' has two possible antonyms: 'young' and 'new'.* ➲ compare SYNONYM

antsy /ˈæntsi/ *adj.* (*NAmE, informal*) impatient; not able to keep still

anus /ˈeɪnəs/ *noun* (*anatomy*) the opening in a person's bottom through which solid waste leaves the body ➲ VISUAL VOCAB page V48 ➲ see also ANAL

anvil /ˈænvɪl/ *noun* an iron block on which a BLACKSMITH puts hot pieces of metal before shaping them with a HAMMER

anx·iety 🔑 /æŋˈzaɪəti/ *noun* (*pl.* -ies) **1** 🔑 [U] ~ (**about/over sth**) the state of feeling nervous or worried that sth bad is going to happen: ***acute/intense/deep anxiety*** ◇ *Some hospital patients experience high levels of anxiety.* **2** 🔑 [C] a worry or fear about sth: *If you're worried about your health, share your anxieties with your doctor.* **3** [U] a strong feeling of wanting to do sth or of wanting sth to happen: ~ **to do sth** *the candidate's anxiety to win the vote* ◇ ~ **for sth** *the people's anxiety for the war to end*

anx·ious 🔑 /ˈæŋkʃəs/ *adj.* **1** 🔑 feeling worried or nervous: ~ (**about sth**) *He seemed anxious about the meeting.* ◇ ~ (**for sb**) *Parents are naturally anxious for their children.* ➲ SYNONYMS at WORRIED **2** 🔑 causing anxiety; showing anxiety: *There were a few anxious moments in the baseball game.* ◇ *an **anxious look/face/expression*** **3** 🔑 wanting sth very much: ~ **to do sth** *She was anxious to finish school and get a job.* ◇ *He was **anxious not to** be misunderstood.* ◇ ~ **for sth** *There are plenty of graduates anxious for work.* ◇ ~ **for sb to do sth** *I'm anxious for her to do as little as possible.* ◇ ~ **that...** *She was anxious that he should meet her father.* ▶ **anx·ious·ly** 🔑 *adv.*: *to **ask/look/wait anxiously*** ◇ *Residents are anxiously awaiting a decision.*

A

any 0-π /'eni/ *det., pron., adv.*
■ ***det.*** **1** 0-π used with uncountable or plural nouns in negative sentences and questions, after *if* or *whether*, and after some verbs such as *prevent, ban, forbid*, etc. to refer to an amount or a number of sth, however large or small: *I didn't eat any meat.* ◇ *Are there any stamps?* ◇ *I've got hardly any money.* ◇ *You can't go out without any shoes.* ◇ *He forbids any talking in class.* ◇ *She asked if we had any questions.* HELP In positive sentences **some** is usually used instead of **any**: *I've got some paper if you want it.* It is also used in questions that expect a positive answer: *Would you like some milk in your tea?* **2** 0-π used with singular countable nouns to refer to one of a number of things or people, when it does not matter which one: *Take any book you like.* ◇ *Any colour will do.* ◇ *Any teacher will tell you that students learn at different rates.* ➲ see also IN ANY CASE at CASE *n.*, IN ANY EVENT at EVENT, AT ANY RATE at RATE *n.* **3 not just ~ sb/sth** used to show that sb/sth is special: *It isn't just any day—it's my birthday!*
■ ***pron.*** **1** 0-π used in negative sentences and in questions and after *if* or *whether* to refer to an amount or a number, however large or small: *We need some more paint; there isn't any left.* ◇ *I need some stamps. Are there any in your bag?* ◇ *Please let me know how many people are coming, if any.* ◇ *She spent hardly any of the money.* ◇ *He returned home without any of the others.* HELP In positive sentences **some** is usually used instead of **any**. It is also used in questions that expect a positive reply: *I've got plenty of paper—would you like some?* **2** 0-π one or more of a number of people or things, especially when it does not matter which: *I'll take any you don't want.* ◇ *'Which colour do you want?' 'Any of them will do.'*
IDM **sb isn't having any (of it)** (*informal*) somebody is not interested or does not agree: *I suggested sharing the cost, but he wasn't having any of it.*
■ ***adv.*** **1** 0-π used to emphasize an adjective or adverb in negative sentences or questions, meaning 'at all': *He wasn't any good at French.* ◇ *I can't run any faster.* ◇ *Is your father feeling any better?* ◇ *I don't want any more.* ◇ *If you don't tell them, nobody will be* ***any the wiser*** (= they will not find out about it). **2** (*NAmE, informal*) used at the end of a negative sentence to mean 'at all': *That won't hurt you any.*

any·body 0-π /'enibɒdi; *NAmE* -bɑːdi; -bʌdi/ *pron.* = ANYONE: *Is there anybody who can help me?* ◇ *Anybody can use the pool—you don't need to be a member.* ◇ *She wasn't anybody before she got that job.*

any·how /'enihaʊ/ *adv.* **1** = ANYWAY **2** in a careless way; not arranged in an order: *She piled the papers in a heap on her desk, just anyhow.*

any 'more (*BrE*) (also **any·more** *NAmE, BrE*) *adv.* often used at the end of negative sentences and at the end of questions, to mean 'any longer': *She doesn't live here any more.* ◇ *Why doesn't he speak to me any more?* ◇ *Now she won't have to go out to work any more.* HELP Do not use 'no more' with this meaning: ~~*She doesn't live here no more.*~~

any·one 0-π /'eniwʌn/ (also **any·body**) *pron.*
1 0-π used instead of *someone* in negative sentences and in questions after *if/whether*, and after verbs such as *prevent, forbid, avoid*, etc.: *Is anyone there?* ◇ *Does anyone else want to come?* ◇ *Did anyone see you?* ◇ *Hardly anyone came.* ◇ *I forbid anyone to touch that clock.* HELP The difference between **anyone** and **someone** is the same as the difference between **any** and **some**. Look at the notes there. **2** 0-π any person at all; it does not matter who: *Anybody can see that it's wrong.* ◇ *The exercises are so simple that almost anyone can do them.* **3** (in negative sentences) an important person: *She wasn't anyone before she got that job.*

any·place /'enipleɪs/ *adv.* (*NAmE*) = ANYWHERE

any·thing 0-π /'eniθɪŋ/ *pron.*
1 0-π used instead of *something* in negative sentences and in questions; after *if/whether*; and after verbs such as *prevent, ban, avoid*, etc.: *Would you like anything else?* ◇ *There's never anything worth watching on TV.* ◇ *If you remember anything at all, please let us know.* ◇ *We hope to prevent anything unpleasant from happening.* HELP The difference between **anything** and **something** is the same as the difference between **any** and **some.** Look at the notes there. **2** 0-π any thing at all, when it does not matter which: *I'm so hungry, I'll eat anything.* **3** any thing of importance: *Is there anything* (= any truth) *in these rumours?*
IDM **anything but** definitely not: *The hotel was anything but cheap.* ◇ *It wasn't cheap. Anything but.* **anything like sb/sth** 0-π (*informal*) (used in questions and negative statements) similar to sb/sth: *He isn't anything like my first boss.* **as happy, quick, etc. as anything** (*informal*) very happy, quick, etc: *I felt as pleased as anything.* **like 'anything** (*BrE, informal*) very much: *They're always slagging me off like anything.* **not anything like as good, much, etc.** used to emphasize that sth is not as good, not enough, etc.: *The book wasn't anything like as good as her first one.* **not for 'anything** (*informal*) definitely not: *I wouldn't give it up for anything.* **or anything** (*informal*) or another thing of a similar type: *If you want to call a meeting or anything, just let me know.*

'any time (*BrE*) (also **any·time** *NAmE, BrE*) *adv.* at a time that is not fixed: *Call me any time.*
IDM **ˌanytime 'soon** (*NAmE*) used in negative sentences and questions to refer to the near future: *Will she be back anytime soon?*

any·way 0-π /'eniweɪ/ (also **any·how**) (also *NAmE informal* **any·ways**) *adv.*
1 0-π used when adding sth to support an idea or argument SYN **besides**: *It's too expensive and anyway the colour doesn't suit you.* ◇ *It's too late now, anyway.* **2** 0-π despite sth; even so: *The water was cold but I took a shower anyway.* ◇ *I'm afraid we can't come, but thanks for the invitation anyway.* **3** 0-π used when changing the subject of a conversation, ending the conversation or returning to a subject: *Anyway, let's forget about that for the moment.* ◇ *Anyway, I'd better go now—I'll see you tomorrow.* **4** 0-π used to correct or slightly change what you have said: *She works in a bank. She did when I last saw her, anyway.*

any·where 0-π /'eniweə(r); *NAmE* -wer/ (*NAmE* also **any·place**) *adv.*
1 0-π used in negative sentences and in questions instead of *somewhere*: *I can't see it anywhere.* ◇ *Did you go anywhere interesting?* ◇ *Many of these animals are not found anywhere else.* ◇ *He's never been anywhere outside Britain.* HELP The difference between **anywhere** and **somewhere** is the same as the difference between **any** and **some**. Look at the notes there. **2** 0-π in, at or to any place, when it does not matter where: *Put the box down anywhere.* ◇ *An accident can happen anywhere.* ▶ **any·where** 0-π *pron.*: *I don't have anywhere to stay.* ◇ *Do you know anywhere I can buy a second-hand computer?*

AOB /ˌeɪ əʊ 'biː; *NAmE* oʊ/ *abbr.* any other business (the things that are discussed at the end of an official meeting that are not on the AGENDA)

A-OK /ˌeɪ əʊ 'keɪ; *NAmE* ˌeɪ oʊ 'keɪ/ *adj.* [not before noun] (*NAmE, informal*) in good condition; in an acceptable manner: *Everything's A-OK now.* ▶ **A-OK** *adv.*: *The party went off A-OK.*

aorta /eɪ'ɔːtə; *NAmE* eɪ'ɔːrtə/ *noun* (*anatomy*) the main ARTERY that carries blood from the heart to the rest of the body once it has passed through the LUNGS

Ao·tea·roa /aʊˌteɪə'rəʊə; *NAmE* -'roʊə/ *noun* (*NZE*) the Maori name for New Zealand, usually translated as 'the land of the long white cloud'

AP /ˌeɪ 'piː/ *abbr.* ASSOCIATED PRESS

apace /ə'peɪs/ *adv.* (*formal*) at a fast speed; quickly: *to* ***continue/grow/proceed/develop apace***

Apa·che /ə'pætʃi/ *noun* (*pl.* **Apa·che** or **Apa·ches**) a member of a Native American people, many of whom live in the south-western US

apart 0-π /ə'pɑːt; *NAmE* ə'pɑːrt/ *adv.*
1 0-π separated by a distance, of space or time: *The two houses stood 500 metres apart.* ◇ *Their birthdays are only three days apart.* ◇ (*figurative*) *The two sides in the talks are still a long way apart* (= are far from reaching an agreement). **2** 0-π not together; separate or separately: *We're living apart now.* ◇ *Over the years, Rosie and I had* ***drifted***

apart. ◇ *She keeps herself apart from other people.* ◇ *I can't* **tell** *the twins* **apart** (= see the difference between them). **3** ⊶ into pieces: *The whole thing just* **came apart** *in my hands.* ◇ *We had to* **take** *the engine* **apart**. ◇ *When his wife died, his world* **fell apart**. **4** used to say that sb/sth is not included in what you are talking about: *Victoria apart, not one of them seems suitable for the job.* IDM see JOKE *v.*, POLE *n.*, RIP *v.*, WORLD

a'part from ⊶ (also **a'side from** especially in *NAmE*) *prep.*
1 ⊶ except for: *I've finished apart from the last question.* ➲ LANGUAGE BANK at EXCEPT **2** ⊶ in addition to; as well as: *Apart from their house in London, they also have a villa in Spain.* ◇ *It was a difficult time. Apart from everything else, we had financial problems.* ◇ *You've got to help. Apart from anything else you're my brother.* ➲ note at BESIDES

apart·heid /ə'pɑːtaɪt; -eɪt; *NAmE* ə'pɑːrtaɪt; -eɪt/ *noun* [U] the former political system in South Africa in which only white people had full political rights and other people, especially black people, were forced to live away from white people, go to separate schools, etc.

apart·ment ⊶ /ə'pɑːtmənt; *NAmE* ə'pɑːrt-/ *noun*
1 ⊶ (*especially NAmE*) a set of rooms for living in, usually on one floor of a building ➲ COLLOCATIONS at HOUSE ➲ compare CONDOMINIUM, FLAT **2** ⊶ a set of rooms used for a holiday/vacation: *self-catering holiday apartments* **3** [usually pl.] (*BrE*) a room in a house, especially a large or famous house: *You can visit the whole palace except for the private apartments.*

a'partment block (*BrE*) (*NAmE* **a'partment building**) *noun* a large building with flats/apartments on each floor ➲ VISUAL VOCAB page V14

a'partment house *noun* (*US*) a small apartment block

apa·thet·ic /ˌæpə'θetɪk/ *adj.* showing no interest or enthusiasm: *The illness made her apathetic and unwilling to meet people.* ▸ **apa·thet·ic·al·ly** /ˌæpə'θetɪkli/ *adv.*

ap·athy /'æpəθi/ *noun* [U] the feeling of not being interested in or enthusiastic about something, or things in general: *There is* **widespread apathy** *among the electorate.*

apato·saurus /əˌpætə'sɔːrəs/ (also **bron·to·saurus**) *noun* a very large DINOSAUR with a long neck and tail

APB /ˌeɪ piː 'biː/ *abbr.* (*NAmE*) ALL-POINTS BULLETIN

ape /eɪp/ *noun, verb*
■ ***noun*** a large animal like a MONKEY, with no tail. There are different types of ape: *the great apes* (= for example, ORANG-UTANS or CHIMPANZEES)
IDM **go 'ape/'apeshit** (*slang, especially NAmE*) to become extremely angry or excited
■ ***verb*** **1 ~ sb/sth** (*BrE, disapproving*) to do sth in the same way as sb else, especially when it is not done very well SYN **imitate**: *For years the British film industry merely aped Hollywood.* **2 ~ sb/sth** (*especially NAmE*) to copy the way sb else behaves or talks, in order to make fun of them SYN **mimic**: *We used to ape the teacher's southern accent.*

ape·man /'eɪpmæn/ *noun* (*pl.* **-men** /-men/) a large animal, half way between an APE and a human

aperi·tif /əˌperə'tiːf/ *noun* (*especially BrE*) a drink, usually one containing alcohol, that people sometimes have just before a meal

aper·ture /'æpətʃə(r); *NAmE* also -tʃʊr/ *noun* **1** (*formal*) a small opening in sth **2** (*technical*) an opening that allows light to reach a LENS, especially in cameras: *For flash photography, set the aperture at f.5.6.*

ape·shit /'eɪpʃɪt/ *noun*
IDM **go 'apeshit** ➲ APE

Apex /'eɪpeks/ (also **APEX**) *abbr.* Advanced Purchase Excursion (a system that offers cheaper travel tickets when they are bought in advance)

apex /'eɪpeks/ *noun* [usually sing.] (*pl.* **apexes**) the top or highest part of sth: *the apex of the roof/triangle* ◇ (*figurative*) *At 37, she'd reached the apex of her career.*

apha·sia /ə'feɪziə/ *noun* [U] (*medical*) the loss of the ability to understand or produce speech, because of brain damage

aphid /'eɪfɪd/ *noun* a very small insect that is harmful to plants. There are several types of aphid, including, for example, GREENFLY.

aph·or·ism /'æfərɪzəm/ *noun* (*formal*) a short phrase that says sth true or wise ▸ **aph·or·is·tic** /ˌæfə'rɪstɪk/ *adj.*

aph·ro·dis·iac /ˌæfrə'dɪziæk/ *noun* a food or drug that is said to give people a strong desire to have sex ▸ **aph·ro·dis·iac** *adj.*: *the aphrodisiac qualities of ginseng*

api·ary /'eɪpiəri; *NAmE* -ieri/ *noun* (*pl.* **-ies**) a place where BEES are kept

apiece /ə'piːs/ *adv.* (used after a noun or number) having, costing or measuring a particular amount each: *Rooney and Walcott scored a goal apiece.* ◇ *The largest stones weigh over five tonnes apiece.*

aplenty /ə'plenti/ *adv., adj.* [after noun] (*formal*) in large amounts, especially more than is needed

aplomb /ə'plɒm; *NAmE* ə'plɑːm/ *noun* [U] (*formal*) if sb does sth **with aplomb**, they do it in a confident and successful way, often in a difficult situation: *with* **considerable/great/remarkable aplomb** ◇ *He delivered the speech with his* **usual aplomb**.

ap·noea (*BrE*) (*NAmE* **ap·nea**) /æp'niːə/ *noun* [U] (*medical*) a condition in which sb stops breathing temporarily while they are sleeping

apoca·lypse /ə'pɒkəlɪps; *NAmE* ə'pɑːk-/ *noun* **1** [sing., U] the destruction of the world: *Civilization is on the brink of apocalypse.* **2 the Apocalypse** [sing.] the end of the world, as described in the Bible **3** [sing.] a situation causing very serious damage and destruction: *an environmental apocalypse*

apoca·lyp·tic /əˌpɒkə'lɪptɪk; *NAmE* əˌpɑːk-/ *adj.* **1** describing very serious damage and destruction in past or future events: *an apocalyptic view of history* ◇ *apocalyptic warnings of the end of society* **2** like the end of the world: *an apocalyptic scene*

apoc·rypha /ə'pɒkrɪfə; *NAmE* ə'pɑːk-/ *noun* [pl.] **1 Apocrypha** Christian religious texts that are related to the Bible but not officially considered to be part of it **2** writings which are not considered to be genuine

apoc·ryph·al /ə'pɒkrɪfl; *NAmE* ə'pɑːk-/ *adj.* (of a story) well known, but probably not true: *Most of the stories about him are apocryphal.*

apo·gee /'æpədʒiː/ *noun* [sing.] **1** (*formal*) the highest point of sth, where it is greatest or most successful **2** (*astronomy*) the point in the ORBIT of the moon, a planet or other object in space when it is furthest from the planet, for example the earth, around which it turns ➲ compare PERIGEE

apol·it·ical /ˌeɪpə'lɪtɪkl/ *adj.* **1** (of a person) not interested in politics; not thinking politics are important **2** not connected with a political party

Apol·lo·nian /ˌæpə'ləʊniən; *NAmE* -'loʊ-/ *adj.* **1** connected with the ancient Greek god Apollo **2** (*formal*) connected with the controlled and reasonable aspects of human nature ➲ compare DIONYSIAC

apolo·get·ic /əˌpɒlə'dʒetɪk; *NAmE* əˌpɑːl-/ *adj.* feeling or showing that you are sorry for doing sth wrong or for causing a problem: *'Sorry,' she said, with an apologetic smile.* ◇ **~ about/for sth** *They were very apologetic about the trouble they'd caused.* ▸ **apolo·get·ic·al·ly** /əˌpɒlə'dʒetɪkli; *NAmE* əˌpɑːl-/ *adv.*: *'I'm sorry I'm late,' he murmured apologetically.*

apo·lo·gia /ˌæpə'ləʊdʒiə; *NAmE* -'loʊ-/ *noun* (*formal*) a formal written defence of your own or sb else's actions or opinions: *His book was seen as an apologia for the war.*

apolo·gist /ə'pɒlədʒɪst; *NAmE* ə'pɑːl-/ *noun* **~ (for sb/sth)** a person who tries to explain and defend sth, especially a political system or religious ideas

apolo·gize ⊶ (*BrE* also **-ise**) /ə'pɒlədʒaɪz; *NAmE* ə'pɑːl-/ *verb* [I]
~ (to sb) (for sth) to say that you are sorry for doing sth

wrong or causing a problem: *Why should I apologize?* ◇ *Go and apologize to her.* ◇ *We apologize for the late departure of this flight.*

apol·ogy /ə'pɒlədʒi; *NAmE* ə'pɑːl-/ *noun* (*pl.* -ies) **1** [C, U] **~ (to sb) (for sth)** a word or statement saying sorry for sth that has been done wrong or that causes a problem: *to **offer/make/demand/accept an apology*** ◇ *You **owe him an apology** for what you said.* ◇ *We should like to offer our apologies for the delay to your flight today.* ◇ *We received a letter of apology.* **2** [C, usually pl.] information that you cannot go to a meeting or must leave early: *The meeting started with apologies* (= the names of people who said they could not go to the meeting). ◇ (*formal*) *She **made her apologies** and left early.*
IDM **make no a'pology/a'pologies for sth** if you say that you **make no apology/apologies for** sth, you mean that you do not feel that you have said or done anything wrong

apo·plec·tic /ˌæpə'plektɪk/ *adj.* **1** very angry: *He was apoplectic with rage at the decision.* **2** (*old-fashioned*) connected with apoplexy: *an **apoplectic attack/fit***

apo·plexy /'æpəpleksi/ *noun* [U] (*old-fashioned*) the sudden loss of the ability to feel or move caused by an injury in the brain SYN **a stroke**

aporia /ə'pɔːriə/ *noun* (*technical*) a situation in which two or more parts of a theory or argument do not agree, meaning that the theory or argument cannot be true

apos·tate /ə'pɒsteɪt; *NAmE* ə'pɑːs-/ *noun* (*formal*) a person who has rejected their religious or political beliefs ▸ **apos·tasy** /ə'pɒstəsi; *NAmE* ə'pɑːs-/ *noun* [U]

a pos·teri·ori /ˌeɪ ˌpɒsteri'ɔːraɪ; *NAmE* ˌpɑːs-/ *adj., adv.* (from *Latin, formal*) analysing sth by starting from known facts and then thinking about the possible causes of the facts, for example saying 'Look, the streets are wet so it must have been raining.' ➲ compare A PRIORI

apos·tle /ə'pɒsl; *NAmE* ə'pɑːsl/ *noun* **1 Apostle** any one of the twelve men that Christ chose to tell people about him and his teachings **2 ~ (of sth)** (*formal*) a person who strongly believes in a policy or an idea and tries to make other people believe in it: *an apostle of free enterprise*

apos·tolic /ˌæpə'stɒlɪk; *NAmE* -'stɑːlɪk/ *adj.* (*technical*) **1** connected with the Apostles or their teaching **2** connected with the Pope or Popes, who are considered to have had authority passed down to them from Christ's Apostles

apos·tro·phe /ə'pɒstrəfi; *NAmE* ə'pɑːs-/ *noun* **1** the mark (') used to show that one or more letters or numbers have been left out, as in *she's* for *she is* and *'63* for *1963* **2** the mark (') used before or after the letter 's' to show that sth belongs to sb, as in *Sam's watch* and *the horses' tails* **3** the mark (') used before the letter 's' to show the plural of a letter or number, as in *How many 3's are there in 9?* and *There are two m's in 'comma'.*

apos·tro·phize (*BrE* also **-ise**) /ə'pɒstrəfaɪz; *NAmE* ə'pɑːs-/ *verb* **1 ~ sb** to address what you are saying, or a poem, a speech in a play, etc. to a particular person **2 ~ sth** to add apostrophes to a piece of writing

apoth·ecary /ə'pɒθəkəri; *NAmE* ə'pɑːθəkeri/ *noun* (*pl.* -ies) a person who made and sold medicines in the past

apothe·osis /əˌpɒθi'əʊsɪs; *NAmE* əˌpɑːθi'oʊ-/ *noun* [usually sing.] (*pl.* **apothe·oses** /-siːz/) (*formal*) **1** the highest or most perfect development of sth **2** the best time in sb's life or career **3** a formal statement that a person has become a god: *the apotheosis of a Roman emperor*

app /æp/ *abbr.* APPLICATION

appa /'ʌpə/ *noun* (*IndE*) = ABBA

appal (*BrE*) (*NAmE* **ap·pall**) /ə'pɔːl/ *verb* (-ll-) to shock sb very much SYN **horrify**: **~ sb** *The brutality of the crime has appalled the public.* ◇ *The idea of sharing a room appalled her.* ◇ **it appals sb that.../to do sth** *It appalled me that they could simply ignore the problem.*

ap·palled /ə'pɔːld/ *adj.* feeling or showing horror or disgust at sth unpleasant or wrong SYN **horrified**: *an **appalled expression/silence*** ◇ *We watched appalled as the child ran in front of the car.* ◇ **~ at sth** *They were appalled at the waste of recyclable material.*

ap·pal·ling /ə'pɔːlɪŋ/ *adj.* **1** (*NAmE, formal* or *BrE*) shocking; extremely bad: *The prisoners were living in appalling conditions.* **2** (*informal*) very bad: *The bus service is appalling now.* ▸ **ap·pal·ling·ly** *adv.*: ***appallingly bad/difficult*** ◇ *The essay was appallingly written.*

app·ar·at /ˌæpə'rɑːt/ *noun* [usually sing.] the system of officials, offices, etc. that a government, especially a Communist government, uses to run a country

ap·par·at·chik /ˌæpə'rɑːtʃɪk/ *noun* (from *Russian, disapproving* or *humorous*) an official in a large political organization: *party apparatchiks*

ap·par·atus /ˌæpə'reɪtəs; *NAmE* -'rætəs/ *noun* (*pl.* **ap·par·atuses**) **1** [U] the tools or other pieces of equipment that are needed for a particular activity or task: *a piece of laboratory apparatus* ◇ *Firefighters needed breathing apparatus to enter the burning house.* ➲ SYNONYMS at EQUIPMENT **2** [C, usually sing.] the structure of a system or an organization, particularly that of a political party or a government: *the power of the state apparatus* **3** [C, usually sing.] (*technical*) a system of organs in the body: *the sensory apparatus*

ap·parel /ə'pærəl/ *noun* [U] **1** (*especially NAmE*) clothing, when it is being sold in shops/stores: *The store sells women's and children's apparel.* **2** (*old-fashioned* or *formal*) clothes, particularly those worn on a formal occasion: *lords and ladies in fine apparel*

ap·par·ent 0-w AW /ə'pærənt/ *adj.*
1 0-w [not usually before noun] easy to see or understand SYN **obvious**: *Their devotion was apparent.* ◇ *Then, **for no apparent reason**, the train suddenly stopped.* ◇ **~ (from sth) (that...)** *It was apparent from her face that she was really upset.* ◇ **~ (to sb) (that...)** ***It** soon **became apparent** to everyone that he couldn't sing.* ➲ SYNONYMS at CLEAR ➲ LANGUAGE BANK at ILLUSTRATE **2** 0-w [usually before noun] that seems to be real or true but may not be SYN **seeming**: *My parents were concerned at my apparent lack of enthusiasm for school.* ➲ see also APPEAR

ap·par·ent·ly 0-w AW /ə'pærəntli/ *adv.*
according to what you have heard or read; according to the way sth appears: *Apparently they are getting divorced soon.* ◇ *I thought she had retired, but apparently she hasn't.* ◇ *He paused, apparently lost in thought.*

ap·par·ition /ˌæpə'rɪʃn/ *noun* a GHOST or an image of a person who is dead

ap·peal 0-w /ə'piːl/ *noun, verb*
■ ***noun*** **1** 0-w [C, U] a formal request to a court or to sb in authority for a judgement or a decision to be changed: (*BrE*) *to lodge an appeal* ◇ (*NAmE*) *to file an appeal* ◇ (*BrE*) *an appeal court/judge* ◇ (*NAmE*) *an appeals court/judge* ◇ **~ against sth** *an appeal against the 3-match ban* ➲ COLLOCATIONS at JUSTICE ➲ see also COURT OF APPEAL **2** 0-w [U] a quality that makes sb/sth attractive or interesting: ***mass/wide/popular appeal*** ◇ *The Beatles have never really **lost their appeal**.* ◇ *The prospect of living in a city **holds little appeal** for me.* ➲ see also SEX APPEAL **3** 0-w [C, U] an urgent and deeply felt request for money, help or information, especially one made by a charity or by the police: *a look of silent appeal* ◇ **~ (to sb) (for sth)** *to launch a TV appeal for donations to the charity* ◇ *The child's mother made an emotional appeal on TV for his return.* ◇ **~ to sb to do sth** *The police made an appeal to the public to remain calm.* **4** [C] **~ to sth** an indirect suggestion that any good, fair or reasonable person would act in a particular way: *I relied on an appeal to his finer feelings.*
■ ***verb*** **1** 0-w [I] **~ (to sb/sth) (against sth)** to make a formal request to a court or to sb in authority for a judgement or a decision to be changed: *He said he would appeal after being found guilty on four counts of murder.* ◇ *The company is appealing against the ruling.* HELP In North American English, the form **appeal (sth) (to sb/sth)** is usually used, without a preposition: *The company has ten days to appeal the decision to the tribunal.* **2** 0-w [I] to attract or interest sb: *The prospect of a long wait in the rain did not appeal.* ◇ **~ to sb** *The design has to appeal to all ages and social groups.*

3 🗝 [I] to make a serious and urgent request: *I am appealing* (= asking for money) *on behalf of the famine victims.* ◇ **~ (to sb) (for sth)** *Community leaders appealed for calm* (= urged people to remain calm). ◇ *Police have appealed for witnesses to come forward.* ◇ **~ to sb to do sth** *Organizers appealed to the crowd not to panic.* **4** [I] **~ (to sth)** to try to persuade sb to do sth by suggesting that it is a fair, reasonable or honest thing to do: *They needed to appeal to his sense of justice.*

ap'peal court *noun* **1** = COURT OF APPEAL **2 Ap'peals Court** [C] (*US*) = COURT OF APPEALS

ap·peal·ing /ə'piːlɪŋ/ *adj.* **1** attractive or interesting: *Spending the holidays in Britain wasn't a prospect that I found particularly appealing.* OPP **unappealing 2** showing that you want people to help you or to show you pity or sympathy: *'Would you really help?' he said with an appealing look.* ▶ **ap·peal·ing·ly** *adv.*: *The dog looked up at her appealingly.*

ap·pear 🗝 /ə'pɪə(r); *NAmE* ə'pɪr/ *verb*
▸ LOOK/SEEM **1** 🗝 *linking verb* (not used in the progressive tenses) to give the impression of being or doing sth SYN **seem: + adj.** *She didn't appear at all surprised at the news.* ◇ ***It appears** unlikely that interest rates will fall further.* ◇ **+ noun** *He appears a perfectly normal person.* ◇ **~ to do sth** *She appeared to be in her late thirties.* ◇ *They appeared not to know what was happening.* ◇ *There appears to have been a mistake.* ◇ **it appears (that)...** *It appears that there has been a mistake.* ◇ ***It would appear that** this was a major problem.* ➲ LANGUAGE BANK at PERHAPS
▸ BE SEEN **2** 🗝 [I] to start to be seen: *Three days later a rash appeared.* ◇ **+ adv./prep.** *A bus appeared around the corner.* ◇ *Smoke appeared on the horizon.*
▸ BEGIN TO EXIST **3** 🗝 [I] (**+ adv./prep.**) to begin to exist or be known or used for the first time: *When did mammals appear on the earth?* ◇ *This problem first appeared in the inner cities.*
▸ OF BOOK/PROGRAMME **4** [I] (**+ adv./prep.**) to be published or broadcast: *His new book will be appearing in the spring.* ◇ *It was too late to prevent the story from appearing in the national newspapers.*
▸ IN MOVIE/PLAY **5** [I] (**+ adv./prep.**) to take part in a film/movie, play, television programme, etc: *He has appeared in over 60 movies.* ◇ *She regularly appears on TV.* ◇ *Next month he will be appearing as Obama in a new play on Broadway.*
▸ ARRIVE **6** [I] (**+ adv./prep.**) to arrive at a place: *By ten o'clock Lee still hadn't appeared.*
▸ BE WRITTEN/MENTIONED **7** [I] (**+ adv./prep.**) to be written or mentioned somewhere: *Your name will appear at the front of the book.*
▸ IN COURT **8** [I] (**+ adv./prep.**) to be present in court in order to give evidence or answer a charge: *A man will appear in court today charged with the murder.* ◇ *She appeared on six charges of theft.* ◇ *He has been asked to appear as a witness for the defence.* **9** [I] **~ for/on behalf of sb** to act as sb's lawyer in court: *Cherie Booth is the lawyer appearing for the defendant.* ➲ compare DISAPPEAR ➲ see also APPARENT

ap·pear·ance 🗝 /ə'pɪərəns; *NAmE* ə'pɪr-/ *noun*
▸ WAY STH LOOKS/SEEMS **1** 🗝 [C, U] the way that sb/sth looks on the outside; what sb/sth seems to be: *the **physical/outward/external appearance** of sth* ◇ *She had never been greatly concerned about her appearance.* ◇ *The dog was similar in general appearance to a spaniel.* ◇ *He **gave every appearance of*** (= seemed very much to be) *enjoying himself.* ◇ *Judging by appearances can be misleading.* ◇ ***To all appearances*** (= as far as people could tell) *he was dead.* ◇ *When she lost all her money, she was determined to **keep up appearances*** (= hide the true situation and pretend that everything was going well).
▸ SB/STH ARRIVING **2** 🗝 [C, usually sing.] the fact of sb/sth arriving, especially when it is not expected: *The sudden appearance of a security guard caused them to drop the money and run.* ◇ *I don't want to go to the party, but I suppose I'd better **put in an appearance*** (= go there for a short time).
3 🗝 [C, usually sing.] the moment at which sth begins to exist or starts to be seen or used: *the early appearance of daffodils in spring* ◇ *the appearance of organic vegetables in the supermarkets*
▸ IN PUBLIC **4** [C] an act of appearing in public, especially as a performer, politician, etc, or in court: *The Dutch player will make his first appearance for Liverpool this Saturday.* ◇ *The singer's first public appearance was at the age of eight.* ◇ *the defendant's appearance in court*
▸ BEING PUBLISHED/BROADCAST **5** [C, usually sing.] an act of being published or broadcast: *the appearance of claims about the minister's private life in the press*

ap·pease /ə'piːz/ *verb* (*formal*, usually *disapproving*) **1 ~ sb** to make sb calmer or less angry by giving them what they want: *The move was widely seen as an attempt to appease critics of the regime.* **2 ~ sb/sth** to give a country what it wants in order to avoid war ▶ **ap·pease·ment** *noun* [U]: *a policy of appeasement*

ap·pel·lant /ə'pelənt/ *noun* (*law*) a person who appeals against a decision made in court

ap·pel·late court /ə'pelət kɔːt; *NAmE* kɔːrt/ *noun* (*technical*) a court in which people can appeal against decisions made in other courts of law

ap·pel·la·tion /ˌæpə'leɪʃn/ *noun* (*formal*) a name or title

ap·pel·la·tive /ə'pelətɪv/ *adj.*, *noun*
■ ***adj.*** (*formal*) relating to the giving of a name
■ ***noun*** (*technical*) a common noun that is used to address a person or thing, for example 'mother' or 'doctor'

ap·pend AW /ə'pend/ *verb* **~ sth (to sth)** (*formal*) to add sth to the end of a piece of writing: *Footnotes have been appended to the document.*

ap·pend·age /ə'pendɪdʒ/ *noun* (*formal*) a smaller or less important part of sth larger

ap·pend·ec·tomy /ˌæpen'dektəmi/ *noun* [C, U] (*pl.* **-ies**) (*medical*) the removal of the APPENDIX by SURGERY

ap·pen·di·citis /əˌpendə'saɪtɪs/ *noun* [U] a painful swelling of the appendix that can be very serious

ap·pen·dix AW /ə'pendɪks/ *noun* (*pl.* **ap·pen·di·ces** /-dɪsiːz/ or **ap·pen·dixes**) **1** a small bag of TISSUE that is attached to the large INTESTINE. In humans, the appendix has no clear function: *He had to have his appendix out* (= removed). ➲ VISUAL VOCAB page V48 **2** a section giving extra information at the end of a book or document: *Full details are given in Appendix 3.*

ap·per·tain /ˌæpə'teɪn; *NAmE* -pər't-/ *verb*
PHR V **apper'tain to sb/sth** (*formal*) to belong or refer to sb/sth: *rights appertaining to the property* ◇ *These figures appertain to last year's sales.*

ap·pe·tite /'æpɪtaɪt/ *noun* **1** [U, C, usually sing.] physical desire for food: *He suffered from headaches and **loss of appetite**.* ◇ *The walk gave me a good appetite.* ◇ *Don't **spoil your appetite** by eating between meals.* **2** [C] a strong desire for sth: *sexual appetites* ◇ *The preview was intended to **whet your appetite*** (= make you want more). ◇ **~ for sth** *The public have an insatiable appetite for scandal.*

ap·pet·izer (*BrE* also **-iser**) /'æpɪtaɪzə(r)/ *noun* a small amount of food or a drink that you have before a meal

ap·pe·tiz·ing (*BrE* also **-is·ing**) /'æpɪtaɪzɪŋ/ *adj.* (of food, etc.) that smells or looks attractive; making you feel hungry or thirsty OPP **unappetizing**

ap·plaud /ə'plɔːd/ *verb* **1** [I, T] to show your approval of sb/sth by clapping your hands: *He started to applaud and the others joined in.* ◇ **~ sb** *They rose to applaud the speaker.* ◇ *She was applauded as she came on stage.* **2** [T] (*formal*) to express praise for sb/sth because you approve of them or it: **~ sth** *We applaud her decision.* ◇ *His efforts to improve the situation are to be applauded.* ◇ **~ sb (for sth)** *I applaud her for having the courage to refuse.*

ap·plause /ə'plɔːz/ *noun* [U] the noise made by a group of people clapping their hands and sometimes shouting to show their approval or enjoyment: *Give her a big **round of applause**!* ◇ *The audience broke into rapturous applause.*

apple 🗝 /'æpl/ *noun*
a round fruit with shiny red or green skin and firm white flesh: *an apple pie* ◇ *apple sauce* ◇ *a garden with three apple*

trees ➲ VISUAL VOCAB page V26 ➲ see also ADAM'S APPLE, BIG APPLE, COOKING APPLE, CRAB APPLE, EATING APPLE, TOFFEE APPLE

IDM **the apple doesn't fall/never falls far from the 'tree** (*saying, especially NAmE*) a child usually behaves in a similar way to his or her parent(s) **the ˌapple of sb's 'eye** a person or thing that is loved more than any other **ˌapples and 'oranges** (*NAmE*) used to describe a situation in which two people or things are completely different from each other: *They really are apples and oranges.* ◇ *They are both great but* ***you can't compare apples and oranges.*** ➲ more at AMERICAN *adj.*, ROTTEN

'apple cart *noun* IDM see UPSET *v.*

ˌapple 'pie *noun* **1** [C, U] apples baked in a dish with PASTRY on the bottom, sides and top: *a slice of apple pie* **2** [U] (*NAmE*) used to represent an idea of perfect home life and comfort: *Who could argue against* ***motherhood and apple pie?*** IDM see AMERICAN *adj.*

ap·plet /'æplət/ *noun* (*computing*) a program that is run from within another program, for example from within an Internet BROWSER

ap·pli·ance /ə'plaɪəns/ *noun* a machine that is designed to do a particular thing in the home, such as preparing food, heating or cleaning: ***electrical/household appliances*** ◇ *They sell a wide range of* ***domestic appliances****—washing machines, dishwashers and so on.* ➲ VISUAL VOCAB page V22

ap·plic·able /ə'plɪkəbl; 'æplɪkəbl/ *adj.* [not usually before noun] that can be said to be true in the case of sb/sth SYN **relevant**: *Give details of children where applicable* (= if you have any). ◇ **~ to sb/sth** *Much of the form was not applicable* (= did not apply) *to me.* ▶ **ap·plic·abil·ity** /əˌplɪkə'bɪləti; ˌæplɪk-/ *noun* [U]: *The new approach had wide applicability to all sorts of different problems.*

ap·pli·cant /'æplɪkənt/ *noun* **~ (for sth)** a person who makes a formal request for sth (= applies for it), especially for a job, a place at a college or university, etc: *There were over 500 applicants for the job.*

ap·pli·ca·tion 🔑 /ˌæplɪ'keɪʃn/ *noun*

▸ FOR JOB/COURSE **1** 🔑 [C, U] a formal (often written) request for sth, such as a job, permission to do sth or a place at a college or university: *a planning/passport application* ◇ *an* ***application form*** (= a piece of paper on which to apply for sth) ◇ **~ for sth/to do sth** *an application for membership/a loan/a licence* ◇ **~ to sb (for sth/to do sth)** *His application to the court for bail has been refused.* ◇ *Further information is available* ***on application*** *to the principal.* ➲ COLLOCATIONS at JOB

▸ PRACTICAL USE **2** 🔑 [U, C] **~ (of sth) (to sth)** the practical use of sth, especially a theory, discovery, etc: *the application of new technology to teaching* ◇ *The invention would have a wide range of applications in industry.*

▸ OF PAINT/CREAM **3** [C, U] an act of putting or spreading sth, such as paint or medical creams, onto sth else: *lotion for external application only* (= to be put on the skin, not swallowed) ◇ *It took three applications of paint to cover the graffiti.*

▸ OF RULE/LAW **4** [U] the act of making a rule, etc. operate or become effective: *strict application of the law*

▸ COMPUTING **5** [C] (*abbr.* **app**) a program designed to do a particular job; a piece of software: *a database application* ◇ *to download an app* ➲ VISUAL VOCAB page V55 ➲ see also KILLER APPLICATION

▸ HARD WORK **6** [U] (*formal*) determination to work hard at sth; great effort: *Success as a writer demands great application.*

ap·pli·ca·tor /'æplɪkeɪtə(r)/ *noun* a small tool that is used to put a substance onto a surface, or to put sth into an object: *Use the applicator to apply cream to the affected area.* ➲ VISUAL VOCAB page V49

ap·plied /ə'plaɪd/ *adj.* [usually before noun] (especially of a subject of study) used in a practical way; not THEORETICAL: *applied mathematics* (= as used by engineers, etc.) ➲ compare PURE (7)

apˌplied lin'guistics *noun* [U] the scientific study of language as it relates to practical problems, in areas such as teaching and dealing with speech problems

ap·pli·qué /ə'pliːkeɪ; *NAmE* ˌæplə'keɪ/ *noun* [U] a type of NEEDLEWORK in which small pieces of cloth are sewn or stuck in a pattern onto a larger piece ▶ **ap·pli·quéd** *adj.*

apply 🔑 /ə'plaɪ/ *verb* (**ap·plies, ap·ply·ing, ap·plied, ap·plied**)

▸ FOR JOB/COURSE **1** 🔑 [I, T] to make a formal request, usually in writing, for sth such as a job, a place at college, university, etc: *You should* ***apply in person/by letter.*** ◇ **~ for sth** *to apply for a job/passport/grant* ◇ **~ to sb/sth (for sth)** *to apply to a company/university* ◇ **~ to do sth** *He has applied to join the army.*

▸ USE **2** 🔑 [T] to use sth or make sth work in a particular situation: **~ sth** *to apply economic sanctions/political pressure* ◇ **~ sth to sth** *The new technology was applied to farming.*

▸ PAINT/CREAM **3** 🔑 [T] **~ sth (to sth)** to put or spread sth such as paint, cream, etc. onto a surface: *Apply the cream sparingly to your face and neck.*

▸ BE RELEVANT **4** 🔑 [I, T] (not used in the progressive tenses) to concern or relate to sb/sth: *Special conditions apply if you are under 18.* ◇ **~ to sb/sth** *What I am saying applies only to some of you.* ◇ **~ sth to sb/sth** *The word 'unexciting' could never be applied to her novels.*

▸ WORK HARD **5** [T] to work at sth or study sth very hard: **~ yourself** *You would pass your exams if you applied yourself.* ◇ **~ yourself/sth to sth/to doing sth** *We applied our minds to finding a solution to our problem.*

▸ PRESS HARD **6** [T] to press on sth hard with your hand, foot, etc. to make sth work or have an effect on sth: **~ sth** *to apply the brakes (of a vehicle)* ◇ **~ sth to sth** *Pressure applied to the wound will stop the bleeding.*

ap·point 🔑 /ə'pɔɪnt/ *verb*

1 🔑 to choose sb for a job or position of responsibility: **~ sb** *They have appointed a new head teacher at my son's school.* ◇ **~ sb to sth** *She has recently been appointed to the committee.* ◇ **~ sb + noun | ~ sb as sth** *They appointed him (as) captain of the English team.* ◇ **~ sb to do sth** *A lawyer was appointed to represent the child.* **2** [usually passive] **~ sth** (*formal*) to arrange or decide on a time or place for doing sth: *A date for the meeting is still to be appointed.* ◇ *Everyone was assembled at the* ***appointed time.***

ap·point·ee /əˌpɔɪn'tiː/ *noun* a person who has been chosen for a job or position of responsibility: *the new appointee to the post*

ap·point·ment 🔑 /ə'pɔɪntmənt/ *noun*

1 🔑 [C] a formal arrangement to meet or visit sb at a particular time, especially for a reason connected with their work: *I've got a* ***dental appointment*** *at 3 o'clock.* ◇ *to make/keep an appointment* ◇ *Viewing is* ***by appointment only*** (= only at a time that has been arranged in advance). ◇ **~ with sb** *an appointment with my lawyer* ◇ **~ for sth** *an appointment for a blood test* ◇ **~ for sb to do sth** *She* ***made an appointment*** *for her son to see the doctor.* **2** 🔑 [C, U] **~ (as/to sth)** the act of choosing a person for a job or position of responsibility; the fact of being chosen for a job, etc: *her recent appointment to the post* ◇ *his appointment as principal* **3** [C] (*especially BrE*) a job or position of responsibility: *a permanent/first appointment* ➲ SYNONYMS at JOB

ap·por·tion /ə'pɔːʃn; *NAmE* ə'pɔːrʃn/ *verb* (*formal*) to divide sth among people; to give a share of sth to sb: **~ sth** *The programme gives the facts but does not* ***apportion blame.*** ◇ **~ sth among/between/to sb** *They apportioned the land among members of the family.* ▶ **ap·por·tion·ment** *noun* [U, sing.] (*formal*): *The apportionment of seats in the House of Representatives is based on the population of each state.*

ap·po·site /'æpəzɪt/ *adj.* **~ (to sth)** (*formal*) very appropriate for a particular situation or in relation to sth

ap·pos·ition /ˌæpə'zɪʃn/ *noun* [U] (*grammar*) the use of a noun phrase immediately after another noun phrase that refers to the same person or thing: *In the phrase 'Paris, the capital of France', 'the capital of France' is in apposition to 'Paris'.*

A

ap·prais·al /ə'preɪzl/ *noun* [C, U] **1** a judgement of the value, performance or nature of sb/sth: *He had read many detailed critical appraisals of her work.* ◇ *She was honest in her appraisal of her team's chances.* **2** (*business*) (*BrE*) a meeting in which an employee discusses with their manager how well they have been doing their job; the system of holding such meetings: *I have my appraisal today.* ◇ ***staff/performance appraisal***

ap·praise /ə'preɪz/ *verb* **1 ~ sb/sth** (*formal*) to consider or examine sb/sth and form an opinion about them or it: *an **appraising glance/look*** ◇ *His eyes coolly appraised the young woman before him.* ◇ *She stepped back to appraise her workmanship.* **2 ~ sb** to make a formal judgement about the value of a person's work, usually after a discussion with them about it: *Managers must appraise all staff.*

ap·prais·er /ə'preɪzə(r)/ *noun* (*NAmE*) a person whose job is to examine a building and say how much it is worth

ap·pre·ciable AW /ə'priːʃəbl/ *adj.* large enough to be noticed or thought important SYN **considerable**: *The new regulations will not make an appreciable difference to most people.* ◇ *an **appreciable effect/increase/amount*** ▶ **ap·pre·ciably** AW /-əbli/ *adv.*: *The risk of infection is appreciably higher among children.*

ap·preci·ate 0- AW /ə'priːʃieɪt/ *verb* **1** 0- [T] (not used in the progressive tenses) **~ sb/sth** to recognize the good qualities of sb/sth: *You can't really appreciate foreign literature in translation.* ◇ *His talents are not **fully appreciated** in that company.* ◇ *Her family doesn't appreciate her.* **2** 0- [T] (not usually used in the progressive tenses) to be grateful for sth that sb has done; to welcome sth: **~ sth** *I'd appreciate some help.* ◇ *Your support is greatly appreciated.* ◇ *Thanks for coming. I **appreciate it**.* ◇ ***I would appreciate it if** you paid in cash.* ◇ **~ doing sth** *I don't appreciate being treated like a second-class citizen.* ◇ **~ sb doing sth** *We would appreciate you letting us know of any problems.* **3** [T] (not used in the progressive tenses) to understand that sth is true SYN **realize**: **~ sth** *What I failed to appreciate was the distance between the two cities.* ◇ **~ how, what, etc...** *I don't think you appreciate how expensive it will be.* ◇ **~ that...** *We didn't **fully appreciate** that he was seriously ill.* **4** [I] to increase in value over a period of time: *Their investments have appreciated over the years.* OPP **depreciate**

ap·pre·ci·ation AW /əˌpriːʃi'eɪʃn/ *noun* **1** [U] pleasure that you have when you recognize and enjoy the good qualities of sb/sth: *She shows little appreciation of good music.* ◇ *The crowd murmured **in appreciation**.* **2** [U, sing.] **~ of sth** a full or sympathetic understanding of sth, such as a situation or a problem, and of what it involves: *I had no appreciation of the problems they faced.* **3** [U] **~ (of/for sth)** the feeling of being grateful for sth: *Please accept this gift **in appreciation of** all you've done for us.* **4** [U, sing.] **~ (in sth)** increase in value over a period of time OPP **depreciation** **5** [C] **~ (of sth)** (*formal*) a piece of writing or a speech in which the strengths and weaknesses of sb/sth, especially an artist or a work of art, are discussed and judged

ap·pre·cia·tive /ə'priːʃətɪv/ *adj.* **1 ~ (of sth)** feeling or showing that you are grateful for sth: *The company was very appreciative of my efforts.* **2** showing pleasure or enjoyment: *an **appreciative audience/smile*** ◇ ***appreciative laughter/comments*** ▶ **ap·pre·cia·tive·ly** *adv.*

ap·pre·hend /ˌæprɪ'hend/ *verb* (*formal*) **1 ~ sb** (of the police) to catch sb and arrest them **2 ~ sth** (*old-fashioned*) to understand or recognize sth

ap·pre·hen·sion /ˌæprɪ'henʃn/ *noun* **1** [U, C] worry or fear that sth unpleasant may happen SYN **anxiety**: *There is growing apprehension that fighting will begin again.* ◇ *He watched the election results **with some apprehension**.* **2** [U] (*formal*) the act of capturing or arresting sb, usually by the police

ap·pre·hen·sive /ˌæprɪ'hensɪv/ *adj.* worried or frightened that sth unpleasant may happen: *an **apprehensive face/glance/look*** ◇ **~ about/of sth** *I was a little apprehensive about the effects of what I had said.* ◇ *You have no reason to be apprehensive of the future.* ◇ **~ that...** *She was deeply apprehensive that something might go wrong.* ▶ **ap·pre·hen·sive·ly** *adv.*

ap·pren·tice /ə'prentɪs/ *noun, verb*

■ ***noun*** a young person who works for an employer for a fixed period of time in order to learn the particular skills needed in their job: *an apprentice electrician/chef*

■ ***verb*** [usually passive] **~ sb (to sb) (as sth)** (*old-fashioned*) to make sb an apprentice

ap·pren·tice·ship /ə'prentɪʃɪp/ *noun* [C, U] a period of time working as an apprentice; a job as an apprentice: *She was in the second year of her apprenticeship as a carpenter.* ◇ *He had **served his apprenticeship** as a plumber.*

ap·prise /ə'praɪz/ *verb* **~ sb of sth** (*formal*) to tell or inform sb of sth

ap·proach 0- AW /ə'prəʊtʃ; *NAmE* ə'proʊtʃ/ *verb, noun*

■ ***verb***

▸ MOVE NEAR **1** 0- [I, T] to come near to sb/sth in distance or time: *We heard the sound of an approaching car/a car approaching.* ◇ *Winter is approaching.* ◇ **~ sb/sth** *As you approach the town, you'll see the college on the left.*

▸ OFFER/ASK **2** 0- [T] to speak to sb about sth, especially to ask them for sth or to offer to do sth: **~ sb** *We have been approached by a number of companies that are interested in our product.* ◇ *I'd like to ask his opinion but I find him difficult to approach* (= not easy to talk to in a friendly way). ◇ **~ sb for sth/about (doing) sth** *She approached the bank for a loan.*

▸ AMOUNT/QUALITY **3** 0- [T] **~ sth** to come close to sth in amount, level or quality: *profits approaching 30 million dollars* ◇ *Few writers approach his richness of language.*

▸ PROBLEM/TASK **4** 0- [T] **~ sth** to start dealing with a problem, task, etc. in a particular way: *What's the best way of approaching this problem?*

■ ***noun***

▸ TO PROBLEM/TASK **1** 0- [C] a way of dealing with sb/sth; a way of doing or thinking about sth such as a problem or a task: *She took the wrong approach in her dealings with them.* ◇ **~ to sth** *The school has decided to adopt a different approach to discipline.*

▸ MOVEMENT NEARER **2** 0- [sing.] movement nearer to sb/sth in distance or time: *She hadn't heard his approach and jumped as the door opened.* ◇ *the approach of spring*

▸ OFFER/REQUEST **3** [C] the act of speaking to sb about sth, especially when making an offer or a request: *The club has **made an approach** to a local company for sponsorship.* ◇ *She resented his persistent approaches.*

▸ PATH/ROAD **4** [C] a path, road, etc. that leads to a place: *All the approaches to the palace were guarded by troops.* ◇ *a new approach road to the port*

▸ OF AIRCRAFT **5** [C] the part of an aircraft's flight immediately before landing: *to begin the final approach to the runway*

▸ STH SIMILAR **6** [sing.] a thing that is like sth else that is mentioned: *That's the **nearest approach** to an apology you'll get from him.* IDM see CARROT

ap·proach·able AW /ə'prəʊtʃəbl; *NAmE* ə'proʊtʃ-/ *adj.* **1** friendly and easy to talk to; easy to understand: *Despite being a big star, she's very approachable.* ◇ *an approachable piece of music* OPP **unapproachable** **2** [not before noun] that can be reached by a particular route or from a particular direction: *The summit was approachable only from the south.*

ap·pro·ba·tion /ˌæprə'beɪʃn/ *noun* [U] (*formal*) approval or agreement

ap·pro·pri·acy AW /ə'prəʊpriəsi; *NAmE* ə'proʊ-/ *noun* [U] **1** the extent to which sth is suitable or acceptable **2** (*linguistics*) the extent to which a word or phrase sounds correct and natural in relation to the situation it is used in

ap·pro·pri·ate 0- AW *adj., verb*

■ ***adj.*** 0- /ə'prəʊpriət; *NAmE* ə'proʊ-/ suitable, acceptable or correct for the particular circumstances: *an appropriate response/measure/method* ◇ *Now that the problem has been identified, appropriate action can be taken.* ◇ *Is now an appropriate time to make a speech?* ◇ *Please debit my Mastercard/Visa/American Express card* (**delete as appropriate**)

(= cross out the options that do not apply). ◇ **~ for sth** *Jeans are not appropriate for a formal party.* ◇ **~ to sth** *The book was written in a style appropriate to the age of the children.* **OPP inappropriate** ▸ **ap·pro·pri·ate·ly** AW *adv.*: *The government has been accused of not responding appropriately to the needs of the homeless.* ◇ *The chain of volcanoes is known, **appropriately enough**, as the 'Ring of Fire'.* **ap·pro·pri·ate·ness** AW *noun* [U]

■ ***verb*** /ə'prəʊprieɪt; *NAmE* ə'proʊ-/ (*formal*) **1 ~ sth** to take sth, sb's ideas, etc. for your own use, especially illegally or without permission: *He was accused of appropriating club funds.* ◇ *Some of the opposition party's policies have been appropriated by the government.* **2 ~ sth** (**for sth**) to take or give sth, especially money for a particular purpose: *Five million dollars have been appropriated for research into the disease.* ➲ compare MISAPPROPRIATE

ap·pro·pri·ation /ə,prəʊpri'eɪʃn; *NAmE* ə,proʊ-/ *noun* **1** [U, sing.] (*formal* or *law*) the act of taking sth that belongs to sb else, especially without permission: *dishonest appropriation of property* ➲ compare MISAPPROPRIATION **2** [U, sing.] (*formal*) the act of keeping or saving money for a particular purpose: *a meeting to discuss the appropriation of funds* **3** [C] (*formal*) a sum of money to be used for a particular purpose, especially by a government or company: *an appropriation of £20 000 for payment of debts*

ap·prov·al 🔑 /ə'pruːvl/ *noun*
1 🔑 [U] the feeling that sb/sth is good or acceptable; a positive opinion of sb/sth: *She desperately wanted to win her father's approval.* ◇ *Do the plans **meet with your approval**?* ◇ *Several people nodded **in approval**.* **OPP disapproval** **2** 🔑 [U, C] agreement to, or permission for sth, especially a plan or request: *The plan will be submitted to the committee for official approval.* ◇ ***parliamentary/congressional/government approval*** ◇ *Senior management have given their **seal of approval** (= formal approval) to the plans.* ◇ *I can't agree to anything without my partner's approval.* ◇ *planning approvals* ◇ *The proposal **is subject to approval** by the shareholders (= they need to agree to it).* ◇ **~ (for sth) (from sb)** *They **required/received approval** for the proposal from the shareholders.* **3** [U] if you buy goods or if goods are sold **on approval**, you can use them for a time without paying, until you decide if you want to buy them or not

ap·prove 🔑 /ə'pruːv/ *verb*
1 🔑 [I] to think that sb/sth is good, acceptable or suitable: *I told my mother I wanted to leave school but she didn't approve.* ◇ **~ of sb/sth** *Do you approve of my idea?* ◇ **~ of sb doing sth** *She doesn't approve of me leaving school this year.* ◇ (*formal*) **~ of sb's doing sth** *She doesn't approve of my leaving school this year.* **OPP disapprove** **2** 🔑 [T] **~ sth** to officially agree to a plan, request, etc: *The committee unanimously approved the plan.* ➲ SYNONYMS at AGREE **3** 🔑 [T, often passive] **~ sth** to say that sth is good enough to be used or is correct: *The course is approved by the Department for Education.*

ap'proved school *noun* (*BrE*) a school where young people who had committed crimes were sent in the past

ap·prov·ing 🔑 /ə'pruːvɪŋ/ *adj.*
showing that you believe that sb/sth is good or acceptable: *He gave me an approving nod.* **OPP disapproving** ▸ **ap·prov·ing·ly** *adv.*: *She looked at him approvingly and smiled.*

approx *abbr.* APPROXIMATE, APPROXIMATELY

ap·proxi·mant /ə'prɒksɪmənt; *NAmE* ə'prɑːks-/ *noun* **1** (*phonetics*) a speech sound made by bringing the parts of the mouth that produce speech close together but not actually touching, for example /r/ and /w/ in *right* and *wet* in many accents of English **2** (*mathematics*) a solution that is close to, but not exactly, the solution of a problem

ap·proxi·mate 🔑 AW *adj.*, *verb*
■ ***adj.*** 🔑 /ə'prɒksɪmət; *NAmE* ə'prɑːk-/ (*abbr.* **approx**) almost correct or accurate, but not completely so: *an **approximate number/total/cost*** ◇ *The cost given is only approximate.* ◇ *Use these figures as an approximate guide in your calculations.* **OPP exact**
■ ***verb*** /ə'prɒksɪmeɪt; *NAmE* ə'prɑːk-/ (*formal*) **1** [T, I] to be similar or close to sth in nature, quality, amount, etc, but not exactly the same: **~ sth** *The animals were reared in conditions which approximated the wild as closely as possible.* ◇ *The total cost will approximate £15 billion.* ◇ **~ to sth** *His story approximates to the facts that we already know.* **2** [T] **~ sth** to calculate or estimate sth fairly accurately: *a formula for approximating the weight of a horse*

ap·proxi·mate·ly 🔑 AW /ə'prɒksɪmətli; *NAmE* ə'prɑːk-/ *adv.*
used to show that sth is almost, but not completely, accurate or correct: *The journey took approximately seven hours.*

Vocabulary Building

Ways of saying approximately

- The flight takes **approximately** three hours.
- The tickets cost **about** £20 each.
- The repairs will cost $200, **give or take** a few dollars.
- How much will it cost, **more or less**?
- We are expecting thirty **or so** people to come.
- She must be 25 **or thereabouts**.
- Profits have fallen by **roughly** 15%.
- You can expect to earn **round about** £40,000 a year.
- The price is **somewhere around** $800.
- She earns **somewhere in the region of** £25,000.

All these words and phrases are used in both speaking and writing; **about** is the most common and **approximately** the most formal.

ap·proxi·ma·tion AW /ə,prɒksɪ'meɪʃn; *NAmE* ə,prɑːk-/ *noun* **1** an estimate of a number or an amount that is almost correct, but not exact: *That's just an approximation, you understand.* **2 ~ (of/to sth)** a thing that is similar to sth else, but is not exactly the same: *Our results should be a good approximation of the true state of affairs.*

ap·pur·ten·ance /ə'pɜːtɪnəns; *NAmE* ə'pɜːrt-/ *noun* [usually pl.] (*formal* or *humorous*) a thing that forms a part of sth larger or more important

APR /,eɪ piː 'ɑː(r)/ *noun* [sing.] the abbreviation for 'annual percentage rate' (the amount of interest a bank charges on money that it lends, calculated for a period of a year): *a rate of 26.4% APR*

après-ski /,æpreɪ 'skiː/ *noun* [U] (from *French*) social activities and entertainments that take place in hotels and restaurants after a day's SKIING

apri·cot /'eɪprɪkɒt; *NAmE* 'æprɪkɑːt/ *noun* **1** [C] a round fruit with yellow or orange skin and a large seed inside: *dried apricots* **2** [U] a yellowish-orange colour ▸ **apri·cot** *adj.*: *The room was painted apricot and white.*

April 🔑 /'eɪprəl/ *noun* [U, C] (*abbr.* **Apr.**)
the fourth month of the year, between March and May: *She was born in April.* ◇ (*BrE*) *The meeting is on the fifth of April/April the fifth.* ◇ (*NAmE*) *The meeting is on April fifth.* ◇ *We went to Japan last April.* ◇ *I arrived at the end of April.* ◇ *last April's election* ◇ *April showers* (= light rain that falls in the spring) ◇ *an April wedding*

,April 'Fool *noun* **1** a trick that is traditionally played on sb on 1 April (called **April Fool's Day** or **All Fools' Day**) **2** a person who has a trick played on them on April Fool's Day

a pri·ori /,eɪ praɪ'ɔːraɪ/ *adj.*, *adv.* (from *Latin*, *formal*) using facts or principles that are known to be true in order to decide what the probable effects or results of sth will be, for example saying 'They haven't eaten anything all day so they must be hungry.' ➲ compare A POSTERIORI

ap·ron /'eɪprən/ *noun* **1** a piece of clothing worn over the front of the body, from the chest or the waist down, and tied around the waist. Aprons are worn over other clothes to keep them clean, for example when cooking. ➲ compare PINAFORE **2** (*technical*) an area with a hard surface at an airport, where aircraft are turned around,

A

loaded, etc. **3** (also **'apron stage**) (*technical*) (in a theatre) the part of the stage that is in front of the curtain

IDM **(tied to) sb's apron strings** (too much under) the influence and control of sb: *The British prime minister is too apt to cling to Washington's apron strings.*

apro·pos /ˌæprəˈpəʊ; *NAmE* -ˈpoʊ/ (also **apro·pos of**) *prep.* concerning or related to sb/sth: *Apropos (of) what you were just saying...*

apse /æps/ *noun* a small area, often in the shape of a SEMI-CIRCLE, usually at the east end of a church

apt /æpt/ *adj.* **1** suitable or appropriate in the circumstances: *a particularly* ***apt description/name/comment*** **2** likely or having a natural tendency to do sth: **~ to be...** *apt to be forgetful/careless* ◇ **~ to do sth** *Babies are apt to put objects into their mouths.* **3 ~ pupil** a person who has a natural ability to learn and understand ▶ **aptly** *adv.*: *the aptly named Grand Hotel* **apt·ness** *noun* [U]

ap·ti·tude /ˈæptɪtjuːd; *NAmE* -tuːd/ *noun* [U, C] natural ability or skill at doing sth SYN **talent**: *an* ***aptitude test*** (= one designed to show whether sb has the natural ability for a particular job or course of education) ◇ **~ for sth** *She showed a natural aptitude for the work.* ◇ **~ for doing sth** *His aptitude for dealing with children got him the job.*

aqua /ˈækwə/ *noun* [U] **1** water (used especially on the labels on packages of food, drinks, medicines, etc. in order to show how much water they contain) **2** a bluish-green colour

aqua·culture /ˈækwəkʌltʃə(r)/ *noun* [U] the growing of plants in water for food

aqua·lung /ˈækwəlʌŋ/ *noun* a piece of breathing equipment that a DIVER wears on his/her back when swimming underwater

aqua·mar·ine /ˌækwəməˈriːn/ *noun* **1** [C, U] a pale greenish-blue SEMI-PRECIOUS STONE **2** [U] a pale greenish-blue colour ▶ **aqua·mar·ine** *adj.*: *an aquamarine sea*

aqua·plane /ˈækwəpleɪn/ *verb, noun*

■ ***verb*** **1** (*BrE*) (*NAmE* **hydro·plane**) [I] (of a motor vehicle) to slide out of control on a wet road **2** [I] to stand on a board that is pulled along on water behind a SPEEDBOAT in the sport of aquaplaning

■ ***noun*** a board that sb stands on in the sport of aquaplaning

aqua·plan·ing /ˈækwəpleɪnɪŋ/ *noun* [U] **1** the sport of being pulled along on a board behind a SPEEDBOAT on water **2** (*BrE*) (*NAmE* **hydro·plan·ing**) the fact of a motor vehicle sliding on a wet surface, so that it is out of control

aquar·ium /əˈkweəriəm; *NAmE* əˈkwer-/ *noun* (*pl.* **aquar·iums** or **aqua·ria** /-riə/) **1** a large glass container in which fish and other water creatures and plants are kept **2** a building where people can go to see fish and other water creatures

Aquar·ius /əˈkweəriəs; *NAmE* əˈkwer-/ (also **the 'Water Bearer, the 'Water Carrier**) *noun* **1** [U] the 11th sign of the ZODIAC **2** [sing.] a person born when the sun is in this sign, that is between 21 January and 19 February ▶ **Aquar·ian** /əˈkweəriən; *NAmE* əˈkwer-/ *noun, adj.*

aqua·robics /ˌækwəˈrəʊbɪks; *NAmE* -ˈroʊ-/ *noun* [U] physical exercises that you do in water, often done in classes ➲ compare AEROBICS

aqua·tic /əˈkwætɪk/ *adj.* [usually before noun] **1** growing or living in, on or near water: ***aquatic plants/life/ecosystems*** **2** connected with water: *aquatic sports*

aqua·tint /ˈækwətɪnt/ *noun* [U, C] (*technical*) a method of producing a picture using acid on a metal plate; a picture produced using this method

aque·duct /ˈækwɪdʌkt/ *noun* a structure for carrying water, usually one built like a bridge across a valley or low ground ➲ VISUAL VOCAB page V12

aque·ous /ˈeɪkwiəs/ *adj.* (*technical*) containing water; like water

ˌaqueous ˈhumour (*especially US* **ˌaqueous ˈhumor**) *noun* [U] (*anatomy*) the clear liquid inside the front part of the eye ➲ compare VITREOUS HUMOUR

aqui·fer /ˈækwɪfə(r)/ *noun* (*geology*) a layer of rock or soil that can absorb and hold water

aquil·ine /ˈækwɪlaɪn/ *adj.* (*formal*) a person with an **aquiline nose** or **aquiline features** has a nose that is thin and curved, similar to the BEAK of an EAGLE

Arab /ˈærəb/ *noun, adj.*

■ ***noun*** **1** a person from the Middle East or N Africa, whose ANCESTORS lived in the Arabian Peninsula **2** a type of horse originally from Arabia

■ ***adj.*** of or connected with Arabia or Arabs: *Arab countries*

ar·ab·esque /ˌærəˈbesk/ *noun* **1** [C] (in BALLET) a position in which the dancer balances on one leg with the other leg lifted and stretched out behind parallel to the ground **2** [C, U] (in art) a type of design where lines wind around each other

Ara·bian /əˈreɪbiən/ *adj.* of or connected with Arabia

HELP **Arabian** is used to describe places: *the Arabian peninsula*. The people are **Arabs** and the adjective to describe them is **Arab**: *Arab children*. The language is **Arabic**: *Arabic script*

Arab·ic /ˈærəbɪk/ *noun, adj.*

■ ***noun*** [U] the language of the Arabs

■ ***adj.*** of or connected with the literature and language of Arab people: *Arabic poetry*

ˌArabic ˈnumeral *noun* any of the symbols 0, 1, 2, 3, 4, etc. used for writing numbers in many countries ➲ compare ROMAN NUMERAL

ar·able /ˈærəbl/ *adj.* connected with growing crops such as WHEAT: ***arable farming/farms/crops*** ◇ ***arable land/fields*** (= used or suitable for growing crops)

arach·nid /əˈræknɪd/ *noun* (*technical*) any small creature of the class that includes spiders, SCORPIONS, MITES and TICKS ➲ VISUAL VOCAB page V11 ➲ compare INSECT

arach·no·pho·bia /əˌræknəˈfəʊbiə; *NAmE* -ˈfoʊ-/ *noun* [U] an extreme fear of spiders

Aran /ˈærən/ *adj.* [only before noun] (*BrE*) (of knitted clothing) with a traditional pattern of lines and diamond shapes made by raised STITCHES: *an Aran sweater*

ar·bi·ter /ˈɑːbɪtə(r); *NAmE* ˈɑːrb-/ *noun* **~ (of sth)** (*formal*) a person with the power or influence to make judgements and decide what will be done or accepted: *The law is the final arbiter of what is considered obscene.* ◇ *an* ***arbiter of taste/style/fashion***

ar·bi·trage /ˈɑːbɪtrɑːʒ; -trɪdʒ; *NAmE* ˈɑːrbətrɑːʒ/ *noun* [U] (*business*) the practice of buying sth (for example, shares or foreign money) in one place and selling it in another place where the price is higher ▶ **ar·bi·tra·geur** /ˌɑːbɪtrɑːˈʒɜː(r); *NAmE* ˌɑːrbətrɑːˈʒɜːr/ (also **ar·bi·trager** /ˈɑːbɪtrɪdʒə(r); *NAmE* ˈɑːrbətrɑːʒər/) *noun*

ar·bi·trary AW /ˈɑːbɪtrəri; ˈɑːbɪtri; *NAmE* ˈɑːrbətreri/ *adj.* **1** (of an action, a decision, a rule, etc.) not seeming to be based on a reason, system or plan and sometimes seeming unfair: *The choice of players for the team seemed completely arbitrary.* ◇ *He makes unpredictable, arbitrary decisions.* **2** (*formal*) using power without restriction and without considering other people: *the arbitrary powers of officials* ▶ **ar·bi·trar·ily** AW /ˌɑːbɪˈtrerəli; ˈɑːbɪtrəli; *NAmE* ˌɑːrbəˈt-/ *adv.*: *The leaders of the groups were chosen arbitrarily.* **ar·bi·trari·ness** AW *noun* [U]

ar·bi·trate /ˈɑːbɪtreɪt; *NAmE* ˈɑːrb-/ *verb* [I, T] to officially settle an argument or a disagreement between two people or groups: **~ (in/on) (sth)** *to arbitrate in a dispute* ◇ **~ between A and B** *A committee was created to arbitrate between management and the unions.*

ar·bi·tra·tion /ˌɑːbɪˈtreɪʃn; *NAmE* ˌɑːrb-/ *noun* [U] the official process of settling an argument or a disagreement by sb who is not involved: *Both sides in the dispute have agreed* ***to go to arbitration***.

ar·bi·tra·tor /ˈɑːbɪtreɪtə(r); *NAmE* ˈɑːrb-/ *noun* a person who is chosen to settle a disagreement

ar·bor·eal /ɑːˈbɔːriəl; *NAmE* ɑːrˈb-/ *adj.* (*technical*) relating to trees; living in trees

ar·bor·etum /ˌɑːbəˈriːtəm; *NAmE* ˌɑːrb-/ *noun* (*pl.* **ar·bor·etums** or **ar·bor·eta** /-tə/) a garden where many different types of tree are grown, for people to look at or for scientific study

ar·bori·cul·ture /ˈɑːbərɪkʌltʃə(r); *NAmE* ˈɑːrb-/ *noun* [U] the study or practice of growing trees and SHRUBS ▸ **ar·bori·cul·tural** /ˌɑːbərɪˈkʌltʃərəl; *NAmE* ˌɑːrb-/ *adj.*: *an arboricultural specialist* **ar·bori·cul·tur·ist** *noun*

ar·bor·ist /ˈɑːbərɪst; *NAmE* ˈɑːrb-/ *noun* (*formal*) = TREE SURGEON

ar·bour (*especially US* **arbor**) /ˈɑːbə(r); *NAmE* ˈɑːrb-/ *noun* a shelter in a garden/yard for people to sit under, made by growing climbing plants over a frame

arc /ɑːk; *NAmE* ɑːrk/ *noun, verb*

■ ***noun*** **1** (*geometry*) part of a circle or a curved line ➲ VISUAL VOCAB page V58 **2** a curved shape: *the arc of a rainbow* ◇ *The beach swept around in an arc.* **3** (*technical*) an electric current passing across a space between two TERMINALS ➲ see also ARC LAMP

■ ***verb*** (**arc·ing** /ˈɑːkɪŋ; *NAmE* ˈɑːrk-/, **arced, arced** /ɑːkt; *NAmE* ɑːrkt/) (*technical*) **1** [I] to move in the shape of an arc **2** [I] to form an electric arc

ar·cade /ɑːˈkeɪd; *NAmE* ɑːrˈk-/ *noun* **1** a covered passage with ARCHES along the side of a row of buildings (usually a row of shops/stores) **2** a covered passage between streets, with shops/stores on either side ➲ VISUAL VOCAB page V2 **3** (also ˈ**shopping arcade**) (both *BrE*) a large building with a number of shops/stores in it ➲ compare SHOPPING MALL **4** (*BrE* also **aˈmusement arcade**) a place where you can play games on machines which you use coins to operate: *arcade games*

Ar·ca·dia /ɑːˈkeɪdiə; *NAmE* ɑːrˈk-/ *noun* [sing.] a part of southern Greece used in poetry and stories to represent an idea of perfect country life

Ar·ca·dian /ɑːˈkeɪdiən; *NAmE* ɑːrˈk-/ *adj.* of or connected with Arcadia or an idea of perfect country life

ar·ca·na /ɑːˈkeɪnə; *NAmE* ɑːrˈk-/ *noun* **1** [pl.] things that are secret or mysterious **2** [sing.] either of the two groups of cards in a TAROT PACK/DECK, the **major arcana** and the **minor arcana**

ar·cane /ɑːˈkeɪn; *NAmE* ɑːrˈk-/ *adj.* (*formal*) secret and mysterious and therefore difficult to understand

arch /ɑːtʃ; *NAmE* ɑːrtʃ/ *noun, verb, adj.*

■ ***noun*** **1** a curved structure that supports the weight of sth above it, such as a bridge or the upper part of a building **2** a structure with a curved top that is supported by straight sides, sometimes forming an entrance or built as a MONUMENT: *Go through the arch and follow the path.* ◇ *Marble Arch is a famous London landmark.* ➲ VISUAL VOCAB page V12 **3** the raised part of the foot formed by a curved section of bones ➲ VISUAL VOCAB page V48 **4** anything that forms a curved shape at the top: *the delicate arch of her eyebrows*

■ ***verb*** **1** [T, I] ~ (**sth**) if you **arch** part of your body, or if it **arches**, it moves and forms a curved shape: *The cat arched its back and hissed.* **2** [I] to be in a curved line or shape across or over sth: *Tall trees arched over the path.*

■ ***adj.*** [usually before noun] (often *disapproving*) seeming amused because you know more about a situation than other people: *an arch tone of voice* ▸ **arch·ly** *adv.*: *'Guess what?' she said archly.*

arch- /ɑːtʃ; *NAmE* ɑːrtʃ/ *combining form* (in nouns) main; most important or most extreme: *archbishop* ◇ *arch-enemy*

archae·olo·gist (*NAmE* also **arche·olo·gist**) /ˌɑːkiˈɒlədʒɪst; *NAmE* ˌɑːrkiˈɑːl-/ *noun* a person who studies archaeology

archae·ology (*NAmE* also **arche·ology**) /ˌɑːkiˈɒlədʒi; *NAmE* ˌɑːrkiˈɑːl-/ *noun* [U] the study of cultures of the past, and of periods of history by examining the remains of buildings and objects found in the ground ➲ see also INDUSTRIAL ARCHAEOLOGY ▸ **arch·aeo·logic·al** (*NAmE* also **arch·eo·logic·al**) /ˌɑːkiəˈlɒdʒɪkl; *NAmE* ˌɑːrkiəˈlɑːdʒ-/ *adj.*: ***archaeological excavations/evidence***

archae·op·teryx /ˌɑːkiˈɒptərɪks; *NAmE* ˌɑːrkiˈɑːptərɪks/ *noun* the oldest known bird, which existed about 150 million years ago

ar·chaic /ɑːˈkeɪɪk; *NAmE* ɑːrˈk-/ *adj.* **1** old and no longer used: *'Thou art' is an archaic form of 'you are'.* **2** very old-fashioned SYN **outdated**: *The system is archaic and unfair and needs changing.* **3** from a much earlier or ancient period of history: *archaic art*

archa·ism /ˈɑːkeɪɪzəm; *NAmE* ˈɑːrk-/ *noun* (*technical*) a very old word or phrase that is no longer used

arch·an·gel /ˈɑːkeɪndʒl; *NAmE* ˈɑːrk-/ *noun* an ANGEL of the highest rank: *the Archangel Gabriel*

arch·bishop /ˌɑːtʃˈbɪʃəp; *NAmE* ˌɑːrtʃ-/ *noun* a BISHOP of the highest rank, responsible for all the churches in a large area: *the Archbishop of Canterbury* (= the head of the Church of England)

arch·bish·op·ric /ˌɑːtʃˈbɪʃəprɪk; *NAmE* ˌɑːrtʃ-/ *noun* **1** the position of an archbishop **2** the district for which an archbishop is responsible

arch·deacon /ˌɑːtʃˈdiːkən; *NAmE* ˌɑːrtʃ-/ *noun* a priest just below the rank of BISHOP, especially in the Anglican Church

arch·dio·cese /ˌɑːtʃˈdaɪəsɪs; *NAmE* ˌɑːrtʃ-/ *noun* a district under the care of an ARCHBISHOP

arch·duch·ess /ˌɑːtʃˈdʌtʃəs; *NAmE* ˌɑːrtʃ-/ *noun* (in the past) the wife of an archduke or a daughter of the EMPEROR of Austria

arch·duke /ˌɑːtʃˈdjuːk; *NAmE* ˌɑːrtʃˈduːk/ *noun* (in the past) a son of the EMPEROR of Austria: *Archduke Franz Ferdinand* ➲ compare GRAND DUKE

arched /ɑːtʃt; *NAmE* ɑːrtʃt/ *adj.* in the shape of an ARCH: *a chair with an arched back*

ˌ**arch-ˈenemy** *noun* a person's main enemy

arche·olo·gist, arche·ology (*NAmE*) = ARCHAEOLOGIST, ARCHAEOLOGY

arch·er /ˈɑːtʃə(r); *NAmE* ˈɑːrtʃ-/ *noun* a person who shoots with a BOW and arrows ➲ VISUAL VOCAB page V34

arch·ery /ˈɑːtʃəri; *NAmE* ˈɑːrtʃ-/ *noun* [U] the art or sport of shooting arrows with a BOW ➲ VISUAL VOCAB page V34

arche·typal /ˌɑːkiˈtaɪpl; *NAmE* ˌɑːrki-/ *adj.* having all the important qualities that make sb/sth a typical example of a particular kind of person or thing: *The Beatles were the archetypal pop group.*

arche·type /ˈɑːkitaɪp/ *noun* (*formal*) the most typical or perfect example of a particular kind of person or thing: *She is the archetype of an American movie star.*

archi·pel·ago /ˌɑːkɪˈpeləɡəʊ; *NAmE* ˌɑːrkɪˈpeləɡoʊ/ *noun* (*pl.* **-os** or **-oes**) a group of islands and the sea surrounding them

archi·tect /ˈɑːkɪtekt; *NAmE* ˈɑːrk-/ *noun* **1** a person whose job is designing buildings, etc. **2** a person who is responsible for planning or creating an idea, an event or a situation: *He was one of the principal architects of the revolution.* ◇ *Jones was the architect of the team's first goal.*

archi·tec·ton·ic /ˌɑːkɪtekˈtɒnɪk; *NAmE* ˌɑːrkɪtekˈtɑːnɪk/ *adj.* (*technical*) of or connected with architecture or architects

archi·tec·tural /ˌɑːkɪˈtektʃərəl; *NAmE* ˌɑːrk-/ *adj.* connected with architecture: *architectural features* ▸ **archi·tec·tur·al·ly** *adv.*: *The house is of little interest architecturally.*

archi·tec·ture /ˈɑːkɪtektʃə(r); *NAmE* ˈɑːrk-/ *noun* **1** [U] the art and study of designing buildings: *to study architecture* **2** [U] the design or style of a building or buildings: *the architecture of the eighteenth century* ◇ *modern architecture* ➲ VISUAL VOCAB page V12 **3** [C, U] (*computing*) the design and structure of a computer system

archi·trave /ˈɑːkɪtreɪv; *NAmE* ˈɑːrk-/ *noun* (*technical*) the frame around a door or window

arch·ive /ˈɑːkaɪv; *NAmE* ˈɑːrk-/ *noun, verb*

■ ***noun*** (also **archives** [pl.]) a collection of historical documents or records of a government, a family, a place or an organization; the place where these records are stored:

the National Sound Archive ◇ *archive film* ◇ *The BBC's archives are bulging with material.*
▪ **verb 1 ~ sth** to put or store a document or other material in an archive **2 ~ sth** (*computing*) to move information that is not often needed to a tape or disk to store it

arch·iv·ist /ˈɑːkɪvɪst; *NAmE* ˈɑːrk-/ *noun* a person whose job is to develop and manage an archive

ˌarch-ˈrival *noun* a person's main opponent

arch·way /ˈɑːtʃweɪ; *NAmE* ˈɑːrtʃ-/ *noun* a passage or an entrance with an ARCH over it: *We went through a stone archway into the courtyard.*

ˈarc lamp (also **ˈarc light**) *noun* a lamp that gives very bright light that is produced by an electric ARC

Arc·tic /ˈɑːktɪk; *NAmE* ˈɑːrk-/ *adj., noun*
▪ **adj. 1** [only before noun] related to or happening in the regions around the North Pole: *Arctic explorers* ➲ compare ANTARCTIC **2 arctic** extremely cold: *TV pictures showed the arctic conditions.*
▪ **noun** [sing.] **the Arctic** the regions of the world around the North Pole

the ˌArctic ˈCircle *noun* [sing.] the line of LATITUDE 66° 33′ North ➲ compare ANTARCTIC CIRCLE

ar·dent /ˈɑːdnt; *NAmE* ˈɑːrdnt/ *adj.* [usually before noun] very enthusiastic and showing strong feelings about sth/sb **SYN** **passionate**: *an ardent supporter of European unity* ▸ **ar·dent·ly** *adv.*

ar·dour (*especially US* **ardor**) /ˈɑːdə(r); *NAmE* ˈɑːrdər/ *noun* [U] (*formal*) very strong feelings of enthusiasm or love **SYN** **passion**

ar·du·ous /ˈɑːdjuəs; -dʒu-; *NAmE* ˈɑːrdʒuəs/ *adj.* involving a lot of effort and energy, especially over a period of time: *an arduous journey across the Andes* ◇ *The work was arduous.* ▸ **ar·du·ous·ly** *adv.*

are[1] /ə(r); *strong form* ɑː(r)/ ➲ BE

are[2] /eə(r); ɑː(r); *NAmE* er; ɑːr/ *noun* a unit for measuring an area of land; 100 square metres

area 0‑w **AW** /ˈeəriə; *NAmE* ˈeriə/ *noun*
▸ PART OF PLACE **1** 0‑w [C] part of a place, town, etc, or a region of a country or the world: *mountainous/desert areas* ◇ *rural/urban/inner-city areas* ◇ *There is heavy traffic in the downtown area tonight.* ◇ *She knows the* ***local area*** *very well.* ◇ *John is the London area manager.* ◇ *Wreckage from the plane was scattered over a* ***wide area****.* ◇ *The farm and* ***surrounding area*** *were flooded.* ➲ see also CATCHMENT AREA, CONSERVATION AREA, DEVELOPMENT AREA, NO-GO AREA **2** 0‑w [C] a part of a room, building or particular space that is used for a special purpose: *the hotel reception area* ◇ *a play/parking/dining area* ➲ SYNONYMS at PLACE ➲ see also REST AREA, SERVICE AREA
▸ PARTICULAR PLACE **3** 0‑w [C] a particular place on an object: *Move the cursor to a blank area of the computer screen.* ◇ *The tumour had not spread to other areas of the body.*
▸ SUBJECT/ACTIVITY **4** 0‑w [C] **~ (of sth)** a particular subject or activity, or an aspect of it: *the areas of training and development* ◇ *Finance is Mark's area.* ◇ *The big* ***growth area*** *of recent years has been in health clubs.* ➲ see also GREY AREA
▸ MEASUREMENT **5** 0‑w [C, U] the amount of space covered by a flat surface or piece of land, described as a measurement: *the area of a triangle* ◇ *The room is 12 square metres in area.*
▸ FOOTBALL **6 the area** (*BrE*) (in football (SOCCER)) = PENALTY AREA: *He shot from just outside the area.*

ˈarea code *noun* the numbers for a particular area or city, which you use when you are making a telephone call from outside the local area ➲ compare DIALLING CODE

arena /əˈriːnə/ *noun* **1** a place with a flat open area in the middle and seats around it where people can watch sports and entertainment: *a concert at Wembley Arena* **2** (*formal*) an area of activity that concerns the public, especially one where there is a lot of opposition between different groups or countries: *the* ***political/international arena***

aren't /ɑːnt; *NAmE* ɑːrnt/ *short form* **1** are not **2** (in questions) am not: *Aren't I clever?*

areola /əˈriːələ/ *noun* (*pl.* **areo·lae** /-liː/) the round area of skin around the NIPPLE

argon /ˈɑːɡɒn; *NAmE* ˈɑːrɡɑːn/ *noun* [U] (*symb.* **Ar**) a chemical element. Argon is a gas that does not react with anything and is used in electric lights.

argot /ˈɑːɡəʊ; *NAmE* ˈɑːrɡət; -ɡoʊ/ *noun* [sing., U] (from *French*) words and phrases that are used by a particular group of people and not easily understood by others **SYN** **jargon**

ar·gu·able /ˈɑːɡjuəbl; *NAmE* ˈɑːrɡ-/ *adj.* (*formal*) **1** that you can give good reasons for: ***It is arguable that*** *giving too much detail may actually be confusing.* **2** not certain; that you do not accept without question **SYN** **debatable**: *It is arguable whether the case should have ever gone to trial* (= perhaps it should not have).

ar·gu·ably /ˈɑːɡjuəbli; *NAmE* ˈɑːrɡ-/ *adv.* used (often before a comparative or superlative adjective) when you are stating an opinion that you believe you could give reasons to support: *He is arguably the best actor of his generation.*

argue 0‑w /ˈɑːɡjuː; *NAmE* ˈɑːrɡ-/ *verb*
1 0‑w [I] to speak angrily to sb because you disagree with them: *My brothers are always arguing.* ◇ **~ (with sb) (about/over sth)** *We're always arguing with each other about money.* ◇ **~ with sb** *I don't want to argue with you—just do it!* **2** 0‑w [I, T] to give reasons why you think that sth is right/wrong, true/not true, etc, especially to persuade people that you are right: **~ for/against sth/doing sth** *They argued for the right to strike.* ◇ **~ sth** *She argued the case for bringing back the death penalty.* ◇ *He was too tired to* ***argue the point*** (= discuss the matter). ◇ *a well-argued article* ◇ **~ that...** *He argued that they needed more time to finish the project.* ◇ ***It could be argued that*** *laws are made by and for men.* ➲ LANGUAGE BANK at NEVERTHELESS, PERHAPS **3** [T] **~ sth** (*formal*) to show clearly that sth exists or is true: *These latest developments argue a change in government policy.*
IDM **ˌargue the ˈtoss** (*BrE, informal*) to continue to disagree about a decision, especially when it is too late to change it or it is not very important
PHR V **ˌargue sb ˈinto/ˈout of doing sth** to persuade sb to do/not do sth by giving them reasons: *They argued him into withdrawing his complaint.* **ˈargue with sth** (usually used in negative sentences) (*informal*) to disagree with a statement: *He's a really successful man—you can't argue with that.*

Language Bank

argue

Verbs for reporting an opinion

- Some critics **argue** that Picasso remained a great master all his life.
- Others **maintain** that there is a significant deterioration in quality in his post-war work.
- Picasso himself **claimed** that good art is created, but great art is stolen.
- As Smith **has noted**, Picasso borrowed imagery from African art.
- As the author **points out**, Picasso borrowed imagery from African art.
- The writer **challenges the notion that** Picasso's sculpture was secondary to his painting.
- **It has been suggested that** Picasso's painting was influenced by jazz music.

➲ Language Banks at ABOUT, ACCORDING TO

ar·gu·ment 0‑w /ˈɑːɡjumənt; *NAmE* ˈɑːrɡ-/ *noun*
1 0‑w [C, U] a conversation or discussion in which two or more people disagree, often angrily: *to* ***win/lose an argument*** ◇ *After some heated argument a decision was finally taken.* ◇ **~ (with sb) (about/over sth)** *We* ***had an argument*** *with the waiter about the bill.* ◇ **~ with sb** *She* ***got into an***

argument with the teacher. **2** 🗝 [C] a reason or set of reasons that sb uses to show that sth is true or correct: *Her main argument was a moral one.* ◇ **~ for/against sth** *There are strong* ***arguments for and against*** *euthanasia.* ◇ **~ that...** *His argument was that public spending must be reduced.* ➲ WRITING TUTOR page WT8 **3** [U] **~ (about sth)** the act of disagreeing in a conversation or discussion using a reason or set of reasons: *Let's assume* ***for the sake of argument*** (= in order to discuss the problem) *that we can't start till March.*

ar·gu·men·ta·tion /ˌɑːgjumən'teɪʃn; *NAmE* ˌɑːrg-/ *noun* [U] logical arguments used to support a theory, an action or an idea

ar·gu·men·ta·tive /ˌɑːgju'mentətɪv; *NAmE* ˌɑːrg-/ *adj.* a person who is **argumentative** likes arguing or often starts arguing

argy-bargy /ˌɑːdʒi 'bɑːdʒi; *NAmE* ˌɑːrdʒi 'bɑːrdʒi/ *noun* [U, C] (*pl.* **ˌargy-'bargies**) (*BrE, informal*) noisy disagreement

ar·gyle /ɑː'gaɪl; *NAmE* 'ɑːrgaɪl/ *noun* [U] a knitted pattern of diamond shapes on a plain background, especially on a sweater or on socks

aria /'ɑːriə/ *noun* a song for one voice, especially in an OPERA or ORATORIO

-arian *suffix* (in nouns and adjectives) believing in; practising: *humanitarian* ◇ *disciplinarian*

arid /'ærɪd/ *adj.* **1** (of land or a climate) having little or no rain; very dry: *arid and semi-arid deserts* **2** (*formal*) with nothing new or interesting in it: *an arid discussion* ▸ **arid·ity** /ə'rɪdəti/ *noun* [U]

Aries /'eəriːz; *NAmE* 'eriːz/ *noun* **1** [U] the first sign of the ZODIAC, the RAM **2** [sing.] a person born when the sun is in this sign, that is between 21 March and 20 April

aright /ə'raɪt/ *adv.* (*old-fashioned*) correctly

arise 🗝 /ə'raɪz/ *verb* (**arose** /ə'rəʊz; *NAmE* ə'roʊz/, **arisen** /ə'rɪzn/)
1 🗝 [I] (rather *formal*) (especially of a problem or a difficult situation) to happen; to start to exist SYN **occur**: *A new crisis has arisen.* ◇ *We keep them informed of any changes as they arise.* ◇ *Children should be disciplined* ***when the need arises*** (= when it is necessary). ◇ *A storm arose during the night.* **2** [I] **~ (out of/from sth)** (rather *formal*) to happen as a result of a particular situation: *injuries arising out of a road accident* ◇ *Emotional or mental problems can arise from a physical cause.* ◇ *Are there any* ***matters arising*** *from the minutes of the last meeting?* **3** [I] (*formal*) to begin to exist or develop: *Several new industries arose in the town.* **4** [I] (*old use* or *literary*) to get out of bed; to stand up: *He arose at dawn.* **5** [I] **~ (against sb/sth)** (*old use*) to come together to protest about sth or to fight for sth: *The peasants arose against their masters.* **6** [I] (*literary*) (of a mountain, a tall building, etc.) to become visible gradually as you move towards it

ar·is·toc·racy /ˌærɪ'stɒkrəsi; *NAmE* -'stɑːk-/ *noun* [C+sing./pl. v.] (*pl.* **-ies**) (in some countries) people born in the highest social class, who have special titles SYN **nobility**: *members of the aristocracy*

ar·is·to·crat /'ærɪstəkræt; *NAmE* ə'rɪst-/ *noun* a member of the aristocracy ➲ compare COMMONER

ar·is·to·crat·ic /ˌærɪstə'krætɪk; *NAmE* əˌrɪstə-/ *adj.* belonging to or typical of the ARISTOCRACY SYN **noble**: *an* ***aristocratic name/family/lifestyle***

Ar·is·to·tel·ian /ˌærɪstə'tiːliən/ *adj.* connected with Aristotle or his philosophy

arith·met·ic /ə'rɪθmətɪk/ *noun* [U] **1** the type of mathematics that deals with the adding, multiplying, etc. of numbers: *He's not very good at arithmetic.* **2** sums involving the adding, multiplying, etc. of numbers: *a quick bit of* ***mental arithmetic*** (= sums you do in your head, without writing anything down) ◇ *I think there's something wrong with your arithmetic.*

arith·met·ic·al /ˌærɪθ'metɪkl/ (also **arith·met·ic**) *adj.* relating to arithmetic: *an arithmetical calculation* ▸ **arith·met·ic·al·ly** /-kli/ *adv.*

arithˌmetic 'mean *noun* (*mathematics*) = MEAN *n.* (2)

arithˌmetic pro'gression (also **arithˌmetic 'series**) *noun* a series of numbers that decrease or increase by the same amount each time, for example 2, 4, 6, 8 ➲ compare GEOMETRIC PROGRESSION

the ark /ɑːk; *NAmE* ɑːrk/ (also **ˌNoah's 'ark**) *noun* [sing.] (in the Bible) a large boat which Noah built to save his family and two of every type of animal from the flood
IDM **out of the 'ark | sth went out with the 'ark** (*BrE, informal*) if sb says that an object or a custom is **out of the ark** or **went out with the ark**, they think that it is very old-fashioned

arm 🗝 /ɑːm; *NAmE* ɑːrm/ *noun, verb*
■ ***noun*** ➲ see also ARMS
▸ PART OF BODY **1** 🗝 either of the two long parts that stick out from the top of the body and connect the shoulders to the hands: *He escaped with only a broken arm.* ◇ *She threw her arms around his neck.* ◇ *The officer grabbed him* ***by the arm*** (= grabbed his arm). ◇ *She touched him gently on the arm.* ◇ *He held the dirty rag* ***at arm's length*** (= as far away from his body as possible). ◇ *They walked along* ***arm in arm*** (= with the arm of one person linked with the arm of the other). ◇ *She cradled the child* ***in her arms.*** ◇ *They fell asleep* ***in each other's arms*** (= holding each other). ◇ *He was carrying a number of files* ***under his arm*** (= between his arm and his body). ◇ *He walked in with a tall blonde* ***on his arm*** (= next to him and holding his arm). ➲ COLLOCATIONS at PHYSICAL ➲ VISUAL VOCAB page V48
▸ OF CLOTHING **2** 🗝 the part of a piece of clothing that covers the arm SYN **sleeve**
▸ OF CHAIR **3** the part of a chair, etc. on which you rest your arms ➲ VISUAL VOCAB pages V18, V56
▸ OF MACHINERY **4** a long narrow part of an object or a piece of machinery, especially one that moves: *a robotic arm*
▸ OF WATER/LAND **5** a long narrow piece of water or land that is joined to a larger area: *A small bridge spans the arm of the river.*
▸ OF ORGANIZATION **6** [usually sing.] **~ (of sth)** a section of a large organization that deals with one particular activity SYN **wing**: *the research arm of the company*
IDM **cost/pay an ˌarm and a 'leg** (*informal*) to cost/pay a lot of money **keep sb at arm's length** to avoid having a close relationship with sb: *He keeps all his clients at arm's length.* ➲ more at AKIMBO, BABE, BEAR *v.*, CHANCE *v.*, FOLD *v.*, LONG *adj.*, OPEN *adj.*, RIGHT *adj.*, SHOT *n.*, TWIST *v.*
■ ***verb*** **1** 🗝 [I, T] to provide weapons for yourself/sb in order to fight a battle or a war: *The country was arming against the enemy.* ◇ **~ yourself/sb (with sth)** *The men armed themselves with sticks and stones.* ◇ (*figurative*) *She had armed herself for the meeting with all the latest statistics.* ➲ see also ARMED **2** [T] **~ sth** to make a bomb, etc. ready to explode ➲ compare DISARM

ar·mada /ɑː'mɑːdə; *NAmE* ɑːr'm-/ *noun* a large group of armed ships sailing together: *The Spanish Armada was sent to attack England in 1588.* ◇ (*figurative*) *a vast armada of football fans*

ar·ma·dillo /ˌɑːmə'dɪləʊ; *NAmE* ˌɑːrmə'dɪloʊ/ *noun* (*pl.* **-os**) an American animal with a hard shell made of pieces of bone, that eats insects and rolls into a ball if sth attacks it

Ar·ma·ged·don /ˌɑːmə'gedn; *NAmE* ˌɑːrm-/ *noun* [sing., U] **1** (in the Bible) a battle between good and evil at the end of the world **2** a terrible war that could destroy the world

Ar·mag·nac /'ɑːmənjæk; *NAmE* 'ɑːr-/ *noun* [U] a type of French BRANDY

Ar·ma·lite™ /'ɑːməlaɪt; *NAmE* 'ɑːrm-/ *noun* a type of light automatic RIFLE

ar·ma·ment /'ɑːməmənt; *NAmE* 'ɑːrm-/ *noun* **1** [C, usually pl.] weapons, especially large guns, bombs, tanks, etc: *the armaments industry* **2** [U] the process of increasing the amount of weapons an army or a country has, especially to prepare for war. ➲ compare DISARMAMENT

A

arma·ture /'ɑːmətʃə(r); *NAmE* 'ɑːrm-/ *noun* (*technical*) a frame that is covered to make a figure: *The figures are made from clay over a wire armature.*

arm·band /'ɑːmbænd; *NAmE* 'ɑːrm-/ *noun* **1** a cloth band worn around the arm as a sign of sth, for example that sb has an official position: *The stewards all wore armbands.* ◇ *Many people at the funeral service were wearing black armbands.* **2** either of two plastic rings that can be filled with air and worn around the arms by sb who is learning to swim

'arm candy *noun* [U] (*informal*) a beautiful woman that a man takes with him when he goes to a public event in order to impress other people

arm·chair *noun, adj.*
■ ***noun*** /'ɑːmtʃeə(r); ɑːm'tʃeə(r); *NAmE* 'ɑːrmtʃer; ɑːrm'tʃer/ a comfortable chair with sides on which you can rest your arms: *to sit in an armchair* ➲ VISUAL VOCAB page V18
■ ***adj.*** /'ɑːmtʃeə(r); *NAmE* 'ɑːrmtʃer/ [only before noun] knowing about a subject through books and television, rather than by doing it for yourself: *an **armchair critic/traveller***

armed 🔑 /ɑːmd; *NAmE* ɑːrmd/ *adj.*
1 🔑 involving the use of weapons: *an armed robbery* ◇ *an international **armed conflict*** (= a war) OPP **unarmed** **2** 🔑 carrying a weapon, especially a gun: *The man is armed and dangerous.* ◇ *armed guards* ◇ *Police were **heavily armed**.* ◇ **~ with a gun, etc.** *He was armed with a rifle.* OPP **unarmed** **3 ~** (**with sth**) knowing sth or carrying sth that you need in order to help you to perform a task: *He was armed with all the facts.*
IDM ˌ**armed to the 'teeth** having many weapons

the ˌarmed 'forces (*BrE* also **the ˌarmed 'services**) *noun* [pl.] a country's army, navy and AIR FORCE

arm·ful /'ɑːmfʊl; *NAmE* 'ɑːrm-/ *noun* a quantity that you can carry in one or both arms

arm·hole /'ɑːmhəʊl; *NAmE* 'ɑːrmhoʊl/ *noun* the place in a coat, shirt, dress, etc. that your arm goes through

ar·mis·tice /'ɑːmɪstɪs; *NAmE* 'ɑːrm-/ *noun* [sing.] a formal agreement during a war to stop fighting and discuss making peace SYN **ceasefire**

arm·lock /'ɑːmlɒk; *NAmE* 'ɑːrmlɑːk/ *noun* (in WRESTLING) a way of holding an opponent's arm so that they cannot move: *He had him in an armlock.*

ar·moire /ɑːm'wɑː(r); *NAmE* ɑːrm'wɑːr/ *noun* (from *French*) a cupboard with drawers or shelves underneath, especially one that has a lot of decoration

ar·mor·ial /ɑː'mɔːriəl; *NAmE* ɑːr'm-/ *adj.* connected with HERALDRY

ar·mour (*especially US* **armor**) /'ɑːmə(r); *NAmE* 'ɑːrm-/ *noun* [U] **1** special metal clothing that soldiers wore in the past to protect their bodies while fighting: *a suit of armour* ◇ (*figurative*) *Monkeys do not have any kind of protective armour and use their brains to solve problems.* **2** metal covers that protect ships and military vehicles such as tanks **3** (*technical*) military vehicles used in war: *an attack by infantry and armour* IDM see CHINK *n.*, KNIGHT *n.*

ar·moured (*especially US* **ar·mored**) /'ɑːməd; *NAmE* 'ɑːrmərd/ *adj.* **1** (especially of a military vehicle) protected by metal covers: *The cruiser was heavily armoured.* ◇ *an armoured car* **2** using armoured vehicles: *an armoured division*

ˌarmoured person'nel carrier (*especially US* **ˌarmored person'nel carrier**) *noun* a military vehicle used to transport soldiers

ar·mour·er (*especially US* **ar·mor·er**) /'ɑːmərə(r); *NAmE* 'ɑːrm-/ *noun* a person who makes or repairs weapons and armour

ˌarmour-'plated (*especially US* **armor-**) *adj.* (of vehicles) covered with sheets of metal to provide protection against bullets, etc.

ar·moury (*especially US* **ar·mory**) /'ɑːməri; *NAmE* 'ɑːrm-/ *noun* (*pl.* **-ies**) **1** a place where weapons and armour are kept SYN **arsenal** **2** (in the US or Canada) a building which is the HEADQUARTERS for training people who are not professional soldiers, for example the National Guard **3** (*formal*) the things that sb has available to help them achieve sth: *Doctors have an armoury of drugs available.* **4** all the weapons and military equipment that a country has: *Britain's nuclear armoury*

arm·pit /'ɑːmpɪt; *NAmE* 'ɑːrm-/ (also *NAmE informal* **pit**) *noun* the part of the body under the arm where it joins the shoulder ➲ VISUAL VOCAB page V48 ➲ see also UNDERARM
IDM **the 'armpit of sth** (*informal, especially NAmE*) the most unpleasant or ugly place in a country or region: *The city has been called the armpit of America.*

arm·rest /'ɑːmrest; *NAmE* 'ɑːrm-/ *noun* the part of some types of seat, especially in planes or cars, which supports your arm

arms 🔑 /ɑːmz; *NAmE* ɑːrmz/ *noun* [pl.]
1 🔑 (*formal*) weapons, especially as used by the army, navy, etc: *arms and ammunition* ◇ *Police officers in the UK do not usually **carry arms**.* ➲ see also FIREARM, SMALL ARMS **2** = COAT OF ARMS: *the King's Arms* (= used as the name of a pub)
IDM **be under 'arms** (*formal*) to have weapons and be ready to fight in a war **lay down your 'arms** (*formal*) to stop fighting **take up arms** (**against sb**) (*formal*) to prepare to fight (**be**) **up in 'arms** (**about/over sth**) (*informal*) (of a group of people) to be very angry about sth and ready to protest strongly about it ➲ more at BEAR *v.*, PRESENT *v.*

'arms control *noun* [U] international agreements to destroy weapons or limit the number of weapons that countries have

'arms race *noun* [sing.] a situation in which countries compete to get the most and best weapons

'arm-twisting *noun* [U] (*informal*) the use of a lot of pressure or even physical force to persuade sb to do sth

'arm-wrestling *noun* [U] a competition to find out which of two people is the strongest, in which they try to force each other's arm down onto a table

army 🔑 /'ɑːmi; *NAmE* 'ɑːrmi/ *noun* (*pl.* **-ies**)
1 🔑 [C+sing./pl. v.] a large organized group of soldiers who are trained to fight on land: *The two opposing armies faced each other across the battlefield.* **2** 🔑 **the army** [sing.+ sing./pl. v.] the part of a country's armed forces that fights on land: *Her husband is **in the army**.* ◇ *After leaving school, Mike **went into the army**.* ◇ *an army officer* ➲ COLLOCATIONS at WAR **3** [C+sing./pl. v.] a large number of people or things, especially when they are organized in some way or involved in a particular activity: *an army of advisers/volunteers* ◇ *An army of ants marched across the path.*

ˌarmy 'surplus *noun* [U] clothing and equipment that the army no longer needs and is sold to the public

ar·nica /'ɑːnɪkə; *NAmE* 'ɑːrn-/ *noun* [U] a natural medicine made from a plant, used to treat BRUISES (= marks that appear on the skin after sb has fallen, been hit, etc.)

'A-road *noun* (in Britain) a road that is less important than a MOTORWAY, but wider and straighter than a B-ROAD

aroma /ə'rəʊmə; *NAmE* ə'roʊmə/ *noun* a pleasant, noticeable smell: *the aroma of fresh coffee*

aroma·ther·apy /əˌrəʊmə'θerəpi; *NAmE* əˌroʊmə-/ *noun* [U] the use of natural oils that smell sweet for controlling pain or for rubbing into the body during MASSAGE
▸ **aroma·ther·ap·ist** *noun*

aro·mat·ic /ˌærə'mætɪk/ *adj.* having a pleasant noticeable smell SYN **fragrant**: ***aromatic oils/herbs***

arose *past tense of* ARISE

around 🔑 /ə'raʊnd/ *adv., prep.*
■ ***adv.*** HELP For the special uses of **around** in phrasal verbs, look at the entries for the verbs. For example **come around to sth** is in the phrasal verb section at **come**.
1 🔑 approximately: *He arrived around five o'clock.* ◇ *The cost would be somewhere around £1500.* **2** 🔑 on every side; surrounding sb/sth: *I could hear laughter all around.* ◇ *a yard with a fence **all around*** **3** 🔑 (*especially NAmE*) (*BrE* usually **round**) moving in a circle: *How do you make the wheels go around?* **4** 🔑 (*especially NAmE*) (*BrE* usually

round) measured in a circle: *an old tree that was at least ten feet around* **5** ⊶ in or to many places: *We were all running around trying to get ready in time.* ◇ *This is our new office—Kay will show you around.* ◇ *There were papers lying around all over the floor.* **6** ⊶ used to describe activities that have no real purpose: *There were several young people sitting around looking bored.* **7** ⊶ present in a place; available: *There was more money around in those days.* ◇ *I knocked but there was no one around.* ◇ *Digital television has been around for some time now.* **8** active and well known in a sport, profession, etc: *a new tennis champion who could be around for a long time* ◇ *She's been around as a film director since the 1980s.* **9** (*especially NAmE*) (*BrE* usually **round**) in a circle or curve to face another way or the opposite way: *She turned the car around and drove off.* ◇ *They looked around when he called.* ➲ see also ABOUT, ROUND

IDM **have been around** to have gained knowledge and experience of the world

■ ***prep.*** (*especially NAmE*) (*BrE* usually **round**) **1** ⊶ surrounding sb/sth; on each side of sth: *The house is built around a central courtyard.* ◇ *He put his arms around her.* **2** ⊶ on, to or from the other side of sb/sth: *Our house is just around the corner.* ◇ *The bus came around the bend.* ◇ *There must be a way around the problem.* **3** ⊶ in a circle: *They walked around the lake.* **4** ⊶ in or to many places in an area: *They walked around the town looking for a place to eat.* **5** to fit in with particular people, ideas, etc: *I can't arrange everything around your timetable!*

Which Word?

around / round / about

- **Around** and **round** can often be used with the same meaning in *BrE*, though **around** is more formal: *The earth goes round/around the sun.* ◇ *They live round/around the corner.* ◇ *We travelled round/around India.* ◇ *She turned round/around when I came in.* In *NAmE* only **around** can be used in these meanings.
- **Around, round** and **about** can also sometimes be used with the same meaning in *BrE*: *The kids were running around/round/about outside.* ◇ *I've been waiting around/round/about to see her all day.* In *NAmE* only **around** can be used in these meanings. **About** or **around** can be used in both *BrE* and *NAmE* to mean 'approximately': *We left around/about 8 o'clock.*

a,round-the-'clock *adj.* = ROUND-THE-CLOCK

arouse /ə'raʊz/ *verb* **1** **~ sth** to make sb have a particular feeling or attitude: *to* ***arouse sb's interest/curiosity/anger*** ◇ *Her strange behaviour aroused our suspicions.* **2** **~ sb** to make sb feel sexually excited SYN **excite** **3** **~ sb** to make you feel more active and want to start doing sth: *The whole community was aroused by the crime.* **4** **~ sb** (**from sth**) (*formal*) to wake sb from sleep ➲ see also ROUSE ▸ **arousal** /ə'raʊzl/ *noun* [U]: ***emotional/sexual arousal***

ar·peg·gio /ɑː'pedʒiəʊ; *NAmE* ɑːr'pedʒioʊ/ *noun* (*pl.* -os) (*music*) the notes of a CHORD played quickly one after the other

arr. *abbr.* **1** (in writing) arrives; arrival: *arr. London 06.00* ➲ compare DEP. **2** (*music*) (in writing) arranged by: *Handel, arr. Mozart*

ar·raign /ə'reɪn/ *verb* [usually passive] **~ sb** (**for sth**) (*law*) to bring sb to court in order to formally accuse them of a crime: *He was arraigned for murder.* ◇ *He was arraigned on a charge of murder.* ▸ **ar·raign·ment** *noun* [C, U]

ar·range ⊶ /ə'reɪndʒ/ *verb*
1 ⊶ [T, I] to plan or organize sth in advance: **~ sth** *The party was arranged quickly.* ◇ *She arranged a loan with the bank.* ◇ *Can I arrange an appointment for Monday?* ◇ *We met at six,* ***as arranged.*** ◇ **~ how, where, etc...** *We've still got to arrange how to get to the airport.* ◇ **~ to do sth** *Have you arranged to meet him?* ◇ **~ that...** *I've arranged that we can borrow their car.* ◇ **~ for sth** (**to do sth**) *We arranged for a car to collect us from the airport.* ◇ **~ with sb** (**about sth**) *I've arranged with the neighbours about feeding the cat while we are away.* **2** ⊶ [T] **~ sth** to put sth in a particular order; to make sth neat or attractive: *The books are arranged alphabetically by author.* ◇ *I must arrange my financial affairs and make a will.* ◇ *She arranged the flowers in a vase.* **3** [T] **~ sth** (**for sth**) to write or change a piece of music so that it is suitable for a particular instrument or voice: *He arranged traditional folk songs for the piano.*

ar,ranged 'marriage *noun* a marriage in which the parents choose the husband or wife for their child

ar·range·ment ⊶ /ə'reɪndʒmənt/ *noun*
1 ⊶ [C, usually pl.] a plan or preparation that you make so that sth can happen: *travel arrangements* ◇ **~ for sth** *I'll* ***make arrangements*** *for you to be met at the airport.* **2** ⊶ [C, usually pl.] the way things are done or organized: *She's happy with her unusual living arrangements.* ◇ *new security arrangements* ◇ *There are special arrangements for people working overseas.* **3** ⊶ [C, U] an agreement that you make with sb that you can both accept: *We can* ***come to an arrangement*** *over the price.* ◇ **~ between A and B** *an arrangement between the school and the parents* ◇ **~ with sb** (**to do sth**) *You can cash cheques here* ***by prior arrangement*** *with the bank.* ◇ **~ that...** *They had an arrangement that the children would spend two weeks with each parent.* **4** ⊶ [C, U] a group of things that are organized or placed in a particular order or position; the act of placing things in a particular order: *plans of the possible seating arrangements* ◇ *the art of flower arrangement* **5** [C, U] a piece of music that has been changed, for example for another instrument to play

ar·ran·ger /ə'reɪndʒə/ *noun* **1** a person who arranges music that has been written by sb different **2** a person who arranges things: *arrangers of care services for the elderly*

ar·rant /'ærənt/ *adj.* [only before noun] (*old-fashioned*) used to emphasize how bad sth/sb is: *arrant nonsense*

array /ə'reɪ/ *noun, verb*
■ ***noun*** **1** [usually sing.] a group or collection of things or people, often one that is large or impressive: *a vast array of bottles of different shapes and sizes* ◇ *a dazzling array of talent* **2** (*computing*) a way of organizing and storing related data in a computer memory **3** (*technical*) a set of numbers, signs or values arranged in rows and columns
■ ***verb*** [usually passive] (*formal*) **1** **~ sth** to arrange a group of things in a pleasing way or so that they are in order: *Jars of all shapes and sizes were arrayed on the shelves.* **2** **~ sb** to arrange soldiers in a position from which they are ready to attack

array·ed /ə'reɪd/ *adj.* [not before noun] **~** (**in sth**) (*literary*) dressed in a particular way, especially in beautiful clothes: *She was arrayed in a black velvet gown.*

ar·rears /ə'rɪəz; *NAmE* ə'rɪrz/ *noun* [pl.] money that sb owes that they have not paid at the right time: ***rent/mortgage/tax arrears***

IDM **be in arrears** | **get/fall into arrears** to be late in paying money that you owe: *We're two months in arrears with the rent.* **in arrears** if money or a person is paid **in arrears** for work, the money is paid after the work has been done

ar·rest ⊶ /ə'rest/ *verb, noun*
■ ***verb*** **1** ⊶ [T, often passive] if the police **arrest** sb, the person is taken to a POLICE STATION and kept there because the police believe they may be guilty of a crime: **~ sb** *A man has been arrested in connection with the robbery.* ◇ **~ sb for sth** *She was arrested for drug-related offences.* ◇ **~ sb for doing sth** *You could* ***get arrested*** *for doing that.* ➲ COLLOCATIONS at JUSTICE **2** [T] **~ sth** (*formal*) to stop a process or a development: *They failed to arrest the company's decline.* **3** [T] **~ sth** (*formal*) to make sb notice sth and pay attention to it: *An unusual noise* ***arrested his attention.*** **4** [I] (*medical*) if sb **arrests**, their heart stops beating: *He arrested on the way to the hospital.*
■ ***noun*** [C, U] **1** ⊶ the act of arresting sb: *The police made several arrests.* ◇ *She was* ***under arrest*** *on suspicion of murder.* ◇ *Opposition leaders were put under* ***house arrest*** (= not

A

allowed to leave their houses). ➲ see also CITIZEN'S ARREST **2** an act of sth stopping or being interrupted: *He died after suffering a **cardiac arrest** (= when his heart suddenly stopped).*

ar,restable of'fence *noun* (*law*) an offence for which sb can be arrested without a WARRANT from a judge

ar·rest·ing /ə'restɪŋ/ *adj.* (*formal*) attracting a lot of attention; very attractive

ar·rival 0‑ /ə'raɪvl/ *noun*
1 0‑ [U, C] an act of coming or being brought to a place: *Guests receive dinner **on/upon arrival** at the hotel.* ◇ *We apologize for the late arrival of the train.* ◇ *the arrival of the mail in the morning* ◇ *daily arrivals of refugees* ◇ *There are 120 **arrivals and departures** every day.* OPP **departure** **2** 0‑ [C] a person or thing that comes to a place: *The first arrivals at the concert got the best seats.* ◇ ***early/late/new arrivals*** ◇ *We're expecting **a new arrival** (= a baby) in the family soon.* **3** 0‑ [U] the time when a new technology or idea is introduced: *the arrival of pay TV*
IDM see DEAD *adj.*

ar·rive 0‑ /ə'raɪv/ *verb*
1 0‑ [I] (*abbr.* arr.) to get to a place, especially at the end of a journey: *I'll wait until they arrive.* ◇ *I was pleased to hear you arrived home safely.* ◇ *to **arrive early/late** for a meeting* ◇ *The police arrived to arrest him.* ◇ **~ at/in/on...** *She'll arrive in New York at noon.* ◇ *The train arrived at the station 20 minutes late.* ◇ *By the time I **arrived on the scene**, it was all over.* ◇ *We didn't arrive back at the hotel until very late.* **2** 0‑ [I] (of things) to be brought to sb: *A letter arrived for you this morning.* ◇ *Send your application to arrive by 31 October.* ◇ *We waited an hour for our lunch to arrive.* ◇ *The new product will arrive on supermarket shelves (= be available) early next year.* **3** 0‑ [I] (of an event or a moment) to happen or to come, especially when you have been waiting for it: *The wedding day finally arrived.* ◇ *The baby arrived (= was born) early.*
IDM **sb has ar'rived** (*informal*) somebody has become successful: *He knew he had arrived when he was shortlisted for the Booker prize.*
PHR V **ar'rive at sth** 0‑ to decide on or find sth, especially after discussion and thought SYN **reach**: *to **arrive at an agreement/a decision/a conclusion*** ◇ *to arrive at the truth*

ar·riv·iste /,æri:'vi:st/ *noun* (from *French, disapproving*) a person who is determined to be accepted as a member of a social group, etc. to which they do not really belong

ar·ro·gance /'ærəgəns/ *noun* [U] the behaviour of a person when they feel that they are more important than other people, so that they are rude to them or do not consider them

ar·ro·gant /'ærəgənt/ *adj.* behaving in a proud, unpleasant way, showing little thought for other people ▸ **ar·ro·gant·ly** *adv.*

ar·ro·gate /'ærəgeɪt/ *verb*
PHR V **arrogate to yourself sth** (*formal*) to claim or take sth that you have no right to: *I do not arrogate to myself the right to decide.*

arrow 0‑ /'ærəʊ; *NAmE* 'æroʊ/ *noun*
1 0‑ a thin stick with a sharp point at one end, which is shot from a BOW: *a **bow and arrow*** ◇ *to **fire/shoot an arrow*** ◇ *The road continues as straight as an arrow.* ➲ VISUAL VOCAB page V34 **2** 0‑ a mark or sign like an arrow (→), used to show direction or position: *Follow the arrows.* ◇ *Use the arrow keys to move the cursor.*

ar·row·head /'ærəʊhed; *NAmE* 'æroʊ-/ *noun* the sharp pointed end of an arrow

ar·row·root /'ærəʊru:t; *NAmE* 'æroʊ-/ *noun* [U] a plant whose roots can be cooked and eaten or made into a type of flour, used especially to make sauces thick; the flour itself

ar·royo /ə'rɔɪəʊ; *NAmE* -oʊ/ *noun* (*pl.* -os) (from *Spanish*) a narrow channel with steep sides cut by a river in a desert region

arse /ɑ:s; *NAmE* ɑ:rs/ *noun, verb*
■ ***noun*** (*BrE, taboo, slang*) **1** (*NAmE* **ass**) the part of the body that you sit on; your bottom: *Get off your arse!* (= stop sitting around doing nothing) **2** (usually following an adjective) a stupid person ➲ see also SMART-ARSE
IDM **My arse!** (*taboo, slang*) used by some people to show they do not believe what sb has said **work your 'arse off** (*taboo, slang*) to work very hard ➲ more at KISS *v.*, KNOW *v.*, LICK *v.*, PAIN *n.*
■ ***verb***
IDM **can't be 'arsed (to do sth)** (*BrE, taboo, slang*) to not want to do sth because it is too much trouble: *I was supposed to do some work this weekend but I couldn't be arsed.*
PHR V **,arse a'bout/a'round** (*BrE, taboo, slang*) to waste time by behaving in a silly way

arse·hole /'ɑ:shəʊl; *NAmE* 'ɑ:rshoʊl/ (*BrE*) (*NAmE* **asshole**) *noun* (*taboo, slang*) **1** the ANUS **2** a stupid or unpleasant person: *What an arsehole!*

'arse-licker (*BrE*) (*NAmE* **'ass-licker**) *noun* (*taboo, slang*) a person who is too friendly to sb in authority and is always ready to do what they want ▸ **'arse-licking** (*BrE*) (*NAmE* **'ass-licking**) *noun* [U]

ar·senal /'ɑ:sənl; *NAmE* 'ɑ:rs-/ *noun* **1** a collection of weapons such as guns and EXPLOSIVES: *Britain's nuclear arsenal* **2** a building where military weapons and EXPLOSIVES are made or stored

ar·senic /'ɑ:snɪk; *NAmE* 'ɑ:rs-/ *noun* [U] (*symb.* As) a chemical element. Arsenic is an extremely poisonous white powder.

arsey /'ɑ:si; *NAmE* 'ɑ:rsi/ *noun* (*AustralE, informal*) very lucky

arson /'ɑ:sn; *NAmE* 'ɑ:rsn/ *noun* [U] the crime of deliberately setting fire to sth, especially a building: *to carry out an **arson attack*** ➲ COLLOCATIONS at CRIME

ar·son·ist /'ɑ:sənɪst; *NAmE* 'ɑ:rs-/ *noun* a person who commits the crime of arson

art 0‑ /ɑ:t; *NAmE* ɑ:rt/ *noun, verb*
■ ***noun*** **1** 0‑ [U] the use of the imagination to express ideas or feelings, particularly in painting, drawing or SCULPTURE: *modern/contemporary/American art* ◇ *an **art critic/historian/lover*** ◇ *Can we call television art?* ◇ *stolen **works of art*** ◇ *Her performance displayed great art.* ➲ see also CLIP ART, FINE ART **2** 0‑ [U] examples of objects such as paintings, drawings or SCULPTURES: *an **art gallery/exhibition*** ◇ *a collection of art and antiques* **3** 0‑ [U] the skill of creating objects such as paintings and drawings, especially when you study it: *She's good at art and design.* ◇ *an **art teacher/student/college/class*** **4** 0‑ **the arts** [pl.] art, music, theatre, literature, etc. when you think of them as a group: *lottery funding for the arts* ➲ see also PERFORMING ARTS **5** [C] a type of VISUAL or performing art: *Dance is a very theatrical art.* **6** 0‑ [C, usually pl.] the subjects you can study at school or university that are not scientific, such as languages, history or literature: *an arts degree* ➲ compare SCIENCE **7** [C, U] an ability or a skill that you can develop with training and practice: *a therapist trained in the art of healing* ◇ *Letter-writing is a lost art nowadays.* ◇ *Appearing confident at interviews is **quite an art** (= rather difficult).*
IDM see FINE *adj.*
■ ***verb*** **thou art** (*old use*) used to mean 'you are', when talking to one person

art deco /,ɑ:t 'dekəʊ; *NAmE* ,ɑ:rt 'dekoʊ/ (also **Art Deco**) *noun* [U] a popular style of decorative art in the 1920s and 1930s that has GEOMETRIC shapes with clear outlines and bright strong colours

'art director *noun* **1** the person who is responsible for the pictures, photos, etc. in a magazine **2** the person who is responsible for the SETS and PROPS when a film/movie is being made

arte·fact (also **ar·ti·fact** especially in *NAmE*) /'ɑ:tɪfækt; *NAmE* 'ɑ:rt-/ *noun* (*technical*) an object that is made by a person, especially sth of historical or cultural interest

ar·teri·ole /ɑ:'tɪəriəʊl; *NAmE* ɑ:r'tɪrioʊl/ *noun* (*anatomy*) a thin branch of an ARTERY that leads off into CAPILLARIES

A

Collocations

Fine arts

Creating art

- **make** a work of art/a drawing/a sketch/a sculpture/a statue/engravings/etchings/prints
- **do** an oil painting/a self-portrait/a line drawing/a rough sketch
- **create** a work of art/an artwork/paintings and sculptures
- **produce** paintings/portraits/oil sketches/his most celebrated work/a series of prints
- **paint** a picture/landscape/portrait/mural/in oils/in watercolours/(*especially US*) in watercolors/on canvas
- **draw** a picture/a portrait/a cartoon/a sketch/a line/a figure/the human form/in charcoal/in ink
- **sketch** a preliminary drawing/a figure/a shape
- **carve** a figure/an image/a sculpture/an altarpiece/reliefs/a block of wood
- **sculpt** a portrait bust/a statue/an abstract figure
- **etch** a line/a pattern/a design/a name into the glass
- **mix** colours/(*especially US*) colors/pigments/paints
- **add/apply** thin/thick layers of paint/colour/(*especially US*) color/pigment
- **use** oil pastels/charcoal/acrylic paint/a can of spray paint
- **work in** bronze/ceramics/stone/oils/pastels/watercolour/a wide variety of media

Describing art

- **paint/depict** a female figure/a biblical scene/a pastoral landscape/a domestic interior
- **depict/illustrate** a traditional/mythological/historical/religious theme
- **create** an abstract composition/a richly textured surface/a distorted perspective
- **paint** dark/rich/skin/flesh tones
- **use** broad brush strokes/loose brushwork/vibrant colours/a limited palette/simple geometric forms
- **develop/adopt/paint** in a stylized manner/an abstract style

Showing and selling art

- **commission** an altarpiece/a bronze bust of sb/a portrait/a religious work/an artist to paint sth
- **frame** a painting/portrait
- **hang** art/a picture/a painting
- **display/exhibit** modern art/sb's work/a collection/original artwork/ drawings/sculptures/a piece
- **be displayed/hung** in a gallery/museum
- **install/place** a sculpture in/at/on sth
- **erect/unveil** a bronze/marble/life-size statue
- **hold/host/mount/open/curate/see** (*especially BrE*) an exhibition/(*NAmE usually*) exhibit
- **be/go on** (*BrE*) exhibition/(*NAmE*) exhibit
- **feature/promote/showcase** a conceptual artist/contemporary works
- **collect** African art/modern British paintings/Japanese prints
- **restore/preserve** a fresco/great works of art

ar·terio·scler·osis /ɑːˌtɪəriəʊskləˈrəʊsɪs; *NAmE* ɑːrˌtɪrioʊskləˈroʊsɪs/ *noun* [U] (*medical*) a condition in which the walls of the arteries become thick and hard, making it difficult for blood to flow

ar·tery /ˈɑːtəri; *NAmE* ˈɑːrt-/ *noun* (*pl.* -ies) **1** any of the tubes that carry blood from the heart to other parts of the body: *blocked arteries* ➲ COLLOCATIONS at ILL ➲ compare VEIN ➲ see also CORONARY ARTERY **2** a large and important road, river, railway/railroad line, etc. ▸ **ar·ter·ial** /ɑːˈtɪəriəl; *NAmE* ɑːrˈtɪr-/ *adj.* [only before noun]: ***arterial blood/disease*** ◇ *an* ***arterial road***

ar·te·sian well /ɑːˌtiːziən ˈwel; *NAmE* ɑːrˈtiːʒn/ *noun* a hole made in the ground through which water rises to the surface by natural pressure

ˈart form *noun* **1** [C] a particular type of artistic activity: *The short story is a difficult art form to master.* **2** [sing.] an activity that sb does very well and gives them the opportunity to show imagination: *She has elevated the dinner party into an art form.*

art·ful /ˈɑːtfl; *NAmE* ˈɑːrtfl/ *adj.* [usually before noun] **1** (*disapproving*) clever at getting what you want, sometimes by not telling the truth SYN **crafty** **2** (of things or actions) designed or done in a clever way ▸ **art·ful·ly** /-fəli/ *adv.*

ˈart gallery (also **gal·lery**) *noun* a building where paintings and other works of art are shown to the public

ˌart ˈhistory *noun* [U] the study of the history of painting, SCULPTURE, etc.

ˈart-house *adj.* [only before noun] **art-house** films/movies are usually made by small companies and are not usually seen by a wide audience

arth·ri·tic /ɑːˈθrɪtɪk; *NAmE* ɑːrˈθ-/ *adj.* suffering from or caused by arthritis: ***arthritic hands/pain***

arth·ritis /ɑːˈθraɪtɪs; *NAmE* ɑːrˈθ-/ *noun* [U] a disease that causes pain and swelling in one or more joints of the body ➲ see also OSTEOARTHRITIS, RHEUMATOID ARTHRITIS

arthro·pod /ˈɑːθrəpɒd; *NAmE* ˈɑːrθrəpɑːd/ *noun* (*biology*) an INVERTEBRATE animal such as an insect, spider, or CRAB, that has its SKELETON on the outside of its body and has joints on its legs

Ar·thur·ian /ɑːˈθjʊəriən; *NAmE* ɑːrˈθʊr-/ *adj.* connected with the stories about Arthur, a king of ancient Britain, his Knights of the Round Table and COURT at Camelot: *Arthurian legends*

ar·ti·choke /ˈɑːtɪtʃəʊk; *NAmE* ˈɑːrtɪtʃoʊk/ *noun* [C, U] **1** (also ˌ**globe ˈarti·choke**) a round vegetable with a lot of thick green leaves. The bottom part of the leaves and the inside of the artichoke can be eaten when cooked. ➲ VISUAL VOCAB page V27 **2** (*BrE*) = JERUSALEM ARTICHOKE

art·icle 🔑 /ˈɑːtɪkl; *NAmE* ˈɑːrt-/ *noun*
1 🔑 **~ (on/about sth)** a piece of writing about a particular subject in a newspaper or magazine: *Have you seen that article about young fashion designers?* ➲ see also LEADING ARTICLE **2** 🔑 (*law*) a separate item in an agreement or a contract: *Article 10 of the European Convention guarantees free speech.* **3** 🔑 (*formal*) a particular item or separate thing, especially one of a set SYN **item**: *articles of clothing* ◇ *toilet articles such as soap and shampoo* ◇ *The articles found in the car helped the police to identify the body.* **4** (*grammar*) the words *a* and *an* (the indefinite article) or *the* (the definite article)

art·icled /ˈɑːtɪkld; *NAmE* ˈɑːrt-/ *adj.* (*BrE*) employed by a group of lawyers, ARCHITECTS or ACCOUNTANTS while training to become qualified: *an articled clerk* (= sb who is training to be a SOLICITOR) ◇ *She* ***was articled to*** *a firm of solicitors.*

ˌarticle of ˈfaith *noun* (*pl.* articles of faith) something you believe very strongly, as if it were a religious belief

ar·ticu·late *verb, adj.*
- ***verb*** /ɑːˈtɪkjuleɪt; *NAmE* ɑːrˈt-/ **1** [T] **~ sth (to sb)** (*formal*) to express or explain your thoughts or feelings clearly in words: *She struggled to articulate her thoughts.* **2** [I, T] to speak, pronounce or play sth in a clear way: *He was too drunk to articulate properly.* ◇ **~ sth** *Every note was carefully articulated.* **3** [I] **~ (with sth)** (*formal*) to be related to sth so that together the two parts form a whole: *These courses are designed to articulate with university degrees.* **4** [I, T] (*technical*) to be joined to sth else by a joint, so that movement is possible; to join sth in this way: **~ (with sth)** *bones that articulate with others* ◇ **~ sth** *a robot with articulated limbs*
- ***adj.*** /ɑːˈtɪkjələt; *NAmE* ɑːrˈt-/ **1** (of a person) good at expressing ideas or feelings clearly in words **2** (of speech)

A

clearly expressed or pronounced: *All we could hear were loud sobs, but no articulate words.* OPP **inarticulate** ▶ **ar·ticu·late·ly** *adv.*

ar·ticu·lated /ɑːˈtɪkjuleɪtɪd; *NAmE* ɑːrˈt-/ *adj.* (*BrE*) (of a vehicle) with two or more sections joined together in a way that makes it easier to turn corners: *an* ***articulated lorry/truck*** ➲ VISUAL VOCAB page V46 ➲ see also TRACTOR-TRAILER

ar·ticu·la·tion /ɑːˌtɪkjuˈleɪʃn; *NAmE* ɑːrˌt-/ *noun* **1** [U] (*formal*) the expression of an idea or a feeling in words: *the articulation of his theory* **2** [U] (*formal*) the act of making sounds in speech or music: *The singer worked hard on the clear articulation of every note.* **3** [U, C, usually sing.] (*technical*) a joint or connection that allows movement

ar·ti·fact (*especially NAmE*) = ARTEFACT

ar·ti·fice /ˈɑːtɪfɪs; *NAmE* ˈɑːrt-/ *noun* [U, C] (*formal*) the clever use of tricks to cheat sb SYN **cunning**

ar·ti·fi·cial 🔑 /ˌɑːtɪˈfɪʃl; *NAmE* ˌɑːrt-/ *adj.*
1 🔑 made or produced to copy sth natural; not real: *an* ***artificial limb/flower/sweetener/fertilizer*** ◊ ***artificial lighting/light*** **2** 🔑 created by people; not happening naturally: *A job interview is a very artificial situation.* ◊ *the artificial barriers of race, class and gender* **3** 🔑 not what it appears to be SYN **fake**: *artificial emotion* ▶ **ar·ti·fi·ci·al·ity** /ˌɑːtɪˌfɪʃiˈæləti; *NAmE* ˌɑːrt-/ *noun* [U] **ar·ti·fi·cial·ly** 🔑 /ˌɑːtɪˈfɪʃəli; *NAmE* ˌɑːrt-/ *adv.*: *artificially created lakes* ◊ *artificially low prices*

Synonyms

artificial

synthetic • false • man-made • fake • imitation

These words all describe things that are not real, or not naturally produced or grown.

artificial made or produced to copy sth natural; not real: *artificial flowers* ◊ *artificial light*

synthetic made by combining chemical substances rather than being produced naturally by plants or animals: *synthetic drugs* ◊ *shoes with synthetic soles*

false not natural: *false teeth* ◊ *a false beard*

man-made made by people; not natural: *man-made fibres such as nylon*

fake made to look like sth else; not real: *a fake-fur jacket*

imitation [only before noun] made to look like sth else; not real: *She would never wear imitation pearls.*

PATTERNS
- artificial/synthetic/man-made **fabrics/fibres/materials/products**
- artificial/synthetic/fake/imitation **fur/leather**
- artificial/synthetic/false/fake/imitation **diamonds/pearls**

ˌartificial insemiˈnation *noun* [U] (*abbr.* AI) the process of making a woman or female animal pregnant by an artificial method of putting male SPERM inside her, and not by sexual activity: *artificial insemination by a donor, abbreviated to 'AID'*

ˌartificial inˈtelligence *noun* [U] (*abbr.* AI) (*computing*) an area of study concerned with making computers copy intelligent human behaviour

ˌartificial ˈlanguage *noun* a language invented for international communication or for use with computers

ˌartificial respiˈration (*BrE* also **ˌartificial ventiˈlation**) *noun* [U] the process of helping a person who has stopped breathing begin to breathe again, usually by blowing into their mouth or nose ➲ compare MOUTH-TO-MOUTH RESUSCITATION

ar·til·lery /ɑːˈtɪləri; *NAmE* ɑːrˈt-/ *noun* **1** [U] large, heavy guns which are often moved on wheels: *The town is under heavy artillery fire.* **2 the artillery** [sing.] the section of an army trained to use these guns

ar·ti·san /ˌɑːtɪˈzæn; *NAmE* ˈɑːrtəzn/ *noun* (*formal*) a person who does skilled work, making things with their hands SYN **craftsman**

art·ist 🔑 /ˈɑːtɪst; *NAmE* ˈɑːrt-/ *noun*
1 🔑 a person who creates works of art, especially paintings or drawings: *an exhibition of work by contemporary British artists* ◊ *a graphic artist* ◊ *a make-up artist* ◊ *Police have issued an artist's impression of her attacker.* ◊ (*figurative*) *Whoever made this cake is a real artist.* ➲ COLLOCATIONS at ART **2** 🔑 (*especially BrE* **ar·tiste** /ɑːˈtiːst; *NAmE* ɑːrˈt-/) a professional entertainer such as a singer, a dancer or an actor: *a* ***recording/solo artist***

art·is·tic 🔑 /ɑːˈtɪstɪk; *NAmE* ɑːrˈt-/ *adj.*
1 🔑 connected with art or artists: *the artistic works of the period* ◊ *a work of great artistic merit* ◊ *the artistic director of the theatre* **2** 🔑 showing a natural skill in or enjoyment of art, especially being able to paint or draw well: ***artistic abilities/achievements/skills/talent*** ◊ *She comes from a very artistic family.* **3** 🔑 done with skill and imagination; attractive or beautiful: *an artistic arrangement of dried flowers* IDM see LICENCE ▶ **art·is·tic·al·ly** 🔑 /ɑːˈtɪstɪkli; *NAmE* ɑːrˈt-/ *adv.*

arˌtistic diˈrector *noun* the person in charge of deciding which plays, OPERAS, etc. a theatre company will perform, and the general artistic policy of the company

art·is·try /ˈɑːtɪstri; *NAmE* ˈɑːrt-/ *noun* [U] the skill of an artist: *He played the piece with effortless artistry.*

art·less /ˈɑːtləs; *NAmE* ˈɑːrt-/ *adj.* (*formal*) **1** simple, natural and honest: *the artless sincerity of a young child* **2** made without skill or art

art nou·veau /ˌɑː(t) nuːˈvəʊ; *NAmE* ˌɑːr(t) nuːˈvoʊ/ (also **Art Nouveau**) *noun* [U] a style of decorative art and ARCHITECTURE popular in Europe and the US at the end of the 19th century and beginning of the 20th century that uses complicated designs and curved patterns based on natural shapes like leaves and flowers

ˌarts and ˈcrafts *noun* [pl.] activities that need both artistic and practical skills, such as making cloth, jewellery and POTTERY

artsy /ˈɑːtsi; *NAmE* ˈɑːrtsi/ (*NAmE*) (*BrE* **arty**) *adj.* (*informal*, usually *disapproving*) seeming or wanting to be very artistic or interested in the arts

artsy-fartsy /ˌɑːtsi ˈfɑːtsi; *NAmE* ˌɑːrtsi ˈfɑːrtsi/ (*especially NAmE*) (*BrE* **arty-farty**) *adj.* (*informal, disapproving*) connected with, or having an interest in, the arts

ˌart ˈtherapy *noun* [U] a type of PSYCHOTHERAPY in which you are encouraged to express yourself using art materials

art·work /ˈɑːtwɜːk; *NAmE* ˈɑːrtwɜːrk/ *noun* **1** [U] photographs and pictures prepared for books, magazines, etc. **2** [C] a work of art, especially one in a museum

arty /ˈɑːti; *NAmE* ˈɑːrti/ (*BrE*) (*NAmE* **artsy**) *adj.* (*informal*, usually *disapproving*) seeming or wanting to be very artistic or interested in the arts: *She hangs out with the arty types she met at drama school.*

arty-farty /ˌɑːti ˈfɑːti; *NAmE* ˌɑːrti ˈfɑːrti/ (*BrE*) (*especially NAmE* **ˌartsy-ˈfartsy**) *adj.* (*informal, disapproving*) connected with, or having an interest in, the arts: *I expect he's out with his arty-farty friends.*

aru·gula /æˈruːgjələ/ (*NAmE*) (*BrE* **rocket**) *noun* [U] a plant with long green leaves that have a strong flavour and are eaten raw in salads

arum lily /ˈeərəm lɪli; *NAmE* ˈerəm/ *noun* (*especially BrE*) an African plant with large white PETALS

arvo /ˈɑːvəʊ; *NAmE* ˈɑːrvoʊ/ *noun* (*pl.* **-os**) (*AustralE, NZE, informal*) afternoon: *See you this arvo!*

-ary *suffix* (in adjectives and nouns) connected with: *planetary* ◊ *budgetary*

Aryan /ˈeəriən; *NAmE* ˈer-/ *noun* **1** a member of the group of people that went to S Asia in around 1500 BC **2** a person who spoke any of the languages of the Indo-European group **3** (especially according to the ideas of the German

Nazi party) a member of a Caucasian, not Jewish, race of people, especially one with fair hair and blue eyes ▶ **Aryan** *adj.*

AS ➲ AS (LEVEL)

Which Word?

as / like

You can use both **as** and **like** to say that things are similar.

- **Like** is a preposition and is used before nouns and pronouns: *He has blue eyes like me.*
- **As** is a conjunction and an adverb and is used before a clause, another adverb or a clause beginning with a preposition: *She enjoys all kinds of music, as I do.* ◇ *Repeat these five steps, as in the last exercise.*
- In informal English **like** is frequently used as a conjunction or an adverb instead of **as**: *Nobody understands him like I do.* ◇ *I don't want to upset him again like before.* It is also used instead of **as if**: *It looks like we're going to be late.* These uses of **like** are common but are not considered correct in formal written English.

You will find more help on the use of **as** and **like** in the entries for particular verbs, such as *act*, *behave*, etc.

as 0-m /əz; *strong form* æz/ *prep., adv., conj.*
■ ***prep.* 1** 0-m used to describe sb/sth appearing to be sb/sth else: *They were all dressed as clowns.* ◇ *The bomb was disguised as a package.* **2** 0-m used to describe the fact that sb/sth has a particular job or function: *She works as a courier.* ◇ *Treat me as a friend.* ◇ *I respect him as a doctor.* ◇ *You can use that glass as a vase.* ◇ *The news came as a shock.* ◇ *She had been there often as a child* (= when she was a child).
■ ***adv.* 1** 0-m **as... as...** used when you are comparing two people or things, or two situations: *You're as tall as your father.* ◇ *He was as white as a sheet.* ◇ *She doesn't play as well as her sister.* ◇ *I haven't known him as long as you* (= as you have known him). ◇ *He doesn't earn as much as me.* ◇ *He doesn't earn as much as I do.* ◇ *It's not as hard as I thought.* ◇ *Run as fast as you can.* ◇ *We'd like it as soon as possible.* **2** 0-m used to say that sth happens in the same way: *As always, he said little.* ◇ *The 'h' in honest is silent, as in 'hour'.*
■ ***conj.* 1** 0-m while sth else is happening: *He sat watching her as she got ready.* ◇ *As she grew older she gained in confidence.* ➲ LANGUAGE BANK at PROCESS **2** 0-m in the way in which: *They did as I had asked.* ◇ *Leave the papers as they are.* ◇ *She lost it, just as I said she would.* **3** 0-m used to state the reason for sth: *As you were out, I left a message.* ◇ *She may need some help as she's new.* **4** used to make a comment or to add information about what you have just said: *As you know, Julia is leaving soon.* ◇ *She's very tall, as is her mother.* **5** used to say that in spite of sth being true, what follows is also true SYN **though**: *Happy as they were, there was something missing.* ◇ *Try as he might* (= however hard he tried), *he couldn't open the door.*
IDM **as against sth** in contrast with sth: *They got 27% of the vote as against 32% at the last election.* **ˌas and ˈwhen** used to say that sth may happen at some time in the future, but only when sth else has happened: *We'll decide on the team as and when we qualify.* ◇ *I'll tell you more as and when* (= as soon as I can). **as for sb/sth** 0-m used to start talking about sb/sth SYN **regarding**: *As for Jo, she's doing fine.* ◇ *As for food for the party, that's all being taken care of.* **as from.../as of...** used to show the time or date from which sth starts: *Our fax number is changing as from May 12.* **as if/as though** 0-m in a way that suggests sth: *He behaved as if nothing had happened.* ◇ *It sounds as though you had a good time.* ◇ *It's my birthday. As if you didn't know!* ◇ *'Don't say anything' '**As if I would!**'* (= surely you do not expect me to) **ˌas it ˈis** considering the present situation; as things are: *We were hoping to finish it by next week—as it is, it may be the week after.* ◇ *I can't help—I've got too much to do as it is* (= already). **as it ˈwere** used when a speaker is giving his or her own impression of a situation or expressing sth in a particular way: *Teachers must put the brakes on, as it were, when they notice students looking puzzled.* **as to sth** | **as regards sth** used when you are referring to sth: *As to tax, that will be deducted from your salary.* **as you ˈdo** used as a comment on sth that you have just said: *He smiled and I smiled back. As you do.* ➲ more at WELL, YET

ASA /ˌeɪ es ˈeɪ/ *abbr.* **1** Advertising Standards Authority (an organization in Britain that controls the standard of advertising) **2** American Standards Association (used especially to show the speed of film): *a 400 ASA film*

asap /ˌeɪ es eɪ ˈpiː/ *abbr.* as soon as possible

as·bes·tos /æsˈbestəs/ *noun* [U] a soft grey mineral that does not burn, used especially in the past in building as a protection against fire or to prevent heat loss

as·bes·tosis /ˌæsbesˈtəʊsɪs; *NAmE* -ˈtoʊ-/ *noun* [U] a disease of the lungs caused by breathing in asbestos dust

ASBO /ˈæzbəʊ; *NAmE* -boʊ/ *noun* the abbreviation for 'anti-social behaviour order' (in the UK, an order made by a court which says that sb must stop behaving in a harmful or annoying way to other people)

as·cend /əˈsend/ *verb* [I, T] (*formal*) to rise; to go up; to climb up: *The path started to ascend more steeply.* ◇ *The air became colder as we ascended.* ◇ *The results, ranked **in ascending order*** (= from the lowest to the highest) *are as follows:* ◇ **~ from sth** *Mist ascended from the valley.* ◇ **~ to sth** (*figurative*) *He ascended to the peak of sporting achievement.* ◇ **~ sth** *Her heart was thumping as she ascended the stairs.* ◇ (*figurative*) *to ascend the throne* (= become king or queen) OPP **descend**

as·cend·ancy (also **as·cend·ency**) /əˈsendənsi/ *noun* [U] **~ (over sb/sth)** (*formal*) the position of having power or influence over sb/sth: ***moral/political/intellectual ascendancy*** ◇ *The opposition party was **in the ascendancy*** (= gaining control).

as·cend·ant (also **as·cend·ent**) /əˈsendənt/ *noun*
IDM **in the ascendant** (*formal*) being or becoming more powerful or popular

as·cen·sion /əˈsenʃn/ *noun* [sing.] **1 the Ascension** (in the Christian religion) the journey of Jesus from the earth into heaven **2** (*formal*) the act of moving up or of reaching a high position: *her ascension to the throne*

Asˈcension Day *noun* (in the Christian religion) the 40th day after Easter when Christians remember when Jesus left the earth and went into heaven

as·cent /əˈsent/ *noun* **1** [C, usually sing.] the act of climbing or moving up; an upward journey: *the first ascent of Mount Everest* ◇ *The cart began its gradual ascent up the hill.* ◇ *The rocket steepened its ascent.* OPP **descent 2** [C, usually sing.] an upward path or slope: *At the other side of the valley was a steep ascent to the top of the hill.* OPP **descent 3** [U] (*formal*) the process of moving forward to a better position or of making progress: *man's ascent to civilization*

as·cer·tain /ˌæsəˈteɪn; *NAmE* ˌæsərˈt-/ *verb* (*formal*) to find out the true or correct information about sth: **~ sth** *It can be difficult to ascertain the facts.* ◇ **~ that...** *I ascertained that the driver was not badly hurt.* ◇ **it is ascertained that...** ***It should be ascertained that*** *the plans comply with the law.* ◇ **~ what, whether, etc...** *The police are trying to ascertain what really happened.* ◇ *Could you ascertain whether she will be coming to the meeting?* ◇ **it is ascertained what, whether, etc...** ***It must be ascertained*** *if the land is still owned by the government.* ▶ **as·cer·tain·able** /ˌæsəˈteɪnəbl; *NAmE* ˌæsərˈt-/ *adj.* **as·cer·tain·ment** /ˌæsəˈteɪnmənt; *NAmE* ˌæsərˈt-/ *noun* [U]

as·cet·ic /əˈsetɪk/ *adj.* [usually before noun] not allowing yourself physical pleasures, especially for religious reasons; related to a simple and strict way of living: *The monks lived a very ascetic life.* ▶ **as·cet·ic** *noun*: *monks, hermits and ascetics* **as·ceti·cism** /əˈsetɪsɪzəm/ *noun* [U]

ASCII /ˈæski/ *noun* [U] (*computing*) the abbreviation for 'American Standard Code for Information Interchange' (a standard code used so that data can be moved between computers that use different programs)

A

as·cor·bic acid /əsˌkɔːbɪk ˈæsɪd; *NAmE* -ˌkɔːrb-/ *noun* [U] = VITAMIN C

ascot /ˈæskɒt; *NAmE* ˈæskɑːt/ *noun* (*NAmE*) = CRAVAT

ascribe /əˈskraɪb/ *verb*
PHR V **aˈscribe sth to sb** to consider or state that a book, etc. was written by a particular person SYN **attribute**: *This play is usually ascribed to Shakespeare.* **aˈscribe sth to sb/sth** (*formal*) **1** to consider that sth is caused by a particular thing or person: *He ascribed his failure to bad luck.* **2** to consider that sb/sth has or should have a particular quality SYN **attribute**: *We ascribe great importance to these policies.* ▶ **ascrib·able** *adj.*: **~ to sb/sth** *Their success is ascribable to the quality of their goods.* **ascrip·tion** /əˈskrɪpʃn/ *noun* [U, C]: **~ (to sb/sth)** *the ascription of meaning to objects and events*

ASEAN /ˈæsiæn/ *abbr.* Association of South East Asian Nations

asep·tic /ˌeɪˈseptɪk/ *adj.* (*medical*) free from harmful bacteria OPP **septic**

asex·ual /ˌeɪˈsekʃuəl/ *adj.* **1** (*technical*) not involving sex; not having sexual organs: *asexual reproduction* **2** not having sexual qualities; not interested in sex: *the tendency to see old people as asexual* ▶ **asex·ual·ly** *adv.*: *to reproduce asexually*

ASH /æʃ/ *abbr.* Action on Smoking and Health (an organization in the UK that tries to make people stop smoking by showing how dangerous it is)

ash /æʃ/ *noun* **1** [U] the grey or black powder that is left after sth, especially TOBACCO, wood or coal, has burnt: *cigarette ash* ◇ *black volcanic ash* **2 ashes** [pl.] what is left after sth has been destroyed by burning: *The town was reduced to ashes in the fighting.* ◇ *the glowing ashes of the campfire* ◇ (*figurative*) *The party had risen, like a phoenix, from the ashes of electoral disaster.* **3 ashes** [pl.] the powder that is left after a dead person's body has been CREMATED (= burned): *She wanted her ashes to be scattered at sea.* **4** [C, U] (also ˈ**ash tree**) a forest tree with grey BARK ➲ VISUAL VOCAB page V8 ➲ see also MOUNTAIN ASH **5** [U] the hard pale wood of the ash tree **6** (*technical*) the letter æ, used in Old English, and as a PHONETIC symbol to represent the vowel sound in *cat* IDM see SACKCLOTH

ashamed 0-w /əˈʃeɪmd/ *adj.* [not before noun]
1 0-w feeling shame or embarrassment about sb/sth or because of sth you have done: **~ of sth** *She was deeply ashamed of her behaviour at the party.* ◇ *Mental illness is* ***nothing to be ashamed of.*** ◇ **~ of sb** *His daughter looked such a mess that he was ashamed of her.* ◇ **~ of yourself** *You should be ashamed of yourself for telling such lies.* ◇ **~ that...** *I feel almost ashamed that I've been so lucky.* ◇ **~ to be sth** *The football riots made me ashamed to be English.* **2** 0-w **~ to do sth** unwilling to do sth because of shame or embarrassment: *I'm* ***ashamed to say*** *that I lied to her.* ◇ *I cried at the end and I'm not ashamed to admit it.*

Which Word?

ashamed / embarrassed

- You feel **ashamed** when you feel guilty because of something wrong that you have deliberately done: *You should be ashamed of treating your daughter like that.* Do not use **ashamed** when you are talking about something that is not very serious or important: *I am sorry that I forgot to buy the milk.* ◇ ~~*I am ashamed that I forgot to buy the milk.*~~
- You feel **embarrassed** when you have made a mistake or done something stupid or feel awkward in front of other people: *I was embarrassed about forgetting his name.*

ˌash ˈblonde *adj.*, *noun*
■ ***adj.*** (also ˌ**ash ˈblond**) **1** (of hair) very pale blonde in colour **2** (of a person) having ash blonde hair
■ ***noun*** a woman with hair that is ash blonde in colour ➲ see also BLONDE

ashen /ˈæʃn/ *adj.* (usually of sb's face) very pale; without colour because of illness or fear: *They listened ashen-faced to the news.* ◇ *His face was ashen and wet with sweat.*

Ash·ken·azi /ˌæʃkəˈnɑːzi/ *noun* (*pl.* **Ash·ken·azim** /-ɪm/) a Jew whose ANCESTORS came from central or eastern Europe ➲ compare SEPHARDI

ashore /əˈʃɔː(r)/ *adv.* towards, onto or on land, having come from an area of water such as the sea or a river: *to* ***come/go ashore*** ◇ *a drowned body found washed ashore on the beach* ◇ *The cruise included several days ashore.*

ash·ram /ˈæʃrəm/ *noun* a place where Hindus who wish to live away from society live together as a group; a place where other Hindus go for a short time to say prayers before returning to society

ash·tray /ˈæʃtreɪ/ *noun* a container into which people who smoke put ASH, cigarette ends, etc.

ˌAsh ˈWednesday *noun* [U, C] the first day of Lent ➲ see also SHROVE TUESDAY

Asia Minor /ˌeɪʃə ˈmaɪnə(r)/ *noun* [sing.] the western PENINSULA of Asia, which now forms most of Turkey

Asian /ˈeɪʃn; ˈeɪʒn/ *noun, adj.*
■ ***noun*** a person from Asia, or whose family originally came from Asia: *British Asians* HELP In *BrE* **Asian** is used especially to refer to people from India, Pakistan and Bangladesh. In *NAmE* it is used especially to refer to people from the Far East.
■ ***adj.*** of or connected with Asia: *Asian music*

ˌAsian Aˈmerican *noun* a person from America whose family come from Asia, especially E Asia ▶ ˌ**Asian-Aˈmerican** *adj.*

Asi·at·ic /ˌeɪʃiˈætɪk; ˌeɪʒi-/ *adj.* (*technical*) of or connected with Asia: *the Asiatic tropics*

ˈA-side *noun* the side of a pop record that was considered more likely to be successful ➲ compare B-SIDE

aside 0-w /əˈsaɪd/ *adv.*, *noun*
■ ***adv.*** **1** 0-w to one side; out of the way: *She pulled the curtain aside.* ◇ ***Stand aside*** *and let these people pass.* ◇ *He* ***took me aside*** (= away from a group of people) *to give me some advice.* ◇ (*figurative*) ***Leaving aside*** (= not considering at this stage) *the cost of the scheme, let us examine its benefits.* ◇ *All our protests were* ***brushed aside*** (= ignored). **2** 0-w to be used later: *We* ***set aside*** *some money for repairs.* **3** used after nouns to say that except for one thing, sth is true: *Money worries aside, things are going well.*
■ ***noun*** **1** (in the theatre) something that a character in a play says to the audience, but which the other characters on stage are not intended to hear **2** a remark, often made in a low voice, which is not intended to be heard by everyone present **3** a remark that is not directly connected with the main subject that is being discussed: *I mention it only as an aside.*

aˈside from 0-w *prep.* (*especially NAmE*)
= APART FROM: *Aside from a few scratches, I'm OK.* ➲ LANGUAGE BANK at EXCEPT

as·in·ine /ˈæsɪnaɪn/ *adj.* (*formal*) stupid or silly SYN **ridiculous**

ask 0-w /ɑːsk; *NAmE* æsk/ *verb*, *noun*
■ ***verb***
▸ QUESTION **1** 0-w [I, T] to say or write sth in the form of a question, in order to get information: *How old are you—if you don't* ***mind me/my asking****?* ◇ **~ about sb/sth** *He asked about her family.* ◇ **~ sth** *Can I* ***ask a question****?* ◇ *Did you ask the price?* ◇ **+ speech** *'Where are you going?' she asked.* ◇ **~ sb + speech** *'Are you sure?' he asked her.* ◇ **~ sb sth** *She asked the students their names.* ◇ *I often* ***get asked*** *that!* ◇ **~ sb (about sth)** *The interviewer asked me about my future plans.* ◇ **~ where, what, etc...** *He asked where I lived.* ◇ **~ sb where, what, etc...** *I had to ask the teacher what to do next.* ◇ *I was asked if/whether I could drive.* HELP You cannot say 'ask to sb': ~~*I asked to my friend what had happened.*~~
▸ REQUEST **2** 0-w [T] to tell sb that you would like them to do sth or that you would like sth to happen: **~ sb to do sth** *All the students were asked to complete a questionnaire.* ◇ *Eric*

A

Synonyms

ask

enquire • demand

These words all mean to say or write sth in the form of a question, in order to get information.

ask to say or write sth in the form of a question, in order to get information: *'Where are you going?' she asked.* ◇ *She asked the students their names.* ◇ *Can I* ***ask a question****?*

enquire/inquire (*rather formal*) to ask sb for information: *I called the station to enquire about train times.*

demand to ask a question very firmly: *'And where have you been?' he demanded angrily.*

PATTERNS

- to ask/enquire **about/after** sb/sth
- to ask/enquire/demand sth **of** sb
- to ask/enquire/demand **what/who/how**, etc.
- to ask/enquire **politely**
- to ask/enquire/demand **angrily**

asked me to marry him. ◇ **~ whether, what, etc...** *I asked whether they could change my ticket.* ◇ **~ sb whether, what, etc...** *She asked me if I would give her English lessons.* ◇ **~ that...** (*formal*) *She asked that she be kept informed of developments.* ◇ (*BrE* also) *She asked that she should be kept informed.* **3** [I, T] to say that you would like sb to give you sth: **~ for sth** *to ask for a job/a drink/an explanation* ◇ *I am writing to ask for some information about courses.* ◇ **~ sth** *Why don't you ask his advice?* ◇ **~ sb for sth** *Why don't you ask him for his advice?* ◇ **~ sth of sb** *Can I ask a favour of you?* ◇ **~ sb sth** *Can I ask you a favour?*
▸ PERMISSION **4** [T] to request permission to do sth: **~ to do sth** *Did you ask to use the car?* ◇ *I asked to see the manager.* ◇ **~ if, whether, etc...** *I'll ask if it's all right to park here.* ◇ **~ sb if, whether, etc...** *She asked her boss whether she could have the day off.*
▸ INVITE **5** [T] to invite sb: **~ sb (+ adv./prep.)** *They've asked me to dinner.* ◇ *I didn't ask them in* (= to come into the house). ◇ *We must ask the neighbours round* (= to our house). ◇ **~ sb to do sth** *She's asked him to come to the party.*
▸ MONEY **6** [T] **~ sth (for sth)** to request a particular amount of money for sth that you are selling: ***He's asking £2 000*** *for the car.*
▸ EXPECT/DEMAND **7** [T] to expect or demand sth: **~ sth** *I know I'm asking a great deal.* ◇ **~ sth of sb** *You're asking too much of him.* ◇ **~ sth to do sth** *I know it's asking a lot to expect them to win again.* ➲ SYNONYMS at DEMAND
IDM **'ask for it** (*informal*) to deserve sth bad that happens to you or that sb does to you **be 'asking for trouble | be 'asking for it** (*informal*) to behave in a way that is very likely to result in trouble **ˌdon't 'ask** (*informal*) if you say **don't ask** to sb, you mean that you do not want to reply to their question, because it would be awkward, embarrassing, etc. **ˌdon't ask 'me** (*informal*) if you say **don't ask me**, you mean that you do not know the answer to a question and are annoyed you have been asked **for the 'asking** if you can have sth **for the asking**, it is very easy for you to get it if you ask for it: *The job is yours for the asking.* **I 'ask you** (*informal*) if you say **I ask you**, you are expressing disapproval, shock or anger about sth/sb **if you ask 'me** (*informal*) in my personal opinion: *Their marriage was a mistake, if you ask me.*
PHR V **'ask after sb** (*BrE*) to say that you would like to know how sb is, what they are doing, etc: *He always asks after you in his letters.* **ˌask a'round** to speak to a number of different people in order to try and get some information: *I don't know of any vacancies in the company but I'll ask around.* **ˌask sb 'back** (*especially BrE*) to invite sb to come back to your house when you are both out together: *I hoped he wouldn't ask me back.* **'ask for sb/sth** to say that you want to speak to sb or be directed to a place: *When you arrive, ask for Jane.* **ˌask sb 'out** to invite sb to go out with you, especially as a way of starting a romantic relationship: *He's too shy to ask her out.*
■ ***noun***
IDM **a big 'ask** (*informal*) a difficult thing to achieve or deal with: *Beating the world champions is certainly a big ask for the team.*

askance /ə'skæns/ *adv.*
IDM **look askance (at sb/sth) | look (at sb/sth) askance** to look at or react to sb/sth with suspicion or doubt, or in a critical way

ask·ari /ə'skɑːri/ *noun* (*EAfrE*) a person who is employed to guard a building, valuable things, etc; a SECURITY GUARD

askew /ə'skjuː/ *adv., adj.* [not before noun] not in a straight or level position SYN **crooked**: *His glasses had been knocked askew by the blow.* ◇ *Her hat was slightly askew.*

'asking price *noun* the price that sb wants to sell sth for ➲ compare SELLING PRICE

aslant /ə'slɑːnt; *NAmE* ə'slænt/ *adv.* not exactly vertical or horizontal; at an angle: *The picture hung aslant.*

asleep /ə'sliːp/ *adj.* [not before noun] sleeping: *The baby was* ***sound asleep*** (= sleeping deeply) *upstairs.* ◇ *I waited until they were all* ***fast asleep*** (= sleeping deeply). ◇ *He was so exhausted that he* ***fell asleep*** *at his desk.* ◇ *She was still* ***half asleep*** (= not fully awake) *when she arrived at work.* ◇ *The police found him asleep in a garage.* OPP **awake**

AS (level) /eɪ 'es levl/ *noun* [C, U] Advanced Subsidiary (level); a British exam usually taken in Year 12 of school or college (= the year before the final year) when students are aged 17. Together with A2 exams, AS levels form the A-level qualification, which is needed for entrance to universities: *AS exams* ◇ *Students will normally take four or five AS subjects.* ◇ *She's* ***doing an AS (level)*** *in French.* ◇ *More than 20 subjects are on offer* ***at AS level*** *at our college.*

asp /æsp/ *noun* **1** a small poisonous snake found in SW Europe **2** a general name for various types of small poisonous snake found in N Africa

as·para·gus /ə'spærəɡəs/ *noun* [U] a plant whose young green or white STEMS are cooked and eaten as a vegetable ➲ VISUAL VOCAB page V27

as·par·tame /ə'spɑːteɪm; *NAmE* 'æspɑːrteɪm/ *noun* [U] a sweet substance used instead of sugar in drinks and food products, especially ones for people who are trying to lose weight

as·pect AW /'æspekt/ *noun*
1 [C] a particular part or feature of a situation, an idea, a problem, etc; a way in which it may be considered: *The book aims to cover all aspects of city life.* ◇ *the most important aspect of the debate* ◇ *She felt she had looked at the problem from every aspect.* ◇ *This was one aspect of her character he hadn't seen before.* **2** [sing., U] (*formal*) the appearance of a place, a situation or a person: *Events began to take on a more sinister aspect.* **3** [C, usually sing.] (*formal*) the direction in which a building, window, piece of land, etc. faces; the side of a building that faces a particular direction SYN **orientation** **4** [U, C] (*grammar*) the form of a verb that shows, for example, whether the action happens once or repeatedly, is completed or still continuing ➲ see also PERFECT *adj.* (7), PROGRESSIVE *adj.*

aspen /'æspən/ *noun* a type of POPLAR tree, with leaves that move even when there is very little wind

Asperger's syndrome /'æspɜːɡəz 'sɪndrəʊm; *NAmE* 'æspɜːrɡərz 'sɪndroʊm/ *noun* [U] a mild type of AUTISM (= a mental condition in which a person finds it very difficult to communicate or form relationships with others)

as·per·gill·osis /ˌæspədʒɪ'ləʊsɪs; *NAmE* ˌæspərdʒɪ'loʊsɪs/ *noun* [U] a serious condition in which parts of the body, usually the lungs, become infected by FUNGI

as·per·ity /æ'sperəti/ *noun* [U] (*formal*) the fact of being rough or severe, especially in the way you speak to or treat sb SYN **harshness**

as·per·sions /ə'spɜːʃnz; *NAmE* ə'spɜːrʒnz/ *noun* [pl.] (*formal*) critical or unpleasant remarks or judgements: *I wouldn't want to* ***cast aspersions on*** *your honesty.*

as·phalt /'æsfælt; *NAmE* -fɔːlt/ *noun* [U] a thick black sticky substance used especially for making the surface of roads

as·phyxia /æs'fɪksiə; əs'f-/ *noun* [U] the state of being unable to breathe, causing death or loss of CONSCIOUSNESS

as·phyxi·ate /əs'fɪksieɪt/ *verb* **~ sb** to make sb become unconscious or die by preventing them from breathing **SYN** **suffocate** ▶ **as·phyxi·ation** /əsˌfɪksi'eɪʃn/ *noun* [U]

aspic /'æspɪk/ *noun* [U] clear jelly which food can be put into when it is being served cold: *chicken breast* ***in aspic***

as·pi·dis·tra /ˌæspɪ'dɪstrə/ *noun* a plant with broad green pointed leaves, often grown indoors

as·pir·ant /ə'spaɪərənt; 'æspərənt/ *noun* **~ (to/for sth)** (*formal*) a person with a strong desire to achieve a position of importance or to win a competition: *aspirants to the title of world champion* ▶ **as·pir·ant** *adj.* [only before noun] = ASPIRING

as·pir·ate *noun, verb*

▪ ***noun*** /'æspərət/ (*phonetics*) the sound /h/, as in *house*: *The word 'hour' is pronounced without an initial aspirate.*

▪ ***verb*** /'æspəreɪt/ **1 ~ sth** (*medical*) to remove liquid from a person's body with a machine **2 ~ sth** (*phonetics*) to pronounce sth with an 'h' sound or with a breath

as·pir·ation /ˌæspə'reɪʃn/ *noun* **1** [C, usually pl., U] a strong desire to have or do sth: *I didn't realize you had political aspirations.* ◇ **~ to do sth** *He has never had any aspiration to earn a lot of money.* ◇ **~ for sth** *What changes are needed to meet women's aspirations for employment?* **2** [U] (*phonetics*) the action of pronouncing a word with a /h/ sound, as in *house*

as·pir·ation·al /ˌæspə'reɪʃənl/ *adj.* wanting very much to achieve success in your career or to improve your social status and standard of living

as·pire /ə'spaɪə(r)/ *verb* [I, T] to have a strong desire to achieve or to become sth: **~ (to sth)** *She aspired to a scientific career.* ◇ **~ to be/do sth** *He aspired to be their next leader.*

as·pirin /'æsprɪn; 'æspərɪn/ *noun* [U, C] (*pl.* **as·pirin** or **as·pir·ins**) a drug used to reduce pain, fever and INFLAMMATION: *Do you have any aspirin?* ◇ *Take two aspirin(s) for a headache.*

as·pir·ing /ə'spaɪərɪŋ/ (also *less frequent* **as·pir·ant**) *adj.* [only before noun] **1** wanting to start the career or activity that is mentioned: *Aspiring musicians need hours of practice every day.* **2** wanting to be successful in life: *He came from an aspiring working-class background.*

ass /æs/ *noun* **1** (*NAmE*) (*BrE* **arse**) (*taboo, slang*) the part of the body that you sit on; your bottom **2** (*BrE, informal*) a stupid person **SYN** **fool**: *Don't be such an ass!* ◇ *I* ***made an ass of myself*** *at the meeting—standing up and then forgetting the question.* **3** (*BrE, old use*) a DONKEY

IDM **get your 'ass in gear | move your 'ass** (*slang, especially NAmE*) a rude way of telling sb to hurry **get your ˌass over/in 'here, etc.** (*slang, especially NAmE*) a rude way of telling sb to come here, etc. ➲ more at BLOW *v.*, COVER *v.*, KICK *v.*, KISS *v.*, PAIN *n.*

as·sa·gai = ASSEGAI

as·sail /ə'seɪl/ *verb* (*formal*) **1 ~ sb/sth** to attack sb/sth violently, either physically or with words: *He was assailed with fierce blows to the head.* ◇ *The proposal was assailed by the opposition party.* ◇ (*figurative*) *A vile smell assailed my nostrils.* **2** [usually passive] **~ sb** to disturb or upset sb severely: *to* ***be assailed by worries/doubts/fears***

as·sail·ant /ə'seɪlənt/ *noun* (*formal*) a person who attacks sb, especially physically **SYN** **attacker**

as·sas·sin /ə'sæsɪn; *NAmE* -sn/ *noun* a person who murders sb important or famous, for money or for political reasons

as·sas·sin·ate /ə'sæsɪneɪt; *NAmE* -sən-/ *verb* [often passive] **~ sb** to murder an important or famous person, especially for political reasons: *The prime minister was assassinated by extremists.* ◇ *a plot to assassinate the president* ▶ **as·sas·sin·ation** /əˌsæsɪ'neɪʃn; *NAmE* -sə'n-/ *noun* [U, C]: *The president survived a number of assassination attempts.* ◇ *the assassination of John F. Kennedy*

as·sault /ə'sɔːlt/ *noun, verb*

▪ ***noun*** **1** [U, C] the crime of attacking sb physically: *Both men were charged with assault.* ◇ *sexual assaults* ◇ **~ on/upon sb** *A significant number of* ***indecent assaults*** *on women go unreported.* ➲ COLLOCATIONS at CRIME **2** [C] **~ (on/upon/against sb/sth)** (by an army, etc.) the act of attacking a building, an area, etc. in order to take control of it **SYN** **attack**: *An assault on the capital was launched in the early hours of the morning.* **3** [C] **~ (on/upon sth)** the act of trying to achieve sth that is difficult or dangerous: *The government has mounted a new assault on unemployment.* ◇ *Three people died during an assault on the mountain* (= while trying to climb it). **4** [C] an act of criticizing sb/sth severely **SYN** **attack**: *The suggested closures* ***came under assault*** *from all parties.* ◇ **~ on/upon/against sb/sth** *The paper's assault on the president was totally unjustified.*

▪ ***verb*** **1 ~ sb** to attack sb violently, especially when this is a crime: *He has been charged with assaulting a police officer.* ◇ *Four women have been* ***sexually assaulted*** *in the area recently.* **2 ~ sth** (*formal*) to affect your senses in a way that is very unpleasant or uncomfortable: *Loud rock music assaulted our ears.*

asˌsault and 'battery *noun* [U] (*law*) the crime of threatening to harm sb and then attacking them physically

as'sault course (*BrE*) (*NAmE* **'obstacle course**) *noun* an area of land with many objects that are difficult to climb, jump over or go through, which is used, especially by soldiers, for improving physical skills and strength

assay /ə'seɪ/ *noun* [C, U] (*technical*) the testing of metals and chemicals for quality, often to see how pure they are ▶ **assay** *verb* **~ sth**

as·se·gai (also **as·sa·gai**) /'æsəgaɪ/ *noun* **1** a weapon consisting of a long stick with a sharp metal point on the end, used mainly in southern Africa **2** a South African tree which produces hard wood

as·sem·blage /ə'semblɪdʒ/ *noun* (*formal, technical*) a collection of things; a group of people: *Tropical rainforests have the most varied assemblage of plants in the world.*

as·sem·ble **AW** /ə'sembl/ *verb* **1** [I, T] to come together as a group; to bring people or things together as a group: *All the students were asked to assemble in the main hall.* ◇ *She then addressed the* ***assembled company*** (= all the people there). ◇ **~ sth** *to assemble evidence/data* ◇ *The manager has assembled a world-class team.* **2** [T] **~ sth** to fit together all the separate parts of sth, for example a piece of furniture: *The shelves are easy to assemble.* **OPP** **disassemble** ➲ SYNONYMS at BUILD

as·sem·bler /ə'semblə(r)/ *noun* **1** a person who assembles a machine or its parts **2** (*computing*) a program for changing instructions into MACHINE CODE **3** (*computing*) = ASSEMBLY LANGUAGE

Asˌsemblies of 'God *noun* [pl.] the largest Pentecostal Church in the US (= one that emphasizes the gifts of the Holy Spirit, such as the power to heal people who are ill/sick)

as·sem·bly **AW** /ə'sembli/ *noun* (*pl.* **-ies**) **1** (also **Assembly**) [C] a group of people who have been elected to meet together regularly and make decisions or laws for a particular region or country: ***state/legislative/federal/local assemblies*** ◇ *Power has been handed over to provincial and regional assemblies.* ◇ *The national assembly has voted to adopt the budget.* ◇ *the California Assembly* ◇ *the UN General Assembly* **2** [U, C] the meeting together of a group of people for a particular purpose; a group of people who meet together for a particular purpose: *They were fighting for freedom of speech and freedom of assembly.* ◇ *He was to address a public assembly on the issue.* ◇ *an* ***assembly point*** (= a place where people have been asked to meet) **3** [C, U] a meeting of the teachers and students in a school, usually at the start of the day, to give information, discuss school

A

events or say prayers together **4** [U] the process of putting together the parts of sth such as a vehicle or piece of furniture: *Putting the bookcase together should be a simple assembly job.* ◇ *a car assembly plant*

as'sembly language *noun* [C, U] (also **as·sem·bler**) (*computing*) the language in which a program is written before it is changed into MACHINE CODE

as'sembly line *noun* = PRODUCTION LINE: *workers on the assembly line*

as·sem·bly·man /ə'semblimən/, **as·sem·bly·wo·man** /ə'sembliwʊmən/ *noun* (*pl.* **-men** /-mən/, **-wo·men** /-wɪmɪn/) a person who is an elected representative in a state assembly in the US

as'sembly room *noun* [usually pl.] (*especially BrE*) a public room or building in which meetings and social events are held

as·sent /ə'sent/ *noun, verb*

■ ***noun*** [U] **~ (to sth)** (*formal*) official agreement to or approval of sth: *The director has* ***given her assent to*** *the proposals.* ◇ *He nodded (his) assent.* ◇ *There were murmurs of both assent and dissent from the crowd.* ◇ *The bill passed in Parliament has now* ***received (the) Royal Assent*** (= been approved by the king/queen).

■ ***verb*** [I] **~ (to sth)** | **(+ speech)** (*formal*) to agree to a request, an idea or a suggestion: *Nobody would assent to the terms they proposed.*

as·sert /ə'sɜːt; *NAmE* ə'sɜːrt/ *verb* **1** to state clearly and firmly that sth is true: **~ that...** *She continued to assert that she was innocent.* ◇ **~ sth** *She continued to assert her innocence.* ◇ **+ speech** *'That is wrong,' he asserted.* ◇ **it is asserted that...** *It is commonly asserted that older people prefer to receive care from family members.* **2 ~ yourself** to behave in a confident and determined way so that other people pay attention to your opinions **3 ~ sth** to make other people recognize your right or authority to do sth, by behaving firmly and confidently: *to* ***assert your independence/rights*** ◇ *I was determined to* ***assert*** *my* ***authority*** *from the beginning.* **4 ~ itself** to start to have an effect: *Good sense asserted itself.*

as·ser·tion /ə'sɜːʃn; *NAmE* ə'sɜːrʃn/ *noun* **1** [C] a statement saying that you strongly believe sth to be true SYN **claim**: *He was correct in his assertion that the minister had been lying.* ◇ *Do you have any evidence to support your assertions?* ➲ SYNONYMS at CLAIM **2** [U, C] the act of stating, using or claiming sth strongly: *the assertion of his authority* ◇ *The demonstration was an assertion of the right to peaceful protest.*

as·sert·ive /ə'sɜːtɪv; *NAmE* ə'sɜːrtɪv/ *adj.* expressing opinions or desires strongly and with confidence, so that people take notice: *You should try and be more assertive.* ◇ *assertive behaviour* OPP **submissive** ▶ **as·sert·ive·ly** *adv.* **as·sert·ive·ness** *noun* [U]: *an assertiveness training course*

as·sess AW /ə'ses/ *verb* **1** to make a judgement about the nature or quality of sb/sth: **~ sb/sth** *It's difficult to assess the effects of these changes.* ◇ *to assess a patient's needs* ◇ **~ sb/sth as sth** *The young men were assessed as either safe or unsafe drivers.* ◇ *I'd assess your chances as low.* ◇ **~ whether, how, etc...** *The committee assesses whether a building is worth preserving.* ◇ *We are trying to assess how well the system works.* **2** to calculate the amount or value of sth SYN **estimate**: **~ sth** *They have assessed the amount of compensation to be paid.* ◇ **~ sth at sth** *Damage to the building was assessed at £40 000.* ▶ **as·sess·able** AW *adj.*

as·sess·ment AW /ə'sesmənt/ *noun* **1** [C] an opinion or a judgement about sb/sth that has been thought about very carefully SYN **evaluation**: *a detailed assessment of the risks involved* ◇ *his assessment of the situation* **2** [U] the act of judging or forming an opinion about sb/sth: *written exams and other forms of assessment* ◇ *Objective assessment of the severity of the problem was difficult.* ➲ see also CONTINUOUS ASSESSMENT **3** [C] an amount that has been calculated and that must be paid: *a tax assessment*

a'ssessment centre (*BrE*) (*NAmE* **a'ssessment center**) *noun* (*business*) (*especially BrE*) an event where people applying for a job are given a number of tests and interviews to find out what their strengths and weaknesses are; the place where this happens: *After the first interview you may be asked back for an assessment centre.*

as·ses·sor /ə'sesə(r)/ *noun* **1** an expert in a particular subject who is asked by a court or other official group to give advice **2** a person who calculates the value or cost of sth or the amount of money to be paid: *an* ***insurance/tax assessor*** **3** a person who judges how well sb has done in an exam, a competition, etc: *College lecturers acted as external assessors of the exam results.*

asset /'æset/ *noun* **1** a person or thing that is valuable or useful to sb/sth: *In his job, patience is an invaluable asset.* ◇ **~ to sb/sth** *She'll be an asset to the team.* **2** [usually pl.] a thing of value, especially property, that a person or company owns, which can be used or sold to pay debts: *the net* ***asset value*** *of the company* ◇ *Her assets include shares in the company and a house in France.* ◇ ***asset sales/management*** ◇ ***financial/capital assets*** ➲ compare LIABILITY

'asset-stripping *noun* [U] (*business*) (usually *disapproving*) the practice of buying a company which is in financial difficulties at a low price and then selling everything that it owns in order to make a profit

ass·hole /'æshəʊl; *NAmE* -hoʊl/ (*NAmE*) (*BrE* **arse·hole**) *noun* (*taboo, slang*) **1** the ANUS **2** a stupid or unpleasant person

as·sidu·ous /ə'sɪdjuəs; *NAmE* -dʒuəs/ *adj.* (*formal*) working very hard and taking great care that everything is done as well as it can be SYN **diligent** ▶ **as·si·du·ity** /ˌæsɪ'djuːəti/ *noun* [U] **as·sidu·ous·ly** *adv.*

as·sign AW /ə'saɪn/ *verb* **1** to give sb sth that they can use, or some work or responsibility: **~ sth (to sb)** *The two large classrooms have been assigned to us.* ◇ *The teacher assigned a different task to each of the children.* ◇ **~ sb sth** *We have been assigned the two large classrooms.* ◇ *The teacher assigned each of the children a different task.* **2** to provide a person for a particular task or position: **~ sb (to sth/as sth)** *They've assigned their best man to the job.* ◇ **~ sb to do sth** *British forces have been assigned to help with peacekeeping.* **3** [usually passive] **~ sb to sb/sth** to send a person to work under the authority of sb or in a particular group: *I was assigned to B platoon.* **4** to say that sth has a particular value or function, or happens at a particular time or place: **~ sth to sth** *Assign a different colour to each different type of information.* ◇ **~ sth sth** *The painting cannot be assigned an exact date.* **5 ~ sth to sb** (*law*) to say that your property or rights now belong to sb else: *The agreement assigns copyright to the publisher.*

as·sig·na·tion /ˌæsɪg'neɪʃn/ *noun* (*formal* or *humorous*) a meeting, especially a secret one, often with a lover

as·sign·ment AW /ə'saɪnmənt/ *noun* **1** [C, U] a task or piece of work that sb is given to do, usually as part of their job or studies: *You will need to complete three written assignments per semester.* ◇ *She is in Greece on an assignment for one of the Sunday newspapers.* ◇ *one of our reporters* ***on assignment*** *in China* ◇ *I had set myself a tough assignment.* **2** [U] the act of giving sth to sb; the act of giving sb a particular task: *his assignment to other duties in the same company*

as·simi·late /ə'sɪməleɪt/ *verb* **1** [T] **~ sth** to fully understand an idea or some information so that you are able to use it yourself: *The committee will need time to assimilate this report.* **2** [I, T] to become, or allow sb to become, a part of a country or community rather than remaining in a separate group: **~ (into/to sth)** *New arrivals find it hard to assimilate.* ◇ **~ sb (into/to sth)** *Immigrants have been successfully assimilated into the community.* **3** [T, often passive] **~ sth into/to sth** to make an idea, a person's attitude, etc. fit into sth or be acceptable: *These changes were gradually assimilated into everyday life.*

as·simi·la·tion /əˌsɪmə'leɪʃn/ *noun* **1** [U] the act of assimilating sb or sth, or being assimilated: *the rapid assimilation of new ideas* ◇ *his assimilation into the community* **2** [U, C] (*phonetics*) the act of making two sounds in speech that are next to each other more similar

A

to each other in certain ways, for example the pronunciation of the /t/ in *football* as a /p/ ; an example of this

as·sist 0- AW /əˈsɪst/ *verb, noun*

■ *verb* (*formal*) **1** 0- [I, T] to help sb to do sth: *Anyone willing to assist can contact this number.* ◇ **~ in/with sth** *We are looking for people who would be willing to assist in the group's work.* ◇ **~ sb** *We'll do all we can to assist you.* ◇ *The play was directed by Mike Johnson, assisted by Sharon Gale.* ◇ **~ sb in doing sth** *We will assist you in finding somewhere to live.* ◇ **~ sb in/with sth** *Two men* ***are assisting the police with their enquiries*** (= are being questioned by the police). ◇ **~ sb to do sth** *a course to assist adults to return to the labour market* **2** 0- [T] **~ sth** to help sth to happen more easily: *activities that will assist the decision-making process*

■ *noun* an action in HOCKEY, BASEBALL, etc. in which a player helps another player on the same team to score a goal or point

as·sist·ance 0- AW /əˈsɪstəns/ *noun* [U] (*formal*) help or support: ***technical/economic/military assistance*** ◇ ***financial assistance*** *for people on low incomes* ◇ *Can I* ***be of any assistance?*** ◇ *Despite his cries, no one* ***came to his assistance.*** ◇ *He can walk only* ***with the assistance of*** *crutches.* ◇ **~ with sth** *She offered me practical assistance with my research.* ◇ **~ in doing sth/to do sth** *The company provides advice and assistance in finding work.*

as·sist·ant 0- AW /əˈsɪstənt/ *noun, adj.*

■ *noun* **1** 0- a person who helps or supports sb, usually in their job: *My assistant will now demonstrate the machine in action.* ◇ *a senior research assistant* ➲ see also PDA, PERSONAL ASSISTANT, TEACHING ASSISTANT **2** 0- (*BrE*) = SALES CLERK, SHOP ASSISTANT: *a sales assistant in a department store* **3** (*BrE*) a student at university or college who spends time in a foreign country teaching his or her own language in a school

■ *adj.* 0- [only before noun] (*abbr.* Asst) (often in titles) having a rank below a senior person and helping them in their work: *the assistant manager* ◇ *Assistant Chief Constable Owen* ◇ *Assistant Attorney General William Weld*

as,sistant proˈfessor *noun* (in the US and Canada) a teacher at a college or university who has a rank just below the rank of an ASSOCIATE PROFESSOR

as,sistant refeˈree (also **referee's assistant**) *noun* (in football (SOCCER)) the official name for a LINESMAN (= an official who helps the REFEREE, for example in deciding whether or where a ball has passed outside the field of play)

ass·is·tant·ship /əˈsɪstəntʃɪp/ *noun* **1** (*BrE*) the position of being an ASSISTANT (3) **2** (*NAmE*) a paid position for a GRADUATE student that involves some teaching or research

as,sisted ˈliving *noun* [U] accommodation for people who need help, for example with tasks like washing and dressing themselves: *assisted living apartments*

as,sisted ˈsuicide *noun* [U] the act of a person killing himself/herself with the help of sb such as a doctor, especially because he/she is suffering from a disease that has no cure

as·sizes /əˈsaɪzɪz/ *noun* a court in the past which travelled to each county of England and Wales ▶ **as·size** *adj.* [only before noun]: *the assize court*

ˈass-kicking *adj.* = KICK-ASS

ˈass-licker (*NAmE*) (*BrE* **ˈarse-licker**) *noun* (*taboo, slang*) a person who is too friendly to sb in authority and is always ready to do what they want ▶ **ˈass-licking** (*NAmE*) (*BrE* **ˈarse-licking**) *noun* [U]

Assoc. *abbr.* (in writing) ASSOCIATION

as·so·ci·ate 0- *verb, adj., noun*

■ *verb* /əˈsəʊʃieɪt; -sieɪt; *NAmE* əˈsoʊ-/ **1** 0- [T] **~ sb/sth (with sb/sth)** to make a connection between people or things in your mind: *I always associate the smell of baking with my childhood.* ◇ *He is closely associated in the public mind with horror movies.* **2** [I] **~ with sb** to spend time with sb, especially a person or people that sb else does not approve of SYN **mix**: *I don't like you associating with those people.* **3** [T] **~ yourself with sth** (*formal*) to show that you support or agree with sth: *I associate myself with the Prime Minister's remarks* (= I agree with them). OPP **dissociate**

■ *adj.* /əˈsəʊʃiət; -siət; *NAmE* əˈsoʊ-/ [only before noun] **1** (often in titles) of a lower rank; having fewer rights in a particular profession or organization: *associate membership of the European Union* ◇ *an* ***associate member/director/editor*** **2** joined to or connected with a profession or an organization: *an associate company in Japan*

■ *noun* /əˈsəʊʃiət; *NAmE* əˈsoʊ-/ **1** a person that you work with, do business with or spend a lot of time with: *business associates* **2** (also **Associate**) an ASSOCIATE *adj.* (1) member **3 Associate** (*US*) a person who has an Associate's degree (= one that is given after completing two years of study at a junior college)

as·so·ci·ated 0- /əˈsəʊʃieɪtɪd; -sieɪt-; *NAmE* əˈsoʊ-/ *adj.*

1 0- if one thing is **associated with** another, the two things are connected because they happen together or one thing causes the other SYN **connected**: *the risks associated with taking drugs* ◇ *Salaries and associated costs have risen substantially.* **2** 0- if a person is **associated with** an organization, etc. they support it: *He no longer wished to be associated with the party's policy on education.* **3 Associated** used in the name of a business company that is made up of a number of smaller companies: *Associated Newspapers*

As,sociated ˈPress *noun* (*abbr.* AP) a US news service. Its offices throughout the world send news to its members which include newspapers and television and radio stations.

as,sociate proˈfessor *noun* (in the US and Canada) a teacher at a college or university who has a rank just below the rank of a professor

as·so·ci·ation 0- /ə,səʊʃiˈeɪʃn; -siˈeɪ-; *NAmE* ə,soʊ-/ *noun*

1 0- [C+sing./pl. v.] (*abbr.* Assoc.) an official group of people who have joined together for a particular purpose SYN **organization**: *Do you belong to any professional or trade associations?* ◇ *the Football Association* ◇ *a residents' association* ➲ see also HOUSING ASSOCIATION **2** 0- [C, U] **~ (with sb/sth)** a connection or relationship between people or organizations: *his alleged association with terrorist groups* ◇ *They have maintained a close association with a college in the US.* ◇ *The book was published* ***in association with*** (= together with) *English Heritage.* ◇ *She became famous through her association with the group of poets.* **3** 0- [C, usually pl.] an idea or a memory that is suggested by sb/sth; a mental connection between ideas: *The seaside had all sorts of pleasant associations with childhood holidays for me.* ◇ *The cat soon made the association between human beings and food.* **4** 0- [C] a connection between things where one is caused by the other: *a proven association between passive smoking and cancer*

As,sociation ˈfootball *noun* [U] (*BrE, formal*) = FOOTBALL (1)

as·so·cia·tive /əˈsəʊʃiətɪv; *NAmE* əˈsoʊ-/ *adj.* **1** relating to the association of ideas or things **2** (*mathematics*) giving the same result no matter what order the parts of a calculation are done, for example $(a \times b) \times c = a \times (b \times c)$

as·son·ance /ˈæsənəns/ *noun* [U] (*technical*) the effect created when two syllables in words that are close together have the same vowel sound, but different consonants, or the same consonants but different vowels, for example, *sonnet* and *porridge* or *cold* and *killed*

as·sort·ed /əˈsɔːtɪd; *NAmE* əˈsɔːrtəd/ *adj.* of various different sorts: *The meat is served with salad or assorted vegetables.* ◇ *The jumper comes in assorted colours.*

as·sort·ment /əˈsɔːtmənt; *NAmE* əˈsɔːrt-/ *noun* [usually sing.] a collection of different things or of different types of the same thing SYN **mixture**: *a wide assortment of gifts to choose from* ◇ *He was dressed in an odd assortment of clothes.*

Asst (also **Asst.** especially in *NAmE*) *abbr.* (in writing) ASSISTANT: *Asst Manager*

as·suage /ə'sweɪdʒ/ *verb* **~ sth** (*formal*) to make an unpleasant feeling less severe

as·sume 0-ᵣ AW /ə'sjuːm; *NAmE* ə'suːm/ *verb* **1** 0-ᵣ to think or accept that sth is true but without having proof of it: **~ (that)...** ***It is reasonable to assume (that)*** *the economy will continue to improve.* ◇ ***Let us assume*** *for a moment that the plan succeeds.* ◇ *She would, he assumed, be home at the usual time.* ◇ **it is assumed (that)...** *It is generally assumed that stress is caused by too much work.* ◇ **~ sth** *Don't always* ***assume the worst*** (= that sth bad has happened). ◇ *In this example we have assumed a unit price of $10.* ◇ **~ sb/sth to be/have sth** *I had assumed him to be a Belgian.* **2 ~ sth** (*formal*) to take or begin to have power or responsibility SYN **take**: *The court assumed responsibility for the girl's welfare.* ◇ *Rebel forces have assumed control of the capital.* **3 ~ sth** (*formal*) to begin to have a particular quality or appearance SYN **take on**: *This matter has assumed considerable importance.* ◇ *In the story the god assumes the form of an eagle.* **4 ~ sth** (*formal*) to pretend to have a particular feeling or quality SYN **put on**: *He assumed an air of concern.*

as·sumed AW /ə'sjuːmd; *NAmE* ə'suːmd/ *adj.* [only before noun] that you suppose to be true or to exist: *the assumed differences between the two states*

as,sumed 'name *noun* a name that sb uses that is not their real name SYN **pseudonym**: *He was living* ***under an assumed name.***

as·sum·ing AW /ə'sjuːmɪŋ; *NAmE* ə'suːmɪŋ/ *conj.* **~ (that)** used to suppose that sth is true so that you can talk about what the results might be: *Assuming (that) he's still alive, how old would he be now?* ◇ *I hope to go to college next year,* ***always assuming*** *I pass my exams.*

as·sump·tion AW /ə'sʌmpʃn/ *noun* **1** [C] a belief or feeling that sth is true or that sth will happen, although there is no proof: *an* ***underlying/implicit assumption*** ◇ *We need to challenge some of the basic assumptions of Western philosophy.* ◇ *We are working* ***on the assumption that*** *everyone invited will turn up.* ◇ *It was impossible to* ***make assumptions about*** *people's reactions.* ◇ *His actions were based on a false assumption.* **2** [C, U] **~ of sth** (*formal*) the act of taking or beginning to have power or responsibility: *their* ***assumption of power/control***

as·sur·ance AW /ə'ʃʊərəns; -ʃɔːr-; *NAmE* ə'ʃʊr-/ *noun* **1** [C] a statement that sth will certainly be true or will certainly happen, particularly when there has been doubt about it SYN **guarantee**, **promise**: *They called for assurances that the government is committed to its education policy.* ◇ *Unemployment seems to be rising, despite repeated* ***assurances to the contrary.*** **2** (also **,self-as'surance**) [U] belief in your own abilities or strengths SYN **confidence**: *There was an air of easy assurance and calm about him.* **3** [U] (*BrE*) a type of insurance in which money is paid out when sb dies or after an agreed period of time: *a life assurance company* ➲ see also QUALITY ASSURANCE

as·sure 0-ᵣ AW /ə'ʃʊə(r); -ʃɔː(r); *NAmE* ə'ʃʊr/ *verb* **1** 0-ᵣ to tell sb that sth is definitely true or is definitely going to happen, especially when they have doubts about it: **~ sb (that)...** *You think I did it deliberately, but I assure you (that) I did not.* ◇ *We were assured that everything possible was being done.* ◇ *She's perfectly safe,* ***I can assure you.*** ◇ **~ sb (of sth)** *We assured him of our support.* ◇ **~ sb + speech** *'He'll come back,' Susan assured her.* **2** (*formal*) to make yourself certain about sth: **~ yourself of sth** *He assured himself of her safety.* ◇ **~ yourself that...** *She assured herself that the letter was still in the drawer.* **3** to make sth certain to happen SYN **guarantee**: **~ sth** *Victory would assure a place in the finals.* ◇ **~ sb sth** *Victory would assure them a place in the finals.* **4 ~ sth** (*BrE*) to INSURE sth, especially against sb's death: *What is the sum assured?* IDM see REST *v.*

as·sured AW /ə'ʃʊəd; ə'ʃɔːd; *NAmE* ə'ʃʊrd/ *adj.* **1** (also **,self-as'sured**) confident in yourself and your abilities: *He spoke in a calm, assured voice.* **2** certain to happen SYN **guaranteed**: *Success seemed assured.* **3 ~ of sth** (of a person) certain to get sth: *You are assured of a warm welcome at this hotel.*

as·sured·ly AW /ə'ʃʊərədli; ə'ʃɔːr-; *NAmE* ə'ʃʊr-/ *adv.* (*formal*) certainly; definitely

AST /,eɪ es 'tiː/ *abbr.* ATLANTIC STANDARD TIME

as·ta·tine /'æstətiːn/ *noun* [U] (*symb.* At) a chemical element. Astatine is a RADIOACTIVE element which is found in small amounts in nature, and is produced artificially for use in medicine.

aster /'æstə(r)/ *noun* a garden plant that has pink, purple, blue or white flowers with many long narrow PETALS

as·ter·isk /'æstərɪsk/ *noun* the symbol (*) placed next to a particular word or phrase to make people notice it or to show that more information is given in another place: *I've placed an asterisk next to the tasks I want you to do first.* ▸ **as·ter·isk** *verb*: **~ sth** *I've asterisked the tasks I want you to do first.*

astern /ə'stɜːn; *NAmE* ə'stɜːrn/ *adv.* (*technical*) **1** in, at or towards the back part of a ship or boat **2** if a ship or boat is moving **astern**, it is moving backwards

as·ter·oid /'æstərɔɪd/ *noun* any one of the many small planets that go around the sun

asthma /'æsmə; *NAmE* 'æzmə/ *noun* [U] a medical condition of the chest that makes breathing difficult: *a severe asthma attack*

asth·mat·ic /æs'mætɪk; *NAmE* æz'mætɪk/ *noun* a person who suffers from asthma ▸ **asth·mat·ic** *adj.*: *asthmatic patients* ◇ *an asthmatic attack*

astig·ma·tism /ə'stɪgmətɪzəm/ *noun* [U] (*medical*) a fault in the shape of a person's eye that prevents them from seeing clearly

as·ton·ish /ə'stɒnɪʃ; *NAmE* ə'stɑːn-/ *verb* to surprise sb very much SYN **amaze** ➲ SYNONYMS at SURPRISE: **~ sb** *The news astonished everyone.* ◇ *She astonished us by saying she was leaving.* ◇ **it astonishes sb (that)...** *It astonishes me (that) he could be so thoughtless.*

as·ton·ished /ə'stɒnɪʃt; *NAmE* ə'stɑːn-/ *adj.* very surprised SYN **amazed**: *The helicopter landed before our astonished eyes.* ◇ **~ at/by sth/sb** *My parents looked astonished at my news.* ◇ **~ (that)...** *She seemed astonished (that) I had never been to Paris.* ◇ **~ to find/hear/learn/see ...** *He was astonished to learn he'd won the competition.*

as·ton·ish·ing /ə'stɒnɪʃɪŋ; *NAmE* ə'stɑːn-/ *adj.* very surprising; difficult to believe SYN **amazing**: *She ran 100m in an astonishing 10.6 seconds.* ◇ *I find it absolutely astonishing that you didn't like it.* ▸ **as·ton·ish·ing·ly** *adv.*: *Jack took the news astonishingly well.* ◇ *Astonishingly, a crowd of several thousands turned out to hear him.*

as·ton·ish·ment /ə'stɒnɪʃmənt; *NAmE* ə'stɑːn-/ *noun* [U] a feeling of very great surprise SYN **amazement**: ***To my utter astonishment,*** *she remembered my name.* ◇ *He stared* ***in astonishment*** *at the stranger.*

as·tound /ə'staʊnd/ *verb* **~ sb** to surprise or shock sb very much SYN **astonish**: *His arrogance astounded her.* ◇ *She was astounded by his arrogance.* ➲ note at SURPRISE

as·tound·ed /ə'staʊndɪd/ *adj.* very surprised or shocked by sth, because it seems very unlikely SYN **astonished**: *an astounded expression* ◇ *How can you say that? I'm absolutely astounded.* ◇ **~ at/by sth** *She looked astounded at the news.* ◇ **~ (that)...** *The doctors were astounded (that) he survived.* ◇ **~ to find/hear/learn/see...** *I was astounded to see her appear from the house.*

as·tound·ing /ə'staʊndɪŋ/ *adj.* so surprising that it is difficult to believe SYN **astonishing**: *There was an astounding 20% increase in sales.* ▸ **as·tound·ing·ly** *adv.*

as·tra·khan /,æstrə'kæn; *NAmE* 'æstrəkən/ *noun* [U] a type of black tightly-curled cloth made from the wool of a particular type of young sheep, used especially for making coats and hats; a type of cloth that is made to look like this

as·tral /'æstrəl/ *adj.* [only before noun] **1** (*technical*) connected with the stars: *astral navigation* **2** connected with the spiritual rather than the physical world of existence: *the astral plane*

astray /əˈstreɪ/ *adv.*

IDM go aˈstray 1 to become lost; to be stolen: *Several letters went astray or were not delivered.* ◇ *We locked up our valuables so they would not go astray.* **2** to go in the wrong direction or to have the wrong result: *Fortunately the gunman's shots went astray.* ◇ *Jack's parents thought the other boys might **lead him astray*** (= make him do things that are wrong).

astride /əˈstraɪd/ *prep., adv.*

■ ***prep.*** with one leg on each side of sth: *to sit **astride a horse/bike/chair*** ◇ (*figurative*) *a town astride the river*

■ ***adv.* 1** with legs or feet wide apart **2** with one leg on each side

astrin·gent /əˈstrɪndʒənt/ *adj., noun*

■ ***adj.* 1** (*technical*) (of a liquid or cream) able to make the skin feel less OILY or to stop the loss of blood from a cut **2** (*formal*) critical in a severe or clever way: ***astringent writers/comments*** **3** (*formal*) (of a taste or smell) slightly bitter but fresh: *the astringent taste of lemon juice* ▸ **astrin·gency** /-ənsi/ *noun* [U]

■ ***noun*** a liquid or cream used in COSMETICS or medicine to make the skin less OILY or to stop the loss of blood from a cut

astro- /ˈæstrəʊ; *NAmE* ˈæstroʊ/ *combining form* (in nouns, adjectives and adverbs) connected with the stars or outer space: *astronaut* ◇ *astrophysics*

astro·labe /ˈæstrəleɪb/ *noun* (*astronomy*) a device used in the past for measuring the distances of stars, planets etc. and for calculating the position of a ship

as·trol·oger /əˈstrɒlədʒə(r); *NAmE* əˈstrɑːl-/ *noun* a person who uses astrology to tell people about their character, about what might happen to them in the future, etc.

as·trol·ogy /əˈstrɒlədʒi; *NAmE* əˈstrɑːl-/ *noun* [U] the study of the positions of the stars and the movements of the planets in the belief that they influence human affairs ▸ **astro·logic·al** /ˌæstrəˈlɒdʒɪkl; *NAmE* -ˈlɑːdʒ-/ *adj.*: *astrological influences*

astro·naut /ˈæstrənɔːt/ *noun* a person whose job involves travelling and working in a SPACECRAFT

as·tron·omer /əˈstrɒnəmə(r); *NAmE* əˈstrɑːn-/ *noun* a scientist who studies astronomy

astro·nom·ic·al /ˌæstrəˈnɒmɪkl; *NAmE* -ˈnɑːm-/ *adj.* **1** connected with ASTRONOMY: *astronomical observations* **2** (also **astro·nom·ic**) (*informal*) (of an amount, a price, etc.) very large: *the astronomical costs of land for building* ◇ *The figures are astronomical.* ▸ **astro·nom·ic·al·ly** /-kli/ *adv.*: *Interest rates are astronomically high.*

astroˌnomical ˈunit *noun* (*abbr.* AU) (*astronomy*) a unit of measurement equal to 149.6 million kilometres, which is the distance from the centre of the earth to the sun

as·tron·omy /əˈstrɒnəmi; *NAmE* əˈstrɑːn-/ *noun* [U] the scientific study of the sun, moon, stars, planets, etc.

astro·phys·ics /ˌæstrəʊˈfɪzɪks; *NAmE* ˌæstroʊ-/ *noun* [U] the scientific study of the physical and chemical structure of the stars, planets, etc. ▸ **astro·physi·cist** /-ˈfɪzɪsɪst/ *noun*

Astro·Turf™ /ˈæstrəʊtɜːf; *NAmE* ˈæstroʊtɜːrf/ *noun* [U] an artificial surface that looks like grass, for playing sports on

ˈA student *noun* (*especially NAmE*) a student who gets or is likely to get the highest marks/grades in his/her work or exams

as·tute /əˈstjuːt; *NAmE* əˈstuːt/ *adj.* very clever and quick at seeing what to do in a particular situation, especially how to get an advantage **SYN shrewd**: *an **astute businessman/politician/observer*** ◇ *It was an astute move to sell the shares then.* ▸ **as·tute·ly** *adv.* **as·tute·ness** *noun* [U]

asun·der /əˈsʌndə(r)/ *adv.* (*old-fashioned* or *literary*) into pieces; apart: *families **rent/torn asunder** by the revolution*

asy·lum /əˈsaɪləm/ *noun* **1** (also *formal* **poˌlitical aˈsylum**) [U] protection that a government gives to people who have left their own country, usually because they were in danger for political reasons: ***to seek/apply for/be granted asylum*** ◇ *There was a nationwide debate on whether the asylum laws should be changed.* **2** [C] (*old use*) a hospital where people who were mentally ill could be cared for, often for a long time

aˈsylum seeker *noun* a person who has been forced to leave their own country because they are in danger and who arrives in another country asking to be allowed to stay there ➲ COLLOCATIONS at RACE

asym·met·ric /ˌeɪsɪˈmetrɪk/ (also **asym·met·ric·al** /ˌeɪsɪˈmetrɪkl/) *adj.* **1** having two sides or parts that are not the same in size or shape: *Most people's faces are asymmetric.* **OPP symmetrical 2** (*technical*) not equal, for example in the way each side or part behaves: *Linguists are studying the asymmetric use of Creole by parents and children* (= parents use one language and children reply in another). ▸ **asym·met·ric·al·ly** /-ɪkli/ *adv.* **asym·met·ry** /ˌeɪˈsɪmətri/ *noun* [C, U]

asymˌmetric ˈbars (*BrE*) (*NAmE* **unˌeven ˈbars**) *noun* [pl.] two bars on posts of different heights that are used by women for doing GYMNASTIC exercises on

asymp·tom·at·ic /ˌeɪsɪmptəˈmætɪk/ *adj.* (*medical*) (of a person or illness) having no SYMPTOMS

asyn·chron·ous /eɪˈsɪŋkrənəs/ *adj.* (*formal*) (of two or more objects or events) not existing or happening at the same time ▸ **asyn·chron·ous·ly** *adv.*

at 🔑 /ət; *strong form* æt/ *prep.*

1 🔑 used to say where sth/sb is or where sth happens: *at the corner of the street* ◇ *We changed at Crewe.* ◇ *They arrived late at the airport.* ◇ *At the roundabout take the third exit.* ◇ *I'll be at home all morning.* ◇ *She's at Tom's* (= at Tom's house). ◇ *I met her at the hospital.* ◇ *How many people were there at the concert?* **2** 🔑 used to say where sb works or studies: *He's been at the bank longer than anyone else.* ◇ *She's at Yale* (= Yale University). **3** 🔑 used to say when sth happens: *We left at 2 o'clock.* ◇ *at the end of the week* ◇ *We woke at dawn.* ◇ *I didn't know at the time of writing* (= when I wrote). ◇ *At night you can see the stars.* ◇ (*BrE*) *What are you doing at the weekend?* **4** 🔑 used to state the age at which sb does sth: *She got married at 25.* ◇ *He left school at the age of 16.* **5** 🔑 in the direction of or towards sb/sth: *What are you looking at?* ◇ *He pointed a gun at her.* ◇ *Somebody threw paint at the prime minister.* **6** used after a verb to show that sb tries to do sth, or partly does sth, but does not succeed or complete it: *He clutched wildly at the rope as he fell.* ◇ *She nibbled at a sandwich* (= ate only small bits of it). **7** 🔑 used to state the distance away from sth: *I held it at arm's length.* ◇ *Can you read a car number plate at fifty metres?* **8** 🔑 used to show the situation sb/sth is in, what sb is doing or what is happening: *The country is now at war.* ◇ *I felt at a disadvantage.* ◇ *I think Mr Harris is at lunch.* **9** 🔑 used to show a rate, speed, etc.: *He was driving at 70 mph.* ◇ *The noise came at two-minute intervals* (= once every two minutes). ◇ *Prices start at $1000.* **10** 🔑 **~ sb's/sth's best/worst, etc.** used to say that sb/sth is as good, bad, etc. as they can be: *This was Murray at his best.* ◇ *The garden's at its most beautiful in June.* **11** 🔑 used with adjectives to show how well sb does sth: *I'm **good at** French.* ◇ *She's hopeless at managing people.* **12** 🔑 used with adjectives to show the cause of sth: *They were impatient at the delay.* ◇ *She was delighted at the result.* **13** (*formal*) in response to sth: *They attended the dinner at the chairman's invitation.* **14** 🔑 (*NAmE*) used when giving a telephone number: *You can reach me at 637-2335, extension 354.* **15** 🔑 (*computing*) the symbol (@) used in email addresses

IDM at that used when you are giving an extra piece of information: *He managed to buy a car after all—and a nice one at that.* **be ˈat it again** to be doing sth, especially sth bad: *Look at all that graffiti—those kids have been at it again.* **ˌwhere it's ˈat** (*informal*) a place or an activity that is very popular or fashionable: *Judging by the crowds waiting to get in, this seems to be where it's at.*

A

at·av·is·tic /ˌætəˈvɪstɪk/ *adj.* (*formal*) related to the attitudes and behaviour of the first humans: ***an atavistic urge/instinct/fear***

ataxia /əˈtæksiə/ (also **ataxy** /əˈtæksi/) *noun* [U] (*medical*) the loss of full control of the body's movements ▸ **ataxic** *adj.*

ate *past tense* of EAT

-ate *suffix* **1** (in adjectives) full of or having the quality of: *passionate* ◇ *Italianate* **2** (in verbs) to give the thing or quality mentioned to: *hyphenate* ◇ *activate* **3** (in nouns) the status or function of: *a doctorate* **4** (in nouns) a group with the status or function of: *the electorate* **5** (*chemistry*) (in nouns) a salt formed by the action of a particular acid: *sulphate*

ˈA-team *noun* [usually sing.] **1** the best sports team in a school, club, etc. **2** a group of the best workers, soldiers, etc.

atel·ier /əˈtelieɪ; *NAmE* ˌætlˈjeɪ/ *noun* a room or building in which an artist works SYN **studio**

atem·poral /ˌeɪˈtempərəl/ *adj.* (*formal*) existing or considered without relation to time

athe·ism /ˈeɪθiɪzəm/ *noun* [U] the belief that God does not exist OPP **theism** ▸ **athe·is·tic** /ˌeɪθiˈɪstɪk/ *adj.*

athe·ist /ˈeɪθiɪst/ *noun* a person who believes that God does not exist ⊃ compare AGNOSTIC

ath·lete /ˈæθliːt/ *noun* **1** a person who competes in sports: *Olympic athletes* **2** (*BrE*) a person who competes in sports such as running and jumping **3** a person who is good at sports and physical exercise: *She is a natural athlete.*

ˌathlete's ˈfoot *noun* [U] an infectious skin disease that affects the feet, especially between the toes

ath·let·ic /æθˈletɪk/ *adj.* **1** physically strong, fit and active: *an* ***athletic figure/build*** ◇ *a tall, slim athletic girl* **2** [only before noun] (*BrE*) connected with sports such as running, jumping and throwing (=athletics): *an* ***athletic club/coach*** ▸ **ath·let·ical·ly** /-ɪkli/ *adv.* **ath·leti·cism** /æθˈletɪsɪzəm/ *noun* [U]: *She moved with great athleticism about the court.*

ath·let·ics /æθˈletɪks/ *noun* [U] **1** (*BrE*) (*NAmE* ˌ**track and ˈfield**) sports that people compete in, such as running and jumping ⊃ **VISUAL VOCAB** page V38 **2** (*NAmE*) any sports that people compete in: *students involved in all forms of college athletics*

athˈletic shoe *noun* (*NAmE*) = TENNIS SHOE

athˌletic supˈporter *noun* (*especially NAmE*) = JOCKSTRAP

at-ˈhome *noun, adj.*
- ***noun*** (*old-fashioned*) a party in sb's home: *We're having an at-home—can you come?*
- ***adj.*** ˌ**at-ˈhome** [only before noun] **1** done or taking place at home: *an at-home job* **2** (of a parent) staying at home rather than going out to work: *at-home dads*

-athon /əθən; *NAmE* əθɑːn/ *suffix* (in nouns) an event in which a particular activity is done for a very long time, especially one organized to raise money for charity: *a swimathon*

athwart /əˈθwɔːt; *NAmE* əˈθwɔːrt/ *prep.* (*literary* or *formal*) **1** across; from one side to the other: *They put a table athwart the doorway.* **2** not agreeing with; opposite to: *His statement ran athwart what was previously said.*

-ation ⊃ -ION

atish·oo /əˈtɪʃuː/ (*BrE*) (also **ah·choo** *NAmE, BrE*) *exclamation* the word for the sound people make when they SNEEZE

-ative *suffix* (in adjectives) doing or tending to do sth: *illustrative* ◇ *talkative* ▸ **-atively** *suffix* (in adverbs): *creatively*

Atkins Diet™ /ˈætkɪnz daɪət/ *noun* a diet in which you eat foods that contain a high level of PROTEIN (meat, eggs, cheese, etc.) and avoid foods that contain a high level of CARBOHYDRATES (bread, rice, fruit, etc.)

Atˌlantic ˈDaylight Time *noun* [U] (*abbr.* ADT) the time used in summer in an area that includes the east of Canada, Puerto Rico and the Virgin Islands, that is five hours earlier than GMT

Atˌlantic ˈStandard Time *noun* [U] (*abbr.* AST) (also **Atˈlantic time**) the time used in winter in an area that includes the east of Canada, Puerto Rico and the Virgin Islands, that is four hours earlier than GMT

At·lan·tis /ætˈlæntɪs/ *noun* [U] (in stories) an island full of beauty and wealth, that was said to have been covered by the sea and lost. There are many stories about people's attempts to find it.

atlas /ˈætləs/ *noun* a book of maps: *a world atlas* ◇ *a road atlas of Europe*

ATM /ˌeɪ tiː ˈem/ *noun* the abbreviation for 'automated teller machine' ⊃ CASH MACHINE

ˌATˈM card (*US*) (*BrE* ˈ**cash card**) *noun* a plastic card used to get money from a CASH MACHINE (= a machine in or outside a bank) ⊃ compare CHEQUE CARD, CREDIT CARD, DEBIT CARD

at·mos·phere 🔑 /ˈætməsfɪə(r); *NAmE* -fɪr/ *noun* **1** 🔑 **the atmosphere** [sing.] the mixture of gases that surrounds the earth: *the upper atmosphere* ◇ *pollution of the atmosphere* **2** 🔑 [C] a mixture of gases that surrounds another planet or a star: *Saturn's atmosphere* **3** 🔑 [C] the air in a room or in a confined space; the air around a place: *a* ***smoky/stuffy atmosphere*** ◇ *These plants love warm, humid atmospheres.* **4** 🔑 [C, sing., U] the feeling or mood that you have in a particular place or situation; a feeling between two people or in a group of people: *a party atmosphere* ◇ *The hotel offers a friendly atmosphere and personal service.* ◇ *Use music and lighting to create a romantic atmosphere.* ◇ *There was an atmosphere of mutual trust between them.* ◇ *The children grew up in an atmosphere of violence and insecurity.* ◇ *The old house is full of atmosphere* (= it's very interesting). IDM see HEAVY *adj.*

at·mos·pher·ic /ˌætməsˈferɪk/ *adj.* **1** [only before noun] related to the earth's atmosphere: ***atmospheric pollution/conditions/pressure*** **2** creating an exciting or emotional mood: *atmospheric music*

at·mos·pher·ics /ˌætməsˈferɪks; *NAmE* also -ˈfɪr-/ *noun* [pl.] **1** qualities in sth that create a particular atmosphere **2** noises that sometimes interrupt a radio broadcast

atoll /ˈætɒl; *NAmE* ˈætɔːl; -tɑːl/ *noun* an island made of CORAL and shaped like a ring with a lake of sea water (called a LAGOON) in the middle

atom 🔑 /ˈætəm/ *noun* the smallest part of a chemical element that can take part in a chemical reaction: *the splitting of the atom* ◇ *Two atoms of hydrogen combine with one atom of oxygen to form a molecule of water.*

ˈatom bomb (also ˈ**A-bomb**) *noun* a bomb that explodes using the energy that is produced when an atom or atoms are split

atom·ic /əˈtɒmɪk; *NAmE* əˈtɑːmɪk/ *adj.* [usually before noun] **1** connected with atoms or an atom: *atomic structure* **2** related to the energy that is produced when atoms are split; related to weapons that use this energy: ***atomic energy/power*** ◇ *the atomic bomb*

aˌtomic ˈclock *noun* an extremely accurate clock that uses the movement of atoms or MOLECULES to measure time

atom·ic·ity /ˌætəmˈɪsɪti/ *noun* (*chemistry*) the number of atoms in one MOLECULE of a substance

aˌtomic ˈmass *noun* (*chemistry*) = RELATIVE ATOMIC MASS

aˌtomic ˈnumber *noun* (*chemistry*) the number of PROTONS in the NUCLEUS (= centre) of an atom, which is characteristic of a chemical element. Elements are placed in the PERIODIC TABLE according to their atomic numbers.

aˌtomic ˈtheory *noun* (*chemistry, physics*) the theory that all elements are made up of small PARTICLES called atoms which are made up of a central NUCLEUS surrounded by moving ELECTRONS

a,tomic 'weight *noun* (*chemistry*) = RELATIVE ATOMIC MASS

atom·ism /ˈætəmɪzəm/ *noun* [U] (*technical*) the idea of analysing sth by separating it into its different parts ➲ compare HOLISM ▸ **atom·is·tic** /ˌætəˈmɪstɪk/ *adj.*

atom·ize (*BrE* also **-ise**) /ˈætəmaɪz/ *verb* **~ sth** to reduce sth to atoms or very small pieces

atom·izer (*BrE* also **-iser**) /ˈætəmaɪzə(r)/ *noun* a container that forces a liquid such as water or paint out as a very fine spray

atonal /eɪˈtəʊnl; *NAmE* eɪˈtoʊnl/ *adj.* (of a piece of music) not written in any particular KEY **OPP tonal** ▸ **aton·al·ity** /ˌeɪtəʊˈnæləti; *NAmE* ˌeɪtoʊˈn-/ *noun* [U]

atone /əˈtəʊn; *NAmE* əˈtoʊn/ *verb* [I] **~ (for sth)** (*formal*) to act in a way that shows you are sorry for doing sth wrong in the past **SYN make amends**: *to atone for a crime* ▸ **atone·ment** *noun* [U]: *to make atonement for his sins* ◇ *Yom Kippur, the Jewish day of atonement*

atop /əˈtɒp; *NAmE* əˈtɑːp/ *prep.* (*especially NAmE*) (*old-fashioned* or *literary* in *BrE*) on top of; at the top of: *a flag high atop a pole* ◇ *a scoop of ice cream atop a slice of apple pie*

atopic /eɪˈtɒpɪk; *NAmE* -ˈtɑːp-/ *adj.* (*medical*) relating to a form of ALLERGY where there is a reaction in a part of the body that does not have direct contact with the thing causing the ALLERGY

-ator *suffix* (in nouns) a person or thing that does sth: *creator* ◇ *percolator*

A to Z /ˌeɪ tə ˈzed; *NAmE* ˌeɪ tə ˈziː/ *noun* [sing.] **1** (*BrE*) a book containing street maps of all the areas of a large city **2** a book containing all the information you need about a subject or place: *an A to Z of needlework*

ATP /ˌeɪ tiː ˈpiː/ *abbr.* (*BrE*) the abbreviation for 'automatic train protection' (a system for automatically stopping a train if the driver does not stop or go slower when a signal tells him/her to)

ˌat-'risk *adj.* [only before noun] (of a person or group) in danger of being attacked or hurt, especially in their own home: *Social services keep lists of* ***at-risk children***.

at·rium /ˈeɪtriəm/ *noun* **1** a large high space, usually with a glass roof, in the centre of a modern building **2** an open space in the centre of an ancient Roman VILLA (= a large house) **3** (*anatomy*) either of the two upper spaces in the heart that are used in the first stage of sending the blood around the body **SYN auricle**

atro·cious /əˈtrəʊʃəs; *NAmE* əˈtroʊ-/ *adj.* **1** very bad or unpleasant **SYN terrible**: *She speaks French with an atrocious accent.* ◇ *Isn't the weather atrocious?* **2** very cruel and shocking: *atrocious acts of brutality* ▸ **atro·cious·ly** *adv.*

atro·city /əˈtrɒsəti; *NAmE* əˈtrɑːs-/ *noun* [C, usually pl., U] (*pl.* -ies) a cruel and violent act, especially in a war

at·ro·phy /ˈætrəfi/ *noun, verb*

■ ***noun*** [U] (*medical*) the condition of losing flesh, muscle, strength, etc. in a part of the body because it does not have enough blood: (*figurative, formal*) *The cultural life of the country will sink into atrophy unless more writers and artists emerge.*

■ ***verb*** (**at·ro·phies, at·ro·phy·ing, at·ro·phied, at·ro·phied**) [I] if a part of the body **atrophies**, it becomes weak because it is not used or because it does not have enough blood: (*figurative*) *Memory can atrophy through lack of use.* ▸ **at·ro·phied** *adj.*: *atrophied muscles* ◇ *atrophied religious values*

at·ta·boy /ˈætəbɔɪ/ *exclamation* (*informal, especially NAmE*) used when you want to encourage sb or show your admiration of them, especially a boy or man ➲ see also ATTAGIRL

at·tach 🔑 **AW** /əˈtætʃ/ *verb*

1 🔑 [T] to fasten or join one thing to another: **~ sth** *I attach a copy of my notes for your information.* ◇ *I attach a copy of the spreadsheet* (= send it with an email). ◇ **~ sth to sth** *Attach the coupon to the front of your letter.* ◇ (*figurative*) *They have attached a number of conditions to the agreement* (= said that the conditions must be part of the agreement). ➲ compare DETACH **2** 🔑 [T] **~ importance, significance, value, weight, etc. (to sth)** to believe that sth is important or worth thinking about: *I attach great importance to this research.* **3** [T] **~ yourself to sb** to join sb for a time, sometimes when you are not welcome or have not been invited: *He attached himself to me at the party and I couldn't get rid of him.* **4** [I, T] (*formal*) to be connected with sb/sth; to connect sth to sth: **~ to sb/sth** *No one is suggesting that any health risks attach to this product.* ◇ *No blame attaches to you.* ◇ **~ sth to sb/sth** *This does not attach any blame to you.*

at·taché /əˈtæʃeɪ; *NAmE* ˌætəˈʃeɪ/ *noun* a person who works at an EMBASSY, usually with a special responsibility for a particular area of activity: *a cultural attaché*

at'taché case *noun* a small hard flat case used for carrying business documents ➲ VISUAL VOCAB page V52 ➲ compare BRIEFCASE

at·tached 🔑 **AW** /əˈtætʃt/ *adj.*

1 🔑 **~ (to sb/sth)** full of affection for sb/sth: *I've never seen two people so attached to each other.* ◇ *We've grown very attached to this house.* ➲ compare UNATTACHED **2** 🔑 [not before noun] **~ to sth** working for or forming part of an organization: *The research unit is attached to the university.* **3** 🔑 **~ (to sth)** joined to sth: *Please complete the attached application form.*

at·tach·ment **AW** /əˈtætʃmənt/ *noun* **1** [C, U] a strong feeling of affection for sb/sth: *a child's strong attachment to its parents* **2** [C, U] belief in and support for an idea or a set of values: *the popular attachment to democratic government* **3** [C] a tool that you can fix onto a machine, to make it do another job: *an electric drill with a range of different attachments* **4** [U, C] the act of joining one thing to another; a thing that joins two things together: *All cars built since 1981 have points for the attachment of safety restraints.* ◇ *They discussed the attachment of new conditions to the peace plans.* ◇ *They had to check the strength of the seat attachments to the floor of the plane.* **5** [U, C] (*BrE*) a short time spent working with an organization such as a hospital, school or part of the armed forces: *She's* ***on attachment*** *to the local hospital.* ◇ *a 4-month training attachment* **6** [C] (*computing*) a document that you send to sb using email ➲ COLLOCATIONS at EMAIL

at·tack 🔑 /əˈtæk/ *noun, verb*

■ ***noun***

▸ VIOLENCE **1** 🔑 [C, U] **~ (on sb)** an act of using violence to try to hurt or kill sb: *a series of racist attacks*

▸ IN WAR **2** 🔑 [C, U] **~ (on sb/sth)** an act of trying to kill or injure the enemy in war, using weapons such as guns and bombs: *to* ***launch/make/mount an attack*** ◇ *The patrol came* ***under attack*** *from all sides.* ➲ COLLOCATIONS at WAR ➲ see also COUNTER-ATTACK

▸ CRITICISM **3** 🔑 [C, U] **~ (on sb/sth)** strong criticism of sb/sth in speech or in writing: *a scathing attack on the government's policies* ◇ *The school has come* ***under attack*** *for failing to encourage bright pupils.*

▸ ACTION TO STOP STH **4** 🔑 [C] **~ (on sth)** an action that you take to try to stop or change sth that you feel is bad: *to launch* ***an all-out attack on*** *poverty/unemployment*

▸ OF ILLNESS **5** 🔑 [C] a sudden, short period of illness, usually severe, especially an illness that you have often: *to suffer an asthma attack* ◇ *an acute attack of food poisoning* ◇ *a panic attack* ◇ (*figurative*) *an attack of the giggles* ➲ see also HEART ATTACK

▸ OF EMOTION **6** 🔑 [C] a sudden period of feeling an emotion such as fear: *an attack of nerves*

▸ DAMAGE **7** [U, C] the action of sth such as an insect, or a disease, that causes damage to sth/sb: *The roof timbers were affected by rot and insect attack.*

▸ IN SPORT **8** 🔑 [sing.] (*BrE*) (*NAmE* **of·fense**) the players in a team whose job is to try to score goals or points: *Germany's attack has been weakened by the loss of some key players through injury.* ➲ compare DEFENCE **9** 🔑 [C, U] the actions that players take to try to score a goal or win the game: *a sustained attack on the Arsenal goal*

■ *verb*
▸ USE VIOLENCE **1** [I, T, often passive] to use violence to try to hurt or kill sb: *Most dogs will not attack unless provoked.* ◇ **~ sb** *A woman was attacked and robbed by a gang of youths.* ◇ **~ sb with sth** *The man attacked him with a knife.*
▸ IN WAR **2** [I, T] to use weapons, such as guns and bombs against an enemy in a war, etc: *The guerrillas attack at night.* ◇ **~ sb/sth** *At dawn the army attacked the town.*
▸ CRITICIZE **3** [T] to criticize sb/sth severely: **~ sb/sth** *a newspaper article attacking the England football manager* ◇ **~ sb/sth for sth/for doing sth** *She has been attacked for ignoring her own party members.*
▸ DAMAGE **4** [T] **~ sth** to have a harmful effect on sth: *a disease that attacks the brain* ◇ *The vines were attacked by mildew.*
▸ DO STH WITH ENERGY **5** [T] **~ sth** to deal with sth with a lot of energy and determination: *Let's attack one problem at a time.*
▸ IN SPORT **6** [I] to go forward in a game in order to try to score goals or points ➲ compare DEFEND: *Spain attacked more in the second half and deserved a goal.*

at'tack dog *noun* **1** a dog that has been trained to attack people or other animals **2** (*disapproving*) a person who often makes strong personal attacks on other people in public: *His image has changed from statesman to attack dog.*

at·tack·er /ə'tækə(r)/ *noun* a person who attacks sb: *She didn't really see her attacker.*

at·ta·girl /'ætəgɜːl; *NAmE* -gɜːrl/ *exclamation* (*informal, especially NAmE*) used when you want to encourage a girl or woman, or show your admiration of them ➲ see also ATTABOY

at·tain AW /ə'teɪn/ *verb* (*formal*) **1 ~ sth** to succeed in getting sth, usually after a lot of effort: *Most of our students attained five 'A' grades in their exams.* **2 ~ sth** to reach a particular age, level or condition: *The cheetah can attain speeds of up to 97 kph.*

at·tain·able AW /ə'teɪnəbl/ *adj.* that you can achieve: ***attainable goals/objectives/targets*** ◇ *This standard is easily attainable by most students.* OPP **unattainable**

at·tain·ment AW /ə'teɪnmənt/ *noun* (*formal*) **1** [C, usually pl.] (*BrE*) something that you achieved: *a young woman of impressive educational attainments* **2** [U] success in achieving sth: *The attainment of his ambitions was still a dream.* ◇ *attainment targets* (= for example in education)

attar /'ætə(r)/ (also **otto**) *noun* an ESSENTIAL OIL usually made from ROSE PETALS

at·tempt /ə'tempt/ *noun, verb*
■ *noun* **1** [C, U] an act of trying to do sth, especially sth difficult, often with no success: *I passed my driving test **at the first attempt**.* ◇ **~ to do sth** *Two factories were closed **in an attempt** to cut costs.* ◇ *They **made no attempt** to escape.* ◇ **~ at sth/at doing sth** *The couple made an unsuccessful attempt at a compromise.* **2** [C] **~** (**on sb/sb's life**) an act of trying to kill sb: *Someone has **made an attempt on** the President's **life**.* **3** [C] **~** (**on sth**) an effort to do better than sth, such as a very good performance in sport: *his attempt on the world land speed record*
■ *verb* to make an effort or try to do sth, especially sth difficult: **~ to do sth** *I will attempt to answer all your questions.* ◇ *Do not attempt to repair this yourself.* ◇ **~ sth** *The prisoners attempted an escape, but failed.*

at·tempted /ə'temptɪd/ *adj.* [only before noun] (of a crime, etc.) that sb has tried to do but without success: ***attempted rape/murder/robbery***

at·tend /ə'tend/ *verb*
1 [I, T] (rather *formal*) to be present at an event: *We'd like as many people as possible to attend.* ◇ **~ sth** *The meeting was attended by 90% of shareholders.* ◇ *to attend a wedding/funeral* **2** [T] **~ sth** (*formal*) to go regularly to a place: *Our children attend the same school.* ◇ *How many people attend church every Sunday?* **3** [I] **~** (**to sb/sth**) (*formal*) to pay attention to what sb is saying or to what you are doing: *She hadn't been attending during the lesson.* **4** [T] **~ sth** (*formal*) to happen at the same time as sth: *She dislikes the loss of privacy that attends TV celebrity.* **5** [T] **~ sb** (*formal*) to be with sb and help them: *The President was attended by several members of his staff.*
PHR V **at'tend to sb/sth** to deal with sb/sth; to take care of sb/sth: *I have some urgent business to attend to.* ◇ *A nurse attended to his needs constantly.* ◇ (*BrE, formal*) *Are you being attended to, Sir?* (= for example, in a shop).

at·tend·ance /ə'tendəns/ *noun* **1** [U, C] the act of being present at a place, for example at school: *Attendance at these lectures is not compulsory.* ◇ *Teachers must keep a record of students' attendances.* **2** [C, U] the number of people present at an organized event: ***high/low/falling/poor attendances*** ◇ *There was an attendance of 42 at the meeting.*
IDM **be in at'tendance** (*formal*) to be present at a special event: *Several heads of state were in attendance at the funeral.* **be in at'tendance** (**on sb**) (*formal*) to be with or near sb in order to help them if necessary: *He always has at least two bodyguards in attendance.* **take at'tendance** (*NAmE*) to check who is present and who is not present at a place and to mark this information on a list of names ➲ more at DANCE *v.*

at'tendance allowance *noun* [U] the money that a very sick or disabled older person receives from the government in Britain if they need sb to care for them at home nearly all the time

at·tend·ant /ə'tendənt/ *noun, adj.*
■ *noun* **1** a person whose job is to serve or help people in a public place: *a **cloakroom/parking/museum attendant*** ➲ see also FLIGHT ATTENDANT **2** a person who takes care of and lives or travels with an important person or a sick or disabled person
■ *adj.* [usually before noun] (*formal*) closely connected with sth that has just been mentioned: ***attendant problems/risks/circumstances*** ◇ **~ upon sth** *We had all the usual problems attendant upon starting a new business.*

at·tend·ee /ˌæten'diː/ *noun* a person who attends a meeting, etc.

at·tend·er /ə'tendə(r)/ (*especially BrE*) (*NAmE* usually **attend·ee**) *noun* a person who goes to a place or an event, often on a regular basis: *She's a regular attender at evening classes.*

at·ten·tion /ə'tenʃn/ *noun, exclamation*
■ *noun*
▸ LISTENING/LOOKING CAREFULLY **1** [U] the act of listening to, looking at or thinking about sth/sb carefully: *the report's attention to detail* ◇ *He turned his attention back to the road again.* ◇ *Small children have a very short **attention span**.* ◇ *Please **pay attention*** (= listen carefully) *to what I am saying.* ◇ *Don't **pay any attention** to what they say* (= don't think that it is important). ◇ *She tried to **attract** the waiter's **attention**.* ◇ *I tried not to **draw attention to*** (= make people notice) *the weak points in my argument.* ◇ *An article in the newspaper **caught my attention**.* ◇ *I couldn't give the programme my **undivided attention**.* ◇ (*formal*) *It **has come to my attention*** (= I have been informed) *that...* ◇ (*formal*) *He **called** (**their**) **attention** to the fact that many files were missing.* ◇ (*formal*) *Can I have your attention please?* ➲ LANGUAGE BANK at EMPHASIS
▸ INTEREST **2** [U] interest that people show in sb/sth: *Films with big stars always **attract** great **attention**.* ◇ *As the youngest child, she was always **the centre of attention**.* **3** [C, usually pl.] things that sb does to try to please you or to show their interest in you: *She tried to escape the unwanted attentions of her former boyfriend.*
▸ TREATMENT **4** [U] special care, action or treatment: *She was in need of medical attention.* ◇ *The roof needs attention* (= needs to be repaired). ◇ ***for the attention of...*** (= written on the envelope of an official letter to say who should deal with it)
▸ SOLDIERS **5** [U] the position soldiers take when they stand very straight with their feet together and their arms at their sides: *to **stand at/to attention*** ➲ compare (STAND) AT EASE at EASE *n.*
■ *exclamation* **1** used for asking people to listen to sth that is being announced: *Attention, please! Passengers for flight*

A

KL412 are requested to go to gate 21 immediately. **2** used for ordering soldiers to stand to attention

at'tention deficit disorder (also **at,tention ,deficit hyperac'tivity disorder**) *noun* [U] (*abbr.* ADD, ADHD) a medical condition, especially in children, that makes it difficult for them to pay attention to what they are doing, to stay still for long and to learn things

at·ten·tive /ə'tentɪv/ *adj.* **1** listening or watching carefully and with interest: *an attentive audience* **2** helpful; making sure that people have what they need: *The hotel staff are friendly and attentive.* ◇ **~ to sb/sth** *Ministers should be more attentive to the needs of families.* ▶ **at·ten·tive·ly** *adv.* **at·ten·tive·ness** *noun* [U] OPP **inattentive**

at·tenu·ate /ə'tenjueɪt/ *verb* **~ sth** (*formal*) to make sth weaker or less effective: *The drug attenuates the effects of the virus.* ▶ **at·tenu·ation** /ə,tenjʊ'eɪʃn/ *noun* [U]

at·tenu·ated /ə'tenjueɪtɪd/ *adj.* (*formal*) **1** made weaker or less effective: *an attenuated form of the virus* **2** (of a person) very thin

at·tenu·ator /ə'tenjueɪtə(r)/ *noun* (*technical*) a device consisting of a number of RESISTORS which reduce the strength of a radio sound or signal

at·test /ə'test/ *verb* (*formal*) **1** [I, T] **~ (to sth)** | **~ (that...)** | **~ (sth)** to show or prove that sth is true SYN **bear witness to**: *Contemporary accounts attest to his courage and determination.* **2** [T] **~ (sth)** | **~ (that...)** to state that you believe that sth is true or genuine, for example in court: *to attest a will* ◇ *The signature was attested by two witnesses.*

attic /'ætɪk/ *noun* a room or space just below the roof of a house, often used for storing things: *furniture stored in the attic* ◇ *an attic bedroom* ➲ compare GARRET, LOFT

at·tire /ə'taɪə(r)/ *noun* [U] (*formal*) clothes: *dressed in formal evening attire*

at·tired /ə'taɪəd; *NAmE* ə'taɪərd/ *adj.* [not before noun] (*formal* or *literary*) dressed in a particular way

at·ti·tude 0‑w AW /'ætɪtju:d; *NAmE* 'ætɪtu:d/ *noun*
1 0‑w [C] **~ (to/towards sb/sth)** the way that you think and feel about sb/sth; the way that you behave towards sb/sth that shows how you think and feel: *changes in public attitudes to marriage* ◇ *the government's attitude towards single parents* ◇ *to* ***have a good/bad/positive/negative attitude towards sb/sth*** ◇ *Youth is simply an* ***attitude of mind.*** ◇ *If you want to pass your exams you'd better change your attitude!* ◇ *You're taking a pretty selfish attitude over this, aren't you?* ◇ *A lot of drivers have a serious* ***attitude problem*** (= they do not behave in a way that is acceptable to other people). **2** [U] confident, sometimes aggressive behaviour that shows you do not care about other people's opinions and that you want to do things in an individual way: *a band* ***with attitude*** ◇ *You'd better get rid of that attitude and shape up, young man.* **3** [C] (*formal*) a position of the body: *Her hands were folded in an attitude of prayer.* IDM see STRIKE *v.*

at·ti·tu·din·al /,ætɪ'tju:dɪnl; *NAmE* -'tu:-/ *adj.* (*formal*) related to the attitudes that people have

attn (also **attn.** especially in *NAmE*) *abbr.* (*business*) (in writing) for the attention of: *Sales Dept, attn C Biggs* ➲ see also FAO

at·tor·ney 0‑w /ə'tɜ:ni; *NAmE* ə'tɜ:rni/ *noun*
1 0‑w (*especially US*) a lawyer, especially one who can act for sb in court ➲ note at LAWYER ➲ see also DISTRICT ATTORNEY **2** a person who is given the power to act on behalf of another in business or legal matters: *She was made her father's attorney when he became ill.* ➲ see also POWER OF ATTORNEY

At,torney 'General *noun* (*pl.* **Attorneys General** or **Attorney Generals**) **1** the most senior legal officer in some countries or states, for example the UK or Canada, who advises the government or head of state on legal matters **2 the At,torney 'General** the head of the US Department of Justice and a member of the President's cabinet (= a group of senior politicians who advise the President)

at·tract 0‑w /ə'trækt/ *verb*
1 0‑w [usually passive] if you are **attracted** by sth, it interests you and makes you want it; if you are **attracted** by sb, you like or admire them: **~ sb** *I had always been attracted by the idea of working abroad.* ◇ **~ sb to sb/sth** *What first attracted me to her was her sense of humour.* **2** 0‑w **~ sb/sth (to sth)** to make sb/sth come somewhere or take part in sth: *The warm damp air attracts a lot of mosquitoes.* ◇ *The exhibition has attracted thousands of visitors.* **3** 0‑w **~ sth** to make people have a particular reaction: *This proposal has* ***attracted a lot of interest.*** ◇ *His comments were bound to* ***attract criticism.*** ◇ *She tried to* ***attract the attention*** *of the waiter.* **4** (*physics*) if a MAGNET or GRAVITY **attracts** sth, it makes it move towards it OPP **repel** IDM see OPPOSITE *n.*

at·tract·ant /ə'træktənt/ *noun* (*technical*) a substance that attracts sth, especially an animal: *This type of trap uses no bait or other attractant.*

at·trac·tion 0‑w /ə'trækʃn/ *noun*
1 0‑w [sing., U] a feeling of liking sb, especially sexually: *She felt an immediate attraction for him.* ◇ *Sexual attraction is a large part of falling in love.* **2** 0‑w [C] an interesting or enjoyable place to go or thing to do: *Buckingham Palace is a major* ***tourist attraction.*** ◇ *The* ***main attraction*** *at Giverny is Monet's garden.* **3** 0‑w [C, U] a feature, quality or person that makes sth seem interesting and enjoyable, and worth having or doing: *I can't see the attraction of sitting on a beach all day.* ◇ *City life holds little attraction for me.* ◇ *She is the star attraction of the show.* **4** [U] (*physics*) a force that pulls things towards each other: ***gravitational/magnetic attraction*** ➲ compare REPULSION

at·tract·ive 0‑w /ə'træktɪv/ *adj.*
1 0‑w (of a person) pleasant to look at, especially in a sexual way: *an attractive woman* ◇ *I like John but I don't* ***find him attractive*** *physically.* ➲ SYNONYMS at BEAUTIFUL **2** 0‑w (of a thing or a place) pleasant: *a big house with an attractive garden* ◇ *That's one of the less attractive aspects of her personality.* **3** 0‑w having features or qualities that make sth seem interesting and worth having SYN **appealing**: *an* ***attractive offer/proposition*** OPP **unattractive** ▶ **at·tract·ive·ly** *adv.*: *The room is arranged very attractively.* ◇ *attractively priced hotel rooms* **at·tract·ive·ness** *noun* [U]: *the attractiveness of travelling abroad*

at·trib·ut·able AW /ə'trɪbjətəbl/ *adj.* [not before noun] **~ to sb/sth** probably caused by the thing mentioned: *Their illnesses are attributable to a poor diet.*

at·tri·bute AW *verb, noun*
▪ ***verb*** /ə'trɪbju:t/ **1 ~ sth to sth** to say or believe that sth is the result of a particular thing: *She attributes her success to hard work and a little luck.* **2** to say or believe that sb is responsible for doing sth, especially for saying, writing or painting sth: **~ sth** *The committee refused to* ***attribute blame*** *without further information.* ◇ **~ sth to sb** *This play is usually attributed to Shakespeare.* ▶ **at·tri·bu·tion** AW /,ætrɪ'bju:ʃn/ *noun* [U]: *The attribution of this painting to Rembrandt has never been questioned.*
▪ ***noun*** /'ætrɪbju:t/ a quality or feature of sb/sth: *Patience is one of the most important attributes in a teacher.*

at·tribu·tive /ə'trɪbjətɪv/ *adj.* (*grammar*) (of adjectives or nouns) used before a noun to describe it: *In 'the blue sky' and 'a family business', 'blue' and 'family' are attributive.* ➲ compare PREDICATIVE ▶ **at·tribu·tive·ly** *adv.*: *Some adjectives can only be used attributively.*

at·tri·tion /ə'trɪʃn/ *noun* [U] (*formal*) **1** a process of making sb/sth, especially your enemy, weaker by repeatedly attacking them or creating problems for them: *It was a* ***war of attrition.*** **2** (*especially NAmE*) (*BrE* also **,natural 'wastage**) the process of reducing the number of people who are employed by an organization by, for example, not replacing people who leave their jobs

at·tuned /ə'tju:nd; *NAmE* ə'tu:nd/ *adj.* [not before noun] **~ (to sb/sth)** familiar with sb/sth so that you can understand or recognize them or it and act in an appropriate way: *She wasn't yet attuned to her baby's needs.*

ATV /,eɪ ti: 'vi:/ *noun* (*especially NAmE*) the abbreviation for 'all-terrain vehicle' (a small open vehicle with one seat and four wheels with very thick tyres, designed especially for use on rough ground without roads) ➲ see also QUAD BIKE

atyp·ical /ˌeɪˈtɪpɪkl/ *adj.* not typical or usual: *atypical behaviour* OPP **typical**

AU /ˌeɪ ˈjuː/ *abbr.* ASTRONOMICAL UNIT

au·ber·gine /ˈəʊbəʒiːn; *NAmE* ˈoʊbərʒiːn/ (*BrE*) (*NAmE* **egg·plant**) *noun* [C, U] a vegetable with shiny dark purple skin and soft white flesh ➲ VISUAL VOCAB page V27

au·burn /ˈɔːbən; *NAmE* ˈɔːbərn/ *adj.* (of hair) reddish-brown in colour ▶ **au·burn** *noun* [U]: *the rich auburn of her hair*

auc·tion /ˈɔːkʃn; ˈɒk-; *NAmE* ˈɔːk-/ *noun, verb*

■ ***noun*** [C, U] a public event at which things are sold to the person who offers the most money for them: *an auction of paintings* ◇ *The house is* ***up for auction*** (= will be sold at an auction). ◇ *A classic Rolls-Royce fetched* (= was sold for) ***£25 000 at auction.*** ◇ *an Internet auction site*

■ ***verb*** [usually passive] **~ sth** to sell sth at an auction: *The costumes from the movie are to be auctioned for charity.*

PHR V **ˌauction sth↔ˈoff** to sell sth at an auction, especially sth that is no longer needed or wanted: *The Army is auctioning off a lot of surplus equipment.*

auc·tion·eer /ˌɔːkʃəˈnɪə(r); ˌɒk-; *NAmE* ˌɔːkʃəˈnɪr/ *noun* a person whose job is to direct an auction and sell the goods

ˈauction house *noun* a company that sells things in auctions

ˈauction room *noun* a building in which AUCTIONS are held

au·da·cious /ɔːˈdeɪʃəs/ *adj.* (*formal*) willing to take risks or to do sth shocking SYN **daring**: *an audacious decision* ▶ **au·da·cious·ly** *adv.*

au·da·city /ɔːˈdæsəti/ *noun* [U] brave but rude or shocking behaviour SYN **nerve**: *He* ***had the audacity*** *to say I was too fat.*

aud·ible /ˈɔːdəbl/ *adj.* that can be heard clearly: *Her voice was* ***barely audible*** *above the noise.* OPP **inaudible** ▶ **audi·bil·ity** /ˌɔːdəˈbɪləti/ *noun* [U] **aud·ibly** /-əbli/ *adv.*

audi·ence 0‑ /ˈɔːdiəns/ *noun*

1 0‑ [C+sing./pl. v.] the group of people who have gathered to watch or listen to sth (a play, concert, sb speaking, etc.): *The audience was/were clapping for 10 minutes.* ◇ *an audience of 10 000* ◇ *The debate was televised in front of a* ***live audience.*** **2** 0‑ [C] a number of people or a particular group of people who watch, read or listen to the same thing: *An audience of millions watched the wedding on TV.* ◇ ***TV/cinema/movie audiences*** ◇ *His book reached an even wider audience when it was made into a movie.* ◇ *The* ***target audience*** *for this advertisement was mainly teenagers.* **3** [C] a formal meeting with an important person: *an audience with the Pope* ➲ SYNONYMS at INTERVIEW

audio /ˈɔːdiəʊ; *NAmE* ˈɔːdioʊ/ *adj.* [only before noun] connected with sound that is recorded: *audio and video cassettes* ▶ **audio** *noun* [U]

audio- /ˈɔːdiəʊ; *NAmE* ˈɔːdioʊ/ *combining form* (in nouns, adjectives and adverbs) connected with hearing or sound: *an audiobook* (= a reading of a book on CASSETTE, CD, etc.) ◇ *audio-visual*

audi·ology /ˌɔːdiˈɒlədʒi; *NAmE* -ˈɑːl-/ *noun* [U] the science and medicine that deals with the sense of hearing ▶ **audi·ologist** *noun*

audi·om·etry /ˌɔːdiˈɒmətri; *NAmE* -ˈɑːm-/ *noun* [U] (*technical*) the measurement of how good a person's sense of hearing is

ˈaudio tape *noun* [U] MAGNETIC tape on which sound can be recorded

ˈaudio typist *noun* a person who types letters or other documents from recordings

ˌaudio-ˈvisual *adj.* (*abbr.* AV) using both sound and pictures: *audio-visual aids for the classroom*

audit /ˈɔːdɪt/ *noun, verb*

■ ***noun*** [C, U] **1** an official examination of business and financial records to see that they are true and correct: *an annual audit* ◇ *a tax audit* **2** an official examination of the quality or standard of sth ➲ see also GREEN AUDIT

■ ***verb*** **1 ~ sth** to officially examine the financial accounts of a company **2 ~ sth** (*NAmE*) to attend a course at college or university but without taking any exams or receiving credit

the ˈAudit Commission *noun* [sing.] (in Britain) an organization that checks that public money is being spent in the best way by local governments

au·di·tion /ɔːˈdɪʃn/ *noun, verb*

■ ***noun*** a short performance given by an actor, a singer, etc, so that sb can decide whether they are suitable to act in a play, sing in a concert, etc.

■ ***verb*** **1** [I] **~ (for sth)** to take part in an audition: *She was auditioning for the role of Lady Macbeth.* **2** [T] **~ sb (for sth)** to watch, listen to and judge sb at an audition: *We auditioned over 200 children for the part.*

au·dit·or /ˈɔːdɪtə(r)/ *noun* **1** a person who officially examines the business and financial records of a company **2** (*NAmE*) a person who attends a college course, but without having to take exams and without receiving credit

audi·tor·ium /ˌɔːdɪˈtɔːriəm/ *noun* (*pl.* **audi·tor·iums** or **audi·toria** /-riə/) **1** the part of a theatre, concert hall, etc. in which the audience sits **2** (*especially NAmE*) a large building or room in which public meetings, concerts, etc. are held

audi·tory /ˈɔːdətri; *NAmE* -tɔːri/ *adj.* (*technical*) connected with hearing: *auditory stimuli*

ˈaudit trail *noun* the detailed record of information on paper or on a computer that can be examined to prove what happened, for example what pieces of business were done and what decisions were made

au fait /ˌəʊ ˈfeɪ; *NAmE* ˌoʊ/ *adj.* [not before noun] **~ (with sth)** (from *French*) completely familiar with sth: *I'm new here so I'm not completely au fait with the system.*

Augean stables /ɔːˌdʒiːən ˈsteɪblz/ *noun* [pl.] (in ancient Greek stories) the very large stables which Hercules cleaned in a day by making a river flow through them

auger /ˈɔːɡə(r)/ *noun* a tool for making holes in wood, that looks like a large CORKSCREW

aught /ɔːt/ *pron.* (*old use*) anything

aug·ment /ɔːɡˈment/ *verb* **~ sth** (*formal*) to increase the amount, value, size, etc. of sth ▶ **aug·men·ta·tion** /ˌɔːɡmenˈteɪʃn/ *noun* [U, C]

aug·men·ta·tive /ˌɔːɡˈmentətɪv/ *adj.* (*linguistics*) (of an AFFIX or a word using an affix) increasing a quality expressed in the original word, especially by meaning 'a large one of its kind'

augur /ˈɔːɡə(r)/ *verb* [I] **~ well/badly** (*formal*) to be a sign that sth will be successful or not successful in the future SYN **bode**: *Conflicts among the various groups do not augur well for the future of the peace talks.*

au·gury /ˈɔːɡjʊri/ *noun* (*pl.* -ies) (*literary*) a sign of what will happen in the future SYN **omen**

Au·gust 0‑ /ˈɔːɡəst/ *noun* [U, C] (*abbr.* **Aug.**) the 8th month of the year, between July and September: (*BrE*) *August Bank Holiday* (= a public holiday on the last Monday in August in Britain) HELP To see how **August** is used, look at the examples at **April**.

au·gust /ɔːˈɡʌst/ *adj.* [usually before noun] (*formal*) impressive, making you feel respect

Au·gust·an /ɔːˈɡʌstən/ *adj.* **1** connected with or happening during the time of the Roman EMPEROR Augustus **2** connected with English literature of the 17th and 18th centuries that was written in a style that was considered CLASSICAL

auk /ɔːk/ *noun* a northern bird with short narrow wings that lives near the sea

auld lang syne /ˌɔːld læŋ ˈsaɪn/ *noun* an old Scottish song expressing feelings of friendship, traditionally sung at midnight on New Year's Eve

A

au nat·urel /ˌəʊ ˌnætju'rel; *NAmE* ˌoʊ/ *adj., adv.* [not before noun] (from *French*) in a natural way: *The fish is served au naturel, uncooked and with nothing added.*

aunt /ɑːnt; *NAmE* ænt/ *noun* **1** the sister of your father or mother; the wife of your uncle: *Aunt Alice* ◇ *My aunt lives in Canada.* **2** (*informal*) used by children, with a first name, to address a woman who is a friend of their parents ➲ see also AGONY AUNT

aun·tie (also **aunty**) /'ɑːnti; *NAmE* 'ænti/ *noun* (*informal*) aunt: *Auntie Mary*

Aunt Sally /ˌɑːnt 'sæli; *NAmE* ˌænt/ *noun* **1** (*BrE*) a game in which people throw balls at a model of a person's head to win prizes **2** a person or thing that a lot of people criticize: *The foreign minister has become everybody's favourite Aunt Sally.*

au pair /ˌəʊ 'peə(r); *NAmE* ˌoʊ 'per/ *noun* (*BrE*) a young person, usually a woman, who lives with a family in a foreign country in order to learn the language. An au pair helps in the house and takes care of children and receives a small wage.

aura /'ɔːrə/ *noun* **~ (of sth)** a feeling or particular quality that is very noticeable and seems to surround a person or place: *She always has an aura of confidence.*

aural /'ɔːrəl/ *adj.* (*technical*) connected with hearing and listening: *aural and visual images* ◇ *aural comprehension tests* ▸ **aur·al·ly** /-əli/ *adv.*

aure·ate /'ɔːriət/ *adj.* (*formal*) **1** decorated in a complicated way: *an aureate style of writing* **2** made of gold or of the colour of gold SYN **golden**

aure·ole /'ɔːriəʊl; *NAmE* -oʊl/ *noun* (*literary*) a circle of light

au re·voir /ˌəʊ rə'vwɑː(r); *NAmE* ˌoʊ/ *exclamation* (from *French*) goodbye (until we meet again)

aur·icle /'ɔːrɪkl/ *noun* (*anatomy*) **1** either of the two upper spaces in the heart used to send blood around the body SYN **atrium** ➲ compare VENTRICLE **2** the outer part of the ear

aur·ora aus·tra·lis /ɔːˌrɔːrə ɒs'trɑːlɪs; ɔːs't-; *NAmE* ɔːs-'t-/ *noun* [sing.] = THE SOUTHERN LIGHTS

aur·ora bor·ealis /ɔːˌrɔːrə ˌbɔːri'eɪlɪs/ *noun* [sing.] = THE NORTHERN LIGHTS

aus·pices /'ɔːspɪsɪz/ *noun* [pl.]
IDM **under the auspices of sb/sth** with the help, support or protection of sb/sth: *The community centre was set up under the auspices of a government initiative.*

aus·pi·cious /ɔː'spɪʃəs/ *adj.* (*formal*) showing signs that sth is likely to be successful in the future SYN **promising**: *an auspicious start to the new school year* OPP **inauspicious**

Aus·sie (also **Oz·zie**) /'ɒzi; *NAmE* 'ɔːzi/ *noun* (*informal*) a person from Australia ▸ **Aus·sie** *adj.*

aus·tere /ɒ'stɪə(r); ɔː'st-; *NAmE* ɔː'stɪr/ *adj.* **1** simple and plain; without any decorations: *her austere bedroom with its simple narrow bed* **2** (of a person) strict and serious in appearance and behaviour: *My father was a distant, austere man.* **3** allowing nothing that gives pleasure; not comfortable: *the monks' austere way of life* ▸ **aus·tere·ly** *adv.*

aus·ter·ity /ɒ'sterəti; ɔː'ster-/ *noun* (*pl.* -ies) **1** [U] a situation when people do not have much money to spend because there are bad economic conditions: *War was followed by many years of austerity.* **2** [U] the quality of being austere: *the austerity of the monks' life* **3** [C, usually pl.] something that is part of an austere way of life: *the austerities of wartime Europe*

aus·tral /'ɒstrəl; 'ɔːs-; *NAmE* 'ɔːs-/ *adj.* (*formal*) relating to the south

Austra·la·sia /ˌɒstrə'leɪʃə; -'leɪʒə; ˌɔːstrə-; *NAmE* ˌɔːstrə-/ *noun* the region including Australia, New Zealand and the islands of the SW Pacific ▸ **Austra·la·sian** *adj., noun*

Australia Day /ɒ'streɪliə deɪ; *NAmE* ɔː'streɪljə; ɑː's-/ *noun* a national public holiday in Australia on 26 January, when people remember the founding of New South Wales on that date in 1788

Aus·tra·lian /ɒ'streɪliən; ɔː'streɪ-/ *adj., noun*
▪ ***adj.*** of or connected with Australia
▪ ***noun*** a person from Australia

Auˌstralian 'Rules (also **Australian ˌRules 'football**) *noun* [U] an Australian game, played by two teams of 18 players, using an OVAL ball, which may be kicked, carried or hit with the hand

Aus·tralo·pith·ecus /ˌɒstrələʊ'pɪθɪkəs; *NAmE* ˌɔːstrəloʊ-/ *noun* [U, C] a creature similar to humans and APES that existed over one million years ago in Africa

Austro- /'ɒstrəʊ-; *NAmE* 'ɔːstroʊ-/ *combining form* (in nouns and adjectives) Austrian: *the Austro-Hungarian border*

aut·archy (also **aut·arky**) /'ɔːtɑːki; *NAmE* 'ɔːtɑːrki/ *noun* (*pl.* -ies) **1** [U, C] = AUTOCRACY **2** [U] (*economics*) economic independence ▸ **aut·arch·ic** (also **aut·ark·ic**) /ɔː'tɑːkɪk; *NAmE* -'tɑːrk-/ *adj.*

au·teur /əʊ'tɜː(r); ɔː't-; *NAmE* oʊ't-/ *noun* a film/movie director who plays such an important part in making their films/movies that they are considered to be the author
ORIGIN From the French word *auteur*, meaning author.

au·then·tic /ɔː'θentɪk/ *adj.* **1** known to be real and genuine and not a copy: *I don't know if the painting is authentic.* OPP **inauthentic** **2** true and accurate: *an authentic account of life in the desert* ◇ *the authentic voice of young black Americans* OPP **inauthentic** **3** made to be exactly the same as the original: *an authentic model of the ancient town* ▸ **au·then·tic·al·ly** /-kli/ *adv.*: *authentically flavoured Mexican dishes*

au·then·ti·cate /ɔː'θentɪkeɪt/ *verb* to prove that sth is genuine, real or true: **~ sth** *The letter has been authenticated by handwriting experts.* ◇ **~ sth as sth** *Experts have authenticated the writing as that of Byron himself.* ▸ **au·then·ti·ca·tion** /ɔːˌθentɪ'keɪʃn/ *noun* [U]

au·then·ti·city /ˌɔːθen'tɪsəti/ *noun* [U] the quality of being genuine or true

author AW /'ɔːθə(r)/ *noun, verb*
▪ ***noun*** **1** a person who writes books or the person who wrote a particular book: *Who is your favourite author?* ◇ *He is the author of three books on art.* ◇ *best-selling author Paul Theroux* ◇ *Who's the author?* ➲ COLLOCATIONS at LITERATURE **2** the person who creates or starts sth, especially a plan or an idea: *As the author of the proposal I cannot agree with you.*
▪ ***verb*** **~ sth** (*formal*) to be the author of a book, report, etc.

author·ess /'ɔːθəres/ *noun* (*old-fashioned*) a woman author

au·thor·ial /ɔː'θɔːriəl/ *adj.* [usually before noun] (*technical*) coming from or connected with the author of sth

author·ing /'ɔːθərɪŋ/ *noun* [U] (*computing*) creating computer programs without using programming language, for use in MULTIMEDIA products

au·thori·tar·ian /ɔːˌθɒrɪ'teəriən; *NAmE* əˌθɔːrə'ter-; əˌθɑːr-/ *adj.* believing that people should obey authority and rules, even when these are unfair, and even if it means that they lose their personal freedom: *an* ***authoritarian regime/government/state*** ▸ **au·thori·tar·ian** *noun*: *Father was a strict authoritarian.* **au·thori·tar·ian·ism** *noun* [U]

au·thori·ta·tive AW /ɔː'θɒrətətɪv; *NAmE* ə'θɔːrəteɪtɪv; ə'θɑːr-/ *adj.* **1** showing that you expect people to obey and respect you: *an authoritative tone of voice* **2** that you can trust and respect as true and correct: *the most authoritative book on the subject* ▸ **au·thori·ta·tive·ly** *adv.*

au·thor·ity AW /ɔː'θɒrəti; *NAmE* ə'θɔːr-; ə'θɑːr-/ *noun* (*pl.* -ies)
▸ POWER **1** [U] the power to give orders to people: *in a position of authority* ◇ *She now* ***has authority over*** *the people who used to be her bosses.* ◇ *Nothing will be done because no one* ***in authority*** (= who has a position of power) *takes the matter seriously.* **2** [U] **~ (to do sth)** the power or right to do sth: *Only the manager has the authority to sign cheques.*

A

▸ PERMISSION **3** [U] official permission to do sth: *It was done without the principal's authority.* ◇ *We acted* ***under the authority of*** *the UN.*
▸ ORGANIZATION **4** [C, usually pl.] the people or an organization who have the power to make decisions or who have a particular area of responsibility in a country or region: *The health authorities are investigating the problem.* ◇ *I have to report this to the authorities.* ➲ see also LOCAL AUTHORITY
▸ KNOWLEDGE **5** [U] the power to influence people because they respect your knowledge or official position: *He spoke* ***with authority*** *on the topic.*
▸ EXPERT **6** [C] **~ (on sth)** a person with special knowledge SYN **specialist**: *She's an authority on criminal law.*
IDM **have sth on good au'thority** to be able to believe sth because you trust the person who gave you the information

au·thor·iza·tion (*BrE* also **-isa·tion**) /ˌɔːθəraɪˈzeɪʃn; *NAmE* ˌɔːθərəˈzeɪʃn/ *noun* **1** [U, C] official permission or power to do sth; the act of giving permission: *You may not enter the security area without authorization.* ◇ *Who gave the authorization to release the data?* **2** [C] a document that gives sb official permission to do sth: *Can I see your authorization?*

au·thor·ize (*BrE* also **-ise**) /ˈɔːθəraɪz/ *verb* [often passive] to give official permission for sth, or for sb to do sth: **~ sth** *I can authorize payments up to £5 000.* ◇ *an authorized biography* ◇ **~ sb to do sth** *I have authorized him to act for me while I am away.* ◇ *The soldiers were authorized to shoot at will.* ➲ see also UNAUTHORIZED

ˌAuthorized ˈVersion *noun* [sing.] an English version of the Bible that was translated in 1611 on the instructions of King James I of England

author·ship AW /ˈɔːθəʃɪp; *NAmE* ˈɔːθərʃɪp/ *noun* [U] **1** the identity of the person who wrote sth, especially a book: *The authorship of the poem is unknown.* **2** the activity or fact of writing a book

aut·ism /ˈɔːtɪzəm/ *noun* [U] a mental condition in which a person finds it very difficult to communicate or form relationships with others ▸ **aut·is·tic** /ɔːˈtɪstɪk/ *adj.*: ***autistic behaviour/children***

auto /ˈɔːtəʊ; *NAmE* ˈɔːtoʊ/ *noun* (*pl.* -os) (*NAmE*) a car: *the auto industry*

auto- /ˈɔːtəʊ; *NAmE* ˈɔːtoʊ/ (also **aut-**) *combining form* (in nouns, adjectives and adverbs) **1** of or by yourself: *autobiography* **2** by itself without a person to operate it: *automatic*

auto·biog·raphy /ˌɔːtəbaɪˈɒɡrəfi; *NAmE* -ˈɑːɡ-/ *noun* [C, U] (*pl.* -ies) the story of a person's life, written by that person; this type of writing ➲ compare BIOGRAPHY ▸ **auto·bio·graph·ic·al** /ˌɔːtəˌbaɪəˈɡræfɪkl/ *adj.*: *an autobiographical novel* (= one that contains many of the writer's own experiences)

ˈauto bra *noun* (*NAmE*) = BRA (2)

auto·clave /ˈɔːtəʊkleɪv; ˈɔːtə-; *NAmE* ˈɔːtoʊ-/ *noun* a strong closed container, used for processes that involve high temperatures or pressure

au·toc·racy /ɔːˈtɒkrəsi; *NAmE* ɔːˈtɑːk-/ *noun* (*pl.* -ies) (also **aut·archy**) **1** [U] a system of government of a country in which one person has complete power **2** [C] a country that is ruled by one person who has complete power

auto·crat /ˈɔːtəkræt/ *noun* **1** a ruler who has complete power SYN **despot 2** a person who expects to be obeyed by other people and does not care about their opinions or feelings ▸ **auto·crat·ic** /ˌɔːtəˈkrætɪk/ *adj.*: *an autocratic manager* **auto·crat·ic·al·ly** /-kli/ *adv.*

auto·cross /ˈɔːtəʊkrɒs; *NAmE* ˈɔːtoʊkrɔːs; ˈɔːtoʊkrɑːs/ *noun* [U] a form of motor racing in which cars are driven over rough ground ➲ compare RALLYCROSS

Auto·cue™ /ˈɔːtəʊkjuː; *NAmE* ˈɔːtoʊ-/ (*BrE*) (also **tele·prompt·er** *NAmE*, *BrE*) *noun* a device used by people who are speaking in public, especially on television, which displays the words that they have to say

auto·didact /ˈɔːtəʊdɪdækt; *NAmE* ˈɔːtoʊ-/ *noun* (*formal*) a person who has taught himself or herself sth rather than having lessons ▸ **auto·didac·tic** /ˌɔːtəʊdɪˈdæktɪk; *NAmE* ˌɔːtoʊ-/ *adj.*

ˌauto-eˈrotic *adj.* relating to the practice of sb getting sexual excitement from their own body

ˌauto-exˈposure *noun* **1** [C] part of a camera that automatically adjusts the amount of light that reaches the film **2** [U] the ability of a camera to do this

auto·focus /ˌɔːtəʊˈfəʊkəs; *NAmE* ˌɔːtoʊˈfoʊkəs/ *noun* **1** [C] part of a camera that automatically adjusts itself, so that the picture will be clear **2** [U] the ability of a camera to do this

auto·genic /ˌɔːtəʊˈdʒenɪk; ˌɔːtə-; *NAmE* ˌɔːtoʊ-/ *adj.* (*formal*) created by or from the thing itself

ˌautogenic ˈtraining *noun* [U] a way of relaxing and dealing with stress using positive thoughts and mental exercises

auto·graph /ˈɔːtəɡrɑːf; *NAmE* -ɡræf/ *noun, verb*
■ ***noun*** a famous person's signature, especially when sb asks them to write it: *Could I have your autograph?*
■ ***verb*** **~ sth** (of a famous person) to sign your name on sth for sb to keep: *The whole team has autographed a football, which will be used as a prize.*

auto·immune /ˌɔːtəʊɪˈmjuːn; *NAmE* ˌɔːtoʊ-/ *adj.* [only before noun] (*medical*) an **autoimmune** disease or medical condition is one that is caused by substances that usually prevent illness

auto·maker /ˈɔːtəʊmeɪkə(r); *NAmE* ˈɔːtoʊ-/ *noun* (*NAmE*) a company that makes cars

auto·mat /ˈɔːtəmæt/ *noun* (*US*) in the past, a restaurant in which food and drink were bought from machines

auto·mate AW /ˈɔːtəmeɪt/ *verb* [usually passive] **~ sth** to use machines and computers instead of people to do a job or task: *The entire manufacturing process has been automated.* ◇ *The factory is now* ***fully automated.***

ˌautomated ˈteller machine *noun* (*abbr.* ATM) = CASH MACHINE

auto·mat·ic AW /ˌɔːtəˈmætɪk/ *adj., noun*
■ ***adj.*** **1** (of a machine, device, etc.) having controls that work without needing a person to operate them: *automatic doors* ◇ *a* ***fully automatic*** *driverless train* ◇ *automatic transmission* (= in a car, etc.) ◇ *an automatic rifle* (= one that continues to fire as long as the TRIGGER is pressed) **2** done or happening without thinking SYN **instinctive**: *Breathing is an automatic function of the body.* ◇ *My reaction was automatic.* **3** always happening as a result of a particular action or situation: *A fine for this offence is automatic.* ▸ **auto·mat·ic·al·ly** AW /-kli/ *adv.*: *The heating switches off automatically.* ◇ *I turned left automatically without thinking.* ◇ *You will automatically get free dental treatment if you are under 18.*
■ ***noun*** **1** a gun that can fire bullets continuously as long as the TRIGGER is pressed **2** (*BrE*) a car with a system of gears that operates without direct action from the driver ➲ compare STICK SHIFT

ˌautomatic ˈpilot (also **auto·pilot**) *noun* a device in an aircraft or a ship that keeps it on a fixed course without the need for a person to control it
IDM **be on ˌautomatic ˈpilot** to do sth without thinking because you have done the same thing many times before: *I got up and dressed on automatic pilot.*

ˌautomatic transˈmission *noun* [U, C] a system in a vehicle that changes the gears for the driver automatically

ˌautomatic ˈwriting *noun* [U] writing which is believed to have been done in an unconscious state or under a SUPERNATURAL influence

auto·ma·tion AW /ˌɔːtəˈmeɪʃn/ *noun* [U] the use of machines to do work that was previously done by people: *Automation meant the loss of many factory jobs.*

au·toma·tism /ɔːˈtɒmətɪzəm; *NAmE* ɔːˈtɑːm-/ *noun* [U] (*art*) a method of painting that avoids conscious thought and allows a free flow of ideas

A

au·toma·ton /ɔː'tɒmətən; *NAmE* ɔː'tɑːm-/ *noun* (*pl.* **au·toma·tons** or **au·tom·ata** /-tə/) **1** a person who behaves like a machine, without thinking or feeling anything SYN **robot 2** a machine that moves without human control; a small ROBOT

auto·mo·bile /'ɔːtəməbiːl/ *noun* (*NAmE*) a car: *the automobile industry* ◇ *an automobile accident*

auto·mo·tive /ˌɔːtə'məʊtɪv; *NAmE* -'moʊ-/ *adj.* (*formal*) connected with vehicles that are driven by engines: *the automotive industry*

auto·nom·ic ner·vous sys·tem /ˌɔːtənɒmɪk 'nɜːvəs sɪstəm; *NAmE* ˌɔːtənɑːmɪk 'nɜːrvəs/ *noun* the part of your NERVOUS SYSTEM that controls processes which are unconscious, for example the process of your heart beating

au·tono·mous /ɔː'tɒnəməs; *NAmE* ɔː'tɑːn-/ *adj.* **1** (of a country, a region or an organization) able to govern itself or control its own affairs SYN **independent**: *an* ***autonomous republic/state/province*** **2** (of a person) able to do things and make decisions without help from anyone else ▶ **au·tono·mous·ly** *adv.*

au·ton·omy /ɔː'tɒnəmi; *NAmE* ɔː'tɑːn-/ *noun* [U] (*formal*) **1** the freedom for a country, a region or an organization to govern itself independently SYN **independence**: *a campaign in Wales for greater autonomy* **2** the ability to act and make decisions without being controlled by anyone else: *giving individuals greater autonomy in their own lives*

auto·pilot /'ɔːtəʊpaɪlət; *NAmE* 'ɔːtoʊ-/ *noun* = AUTOMATIC PILOT

aut·opsy /'ɔːtɒpsi; *NAmE* 'ɔːtɑːpsi/ *noun* (*pl.* -ies) an official examination of a dead body by a doctor in order to discover the cause of death SYN **post-mortem**: *an autopsy report* ◇ *to perform an autopsy*

'auto racing *noun* [U] (*NAmE*) = MOTOR RACING

'auto-rickshaw *noun* a covered motor vehicle with three wheels, a driver's seat in front and a seat for passengers at the back, used especially in some Asian countries

auto·save /'ɔːtəʊseɪv; *NAmE* 'ɔːtoʊ-/ *noun* [sing.] (*computing*) the fact that changes to a document are saved automatically as you work ▶ **auto·save** *verb* **~ sth**

ˌauto-sug'gestion *noun* [U] (*psychology*) a process that makes you believe sth or act in a particular way according to ideas that come from within yourself without you realizing it

auto·wind /'ɔːtəʊwaɪnd; *NAmE* 'ɔːtoʊ-/ (also **auto·wind·er** /'ɔːtəʊwaɪndə(r); *NAmE* 'ɔːtoʊ-/) *noun* **1** [sing.] part of a camera which automatically winds the film forwards so that you can take the next picture **2** [U] the ability of a camera to do this ▶ **auto·wind** *verb* [I]

au·tumn 0-w /'ɔːtəm/ (*especially BrE*) (*NAmE* usually **fall**) *noun* [U, C]
the season of the year between summer and winter, when leaves change colour and the weather becomes colder: *in the autumn of 2010* ◇ *in* ***early/late autumn*** ◇ *the autumn term* (= for example at a school or college in Britain) ◇ ***autumn colours/leaves*** ◇ *It's been a very mild autumn this year.*

au·tum·nal /ɔː'tʌmnəl/ *adj.* [usually before noun] like or connected with autumn: *autumnal colours*

aux·il·iary /ɔːg'zɪliəri/ *adj.*, *noun*
■ ***adj.*** **1** (of workers) giving help or support to the main group of workers SYN **ancillary**: ***auxiliary nurses/workers/services*** **2** (*technical*) (of a piece of equipment) used if there is a problem with the main piece of equipment
■ ***noun*** (*pl.* -ies) **1** (also **auˌxiliary 'verb**) (*grammar*) a verb such as *be, do* and *have* used with main verbs to show tense, etc. and to form questions and negatives **2** a worker who gives help or support to the main group of workers: *nursing auxiliaries*

auxin /'ɔːksɪn/ *noun* [U] a HORMONE found in plants

AV /ˌeɪ 'viː/ *abbr.* AUDIO-VISUAL

avail /ə'veɪl/ *noun, verb*
■ ***noun***
IDM **to little/no a'vail** (*formal*) with little or no success: *The doctors tried everything to keep him alive but to no avail.* **of little/no a'vail** (*formal*) of little or no use: *Your ability to argue is of little avail if the facts are wrong.*
■ ***verb*** **1** [T] **~ sb (sth)** | **~ sth** (*formal* or *old-fashioned*) to be helpful or useful to sb **2** [T, I] (*IndE, non-standard*) to make use of sth, especially an opportunity or offer: **~ sth** *To avail all these benefits, just register online.* ◇ **~ of sth** *Why not avail of our special offers?*
PHR V **a'vail yourself of sth** (*formal*) to make use of sth, especially an opportunity or offer: *Guests are encouraged to avail themselves of the full range of hotel facilities.*

avail·able 0-w AW /ə'veɪləbl/ *adj.*
1 0-w (of things) that you can get, buy or find: *available resources/facilities* ◇ ***readily/freely/publicly/generally available*** ◇ *Tickets are available free of charge from the school.* ◇ *When will the information be* ***made available****?* ◇ *Further information is available on request.* ◇ *This was the only room available.* ◇ *We'll send you a copy as soon as it* ***becomes available.*** ◇ *Every available doctor was called to the scene.* **2** 0-w (of a person) free to see or talk to people: *Will she be available this afternoon?* ◇ *The director was not available for comment.* ▶ **avail·abil·ity** AW /əˌveɪlə'bɪləti/ *noun* [U]: *the availability of cheap flights* ◇ (*BrE*) *This offer is* ***subject to availability.***

ava·lanche /'ævəlɑːnʃ; *NAmE* 'ævəlæntʃ/ (*NAmE* also **snow·slide**) *noun* a mass of snow, ice and rock that falls down the side of a mountain: *alpine villages destroyed in an avalanche* ◇ (*figurative*) *We received an avalanche of letters in reply to our advertisement.*

avant- /'ævɒ̃; *NAmE* 'ævɑ̃ː/ *combining form* (used especially with types of popular music) in a style that is modern and very different from what has been done before: *experimental music like avant-rock* ◇ *avant-jazz* ◇ *avant-pop*

the avant-garde /ˌævɒ̃ 'gɑːd; *NAmE* ˌævɑ̃ː 'gɑːrd/ *noun* (from *French*) **1** [sing.] new and very modern ideas in art, music or literature that are sometimes surprising or shocking **2** [sing.+ sing./pl. v.] a group of artists, etc. who introduce new and very modern ideas ▶ **avant-garde** *adj.*

avar·ice /'ævərɪs/ *noun* [U] (*formal*) extreme desire for wealth SYN **greed** ▶ **avar·icious** /ˌævə'rɪʃəs/ *adj.*

ava·tar /'ævətɑː(r)/ *noun* **1** (in Hinduism and Buddhism) a god appearing in a physical form **2** a picture of a person or an animal that represents a particular computer user, on a computer screen, especially in a computer game or CHAT ROOM

Ave. (*NAmE* also **Av.**) *abbr.* (used in written addresses) AVENUE: *Fifth Ave.*

avenge /ə'vendʒ/ *verb* (*formal*) to punish or hurt sb in return for sth bad or wrong that they have done to you, your family or friends: **~ sth** *He promised to avenge his father's murder.* ◇ **~ yourself on sb** *She was determined to avenge herself on the man who had betrayed her.* ▶ **aven·ger** *noun*

Grammar Point

avenge / revenge

Avenge is a verb; **revenge** is (usually) a noun.

- People **avenge** something or **avenge** themselves **on** somebody: *She vowed to avenge her brother's death.* ◇ *He later avenged himself on his wife's killers.* You **take revenge on** a person.
- In more formal or literary English, **revenge** can also be a verb. People **revenge** themselves **on** somebody or **are revenged on** them (with the same meaning): *He was later revenged on his wife's killers.* You cannot **revenge** something: ~~*She vowed to revenge her brother's death.*~~

av·enue /'ævənjuː; *NAmE* -nuː/ *noun* **1** (*abbr.* **Ave.**, **Av.**) a street in a town or city: *a hotel on Fifth Avenue* **2** (*BrE*) a wide straight road with trees on both sides, especially one leading to a big house **3** a choice or way of making progress towards sth: *Several avenues are open to us.* ◇ *We will explore every avenue until we find an answer.*

aver /ə'vɜː(r)/ *verb* (-rr-) **~ that...** | **~ sth** | **+ speech** (*formal*) to state firmly and strongly that sth is true **SYN** **assert, declare**: *She averred that she had never seen the man before.*

aver·age 0⁻ /'ævərɪdʒ/ *adj., noun, verb*

■ ***adj.*** **1** 0⁻ [only before noun] calculated by adding several amounts together, finding a total, and dividing the total by the number of amounts: *an **average rate/cost/price** ◇ Average earnings are around £20 000 per annum. ◇ at an average speed of 100 miles per hour* **2** 0⁻ typical or normal: *40 hours is a fairly average working week for most people. ◇ children of **above/below average** intelligence ◇ £20 for dinner is about average.* **3** 0⁻ ordinary; not special: *I was just an average sort of student.* ▶ **aver·age·ly** *adv.*: *He was attractive and averagely intelligent.*

■ ***noun*** [C, U] **1** 0⁻ the result of adding several amounts together, finding a total, and dividing the total by the number of amounts: *The average of 4, 5 and 9 is 6. ◇ Parents spend **an average of** $220 a year on toys. ◇ If I get an A on this essay, that will bring my average* (= average mark/grade) *up to a B+.* ➲ see also GRADE POINT AVERAGE **2** 0⁻ a level which is usual: *Temperatures are **above/below average** for the time of year. ◇ 400 people a year die of this disease **on average**. ◇ Class sizes in the school are below **the national average**.* **IDM** see LAW

■ ***verb*** **1** [T] **~ sth** [no passive] to be equal to a particular amount as an average: *Economic growth is expected to average 2% next year. ◇ Drivers in London can expect to average about 12 miles per hour* (= to have that as their average speed). **2** [T, I] **~ (sth)** to calculate the average of sth: *Earnings are averaged over the whole period.*

PHR V **,average 'out (at sth)** to result in an average amount over a period of time or when several things are considered: *The cost should average out at about £6 per person. ◇ Sometimes I pay, sometimes he pays—it seems to average out* (= result in us paying the same amount). **,average sth↔'out (at sth)** to calculate the average of sth

averse /ə'vɜːs; *NAmE* ə'vɜːrs/ *adj.* [not before noun] **1 not ~ to sth / to doing sth** liking sth or wanting to do sth; not opposed to doing sth: *I mentioned it to Kate and she wasn't averse to the idea.* **2 ~ to sth / to doing sth** (*formal*) not liking sth or wanting to do sth; opposed to doing sth: *He was averse to any change.*

aver·sion /ə'vɜːʃn; *NAmE* ə'vɜːrʒn/ *noun* [C, U] a strong feeling of not liking sb/sth: *a strong aversion* ◇ **~ to sb/sth** *He had an aversion to getting up early.*

a'version therapy *noun* [U] a way of helping sb to lose a bad habit, by making the habit seem to be associated with an effect that is not pleasant

avert /ə'vɜːt; *NAmE* ə'vɜːrt/ *verb* **1 ~ sth** to prevent sth bad or dangerous from happening: *A disaster was narrowly averted. ◇ He did his best to avert suspicion.* **2 ~ your eyes/gaze/face (from sth)** to turn your eyes, etc. away from sth that you do not want to see: *She averted her eyes from the terrible scene in front of her.*

avian /'eɪviən/ *adj.* [usually before noun] (*technical*) of or connected with birds

'avian flu *noun* [U] (*formal*) = BIRD FLU

avi·ary /'eɪviəri; *NAmE* 'eɪvieri/ *noun* (*pl.* -ies) a large CAGE or building for keeping birds in, for example in a ZOO

avi·ation /,eɪvi'eɪʃn/ *noun* [U] the designing, building and flying of aircraft: ***civil/military aviation** ◇ the **aviation business/industry***

avi·ator /'eɪvieɪtə(r)/ *noun* (*old-fashioned*) a person who flies an aircraft

avid /'ævɪd/ *adj.* **1** [usually before noun] very enthusiastic about sth (often a hobby) **SYN** **keen**: *an **avid reader/collector** ◇ She has **taken an avid interest in** the project* (= she is extremely interested in it). **2 ~ for sth** wanting to get sth very much: *He was avid for more information.* ▶ **avid·ity** /ə'vɪdəti/ *noun* [U] **avid·ly** *adv.*: *She reads avidly.*

avi·on·ics /,eɪvi'ɒnɪks; *NAmE* -'ɑːn-/ *noun* **1** [U] the science of ELECTRONICS when used in designing and making aircraft **2** [pl.] the electronic devices in an aircraft or a SPACECRAFT ▶ **avi·on·ic** *adj.*

avo·cado /,ævə'kɑːdəʊ; *NAmE* -'kɑːdoʊ/ *noun* (*pl.* -os) (*BrE* also **,avocado 'pear**) a tropical fruit with hard, dark green skin, soft, light green flesh and a large seed inside. Avocados are not sweet and are sometimes eaten at the beginning of a meal. ➲ VISUAL VOCAB page V26

avo·ca·tion /,ævəʊ'keɪʃn; *NAmE* ,ævoʊ-/ *noun* (*formal*) a hobby or other activity that you do for interest and enjoyment

avo·cet /'ævəset/ *noun* a bird that lives on or near water, with long legs and black and white feathers

avoid 0⁻ /ə'vɔɪd/ *verb*

1 0⁻ to prevent sth bad from happening: **~ sth** *The accident could have been avoided. ◇ They **narrowly avoided** defeat. ◇ The name was changed to avoid confusion with another firm.* ◇ **~ doing sth** *They built a wall to avoid soil being washed away.* **2** 0⁻ to keep away from sb/sth; to try not to do sth: **~ sb/sth** *He's been avoiding me all week. ◇ She kept avoiding my eyes* (= avoided looking at me). *◇ I left early to avoid the rush hour.* ◇ **~ doing sth** *I've been avoiding getting down to work all day. ◇ You should avoid mentioning his divorce.* **3** 0⁻ **~ sth** to prevent yourself from hitting sth: *The car swerved to avoid a cat.*

IDM **avoid sb/sth like the 'plague** (*informal*) to try very hard not to meet sb, do sth, etc. ➲ more at TRAP *n.*

avoid·able /ə'vɔɪdəbl/ *adj.* that can be prevented: *Many deaths from heart disease are actually avoidable.* **OPP** **unavoidable**

avoid·ance /ə'vɔɪdəns/ *noun* [U] **~ (of sth)** not doing sth; preventing sth from existing or happening: *A person's health improves with the avoidance of stress.* ➲ see also TAX AVOIDANCE

avoir·du·pois /,ævədə'pɔɪz; ,ævwɑːdjuː'pwɑː; *NAmE* ,ævərdə'pɔɪz/ *noun* [U] the system of weights based on the pound

avow /ə'vaʊ/ *verb* **~ that...** | **~ sth** | **+ speech** (*formal*) to say firmly and often publicly what your opinion is, what you think is true, etc: *An aide avowed that the President had known nothing of the deals.* ▶ **avow·al** /ə'vaʊəl/ *noun*: (*formal*) *an avowal of love*

avowed /ə'vaʊd/ *adj.* [only before noun] (*formal*) that has been admitted or stated in public: *an avowed atheist ◇ an **avowed aim/intention/objective/purpose*** ▶ **avow·ed·ly** /ə'vaʊɪdli/ *adv.*

avun·cu·lar /ə'vʌŋkjələ(r)/ *adj.* (*formal*) behaving in a kind and friendly way towards young people, similar to the way an uncle treats his nieces or nephews

aw /ɔː/ *exclamation* (*especially NAmE*) used to express disapproval, protest or sympathy: *Aw, come on, Andy!*

await /ə'weɪt/ *verb* (*formal*) **1 ~ sb/sth** to wait for sb/sth: *He is in custody **awaiting trial**. ◇ Her latest novel is eagerly awaited.* **2 ~ sb** to be going to happen to sb: *A warm welcome awaits all our guests.*

awake 0⁻ /ə'weɪk/ *adj., verb*

■ ***adj.*** 0⁻ [not before noun] not asleep (especially immediately before or after sleeping): *to be **half/fully awake** ◇ to be **wide awake*** (= fully awake) *◇ I was still awake when he came to bed. ◇ The noise was **keeping** everyone **awake**. ◇ I was finding it hard to **stay awake**. ◇ He **lies awake** at night worrying about his job. ◇ She was awake* (= not unconscious) *during the operation on her leg.*

■ ***verb*** (**awoke** /ə'wəʊk; *NAmE* ə'woʊk/, **awoken** /ə'wəʊkən; *NAmE* ə'woʊkən/) (*formal*) **1** [I, T] to wake up; to make sb wake up: **~ (sb) (from/to sth)** *I awoke from a deep sleep.* ◇ **~ to do sth** *He awoke to find her gone.* ◇ **~ sb** *Her voice awoke the sleeping child.* **2** [I, T] **~ (sth)** if an emotion **awakes** or sth **awakes** an emotion, you start to feel that emotion: *His speech is bound to awake old fears and hostilities.*

PHR V **a'wake to sth** to become aware of sth and its possible effects or results: *It took her some time to awake to the dangers of her situation.* ➲ compare WAKE

Which Word?

awake / awaken / wake up / waken

- **Wake (up)** is the most common of these verbs. It can mean somebody has finished sleeping: *What time do you usually wake up?* or that somebody or something has disturbed your sleep: *The children woke me up.* ◇ *I was woken (up) by the telephone.*
- The verb **awake** is usually only used in writing and in the past tense **awoke**: *She awoke to a day of brilliant sunshine.* **Waken** and **awaken** are much more formal. **Awaken** is used especially in literature: *The Prince awakened Sleeping Beauty with a kiss.*
- **Awake** is also an adjective: *I was awake half the night worrying.* ◇ *Is the baby awake yet?* **Waking** is not used in this way.
- Look also at ASLEEP and the verb SLEEP.

awaken /ə'weɪkən/ *verb* (*formal*) **1** [I, T, often passive] to wake up; to make sb wake up: **~ (sb) (from/to sth)** *She awakened to the sound of birds singing.* ◇ **~ to do sth** *We awakened to find the others gone.* ◇ **~ sb** *He was awakened at dawn by the sound of crying.* ➲ note at AWAKE **2** [I, T] **~ (sth)** if an emotion **awakens** or sth **awakens** an emotion, you start to feel that emotion: *The dream awakened terrible memories.*

PHR V **a'waken (sb) to sth** to become aware or to make sb aware of sth and its possible effects or results: *I gradually awakened to the realization that our marriage was over.* ➲ compare WAKEN

awaken·ing /ə'weɪkənɪŋ/ *noun* **1** [C, usually sing.] an occasion when you realize sth or become aware of sth: *If they had expected a warm welcome, they were in for a* ***rude awakening*** (= they would soon realize that it would not be warm). **2** [C, U] the act of beginning to understand or feel sth; the act of sth starting or waking: *sexual awakening* ◇ *the awakening of interest in the environment*

award 🔑 /ə'wɔːd; *NAmE* ə'wɔːrd/ *noun, verb*

■ ***noun*** **1** 🔑 [C] (often in names of particular awards) a prize such as money, etc. for sth that sb has done: *He was nominated for the best actor award.* ◇ *an* ***award presentation/ceremony*** ◇ *the Housing Design Award* ◇ **~ for sth** *to* ***win/receive/get an award*** *for sth* ➲ see also ACADEMY AWARD **2** [C] an increase in the amount of money sb earns: *an annual pay award* **3** [C, U] the amount of money that a court decides should be given to sb who has won a case; the decision to give this money: *an award of £600 000 in libel damages* **4** [U] the official decision to give sth (such as a DIPLOMA) to sb: *Satisfactory completion of the course will lead to the award of the Diploma of Social Work.* **5** [C] (*BrE*) money that students get to help pay for living costs while they study or do research

■ ***verb*** 🔑 [T] to make an official decision to give sth to sb as a payment, prize, etc: **~ sth (to sb)** *The judges awarded equal points to both finalists.* ◇ **~ (sb) sth** *The judges awarded both finalists equal points.* ◇ *He was awarded damages of £50 000.*

award·ee /ə,wɔː'diː; *NAmE* ə,wɔːr'diː/ *noun* a person who is awarded sth, such as a prize

a'ward-winning *adj.* [only before noun] having won a prize: *the award-winning TV drama*

aware 🔑 AW /ə'weə(r); *NAmE* ə'wer/ *adj.*
1 🔑 [not before noun] knowing or realizing sth: *As you're aware, this is not a new problem.* ◇ ***As far as I'm aware,*** *nobody has done anything about it.* ◇ ***acutely/painfully*** (= very) ***aware*** ◇ **~ of sth** *I don't think people are really aware of just how much it costs.* ◇ *He was* ***well aware*** *of the problem.* ◇ *Everybody should* ***be made aware of*** *the risks involved.* ◇ **~ that...** *Were you aware that something was wrong?* **2** 🔑 [not before noun] noticing that sth is present, or that sth is happening: **~ of sb/sth** *She slipped away without him being aware of it.* ◇ *They suddenly became aware of people looking at them.* ◇ **~ that...** *I was aware that she was trembling.* **3** (used with an adverb) interested in and knowing about sth, and thinking it is important: *Young people are very environmentally aware.* OPP **unaware**

aware·ness AW /ə'weənəs; *NAmE* ə'wer-/ *noun* [U, sing.] **~ (of sth)** | **~ (that...)** knowing sth; knowing that sth exists and is important; being interested in sth: *an awareness of the importance of eating a healthy diet* ◇ *There was an almost complete* ***lack of awareness*** *of the issues involved.* ◇ *It is important that students* ***develop an awareness of*** *how the Internet can be used.* ◇ *to* ***raise/heighten/increase*** *public* ***awareness*** *of sth* ◇ ***a greater/a growing/an increasing awareness*** *of sth* ◇ *environmental awareness* (= knowing that looking after the environment is important) ◇ *Energy Awareness Week* ◇ *There seems to be a general awareness that this is not the solution.*

awash /ə'wɒʃ; *NAmE* ə'wɔːʃ; ə'wɑːʃ/ *adj.* [not before noun] **1 ~ (with water)** covered with water **2 ~ with sth** having sth in large quantities: *The city is awash with drugs.*

away 🔑 /ə'weɪ/ *adv.*
HELP For the special uses of **away** in phrasal verbs, look at the entries for the verbs. For example **get away with sth** is in the phrasal verb section at **get.** **1** 🔑 to or at a distance from sb/sth in space or time: *The beach is a mile away.* ◇ *Christmas is still months away.* ◇ **~ from sb/sth** *The station is a few minutes' walk away from here.* **2** 🔑 to a different place or in a different direction: *Go away!* ◇ *Put your toys away.* ◇ *The bright light made her look away.* **3** 🔑 not present SYN **absent**: *There were ten children away yesterday.* ◇ *Sorry, he's away.* ◇ **~ from sb/sth** *She was away from work for a week.* **4** used after verbs to say that sth is done continuously or with a lot of energy: *She was still writing away furiously when the bell went.* ◇ *They were soon chatting away like old friends.* **5** until disappearing completely: *The water boiled away.* ◇ *The music faded away.* ◇ *They danced the night away* (= all night). **6** (*sport*) at the opponent's ground or STADIUM: *Chelsea are playing away this Saturday.* ◇ *an* ***away match/game*** ➲ compare HOME

IDM **away with...** (*literary*) used to say that you would like to be rid of sb/sth: *Away with all these rules and regulations!* ➲ more at COBWEBS, DANCE *v.*, FAR *adv.*, RIGHT *adv.*, STRAIGHT *adv.*

away·day /ə'weɪdeɪ/ *noun* (*BrE, business*) a day that a group of workers spend together away from their usual place of work in order to discuss ideas or plans: *The management are having an awayday to discuss strategy.* ◇ *We talked about it at the awayday.*

awe /ɔː/ *noun, verb*

■ ***noun*** [U] feelings of respect and slight fear; feelings of being very impressed by sth/sb: *awe and respect* ◇ *awe and wonder* ◇ *He speaks of her* ***with awe.*** ◇ *'It's magnificent,' she whispered* ***in awe.***

IDM **be/stand in 'awe of sb/sth** to admire sb/sth and be slightly frightened of them/it: *While Diana was in awe of her grandfather, she adored her grandmother.*

■ ***verb*** **~ sb** [usually passive] (*formal*) to fill sb with awe: *She seemed awed by the presence of so many famous people.* ▸ **awed** *adj.*: *We watched in awed silence.*

'awe-inspir·ing *adj.* impressive; making you feel respect and admiration: *The building was awe-inspiring in size and design.*

awe·some /'ɔːsəm/ *adj.* **1** very impressive or very difficult and perhaps rather frightening: *an awesome sight* ◇ *awesome beauty/power* ◇ *They had an awesome task ahead.* **2** (*especially NAmE, informal*) very good, enjoyable, etc: *I just bought this awesome new CD!* ◇ *Wow! That's totally awesome!* ➲ SYNONYMS at GREAT ▸ **awe·some·ly** *adv.*: *awesomely beautiful*

awe·struck /'ɔːstrʌk/ *adj.* (*literary*) feeling very impressed by sth: *People were awestruck by the pictures the satellite sent back to Earth.*

awful 🔑 /'ɔːfl/ *adj., adv.*

■ ***adj.*** **1** 🔑 (*informal*) very bad or unpleasant: *That's an awful colour.* ◇ *'They didn't even offer to pay.' 'Oh that's awful.'* ◇ *It's awful, isn't it?* ◇ *The weather last summer was awful.* ◇ *I feel awful about forgetting her birthday.* ◇ ***to look/feel awful*** (= to look/feel ill) ◇ *There's an awful smell in here.* ◇ *The awful thing is, it was my fault.* ➲ note at TERRIBLE **2** 🔑 (*informal*) used to emphasize sth, especially that

there is a large amount or too much of sth: *It's going to cost **an awful lot of** money.* ◇ *There's not an awful lot of room.* ◇ *I feel an awful lot better than I did yesterday.* ◇ (*BrE*) *I had an awful job persuading him to come* (= it was very difficult). **3** ⊶ very shocking SYN **terrible**: *the awful horrors of war* ▸ **aw·ful·ness** *noun* [U]: *the sheer awfulness of the situation*
■ ***adv.*** (*informal, especially NAmE*) very; extremely: *Clint is awful smart.*

aw·ful·ly ⊶ /ˈɔːfli/ *adv.* very; extremely SYN **terribly**: *I'm awfully sorry about that problem the other day.*

awhile /əˈwaɪl/ *adv.* (*formal* or *literary*) for a short time

awk·ward ⊶ /ˈɔːkwəd; *NAmE* -wərd/ *adj.* **1** ⊶ making you feel embarrassed: *There was an awkward silence.* **2** ⊶ difficult to deal with SYN **difficult**: *Don't ask awkward questions.* ◇ *You've put me in an awkward position.* ◇ *an awkward customer* (= a person who is difficult to deal with) ◇ *Please don't be awkward about letting him come.* **3** ⊶ not convenient SYN **inconvenient**: *Have I come at an awkward time?* **4** ⊶ difficult or dangerous because of its shape or design: *This box is very awkward for one person to carry.* **5** ⊶ not moving in an easy way; not comfortable: *He tried to dance, but he was too clumsy and awkward.* ◇ *I must have slept in an awkward position—I'm aching all over.* ▸ **awk·ward·ly** ⊶ *adv.*: *'I'm sorry,' he said awkwardly.* ◇ *She fell awkwardly and broke her ankle.* ◇ *an awkwardly shaped room* **awk·ward·ness** *noun* [U]: *She laughed to cover up her feeling of awkwardness.*

awl /ɔːl/ *noun* a small pointed tool used for making holes, especially in leather

awn·ing /ˈɔːnɪŋ/ *noun* a sheet of strong cloth that stretches out from above a door or window to keep off the sun or rain ➲ VISUAL VOCAB page V2

awoke *past tense* of AWAKE

awoken *past part.* of AWAKE

AWOL /ˈeɪwɒl; *NAmE* ˈeɪwɔːl/ *abbr.* absent without leave (used especially in the armed forces when sb has left their group without permission): *He's **gone AWOL** from his base.* ◇ (*humorous*) *The guitarist went AWOL in the middle of the recording.*

awry /əˈraɪ/ *adv., adj.* **1** if sth **goes awry**, it does not happen in the way that was planned: *All my plans for the party had gone awry.* **2** not in the right position SYN **untidy**: *She rushed out, her hair awry.*

axe

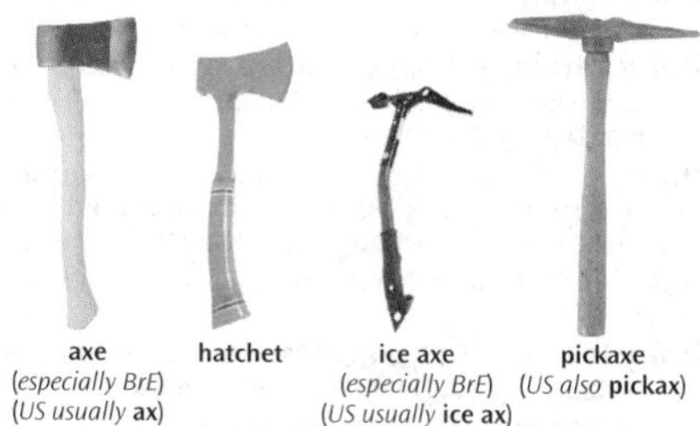

axe (*especially BrE*) (*US usually* **ax**)

hatchet

ice axe (*especially BrE*) (*US usually* **ice ax**)

pickaxe (*US also* **pickax**)

axe /æks/ *noun, verb*
■ ***noun*** (*especially BrE*) (*US* usually **ax**) **1** a tool with a wooden handle and a heavy metal blade, used for chopping wood, cutting down trees, etc. ➲ see also BATTLEAXE, ICE AXE, PICKAXE **2 the axe** [sing.] (*informal*) (often used in newspapers) if sb gets **the axe**, they lose their job; if an institution or a project gets **the axe**, it is closed or stopped, usually because of a lack of money: *Up to 300 workers are **facing the axe** at a struggling Merseyside firm.* ◇ *Patients are delighted their local hospital has been saved from the axe.*
IDM ˌ**have an ˈaxe to grind** to have private reasons for being involved in sth or for arguing for a particular cause: *She had no axe to grind and was only acting out of concern for their safety.*
■ ***verb*** (*BrE*) (*US* **ax**) [often passive] **1 ~ sth** (*informal*) (often used in newspapers) to get rid of a service, system, etc. or to reduce the money spent on it by a large amount: *Other less profitable services are to be axed later this year.* **2 ~ sb** (*informal*) (often used in newspapers) to remove sb from their job: *Jones has been axed from the team.* **3 ~ sb** to kill sb with an axe

axel /ˈæksl/ *noun* a jump in SKATING in which you jump from the front outside edge of one foot, turn in the air, and land on the outside edge of your other foot

axe·man /ˈæksmən/ (*especially BrE*) (*NAmE* usually **axman**) (*pl.* **-men** /-mən/) *noun* (*informal*) a man who attacks other people with an axe

axial /ˈæksiəl/ *adj.* of or related to an AXIS: *an axial road*

axiom /ˈæksiəm/ *noun* (*formal*) a rule or principle that most people believe to be true

axio·mat·ic /ˌæksiəˈmætɪk/ *adj.* [not usually before noun] (*formal*) true in such an obvious way that you do not need to prove it SYN **self-evident**: *It is axiomatic that life is not always easy.* ▸ **axio·mat·ic·al·ly** *adv.*

axis

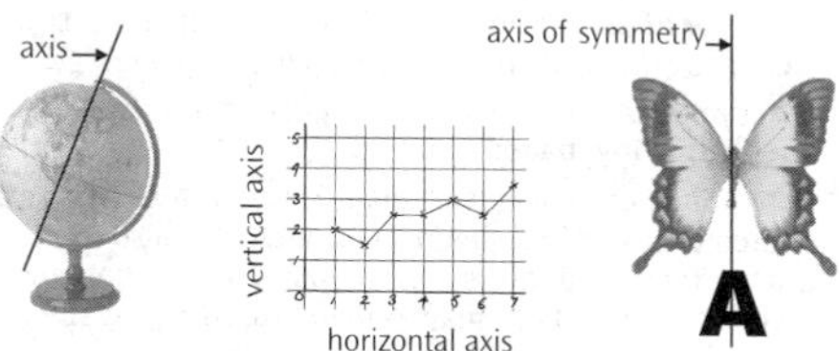

axis /ˈæksɪs/ *noun* (*pl.* **axes** /ˈæksiːz/) **1** an imaginary line through the centre of an object, around which the object turns: *Mars takes longer to revolve on its axis than the Earth.* **2** (*technical*) a fixed line against which the positions of points are measured, especially points on a GRAPH: *the **vertical/horizontal axis*** **3** (*geometry*) a line that divides a shape into two equal parts: *an axis of symmetry* ◇ *The axis of a circle is its diameter.* **4** [usually sing.] (*formal*) an agreement or ALLIANCE between two or more countries: *the Franco-German axis*

axle /ˈæksl/ *noun* a long straight piece of metal that connects a pair of wheels on a vehicle: *the **front/rear axle***

axman (*US*) = AXEMAN

axon /ˈæksɒn; *NAmE* ˈæksɑːn/ *noun* (*biology*) the long thin part of a nerve cell along which signals are sent to other cells ➲ compare DENDRITE

ayah /ˈaɪə/ *noun* (*IndE*) **1** a woman whose job is caring for children, doing domestic work, etc. **2** a person whose job is caring for sb who is ill/sick

aya·tol·lah /ˌaɪəˈtɒlə; *NAmE* -ˈtoʊlə/ *noun* a religious leader of Shiite Muslims in Iran

aye /aɪ/ *exclamation* (*old use* or *dialect*) **1** yes: *'Did you see what happened?' 'Oh aye, I was there.'* **2** always; still

ayes /aɪz/ *noun* [pl.] the total number of people voting 'yes' in a formal debate, for example in a parliament: *The ayes have it* (= more people have voted for sth than against it). OPP **noes**

Ayur·vedic medicine /ˌaɪəveɪdɪk ˈmedsn; *NAmE* ˌɑːjʊr-/ *noun* [U] a type of traditional Hindu medicine that treats illnesses using a combination of foods, HERBS and breathing exercises

aza·lea /əˈzeɪliə/ *noun* a plant or bush with large flowers that may be pink, purple, white or yellow, grown in a pot or in a garden

azi·muth /ˈæzɪməθ/ *noun* (*astronomy*) an angle related to a distance around the earth's HORIZON, used to find out the position of a star, planet, etc.

AZT™ /ˌeɪ zed ˈtiː; *NAmE* ziː/ *noun* [U] a drug that is used to treat AIDS

azure /ˈæʒə(r); *BrE* also ˈæzjʊə(r)/ *adj.* bright blue in colour like the sky ▸ **azure** *noun* [U]

Bb

B /biː/ *noun, symbol*

■ ***noun*** (also **b**) (*pl.* Bs, B's, b's /biːz/) **1** [C, U] the second letter of the English alphabet: *'Butter' begins with (a) B/'B'.* **2 B** [C, U] (*music*) the 7th note in the SCALE of C MAJOR **3 B** [C, U] the second highest mark/grade that a student can get for a piece of work: *She got (a)* ***B in/for*** *History.* **4 B** [U] used to represent the second of two or more possibilities: *Shall we go for plan A or plan B?* **5 B** [U] used to represent a person, for example in an imagined situation or to hide their identity: *Let's pretend A meets B in the park.* ➲ see also B-ROAD **IDM** see A

■ ***symbol*** used in Britain before a number to refer to a particular secondary road: *the B1224 to York*

b. *abbr.* (in writing) born: *Emily Clifton, b. 1800*

B2B /ˌbiː tə ˈbiː/ *abbr.* BUSINESS-TO-BUSINESS

BA (*BrE*) (*NAmE* **B.A.**) /ˌbiː ˈeɪ/ *noun* the abbreviation for 'Bachelor of Arts' (a first university degree in an ARTS subject): *to* ***be/have/do a BA*** ◇ *(BrE) Darren Green BA*

baa /bɑː/ *noun* the sound made by sheep or LAMBS ▶ **baa** *verb* [I] (**baa·ing, baaed** or **baa'd**)

baba /ˈbɑːbɑː/ *noun* **1** a small cake, often with RUM poured over it **2** (*IndE, EAfrE*) a father (often also used as a title or form of address for any older man, showing respect) **3** (*IndE*) a holy man **4** (*IndE*) (used especially as a form of address) a small child

Bab·bitt /ˈbæbɪt/ *noun* (*NAmE*) a person who is satisfied with a narrow set of values and thinks mainly about possessions and making money **ORIGIN** From the name of the main character in the novel *Babbitt* by Sinclair Lewis.

bab·ble /ˈbæbl/ *noun, verb*

■ ***noun*** [sing.] **1** the sound of many people speaking at the same time: *a babble of voices* **2** talking that is confused or silly and is difficult to understand: *I can't listen to his constant babble.* **3** the sounds a baby makes before beginning to say actual words ➲ see also PSYCHOBABBLE

■ ***verb*** **1** [I, T] **~ (away/on) (sth)** to talk quickly in a way that is difficult to understand: *They were all babbling away in a foreign language.* ◇ *I realized I was babbling like an idiot.* **2** [I] to make the sound of water flowing over rocks, like a stream: *a babbling brook*

babby /ˈbæbi/ *noun* (*pl.* -ies) (*BrE, dialect*) a baby

babe /beɪb/ *noun* **1** (*old use*) a baby **2** (*slang*) a word used to address a young woman, or your wife, husband or lover, usually expressing affection but sometimes considered offensive if used by a man to a woman he does not know: *What're you doing tonight, babe?* **3** (*informal*) an attractive young woman

IDM **a ˌbabe in ˈarms** (*old-fashioned*) a very small baby that cannot yet walk ➲ more at MOUTH *n.*

babel /ˈbeɪbl/ *noun* [sing.] (*formal*) the sound of many voices talking at one time, especially when more than one language is being spoken **ORIGIN** From the Bible story in which God punished the people who were trying to build a tower to reach heaven (the **tower of Babel**) by making them unable to understand each others' languages.

ˈbabe magnet *noun* (*slang, especially NAmE*) a man or a man's possession that is considered to be attractive to women: *Bob's such a babe magnet.* ◇ *A sports car like that is a complete babe magnet.*

ˌbabes in the ˈwood *noun* [pl.] innocent people who are easily tricked or harmed **ORIGIN** From a children's story about a boy and a girl who are left alone in a wood where they die and a bird covers them with leaves.

ba·boon /bəˈbuːn; *NAmE* bæˈb-/ *noun* a large African or Asian MONKEY with a long face like a dog's

babu /ˈbɑːbuː/ *noun* (*IndE*) a person who works in an office

ba·bushka /bəˈbʊʃkə; ˈbæbʊʃkə/ *noun* (from *Russian*) **1** a Russian old woman or grandmother **2** a traditional Russian woman's HEADSCARF, tied under the chin

baby 0‑w /ˈbeɪbi/ *noun, adj., verb*

■ ***noun*** (*pl.* -ies) **1** 0‑w a very young child or animal: *The baby's crying!* ◇ *a newborn baby* ◇ *My sister's* ***expecting a baby*** = she is pregnant. ◇ *She* ***had a baby*** *last year.* ◇ ***a baby boy/girl*** ◇ ***baby food/clothes*** ◇ *a baby monkey/blackbird* ➲ COLLOCATIONS at CHILD **2** (*informal*) the youngest member of a family or group: *He's the baby of the team.* **3** (*disapproving*) a person who behaves like a young child and is easily upset: *Stop crying and don't be such a baby.* **4** (*slang, especially NAmE*) a word used to address sb, especially your wife, husband or lover, in a way that expresses affection but that can be offensive if used by a man to a woman he does not know

IDM **be your/sb's baby** (*informal*) to be a plan or project that sb is responsible for and cares about because they have created it **leave sb holding the ˈbaby** (*informal*) to suddenly make sb responsible for sth important that is really your responsibility: *He changed to another job and we were left holding the baby.* **throw the baby out with the ˈbathwater** (*informal*) to lose sth that you want at the same time as you are trying to get rid of sth that you do not want ➲ more at CANDY, SLEEP *v.*

■ ***adj.*** [only before noun] **baby** vegetables are a very small version of particular vegetables, or are picked when they are very small: *baby carrots*

■ ***verb*** (**ba·bies, baby·ing, ba·bied, ba·bied**) **~ sb** to treat sb with too much care, as if they were a baby

ˌbaby ˈblue *adj.* very pale blue in colour ▶ **ˌbaby ˈblue** *noun* [U]

ˈbaby blues *noun* [pl.] (*informal*) a depressed feeling that some women get after the birth of a baby **SYN** **post-natal depression**

ˈbaby boom *noun* a period when many more babies are born than usual

ˈbaby boomer (*NAmE* also **boom·er**) *noun* a person born during a baby boom, especially after the Second World War

ˈbaby bouncer *noun* (*BrE*) a type of seat that hangs from pieces of ELASTIC, in which a baby can sit and BOUNCE up and down

ˈbaby buggy *noun* **1** **ˈBaby Buggy™** (*BrE*) = BUGGY **2** (*old-fashioned, NAmE*) = BABY CARRIAGE

ˈbaby carriage (*NAmE*) (*BrE* **pram**) *noun* a small vehicle on four wheels for a baby to go out in, pushed by a person on foot ➲ picture at PUSHCHAIR

ˌbaby-ˈdoll *adj.* used to describe a style of women's dress or NIGHTDRESS that is short with a high waist and is similar to the type of dress traditionally worn by DOLLS

ˈbaby-faced *adj.* with a face that looks young and innocent

ˈbaby fat (*NAmE*) (*BrE* **ˈpuppy fat**) *noun* [U] fat on a child's body that disappears as the child grows older

ˌbaby ˈgrand *noun* a small GRAND PIANO

Baby·gro™ /ˈbeɪbigrəʊ; *NAmE* -groʊ/ *noun* (*pl.* -os) (*BrE*) a piece of clothing for babies, usually covering the whole body except the head and hands, made of a type of cloth that stretches easily ➲ compare ONESIE

ba·by·hood /ˈbeɪbihʊd/ *noun* [U] the period of your life when you are a baby

baby·ish /ˈbeɪbiɪʃ/ *adj.* (usually *disapproving*) typical of or suitable for a baby

ˈbaby shower *noun* (*especially NAmE*) a party given for a woman who is going to have a baby, at which her friends give her presents for the baby

baby·sit /ˈbeɪbisɪt/ *verb* (**baby·sit·ting, baby·sat, baby·sat**) (also **sit**) [I, T] to take care of babies or children for a short time while their parents are out: **~ (for sb)** *She regularly babysits for us.* ◇ **~ sb** *He's babysitting the neighbour's children.* ▶ **baby·sit·ting** *noun* [U]

baby·sit·ter /ˈbeɪbisɪtə(r)/ (also **sit·ter** especially in *NAmE*) *noun* a person who takes care of babies or children while their parents are away from home and is usually paid to do this: *I can't find a babysitter for tonight.* ➲ see also CHILDMINDER

ˈ**baby talk** *noun* [U] the words or sounds a baby says when it is learning to talk; the special language adults sometimes use when talking to babies

ˈ**baby tooth** (*BrE* also ˈ**milk tooth**) *noun* any of the first set of teeth in young children that drop out and are replaced by others

ˈ**baby walker** (*BrE*) (*NAmE* **walk·er**) *noun* a frame with wheels and a HARNESS for a baby who can walk around a room, supported by the frame

bac·ca·laur·eate /ˌbækəˈlɔːriət/ *noun* **1** the last SECONDARY SCHOOL exam in France and other countries, and in some international schools: ***to sit/take/pass/fail your baccalaureate*** ➲ see also INTERNATIONAL BACCALAUREATE **2** (in the US) a religious service or talk for students who have completed HIGH SCHOOL or college

bac·carat /ˈbækərɑː/ *noun* [U] a card game in which players hold two or three cards each and bet on whose cards will have the highest number left over when their value is divided by ten

bac·chan·al·ian /ˌbækəˈneɪliən/ *adj.* (*formal*) (of a party, etc.) wild and involving large amounts of alcohol ORIGIN From the name of the Greek god **Bacchus** (also called Dionysus), the god of wine and wild enjoyment.

baccy /ˈbæki/ *noun* [U] (*BrE, informal*) TOBACCO

bach /bætʃ/ *noun* (*NZE*) a small holiday house

bach·elor /ˈbætʃələ(r)/ *noun* **1** a man who has never been married: *an eligible bachelor* (= one that many people want to marry, especially because he is rich) ◇ ***a confirmed bachelor*** (= a person who does not intend to marry; often used in newspapers to refer to a HOMOSEXUAL man) ➲ compare SPINSTER **2** (usually **Bachelor**) a person who has a Bachelor's degree (= a first university degree): *a **Bachelor of Arts/Engineering/Science*** ➲ see also BA, BEd, BSc **3** (*CanE*) = BACHELOR APARTMENT

ˈ**bachelor apartment** *noun* a small flat/apartment suitable for a person living alone

ba·chelor·ette /ˌbætʃələˈret/ *noun* (*NAmE*) a young woman who is not married

ˈ**bachelor girl** *noun* an independent young woman who is not married

bach·elor·hood /ˈbætʃələhʊd; *NAmE* -lərh-/ *noun* [U] the time in a man's life before he is married

ˈ**bachelor pad** *noun* a house or flat/apartment in which a man who is not married enjoys a lifestyle without family responsibilities

ˈ**bachelor party** (*NAmE*) (*BrE* ˈ**stag night**, ˈ**stag party**) *noun* a party that a man has with his male friends just before he gets married, often the night before

ba·cil·lus /bəˈsɪləs/ *noun* (*pl.* **ba·cilli** /bəˈsɪlaɪ/) a type of bacteria. There are several types of bacillus, some of which cause disease.

back ⚿ /bæk/ *noun, adj., adv., verb*

■ ***noun***

▸ PART OF BODY **1** ⚿ the part of the human body that is on the opposite side to the chest, between the neck and the tops of the legs; the part of an animal's body that CORRESPONDS to this: *Do you sleep on your back or your front?* ◇ *He stood with his back to the door.* ◇ *They had their hands tied behind their backs.* ◇ *back pain* ◇ *a back massage* ◇ *A small boy rode on the elephant's back.* ➲ COLLOCATIONS at PHYSICAL ➲ VISUAL VOCAB page V48 ➲ see also BAREBACK, HORSEBACK **2** ⚿ the row of bones in the middle of the back SYN **backbone, spine**: *She broke her back in a riding accident.* ◇ *He **put his back out*** (=DISLOCATED sth in his back) *lifting the crates.*

▸ PART FURTHEST FROM FRONT **3** ⚿ [usually sing.] **~ (of sth)** the part or area of sth that is furthest from the front: *We could only get seats **at the back*** (= of the room). ◇ *I found some old photos at the back of the drawer.* ◇ *He was shot in the back of the knee.* ◇ *The house has three bedrooms at the front and two **at the back**.* ◇ (*BrE*) *There's room for three people **in the back**.* ◇ (*NAmE*) *There's room for three people **in back*** = of a car, etc.. ◇ (*BrE*) *If you'd like to come **round the back*** (= to the area behind the house), *I'll show you the garden.* ➲ see also HARDBACK, PAPERBACK, SHORT BACK AND SIDES

▸ OF PIECE OF PAPER **4** ⚿ [usually sing.] **~ (of sth)** the part of a piece of paper, etc. that is on the opposite side to the one that has information or the most important information on it: *Write your name on the back of the cheque.*

▸ OF BOOK **5** ⚿ [usually sing.] **~ (of sth)** the last few pages of a book, etc: *The television guide is at the back of the paper.*

▸ OF CHAIR **6** the part of a chair, etc. against which you lean your back ➲ VISUAL VOCAB page V18

▸ -BACKED **7** (in adjectives) used to describe furniture that has the type of back mentioned: *a high-backed sofa*

▸ IN SPORT **8** (in sports) a player whose main role is to defend their team's goal ➲ compare FORWARD *n.* ➲ see also FULLBACK, HALFBACK

IDM **at/in the back of your mind** if a thought, etc. is **at the back of your mind**, you are aware of it but it is not what you are mainly thinking about **the ˌback of beˈyond** (*informal*) a place that is a long way from other houses, towns, etc. ˌ**back to ˈback 1** if two people stand **back to back**, they stand with their backs facing or touching each other ➲ see also BACK-TO-BACK **2** if two or more things happen **back to back**, they happen one after the other ˌ**back to ˈfront** ⚿ (*BrE*) (*NAmE* **back·wards**) if you put on a piece of clothing **back to front**, you make a mistake and put the back where the front should be: *I think you've got that sweater on back to front.* ➲ compare INSIDE OUT at INSIDE *n.* **be glad, etc. to see the back of sb/sth** (*informal, especially BrE*) to be happy that you will not have to deal with or see sb/sth again because you do not like them or it: *Was I pleased to see the back of her!* **behind sb's ˈback** ⚿ without sb's knowledge or permission: *Have you been talking about me behind my back?* ◇ *They went ahead and sold it behind my back.* ➲ compare TO SB'S FACE at FACE *n.* **be on sb's ˈback** (*informal*) to keep asking or telling sb to do sth that they do not want to do, in a way that they find annoying **break the ˈback of sth** to finish the largest or most important part of a task **get/put sb's ˈback up** (*informal*) to annoy sb: *That sort of attitude really gets my back up!* **get off sb's ˈback** (*informal*) to stop annoying sb, for example by criticizing them, or asking them to do sth: *Just get off my back, will you!* **have (got) sb's ˈback** (*NAmE, informal*) to protect and support sb: *Don't worry, I've got your back.* **have your ˌback to the ˈwall** (*informal*) to be in a difficult situation in which you are forced to do sth but are unable to make the choices that you would like **off the ˌback of a ˈlorry** (*BrE, informal, humorous*) goods that **fell off the back of a lorry** were probably stolen. People say or accept that they came 'off the back of a lorry' to avoid saying or asking where they really came from. **on the back of sth** as a result of an achievement or a success: *The profits growth came on the back of a 26 per cent rise in sales.* **(flat) on your back** (*informal*) in bed because you are ill/sick: *She's been flat on her back for over a week now.* ◇ (*figurative*) *The UK market was flat on its back* (= business was very bad). **put your ˈback into sth** to use a lot of effort and energy on a particular task **turn your back** ⚿ to turn so that you are facing in the opposite direction **turn your back on sb/sth 1** ⚿ to move so that you are standing or sitting with your back facing sb/sth: *When on stage, try not to turn your back on the audience.* **2** ⚿ to reject sb/sth that you have previously been connected with: *She turned her back on them when they needed her.* ➲ more at COVER *v.*, EYE *n.*, KNOW *v.*, PAT *n.*, PAT *v.*, PUSH *v.*, ROD, SCRATCH *v.*, SHIRT, STAB *n.*, STAB *v.*, STRAW, WATER *n.*

■ ***adj.*** [only before noun]

▸ AWAY FROM FRONT **1** ⚿ located behind or at the back of sth: *We were sitting in the back row.* ◇ *back teeth* ◇ *a back room* (= one at the back of a building) ◇ *the back page of a newspaper* ➲ compare FRONT *adj.*

B

▸ FROM PAST **2** of or from a past time: *a back number of the magazine*
▸ OWED **3** owed for a time in the past: ***back pay/taxes/rent***
▸ PHONETICS **4** (*phonetics*) (of a vowel) produced with the back of the tongue in a higher position than the front, for example /ɑː/ in English ⊃ compare CENTRAL, FRONT

IDM **on the back 'burner** (*informal*) (of an idea, a plan, etc.) left for the present time, to be done or considered later ⊃ compare ON THE FRONT BURNER ⊃ see also BACK-BURNER at FRONT *adj.*

■ ***adv.*** HELP For the special uses of **back** in phrasal verbs, look at the entries for the verbs. For example **pay sb back** is in the phrasal verb section at **pay**.
▸ AWAY FROM FRONT **1** away from the front or centre; behind you: *I stepped back to let them pass.* ◇ *Sit back and relax.* ◇ *You've combed your hair back.* ◇ *He turned and looked back.* ◇ *She fell back towards the end of the race.* OPP **forward**
▸ AT A DISTANCE **2** at a distance away from sth: *The barriers kept the crowd back.* ◇ *Stand back and give me some room.*
▸ UNDER CONTROL **3** under control; prevented from being expressed or coming out: *He could no longer hold back his tears.*
▸ AS BEFORE **4** to or into the place, condition, situation or activity where sb/sth was before: *Put the book back on the shelf.* ◇ *Please give me my ball back.* ◇ *He'll be back on Monday.* ◇ *It takes me an hour to walk* ***there and back***. ◇ *Could you go back to the beginning of the story?* ◇ *She woke up briefly and then went back to sleep.* ◇ *We were right* ***back where we started****, only this time without any money.*
▸ IN PAST **5** in or into the past; ago: *The village has a history going back to the Middle Ages.* ◇ *She left* ***back in*** *November.* ◇ *That was a few years back.*
▸ AT A PREVIOUS PLACE **6** at a place previously left or mentioned: *We should have turned left five kilometres back.* ◇ *Back at home, her parents were worried.* ◇ *I can't wait to get back home.*
▸ IN RETURN **7** in return or reply: *If he kicks me, I'll kick him back.* ◇ *Could you call back later, please?*

IDM ˌ**back and 'forth** from one place to another and back again repeatedly: *ferries sailing back and forth between the islands* ˌ**back in the 'day** in the past: *My dad's always talking about how great everything was back in the day.* ˌ**back in the 'days** at a particular time in the past: *I was a fan back in the days when the band wasn't yet famous.* **back of sth** (*NAmE, informal*) behind sth: *the houses back of the church* ⊃ more at EARTH *n.*, SQUARE *n.*

■ ***verb***
▸ MOVE BACKWARDS **1** [I, T] to move or make sth move backwards: **+ adv./prep.** *He backed against the wall, terrified.* ◇ **~ sth + adv./prep.** *If you can't drive in forwards, try backing it in.* ⊃ compare REVERSE
▸ SUPPORT **2** [T] **~ sb/sth** to give help or support to sb/sth: *Her parents backed her in her choice of career.* ◇ *Doctors have backed plans to raise the tax on cigarettes.* ◇ *The programme of economic reform is backed* (= given financial support) *by foreign aid.* ◇ *a United Nations-backed peace plan*
▸ BET MONEY **3** [T] **~ sth** to bet money on a horse in a race, a team in a competition, etc: *I backed the winner and won fifty pounds.*
▸ MUSIC **4** [T] **~ sth** to play or sing music that supports the main singer or instrument ⊃ see also BACKING
▸ COVER BACK **5** [T] **~ sth (with sth)** [usually passive] to cover the back of sth in order to support or protect it
▸ BE BEHIND **6** [T, usually passive] **~ sth** (*BrE*) to be located behind sth: *The house is backed by fields.*

IDM ˌ**back the wrong 'horse** (*BrE*) to support sb/sth that is not successful

PHR V ˌ**back a'way (from sb/sth)** to move away backwards from sb/sth that is frightening or unpleasant; to avoid doing sth that is unpleasant ˌ**back 'down (on/from sth)** (*NAmE* also ˌ**back 'off**) to take back a demand, an opinion, etc. that other people are strongly opposed to; to admit defeat: *She refused to back down on a point of principle.* ˌ**back 'off 1** to move backwards in order to get away from sb/sth frightening or unpleasant: *As the riot police approached, the crowd backed off.* **2** to stop threatening, criticizing or annoying sb: *Back off! There's no need to yell at me.* ◇ *The press have agreed to back off and leave the couple alone.* ˌ**back 'off (from sth)** to choose not to take action, in order to avoid a difficult situation: *The government backed off from a confrontation.* ˌ**back 'onto sth** (*BrE*) (of a building) to have sth directly behind it: *Our house backs onto the river.* ˌ**back 'out (of sth)** to decide that you are no longer going to take part in sth that has been agreed: *He lost confidence and backed out of the deal at the last minute.* ˌ**back 'up** | ˌ**back sth↔'up** to move backwards, especially in a vehicle: *You can back up another two feet or so.* ◇ *I backed the car up to the door.* ˌ**back sb/sth↔'up 1** to support sb/sth; to say that what sb says, etc. is true: *I'll back you up if they don't believe you.* ◇ *The writer doesn't back up his opinions with examples.* **2** to provide support for sb/sth: *two doctors backed up by a team of nurses* ◇ *The rebels backed up their demands with threats.* ⊃ related noun BACKUP ˌ**back sth↔'up** (*computing*) to prepare a second copy of a file, program, etc. that can be used if the main one fails or needs extra support ⊃ related noun BACKUP

Which Word?

at the back / at the rear / behind

■ **At the back** and **at the rear** have a similar meaning, but **at the rear** is used more in formal or official language: *What's that at the back of the fridge?* ◇ *Smoking is only allowed at the rear of the aircraft.* It is more usual to talk about the **back door** of a house but the **rear exit** of an aircraft or public building. If something is **behind** something else it is near to the back of it but not part of it. Compare: *Our room was at the back of the hotel* and *There's a lovely wood just behind our hotel.*

back·ache /ˈbækeɪk/ *noun* [U, C] a continuous pain in the back: (*BrE*) *to have backache/a backache* ◇ (*NAmE*) *to have a backache*

ˌ**back 'alley** *noun* a narrow passage behind or between buildings

ˌ**back-'alley** *adj.* [only before noun] happening or done secretly, often illegally: *a back-alley abortion*

back·beat /ˈbækbiːt/ *noun* (*music*) a strong emphasis on one or two of the beats that are not normally emphasized, used especially in JAZZ and rock music

ˌ**back 'bench** *noun* [usually pl.] (in the House of Commons in Britain, and in certain other parliaments) any of the seats for Members of Parliament who do not have senior positions in the government or the other parties: *He resigned as Home Secretary and returned to the back benches.* ◇ *back-bench MPs* ⊃ compare THE FRONT BENCH

back·bench·er /ˌbækˈbentʃə(r)/ *noun* (in the British and certain other parliaments) a member who sits in the rows of seats at the back, and who does not have an important position in the government or the opposition ⊃ compare FRONTBENCHER

back·bit·ing /ˈbækbaɪtɪŋ/ *noun* [U] unpleasant and unkind talk about sb who is not present

back·board /ˈbækbɔːd; *NAmE* -bɔːrd/ *noun* the board behind the BASKET in the game of BASKETBALL

back·bone /ˈbækbəʊn; *NAmE* -boʊn/ *noun* **1** [C] the row of small bones that are connected together down the middle of the back SYN **spine** ⊃ VISUAL VOCAB page V48 **2** [sing.] the most important part of a system, an organization, etc. that gives it support and strength: *Agriculture forms the backbone of the rural economy.* **3** [U] the strength of character that you need to do sth difficult: *He doesn't have the backbone to face the truth.*

ˈ**back-breaking** *adj.* (of physical work) very hard and tiring

ˌ**back-ˈburn·er** *verb* **~ sth** (*informal, especially NAmE*) to leave an idea or a plan for a time, to be done or considered later ➲ compare ON THE BACK BURNER at BACK *adj.*

ˈ**back catalogue** (*NAmE* also **back catalog**) *noun* all the recorded music previously produced by a musician: *The entire Beatles' back catalogue has been put online.*

back·channel /ˈbæktʃænl/ *noun* **1** a secret or unusual way of passing information to other people **2** (*linguistics*) a sound or sign that sb makes to show that they are listening to the person who is talking to them

back·chat /ˈbæktʃæt/ (*BrE*) (*NAmE* ˈ**back talk**) *noun* [U] (*informal*) a way of answering that shows no respect for sb in authority

back·cloth /ˈbækklɒθ; *NAmE* -klɔːθ; -klɑːθ/ *noun* (*BrE*) = BACKDROP

back·comb /ˈbækkəʊm; *NAmE* -koʊm/ (*BrE*) (*NAmE* **tease**) *verb* **~ sth** to COMB your hair in the opposite direction to the way it grows so that it looks thicker

ˌ**back ˈcopy** *noun* (*BrE*) = BACK ISSUE

back·coun·try /ˈbækkʌntri/ *noun* [U] (*NAmE*) an area away from roads and towns, especially in the mountains

back·court /ˈbækkɔːt; *NAmE* -kɔːrt/ *noun* **1** (in TENNIS, BASKETBALL, etc.) the area at either end of the COURT **2** (in BASKETBALL) the players who form the defence **3** (*ScotE*) an area surrounded by walls but with no roof at the back of a building

back·crawl /ˈbækkrɔːl/ *noun* [U, sing.] (*BrE*) = BACKSTROKE

back·date /ˌbækˈdeɪt/ *verb* **1 ~ sth** to write a date on a cheque or other document that is earlier than the actual date ➲ compare POST-DATE **2 ~ sth** (*BrE*) to make sth, especially a payment, take effect from an earlier date: *Postal workers are getting a 5.2% pay rise, backdated to February.*

ˌ**back ˈdoor** *noun* the door at the back or side of a building

IDM **by/through the back door** in an unfair or indirect way: *He used his friends to help him get into the civil service by the back door.*

ˌ**back-ˈdoor** *adj.* [only before noun] using indirect or secret means in order to achieve sth

back·draught (also **back·draft**) /ˈbækdrɑːft; *NAmE* -dræft/ *noun* **1** a current of air that flows backwards down a CHIMNEY, pipe, etc. **2** an explosion caused by more OXYGEN being supplied to a fire, for example by a door being opened

back·drop /ˈbækdrɒp; *NAmE* -drɑːp/ (*BrE* also **back·cloth**) *noun* **1** a painted piece of cloth that is hung behind the stage in a theatre as part of the SCENERY **2** everything that can be seen around an event that is taking place, but which is not part of that event: *The mountains provided a dramatic backdrop for our picnic.* **3** the general conditions in which an event takes place, which sometimes help to explain that event: *It was* ***against this backdrop*** *of racial tension that the civil war began.*

ˌ**back ˈend** *noun* (*especially BrE*) **1** the end of a period or process: *the back end of last year* **2** the part of sth which is behind the part that you can see **3** (*informal*) a person's bottom (= the part they sit on)

ˈ**back-end** *adj.* [only before noun] **1** relating to the end of a period or process **2** (*computing*) (of a device or program) not used directly by a user, but used by a program or computer ➲ compare FRONT-END

back·er /ˈbækə(r)/ *noun* a person or company that gives support to sb/sth, especially financial support

back·field /ˈbækfiːld/ *noun* [sing., U] **1** (in AMERICAN FOOTBALL) the area of play behind the line of SCRIMMAGE **2** the players who play in or around this area

back·fill /ˈbækfɪl/ *verb* **~ sth** to fill a hole with the material that has been dug out of it

back·fire /ˌbækˈfaɪə(r)/ *verb* **1** [I] **~ (on sb)** to have the opposite effect to the one intended, with bad or dangerous results: *Unfortunately the plan backfired.* **2** [I] (of an engine or a vehicle) to make a sudden noise like an explosion ➲ compare MISFIRE

back·flip /ˈbækflɪp/ *noun* if sb does a **backflip**, they turn their body over backwards in the air and land on their feet again

ˈ**back-formation** *noun* [U, C] (*linguistics*) a word formed by removing or changing the beginning or end of a word that already exists. For example, *cheeseburger* is a back-formation from *hamburger*.

back·gam·mon /ˈbækgæmən; ˌbækˈgæmən/ *noun* [U] a game for two people played on a board marked with long thin triangles. Players throw DICE and move pieces around the board. ➲ VISUAL VOCAB page V33

back·ground 🔑 /ˈbækgraʊnd/ *noun*

▸ FAMILY/EDUCATION, ETC. **1** 🔑 [C] the details of a person's family, education, experience, etc: *a person's* ***family/social/cultural/educational/class background*** ◇ *The job would suit someone with a business background.*

▸ PAST **2** 🔑 [C, usually sing., U] the circumstances or past events that help explain why sth is how it is; information about these: *the historical background to the war* ◇ ***background information/knowledge*** ◇ *The elections are taking place* ***against a background*** *of violence.* ◇ *Can you give me more background on the company?*

▸ OF PICTURE/PHOTO **3** 🔑 [C, usually sing.] the part of a picture, photograph or view behind the main objects, people, etc: *a photograph with trees* ***in the background*** ➲ SYNONYMS at ENVIRONMENT ➲ compare FOREGROUND

▸ LESS IMPORTANT POSITION **4** 🔑 [sing.] a position in which people are not paying attention to sb/sth or not as much attention as they are paying to sb/sth else: *He prefers to remain* ***in the background*** *and let his assistant talk to the press.* ◇ *A piano tinkled gently* ***in the background.*** ◇ ***background music*** ◇ *There was a lot of* ***background noise*** (= that you could hear, but were not listening to). ➲ compare FOREGROUND

▸ COLOUR UNDER STH **5** [C, usually sing.] a colour or design on which sth is painted, drawn, etc: *The name of the company is written in red on a white background.*

IDM **in the ˈbackground** (*computing*) (of a computer program) not being used at the present time and appearing on the screen behind programs that are being used ➲ compare IN THE FOREGROUND ➲ more at MERGE

back·hand /ˈbækhænd/ *noun* [usually sing.] (in TENNIS, etc.) a stroke played with the back of the hand turned in the direction towards which the ball is hit: *He has a good backhand* (= he can make good backhand strokes). ◇ *a* ***backhand volley/drive*** ➲ compare FOREHAND

back·han·ded /ˌbækˈhændɪd/ *adj.* having a meaning that is not directly or clearly expressed, or that is not intended

IDM **a ˌbackhanded ˈcompliment** (*NAmE* also ˌ**left-handed ˈcompliment**) a remark that seems to express admiration but could also be understood as an insult

back·hand·er /ˈbækhændə(r)/ *noun* (*BrE, informal*) a secret and illegal payment made to sb in exchange for a favour SYN **bribe**

ˌ**back-ˈheel** *verb* **~ sth** to kick a ball using the heel: *He back-heeled the ball towards goal.* ▸ ˌ**back-ˈheel** *noun*

back·hoe /ˈbækhəʊ; *NAmE* -hoʊ/ *noun* a large vehicle with machinery for digging, used in building roads, etc. ➲ VISUAL VOCAB page V47

back·ing /ˈbækɪŋ/ *noun* **1** [U] help SYN **support**: *financial backing* ◇ *The police gave the proposals their full backing.* **2** [U, C] material attached to the back of sth in order to protect it or make it stronger **3** [U, C, usually sing.] (especially in pop music) music that accompanies the main singer or tune: *a* ***backing group/singer/track***

ˌ**back ˈissue** (*BrE* also ˌ**back ˈcopy**, ˌ**back ˈnumber**) *noun* a copy of a newspaper or magazine from a date in the past

back·lash /ˈbæklæʃ/ *noun* [sing.] **~ (against sth)** | **~ (from sb)** a strong negative reaction by a large number of people, for example to sth that has recently changed in

B

society: *The government is facing an angry backlash from voters over the new tax.*

back·less /ˈbækləs/ *adj.* (of a dress) not covering most of the back

back·light /ˈbæklaɪt/ *noun, verb*
■ *noun* [U] light from behind sth in a photograph or painting
■ *verb* (*pt, pp* -lit or -lighted) **~ sth** to shine light on sth from behind ▸ **back·lit** *adj.*: *a backlit photograph*

back·list /ˈbæklɪst/ *noun* the list of books that have been published by a company in the past and are still available

back·log /ˈbæklɒg; *NAmE* -lɔːg; -lɑːg/ *noun* a quantity of work that should have been done already, but has not yet been done

back·lot /ˈbæklɒt; *NAmE* -lɑːt/ *noun* an outdoor area in a film/movie studio, where pieces of SCENERY are made and some scenes are filmed

back·mark·er /ˈbækmɑːkə(r); *NAmE* -mɑːrk-/ *noun* (*BrE*) the person, horse, etc. who is in last position in a race

back·most /ˈbækməʊst; *NAmE* -moʊst/ *adj.* [usually before noun] furthest back: *the backmost teeth*

ˌ**back ˈnumber** *noun* (*BrE*) = BACK ISSUE

ˌ**back ˈoffice** *noun* (*business*) the part of a business company which does not deal directly with the public

back·pack /ˈbækpæk/ *noun, verb*
■ *noun* (*especially NAmE*) (*BrE* also **ruck·sack**) a large bag, often supported on a light metal frame, carried on the back and used especially by people who go climbing or walking ➲ VISUAL VOCAB pages V52, V57
■ *verb* [I] (usually **go backpacking**) to travel on holiday/vacation carrying your equipment and clothes in a backpack: *They went backpacking in Spain last year.* ▸ **back·pack·er** *noun*

ˌ**back ˈpassage** *noun* (*BrE*) a polite way of referring to sb's RECTUM (= the part of the body where solid waste leaves the body)

ˌ**back-ˈpedal** *verb* (-ll-, *NAmE* -l-) **1** [I] **~ (on sth)** to change an earlier statement or opinion; to not do sth that you promised to do: *The protests have forced the government to back-pedal on the new tax.* **2** [I] to PEDAL backwards on a bicycle; to walk or run backwards

back·plane /ˈbækpleɪn/ *noun* (*computing*) a CIRCUIT BOARD that other devices can be connected to

ˈ**back-projec·tion** *noun* **1** [U] the process of shining an image onto the back of a screen **2** [C] an image that has been shone onto the back of a screen

back·rest /ˈbækrest/ *noun* part of a seat that supports sb's back

ˌ**back ˈroom** *noun* a room at the back of a building, away from the entrance, often where secret activities take place

ˈ**back-room boys** *noun* [pl.] (*BrE*) people who do important work for a person or an organization but who are not well known themselves

back·scratch·ing /ˈbækskrætʃɪŋ/ *noun* [U] (*informal*, often *disapproving*) the fact of giving sb help in return for help that they have given you, often in connection with sth that might be illegal

ˌ**back ˈseat** *noun* a seat at the back of a vehicle
IDM **take a back seat** to allow sb else to play a more active and important role in a particular situation than you do

ˌ**back-seat ˈdriver** *noun* (*disapproving*) **1** a passenger in a vehicle who keeps giving advice to the driver about how he or she should drive **2** a person who wants to be in control of sth that is not really their responsibility

back·sheesh = BAKSHEESH

back·shift /ˈbækʃɪft/ *noun* [U] (*linguistics*) the changing of a tense when reporting what sb said, for example when reporting the words 'What *are* you doing?' as 'He asked me what I *was* doing'

back·side /ˈbæksaɪd/ *noun* (*informal*) the part of the body that you sit on SYN **behind, bottom**: *Get up off your backside and do some work!* IDM see PAIN *n.*

back·slap·ping /ˈbækslæpɪŋ/ *noun* [U] loud and enthusiastic behaviour when people are praising each other for sth good they have done ▸ **back·slap·ping** *adj.* [only before noun]: *backslapping tributes*

back·slash /ˈbækslæʃ/ *noun* a mark (\), used in computer commands ➲ compare FORWARD SLASH

back·slid·ing /ˈbækslaɪdɪŋ/ *noun* [U] the situation when sb fails to do sth that they agreed to do and returns to their former bad behaviour

back·space /ˈbækspeɪs/ *noun, verb*
■ *noun* the key on the keyboard of a computer or TYPEWRITER which allows you to move backwards. On a computer keyboard this key also removes the last letter that you typed.
■ *verb* [I] to use the backspace key on a computer keyboard or on a TYPEWRITER

back·spin /ˈbækspɪn/ *noun* [U] a backward spinning movement of a ball that has been hit, which makes it go less far than it normally would

ˈ**back-stabbing** *noun* [U] the action of criticizing sb when they are not there, while pretending to be their friend at other times

back·stage /ˌbækˈsteɪdʒ/ *adv.* **1** in the part of a theatre where the actors and artists get ready and wait to perform: *After the show, we were allowed to go backstage to meet the cast.* **2** away from the attention of the public; in secret: *I'd like to know what really goes on backstage in government.* ▸ **back·stage** *adj.*

back·stairs /ˈbæksteəz; *NAmE* -sterz/ *noun, adj.*
■ *noun* [pl.] stairs at the back or side of a building, sometimes used by servants
■ *adj.* secret or dishonest: *backstairs deals between politicians*

back·stitch /ˈbækstɪtʃ/ *noun* [U, C] a method of sewing in which each STITCH begins at the middle of the previous one

back·story /ˈbækstɔːri/ *noun* (*pl.* -ies) [C, U] **1** the things that are supposed to have happened to the characters in a film/movie, novel, etc, before the film/movie, etc. starts: *The film spends too long establishing the characters' backstories.* **2** (especially in journalism) the background to a news story: *First, some backstory:...*

back·street /ˈbækstriːt/ *noun, adj.*
■ *noun* a small quiet street, usually in a poor part of a town or city, away from main roads
■ *adj.* [only before noun] acting or happening secretly, often dishonestly or illegally: *backstreet dealers* ◇ *backstreet abortions*

back·stroke /ˈbækstrəʊk; *NAmE* -stroʊk/ (*BrE* also **back·crawl**) *noun* [U, sing.] a style of swimming in which you lie on your back: *Can you do (the) backstroke?* ◇ *He won the 100 metres backstroke* (= the race). ➲ VISUAL VOCAB page V37

back·swing /ˈbækswɪŋ/ *noun* (*sport*) the backwards movement of your arm or arms before you hit the ball

ˈ**back talk** (*NAmE*) (*BrE* **back·chat**) *noun* [U] (*informal*) a way of answering that shows no respect for sb in authority

ˌ**back-to-ˈback** *noun* (*BrE*) a house in a row of houses that share walls with the houses on each side and behind: *back-to-backs built for the poor in the 19th century*

back·track /ˈbæktræk/ *verb* **1** [I] to go back along the same route that you have just come along **2** [I] to change an earlier statement, opinion or promise because of pressure from sb/sth

back·up /ˈbækʌp/ *noun* [U, C] **1** extra help or support that you can get if necessary: *The police had backup from the army.* ◇ *We can use him as a backup if one of the other players drops out.* ◇ *a backup power supply* **2** (*computing*) a copy of a file, etc. that can be used if the original is lost or damaged: *Always make a backup of your work.* ◇ *a backup copy* ➲ see also BACK UP

ˈ**backup light** (*NAmE*) (*BrE* **reˈversing light**) *noun* a white light at the back of a vehicle that comes on when the vehicle moves backwards

back·ward /ˈbækwəd; *NAmE* -wərd/ *adj.*
1 [only before noun] directed or moving towards the back: *She strode past him* ***without a backward glance***. **2** moving in a direction that means that no progress is being made SYN **retrograde**: *She felt that going back to live in her home town would be a backward step.* **3** having made less progress than normal; developing slowly: *a backward part of the country, with no paved roads and no electricity* ◊ *a backward child* ◊ (*BrE, informal*) *She's not* ***backward in coming forward*** (= she's not shy). ⮌ compare FORWARD

ˌ**backward ˈclasses** *noun* [pl.] (in India) the people in a CASTE (= division of society) or community who are recommended by each state authority for special help in education and employment

ˈ**backward-looking** *adj.* (*disapproving*) opposed to progress or change

back·ward·ness /ˈbækwədnəs; *NAmE* -wərd-/ *noun* [U] the state of having made less progress than normal

back·wards /ˈbækwədz; *NAmE* -wərdz/ (also **back·ward** especially in *NAmE*) *adv.*
1 towards a place or position that is behind: *I lost my balance and fell backwards.* ◊ *He took a step backwards.* OPP **forward** **2** in the opposite direction to the usual one: *'Ambulance' is written backwards so you can read it in the mirror.* ◊ *In the movie they take a journey backwards through time.* **3** towards a worse state: *I felt that going to live with my parents would be a step backwards.* OPP **forward** **4** (*NAmE*) (*BrE* ˌ**back to ˈfront**) if you put on a piece of clothing **backwards**, you make a mistake and put the back where the front should be
IDM ˌ**backward(s) and ˈforward(s)** from one place or position to another and back again many times: *She rocked backwards and forwards on her chair.* **bend/lean over ˈbackwards (to do sth)** to make a great effort, especially in order to be helpful or fair: *I've bent over backwards to help him.* ⮌ more at KNOW *v.*

ˌ**backwards comˈpatible** (also ˌ**backward comˈpatible**) *adj.* (*computing*) able to be used with systems, machines or programs which are older

back·wash /ˈbækwɒʃ; *NAmE* -wɔːʃ; -wɑːʃ/ *noun* [sing.] **1** the unpleasant result of an event **2** waves caused by a boat moving through water; the movement of water back into the sea after a wave has hit the beach

back·water /ˈbækwɔːtə(r)/ *noun* **1** a part of a river away from the main part, where the water only moves slowly **2** (often *disapproving*) a place that is away from the places where most things happen, and is therefore not affected by events, progress, new ideas, etc: *a* ***sleepy/quiet/rural backwater***

back·woods /ˈbækwʊdz/ *noun* [pl.] a place that is away from any big towns and from the influence of modern life

back·woods·man /ˈbækwʊdzmən/ *noun* (*pl.* **-men** /-mən/) (*NAmE*) a person who lives in a region far from towns where not many people live, especially one who does not have much education or good manners

back·yard /ˌbækˈjɑːd; *NAmE* -ˈjɑːrd/ *noun* **1** (*BrE*) an area with a hard surface behind a house, often surrounded by a wall **2** (*NAmE*) the whole area behind and belonging to a house, including an area of grass and the garden: *a backyard barbecue* ⮌ see also YARD
IDM **in your (own) backyard** in or near the place where you live or work: *The residents didn't want a new factory in their backyard.* ◊ *The party leader is facing opposition in his own backyard* (= from his own members). ⮌ see also NIMBY

bac·lava = BAKLAVA

bacon /ˈbeɪkən/ *noun* [U] meat from the back or sides of a pig that has been CURED (= preserved using salt or smoke), usually served in thin slices: *a rasher of bacon* ◊ *bacon and eggs* ◊ ***smoked/unsmoked bacon*** ⮌ compare GAMMON, HAM (1), PORK IDM see HOME *adv.*, SAVE *v.*

bac·teria /bækˈtɪəriə; *NAmE* -ˈtɪr-/ *noun* [pl.] (*sing.* **bac·ter·ium** /-iəm/) the simplest and smallest forms of life. Bacteria exist in large numbers in air, water and soil, and also in living and dead creatures and plants, and are often a cause of disease ⮌ COLLOCATIONS at LIFE ▸ **bac·ter·ial** /-riəl/ *adj.*: ***bacterial infections/growth***

bac·teri·ology /bækˌtɪəriˈɒlədʒi; *NAmE* -ˌtɪriˈɑːl-/ *noun* [U] the scientific study of bacteria ▸ **bac·terio·logic·al** /bækˌtɪəriəˈlɒdʒɪkl; *NAmE* -ˌtɪriəˈlɑːdʒ-/ *adj.* **bac·teri·olo·gist** *noun*

bad /bæd/ *adj., noun, adv.*
■ ***adj.*** (**worse** /wɜːs; *NAmE* wɜːrs/, **worst** /wɜːst; *NAmE* wɜːrst/)
▸ UNPLEASANT **1** unpleasant; full of problems: *bad news/weather/dreams/habits* ◊ *I'm having a really bad day.* ◊ *It was the worst experience of her life.* ◊ *Smoking gives you bad breath.* ◊ *Things are* ***bad enough*** *without our own guns shelling us.*
▸ POOR QUALITY **2** of poor quality; below an acceptable standard: *bad conditions/driving* ◊ *a bad copy/diet* ◊ *I thought it was a very bad article.* ◊ *This isn't as bad as I thought.* ◊ *That's not a bad idea.*
▸ NOT GOOD AT STH **3** **~ at sth/at doing sth** (of a person) not able to do sth well or in an acceptable way SYN **poor**: *a bad teacher* ◊ *You're a bad liar!* ◊ *He's a bad loser* (= he complains when he loses a game). ◊ *She is so bad at keeping secrets.*
▸ SERIOUS **4** serious; severe: *You're heading for a bad attack of sunburn.* ◊ *The engagement was a bad mistake.* ◊ *My headache is getting worse.*
▸ NOT APPROPRIATE **5** [only before noun] not appropriate in a particular situation: *I know that this is a bad time to ask for help.* ◊ *He now realized that it had been a bad decision on his part.*
▸ WICKED **6** morally unacceptable: *The hero gets to shoot all the bad guys.* ◊ *He said I must have done something bad to deserve it.*
▸ CHILDREN **7** [usually before noun] (especially of children) not behaving well SYN **naughty**: *Have you been a bad boy?*
▸ HARMFUL **8** [not before noun] **~ for sb/sth** harmful; causing or likely to cause damage: *Those shoes are bad for her feet.* ◊ *Weather like this is bad for business.*
▸ PAINFUL **9** [usually before noun] (of parts of the body) not healthy; painful: *I've got a bad back.*
▸ FOOD **10** not safe to eat because it has decayed: *Put the meat in the fridge so it doesn't* ***go bad***.
▸ TEMPER/MOOD **11** **~ temper/mood** the state of feeling annoyed or angry: *It put me in a bad mood for the rest of the day.*
▸ GUILTY/SORRY **12** **feel ~** to feel guilty or sorry about sth: *She felt bad about leaving him.* ◊ *Why should I want to make you feel bad?*
▸ ILL/SICK **13** **feel/look ~** to feel or look ill/sick: *I'm afraid I'm feeling pretty bad.*
▸ EXCELLENT **14** (**bad·der, bad·dest**) (*slang, especially NAmE*) good; excellent
IDM Most idioms containing **bad** are at the entries for the nouns and verbs in the idioms, for example **be bad news (for sb/sth)** is at **news**. **can't be bad** (*informal*) used to try to persuade sb to agree that sth is good: *You'll save fifty dollars, which can't be bad, can it?* **have got it ˈbad** (*informal, humorous*) to be very much in love: *You're not seeing him again tonight, are you? That's five times this week—you've got it bad!* **not ˈbad** (*informal*) quite good; better than you expected: *'How are you?' 'Not too bad.'* ◊ *That wasn't bad for a first attempt.* **too bad** (*informal*) **1** (*ironic*) used to say 'bad luck' or 'it's a shame' when you do not really mean it: *If sometimes they're the wrong decisions, too bad.* **2** a shame; a pity: *Too bad every day can't be as good as this.* **3** (*old-fashioned*) annoying: *Really, it was too bad of you to be so late.*
■ ***noun*** **the bad** [U] bad people, things, or events: *You will always have the bad as well as the good in the world.*
IDM ˌ**go to the ˈbad** (*old-fashioned*) to begin behaving in an immoral way: *I hate to see you going to the bad.* ˈ**my bad**

(*NAmE, informal*) used when you are admitting that sth is your fault or that you have made a mistake: *I'm sorry—my bad.* **take the ˌbad with the ˈgood** to accept the bad aspects of sth as well as the good ones **to the ˈbad** (*BrE*) used to say that sb now has a particular amount less money than they did before: *After the sale they were £300 to the bad.*

■ ***adv.*** (*NAmE, informal*) badly: *She wanted it real bad.* ◇ *Are you hurt bad?*

Vocabulary Building

Bad and very bad

Instead of saying that something is **bad** or **very bad**, try to use more precise and interesting adjectives to describe things:

- an **unpleasant**/a **foul**/a **disgusting** smell
- **appalling/dreadful/severe** weather
- an **unpleasant**/a **frightening**/a **traumatic** experience
- **poor/weak** eyesight
- a **terrible/serious/horrific** accident
- a **wicked**/an **evil**/an **immoral** person
- an **awkward**/an **embarrassing**/a **difficult** situation
- We were working in **difficult/appalling** conditions.

To refer to your health, you can say: *I feel* ***unwell/sick/ terrible*** ◇ *I don't feel (very)* ***well***.

In conversation, words like **terrible**, **horrible**, **awful** and **dreadful** can be used in most situations to mean 'very bad'.

bad·ass /ˈbædæs/ *adj.* (*NAmE, informal*) (of a person) tough and aggressive ▸ **bad·ass** *noun*

ˌbad ˈbreath *noun* [U] breath that smells unpleasant SYN **halitosis**: *Have I got bad breath?*

ˌbad ˈdebt *noun* [C, U] a debt that is unlikely to be paid

baddy /ˈbædi/ *noun* (*pl.* -ies) (*BrE, informal*) a bad or evil character in a film/movie, book, play, etc: *As usual, the cops get the baddies in the end.* OPP **goody**

bade *past tense* of BID

badge /bædʒ/ *noun* **1** a small piece of metal or plastic, with a design or words on it, that a person wears to show that they belong to an organization, support sth, have achieved sth, have a particular rank, etc: *She wore a badge saying 'Vote for Coates'.* ◇ *All employees have to wear name badges.* ➲ VISUAL VOCAB page V53 ➲ compare BUTTON **2** (*BrE*) (*NAmE* **patch**) a piece of material that you sew onto clothes as part of a uniform: *the school badge* **3** a small piece of metal that you carry or wear to prove who you are, used, for example, by police officers: *He pulled out a badge and said he was a cop.* **4** (*formal*) something that shows that a particular quality is present: *His gun was a badge of power for him.*

badger /ˈbædʒə(r)/ *noun, verb*

■ ***noun*** an animal with grey fur and wide black and white lines on its head. Badgers are NOCTURNAL (= active mostly at night) and live in holes in the ground.

■ ***verb*** to put pressure on sb by repeatedly asking them questions or asking them to do sth SYN **pester**: **~ sb (into doing sth)** *I finally badgered him into coming with us.* ◇ **~ sb about sth** *Reporters constantly badger her about her private life.* ◇ **~ sb to do sth** *His daughter was always badgering him to let her join the club.*

ˌbad ˈhair day *noun* (*informal*) a day on which everything seems to go wrong

bad·in·age /ˈbædɪnɑːʒ; *NAmE* ˌbædənˈɑːʒ/ *noun* [U] (from *French, literary*) friendly joking between people SYN **banter**

bad·lands /ˈbædlændz/ *noun* [pl.] **1** large areas of land that have been farmed too much with the result that plants will not grow there **2 the Badlands** a large area of land in the western US where plants will not grow

ˌbad ˈlanguage *noun* [U] words that many people find offensive SYN **swear words**

badly 0‑w /ˈbædli/ *adv.* (worse, worst)

1 0‑w not skilfully or not carefully: *to play/sing badly* ◇ *badly designed/organized* OPP **well 2** 0‑w not successfully: *Things have been* ***going badly***. ◇ *I* ***did badly*** (= was not successful) *in my exams.* OPP **well 3** 0‑w not in an acceptable way: *to behave/sleep badly* ◇ *badly paid/treated* ◇ *The kids took the dog's death very badly* (= they were very unhappy). OPP **well 4** 0‑w in a way that makes people get a bad opinion about sth: *The economic crisis reflects badly on the government's policies.* ◇ *She's only trying to help, so don't* ***think badly of*** *her.* OPP **well 5** 0‑w used to emphasize how much you want, need, etc. sb/sth: *The building is* ***badly in need of*** *repair.* ◇ *They wanted to win so badly.* ◇ *I miss her badly.* **6** 0‑w used to emphasize how serious a situation or an event is: ***badly damaged/injured/hurt*** ◇ *The country has been badly affected by recession.* ◇ *Everything's* ***gone badly wrong!***

badly ˈoff *adj.* (worse ˈoff, worst ˈoff) **1** not having much money SYN **poor**: *We aren't too badly off but we can't afford a house like that.* OPP **well off 2** not in a good situation: *I've got quite a big room so I'm not too badly off.* OPP **well off**

IDM **be badly ˈoff for sth** (*BrE*) to not have enough of sth

bad·mash /bʌdˈmɑːʃ/ *noun* (*IndE*) a dishonest man

bad·min·ton /ˈbædmɪntən/ *noun* [U] a game like TENNIS played by two or four people, usually indoors. Players hit a small light kind of ball, originally with feathers around it (= a SHUTTLECOCK) across a high net using a RACKET. ➲ VISUAL VOCAB page V37

ˈbad-mouth *verb* **~ sb** (*informal*) to say unpleasant things about sb: *No one wants to employ somebody who badmouths their former employer.*

bad·ness /ˈbædnəs/ *noun* [U] the fact of being morally bad: *There was not a hint of badness in him.*

ˌbad-ˈtempered 0‑w *adj.* often angry; in an angry mood: *She gets very bad-tempered when she's tired.*

Ba·fana Ba·fana /bəˌfɑːnə bəˈfɑːnə/ *noun* (*SAfrE*) a popular name for the South African national men's football (SOCCER) team

baf·fle /ˈbæfl/ *verb, noun*

■ ***verb*** to confuse sb completely; to be too difficult or strange for sb to understand or explain: **~ sb** *His behaviour baffles me.* ◇ **be baffled (as to) why, how, where, etc...** *I'm baffled as to why she hasn't called.* ◇ *I'm baffled why she hasn't called.* ▸ **baffle·ment** *noun* [U]: *His reaction was one of bafflement.* **baf·fling** *adj.*

■ ***noun*** (*technical*) a screen used to control or prevent the flow of sound, light or liquid

BAFTA /ˈbæftə/ *abbr., noun*

■ ***abbr.*** British Academy of Film and Television Arts

■ ***noun*** an award presented by the British Academy of Film and Television Arts: *He won a BAFTA for the role.*

bag 0‑w /bæg/ *noun, verb*

■ ***noun***

▸ CONTAINER **1** 0‑w [C] (often in compounds) a container made of paper or plastic, that opens at the top, used especially in shops/stores: *a* ***plastic/polythene/paper bag*** ◇ *a* ***laundry/mail bag*** ◇ *a black plastic* ***rubbish/garbage bag*** **2** 0‑w [C] a strong container made from cloth, plastic, leather, etc, usually with one or two handles, used to carry things in when shopping or travelling: *a shopping bag* ◇ *a make-up bag* ◇ *He's upstairs unpacking his bags.* ◇ *She opened her bag* (= her HANDBAG) *and took out her comb.* ➲ VISUAL VOCAB pages V52, V57 ➲ see also AIRBAG, BEANBAG, BUMBAG, GOODY BAG, PUNCHBAG, SANDBAG, TEA BAG

▸ AMOUNT **3** [C] **~ (of sth)** the amount contained in a bag: *She ate a bag of chips.* ➲ VISUAL VOCAB page V29 ➲ see also MIXED BAG, RAGBAG **4 bags** [U, pl.] **~ (of sth)** (*BrE, informal*) a large amount or a large number of sth: *Get in! There's bags of room.*

▸ UNDER EYES **5 bags** [pl.] dark circles or loose folds of skin under the eyes, as a result of getting old or lack of sleep
▸ UNPLEASANT WOMAN **6** [C] (*informal, especially BrE*) an insulting word for an unpleasant or bad-tempered older woman ➲ see also RATBAG, SCUMBAG, WINDBAG
▸ BIRDS/ANIMALS **7** [C, usually sing.] all the birds, animals, etc. shot or caught on one occasion HELP There are many other compounds ending in **bag**. You will find them at their place in the alphabet.
IDM **ˌbag and ˈbaggage** with all your possessions, especially secretly or suddenly: *He threw her out onto the street, bag and baggage.* **a ˌbag of ˈbones** (*informal*) a very thin person or animal **be in the ˈbag** (*informal*) if sth is **in the bag**, it is almost certain to be won or achieved **leave sb holding the ˈbag** (*NAmE, informal*) to suddenly make sb responsible for sth important, such as finishing a difficult job, that is really your responsibility **(not) sb's ˈbag** (*informal*) (not) sth that you are interested in or good at: *Poetry isn't really my bag.* ➲ more at CAT, NERVE *n.*, PACK *v.*, TRICK *n.*
■ *verb* (-gg-)
▸ PUT INTO BAGS **1 ~ sth (up)** to put sth into bags: *The fruit is washed, sorted and bagged at the farm.*
▸ CATCH ANIMAL **2 ~ sth** (*informal*) to catch or kill an animal
▸ IN SPORT **3 ~ sth** (*informal*) to score a goal, point, etc: *Dublin bagged two goals in last night's win.*
▸ CLAIM STH **4 ~ sth** (*BrE, informal*) to claim sth as yours before sb else claims it; to take sth before sb else can get it: *Sally had managed to bag the two best seats.* ◇ *Quick, bag that table over there!*
▸ CRITICIZE SB/STH **5 ~ sb/sth** (*AustralE, NZE, informal*) to criticize sb/sth
▸ DECIDE NOT TO DO STH **6 ~ sth** (*NAmE, informal*) to decide not to do sth because you think it will not be successful or because you think it will be better to do it later: *They decided to bag the trip because they were short of cash.*
IDM **bags (I)...** (*BrE*) (*NAmE* **ˈdibs on...**) used to claim sth as yours before sb else can claim it: *Bags I sit in the front seat!*

baga·telle /ˌbægəˈtel/ *noun* **1** [U] a game played on a board with small balls that you try to hit into holes **2** [C, usually sing.] (*literary*) a small and unimportant thing or amount: *It cost a mere bagatelle.*

bagel /ˈbeɪɡl/ *noun* a hard bread roll shaped like a ring

bag·gage 🔑 /ˈbægɪdʒ/ *noun* [U]
1 🔑 (*especially NAmE*) = LUGGAGE: *excess baggage* (= weighing more than the limit allowed on a plane) ◇ *baggage handlers* (= people employed to load and unload baggage at airports) ◇ (*NAmE*) *We loaded our baggage into the car.* ➲ COLLOCATIONS at TRAVEL **2** the beliefs and attitudes that sb has as a result of their past experiences: *She was carrying a lot of* **emotional baggage**. IDM see BAG *n.*

Which Word?

baggage / luggage

- **Luggage** is the usual word in *BrE*, but **baggage** is also used, especially in the context of the bags and cases that passengers take on a flight. In *NAmE* **baggage** is usually used.
- Both these words are uncountable nouns: *Do you have a lot of luggage?* ◇ *Two pieces of luggage have gone missing.* ◇ *Never leave baggage unattended.*

ˈbaggage car (*NAmE*) (*BrE* **ˈluggage van**) *noun* a coach/car on a train for carrying passengers' luggage

ˈbaggage reclaim (*BrE*) (*NAmE* **ˈbaggage claim**) *noun* [U] the place at an airport where you get your suitcases, etc. again after you have flown

Bag·gie™ /ˈbægi/ *noun* (*NAmE*) a small bag made of clear plastic that is used for storing SANDWICHES, etc.

baggy /ˈbægi/ *adj.* (**bag·gier**, **bag·gi·est**) (of clothes) fitting loosely: *a baggy T-shirt* OPP **tight**

ˈbag lady *noun* a woman who has no home and who walks around carrying her possessions with her

ˈbag lunch *noun* (*NAmE*) a meal of SANDWICHES, fruit, etc. that you take to school, work, etc. in a bag ➲ compare BOX LUNCH, PACKED LUNCH

bag·pipes /ˈbægpaɪps/ (also **pipes**) *noun* [pl.] (*NAmE* also **bag·pipe** [sing.]) a musical instrument played especially in Scotland. The player blows air into a bag held under the arm and then slowly forces the air out through pipes to produce a noise. ➲ picture at PIPE ▸ **bag·pipe** *adj.*: *bagpipe music*

ba·guette /bæˈget/ *noun* **1** (also **ˌFrench ˈloaf**, **ˌFrench ˈstick**) a LOAF of white bread in the shape of a long thick stick that is crisp on the outside and soft inside **2** a small baguette or part of one that is filled with food and eaten as a SANDWICH: *a cheese baguette*

bah /bɑː/ *exclamation* used to show a sound that people make to express disapproval

Baha'i (also **Bahai**) /bɑːˈhɑːi; bəˈhaɪ/ *noun* [U] a religion that teaches that people and religions are the same, and that there should be peace

Ba·hasa In·do·nesia /bəˌhɑːsə ɪndəˈniːʒə/ *noun* [U] the official language of Indonesia

Ba·hasa Ma·lay·sia /bəˌhɑːsə məˈleɪʒə/ *noun* [U] the official language of Malaysia

bail /beɪl/ *noun, verb*
■ *noun* **1** [U] money that sb agrees to pay if a person accused of a crime does not appear at their trial. When bail has been arranged, the accused person is allowed to go free until the trial: *Can anyone* **put up bail** *for you?* ◇ *She was released* **on £2 000 bail**. ◇ *Bail was set at $1 million.* ◇ *He committed another offence while he was out* **on bail** (= after bail had been agreed). ◇ *The judge* **granted/refused bail**. ◇ *She* **jumped/skipped bail** (= did not appear at her trial). ➲ COLLOCATIONS at JUSTICE **2** [C, usually pl.] (in CRICKET) either of the two small pieces of wood on top of each set of three wooden posts (called STUMPS)
■ *verb* (*BrE* also **bale**) **1** [T] **~ sb (to do sth)** to release sb on bail: *He was* **bailed to appear** *in court on 15 March.* **2** [I] (*NAmE, informal*) to leave a place, especially quickly: *Sorry, I really have to bail.* **3** [T] **~ sb (up)** (*AustralE, NZE, informal*) to approach sb and talk to them, often when they do not want this
PHR V **ˌbail ˈout (of sth)** **1** to jump out of a plane that is going to crash **2** to escape from a situation that you no longer want to be involved in: *I'd understand if you wanted to bail out of this relationship.* **ˌbail ˈout | ˌbail (sth)↔ˈout** to empty water from sth by lifting it out with your hand or a container: *He had to stop rowing to bail water out of the boat.* ◇ *The boat will sink unless we bail out.* **ˌbail sb↔ˈout** to pay sb's bail for them **ˌbail sb↔ˈout (of sth)** to rescue sb from a difficult situation: *The government had to bail the company out of financial difficulty.* ◇ *Ryan's late goal bailed out his team.* ➲ SYNONYMS at SAVE

bai·ley /ˈbeɪli/ *noun* the open area of a castle, inside the outer wall

bail·iff /ˈbeɪlɪf/ *noun* **1** (*BrE*) a law officer whose job is to take the possessions and property of people who cannot pay their debts **2** (*BrE*) a person employed to manage land or a large farm for sb else **3** (*NAmE*) an official who keeps order in court, takes people to their seats, watches prisoners, etc.

bail·out /ˈbeɪlaʊt/ *noun* an act of giving money to a company, a foreign country, etc. that has very serious financial problems

bain-marie /ˌbæn məˈriː/ *noun* (from *French*) a pan of hot water in which a bowl of food is cooked or warmed slowly

bairn /beən; *NAmE* bern/ *noun* (*ScotE, NEngE*) a child

bait /beɪt/ *noun, verb*
■ *noun* [U, C] **1** food put on a hook to catch fish or in nets, traps, etc. to catch animals or birds: *The fish took the bait.* **2** a person or thing that is used to catch sb or to attract them, for example to make them do what you want
■ *verb* **1 ~ sth (with sth)** to place food on a hook, in a trap,

etc. in order to attract or catch an animal: *He baited the trap with a piece of meat.* **2 ~ sb** to deliberately try to make sb angry by making cruel or insulting remarks **3 -baiting** (in compound nouns) the activity of attacking a wild animal with dogs: *bear-baiting*

ˌbait-and-ˈswitch *noun* [C, usually sing.] a selling method where advertisements for low-priced products are used to attract customers, who are then persuaded to buy sth more expensive

baize /beɪz/ *noun* [U] a type of thick cloth made of wool that is usually green, used especially for covering card tables and BILLIARD, SNOOKER or POOL tables

bake 🔑 /beɪk/ *verb*
1 🔑 [T, I] to cook food in an oven without extra fat or liquid; to be cooked in this way: **~ (sth)** *baked apples* ◇ *the delicious smell of baking bread* ◇ **~ sth for sb** *I'm baking a birthday cake for Alex.* ◇ **~ sb sth** *I'm baking Alex a cake.* ➲ COLLOCATIONS at COOKING ➲ VISUAL VOCAB page V24 **2** [I, T] to become or to make sth become hard by heating: *The bricks are left in the kiln to bake.* ◇ **~ sth (+ adj.)** *The sun had baked the ground hard.* **3** [I] (*informal*) to be or become very hot: *We sat baking in the sun.* ➲ see also HALF-BAKED

baked Al·aska /ˌbeɪkt əˈlæskə/ *noun* [C, U] a DESSERT made of cake and ice cream covered in MERINGUE and cooked quickly in a very hot oven

baked ˈbeans *noun* [pl.] **1** (*especially BrE*) small white BEANS cooked in a tomato sauce and usually sold in cans **2** (*NAmE*) = BOSTON BAKED BEANS

ˌbaked poˈtato (also **ˌjacket poˈtato**) *noun* a potato cooked in its skin in an oven: *a baked potato and beans*

bake·house /ˈbeɪkhaʊs/ *noun* (*old-fashioned*) a building or an area where bread is made

Bake·lite™ /ˈbeɪkəlaɪt; *NAmE* also ˈbeɪkl-/ *noun* [U] a type of hard plastic used in the past for electrical equipment, etc.

baker /ˈbeɪkə(r)/ *noun* **1** a person whose job is baking and selling bread and cakes **2 baker's** (*pl.* **bakers**) (*BrE*) a shop that sells bread and cakes: *I'm just going to the baker's.*

ˌbaker's ˈdozen *noun* [sing.] (*old-fashioned*) a group of thirteen (= one more than a dozen, which is twelve) **ORIGIN** This phrase comes from bakers' old custom of adding one extra loaf to an order of a dozen.

bakery /ˈbeɪkəri/ *noun* (*pl.* -ies) (*NAmE* also **bake·shop**) a place where bread and cakes are made and/or sold

ˈbake sale *noun* (*NAmE*) an event at which cakes, etc. are baked and sold to make money, usually for a school or charity

bake·shop /ˈbeɪkʃɒp; *NAmE* -ʃɑːp/ *noun* (*NAmE*) = BAKERY

bake·ware /ˈbeɪkweə(r); *NAmE* -wer/ *noun* [U] tins and other containers used for baking

bak·ing /ˈbeɪkɪŋ/ *noun, adj.*
■ ***noun*** [U] the process of cooking using dry heat in an oven: *a* ***baking dish/tin***
■ ***adj.*** (also **ˌbaking ˈhot**) extremely hot

ˈbaking flour *noun* [U] (*US*) = SELF-RISING FLOUR

ˈbaking powder *noun* [U] a mixture of powders that are used to make cakes rise and become light as they are baked

ˈbaking sheet (also **ˈbaking tray**) (both *BrE*) (*NAmE* **ˈcookie sheet**) *noun* a small sheet of metal used for baking food on

ˈbaking soda *noun* [U] = SODIUM BICARBONATE

bak·kie /ˈbʌki/ *noun* (*SAfrE*) a motor vehicle with low sides and no roof at the back, used for transporting goods or people, or as a car ➲ compare PICKUP

bak·lava (also **bac·lava**) /ˈbɑːkləvə; *NAmE* ˌbɑːkləˈvɑː/ *noun* [C, U] a sweet dish from the Middle East, made from very thin PASTRY, nuts, and HONEY

bak·sheesh (also **back·sheesh**) /ˌbækˈʃiːʃ/ *noun* [U] (*informal*) (in some Asian countries) a small amount of money that is given as a gift to poor people, or given to sb to thank them or to persuade them to help you

bala·clava /ˌbæləˈklɑːvə/ (also **ˌbalaclava ˈhelmet**) *noun* (*especially BrE*) a type of hat made of wool that covers most of the head, neck and face

bala·fon /ˈbæləfɒn; *NAmE* -fɑːn/ *noun* a large type of XYLOPHONE (= a musical instrument with rows of wooden bars that you hit) that is used in W African music

bala·laika /ˌbæləˈlaɪkə/ *noun* a musical instrument like a GUITAR with a body shaped like a triangle and two, three, or four strings, popular especially in Russia ➲ VISUAL VOCAB page V31

bal·ance 🔑 /ˈbæləns/ *noun, verb*
■ ***noun***
▸ EQUAL AMOUNTS **1** 🔑 [U, sing.] a situation in which different things exist in equal, correct or good amounts ➲ see also IMBALANCE: *This newspaper maintains a good balance in its presentation of different opinions.* ◇ *Tourists often disturb the delicate balance of nature on the island.* ◇ *His wife's death disturbed the* ***balance of his mind.*** ◇ **~ between A and B** *Try to keep a balance between work and relaxation.*
▸ OF BODY **2** 🔑 [U] the ability to keep steady with an equal amount of weight on each side of the body: *Athletes need a good sense of balance.* ◇ *I struggled to* ***keep my balance*** *on my new skates.* ◇ *She cycled round the corner,* ***lost her balance*** *and fell off.*
▸ MONEY **3** 🔑 [C, usually sing.] the amount that is left after taking numbers or money away from a total: *to check your* ***bank balance*** (= to find out how much money there is in your account) **4** 🔑 [C, usually sing.] an amount of money still owed after some payment has been made: *The balance of $500 must be paid within 90 days.*
▸ INSTRUMENT FOR WEIGHING **5** [C] an instrument for weighing things, with a bar that is supported in the middle and has dishes hanging from each end

IDM **(on) the balance of ˈevidence/probaˈbility** (*formal*) (considering) the evidence on both sides of an argument, to find the most likely reason for or result of sth **(be/hang) in the ˈbalance** if the future of sth/sb, or the result of sth is/hangs **in the balance**, it is uncertain: *The long-term future of the space programme hangs in the balance.* **(catch/throw sb) off ˈbalance 1** to make sb/sth unsteady and in danger of falling: *I was thrown off balance by the sudden gust of wind.* **2** to make sb surprised and no longer calm: *The senator was clearly caught off balance by the unexpected question.* **on ˈbalance** after considering all the information: *On balance, the company has had a successful year.* ➲ more at REDRESS *v.*, STRIKE *v.*, SWING *v.*, TIP *v.*

■ ***verb***
▸ KEEP STEADY **1** 🔑 [I, T] to put your body or sth else into a position where it is steady and does not fall: **~ (on sth)** *How long can you balance on one leg?* ◇ **~ sth (on sth)** *The television was precariously balanced on top of a pile of books.* ◇ *She balanced the cup on her knee.*
▸ BE/KEEP EQUAL **2** 🔑 [I, T] to be equal in value, amount, etc. to sth else that has the opposite effect **SYN** **offset**: **~ out** *The good and bad effects of any decision will usually balance out.* ◇ **~ sth (out)** *This year's profits will balance our previous losses.* ◇ *His lack of experience was balanced by a willingness to learn.* **3** 🔑 [T] **~ A with/and B** to give equal importance to two contrasting things or parts of sth: *She tries to balance home life and career.*
▸ COMPARE **4** [T] **~ A against B** to compare the relative importance of two contrasting things: *The cost of obtaining legal advice needs to be balanced against its benefits.*
▸ MONEY **5** [T] **~ sth** (*finance*) to show that in an account the total money spent is equal to the total money received; to calculate the difference between the two totals

ˈbalance beam *noun* (*NAmE*) = BEAM *n.* (3)

bal·anced /ˈbælənst/ *adj.* [usually before noun] (*approving*) keeping or showing a balance so that different things or different parts of sth exist in equal or correct amounts: *The programme presented a balanced view of the two sides of the conflict.* ◇ *a balanced diet* (= one with the quantity and variety of food needed for good health)

ˌbalance of ˈpayments *noun* [sing.] the difference between the amount a country pays for imports and the amount it receives for exports in a particular period of time

ˌbalance of ˈpower *noun* [sing.] **1** a situation in which political or military strength is divided between two countries or groups of countries ➲ COLLOCATIONS at INTERNATIONAL **2** the power held by a small group which can give its support to either of two larger and equally strong groups

ˌbalance of ˈtrade (also ˈ**trade balance**) *noun* [sing.] the difference in value between imports and exports: *a balance-of-trade deficit* (= when a country spends more on imports than it earns from exports)

ˈ**balance sheet** *noun* (*finance*) a written statement showing the amount of money and property that a company has and listing what has been received and paid out

ˈ**bal·an·cing act** *noun* a process in which sb tries to please two or more people or groups who want different things: *The UN must perform a delicate balancing act between the different sides in the conflict.*

bal·cony /ˈbælkəni/ *noun* (*pl.* -ies) **1** a platform that is built on the upstairs outside wall of a building, with a wall or rail around it. You can get out onto a balcony from an upstairs room. ➲ VISUAL VOCAB page V15 **2** an area of seats upstairs in a theatre ➲ see also CIRCLE, FIRST BALCONY

bald /bɔːld/ *adj.* **1** having little or no hair on the head: *He started **going bald** in his twenties.* ➲ VISUAL VOCAB page V49 **2** without any of the usual hair, marks, etc. covering the skin or surface of sth: *Our dog has a bald patch on its leg.* ◇ *a bald tyre* (= a tyre whose surface has become smooth) **3** without any extra explanation or detail to help you understand or accept what is being said: *The bald fact is that we don't need you any longer.* ◇ *The letter was a bald statement of our legal position.* ➲ see also BALDLY ▸ **bald·ness** *noun* [U]

IDM (**as**) **bald as a coot** (*BrE, informal*) completely bald

ˌbald ˈeagle *noun* a N American BIRD OF PREY (= a bird that kills other creatures for food) with a white head and white tail feathers. It is used as a symbol of the US.

bal·der·dash /ˈbɔːldədæʃ; *NAmE* -dərd-/ *noun* [U] (*old-fashioned*) nonsense

ˌbald-ˈfaced *adj.* (*disapproving, especially NAmE*) making no attempt to hide your dishonest behaviour SYN **barefaced, blatant**: *bald-faced lies*

bald·ing /ˈbɔːldɪŋ/ *adj.* starting to lose the hair on your head: *a short balding man with glasses*

bald·ly /ˈbɔːldli/ *adv.* in a few words with nothing extra or unnecessary: *'You're lying,' he said baldly.*

baldy (also **baldie**) /ˈbɔːldi/ *noun* (*pl.* -ies) (*informal, offensive*) a person who has no hair or almost no hair on their head

bale /beɪl/ *noun, verb*

■ ***noun*** a large amount of a light material pressed tightly together and tied up: ***bales of hay/straw/cotton/wool***

■ ***verb*** **1** ~ **sth** to make sth into bales: *The waste paper is baled, then sent for recycling.* **2** ~ **sb** (**to do sth**) (*BrE*) = BAIL

PHR V **ˌbale ˈout** | **ˌbale sth↔ˈout** | **ˌbale sb↔ˈout** (*BrE*) = BAIL OUT, BAIL STH OUT, BAIL SB OUT

bale·ful /ˈbeɪlfl/ *adj.* (*literary*) threatening to do sth evil or to hurt sb: *a **baleful look/influence*** ▸ **bale·ful·ly** /ˈbeɪlfəli/ *adv.*

baler /ˈbeɪlə(r)/ *noun* a machine for making paper, cotton, HAY, etc. into BALES

balk (*especially NAmE*) = BAULK

Bal·kan·ize /ˈbɔːlkənaɪz; *BrE* also ˈbɒl-/ *verb* **~ sth** to divide a region into smaller regions which are unfriendly or aggressive towards each other ▸ **Bal·kan·iza·tion** /ˌbɔːlkənaɪˈzeɪʃn; *BrE* also ˌbɒl-/ *noun* [U]

the Bal·kans /ˈbɔːlkənz; *BrE* also ˈbɒl-/ *noun* [pl.] a region of SE Europe, including the countries to the south of the rivers Sava and Danube ▸ **Bal·kan** *adj.*: *the Balkan Peninsula*

balky /ˈbɔːlki; ˈbɔːki/ *adj.* (*NAmE*) (of a person or machine) refusing or failing to do what you want them to do

ball 🔑 /bɔːl/ *noun, verb*

■ ***noun*** **1** 🔑 a round object used for throwing, hitting or kicking in games and sports: *a **golf/tennis/cricket ball*** ◇ *Bounce the ball and try and hit it over the net.* ➲ VISUAL VOCAB page V36 **2** 🔑 a round object or a thing that has been formed into a round shape: *The sun was a huge ball of fire low on the horizon.* ◇ *a ball of string* ◇ *Some animals roll themselves into a ball for protection.* **3** a kick, hit or throw of the ball in some sports: *He sent over a high ball.* **4** (in BASEBALL) a throw by the PITCHER that is outside the STRIKE ZONE (= the area between the BATTER's upper arms and knees **5 ~ of the foot/hand** the part underneath the big toe or the thumb ➲ VISUAL VOCAB page V48 **6** [usually pl.] (*taboo, informal*) a TESTICLE ➲ see also BALLS **7** a large formal party with dancing

IDM **a ˌball and ˈchain** (*BrE*) a problem that prevents you from doing what you would like to do **the ball is in your/sb's ˈcourt** it is your/sb's responsibility to take action next: *They've offered me the job, so the ball's in my court now.* **a ˌball of ˈfire** (*informal*) a person who is full of energy and enthusiasm **get/set/start/keep the ball ˈrolling** to make sth start happening; to make sure that sth continues to happen **have a ˈball** (*informal*) to enjoy yourself a lot **have something/a lot on the ˈball** (*US, informal*) to be capable of doing a job very well; to be intelligent (**be**) **on the ˈball** to be aware of and understand what is happening and able to react quickly: *The new publicity manager is really on the ball.* **pick up/take the ˌball and ˈrun with it** (*especially NAmE*) to develop an idea or plan that already exists: *It's up to the private sector to take the ball and run with it.* **play ˈball** (**with sb**) **1** (*NAmE*) to play with a ball: *Chris was in the park playing ball with the kids.* **2** (*informal*) to be willing to work with other people in a helpful way, especially so that sb can get what they want **the whole ball of ˈwax** (*NAmE, informal*) the whole thing; everything: *I panicked, I cried—the whole ball of wax.* ➲ more at CARRY *v.*, DROP *v.*, EYE *n.*

■ ***verb*** **1** [I, T] to form sth or be formed into the shape of a ball: **~** (**into sth**) *Her hands balled into fists.* ◇ **~ sth** (**into sth**) *My hands were balled into fists.* **2** [T] **~ sb** (*NAmE, taboo, slang*) (of a man) to have sex with a woman

bal·lad /ˈbæləd/ *noun* **1** a song or poem that tells a story: *a medieval ballad about a knight and a lady* **2** a slow song about love: *Her latest single is a ballad.* ➲ COLLOCATIONS at MUSIC

bal·lad·eer /ˌbæləˈdɪə(r); *NAmE* -ˈdɪr/ *noun* a person who sings or writes ballads

ball-and-socket joint

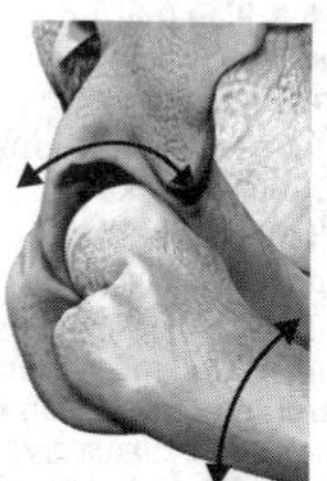

ˌball-and-ˈsocket joint *noun* (*anatomy*) a joint such as the hip joint, in which a ball-shaped part moves inside a curved hollow part

bal·last /ˈbæləst/ *noun* [U] **1** heavy material placed in a ship or HOT-AIR BALLOON to make it heavier and keep it steady **2** a layer of stones that makes a strong base on which a road, railway/railroad, etc. can be built

ball bearing

ˌball ˈbearing *noun* a ring of small metal balls used in a machine to enable the parts to turn smoothly; one of these small metal balls

ball·boy /ˈbɔːlbɔɪ/ *noun* a boy who picks up the balls for the players in a TENNIS match ➲ see also BALLGIRL

ˈ**ball-breaker** *noun* (*informal*) a sexually aggressive woman who destroys men's confidence ▸ ˈ**ball-breaking** *adj.*

B

ball·cock /ˈbɔːlkɒk; *NAmE* -kɑːk/ *noun* a device with a floating ball that controls the amount of water going into a container, for example the water tank of a toilet

bal·ler·ina /ˌbæləˈriːnə/ *noun* a female dancer in BALLET ➲ see also PRIMA BALLERINA

bal·let /ˈbæleɪ/ *noun* **1** [U] a style of dancing that tells a dramatic story with music but no talking or singing: *She wants to be a* ***ballet dancer.*** ◇ *ballet shoes* **2** [C] a story or work of art performed by a group of ballet dancers: *'Swan Lake' is one of the great classical ballets.* **3** [C+sing./pl. v.] a group of dancers who work and perform ballet together: *members of the Royal Ballet*

bal·let·ic /bæˈletɪk/ *adj.* (*formal, approving*) smooth and elegant, like a movement or a dancer in ballet

ˈ**ball game** *noun* **1** any game played with a ball **2** (*NAmE*) a game of BASEBALL: *Are you going to the ball game?*
IDM **a (whole) different/new ˈball game** (*informal*) a completely different kind of situation

ball·girl /ˈbɔːlɡɜːl; *NAmE* -ɡɜːrl/ *noun* a girl who picks up the balls for the players in a TENNIS match ➲ see also BALLBOY

ball·hawk /ˈbɔːlhɔːk/ *noun* (*US, informal*) a player who is good at getting or catching balls, especially in AMERICAN FOOTBALL, BASEBALL or BASKETBALL

ˈ**ball hockey** *noun* [U] (*CanE*) a version of ICE HOCKEY played on a hard surface without ice, and with a ball instead of a PUCK

bal·listic /bəˈlɪstɪk/ *adj.* connected with ballistics
IDM **go balˈlistic** (*informal*) to become very angry: *He went ballistic when I told him.*

balˌlistic ˈmissile *noun* a MISSILE that is fired into the air at a particular speed and angle in order to fall in the right place

bal·lis·tics /bəˈlɪstɪks/ *noun* [U] the scientific study of things that are shot or fired through the air, such as bullets and MISSILES

bal·loon /bəˈluːn/ *noun, verb*
■ ***noun*** **1** a small bag made of very thin rubber that becomes larger and rounder when you fill it with air or gas. Balloons are brightly coloured and used as decorations or toys: ***to blow up/burst/pop a balloon*** ➲ compare TRIAL BALLOON **2** (also **hot-ˈair balloon**) a large balloon made of strong material that is filled with hot air or gas to make it rise in the air, usually carrying a BASKET for passengers ➲ VISUAL VOCAB page V43
IDM **when the balˈloon goes up** (*BrE, informal*) when the trouble that you are expecting begins ➲ more at LEAD[2]
■ ***verb*** **1** [I] ~ **(out/up)** to suddenly swell out or get bigger: *Her skirt ballooned out in the wind.* **2** [I] (usually **go ballooning**) to travel in a HOT-AIR BALLOON as a sport

bal·loon·ist /bəˈluːnɪst/ *noun* a person who travels in a balloon as a sport

balˈloon whisk *noun* a WHISK that you hold in your hand, made of thin pieces of curved wire

bal·lot /ˈbælət/ *noun, verb*
■ ***noun*** **1** [U, C] the system of voting in writing and usually in secret; an occasion on which a vote is held: *The chairperson is chosen by* ***secret ballot.*** ◇ *The union cannot call a strike unless it* ***holds a ballot*** *of members.* ➲ SYNONYMS at ELECTION ➲ COLLOCATIONS at VOTE **2** (*BrE* also **ˈballot paper**) [C] the piece of paper on which sb marks who they are voting for: *What percentage of eligible voters* ***cast their ballots?*** **3 the ballot** [sing.] the total number of votes in an election: *She won 58.8% of the ballot.* ➲ see also POLL
■ ***verb*** **1** [T] ~ **sb (on sth)** to ask sb to vote in writing and secretly about sth SYN **poll**: *The union balloted its members on the proposed changes.* **2** [I] to vote secretly about sth: *The workers balloted for a strike.*

ˈ**ballot box** *noun* **1** [C] a box in which people put their ballots after voting **2 the ballot box** [sing.] the system of voting in an election: *The people make their wishes known through the ballot box.*

ˈ**ballot paper** *noun* (*BrE*) = BALLOT (2)

ball·park /ˈbɔːlpɑːk; *NAmE* -pɑːrk/ *noun* **1** [C] (*especially NAmE*) a place where BASEBALL is played **2** [sing.] an area or a range within which an amount is likely to be correct or within which sth can be measured: *The offers for the contract were all* ***in the same ballpark.*** ◇ *If you said five million you'd be* ***in the ballpark.*** ◇ *Give me a* ***ballpark figure*** (= a number that is approximately right).

ball·point /ˈbɔːlpɔɪnt/ (also **ˌballpoint ˈpen**) *noun* a pen with a very small metal ball at its point, that rolls ink onto the paper ➲ VISUAL VOCAB page V56 ➲ compare BIRO

ball·room /ˈbɔːlruːm; -rʊm/ *noun* a very large room used for dancing on formal occasions ➲ compare DANCE HALL

ˌ**ballroom ˈdancing** *noun* [U] a type of dancing done with a partner and using particular fixed steps and movements to particular types of music such as the WALTZ

balls /bɔːlz/ *noun, verb*
■ ***noun*** (*taboo, slang*) **1** [U] (*BrE*) nonsense: *That's a load of balls!* **2** [pl.] courage: *She's got balls, I'll say that for her.* ◇ *It took a lot of balls to do that.* **3 Balls!** (*BrE*) *exclamation* used as a swear word when you are disagreeing with sth, or when you are angry about sth HELP Less offensive ways to express this are 'Nonsense!', or 'Come off it!' **4** [pl.] TESTICLES
IDM **go ˈballs out** to do sth in a very determined or extreme way, especially when it means taking risks: *The team went balls out in the final.*
■ ***verb***
PHR V **ˌballs sth↔ˈup** (*BrE, taboo, slang*) to spoil sth; to do sth very badly ➲ related noun BALLS-UP HELP A more polite way of saying this is **foul sth up**, **mess sth up**, or **bungle sth.** ➲ see also BALL (6)

ˈ**balls-out** *adj.* (*taboo, slang*) very determined or extreme: *a balls-out attack* ◇ *It's a balls-out shoot-'em-up action movie.*

ˈ**balls-up** *noun* (*taboo, slang, especially BrE*) something that has been done very badly: *I made a real balls-up of my exams.*

ballsy /ˈbɔːlzi/ *adj.* (*informal, especially NAmE*) showing a lot of courage and determination: *She is one ballsy lady!*

bally·hoo /ˌbæliˈhuː; *NAmE* ˈbælihuː/ *noun* [U] (*informal, disapproving*) unnecessary noise and excitement

balm /bɑːm/ *noun* [U, C, usually sing.] **1** (also **bal·sam**) oil with a pleasant smell that is obtained from some types of trees and plants, used in the past to help heal wounds, for example **2** a liquid, cream, etc. that has a pleasant smell and is used to make wounds less painful or skin softer: *lip balm* **3** (*literary*) something that makes you feel calm or relaxed

bal·moral /bælˈmɒrəl; *NAmE* -ˈmɔːr-/ *noun* **1** a type of round hat without a BRIM, often with RIBBONS attached, worn by some Scottish soldiers as part of their uniform **2** a strong heavy walking boot

balmy /ˈbɑːmi/ *adj.* (*approving*) (of the air, weather, etc.) warm and pleasant SYN **mild**: *a balmy summer evening*

ba·lo·ney /bəˈləʊni; *NAmE* -ˈloʊ-/ *noun* [U] **1** (*informal, especially NAmE*) nonsense; lies: *Don't give me that baloney!* **2** (*NAmE*) = BOLOGNA

balsa /ˈbɔːlsə/ (also **ˈbalsa wood**) *noun* [U] the light wood of the tropical American **balsa tree**, used especially for making models

bal·sam /ˈbɔːlsəm/ *noun* **1** [U, C] = BALM **2** [C] any plant or tree from which BALM is obtained

bal·sam·ic vin·egar /bɔːlˌsæmɪk ˈvɪnɪɡə(r)/ *noun* [U] a dark sweet Italian VINEGAR, stored in BARRELS (= round wooden containers) to give it flavour

balti /ˈbɔːlti; ˈbɒlti; *NAmE* ˈbɑːlti/ *noun* [C, U] a type of meat or vegetable dish cooked in Pakistani style, usually served in a round metal pan which gives its name to the dish

Bal·tic /ˈbɔːltɪk/ *adj.* relating to the Baltic Sea in northern Europe and the countries surrounding it: *the Baltic republics of Estonia, Latvia and Lithuania*

bal·us·ter /ˈbæləstə(r)/ *noun* any of the short posts that form a balustrade

bal·us·trade /ˌbæləˈstreɪd/ *noun* a row of posts, joined together at the top, built along the edge of a BALCONY, bridge, etc. to prevent people from falling off, or as a decoration

bam /bæm/ *exclamation* (*informal*) **1** used to represent the sound of a sudden loud hit or a gun being fired: *She pointed the gun at him and—bam!* **2** used to show that sth happens very suddenly: *I saw him yesterday and—bam!—I realized I was still in love with him.*

bam·boo /ˌbæmˈbuː/ *noun* [C, U] (*pl.* **-oos**) a tall tropical plant that is a member of the grass family and has hard hollow STEMS that are used for making furniture, poles, etc: *a bamboo grove* ◇ *a bamboo chair* ◇ *bamboo shoots* (= young bamboo plants that can be eaten) ⊃ VISUAL VOCAB page V9

bam·boo·zle /bæmˈbuːzl/ *verb* **~ sb** (*informal*) to confuse sb, especially by tricking them

ban 🔑 /bæn/ *verb, noun*

■ ***verb*** (-nn-) **1** 🔑 **~ sth** to decide or say officially that sth is not allowed SYN **prohibit**: *Chemical weapons are banned internationally.* **2** 🔑 [usually passive] to order sb not to do sth, go somewhere, etc, especially officially: **~ sb from sth** *He was banned from the meeting.* ◇ **~ sb from doing sth** *She's been banned from leaving Greece while the allegations are investigated.* ◇ (*BrE*) *He was banned from driving for six months.*

■ ***noun*** 🔑 **~ (on sth)** an official rule that says that sth is not allowed: *There is to be a total ban on smoking in the office.* ◇ *to* ***impose/lift a ban***

banal /bəˈnɑːl; *NAmE* also ˈbeɪnl/ *adj.* (*disapproving*) very ordinary and containing nothing that is interesting or important

ban·al·ity /bəˈnæləti/ *noun* (*pl.* **-ies**) [U, C] (*disapproving*) the quality of being banal; things, remarks, etc. that are banal: *the banality of modern city life* ◇ *They exchanged banalities for a couple of minutes.*

ba·nana /bəˈnɑːnə; *NAmE* bəˈnænə/ *noun* a long curved fruit with a thick yellow skin and soft flesh, that grows on trees in hot countries: *a bunch of bananas* ⊃ VISUAL VOCAB page V26

IDM **go baˈnanas** (*slang*) to become angry, crazy or silly

baˈnana belt *noun* (*NAmE, informal*) a region where the weather is warm

baˌnana reˈpublic *noun* (*disapproving, offensive*) a poor country with a weak government, that depends on foreign money

baˈnana skin *noun* (*BrE, informal*) something that could cause difficulty or embarrassment, especially to sb in a public position

baˌnana ˈsplit *noun* a cold DESSERT (= a sweet dish) made from a BANANA that is cut in half along its length and filled with ice cream, nuts, etc.

band 🔑 /bænd/ *noun, verb*

■ ***noun***

▸ GROUP OF MUSICIANS **1** 🔑 [C+sing./pl. v.] a small group of musicians who play popular music together, often with a singer or singers: *a* ***rock/jazz band*** ◇ *She's a singer with a band.* ⊃ see also BOY BAND, GIRL BAND **2** 🔑 [C+sing./pl. v.] a group of musicians who play BRASS and PERCUSSION instruments: *a military band* ⊃ see also BRASS BAND, MARCHING BAND, ONE-MAN BAND

▸ GROUP OF PEOPLE **3** 🔑 [C+sing./pl. v.] a group of people who do sth together or who have the same ideas: *a band of outlaws* ◇ *He persuaded a small band of volunteers to help.*

▸ STRIP OF MATERIAL/COLOUR **4** 🔑 [C] a thin flat strip or circle of any material that is put around things, for example to hold them together or to make them stronger: *She always ties her hair back in a band.* ◇ *All babies in the hospital have name bands on their wrists.* ◇ *She wore a simple band of gold = a ring on her finger.* ⊃ VISUAL VOCAB page V53 ⊃ see also ARMBAND, HAIRBAND, HATBAND, RUBBER BAND, SWEATBAND, WAISTBAND **5** 🔑 [C] a strip of colour or material on sth that is different from what is around it: *a white plate with a blue band around the edge*

▸ OF RADIO WAVES **6** (also **wave·band**) [C] a range of radio waves: *Short-wave radio uses the 20-50 metre band.*

▸ RANGE **7** [C] a range of numbers, ages, prices, etc. within which people or things are counted or measured: *the 25-35 age band* ◇ *tax bands*

■ ***verb***

▸ WITH COLOUR/MATERIAL **1** [usually passive] **be banded** (**+ adj.**) to put a band of a different colour or material around sth: *Many insects are banded black and yellow.*

▸ PUT INTO RANGE **2** [usually passive] **~ sth** (*BrE*) to be organized into bands of price, income, etc: *Tax is banded according to income.*

PHR V **ˌband toˈgether** to form a group in order to achieve sth: *Local people banded together to fight the drug dealers.*

ban·dage 🔑 /ˈbændɪdʒ/ *noun, verb*

■ ***noun*** 🔑 a strip of cloth used for tying around a part of the body that has been hurt in order to protect or support it

■ ***verb*** 🔑 **~ sth** (**up**) to wrap a bandage around a part of the body in order to protect it because it is injured ⊃ COLLOCATIONS at INJURY

ˈBand-Aid™ *noun* (*especially NAmE*) **1** (*BrE* also **plas·ter**, **ˈsticking plaster**) [C, U] material that can be stuck to the skin to protect a small wound or cut; a piece of this **2** (*disapproving*) a temporary solution to a problem that does not really solve it at all

ban·dana (also **ban·danna**) /bænˈdænə/ *noun* a piece of brightly coloured cloth worn around the neck or head

B and B (also **B & B**, **b and b**, **b & b**) /ˌbiː ən ˈbiː/ *abbr.* (*informal, especially BrE*) BED AND BREAKFAST

ˈband council *noun* (*CanE*) a local form of Aboriginal government in Canada, consisting of an elected chief and COUNCILLORS

ban·deau /ˈbændəʊ; *NAmE* -doʊ/ *noun* **1** a narrow band worn around the head to hold the hair in place **2** a piece of women's clothing that is tied around the body to cover the breasts: *a bandeau bikini top*

bandh /bʌnd/ *noun* (*IndE*) a general strike

bandi·coot /ˈbændɪkuːt/ *noun* **1** a small Australasian animal with a long nose and long tail, which eats mainly insects **2** (also **ˌbandicoot ˈrat**) an Asian RAT

band·ing /ˈbændɪŋ/ (also **stream·ing** especially in *BrE*) *noun* [U] the policy of dividing school students into groups of the same level of ability

ban·dit /ˈbændɪt/ *noun* a member of an armed group of thieves who attack travellers

ban·dito /bænˈdiːtəʊ; *NAmE* -toʊ/ (also **ban·dido**) /-dəʊ; *NAmE* -doʊ/ *noun* (*NAmE*, from *Spanish*) (*pl.* **-os**) a Mexican BANDIT

ban·dit·ry /ˈbændɪtri/ *noun* [U] (*formal*) acts of stealing and violence by bandits

band·leader /ˈbændliːdə(r)/ *noun* a player who is in charge of a band, especially a JAZZ band

band·mas·ter /ˈbændmɑːstə(r); *NAmE* -mæs-/ *noun* a person who CONDUCTS a military or BRASS band

bando·bast /ˈbʌndəbʌst/ *noun* [U, C, usually sing.] (*IndE*) preparation or an arrangement for dealing with sth: *The* ***police bandobast*** *was very effective.*

ban·do·lier (also **ban·do·leer**) /ˌbændəˈlɪə(r); *NAmE* -ˈlɪr/ *noun* a belt made for carrying bullets and worn over the shoulder

bands·man /ˈbændzmən/ *noun* (*pl.* **-men** /-mən/) a musician who plays in a military or BRASS band

band·stand /ˈbændstænd/ *noun* a covered platform outdoors, where musicians, especially a BRASS or military band, can stand and play

band·wagon /ˈbændwægən/ *noun* [usually sing.] an activity that more and more people are becoming involved in: *The World Cup bandwagon is starting to roll.*

IDM **climb/jump on the ˈbandwagon** (*informal, disapproving*) to join others in doing sth that is becoming fashionable because you hope to become popular or successful yourself: *politicians eager to jump on the environmental bandwagon* ORIGIN In the US, political PARADES often included a band on a wagon. Political leaders would join them in the hope of winning popular support.

B

band·width /ˈbændwɪdθ/ *noun* [C, U] (*computing*) **1** a band of FREQUENCIES used for sending electronic signals **2** a measurement of the amount of information that a particular computer network or Internet connection can send in a particular time. It is often measured in BITS per second.

bandy /ˈbændi/ *adj., verb*

■ ***adj.*** (of the legs) curving, with the knees wide apart: *to be bandy-legged*

■ ***verb*** (**ban·dies**, **bandy·ing**, **ban·died**, **ban·died**)

IDM **bandy ˈwords** (**with sb**) (*old-fashioned*) to argue with sb or speak rudely to them

PHR V ˌ**bandy sth↔aˈbout/aˈround** [usually passive] if a name, a word, a story, etc, is **bandied about/around**, it is mentioned frequently by many people: *His name was being bandied about as a future prime minister.*

bane /beɪn/ *noun* [sing.] **the ~ of sb/sth** something that causes trouble and makes people unhappy: *The neighbours' kids are the **bane of my life**.*

bane·ful /ˈbeɪnfl/ *adj.* (*literary*) evil or causing evil

bang /bæŋ/ *verb, noun, adv., exclamation*

■ ***verb*** **1** [I, T] to hit sth in a way that makes a loud noise: **~ on sth** *She banged on the door angrily.* ◇ **~ sth** (**with sth**) *The baby was banging the table with his spoon.* ➲ SYNONYMS at HIT **2** [I, T] to close sth or to be closed with a loud noise SYN **slam**: *A window was banging somewhere* (= opening and closing noisily). ◇ **+ adj.** *The door banged shut behind her.* ◇ **~ sth** *Don't bang the door when you go out!* **3** [T] **~ sth + adv./prep.** to put sth somewhere suddenly and violently SYN **slam**: *He banged the money down on the counter.* ◇ *She banged saucepans around irritably.* **4** [T] **~ sth** (**+ adv./prep.**) to hit sth, especially a part of the body, against sth by accident SYN **bump**: *She tripped and banged her knee on the desk.* **5** [T] **~ sb** (*taboo, slang*) (of a man) to have sex with a woman IDM see DRUM *n.*, HEAD *n.*

PHR V ˌ**bang aˈbout/aˈround** to move around noisily: *We could hear the kids banging around upstairs.* ˌ**bang ˈinto sth** to crash into or hit sth by mistake: *I banged into a chair and hurt my leg.* ˌ**bang ˈon about sth** (*BrE, informal*) to talk a lot about sth in a boring way SYN **go on**: *He keeps banging on about his new job.* ˌ**bang sb↔ˈup** (*BrE, informal*) to put sb in prison ˌ**bang sth↔ˈup** (*NAmE, informal*) to damage or injure sth

■ ***noun*** **1** a sudden loud noise: *The door swung shut with a bang.* ◇ *Suddenly there was a loud bang and a puff of smoke.* ➲ see also BIG BANG **2** a sudden painful blow on a part of the body: *a bang on the head* **3 bangs** [pl.] (*NAmE*) (*BrE* **fringe**) the front part of sb's hair that is cut so that it hangs over their FOREHEAD ➲ VISUAL VOCAB page V49 **4** = BHANG **5** (*informal, computing*) the symbol (!)

IDM ˌ**bang for your ˈbuck** (*especially NAmE, informal*) if you get more, better, etc. **bang for your buck**, you get better value for the money you spend or the effort you put in to sth **with a ˈbang** (*informal*) **1** very successfully: *The party **went with a bang**.* **2** in a way that everyone notices; with a powerful effect: *The team won their last four games, ending the season with a bang.* ➲ more at EARTH *n.*, SLAP *adv.*

■ ***adv.*** (*informal, especially BrE*) exactly; completely: *Our computers are **bang up to date**.* ◇ *My estimate was bang on target.* ◇ *You're bang on time, as usual* ➲ see also SLAP BANG

IDM **bang goes sth** (*BrE, informal*) used when you say that sth you hoped to have or achieve is no longer possible: *Bang went my hopes of promotion.* **go ˈbang** (*informal*) to burst or explode with a loud noise; to make a sudden loud noise: *A balloon suddenly went bang.* IDM see RIGHT *n.*

■ ***exclamation*** used to show the sound of sth loud, like a gun: *'Bang, bang, you're dead!' shouted the little boy.*

ˌ**banged ˈup** *adj.* (*NAmE, informal*) injured or damaged: *Two days after the accident she still looked pretty banged up.*

bang·er /ˈbæŋə(r)/ *noun* (*BrE, informal*) **1** a SAUSAGE: *bangers and mash* **2** (*NAmE* **beat·er**) an old car that is in bad condition **3** a FIREWORK that makes a loud noise when it explodes

Bangla /ˈbʌŋlɜː/ *noun* [U] **1** the Bengali language **2** Bangladesh

ban·gle /ˈbæŋgl/ *noun* a piece of jewellery in the form of a large ring of gold, silver, etc. worn loosely around the wrist ➲ VISUAL VOCAB page V53

ˈ**bang-up** *adj.* (*NAmE, informal*) very good

bania /ˈbʌnjə/ *noun* (*IndE*) **1** a person who sells things **2** (*disapproving*) a person who is interested in making money

ban·ish /ˈbænɪʃ/ *verb* **1** [usually passive] **~ sb** (**from...**) (**to ...**) to order sb to leave a place, especially a country, as a punishment SYN **exile**: *He was banished to Australia, where he died five years later.* ◇ *The children were banished from the dining room.* **2 ~ sb/sth** (**from sth**) to make sb/sth go away; to get rid of sb/sth: *The sight of food banished all other thoughts from my mind.*

ban·ish·ment /ˈbænɪʃmənt/ *noun* [U] the punishment of being sent away from a place, especially from a country

ban·is·ter (also **ban·nis·ter**) /ˈbænɪstə(r)/ *noun* (*BrE* also **ban·is·ters** [pl.]) the posts and rail which you can hold for support when going up or down stairs: *to hold on to the banister/banisters* ➲ picture at STAIRCASE

banjo /ˈbændʒəʊ; *NAmE* ˈbændʒoʊ/ *noun* (*pl.* **-os**) a musical instrument like a GUITAR, with a long neck, a round body and four or more strings ➲ VISUAL VOCAB page V31

bank 0→ /bæŋk/ *noun, verb*

■ ***noun***

▸ FOR MONEY **1** 0→ an organization that provides various financial services, for example keeping or lending money: *My salary is paid directly into my bank.* ◇ *I need to go to the bank* (= the local office of a bank). ◇ *a bank loan* ◇ *a bank manager* ➲ COLLOCATIONS at FINANCE ➲ see also INVESTMENT BANK, MERCHANT BANK

▸ IN GAMBLING **2** a supply of money or things that are used as money in some games, especially those in which gambling is involved

▸ STH COLLECTED/STORED **3** an amount of sth that is collected; a place where sth is stored ready for use: *a bank of knowledge* ◇ *a **blood/sperm bank*** ➲ see also DATABANK

▸ OF RIVER/CANAL **4** 0→ the side of a river, CANAL, etc. and the land near it: *He jumped in and swam to the opposite bank.* ◇ *It's on the north bank of the Thames.* ◇ *a house on the banks of the River Severn* (= on land near the river)

▸ SLOPE **5** a raised area of ground that slopes at the sides, often at the edge of sth or dividing sth: *There were low banks of earth between the rice fields.* ◇ *The girls ran down the steep grassy bank.* **6** an artificial slope built at the side of a road, so that cars can drive fast around bends

▸ OF CLOUD/SNOW, ETC. **7** a mass of cloud, snow, etc, especially one formed by the wind: *The sun disappeared behind a bank of clouds.*

▸ OF MACHINES, ETC. **8** a row or series of similar objects, especially machines: *a **bank of lights/switches/computers***

IDM **not ˌbreak the ˈbank** (*informal, humorous*) if you say sth **won't break the bank**, you mean that it won't cost a lot of money, or more than you can afford ➲ more at LAUGH *v.*

■ ***verb***

▸ MONEY **1** [T] **~ sth** to put money into a bank account: *She is believed to have banked* (= been paid) *£10 million in two years.* **2** [I] **~** (**with/at...**) to have an account with a particular bank: *The family had banked with Coutts for generations.*

▸ OF PLANE **3** [I] to travel with one side higher than the other when turning: *The plane banked steeply to the left.*

▸ FORM PILES **4** [T] **~ sth** (**up**) to form sth into piles: *They banked the earth* (*up*) *into a mound.*

▸ A FIRE **5** [T] **~ sth** (**up**) to pile coal, etc. on a fire so that the fire burns slowly for a long time: *The fire was banked up as high as if it were midwinter.*

PHR V ˈ**bank on sb/sth** to rely on sb/sth: *I'm banking on your help.* ◇ *'I'm sure he'll help.' '**Don't bank on it*** (= it is not likely to happen).' ◇ **~ to do sth** *I'm banking on you to help me.* ◇ **~ doing sth** *I was banking on getting something to eat on the train.* ˌ**bank ˈup** to form into piles, especially because of the wind: *The snow had banked up against the wall.*

bank·able /ˈbæŋkəbl/ *adj.* (*informal*) likely to make money for sb: *The movie's success has made her one of the world's most bankable stars.*

ˈ**bank account** *noun* an arrangement that you have with a bank that allows you to keep your money there, to pay in or take out money, etc: *to* ***open/close a bank account***

ˈ**bank balance** *noun* the amount of money that sb has in their bank account at a particular time

ˈ**bank card** *noun* **1** (also ˈ**banker's card**) (both *BrE*) a plastic card provided by your bank that may be used as a CHEQUE CARD or DEBIT CARD or to get money from your account out of a machine **2** (*NAmE*) a credit card provided by your bank, that can also be used as a DEBIT CARD and to get money from your account out of a machine

ˈ**bank draft** (also ˈ**banker's draft**) *noun* a cheque paid by a bank to another bank or to a particular person or organization

bank·er /ˈbæŋkə(r)/ *noun* **1** a person who owns a bank or has an important job at a bank: *a merchant banker* **2** a person who is in charge of the money in particular games

ˌ**banker's ˈorder** *noun* (*BrE*) an instruction to your bank to pay money to sb directly from your bank account ➲ compare STANDING ORDER

ˌ**bank ˈholiday** (*BrE*) *noun* a public holiday, for example Christmas Day, New Year's Day, etc: *Bank Holiday Monday* ◇ *a bank holiday weekend* (= a weekend followed by a Monday which is a holiday) ➲ compare LEGAL HOLIDAY, PUBLIC HOLIDAY ➲ see also HOLIDAY

bank·ing /ˈbæŋkɪŋ/ *noun* [U] the business activity of banks: *She's thinking about a career in banking.*

bank·note /ˈbæŋknəʊt; *NAmE* -noʊt/ *noun* (*especially BrE*) = NOTE: *forged* (= illegally copied) *banknotes*

ˈ**bank rate** *noun* the rate of interest charged by a bank for lending money, which is fixed by a central bank in a country

bank·roll /ˈbæŋkrəʊl; *NAmE* -roʊl/ *verb, noun*

▪ ***verb*** **~ sb/sth** (*informal, especially NAmE*) to support sb/sth by giving money **SYN** **finance**: *They claimed his campaign had been bankrolled with drug money.*

▪ ***noun*** (*especially NAmE*) a supply of money: *He is the candidate with the biggest campaign bankroll.*

bank·rupt /ˈbæŋkrʌpt/ *adj., noun, verb*

▪ ***adj.*** **1** without enough money to pay what you owe **SYN** **insolvent**: *They* ***went bankrupt*** *in 2009.* ◇ *The company was* ***declared bankrupt*** *in the High Court.* **2 ~ (of sth)** (*formal, disapproving*) completely lacking in anything that has value: *a government bankrupt of new ideas* ◇ *a society that is morally bankrupt*

▪ ***noun*** (*law*) a person who has been judged by a court to be unable to pay his or her debts

▪ ***verb*** **~ sb** to make sb bankrupt: *The company was almost bankrupted by legal costs.*

bank·rupt·cy /ˈbæŋkrʌptsi/ *noun* [U, C] (*pl.* -ies) the state of being bankrupt **SYN** **insolvency**: *The company* ***filed for bankruptcy*** (= asked to be officially bankrupt) *in 2009.* ◇ ***moral/political bankruptcy*** ◇ *There could be further bankruptcies among small farmers.* ➲ COLLOCATIONS at BUSINESS

ˈ**bank statement** (also **state·ment**) *noun* a printed record of all the money paid into and out of a customer's bank account within a particular period

ban·ner /ˈbænə(r)/ *noun* a long piece of cloth with a message on it that is carried between two poles or hung in a public place to show support for sth: *Protesters carried a banner reading 'Save our Wildlife'.* ➲ VISUAL VOCAB page V2

ˈ**banner ad** *noun* an advertisement across the top or bottom or down the side of a page on the Internet

ˌ**banner ˈheadline** *noun* a line of words printed in large letters across the front page of a newspaper

ˌ**banner ˈyear** *noun* (*NAmE*) a year in which sth is especially successful

ban·nis·ter = BANISTER

banns /bænz/ *noun* [pl.] a public statement in church that two people intend to marry each other

ban·offi pie (also **baˌn·offee ˈpie**) /bəˌnɒfi ˈpaɪ; *NAmE* bəˌnɔːfi; -ˌnɑːf-/ *noun* a sweet food made with TOFFEE, BANANAS and cream

ban·quet /ˈbæŋkwɪt/ *noun* **1** a formal meal for a large number of people, usually for a special occasion, at which speeches are often made: *a state banquet in honour of the visiting President* **2** a large impressive meal

ban·quet·ing /ˈbæŋkwɪtɪŋ/ *adj.* connected with banquets: *a banqueting hall*

ban·quette /bæŋˈket/ *noun* a long soft seat along a wall in a restaurant, etc.

ban·shee /bænˈʃiː; ˈbænʃiː/ *noun* (in Irish stories) a female spirit who gives a long sad cry as a warning to people that sb in their family is going to die soon

ban·tam /ˈbæntəm/ *noun* a type of small chicken

ban·tam·weight /ˈbæntəmweɪt/ *noun* a BOXER weighing between 51 and 53.5 kilograms, or a WRESTLER who weighs between 52 and 57 kilograms, heavier than a FLYWEIGHT: *a bantamweight champion*

ban·ter /ˈbæntə(r)/ *noun, verb*

▪ ***noun*** [U] friendly remarks and jokes: *He enjoyed exchanging banter with the customers.*

▪ ***verb*** [I] **~ (with sb)** to joke with sb: *He bantered with reporters and posed for photographers.*

ban·ter·ing /ˈbæntərɪŋ/ *adj.* (of a way of talking) amusing and friendly: *There was a friendly, bantering tone in his voice.*

ban·yan /ˈbænjən/ (also ˈ**banyan tree**) *noun* a S Asian tree with structures that grow down from the branches to the ground and then grow into new roots and TRUNKS

bao·bab /ˈbeɪəʊbæb; *NAmE* ˈbeɪoʊ-/ *noun* a short thick tree, found especially in Africa and Australia, that lives for many years

bap /bæp/ *noun* (*BrE*) a round flat bread roll ➲ see also BUN

bap·tism /ˈbæptɪzəm/ *noun* a Christian ceremony in which a few drops of water are poured on sb or they are covered with water, to welcome them into the Christian Church and often to name them ➲ compare CHRISTENING

IDM ➤ **a ˌbaptism of ˈfire** a difficult introduction to a new job or activity

bap·tis·mal /bæpˈtɪzməl/ *adj.* [only before noun] connected with baptism: *a* ***baptismal service/ceremony***

Bap·tist /ˈbæptɪst/ *noun* a member of a Christian Protestant Church that believes that baptism should take place when a person is old enough to understand what it means, and not as a baby ▸ **Bap·tist** *adj.* [usually before noun]: *a Baptist church*

bap·tize (*BrE* also **-ise**) /bæpˈtaɪz/ *verb* [usually passive] **~ sb (+ noun)** to give sb BAPTISM: *She was baptized Mary.* ◇ *I was baptized a Catholic.* ➲ see also CHRISTEN

Bapu /ˈbɑːpuː/ *noun* (*IndE*) **1** (used especially as a form of address) a father **2** a name by which Mahatma Gandhi is referred to, showing affection

bar 🔑 /bɑː(r)/ *noun, verb, prep.*

▪ ***noun***

▸ FOR DRINKS/FOOD **1** 🔑 [C] a place where you can buy and drink alcoholic and other drinks: *We met at a bar called the Flamingo.* ◇ *the island's only* ***licensed bar*** (= one that is allowed to sell alcoholic drinks) ◇ *a cocktail bar* ◇ (*BrE*) *I found David in the bar of the Red Lion* (= a room in a pub where drinks are served). ➲ see also BARROOM, LOUNGE BAR, MINIBAR, PUBLIC BAR, SALOON BAR **2** 🔑 [C] a long wide wooden surface where drinks, etc. are served: *She was sitting at the bar.* ◇ *It was so crowded I couldn't get to the bar.* **3** 🔑 [C] (especially in compounds) a place in which a particular kind of food or drink is the main thing that is served: *a sandwich bar* ◇ *a coffee bar* ➲ see also OXYGEN BAR, SNACK BAR, WINE BAR

▸ OF CHOCOLATE/SOAP **4** 🔑 [C] a piece of sth with straight sides: *a* ***bar of chocolate/soap*** ◇ *candy bars*
▸ OF METAL/WOOD **5** 🔑 [C] a long straight piece of metal or wood. Bars are often used to stop sb from getting through a space: *He smashed the window with an iron bar.* ◇ *All the ground floor windows were fitted with bars.* ◇ *a five-bar gate* (= one made with five horizontal bars of wood) ➲ VISUAL VOCAB page V38 ➲ see also BULL BARS, ROLL BAR, SPACE BAR, TOW BAR
▸ IN ELECTRIC FIRE **6** [C] a piece of metal with wire wrapped around it that becomes red and hot when electricity is passed through it
▸ IN SPORTS **7 the bar** [sing.] the CROSSBAR of a goal: *His shot hit the bar.*
▸ OF COLOUR/LIGHT **8** [C] a band of colour or light: *Bars of sunlight slanted down from the tall narrow windows.*
▸ THAT PREVENTS STH **9** [C, usually sing.] **~ (to sth)** a thing that stops sb from doing sth: *At that time being a woman was a bar to promotion in most professions.* ➲ see also COLOUR BAR
▸ IN MUSIC **10** (*BrE*) (*NAmE* **meas·ure**) [C] one of the short sections of equal length that a piece of music is divided into, and the notes that are in it: *four beats to the bar* ◇ *the opening bars of a piece of music* ➲ picture at MUSIC
▸ LAW **11 the Bar** [sing.] (*BrE*) the profession of BARRISTER (= a lawyer in a higher court): *to* ***be called to the Bar*** (= allowed to work as a qualified BARRISTER) **12 the Bar** [sing.] (*NAmE*) the profession of any kind of lawyer
▸ MEASUREMENT **13** a unit for measuring the pressure of the atmosphere, equal to a hundred thousand NEWTONS per square metre ➲ see also MILLIBAR
IDM **not have a 'bar of sth** (*AustralE, NZE*) to have nothing to do with sth: *If he tries to sell you his car, don't have a bar of it.* **be,hind 'bars** (*informal*) in prison: *The murderer is now safely behind bars.* **set the 'bar** to set a standard of quality or performance: *The show really sets the bar for artistic invention.* ➲ more at LOWER *v.*, RAISE *v.*
■ *verb* (-rr-)
▸ CLOSE WITH BARS **1** [usually passive] **~ sth** to close sth with a bar or bars: *All the doors and windows were barred.*
▸ BLOCK **2 ~ sth** to block a road, path, etc. so that nobody can pass: *Two police officers were barring her exit.* ◇ *We found our way barred by rocks.*
▸ PREVENT **3 ~ sb (from sth/from doing sth)** to ban or prevent sb from doing sth: *The players are barred from drinking alcohol the night before a match.* IDM see HOLD *n.*
■ ***prep.*** (*especially BrE*) except for sb/sth: *The students all attended, bar two who were ill.* ◇ *It's the best result we've ever had,* ***bar none*** (= none was better). IDM see SHOUTING

Vocabulary Building

A bar of chocolate

If you want to describe a whole unit of a particular substance, or a group of things that are normally together, for example when you buy them, you need to use the correct word.

- a **bar** of soap/chocolate; a candy **bar**
- a **block** of ice/stone/wood
- a **bolt/roll/length** of fabric
- a **cube** of ice/sugar; an ice/sugar **cube**
- a **loaf** of bread
- a **roll** of film/carpet
- a **slab** of marble/concrete
- a **stick** of gum
- a **bunch** of bananas/grapes
- a **bunch/bouquet** of flowers
- a **bundle** of sticks
- a **set/bunch** of keys
- a **set** of chairs/glasses/clothes/guitar strings

bars

bar

sandwich bar

five-bar gate

bars on a window

bar of chocolate

bar of soap

barcode

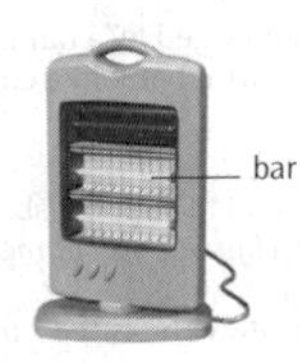

bars on an electric fire

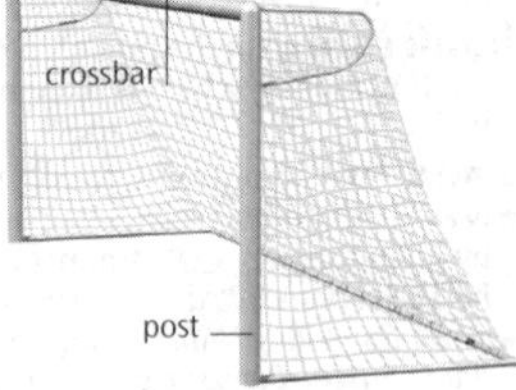

crossbar

bar of music

bar·aza /bəˈrɑːzə/ *noun* (*EAfrE*) a public meeting that is held in order to discuss important matters affecting the community

barb /bɑːb; *NAmE* bɑːrb/ *noun* **1** the point of an arrow or a hook that is curved backwards to make it difficult to pull out **2** a remark that is meant to hurt sb's feelings ➲ see also BARBED

bar·bar·ian /bɑːˈbeəriən; *NAmE* bɑːrˈber-/ *noun* **1** a person long ago in the past who belonged to a European people which was considered wild and UNCIVILIZED: *barbarian invasions of the fifth century* **2** a person who behaves very badly and has no respect for art, education, etc.

bar·bar·ic /bɑːˈbærɪk; *NAmE* bɑːrˈb-/ *adj.* **1** cruel and violent and not as expected from people who are educated and respect each other: *a* ***barbaric act/custom/ritual*** ◇ *The way these animals are killed is barbaric.* **2** connected with BARBARIANS (1) ▸ **bar·bar·ic·al·ly** /-kli/ *adv.*

bar·bar·ism /ˈbɑːbərɪzəm; *NAmE* ˈbɑːrb-/ *noun* [U] **1** a state of not having any education, respect for art, etc. **2** cruel or violent behaviour: *the barbarism of war*

bar·bar·ity /bɑːˈbærəti; *NAmE* bɑːrˈb-/ *noun* (*pl.* -ies) [U, C] behaviour that deliberately causes extreme pain or suffering to others

B

bar·bar·ous /ˈbɑːbərəs; *NAmE* ˈbɑːrb-/ *adj.* (*formal*) **1** extremely cruel and shocking: *the barbarous treatment of these prisoners of war* **2** showing a lack of education and good manners ▸ **bar·bar·ous·ly** *adv.*

bar·be·cue /ˈbɑːbɪkjuː; *NAmE* ˈbɑːrb-/ *noun, verb*
■ ***noun*** (*abbr.* **BBQ**) (also *informal* **bar·bie** *BrE, AustralE*) **1** a metal frame for cooking food on over an open fire outdoors: *I put another steak on the barbecue.* ◇ *a barbecue sausage* (= cooked in this way) ➲ VISUAL VOCAB pages V16, V24 **2** an outdoor meal or party when food is cooked in this way: *Let's have a barbecue!* ➲ compare COOKOUT
■ ***verb*** [T, I] **~ (sth)** to cook food on a barbecue ➲ compare BROIL

ˌ**barbecue ˈsauce** *noun* [C, U] a spicy sauce served with food that has been cooked on a barbecue

barbed /bɑːbd; *NAmE* bɑːrbd/ *adj.* **1** (of an ARROW or a hook) having a point that is curved backwards (called a BARB) **2** (of a remark or comment) meant to hurt sb's feelings

ˌ**barbed ˈwire** *noun* [U] strong wire with short sharp points on it, used especially for fences: *a barbed wire fence*

barbed wire

bar·bell /ˈbɑːbel; *NAmE* ˈbɑːrbel/ *noun* a long metal bar with weights at each end, used in the sport of WEIGHTLIFTING and for exercise ➲ VISUAL VOCAB page V35

bar·ber /ˈbɑːbə(r); *NAmE* ˈbɑːrb-/ *noun* **1** a person whose job is to cut men's hair and sometimes to shave them **2** (also **barber's**) (both *BrE*) (*pl.* **bar·bers**) a shop where men can have their hair cut ➲ compare HAIRDRESSER

bar·ber·shop /ˈbɑːbəʃɒp; *NAmE* ˈbɑːrbərʃɑːp/ *noun* **1** (*especially NAmE*) (*BrE* usually **barber's**) [C] a place where a barber works **2** [U] a type of light music for four parts sung by men, without instruments: *a barbershop quartet*

ˌ**barber's ˈpole** *noun* a pole painted with a SPIRAL of red and white that is traditionally hung outside a barber's shop

bar·bie /ˈbɑːbi; *NAmE* ˈbɑːrbi/ *noun* (*BrE, AustralE, informal*) = BARBECUE

ˈ**Barbie doll™** (also **Barbie**) *noun* **1** a DOLL that looks like an attractive young woman **2** (*informal*) a woman who is sexually attractive, especially one who is thought to be stupid or boring

ˌ**bar ˈbilliards** *noun* [U] (*BrE*) a game played on a small table, in which you try to hit balls into holes without knocking down the small wooden objects that stand in front of the holes

bar·bit·ur·ate /bɑːˈbɪtʃʊrət; *NAmE* bɑːrˈb-/ *noun* a powerful drug that makes you feel calm and relaxed or puts you to sleep. There are several types of barbiturate.

Bar·bour™ /ˈbɑːbə(r); *NAmE* ˈbɑːrbər/ *noun* a type of coat, usually dark green, made of special cotton with WAX on it that protects against rain and wind

ˈ**bar chart** (also ˈ**bar graph**) *noun* a diagram that uses lines or narrow RECTANGLES (= bars) of different heights (but equal widths) to show different amounts, so that they can be compared ➲ WRITING TUTOR page WT16 ➲ compare HISTOGRAM

bar·code /ˈbɑːkəʊd; *NAmE* ˈbɑːrkoʊd/ *noun* a pattern of thick and thin lines that is printed on things you buy. It contains information that a computer can read. ➲ picture at BAR

bard /bɑːd; *NAmE* bɑːrd/ *noun* (*literary*) a person who writes poems

bare /beə(r); *NAmE* ber/ *adj., verb*
■ ***adj.*** (**barer, bar·est**) **1** not covered by any clothes: *She likes to walk around in* ***bare feet.*** ➲ see also BAREFOOT **2** (of trees or countryside) not covered with leaves; without plants or trees: *the bare branches of winter trees* ◇ *a bare mountainside* **3** (of surfaces) not covered with or protected by anything: *bare wooden floorboards* ◇ *Bare wires were sticking out of the cable.* ◇ *The walls were bare except for a clock.* **4** (of a room, cupboard, etc.) empty: *The fridge was completely bare.* ◇ *bare shelves* **5** [only before noun] just enough; the most basic or simple: *The family was short of even the* ***bare necessities*** *of life.* ◇ *We only had the* ***bare essentials*** *in the way of equipment.* ◇ *He did the* ***bare minimum*** *of work but still passed the exam.* ◇ *She gave me only the bare facts of the case.* ◇ *It was the barest hint of a smile.* ➲ SYNONYMS at NAKED, PLAIN ▸ **bare·ness** *noun* [U]
IDM **the bare ˈbones (of sth)** the basic facts: *the bare bones of the story* **with your bare ˈhands** without weapons or tools: *He was capable of killing a man with his bare hands.* **lay sth ˈbare** (*formal*) to show sth that was covered or to make sth known that was secret: *Every aspect of their private lives has been laid bare.* ➲ more at CUPBOARD
■ ***verb*** **~ sth** to remove the covering from sth, especially from part of the body: *She was paid several thousand dollars to* ***bare all*** (= take all her clothes off) *for the magazine.*
IDM **bare your ˈsoul (to sb)** to tell sb your deepest and most private feelings **bare your ˈteeth** to show your teeth in an aggressive and threatening way: *The dog bared its teeth and growled.*

bare·back /ˈbeəbæk; *NAmE* ˈberb-/ *adj., adv.* on a horse without a SADDLE: *a bareback rider* ◇ *riding bareback*

bare·faced /ˈbeəfeɪst; *NAmE* ˈberf-/ *adj.* [only before noun] (*disapproving*) showing that you do not care about offending sb or about behaving badly SYN **bald-faced, blatant**: *a barefaced lie* ◇ *barefaced cheek*

bare·foot /ˈbeəfʊt; *NAmE* ˈberf-/ (also *less frequent* **bare·foot·ed**) *adj., adv.* not wearing anything on your feet: *poor children going barefoot in the street*

bare·head·ed /ˌbeəˈhedɪd; *NAmE* ˌberˈh-/ *adj., adv.* not wearing anything to cover your head

ˌ**bare-ˈknuckle** (also ˌ**bare-ˈknuckled**) *adj.* [only before noun] (of a BOXER OR BOXING match) without gloves

bare·ly /ˈbeəli; *NAmE* ˈberli/ *adv.* **1** in a way that is just possible but only with difficulty: *The music was barely audible.* ◇ *She was barely able to stand.* ◇ *We barely had time to catch the train.* **2** in a way that almost does not happen or exist: *She barely acknowledged his presence.* ◇ *There was barely any smell.* **3** just; certainly not more than (a particular amount, age, time, etc.): *Barely 50% of the population voted.* ◇ *He was barely 20 years old and already running his own company.* ◇ *They arrived barely a minute later.* **4** only a very short time before: *I had barely started speaking when he interrupted me.* ➲ note at HARDLY

barf /bɑːf; *NAmE* bɑːrf/ *verb* [I] (*NAmE, informal*) to VOMIT ▸ **barf** *noun* [U]

bar·fly /ˈbɑːflaɪ; *NAmE* ˈbɑːr-/ *noun* (*pl.* **-ies**) (*informal*) a person who spends a lot of time drinking in bars

bar·gain 0‑ /ˈbɑːgən; *NAmE* ˈbɑːrgən/ *noun, verb*
■ ***noun*** **1** 0‑ a thing bought for less than the usual price: *I picked up a few good bargains in the sale.* ◇ *The car was a bargain at that price.* ◇ *bargain prices* ➲ COLLOCATIONS at SHOPPING **2 ~ (with sb)** an agreement between two or more people or groups, to do sth for each other: *He and his partner had* ***made a bargain*** *to tell each other everything.* ◇ *I've done what I promised and I expect you to* ***keep your side of the bargain*** (= do what you agreed in return). ◇ *Finally the two sides* ***struck a bargain*** (= reached an agreement).
IDM **into the ˈbargain** (*BrE*) (*NAmE* **in the ˈbargain**) (used to emphasize an extra piece of information) also; as well: *Volunteers learn a lot and enjoy themselves into the bargain.* ➲ more at HARD *adj.*, STRIKE *v.*
■ ***verb*** [I] to discuss prices, conditions, etc. with sb in order to reach an agreement that is acceptable SYN **negotiate**: **~ (with sb) (about/over/for sth)** *In the market dealers were bargaining with growers over the price of coffee.* ◇ *He said he wasn't prepared to bargain.*
PHR V ˌ**bargain sth↔aˈway** to give sth away and not get

sth of equal value in return: *They felt that their leaders had bargained away their freedom.* ˈ**bargain for/on sth** (usually in negative sentences) to expect sth to happen and be prepared for it: *We hadn't bargained for this sudden change in the weather.* ◇ *When he agreed to answer a few questions, **he got more than he bargained for*** (= he got more questions, or more difficult ones, than he had expected). ◇ **~ doing sth** *I didn't bargain on finding them here as well.* ◇ **~ sb doing sth** *I hadn't bargained on them being here.*

ˌbargain ˈbasement *noun* a part of a large shop/store, usually in the floor below street level, where goods are sold at reduced prices: *bargain-basement prices*

ˈbargain hunter *noun* a person who is looking for goods that are good value for money, usually because they are being sold at prices that are lower than usual ▸ **ˈbargain hunting** *noun* [U]

bar·gain·ing /ˈbɑːɡənɪŋ; *NAmE* ˈbɑːrɡ-/ *noun* [U] discussion of prices, conditions, etc. with the aim of reaching an agreement that is acceptable SYN **negotiation**: *After much **hard bargaining** we reached an agreement.* ◇ *wage bargaining* ◇ *Exporters are in a strong **bargaining position** at the moment.* ➲ see also COLLECTIVE BARGAINING, PLEA-BARGAINING

ˈbargaining chip (*BrE* also ˈ**bargaining counter**) *noun* a fact or a thing that a person or a group of people can use to get an advantage for themselves when they are trying to reach an agreement with another group

ˈbargaining power *noun* [U] the amount of control a person or group has when trying to reach an agreement with another group in a business or political situation

barge /bɑːdʒ; *NAmE* bɑːrdʒ/ *noun, verb*

■ ***noun*** a large boat with a flat bottom, used for carrying goods and people on CANALS and rivers

■ ***verb*** [I, T] **+ adv./prep.** to move in an awkward way, pushing people out of the way or crashing into them SYN **push**: *He barged past me to get to the bar.* ◇ *They **barged their way** through the crowds.*

PHR V **ˌbarge ˈin (on sb/sth)** to enter a place or join a group of people, rudely interrupting what sb else is doing or saying: *I hope you don't mind me barging in like this.* ◇ *He barged in on us while we were having a meeting.*

barge·board /ˈbɑːdʒbɔːd; *NAmE* ˈbɑːrdʒbɔːrd/ *noun* a board that is fixed to the end of a roof to hide the ends of the wooden roof BEAMS

bar·gee /bɑːˈdʒiː; *NAmE* bɑːrˈdʒiː/ *noun* a person who controls or works on a BARGE

barge·pole /ˈbɑːdʒpəʊl; *NAmE* ˈbɑːrdʒpoʊl/ *noun* IDM see TOUCH *v.*

ˈbar graph *noun* = BAR CHART

ˈbar-hop *verb* [I] (-pp-) (*NAmE, informal*) to drink in a series of bars in a single day or evening

bar·is·ta (also **Bar·is·ta™**) /bəˈriːstə; -ˈrɪs-/ *noun* a person who works in a COFFEE BAR

bari·tone /ˈbærɪtəʊn; *NAmE* -toʊn/ *noun* **1** a man's singing voice with a range between TENOR and BASS; a man with a baritone voice **2** a musical instrument that is second lowest in PITCH in its family ▸ **bari·tone** *adj.* ➲ compare ALTO, BASS, TENOR

bar·ium /ˈbeəriəm; *NAmE* ˈber-/ *noun* [U] (*symb.* Ba) a chemical element. Barium is a soft silver-white metal

ˌbarium ˈmeal *noun* a substance containing barium that a doctor gives sb to swallow before an X-RAY because it makes organs in the body easier to see

bark /bɑːk; *NAmE* bɑːrk/ *noun, verb*

■ ***noun*** [U, C] **1** the outer covering of a tree ➲ VISUAL VOCAB page V8 **2** the short loud sound made by dogs and some other animals **3** a short loud sound made by a gun or a voice: *a bark of laughter*

IDM **sb's bark is worse than their bite** (*informal*) used to say that sb is not really as angry or as aggressive as they sound

■ ***verb*** **1** [I] **~ (at sb/sth)** when a dog **barks**, it makes a short loud sound: *The dog suddenly started barking at us.* **2** [T] to give orders, ask questions, etc. in a loud, unfriendly way: **~ out sth** *She barked out an order.* ◇ **~ sth (at sb)** *He barked questions at her.* ◇ **+ speech** *'Who are you?' he barked.* **3** [T] **~ sth** (*especially BrE*) to rub the skin off your knee, etc. by falling or by knocking against sth SYN **graze**

IDM **be barking up the wrong ˈtree** (*informal*) to have the wrong idea about how to get or achieve sth: *You're barking up the wrong tree if you're expecting us to lend you any money.* IDM see DOG *n.*

bark·er /ˈbɑːkə(r); *NAmE* ˈbɑːrk-/ *noun* a person who stands outside a place where there is entertainment and shouts to people to go in

ˌbark·ing ˈmad (also **bark·ing**) *adj.* (*BrE, informal*) completely crazy

bar·ley /ˈbɑːli; *NAmE* ˈbɑːrli/ *noun* [U] a plant grown for its grain that is used for making food, beer and WHISKY; the grains of this plant ➲ VISUAL VOCAB page V28

ˈbarley sugar *noun* [U] a hard clear sweet/candy made from boiled sugar

ˈbarley water *noun* [U] (*BrE*) a drink made by boiling BARLEY in water. It is usually flavoured with orange or lemon: *lemon barley water*

ˌbarley ˈwine *noun* [U] a strong English beer

ˈbar line *noun* (*music*) a vertical line used in written music to mark a division between BARS/MEASURES

bar·maid /ˈbɑːmeɪd; *NAmE* ˈbɑːrm-/ (*BrE*) (*NAmE* **bar·tend·er**) *noun* a woman who works in a bar, serving drinks

bar·man /ˈbɑːmən; *NAmE* ˈbɑːrmən/ *noun* (*pl.* **-men** /-mən/) (*especially BrE*) (*NAmE* usually **bar·tend·er**) a man who works in a bar, serving drinks

bar mitz·vah /ˌbɑː ˈmɪtsvə; *NAmE* ˌbɑːr/ *noun* **1** a ceremony and celebration for a Jewish boy who has reached the age of 13, at which he accepts the religious responsibilities of an adult **2** the boy who is celebrating this occasion ➲ compare BAT MITZVAH

barmy /ˈbɑːmi; *NAmE* ˈbɑːrmi/ *adj.* (*BrE, informal*) slightly crazy

barn /bɑːn; *NAmE* bɑːrn/ *noun* **1** a large farm building for storing grain or keeping animals in: *a hay barn* ◇ *They live in a converted barn* (= a barn that has been turned into a house). ➲ VISUAL VOCAB pages V2, V13 ➲ see also DUTCH BARN **2** a large plain ugly building: *They live in a great barn of a house.* **3** (*NAmE*) a building in which buses, trucks, etc. are kept when not being used

IDM **close, etc. the barn door after the horse has eˈscaped** (*NAmE*) ➲ STABLE DOOR

bar·nacle /ˈbɑːnəkl; *NAmE* ˈbɑːrn-/ *noun* a small SHELLFISH that attaches itself to objects underwater, for example to rocks and the bottoms of ships

Bar·nardo's /bəˈnɑːdəʊz; *NAmE* bərˈnɑːrdoʊz/ *noun* a British charity that helps children with social, physical and mental problems ORIGIN From Dr Thomas Barnardo, who opened a home for poor children without parents in London in 1870.

ˈbarn dance *noun* an informal social event at which people dance traditional COUNTRY DANCES

bar·net /ˈbɑːnɪt; *NAmE* ˈbɑːrn-/ *noun* (*BrE, informal*) a person's hair

bar·ney /ˈbɑːni; *NAmE* ˈbɑːrni/ *noun* (*BrE, informal*) an argument

ˈbarn owl *noun* a BIRD OF PREY (= a bird that kills other creatures for food) of the OWL family, that often makes its nest in BARNS and other buildings ➲ VISUAL VOCAB page V10

barn·storm /ˈbɑːnstɔːm; *NAmE* ˈbɑːrnstɔːrm/ *verb* [I, T] **~ (sth)** (*especially NAmE*) to travel quickly through an area making political speeches, or getting a lot of attention for your organization, ideas, etc: *He barnstormed across the southern states in an attempt to woo the voters.*

barn·storm·ing /ˈbɑːnstɔːmɪŋ; *NAmE* ˈbɑːrnstɔːrmɪŋ/ *adj.* [only before noun] a **barnstorming** performance or show of skill in a sports game, etc. is one that people find very exciting to watch

barn·yard /ˈbɑːnjɑːd; *NAmE* ˈbɑːrnjɑːrd/ *noun* an area on a farm that is surrounded by farm buildings

bar·om·eter /bəˈrɒmɪtə(r); *NAmE* -ˈrɑːm-/ *noun* **1** an instrument for measuring air pressure to show when the weather will change: *The barometer is falling* (= showing that it will probably rain). **2** something that shows the changes that are happening in an economic, social or political situation: *Infant mortality is a reliable barometer of socio-economic conditions.* ▸ **baro·metric** /ˌbærəˈmetrɪk/ *adj.*: *barometric pressure*

baron /ˈbærən/ *noun* **1** a NOBLEMAN of the lowest rank. In Britain, barons use the title *Lord*; in other countries they use the title *Baron*. **2** a person who owns or controls a large part of a particular industry: *a press baron* ◇ *drug barons*

bar·on·ess /ˈbærənəs; *NAmE* ˌbærəˈnes/ *noun* **1** a woman who has the same rank as a baron. In Britain, baronesses use the title *Lady* or *Baroness*: *Baroness Thatcher* **2** the wife of a baron

bar·onet /ˈbærənət/ *noun* (*abbr.* **Bart**, **Bt**) (in Britain) a man who has the lowest rank of honour that can be passed from a father to his son when he dies. Baronets use the title *Sir*. ➲ compare KNIGHT (2)

bar·on·et·cy /ˈbærənətsi/ *noun* (*pl.* -ies) the rank or position of a baronet

bar·on·ial /bəˈrəʊniəl; *NAmE* -ˈroʊ-/ *adj.* [usually before noun] connected with or typical of a BARON: *a baronial hall*

bar·ony /ˈbærəni/ *noun* (*pl.* -ies) **1** the rank or position of a BARON **2** an area of land that is owned and controlled by a BARON

bar·oque /bəˈrɒk; *NAmE* bəˈroʊk/ (also **Baroque**) *adj.* [usually before noun] used to describe European ARCHITECTURE, art and music of the 17th and early 18th centuries that has a grand and highly decorated style: ***baroque churches/music*** ◇ *the baroque period* ▸ **bar·oque** (also **Baroque**) *noun* [sing.]: *paintings representative of the baroque*

barque /bɑːk; *NAmE* bɑːrk/ *noun* a sailing ship with three or more MASTS (= posts that support the sails)

bar·rack /ˈbærək/ *verb* **1** [I, T] **~ (sb)** (*BrE*) to shout criticism at players in a game, speakers at a meeting, performers, etc. **2** [I, T] **~ (for) sb** (*AustralE, NZE*) to shout encouragement to a person or team that you support ▸ **bar·rack·ing** *noun* [U]

bar·racks /ˈbærəks/ *noun* [C+sing./pl. v.] (*pl.* **bar·racks**) **1** a large building or group of buildings for soldiers to live in: *an army barracks* ◇ *The troops were ordered* ***back to barracks***. **2** any large ugly building or buildings ▸ **bar·rack** *adj.* [only before noun]: *a barrack unit*

bar·ra·cuda /ˌbærəˈkjuːdə; *NAmE* -ˈkuːdə/ *noun* a large aggressive fish with sharp teeth that lives in warm seas

bar·rage /ˈbærɑːʒ; *NAmE* bəˈrɑːʒ/ *noun* **1** [C, usually sing.] the continuous firing of a large number of guns in a particular direction, especially to protect soldiers while they are attacking or moving towards the enemy **2** [sing.] **~ (of sth)** a large number of sth, such as questions or comments, that are directed at sb very quickly, one after the other, often in an aggressive way: *a* ***barrage of questions/criticisms/complaints*** **3** / *NAmE* ˈbɑːrɪdʒ/ [C] a wall or barrier built across a river to store water, prevent a flood, etc.

ˈbarrage balloon *noun* a large BALLOON that floats in the air and is held in place by cables, used in the past to make the progress of enemy aircraft more difficult

bar·ra·mundi /ˌbærəˈmʌndi/ *noun* (*pl.* **bar·ra·mundi**) a large fish found in rivers in Australia and SE Asia

bar·rel /ˈbærəl/ *noun, verb*

▪ ***noun*** **1** a large round container, usually made of wood or metal, with flat ends and, usually, curved sides: *a* ***beer/wine barrel*** **2** the contents of or the amount contained in a barrel; a unit of measurement in the oil industry equal to between 120 and 159 litres: *They got through two barrels of beer.* ◇ *Oil prices fell to $9 a barrel.* **3** the part of a gun like a tube through which the bullets are fired

IDM **a barrel of ˈlaughs** (often *ironic*) very amusing; a lot of fun: *Life hasn't exactly been a barrel of laughs lately.* **(get/have sb) over a barrel** (*informal*) (to put/have sb) in a situation in which they must accept or do what you want: *They've got us over a barrel. Either we agree to their terms or we lose the money.* ➲ more at LOCK *n.*, SCRAPE *v.*, SHOOT *v.*

▪ ***verb*** (-ll-) [I] **+ adv./prep.** (*NAmE, informal*) to move very fast in a particular direction, especially in a way that you cannot control: *He came barreling down the hill and smashed into a phone booth.*

ˌbarrel-ˈchested *adj.* (of a man) having a large rounded chest

ˈbarrel organ *noun* a musical instrument that is played by turning a handle, usually played in the streets for money ➲ see also ORGAN-GRINDER

bar·ren /ˈbærən/ *adj.* **1** (of land or soil) not good enough for plants to grow on it: *a barren desert* ◇ *a barren landscape* (= one that is empty, with few plants) **2** (of plants or trees) not producing fruit or seeds SYN **infertile** **3** (*old-fashioned* or *formal*) (of women or female animals) not able to produce children or young animals SYN **infertile** **4** [usually before noun] not producing anything useful or successful: *The team will come through this* ***barren patch*** *and start to win again.* ▸ **bar·ren·ness** /ˈbærənnəs/ *noun* [U]

bar·rette /bæˈret/ (*NAmE*) (*BrE* **hair·slide**, **slide**) *noun* a small decorative piece of metal or plastic used by women for holding their hair in place

bar·ri·cade /ˌbærɪˈkeɪd/ *noun, verb*

▪ ***noun*** a line of objects placed across a road, etc. to stop people from getting past: *The police stormed the barricades the demonstrators had put up.*

▪ ***verb*** **~ sth** to defend or block sth by building a barricade: *They barricaded all the doors and windows.*

PHR V **barriˌcade yourself ˈin/inˈside (sth)** to build a barricade in front of you in order to prevent anyone from coming in: *He had barricaded himself in his room.*

bar·rier 🔑 /ˈbæriə(r)/ *noun*

1 🔑 an object like a fence that prevents people from moving forward from one place to another: *The crowd had to stand behind barriers.* ◇ *Show your ticket at the barrier.* ➲ see also CRASH BARRIER **2** 🔑 a problem, rule or situation that prevents sb from doing sth, or that makes sth impossible: *the removal of trade barriers* ◇ **~ to sth** *Lack of confidence is a psychological barrier to success.* ➲ COLLOCATIONS at INTERNATIONAL **3** 🔑 something that exists between one thing or person and another and keeps them separate: *The Yangtze river is a natural barrier to the north-east.* ◇ *the* ***language barrier*** (= when people cannot communicate because they do not speak the same language) ◇ **~ between A and B** *There was no real barrier between reality and fantasy in his mind.* ◇ **~ against sth** *Ozone is the earth's barrier against ultra-violet radiation.* **4** a particular amount, level or number that it is difficult to get past: *the first player whose earnings passed the $10 million barrier*

ˈbarrier method *noun* a method of avoiding becoming pregnant by stopping the SPERM from reaching the egg, for example by using a CONDOM

ˌbarrier ˈreef *noun* a line of rock and CORAL in the sea, often not far from land

bar·ring /ˈbɑːrɪŋ/ *prep.* except for; unless there is/are: *Barring accidents, we should arrive on time.*

bar·rio /ˈbæriəʊ; *NAmE* ˈbɑːrioʊ/ *noun* (from *Spanish*) (*pl.* -os) **1** a district of a city in Spain or in another Spanish-speaking country **2** (*US*) a district of a city in the US where a lot of Spanish-speaking people live

bar·ris·ter /ˈbærɪstə(r)/ *noun* a lawyer in Britain who has the right to argue cases in the higher courts of law ➲ note at LAWYER

bar·room /ˈbɑːruːm; -rʊm/ *noun* a room in which alcoholic drinks are served at a bar: *a topic much discussed in barrooms across the country* ◇ *a barroom brawl*

B

bar·row /ˈbærəʊ; *NAmE* -roʊ/ *noun* **1** (*BrE*) a small open vehicle with two wheels from which fruit, vegetables, etc. are sold in the street **2** a large pile of earth built over a place where people were buried in ancient times **3** = WHEELBARROW

ˈ**barrow boy** *noun* (*BrE*) a man or boy who sells things from a barrow in the street

ˈ**bar stool** *noun* a tall seat for customers at a bar to sit on

Bart /bɑːt; *NAmE* bɑːrt/ *abbr.* BARONET

bar·tend·er /ˈbɑːtendə(r); *NAmE* ˈbɑːrt-/ *noun* (*especially NAmE*) **1** (*BrE* also **bar·maid**) a woman who works in a bar, serving drinks **2** = BARMAN

bar·ter /ˈbɑːtə(r); *NAmE* ˈbɑːrt-/ *verb* [I, T] to exchange goods, property, services, etc. for other goods, etc. without using money: **~ (with sb) (for sth)** *The prisoners tried to barter with the guards for items like writing paper and books.* ◇ **~ sth (for sth)** *The local people bartered wheat for tools.* ▶ **bar·ter** *noun* [U]: *The islanders use a system of barter instead of money.*

basal /ˈbeɪsl/ *adj.* (*technical*) forming or belonging to a bottom layer or base: *basal cells of the skin*

bas·alt /ˈbæsɔːlt; *NAmE* bəˈsɔːlt/ *noun* [U] a type of dark rock that comes from VOLCANOES

base 0‑w /beɪs/ *noun, verb, adj.*

■ *noun*

▸ LOWEST PART **1** 0‑w [C, usually sing.] the lowest part of sth, especially the part or surface on which it rests or stands: *the base of a column/glass* ◇ *a pain at the base of the spine* ◇ *The lamp has a heavy base.* ➲ VISUAL VOCAB page V12, V20 ➲ SYNONYMS at BOTTOM

▸ ORIGINAL IDEA/SITUATION **2** 0‑w [C] an idea, a fact, a situation, etc. from which sth is developed SYN **basis**: *She used her family's history as a base for her novel.* ◇ *His arguments have a sound economic base.* ➲ SYNONYMS at BASIS

▸ OF SUPPORT/INCOME/POWER **3** [C, usually sing.] the people, activity, etc. from which sb/sth gets most of their support, income, power, etc: *These policies have a broad base of support.* ◇ *an economy with a solid* ***manufacturing base*** ➲ see also CUSTOMER BASE, POWER BASE **4** (*especially NAmE*) (*BrE* usually **basic**) **~ pay/salary/wage** the pay that you get before anything extra is added: *All we got was base pay—we didn't reach profitability levels to award a bonus.*

▸ FIRST/MAIN SUBSTANCE **5** [C, usually sing.] the first or main part of a substance to which other things are added: *a drink with a rum base* ◇ *Put some moisturizer on as a base before applying your make-up.*

▸ MAIN PLACE **6** 0‑w [C] the main place where you live or stay or where a business operates from: *I spend a lot of time in Britain but Paris is still my base.* ◇ *The town is an ideal base for touring the area.* ◇ *The company has its base in New York, and branch offices all over the world.*

▸ OF ARMY, NAVY, ETC. **7** 0‑w [C, U] a place where an army, a navy, etc. operates from: *a* ***military/naval base*** ◇ *an* ***air base*** ◇ *After the attack, they returned to base.*

▸ CHEMISTRY **8** [C] a chemical substance, for example an ALKALI, that can combine with an acid to form a salt

▸ MATHEMATICS **9** [C, usually sing.] a number on which a system of counting and expressing numbers is built up, for example 10 in the DECIMAL system and 2 in the BINARY system

▸ IN BASEBALL/ROUNDERS **10** [C] one of the four positions that a player must reach in order to score points ➲ see also DATABASE

IDM **off base** (*NAmE, informal*) completely wrong about sth: *If that's what you think, you're way off base.* ➲ more at COVER *v.*, FIRST BASE, TOUCH *v.*

■ *verb* 0‑w [usually passive] **~ sb/sth/yourself in...** to use a particular city, town, etc. as the main place for a business, holiday/vacation, etc: *They decided to base the new company in York.* ◇ *We're going to base ourselves in Tokyo and make trips from there.*

PHR V ˈ**base sth on/upon sth** 0‑w to use an idea, a fact, a situation, etc. as the point from which sth can be developed: *What are you basing this theory on?* ➲ see also BASED

■ *adj.* (**baser, bas·est**) (*formal*) not having moral principles or rules: *He acted from base motives.* ▶ **base·ly** *adv.*

base·ball /ˈbeɪsbɔːl/ *noun* **1** [U] a game played especially in the US by two teams of nine players, using a BAT and ball. Each player tries to hit the ball and then run around four BASES before the other team can return the ball: *a baseball bat/team/stadium* ◇ *a pair of baseball boots* ➲ compare ROUNDERS ➲ VISUAL VOCAB page V36 **2** [C] the ball used in this game

ˈ**baseball cap** *noun* a cap with a long PEAK (= a curved part sticking out in front), originally worn by BASEBALL players ➲ VISUAL VOCAB page V53

base·board /ˈbeɪsbɔːd; *NAmE* -bɔːrd/ (*NAmE*) (*BrE* ˈ**skirting board, skirt·ing**) *noun* a narrow piece of wood that is fixed along the bottom of the walls in a house

ˈ**base camp** *noun* a camp where people start their journey when climbing high mountains

based 0‑w /beɪst/ *adj.* [not before noun]
1 0‑w **~ (on sth)** if one thing is **based** on another, it uses it or is developed from it: *The movie is based on a real-life incident.* ◇ *The report is based on figures from six different European cities.* **2** 0‑w (also in compounds) if a person or business is **based** in a particular place, that is where they live or work, or where the work of the business is done: *We're based in Chicago.* ◇ *a Chicago-based company* **3** 0‑w **-based** (in compounds) containing sth as an important part or feature: *lead-based paints* ◇ *a class-based society* ➲ see also BROAD-BASED

ˈ**base form** *noun* (*grammar*) the basic form of a word to which endings can usually be added, for example *wall* is the base form of *walls* and *walled*. The base form is the form in which words in the dictionary are usually shown.

ˈ**base jumping** (also **BASE jumping**) *noun* [U] the sport of jumping with a PARACHUTE from a high place such as a building or a bridge ▶ ˈ**base jumper** *noun*

base·less /ˈbeɪsləs/ *adj.* (*formal*) not supported by good reasons or facts SYN **unfounded**: *The rumours were completely baseless.*

base·line /ˈbeɪslaɪn/ *noun* [usually sing.] **1** (*sport*) a line marking each end of the COURT in TENNIS or the edge of the area where a player can run in BASEBALL **2** (*technical*) a line or measurement that is used as a starting point when comparing facts: *The figures for 2009 were used as a baseline for the study.*

base·man /ˈbeɪsmæn/ *noun* (*pl.* **-men** /-mən/) (in BASEBALL) a player who defends first, second or third base

base·ment /ˈbeɪsmənt/ *noun* a room or rooms in a building, partly or completely below the level of the ground: *Kitchen goods are sold in the basement.* ◇ *a* ***basement flat/apartment*** ➲ VISUAL VOCAB page V15 ➲ see also BARGAIN BASEMENT

ˌ**base ˈmetal** *noun* a metal, for example iron or LEAD, that is not a PRECIOUS METAL such as gold

ˈ**base rate** *noun* (*finance*) a rate of interest, set by a central bank, that banks in Britain use when calculating the amount of interest that they charge on money they lend ➲ compare PRIME RATE

bases **1** *pl.* of BASIS **2** *pl.* of BASE

bash /bæʃ/ *verb, noun*

■ *verb* (*informal*) **1** [T, I] to hit sb/sth very hard: **~ sb/sth** *He bashed her over the head with a hammer.* ◇ **~ into sb/sth** *I braked too late and bashed into the car in front.* ➲ SYNONYMS at HIT **2** [T] **~ sb/sth** to criticize sb/sth strongly: *Bashing politicians is normal practice in the press.* ◇ *a liberal-bashing administration* ➲ see also BASHING

PHR V ˌ**bash aˈway (on/at sth)** | ˌ**bash ˈon (with sth)** (*BrE*) to continue working hard at sth: *He sat bashing away at his essay all day.* ◇ *We'll never get finished at this rate. We'd better bash on.* ˌ**bash sth↔ˈdown/ˈin** to destroy sth by hitting it very hard and often: *The police bashed the door down.* ◇ *I'll bash your head in if you do that again.* ˌ**bash sth↔ˈout** (*informal*) to produce sth quickly and in large quantities, but not of very good quality SYN **knock out**: *She bashed* *out about four books a year.* ˌ**bash sb ˈup** (*BrE, informal*) to attack sb violently

▪ **noun** (*informal*) **1** a hard hit: *He gave Mike a bash on the nose.* **2** a large party or celebration: *a birthday bash*

IDM **have a bash** (**at sth**) (*BrE, informal*) to try to do sth, especially when you are not sure if you will succeed: *I'm not sure I'll be any good but I'll have a bash.*

bash·ful /ˈbæʃfl/ *adj.* shy and easily embarrassed ▸ **bash·ful·ly** /-fəli/ *adv.*: *She smiled bashfully.* **bash·ful·ness** *noun* [U]

bash·ing /ˈbæʃɪŋ/ *noun* [U, C] (often in compounds) **1** (used especially in newspapers) very strong criticism of a person or group: *union-bashing* **2** a physical attack, or a series of attacks, on a person or group of people: *gay-bashing* (= attacking HOMOSEXUALS) ◇ *to give sb a bashing*

basic 0-w /ˈbeɪsɪk/ *adj.*
1 0-w forming the part of sth that is most necessary and from which other things develop: *basic information/facts/ideas* ◇ *the basic principles of law* ◇ **~ to sth** *Drums are basic to African music.* **2** 0-w of the simplest kind or at the simplest level: *The campsite provided only basic facilities.* ◇ *My knowledge of French is pretty basic.* **3** 0-w [only before noun] necessary and important to all people: *basic human rights* ◇ *the cost of basic foods* **4** (*especially BrE*) (*NAmE* usually **base**) before anything extra is added: *The* **basic pay** *of the average worker has risen by 3 per cent.*

BASIC /ˈbeɪsɪk/ *noun* [U] a simple language, using familiar English words, for writing computer programs

ba·sic·ally 0-w /ˈbeɪsɪkli/ *adv.*
1 0-w in the most important ways, without considering things that are less important SYN **essentially**: *Yes, that's basically correct.* ◇ *The two approaches are basically very similar.* ◇ *There have been some problems but basically it's a good system.* **2** 0-w used when you are giving your opinion or stating what is important about a situation: *Basically, there's not a lot we can do about it.* ◇ *He basically just sits there and does nothing all day.* ◇ *And that's it, basically.*

ˌ**Basic ˈEnglish** *noun* [U] a set of 850 carefully chosen words of English, used for international communication

basics /ˈbeɪsɪks/ *noun* [pl.] **1 ~ (of sth)** the most important and necessary facts, skills, ideas, etc. from which other things develop: *the basics of computer programming* **2** the simplest and most important things that people need in a particular situation: *Some schools lack money for basics like books and pencils.*

IDM **go/get back to ˈbasics** to think about the simple or most important ideas within a subject or an activity instead of new ideas or complicated details

basil /ˈbæzl; *NAmE* also ˈbeɪzl/ *noun* [U] a plant with shiny green leaves that smell sweet and are used in cooking as a HERB ⇨ VISUAL VOCAB page V28

ba·sil·ica /bəˈzɪlɪkə/ *noun* a large church or hall with a curved end and two rows of columns inside

basi·lisk /ˈbæzɪlɪsk/ *noun* (in ancient stories) a creature like a snake, which can kill people by looking at them or breathing on them

basin /ˈbeɪsn/ *noun* **1** (*especially BrE*) = WASHBASIN **2** a large round bowl for holding liquids or (in British English) for preparing foods in; the amount of liquid, etc. in a basin: *a pudding basin* **3** an area of land around a large river with streams running down into it: *the Amazon Basin* **4** (*technical*) a place where the earth's surface is lower than in other areas of the world: *the Pacific Basin* **5** a sheltered area of water providing a safe HARBOUR for boats: *a yacht basin*

basis 0-w /ˈbeɪsɪs/ *noun* (*pl.* **bases** /ˈbeɪsiːz/)
1 0-w [sing.] the reason why people take a particular action: *She was chosen for the job* **on the basis of** *her qualifications.* ◇ *Some movies have been banned* **on the basis that** *they are too violent.* ⇨ SYNONYMS at REASON **2** 0-w [sing.] the way things are organized or arranged: *on a* **regular/permanent/part-time/temporary basis** ◇ *on a* **daily/day-to-day/weekly basis** **3** 0-w [C, usually sing., U] the important facts, ideas or events that support sth and that it can develop from: *The basis of a good marriage is trust.* ◇ *This article will* **form the basis for** *our discussion.* ◇ *The theory seems to have no basis in fact.*

B

Synonyms

basis

foundation • **base**

These are all words for the ideas or facts that sth is based on.

basis [usually sing.] a principle, an idea or a fact that supports sth and that it can develop from: *This article will form the basis for our discussion.*

foundation [C, U] a principle, an idea or a fact that supports sth and that it develops from: *Respect and friendship provide a solid foundation for marriage.* ◇ *The rumour is totally without foundation* (= is not based on any facts).

BASIS OR FOUNDATION?

Foundation is often used to talk about larger or more important things than **basis**: *He laid the foundations of Japan 's modern economy.* ◇ *These figures formed the basis of their pay claim.*

base [usually sing.] an idea, a fact or a situation from which sth is developed: *His arguments have a sound economic base.*

PATTERNS

- a/the basis/foundation/base **for/of** sth
- a **secure/solid/sound/strong/weak** basis/foundation/base
- to **form** the basis/foundation/base of sth
- to **be without** basis/foundation

bask /bɑːsk; *NAmE* bæsk/ *verb* [I] **~ (in sth)** to enjoy sitting or lying in the heat or light of sth, especially the sun: *We sat basking in the warm sunshine.*

PHR V ˈ**bask in sth** to enjoy the good feelings that you have when other people praise or admire you, or when they give you a lot of attention: *He had always basked in his parents' attention.* ◇ *I never minded* **basking in** *my wife's* **reflected glory** (= enjoying the praise, attention, etc. she got).

baskets

shopping basket

washing basket

clothes basket (*BrE*) **hamper** (*NAmE*)

picnic basket (*BrE also* **hamper**)

hanging basket

waste-paper basket (*BrE*) **wastebasket** (*NAmE*)

bas·ket /ˈbɑːskɪt; *NAmE* ˈbæs-/ *noun* **1** a container for holding or carrying things. Baskets are made of thin strips of material that bends and twists easily, for example plastic, wire or WICKER: *a* **shopping basket** ◇ *a* **picnic basket** ◇ *a* **clothes/laundry basket** (= in which dirty clothes are put before being washed) ◇ *a* ***wicker/ wire basket*** ◇ *a* ***cat/dog basket*** (= in which a cat or dog sleeps or is carried around) ➲ VISUAL VOCAB page V43 ➲ see also WASTE-PAPER BASKET **2** the amount contained in a basket: *a basket of fruit* **3** the net and the metal ring it hangs from, high up at each end of a BASKETBALL COURT; a point that is scored by throwing the ball through this net: *to* ***make/shoot a basket*** ➲ VISUAL VOCAB page V36 **4** (*economics*) a number of different goods or CURRENCIES: *the value of the rupee against a basket of currencies* IDM see EGG *n.*

bas·ket·ball /ˈbɑːskɪtbɔːl; *NAmE* ˈbæs-/ *noun* **1** [U] a game played by two teams of five players, using a large ball which players try to throw into a high net hanging from a ring: *a* ***basketball game/coach/team*** ➲ VISUAL VOCAB page V36 **2** [C] the ball used in this game

ˈbasket case *noun* (*informal*) **1** a country or an organization whose economic situation is very bad **2** a person who is slightly crazy and who has problems dealing with situations

basket·work /ˈbɑːskɪtwɜːk; *NAmE* ˈbæskɪtwɜːrk/ *noun* [U] **1** material twisted together in the style of a basket **2** the craft of making baskets, etc.

bas·mati /bæsˈmæti; bæz-/ (also **basˌmati ˈrice**) *noun* [U] a type of rice with long grains and a delicate flavour

bas mitzvah /ˌbæs ˈmɪtsvə/ *noun* = BAT MITZVAH

Basque /bɑːsk; bæsk; *NAmE* bæsk/ *noun, adj.*

■ ***noun*** **1** [C] a person who was born in the Basque country **2** [U] the language of the people living in the Basque country of France and Spain

■ ***adj.*** connected with these people or their language

basque /bɑːsk; bæsk; *NAmE* bæsk/ *noun* a piece of women's underwear that covers the body from just under the arms to the tops of the legs

bas-relief /ˌbæs rɪˈliːf/ *noun* [U, C] a form of SCULPTURE in which the shapes are cut so that they are slightly raised from the background; a SCULPTURE made in this way

bass¹ /beɪs/ *noun, adj.* ➲ see also BASS²

■ ***noun*** **1** [U] the lowest tone or part in music, for instruments or voices: *He always plays his stereo with the bass turned right up.* ◇ *He sings bass.* ◇ *a pounding bass line* ➲ compare TREBLE ➲ see also DRUM AND BASS **2** [C] a man's singing voice with a low range; a man with a bass voice ➲ compare ALTO, BARITONE, TENOR **3** [sing.] a musical part that is written for a bass voice **4** (also ˌ**bass guiˈtar**) [C] an electric GUITAR that plays very low notes: *a bass player* ◇ *bass and drums* ◇ *Eilís Phillips on* (= playing) *bass* **5** [C] = DOUBLE BASS

■ ***adj.*** [only before noun] low in tone: *a bass voice* ◇ *the* ***bass clef*** (= the symbol in music showing that the notes following it are low) ➲ picture at MUSIC ➲ compare TREBLE

bass² /bæs/ *noun* [C, U] (*pl.* **bass**) a sea or FRESHWATER fish that is used for food ➲ see also BASS¹

ˌ**bass ˈdrum** *noun* a large drum that makes a very low sound, used in ORCHESTRAS ➲ VISUAL VOCAB page V30

bas·set /ˈbæsɪt/ (also ˈ**basset hound**) *noun* a dog with short legs, a long body and long ears

bas·sinet /ˌbæsɪˈnet/ (*especially NAmE*) (*BrE* usually **Moses basket**) *noun* a small bed for a baby, that looks like a BASKET

bass·ist /ˈbeɪsɪst/ *noun* a person who plays the BASS GUITAR or the DOUBLE BASS

bas·soon /bəˈsuːn/ *noun* a musical instrument of the WOODWIND group. It is shaped like a large wooden tube with a double REED that you blow into, and produces notes with a low sound. ➲ VISUAL VOCAB page V30

bas·soon·ist /bəˈsuːnɪst/ *noun* a person who plays the bassoon

bas·tard /ˈbɑːstəd; ˈbæs-; *NAmE* ˈbæstərd/ *noun* **1** (*taboo, slang*) used to insult sb, especially a man, who has been rude, unpleasant or cruel: *He's a real bastard.* ◇ *You bastard! You've made her cry.* **2** (*BrE, slang*) a word that some people use about or to sb, especially a man, who they feel very jealous of or sorry for: *What a lucky bastard!* ◇ *You poor bastard!* **3** (*BrE, slang*) used about sth that causes difficulties or problems: *It's a bastard of a problem.* **4** (*old-fashioned, disapproving*) a person whose parents were not married to each other when he or she was born

bas·tard·ize (*BrE* also **-ise**) /ˈbɑːstədaɪz; ˈbæs-; *NAmE* ˈbæstərd-/ *verb* **~ sth** (*formal*) to copy sth, but change parts of it so that it is not as good as the original

baste /beɪst/ *verb* **1 ~ sth** to pour liquid fat or juices over meat, etc. while it is cooking **2 ~ sth** to sew pieces of cloth together temporarily with long loose STITCHES

ˈ**basting brush** *noun* a brush used for brushing liquid fat or juices over meat, etc. while it is cooking ➲ VISUAL VOCAB page V23

bas·tion /ˈbæstiən/ *noun* **1** (*formal*) a group of people or a system that protects a way of life or a belief when it seems that it may disappear: *a bastion of male privilege* ◇ *a bastion of freedom* **2** a place that military forces are defending

bat /bæt/ *noun, verb*

■ ***noun*** **1** a piece of wood with a handle, made in various shapes and sizes, and used for hitting the ball in games such as BASEBALL, CRICKET and TABLE TENNIS: *a* ***baseball/cricket bat*** ➲ VISUAL VOCAB pages V36, V37 ➲ compare RACKET **2** an animal like a mouse with wings, that flies and feeds at night (= it is NOCTURNAL). There are many types of bat. ➲ VISUAL VOCAB page V10 ➲ see also FRUIT BAT, OLD BAT, VAMPIRE BAT

IDM **like a bat out of ˈhell** (*informal*) very fast **off your own ˈbat** (*BrE, informal*) if you do sth **off your own bat**, it is your own idea and you do it without help or encouragement from anyone else ➲ more at BLIND *adj.*, RIGHT *adv.*

■ ***verb*** (-tt-) **1** [I, T] **~ (sth)** to hit a ball with a bat, especially in a game of CRICKET or BASEBALL: *He bats very well.* ◇ *Who's batting first for the Orioles?* **2** [T] **~ sth + adv./prep.** to hit sth small that is flying through the air: *He batted the wasp away.*

IDM ˌ**bat your ˈeyes/ˈeyelashes** to open and close your eyes quickly, in a way that is supposed to be attractive **bat a ˈthousand** (*NAmE, informal*) to be very successful **go to ˈbat for sb** (*NAmE, informal*) to give sb help and support **not bat an ˈeyelid** (*BrE*) (*NAmE* **not bat an ˈeye**) (*informal*) to show no surprise or embarrassment when sth unusual happens: *She didn't bat an eyelid when I told her my news.*

PHR V ˌ**bat sth↔aˈround** (*informal*) to discuss whether an idea or a plan is good or not, before deciding what to do: *It's just an idea we've been batting around.*

batch /bætʃ/ *noun, verb*

■ ***noun*** **1** a number of people or things that are dealt with as a group: *Each summer a new batch of students tries to find work.* ◇ *We deliver the goods* ***in batches.*** **2** an amount of food, medicine, etc. produced at one time: *a batch of cookies* **3** (*computing*) a set of jobs that are processed together on a computer: *to process a batch job* ◇ *a* ***batch file/program***

■ ***verb*** [T, I] **~ (sth)** to put things into groups in order to deal with them: *The service will be improved by batching and sorting enquiries.*

batch·mate /ˈbætʃmeɪt/ *noun* (*IndE*) a person who is or was in the same year group as you at school or college

ˌ**batch ˈprocessing** *noun* [U] (*computing*) a way of running a group of programs at the same time, usually automatically

bated /ˈbeɪtɪd/ *adj.*

IDM **with bated ˈbreath** (*formal*) feeling very anxious or excited: *We waited with bated breath for the winner to be announced.*

bath 🔑 /bɑːθ; *NAmE* bæθ/ *noun, verb*

■ ***noun*** (*pl.* **baths** /bɑːðz; *NAmE* bæðz/) **1** 🔑 [C] (*BrE*) (also **bath·tub**, *informal* **tub** *NAmE, BrE*) a large, long container that you put water in and then get into to wash your whole body ➲ VISUAL VOCAB page V21 ➲ see also BIRD BATH **2** 🔑 [C] (*BrE*) the water in a bath/BATHTUB, ready to use: *a long soak in a hot bath* ◇ *Please* ***run a bath*** *for me* (= fill the bath with water). **3** 🔑 [C] an act of washing your whole body by sitting or lying in water: *I think I'll **have a bath** and go to bed.* ◇ *(especially NAmE) to **take a bath*** ➲ see also BUBBLE BATH **4 baths** [pl.] (*old-fashioned, BrE*) a public building where you can go to swim ➲ see also SWIMMING BATH, SWIMMING POOL **5** [C, usually pl.] a public place where people went in the past to wash or have a bath: *Roman villas and baths* ➲ see also TURKISH BATH **6** [C] (*technical*) a container with a liquid such as water or a DYE in it, in which sth is washed or placed for a period of time. Baths are used in industrial, chemical and medical processes. ➲ see also BLOODBATH

IDM **take a 'bath** (*NAmE*) to lose money on a business agreement

■ ***verb*** (*BrE*) (*NAmE* **bathe**) **1** [T] **~ sb** to give a bath to sb: *It's your turn to bath the baby.* **2** [I] (*old-fashioned*) to have a bath

Which Word?

bath / bathe / swim / sunbathe

- When you wash yourself you can say that you **bath** (*BrE*) or **bathe** (*NAmE*), but it is much more common to say **have a bath** (*BrE*) or **take a bath** (*NAmE*).
- You can also **bath** (*BrE*) or **bathe** (*NAmE*) another person, for example a baby.
- You **bathe** a part of your body, especially to clean a wound.
- When you go swimming it is old-fashioned to say that you **bathe**, and you cannot say that you *bath* or *take a bath*. It is more common to **swim**, **go for a swim**, **have a swim** or **go swimming**: *Let's go for a quick swim in the pool.* ◇ *She goes swimming every morning before breakfast.* What you wear for this activity is usually called a **swimming costume** in *BrE* and a **bathing suit** in *NAmE*.
- When you lie in the sun in order to go brown you **sunbathe**.

,bath 'chair *noun* a special chair with wheels, used in the past for moving a person who was sick or old

bathe /beɪð/ *verb, noun*

■ ***verb*** **1** [T] **~ sth** to wash sth with water, especially a part of your body: *Bathe the wound and apply a clean dressing.* **2** [T, I] **~ (sb)** (*NAmE*) = BATH: *Have you bathed the baby yet?* ◇ *I bathe every day.* ➲ note at BATH **3** [I] (*old-fashioned*) to go swimming in the sea, a river, etc. for enjoyment ➲ see also SUNBATHE **4** [T] **~ sth (in sth)** (*literary*) to fill or cover sth with light: *The moon bathed the countryside in a silver light.*

■ ***noun*** [sing.] (*BrE, formal*) an act of swimming in the sea, a river, etc: *to go for a bathe*

bathed /beɪðd/ *adj.* **1 ~ in sth** (*literary*) covered with light: *The castle was bathed in moonlight.* **2 ~ in sth** wet because covered with sweat or tears: *I was so nervous that I was bathed in perspiration.*

bather /'beɪðə(r)/ *noun* **1** [C] (*BrE*) a person who is swimming in the sea, a river, etc. **2 bathers** [pl.] (*AustralE*) = SWIMMING COSTUME, SWIMMING TRUNKS

bath·house /'bɑ:θhaʊs; *NAmE* 'bæθ-/ *noun* **1** a public building in which there are baths, steam rooms, etc. **2** (*NAmE*) a building in which you change your clothes for swimming

bath·ing /'beɪðɪŋ/ *noun* [U] (*BrE*) the activity of going into the sea, a river, etc. to swim: *facilities for bathing and boating* ◇ *a safe bathing beach*

'bathing cap (*especially NAmE*) (*BrE* also **'swimming cap**, **'swimming hat**) *noun* a soft rubber or plastic cap that fits closely over your head to keep your hair dry while you are swimming

'bathing costume *noun* (*BrE, old-fashioned*) = SWIMMING COSTUME

'bathing machine *noun* a shelter with wheels that people in the past went into to put swimming clothes on, which was then pulled to the edge of the sea so they could swim from it

'bathing suit *noun* (*NAmE* or *old-fashioned*) = SWIMSUIT

'bath mat *noun* **1** a piece of material that you put beside the bath/BATHTUB to stand on when you get out ➲ VISUAL VOCAB page V21 **2** a piece of rubber that you put on the bottom of the bath/BATHTUB so that you do not slip

bathos /'beɪθɒs; *NAmE* -θɑ:s/ *noun* [U] (*formal*) (in writing or speech) a sudden change, that is not always intended, from a serious subject or feeling to sth that is silly or not important

bath·robe /'bɑ:θrəʊb; *NAmE* 'bæθroʊb/ (also **robe**) *noun* **1** a loose piece of clothing worn before and after taking a bath ➲ VISUAL VOCAB page V21 **2** (*NAmE*) (*BrE* **'dressing gown**) a long loose piece of clothing, usually with a belt, worn indoors over night clothes, for example when you first get out of bed ➲ VISUAL VOCAB page V51

bath·room 🔑 /'bɑ:θru:m; -rʊm; *NAmE* 'bæθ-/ *noun* **1** 🔑 a room in which there is a bath/BATHTUB, a WASHBASIN and often a toilet: *Go and wash your hands in the bathroom.* ➲ VISUAL VOCAB page V21 **2** 🔑 (*NAmE*) a room in which there is a toilet, a SINK and sometimes a bath/BATHTUB or shower: *I have to **go to the bathroom*** (= use the toilet). ◇ *Where's the bathroom?* (= for example in a restaurant) ➲ note at TOILET

bath·tub /'bɑ:θtʌb; *NAmE* bæθ-/ (also *informal* **tub**) (both *especially NAmE*) (*BrE* also **bath**) *noun* a large, long container that you put water in and then get into to wash your whole body ➲ VISUAL VOCAB page V21

bath·water /'bɑ:θwɔ:tə(r); *NAmE* 'bæθwɔ:tər; -wɑ:t-/ *noun* [U] water in a bath/BATHTUB IDM see BABY *n.*

batik /bə'ti:k/ *noun* [U, C] a method of printing patterns on cloth using WAX (= a solid substance made from fat or oil) on the parts that will not have any colour; a piece of cloth printed in this way

bat·man /'bætmən/ *noun* (*pl.* **-men** /-mən/) (*BrE*) the personal servant of an officer in the armed forces

bat mitzvah /,bæt 'mɪtsvə/ (also **,bas 'mitzvah**) *noun* **1** a ceremony and celebration that is held for a Jewish girl between the ages of 12 and 14 at which she accepts the religious responsibilities of an adult **2** the girl who is celebrating this occasion ➲ compare BAR MITZVAH

baton /'bætɒn; -tõ; *NAmE* bə'tɑ:n/ *noun* **1** (*especially BrE*) = TRUNCHEON: *a **baton charge*** (= one made by police carrying batons, to force a crowd back) **2** a thin light stick used by the person (called a CONDUCTOR) who is in control of an ORCHESTRA, etc. **3** a short light stick that one member of a team in a RELAY race passes to the next person to run: *to **pass/hand over the baton*** ◇ (*figurative*) *The President **handed over the baton*** (= passed responsibility) *to his successor.* **4** a long stick that is held and thrown in the air by a person marching in front of a band, or by a MAJORETTE

'baton round *noun* (*BrE*) a rubber or plastic bullet that is fired to control a crowd that has become violent

bats·man /'bætsmən/ *noun* (*pl.* **-men** /-mən/) (in CRICKET) the player who is hitting the ball ➲ VISUAL VOCAB page V36

bat·tal·ion /bə'tæliən/ *noun* **1** (*BrE*) a large group of soldiers that form part of a BRIGADE **2** (*formal*) a large group of people, especially an organized group with a particular purpose: *a battalion of supporters*

bat·ten /'bætn/ *noun, verb*

■ ***noun*** (*technical*) a long strip of wood that is used to keep other building materials in place on a wall or roof

■ ***verb***

IDM **,batten down the 'hatches 1** to prepare yourself for a period of difficulty or trouble **2** (on a ship) to firmly shut all the entrances to the lower part, especially because a storm is expected

PHR V **,batten sth↔'down** to fix sth firmly in position with wooden boards: *He was busy battening down all the shutters and doors.* **'batten on sb** (*BrE, disapproving, formal*) to live well by using other people's money, etc.

bat·ter /ˈbætə(r)/ *verb, noun*
■ ***verb*** [I, T, often passive] to hit sb/sth hard many times, especially in a way that causes serious damage: **~ at/on sth** *She battered at the door with her fists.* ◇ **~ sb** *He had been badly battered about the head and face.* ◇ *Her killer had **battered** her **to death**.* ◇ **~ sth** *Severe winds have been battering the north coast.* ➲ SYNONYMS at BEAT
PHR V ˌ**batter sth↔ˈdown** to hit sth hard many times until it breaks or comes down
■ ***noun*** **1** [U, C] a mixture of eggs, milk and flour used in cooking to cover food such as fish or chicken before you fry it, or to make PANCAKES **2** [U, C] (*NAmE*) a mixture of eggs, milk, flour, etc. used for making cakes **3** [C] (*NAmE*) (in BASEBALL) the player who is hitting the ball ➲ VISUAL VOCAB page V36

bat·tered /ˈbætəd; *NAmE* -tərd/ *adj.* **1** old, used a lot, and not in very good condition: *a battered old car* **2** [usually before noun] attacked violently and injured; attacked and badly damaged by weapons or by bad weather: ***battered women/children*** ◇ *The child had suffered what has become known as 'battered baby syndrome.'* ◇ *Rockets and shells continued to hit the battered port.*

bat·ter·ing /ˈbætərɪŋ/ *noun* [U, sing.] a violent attack that injures or damages sb/sth: *wife battering* ◇ (*figurative*) *The film **took a battering** from critics in the US.*

ˈ**battering ram** *noun* a long, heavy piece of wood used in war in the past for breaking down doors and walls

bat·tery 0→ /ˈbætri; -təri/ *noun* (*pl.* -ies)
1 0→ [C] a device that is placed inside a car engine, clock, radio, etc. and that produces the electricity that makes it work: *to replace the batteries* ◇ *a rechargeable battery* ◇ ***battery-powered/-operated*** ◇ *a car battery* ◇ *The battery is flat* (= it is no longer producing electricity). **2** [C] **~ (of sth)** a large number of things or people of the same type: *He faced a battery of questions.* ◇ *a battery of reporters* **3** [C] (*technical*) a number of large guns that are used together **4** [C] (*BrE*) (often used as an adjective) a large number of small CAGES that are joined together and are used for keeping chickens, etc. in on a farm: *a battery hen* ◇ *battery eggs* ➲ compare FREE-RANGE **5** [U] (*law*) the crime of attacking sb physically ➲ see also ASSAULT AND BATTERY
IDM see RECHARGE

ˈ**battery farm** *noun* (*BrE*) a farm where large numbers of chickens or other animals are kept in very small CAGES or crowded conditions ➲ compare FACTORY FARM, FREE-RANGE ▶ ˈ**battery farming** *noun* [U]

bat·tle 0→ /ˈbætl/ *noun, verb*
■ ***noun*** **1** 0→ [C, U] a fight between armies, ships or planes, especially during a war; a violent fight between groups of people: *the battle of Waterloo* ◇ *to be killed **in battle*** ◇ *a gun battle* ➲ see also PITCHED BATTLE **2** 0→ [C] **~ (with sb) (for sth)** a competition, an argument or a struggle between people or groups of people trying to win power or control: *a legal battle for compensation* ◇ *a battle with an insurance company* ◇ *a **battle of wits*** (= when each side uses their ability to think quickly to try to win) ◇ *a **battle of wills*** (= when each side is very determined to win) ➲ SYNONYMS at CAMPAIGN **3** 0→ [C, usually sing.] a determined effort that sb makes to solve a difficult problem or succeed in a difficult situation: **~ (against sth)** *her long battle against cancer* ◇ *to fight an uphill battle against prejudice* ◇ **~ (for sth)** *a battle for survival* ◇ **~ (with sth)** *his battle with alcoholism*
IDM **the battle lines are ˈdrawn** used to say that people or groups have shown which side they intend to support in an argument or contest that is going to begin **do ˈbattle (with sb) (over sth)** to fight or argue with sb **half the ˈbattle** the most important or difficult part of achieving sth ➲ more at FIGHT *v.*, JOIN *v.*
■ ***verb*** [I, T] to try very hard to achieve sth difficult or to deal with sth unpleasant or dangerous: *Both teams battled hard.* ◇ *I had to battle hard just to stay afloat.* ◇ **~ with/against sb/sth (for sth)** *She's still battling with a knee injury.* ◇ **~ for sth** *The two leaders are battling for control of the government.* ◇ *The two sides will **battle it out** in the final next week.* ◇ **~ sth** (*NAmE*) *He battled cancer for four years.*

battle·axe (*BrE*) (*US* also **battle·ax**) /ˈbætlæks/ *noun* **1** (*informal, disapproving*) an aggressive and unpleasant older woman **2** a heavy AXE with a long handle, used in the past as a weapon

battle·cruiser /ˈbætlkruːzə(r)/ *noun* a large fast ship used in war in the past, faster and lighter than a BATTLESHIP

ˈ**battle cry** *noun* **1** a shout that soldiers used to give in battle to encourage their own army or to frighten the enemy **2** a word or phrase used by a group of people who work together for a particular purpose, especially a political one

battle·dress /ˈbætldres/ *noun* [U] (*BrE*) the uniform that soldiers wear for training and when they go to fight

ˈ**battle fatigue** *noun* [U] = COMBAT FATIGUE

ˈ**battle fatigues** *noun* [pl.] = COMBAT FATIGUES

battle·field /ˈbætlfiːld/ (also **battle·ground** /ˈbætlɡraʊnd/) *noun* **1** a place where a battle is being fought or has been fought **2** a subject that people feel strongly about and argue about

ˈ**battle-hardened** *adj.* (of soldiers) having experience of war and therefore effective at fighting battles

battle·ments /ˈbætlmənts/ *noun* [pl.] a low wall around the top of a castle with spaces in it that people inside could shoot through ➲ VISUAL VOCAB page V13

ˈ**battle-scarred** *adj.* a person or place that is **battle-scarred** has been in a war or fight and shows the signs of injury or damage

battle·ship /ˈbætlʃɪp/ *noun* a very large ship used in war, with big guns and heavy ARMOUR (= metal plates that cover the ship to protect it)

batty /ˈbæti/ *adj.* (*informal, especially BrE*) (of people or ideas) slightly crazy, in a harmless way ➲ SYNONYMS at MAD

bau·ble /ˈbɔːbl/ *noun* **1** a piece of jewellery that is cheap and has little artistic value **2** (*BrE*) a decoration for a Christmas tree in the shape of a ball

baud /bɔːd/ *noun* (*computing*) a unit for measuring the speed at which electronic signals and information are sent from one computer to another

Bau·haus /ˈbaʊhaʊs/ *noun* [U] (from *German*) a style and movement in German ARCHITECTURE and design in the early 20th century that was influenced by the methods and materials used in industry and placed emphasis on how things would be used

baulk (*BrE*) (*NAmE* usually **balk**) /bɔːk/ *verb* **1** [I] **~ (at sth)** to be unwilling to do sth or become involved in sth because it is difficult, dangerous, etc: *Many parents may baulk at the idea of paying $100 for a pair of shoes.* **2** [I] **~ (at sth)** (of a horse) to stop suddenly and refuse to jump a fence, etc. **3** [T] **~ sb (of sth)** [usually passive] (*formal*) to prevent sb from getting sth or doing sth: *She looked like a lion baulked of its prey.*

baux·ite /ˈbɔːksaɪt/ *noun* [U] a soft mineral from which ALUMINIUM/ALUMINUM is obtained

bawd /bɔːd/ *noun* (*old use*) a woman who was in charge of a BROTHEL (= a house where men pay to have sex)

bawdy /ˈbɔːdi/ *adj.* (**bawd·ier, bawd·iest**) (*old-fashioned*) (of songs, plays, etc.) loud, and dealing with sex in an amusing way

bawl /bɔːl/ *verb* **1** [I, T] to shout loudly, especially in an unpleasant or angry way: **~ (at sb)** *She bawled at him in front of everyone.* ◇ **~ (out) sth (at sb)** *He sat in his office bawling orders at his secretary.* ◇ **+ speech (+ out)** *'Get in here now!' she bawled out.* **2** [I, T] (**+ speech**) to cry loudly, especially in an unpleasant and annoying way: *A child was bawling in the next room.* ◇ *He was **bawling his eyes out*** (= crying very loudly).
PHR V ˌ**bawl sb↔ˈout** (*informal*) to speak angrily to sb because they have done sth wrong: *The teacher bawled him out for being late.*

bay 0-ᴡ /beɪ/ *noun, verb, adj.*

■ ***noun* 1** 0-ᴡ [C] a part of the sea, or of a large lake, partly surrounded by a wide curve of the land: *the Bay of Bengal* ◇ *Hudson Bay* ◇ *a magnificent view across the bay* ➲ VISUAL VOCAB page V4 **2** [C] a marked section of ground either inside or outside a building, for example for a vehicle to park in, for storing things, etc: *a **parking/loading bay*** ◇ *Put the equipment in No 3 bay.* ➲ see also SICKBAY **3** [C] a curved area of a room or building that sticks out from the rest of the building **4** [C] a horse of a dark brown colour: *He was riding a big bay.* **5** [C] a deep noise, especially the noise made by dogs when hunting **6** (also **'sweet bay**) [C] = BAY TREE **7** [U] a HERB used to give flavour to food, made of the leaves of the BAY TREE ➲ VISUAL VOCAB page V28

IDM **at 'bay** when an animal that is being hunted is **at bay**, it must turn and face the dogs and HUNTERS because it is impossible to escape from them **hold/keep sb/sth at 'bay** to prevent an enemy from coming close or a problem from having a bad effect SYN **ward off**: *I'm trying to keep my cred-itors at bay.* ◇ *Charlotte bit her lip to hold the tears at bay.*

■ ***verb* 1** [I] (of a dog or WOLF) to make a long deep sound, especially while hunting SYN **howl**: *a pack of baying hounds* **2** [I] **~ (for sth)** (usually used in the progressive tenses) to demand sth in a loud and angry way: *The refer-ee's decision left the crowd **baying for blood*** (= threatening violence towards him).

■ ***adj.*** (of a horse) dark brown in colour: *a bay mare*

'bay leaf *noun* the dried leaf of the BAY TREE that is used in cooking as a HERB

bay·onet *noun, verb*

■ ***noun*** /'beɪənət/ a long, sharp knife that is fastened onto the end of a RIFLE and used as a weapon in battle

■ ***verb*** /'beɪənət; ˌbeɪə'net/ **~ sb** to push a bayonet into sb in order to kill them

bayou /'baɪuː/ *noun* a branch of a river in the southern US that moves very slowly and has many plants growing in it

'bay tree (also **bay**) *noun* a small tree with dark green leaves with a sweet smell that are used in cooking ➲ see also BAY LEAF

ˌbay 'window *noun* a large window, usually with glass on three sides, that sticks out from the outside wall of a house ➲ VISUAL VOCAB page V15

ba·zaar /bə'zɑː(r)/ *noun* **1** (in some Eastern countries) a street or an area of a town where there are many small shops **2** (in Britain, the US, etc.) a sale of goods, often items made by hand, to raise money for a charity or for people who need help

ba·zooka /bə'zuːkə/ *noun* a long gun, shaped like a tube, which is held on the shoulder and used to fire ROCKETS at military vehicles

ba·zoom /bə'zuːm/ *noun* [usually pl.] (*informal, especially NAmE*) a woman's breast

BBC /ˌbiː biː 'siː/ *abbr.* British Broadcasting Corporation (a national organization which broadcasts television and radio programmes and which is paid for by the public and not by advertising): *The news is on BBC One at 6.* ◇ *BBC Radio 4*

the ˌBBC World 'Service *noun* [sing.] a department of the BBC which broadcasts programmes, including news programmes, in English and many other languages to other countries

BBQ *abbr.* BARBECUE

BBS /ˌbiː ˌbiː 'es/ *noun* [C, U] (*computing*) bulletin board sys-tem (a system which allows a group of people to leave mes-sages which the others in the group can read and reply to)

BC (*BrE*) (*US* **B.C.**) /ˌbiː 'siː/ *abbr.* before Christ (used in the Christian CALENDAR to show a particular number of years before the year when Christ is believed to have been born): *in (the year) 2000 BC* ◇ *the third century BC* ➲ compare AD, AH, BCE, CE

BCE /ˌbiː siː 'iː/ (also **B.C.E.** especially in *NAmE*) *abbr.* before the Common Era (before the birth of Christ, when the Christian CALENDAR starts counting years. BCE can be used to give dates in the same way as BC): *in (the year) 2 000 BCE* ◇ *the third century BCE* ➲ compare AD, BC, CE

be 0-ᴡ /bi; *strong form* biː/ *verb, auxiliary verb*
➲ IRREGULAR VERBS

■ ***verb* 1** 0-ᴡ *linking verb* **there is/are + noun** to exist; to be present: *Is there a God?* ◇ *Once upon a time there was a prin-cess...* ◇ *I tried phoning but there was no answer.* ◇ *There's a bank down the road.* ◇ *Was there a pool at the hotel?* **2** 0-ᴡ [I] **+ adv./prep.** to be located; to be in a place: *The town is three miles away.* ◇ *If you're looking for your file, it's on the table.* ◇ *Mary's upstairs.* **3** 0-ᴡ [I] **+ adv./prep.** to happen at a time or in a place: *The party is on Friday evening.* ◇ *The meetings are always in the main conference room.* **4** 0-ᴡ [I] **+ adv./prep.** to remain in a place: *She has been in her room for hours.* ◇ *They're here till Christmas.* **5** 0-ᴡ [I] **+ adv./prep.** to attend an event; to be present in a place: *I'll be at the party.* ◇ *He'll be here soon* (= will arrive soon). **6** 0-ᴡ [I] (only used in the perfect tenses) **+ adv./prep.** to visit or call: *I've never been to Spain.* ◇ *He had been abroad many times.* ◇ (*BrE*) *Has the postman been yet?* HELP In *NAmE*, **come** is used instead: *Has the mailman come yet?* **7** 0-ᴡ [I] **~ from ...** used to say where sb was born or where their home is: *She's from Italy.* **8** 0-ᴡ *linking verb* used when you are nam-ing people or things, describing them or giving more infor-mation about them: **+ noun** *Today is Monday.* ◇ *'Who is that?' 'It's my brother.'* ◇ *She's a great beauty.* ◇ *Susan is a doctor.* ◇ *He wants to be* (= become) *a pilot when he grows up.* ◇ **+ adj.** *It's beautiful!* ◇ *Life is unfair.* ◇ *He is ten years old.* ◇ *'How are you?' 'I'm very well, thanks.'* ◇ *Be quick!* ◇ **~ (that)...** ***The fact is*** *(that) we don't have enough money.* ◇ **~ doing sth** *The problem is getting it all done in the time available.* ◇ **~ to do sth** *The problem is to get it all done in the time available.* **9** 0-ᴡ *linking verb* **it is/was** used when you are describing a situation or saying what you think about it: **+ adj.** *It was really hot in the sauna.* ◇ *It's strange how she never comes to see us any more.* ◇ *He thinks it's clever to make fun of people.* ◇ **+ noun** *It would be a shame if you lost it.* ◇ *It's going to be a great match.* **10** 0-ᴡ *linking verb* **it is/was** used to talk about time: **+ noun** *It's two thirty.* ◇ **+ adj.** *It was late at night when we finally arrived.* **11** 0-ᴡ *linking verb* **+ noun** used to say what sth is made of: *Is your jacket real leather?* **12** 0-ᴡ *linking verb* [I] used to say who sth belongs to or who it is intended for: **~ mine, yours, etc.** *The money's not yours, it's John's.* ◇ **~ for me, you, etc.** *This package is for you.* **13** 0-ᴡ *linking verb* **+ noun** to cost: *'How much is that dress?' 'Eighty dollars.'* **14** 0-ᴡ *linking verb* **+ noun** to be equal to: *Three and three is six.* ◇ *How much is a thousand pounds in euros?* ◇ *Let x be the sum of a and b.* ◇ *London is not England* (= do not think that all of England is like London). **15** 0-ᴡ *linking verb* **~ everything, nothing, etc. (to sb)** used to say how im-portant sth is to sb: *Money isn't everything* (= it is not the only important thing). ◇ *A thousand dollars is nothing to somebody as rich as he is.*

IDM Most idioms containing **be** are at the entries for the nouns and adjectives in the idioms, for example **be the death of sb** is at **death**. **the ˌbe-all and 'end-all (of sth)** (*informal*) the most important part; all that matters: *Her career is the be-all and end-all of her existence.* **as/that was** as sb/sth used to be called: *Jill Davis that was* (= be-fore her marriage) ◇ *the Soviet Union, as was* **(he, she, etc. has) been and 'done sth** (*BrE, informal*) used to show that you are surprised and annoyed by sth that sb has done: *Someone's been and parked in front of the entrance!* ➲ see also GO AND DO STH **if it wasn't/weren't for...** 0-ᴡ used to say that sb/sth stopped sb/sth from happening: *If it weren't for you, I wouldn't be alive today.* **ˌleave/ˌlet sb/sth 'be** to leave sb/sth alone without disturbing them or it: *Leave her be, she obviously doesn't want to talk about it.* ◇ *Let the poor dog be* (= don't annoy it). **-to-be** (in com-pounds) future: *his bride-to-be* ◇ *mothers-to-be* (= pregnant women)

■ ***auxiliary verb* 1** 0-ᴡ used with a past participle to form the passive: *He was killed in the war.* ◇ *Where were they made?* ◇ *The house was still being built.* ◇ *You will be told what to do.* **2** 0-ᴡ used with a present participle to form progressive tenses: *I am studying Chinese.* ◇ *I'll be seeing him soon.* ◇ *What have you been doing this week?* ◇ *I'm always being*

B

criticized. **3** used to make QUESTION TAGS (= short questions added to the end of statements): *You're not hungry, are you?* ◇ *Ben's coming, isn't he?* ◇ *The old theatre was pulled down, wasn't it?* **4** used to avoid repeating the full form of a verb in the passive or a progressive tense: *Karen wasn't beaten in any of her games, but all the others were.* ◇ *'Are you coming with us?' 'No, I'm not.'* **5** **~ to do sth** used to say what must or should be done: *I am to call them once I reach the airport.* ◇ *You are to report this to the police.* ◇ *What is to be done about this problem?* **6** **~ to do sth** used to say what is arranged to happen: *They are to be married in June.* **7** **~ to do sth** used to say what happened later: *He was to regret that decision for the rest of his life* (= he did regret it). **8** **~ not, never, etc. to be done** used to say what could not or did not happen: *Anna was nowhere to be found* (= we could not find her anywhere). ◇ *He was never to see his wife again* (= although he did not know it would be so at the time, he did not see her again). ◇ *She wanted to write a successful novel, but **it was not to be*** (= it turned out never to happen). **9** **if sb/it were to do sth ... | were sb/it to do sth...** (*formal*) used to express a condition: *If we were to offer you more money, would you stay?* ◇ *Were we to offer you more money, would you stay?*

be- /bɪ-/ *prefix* **1** (in verbs) to make or treat sb/sth as: *Don't belittle his achievements* (= say they are not important). ◇ *An older girl befriended me.* **2** (in adjectives ending in *-ed*) wearing or covered with: *heavily bejewelled fingers* ◇ *bespattered with mud* **3** (in verbs and adjectives ending in *-ed*) to cause sth to be: *The ship was becalmed.* (= there was no wind so it could not move) ◇ *The rebels besieged the fort.* **4** used to turn INTRANSITIVE verbs (= without an object) into TRANSITIVE verbs (= with an object): *She is always bemoaning her lot.*

beach /biːtʃ/ *noun, verb*
- ***noun*** an area of sand or small stones (called SHINGLE), beside the sea or a lake: *tourists sunbathing on the beach* ◇ *a **sandy/pebble/shingle beach*** ◇ *a beach bar* ➲ SYNONYMS at COAST ➲ VISUAL VOCAB page V4
- ***verb*** [T, I] **~ (sth)** to come or bring sth out of the water and onto the beach: *He beached the boat and lifted the boy onto the shore.* ◇ *a beached whale* (= one that has become stuck on land and cannot get back into the water)

ˈbeach ball *noun* a large, light, coloured plastic ball that people play games with on the beach

ˈbeach buggy (also **ˈdune buggy**) *noun* a small car used for driving on sand

beach·comb·er /ˈbiːtʃkəʊmə(r); *NAmE* -koʊm-/ *noun* a person who walks along beaches collecting interesting or valuable things, either for pleasure or to sell

beach·front /ˈbiːtʃfrʌnt/ (often **the beachfront**) *noun* [sing.] (*especially NAmE*) the part of a town facing the beach: *beachfront hotels/apartments*

beach·head /ˈbiːtʃhed/ *noun* a strong position on a beach from which an army that has just landed prepares to go forward and attack ➲ see also BRIDGEHEAD

ˌbeach ˈvolleyball *noun* [U] a form of VOLLEYBALL played on sand by teams of two players

beach·wear /ˈbiːtʃweə(r); *NAmE* -wer/ *noun* [U] (used especially in shops/stores) clothes for wearing on the beach

bea·con /ˈbiːkən/ *noun* **1** a light that is placed somewhere to guide vehicles and warn them of danger: *a navigation beacon* ◇ (*figurative*) *He was **a beacon of hope** for the younger generation.* ➲ see also BELISHA BEACON **2** a radio station whose signal helps ships and aircraft to find their position **3** (in the past) a fire lit on top of a hill as a signal

ˌBeacon ˈHill *noun* an old, fashionable area of Boston in the US, where many rich families and politicians live

bead /biːd/ *noun* **1** [C] a small piece of glass, wood, etc. with a hole through it, that can be put on a string with others of the same type and worn as jewellery, etc: *a necklace of wooden beads* ◇ *A bead curtain separated the two rooms.* ➲ VISUAL VOCAB page V53 ➲ see also WORRY BEADS **2** **beads** [pl.] a ROSARY **3** [C] a small drop of liquid: *There were beads of sweat on his forehead.*
IDM **draw/get a ˈbead on sb/sth** (*especially NAmE*) to aim carefully at sb/sth before shooting a gun

bead·ed /ˈbiːdɪd/ *adj.* **1** decorated with beads: *a beaded dress* **2** **~ with sth** with small drops of a liquid on it: *His face was beaded with sweat.*

bead·ing /ˈbiːdɪŋ/ *noun* [U] **1** a strip of wood, stone or plastic with a pattern on it, used for decorating walls, doors and furniture **2** BEADS that are sewn together and used as a decoration on clothes

beady /ˈbiːdi/ *adj.* (of eyes) small, round and bright; watching everything closely or with suspicion: (*BrE*) *I shall certainly **keep a beady eye** on his behaviour.*

ˌbeady-ˈeyed *adj.* (*informal*) watching carefully and noticing every small detail

bea·gle /ˈbiːɡl/ *noun* a small dog with short legs, used in hunting

beak /biːk/ *noun*
1 the hard pointed or curved outer part of a bird's mouth SYN **bill**: *The gull held the fish in its beak.* ➲ VISUAL VOCAB page V10 **2** (*humorous*) a person's nose, especially when it is large and/or pointed **3** (*old-fashioned, BrE, slang*) a person in a position of authority, especially a judge

beaked /biːkt/ *adj.* (usually in compounds) having a beak, or the type of beak mentioned: *flat-beaked*

bea·ker /ˈbiːkə(r)/ *noun* **1** (*BrE*) a plastic or paper cup, often without a handle, used for drinking from ➲ VISUAL VOCAB pages V19, V21 **2** (*BrE*) the amount contained in a beaker: *a beaker of coffee* **3** a glass cup with straight sides and a lip, used in chemistry, for example for measuring liquids ➲ VISUAL VOCAB page V57

beam /biːm/ *noun, verb*
- ***noun*** **1** a line of light, electric waves or PARTICLES: *narrow **beams of light/sunlight*** ◇ *the **beam of a torch/flashlight*** ◇ *a **laser/electron beam*** ◇ (*BrE*) *The car's headlights were on **full beam*** (= shining as brightly as possible and not directed downwards). ◇ (*NAmE*) *a car with its **high beams** on* **2** a long piece of wood, metal, etc. used to support weight, especially as part of the roof in a building: *The cottage had exposed oak beams.* **3** (*especially BrE*) (*NAmE* usually **ˈbalance beam**) a wooden bar that is used in the sport of GYMNASTICS for people to move and balance on **4** a wide and happy smile: *a beam of satisfaction*
IDM **off ˈbeam** (*informal*) not correct; wrong: *Your calculation is way off beam.*
- ***verb*** **1** [I, T, no passive] to have a big happy smile on your face: **~ (at sb)** *He beamed at the journalists.* ◇ **~ (with sth)** *She was positively beaming with pleasure.* ◇ **~ sth (at sb)** *The barman beamed a warm smile at her.* ◇ *'I'd love to come,' she beamed* (= said with a large smile). **2** [T] **+ adv./prep.** to send radio or television signals over long distances using electronic equipment: *Live pictures of the ceremony were beamed around the world.* **3** [I] **+ adv./prep.** to produce a stream of light and/or heat: *The morning sun beamed down on us.* ◇ *Light beamed through a hole in the curtain.*
IDM see EAR
PHR V **ˌbeam sb ˈdown/ˈup** (in SCIENCE FICTION stories) to transport sb to or from a SPACESHIP using special electronic equipment ORIGIN From the American television series *Star Trek*.

beamed /biːmd/ *adj.* having beams of wood: *a high beamed ceiling*

bean /biːn/ *noun, verb*
- ***noun*** **1** a seed, or POD containing seeds, of a climbing plant, eaten as a vegetable. There are several types of bean and the plants that they grow on are also called beans: *broad beans* ◇ *runner beans* ◇ *beans* (=BAKED BEANS) *on toast* ➲ VISUAL VOCAB page V27 **2** (usually in compounds) a seed from a coffee plant, or some other plants: ***coffee/cocoa beans*** ➲ see also JELLY BEAN
IDM **full of ˈbeans/ˈlife** (of a person) having a lot of energy **not have a ˈbean** (*BrE, informal*) to have no money ➲ more at HILL, KNOW *v.*, SPILL *v.*
- ***verb*** **~ sb** (*NAmE, informal*) to hit sb on the head: *I got beaned by a rock someone threw.*

bean·bag /ˈbiːnbæɡ/ *noun* **1** a very large bag made of cloth and filled with small pieces of plastic, used for sitting on **2** a small bag made of cloth filled with BEANS or small pieces of plastic and used as a ball

ˈbean counter *noun* (*informal, disapproving*) a person who works with money, for example as an ACCOUNTANT and who wants to keep strict control of how much money a company spends

ˈbean curd *noun* [U] = TOFU

bean·feast /ˈbiːnfiːst/ *noun* (*old-fashioned, BrE*) a party or celebration

beanie /ˈbiːni/ *noun* a small, round close-fitting hat ➲ VISUAL VOCAB page V53

beano /ˈbiːnəʊ; *NAmE* -noʊ/ *noun* (*pl.* -os) (*BrE, informal*) a party

bean·pole /ˈbiːnpəʊl; *NAmE* -poʊl/ *noun* (*informal, usually disapproving*) a tall thin person

ˈbean sprouts *noun* [pl.] BEAN seeds that are just beginning to grow, often eaten raw ➲ VISUAL VOCAB page V27

bean·stalk /ˈbiːnstɔːk/ *noun* the tall fast-growing STEM of a BEAN plant

bear 🔑 /beə(r); *NAmE* ber/ *verb, noun*

■ ***verb*** (**bore** /bɔː(r)/, **borne** /bɔːn; *NAmE* bɔːrn/)

▸ ACCEPT/DEAL WITH **1** 🔑 [T] (used with *can/could* in negative sentences and questions) to be able to accept and deal with sth unpleasant SYN **stand**: **~ sth** *The pain was almost more than he could bear.* ◇ *She* ***couldn't bear the thought*** *of losing him.* ◇ **~ doing sth** *I can't bear having cats in the house.* ◇ *He can't bear being laughed at.* ◇ **~ to do sth** *He can't bear to be laughed at.* ◇ **~ sb doing sth** *I can't bear you doing that.* ➲ SYNONYMS at HATE

▸ NOT BE SUITABLE **2** [T] **not ~** to not be suitable for sth: **~ sth** *Her later work* ***does not bear comparison*** *with her earlier novels* (= because it is not nearly as good). ◇ *The plan* ***won't bear*** *close* ***inspection*** (= it will be found to be unacceptable when carefully examined). ◇ **~ doing sth** *The joke* ***doesn't bear repeating*** (= because it is not funny or may offend people). ◇ *His sufferings* ***don't bear thinking about*** (= because they are so terrible).

▸ BE RESPONSIBLE FOR STH **3** 🔑 [T] **~ sth** (*formal*) to take responsibility for sth: *She* ***bore the responsibility*** *for most of the changes.* ◇ *Do parents have to* ***bear the*** *whole* ***cost*** *of tuition fees?* ◇ *You shouldn't have to* ***bear the blame*** *for other people's mistakes.*

▸ NEGATIVE FEELING **4** [T] to have a feeling, especially a negative feeling: **~ sth (against/towards sb)** *He* ***bears no resentment*** *towards them.* ◇ *He's* ***borne a grudge*** *against me ever since that day.* ◇ **~ sb sth** *He's* ***borne me a grudge*** *ever since that day.* ◇ *She* ***bore him no ill will.***

▸ SUPPORT WEIGHT **5** 🔑 [T] **~ sth** to support the weight of sb/sth: *The ice is too thin to bear your weight.*

▸ SHOW **6** [T] **~ sth** (*formal*) to show sth; to carry sth so that it can be seen: *The document bore her signature.* ◇ *He was badly wounded in the war and still bears the scars.* ◇ *She* ***bears little resemblance to*** (= is not much like) *her mother.* ◇ *The title of the essay* ***bore little relation to*** (= was not much connected with) *the contents.*

▸ NAME **7** [T] **~ sth** (*formal*) to have a particular name: *a family that bore an ancient and honoured name*

▸ CARRY **8** [T] **~ sb/sth** (*old-fashioned* or *formal*) to carry sb/sth, especially while moving: *three kings bearing gifts*

▸ YOURSELF **9** [T] **~ yourself well, etc.** (*formal*) to move, behave or act in a particular way: *He bears himself* (= stands, walks, etc.) *proudly, like a soldier.* ◇ *She bore herself with dignity throughout the funeral.*

▸ CHILD **10** [T] (*formal*) to give birth to a child: **~ sth** *She was not able to bear children.* ◇ **~ sb sth** *She had borne him six sons.*

▸ OF TREES/PLANTS **11** [T] **~ sth** (*formal*) to produce flowers or fruit

▸ TURN **12** [I] **~ (to the) left, north, etc.** to go or turn in the direction mentioned: *When you get to the fork in the road, bear right.*

IDM **bear ˈarms** (*old use*) to be a soldier; to fight **bear ˈfruit** to have a successful result **bear ˈhard, ˈheavily, seˈverely, etc. on sb** (*formal*) to be a cause of difficulty or suffering to sb: *Taxation bears heavily on us all.* **be borne ˈin on sb** (*formal, especially BrE*) to be realized by sb, especially after a period of time: *It was gradually borne in on us that defeat was inevitable.* **bring sth to bear (on sb/sth)** (*formal*) to use energy, pressure, influence, etc. to try to achieve sth or make sb do sth: *We must bring all our energies to bear upon the task.* ◇ ***Pressure was brought to bear*** *on us to finish the work on time.* ➲ more at BRUNT, CROSS *n.*, GRIN *v.*, MIND *n.*, WITNESS *n.*

PHR V **ˌbear ˈdown on sb/sth 1** (*especially BrE*) to move quickly towards sb/sth in a determined or threatening way **2** (*especially NAmE*) to press on sb/sth: *Bear down on it with all your strength so it doesn't move.* **ˈbear on sth** (*formal*) to relate to sth SYN **affect**: *These are matters that bear on the welfare of the community.* **ˌbear sb/sth↔ˈout** (*especially BrE*) to show that sb is right or that sth is true: *The other witnesses will bear me out.* ◇ *The other witnesses will bear out what I say.* **ˌbear ˈup (against/under sth)** to remain as cheerful as possible during a difficult time: *He's bearing up well under the strain of losing his job.* ◇ *'How are you?' 'Bearing up.'* **ˈbear with sb/sth** to be patient with sb/sth: *She's under a lot of strain. Just bear with her.* ◇ *If you will bear with me* (= be patient and listen to me) *a little longer, I'll answer your question.*

■ ***noun*** **1** a heavy wild animal with thick fur and sharp CLAWS (= pointed parts on the ends of its feet). There are many types of bear: *a black bear* ➲ see also GRIZZLY BEAR, POLAR BEAR, TEDDY BEAR **2** (*finance*) a person who sells shares in a company, etc, hoping to buy them back later at a lower price ➲ compare BULL ➲ see also BEARISH

IDM **like a bear with a sore ˈhead** (*informal*) bad-tempered or in a bad-tempered way

bear·able /ˈbeərəbl; *NAmE* ˈber-/ *adj.* a person or thing that is **bearable** can be accepted or dealt with: *She was the only thing that made life bearable.* OPP **unbearable**

beard 🔑 /bɪəd; *NAmE* bɪrd/ *noun, verb*

■ ***noun*** 🔑 [C, U] hair that grows on the chin and cheeks of a man's face; similar hair that grows on some animals: *He has decided to grow a beard and a moustache.* ◇ *a week's growth of beard* ◇ *a goat's beard* ➲ COLLOCATIONS at PHYSICAL ➲ VISUAL VOCAB page V49 ➲ compare MOUSTACHE ▸ **beard·ed** *adj.*: *a* ***bearded face/man***

■ ***verb***

IDM **to beard the lion in his ˈden** to go to see an important or powerful person to tell them that you disagree with them, that you want sth, etc.

beardie /ˈbɪədi; *NAmE* ˈbɪrdi/ *noun* (*BrE, informal, disapproving*) a man with a beard

bear·er /ˈbeərə(r); *NAmE* ˈber-/ *noun* **1** a person whose job it is to carry sth, especially at a ceremony: *coffin bearers* ➲ see also PALL-BEARER, RING BEARER, STANDARD-BEARER, STRETCHER-BEARER **2** a person who brings a message, a letter, etc: *I'm sorry to be the bearer of bad news.* **3** (*formal*) a person who has sth with them or is the official owner of sth, such as a document: *A pass will allow the bearer to enter the building.* **4** a person who has knowledge of sth, such as an idea or a tradition, and makes sure that it is not forgotten, by teaching others about it

ˈbear hug *noun* an act of showing affection for sb by holding them very tightly and strongly in your arms

bear·ing /ˈbeərɪŋ; *NAmE* ˈber-/ *noun* **1** [U] **~ on sth** the way in which sth is related to sth or influences it: *Recent events had no bearing on our decision.* ◇ *Regular exercise has a direct bearing on fitness and health.* **2** [sing.] the way in which you stand, walk or behave: *Her whole bearing was alert.* **3** [C] (*technical*) a direction measured from a fixed point using a COMPASS **4** [C] (*technical*) a part of a machine that supports a moving part, especially one that is turning ➲ see also BALL BEARING

IDM **get/find/take your ˈbearings** to make yourself familiar with your surroundings in order to find out where you are or to feel comfortable in a place **lose your ˈbearings** to become lost or confused

bear·ish /ˈbeərɪʃ; *NAmE* ˈber-/ *adj.* (*finance*) showing or expecting a fall in the prices of shares: *a bearish market* ◇ *Japanese banks remain bearish.* ➲ compare BULLISH

B

ˈ**bear market** *noun* (*finance*) a period during which people are selling shares, etc. rather than buying, because they expect the prices to fall ➲ compare BULL MARKET

bear·skin /ˈbeəskɪn; *NAmE* ˈbers-/ *noun* **1** the skin and fur of a BEAR: *a bearskin rug* **2** a tall hat of black fur worn for special ceremonies by some British soldiers

beast /biːst/ *noun* **1** (*old-fashioned* or *formal*) an animal, especially one that is large or dangerous, or one that is unusual: ***wild/savage/ferocious beasts*** ◇ ***mythical beasts*** *such as unicorns and dragons* **2** a person who is cruel and whose behaviour is uncontrolled SYN **animal 3** (*informal*, often *humorous*) an unpleasant person or thing: *The maths exam was a real beast.* **4** (*informal*) a thing of a particular kind SYN **animal**: *His new guitar is a very expensive beast.*

beast·ly /ˈbiːstli/ *adj.* (*old-fashioned, BrE, informal*) unpleasant SYN **horrible, nasty** ▸ **beast·li·ness** *noun* [U]

ˌ**beast of ˈburden** *noun* an animal used for heavy work such as carrying or pulling things

Synonyms

beat

batter • pound • lash • hammer

These words all mean to hit sb/sth many times, especially hard.

beat to hit sb/sth a lot of times, especially very hard: *Someone was beating at the door.* ◇ *A young man was found beaten to death last night.* ◇ *At that time, children were often beaten for quite minor offences* (= as a punishment).

batter to hit sb/sth hard a lot of times, especially in way that causes serious damage: *He had been badly battered around the head and face.* ◇ *Severe winds have been battering the coast.*

pound to hit sb/sth hard a lot of times, especially in a way that makes a lot of noise: *Heavy rain pounded on the roof.*

lash to hit sb/sth with a lot of force: *The rain lashed at the window.* NOTE The subject of **lash** is often *rain, wind, hail, sea* or *waves*.

hammer to hit sb/sth hard a lot of times, in a way that is noisy or violent: *He hammered the door with his fists.*

POUND OR HAMMER?

There is not much difference in meaning between these two, but to **pound** is sometimes a steadier action. To **hammer** can be more violent and it is often used figuratively.

PATTERNS

- to beat/batter/pound/lash/hammer sb/sth **with** sth
- to beat/batter/pound/lash/hammer **against** sth
- to beat/batter/pound/hammer **on** sth
- to beat/batter/hammer sth **down**
- the **rain/wind/sea** beats/batters/pounds/lashes (at) sth

beat 0‑ˉ /biːt/ *verb, noun, adj.*

■ ***verb*** (**beat, beaten** /ˈbiːtn/)

▸ IN GAME **1** 0‑ˉ [T] **~ sb (at sth)** to defeat sb in a game or competition: *He beat me at chess.* ◇ *Their recent wins have proved they're still* ***the ones to beat*** (= the most difficult team to beat).

▸ CONTROL **2** 0‑ˉ [T] **~ sth** (*informal*) to get control of sth SYN **defeat**: *The government's main aim is to beat inflation.*

▸ BE TOO DIFFICULT **3** 0‑ˉ [T] (*informal*) to be too difficult for sb SYN **defeat**: **~ sb** *a problem that beats even the experts* ◇ **~ sb why, how, etc...** ***It beats me*** (= I don't know) *why he did it.* ◇ ***What beats me*** *is how it was done so quickly* (= I don't understand how).

▸ BE BETTER **4** 0‑ˉ [T] **~ sth** (rather *informal*) to do or be better than sth: ***Nothing beats*** *home cooking.* ◇ ***You can't beat*** *Italian shoes.* ◇ *They want to* ***beat the*** *speed* ***record*** (= go faster than anyone before).

▸ AVOID **5** [T] **~ sth** (*informal*) to avoid sth: *If we go early we should beat the traffic.* ◇ *We were up and off early to* ***beat the heat***.

▸ HIT **6** 0‑ˉ [I, T] to hit sb/sth many times, usually very hard: **+ adv./prep.** *Somebody was beating at the door.* ◇ *Hailstones beat against the window.* ◇ **~ sth** *Someone was beating a drum.* ◇ **~ sth + adv./prep.** *She was beating dust out of the carpet* (= removing dust from the carpet by beating it). ◇ **~ sb** *At that time children were regularly beaten for quite minor offences* (= a punishment). ◇ **~ sb + adv./prep.** *An elderly man was found* ***beaten to death***. ◇ **~ sb + adj.** *They beat him unconscious* (= hit him until he became unconscious).

▸ OF HEART/DRUMS/WINGS **7** 0‑ˉ [I, T] to make, or cause sth to make, a regular sound or movement: *She's alive—her* ***heart is still beating***. ◇ *We heard the* ***drums beating***. ◇ *The bird was* ***beating its wings*** (= moving them up and down) *frantically.*

▸ MIX **8** 0‑ˉ [T] to mix sth with short quick movements with a fork, etc: **~ sth (up)** *Beat the eggs up to a frothy consistency.* ◇ **~ A and B together** *Beat the flour and milk together.*

▸ SHAPE METAL **9** [T] to change the shape of sth, especially metal, by hitting it with a hammer, etc: **~ sth (out) (into sth)** *beaten silver* ◇ *The gold is beaten out into thin strips.* ◇ **~ sth + adj.** *The metal had been beaten flat.*

▸ MAKE PATH **10** [T] **~ sth (through, across, along, etc. sth)** to make a path, etc. by walking somewhere or by pressing branches down and walking over them: *a well-beaten track* (= one that has been worn hard by much use) ◇ *The hunters beat a path through the undergrowth.*

IDM **beat about the ˈbush** (*BrE*) (*NAmE* **beat around the ˈbush**) to talk about sth for a long time without coming to the main point: *Stop beating about the bush and tell me what you want.* **beat sb at their own ˈgame** to defeat or do better than sb in an activity which they have chosen or in which they think they are strong **beat your ˈbrains out** (*informal, especially NAmE*) to think very hard about sth for a long time **beat your ˈbreast** to show that you feel sorry about sth that you have done, especially in public and in an exaggerated way **beat the ˈclock** to finish a task, race, etc. before a particular time ˈ**beat it** (*slang*) (usually used in orders) to go away immediately: *This is private land, so beat it!* **beat a path to sb's ˈdoor** if a lot of people **beat a path to sb's door**, they are all interested in sth that person has to sell, or can do or tell them: *Top theatrical agents are beating a path to the teenager's door.* **beat the ˈrap** (*NAmE, slang*) to escape without being punished **beat a (hasty) reˈtreat** to go away or back quickly, especially to avoid sth unpleasant **beat ˈtime (to sth)** to mark or follow the rhythm of music, by waving a stick, tapping your foot, etc: *She beat time with her fingers.* **beat sb to the ˈpunch** (*informal*) to get or do sth before sb else can **can you beat that/it!** (*informal*) used to express surprise or anger **if you can't beat them, ˈjoin them** (*saying*) if you cannot defeat sb or be as successful as they are, then it is more sensible to join them in what they are doing and perhaps get some advantage for yourself by doing so ˌ**off the** ˌ**beaten ˈtrack** far away from other people, houses, etc: *They live miles off the beaten track.* **a rod/stick to ˈbeat sb with** a fact, an argument, etc. that is used in order to blame or punish sb **take some ˈbeating** to be difficult to beat: *That score is going to take some beating.* ◇ *For sheer luxury, this hotel takes some beating.* ➲ more at BLACK *adj.*, DAYLIGHTS, DRUM *n.*, HELL

PHR V ˌ**beat sth↔ˈdown** to hit a door, etc. many times until it breaks open ˌ**beat ˈdown (on sb/sth)** if the sun **beats down** it shines with great heat ˌ**beat sb/sth ˈdown (to sth)** to persuade sb to reduce the price at which they are selling sth: *He wanted $8 000 for the car but I beat him down to $6 000.* ◇ *I beat down the price to $6 000.* ˌ**beat ˈoff** (*NAmE, taboo, slang*) to MASTURBATE ˌ**beat sb/sth↔ˈoff** to force sb/sth back or away by fighting: *The attacker was beaten off.* ◇ *She beat off a challenge to her leadership.* ˈ**beat on sb** = BEAT UP ON SB ˌ**beat sth↔ˈout 1** to produce a rhythm by hitting sth many times **2** to put a fire out by beating: *We beat the flames out.* **3** to remove sth by hitting it with a HAMMER, etc: *They can beat out the dent in the* *car's wing.* ˌ**beat sth ˈout of sb** to hit sb until they tell you what you want to know ˈ**beat sb out of sth** (*NAmE, informal*) to cheat sb by taking sth from them: *Her brother beat her out of $200.* ˈ**beat sb to sth/...** | ˌ**beat sb ˈto it** to get somewhere or do sth before sb else: *She beat me to the top of the hill.* ◇ *I was about to take the last cake, but he beat me to it.* ˌ**beat sb↔ˈup** 🔑 to hit or kick sb hard, many times: *He was badly beaten up by a gang of thugs.* ˌ**beat ˈup on sb** (also ˈ**beat on sb**) (*NAmE*) to blame sb too much for sth: *Don't beat up on Paul, he tried his best.* ˌ**beat yourself ˈup (about/over sth)** (also ˌ**beat ˈup on yourself (about/over sth)**) (*NAmE, informal*) to blame yourself too much for sth: *Look, there's no need to beat yourself up over this.*

■ ***noun***

▸ OF DRUMS/HEART/WINGS **1** 🔑 [C] a single blow to sth, such as a drum, or a movement of sth, such as your heart; the sound that this makes: *several loud beats on the drum* ◇ (*figurative*) *His heart missed a beat when he saw her.* **2** 🔑 [sing.] a series of regular blows to sth, such as a drum; the sound that this makes: *the steady beat of the drums* ➲ see also HEARTBEAT

▸ RHYTHM **3** 🔑 [C] the main rhythm, or a unit of rhythm, in a piece of music, a poem, etc: *This type of music has a strong beat to it.* ◇ *The piece has four beats to the bar.*

▸ OF POLICE OFFICER **4** [C, usually sing.] the area that a police officer walks around regularly and which he or she is responsible for: *More police officers out* ***on the beat*** *may help to cut crime.* IDM see HEART, MARCH, WALK *v.*

■ ***adj.*** [not before noun] (*informal*) = DEAD BEAT

beat·box /ˈbiːtbɒks; *NAmE* -bɑːks/ *noun, verb*

■ ***noun* 1** [C] (*informal*) an electronic machine that produces drum sounds **2** [C] (*informal*) a radio, CD player, etc. that can be carried around and is used for playing loud music **3** (also **beat·boxer**) [C] a person who uses the voice to make sounds in HIP HOP **4** [U] music that is created using sounds made with the human voice

■ ***verb*** [I] to imitate the sound of a drum with the voice

beat·box·ing /ˈbiːtbɒksɪŋ; *NAmE* -bɑːks-/ *noun* [U] the use of the human voice to create the beat in HIP HOP: *an amazing beatboxing performance*

ˌ**beaten-ˈup** *adj.* = BEAT-UP

beat·er /ˈbiːtə(r)/ *noun* **1** (often in compounds) a tool used for beating things: *a carpet beater* ◇ *an egg beater* **2** a person employed to drive birds and animals out of bushes, etc, into the open, so they can be shot for sport **3 -beater** (in compounds) a person who hits someone: *a wife-beater* **4** (*NAmE*) (*BrE* **bang·er**) (*informal*) an old car that is in bad condition ➲ see also WORLD-BEATER

the ˈbeat generation *noun* [sing.] a group of young people in the 1950s and early 1960s who rejected the way most people lived in society, wanted to express themselves freely, and liked modern JAZZ

bea·tif·ic /ˌbiːəˈtɪfɪk/ *adj.* (*formal*) showing great joy and peace: *a* ***beatific smile/expression***

be·atify /biˈætɪfaɪ/ *verb* (**be·ati·fies, be·ati·fy·ing, be·ati·fied, be·ati·fied**) **~ sb** (of the Pope) to give a dead person a special honour by stating officially that he/she is very holy ➲ compare BLESS, CANONIZE ▸ **be·ati·fi·ca·tion** /biˌætɪfɪˈkeɪʃn/ *noun* [C, U]

beat·ing /ˈbiːtɪŋ/ *noun* **1** [C] an act of hitting sb hard and repeatedly, as a punishment or in a fight: *to give sb a beating* **2** [C] (*informal*) a very heavy defeat: *The team has* ***taken*** *a few* ***beatings*** *this season.* **3** [U] a series of regular blows to sth such as a drum, or movements of sth, such as your heart; the sound that this makes: *He could hear the beating of his own heart.* ◇ *the* ***beating of drums/wings***

IDM **take some ˈbeating** (*BrE*) to be difficult to do or be better than: *As a place to live, Oxford takes some beating.*

be·ati·tude /biˈætɪtjuːd; *NAmE* -tuːd/ *noun* **the Beati·tudes** [pl.] (in the Bible) the eight statements made by Christ about people who are BLESSED

beat·nik /ˈbiːtnɪk/ *noun* a young person in the 1950s and early 1960s who rejected the way of life of ordinary society and showed this by behaving and dressing in a different way from most people

ˌ**beat-ˈup** (also ˌ**beaten-ˈup**) *adj.* [usually before noun] (*informal*) old and damaged: *a beat-up old truck*

beau /bəʊ; *NAmE* boʊ/ *noun* (*pl.* **beaux** or **beaus** /bəʊz; *NAmE* boʊz/) (*old-fashioned*) a woman's male lover or friend

beau·coup /ˈbəʊkuː; *NAmE* ˈboʊ-/ *det.* (*US, informal*, from *French*) many or a lot: *You can spend beaucoup bucks* (= a lot of money) *on software.*

the Beau·fort scale /ˈbəʊfət skeɪl; *NAmE* ˈboʊfərt/ *noun* [sing.] a range of numbers used for measuring how strongly the wind is blowing. The lowest number 0 means that there is no wind and the highest number 12 means that there is a HURRICANE (= a violent storm with very strong winds): *The storm measured 10* ***on the Beaufort scale.*** ORIGIN From Sir Francis Beaufort, the English admiral who invented it.

Beau·jo·lais /ˈbəʊʒəleɪ; *NAmE* ˌboʊʒəˈleɪ/ *noun* (*pl.* **Beau·jo·lais**) [C, U] a light wine, usually red, from the Beaujolais district of France

beaut /bjuːt/ *noun, adj., exclamation*

■ ***noun*** (*NAmE, AustralE, NZE, informal*) an excellent or beautiful person or thing

■ ***adj., exclamation*** (*AustralE, informal*) excellent; very good

beaut·eous /ˈbjuːtiəs/ *adj.* (*literary*) beautiful

beaut·ician /bjuːˈtɪʃn/ *noun* a person, usually a woman, whose job is to give beauty treatments to the face and body

beau·ti·ful 🔑 /ˈbjuːtɪfl/ *adj.*

1 🔑 having beauty; pleasing to the senses or to the mind: *a beautiful woman/face/baby/voice/poem/smell/evening* ◇ *beautiful countryside/weather/music* **2** 🔑 very good or skilful: *What beautiful timing!*

beau·ti·ful·ly 🔑 /ˈbjuːtɪfli/ *adv.*

1 🔑 in a beautiful way: *She sings beautifully.* ◇ *a beautifully decorated house* **2** 🔑 very well; in a pleasing way: *It's all working out beautifully.*

beaut·ify /ˈbjuːtɪfaɪ/ *verb* (**beau·ti·fies, beau·ti·fy·ing, beau·ti·fied, beau·ti·fied**) **~ sb/sth** to make sb/sth beautiful or more beautiful

beauty 🔑 /ˈbjuːti/ *noun* (*pl.* -ies)

1 🔑 [U] the quality of being pleasing to the senses or to the mind: *the* ***beauty of*** *the sunset/of poetry/of his singing* ◇ *a woman of great beauty* ◇ *The woods were designated an* ***area of outstanding natural beauty.*** ◇ ***beauty products/treatment*** (= intended to make a person more beautiful) **2** [C] a person or thing that is beautiful: *She had been a beauty in her day.* **3** [C] an excellent example of its type: *That last goal was a beauty!* **4** [C] a pleasing feature SYN **advantage**: *One of the beauties of living here is that it's so peaceful.* ◇ *The project will require very little work to start up;* ***that's the beauty of it.***

IDM **beauty is in the eye of the ˈbeholder** (*saying*) people all have different ideas about what is beautiful **beauty is only skin-ˈdeep** (*saying*) how a person looks is less important than their character

ˌ**Beauty and the ˈBeast** *noun* **1** a traditional story about a young girl who saves a large ugly creature from a magic SPELL by her love. He becomes a HANDSOME prince and they get married. **2** (*informal, humorous*) two people of whom one is much more attractive than the other

ˈ**beauty contest** *noun* (*BrE*) **1** a competition to choose the most beautiful from a group of women ➲ compare PAGEANT **2** (*US* ˌ**beauty paˈrade**) an occasion on which several competing companies or people try to persuade sb to use their services

ˈ**beauty mark** *noun* (*NAmE*) = BEAUTY SPOT

ˈ**beauty queen** *noun* a woman who is judged to be the most beautiful in a BEAUTY CONTEST

ˈ**beauty salon** (also ˈ**beauty parlour**) (*US* also ˈ**beauty shop**) *noun* a place where you can pay for treatment to your face, hair, nails, etc, which is intended to make you more beautiful

B

Synonyms

beautiful

pretty • handsome • attractive • lovely • good-looking • gorgeous

These words all describe people who are pleasant to look at.

beautiful (especially of a woman or girl) very pleasant to look at: *She looked stunningly beautiful that night.*

pretty (especially of a girl or woman) pleasant to look at: *She's got a very pretty face.* NOTE **Pretty** is used most often to talk about girls. When it is used to talk about a woman, it usually suggests that she is like a girl, with small, delicate features.

handsome (of a man) pleasant to look at; (of a woman) pleasant to look at, with large strong features rather than small delicate ones: *He was described as* ***'tall, dark and handsome'****.*

attractive (of a person) pleasant to look at, especially in a sexual way: *She's a very attractive woman.*

lovely (of a person) beautiful; very attractive: *She looked particularly lovely that night.* NOTE When you describe sb as **lovely**, you are usually showing that you also have a strong feeling of affection for them.

good-looking (of a person) pleasant to look at, often in a sexual way: *She arrived with a very good-looking man.*

gorgeous (*informal*) (of a person) extremely attractive, especially in a sexual way: *You look gorgeous!*

ATTRACTIVE OR GOOD-LOOKING?

If you describe sb as **attractive** you often also mean that they have a pleasant personality as well as being pleasant to look at; **good-looking** just describes sb's physical appearance.

PATTERNS

- a(n) beautiful/pretty/handsome/attractive/lovely/good-looking/gorgeous **girl/woman**
- a(n) beautiful/handsome/attractive/good-looking/gorgeous **boy/man**
- a(n) beautiful/pretty/handsome/attractive/lovely/good-looking **face**

ˈbeauty school *noun* (*NAmE*) a place that trains people to cut hair, take care of nails, etc. as a job

ˈbeauty sleep *noun* [U] (*humorous*) enough sleep at night to make sure that you look and feel healthy and beautiful

ˈbeauty spot *noun* **1** (*BrE*) a place in the countryside which is famous because it is beautiful **2** (*NAmE* also **ˈbeauty mark**) a small dark spot on a woman's face, which used to be thought to make her more beautiful

beaux *pl.* of BEAU

bea·ver /ˈbiːvə(r)/ *noun, verb*

■ ***noun*** **1** [C] an animal with a wide flat tail and strong teeth. Beavers live in water and on land and can build DAMS (= barriers across rivers), made of pieces of wood and mud. It is an official symbol of Canada. ➲ **VISUAL VOCAB** page V10 ➲ see also EAGER BEAVER **2** [U] the fur of the beaver, used in making hats and clothes **3** [C] (*taboo, slang, especially NAmE*) the area around a woman's sex organs

■ ***verb***

PHR V **ˌbeaver aˈway (at sth)** (*informal*) to work very hard at sth: *He's been beavering away at the accounts all morning.*

bebop /ˈbiːbɒp; *NAmE* -bɑːp/ (also **bop**) *noun* [U] a type of JAZZ with complicated rhythms

BEC /bek/ *abbr.* Business English Certificate (British tests, set by the University of Cambridge, in English as a foreign language for students who are preparing for a career in business)

be·calmed /bɪˈkɑːmd/ *adj.* (of a ship with a sail) unable to move because there is no wind

be·came *past tense* of BECOME

be·cause 0‑ /bɪˈkɒz; -ˈkəz; *NAmE* -ˈkɔːz; -ˈkʌz/ *conj.* for the reason that: *I did it because he told me to.* ◇ *Just because I don't complain, people think I'm satisfied.* ▸ **because of** 0‑ *prep.*: *They are here because of us.* ◇ *He walked slowly because of his bad leg.* ◇ *Because of his wife ('s) being there, I said nothing about it.*

Language Bank

because of

Explaining reasons

- The number of people with diabetes is growing, partly **because of** an increase in levels of obesity.
- The number of overweight children has increased dramatically in recent years, largely **as a result of** changes in diet and lifestyle.
- The increase in childhood obesity is largely **due to/the result of** changes in lifestyle and diet over the last twenty years.
- Many obese children are bullied at school **on account of** their weight.
- Part of the problem with treating childhood obesity **stems from** the fact that parents do not always recognize that their children are obese.
- Childhood obesity may be **caused by** genetic factors, as well as environmental ones.

➲ Language Banks at CAUSE, CONSEQUENTLY, THEREFORE

béch·amel /ˈbeɪʃəmel/ (also **ˌbéchamel ˈsauce**) *noun* [U] a thick sauce made with milk, flour and butter SYN **white sauce**

beck /bek/ *noun* (*BrE, dialect*) a small river SYN **stream**

IDM **at sb's ˌbeck and ˈcall** always ready to obey sb's orders: *Don't expect to have me at your beck and call.*

beckon /ˈbekən/ *verb* **1** [I, T] to give sb a signal using your finger or hand, especially to tell them to move nearer or to follow you SYN **signal**: **~ to sb** (**to do sth**) *He beckoned to the waiter to bring the bill.* ◇ **~ sb** (**+ adv./prep.**) *He beckoned her over with a wave.* ◇ *The boss beckoned him into her office.* ◇ **~ sb to do sth** *She beckoned him to come and join them.* **2** [I, T] to appear very attractive to sb: *The clear blue sea beckoned.* ◇ **~ sb** *The prospect of a month without work was beckoning her.* **3** [I] to be sth that is likely to happen or will possibly happen to sb in the future: *For many kids leaving college the prospect of unemployment beckons.*

Synonyms

become / get / go / turn

These verbs are used frequently with the following adjectives:

become ~	get ~	go ~	turn ~
involved	used to	wrong	blue
clear	better	right	sour
accustomed	worse	bad	bad
pregnant	pregnant	white	red
extinct	tired	crazy	cold
famous	angry	bald	
ill	dark	blind	

- **Become** is more formal than **get**. Both describe changes in people's emotional or physical state, or natural or social changes.
- **Go** is usually used for negative changes.
- **Go** and **turn** are both used for changes of colour.
- **Turn** is also used for changes in the weather.

be·come 0-w /bɪˈkʌm/ *verb* (**be·came** /bɪˈkeɪm/, **be·come**)
1 0-w *linking verb* to start to be sth: **+ adj.** *It was becoming more and more difficult to live on his salary.* ◇ *It soon became apparent that no one was going to come.* ◇ *She was becoming confused.* ◇ **+ noun** *She became queen in 1952.* ◇ *The bill will become law next year.* **2** [T, no passive] (not used in the progressive tenses) **~ sb** (*formal*) to be suitable for sb: *Such behaviour did not become her.* **3** [T, no passive] (not used in the progressive tenses) **~ sb** (*formal*) to look attractive on sb SYN **suit**: *Short hair really becomes you.*
IDM **what became, has become, will become of sb/sth?** used to ask what has happened or what will happen to sb/sth: *What became of that student who used to live with you?* ◇ *I dread to think what will become of them if they lose their home.*

be·com·ing /bɪˈkʌmɪŋ/ *adj.* (*formal*) **1** (of clothes, etc.) making the person wearing them look more attractive SYN **flattering** **2** suitable or appropriate for sb or their situation SYN **fitting**: *It was not very becoming behaviour for a teacher.* OPP **unbecoming**

bec·que·rel /ˈbekərel/ *noun* (*abbr.* **Bq**) (*physics*) a unit for measuring RADIOACTIVITY

BEd (also **B.Ed.** especially in *NAmE*) /ˌbiː ˈed/ *noun* the abbreviation for 'Bachelor of Education' (a first university degree in education): (*BrE*) *Sarah Wells BEd*

bed 0-w /bed/ *noun, verb*
■ ***noun***
▸ FURNITURE **1** 0-w [C, U] a piece of furniture for sleeping on: *a* ***single/double bed*** ◇ *She lay* ***on the bed*** (= on top of the covers). ◇ *He lay* ***in bed*** (= under the covers). ◇ *I'm tired—I'm* ***going to bed.*** ◇ *It's* ***time for bed*** (= time to go to sleep). ◇ *I'll just* ***put*** *the kids* ***to bed.*** ◇ *He likes to have a mug of cocoa before bed* (= before going to bed). ◇ *to* ***get into/out of bed*** ◇ *to* ***make the bed*** (= arrange the covers in a tidy way) ◇ *Could you give me a bed for the night* (= somewhere to sleep)? ◇ *There's a shortage of hospital beds* (= not enough room for patients to be admitted). ◇ *He has been* ***confined to bed*** *with flu for the past couple of days.* ➲ VISUAL VOCAB page V20 ➲ see also AIRBED, CAMP BED, SOFA BED, TWIN BED, WATERBED
▸ OF RIVER/LAKE/SEA **2** 0-w [C] the bottom of a river, the sea, etc: *the ocean bed* ◇ *oyster beds* (= an area in the sea where there are many OYSTERS)
▸ FOR FLOWERS/VEGETABLES **3** [C] an area of ground in a garden/yard or park for growing flowers, vegetables, etc: *flower beds* ➲ see also SEEDBED
▸ BOTTOM LAYER **4** [C] **~ of sth** a layer of sth that other things lie or rest on: *grilled chicken, served on a bed of rice* ◇ *The blocks should be laid on a bed of concrete.*
▸ GEOLOGY **5** [C] a layer of CLAY, rock, etc. in the ground ➲ see also BEDROCK
IDM **(not) a bed of ˈroses** (not) an easy or a pleasant situation: *Their life together hasn't exactly been a bed of roses.* **get out of bed on the wrong side** (*BrE*) (*NAmE* **get up on the wrong side of the bed**) to be bad-tempered for the whole day for no particular reason **go to bed with sb** (*informal*) to have sex with sb **in bed** used to refer to sexual activity: *What's he like in bed?* ◇ *I caught them in bed together* (= having sex). **you've made your bed and you must ˈlie in/on it** (*saying*) you must accept the results of your actions **take to your ˈbed** to go to bed and stay there because you are ill/sick ➲ more at DIE *v.*, WET *v.*
■ ***verb*** (-dd-) **1 ~ sth (in sth)** to fix sth firmly in sth: *The bricks were bedded in sand to improve drainage.* ◇ *Make sure that you bed the roots firmly in the soil.* **2 ~ sb** (*old-fashioned*) to have sex with sb
PHR V **ˌbed ˈdown** to sleep in a place where you do not usually sleep: *You have my room and I'll bed down in the living room.*

ˌbed and ˈboard *noun* [U] (*BrE*) a room to sleep in and food

ˌbed and ˈbreakfast *noun* (*abbr.* **B and B, B & B**) **1** [U] (*BrE*) a service that provides a room to sleep in and a meal the next morning in private houses and small hotels: *Do you do bed and breakfast?* ◇ *Bed and breakfast costs £50 a night.* ➲ compare EUROPEAN PLAN, FULL BOARD, HALF BOARD **2** [C] a place that provides this service: *There were several good bed and breakfasts in the area.*

be·dazzle /bɪˈdæzl/ *verb* [usually passive] **~ sb** to impress sb very much with intelligence, beauty, etc: *He was so bedazzled by her looks that he couldn't speak.* ▸ **be·dazzle·ment** /bɪˈdæzlmənt/ *noun* [U]

bed·bug /ˈbedbʌɡ/ *noun* a small flat insect that lives especially in beds, where it bites people and sucks their blood

bed·cham·ber /ˈbedtʃeɪmbə(r)/ *noun* (*old use*) a bedroom: *the royal bedchamber*

bed·clothes /ˈbedkləʊðz; *NAmE* -kloʊðz/ (*BrE* also **bedcovers**) *noun* [pl.] the sheets and other covers that you put on a bed

bed·cover /ˈbedkʌvə(r)/ *noun* (*BrE*) **1** = BEDSPREAD **2 bedcovers** = BEDCLOTHES

bed·ding /ˈbedɪŋ/ *noun* [U] **1** the sheets and covers that you put on a bed, often also the MATTRESS and the PILLOWS ➲ VISUAL VOCAB page V20 **2** STRAW, etc. for animals to sleep on

ˈbedding plant *noun* a plant that is planted out in a garden bed, usually just before it gets flowers. It usually grows and dies within one year.

beddy-byes /ˈbedi baɪz/ (*BrE*) (*NAmE* **ˈbeddy-bye**) *noun* [U] a child's word for bed, used when talking about the time sb goes to bed: *Time for beddy-byes.*

be·deck /bɪˈdek/ *verb* [usually passive] **~ sth/sb (with/in sth)** (*literary*) to decorate sth/sb with flowers, flags, PRECIOUS STONES, etc.

be·devil /bɪˈdevl/ *verb* (-ll-, *especially US* -l-) **~ sb/sth** (*formal*) to cause a lot of problems for sb/sth over a long period of time SYN **beset**: *The expedition was bedevilled by bad weather.*

bed·fel·low /ˈbedfeləʊ; *NAmE* -feloʊ/ *noun* a person or thing that is connected with or related to another, often in a way that you would not expect: ***strange/unlikely bedfellows***

bed·head /ˈbedhed/ *noun* the part of the bed that is at the end, behind the head of the person sleeping on it

bed·jacket /ˈbeddʒækɪt/ *noun* a short jacket worn when sitting up in bed

bed·lam /ˈbedləm/ *noun* [U] a scene full of noise and confusion SYN **chaos**: ***It was bedlam*** *at our house on the morning of the wedding.*

bed·linen /ˈbedlɪnɪn/ *noun* [U] sheets and PILLOWCASES for a bed

Bed·ouin /ˈbedʊɪn/ *noun* (*pl.* **Bed·ouin**) a member of an Arab people that traditionally lives in tents in the desert

bed·pan /ˈbedpæn/ *noun* a container used as a toilet by a person who is too ill/sick to get out of bed

bed·post /ˈbedpəʊst; *NAmE* -poʊst/ *noun* one of the four vertical supports at the corners of a bed (especially an old type of bed with a wooden or metal frame) ➲ VISUAL VOCAB page V20

be·drag·gled /bɪˈdræɡld/ *adj.* made wet, dirty or untidy by rain, mud, etc: ***bedraggled hair/clothes***

bed·rid·den /ˈbedrɪdn/ *adj.* having to stay in bed all the time because you are sick, injured or old

bed·rock /ˈbedrɒk; *NAmE* -rɑːk/ *noun* **1** [sing.] a strong base for sth, especially the facts or the principles on which it is based: *The poor suburbs traditionally* ***formed the bedrock of*** *the party's support.* ◇ *Honesty is the bedrock of any healthy relationship.* **2** [U] the solid rock in the ground below the loose soil and sand

bed·roll /ˈbedrəʊl; *NAmE* -roʊl/ *noun* (*especially NAmE*) a thick piece of material or a SLEEPING BAG that you can roll up for carrying and use for sleeping on or in, for example when you are camping

bed·room 0-w /ˈbedruːm; -rʊm/ *noun, adj.*
■ ***noun*** **1** 0-w a room for sleeping in: *the spare bedroom* ◇ *a*

hotel with 20 bedrooms ◇ *This is the* ***master bedroom*** (= the main bedroom of the house). **2 -bedroomed** having the number of bedrooms mentioned: *a three-bedroomed house*
■ ***adj.*** [only before noun] used as a way of referring to sexual activity: *the bedroom scenes in the movie*

ˈbedroom community (also **ˈbedroom suburb**) (both *NAmE*) (*BrE* **ˈdormitory town**) *noun* a town that people live in and from where they travel to work in a bigger town or city

bed·side /ˈbedsaɪd/ *noun* [usually sing.] the area beside a bed: *His mother has been* ***at his bedside*** *throughout his illness.* ◇ *a bedside lamp*

ˌbedside ˈmanner *noun* [sing.] the way in which a doctor or other person talks to sb who is ill/sick

ˌbedside ˈtable (*especially BrE*) (*NAmE* usually **night·stand**, **ˈnight table**) *noun* a small table beside a bed ➲ VISUAL VOCAB page V20

bed·sit /ˈbedsɪt/ (also **bed·sit·ter** /ˈbedsɪtə(r)/) (also *formal* **ˌbedˈsitting room**) *noun* (all *BrE*) a room that a person rents and uses for both living and sleeping in ➲ COLLOCATIONS at HOUSE

bed·sore /ˈbedsɔː(r)/ *noun* a painful and sometimes infected place on a person's skin, caused by lying in bed for a long time

bed·spread /ˈbedspred/ (*BrE* also **bed·cover**) (*NAmE* also **spread**) *noun* an attractive cover put on top of all the sheets and covers on a bed ➲ VISUAL VOCAB page V20

bed·stead /ˈbedsted/ *noun* the wooden or metal frame of an old-fashioned type of bed

bed·time /ˈbedtaɪm/ *noun* [U] the time when sb usually goes to bed: *It's way past your bedtime.* ◇ *Will you read me a bedtime story?*

ˈbed-wetting *noun* [U] the problem of URINATING in bed, usually by children while they are asleep

bee /biː/ *noun* **1** a black and yellow flying insect that can sting. Bees live in large groups and make HONEY (= a sweet sticky substance that is good to eat): *a swarm of bees* ◇ *a bee sting* ◇ *Bees were buzzing in the clover.* ➲ see also BEEHIVE, BEESWAX, BUMBLEBEE, QUEEN BEE **2** (*NAmE*) a meeting in a group where people combine work, competition and pleasure: *a sewing bee* ➲ see also SPELLING BEE
IDM **the ˌbee's ˈknees** (*informal*) an excellent person or thing: *She thinks she's the bee's knees* (= she has a very high opinion of herself). **have a ˈbee in your bonnet (about sth)** (*informal*) to think or talk about sth all the time and to think that it is very important ➲ more at BIRD, BUSY *adj.*

the Beeb /biːb/ *noun* [sing.] an informal name for the BBC

beech /biːtʃ/ *noun* **1** [U, C] (also **ˈbeech tree** [C]) a tall forest tree with smooth grey BARK, shiny leaves and small nuts: *forests planted with beech* ◇ *beech hedges* ◇ *The great beeches towered up towards the sky.* ➲ VISUAL VOCAB page V8 ➲ see also COPPER BEECH **2** (also **ˈbeech·wood** /ˈbiːtʃwʊd/) [U] the wood of the beech tree

beef 0-π /biːf/ *noun, verb*
■ ***noun*** **1** 0-π [U] meat that comes from a cow: ***roast/minced beef*** ◇ *beef and dairy cattle* ➲ see also CORNED BEEF **2** [C] (*informal*) a complaint: *What's his latest beef?*
■ ***verb*** [I] **~ (about sb/sth)** (*informal*) to complain a lot about sb/sth
PHR V **ˌbeef sth↔ˈup** (*informal*) to make sth bigger, better, more interesting, etc.

beef·bur·ger /ˈbiːfbɜːɡə(r); *NAmE* -bɜːrɡ-/ *noun* (*BrE*) = HAMBURGER

beef·cake /ˈbiːfkeɪk/ *noun* [U] (*slang*) attractive men with big muscles, especially those that appear in magazines

beef·eater /ˈbiːfiːtə(r)/ *noun* a guard who dresses in a traditional uniform at the Tower of London

beef·steak /ˈbiːfsteɪk/ *noun* [C, U] = STEAK

ˌbeef ˈtea *noun* [U] (*BrE*) a hot drink made by boiling beef in water. It used to be given to people who were sick.

ˌbeef toˈmato (also **ˌbeefsteak toˈmato** especially in *NAmE*) *noun* a type of large tomato

beefy /ˈbiːfi/ *adj.* (**beef·ier, beefi·est**) (*informal*) (of a person or their body) big or fat: ***beefy men/arms/thighs***

bee·hive /ˈbiːhaɪv/ *noun* **1** = HIVE **2** a HAIRSTYLE for women, with the hair piled high on top of the head

ˈbee-keeper *noun* a person who owns and takes care of BEES ▸ **ˈbee-keeping** *noun* [U]

bee·line /ˈbiːlaɪn/ *noun*
IDM **make a ˈbeeline for sth/sb** (*informal*) to go straight towards sth/sb as quickly as you can

Be·el·ze·bub /bɪˈelzɪbʌb/ *noun* a name for the DEVIL

been /biːn; bɪn; *NAmE* bɪn/ ➲ BE ➲ see also GO

ˈbeen-to *noun* (*WAfrE*) a person who returns to his or her home in Africa after studying, working, etc. in a foreign country. People are often identified as **been-tos** because they have a different accent.

beep /biːp/ *noun, verb*
■ ***noun*** a short high sound such as that made by a car horn or by electronic equipment
■ ***verb*** **1** [I] (of an electronic machine) to make a short high sound: *The microwave beeps to let you know when it has finished.* **2** [I, T] when a car horn, etc. **beeps** or when you **beep** it, it makes a short noise: *The car behind started beeping at us.* ◇ **~ sth** *He beeped his horn at the cyclist.* **3** (*NAmE*) (*BrE* **bleep**) [T] **~ sb** to call sb on their beeper

beep·er /ˈbiːpə(r)/ *noun* (*especially NAmE*) = BLEEPER

beer 0-π /bɪə(r); *NAmE* bɪr/ *noun*
1 0-π [U, C] an alcoholic drink made from MALT and flavoured with HOPS. There are many types of beer: ***a barrel/bottle/glass of beer*** ◇ *beers brewed in Germany* ◇ *a beer glass* ◇ *Are you a beer drinker?* **2** 0-π [C] a glass, bottle or can of beer: *Shall we have a beer?* ➲ see also GINGER BEER, GUEST BEER, KEG BEER, ROOT BEER, SMALL BEER

ˈbeer belly (also **ˈbeer gut**) *noun* (*informal*) a man's very fat stomach, caused by drinking a lot of beer over a long period

ˈbeer cellar *noun* **1** a room for storing beer below a pub or bar **2** a pub or bar that is underground or partly underground

ˈbeer garden *noun* an outdoor area at a pub or bar with tables and chairs

ˈbeer mat *noun* (*BrE*) a small piece of cardboard that you put under a glass, usually in a bar, etc. in order to protect the surface below

beery /ˈbɪəri; *NAmE* ˈbɪri/ *adj.* smelling of beer; influenced by the drinking of beer

bees·wax /ˈbiːzwæks/ *noun* [U] a yellow sticky substance that is produced by BEES and is used especially for making CANDLES and polish for wood

beet /biːt/ *noun* [C, U] **1** a plant with a root that is used as a vegetable, especially for feeding animals or making sugar ➲ see also SUGAR BEET **2** (*NAmE*) (*BrE* **beet·root**) a plant with a round dark red root that is cooked and eaten as a vegetable ➲ VISUAL VOCAB page V27

bee·tle /ˈbiːtl/ *noun, verb*
■ ***noun*** **1** an insect, often large and black, with a hard case on its back, covering its wings. There are several types of beetle. ➲ VISUAL VOCAB page V11 ➲ see also DEATH-WATCH BEETLE **2 Beetle™** (*NAmE* also **bug**) the English names for the original Volkswagen small car with a round shape at the front and the back
■ ***verb*** [I] **+ adv./prep.** (*BrE, informal*) to move somewhere quickly SYN **scurry**: *I last saw him beetling off down the road.*

beet·root /ˈbiːtruːt/ (*BrE*) (*NAmE* **beet**) *noun* [U, C] a plant with a round dark red root that is cooked and eaten as a vegetable ➲ VISUAL VOCAB page V27

be·fall /bɪˈfɔːl/ *verb* (**be·fell** /bɪˈfel/, **be·fallen** /bɪˈfɔːlən/) **~ sb** (used only in the third person) (*literary*) (of sth unpleasant) to happen to sb: *They were unaware of the fate that was to befall them.*

befit /bɪˈfɪt/ *verb* (**-tt-**) (used only in the third person and in participles) **sth befits sb** (*formal*) to be suitable and good enough for sb/sth: *It was a lavish reception* **as befitted** *a visitor of her status.* ◇ *He lived in the style befitting a gentleman.*

befog /bɪˈfɒg; *NAmE* -ˈfɑːg/ *verb* **~ sb** to make sb confused: *Her brain was befogged by lack of sleep.*

be·fore 0→ /bɪˈfɔː(r)/ *prep., conj., adv.*

■ ***prep.*** **1** 0→ earlier than sb/sth: *before lunch* ◇ *the day before yesterday* ◇ *The year before last he won a gold medal, and the year before that he won a silver.* ◇ *She's lived there since before the war.* ◇ *He arrived before me.* ◇ *She became a lawyer as her father had before her.* ◇ *Leave your keys at reception before departure.* ◇ *Something ought to have been done before now.* ◇ *We'll know* **before long** (= soon). ◇ *Turn left just before* (= before you reach) *the bank.* **2** (rather *formal*) used to say that sb/sth is in a position in front of sb/sth: *They knelt before the throne.* ◇ *Before you is a list of the points we have to discuss.* ➲ compare BEHIND **3** 0→ used to say that sb/sth is ahead of sb/sth in an order or arrangement: *Your name is before mine on the list.* ◇ *He puts his work before everything* (= regards it as more important than anything else). **4** 0→ used to say that sth is facing sb in the future: *The task before us is a daunting one.* ◇ *The whole summer lay before me.* **5** in the presence of sb who is listening, watching, etc: *He was brought before the judge.* ◇ *She said it before witnesses.* ◇ *They had the advantage of playing before their home crowd.* **6** (*formal*) used to say how sb reacts when they have to face sb/sth: *They retreated before the enemy.*

■ ***conj.*** **1** 0→ earlier than the time when: *Do it before you forget.* ◇ *Did she leave a message before she went?* **2** 0→ until: *It may be many years before the situation improves.* ◇ *It was some time before I realized the truth.* **3** 0→ used to warn or threaten sb that sth bad could happen: *Put that away before it gets broken.* **4** (*formal*) rather than: *I'd die before I apologized!*

■ ***adv.*** 0→ at an earlier time; in the past; already: *You should have told me so before.* ◇ *It had been fine the week before* (= the previous week). ◇ *That had happened long before* (= a long time earlier). ◇ *I think we've met before.*

be·fore·hand /bɪˈfɔːhænd; *NAmE* -ˈfɔːrh-/ *adv.* earlier; before sth else happens or is done: *two weeks/three days/a few hours beforehand* ◇ *I wish we'd known about it beforehand.*

be·friend /bɪˈfrend/ *verb* [usually passive] **~ sb** to become a friend of sb, especially sb who needs your help: *Shortly after my arrival at the school, I was befriended by an older girl.*

be·fud·dled /bɪˈfʌdld/ *adj.* confused and unable to think normally: *He was befuddled by drink.*

beg /beg/ *verb* (-gg-) **1** [I, T] to ask sb for sth especially in an anxious way because you want or need it very much: **~ (for sth)** *He wants to see them beg for mercy.* ◇ **~ sb (for sth)** *They begged him for help.* ◇ **~ sth (of/from sb)** *She begged permission to leave.* ◇ *I managed to beg a lift from a passing motorist.* ◇ **~ (sb) + speech** *'Give me one more chance,' he begged (her).* ◇ **~ sb to do sth** *She begged him not to go.* ◇ **~ to do sth** *He begged to be told the truth.* ◇ **~ that...** (*formal*) *She begged that she be allowed to go.* ◇ (*BrE* also) *She begged that she should be allowed to go.* ◇ **~ of sb** (*formal*) *Don't leave me here, I beg of you!* **2** [I, T] to ask sb for money, food, etc, especially in the street: *London is full of homeless people begging in the streets.* ◇ *a begging letter* (= one that asks sb for money) ◇ **~ for sth (from sb)** *The children were begging for food.* ◇ **~ sth (from sb)** *We managed to beg a meal from the cafe owner.* **3** [I] if a dog **begs**, it sits on its back legs with its front legs in the air, waiting to be given sth

IDM **beg ˈleave to do sth** (*formal*) to ask sb for permission to do sth **be going ˈbegging** (*BrE, informal*) if sth **is going begging**, it is available because nobody else wants it **beg sb's ˈpardon** (*formal, especially BrE*) to ask sb to forgive you for sth you have said or done **beg the ˈquestion 1** to make sb want to ask a question that has not yet been answered: *All of which begs the question as to who will fund the project.* **2** to talk about sth as if it were definitely true, even though it might not be: *These assumptions beg the question that children learn languages more easily than adults.* **I beg to differ** used to say politely that you do not agree with sth that has just been said **I beg your pardon 1** (*formal*) used to tell sb that you are sorry for sth you have said or done: *I beg your pardon, I thought that was my coat.* **2** used to ask sb to repeat what they have just said because you did not hear: *'It's on Duke Street.' 'I beg your pardon.' 'Duke Street.'* **3** (*especially BrE*) used to tell sb that you are offended by what they have just said or by the way that they have said it: *'Just go away.' 'I beg your pardon!'*

PHR V **ˌbeg ˈoff** to say that you are unable to do sth that you have agreed to do: *He's always begging off at the last minute.*

begad /bɪˈgæd/ *exclamation* (*old use*) used to express surprise or for emphasis

began *past tense of* BEGIN

beget /bɪˈget/ *verb* (**be·get·ting**, **begot**, **begot** /bɪˈgɒt; *NAmE* -gɑːt/ HELP In sense 1 **begat** /bɪˈgæt/ is used for the past tense, and **be·got·ten** /bɪˈgɒtn/ /-ˈgɑːtn/ is used for the past participle.) **1** (old use, for example in the Bible) **~ sb** to become the father of a child: *Isaac begat Jacob.* **2 ~ sth** (*formal* or *old-fashioned*) to make sth happen: *Violence begets violence.* ► **be·get·ter** *noun*

beg·gar /ˈbegə(r)/ *noun, verb*

■ ***noun*** **1** a person who lives by asking people for money or food **2** (*BrE, informal*) used with an adjective to describe sb in a particular way: *Aren't you dressed yet, you lazy beggar?*

IDM **ˌbeggars can't be ˈchoosers** (*saying*) people say **beggars can't be choosers** when there is no choice and sb must be satisfied with what is available ➲ more at WISH *n.*

■ ***verb*** **~ sb/sth/yourself** to make sb/sth very poor: *Why should I beggar myself for you?*

IDM **beggar beˈlief/deˈscription** to be too extreme, shocking, etc. to believe/describe: *It beggars belief how things could have got this bad.*

beg·gar·ly /ˈbegəli; *NAmE* -gərli/ *adj.* (*literary*) very small in amount

ˈbegging bowl *noun* a bowl held out by sb asking for food or money: (*figurative*) *He is taking round the begging bowl on behalf of the party's campaign fund.*

begin 0→ /bɪˈgɪn/ *verb* (**be·gin·ning**, **began** /bɪˈgæn/, **begun** /bɪˈgʌn/)

1 0→ [I, T] to start doing sth; to do the first part of sth: *Shall I begin?* ◇ **~ at/with sth** *Let's begin at page 9.* ◇ **~ by doing sth** *She began by thanking us all for coming.* ◇ **~ sth** *We began work on the project in May.* ◇ *I began* (= started reading) *this novel last month and I still haven't finished it.* ◇ **~ sth at/with sth** *He always begins his lessons with a warm-up exercise.* ◇ **~ sth as sth** *He began his political career as a student* (= when he was a student). ◇ **~ to do sth** *I began to feel dizzy.* ◇ *At last the guests began to arrive.* ◇ *She began to cry.* ◇ *It was beginning to snow.* ◇ *I was beginning to think you'd never come.* ◇ **~ doing sth** *Everyone began talking at once.* ◇ *When will you begin recruiting?* ➲ SYNONYMS at START ➲ LANGUAGE BANK at FIRST **2** 0→ [I] to start to happen or exist, especially from a particular time: *When does the concert begin?* ◇ *Work on the new bridge is due to begin in September.* ◇ *The evening began well.* **3** 0→ [I] **~ as sth** to be sth first, before becoming sth else: *He began as an actor, before starting to direct films.* ◇ *What began as a minor scuffle turned into a full-scale riot.* **4** 0→ [I] to have sth as the first part or the point where sth starts: *Where does Europe end and Asia begin?* ◇ **~ with sth** *Use 'an' before words beginning with a vowel.* ◇ *'I'm thinking of a country in Asia.' 'What does it begin with* (= what is the first letter)*?'* ◇ *Each chapter begins with a quotation.* ◇ **~ at...** *The path begins at Livingston village.* **5** 0→ [T] **+ speech** to start speaking: *'Ladies and gentlemen,' he began, 'welcome to the Town Hall.'* **6** 0→ [I, T] to start or make sth start for the first time: *The school began in 1920, with only ten pupils.* ◇ **~ sth** *He began a new magazine on post-war architecture.* **7** [T] **not ~ to do sth** to make no attempt to do sth or have no chance of doing sth: *I* ***can't begin to*** *thank you enough.* ◇ *He didn't even begin to understand my problem.*

IDM **to beˈgin with 1** 0→ at first: *I found it tiring to begin with but I soon got used to it.* ◇ *We'll go slowly to begin with.*

2 used to introduce the first point you want to make: *'What was it you didn't like?' 'Well, to begin with, our room was far too small.'* ➲ more at CHARITY

B

Which Word?

begin / start

- There is not much difference in meaning between **begin** and **start**, though **start** is more common in spoken English: *What time does the concert start/begin?* ◇ *She started/began working here three months ago.* **Begin** is often used when you are describing a series of events: *The story begins on the island of Corfu.* **Start**, but not **begin**, can also mean 'to start a journey', 'to start something happening' or 'to start a machine working': *We'll need to start at 7.00.* ◇ *Who do you think started the fire?* ◇ *The car won't start.*
- You can use either an infinitive or a form with *-ing* after **begin** and **start**, with no difference in meaning: *I didn't start worrying/to worry until she was 2 hours late.*
- After the forms **beginning** and **starting**, the *-ing* form of the verb is not normally used: *It's starting/beginning to rain.* ◇ ~~*It's starting/beginning raining.*~~

be·gin·ner /bɪˈɡɪnə(r)/ *noun* a person who is starting to learn sth and cannot do it very well yet: *She's in the beginners' class.*

be,ginner's 'luck *noun* [U] good luck or unexpected success when you start to do sth new

be·gin·ning /bɪˈɡɪnɪŋ/ *noun*
1 [C, usually sing.] **~ (of sth)** the time when sth starts; the first part of an event, a story, etc: *We're going to Japan* ***at the beginning of*** *July.* ◇ *She's been working there* ***since the beginning of*** *last summer.* ◇ *We missed the beginning of the movie.* ◇ *Let's start again* ***from the beginning.*** ◇ *The birth of their first child* ***marked the beginning of*** *a new era in their married life.* ◇ *I've read the whole book* ***from beginning to end*** *and still can't understand it.* HELP **At the beginning (of)** is used for the time and place when something begins. **In the beginning**=**at first** and suggests a contrast with a later situation. **2 beginnings** [pl.] the first or early ideas, signs or stages of sth: *Did democracy have its beginnings in ancient Greece?* ◇ *He built up his multimillion-pound music business* ***from small beginnings.***
IDM **the beginning of the 'end** the first sign of sth ending

be·gone /bɪˈɡɒn; *NAmE* -ˈɡɔːn; -ˈɡɑːn/ *exclamation* (*old use*) a way of telling sb to go away immediately

be·go·nia /bɪˈɡəʊniə; *NAmE* -ˈɡoʊ-/ *noun* a plant with large shiny flowers that may be pink, red, yellow or white, grown indoors or in a garden

be·gorra /bɪˈɡɒrə; *NAmE* bɪˈɡɔːrə; -ˈɡɑːr-/ *exclamation* (*IrishE*, *old-fashioned*) used to express surprise

begot *past tense* of BEGET

be·got·ten *past part.* of BEGET

be·grudge /bɪˈɡrʌdʒ/ *verb* (often used in negative sentences) **1** to feel unhappy that sb has sth because you do not think that they deserve it: **~ sb sth** *You surely don't begrudge him his happiness.* ◇ **~ sb doing sth** *I don't begrudge her being so successful.* **2** to feel unhappy about having to do, pay or give sth: **~ sth** *I begrudge every second I spent trying to help him.* ◇ **~ doing sth** *They begrudge paying so much money for a second-rate service.*

be·grudg·ing·ly /bɪˈɡrʌdʒɪŋli/ *adv.* = GRUDGINGLY

be·guile /bɪˈɡaɪl/ *verb* (*formal*) **1 ~ sb (into doing sth)** to trick sb into doing sth, especially by being nice to them: *She beguiled them into believing her version of events.* **2 ~ sb** to attract or interest sb: *He was beguiled by her beauty.*

be·guil·ing /bɪˈɡaɪlɪŋ/ *adj.* (*formal*) attractive and interesting but sometimes mysterious or trying to trick you: *beguiling advertisements* ◇ *Her beauty was beguiling.* ▸ **be·guil·ing·ly** *adv.*

begum /ˈbeɪɡəm/ *noun* a title of respect used for a Muslim woman of high rank and for a married Muslim woman: *Begum Zia*

begun *past part.* of BEGIN

be·half AW /bɪˈhɑːf; *NAmE* bɪˈhæf/ *noun*
IDM **in behalf of sb | in sb's behalf** (*US*) in order to help sb: *We collected money in behalf of the homeless.* **on behalf of sb | on sb's behalf 1** as the representative of sb or instead of them: *On behalf of the department I would like to thank you all.* ◇ *Mr Knight cannot be here, so his wife will accept the prize on his behalf.* **2** in order to help sb: *They campaigned on behalf of asylum seekers.* **3** because of sb; for sb: *Don't worry on my behalf.*

be·have /bɪˈheɪv/ *verb*
1 [I] **+ adv./prep.** to do things in a particular way SYN **act**: *The doctor behaved very unprofessionally.* ◇ *They behaved very badly towards their guests.* ◇ *He behaved like a true gentleman.* ◇ *She behaved with great dignity.* ◇ *He* ***behaved as if/though*** *nothing had happened.* ◇ *They behave differently when you're not around.* HELP In spoken English people often use **like** instead of **as if** or **as though**, especially in *NAmE*: *He behaved like nothing had happened.* This is not considered correct in written *BrE*. **2** [I, T] to do things in a way that people think is correct or polite: *Will you kids just behave!* ◇ *She doesn't know how to behave in public.* ◇ **~ yourself** *I want you to behave yourselves while I'm away.* OPP **misbehave 3 -behaved** (in adjectives) behaving in the way mentioned: ***well-/badly-behaved*** *children* **4** [I] **+ adv./prep.** (*technical*) to naturally react, move, etc. in a particular way: *a study of how metals behave under pressure* IDM see OWN *v.*

be·hav·iour (*especially US* **be·hav·ior**) /bɪˈheɪvjə(r)/ *noun*
1 [U] the way that sb behaves, especially towards other people: ***good/bad behaviour*** ◇ ***social/sexual/criminal behaviour*** ◇ *His behaviour towards her was becoming more and more aggressive.* **2** [U, C] the way a person, an animal, a plant, a chemical, etc. behaves or functions in a particular situation: *the behaviour of dolphins/chromosomes* ◇ *studying human and animal behaviour* ◇ (*technical*) *to study learned behaviours* ▸ **be·hav·iour·al** (*especially US* **be·hav·ior·al** /-jərəl/) *adj.*: *children with behavioural difficulties* ◇ *behavioural science* (= the study of human behaviour) **be·hav·iour·al·ly** (*especially US* **be·hav·ior·al·ly**) *adv.*
IDM **be on your best be'haviour** to behave in the most polite way you can

be·hav·iour·ism (*especially US* **be·hav·ior·ism**) /bɪˈheɪvjərɪzəm/ *noun* [U] (*psychology*) the theory that all human behaviour is learnt by adapting to outside conditions and that learning is not influenced by thoughts and feelings ▸ **be·hav·iour·ist** (*especially US* **be·hav·ior·ist**) /-jərɪst/ *noun*

be·head /bɪˈhed/ *verb* [usually passive] **~ sb** to cut off sb's head, especially as a punishment SYN **decapitate**

be·held *past tense, past part.* of BEHOLD

be·he·moth /bɪˈhiːmɒθ; ˈbiːhɪmɒθ; *NAmE* -mɔːθ/ *noun* (*formal*) a very big and powerful company or organization

be·hest /bɪˈhest/ *noun* [sing.]
IDM **at sb's be'hest** (*old use* or *formal*) because sb has ordered or requested it

be·hind /bɪˈhaɪnd/ *prep., adv., noun*
■ ***prep.* 1** at or towards the back of sb/sth, and often hidden by it or them: *Who's the girl standing behind Jan?* ◇ *Stay close behind me.* ◇ *a small street behind the station* ◇ *She glanced behind her.* ◇ *Don't forget to lock the door behind you* (= when you leave). ◇ *The sun disappeared behind the clouds.* ➲ note at BACK ➲ compare IN FRONT OF **2** making less progress than sb/sth: *He's behind the rest of the class in reading.* ◇ *We're* ***behind schedule*** (= late). **3** giving support to or approval of sb/sth: *She knew that, whatever she decided, her family was right behind her.* **4** responsible for starting or developing sth: *What's behind that happy smile* (= what is causing it)? ◇ *He was the man behind the plan to build a new hospital.* **5** used to say that sth is in sb's past: *The accident is behind you now, so try to forget it.* ◇ *She has ten years' useful experience behind her.*

■ ***adv.*** **1** at or towards the back of sb/sth; further back: *She rode off down the road with the dog running behind.* ◇ *The others are a long way behind.* ◇ *He was shot from behind as he ran away.* ◇ *I had fallen so far behind that it seemed pointless trying to catch up.* **2** in the place where sb/sth is or was: *I was told to **stay behind** after school* (= remain in school). ◇ *This bag was **left behind** after the class.* **3** late in paying money or completing work: **~ (with sth)** *She's **fallen behind** with the payments.* ◇ **~ (in sth)** *He was terribly behind in his work.*

■ ***noun*** (*informal*) a person's bottom. People often say 'behind' to avoid saying 'bottom'. SYN **backside**: *The dog bit him on his behind.*

be·hind·hand /bɪˈhaɪndhænd/ *adj.* [not before noun] **~ (with/in sth)** late in doing sth or in paying money that is owed: *They were behindhand in settling their debts.*

be·hold /bɪˈhəʊld; *NAmE* bɪˈhoʊld/ *verb* (**be·held** /bɪˈheld/, **be·held**) **~ sb/sth** (*old use* or *literary*) to look at or see sb/sth: *Her face was a joy to behold.* ◇ *They beheld a bright star shining in the sky.* IDM see LO

be·holden /bɪˈhəʊldən; *NAmE* -ˈhoʊld-/ *adj.* **~ to sb (for sth)** (*formal*) owing sth to sb because of sth that they have done for you: *She didn't like to be beholden to anyone.*

be·hold·er /bɪˈhəʊldə(r); *NAmE* -ˈhoʊld-/ *noun* IDM see BEAUTY

be·hove /bɪˈhəʊv; *NAmE* bɪˈhoʊv/ (*BrE*) (*NAmE* **be·hoove** /bɪˈhuːv/) *verb*

IDM **it behoves sb to do sth** (*formal*) it is right or necessary for sb to do sth: *It behoves us to study these findings carefully.*

beige /beɪʒ/ *adj.* light yellowish-brown in colour ▸ **beige** *noun* [U]

being /ˈbiːɪŋ/ *noun* **1** [U] existence: *The Irish Free State **came into being** in 1922.* ◇ *A new era was **brought into being** by the war.* ➲ see also WELL-BEING **2** [C] a living creature: *human beings* ◇ *a strange being from another planet* **3** [U] (*formal*) your mind and all of your feelings: *I hated him with my whole being.* ➲ see also BE *v.*

be·jew·elled (*BrE*) (*US* **be·jew·eled**) /bɪˈdʒuːəld/ *adj.* (*literary*) decorated with PRECIOUS STONES; wearing jewellery

bel /bel/ *noun* (*technical*) a measurement of sound equal to 10 DECIBELS

be·la·bour (*especially US* **be·la·bor**) /bɪˈleɪbə(r)/ *verb*

IDM **belabour the ˈpoint** (*formal*) to repeat an idea, argument, etc. many times to emphasize it, especially when it has already been mentioned or understood

be·lated /bɪˈleɪtɪd/ *adj.* coming or happening late: *a belated birthday present* ▸ **be·lated·ly** *adv.*

belay /ˈbiːleɪ; bɪˈleɪ/ *verb* [I, T] **~ (sth/sb)** (*technical*) (in climbing) to attach a rope to a rock, etc; to make a person safe while climbing by attaching a rope to the person and to a rock, etc.

bel canto /ˌbel ˈkæntəʊ; *NAmE* -toʊ/ *noun* [U] (*music*) a style of OPERA or opera singing in the 19th century in which producing a beautiful tone was considered very important

belch /beltʃ/ *verb* **1** [I] to let air come up noisily from your stomach and out through your mouth: *He wiped his hand across his mouth, then belched loudly.* SYN **burp** **2** [I, T] **~ (out/forth) (sth)** to send out large amounts of smoke, flames, etc; to come out of sth in large amounts SYN **spew out** ▸ **belch** *noun*: *He sat back and gave a loud belch.*

be·lea·guered /bɪˈliːɡəd; *NAmE* -ɡərd/ *adj.* **1** (*formal*) experiencing a lot of criticism and difficulties: *The beleaguered party leader was forced to resign.* **2** surrounded by an enemy: *supplies for the beleaguered city*

bel·fry /ˈbelfri/ *noun* (*pl.* **-ies**) a tower in which bells hang, especially as part of a church

belie /bɪˈlaɪ/ *verb* (**be·lies**, **be·ly·ing**, **be·lied**, **be·lied**) (*formal*) **1** **~ sth** to give a false impression of sb/sth: *Her energy and youthful good looks belie her 65 years.* **2** **~ sth** to show that sth cannot be true or correct: *Government claims that there is no poverty are belied by the number of homeless people on the streets.*

be·lief /bɪˈliːf/ *noun*
1 [U] **~ (in sth/sb)** a strong feeling that sth/sb exists or is true; confidence that sth/sb is good or right: *I admire his passionate belief in what he is doing.* ◇ *belief in God/democracy* **2** [sing., U] **~ (that...)** an opinion about sth; sth that you think is true: *She acted **in the belief that** she was doing good.* ◇ ***Contrary to popular belief*** (= in spite of what people may think), *he was not responsible for the tragedy.* ◇ *There is a general belief that things will soon get better.* **3** [C, usually pl.] something that you believe, especially as part of your religion: ***religious/political beliefs*** ➲ compare DISBELIEF, UNBELIEF

IDM **beyond beˈlief** (in a way that is) too great, difficult, etc. to be believed: *Dissatisfaction with the government has grown beyond belief.* ◇ *icy air that was cold beyond belief* ➲ more at BEGGAR *v.*, BEST *n.*

be·liev·able /bɪˈliːvəbl/ *adj.* that can be believed SYN **plausible**: *Her explanation certainly sounded believable.* ◇ *a play with believable characters* OPP **unbelievable**

be·lieve /bɪˈliːv/ *verb* (not used in the progressive tenses)

▸ FEEL CERTAIN **1** [T] to feel certain that sth is true or that sb is telling you the truth: **~ sb** *I don't believe you!* ◇ *The man claimed to be a social worker and the old woman believed him.* ◇ *Believe me, she's not right for you.* ◇ **~ sth** *I believed his lies for years.* ◇ *I find that **hard to believe**.* ◇ ***Don't believe a word of it*** (= don't believe any part of what sb is saying). ◇ **~ (that)...** *People used to believe (that) the earth was flat.* ◇ *He refused to believe (that) his son was involved in drugs.* ◇ ***I do believe** you're right* (= I think sth is true, even though it is surprising).

▸ THINK POSSIBLE **2** [I, T] to think that sth is true or possible, although you are not completely certain: *'Where does she come from?' 'Spain, I believe.'* ◇ *'Does he still work there?' '**I believe so/not**.'* ◇ **~ (that)...** *Police believe (that) the man may be armed.* ◇ **it is believed (that)...** *It is believed that the couple have left the country.* ◇ **~ sb/sth to be, have, etc. sth** *The vases are believed to be worth over $20 000 each.* ◇ **~ sb/sth + adj.** *Three sailors are missing, believed drowned.* ➲ SYNONYMS at THINK

▸ HAVE OPINION **3** [T] **~ (that)...** to have the opinion that sth is right or true: *The party believes (that) education is the most important issue facing the government.* ➲ LANGUAGE BANK at ACCORDING TO, OPINION

▸ BE SURPRISED/ANNOYED **4** [T] **don't/can't ~** used to say that you are surprised or annoyed at sth: **~ (that)...** *She couldn't believe (that) it was all happening again.* ◇ **~ how, what, etc...** *I can't believe how much better I feel.*

▸ RELIGION **5** [I] to have a religious faith: *The god appears only to those who believe.*

IDM **believe it or ˈnot** (*informal*) used to introduce information that is true but that may surprise people: *Believe it or not, he asked me to marry him!* **believe (you) ˈme** (*informal*) used to emphasize that you strongly believe what you are saying: *You haven't heard the last of this, believe you me!* **don't you beˈlieve it!** (*informal*) used to tell sb that sth is definitely not true **I don't beˈlieve it!** (*informal*) used to say that you are surprised or annoyed about sth: *I don't believe it! What are you doing here?* **if you believe that, you'll believe ˈanything** (*informal*) used to say that you think sb is stupid if they believe that sth is true **make believe (that...)** to pretend that sth is true ➲ related noun MAKE-BELIEVE **not believe your ˈears/ˈeyes** (*informal*) to be very surprised at sth you hear/see: *I couldn't believe my eyes when she walked in.* **seeing is beˈlieving** (*saying*) used to say that sb will have to believe that sth is true when they see it, although they do not think it is true now **would you beˈlieve (it)?** (*informal*) used to show that you are surprised and annoyed about sth: *And, would you believe, he didn't even apologize!* **you/you'd better beˈlieve it!** (*informal*) used to tell sb that sth is definitely true ➲ more at GIVE *v.*

PHR V **beˈlieve in sb/sth** to feel certain that sb/sth ex-

B

ists: *Do you believe in God?* **be'lieve in sb** ⚷ to feel that you can trust sb and/or that they will be successful: *They need a leader they can believe in.* ➲ SYNONYMS at TRUST **be'lieve in sth** ⚷ to think that sth is good, right or acceptable: **~ doing sth** *I don't believe in hitting children.* **be'lieve sth of sb** to think that sb is capable of sth: *Are you sure he was lying? I can't believe that of him.*

be·liever /bɪ'liːvə(r)/ *noun* a person who believes in the existence or truth of sth, especially sb who believes in a god or religious faith OPP **unbeliever**
IDM **be a (great/firm) believer in sth** to believe strongly that sth is good, important or valuable

Be·li·sha bea·con /bəˌliːʃə 'biːkən/ *noun* (in Britain) a post with an orange flashing light on top marking a place where cars must stop to allow people to cross the road

be·lit·tle /bɪ'lɪtl/ *verb* **~ sb/sth** to make sb or the things that sb does seem unimportant: *She felt her husband constantly belittled her achievements.*

bell ⚷ /bel/ *noun*
1 ⚷ a hollow metal object, often shaped like a cup, that makes a ringing sound when hit by a small piece of metal inside it; the sound that it makes: *A peal of church bells rang out in the distance.* ◇ *a bicycle bell* ◇ *His voice came down the line* **as clear as a bell**. ◇ *the bell of a trumpet* (= the bell-shaped part at the end of it) ◇ *a bell-shaped flower* ➲ VISUAL VOCAB page V30 **2** ⚷ an electrical device which makes a ringing sound when a button on it is pushed; the sound that it makes, used as a signal or a warning: ***Ring the bell*** *to see if they're in.* ◇ *The* ***bell's ringing!*** ◇ *The bell went for the end of the lesson.* ◇ *An* ***alarm bell*** *went off.* ◇ (*figurative*) ***Warning bells*** *started ringing in her head as she sensed that something was wrong.*
IDM **give sb a 'bell** (*BrE, informal*) to call sb by telephone ➲ more at ALARM *n.*, PULL *v.*, RING *v.*, SOUND *adj.*

bella·donna /ˌbelə'dɒnə; *NAmE* -'dɑːnə/ *noun* [U] **1** = DEADLY NIGHTSHADE **2** a poisonous drug made from DEADLY NIGHTSHADE

'bell-bottoms *noun* [pl.] trousers/pants with legs that become very wide below the knee

bell·boy /'belbɔɪ/ (*especially NAmE*) (*NAmE* also **bell·hop**) *noun* a person whose job is to carry people's cases to their rooms in a hotel

'bell curve *noun* (*mathematics*) a line on a GRAPH that rises to a high round curve in the middle, showing NORMAL DISTRIBUTION

belle /bel/ *noun* (*old-fashioned*) a beautiful woman; the most beautiful woman in a particular place

belles-lettres /ˌbel 'letrə/ *noun* [U+sing./pl. v.] (from *French, old-fashioned*) studies or writings on the subject of literature or art, contrasted with those on technical or scientific subjects

bell·hop /'belhɒp; *NAmE* -hɑːp/ *noun* (*NAmE*) = BELLBOY

bel·li·cose /'belɪkəʊs; -kəʊz; *NAmE* -koʊs; -koʊz/ *adj.* (*formal*) having or showing a desire to argue or fight SYN **aggressive, warlike** ▸ **bel·li·cos·ity** /ˌbelɪ'kɒsəti; *NAmE* -'kɑːs-/ *noun* [U]

-bellied ➲ BELLY

bel·liger·ent /bə'lɪdʒərənt/ *adj., noun*
■ ***adj.*** **1** unfriendly and aggressive SYN **hostile**: *a belligerent attitude* **2** [only before noun] (*formal*) (of a country) fighting a war: *the* ***belligerent*** ***countries/states/nations*** ▸ **bel·liger·ence** /-əns/ *noun* [U] **bel·liger·ent·ly** *adv.*
■ ***noun*** (*formal*) a country or group that is fighting a war

'bell jar *noun* a tall round glass cover, used by scientists

bel·low /'beləʊ; *NAmE* -loʊ/ *verb* **1** [I, T] to shout in a loud deep voice, especially because you are angry SYN **yell**: **~ (at sb)** *They bellowed at her to stop.* ◇ **~ sth (at sb)** *The coach bellowed instructions from the sidelines.* ◇ **+ speech** *'Get over here!' he bellowed.* ➲ SYNONYMS at SHOUT **2** [I] when a large animal such as a BULL **bellows**, it makes a loud deep sound ▸ **bel·low** *noun*: *to let out a* ***bellow of rage/pain***

bel·lows /'beləʊz; *NAmE* -loʊz/ *noun* (*pl.* **bel·lows**) [C+sing./pl. v.] a piece of equipment for blowing air into or through sth. Bellows are used for making a fire burn better or for producing sound in some types of musical instruments: *a pair of bellows* (= a small bellows with two handles to be pushed together)

bellows

'bell pepper (*NAmE*) (also **ˌsweet 'pepper** *BrE, NAmE*) (*BrE* **pep·per**) *noun* a hollow fruit, usually red, green or yellow, eaten as a vegetable either raw or cooked ➲ VISUAL VOCAB page V27

'bell pull *noun* a rope or handle that you pull to make a bell ring, for example to make sb in another room hear you

'bell push *noun* (*BrE*) a button that you press to make an electric bell ring

'bell-ringer (also **ringer**) *noun* a person who rings church bells as a hobby ▸ **'bell-ringing** *noun* [U] ➲ see also CAMPANOLOGIST, CAMPANOLOGY

ˌbells and 'whistles *noun* [pl.] (*computing*) attractive extra features

bell·wether /'belweðə(r)/ *noun* [usually sing.] something that is used as a sign of what will happen in the future: *University campuses are often the bellwether of change.*

belly /'beli/ *noun, verb*
■ ***noun*** (*pl.* **-ies**) **1** the part of the body below the chest SYN **stomach, gut**: *They crawled along on their bellies.* ➲ see also BEER BELLY, POT BELLY **2** (*literary*) the round or curved part of an object: *the belly of a ship* ➲ VISUAL VOCAB page V30 **3 -bellied** (in adjectives) having the type of belly mentioned: *swollen-bellied* ◇ *round-bellied*
IDM **go belly 'up** (*informal*) to fail completely: *Last year the business went belly up after one of the partners resigned.*
■ ***verb*** (**bel·lies, belly·ing, bel·lied, bel·lied**) [I] **~ (out)** (especially of sails) to fill with air and become rounder

belly·ache /'belieɪk/ *noun, verb*
■ ***noun*** [C, U] (*informal*) a pain in the stomach: *I've got (a) bellyache.*
■ ***verb*** [I] (*informal*) to complain a lot about sth in an annoying or unreasonable way

'belly button *noun* (*informal*) = NAVEL

'belly dance *noun* a dance, originally from the Middle East, in which a woman moves her belly and hips around ▸ **'belly dancer** *noun*

belly·flop /'beliflɒp; *NAmE* -flɑːp/ *noun* (*informal*) a bad DIVE into water, in which the front of the body hits the water flat

belly·ful /'belifʊl/ *noun*
IDM **have had a 'bellyful of sb/sth** (*informal*) to have had more than enough of sb/sth, so that you cannot deal with any more: *I've had a bellyful of your moaning.*

'belly laugh *noun* (*informal*) a deep loud laugh

be·long ⚷ /bɪ'lɒŋ; *NAmE* -lɔːŋ/ *verb* (not used in the progressive tenses)
1 ⚷ [I] **+ adv./prep.** to be in the right or suitable place: *Where do these plates belong* (= where are they kept)? ◇ *Are you sure these documents belong together?* **2** ⚷ [I] to feel comfortable and happy in a particular situation or with a particular group of people: *I don't feel as if I belong here.* ▸ **be·long·ing** *noun* [U]: *to feel a sense of belonging*
PHR V **be'long to sb 1** ⚷ to be owned by sb: *Who does this watch belong to?* ◇ *The islands belong to Spain.* **2** an event, a competition, etc. that **belongs to** sb is one in which they are the most successful or popular: *British actors did well at the award ceremony, but the evening belonged to the Americans.* **be'long to sth 1** ⚷ to be a member of a club, an organization, etc: *Have you ever belonged to a political party?* **2** ⚷ to be part of a particular group type, or system: *Lions and tigers belong to the cat family.*

be·long·ings /bɪ'lɒŋɪŋz; *NAmE* -'lɔːŋ-/ *noun* [pl.] the things that you own which can be moved, for example not land or buildings SYN **possessions**: *insurance of prop-*

erty and personal belongings ◊ *She packed her few belongings in a bag and left.* ➲ SYNONYMS at THING

be·loved *adj., noun*
■ **adj.** (*formal*) **1** /bɪˈlʌvd/ **~ by/of sb** loved very much by sb; very popular with sb: *the deep purple flowers so beloved by artists* **2** /bɪˈlʌvɪd/ [only before noun] loved very much: *in memory of our dearly beloved son, John*
■ **noun** /bɪˈlʌvɪd/ (*old use* or *literary*) a person who is loved very much by sb: *It was a gift from her beloved.*

below 🔑 /bɪˈləʊ; *NAmE* bɪˈloʊ/ *prep., adv.*
■ **prep. 1** 🔑 at or to a lower level or position than sb/sth: *He dived below the surface of the water.* ◊ *Please do not write below this line.* ◊ *Skirts will be worn below* (= long enough to cover) *the knee.* **2** 🔑 of a lower amount or standard than sb/sth: *The temperatures remained below freezing all day.* ◊ *Her work was well below average for the class.* **3** 🔑 of a lower rank or of less importance than sb/sth: *A police sergeant is below an inspector.*
■ **adv. 1** 🔑 at or to a lower level, position or place: *They live on the floor below.* ◊ *I could still see the airport buildings far below.* ◊ *See below* (= at the bottom of the page) *for references.* ◊ *The passengers who felt seasick stayed below* (= on a lower DECK). **2** (of a temperature) lower than zero: *The thermometer had dropped to a record 40 below* (= −40 degrees). **3** at a lower rank: *This ruling applies to the ranks of Inspector and below.*

beˌlow-the-ˈfold *adj.* not in a position where it is seen first, for example on the bottom part of a newspaper page or web page: *below-the-fold links* ◊ *That story would have been better in a less prominent, below-the fold-position.* ➲ compare ABOVE-THE-FOLD **IDM** see FOLD *n.*

belt 🔑 /belt/ *noun, verb*
■ **noun 1** 🔑 a long narrow piece of leather, cloth, etc. that you wear around the waist: *to* **do up/fasten/tighten a belt** ◊ *a belt buckle* ➲ VISUAL VOCAB page V51 ➲ see also BLACK BELT, LIFEBELT, SEAT BELT, SUSPENDER BELT **2** a continuous band of material that moves round and is used to carry things along or to drive machinery ➲ see also CONVEYOR BELT, FAN BELT **3** an area with particular characteristics or where a particular group of people live: *the country's* **corn/industrial belt** ◊ *We live in the* **commuter belt**. ◊ *a belt of rain moving across the country* ➲ see also GREEN BELT **4** (*informal*) an act of hitting sth/sb hard: *She gave the ball a terrific belt.*
IDM **below the ˈbelt** (of a remark) unfair or cruel: *That was distinctly below the belt!* **ˌbelt and ˈbraces** (*informal*) taking more actions than are really necessary to make sure that sth succeeds or works as it should: *a belt-and-braces policy* **have sth under your ˈbelt** (*informal*) to have already achieved or obtained sth: *She already has a couple of good wins under her belt.* ➲ more at TIGHTEN
■ **verb 1 ~ sb/sth** (*informal*) to hit sb/sth hard: *He belted the ball right out of the park.* ◊ *I'll belt you if you do that again.* **2** [I] **+ adv./prep.** (*informal, especially BrE*) to move very fast **SYN** **tear**: *A truck came belting up behind us.* **3** [T] **~ sth** to fasten a belt around sth: *The dress was belted at the waist.*
PHR V **ˌbelt sth↔ˈout** (*informal*) to sing a song or play music loudly **ˌbelt ˈup** (*BrE*) **1** (*NAmE* **ˌbuckle ˈup**) (*informal*) to fasten your SEAT BELT (= a belt worn by a passenger in a vehicle) **2** (*informal*) used to tell sb rudely to be quiet **SYN** **shut up**: *Just belt up, will you!*

belt·ed /ˈbeltɪd/ *adj.* with a belt around it: *a belted jacket*

belt·way /ˈbeltweɪ/ *noun* (*US*) a RING ROAD, especially the one around Washington DC

be·luga /bəˈluːɡə/ (*pl.* **be·luga** or **be·lugas**) *noun* **1** [C] a type of small WHALE **2** [C] a type of large fish that lives in rivers and lakes in eastern Europe **3** (also **beˌluga ˈcaviar**) [U] a type of CAVIAR (= fish eggs), from a beluga

be·moan /bɪˈməʊn; *NAmE* bɪˈmoʊn/ *verb* **~ sth** (*formal*) to complain or say that you are not happy about sth: *They sat bemoaning the fact that no one would give them a chance.*

be·mused /bɪˈmjuːzd/ *adj.* showing that you are confused and unable to think clearly **SYN** **bewildered**: *a* **bemused expression/smile** ▸ **be·muse** *verb* **~ sb** **be·mus·ed·ly** /bɪˈmjuːzɪdli/ *adv.*

bench /bentʃ/ *noun* **1** [C] a long seat for two or more people, usually made of wood: *a park bench* ➲ VISUAL VOCAB page V16 **2 the bench** [sing.] (*law*) a judge in court or the seat where he/she sits; the position of being a judge or MAGISTRATE: *His lawyer turned to address the bench.* ◊ *She has recently been appointed to the bench.* **3** [C, usually pl.] (in the British Parliament) a seat where a particular group of politicians sit: *There was cheering from the Opposition benches.* ➲ see also BACK BENCH, THE FRONT BENCH **4 the bench** [sing.] (*sport*) the seats where players sit when they are not playing in the game: *the substitutes' bench* **5** [C] = WORKBENCH: *a carpenter's bench*

bench·mark /ˈbentʃmɑːk; *NAmE* -mɑːrk/ *noun, verb*
■ **noun** something that can be measured and used as a standard that other things can be compared with: *Tests at the age of seven provide a benchmark against which the child's progress at school can be measured.*
■ **verb ~ sth** (**against sth**) to judge the quality of sth in relation to that of other similar things: *Projects are assessed and benchmarked against the targets.*

ˈbench press *noun* an exercise in which you lie on a raised surface with your feet on the floor and raise a weight with both arms

bench·warm·er /ˈbentʃwɔːmə(r); *NAmE* -wɔːrm-/ *noun* (*NAmE, informal*) a sports player who is not chosen to play in a particular game, but is available if their team needs them **SYN** **substitute**

bend 🔑 /bend/ *verb, noun*
■ **verb** (**bent, bent** /bent/) **1** 🔑 [I, T] (especially of sb's body or head) to lean, or make sth lean, in a particular direction: *He bent and kissed her.* ◊ **+ adv./prep.** *fields of poppies bending in the wind* ◊ *His dark head bent over her.* ◊ *She bent forward to pick up the newspaper.* ◊ *Slowly bend from the waist and bring your head down to your knees.* ◊ **~ sth** (**+ adv./prep.**) *He bent his head and kissed her.* ◊ *She was bent over her desk writing a letter.* **2** 🔑 [T, I] **~** (**sth**) if you **bend** your arm, leg, etc. or if it **bends**, you move it so that it is no longer straight: *Bend your knees, keeping your back straight.* ◊ *Lie flat and let your knees bend.* **3** 🔑 [T] **~ sth** to force sth that was straight into an angle or a curve: *Mark the pipe where you want to bend it.* ◊ *The knives were bent out of shape.* ◊ *He bent the wire into the shape of a square.* **4** 🔑 [I, T] to change direction to form a curve or an angle; to make sth change direction in this way: *The road bent sharply to the right.* ◊ **~ sth** *Glass and water both bend light.*
IDM **bend sb's ˈear** (**about sth**) (*informal*) to talk to sb a lot about sth, especially about a problem that you have **bend your ˈmind/ˈefforts to sth** (*formal*) to think very hard about or put a lot of effort into one particular thing **bend the ˈtruth** to say sth that is not completely true **on bended ˈknee**(**s**) if you ask for sth **on bended knee**(**s**), you ask for it in a very anxious and/or HUMBLE way ➲ more at BACKWARDS, RULE *n.*
PHR V **ˈbend sb to sth** (*formal*) to force or persuade sb to do what you want or to accept your opinions: *He manipulates people and tries to* **bend them to his will** (= make them do what he wants).
■ **noun 1** 🔑 [C] a curve or turn, especially in a road or river: *a sharp bend in the road* ➲ see also HAIRPIN BEND **2 the bends** [pl.] severe pain and difficulty in breathing experienced by a DIVER who comes back to the surface of the water too quickly
IDM **round the bend/twist** (*informal, especially BrE*) crazy: *She's gone completely round the bend.* ◊ *The kids have been* **driving me round the bend** *today* (= annoying me very much).

bend·er /ˈbendə(r)/ *noun* (*slang*) a period of drinking a lot of alcohol or taking a lot of drugs: *to go on a bender*

bendy /ˈbendi/ *adj.* (*BrE, informal*) **1** that can be bent easily **SYN** **flexible** **2** with many bends: *a bendy road*

ˈbendy bus *noun* (*BrE, informal*) a long bus that bends in the middle so that it can turn corners more easily

be·neath 🔑 /bɪˈniːθ/ *prep.* (*formal*)
1 🔑 in or to a lower position than sb/sth; under sb/sth:

B

They found the body buried beneath a pile of leaves. ◇ *The boat sank beneath the waves.* **2** not good enough for sb: *He considers such jobs beneath him.* ◇ *They thought she had married beneath her* (= married a man of lower social status). ▸ **be·neath** ⊶ *adv.*: *Her careful make-up hid the signs of age beneath.*

Bene·dic·tine /ˌbenɪˈdɪktɪn/ *noun* a member of a Christian group of MONKS or NUNS following the rules of St Benedict ▸ **Bene·dic·tine** *adj.*: *a Benedictine monastery*

bene·dic·tion /ˌbenɪˈdɪkʃn/ *noun* [C, U] (*formal*) a Christian prayer of BLESSING

bene·fac·tion /ˌbenɪˈfækʃn/ *noun* (*formal*) a gift, usually of money, that is given to a person or an organization in order to do good

bene·fac·tor /ˈbenɪfæktə(r)/ *noun* (*formal*) a person who gives money or other help to a person or an organization such as a school or charity

bene·fice /ˈbenɪfɪs/ *noun* the paid position of a Christian priest in charge of a PARISH

be·nefi·cent /bɪˈnefɪsnt/ *adj.* (*formal*) giving help; showing kindness SYN **generous** ▸ **be·nefi·cence** /bɪˈnefɪsns/ *noun* [U]

bene·fi·cial AW /ˌbenɪˈfɪʃl/ *adj.* **~ (to sth/sb)** (*formal*) improving a situation; having a helpful or useful effect SYN **advantageous, favourable**: *A good diet is beneficial to health.* OPP **detrimental**

bene·fi·ciary AW /ˌbenɪˈfɪʃəri; *NAmE* -ˈfɪʃieri/ *noun* (*pl.* -ies) **1 ~ (of sth)** a person who gains as a result of sth: *Who will be the main beneficiary of the cuts in income tax?* **2 ~ (of sth)** a person who receives money or property when sb dies

bene·fit ⊶ AW /ˈbenɪfɪt/ *noun, verb*

■ ***noun*** **1** ⊶ [U, C] an advantage that sth gives you; a helpful and useful effect that sth has: *I've* ***had the benefit of*** *a good education.* ◇ *The new regulations will be* ***of benefit to*** *everyone concerned.* ◇ *It will be* ***to your benefit*** *to arrive early.* ◇ *He couldn't see the benefit of arguing any longer.* ◇ *the benefits of modern medicine* ◇ *It was good to see her finally* ***reaping the benefits*** (= enjoying the results) *of all her hard work.* ➲ see also COST-BENEFIT, FRINGE BENEFIT **2** [U, C] (*BrE*) money provided by the government to people who need financial help because they are unemployed, ill/sick, etc. ➲ see also CHILD BENEFIT, HOUSING BENEFIT, SICKNESS BENEFIT **3** [C, usually pl.] an advantage that you get from a company in addition to the money that you earn; money from an insurance company: *The insurance plan will provide substantial cash benefits to your family in case of your death.* ➲ see also FRINGE BENEFIT **4** [C] an event such as a performance, a dinner, etc, organized in order to raise money for a particular person or charity: *a* ***benefit match/concert***

IDM **for sb's benefit** ⊶ especially in order to help or be useful to sb: *I have typed out some lecture notes for the benefit of those people who were absent last week.* ◇ *Don't go to any trouble for my benefit!* **give sb the ˌbenefit of the ˈdoubt** to accept that sb has told the truth or has not done sth wrong because you cannot prove that they have not

■ ***verb*** (-t- or -tt-) **1** ⊶ [T] **~ sb** to be useful to sb or improve their life in some way: *We should spend the money on something that will benefit everyone.* **2** ⊶ [I] **~ (from/by sth)** to be in a better position because of sth: *Who exactly* ***stands to benefit*** *from these changes?*

Bene·lux /ˈbenɪlʌks/ *noun* [U] a name for Belgium, the Netherlands and Luxembourg, when they are thought of as a group

be·nevo·lent /bəˈnevələnt/ *adj.* **1** (*formal*) (especially of people in authority) kind, helpful and generous: *a benevolent smile/attitude* ◇ *belief in the existence of a benevolent god* OPP **malevolent 2** used in the names of some organizations that give help and money to people in need: *the RAF Benevolent Fund* ▸ **be·nevo·lence** /bəˈnevələns/ *noun* [U] **be·nevo·lent·ly** *adv.*

Ben·gali /beŋˈɡɔːli; *NAmE* -ˈɡɑːli/ *noun* **1** [C] a person from Bangladesh or West Bengal in eastern India **2** [U] the language of people from Bangladesh or West Bengal in eastern India ▸ **Ben·gali** *adj.*

be·night·ed /bɪˈnaɪtɪd/ *adj.* (*old-fashioned*) **1** (of people) without understanding **2** (of places) without the benefits of modern life

be·nign /bɪˈnaɪn/ *adj.* **1** (*formal*) (of people) kind and gentle; not hurting anybody **2** (*medical*) (of TUMOURS growing in the body) not dangerous or likely to cause death OPP **malignant** ▸ **be·nign·ly** *adv.*: *He smiled benignly.*

bent ⊶ /bent/ *adj., noun* ➲ see also BEND

■ ***adj.*** **1** ⊶ not straight: *a piece of bent wire* ◇ *Do this exercise with your knees bent* (= not with your legs straight). ➲ picture at CURVED **2** ⊶ (of a person) not able to stand up straight, usually as a result of being old or ill/sick: *a small bent old woman* ◇ *He was* ***bent double*** *with laughter.* **3** (*BrE, informal*) (of a person in authority) dishonest

IDM **ˈbent on sth/on doing sth** determined to do sth (usually sth bad): *She seems bent on making life difficult for me.* ➲ see also HELL-BENT **get bent out of ˈshape (about/over sth)** (*NAmE, informal*) to become angry, anxious or upset: *Don't get bent out of shape about it. It was just a mistake!*

■ ***noun*** [usually sing.] **~ (for sth)** a natural skill or interest in sth: *She has a bent for mathematics.*

bent·wood /ˈbentwʊd/ *noun* [U] wood that is artificially shaped for making furniture: *bentwood chairs*

ben·zene /ˈbenziːn/ *noun* [U] a clear liquid obtained from PETROLEUM and COAL TAR, used in making plastics and many chemical products

be·queath /bɪˈkwiːð/ *verb* (*formal*) **1** to say in a WILL that you want sb to have your property, money, etc. after you die SYN **leave**: **~ sth (to sb)** *He bequeathed his entire estate* (= all his money and property) *to his daughter.* ◇ **~ sb sth** *He bequeathed his daughter his entire estate.* **2 ~ sth (to sb)** | **~ sb sth** to leave the results of your work, knowledge, etc. for other people to use or deal with, especially after you have died

be·quest /bɪˈkwest/ *noun* (*formal*) money or property that you ask to be given to a particular person when you die: *He left a bequest to each of his grandchildren.*

be·rate /bɪˈreɪt/ *verb* **~ sb/yourself** (*formal*) to criticize or speak angrily to sb because you do not approve of sth they have done

be·reave /bɪˈriːv/ *verb* **be bereaved** if sb **is bereaved**, a relative or close friend has just died: *The ceremony was an ordeal for those who had been recently bereaved.*

be·reaved /bɪˈriːvd/ *adj.* (*formal*) **1** having lost a relative or close friend who has recently died: *recently bereaved families* **2 the bereaved** *noun* (*pl.* **the bereaved**) a person who is bereaved: *an organization offering counselling for the bereaved*

be·reave·ment /bɪˈriːvmənt/ *noun* **1** [U] the state of having lost a relative or close friend because they have died: *the pain of an emotional crisis such as divorce or bereavement* **2** [C] the death of a relative or close friend: *A family bereavement meant that he could not attend the conference.*

be·reft /bɪˈreft/ *adj.* [not before noun] (*formal*) **1 ~ of sth** completely lacking sth; having lost sth: *bereft of ideas/hope* **2** (of a person) sad and lonely because you have lost sth: *He was utterly bereft when his wife died.*

beret /ˈbereɪ; *NAmE* bəˈreɪ/ *noun* a round flat cap made out of soft cloth and with a tight band around the head ➲ VISUAL VOCAB page V53

berg /bɜːɡ; *NAmE* bɜːrɡ/ *noun* (*SAfrE*) **1** a mountain or group of mountains **2 the Berg** [sing.] the Drakensberg, a group of tall mountains in South Africa

ber·ga·mot /ˈbɜːɡəmɒt; *NAmE* ˈbɜːrɡəmɑːt/ *noun* [U] **1** (also ˈ**bergamot oil**) oil from the skin of a small orange **2** a type of HERB

berg·schrund /ˈbɜːɡʃrʊnd; *NAmE* ˈbɜːrkʃrʊnt/ *noun* (*geology*) a deep crack formed where a GLACIER (= a large moving mass of ice) meets the side of a mountain

ber·i·ber·i /ˌberiˈberi/ *noun* [U] a disease that affects the nerves and heart, caused by a lack of VITAMIN B

berk /bɜːk; *NAmE* bɜːrk/ *noun* (*old-fashioned, BrE, slang*) a stupid person SYN **idiot**

ber·ke·lium /bɜːˈkiːliəm; ˈbɜːkliəm; *NAmE* ˈbɜːrkliəm/ *noun* [U] (*symb.* **Bk**) a chemical element. Berkelium is a RADIOACTIVE metal that is produced artificially from AMERICIUM and HELIUM.

Ber·lin·er /ˌbɜːˈlɪnə(r); *NAmE* ˌbɜːr-/ *adj.* (*BrE*) (of a newspaper) printed on pages measuring 470mm by 315mm, smaller than a BROADSHEET and larger than a TABLOID

berm /bɜːm; *NAmE* bɜːrm/ *noun* (*technical*) **1** an area of ground at the side of a road; a raised area of ground at the side of a river or CANAL **2** a narrow raised area of sand formed on a beach by the waves coming in from the sea

Bermuda shorts /bəˌmjuːdə ˈʃɔːts; *NAmE* bərˌmjuːdə ˈʃɔːrts/ (also **Ber·mu·das** /bəˈmjuːdəz; *NAmE* bərˈm-/) *noun* [pl.] SHORTS (= short trousers/pants) that come down to just above the knee: *a pair of Bermudas*

the Berˌmuda ˈTriangle *noun* [sing.] an area in the Atlantic Ocean between Bermuda, Florida and Puerto Rico where a large number of ships and aircraft are believed to have disappeared in a mysterious way: *This area of town is known as the Bermuda Triangle because drinkers can disappear into the pubs and clubs and be lost to the world.*

berry /ˈberi/ *noun* (*pl.* **-ies**) (often in compounds) a small fruit that grows on a bush. There are several types of berry, some of which can be eaten: *Birds feed on nuts and berries in the winter.* ◇ *blackberries/raspberries* ➲ VISUAL VOCAB pages V8, V26

ber·serk /bəˈzɜːk; -ˈsɜːk; *NAmE* bərˈzɜːrk; -ˈsɜːrk/ *adj.* [not usually before noun] (*informal*) **1** very angry, often in a violent or uncontrolled way: *He* **went berserk** *when he found out where I'd been.* **2** very excited: *People were going berserk with excitement.*

berth /bɜːθ; *NAmE* bɜːrθ/ *noun, verb*

■ ***noun*** **1** a place to sleep on a ship or train, or in a CARAVAN/CAMPER SYN **bunk** **2** a place where a ship or boat can stop and stay, usually in a HARBOUR IDM see WIDE *adj.*

■ ***verb*** [T, I] **~ (sth)** to put a ship in a berth or keep it there; to sail into a berth: *The ship is berthed at Southampton.*

beryl /ˈberəl/ *noun* [U] a transparent pale green, blue or yellow SEMI-PRECIOUS STONE, used in making jewellery

beryl·lium /bəˈrɪliəm/ *noun* [U] (*symb.* **Be**) a chemical element. Beryllium is a hard grey metal found mainly in the mineral BERYL.

besan /ˈbeɪsʌn/ *noun* = GRAM FLOUR

be·seech /bɪˈsiːtʃ/ *verb* (**be·sought**, **be·sought** /bɪˈsɔːt/) or (**be·seeched**, **be·seeched**) **~ sb (to do sth)** (*formal*) to ask sb for sth in an anxious way because you want or need it very much SYN **implore**, **beg**: *Let him go, I beseech you!*

be·seech·ing /bɪˈsiːtʃɪŋ/ *adj.* [only before noun] (*formal*) (of a look, tone of voice, etc.) showing that you want sth very much ▸ **be·seech·ing·ly** *adv.*

beset /bɪˈset/ *verb* (**be·set·ting**, **beset**, **beset**) [usually passive] **~ sb/sth** (*formal*) to affect sb/sth in an unpleasant or harmful way: *The team was beset by injury all season.* ◇ *It's one of the most difficult problems besetting our modern way of life.*

be·side 0‑w /bɪˈsaɪd/ *prep.*

1 0‑w next to or at the side of sb/sth: *He sat beside her all night.* ◇ *a mill beside a stream* **2** compared with sb/sth: *My painting looks childish beside yours.*

IDM **be beside the ˈpoint** to not be important or closely related to the main thing you are talking about: *Yes, I know it was an accident, but that's beside the point.* **beˈside yourself (with sth)** unable to control yourself because of the strength of emotion you are feeling: *He was beside himself with rage when I told him what I had done.*

Which Word?

beside / besides

- The preposition **beside** usually means 'next to something/somebody' or 'at the side of something/somebody': *Sit here beside me.* **Besides** means 'in addition to something': *What other sports do you play besides hockey?* Do not use **beside** with this meaning.
- The adverb **besides** is not usually used on its own with the same meaning as the preposition. It is mainly used to give another reason or argument for something: *I don't think I'll come on Saturday. I have a lot of work to do. Besides, I don't really like parties.* ◇ ~~*She likes football. Besides, she likes tennis and basketball.*~~

be·sides /bɪˈsaɪdz/ *prep., adv.*

■ ***prep.*** in addition to sb/sth; apart from sb/sth: *We have lots of things in common besides music.* ◇ *Besides working as a doctor, he also writes novels in his spare time.* ◇ *I've got no family besides my parents.* ➲ LANGUAGE BANK at EXCEPT ➲ note at BESIDE

■ ***adv.*** **1** used for making an extra comment that adds to what you have just said: *I don't really want to go. Besides, it's too late now.* ➲ LANGUAGE BANK at ADDITION ➲ note at BESIDE **2** in addition; also: *discounts on televisions, stereos and much more besides*

Which Word?

besides / apart from / except

- The preposition **besides** means 'in addition to': *What other sports do you like besides football?* You use **except** when you mention the only thing that is not included in a statement: *I like all sports except football.* You can use **apart from** with both these meanings: *What other sports do you like apart from football?* ◇ *I like all sports apart from football.*

be·siege /bɪˈsiːdʒ/ *verb* **1 ~ sth** to surround a building, city, etc. with soldiers until the people inside are forced to let you in SYN **lay siege to**: *Paris was besieged for four months and forced to surrender.* ◇ (*figurative*) *Fans besieged the box office to try and get tickets for the concert.* **2** [usually passive] **~ sb/sth** (especially of sth unpleasant or annoying) to surround sb/sth in large numbers: *The actress was besieged by reporters at the airport.* **3 ~ sb (with sth)** to send so many letters, ask so many questions, etc. that it is difficult for sb to deal with them all: *The radio station was besieged with calls from angry listeners.*

be·smirch /bɪˈsmɜːtʃ; *NAmE* bɪˈsmɜːrtʃ/ *verb* **~ sb/sth** (*formal*) to damage the opinion that people have of sb/sth SYN **sully**

besom /ˈbiːzəm/ *noun* a brush for sweeping floors, made from sticks tied onto a long handle

be·sot·ted /bɪˈsɒtɪd; *NAmE* -ˈsɑːt-/ *adj.* **~ (by/with sb/sth)** loving sb/sth so much that you do not behave in a sensible way: *He is completely besotted with his new girlfriend.*

be·sought *past tense, past part.* of BESEECH

be·spat·ter /bɪˈspætə(r)/ *verb* **~ sth** (*literary*) to accidentally cover sth with small drops of water

be·speak /bɪˈspiːk/ *verb* (**be·spoke** /-ˈspəʊk; *NAmE* -ˈspoʊk/, **be·spoken** /-ˈspəʊkən; *NAmE* -ˈspoʊ-/) **~ sth** (*literary*) to show or suggest sth: *His style of dressing bespoke great self-confidence.*

be·spec·tacled /bɪˈspektəkld/ *adj.* (*formal*) wearing SPECTACLES

be·spoke /bɪˈspəʊk; *NAmE* bɪˈspoʊk/ *adj.* [usually before noun] (*especially BrE, formal*) **1** (*NAmE* usually ˌ**customˈmade**) (of a product) made specially, according to the needs of an individual customer SYN **tailor-made**: *bespoke software* ◇ *a bespoke suit* **2** making products specially, according to the needs of an individual customer: *a bespoke tailor*

best 0─ /best/ *adj., adv., noun, verb*

■ ***adj.*** (superlative of *good*) **1** 0─ of the most excellent type or quality: *That's the best movie I've ever seen!* ◇ *She was one of the best tennis players of her generation.* ◇ *Is that your best suit?* ◇ *They've been* ***best friends*** (= closest friends) *since they were children.* ◇ *the company's* ***best-ever*** *results* ◇ *We want the kids to have the* ***best possible*** *education.* **2** 0─ most enjoyable; happiest: *Those were the best years of my life.* **3** 0─ most suitable or appropriate: *What's the best way to cook steak?* ◇ *The best thing to do would be to apologize.* ◇ *He's the best man for the job.* ◇ ***It's best*** *if you go now.* ◇ *I'm not in the best position to advise you.*

IDM Idioms containing **best** *adj.* are at the entries for the nouns and verbs in the idioms, for example **on your best behaviour** is at **behaviour**.

■ ***adv.*** (superlative of *well*, often used in adjectives) **1** 0─ most; to the greatest extent: *Which one do you like best?* ◇ *Well-drained soil suits the plant best.* ◇ *her* ***best-known*** *poem* **2** 0─ in the most excellent way; to the highest standard: *He works best in the mornings.* ◇ *Britain's* ***best-dressed*** *woman* ◇ *The beaches are beautiful, but,* ***best of all***, *there are very few tourists.* **3** 0─ in the most suitable or appropriate way: *Painting is best done in daylight.* ◇ *Do as you* ***think best*** (= what you think is the most suitable thing to do).

IDM **as ˌbest you ˈcan** not perfectly but as well as you are able: *We'll manage as best we can.*

■ ***noun*** [sing.] (usually **the best**) **1** 0─ the most excellent thing or person: *We all want the best for our children.* ◇ *They only buy the best.* ◇ *They're all good players, but she's the best of all.* ◇ *We're* ***the best of friends*** (= very close friends). **2** 0─ the highest standard that sb/sth can reach: *She always brings out the best in people.* ◇ *The town* ***looks its best*** (= is most attractive) *in the spring.* ◇ *Don't worry about the exam—just* ***do your best.*** ◇ *The roses are* ***past their best*** *now.* ◇ *I don't really feel* ***at my best*** *today.* **3** 0─ something that is as close as possible to what you need or want: *Fifty pounds is the best I can offer you.* ◇ *The best we can hope for in the game is a draw.* **4** the highest standard that a particular person has reached, especially in a sport: *She won the race with a* ***personal best*** *of 2 minutes 22.*

IDM **all the ˈbest** (*informal*) used when you are saying goodbye to sb or ending a letter, to give sb your good wishes **at ˈbest** used for saying what is the best opinion you can have of sb/sth, or the best thing that can happen, when the situation is bad: *Their response to the proposal was, at best, cool.* ◇ *We can't arrive before Friday at best.* **be (all) for the ˈbest** used to say that although sth appears bad or unpleasant now, it will be good in the end: *I don't want you to leave, but perhaps it's for the best.* **the best of a bad ˈbunch** (*BrE* also **the best of a bad ˈlot**) (*informal*) a person or thing that is a little better than the rest of a group, although none are very good **the best of ˈthree, ˈfive, etc.** (especially in games and sports) up to three, five, etc. games played to decide who wins, the winner being the person who wins most of them **the best that money can ˈbuy** the very best: *We make sure our clients get the best that money can buy.* **do, mean, etc. sth for the ˈbest** to do or say sth in order to achieve a good result or to help sb: *I just don't know what to do for the best.* ◇ *I'm sorry if my advice offended you—I meant it for the best.* **have/get the ˈbest of sth** to gain more advantage from sth than sb else: *I thought you had the best of that discussion.* **make the best of sth/it | make the best of things | make the best of a bad job** to accept a bad or difficult situation and do as well as you can **to the best of your ˈknowledge/beˈlief** as far as you know: *He never made a will, to the best of my knowledge.* **with the ˈbest (of them)** as well as anyone: *He'll be out there, dancing with the best of them.* ➲ more at BUNCH *n.*, HOPE *v.*, LUCK *n.*, SUNDAY

■ ***verb*** [usually passive] **~ sb** (*formal*) to defeat or be more successful than sb

ˌbest-beˈfore date *noun* (*BrE*) a date printed on a container or package, advising you to use food or drink before this date as it will not be of such good quality after that

bes·tial /ˈbestiəl; *NAmE* ˈbestʃəl/ *adj.* (*formal*) cruel and disgusting; of or like a BEAST: ***bestial acts/cruelty/noises***

bes·ti·al·ity /ˌbestiˈæləti; *NAmE* ˌbestʃi-/ *noun* [U] **1** (*technical*) sexual activity between a human and an animal **2** (*formal*) cruel or disgusting behaviour

bes·tiary /ˈbestɪəri; *NAmE* -eri/ *noun* (*pl.* -ies) a collection of descriptions of, or stories about, various types of animal, especially one written in the Middle Ages

be·stir /bɪˈstɜː(r)/ *verb* (-rr-) **~ yourself** (*formal* or *humorous*) to start doing things after a period during which you have been doing nothing SYN **rouse**

ˌbest ˈman *noun* [sing.] a male friend or relative of the BRIDEGROOM at a wedding, who helps him during the wedding ceremony ➲ compare BRIDESMAID

be·stow /bɪˈstəʊ; *NAmE* bɪˈstoʊ/ *verb* **~ sth (on/upon sb)** (*formal*) to give sth to sb, especially to show how much they are respected: *It was a title bestowed upon him by the king.*

ˌbest ˈpractice *noun* [U, C] a way of doing sth that is seen as a very good example of how it should be done and can be copied by other companies or organizations

be·stride /bɪˈstraɪd/ *verb* **~ sth** (*literary*) to sit with one leg on either side of sth: *He bestrode his horse.*

ˌbest-ˈseller (also **best·seller**) /ˌbestˈselə(r)/ *noun* a product, usually a book, which is bought by large numbers of people: *the best-seller list* ▸ **ˌbest-ˈselling** *adj.*: *a* ***best-selling novel/author***

be·suit·ed /bɪˈsuːtɪd; *BrE* also -sjuːt-/ *adj.* (*formal*) wearing a suit: *besuited businessmen*

bet 0─ /bet/ *verb, noun*

■ ***verb*** (**bet·ting, bet, bet**) **1** 0─ [I, T] to risk money on a race or an event by trying to predict the result: *You have to be over 16 to bet.* ◇ **~ on/against sth** *I wouldn't bet on them winning the next election.* ◇ **~ sth (on sth)** *He bet $2 000 on the final score of the game.* ◇ **~ (sb) (sth) (that...)** *She bet me £20 that I wouldn't do it.* ➲ see also BETTING, GAMBLE **2** 0─ [T] (*informal*) used to say that you are almost certain that sth is true or that sth will happen: **~ (that)...** *I bet (that) we're too late.* ◇ *You can bet (that) the moment I sit down, the phone will ring.* ◇ **~ sb (that)...** *I'll bet you (that) he knows all about it.*

IDM **I/I'll bet!** (*informal*) **1** used to show that you can understand what sb is feeling, describing, etc.: *'I nearly died when he told me.' 'I bet!'* **2** used to tell sb that you do not believe what they have just said: *'I'm going to tell her what I think of her.' 'Yeah, I bet!'* **I wouldn't ˈbet on it | don't ˈbet on it** (*informal*) used to say that you do not think that sth is very likely: *'She'll soon get used to the idea.' 'I wouldn't bet on it.'* **you ˈbet!** (*informal*) used instead of 'yes' to emphasize that sb has guessed sth correctly or made a good suggestion: *'Are you nervous?' 'You bet!'* **you can bet your ˈlife/your bottom ˈdollar (on sth/(that)...)** (*informal*) used to say that you are certain that sth will happen: *You can bet your bottom dollar that he'll be late.*

■ ***noun*** **1** 0─ an arrangement to risk money, etc. on the result of a particular event; the money that you risk in this way: *to* ***win/lose a bet*** ◇ **~ on sth** *We've got a bet on who's going to arrive first.* ◇ *He had a bet on the horses.* ◇ *They all put a bet on the race.* ◇ *I hear you're taking bets on whether she'll marry him.* ◇ *I did it* ***for a bet*** (= because sb had agreed to pay me money if I did). ◇ *'Liverpool are bound to win.'* ***'Do you want a bet?'*** (= I disagree with you, I don't think they will.) **2** (*informal*) an opinion about what is likely to happen or to have happened: *My bet is that they've been held up in traffic.*

IDM **all bets are ˈoff** used to say that if a particular event happens then your current forecast, agreement, etc. will no longer apply: *We expect shares to rise unless the economy slows down again, in which case all bets are off.* **the/your best bet** (*informal*) used to tell sb what is the best action for them to take to get the result they want: *If you want to get around London fast, the Underground is your best bet.* **a ˌgood/ˌsafe ˈbet** something that is likely to happen, to succeed or to be suitable: *Clothes are a safe bet as a present for a teenager.* ➲ more at HEDGE *v.*

beta /ˈbiːtə; *NAmE* ˈbeɪtə/ *noun* the second letter of the Greek alphabet (Β, β) '**beta blocker** *noun* a drug used to control heart rhythm, treat severe chest pain and reduce high blood pressure

ˌ**beta-'carotene** *noun* [U] a substance found in carrots and other plants, which is needed by humans

'**beta decay** *noun* [sing.] (*physics*) the breaking up of an atom in which an ELECTRON is given off

be·take /bɪ'teɪk/ *verb* (**be·took** /-'tʊk/, **be·taken** /-'teɪkən/) **~ yourself + adv./prep.** (*literary*) to go somewhere: *He betook himself to his room.*

'**beta particle** (also '**beta ray**) *noun* (*physics*) a fast-moving ELECTRON that is produced when some RADIOACTIVE substances decay

'**beta test** *noun* a test on a new product, done by sb who does not work for the company that is developing the product ➲ compare ALPHA TEST ▶ '**beta-test** *verb* **~ sth**

'**beta version** *noun* [usually sing.] the version of a new product, especially computer software, that is almost ready for the public to buy or use, but is given to a few customers to test first

betel /'bi:tl/ *noun* [U] the leaves of a climbing plant, also called betel, chewed by people in Asia

'**betel nut** *noun* the slightly bitter nut of a tropical Asian PALM, that is cut into small pieces, wrapped in betel leaves, and chewed

bête noire /ˌbet 'nwɑ:(r)/ *noun* (*pl.* **bêtes noires** /ˌbet 'nwɑ:(r); *NAmE* also 'nwɑ:rz/) (from *French*) a person or thing that particularly annoys you and that you do not like

be·tide /bɪ'taɪd/ *verb* IDM see WOE

be·token /bɪ'təʊkən; *NAmE* -'toʊ-/ *verb* **~ sth** (*literary*) to be a sign of sth: *a clear blue sky betokening a fine day*

be·tray /bɪ'treɪ/ *verb* **1** to give information about sb/sth to an enemy: **~ sb/sth** *He was offered money to betray his colleagues.* ◇ **~ sb/sth to sb** *For years they had been betraying state secrets to Russia.* **2 ~ sb/sth** to hurt sb who trusts you, especially by not being loyal or faithful to them: *She felt betrayed when she found out the truth about him.* ◇ *She* ***betrayed his trust*** *over and over again.* ◇ *I have never known her to* ***betray a confidence*** (= tell other people sth that should be kept secret). ➲ SYNONYMS at CHEAT **3 ~ sth** to ignore your principles or beliefs in order to achieve sth or gain an advantage for yourself: *He has been accused of betraying his former socialist ideals.* **4** to tell sb or make them aware of a piece of information, a feeling, etc, usually without meaning to SYN **give away**: **~ sth** *His voice betrayed the worry he was trying to hide.* ◇ **~ yourself** *She was terrified of saying something that would make her betray herself* (= show her feelings or who she was).

be·tray·al /bɪ'treɪəl/ *noun* [U, C] the act of betraying sb/sth or the fact of being betrayed: *a* ***sense/a feeling/an act of betrayal*** ◇ *I saw her actions as a betrayal of my trust.* ◇ *the many disappointments and betrayals in his life*

be·troth·al /bɪ'trəʊðl; *NAmE* -'troʊ-/ *noun* **~ (to sb)** (*formal* or *old-fashioned*) an agreement to marry sb SYN **engagement**

be·trothed /bɪ'trəʊðd; *NAmE* -'troʊ-/ *adj.* (*formal* or *old-fashioned*) **1 ~ (to sb)** having promised to marry sb SYN **engaged 2 sb's betrothed** *noun* [sing.] the person that sb has promised to marry

bet·ter 0-w /'betə(r)/ *adj., adv., noun, verb*

■ ***adj.*** (comparative of *good*) **1** 0-w of a higher standard or less poor quality; not as bad as sth else: *We're hoping for better weather tomorrow.* ◇ *Her work is getting* ***better and better.*** ◇ *He is in a much better mood than usual.* ◇ *The meal couldn't have been better.* ◇ *There's nothing better than a long soak in a hot bath.* ◇ *If you can only exercise once a week, that's* ***better than nothing*** (= better than taking no exercise at all). **2** 0-w more able or skilled: *She's far better at science than her brother.* **3** 0-w more suitable or appropriate: *Can you think of a better word than 'nice'?* ◇ *It would be better for him to talk to his parents about his problems.* ◇ ***You'd be better*** *going by bus.* **4** 0-w less ill/sick or unhappy: *She's a lot better today.* ◇ *His leg was getting better.* ◇ *You'll feel* ***all the better for*** *a good night's sleep.* **5** fully recovered after an illness; in good health again: *Don't go back to work until you are better.* ➲ see also WELL *adj.*

IDM Most idioms containing **better** are at the entries for the nouns and verbs in the idioms, for example **better luck next time** is at **luck**. **little/no better than** almost or just the same as; almost or just as bad as: *The path was no better than a sheep track.* **that's (much) 'better 1** used to give support to sb who has been upset and is trying to become calmer: *Dry your eyes now. That's better.* **2** used to praise sb who has made an effort to improve: *That's much better—you played the right notes this time.* **the ˌbigger, ˌsmaller, ˌfaster, ˌslower, etc. the 'better** used to say that sth should be as big, small, etc. as possible: *As far as the hard disk is concerned, the bigger the better.* ➲ more at DISCRETION, HEAD *n.*, PART *n.*, PREVENTION

■ ***adv.*** (comparative of *well*) **1** 0-w in a more excellent or pleasant way; not as badly: *She sings much better than I do.* ◇ *Sound travels better in water than in air.* ◇ *People are better educated now.* **2** 0-w more; to a greater degree: *You'll like her when you know her better.* ◇ *A cup of tea? There's nothing I'd like better!* ◇ *Fit people are better able to cope with stress.* **3** used to suggest that sth would be a suitable or appropriate thing to do: *The money could be better spent on more urgent cases.* ◇ *Some things are better left unsaid.* ◇ *You'd* ***do better to*** *tell her everything before she finds out from someone else.*

IDM Most idioms containing **better** are at the entries for the nouns, adjectives and verbs in the idioms, for example **better the devil you know** is at **devil**. **be better 'off** 0-w to have more money: *Families will be better off under the new law.* ◇ *Her promotion means she's $100 a week better off.* OPP **be worse off** **be better off (doing sth)** used to say that sb is/would be happier or more satisfied if they were in a particular position or did a particular thing: *She's better off without him.* ◇ *The weather was so bad we'd have been better off staying at home.* **had better/best (do sth)** 0-w used to tell sb what you think they should do.: *You'd better go to the doctor about your cough.* ◇ *We'd better leave now or we'll miss the bus.* ◇ *You'd better not do that again.* ◇ *'I'll give you back the money tomorrow.' 'You'd better!'* (= as a threat) ➲ note at SHOULD

■ ***noun*** **1** 0-w [sing., U] something that is better: *the better of the two books* ◇ *I expected better of him* (= I thought he would have behaved better). **2 your betters** [pl.] (*old-fashioned*) people who are more intelligent or more important than you

IDM **for ˌbetter or (for) 'worse** used to say that sth cannot be changed, whether the result is good or bad **get the better of sb/sth** to defeat sb/sth or gain an advantage: *No one can get the better of her in an argument.* ◇ *She always gets the better of an argument.* ◇ *His curiosity got the better of him* (= he didn't intend to ask questions, but he wanted to know so badly that he did). **so much the 'better/'worse** used to say that sth is even better/worse: *We don't actually need it on Tuesday, but if it arrives by then, so much the better.* ➲ more at CHANGE *n.*, ELDER *n.*, THINK *v.*

■ ***verb*** **1** [often passive] **~ sth** to be better or do sth better than sb/sth else: *The work he produced early in his career has never really been bettered.* **2 ~ yourself** to improve your social position through education, a better job, etc: *Thousands of Victorian workers joined educational associations in an attempt to better themselves.*

ˌ**better 'half** *noun* = OTHER HALF

bet·ter·ment /'betəmənt; *NAmE* 'betərm-/ *noun* [U] (*formal*) the process of becoming or making sth/sb better SYN **improvement**

bet·ting 0-w /'betɪŋ/ *noun* [U] the act of risking money, etc. on the unknown result of an event: *illegal betting* ➲ see also SPREAD BETTING

IDM **what's the betting...? | the betting is that...** (*informal*) it seems likely that...: *What's the betting that he gets his own way?* ◇ *The betting is that he'll get his own way.*

'**betting shop** *noun* (*BrE*) a shop where you can bet on horse races and other competitions

be·tween 0-w /bɪ'twi:n/ *prep., adv.*

■ ***prep.*** **1** 0-w in or into the space separating two or more points, objects, people, etc: *Q comes between P and R in*

B

the English alphabet. ◇ *I sat down between Jo and Diana.* ◇ *Switzerland lies between France, Germany, Austria and Italy.* ◇ *The paper had fallen down between the desk and the wall.* ◇ *(figurative) My job is somewhere between a secretary and a personal assistant.* **2** 🔑 in the period of time that separates two days, years, events, etc: *It's cheaper between 6 p.m. and 8 a.m.* ◇ *Don't eat between meals.* ◇ *Children must attend school between the ages of 5 and 16.* ◇ *Many changes took place between the two world wars.* **3** 🔑 at some point along a scale from one amount, weight, distance, etc. to another: *It weighed between nine and ten kilos.* ◇ *The temperature remained between 25 °C and 30 °C all week.* **4** 🔑 (of a line) separating one place from another: *the border between Sweden and Norway* **5** 🔑 from one place to another: *We fly between Rome and Paris twice daily.* **6** 🔑 used to show a connection or relationship: *a difference/distinction/contrast between two things* ◇ *a link between unemployment and crime* ◇ *There's a lot of bad feeling between them.* ◇ *I had to choose between the two jobs.* **7** 🔑 shared by two or more people or things: *We ate a pizza between us.* ◇ *This is just* ***between you and me/between ourselves*** (= it is a secret). **8** 🔑 by putting together the efforts or actions of two or more people or groups: *We ought to be able to manage it between us.* **9 ~ doing sth** used to show that several activities are involved: *Between working full-time and taking care of the kids, he didn't have much time for hobbies.*
■ ***adv.*** 🔑 (usually **in between**) in the space or period of time separating two or more points, objects, etc. or two dates, events, etc: *The house was near a park but there was a road in between.* ◇ *I see her most weekends but not very often in between.* IDM see BETWIXT

be·twixt /bɪˈtwɪkst/ *adv., prep.* (*literary* or *old use*) between
IDM **beˌtwixt and beˈtween** (*old-fashioned*) in a middle position; neither one thing nor the other

bevel /ˈbevl/ *noun* **1** a sloping edge or surface, for example at the side of a picture frame or sheet of glass **2** a tool for making sloping edges on wood or stone

bev·elled (*especially US* **bev·eled**) /ˈbevld/ *adj.* [usually before noun] having a sloping edge or surface

bevelled (*epecially US* **beveled**)

bev·er·age /ˈbevərɪdʒ/ *noun* (*formal*) any type of drink except water: *laws governing the sale of alcoholic beverages*

bevvy /ˈbevi/ *noun* (*pl.* -ies) (*BrE, informal*) an alcoholic drink, especially beer: *We went out for a few bevvies last night.*

bevy /ˈbevi/ *noun* [sing.] (*informal*) a large group of people or things of the same kind: *a bevy of beauties* (= beautiful young women)

be·wail /bɪˈweɪl/ *verb* **~ sth** (*formal* or *humorous*) to express great sadness about sth

be·ware /bɪˈweə(r); *NAmE* -ˈwer/ *verb* [I, T] (used only in infinitives and in orders) if you tell sb to **beware**, you are warning them that sb/sth is dangerous and that they should be careful: **~ of sb/sth** *Motorists have been warned to beware of icy roads.* ◇ **~ (of) doing sth** *Beware of saying anything that might reveal where you live.* ◇ **~ sb/sth** *It's a great place for swimming, but beware dangerous currents.*

be·wigged /bɪˈwɪgd/ *adj.* (*formal*) (of a person) wearing a WIG

be·wil·der /bɪˈwɪldə(r)/ *verb* [usually passive] **~ sb** to confuse sb: *She was totally bewildered by his sudden change of mood.* ▶ **be·wil·dered** *adj.*: *He turned around, with a bewildered look on his face.*

be·wil·der·ing /bɪˈwɪldərɪŋ/ *adj.* making you feel confused because there are too many things to choose from or because sth is difficult to understand SYN **confusing**: *a* ***bewildering array/range*** ◇ *There is a* ***bewildering variety*** *of software available.* ▶ **be·wil·der·ing·ly** *adv.*: *All the houses looked bewilderingly similar.*

be·wil·der·ment /bɪˈwɪldəmənt; *NAmE* -dərm-/ *noun* [U] a feeling of being completely confused SYN **confusion**: *to* ***look/stare in bewilderment***

be·witch /bɪˈwɪtʃ/ *verb* **1** [often passive] **~ sb** to attract or impress sb so much that they cannot think in a sensible way: *He was completely bewitched by her beauty.* **2 ~ sb** to put a magic SPELL on sb SYN **enchant**

be·witch·ing /bɪˈwɪtʃɪŋ/ *adj.* so beautiful or interesting that you cannot think about anything else: *a bewitching girl/smile* ◇ *a bewitching performance*

be·yond 🔑 /bɪˈjɒnd; *NAmE* bɪˈjɑːnd/ *prep., adv.*
■ ***prep.*** **1** 🔑 on or to the further side of sth: *The road continues beyond the village up into the hills.* **2** 🔑 later than a particular time: *It won't go on beyond midnight.* ◇ *I know what I'll be doing for the next three weeks but I haven't thought beyond that.* **3** 🔑 more than sth: *Our success was far beyond what we thought possible.* ◇ *She's got nothing beyond her state pension.* **4** 🔑 used to say that sth is not possible: *The bicycle was beyond repair* (= is too badly damaged to repair). ◇ *The situation is beyond our control.* **5** 🔑 too far or too advanced for sb/sth: *The handle was just beyond my reach.* ◇ *The exercise was beyond the abilities of most of the class.*
IDM **be beyond sb** (*informal*) to be impossible for sb to imagine, understand or do: *It's beyond me why she wants to marry Jeff.*
■ ***adv.*** 🔑 on the other side; further on: *Snowdon and the mountains beyond were covered in snow.* ◇ *The immediate future is clear, but it's hard to tell what lies beyond.* ◇ *the year 2010 and beyond* IDM see BACK *n.*, DOUBT *n.*

bez·el /ˈbezl/ *noun* (*technical*) a ring with a long narrow cut around the inside, used to hold sth in place, such as the cover of a watch or mobile/cell phone

Bhag·wan /bʌgˈwɑːn/ *noun* (*IndE*) **1** God: *'May Bhagwan bless you,' he said.* **2** a title for a GURU or a god in the form of a man: *Bhagwan Rajneesh*

bhai /baɪ/ *noun* (*IndE*) **1** a brother **2** used as a polite form of address to a man; in western India, often added to the first or last name: *Suresh Bhai* ◇ *Gandhi Bhai*

bhaji /ˈbɑːdʒi/ (also **bha·jia** /ˈbɑːdʒiə/) *noun* (*pl.* **bhajis**, **bha·jia**) **1** [C] a spicy S Asian food consisting of vegetables fried in BATTER (= a mixture of flour and liquid) **2** [U] a S Asian dish of spicy fried vegetables

bhang (also **bang**) /bæŋ/ *noun* [U] the leaves and flower tops of the CANNABIS plant, used as a drug

bhangra /ˈbɑːŋgrə/ *noun* [U] a type of dance music that combines traditional Punjabi music from India and Pakistan with Western pop music

Bha·rata·na·tyam /ˌbʌrətəˈnɑːtjəm/ *noun* [U] a CLASSICAL dance form from southern India

bha·van /ˈbʌvən/ *noun* (*IndE*) a building made or used for a special purpose, for example for meetings or concerts

bhindi /ˈbɪndi/ *noun* (*pl.* **bhindi** or **bhindis**) [C, U] (*IndE*) = OKRA

bi /baɪ/ *adj.* (*informal*) = BISEXUAL

bi- /baɪ/ *combining form* (in nouns and adjectives) two; twice; double: *bilingual* ◇ *bicentenary* HELP **Bi-** with a period of time can mean either 'happening twice' in that period of time, or 'happening once in every two' periods.

bi·an·nual /baɪˈænjuəl/ *adj.* [only before noun] happening twice a year ➔ compare ANNUAL ➔ see also BIENNIAL

bias AW /ˈbaɪəs/ *noun, verb*
■ ***noun*** **1** [U, C, usually sing.] a strong feeling in favour of or against one group of people, or one side in an argument, often not based on fair judgement: *accusations of political bias in news programmes* (= that reports are unfair and show favour to one political party) ◇ *Employers must consider all candidates impartially and without bias.* ◇ *Some institutions still have a strong bias against women.* ➔ COLLOCATIONS at RACE **2** [C, usually sing.] an interest in one thing more than others; a special ability: *The course has a strong practical bias.* **3** [U, sing.] the **bias** of a piece of cloth is an edge cut DIAGONALLY across the threads: *The skirt is cut on the bias.*
■ ***verb*** (-s- or -ss-) **1 ~ sb/sth (towards/against/in favour of**

sb/sth) to unfairly influence sb's opinions or decisions **SYN prejudice**: *The newspapers have biased people against her.* **2 ~ sth** to have an effect on the results of research or an experiment so that they do not show the real situation: *The experiment contained an error which could bias the results.*

'bias-cut *adj.* (of cloth or of an item of clothing) cut across the natural direction of the lines in the cloth

biased AW (also **biassed**) /'baɪəst/ *adj.* **1 ~ (toward(s)/against/in favour of sb/sth)** having a tendency to show favour towards or against one group of people or one opinion for personal reasons; making unfair judgements: *biased information/sources/press reports* ◇ *a biased jury/witness* OPP **unbiased** **2 ~ toward(s) sth/sb** having a particular interest in one thing more than others: *a school biased towards music and art*

bi·ath·lon /baɪ'æθlən/ *noun* a sporting event that combines CROSS-COUNTRY SKIING and RIFLE shooting ➲ compare DECATHLON, HEPTATHLON, PENTATHLON, TETRATHLON, TRIATHLON

bib /bɪb/ *noun* **1** a piece of cloth or plastic that you put under a baby's chin to protect its clothes while it is eating **2** (*especially BrE*) a piece of cloth or plastic with a number or special colours on it that people wear on their chests and backs when they are taking part in a sport, so that people know who they are
IDM **your best bib and 'tucker** (*humorous*) your best clothes that you only wear on special occasions

bible /'baɪbl/ *noun* **1 the Bible** [sing.] the holy book of the Christian religion, consisting of the Old Testament and the New Testament **2 the Bible** [sing.] the holy book of the Jewish religion, consisting of the Torah (or Law), the PROPHETS and the Writings **3** [C] a copy of the holy book of the Christian or Jewish religion **4** [C] a book containing important information on a subject, that you refer to very often: *the stamp-collector's bible*

'Bible-bashing (also **'Bible-thumping**) *noun* [U] (*informal, disapproving*) the act of teaching or talking about the Bible in public in a very enthusiastic or aggressive way ▸ **'Bible-basher, 'Bible-thumper** *noun*

the 'Bible Belt *noun* [sing.] an area of the southern and middle western US where people have strong and strict Christian beliefs

bib·lical /'bɪblɪkl/ (also **Biblical**) *adj.* **1** connected with the Bible; in the Bible: ***biblical scholarship/times/scenes*** ◇ ***biblical stories/passages*** **2** very great; on a large scale: *a thunderstorm **of biblical proportions***
IDM **know sb in the 'biblical sense** (*humorous*) to have had sex with sb: *He had known her—but not in the biblical sense.*

biblio- /'bɪbliəʊ; *NAmE* -lioʊ/ *combining form* (in nouns, adjectives and adverbs) connected with books: *bibliophile*

bibli·og·raphy /ˌbɪbli'ɒɡrəfi; *NAmE* -'ɑːɡ-/ *noun* (*pl.* -ies) **1** [C] a list of books or articles about a particular subject or by a particular author; the list of books, etc. that have been used by sb writing an article, etc. ➲ WRITING TUTOR page WT11 **2** [U] the study of the history of books and their production ▸ **bibli·og·raph·er** /-'ɒɡrəfə(r); *NAmE* -'ɑːɡ-/ *noun* **bib·lio·graph·ic·al** /ˌbɪbliə'ɡræfɪkl/ (also **bib·lio·graph·ic** /ˌbɪbliə'ɡræfɪk/) *adj.*

bib·lio·phile /'bɪbliəfaɪl/ *noun* (*formal*) a person who loves or collects books

'bib overalls *noun* [pl.] (*NAmE*) = OVERALLS (3)

bibu·lous /'bɪbjələs/ *adj.* (*old-fashioned* or *humorous*) liking to drink too much alcohol

bi·cam·eral /ˌbaɪ'kæmərəl/ *adj.* (*technical*) (of a parliament) having two main parts, such as the Senate and the House of Representatives in the US, and the House of Commons and the House of Lords in Britain

bi·carb /'baɪkɑːb; *NAmE* -kɑːrb/ *noun* [U] (*informal*) = SODIUM BICARBONATE

bi·car·bon·ate /ˌbaɪ'kɑːbənət; *NAmE* -'kɑːrb-/ *noun* [U] (*chemistry*) a salt made from CARBONIC ACID containing CARBON, HYDROGEN and OXYGEN together with another element

biˌcarbonate of 'soda *noun* [U] = SODIUM BICARBONATE

bi·cen·ten·ary /ˌbaɪsen'tiːnəri; *NAmE* -'ten-/ *noun* (*pl.* -ies) (*BrE*) (*NAmE* **bi·cen·ten·nial**) the year, or the day, when you celebrate an important event that happened exactly 200 years earlier ▸ **bi·cen·ten·ary** *adj.* [only before noun]: *bicentenary celebrations*

bi·cen·ten·nial /ˌbaɪsen'teniəl/ (*NAmE*) (*BrE* **bi·cen·ten·ary**) *noun* the year, or the day, when you celebrate an important event that happened exactly 200 years earlier ▸ **bi·cen·ten·nial** *adj.* [only before noun]: (*especially NAmE*) *bicentennial celebrations*

bi·ceps /'baɪseps/ *noun* (*pl.* **bi·ceps**) the main muscle at the front of the top part of the arm ➲ compare TRICEPS

bicker /'bɪkə(r)/ *verb* [I] **~ (about/over sth)** to argue about things that are not important SYN **squabble**: *The children are always bickering about something or other.* ▸ **bicker·ing** *noun* [U]

bicky (also **bikky**) /'bɪki/ *noun* (*pl.* -ies) (*informal*) a biscuit
IDM **big 'bickies** (*AustralE, NZE, informal*) a large sum of money

bi·coast·al /ˌbaɪ'kəʊstl; *NAmE* -'koʊstl/ *adj.* (*NAmE*) involving people and places on both the east and west coasts of the US

bi·cycle 0-w /'baɪsɪkl/ *noun, verb*
■ ***noun*** 0-w (also *informal* **bike**) a road vehicle with two wheels that you ride by pushing the PEDALS with your feet: *He got on his bicycle and rode off.* ◇ *We went for a **bicycle ride** on Sunday.* ➲ VISUAL VOCAB pages V7, V41
■ ***verb*** [I] (+ **adv./prep.**) (*old-fashioned*) to go somewhere on a bicycle ➲ compare BIKE, CYCLE

'bicycle clip *noun* one of the two bands that people wear around their ankles when they are riding a bicycle to stop their trousers/pants getting caught in the chain

'bicycle lane (also *informal* **'bike lane**) (both *NAmE*) (*BrE* **'cycle lane**) *noun* a part of a road that only bicycles are allowed to use ➲ VISUAL VOCAB page V3

bi·cyc·list /'baɪsɪklɪst/ *noun* (*old-fashioned* in British English, *formal* in North American English) a person who rides a bicycle ➲ compare CYCLIST

bid[1] 0-w /bɪd/ *verb, noun* ➲ see also BID[2]
■ ***verb*** (**bid·ding, bid, bid**) **1** 0-w [I, T] to offer to pay a particular price for sth, especially at an AUCTION: **~ (sth) (for sth)** *I bid £2 000 for the painting.* ◇ **~ (against sb)** *We wanted to buy the chairs but another couple were bidding against us.* **2** 0-w [I] **~ (for sth)** | (*NAmE* also) **~ (on sth)** | **~ (to do sth)** to offer to do work or provide a service for a particular price, in competition with other companies, etc. SYN **tender**: *A French firm will be bidding for the contract.* **3** [T] **~ to do sth** (used especially in newspapers) to try to do, get or achieve sth SYN **attempt**: *The team is bidding to retain its place in the league.* **4** [T, I] **~ (sth)** (in some card games) to say how many points you expect to win: *She bid four hearts.*
IDM **what am I 'bid?** used by an AUCTIONEER when he or she is selling sth: *What am I bid for this vase?*
■ ***noun*** **1** 0-w **~ (for sth)** an offer by a person or a company to pay a particular amount of money for sth: *Granada mounted a hostile **takeover bid** for Forte.* ◇ *At the auction* (= a public sale where things are sold to the person who offers the most), *the highest bid for the picture was £200.* ◇ *Any more bids?* **2** 0-w **~ (for sth)** | (*NAmE* also) **~ (on sth)** an offer to do work or provide a service for a particular price, in competition with other companies, etc. SYN **tender**: *The company submitted a bid for the contract to clean the hospital.* **3** (used especially in newspapers) an effort to do sth or to obtain sth: **~ for sth** *a bid for power* ◇ **~ to do sth** *a desperate bid to escape from his attackers* **4** (in some card games) a statement of the number of points a player thinks he or she will win

bid[2] /bɪd/ *verb* ➲ see also BID[1] (**bid·ding, bade** /beɪd; bæd/, **bidden** /'bɪdn/) or (**bid·ding, bid, bid**) **1 ~ (sb) good morning, farewell, etc.** (*formal*) to say 'good morning',

B

etc. to sb: *I bade farewell to all the friends I had made in Paris.* ◇ *I bade all my friends farewell.* **2 ~ sb (do sth)** (*old use or literary*) to tell sb to do sth: *He bade me come closer.*

bid·dable /ˈbɪdəbl/ *adj.* (*formal, especially BrE*) (of people) willing to obey and to do what they are told to

bid·der /ˈbɪdə(r)/ *noun* **1** a person or group that offers to pay an amount of money to buy sth: *It went to the highest bidder* (= the person who offered the most money). **2** a person or group that offers to do sth or to provide sth for a particular amount of money, in competition with others: *There were six bidders for the catering contract.*

bid·ding /ˈbɪdɪŋ/ *noun* [U] **1** the act of offering prices, especially at an AUCTION: *There was fast bidding between private collectors and dealers.* ◇ *Several companies remained* ***in the bidding.*** **2** the act of offering to do sth or to provide sth for a particular price: *competitive bidding for the contract* **3** (in some card games) the process of stating the number of points that players think they will win **4** (*old-fashioned* or *formal*) what sb asks or orders you to do: ***to do sb's bidding*** (= to obey sb)

biddy /ˈbɪdi/ *noun* (*pl.* -ies) (*informal, disapproving*) an old woman, especially an annoying one

bide /baɪd/ *verb* [I] (*old use*) = ABIDE

IDM **bide your ˈtime** to wait for the right time to do sth

bidet /ˈbiːdeɪ; *NAmE* bɪˈdeɪ/ *noun* a low bowl in the bathroom, usually with taps/faucets, that you fill with water and sit on to wash your bottom ➲ VISUAL VOCAB page V21

bi·di·rec·tion·al /ˌbaɪdəˈrekʃənl; -dɪ-; -daɪ-/ *adj.* (*technical*) functioning in two directions

bi·en·nial /baɪˈeniəl/ *adj., noun*

■ ***adj.*** [usually before noun] happening once every two years: *a biennial convention* ▶ **bi·en·ni·al·ly** *adv.* ➲ see also ANNUAL, BIANNUAL

■ ***noun*** any plant that lives for two years, producing flowers in the second year ➲ compare ANNUAL, PERENNIAL

bier /bɪə(r); *NAmE* bɪr/ *noun* a frame on which the dead body or the COFFIN is placed or carried at a funeral

biff /bɪf/ *verb* **~ sb** (*old-fashioned, informal*) to hit sb hard with your FIST: *He biffed me on the nose.* ▶ **biff** *noun*

bi·focals /ˌbaɪˈfəʊklz; *NAmE* -ˈfoʊ-/ *noun* [pl.] a pair of glasses with each LENS made in two parts. The upper part is for looking at things at a distance, and the lower part is for looking at things that are close to you. ➲ compare VARIFOCALS ▶ **bi·focal** *adj.*

bi·fur·cate /ˈbaɪfəkeɪt; *NAmE* -fərk-/ *verb* [I] (*formal*) (of roads, rivers, etc.) to divide into two separate parts ▶ **bi·fur·ca·tion** /ˌbaɪfəˈkeɪʃn; *NAmE* -fərˈk-/ *noun* [C, U]

big 0⊸ /bɪg/ *adj., adv., verb* ➲ see also BIGS *n.*

■ ***adj.*** (**big·ger, big·gest**)

▸ LARGE **1** 0⊸ large in size, degree, amount, etc: *a big man/house/increase* ◇ *This shirt isn't big enough.* ◇ *It's the world's biggest computer company.* ◇ (*informal*) *He had this* ***great big*** *grin on his face.* ◇ *They were earning big money.* ◇ *The news came as a big blow.*

▸ OLDER **2** 0⊸ (*informal*) older: *my big brother* ◇ *You're a big girl now.*

▸ IMPORTANT **3** 0⊸ [only before noun] (rather *informal*) important; serious: *a big decision* ◇ *Tonight is the biggest match of his career.* ◇ *You are making a big mistake.* ◇ *She took the stage for her* ***big moment.*** ◇ (*informal*) *Do you really think we can take on the* ***big boys*** (= compete with the most powerful people)?

▸ AMBITIOUS **4** (*informal*) (of a plan) needing a lot of effort, money or time to succeed: *They're full of big ideas.*

▸ POPULAR **5** (*informal*) popular with the public; successful: *Orange is the big colour this year.* ◇ **~ in...** *The band's very big in Japan.*

▸ ENTHUSIASTIC **6** (*informal*) enthusiastic about sb/sth: *I'm a big fan of hers.*

▸ DOING STH A LOT **7** doing sth often or to a large degree: *a big eater/drinker/spender*

▸ GENEROUS **8 ~ of sb** (usually *ironic*) kind or generous: *He gave me an extra five pounds for two hours' work. I thought 'That's big of you'.*

▶ **big·ness** *noun* [U]

IDM **be/get too big for your ˈboots** to be/become too proud of yourself; to behave as if you are more important than you really are **a ˌbig ˈcheese** (*informal, humorous*) an important and powerful person, especially in an organization **ˌbig ˈdeal!** (*informal, ironic*) used to say that you are not impressed by sth: *So he earns more than me. Big deal!* **the big enchiˈlada** (*NAmE, informal, humorous*) the most important person or thing **a big fish (in a small pond)** an important person (in a small community) **a ˌbig girl's ˈblouse** (*BrE, informal*) a weak man, who is not brave or confident **a big noise/shot/name** an important person **the big ˈpicture** (*informal, especially NAmE*) the situation as a whole: *Right now forget the details and take a look at the big picture.* **the big ˈstick** (*informal*) the use or threat of force or power: *The authorities used quiet persuasion instead of the big stick.* **the big three, four, etc.** the three, four, etc. most important countries, people, companies, etc: *She works for one of the Big Six.* **give sb/get a big ˈhand** to show your approval of sb by clapping your hands; to be APPLAUDED in this way: *Ladies and gentlemen, let's give a big hand to our special guests tonight.* **have a big ˈmouth 1** to be bad at keeping secrets **2** to talk too much, especially about your own abilities and achievements **me and my big ˈmouth** (*informal*) used when you realize that you have said sth that you should not have said **no big ˈdeal** (*informal*) used to say that sth is not important or not a problem: *If I don't win it's no big deal.* ➲ more at EYE *n.*, FISH *n.*, THING, WAY *n.*

■ ***adv.*** in an impressive way: *We need to think big.*

IDM **go over ˈbig (with sb)** (*informal*) to make a good impression on sb; to be successful: *This story went over big with my kids.* **make it ˈbig** to be very successful: *He's hoping to make it big on TV.* ➲ more at HIT *v.*

■ ***verb*** (-gg-)

PHR V **ˌbig sb/sth↔ˈup** (*BrE, slang*) to praise or recommend sb/sth strongly: *He's been bigging up the CD on his radio show.*

Synonyms

big / large / great

These adjectives are frequently used with the following nouns:

big ~	large ~	great ~
man	numbers	success
house	part	majority
car	area	interest
boy	room	importance
dog	company	difficulty
smile	eyes	problem
problem	family	pleasure
surprise	volume	beauty
question	population	artist
difference	problem	surprise

- **Large** is more formal than **big** and should be used in writing unless it is in an informal style. It is not usually used to describe people, except to avoid saying 'fat'.
- **Great** often suggests quality and not just size. Note also the phrases: *a large amount of* ◇ *a large number of* ◇ *a large quantity of* ◇ *a great deal of* ◇ *in great detail* ◇ *a person of great age.*

bigam·ist /ˈbɪgəmɪst/ *noun* a person who commits the crime of bigamy

big·amy /ˈbɪgəmi/ *noun* [U] the crime of marrying sb when you are still legally married to sb else ➲ compare MONOGAMY, POLYGAMY ▶ **big·am·ous** /ˈbɪgəməs/ *adj.*: *a bigamous relationship*

the ˌBig ˈApple *noun* [sing.] (*informal*) New York City

B

the ˌBig Bad ˈWolf *noun* [sing.] (*informal*) a dangerous and frightening enemy ORIGIN From the wolf in several children's stories and the song *Who's Afraid of the Big Bad Wolf?*

ˈbig band *noun* a large group of musicians playing JAZZ or dance music: *the big-band sound*

ˌBig ˈBang *noun* [sing.] (usually **the Big Bang**) the single large explosion that some scientists suggest created the universe

ˌbig ˈbox (also **ˌbig-box ˈstore**) *noun* (*NAmE, informal*) a very large shop/store, built on one level and located outside a town, which sells goods at low prices: *When a big-box store opens, smaller retailers often go out of business.* ◇ *Efforts were made to limit big-box expansion.*

ˌBig ˈBrother *noun* [sing.] a leader, a person in authority or a government that tries to control people's behaviour and thoughts, but pretends to act for their benefit ORIGIN From George Orwell's novel *Nineteen Eighty-Four*, in which the leader of the government, **Big Brother**, had total control over the people. The slogan 'Big Brother is watching you' reminded people that he knew everything they did.

ˌbig ˈbucks *noun* [pl.] (*NAmE, informal*) a large amount of money

ˌbig ˈbusiness *noun* [U] **1** large companies that have a lot of power, considered as a group: *links between politics and big business* **2** something that has become important because people are willing to spend a lot of money on it: *Health and fitness have become big business.*

ˌbig ˈcat *noun* any large wild animal of the cat family. LIONS, TIGERS and LEOPARDS are all big cats.

ˌBig ˈChief *noun* (*informal*) the person in charge of a business or other organization

ˌbig ˈdipper *noun* **1** (*old-fashioned, BrE*) a small train at an AMUSEMENT PARK, which goes very quickly up and down a steep track and around bends ➲ see also ROLLER COASTER **2 the ˌBig ˈDipper** (*NAmE*) (*BrE* **the Plough**) [sing.] a group of seven bright stars that can only be seen from the northern half of the world

ˌbig ˈend *noun* (in a car engine) the end of a connecting ROD that fits around the CRANKSHAFT

Big·foot /ˈbɪgfʊt/ *noun* (*pl.* **Big·feet**) (also **Sas·quatch**) a large creature covered with hair like an APE, which some people believe lives in western N America

ˌbig ˈgame *noun* [U] large wild animals that people hunt for sport, for example ELEPHANTS and LIONS

big·gie /ˈbɪgi/ *noun* (*informal*) an important thing, person or event

ˌbig ˈgovernment *noun* [U] (*disapproving*) a type of government that has a lot of control over people's lives and the economy

ˌbig ˈgun *noun* (*informal*) a person who has a lot of power or influence

ˌbig ˈhair *noun* [U] hair in a style that makes a large shape around the head

ˌbig-ˈheaded *adj.* (*informal, disapproving*) having a very high opinion of how important and clever you are; too proud ▸ **ˈbig-head** *noun*

ˌbig-ˈhearted *adj.* very kind; generous

ˌbig ˈhitter *noun* (*informal*) a person who is successful and has a lot of influence: *They've appointed one of the industry's big hitters to the board.*

bight /baɪt/ *noun* a long curved part of a coast or river: *the Great Australian Bight*

ˈbig league *noun* (*NAmE*) **1** [C] a group of teams in a professional sport, especially BASEBALL, that play at the highest level **2 the big league** [sing.] (*informal*) a very successful and important group: *Over the past year, the company has joined the big league.*

ˈbig-league *adj.* (*NAmE*) **1** connected with sports teams that are in a big league **2** very important and successful

ˌBig Man on ˈCampus *noun* (*abbr.* BMOC) (*NAmE, informal*) a successful popular male student at a college or university

ˈbig mouth *noun* (*informal*) a person who talks a lot, especially about him- or herself, and who cannot keep secrets ▸ **ˈbig-mouthed** *adj.*

ˌBig ˈMuddy *noun* (*US, informal*) **1** the Mississippi River **2** a name for Vietnam used especially by US soldiers who fought there

bigot /ˈbɪgət/ *noun* a person who has very strong, unreasonable beliefs or opinions about race, religion or politics and who will not listen to or accept the opinions of anyone who disagrees: *a **religious/racial bigot***

big·ot·ed /ˈbɪgətɪd/ *adj.* showing strong, unreasonable beliefs or opinions and a refusal to change them

big·ot·ry /ˈbɪgətri/ *noun* [U] the state of feeling, or the act of expressing, strong, unreasonable beliefs or opinions

bigs /bɪgz/ *noun* [pl.] (*NAmE, informal*) **1 the bigs** the major league in a professional sport **2** large companies with a lot of money and influence: *software bigs* ◇ *the Internet travel bigs*

the ˌbig ˈscreen *noun* [sing.] the cinema (when contrasted with television): *The movie hits the big screen in July.* ◇ *her first big-screen success*

the ˌbig ˈsmoke *noun* (*BrE, informal*) London, or another large city

ˌbig ˈtent *noun* a group or philosophy that accepts and includes individuals and organizations that have a wide variety of opinions or styles SYN **broad church**: *The movement soon became a big tent under which many campaign groups gathered.*

ˈbig-ticket *adj.* [only before noun] (*NAmE*) costing a lot of money: *big-ticket items*

ˈbig time *noun, adv.* (*informal*)
- ***noun* the big time** great success in a profession, especially the entertainment business: *a bit-part actor who finally **made/hit the big time*** ➲ compare SMALL-TIME
- ***adv.*** on a large scale; to a great extent: *This time they've messed up big time!*

ˌbig ˈtoe *noun* the largest toe on a person's foot ➲ VISUAL VOCAB page V48

ˌbig ˈtop (usually **the big top**) *noun* the large tent in which a CIRCUS gives performances

ˌbig ˈwheel *noun* **1** (usually **the Big Wheel**) (*BrE*) (also **Fer·ris wheel** *NAmE, BrE*) a large wheel which stands in a vertical position at an AMUSEMENT PARK, with seats hanging at its edge for people to ride in **2** (*NAmE, informal*) an important person in a company or an organization

big·wig /ˈbɪgwɪg/ *noun* (*informal*) an important person: *She had to entertain some boring local bigwigs.*

bijou /ˈbiːʒuː/ *adj.* [only before noun] (*BrE*, sometimes *ironic*) (of a building or a garden) small but attractive and fashionable: *The house was terribly small and cramped, but the agent described it as a bijou residence.*

bike 0-w /baɪk/ *noun, verb*
- ***noun*** (*informal*) **1** 0-w a bicycle: *She got on her bike and rode off.* ◇ *I usually go to work **by bike**.* ➲ VISUAL VOCAB page V41 ➲ see also MOUNTAIN BIKE, PUSHBIKE, QUAD BIKE **2** 0-w a motorcycle

IDM **on your bike!** (*BrE, informal*) a rude way of telling sb to go away
- ***verb*** **1** [I] (+ **adv./prep.**) (*informal*) to go somewhere on a bicycle or motorcycle: *My dad bikes to work every day.* **2** [T] **~ sth** (+ **adv./prep.**) (*informal*) to send sth to sb by motorcycle: *I'll bike the contract over to you this afternoon.* ▸ **bik·ing** *noun* [U]: *The activities on offer include sailing and **mountain biking**.* ➲ compare BICYCLE, CYCLE

ˈbike lane *noun* (*NAmE, informal*) = BICYCLE LANE

biker /ˈbaɪkə(r)/ *noun* **1** a person who rides a motorcycle, usually as a member of a large group **2** a person who rides a bicycle, especially a MOUNTAIN BIKE

bikie /ˈbaɪki/ *noun* (*AustralE, NZE, informal*) a member of a group of people who ride motorcycles

B

bi·kini /bɪˈkiːni/ *noun* a piece of clothing in two pieces that women wear for swimming and lying in the sun

biˈkini line *noun* the area of skin around the bottom half of a BIKINI and the hair that grows there, which some women remove

bikky = BICKY

bi·la·bial /ˌbaɪˈleɪbiəl/ *noun* (*phonetics*) a speech sound made by using both lips, such as /b/ /p/ and /m/ in /buy/ /pie/ and /my/ ▸ **bi·la·bial** *adj.*

bi·lat·eral /ˌbaɪˈlætərəl/ *adj.* **1** involving two groups of people or two countries: ***bilateral relations/agreements/trade/talks*** **2** (*medical*) involving both of two parts or sides of the body or brain ▸ **bi·lat·eral·ly** *adv.* ➲ compare MULTILATERAL, TRILATERAL, UNILATERAL

bil·berry /ˈbɪlbəri; *NAmE* -beri/ (also **whortle·berry**) *noun* (*pl.* **-ies**) a small dark blue BERRY that grows on bushes on hills and in woods in northern Europe and can be eaten. The bush is also called a bilberry. ➲ compare BLUEBERRY

bilby /ˈbɪlbi/ *noun* (*pl.* **-ies**) a small Australasian animal with a long nose, a long tail and big ears

bile /baɪl/ *noun* [U] **1** the greenish brown liquid with a bitter unpleasant taste that is produced by the LIVER to help the body to deal with the fats we eat, and that can come into your mouth when you VOMIT with an empty stomach **2** (*formal*) anger or hatred: *The critic's review of the play was just a paragraph of bile.*

ˈbile duct *noun* the tube that carries bile from the LIVER and the GALL BLADDER to the DUODENUM ➲ VISUAL VOCAB page V48

bilge /bɪldʒ/ *noun* **1** [C] (also **bilges** [pl.]) the almost flat part of the bottom of a boat or a ship, inside or outside **2** (also **ˈbilge water**) [U] dirty water that collects in a ship's bilge

bil·har·zia /bɪlˈhɑːtsiə; *NAmE* -ˈhɑːrt-/ *noun* [U] a serious disease, common in parts of Africa and S America, caused by small WORMS that get into the blood

bil·iary /ˈbɪliəri; *NAmE* -eri/ *adj.* (*medical*) relating to BILE or to the BILE DUCT

bi·lin·gual /ˌbaɪˈlɪŋɡwəl/ *adj.* **1** able to speak two languages equally well: *She is bilingual in English and Punjabi.* **2** using two languages; written in two languages: ***bilingual education/communities*** ◇ *a bilingual dictionary* ▸ **bi·lin·gual** *noun*: *Welsh/English bilinguals* ➲ compare MONOLINGUAL, MULTILINGUAL

bili·ous /ˈbɪliəs/ *adj.* **1** feeling as if you might VOMIT soon **2** (of colours, usually green or yellow) creating an unpleasant effect: *a bilious green dress* **3** (*formal*) bad-tempered; full of anger

bili·ru·bin /ˌbɪlɪˈruːbɪn/ *noun* [U] (*medical*) an orange substance produced in the LIVER

bilk /bɪlk/ *verb* (*informal, especially NAmE*) **~ sb** (**out of sth**) | **~ sth** (**from sb**) to cheat sb, especially by taking money from them: *a con man who bilked investors out of millions of dollars*

bill 🔑 /bɪl/ *noun, verb*

■ ***noun***

▸ FOR PAYMENT **1** 🔑 a piece of paper that shows how much you owe sb for goods or services: *the* ***telephone/electricity/gas bill*** ◇ *We* ***ran up a*** *massive hotel* ***bill***. ◇ *She always* ***pays*** *her* ***bills*** *on time.* ◇ *The bills are piling up* (= there are more and more that have still not been paid). ➲ COLLOCATIONS at FINANCE **2** 🔑 (*especially BrE*) (*NAmE* usually **check**) a piece of paper that shows how much you have to pay for the food and drinks that you have had in a restaurant: *Let's ask for the bill.* ➲ COLLOCATIONS at RESTAURANT

▸ MONEY **3** 🔑 (*NAmE*) = NOTE (6): *a ten-dollar bill*

▸ IN PARLIAMENT **4** 🔑 a written suggestion for a new law that is presented to a country's parliament so that its members can discuss it: *to* ***introduce/approve/reject a bill*** ◇ *the Education Reform Bill*

▸ AT THEATRE, ETC. **5** a programme of entertainment at a theatre, etc: *a horror* ***double bill*** (= two horror films/movies shown one after the other) ◇ ***Topping the bill*** (= the most important performer) *is Paul Simon.*

▸ ADVERTISEMENT **6** a notice in a public place to advertise an event SYN **poster** ➲ see also HANDBILL

▸ OF BIRDS **7** the hard pointed or curved outer part of a bird's mouth SYN **beak** ➲ VISUAL VOCAB page V10 **8 -billed** (in adjectives) having the type of bill mentioned: *long-billed waders*

▸ ON HAT **9** (also **visor**) (both *NAmE*) (*BrE* **peak**) the stiff front part of a cap that sticks out above your eyes ➲ VISUAL VOCAB page V53 ➲ see also THE OLD BILL

IDM **fill/fit the ˈbill** to be what is needed in a particular situation or for a particular purpose: *On paper, several of the applicants fit the bill.* ➲ more at CLEAN *adj.*, FOOT *v.*

■ ***verb***

▸ ASK FOR PAYMENT **1 ~ sb** (**for sth**) to send sb a bill for sth: *Please bill me for the books.*

▸ ADVERTISE **2** [usually passive] **~ sb/sth as sth** to advertise or describe sb/sth in a particular way: *He was billed as the new Tom Cruise.* **3** [usually passive] **~ sb/sth to do sth** to advertise that sb/sth will do sth: *She was billed to speak on 'China—Yesterday and Today'.*

IDM **bill and ˈcoo** (*old-fashioned, informal*) if two people who are in love **bill and coo**, they kiss and speak in a loving way to each other

Synonyms

bill

account • invoice • check

These are all words for a record of how much you owe for goods or services you have bought or used.

bill a list of goods that you have bought or services that you have used, showing how much you owe; the price or cost of sth: *the gas bill*

account an arrangement with a shop/store or business to pay bills for goods or services at a later time, for example in regular amounts every month: *Put it on my account please.*

invoice (*rather formal*) a bill for goods that sb has bought or work that has been done for sb: *The builders sent an invoice for £250.*

BILL OR INVOICE?

You would get a **bill** in a restaurant, bar or hotel; from a company that supplies you with gas, electricity, etc; or from sb whose property you have damaged. An **invoice** is for goods supplied or work done as agreed between a customer and supplier.

check (*NAmE*) a piece of paper that shows how much you have to pay for the food and drinks that you have had in a restaurant: *Can I have the check, please?* NOTE In British English the usual word for this is **bill**.

PATTERNS

- the bill/invoice/check **for** sth
- to **pay/settle** a(n) bill/account/invoice/check
- to **put sth on** the/sb's bill/account/invoice/check

billa·bong /ˈbɪləbɒŋ; *NAmE* -bɔːŋ/ *noun* (in Australia) a lake that is formed when a river floods

bill·board /ˈbɪlbɔːd; *NAmE* -bɔːrd/ (*especially NAmE*) (*BrE* also **hoard·ing**) *noun* a large board on the outside of a building or at the side of the road, used for putting advertisements on

bil·let /ˈbɪlɪt/ *noun, verb*

■ ***noun*** a place, often in a private house, where soldiers live temporarily

■ ***verb*** [T, usually passive] **+ adv./prep.** to send soldiers to live somewhere temporarily, especially in private houses during a war

billet-doux /ˌbɪleɪ ˈduː/ *noun* (*pl.* **billets-doux** /ˌbɪleɪ ˈduːz/) (from *French, humorous* or *literary*) a love letter

bill·fold /ˈbɪlfəʊld; NAmE -foʊld/ *noun* (*NAmE*) = WALLET

bill·hook /ˈbɪlhʊk/ *noun* a tool with a long handle and a curved blade, used for cutting the small branches off trees

bil·liards /ˈbɪliədz; NAmE ˈbɪljərdz/ *noun* [U] a game for two people played with CUES (= long sticks) and three balls on a long table covered with green cloth. Players try to hit the balls against each other and into pockets at the edge of the table: *a game of billiards* ➲ compare POOL, SNOOKER ▸ **bil·liard** *adj.* [only before noun]: *a billiard cue*

bill·ing /ˈbɪlɪŋ/ *noun* **1** [U] the position, especially an important one, that sb is advertised or described as having in a show, etc: *to have* ***top/star billing*** **2** [U] the act of preparing and sending bills to customers **3** [C, usually pl.] the total amount of business that a company does in a particular period of time: *billings around $7 million*

bil·lion 0➜ /ˈbɪljən/ *number* (*plural verb*)
1 0➜ (*abbr.* bn) 1 000 000 000; one thousand million: *Worldwide sales reached 2.5 billion.* ◇ *half a billion dollars* ◇ *They have spent billions on the problem* (= billions of dollars, etc.). HELP You say **a, one, two, several, etc. billion** without a final 's' on 'billion'. **Billions (of...)** can be used if there is no number or quantity before it. Always use a plural verb with **billion** or **billions**, except when an amount of money is mentioned: *Two billion (people) worldwide are expected to watch the game.* ◇ *Two billion (dollars) was withdrawn from the account.* There are more examples of how to use numbers at the entry for **hundred**. **2** 0➜ **a billion** or **billions** (**of...**) (*informal*) a very large amount: *Our immune systems are killing billions of germs right now.* **3** (*old-fashioned, BrE*) 1 000 000 000 000; one million million SYN **trillion**

bil·lion·aire /ˌbɪljəˈneə(r); NAmE -ˈner/ *noun* an extremely rich person, who has at least a thousand million pounds, dollars, etc. in money or property

ˌbill of ˈcosts *noun* (*BrE, law*) a list of the charges and expenses that sb must pay to a lawyer or to sb who has won a legal case

ˌbill of exˈchange *noun* (*pl.* **bills of exchange**) (*business*) a written order to pay a sum of money to a particular person on a particular date

ˌbill of ˈfare *noun* (*pl.* **bills of fare**) (*old-fashioned*) a list of the food that can be ordered in a restaurant SYN **menu**

ˌbill of ˈlad·ing /ˌbɪl əv ˈleɪdɪŋ; NAmE ˌbɪl əv ˈleɪdɪŋ/ *noun* (*pl.* **bills of lad·ing**) (*business*) a list giving details of the goods that a ship, etc. is carrying

ˌbill of ˈrights *noun* [sing.] a written statement of the basic rights of the citizens of a country

ˌbill of ˈsale *noun* (*pl.* **bills of sale**) (*business*) an official document showing that sth has been bought

bil·low /ˈbɪləʊ; NAmE -loʊ/ *verb, noun*
■ ***verb*** **1** [I] (of a sail, skirt, etc.) to fill with air and swell out: *The curtains billowed in the breeze.* **2** [I] if smoke, cloud, etc. **billows**, it rises and moves in a large mass: *A great cloud of smoke billowed out of the chimney.*
■ ***noun*** [usually pl.] a moving mass or cloud of smoke, steam, etc. like a wave

billy /ˈbɪli/ *noun* (*pl.* **-ies**) (also **billy·can** /ˈbɪlikæn/) (both *BrE*) a metal can with a lid and a handle used for boiling water or for cooking when you are camping

ˈbilly club *noun* (*NAmE*) a short wooden stick used as a weapon by police officers

ˈbilly goat *noun* a male GOAT ➲ compare NANNY GOAT

billy-o /ˈbɪliəʊ; NAmE -oʊ/ *noun*
IDM **like ˈbilly-o** (*BrE, informal*) very hard or fast: *I ran like billy-o.*

bil·tong /ˈbɪltɒŋ; ˈbəl-; NAmE ˈbɪltɔːŋ/ *noun* [U] (*SAfrE*) raw dry meat that is eaten in small pieces. Biltong is preserved by being treated with salt.

bimbo /ˈbɪmbəʊ; NAmE -boʊ/ *noun* (*pl.* **-os**) (*informal, disapproving*) a young person, usually a woman, who is sexually attractive but not very intelligent: *He's going out with an empty-headed bimbo half his age.*

bi·month·ly /ˌbaɪˈmʌnθli/ *adj., adv.* produced or happening every two months or twice each month

bin 0➜ /bɪn/ *noun, verb*
■ ***noun*** **1** 0➜ a container that you put waste in: *a rubbish bin* ➲ see also DUSTBIN, WASTE BIN **2** a large container, usually with a lid, for storing things in: *a bread bin*
■ ***verb*** (-nn-) **~ sth** (*BrE, informal*) to throw sth away: *Do you need to keep these letters or shall we bin them?*

bin·ary /ˈbaɪnəri/ *adj.* **1** (*computing, mathematics*) using only 0 and 1 as a system of numbers: *the* ***binary system*** ◇ *binary arithmetic* **2** (*technical*) based on only two numbers; consisting of two parts: ***binary code/numbers*** ➲ compare UNARY ▸ **bin·ary** *noun* [U]: *The computer performs calculations in binary and converts the results to decimal.*

ˈbin bag *noun* (*BrE, informal*) a large plastic bag for putting rubbish/garbage in

bind /baɪnd/ *verb, noun*
■ ***verb*** (**bound, bound** /baʊnd/)
▸ TIE WITH ROPE/CLOTH **1** [T] (*formal*) to tie sb/sth with rope, string, etc. so that they cannot move or are held together firmly: **~ sb/sth to sth** *She was bound to a chair.* ◇ **~ sb/sth together** *They bound his hands together.* ◇ **~ sb/sth** *He was left* ***bound and gagged*** (= tied up and with a piece of cloth tied over his mouth). **2** [T] **~ sth** (**up**) (*formal*) to tie a long thin piece of cloth around sth: *She bound up his wounds.*
▸ UNITE **3** [T] to unite people, organizations, etc. so that they live or work together more happily or effectively: **~ A** (**and B**) (**together**) *Organizations such as schools and clubs bind a community together.* ◇ **~ A to B** *She thought that having his child would bind him to her forever.*
▸ MAKE SB DO STH **4** [T, usually passive] to force sb to do sth by making them promise to do it or by making it their duty to do it: **~ sb** (**to sth**) *He had been bound to secrecy* (= made to promise not to tell people about sth). ◇ **~ sb to do sth** *The agreement binds her to repay the debt within six months.* ➲ see also BINDING, BOUND
▸ STICK TOGETHER **5** [I, T] to stick together or to make things stick together in a solid mass: **~** (**together**) *Add an egg yolk to make the mixture bind.* ◇ **~ sth** (**together**) *Add an egg yolk to bind the mixture together.*
▸ BOOK **6** [T, usually passive] **~ sth** (**in sth**) to fasten the pages of a book together and put them inside a cover: *two volumes bound in leather*
▸ SEW EDGE **7** [T, often passive] **~ sth** (**with sth**) to sew a piece of material to the edge of sth to decorate it or to make it stronger: *The blankets were bound with satin.* IDM see HAND *n.*
PHR V **ˌbind sb ˈover** [usually passive] **1** (*NAmE, law*) to give sb BAIL while they are waiting to go to trial: *He was bound over for trial.* **2** (*BrE, law*) to give sb a formal warning that if they break the law again they will be punished: *She was* ***bound over to keep the peace*** *for a year.*
■ ***noun*** [sing.] (*BrE, informal*) an annoying situation that is often difficult to avoid ➲ see also DOUBLE BIND
IDM **in a ˈbind** (*NAmE*) in a difficult situation that you do not know how to get out of

bind·er /ˈbaɪndə(r)/ *noun* **1** [C] a hard cover for holding sheets of paper, magazines, etc. together: *a ring binder* ➲ VISUAL VOCAB page V56 **2** [C] a person or machine that puts covers on books **3** [C, U] a substance that makes things stick or mix together in a solid form **4** [C] a machine that fastens WHEAT into bunches after it has been cut

bindi /ˈbɪndi/ *noun* a decorative mark worn in the middle of the FOREHEAD, usually by Hindu women

bind·ing /ˈbaɪndɪŋ/ *adj., noun*
■ ***adj.*** **~** (**on/upon sb**) that must be obeyed because it is accepted in law: *a* ***binding promise/agreement/contract***
■ ***noun*** **1** [C, U] the cover that holds the pages of a book together **2** [C, U] cloth that is fastened to the edge of sth to protect or decorate it **3** [C] a device on a SKI that holds the heel and toe of your boot in place and releases the boot automatically if you fall ➲ VISUAL VOCAB page V39

ˈbinding theory *noun* ➲ GOVERNMENT AND BINDING THEORY

bind·weed /ˈbaɪndwiːd/ *noun* [U] a wild plant that twists itself around other plants

B

binge /bɪndʒ/ *noun, verb*

- ***noun*** (*informal*) a short period of time when sb does too much of a particular activity, especially eating or drinking alcohol: *to go on a binge* ◇ *One of the symptoms is **binge eating**.*
- ***verb*** (**binge·ing** or **bin·ging, binged, binged**) [I] **~ (on sth)** to eat or drink too much, especially without being able to control yourself: *When she's depressed she binges on chocolate.*

bingo /ˈbɪŋɡəʊ; *NAmE* -ɡoʊ/ *noun, exclamation*

- ***noun*** [U] a game in which each player has a card with numbers on. Numbers are called out in no particular order and the first player whose numbers are all called out, or who has a line of numbers called out, wins a prize: *to play bingo* ◇ *a bingo hall*
- ***exclamation*** used to express pleasure and/or surprise because you have found sth that you were looking for, or done sth that you were trying to do: *The computer program searches, and bingo! We've got a match.*

ˈ**bingo wings** *noun* [pl.] (*BrE, informal, humorous*) long folds of loose skin and fat that hang down from the upper arms, especially of older people

ˈ**bin liner** *noun* (*BrE*) a plastic bag that is placed inside a container for holding waste

bin·man /ˈbɪnmæn/ *noun* (*pl.* **-men** /-men/) (*BrE, informal*) = DUSTMAN

bin·ocu·lar /bɪˈnɒkjələ(r); *NAmE* bɪˈnɑːkjələr/ *adj.* (*technical*) using two eyes to see: *binocular vision*

bin·ocu·lars /bɪˈnɒkjələz; *NAmE* bɪˈnɑːkjələrz/ (also ˈ**field glasses**) *noun* [pl.] an instrument, like two small TELESCOPES fixed together, that makes objects that are far away seem nearer when you look through it: *a pair of binoculars* ◇ *We looked at the birds through binoculars.*

binoculars

eyepiece

telescope

bi·no·mial /baɪˈnəʊmiəl; *NAmE* -ˈnoʊ-/ *noun* **1** (*mathematics*) an expression that has two groups of numbers or letters, joined by the sign + or − **2** (*linguistics*) a pair of nouns joined by a word like 'and', where the order of the nouns is always the same, for example 'knife and fork' ▸ **bi·no·mial** *adj.*

bint /bɪnt/ *noun* (*BrE, slang*) an offensive way of referring to a woman: *a posh bint*

bio- /ˈbaɪəʊ; *NAmE* ˈbaɪoʊ/ *combining form* (in nouns, adjectives and adverbs) connected with living things or human life: *biodegradable* ◇ *biography*

bio·break /ˈbaɪəʊbreɪk; *NAmE* ˈbaɪoʊ-/ *noun* a short period of time when you leave your computer or a meeting in order to go to the toilet/bathroom: *I need to take a biobreak.*

bio·chem·ist /ˌbaɪəʊˈkemɪst; *NAmE* ˌbaɪoʊ-/ *noun* a scientist who studies biochemistry

bio·chem·is·try /ˌbaɪəʊˈkemɪstri; *NAmE* ˌbaɪoʊ-/ *noun* **1** [U] the scientific study of the chemistry of living things **2** [U, C] the chemical structure and behaviour of a living thing ▸ **bio·chem·ical** /ˌbaɪəʊˈkemɪkl; *NAmE* ˌbaɪoʊ-/ *adj.*

bio·data /ˈbaɪəʊdeɪtə; *NAmE* ˈbaɪoʊ-; -dætə/ *noun* [U, pl.] information about a person and about what they have done in their life

bio·degrad·able /ˌbaɪəʊdɪˈɡreɪdəbl; *NAmE* ˌbaɪoʊ-/ *adj.* a substance or chemical that is **biodegradable** can be changed to a harmless natural state by the action of bacteria, and will therefore not damage the environment OPP **non-biodegradable** ➲ COLLOCATIONS at ENVIRONMENT

bio·de·grade /ˌbaɪəʊdɪˈɡreɪd; *NAmE* ˌbaɪoʊ-/ *verb* [I] (of a substance or chemical) to change back to a harmless natural state by the action of bacteria

bio·diesel /ˈbaɪəʊdiːzl; *NAmE* ˈbaɪoʊ-/ *noun* [U] a type of fuel made from plant or animal material and used in engines

bio·di·ver·sity /ˌbaɪəʊdaɪˈvɜːsəti; *NAmE* ˌbaɪoʊdaɪˈvɜːrs-/ (also *less frequent* ˌ**bioˌlogical diˈversity**) *noun* [U] the existence of a large number of different kinds of animals and plants which make a balanced environment ➲ COLLOCATIONS at ENVIRONMENT

bio·engin·eer·ing /ˌbaɪəʊˌendʒɪˈnɪərɪŋ; *NAmE* ˌbaɪoʊˌendʒɪˈnɪrɪŋ/ *noun* [U] the use of engineering methods to solve medical problems, for example the use of artificial arms and legs

bio·eth·ics /ˌbaɪəʊˈeθɪks; *NAmE* ˌbaɪoʊ-/ *noun* [U] (*technical*) the moral principles that influence research in medicine and biology

bio·feed·back /ˌbaɪəʊˈfiːdbæk; *NAmE* ˌbaɪoʊ-/ *noun* [U] (*technical*) the use of electronic equipment to record and display activity in the body that is not usually under your conscious control, for example your heart rate, so that you can learn to control that activity

bio·fuel /ˈbaɪəʊfjuːəl; *NAmE* ˈbaɪoʊ-/ *noun* [C, U] fuel made from plant or animal sources and used in engines: *biofuels made from sugar cane and sugar beet*

bio·gas /ˈbaɪəʊɡæs; *NAmE* ˈbaɪoʊ-/ *noun* [U] gas, especially METHANE, that is produced by dead plants and that can be burned to produce heat

biog·raph·er /baɪˈɒɡrəfə(r); *NAmE* -ˈɑːɡ-/ *noun* a person who writes the story of another person's life

biog·raphy /baɪˈɒɡrəfi; *NAmE* -ˈɑːɡ-/ *noun* [C, U] (*pl.* **-ies**) the story of a person's life written by sb else; this type of writing: *Boswell's biography of Johnson* ➲ compare AUTOBIOGRAPHY ▸ **bio·graph·ic·al** /ˌbaɪəˈɡræfɪkl/ *adj.*

bio·hazard /ˈbaɪəʊhæzəd; *NAmE* ˈbaɪoʊhæzərd/ *noun* a risk to human health or to the environment, from a BIOLOGICAL source

bio·logic·al /ˌbaɪəˈlɒdʒɪkl; *NAmE* -ˈlɑːdʒ-/ *adj.* **1** connected with the science of biology: *the biological sciences* **2** connected with the processes that take place within living things: *the biological effects of radiation* ◇ *the **biological control** of pests* (= using living ORGANISMS to destroy them, not chemicals) ◇ *a child's **biological parents*** (= natural parents, not the people who adopted him/her) **3** (of washing powder, etc.) using ENZYMES (= chemical substances that are found in plants and animals) to get clothes, etc. clean: *biological and non-biological powders* ▸ **bio·logic·al·ly** /-kli/ *adv.*

ˌ**bioˌlogical ˈclock** *noun* (*technical*) a natural system in living things that controls regular physical activities such as sleeping: (*figurative*) *At 35, Kate's biological clock was ticking* (= she was beginning to think that she would soon be too old to have children).

ˌ**bioˌlogical diˈversity** *noun* = BIODIVERSITY

ˌ**bioˌlogical ˈwarfare** (also ˌ**germ ˈwarfare**) *noun* [U] the use of harmful bacteria as weapons of war

ˌ**bioˌlogical ˈweapon** *noun* a weapon of war that uses harmful bacteria ➲ compare CHEMICAL WEAPON

biolo·gist /baɪˈɒlədʒɪst; *NAmE* -ˈɑːl-/ *noun* a scientist who studies biology

biol·ogy 0-w /baɪˈɒlədʒi; *NAmE* -ˈɑːl-/ *noun* [U] **1** 0-w the scientific study of the life and structure of plants and animals: *a degree in biology* ➲ compare BOTANY, ZOOLOGY **2** 0-w the way in which the body and cells of a living thing behave: *How far is human nature determined by biology?* ◇ *the biology of marine animals*

bio·lu·min·es·cence /ˌbaɪəʊluːmɪˈnesns; *NAmE* ˌbaɪoʊ-/ *noun* [U] (*biology*) the natural production of light by living creatures such as GLOW-WORMS

bio·mass /ˈbaɪəʊmæs; *NAmE* ˈbaɪoʊ-/ *noun* [U, sing.] (*technical*) **1** the total quantity or MASS (= weight) of plants and animals in a particular area or volume **2** natural materials from living or recently dead plants, trees and animals, used as fuel and in industrial production, especially in the generation of electricity: *biomass crops* ⊃ compare FOSSIL FUEL

biome /ˈbaɪəʊm; *NAmE* ˈbaɪoʊm/ *noun* (*biology*) the characteristic plants and animals that exist in a particular type of environment, for example in a forest or desert

bio·mech·an·ics /ˌbaɪəʊməˈkænɪks; *NAmE* ˌbaɪoʊ-/ *noun* [U] the scientific study of the physical movement and structure of living creatures

bio·med·ical /ˌbaɪəʊˈmedɪkl; *NAmE* ˌbaɪoʊ-/ *adj.* [usually before noun] relating to how biology affects medicine

bio·metric /ˌbaɪəʊˈmetrɪk; *NAmE* ˌbaɪoʊ-/ *adj.* [usually before noun] using measurements of human features, such as fingers or eyes, in order to identify people

bi·onic /baɪˈɒnɪk; *NAmE* -ˈɑːnɪk/ *adj.* having parts of the body that are electronic, and therefore able to do things that are not possible for normal humans

bio·phys·ics /ˌbaɪəʊˈfɪzɪks; *NAmE* ˌbaɪoʊ-/ *noun* [U] the science that uses the laws and methods of physics to study biology

bio·pic /ˈbaɪəʊpɪk; *NAmE* ˈbaɪoʊ-/ *noun* a film/movie about the life of a particular person

bi·opsy /ˈbaɪɒpsi; *NAmE* -ɑːpsi/ *noun* (*pl.* -ies) the removal and examination of TISSUE from the body of sb who is ill/sick, in order to find out more about their disease

Collocations

Biotechnology

GM crops: for

- **face/suffer from/alleviate** food shortages
- **begin/do/conduct** field trials of GM crops
- **grow/develop** GM crops/seeds/plants/foods
- **improve/increase** food security/crop yields
- **label** food that contains GMOs (= genetically modified organisms)
- **fund/invest in** genetic engineering/research
- **promote/support/be in favour of** GM food/GM crops/genetic engineering
- **embrace** biotechnology/GM technology

GM crops: against

- **oppose/be against** GM technology/food/crops/trials
- **call for/introduce/impose** a ban on genetic modification/a moratorium on the release of GMOs
- **ban/prohibit/outlaw** the use of pesticides/chemical fertilizers/GMOs/so-called 'Frankenfoods'
- **stop/halt/wreck/destroy** GM crop trials
- **promote/support/be in favour of** organic farming

Biotechnology in medicine: for

- **grow/obtain/harvest** human organs/stem cells from human embryos
- **transplant** organs/genes/tissue/cells (into mice/animals/embryos)
- **use** biotechnology/gene therapy to treat/repair/cure sth
- **fund/invest in/ promote/support/be in favour of** (embryonic) stem cell research
- **successfully clone/succeed in cloning** a sheep/a human embryo/a human being

Biotechnology in medicine: against

- **create/produce** 'designer babies'
- **consider/explore/address** the ethical issues raised by/related to/surrounding sth
- **oppose/be against** human cloning/stem cell research
- **call for/introduce/impose** a ban on human cloning/a moratorium on xenotransplantation
- **ban/prohibit/outlaw** human cloning/stem cell research/xenotransplantation

bio·rhythm /ˈbaɪəʊrɪðəm; *NAmE* ˈbaɪoʊ-/ *noun* [usually pl.] the changing pattern of how physical processes happen in the body, that some people believe affects human behaviour

bio·sci·ence /ˌbaɪəʊˈsaɪəns; *NAmE* ˌbaɪoʊ-/ *noun* [C, U] any of the LIFE SCIENCES (= sciences concerned with studying humans, animals or plants)

bio·se·cur·ity /ˌbaɪəʊsɪˈkjʊərəti; *NAmE* ˌbaɪoʊsəˈkjʊr-/ *noun* [U] the activities involved in preventing the spread of animal and plant diseases from one area to another

bio·sphere /ˈbaɪəʊsfɪə(r); *NAmE* ˈbaɪoʊsfɪr/ *noun* [sing.] (*technical*) the part of the earth's surface and atmosphere in which plants and animals can live

bio·tech·nol·ogy /ˌbaɪəʊtekˈnɒlədʒi; *NAmE* ˌbaɪoʊtekˈnɑːl-/ (also *informal* **bio·tech** /ˈbaɪəʊtek; *NAmE* ˈbaɪoʊ-/) *noun* [U] (*technical*) the use of living cells and bacteria in industrial and scientific processes ▸ **bio·tech·no·logic·al** /ˌbaɪəʊteknəˈlɒdʒɪkl; *NAmE* ˌbaɪoʊteknəˈlɑːdʒɪkl/: *biotechnological research*

bi·ot·ic /baɪˈɒtɪk; *NAmE* baɪˈɑːtɪk/ *adj.* (*biology*) of or related to living things

bio·type /ˈbaɪəʊtaɪp; *NAmE* ˈbaɪoʊ-/ *noun* (*biology*) a group of living things with exactly the same combination of GENES

bi·par·tisan /ˌbaɪpɑːtɪˈzæn; *NAmE* ˌbaɪˈpɑːrtɪzn/ *adj.* involving two political parties: *a bipartisan policy*

bi·par·tite /baɪˈpɑːtaɪt; *NAmE* -ˈpɑːrt-/ *adj.* (*technical*) involving or made up of two separate parts

biped /ˈbaɪped/ *noun* (*technical*) any creature with two feet ⊃ compare QUADRUPED

bi·pedal /ˌbaɪˈpiːdl; *NAmE* also -ˈpedl/ *adj.* (*technical*) (of animals) using only two legs for walking

bi·plane /ˈbaɪpleɪn/ *noun* an early type of plane with two sets of wings, one above the other ⊃ VISUAL VOCAB page V43 ⊃ compare MONOPLANE

bi·polar /ˌbaɪˈpəʊlə(r); *NAmE* -ˈpoʊlər/ (also ˌ**manic-deˈpressive**) *adj.* (*psychology*) suffering from or connected with bipolar disorder ▸ **bi·polar** (also ˌ**manic-deˈpressive**) *noun*

ˌ**biˌpolar disˈorder** (also **biˌpolar afˌfective disˈorder**) *noun* [U, C] (also ˌ**manic-deˈpression** [U]) (*psychology*) a mental illness causing sb to change suddenly from being extremely depressed to being extremely happy

bi·racial /ˌbaɪˈreɪʃl/ *adj.* (*NAmE*) (*especially BrE* **mixed race**) concerning or containing members of two different races

birch /bɜːtʃ; *NAmE* bɜːrtʃ/ *noun* **1** [C, U] (also ˈ**birch tree** [C]) a tree with smooth BARK and thin branches, that grows in northern countries ⊃ see also SILVER BIRCH **2** (also **birch·wood** /ˈbɜːtʃwʊd; *NAmE* ˈbɜːrtʃ-/) [U] the hard pale wood of the birch tree **3 the birch** [sing.] the practice of hitting sb with a bunch of birch sticks, as a punishment

bird 0-ᴡ /bɜːd; *NAmE* bɜːrd/ *noun, verb*

■ ***noun*** **1** 0-ᴡ a creature that is covered with feathers and has two wings and two legs. Most birds can fly: *a bird's nest with two eggs in it* ◇ *a species of bird* ◇ *The area has a wealth of bird life.* ⊃ COLLOCATIONS at LIFE ⊃ VISUAL VOCAB page V10 ⊃ see also GAME BIRD, SEABIRD, SONGBIRD, WATERBIRD **2** (*BrE, slang*, sometimes *offensive*) a way of referring to a young woman ⊃ see also DOLLY BIRD **3** (*informal*) a person of a particular type, especially sb who is strange or unusual in some way: *a wise old bird* ◇ *She is that rare bird: a politician with a social conscience.*

IDM **be (strictly) for the birds** (*informal*) to not be important or practical **the bird has ˈflown** the wanted person has escaped **a bird in the ˈhand is worth two in the ˈbush** (*saying*) it is better to keep sth that you already have than to risk losing it by trying to get much more **the birds and the ˈbees** (*humorous*) the basic facts about sex, especially as told to children **a ˌbird's-ˌeye ˈview (of sth)** a view of sth from a high position looking down **birds of a** 'feather (flock to'gether) (*saying*) people of the same sort (are found together) **give sb/get the 'bird** (*informal*) **1** (*BrE*) to shout at sb as a sign of disapproval; to be shouted at **2** (*NAmE*) to make a rude sign at sb with your middle finger; to have this sign made at you ➲ more at EARLY *adj.*, KILL *v.*, LITTLE *adj.*

■ ***verb*** [I, T] (*NAmE, informal*) **~ (sth)** to go BIRDWATCHING

'bird bath *noun* a bowl filled with water for birds to wash in and drink from, usually in a garden/yard

bird·brain /'bɜːdbreɪn; *NAmE* 'bɜːrd-/ *noun* (*especially NAmE*) a stupid person

bird·cage /'bɜːdkeɪdʒ; *NAmE* 'bɜːrd-/ *noun* a CAGE in which birds are kept, usually one in a house

'bird dog *noun* (*NAmE, informal*) **1** a dog used in hunting to bring back birds that have been shot **2** a person whose job involves searching for good players for a sports team

bird·er /'bɜːdə(r); *NAmE* 'bɜːrdər/ (*informal*) = BIRDWATCHER ➲ compare ORNITHOLOGIST

'bird feeder *noun* a container or platform in a garden in/on which people put food for birds

'bird flu (also **'chicken flu**) (also *formal* **'avian flu**) *noun* [U] a serious illness that affects birds, especially chickens, that can be spread from birds to humans and that can cause death: *Ten new cases of bird flu were reported yesterday.*

bir·die /'bɜːdi; *NAmE* 'bɜːrdi/ *noun* **1** (*informal*) a child's word for a little bird **2** (in GOLF) a score of one stroke less than PAR (= the standard score for a hole) ➲ compare BOGEY, EAGLE **3** (*NAmE*) = SHUTTLECOCK

bird·ing /'bɜːdɪŋ; *NAmE* 'bɜːrd-/ (*informal*) = BIRDWATCHING

ˌbird of 'paradise *noun* (*pl.* **birds of paradise**) a bird with very bright feathers, found mainly in New Guinea

ˌbird of 'passage *noun* (*pl.* **birds of passage**) **1** a bird that travels regularly from one part of the world to another at different seasons of the year **2** a person who passes through a place without staying there long

ˌbird of 'prey *noun* (*pl.* **birds of prey**) a bird that hunts and kills other creatures for food. EAGLES, HAWKS and OWLS are all birds of prey. ➲ VISUAL VOCAB page V10

bird·seed /'bɜːdsiːd; *NAmE* 'bɜːrd-/ *noun* [U] special seeds for feeding birds

bird·song /'bɜːdsɒŋ; *NAmE* 'bɜːrdsɔːŋ/ *noun* [U] the musical sounds made by birds

'bird strike *noun* an occasion when a bird hits an aircraft

'bird table *noun* (*BrE*) a wooden platform in a garden/yard on which people put food for birds ➲ VISUAL VOCAB page V16

bird·watch·er /'bɜːdwɒtʃə(r); *NAmE* 'bɜːrdwɑːtʃər/ (also *informal* **birder**) *noun* a person who watches birds in their natural environment and identifies different breeds, as a hobby ➲ compare ORNITHOLOGIST ▸ **bird·watch·ing** (also *informal* **birding**) *noun* [U]

bi·retta /bɪ'retə/ *noun* a square cap worn by Roman Catholic priests

biri·ani = BIRYANI

Biro™ /'baɪrəʊ; *NAmE* 'baɪroʊ/ *noun* (*pl.* -os) (*BrE*) a plastic pen with a metal ball at the top that rolls ink onto the paper ➲ VISUAL VOCAB page V56 ➲ compare BALLPOINT

birth 0‑w /bɜːθ; *NAmE* bɜːrθ/ *noun*

1 0‑w [U, C] the time when a baby is born; the process of being born: *The baby weighed three kilos* ***at birth.*** ◇ *John was present at the birth of both his children.* ◇ *It was a difficult birth.* ◇ *a* ***hospital/home birth*** ◇ *Mark has been blind* ***from birth.*** ◇ *Please state your* ***date and place of birth.*** ➲ COLLOCATIONS at CHILD **2** 0‑w [sing.] the beginning of a new situation, idea, place, etc: *the birth of a new society in South Africa* **3** 0‑w [U] a person's origin or the social position of their family: *Anne was French* ***by birth*** *but lived most of her life in Italy.* ◇ *a woman of noble birth*

IDM **give 'birth (to sb/sth)** 0‑w to produce a baby or young animal: *She died shortly after giving birth.* ◇ *Mary gave birth to a healthy baby girl.* ◇ (*figurative*) *It was the study of history that gave birth to the social sciences.*

'birth certificate *noun* an official document that shows when and where a person was born

'birth control *noun* [U] the practice of controlling the number of children a person has, using various methods of CONTRACEPTION: *a reliable method of birth control*

birth·day 0‑w /'bɜːθdeɪ; *NAmE* 'bɜːrθ-/ *noun*

the day in each year which is the same date as the one on which you were born: *Happy Birthday!* ◇ *Oliver's 13th birthday* ◇ *a* ***birthday card/party/present***

IDM **in your 'birthday suit** (*humorous*) not wearing any clothes

birth·ing /'bɜːθɪŋ; *NAmE* 'bɜːrθ-/ *noun* [U] the action or process of giving birth: *a birthing pool*

birth·mark /'bɜːθmɑːk; *NAmE* 'bɜːrθmɑːrk/ *noun* a red or brown mark on a person's skin that has been there since they were born

'birth mother *noun* the woman who gave birth to a child who has been adopted

'birth partner *noun* a person whom a woman chooses to be with her when she is giving birth to a baby

birth·place /'bɜːθpleɪs; *NAmE* 'bɜːrθ-/ *noun* **1** the house or area where a person was born, especially a famous person **2** the place where sth first happened: *Hawaii was the birthplace of surfing.*

'birth rate *noun* the number of births every year for every 1 000 people in the population of a place: *a* ***low/high birth rate***

birth·right /'bɜːθraɪt; *NAmE* 'bɜːrθraɪt/ *noun* (*formal*) a thing that sb has a right to because of the family or country they were born in, or because it is a basic right of all humans: *The property is the birthright of the eldest child.* ◇ *Education is every child's birthright.*

birth·stone /'bɜːθstəʊn; *NAmE* 'bɜːrθstoʊn/ *noun* a SEMI-PRECIOUS STONE that is associated with the month of sb's birth or their sign of the ZODIAC

birth·weight /'bɜːθweɪt; *NAmE* 'bɜːrθ-/ *noun* [U, C] the recorded weight of a baby when it is born

biry·ani (also **biri·ani, biri·yani**) /ˌbɪri'ɑːni/ *noun* [U, C] a S Asian dish made from rice with meat, fish or vegetables: *chicken biryani*

bis /bɪs/ *adv.* (*music*) (used as an instruction) again

bis·cuit 0‑w /'bɪskɪt/ *noun*

1 0‑w [C] (*BrE*) a small flat dry cake for one person, usually sweet, and baked until crisp: *a packet of chocolate biscuits* ◇ *a selection of cheese biscuits* ➲ compare COOKIE ➲ see also DIGESTIVE BISCUIT, DOG BISCUIT **2** [C] (*NAmE*) a soft bread roll, often eaten with GRAVY **3** [U] a pale yellowish-brown colour

IDM **take the 'biscuit** (*BrE*) (also **take the 'cake** *NAmE, BrE*) (*informal*) to be the most surprising, annoying, etc. thing that has happened or that sb has done: *You've done some stupid things before, but this really takes the biscuit!*

bi·sect /baɪ'sekt/ *verb* **~ sth** (*technical*) to divide sth into two equal parts

bi·sex·ual /ˌbaɪ'sekʃuəl/ *adj., noun*

■ ***adj.*** **1** (also *informal* **bi**) sexually attracted to both men and women **2** (*biology*) having both male and female sexual organs ▸ **bi·sexu·al·ity** /ˌbaɪˌsekʃu'æləti/ *noun* [U]

■ ***noun*** a person who is bisexual ➲ compare HETEROSEXUAL, HOMOSEXUAL

bishop /'bɪʃəp/ *noun* **1** a senior priest in charge of the work of the Church in a city or district: *the Bishop of Oxford* ◇ *Bishop Harries* ➲ see also ARCHBISHOP **2** a piece used in the game of CHESS that is shaped like a bishop's hat and can move any number of squares in a DIAGONAL line ➲ VISUAL VOCAB page V33

bish·op·ric /'bɪʃəprɪk/ *noun* **1** the position of a bishop **2** the district for which a bishop is responsible SYN **diocese**

bis·muth /ˈbɪzməθ/ *noun* [U] (*symb.* **Bi**) a chemical element. Bismuth is a reddish-white metal that breaks easily and is used in medicine.

bison /ˈbaɪsn/ *noun* (*pl.* **bison**) a large wild animal of the cow family that is covered with hair. There are two types of bison, the N American (also called BUFFALO) and the European: *a herd of bison*

bisque /bɪsk; biːsk/ *noun* [U, C] a thick soup, especially one made from SHELLFISH: *lobster bisque* ➲ see also CHOWDER

bis·tro /ˈbiːstrəʊ; *NAmE* -stroʊ/ *noun* (*pl.* **-os**) a small informal restaurant

bit 0-ᴡ /bɪt/ *noun*

▸ SMALL AMOUNT **1** 0-ᴡ **a bit** [sing.] (used as an adverb) (*especially BrE*) rather SYN **a little**: *These trousers are a bit tight.* ◇ *'Are you tired?' 'Yes, I am a bit.'* ◇ *It costs a bit more than I wanted to spend.* ◇ *I can lend you fifty pounds, if you want. That should help a bit.* **2** 0-ᴡ **a bit** [sing.] (*especially BrE*) a short time or distance: *Wait a bit!* ◇ *Can you move up a bit?* ◇ *Greg thought for a bit before answering.* **3** 0-ᴡ [C] **~ of sth** (*especially BrE*) a small amount or piece of sth: *some useful bits of information* ◇ *With **a bit of luck**, we'll be there by 12.* ◇ *I've got a bit of shopping to do.* ◇ *a bit of cake* ◇ *bits of grass/paper*

▸ PART OF STH **4** 0-ᴡ [C] (*especially BrE*) a part of sth larger: *The best bit of the holiday was seeing the Grand Canyon.* ◇ *The school play was a huge success—the audience roared with laughter at all the funny bits.*

▸ LARGE AMOUNT **5** [sing.] **a ~ (of sth)** (*informal, especially BrE*) a large amount: *'How much does he earn?' **'Quite a bit!'*** ◇ *The new system will **take a bit of** getting used to* (= it will take a long time to get used to).

▸ COMPUTING **6** [C] the smallest unit of information used by a computer

▸ FOR HORSE **7** [C] a metal bar that is put in a horse's mouth so that the rider can control it

▸ TOOL **8** [C] a tool or part of a tool for DRILLING (= making) holes ➲ VISUAL VOCAB page V17 ➲ see also DRILL

▸ MONEY **9** [C] (*NAmE, informal*) an amount of money equal to 12½ cents

▸ SEXUAL ORGANS **10 bits** [pl.] (*BrE, informal*) a person's sexual organs ➲ see also BITE, BIT, BITTEN *v.*

IDM **be in ˈbits** (*BrE, informal*) to be very sad or worried: *Inside I'm in bits because I miss him so much.* **the (whole)... bit** (*informal, disapproving*) behaviour or ideas that are typical of a particular group, type of person or activity: *She couldn't accept the whole drug-culture bit.* **bit by ˈbit** a piece at a time; gradually: *He assembled the model aircraft bit by bit.* ◇ *Bit by bit memories of the night came back to me.* **a bit ˈmuch** (*informal*) not fair or not reasonable: *It's a bit much calling me at three in the morning.* **a bit of a...** (*informal, especially BrE*) used when talking about unpleasant or negative things or ideas, to mean 'rather a...': *We may have a bit of a problem on our hands.* ◇ *The rail strike is a bit of a pain.* **a bit of all ˈright** (*BrE, slang*) a person that you think is sexually attractive **a bit of ˈrough** (*BrE, slang*) a person of a low social class who has a sexual relationship with sb of a higher class **a bit on the ˈside** (*BrE, slang*) the boyfriend or girlfriend of sb who is already married or in a steady sexual relationship with sb else **ˌbits and ˈpieces/ˈbobs** (*BrE, informal*) small objects or items of various kinds: *She stuffed all her bits and pieces into a bag and left.* **do your ˈbit** (*informal*) to do your share of a task: *We can finish this job on time if everyone does their bit.* **every bit as good, bad, etc. (as sb/sth)** just as good, bad, etc; equally good, bad, etc: *Rome is every bit as beautiful as Paris.* **get the bit between your teeth** (*informal*) to become very enthusiastic about sth that you have started to do so that you are unlikely to stop until you have finished **not a ˈbit | not one (little) ˈbit** not at all; not in any way: *'Are you cold?' 'Not a bit.'* ◇ *It's not a bit of use* (= there's no point in) *complaining.* ◇ *I don't like that idea one bit.* **not a ˈbit of it!** (*informal, BrE*) used for saying that sth that you had expected to happen did not happen: *You'd think she'd be tired after the journey but not a bit of it!* **to bits 1** into small pieces: *The book fell to bits in my hands.* ◇ *She took the engine to bits, then carefully put it together again.* **2** (*informal*) very much: *I love my kids to bits.* ◇ *She was **thrilled to bits** when I said I'd come.* ➲ more at BLIND *adj.*, CHAMP *v.*

British/American

a bit / a little

- In *BrE* it is common to use **a bit** to mean 'slightly' or 'to a small extent': *These shoes are a bit tight.* ◇ *I'll be a bit later home tomorrow.* ◇ *Can you turn the volume up a bit?*
- It is more common in *NAmE* to say **a little**, or (*informal*) **a little bit**. You can also use these phrases in *BrE*: *These shoes are a little bit too tight.* ◇ *I'll be a little later home tomorrow.* ◇ *Can you turn the volume up a little bit?*

bitch /bɪtʃ/ *noun, verb*

■ *noun* **1** [C] a female dog: *a greyhound bitch* **2** [C] (*slang, disapproving*) an offensive way of referring to a woman, especially an unpleasant one: *You stupid little bitch!* ◇ *She can be a real bitch.* **3** [sing.] (*slang*) a thing that causes problems or difficulties: ***Life's a bitch.*** **4** [sing.] **~ (about sb/sth)** (*informal*) a complaint about sb/sth or a conversation in which you complain about them: *We've been having a bitch about our boss.* ➲ see also SON OF A BITCH

■ *verb* [I] **~ (about sb/sth)** (*informal*) to make unkind and critical remarks about sb/sth, especially when they are not there

bitch·in' (also **bitch·ing**) /ˈbɪtʃɪn/ *adj.* (*slang, especially NAmE*) very good

bitchy /ˈbɪtʃi/ *adj.* (*informal*) (**bitch·ier**, **bitchi·est**) saying unpleasant and unkind things about other people: *bitchy remarks* ▸ **bitchi·ness** *noun* [U]

bite 0-ᴡ /baɪt/ *verb, noun*

■ *verb* (**bit** /bɪt/, **bit·ten** /ˈbɪtn/)

▸ USE TEETH **1** 0-ᴡ [I, T] to use your teeth to cut into or through sth: *Does your dog bite?* ◇ *Come here! I won't bite!* (= you don't need to be afraid) ◇ **~ into/through sth** *She bit into a ripe juicy pear.* ◇ **~ sb/sth** *She was bitten by the family dog.* ◇ *Stop biting your nails!* ◇ **~ off sth/sth off** *He bit off a large chunk of bread/He bit a large chunk of bread off.*

▸ OF INSECT/SNAKE **2** 0-ᴡ [I, T] to wound sb by making a small hole or mark in their skin: *Most European spiders don't bite.* ◇ **~ sb** *We were badly bitten by mosquitoes.*

▸ OF FISH **3** [I] if a fish **bites**, it takes food from the hook of a FISHING LINE and may get caught

▸ HAVE EFFECT **4** [I] to have an unpleasant effect: *The recession is beginning to bite.*

IDM **be bitten by sth** to develop a strong interest in or enthusiasm for sth: *He's been **bitten by the** travel **bug**.* **bite the ˈbullet** (*informal*) to start to deal with an unpleasant or difficult situation which cannot be avoided ORIGIN From the custom of giving soldiers a bullet to bite on during a medical operation without anaesthetic. **bite the ˈdust** (*informal*) **1** to fail, or to be defeated or destroyed: *Thousands of small businesses bite the dust every year.* **2** (*humorous*) to die **bite the hand that ˈfeeds you** to harm sb who has helped you or supported you **bite your ˈlip** to stop yourself from saying sth or from showing an emotion **bite off more than you can ˈchew** to try to do too much, or sth that is too difficult **bite your ˈtongue** to stop yourself from saying sth that might upset sb or cause an argument, although you want to speak: *I didn't believe her explanation but I bit my tongue.* ➲ more at HAIR, HEAD *n.*, ONCE *adv.*

PHR V **ˌbite ˈback (at sb/sth)** to react angrily, especially when sb has criticized or harmed you **ˌbite sth↔ˈback** to stop yourself from saying sth or from showing your feelings: *She bit back her anger.* **ˌbite ˈinto sth** to cut into the surface of sth: *The horses' hooves bit deep into the soft earth.*

■ *noun*

▸ USING TEETH **1** 0-ᴡ [C] an act of biting: *The dog gave me a playful bite.* ◇ *He has to wear a brace to correct his bite* (= the way the upper and lower teeth fit together).

▸ FOOD **2** 0-ᴡ [C] a small piece of food that you can bite from a

larger piece: *She took a couple of bites of the sandwich.* ◇ *He didn't eat a bite of his dinner* (= he ate nothing). **3 a ~ (to eat)** [sing.] (*informal*) a small amount of food; a small meal: *How about a bite of lunch?* ◇ *We just have time for **a bite to eat** before the movie.*
▸ OF INSECT/ANIMAL **4** 🔑 [C] a wound made by an animal or insect: *Dog bites can get infected.* ◇ *a mosquito/snake bite*
▸ STRONG TASTE **5** [U] a pleasant strong taste: *Cheese will add extra bite to any pasta dish.*
▸ COLD **6** [sing.] a sharp cold feeling: *There's a bite in the air tonight.*
▸ POWERFUL EFFECT **7** [U] a quality that makes sth effective or powerful: *The performance had no bite to it.*
▸ OF FISH **8** [C] the act of a fish biting food on a hook ➲ see also FROSTBITE, LOVE BITE, SOUND BITE
IDM **a bite at/of the 'cherry** (*BrE*) an opportunity to do sth: *They were eager for a second bite of the cherry.* ➲ more at BARK *n.*

'bite-sized (also **'bite-size**) *adj.* [usually before noun] **1** small enough to put into the mouth and eat: *Cut the meat into bite-sized pieces.* **2** (*informal*) very small or short: *The exams are taken in bite-size chunks over two years.*

bit·ing /'baɪtɪŋ/ *adj.* **1** (of a wind) very cold and unpleasant **2** (of remarks) cruel and critical: ***biting sarcasm/wit*** ▸ **bit·ing·ly** *adv.*

bit·map /'bɪtmæp/ *noun* (*computing*) a way in which an image is stored with a fixed number of BITS (= units of information) for each unit of the image ▸ **bit·map** *verb* (-pp-) **~ sth**

bi·tonal /ˌbaɪ'təʊnl; *NAmE* -'toʊ-/ *adj.* (*music*) having parts in two different KEYS sounding together ▸ **bi·ton·al·ity** /ˌbaɪtəʊ'næləti; *NAmE* -toʊ-/ *noun* [U]

'bit part *noun* a small part in a film/movie

'bit player *noun* **1** an actor with a small part in a film/movie **2** a person or an organization that is involved in a situation but does not have an important role and has little influence

bit·stream /'bɪtstriːm/ *noun* (*computing*) a flow of data in BINARY form

bit·ten *past part.* of BITE

bit·ter 🔑 /'bɪtə(r)/ *adj.*, *noun*
■ ***adj.*** HELP **more bitter** and **most bitter** are the usual comparative and superlative forms, but **bitterest** can also be used. **1** 🔑 (of arguments, disagreements, etc.) very serious and unpleasant, with a lot of anger and hatred involved: *a long and bitter dispute* **2** 🔑 (of people) feeling angry and unhappy because you feel that you have been treated unfairly: *She is very bitter about losing her job.* **3** 🔑 [usually before noun] making you feel very unhappy; caused by great unhappiness: *to **weep/shed bitter tears*** ◇ *Losing the match was **a bitter disappointment** for the team.* ◇ *I've learnt from **bitter experience** not to trust what he says.* **4** 🔑 (of food, etc.) having a strong, unpleasant taste; not sweet: *Black coffee leaves a bitter taste in the mouth.* ➲ compare SWEET **5** 🔑 (of weather conditions) extremely cold and unpleasant: *bitter cold* ◇ *a bitter wind* ◇ *It's really bitter out today.* ▸ **bit·ter·ness** *noun* [U]: *The pay cut caused bitterness among the staff.* ◇ *The flowers of the hop plant add bitterness to the beer.*
IDM **a bitter 'pill (for sb) (to swallow)** a fact or an event that is unpleasant and difficult to accept **to/until the bitter 'end** continuing until you have done everything you can, or until sth is completely finished, despite difficulties and problems: *They were prepared to fight to the bitter end for their rights.*
■ ***noun*** (*BrE*) **1** [U, C] a type of beer with a dark colour and a strong bitter taste, that is very popular in Britain: *A pint of bitter, please.* ➲ compare MILD **2 bitters** [U+sing./pl. v.] a strong bitter alcoholic liquid that is made from plants and added to other alcoholic drinks to give flavour: *gin with a dash of bitters*

ˌbitter 'lemon *noun* [U] (*BrE*) a FIZZY drink (= with bubbles) that tastes of lemon and is slightly bitter

Synonyms

bitter

pungent • sour • acrid • sharp • acid

These words all describe a strong, unpleasant taste or smell.

bitter (of a taste or smell) strong and usually unpleasant; (of food or drink) having a bitter taste.

pungent (of a smell or taste) strong and usually unpleasant; (of food or smoke) having a pungent smell or taste: *the pungent smell of burning rubber*

sour (of a taste) bitter like the taste of a lemon or of fruit that is not ripe; (of food or drink) having a sour taste: *Too much pulp produces a sour wine.*

acrid (of a smell or taste) strong and unpleasant; (of smoke) having an acrid smell: *acrid smoke from burning tyres*

sharp (of a taste or smell) strong and slightly bitter; (of food or drink) having a sharp taste: *The cheese has a distinctively sharp taste.*

acid (of a taste or smell) bitter, like the taste of a lemon or of fruit that is not ripe; (of food or drink) having an acid taste.

WHICH WORD?

A **bitter** taste is usually unpleasant, but some people enjoy the bitter flavour of coffee or chocolate. No other word can describe this flavour. A **sharp** or **pungent** flavour is more strong than unpleasant, especially when describing cheese. **Sharp**, **sour** and **acid** all describe the taste of a lemon or a fruit that is not ripe. An **acrid** smell is strong and unpleasant, especially the smell of smoke or burning, but not the smell of food.

PATTERNS

- a(n) bitter/pungent/sour/acrid/sharp/acid **taste/flavour**
- a(n) bitter/pungent/acrid/sharp/acid **smell/odour**
- a(n) bitter/sour/sharp/acid **fruit**
- pungent/sharp **cheese**
- pungent/acrid **smoke**

bit·ter·ly 🔑 /'bɪtəli; *NAmE* -tərli/ *adv.* **1** 🔑 in a way that shows feelings of sadness or anger: *She wept bitterly.* ◇ *They complained bitterly.* ◇ *The development was bitterly opposed by the local community.* **2** 🔑 (describing unpleasant or sad feelings) extremely: ***bitterly disappointed/ashamed*** **3** 🔑 **~ cold** very cold

bit·tern /'bɪtən; *NAmE* -tərn/ *noun* a European bird of the HERON family, that lives on wet ground and has a loud call

ˌbitter-'sweet *adj.* (*BrE*) **1** bringing pleasure mixed with sadness: *bitter-sweet memories* **2** (of tastes or smells) bitter and sweet at the same time

bitty /'bɪti/ *adj.* (*BrE, informal*) (**bit·tier**, **bit·ti·est**) made up of many small separate parts, which do not seem to fit together well

bitu·men /'bɪtʃəmən; *NAmE* bə'tuːmən; -'tjuː-/ *noun* [U] **1** a black sticky substance obtained from oil, used for covering roads or roofs **2** (*AustralE, informal*) the surface of a road that is covered with TAR: *a kilometre and a half of bitumen*

bi·tu·min·ous /bɪ'tjuːmɪnəs; *NAmE* bə'tuː-/ *adj.* containing bitumen

bit·zer /'bɪtsə(r)/ *noun* (*AustralE, NZE, informal*) **1** a thing that is made from parts that originally did not belong together **2** a dog that is a mixture of different breeds SYN **mongrel**

bi·valve /'baɪvælv/ *noun* (*technical*) any SHELLFISH with a shell in two parts, for example a MUSSEL ➲ compare MOLLUSC

biv·ouac /'bɪvuæk/ *noun, verb*
■ ***noun*** a temporary camp or shelter, without using a tent,

that is made and used especially by people climbing mountains or by soldiers
■ ***verb*** (-ck-) [I] to spend the night in a bivouac

bivvy /ˈbɪvi/
■ ***noun*** (*pl.* **biv·vies**) a tent or temporary shelter
■ ***verb*** (*third person sing. pres. t.* **biv·vies** *pres. part.* **bivvy·ing** *pt, pp* **biv·vied**) [I] to sleep in a tent or temporary shelter

the biz /bɪz/ *noun* [sing.] (*informal*) a particular type of business, especially one connected with entertainment: *people in the music biz*
IDM **be the ˈbiz** (*informal*) to be very good

bi·zarre /bɪˈzɑː(r)/ *adj.* very strange or unusual SYN **weird**: *a bizarre situation/incident/story* ◇ *bizarre behaviour* ▶ **bi·zarre·ly** *adv.*: *bizarrely dressed*

blab /blæb/ *verb* (-bb-) [I, T] **~ (to sb) (about sth)** | **~ (sth) (to sb)** (*informal*) to tell sb information that should be kept secret: *Someone must have blabbed to the police.*

blab·ber /ˈblæbə(r)/ *verb* [I] **~ (on) (about sth)** (*informal*) to talk in a way that other people think is silly and annoying: *What was she blabbering on about this time?*

blab·ber·mouth /ˈblæbəmaʊθ; *NAmE* -bərm-/ *noun* (*informal, disapproving*) a person who tells secrets because they talk too much

black 0‑ /blæk/ *adj., noun, verb*
■ ***adj.*** (**black·er, black·est**)
▸ COLOUR **1** 0‑ having the very darkest colour, like night or coal: *a shiny black car* ◇ *black storm clouds*
▸ WITH NO LIGHT **2** 0‑ without light; completely dark: *a black night*
▸ PEOPLE **3** 0‑ (also **Black**) belonging to a race of people who have dark skin; connected with black people: *a black woman writer* ◇ *black culture* HELP **Black** is the word most widely used and generally accepted in Britain. In the US the currently accepted term is **African American**.
▸ TEA/COFFEE **4** 0‑ without milk: *Two black coffees, please.* ➲ compare WHITE
▸ DIRTY **5** 0‑ very dirty; covered with dirt: *chimneys black with smoke* ◇ *Go and wash your hands; they're absolutely black!*
▸ ANGRY **6** full of anger or hatred: *She's been in a really black mood all day.* ◇ *Rory shot her a black look.*
▸ DEPRESSING **7** without hope; very depressing: *The future looks pretty black.* ◇ *It's been another black day for the north-east with the announcement of further job losses.*
▸ EVIL **8** (*literary*) evil or immoral: *black deeds/lies*
▸ HUMOUR **9** dealing with unpleasant or terrible things, such as murder, in a humorous way: *'Good place to bury the bodies,' she joked with* ***black humour.*** ◇ *The play is a* ***black comedy.*** ➲ see also BLACKLY
▶ **black·ness** *noun* [U, sing.]: *She peered out into the blackness of the night.*
IDM **(beat sb) black and ˈblue** (to hit sb until they are) covered with BRUISES (= blue, brown or purple marks on the body) **not as black as he/she/it is ˈpainted** not as bad as people say he/she/it is: *He's not very friendly, but he's not as black as he's painted.* ➲ more at POT *n.*
■ ***noun***
▸ COLOUR **1** 0‑ [U] the very darkest colour, like night or coal: *the black of the night sky* ◇ *Everyone at the funeral was dressed in black.*
▸ PEOPLE **2** 0‑ (also **Black**) [C, usually pl.] a member of a race of people who have dark skin HELP In this meaning **black** is more common in the plural. It can sound offensive in the singular. Instead, you can use the adjective ('a black man/woman') or, in the US, **African American.**
IDM **be in the ˈblack** to have money, for example in your bank account ➲ compare BE IN THE RED at RED **ˌblack and ˈwhite** 0‑ having no colours except black, white and shades of grey (in photographs, on television, etc.): *a film made in black and white* ◇ *black-and-white photos* **in black and white** in writing or in print: *I never thought they'd put it in black and white on the front page.* **(in) black and white** in a way that makes people or things seem completely bad or good, or completely right or wrong: *It's a complex issue, but he only sees it in black and white.* ◇ *This is not a black-and-white decision* (= where the difference between two choices is completely clear).
■ ***verb*** **1 ~ sth/sb** (*BrE*) to refuse to deal with goods or to do business with sb as a political protest SYN **boycott**: *The unions have blacked all imports from the country.* **2 ~ sth** to make sth black SYN **blacken**
PHR V **ˌblack ˈout** to become unconscious for a short time SYN **faint**: *The driver had probably blacked out at the wheel.* ➲ related noun BLACKOUT **ˌblack sth↔ˈout 1** to make a place dark by turning off lights, covering windows, etc: *A power failure blacked out the city last night.* ◇ *a house with blacked out windows* ➲ related noun BLACKOUT **2** to prevent sth such as a piece of writing or a television broadcast from being read or seen: *Some lines of the document have been blacked out for security reasons.*

black·amoor /ˈblækəmɔː(r)/ *noun* (*old use, taboo*) an offensive word for a black person

the ˌblack ˈarts *noun* [pl.] = BLACK MAGIC

black·ball /ˈblækbɔːl/ *verb* **~ sb** to prevent sb from joining a club or a group by voting against them

ˌblack ˈbelt *noun* **1** a belt that you can earn in a sport such as JUDO or KARATE which shows that you have reached a very high standard **2** a person who has gained a black belt

Black·Berry™ /ˈblækbəri; *NAmE* -beri/ *noun* (*pl.* **-ies**) a very small computer that you can hold in your hand and that you can use for storing information, sending and receiving emails and TEXT MESSAGES, making and receiving phone calls and looking at the Internet: *Check your emails via your BlackBerry.* ◇ *a BlackBerry handset*

black·berry /ˈblækbəri; *NAmE* -beri/ (*pl.* **-ies**) (*BrE* also **bram·ble**) *noun* a small soft black fruit that grows on a bush with THORNS in gardens/yards or in the countryside. The bush is also called a blackberry/bramble: *blackberry and apple pie* ➲ VISUAL VOCAB page V26

black·berry·ing /ˈblækbəriɪŋ; *NAmE* -beriɪŋ/ *noun* [U] the act of picking blackberries: *Shall we* ***go blackberrying?***

black·bird /ˈblækbɜːd; *NAmE* -bɜːrd/ *noun* **1** a European bird: the male is black with a yellow beak and the female is brown with a brown beak **2** a black N American bird, larger than the European blackbird, related to the STARLING

black·board /ˈblækbɔːd; *NAmE* -bɔːrd/ (also **chalk·board** especially in *NAmE*) *noun* a large board with a smooth black or dark green surface that teachers write on with a piece of CHALK: *to write on the blackboard* ➲ compare WHITEBOARD

ˌblack ˈbox *noun* **1** (also **ˈflight recorder**) a small machine in a plane that records all the details of each flight and is useful for finding out the cause of an accident **2** [usually sing.] (*technical*) a complicated piece of equipment, usually electronic, that you know produces particular results, but that you do not completely understand

ˌblack ˈcab *noun* (*BrE*) a traditional type of taxi in London and some other British cities. Its driver is licensed by the city to stop and pick up passengers in the street: *a queue of black cabs at the station*

the ˈBlack Country *noun* [sing.] an area in the West Midlands of England where there used to be a lot of heavy industry

black·cur·rant /ˌblækˈkʌrənt; ˈblækkʌrənt; *NAmE* -kɜːr-/ *noun* a small black BERRY that grows in bunches on a garden bush and can be eaten: *blackcurrant jam* ◇ *a blackcurrant bush*

the ˌBlack ˈDeath *noun* [sing.] the name used for the very serious infectious disease, (called BUBONIC PLAGUE), which killed millions of people in Europe and Asia in the 14th century

ˌblack ˈdiamond *noun* **1** [C] (*BrE, informal*) a lump of coal **2** [U, C] a dark form of diamond **3** [C] (*NAmE*) a slope that is difficult to SKI down: *a black diamond run*

the ˌblack eˈconomy (*BrE*) (*NAmE* **the ˌunderground eˈconomy**) *noun* [sing.] business activity or work

B

that is done without the knowledge of the government or other officials so that people avoid paying tax on the money they earn

ˌblack emˈpowerment (also **ˌblack ecoˌnomic emˈpowerment**) *noun* [U] in southern Africa, a policy which aims to give black people the chance to earn more money, own more property, etc, and have a greater role in the economy than they did before

black·en /ˈblækən/ *verb* **1** [T, I] **~ (sth)** to make sth black; to become black: *Their faces were blackened with soot.* ◇ *Smoke had blackened the walls.* **2** [T] **~ sb's name/reputation/character** to say unpleasant things that give people a bad opinion of sb: *He accused the newspaper of trying to blacken his name.*

ˌBlack ˈEnglish *noun* [U] any of various forms of English spoken by black people, especially a form spoken in US cities

ˌblack ˈeye *noun* an area of dark skin (called a BRUISE), that can form around sb's eye when they receive a blow on it

black·face /ˈblækfeɪs/ *noun* **1** [C] a type of sheep with a black face **2** [U] a dark substance used by actors to make their skin look dark

ˌblack ˈflag *noun* **1** a black flag used in motor racing to stop a driver who has done sth wrong **2** a flag with a SKULL AND CROSSBONES on it

black·fly /ˈblækflaɪ/ *noun* (*pl.* **black·fly** or **black·flies**) **1** a small black or dark green insect that damages plants **2** (also ˈ**black fly**) a small black fly that sucks blood from humans and animals

Black·foot /ˈblækfʊt/ *noun* (*pl.* **Black·feet** /ˈblækfiːt/ or **Black·foot**) a member of a Native American people, many of whom live in the US state of Montana and in Alberta in Canada

ˌBlack Forest ˈgateau *noun* a type of chocolate cake with layers of CHERRIES and cream

ˌblack ˈgold *noun* [U] (*NAmE, informal*) oil

black·guard /ˈblægɑːd; *NAmE* -gɑːrd/ *noun* (*old-fashioned, BrE*) a man who is dishonest and has no sense of what is right and what is wrong

black·head /ˈblækhed/ *noun* a small spot on the skin, often on the face, with a black top

ˌblack ˈhole *noun* an area in space that nothing, not even light, can escape from, because GRAVITY (= the force that pulls objects in space towards each other) is so strong there: (*figurative*) *The company viewed the venture as a financial black hole* (= it would use a lot of the company's money with no real result).

ˌblack ˈice *noun* [U] ice in a thin layer on the surface of a road

black·jack /ˈblækdʒæk/ *noun* **1** (*BrE* also **pon·toon**) [U] a card game in which players try to collect cards with a total value of 21 and no more **2** [C] (*especially NAmE*) a type of CLUB used as a weapon, especially a metal pipe covered with leather

black·leg /ˈblækleg/ *noun* (*BrE, disapproving*) a person who continues to work when the people they work with are on strike; a person who is employed to work instead of those who are on strike ➲ compare STRIKE-BREAKER ➲ see also SCAB

ˌblack ˈlight *noun* [U] ULTRAVIOLET or INFRARED RAYS, which cannot be seen

black·list /ˈblæklɪst/ *noun, verb*

■ ***noun*** a list of the names of people, companies, products or countries that an organization or a government considers unacceptable and that must be avoided

■ ***verb*** **~ sb/sth** to put the name of a person, a company, a product or a country on a blacklist: *She was blacklisted by all the major Hollywood studios because of her political views.*

ˌblack ˈlung *noun* [U] (*NAmE*) a lung disease caused by breathing in coal dust over a long period of time

black·ly /ˈblækli/ *adv.* **~ comic/funny/humorous/satirical** dealing with unpleasant or terrible things, such as murder, in a humorous way: *The movie takes a blackly humorous look at death.*

ˌblack ˈmagic *noun* [U] (also **the black ˈarts**) a type of magic which is believed to use the power of the DEVIL in order to do evil

black·mail /ˈblækmeɪl/ *noun, verb*

■ ***noun*** [U] **1** the crime of demanding money from a person by threatening to tell sb else a secret about them **2** the act of putting pressure on a person or a group to do sth they do not want to do, for example by making threats or by making them feel guilty: ***emotional/moral blackmail***

■ ***verb*** to force sb to give you money or do sth for you by threatening them, for example by saying you will tell people a secret about them: **~ sb** *She blackmailed him for years by threatening to tell the newspapers about their affair.* ◇ **~ sb into doing sth** *The President said he wouldn't be blackmailed into agreeing to the terrorists' demands.*

black·mail·er /ˈblækmeɪlə(r)/ *noun* a person who commits blackmail

Black Maria /ˌblæk məˈraɪə/ *noun* (*old-fashioned, slang*) a police van that was used in the past for transporting prisoners in

ˌblack ˈmark *noun* (*BrE*) a note, either in writing on an official record, or in sb's mind, of sth you have done or said that makes people think badly of you: *She earned a black mark for opposing company policy.* ◇ *The public scandal was a black mark against him.*

ˌblack ˈmarket *noun* [usually sing.] an illegal form of trade in which foreign money, or goods that are difficult to obtain, are bought and sold: *to buy or sell goods* ***on the black market*** ◇ *a flourishing black market in foreign currency*

ˌblack markeˈteer *noun* a person who sells goods on the black market

ˌblack ˈmass *noun* a ceremony in which people worship the DEVIL

ˌBlack ˈMuslim *noun* a member of a group of black people, especially in the US, who follow the religion of Islam and want a separate black society

black·out /ˈblækaʊt/ *noun* **1** a period when there is no light as a result of an electrical power failure **2** a situation when the government or the police will not allow any news or information on a particular subject to be given to the public **3** [usually sing.] (*especially BrE*) a period of time during a war when all lights must be put out or covered at night, so that they cannot be seen by an enemy attacking by air **4** [usually pl.] (*BrE*) a covering for windows that stops light being seen from outside, or light from outside from coming into a room **5** a temporary loss of CONSCIOUSNESS, sight or memory: *She had a blackout and couldn't remember anything about the accident.*

ˌblack ˈpepper *noun* [U] a black powder made from dried BERRIES (called PEPPERCORNS), used to give a spicy flavour to food: *salt and freshly ground black pepper*

ˌBlack ˈPower *noun* [U] a movement supporting rights and political power for black people

ˌblack ˈpudding (*BrE*) (*NAmE* ˈ**blood sausage**) (also **ˌblood ˈpudding** *BrE, NAmE*) *noun* [U, C] a type of large dark SAUSAGE made from pig's blood, fat and grain

ˌBlack ˈRod *noun* [U] an official who takes part in the opening ceremony of the British parliament

ˌblack ˈsheep *noun* [usually sing.] a person who is different from the rest of their family or another group, and who is considered bad or embarrassing: *the black sheep of the family*

black·shirt /ˈblækʃɜːt; *NAmE* -ʃɜːrt/ (also **Blackshirt**) *noun* a member of a FASCIST organization, especially in the 1920s and 30s

black·smith /ˈblæksmɪθ/ (also **smith**) *noun* a person whose job is to make and repair things made of iron, especially HORSESHOES ➲ compare FARRIER

B

ˈ**black spot** *noun* (*BrE*) a place, a situation or an event that is a problem or that causes a lot of problems: *an environmental black spot* ◇ *That corner is a notorious accident black spot* (= a lot of accidents happen there).

black·thorn /ˈblækθɔːn; *NAmE* -θɔːrn/ *noun* [U] a bush with THORNS with black branches, white flowers and sour purple fruit called SLOES

ˌ**black** ˈ**tie** *noun* a black BOW TIE worn with a DINNER JACKET ▶ ˌ**black** ˈ**tie** *adj.*: *The party is black tie* (= dinner jackets should be worn). ◇ *a black-tie dinner*

black·top /ˈblæktɒp; *NAmE* -tɑːp/ *noun, verb* (*NAmE*) = TARMAC

ˌ**black** ˈ**widow** *noun* a poisonous American spider. The female black widow often eats the male.

blad·der /ˈblædə(r)/ *noun* **1** an organ that is shaped like a bag in which liquid waste (=URINE) collects before it is passed out of the body ➲ see also GALL BLADDER ➲ **VISUAL VOCAB** page V48 **2** a bag made of rubber, leather, etc. that can be filled with air or liquid, such as the one inside a football

blad·dered /ˈblædəd; *NAmE* ˈblædərd/ *adj.* [not before noun] (*BrE, slang*) drunk

blade 🗝 /bleɪd/ *noun*
1 🗝 the flat part of a knife, tool or machine, which has a sharp edge or edges for cutting ➲ **VISUAL VOCAB** pages V17, V19, V21, V23 ➲ see also RAZOR BLADE, SWITCHBLADE **2** one of the flat parts that turn around in an engine or on a HELICOPTER: *the blades of a propeller* ◇ *rotor blades on a helicopter* ➲ **VISUAL VOCAB** page V43 **3** the flat wide part of an OAR (= one of the long poles that are used to ROW a boat) that goes in the water ➲ **VISUAL VOCAB** page V45 **4** a single flat leaf of grass **5** the flat metal part on the bottom of an ICE SKATE ➲ see also SHOULDER BLADE

blades

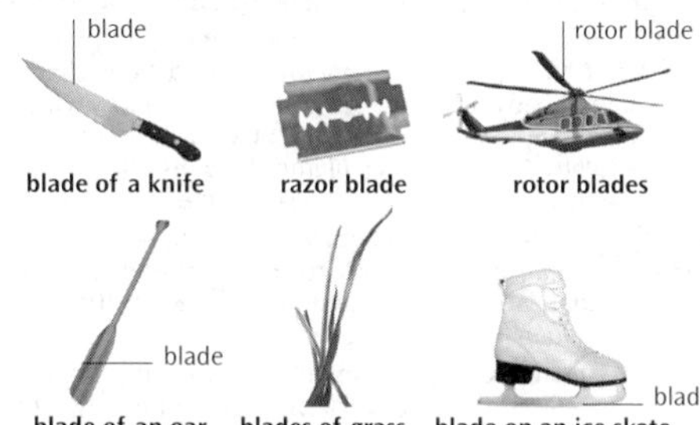

blad·ing /ˈbleɪdɪŋ/ *noun* [U] the sport of moving on ROLLERBLADES

blag /blæg/ *verb* (-gg-) **~ sth** (*BrE, informal*) to persuade sb to give you sth, or to let you do sth, by talking to them in a clever or amusing way: *I blagged some tickets for the game.* ◇ *We* ***blagged our way*** *into the reception by saying that we were from the press.*

blah /blɑː/ *noun, adj.*
■ ***noun*** [U] (*informal*) people say **blah, blah, blah**, when they do not want to give the exact words that sb has said or written because they think they are not important or are boring: *They said, 'Come in, sit down, blah, blah, blah, sign here'.*
■ ***adj.*** (*NAmE, informal*) **1** not interesting: *The movie was pretty blah.* **2** not feeling well; feeling slightly unhappy

blame 🗝 /bleɪm/ *verb, noun*
■ ***verb*** 🗝 to think or say that sb/sth is responsible for sth bad: **~ sb/sth (for sth)** *She doesn't blame anyone for her father's death.* ◇ *A dropped cigarette is being blamed for the fire.* ◇ **~ sth on sb/sth** *Police are blaming the accident on dangerous driving.*
IDM **be to blame (for sth)** 🗝 to be responsible for sth bad: *If anyone's to blame, it's me.* ◇ *Which driver was to blame for the accident?* **don't blame** ˈ**me** (*informal*) used to advise sb not to do sth, when you think they will do it despite your advice: *Call her if you like, but don't blame me if she's angry.* **I don't** ˈ**blame you/her, etc. (for doing sth)** (*informal*) used to say that you think that what sb did was reasonable and the right thing to do: *'I just slammed the phone down when he said that.' 'I don't blame you!'* **only have yourself to** ˈ**blame** used to say that you think sth is sb's own fault: *If you lose your job, you'll only have yourself to blame.*
■ ***noun*** 🗝 [U] **~ (for sth)** responsibility for doing sth badly or wrongly; saying that sb is responsible for sth: *to* ***lay/put the blame*** *for sth on sb* ◇ *The government will have* ***to take the blame*** *for the riots.* ◇ *Why do I always* ***get the blame*** *for everything that goes wrong?* ➲ compare CREDIT *n.* (7)

blame·less /ˈbleɪmləs/ *adj.* doing no wrong; free from responsibility for doing sth bad **SYN** **innocent**: *to lead a blameless life* ◇ *None of us is entirely blameless in this matter.* ▶ **blame·less·ly** *adv.*

blame·worthy /ˈbleɪmwɜːði; *NAmE* -wɜːrði/ *adj.* (*formal*) deserving disapproval and criticism; responsible for doing sth wrong

blanch /blɑːntʃ; *NAmE* blæntʃ/ *verb* **1** [I] **~ (at sth)** (*formal*) to become pale because you are shocked or frightened **2** [T] **~ sth** to prepare food, especially vegetables, by putting it into boiling water for a short time

blanc·mange /bləˈmɒnʒ; *NAmE* -ˈmɑːnʒ/ *noun* [C, U] (*BrE*) a cold DESSERT (= a sweet dish) that looks like jelly, made with milk and flavoured with fruit

bland /blænd/ *adj.* (**bland·er**, **bland·est**) **1** with little colour, excitement or interest; without anything to attract attention **SYN** **nondescript**: *bland background music* **2** not having a strong or interesting taste: *a rather bland diet of soup, fish and bread* **3** showing no strong emotions or excitement; not saying anything very interesting: *a bland smile* ◇ *After the meeting, a bland statement was issued.* ▶ **bland·ly** *adv.* **bland·ness** *noun* [U]

bland·ish·ments /ˈblændɪʃmənts/ *noun* [pl.] (*formal*) pleasant things that you say to sb or do for them to try to persuade them to do sth

blank 🗝 /blæŋk/ *adj., noun, verb*
■ ***adj.*** **1** 🗝 empty, with nothing written, printed or recorded on it: *Sign your name in the blank space below.* ◇ *a blank CD* ◇ *Write on one side of the paper and leave the other side blank.* ◇ *She turned to a blank page in her notebook.* **2** 🗝 (of a wall or screen) empty; with no pictures, marks or decoration: *blank whitewashed walls* ◇ *Suddenly the screen* ***went blank***. **3** showing no feeling, understanding or interest: *She stared at me with a blank expression on her face.* ◇ *Steve* ***looked blank*** *and said he had no idea what I was talking about.* ◇ *Suddenly* ***my mind went blank*** (= I could not remember anything). **4** [only before noun] (of negative things) complete and total: *a* ***blank refusal/denial*** ➲ see also POINT-BLANK ▶ **blank·ly** *adv.*: *She stared blankly into space, not knowing what to say next.* **blank·ness** *noun* [U]
■ ***noun*** **1** 🗝 [C] an empty space on a printed form or document for you to write answers, information, etc. in: *Please* ***fill in the blanks***. ◇ *If you can't answer the question, leave a blank.* **2** [sing.] a state of not being able to remember anything: *My* ***mind was a blank*** *and I couldn't remember her name.* **3** [C] (also ˌ**blank** ˈ**cartridge**) a CARTRIDGE in a gun that contains an EXPLOSIVE but no bullet: *The troops fired blanks in the air.* **IDM** see DRAW *v.*
■ ***verb*** **1** [T] **~ sb** (*BrE, informal*) to ignore sb completely: *I saw her on the bus this morning, but she totally blanked me.* **2** [I] (*NAmE*) to be suddenly unable to remember or think of sth: *I knew the answer, but I totally blanked during the test.*
PHR V ˌ**blank** ˈ**out** to suddenly become empty: *The screen blanked out.* ˌ**blank sth**↔ˈ**out 1** to cover sth completely so that it cannot be seen: *All the names in the letter had been blanked out.* **2** to deliberately forget sth unpleasant: *She had tried to blank out the whole experience.*

ˌ**blank** ˈ**cheque** (*BrE*) (*NAmE* ˌ**blank** ˈ**check**) *noun* **1** a cheque that is signed but which does not have the amount of money to be paid written on it **2** permission or authority to do sth that is necessary in a particular situation: *The President was **given a blank check** by Congress to continue the war.*

B

blan·ket /'blæŋkɪt/ *noun, adj., verb*

■ ***noun*** **1** a large cover, often made of wool, used especially on beds to keep people warm ➲ VISUAL VOCAB page V20 ➲ see also ELECTRIC BLANKET **2** [usually sing.] **~ of sth** a thick layer or covering of sth: *a **blanket of fog/snow/cloud*** ◇ (*figurative*) *The trial was conducted under a blanket of secrecy.* ➲ see also WET BLANKET

■ ***adj.*** [only before noun] including or affecting all possible cases, situations or people: *a **blanket ban** on tobacco advertising* ◇ *a blanket refusal*

■ ***verb*** [often passive] **~ sth** (*formal*) to cover sth completely with a thick layer: *Snow soon blanketed the frozen ground.*

'blanket bath *noun* (*BrE*) an act of washing the whole of sb's body when they cannot get out of bed because they are sick, injured or old

blankety-blank /ˌblæŋkəti 'blæŋk/ *adj.* [only before noun] (*informal*) used in place of a rude word that the speaker does not want to say: *It's not my blankety-blank fault!*

ˌblank 'verse *noun* [U] (*technical*) poetry that has a regular rhythm, usually with ten syllables and five stresses in each line, but which does not RHYME ➲ compare FREE VERSE

blare /bleə(r); *NAmE* bler/ *verb, noun*

■ ***verb*** [I, T] to make a loud unpleasant noise: *police cars with lights flashing and sirens blaring* ◇ **~ out** *Music blared out from the open window.* ◇ **~ sth** (**out**) *The radio was blaring (out) rock music.*

■ ***noun*** [sing.] a loud unpleasant noise: *the blare of car horns*

blar·ney /'blɑːni; *NAmE* 'blɑːrni/ *noun* [U] (*informal*) talk that is friendly and amusing but probably not true, and which may be used to persuade or trick you ORIGIN From **Blarney**, a castle in Ireland where there is a stone which is said to have magic powers: anyone who kisses the 'Blarney stone' is given the gift of speaking persuasively ('the gift of the gab').

blasé /'blɑːzeɪ; *NAmE* blɑː'zeɪ/ *adj.* **~ (about sth)** not impressed, excited or worried about sth, because you have seen or experienced it many times before

blas·pheme /blæs'fiːm/ *verb* [I, T] **~ (sb/sth)** to speak about God or the holy things of a particular religion in an offensive way; to swear using the names of God or holy things ▶ **blas·phemer** *noun*

blas·phemy /'blæsfəmi/ *noun* (*pl.* -ies) [U, C] behaviour or language that insults or shows a lack of respect for God or religion ▶ **blas·phem·ous** /'blæsfəməs/ *adj.*: *Many people found the film blasphemous.* **blas·phem·ous·ly** *adv.*

blast /blɑːst; *NAmE* blæst/ *noun, verb, exclamation*

■ ***noun***

▸ EXPLOSION **1** [C] an explosion or a powerful movement of air caused by an explosion: *a bomb blast* ◇ *27 schoolchildren were injured in the blast.*

▸ OF AIR **2** [C] a sudden strong movement of air: *A blast of hot air hit us as we stepped off the plane.* ◇ *the wind's icy blasts*

▸ LOUD NOISE **3** [C] a sudden loud noise, especially one made by a musical instrument that you blow, or by a whistle or a car horn: *three short blasts on the ship's siren*

▸ CRITICISM **4** [C] (used especially in newspapers) strong criticism: *Blast for prison governors in judge's report.*

▸ FUN **5** [sing.] (*informal, especially NAmE*) a very enjoyable experience that is a lot of fun: *The party was a blast.* ◇ *We had a blast at the party.*

▸ EMAIL **6** [C] (*NAmE, informal*) advertising or information that is sent to a large number of people at the same time by email

IDM **a ˌblast from the 'past** (*informal*) a person or thing from your past that you see, hear, meet, etc. again in the present (**at**) **full 'blast** with the greatest possible volume or power: *She had the car stereo on at full blast.*

■ ***verb***

▸ EXPLODE **1** [T, I] **~ (sth)** (**+ adv./prep.**) to violently destroy or break sth into pieces, using EXPLOSIVES: *They blasted a huge crater in the runway.* ◇ *They had to blast a tunnel through the mountain.* ◇ *All the windows were blasted inwards with the force of the explosion.* ◇ *The jumbo jet was blasted out of the sky.* ◇ *Danger! Blasting in Progress!*

▸ MAKE LOUD NOISE **2** [I, T] to make a loud unpleasant noise, especially music: **~ (out)** *Music suddenly blasted out from the speakers.* ◇ **~ sth (out)** *The radio blasted out rock music at full volume.*

▸ CRITICIZE **3** [T] **~ sb/sth (for sth/for doing sth)** (*informal*) to criticize sb/sth severely: *The movie was blasted by all the critics.*

▸ HIT/KICK/SHOOT **4** [T] **~ sb/sth (+ adv./prep.)** (*informal*) to hit, kick or shoot sb/sth with a lot of force: *He blasted the ball past the goalie.* ◇ *He blasted* (= shot) *the policeman right between the eyes.*

▸ AIR/WATER **5** [T] **~ sb/sth (+ adv./prep.)** to direct air, water, etc. at sb/sth with a lot of force: *Police blasted the demonstrators with water cannons.*

▸ DESTROY WITH DISEASE, ETC. **6** [T, usually passive] **~ sth** to destroy sth such as a plant with disease, cold, heat, etc: *Their whole crop had been blasted by a late frost.*

PHR V **ˌblast a'way** if a gun or sb using a gun **blasts away**, the gun fires continuously and loudly **ˌblast 'off** (of SPACECRAFT) to leave the ground SYN **lift off, take off** ➲ related noun BLAST-OFF

■ ***exclamation*** (*informal, especially BrE*) people sometimes say **Blast!** when they are annoyed about sth: *Oh blast! The car won't start.*

blast·ed /'blɑːstɪd; *NAmE* 'blæs-/ *adj.* [only before noun] (*informal*) used when you are very annoyed about sth: *Make your own blasted coffee!*

'blast furnace *noun* a large structure like an oven in which iron ORE (= rock containing iron) is melted in order to take out the metal

'blast-off *noun* [U] the moment when a SPACECRAFT leaves the ground

bla·tant /'bleɪtnt/ *adj.* (*disapproving*) (of actions that are considered bad) done in an obvious and open way without caring if people are shocked SYN **flagrant**: *a blatant attempt to buy votes* ◇ *It was a blatant lie.* ▶ **bla·tant·ly** *adv.*: *a blatantly unfair decision* ◇ *He just blatantly lied about it.*

blather /'blæðə(r)/ (also **bleth·er**) *verb* [I] **~ (on) (about sth)** (*informal, especially BrE*) to talk continuously about things that are silly or unimportant ▶ **blather** (also **blether**) *noun* [U]

blax·ploit·ation /ˌblæksplɔɪ'teɪʃn/ *noun* [U] the use of black people in films/movies, especially in a way which shows them in fixed ways that are different from real life

blaze /bleɪz/ *verb, noun*

■ ***verb*** **1** [I] to burn brightly and strongly: *A huge fire was blazing in the fireplace.* ◇ *Within minutes the whole building was blazing.* ◇ *He rushed back into the blazing house.* **2** [I] to shine brightly: *The sun blazed down from a clear blue sky.* ◇ *The garden blazed with colour.* **3** [I] **~ (with sth)** (*formal*) if sb's eyes **blaze**, they look extremely angry: *Her eyes were blazing with fury.* **4** (also **blazon**) [T, usually passive] **~ sth (across/all over sth)** to make news or information widely known by telling people about it in a way they are sure to notice: *The story was blazed all over the daily papers.* **5** [I] **~ (away)** if a gun or sb using a gun **blazes**, the gun fires continuously: *In the distance machine guns were blazing.*

IDM **blaze a 'trail** to be the first to do or to discover sth that others follow: *The department is blazing a trail in the field of laser surgery.* ➲ compare TRAILBLAZER ➲ more at GUN *n.*

PHR V **ˌblaze 'up 1** to suddenly start burning very strongly **2** to suddenly become very angry

■ ***noun*** **1** [C] (used especially in newspapers) a very large fire, especially a dangerous one: *Five people died in the blaze.* **2** [sing.] strong bright flames in a fire: *Dry wood makes a good blaze.* **3** [sing.] **a ~ of sth** a very bright show of lights or colour; an impressive or noticeable show of sth: *The gardens are a blaze of colour.* ◇ *a blaze of lights in the city centre* ◇ *the bright blaze of the sun* ◇ *a blaze of glory* ◇ *They got married in a blaze of publicity.* **4** [sing.] (**a**) **~ of sth** a sudden show of very strong feeling: *a **blaze of anger/***

passion/hate **5** [C, usually sing.] a white mark on an animal's face

IDM **what/where/who the 'blazes...?** (*old-fashioned, informal*) used to emphasize that you are annoyed and surprised, to avoid using the word 'hell': *What the blazes have you done?* **like blazes** (*old-fashioned, informal*) very hard; very fast

blazer /'bleɪzə(r)/ *noun* a jacket, not worn with matching trousers/pants, often showing the colours or BADGE of a club, school, team, etc.

blaz·ing /'bleɪzɪŋ/ *adj.* [only before noun] **1** (also ˌ**blazing 'hot**) extremely hot: *blazing heat* ◇ *a blazing hot day* **2** extremely angry or full of strong emotion: *She had a* ***blazing row*** *with Eddie and stormed out of the house.*

blazon /'bleɪzn/ *verb* **1** [usually passive] **~ sth (on/across/over sth)** = EMBLAZON: *He had the word 'Cool' blazoned across his chest.* **2** = BLAZE (4)

bleach /bliːtʃ/ *verb, noun*

▪ ***verb*** [I, T] to become white or pale by a chemical process or by the effect of light from the sun; to make sth white or pale in this way: *bones of animals bleaching in the sun* ◇ **~ sth** *His hair* ***was bleached by the sun.*** ◇ *bleached cotton/paper* ◇ **~ sth + adj.** *She bleached her hair blonde.*

▪ ***noun*** [U, C] a chemical that is used to make sth become white or pale and as a DISINFECTANT (= to prevent infection from spreading)

bleach·ers /'bliːtʃəz; *NAmE* -tʃərz/ *noun* [pl.] (*NAmE*) rows of seats at a sports ground ▸ **bleach·er** *adj.* [only before noun]: *bleacher seats*

bleak /bliːk/ *adj.* (**bleak·er, bleak·est**) **1** (of a situation) not encouraging or giving any reason to have hope: *a* ***bleak outlook/prospect*** ◇ ***The future looks bleak*** *for the fishing industry.* ◇ *The medical prognosis was bleak.* **2** (of the weather) cold and unpleasant: *a bleak winter's day* **3** (of a place) exposed, empty, or with no pleasant features: *a* ***bleak landscape/hillside/moor*** ◇ *bleak concrete housing* ▸ **bleak·ly** *adv.*: *'There seems no hope,' she said bleakly.* ◇ *bleakly lit corridors* **bleak·ness** *noun* [U]

blear·ily /'blɪərəli; *NAmE* 'blɪr-/ *adv.* with bleary eyes; in a tired way: *'I was asleep,' she explained blearily.*

bleary /'blɪəri; *NAmE* 'blɪri/ *adj.* (of eyes) not able to see clearly, especially because you are tired: *She had bleary red eyes from lack of sleep.*

ˌ**bleary-'eyed** *adj.* with bleary eyes and seeming tired: *He appeared at breakfast bleary-eyed and with a hangover.*

bleat /bliːt/ *verb* **1** [I] to make the sound that sheep and GOATS make **2** [I, T] **~ (on) (about sth)** | **~ that...** | **+ speech** to speak in a weak or complaining voice: *'But I've only just got here,' he bleated feebly.* ▸ **bleat** *noun*: *The lamb gave a faint bleat.* **bleat·ing** *noun* [U, C]: *the distant bleating of sheep*

bleed /bliːd/ *verb* (**bled, bled** /bled/) **1** [I] to lose blood, especially from a wound or an injury: *My finger's bleeding.* ◇ *She slowly* ***bled to death.*** ◇ *He was bleeding from a gash on his head.* **2** [T] **~ sb** (in the past) to take blood from sb as a way of treating disease **3** [T] **~ sb (for sth)** (*informal*) to force sb to pay a lot of money over a period of time: *My ex-wife is bleeding me for every penny I have.* **4** [T] **~ sth** to remove air or liquid from sth so that it works correctly **5** [I] **~ (into sth)** to spread from one area of sth to another area: *Keep the paint fairly dry so that the colours don't bleed into each other.*

IDM **bleed sb 'dry** (*disapproving*) to take away all sb's money: *The big corporations are bleeding some of these small countries dry.* ➲ more at HEART

bleed·er /'bliːdə(r)/ *noun* (*old-fashioned, BrE, informal*) a rude way of referring to a person

bleed·ing /'bliːdɪŋ/ *adj., noun*

▪ ***adj.*** [only before noun] (*BrE, slang*) = BLOODY

▪ ***noun*** [U] the process of losing blood from the body: *Press firmly on the wound to stop the bleeding.*

ˌ**bleeding 'edge** *noun* [sing.] **the ~ (of sth)** (*computing*) technology that is so advanced that there may be problems when you use it: *They were working at the bleeding edge of chip design.* ➲ compare CUTTING EDGE

ˌ**bleeding 'heart** *noun* (*disapproving*) a person who is too kind and sympathetic towards people that other people think do not deserve kindness: *a bleeding-heart liberal*

bleep /bliːp/ *noun, verb*

▪ ***noun*** a short high sound made by a piece of electronic equipment

▪ ***verb*** **1** [I] to make a short high electronic sound: *The microwave will bleep when your meal is ready.* **2** (*BrE*) (*NAmE* **beep**) [T] **~ sb** to call sb on their bleeper: *Please bleep the doctor on duty immediately.* **3** [T] **~ sth (out)** to broadcast a short high electronic sound in place of a SWEAR WORD on a television or radio show, so that people will not be offended

bleep·er /'bliːpə(r)/ (*NAmE* **beep·er**) *noun* a small electronic device that you carry around with you and that lets you know when sb is trying to contact you, by making a sound

blem·ish /'blemɪʃ/ *noun, verb*

▪ ***noun*** a mark on the skin or on an object that spoils it and makes it look less beautiful or perfect: *make-up to cover blemishes* ◇ (*figurative*) *His reputation is without a blemish.*

▪ ***verb*** [usually passive] **~ sth** (*formal*) to spoil sth that is beautiful or perfect in all other ways

blench /blentʃ/ *verb* [I] (*BrE, formal*) to react to sth in a way that shows you are frightened

blend /blend/ *verb, noun*

▪ ***verb*** **1** [T] to mix two or more substances together: **~ A with B** *Blend the flour with the milk to make a smooth paste.* ◇ **~ A and B (together)** ***Blend together*** *the eggs, sugar and flour.* ➲ SYNONYMS at MIX **2** [I] to form a mixture with sth: **~ with sth** *Oil does not blend with water.* ◇ **~ (together)** *Oil and water do not blend.* **3** [I, T] to combine with sth in an attractive or effective way; to combine sth in this way: **~ (sth) (together)** *The old and new buildings blend together perfectly.* ◇ **~ sth (and/with sth)** *Their music blends traditional and modern styles.* **4** [T, usually passive] **~ sth** to produce sth by mixing different types together: ***blended whisky/tea*** IDM see WOODWORK

PHR V ˌ**blend 'in (with sth/sb)** if sth **blends in**, it is similar to its surroundings or matches its surroundings: *Choose curtains that blend in with your decor.* ◇ *The thieves soon blended in with the crowd and got away.* ˌ**blend sth↔'in** (in cooking) to add another substance and mix it in with the others: *Beat the butter and sugar; then blend in the egg.* ˌ**blend 'into sth** to look so similar to the background that it is difficult for you to see it separately: *He blended into the crowd.*

▪ ***noun*** **1** a mixture of different types of the same thing: *a blend of tea* **2** [usually sing.] a pleasant or useful combination of different things: *a blend of youth and experience*

ˌ**blended 'family** *noun* (*especially NAmE*) a family that consists of two people and their children from their own relationship and from previous ones

ˌ**blended 'learning** *noun* [U] a way of studying a subject that combines being taught in class with the use of different technologies, including learning over the Internet: *Blended learning is a cost-effective way of delivering training.*

blend·er /'blendə(r)/ (*BrE* also **li·quid·izer**) *noun* an electric machine for mixing soft food or liquid ➲ VISUAL VOCAB page V22

bless /bles/ *verb, exclamation*

▪ ***verb*** (**blessed, blessed** /blest/) **1 ~ sb/sth** to ask God to protect sb/sth: *They brought the children to Jesus and he blessed them.* ◇ *God bless you!* **2 ~ sth** to make sth holy by saying a prayer over it: *The priest blessed the bread and wine.* **3 ~ sb/sth** (*formal*) to call God holy; to praise God: *We bless your holy name, O Lord.* **4 ~ sb/sth** (*old-fashioned, informal*) used to express surprise: *Bless my soul! Here comes Bill!* ◇ *'Where's Joe?' 'I'm blessed if I know!'* (= I don't know)

IDM **be blessed with sth/sb** to have sth good such as ability, great happiness, etc: *She's blessed with excellent health.*

◇ *We're blessed with five lovely grandchildren.* ˈ**bless you** said to sb after they have SNEEZED ˈ**bless you, her, him, etc.** (*informal*) used to show that you are pleased with sb, especially because of sth they have done: *Sarah, bless her, had made a cup of tea.* ➲ more at GOD

■ ***exclamation*** (*BrE*, sometimes *humorous*) used to show affection towards sb because of sth they have done: *'He bought us all a present.' 'Oh, bless!'*

blessed /ˈblesɪd/ *adj.* **1 Blessed** holy: *the Blessed Virgin Mary* **2** (in religious language) lucky: *Blessed are the poor.* **3** [only before noun] enjoyable in a way that gives you a sense of peace or a feeling of freedom from anxiety or pain: *a moment of blessed calm* **4** [only before noun] (*old-fashioned, informal*) used to express mild anger: *I can't see a blessed thing without my glasses.* ▶ **bless·ed·ly** *adv.*: *The kitchen was warm and blessedly familiar.* **bless·ed·ness** /ˈblesɪdnəs/ *noun* [U]

bless·ing /ˈblesɪŋ/ *noun* **1** [usually sing.] God's help and protection, or a prayer asking for this: *to pray for God's blessing* ◇ *The bishop said the blessing.* ➲ COLLOCATIONS at RELIGION **2** [usually sing.] approval of or permission for sth: *The government **gave its blessing** to the new plans.* ◇ *He went **with** his parents' **blessing**.* **3** something that is good or helpful: *Lack of traffic is one of the blessings of country life.* ◇ ***It's a blessing** that nobody was in the house at the time.* ➲ see also MIXED BLESSING

IDM **a blessing in disˈguise** something that seems to be a problem at first, but that has good results in the end ➲ more at COUNT *v.*

blether /ˈbleðə(r)/ *verb, noun* = BLATHER

blew *past tense of* BLOW

blight /blaɪt/ *verb, noun*

■ ***verb*** **~ sth** to spoil or damage sth, especially by causing a lot of problems: *His career has been blighted by injuries.* ◇ *an area blighted by unemployment*

■ ***noun*** **1** [U, C] any disease that kills plants, especially crops: *potato blight* **2** [sing., U] **~ (on sb/sth)** something that has a bad effect on a situation, a person's life or the environment: *His death **cast a blight on** the whole of that year.* ◇ ***urban blight*** (= areas in a city that are ugly or not cared for well)

blight·er /ˈblaɪtə(r)/ *noun* (*old-fashioned, BrE, informal*) a way of referring to a person (usually a man) that you either find unpleasant or that you feel some sympathy for

Blighty /ˈblaɪti/ *noun* [U] (*BrE*) a name for Britain or England, used especially by soldiers in the First and Second World Wars, and now sometimes used in a humorous way

bli·mey /ˈblaɪmi/ (also ˌ**cor** ˈ**bli·mey**) *exclamation* (*BrE, informal, slang*) used to express surprise or anger: *Blimey, it's hot today.*

blimp /blɪmp/ *noun* **1** (*especially NAmE*) a small AIRSHIP (= an aircraft without wings) **2** (also ˌ**Colonel** ˈ**Blimp**) (*old-fashioned, BrE, disapproving*) an older person, especially an old army officer, with very old-fashioned political opinions ▶ **blimp·ish** *adj.*

blind 0-w /blaɪnd/ *adj., verb, noun, adv.*

■ ***adj.*** (**blind·er**, **blind·est**) **1** 0-w not able to see: *Doctors think he will **go blind**.* ◇ *blind and partially sighted people* ◇ *One of her parents is blind.* **2 the blind** *noun* [pl.] people who are blind: *recorded books for the blind* ◇ *guide dogs for the blind* **3 ~ (to sth)** not noticing or realizing sth: *She is blind to her husband's faults.* ◇ *I must have been blind not to realize the danger we were in.* **4** [usually before noun] (of strong feelings) seeming to be unreasonable, and accepted without question; seeming to be out of control: ***blind faith/obedience*** ◇ *It was a moment of **blind panic**.* **5** [usually before noun] (of a situation or an event) that cannot be controlled by reason: *blind chance* ◇ *the blind force of nature* **6** that a driver in a car cannot see, or cannot see around: *a blind driveway* ◇ *a **blind bend/corner*** ▶ **blind·ness** *noun* [U]: ***total/temporary/partial blindness*** ➲ see also BLINDLY

IDM (**as**) **blind as a ˈbat** (*humorous*) not able to see well **the blind leading the ˈblind** a situation in which people with almost no experience or knowledge give advice to others who also have no experience or knowledge **not a blind bit/the blindest bit of…** (*BrE, informal*) not any: *He didn't **take a blind bit of notice** of me* (= he ignored me). ◇ *It won't **make the blindest bit of difference*** (= it will make no difference at all). **turn a blind ˈeye (to sth)** to pretend not to notice sth bad that is happening, so you do not have to do anything about it ➲ more at LOVE *n.*

■ ***verb*** **1 ~ sb** to permanently destroy sb's ability to see: *She was blinded in the explosion.* **2 ~ sb/sth** to make it difficult for sb to see for a short time: *When she went outside she was temporarily blinded by the sun.* **3 ~ sb (to sth)** to make sb no longer able to think clearly or behave in a sensible way: *His sense of loyalty blinded him to the truth.*

IDM **blind sb with science** to confuse sb by using technical or complicated language that they do not understand ➲ more at EFF

■ ***noun*** **1** (*NAmE* also **shade**, ˈ**window shade**) [C] a covering for a window, especially one made of a roll of cloth that is fixed at the top of the window and can be pulled up and down ➲ see also VENETIAN BLIND **2** [sing.] something people say or do to hide the truth about sth in order to trick other people

■ ***adv.*** (in connection with flying) without being able to see; using instruments only

IDM **blind ˈdrunk** extremely drunk ➲ more at ROB, SWEAR

Which Word?

blind / blindly

■ There are two adverbs that come from the adjective **blind**. **Blindly** means 'not being able to see what you are doing' or 'not thinking about something'. The adverb **blind** is mainly used in the context of flying and means 'without being able to see', 'using instruments only'.

ˌ**blind ˈalley** *noun* a way of doing sth that seems useful at first, but does not produce useful results, like following a path that suddenly stops

ˌ**blind ˈdate** *noun* a meeting between two people who have not met each other before. The meeting is sometimes organized by their friends because they want them to develop a romantic relationship.

blind·er /ˈblaɪndə(r)/ *noun* **1** [C, usually sing.] (*BrE, informal*) something which is excellent, especially in sport: *a blinder of a game* **2 blinders** [pl.] (*NAmE*) = BLINKERS

blind·fold /ˈblaɪndfəʊld; *NAmE* -foʊld/ *noun, verb, adj., adv.*

■ ***noun*** something that is put over sb's eyes so they cannot see

■ ***verb*** **~ sb** to cover sb's eyes with a piece of cloth or other covering so that they cannot see: *The hostages were tied up and blindfolded.*

■ ***adj., adv.*** (*BrE*) (also **blind·fold·ed** *BrE, NAmE*) with the eyes covered: *The reporter was taken blindfold to a secret location.* ◇ *I knew the way home blindfold* (= because it was so familiar). ◇ *I could do that blindfold* (= very easily, with no problems).

blind·ing /ˈblaɪndɪŋ/ *adj.* [usually before noun] **1** very bright; so strong that you cannot see: *a blinding flash of light* ◇ (*figurative*) *a blinding* (= very bad) *headache* **2** (*BrE, informal*) very good or enjoyable

blind·ing·ly /ˈblaɪndɪŋli/ *adv.* very; extremely: *The reason is **blindingly obvious**.* ◇ *The latest computers can work at a **blindingly fast** speed.*

blind·ly /ˈblaɪndli/ *adv.* **1** without being able to see what you are doing: *She groped blindly for the light switch in the dark room.* **2** without thinking about what you are doing: *He wanted to decide for himself instead of blindly following his parents' advice.* ➲ note at BLIND

ˌ**blind man's ˈbuff** (*BrE*) (*NAmE* ˌ**blind man's ˈbluff**) *noun* [U] a children's game in which a player whose eyes are covered with a piece of cloth tries to catch and identify the other players

ˈblind side *noun* a direction in which sb cannot see very much, especially approaching danger

blind·side /ˈblaɪndsaɪd/ *verb* (*NAmE*) **1 ~ sb** to attack sb from the direction where they cannot see you coming **2** [usually passive] **~ sb** to give sb an unpleasant surprise: *Just when it seemed life was going well, she was blindsided by a devastating illness.*

ˈblind spot *noun* **1** an area that sb cannot see, especially an area of the road when they are driving a car **2** if sb has a **blind spot** about sth, they ignore it or they are unwilling or unable to understand it **3** the part of the RETINA in the eye that is not sensitive to light **4** an area where a radio signal cannot be received

ˌblind ˈtest *noun* a way of deciding which product out of a number of competing products is the best or most popular, or how a new product compares with others. People are asked to try the different products and to say which ones they prefer, but they are not told the names of the products.

ˌblind ˈtrust *noun* a type of TRUST that takes care of sb's investments, without the person knowing how their money is being invested. It is used by politicians, for example, so that their private business does not influence their political decisions.

bling /blɪŋ/ (also **ˌbling-ˈbling**) *noun* (*informal*) expensive shiny jewellery and bright fashionable clothes worn in order to attract attention to yourself ▶ **bling** (also **ˌbling-ˈbling**) *adj.*: *women with big hair and bling jewellery* ◇ *bling culture/lifestyles*

blini /ˈblɪni; ˈbliːni/ (also **blinis**) *noun* [pl.] (*sing.* **blin**) small Russian PANCAKES (= thin flat round cakes), served with SOUR CREAM

blink /blɪŋk/ *verb, noun*

■ ***verb*** **1** [I, T] **~ (sth)** when you **blink** or **blink your eyes** or **your eyes blink**, you shut and open your eyes quickly: *He blinked in the bright sunlight.* ◇ *I'll be back* ***before you can blink*** (= very quickly). ◇ *When I told him the news he* ***didn't even blink*** (= showed no surprise at all). ➲ compare WINK **2** [I] to shine with an unsteady light; to flash on and off: *Suddenly a warning light blinked.*

PHR V **ˌblink sth↔aˈway/ˈback** to try to control tears or clear your eyes by blinking: *She bravely blinked back her tears.*

■ ***noun*** [usually sing.] the act of shutting and opening your eyes very quickly

IDM **in the blink of an ˈeye** very quickly; in a short time **on the ˈblink** (*informal*) (of a machine) no longer working correctly

blink·er /ˈblɪŋkə(r)/ *noun* **1** [C] (*informal*) = INDICATOR (3), TURN SIGNAL **2 blinkers** (*NAmE* also **blind·ers**) [pl.] pieces of leather that are placed at the side of a horse's eyes to stop it from looking sideways: (*figurative*) *We need to have a fresh look at the plan, without blinkers* (= we need to consider every aspect of it).

blink·ered /ˈblɪŋkəd; *NAmE* -kərd/ *adj.* (*disapproving*) not aware of every aspect of a situation; not willing to accept different ideas about sth **SYN** **narrow-minded**: *a blinkered* ***policy/attitude/approach***

blink·ing /ˈblɪŋkɪŋ/ *adj., adv.* (*BrE, old-fashioned, informal*) a mild swear word that some people use when they are annoyed, to avoid saying 'bloody': *Shut the blinking door!*

blip /blɪp/ *noun* **1** a change in a process or situation, usually when it gets worse for a short time before it gets better; a temporary problem: *a temporary blip* **2** a short high sound made by an electronic device **3** a small flashing point of light on a RADAR screen, representing an object

bliss /blɪs/ *noun, verb*

■ ***noun*** [U] extreme happiness: ***married/wedded/domestic bliss*** ◇ *My idea of bliss is a month in the Bahamas.* ◇ *Swimming on a hot day is* ***sheer bliss.*** **IDM** see IGNORANCE

■ ***verb***

PHR V **ˌbliss ˈout** (also **be ˌblissed ˈout**) (*especially BrE*) to reach a state of perfect happiness, when you are not aware of anything else

bliss·ful /ˈblɪsfl/ *adj.* extremely happy; showing happiness: *We spent three blissful weeks away from work.* ◇ *a blissful smile* ◇ *We preferred to remain in* ***blissful ignorance*** *of* (= not to know) *what was going on.* ➲ SYNONYMS at HAPPY ▶ **bliss·ful·ly** /-fəli/ *adv.*: *blissfully happy* ◇ ***blissfully ignorant/unaware***

ˈB-list *adj.* [usually before noun] used to describe the group of people who are considered to be fairly famous, successful or important, but not as much as the A-LIST people: *a TV chat show full of* ***B-list celebrities***

blis·ter /ˈblɪstə(r)/ *noun, verb*

■ ***noun*** **1** a swelling on the surface of the skin that is filled with liquid and is caused, for example, by rubbing or burning ➲ see also FEVER BLISTER **2** a similar swelling, filled with air or liquid, on metal, painted wood or another surface

■ ***verb*** **1** [I, T] to form blisters; to make sth form blisters: *His skin was beginning to blister.* ◇ **~ sth** *Her face had been blistered by the sun.* **2** [I, T] **~ (sth)** when a surface **blisters** or sth **blisters** it, it swells and cracks **3** [T] **~ sb** (*NAmE*) to criticize sb strongly ▶ **blis·tered** *adj.*: *cracked and blistered skin* ◇ *blistered paintwork*

blis·ter·ing /ˈblɪstərɪŋ/ *adj.* [usually before noun] **1** (describing actions in sport) done very fast or with great energy: *The runners set off at a blistering pace.* **2** extremely hot in a way that is uncomfortable **SYN** **baking**: *a blistering July day* ◇ *blistering heat* **3** very critical: *a blistering attack* ▶ **blis·ter·ing·ly** *adv.*

ˈblister pack (also **ˈbubble pack**) *noun* a pack in which small goods, such as tablets, are sold, with each individual item in its own separate plastic or FOIL section on a piece of card ➲ VISUAL VOCAB page V29

blithe /blaɪð/ *adj.* [usually before noun] **1** (*disapproving*) showing you do not care or are not anxious about what you are doing: *He drove with blithe disregard for the rules of the road.* **2** (*literary*) happy; not anxious: *a blithe and carefree girl* ▶ **blithe·ly** *adv.*: *He was blithely unaware of the trouble he'd caused.* ◇ *'It'll be easy,' she said blithely.*

blith·er·ing /ˈblɪðərɪŋ/ *adj.* [only before noun] (*old-fashioned, BrE, informal*) complete: *He was a* ***blithering idiot.***

BLitt (*NAmE* **B.Litt**) /ˌbiː ˈlɪt/ *noun* the abbreviation for 'Bachelor of Letters' or 'Bachelor of Literature' (a university degree in an ARTS subject that may be a first or second degree)

blitz /blɪts/ *noun, verb*

■ ***noun*** **1** [C, usually sing.] something which is done with a lot of energy: *an* ***advertising/a media blitz*** (= a lot of information about sth on television, in newspapers, etc.) **2** [C, usually sing.] a sudden attack: *Five shops were damaged in a firebomb blitz.* ◇ **~ on sth** (*figurative*) *a blitz on passengers who avoid paying fares* ◇ (*figurative*) *I've had a blitz on the house* (= cleaned it very thoroughly). **3 the Blitz** [sing.] the German air attacks on the United Kingdom in 1940–41

■ ***verb*** **~ sth** to attack or damage a city by dropping a large number of bombs on it in a short time

blitz·krieg /ˈblɪtskriːg/ *noun* (from *German*) a sudden military attack intended to win a quick victory

bliz·zard /ˈblɪzəd; *NAmE* -zərd/ *noun* **1** a SNOWSTORM with very strong winds: *blizzard conditions* ◇ *a* ***raging/howling blizzard*** ➲ COLLOCATIONS at WEATHER **2** a large quantity of things that may seem to be attacking you: *a blizzard of documents*

bloat /bləʊt; *NAmE* bloʊt/ *verb* [T, I] **~ sth** to swell or make sth swell, especially in an unpleasant way: *Her features had been bloated by years of drinking.*

bloat·ed /ˈbləʊtɪd; *NAmE* ˈbloʊ-/ *adj.* **1** full of liquid or gas and therefore bigger than normal, in a way that is unpleasant: *a bloated body floating in the canal* ◇ (*figurative*) *a bloated organization* (= with too many people in it) **2** full of food and feeling uncomfortable: *I felt bloated after the huge meal they'd served.*

B

bloat·er /ˈbləʊtə(r); *NAmE* ˈbloʊ-/ *noun* (*BrE*) a HERRING (a type of fish) that has been left in salt water and then smoked

blob /blɒb; *NAmE* blɑːb/ *noun* a small amount or drop of sth, especially a liquid; a small area of colour: *a blob of ink* ◇ *a pink blob*

bloc /blɒk; *NAmE* blɑːk/ *noun* a group of countries that work closely together because they have similar political interests ➲ COLLOCATIONS at INTERNATIONAL ➲ see also EN BLOC

block 🔑 /blɒk; *NAmE* blɑːk/ *noun, verb*

■ ***noun***

▸ SOLID MATERIAL **1** 🔑 [C] a large piece of a solid material that is square in shape and usually has flat sides: *a block of ice/concrete/stone* ◇ *a chopping block* (= for cutting food on) ➲ see also BREEZE BLOCK, BUILDING BLOCK, CINDER BLOCK

▸ BUILDING **2** 🔑 [C] (*BrE*) a tall building that contains flats or offices; buildings that form part of a school, hospital, etc. which are used for a particular purpose: *a tower block* ◇ *a block of flats* ◇ *an office block* ◇ *the university's science block* ➲ VISUAL VOCAB page V14 ➲ SYNONYMS at BUILDING

▸ STREETS **3** 🔑 [C] a group of buildings with streets on all sides: *She took the dog for a walk around the block.* **4** 🔑 [C] (*NAmE*) the length of one side of a piece of land or group of buildings, from the place where one street crosses it to the next: *His apartment is three blocks away from the police station.*

▸ AREA OF LAND **5** [C] (*especially NAmE*) a large area of land **6** [C] (*AustralE*) an area of land for building a house on

▸ AMOUNT **7** [C] a quantity of sth or an amount of time that is considered as a single unit: *a block of shares* ◇ *a block of text in a document* ◇ (*BrE*) *The theatre gives discounts for* ***block bookings*** (= a large number of tickets bought at the same time). ◇ *The three-hour class is divided into four blocks of 45 minutes each.*

▸ THAT STOPS PROGRESS **8** [C, usually sing.] something that makes movement or progress difficult or impossible SYN **obstacle**: *Lack of training acts as a block to progress in a career.* ➲ see also ROADBLOCK, STUMBLING BLOCK, WRITER'S BLOCK

▸ IN SPORT **9** [C] a movement that stops another player from going forward **10 the blocks** [pl.] = STARTING BLOCKS

▸ FOR PUNISHMENT **11 the block** [sing.] (in the past) the piece of wood on which a person's head was cut off as a punishment

IDM **go on the ˈblock** to be sold, especially at an AUCTION (= a sale in which items are sold to the person who offers the most money) **have been around the ˈblock (a few times)** (*informal*) to have a lot of experience **put/lay your head/neck on the block** to risk losing your job, damaging your reputation, etc. by doing or saying sth ➲ more at CHIP *n.*, KNOCK *v.*, NEW

■ ***verb*** **1** 🔑 **~ sth** to stop sth from moving or flowing through a pipe, a passage, a road, etc. by putting sth in it or across it: *After today's heavy snow, many roads are still blocked.* ◇ *a blocked sink* **2** 🔑 **~ the/sb's way, exit, view, etc.** to stop sb from going somewhere or seeing sth by standing in front of them or in their way: *One of the guards moved to block her path.* ◇ *An ugly new building blocked the view from the window.* **3** 🔑 **~ sth** to prevent sth from happening, developing or making progress: *The proposed merger has been blocked by the government.* **4 ~ sth** to stop a ball, blow, etc. from reaching somewhere by moving in front of it: *His shot was blocked by the goalie.*

PHR V ˌ**block sb/sth↔ˈin** to prevent a car from being able to be driven away by parking too close to it ˌ**block sth↔ˈin** to draw or paint sth roughly, without showing any detail: *I have blocked in the shapes of the larger buildings.* ˌ**block sth↔ˈoff** to close a road or an opening by placing a barrier at one end or in front of it ˌ**block sth↔ˈout 1** to stop light or noise from coming in: *Black clouds blocked out the sun.* **2** to stop yourself from thinking about or remembering sth unpleasant: *Over the years she had tried to block out that part of her life.* ˌ**block sth↔ˈup** to completely fill a hole or an opening and so prevent anything from passing through it: *One door had been blocked up.* ◇ *My nose is blocked up.*

block·ade /blɒˈkeɪd; *NAmE* blɑːˈk-/ *noun, verb*

■ ***noun*** **1** the action of surrounding or closing a place, especially a port, in order to stop people or goods from coming in or out: *a naval blockade* ◇ *to* ***impose/lift a blockade*** ◇ *an economic blockade* (= stopping goods from entering or leaving a country) **2** a barrier that stops people or vehicles from entering or leaving a place: *The police set up blockades on highways leading out of the city.*

■ ***verb*** **~ sth** to surround a place, especially a port, in order to stop people or goods from coming in or out

block·age /ˈblɒkɪdʒ; *NAmE* ˈblɑːk-/ *noun* **1** a thing that blocks flow or movement, for example of a liquid in a narrow place SYN **obstruction**: *a blockage in an artery/a pipe/a drain* **2** the state of being blocked: *to* ***cause/clear the blockage***

ˌ**block and ˈtackle** *noun* [sing.] a piece of equipment for lifting heavy objects, which works by a system of ropes and PULLEYS (= small wheels around which the ropes are stretched)

block and tackle

block·bust·er /ˈblɒkbʌstə(r); *NAmE* ˈblɑːk-/ *noun* (*informal*) something very successful, especially a very successful book or film/movie: *a Hollywood blockbuster* ▸ **block·bust·ing** *adj.*: *a blockbusting performance*

ˌ**block ˈcapitals** (also ˌ**block ˈlet·ters**) *noun* [pl.] separate capital letters: *Please fill out the form in block capitals.*

block·head /ˈblɒkhed; *NAmE* ˈblɑːk-/ *noun* (*informal*) a very stupid person

block·house /ˈblɒkhaʊs; *NAmE* ˈblɑːk-/ *noun* **1** a strong concrete shelter used by soldiers, for example during a battle **2** (*NAmE*) a house made of LOGS (= thick pieces of wood)

ˌ**block ˈvote** *noun* a voting system in which each person who votes represents a number of people

blog /blɒg; *NAmE* blɑːg/ *noun, verb*

■ ***noun*** (also **web·log**) a website where a person writes regularly about recent events or topics that interest them, usually with photos and links to other websites that they find interesting ➲ COLLOCATIONS at EMAIL

■ ***verb*** (-gg-) [I] to keep a blog ▸ **blog·ger** *noun* **blog·ging** *noun* [U]

blogo·sphere /ˈblɒgəsfɪə(r); *NAmE* ˈblɑːgəsfɪr/ *noun* (usually **the blogosphere**) [sing.] (*informal*) all the personal websites that exist on the Internet, viewed as a network of people communicating with each other: *It's one of the top stories in the blogosphere.* ◇ *the growing influence of the political blogosphere*

blog·roll /ˈblɒgrəʊl; *NAmE* ˈblɑːgroʊl/ *noun* (*computing*) a list on a website of other linked websites that the website owner thinks are useful or interesting

bloke /bləʊk; *NAmE* bloʊk/ *noun* (*BrE, informal*) a man: *He seemed like a nice bloke.*

bloke·ish (also **blok·ish**) /ˈbləʊkɪʃ; *NAmE* ˈbloʊk-/ *adj.* (*BrE, informal*) behaving in a way that is supposed to be typical of men, especially men enjoying themselves in a group

blonde 🔑 /blɒnd; *NAmE* blɑːnd/ *adj., noun*

■ ***adj.*** (also **blond**) HELP In British English it is usual to spell this word **blonde** when writing about a woman or girl and **blond** when writing about a man or boy, although the spelling **blonde** is sometimes used for men and boys too. In American English the spelling **blond** is often preferred for either sex. **Blonde** may be used to describe a woman's hair, but it is sometimes considered offensive to refer to a woman as 'a blonde' because hair colour is not a whole person. **1** 🔑 (of hair) pale gold in colour **2** 🔑 (of a person) having blonde hair: *a small, blond boy*

■ ***noun*** 🔑 (sometimes *offensive*) a woman with hair that is pale gold in colour: *Is she a natural blonde* (= Is her hair naturally blonde)? ➲ compare BRUNETTE, REDHEAD

blood 0‐ /blʌd/ *noun, verb*

■ ***noun* 1** 0‐ [U] the red liquid that flows through the bodies of humans and animals: *He lost a lot of blood in the accident.* ◇ *Blood was pouring out of a cut on her head.* ◇ *to **give blood*** (= to have blood taken from you so that it can be used in the medical treatment of other people) ◇ *to **draw blood*** (= to wound a person so that they lose blood) ◇ *a **blood cell/sample*** **2 -blooded** (in adjectives) having the type of blood mentioned: *cold-blooded reptiles* ➲ see also BLUE-BLOODED, HOT-BLOODED, RED-BLOODED **3** [U] (*formal*) family origins: *She is of noble blood.* **4** [C] (*old-fashioned, BrE*) a rich and fashionable man

IDM **bad 'blood (between A and B)** (*old-fashioned*) feelings of hatred or strong dislike **be after/out for sb's 'blood** (*informal*, often *humorous*) to be angry with sb and want to hurt or punish them **be/run in your 'blood** to be a natural part of your character and of the character of other members of your family **blood is thicker than 'water** (*saying*) family relationships are stronger than any others **sb's 'blood is up** (*BrE*) somebody is very angry and ready to argue or fight **blood, sweat and 'tears** very hard work; a lot of effort **have sb's 'blood on your hands** to be responsible for sb's death: *a dictator with the blood of thousands on his hands* **like getting blood out of/from a 'stone** almost impossible to obtain: *Getting an apology from him was like getting blood from a stone.* **make sb's 'blood boil** to make sb extremely angry **make sb's blood run cold** to make sb very frightened or fill them with horror **new/fresh 'blood** new members or employees, especially young ones, with new ideas or ways of doing things ➲ more at COLD *adj.*, FLESH *n.*, FREEZE *v.*, SPILL *v.*, SPIT *v.*, STIR *v.*, SWEAT *v.*

■ ***verb* ~ sb** (*especially BrE*) to give sb their first experience of an activity

'blood bank *noun* a place where blood is kept for use in hospitals, etc.

blood·bath /'blʌdbɑːθ; *NAmE* -bæθ/ *noun* [sing.] a situation in which many people are killed violently SYN **massacre**

'blood brother *noun* a man who has promised to treat another man as his brother, usually in a ceremony in which their blood is mixed together

'blood clot (also **clot**) *noun* a lump that is formed when blood dries or becomes thicker: *a blood clot on the brain*

'blood count *noun* the number of red and white cells in sb's blood; a medical test to count these

'blood-curdling *adj.* (of a sound or a story) filling you with horror; extremely frightening: *a **blood-curdling** scream/story*

'blood donor *noun* a person who gives some of his or her blood to be used in the medical treatment of other people

'blood group (also **'blood type** especially in *NAmE*) *noun* any of the different types that human blood is separated into for medical purposes: (*BrE*) *What blood group are you?* ◇ (*NAmE*) *What blood type do you have?* ◇ *blood group/type O*

'blood heat *noun* [U] the normal temperature of a human body

blood·hound /'blʌdhaʊnd/ *noun* a large dog with a very good sense of smell, used to follow or look for people

blood·ied /'blʌdid/ *adj.* covered in blood: *his bruised and bloodied nose*

blood·less /'blʌdləs/ *adj.* **1** without any killing: *a **bloodless coup/revolution*** **2** (of a person or a part of the body) very pale: *bloodless lips* **3** lacking human emotion SYN **cold, unemotional**

blood·let·ting /'blʌdletɪŋ/ *noun* [U] **1** (*formal*) the killing or wounding of people SYN **bloodshed 2** a medical treatment used in the past in which some of a patient's blood was removed

blood·line /'blʌdlaɪn/ *noun* (*technical*) the set of ANCESTORS of a person or an animal

blood·lust /'blʌdlʌst/ *noun* [U] a strong desire to kill or be violent

'blood money *noun* [U] (*disapproving*) **1** money paid to a person who is hired to murder sb **2** money paid to the family of a murdered person

'blood orange *noun* a type of orange with red flesh

'blood poisoning *noun* an illness where the blood becomes infected with harmful bacteria

'blood pressure *noun* [U] the pressure of blood as it travels around the body: *to have **high/low blood pressure*** ◇ *to **take*** (= measure) ***sb's blood pressure*** ➲ COLLOCATIONS at DIET

,blood-'red *adj.* bright red in colour, like fresh blood

'blood relation (also **'blood relative**) *noun* a person related to sb by birth rather than by marriage

'blood sausage (*NAmE*) (*BrE* **,black 'pudding**) *noun* [U, C] a type of large dark SAUSAGE made from pig's blood, fat and grain

blood·shed /'blʌdʃed/ *noun* [U] the killing or wounding of people, usually during fighting or a war: *The two sides called a truce to avoid further bloodshed.*

blood·shot /'blʌdʃɒt; *NAmE* -ʃɑːt/ *adj.* (of eyes) with the part that is usually white full of red lines because of lack of sleep, etc.

'blood sport *noun* [usually pl.] a sport in which animals or birds are killed

blood·stain /'blʌdsteɪn/ *noun* a mark or spot of blood on sth ▸ **blood·stained** *adj.*: *a bloodstained shirt*

blood·stock /'blʌdstɒk; *NAmE* -stɑːk/ *noun* [U] horses of pure breed, bred especially for racing

blood·stream /'blʌdstriːm/ *noun* [sing.] the blood flowing through the body: *They injected the drug directly into her bloodstream.*

blood·sucker /'blʌdsʌkə(r)/ *noun* **1** an animal or insect that sucks blood from people or animals **2** (*informal, disapproving*) a person who takes advantage of other people in order to gain financial benefit ▸ **blood·suck·ing** /'blʌdsʌkɪŋ/ *adj.* [only before noun]: *bloodsucking insects* ◇ (*disapproving*) *bloodsucking lawyers*

,blood 'sugar *noun* [U] the amount of GLUCOSE in your blood

'blood test *noun* an examination of a small amount of your blood by doctors in order to make judgements about your medical condition

blood·thirsty /'blʌdθɜːsti; *NAmE* -θɜːrsti/ *adj.* **1** wanting to kill or wound; enjoying seeing or hearing about killing and violence **2** (of a book, film/movie, etc.) describing or showing killing and violence

'blood transfusion (also **transfusion**) *noun* [C, U] the process of putting new blood into the body of a person or an animal: *He was given a blood transfusion.*

'blood type *noun* (*especially NAmE*) = BLOOD GROUP

'blood vessel *noun* any of the tubes through which blood flows through the body ➲ see also ARTERY, CAPILLARY, VEIN

bloody[1] /'blʌdi/ *adj.* [only before noun], *adv.* ➲ see also BLOODY[2] (*BrE, taboo, slang*) a swear word that many people find offensive that is used to emphasize a comment or an angry statement: *Don't be such a bloody fool.* ◇ *That was a bloody good meal!* ◇ *What bloody awful weather!* ◇ *She did bloody well to win that race.* ◇ *He doesn't bloody care about anybody else.* ◇ *'Will you apologize?' 'Not bloody likely!'* (= Certainly not)

IDM **bloody well** (*BrE, taboo*) used to emphasize an angry statement or an order: *You can bloody well keep your job—I don't want it !*

bloody[2] /'blʌdi/ *adj.* ➲ see also BLOODY[1] (**blood·ier, bloodi·est**) **1** involving a lot of violence and killing: *a bloody battle* ◇ *The terrorists have halted their bloody campaign of violence.* **2** covered with blood; BLEEDING: *to give* *sb a bloody nose* (= in a fight) ▸ **blood·ily** *adv.* IDM see SCREAM *v.*

B

Bloody Mary /ˌblʌdi ˈmeəri; *NAmE* ˈmeri/ *noun* (*pl.* Bloody Marys) an alcoholic drink made by mixing VODKA with tomato juice

ˌbloody-ˈminded *adj.* (*BrE, informal*) behaving in a way that makes things difficult for other people; refusing to be helpful ▸ **ˌbloody-ˈminded·ness** *noun* [U]

bloom /bluːm/ *noun, verb*

■ ***noun*** (*formal* or *technical*) **1** [C] a flower (usually one on a plant that people admire for its flowers): *the exotic blooms of the orchid* **2** [sing., U] a healthy fresh appearance: *the bloom in her cheeks*

IDM **in (full) bloom** (of trees, plants, gardens, etc.) with the flowers fully open

■ ***verb*** **1** [I] to produce flowers SYN **flower**: *Most roses will begin to bloom from late May.* **2** [I] to become healthy, happy or confident SYN **blossom**: *The children had bloomed during their stay on the farm.*

bloom·er /ˈbluːmə(r)/ *noun* (*old-fashioned, BrE, informal*) a mistake

bloom·ers /ˈbluːməz; *NAmE* -ərz/ *noun* [pl.] **1** (*informal*) an old-fashioned piece of women's underwear like long loose UNDERPANTS **2** short loose trousers/pants that fit tightly at the knee, worn in the past by women for games, riding bicycles, etc: *a pair of bloomers*

bloom·ing /ˈbluːmɪŋ; ˈblʊm-/ *adj.* [only before noun], *adv.* (*BrE, informal*) a mild swear word, used to emphasize a comment or a statement, especially an angry one: *What blooming awful weather!*

bloop /bluːp/ *verb* [I] (*NAmE, informal*) to make a mistake

bloop·er /ˈbluːpə(r)/ *noun* (*NAmE*) an embarrassing mistake that you make in public

blos·som /ˈblɒsəm; *NAmE* ˈblɑːs-/ *noun, verb*

■ ***noun*** [C, U] a flower or a mass of flowers, especially on a fruit tree or bush: *cherry/orange/apple blossom* ◇ *The trees are* ***in blossom***. ➲ VISUAL VOCAB page V8

■ ***verb*** **1** [I] (of a tree or bush) to produce blossom **2** [I] to become more healthy, confident or successful: *She has visibly blossomed over the last few months.* ◇ **~ into sth** *Their friendship blossomed into love.*

blot /blɒt; *NAmE* blɑːt/ *verb, noun*

■ ***verb*** (-tt-) **1 ~ sth (up)** to remove liquid from a surface by pressing soft paper or cloth on it **2 ~ sth** to make a spot or spots of ink fall on paper

IDM **blot your ˈcopybook** (*old-fashioned, informal*) to do sth to spoil the opinion that other people have of you

PHR V **ˌblot sth↔ˈout 1** to cover or hide sth completely: *Clouds blotted out the sun.* **2** to deliberately try to forget an unpleasant memory or thought: *He tried to blot out the image of Helen's sad face.*

■ ***noun*** **1** a spot or dirty mark on sth, made by ink, etc. ➲ SYNONYMS at MARK **2 ~ (on sth)** something that spoils the opinion that other people have of you, or your happiness: *Her involvement in the fraud has left a serious blot on her character.*

IDM **a blot on the ˈlandscape** an object, especially an ugly building, that spoils the beauty of a place

blotch /blɒtʃ; *NAmE* blɑːtʃ/ *noun* a mark, usually not regular in shape, on skin, plants, material, etc: *He had come out in* (= become covered in) *dark red blotches.*

blotchy /ˈblɒtʃi; *NAmE* ˈblɑː-/ (*BrE* also **blotched**) *adj.* covered in blotches: *her blotchy and swollen face*

blot·ter /ˈblɒtə(r); *NAmE* ˈblɑːt-/ *noun* **1** a large piece of blotting paper in a cover with a stiff back which is kept on a desk **2** (*NAmE*) the record of arrests in a police district

ˈblotting paper *noun* [U] soft thick paper used for drying ink after you have written sth on a piece of paper

blotto /ˈblɒtəʊ; *NAmE* ˈblɑːtoʊ/ *adj.* [not before noun] (*old-fashioned, informal*) very drunk

blouse /blaʊz; *NAmE* blaʊs/ *noun* a piece of clothing like a shirt, worn by women ➲ VISUAL VOCAB page V50 IDM see BIG *adj.*

blouson /ˈbluːzɒn; *NAmE* ˈblaʊsɑːn/ *noun* a short loose jacket that is gathered together at the waist

blo·vi·ate /ˈbləʊvieɪt; *NAmE* ˈbloʊ-/ [I] (*NAmE, informal, disapproving*) to talk or write in a way that shows that you think you know a lot and have sth important to say, when in fact you do not know much and have nothing important to say

blow 0‑w /bləʊ; *NAmE* bloʊ/ *verb, noun, exclamation*

■ ***verb*** (**blew** /bluː/, **blown** /bləʊn; *NAmE* bloʊn/ HELP In sense 13 **blowed** is used for the past participle.)

▸ FROM MOUTH **1** 0‑w [I, T] to send out air from the mouth: **+ adv./prep.** *You're not blowing hard enough!* ◇ *The policeman asked me to blow into the breathalyser.* ◇ **~ sth + adv./prep.** *He drew on his cigarette and blew out a stream of smoke.*

▸ OF WIND **2** 0‑w [I, T] (**+ adv./prep.**) when the wind or a current of air **blows**, it is moving; when **it blows**, the wind is blowing: *A cold wind blew from the east.* ◇ *It was blowing hard.* ◇ *It was* ***blowing a gale*** (= there was a strong wind).

▸ MOVE WITH WIND/BREATH **3** 0‑w [I, T] to be moved by the wind, sb's breath, etc; to move sth in this way: **+ adv./prep.** *My hat blew off.* ◇ **+ adj.** *The door blew open.* ◇ **~ sth + adv./prep.** *I was almost blown over by the wind.* ◇ *She blew the dust off the book.* ◇ *The ship was blown onto the rocks.* ◇ **~ sth + adj.** *The wind blew the door shut.*

▸ WHISTLE/INSTRUMENT **4** 0‑w [T, I] **~ (sth)** if you **blow** a whistle, musical instrument, etc. or if a whistle, etc. **blows**, you produce a sound by blowing into the whistle, etc: *The referee blew his whistle.* ◇ *the sound of trumpets blowing*

▸ YOUR NOSE **5** 0‑w [T] **~ your nose** to clear your nose by blowing strongly through it into a TISSUE or HANDKERCHIEF

▸ A KISS **6** [T] **~ (sb) a kiss** to kiss your hand and then pretend to blow the kiss towards sb

▸ SHAPE STH **7** [T] **~ sth** to make or shape sth by blowing: *to blow smoke rings* ◇ *to* ***blow bubbles*** (= for example, by blowing onto a thin layer of water mixed with soap) ◇ *to* ***blow glass*** (= to send a current of air into melted glass to shape it)

▸ ELECTRICITY **8** [I, T] **~ (sth)** if a FUSE **blows** or you **blow** a FUSE, the electricity stops flowing suddenly because the FUSE (= a thin wire) has melted because the current was too strong

▸ TYRE **9** [I, T] to break open or apart, especially because of pressure from inside; to make a tyre break in this way: *The car spun out of control when a tyre blew.* ◇ *The truck blew a tyre and lurched off the road.*

▸ WITH EXPLOSIVES **10** [T] **~ sth** to break sth open with EXPLOSIVES: *The safe had been blown by the thieves.*

▸ SECRET **11** [T] **~ sth** (*informal*) to make known sth that was secret: *One mistake could* ***blow your cover*** (= make your real name, job, intentions, etc. known).

▸ MONEY **12** [T] **~ sth (on sth)** (*informal*) to spend or waste a lot of money on sth: *He inherited over a million dollars and blew it all on drink and gambling.*

▸ OPPORTUNITY **13** [T] **~ sth** (*informal*) to waste an opportunity: *She* ***blew her chances*** *by arriving late for the interview.* ◇ *You had your chance and you* ***blew it***.

▸ EXCLAMATION **14** [T] **~ sb/sth** (*BrE, informal*) used to show that you are annoyed, surprised or do not care about sth: *Blow it! We've missed the bus.* ◇ *Well, blow me down! I never thought I'd see you again.* ◇ ***I'm blowed if*** *I'm going to* (= I certainly will not) *let him treat you like that.* ◇ *Let's take a taxi and blow* (= never mind) *the expense.*

▸ LEAVE SUDDENLY **15** [T, I] **~ (sth)** (*NAmE, slang*) to leave a place suddenly: *Let's blow this joint.*

IDM **blow your/sb's ˈbrains out** to kill yourself/sb by shooting yourself/them in the head **blow ˈchunks** (*NAmE, slang*) to VOMIT **blow a ˈfuse** (*informal*) to get very angry **blow the ˈgaff (on sb/sth)** (*BrE, informal*) to tell sth secret, especially by mistake **blow hot and ˈcold (about sth)** (*informal*) to change your opinion about sth often **blow sb/sth out of the ˈwater** (*informal*) **1** to destroy sb/sth completely **2** to show that sb/sth is not good by being very much better than it/them: *A DVD music system plays discs that look like CDs, but blows them out of the water.* **blow** '**smoke** (**up sb's ass**) (*taboo, NAmE, slang*) to try to trick sb or lie to sb, particularly by saying sth is better than it really is **blow your 'mind** (*informal*) to produce a very strong pleasant or shocking feeling: *Wait till you hear this. It'll blow your mind.* ➲ see also MIND-BLOWING **blow your own 'trumpet** (*especially BrE*) (*NAmE* usually **blow/toot your own 'horn**) (*informal*) to praise your own abilities and achievements SYN **boast** ORIGIN This phrase refers to the custom of announcing important guests by blowing a horn. **blow your 'top** (*BrE*) (*NAmE* **blow your 'stack**) (*informal*) to get very angry **blow up in sb's 'face** if a plan, etc. **blows up in your face**, it goes wrong in a way that causes you damage, embarrassment, etc. **blow the 'whistle on sb/sth** (*informal*) to tell sb in authority about sth wrong or illegal that sb is doing ➲ see also WHISTLE-BLOWER IDM see COBWEB, ILL *adj.*, KINGDOM, LARK *n.*, LID, PUFF *v.*, SOCK *n.*, WAY *n.*

PHR V ,**blow sth↔a'part 1** to completely destroy sth in an explosion **2** to show that an idea is completely false: *What we discovered blew apart all our preconceptions about this fascinating species.* ,**blow sb↔a'way** (*informal, especially NAmE*) **1** to kill sb by shooting them **2** to impress sb a lot or to make them very happy **3** to defeat sb easily ,**blow 'in** | ,**blow 'into sth** (*informal*) to arrive or enter a place suddenly: *Look who's just blown in!* ◇ *Have you heard who's* ***blown into town***? ,**blow 'off** (*BrE, informal*) a rude way of saying 'BREAK WIND' (= release gas through your bottom) ,**blow sb↔'off** (*NAmE*) to deliberately not meet sb when you said you would; to end a romantic relationship with sb ,**blow sth↔'off** (*NAmE*) to deliberately not do sth that you said you would: *He looks for any excuse he can to blow off work.* ,**blow 'out 1** if a flame, etc. **blows out**, it is put out by the wind, etc: *Somebody opened the door and the candle blew out.* **2** if an oil or gas WELL **blows out**, it sends out gas suddenly and with force ➲ related noun BLOWOUT ,**blow itself 'out** when a storm **blows itself out**, it finally loses its force ,**blow sb↔'out** (*NAmE, informal*) to defeat sb easily ,**blow sth↔'out** 🔑 to put out a flame, etc. by blowing ,**blow 'over** to go away without having a serious effect: *The storm blew over in the night.* ◇ *The scandal will soon blow over.* ,**blow 'up 1** 🔑 to explode; to be destroyed by an explosion: *The bomb blew up.* ◇ *A police officer was killed when his car blew up.* ➲ SYNONYMS at EXPLODE **2** to start suddenly and with force: *A storm was blowing up.* ◇ *A crisis has blown up over the President's latest speech.* ,**blow sth↔'up 1** to destroy sth by an explosion: *The police station was blown up by terrorists.* ➲ SYNONYMS at EXPLODE **2** 🔑 to fill sth with air or gas so that it becomes firm: *The tyres on my bike need blowing up.* **3** to make a photograph bigger SYN **enlarge** ➲ related noun BLOW-UP **4** to make sth seem more important, better, worse, etc. than it really is: *The whole affair was* ***blown up out of all proportion***. ,**blow 'up** (**at sb**) (*informal*) to get angry with sb SYN **lose your temper**: *I'm sorry I blew up at you.* ➲ related noun BLOW-UP

■ ***noun*** **1** 🔑 a hard hit with the hand, a weapon, etc: *She received a severe blow on the head.* ◇ *He was knocked out by a single blow to the head.* ◇ *The two men were* ***exchanging blows***. ◇ *He* ***landed a blow*** *on Hill's nose.* **2** 🔑 **~** (**to sb/sth**) a sudden event which has damaging effects on sb/sth, causing sadness or disappointment: *Losing his job* ***came as a*** *terrible* ***blow*** *to him.* ◇ *It was a shattering blow to her pride.* ➲ see also BODY BLOW **3** 🔑 the action of blowing: *Give your nose a good blow* (= clear it completely).

IDM **a** ,**blow-by-,blow ac'count, de'scription, etc.** (**of sth**) (*informal*) a description of an event which gives you all the details in the order in which they happen **come to 'blows** (**over sth**) to start fighting because of sth **soften/cushion the 'blow** to make sth that is unpleasant seem less unpleasant and easier to accept ➲ more at DEAL *v.*, STRIKE *v.*

■ ***exclamation*** (*old-fashioned, BrE*) used to show that you are annoyed about sth: *Blow! I completely forgot it.*

blow·back /ˈbləʊbæk; *NAmE* ˈbloʊbæk/ *noun* [U, C] **1** a process in which gases expand or travel in a direction that is opposite to the usual one: *blowback gas* ◇ *Blowback may be caused by a defective mechanism.* **2** (*especially NAmE*) the results of a political action or situation that are not what was intended or wanted: *The policy has led to blowback.* ◇ *The war created a ferocious blowback.*

'**blow-dry** *verb* **~ sth** to dry hair with a HAIRDRYER and shape it into a particular style ► '**blow-dry** *noun*: *a cut and blow-dry*

blow·er /ˈbləʊə(r); *NAmE* ˈbloʊ-/ *noun* **1** [C] a device that produces a current of air: *a hot-air blower* **2 the blower** [sing.] (*old-fashioned, BrE, informal*) the telephone ➲ see also WHISTLE-BLOWER

blow·fly /ˈbləʊflaɪ; *NAmE* ˈbloʊ-/ *noun* (*pl.* **blow·flies**) a large fly that lays its eggs on meat and other food

blow·hard /ˈbləʊhɑːd; *NAmE* ˈbloʊhɑːrd/ *noun* (*NAmE, informal, disapproving*) a person who talks too proudly about sth they own or sth they have done

blow·hole /ˈbləʊhəʊl; *NAmE* ˈbloʊhoʊl/ *noun* **1** a hole in the top of a WHALE's head through which it breathes ➲ VISUAL VOCAB page V10 **2** a hole in a large area of ice, through which SEALS, etc. breathe

blowie /ˈbləʊi; *NAmE* ˈbloʊi/ *noun* (*AustralE, NZE, informal*) a BLOWFLY

'**blow-in** *noun* (*AustralE, informal*) a person who has recently arrived somewhere

'**blow job** *noun* (*taboo, slang*) the act of touching a man's PENIS with the tongue and lips to give sexual pleasure SYN **fellatio**

blow·lamp /ˈbləʊlæmp; *NAmE* ˈbloʊ-/ (*BrE*) (*US* '**blow-torch, torch**) *noun* a tool for directing a very hot flame onto part of a surface, for example to remove paint

blown *past part.* of BLOW

blow·out /ˈbləʊaʊt; *NAmE* ˈbloʊ-/ *noun* **1** an occasion when a tyre suddenly bursts on a vehicle while it is moving SYN **puncture**: *to have a blowout* **2** [usually sing.] (*informal*) a large meal at which people eat too much: *a four-course blowout* **3** (*NAmE, informal*) a large party or social occasion: *We're going to have a huge blowout for Valentine's Day.* **4** (*NAmE, informal*) an easy victory: *The game was a blowout, 8–1.* **5** a sudden escape of oil or gas from an OIL WELL

blow·pipe /ˈbləʊpaɪp; *NAmE* ˈbloʊ-/ *noun* **1** a weapon consisting of a long tube through which an arrow is blown **2** a long tube for blowing glass into a particular shape

blowsy (also **blowzy**) /ˈblaʊzi/ *adj.* (*BrE, informal, disapproving*) a woman who is **blowsy** is big and fat and looks untidy

blow·torch /ˈbləʊtɔːtʃ; *NAmE* ˈbloʊtɔːrtʃ/ (also **torch**) (both *NAmE*) (*BrE* **blow·lamp**) *noun* a tool for directing a very hot flame onto part of a surface, for example to remove paint

'**blow-up** *noun* **1** an ENLARGEMENT of a photograph, picture or design: *Can you do me a blow-up of his face?* **2** (*NAmE*) an occasion when sb suddenly becomes angry

BLT /ˌbiː el ˈtiː/ *noun* the abbreviation for 'bacon, lettuce and tomato' (used to refer to a SANDWICH filled with this): *I'll have a BLT with extra mayonnaise.*

blub /blʌb/ *verb* (**-bb-**) [I] (*BrE, informal*) to cry

blub·ber /ˈblʌbə(r)/ *noun, verb*

■ ***noun*** [U] the fat of WHALES and other sea animals

■ ***verb*** [I, T] (+ **speech**) (*informal, disapproving*) to cry noisily: *There he sat, blubbering like a baby.*

bludge /blʌdʒ/ *verb, noun* (*AustralE, NZE, informal*)

■ ***verb*** **1** [I] to not do any work and live from what other people give you **2** [T] **~ sth** to ask sb for sth especially because you cannot or do not want to pay for it yourself SYN **cadge**: *The girls bludged smokes.*

■ ***noun*** an easy job

bludg·eon /ˈblʌdʒən/ *verb* **1 ~ sb** to hit sb several times with a heavy object **2 ~ sb** (**into sth/into doing sth**) to force sb to do sth, especially by arguing with them: *They tried to bludgeon me into joining their protest.*

bludger /ˈblʌdʒə(r)/ *noun* (*AustralE, NZE, informal*) **1** a lazy person **2** a person who asks other people for sth because they cannot or do not want to pay for it **SYN** **scrounger**

B

blue 0━ /bluː/ *adj., noun*

■ ***adj.*** (bluer, blu·est) **1** 0━ having the colour of a clear sky or the sea/ocean on a clear day: *piercing blue eyes* ◇ *a blue shirt* **2** 0━ (of a person or part of the body) looking slightly blue in colour because the person is cold or cannot breathe easily: *Her hands were blue with cold.* **3** (*informal*) sad **SYN** **depressed**: *He'd been feeling blue all week.* **4** films/movies, jokes or stories that are **blue** are about sex: *a blue movie* **5** (*politics*) (of an area in the US) having more people who vote for the DEMOCRATIC candidate than the REPUBLICAN one: *blue states/counties* **OPP** **red** ➲ see also TRUE-BLUE ▸ **blue·ness** *noun* [U, sing.]: *the blueness of the water*

IDM **do sth till you are blue in the 'face** (*informal*) to try to do sth as hard and as long as you possibly can but without success: *You can argue till you're blue in the face, but you won't change my mind.* ➲ more at BLACK *adj.*, DEVIL, ONCE *adv.*, SCREAM *v.*

■ ***noun*** ➲ see also BLUES **1** 0━ [C, U] the colour of a clear sky or the sea/ocean on a clear day: ***bright/dark/light/pale blue*** ◇ *The room was decorated in vibrant blues and yellows.* ◇ *She was dressed in blue.* **2** [C] (*BrE*) a person who has played a particular sport for Oxford or Cambridge University; a title given to them **3** [C] (*AustralE, NZE, informal*) a mistake **4** [C] (*AustralE, NZE, informal*) a name for a person with red hair **5** [C] (*AustralE, NZE, informal*) a fight

IDM **out of the 'blue** unexpectedly; without warning: *The decision came out of the blue.* ➲ more at BOLT *n.*, BOY *n.*

ˌblue 'baby *noun* a baby whose skin is slightly blue at birth because there is sth wrong with its heart

blue·bell /'bluːbel/ *noun* **1** a garden or wild flower with a short STEM and small blue or white flowers shaped like bells ➲ **VISUAL VOCAB** page V9 **2** (*ScotE*) = HAREBELL

blue·berry /'bluːbəri; *NAmE* -beri/ *noun* (*pl.* -ies) a dark blue BERRY that grows on bushes in N America and can be eaten ➲ compare BILBERRY

blue·bird /'bluːbɜːd; *NAmE* -bɜːrd/ *noun* a small N American bird with blue feathers on its back or head

ˌblue-'blooded *adj.* from a royal or NOBLE family ▸ **ˌblue 'blood** *noun* [U]

'blue book *noun* **1** (*US*) a book with a blue cover used by students for writing the answers to examination questions **2** (*NAmE*) a book that lists the prices that people should expect to pay for used cars

blue·bot·tle /'bluːbɒtl; *NAmE* -bɑːtl/ *noun* a large fly with a blue body

ˌblue 'cheese *noun* [U, C] cheese with lines of blue MOULD in it

ˌblue-'chip *adj.* [only before noun] (*finance*) a **blue-chip** investment is thought to be safe and likely to make a profit: *blue-chip companies*

ˌblue-'collar *adj.* [only before noun] connected with people who do physical work in industry: ***blue-collar workers/voters/votes*** ➲ compare PINK-COLLAR, WHITE-COLLAR

ˌblue 'crane *noun* a type of CRANE (= a large bird with long legs and a long neck) that has blue-grey feathers. It is the national bird of South Africa.

ˌblue-eyed 'boy *noun* [usually sing.] (*BrE, informal*, often *disapproving*) a person treated with special favour by sb: *He's the manager's blue-eyed boy.*

ˌblue 'flag *noun* **1** (*BrE*) a blue flag used in motor racing to show that a driver who is much further ahead is trying to pass **2** an award given to beaches in Europe that are clean and safe

ˌblue 'funk *noun* (*old-fashioned, informal*) = FUNK

blue·grass /'bluːgrɑːs; *NAmE* -græs/ *noun* [U] a type of traditional American country music played on GUITARS and BANJOS

ˌblue 'helmet *noun* a member of a United Nations force that is trying to prevent war or violence in a place

blue·jay /'bluːdʒeɪ/ *noun* a large N American bird with blue feathers on its back and a row of feathers (called a CREST) standing up on its head

'blue jeans *noun* [pl.] (*especially NAmE*) trousers/pants made of blue DENIM

'blue law *noun* [usually pl.] (in the US) a law that bans business and certain other activities, such as sports, on Sundays

ˌblue-on-'blue *adj.* [only before noun] (*BrE*) in a war, used to describe an accident or attack in which people are hit by a bomb or weapon that is fired by their own side ➲ compare FRIENDLY FIRE

ˌblue 'pages *noun* [pl.] (in the US) the blue pages in a TELEPHONE DIRECTORY that give a list of government departments and their telephone numbers

blue·print /'bluːprɪnt/ *noun* **1** a PHOTOGRAPHIC print of a plan for a building or a machine, with white lines on a blue background **2** ~ (**for sth**) a plan which shows what can be achieved and how it can be achieved: *a blueprint for the privatization of health care* **3** (*technical*) the pattern in every living cell, which decides how the plant, animal or person will develop and what it will look like: *DNA carries the* ***genetic blueprint*** *which tells any organism how to build itself.*

blue riband /ˌbluː 'rɪbənd/ (*BrE*) (also **ˌblue 'ribbon** *NAmE, BrE*) *noun* an honour (sometimes in the form of a blue RIBBON) given to the winner of the first prize in a competition: *a blue-riband event* (= a very important one)

blues /bluːz/ *noun* **1** (often **the blues**) [U] a type of slow sad music with strong rhythms, developed by African American musicians in the southern US: *a* ***blues band/singer*** **2** [C] (*pl.* **blues**) a blues song **3 the blues** [pl.] (*informal*) feelings of sadness: *the Monday morning blues* ➲ see also BABY BLUES

ˌblue-'sky *adj.* [only before noun] involving new and interesting ideas which are not yet possible or practical: *The government has been doing some* ***blue-sky thinking*** *on how to improve school standards.*

blue·stock·ing /'bluːstɒkɪŋ; *NAmE* -stɑːk-/ *noun* (*old-fashioned, BrE*, sometimes *disapproving*) a well-educated woman who is more interested in ideas and studying than in traditionally FEMININE things

bluesy /'bluːzi/ *adj.* having the slow strong rhythms and sad mood of blues music: *a* ***bluesy sound/voice***

'blue tit *noun* a small European bird of the TIT family, with a blue head, wings and tail and yellow parts underneath

Blue·tooth™ /'bluːtuːθ/ *noun* [U] a radio technology that makes it possible for mobile phones/cell phones, computers and other electronic devices to be linked over short distances, without needing to be connected by wires: *Bluetooth-enabled devices*

ˌblue 'whale *noun* a type of WHALE that is the largest known living animal

bluff /blʌf/ *verb, noun, adj.*

■ ***verb*** [I, T] ~ (**sth**) to try to make sb believe that you will do sth that you do not really intend to do, or that you know sth that you do not really know: *I don't think he'll shoot—I think he's just bluffing.*

PHR V **'bluff sb into doing sth** to make sb do sth by tricking them, especially by pretending you have more experience, knowledge, etc. than you really have **ˌbluff it 'out** to get out of a difficult situation by continuing to tell lies, especially when they suspect you are not being honest **ˌbluff your way 'in/'out/'through** | **ˌbluff your way 'into/'out of/'through sth** to succeed in dealing with a difficult situation by making other people believe sth which is not true: *She successfully bluffed her way through the interview.*

■ ***noun*** **1** [U, C] an attempt to trick sb by making them believe that you will do sth when you really have no intention of doing it, or that you know sth when you do not, in fact, know it: *It was just a game of bluff.* ◇ *He said he would resign if he didn't get more money, but it was only a bluff.* ➲ see also DOUBLE BLUFF **2** [C] a steep CLIFF or slope, especially by the sea or a river **IDM** see CALL *v.*

■ ***adj.*** (of people or their manner) very direct and cheerful, with good intentions, although not always very polite: *Beneath his bluff exterior he was a sensitive man.*

blu·ish /ˈbluːɪʃ/ *adj.* fairly blue in colour: *a bluish-green carpet*

blun·der /ˈblʌndə(r)/ *noun, verb*

▪ ***noun*** a stupid or careless mistake: *to make a terrible blunder* ◇ *a series of political blunders*

▪ ***verb*** [I] to make a stupid or careless mistake: *The government had blundered in its handling of the affair.* PHR V **ˌblunder aˈbout, aˈround, etc.** to move around in an awkward way, knocking into things, as if you cannot see where you are going **ˌblunder ˈinto sth 1** to knock into sth because you are awkward or are not able to see **2** to find yourself in a difficult or unpleasant situation by accident **ˌblunder ˈon** to continue doing sth in a careless or stupid way

blun·der·buss /ˈblʌndəbʌs; *NAmE* -dərb-/ *noun* an old type of gun with a wide end

blunt /blʌnt/ *adj., verb*

▪ ***adj.*** (**blunt·er, blunt·est**) **1** without a sharp edge or point: *a blunt knife* ◇ *This pencil's blunt !* ◇ *The police said he had been hit with a* ***blunt instrument.*** OPP **sharp 2** (of a person or remark) very direct; saying exactly what you think without trying to be polite: *She has a reputation for blunt speaking.* ◇ *To be blunt, your work is appalling.* ➲ SYNONYMS at HONEST ▸ **blunt·ness** *noun* [U]

▪ ***verb*** **1 ~ sth** to make sth weaker or less effective: *Age hadn't blunted his passion for adventure.* **2 ~ sth** to make a point or an edge less sharp

blunt·ly /ˈblʌntli/ *adv.* in a very direct way, without trying to be polite or kind: ***To put it bluntly,*** *I want a divorce.* ◇ *'Is she dead?' he asked bluntly.*

blur /blɜː(r)/ *noun, verb*

▪ ***noun*** [usually sing.] **1** a shape that you cannot see clearly, often because it is moving too fast: *His arm was a rapid blur of movement as he struck.* ◇ *Everything is a blur when I take my glasses off.* **2** something that you cannot remember clearly: *The events of that day were just a blur.*

▪ ***verb*** (-rr-) **1** [I, T] if the shape or outline of sth **blurs**, or if sth **blurs** it, it becomes less clear and sharp: *The writing blurred and danced before his eyes.* ◇ **~ sth** *The mist blurred the edges of the buildings.* **2** [T, I] **~ (sth)** if sth **blurs** your eyes or vision, or your eyes or vision **blur**, you cannot see things clearly: *Tears blurred her eyes.* **3** [I, T] to become or make sth become difficult to distinguish clearly: *The differences between art and life seem to have blurred.* ◇ **~ sth** *She tends to* ***blur the distinction*** *between her friends and her colleagues.*

Blu-ray /ˈbluː reɪ/ *noun* [U] technology that uses a blue LASER (= a very strong line of light) to record and play large amounts of high quality data on a type of CD: *These high definition movies are all out on Blu-Ray.*

ˈBlu-ray Disc™ *noun* (*abbr.* **BD, BD-ROM**) a type of CD on which large amounts of data can be stored, used especially to play high quality video

blurb /blɜːb; *NAmE* blɜːrb/ *noun* a short description of a book, a new product, etc, written by the people who have produced it, that is intended to attract your attention and make you want to buy it

blurred /blɜːd; *NAmE* blɜːrd/ *adj.* **1** not clear; without a clear outline or shape: *She suffered from dizziness and blurred vision.* ◇ *a* ***blurred image/picture*** **2** difficult to remember clearly: *blurred memories* **3** difficult to distinguish, so that differences are not clear: ***blurred distinctions/boundaries***

blurry /ˈblɜːri/ *adj.* (*informal*) without a clear outline; not clear: *blurry, distorted photographs* ◇ (*figurative*) *a blurry policy*

blurt /blɜːt; *NAmE* blɜːrt/ *verb* **~ sth (out)** | **~ that...** | **~ what, how, etc...** | **+ speech** to say sth suddenly and without thinking carefully enough: *She blurted it out before I could stop her.* ➲ SYNONYMS at CALL

blush /blʌʃ/ *verb, noun*

▪ ***verb*** **1** [I] to become red in the face because you are embarrassed or ashamed SYN **go red: ~ (with sth) (at sth)** *to blush with embarrassment/shame* ◇ *She blushed furiously at the memory of the conversation.* ◇ **+ adj./noun** *He blushed scarlet at the thought.* **2** [T] **~ to do sth** to be ashamed or embarrassed about sth: *I blush to admit it, but I quite like her music.*

▪ ***noun*** **1** [C] the red colour that spreads over your face when you are embarrassed or ashamed: *She felt a warm blush rise to her cheeks.* ◇ *He turned away to hide his blushes.* **2** [U, C] (*NAmE*) = BLUSHER IDM see SPARE *v.*

blush·er /ˈblʌʃə(r)/ (*NAmE* also **blush**) *noun* [U, C] a coloured cream or powder that some people put on their cheeks to give them more colour ➲ VISUAL VOCAB page V49

blus·ter /ˈblʌstə(r)/ *verb* **1** [T, I] **~ (sth)** | **+ speech** to talk in an aggressive or threatening way, but with little effect: *'I don't know what you're talking about,' he blustered.* ◇ *a blustering bully* **2** [I] (of the wind) to blow violently ▸ **blus·ter** *noun* [U]: *I wasn't frightened by what he said—it was all bluster.*

blus·tery /ˈblʌstəri/ *adj.* (of weather) with strong winds: ***blustery winds/conditions*** ◇ *The day was cold and blustery.*

Blu-tack™ /ˈbluː tæk/ *noun* [U] a blue sticky material used to attach paper to walls

Blvd. *abbr.* (used in written addresses) BOULEVARD

BMI /ˌbiː em ˈaɪ/ *abbr.* BODY MASS INDEX

BMOC /ˌbiː em əʊ ˈsiː; *NAmE* oʊ/ *abbr.* (*US*) BIG MAN ON CAMPUS

ˈB-movie (also **ˈB-picture**) *noun* a film/movie which is made cheaply and is not very good: *a B-movie actress*

BMus (*NAmE* **B.Mus**) /ˌbiː ˈmʌz/ *noun* the abbreviation for 'Bachelor of Music' (a university degree in music that is usually a first degree)

BMX /ˌbiː em ˈeks/ *noun* **1** [C] a strong bicycle which can be used for riding on rough ground **2** (also **BMXing**) [U] the sport of racing BMX bicycles on rough ground

bn *abbr.* (*BrE*) (in writing) BILLION

the BNP /ˌbiː en ˈpiː/ *abbr.* the British National Party (a small British political party on the extreme right)

BO /ˌbiː ˈəʊ; *NAmE* ˈoʊ/ *noun* [U] the abbreviation for 'body odour/odor' (an unpleasant smell from a person's body, especially of sweat): *She's got BO.*

boa /ˈbəʊə; *NAmE* ˈboʊə/ *noun* **1** = BOA CONSTRICTOR **2** = FEATHER BOA

boa constrictor /ˈbəʊə kənstrɪktə(r); *NAmE* ˈboʊə/ (also **boa**) *noun* a large S American snake that kills animals for food by winding its long body around them and crushing them

boar /bɔː(r)/ *noun* (*pl.* **boar** or **boars**) **1** (also **ˌwild ˈboar**) a wild pig **2** a male pig that has not been CASTRATED ➲ compare HOG, SOW

board 0‑ᵚ /bɔːd; *NAmE* bɔːrd/ *noun, verb*

▪ ***noun***

▸ PIECE OF WOOD ETC. **1** 0‑ᵚ [C, U] a long thin piece of strong hard material, especially wood, used, for example, for making floors, building walls and roofs and making boats: *He had ripped up the carpet, leaving only the bare boards.* ➲ see also CHIPBOARD, FLOORBOARD, HARDBOARD, SKIRTING BOARD **2** 0‑ᵚ [C] (especially in compounds) a piece of wood, or other strong material, that is used for a special purpose: *a blackboard* ◇ *I'll write it up on the board.* ◇ (*BrE*) *a noticeboard* ◇ (*NAmE*) *a bulletin board* ◇ *The exam results went up on the board.* ◇ *a diving board* ◇ *She jumped off the top board.* ◇ *a chessboard* ◇ *He removed the figure from the board.* ➲ see also MESSAGE BOARD

▸ IN WATER SPORTS **3** [C] = BODYBOARD, SAILBOARD, SURFBOARD

▸ GROUP OF PEOPLE **4** 0‑ᵚ [C+sing./pl. v.] a group of people who have power to make decisions and control a company or other organization: *She has a seat on the board of directors.* ◇ *The board is/are unhappy about falling sales.* ◇ *members of the board* ◇ *discussions at board level* ◇ *the* ***academic board*** (= for example, of a British university) ◇ (*NAmE*) *the* ***Board***

B

of Education (= a group of elected officials who are in charge of all the public schools in a particular area)
▸ ORGANIZATION **5** [C] used in the name of some organizations: *the Welsh Tourist Board* (= responsible for giving tourist information)
▸ MEALS **6** [U] the meals that are provided when you stay in a hotel, GUEST HOUSE, etc; what you pay for the meals: *He pays £90 a week board and lodging.* ➲ see also BED AND BOARD, FULL BOARD, HALF BOARD
▸ EXAMS **7 boards** [pl.] (*old-fashioned, US*) exams that you take when you apply to go to college in the US
▸ IN THEATRE **8 the boards** [pl.] (*old-fashioned, informal*) the stage in a theatre: *His play is on the boards on Broadway.* ◇ *She's treading the boards* (= working as an actress).
▸ ICE HOCKEY **9 the boards** [pl.] (*NAmE*) the low wooden wall surrounding the area where a game of ICE HOCKEY is played: *The puck went wide, hitting the boards.* **HELP** There are many other compounds ending in **board**. You will find them at their place in the alphabet.
IDM **a,cross the 'board** involving everyone or everything in a company, an industry, etc: *The industry needs more investment across the board.* ◇ *an across-the-board wage increase* **,go by the 'board** (*BrE*) (of plans or principles) to be rejected or ignored; to be no longer possible: *All her efforts to be polite went by the board and she started to shout.* **on 'board** 🔑 **1** on or in a ship, an aircraft or a train **SYN** **aboard**: *Have the passengers gone on board yet?* **2** giving your support to an idea or a project: *We must get more sponsors on board.* ◇ *You need to bring the whole staff on board.* **take sth on 'board** to accept and understand an idea or a suggestion: *I told her what I thought, but she didn't take my advice on board.* ➲ more at SWEEP *v.*
■ ***verb***
▸ GET ON PLANE/SHIP, ETC. **1** 🔑 [I, T] (*formal*) to get on a ship, train, plane, bus, etc: *Passengers are waiting to board.* ◇ **~ sth** *The ship was boarded by customs officials.* **2** 🔑 [I] **be boarding** when a plane or ship **is boarding**, it is ready for passengers to get on: *Flight BA193 for Paris is now boarding at Gate 37.*
▸ LIVE SOMEWHERE **3** [I] **~ at.../with sb** to live and take meals in sb's home, in return for payment: *She always had one or two students boarding with her.* **4** [I] to live at a school during the school year
PHR V **,board sb 'out** (*BrE*) to arrange for sb to live somewhere away from their place of work, school, etc. in return for payment **,board sth↔'up** to cover a window, door, etc. with wooden boards

board·er /ˈbɔːdə(r); *NAmE* ˈbɔːrd-/ *noun* (*especially BrE*) **1** a child who lives at school and goes home for the holidays: *boarders and day pupils* **2** a person who pays money to live in a room in sb else's house **SYN** **lodger**

'board game *noun* any game played on a board, often using DICE and small pieces that are moved around

board·ing /ˈbɔːdɪŋ; *NAmE* ˈbɔːrd-/ *noun* [U] **1** (*BrE*) long pieces of wood that are put together to make a wall, etc. **2** the arrangement by which school students live at their school, going home during the holidays: *boarding fees*

'boarding card (*BrE*) (also **'boarding pass** *NAmE, BrE*) *noun* a card that you show before you get on a plane or boat

'boarding house *noun* a private house where people can pay for accommodation and meals

'boarding kennel *noun* [usually pl.] (*BrE*) a place where people can leave their dogs to be taken care of when they go on holiday/vacation ➲ see also KENNEL (2)

'boarding school *noun* a school where children can live during the school year ➲ compare DAY SCHOOL

board·room /ˈbɔːdruːm; -rʊm; *NAmE* ˈbɔːrd-/ *noun* a room in which the meetings of the board of a company (= the group of people who control it) are held: *a boardroom row*

board·sail·ing /ˈbɔːdseɪlɪŋ; *NAmE* ˈbɔːrd-/ *noun* [U] = WINDSURFING

board·walk /ˈbɔːdwɔːk; *NAmE* ˈbɔːrd-/ *noun* (*especially NAmE*) a path made of wooden boards, especially on a beach or near water

boast /bəʊst; *NAmE* boʊst/ *verb, noun*
■ ***verb*** **1** [I, T] to talk with too much pride about sth that you have or can do: *I don't want to boast, but I can actually speak six languages.* ◇ **~ about sth** *She is always boasting about how wonderful her children are.* ◇ **~ of sth** *He openly boasted of his skill as a burglar.* ◇ **~ that...** *Sam boasted that she could beat anyone at poker.* ◇ **+ speech** *'I won!' she boasted.* **2** [T] (not used in the progressive tenses) **~ sth** to have sth that is impressive and that you can be proud of: *The hotel also boasts two swimming pools and a golf course.*
■ ***noun*** **~ (that...)** (often *disapproving*) something that a person talks about in a very proud way, often to seem more important or clever: *Despite his boasts that his children were brilliant, neither of them went to college.* ◇ *It was her* ***proud boast*** *that she had never missed a day's work because of illness.*

boast·ful /ˈbəʊstfl; *NAmE* ˈboʊstfl/ *adj.* (*disapproving*) talking about yourself in a very proud way: *I tried to emphasize my good points without sounding boastful.*

boat 🔑 /bəʊt; *NAmE* boʊt/ *noun*
1 🔑 a vehicle (smaller than a ship) that travels on water, moved by OARS, sails or a motor: *a* ***rowing/sailing boat*** ◇ *a fishing boat* ◇ *You can take a* ***boat trip*** *along the coast.* ➲ see also CANAL BOAT, LIFEBOAT, MOTORBOAT, POWERBOAT, SPEEDBOAT, STEAMBOAT **2** 🔑 any ship: *'How are you going to France?' 'We're going* ***by boat*** (= by FERRY).*'* ➲ VISUAL VOCAB pages V44, V45 ➲ see also GRAVY BOAT, SAUCE BOAT
IDM **be in the same 'boat** to be in the same difficult situation ➲ more at BURN *v.*, FLOAT *v.*, MISS *v.*, PUSH *v.*, ROCK *v.*

boat·er /ˈbəʊtə(r); *NAmE* ˈboʊt-/ *noun* a hard STRAW hat with a flat top ➲ VISUAL VOCAB page V52

boat·hook /ˈbəʊthʊk; *NAmE* ˈboʊt-/ *noun* a long pole with a hook at one end, used for pulling or pushing boats

boat·house /ˈbəʊthaʊs; *NAmE* ˈboʊt-/ *noun* a building beside a river or lake for keeping a boat in

boat·ing /ˈbəʊtɪŋ; *NAmE* ˈboʊtɪŋ/ *noun* [U] the activity of using a small boat for pleasure: *to* ***go boating*** ◇ *Local activities include walking, boating and golf.*

boat·man /ˈbəʊtmən; *NAmE* ˈboʊt-/ *noun* (*pl.* **-men** /-mən/) a man who earns money from small boats, either by carrying passengers or goods on them, or by renting them out

'boat people *noun* [pl.] people who escape from their own country in small boats to try to find safety in another country

boat·swain /ˈbəʊsn; *NAmE* ˈboʊ-/ *noun* = BOSUN

'boat train *noun* a train that takes passengers to or from a place where a boat arrives or leaves

boat·yard /ˈbəʊtjɑːd; *NAmE* ˈboʊtjɑːrd/ *noun* a place where boats are built, repaired or kept

Bob /bɒb; *NAmE* bɑːb/ *noun*
IDM **Bob's your 'uncle** (*BrE, informal*) used to say how easy and quick it is to do a particular task: *Press here and Bob's your uncle! It's disappeared.*

bob /bɒb; *NAmE* bɑːb/ *verb, noun*
■ ***verb*** (**-bb-**) **1** [I, T] to move or make sth move quickly up and down, especially in water: **~ up and down** *Tiny boats bobbed up and down in the harbour.* ◇ **~ sth (up and down)** *She bobbed her head nervously.* **2** [T] **~ sth** to cut sb's hair so that it is the same length all the way around
PHR V **,bob 'up** to come to the surface suddenly: *The dark head of a seal bobbed up a few yards away.*
■ ***noun*** **1** a quick movement down and up of your head and body: *a bob of the head* **2** a style of a woman's hair in which it is cut the same length all the way around: *She wears her hair in a bob.* ➲ VISUAL VOCAB page V49 **3** (*pl.* **bob**) (*informal*) an old British coin, the SHILLING, worth 12 old pence: *That'll cost a few bob* (= a lot of money). **4** = BOBSLEIGH **IDM** see BIT

bobbed /bɒbd; *NAmE* bɑːbd/ *adj.* (of hair) cut so that it hangs loosely to the level of the chin all around the back and sides

bob·ber /ˈbɒbə(r); *NAmE* ˈbɑːb-/ *noun* **1** a floating object used in fishing to hold the hook at the right depth **2** (*BrE*) a person who rides on a BOBSLEIGH

bob·bin /ˈbɒbɪn; *NAmE* ˈbɑːbɪn/ *noun* a small device on which you wind thread, used, for example, in a sewing machine

bob·ble /ˈbɒbl; *NAmE* ˈbɑːbl/ *noun, verb*
- ***noun*** (*BrE*) a small, soft ball, usually made of wool, that is used especially for decorating clothes SYN **pompom**: *a woolly hat with a bobble on top* ➲ VISUAL VOCAB page V53
- ***verb*** (*informal*) **1** [I] + **adv./prep.** to move along the ground with small BOUNCES: *The ball somehow bobbled into the net.* **2** [T] **~ sth** (*NAmE*) to drop a ball or to fail to stop it: *She tried to catch the ball but bobbled it.* **3** [I] (*BrE, informal*) (of a piece of clothing, especially one made of wool) to become covered in very small balls of FIBRE

bobby /ˈbɒbi; *NAmE* ˈbɑːbi/ *noun* (*pl.* -ies) (*old-fashioned, BrE, informal*) a police officer ORIGIN Named after Sir Robert Peel, the politician who created London's police force in the 19th century. **Bobby** is a familiar form of 'Robert'.

ˌ**bobby-ˈdazzler** *noun* (*old-fashioned, BrE, informal*) an excellent or very special person or thing

ˈ**bobby pin** (*NAmE*) (*BrE* **hair·grip**, **grip**, **kirby grip**) *noun* a small thin piece of metal or plastic folded in the middle, used by women for holding their hair in place ➲ compare HAIRPIN

ˈ**bobby socks** *noun* [pl.] short white socks worn with a dress or skirt, especially by girls and young women in the US in the 1940s and 50s

bob·cat /ˈbɒbkæt; *NAmE* ˈbɑːb-/ *noun* a N American wild cat

bobs /bɒbz; *NAmE* bɑːbz/ *noun* [pl.] IDM see BIT *n.*

bob·sleigh /ˈbɒbsleɪ; *NAmE* ˈbɑːb-/ (*BrE*) (*NAmE* **bob·sled** /ˈbɒbsled; *NAmE* ˈbɑːb-/) (also **bob**) *noun* a racing(= a vehicle for two or more people that slides over snow) SLEDGE ➲ VISUAL VOCAB page V39

bob·tail /ˈbɒbteɪl; *NAmE* ˈbɑːbteɪl/ *noun* **1** a dog, cat or horse with a tail that has been cut short **2** a tail that has been cut short

bod /bɒd; *NAmE* bɑːd/ *noun* (*informal*) **1** (*BrE*) a person: *She's a bit of an odd bod* (= rather strange). **2** a person's body: *He's got a great bod.*

bo·da·cious /bəʊˈdeɪʃəs; *NAmE* boʊ-/ *adj.* (*informal, especially NAmE*) **1** excellent; extremely good **2** willing to take risks or to do sth shocking SYN **audacious**

bode /bəʊd; *NAmE* boʊd/ *verb*
IDM **bode ˈwell/ˈill** (**for sb/sth**) (*formal*) to be a good/bad sign for sb/sth SYN **augur**: *These figures do not bode well for the company's future.*

bodge /bɒdʒ; *NAmE* bɑːdʒ/ *verb* **~ sth** (**up/together**) (*BrE, informal*) to make or repair sth in a way that is not as good as it should be

Bodhi·sat·tva /ˌbɒdɪˈsɑːtvə; *NAmE* ˌboʊd-/ *noun* (in Mahayana Buddhism) a person who is able to reach NIRVANA (= a state of peace and happiness) but who delays doing this because of the suffering of other humans

bodh·rán /ˈbaʊrɑːn; *NAmE* ˈbɔːr-/ *noun* (*IrishE*) a shallow Irish drum that you hold sideways in your hand and play with a short wooden stick

bod·ice /ˈbɒdɪs; *NAmE* ˈbɑːdɪs/ *noun* the top part of a woman's dress, above the waist

ˈ**bodice-ripper** *noun* (*informal*) a romantic novel or film/movie with a lot of sex in it, which is set in the past

bod·ily /ˈbɒdɪli; *NAmE* ˈbɑːd-/ *adj., adv.*
- ***adj.*** [only before noun] connected with the human body: *bodily functions/changes/needs* ◇ *bodily fluids* ◇ *bodily harm* (= physical injury)
- ***adv.*** **1** by moving the whole of sb's body; by force: *The force of the blast hurled us bodily to the ground.* ◇ *He lifted her bodily into the air.* **2** in one piece; completely: *The monument was moved bodily to a new site.*

bod·kin /ˈbɒdkɪn; *NAmE* ˈbɑːd-/ *noun* a thick needle with no point

Vocabulary Building

Actions expressing emotions

Often parts of the body are closely linked to particular verbs. The combination of the verb and part of the body expresses an emotion or attitude.

action	part of body	you are...
bite	lips	nervous
clench	fist	angry, aggressive
click	fingers	trying to remember sth
click	tongue	annoyed
drum/tap	fingers	impatient
hang	head	ashamed
lick	lips	anticipating sth good, nervous
nod	head	agreeing
purse	lips	disapproving
raise	eyebrows	enquiring, surprised
scratch	head	puzzled
shake	head	disagreeing
shrug	shoulders	doubtful, indifferent
stamp	foot	angry
wrinkle	nose	feeling dislike or distaste
wrinkle	forehead	puzzled

For example: *She bit her lip nervously.* ◇ *He scratched his head and looked thoughtful.* ◇ *I wrinkled my nose in disgust.* ◇ *She raised questioning eyebrows.*

body 🔑 /ˈbɒdi; *NAmE* ˈbɑːdi/ *noun* (*pl.* -ies)
- ▸ OF PERSON/ANIMAL **1** 🔑 [C] the whole physical structure of a human or an animal: *a **human/female/male/naked body*** ◇ *parts of the body* ◇ *His whole body was trembling.* ◇ ***body fat/weight/temperature/size/heat*** **2** 🔑 [C] the main part of a body not including the head, or not including the head, arms and legs: *She had injuries to her head and body.* ◇ *He has a large body, but thin legs.* **3** 🔑 [C] the body of a dead person or animal: *a dead body* ◇ *The family of the missing girl has been called in by the police to identify the body.*
- ▸ MAIN PART **4** [sing.] **the ~ of sth** the main part of sth, especially a building, a vehicle or a book, an article, etc: *the body of a plane* (= the central part where the seats are) ◇ *the **main body** of the text*
- ▸ GROUP OF PEOPLE **5** 🔑 [C+sing./pl. v.] a group of people who work or act together, often for an official purpose, or who are connected in some other way: *a **regulatory/an advisory/a review body*** ◇ *The governing body of the school is/are concerned about discipline.* ◇ *recognized professional bodies such as the Law Association* ◇ *An independent body has been set up to investigate the affair.* ◇ *A large body of people will be affected by the tax cuts.* ◇ *The protesters marched **in a body*** (= all together) *to the White House.* ◇ *a meeting of representatives of the student body and teaching staff*
- ▸ LARGE AMOUNT **6** [C] **~ of sth** a large amount or collection of sth: *a vast **body of evidence/information/research*** ◇ *large bodies of water* (= lakes or seas) ◇ *There is a powerful body of opinion against the ruling.*
- ▸ OBJECT **7** [C] (*formal*) an object: ***heavenly bodies*** (= stars, planets, etc.) ◇ *an operation to remove a **foreign body*** (= sth that would not usually be there) *from a wound*
- ▸ OF DRINK/HAIR **8** [U] the full strong flavour of alcoholic drinks or the thick healthy quality of sb's hair: *a wine with plenty of body* ◇ *Regular use of conditioner is supposed to give your hair more body.*
- ▸ -BODIED **9** (in adjectives) having the type of body men-

tioned: *full-bodied red wines* ◇ *soft-bodied insects* ➲ see also ABLE-BODIED
▸ CLOTHING **10** [C] (*BrE*) (*NAmE* **body·suit**) a piece of clothing which fits tightly over a woman's upper body and bottom, usually fastening between the legs
IDM **body and 'soul** with all your energy: *She committed herself body and soul to fighting for the cause.* **keep body and 'soul together** to stay alive with just enough of the food, clothing, etc. that you need SYN **survive**: *They barely have enough money to keep body and soul together.* ➲ more at BONE *n.*, DEAD *adj.*, SELL *v.*

'body armour (*especially US* **'body armor**) *noun* [U] clothing worn by the police, etc. to protect themselves

'body bag *noun* a bag for carrying a dead body in, for example in a war

'body blow *noun* something which has damaging effects on sb/sth, creating problems or causing severe disappointment

body·board /'bɒdibɔːd; *NAmE* 'bɑːdibɔːrd/ *noun* a short light type of SURFBOARD that you ride lying on your front ▸ **body·board·ing** *noun* [U] ➲ VISUAL VOCAB page V40

body·build·ing /'bɒdibɪldɪŋ; *NAmE* 'bɑːdi-/ *noun* [U] the activity of doing regular exercises in order to make your muscles bigger and stronger ▸ **body·build·er** *noun*

'body-check *noun* (in ICE HOCKEY) an attempt to prevent a player's movement by blocking them with your shoulder or hip

'body clock *noun* the natural tendency that your body has to sleep, eat, etc. at particular times of the day

'body double *noun* a person who takes part in a film/movie in place of an actor when the scene involves being naked, or using special or dangerous skills

body·guard /'bɒdigɑːd; *NAmE* 'bɑːdigɑːrd/ *noun* [C+sing./ pl. v.] a person or a group of people who are employed to protect sb: *The President's bodyguard is/are armed.*

'body language *noun* [U] the process of communicating what you are feeling or thinking by the way you place and move your body rather than by words

body mass index *noun* (*abbr.* BMI) an approximate measure of whether sb weighs too much or too little, calculated by dividing their weight in kilograms by their height in metres squared

'body odour (*especially US* **'body odor**) *noun* [U] (*abbr.* BO) an unpleasant smell from a person's body, especially of sweat

'body piercing (also **pier·cing**) *noun* [U] the making of holes in parts of the body as a decoration: *tattooing and body piercing*

the ˌbody 'politic *noun* [sing.] (*formal*) all the people of a particular nation considered as an organized political group

'body-popping *noun* [U] a way of dancing in which you make stiff movements like a ROBOT

'body search *noun* a search of a person's body, for example by the police or by a customs official, for drugs, weapons, etc.

'body shop *noun* **1** the part of a car factory where the main bodies of the cars are made **2** a place where repairs are made to the main bodies of cars

body·snatch·er /'bɒdisnætʃə(r); *NAmE* 'bɑːdi-/ *noun* a person who stole bodies from GRAVEYARDS in the past, especially to sell for medical experiments

'body stocking *noun* a piece of clothing that fits closely over the whole body from the neck to the ankles, often including the arms, worn for example by dancers

body·suit /'bɒdisuːt; *NAmE* 'bɑːdisuːt; *BrE* also -sjuːt/ **1** (*NAmE*) (*BrE* **body**) *noun* a piece of clothing which fits tightly over a woman's upper body and bottom, usually fastening between the legs **2** a piece of clothing that fits closely over the body, including the arms and legs, worn by men and women for sports

'body swerve *noun* a sudden movement that you make to the side when running to avoid crashing into sb/sth

'body warmer *noun* (*BrE*) a thick warm jacket without sleeves that you wear outdoors ➲ VISUAL VOCAB page V50

body·work /'bɒdiwɜːk; *NAmE* 'bɑːdiwɜːrk/ *noun* [U] the main outside structure of a vehicle, usually made of painted metal

Boer /bɔː(r)/ *noun* **1** a South African whose family originally came from the Netherlands: *the Boer War* (= the war between the Boers and the British, 1899-1902) ➲ see also AFRIKANER **2 boer** (*SAfrE*) a farmer **3 boer** (*SAfrE, disapproving*) used to refer to a member of the police or the army, especially in the past

boere·wors /'buːrəvɔːs; 'bʊ-; *NAmE* -vɔːrs/ *noun* [U] (*SAfrE*) a spicy SAUSAGE that is prepared in a long piece and sold usually wound into a COIL (= a series of circles)

bof·fin /'bɒfɪn; *NAmE* 'bɑːfən/ *noun* (*BrE, informal*) a scientist, especially one doing research

bog /bɒg; *NAmE* bɑːg; bɔːg/ *noun, verb*
▪ ***noun*** **1** [C, U] (an area of) wet soft ground, formed of decaying plants: *a peat bog* ➲ see also BOGGY **2** [C] (*BrE, slang*) a toilet/bathroom: *Have you got any* ***bog roll*** (= toilet paper)?
▪ ***verb*** (-gg-)
PHR V **ˌbog sth/sb 'down (in sth)** [usually passive] **1** to make sth sink into mud or wet ground: *The tank became bogged down in mud.* **2** to prevent sb from making progress in an activity: *We mustn't* ***get bogged down*** *in details.* **ˌbog 'off** (*BrE, taboo, slang*) only used in orders, to tell sb to go away: *Bog off, I'm trying to sleep!*

bogan /'bəʊgən; *NAmE* 'boʊ-/ *noun* (*AustralE, NZE, informal*) a rude or socially unacceptable person

bogey /'bəʊgi; *NAmE* 'boʊgi/ *noun* **1** (also **bogy**) a thing that causes fear, often without reason **2** (also **bogy**) (both *BrE*) (*NAmE* **boo·ger**) (*informal*) a piece of dried MUCUS from inside your nose **3** (also **bogy**) (*BrE*) = BOGEYMAN **4** (in GOLF) a score of one stroke over PAR (= the standard score for a hole) ➲ compare BIRDIE, EAGLE

bo·gey·man (also **bogy·man**) /'bəʊgimæn; *NAmE* 'boʊgi-/ *noun* (*BrE* also **bogey, bogy**) (*NAmE* usually **boo·gey·man**) (*pl.* -men /-men/) an imaginary evil spirit that is used to frighten children: *The bogeyman's coming!*

bog·gle /'bɒgl; *NAmE* 'bɑːgl/ *verb* [I] **~ (at sth)** (*informal*) to be slow to do or accept sth because you are surprised or shocked by it: *Even I boggle at the idea of spending so much money.*
IDM **sth boggles the 'mind** (also **the mind 'boggles**) (*informal*) if sth **boggles the mind** or **the mind boggles** at it, it is so unusual that people find it hard to imagine or accept: *The vastness of space really boggles the mind.* ◇ *'He says he's married to his cats!' 'The mind boggles!'* ➲ compare MIND-BOGGLING

boggy /'bɒgi; *NAmE* 'bɑːgi; 'bɔːgi/ *adj.* (**bog·gier, bog·gi·est**) (of land) soft and wet, like a BOG: *boggy ground*

bogie /'bəʊgi; *NAmE* 'boʊgi/ *noun* **1** (*especially BrE*) a frame with four or six wheels that forms part of a railway carriage/railroad car. The main body of the carriage/car usually rests on two bogies, one at each end. **2** (*IndE*) a railway carriage/railroad car

BOGOF /'bɒgɒf; *NAmE* 'bɑːgɑːf/ *abbr.* (*BrE, informal*) buy one, get one free (a type of special offer used in shops/stores): *BOGOF offers and bargains*

ˌbog-'standard *adj.* (*BrE, informal*) ordinary; with no special features SYN **average**

bogus /'bəʊgəs; *NAmE* 'boʊ-/ *adj.* pretending to be real or genuine SYN **false**: *a bogus doctor/contract* ◇ *bogus claims of injury by workers*

bogy, bogy·man = BOGEY, BOGEYMAN

bo·he·mian /bəʊ'hiːmiən; *NAmE* boʊ'h-/ *noun* a person, often sb who is involved with the arts, who lives in a very informal way without following accepted rules of behaviour ▸ **bo·he·mian** *adj.*: *a* ***bohemian existence/lifestyle***

B

boho /ˈbəʊhəʊ; *NAmE* ˈboʊhoʊ/ (also ˈ**boho chic**) *noun* [U] a style of women's fashion that was popular at the beginning of the 21st century. It included loose tops, long skirts, wide belts and boots.

boh·rium /ˈbɔːriəm/ *noun* [U] (*symb.* **Bh**) a RADIOACTIVE chemical element. Bohrium is produced when atoms COLLIDE (= crash into each other)

boil /bɔɪl/ *verb, noun*

■ ***verb*** **1** [I, T] when a liquid **boils** or when you **boil** it, it is heated to the point where it forms bubbles and turns to steam or VAPOUR: *The water was bubbling and boiling away.* ◇ **~ sth** *Boil plenty of salted water, then add the spaghetti.* ➲ VISUAL VOCAB page V24 **2** [I, T] when a KETTLE, pan, etc. **boils** or when you **boil** a KETTLE, etc, it is heated until the water inside it **boils**: (*BrE*) *The kettle's boiling.* ◇ **~ sth** *I'll boil the kettle and make some tea.* ◇ **+ adj.** *She left the gas on by mistake and the pan* ***boiled dry*** (= the water boiled until there was none left). **3** [I, T] to cook or wash sth in boiling water; to be cooked or washed in boiling water: *She put some potatoes on to boil.* ◇ **~ sth** *boiled carrots/cabbage* ◇ *to boil an egg for sb* ◇ **~ sb sth** *to boil sb an egg* ➲ COLLOCATIONS at COOKING **4** [I] **~ (with sth)** if you **boil** with anger, etc. or anger, etc. **boils** inside you, you are very angry: *He was boiling with rage.* IDM see BLOOD *n.*, WATCH *v.*

PHR V ˌ**boil** ˈ**down** | ˌ**boil sth**↔ˈ**down** to be reduced or to reduce sth by boiling ˌ**boil sth** ˈ**down** (**to sth**) to make sth, especially information, shorter by leaving out the parts that are not important: *The original speech I had written got boiled down to about ten minutes.* ˌ**boil** ˈ**down to sth** (not used in the progressive tenses) (of a situation, problem, etc.) to have sth as a main or basic part: *In the end,* ***what it all boils down to*** *is money, or the lack of it.* ˌ**boil** ˈ**over 1** (of liquid) to boil and flow over the side of a pan, etc. **2** (*informal*) to become very angry **3** (of a situation, an emotion, etc.) to change into sth more dangerous or violent SYN **explode**: *Racial tension finally boiled over in the inner city riots.* ˌ**boil** ˈ**up** if a situation or an emotion **boils up**, it becomes dangerous, worrying, etc: *I could feel anger boiling up inside me.* ˌ**boil sth**↔ˈ**up** to heat a liquid or some food until it boils

■ ***noun*** **1** [sing.] a period of boiling; the point at which liquid boils: (*BrE*) ***Bring*** *the soup* ***to the boil****, then allow it to simmer for five minutes.* ◇ (*NAmE*) ***Bring*** *the soup* ***to a boil.*** **2** [C] a painful infected swelling under the skin which is full of a thick yellow liquid (called PUS)

IDM **off the** ˈ**boil** (*BrE*) less good than before: *The second series of the show really went off the boil.* **on the** ˈ**boil** very active: *We have several projects all on the boil at once.*

ˌ**boiled** ˈ**sweet** (*BrE*) (*NAmE* ˌ**hard** ˈ**candy**) *noun* a hard sweet/candy made from boiled sugar, often with fruit flavours

boil·er /ˈbɔɪlə(r)/ (also **fur·nace** especially in *NAmE*) *noun* a container in which water is heated to provide hot water and heating in a building or to produce steam in an engine

boiler·maker /ˈbɔɪləmeɪkə(r); *NAmE* -lərm-/ *noun* **1** a person or company that makes boilers **2** (*NAmE*) a person who makes and repairs metal objects for industry **3** (*NAmE*) a drink of WHISKY followed immediately by a glass of beer

boil·er·plate /ˈbɔɪləpleɪt; *NAmE* -lər-/ *noun* [C, U] (*NAmE*) a standard form of words that can be used as a model for writing parts of a business document, legal agreement, etc.

ˈ**boiler room** *noun* **1** a room in a building or ship containing the boiler **2** (*NAmE*) a room or office used by people using telephones to sell sth, especially shares, in an aggressive or a dishonest way

ˈ**boiler suit** *noun* (*especially BrE*) (*NAmE* usually **cov·er·alls**) a piece of clothing like trousers/pants and a jacket in one piece, worn for doing dirty work ➲ compare OVERALLS

boil·ing /ˈbɔɪlɪŋ/ (also ˌ**boiling** ˈ**hot**) *adj.* very hot SYN **baking**: *You must be boiling in that sweater!* ◇ *a boiling hot day* OPP **freezing**

ˈ**boiling point** *noun* [U, C] **1** the temperature at which a liquid starts to boil **2** the point at which a person becomes very angry, or a situation is likely to become violent: *Racial tension has* ***reached boiling point.***

bois·ter·ous /ˈbɔɪstərəs/ *adj.* (of people, animals or behaviour) noisy and full of life and energy: *It was a challenge, keeping ten boisterous seven-year-olds amused.* ▸ **bois·ter·ous·ly** *adv.*

bok choy /ˌbɒk ˈtʃɔɪ; *NAmE* ˌbɑːk/ (*NAmE*) (*BrE* **pak choi**) *noun* [U] a type of CHINESE CABBAGE with long dark green leaves and thick white STEMS

bold /bəʊld; *NAmE* boʊld/ *adj., noun*

■ ***adj.*** (**bold·er**, **bold·est**) **1** (of people or behaviour) brave and confident; not afraid to say what you feel or to take risks: *It was a bold move on their part to open a business in France.* ◇ *The wine made him bold enough to approach her.* **2** (of shape, colour, lines, etc.) that can be easily seen; having a strong clear appearance: *the bold outline of a mountain against the sky* ◇ *She paints with bold strokes of the brush.* **3** (*technical*) (of printed words or letters) in a thick, dark TYPE: *Highlight the important words in bold type.* ◇ *bold lettering* ▸ **bold·ly** *adv.* **bold·ness** *noun* [U]

IDM **be/make so bold** (**as to do sth**) (*formal*) used especially when politely asking a question or making a suggestion which you hope will not offend anyone (although it may criticize them slightly): *If I may be so bold as to suggest that he made a mistake in his calculations...* (**as**) **bold as** ˈ**brass** (*BrE, informal*) without showing any respect, shame or fear

■ ***noun*** (also **bold·face** /ˈbəʊldfeɪs; *NAmE* ˈboʊld-/) [U] (*technical*) thick, dark TYPE used for printing words or letters: *Headwords are printed* ***in bold.***

bole /bəʊl; *NAmE* boʊl/ *noun* the main STEM of a tree SYN **trunk**

bol·ero /bəˈleərəʊ; *NAmE* bəˈleroʊ/ *noun* (*pl.* **-os**) **1** a traditional Spanish dance; a piece of music for this dance **2** /*BrE* also ˈbɒlərəʊ/ a women's short jacket that is not fastened at the front

bol·etus /bəˈliːtəs/ (also **bol·ete** /bəˈliːt/) *noun* [C, U] a MUSHROOM with small round holes under the top part. Some types of boletus can be eaten.

boll /bəʊl; *NAmE* boʊl/ *noun* the part of the cotton plant that contains the seeds

bol·lard /ˈbɒlɑːd; *NAmE* ˈbɑːlərd/ *noun* **1** (*BrE*) a short thick post that is used to stop vehicles from going on to a road or part of a road ➲ VISUAL VOCAB page V3 **2** a short thick post on a ship, or on land close to water, to which a ship's rope may be tied

bol·lock·ing /ˈbɒləkɪŋ; *NAmE* ˈbɑːl-/ *noun* (*BrE, taboo*) an occasion when sb tells you that they are very angry with you, often by shouting at you: *to give sb a bollocking* ◇ *to get a bollocking* HELP There are more polite ways to express this, for example **to give sb/to get a rocket**, or **to tear a strip off sb**.

bol·locks /ˈbɒləks; *NAmE* ˈbɑːl-/ *noun* (*BrE, taboo, slang*) **1** [U] nonsense: *You're talking a load of bollocks!* **2** [pl.] a man's TESTICLES **3 Bollocks!** *exclamation* used as a swear word when sb is disagreeing with sth, or when they are angry about sth: *Bollocks! He never said that!*

ˈ**boll weevil** *noun* an insect that damages cotton plants

Bol·ly·wood /ˈbɒliwʊd; *NAmE* ˈbɑːl-/ *noun* [U] (*informal*) used to refer to the Hindi film/movie industry, which mainly takes place in the Indian city of Mumbai (formerly called Bombay)

bol·ogna /bəˈləʊnjə; bəˈlɒnjə; *NAmE* -ˈloʊ-/ (also **ba·lo·ney**) *noun* [U] (*NAmE*) a type of SAUSAGE that is put in SANDWICHES, made of a mixture of meats

bolo tie /ˈbəʊləʊ taɪ; *NAmE* ˈboʊloʊ/ *noun* (*NAmE*) a string worn around the neck and fastened with a decorative CLASP or bar ➲ see also BOOTLACE TIE

Bol·shevik /ˈbɒlʃɪvɪk; *NAmE* ˈboʊl-/ *noun* a member of the group in Russia that took control after the 1917 Revolution ▸ **Bol·shevik** *adj.* **Bol·shevism** /ˈbɒlʃɪvɪzəm; *NAmE* ˈboʊl-/ *noun* [U]

B

bol·shie (also **bol·shy**) /ˈbɒlʃi; *NAmE* ˈboʊl-/ *adj.* (*BrE, informal, disapproving*) (of a person) creating difficulties or arguments deliberately, and refusing to be helpful

bol·ster /ˈbəʊlstə(r); *NAmE* ˈboʊl-/ *verb, noun*
- ***verb*** to improve sth or make it stronger: **~ sth** *to* ***bolster sb's confidence/courage/morale*** ◇ **~ sth up** *Falling interest rates may help to bolster up the economy.*
- ***noun*** a long thick PILLOW that is placed across the top of a bed under the other pillows

bolt /bəʊlt; *NAmE* boʊlt/ *noun, verb, adv.*
- ***noun*** **1** a long, narrow piece of metal that you slide across the inside of a door or window in order to lock it **2** a piece of metal like a screw without a point which is used with a circle of metal (= a NUT) to fasten things together: *nuts and bolts* ➲ VISUAL VOCAB page V17 **3 ~ of lightning** a sudden flash of LIGHTNING in the sky, appearing as a line **4** a short heavy arrow shot from a CROSSBOW **5** a long piece of cloth wound in a roll around a piece of cardboard

IDM **a ˌbolt from the ˈblue** an event or a piece of news which is sudden and unexpected; a complete surprise: *Her dismissal came as a bolt from the blue.* **make a ˈbolt for sth | make a ˈbolt for it** to run away very fast, in order to escape ➲ more at NUT *n.*, SHOT *v.*
- ***verb*** **1** [T, I] **~ (sth)** to fasten sth such as a door or window by sliding a bolt across; to be able to be fastened in this way: *Don't forget to bolt the door.* ◇ *The gate bolts on the inside.* **2** [T] to fasten things together with a bolt: **~ A to B** *The vice is bolted to the workbench.* ◇ **~ A and B together** *The various parts of the car are then bolted together.* **3** [I] if an animal, especially a horse, **bolts**, it suddenly runs away because it is frightened **4** [I] (**+ adv./prep.**) (of a person) to run away, especially in order to escape: *When he saw the police arrive, he bolted down an alley.* **5** [T] **~ sth** (**down**) to eat sth very quickly: *Don't bolt your food!* **6** (*NAmE*) [T, I] **~ (sth)** to stop supporting a particular group or political party: *Many Democrats bolted the party to vote Republican.* **7** [I] (of a plant, especially a vegetable) to grow too quickly and start producing seeds and so become less good to eat

IDM see STABLE DOOR *n.*
- ***adv.***

IDM **sit/stand bolt ˈupright** to sit or stand with your back straight

bolts

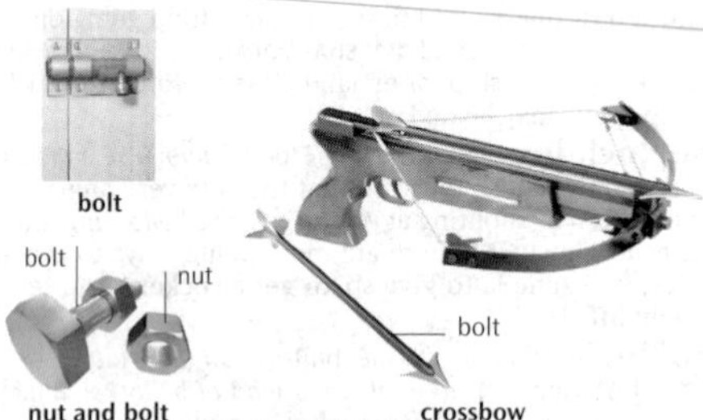

ˈbolt-action *adj.* (of a gun) having a back part that is opened by turning a BOLT and sliding it back

ˈbolt-hole *noun* (*BrE*) a place that you can escape to, for example when you are in a difficult situation

ˈbolt-on *adj.* [only before noun] able to be easily added to a machine, etc. to make it able to do sth new

bolus /ˈbəʊləs; *NAmE* ˈboʊləs/ *noun* **1** (*medical*) a single amount of a drug that is given at one time SYN **dose** **2** (*technical*) a small round mass of substance, especially chewed food that is swallowed

boma /ˈbəʊmə; *NAmE* ˈboʊ-/ *noun* (*EAfrE, SAfrE*) (in wild country) an area surrounded by a fence, often made of sticks, used to protect animals or people

bomb 0‒ /bɒm; *NAmE* bɑːm/ *noun, verb*
- ***noun*** **1** 0‒ [C] a weapon designed to explode at a particular time or when it is dropped or thrown: *a* ***bomb attack/blast/explosion*** ◇ *a* ***bomb goes off/explodes*** ◇ *extensive bomb damage* ◇ *Hundreds of bombs were dropped on the city.* ➲ see also DIRTY BOMB **2 the bomb** [sing.] nuclear weapons (ATOMIC or HYDROGEN bombs): *countries which have the bomb* **3 a bomb** [sing.] (*BrE, informal*) a lot of money: *That dress must have cost a bomb!* **4 a bomb** [sing.] (*NAmE, informal*) a complete failure: *The musical was a complete bomb on Broadway.* **5** [C] (*NAmE*) (in AMERICAN FOOTBALL) a long forward throw of the ball **6** [C] (*NAmE*) a container in which a liquid such as paint or insect poison is kept under pressure and released as a spray or as FOAM: *a bug bomb* (= used for killing insects)

IDM **be the ˈbomb** (*NAmE*) to be very good; to be the best: *Check out the new website. It's the bomb!* **go down a ˈbomb | go (like) a ˈbomb** (*BrE*) to be very successful: *Our performance went down a bomb.* ◇ *The party was really going (like) a bomb.* **go like a ˈbomb** (*BrE*) (of a vehicle) to go very fast
- ***verb*** **1** 0‒ [T] **~ sth** to attack sb/sth by leaving a bomb in a place or by dropping bombs from a plane: *Terrorists bombed several army barracks.* ◇ *The city was heavily bombed in the war.* **2** [I] **+ adv./prep.** (*BrE, informal*) to move very fast, especially in a vehicle, in a particular direction: *They were bombing down the road at about 80 miles an hour.* **3** [T, I] **~ (sth)** (*NAmE, informal*) to fail a test or an exam very badly: *The exam was impossible! I definitely bombed it.* **4** [I] (*informal*) (of a play, show, etc.) to fail very badly: *His latest musical bombed and lost thousands of dollars.*

PHR V **be ˌbombed ˈout (of sth)** **1** if you are **bombed out**, your home is destroyed by bombs **2** if a building is **bombed out**, it has been destroyed by bombs

ˈbomb alert *noun* (*BrE*) = BOMB SCARE

bom·bard /bɒmˈbɑːd; *NAmE* bɑːmˈbɑːrd/ *verb* **1 ~ sb/sth (with sth)** to attack a place by firing large guns at it or dropping bombs on it continuously **2 ~ sb/sth (with sth)** to attack sb with a lot of questions, criticisms, etc. or by giving them too much information: *We have been bombarded with letters of complaint.* ▶ **bom·bard·ment** *noun* [U, C]: *The city came under heavy bombardment.*

bom·bard·ier /ˌbɒmbəˈdɪə(r); *NAmE* ˌbɑːmbərˈdɪr/ *noun* **1** the person on a military plane in the US AIR FORCE who is responsible for aiming and dropping bombs **2** a member of a low rank in the Royal Artillery (= a part of the British army that uses large guns)

bom·bast /ˈbɒmbæst; *NAmE* ˈbɑːm-/ *noun* [U] (*formal*) words which sound important but have little meaning, used to impress people ▶ **bom·bas·tic** /bɒmˈbæstɪk; *NAmE* bɑːm-/ *adj.*: *a bombastic speaker*

Bombay mix /ˌbɒmbeɪ ˈmɪks; *NAmE* ˌbɑːm-/ *noun* [U] an Indian food consisting of LENTILS, PEANUTS and spices, eaten as a SNACK

ˈbomb bay *noun* a part of an aircraft in which bombs are held and from which they can be dropped

ˈbomb disposal *noun* [U] the job of removing or exploding bombs in order to make an area safe: *a* ***bomb disposal expert/squad/team***

bombed /bɒmd; *NAmE* bɑːmd/ *adj.* [not before noun] (*informal*) extremely drunk

bomb·er /ˈbɒmə(r); *NAmE* ˈbɑːm-/ *noun* **1** a plane that carries and drops bombs **2** a person who puts a bomb somewhere illegally

ˈbomber jacket *noun* a short jacket that fits tightly around the waist and fastens with a ZIP/ZIPPER

bomb·ing /ˈbɒmɪŋ; *NAmE* ˈbɑːm-/ *noun* [C, U] an occasion when a bomb is dropped or left somewhere; the act of doing this: *recent bombings in major cities* ◇ *enemy bombing*

bom·bora /bɒmˈbɔːrə; *NAmE* bɑːm-/ *noun* (*AustralE*) **1** a wave which forms over an underwater rock, sometimes producing a dangerous area of broken water **2** an area of rock underwater

bomb·proof /ˈbɒmpruːf; *NAmE* ˈbɑːm-/ *adj.* strong enough to give protection against an attack by a bomb

ˈbomb scare (also **ˈbomb threat** especially in *NAmE*) (*BrE* also **ˈbomb alert**) *noun* an occasion when sb says that they have put a bomb somewhere and everyone has to leave the area

bomb·shell /ˈbɒmʃel; *NAmE* ˈbɑːm-/ *noun* [usually sing.] (*informal*) **1** an event or a piece of news which is unexpected and usually unpleasant: *The news of his death came as a bombshell.* ◇ *She* **dropped a bombshell** *at the meeting and announced that she was leaving.* **2 a blond(e) bombshell** a very attractive woman with blonde hair

ˈbomb site *noun* an area where all the buildings have been destroyed by bombs

bona fide /ˌbəʊnə ˈfaɪdi; *NAmE* ˌboʊnə/ *adj.* [usually before noun] (from *Latin*) genuine, real or legal; not false: *a bona fide reason* ◇ *Is it a bona fide, reputable organization?*

bona fides /ˌbəʊnə ˈfaɪdiːz; *NAmE* ˌboʊnə/ *noun* [pl.] (from *Latin*) evidence that sb is who they say that they are; evidence that sb/sth is honest

bon·anza /bəˈnænzə/ *noun* [sing.] **1** a situation in which people can make a lot of money or be very successful: *a cash bonanza for investors* ◇ *a bonanza year for the computer industry* **2** a situation where there is a large amount of sth pleasant: *the usual bonanza of sport in the summer*

bon·bon /ˈbɒnbɒn; *NAmE* ˈbɑːnbɑːn/ *noun* a sweet/candy, especially one with a soft centre

bonce /bɒns; *NAmE* bɑːns/ *noun* (*BrE, informal*) a person's head

bond AW /bɒnd; *NAmE* bɑːnd/ *noun, verb*

■ ***noun***

▸ STRONG CONNECTION **1** [C] **~ (between A and B)** something that forms a connection between people or groups, such as a feeling of friendship or shared ideas and experiences: *A bond of friendship had been forged between them.* ◇ *The agreement strengthened the bonds between the two countries.* ◇ *the special bond between mother and child*

▸ MONEY **2** [C] an agreement by a government or a company to pay you interest on the money you have lent; a document containing this agreement ➔ see also JUNK BOND **3** [U] (*law*) (*especially NAmE*) a sum of money that is paid as BAIL: *He was released on $5 000 bond.* **4** [C] (also **ˈmortgage bond**) (*SAfrE*) a legal agreement by which a bank lends you money to buy a house, etc. which you pay back over many years; the sum of money that is lent: *to pay off a bond* ◇ *We had to take out a second bond on the property.* ◇ *bond rates* (= of interest)

▸ ROPES/CHAINS **5 bonds** [pl.] (*formal*) the ropes or chains keeping sb prisoner; anything that stops you from being free to do what you want: *to release sb from their bonds* ◇ *the* ***bonds of oppression/injustice***

▸ LEGAL AGREEMENT **6** [C] (*formal*) a legal written agreement or promise: *We entered into a solemn bond.*

▸ JOIN **7** [C] the way in which two things are joined together: *a firm bond between the two surfaces*

▸ CHEMISTRY **8** [C] the way in which atoms are held together in a chemical COMPOUND IDM see WORD *n.*

■ ***verb***

▸ JOIN FIRMLY **1** [T, I] to join two things firmly together; to join firmly to sth else: **~ sth** *This new glue bonds a variety of surfaces in seconds.* ◇ **~ (A) to B** *It cannot be used to bond wood to metal.* ◇ **~ (A and B) together** *The atoms bond together to form a molecule.*

▸ DEVELOP RELATIONSHIP **2** [I, T] **~ (with sb)** to develop or create a relationship of trust with sb: *Mothers who are depressed sometimes fail to bond with their children.*

bond·age /ˈbɒndɪdʒ; *NAmE* ˈbɑːn-/ *noun* **1** (*old-fashioned* or *formal*) the state of being a SLAVE or prisoner SYN **slavery**: (*figurative*) *women's liberation from the bondage of domestic life* **2** the practice of being tied with ropes, chains, etc. in order to gain sexual pleasure

ˌbonded ˈlabour (*especially US* **ˌbonded ˈlabor**) *noun* [U] forced work for an employer for a fixed time without being paid, often as a way of paying a debt: *Many of the immigrants are used as bonded labour.* ▸ **ˌbonded ˈlabourer** (*especially US* **ˌbonded ˈlaborer**) *noun*

ˌbonded ˈwarehouse *noun* (*BrE*) a government building where imported goods are stored until tax has been paid on them

bond·ing AW /ˈbɒndɪŋ; *NAmE* ˈbɑːn-/ *noun* [U] **1** the process of forming a special relationship with sb or with a group of people: *mother-child bonding* ◇ *male bonding* **2** (*chemistry*) the process of atoms joining together: *hydrogen bonding*

bone 🔑 /bəʊn; *NAmE* boʊn/ *noun, verb*

■ ***noun*** **1** 🔑 [C] any of the hard parts that form the SKELETON of the body of a human or an animal: *He survived the accident with no broken bones.* ◇ *This fish has a lot of bones in it.* **2** [U] the hard substance that bones are made of: *knives with bone handles* **3 -boned** (in adjectives) having bones of the type mentioned: *fine-boned*

IDM **a bone of conˈtention** a subject which causes disagreement and arguments between people **close to the ˈbone** (*BrE, informal*) (of a remark, joke, story, etc.) so honest or clearly expressed that it is likely to cause offence to some people **cut, pare, etc. sth to the ˈbone** to reduce sth, such as costs, as much as you possibly can **have a ˈbone to pick with sb** (*informal*) to be angry with sb about sth and want to discuss it with them **make no bones about (doing) sth** to be honest and open about sth; to not hesitate to do sth: *She made no bones about telling him exactly what she thought of him.* **not have a ... bone in your body** to have none of the quality mentioned: *She was honest and hard-working, and didn't have an unkind bone in her body.* **throw sb a ˈbone** to give sb a small part of what they want as a way of showing that you want to help them, without offering them the main thing they want **to the ˈbone** affecting you very strongly: *His threats chilled her to the bone.* ➔ more at BAG *n.*, BARE *adj.*, FEEL *v.*, FINGER *n.*, FLESH *n.*, SKIN *n.*

■ ***verb*** **~ sth** to take the bones out of fish or meat

PHR V **ˌbone ˈup on sth** (*informal*) to try to learn about sth or to remind yourself of what you already know about it: *She had boned up on the city's history before the visit.*

ˌbone ˈchina *noun* [U] thin delicate CHINA made of CLAY mixed with crushed bone; cups, plates, etc. made of this

ˌbone ˈdry *adj.* [not usually before noun] completely dry

bone·head /ˈbəʊnhed; *NAmE* ˈboʊn-/ *noun* (*informal*) a stupid person

ˌbone ˈidle *adj.* (*old-fashioned, BrE, informal*) very lazy

bone·less /ˈbəʊnləs; *NAmE* ˈboʊn-/ *adj.* (of meat or fish) without any bones: *boneless chicken breasts*

ˈbone marrow (also **mar·row**) *noun* [U] a soft substance that fills the hollow parts of bones: *a bone marrow transplant*

bone·meal /ˈbəʊnmiːl; *NAmE* ˈboʊn-/ *noun* [U] a substance made from crushed animal bones which is used to make soil richer

boner /ˈbəʊnə(r); *NAmE* ˈboʊn-/ *noun* (*NAmE, informal*) **1** (*taboo*) an ERECTION of the PENIS **2** an embarrassing mistake

bone·shaker /ˈbəʊnʃeɪkə(r); *NAmE* ˈboʊn-/ *noun* (*BrE, informal*) **1** an old vehicle that is in bad condition **2** an old type of bicycle without rubber tyres

bon·fire /ˈbɒnfaɪə(r); *NAmE* ˈbɑːn-/ *noun* a large outdoor fire for burning waste or as part of a celebration

ˈBonfire Night (also **ˌGuy ˈFawkes night**) *noun* [U, C] the night of 5 November, when there is a tradition in Britain that people light bonfires and have FIREWORKS to celebrate the failure of the plan in 1605 to destroy the parliament buildings with EXPLOSIVES

bong /bɒŋ; *NAmE* bɑːŋ/ *noun* **1** the sound made by a large bell: *the bongs of Big Ben* **2** a long pipe for smoking CANNABIS and other drugs, which passes the smoke through a container of water

bongo /ˈbɒŋgəʊ; *NAmE* ˈbɑːŋgoʊ; ˈbɔːŋgoʊ/ (*pl.* -os) (also **ˈbongo drum**) *noun* a small drum, usually one of a pair, that you play with your fingers

bon·homie /ˈbɒnəmi; *NAmE* ˌbɑːnəˈmiː/ *noun* [U] (from *French, formal*) a feeling of cheerful friendship

B

bonk /bɒŋk; *NAmE* bɑːŋk/ *noun, verb*
■ ***noun*** (*BrE, informal*) **1** [sing.] an act of having sex with sb **2** [C] the act of hitting sb on the head or of hitting your head on sth
■ ***verb*** (*BrE, informal*) **1** [T, I] **~ (sb)** to have sex with sb: *He's been bonking one of his students.* **2** [T] **~ sth** to hit sb lightly on the head or to hit yourself by mistake: *I bonked my head on the doorway.*

bonk·buster /ˈbɒŋkbʌstə(r); *NAmE* ˈbɑːŋk-/ *noun* (*BrE, informal*) a type of popular novel in which there is a lot of sex or romantic love

bonk·ers /ˈbɒŋkəz; *NAmE* ˈbɑːŋkərz/ *adj.* [not before noun] (*informal*) completely crazy and silly: *I'll* ***go bonkers*** *if I have to wait any longer.* IDM see RAVING *adv.*

bon mot /ˌbɒn ˈməʊ; *NAmE* ˌbɑːn ˈmoʊ; ˌbɔːn ˈmoʊ/ *noun* (*pl.* **bons mots** /ˌbɒn ˈməʊ; *NAmE* ˌbɑːn ˈmoʊ; ˌbɔːn ˈmoʊ/) (from *French, formal*) a funny and clever remark

bon·net /ˈbɒnɪt; *NAmE* ˈbɑːnət/ *noun* **1** a hat tied with strings under the chin, worn by babies and, especially in the past, by women **2** (*BrE*) (*NAmE* **hood**) the metal part over the front of a vehicle, usually covering the engine ➲ COLLOCATIONS at DRIVING ➲ VISUAL VOCAB page V42 IDM see BEE

bonny (also **bonnie**) /ˈbɒni; *NAmE* ˈbɑːni/ *adj.* (**bon·nier, bon·ni·est**) (*dialect, especially ScotE*) very pretty; attractive: *a* ***bonny baby/lass***

bon·sai /ˈbɒnsaɪ; *NAmE* ˈbɑːn-/ *noun* (*pl.* **bonsai**) **1** [C] a small tree that is grown in a pot and prevented from reaching its normal size **2** [U] the Japanese art of growing bonsai

bonsai

bon·sella /bɒnˈselə; *NAmE* bɑːn-/ *noun* (*SAfrE, informal*) something that you receive as a present or reward, especially money

bonus /ˈbəʊnəs; *NAmE* ˈboʊ-/ *noun* (*pl.* **-es**) **1** an extra amount of money that is added to a payment, especially to sb's wages as a reward: *a £100 Christmas bonus* ◇ *productivity bonuses* **2** anything pleasant that is extra and more or better than you were expecting: *Being able to walk to work is an* ***added bonus*** *of the new job.* ➲ see also NO-CLAIMS BONUS

bon viv·ant /ˌbɒ̃ viːˈvɒ̃; *NAmE* ˌbɑːn viːˈvɑːnt/ (also **bon viv·eur** /-ˈvɜː(r)/) *noun* (from *French*) a person who enjoys going out with friends and eating good food, drinking good wine, etc.

bon voy·age /ˌbɒn vɔɪˈɑːʒ; *NAmE* ˌbɑːn/ *exclamation* (from *French*) said to sb who is leaving on a journey, to wish them a good journey

bony /ˈbəʊni; *NAmE* ˈboʊni/ *adj.* (**boni·er, boni·est**) **1** (of a person or part of the body) very thin so that the bones can be seen under the skin **2** (of fish) full of small bones **3** consisting of or like bone

bon·zer /ˈbɒnzə(r); *NAmE* ˈbɑːn-/ *adj.* (*AustralE, NZE, informal*) excellent

boo /buː/ *exclamation, noun, verb*
■ ***exclamation, noun*** **1** a sound that people make to show that they do not like an actor, speaker, etc: *'Boo!' they shouted, 'Get off!'* ◇ *The speech was greeted with loud boos from the audience.* **2** people shout **Boo!** when they want to surprise or frighten sb IDM see SAY *v.*
■ ***verb*** [I, T] to show that you do not like a person, performance, idea, etc. by shouting 'boo': *The audience booed as she started her speech.* ◇ **~ sb** *He was* ***booed off the stage.***

boob /buːb/ *noun, verb*
■ ***noun*** **1** (*slang*) a woman's breast **2** (*BrE, informal*) a stupid mistake: *I made a bit of a boob throwing that file away.* **3** (*NAmE*) a stupid person
■ ***verb*** [I] (*informal*) to make a stupid mistake

ˈboo-boo *noun* **1** (*informal*) a stupid mistake: *I think I've made a boo-boo.* **2** (*NAmE*) a child's word for a small cut or injury

ˈboob tube *noun* **1** (*BrE, informal*) (*NAmE* **ˈtube top**) a piece of women's clothing that is made of cloth that stretches and covers the chest **2** (*NAmE, informal, disapproving*) the television

booby /ˈbuːbi/ *noun* (*pl.* **-ies**) **1** (*informal*) a stupid person: *Don't be such a booby!* **2** [usually pl.] (*informal*) a word for a woman's breast, used especially by children **3** a large tropical bird with brightly coloured feet that lives near the sea

ˈbooby prize *noun* a prize that is given as a joke to the person who is last in a competition

ˈbooby trap *noun* **1** a hidden bomb that explodes when the object that it is connected to is touched **2** a hidden device that is meant as a joke to surprise sb, for example an object placed above a door so that it will fall on the first person who opens the door

ˈbooby-trap *verb* (**-pp-**) **~ sth** to place a booby trap in or on sth

boof·head /ˈbuːfhed/ *noun* (*AustralE, informal*) a stupid person

boo·ger /ˈbuːgə(r)/ (*NAmE*) (*BrE* **bogey, bogy**) *noun* (*informal*) a piece of dried MUCUS from inside your nose

boo·gey·man /ˈbuːgimæn/ *noun* (*NAmE*) = BOGEYMAN

boo·gie /ˈbuːgi; *NAmE* ˈbʊgi/ *noun, verb*
■ ***noun*** (also ˌ**boogie-ˈwoogie** /-ˈwuːgi; *NAmE* -ˈwʊgi/) [U] a type of blues music played on the piano, with a fast strong rhythm
■ ***verb*** [I] (*informal*) to dance to fast pop music

ˈboogie board *noun* a small board used for riding on waves in a lying position

boo·hoo /ˈbuːhuː; ˌbuːˈhuː/ *exclamation* used in written English to show the sound of sb crying

book 🔑 /bʊk/ *noun, verb*
■ ***noun***
▸ PRINTED WORK **1** 🔑 [C] a set of printed pages that are fastened inside a cover so that you can turn them and read them: *a pile of books* ◇ ***hardback/paperback books*** **2** 🔑 [C] a written work published in printed or electronic form: *a book by Stephen King* ◇ *a* ***book about/on*** *wildlife* ◇ ***reference/children's/library books*** ➲ COLLOCATIONS at LITERATURE
▸ FOR WRITING IN **3** 🔑 [C] a set of sheets of paper that are fastened together inside a cover and used for writing in: *an exercise book* ◇ *a notebook* ➲ see also ADDRESS BOOK
▸ OF STAMPS/TICKETS/MATCHES, ETC. **4** 🔑 [C] a set of things that are fastened together like a book: *a* ***book of stamps/tickets/matches*** ◇ *a chequebook*
▸ ACCOUNTS **5 the books** [pl.] the written records of the financial affairs of a business SYN **accounts**: *to do the books* (= to check the accounts)
▸ SECTION OF BIBLE, ETC. **6** [C] a section of a large written work: *the books of the Bible*
▸ FOR BETTING **7** [C] (*BrE*) a record of bets made on whether sth will happen, sb will win a race, etc.
IDM **be in sb's good/bad ˈbooks** (*informal*) used to say that sb is pleased/annoyed with you: *I'm in her good books at the moment because I cleared up the kitchen.* **bring sb to ˈbook (for sth)** (*formal, especially BrE*) to punish sb for doing sth wrong and make them explain their behaviour **by the ˈbook** following rules and instructions in a very strict way: *She always does everything by the book.* **in my ˈbook** (*informal*) used when you are giving your opinion: *That's cheating in my book.* **(be) on sb's ˈbooks** (to be) on an organization's list, for example of people who are available for a particular type of work: *We have very few nurses on our books at the moment.* ◇ *Most of the houses on our books are in the north of the city.* **throw the ˈbook at sb** (*informal*) to punish sb who has committed an offence as severely as possible ➲ more at CLOSE[1] *v.*, CLOSED, COOK *v.*, HISTORY, JUDGE *v.*, LEAF *n.*, OPEN *adj.*, READ *v.*, SUIT *v.*, TRICK *n.*
■ ***verb*** **1** 🔑 [I, T] to arrange to have or use sth on a particular date in the future; to buy a ticket in advance: *Book early to*

avoid disappointment. ◇ **~ sth** *She booked a flight to Chicago.* ◇ *The performance is* **booked up** (= there are no more tickets available). ◇ *I'm sorry—we're* ***fully booked.*** ◇ (*BrE*) *I'd like to book a table for two for 8 o'clock tonight.* **HELP** In American English **book** is not used if you do not have to pay in advance; instead use **make a reservation**:*NAmE: I'd like to make a reservation for 8 o'clock tonight.* ➲ compare RESERVE **2** [T] to arrange for sb to have a seat on a plane, etc: **~ sb + adv./prep.** *I've booked you on the 10 o'clock flight.* ◇ **~ sb sth** (**+ adv./prep.**) *I've booked you a room at the Park Hotel.* **3** [T] **~ sb/sth** (**for sth**) to arrange for a singer, etc. to perform on a particular date: *We've booked a band for the wedding reception.* **4** [T] **~ sb** (**for sth**) (*informal*) to write down sb's name and address because they have committed a crime or an offence: *He was booked for possession of cocaine.* **5** [T] **~ sb** (*BrE, informal*) (of a REFEREE) to write down in an official book the name of a player who has broken the rules of the game

PHR V ˌ**book ˈin/ˈinto sth** (*BrE*) to arrive at a hotel, etc. and arrange to stay there: *I got in at ten and booked straight into a hotel.* ˌ**book sb ˈin/ˈinto sth** to arrange for sb to have a room at a hotel, etc.

book·able /ˈbʊkəbl/ *adj.* **1** tickets, etc. that are **bookable** can be ordered in advance **2** (*BrE*) if an offence in football (SOCCER) is **bookable**, the name of the player responsible is written down in a book by the REFEREE as a punishment **3** (*NAmE*) if a crime is a **bookable** offence, the person responsible can be arrested

book·bind·er /ˈbʊkbaɪndə(r)/ *noun* a person whose job is fastening the pages of books together and putting covers on them ▸ **book·bind·ing** *noun* [U]

book·case /ˈbʊkkeɪs/ *noun* a piece of furniture with shelves for keeping books on ➲ VISUAL VOCAB page V18

ˈ**book club** *noun* **1** an organization that sells books cheaply to its members **2** = BOOK GROUP

book·cross·ing /ˈbʊkkrɒsɪŋ; *NAmE* -krɔːs-/ *noun* [U] the practice of leaving a book in a public place so that another person can find it, read it and then leave it where sb else will find it

book·end /ˈbʊkend/ *noun* [usually pl.] one of a pair of objects used to keep a row of books standing up ➲ VISUAL VOCAB page V18

ˈ**book group** (also ˈ**book club**, ˈ**reading group**) *noun* a group of people who meet together regularly to discuss a book they have all read

bookie /ˈbʊki/ *noun* (*informal*) = BOOKMAKER

book·ing /ˈbʊkɪŋ/ *noun* **1** [C, U] (*especially BrE*) an arrangement that you make in advance to buy a ticket to travel somewhere, go to the theatre, etc: *a* ***booking form/hall/clerk*** ◇ *Can I* ***make a booking*** *for Friday?* ◇ ***Early booking*** *is recommended.* ◇ *No* ***advance booking*** *is necessary.* ◇ *We can't take any more bookings.* ➲ compare RESERVATION **2** [C] an arrangement for sb to perform at a theatre, in a concert, etc. **3** [C] (*BrE*) (in football (SOCCER)) an act of the REFEREE writing a player's name in a book, as a punishment because an offence has been committed

ˈ**booking office** *noun* (*BrE*) a place where you can buy tickets, at a train or bus station or at a theatre

book·ish /ˈbʊkɪʃ/ *adj.* (often *disapproving*) interested in reading and studying, rather than in more active or practical things

book·keep·er /ˈbʊkkiːpə(r)/ *noun* a person whose job is to keep an accurate record of the accounts of a business ▸ **book·keep·ing** *noun* [U]

ˈ**book learning** *noun* [U] knowledge from books or study rather than from experience

book·let /ˈbʊklət/ *noun* a small thin book with a paper cover that contains information about a particular subject

book·maker /ˈbʊkmeɪkə(r)/ (also *informal* **bookie**) (also *BrE formal* ˈ**turf accountant**) *noun* a person whose job is to take bets on the result of horse races, etc. and pay out money to people who win ▸ **book·mak·ing** *noun* [U]

book·mark /ˈbʊkmɑːk; *NAmE* -mɑːrk/ *noun* **1** a strip of paper, etc. that you put between the pages of a book when you finish reading so that you can easily find the place again **2** (*computing*) a record of the address of a file, a page on the Internet, etc. that enables you to find it quickly ▸ **book·mark** *verb*: **~ sth** *Do you want to bookmark this site?*

B

book·mobile /ˈbʊkməbiːl/ (*NAmE*) (*BrE* ˌ**mobile ˈlibrary**) *noun* a van/truck that contains a library and travels from place to place so that people in different places can borrow books

book·plate /ˈbʊkpleɪt/ *noun* a decorative piece of paper that is stuck in a book to show the name of the person who owns it

book·sel·ler /ˈbʊkselə(r)/ *noun* a person whose job is selling books

book·shelf /ˈbʊkʃelf/ *noun* (*pl.* **book·shelves** /ˈbʊkʃelvz/) a shelf that you keep books on

book·shop /ˈbʊkʃɒp; *NAmE* -ʃɑːp/ (*especially BrE*) (*NAmE* usually **book·store** /ˈbʊkstɔː(r)/) *noun* a shop/store that sells books

ˈ**book-smart** *adj.* (*NAmE*, becoming *old-fashioned*, often *disapproving*) having a lot of academic knowledge learned from books and studying, but not necessarily knowing much about people and living in the real world: *He's book smart but he's got no common sense.* ➲ compare STREET-SMART

book·stall /ˈbʊkstɔːl/ (*especially BrE*) (*NAmE* usually **news-stand**) *noun* a small shop/store that is open at the front, where you can buy books, newspapers or magazines, for example at a station or an airport

ˈ**book token** *noun* (*BrE*) a card, usually given as a gift, that you can exchange for books of a particular value

book·worm /ˈbʊkwɜːm; *NAmE* -wɜːrm/ *noun* a person who likes reading very much

Bool·ean /ˈbuːliən/ *adj.* (*mathematics, computing*) connected with a system, used especially in COMPUTING and ELECTRONICS, that uses only the numbers 1 (to show sth is true) and 0 (to show sth is false)

ˌ**Boolean ˈoperator** *noun* (*computing*) a symbol or word such as 'or' or 'and', used in computer programs and searches to show what is or is not included

boom /buːm/ *noun, verb*

■ ***noun***

▸ IN BUSINESS/ECONOMY **1** a sudden increase in trade and economic activity; a period of wealth and success: *Living standards improved rapidly during the post-war boom.* ◇ **~ in sth** *a boom in car sales* ◇ *a* ***boom year*** (*for trade, exports, etc.*) ◇ *a* ***property/housing boom*** ◇ *a chaotic period of* ***boom and bust*** ➲ COLLOCATIONS at ECONOMY ➲ compare SLUMP ➲ see also BABY BOOM

▸ POPULAR PERIOD **2** [usually sing.] a period when sth such as a sport or a type of music suddenly becomes very popular and successful: *The only way to satisfy the golf boom was to build more courses.*

▸ ON BOAT **3** a long pole that the bottom of a sail is attached to and that you move to change the position of the sail ➲ VISUAL VOCAB page V45

▸ SOUND **4** [usually sing.] a loud deep sound: *the distant boom of the guns* ➲ see also SONIC BOOM

▸ IN RIVER/HARBOUR **5** a floating barrier that is placed across a river or the entrance to a HARBOUR to prevent ships or other objects from coming in or going out

▸ FOR MICROPHONE **6** a long pole that carries a MICROPHONE or other equipment

■ ***verb***

▸ MAKE LOUD SOUND **1** [I] to make a loud deep sound: *Outside, thunder boomed and crashed.* **2** [T, I] to say sth in a loud deep voice: **+ speech** *'Get out of my sight!' he boomed.* ◇ **~** (**out**) *A voice boomed out from the darkness.* ◇ *He had a* ***booming voice.***

▸ OF BUSINESS/ECONOMY **3** [I] to have a period of rapid growth; to become bigger, more successful, etc: *By the 1980s, the computer industry was booming.* ◇ *Business is booming!*

ˈ**boom box** *noun* (*especially NAmE*) = GHETTO BLASTER

B

boom·er /ˈbuːmə(r)/ *noun* **1** (*NAmE*) = BABY BOOMER **2** a large male KANGAROO

boom·er·ang /ˈbuːməræŋ/ *noun, verb*

■ ***noun*** a curved flat piece of wood that you throw and that can fly in a circle and come back to you. Boomerangs were first used by Australian Aborigines as weapons when they were hunting.

boomerang

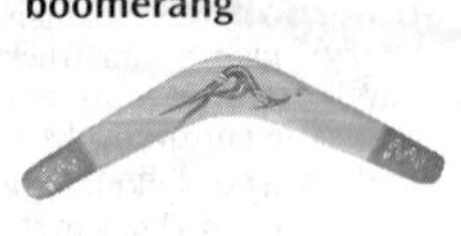

■ ***verb*** [I] if a plan **boomerangs** on sb, it hurts them instead of the person it was intended to hurt SYN **backfire**

ˈ**boomerang kid** (also ˈ**boomerang child**) *noun* (*informal*) an adult child who returns home to live with his or her parents after being away for some time

ˈ**boom town** *noun* a town that has become rich and successful because trade and industry has developed there

boon /buːn/ *noun* **~** (**to/for sb**) something that is very helpful and makes life easier for you: *The new software will prove a boon to Internet users.*

ˌ**boon comˈpanion** *noun* (*literary*) a very good friend

boon·docks /ˈbuːndɒks; *NAmE* -dɑːks/ (also **boon·ies**) *noun* [pl.] (*NAmE, informal, disapproving*) an area far away from cities or towns

boon·dog·gle /ˈbuːndɒgl; *NAmE* -dɑːgl; -dɔːgl/ *noun* (*NAmE, informal*) a piece of work that is unnecessary and that wastes time and/or money

boor /bʊə(r); bɔː(r); *NAmE* bʊr/ *noun* (*old-fashioned*) a rude unpleasant person

boor·ish /ˈbʊərɪʃ; ˈbɔːr-; *NAmE* ˈbʊr-/ *adj.* (of people and their behaviour) very unpleasant and rude

boost /buːst/ *verb, noun*

■ ***verb* 1 ~ sth** to make sth increase, or become better or more successful: *to boost exports/profits* ◇ *The movie helped boost her screen career.* ◇ *to **boost sb's confidence/morale*** ◇ *Getting that job did a lot to **boost his ego*** (= make him feel more confident). **2 ~ sth** (*NAmE, informal*, becoming *old-fashioned*) to steal sth

■ ***noun*** [usually sing.] **1** something that helps or encourages sb/sth: *a **great/tremendous/welcome boost*** ◇ *The tax cuts will give a much needed boost to the economy.* ◇ *Winning the competition was a wonderful boost for her morale.* **2** an increase in sth: *a boost in car sales* **3** an increase in power in an engine or a piece of electrical equipment **4** (*especially NAmE*) an act of pushing sb up from behind: *He gave her a boost over the fence.*

boost·er /ˈbuːstə(r)/ *noun* **1** (also ˈ**booster rocket**) a ROCKET that gives a SPACECRAFT extra power when it leaves the earth, or that makes a MISSILE go further **2** a device that gives extra power to a piece of electrical equipment **3** an extra small amount of a drug that is given to increase the effect of one given earlier, for example to protect you from a disease for longer: *a tetanus booster* **4** a thing that helps, encourages or improves sb/sth: *a **morale/confidence booster*** **5** (*especially NAmE*) a person who gives their support to sb/sth, especially in politics: *a meeting of Republican boosters*

ˈ**booster seat** *noun* a seat that you put on a car seat, or on a chair at a table, so that a small child can sit higher

boot 🔑 /buːt/ *noun, verb*

■ ***noun* 1** 🔑 a strong shoe that covers the foot and ankle and often the lower part of the leg: (*BrE*) *walking boots* ◇ (*NAmE*) *hiking boots* ◇ *a pair of black leather boots* ◇ *cowboy boots* ➲ VISUAL VOCAB page V52 ➲ see also DESERT BOOT, FOOTBALL BOOT, WELLINGTON **2** (*BrE*) (*NAmE* **trunk**) the space at the back of a car that you put bags, cases, etc. in: *I'll put the luggage in the boot.* ➲ VISUAL VOCAB page V42 ➲ see also CAR BOOT SALE **3** [usually sing.] (*informal*) a quick hard kick: *He gave the ball a tremendous boot.* **4** (*NAmE*) = DENVER BOOT

IDM **be given the ˈboot** | **get the ˈboot** (*informal*) to be told that you must leave your job or that a relationship you are having with sb is over **the boot is on the other ˈfoot** (*BrE*) (*NAmE* **the shoe is on the other ˈfoot**) used to say that a situation has changed so that sb now has power or authority over the person who used to have power or authority over them **put/stick the ˈboot in** (*BrE, informal*) **1** to kick sb very hard, especially when they are on the ground **2** to attack sb by criticizing them when they are in a difficult situation **to boot** (*old-fashioned* or *humorous*) used to add a comment to sth that you have said: *He was a vegetarian, and a fussy one to boot.* ➲ more at BIG *adj.*, FILL *v.*, LICK *v.*, TOUGH *adj.*

■ ***verb* 1** [T] **~ sth + adv./prep.** to kick sb/sth hard with your foot: *He booted the ball clear of the goal.* **2** [I, T] **~ (sth) (up)** (*computing*) to prepare a computer for use by loading its OPERATING SYSTEM; to be prepared in this way **3** [T] **be/get booted** (*NAmE, informal*) if you or your car is **booted**, a piece of equipment is fixed to the car's wheel so that you cannot drive it away, usually because the car is illegally parked ➲ see also CLAMP

PHR V ˌ**boot sb↔ˈout** (**of sth**) (*informal*) to force sb to leave a place or job SYN **throw out**

boot·boy /ˈbuːtbɔɪ/ *noun* (*BrE*) **1** (*informal*) a violent young man, especially one with very short hair and big heavy boots **2** in the past, a boy employed to clean boots and shoes

ˈ**boot camp** *noun* **1** a training camp for new members of the armed forces, where they have to work hard **2** a type of prison for young criminals where there is strict discipline

ˈ**boot-cut** *adj.* [usually before noun] **boot-cut** trousers/pants are slightly wider at the bottom of the legs where the material goes over the feet or shoes

bootee (also **bootie**) /buːˈtiː/ *noun* **1** a baby's sock, worn instead of shoes: *a pair of bootees* **2** a woman's short boot

booth /buːð; *NAmE* buːθ/ *noun* **1** a small confined place where you can do sth privately, for example make a telephone call, or vote: *a phone booth* ◇ *a polling/voting booth* ➲ see also PHOTO BOOTH, TOLLBOOTH **2** a small tent or temporary structure at a market, an exhibition or a FAIRGROUND, where you can buy things, get information or watch sth **3** a place to sit in a restaurant which consists of two long seats with a table between them

ˌ**Boot ˈHill** *noun* [U] (*US, informal, humorous*) (in the Wild West) a place where people are buried

boot·lace /ˈbuːtleɪs/ *noun* [usually pl.] a long thin piece of leather or string used to fasten boots or shoes

boot·leg /ˈbuːtleg/ *adj., verb*

■ ***adj.*** [only before noun] made and sold illegally: *a bootleg CD* (= for example, one recorded illegally at a concert) ➲ see also PIRATE ▸ **boot·leg** *noun*: *a bootleg of the concert*

■ ***verb*** (-gg-) **~ sth** to make or sell goods, especially alcohol, illegally ▸ **boot·leg·ger** *noun* **boot·leg·ging** *noun* [U]

boot·lick·er /ˈbuːtlɪkə(r)/ *noun* (*informal, disapproving*) a person who is too friendly to sb in authority and is always ready to do what they want ▸ **boot·lick·ing** /ˈbuːtlɪkɪŋ/ *noun* [U]

boot·strap /ˈbuːtstræp/ *noun*

IDM **pull/drag yourself up by your** (**own**) ˈ**bootstraps** (*informal*) to improve your situation yourself, without help from other people

booty /ˈbuːti/ (*pl.* -ies) *noun* **1** [U] valuable things that are stolen, especially by soldiers in a time of war SYN **loot** **2** [U] (*informal*) valuable things that sb wins, buys or obtains: *When we got home from our day's shopping, we laid all our booty out on the floor.* **3** [C] (*informal, especially NAmE*) the part of the body that you sit on SYN **buttocks**: *to shake your booty* (= to dance with great energy)

boo·ty·li·cious /ˌbuːtɪˈlɪʃəs/ *adj.* (*informal, especially NAmE*) sexually attractive

booze /buːz/ *noun, verb*

■ ***noun*** [U] (*informal*) alcoholic drink

■ ***verb*** [I] (*informal*) (usually used in the progressive tenses) to drink alcohol, especially in large quantities: *He's out boozing with his mates.*

ˈ**booze cruise** *noun* (*informal, humorous*) **1** (*BrE*) a short trip by FERRY from Britain to France or Belgium in order to buy alcohol or cigarettes cheaply: *to go on a booze cruise* **2** (*especially NAmE*) a social occasion when people travel on a ship or boat and enjoy themselves by drinking alcohol, eating and dancing

boozer /ˈbuːzə(r)/ *noun* (*informal*) **1** (*BrE*) a pub **2** a person who drinks a lot of alcohol

ˈ**booze-up** *noun* (*BrE, informal*) an occasion when people drink a lot of alcohol

boozy /ˈbuːzi/ *adj.* (*informal*) liking to drink a lot of alcohol; involving a lot of alcoholic drink: *one of my boozy friends* ◇ *a boozy lunch*

bop /bɒp; *NAmE* bɑːp/ *noun, verb*
- **noun 1** [C] (*BrE, informal*) a dance to pop music; a social event at which people dance to pop music **2** [U] = BEBOP
- **verb** (-pp-) **1** [I] (*BrE, informal*) to dance to pop music **2** [T] **~ sb** to hit sb lightly

bor·age /ˈbɒrɪdʒ; *NAmE* ˈbɔːrɪdʒ; ˈbɑːrɪdʒ/ *noun* [U] a Mediterranean plant with blue flowers that are shaped like stars, and leaves covered with small hairs. Borage leaves are eaten raw as a salad vegetable.

borax /ˈbɔːræks/ *noun* [U] a white mineral, usually in powder form, used in making glass and as an ANTISEPTIC (= a substance that helps to prevent infection in wounds)

bor·dello /bɔːˈdeləʊ; *NAmE* bɔːrˈdeloʊ/ *noun* (*pl.* -os) (*especially NAmE*) = BROTHEL

Synonyms

border

boundary • frontier

These are all words for a line that marks the edge of sth and separates it from other areas or things.

border the line that separates two countries or areas; the land near this line: *a national park on the border between Kenya and Tanzania*

boundary a line that marks the edges of an area of land and separates it from other areas: *The fence marked the boundary between my property and hers.*

frontier (*BrE*) the line that separates two countries or areas; the land near this line: *The river formed the frontier between the land of the Saxons and that of the Danes.*

WHICH WORD?

The point where you cross from one country to another is usually called the **border**. In British English it can also be called the **frontier**, but this is often in a context of wildness, danger and uncertainty: *The rebels control the frontier and the surrounding area.* The line on a map that shows the border of a country can be called the **boundary** but 'boundary' is not used when you cross from one country to another: *After the war the national boundaries were redrawn.* ◇ ~~*Thousands of immigrants cross the boundary every day.*~~ **Boundary** can also be a physical line between two places, for example between property belonging to two different people, marked by a fence or wall: *the boundary fence/wall between the properties*

PATTERNS
- **across/along/on/over** a/the border/boundary/frontier
- **at** the boundary/frontier
- the border/boundary/frontier **with** a place
- the **northern/southern/eastern/western** border/boundary/frontier
- a **national/common/disputed** border/boundary/frontier

bor·der 🔑 /ˈbɔːdə(r); *NAmE* ˈbɔːrd-/ *noun, verb*
- **noun 1** 🔑 the line that divides two countries or areas; the land near this line: *a national park on the border between Kenya and Tanzania* ◇ *Denmark's border with Germany* ◇ *in the US, near the Canadian border* ◇ *Nevada's northern border* ◇ *to cross the border* ◇ *to flee* ***across/over the border*** ◇ ***border guards/controls*** ◇ *a* ***border dispute/incident*** ◇ *a* ***border town/state*** ◇ (*figurative*) *It is difficult to define the border between love and friendship.* ➲ COLLOCATIONS at INTERNATIONAL **2** 🔑 a strip around the edge of sth such as a picture or a piece of cloth: *a pillowcase with a lace border* ➲ picture at EDGE **3** (in a garden) a strip of soil which is planted with flowers, along the edge of the grass ➲ VISUAL VOCAB page V16
- **verb 1 ~ sth** (of a country or an area) to share a border with another country or area: *the countries bordering the Baltic* **2 ~ sth** to form a line along or around the edge of sth: *Meadows bordered the path to the woods.* ◇ *The large garden is bordered by a stream.*

PHR V ˈ**border on sth 1** to come very close to being sth, especially a strong or unpleasant emotion or quality: *She felt an anxiety bordering on hysteria.* **2** to be next to sth: *areas bordering on the Black Sea*

ˌ**Border** ˈ**collie** *noun* a medium-sized black and white dog, often used as a SHEEPDOG

bor·der·land /ˈbɔːdəlænd; *NAmE* ˈbɔːrdər-/ *noun* **1** [C] an area of land close to a border between two countries **2** [sing.] an area between two qualities, ideas or subjects that has features of both but is not clearly one or the other: *the murky borderland between history and myth*

bor·der·line /ˈbɔːdəlaɪn; *NAmE* ˈbɔːrdər-/ *adj., noun*
- **adj.** not clearly belonging to a particular condition or group; not clearly acceptable: *In* ***borderline cases*** *teachers will take the final decision, based on the student's previous work.* ◇ *a* ***borderline pass/fail*** *in an exam*
- **noun** the division between two qualities or conditions: *This biography sometimes crosses the borderline between fact and fiction.*

bore 🔑 /bɔː(r)/ *verb, noun* ➲ see also BEAR, BORE, BORNE *V.*
- **verb 1** 🔑 [T] to make sb feel bored, especially by talking too much: **~ sb** *I'm not boring you, am I?* ◇ **~ sb with sth** *Has he been boring you with his stories about his trip?* **2** [I, T] to make a long deep hole with a tool or by digging: **~ into/through sth** *The drill is strong enough to bore through solid rock.* ◇ **~ sth** (**in/through sth**) *to bore a hole in sth* **3** [I] **~ into sb/sth** (of eyes) to stare in a way that makes sb feel uncomfortable: *His blue eyes seemed to bore into her.*
- **noun 1** [C] a person who is very boring, usually because they talk too much **2** [sing.] a situation or thing that is boring or that annoys you: *It's such a bore having to stay late this evening.* **3** [C] (also **gauge** especially in *NAmE*) the hollow inside of a tube, such as a pipe or a gun; the width of the hole: *a tube with a* ***wide/narrow bore*** ◇ *a twelve-bore shotgun* **4** [C] a strong, high wave that rushes along a river from the sea at particular times of the year **5** [C] (also **bore·hole**) a deep hole made in the ground, especially to find water or oil IDM see CRASH *V.*

bored 🔑 /bɔːd; *NAmE* bɔːrd/ *adj.* feeling tired and impatient because you have lost interest in sb/sth or because you have nothing to do: *There was a bored expression on her face.* ◇ **~ with sb/sth** | **~ with doing sth** *The children quickly* ***got bored*** *with staying indoors.*

IDM **bored** ˈ**stiff** | **bored to** ˈ**death/**ˈ**tears** | **bored out of your** ˈ**mind** extremely bored ➲ more at WITLESS

bore·dom /ˈbɔːdəm; *NAmE* ˈbɔːrdəm/ *noun* [U] the state of feeling bored; the quality of being very boring: *I started to eat too much out of sheer boredom.* ◇ *Television helps to relieve the boredom of the long winter evenings.*

bore·hole /ˈbɔːhəʊl; *NAmE* ˈbɔːrhoʊl/ *noun* = BORE (5)

bore·well /ˈbɔːwel; *NAmE* ˈbɔːrwel/ *noun* (*IndE*) a pipe that is put into a hole that has been BORED in the ground, and used with a PUMP in order to get water from under the ground

bor·ing 🔑 /ˈbɔːrɪŋ/ *adj.* not interesting; making you feel tired and impatient: *a boring man* ◇ *a boring job/book/evening* ▶ **bor·ing·ly** *adv.*: *boringly normal*

born 🔑 /bɔːn; *NAmE* bɔːrn/ *verb, adj.*
- **verb be born** (used only in the passive, without *by*) **1** 🔑

B

Synonyms

boring

dull • tedious

These words all describe a subject, activity, person or place that is not interesting or exciting.

boring not interesting; making you feel tired and impatient: *He's such a boring man! ◇ She found her job very boring.*

dull not interesting or exciting: *Life in a small town could be deadly dull.*

tedious lasting or taking too long and not interesting, so that you feel bored and impatient: *The journey soon became tedious.*

PATTERNS

- to be boring/dull/tedious **for** sb
- boring/dull/tedious **subjects/books**
- boring/dull/tedious **jobs/work/games**
- a boring/dull **place/man/woman/person**
- **deadly** boring/dull

(*abbr.* **b.**) to come out of your mother's body at the beginning of your life: *I was born in 1976. ◇ She was born with a weak heart.* ◇ **~ into sth** *She was born into a very musical family.* ◇ **~ of/to sb** *He was born of/to German parents.* ◇ **+ adj.** *Her brother was* **born blind** (= was blind when he was born). ◇ **+ noun** *John Wayne was born Marion Michael Morrison* (= that was his name at birth). ➲ COLLOCATIONS at AGE **2** 0━ (of an idea, an organization, a feeling, etc.) to start to exist: *the city where the protest movement was born* ◇ **~ (out) of sth** *She acted with a courage born (out) of desperation.* **3 -born** (in compounds) born in the order, way, place, etc. mentioned: *firstborn ◇ nobly-born ◇ French-born* ➲ see also NEWBORN

IDM **be 'born to be/do sth** to have sth as your DESTINY (= what is certain to happen to you) from birth: *He was born to be a great composer.* **ˌborn and 'bred** born and having grown up in a particular place with a particular background and education: *He was born and bred in Boston. ◇ I'm a Londoner, born and bred.* **born with a silver 'spoon in your mouth** (*saying*) having rich parents **in all my born 'days** (*old-fashioned, informal*) used when you are very surprised at sth you have never heard or seen before: *I've never heard such nonsense in all my born days.* **not be born 'yesterday** (*informal*) used to say that you are not stupid enough to believe what sb is telling you: *Oh yeah? I wasn't born yesterday, you know.* **there's one born every 'minute** (*saying*) used to say that sb is very stupid ➲ more at KNOW *v.*, MANNER, WAY *n.*

■ ***adj.*** [only before noun] having a natural ability or skill for a particular activity or job: *a* ***born athlete/writer/leader*** ◇ *a* ***born loser*** (= a person who always loses or is unsuccessful)

ˌborn-a'gain *adj.* [usually before noun] having come to have a strong belief in a particular religion (especially EVANGELICAL Christianity) or idea, and wanting other people to have the same belief: *a born-again Christian ◇ a born-again vegetarian*

borne /bɔːn; *NAmE* bɔːrn/ **1** *past part.* of BEAR **2 -borne** (in adjectives) carried by: *waterborne diseases*

boron /ˈbɔːrɒn; *NAmE* -rɑːn/ *noun* [U] (*symb.* **B**) a chemical element. Boron is a solid substance used in making steel ALLOYS and parts for nuclear REACTORS.

bor·ough /ˈbʌrə; *NAmE* ˈbɜːroʊ/ *noun* a town or part of a city that has its own local government: *the London borough of Westminster ◇ The Bronx is one of the five boroughs of New York. ◇ a borough council*

bor·row 0━ /ˈbɒrəʊ; *NAmE* ˈbɑːroʊ; ˈbɔːr-/ *verb* **1** 0━ [T] to take and use sth that belongs to sb else, and return it to them at a later time: **~ sth** *Can I borrow your umbrella?* ◇ **~ sth from sb/sth** *Members can borrow up to ten books from the library at any one time.* ◇ (*BrE, informal*) **~ sth off sb** *I borrowed the DVD off my brother.* ➲ compare LEND **2** 0━ [T, I] to take money from a person or bank and agree to pay it back to them at a later time: **~ sth (from sb/sth)** *She borrowed £2 000 from her parents.* ◇ **~ (from sb/sth)** *I don't like to borrow from friends.* ◇ **~ sth off sb** (*informal*) *I had to borrow the money off a friend.* ➲ compare LEND **3** [I, T] to take words, ideas, etc. from another language, person, etc. and use them, as your own: **~ (from sb/sth)** *The author borrows heavily from Henry James.* ◇ **~ sth (from sb/sth)** *Some musical terms are borrowed from Italian.*

IDM **be (living) on borrowed 'time** **1** to still be alive after the time when you were expected to die **2** to be doing sth that other people are likely to soon stop you from doing

Which Word?

borrow / lend

- These two words are often confused. You **borrow** something from someone else, while they **lend** it to you: *Can I borrow your pen? ◇ Can I borrow a pen from you? ◇ Here, I'll lend you my pen.*

bor·row·er /ˈbɒrəʊə(r); *NAmE* ˈbɑːroʊər; ˈbɔːr-/ *noun* a person or an organization that borrows money, especially from a bank ➲ compare LENDER

bor·row·ing /ˈbɒrəʊɪŋ; *NAmE* ˈbɑːroʊɪŋ; ˈbɔːr-/ *noun* **1** [C, U] the money that a company, an organization or a person borrows; the act of borrowing money: *an attempt to reduce bank borrowings ◇ High interest rates help to keep borrowing down.* ➲ COLLOCATIONS at ECONOMY **2** [C] a word, a phrase or an idea that sb has taken from another person's work or from another language and used in their own

borscht /bɔːʃt; *NAmE* bɔːrʃt/ (*BrE* also **borsch** /bɔːʃ; *NAmE* bɔːrʃ/) *noun* [U] a Russian or Polish soup made from BEETROOT (= a dark red root vegetable)

bor·stal /ˈbɔːstl; *NAmE* ˈbɔːrstl/ *noun* [C, U] (in Britain in the past) a type of prison for young criminals ➲ see also YOUTH CUSTODY

bor·zoi /ˈbɔːzɔɪ; *NAmE* ˈbɔːr-/ *noun* a large Russian dog with soft white hair

bos·ber·aad /ˈbɒsbərɑːt; ˈbɔːs-; ˈbɑːs-/ *noun* (*SAfrE*) a meeting of business leaders, politicians, etc. at a place that is a long way from a town, in order to discuss important matters

bosom /ˈbʊzəm/ *noun* **1** [C] a woman's chest or breasts: *her ample bosom ◇ She pressed him to her bosom.* **2** [C] the part of a piece of clothing that covers a woman's bosom: *a rose pinned to her bosom* **3 the ~ of sth** [sing.] a situation in which you are with people who love and protect you: *to live in the bosom of your family*

ˌbosom 'friend (*NAmE* also **ˌbosom 'buddy**) *noun* a very close friend

bos·omy /ˈbʊzəmi/ *adj.* (*old-fashioned, BrE, informal*) (of a woman) having large breasts

boss 0━ /bɒs; *NAmE* bɔːs; bɑːs/ *noun, verb, adj.*

■ ***noun*** **1** 0━ a person who is in charge of other people at work and tells them what to do: *I'll ask my boss if I can have the day off. ◇ I like being* **my own boss** (= working for myself and making my own decisions). ◇ *Who's the boss* (= who's in control) *in this house?* **2** 0━ (*informal*) a person who is in charge of a large organization: *the new boss at IBM ◇ Hospital bosses protested at the decision.* IDM see SHOW *v.*

■ ***verb*** **~ sb (about/around)** to tell sb what to do in an aggressive and/or annoying way: *I'm sick of you bossing me around!*

■ ***adj.*** (*slang*) very good

bossa nova /ˌbɒsə ˈnəʊvə; *NAmE* ˌbɑːsə ˈnoʊvə; ˌbɔːsə ˈnoʊvə/ *noun* [U, C] a style of Brazilian popular music, popular in the 1960s

bossy /ˈbɒsi; *NAmE* ˈbɔːsi; ˈbɑːsi/ *adj.* (*disapproving*) (boss·ier, bossi·est) always telling people what to do ▸ **boss·ily** *adv.* **bossi·ness** *noun* [U]

bossy·boots /ˈbɒsibuːts; *NAmE* ˈbɔːs-/ *noun* (*pl.* bossy·boots) (*informal, disapproving*) a person who always tells people what they should do

ˌBoston baked ˈbeans (also **baked ˈbeans**) *noun* [pl.] (*NAmE*) small white beans baked with pork and brown sugar or MOLASSES (= a dark, sweet, thick liquid obtained from sugar)

bo·sun (also **bo'sun, boat·swain**) /ˈbəʊsn; *NAmE* ˈboʊ-/ *noun* an officer on a ship whose job is to take care of the equipment and the people who work on the ship

bot /bɒt; *NAmE* bɑːt/ *noun* (*computing*) a computer program that performs a particular task again and again many times

bo·tan·ic·al /bəˈtænɪkl/ *adj.* connected with the science of botany

boˌtanical ˈgarden (also **boˌtanic ˈgarden**) *noun* [usually pl.] a park where plants, trees and flowers are grown for scientific study

bot·an·ist /ˈbɒtənɪst; *NAmE* ˈbɑːt-/ *noun* a scientist who studies botany

bot·any /ˈbɒtəni; *NAmE* ˈbɑːt-/ *noun* [U] the scientific study of plants and their structure ➲ compare BIOLOGY, ZOOLOGY

botch /bɒtʃ; *NAmE* bɑːtʃ/ *verb, noun*

▪ ***verb*** **~ sth (up)** (*informal*) to spoil sth by doing it badly: *He completely botched up the interview.* ◇ *The work they did on the house was a botched job.*

▪ ***noun*** (also **ˈbotch-up**) (*BrE, informal*) a piece of work or a job that has been done badly: *I've made a real botch of the decorating.*

both 0-ᵯ /bəʊθ; *NAmE* boʊθ/ *det., pron.*
1 0-ᵯ used with plural nouns to mean 'the two' or 'the one as well as the other': *Both women were French.* ◇ *Both the women were French.* ◇ *Both of the women were French.* ◇ *I talked to the women. Both of them were French/They were both French.* ◇ *I liked them both.* ◇ *We were both tired.* ◇ *Both of us were tired.* ◇ *We have both seen the movie.* ◇ *I have two sisters. Both of them live in London/They both live in London.* ◇ *Both (my) sisters live in London.* **2** 0-ᵯ **both... and...** not only... but also...: *Both his mother and his father will be there.* ◇ *For this job you will need a good knowledge of both Italian and Spanish.* ➲ LANGUAGE BANK at SIMILARLY

bother 0-ᵯ /ˈbɒðə(r); *NAmE* ˈbɑːð-/ *verb, noun, exclamation*

▪ ***verb*** **1** 0-ᵯ [I, T] (often used in negative sentences and questions) to spend time and/or energy doing sth: *'Shall I wait?' 'No, don't bother'.* ◇ *I don't know why I bother! Nobody ever listens!* ◇ **~ with/about sth** *It's not worth bothering with (=* using) *an umbrella—the car's just outside.* ◇ *I don't know why you bother with that crowd* (= why you spend time with them). ◇ **~ to do sth** *He didn't even bother to let me know he was coming.* ◇ **~ doing sth** *Why bother asking if you're not really interested?* **2** 0-ᵯ [T] to annoy, worry or upset sb; to cause sb trouble or pain: **~ sb** *The thing that bothers me is...* ◇ *That sprained ankle is still bothering her* (= hurting). ◇ *'I'm sorry he was so rude to you.' 'It doesn't bother me.'* ◇ **~ sb with sth** *I don't want to bother her with my problems at the moment.* ◇ **be bothered about sth** *You don't sound too bothered about it.* ◇ **~ sb that...** *Does it bother you that she earns more than you?* ◇ **it bothers sb to do sth** *It bothers me to think of her alone in that big house.* **3** 0-ᵯ [T] to interrupt sb; to talk to sb when they do not want to talk to you: **~ sb** *Stop bothering me when I'm working.* ◇ *Let me know if he bothers you again.* ◇ ***Sorry to bother you,*** *but there's a call for you on line two.*

IDM **be bothered (about sb/sth)** 0-ᵯ (*informal, especially BrE*) to think that sb/sth is important: *I'm not bothered about what he thinks.* ◇ *'Where shall we eat?' 'I'm not bothered.'* (= I don't mind where we go). **can't be bothered (to do sth)** 0-ᵯ used to say that you do not want to spend time and/or energy doing sth: *I should really do some work this weekend but I can't be bothered.* ◇ *All this has happened because you couldn't be bothered to give me the message.* **not bother yourself/your head with/about sth** (*especially BrE*) to not spend time/effort on sth, because it is not important or you are not interested in it ➲ more at HOT *adj.*

▪ ***noun*** **1** [U] trouble or difficulty: *You seem to have got yourself into a* ***spot of bother.*** ◇ *I don't want to* ***put you to any bother*** (= cause you any trouble). ◇ ***Don't go to the bother*** *of tidying up on my account* (= don't make the effort to do it). ◇ *'Thanks for your help!' 'It was no bother.'* ◇ *Call them and save yourself the bother of going round.* **2 a bother** [sing.] (*BrE*) an annoying situation, thing or person **SYN** **nuisance**: *I hope I haven't been a bother.*

▪ ***exclamation*** (*BrE*) used to express the fact that you are annoyed about sth/sb: *Bother! I've left my wallet at home.* ◇ *Oh, bother him! He's never around when you need him.*

both·er·ation /ˌbɒðəˈreɪʃn; *NAmE* ˈbɑːð-/ *exclamation* (*old-fashioned*) a word that people use to show that they are annoyed

both·er·some /ˈbɒðəsəm; *NAmE* ˈbɑːðərsəm/ *adj.* (*old-fashioned*) causing trouble or difficulty **SYN** **annoying**

bothy /ˈbɒθi; *NAmE* ˈbɔːθi/ *noun* (*pl.* -ies) a small building in Scotland for farm workers to live in or for people to shelter in

bot·net /ˈbɒtnet; *NAmE* ˈbɑːt-/ *noun* (*computing*) a group of computers that are controlled by MALWARE (= software such as a virus that the users do not know about or want)

Bo·tox™ /ˈbəʊtɒks; *NAmE* ˈboʊtɑːks/ *noun* [U] a substance that makes muscles relax. It is sometimes INJECTED into the skin around sb's eyes to remove lines and make the skin look younger. ▸ **Bo·tox** *verb* **~ sb/sth** [usually passive]: *Do you think she's been Botoxed?*

bot·tle 0-ᵯ /ˈbɒtl; *NAmE* ˈbɑːtl/ *noun, verb*

▪ ***noun*** **1** 0-ᵯ [C] a glass or plastic container, usually round with straight sides and a narrow neck, used especially for storing liquids: *a* ***wine/beer/milk bottle*** ◇ *Put the top back on the bottle.* ➲ VISUAL VOCAB page V29 **2** 0-ᵯ [C] (also **bottle·ful** /-fʊl/) the amount contained in a bottle: *He drank a whole bottle of wine.* **3 the bottle** [sing.] (*informal*) alcoholic drink: *After his wife died, he really* ***hit the bottle*** (= started drinking heavily). **4** [C, usually sing.] a bottle used to give milk to a baby; the milk from such a bottle (used instead of mother's milk): *It's time for her bottle.* **5** [U] (*BrE, informal*) courage or confidence, for example to do sth that is dangerous or unpleasant **SYN** **nerve**: *It took a lot of bottle to do that.*

▪ ***verb*** **1 ~ sth** to put a liquid into a bottle: *The wines are bottled after three years.* **2 ~ sth** to put fruit or vegetables into glass containers in order to preserve them ▸ **bot·tled** *adj.*: ***bottled beer/water/pickles*** ◇ ***bottled gas*** (= sold in metal containers for use in heating and cooking)

IDM **ˈbottle it** (*BrE, informal*) to not do sth, or not finish sth, because you are frightened

PHR V **ˌbottle ˈout (of sth/doing sth)** (*BrE, informal*) to not do sth that you had intended to do because you are too frightened **ˌbottle sth↔ˈup** to not allow other people to see that you are unhappy, angry, etc, especially when this happens over a long period of time: *Try not to bottle up your emotions.*

ˈbottle bank *noun* (*BrE*) a large container in a public place where people can leave their empty bottles so that the glass can be used again (=RECYCLED); a public place with several of these containers ➲ VISUAL VOCAB page V7

ˌbottle ˈblonde (also **ˌbottle ˈblond**) *adj.* (*disapproving*) (of hair) artificially coloured blonde ▸ **ˌbottle ˈblonde** *noun*

ˈbottle-feed *verb* [T, I] **~ (sb)** to feed a baby with artificial milk from a bottle ➲ compare BREASTFEED

ˌbottle-ˈgreen *adj.* (*especially BrE*) dark green in colour: *a bottle-green coat* ▸ **ˌbottle ˈgreen** *noun* [U]

bottle·neck /ˈbɒtlnek; *NAmE* ˈbɑːtl-/ *noun* **1** a narrow or busy section of road where the traffic often gets slower and stops **2** anything that delays development or progress, particularly in business or industry **SYN** **logjam**

B

'**bottle opener** *noun* a small tool for opening bottles with metal tops, for example beer bottles ➲ VISUAL VOCAB page V23

'**bottle party** *noun* (*BrE*) a party to which the people who have been invited are asked to bring a bottle, usually of wine

'**bottle store** (also '**bottle shop**) *noun* (*AustralE, NZE, SAfrE*) a shop/store that sells a variety of alcoholic drinks in bottles, cans, etc. to take away ➲ compare OFF-LICENCE

Synonyms

bottom

base • foundation • foot

These are all words for the lowest part of sth.

bottom [usually sing.] the lowest part of sth: *Footnotes are given at the bottom of each page.* ◊ *I waited for them at the bottom of the hill.*

base [usually sing.] the lowest part of sth, especially the part or surface on which it rests or stands: *The lamp has a heavy base.*

foundation [usually pl.] a layer of bricks, concrete, etc. that forms the solid underground base of a building: *to lay the foundations of the new school*

foot [sing.] the lowest part of sth: *At the foot of the stairs she turned to face him.*

BOTTOM OR FOOT?

Foot is used to talk about a limited number of things: it is used most often with *tree, hill/mountain, steps/stairs* and *page*. **Bottom** can be used to talk about a much wider range of things, including those mentioned above for **foot**. **Foot** is generally used in more literary contexts.

PATTERNS

- **at/near/towards** the bottom/base/foot of sth
- **on** the bottom/base of sth
- (a) **firm/solid/strong** base/foundation(s)

bot·tom 🔑 /ˈbɒtəm; *NAmE* ˈbɑːtəm/ *noun, adj., verb*

■ ***noun***

▸ LOWEST PART **1** 🔑 [C, usually sing.] **~ (of sth)** the lowest part of sth: *Footnotes are given at the bottom of each page.* ◊ *I waited for them at the bottom of the hill.* ◊ *The book I want is right at the bottom* (= of the pile). OPP **top 2** 🔑 [C, usually sing.] **~ (of sth)** the part of sth that faces downwards and is not usually seen: *The manufacturer's name is on the bottom of the plate.*

▸ OF CONTAINER **3** 🔑 [C, usually sing.] **~ (of sth)** the lowest surface on the inside of a container: *I found some coins at the bottom of my bag.*

▸ OF RIVER/POOL **4** 🔑 [sing.] the ground below the water in a lake, river, swimming pool, etc: *He dived in and hit his head on the bottom.*

▸ END OF STH **5** 🔑 **the ~ (of sth)** [sing.] (*especially BrE*) the part of sth that is furthest from you, your house, etc: *I went to the school at the bottom of our street.* ◊ *There was a stream at the bottom of the garden.*

▸ LOWEST POSITION **6** 🔑 [sing.] **~ (of sth)** the lowest position in a class, on a list, etc; a person, team, etc. that is in this position: *a battle between the teams at the bottom of the league* ◊ *You have to be prepared to start at the bottom and work your way up.* ◊ *I was always bottom of the class in math.* OPP **top**

▸ PART OF BODY **7** 🔑 [C] (*especially BrE*) the part of the body that you sit on SYN **backside, behind**

▸ CLOTHING **8** [C, usually pl.] the lower part of a set of clothes that consists of two pieces: *a bikini bottom* ◊ *a pair of pyjama/tracksuit bottoms* ➲ compare TOP

▸ OF SHIP **9** [C] the lower part of a ship that is below the surface of the water SYN **hull**

▸ **-BOTTOMED 10** (in adjectives) having the type of bottom mentioned: *a flat-bottomed boat*

IDM **at bottom** used to say what sb/sth is really like: *Their offer to help was at bottom self-centred.* **be/lie at the bottom of sth** to be the original cause of sth, especially sth unpleasant **the bottom drops/falls out (of sth)** people stop buying or using the products of a particular industry: *The bottom has fallen out of the travel market.* **bottoms 'up!** (*informal*) used to express good wishes when drinking alcohol, or to tell sb to finish their drink **get to the bottom of sth** to find out the real cause of sth, especially sth unpleasant ➲ more at HEAP *n.*, HEART, PILE *n.*, SCRAPE *v.*, TOP *n.*, TOUCH *v.*

■ ***adj.*** 🔑 [only before noun] in the lowest, last or furthest place or position: *the bottom line (on a page)* ◊ *your bottom lip* ◊ *the bottom step (of a flight of stairs)* ◊ *on the bottom shelf* ◊ *Put your clothes in the bottom drawer.* ◊ *Their house is at the bottom end of Bury Road* (= the end furthest from where you enter the road). ◊ *in the bottom right-hand corner of the page* ◊ *the bottom end of the price range* ◊ *to go up a hill in bottom gear* ◊ *We* ***came bottom*** (= got the worst result) *with 12 points.* IDM see BET *v.* ➲ see also ROCK-BOTTOM

■ ***verb***

PHR V ˌ**bottom 'out** (of prices, a bad situation, etc.) to stop getting worse: *The recession is finally beginning to show signs of bottoming out.*

ˌ**bottom 'drawer** *noun* (*BrE*) items for the house collected by a woman, especially in the past, in preparation for her marriage (and often kept in a drawer) ➲ compare HOPE CHEST

'**bottom feeder** *noun* **1** (*NAmE, informal*) a person who earns money by taking advantage of bad things that happen to other people or by using things that other people throw away **2** a fish that feeds at the bottom of a river, lake or the sea

bot·tom·less /ˈbɒtəmləs; *NAmE* ˈbɑːt-/ *adj.* (*formal*) very deep; seeming to have no bottom or limit

IDM **a bottomless 'pit (of sth)** a thing or situation which seems to have no limits or seems never to end: *There isn't a bottomless pit of money for public spending.* ◊ *the bottomless pit of his sorrow*

ˌ**bottom 'line** *noun* [sing.] **1 the bottom line** the most important thing that you have to consider or accept; the essential point in a discussion, etc: *The bottom line is that we have to make a decision today.* **2** (*business*) the amount of money that is a profit or a loss after everything has been calculated: *The bottom line for 2008 was a pre-tax profit of £85 million.* **3** the lowest price that sb will accept: *Two thousand—and that's my bottom line!*

ˌ**bottom-'up** *adj.* (of a plan, project, etc.) starting with details and then later moving on to more general principles: *a bottom-up approach to tackling the problem* ➲ compare TOP-DOWN

botu·lin /ˈbɒtjulɪn; *NAmE* ˈbɑːtʃə-/ *noun* [U] the poisonous substance in the bacteria that cause BOTULISM

botu·lism /ˈbɒtjulɪzəm; *NAmE* ˈbɑːtʃə-/ *noun* [U] a serious illness caused by bacteria in badly preserved food

bou·doir /ˈbuːdwɑː(r)/ *noun* (*old-fashioned*) a woman's small private room or bedroom

bouf·fant /ˈbuːfɒ̃; *NAmE* buːˈfɑːnt/ *adj.* (of a person's hair) in a style that raises it up and back from the head in a high round shape

bou·gain·vil·lea (also **bou·gain·vil·laea**) /ˌbuːgənˈvɪliə/ *noun* a tropical climbing plant with red, purple, white or pink flowers

bough /baʊ/ *noun* (*formal* or *literary*) a large branch of a tree

bought *past tense, past part.* of BUY

bouil·la·baisse /ˈbuːjəbeɪs/ *noun* [U] (from *French*) a spicy fish soup from the south of France

bouil·lon /ˈbuːjɒn; -jɒ̃; *NAmE* -jɑːn/ *noun* [U, C] a liquid made by boiling meat or vegetables in water, used for making clear soups or sauces

B

boul·der /ˈbəʊldə(r); *NAmE* ˈboʊl-/ *noun* a very large rock which has been shaped by water or the weather ➲ VISUAL VOCAB page V4

boul·der·ing /ˈbəʊldərɪŋ; *NAmE* ˈboʊl-/ *noun* [U] the sport or activity of climbing on large rocks

boule (also **boules**) /buːl/ *noun* [U] a French game in which players take turns to roll metal balls as near as possible to a small ball

boule·vard /ˈbuːləvɑːd; *NAmE* ˈbʊləvɑːrd/ *noun* **1** (*BrE*) a wide city street, often with trees on either side **2** (*abbr.* Blvd.) (*NAmE*) a wide main road (often used in the name of streets): *Sunset Boulevard*

bounce /baʊns/ *verb, noun*

■ ***verb***

▸ MOVE OFF SURFACE **1** [I, T] if sth **bounces** or you **bounce** it, it moves quickly away from a surface it has just hit or you make it do this: *The ball bounced twice before he could reach it.* ◇ **~ off sth** *Short sound waves bounce off even small objects.* ◇ *The light bounced off the river and dazzled her.* ◇ **~ sth (against/on/off sth)** *She bounced the ball against the wall.*

▸ MOVE UP AND DOWN **2** [I] **~ (up and down) (on sth)** (of a person) to jump up and down on sth: *She bounced up and down excitedly on the bed.* **3** [T] **~ sb (up and down) (on sth)** to move a child up and down while he or she is sitting on your knee in order to entertain him or her **4** [I, T] **~ (sth) (up and down)** to move up and down; to move sth up and down: *Her hair bounced as she walked.* **5** [I] **+ adv./prep.** to move up and down in a particular direction: *The bus bounced down the hill.*

▸ MOVE WITH ENERGY **6** [I] **+ adv./prep.** (of a person) to move somewhere in a lively and cheerful way: *He bounced across the room to greet them.*

▸ CHEQUE **7** [I, T] **~ (sth)** (*informal*) if a cheque **bounces**, or a bank **bounces** it, the bank refuses to accept it because there is not enough money in the account

▸ IDEAS **8** [T] **~ ideas (off sb)/(around)** to tell sb your ideas in order to find out what they think about them: *He bounced ideas off colleagues everywhere he went.*

▸ COMPUTING **9** [I, T] **~ (sth) (back)** if an email **bounces** or the system **bounces** it, it returns to the person who sent it because the system cannot deliver it

▸ MAKE SB LEAVE **10** [T] **~ sb (from sth)** (*informal, especially NAmE*) to force sb to leave a job, team, place, etc: *He was soon bounced from the post.*

IDM **be ˈbouncing off the walls** (*informal*) to be so full of energy or so excited that you cannot keep still

PHR V ˌ**bounce ˈback** to become healthy, successful or confident again after being ill/sick or having difficulties SYN **recover**: *He's had a lot of problems, but he always seems to bounce back pretty quickly.* ˌ**bounce ˈback** | ˌ**bounce sth**↔ ˈ**back** (*computing*) if an email **bounces back**, or the system **bounces** it **back**, it returns to the person who sent it because the system cannot deliver it ˌ**bounce ˈback (from sth)** (*business*) (of prices, shares, etc.) to return to their previous high level or value after a period of difficulty: *The airline's shares have bounced back from two days of heavy losses.* ˌ**bounce sb ˈinto sth** (*BrE*) to make sb do sth without giving them enough time to think about it

■ ***noun***

▸ MOVEMENT **1** [C] the action of bouncing: *one bounce of the ball* ◇ (*NAmE*) *a bounce* (= increase) *in popularity* **2** [U] the ability to bounce or to make sth bounce: *There's not much bounce left in these balls.* ◇ *Players complained about the uneven bounce of the tennis court.*

▸ ENERGY **3** [U, C] the energy that a person has: *All her old bounce was back.* ◇ *There was a bounce to his step.*

▸ OF HAIR **4** [U] the quality in a person's hair that shows that it is in good condition and means that it does not lie flat: *thin fine hair, lacking in bounce*

IDM **on the ˈbounce** (*BrE, informal*) one after the other, without anything else coming between: *We've won six matches on the bounce.*

bounce·back·abil·ity /ˌbaʊnsbækəˈbɪləti/ *noun* (*BrE*) [U] (*informal*) (especially in sport) the ability to be successful again after playing or performing badly for a time: *The team have shown great bouncebackability.* ◇ *This will be a test of their famous bouncebackability.*

boun·cer /ˈbaʊnsə(r)/ *noun* **1** a person employed to stand at the entrance to a club, pub, etc. to stop people who are not wanted from going in, and to throw out people who are causing trouble inside **2** (in CRICKET) a ball thrown very fast that rises high after it hits the ground **3** (also **inˌflatable ˈbouncer**) (both *NAmE*) (*BrE* ˌ**bouncy ˈcastle**) a plastic castle or other shape which is filled with air and which children can jump and play on

boun·cing /ˈbaʊnsɪŋ/ *adj.* **~ (with sth)** healthy and full of energy: *a bouncing baby boy*

bouncy /ˈbaʊnsi/ *adj.* (**boun·cier, boun·ci·est**) **1** that bounces well or that has the ability to make sth bounce: *a very bouncy ball* ◇ *his bouncy blond curls* **2** lively and full of energy

ˌ**bouncy ˈcastle** (*BrE*) (*NAmE* **bouncer, inˌflatable ˈbouncer**) *noun* a plastic castle or other shape which is filled with air and which children can jump and play on

bound 0‑ /baʊnd/ *adj., verb, noun* ➲ see also BIND *v.*

■ ***adj.*** [not before noun] **1** 0‑ **~ to do/be sth** certain or likely to happen, or to do or be sth: *There are bound to be changes when the new system is introduced.* ◇ *It's bound to be sunny again tomorrow.* ◇ *You've done so much work—you're bound to pass the exam.* ◇ *It was bound to happen sooner or later* (= we should have expected it). ◇ *You're bound to be nervous the first time* (= it's easy to understand). ➲ SYNONYMS at CERTAIN **2** forced to do sth by law, duty or a particular situation: **~ by sth** *We are not bound by the decision.* ◇ *You are bound by the contract to pay before the end of the month.* ◇ **~ (by sth) to do sth** (*BrE, formal*) *I am* **bound to say** *I disagree with you on this point.* **3** (in compounds) prevented from going somewhere or from working normally by the conditions mentioned: *Strike-bound travellers face long delays.* ◇ *fogbound airports* **4** (also in compounds) travelling, or ready to travel, in a particular direction or to a particular place: *homeward bound* (= going home) ◇ *Paris-bound* ◇ ***northbound/southbound/eastbound/westbound*** ◇ **~ for...** *a plane bound for Dublin*

IDM **be bound ˈup in sth** very busy with sth; very interested or involved in sth: *He's too bound up in his work to have much time for his children.* **bound and deˈtermined** (*NAmE*) very determined to do sth **be bound toˈgether by/in sth** to be closely connected: *communities bound together by customs and traditions* **bound ˈup with sth** closely connected with sth: *From that moment my life became inextricably bound up with hers.* ˈ**I'll be bound** (*old-fashioned, BrE, informal*) I feel sure ➲ more at HONOUR *n.*

■ ***verb*** **1** [I] **+ adv./prep.** to run with long steps, especially in an enthusiastic way: *The dogs bounded ahead.* **2** [T, usually passive] **~ sth** (*formal*) to form the edge or limit of an area: *The field was bounded on the left by a wood.*

■ ***noun*** (*formal*) a high or long jump ➲ see also BOUNDS IDM see LEAP *n.*

bound·ary /ˈbaʊndri/ *noun* (*pl.* -ies) **1** a real or imagined line that marks the limits or edges of sth and separates it from other things or places; a dividing line: *national boundaries* ◇ (*BrE*) *county boundaries* ◇ ***boundary changes/disputes*** ◇ *The fence marks the boundary between my property and hers.* ◇ *Scientists continue to* ***push back the boundaries*** *of human knowledge.* ◇ *the boundary between acceptable and unacceptable behaviour* ➲ SYNONYMS at BORDER **2** (in CRICKET) a hit of the ball that crosses the boundary of the playing area and scores extra points

bound·en /ˈbaʊndən/ *adj.*

IDM **a/your bounden ˈduty** (*old-fashioned, formal*) something that you feel you must do; a responsibility which cannot be ignored

bound·er /ˈbaʊndə(r)/ *noun* (*old-fashioned, BrE, informal*) a man who behaves badly and cannot be trusted

bound·less /ˈbaʊndləs/ *adj.* without limits; seeming to have no end SYN **infinite**

B

bounds /baʊndz/ *noun* [pl.] the accepted or furthest limits of sth: ***beyond/outside/within the bounds of*** *decency* ◇ *Public spending must be kept within reasonable bounds.* ◇ *It was not* ***beyond the bounds of possibility*** *that they would meet again one day.* ◇ *His enthusiasm* ***knew no bounds*** (= was very great).
IDM **out of ˈbounds 1** (in some sports) outside the area of play which is allowed: *His shot went out of bounds.* **2** (*NAmE*) not reasonable or acceptable: *His demands were out of bounds.* **out of ˈbounds (to/for sb)** (*especially BrE*) if a place is **out of bounds**, people are not allowed to go there ➲ see also OFF-LIMITS ➲ more at LEAP *n.*

boun·teous /ˈbaʊntiəs/ *adj.* (*formal* or *literary*) giving very generously

boun·ti·ful /ˈbaʊntɪfl/ *adj.* (*formal* or *literary*) **1** in large quantities; large: *a bountiful supply of food* **2** giving generously SYN **generous**: *belief in a bountiful god*

bounty /ˈbaʊnti/ *noun* (*pl.* -ies) **1** [U, C] (*literary*) generous actions; sth provided in large quantities **2** [C] money given as a reward: *a* ***bounty hunter*** (= sb who catches criminals or kills people for a reward)

bou·quet /buˈkeɪ/ *noun* **1** [C] a bunch of flowers arranged in an attractive way so that it can be carried in a ceremony or presented as a gift: *The little girl presented the princess with a large* ***bouquet of flowers***. **2** [C, U] the pleasant smell of a type of food or drink, especially of wine

bou·quet garni /ˌbuːkeɪ ɡɑːˈniː; *NAmE* ɡɑːrˈniː; *NAmE* also boʊˌkeɪ/ *noun* (*pl.* **bou·quets gar·nis** /ˌbuːkeɪ ɡɑːˈniː; *NAmE* ɡɑːrˈniː; *NAmE* also boʊˌkeɪ/) (from *French*) a bunch of different HERBS in a small bag, used in cooking to give extra flavour to food

bour·bon /ˈbɜːbən; *NAmE* ˈbɜːrbən/ *noun* **1** [U, C] a type of American WHISKY made with CORN (MAIZE) and RYE **2** [C] a glass of bourbon

bour·geois /ˈbʊəʒwɑː; ˌbʊəˈʒwɑː; *NAmE* ˌbʊrˈʒ-; ˈbʊrʒ-/ *adj.* **1** belonging to the middle class: *a traditional bourgeois family* ➲ see also PETIT BOURGEOIS **2** (*disapproving*) interested mainly in possessions and social status and supporting traditional values: ***bourgeois attitudes/tastes*** ◇ *They've become very bourgeois since they got married.* **3** (*politics*) supporting the interests of CAPITALISM: *bourgeois ideology* ► **bour·geois** *noun* (*pl.* **bour·geois**)

bour·geoisie /ˌbʊəʒwɑːˈziː; *NAmE* ˌbʊrʒ-/ *noun* **the bourgeoisie** [sing.+ sing./pl. v.] **1** the middle classes in society: *the rise of the bourgeoisie in the nineteenth century* **2** (*politics*) the CAPITALIST class: *the proletariat and the bourgeoisie*

Bourke /bɜːk; *NAmE* bɜːrk/ *noun*
IDM **back of Bourke** (*AustralE*) (in) the country, a long way from the coast and towns; in the OUTBACK ORIGIN From the name of the town in New South Wales.

bourse /bʊəs; *NAmE* bʊrs/ *noun* (from *French*) a STOCK EXCHANGE, especially the one in Paris

bout /baʊt/ *noun* **1** a short period of great activity; a short period during which there is a lot of a particular thing, usually sth unpleasant: *a drinking bout* ◇ **~ of sth/of doing sth** *the latest bout of inflation* **2 ~ (of sth)** an attack or period of illness: *a severe bout of flu/coughing* ◇ *He suffered occasional bouts of depression.* ◇ (*NAmE*) *a bout with the flu* **3** a BOXING or WRESTLING match

bou·tique /buːˈtiːk/ *noun, adj.*
■ ***noun*** a small shop/store that sells fashionable clothes or expensive gifts
■ ***adj.*** [only before noun] (of a business) small and offering products or services of a high quality to a small number of customers: *a boutique hotel that offers an escape from the outside world* ◇ *a boutique investment bank*

bou·ton·nière /ˌbuːtɒnˈjeə(r); *NAmE* ˌbuːtnˈɪr; -tənˈjer/ (*NAmE*, from *French*) (*BrE* **but·ton·hole**) *noun* a flower that is worn in the BUTTONHOLE of a coat or jacket

bou·zou·ki /bʊˈzuːki/ *noun* a Greek musical instrument with strings that are played with the fingers

bo·vine /ˈbəʊvaɪn; *NAmE* ˈboʊ-/ *adj.* [usually before noun] **1** (*technical*) connected with cows: *bovine diseases* **2** (*disapproving*) (of a person) stupid and slow

Bov·ril™ /ˈbɒvrɪl; *NAmE* ˈbɑːv-/ *noun* **1** [U] a dark substance made from beef, used in cooking and for making drinks **2** [U, C] a hot drink made by mixing Bovril with water

bow

bow of a ship — take a bow

bow¹ /baʊ/ *verb, noun* ➲ see also BOW²
■ ***verb* 1** [I] to move your head or the top half of your body forwards and downwards as a sign of respect or to say hello or goodbye: **~ (to/before sb/sth)** *He bowed low to the assembled crowd.* ◇ **~ down (to/before sb/sth)** *The people all bowed down before the Emperor.* **2** [T] **~ your head** to move your head forwards and downwards: *She bowed her head in shame.* ◇ *They stood in silence with their heads bowed.* **3** [I, T] to bend or make sth bend: **(+ adv./prep)** *The pines bowed in the wind.* ◇ **~ sth (+ adv./prep)** *Their backs were bowed under the weight of their packs.*
IDM **ˌbow and ˈscrape** (*disapproving*) to be too polite to an important person in order to gain their approval
PHR V **ˌbow ˈdown to sb/sth** (*disapproving*) to allow sb to tell you what to do **ˌbow ˈout (of sth)** to stop taking part in an activity, especially one in which you have been successful in the past: *She has finally decided it's time to bow out of international tennis.* **ˈbow to sth** to agree unwillingly to do sth because other people want you to: *They finally bowed to pressure from the public.* ◇ *She* ***bowed to the inevitable*** (= accepted a situation in which she had no choice) *and resigned.*
■ ***noun* 1** the act of bending your head or the upper part of your body forward in order to say hello or goodbye to sb or to show respect **2** (also **bows** [pl.]) the front part of a boat or ship ➲ VISUAL VOCAB page V44 ➲ compare STERN *n.*
IDM **take a/your ˈbow** (of a performer) to bow to the audience as they are APPLAUDING you ➲ more at SHOT *n.*

bow² /bəʊ; *NAmE* boʊ/ *noun, verb* ➲ see also BOW¹
■ ***noun* 1** a weapon used for shooting arrows, consisting of a long curved piece of wood with a tight string joining its ends: *He was armed with a* ***bow and arrow***. ➲ VISUAL VOCAB page V34 **2** a knot with two LOOPS and two loose ends which is used for decoration on clothes, in hair, etc. or for tying shoes: *to tie your shoelaces in a bow* ◇ *Her hair was tied back in a neat bow.* ➲ picture at KNOT **3** a long

bows

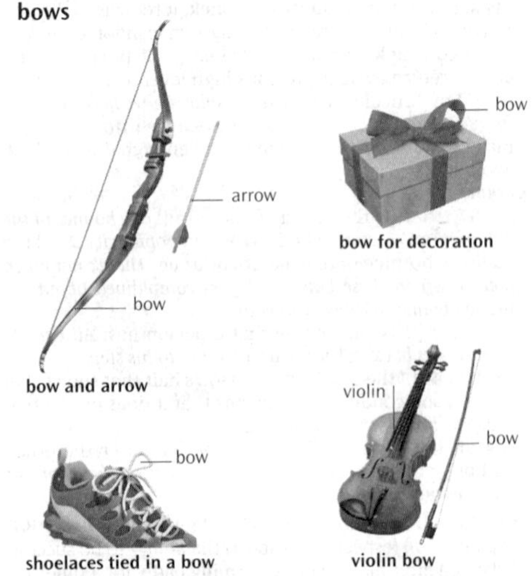

bow and arrow — bow for decoration — shoelaces tied in a bow — violin bow thin piece of wood with thin string stretched along it, used for playing musical instruments such as the VIOLIN ➲ VISUAL VOCAB page V30 IDM see STRING *n.*

■ *verb* [I, T] ~ (sth) to use a bow to play a musical instrument that has strings

bowd·ler·ize (*BrE* also **-ise**) /ˈbaʊdləraɪz/ *verb* **~ sth** (usually *disapproving*) to remove the parts of a book, play, etc. that you think are likely to shock or offend people SYN **expurgate** ORIGIN Named after Dr Thomas **Bowdler**, who in 1818 produced a version of Shakespeare from which he had taken out all the material which he considered not suitable for family use.

bowel /ˈbaʊəl/ *noun* **1** [C, usually pl.] the tube along which food passes after it has been through the stomach, especially the end where waste is collected before it is passed out of the body: (*medical*) *to* ***empty/move/open your bowels*** (= to pass solid waste out of the body) ◇ *bowel cancer/cancer of the bowel* **2 the bowels of sth** [pl.] (*literary*) the part that is deepest inside sth: *A rumble came from* ***the bowels of the earth*** (= deep underground).

ˈ**bowel movement** (also **movement**) *noun* (*medical*) an act of emptying waste material from the bowels; the waste material that is emptied

bower /ˈbaʊə(r)/ *noun* (*literary*) a pleasant place in the shade under trees or climbing plants in a wood or garden/yard

bower·bird /ˈbaʊəbɜːd; *NAmE* ˈbaʊərbɜːrd/ *noun* a bird found in Australia, the male of which decorates a place with shells, feathers, etc. to attract females

bow·fin /ˈbəʊfɪn; *NAmE* ˈboʊ-/ *noun* (*pl.* **bow·fin** or **bow·fins**) an American fish with a large head that can survive for a long time out of water

bow·ie knife /ˈbəʊi naɪf; *NAmE* ˈboʊi/ *noun* a large heavy knife with a long blade, used in hunting

bowl 🔑 /bəʊl; *NAmE* boʊl/ *noun, verb*

■ ***noun***

▸ CONTAINER **1** 🔑 [C] (especially in compounds) a deep round dish with a wide open top, used especially for holding food or liquid: *a* ***salad/fruit/sugar, etc. bowl*** ◇ *a* ***washing-up bowl*** ➲ VISUAL VOCAB page V19

▸ AMOUNT **2** 🔑 [C] (also **bowl·ful** /-fʊl/) the amount contained in a bowl: *a bowl of soup*

▸ SHAPE **3** [C] the part of some objects that is shaped like a bowl: *the bowl of a spoon* ◇ *a* ***toilet/lavatory bowl*** ➲ VISUAL VOCAB page V19

▸ THEATRE **4** [C] (*especially NAmE*) (in names) a large round theatre without a roof, used for concerts, etc. outdoors: *the Hollywood Bowl*

▸ BALL **5** [C] a heavy wooden ball that is used in the games of BOWLS and BOWLING

▸ GAME **6 bowls** [U] (*NAmE* also ˈ**lawn bowling**) a game played on an area of very smooth grass, in which players take turns to roll bowls as near as possible to a small ball ➲ VISUAL VOCAB page V34

▸ FOOTBALL GAME **7** [C] (*NAmE*) (in names) a game of AMERICAN FOOTBALL played after the main season between the best teams: *the Super Bowl*

■ ***verb***

▸ ROLL BALL **1** [I, T] ~ (sth) to roll a ball in the games of bowls and BOWLING

▸ IN CRICKET **2** [I, T] ~ (sth) to throw a ball to the BATSMAN (= the person who hits the ball) ➲ SYNONYMS at THROW **3** [T] **~ sb** (**out**) to make the BATSMAN have to leave the field by throwing a ball that hits the WICKET

▸ MOVE QUICKLY **4** [I] **+ adv./prep.** (*BrE*) to move quickly in a particular direction, especially in a vehicle: *Soon we were bowling along the country roads.*

PHR V ˌ**bowl sb** ˈ**over 1** to run into sb and knock them down **2** to surprise or impress sb a lot

bow legs /ˌbəʊ ˈlegz; *NAmE* ˌboʊ/ *noun* [pl.] legs that curve out at the knees ▸ **bow-legged** /ˌbəʊ ˈlegɪd; *NAmE* ˌboʊ/ *adj.*

bowl·er /ˈbəʊlə(r); *NAmE* ˈboʊ-/ *noun* **1** (in CRICKET) a player who throws the ball towards the BATSMAN **2** (also ˌ**bowler** ˈ**hat**) (both *especially BrE*) (*NAmE* usually **derby**) a hard black hat with a curved BRIM and round top, worn, for example, in the past by men in business in Britain ➲ VISUAL VOCAB page V53

bow·line[1] /ˈbaʊlaɪn/ *noun* a rope that attaches one side of a sail to the BOW of a boat

bow·line[2] /ˈbəʊlɪn; *NAmE* ˈboʊlən/ *noun* a type of knot, used for making a LOOP at the end of a rope

bowl·ing /ˈbəʊlɪŋ; *NAmE* ˈboʊ-/ *noun* [U] a game in which players roll heavy balls (called BOWLS) along a special track towards a group of PINS (= bottle-shaped objects) and try to knock over as many of them as possible ➲ compare BOWLS ➲ VISUAL VOCAB page V34

ˈ**bowling alley** *noun* a building or part of a building where people can go bowling

ˈ**bowling green** *noun* an area of grass that has been cut short on which the game of BOWLS is played ➲ VISUAL VOCAB page V34

bow·man /ˈbəʊmən; *NAmE* ˈboʊ-/ *noun* (*pl.* **-men** /-mən/) (*old-fashioned*) = ARCHER

bow·ser™ /ˈbaʊzə(r)/ *noun* (*especially BrE*) a container, often on wheels, used for holding liquids such as water or fuel, often because the normal supply is not available

bow·sprit /ˈbəʊsprɪt; *NAmE* ˈboʊ-/ *noun* a thick pole that sticks forward at the front of a ship

bow·string /ˈbəʊstrɪŋ; *NAmE* ˈboʊ-/ *noun* the string on a BOW[2] which is pulled back to shoot arrows

bow tie /ˌbəʊ ˈtaɪ; *NAmE* ˌboʊ/ *noun* a man's tie that is tied in the shape of a bow and that does not hang down ➲ VISUAL VOCAB page V50

bow-wow /ˈbaʊ waʊ/ *noun* a child's word for a dog

box 🔑 /bɒks; *NAmE* bɑːks/ *noun, verb*

■ ***noun***

▸ CONTAINER **1** 🔑 [C] (especially in compounds) a container made of wood, cardboard, metal, etc. with a flat stiff base and sides and often a lid, used especially for holding solid things: *She kept all the letters in a box.* ◇ *a money box* ◇ *cardboard boxes* ◇ *a toolbox* ◇ *a matchbox* ➲ VISUAL VOCAB page V29 **2** 🔑 [C] a box and its contents: *a* ***box of chocolates/matches*** ➲ VISUAL VOCAB page V29

▸ IN THEATRE/COURT **3** [C] a small area in a theatre or court separated off from where other people sit: *a box at the opera* ◇ *the* ***witness/jury box***

▸ SHELTER **4** [C] a small shelter used for a particular purpose: *a* ***sentry/signal box*** ◇ (*BrE*) *a telephone box* ◇ *I called him from the phone box on the corner.*

▸ SHAPE **5** 🔑 [C] a small square or RECTANGLE drawn on a page for people to write information in: *Put a cross in the appropriate box.* ◇ *to* ***tick/check a box***

▸ TELEVISION **6 the box** [sing.] (*informal, especially BrE*) the television: *What's on the box tonight?*

▸ ON ROAD **7** [C] (*BrE*) = BOX JUNCTION: *Only traffic turning right may enter the box.*

▸ IN SPORT **8** [C] an area on a sports field that is marked by lines and used for a particular purpose: (*BrE*) *He was fouled in the box* (= the penalty box).

▸ FOR MAIL **9** [C] = BOX NUMBER ➲ see also PO BOX

▸ PROTECTION **10** [C] (*BrE*) a piece of plastic that a man wears over his sex organs to protect them while he is playing a sport, especially CRICKET

▸ TREE/WOOD **11** [C, U] a small EVERGREEN tree or bush with thick dark leaves, used especially for garden HEDGES **12** (also **box·wood**) [U] the hard wood of this bush

IDM **give sb a box on the** ˈ**ears** (*old-fashioned*) to hit sb with your hand on the side of their head as a punishment ➲ more at THINK *v.*, TICK *v.*, TRICK *n.*

■ ***verb***

▸ FIGHT **1** [I, T] ~ (sb) to fight sb in the sport of BOXING

▸ PUT IN CONTAINER **2** [T] **~ sth** (**up**) to put sth in a box

IDM **box** ˈ**clever** (*BrE, informal*) to act in a clever way to get what you want, sometimes tricking sb **box sb's** ˈ**ears** (*old-fashioned*) to hit sb with your hand on the side of their head as a punishment

PHR V ˌ**box sb/sth** ˈ**in 1** to prevent sb/sth from being able to move by surrounding them with people, vehicles, etc:

B

Someone had parked behind us and boxed us in. **2** [usually passive] (of a situation) to prevent sb from doing what they want by creating unnecessary problems: *She felt boxed in by all their petty rules.*

box·car /ˈbɒkskɑː(r); *NAmE* ˈbɑːks-/ *noun* (*especially NAmE*) a closed coach/car on a train, with a sliding door, used for carrying goods

boxed /bɒkst; *NAmE* bɑːkst/ *adj.* put and/or sold in a box: *a boxed set of original recordings*

boxer /ˈbɒksə(r); *NAmE* ˈbɑːk-/ *noun* **1** a person who boxes, especially as a job: *a* ***professional/amateur/heavyweight boxer*** **2** a large dog with smooth hair, a short flat nose and a tail that has usually been cut very short

Bo·xer·cise™ /ˈbɒksəsaɪz; *NAmE* ˈbɑːksər-/ *noun* [U] (*BrE*) a form of exercise that uses movements and equipment used in BOXING

ˈ**boxer shorts** (also **boxers**) (*NAmE* also **shorts**) *noun* [pl.] men's UNDERPANTS similar to the SHORTS worn by boxers: *a pair of boxer shorts*

box·ful /ˈbɒksfʊl; *NAmE* ˈbɑːksfʊl/ *noun* a full box (of sth)

box·ing /ˈbɒksɪŋ; *NAmE* ˈbɑːks-/ *noun* [U] a sport in which two people fight each other with their hands, while wearing very large thick gloves (called **boxing gloves**): *a* ***boxing champion/match*** ◇ *heavyweight boxing* ➲ VISUAL VOCAB page V39

ˈ**Box·ing Day** *noun* [U, C] (*BrE*) the first day after Christmas Day that is not a Sunday. Boxing Day is an official holiday in Britain and some other countries.

ˈ**box junction** (also **box**) *noun* (*BrE*) a place where two roads cross or join, marked with a pattern of yellow lines to show that vehicles must not stop

ˈ**box kite** *noun* a KITE in the shape of a long box which is open at both ends

ˈ**box lunch** *noun* (*NAmE*) a meal of SANDWICHES, fruit, etc. that you take to school, work, etc. in a box ➲ compare BAG LUNCH, PACKED LUNCH

ˈ**box number** (also **box**) *noun* a number used as an address, especially one given in newspaper advertisements to which replies can be sent

ˈ**box office** *noun* the place at a theatre, cinema/movie theater, etc. where the tickets are sold: *The movie has been a huge* ***box-office success*** (= many people have been to see it). ➲ COLLOCATIONS at CINEMA

ˈ**box room** *noun* (*BrE*) a small room in a house for storing things in

ˈ**box score** *noun* the results of a BASEBALL game or other sporting event shown in the form of rows and columns which include details of each player's performance

ˈ**box seat** *noun*
IDM **in the ˈbox seat** (*AustralE, NZE, informal*) in a position in which you have an advantage

box·wood /ˈbɒkswʊd; *NAmE* ˈbɑːks-/ *noun* [U] = BOX (12)

boxy /ˈbɒksi; *NAmE* ˈbɑːksi/ *adj.* having a square shape: *a boxy car*

boy 🔑 /bɔɪ/ *noun, exclamation*
■ ***noun*** **1** 🔑 [C] a male child or a young male person: ***a little/small/young boy*** ◇ *I used to play here as a boy.* ◇ *The older boys at school used to tease him.* ◇ *Now she's a teenager, she's starting to be interested in boys.* ➲ see also OLD BOY, TOY BOY **2** 🔑 [C] a young son: *They have two boys and a girl.* ◇ *Her eldest boy is at college.* **3** [C] (in compounds; offensive when used of an older man) a boy or young man who does a particular job: *a delivery boy* ➲ see also BACK-ROOM BOYS, BARROW BOY, BEST BOY **4** [C] a way of talking about sb who comes from a particular place, etc.: *He's a* ***local boy.*** ◇ *a* ***city/country boy*** **5 the boys** [pl.] (*informal*) a group of male friends who often go out together: *a night out with the boys* **6 our boys** [pl.] a way of talking with affection about your country's soldiers **7** [C] (*NAmE, taboo*) used as an offensive way of addressing a black man, especially in the past
IDM **the boys in ˈblue** (*informal*) the police ˌ**boys ˌwill be ˈboys** (*saying*) you should not be surprised when boys or men behave in a noisy or rough way as this is part of typical male behaviour ➲ more at JOB *n.*, MAN *n.*, WORK *n.*
■ ***exclamation*** (*informal, especially NAmE*) used to express feelings of surprise, pleasure, pain, etc.: *Boy, it sure is hot!* ◇ *Oh boy! That's great!*

ˈ**boy band** *noun* a group of attractive young men who sing pop music and dance, and who are especially popular with girls

boy·cott /ˈbɔɪkɒt; *NAmE* -kɑːt/ *verb, noun*
■ ***verb*** **~ sth** to refuse to buy, use or take part in sth as a way of protesting: *We are asking people to boycott goods from companies that use child labour.*
■ ***noun*** an act of boycotting sb/sth: **~ (of sth)** *a trade boycott of British goods* ◇ **~ (on sth)** *a boycott on the use of tropical wood*

boyf /bɔɪf/ *noun* (*BrE, informal*) a boyfriend

boy·friend 🔑 /ˈbɔɪfrend/ *noun* a man or boy that sb has a romantic or sexual relationship with

boy·hood /ˈbɔɪhʊd/ *noun* [U] (becoming *old-fashioned*) the time in a man's life when he is a boy: ***boyhood days/memories/friends***

boy·ish /ˈbɔɪɪʃ/ *adj.* (*approving*) looking or behaving like a boy, in a way that is attractive: ***boyish charm/enthusiasm*** ◇ *her slim boyish figure* ▸ **boy·ish·ly** *adv.*

boyo /ˈbɔɪəʊ; *NAmE* ˈbɔɪoʊ/ *noun* (*informal*) used for addressing a boy or a man in Wales

ˌ**boy ˈracer** *noun* (*BrE, informal, disapproving*) a man, especially a young man, who drives his car too fast and without care

ˌ**Boy ˈScout** *noun* (*US* or *old-fashioned*) a boy who is a member of the SCOUTS

boy·sen·berry /ˈbɔɪznbəri; *NAmE* -beri/ *noun* (*pl.* **-ies**) a large red fruit like a BLACKBERRY. The bush it grows on is also called a boysenberry.

ˈ**boy shorts** *noun* [pl.] a piece of women's underwear that covers the body from the hips to the top of the legs

ˈ**boy toy** *noun* (*NAmE, informal*) **1** (*BrE* ˈ**toy boy**) (*humorous*) a woman's male lover who is much younger than she is **2** (*disapproving*) a young woman who is happy to be considered only for her sexual attraction and not for her character or intelligence

ˌ**boy ˈwonder** *noun* (*informal, humorous*) a boy or young man who is extremely good at sth

bozo /ˈbəʊzəʊ; *NAmE* ˈboʊzoʊ/ *noun* (*pl.* **-os**) (*informal, especially NAmE*) a stupid person

BPhil (*NAmE* **B.Phil**) /ˌbiː ˈfɪl/ *noun* the abbreviation for 'Bachelor of Philosophy'(a university degree in philosophy that is usually a second degree)

bpi /ˌbiː piː ˈaɪ/ *abbr.* (*computing*) bits per inch (a measure of the amount of data that can fit onto a tape or disk)

ˈ**B-picture** = B-MOVIE

bps /ˌbiː piː ˈes/ *abbr.* (*computing*) bits per second (a measure of the speed at which data is sent or received)

Bq *abbr.* = BECQUEREL

Br. *abbr.* (in writing) British

bra /brɑː/ *noun* **1** (also *formal* **brassière**) a piece of women's underwear worn to cover and support the breasts **2** (also ˈ**car bra**, ˈ**auto bra**) a tightly fitting cover that is put over the front end of a car to protect it, sometimes made of a material that absorbs the waves from police RADAR equipment, so that it is more difficult to tell if a driver is going too fast

braai /braɪ/ *noun, verb* (*SAfrE*)
■ ***noun*** **1** (also **braai·vleis**) a social event at which food is cooked outdoors over an open fire: *We're having a braai at our place next Saturday.* ◇ *a bring-and-braai* (= everyone brings their own meat) **2** the surface or piece of equipment where the fire is made

▪ ***verb*** (**braais**, **braai·ing** or **braaing**, **braaied**) [T, I] **~ (sth)** to cook food over an open fire, especially as part of a social event ➲ compare BARBECUE

braai·vleis /ˈbraɪfleɪs/ *noun* (*SAfrE*) **1** = BRAAI (1) **2** [U] meat that is cooked over an open fire

brace /breɪs/ *noun, verb*

▪ ***noun*** **1** [C] a device that holds things firmly together or holds and supports them in position: *a neck brace* (= worn to support the neck after an injury) **2** [C] (*NAmE* **braces** [pl.]) a metal device that children wear inside the mouth to help their teeth grow straight **3 braces** (*BrE*) (*NAmE* **sus·pend·ers**) [pl.] long narrow pieces of cloth, leather, etc. for holding trousers/pants up. They are fastened to the top of the trousers/pants at the front and back and passed over the shoulders: *a pair of braces* ➲ VISUAL VOCAB page V50 **4** (*NAmE*) (*BrE* **cal·li·per**) [C, usually pl.] a metal support for weak or injured legs **5** [C] either of the two marks, { }, used to show that the words, etc. between them are connected ➲ compare BRACKET **6** [C] (*pl.* **brace**) a pair of birds or animals that have been killed in hunting IDM see BELT *n.*

▪ ***verb*** **1 ~ sb/yourself** (**for sth**) | **~ sb/yourself** (**to do sth**) to prepare sb/yourself for sth difficult or unpleasant that is going to happen: *UN troops are braced for more violence.* ◇ *They are bracing themselves for a long legal battle.* **2 ~ sth/yourself** (**against sth**) to press your body or part of your body firmly against sth in order to stop yourself from falling: *They braced themselves against the wind.* **3 ~ sth** to contract the muscles in your body or part of your body before doing sth that is physically difficult: *He stood with his legs and shoulders braced, ready to lift the weights.* **4 ~ sth** (*technical*) to make sth stronger or more solid by supporting it with sth: *The roof was braced by lengths of timber.*

brace·let /ˈbreɪslət/ *noun* a piece of jewellery worn around the wrist or arm ➲ VISUAL VOCAB page V53

bracer /ˈbreɪsə(r)/ *noun* a drink, usually alcoholic, which is intended to give strength to the person who drinks it

bra·chio·pod /ˈbrækiəpɒd; *NAmE* -pɑːd/ *noun* (*biology*) a shellfish that has two joined shells and uses small TENTACLES (= long thin parts) to find food

bra·chio·saurus /ˌbrækiəˈsɔːrəs/ *noun* a very large DINOSAUR whose front legs were much longer than its back legs

brac·ing /ˈbreɪsɪŋ/ *adj.* (especially of weather) making you feel full of energy because it is cold: *bracing sea air*

bracken /ˈbrækən/ *noun* [U] a wild plant with large leaves that grows thickly on hills and in woods and turns brown in the autumn/fall

bracket /ˈbrækɪt/ *noun, verb*

▪ ***noun*** **1** (also ˈ**round bracket**) (both *BrE*) (also **par·en·thesis** *NAmE* or *formal*) [usually pl.] either of a pair of marks, ( ) placed around extra information in a piece of writing or part of a problem in mathematics: *Publication dates are given* ***in brackets*** *after each title.* ◇ *Add the numbers in brackets first.* ➲ see also ANGLE BRACKET ➲ compare BRACE **2** (*NAmE*) (*BrE* ˌ**square** ˈ**bracket**) [usually pl.] either of a pair of marks, [ ], placed at the beginning and end of extra information in a text, especially comments made by an editor **3 price, age, income, etc. ~** prices, etc. within a particular range: *people in the lower income bracket* ◇ *Most of the houses are out of our price bracket.* ◇ *the 30–34 age bracket* (= people aged between 30 and 34) **4** a piece of wood, metal or plastic fixed to the wall to support a shelf, lamp, etc.

▪ ***verb*** **1 ~ sth** to put words, information, etc. between brackets **2 ~ A and B** (**together**) | **~ A** (**together**) **with B** [often passive] to consider people or things to be similar or connected in some way: *It is unfair to bracket together those who cannot work with those who will not.*

brack·ish /ˈbrækɪʃ/ *adj.* (of water) salty in an unpleasant way: ***brackish lakes/lagoons/marshes***

brad /bræd/ *noun* a small thin nail with a small head and a flat tip

brad·awl /ˈbrædɔːl/ *noun* a small pointed tool used for making holes ➲ VISUAL VOCAB page V17

brae /breɪ/ *noun* (*ScotE*) (often in place names) a steep slope or hill

brag /bræg/ *verb, noun*

▪ ***verb*** [I, T] (**-gg-**) **~ (to sb) (about/of sth)** | **~ that...** | **+ speech** (*disapproving*) to talk too proudly about sth you own or sth you have done SYN **boast**: *He bragged to his friends about the crime.*

▪ ***noun*** [U] a card game which is a simple form of POKER

brag·ga·docio /ˌbrægəˈdəʊʃiəʊ; *NAmE* -ˈdoʊʃioʊ/ *noun* [U] (*literary*) behaviour that seems too proud or confident

brag·gart /ˈbrægət; *NAmE* -gərt/ *noun* (*old-fashioned*) a person who brags

Brah·man /ˈbrɑːmən/ (also **Brah·min**) *noun* a Hindu who belongs to the CASTE (= division of society) that is considered the highest, originally that of priests

Brah·min /ˈbrɑːmɪn/ *noun* **1** = BRAHMAN **2** (*NAmE*) a person who is rich and has a lot of influence in society, especially sb from New England whose family belongs to the highest social class: *a Boston Brahmin*

braid /breɪd/ *noun, verb*

▪ ***noun*** **1** [U] thin coloured rope that is used to decorate furniture and military uniforms: *The general's uniform was trimmed with gold braid.* **2** (*especially NAmE*) (*BrE* also **plait**) [C] a long piece of sth, especially hair, that is divided into three parts and twisted together: *She wears her hair in braids.* ➲ VISUAL VOCAB page V49

▪ ***verb*** **~ sth** (*especially NAmE*) (*BrE* also **plait**) to twist three or more long pieces of hair, rope, etc. together to make one long piece: *She'd braided her hair.*

Braille /breɪl/ (also **braille**) *noun* [U] a system of printing for blind people in which the letters of the alphabet and the numbers are printed as raised dots that can be read by touching them

brain 🔑 /breɪn/ *noun, verb*

▪ ***noun***

▸ IN HEAD **1** 🔑 [C] the organ inside the head that controls movement, thought, memory and feeling: *damage to the brain* ◇ *brain cells* ◇ *She died of a brain tumour.* ◇ *a device to measure brain activity during sleep* ➲ VISUAL VOCAB page V48

▸ FOOD **2 brains** [pl.] the brain of an animal, eaten as food: *sheep's brains*

▸ INTELLIGENCE **3** 🔑 [U, C, usually pl.] the ability to learn quickly and think about things in a logical and intelligent way: *It doesn't take much brain to work out that both stories can't be true.* ◇ *Teachers spotted that he had a good brain at an early age.* ◇ *You need brains as well as brawn* (= intelligence as well as strength) *to do this job.* ➲ see also NO-BRAINER

▸ INTELLIGENT PERSON **4** [C, usually pl.] (*informal*) an intelligent person: *one of the best scientific brains in the country* **5 the brains** [sing.] the most intelligent person in a particular group; the person who is responsible for thinking of and organizing sth: *He's always been the brains of the family.* ◇ *The band's drummer is* ***the brains behind*** *their latest venture.*

IDM **have sth on the brain** (*informal*) to think about sth all the time, especially in a way that is annoying: *He has sex on the brain.* ➲ more at BEAT *v.*, BLOW *v.*, CUDGEL *v.*, PICK *v.*, RACK *v.*

▪ ***verb*** **~ sb/sth/yourself** (*informal*) to kill a person or an animal by hitting them very hard on the head: *I nearly brained myself on that low beam.*

brain·box /ˈbreɪnbɒks; *NAmE* -bɑːks/ *noun* (*BrE, informal*) a person who is very intelligent

brain·child /ˈbreɪntʃaɪld/ *noun* [sing.] an idea or invention of one person or a small group of people

ˈ**brain damage** *noun* [U] permanent damage to the brain caused by illness or an accident ▶ ˈ**brain-damaged** *adj.*

ˈ**brain-dead** *adj.* **1** suffering from serious damage to the brain and needing machines to stay alive **2** (*humorous*) very stupid and boring; not intelligent

B

ˈ**brain death** *noun* [U] very serious damage to the brain that cannot be cured. A person who is suffering from brain death needs machines to keep them alive, even though their heart is still beating.

ˈ**brain drain** *noun* [sing.] (*informal*) the movement of highly skilled and qualified people to a country where they can work in better conditions and earn more money

brain·iac /ˈbreɪniæk/ *noun* (*NAmE, informal*) a very intelligent person ORIGIN From the name of a character in the *Superman* stories.

brain·less /ˈbreɪnləs/ *adj.* stupid; not able to think or talk in an intelligent way

brain·power /ˈbreɪnpaʊə(r)/ *noun* [U] the ability to think; intelligence

brain·stem /ˈbreɪnstem/ *noun* (*anatomy*) the central part of the brain, which continues downwards to form the SPINAL CORD

brain·storm /ˈbreɪnstɔːm; *NAmE* -stɔːrm/ *noun* [sing.] **1** (*BrE*) a sudden inability to think clearly which causes unusual behaviour: *She had a brainstorm in the exam and didn't answer a single question.* **2** (*NAmE*) = BRAINWAVE

brain·storm·ing /ˈbreɪnstɔːmɪŋ; *NAmE* -stɔːrm-/ *noun* [U] a way of making a group of people all think about sth at the same time, often in order to solve a problem or to create good ideas: *a brainstorming session* ▸ **brain·storm** *verb* [T, I]: **~ (sth)** *Brainstorm as many ideas as possible.*

ˈ**brain surgery** *noun* [U]
IDM **it's not ˈbrain surgery** (*informal*) used to emphasize that sth is easy to do or understand SYN **rocket science**: *Look, this isn't brain surgery we're doing here.*

ˈ**brain-teaser** *noun* a problem that is difficult but fun to solve

brain·wash /ˈbreɪnwɒʃ; *NAmE* -wɔːʃ; -wɑːʃ/ *verb* to force sb to accept your ideas or beliefs, for example by repeating the same thing many times or by preventing the person from thinking clearly: **~ sb** *The group is accused of brainwashing its young members.* ◇ **~ sb into doing sth** *Women have been brainwashed into thinking that they must go out to work in order to fulfil themselves.* ▸ **brain·wash·ing** *noun* [U]: *the victims of brainwashing and torture*

brain·wave /ˈbreɪnweɪv/ *noun* **1** (*NAmE* also **brainstorm**) a sudden good idea: *I've had a brainwave!* **2** an electrical signal in the brain

brainy /ˈbreɪni/ *adj.* (*informal*) (**brain·ier, braini·est**) very intelligent

braise /breɪz/ *verb* **~ sth** to cook meat or vegetables very slowly with a little liquid in a closed container: *braising steak* (= that is suitable for braising)

brake /breɪk/ *noun, verb*
■ *noun* **1** a device for slowing or stopping a vehicle: *to* **put/slam** *on the* **brakes** ◇ *the brake pedal* ➲ COLLOCATIONS at DRIVING ➲ VISUAL VOCAB pages V41, V42 ➲ see also AIR BRAKE, DISC BRAKE, FOOTBRAKE, HANDBRAKE **2 ~ (on sth)** a thing that stops sth or makes it difficult: *High interest rates are a brake on the economy.* IDM see JAM *v.*
■ *verb* [I, T] to go slower or make a vehicle go slower using the brake: *The car braked and swerved.* ◇ *The truck* **braked to a halt**. ◇ *You don't need to brake at every bend.* ◇ *She had to brake hard to avoid running into the car in front.* ◇ **~ sth** *He braked the car and pulled in to the side of the road.*

ˈ**brake fluid** *noun* [U] liquid used in BRAKES to make the different parts move smoothly

ˈ**brake light** (*NAmE* also ˈ**stop light**) *noun* a red light on the back of a vehicle that comes on when the brakes are used

ˈ**brake pad** *noun* a thin block that presses onto the disc in a DISC BRAKE in a vehicle, in order to stop the vehicle

bram·ble /ˈbræmbl/ *noun* **1** (*especially BrE*) a wild bush with THORNS on which BLACKBERRIES grow **2** (*BrE*) = BLACKBERRY

bran /bræn/ *noun* [U] the outer covering of grain which is left when the grain is made into flour

branch 0-w /brɑːntʃ; *NAmE* bræntʃ/ *noun, verb*
■ *noun*
▸ OF TREE **1** 0-w a part of a tree that grows out from the main STEM and on which leaves, flowers and fruit grow ➲ VISUAL VOCAB page V8
▸ OF COMPANY **2** 0-w a local office or shop/store belonging to a large company or organization: *The bank has branches all over the country.* ◇ *Our New York branch is dealing with the matter.*
▸ OF GOVERNMENT **3** 0-w a part of a government or other large organization that deals with one particular aspect of its work SYN **department**: *the anti-terrorist branch*
▸ OF KNOWLEDGE **4** 0-w a division of an area of knowledge or a group of languages: *the branch of computer science known as 'artificial intelligence'*
▸ OF RIVER/ROAD **5** a smaller or less important part of a river, road, railway/railroad, etc. that leads away from the main part: *a branch of the Rhine* ◇ *a* **branch line** (= a small line off a main railway line, often in country areas)
▸ OF FAMILY **6** a group of members of a family who all have the same ANCESTORS: *My uncle's branch of the family emigrated to Canada.* IDM see ROOT *n.*
■ *verb* [I] to divide into two or more parts, especially smaller or less important parts: *The accident happened where the road branches.*
PHRV ˌ**branch ˈoff 1** (of a road or river) to be joined to another road or river but lead in a different direction: *Just after the lake, the path branches off to the right.* **2** (of a person) to leave a road or path and travel in a different direction ˌ**branch ˈout (into sth)** to start to do an activity that you have not done before, especially in your work or business SYN **diversify**: *The company branched out into selling insurance.* ◇ *I decided to* **branch out on my own**.

brand 0-w /brænd/ *noun, verb*
■ *noun* **1** 0-w a type of product made by a particular company: *Which brand of toothpaste do you use?* ◇ (*BrE*) *You pay less for the supermarket's* **own brand**. ◇ (*NAmE*) *You pay less for the* **store brand**. ◇ **brand loyalty** (= the tendency of customers to continue buying the same brand) ◇ *Champagne houses owe their success to* **brand image**. ◇ *the* **leading brand** *of detergent* ➲ see also OWN-BRAND **2** a particular type or kind of sth: *an unorthodox brand of humour* **3** a mark made with a piece of hot metal, especially on farm animals to show who owns them
■ *verb* [often passive] **1** to describe sb as being sth bad or unpleasant, especially unfairly: **~ sb as sth** *They were branded as liars and cheats.* ◇ **~ sb + noun/adj.** *The newspapers branded her a hypocrite.* **2 ~ sth (with sth)** to mark an animal with a BRAND *n.* (3) to show who owns it

brand·ed /ˈbrændɪd/ *adj.* [only before noun] (of a product) made by a well-known company and having that company's name on it: ***branded drugs/goods/products***

brand·ing /ˈbrændɪŋ/ *noun* [U] the activity of giving a particular name and image to goods and services so that people will be attracted to them and want to buy them

ˈ**branding iron** *noun* a metal tool that is heated and used to BRAND farm animals

bran·dish /ˈbrændɪʃ/ *verb* **~ sth** to hold or wave sth, especially a weapon, in an aggressive or excited way

ˈ**brand name** (also ˈ**trade name**) *noun* the name given to a product by the company that produces it

ˌ**brand ˈnew** *adj.* completely new: *a brand new computer* ◇ *She bought her car brand new.*

brandy /ˈbrændi/ *noun* (*pl.* **-ies**) **1** [U, C] a strong alcoholic drink made from wine. **2** [C] a glass of brandy

ˌ**brandy ˈbutter** *noun* [U] a very thick sweet sauce made with butter, sugar and brandy, often eaten with CHRISTMAS PUDDING

ˈ**brandy snap** *noun* (*especially BrE*) a thin crisp biscuit/cookie in the shape of a tube, flavoured with GINGER and often filled with cream

ˈ**bran tub** *noun* (*BrE*) a container that holds prizes hidden in BRAN, paper, etc, which children have to find as a game

brash /bræʃ/ *adj.* (*disapproving*) **1** confident in an aggressive way: *Beneath his brash exterior, he's still a little boy inside.* **2** (*BrE*) (of things and places) too bright or too noisy in a way that is not attractive ▶ **brash·ly** *adv.* **brash·ness** *noun* [U]

brass /brɑːs; *NAmE* bræs/ *noun*
▸ METAL **1** [U] a bright yellow metal made by mixing COPPER and ZINC; objects made of brass: *solid* ***brass fittings/door handles*** ◊ *a* ***brass plate*** (= a sign outside a building giving the name and profession of the person who works there) ◊ *to* ***clean/polish the brass***
▸ MUSICAL INSTRUMENTS **2** [U+sing./pl. v.] the musical instruments made of metal, such as TRUMPETS or FRENCH HORNS, that form a band or section of an ORCHESTRA; the people who play them: *music for piano, strings and brass* ➲ compare PERCUSSION, STRINGS, WOODWIND, WIND INSTRUMENT ➲ VISUAL VOCAB page V30
▸ FOR A HORSE **3** [C] (*BrE*) a decorated piece of brass used as a decorative object, especially a round flat piece attached to a horse's HARNESS
▸ IN CHURCH **4** [C] (*especially BrE*) a flat piece of brass with words or a picture on it, fixed to the floor or wall of a church in memory of sb who has died
▸ IMPORTANT PEOPLE **5** (*especially NAmE*) (also *BrE informal* ˌ**top** ˈ**brass**) [U+sing./pl. v.] the people who are in the most important positions in a company, an organization, etc.
▸ MONEY **6** [U] (*old-fashioned, BrE, informal*) money ➲ see also BRASSY
IDM ˌ**brass** ˈ**monkeys** | ˌ**brass** ˈ**monkey weather** (*BrE, slang*) if you say that it is **brass monkeys** or **brass monkey weather**, you mean that it is very cold weather ˌ**brass** ˈ**neck**/ˈ**nerve** (*BrE, informal*) a combination of confidence and lack of respect: *I didn't think she would have the brass neck to do that.* **the** ˌ**brass** ˈ**ring** (*NAmE, informal*) the opportunity to be successful; success that you have worked hard to get: *The girls' outdoor track team has* ***grabbed the brass ring*** *seven times.* ORIGIN From the custom of giving a free ride to any child who grabbed one of the rings hanging around the side of a merry-go-round at a fairground. (**get down to**) **brass** ˈ**tacks** (*informal*) (to start to consider) the basic facts or practical details of sth ➲ more at BOLD, MUCK *n.*

ˌ**brass** ˈ**band** *noun* [C+sing./pl. v.] a group of musicians who play brass instruments

ˌ**brassed** ˈ**off** *adj.* (*BrE, slang*) annoyed SYN **fed up**

bras·serie /ˈbræsəri; *NAmE* ˌbræsəˈriː/ *noun* a type of restaurant, often one in a French style that is not very expensive

bras·sica /ˈbræsɪkə/ *noun* a plant of a type that includes CABBAGE, RAPE and MUSTARD

brass·ière /ˈbræziə(r); *NAmE* brəˈzɪr/ *noun* (*formal*) = BRA

ˌ**brass** ˈ**knuckles** *noun* [pl.] (*NAmE*) = KNUCKLEDUSTER

ˈ**brass rubbing** *noun* [U, C] the art of rubbing a soft pencil or CHALK on a piece of paper placed over a BRASS in a church; the pattern you get by doing this

brassy /ˈbrɑːsi; *NAmE* ˈbræsi/ *adj.* **1** (sometimes *disapproving*) (of music) loud and unpleasant **2** (*informal, disapproving*) (of a woman) dressing in a way that makes her sexual attraction obvious, but without style: *the brassy blonde behind the bar* **3** like BRASS (1) in colour; too yellow and bright **4** (*NAmE, informal*) saying what you think, without caring about other people

brat /bræt/ *noun* (*informal, disapproving*) a person, especially a child, who behaves badly: *a* ***spoiled/spoilt brat*** ▶ **bratty** /ˈbræti/ *adj.*: *a bratty kid*

the ˈ**brat pack** *noun* [usually sing.] a group of famous young people, especially film/movie actors, who sometimes behave badly

bra·vado /brəˈvɑːdəʊ; *NAmE* -doʊ/ *noun* [U] a confident way of behaving that is intended to impress people, sometimes as a way of hiding a lack of confidence: *an act of sheer bravado*

brave 0‑ /breɪv/ *adj., verb, noun*
■ *adj.* (**braver**, **brav·est**) **1** 0‑ (of a person) willing to do things which are difficult, dangerous or painful; not afraid SYN **courageous**: *brave men and women* ◊ *Be brave!* ◊ *I wasn't brave enough to tell her what I thought of her.* **2** 0‑ (of an action) requiring or showing courage: *a brave decision* ◊ *She died after a brave fight against cancer.* ◊ *He felt homesick, but made a brave attempt to appear cheerful.* **3** ~ **new** (sometimes *ironic*) new in an impressive way: *a vision of a brave new Britain* ▶ **brave·ly** *adv.* **bravery** /ˈbreɪvəri/ *noun* [U] SYN **courage**: *an award for outstanding bravery* ◊ *acts of skill and bravery*
IDM (**a**) ˌ**brave new** ˈ**world** a situation or society that changes in a way that is meant to improve people's lives but is often a source of extra problems: *the brave new world of technology* **put on a brave** ˈ**face** | **put a brave** ˈ**face on sth** to pretend that you feel confident and happy when you do not
■ *verb* ~ **sb/sth** to have to deal with sth difficult or unpleasant in order to achieve sth: *He did not feel up to braving the journalists at the airport.* ◊ *Over a thousand people* ***braved the elements*** (= went outside in spite of the bad weather) *to attend the march.*
■ *noun* **1 the brave** [pl.] people who are brave: *America, the land of the free and the home of the brave* **2** [C] (*old-fashioned*) a Native American WARRIOR

bravo /ˌbrɑːˈvəʊ; *NAmE* -ˈvoʊ/ *exclamation* (becoming *old-fashioned*) people say **Bravo!** at the end of sth they have enjoyed, such as a play at the theatre

bra·vura /brəˈvjʊərə; *NAmE* -ˈvjʊrə/ *noun* [U] (*formal*) great skill and enthusiasm in doing sth artistic: *a bravura performance*

braw /brɔː/ *adj.* (*ScotE*) fine: *braw lads and bonny lasses* ◊ *It was a braw day.*

brawl /brɔːl/ *noun, verb*
■ *noun* a noisy and violent fight involving a group of people, usually in a public place: *a drunken brawl* ➲ SYNONYMS at FIGHT
■ *verb* [I] to take part in a noisy and violent fight, usually in a public place: *They were arrested for brawling in the street.* ▶ **brawl·er** *noun*

brawn /brɔːn/ *noun* [U] **1** physical strength: *In this job you need brains as well as brawn.* **2** (*BrE*) (*NAmE* **head-cheese**) meat made from the head of a pig or CALF that has been boiled and pressed into a container, served cold in thin slices

brawny /ˈbrɔːni/ *adj.* (*informal*) having strong muscles SYN **burly**: *He was a great brawny brute of a man.*

bray /breɪ/ *verb* **1** [I] when a DONKEY **brays**, it makes a loud unpleasant sound **2** [I] (of a person) to talk or laugh in a loud unpleasant voice: *He brayed with laughter.* ◊ *a braying voice* ▶ **bray** *noun*

bra·zen /ˈbreɪzn/ *adj., verb*
■ *adj.* **1** (*disapproving*) open and without shame, usually about sth that people find shocking SYN **shameless**: *She had become brazen about the whole affair.* ◊ *his brazen admission that he was cheating* **2** made of, or the colour of, BRASS (1) ▶ **brazen·ly** *adv.*: *She had brazenly admitted allowing him back into the house.* **brazen·ness** *noun* [U]
■ *verb*
PHR V ˌ**brazen it** ˈ**out** to behave as if you are not ashamed or embarrassed about sth even though you should be: *Now that everyone knew the truth, the only thing to do was to brazen it out.*

bra·zier /ˈbreɪziə(r)/ *noun* a large metal container that holds a fire and is used to keep people warm when they are outside

bra·zil /brəˈzɪl/ (also **braˈzil nut**) *noun* the curved nut of a large S American tree. It has a hard shell with three sides. ➲ VISUAL VOCAB page V28

Bra·zil·ian /brəˈzɪliən/ *adj., noun*
■ *adj.* from or connected with Brazil
■ *noun* a person from Brazil

Braˌ**zilian** ˈ**wax** *noun* a style of removing a woman's PUBIC hair using WAX, in which almost all the hair is removed with only a very small central strip remaining

B

breach /briːtʃ/ *noun, verb*
■ *noun* (*formal*) **1** [C, U] **~ of sth** a failure to do sth that must be done by law: *a* ***breach of*** *contract/copyright/warranty* ◇ *They are* ***in breach of*** *Article 119.* ◇ (*BrE*) (*a*) ***breach of the peace*** (= the crime of behaving in a noisy or violent way in public) **2** [C, U] **~ of sth** an action that breaks an agreement to behave in a particular way: *a* ***breach of confidence/trust*** ◇ *a breach of security* (= when sth that is normally protected is no longer secure) **3** [C] a break in a relationship between people or countries: *a breach in Franco-German relations* **4** [C] an opening that is created during a military attack or by strong winds or seas: *They escaped through a breach in the wire fence.* IDM see STEP *v.*
■ *verb* (*formal*) **1 ~ sth** to not keep to an agreement or not keep a promise SYN **break**: *The government is accused of breaching the terms of the treaty.* **2 ~ sth** to make a hole in a wall, fence, etc. so that sb/sth can go through it: *The dam had been breached.*

bread 🔑 /bred/ *noun* [U]
1 🔑 a type of food made from flour, water and usually YEAST mixed together and baked: *a* ***loaf/slice/piece of bread*** ◇ ***white/brown/wholemeal bread*** ➲ see also CRISPBREAD, FRENCH BREAD, GINGERBREAD **2** (*old-fashioned, slang*) money
IDM **take the bread out of sb's 'mouth** to take away sb's job so that they are no longer able to earn enough money to live ➲ more at DAILY *adj.*, HALF *det.*, KNOW *v.*, SLICED

ˌbread and 'butter *noun* [U] **1** slices of bread that have been spread with butter: *a piece of bread and butter* **2** (*informal*) a person or company's main source of income

ˌbread-and-'butter *adj.* [only before noun] basic; very important: *Employment and taxation are the bread-and-butter issues of politics.*

ˌbread-and-butter 'pudding *noun* [U, C] a DESSERT (= sweet dish) consisting of layers of bread with butter on, cooked with dried fruit in a mixture of eggs and milk

bread·bas·ket /ˈbredbɑːskɪt; *NAmE* -bæs-/ *noun* [sing.] (*especially NAmE*) the part of a country or region that produces large amounts of food, especially grain, for the rest of the country or region

'bread bin (*BrE*) (*NAmE* **bread·box** /ˈbredbɒks; *NAmE* -bɑːks/) *noun* a wooden, metal or plastic container for keeping bread in so that it stays fresh

bread·board /ˈbredbɔːd; *NAmE* -bɔːrd/ *noun* a flat board used for cutting bread on

bread·crumbs /ˈbredkrʌmz/ *noun* [pl.] very small pieces of bread that can be used in cooking

bread·ed /ˈbredɪd/ *adj.* covered in breadcrumbs

bread·fruit /ˈbredfruːt/ *noun* [C, U] (*pl.* **bread·fruit**) a large tropical fruit with a thick skin, that tastes and feels like bread when it is cooked. It grows on a tree which is called a breadfruit tree.

bread·line /ˈbredlaɪn/ *noun* **1** [sing.] the lowest level of income on which it is possible to live: *Many people without jobs are living* ***on the breadline*** (= are very poor). **2** [C] (*NAmE*) (in the past) a line of people waiting to receive free food

ˌbread 'roll *noun* = ROLL

bread·stick /ˈbredstɪk/ *noun* **1** a long thin piece of bread, which is dry like a biscuit **2** a piece of fresh bread, baked in the shape of a small stick

breadth /bredθ/ *noun* [U, C] **1** the distance or measurement from one side to the other; how broad or wide sth is SYN **width**: *She estimated the breadth of the lake to be 500 metres.* ➲ compare LENGTH **2** a wide range (of knowledge, interests, etc.): *He was surprised at her breadth of reading.* ◇ *The curriculum needs breadth and balance.* ◇ *a new political leader whose* ***breadth of vision*** (= willingness to accept new ideas) *can persuade others to change* IDM see LENGTH

'bread tree (also **'bread palm**) *noun* a large plant found in tropical and southern Africa whose thick main STEM can be made into a type of flour

bread·win·ner /ˈbredwɪnə(r)/ *noun* a person who supports their family with the money they earn

break 🔑 /breɪk/ *verb, noun*
■ *verb* (**broke** /brəʊk; *NAmE* broʊk/, **broken** /ˈbrəʊkən; *NAmE* ˈbroʊkən/)
▸ IN PIECES **1** 🔑 [I, T] to be damaged and separated into two or more parts, as a result of force; to damage sth in this way: *All the windows broke with the force of the blast.* ◇ **~ in/into sth** *She dropped the plate and it* ***broke into pieces.*** ◇ **~ sth** *to break a cup/window* ◇ *She fell off a ladder and broke her arm.* ◇ **~ sth in/into sth** *He* ***broke*** *the chocolate* ***in two.*** ➲ COLLOCATIONS at INJURY
▸ STOP WORKING **2** 🔑 [I, T] to stop working as a result of being damaged; to damage sth and stop it from working: *My watch has broken.* ◇ **~ sth** *I think I've broken the washing machine.*
▸ SKIN **3** [T] **~ sth** to cut the surface of the skin and make it BLEED: *The dog bit me but didn't break the skin.*
▸ LAW/PROMISE **4** 🔑 [T] **~ sth** to do sth that is against the law; to not keep a promise, etc: *to break the law/rules/conditions* ◇ *to break an agreement/a contract/a promise/your word* ◇ *to break an appointment* (= not to come to it) ◇ *He was breaking the speed limit* (= travelling faster than the law allows).
▸ STOP FOR SHORT TIME **5** 🔑 [I, T] to stop doing sth for a while, especially when it is time to eat or have a drink: **~ (for sth)** *Let's break for lunch.* ◇ **~ sth** *a broken night's sleep* (= a night during which you often wake up) ◇ (*especially BrE*) *We* ***broke our journey*** *in Oxford* (= stopped in Oxford on the way to the place we were going to).
▸ END STH **6** [T] **~ sth** to interrupt sth so that it ends suddenly: *She* ***broke the silence*** *by coughing.* ◇ *A tree* ***broke his fall*** (= stopped him as he was falling). ◇ *The phone rang and broke my train of thought.* **7** [T] **~ sth** to make sth end by using force or strong action: *an attempt to break the year-long siege* ◇ *Management has not succeeded in* ***breaking the strike.*** **8** [T] **~ sth** to end a connection with sth or a relationship with sb: *He broke all ties with his parents.*
▸ ESCAPE **9** [I] **~ free (from sb/sth)** (of a person or an object) to get away from or out of a position in which they are stuck or trapped: *He finally managed to break free from his attacker.*
▸ DESTROY, BE DESTROYED **10** [T, I] **~ (sb/sth)** to destroy sth or make sb/sth weaker; to become weak or be destroyed: *to break sb's morale/resistance/resolve/spirit* ◇ *The government was determined to break the power of the trade unions.* ◇ *The scandal broke him* (= ruined his reputation and destroyed his confidence). ◇ *She broke under questioning* (= was no longer able to bear it) *and confessed to everything.*
▸ MAKE SB FEEL BAD **11** [T] **~ sb** to make sb feel so sad, lonely, etc. that they cannot live a normal life: *The death of his wife broke him completely.*
▸ OF WEATHER **12** [I] to change suddenly, usually after a period when it has been fine
▸ SHOW OPENING **13** [I] to show an opening: *The clouds broke and the sun came out.*
▸ OF DAY/DAWN/STORM **14** [I] when the day or DAWN or a storm **breaks**, it begins: *Dawn was breaking when they finally left.* ➲ see also DAYBREAK
▸ OF NEWS **15** [I] if a piece of news **breaks**, it becomes known: *There was a public outcry when the scandal broke.* ◇ ***breaking news*** (= news that is arriving about events that have just happened) **16** [T] **~ it/the news to sb** to be the first to tell sb some bad news: *Who's going to break it to her?* ◇ *I'm sorry to be the one to break the news to you.*
▸ OF VOICE **17** [I] if sb's voice **breaks**, it changes its tone because of emotion: *Her voice broke as she told us the dreadful news.* **18** [I] when a boy's voice **breaks**, it becomes permanently deeper at about the age of 13 or 14
▸ A RECORD **19** 🔑 [T] **~ a record** to do sth better, faster, etc. than anyone has ever done it before: *She had broken the world 100 metres record.* ◇ *The movie broke all box-office records.*
▸ OF WAVES **20** [I] when waves **break**, they fall and are dissolved into FOAM, usually near land: *the sound of waves*

breaking on the beach ◇ *The sea was breaking over the wrecked ship.*

▸ STH SECRET **21** [T] **~ a code/cipher** to find the meaning of sth secret: *to break a code*

▸ MONEY **22** [T] **~ sth** (*especially NAmE*) to change a BANKNOTE for coins: *Can you break a twenty-dollar bill?*

IDM Idioms containing **break** are at the entries for the nouns and adjectives in the idioms, for example **break sb's heart** is at **heart**.

PHR V **ˌbreak aˈway (from sb/sth) 1** to escape suddenly from sb who is holding you or keeping you prisoner: *The prisoner broke away from his guards.* **2** to leave a political party, state, etc, especially to form a new one: *The people of the province wished to break away and form a new state.* ➲ related noun BREAKAWAY **3** to move away from a crowd or group, especially in a race: *She broke away from the pack and opened up a two-second lead.*

ˌbreak ˈdown 1 🔑 (of a machine or vehicle) to stop working because of a fault: *The telephone system has broken down.* ◇ *We (= the car) broke down on the freeway.* ➲ related noun BREAKDOWN **2** 🔑 to fail: *Negotiations between the two sides have broken down.* ➲ related noun BREAKDOWN **3** to become very bad: *Her health broke down under the pressure of work.* ➲ see also NERVOUS BREAKDOWN **4** 🔑 to lose control of your feelings and start crying: *He broke down and wept when he heard the news.* **5** to divide into parts to be analysed: *Expenditure on the project breaks down as follows: wages $10m, plant $4m, raw materials $5m.* ➲ related noun BREAKDOWN ➲ LANGUAGE BANK at ILLUSTRATE **ˌbreak sth↔ˈdown 1** 🔑 to make sth fall down, open, etc. by hitting it hard: *Firefighters had to break the door down to reach the people trapped inside.* **2** to destroy sth or make it disappear, especially a particular feeling or attitude that sb has: *to break down resistance/opposition* ◇ *to break down sb's reserve/shyness* ◇ *Attempts must be made to break down the barriers of fear and hostility which divide the two communities.* **3** to divide sth into parts in order to analyse it or make it easier to do: *Break your expenditure down into bills, food and other.* ◇ *Each lesson is broken down into several units.* ➲ related noun BREAKDOWN **4** to make a substance separate into parts or change into a different form in a chemical process: *Sugar and starch are broken down in the stomach.* ➲ related noun BREAKDOWN

ˈbreak for sth to suddenly run towards sth when you are trying to escape: *She had to hold him back as he tried to break for the door.*

ˌbreak ˈin 🔑 to enter a building by force: *Burglars had broken in while we were away.* ➲ related noun BREAK-IN

ˌbreak sb/sth ˈin 1 to train sb/sth in sth new that they must do: *to break in new recruits* ◇ *The young horse was not yet broken in* (= trained to carry a rider). **2** to wear sth, especially new shoes, until they become comfortable

ˌbreak ˈin (on sth) to interrupt or disturb sth: *She longed to break in on their conversation but didn't want to appear rude.* ◇ **+ speech** *'I didn't do it!' she broke in.*

ˌbreak ˈinto sth 1 🔑 to enter a building by force; to open a car, etc. by force: *We had our car broken into last week.* ➲ related noun BREAK-IN **2** to begin laughing, singing, etc. suddenly: *As the President's car drew up, the crowd broke into loud applause.* **3** to suddenly start running; to start running faster than before: *He broke into a run when he saw the police.* ◇ *Her horse broke into a trot.* **4** (*BrE*) to use a BANKNOTE of high value to buy sth that costs less: *I had to break into a £20 to pay the bus fare.* **5** to open and use sth that has been kept for an emergency: *They had to break into the emergency food supplies.* **6** to be successful when you get involved in sth: *The company is having difficulty breaking into new markets.*

ˌbreak ˈoff 1 🔑 to become separated from sth as a result of force: *The back section of the plane had broken off.* **2** to stop speaking or stop doing sth for a time: *He broke off in the middle of a sentence.* **ˌbreak sth↔ˈoff** 🔑 **1** to separate sth, using force: *She broke off a piece of chocolate and gave it to me.* **2** 🔑 to end sth suddenly: *Britain threatened to break off diplomatic relations.* ◇ *They've broken off their engagement.*

ˌbreak ˈout 🔑 (of war, fighting or other unpleasant events) to start suddenly: *They had escaped to America shortly before war broke out in 1939.* ◇ *Fighting had broken out between rival groups of fans.* ◇ *Fire broke out during the night.* ➲ related noun OUTBREAK **ˌbreak ˈout (of sth)** to escape from a place or situation: *Several prisoners broke out of the jail.* ◇ *She needed to break out of her daily routine and do something exciting.* ➲ related noun BREAKOUT

ˌbreak ˈout in sth to suddenly become covered in sth: *Her face broke out in a rash.* ◇ *He broke out in a cold sweat* (= for example, through fear).

ˌbreak ˈthrough to make new and important discoveries: *Scientists think they are beginning to break through in the fight against cancer.* ➲ related noun BREAKTHROUGH

ˌbreak ˈthrough | ˌbreak ˈthrough sth 1 to make a way through sth using force: *Demonstrators broke through the police cordon.* **2** (of the sun or moon) to appear from behind clouds: *The sun broke through at last in the afternoon.*

ˌbreak ˈthrough sth to succeed in dealing with an attitude that sb has and the difficulties it creates SYN **overcome**: *He had finally managed to break through her reserve.*

ˌbreak ˈup 1 🔑 to separate into smaller pieces: *The ship broke up on the rocks.* **2** 🔑 to come to an end: *Their marriage has broken up.* ➲ related noun BREAK-UP **3** to go away in different directions: *The meeting broke up at eleven o'clock.* **4** (*especially BrE*) to begin the holidays when school closes at the end of a term: *When do you break up for Christmas?* **5** (*BrE*) to become very weak: *He was breaking up under the strain.* **6** (*NAmE*) to laugh very hard: *Woody Allen makes me just break up.* **7** when a person who is talking on a mobile/cell phone **breaks up**, you can no longer hear them clearly because the signal has been interrupted

ˌbreak sth↔ˈup 1 🔑 to make sth separate into smaller pieces; to divide sth into smaller parts: *The ship was broken up for scrap metal.* ◇ *Sentences can be broken up into clauses.* **2** to end a relationship, a company, etc: *They decided to break up the partnership.* ➲ related noun BREAK-UP **3** to make people leave sth or stop doing sth, especially by using force: *Police were called in to break up the fight.*

ˌbreak ˈup (with sb) 🔑 to end a relationship with sb: *She's just broken up with her boyfriend.* ➲ related noun BREAK-UP

ˈbreak with sth to end a connection with sth: *to* ***break with tradition/old habits/the past***

■ ***noun***

▸ SHORT STOP/PAUSE **1** 🔑 [C] a short period of time when you stop what you are doing and rest, eat, etc: *a* ***coffee/lunch/tea break*** ◇ *Let's* ***take a break.*** ◇ *a break for lunch* ◇ *She worked all day without a break.* ➲ SYNONYMS at REST **2** (also **ˈbreak time**) (both *BrE*) (*NAmE* **re·cess**) [U] a period of time between lessons at school: *Come and see me at break.* **3** 🔑 [C] a pause or period of time when sth stops before starting again: *a break in my daily routine* ◇ *She wanted to take a* ***career break*** *in order to have children.* **4** 🔑 [C] a pause for advertisements in the middle of a television or radio programme: *More news after the break.*

▸ HOLIDAY/VACATION **5** 🔑 [C] a short holiday/vacation: *We had a weekend break in New York.* ◇ *a well-earned break*

▸ CHANGE IN SITUATION **6** [sing.] the moment when a situation or a relationship that has existed for a time changes, ends or is interrupted: **~ (with sb/sth)** *He needed to make a complete break with the past.* ◇ *a* ***break with tradition/convention*** (= a change from what is accepted, in sth such as art, behaviour, etc.) ◇ **~ (in sth)** *a* ***break in the weather*** (= a change from one type of weather to a different one) ◇ *a break in diplomatic relations*

▸ OPENING/SPACE **7** [C] **~ (in sth)** a space or an opening between two or more things: *We could see the moon through a break in the clouds.*

▸ OPPORTUNITY **8** [C] (*informal*) an opportunity to do sth, usually to get sth that you want or to achieve success: *I got my* ***lucky break*** *when I won a 'Young Journalist of the Year' competition.* ◇ *We've had a few bad breaks* (= pieces of bad luck) *along the way.*

▸ OF BONE **9** [C] a place where sth, especially a bone in your body, has broken: *The X-ray showed there was no break in his leg.*

▸ IN TENNIS **10** (also **break of 'serve**) [C] a win in a game in which your opponent is SERVING: *It was her second break in the set.* ◇ ***break point*** (= a situation in which, if you win the next point, you win the game)
▸ IN BILLIARDS/SNOOKER **11** [C] a series of successful shots by one player; the number of points scored in a series of successful shots: *He's put together a magnificent break.* ◇ *a 147 break* (= the highest possible break in SNOOKER)
IDM **break of 'day/'dawn** (*literary*) the moment in the early hours of the morning when it begins to get light **give me a 'break!** (*informal*) used when sb wants sb else to stop doing or saying sth that is annoying, or to stop saying sth that is not true **give sb a 'break** to give sb a chance; to not judge sb too severely: *Give the lad a break—it's only his second day on the job.* **make a 'break for sth/for it** to run towards sth in order to try and escape: *He suddenly leapt up and made a break for the door.* ◇ *They decided to make a break for it* (= to try and escape) *that night.* ➲ more at CLEAN *adj.*

Vocabulary Building

Words that mean 'break'

burst	*The balloon hit a tree and burst.*
crack	*The ice started to crack.*
crumble	*Crumble the cheese into a bowl.*
cut	*Now cut the wire in two.*
fracture	*He fell and fractured his hip.*
shatter	*The vase hit the floor and shattered.*
smash	*Vandals had smashed two windows.*
snap	*I snapped the pencil in half.*
split	*The bag had split open on the way home.*
tear	*She tore the letter into pieces.*

All these verbs, except **cut**, can be used with or without an object.

break·able /'breɪkəbl/ *adj.* likely to break; easily broken

break·age /'breɪkɪdʒ/ *noun* **1** [C, usually pl.] an object that has been broken: *The last time we moved house there were very few breakages.* **2** [U, C] the act of breaking sth: *Wrap it up carefully to protect against breakage.*

break·away /'breɪkəweɪ/ *adj., noun*
■ ***adj.*** [only before noun] (of a political group, an organization, or a part of a country) having separated from a larger group or country: *a* ***breakaway faction/group/section*** ◇ *a breakaway republic*
■ ***noun*** [sing.] **1** an occasion when members of a political party or an organization leave it in order to form a new party, etc. **2** a change from an accepted style: *a breakaway from his earlier singing style*

break·beat /'breɪkbi:t/ *noun* **1** [C] a series of drum beats that are repeated to form the rhythm of a piece of dance music **2** [U] dance music, for example HIP HOP, that uses breakbeats

break·bone fever /'breɪkbəʊn fi:və(r); *NAmE* -boʊn/ *noun* [U] = DENGUE

'break-dancing *noun* [U] a style of dancing with ACROBATIC movements, often performed in the street ▸ **'break-dance** *verb* [I] **'break-dancer** *noun*

break·down /'breɪkdaʊn/ *noun* **1** [C] an occasion when a vehicle or machine stops working: *a breakdown on the motorway* ◇ *a breakdown recovery service* **2** [C, U] a failure of a relationship, discussion or system: *the breakdown of a marriage* ◇ *marriage breakdown* ◇ *a breakdown in communications* ◇ *The breakdown of the negotiations was not unexpected.* ◇ *the breakdown of law and order* **3** [C, usually sing.] detailed information that you get by studying a set of figures: *First, let's look at a breakdown of the costs.* **4** [U] (*technical*) the breaking of a substance into the parts of which it is made: *the breakdown of proteins in the digestive system* **5** [C] = NERVOUS BREAKDOWN: *She's still recovering from her breakdown.*

'breakdown lane (*US*) (*BrE* ˌ**hard 'shoulder**) *noun* a strip of ground with a hard surface beside a major road such as a MOTORWAY or INTERSTATE where vehicles can stop in an emergency

'breakdown truck (*BrE*) (also **'tow truck** *NAmE, BrE*) *noun* a truck that is used for taking cars away to be repaired when they have had a breakdown ➲ VISUAL VOCAB page V46

break·er /'breɪkə(r)/ *noun* a large wave covered with white bubbles that is moving towards land ➲ see also CIRCUIT-BREAKER, ICEBREAKER, HOUSEBREAKER, LAWBREAKER, RECORD-BREAKER, STRIKE-BREAKER, TIE-BREAKER

'break-even *noun* [U] (*business*) a time when a company or piece of business earns just enough money to pay for its costs: *The company expects to reach break-even next year.* ➲ see also EVEN *adj.*

break·fast 0‑w /'brekfəst/ *noun, verb*
■ ***noun*** 0‑w [C, U] the first meal of the day: *a* ***big/hearty/light breakfast*** ◇ (*especially BrE*) *a cooked breakfast* ◇ *Do you want bacon and eggs* ***for breakfast***? ◇ *They were having breakfast when I arrived.* ◇ *She doesn't eat much breakfast.* ➲ see also BED AND BREAKFAST, CONTINENTAL BREAKFAST, ENGLISH BREAKFAST, POWER BREAKFAST, WEDDING BREAKFAST IDM see DOG *n.*
■ ***verb*** [I] ~ **(on sth)** (*formal*) to eat breakfast

'break-in *noun* an entry into a building using force, usually to steal sth

ˌ**breaking and 'entering** *noun* [U] (*NAmE* or *old-fashioned*) the crime of entering a building illegally and using force

'breaking point (also **'break point**) *noun* [U] the time when problems become so great that a person, an organization or a system can no longer deal with them: *to* ***be at/to reach breaking point*** ◇ *to be stretched to breaking point*

break·neck /'breɪknek/ *adj.* [only before noun] very fast and dangerous: *to drive, etc.* ***at breakneck speed***

break·out /'breɪkaʊt/ *noun, adj.*
■ ***noun*** an escape from prison, usually by a group of prisoners: *a mass breakout from a top security prison*
■ ***adj.*** [only before noun] **1** (*NAmE, informal*) suddenly and extremely popular and successful; establishing sb's reputation: *a breakout hit/movie* **2** (*especially NAmE*) taking place separately from the main meeting with a smaller number of people: *a* ***breakout session*** *before the plenary* ◇ *a* ***breakout group*** *on ethical issues*

'break point *noun* **1** the point where sth, especially a computer program, is interrupted **2** ˌ**break 'point** (especially in TENNIS) a point that the person who is SERVING must win in order not to lose a game **3** = BREAKING POINT

break·through /'breɪkθru:/ *noun, adj.*
■ ***noun*** an important development that may lead to an agreement or achievement: *to* ***make/achieve a breakthrough*** ◇ *a significant breakthrough in negotiations* ◇ *a major breakthrough in cancer research*
■ ***adj.*** [only before noun] in which a performer or type of product is successful for the first time, when it is likely to be even more successful in the future: *It was a breakthrough album for the band.* ◇ *breakthrough technology/products*

'break time *noun* [U] (*BrE*) = BREAK

'break-up *noun* **1** the ending of a relationship or an association: *the break-up of their marriage* ◇ *family break-ups* **2** the division of a large organization or country into smaller parts

break·water /'breɪkwɔ:tə(r)/ *noun* a wall built out into the sea to protect the SHORE or HARBOUR from the force of the waves ➲ VISUAL VOCAB page V4

bream /bri:m/ *noun* (*pl.* **bream**) a FRESHWATER or sea fish that is used for food

breast ⊶ /brest/ *noun, verb*
■ ***noun***
▸ PART OF BODY **1** ⊶ [C] either of the two round soft parts at the front of a woman's body that produce milk when she has had a baby: *She put the baby to her breast.* ◇ *breast cancer* ◇ *breast milk* **2** ⊶ [C] the similar, smaller part on a man's body, which does not produce milk **3** [C] (*literary*) the top part of the front of your body, below your neck **SYN** **chest**: *He cradled the child against his breast.*
▸ CLOTHING **4** [C] the part of a piece of clothing that covers your chest: *A row of medals was pinned to the breast of his coat.*
▸ OF BIRD **5** [C] the front part of a bird's body: *breast feathers* ◇ *The robin has a red breast.*
▸ MEAT **6** [C, U] meat from the front part of the body of a bird or an animal: ***chicken/turkey breasts*** ◇ *breast of lamb*
▸ -BREASTED **7** (in adjectives) having the type of chest or breasts mentioned: *a* ***small-breasted/full-breasted*** *woman* ◇ *bare-breasted* ◇ *the yellow-breasted male of the species* ➲ see also DOUBLE-BREASTED, SINGLE-BREASTED
▸ HEART **8** [C] (*literary*) the part of the body where the feelings and emotions are thought to be: *a troubled breast* ➲ see also CHIMNEY BREAST **IDM** see BEAT *v.*, CLEAN *adj.*
■ ***verb*** (*formal*) **1** **~ sth** to reach the top of a hill, etc: *As they breasted the ridge, they saw the valley and lake before them.* **2** **~ sth** to push through sth, touching it with your chest: *He strode into the ocean, breasting the waves.*

breast·bone /ˈbrestbəʊn; *NAmE* -boʊn/ *noun* the long flat bone in the chest that the seven top pairs of RIBS are connected to **SYN** **sternum** ➲ VISUAL VOCAB page V48

breast·feed /ˈbrestfiːd/ *verb* (**breast·fed**, **breast·fed** /-fed/) [I, T] **~ (sb)** when a woman **breastfeeds**, she feeds her baby with milk from her breasts. ➲ compare BOTTLE-FEED, NURSE *v.* (6)

breast·plate /ˈbrestpleɪt/ *noun* a piece of ARMOUR worn by soldiers in the past to protect the upper front part of the body

ˌ**breast ˈpocket** *noun* a pocket on a shirt, or on the outside or inside of the part of a jacket that covers the chest ➲ VISUAL VOCAB page V51

ˈ**breast pump** *noun* a device for getting milk from a woman's breasts, so that her baby can be fed later from a bottle

breast·stroke /ˈbreststrəʊk; *NAmE* -stroʊk/ *noun* [U, sing.] a style of swimming that you do on your front, moving your arms and legs away from your body and then back towards it in a circle ➲ VISUAL VOCAB page V37

breath ⊶ /breθ/ *noun*
1 ⊶ [U] the air that you take into your lungs and send out again: *His breath smelt of garlic.* ◇ *bad breath* (= that smells bad) ◇ *We had to stop for breath before we got to the top.* ◇ *She was very* ***short of breath*** (= had difficulty breathing). **2** ⊶ [C] an amount of air that enters the lungs at one time: *to take a deep breath* ◇ *He recited the whole poem in one breath.* **3** [sing.] **~ of sth** (*formal*) a small amount of sth; slight evidence of sth: *a* ***breath of suspicion/scandal*** **4** [sing.] **a ~ of air/wind** (*literary*) a slight movement of air
IDM **a breath of (fresh) ˈair** clean air breathed in after being indoors or in a dirty atmosphere: *We'll get a breath of fresh air at lunchtime.* **a breath of fresh ˈair** a person, thing or place that is new and different and therefore interesting and exciting **the breath of ˈlife to/for sb** (*literary*) an essential part of a person's existence **get your ˈbreath (again/back)** (*BrE*) (also **catch your ˈbreath** *NAmE, BrE*) to breathe normally again after running or doing some tiring exercise **hold your ˈbreath** **1** to stop breathing for a short time: *Hold your breath and count to ten.* **2** to be anxious while you are waiting for sth that you are worried about: *He held his breath while the results were read out.* **3** (*informal*) people say **don't hold your breath!** to emphasize that sth will take a long time or may not happen: *She said she'd do it this week, but don't hold your breath!* **in the same ˈbreath** immediately after saying sth that suggests the opposite intention or meaning: *He praised my work and in the same breath told me I would have to leave.* **his/her last/dying ˈbreath** the last moment of a person's life **out of ˈbreath** ⊶ having difficulty breathing after exercise: *We were out of breath after only five minutes.* **say sth, speak, etc. under your ˈbreath** to say sth quietly so that people cannot hear: *'Rubbish!' he murmured under his breath.* **take sb's ˈbreath away** to be very surprising or beautiful: *My first view of the island from the air took my breath away.* ➲ more at BATED, CATCH *V.*, DRAW *V.*, SAVE *V.*, WASTE *V.*

breath·able /ˈbriːðəbl/ *adj.* (*technical*) (of material used in making clothes) allowing air to pass through: *Breathable, waterproof clothing is essential for most outdoor sports.*

breath·alyse (*BrE*) (*NAmE* **breath·alyze**) /ˈbreθəlaɪz/ *verb* [usually passive] **~ sb** to check how much alcohol a driver has drunk by making him or her breathe into a breathalyser: *Both drivers were breathalysed at the scene of the accident.*

breath·alyser (*BrE*) (*NAmE* **Breath·alyzer™**) /ˈbreθəlaɪzə(r)/ *noun* a device used by the police to measure the amount of alcohol in a driver's breath

breathe ⊶ /briːð/ *verb*
▸ AIR/BREATH **1** ⊶ [I, T] to take air into your lungs and send it out again through your nose or mouth: *He breathed deeply before speaking again.* ◇ *The air was so cold we could hardly breathe.* ◇ *She was beginning to breathe more easily.* ◇ **~ sth** *Most people don't realize that they are breathing polluted air.* **2** [T] **~ sth (+ adv./prep.)** to send air, smoke or a particular smell out of your mouth: *He came up close, breathing alcohol fumes all over me.*
▸ SAY QUIETLY **3** [T] **~ sth** | **+ speech** (*literary*) to say sth quietly: *'I'm over here,' she breathed.*
▸ OF WINE **4** [I] if you allow wine to **breathe**, you open the bottle and let air get in before you drink it
▸ OF CLOTH/SKIN **5** [I] if cloth, leather, skin, etc. can **breathe**, air can move around or through it: *Cotton clothing allows your skin to breathe.*
▸ FEELING/QUALITY **6** [T] **~ sth** (*formal*) to be full of a particular feeling or quality: *Her performance breathed wit and charm.*
IDM **breathe (easily/freely) again** to feel calm again after sth unpleasant or frightening has ended **breathe down sb's ˈneck** (*informal*) to watch closely what sb is doing in a way that makes them feel anxious and/or annoyed ˌ**breathe (new) ˈlife into sth** to improve sth by introducing new ideas and making people more interested in it **breathe your ˈlast** (*literary*) to die ➲ more at EASY *adj.*, LIVE[1]
PHR V ˌ**breathe ˈin** ⊶ to take air into your lungs through your nose or mouth **SYN** **inhale** ˌ**breathe sth↔ˈin** to take air, smoke, etc. into your lungs through your nose or mouth: *His illness is a result of breathing in paint fumes over many years.* ˌ**breathe ˈout** ⊶ to send air out of your lungs through your nose or mouth **SYN** **exhale** ˌ**breathe sth↔ˈout** to send air, smoke, etc. out of your lungs through your nose or mouth: *Humans take in oxygen and breathe out carbon dioxide.*

breather /ˈbriːðə(r)/ *noun* (*informal*) a short pause for rest or to relax: *to* ***take/have a breather*** ◇ *Tell me when you need a breather.* ◇ *a five-minute breather* ➲ see also HEAVY BREATHER

breath·ing ⊶ /ˈbriːðɪŋ/ *noun* [U] the action of taking air into the lungs and sending it out again: *Her breathing became steady and she fell asleep.* ◇ *Deep breathing exercises will help you relax.* ◇ *Heavy* (= loud) *breathing was all I could hear.*

ˈ**breathing space** *noun* [C, U] a short rest in the middle of a period of mental or physical effort ➲ SYNONYMS at REST

breath·less /ˈbreθləs/ *adj.* **1** having difficulty in breathing; making it difficult for sb to breathe: *He arrived breathless at the top of the stairs.* ◇ *They maintained a breathless* (= very fast) *pace for half an hour.* **2** (*formal*) experiencing, or making sb experience, a strong emotional reaction: *the breathless excitement of seeing each other again* ◇ **~ with sth** *breathless with terror* **3** (*formal*) with no air or wind: *the* *breathless heat of a summer afternoon* ▸ **breath·less·ly** *adv.* **breath·less·ness** *noun* [U]

B

breath·tak·ing /ˈbreθteɪkɪŋ/ *adj.* very exciting or impressive (usually in a pleasant way); very surprising: *a breathtaking view of the mountains* ◇ *The scene was one of breathtaking beauty.* ◇ *He spoke with breathtaking arrogance.* ▸ **breath·tak·ing·ly** *adv.*: *a breathtakingly expensive diamond*

ˈ**breath test** *noun* a test used by the police to show the amount of alcohol in a driver's breath

breathy /ˈbreθi/ *adj.* speaking or singing with a noticeable sound of breathing

bred *past tense, past part.* of BREED

breech /briːtʃ/ *noun* the part of a gun at the back where the bullets are loaded

ˈ**breech birth** (also ˌ**breech deˈlivery**) *noun* a birth in which the baby's bottom or feet come out of the mother first

breeches /ˈbrɪtʃɪz/ *noun* [pl.] short trousers/pants fastened just below the knee: *a pair of breeches* ◇ *riding breeches*

breed 0➡ /briːd/ *verb, noun*

■ ***verb*** (**bred, bred** /bred/) **1** 0➡ [I] (of animals) to have sex and produce young: *Many animals breed only at certain times of the year.* ➲ see also INTERBREED **2** 0➡ [T] **~ sth** (**for/as sth**) to keep animals or plants in order to produce young ones in a controlled way: *The rabbits are bred for their long coats.* ➲ COLLOCATIONS at FARMING ➲ see also CROSS-BREED, PURE-BRED, THOROUGHBRED **3** [T] **~ sth** to be the cause of sth: *Nothing breeds success like success.* **4** [T, usually passive] **~ sth into sb** to educate sb in a particular way as they are growing up: *Fear of failure was bred into him at an early age.* ➲ see also WELL BRED IDM see BORN *V.*, FAMILIARITY

■ ***noun*** **1** 0➡ a particular type of animal that has been developed by people in a controlled way, especially a type of dog, cat or farm animal: *Labradors and other large breeds of dog* ◇ *a* ***breed of cattle/sheep*** **2** [usually sing.] a type of person: *He represents a new breed of politician.* ◇ *Players as skilful as this are* ***a rare breed.***

breed·er /ˈbriːdə(r)/ *noun* a person who breeds animals: *a dog/horse/cattle, etc. breeder*

breed·ing /ˈbriːdɪŋ/ *noun* [U] **1** the keeping of animals in order to breed from them: *the breeding of horses* **2** the producing of young animals, plants, etc: *the breeding season* **3** the family or social background that is thought to result in good manners: *a sign of good breeding*

ˈ**breeding ground** *noun* **1** [usually pl.] a place where wild animals go to produce their young **2 ~** (**for sth**) [usually sing.] a place where sth, especially sth bad, is able to develop: *This area of the city has become a breeding ground for violent crime.*

breeze /briːz/ *noun, verb*

■ ***noun*** **1** [C] a light wind: *a sea breeze* ◇ *The flowers were gently swaying* ***in the breeze.*** ◇ *A light breeze was blowing.* ➲ COLLOCATIONS at WEATHER **2** [sing.] (*informal*) a thing that is easy to do: *It was a breeze.* IDM see SHOOT *V.*

■ ***verb*** [I] **+ adv./prep.** to move in a cheerful and confident way in a particular direction: *She just breezed in and asked me to help.*

PHR V ˌ**breeze ˈthrough sth** to do sth successfully and easily: *He breezed through the tests.*

ˈ**breeze block** (*BrE*) (*NAmE* ˈ**cinder block**) *noun* a light building block, made of sand, coal ASHES and CEMENT

breeze·way /ˈbriːzweɪ/ *noun* (*NAmE*) an outside passage with a roof and open sides between two separate parts of a building

breezy /ˈbriːzi/ *adj.* (**breez·ier, breezi·est**) **1** with the wind blowing quite strongly: *It was a bright, breezy day.* ◇ *the breezy east coast* **2** having or showing a cheerful and relaxed manner: *You're very bright and breezy today!* ▸ **breez·ily** /ˈbriːzɪli/ *adv.*: *'Hi folks,' he said breezily.* **breezi·ness** /ˈbriːzinəs/ *noun* [U]

breth·ren /ˈbreðrən/ *noun* [pl.] (*old-fashioned*) **1** used to talk to people in church or to talk about the members of a male religious group: *Let us pray, brethren.* **2** people who are part of the same society as yourself: *We should do all we can to help our less fortunate brethren.*

Bre·ton /ˈbretən/ *noun, adj.*

■ ***noun*** **1** [U] the Celtic language of Brittany in NW France **2** [C] a person who was born in Brittany or who lives in Brittany

■ ***adj.*** connected with Brittany or its language or culture

breve /briːv/ *noun* (*music*) a note that lasts as long as eight CROTCHETS/QUARTER NOTES, which is rarely used in modern music

brev·ity AW /ˈbrevəti/ *noun* [U] (*formal*) **1** the quality of using few words when speaking or writing SYN **conciseness**: *The report is a masterpiece of brevity.* **2** the fact of lasting a short time: *the brevity of human life* ➲ see also BRIEF

brew /bruː/ *verb, noun*

■ ***verb*** **1** [T, I] **~ sth** to make beer: *This beer is brewed in the Czech Republic.* **2** [T] **~ sth** to make a hot drink of tea or coffee: *freshly brewed coffee* **3** [I] (*especially BrE*) (of tea or coffee) to be mixed with hot water and become ready to drink: *Always let tea brew for a few minutes.* **4** [I] **~** (**up**) (usually used in the progressive tenses) if sth unpleasant **is brewing** or **brewing up**, it seems likely to happen soon

PHR V ˌ**brew ˈup** | ˌ**brew sth↔ˈup** (*BrE, informal*) to make a hot drink of tea or coffee: *Whose turn is it to brew up?* ➲ related noun BREW-UP

■ ***noun*** **1** [C, U] a type of beer, especially one made in a particular place: *I thought I'd try the local brew.* ◇ *home brew* (= beer made at home) **2** [C, usually sing.] (*BrE, informal*) an amount of tea made at one time: *I'll make a fresh brew.* ◇ *Let's have a brew.* **3** [C, usually sing.] a mixture of different ideas, events, etc: *The movie is a potent brew of adventure, sex and comedy.* ◇ *His music is* ***a heady brew*** (= a powerful mixture) *of heavy metal and punk.*

IDM **a witch's/an evil ˈbrew** (*BrE*) an unpleasant drink that is a mixture of different things

brew·er /ˈbruːə(r)/ *noun* a person or company that makes beer

brew·ery /ˈbruːəri/ *noun* (*pl.* **-ies**) a factory where beer is made; a company that makes beer

brew·house /ˈbruːhaʊs/ *noun* a factory where beer is made SYN **brewery**

ˈ**brew-up** *noun* (*BrE, informal*) an act of making tea: *We always have a brew-up at 11 o'clock.*

briar (also **brier**) /ˈbraɪə(r)/ *noun* **1** a wild bush with THORNS, especially a wild ROSE bush **2** a bush with a hard root that is used for making TOBACCO pipes; a tobacco pipe made from this root

bribe /braɪb/ *noun, verb*

■ ***noun*** a sum of money or sth valuable that you give or offer to sb to persuade them to help you, especially by doing sth dishonest: *It was alleged that he had* ***taken bribes*** *while in office.* ◇ *She had been offered a $50 000 bribe to drop the charges.* ➲ COLLOCATIONS at CRIME

■ ***verb*** to give sb money or sth valuable in order to persuade them to help you, especially by doing sth dishonest: **~ sb** (**with sth**) *They bribed the guards with cigarettes.* ◇ **~ sb into doing sth** *She was bribed into handing over secret information.* ◇ **~ sb to do sth** *She bribed him to sign the certificate.* ◇ **~ your way...** *He managed to* ***bribe his way*** *onto the ship .*

brib·ery /ˈbraɪbəri/ *noun* [U] the giving or taking of bribes: *She was arrested on bribery charges.* ◇ *allegations of bribery and corruption*

bric-a-brac /ˈbrɪk ə bræk/ *noun* [U] ORNAMENTS and other small decorative objects of little value: *market stalls selling cheap bric-a-brac*

brick 0➡ /brɪk/ *noun, verb*

■ ***noun*** **1** 0➡ [C, U] baked CLAY used for building walls, houses and other buildings; an individual block of this: *The school is built of brick.* ◇ *a pile of bricks* ◇ *a brick wall* ➲ see also RED-BRICK ➲ VISUAL VOCAB page V15 **2** [C] a plastic or wooden block, used as a toy for young children to build things with **3** [C, usually sing.] (*old-fashioned*, *BrE*, *informal*) a friend that you can rely on when you need help

IDM **be up against a brick 'wall** to be unable to make any progress because there is a difficulty that stops you **bricks and 'mortar** buildings, when you are thinking of them in connection with how much they cost to build or how much they are worth: *They put their money into bricks and mortar.* ◇ (*business*) *a new Internet company without a lot of bricks-and-mortar businesses* (= businesses with buildings that customers go to) ◇ (*NAmE* also) *brick-and-mortar businesses* **make bricks without 'straw** (*BrE*) to try to work without the necessary material, money, information, etc. ➲ more at CAT *n.*, DROP *v.*, HEAD *n.*, TON *n.*

■ ***verb***

PHR V **,brick sth↔'in/'up** to fill an opening in a wall with bricks: *The windows had been bricked up.*

brick·bat /'brɪkbæt/ *noun* [usually pl.] an insulting remark made in public

brick·lay·er /'brɪkleɪə(r)/ (also *BrE informal* **brickie**) *noun* a person whose job is to build walls, etc. with bricks ▸ **brick·lay·ing** *noun* [U]

brick·work /'brɪkwɜːk; *NAmE* -wɜːrk/ *noun* **1** [U] the bricks in a wall, building, etc: *Plaster had fallen away in places, exposing the brickwork.* **2 brick·works** [C] (*pl.* **brick·works**) (*BrE*) a place where bricks are made

bri·dal /'braɪdl/ *adj.* [only before noun] connected with a bride or a wedding: *a bridal gown* ◇ *the* ***bridal party*** (= the bride and the bridegroom and the people helping them at their wedding, sometimes used to refer only to the bride and those helping her) ◇ *a* ***bridal suite*** (= a set of rooms in a hotel for a couple who have just got married) ◇ (*NAmE*) *a* ***bridal shower*** (= a party for a woman who will get married soon)

bride /braɪd/ *noun* a woman on her wedding day, or just before or just after it: *a toast to the* ***bride and groom*** ◇ *He introduced his new bride.*

bride·groom /'braɪdgruːm/ (also **groom**) *noun* a man on his wedding day, or just before or just after it

brides·maid /'braɪdzmeɪd/ *noun* a young woman or girl who helps a BRIDE before and during the marriage ceremony ➲ compare BEST MAN, PAGEBOY

bridge 0‑w /brɪdʒ/ *noun*, *verb*

■ ***noun***

▸ OVER ROAD/RIVER **1** 0‑w [C] a structure that is built over a road, railway/railroad, river, etc. so that people or vehicles can cross from one side to the other: *We crossed the bridge over the river Windrush.* ➲ **VISUAL VOCAB** pages V3, V12 ➲ see also SUSPENSION BRIDGE, SWING BRIDGE

▸ CONNECTION **2** 0‑w [C] a thing that provides a connection or contact between two different things: *Cultural exchanges are a way of* ***building bridges*** *between countries.*

▸ OF SHIP **3** [C, usually sing.] (usually **the bridge**) the part of a ship where the captain and other officers stand when they are controlling and steering the ship ➲ **VISUAL VOCAB** page V44

▸ CARD GAME **4** [U] a card game for two pairs of players who have to predict how many cards they will win. They score points if they succeed in winning that number of cards and lose points if they fail. ➲ see also CONTRACT BRIDGE

▸ OF NOSE **5 the ~ of sb's nose** [sing.] the hard part at the top of the nose, between the eyes ➲ **VISUAL VOCAB** page V48

▸ OF GLASSES **6** [C] the part of a pair of glasses that rests on your nose

▸ OF GUITAR/VIOLIN **7** [C] a small piece of wood on a GUITAR, VIOLIN, etc. over which the strings are stretched ➲ **VISUAL VOCAB** page V31

▸ FALSE TEETH **8** [C] a false tooth or false teeth, held permanently in place by being fastened to natural teeth on either side **IDM** see BURN *v.*, CROSS *v.*, WATER *n.*

■ ***verb***

▸ BUILD/FORM BRIDGE **~ sth** to build or form a bridge over sth: *The valley was originally bridged by the Romans.* ◇ *A plank of wood bridged the stream.*

IDM **bridge the 'gap/'gulf/di'vide** (**between A and B**) to reduce or get rid of the differences that exist between two things or groups of people

B

bridges

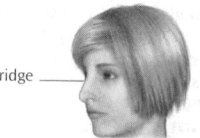

bridge over a river

bridge of the nose

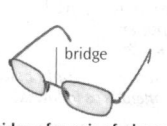

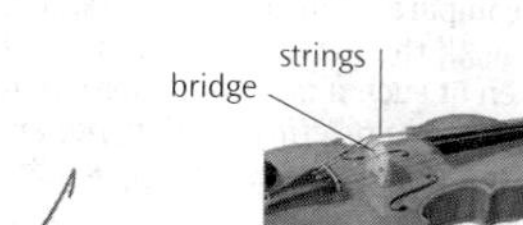

bridge of a pair of glasses

bridge of a violin

'bridge-building *noun* [U] activities intended to make relations between two groups, countries, etc. friendlier

bridge·head /'brɪdʒhed/ *noun* **1** a strong position that an army has captured in enemy land, from which it can go forward or attack the enemy **2** [usually sing.] a good position from which to make progress

bridge·work /'brɪdʒwɜːk; *NAmE* -wɜːrk/ *noun* [U] **1** artificial teeth and the parts that keep them in place in the mouth **2** the work of making these teeth or putting them in place

'bridging loan (*BrE*) (*NAmE* **'bridge loan**) *noun* an amount of money that a bank lends you for a short time, especially so that you can buy a new house while you are waiting to sell your old one

bri·die /'braɪdi/ *noun* (*ScotE*) a small PIE containing meat

bridle /'braɪdl/ *noun*, *verb*

■ ***noun*** a set of leather bands, attached to REINS, which is put around a horse's head and used for controlling it

■ ***verb*** **1** [T] **~ sth** to put a bridle on a horse **2** [I] **~ (at sth)** (*literary*) to show that you are annoyed and/or offended at sth, especially by moving your head up and backwards in a proud way: *She bridled at the suggestion that she was lying.*

'bridle path (*BrE* also **bridle·way** /'braɪdlweɪ/) *noun* a rough path that is suitable for people riding horses or walking, but not for cars

Brie /briː/ *noun* [U, C] a type of soft French cheese

brief 0‑w **AW** /briːf/ *adj.*, *noun*, *verb*

■ ***adj.*** (**brief·er**, **brief·est**) **1** 0‑w lasting only a short time; short: *a brief visit/meeting/conversation* ◇ *a brief pause/silence* ◇ *Mozart's life was brief.* **2** 0‑w using few words: *a brief description/summary/account* ◇ *Please* ***be brief*** (= say what you want to say quickly). **3** (of clothes) short and not covering much of the body: *a brief skirt* ➲ see also BREVITY, BRIEFLY

IDM **in brief** in a few words, without details: *In brief, the meeting was a disaster.* ◇ *Now the rest of the news in brief.*

■ ***noun*** ➲ see also BRIEFS **1** (*BrE*) the instructions that a person is given explaining what their job is and what their duties are: *It wasn't part of his brief to speak to the press.* ◇ *I was* ***given the brief*** *of reorganizing the department.* ◇ ***to stick to your brief*** (= to only do what you are asked to do) ◇ *to* ***prepare/produce a brief*** *for sb* **2** (*BrE*, *law*) a legal case that is given to a lawyer to argue in court; a piece of work for a BARRISTER **3** (*NAmE*, *law*) a written summary of the facts that support one side of a legal case, that will be presented to a court **4** (*BrE*, *informal*) a SOLICITOR or a defence lawyer: *I want to see my brief.* **5** (*especially NAmE*) = BRIEFING (2): *Officials are pushing for this target to be included in the next presidential brief.*

IDM **hold no brief for sb/sth** (*BrE*, *formal*) to not support or be in favour of sb/sth: *I hold no brief for either side in this war.*

■ ***verb*** **1** to give sb information about sth so that they are prepared to deal with it: **~ sb** *I expect to be kept fully briefed at all times.* ◇ **~ sb on/about sth** *The officer briefed her on what to expect.* ➲ compare DEBRIEF **2 ~ sb (to do sth)** (*BrE*,

B

law) to give a lawyer, especially a BARRISTER, the main facts of a legal case so that it can be argued in court

brief·case /ˈbriːfkeɪs/ *noun* a flat case used for carrying papers and documents ➲ VISUAL VOCAB page V52 ➲ compare ATTACHÉ CASE

brief·ing AW /ˈbriːfɪŋ/ *noun* **1** [C] a meeting in which people are given instructions or information: *a press briefing* ➲ compare DEBRIEFING **2** (also **brief** especially in *NAmE*) [C, U] the detailed instructions or information that are given at such a meeting: *Captain Trent gave his men a full briefing.* ◇ *a* ***briefing session/paper***

brief·ly 0-π AW /ˈbriːfli/ *adv.* **1** 0-π for a short time: *He had spoken to Emma* ***only briefly***. **2** 0-π in few words: *Briefly, the argument is as follows…* ◇ *Let me tell you briefly what happened.*

briefs /briːfs/ *noun* [pl.] men's UNDERPANTS or women's KNICKERS: *a pair of briefs*

brier = BRIAR

brig /brɪɡ/ *noun* **1** a ship with two MASTS (= posts that support the sails) and square sails **2** (*NAmE*) a prison, especially one on a WARSHIP

Brig. *abbr.* (in writing) BRIGADIER

bri·gade /brɪˈɡeɪd/ *noun* **1** a large group of soldiers that forms a unit of an army **2** [usually sing.] (often *disapproving*) used, always with a word or phrase in front of it, to describe a group of people who share the same opinions or are similar in some other way: *the anti-smoking brigade* ➲ see also FIRE BRIGADE IDM see HEAVY *adj.*

briga·dier /ˌbrɪɡəˈdɪə(r); *NAmE* -ˈdɪr/ *noun* (*abbr.* Brig.) an officer of high rank in the British army: *Brigadier Michael Swift*

ˌbrigadier ˈgeneral *noun* an officer of high rank in the US army, AIR FORCE or MARINES

brig·and /ˈbrɪɡənd/ *noun* (*old-fashioned*) a member of a group of criminals that steals from people, especially one that attacks travellers SYN **bandit**

bright 0-π /braɪt/ *adj., adv., noun*

■ ***adj.*** (**bright·er**, **bright·est**) **1** 0-π full of light; shining strongly: ***bright light/sunshine*** ◇ *a bright room* ◇ *Her eyes were bright with tears.* ◇ *a bright morning* (= with the sun shining) **2** 0-π (of a colour) strong and easy to see: *I like bright colours.* ◇ *a bright yellow dress* ◇ *Jack's face turned* ***bright red***. **3** 0-π cheerful and lively: *His eyes were bright and excited.* ◇ *She gave me a bright smile.* ◇ *Why are you so* ***bright and cheerful*** *today?* ◇ *His face was* ***bright with*** *excitement.* **4** 0-π intelligent; quick to learn: *the brightest pupil in the class* ◇ *Do you have any* ***bright ideas*** (= clever ideas)? ➲ SYNONYMS at INTELLIGENT **5** giving reason to believe that good things will happen; likely to be successful: *This young musician has* ***a bright future***. ◇ *Prospects for the coming year look bright.* ◇ *a bright start to the week* ▸ **bright·ly** 0-π *adv.*: *a brightly lit room* ◇ *'Hi!' she called brightly.* **bright·ness** *noun* [U]

IDM **bright and ˈearly** very early in the morning: *You're up bright and early today!* (**as**) **bright as a ˈbutton** (*BrE*) intelligent and quick to understand **the bright ˈlights** the excitement of city life: *Although he grew up in the country, he's always had a taste for the bright lights.* **a bright ˈspark** (*BrE, informal*, often *ironic*) a lively and intelligent person, especially sb young: *Some bright spark* (= stupid person) *left the tap running all night.* **a/the ˈbright spot** a good or pleasant part of sth that is unpleasant or bad in all other ways: *The win last week was the only bright spot in their last ten games.* **look on the ˈbright side** to be cheerful or positive about a bad situation, for example by thinking only of the advantages and not the disadvantages

■ ***adv.*** (**bright·er**, **bright·est**) (*literary*) (usually with the verbs *burn* and *shine*) brightly: *The stars were shining bright.*

■ ***noun*** **brights** [pl.] (*NAmE*) the HEADLIGHTS on a vehicle set to a position in which they are shining as brightly as possible and not directed downwards

Synonyms

bright

brilliant • vivid • vibrant

These words all describe things that are shining or full of light or colours that are strong and easy to see.

bright full of light; shining strongly; (of colours) strong and easy to see: *a bright yellow dress*

brilliant very bright: *The sky was a brilliant blue.*

vivid (*approving*) (of colours) bright and strong: *His eyes were a vivid green.*

vibrant (*approving*) (of colours) bright and strong: *The room was decorated in vibrant blues and greens.*

VIVID OR VIBRANT?

These two words are very similar, but **vivid** emphasizes how bright a colour is, while **vibrant** suggests a more lively and exciting colour or combination of colours.

PATTERNS

- bright/brilliant/vivid/vibrant **colours**
- bright/brilliant **light/sunlight/sunshine/eyes**

bright·en /ˈbraɪtn/ *verb* **1** [I, T] to become or make sth lighter or brighter in colour: *In the distance, the sky was beginning to brighten.* ◇ **~ sth** *a shampoo to brighten and condition your hair* **2** [I, T] to become, feel or look happier; to make sb look happier: *Her eyes brightened.* ◇ **~ up** *He brightened up at their words of encouragement.* ◇ **~ sth** (**up**) *A smile brightened her face.* **3** [T, I] **~ (sth)** (**up**) to become or make sth become more pleasant or enjoyable; to bring hope: *A personal letter will usually brighten up a person's day.* **4** [T] **~ sth** (**up**) to make sth look more brightly coloured and attractive: *Fresh flowers will brighten up any room in the house.* **5** [I] **~** (**up**) (of the weather) to improve and become brighter: *According to the forecast, it should brighten up later.*

ˌbright-ˈeyed (also **ˌbright-eyed and ˌbushy-ˈtailed**) *adj.* (of a person) full of interest and enthusiasm

ˌbright young ˈthing *noun* an enthusiastic and intelligent young person who wants to be successful in their career ORIGIN From the name used in the 1920s for rich young people whose behaviour was considered shocking.

brill /brɪl/ *adj.* (*BrE, informal*) very good

bril·liant 0-π /ˈbrɪliənt/ *adj.* **1** 0-π extremely clever or impressive: *What a brilliant idea!* ◇ *a brilliant performance/invention* **2** 0-π very successful: *a brilliant career* ◇ *The play was a brilliant success.* **3** 0-π very intelligent or skilful: *a brilliant young scientist* ◇ *She has one of the most brilliant minds in the country.* ➲ SYNONYMS at INTELLIGENT **4** 0-π (of light or colours) very bright: *brilliant sunshine* ◇ *brilliant blue eyes* ➲ SYNONYMS at BRIGHT **5** 0-π (*BrE, informal*) very good; excellent: *'How was it?' 'Brilliant!'* ◇ *Thanks. You've been brilliant* (= very helpful). ➲ SYNONYMS at GREAT ▸ **bril·liance** /ˈbrɪliəns/ *noun* [U] **bril·li·ant·ly** *adv.*: *The plan worked brilliantly.* ◇ *It was brilliantly sunny.*

bril·lian·tine /ˈbrɪliəntiːn/ *noun* [U] oil used in the past to make men's hair shiny

brim /brɪm/ *noun, verb*

■ ***noun*** **1** the top edge of a cup, bowl, glass, etc: *two wine glasses,* ***filled to the brim*** **2** the flat edge around the bottom of a hat that sticks out ➲ VISUAL VOCAB page V53 **3 -brimmed** (in adjectives) having the type of brim mentioned: *a wide-brimmed hat*

■ ***verb*** (-mm-) [I] to be full of sth; to fill sth: *Tears brimmed in her eyes.* ◇ **~ with sth** *Her eyes brimmed with tears.* ◇ *The team were brimming with confidence before the game.*

PHR V **ˌbrim ˈover** (**with sth**) (of a cup, container, etc.) to be so full of a liquid that it flows over the edge SYN **overflow**: (*figurative*) *Her heart was brimming over with happiness.*

brim·ful /ˈbrɪmfʊl/ *adj.* **~ of sth** completely full of sth: *She's certainly brimful of energy.* ◇ *a jug brimful of cream*

brim·stone /ˈbrɪmstəʊn; *NAmE* -stoʊn/ *noun* (*old use*) the chemical element SULPHUR

brin·dle /ˈbrɪndl/ (also **brin·dled** /ˈbrɪndld/) *adj.* (of dogs, cats and cows) brown with bands or marks of another colour

brine /braɪn/ *noun* [U] very salty water, used especially for preserving food ➲ see also BRINY

bring 0‑w /brɪŋ/ *verb* (**brought**, **brought** /brɔːt/)
▸ COME WITH SB/STH **1** 0‑w to come to a place with sb/sth: **~ sb/sth** (**with you**) *Don't forget to bring your books with you.* ◇ **~ sb/sth to sth** *She brought her boyfriend to the party.* ◇ **~ sth for sb** *Bring a present for Helen.* ◇ **~ sb sth** *Bring Helen a present.*
▸ PROVIDE **2** 0‑w to provide sb/sth with sth: **~ sb/sth sth** *His writing brings him $10 000 a year.* ◇ **~ sth to sb/sth** *The team's new manager brings ten years' experience to the job.*
▸ CAUSE **3** 0‑w **~ sth** to cause sth: *The revolution brought many changes.* ◇ *The news* **brought tears to his eyes** (= made him cry). ◇ *Retirement usually* **brings with it** *a massive drop in income.* **4** 0‑w **~ sb/sth + adv./prep.** to cause sb/sth to be in a particular condition or place: *to* **bring** *a meeting* **to an end** ◇ **Bring** *the water* **to the boil**. ◇ *The article brought her into conflict with the authorities.* ◇ *Hello Simon! What brings you here?*
▸ MAKE SB/STH MOVE **5** to make sb/sth move in a particular direction or way: **~ sb/sth + adv./prep.** *The judge brought his hammer down on the table.* ◇ **~ sb/sth running** *Her cries brought the neighbours running* (= made them run to her).
▸ ACCUSATION **6 ~ sth** (**against sb**) to officially accuse sb of a crime: *to* **bring a charge/a legal action/an accusation** *against sb*
▸ FORCE YOURSELF **7 ~ yourself to do sth** to force yourself to do sth: *She could not bring herself to tell him the news.*

IDM Idioms containing **bring** are at the entries for the nouns and adjectives in the idioms, for example **bring sb/sth to heel** is at **heel**.

PHR V ˌ**bring sth↔aˈbout** to make sth happen SYN **cause**: *What brought about the change in his attitude?* ➲ LANGUAGE BANK at CAUSE

ˌ**bring sb aˈround** (*NAmE*) = BRING SB ROUND ˌ**bring sth aˈround to sth** (*NAmE*) = BRING STH ROUND TO STH

ˌ**bring sb/sth↔ˈback** 0‑w to return sb/sth: *Please bring back all library books by the end of the week.* ◇ *He brought me back* (= gave me a ride home) *in his car.* ˌ**bring sth↔ˈback 1** to make sb remember sth or think about it again: *The photographs brought back many pleasant memories.* **2** to make sth that existed before be introduced again SYN **reintroduce**: *Most people are against bringing back the death penalty.* ˌ**bring sb sth↔ˈback** | ˌ**bring sth↔ˈback** (**for sb**) to return with sth for sb: *What did you bring the kids back from Italy?* ◇ *I brought a T-shirt back for Mark.*

ˈ**bring sb/sth before sb** (*formal*) to present sb/sth for discussion or judgement: *The matter will be brought before the committee.* ◇ *He was brought before the court and found guilty.*

ˌ**bring sb↔ˈdown 1** to make sb lose power or be defeated: *The scandal may bring down the government.* **2** (in sports) to make sb fall over: *He was brought down in the penalty area.* ˌ**bring sth↔ˈdown 1** 0‑w to reduce sth: *We aim to bring down prices on all our computers.* **2** to land an aircraft: *The pilot managed to bring the plane down in a field.* **3** to make an aircraft fall out of the sky: *Twelve enemy fighters had been brought down.* **4** to make an animal or a bird fall down or fall out of the sky by killing or wounding it: *He brought down the bear with a single shot.*

ˌ**bring sb/sth↔ˈforth** (*old use* or *formal*) to give birth to sb; to produce sth: *She brought forth a son.* ◇ *trees bringing forth fruit*

ˌ**bring sth↔ˈforward 1** 0‑w to move sth to an earlier date or time: *The meeting has been brought forward from 10 May to 3 May.* **2** to suggest sth for discussion: *Please bring the matter forward at the next meeting.* **3** to move a total sum from the bottom of one page or column of numbers to the top of the next: *A credit balance of $50 was brought forward from his September account.*

ˌ**bring sb↔ˈin 1** to ask sb to do a particular job or to be involved in sth: *Local residents were angry at not being brought in on* (= asked for their opinion about) *the new housing proposal.* ◇ **~ to do sth** *Experts were brought in to advise the government.* **2** (of the police) to bring sb to a police station in order to ask them questions or arrest them: *Two men were brought in for questioning.* ˌ**bring sb/sth↔ˈin 1** to introduce a new law: *They want to bring in a bill to limit arms exports.* **2** to attract sb/sth to a place or business: *We need to bring in a lot more new business.* **3** to give a decision in court: *The jury brought in a verdict of guilty.* ˌ**bring sb ˈin sth** | ˌ**bring ˈin sth** to make or earn a particular amount of money: *His freelance work brings him in about $20 000 a year.* ◇ *How much does she bring in now?*

ˌ**bring sth↔ˈoff** to succeed in doing sth difficult SYN **pull off**: *It was a difficult task but we brought it off.* ◇ *The goalie brought off a superb save.*

ˌ**bring sb↔ˈon** to help sb develop or improve while they are learning to do sth ˌ**bring sth↔ˈon 1** to make sth develop, usually sth unpleasant SYN **cause**: *He was suffering from stress brought on by overwork.* **2** to make crops, fruit, etc. grow well ˈ**bring sth on yourself/sb** to be responsible for sth unpleasant that happens to you/sb: *I have no sympathy—you brought it all on yourself.*

ˌ**bring sb↔ˈout** (*BrE*) to make people go on strike ˌ**bring sb ˈout of himself, herself, etc.** to help sb to feel more confident: *She's a shy girl who needs friends to bring her out of herself.* ˌ**bring sth↔ˈout 1** 0‑w to make sth appear: *A crisis* **brings out the best in her.** **2** to make sth easy to see or understand: *That dress really brings out the colour of your eyes.* **3** 0‑w to produce sth; to publish sth: *The band have just brought out their second album.* ˌ**bring sb ˈout in sth** to make sb's skin be covered in spots, etc: *The heat brought him out in a rash.*

ˌ**bring sb ˈround** (*BrE*) (*NAmE* ˌ**bring sb aˈround**) (also ˌ**bring sb ˈto**) to make sb who is unconscious become conscious again ˌ**bring sb ˈround** (**to...**) (*BrE*) (*NAmE* ˌ**bring sb aˈround**) to bring sb to sb's house: *Bring the family round one evening. We'd love to meet them.* ˌ**bring sb ˈround** (**to sth**) (*BrE*) (*NAmE* ˌ**bring sb aˈround**) to persuade sb to agree to sth: *He didn't like the plan at first, but we managed to bring him round.* ˌ**bring sth ˈround to sth** (*BrE*) (*NAmE* ˌ**bring sth aˈround to sth**) to direct a conversation to a particular subject

ˌ**bring sb ˈto** = BRING SB ROUND

ˌ**bring A and B toˈgether** to help two people or groups to end a disagreement: *The loss of their son brought the two of them together.*

ˌ**bring sb↔ˈup 1** 0‑w [often passive] to care for a child, teaching him or her how to behave, etc. SYN **raise**: *She brought up five children.* ◇ *He was brought up by his aunt.* ◇ *a* **well/badly brought up** *child* ◇ **~ to do sth** *They were brought up to* (= taught as children to) *respect authority.* ◇ **+ noun** *I was brought up a Catholic.* ➲ related noun UPBRINGING **2** (*law*) to make sb appear for trial: *He was brought up on a charge of drunken driving.* ˌ**bring sth↔ˈup 1** 0‑w to mention a subject or start to talk about it SYN **raise**: *Bring it up at the meeting.* **2** (*BrE*) to VOMIT: *to bring up your lunch* **3** to make sth appear on a computer screen: *Click with the right mouse button to bring up a new menu.* ˌ**bring sb ˈup against sth** to force sb to know about sth and have to deal with it: *Working in the slums brought her up against the realities of poverty.*

ˌ**bring-and-ˈbuy sale** *noun* (*BrE*) a sale, usually for charity, at which people bring things for sale and buy those brought by others

brin·jal /ˈbrɪndʒl/ *noun* [C, U] (*IndE, SAfrE*) an AUBERGINE/EGGPLANT (= a vegetable with shiny dark purple skin and soft white flesh)

brink /brɪŋk/ *noun* [sing.] **1 the ~** (**of sth**) if you are on the **brink** of sth, you are almost in a very new, dangerous or exciting situation: *on the* **brink of collapse/war/death/disaster** ◇ *Scientists are on the brink of making a major new discovery.* ◇ *He's pulled the company* **back from the brink** (= he has saved it from disaster). **2** (*literary*) the extreme edge of land, for example at the top of a CLIFF or by a river: *the brink of the precipice* IDM see TEETER

brink·man·ship /ˈbrɪŋkmənʃɪp/ (*NAmE* also **brinks·man·ship** /ˈbrɪŋks-/) *noun* [U] the activity, especially in politics, of getting into a situation that could be very dangerous in order to frighten people and make them do what you want

B

briny /ˈbraɪni/ *adj.* (of water) containing a lot of salt SYN salty ➲ see also BRINE

brio /ˈbriːəʊ; *NAmE* ˈbriːoʊ/ *noun* [U] (*formal*) enthusiasm and individual style

bri·oche /briˈɒʃ; *NAmE* briˈoʊʃ/ *noun* [C, U] a type of sweet bread made from flour, eggs and butter, usually in the shape of a small bread roll

bri·quette /brɪˈket/ *noun* a small hard block made from coal dust and used as fuel

brisk /brɪsk/ *adj.* (*comparative* **brisk·er**, no *superlative*) **1** quick; busy: *a brisk walk* ◊ *to set off at a brisk pace* ◊ *Ice-cream vendors were doing a brisk trade* (= selling a lot of ice cream). **2** (of a person, their voice or manner) practical and confident; showing a desire to get things done quickly: *His tone became brisk and businesslike.* **3** (of wind and the weather) cold but pleasantly fresh: *a* ***brisk wind/breeze*** ▶ **brisk·ly** *adv.* **brisk·ness** *noun* [U]

bris·ket /ˈbrɪskɪt/ *noun* [U] meat that comes from the chest of an animal, especially a cow

bris·tle /ˈbrɪsl/ *noun, verb*

■ ***noun*** **1** a short stiff hair: *the bristles on his chin* **2** one of the short stiff hairs or wires in a brush

■ ***verb*** **1** [I] **~** (**with sth**) (**at sth**) to suddenly become very annoyed or offended at what sb says or does: *His lies made her bristle with rage.* **2** [I] (of an animal's fur) to stand up on the back and neck because the animal is frightened or angry

PHR V **ˈbristle with sth** to contain a large number of sth: *The whole subject bristles with problems.*

brist·ly /ˈbrɪsli/ *adj.* like or full of bristles; rough: *a* ***bristly chin/moustache***

ˈBristol fashion *adj.* (*old-fashioned*) [not before noun] (*BrE, informal*) in good order or neat and clean: *all shipshape and Bristol fashion*

bris·tols /ˈbrɪstlz/ *noun* [pl.] (*BrE, slang*) a woman's breasts

Brit /brɪt/ *noun* (*informal*) a person from Britain ➲ note at BRITISH

Brit·ain /ˈbrɪtn/ *noun* [sing.] the island containing England, Scotland and Wales ➲ see also GREAT BRITAIN, UNITED KINGDOM

Bri·tan·nia /brɪˈtænjə/ *noun* [sing.] a figure of a woman used as a symbol of Britain. She is usually shown sitting down wearing a HELMET and holding a SHIELD and a TRIDENT (= a long weapon with three points).

Bri·tan·nic /brɪˈtænɪk/ *adj.* (*old-fashioned, formal*) (used mainly in names or titles) relating to Britain or the British Empire: *her Britannic Majesty* (= the Queen)

Brit·ish /ˈbrɪtɪʃ/ *adj.* **1** (*abbr.* **Br.**) connected with the United Kingdom of Great Britain and Northern Ireland or the people who live there: *the British Government* ◊ *He was born in France but his parents are British.* ◊ *British-based/British-born/British-made* **2 the British** *noun* [pl.] the people of the United Kingdom ▶ **Brit·ish·ness** *noun* [U]

More About

the British

- There is no singular noun which is commonly used to refer to a person from Britain. Instead the adjective **British** is used: *She's British.* ◊ *The British have a very odd sense of humour.* The adjective **English** refers only to people from England, not the rest of the United Kingdom.
- The noun **Briton** is used mainly in newspapers: *The survivors of the avalanche included 12 Britons.* It also describes the early inhabitants of Britain: *the ancient Britons.* **Brit** is informal and can sound negative. **Britisher** is now very old-fashioned.

➲ note at SCOTTISH

the ˌBritish ˈCouncil *noun* [sing.] an organization that represents British culture in other countries and develops closer cultural relations with them

ˌBritish ˈEnglish *noun* [U] the English language as spoken in Britain and certain other countries

Brit·ish·er /ˈbrɪtɪʃə(r)/ *noun* (*old-fashioned, NAmE, informal*) a person from Britain

the ˌBritish ˈLions *noun* [pl.] a RUGBY team of the best players from England, Ireland, Scotland and Wales that plays abroad

ˌBritish ˌoverseas ˈterritory *noun* (*BrE*) an island or group of islands in which the British government is responsible for defence and relations with other countries

ˌBritish ˈSummer Time *noun* [U] (*abbr.* **BST**) the time used in the UK in summer that is one hour ahead of GMT

Briton /ˈbrɪtn/ *noun* (*formal*) a person from Britain: *the ancient Britons* ◊ *the first Briton to climb Everest without oxygen* ➲ note at BRITISH

brit·tle /ˈbrɪtl/ *adj.* **1** hard but easily broken: ***brittle bones/nails*** **2** a **brittle** mood or state of mind is one that appears to be happy or strong but is actually nervous and easily damaged: *a brittle temperament* **3** (of a sound) hard and sharp in an unpleasant way: *a brittle laugh* ▶ **brittle·ness** *noun* [U]

ˌbrittle ˈbone disease *noun* [U] (*medical*) **1** a rare disease in which sb's bones break extremely easily **2** = OSTEOPOROSIS

Brit·ton·ic /brɪˈtɒnɪk; *NAmE* -ˈtɑːn-/ *adj.* = BRYTHONIC

bro /brəʊ; *NAmE* broʊ/ *noun* (*pl.* **bros**) (*informal*) **1** a brother **2** (*especially NAmE*) a friendly way of addressing a male person: *Thanks, bro!*

broach /brəʊtʃ; *NAmE* broʊtʃ/ *verb* **~ sth** (**to/with sb**) to begin talking about a subject that is difficult to discuss, especially because it is embarrassing or because people disagree about it: *She was dreading having to* ***broach the subject*** *of money to her father.*

ˈB-road *noun* (in Britain) a road that is less important than an A-ROAD and usually joins small towns and villages

broad 🔑 /brɔːd/ *adj., noun*

■ ***adj.*** (**broad·er**, **broad·est**)

WORD FAMILY
broad *adj.*
broadly *adv.*
broaden *verb*
breadth *noun*

▸ WIDE **1** 🔑 wide: *a broad street/avenue/river* ◊ *broad shoulders* ◊ *He is tall, broad and muscular.* ◊ *a* ***broad smile/grin*** (= one in which your mouth is stretched very wide because you are very pleased or amused) OPP **narrow** (1) **2** used after a measurement of distance to show how wide sth is: *two metres broad and one metre high*

▸ WIDE RANGE **3** including a great variety of people or things: *a broad range of products* ◊ *a broad spectrum of interests* ◊ *There is broad support for the government's policies.* ◊ *She* ***took a broad view*** *of the duties of being a teacher* (= she believed her duties included a wide range of things). OPP **narrow**

▸ GENERAL **4** 🔑 [only before noun] general; not detailed: *the broad outline of a proposal* ◊ *The negotiators were in broad agreement on the main issues.* ◊ *She's a feminist, in the* ***broadest sense of the word.*** ◊ *In* ***broad terms****, the paper argues that each country should develop its own policy.*

▸ LAND/WATER **5** 🔑 covering a wide area: *a broad expanse of water*

▸ ACCENT **6** if sb has a **broad accent**, you can hear very easily which area they come from SYN **strong**

▸ HINT **7** if sb gives a **broad hint**, they make it very clear what they are thinking or what they want

▸ HUMOUR **8** (*NAmE*) dealing with sex in an amusing way: *The movie mixes broad humor with romance.* ➲ note at WIDE

IDM **a broad ˈchurch** (*BrE*) an organization that accepts a wide range of opinions SYN **big tent** (**in**) **broad ˈdaylight** (in) the clear light of day, when it is easy to see: *The robbery occurred in broad daylight, in a crowded street.* **it's as ˌbroad as it's ˈlong** (*BrE, informal*) it makes no real differ-

ence which of two possible choices you make ➲ more at PAINT v.
■ **noun** (*old-fashioned, NAmE, slang*) an offensive way of referring to a woman

broad·band /ˈbrɔːdbænd/ *noun* [U] **1** (*technical*) signals that use a wide range of FREQUENCIES ➲ compare NARROWBAND **2** a way of connecting a computer to the Internet, which allows you to receive information, including pictures, etc, very quickly: *We have broadband at home now.* ➲ COLLOCATIONS at EMAIL

ˌ**broad-ˈbased** (also ˌ**broadly-ˈbased**) *adj.* based on a wide variety of people, things or ideas; not limited

ˌ**broad ˈbean** (*BrE*) (*NAmE* ˈ**fava bean**) *noun* a type of round, pale green BEAN. Several broad beans grow together inside a fat POD.

ˌ**broad-ˈbrush** *adj.* [only before noun] dealing with a subject or problem in a general way rather than considering details: *a broad-brush approach*

broad·cast 0-w /ˈbrɔːdkɑːst; *NAmE* -kæst/ *verb, noun*
■ **verb** (**broad·cast, broad·cast** or **broad·cast, broad·casted**) **1** 0-w [T, I] **~ (sth)** to send out programmes on television or radio: *The concert will be* ***broadcast live*** (= at the same time as it takes place) *tomorrow evening.* ◇ *They began broadcasting in 1922.* ➲ COLLOCATIONS at TELEVISION **2** [T] **~ sth** to tell a lot of people about sth: *I don't like to* ***broadcast the fact*** *that my father owns the company.*
■ **noun** 0-w a radio or television programme: (*BrE*) *a party political broadcast* (= for example, before an election) ◇ *We watched a* ***live broadcast*** *of the speech* (= one shown at the same time as the speech was made).

broad·cast·er /ˈbrɔːdkɑːstə(r); *NAmE* -kæst-/ *noun* **1** a person whose job is presenting or talking on television or radio programmes **2** a company that sends out television or radio programmes

broad·cast·ing /ˈbrɔːdkɑːstɪŋ; *NAmE* -kæst-/ *noun* [U] the business of making and sending out radio and television programmes: *to work in broadcasting* ◇ *the British Broadcasting Corporation* (= the BBC)

broad·en /ˈbrɔːdn/ *verb* **1** [I] to become wider: *Her smile broadened.* **2** [T, I] **~ (sth)** to affect or make sth affect more people or things: *a promise to broaden access to higher education* ◇ *The party needs to broaden its appeal to voters.* **3** [T] **~ sth** to increase your experience, knowledge, etc: *Few would disagree that travel* ***broadens the mind*** (= helps you to understand other people's customs, etc.). ◇ *Spending a year working in the city helped to* ***broaden his horizons.***
PHR V ˌ**broaden ˈout** (of a road, river, etc.) to become wider SYN **widen out**

the ˈbroad jump *noun* [sing.] (*NAmE*) = THE LONG JUMP

broad·leaved /ˈbrɔːdliːvd/ (also *less frequent* **broad·leaf** /ˈbrɔːdliːf/) *adj.* (*technical*) (of plants) having broad flat leaves

broad·ly 0-w /ˈbrɔːdli/ *adv.*
1 0-w generally, without considering details: ***Broadly speaking,*** *I agree with you.* ◇ ***broadly similar/comparable/equivalent/consistent*** **2** 0-w if you smile **broadly**, you smile with your mouth stretched very wide because you are very pleased or amused

ˌ**broad-ˈminded** *adj.* willing to listen to other people's opinions and accept behaviour that is different from your own SYN **tolerant** OPP **narrow-minded** ▸ ˌ**broad-ˈminded·ness** *noun* [U]

Broad·moor /ˈbrɔːdmɔː(r)/ *noun* a special hospital in southern England for criminals who are mentally ill and considered very dangerous

broad·ness /ˈbrɔːdnəs/ *noun* [U] the quality of being broad

broad·scale /ˈbrɔːdskeɪl/ *adj.* on a large scale: *The broadscale cutting down of trees is damaging the environment.*

broad·sheet /ˈbrɔːdʃiːt/ *noun* **1** a newspaper printed on a large size of paper, generally considered more serious than smaller newspapers ➲ compare TABLOID **2** a large piece of paper printed on one side only with information or an advertisement

broad·side /ˈbrɔːdsaɪd/ *noun, adv., verb*
■ **noun** an aggressive attack in words, whether written or spoken: *The prime minister* ***fired a broadside*** *at his critics.*
■ **adv.** with one side facing sth SYN **sideways**: *The car skidded and crashed broadside into another car.* ◇ (*BrE*) *The boat swung* ***broadside on*** *to the current of the river.*
■ **verb ~ sth** (*NAmE*) to crash into the side of sth: *The driver ran a stop light and broadsided the truck.*

ˌ**broad-ˈspectrum** *adj.* [only before noun] (*technical*) (of a drug or chemical) effective against a large variety of bacteria, insects, etc.

broad·sword /ˈbrɔːdsɔːd; *NAmE* -sɔːrd/ *noun* a large SWORD with a broad flat blade

Broad·way /ˈbrɔːdweɪ/ *noun* [U] a street in New York City where there are many theatres, sometimes used to refer to the US theatre industry in general: *a Broadway musical* ◇ *The play opened* ***on Broadway*** *in 2008.* ➲ see also OFF-BROADWAY

bro·cade /brəˈkeɪd/ *noun* [U, C] a type of thick heavy cloth with a raised pattern made especially from gold or silver silk thread

bro·caded /brəˈkeɪdɪd/ *adj.* [usually before noun] made of or decorated with brocade

Broca's area /ˈbrəʊkəz eəriə; *NAmE* ˈbroʊkəz eriə/ *noun* (*anatomy*) an area in the front part of the brain connected with speech

broc·coli /ˈbrɒkəli; *NAmE* ˈbrɑːk-/ *noun* [U] a vegetable with a thick green STEM and several dark green or purple flower heads ➲ VISUAL VOCAB page V27

bro·chette /brɒˈʃet; *NAmE* broʊ-/ *noun* (from *French*) **1** [C, U] a dish consisting of pieces of food cooked on a thin stick over a fire **2** [C] one of the sticks used for cooking food in this way

bro·chure /ˈbrəʊʃə(r); *NAmE* broʊˈʃʊr/ *noun* a small magazine or book containing pictures and information about sth or advertising sth: *a travel brochure*

bro·derie ang·laise /ˌbrəʊdəri ˈɒŋgleɪz; *NAmE* ˌbroʊdəri ˈɑːŋgleɪz/ *noun* [U] (from *French*) decoration with sewing on fine white cloth; the cloth decorated in this way

broer /ˈbruːə(r)/ *noun* (*SAfrE, informal*) **1** a brother **2** (used of a boy or man) a friend **3** a friendly form of address that is used by one boy or man to another: *How's it going, my broer?*

brogue /brəʊg; *NAmE* broʊg/ *noun* **1** [usually pl.] a strong shoe which usually has a pattern in the leather: *a pair of brogues* ➲ VISUAL VOCAB page V52 **2** [usually sing.] the accent that sb has when they are speaking, especially the accent of Irish or Scottish speakers of English

broil /brɔɪl/ *verb* **1** [T] **~ sth** (*NAmE*) to cook meat or fish under direct heat or over heat on metal bars: *broiled chicken* ➲ compare BARBECUE, GRILL **2** [I, T] **~ (sb)** to become or make sb become very hot: *They lay broiling in the sun.*

broil·er /ˈbrɔɪlə(r)/ *noun* **1** (also ˈ**broiler chicken**) (*especially NAmE*) a young chicken suitable for broiling or ROASTING **2** (*NAmE*) the part inside the oven of a cooker/stove that directs heat downwards to cook food that is placed underneath it ➲ compare GRILL

broke /brəʊk; *NAmE* broʊk/ *adj.* [not before noun] (*informal*) having no money: *I'm always broke by the end of the month.* ◇ *During the recession thousands of small businesses* ***went broke*** (= had to stop doing business). ◇ ***flat/stony broke*** (= completely broke) ➲ see also BREAK
IDM **go for ˈbroke** (*informal*) to risk everything in one determined effort to do sth ➲ more at AIN'T

broken 0-w /ˈbrəʊkən; *NAmE* ˈbroʊ-/ *adj.*
▸ DAMAGED **1** 0-w that has been damaged or injured; no longer whole or working correctly: *a broken window/plate* ◇ *a broken leg/arm* ◇ *pieces of broken glass* ◇ *How did this dish* ***get broken?*** ◇ *The TV's broken.* ➲ see also BROKEN HEART
▸ RELATIONSHIP **2** 0-w [usually before noun] ended or des-

troyed: *a* **broken** ***marriage/engagement*** ➲ see also BROKEN HOME

▸ PROMISE/AGREEMENT **3** 🗝 [usually before noun] not kept

▸ NOT CONTINUOUS **4** 🗝 [usually before noun] not continuous; disturbed or interrupted: *a night of broken sleep* ◇ *a single broken white line across the road*

▸ PERSON **5** [only before noun] made weak and tired by illness or difficulties: *He was a broken man after the failure of his business.*

▸ LANGUAGE **6** [only before noun] (of a language that is not your own) spoken slowly and with a lot of mistakes; not FLUENT: *to speak in broken English*

▸ GROUND **7** having a rough surface: *an area of broken, rocky ground* ➲ see also BREAK, BROKE, BROKEN *v.*

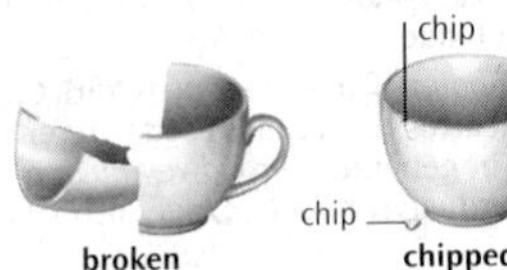

ˌbroken-ˈdown *adj.* [usually before noun] in a very bad condition; not working correctly; very tired and sick: *a broken-down old car/horse*

ˌbroken ˈheart *noun* a feeling of great sadness, especially when sb you love has died or left you: *No one ever died of a broken heart.* ▸ **ˌbroken-ˈhearted** *adj.*: *He was broken-hearted when his wife died.* ➲ compare HEARTBROKEN

ˌbroken ˈhome *noun* a family in which the parents are divorced or separated: *She comes from a broken home.*

broken·ly /ˈbrəʊkənli; *NAmE* ˈbroʊ-/ *adv.* (*formal*) (of sb's manner of speaking) in phrases that are very short or not complete, with a lot of pauses; not FLUENTLY

broker /ˈbrəʊkə(r); *NAmE* ˈbroʊ-/ *noun, verb*

▪ ***noun*** **1** a person who buys and sells things for other people: *an insurance broker* **2** = STOCKBROKER ➲ see also HONEST BROKER, PAWNBROKER, POWER BROKER

▪ ***verb*** **~ sth** to arrange the details of an agreement, especially between different countries: *a peace plan brokered by the UN*

broker·age /ˈbrəʊkərɪdʒ; *NAmE* ˈbroʊ-/ *noun* [U] **1** the business of being a broker: *a* ***brokerage firm/house*** **2** an amount of money charged by a broker for work that he/she does

ˈbroker-dealer *noun* (*finance*) a person who works on the Stock Exchange buying shares from and selling shares to BROKERS and the public ➲ compare JOBBER

brolly /ˈbrɒli; *NAmE* ˈbrɑːli/ *noun* (*pl.* -ies) (*BrE, informal*) = UMBRELLA

brom·ide /ˈbrəʊmaɪd; *NAmE* ˈbroʊ-/ *noun* [C, U] a chemical which contains BROMINE, used, especially in the past, to make people feel calm

brom·ine /ˈbrəʊmiːn; *NAmE* ˈbroʊ-/ *noun* [U] (*symb.* Br) a chemical element. Bromine is a dark red poisonous liquid and has a very strong unpleasant smell. It is mainly found in the form of salts in sea water.

bron·chial /ˈbrɒŋkiəl; *NAmE* ˈbrɑːŋ-/ *adj.* [usually before noun] (*medical*) of or affecting the two main branches of the WINDPIPE (called **bronchial tubes**) leading to the lungs: *bronchial pneumonia* ➲ VISUAL VOCAB page V48

bron·chitis /brɒŋˈkaɪtɪs; *NAmE* brɑːŋ-/ *noun* [U] an illness that affects the bronchial tubes leading to the lungs: *He was suffering from chronic bronchitis.* ▸ **bron·chit·ic** /brɒŋˈkɪtɪk; *NAmE* brɑːŋ-/ *adj.*: *a bronchitic cough*

bron·chus /ˈbrɒŋkəs; *NAmE* ˈbrɑːŋ-/ *noun* (*pl.* **bron·chi** /ˈbrɒŋkaɪ; *NAmE* ˈbrɑːŋ-/) (*anatomy*) any one of the system of tubes which make up the main branches of the WINDPIPE through which air passes in and out of the lungs

bronco /ˈbrɒŋkəʊ; *NAmE* ˈbrɑːŋkoʊ/ *noun* (*pl.* -os) a wild horse of the western US: *a bucking bronco in the rodeo*

bron·to·saurus /ˌbrɒntəˈsɔːrəs; *NAmE* ˌbrɑːn-/ *noun* = APATOSAURUS

Bronx cheer /ˌbrɒŋks ˈtʃɪə(r); *NAmE* ˌbrɑːŋks ˈtʃɪr/ *noun* (*NAmE, informal*) = RASPBERRY (2)

bronze /brɒnz; *NAmE* brɑːnz/ *noun, adj.*

▪ ***noun*** **1** [U] a dark reddish-brown metal made by mixing COPPER and tin: *a bronze statue* ◇ *a figure cast in bronze* **2** [U] a dark reddish-brown colour, like bronze **3** [C] a work of art made of bronze, for example a statue **4** [C, U] = BRONZE MEDAL

▪ ***adj.*** dark reddish-brown in colour: *bronze skin*

the ˈBronze Age *noun* [sing.] the period in history between the Stone Age and the Iron Age when people used tools and weapons made of bronze

bronzed /brɒnzd; *NAmE* brɑːnzd/ *adj.* having skin that has been turned brown in an attractive way by the sun SYN **tanned**

ˌbronze ˈmedal (also **bronze**) *noun* [C, U] a MEDAL given as third prize in a competition or race: *an Olympic bronze medal winner* ◇ *She won (a) bronze at the Olympics.* ➲ compare GOLD MEDAL, SILVER MEDAL ▸ **ˌbronze ˈmedallist** (*BrE*) (*NAmE* **ˌbronze ˈmedalist**) *noun*: *She's an Olympic bronze medallist.*

brooch /brəʊtʃ; *NAmE* broʊtʃ/ (*especially BrE*) (*NAmE* usually **pin**) *noun* a piece of jewellery with a pin on the back of it, that can be fastened to your clothes ➲ VISUAL VOCAB page V53

brood /bruːd/ *verb, noun*

▪ ***verb*** **1** [I] **~ (over/on/about sth)** to think a lot about sth that makes you annoyed, anxious or upset: *You're not still brooding over what he said, are you?* **2** [I, T] **~ (sth)** if a bird **broods**, or **broods** its eggs, it sits on the eggs in order to HATCH them (= make the young come out of them)

▪ ***noun*** [C+sing./pl. v.] **1** all the young birds or creatures that a mother produces at one time SYN **clutch 2** (*humorous*) a large family of children

brood·ing /ˈbruːdɪŋ/ *adj.* (*literary*) sad and mysterious or threatening: *dark, brooding eyes* ◇ *a brooding silence* ◇ *Ireland's brooding landscape*

ˈbrood mare *noun* a female horse kept for breeding

broody /ˈbruːdi/ *adj.* **1** (of a woman) wanting very much to have a baby: *I reached the age of 27 and suddenly started to feel broody.* **2** (of a female bird) wanting to lay eggs and sit on them: *a broody hen* **3** quiet and thinking about sth because you are unhappy or disappointed ▸ **broodi·ness** *noun* [U]

brook /brʊk/ *noun, verb*

▪ ***noun*** a small river

▪ ***verb*** **not brook sth/not brook sb doing sth/brook no...** (*formal*) to not allow sth: *The tone in his voice brooked no argument.*

broom /bruːm/ *noun* **1** [C] a brush on the end of a long handle, used for sweeping floors ➲ VISUAL VOCAB page V17 ➲ see also NEW BROOM **2** [U] a wild bush with small yellow flowers IDM see NEW

ˈbroom cupboard *noun* (*BrE*) **1** a large built-in cupboard used for keeping cleaning equipment, etc. in **2** (often *humorous*) a very small room: *I couldn't afford more than a broom cupboard to set up office in.*

broom·stick /ˈbruːmstɪk/ *noun* a broom with a long handle and small thin sticks at the end, or the handle of a broom. In stories WITCHES (= women with evil magic powers) ride through the air on broomsticks.

Bros (also **Bros.** especially in *NAmE*) *abbr.* (used in the name of a company) Brothers: *Warner Bros*

broth /brɒθ; *NAmE* brɑːθ; brɔːθ/ *noun* [U, C] thick soup made by boiling meat or fish and vegetables in water: *chicken broth* ➲ see also SCOTCH BROTH IDM see COOK *n.*

brothel /ˈbrɒθl; *NAmE* ˈbrɑːθl; ˈbrɔːθl/ (also **bor·dello** especially in *NAmE*) *noun* a house where people pay to have sex with PROSTITUTES

ˈbrothel creepers *noun* [pl.] (*BrE, informal*) SUEDE shoes with thick soft SOLES, popular in the 1950s

brother 🗝 /ˈbrʌðə(r)/ *noun, exclamation*

▪ ***noun***

▸ IN FAMILY **1** 🗝 a boy or man who has the same mother and

father as another person: *We're brothers.* ◇ *He's my brother.* ◇ *an* ***older/younger brother*** ◇ *a* ***twin brother*** ◇ *Does she have any* ***brothers and sisters?*** ◇ *Edward was the youngest of the Kennedy brothers.* ◇ *He was like a brother to me* (= very close). ➲ see also HALF-BROTHER, STEPBROTHER
▸ OTHER MEN **2** (*pl.* **brothers** or *old-fashioned* **brethren**) used for talking to or talking about other male members of an organization or other men who have the same ideas, purpose, etc. as yourself: *We must work together, brothers!* ◇ *He was greatly respected by his brother officers.* ◇ *We must support our weaker brethren.*
▸ IN RELIGIOUS GROUP **3** (also **Brother**) (*pl.* **brethren** or **brothers**) a male member of a religious group, especially a MONK: *Brother Luke* ◇ *The Brethren meet regularly for prayer.*
▸ FORM OF ADDRESS **4** (*NAmE, informal*) used by black people as a form of address for a black man
▸ AT COLLEGE/UNIVERSITY **5** (in the US) a member of a FRATERNITY (= a club for a group of male students at a college or university)
■ ***exclamation*** (*old-fashioned, especially NAmE*) used to express the fact that you are annoyed or surprised: *Oh brother!*

brother·hood /ˈbrʌðəhʊd; *NAmE* -ðərh-/ *noun* **1** [U] friendship and understanding between people: *to live in peace and brotherhood* **2** [C+sing./pl. v.] an organization formed for a particular purpose, especially a religious society or political organization **3** [U] the relationship of brothers: *the ties of brotherhood*

ˈ**brother-in-law** (*pl.* **brothers-in-law**) *noun* the brother of your husband or wife; your sister's husband; the husband of your husband or wife's sister ➲ compare SISTER-IN-LAW

brother·ly /ˈbrʌðəli; *NAmE* -ðərli/ *adj.* [usually before noun] showing feelings of affection and kindness that you would expect a brother to show: ***brotherly love/advice*** ◇ *He gave her a brotherly kiss on the cheek.*

brougham /ˈbruːəm/ *noun* a type of CARRIAGE used in the past, which had a closed roof and four wheels and was pulled by one horse

brought *past tense, past part.* of BRING **IDM** see LOW *adj.*

brou·haha /ˈbruːhɑːhɑː/ *noun* [U, sing.] (*old-fashioned, informal*) noisy excitement or complaints about sth

brow /braʊ/ *noun* **1** (*literary*) the part of the face above the eyes and below the hair **SYN** **forehead**: *The nurse mopped his fevered brow.* ◇ *Her* ***brow furrowed*** *in concentration.* **2** [usually pl.] = EYEBROW: *One dark brow rose in surprise.* **3** [usually sing.] the top part of a hill: *The path disappeared over the brow of the hill.* ➲ see also HIGHBROW, MIDDLEBROW, LOWBROW **IDM** see KNIT *v.*

brow·beat /ˈbraʊbiːt/ *verb* (**brow·beat**, **brow·beat·en** /ˈbraʊbiːtn/) **~ sb** (**into doing sth**) to frighten or threaten sb in order to make them do sth **SYN** **intimidate**: *They were browbeaten into accepting the offer.*

brown 0‑ᵣ /braʊn/ *adj., noun, verb*
■ ***adj.*** (**brown·er**, **brown·est**) **1** 0‑ᵣ having the colour of earth or coffee: *brown eyes* ◇ *brown bread* ◇ *dark brown shoe polish* ◇ *a package wrapped in brown paper* **2** 0‑ᵣ having skin that is naturally brown or has been made brown by the sun: (*BrE*) *I don't go brown very easily.* ◇ *After the summer in Spain, the children were* ***brown as berries.***
IDM **in a brown ˈstudy** (*old-fashioned, BrE*) thinking deeply so that you do not notice what is happening around you
■ ***noun*** 0‑ᵣ [U, C] the colour of earth or coffee: *leaves of various shades of brown* ◇ *Brown doesn't* (= brown clothes do not) *suit you.*
■ ***verb*** [I, T] to become brown; to make sth brown: *Heat the butter until it browns.* ◇ *The grass was browning in patches.* ◇ **~ sth** *Brown the onions before adding the meat.*
IDM ˌ**browned ˈoff** (**with sb/sth**) (*BrE, informal*) bored, unhappy and/or annoyed **SYN** **fed up**: *By now the passengers were getting browned off with the delay.*

ˌ**brown ˈale** *noun* (*BrE*) **1** [U, C] a type of mild sweet dark beer sold in bottles **2** [C] a bottle or glass of brown ale

ˈ**brown-bag** *verb* (-gg-) **~ sth** (*NAmE, informal*) to bring your lunch with you to work or school, usually in a brown paper bag: *My kids have been* ***brown-bagging it*** *this week.*

ˌ**brown ˈdwarf** *noun* (*astronomy*) an object in space that is between a large planet and a small star in size, and produces heat

brown·field /ˈbraʊnfiːld/ *adj.* [only before noun] (*BrE*) used to describe an area of land in a city that was used by industry or for offices in the past and that may now be cleared for new building development: *a brownfield site*

ˈ**brown goods** *noun* [pl.] small electrical items such as televisions, radios, music and video equipment ➲ compare WHITE GOODS

Brown·ian motion /ˈbraʊniən məʊʃn; *NAmE* moʊʃn/ *noun* [U] (*physics*) the movement without any regular pattern made by very small pieces of matter in a liquid or gas

brownie /ˈbraʊni/ *noun* **1** [C] a thick soft flat cake made with chocolate and sometimes nuts and served in small squares: *a fudge brownie* **2** **the Brownies** [pl.] a branch of the SCOUT ASSOCIATION for girls between the ages of seven and ten or eleven: *to join the Brownies* **3** [C] **Brownie** (*BrE* also ˈ**Brownie Guide**) a member of the Brownies ➲ compare CUB, GUIDE, SCOUT

ˈ**brownie point** *noun* [usually pl.] (*informal*) if sb does sth to earn **brownie points**, they do it to make sb in authority have a good opinion of them **ORIGIN** The Brownies is a club for young girls who are not yet old enough to be Guides. They are awarded points for good behaviour and achievements.

brown·ish /ˈbraʊnɪʃ/ (also *less frequent* **browny** /ˈbraʊni/) *adj.* fairly brown in colour: *You can't see in this light, but my new coat is a sort of brownish colour.*

ˈ**brown-nose** *verb* [I] (*informal, disapproving*) to treat sb in authority with special respect in order to make them approve of you or treat you better

ˈ**brown-out** *noun* (*especially NAmE*) a period of time when the amount of electrical power that is supplied to an area is reduced

ˌ**brown ˈrat** (also ˌ**common ˈrat**, ˌ**Norway ˈrat**) *noun* a common type of RAT

ˌ**brown ˈrice** *noun* [U] rice that is light brown because it has not had all of its outside part removed

ˌ**brown ˈsauce** *noun* [U] **1** (*BrE*) a sauce made with VINEGAR and spices, sold in bottles **2** (*NAmE*) a sauce made with fat and flour, cooked until it becomes brown

brown·stone /ˈbraʊnstəʊn; *NAmE* -stoʊn/ *noun* (*NAmE*) a house built of, or with a front made of, a type of reddish-brown stone, which is also called brownstone: *New York brownstones*

ˌ**brown ˈsugar** *noun* [U] sugar that has a brown colour and has only been partly REFINED

ˌ**Brown v Board of Eduˈcation** *noun* a law case in 1954 which led to a decision of the US Supreme Court that made separate education for black and white children illegal

browse /braʊz/ *verb* **1** [I, T] to look at a lot of things in a shop/store rather than looking for one particular thing: *You are welcome to come in and browse.* ◇ **~ sth** *She browsed the shelves for something interesting to read.* **2** [I, T] **~** (**through**) **sth** to look through the pages of a book, newspaper, etc. without reading everything: *I found the article while I was browsing through some old magazines.* **3** [I, T] **~** (**sth**) (*computing*) to look for information on a computer, especially on the Internet **4** [I] **~** (**on sth**) (of cows, GOATS, etc.) to eat leaves, etc. that are growing high up ▸ **browse** *noun* [sing.]: *The gift shop is well worth a browse.*

browser /ˈbraʊzə(r)/ *noun* **1** (*computing*) a program that lets you look at or read documents on the Internet: *a Web browser* ➲ COLLOCATIONS at EMAIL ➲ VISUAL VOCAB page V55 **2** a person who looks through books, magazines, etc. or at things for sale, but may not seriously intend to buy anything

B

brrr /brrr/ *exclamation* a sound that people make to show that they are very cold: *Brrr, it's freezing here.*

bru·cel·losis /ˌbruːsəˈləʊsɪs; *NAmE* -ˈloʊs-/ *noun* [U] a disease caused by bacteria that affects cows and that can cause fever in humans

bruise /bruːz/ *verb, noun*

■ *verb* **1** [I, T] to develop a bruise, or make a bruise or bruises appear on the skin of sb/sth: *Strawberries bruise easily.* ◇ **~ sth** *She had slipped and badly bruised her face.* ➲ SYNONYMS at INJURE ➲ COLLOCATIONS at INJURY **2** [T, usually passive] **~ sb** to affect sb badly and make them feel unhappy and less confident: *They had been badly bruised by the defeat.* ▶ **bruised** *adj.*: *He suffered badly bruised ribs in the crash.* ◇ *bruised fruit* ◇ *a bruised ego* **bruis·ing** *noun* [U]: *She suffered severe bruising, but no bones were broken.* ◇ *internal bruising* ➲ see also BRUISING *adj.*

■ *noun* **1** a blue, brown or purple mark that appears on the skin after sb has fallen, been hit, etc: *to be covered in bruises* ◇ *cuts and bruises* ➲ SYNONYMS at INJURE **2** a mark on a fruit or vegetable where it is damaged

bruiser /ˈbruːzə(r)/ *noun* (*informal*) a large strong aggressive man

bruis·ing /ˈbruːzɪŋ/ *adj.* difficult and unpleasant, making you feel tired or weak: *a* ***bruising meeting/experience***

bruit /bruːt/ *verb* **~ sth** (**about**) (*formal*) to spread a piece of news widely: *This rumour has been bruited about for years.*

Brum·mie /ˈbrʌmi/ *noun* (*BrE, informal*) a person from the city of Birmingham in England ▶ **Brum·mie** *adj.*: *a Brummie accent*

brunch /brʌntʃ/ *noun* [C, U] a meal that you eat in the late morning as a combination of breakfast and lunch

bru·nette /bruːˈnet/ *noun* (sometimes *offensive*) a white-skinned woman with dark brown hair ➲ compare BLONDE, REDHEAD

brunt /brʌnt/ *noun*

IDM **bear, take, etc. the ˈbrunt of sth** to receive the main force of sth unpleasant: *Schools will bear the brunt of cuts in government spending.*

brus·chetta /bruˈsketə/ *noun* [U] (from *Italian*) an Italian dish consisting of pieces of warm bread covered with oil and chopped raw tomatoes: *a first course of bruschetta*

brush 0‑ᴡ /brʌʃ/ *noun, verb*

■ *noun* **1** 0‑ᴡ [C] an object made of short stiff hairs (called BRISTLES) or wires set in a block of wood or plastic, usually attached to a handle. Brushes are used for many different jobs, such as cleaning, painting and tidying your hair: *a paintbrush* ◇ *a hairbrush* ◇ *a toothbrush* ◇ *brush strokes* (= the marks left by a brush when painting) ◇ *a dustpan and brush* ◇ *Apply the paint with a fine brush.* ➲ VISUAL VOCAB pages V17, V49 **2** [sing.] an act of brushing: *to give your teeth a good brush* **3** [sing.] a light touch made in passing sth/sb: *the brush of his lips on her cheek* **4** [C] **~ with sb/sth** a short unfriendly meeting with sb; an occasion when you nearly experience sth unpleasant: *She had a nasty brush with her boss this morning.* ◇ *In his job he's had frequent brushes with death.* ◇ *a brush with the law* **5** [U] land covered by small trees or bushes: *a brush fire* **6** [C] the tail of a FOX IDM see DAFT *adj.*, PAINT *v.*, TAR *v.*

■ *verb* **1** 0‑ᴡ [T] to clean, polish, or make smooth with a brush: **~ sth** *to brush your hair/teeth/shoes* ◇ **~ sth + adj.** *A tiled floor is easy to brush clean.* **2** [T] to put sth, for example oil, milk or egg, on sth using a brush: **~ A with B** *Brush the pastry with beaten egg.* ◇ **~ B over A** *Brush beaten egg over the pastry.* **3** 0‑ᴡ [T] **~ sth + adv./prep.** to remove sth from a surface with a brush or with your hand: *He brushed the dirt off his jacket.* ◇ *She brushed the fly away.* **4** [I, T] to touch sb/sth lightly while moving close to them/it: **~ against/by/past sb/sth** *She brushed past him.* ◇ *His hand accidentally brushed against hers.* ◇ **~ sth** *The leaves brushed her cheek.* ◇ **~ sth with sth** *He brushed her lips with his.*

PHR V **ˌbrush sb/sth↔aˈside** to ignore sb/sth; to treat sb/sth as unimportant SYN **dismiss**: *He brushed aside my fears.* **ˌbrush sb/yourself ˈdown** (*BrE*) = BRUSH SB/YOURSELF OFF **ˌbrush sth↔ˈdown** to clean sth by brushing it: *to brush a coat/horse down* **ˌbrush ˈoff** to be removed by brushing: *Mud brushes off easily when it is dry.* **ˌbrush sb↔ˈoff** to rudely ignore sb or refuse to listen to them: *She brushed him off impatiently.* ➲ related noun BRUSH-OFF **ˌbrush sb/yourself ˈoff** (*BrE* **ˌbrush sb/yourself ˈdown**) to make sb/yourself tidy, especially after you have fallen, by brushing your clothes, etc. with your hands **ˌbrush sth↔ˈup** | **ˌbrush ˈup on sth** to quickly improve a skill, especially when you have not used it for a time: *I must brush up on my Spanish before I go to Seville.*

ˈbrush-off *noun* [sing.] (*informal*) rude or unfriendly behaviour that shows that a person is not interested in sb: *Paul asked Tara out to dinner but she* ***gave him the brush-off.***

brush·wood /ˈbrʌʃwʊd/ *noun* [U] small broken or dead branches of trees, often used to make fires

brush·work /ˈbrʌʃwɜːk; *NAmE* -wɜːrk/ *noun* [U] the particular way in which an artist uses a brush to paint ➲ COLLOCATIONS at ART

brusque /bruːsk; brʊsk; *NAmE* brʌsk/ *adj.* using very few words and sounding rude SYN **abrupt, curt**: *The doctor spoke in a brusque tone.* ▶ **brusque·ly** *adv.*: *'What's your name?' he asked brusquely.* **brusque·ness** *noun* [U]

Brus·sels sprout /ˌbrʌslz ˈspraʊt/ (also **Brussel sprout, sprout**) *noun* a small round green vegetable like a very small CABBAGE ➲ VISUAL VOCAB page V27

bru·tal /ˈbruːtl/ *adj.* **1** violent and cruel: *a brutal attack/murder/rape/killing* **2** direct and clear about sth unpleasant; not thinking of people's feelings: *With brutal honesty she told him she did not love him.* ▶ **bru·tal·ity** /bruːˈtæləti/ *noun* [U, C] (*pl.* **-ies**): *police brutality* ◇ *the brutalities of war* **bru·tal·ly** /-təli/ *adv.*: *He was brutally assaulted.* ◇ *Let me be brutally frank about this.*

bru·tal·ism /ˈbruːtəlɪzəm/ *noun* [U] (*architecture*) (sometimes *disapproving*) a style of architecture used especially in the 1950s and 60s which uses large concrete blocks, steel, etc, and is sometimes considered ugly and unpleasant ▶ **bru·tal·ist** /ˈbruːtəlɪst/ *adj.*, *noun*

bru·tal·ize (*BrE* also **-ise**) /ˈbruːtəlaɪz/ *verb* **1** [usually passive] **~ sb** to make sb unable to feel normal human emotions such as pity: *soldiers brutalized by war* **2 ~ sb** to treat sb in a cruel or violent way

brute /bruːt/ *noun, adj.*

■ *noun* **1** (sometimes *humorous*) a man who treats people in an unkind, cruel way: *His father was a drunken brute.* ◇ *You've forgotten my birthday again, you brute!* **2** a large strong animal **3** a thing which is awkward and unpleasant

■ *adj.* [only before noun] **1** involving physical strength only and not thought or intelligence: ***brute force/strength*** **2** basic and unpleasant: *the brute facts of inequality*

bru·tish /ˈbruːtɪʃ/ *adj.* unkind and violent and not showing thought or intelligence ▶ **bru·tish·ness** *noun* [U]

BS (*NAmE* also **B.S.**) /ˌbiː ˈes/ *abbr.* **1** (*NAmE*) = BSc **2** (*BrE*) Bachelor of Surgery (a university degree in medicine) **3** British Standard (used on labels, etc. showing a number given by the British Standards Institution which controls the quality of products): *produced to BS4353* **4** (*US, taboo, slang*) BULLSHIT: *That guy's full of BS.*

BSc /ˌbiː es ˈsiː/ (*BrE*) (*NAmE* **B.S., BS**) *noun* the abbreviation for 'Bachelor of Science' (a first university degree in science): (*BrE*) *to* ***be/have/do a BSc*** *in Zoology* ◇ (*BrE*) *Jill Ayres BSc*

BSE /ˌbiː es ˈiː/ (also *informal* **ˌmad ˈcow disease**) *noun* [U] the abbreviation for 'bovine spongiform encephalopathy' (a brain disease of cows that causes death)

BSI /ˌbiː es ˈaɪ/ *abbr.* the British Standards Institution (the organization that decides the standard sizes for goods produced in Britain, and tests the safety of electrical goods, children's toys, etc.)

ˈB-side *noun* the side of a pop record that was considered less likely to be successful ➲ compare A-SIDE

BST /ˌbiː es ˈtiː/ *abbr.* BRITISH SUMMER TIME

BTEC /ˈbiːtek/ *noun* used to refer to any of a large group of British qualifications that can be taken in many different subjects at several levels (the abbreviation for 'Business and Technology Education Council'): *a BTEC Higher National Diploma in Public Service Studies*

BTW *abbr.* used in writing to mean 'by the way'

bub·ble /ˈbʌbl/ *noun, verb*
■ *noun* **1** a ball of air or gas in a liquid, or a ball of air inside a solid substance such as glass: *champagne bubbles* ◇ *a bubble of oxygen* ◇ *blowing bubbles into water through a straw* ➲ picture at FROTH ➲ see also SPEECH BUBBLE **2** a round ball of liquid, containing air, produced by soap and water: *The children like to have bubbles in their bath.* **3** a small amount of a feeling that sb wants to express: *a* ***bubble of laughter/hope/enthusiasm*** **4** a good or lucky situation that is unlikely to last long: *At the time the telecoms bubble was at its height.*
IDM **the bubble ˈbursts** there is a sudden end to a good or lucky situation: *When the bubble finally burst, hundreds of people lost their jobs.* ➲ more at BURST *v.*
■ *verb* **1** [I] to form bubbles: *The water in the pan was beginning to bubble.* ◇ *Add the white wine and let it* ***bubble up***. **2** [I] (+ **adv./prep.**) to make a bubbling sound, especially when moving in the direction mentioned: *I could hear the soup bubbling away.* ◇ *A stream came bubbling between the stones.* **3** [I] **~ (over) with sth** to be full of a particular feeling: *She was bubbling over with excitement.* **4** [I] + **adv./prep.** (of a feeling) to be felt strongly by a person; to be present in a situation: *Laughter bubbled up inside him.* ◇ *the anger that bubbled beneath the surface*
PHR V **ˌbubble ˈunder** (*especially BrE*) (*NAmE* usually **ˌbubble under the ˈradar**) (*informal*) to be likely to be very successful or popular soon: *Here are two records that are bubbling under.*

ˌbubble and ˈsqueak *noun* [U] a type of British food made from cold cooked potatoes and CABBAGE that are mixed together and fried

ˈbubble bath *noun* **1** [U] a liquid soap that smells pleasant and makes a lot of bubbles when it is added to bath water **2** [C] a bath with bubble bath in the water

bubble·gum /ˈbʌblɡʌm/ *noun, adj.*
■ *noun* [U] a type of CHEWING GUM that can be blown into bubbles
■ *adj.* [only before noun] simple in style, not serious and liked mainly by young people: *This CD is pure bubblegum pop.*

bubble·jet printer /ˈbʌbldʒet prɪntə(r)/ *noun* a type of printer that uses bubbles of air to blow small dots of ink in order to form letters, numbers, etc. on paper

ˈbubble pack *noun* = BLISTER PACK

ˈbubble wrap (*BrE*) (*NAmE* **ˈBubble Wrap™**) *noun* [U] a sheet of plastic which has lots of small raised parts filled with air, used for protecting things that are being carried or sent by post/mail

bubb·ly /ˈbʌbli/ *adj.* (**bub·blier, bub·bli·est**) *noun*
■ *adj.* **1** full of bubbles **2** (*informal*) (of a person) always cheerful, friendly and enthusiastic
■ *noun* [U] (*informal*) = CHAMPAGNE

bu·bon·ic plague /bjuːˌbɒnɪk ˈpleɪɡ; *NAmE* -ˌbɑːnɪk/ (also **the plague**) *noun* [U] a disease spread by RATS that causes fever, swellings on the body and usually death

buc·can·eer /ˌbʌkəˈnɪə(r); *NAmE* -ˈnɪr/ *noun* **1** (in the past) a sailor who attacked ships at sea and stole from them SYN **pirate** **2** (especially in business) a person who achieves success in a skilful but not always honest way

bucc·an·eer·ing /ˌbʌkəˈnɪərɪŋ; *NAmE* -ˈnɪrɪŋ/ *adj.* enjoying taking risks, especially in business: *Virgin's buccaneering founder, Richard Branson*

buck /bʌk/ *noun, verb*
■ *noun* **1** [C] (*informal*) a US, Australian or New Zealand dollar; a South African RAND; an Indian RUPEE: *They cost ten bucks.* ◇ *We're talking* ***big bucks*** (= a lot of money) *here.* **2** [C] a male DEER, HARE or RABBIT (also called a **buck rabbit**) ➲ compare DOE, HART, STAG **3** [C] (*pl.* **buck**) (*SAfrE*) a DEER, whether male or female: *a herd of buck* **4** [C] (*old-fashioned, informal*) a young man **5 the buck** [sing.] used in some expressions to refer to the responsibility or blame for sth: *It was my decision.* ***The buck stops here*** (= nobody else can be blamed). ◇ *I was tempted to* ***pass the buck*** (= make sb else responsible). ORIGIN From **buck**, an object which in a poker game is placed in front of the player whose turn it is to deal.
IDM **make a fast/quick buck** (*informal*, often *disapproving*) to earn money quickly and easily ➲ more at BANG *n.*, MILLION
■ *verb* **1** [I] (of a horse) to jump with the two back feet or all four feet off the ground **2** [I] to move up and down suddenly or in a way that is not controlled: *The boat bucked and heaved beneath them.* **3** [T] **~ sth** (*informal*) to resist or oppose sth: *One or two companies have managed to* ***buck the trend*** *of the recession.* ◇ *He admired her willingness to* ***buck the system*** (= oppose authority or rules).
IDM **buck your iˈdeas up** (*BrE, informal*) to start behaving in a more acceptable way, so that work gets done better, etc.
PHR V **ˌbuck ˈup** (*informal*) **1** (often in orders) to become more cheerful SYN **cheer up**: *Buck up, kid! It's not the end of the game.* **2 buck up!** (*old-fashioned*) used to tell sb to hurry SYN **hurry up** **ˌbuck sb ˈup** (*BrE, informal*) to make sb more cheerful SYN **cheer up**: *The good news bucked us all up.*

bucket /ˈbʌkɪt/ *noun, verb*
■ *noun* **1** (*NAmE* also **pail**) [C] an open container with a handle, used for carrying or holding liquids, sand, etc: *a plastic bucket* ◇ (*BrE*) *They were playing on the beach with their* ***buckets and spades***. ➲ VISUAL VOCAB page V17 **2** [C] a large container that is part of a CRANE or DIGGER and is used for lifting things ➲ VISUAL VOCAB page V47 **3** (also **bucket·ful** /-fʊl/) (*NAmE* also **pail, pail·ful**) [C] the amount contained in a bucket: *two buckets/bucketfuls of water* ◇ *They used to drink tea* ***by the bucket/bucketful*** (= in large quantities). **4 buckets** [pl.] (*informal*) a large amount: *To succeed in show business, you need buckets of confidence.* ◇ *We* ***wept buckets***. ◇ *He was* ***sweating buckets*** *by the end of the race.* ◇ *The rain was coming down* ***in buckets*** (= it was raining very heavily). IDM see DROP *n.*, KICK *v.*
■ *verb*
PHR V **ˈbucket down** (*BrE, informal*) to rain heavily SYN **pour**: *It's bucketing down.*

ˈbucket seat *noun* a seat with a curved back for one person, especially in a car

ˈbucket shop *noun* (*informal, especially BrE*) a place that sells cheap plane tickets

buck·eye /ˈbʌkaɪ/ *noun* **1** a N American tree that has bright red or white flowers and produces nuts **2** an orange and brown BUTTERFLY with large spots on its wings that look like eyes **3 Buckeye** (*US, informal*) a person from the US state of Ohio

ˌBuck ˈHouse *noun* (*BrE*, often *ironic*) an informal name for Buckingham Palace: *We stayed at Tom's place. It isn't exactly Buck House, but it's comfortable enough.*

Buck·ing·ham Pal·ace /ˌbʌkɪŋəm ˈpæləs/ *noun* **1** the official home of the British royal family in London **2** the British royal family or the people who advise them: *Buckingham Palace refused to comment.*

buckle /ˈbʌkl/ *verb, noun*
■ *verb* **1** [T, I] to fasten sth or be fastened with a buckle: **~ (sth)** *She buckled her belt.* ◇ **~ (sth on/up)** *He buckled on his sword.* ◇ *These shoes buckle at the side.* **2** [I, T] to become crushed or bent under a weight or force; to crush or bend sth in this way: *The steel frames began to buckle under the strain.* ◇ (*figurative*) *A weaker man would have buckled under the pressure.* ◇ **~ sth** *The crash buckled the front of my car.* **3** [I] when your knees or legs **buckle** or when you **buckle** at the knees, your knees become weak and you start to fall
PHR V **ˌbuckle ˈdown (to sth)** (*informal*) to start to do sth seriously: *I'd better buckle down to those reports.* **ˌbuckle ˈup** (*NAmE*) (*BrE* **ˌbelt ˈup**) (*informal*) to fasten your SEAT BELT (= a belt worn by a passenger in a vehicle)

B

■ *noun* a piece of metal or plastic used for joining the ends of a belt or for fastening a part of a bag, shoe, etc. ➲ VISUAL VOCAB pages V51, V52

Buck·ley's /ˈbʌkliz/ *noun*
IDM **not have Buckley's (chance)** (*AustralE, NZE, informal*) used to suggest that sb has little or no hope of achieving a particular aim

buck 'naked *adj.* (*NAmE, informal*) (of a person) not wearing any clothes at all

buck·ram /ˈbʌkrəm/ *noun* [U] a type of stiff cloth made especially from cotton or LINEN, used in the past for covering books and for making clothes stiffer

,Buck's 'Fizz (*BrE*) (*NAmE* **mi·mosa**) *noun* [U, C] an alcoholic drink made by mixing SPARKLING white wine (= with bubbles) with orange juice

buck·shot /ˈbʌkʃɒt; *NAmE* -ʃɑːt/ *noun* [U] balls of LEAD that are fired from a SHOTGUN

buck·skin /ˈbʌkskɪn/ *noun* [U] soft leather made from the skin of DEER or GOATS, used for making gloves, bags, etc.

,buck 'teeth *noun* [pl.] top teeth that stick forward ▶ **,buck-'toothed** *adj.*

buck·wheat /ˈbʌkwiːt/ *noun* [U] small dark grain that is grown as food for animals and for making flour

bu·col·ic /bjuːˈkɒlɪk; *NAmE* -ˈkɑːlɪk/ *adj.* (*literary*) connected with the countryside or country life

bud /bʌd/ *noun, verb*
■ *noun* **1** a small lump that grows on a plant and from which a flower, leaf or STEM develops: *the first buds appearing in spring* ◇ *The tree is* ***in bud*** *already.* ➲ COLLOCATIONS at LIFE ➲ VISUAL VOCAB page V8 **2** a flower or leaf that is not fully open ➲ VISUAL VOCAB page V9 **3** (*NAmE, informal*) = BUDDY: *Listen, bud, enough of the wisecracks, OK?* ➲ see also COTTON BUD, ROSEBUD, TASTE BUD IDM see NIP *v.*
■ *verb* [I] to produce buds

Bud·dha /ˈbʊdə/ *noun* **1** (also **the Buddha**) [sing.] the person on whose teachings the Buddhist religion is based **2** [C] a statue or picture of the Buddha **3** [C] a person who has achieved ENLIGHTENMENT (= spiritual knowledge) in Buddhism

Bud·dhism /ˈbʊdɪzəm/ *noun* [U] an Asian religion based on the teaching of Siddhartha Gautama (or Buddha) ▶ **Bud·dhist** /ˈbʊdɪst/ *noun*: *a devout Buddhist* **Bud·dhist** /ˈbʊdɪst/ *adj.* [usually before noun]: *a* ***Buddhist monk/temple***

bud·ding /ˈbʌdɪŋ/ *adj.* [only before noun] beginning to develop or become successful: *a* ***budding artist/writer*** ◇ *our budding romance*

bud·dleia /ˈbʌdliə/ *noun* [C, U] a bush with purple or white flowers that grow in groups

buddy /ˈbʌdi/ *noun, verb*
■ *noun* (*pl.* -ies) **1** (*NAmE* also **bud**) (*informal*) a friend: *an old college buddy of mine* **2** (also **bud**) (both *NAmE, informal*) used to speak to a man you do not know: *'Where to, buddy?' the driver asked.* **3** (*especially NAmE*) a partner who does an activity with you so that you can help each other: *The school uses a* ***buddy system*** *to pair newcomers with older students.*
■ *verb* (**bud·dies, buddy·ing, bud·died, bud·died**)
PHR V **,buddy 'up (to/with sb)** (*NAmE*) **1** (*BrE* **,pal 'up (with sb)**) (*informal*) to become friendly with sb: *You and your neighbour might want to buddy up to make the trip more enjoyable.* **2** to become friendly with sb in order to get an advantage for yourself

'buddy movie *noun* (*informal*) a film/movie in which there is a close friendship between two people

budge /bʌdʒ/ *verb* (usually used in negative sentences) (rather *informal*) **1** [I, T] to move slightly; to make sth/sb move slightly: *She pushed at the door but it wouldn't budge.* ◇ *The dog refused to budge.* ◇ **~ sth** *I heaved with all my might but still couldn't budge it.* **2** [I, T] to change your opinion about sth; to make sb change their opinion: *He* ***won't budge an inch*** *on the issue.* ◇ **~ sb** *He was not to be budged on the issue.*
PHR V **,budge 'up** (*BrE, informal*) to move, so that there is room for other people SYN **move up**: *Budge up a bit!*

budg·eri·gar /ˈbʌdʒərigɑː(r)/ *noun* (also *informal* **budgie**) (both *BrE*) a small bird of the PARROT family, often kept in a CAGE as a pet

budget 0-w /ˈbʌdʒɪt/ *noun, verb, adj.*
■ *noun* **1** 0-w [C, U] the money that is available to a person or an organization and a plan of how it will be spent over a period of time: *a* ***monthly/an annual/a family budget*** ◇ *the* ***education/defence budget*** (= the amount of money that can be spent on this) ◇ *an advertising budget of $2 million* ◇ *a big-budget movie* ◇ *We decorated the house* ***on a tight budget*** (= without much money to spend). ◇ *The work was finished on time and* ***within budget*** (= did not cost more money than was planned). ◇ *They went* ***over budget*** (= spent too much money). ◇ *budget cuts* ➲ COLLOCATIONS at BUSINESS, FINANCE **2** (*BrE* also **Budget**) [C, usually sing.] an official statement by the government of a country's income from taxes, etc. and how it will be spent: *tax cuts in this year's budget* ◇ *a budget deficit* (= when the government spends more money than it earns) ➲ COLLOCATIONS at BUDGET
■ *verb* [I, T] to be careful about the amount of money you spend; to plan to spend an amount of money for a particular purpose: *If we budget carefully we'll be able to afford the trip.* ◇ **~ for sth** *I've budgeted for two new members of staff.* ◇ **~ sth (for sth)** *Ten million francs has been budgeted for the project.* ◇ **~ sth (at sth)** *The project has been budgeted at ten million francs.* ➲ SYNONYMS at SAVE ▶ **budget·ing** *noun* [U]
■ *adj.* [only before noun] (used in advertising, etc.) low in price: *a* ***budget flight/hotel*** ➲ SYNONYMS at CHEAP

'budget account *noun* (*BrE*) an arrangement with a shop/store or company to pay your bills in fixed regular amounts and not as one large payment

budget·ary /ˈbʌdʒɪtəri; *NAmE* -teri/ *adj.* connected with a budget: ***budgetary control/policies/reform*** ➲ SYNONYMS at ECONOMIC

budgie /ˈbʌdʒi/ *noun* (*BrE, informal*) = BUDGERIGAR

buff /bʌf/ *noun, adj., verb*
■ *noun* **1** [C] (used in compounds) a person who is very interested in a particular subject or activity and knows a lot about it: *an opera buff* **2** [U] a pale yellow-brown colour SYN **beige** **3** [U] soft strong yellowish-brown leather ➲ see also BLIND MAN'S BUFF
IDM **in the 'buff** (*informal*) wearing no clothes SYN **naked**
■ *adj.* **1** pale yellow-brown in colour SYN **beige**: *a buff envelope* **2** (*slang*) physically fit and attractive with big muscles
■ *verb* **~ sth (up)** to polish sth with a soft cloth
PHR V **,buff 'up | ,buff yourself 'up** (*slang*) to make yourself more attractive, especially by exercising in order to make your muscles bigger: *He buffed up to take the role of the commando captain.* **,buff sb/sth 'up** (*informal*) to work on sb/sth to make them/it seem more attractive or impressive: *The team will have to buff up their tarnished image.*

buf·falo /ˈbʌfələʊ; *NAmE* -loʊ/ *noun* (*pl.* **buf·falo** or **buf·faloes**) **1** a large animal of the cow family. There are two types of buffalo, the African and the Asian, which has wide, curved horns. ➲ see also WATER BUFFALO **2** = BISON

buf·fer /ˈbʌfə(r)/ *noun, verb*
■ *noun* **1** a thing or person that reduces a shock or protects sb/sth against difficulties: **~ (against sth)** *Support from family and friends acts as a buffer against stress.* ◇ **~ (between sth and sth)** *She often had to act as a buffer between father and son.* ◇ *a* ***buffer state*** (= a small country between two powerful states that helps keep peace between them) ◇ *a* ***buffer zone*** (= an area of land between two opposing armies or countries) **2** (*BrE*) one of two round metal devices on the front or end of a train, or at the end of a railway/railroad track, that reduce the shock if the train hits sth **3** (*computing*) an area in a computer's memory where data can be stored for a short time **4** (also **old 'buffer**) (*old-fashioned, BrE*) a silly old man IDM see HIT *v.*

■ ***verb* 1 ~ sth** to reduce the harmful effects of sth: *to buffer the effects of stress on health* **2 ~ sb (against sth)** to protect sb from sth: *They tried to buffer themselves against problems and uncertainties.* **3 ~ sth** (*computing*) (of a computer) to hold data for a short time before using it

buf·fet¹ /ˈbʊfeɪ; ˈbʌfeɪ; *NAmE* bəˈfeɪ/ *noun* ➲ see also BUFFET² **1** a meal at which people serve themselves from a table and then stand or sit somewhere else to eat: *a* ***buffet lunch/supper*** ◇ *Dinner will be a cold buffet, not a sit-down meal.* **2** a place, for example in a train or bus station, where you can buy food and drinks to eat or drink there, or to take away **3** (*BrE*) = BUFFET CAR **4** (*especially NAmE*) = SIDEBOARD (1)

buf·fet² /ˈbʌfɪt/ ➲ see also BUFFET¹ *verb* [often passive] **~ sb/sth** to knock or push sb/sth roughly from side to side: *to be buffeted by the wind* ◇ (*figurative, formal*) *The nation had been buffeted by a wave of strikes.* ▸ **buf·fet·ing** *noun* [U, C, usually sing.]

buffet car /ˈbʊfeɪ kɑː(r); ˈbʌfeɪ; *NAmE* bəˈfeɪ/ (also **buffet**) *noun* (*BrE*) the part of a train where you can buy sth to eat and drink

buf·foon /bəˈfuːn/ *noun* (*old-fashioned*) a person who does silly but amusing things ▸ **buf·foon·ery** /-əri/ *noun* [U]

bug /bʌg/ *noun, verb*

■ ***noun* 1** [C] (*especially NAmE*) any small insect **2** [C] (*informal*) an infectious illness that is usually fairly mild: *a flu bug* ◇ *There's a stomach* ***bug going round*** (= people are catching it from each other). ◇ *I picked up a bug in the office.* ➲ SYNONYMS at DISEASE ➲ COLLOCATIONS at ILL **3** (usually **the... bug**) [sing.] (*informal*) an enthusiastic interest in sth such as a sport or a hobby: *the travel bug* ◇ *She was never interested in fitness before but now* ***she's been bitten by the bug.*** **4** [C] (*informal*) a small hidden device for listening to other people's conversations **5** [C] a fault in a machine, especially in a computer system or program **6** [C] (*NAmE*) = BEETLE

■ ***verb*** (-gg-) **1 ~ sth** to put a special device (= a bug) somewhere in order to listen secretly to other people's conversations: *They bugged her hotel room.* ◇ *They were bugging his telephone conversations.* ◇ *a bugging device* **2 ~ sb** (*informal*) to annoy or irritate sb: *Stop bugging me!* ◇ *It's something that's been bugging me a lot recently.*

IDM ˌ**bug the ˈhell/ˈcrap/ˈshit out of sb** (*taboo, slang*) to annoy sb very much: *The song just bugs the hell out of me.*

PHR V **bug ˈoff!** (*NAmE, informal*) a rude way of telling sb to go away ˌ**bug ˈout** (*informal*) **1** (*NAmE*) (especially of sb's eyes) to be wide open and stick out: *Their eyes were bugging out of their heads when they saw it.* **2** (*NAmE, AustralE*) to leave a place or situation, especially because it is becoming dangerous: *We should bug out now before it's too late.* **3** (*NAmE*) to become too frightened to do sth: *Susan started to bug out when she heard a noise in the bushes.*

bug·a·boo /ˈbʌgəbuː/ *noun* (*NAmE, informal*) a thing that people are afraid of

bug·bear /ˈbʌgbeə(r); *NAmE* -ber/ *noun* (*especially BrE*) a thing that annoys people and that they worry about: *Inflation is the government's main bugbear.*

ˈ**bug-eyed** *adj.* (*informal*) having eyes that stick out

bug·ger /ˈbʌgə(r)/ *noun, verb*

■ ***noun*** (*BrE, taboo, slang*) **1** an offensive word used to insult sb, especially a man, and to show anger or dislike: *Come here, you little bugger!* ◇ *You stupid bugger! You could have run me over!* **2** used to refer to a person, especially a man, that you like or feel sympathy for: *Poor bugger! His wife left him last week.* ◇ *He's a tough old bugger.* **3** [usually sing.] a thing that is difficult or causes problems: *This door's a bugger to open.* ◇ *Question 6 is a real bugger.*
IDM see SILLY *adj.*

■ ***verb* 1** [I, T] (*BrE, taboo, slang*) used as a swear word when sb is annoyed about sth or to show that they do not care about sth at all: *Bugger! I've left my keys at home.* ◇ **~ sth** *Bugger it! I've burnt the toast.* ◇ *Oh, bugger the cost! Let's get it anyway.* **2** [T] **~ sth** (*BrE, taboo, slang*) to break or ruin sth: *I think I've buggered the computer.* **3** [T] **~ sb** (*taboo* or *law*) to have ANAL sex with sb

IDM ˌ**bugger ˈme** (*BrE, taboo, slang*) used to express surprise: *Bugger me! Did you see that?*

PHR V ˌ**bugger aˈbout/aˈround** (*BrE, taboo, slang*) to waste time by behaving in a silly way or with no clear purpose: *Stop buggering about and get back to work.* **HELP** A more polite, informal way of saying this is **mess about** (*BrE*) or **mess around** (*NAmE, BrE*). ˌ**bugger sb aˈbout/aˈround** (*BrE, taboo, slang*) to treat sb in a way that is deliberately not helpful to them or wastes their time: *I'm sick of being buggered about by the company.* **HELP** A more polite, informal way of saying this is **mess sb about/around.** ˌ**bugger ˈoff** (*BrE, taboo, slang*) (often used in orders) to go away: *Bugger off and leave me alone.* ◇ *Where is everyone? They've all buggered off.* ˌ**bugger sth↔ˈup** (*BrE, taboo, slang*) to do sth badly or spoil sth: *I buggered up the exam.* ◇ *Sorry for buggering up your plans.* **HELP** A more polite, informal way of saying this is **foul sth up, mess sth up** or **bungle sth.**

ˌ**bugger ˈall** *noun* [U] (*BrE, taboo, slang*) nothing at all; none at all: *There's bugger all on TV tonight.* ◇ *Well, she was bugger all help* (= no help at all).

bug·gered /ˈbʌgəd; *NAmE* -gərd/ *adj.* [not before noun] (*BrE, taboo, slang*) **1** very tired **2** broken or ruined: *Oh no, the TV's buggered.*

IDM **I'll be buggered** (*BrE, taboo, slang*) used to express great surprise: *Well, I'll be buggered! Look who's here.* **I'm ˈbuggered if...** (*BrE, taboo, slang*) used to say that you do not know sth or to refuse to do sth: *'What's this meeting all about?' 'I'm buggered if I know.'* ◇ *Well I'm buggered if I'm going to help her after what she said to me.*

bug·gery /ˈbʌgəri/ *noun* [U] (*BrE, taboo, slang* or *law*) ANAL SEX

Bug·gins' turn /ˈbʌgɪnz tɜːn; ˈbʌgɪnzɪz; *NAmE* tɜːrn/ *noun* [U] (*BrE, informal*) used to refer to the way in which it sometimes seems that people get jobs or are promoted not because they are good at what they do, but because they have been doing it for longer than anybody else

buggy /ˈbʌgi/ *noun* (*pl.* -ies) **1** (*BrE*) (*NAmE* **cart**) a small car, often without a roof or doors, used for a particular purpose: *a* ***garden/golf buggy*** ➲ see also BEACH BUGGY **2** (also ˈ**Baby Buggy™**) (both *BrE*) (*NAmE* **strol·ler**) a type of light folding chair on wheels in which a baby or small child is pushed along ➲ compare PUSHCHAIR **3** a light CARRIAGE for one or two people, pulled by one horse

bugle /ˈbjuːgl/ *noun* a musical instrument like a small TRUMPET, used in the army for giving signals

bu·gler /ˈbjuːglə(r)/ *noun* a person who plays the bugle

bui·bui /ˈbʊibʊi/ *noun* (*EAfrE*) an item of clothing worn by some Muslim women, consisting of a long black dress and piece of black cloth that covers the head showing only the face or eyes

build 🔑 /bɪld/ *verb, noun*

■ ***verb*** (**built, built** /bɪlt/) **1** 🔑 [T, I] to make sth, especially a building, by putting parts together: **~ (sth)** *They have permission to build 200 new houses.* ◇ *Robins build nests almost anywhere.* ◇ *They're going to build on the site of the old power station.* ◇ **~ sth of/in/from sth** *a house built of stone* ◇ **~ sth for sb** *They had a house built for them.* ◇ **~ sb sth** *David built us a shed in the back yard.* **2** 🔑 [T] **~ sth** to create or develop sth: *She's built a new career for herself.* ◇ *We want to build a better life.* ◇ *This information will help us build a picture of his attacker.* **3** [I] (of a feeling) to become gradually stronger: *The tension and excitement built gradually all day.* **IDM** see CASTLE, ROME

PHR V ˌ**build sth aˈround sth** [usually passive] to create sth, using sth else as a basis: *The story is built around a group of high school dropouts.* ˌ**build sth↔ˈin** | ˌ**build sth ˈinto sth** [often passive] **1** to make sth a permanent part of a larger structure: *We're having new wardrobes built in.* ◇ *The pipes were built into the concrete.* **2** to make sth a permanent part of a system, plan, etc: *A certain amount of flexibility is built into the system.* ➲ see also BUILT-IN ˈ**build on sth** to use sth as a basis for further progress: *This study builds on earlier work.* ˈ**build sth on sth** [usually passive] to base sth on sth: *an argument built on sound logic* ˌ**build**

B

sth↔'on | ˌ**build sth 'onto sth** to add sth (for example, an extra room) to an existing structure by building: *They've built an extension on.* ◇ *The new wing was built onto the hospital last year.* ˌ**build 'up (to sth)** 0➡ to become greater, more powerful or larger in number: *All the pressure built up and he was off work for weeks with stress.* ◇ *The music builds up to a rousing climax.* ➲ related noun BUILD-UP (1) ˌ**build 'up to sth** | ˌ**build yourself 'up to sth** to prepare for a particular moment or event: *Build yourself up to peak performance on the day of the exam.* ➲ related noun BUILD-UP (2) ˌ**build sb/sth 'up** [usually passive] to give a very positive and enthusiastic description of sb/sth, often exaggerating your claims: *The play was built up to be a masterpiece but I found it very disappointing.* ➲ related noun BUILD-UP (3) ˌ**build sb/yourself↔'up** to make sb/yourself healthier or stronger: *You need more protein to build you up.* ˌ**build sth↔'up 1** 0➡ to create or develop sth: *She's built up a very successful business.* ◇ *These finds help us* ***build up a picture*** *of life in the Middle Ages.* ◇ *I am anxious not to* ***build up false hopes*** (= to encourage people to hope for too much). **2** to make sth higher or stronger than it was before

■ ***noun*** [U, C, usually sing.] the shape and size of the human body: *a man of average build*

Synonyms

build

construct • assemble • erect • put sth up

These words all mean to make sth, especially by putting different parts together.

build to make sth, especially a building, by putting parts together: *a house built of stone* ◇ *They're going to build on the site of the old power station.*

construct [often passive] (*rather formal*) to build sth such as a road, building or machine

assemble (*rather formal*) to fit together all the separate parts of sth such as a piece of furniture or a machine: *The cupboard is easy to assemble.*

erect (*formal*) to build sth; to put sth in position and make it stand upright: *Police had to erect barriers to keep crowds back.*

put sth up to build sth or place sth somewhere: *They're putting up new hotels in order to boost tourism in the area.*

PATTERNS

- to build/construct/erect/put up a **house/wall**
- to build/construct/erect/put up some **shelves**
- to build/construct/erect/put up a **barrier/fence/shelter**
- to build/construct/assemble a(n) **engine/machine**
- to build/construct a **road/railway/railroad/tunnel**
- to erect/put up a **tent/statue/monument**

build·er /ˈbɪldə(r)/ *noun* **1** a person or company whose job is to build or repair houses or other buildings **2** (usually in compounds) a person or thing that builds, creates or develops sth: *a shipbuilder* ◇ *a confidence builder* ➲ see also BODYBUILDER

ˈ**builders' merchant** *noun* a person or shop that supplies materials to the building trade

build·ing 0➡ /ˈbɪldɪŋ/ *noun*
1 0➡ [C] a structure such as a house or school that has a roof and walls: *tall/old/historic buildings* ➲ COLLOCATIONS at DECORATE ➲ VISUAL VOCAB page V13 **2** 0➡ [U] the process and work of building: *the building of the school* ◇ *There's building work going on next door.* ◇ *the building trade* ◇ ***building materials/costs/regulations***

Synonyms

building

property • premises • complex • structure • block

These are all words for a structure such as a house, office block or factory that has a roof and four walls

building a structure such as a house, office block or factory that has a roof and four walls

property a building or buildings and the surrounding land; land and buildings: *We have a buyer who would like to view the property.* ◇ *The price of property has risen enormously.* NOTE This word is often used when talking about buying/selling houses or other buildings and land.

premises [pl.] the building or buildings and surrounding land that a business owns or uses: *The company is looking for larger premises.*

complex a group of buildings of a similar type together in one place: *a leisure complex*

structure a thing that is made of several parts, especially a building: *The pier is a wooden structure.*

block (*BrE*) a tall building that contains flats or offices; a building that forms part of a school, hospital, etc. and is used for a particular purpose: *a block of flats* ◇ *the school's science block*

PATTERNS

- a(n) **commercial/industrial/residential** building/property/premises/complex/block
- an **apartment** building/complex/block
- a/the **school** building/premises
- to **build** a(n) property/complex/structure/block
- to **put up** a building/property/structure/block
- to **demolish/pull down** a(n) building/property/complex/structure/block

ˈ**building block** *noun* **1** [C] a piece of wood or plastic used as a toy for children to build things with ➲ VISUAL VOCAB page V32 **2 building blocks** [pl.] parts that are joined together in order to make a large thing exist: *Single words are the building blocks of language.*

ˈ**building site** (*especially BrE*) (*NAmE* usually **conˈstruction site**) *noun* an area of land where sth is being built

ˈ**building society** *noun* (*BrE*) (*US* ˌ**savings and ˈloan association**) an organization like a bank that lends money to people who want to buy a house. People also save money with a building society.

ˈ**build-up** *noun* **1** [sing., U] an increase in the amount of sth over a period of time: *a steady build-up of traffic in the evenings* **2** [C, usually sing.] **~ (to sth)** the time before an important event, when people are preparing for it: *the build-up to the President's visit* **3** [C, usually sing.] a very positive and enthusiastic description of sth that is going to happen, that is intended to make people excited about it: *The media have given the show a huge build-up.*

built /bɪlt/ *combining form* (after adverbs and in compound adjectives) made in the particular way that is mentioned: *a newly built station* ◇ *American-built cars* ➲ see also PURPOSE-BUILT, WELL BUILT

ˌ**built-ˈin** (also *less frequent* ˌ**in-ˈbuilt**) *adj.* [only before noun] included as part of sth and not separate from it: *built-in cupboards* ➲ compare INBUILT

ˌ**built-ˈup** *adj.* [usually before noun] (*especially BrE*) (of an area of land) covered in buildings, roads, etc: *to reduce the speed limit in built-up areas*

bulb /bʌlb/ *noun* **1** (also ˈ**light bulb**) the glass part that fits into an electric lamp, etc. to give light when it is switched on: *a 60-watt bulb* ◇ *a room lit by bare bulbs* (= with no decorative cover) ➲ VISUAL VOCAB page V18 **2** the round underground part of some plants, shaped like an onion, that grows into a new plant every year ➲ VISUAL VOCAB page V9 **3** an object shaped like a bulb, for example the end of a THERMOMETER

bulb·ous /ˈbʌlbəs/ *adj.* shaped like a bulb; round and fat in an ugly way: *a bulbous red nose*

bul·gar (also **bul·gur**) /ˈbʌlɡə(r)/ (also ˈ**bulgar wheat**) *noun* [U] a type of food consisting of grains of WHEAT that are boiled then dried

bulge /bʌldʒ/ *verb, noun*

■ *verb* **1** [I] ~ (**with sth**) (usually used in the progressive tenses) to be completely full (of sth): *Her pockets were bulging with presents.* ◇ *a bulging briefcase* **2** [I] to stick out from sth in a round shape: *His eyes bulged.* IDM see SEAM

■ *noun* **1** a lump that sticks out from sth in a round shape: *the bulge of a gun in his pocket* **2** (*informal*) fat on the body that sticks out in a round shape: *That skirt's too tight. It shows all your bulges.* **3** a sudden temporary increase in the amount of sth: *After the war there was a bulge in the birth rate.*

bul·ging /ˈbʌldʒɪŋ/ *adj.* that sticks out from sth in a round shape: *bulging eyes*

bu·limia /buˈlɪmiə; bju-; -ˈliːmiə/ (also **bulimia nervosa** /buˌlɪmiə nɜːˈvəʊsə; *NAmE* nɜːrˈvoʊsə/) *noun* [U] an emotional DISORDER in which a person repeatedly eats too much and then forces him- or herself to VOMIT ➲ COLLOCATIONS at DIET ➲ compare ANOREXIA ▶ **bu·lim·ic** /buˈlɪmɪk; bju-; -ˈliːmɪk/ *adj., noun*

bulk AW /bʌlk/ *noun, verb*

■ *noun* **1** [sing.] **the** ~ (**of sth**) the main part of sth; most of sth: *The bulk of the population lives in cities.* **2** [U] the (large) size or quantity of sth: *Despite its bulk and weight, the car is extremely fast.* ◇ *a* ***bulk order*** (= one for a large number of similar items) ◇ ***bulk buying*** (= buying in large amounts, often at a reduced price) ◇ *It's cheaper to buy* ***in bulk***. **3** [sing.] the weight or shape of sb/sth large: *She heaved her bulk out of the chair.*

■ *verb*

IDM **bulk ˈlarge** (*BrE, formal*) to be the most important part of sth

PHR V ˌ**bulk sth**↔ˈ**out**/ˈ**up** to make sth bigger, thicker or heavier

bulk·head /ˈbʌlkhed/ *noun* (*technical*) a wall that divides a ship or an aircraft into separate parts

bulky AW /ˈbʌlki/ *adj.* (**bulk·ier, bulki·est**) **1** (of a thing) large and difficult to move or carry: *Bulky items will be collected separately.* **2** (of a person) tall and heavy: *The bulky figure of Inspector Jones appeared at the door.*

bull /bʊl/ *noun* **1** [C] the male of any animal in the cow family: *a bull neck* (= a short thick neck like a bull's) ➲ compare BULLOCK, COW, OX, STEER **2** [C] the male of the ELEPHANT, WHALE and some other large animals ➲ compare COW **3** [C] (*finance*) a person who buys shares in a company, hoping to sell them soon afterwards at a higher price ➲ compare BEAR **4** [C] an official order or statement from the POPE (= the head of the Roman Catholic Church): *a papal bull* **5** [U] (*slang*) = BULLSHIT: *That's a load of bull!* **6** [C] = BULLSEYE ➲ see also COCK AND BULL STORY

IDM **a bull in a ˈchina shop** a person who is careless, or who moves or acts in a rough or awkward way, in a place or situation where skill and care are needed **take the bull by the ˈhorns** to face a difficult or dangerous situation directly and with courage ➲ more at RED *adj.*, SHOOT *v.*

ˈ**bull bars** *noun* [pl.] (*BrE*) a set of strong metal bars fixed to the front of a large vehicle to protect it from damage

bull·dog /ˈbʊldɒɡ; *NAmE* -dɔːɡ/ *noun* a short strong dog with a large head, a short flat nose and a short thick neck

ˈ**Bulldog clip™** *noun* (*BrE*) a metal device for holding papers together ➲ VISUAL VOCAB page V56

bull·doze /ˈbʊldəʊz; *NAmE* -doʊz/ *verb* **1** [T] ~ **sth** to destroy buildings, trees, etc. with a bulldozer: *The trees are being bulldozed to make way for a new superstore.* **2** [I, T] to force your way somewhere; to force sth somewhere: **+ adv./prep.** *Rooney bulldozed through to score.* ◇ ~ **sth + adv./prep.** *They bulldozed the tax through Parliament.* ◇ *He* ***bulldozed his way*** *to victory.* **3** [T] ~ **sb** (**into doing sth**) to force sb to do sth SYN **railroad**: *They bulldozed him into selling.*

bull·dozer /ˈbʊldəʊzə(r); *NAmE* -doʊz-/ *noun* a powerful vehicle with a broad steel blade in front, used for moving earth or knocking down buildings ➲ VISUAL VOCAB page V47

bull·dyke (also **bull·dike**) /ˈbʊldaɪk/ *noun* (*offensive*) a LESBIAN who is thought to look very male or to act in a typically male way

bul·let 🔑 /ˈbʊlɪt/ *noun*
a small metal object that is fired from a gun: *bullet wounds* ◇ *There were bullet holes in the door.* ◇ *He was killed by a bullet in the head.* ➲ see also MAGIC BULLET, PLASTIC BULLET, RUBBER BULLET IDM see BITE *v.*

bul·letin /ˈbʊlətɪn/ *noun* **1** a short news report on the radio or television **2** an official statement about sth important: *a bulletin on the President's health* **3** a printed report that gives news about an organization or a group

ˈ**bulletin board** *noun* **1** (*NAmE*) (*BrE* **no·tice·board**) (also **board** *BrE, NAmE*) a board for putting notices on ➲ VISUAL VOCAB page V56 **2** (*computing*) a place in a computer system where any user can write or read messages

ˈ**bullet point** *noun* an item in a list in a document, that is printed with a square, diamond or circle in front of it in order to show that it is important. The square, etc. is also called a bullet point.

bul·let·proof /ˈbʊlɪtpruːf/ *adj.* that can stop bullets from passing through it: *a bulletproof vest*

ˈ**bullet train** *noun* (*informal*) a Japanese train that carries passengers at high speeds

bull·fight /ˈbʊlfaɪt/ *noun* a traditional public entertainment, popular especially in Spain, in which BULLS are fought and usually killed ▶ **bull·fight·er** *noun* **bull·fight·ing** *noun* [U] ➲ see also MATADOR

bull·finch /ˈbʊlfɪntʃ/ *noun* a small European bird of the FINCH family, with a strong curved beak and a pink breast

bull·frog /ˈbʊlfrɒɡ; *NAmE* -frɔːɡ; -frɑːɡ/ *noun* a large American FROG with a loud CROAK

bull·head·ed /ˌbʊlˈhedɪd/ *adj.* (*NAmE*) unwilling to change your opinion about sth, in a way that other people think is annoying and unreasonable SYN **obstinate, stubborn** ▶ **bull·head·ed·ness** *noun* [U]

bull·horn /ˈbʊlhɔːn; *NAmE* -hɔːrn/ (*NAmE*) (*BrE* **loud·hail·er**) *noun* an electronic device, shaped like a horn, with a MICROPHONE at one end, that you speak into in order to make your voice louder so that it can be heard at a distance ➲ compare MEGAPHONE

bul·lion /ˈbʊliən/ *noun* [U] gold or silver in large amounts or in the form of bars: *gold bullion*

bull·ish /ˈbʊlɪʃ/ *adj.* **1** feeling confident and positive about the future: *in a bullish mood* **2** (*finance*) causing, or connected with, an increase in the price of shares: *a bullish market* ➲ compare BEARISH

ˈ**bull market** *noun* (*finance*) a period during which share prices are rising and people are buying shares ➲ compare BEAR MARKET

ˌ**bull ˈmastiff** *noun* a large strong dog with short smooth hair

bul·lock /ˈbʊlək/ *noun* a young BULL (= a male cow) that has been CASTRATED (= had part of its sex organs removed) ➲ compare OX, STEER

bull·pen /ˈbʊlpen/ *noun* (*NAmE*) **1** the part of a BASEBALL field where players practise PITCHING (= throwing) before the game **2** extra PITCHERS (= players who throw the ball) in a BASEBALL team who are used, if necessary, to replace the usual pitchers: *The team's bullpen is solid this year.* **3** a type of large office which is OPEN-PLAN (= it does not have walls dividing the office area) **4** a room where prisoners wait before they go into the court for their trial

bull·ring /ˈbʊlrɪŋ/ *noun* the large round area, like an outdoor theatre, where BULLFIGHTS take place

bull·rush = BULRUSH

B

ˈbull session *noun* (*NAmE, informal*) an occasion when people meet and talk in an informal way

bulls·eye /ˈbʊlzaɪ/ (also **bull**) *noun* [usually sing.] the centre of the target that you shoot or throw at in shooting, ARCHERY or DARTS; a shot or throw that hits this: *He scored a bullseye.* ➲ VISUAL VOCAB page V34

bull·shit /ˈbʊlʃɪt/ *noun, verb*
■ ***noun*** [U] (*taboo, slang*) (also *informal* **bull**) (*abbr.* **BS**) nonsense: *That's just bullshit.*
■ ***verb*** (-tt-) [I, T] (*taboo, slang*) to say things that are not true, especially in order to trick sb: *She's just bullshitting.* ◇ **~ sb** *Don't try to bullshit me!* ▶ **bull·shit·ter** *noun*

ˌbull ˈterrier *noun* a strong dog with short hair, a thick neck and a long nose ➲ see also PIT BULL TERRIER

bully /ˈbʊli/ *noun, verb, exclamation*
■ ***noun*** (*pl.* **-ies**) a person who uses their strength or power to frighten or hurt weaker people: *the school bully*
■ ***verb*** (**bul·lies, bully·ing, bul·lied, bul·lied**) to frighten or hurt a weaker person; to use your strength or power to make sb do sth: **~ sb** *My son is being bullied at school.* ◇ **~ sb into sth/into doing sth** *I won't be bullied into signing anything.* ▶ **bully·ing** *noun* [U]: *Bullying is a problem in many schools.* ◇ *He refused to give in to bullying and threats.* ◇ ***bullying behaviour/tactics*** ➲ COLLOCATIONS at EDUCATION
■ ***exclamation***
IDM **bully for you, etc.** (*informal*) used to show that you do not think that what sb has said or done is very impressive: *He's got a job in New York? Well, bully for him!*

ˈbully boy *noun* (*BrE, informal*) an aggressive violent man: *The group have frequently used bully-boy tactics.*

ˈbully pulpit *noun* [sing.] (*NAmE*) a position of authority that gives sb the opportunity to speak in public about an issue

bul·rush (also **bull·rush**) /ˈbʊlrʌʃ/ *noun* a tall plant with long narrow leaves and a long brown head of flowers, that grows in or near water ➲ VISUAL VOCAB page V9

bul·wark /ˈbʊlwək; *NAmE* -wɜːrk/ *noun* **1** [usually sing.] **~ (against sth)** (*formal*) a person or thing that protects or defends sth: *a bulwark against extremism* **2** [C] a wall built as a defence **3** [usually pl.] the part of a ship's side that is above the level of the DECK

bum /bʌm/ *noun, verb, adj.*
■ ***noun*** (*informal*) **1** (*BrE*) the part of the body that you sit on SYN **backside, behind, bottom 2** (*especially NAmE*) a person who has no home or job and who asks other people for money or food: *a beach bum* (= sb who spends all their time on the beach, without having a job) **3** a lazy person who does nothing for other people or for society: *He's nothing but a no-good bum!*
IDM **bums on ˈseats** (*BrE, informal*) used to refer to the number of people who attend a show, talk, etc, especially when emphasizing the need or desire to attract a large number: *They're not bothered about attracting the right audience—they just want bums on seats.* **give sb/get the ˌbum's ˈrush** (*informal, especially NAmE*) to force sb/be forced to leave a place quickly: *He was soon given the bum's rush from the club.*
■ ***verb*** (-mm-) **1 ~ sth (off sb)** (*informal*) to get sth from sb by asking SYN **cadge**: *Can I bum a cigarette off you?* **2 ~ sb (out)** (*NAmE, informal*) to make sb feel upset or disappointed
PHR V **ˌbum aˈround/aˈbout** (*informal*) to travel around or spend your time with no particular plans: *He bummed around the world for a year.*
■ ***adj.*** [only before noun] (*informal*) of bad quality; wrong or useless: *He didn't play one bum note.* ◇ *a* ***bum deal*** (= a situation where you do not get what you deserve or have paid for)

bum·bag /ˈbʌmbæg/ (*BrE*) (*NAmE* ˈ**fanny pack**) *noun* (*informal*) a small bag attached to a belt and worn around the waist, to keep money, etc. in ➲ VISUAL VOCAB page V52

bum·ble /ˈbʌmbl/ *verb* [I] **+ adv./prep.** to act or move in an awkward or confused way: *I could hear him bumbling around in the kitchen.*

bumble·bee /ˈbʌmblbiː/ *noun* a large BEE covered with small hairs that makes a loud noise as it flies ➲ VISUAL VOCAB page V11

bum·bling /ˈbʌmblɪŋ/ *adj.* [only before noun] behaving in an awkward confused way, often making careless mistakes

bumf (also **bumph**) /bʌmf/ *noun* [U] (*BrE, informal*) written information, especially advertisements, official documents, forms, etc, that seem boring or unnecessary: *He threw away my letter, thinking it was just more election bumf.*

bum·fluff /ˈbʌmflʌf/ *noun* [U] (*informal*) the soft hair that grows on the upper lip and chin of a boy, as his beard begins to grow

bum·mer /ˈbʌmə(r)/ *noun* **a bummer** [sing.] (*informal*) a disappointing or unpleasant situation: *It's a real bummer that she can't come.*

bump /bʌmp/ *verb, noun*
■ ***verb*** **1** [I] to hit sb/sth by accident: **~ into sb/sth** *In the dark I bumped into a chair.* ◇ **~ against sb/sth** *The car bumped against the kerb.* ➲ SYNONYMS at HIT **2** [T] **~ sth (against/on sth)** to hit sth, especially a part of your body, against or on sth: *Be careful not to bump your head on the beam when you stand up.* **3** [I, T] to move across a rough surface: **+ adv./prep.** *The jeep bumped along the dirt track.* ◇ **~ sth + adv./prep.** *The car* ***bumped its way*** *slowly down the drive.* **4** [T] **~ sb + adv./prep.** to move sb from one group or position to another; to remove sb from a group: *The airline apologized and bumped us up to first class.* ◇ *If you are bumped off an airline because of overbooking, you are entitled to compensation.* ◇ *The coach told him he had been bumped from the crew.*
PHR V **ˌbump ˈinto sb** (*informal*) to meet sb by chance **ˌbump sb↔ˈoff** (*informal*) to murder sb **ˌbump sth↔ˈup** (*informal*) to increase or raise sth **ˌbump ˈup against sth** to experience a problem or factor that you did not expect: *We kept bumping up against inflexible regulations.*
■ ***noun*** **1** [C] the action or sound of sth hitting a hard surface: *He fell to the ground* ***with a bump.*** ◇ *We could hear loud bumps from upstairs where the children were playing.* **2** [C] a swelling on the body, often caused by a blow SYN **lump**: *She was covered in bumps and bruises.* ◇ *How did you get that bump on your forehead?* **3** [C] a part of a flat surface that is not even, but raised above the rest of it: *a bump in the road* ➲ see also BUMPY **4** [C] a slight accident in which your vehicle hits sth **5 the bumps** [pl.] (*BrE*) (on a child's birthday) the act of lifting the child in the air and then putting them down on the ground, once for every year of their age: *We gave her the bumps.* IDM see EARTH *n.*, THING

bump·er /ˈbʌmpə(r)/ *noun, adj.*
■ ***noun*** a bar fixed to the front and back of a car, etc. to reduce the effect if it hits anything: *a* ***bumper sticker*** (= a sign that people stick on the bumper of their cars with a message on it) ◇ *The cars were* ***bumper to bumper*** *on the road to the coast* (= so close that their bumpers were nearly touching). ➲ VISUAL VOCAB page V42
■ ***adj.*** [only before noun] (*approving*) unusually large; producing an unusually large amount: *a bumper issue* (= of a magazine, etc.) ◇ *a* ***bumper crop/harvest/season/year***

ˈbumper car (*especially NAmE*) (*BrE* also **dodgem, ˈdodgem car**) *noun* one of the small electric cars that you drive in the dodgems

bumph = BUMF

bump·kin /ˈbʌmpkɪn/ *noun* = COUNTRY BUMPKIN

bump·tious /ˈbʌmpʃəs/ *adj.* (*disapproving*) showing that you think that you are very important; often giving your opinions in a loud, confident and annoying way

bumpy /ˈbʌmpi/ *adj.* (**bump·ier, bumpi·est**) **1** (of a surface) not even; with a lot of bumps: *a bumpy road/track* ◇ *bumpy ground* **2** (of a journey) uncomfortable with a lot of sudden unpleasant movements caused by the road surface, weather conditions, etc: ***a bumpy ride/flight***

IDM **have/give sb a bumpy 'ride** to have a difficult time; to make a situation difficult for sb

bun /bʌn/ *noun* **1** [C] (*BrE*) a small round sweet cake: *an iced bun* ➲ see also HOT CROSS BUN **2** [C] (*BrE* also **bap**) a small round flat bread roll: *a hamburger bun* ➲ compare ROLL **3** [C] long hair that has been twisted into a round shape and is worn on top or at the back of the head: *She wore her hair in a bun.* ➲ VISUAL VOCAB page V49 **4 buns** [pl.] (*slang, especially NAmE*) the two sides of a person's bottom

IDM **have a 'bun in the oven** (*informal, humorous*) to be pregnant

bunch 🔑 /bʌntʃ/ *noun, verb*

■ ***noun*** **1** 🔑 [C] **~ of sth** a number of things of the same type which are growing or fastened together: *a bunch of bananas/grapes, etc.* ◇ *a bunch of keys* ◇ *She picked me a* ***bunch of flowers.*** ➲ VISUAL VOCAB page V26 **2** [sing.] **a ~ (of sth)** (*informal, especially NAmE*) a large amount of sth; a large number of things or people: *I have* ***a whole bunch of*** *stuff to do this morning.* **3** [sing.] (*informal*) a group of people: *The people that I work with are a great bunch.* **4 bunches** [pl.] (*BrE*) long hair that is divided in two and tied at each side of the head: *She wore her hair in bunches.* ➲ VISUAL VOCAB page V49

IDM **the best/pick of the 'bunch** the best out of a group of people or things ➲ more at BEST

■ ***verb*** [I, T] to become tight or to form tight folds; to make sth do this: *His muscles bunched under his shirt.* ◇ **~ (sth) up** *Her skirt had bunched up round her waist.* ◇ **~ sth** *His forehead was bunched in a frown.*

PHR V **,bunch 'up/to'gether | ,bunch sb/sth 'up/to'gether** to move closer and form into a group; to make people or things do this: *The sheep bunched together as soon as they saw the dog.*

bun·dle /'bʌndl/ *noun, verb*

■ ***noun*** **1** [C] a number of things tied or wrapped together; sth that is wrapped up: *a* ***bundle of rags/papers/firewood*** ◇ *She held her little bundle* (= her baby) *tightly in her arms.* **2** [C] a number of things that belong, or are sold together: *a bundle of ideas* ◇ *a bundle of graphics packages for your PC* **3** [sing.] **a ~ of laughs, fun, etc.** (*informal*) a person or thing that makes you laugh: *He wasn't exactly a bundle of laughs* (= a happy person to be with) *last night.* ➲ see also BUNDLE OF JOY **4 a bundle** [sing.] (*informal*) a large amount of money: *That car must have cost a bundle.*

IDM **not go a bundle on sb/sth** (*BrE, informal*) to not like sb/sth very much ➲ more at DROP *v.*, NERVE *n.*

■ ***verb*** **1** [T] **~ sb + adv./prep.** to push or send sb somewhere quickly and not carefully: *They bundled her into the back of a car.* ◇ *He was bundled off to boarding school.* **2** [I] **+ adv./prep.** to move somewhere quickly in a group: *We bundled out onto the street.* **3** [T] **~ sth (with sth)** to supply extra equipment, especially software when selling a new computer, at no extra cost: *A further nine applications are bundled with the system.*

PHR V **,bundle sth↔'up | ,bundle sth↔to'gether** to make or tie sth into a bundle: *He bundled up the dirty clothes and stuffed them into the bag.* ◇ *The papers were all bundled together, ready to be thrown out.* **,bundle sb 'up (in sth)** to put warm clothes or coverings on sb: *I bundled her up in a blanket and gave her a hot drink.*

,bun·dle of 'joy *noun* (*informal, humorous*, sometimes *ironic*) a baby son or daughter: *Here are the latest pictures of our little bundle of joy.*

bun·fight /'bʌnfaɪt/ *noun* (*BrE, informal*) **1** an impressive or important party or other social event **2** an angry argument or discussion

bung /bʌŋ/ *verb, noun, adj.*

■ ***verb*** **~ sth + adv./prep.** (*BrE, informal*) to put or throw sth somewhere, carelessly and quickly: *Bung this in the bin, can you?*

PHR V **,bung sth 'up (with sth)** [usually passive] to block sth: *My nose is all bunged up.* ◇ *The drains are bunged up with dead leaves.*

■ ***noun*** **1** a round piece of wood, rubber, etc. used for closing the hole in a container such as a BARREL or JAR **2** (*BrE, informal*) an amount of money that is given to sb to persuade them to do sth illegal

■ ***adj.*** (*AustralE, NZE, informal*) broken

bun·ga·low /'bʌŋgələʊ; *NAmE* -loʊ/ *noun* **1** (*BrE*) a house built all on one level, without stairs ➲ VISUAL VOCAB page V14 ➲ compare RANCH HOUSE **2** (in some Asian countries) a large house, sometimes on more than one level, that is not joined to another house on either side

bun·gee /'bʌndʒi/ *noun* **1** a long rope which can stretch, that people tie to their feet when they do bungee jumping ➲ VISUAL VOCAB page V40 **2** (*NAmE*) a thick ELASTIC rope with a hook at each end that can be used to hold packages together, keep things in position, etc.

bun·gee jump·ing *noun* [U] a sport in which a person jumps from a high place, such as a bridge or a CLIFF, with a bungee tied to their feet: *to go bungee jumping* ➲ VISUAL VOCAB page V40 ▸ **bun·gee jump** *noun*: *to do a bungee jump*

bun·gle /'bʌŋgl/ *verb, noun*

■ ***verb*** [T, I] **~ (sth)** to do sth badly or without skill; to fail at sth SYN **botch**: *They bungled the job.* ◇ *a* ***bungled robbery/raid/attempt*** ▸ **bun·gler** /'bʌŋglə(r)/ *noun* **bun·gling** *adj.*: *bungling incompetence*

■ ***noun*** [usually sing.] something that is done badly and that causes problems: *Their pay was late because of a computer bungle.*

bun·ion /'bʌnjən/ *noun* a painful swelling on the foot, usually on the big toe

bunk /bʌŋk/ *noun, verb*

■ ***noun*** **1** [C] a narrow bed that is fixed to a wall, especially on a ship or train **2** [C] (also **'bunk bed**) one of two beds that are fixed together, one above the other, especially for children ➲ VISUAL VOCAB page V20 **3** [U] (*old-fashioned, informal*) nonsense SYN **bunkum**

IDM **do a 'bunk** (*BrE, informal*) to run away from a place without telling anyone

■ ***verb***

PHR V **,bunk 'off | ,bunk off 'school/'work** (*BrE, informal*) to stay away from school or work when you should be there; to leave school or work early SYN **skive, play truant**

bun·ker /'bʌŋkə(r)/ *noun, verb*

■ ***noun*** **1** a strongly built shelter for soldiers or guns, usually underground: *a* ***concrete/underground/secret bunker*** **2** a container for storing coal, especially on a ship or outside a house: *a coal bunker* **3** (*NAmE* also **'sand trap, trap**) a small area filled with sand on a GOLF COURSE ➲ VISUAL VOCAB page V34

■ ***verb*** **be bunkered** (in GOLF) to have hit your ball into a bunker (and therefore to be in a difficult position)

bunk·house /'bʌŋkhaʊs/ *noun* a building for workers to sleep in

bun·kum /'bʌŋkəm/ *noun* [U] (*old-fashioned, informal*) nonsense SYN **bunk**

bunny /'bʌni/ *noun* (*pl.* -ies) (also **'bunny rabbit**) a child's word for a RABBIT IDM see HAPPY *adj.*

'bunny-hop *noun* a small jump forward in a CROUCHING position ▸ **'bunny-hop** *verb* (-pp-) [I]

'bunny slope (*NAmE*) (*BrE* **'nursery slope**) *noun* a slope that is not very steep and is used by people who are learning to SKI

Bun·sen burn·er /,bʌnsn 'bɜːnə(r); *NAmE* 'bɜːrn-/ *noun* an instrument used in scientific work that produces a hot gas flame ➲ VISUAL VOCAB page V57

bunt /bʌnt/ *verb* [T, I] **~ (sth)** (*NAmE*) (in BASEBALL) to deliberately hit the ball only a short distance ▸ **bunt** *noun*

bunt·ing /'bʌntɪŋ/ *noun* **1** [U] coloured flags or paper used for decorating streets and buildings in celebrations **2** [C] a small bird related to the FINCH and SPARROW families. There are several types of bunting: *a* ***corn/reed/snow bunting***

bun·yip /'bʌnjɪp/ *noun* (*AustralE*) (in stories) a MONSTER that lives in or near water

B

buoy /bɔɪ; *NAmE* also 'bu:i/ *noun, verb*
■ **noun** an object which floats on the sea or a river to mark the places where it is dangerous and where it is safe for boats to go ➲ see also LIFEBUOY
■ **verb** [usually passive] **1** ~ **sb** (**up**) to make sb feel cheerful or confident: *Buoyed by their win yesterday the team feel confident of further success.* **2** ~ **sb/sth** (**up**) to keep sb/sth floating on water **3** ~ **sth** (**up**) to keep prices at a high or acceptable level

buoy·ant /'bɔɪənt; *NAmE* 'bu:jənt/ *adj.* **1** (of prices, business activity, etc.) tending to increase or stay at a high level, usually showing financial success: *a **buoyant economy/market*** ◇ ***buoyant sales/prices*** ◇ *a buoyant demand for homes* **2** cheerful and feeling sure that things will be successful: *They were all in buoyant mood.* **3** floating, able to float or able to keep things floating: *The boat bobbed like a cork on the waves: light and buoyant.* ◇ *Salt water is more buoyant than fresh water.* ▶ **buoy·ancy** /-ənsi/ *noun* [U]: *the buoyancy of the market* ◇ *a mood of buoyancy* ◇ *a buoyancy aid* (= sth to help you float)

bup·pie (also **buppy**) /'bʌpi/ (*pl.* -ies) *noun* (*SAfrE, informal*) a black person who is a YUPPIE

bur = BURR

Bur·berry™ /'bɜ:bəri; *NAmE* 'bɜ:rberi/ *noun* (*pl.* -ies) a type of RAINCOAT

bur·ble /'bɜ:bl; *NAmE* 'bɜ:rbl/ *verb* **1** [I, T] ~ (**on**) (**about sth**) | + **speech** (*BrE, disapproving*) to speak in a confused or silly way that is difficult to hear or understand: *What's he burbling about?* **2** [I] to make the gentle sound of a stream flowing over stones

burbs /bɜ:bz; *NAmE* bɜ:rbz/ *noun* **the burbs** [pl.] (*NAmE, informal*) = SUBURBS

bur·den /'bɜ:dn; *NAmE* 'bɜ:rdn/ *noun, verb*
■ **noun 1 the** ~ (**of sth**) | **a** ~ (**on/to sb**) a duty, responsibility, etc. that causes worry, difficulty or hard work: *to **bear/carry/ease/reduce/share the burden*** ◇ *The main burden of caring for old people falls on the state.* ◇ *the heavy tax burden on working people* ◇ *I don't want to become a burden to my children when I'm old.* **2** (*formal*) a heavy load that is difficult to carry ➲ see also BEAST OF BURDEN
■ **verb 1** ~ **sb/yourself** (**with sth**) to give sb a duty, responsibility, etc. that causes worry, difficulty or hard work: *They have burdened themselves with a high mortgage.* ◇ *I don't want to burden you with my worries.* ◇ *to be burdened by high taxation* OPP **unburden 2 be burdened with sth** to be carrying sth heavy: *She got off the bus, burdened with two heavy suitcases.*

the ˌburden of ˈproof *noun* [sing.] (*law*) the task or responsibility of proving that sth is true

bur·den·some /'bɜ:dnsəm; *NAmE* 'bɜ:rd-/ *adj.* (*formal*) causing worry, difficulty or hard work SYN **onerous**

bur·dock /'bɜ:dɒk; *NAmE* 'bɜ:rdɑ:k/ *noun* [U] a plant with flowers that become PRICKLY and stick to passing animals

bur·eau /'bjʊərəʊ; *NAmE* 'bjʊroʊ/ *noun* (*pl.* **bur·eaux** or **bur·eaus** /-rəʊz; *NAmE* -roʊz/) **1** (*BrE*) a desk with drawers and usually a top that opens down to make a table to write on **2** (*NAmE*) = CHEST OF DRAWERS **3** an office or organization that provides information on a particular subject: *an employment bureau* **4** (in the US) a government department or part of a government department: *the Federal Bureau of Investigation*

bur·eau·cracy /bjʊə'rɒkrəsi; *NAmE* bjʊ'rɑ:k-/ *noun* (*pl.* -ies) **1** [U] (often *disapproving*) the system of official rules and ways of doing things that a government or an organization has, especially when these seem to be too complicated: ***unnecessary/excessive bureaucracy*** **2** [U, C] a system of government in which there are a large number of state officials who are not elected; a country with such a system: *the power of the state bureaucracy* ◇ *living in a modern bureaucracy*

bur·eau·crat /'bjʊərəkræt; *NAmE* 'bjʊr-/ *noun* (often *disapproving*) an official working in an organization or a government department, especially one who follows the rules of the department too strictly

bur·eau·crat·ic /ˌbjʊərə'krætɪk; *NAmE* ˌbjʊr-/ *adj.* (often *disapproving*) connected with a bureaucracy or bureaucrats and involving complicated official rules which may seem unnecessary: ***bureaucratic power/control/procedures/organizations*** ◇ *The report revealed a great deal of bureaucratic inefficiency.* ▶ **bur·eau·crat·ic·al·ly** /-ɪkli/ *adv.*

bur·eau de change /ˌbjʊərəʊ də 'ʃɑ:nʒ; *NAmE* ˌbjʊroʊ/ *noun* (*pl.* **bur·eaux de change** /ˌbjʊərəʊ; *NAmE* ˌbjʊroʊ/) (from *French*) an office at a hotel, in an airport, etc, where you can exchange money from one country for that from another

bur·ette (*US* also **buret**) /bju'ret/ *noun* a glass tube with measurements on it and a tap/faucet at one end, used, for example, in chemical experiments for measuring out amounts of a liquid ➲ VISUAL VOCAB page V57

burg /bɜ:g; *NAmE* bɜ:rg/ *noun* (*NAmE, informal*) a town or city

bur·geon /'bɜ:dʒən; *NAmE* 'bɜ:rdʒən/ *verb* [I] (*formal*) to begin to grow or develop rapidly ▶ **bur·geon·ing** *adj.*: *a burgeoning population* ◇ *burgeoning demand*

bur·ger /'bɜ:gə(r); *NAmE* 'bɜ:rg-/ *noun* **1** = HAMBURGER **2 -bur·ger** (in compounds) finely chopped fish, vegetables, nuts, etc. made into flat round shapes like HAMBURGERS: *a spicy beanburger* ➲ see also CHEESEBURGER, VEGGIE BURGER

burgh /'bʌrə/ *noun* (*old-fashioned* or *ScotE*) a town or part of a city that has its own local government

bur·gher /'bɜ:gə(r); *NAmE* 'bɜ:rg-/ *noun* (*old use* or *humorous*) a citizen of a particular town

burg·lar /'bɜ:glə(r); *NAmE* 'bɜ:rg-/ *noun* a person who enters a building illegally in order to steal

ˈburglar alarm *noun* an electronic device, often fixed to a wall, that rings a loud bell if sb tries to enter a building by force ➲ VISUAL VOCAB page V15

burg·lary /'bɜ:gləri; *NAmE* 'bɜ:rg-/ *noun* [U, C] (*pl.* -ies) the crime of entering a building illegally and stealing things from it SYN **housebreaking**: *The youth was charged with three counts of burglary.* ◇ *a rise in the number of burglaries committed in the area* ➲ compare ROBBERY, THEFT

bur·gle /'bɜ:gl; *NAmE* 'bɜ:rgl/ (*BrE*) (*NAmE* **burg·lar·ize** /'bɜ:gləraɪz; *NAmE* 'bɜ:rg-/) *verb* ~ **sb/sth** to enter a building illegally, usually using force, and steal from it: *We were burgled while we were away* (= our house was burgled). ◇ *The house next door was burgled.* ➲ COLLOCATIONS at CRIME

bur·goo /bɜ:'gu:; *NAmE* bɜ:r'gu:/ *noun* (*pl.* -oos) (*NAmE*) **1** [U] a type of thick soup, especially one eaten outdoors **2** [C] an event at which burgoo is eaten outdoors

bur·gundy /'bɜ:gəndi; *NAmE* 'bɜ:rg-/ *noun* **1 Burgundy** [U, C] (*pl.* -ies) a red or white wine from the Burgundy area of eastern France. **2** [U] a dark red colour ▶ **bur·gundy** *adj.*: *a burgundy leather briefcase*

bur·ial /'beriəl/ *noun* [U, C] the act or ceremony of burying a dead body: *a **burial place/mound/site*** ◇ *Her body was sent home for burial.* ◇ *His family insisted he should be given a proper burial.*

ˈburial ground *noun* a place where dead bodies are buried, especially an ancient place

burka (also **burkha**) /'bʊəkə; 'bɜ:kə; *NAmE* 'bɜ:rkə/ *noun* a long loose piece of clothing that covers the whole body, including the head and face, worn in public by Muslim women in some countries

bur·lap /'bɜ:læp; *NAmE* 'bɜ:rl-/ *noun* [U] (*NAmE*) = HESSIAN

bur·lesque /bɜ:'lesk; *NAmE* bɜ:r'l-/ *noun* **1** [C] a performance or piece of writing which tries to make sth look ridiculous by representing it in a humorous way SYN **parody**: *a burlesque of literary life* **2** [U] (*NAmE*) a type of entertainment, popular in the past in the US, involving humorous acts, singing, dancing, etc. and often including STRIPTEASE ▶ **bur·lesque** *adj.* [usually before noun]

burly /'bɜ:li; *NAmE* 'bɜ:rli/ *adj.* (**bur·lier, bur·li·est**) (of a man or a man's body) big, strong and heavy SYN **brawny**

burn 0‑ /bɜːn; *NAmE* bɜːrn/ *verb, noun*

■ ***verb*** (**burnt**, **burnt** /bɜːnt; *NAmE* bɜːrnt/) or (**burned**, **burned** /bɜːnd; *NAmE* bɜːrnd/)

▸ FIRE **1** 0‑ [I] to produce flames and heat: *A welcoming fire was burning in the fireplace.* ◇ *Fires were burning all over the city.* **2** 0‑ [I] (used especially in the progressive tenses) to be on fire: *By nightfall the whole city was burning.* ◇ *Two children were rescued from the burning car.* ◇ *The smell of burning rubber filled the air.* **3** 0‑ [T, I] to destroy, damage, injure or kill sb/sth by fire; to be destroyed, etc. by fire: **~ (sb/sth)** *to burn waste paper/dead leaves* ◇ *All his belongings were burnt in the fire.* ◇ *The cigarette burned a hole in the carpet.* ◇ *The house was* **burnt to the ground** (= completely destroyed). ◇ *The house* **burned to the ground.** ◇ *Ten people* **burned to death** *in the hotel fire.* ◇ **~ sb/sth + adj.** *His greatest fear is of being* **burnt alive.**

▸ FUEL **4** 0‑ [T, I] **~ (sth)** if you **burn** a fuel, or a fuel **burns**, it produces heat, light or energy: *a furnace that burns gas/oil/coke* ◇ (*figurative*) *Some people burn calories* (= use food to produce energy) *faster than others.* ◇ *Which fuel burns most efficiently?*

▸ FOOD **5** 0‑ [I, T] if food **burns**, or if you **burn** it, it is spoiled because it gets too hot: *I can smell something burning in the kitchen.* ◇ **~ sth** *Sorry—I burnt the toast.*

▸ SUN/HEAT/ACID **6** 0‑ [I, T] to be damaged or injured by the sun, heat, acid, etc; to damage or injure sb/sth in this way: *My skin burns easily* (= in the sun). ◇ **~ sb** *I got badly burned by the sun yesterday.* ◇ **~ sth** *The soup's hot. Don't burn your mouth.* ◇ **~ yourself** *I burned myself on the stove.*

▸ OF PART OF BODY **7** [I] if part of your body **burns** or **is burning**, it feels very hot and painful: *Your forehead's burning. Have you got a fever?* ◇ *Her cheeks burned with embarrassment.* ➲ SYNONYMS at HURT

▸ OF A LIGHT **8** [I] to produce light: *Lights were burning upstairs, but no one answered the door.*

▸ FEEL EMOTION/DESIRE **9** [I, T] (*literary*) to feel a very strong emotion or desire: **~ with sth** *to be burning with rage/ambition/love* ◇ **~ to do sth** *He was burning to go climbing again.*

▸ GO FAST **10** [I] **+ adv./prep.** (*informal*) to move very fast in a particular direction: *The car was burning down the road.*

▸ MAKE ANGRY **11** [T] **~ sb** (*NAmE, informal*) to make sb very angry: *So you did it just to burn me?*

▸ CD, ETC. **12** [T, I] **~ (sth)** (**to sth**) to put information onto a CD, etc.

IDM **burn your 'bridges** (*BrE* also **burn your 'boats**) to do sth that makes it impossible to return to the previous situation later: *Think carefully before you resign—you don't want to burn your bridges.* **burn the candle at both 'ends** to become very tired by trying to do too many things and going to bed late and getting up early **burn your 'fingers | get your 'fingers burnt** to suffer as a result of doing sth without realizing the possible bad results, especially in business: *He got his fingers badly burnt dabbling in the stock market.* **burn a 'hole in your pocket** if money **burns a hole in your pocket**, you want to spend it as soon as you have it **burn the midnight 'oil** to study or work until late at night **burn 'rubber** (*informal*) to drive very fast **burn sth to a 'cinder/'crisp** to cook sth for too long or with too much heat, so that it becomes badly burnt ➲ more at EAR, FEEL *v.*, MONEY

PHR V **,burn a'way | ,burn sth↔a'way** to disappear as a result of burning; to make sth do this: *Half the candle had burnt away.* ◇ *The clothing on his back got burnt away in the fire.* **,burn 'down** if a fire **burns down**, it becomes weaker and has smaller flames **,burn 'down | ,burn sth↔'down** 0‑ to be destroyed, or to destroy sth, by fire: *The house burned down in 1895.* **,burn sth↔'off 1** to remove sth by burning: *Burn off the old paint before repainting the door.* **2** to use energy by doing exercise: *This workout helps you to burn off fat and tone muscles.* **,burn 'out | ,burn itself 'out** (of a fire) to stop burning because there is nothing more to burn: *The fire had burnt (itself) out before the fire engines arrived.* **,burn 'out | ,burn sth↔'out** to stop working or to make sth stop working because it gets too hot or is used too much: *The clutch has burnt out.* **,burn 'out | ,burn yourself/sb 'out** to become extremely tired or sick by working too hard over a period of time: *If he doesn't stop working so hard, he'll burn himself out.* ◇ *By the age of 25 she was completely burned out and retired from the sport.* ➲ related noun BURNOUT **,burn sth 'out** [usually passive] to destroy sth completely by fire so that only the outer frame remains: *The hotel was completely burnt out.* ◇ *the burnt-out wreck of a car* **,burn 'up 1** to be destroyed by heat: *The spacecraft burned up as it entered the earth's atmosphere.* **2** (usually used in the progressive tenses) (*informal*) to have a high temperature: *You're burning up—have you seen a doctor?* **3** (of a fire) to burn more strongly and with larger flames **,burn sb 'up** (*NAmE, informal*) to make sb very angry: *The way he treats me really burns me up.* **,burn sth↔'up 1** to get rid of or destroy sth by burning: *The fire burned up 1 500 acres of farmland.* **2** to use CALORIES or energy by doing exercise: *Which burns up more calories—swimming or cycling?*

■ ***noun***

▸ INJURY **1** [C] an injury or a mark caused by fire, heat or acid: ***minor/severe/third-degree burns*** ◇ *cigarette burns on the furniture* ◇ *burn marks* ◇ *a specialist burns unit in a hospital*

▸ IN MUSCLES **2 the burn** [sing.] the feeling that you get in your muscles when you have done a lot of exercise

▸ RIVER **3** [C] (*ScotE*) a small river SYN **stream** IDM see SLOW *adj.*

Synonyms

burn

char • scald • scorch • singe

These words all mean to damage, injure, destroy or kill sb/sth with heat or fire.

burn to damage, injure, destroy or kill sb/sth with fire, heat or acid; to be damaged, etc. by fire, heat or acid: *She burned all his letters.* ◇ *The house* ***burned down*** *in 1995.*

char [usually passive] to make sth black by burning it; to become black by burning: *The bodies had been charred beyond recognition.*

scald to burn part of your body with very hot liquid or steam.

scorch to burn and slightly damage a surface by making it too hot: *I scorched my dress when I was ironing it.*

singe to burn the surface of sth slightly, usually by mistake; to be burnt in this way: *He singed his hair as he tried to light his cigarette.*

SCORCH OR SINGE?

Things are **scorched** by heat or fire. Things can only be **singed** by fire or a flame.

PATTERNS

- to burn/scald **yourself/your hand**
- to burn/scorch/singe your **hair/clothes**
- burned out/charred/scorched **remains/ruins/buildings**

burn·er /ˈbɜːnə(r); *NAmE* ˈbɜːrn-/ *noun* **1** the part of a cooker/stove, etc. that produces a flame ➲ VISUAL VOCAB page V22 **2** a large, solid, metal piece of equipment for burning wood or coal, used for heating a room: *a wood burner* ➲ see also BUNSEN BURNER IDM see BACK *adj.*, FRONT *adj.*

burn·ing /ˈbɜːnɪŋ; *NAmE* ˈbɜːrn-/ *adj., adv.*

■ ***adj.*** [only before noun] **1** (of feelings, etc.) very strong; extreme: *a* ***burning desire*** *to win* ◇ *He's always had a* ***burning ambition*** *to start his own business.* **2 a ~ issue/question** a very important and urgent problem **3** (of pain, etc.) very strong and giving a feeling of burning ➲ SYNONYMS at PAINFUL **4** very hot; looking and feeling very hot: *the burning sun* ◇ *her burning face* **5 ~ eyes** (*literary*) eyes that seem to be staring at you very hard

■ ***adv.*** **burning hot** very hot

B

bur·nish /ˈbɜːnɪʃ; *NAmE* ˈbɜːrnɪʃ/ *verb* **~ sth** (*formal*) to polish metal until it is smooth and shiny ▸ **bur·nished** *adj.* [usually before noun]: ***burnished gold/copper***

bur·nous (*NAmE* usually **bur·noose**) /bɜːˈnuːs; *NAmE* bɜːrˈn-/ *noun* a long loose item of outer clothing with a HOOD (= covering for the head), worn by Arabs

burn·out /ˈbɜːnaʊt; *NAmE* ˈbɜːrn-/ *noun* [C, U] **1** the state of being extremely tired or ill, either physically or mentally, because you have worked too hard **2** the point at which a ROCKET has used all of its fuel and has no more power

ˈ**Burns Night** *noun* [U, C] the evening of 25 January when Scottish people celebrate the birthday of the Scottish POET, Robert Burns, with traditional Scottish music, WHISKY and dishes such as HAGGIS

burnt 0‑ /bɜːnt; *NAmE* bɜːrnt/ *adj.* damaged or injured by burning: *burnt toast* ◊ *Your hand looks badly burnt.*

ˌ**burnt ˈochre** *noun* [U] **1** a deep yellow-brown colour **2** a yellow-brown PIGMENT, used in art

ˌ**burnt ˈoffering** *noun* **1** something (usually an animal) that is burnt in a religious ceremony as a gift offered to a god **2** (*BrE, humorous*) food that has been badly burnt by accident

ˌ**burnt-ˈout** (*NAmE* ˌ**burned-ˈout**) *adj.* **1** destroyed or badly damaged by fire: *a burnt-out car* **2** feeling as if you have done sth for too long and need to have a rest: *I'm feeling burnt-out at work—I need a holiday.*

burnt sienna /ˌbɜːnt siˈenə; *NAmE* ˌbɜːrnt/ *noun* [U] **1** a deep red-brown colour **2** a deep red-brown PIGMENT, used in art

burnt umber /ˌbɜːnt ˈʌmbə(r); *NAmE* ˌbɜːrnt/ *noun* [U] **1** a dark brown colour **2** a dark brown PIGMENT, used in art

burp /bɜːp; *NAmE* bɜːrp/ *verb* (*informal*) **1** [I] to let out air from the stomach through the mouth, making a noise SYN **belch** **2** [T] **~ sb** to make a baby bring up air from the stomach, especially by rubbing or PATTING its back ▸ **burp** *noun*

burr /bɜː(r)/ *noun* **1** [usually sing.] a strong pronunciation of the 'r' sound, typical of some accents in English; an accent with this type of pronunciation: *She speaks with a soft West Country burr.* **2** [usually sing.] the soft regular noise made by parts of a machine moving quickly SYN **whirr** **3** (also **bur**) [C] the seed container of some plants which is covered in very small hooks that stick to clothes or fur

bur·rito /bʊˈriːtəʊ; *NAmE* -toʊ/ *noun* (*pl.* -os) (from *Spanish*) a Mexican dish consisting of a TORTILLA filled with meat or BEANS

burro /ˈbʊrəʊ; *NAmE* ˈbɜːroʊ/ *noun* (*pl.* -os) (*NAmE*, from *Spanish*) a small DONKEY

bur·row /ˈbʌrəʊ; *NAmE* ˈbɜːroʊ/ *verb, noun*

■ ***verb*** **1** [I, T] to make a hole or a tunnel in the ground by digging SYN **dig**: (**+ adv./prep.**) *Earthworms burrow deep into the soil.* ◊ **~ sth + adv./prep.** *The rodent* ***burrowed its way*** *into the sand.* **2** [I, T] to press yourself close to sb or under sth: **+ adv./prep.** *He burrowed down beneath the blankets.* ◊ **~ sth + adv./prep.** *She burrowed her face into his chest.* **3** [I] **+ adv./prep.** to search for sth under or among things: *She burrowed in the drawer for a pair of socks.* ◊ *He was afraid that they would burrow into his past.*

■ ***noun*** a hole or tunnel in the ground made by animals such as RABBITS for them to live in

bursa /ˈbɜːsə; *NAmE* ˈbɜːrsə/ *noun* (*pl.* **bur·sae** /-siː/ or **bur·sas**) (*anatomy*) a part inside the body like a bag or sleeve, which is filled with liquid, especially around a joint so that it can work smoothly

bur·sar /ˈbɜːsə(r); *NAmE* ˈbɜːrs-/ *noun* (*especially BrE*) a person whose job is to manage the financial affairs of a school or college

bur·sary /ˈbɜːsəri; *NAmE* ˈbɜːrs-/ *noun* (*pl.* -ies) (*especially BrE*) an amount of money that is given to sb so that they can study, usually at a college or university SYN **grant, scholarship**

bur·sitis /ˌbɜːˈsaɪtɪs; *NAmE* ˌbɜːr-/ *noun* [U] (*medical*) a condition in which a bursa becomes swollen and sore

burst 0‑ /bɜːst; *NAmE* bɜːrst/ *verb, noun*

■ ***verb*** (**burst, burst**) **1** 0‑ [I, T] to break open or apart, especially because of pressure from inside; to make sth break in this way: *That balloon will burst if you blow it up any more.* ◊ *The dam burst under the weight of water.* ◊ *Shells were bursting* (= exploding) *all around us.* ◊ (*figurative*) *He felt he would burst with anger and shame.* ◊ *a burst pipe* ◊ **~ sth** *Don't burst that balloon!* ◊ *The river* ***burst its banks*** *and flooded nearby towns.* ➲ SYNONYMS at EXPLODE **2** 0‑ [I] **+ adv./prep.** to go or move somewhere suddenly with great force; to come from somewhere suddenly: *He burst into the room without knocking.* ◊ *The sun burst through the clouds.* ◊ *The words burst from her in an angry rush.* **3** [I] **be bursting** (**with sth**) to be very full of sth; to be very full and almost breaking open: *The roads are bursting with cars.* ◊ *to* ***be bursting with ideas/enthusiasm/pride*** ◊ *The hall was filled to* ***bursting point.*** ◊ *The hall was* ***full to bursting.*** ◊ (*informal*) ***I'm bursting*** (*for a pee*)*!* (= I need to use the toilet right now).

IDM **be bursting to do sth** to want to do sth so much that you can hardly stop yourself: *She was bursting to tell him the good news.* ˌ**burst sb's ˈbubble** to bring an end to sb's hopes, happiness, etc. ˌ**burst ˈopen** | ˌ**burst** (**sth**) ˈ**open** to open suddenly or violently; to make sth open in this way: *The door burst open.* ◊ *Firefighters burst the door open and rescued them.* ➲ more at BUBBLE *n.*, SEAM

PHR V ˌ**burst ˈin** | ˌ**burst into a ˈroom, ˈbuilding, etc.** to enter a room or building suddenly and noisily ˌ**burst ˈin on sb/sth** to interrupt sb/sth by entering a place suddenly and noisily: *He burst in on the meeting.* ˈ**burst into sth** 0‑ to start producing sth suddenly and with great force: *The aircraft crashed and* ***burst into flames*** (= suddenly began to burn). ◊ *She* ***burst into tears*** (= suddenly began to cry). ˈ**burst on/onto sth** to appear somewhere suddenly in a way that is very noticeable: *A major new talent has* ***burst onto the*** *literary* ***scene.*** ˌ**burst ˈout 1** to speak suddenly, loudly and with strong feeling: **+ speech** *'For heavens' sake!' he burst out.* ➲ related noun OUTBURST ➲ SYNONYMS at CALL **2** 0‑ to begin doing sth suddenly: **~ doing sth** *Karen* ***burst out laughing.***

■ ***noun*** **1** a short period of a particular activity or strong emotion that often starts suddenly: *a sudden* ***burst of activity/energy/anger/enthusiasm*** ◊ *Her breath was coming* ***in short bursts.*** ◊ *I tend to work* ***in bursts.*** ◊ *spontaneous bursts of applause* **2** an occasion when sth bursts; the hole left where sth has burst: *a burst in a water pipe* **3** a short series of shots from a gun: *frequent bursts of machine-gun fire*

bursty /ˈbɜːsti; *NAmE* ˈbɜːrsti/ *adj.* (**burst·ier, bursti·est**) **1** (*technical*) used to describe data that is sent in small, sudden groups of signals: *a bursty connection* ◊ *bursty Internet traffic* **2** (*informal*) occurring at intervals, for short periods of time

bur·ton /ˈbɜːtn; *NAmE* ˈbɜːrtn/ *noun*

IDM **gone for a ˈburton** (*old-fashioned, BrE, informal*) lost or destroyed

bury 0‑ /ˈberi/ *verb* (**bur·ies, bury·ing, bur·ied, bur·ied**)

▸ DEAD PERSON **1** 0‑ **~ sb/sth** to place a dead body in a grave: *He was buried in Highgate Cemetery.* ◊ (*figurative*) *Their ambitions were finally* ***dead and buried.*** **2** **~ sb** (*old-fashioned*) to lose sb by death: *She's 85 and has buried three husbands.*

▸ HIDE IN GROUND **3** 0‑ **~ sth** to hide sth in the ground: *buried treasure* ◊ *The dog had buried its bone in the garden.*

▸ COVER **4** 0‑ [often passive] to cover sb/sth with soil, rocks, leaves, etc: **~ sb/sth** *The house was buried under ten feet of snow.* ◊ **~ sb/sth + adj.** *The miners were* ***buried alive*** *when the tunnel collapsed.* **5** 0‑ **~ sth** to cover sth so that it cannot be seen: *Your letter got buried under a pile of papers.* ◊ *He buried his face in his hands and wept.*

▸ HIDE FEELING **6** **~ sth** to ignore or hide a feeling, a mistake, etc: *She had learnt to bury her feelings.*

▸ PUT DEEPLY INTO STH **7** **~ sth** (**in sth**) to put sth deeply into sth else: *He walked slowly, his hands buried in his pockets.* ◇ *She always has her head buried in a book.*

IDM ˌ**bury the ˈhatchet** | ˌ**bury your ˈdifferences** to stop being unfriendly and become friends again ➲ more at HEAD *n.*

PHR V ˈ**bury yourself in sth** **1** to give all your attention to sth: *Since she left, he's buried himself in his work.* **2** to go to or be in a place where you will not meet many people: *She buried herself in the country to write a book.*

bus 0‑ /bʌs/ *noun, verb*

■ ***noun*** (*pl.* **buses**, *US* also **busses**) **1** 0‑ a large road vehicle that carries passengers, especially one that travels along a fixed route and stops regularly to let people get on and off: *Shall we walk or go* ***by bus****?* ◇ *A regular bus service connects the train station with the town centre.* ◇ *a* ***bus company/driver*** ◇ *a school bus* ➲ VISUAL VOCAB page V46 ➲ compare COACH ➲ see also BUS LANE, BUS SHELTER, BUS STATION, BUS STOP, MINIBUS, TROLLEYBUS **2** (*computing*) a set of wires that carries information from one part of a computer system to another

■ ***verb*** (**-s-** or **-ss-**) **1** **~ sb (from/to...)** to transport sb by bus: *We were bussed from the airport to our hotel.* **2** **~ sb** (*NAmE*) to transport young people by bus to another area so that students of different races can be educated together **3** **~ sth** (*NAmE*) to take the dirty plates, etc. off the tables in a restaurant, as a job

bus·boy /ˈbʌsbɔɪ/ *noun* (*NAmE*) a person who works in a restaurant and whose job is to clear the dirty dishes, etc.

busby /ˈbʌzbi/ *noun* (*pl.* **-ies**) a tall fur hat worn by some British soldiers for special ceremonies

bush 0‑ /bʊʃ/ *noun*

1 0‑ [C] a plant that grows thickly with several hard STEMS coming up from the root: *a rose bush* ◇ *holly bushes* ➲ compare TREE **2** [C] a thing that looks like a bush, especially an area of thick hair or fur **3** (often **the bush**) [U] an area of wild land that has not been cleared, especially in Africa and Australia; in New Zealand an area where the forest has not been cleared IDM see BEAT *v.*, BIRD

bush·baby /ˈbʊʃbeɪbi/ *noun* (*pl.* **-ies**) a small African animal with large eyes, which lives in trees

bushed /bʊʃt/ *adj.* [not before noun] (*informal*) very tired SYN **exhausted**

bushel /ˈbʊʃl/ *noun* **1** [C] a unit for measuring grain and fruit (equal in volume to 8 gallons) **2** **bushels** [pl.] **~ (of sth)** (*NAmE, informal*) a large amount of sth IDM see HIDE *v.*

ˈ**bush fire** *noun* a fire in a large area of rough open ground, especially one that spreads quickly

bush·fowl /ˈbʊʃfaʊl/ *noun* [C, U] (**bush·fowl** or **bush·fowls**) (*WAfrE*) a bird with a large body and brown and white feathers that walks a lot on the ground and is often used for food

bu·shido /ˈbʊʃiːdəʊ; bʊˈʃiːdəʊ; *NAmE* -doʊ/ *noun* [U] (from *Japanese*) the system of honour and morals of the Japanese SAMURAI

ˈ**bush-league** *adj.* (*NAmE, informal*) of very low quality

Bush·man /ˈbʊʃmən/ *noun* (*pl.* **-men** /-mən/) **1** a member of one of the races of people from southern Africa who live and hunt in the African BUSH **2** **bushman** a person who lives, works or travels in the Australian BUSH

bush·meat /ˈbʊʃmiːt/ *noun* [U] the meat of wild animals used as food, for example African animals

bush·ran·ger /ˈbʊʃreɪndʒə(r)/ *noun* (*AustralE, NZE*) (in the past) an OUTLAW (= a person who has done sth illegal and is hiding to avoid being caught) who lives in the bush (= areas of wild land far away from large towns)

ˈ**bush rat** *noun* [C, U] (*pl.* **bush rat** or **bush rats**) (in W Africa) a type of large RODENT similar to a RAT that is found in wild areas and used for food

ˌ**bush ˈtelegraph** *noun* [U, sing.] (*informal, humorous*) the process by which information and news are passed quickly from person to person

bush·whack /ˈbʊʃwæk/ *verb* **1** [I] to live or travel in wild country **2** [I] **+ adv./prep.** to cut your way through bushes, plants, etc. in wild country: *We had to bushwhack through undergrowth.* **3** [T] **~ sb** to attack sb very suddenly from a hidden position SYN **ambush** **4** [I] to fight as a GUERRILLA ▸ **bush·whacking** *noun* [U]

bush·whack·er /ˈbʊʃwækə(r)/ *noun* **1** a person who lives or travels in an area of wild country **2** a person who fights in a GUERRILLA war

bushy /ˈbʊʃi/ *adj.* (**bush·ier**, **bushi·est**) **1** (of hair or fur) growing thickly: *a* ***bushy beard/tail*** ◇ *bushy eyebrows* **2** (of plants) growing thickly, with a lot of leaves

ˌ**bushy-ˈtailed** *adj.* ➲ BRIGHT-EYED

busily ➲ BUSY

busi·ness 0‑ /ˈbɪznəs/ *noun*

▸ TRADE **1** 0‑ [U] the activity of making, buying, selling or supplying goods or services for money SYN **commerce**, **trade**: *business contacts/affairs/interests* ◇ *a business investment* ◇ *It's been a pleasure to* ***do business with*** *you.* ◇ *She has set up* ***in business*** *as a hairdresser.* ◇ *When he left school, he* ***went into business*** *with his brother.* ◇ *She works in the computer business.* ➲ see also AGRIBUSINESS, BIG BUSINESS, SHOW BUSINESS

▸ WORK **2** 0‑ [U] work that is part of your job: *Is the trip to Rome* ***business or pleasure****?* ◇ *a business lunch* ◇ *He's away* ***on business****.* **3** 0‑ [U] the amount of work done by a company, etc; the rate or quality of this work: *Business was bad.* ◇ *Business was booming.* ◇ *Her job was to drum up* (= increase) *business.* ◇ *How's business?*

▸ COMPANY **4** 0‑ [C] a commercial organization such as a company, shop/store or factory: *to* ***have/start/run a business*** ◇ *business premises* ◇ *She works in the family business.* ◇ *They've got a small catering business.*

▸ RESPONSIBILITY **5** 0‑ [U] something that concerns a particular person or organization: *It is the business of the police to protect the community.* ◇ *I shall* ***make it my business*** *to find out who is responsible.* ◇ *My private life is* ***none of your business*** (= does not concern you). ◇ *It's* ***no business of yours*** *who I invite to the party.*

▸ IMPORTANT MATTERS **6** 0‑ [U] important matters that need to be dealt with or discussed: *the main business of the meeting* ◇ *He has some* ***unfinished business*** *to deal with.*

▸ EVENT **7** [sing.] (usually with an adjective) a matter, an event or a situation: *That plane crash was a terrible business.* ◇ *I found the whole business very depressing.* ◇ *The business of the missing tickets hasn't been sorted out.*

▸ BEING A CUSTOMER **8** (*especially NAmE*) (also *BrE formal* **custom**) [U] the fact of a person or people buying goods or services at a shop/store or business: *We're grateful for your business.*

IDM **any other ˈbusiness** the things that are discussed at the end of an official meeting that do not appear on the AGENDA: *I think we've finished item four. Now is there any other business?* ➲ see also AOB **be in ˈbusiness** (*informal*) to have everything that you need in order to be able to start sth immediately: *All we need is a car and we'll be in business.* **be the ˈbusiness** (*informal*) to be very good **business as ˈusual** a way of saying that things will continue as normal despite a difficult situation ˌ**business is ˈbusiness** a way of saying that financial and commercial matters are the important things to consider and you should not be influenced by friendship, etc. **get down to ˈbusiness** to start dealing with the matter that needs to be dealt with, or doing the work that needs to be done **go about your ˈbusiness** to do the things that you normally do: *streets filled with people going about their daily business* **have no business doing sth** | **have no business to do sth** to have no right to do sth: *You have no business being here.* **like ˈnobody's business** (*BrE, informal*) very much, very fast, very well, etc: *I've been working like nobody's business to get it finished in time.* **not be in the business of doing sth** not intending to do sth (which it would be surprising for you to do): *I'm not in the business of getting other people to do my work for me.* **out of ˈbusiness** having stopped operating as a business because there is no more money or work available: *The new regulations will* ***put*** *many small businesses* ***out of business****.* ◇ *Some travel companies will* probably **go out of business** this summer. ➲ more at MEAN *v.*, MIND *v.*, PLY *v.*

B

Collocations

Business

Running a business

- **buy/acquire/own/sell** a company/firm/franchise
- **set up/establish/ start/start up/launch** a business/ company
- **run/operate** a business/company/franchise
- **head/run** a firm/department/team
- **make/secure/win/block** a deal
- **expand/grow/build** the business
- **boost/increase** investment/spending/sales/turnover/ earnings/exports/trade
- **increase/expand** production/output/sales
- **boost/maximize** production/productivity/efficiency/ income/revenue/profit/profitability
- **achieve/maintain/sustain** growth/profitability
- **cut/reduce/bring down/lower/slash** costs/prices
- **announce/impose/make** cuts/cutbacks

Sales and marketing

- **break into/enter/capture/dominate** the market
- **gain/grab/take/win/boost/lose** market share
- **find/build/create** a market for sth
- **start/launch** an advertising/a marketing campaign
- **develop/launch/promote** a product/website
- **create/generate** demand for your product
- **attract/get/retain/help** customers/clients
- **drive/generate/boost/increase** demand/sales
- **beat/keep ahead of/out-think/outperform** the competition
- **meet/reach/exceed/miss** sales targets

Finance

- **draw up/set/present/agree/approve** a budget
- **keep to/balance/cut/reduce/slash** the budget
- **be/come in below/under/over/within** budget
- **generate** income/revenue/profit/funds/business
- **fund/finance** a campaign/a venture/an expansion/ spending/a deficit
- **provide/raise/allocate** capital/funds
- **attract/encourage** investment/investors
- **recover/recoup** costs/losses/an investment
- **get/obtain/offer sb/grant sb** credit/a loan
- **apply for/raise/secure/arrange/provide** finance

Failure

- **lose** business/trade/customers/sales/revenue
- **accumulate/accrue/incur/run up** debts
- **suffer/sustain** enormous/heavy/serious losses
- **face** cuts/a deficit/redundancy/bankruptcy
- **file for**/(*NAmE*) **enter/avoid/escape** bankruptcy
- (*BrE*) **go into** administration/liquidation
- **liquidate/wind up** a company
- **survive/weather** a recession/downturn
- **propose/seek/block/oppose** a merger
- **launch/make/accept/defeat** a takeover bid

ˈbusiness administration *noun* [U] the study of how to manage a business: *a master's degree in business administration* (= *an MBA*)

ˈbusiness card (also **card**) *noun* a small card printed with sb's name and details of their job and company ➲ compare VISITING CARD

ˈbusiness class (*BrE* also **ˈclub class**) *noun* [U] the part of a plane where passengers have a high level of comfort and service, designed for people travelling on business, and less expensive than first class ▶ **ˈbusiness class** (*BrE* also **ˈclub class**) *adv.*: *I always fly business class.*

the ˈbusiness end *noun* [sing.] **~ (of sth)** (*informal*) the end of a tool or weapon which performs its main function

ˈbusiness hours *noun* [pl.] the hours in a day that a shop/store or company is open

busi·ness·like /ˈbɪznəslaɪk/ *adj.* (of a person) working in an efficient and organized way and not wasting time or thinking about personal things: *She adopted a brisk businesslike tone.*

busi·ness·man 🔑 /ˈbɪznəsmæn; -mən/, **busi·ness·woman** /ˈbɪznəswʊmən/ *noun* (*pl.* **-men** /-men; -mən/, **-women** /-wɪmɪn/)
1 🔑 a person who works in business, especially at a high level **2** 🔑 a person who is skilful in business and financial matters: *I should have got a better price for the car, but I'm not much of a businessman.* ➲ note at GENDER

ˈbusiness park *noun* an area of land that is specially designed for offices and small factories

ˈbusiness person *noun* a person who works in business, especially at a high level

ˈbusiness school *noun* a part of a college or university that teaches business, often to GRADUATES (= people who already have a first degree)

ˈbusiness studies *noun* [U+sing./pl. v.] the study of subjects connected with money and managing a business: *a degree in business studies*

ˌbusiness-to-ˈbusiness *adj.* [usually before noun] (*abbr.* **B2B**) done between one business and another rather than between a business and its ordinary customers

bus·ing (*NAmE*) = BUSSING

busk /bʌsk/ *verb* [I] to perform music in a public place and ask for money from people passing by ▶ **busk·er** *noun* ➲ VISUAL VOCAB page V2 **busk·ing** *noun* [U]

ˈbus lane *noun* a part of a road that only buses are allowed to use

bus·load /ˈbʌsləʊd; *NAmE* -loʊd/ *noun* (*especially NAmE*) a large group of people on a bus

ˌbus·man's ˈholi·day *noun* [sing.] a holiday that is spent doing the same thing that you do at work

ˈbus pass *noun* **1** a ticket that allows you to travel on any bus within a particular area for a fixed period of time **2** a ticket that allows people from particular groups (for example, students or old people) to travel free or at a reduced cost: (*BrE, humorous*) *I'm not old enough for my bus pass yet!*

ˈbus shelter *noun* a structure with a roof where people can stand while they are waiting for a bus

buss·ing (also *NAmE* **bus·ing**) /ˈbʌsɪŋ/ *noun* [U] (in the US) a system of transporting young people by bus to another area so that students of different races can be educated together

ˈbus station *noun* the place in a town or city where buses (especially to or from other towns) leave and arrive

ˈbus stop *noun* a place at the side of a road that is marked with a sign, where buses stop ➲ VISUAL VOCAB page V3

bust /bʌst/ *verb, noun, adj.*
■ ***verb*** (**bust**, **bust** or **bust·ed**, **bust·ed**) (*informal*) **1 ~ sth** to break sth: *I bust my camera.* ◊ *The lights are busted.* ◊ *Come out, or I'll bust the door down!* **2 ~ sb/sth (for sth)** (of the police) to suddenly enter a place and search it or arrest sb: *He's been busted for drugs.* **3 ~ sb** (*especially NAmE*) to make sb lower in military rank as a punishment SYN **demote**
IDM **bust a ˈgut (doing sth/to do sth)** (*informal*) to make a great effort to do sth **... or ˈbust** (*informal*) used to say that you will try very hard to get somewhere or achieve sth: *For him it's the Olympics or bust.*
PHR V **ˌbust ˈup** (*informal*) (of a couple, friends, partners, etc.) to have an argument and separate SYN **break up**: *They bust up after five years of marriage.* ➲ related noun BUST-UP **ˌbust sth↔ˈup** (*informal*) to make sth end by disturbing or ruining it SYN **break sth up**: *It was his drinking that bust up his marriage.*

■ ***noun*** **1** a stone or metal model of a person's head, shoulders and chest **2** (used especially when talking about clothes or measurements) a woman's breasts or the measurement around the breasts and back: *What is your bust measurement, Madam?* **3** (*informal*) an unexpected visit made by the police in order to arrest people for doing sth illegal: *a drug bust* **4** (*NAmE*) a thing that is not good: *As a show it was a bust.*

■ ***adj.*** [not usually before noun] (*informal*) **1** (*BrE*) broken: *My watch is bust.* **2** (of a person or business) failed because of a lack of money SYN **bankrupt**: *We're bust!* ◇ *We lost our money when the travel company* ***went bust***.

bus·tard /ˈbʌstəd; *NAmE* ˈbʌstərd/ *noun* a large European bird that can run fast

busted /ˈbʌstɪd/ *adj.* [not before noun] (*NAmE, informal*) caught in the act of doing sth wrong and likely to be punished: *You are so busted!*

bus·ter /ˈbʌstə(r)/ *noun* **1** (*NAmE, informal*) used to speak to a man you do not like: *Get lost, buster!* **2** (usually in compounds; often used in newspapers) a person or thing that stops or gets rid of sth: *crime-busters*

bus·tier /ˈbʌstieɪ/ *noun* a woman's tight top which does not cover the arms or shoulders

bus·tle /ˈbʌsl/ *verb, noun*

■ ***verb*** [I, T] to move around in a busy way or to hurry sb in a particular direction: **+ adv./prep.** *She bustled around in the kitchen.* ◇ **~ sb + adv./prep.** *The nurse bustled us out of the room.*

■ ***noun*** **1** [U] busy and noisy activity: *the* ***hustle and bustle*** *of city life* **2** [C] a frame that was worn under a skirt by women in the past in order to hold the skirt out at the back

bust·ling /ˈbʌslɪŋ/ *adj.* full of people moving about in a busy way: *a bustling city* ◇ **~ with sth** *The market was bustling with life.*

ˈ**bust-up** *noun* (*informal, especially BrE*) **1** a bad argument or very angry disagreement SYN **row**: *Sue and Tony had a bust-up and aren't speaking to each other.* **2** the end of a relationship SYN **break-up**: *the final bust-up of their marriage*

busty /ˈbʌsti/ *adj.* (*informal*) (of a woman) having large breasts

bus·way /ˈbʌsweɪ/ *noun* (*BrE*) a road or section of a road that can only be used by buses, especially one with special tracks for guiding the buses

busy 0-w /ˈbɪzi/ *adj., verb*

■ ***adj.*** (**busier, busi·est**)

▸ DOING STH **1** 0-w having a lot to do; perhaps not free to do sth else because you are working on sth: *Are you busy tonight?* ◇ *I'm afraid the doctor is busy at the moment. Can he call you back?* ◇ *I'll be too busy to come to the meeting.* ◇ *The principal is a very busy woman.* ◇ *She was always too busy to listen.* ◇ *a very busy life* ◇ **~ with sth/sb** *Kate's busy with her homework.* **2** 0-w **~ (doing sth)** spending a lot of time on sth: *James is busy practising for the school concert.* ◇ *Let's get busy with the clearing up.*

▸ PLACE **3** 0-w full of people, activity, vehicles, etc: *a busy main road* ◇ *Victoria is one of London's busiest stations.*

▸ PERIOD OF TIME **4** 0-w full of work and activity: *Have you had a busy day?* ◇ *This is one of the busiest times of the year for the department.*

▸ TELEPHONE **5** 0-w (*especially NAmE*) being used SYN **engaged**: *The line is busy—I'll try again later.* ◇ *the busy signal* ➲ COLLOCATIONS at PHONE

▸ PATTERN/DESIGN **6** too full of small details

▸ **busily** *adv.*: *He was busily engaged repairing his bike.*

IDM **as busy as a ˈbee** very busy **keep yourself ˈbusy** to find enough things to do: *Since she retired she's kept herself very busy.*

■ ***verb*** (**busies, busy·ing, busied, busied**) to fill your time doing an activity or a task: **~ yourself (with sth)** *She busied herself with the preparations for the party.* ◇ **~ yourself (in/with) doing sth** *While we talked, Bill busied himself fixing lunch.*

busy·body /ˈbɪzibɒdi; *NAmE* -bɑːdi/ *noun* (*pl.* **-ies**) (*disapproving*) a person who is too interested in what other people are doing: *He's an interfering old busybody!*

busy Lizzie /ˌbɪzi ˈlɪzi/ *noun* a small plant with a lot of red, pink or white flowers, often grown indoors or in gardens

busy·work /ˈbɪziwɜːk; *NAmE* -wɜːrk/ *noun* [U] (*NAmE*) work that is given to sb to keep them busy, without really being useful

but 0-w /bət; *strong form* bʌt/ *conj., prep., adv., noun*

■ ***conj.*** **1** 0-w used to introduce a word or phrase that contrasts with what was said before: *I got it wrong. It wasn't the red one but the blue one.* ◇ *His mother won't be there, but his father might.* ◇ *It isn't that he lied exactly, but he did tend to exaggerate.* **2** 0-w however; despite this: *I'd asked everybody but only two people came.* ◇ *By the end of the day we were tired but happy.* ➲ LANGUAGE BANK at NEVERTHELESS **3** 0-w used when you are saying sorry about sth: *I'm sorry but I can't stay any longer.* **4** 0-w used to introduce a statement that shows that you are surprised or annoyed, or that you disagree: *But that's not possible!* ◇ *'Here's the money I owe you.' 'But that's not right—it was only £10.'* **5** except: *I had no choice but to sign the contract.* **6** used before repeating a word in order to emphasize it: *Nothing, but nothing would make him change his mind.* **7** (*literary*) used to emphasize that sth is always true: *She never passed her old home but she thought of the happy years she had spent there* (= she always thought of them).

IDM **but for 1** if it were not for: *He would have played but for a knee injury.* **2** except for: *The square was empty but for a couple of cabs.* **but then (again) 1** however; on the other hand: *He might agree. But then again he might have a completely different opinion.* **2** used before a statement that explains or gives a reason for what has just been said: *She speaks very good Italian. But then she did live in Rome for a year* (= so it's not surprising). **you cannot/could not but ...** (*formal*) used to show that everything else is impossible except the thing that you are saying: *What could he do but forgive her?* (= that was the only thing possible)

■ ***prep.*** except; apart from: *We've had nothing but trouble with this car.* ◇ *The problem is anything but easy.* ◇ *Who but Rosa could think of something like that?* ◇ *Everyone was there but him.* ◇ *I came* ***last but one*** *in the race* (= I wasn't last but next to last). ◇ *Take the first turning but one* (= not the first one but the one after it).

■ ***adv.*** only: *I don't think we'll manage it. Still, we can but try.* ◇ *There were a lot of famous people there: Tom Hanks and Julia Roberts, to name but two.*

■ ***noun*** /bʌt/ [usually pl.] a reason that sb gives for not doing sth or not agreeing: *'Let us have no buts,' he said firmly. 'You are coming.'* ◇ *With so many* ***ifs and buts***, *it is easier to wait and see.*

bu·tane /ˈbjuːteɪn/ *noun* [U] a gas produced from PETROLEUM, used in liquid form as a fuel for cooking etc.

butch /bʊtʃ/ *adj.* (*informal*) **1** (of a woman) behaving or dressing like a man ➲ compare FEMME **2** (of a man) big, and often behaving in an aggressive way

butcher /ˈbʊtʃə(r)/ *noun, verb*

■ ***noun*** **1** a person whose job is cutting up and selling meat in a shop/store or killing animals for this purpose **2 butcher's** (*pl.* **butchers**) a shop/store that sells meat: *He owns the butcher's in the main street.* **3** a person who kills people in a cruel and violent way

IDM **have/take a ˈbutcher's** (*BrE, slang*) to have a look at sth ORIGIN From rhyming slang, in which **butcher's hook** stands for 'look'.

■ ***verb*** **1 ~ sb** to kill people in a very cruel and violent way **2 ~ sth** to kill animals and cut them up for use as meat **3 ~ sth** (*especially NAmE*) to spoil sth by doing it very badly: *The script was good, but those guys butchered it.*

ˈ**butcher block** *noun* [U] (*NAmE*) a material used for surfaces in kitchens, especially those that you work on

ˈ**butcher's block** *noun* a thick block of wood on which a butcher cuts meat, also used in kitchens as a surface for cutting food on

butch·ery /ˈbʊtʃəri/ *noun* [U] **1** cruel, violent and unnecessary killing **2** the work of preparing meat to be sold

B

but·ler /ˈbʌtlə(r)/ *noun* the main male servant in a large house

butt /bʌt/ *verb, noun*

■ ***verb* 1 ~ sb/sth** to hit or push sb/sth hard with your head **2 ~ sb/sth** if an animal **butts** sb/sth, it hits them or it hard with its horns and head

PHR V **ˌbutt ˈin (on sb/sth) 1** to interrupt a conversation rudely: *How can I explain if you keep butting in?* ◇ **+ speech** *'Is that normal?' Josie butted in.* **2** (*informal*) to become involved in a situation that does not concern you SYN **interfere (in)**: *I didn't ask you to butt in on my private business.* **ˌbutt ˈout** (*informal, especially NAmE*) used to tell sb rudely to go away or to stop INTERFERING in sth that does not concern them: *Butt out, Neil! This is none of your business.*

■ ***noun* 1** the thick end of a weapon or tool: *a rifle butt* **2** the part of a cigarette or CIGAR that is left after it has been smoked **3** (*BrE*) a large round container for storing or collecting liquids: *a water butt* **4** (*informal, especially NAmE*) the part of the body that you sit on SYN **buttocks**: *Get off your butt and do some work!* ◇ *Get your butt over here!* (= Come here!) **5** the act of hitting sb with your head: *a butt from his head* ➲ see also HEADBUTT

IDM **be the butt of sth** to be the person or thing that other people often joke about or criticize SYN **target**: *She was the butt of some very unkind jokes.* ➲ more at PAIN *n.*

butte /bjuːt/ *noun* (*especially NAmE*) a hill that is flat on top and is separate from other high ground

but·ter 0‑w /ˈbʌtə(r)/ *noun, verb*

■ ***noun*** 0‑w [U] a soft yellow food made from cream, used in cooking and for spreading on bread: *Fry the onions in butter.* ➲ see also BREAD AND BUTTER, PEANUT BUTTER

IDM **butter wouldn't melt (in sb's ˈmouth)** (*informal*) used to say that sb seems to be innocent, kind, etc. when they are not really ➲ more at KNIFE *v.*

■ ***verb* ~ sth** to spread butter on sth: *She buttered four thick slices of bread.* IDM see KNOW *v.*

PHR V **ˌbutter sb↔ˈup** (*informal*) to say nice things to sb so that they will help you or give you sth

ˈbutter bean *noun* a large pale yellow BEAN. Butter beans are often sold dried.

but·ter·cream /ˈbʌtəkriːm; *NAmE* -tərk-/ *noun* [U] a soft mixture of butter and sugar, used inside and on top of cakes

but·ter·cup /ˈbʌtəkʌp; *NAmE* -tərk-/ *noun* a wild plant with small shiny yellow flowers that are shaped like cups ➲ VISUAL VOCAB page V9

but·ter·fat /ˈbʌtəfæt; *NAmE* ˈbʌtər-/ *noun* [U] the natural fat contained in milk and milk products

but·ter·fin·gers /ˈbʌtəfɪŋɡəz; *NAmE* ˈbʌtərfɪŋɡərz/ *noun* [sing.] (*informal*) a person who often drops things

but·ter·fly /ˈbʌtəflaɪ; *NAmE* -tərf-/ *noun* (*pl.* **-ies**) **1** [C] a flying insect with a long thin body and four large, usually brightly coloured, wings: *butterflies and moths* ◇ *She's like a butterfly. She flits in and out of people's lives.* ➲ VISUAL VOCAB page V11 **2** [U] a swimming stroke in which you swim on your front and lift both arms forward at the same time while your legs move up and down together: *She was third in the 200m butterfly* (= a swimming race). ➲ VISUAL VOCAB page V37

IDM **have ˈbutterflies (in your stomach)** (*informal*) to have a nervous feeling in your stomach before doing sth

ˈbutter knife *noun* a knife that has a flat blade with a round end, used for spreading butter on bread ➲ VISUAL VOCAB page V19

but·ter·milk /ˈbʌtəmɪlk; *NAmE* -tərm-/ *noun* [U] the liquid that remains after butter has been separated from milk, used in cooking or as a drink

but·ter·nut /ˈbʌtənʌt; *NAmE* ˈbʌtər-/ *noun* a N American tree grown as a decoration and for its wood

but·ter·nut squash *noun* [C, U] a long vegetable that grows on the ground, has a hard yellow skin and orange flesh and is fatter at one end than the other

but·ter·scotch /ˈbʌtəskɒtʃ; *NAmE* ˈbʌtərskɑːtʃ/ *noun* [U] **1** a type of hard pale brown sweet/candy made by boiling butter and brown sugar together **2** (*especially NAmE*) a sauce flavoured with butterscotch, used for pouring on ice cream, etc.

but·tery /ˈbʌtəri/ *adj.* like, containing or covered with butter

but·tock /ˈbʌtək/ *noun* [usually pl.] either of the two round soft parts at the top of a person's legs ➲ VISUAL VOCAB page V48

but·ton 0‑w /ˈbʌtn/ *noun, verb*

■ ***noun* 1** 0‑w a small round piece of metal, plastic, etc. that is sewn onto a piece of clothing and used for fastening two parts together: (*BrE*) *to* ***do up/undo your buttons*** ◇ (*NAmE*) *to* ***button/unbutton your buttons*** ◇ *to sew on a button* ◇ *shirt buttons* ➲ VISUAL VOCAB page V51 **2** 0‑w a small part of a machine that you press to make it work: *the* ***play/stop/rewind button*** ◇ *Adam pressed a button and waited for the lift.* ◇ *Choose 'printer' from the menu and click with the right mouse button.* ◇ *The windows slide down* ***at the touch of a button****.* ➲ picture at HANDLE ➲ see also PUSH-BUTTON **3** a small area on a computer screen that you click on to make it do sth: *Click on the back button to go back to the previous screen.* **4** (*especially NAmE*) a BADGE, especially one with a message printed on it ➲ VISUAL VOCAB page V53 ➲ see also BELLY BUTTON

IDM **on the ˈbutton** (*informal, especially NAmE*) **1** at exactly the right time or at the exact time mentioned: *We arrived at 4 o'clock on the button.* **2** exactly right: *You're on the button there!* **ˌpush all the (right) ˈbuttons** (also **ˌpress all the (right) ˈbuttons** especially in *BrE*) (*informal*) to do exactly the right things to please sb: *a new satirical comedy show that pushes all the right buttons* **ˌpush sb's ˈbuttons** (also **ˌpress sb's ˈbuttons** especially in *BrE*) (*informal*) to make sb react in either a positive or a negative way: *I've known him for years, but I still don't know what pushes his buttons.* ➲ more at BRIGHT *adj.*

■ ***verb* 1** [T] **~ sth (up)** to fasten sth with buttons: *She hurriedly buttoned (up) her blouse.* **2** [I] **~ (up)** to be fastened with buttons: *The dress buttons (up) at the back.*

IDM **ˈbutton it!** (*BrE, informal*) used to tell sb rudely to be quiet

ˌbutton-ˈdown *adj.* a **button-down** COLLAR, shirt, etc. has the ends of the COLLAR fastened to the shirt with buttons ➲ VISUAL VOCAB page V51

ˌbuttoned-ˈup *adj.* (*informal, especially BrE*) not expressing your emotions openly

but·ton·hole /ˈbʌtnhəʊl; *NAmE* -hoʊl/ *noun, verb*

■ ***noun* 1** a hole on a piece of clothing for a button to be put through ➲ VISUAL VOCAB page V51 **2** (*BrE*) (*NAmE* **bou·ton·nière**) a flower that is worn in the buttonhole of a coat or jacket

■ ***verb* ~ sb** (*informal*) to make sb stop and listen to you, especially when they do not want to

ˈbutton lift (*BrE*) (also **Poma™**) *noun* a machine with poles which pulls people up the mountain on their SKIS

ˌbutton ˈmushroom *noun* a small young MUSHROOM used in cooking

but·tress /ˈbʌtrəs/ *noun, verb*

■ ***noun*** a stone or brick structure that supports a wall

■ ***verb* ~ sb/sth** (*formal*) to support or give strength to sb/sth: *The sharp increase in crime seems to buttress the argument for more police officers on the street.*

butty /ˈbʌti/ *noun* (*pl.* **-ies**) **1** (*BrE, informal*) a SANDWICH: *a jam butty* **2** (*WelshE, informal*) a friend; a person that you work with

buxom /ˈbʌksəm/ *adj.* (of a woman) large in an attractive way, and with large breasts

buy 0‑w /baɪ/ *verb, noun*

■ ***verb*** (**bought, bought** /bɔːt/)

▸ WITH MONEY **1** 0‑w [T, I] to obtain sth by paying money for it: **~ (sth)** *Where did you buy that dress?* ◇ *If you're thinking of getting a new car, now is a good time to buy.* ◇ **~ sth from sb** *I bought it from a friend for £10.* ◇ **~ sb sth** *He bought me a new coat.* ◇ **~ sth for sb** *He bought a new coat for me.* ◇ **~ sth + adj.** *I bought my car second-hand.* OPP **sell 2** [T] **~ sth** (of

money) to be enough to pay for sth: *He gave his children the best education that money can buy.* ◇ *Five pounds doesn't buy much nowadays.* **3** [T] **~ sb** to persuade sb to do sth dishonest in return for money SYN **bribe**: *He can't be bought* (= he's too honest to accept money in this way).
▸ OBTAIN **4** [T, usually passive] **~ sth** to obtain sth by losing sth else of great value: *Her fame was bought at the expense of her marriage.*
▸ BELIEVE **5** [T] **~ sth** (*informal*) to believe that sth is true, especially sth that is not very likely: *You could say you were ill but I don't think they'd* **buy it** (= accept the explanation).
IDM **(have) 'bought it** (*informal*) to be killed, especially in an accident or a war **buy the 'farm** (*NAmE, informal*) to die **buy 'time** to do sth in order to delay an event, a decision, etc. ➲ more at BEST *n.*, PIG *n.*, PUP
PHR V **,buy sth↔'in** (*BrE*) to buy sth in large quantities **,buy 'into sth 1** to buy shares in a company, especially in order to gain some control over it **2** (*informal*) to believe sth, especially an idea that many other people believe in: *She had never bought into the idea that to be attractive you have to be thin.* ➲ related noun BUY-IN **,buy sb↔'off** to pay sb money, especially dishonestly, to prevent them from doing sth you do not want them to do **,buy sb↔'out 1** to pay sb for their share in a business, usually in order to get total control of it for yourself ➲ related noun BUYOUT **2** to pay money so that sb can leave an organization, especially the army, before the end of an agreed period **,buy sth↔'up** to buy all or as much as possible of sth: *Developers are buying up all the land on the island.*
■ ***noun***
▸ STH BOUGHT **1 a good, better, etc. ~** a thing that is worth the money that you pay for it: *That jacket was a really good buy.* ◇ *Best buys this week are carrots and cabbages.* **2** something that is bought or that is for sale; the act of buying sth: *Computer games are a popular buy this Christmas.*

buyer 0‑w /'baɪə(r)/ *noun*
1 0‑w a person who buys sth, especially sth expensive: *Have you found a buyer for your house ?* ➲ compare PURCHASER OPP **seller, vendor 2** a person whose job is to choose goods that will be sold in a large shop/store
IDM **a ,buyer's 'market** a situation in which there is a lot of a particular item for sale, so that prices are low and people buying have a choice

,buyer's re'morse *noun* [U] (*NAmE*) the feeling of disappointment sb has after they have bought sth when they think they have made a mistake

'buy-in *noun* [U] (*business*) the fact of accepting a policy or change because you agree with it: *If you want to make major changes you need buy-in from everyone in the organization.* ◇ *You need to win people's buy-in.* ➲ see also BUY *v.*

buy·out /'baɪaʊt/ *noun* a situation in which a person or group gains control of a company by buying all or most of its shares: *a management buyout*

buzz /bʌz/ *verb, noun*
■ ***verb* 1** [I] (of a BEE) to make a continuous low sound: *Bees buzzed lazily among the flowers.* **2** [I] to make a sound like a BEEbuzzing: *The doorbell buzzed loudly.* ◇ *My ears were buzzing* (= were filled with a continuous sound). **3** [I] to be full of excitement, activity, etc: *New York buzzes from dawn to dusk.* ◇ *My head was still buzzing after the day's events.* ◇ **~ with sth** *The place was buzzing with journalists.* **4** [I, T] **~ (sth) (for sb/sth)** to call sb to come by pressing a BUZZER: *The doctor buzzed for the next patient to come in.* **5** [T] **~ sb/sth** (*informal*) to fly very close to sb/sth, especially as a warning or threat
PHR V **,buzz a'bout/a'round** to move around quickly, especially because you are very busy: *I've been buzzing around town all day sorting out my trip.* **,buzz 'off** (*informal*) used to tell sb rudely to go away: *Just buzz off and let me get on with my work.*
■ ***noun* 1** [C, usually sing.] (also **buzz·ing** [U, sing.]) a continuous sound like the one that a BEE, a BUZZER or other electronic device makes: *the buzz of bees hunting nectar* ◇ *The buzz of the Entryphone interrupted our conversation.* ◇ *hums and buzzes from the amplifier* **2** [sing.] the sound of people talking, especially in an excited way: *The buzz of conversation suddenly stopped when she came into the room.* **3** [sing.] (*informal*) a strong feeling of pleasure, excitement or achievement: *a* **buzz of excitement/expectation** ◇ *She* **gets a buzz** *out of her work.* ◇ *Flying* **gives me a real buzz.** ◇ *You can sense the creative buzz in the city.* **4 the buzz** [sing.] (*informal*) news that people tell each other that may or may not be true SYN **rumour**
IDM **give sb a 'buzz** (*informal*) to telephone sb: *I'll give you a buzz on Monday, OK?*

buz·zard /'bʌzəd; *NAmE* -zərd/ *noun* **1** (*BrE*) a large European BIRD OF PREY (= a bird that kills other creatures for food) of the HAWK family **2** (*NAmE*) a large American bird like a VULTURE that eats the flesh of animals that are already dead

'buzz cut *noun* a style of cutting the hair in which all the hair is cut very short, close to the skin of the head

buzz·er /'bʌzə(r)/ *noun* an electrical device that produces a BUZZING sound as a signal
IDM **at the 'buzzer** (*NAmE*) at the end of a game or period of play: *He missed a three-point attempt at the buzzer.*

'buzz group *noun* one of the small groups of people that a large group can be divided into in order to discuss and give their opinions about a particular subject. The information obtained is used by people doing MARKET RESEARCH.

'buzz saw *noun* (*NAmE*) = CIRCULAR SAW

buzz·word /'bʌzwɜːd; *NAmE* -wɜːrd/ *noun* a word or phrase, especially one connected with a particular subject, that has become fashionable and popular and is used a lot in newspapers, etc.

b/w *abbr.* (in writing) black and white

bwana /'bwɑːnə/ *noun* a word used in parts of E Africa to address a man who has authority over you, for example your employer

by 0‑w /baɪ/ *prep., adv.*
■ ***prep.* 1** 0‑w near sb/sth; at the side of sb/sth; beside sb/sth: *a house by the river* ◇ *The telephone is by the window.* ◇ *Come and sit by me.* **2** 0‑w used, usually after a passive verb, to show who or what does, creates or causes sth: *He was knocked down by a bus.* ◇ *a play by Ibsen* ◇ *Who's that book by?* ◇ *I was frightened by the noise.* **3** 0‑w used for showing how or in what way sth is done: *The house is heated by gas.* ◇ *May I pay by cheque?* ◇ *I will contact you by letter.* ◇ *to travel* **by boat/bus/car/plane** ◇ *to travel* **by air/land/sea** ◇ *Switch it on by pressing this button.* **4** 0‑w used before particular nouns without *the*, to say that sth happens as a result of sth: *They met by chance.* ◇ *I did it by mistake.* ◇ *The coroner's verdict was 'death by misadventure'.* **5** 0‑w not later than the time mentioned; before: *Can you finish the work by five o'clock?* ◇ *I'll have it done by tomorrow.* ◇ *By this time next week we'll be in New York.* ◇ *He ought to have arrived* **by now/by this time.** ◇ **By the time (that)** *this letter reaches you I will have left the country.* **6** 0‑w past sb/sth: *He walked by me without speaking.* **7** 0‑w during sth; in a particular situation: *to travel* **by day/night** ◇ *We had to work by candlelight.* **8** 0‑w used to show the degree or amount of sth: *The bullet missed him by two inches.* ◇ *House prices went up by 10%.* ◇ *It would be better by far* (= much better) *to...* **9** 0‑w from what sth shows or says; according to sth: *By my watch it is two o'clock.* ◇ *I could tell by the look on her face that something terrible had happened.* ◇ *By law, you are a child until you are 18.* **10** 0‑w used to show the part of sb/sth that sb touches, holds, etc.: *I took him by the hand.* ◇ *She seized her by the hair.* ◇ *Pick it up by the handle!* **11** 0‑w used with *the* to show the period or quantity used for buying, selling or measuring sth: *We rented the car by the day.* ◇ *They're paid by the hour.* ◇ *We only sell it by the metre.* **12** 0‑w used to state the rate at which sth happens: *They're improving day by day.* ◇ *We'll do it bit by bit.* ◇ *It was getting worse by the minute* (= very fast). ◇ *The children came in two by two* (= in groups of two). **13** 0‑w used to show the measurements of sth: *The room measures fifteen feet by twenty feet.* **14** 0‑w used when multiplying or dividing: *6 multiplied by 2 equals 12.* ◇ *6 divided by 2 equals 3.* **15** used for giving more information about where sb comes from, what sb does, etc.: *He's German by birth.* ◇

They're both doctors by profession. **16** used when swearing to mean 'in the name of': *I swear by Almighty God...*
IDM **by the 'by/'bye** = BY THE WAY at WAY
■ ***adv.*** **1** past: *Just drive by. Don't stop.* ◇ *He hurried by without speaking to me.* ◇ *Excuse me, I can't get by.* ◇ *Time goes by so quickly.* **2** used to say that sth is saved so that it can be used in the future: *I've put some money by for college fees.* **3** in order to visit sb for a short time: *I'll come by this evening and pick up the books.*
IDM **by and 'by** (*old-fashioned*) before long; soon: *By and by she met an old man with a beard.*

by- (also **bye-**) /baɪ/ *prefix* (in nouns and verbs) **1** less important: *a by-product* **2** near: *a bystander*

by·catch /'baɪkætʃ/ *noun* [U] fish that are caught by ships by accident when other types of fish are being caught: *Thousands of small fish are thrown back into the sea as by-catch.*

bye /baɪ/ *exclamation, noun*
■ ***exclamation*** (also ˌ**bye-'bye**, **'bye-bye**) (*informal*) goodbye: *Bye! See you next week.* ◇ *She waved bye-bye and got into the car.* ◇ *Bye for now Dad!*
■ ***noun*** (*sport*) a situation in which a player or team does not have an opponent in one part of the competition and continues to the next part as if they had won IDM see BY

'bye-byes *noun*
IDM **go (to) 'bye-byes** (*BrE, informal*) used by small children or to small children, to mean 'go to sleep'

'bye-law = BY-LAW

'by-election *noun* (*BrE*) an election of a new Member of Parliament to replace sb who has died or left parliament ➲ compare GENERAL ELECTION

by·gone /'baɪgɒn; *NAmE* -gɔːn/ *adj.* [only before noun] happening or existing a long time ago: *a* ***bygone age/era***

by·gones /'baɪgɒnz; *NAmE* -gɔːnz/ *noun* [pl.]
IDM **let ˌbygones be 'bygones** to decide to forget about disagreements that happened in the past

'by-law (also **'bye-law**) *noun* **1** (*BrE*) a law that is made by a local authority and that applies only to that area **2** (*NAmE*) a law or rule of a club or company

by·line /'baɪlaɪn/ *noun* a line at the beginning or end of a piece of writing in a newspaper or magazine that gives the writer's name

by·name /'baɪneɪm/ *noun* a name given to sb who has the same first name as sb else, so that it is clear who is being referred to

by·pass /'baɪpɑːs/ *noun, verb*
■ ***noun*** **1** (*especially BrE*) a road that passes around a town or city rather than through the centre **2** a medical operation on the heart in which blood is directed along a different route so that it does not flow through a part that is damaged or blocked; the new route that the blood takes: *heart bypass surgery* ◇ *a triple bypass operation*
■ ***verb*** **1 ~ sth** to go around or avoid a place: *A new road now bypasses the town.* **2 ~ sth** to ignore a rule, an official system or sb in authority, especially in order to get sth done quickly

'by-product *noun* **1** a substance that is produced during the process of making or destroying sth else: *When burnt, plastic produces dangerous by-products.* **2** a thing that happens, often unexpectedly, as the result of sth else: *One of the by-products of unemployment is an increase in crime.*

byre /'baɪə(r)/ *noun* (*old-fashioned, BrE*) a farm building in which cows are kept SYN **cowshed**

by·road /'baɪrəʊd; *NAmE* -roʊd/ *noun* a minor road

by·stand·er /'baɪstændə(r)/ *noun* a person who sees sth that is happening but is not involved SYN **onlooker**: ***innocent bystanders*** *at the scene of the accident* ➲ SYNONYMS at WITNESS

byte /baɪt/ *noun* a unit of information stored in a computer, equal to 8 BITS. A computer's memory is measured in bytes.

byway /'baɪweɪ/ *noun* **1** [C] a small road that is not used very much **2 byways** [pl.] the less important areas of a subject

by·word /'baɪwɜːd; *NAmE* -wɜːrd/ *noun* [usually sing.] **1 a ~ for sth** a person or thing that is a well-known or typical example of a particular quality: *The name Chanel became a byword for elegance.* **2** (*especially NAmE*) a word or phrase that is well known or often used

By·zan·tine /baɪ'zæntaɪn; bɪ-; -tiːn; *NAmE* 'bɪzəntiːn/ *adj.* [usually before noun] **1** connected with Byzantium or the Eastern Roman Empire **2** used to describe ARCHITECTURE of the 5th to the 15th centuries in the Byzantine Empire, especially churches with high central DOMES and MOSAICS **3** (also **byzantine**) (*formal*) (of an idea, a system, etc.) complicated, secret and difficult to change: *an organization of byzantine complexity*

Cc

C /siː/ *noun, abbr., symbol*
■ ***noun*** (also **c**) [C, U] (*pl.* **Cs**, **C's**, **c's** /siːz/) **1** the third letter of the English alphabet: *'Cat' begins with (a) C/'C'.* **2** **C** (*music*) the first note in the SCALE of C MAJOR ➲ see also MIDDLE C **3** **C** the third highest mark/grade that a student can get for a piece of work: *She got (a)* ***C/'C' in/for*** *Physics.*
■ ***abbr.*** **1** **C.** CAPE: *C. Horn* (= for example, on a map) **2** CELSIUS, CENTIGRADE: *Water freezes at 0° C.* **3** (also ©) (*NAmE* also **C.**) COPYRIGHT: *© Oxford University Press 2010* ➲ see also C. OF E., C. & W.
■ ***symbol*** **1** (also **c**) the number 100 in ROMAN NUMERALS **2** the symbol for the chemical element CARBON

c (*BrE*) (also **c.** *NAmE, BrE*) *abbr.* **1** (in writing) CENT(s) **2** (also **C**) (in writing) century: *in the 19th c* ◇ (*NAmE*) *a C19th church* ➲ see also CENT. **3** (also **ca**) (especially before dates)about; approximately (from Latin *circa*): *c1890* **4** (*NAmE*) (in cooking) cup: *add 2c. flour*

cab /kæb/ *noun* **1** a taxi ➲ VISUAL VOCAB page V47 **2** the place where the driver sits in a bus, train or lorry/truck ➲ VISUAL VOCAB page V46

cabal /kəˈbæl; *NAmE* also -ˈbɑːl/ *noun* (*formal*, usually *disapproving*) a small group of people who are involved in secret plans to get political power

Ca·bala = KABBALAH

caba·ret /ˈkæbəreɪ; *NAmE* ˌkæbəˈreɪ/ *noun* **1** [C, U] entertainment with singing and dancing that is performed in restaurants or clubs in the evenings: *a* ***cabaret act/singer/band*** **2** [C] a restaurant or club where cabaret entertainment is performed

cab·bage /ˈkæbɪdʒ/ *noun* **1** [U, C] a round vegetable with large green, purplish-red or white leaves that can be eaten raw or cooked: *Do you like cabbage?* ◇ *two cabbages* ◇ ***white/red cabbage*** ➲ see also CHINESE CABBAGE, PAK CHOI ➲ VISUAL VOCAB page V27 **2** [C] (*BrE*) = VEGETABLE (2)

cab·bal·is·tic /ˌkæbəˈlɪstɪk/ *adj.* relating to secret or MYSTICAL beliefs

cabby (also **cab·bie**) /ˈkæbi/ *noun* (*pl.* -ies) (*informal*) a person who drives a taxi

caber /ˈkeɪbə(r)/ *noun* a long heavy wooden pole that is thrown into the air as a test of strength in the traditional Scottish sport of **tossing the caber**

cabin /ˈkæbɪn/ *noun* **1** a small room on a ship in which you live or sleep **2** one of the areas for passengers to sit in a plane ➲ VISUAL VOCAB page V43 **3** a small house or shelter, usually made of wood: *a log cabin* ➲ VISUAL VOCAB page V13

ˈ**cabin boy** *noun* a boy or young man who works as a servant on a ship

ˈ**cabin crew** *noun* [C+sing./pl. v.] the people whose job is to take care of passengers on a plane

ˈ**cabin cruiser** *noun* = CRUISER

cab·inet 🔑 /ˈkæbɪnət/ *noun*
1 🔑 (usually **the Cabinet**) [C+sing./pl. v.] a group of chosen members of a government, which is responsible for advising and deciding on government policy: *a cabinet meeting* ◇ (*BrE*) *a cabinet minister* ◇ (*BrE*) *the shadow Cabinet* (= the most important members of the opposition party) **2** 🔑 [C] a piece of furniture with doors, drawers and/or shelves, that is used for storing or showing things: *kitchen cabinets* ◇ *a medicine cabinet* ◇ *The china was displayed in a glass cabinet.* ➲ see also FILING CABINET ➲ VISUAL VOCAB page V21

cab·inet·maker /ˈkæbɪnətmeɪkə(r)/ *noun* a person who makes fine wooden furniture, especially as a job

the ˈCabinet Office *noun* [sing.] (in Britain) a government department that is responsible for the work of the Cabinet and the CIVIL SERVICE

cab·in·et·ry /ˈkæbɪnətri/ *noun* [U] (*NAmE*) CABINETS (= cupboards, especially fitted in a kitchen)

cable 🔑 /ˈkeɪbl/ *noun, verb*
■ ***noun*** **1** 🔑 [U, C] thick strong metal rope used on ships, for supporting bridges, etc. ➲ picture at CORD **2** 🔑 [C, U] a set of wires, covered in plastic or rubber, that carries electricity, telephone signals, etc: ***overhead/underground cables*** ◇ *a 10 000 volt cable* ◇ *fibre-optic cable* **3** [U] = CABLE TELEVISION: *We can receive up to 500 cable channels.* **4** [C] (*old-fashioned*) a message sent by electrical signals and printed out
■ ***verb*** [T, I] **~ (sb)** (*old-fashioned*) to send sb a CABLE *n.* (4)

ˈ**cable car** *noun* **1** a vehicle that hangs from and is pulled by a moving cable and that carries people up and down a mountain **2** (*especially NAmE*) a vehicle that runs on tracks and is pulled by a moving cable ➲ VISUAL VOCAB page V47

ˌ**cable ˈtelevision** (also **cable**, ˌ**cable TˈV**) *noun* [U] a system of broadcasting television programmes along wires rather than by radio waves

cab·ling /ˈkeɪblɪŋ/ *noun* [U] all the cables that are required for particular equipment or a particular system

ca·boo·dle /kəˈbuːdl/ *noun*
IDM **the whole (kit and) caˈboodle** (*informal*) everything: *I had new clothes, a new hairstyle—the whole caboodle.*

ca·boose /kəˈbuːs/ *noun* (*NAmE*) the part at the back of a train where the person who is in charge of the train rides

cab·ri·olet /ˈkæbriəʊleɪ; *NAmE* -oʊleɪ/ *noun* a car with a roof that can be folded down or removed SYN **convertible** ➲ compare SOFT TOP

ca·cao /kəˈkaʊ/ *noun* [U] a tropical tree with seeds that are used to make chocolate and COCOA; the seeds from this tree

cache /kæʃ/ *noun, verb*
■ ***noun*** **1** a hidden store of things such as weapons: *an arms cache* **2** (*computing*) a part of a computer's memory that stores copies of data that is often needed while a program is running. This data can be accessed very quickly.
■ ***verb*** **1 ~ sth** to store things in a secret place, especially weapons **2 ~ sth** (*computing*) to store data in a cache: *This page is cached.*

cachet /ˈkæʃeɪ; *NAmE* kæˈʃeɪ/ *noun* [U, sing.] (*formal*) if sth has **cachet**, it has a special quality that people admire and approve of SYN **prestige**

cack /kæk/ *noun* [U] (*BrE, slang*) solid waste matter that is passed from the body through the BOWELS

cack-handed /ˌkæk ˈhændɪd/ *adj.* (*BrE, informal, disapproving*) a **cack-handed** person often drops or breaks things or does things badly SYN **clumsy**

cackle /ˈkækl/ *verb, noun*
■ ***verb*** **1** [I] (of a chicken) to make a loud unpleasant noise **2** [I, T] (**+ speech**) to laugh in a loud unpleasant way: *They all cackled with delight.*
■ ***noun*** **1** the loud noise that a HEN makes **2** a loud unpleasant laugh

cac·oph·ony /kəˈkɒfəni; *NAmE* -ˈkɑːf-/ *noun* [U, sing.] (*formal*) a mixture of loud unpleasant sounds ▸ **cac·oph·on·ous** /-nəs/ *adj.*

cac·tus /ˈkæktəs/ *noun* (*pl.* **cac·tuses** or **cacti** /ˈkæktaɪ/) a plant that grows in hot dry regions, especially one with thick STEMS covered in SPINES but without leaves. There are many different types of cactus. ➲ VISUAL VOCAB page V9

CAD /kæd; ˌsiː eɪ ˈdiː/ *noun* [U] the abbreviation for 'computer-aided design' (the use of computers to design machines, buildings, vehicles, etc.)

cad /kæd/ *noun* (*old-fashioned*) a man who behaves in a dishonest or unfair way

ca·da·ver /kəˈdævə(r)/ *noun* (*technical*) a dead human body SYN **corpse**

ca·da·ver·ous /kəˈdævərəs/ *adj.* (*literary*) (of a person) extremely pale, thin and looking ill/sick

cad·die (also **caddy**) /ˈkædi/ *noun, verb*
■ ***noun*** (*pl.* -ies) (in GOLF) a person who helps a player by carrying his or her CLUBS and equipment during a game
■ ***verb*** (**cad·dies, caddy·ing, cad·died, cad·died**) [I] to act as a caddie in the game of GOLF

C

cad·dis /ˈkædɪs/ (also ˈ**caddis fly**) *noun* a small insect. The young forms, called **caddis worms**, are often used for catching fish.

caddy /ˈkædi/ *noun* (*pl.* -ies) **1** (*especially BrE*) = TEA CADDY **2** (*NAmE*) a small bag for storing or carrying small objects: *a **sewing/make-up caddy*** **3** = CADDIE

ca·dence /ˈkeɪdns/ *noun* **1** (*formal*) the rise and fall of the voice in speaking: *He delivered his words in slow, measured cadences.* **2** the end of a musical phrase

ca·denza /kəˈdenzə/ *noun* **1** (*music*) a short passage, usually near the end of a piece of CLASSICAL music, which is played or sung by the SOLOIST alone, and intended to show the performer's skill **2** (*SAfrE*) if sb has a **cadenza**, they react suddenly and angrily to sth, especially in a way that seems unreasonable or humorous

cadet /kəˈdet/ *noun* a young person who is training to become an officer in the police or armed forces

cadge /kædʒ/ *verb* [T, I] **~ (sth) (from/off sb)** (*BrE, informal*) to ask sb for food, money, etc. especially because you cannot or do not want to pay for sth yourself: *I managed to cadge some money off my dad.* ▸ **cadger** *noun*

Cad·il·lac™ /ˈkædɪlæk/ *noun* **1** a large and expensive US make of car **2 the ~ of sth** (*NAmE*) something that is thought of as an example of the highest quality of a type of thing: *This is the Cadillac of watches.*

cad·mium /ˈkædmiəm/ *noun* [U] (*symb.* **Cd**) a chemical element. Cadmium is a soft, poisonous, bluish-white metal that is used in batteries and nuclear REACTORS.

cadre /ˈkɑːdə(r); *NAmE* ˈkædri/ *noun* (*formal*) **1** [C+sing./pl. v.] a small group of people who are specially chosen and trained for a particular purpose **2** [C] a member of this kind of group

CAE /ˌsiː eɪ ˈiː/ *noun* [U] the abbreviation for 'Certificate in Advanced English' (a British test that measures a person's ability to speak and write English as a foreign language at an advanced level)

cae·cum (*BrE*) (*NAmE* **cecum**) /ˈsiːkəm/ *noun* (*pl.* cae·ca, ceca /ˈsiːkə/) a small bag which is part of the INTESTINE, between the small and the large intestine

Cae·sar·ean /sɪˈzeəriən; *NAmE* -ˈzer-/ (also **Cae·sar·ian, Caeˌsarean ˈsection, Caeˌsarian ˈsection**) (*US* also **ce·sar·ean, ce·sar·ian, ˈC-section**) *noun* [C, U] a medical operation in which an opening is cut in a woman's body in order to take out a baby: *an emergency Caesarean* ◇ *The baby was born by Caesarean section.* ◇ *She had to have a Caesarean.*

Caesar salad /ˌsiːzə ˈsæləd; *NAmE* ˌsiːzər/ *noun* [U, C] a salad of LETTUCE and CROUTONS served with a mixture of oil, lemon juice, egg, etc.

cae·sium (*BrE*) (*NAmE* **ces·ium**) /ˈsiːziəm/ *noun* [U] (*symb.* **Cs**) a chemical element. Caesium is a soft silver-white metal that reacts strongly in water, used in PHOTOELECTRIC CELLS.

caes·ura /sɪˈzjʊərə; *NAmE* sɪˈzjʊrə/ *noun* (*technical*) a pause near the middle of a line of poetry ➲ compare ENJAMBEMENT

cafe (also **café**) /ˈkæfeɪ; *NAmE* kæˈfeɪ/ *noun* **1** a place where you can buy drinks and simple meals. Alcohol is not usually served in British or American cafes. ➲ compare RESTAURANT ➲ VISUAL VOCAB page V2 **2** (*SAfrE*) a small shop/store that sells sweets, newspapers, food, etc. and usually stays open later than other shops/stores

cafe·teria /ˌkæfəˈtɪəriə; *NAmE* -ˈtɪr-/ *noun* a restaurant where you choose and pay for your meal at a counter and carry it to a table. Cafeterias are often found in factories, colleges, hospitals, etc.

cafe·tière /ˌkæfəˈtjeə(r); *NAmE* -ˈtjer/ (*BrE*) (*NAmE* ˌ**French ˈpress**) *noun* a special glass container for making coffee with a metal FILTER that you push down ➲ VISUAL VOCAB page V22

caff /kæf/ *noun* (*BrE, informal*) a CAFE serving simple, basic food: *a transport caff*

caf·fein·ated /ˈkæfɪneɪtɪd/ *adj.* (of coffee or tea) containing caffeine ➲ compare DECAFFEINATED

caf·feine /ˈkæfiːn/ *noun* [U] a drug found in coffee and tea that makes you feel more active ➲ COLLOCATIONS at DIET ➲ see also DECAFFEINATED

caffè latte /ˌkæfeɪ ˈlɑːteɪ/ (also **latte**) *noun* (from *Italian*) a drink made by adding a small amount of strong coffee to a glass or cup of FROTHY steamed milk

caf·tan *noun* = KAFTAN

cage /keɪdʒ/ *noun, verb*
■ ***noun*** a structure made of metal bars or wire in which animals or birds are kept: *a birdcage* ➲ see also RIBCAGE
IDM see RATTLE *v.*
■ ***verb*** [usually passive] **~ sth (up)** to put or keep an animal in a cage: *The dogs are caged (up) at night.* ▸ **caged** *adj.*: *He paced the room like a **caged animal**.*

cagey /ˈkeɪdʒi/ *adj.* (**cagi·er, cagi·est**) **~ (about sth)** (*informal*) not wanting to give sb information SYN **evasive, secretive**: *Tony is very cagey about his family.* ▸ **cagi·ly** *adv.*

ca·goule (also **ka·goul**) /kəˈguːl/ *noun* (*BrE*) a long light jacket with a HOOD, worn to give protection from wind and rain

ca·hoots /kəˈhuːts/ *noun*
IDM **be in cahoots (with sb)** (*informal*) to be planning or doing sth dishonest with sb else SYN **be in collusion**

cai·man (also **cay·man**) /ˈkeɪmən/ *noun* (*pl.* -mans) a N and S American REPTILE similar to an ALLIGATOR

cairn /keən; *NAmE* kern/ *noun* a pile of stones which mark a special place such as the top of a mountain or a place where sb is buried

ca·jole /kəˈdʒəʊl; *NAmE* kəˈdʒoʊl/ *verb* [T, I] to make sb do sth by talking to them and being very nice to them SYN **coax**: **~ sb (into sth/into doing sth)** *He cajoled me into agreeing to do the work.* ◇ **~ sth out of sb** *I managed to cajole his address out of them.* ◇ **(+ speech)** *'Please say yes,' she cajoled.*

Cajun /ˈkeɪdʒn/ *noun, adj.*
■ ***noun*** **1** [C] a person of French origin from Louisiana who speaks an old form of French, also called Cajun **2** [U] a type of music originally played by Cajuns, that is a mixture of BLUES and FOLK MUSIC
■ ***adj.*** connected with the Cajuns, their language, music or spicy cooking: *Cajun chicken/cuisine*

cake 🔑 /keɪk/ *noun, verb*
■ ***noun*** **1** 🔑 [C, U] a sweet food made from a mixture of flour, eggs, butter, sugar, etc. that is baked in an oven. Cakes are made in various shapes and sizes and are often decorated, for example with cream or ICING: *a **piece/slice of cake*** ◇ *to **make/bake a cake*** ◇ *a chocolate cake* ◇ *a birthday cake* ◇ (*BrE*) *a cake tin* (= for cooking a cake in) ◇ (*NAmE*) *a cake pan* ➲ see also ANGEL FOOD CAKE, CHRISTMAS CAKE, FRUIT CAKE, SPONGE CAKE, WEDDING CAKE **2** [C] a food mixture that is cooked in a round flat shape: *potato cakes* ➲ see also CATTLE CAKE, FISHCAKE
IDM **have your cake and ˈeat it** (*BrE*) (also **have your cake and eat it too** *NAmE, BrE*) to have the advantages of sth without its disadvantages; to have both things that are available **a slice/share of the ˈcake** (*BrE*) (*NAmE* **a piece/slice/share of the ˈpie**) a share of the available money or benefits that you believe you have a right to **take the ˈcake** (*especially NAmE*) (*BrE* also **take the ˈbiscuit**) (*informal*) to be the most surprising, annoying, etc. thing that has happened or that sb has done ➲ more at HOT *adj.*, ICING, PIECE *n.*
■ ***verb*** **1** [T, usually passive] **~ sth (in/with sth)** to cover sth with a thick layer of sth soft that becomes hard when it dries: *Her shoes were caked with mud.* **2** [I] if a substance **cakes**, it becomes hard when it dries ▸ **caked** *adj.*: *caked blood*

C

cake·walk /ˈkeɪkwɔːk/ *noun* [sing.] (*informal*) something that is extremely easy to do

CAL /kæl/ *abbr.* computer assisted learning ➲ compare CALL

cala·bash /ˈkæləbæʃ/ *noun* **1** a container made from the hard covering of a fruit or vegetable; the fruit or vegetable from which a calabash is made ➲ see also GOURD **2** (also **ˈcalabash tree**) a tropical tree that produces a large round fruit with very hard skin, also called calabash

cala·brese /ˈkæləbriːs; ˌkæləˈbriːs/ *noun* [U] a type of BROCCOLI (= a vegetable with a thick green STEM and green or purple flower heads)

cala·mine /ˈkæləmaɪn/ (also **ˈcalamine lotion**) *noun* [U] a pink liquid that you put on burnt or sore skin to make it less painful

ca·lami·t·ous /kəˈlæmɪtəs/ *adj.* (*formal*) causing great damage to people's lives, property, etc. SYN **disastrous**

ca·lam·ity /kəˈlæməti/ *noun* [C, U] (*pl.* -ies) an event that causes great damage to people's lives, property, etc. SYN **disaster**

cal·cify /ˈkælsɪfaɪ/ *verb* (**cal·ci·fies, cal·ci·fy·ing, cal·ci·fied, cal·ci·fied**) [I, T] **~ (sth)** (*technical*) to become hard or make sth hard by adding CALCIUM salts ▸ **cal·ci·fi·ca·tion** /ˌkælsɪfɪˈkeɪʃn/ *noun* [U]

cal·cite /ˈkælsaɪt/ *noun* [U] (*chemistry*) a white or clear mineral consisting of CALCIUM CARBONATE. It forms a major part of rocks such as LIMESTONE, MARBLE and CHALK.

cal·cium /ˈkælsiəm/ *noun* [U] (*symb.* Ca) a chemical element. Calcium is a soft silver-white metal that is found in bones, teeth and CHALK.

ˌcalcium ˈcarbonate *noun* [U] (*symb.* $CaCO_3$) (*chemistry*) a white solid substance that exists naturally as CHALK, LIMESTONE and MARBLE

cal·cul·able /ˈkælkjələbl/ *adj.* that can be calculated: *a calculable risk* ➲ compare INCALCULABLE

cal·cu·late 🔑 /ˈkælkjuleɪt/ *verb*
1 🔑 to use numbers to find out a total number, amount, distance, etc. SYN **work out**: **~ sth** *Use the formula to calculate the volume of the container.* ◇ *Benefit is calculated on the basis of average weekly earnings.* ◇ **~ how much, what, etc.** *You'll need to calculate how much time the assignment will take.* ◇ **it is calculated that…** *It has been calculated that at least 47 000 jobs were lost last year.* **2** 🔑 to guess sth or form an opinion by using all the information available SYN **estimate**: **~ that…** *Conservationists calculate that hundreds of species could be lost in this area.* ◇ **~ how much, what, etc.** *It is impossible to calculate what influence he had on her life.*

cal·cu·lated /ˈkælkjuleɪtɪd/ *adj.* [usually before noun] carefully planned to get what you want: *a calculated insult* ◇ *He took **a calculated risk*** (= a risk that you decide is worth taking even though you know it might have bad results).
IDM **be calculated to do sth** to be intended to do sth; to be likely to do sth: *Her latest play is calculated to shock.* ◇ *This sort of life is not calculated to appeal to a young man of 20.*

cal·cu·lat·ing /ˈkælkjuleɪtɪŋ/ *adj.* (*disapproving*) good at planning things so that you have an advantage, without caring about other people: *a cold and calculating killer* ◇ *I never realized you could be so calculating.*

cal·cu·la·tion 🔑 /ˌkælkjuˈleɪʃn/ *noun*
1 🔑 [C, U] the act or process of using numbers to find out an amount: *Cathy did a rough calculation.* ◇ *By my calculation(s), we made a profit of £20 000 last year.* ◇ *Our guess was confirmed by calculation.* ➲ COLLOCATIONS at SCIENTIFIC **2** [C, U] the process of using your judgement to decide what the results would be of doing sth **3** [U] (*disapproving*) careful planning for yourself without caring about other people: *an act of cold calculation*

cal·cu·la·tor /ˈkælkjuleɪtə(r)/ *noun* a small electronic device for calculating with numbers ➲ VISUAL VOCAB page V56: *a pocket calculator*

cal·cu·lus /ˈkælkjələs/ *noun* [U] the type of mathematics that deals with rates of change, for example in the slope of a curve or the speed of a falling object

cal·dera /kɒlˈdeərə; *NAmE* kɔːlˈdɪərə; -ˈderə; -ˈdɪrə/ *noun* (*technical*) a very large hole in the top of a VOLCANO, usually caused by an ERUPTION

cal·dron (*US*) = CAULDRON

Cale·do·nian /ˌkælɪˈdəʊniən; *NAmE* -ˈdoʊ-/ *adj.* connected with Scotland

cal·en·dar /ˈkælɪndə(r)/ *noun* **1** a page or series of pages showing the days, weeks and months of a particular year, especially one that you hang on a wall: *a calendar for 2010* ➲ VISUAL VOCAB page V56 ➲ see also ADVENT CALENDAR **2** (*NAmE*) a record of what you have to do each day; the book in which you write this down **3** [usually sing.] a list of important events or dates of a particular type during the year: *This is one of the biggest weeks in the racing calendar.* **4** a system by which time is divided into fixed periods, showing the beginning and end of a year: *the Islamic calendar*

ˌcalendar ˈmonth *noun* (*technical*) **1** one of the twelve months of the year ➲ compare LUNAR MONTH **2** a period of time from a particular date in one month to the same date in the next one

ˌcalendar ˈyear *noun* (*technical*) the period of time from 1 January to 31 December in the same year

calf /kɑːf; *NAmE* kæf/ *noun* (*pl.* **calves** /kɑːvz; *NAmE* kævz/) **1** [C] the back part of the leg between the ankle and the knee: *I've torn a calf muscle.* ➲ VISUAL VOCAB page V48 **2** [C] a young cow **3** [C] a young animal of some other type such as a young ELEPHANT or WHALE **4** [U] = CALFSKIN
IDM **in/with ˈcalf** (of a cow) pregnant

calf·skin /ˈkɑːfskɪn; *NAmE* ˈkæf-/ (also **calf**) *noun* [U] soft thin leather made from the skin of calves, used especially for making shoes and clothing

cali·brate /ˈkælɪbreɪt/ *verb* **~ sth** (*technical*) to mark units of measurement on an instrument such as a THERMOMETER so that it can be used for measuring sth accurately

cali·bra·tion /ˌkælɪˈbreɪʃn/ *noun* (*technical*) **1** [U] the act of calibrating: *a calibration error* **2** [C] the units of measurement marked on a THERMOMETER or other instrument

cali·bre (*especially US* **cali·ber**) /ˈkælɪbə(r)/ *noun* **1** [U] the quality of sth, especially a person's ability SYN **standard**: *He was impressed by the **high calibre of** applicants for the job.* ◇ *The firm needs more people of your calibre.* **2** [C] the width of the inside of a tube or gun; the width of a bullet

cal·ico /ˈkælɪkəʊ; *NAmE* -koʊ/ *noun* [U] **1** (*especially BrE*) a type of heavy cotton cloth that is usually plain white **2** (*especially NAmE*) a type of rough cotton cloth that has a pattern printed on it

ˈcalico cat *noun* (*NAmE*) = TORTOISESHELL (2)

cali·for·nium /ˌkælɪˈfɔːniəm; *NAmE* -ˈfɔːrn-/ *noun* [U] (*symb.* Cf) a chemical element. Californium is a RADIOACTIVE metal produced artificially with CURIUM or AMERICIUM.

cali·per (*especially NAmE*) = CALLIPER

ca·liph /ˈkeɪlɪf/ *noun* a title used by Muslim rulers, especially in the past

ca·liph·ate /ˈkælɪfeɪt; ˈkeɪl-; *NAmE* ˈkeɪl-/ *noun* **1** the position of a caliph **2** an area of land that is ruled over by a caliph

cal·is·then·ics *noun* (*NAmE*) = CALLISTHENICS

CALL /kɔːl/ *abbr.* computer assisted language learning ➲ compare CAL

call 🔑 /kɔːl/ *verb, noun*
▪ *verb*
▸ GIVE NAME **1** 🔑 [T] to give sb/sth a particular name; to use a particular name or title when you are talking to sb: **~ sb/sth + noun** *They decided to call the baby Mark.* ◇ *His name's Hiroshi but everyone calls him Hiro.* ◇ *What do they call that*

C

new fabric? ◇ **~ sb** *They called their first daughter after her grandmother.* ◇ *We call each other by our first names here.* ➲ see also CALLED

▸ DESCRIBE **2** [T] to describe sb/sth in a particular way; to consider sb/sth to be sth: **~ sb/sth + noun** *I wouldn't call German an easy language.* ◇ *Are you calling me a liar?* ◇ *He was in the front room, or the lounge or whatever you want to call it.* ◇ *I make it ten pounds forty-three you owe me. Let's call it ten pounds.* ◇ **~ sb/sth + adj.** *Would you call it blue or green?* ➲ SYNONYMS at REGARD **3** [T] **~ yourself + noun** to claim that you are a particular type of person, especially when other people question whether this is true: *Call yourself a friend? So why won't you help me, then?* ◇ *She's no right to call herself a feminist.*

▸ SHOUT **4** [I, T] to shout or say sth loudly to attract sb's attention: *I thought I heard somebody calling.* ◇ **~ (out) to sb (for sth)** *She called out to her father for help.* ◇ **~ (sth) out** *He called out a warning from the kitchen.* ◇ **~ sth** *Did somebody call my name?* ◇ **+ speech** *'See you later!' she called.* **5** [T, I] **~ (sb)** to ask sb to come by shouting or speaking loudly: *Will you call the kids in for lunch?* ◇ *Did you call?*

▸ TELEPHONE **6** [T] to ask sb/sth to come quickly to a particular place by telephoning: **~ sb/sth** *to call the fire department/the police/a doctor/an ambulance* ◇ *The doctor has been called to an urgent case.* ◇ *I'll call a taxi for you.* ◇ **~ sb sth** *I'll call you a taxi.* **7** [I, T] to telephone sb: *I'll call again later.* ◇ **~ sb/sth** *I called the office to tell them I'd be late.* ◇ *My brother called me from Spain last night.* ➲ note at PHONE

▸ ORDER SB TO COME **8** [T, usually passive] **+ adv./prep.** (*formal*) to order sb to come to a place: *Several candidates were called for a second interview.* ◇ *The ambassador was called back to London by the prime minister.* ◇ *He felt called to the priesthood* (= had a strong feeling that he must become a priest).

▸ VISIT **9** [I] (*especially BrE*) to make a short visit to a person or place: *I'll call round and see you on my way home.* ◇ **~ on sb** *Let's call on John.* ◇ **~ to do sth** *He was out when I called to see him.*

▸ MEETING/STRIKE, ETC. **10** [T] **~ sth** to order sth to happen; to announce that sth will happen: *to* ***call a meeting/an election/a strike***

▸ OF BIRD/ANIMAL **11** [I] to make the cry that is typical for it

▸ IN GAMES **12** [T, I] **~ (sth)** to say which side of a coin you think will face upwards after it is thrown: *to* ***call heads/tails***

IDM **call sb's 'bluff** to tell sb to do what they are threatening to do, because you believe that they will not be cruel or brave enough to do it **call sth into 'play** (*formal*) to make use of sth: *Chess is a game that calls into play all your powers of concentration.* **call sth into 'question** to doubt sth or make others doubt sth SYN **question**: *His honesty has never been called into question.* **call it a 'day** (*informal*) to decide or agree to stop doing sth: *After forty years in politics I think it's time for me to call it a day* (= to retire). **call it 'quits** (*informal*) **1** to agree to end a contest, disagreement, etc. because both sides seem equal **2** to decide to stop doing sth **call sb 'names** to use insulting words about sb **call the 'shots/'tune** (*informal*) to be the person who controls a situation **call a spade a 'spade** to say exactly what you think without trying to hide your opinion **call 'time (on sth)** (*BrE*) to say or decide that it is time for sth to finish **call sb to ac'count (for/over sth)** to make sb explain a mistake, etc. because they are responsible for it **call sb/sth to 'order** to ask people in a meeting to be quiet so that the meeting can start or continue ➲ more at CARPET *n.*, MIND *n.*, PAY *v.*, POT *n.*, WHAT

PHR V **'call at...** (*BrE*) (of a train, etc.) to stop at a place for a short time: *This train calls at Didcot and Reading.* **,call sb a'way** to ask sb to stop what they are doing and to go somewhere else: *She was called away from the meeting to take an urgent phone call.* **,call 'back** | **,call sb 'back** to telephone sb again or to telephone sb who telephoned you earlier: *She said she'd call back.* ◇ *I'm waiting for someone to call me back with a price.* **'call for sb** (*especially BrE*) to collect sb in order to go somewhere: *I'll call for you at 7 o'clock.* **'call for sth 1** to need sth: *The situation calls for prompt action.* ◇ *'I've been promoted.' 'This calls for a celebration!'* ➲ see also UNCALLED FOR **2** to publicly ask for sth to happen: *They called for the immediate release of the hostages.* ◇ *The opposition have called for him to resign.* **,call sth↔'forth** (*formal*) to produce a particular reaction: *His speech called forth an angry response.* **,call 'in** to telephone a place, especially the place where you work: *Several people have* ***called in sick*** *today.* **,call sb↔'in** to ask for the services of sb: *to call in a doctor/the police* **,call sth↔'in** to order or ask for the return of sth: *Cars with serious faults have been called in by the manufacturers.* **,call sb/sth↔'off** to order a dog or a person to stop attacking, searching, etc. **,call sth↔'off** to cancel sth; to decide that sth will not happen: *to call off a deal/trip/strike* ◇ *They have called off their engagement* (= decided not to get married). ◇ *The game was called off because of bad weather.* **'call on/upon sb** (*formal*) **1** to formally invite or ask sb to speak, etc: *I now call upon the chairman to address the meeting.* **2** to ask or demand that sb do sth: *I feel called upon* (= feel that I ought) *to warn you that...* **,call sb 'out 1** to ask sb to come, especially to an emergency: *to call out an engineer/a plumber/the troops* **2** to order or advise workers to stop work as a protest ➲ related noun CALL-OUT **,call sb↔'up 1** (*especially NAmE*) to make a telephone call to sb **2** to make sb do their training in the army, etc. or fight in a war SYN **conscript**, **draft 3** to give sb the opportunity to play in a sports team, especially for their country ➲ related noun CALL-UP **,call sth↔'up 1** to bring sth back to your mind SYN **recall**: *The smell of the sea called up memories of her childhood.* **2** to use sth that is stored or kept available: *I called his address up on the computer.* ◇ *She called up her last reserves of strength.*

Synonyms

call

cry out • exclaim • blurt • burst out

These words all mean to shout or say sth loudly or suddenly.

call to shout or say sth loudly to attract sb's attention: *I thought I heard someone calling.*

cry out (sth) to shout sth loudly, especially when you need help or are in trouble: *She cried out for help.* ◇ *I cried out his name.*

exclaim to say sth suddenly and loudly, especially because of a strong emotion: *'It isn't fair!' he exclaimed angrily.*

blurt to say sth suddenly and without thinking carefully enough: *He* ***blurted out*** *the answer without thinking.*

burst out to say sth suddenly and loudly, especially with a lot of emotion: *'He's a bully!' the little boy burst out.*

PATTERNS

- to call/cry out/exclaim/blurt out (sth) **to** sb
- to call/cry out **for** sth
- to cry out/exclaim/blurt out/burst out **in/with** sth
- to call/cry out/exclaim/blurt out/burst out **suddenly**
- to call/cry out/exclaim/burst out **loudly**

■ ***noun***

▸ ON TELEPHONE **1** [C] (also **'phone call**) the act of speaking to sb on the telephone: *to* ***get/have/receive a call*** *from sb* ◇ *to* ***give sb/to make a call*** ◇ *Were there any calls for me while I was out?* ◇ *I'll* ***take*** (= answer) ***the call*** *upstairs.* ◇ *I left a message but he didn't* ***return my call.*** ◇ *a* ***local call*** ◇ *a* ***long-distance call*** ➲ note at PHONE ➲ see also WAKE-UP CALL

▸ LOUD SOUND **2** [C] a loud sound made by a bird or an animal, or by a person to attract attention: *the distinctive call of the cuckoo* ◇ *a call for help*

▸ VISIT **3** [C] a short visit to sb's house: *The doctor has five calls to make this morning.* ◇ (*old-fashioned*) ***to pay a call*** *on an old friend*

▸ REQUEST/DEMAND **4** [C] **~ (for sth)** a request, an order or a demand for sb to do sth or to go somewhere: *calls for the* *minister to resign* ◇ *calls for national unity* ◇ *This is the last call for passengers travelling on British Airways flight 199 to Rome.* ◇ (*formal*) *a* ***call to arms*** (= a strong request to fight in the army, etc.) ➲ see also CURTAIN CALL **5** [U] **no ~ for sth | no ~ (for sb) to do sth** no demand for sth; no reason for sb's behaviour: *There isn't a lot of call for small specialist shops nowadays.* **6** [C] **~ on sb/sth** a demand or pressure placed on sb/sth: *She is a busy woman with many calls on her time.*

▸ OF A PLACE **7** [sing.] **~ (of sth)** (*literary*) a strong feeling of attraction that a particular place has for you: *the call of the sea/your homeland*

▸ TO A PARTICULAR JOB **8** [sing.] **~ (to do sth)** a strong feeling that you want to do sth, especially a particular job

▸ DECISION **9** [C] (*informal*) a decision: *It's your call!* ◇ *a* ***good/bad*** *call* ◇ *That's a tough call.*

▸ IN TENNIS **10** [C] a decision made by the UMPIRE: *There was a disputed call in the second set.*

▸ IN CARD GAMES **11** [C] a player's BID or turn to BID

IDM **the call of ˈnature** (*humorous*) the need to go to the toilet **have first ˈcall (on sb/sth)** to be the most important person or thing competing for sb's time, money, etc. and to be dealt with or paid for before other people or things: *The children always have first call on her time.* **(be) on ˈcall** (of a doctor, police officer, etc.) available for work if necessary, especially in an emergency: *I'll be on call the night of the party.* ➲ see also ON-CALL *adj.* ➲ more at BECK, CLOSE² *adj.*

call·back /ˈkɔːlbæk/ *noun* **1** [C] a telephone call which you make to sb who has just called you **2 Callback™** [U, C] = RINGBACK **3** [U, C] (*computing*) a process by which the user of a computer or telephone system proves their identity by contacting a computer, which then contacts them **4** [C] (*especially NAmE*) an occasion when you are asked to return somewhere, for example for a second interview when you are trying to get a job **5** [C] an occasion when people are asked to return goods that they have bought, usually because they are not safe

ˈcall box *noun* **1** (*BrE*) = PHONE BOX **2** (*NAmE*) a small box beside a road, with a telephone in it, to call for help after an accident, etc.

ˈcall centre (*BrE*) (*NAmE* **ˈcall center**) *noun* an office in which a large number of people work using telephones, for example arranging insurance for people, or taking customers' orders and answering questions

called 🔑 /kɔːld/ *adj.* [not before noun] having a particular name: *What's their son called?* ◇ *I don't know anyone called Scott.* ◇ *I've forgotten what the firm he works for is called.* ◇ *What's it called again? Yeah, that's right. A modem.* ➲ see also SO-CALLED

call·er /ˈkɔːlə(r)/ *noun* **1** a person who is making a telephone call: *The caller hung up.* ◇ *an anonymous caller* **2** a person who goes to a house or a building **3** a person who shouts out the steps for people performing a SQUARE DANCE or COUNTRY DANCE

ˈcaller ID *noun* [U] a system that uses a device on your telephone to identify and display the telephone number of the person who is calling you

ˈcall girl *noun* a PROSTITUTE who makes her arrangements by telephone

cal·lig·raphy /kəˈlɪgrəfi/ *noun* [U] beautiful HANDWRITING that you do with a special pen or brush; the art of producing this ▸ **cal·lig·raph·er** *noun*

ˈcall-in (*NAmE*) (*BrE* **ˈphone-in**) *noun* a radio or television programme in which people can telephone and make comments or ask questions about a particular subject

call·ing /ˈkɔːlɪŋ/ *noun* **1** a strong desire or feeling of duty to do a particular job, especially one in which you help other people SYN **vocation**: *He realized that his calling was to preach the gospel.* **2** (*formal*) a profession or career

ˈcalling card *noun* (*NAmE*) **1** (*BrE* **ˈvisiting card**) (also **card** *BrE, NAmE*) (especially in the past) a small card with your name on it which you leave with sb after, or instead of, a formal visit **2** = PHONECARD

cal·li·per *noun* (*BrE*) (also **cali·per** *NAmE, BrE*) /ˈkælɪpə(r)/ **1 callipers** [pl.] an instrument with two long thin parts joined at one end, used for measuring the DIAMETER of tubes and round objects (= the distance across them): *a pair of callipers* **2** (*BrE*) (*NAmE* **brace**) [C, usually pl.] a metal support for weak or injured legs

C

cal·lis·then·ics (*BrE*) (*NAmE* **cal·is·then·ics**) /ˌkælɪsˈθenɪks/ *noun* [U+sing./pl. v.] physical exercises intended to develop a strong and attractive body

ˈcall letters *noun* [pl.] (*NAmE*) the letters that are used to identify a radio or television station: *the call letters WNBC*

cal·lous /ˈkæləs/ *adj.* not caring about other people's feelings or suffering SYN **cruel, unfeeling**: *a* ***callous killer/attitude/act*** ◇ *a* ***callous disregard*** *for the feelings of others* ▸ **cal·lous·ly** *adv.* **cal·lous·ness** *noun* [U]

cal·loused (also **cal·lused**) /ˈkæləst/ *adj.* (of the skin) made rough and hard, usually by hard work: *calloused hands*

ˈcall-out *noun* an occasion when sb is called to do repairs, rescue sb, etc: *a call-out charge* ◇ *ambulance call-outs*

cal·low /ˈkæləʊ; *NAmE* -loʊ/ *adj.* (*formal, disapproving*) young and without experience SYN **inexperienced**: *a callow youth*

ˈcall sign *noun* the letters and numbers used in radio communication to identify the person who is sending a message

ˈcall-up (*BrE*) *noun* **1** [U, C, usually sing.] an order to join the armed forces SYN **conscription, the draft**: *to receive your* ***call-up papers*** **2** [C] the opportunity to play in a sports team, especially for your country: *His recent form has earned him a call-up to the England squad.*

cal·lus /ˈkæləs/ *noun* an area of thick hard skin on a hand or foot, usually caused by rubbing

cal·lused = CALLOUSED

ˈcall waiting *noun* [U] a telephone service that tells you if sb is trying to call you when you are using the telephone

calm 🔑 /kɑːm/ *adj., verb, noun*

■ ***adj.*** (**calm·er, calm·est**) **1** 🔑 not excited, nervous or upset: *It is important to* ***keep calm*** *in an emergency.* ◇ *Try to* ***remain calm.*** ◇ *Her voice was surprisingly calm.* ◇ *The city is calm again* (= free from trouble and fighting) *after yesterday's riots.* **2** 🔑 (of the sea) without large waves **3** 🔑 (of the weather) without wind: *a calm, cloudless day* ▸ **calm·ly** 🔑 *adv.*: *'I'll call the doctor,' he said calmly.* **calm·ness** *noun* [U]

■ ***verb*** 🔑 **~ sb/sth** to make sb/sth become quiet and more relaxed, especially after strong emotion or excitement: *Have some tea; it'll calm your nerves.* ◇ *His presence had* ***a calming influence.*** ➲ see also TRAFFIC CALMING

PHR V **ˌcalm ˈdown | ˌcalm sb/sth↔ˈdown** 🔑 to become or make sb become calm: *Look, calm down! We'll find her.* ◇ *We waited inside until things calmed down.* ◇ *He took a few deep breaths to calm himself down.*

■ ***noun*** [C, U] **1** 🔑 a quiet and peaceful time or situation: *the calm of a summer evening* ◇ *The police* ***appealed for calm.*** **2** a quiet and relaxed manner: *Her previous calm gave way to terror.*

IDM **the calm before the storm** a calm time immediately before an expected period of violent activity or argument

Which Word?

calm / calmness

- The noun **calm** is usually used to talk about a peaceful time or situation: *There was a short period of uneasy calm after the riot.* It can also be used to describe a person's manner: *She spoke with icy calm.* **Calmness** is usually used to talk about a person: *We admired his calmness under pressure.*

Calor gas™ /ˈkælə gæs; *NAmE* ˈkælər/ (*BrE*) (*US* ˈ**cooking gas**) *noun* [U] a type of gas stored as a liquid under pressure in metal containers and used for heating and cooking in places where there is no gas supply

C

cal·orie /ˈkæləri/ *noun* **1** a unit for measuring how much energy food will produce: *No sugar for me, thanks—I'm* ***counting my calories.*** ◇ *a* ***low-calorie drink/diet*** ➲ COLLOCATIONS at DIET **2** (*technical*) a unit for measuring a quantity of heat; the amount of heat needed to raise the temperature of a gram of water by one degree Celsius

cal·or·if·ic /ˌkæləˈrɪfɪk/ *adj.* [usually before noun] **1** (*technical*) relating to the amount of energy contained in food or fuel: *the calorific value of food* (= the quantity of heat or energy produced by a particular amount of food) **2** (of food and drink) containing a lot of calories and likely to make you fat: *calorific chocolate cake*

cal·or·im·eter /ˌkæləˈrɪmɪtə(r)/ *noun* (*technical*) a device which measures the amount of heat in a chemical reaction

calque /kælk/ (also ˈ**loan translation**) *noun* (*linguistics*) a word or expression in a language that is a translation of a word or expression in another language: *'Traffic calming' is a calque of the German 'Verkehrsberuhigung'.*

cal·umny /ˈkæləmni/ *noun* (*pl.* -ies) (*formal*) **1** [C] a false statement about a person that is made to damage their reputation **2** [U] the act of making such a statement SYN **slander**

Cal·va·dos /ˈkælvədɒs; *NAmE* ˌkælvəˈdoʊs/ *noun* [U] a French drink made by DISTILLING apple juice

calve /kɑːv; *NAmE* kæv/ *verb* [I] (of a cow) to give birth to a CALF

calves *pl.* of CALF

Cal·vin·ist /ˈkælvɪnɪst/ (also **Cal·vin·is·tic**) *adj.* **1** connected with a Church that follows the teachings of the French Protestant, John Calvin **2** having very strict moral attitudes ▸ **Cal·vin·ism** *noun* [U] **Cal·vin·ist** *noun*

ca·lypso /kəˈlɪpsəʊ; *NAmE* -soʊ/ *noun* [C, U] (*pl.* -os) a Caribbean song about a subject of current interest; this type of music

calyx /ˈkeɪlɪks/ *noun* (*pl.* **ca·lyxes** or **ca·ly·ces** /ˈkeɪlɪsiːz/) (*technical*) the ring of small green leaves (called SEPALS) that protect a flower before it opens

CAM /kæm/ *abbr.* computer aided manufacturing

cam /kæm/ *noun* a part on a wheel that sticks out and changes the CIRCULAR movement of the wheel into up-and-down or backwards-and-forwards movement

cama·rad·erie /ˌkæməˈrɑːdəri; *NAmE* ˌkɑːməˈrɑːdəri/ *noun* [U] a feeling of friendship and trust among people who work or spend a lot of time together

cam·ber /ˈkæmbə(r)/ *noun* a slight downward curve from the middle of a road to each side

cam·bric /ˈkæmbrɪk/ *noun* [U] a type of thin white cloth made from cotton or LINEN

cam·cord·er /ˈkæmkɔːdə(r); *NAmE* -kɔːrd-/ *noun* a video camera that records pictures and sound and that can be carried around

came *past tense* of COME

camel /ˈkæml/ *noun* **1** [C] an animal with a long neck and one or two HUMPS on its back, used in desert countries for riding on or for carrying goods ➲ compare DROMEDARY **2** [U] = CAMEL HAIR: *a camel coat* IDM see STRAW

ˈ**camel hair** *noun* [U] (also **camel**) a type of thick soft pale brown cloth made from camel's hair or a mixture of camel's hair and wool, used especially for making coats: *a camel-hair coat*

cam·el·lia /kəˈmiːliə/ *noun* a bush with shiny leaves and white, red or pink flowers that look like ROSES and are also called camellias

Cam·em·bert /ˈkæməmbeə(r); *NAmE* -ber/ *noun* [U, C] a type of soft French cheese with a strong flavour

cameo /ˈkæmiəʊ; *NAmE* -mioʊ/ *noun* (*pl.* -os) **1** a small part in a film/movie or play for a famous actor: *a* ***cameo role/appearance*** **2** a short piece of writing that gives a good description of sb/sth **3** a piece of jewellery that consists of a raised design, often of a head, on a background of a different colour: *a* ***cameo brooch/ring***

cam·era 0‒ /ˈkæmərə/ *noun* a piece of equipment for taking photographs, moving pictures or television pictures: *Just point the camera and press the button.* ◇ *Cameras started clicking as soon as she stepped out of the car.* ◇ *a* ***TV/video camera*** ◇ *a camera crew*
IDM **in** ˈ**camera** (*law*) in a judge's private room, without the press or the public being present: *The trial was held in camera.* **on** ˈ**camera** being filmed or shown on television: *Are you prepared to tell your story on camera?*

cam·era·man /ˈkæmrəmæn/, **came·ra·woman** /ˈkæmrəwʊmən/ *noun* (*pl.* -men /-men/, -women /-wɪmɪn/) a person whose job is operating a camera for making films/movies or television programmes ➲ note at GENDER

camera obscura /ˌkæmərə əbˈskjʊərə; *NAmE* -skjʊrə/ *noun* an early form of camera consisting of a dark box with a tiny hole or LENS in the front and a small screen inside, on which the image appears

ˈ**camera operator** *noun* (also ˈ**camera person** *pl.* ˈ**camera people**) a person whose job is operating a camera for making films/movies or television programmes

cam·era·work /ˈkæmrəwɜːk; *NAmE* -wɜːrk/ *noun* [U] the style in which sb takes photographs or uses a film/movie camera

cami·sole /ˈkæmɪsəʊl; *NAmE* -soʊl/ *noun* a short piece of women's underwear that is worn on the top half of the body and is held up with narrow strips of material over the shoulders

camo·mile (*especially BrE*) (also **chamo·mile** especially in *NAmE*) /ˈkæməmaɪl/ *noun* [U] a plant with a sweet smell and small white and yellow flowers. Its dried leaves and flowers are used to make tea, medicine, etc: *camomile tea*

cam·ou·flage /ˈkæməflɑːʒ/ *noun, verb*
■ ***noun*** **1** [U] a way of hiding soldiers and military equipment, using paint, leaves or nets, so that they look like part of their surroundings: *a camouflage jacket* (= covered with green and brown marks and worn by soldiers) ◇ *troops dressed in camouflage* **2** [U, sing.] the way in which an animal's colour or shape matches its surroundings and makes it difficult to see **3** [U, sing.] behaviour that is deliberately meant to hide the truth: *Her angry words were camouflage for the way she felt.*
■ ***verb*** **~ sth (with sth)** to hide sb/sth by making them or it look like the things around, or like sth else: *The soldiers camouflaged themselves with leaves.* ◇ *Her size was camouflaged by the long loose dress she wore.* ➲ SYNONYMS at HIDE

camp 0‒ /kæmp/ *noun, verb, adj.*
■ ***noun***
▸ IN TENTS **1** 0‒ [C, U] a place where people live temporarily in tents or temporary buildings: *Let's return to camp.* ◇ *to* ***pitch/make camp*** (= put up tents) ◇ *to break camp* (= to take down tents) ➲ see also HOLIDAY CAMP
▸ HOLIDAY/VACATION **2** 0‒ [C, U] a place where young people go on holiday/vacation and take part in various activities or a particular activity: *a tennis camp* ◇ *He spent two weeks at camp this summer.* ◇ *summer camp* ➲ see also FAT CAMP
▸ PRISON, ETC. **3** 0‒ [C] (used in compounds) a place where people are kept in temporary buildings or tents, especially by a government and often for long periods: *a refugee camp* ◇ *a camp guard* ➲ see also CONCENTRATION CAMP, PRISON CAMP, TRANSIT CAMP
▸ ARMY **4** [C, U] a place where soldiers live while they are training or fighting: *an army camp*
▸ GROUP OF PEOPLE **5** [C] a group of people who have the same ideas about sth and oppose people with other ideas: *the socialist camp* ◇ *We were in opposing camps.* **6** [C] one of the sides in a competition and the people connected with it: *There was an air of confidence in the England camp.*
IDM see FOOT *n.*
■ ***verb***
▸ LIVE IN TENT **1** 0‒ [I] to put up a tent and live in it for a short

time: *I camped overnight in a field.* **2** 0- [I] **go camping** to stay in a tent, especially while you are on holiday/vacation: *They go camping in France every year.*
▸ STAY FOR SHORT TIME **3** [I] **~ (out)** to live in sb's house for a short time, especially when you do not have a bed there: *I'm camping out at a friend's apartment at the moment.*
PHR V **ˌcamp ˈout** to live outside for a short time: *Dozens of reporters camped out on her doorstep.* **ˌcamp it ˈup** (*BrE, informal*) to behave in a very exaggerated manner, especially to attract attention to yourself or to make people laugh
■ ***adj.*** **1** (of a man or his manner) deliberately behaving in a way that some people think is typical of a HOMOSEXUAL SYN **effeminate** **2** exaggerated in style, especially in a deliberately amusing way: *The movie is a camp celebration of the fashion industry.*

Synonyms

campaign

battle • struggle • drive • war • fight

These are all words for an effort made to achieve or prevent sth.

campaign a series of planned activities that are intended to achieve a particular social, commercial or political aim: *the campaign for parliamentary reform ◇ an advertising campaign*

battle a competition or argument between people or groups of people trying to win power or control: *She finally won the legal battle for compensation. ◇ the endless battle between man and nature*

struggle a competition or argument between people or groups of people trying to win power or control: *the struggle for independence ◇ the struggle between good and evil*

BATTLE OR STRUGGLE?

A **struggle** is always about things that seem absolutely necessary, such as life and death or freedom. A **battle** can also be about things that are not absolutely necessary, just desirable, or about the pleasure of winning: *the battle/struggle between good and evil ◇ ~~a legal struggle for compensation~~ ◇ ~~a struggle of wills/wits~~.*

drive an organized effort by a group of people to achieve sth: *the drive for greater efficiency ◇ a drive to reduce energy consumption*

CAMPAIGN OR DRIVE?

A **campaign** is usually aimed at getting other people to do sth; a **drive** may be an attempt by people to get themselves to do sth: *From today, we're going on an* ***economy drive*** (= we must spend less). A **campaign** may be larger, more formal and more organized than a **drive**.

war [sing.] an effort over a long period of time to get rid of or stop sth bad: *the war against crime*

fight [sing.] the work of trying to stop or prevent sth bad or achieve sth good; an act of competing, especially in a sport: *Workers won their fight to stop compulsory redundancies.*

WAR OR FIGHT?

A **war** is about stopping things, like drugs and crime, that everyone agrees are bad. A **fight** can be about achieving justice for yourself.

PATTERNS

- a campaign/battle/struggle/drive/war/fight **against** sth
- a campaign/battle/struggle/drive/fight **for** sth
- a **one-man/one-woman/personal** campaign/battle/struggle/war
- a **bitter** campaign/battle/struggle/drive/war/fight
- to **launch/embark on** a campaign/battle/drive
- to **lead/continue** the campaign/battle/struggle/drive/fight
- to **win/lose** a battle/struggle/war/fight

cam·paign 0- /kæmˈpeɪn/ *noun, verb*
■ ***noun*** **1** 0- **~ (against/for sth)** a series of planned activities that are intended to achieve a particular social, commercial or political aim: *to* ***conduct a campaign*** *◇ a campaign against ageism in the workplace ◇ the campaign for parliamentary reform ◇ an anti-smoking campaign ◇ Today police* ***launched*** (= began) ***a campaign*** *to reduce road accidents. ◇ an advertising campaign ◇ an election campaign ◇ the President's* ***campaign team/manager*** ➲ COLLOCATIONS at VOTE **2** a series of attacks and battles that are intended to achieve a particular military aim during a war
■ ***verb*** [I, T] to take part in or lead a campaign, for example to achieve political change or in order to win an election: *The party* ***campaigned vigorously*** *in the north of the country.* ◇ **~ for/against sb/sth** *We have campaigned against whaling for the last 15 years.* ◇ **~ to do sth** *They are campaigning to save the area from building development.* ▸ **cam·paign·ing** *noun* [U]

cam·paign·er /kæmˈpeɪnə(r)/ *noun* a person who leads or takes part in a campaign, especially one for political or social change: *a leading human rights campaigner ◇ a campaigner on environmental issues ◇ a campaigner for women priests ◇ an* ***old/veteran/seasoned campaigner*** (= a person with a lot of experience of a particular activity) ◇ (*especially NAmE*) *Obama campaigners* (= people working for Obama in a campaign)

cam·pa·nile /ˌkæmpəˈniːli/ *noun* a tower that contains a bell, especially one that is not part of another building

cam·pan·ology /ˌkæmpəˈnɒlədʒi; *NAmE* -ˈnɑːl-/ *noun* [U] (*formal*) the study of bells and the art of ringing bells ▸ **cam·pan·olo·gist** /-ədʒɪst/ *noun* ➲ see also BELL-RINGER

ˌcamp ˈbed (*BrE*) (*NAmE* **cot**) *noun* a light narrow bed that you can fold up and carry easily ➲ VISUAL VOCAB page V20

camp·er /ˈkæmpə(r)/ *noun* **1** a person who spends a holiday/vacation living in a tent or at a holiday camp **2** (also **ˈcamper van**) (both *BrE*) (*NAmE* **RV**, **reˌcreˌational ˈvehicle**) (also **motor·home** *NAmE, BrE*) a large vehicle designed for people to live and sleep in when they are travelling ➲ VISUAL VOCAB page V47 **3** (*NAmE*) (*BrE* **caravan**) a road vehicle without an engine that is pulled by a car, designed for people to live and sleep in, especially when they are on holiday/vacation ➲ VISUAL VOCAB page V47 IDM see HAPPY *adj.*

camp·fire /ˈkæmpfaɪə(r)/ *noun* an outdoor fire made by people who are sleeping outside or living in a tent

ˌcamp ˈfollower *noun* **1** a person who supports a particular group or political party but is not a member of it **2** (in the past) a person who was not a soldier but followed an army from place to place to sell goods or services

camp·ground /ˈkæmpgraʊnd/ (*NAmE*) (*BrE* **camp·site**, **ˈcamping site**) *noun* a place where people on holiday/vacation can put up their tents, park their CARAVAN/CAMPER, etc, often with toilets, water, etc.

cam·phor /ˈkæmfə(r)/ *noun* [U] a white substance with a strong smell, used in medicine, for making plastics and to keep insects away from clothes

camp·ing 0- /ˈkæmpɪŋ/ *noun* [U] living in a tent, etc. on holiday/vacation: *Do you* ***go camping****? ◇ a camping trip*

camp·site /ˈkæmpsaɪt/ *noun* **1** (also **ˈcamping site**) (both *BrE*) (*NAmE* **ˈcamp·ground**) a place where people on holiday/vacation can put up their tents, park their CARAVAN/CAMPER, etc, often with toilets, water, etc. **2** (*NAmE*) a place in a CAMPGROUND where you can put up one tent or park one CAMPER, etc.

cam·pus /ˈkæmpəs/ *noun* the buildings of a university or college and the land around them: *She lives* ***on campus*** (= within the main university area). ◇ *campus life*

cam·shaft /ˈkæmʃɑːft; *NAmE* -ʃæft/ *noun* a long straight piece of metal with a CAM on it joining parts of machinery, especially in a vehicle

C

can[1] **0-w** /kən; *strong form* kæn/ *modal verb* ➲ see also CAN[2] (*negative* **can·not** /ˈkænɒt; *NAmE* -nɑːt/, *short form* **can't** /kɑːnt; *NAmE* kænt/, *pt* **could** /kəd; *strong form* kʊd/, *negative* **could not**, *short form* **couldn't** /ˈkʊdnt/)
1 0-w used to say that it is possible for sb/sth to do sth, or for sth to happen: *I can run fast.* ◇ *Can you call back tomorrow?* ◇ *He couldn't answer the question.* ◇ *The stadium can be emptied in four minutes.* ◇ *I can't promise anything, but I'll do what I can.* ◇ *Please let us know if you cannot attend the meeting.* **2** 0-w used to say that sb knows how to do sth: *She can speak Spanish.* ◇ *Can he cook?* ◇ *I could drive a car before I left school.* **3** 0-w used with the verbs 'feel', 'hear', 'see', 'smell', 'taste': *She could feel a lump in her breast.* ◇ *I can hear music.* **4** 0-w used to show that sb is allowed to do sth: *You can take the car, if you want.* ◇ *We can't wear jeans at work.* **5** 0-w (*informal*) used to ask permission to do sth: *Can I read your newspaper?* ◇ *Can I take you home?* **6** 0-w (*informal*) used to ask sb to help you: *Can you help me with this box?* ◇ *Can you feed the cat, please?* **7** 0-w used in the negative for saying that you are sure sth is not true: *That can't be Mary—she's in New York.* ◇ *He can't have slept through all that noise.* **8** 0-w used to express doubt or surprise: *What can they be doing?* ◇ *Can he be serious?* ◇ *Where can she have put it?* **9** 0-w used to say what sb/sth is often like: *He can be very tactless sometimes.* ◇ *It can be quite cold here in winter.* **10** 0-w used to make suggestions: *We can eat in a restaurant, if you like.* ◇ *I can take the car if necessary.* **11** (*informal*) used to say that sb must do sth, usually when you are angry: *You can shut up or get out!* ➲ note at MODAL
IDM **can't be doing with sb/sth/sb doing sth** (*informal*) used to say that you do not like sth and are unwilling to accept it: *I can't be doing with people who complain all the time.* **no can ˈdo** (*informal*) used to say that you are not able or willing to do sth: *Sorry, no can do. I just don't have the time.*

Which Word?

can / may

- **Can** and **cannot** (or **can't**) are the most common words used for asking for, giving or refusing permission: *Can I borrow your calculator?* ◇ *You can come with us if you want to.* ◇ *You can't park your car there.*
- **May** (negative **may not**) is used as a polite and fairly formal way to ask for or give permission: *May I borrow your newspaper?* ◇ *You may come if you wish.* It is often used in official signs and rules: *Visitors may use the swimming pool between 7 a.m. and 7 p.m.* ◇ *Students may not use the college car park.* The form **mayn't** is hardly ever used in modern English.

can[2] **0-w** /kæn/ *noun, verb* ➲ see also CAN[1]
■ ***noun*** **1** 0-w (*BrE* also **tin**) [C] a metal container in which food and drink is sold: *a can of beans* ◇ *a beer/paint can* ➲ VISUAL VOCAB page V29 HELP In *NAmE* **can** is the usual word used for both food and drink. In *BrE* **can** is always used for drink, but **tin** or **can** can be used for food, paint, etc. **2** 0-w [C] the amount contained in a can: *We drank a can of Coke each.* **3** [C] a metal or plastic container for holding or carrying liquids: *an oil can* ◇ *a watering can* **4** [C] a metal container in which liquids are kept under pressure and let out in a fine spray when you press a button on the lid: *a can of hairspray* ➲ VISUAL VOCAB page V29 **5 the can** [sing.] (*NAmE, slang*) prison **6 the can** [sing.] (*NAmE, slang*) the toilet
IDM **a can of ˈworms** (*informal*) if you open up **a can of worms**, you start doing sth that will cause a lot of problems and be very difficult **be in the ˈcan** (*informal*) (especially of filmed or recorded material) to be completed and ready for use ➲ more at CARRY
■ ***verb*** (-nn-) **1 ~ sth** (*especially NAmE*) to preserve food by putting it in a can **2 ~ sb** (*NAmE, informal*) to dismiss sb from their job SYN **fire, sack**

Grammar Point

can / could / be able to / manage

- **Can** is used to say that somebody knows how to do something: *Can you play the piano?* It is also used with verbs of seeing, noticing, etc: *I can hear someone calling*, and with passive infinitives: *The DVD can be rented from your local store.*
- **Can** or **be able to** are used to say that something is possible or that somebody has the opportunity to do something: *Can you/are you able to come on Saturday?*
- You use **be able to** to form the future and perfect tenses and the infinitive: *You'll be able to get a taxi outside the station.* ◇ *I haven't been able to get much work done today.* ◇ *She'd love to be able to play the piano.*
- **Could** is used to talk about what someone was generally able to do in the past: *Our daughter could walk when she was nine months old.*
- You use **was/were able to** or **manage** (but not **could**) when you are saying that something was possible on a particular occasion in the past: *I was able to/managed to find some useful books in the library.* ◇ ~~*I could find some useful books in the library.*~~ In negative sentences, **could not** can also be used: *We weren't able to/didn't manage to/couldn't get there in time.* **Could** is also used with this meaning with verbs of seeing, noticing, understanding, etc: *I could see there was something wrong.*
- **Could have** is used when you are saying that it was possible for somebody to do something in the past but they did not try: *I could have won the game but decided to let her win.*

ˈCanada Day *noun* (in Canada) a national holiday held on 1 July to celebrate the original joining together of PROVINCES to form Canada in 1867

ˌCanada ˈgoose *noun* a common N American GOOSE with a black head and neck

Can·adian /kəˈneɪdiən/ *adj., noun*
■ ***adj.*** from or connected with Canada
■ ***noun*** a person from Canada

canal /kəˈnæl/ *noun* **1** a long straight passage dug in the ground and filled with water for boats and ships to travel along; a smaller passage used for carrying water to fields, crops, etc: *the Panama/Suez Canal* ◇ *an irrigation canal* **2** a tube inside the body through which liquid, food or air can pass ➲ see also ALIMENTARY CANAL

caˈnal boat *noun* a long narrow boat used on canals ➲ VISUAL VOCAB page V44

can·al·ize (*BrE* also **-ise**) /ˈkænəlaɪz/ *verb* **1 ~ sth** (*technical*) to make a river wider, deeper or straighter; to make a river into a canal **2 ~ sth** (*formal*) to control an emotion, activity, etc. so that it is aimed at a particular purpose SYN **channel** ▶ **can·al·iza·tion, -isa·tion** /ˌkænəlaɪˈzeɪʃn; *NAmE* -nələˈz-/ *noun* [U]

can·apé /ˈkænəpeɪ; *NAmE* ˌkænəˈpeɪ/ *noun* [usually pl.] a small biscuit or piece of bread with cheese, meat, fish, etc. on it, usually served with drinks at a party

can·ard /kæˈnɑːd; ˈkænɑːd; *NAmE* kəˈnɑːrd; ˈkænɑːrd/ *noun* (*formal*) a false report or piece of news

can·ary /kəˈneəri; *NAmE* -ˈneri/ *noun* (*pl.* **-ies**) a small yellow bird with a beautiful song, often kept in a CAGE as a pet IDM see CAT

can·asta /kəˈnæstə/ *noun* [U] a card game played with two packs of cards, in which players try to collect sets of cards

can·can /ˈkænkæn/ *noun* (often **the cancan**) [sing.] a fast dance in which a line of women kick their legs high in the air

can·cel **0-w** /ˈkænsl/ *verb* (-ll-, *US* -l-)
1 0-w [T] **~ sth** to decide that sth that has been arranged

will not now take place: *All flights have been cancelled because of bad weather.* ◇ *Don't forget to cancel the newspaper* (= arrange for it not to be delivered) *before going away.* ➲ compare POSTPONE **2** [T, I] **~ (sth)** to say that you no longer want to continue with an agreement, especially one that has been legally arranged: *to cancel a policy/subscription* ◇ *Is it too late to cancel my order?* ◇ *The US has agreed to cancel debts* (= say that they no longer need to be paid) *totalling $10 million.* ◇ *No charge will be made if you cancel within 10 days.* **3** [T] **~ sth** to mark a ticket or stamp so that it cannot be used again

PHR V **,cancel 'out | ,cancel sth↔'out** if two or more things **cancel out** or one **cancels out** the other, they are equally important but have an opposite effect on a situation so that the situation does not change: *Recent losses have cancelled out any profits made at the start of the year.* ◇ *The advantages and disadvantages would appear to* ***cancel each other out.***

can·cel·la·tion /ˌkænsəˈleɪʃn/ (US **can·cel·ation**) *noun* **1** [U, C] a decision to stop sth that has already been arranged from happening; a statement that sth will not happen: *We need at least 24 hours' notice of cancellation.* ◇ *a cancellation fee* ◇ *Heavy seas can cause cancellation of ferry services.* ◇ *Cancellations must be made in writing.* **2** [C] something that has been cancelled: *Are there any cancellations for this evening's performance?* (= tickets that have been returned) **3** [U] the fact of making sth no longer valid: *the cancellation of the contract*

Can·cer /ˈkænsə(r)/ *noun* **1** [U] the fourth sign of the ZODIAC, the CRAB **2** [sing.] a person born when the sun is in this sign, that is between 22 June and 22 July, approximately ▸ **Can·cer·ian** /kænˈsɪəriən; *NAmE* -ˈsɪr-/ *noun, adj.*

can·cer /ˈkænsə(r)/ *noun*
1 [U, C] a serious disease in which GROWTHS of cells, also called cancers, form in the body and kill normal body cells. The disease often causes death: *lung/breast cancer* ◇ *cancer of the bowel/stomach* ◇ *Most skin cancers are completely curable.* ◇ *The cancer has spread to his stomach.* ◇ *cancer patients* ◇ *cancer research* ➲ COLLOCATIONS at ILL **2** [C] (*literary*) an evil or dangerous thing that spreads quickly: *Violence is a cancer in our society.* ▸ **can·cer·ous** /ˈkænsərəs/ *adj.*: *to become cancerous* ◇ ***cancerous cells/growths/tumours***

can·dela /kænˈdelə; -ˈdiːlə; ˈkændɪlə/ *noun* (*physics*) (*abbr.* cd) a unit for measuring the amount of light that shines in a particular direction

can·de·la·bra /ˌkændəˈlɑːbrə/ (also *less frequent* **can·de·la·brum** /ˌkændəˈlɑːbrəm/) *noun* (*pl.* **can·de·la·bra, can·de·la·bras**, *US* also **can·de·la·brums**) an object with several branches for holding CANDLES or lights

can·did /ˈkændɪd/ *adj.* **1** saying what you think openly and honestly; not hiding your thoughts: *a candid statement/interview* ➲ see also CANDOUR **2** a **candid** photograph is one that is taken without the person in it knowing that they are being photographed ▸ **can·did·ly** *adv.*

can·dida /ˈkændɪdə/ *noun* [U] (*medical*) the FUNGUS that can cause an infection of THRUSH

can·di·dacy /ˈkændɪdəsi/ *noun* [C, U] (*pl.* -ies) (also **can·di·da·ture** especially in *BrE*) the fact of being a candidate in an election: *to* ***announce/declare/withdraw your candidacy*** *for the post*

can·di·date /ˈkændɪdət; -deɪt/ *noun*
1 **~ (for sth)** a person who is trying to be elected or is applying for a job: *one of the leading candidates for the presidency* ◇ *a presidential candidate* ◇ (*BrE*) *He stood as a candidate in the local elections.* ◇ *There were a large number of candidates for the job.* ➲ COLLOCATIONS at VOTE **2** (*BrE*) a person taking an exam: *a candidate for the degree of MPhil* **3** **~ (for sth)** a person or group that is considered suitable for sth or that is likely to get sth or to be sth: *Our team is a* ***prime candidate for*** *relegation this year.* ◇ *Your father is an obvious candidate for a heart attack.*

can·di·da·ture /ˈkændɪdətʃə(r)/ *noun* (*especially BrE*) = CANDIDACY

can·died /ˈkændid/ *adj.* [only before noun] (of fruit or other food) preserved by boiling in sugar; cooked in sugar: *candied fruit*

can·dle /ˈkændl/ *noun* a round stick of WAX with a piece of string (called a WICK) through the middle which is lit to give light as it burns ➲ VISUAL VOCAB page V19

IDM **cannot hold a candle to sb/sth** is not as good as sb or sth else: *His singing can't hold a candle to Bocelli's.* ➲ more at BURN *v.*, WORTH *adj.*

candle·light /ˈkændllaɪt/ *noun* [U] the light that a candle produces: *to read by candlelight*

candle·lit /ˈkændllɪt/ *adj.* [only before noun] lit by candles: *a romantic candlelit dinner*

candle·stick /ˈkændlstɪk/ *noun* an object for holding a candle ➲ VISUAL VOCAB page V19

candle·wick /ˈkændlwɪk/ *noun* [U] a type of soft cotton cloth with a raised pattern of threads, used especially for making BEDSPREADS

ˌcan-ˈdo *adj.* [only before noun] (*informal*) willing to try new things and expecting that they will be successful: ***a can-do attitude/spirit***

cand·our (*especially US* **can·dor**) /ˈkændə(r)/ *noun* [U] the quality of saying what you think openly and honestly SYN **frankness**: *'I don't trust him,' he said in a rare moment of candour.* ➲ see also CANDID

C & W *abbr.* COUNTRY AND WESTERN

candy /ˈkændi/ *noun* [U, C] (*pl.* -ies) (*NAmE*) sweet food made of sugar and/or chocolate, eaten between meals; a piece of this SYN **sweet**: *a box of candy* ◇ *a candy store* ◇ *a candy bar* ◇ *Who wants the last piece of candy?* ➲ see also ARM CANDY, EYE CANDY

IDM **be like taking ˌcandy from a ˈbaby** (*informal*) used to emphasize how easy it is to do sth

ˈcandy apple (*NAmE*) (*BrE* **ˈtoffee apple**) *noun* an apple covered with a thin layer of hard toffee and fixed on a stick

candy·floss /ˈkændiflɒs; *NAmE* -flɔːs; -flɑːs/ (*BrE*) (*NAmE* **ˌcotton ˈcandy**) *noun* [U] a type of sweet/candy in the form of a mass of sticky threads made from melted sugar and served on a stick, especially at FAIRGROUNDS

candy·man /ˈkændimæn/ *noun* (*US, slang*) a person who sells illegal drugs

ˈcandy-striped *adj.* (of cloth or clothes) with a pattern of stripes in white and another colour, especially pink

cane /keɪn/ *noun, verb*
■ ***noun*** **1** [C] the hard hollow STEM of some plants, for example BAMBOO or sugar ➲ VISUAL VOCAB page V16 **2** [U] these STEMS used as a material for making furniture, etc: *a cane chair* **3** [C] a piece of cane or a thin stick, used as a support for plants **4** [C] a piece of cane or a thin stick, used to help sb to walk ➲ see also WALKING STICK **5** [C] a piece of cane or a thin stick, used in the past in some schools for beating children as a punishment: *to* ***get the cane*** (= be punished with a cane)
■ ***verb*** **~ sb** to hit a child with a cane as a punishment ▸ **can·ing** *noun* [U, C]: *the abolition of caning in schools*

ˈcane rat *noun* a type of large RODENT found in wild areas of Africa, which can be used for food ➲ see also CUTTING GRASS

ˈcane sugar *noun* [U] sugar obtained from the juice of SUGAR CANE

ca·nine /ˈkeɪnaɪn/ *adj., noun*
■ ***adj.*** connected with dogs
■ ***noun*** **1** (also **ˈcanine tooth**) one of the four pointed teeth in the front of a human's or animal's mouth ➲ compare INCISOR, MOLAR **2** (*formal*) a dog

can·is·ter /ˈkænɪstə(r)/ *noun* **1** a container with a lid for holding tea, coffee, etc. **2** a strong metal container containing gas or a chemical substance, especially one that bursts when it is fired from a gun or thrown: *tear-gas can-*

C

isters **3** a flat round metal container used for storing film: *a film canister*

can·ker /ˈkæŋkə(r)/ *noun* **1** [U] a disease that destroys the wood of plants and trees **2** [U] a disease that causes sore areas in the ears of animals, especially dogs and cats **3** [C] (*literary*) an evil or dangerous influence that spreads and affects people's behaviour

ˈcanker sore (*NAmE*) (*BrE* **ˈmouth ulcer**) *noun* a small sore area in the mouth

can·na·bis /ˈkænəbɪs/ *noun* [U] a drug made from the dried leaves and flowers or RESIN of the HEMP plant, which is smoked or eaten and which gives the user a feeling of being relaxed. Use of the drug is illegal in many countries.

canned /kænd/ *adj.* **1** (*BrE* also **tinned**) (of food) preserved in a can: *canned food/soup* **2 ~ laughter/music** the sound of people laughing or music that has been previously recorded and used in television and radio programmes

can·nel·loni /ˌkænəˈləʊni; *NAmE* -ˈloʊni/ *noun* [U] (from *Italian*) large tubes of PASTA that are served filled with meat or cheese

can·nery /ˈkænəri/ *noun* (*pl.* -ies) a factory where food is put into cans

can·ni·bal /ˈkænɪbl/ *noun* **1** a person who eats human flesh: *a tribe of cannibals* **2** an animal that eats the flesh of other animals of the same kind ▸ **can·ni·bal·ism** /ˈkænɪbəlɪzəm/ *noun* [U]: *to practise cannibalism* **can·ni·bal·is·tic** /ˌkænɪbəˈlɪstɪk/ *adj.*

can·ni·bal·ize (*BrE* also **-ise**) /ˈkænɪbəlaɪz/ *verb* **1 ~ sth** to take the parts of a machine, vehicle, etc. and use them to repair or build another **2 ~ sth** (*business*) (of a company) to reduce the sales of one of its products by introducing a similar new product ▸ **can·ni·bal·iza·tion, -isa·tion** /ˌkænɪbəlaɪˈzeɪʃn; *NAmE* -ləˈz-/ *noun* [U]

can·non /ˈkænən/ *noun, verb*

■ ***noun*** (*pl.* **can·non** or **can·nons**) **1** an old type of large heavy gun, usually on wheels, that fires solid metal or stone balls ➲ see also LOOSE CANNON, WATER CANNON **2** an automatic gun that is fired from an aircraft

■ ***verb*** [I] **+ adv./prep.** to hit sb/sth with a lot of force while you are moving: *He ran around the corner, cannoning into a group of kids.*

can·non·ade /ˌkænəˈneɪd/ *noun* a continuous firing of large guns

can·non·ball /ˈkænənbɔːl/ *noun* a large metal or stone ball that is fired from a CANNON

ˈcannon fodder *noun* [U] soldiers who are thought of not as people whose lives are important, but as material to be used up in war

can·not 0‑ /ˈkænɒt; *NAmE* -nɑːt/ = CAN NOT: *I cannot believe the price of the tickets!*

can·nula /ˈkænjʊlə/ *noun* (*pl.* **can·nulae** /-liː/ or **can·nulas**) (*medical*) a thin tube that is put into a VEIN or other part of the body, for example to give sb medicine

canny /ˈkæni/ *adj.* intelligent, careful and showing good judgement, especially in business or politics: *a canny politician* ◇ *a canny move* ▸ **can·nily** *adv.*

canoe /kəˈnuː/ *noun, verb*

■ ***noun*** a light narrow boat which you move along in the water with a PADDLE ➲ VISUAL VOCAB page V45 ➲ see also KAYAK

■ ***verb*** (**ca·noe·ing, ca·noed, ca·noed**) [I] (often **go canoeing**) to travel in a canoe

ca·noe·ing /kəˈnuːɪŋ/ *noun* [U] the sport of travelling in or racing a CANOE: *to go canoeing*

ca·noe·ist /kəˈnuːɪst/ *noun* a person travelling in a canoe

can·ola /kəˈnəʊlə; *NAmE* -ˈnoʊ-/ *noun* [U] a type of cooking oil made from a variety of RAPESEED that was developed in Canada and is grown widely in N America. The plant is also referred to as **canola**.

canon /ˈkænən/ *noun* **1** a Christian priest with special duties in a CATHEDRAL **2** (*formal*) a generally accepted rule, standard or principle by which sth is judged **3** a list of the books or other works that are generally accepted as the genuine work of a particular writer or as being important: *the Shakespeare canon* ◇ *'Wuthering Heights' is a central book in the canon of English literature.* **4** a piece of music in which singers or instruments take it in turns to repeat the MELODY (= tune)

ca·non·ic·al /kəˈnɒnɪkl; *NAmE* -ˈnɑːn-/ (also **ca·non·ic**) *adj.* **1** included in a list of holy books that are accepted as genuine; connected with works of literature that are highly respected **2** according to the law of the Christian Church **3** (*technical*) in the simplest accepted form in mathematics

caˈnonical form *noun* (*linguistics*) the most basic form of a GRAMMATICAL structure or expression, for example the infinitive in the case of a verb

can·on·ize (*BrE* also **-ise**) /ˈkænənaɪz/ *verb* [usually passive] **~ sb** (of the POPE) to state officially that sb is now a SAINT ➲ compare BEATIFY ▸ **can·on·iza·tion, -isa·tion** /ˌkænənaɪˈzeɪʃn; *NAmE* -nəˈz-/ *noun* [C, U]

ˌcanon ˈlaw *noun* [U] the law of the Christian church

ca·noo·dle /kəˈnuːdl/ *verb* [I] (*BrE, old-fashioned, informal*) (of two people) to kiss and touch each other in a sexual way

ˈcan opener (*especially NAmE*) (*BrE* also **ˈtin opener**) *noun* a kitchen UTENSIL (= a tool) for opening cans of food ➲ VISUAL VOCAB page V23

can·opy /ˈkænəpi/ *noun* (*pl.* -ies) **1** a cover that is fixed or hangs above a bed, seat, etc. as a shelter or decoration ➲ VISUAL VOCAB page V20 ➲ picture at PUSHCHAIR **2** a layer of sth that spreads over an area like a roof, especially branches of trees in a forest **3** (*especially NAmE*) a roof that is supported on posts and is sometimes also attached at one side to a building: *a new steel entrance canopy for the building* ◇ *a fabric canopy to provide shade in the backyard* **4** a cover for the COCKPIT of an aircraft

canst /kænst/ *verb* **thou canst** (*old use*) used to mean 'you can', when talking to one person

cant /kænt/ *noun, verb*

■ ***noun*** [U] statements, especially about moral or religious issues, that are not sincere and that you cannot trust **SYN hypocrisy**

■ ***verb*** [I, T] **~ (sth)** (*formal*) to be or put sth in a sloping position

can't /kɑːnt; *NAmE* kænt/ *short form* cannot

Cantab /ˈkæntæb/ *abbr.* (used after degree titles) of Cambridge University: *James Cox MA (Cantab)*

Can·ta·bri·gian /ˌkæntəˈbrɪdʒiən/ *adj.* (*formal* or *humorous*) relating to Cambridge in England, or to Cambridge University

can·ta·loupe /ˈkæntəluːp/ *noun* a MELON (= a type of fruit) with a green skin and orange flesh

can·tan·ker·ous /kænˈtæŋkərəs/ *adj.* bad-tempered and always complaining: *a cantankerous old man*

can·tata /kænˈtɑːtə/ *noun* a short musical work, often on a religious subject, sung by SOLO singers, often with a CHOIR and ORCHESTRA ➲ compare MOTET, ORATORIO

can·teen /kænˈtiːn/ *noun* **1** (*especially BrE*) a place where food and drink are served in a factory, a school, etc. **2** a small container used by soldiers, travellers, etc. for carrying water or other liquid **3 ~ of cutlery** (*BrE*) a box containing a set of knives, forks and spoons

canˈteen culture *noun* [U] (*BrE, disapproving*) a set of old-fashioned and unfair attitudes that are said to exist among police officers

can·ter /ˈkæntə(r)/ *noun, verb*

■ ***noun*** [usually sing.] a movement of a horse at a speed that is fairly fast but not very fast; a ride on a horse moving at this speed: *She set off at a canter.*

■ ***verb*** [I, T] **~ (sth)** (of a horse or rider) to move or make a horse move at a canter: *We cantered along the beach.* ➲ compare GALLOP, TROT

can·ticle /ˈkæntɪkl/ *noun* a religious song with words taken from the Bible

can·ti·lever /ˈkæntɪliːvə(r)/ *noun* a long piece of metal or wood that sticks out from a wall to support the end of a bridge or other structure: *a cantilever bridge* ➲ VISUAL VOCAB page V12

canto /ˈkæntəʊ; *NAmE* -toʊ/ *noun* (*pl.* -os) one of the sections of a long poem

can·ton /ˈkæntɒn; *NAmE* -tən; -tɑːn/ *noun* one of the official regions which some countries, such as Switzerland, are divided into

Can·ton·ese /ˌkæntəˈniːz/ *noun, adj.*
▪ ***noun*** **1** (also **Yue**) [U] a form of Chinese spoken mainly in southern China, including Hong Kong **2** [C] (*pl.* **Can·ton·ese**) a person whose first language is Cantonese
▪ ***adj.*** of or relating to people who speak Cantonese, or their language or culture: *Cantonese cooking*

can·ton·ment /kænˈtɒnmənt; -ˈtuːn-; *NAmE* kænˈtɑːn-/ *noun* a military camp, especially a permanent British military camp in India in the past

Can·to·pop /ˈkæntəʊpɒp; *NAmE* ˈkæntoʊpɑːp/ *noun* [U] (*SEAsianE*) a type of pop music that combines Cantonese words and Western pop music

can·tor /ˈkæntɔː(r)/ *noun* the person who leads the singing in a SYNAGOGUE or in a church CHOIR

Ca·nuck /kəˈnʌk/ *noun* (*NAmE, informal*) a person from Canada, especially sb whose first language is French. In the US this term is often offensive.

Ca·nute /kəˈnjuːt; *NAmE* -ˈnuːt/ *noun* used to describe a person who tries to stop sth from happening but will never succeed: *His efforts to stem the tide of violent crime have been as effective as Canute's.* ORIGIN From the story of a Danish king of England who was said to have stood in front of the sea and shown people that he was not able to order the water that was moving in towards the land to turn back. The story is often changed to suggest that Canute really thought that he could turn back the sea.

can·vas /ˈkænvəs/ *noun* **1** [U] a strong heavy rough material used for making tents, sails, etc. and by artists for painting on ➲ COLLOCATIONS at ART **2** [C] a piece of canvas used for painting on; a painting done on a piece of canvas, using oil paints: *a sale of the artist's early canvases* ➲ VISUAL VOCAB page V35
IDM **under ˈcanvas** in a tent

can·vass /ˈkænvəs/ *verb* **1** [I, T] to ask sb to support a particular person, political party, etc, especially by going around an area and talking to people: **~ (for sth)** *He spent the whole month canvassing for votes.* ◇ **~ sb (for sth)** *Party workers are busy canvassing local residents.* **2** [T] to ask people about sth in order to find out what they think about it: **~ sth** *He has been canvassing opinion on the issue.* ◇ **~ sb** *People are being canvassed for their views on the proposed new road.* **3** [T] **~ support** to try and get support from a group of people SYN **drum up** **4** [T] **~ sth** to discuss an idea thoroughly: *The proposal is currently being canvassed.* ▸ **can·vass** *noun*: *to carry out a canvass* **can·vass·er** *noun*

can·yon /ˈkænjən/ *noun* a deep valley with steep sides of rock SYN **gorge** ➲ VISUAL VOCAB page V4

can·yon·ing /ˈkænjənɪŋ/ *noun* [U] a sport in which you jump into a mountain stream and allow yourself to be carried down at high speed

CAP /ˌsiː eɪ ˈpiː/ *abbr.* Common Agricultural Policy (of the European Union)

cap 0‑ /kæp/ *noun, verb*
▪ ***noun***
▸ HAT **1** 0‑ a type of soft flat hat with a PEAK (= a hard curved part sticking out in front). Caps are worn especially by men and boys, often as part of a uniform: *a school cap* ➲ see also BASEBALL CAP, CLOTH CAP, MOB CAP ➲ VISUAL VOCAB page V53 **2** 0‑ (usually in compounds) a soft hat that fits closely and is worn for a particular purpose: *a shower cap* **3** a soft hat with a square flat top worn by some university teachers and students at special ceremonies ➲ compare MORTAR BOARD
▸ IN SPORT **4** (*BrE*) a cap given to sb who is chosen to play for a school, country, etc; a player chosen to play for their country, etc: *He won his first cap* (= was first chosen to play) *for England against France.* ◇ *There are three new caps in the side.*
▸ ON PEN/BOTTLE **5** a cover or top for a pen, bottle, etc: *a lens cap* ➲ VISUAL VOCAB page V29 ➲ see also FILLER CAP, HUBCAP ➲ SYNONYMS at LID
▸ LIMIT ON MONEY **6** an upper limit on an amount of money that can be spent or borrowed by a particular institution or in a particular situation: *The government has placed a cap on local council spending.*
▸ IN TOY GUNS **7** a small paper container with EXPLOSIVE powder inside it, used especially in toy guns
▸ FOR WOMAN **8** (*BrE*) = DIAPHRAGM (2) ➲ see also ICE CAP, THINKING CAP
IDM **go cap in ˈhand (to sb)** (*BrE*) (*US* **go hat in ˈhand**) to ask sb for sth, especially money, in a very polite way that makes you seem less important **if the cap fits (, wear it)** (*BrE*) (*NAmE* **if the shoe fits (, wear it)**) (*informal*) if you feel that a remark applies to you, you should accept it and take it as a warning or criticism: *I didn't actually say that you were lazy, but if the cap fits…* ➲ more at FEATHER *n.*
▪ ***verb*** (-pp-)
▸ COVER TOP **1** [usually passive] **~ sth (with sth)** to cover the top or end of sth with sth: *mountains capped with snow* ◇ *snow-capped mountains*
▸ LIMIT MONEY **2** [often passive] **~ sth** (*especially BrE*) to limit the amount of money that can be charged for sth or spent on sth: *a capped mortgage*
▸ BEAT **3** **~ sth** (*especially BrE*) to say or do sth that is funnier, more impressive, etc. than sth that has been said or done before: *What an amazing story. Can anyone cap that?*
▸ TOOTH **4** [usually passive] **~ sth** to put an artificial covering on a tooth to make it look more attractive SYN **crown**: *He's had his front teeth capped.*
▸ IN SPORT **5** [usually passive] **~ sb** (*BrE*) to choose sb to play in their country's national team for a particular sport: *He has been capped more than 30 times for Wales.*
IDM **to cap/top it ˈall** (*informal*) used to introduce the final piece of information that is worse than the other bad things that you have just mentioned

cap·abil·ity AW /ˌkeɪpəˈbɪləti/ *noun* [C, U] (*pl.* -ies) **1** **~ (to do sth/of doing sth)** the ability or qualities necessary to do sth: *Animals in the zoo have lost the capability to catch/of catching food for themselves.* ◇ ***beyond/within the capabilities*** *of current technology* ◇ *Age affects the range of a person's capabilities.* **2** the power or weapons that a country has for war or for military action: *Britain's* ***nuclear/military capability***

cap·able 0‑ AW /ˈkeɪpəbl/ *adj.*
1 0‑ having the ability or qualities necessary for doing sth: **~ of sth** *You are capable of better work than this.* ◇ **~ of doing sth** *He's quite capable of lying to get out of trouble.* ◇ *I'm perfectly capable of doing it myself, thank you.* **2** 0‑ having the ability to do things well SYN **skilled, competent**: *She's a very capable teacher.* ◇ *I'll leave the organization in your capable hands.* OPP **incapable** ▸ **cap·ably** *adv.*

cap·acious /kəˈpeɪʃəs/ *adj.* (*formal*) having a lot of space to put things in SYN **roomy**: *capacious pockets*

cap·aci·tance /kəˈpæsɪtəns/ *noun* [U] (*physics*) **1** the ability of a system to store an electrical charge **2** a comparison between change in electrical charge and change in electrical POTENTIAL

cap·aci·tor /kəˈpæsɪtə(r)/ *noun* (*physics*) a device used to store an electrical charge

cap·acity 0‑ AW /kəˈpæsəti/ *noun* (*pl.* -ies)
▸ OF CONTAINER **1** 0‑ [U, C, usually sing.] the number of things or people that a container or space can hold: *The theatre has a seating capacity of 2 000.* ◇ *a fuel tank with a capacity of 50 litres* ◇ *The hall was filled* ***to capacity*** (= was completely full). ◇ *They played to a* ***capacity crowd*** (= one that filled all the space or seats).
▸ ABILITY **2** 0‑ [C, usually sing., U] the ability to understand or

to do sth: *intellectual capacity* ◇ **~ for sth** *She has an enormous capacity for hard work.* ◇ **~ for doing sth** *Limited resources are restricting our capacity for developing new products.* ◇ **~ to do sth** *your capacity to enjoy life*

▸ ROLE **3** [C, usually sing.] the official position or function that sb has SYN **role**: *acting **in her capacity as** manager* ◇ *We are simply involved in an **advisory capacity** on the project.*

▸ OF FACTORY/MACHINE **4** [sing., U] the quantity that a factory, machine, etc. can produce: *The factory is working at full capacity.*

▸ OF ENGINE **5** [C, U] the size or power of a piece of equipment, especially the engine of a vehicle: *an engine with a capacity of 1 600 cc*

ca·pari·soned /kəˈpærɪsnd/ *adj.* in the past a **caparisoned** horse or other animal was one covered with a decorated cloth

cape /keɪp/ *noun* **1** a loose outer piece of clothing that has no sleeves, fastens at the neck and hangs from the shoulders, like a CLOAK but shorter: *a bullfighter's cape* **2** (*abbr.* C.) (often in place names) a piece of high land that sticks out into the sea: *Cape Horn*

caped /keɪpt/ *adj.* wearing a cape

caper /ˈkeɪpə(r)/ *noun, verb*

■ ***noun*** **1** [usually pl.] the small green flower BUD of a Mediterranean bush, preserved in VINEGAR and used to flavour dishes and sauces **2** (*informal*) an activity, especially one that is illegal or dangerous: *A call to the police should put an end to their little caper.* **3** an amusing film/movie that contains a lot of action: *a British spy caper* **4** a short jumping or dancing movement: *He **cut a** little celebratory **caper*** (= jumped or danced a few steps) *in the middle of the road.*

■ ***verb*** [I] (+ **adv./prep.**) (*formal*) to run or jump around in a happy and excited way

cap·er·cail·lie /ˌkæpəˈkeɪli; *NAmE* ˌkæpər-/ *noun* a large GROUSE (= a type of large bird) similar to a TURKEY, the male of which spreads out his tail feathers to attract females

ca·pil·lary /kəˈpɪləri; *NAmE* ˈkæpəleri/ *noun* (*pl.* -ies) (*anatomy*) any of the smallest tubes in the body that carry blood ➲ VISUAL VOCAB page V48

caˈpillary action *noun* [U] (*technical*) the force that makes a liquid move up a narrow tube

cap·ital /ˈkæpɪtl/ *noun, adj.*

■ ***noun***

▸ CITY **1** (also ˌ**capital ˈcity**) [C] the most important town or city of a country, usually where the central government operates from: *Cairo is the capital of Egypt.* ◇ (*figurative*) *Paris, the fashion capital of the world*

▸ MONEY **2** [sing.] a large amount of money that is invested or is used to start a business: *to set up a business with a **starting capital** of £100 000* **3** [U] wealth or property that is owned by a business or a person: *capital assets* ◇ *capital expenditure* (= money that an organization spends on buildings, equipment, etc.) **4** [U] (*technical*) people who use their money to start businesses, considered as a group: *capital and labour*

▸ LETTER **5** (also ˌ**capital ˈletter**) [C] a letter of the form and size that is used at the beginning of a sentence or a name (= A,B,C rather than a,b,c): *Use **block capitals*** (= separate capital letters). ◇ *Please write **in capitals/in capital letters**.*

▸ ARCHITECTURE **6** the top part of a column ➲ VISUAL VOCAB page V12

IDM **make capital (out) of sth** to use a situation for your own advantage: *The opposition parties are making political capital out of the government's problems.*

■ ***adj.***

▸ PUNISHMENT **1** [only before noun] involving punishment by death: *a capital offence*

▸ LETTER **2** [only before noun] (of letters of the alphabet) having the form and size used at the beginning of a sentence or a name: *English is written with a capital 'E'.* ➲ compare LOWER CASE

▸ EXCELLENT **3** (*old-fashioned, BrE*) excellent

IDM **with a capital A, B, etc.** used to emphasize that a word has a stronger meaning than usual in a particular situation: *He was romantic with a capital R.*

ˌ**capital ˈgains** *noun* [pl.] profits that you make from selling sth, especially property: *to pay **capital gains tax***

ˈ**capital goods** *noun* [pl.] (*business*) goods such as factory machines that are used for producing other goods ➲ compare CONSUMER GOODS

ˌ**capital-inˈtensive** *adj.* (of a business, an industry, etc.) needing large amounts of money in order to operate well ➲ compare LABOUR-INTENSIVE

cap·it·al·ism /ˈkæpɪtəlɪzəm/ *noun* [U] an economic system in which a country's businesses and industry are controlled and run for profit by private owners rather than by the government ➲ compare SOCIALISM

cap·it·al·ist /ˈkæpɪtəlɪst/ *noun, adj.*

■ ***noun*** **1** a person who supports capitalism **2** a person who owns or controls a lot of wealth and uses it to produce more wealth

■ ***adj.*** (also *less frequent* **cap·it·al·is·tic** /ˌkæpɪtəˈlɪstɪk/) based on the principles of capitalism: *a **capitalist society/system/economy***

cap·it·al·ize (*BrE* also **-ise**) /ˈkæpɪtəlaɪz/ *verb* **1** **~ sth** to write or print a letter of the alphabet as a capital; to begin a word with a capital letter **2** **~ sth** (*business*) to sell possessions in order to change them into money **3** [usually passive] **~ sth** (*business*) to provide a company etc. with the money it needs to function ▸ **cap·it·al·iza·tion, -isa·tion** /ˌkæpɪtəlaɪˈzeɪʃn; *NAmE* -ləˈz-/ *noun* [U, sing.]

PHR V ˈ**capitalize on/upon sth** to gain a further advantage for yourself from a situation SYN **take advantage of sth**: *The team failed to capitalize on their early lead.*

ˌ**capital ˈletter** *noun* = CAPITAL (5)

ˌ**capital ˈpunishment** *noun* [U] punishment by death

ˌ**capital ˈsum** *noun* a single payment of money that is made to sb, for example by an insurance company

capi·ta·tion /ˌkæpɪˈteɪʃn/ *noun* [C, U] (*technical*) a tax or payment of an equal amount for each person; the system of payments of this kind: *a capitation fee for each pupil*

cap·itol /ˈkæpɪtl/ *noun* **1** (usually **the Capitol**) [sing.] the building in Washington DC where the US Congress (= the national parliament) meets to work on new laws **2** [usually sing.] a building in each US state where politicians meet to work on new laws: *the California state capitol*

ˌ**Capitol ˈHill** (also *informal* **the Hill**) *noun* [sing.] used to refer to the US Capitol and the activities that take place there

ca·pitu·late /kəˈpɪtʃuleɪt/ *verb* **1** [I] **~ (to sb/sth)** to agree to do sth that you have been refusing to do for a long time SYN **give in, yield**: *They were finally forced to capitulate to the terrorists' demands.* **2** [I] **~ (to sb/sth)** to stop resisting an enemy and accept that you are defeated SYN **surrender**: *The town capitulated after a three-week siege.* ▸ **ca·pitu·la·tion** /kəˌpɪtʃuˈleɪʃn/ *noun* [C, U]

Cap·let™ /ˈkæplət/ *noun* a long narrow tablet of medicine, with rounded ends, that you swallow

capo·eira /ˌkæpʊˈeɪrə/ *noun* [U] a Brazilian system of movements which is similar to dance and MARTIAL ARTS

capon /ˈkeɪpɒn; ˈkeɪpən; *NAmE* -pɑːn/ *noun* a male chicken that has been CASTRATED (= had part of its sex organs removed) and made fat for eating

cap·pella ➲ A CAPPELLA

cap·puc·cino /ˌkæpuˈtʃiːnəʊ; *NAmE* -noʊ/ *noun* (*pl.* -os) **1** [U] a type of coffee made with hot FROTHY milk and sometimes with chocolate powder on the top **2** [C] a cup of cappuccino

ca·price /kəˈpriːs/ *noun* (*formal*) **1** [C] a sudden change in attitude or behaviour for no obvious reason SYN **whim** **2** [U] the tendency to change your mind suddenly or behave unexpectedly

ca·pri·cious /kəˈprɪʃəs/ *adj.* (*formal*) **1** showing sudden changes in attitude or behaviour SYN **unpredictable** **2** changing suddenly and quickly SYN **changeable**: *a ca-*

pricious climate ▸ **ca·pri·cious·ly** *adv.* **ca·pri·cious·ness** *noun* [U]

Cap·ri·corn /ˈkæprɪkɔːn; *NAmE* -kɔːrn/ *noun* **1** [U] the 10th sign of the ZODIAC, the Goat **2** [C] a person born when the sun is in this sign, that is between 21 December and 20 January, approximately

ca·pri pants /kəˈpriː pænts/ (also **ca·pris**) *noun* [pl.] a type of trousers/pants for women ending between the knee and the foot

caps /kæps/ *noun* [pl.] (*technical*) capital letters: *a title printed in bold caps*

cap·sicum /ˈkæpsɪkəm/ *noun* (*technical*) a type of plant which has hollow fruits. Some types of these are eaten as vegetables, either raw or cooked, for example SWEET PEPPERS or CHILLIES.

cap·size /kæpˈsaɪz; *NAmE* ˈkæpsaɪz/ *verb* [I, T] **~ (sth)** if a boat **capsizes** or sth **capsizes** it, it turns over in the water

cap·stan /ˈkæpstən/ *noun* a thick CYLINDER that winds up a rope, used for lifting heavy objects such as an ANCHOR on a ship

cap·stone /ˈkæpstəʊn; *NAmE* -stoʊn/ *noun* **1** a stone placed at the top of a building or wall **2** (*especially NAmE*) the best and final thing that sb achieves, thought of as making their career or life complete

cap·sule /ˈkæpsjuːl; *NAmE* also ˈkæpsl/ *noun* **1** a small container which has a measured amount of a medicine inside and which dissolves when you swallow it **2** a small plastic container with a substance or liquid inside **3** the part of a SPACECRAFT in which people travel and that often separates from the main ROCKET **4** (*technical*) a shell or container for seeds or eggs in some plants and animals ➲ see also TIME CAPSULE

Capt. *abbr.* captain

cap·tain 🔑 /ˈkæptɪn/ *noun, verb*

■ ***noun*** **1** 🔑 the person in charge of a ship or commercial aircraft: *Captain Cook* ◇ *The captain gave the order to abandon ship.* **2** 🔑 an officer of fairly high rank in the navy, the army and the US AIR FORCE: *Captain Lance Price* ➲ see also GROUP CAPTAIN **3** 🔑 the leader of a group of people, especially a sports team: *She was captain of the hockey team at school.* **4** an officer of high rank in a US police or fire department

■ ***verb*** **~ sth** to be a captain of a sports team or a ship

cap·tain·cy /ˈkæptənsi/ *noun* [C, usually sing., U] (*pl.* -ies) the position of captain of a team; the period during which sb is captain

ˌcaptain of ˈindustry *noun* (*pl.* captains of industry) used in newspapers, etc. to describe a person who manages a large business company

cap·tion /ˈkæpʃn/ *noun, verb*

■ ***noun*** words that are printed underneath a picture, CARTOON, etc. that explain or describe it ➲ see also CLOSED-CAPTIONED

■ ***verb*** [usually passive] **~ sth** to write a caption for a picture, photograph, etc.

cap·tiv·ate /ˈkæptɪveɪt/ *verb* [often passive] **~ sb** to keep sb's attention by being interesting, attractive, etc. SYN **enchant**: *The children were captivated by her stories.*

cap·tiv·at·ing /ˈkæptɪveɪtɪŋ/ *adj.* taking all your attention; very attractive and interesting SYN **enchanting**: *He found her captivating.*

cap·tive /ˈkæptɪv/ *adj., noun*

■ ***adj.*** **1** kept as a prisoner or in a confined space; unable to escape: *captive animals* ◇ *They were* ***taken captive*** *by masked gunmen.* ◇ *captive breeding* (= the catching and breeding of wild animals) **2** [only before noun] not free to leave a particular place or to choose what you want do to: *A salesman loves to have a* ***captive audience*** (= listening because they have no choice).

■ ***noun*** a person who is kept as a prisoner, especially in a war

cap·tiv·ity /kæpˈtɪvəti/ *noun* [U] the state of being kept as a prisoner or in a confined space: *He was held* ***in captivity*** *for three years.* ◇ *The bird had escaped from captivity.*

cap·tor /ˈkæptə(r)/ *noun* (*formal*) a person who captures a person or an animal and keeps them as a prisoner

cap·ture 🔑 /ˈkæptʃə(r)/ *verb, noun*

■ ***verb***

▸ CATCH **1** 🔑 to catch a person or an animal and keep them as a prisoner or in a confined space: **~ sb** *Allied troops captured over 300 enemy soldiers.* ◇ **~ sth** *The animals are captured in nets and sold to local zoos.*

▸ TAKE CONTROL **2** 🔑 **~ sth** to take control of a place, building, etc. using force: *The city was captured in 1941.* **3** 🔑 **~ sth** to succeed in getting control of sth that other people are also trying to control: *The company has captured 90% of the market.*

▸ MAKE SB INTERESTED **4 ~ sb's attention/imagination/interest** to make sb interested in sth: *They use puppets to capture the imagination of younger audiences.*

▸ FEELING/ATMOSPHERE **5 ~ sth** to succeed in accurately expressing a feeling, an atmosphere, etc. in a picture, piece of writing, film/movie, etc. SYN **catch**: *The article captured the mood of the nation.*

▸ FILM/RECORD/PAINT **6** [often passive] **~ sb/sth on film/tape/canvas, etc.** to film/record/paint, etc. sb/sth: *The attack was captured on film by security cameras.*

▸ SB'S HEART **7 ~ sb's heart** to make sb love you

▸ COMPUTING **8 ~ sth** to put sth into a computer in a form it can use

■ ***noun*** 🔑 [U] the act of capturing sb/sth or of being captured: *the capture of enemy territory* ◇ *He evaded capture for three days.* ◇ *data capture*

capy·bara /ˌkæpɪˈbɑːrə; *NAmE* ˌkæpəˈberə/ *noun* (*pl.* capy·bara or capy·baras) an animal like a very large RABBIT with thick legs and small ears, which lives near water in S and Central America

car 🔑 /kɑː(r)/ *noun*

1 🔑 (also *BrE formal* ˈ**motor car**) (*NAmE* also **auto·mo·bile**) a road vehicle with an engine and four wheels that can carry a small number of passengers: *Paula got into the car and drove off.* ◇ *'How did you come?' '****By car****.'* ◇ *Are you going* ***in the car****?* ◇ *a* ***car driver/manufacturer/dealer*** ◇ *a* ***car accident/crash*** ◇ *Where can I park the car?* ➲ COLLOCATIONS at DRIVING ➲ VISUAL VOCAB page V42 ➲ see also COMPANY CAR **2** 🔑 (also **rail·car** both *NAmE*) a separate section of a train: *Several cars went off the rails.* ➲ VISUAL VOCAB page V47 **3** (*BrE*) (in compounds) a coach/car on a train of a particular type: *a* ***sleeping/dining car***

ca·rafe /kəˈræf/ *noun* a glass container with a wide neck in which wine or water is served at meals; the amount contained in a carafe ➲ VISUAL VOCAB page V19

cara·mel /ˈkærəmel/ *noun* **1** [U, C] a type of hard sticky sweet/candy made from butter, sugar and milk; a small piece of this **2** [U] burnt sugar used for adding colour and flavour to food ➲ see also CRÈME CARAMEL **3** [U] a light brown colour

cara·mel·ize (*BrE* also **-ise**) /ˈkærəməlaɪz/ *verb* **1** [I] (of sugar) to turn into caramel **2** [T] **~ sth** to cook sth, especially fruit, with sugar so that it is covered with caramel

cara·pace /ˈkærəpeɪs/ *noun* (*technical*) the hard shell on the back of some animals such as CRABS, that protects them

carat /ˈkærət/ *noun* (*abbr.* ct) **1** a unit for measuring the weight of diamonds and other PRECIOUS STONES, equal to 200 milligrams **2** (*especially BrE*) (*NAmE* usually **karat**) a unit for measuring how pure gold is. The purest gold is 24 carats: *an 18-carat gold ring*

cara·van /ˈkærəvæn/ *noun* **1** (*BrE*) (*NAmE* **camp·er**) a road vehicle without an engine that is pulled by a car, designed for people to live and sleep in, especially when they are on holiday/vacation: *a* ***caravan site/park*** ➲ VISUAL VOCAB page V47 **2** (*BrE*) a covered vehicle that is pulled by a horse and used for living in: *a Gypsy caravan* **3** a group of people with vehicles or animals who are travelling together, especially across the desert

C

cara·van·ning /ˈkærəvænɪŋ/ *noun* [U] (*BrE*) the activity of spending a holiday/vacation in a caravan

cara·van·serai /ˌkærəˈvænsəraɪ; -ri/ (*especially US* **cara·van·sary** /ˌkærəˈvænsəri/ *pl.* **-ies**) *noun* **1** in the past, a place where travellers could stay in desert areas of Asia and N Africa **2** (*formal*) a group of people travelling together

cara·way /ˈkærəweɪ/ *noun* [U] the dried seeds of the caraway plant, used to give flavour to food: *caraway seeds*

carb /kɑːb; *NAmE* kɑːrb/ *noun* = CARBOHYDRATE

car·bine /ˈkɑːbaɪn; *NAmE* ˈkɑːrb-/ *noun* a short light RIFLE

carbo·hy·drate /ˌkɑːbəʊˈhaɪdreɪt; *NAmE* ˌkɑːrboʊ-/ *noun* **1** (also *informal* **carb**) [C, U] a substance such as sugar or STARCH that consists of CARBON, HYDROGEN and OXYGEN. Carbohydrates in food provide the body with energy and heat. **2 carbohydrates** (also *informal* **carbs**) [pl.] foods such as bread, potatoes and rice that contain a lot of carbohydrate

car·bol·ic /kɑːˈbɒlɪk; *NAmE* kɑːrˈbɑːlɪk/ (also **carˌbolic ˈacid**) *noun* [U] a chemical that kills bacteria, used as an ANTISEPTIC and as a DISINFECTANT (= to prevent infection from spreading): *carbolic soap*

ˈcar bomb *noun* a bomb hidden inside or under a car

car·bon /ˈkɑːbən; *NAmE* ˈkɑːrb-/ *noun* **1** [U] (*symb.* C) a chemical element. Carbon is found in all living things, existing in a pure state as diamond, GRAPHITE and BUCKMINSTERFULLERENE: *carbon fibre* **2** [U] used when referring to the gas CARBON DIOXIDE in terms of the effect it has on the earth's climate in causing GLOBAL WARMING: *carbon emissions/levels/taxes* ◇ (*BrE*) *How do we move to a low carbon economy?* **3** [C] = CARBON COPY **4** [C] a piece of CARBON PAPER

car·bon·ate /ˈkɑːbəneɪt; *NAmE* ˈkɑːrbənət/ *noun* (*chemistry*) a salt that contains CARBON and OXYGEN together with another chemical

car·bon·ated /ˈkɑːbəneɪtɪd; *NAmE* ˈkɑːrb-/ *adj.* (*technical*) (of a drink) containing small bubbles of CARBON DIOXIDE SYN **fizzy**

ˌcarbon ˈcopy (also **car·bon**) *noun* **1** a copy of a document, letter, etc. made with CARBON PAPER ➔ see also CC **2** a person or thing that is very similar to sb/sth else: *She is a carbon copy of her sister.*

ˈcarbon credit *noun* **1** a key element in the system of national and international CARBON TRADING. A country or organization has the right to produce a particular amount of CARBON DIOXIDE and other gases that cause GLOBAL WARMING, which is expressed in terms of **carbon credits**, which may be traded between countries or organizations: *The sale of carbon credits can finance renewable energy projects.* **2** a CARBON OFFSET, which a person or company may choose to buy as a way of reducing the level of CARBON DIOXIDE for which they are responsible: *Wind energy companies sell carbon credits to consumers.*

ˈcarbon cycle *noun* [C, U] the processes by which carbon is changed from one form to another within the environment, for example in plants and when wood or oil is burned

ˌcarbon ˈdating (also *formal* **ˌradiocarbon ˈdating**) *noun* [U] a method of calculating the age of very old objects by measuring the amounts of different forms of carbon in them

ˌcarbon diˈoxide *noun* [U] (*symb.* CO_2) a gas breathed out by people and animals from the lungs or produced by burning CARBON

ˌcarbon ˈfootprint *noun* a measure of the amount of carbon dioxide that is produced by the daily activities of a person or company: *Flying is the biggest contribution to my carbon footprint.* ➔ **COLLOCATIONS** at ENVIRONMENT

car·bon·ic acid /kɑːˌbɒnɪk ˈæsɪd; *NAmE* kɑːrˌbɑːnɪk/ *noun* [U] (*chemistry*) a very weak acid that is formed when carbon dioxide is dissolved in water

car·bon·ifer·ous /ˌkɑːbəˈnɪfərəs; *NAmE* ˌkɑːrb-/ *adj.* (*geology*) **1** producing or containing coal **2 Carboniferous** of the period in the earth's history when layers of coal were formed underground

car·bon·ize (*BrE* also **-ise**) /ˈkɑːbənaɪz; *NAmE* ˈkɑːrb-/ *verb* **1** [I, T] **~ (sth)** to become CARBON, or to make sth become carbon **2** [T] **~ sth** to cover sth with CARBON ▸ **car·bon·iza·tion, -isa·tion** /ˌkɑːbənaɪˈzeɪʃn; *NAmE* ˈkɑːrb-/ *noun* [U]

ˌcarbon monˈoxide /ˌkɑːbən mənˈɒksaɪd; *NAmE* ˌkɑːrbən mənˈɑːksaɪd/ *noun* [U] (*symb.* CO) a poisonous gas formed when CARBON burns partly but not completely. It is produced when petrol/gas is burnt in car engines.

ˌcarbon ˈneu·tral *adj.* in which the amount of CARBON DIOXIDE produced has been reduced to nothing or is balanced by actions that protect the environment SYN **zero-carbon**: *All of these fuels are renewable and carbon neutral.*

ˌcarbon ˈoffset *noun* [C, U] a way for a company or person to reduce the level of CARBON DIOXIDE for which they are responsible by paying money to a company that works to reduce the total amount produced in the world, for example by planting trees: *carbon offset initiatives for air travellers* ➔ compare CARBON CREDIT

ˈcarbon paper *noun* thin paper with a dark substance on one side, that is used between two sheets of paper for making copies of written or typed documents

ˈcarbon trading (also **eˈmissions trading**) *noun* [U] a system that gives countries and organizations the right to produce a particular amount of CARBON DIOXIDE and other gases that cause GLOBAL WARMING, and allows them to sell this right

ˌcar ˈboot sale *noun* (*BrE*) an outdoor sale where people sell things that they no longer want, using tables or the backs of their cars to put the goods on

Car·bor·un·dum™ /ˌkɑːbəˈrʌndəm; *NAmE* ˌkɑːrb-/ *noun* [U] (*chemistry*) a very hard black solid substance, used as an ABRASIVE

car·boy /ˈkɑːbɔɪ; *NAmE* ˈkɑːrbɔɪ/ *noun* a large round bottle, usually protected by an outer frame of wood and used for storing and transporting dangerous liquids

ˈcar bra *noun* = BRA (2)

car·bun·cle /ˈkɑːbʌŋkl; *NAmE* ˈkɑːrb-/ *noun* **1** a large painful swelling under the skin **2** a bright red JEWEL, usually cut into a round shape

car·bur·et·tor (*BrE*) (*NAmE* **car·bur·etor**) /ˌkɑːbəˈretə(r); *NAmE* ˈkɑːrbəreɪtər/ *noun* the part of an engine, for example in a car, where petrol/gas and air are mixed together

car·cass (*BrE* also *less frequent* **car·case**) /ˈkɑːkəs; *NAmE* ˈkɑːrkəs/ *noun* the dead body of an animal, especially of a large one or of one that is ready for cutting up as meat

car·cino·gen /kɑːˈsɪnədʒən; *NAmE* kɑːrˈs-/ *noun* a substance that can cause cancer

car·cino·gen·ic /ˌkɑːsɪnəˈdʒenɪk; *NAmE* ˌkɑːrs-/ *adj.* likely to cause cancer

car·cin·oma /ˌkɑːsɪˈnəʊmə; *NAmE* ˌkɑːrsɪˈnoʊmə/ *noun* (*medical*) a cancer that affects the top layer of the skin or the LINING of the body's internal organs

card 🔑 /kɑːd; *NAmE* kɑːrd/ *noun, verb*

■ ***noun***

▸ PAPER **1** 🔑 [U] (*BrE*) thick stiff paper: *a piece of card* ◇ *The model of the building was made of card.*

▸ WITH INFORMATION **2** 🔑 [C] a small piece of stiff paper or plastic with information on it, especially information about sb's identity: *a membership card* ◇ *an appointment card* ➔ see also GREEN CARD, IDENTITY CARD, LOYALTY CARD, RED CARD, REPORT CARD, YELLOW CARD **3** [C] = BUSINESS CARD: *Here's my card if you need to contact me again.* **4** [C] = VISITING CARD

▸ FOR MONEY **5** 🔑 [C] a small piece of plastic, especially one given by a bank or shop/store, used for buying things or obtaining money: *I put the meal on* (= paid for it using) *my card.* ➔ see also CASH CARD, CHARGE CARD, CHEQUE CARD, CHIP CARD, CREDIT CARD, DEBIT CARD, PHONECARD, SIM CARD, SMART CARD, SWIPE CARD

▸ WITH A MESSAGE **6** 🔑 [C] a piece of stiff paper that is folded in the middle and has a picture on the front of it, used for sending sb a message with your good wishes, an invitation, etc: *a* ***birthday/get-well/good luck card*** ➲ see also CHRISTMAS CARD, GREETINGS CARD **7** [C] = POSTCARD: *Did you get my card from Italy?*
▸ IN GAMES **8** 🔑 [C] = PLAYING CARD: (*BrE*) *a pack of cards* ◇ (*NAmE*) *a deck of cards* ➲ VISUAL VOCAB page V32 ➲ see also TRUMP CARD, WILD CARD **9** 🔑 **cards** [pl.] a game or games in which PLAYING CARDS are used: *Who wants to play cards?* ◇ *I've never been very good at cards.* ◇ *Let's have a game of cards.* ◇ *She won £20 at cards.*
▸ COMPUTING **10** [C] a small device containing an electronic CIRCUIT that is part of a computer or added to it, enabling it to perform particular functions: *a printed circuit card* ◇ *a* ***graphics/network/sound card*** ➲ see also EXPANSION CARD
▸ PERSON **11** [C] (*old-fashioned, informal*) an unusual or amusing person
▸ HORSE RACES **12** [C] a list of all the races at a particular RACE MEETING (= a series of horse races)
▸ FOR WOOL/COTTON **13** [C] (*technical*) a machine or tool used for cleaning and COMBING wool or cotton before it is spun
IDM **sb's best/strongest/winning 'card** something that gives sb an advantage over other people in a particular situation **get your 'cards** (*BrE, informal*) to be told to leave a job **give sb their 'cards** (*BrE, informal*) to make sb leave their job **have a card up your 'sleeve** to have an idea, a plan, etc. that will give you an advantage in a particular situation and that you keep secret until it is needed **hold all the 'cards** (*informal*) to be able to control a particular situation because you have an advantage over other people **hold/keep/play your cards close to your 'chest** to keep your ideas, plans, etc. secret **lay/put your cards on the 'table** to tell sb honestly what your plans, ideas, etc. are **on the 'cards** (*BrE*) (*NAmE* **in the 'cards**) (*informal*) likely to happen: *The merger has been on the cards for some time now.* **play the ... card** to mention a particular subject, idea or quality in order to gain an advantage: *He accused his opponent of playing the immigration card during the campaign.* ➲ see also RACE CARD **play your 'cards right** to deal successfully with a particular situation so that you achieve some advantage or sth that you want ➲ more at SHOW *v.*, STACKED
■ ***verb*** **1 ~ sth** (*technical*) to clean wool using a wire instrument **2 ~ sb** (*NAmE, informal*) to ask a person to show their identity card as a means of checking how old they are, for example if they want to buy alcohol

car·da·mom /ˈkɑːdəməm; *NAmE* ˈkɑːrd-/ *noun* [U] the dried seeds of a SE Asian plant, used in cooking as a spice ➲ VISUAL VOCAB page V28

card·board 🔑 /ˈkɑːdbɔːd; *NAmE* ˈkɑːrdbɔːrd/ *noun, adj.*
■ ***noun*** 🔑 [U] stiff material like very thick paper, often used for making boxes: *a cardboard box* ◇ *a piece of cardboard*
■ ***adj.*** [only before noun] not seeming real or genuine: *a novel with superficial cardboard characters*

ˌcardboard ˈcity *noun* an area of a city where people who have nowhere to live sleep outside, protected only by cardboard boxes

ˈcard-carrying *adj.* [only before noun] known to be an official and usually active member of a political organization: *a card-carrying member of the Conservative party*

ˈcard catalog (*NAmE*) (*BrE* **ˈcard index, index**) *noun* a box of cards with information on them, arranged in alphabetical order ➲ VISUAL VOCAB page V56

ˈcard game *noun* a game in which playing cards are used

card·hold·er /ˈkɑːdhəʊldə(r); *NAmE* ˈkɑːrdhoʊl-/ *noun* a person who has a credit card from a bank, etc.

car·diac /ˈkɑːdiæk; *NAmE* ˈkɑːrd-/ *adj.* [only before noun] (*medical*) connected with the heart or heart disease: ***cardiac disease/failure/surgery*** ◇ *to suffer* ***cardiac arrest*** (= an occasion when a person's heart stops temporarily or permanently)

car·di·gan /ˈkɑːdɪɡən; *NAmE* ˈkɑːrd-/ (*NAmE* also **ˌcardigan ˈsweater**) *noun* a knitted jacket made of wool, usually with no COLLAR and fastened with buttons at the front ➲ VISUAL VOCAB page V51

car·din·al /ˈkɑːdɪnl; *NAmE* ˈkɑːrd-/ *noun, adj.*
■ ***noun*** **1** a priest of the highest rank in the Roman Catholic Church. Cardinals elect and advise the POPE: *Cardinal Brady* **2** (also **ˌcardinal ˈnumber**) a number, such as 1, 2 and 3, used to show quantity rather than order ➲ compare ORDINAL **3** a N American bird. The male cardinal is bright red.
■ ***adj.*** [only before noun] (*formal*) most important; having other things based on it: *Respect for life is a cardinal principle of English law.*

ˌcardinal ˈpoints *noun* [pl.] (*technical*) the four main points (North, South, East and West) of the COMPASS

ˌcardinal ˈsin *noun* **1** (sometimes *humorous*) an action that is a serious mistake or that other people disapprove of: *He committed the cardinal sin of criticizing his teammates.* **2** a serious SIN in the Christian Church

ˈcard index (also **index**) (both *BrE*) (*NAmE* **ˈcard catalog**) *noun* a box of cards with information on them, arranged in alphabetical order ➲ VISUAL VOCAB page V56

cardio /ˈkɑːdiəʊ; *NAmE* ˈkɑːrdioʊ/ *noun* [U] (*informal*) exercises to make your heart work harder, that you do to keep yourself fit: *Cardio is the answer if you want to lose weight.* ◇ *cardio exercise/workouts* ➲ see also CARDIOVASCULAR

cardio- /ˈkɑːdiəʊ; *NAmE* ˈkɑːrdioʊ/ *combining form* (in nouns, adjectives and adverbs) connected with the heart: *cardiogram*

car·di·olo·gist /ˌkɑːdiˈɒlədʒɪst; *NAmE* ˌkɑːrdiˈɑːl-/ *noun* a doctor who studies and treats heart diseases ▸ **car·di·ology** /-dʒi/ *noun* [U]

car·dio·vas·cu·lar /ˌkɑːdiəʊˈvæskjələ(r); *NAmE* ˌkɑːrdioʊ-/ *adj.* (*medical*) connected with the heart and the BLOOD VESSELS (= the tubes that carry blood around the body)

card·phone /ˈkɑːdfəʊn; *NAmE* ˈkɑːrdfoʊn/ *noun* (*BrE*) a public telephone in which you use a plastic card (= a PHONECARD) instead of money

ˈcard sharp *noun* a person who cheats in games of cards in order to make money

ˈcard swipe *noun* an electronic device through which you pass a credit card, etc. in order to record the information on it, open a door, etc.

ˈcard table *noun* a small table for playing card games on, especially one that you can fold

care 🔑 /keə(r); *NAmE* ker/ *noun, verb*
■ ***noun*** **1** 🔑 [U] the process of caring for sb/sth and providing what they need for their health or protection: *medical/patient care* ◇ *How much do men share housework and the care of the children?* ◇ *the provision of care for the elderly* ◇ ***skin/hair care*** *products* ➲ see also COMMUNITY CARE, DAY CARE, EASY-CARE, HEALTH CARE, INTENSIVE CARE **2** 🔑 [U] attention or thought that you give to sth that you are doing so that you will do it well and avoid mistakes or damage: *She chose her words* ***with care.*** ◇ *Great care is needed when choosing a used car.* ◇ *Fragile—handle with care* (= written on a container holding sth which is easily broken or damaged) **3** [C, usually pl., U] (*formal*) a feeling of worry or anxiety; something that causes problems or anxiety: *I felt free from the cares of the day as soon as I left the building.* ◇ *Sam looked as if he* ***didn't have a care in the world.***

> **WORD FAMILY**
> **care** *noun, verb*
> **careful** *adj.* (≠ careless)
> **carefully** *adv.* (≠ carelessly)
> **caring** *adj.* (≠ uncaring)

IDM **ˈcare of sb** (*NAmE* also **in ˈcare of sb**) (*abbr.* c/o) used when writing to sb at another person's address: *Write to him care of his lawyer.* **in ˈcare** (*BrE*) (of children) living in an institution run by the local authority rather than with their parents: *The two girls were* ***taken into care*** *after their parents were killed.* **in the care of sb/in sb's care** being cared for by sb: *The child was left in the care of friends.* **take** '**care** (*informal*) used when saying goodbye: *Bye! Take care!* **take care (that…/to do sth)** to be careful: *Take care (that) you don't drink too much!* ◇ *Care should be taken to close the lid securely.* **take care of sb/sth/yourself 1** 🔑 to care for sb/sth/yourself; to be careful about sth: *Who's taking care of the children while you're away?* ◇ *She takes great care of her clothes.* ◇ *He's old enough to take care of himself.* **2** 🔑 to be responsible for or to deal with a situation or task: *Don't worry about the travel arrangements. They're all being taken care of.* ◇ *Celia takes care of the marketing side of things.* **under the care of sb** receiving medical care from sb: *He's under the care of Dr Parks.*

■ ***verb*** (not used in the progressive tenses) **1** 🔑 [I, T] to feel that sth is important and worth worrying about: ***I don't care*** (= I will not be upset) *if I never see him again!* ◇ *He threatened to fire me,* ***as if I cared!*** ◇ **~ about sth** *She cares deeply about environmental issues.* ◇ **~ what/whether, etc.** *I don't care what he thinks.* ◇ **~ that…** *She doesn't seem to care that he's been married four times before.* **2** 🔑 [I] **~ (about sb)** to like or love sb and worry about what happens to them: *He genuinely cares about his employees.* **3** [T] **~ to do sth** to make the effort to do sth: *I've done this job more times than I care to remember.*

IDM **couldn't care 'less** (*informal*) used to say, often rudely, that you do not think that sb/sth is important or worth worrying about: *Quite honestly, I couldn't care less what they do.* **for all you, I, they, etc. care** (*informal*) used to say that a person is not worried about or interested in what happens to sb/sth: *I could be dead for all he cares!* **who 'cares? | What do I, you, etc. care?** (*informal*) used to say, often rudely, that you do not think that sth is important or interesting: *Who cares what she thinks?* **Would you care for sth? | Would you care to do sth?** (*formal*) used to ask sb politely if they would like sth or would like to do sth, or if they would be willing to do sth: *Would you care for another drink?* ◇ *If you'd care to follow me, I'll show you where his office is.* ➲ note at WANT ➲ more at DAMN *n.*, FIG *n.*, HOOT *n.*, TUPPENCE

PHR V **'care for sb 1** 🔑 to look after sb who is sick, very old, very young, etc. SYN **take care of**: *She moved back home to care for her elderly parents.* ➲ see also UNCARED FOR **2** to love or like sb very much: *He cared for her more than she realized.* ➲ SYNONYMS at LOVE **not 'care for sb/sth** (*formal*) to not like sb/sth: *He didn't much care for her friends.*

Synonyms

care

caution • **prudence**

These are all words for attention or thought that you give to sth in order to avoid mistakes or accidents.

care attention or thought that you give to sth that you are doing so that you will do it well and avoid mistakes or damage: *She chose her words with care.*

caution care that you take in order to avoid danger or mistakes; not taking any risks: *The utmost caution must be exercised when handling explosives.*

prudence (*rather formal*) being sensible and careful when you make judgements and decisions; avoiding unnecessary risks: *As a matter of prudence, keep a record of all your financial transactions.* NOTE **Prudence** is used particularly in financial contexts.

PATTERNS
- to do sth **with** care/caution/prudence
- **great/extreme** care/caution/prudence
- to **use/exercise** care/caution/prudence
- to **proceed with** care/caution

'**care assistant** *noun* (*BrE*) = CARE WORKER

Which Word?

take care of / look after / care for

- You can **take care of** or, especially in *BrE*, **look after** someone who is very young, very old, or sick, or something that needs keeping in good condition: *We've asked my mother to take care of/look after the kids while we're away.* ◇ *You can borrow my camera if you promise to take care of/look after it.*
- In more formal language you can also **care for** someone: *She does some voluntary work, caring for the elderly,* but **care for** is more commonly used to mean 'like': *I don't really care for spicy food.*

car·een /kəˈriːn/ *verb* [I] **+ adv./prep.** (*especially NAmE*) (of a person or vehicle) to move forward very quickly especially in a way that is dangerous or uncontrolled SYN **hurtle**

car·eer 🔑 /kəˈrɪə(r); *NAmE* kəˈrɪr/ *noun, verb*

■ ***noun* 1** 🔑 the series of jobs that a person has in a particular area of work, usually involving more responsibility as time passes: *a* ***career in*** *politics* ◇ *a teaching career* ◇ *What made you decide on a* ***career as*** *a vet?* ◇ *She has been concentrating on her career.* ◇ *a change of career* ◇ *That will be a good* ***career move*** (= something that will help your career). ◇ *a* ***career soldier/diplomat*** (= a professional one) ◇ (*BrE*) *a* ***careers adviser/officer*** (= a person whose job is to give people advice and information about jobs) ➲ SYNONYMS at WORK ➲ COLLOCATIONS at JOB **2** 🔑 the period of time that you spend in your life working or doing a particular thing: *She started her career as an English teacher.* ◇ *He is playing the best tennis of his career.* ◇ *My school career was not very impressive.*

■ ***verb*** [I] **+ adv./prep.** (of a person or vehicle) to move forward very quickly, especially in an uncontrolled way SYN **hurtle**: *The vehicle careered across the road and hit a cyclist.*

ca'reer break *noun* a period of time when you do not do your usual job, for example because you have children to care for

car·eer·ist /kəˈrɪərɪst; *NAmE* -ˈrɪr-/ *noun* (often *disapproving*) a person whose career is more important to them than anything else ▶ **car·eer·ism** *noun* [U]

ca'reer woman *noun* a woman whose career is more important to her than getting married and having children

care·free /ˈkeəfriː; *NAmE* ˈkerf-/ *adj.* having no worries or responsibilities: *He looked happy and carefree.* ◇ *a* ***carefree attitude/life***

care·ful 🔑 /ˈkeəfl; *NAmE* ˈkerfl/ *adj.*

1 🔑 [not before noun] giving attention or thought to what you are doing so that you avoid hurting yourself, damaging sth or doing sth wrong: *Be careful!* ◇ **~ to do sth** *He was careful to keep out of sight.* ◇ **~ not to do sth** *Be careful not to wake the baby.* ◇ **~ when/what/how, etc.** *You must be careful when handling chemicals.* ◇ **~ of/about/with sth** *Be careful of the traffic.* ◇ *Please be careful with my glasses* (= Don't break them). ◇ **~ (that)…** *Be careful you don't bump your head.* **2** 🔑 giving a lot of attention to details: *a careful piece of work* ◇ *a careful examination of the facts* ◇ *After careful consideration we have decided to offer you the job.* OPP **careless** ▶ **care·ful·ly** 🔑 /ˈkeəfəli; *NAmE* ˈker-/ *adv.*: *Please listen carefully.* ◇ *She put the glass down carefully.* ◇ *Drive carefully.* OPP **carelessly** ▶ **care·ful·ness** *noun* [U]

IDM **you can't be too 'careful** used to warn sb that they should take care to avoid danger or problems: *Don't stay out in the sun for too long—you can't be too careful.* **careful with money** not spending money on unimportant things

care·giver /ˈkeəgɪvə(r); *NAmE* ˈkerg-/ (*NAmE*) (*BrE* **carer**) *noun* a person who takes care of a sick or old person at home

'**care home** *noun* (*BrE*) a place where people live and are cared for when they cannot live at home or look after themselves: *a care home for the elderly*

ˌ**care in the com'munity** *noun* [U] = COMMUNITY CARE

ˈ**care label** *noun* a label attached to the inside of a piece of clothing, giving instructions about how it should be washed and ironed

care·less 0➡ /ˈkeələs; *NAmE* ˈkerləs/ *adj.* **1** 0➡ not giving enough attention and thought to what you are doing, so that you make mistakes: *It was careless of me to leave the door open.* ◇ *Don't be so **careless about/with** spelling.* ◇ *a careless worker/driver* OPP **careful 2** 0➡ resulting from a lack of attention and thought: *a **careless mistake/error*** **3 ~ of sth** (*formal*) not at all worried about sth: *He seemed careless of his own safety.* **4** not showing interest or effort SYN **casual**: *She gave a careless shrug.* ◇ *a **careless laugh/smile*** ▸ **care·less·ly** 0➡ *adv.*: *Someone had carelessly left a window open.* ◇ *She threw her coat carelessly onto the chair.* ◇ *'I don't mind,' he said carelessly.* **care·less·ness** *noun* [U]: *a moment of carelessness*

care·line /ˈkeəlaɪn; *NAmE* ˈkerl-/ *noun* a telephone service that you can call to get advice or information on a company's products: *Call our customer careline for advice.*

carer /ˈkeərə(r); *NAmE* ˈker-/ (*BrE*) (*NAmE* **care·giver**) *noun* a person who takes care of a sick or old person at home

ca·ress /kəˈres/ *verb, noun*
▪ ***verb* ~ sb/sth** to touch sb/sth gently, especially in a sexual way or in a way that shows affection: *His fingers caressed the back of her neck.*
▪ ***noun*** a gentle touch or kiss to show you love sb

caret /ˈkærət/ *noun* a mark (^) placed below a line of printed or written text to show that words or letters should be added at that place in the text

care·taker /ˈkeəteɪkə(r); *NAmE* ˈkert-/ *noun, adj.*
▪ ***noun*** **1** (*BrE*) (*NAmE, ScotE* **jani·tor**) (*NAmE* also **cus·to·dian**) a person whose job is to take care of a building such as a school or a block of flats or an apartment building **2** (*especially NAmE*) a person who takes care of a house or land while the owner is away **3** (*especially NAmE*) a person such as a teacher, parent, nurse, etc, who takes care of other people
▪ ***adj.*** [only before noun] in charge for a short time, until a new leader or government is chosen: *a **caretaker manager/government***

ˈ**care worker** (also ˈ**care assistant**) (both *BrE*) *noun* a person whose job is to help and take care of people who are mentally ill, sick or disabled, especially those who live in special homes or hospitals

care·worn /ˈkeəwɔːn; *NAmE* ˈkerwɔːrn/ *adj.* looking tired because you have a lot of worries

cargo /ˈkɑːɡəʊ; *NAmE* ˈkɑːrɡoʊ/ *noun* [C, U] (*pl.* **-oes**, *NAmE* also **-os**) the goods carried in a ship or plane: *The tanker began to spill its cargo of oil.* ◇ *a cargo ship*

ˈ**cargo pants** (also **car·goes**) (*BrE* also **com·bats**, ˈ**com·bat trousers**) *noun* [pl.] loose trousers that have pockets in various places, for example on the side of the leg above the knee ➲ VISUAL VOCAB page V51

Carib·bean /ˌkærɪˈbiːən; kəˈrɪbiən/ *noun, adj.*
▪ ***noun* the Caribbean** the region consisting of the Caribbean Sea and its islands, including the West Indies, and the coasts which surround it
▪ ***adj.*** connected with the Caribbean

cari·bou /ˈkærɪbuː/ *noun* (*pl.* **cari·bou**) a N American REINDEER

cari·ca·ture /ˈkærɪkətʃʊə(r); *NAmE* -tʃər; -tʃʊr/ *noun, verb*
▪ ***noun*** **1** [C] a funny drawing or picture of sb that exaggerates some of their features **2** [C] a description of a person or thing that makes them seem ridiculous by exaggerating some of their characteristics: *He had unfairly presented a caricature of my views.* **3** [U] the art of drawing or writing caricatures ▸ **cari·ca·tur·ist** *noun*
▪ ***verb*** [often passive] **~ sb/sth (as sth)** to produce a caricature of sb; to describe or present sb as a type of person you would laugh at or not respect: *She was unfairly caricatured as a dumb blonde.*

car·ies /ˈkeəriːz; *NAmE* ˈker-/ *noun* [U] (*medical*) decay in teeth or bones: *dental caries*

car·il·lon /kəˈrɪljən; *NAmE* ˈkærəlɑːn/ *noun* **1** a set of bells on which tunes can be played, sometimes using a keyboard **2** a tune played on bells

car·ing /ˈkeərɪŋ; *NAmE* ˈker-/ *adj.* [usually before noun] kind, helpful and showing that you care about other people: *He's a very caring person.* ◇ *Children need a caring environment.* ◇ (*BrE*) *a **caring profession*** (= a job that involves looking after or helping other people)

car·jack·ing /ˈkɑːdʒækɪŋ; *NAmE* ˈkɑːrdʒ-/ *noun* [U, C] the crime of forcing the driver of a car to take you somewhere or give you their car, using threats and violence ➲ compare HIJACKING ▸ **car·jack** *verb* **~ sth car·jack·er** *noun*

car·load /ˈkɑːləʊd; *NAmE* ˈkɑːrloʊd/ *noun* the number of people or things that a car is carrying or is able to carry

car·mine /ˈkɑːmaɪn; *NAmE* ˈkɑːrm-/ *adj.* (*formal*) dark red in colour ▸ **car·mine** *noun* [U]

carn·age /ˈkɑːnɪdʒ; *NAmE* ˈkɑːrn-/ *noun* [U] the violent killing of a large number of people SYN **slaughter**: *a scene of carnage*

car·nal /ˈkɑːnl; *NAmE* ˈkɑːrnl/ *adj.* [usually before noun] (*formal* or *law*) connected with the body or with sex: ***carnal desires/appetites*** ▸ **car·nal·ly** /ˈkɑːnəli; *NAmE* ˈkɑːrn-/ *adv.*

ˌ**carnal** ˈ**knowledge** *noun* [U] (*old-fashioned* or *law*) = SEXUAL INTERCOURSE

car·na·tion /kɑːˈneɪʃn; *NAmE* kɑːrˈn-/ *noun* a white, pink, red or yellow flower, often worn as a decoration on formal occasions: *He was wearing a carnation in his buttonhole.* ➲ VISUAL VOCAB page V9

car·ne·lian /kɑːˈniːliən; *NAmE* kɑːrˈn-/ (also **cor·nel·ian**) *noun* [C, U] a red, brown or white stone, used in jewellery

car·ni·val /ˈkɑːnɪvl; *NAmE* ˈkɑːrn-/ *noun* **1** [C, U] a public festival, usually one that happens at a regular time each year, that involves music and dancing in the streets, for which people wear brightly coloured clothes: *There is a local carnival every year.* ◇ *the carnival in Rio* ◇ *a carnival atmosphere* **2** [C] (*NAmE*) = FAIR *n.* (1) **3** (*NAmE*) (*BrE* **fete**, **fair**) [C] an outdoor entertainment at which people can play games to win prizes, buy food and drink, etc, usually arranged to make money for a special purpose **4** [sing.] **~ of sth** (*formal*) an exciting or brightly coloured mixture of things: *this summer's carnival of sport*

car·ni·vore /ˈkɑːnɪvɔː(r); *NAmE* ˈkɑːrn-/ *noun* any animal that eats meat ➲ compare HERBIVORE, INSECTIVORE, OMNIVORE ▸ **car·ni·vor·ous** /kɑːˈnɪvərəs; *NAmE* kɑːrˈn-/ *adj.*: *a carnivorous diet* ➲ compare OMNIVOROUS

carob /ˈkærəb/ (also ˈ**carob tree**) *noun* a southern European tree with dark brown fruit that can be made into a powder that tastes like chocolate

carol /ˈkærəl/ *noun, verb*
▪ ***noun*** (also ˌ**Christmas** ˈ**carol**) a Christian religious song sung at Christmas
▪ ***verb*** (**-ll-**, *US* **-l-**) [I, T] **~ (sth)** | **+ speech** to sing sth in a cheerful way

ˈ**carol singing** *noun* [U] the singing of Christmas carols especially in a church or outdoors, often to collect money for charity ▸ ˈ**carol singer** *noun*

carom /ˈkærəm/ *verb* [I] (*especially NAmE*) to hit a surface and come off it fast at a different angle

car·ot·ene /ˈkærətiːn/ *noun* [U] a red or orange substance found in carrots and other plants ➲ see also BETA-CAROTENE

ca·rotid ar·tery /kəˈrɒtɪd ɑːtəri; *NAmE* -ˈrɑːt- ɑːrt-/ *noun* (*anatomy*) either of the two large ARTERIES in the neck that carry blood to the head

ca·rouse /kəˈraʊz/ *verb* [I] (*literary*) to spend time drinking alcohol, laughing and enjoying yourself in a noisy way with other people

car·ou·sel /ˌkærəˈsel/ *noun* **1** (*especially NAmE*) = MERRY-GO-ROUND (1) ➲ picture at ROUNDABOUT **2** a moving belt from which you collect your bags at an airport

carp /kɑːp; *NAmE* kɑːrp/ *noun, verb*
■ *noun* [C, U] (*pl.* **carp**) a large FRESHWATER fish that is used for food
■ *verb* [I] **~ (at sb) (about sth)** to keep complaining about sb/sth in an annoying way

car·pal /ˈkɑːpl; *NAmE* ˈkɑːrpl/ *noun* (*anatomy*) any of the eight small bones that form the wrist

car·pal tun·nel syn·drome /ˌkɑːpl ˈtʌnl sɪndrəʊm; *NAmE* ˌkɑːrpl ˈtʌnl sɪndroʊm/ *noun* [U] (*medical*) a painful condition of the hand and fingers caused by pressure on a nerve because of repeated movements over a long period

ˈ**car park** *noun* (*BrE*) an area or a building where people can leave their cars ➲ see also GARAGE, MULTI-STOREY CAR PARK ➲ compare PARKING LOT

carpe diem /ˌkɑːpeɪ ˈdiːem; ˈdaɪem; *NAmE* ˌkɑːrpeɪ/ *exclamation* (from *Latin*) an expression used when you want to say that sb should not wait, but should take an opportunity as soon as it appears

car·pel /ˈkɑːpl; *NAmE* ˈkɑːrpl/ *noun* (*biology*) the part of a plant in which seeds are produced ➲ VISUAL VOCAB page V9

car·pen·ter /ˈkɑːpəntə(r); *NAmE* ˈkɑːrp-/ *noun* a person whose job is making and repairing wooden objects and structures ➲ compare JOINER

car·pen·try /ˈkɑːpəntri; *NAmE* ˈkɑːrp-/ *noun* [U] **1** the work of a carpenter **2** things made by a carpenter

car·pet 0‑ˉ /ˈkɑːpɪt; *NAmE* ˈkɑːrpɪt/ *noun, verb*
■ *noun* **1** 0‑ˉ [U] a thick WOVEN material made of wool, etc. for covering floors or stairs: *a roll of carpet* **2** 0‑ˉ [C] a piece of carpet used as a floor covering, especially when shaped to fit a room: *to lay a carpet* ◇ *a bedroom carpet* ◇ (*BrE*) *We have* ***fitted carpets*** (= carpets from wall to wall) *in our house.* ➲ VISUAL VOCAB page V20 ➲ see also CARPETING, RED CARPET, RUG **3** [C] **~ (of sth)** (*literary*) a thick layer of sth on the ground: *a carpet of snow*
IDM **(be/get called) on the ˈcarpet** (*informal, especially NAmE*) called to see sb in authority because you have done sth wrong: *I got called on the carpet for being late.* ➲ more at SWEEP *v.*
■ *verb* [usually passive] **1 ~ sth** to cover the floor of a room with a carpet: *The hall was carpeted in blue.* **2 ~ sth (with/in sth)** (*literary*) to cover sth with a thick layer of sth: *The forest floor was carpeted with wild flowers.* **3 ~ sb** (*informal, especially BrE*) to speak angrily to sb because they have done sth wrong SYN **reprimand**

ˈ**carpet bag** *noun* a bag used in the past for carrying your things when travelling

car·pet·bag·ger /ˈkɑːpɪtbægə(r); *NAmE* ˈkɑːrp-/ *noun* **1** (*disapproving*) a politician who tries to be elected in an area where he or she is not known and is therefore not welcome **2** a person from the northern states of the US who went to the South after the Civil War in order to make money or get political power

ˈ**carpet-bomb** *verb* **1 ~ sth** to drop a large number of bombs onto every part of an area **2 ~ sb** (*business*) to send an advertisement to a very large number of people, especially by email ▸ ˈ**carpet-bombing** *noun* [U]

car·pet·ing /ˈkɑːpɪtɪŋ; *NAmE* ˈkɑːrp-/ *noun* **1** [U] carpets in general or the material used for carpets: *new offices with wall-to-wall carpeting* ◇ (*NAmE*) *We need new carpeting* (= a new carpet) *in the living room.* **2** [C] (*BrE, informal*) an act of speaking angrily to sb because they have done sth wrong

ˈ**carpet slipper** *noun* [usually pl.] (*old-fashioned, BrE*) a type of SLIPPER (= a shoe that you wear in the house), with the upper part made of cloth

ˈ**carpet sweeper** *noun* a simple machine for cleaning carpets, with a long handle and brushes that go around

ˈ**car phone** *noun* a radio telephone for use in a car

ˈ**car pool** *noun* **1** a group of car owners who take turns to drive everyone in the group to work, so that only one car is used at a time **2** (*BrE*) (also ˈ**motor pool** *US, BrE*) a group of cars owned by a company or an organization, that its staff can use

car·pool /ˈkɑːpuːl; *NAmE* ˈkɑːr-/ *verb* [I] if a group of people **carpool**, they travel to work together in one car and divide the cost between them

car·port /ˈkɑːpɔːt; *NAmE* ˈkɑːrpɔːrt/ *noun* a shelter for a car, usually built beside a house and consisting of a roof supported by posts

car·rel /ˈkærəl/ *noun* a small area with a desk, separated from other desks by a dividing wall or screen, where one person can work in a library

car·riage /ˈkærɪdʒ/ *noun* **1** (also **coach**) (both *BrE*) (*NAmE* **car**) [C] a separate section of a train for carrying passengers: *a railway carriage* ➲ VISUAL VOCAB page V47 **2** [C] a road vehicle, usually with four wheels, that is pulled by one or more horses and was used in the past to carry people: *a horse-drawn carriage* **3** (*BrE*) (also **handling** *NAmE, BrE*) [U] (*formal*) the act or cost of transporting goods from one place to another: *£16.95 including VAT and carriage* **4** [C] a moving part of a machine that supports or moves another part, for example on a TYPEWRITER: *a carriage return* (= the act of starting a new line when typing) **5** [sing.] (*old-fashioned*) the way in which sb holds and moves their head and body SYN **bearing** ➲ see also BABY CARRIAGE, UNDERCARRIAGE

ˈ**carriage clock** *noun* a small clock inside a case with a handle on top

ˈ**carriage house** (*US*) (*BrE* ˈ**mews house**) *noun* a house in a row of houses converted from stables (= buildings used to keep horses in)

car·riage·way /ˈkærɪdʒweɪ/ *noun* (*BrE*) **1** one of the two sides of a MOTORWAY or other large road, used by traffic moving in the same direction: *the eastbound carriageway of the M50* ➲ see also DUAL CARRIAGEWAY **2** the part of a road intended for vehicles, not people walking, etc.

car·rier /ˈkæriə(r)/ *noun* **1** a company that carries goods or passengers from one place to another, especially by air **2** a military vehicle or ship that carries soldiers or equipment from one place to another: *an armoured personnel carrier* ➲ see also AIRCRAFT CARRIER, PEOPLE CARRIER **3** a person or animal that passes a disease to other people or animals but does not suffer from it **4** a metal frame that is fixed to a bicycle and used for carrying bags **5** a person or thing that carries sth: *Aquarius, the Water Carrier* ◇ *a baby carrier* (= for carrying a baby on your back or in front of you) **6** (*BrE*) = CARRIER BAG **7** a company that provides a telephone or Internet service: *a telecoms carrier*

ˈ**carrier bag** (also **car·rier**) (both *BrE*) (*NAmE* ˈ**shopping bag**) *noun* a paper or plastic bag for carrying shopping ➲ VISUAL VOCAB page V29

ˈ**carrier pigeon** *noun* a PIGEON (= a type of bird) that has been trained to carry messages

car·rion /ˈkæriən/ *noun* [U] the decaying flesh of dead animals: *crows feeding on carrion* ➲ VISUAL VOCAB page V10

ˈ**carrion crow** *noun* a type of medium-sized CROW

car·rot 0‑ˉ /ˈkærət/ *noun*
1 0‑ˉ [U, C] a long pointed orange root vegetable: *grated carrot* ◇ *a pound of carrots* ➲ VISUAL VOCAB page V27 **2** [C] a reward promised to sb in order to persuade them to do sth SYN **incentive**: *They are holding out a carrot of $120 million in economic aid.*
IDM **the carrot and (the) stick (approach)** if you use **the carrot and stick approach**, you persuade sb to try harder by offering them a reward if they do, or a punishment if they do not

car·roty /ˈkærəti/ *adj.* (sometimes *disapproving*) (of hair) orange in colour

carry 0‑ˉ /ˈkæri/ *verb* (**car·ries**, **carry·ing**, **car·ried**, **car·ried**)
▸ TAKE WITH YOU **1** 0‑ˉ [T] **~ sb/sth** to support the weight of sb/sth and take them or it from place to place; to take sb/

sth from one place to another: *He was carrying a suitcase.* ◇ *She carried her baby in her arms.* ◇ *The injured were carried away on stretchers.* ◇ *a train carrying commuters to work* **2** [T] **~ sth** to have sth with you and take it wherever you go: *Police in many countries carry guns.* ◇ *I never carry much money on me.*

▸ OF PIPES/WIRES **3** [T] **~ sth** to contain and direct the flow of water, electricity, etc: *a pipeline carrying oil* ◇ *The veins carry blood to the heart.*

▸ DISEASE **4** [T] **~ sth** if a person, an insect, etc. **carries** a disease, they are infected with it and might spread it to others although they might not become sick themselves: *Ticks can carry a nasty disease which affects humans.*

▸ REMEMBER **5** [T] **~ sth in your head/mind** to be able to remember sth

▸ SUPPORT WEIGHT **6** [T] **~ sth** to support the weight of sth: *A road bridge has to carry a lot of traffic.*

▸ RESPONSIBILITY **7** [T] **~ sth** to accept responsibility for sth; to suffer the results of sth: *He is carrying the department* (= it is only working because of his efforts). ◇ *Their group was targeted to* ***carry the burden*** *of job losses.*

▸ HAVE AS QUALITY/FEATURE **8** [T] **~ sth** to have sth as a quality or feature: *Her speech carried the ring of authority.* ◇ *My views don't* ***carry much weight*** *with* (= have much influence on) *the boss.* ◇ *Each bike carries a ten-year guarantee.* **9** [T] **~ sth** to have sth as a result: *Crimes of violence carry heavy penalties.* ◇ *Being a combat sport, karate* ***carries with it*** *the risk of injury.*

▸ OF THROW/KICK **10** [I] **+ noun + adv./prep.** if sth that is thrown, kicked, etc. **carries** a particular distance, it travels that distance before stopping: *The fullback's kick carried 50 metres into the crowd.*

▸ OF SOUND **11** [I] (**+ adv./prep.**) if a sound **carries**, it can be heard a long distance away

▸ TAKE TO PLACE/POSITION **12** [T] **~ sth/sb to/into sth** to take sth/sb to a particular point or in a particular direction: *The war was carried into enemy territory.* ◇ *Her abilities carried her to the top of her profession.*

▸ APPROVAL/SUPPORT **13** [T, usually passive] **~ sth** to approve of sth by more people voting for it than against it: *The resolution was carried by 340 votes to 210.* **14** [T] to win the support or sympathy of sb; to persuade people to accept your argument: **~ sb** *His moving speech was enough to carry the audience.* ◇ **~ sth** *She nodded in agreement, and he saw he had carried his point.*

▸ HAVE LABEL **15** [T] **~ sth** to have a particular label or piece of information attached: *Cigarettes carry a health warning.*

▸ NEWS STORY **16** [T] **~ sth** if a newspaper or broadcast **carries** a particular story, it publishes or broadcasts it

▸ ITEM IN STORE **17** [T] **~ sth** if a shop/store **carries** a particular item, it has it for sale: *We* ***carry a range*** *of educational software.*

▸ BABY **18** [T] **be carrying sb** to be pregnant with sb: *She was carrying twins.*

▸ YOURSELF **19** [T] **~ yourself + adv./prep.** to hold or move your head or body in a particular way: *to carry yourself well*

▸ ADDING NUMBERS **20** [T] **~ sth** to add a number to the next column on the left when adding up numbers, for example when the numbers add up to more than ten

IDM **be/get carried a'way** to get very excited or lose control of your feelings: *I got carried away and started shouting at the television.* **carry all/everything be'fore you** to be completely successful **carry the 'ball** (*US, informal*) to take responsibility for getting sth done: *My co-worker was sick, so I had to carry the ball.* **carry the 'can (for sb/sth)** (*BrE, informal*) to accept the blame for sth, especially when it is not your fault **carry a torch for sb** to be in love with sb, especially sb who does not love you in return ⇨ more at DAY, FAR *adv.*, FAST *adv.*, FETCH

PHR V **ˌcarry sb 'back (to sth)** to make sb remember a time in the past: *The smell of the sea carried her back to her childhood.* **ˌcarry sth↔'forward** (also **ˌcarry sth↔'over**) to move a total amount from one column or page to the next **ˌcarry sth↔'off** **1** to win sth: *He carried off most of the prizes.* **2** to succeed in doing sth that most people would find difficult: *She's had her hair cut really short, but she can* ***carry it off.*** **ˌcarry 'on** **1** (*especially BrE*) to continue moving: *Carry on until you get to the junction, then turn left.* **2** (*informal*) to argue or complain noisily: *He was shouting and carrying on.* ⇨ related noun CARRY-ON **ˌcarry 'on (with sth)** | **ˌcarry sth↔'on** to continue doing sth: *Carry on with your work while I'm away.* ◇ *After he left I just tried to carry on as normal* (= do the things I usually do). ◇ *Carry on the good work!* ◇ **~ doing sth** *He carried on peeling the potatoes.* **ˌcarry 'on (with sb)** (*old-fashioned*) to have a sexual relationship with sb when you should not: *His wife found out he'd been carrying on with another woman.* **ˌcarry sth↔'out** **1** to do sth that you have said you will do or have been asked to do: *to carry out a promise/a threat/a plan/an order* **2** to do and complete a task: *to carry out an inquiry/an investigation/a survey* ◇ *Extensive tests have been carried out on the patient.* **ˌcarry 'over** to continue to exist in a different situation: *Attitudes learned at home carry over into the playground.* **ˌcarry sth↔'over** **1** to keep sth from one situation and use it or deal with it in a different situation **2** to delay sth until a later time: *The match had to be carried over until Sunday.* **3** = CARRY STH FORWARD **ˌcarry sb 'through** | **ˌcarry sb 'through sth** to help sb to survive a difficult period: *His determination carried him through the ordeal.* **ˌcarry sth 'through** to complete sth successfully: *It's a difficult job but she's the person to carry it through.* **ˌcarry 'through (on/with sth)** (*NAmE*) to do what you have said you will do: *He has proved he can carry through on his promises.*

carry·cot /'kærikɒt; *NAmE* -kɑːt/ *noun* (*BrE*) a small bed for a baby, with handles at the sides so you can carry it ⇨ picture at PUSHCHAIR

'carry-on *noun* **1** [usually sing.] (*BrE, informal*) a display of excitement, anger or silly behaviour over sth unimportant: *What a carry-on!* **2** (*NAmE*) a small bag or case that you carry onto a plane with you: *Only one carry-on is allowed.* ◇ *carry-on baggage*

'carry-out *noun* (*US, ScotE*) = TAKEAWAY: *Let's get a carry-out.* ◇ *carry-out coffees*

'carry-over *noun* **1** [usually sing.] something that remains or results from a situation in the past: *His neatness is a carry-over from his army days.* **2** an amount of money that has not been used and so can be used later: *The £20 million included a £7 million carry-over from last year's underspend.*

'car seat *noun* **1** (also **'child seat**) a special safety seat for a child, that can be fitted into a car **2** a seat in a car

car·sick /'kɑːsɪk; *NAmE* 'kɑːrsɪk/ *adj.* [not usually before noun] feeling ill/sick because you are travelling in a car: *Do you get carsick?* ▸ **car·sick·ness** *noun* [U]

cart /kɑːt; *NAmE* kɑːrt/ *noun, verb*

■ ***noun*** **1** a vehicle with two or four wheels that is pulled by a horse and used for carrying loads: *a horse and cart* **2** (also **hand·cart**) a light vehicle with wheels that you pull or push by hand **3** (*NAmE*) (*BrE* **trol·ley**) a small vehicle with wheels that can be pushed or pulled along and is used for carrying things: *a* ***shopping/baggage cart*** ◇ *a serving cart* **4** (*NAmE*) (*BrE* **buggy**) a small car, often without a roof or doors, used for a particular purpose: *a golf cart*

IDM **put the ˌcart before the 'horse** to put or do things in the wrong order

■ ***verb*** **1** **~ sth** (**+ adv./prep.**) to carry sth in a cart or other vehicle: *The rubbish is then carted away for recycling.* **2** **~ sth + adv./prep.** (*informal*) to carry sth that is large, heavy or awkward in your hands: *We had to cart our luggage up six flights of stairs.* **3** **~ sb + adv./prep.** (*informal*) to take sb somewhere, especially with difficulty: *The demonstrators were carted off to the local police station.*

carte blanche /ˌkɑːt 'blɑːnʃ; *NAmE* ˌkɑːrt/ *noun* [U] (from *French*) **~** (**to do sth**) the complete freedom or authority to do whatever you like

car·tel /kɑː'tel; *NAmE* kɑːr'tel/ *noun* [C+sing./pl. v.] a group of separate companies that agree to increase profits by fixing prices and not competing with each other

C

Car·te·sian /kɑːˈtiːziən; -ʒən; *NAmE* kɑːrˈt-/ *adj.* connected with the French PHILOSOPHER Descartes and his ideas about philosophy and mathematics

cart·horse /ˈkɑːthɔːs; *NAmE* ˈkɑːrthɔːrs/ *noun* a large strong horse used especially in the past for heavy work on farms

car·til·age /ˈkɑːtɪlɪdʒ; *NAmE* ˈkɑːrt-/ *noun* [U, C] the strong white TISSUE that is important in support and especially in joints to prevent the bones rubbing against each other ➲ VISUAL VOCAB page V48

car·ti·la·gin·ous /ˌkɑːtɪˈlædʒɪnəs; *NAmE* ˌkɑːrt-/ *adj.* (*anatomy*) made of cartilage

cart·load /ˈkɑːtləʊd; *NAmE* ˈkɑːrtloʊd/ *noun* **1** the amount of sth that fills a CART **2** [usually pl.] (*informal*) a large amount of sth

car·tog·raph·er /kɑːˈtɒɡrəfə(r); *NAmE* kɑːrˈtɑːɡ-/ *noun* a person who draws or makes maps

car·tog·raphy /kɑːˈtɒɡrəfi; *NAmE* kɑːrˈtɑːɡ-/ *noun* [U] the art or process of drawing or making maps ▸ **carto·graph·ic** /ˌkɑːtəˈɡræfɪk; *NAmE* ˌkɑːrt-/ *adj.*

car·ton /ˈkɑːtn; *NAmE* ˈkɑːrtn/ *noun* **1** a light cardboard or plastic box or pot for holding goods, especially food or liquid; the contents of a carton: *a milk carton/a carton of milk* ➲ VISUAL VOCAB page V29 **2** (*NAmE*) a large container in which goods are packed in smaller containers: *a carton of cigarettes* ➲ VISUAL VOCAB page V29

car·toon /kɑːˈtuːn; *NAmE* kɑːrˈt-/ *noun* **1** an amusing drawing in a newspaper or magazine, especially one about politics or events in the news ➲ WRITING TUTOR page WT22 **2** = COMIC STRIP **3** (also ˌ**animated carˈtoon**) a film/movie made by photographing a series of gradually changing drawings or models, so that they look as if they are moving: *a Walt Disney cartoon* ◇ *a cartoon character* **4** (*technical*) a drawing made by an artist as a preparation for a painting

car·toon·ist /kɑːˈtuːnɪst; *NAmE* kɑːrˈt-/ *noun* a person who draws cartoons

car·touche /kɑːˈtuːʃ; *NAmE* kɑːr-/ *noun* an OBLONG or OVAL shape which contains a set of ancient Egyptian HIEROGLYPHS, often representing the name and title of a king or queen

cart·ridge /ˈkɑːtrɪdʒ; *NAmE* ˈkɑːrt-/ *noun* **1** (*NAmE* also **shell**) a tube or case containing EXPLOSIVE and a bullet or SHOT, for shooting from a gun **2** a case containing sth that is used in a machine, for example film for a camera, ink for a printer, etc. Cartridges are put into the machine and can be removed and replaced when they are finished or empty. **3** a thin tube containing ink which you put inside a pen

ˈ**cartridge paper** *noun* [U] (*BrE*) thick strong paper for drawing on

ˈ**cart track** *noun* (*BrE*) a rough track that is not suitable for ordinary cars, etc.

cart·wheel /ˈkɑːtwiːl; *NAmE* ˈkɑːrt-/ *noun* **1** a fast physical movement in which you turn in a circle sideways by putting your hands on the ground and bringing your legs, one at a time, over your head: *to* ***do/turn cartwheels*** **2** the wheel of a CART ▸ **cart·wheel** *verb* [I]

carve /kɑːv; *NAmE* kɑːrv/ *verb* **1** [T, I] to make objects, patterns, etc. by cutting away material from wood or stone: **~ sth** *a carved doorway* ◇ **~ sth from/out of sth** *The statue was carved out of a single piece of stone.* ◇ **~ sth into/in sth** *The wood had been carved into the shape of a flower.* ◇ **~ in sth** *She carves in both stone and wood.* ➲ COLLOCATIONS at ART **2** [T] **~ sth (on sth)** to write sth on a surface by cutting into it: *They carved their initials on the desk.* **3** to cut a large piece of cooked meat into smaller pieces for eating: [T, I] **~ (sth)** | **~ (sb) sth** *Who's going to carve the turkey?* **4** [T, no passive] to work hard in order to have a successful career, reputation, etc: **~ sth (out)** *He succeeded in carving out a career in the media.* ◇ **~ sth (out) for yourself** *She has carved a place for herself in the fashion world.* IDM see STONE

PHR V ˌ**carve sth↔ˈup** (*disapproving*) to divide a company, an area of land, etc. into smaller parts in order to share it between people

car·very /ˈkɑːvəri; *NAmE* ˈkɑːrv-/ *noun* (*pl.* -ies) (*BrE*) a restaurant that serves ROAST meat

ˈ**carve-up** *noun* [sing.] (*BrE, informal*) the dividing of sth such as a company or a country into separate parts

carv·ing /ˈkɑːvɪŋ; *NAmE* ˈkɑːrvɪŋ/ *noun* **1** [C, U] an object or a pattern made by cutting away material from wood or stone **2** [U] the art of making objects in this way ➲ VISUAL VOCAB page V35

ˈ**carving knife** *noun* a large sharp knife for cutting cooked meat ➲ VISUAL VOCAB page V23

ˈ**car wash** *noun* a place with special equipment, where you can pay to have your car washed

cary·atid /ˌkæriˈætɪd/ *noun* (*architecture*) a statue of a female figure used as a supporting PILLAR in a building

Casa·nova /ˌkæsəˈnəʊvə; ˌkæzə-; *NAmE* -ˈnoʊvə/ *noun* a man who has sex with a lot of women ORIGIN From Giovanni Jacopo Casanova, an Italian man in the 18th century who was famous for having sex with many women.

cas·bah = KASBAH

cas·cade /kæˈskeɪd/ *noun, verb*

■ ***noun*** **1** a small WATERFALL, especially one of several falling down a steep slope with rocks **2** a large amount of water falling or pouring down: *a cascade of rainwater* **3** (*formal*) a large amount of sth hanging down: *Her hair tumbled in a cascade down her back.* **4** (*formal*) a large number of things falling or coming quickly at the same time: *He crashed to the ground in a cascade of oil cans.*

■ ***verb*** **1** [I] **+ adv./prep.** to flow downwards in large amounts: *Water cascaded down the mountainside.* **2** [I] **+ adv./prep.** (*formal*) to fall or hang in large amounts: *Blonde hair cascaded over her shoulders.*

case 0‒ /keɪs/ *noun, verb*

■ ***noun***

▸ SITUATION **1** 0‒ [C] a particular situation or a situation of a particular type: *In some cases people have had to wait several weeks for an appointment.* ◇ *The company only dismisses its employees in cases of gross misconduct.* ◇ *It's a* ***classic case*** (= a very typical case) *of bad planning.* ➲ see also WORST-CASE ➲ SYNONYMS at EXAMPLE, SITUATION **2** 0‒ **the case** [sing.] **~ (that...)** the true situation: *If that is the case* (= if the situation described is true), *we need more staff.* ◇ *It is simply not the case that prison conditions are improving.* **3** 0‒ [C, usually sing.] a situation that relates to a particular person or thing: *In your case, we are prepared to be lenient.* ◇ *I cannot make an exception in your case* (= for you and not for others). ◇ *Every application will be decided* ***on a case-by-case basis*** (= each one will be considered separately). ➲ SYNONYMS at EXAMPLE

▸ POLICE INVESTIGATION **4** 0‒ [C] a matter that is being officially investigated, especially by the police: *a murder case* ◇ *a case of theft* ➲ COLLOCATIONS at CRIME

▸ IN COURT **5** 0‒ [C] a question to be decided in court: *The case will be heard next week.* ◇ *a court case* ◇ *to* ***win/lose a case*** ➲ see also TEST CASE

▸ ARGUMENTS **6** 0‒ [C, usually sing.] **~ (for/against sth)** a set of facts or arguments that support one side in a trial, a discussion, etc: *the* ***case for the defence/prosecution*** ◇ *Our lawyer didn't think we* ***had a case*** (= had enough good arguments to win in a court of law). ◇ *the* ***case for/against*** *private education* ◇ *The report* ***makes out a*** *strong* ***case*** (= gives good arguments) *for spending more money on hospitals.* ◇ *You will each be given the chance to* ***state*** *your* ***case***.

▸ CONTAINER **7** 0‒ [C] (often in compounds) a container or covering used to protect or store things; a container with its contents or the amount that it contains: *a pencil case* ◇ *a jewellery case* ◇ *a packing case* (= a large wooden box for packing things in) ◇ *The museum was full of stuffed animals in glass cases.* ◇ *a case* (= 12 bottles) *of champagne* ➲ picture at CLOCK ➲ see also VANITY CASE **8** 0‒ [C] = SUITCASE: *Let me carry your case for you.*

▸ OF DISEASE **9** 0‒ [C] the fact of sb having a disease or an injury; a person suffering from a disease or an injury: *a severe case of typhoid* ◇ *The most serious cases were treated at the scene of the accident.*

▸ PERSON **10** [C] a person who needs, or is thought to need, special treatment or attention: *He's a hopeless case.*
▸ GRAMMAR **11** [C, U] the form of a noun, an adjective or a pronoun in some languages, that shows its relationship to another word: *the* ***nominative/accusative/genitive case*** ◇ *Latin nouns have case, number and gender.*
IDM **as the ˌcase may ˈbe** used to say that one of two or more possibilities is true, but which one is true depends on the circumstances: *There may be an announcement about this tomorrow—or not, as the case may be.* **be on sb's ˈcase** (*informal*) to criticize sb all the time: *She's always on my case about cleaning my room.* **be on the ˈcase** to be dealing with a particular matter, especially a criminal investigation: *We have two agents on the case.* **get off my ˈcase** (*informal*) used to tell sb to stop criticizing you **a case in ˈpoint** a clear example of the problem, situation, etc. that is being discussed ➲ LANGUAGE BANK at E.G. **in ˈany case** whatever happens or may have happened: *There's no point complaining now—we're leaving tomorrow in any case.* **(just) in case (...)** because of the possibility of sth happening: *You'd better take the keys in case I'm out.* ◇ *You probably won't need to call—but take my number, just in case.* ◇ *In case* (= if it is true that) *you're wondering why Jo's here—let me explain...* **in case of sth** (often on official notices) if sth happens: *In case of fire, ring the alarm bell.* **in ˈthat case** if that happens or has happened; if that is the situation: *'I've made up my mind.' 'In that case, there's no point discussing it.'* ➲ more at DOG *n.*, REST *v.*
■ *verb*
IDM **case the joint** (*informal*) to look carefully around a building so that you can plan how to steal things from it at a later time

case·book /ˈkeɪsbʊk/ *noun* a written record kept by doctors, lawyers, etc. of cases they have dealt with

cased /keɪst/ *adj.* **~ in sth** completely covered with a particular material: *The towers are made of steel cased in granite.* ➲ see also CASING

ˌcase ˈhistory *noun* a record of a person's background, past illnesses, etc. that a doctor or SOCIAL WORKER studies

ˈcase law *noun* [U] (*law*) law based on decisions made by judges in earlier cases ➲ compare COMMON LAW, STATUTE LAW ➲ see also TEST CASE

case·load /ˈkeɪsləʊd; *NAmE* -loʊd/ *noun* all the people that a doctor, SOCIAL WORKER, etc. is responsible for at one time: *a heavy caseload* (= a large number of people)

case·ment /ˈkeɪsmənt/ (also **ˌcasement ˈwindow**) *noun* a window that opens on HINGES like a door ➲ VISUAL VOCAB page V15

ˌcase-ˈsensitive *adj.* (*computing*) a program which is **case-sensitive** recognizes the difference between capital letters and small letters

ˈcase study *noun* a detailed account of the development of a person, a group of people or a situation over a period of time

case·work /ˈkeɪswɜːk; *NAmE* -wɜːrk/ *noun* [U] social work (= work done to help people in the community with special needs) involving the study of a particular person's family and background

case·work·er /ˈkeɪswɜːkə(r); *NAmE* -wɜːrk-/ *noun* (*especially NAmE*) a SOCIAL WORKER who helps a particular person or family in the community with special needs

cash 0-w /kæʃ/ *noun, verb*
■ *noun* [U] **1** 0-w money in the form of coins or notes/bills: *How much cash do you have on you?* ◇ *Payments can be made by cheque or* ***in cash***. ◇ *Customers are offered a 10% discount if they* ***pay cash***. ◇ *The thieves stole £500* ***in cash***. ➲ COLLOCATIONS at FINANCE ➲ picture at MONEY ➲ see also HARD CASH, PETTY CASH ➲ SYNONYMS at MONEY **2** 0-w (*informal*) money in any form: *The museum needs to find ways of raising cash.* ◇ *I'm short of cash right now.* ◇ *I'm constantly* ***strapped for cash*** (= without enough money).
IDM **cash ˈdown** (*BrE*) (also **ˌcash up ˈfront** *NAmE, BrE*) with immediate payment of cash: *to pay for sth cash down* **ˌcash in ˈhand** (*BrE, informal*) if you pay for goods and services **cash in hand**, you pay in cash, especially so that the person being paid can avoid paying tax on the amount **ˌcash on deˈlivery** (*abbr.* **COD**) a system of paying for goods when they are delivered
■ *verb* **~ a cheque/check** to exchange a cheque/check for the amount of money that it is worth
IDM **cash in your ˈchips** (*informal*) to die
PHR V **ˌcash ˈin (on sth)** (*disapproving*) to gain an advantage for yourself from a situation, especially in a way that other people think is wrong or immoral: *The film studio is being accused of cashing in on the singer's death.* **ˌcash sth↔ˈin** to exchange sth, such as an insurance policy, for money before the date on which it would normally end **ˌcash ˈup** (*BrE*) (*NAmE* **ˌcash ˈout**) to add up the amount of money that has been received in a shop/store, club, etc, especially at the end of the day

ˌcash and ˈcarry *noun* [C, U] a large WHOLESALE shop/store that sells goods in large quantities at low prices to customers from other businesses who pay in cash and take the goods away themselves; the system of buying and selling goods in this way

cash·back (*BrE*) (*US* **cash-back**) /ˈkæʃbæk/ *noun* **1** [U] if you ask for **cashback** when you are paying for goods in a shop/store with a DEBIT CARD (= a plastic card that takes money directly from your bank account), you get a sum of money in cash, that is added to your bill **2** [U, C] a sum of money that is offered to people who buy particular products or services: *There's £200 cashback on this computer if you buy before January 31.*

ˈcash bar *noun* a bar at a wedding, party, etc, at which the guests have to pay for their own drinks rather than getting them free

ˈcash box *noun* a box with a lock for keeping money in, usually made of metal

ˈcash card *noun* (*BrE*) (*US* **ATˈM card**) a plastic card used to get money from a CASH MACHINE (= a machine in or outside a bank) ➲ compare CHEQUE CARD, CREDIT CARD, DEBIT CARD

ˈcash cow *noun* (*business*) the part of a business that always makes a profit and that provides money for the rest of the business

ˈcash crop *noun* a crop grown for selling, rather than for use by the person who grows it ➲ compare SUBSISTENCE

ˈcash desk *noun* (*BrE*) the place in a shop/store where you pay for goods that you have bought

ˈcash dispenser *noun* (*BrE*) = CASH MACHINE

ˌcashed ˈup *adj.* (*informal, especially AustralE*) very rich: *Mark was cashed up that night, so he got the drinks.* ◇ *support from cashed-up investors*

cashew /ˈkæʃuː; kæˈʃuː/ (also **ˈcashew nut**) *noun* the small curved nut of the tropical American **cashew tree**, used in cooking and often eaten salted with alcoholic drinks ➲ VISUAL VOCAB page V28

ˈcash flow *noun* [C, U] the movement of money into and out of a business as goods are bought and sold: *a healthy cash flow* (= having enough money to make payments when necessary) ◇ *cash-flow problems*

cash·ier /kæˈʃɪə(r); *NAmE* -ˈʃɪr/ *noun, verb*
■ *noun* a person whose job is to receive and pay out money in a bank, shop/store, hotel, etc.
■ *verb* [usually passive] **~ sb** to make sb leave the army, navy, etc. because they have done sth wrong

cash·less /ˈkæʃləs/ *adj.* done or working without using cash: *We are moving towards the cashless society.*

ˈcash machine (*BrE* also **ˈcash dispenser**, **ˈcashpoint™**) (also **ATM** *NAmE, BrE*) (also **ABM** *CanE*) *noun* a machine in or outside a bank, etc, from which you can get money from your bank account using a special plastic card ➲ COLLOCATIONS at FINANCE

cash·mere /ˈkæʃmɪə(r); ˌkæʃˈm-; *NAmE* ˈkæʒmɪr; ˈkæʃ-/ *noun* [U] fine soft wool made from the long hair of a type of GOAT, used especially for making expensive clothes

'cash register (*BrE* also **till**) (*NAmE* also **regis·ter**) *noun* a machine used in shops/stores, restaurants, etc. that has a drawer for keeping money in, and that shows and records the amount of money received for each thing that is sold

'cash-starved *adj.* [only before noun] without enough money, usually because another organization, such as the government, has failed to provide it: *cash-starved public services*

'cash-strapped *adj.* [only before noun] without enough money: ***cash-strapped governments/shoppers***

cas·ing /'keɪsɪŋ/ *noun* [C, U] a covering that protects sth

ca·sino /kə'siːnəʊ; *NAmE* -noʊ/ *noun* (*pl.* -os) a public building or room where people play gambling games for money

cask /kɑːsk; *NAmE* kæsk/ *noun* a small wooden BARREL used for storing liquids, especially alcoholic drinks; the amount contained in a cask: *a wine cask/a cask of wine*

cas·ket /'kɑːskɪt; *NAmE* 'kæs-/ *noun* **1** a small decorated box for holding jewellery or other valuable things, especially in the past **2** (*NAmE*) (also **coffin** especially in *BrE*) a box in which a dead body is buried or CREMATED

Cas·san·dra /kə'sændrə/ *noun* a person who predicts that sth bad will happen, especially a person who is not believed ORIGIN From the name of a princess in ancient Greek stories to whom Apollo gave the ability to predict the future. After she tricked him, he stopped people from believing her.

cas·sava /kə'sɑːvə/ (also **man·ioc**) *noun* [U] **1** a tropical plant with many branches and long roots that you can eat **2** the roots of this plant, which can be boiled, fried, ROASTED or made into flour

cas·ser·ole /'kæsərəʊl; *NAmE* -roʊl/ *noun* **1** [C, U] a hot dish made with meat, vegetables, etc. that are cooked slowly in liquid in an oven: *a chicken casserole* ◇ *Is there any casserole left?* **2** [C] (also **'casserole dish**) a container with a lid used for cooking meat, etc. in liquid in an oven ➲ VISUAL VOCAB page V24 ▸ **cas·ser·ole** *verb* **~ sth** ➲ VISUAL VOCAB page V24

cas·sette /kə'set/ *noun* **1** a small flat plastic case containing tape for playing or recording music or sound: *a* ***cassette recorder/player*** ◇ *available* ***on cassette*** ◇ *a video cassette* (= for recording sound and pictures) **2** a plastic case containing film that can be put into a camera

cas·sock /'kæsək/ *noun* a long piece of clothing, usually black or red, worn by some Christian priests and other people with special duties in a church

cas·sou·let /'kæsʊleɪ/ *noun* [U] (from *French*) a dish consisting of meat and BEANS cooked slowly in liquid

cas·so·wary /'kæsəwəri; -weəri; *NAmE* -weri/ *noun* (*pl.* -ies) a very large bird related to the EMU, that does not fly. It is found mainly in New Guinea.

cast 0-w /kɑːst; *NAmE* kæst/ *verb, noun*

■ ***verb*** (cast, cast)

▸ A LOOK/GLANCE/SMILE **1** [T] **~ (sb) sth** to look, smile, etc. in a particular direction: *She cast a welcoming smile in his direction.*

▸ LIGHT/A SHADOW **2** [T] **~ sth (over sth)** to make light, a shadow, etc. appear in a particular place: *The setting sun cast an orange glow over the mountains.* ◇ (*figurative*) *The sad news cast a shadow over the proceedings* (= made people feel unhappy).

▸ DOUBT **3** [T] **~ doubt/aspersions (on/upon sth)** to say, do or suggest sth that makes people doubt sth or think that sb is less honest, good, etc: *This latest evidence casts serious doubt on his version of events.*

▸ FISHING LINE **4** [I, T] **~ (sth)** to throw one end of a FISHING LINE into a river, etc.

▸ THROW **5** [T] **~ sb/sth** (*literary*) to throw sb/sth somewhere, especially using force: *The priceless treasures had been cast into the Nile.* ◇ *They cast anchor at nightfall.*

▸ SKIN **6** [T] **~ sth** when a snake **casts** its skin, the skin comes off as part of a natural process SYN **shed**

▸ SHOE **7** [T] **~ sth** if a horse **casts** a shoe, the shoe comes off by accident

▸ ACTORS **8** [T] to choose actors to play the different parts in a film/movie, play, etc; to choose an actor to play a particular role: **~ sth** *The play is being cast in both the US and Britain.* ◇ **~ sb (as sb)** *He has cast her as an ambitious lawyer in his latest movie.*

▸ DESCRIBE **9** [T] to describe or present sb/yourself in a particular way: **~ sb/yourself (as sth)** *He cast himself as the innocent victim of a hate campaign.* ◇ **~ sb/yourself (in sth)** *The press were quick to cast her in the role of 'the other woman'.*

▸ VOTE **10** [T] **~ a/your vote/ballot (for sb/sth)** to vote for sb/sth

▸ SHAPE METAL **11** [T] **~ sth (in sth)** to shape hot liquid metal, etc. by pouring it into a hollow container (called a MOULD): *a statue cast in bronze* ◇ (*figurative*) *an artist* ***cast in the mould of*** (= very similar to) *Miró*

IDM **cast your mind back (to sth)** to make yourself think about sth that happened in the past: *I want you to cast your minds back to the first time you met.* **cast your net wide** to consider a lot of different people, activities, possibilities, etc. when you are looking for sth **cast a 'spell (on sb/sth)** to use words that are thought to be magic and have the power to change or influence sb/sth ➲ more at ADRIFT, CAUTION *n.*, DIE *n.*, EYE *n.*, LIGHT *n.*, LOT *n.*

PHR V ,**cast a'bout/a'round for sth** to try hard to think of or find sth, especially when this is difficult: *She cast around desperately for a safe topic of conversation.* ,**cast sb/sth↔a'side** (*formal*) to get rid of sb/sth because you no longer want or need them SYN **discard** **be ,cast a'way** to be left somewhere after a SHIPWRECK ➲ related noun CASTAWAY **be ,cast 'down (by sth)** (*literary*) to be sad or unhappy about sth ➲ see also DOWNCAST ,**cast 'off** | ,**cast sth↔'off** **1** to undo the ropes that are holding a boat in a fixed position, in order to sail away **2** (in knitting) to remove STITCHES from the needles in a way that forms an edge that will not come undone ,**cast sth↔'off** (*formal*) to get rid of sth because you no longer want or need it: *The town is still trying to cast off its dull image.* ,**cast 'on** | ,**cast sth↔'on** (in knitting) to put the first row of STITCHES on a needle ,**cast sb/sth↔'out** (*literary*) to get rid of sb/sth, especially by using force: *He claimed to have the power to cast out demons.* ➲ related noun OUTCAST

■ ***noun***

▸ ACTORS **1** 0-w [C+sing./pl. v.] all the people who act in a play or film/movie: *The whole cast performs/perform brilliantly.* ◇ *members of the cast* ◇ *an* ***all-star cast*** (= including many well-known actors) ◇ *the* ***supporting cast*** (= not the main actors, but the others) ◇ *a cast list*

▸ IN SHAPING METAL **2** [C] an object that is made by pouring hot liquid metal, etc. into a MOULD (= a specially shaped container) **3** [C] a shaped container used to make an object SYN **mould**

▸ APPEARANCE **4** [sing.] (*BrE, formal*) the way that a person or thing is or appears: *He has an unusual* ***cast of mind.*** ◇ *I disliked the arrogant cast to her mouth.*

▸ THROW **5** [C] an act of throwing sth, especially a fishing line

▸ ON ARM/LEG **6** [C] = PLASTER CAST: *Her leg's* ***in a cast.*** ➲ see also OPENCAST

cas·ta·nets /,kæstə'nets/ *noun* [pl.] a musical instrument that consists of two small round pieces of wood that you hold in the hand and hit together with the fingers to make a noise. Castanets are used especially by Spanish dancers. ➲ VISUAL VOCAB page V30

cast·away /'kɑːstəweɪ; *NAmE* 'kæst-/ *noun* a person whose ship has sunk (= who has been SHIPWRECKED) and who has had to swim to a lonely place, usually an island

caste /kɑːst; *NAmE* kæst/ *noun* **1** [C] any of the four main divisions of Hindu society, originally those made according to functions in society: *the caste system* ◇ *high-caste Brahmins* **2** [C] a social class, especially one whose members do not allow others to join it: *the ruling caste* **3** [U] the system of dividing society into classes based on differences in family origin, rank or wealth

cas·tel·lated /ˈkæstəleɪtɪd/ *adj.* (*architecture*) built in the style of a castle with BATTLEMENTS

cas·tel·la·tions /ˌkæstəˈleɪʃnz/ *noun* [pl.] the top edge of a castle wall, that has regular spaces along it

cas·ter (*NAmE*) (*BrE* **cas·tor**) /ˈkɑːstə(r); *NAmE* ˈkæs-/ *noun* one of the small wheels fixed to the bottom of a piece of furniture so that it can be moved easily

ˌcaster ˈsugar (also **ˌcastor ˈsugar**) *noun* [U] (*BrE*) white sugar in the form of very fine grains, used in cooking

cas·ti·gate /ˈkæstɪgeɪt/ *verb* **~ sb/sth/yourself** (**for sth**) (*formal*) to criticize sb/sth severely: *He castigated himself for being so stupid.* ▸ **cas·ti·ga·tion** /ˌkæstɪˈgeɪʃn/ *noun* [U]

cast·ing /ˈkɑːstɪŋ; *NAmE* ˈkæst-/ *noun* **1** [U] the process of choosing actors for a play or film/movie **2** [C] an object made by pouring hot liquid metal, etc. into a MOULD (= a specially shaped container)

ˈcasting couch *noun* used to refer to a process in which actors are chosen for a film/movie, etc. if they have sex with the person in charge of choosing the actors

ˌcasting ˈvote *noun* [usually sing.] the vote given by the person in charge of an official meeting to decide an issue when votes on each side are equal

ˌcast ˈiron *noun* [U] a hard type of iron that does not bend easily and is shaped by pouring the hot liquid metal into a MOULD (= a specially shaped container)

ˌcast-ˈiron *adj.* **1** made of cast iron: *a cast-iron bridge* **2** (*BrE*) very strong or certain; that cannot be broken or fail: *a* ***cast-iron guarantee/promise*** ◇ *a* ***cast-iron excuse/alibi*** ➲ compare IRONCLAD

cas·tle 0‑ᵚ /ˈkɑːsl; *NAmE* ˈkæsl/ *noun*
1 0‑ᵚ a large strong building with thick high walls and towers, built in the past by kings or queens, or other important people, to defend themselves against attack ➲ VISUAL VOCAB page V13 ➲ see also SANDCASTLE **2** (also **rook**) (in CHESS) any of the four pieces placed in the corner squares of the board at the start of the game, usually made to look like a castle ➲ VISUAL VOCAB page V33
IDM **(build) castles in the ˈair** (*BrE*) (to have) plans or dreams that are not likely to happen or come true ➲ more at ENGLISHMAN

ˈcast-off (*especially BrE*) (also **ˈhand-me-down** especially in *NAmE*) *noun* [usually pl.] a piece of clothing that the original owner no longer wants to wear ▸ **ˈcast-off** (also **ˈhand-me-down**) *adj.*: *a cast-off overcoat*

cas·tor (*BrE*) (*NAmE* **cas·ter**) /ˈkɑːstə(r); *NAmE* ˈkæs-/ *noun* one of the small wheels fixed to the bottom of a piece of furniture so that it can be moved easily ➲ VISUAL VOCAB page V56

ˌcastor ˈoil *noun* [U] a thick yellow oil obtained from a tropical plant and used in the past as a type of medicine, usually as a LAXATIVE

ˌcastor ˈsugar *noun* [U] = CASTER SUGAR

cas·trate /kæˈstreɪt; *NAmE* ˈkæstreɪt/ *verb* **~ sb/sth** to remove the TESTICLES of a male animal or person ▸ **cas·tra·tion** /kæˈstreɪʃn/ *noun* [U, C]

cas·ual /ˈkæʒuəl/ *adj.*, *noun*
■ ***adj.***
▸ WITHOUT CARE/ATTENTION **1** [usually before noun] not showing much care or thought; seeming not to be worried; not wanting to show that sth is important to you: *a casual manner* ◇ *It was just a casual remark—I wasn't really serious.* ◇ *He tried to sound casual, but I knew he was worried.* ◇ *They have a casual attitude towards safety* (= they don't care enough). **2** [usually before noun] without paying attention to detail: *a casual glance* ◇ *It's obvious even to the casual observer.*
▸ NOT FORMAL **3** not formal: *casual clothes* (= comfortable clothes that you choose to wear in your free time) ◇ *family parties and other casual occasions*
▸ WORK **4** [usually before noun] (*BrE*) not permanent; not done, or doing sth regularly: ***casual workers/labour*** ◇ *Students sometimes do casual work in the tourist trade.* ◇ *They are employed* ***on a casual basis*** (= they do not have a permanent job with the company).
▸ RELATIONSHIP **5** [usually before noun] without deep affection: *a casual acquaintance* ◇ *a casual friendship* ◇ *to have casual sex* (= to have sex without having a steady relationship with that partner)
▸ BY CHANCE **6** [only before noun] happening by chance; doing sth by chance: *a* ***casual encounter/meeting*** ◇ *a casual passer-by* ◇ *The exhibition is interesting to both the enthusiast and the casual visitor.* ◇ *The disease is not spread by casual contact.*
▸ **cas·ual·ly** *adv.*: *'What did he say about me?' she asked as casually as she could.* ◇ *They chatted casually on the phone.* ◇ *dressed casually in jeans and T-shirt* **cas·ual·ness** *noun* [U]: *He was sure that the casualness of the gesture was deliberate.*
■ ***noun*** (*BrE*)
▸ CLOTHES **1** **casuals** [pl.] informal clothes or shoes: *dressed in casuals*
▸ WORKER **2** [C] a casual worker (= one who does not work permanently for a company)

casu·al·iza·tion /ˌkæʒuəlaɪˈzeɪʃn/ *noun* [U] the practice of employing temporary staff for short periods instead of permanent staff, in order to save costs

casu·alty /ˈkæʒuəlti/ *noun* (*pl.* -ies) **1** [C] a person who is killed or injured in war or in an accident: *road casualties* ◇ *Both sides had suffered* ***heavy casualties*** (= many people had been killed). ➲ COLLOCATIONS at WAR **2** [C] a person that suffers or a thing that is destroyed when sth else takes place SYN **victim**: *She became a casualty of the reduction in part-time work* (= she lost her job). ◇ *Small shops have been a casualty of the recession.* **3** [U] (also **ˈcasualty department**, **ˌaccident and eˈmergency**) (all *BrE*) (*NAmE* **eˈmergency room**) the part of a hospital where people who need urgent treatment are taken: *The victims were rushed to casualty.*

casu·is·try /ˈkæʒuɪstri/ *noun* [U] (*formal*, *disapproving*) a way of solving moral or legal problems by using clever arguments that may be false

casus belli /ˌkeɪsəs ˈbelaɪ; ˌkɑːsʊs ˈbeliː/ *noun* (*pl.* **casus belli**) (*formal*) an act or situation that is used to justify a war

cat 0‑ᵚ /kæt/ *noun*
1 0‑ᵚ a small animal with soft fur that people often keep as a pet. Cats catch and kill birds and mice: *cat food* ➲ see also KITTEN, TOMCAT **2** a wild animal of the cat family: *the big cats* (= LIONS, TIGERS, etc.) ➲ see also FAT CAT, WILDCAT
IDM **be the cat's ˈwhiskers/pyˈjamas** (*informal*) to be the best thing, person, idea, etc: *He thinks he's the cat's whiskers* (= he has a high opinion of himself). **let the ˈcat out of the bag** to tell a secret carelessly or by mistake: *I wanted it to be a surprise, but my sister let the cat out of the bag.* **like a ˌcat on hot ˈbricks** (*BrE*) very nervous: *She was like a cat on hot bricks before her driving test.* **like a cat that's got the ˈcream** (*BrE*) (*US* **like the cat that got/ate/swallowed the canˈary**) very pleased with yourself SYN **smug** **look like sth the ˈcat brought/dragged in** (*informal*) (of a person) to look dirty and untidy **not have/stand a cat in ˈhell's chance** (**of doing sth**) to have no chance at all **play** (**a game of**) **ˌcat and ˈmouse with sb** | **play a ˌcat-and-ˈmouse game with sb** to play a cruel game with sb in your power by changing your behaviour very often, so that they become nervous and do not know what to expect **put/set the cat among the ˈpigeons** (*BrE*) to say or do sth that is likely to cause trouble **when the cat's aˈway the mice will ˈplay** (*saying*) people enjoy themselves more and behave with greater freedom when the person in charge of them is not there ➲ more at CURIOSITY, RAIN *v.*, ROOM *n.*, WAY *n.*

ca·tab·ol·ism (also **ka·tab·ol·ism**) /kəˈtæbəlɪzəm/ *noun* [U] (*biology*) the process by which chemical structures are broken down and energy is released

cata·clysm /ˈkætəklɪzəm/ *noun* (*formal*) a sudden disaster or a violent event that causes change, for example a flood or a war ▸ **cata·clys·mic** /ˌkætəˈklɪzmɪk/ *adj.* [usually before noun]

C

cata·combs /ˈkætəkuːmz; *NAmE* -koʊmz/ *noun* [pl.] a series of underground tunnels used for burying dead people, especially in ancient times

cata·falque /ˈkætəfælk/ *noun* a decorated platform on which the dead body of a famous person is placed before a funeral

C

Cata·lan /ˈkætəlæn/ *noun, adj.*
- ***noun* 1** [U] a language spoken in Catalonia, Andorra, the Balearic Islands and parts of southern France **2** [C] a person who was born in or who lives in Catalonia
- ***adj.*** connected with Catalonia, its people, its language, or its culture

cata·lepsy /ˈkætəlepsi/ *noun* [U] (*medical*) a condition in which sb's body becomes stiff and they temporarily become unconscious ▶ **cata·lep·tic** /ˌkætəˈleptɪk/ *adj.*

cata·logue (*NAmE* also **cata·log**) /ˈkætəlɒg; *NAmE* -lɔːg; -lɑːg/ *noun, verb*
- ***noun* 1** a complete list of items, for example of things that people can look at or buy: *a mail-order catalogue* (= a book showing goods for sale to be sent to people's homes) ◇ *to consult the library catalogue* ◇ *An illustrated catalogue accompanies the exhibition.* ◇ *an online catalogue* **2** a long series of things that happen (usually bad things): *a **catalogue of disasters/errors/misfortunes***
- ***verb* 1 ~ sth** to arrange a list of things in order in a catalogue; to record sth in a catalogue **2 ~ sth** to give a list of things connected with a particular person, event, etc: *Interviews with the refugees catalogue a history of discrimination and violence.*

cata·lyse (*BrE*) (*NAmE* **cata·lyze**) /ˈkætəlaɪz/ *verb* **~ sth** (*chemistry*) to make a chemical reaction happen faster

cata·lyst /ˈkætəlɪst/ *noun* **1** (*chemistry*) a substance that makes a chemical reaction happen faster without being changed itself **2 ~ (for sth)** a person or thing that causes a change: *I see my role as being a catalyst for change.*

cata·lyt·ic con·vert·er /ˌkætəˌlɪtɪk kənˈvɜːtə(r); *NAmE* -ˈvɜːrt-/ *noun* a device used in the EXHAUST system of vehicles to reduce the damage caused to the environment

cata·ma·ran /ˌkætəməˈræn/ *noun* a fast sailing boat with two HULLS ➲ VISUAL VOCAB page V44 ➲ compare TRIMARAN

cata·mite /ˈkætəmaɪt/ *noun* (*old use*) a boy kept as a SLAVE for a man to have sex with

cata·pult /ˈkætəpʌlt/ *noun, verb*
- ***noun* 1** (*BrE*) (*NAmE* **sling·shot**) a stick shaped like a Y with a rubber band attached to it, used by children for shooting stones **2** a weapon used in the past to throw heavy stones **3** a machine used for sending planes up into the air from a ship

catapult (*BrE*)
slingshot (*NAmE*)

- ***verb*** [T, I] to throw sb/sth or be thrown suddenly and violently through the air: **~ (sb/sth) + adv./prep.** *She was catapulted out of the car as it hit the wall.* ◇ (*figurative*) *The movie catapulted him to international stardom.*

cat·ar·act /ˈkætərækt/ *noun* **1** a medical condition that affects the LENS of the eye and causes a gradual loss of sight **2** (*literary*) a large steep WATERFALL

ca·tarrh /kəˈtɑː(r)/ *noun* [U] thick liquid (called PHLEGM) that you have in your nose and throat because, for example, you have a cold

ca·tas·trophe /kəˈtæstrəfi/ *noun* **1** a sudden event that causes many people to suffer **SYN** **disaster**: *Early warnings of rising water levels prevented another major catastrophe.* **2** an event that causes one person or a group of people personal suffering, or that makes difficulties: *The attempt to expand the business was a catastrophe for the firm.* ◇ *We've had a few catastrophes with the food for the party.* ▶ **cata·stroph·ic** /ˌkætəˈstrɒfɪk; *NAmE* -ˈstrɑː-/ **SYN** **disastrous** *adj.*: *catastrophic effects/losses/results* ◇ (*US*) *a catastrophic illness* (= one that costs a very large amount to treat) **cata·stroph·ic·al·ly** /-kli/ *adv.*

cata·to·nia /ˌkætəˈtəʊniə; *NAmE* -ˈtoʊ-/ *noun* [U] (*medical*) a condition resulting from a mental illness, especially SCHIZOPHRENIA, in which a person does not move for long periods

cata·ton·ic /ˌkætəˈtɒnɪk; *NAmE* -ˈtɑːnɪk/ *adj.* (*medical*) not able to move or show any reaction to things because of illness, shock, etc.

cat·bird seat /ˈkætbɜːd siːt; *NAmE* -bɜːrd/ *noun*
IDM **be in the ˈcatbird seat** (*NAmE*) to have an advantage over other people or be in control of a situation

ˈcat burglar *noun* a thief who climbs up the outside of a building in order to enter it and steal sth

cat·call /ˈkætkɔːl/ *noun* [usually pl.] a noise or shout expressing anger at or disapproval of sb who is speaking or performing in public

catch 🗝 /kætʃ/ *verb, noun*
- ***verb*** (**caught, caught** /kɔːt/)
- ▸ HOLD **1** 🗝 [T] **~ sth** to stop and hold a moving object, especially in your hands: *She managed to catch the keys as they fell.* ◇ *'Throw me over that towel, will you?' 'OK. Catch!'* ◇ *The dog caught the stick in its mouth.* **2** 🗝 [T] **~ sth** to hold a liquid when it falls: *The roof was leaking and I had to use a bucket to catch the drips.* **3** 🗝 [T] **~ sb/sth (+ adv./prep.)** to take hold of sb/sth: *He **caught hold of** her arm as she tried to push past him.*
- ▸ CAPTURE **4** 🗝 [T] **~ sb/sth** to capture a person or an animal that tries or would try to escape: *The murderer was never caught.* ◇ *Our cat is hopeless at catching mice.* ◇ *How many fish did you catch?*
- ▸ SB DOING STH **5** 🗝 [T] to find or discover sb doing sth, especially sth wrong: **~ sb doing sth** *I caught her smoking in the bathroom.* ◇ ***You wouldn't catch me** working* (= I would never work) *on a Sunday!* ◇ **~ yourself doing sth** *She caught herself wondering whether she had made a mistake.* ◇ **~ sb + adv./prep.** *He was caught with bomb-making equipment in his home.* ◇ *Mark walked in and **caught them at it*** (= in the act of doing sth wrong). ◇ *thieves **caught in the act*** ◇ *You've caught me at a bad time* (= at a time when I am busy).
- ▸ BUS/TRAIN/PLANE **6** 🗝 [T] **~ sth** to be in time for a bus, train, plane, etc. and get on it: *We caught the 12.15 from Oxford.* ◇ *I must go—I have a train to catch.*
- ▸ BE IN TIME **7** [T] **~ sb/sth** to be in time to do sth, talk to sb, etc: *I caught him just as he was leaving the building.* ◇ *I was hoping to catch you at home* (= to telephone you at home when you were there). ◇ *The illness can be treated provided it's caught* (= discovered) *early enough.* ◇ (*BrE*) *to **catch the post*** (= post letters before the box is emptied) ◇ (*BrE, informal*) *Bye for now! I'll **catch you later*** (= speak to you again later).
- ▸ SEE/HEAR **8** [T] **~ sth** (*informal, especially NAmE*) to see or hear sth; to attend sth: *Let's eat now and maybe we could catch a movie later.* ➲ SYNONYMS at SEE
- ▸ HAPPEN UNEXPECTEDLY **9** 🗝 [T] **~ sb** to happen unexpectedly and put sb in a difficult situation: *His arrival **caught** me **by surprise**.* ◇ *She **got caught in** a thunderstorm.*
- ▸ ILLNESS **10** 🗝 [T] to get an illness: **~ sth** *to catch measles* ◇ **~ sth from sb** *I think I must have caught this cold from you.*
- ▸ BECOME STUCK **11** 🗝 [I, T] to become stuck in or on sth; to make sth become stuck: **~ (in/on sth)** *Her dress caught on a nail.* ◇ **~ sth (in/on sth)** *He caught his thumb in the door.*
- ▸ HIT **12** [T] to hit sb/sth: **~ sb/sth + adv./prep.** *The stone caught him on the side of the head.* ◇ **~ sb sth + adv./prep.** *She caught him a blow on the chin.*
- ▸ NOTICE **13** [T] **~ sth** to notice sth only for a moment: *She **caught sight** of a car in the distance.* ◇ *He **caught a glimpse** of himself in the mirror.* ◇ *I caught a look of surprise on her face.* ◇ *He **caught a whiff** of her perfume.*
- ▸ HEAR/UNDERSTAND **14** 🗝 [T] **~ sth** to hear or understand sth: *Sorry, I didn't quite catch what you said.*
- ▸ INTEREST **15** 🗝 [T] **~ sb's interest, imagination, attention, etc.** if sth **catches** your interest, etc, you notice it and feel interested in it
- ▸ SHOW ACCURATELY **16** [T] **~ sth** to show or describe sth ac-

curately **SYN capture**: *The artist has caught her smile perfectly.*

▸ LIGHT **17** [T] **~ sth** if sth **catches** the light or the light **catches** it, the light shines on it and makes it shine too: *The knife gleamed as it **caught the light**.*

▸ THE SUN **18** [T] **~ the sun** (*informal*) if you **catch the sun**, you become red or brown because of spending time in the sun

▸ BURN **19** [T, I] **~ (fire)** to begin to burn: *The wooden rafters caught fire.* ◇ *These logs are wet: they won't catch.*

▸ IN CRICKET **20** [T] **~ sb** to make a player unable to continue BATTING by catching the ball they have hit before it touches the ground

IDM **catch your 'breath 1** to stop breathing for a moment because of fear, shock, etc. **2** to breathe normally again after running or doing some tiring exercise **catch your 'death (of 'cold)** (*old-fashioned, informal*) to catch a very bad cold **catch sb's 'eye** to attract sb's attention: *Can you catch the waiter's eye?* **'catch it** (*BrE*) (*NAmE* **catch 'hell, 'get it**) (*informal*) to be punished or spoken to angrily about sth: *If your dad finds out you'll really catch it!* **catch sb 'napping** (*BrE*) to get an advantage over sb by doing sth when they are not expecting it and not ready for it **catch sb on the 'hop** (*informal*) to surprise sb by doing sth when they are not expecting it and not ready for it **catch sb red-'handed** to catch sb in the act of doing sth wrong or committing a crime **catch sb with their 'pants down** (*BrE* also **catch sb with their 'trousers down**) (*informal*) to arrive or do sth when sb is not expecting it and not ready, especially when they are in an embarrassing situation ⇨ more at BALANCE *n.*, CLEFT *adj.*, EARLY *adj.*, FANCY *n.*, RAW *n.*, ROCK *n.*, SHORT *adj.*

PHR V **'catch at sth** = CLUTCH AT STH **,catch 'on** to become popular or fashionable: *He invented a new game, but it never really caught on.* **,catch 'on (to sth)** (*informal*) to understand sth: *He is very quick to catch on to things.* **,catch sb 'out 1** to surprise sb and put them in a difficult position: *Many investors were caught out by the fall in share prices.* **2** to show that sb does not know much or is doing sth wrong: *They tried to catch her out with a difficult question.* **,catch 'up on sth 1** to spend extra time doing sth because you have not done it earlier: *I have a lot of work to catch up on.* **2** to find out about things that have happened: *We spent the evening catching up on each other's news.* **be/get ,caught 'up in sth** to become involved in sth, especially when you do not want to be: *Innocent passers-by got caught up in the riots.* **,catch 'up (with sb)** (*BrE* also **,catch sb 'up**) **1** 🔑 to reach sb who is ahead by going faster: *Go on ahead. I'll catch up with you.* ◇ *I'll catch you up.* **2** 🔑 to reach the same level or standard as sb who was better or more advanced: *After missing a term through illness he had to work hard to catch up with the others.* **,catch 'up with sb 1** to finally start to cause problems for sb after they have managed to avoid this for some time: *She was terrified that one day her past problems would catch up with her.* **2** if the police or authorities **catch up with** sb, they find and punish them after some time: *The law caught up with him years later when he had moved to Spain.*

■ ***noun***

▸ OF BALL **1** [C] an act of catching sth, for example a ball: *to make a catch*

▸ AMOUNT CAUGHT **2** [C] the total amount of things that are caught: *a huge catch of fish*

▸ FASTENING **3** [C] a device used for fastening sth: *a catch on the door* ◇ *safety catches for the windows*

▸ DIFFICULTY **4** [C, usually sing.] (*informal*) a hidden difficulty or disadvantage: *All that money for two hours' work—what's the catch?*

▸ CHILD'S GAME **5** [U] a child's game in which two people throw a ball to each other

▸ PERSON **6** [sing.] (*old-fashioned*) a person that other people see as a good person to marry, employ, etc.

IDM **(a) catch-22 | a catch-22 situation** (*informal*) a difficult situation from which there is no escape because you need to do one thing before doing a second, and you cannot do the second thing before doing the first: *I can't get a job because I haven't got anywhere to live but I can't afford a place to live until I get a job—it's a catch-22 situation.*

'catch-all *noun* **1** (*especially NAmE*) a thing for holding many small objects **2** a group or description that includes different things and that does not state clearly what is included or not ▸ **'catch-all** *adj.* [only before noun]: ***a catch-all phrase/term***

catch·er /ˈkætʃə(r)/ *noun* **1** (in BASEBALL) the player who stands behind the BATTER and catches the ball if he or she does not hit it ⇨ VISUAL VOCAB page V36 **2** (usually in compounds) a person or thing that catches sth: *a rat catcher*

catch·ing /ˈkætʃɪŋ/ *adj.* [not before noun] **1** (of a disease) easily caught by one person from another **SYN infectious** **2** (of an emotion or a mood) passing quickly from one person to another **SYN infectious**: *Try to be as enthusiastic as possible (enthusiasm is catching)!*

catch·line /ˈkætʃlaɪn/ *noun* **1** (*technical*) a short line of text which can be easily noticed, for example at the top of a page **2** a phrase used in an advertisement

catch·ment area /ˈkætʃmənt eəriə; *NAmE* eriə/ *noun* **1** (*BrE*) the area from which a school takes its students, a hospital its patients, etc. **2** (also **catch·ment**) (*technical*) the area from which rain flows into a particular river or lake

catch·penny /ˈkætʃpeni/ *adj.* (*old-fashioned*) (of a product or service) produced or provided just to make money, without being of good quality

catch·phrase /ˈkætʃfreɪz/ *noun* a popular phrase that is connected with the politician or entertainer who used it and made it famous

'catch-up *noun* **1** [U] the act of trying to reach the same level or standard as sb who is ahead of you: *It was a month of catch-up for them.* **2** [C, sing.] an occasion when two or more people meet to discuss what has happened since the last time they met: *We must get together for a catch-up.*

IDM **play 'catch-up** to try to equal sb that you are competing against in a sport or game: *After our bad start to the season we were always playing catch-up.*

catchy /ˈkætʃi/ *adj.* (*informal*) (**catch·ier, catchi·est**) (of music or the words of an advertisement) pleasing and easily remembered: *a **catchy tune/slogan***

'cat door (*NAmE*) (*BrE* **'cat flap**) *noun* a hole cut in the bottom of the door to a house, covered by a piece of plastic that swings, so a pet cat can go in and out

cat·ech·ism /ˈkætəkɪzəm/ *noun* [usually sing.] a set of questions and answers that are used for teaching people about the beliefs of the Christian religion

cat·egor·ic·al /ˌkætəˈɡɒrɪkl; *NAmE* -ˈɡɔːr-/ *adj.* [usually before noun] (*formal*) expressed clearly and in a way that shows that you are very sure about what you are saying: *to make a categorical statement* ◇ *to give a categorical assurance* ▸ **cat·egor·ic·al·ly** /-kli/ *adv.*: *He categorically rejected our offer.*

cat·egor·ize (*BrE* also **-ise**) **AW** /ˈkætəɡəraɪz/ *verb* to put people or things into groups according to what type they are **SYN classify**: **~ sb/sth** *Participants were categorized according to age.* ◇ **~ sb/sth as sth** *His latest work cannot be categorized as either a novel or an autobiography.* ▸ **cat·egor·iza·tion, -isa·tion** **AW** /ˌkætəɡəraɪˈzeɪʃn/ *noun* [U, C]

cat·egory 🔑 **AW** /ˈkætəɡəri; *NAmE* -ɡɔːri/ *noun* (*pl.* -ies)

a group of people or things with particular features in common **SYN class**: *Students over 25 **fall into a** different **category**.* ◇ *The results can be divided into three **main categories**.*

cater /ˈkeɪtə(r)/ *verb* [I, T] to provide food and drinks for a social event: (*BrE*) **~ for sb/sth** *Most of our work now involves catering for weddings.* ◇ (*NAmE*) **~ sth** *Who will be catering the wedding?*

PHR V **'cater for sb/sth** to provide the things that a particular person or situation needs or wants: *The class caters for all ability ranges.* **'cater to sb/sth** to provide the things

C

that a particular type or person wants, especially things that you do not approve of: *They only publish novels which cater to the mass market.*

cater·er /ˈkeɪtərə(r)/ *noun* a person or company whose job is to provide food and drinks at a business meeting or for a special occasion such as a wedding

cater·ing /ˈkeɪtərɪŋ/ *noun* [U] the work of providing food and drinks for meetings or social events: *Who did the catering for your son's wedding?*

cat·er·pil·lar /ˈkætəpɪlə(r); *NAmE* -tərp-/ *noun* a small creature like a WORM with legs, that develops into a BUTTERFLY or MOTH (= flying insects with large, sometimes brightly coloured, wings). Caterpillars eat the leaves of plants. ➲ VISUAL VOCAB page V11

ˈ**Caterpillar track™** (*especially BrE*) (also ˈ**tank tread** especially in *NAmE*) *noun* a metal belt fastened around the wheels of a heavy vehicle, used for travelling over rough or soft ground ➲ VISUAL VOCAB page V47

cat·er·waul /ˈkætəwɔːl; *NAmE* ˈkætər-/ *verb* [I] to make the loud unpleasant noise that is typical of a cat

cat·fight /ˈkætfaɪt/ *noun* (*informal*) a fight between women

cat·fish /ˈkætfɪʃ/ *noun* (*pl.* cat·fish) a large fish with long stiff hairs, like a cat's WHISKERS, around its mouth. There are several types of catfish, most of which are FRESHWATER fish.

ˈ**cat flap** (*BrE*) (*NAmE* ˈ**cat door**) *noun* a hole cut in the bottom of the door to a house, covered by a piece of plastic that swings, so a pet cat can go in and out

cat·gut /ˈkætɡʌt/ (also **gut**) *noun* [U] thin strong string made from animals' INTESTINES and used in making musical instruments

cath·ar·sis /kəˈθɑːsɪs; *NAmE* -ˈθɑːrs-/ *noun* [U, C] (*pl.* cath·arses /-siːz/) (*technical*) the process of releasing strong feelings, for example through plays or other artistic activities, as a way of providing relief from anger, suffering, etc. ▶ **cath·ar·tic** /kəˈθɑːtɪk; *NAmE* -ˈθɑːrt-/ *adj.*: *It was a cathartic experience.*

cath·edral /kəˈθiːdrəl/ *noun* the main church of a district, under the care of a BISHOP (= a priest of high rank): *St Paul's Cathedral* ◇ (*BrE*) *a cathedral city*

Cath·er·ine wheel /ˈkæθrɪn wiːl/ (*especially BrE*) (*NAmE* usually **pin·wheel**) *noun* a round flat FIREWORK that spins around when lit

cath·eter /ˈkæθɪtə(r)/ *noun* a thin tube that is put into the body in order to remove liquid such as URINE

cath·ode /ˈkæθəʊd; *NAmE* -oʊd/ *noun* (*technical*) the ELECTRODE in an electrical device where REDUCTION occurs; the negative electrode in an ELECTROLYTIC cell and the positive electrode in a battery ➲ compare ANODE

ˌ**cathode ˈray tube** *noun* a VACUUM tube inside a television or computer screen, etc. from which a stream of ELECTRONS produces images on the screen

Cath·olic /ˈkæθlɪk/ *noun* = ROMAN CATHOLIC: *They're Catholics.* ▶ **Cath·oli·cism** /kəˈθɒləsɪzəm; *NAmE* -ˈθɑːlə-/ *noun* [U] = ROMAN CATHOLICISM

cath·olic /ˈkæθlɪk/ *adj.* **1 Catholic** = ROMAN CATHOLIC: *Are they Catholic or Protestant?* ◇ *a Catholic church* **2** (often **Catholic**) (*technical*) connected with all Christians or the whole Christian Church **3** (*formal*) including many or most things: *to have catholic tastes* (= to like many different things)

cat·ion /ˈkætaɪən/ *noun* (*chemistry, physics*) an ION with a positive electrical CHARGE ➲ compare ANION

cat·kin /ˈkætkɪn/ *noun* a long thin hanging bunch, or short standing group, of soft flowers on the branches of trees such as the WILLOW ➲ VISUAL VOCAB page V8

cat·mint /ˈkætmɪnt/ (*BrE*) (also **cat·nip** /ˈkætnɪp/ *NAmE, BrE*) *noun* [U] a plant that has white flowers with purple spots, leaves covered with small hairs and a smell that is attractive to cats

cat·nap /ˈkætnæp/ *noun* a short sleep ▶ **cat·nap** *verb* (-pp-) [I]

cat-o'-nine-tails /ˌkæt ə ˈnaɪn teɪlz/ *noun* [sing.] a WHIP made of nine strings with knots in them, that was used to punish prisoners in the past

CAT scan /ˈkæt skæn/ (also ˌ**CˈT scan**) *noun* a medical examination that uses a computer to produce an image of the inside of sb's body from X-RAY or ULTRASOUND pictures

ˌ**cat's ˈcradle** *noun* **1** [U] a game in which you wrap string around the fingers of both hands to make different patterns **2** [C] a pattern made with string in a game of cat's cradle

cat's cradle

Cats·eye™ /ˈkætsaɪ/ *noun* (*BrE*) one of a line of small objects that are fixed into a road and that reflect a car's lights in order to guide traffic at night

cat·suit /ˈkætsuːt; *BrE* also -sjuːt/ *noun* a piece of women's clothing that fits closely and covers the body and legs

cat·tery /ˈkætəri/ *noun* (*pl.* -ies) (*BrE*) a place where people can pay to leave their cats to be cared for while they are away

cat·tle /ˈkætl/ *noun* [pl.] cows and BULLS that are kept as farm animals for their milk or meat: *a herd of cattle* ◇ *twenty **head of cattle*** (= twenty cows) ◇ ***dairy/beef cattle*** ➲ COLLOCATIONS at FARMING ➲ VISUAL VOCAB page V6

cat·tle duff·ing /ˈkætl dʌfɪŋ/ *noun* (*AustralE*) the stealing of cows

ˈ**cattle grid** (*BrE*) (*NAmE* ˈ**cattle guard**) *noun* metal bars that are placed over a hole that has been made in the road. Cars can pass over the metal bars but animals such as sheep and cows cannot.

ˈ**cattle plague** *noun* [U] (*BrE*) = RINDERPEST

catty /ˈkæti/ *adj.* (*informal*) (cat·tier, cat·ti·est) (of a woman) saying unkind things about other people **SYN** **bitchy, spiteful**: *a catty comment* ▶ **cat·ti·ness** *noun* [U]

ˌ**catty-ˈcorner(ed)** (also ˌ**kitty-ˈcorner(ed)**) *adj., adv.* (*NAmE, informal*) opposite and at a DIAGONAL angle from sth/sb: *a restaurant catty-corner from the theater* ◇ *Motorcyclists cut catty-cornered across his yard.*

cat·walk /ˈkætwɔːk/ *noun* **1** (*NAmE* also **run·way**) the long stage that models walk on during a fashion show ➲ COLLOCATIONS at FASHION **2** a narrow platform for people to walk on, for example along the outside of a building or a bridge

Cau·ca·sian /kɔːˈkeɪziən; kɔːˈkeɪʒn/ *noun* a member of any of the races of people who have pale skin ▶ **Cau·ca·sian** *adj.*

cau·cus /ˈkɔːkəs/ *noun, verb*

■ ***noun*** (*especially NAmE*) **1** a meeting of the members or leaders of a political party to choose candidates or to decide policy; the members or leaders of a political party as a group **2** a group of people with similar interests, often within a larger organization or political party: *the Congressional Black Caucus*

■ ***verb*** [I, T] (*NAmE*) **~ (sb)** to meet in a caucus or other group to discuss sth

caught *past tense, past part.* of CATCH

caul·dron (*US* also **cal·dron**) /ˈkɔːldrən/ *noun* a large deep pot for boiling liquids or cooking food over a fire: *a witch's cauldron* ◇ (*figurative*) *The stadium was a seething cauldron of emotion.*

cauli·flower /ˈkɒliflaʊə(r); *NAmE* ˈkɔːli-; ˈkɑːli-/ *noun* [U, C] a vegetable with green leaves around a large hard white head of flowers: *Do you like cauliflower?* ◇ *two cauliflowers* ➲ VISUAL VOCAB page V27

ˌ**cauliflower ˈcheese** (*BrE*) (*NAmE* ˌ**cauliflower with ˈcheese**) *noun* [U] a hot dish of cauliflower cooked and served in a cheese sauce

ˌ**cauliflower ˈear** *noun* an ear that is permanently swollen because it has been hit many times

caulk /kɔːk/ *verb* **~ sth** to fill the holes or cracks in sth, especially a ship, with a substance that keeps out water

causal /ˈkɔːzl/ *adj.* **1** (*formal*) connected with the relationship between two things, where one causes the other to happen: *the causal relationship between poverty and disease* **2 ~ conjunction/connective** (*grammar*) a word such as *because* that introduces a statement about the cause of sth ▶ **caus·al·ly**: *Are the two factors causally connected?*

caus·al·ity /kɔːˈzæləti/ (also **caus·ation**) *noun* [U] (*formal*) the relationship between sth that happens and the reason for it happening; the principle that nothing can happen without a cause

caus·ation /kɔːˈzeɪʃn/ *noun* [U] (*formal*) **1** the process of one event causing or producing another event **2** = CAUSALITY

causa·tive /ˈkɔːzətɪv/ *adj.* **1** (*formal*) acting as the cause of sth: *Smoking is a causative factor in several major diseases.* **2** (*grammar*) a **causative verb** expresses a cause, for example *blacken* which means 'to cause to become black' ➲ compare ERGATIVE, INCHOATIVE

cause 🗝 /kɔːz/ *noun, verb*

▪ ***noun*** **1** 🗝 [C] the person or thing that makes sth happen: *Unemployment is a major cause of poverty.* ◇ *There was discussion about the fire and its likely cause.* ◇ *Drinking and driving is one of the most common causes of traffic accidents.* **2** 🗝 [U] **~ (for sth)** a reason for having particular feelings or behaving in a particular way: *There is no* ***cause for concern.*** ◇ *The food was excellent—I had no* ***cause for complaint.*** ◇ ***with/without good cause*** (= with/without a good reason) **3** 🗝 [C] an organization or idea that people support or fight for: *Animal welfare campaigners raised £70 000 for their cause last year.* ◇ *a* ***good cause*** (= an organization that does good work, such as a charity) ◇ *fighting for the Republican cause* ➲ see also LOST CAUSE **4** [C] (*law*) a case that goes to court

IDM **be for/in a good ˈcause** worth doing, because it is helping other people ➲ more at COMMON *adj.*

▪ ***verb*** 🗝 to make sth happen, especially sth bad or unpleasant: **~ sth** *Do they know what caused the fire?* ◇ *Are you* ***causing trouble*** *again?* ◇ *deaths caused by dangerous driving* ◇ **~ sth for sb** *The bad weather is causing problems for many farmers.* ◇ **~ sb sth** *The project is still causing him a lot of problems.* ◇ **~ sth to do sth** *The poor harvest caused prices to rise sharply.*

Language Bank

cause

X causes Y

- Childhood obesity can **cause/lead to** long-term health problems.
- Changes in lifestyle and diet over the last twenty years have **caused/led to/resulted in** a sharp increase in childhood obesity.
- Several factors, including changes in diet and lifestyle, **have contributed to** the increase in childhood obesity.
- Research suggests that fast food and soft drinks directly **contribute to** childhood obesity.
- Genetics, lifestyle and diet **are** all important **factors** in cases of childhood obesity.
- Even small changes in lifestyle and diet can **bring about** significant weight loss.

➲ Language Banks at BECAUSE OF, CONSEQUENTLY, THEREFORE

ˈcause *conj.* = COS[1]

cause cé·lèbre /ˌkɔːz seˈlebrə/ *noun* (from *French*) (*pl.* **causes cé·lèbres** /ˌkɔːz seˈlebrə/) an issue that attracts a lot of attention and is supported by a lot of people

cause·way /ˈkɔːzweɪ/ *noun* a raised road or path across water or wet ground

caus·tic /ˈkɔːstɪk/ *adj.* **1** (of a chemical substance) able to destroy or dissolve other substances **SYN** **corrosive** **2** critical in a bitter or SARCASTIC way **SYN** **scathing**: ***caustic comments/wit*** ▶ **caus·tic·al·ly** /-kli/ *adv.*

ˌ**caustic ˈsoda** *noun* [U] a chemical used in making paper and soap

caut·er·ize (*BrE* also **-ise**) /ˈkɔːtəraɪz/ *verb* **~ sth** (*medical*) to burn a wound, using a chemical or heat, in order to stop the loss of blood or to prevent infection

cau·tion /ˈkɔːʃn/ *noun, verb*

▪ ***noun*** **1** [U] care that you take in order to avoid danger or mistakes; not taking any risks: ***extreme/great caution*** ◇ *Statistics should be treated* ***with caution.*** ➲ SYNONYMS at CARE **2** [C] (*BrE*) a warning that is given by the police to sb who has committed a crime that is not too serious: *As a first offender, she got off with a caution.* **3** [U, C] (*formal*) a warning or a piece of advice about a possible danger or risk: *a* ***word/note of caution*** ◇ *Some cautions must be mentioned—for example good tools are essential to do the job well.*

IDM **throw/cast caution to the ˈwind(s)** to stop caring about how dangerous sth might be; to start taking risks

▪ ***verb*** **1** [I, T] to warn sb about the possible dangers or problems of sth: **~ against sth** *I would caution against getting too involved.* ◇ **~ sb against/about sth** *Sam cautioned him against making a hasty decision.* ◇ **~ (sb) that...** *The government cautioned that pay increases could lead to job losses.* ◇ **~ sb to do sth** *Employees were cautioned to be careful about what they said to people outside the company.* ◇ **~ (sb) + speech** *'I'd take care if I were you,' she cautioned (him).* **2** [T] **~ sb** (*BrE, law*) to warn sb officially that anything they say may be used as evidence against them in court: *Suspects must be cautioned before any questions are asked.* **3** [T, usually passive] (*BrE, law*) **~ sb (for sth)** to warn sb officially that they will be punished if they do sth wrong or illegal again: *She wasn't sent to the juvenile court; instead she was cautioned.*

cau·tion·ary /ˈkɔːʃənəri; *NAmE* -neri/ *adj.* giving advice or a warning: *a* ***cautionary tale*** *about the problems of buying a computer* ◇ *In her conclusion, the author sounds a* ***cautionary note.***

cau·tious /ˈkɔːʃəs/ *adj.* being careful about what you say or do, especially to avoid danger or mistakes; not taking any risks: *The government has been cautious in its response to the report.* ◇ *They've taken a very* ***cautious approach.*** ◇ *They expressed cautious optimism about a solution to the crisis.* ◇ **~ about sb/sth | ~ about doing sth** *He was very cautious about committing himself to anything.* ▶ **cau·tious·ly** *adv.*: *She looked cautiously around and then walked away from the house.* ◇ *I'm cautiously optimistic.* **cau·tious·ness** *noun* [U]

Which Word?

cautious / careful

- A **cautious** person is nervous that something may be dangerous or unwise, so they only do it very slowly or after a lot of thought. (opposite= **rash**)
- A **careful** person is not nervous but does take extra care to make sure that everything is correct or nothing goes wrong. (opposite= **careless**)
- Notice also:

Be careful/Take care *when you drive on icy roads.*
Caution/Warning *- thin ice.*

cava /ˈkɑːvə/ *noun* [U, C] a type of SPARKLING white wine (= with bubbles) from Spain

cav·al·cade /ˌkævlˈkeɪd/ *noun* a line of people on horses or in vehicles forming part of a ceremony

Cava·lier /ˌkævəˈlɪə(r); *NAmE* -ˈlɪr/ *noun* a supporter of the King in the English Civil War (1642-49) ➲ compare ROUNDHEAD

C

cava·lier /ˌkævəˈlɪə(r); *NAmE* -ˈlɪr/ *adj.* [usually before noun] not caring enough about sth important or about the feelings of other people: *The government takes a **cavalier attitude** to the problems of prison overcrowding.* ▸ **cava·lier·ly** *adv.*

cav·alry /ˈkævlri/ *noun* (usually **the cavalry**) [sing.+ sing./pl. v.] (in the past) the part of the army that fought on horses; the part of the modern army that uses ARMOURED vehicles

cave /keɪv/ *noun, verb*
■ ***noun*** a large hole in the side of a hill or under the ground: *the mouth* (= the entrance) *of the cave* ◇ *a **cave-dweller*** (= a person who lives in a cave) ➲ VISUAL VOCAB page V4
■ ***verb***
PHR V ˌ**cave** ˈ**in** (**on sb/sth**) (of a roof, wall, etc.) to fall down and towards the centre: *The ceiling suddenly caved in on top of them.* ➲ related noun CAVE-IN ˌ**cave** ˈ**in** (**to sth**) to finally do what sb wants after you have been strongly opposing them: *The President is unlikely to cave in to demands for a public inquiry.* ➲ see also CAVING

cav·eat /ˈkæviæt/ *noun* (*formal*, from *Latin*) a warning that particular things need to be considered before sth can be done

cav·eat emp·tor /ˌkæviæt ˈemptɔː(r)/ *noun* (from *Latin*) the principle that a person who buys sth is responsible for finding any faults in the thing they buy

ˈ**cave-in** *noun* the fact of sth suddenly collapsing

cave·man /ˈkeɪvmæn/ *noun* (*pl.* -men /-men/) **1** a person who lived in a CAVE thousands of years ago **2** (*informal*) a man who behaves in an aggressive way

ˈ**cave painting** *noun* a PREHISTORIC painting on the walls of a CAVE, often showing animals and hunting scenes

caver /ˈkeɪvə(r)/ (also **pot·holer**) (both *BrE*) (*NAmE* **spe·lunk·er**) *noun* a person who goes into CAVES under the ground as a sport or hobby ➲ compare SPELEOLOGIST

cav·ern /ˈkævən; *NAmE* -vərn/ *noun* a CAVE, especially a large one

cav·ern·ous /ˈkævənəs; *NAmE* -vərn-/ *adj.* (*formal*) (of a room or space) very large and often empty and/or dark; like a CAVE

cav·iar (also **cavi·are**) /ˈkæviɑː(r)/ *noun* [U] the eggs of some types of fish, especially the STURGEON, that are preserved using salt and eaten as a very special and expensive type of food

cavil /ˈkævl/ *verb* (-ll-, *especially US* -l-) [I] **~ (at sth)** (*formal*) to make unnecessary complaints about sth **SYN** **quibble**

cav·ing /ˈkeɪvɪŋ/ (also **pot·hol·ing**) (both *BrE*) (*NAmE* **spe·lunk·ing**) *noun* [U] the sport or activity of going into CAVES under the ground: *He had always wanted to **go caving**.* ➲ VISUAL VOCAB page V34

cav·ity /ˈkævəti/ *noun* (*pl.* -ies) (*formal* or *technical*) **1** a hole or empty space inside sth solid: *the abdominal cavity* **2** a hole in a tooth

ˌ**cavity** ˈ**wall** *noun* a wall consisting of two walls with a space between them, designed to prevent heat from escaping: *cavity wall insulation*

ca·vort /kəˈvɔːt; *NAmE* kəˈvɔːrt/ *verb* [I] **+ adv./prep.** to jump or move around in a noisy, excited and often sexual way: *The photos showed her cavorting on the beach with her new lover.*

caw /kɔː/ *noun* the loud, unpleasant sound that is made by birds such as CROWS and ROOKS ▸ **caw** *verb* [I]

cay·enne /keɪˈen/ (also ˌ**cayenne** ˈ**pepper**) *noun* [U] a type of red pepper used in cooking to give a hot flavour to food

cay·man = CAIMAN

CB /ˌsiː ˈbiː/ *noun* [U] the abbreviation for 'Citizens' Band' (a range of waves on a radio on which people can talk to each other over short distances, especially when driving): *A truck driver used his CB radio to call for help.*

CBE /ˌsiː biː ˈiː/ *noun* the abbreviation for 'Commander (of the Order) of the British Empire' (an award given in Britain to some people for a special achievement): *He was made a CBE in 2006.* ◇ *Shami Chakrabarti CBE*

CBI /ˌsiː biː ˈaɪ/ *abbr.* Confederation of British Industry (an important organization to which businesses and industries belong)

CBS /ˌsiː biː ˈes/ *abbr.* Columbia Broadcasting System (an American recording and broadcasting company that produces records, television programmes, etc.)

cc /ˌsiː ˈsiː/ *abbr., verb*
■ ***abbr.*** **1** carbon copy (to) (used on business letters and emails to show that a copy is being sent to another person): *to Luke Peters, cc Janet Gold* **2** cubic centimetre(s): *an 850cc engine*
■ ***verb*** (cc's, cc'ing, cc'ed, cc'ed /ˌsiː ˈsiːd/) **~ sth** (**to sb**) | **~ sb sth** (*informal*) to send sb a copy of a letter or email message that you are sending to sb else: *Her message was sent to the company president and cc'ed to us.*

CCRA /ˌsiː siː ɑːr ˈeɪ/ *abbr.* Canada Customs and Revenue Agency (the department of the Canadian government that deals with personal income tax, and with taxes on goods that are bought and sold)

CCTV /ˌsiː siː tiː ˈviː/ *abbr.* CLOSED-CIRCUIT TELEVISION

CD 0‑ /ˌsiː ˈdiː/ (also **disc**) *noun*
the abbreviation for 'compact disc' (a small disc on which sound or information is recorded. CDs are played on a special machine called a **CD player**): *His albums are available **on CD** and online.* ➲ COLLOCATIONS at MUSIC

ˌ**C'D burn·er** (also ˌ**C'D writer**) *noun* a piece of equipment used for copying sound or information from a computer onto a CD

CD-I (*US* **CDI**™) /ˌsiː diː ˈaɪ/ *noun* **1** [U] the abbreviation for 'compact disc interactive' (a MULTIMEDIA system which uses CDs that can react to instructions given by the user) **2** [C] the type of CD that this type of system uses

CD-R™ /ˌsiː diː ˈɑː(r)/ *noun* [C, U] the abbreviation for 'compact disc recordable' (a CD on which information, sound and pictures can be recorded once only)

Cdr (also **Cdr.** especially in *US*) *abbr.* (in writing) COMMANDER: *Cdr (John) Stone*

CD-ROM /ˌsiː diː ˈrɒm; *NAmE* ˈrɑːm/ *noun* [C, U] the abbreviation for 'compact disc read-only memory' (a CD on which large amounts of information, sound and pictures can be stored, for use on a computer): *The software package contains 5 CD-ROMs.* ◇ *The encyclopedia is available on CD-ROM.* ◇ *a CD-ROM drive* (= in a computer) ➲ VISUAL VOCAB page V54 ➲ compare ROM

CD-RW /ˌsiː diː ɑː ˈdʌbljuː; *NAmE* ɑːr/ *noun* [C, U] the abbreviation for 'compact disc rewritable' (a CD on which information, sound and pictures can be recorded and removed more than once)

CDT /ˌsiː diː ˈtiː/ *abbr.* **1** (*BrE*) Craft, Design and Technology (taught as a subject in schools) **2** CENTRAL DAYLIGHT TIME

ˌ**C'D writer** *noun* = CD BURNER

CE /ˌsiː ˈiː/ *abbr.* **1** (in Britain) Church of England **2** (also **C.E.** especially in *NAmE*) Common Era (the period since the birth of Christ when the Christian CALENDAR starts counting years). CE can be used to give dates in the same way as AD. ➲ compare AD, BC, BCE

cease 0‑ **AW** /siːs/ *verb* [I, T] (*formal*)
to stop happening or existing; to stop sth from happening or existing: *Welfare payments cease as soon as an individual starts a job.* ◇ **~ to do sth** *You never cease to amaze me!* ◇ **~ sth** *They voted to cease strike action immediately.* ◇ *He ordered his men to cease fire* (= stop shooting). ◇ **~ doing sth** *The company ceased trading in June.* ➲ see also CESSATION **IDM** see WONDER *n.*

cease·fire /ˈsiːsfaɪə(r)/ *noun* a time when enemies agree to stop fighting, usually while a way is found to end the fighting permanently **SYN** **truce**: *a call for an immediate ceasefire* ◇ *Observers have reported serious violations of the ceasefire.* ➲ COLLOCATIONS at WAR

cease·less AW /ˈsiːsləs/ *adj.* (*formal*) not stopping; seeming to have no end SYN **constant**, **interminable** ▶ **cease·less·ly** *adv.*

cecum (*NAmE*) (*BrE* **cae·cum**) /ˈsiːkəm/ *noun* (*pl.* ceca /ˈsiːkə/) a small bag which is part of the INTESTINE, between the small and the large intestine

cedar /ˈsiːdə(r)/ *noun* **1** (also ˈ**cedar tree**) [C] a tall EVERGREEN tree with wide spreading branches **2** (also **cedarwood**) [U] the hard red wood of the cedar tree, which has a sweet smell

cede /siːd/ *verb* **~ sth** (**to sb**) (*formal*) to give sb control of sth or give them power, a right, etc, especially unwillingly: *Cuba was ceded by Spain to the US in 1898.* ➲ see also CESSION

ce·dilla /sɪˈdɪlə/ *noun* the mark placed under the letter *c* in French, Portuguese, etc. to show that it is pronounced like an *s* rather than a *k*, as in *français*; a similar mark under *s* in Turkish and some other languages

cei·lidh /ˈkeɪli/ *noun* a social occasion with music and dancing, especially in Scotland and Ireland

ceil·ing 🔑 /ˈsiːlɪŋ/ *noun*
1 🔑 the top inside surface of a room: *She lay on her back staring up at the ceiling.* ◇ *a large room with a high ceiling* **2** the highest limit or amount of sth: *price ceilings* ➲ compare FLOOR **3** (*technical*) the greatest height at which a particular aircraft is able to fly ➲ see also GLASS CEILING IDM see HIT *v.*

ˈ**ceiling rose** (also **rose**) *noun* (*technical*) a round object that is fixed to the ceiling of a room for the wires of an electric light to go through

celeb /səˈleb/ *noun* (*informal*) = CELEBRITY

cele·brant /ˈselɪbrənt/ *noun* **1** a priest who leads a church service, especially the COMMUNION service; a person who attends a service **2** (*NAmE*) a person who is celebrating sth, for example at a party

cele·brate 🔑 /ˈselɪbreɪt/ *verb*
1 🔑 [I, T] to show that a day or an event is important by doing sth special on it: *Jake's passed his exams. We're going out to celebrate.* ◇ **~ sth** *We celebrated our 25th wedding anniversary in Florence.* ◇ *How do people celebrate New Year in your country?* **2** [T] **~ sth** to perform a religious ceremony, especially the Christian COMMUNION service **3** [T] **~ sb/sth** (*formal*) to praise sb/sth: *a movie celebrating the life and work of Martin Luther King*

cele·brated /ˈselɪbreɪtɪd/ *adj.* famous for having good qualities: *a celebrated painter*

cele·bra·tion 🔑 /ˌselɪˈbreɪʃn/ *noun*
1 🔑 [C] a special event that people organize in order to celebrate sth: *birthday/wedding celebrations* **2** 🔑 [U, C] the act of celebrating sth: *Her triumph was a* ***cause for celebration.*** ◇ *a party* ***in celebration of*** *their fiftieth wedding anniversary* ◇ *The service was a celebration of his life* (= praised what he had done in his life).

cele·bra·tory /ˌseləˈbreɪtəri; *NAmE* ˈseləbrətɔːri/ *adj.* celebrating sth or marking a special occasion: *a* ***celebratory drink/dinner***

ce·leb·rity /səˈlebrəti/ *noun* (*pl.* -ies) **1** (also *informal* **celeb**) [C] a famous person: *TV celebrities* **2** [U] the state of being famous SYN **fame**: *Does he find his new celebrity intruding on his private life?*

cel·eri·ac /səˈleriæk/ *noun* [U] a large white root vegetable which is a type of CELERY and which is eaten raw or cooked

cel·ery /ˈseləri/ *noun* [U] a vegetable with long crisp light green STEMS that are often eaten raw: (*BrE*) *a stick of celery* ◇ (*NAmE*) *a stalk of celery* ➲ VISUAL VOCAB page V27

cel·esta /səˈlestə/ (also **ce·leste** /səˈlest/) *noun* a small musical instrument with a keyboard, that produces a sound like bells

ce·les·tial /səˈlestiəl; *NAmE* -tʃl/ *adj.* [usually before noun] (*formal* or *literary*) of the sky or of heaven: ***celestial bodies*** (= the sun, moon, stars, etc.) ◇ *celestial light/music* ➲ compare TERRESTRIAL

ce·liac dis·ease (*NAmE*) (*BrE* **coel·iac disease**) /ˈsiːliæk dɪziːz/ a disease in which sb cannot DIGEST food (= break it down in their body) because their body is very sensitive to GLUTEN (= a PROTEIN that is found in WHEAT)

celi·bate /ˈselɪbət/ *adj.*, *noun*
▪ ***adj.*** **1** not married and not having sex, especially for religious reasons: *celibate priests* **2** not having sex: *I've been celibate for the past six months.* ▶ **celi·bacy** /ˈselɪbəsi/ *noun* [U]: *a vow of celibacy*
▪ ***noun*** (*formal*) a person who has chosen not to marry; a person who never has sex

cell 🔑 /sel/ *noun*
1 🔑 a room for one or more prisoners in a prison or police station ➲ see also PADDED CELL **2** a small room without much furniture in which a MONK or NUN lives **3** 🔑 the smallest unit of living matter that can exist on its own. All plants and animals are made up of cells: *blood cells* ◇ *the nucleus of a cell* ➲ see also STEM CELL **4** each of the small sections that together form a larger structure, for example a HONEYCOMB **5** a device for producing an electric current, for example by the action of chemicals or light: *a photoelectric cell* **6** a small group of people who work as part of a larger political organization, especially secretly: *a terrorist cell* **7** one of the small squares in a SPREADSHEET computer program in which you enter a single piece of data **8** (*informal, especially NAmE*) = CELL PHONE

cel·lar /ˈselə(r)/ *noun* **1** an underground room often used for storing things: *a coal cellar* **2** = WINE CELLAR ➲ see also SALT CELLAR

cell·ist /ˈtʃelɪst/ *noun* a person who plays the CELLO

cell·mate /ˈselmeɪt/ *noun* a prisoner with whom another prisoner shares a cell

cello /ˈtʃeləʊ; *NAmE* -loʊ/ (also *formal* **vio·lon·cello**) *noun* (*pl.* -os) a musical instrument with strings, shaped like a large VIOLIN. The player sits down and holds the cello between his or her knees. ➲ VISUAL VOCAB page V30

Cel·lo·phane™ /ˈseləfeɪn/ *noun* [U] a thin transparent plastic material used for wrapping things

ˈ**cell phone** 🔑 (also ˌ**cellular** ˈ**phone**, *informal* **cell**) (*especially NAmE*) (*BrE* usually ˌ**mobile** ˈ**phone**, **mo·bile**) *noun*
a telephone that does not have wires and works by radio, that you can carry with you and use anywhere: *cell phone users* ◇ *I talked to her on my cell phone.* ◇ *The use of cellular phones is not permitted on most aircraft.* ➲ COLLOCATIONS at PHONE

cel·lu·lar /ˈseljələ(r)/ *adj.* **1** connected with or consisting of the cells of plants or animals: ***cellular structure/processes*** **2** connected with a telephone system that works by radio instead of wires: *a cellular network* ◇ *cellular radio* **3** (*BrE*) (of cloth) loosely WOVEN for extra warmth: *cellular blankets*

cel·lu·lite /ˈseljulaɪt/ *noun* [U] a type of fat that some people get below their skin, which stops the surface of the skin looking smooth

cel·lu·loid /ˈseljulɔɪd/ *noun* [U] **1** a thin transparent plastic material made in sheets, used in the past for cinema film **2** (*old-fashioned*) used as a way of referring to films/movies

cel·lu·lose /ˈseljuləʊs; *NAmE* -loʊs/ *noun* [U] **1** a natural substance that forms the cell walls of all plants and trees and is used in making plastics, paper, etc. **2** any COMPOUND of cellulose used in making paint, LACQUER, etc.

Cel·sius /ˈselsiəs/ (also **centi·grade**) *adj.* (*abbr.* C) of or using a scale of temperature in which water freezes at 0° and boils at 100°: *It will be a mild night, around nine degrees Celsius.* ◇ *the Celsius Scale* ▶ **Cel·sius** *noun* [U]: *temperatures in Celsius and Fahrenheit*

Celt /kelt/ *noun* **1** a member of a race of people from western Europe who settled in ancient Britain before the Romans came **2** a person whose ANCESTORS were Celts, especially one from Ireland, Wales, Scotland, Cornwall or Brittany

CELTA /ˈseltə/ *noun* [U] the abbreviation for 'Certificate in English Language Teaching to Adults' (a British qualification from the University of Cambridge for teachers with little or no experience of teaching English as a foreign language)

Cel·tic /ˈkeltɪk/ *adj.* connected with the Celts or their language: *Celtic history*

ˌCeltic ˈcross *noun* a cross with the vertical part longer than the horizontal part and a circle round the centre

the ˌCeltic ˈfringe *noun* [sing.] (*BrE*) the people in Ireland and western parts of Britain whose ANCESTORS were CELTS, often used to refer to Ireland, Scotland and Wales

ce·ment /sɪˈment/ *noun, verb*

- ***noun*** [U] **1** a grey powder made by burning CLAY and LIME that sets hard when it is mixed with water. Cement is used in building to stick bricks together and to make very hard surfaces. **2** the hard substance that is formed when cement becomes dry and hard: *a floor of cement* ◇ *a cement floor* ➲ see also CONCRETE, MORTAR **3** a soft substance that becomes hard when dry and is used for sticking things together or filling in holes: *dental cement* (= for filling holes in teeth) **4** (*formal*) something that unites people in a common interest: *values which are the cement of society*
- ***verb*** **1** [often passive] **~ A and B** (**together**) to join two things together using cement, glue, etc. **2 ~ sth** to make a relationship, an agreement, etc. stronger SYN **strengthen**: *The President's visit was intended to cement the alliance between the two countries.*

cemen·ta·tion /ˌsiːmenˈteɪʃn/ *noun* [U] **1** (*chemistry*) the process of changing a metal by heating it together with a powder **2** (*geology*) the process of grains of sand, etc. sticking together to form SEDIMENTARY rocks

ceˈment mixer (also **ˈconcrete mixer**) *noun* a machine with a drum that holds sand, water and cement and turns to mix them together ➲ VISUAL VOCAB page V47

cem·et·ery /ˈsemətri; *NAmE* -teri/ *noun* (*pl.* -ies) an area of land used for burying dead people, especially one that is not beside a church ➲ compare CHURCHYARD, GRAVEYARD

ceno·taph /ˈsenətɑːf; *NAmE* -tæf/ *noun* a MONUMENT built in memory of soldiers killed in war who are buried somewhere else

cen·ser /ˈsensə(r)/ *noun* a container for holding and burning INCENSE (= a substance that produces a pleasant smell), used especially during religious ceremonies

cen·sor /ˈsensə(r)/ *noun, verb*

- ***noun*** a person whose job is to examine books, films/movies, etc. and remove parts which are considered to be offensive, immoral or a political threat
- ***verb* ~ sth** to remove the parts of a book, film/movie, etc. that are considered to be offensive, immoral or a political threat: *The news reports had been* ***heavily censored***.

cen·sori·ous /senˈsɔːriəs/ *adj.* (*formal*) tending to criticize people or things a lot SYN **critical**

cen·sor·ship /ˈsensəʃɪp; *NAmE* -sərʃ-/ *noun* [U] the act or policy of CENSORING books, etc: *press censorship* ◇ *The decree imposed strict censorship of the media.*

cen·sure /ˈsenʃə(r)/ *noun, verb*

- ***noun*** [U] (*formal*) strong criticism: *a vote of censure on the government's foreign policy*
- ***verb* ~ sb** (**for sth**) (*formal*) to criticize sb severely, and often publicly, because of sth they have done SYN **rebuke**: *He was censured for leaking information to the press.*

cen·sus /ˈsensəs/ *noun* (*pl.* **cen·suses**) the process of officially counting sth, especially a country's population, and recording various facts

cent 🔑 /sent/ *noun* (*abbr.* c, ct) a coin and unit of money worth 1% of the main unit of money in many countries, for example of the US dollar or of the euro ➲ see also PER CENT, RED CENT

IDM **put in your two ˈcents' worth** (*NAmE*) (*BrE* **put in your two ˈpennyworth, put in your two ˈpenn'orth**) (*informal*) to give your opinion about sth, even if other people do not want to hear it

cent. *abbr.* century: *in the 20th cent.*

cen·taur /ˈsentɔː(r)/ *noun* (in ancient Greek stories) a creature with a man's head, arms and upper body on a horse's body and legs

cen·ten·ar·ian /ˌsentɪˈneəriən; *NAmE* -ˈner-/ *noun* a person who is 100 years old or more

cen·ten·ary /senˈtiːnəri; *NAmE* -ˈtenəri/ (*pl.* -ies) (*BrE*) (also **cen·ten·nial** *NAmE, BrE*) *noun* the 100th anniversary of an event: *The club will celebrate its centenary next year.* ◇ *the centenary year* ➲ see also BICENTENARY, TERCENTENARY

cen·ten·nial /senˈteniəl/ (*especially NAmE*) (*BrE* also **cen·ten·ary**) *noun* the 100th anniversary of an event: *The year 1889 was the centennial of the inauguration of George Washington.* ➲ see also BICENTENNIAL

cen·ter (*US*) = CENTRE

cen·ter·board, cen·tered, cen·ter·fold, cen·ter·piece (*US*) = CENTREBOARD, CENTRED, CENTREFOLD, CENTREPIECE

centi- /ˈsentɪ-/ *combining form* (in nouns) **1** hundred: *centipede* **2** (often used in units of measurement) one hundredth: *centimetre*

centi·grade /ˈsentɪɡreɪd/ *adj.* = CELSIUS: *a temperature of 40 degrees centigrade* ▸ **centi·grade** *noun* [U]: *temperatures in centigrade and Fahrenheit*

centi·gram (also **centi·gramme**) /ˈsentɪɡræm/ *noun* a unit for measuring weight. There are 100 centigrams in a gram.

centi·litre (*especially US* **centi·liter**) /ˈsentɪliːtə(r)/ *noun* (*abbr.* cl) a unit for measuring liquids. There are 100 centilitres in a litre.

centi·metre 🔑 (*especially US* **centi·meter**) /ˈsentɪmiːtə(r)/ *noun* (*abbr.* cm) a unit for measuring length. There are 100 centimetres in a metre.

centi·pede /ˈsentɪpiːd/ *noun* a small creature like an insect, with a long thin body and many legs

cen·tral 🔑 /ˈsentrəl/ *adj.*

1 🔑 most important: *The central issue is that of widespread racism.* ◇ *She has been a central figure in the campaign.* ◇ *Prevention also plays a central role in traditional medicine.* ◇ *Reducing inflation is* ***central to*** (= is an important part of) *the government's economic policy.* ➲ SYNONYMS at MAIN **2** 🔑 having power or control over other parts: *the central committee* (= of a political party) ◇ *The organization has a central office in York.* **3** 🔑 in the centre of an area or object: *central London* ◇ *Central America/Europe/Asia* ◇ *the central area of the brain* **4** 🔑 easily reached from many areas: *The flat is very central—just five minutes from Princes Street.* ◇ *a central location* **5** (*phonetics*) (of a vowel) produced with the centre of the tongue in a higher position than the front or the back, for example /ɜː/ in *bird* ➲ compare BACK, FRONT ▸ **cen·tral·ity** /senˈtræləti/ *noun* [U]: (*formal*) *the centrality of the family as a social institution* **cen·tral·ly** /ˈsentrəli/ *adv.*: *The hotel is centrally located for all major attractions.* ◇ *a centrally planned economy* ◇ *Is the house centrally heated* (= does it have central heating)?

ˌCentral Aˈmerica *noun* [U] the part of N America that consists of Guatemala, Belize, Honduras, El Salvador, Nicaragua, Costa Rica and Panama ▸ **ˌCentral Aˈmerican** *adj., noun*

ˌcentral ˈbank *noun* a national bank that does business with the government and other banks, and issues the country's coins and paper money

ˌCentral ˈDaylight Time *noun* [U] (*abbr.* CDT) the time used in summer in the central US and Canada, which is five hours earlier than GMT

ˌCentral Euroˈpean Time *noun* [U] (*abbr.* CET) the time used in central and part of western Europe, which is one hour later than GMT

ˌcentral ˈgovernment *noun* [U, C] the government of a whole country, rather than LOCAL GOVERNMENT which is concerned with smaller areas

ˌcentral ˈheating *noun* [U] a system for heating a building from one source which then sends the hot water or hot air around the building through pipes ➲ COLLOCATIONS at DECORATE

the ˌCentral Inˈtelligence Agency *noun* [sing.] = CIA

cen·tral·ism /ˈsentrəlɪzəm/ *noun* [U] a way of organizing sth, such as government or education, that involves one central group of people controlling the whole system ▸ **cen·tral·ist** *adj.*: *centralist control of schools*

cen·tral·ize (*BrE* also **-ise**) /ˈsentrəlaɪz/ *verb* **~ sth** to give the control of a country or an organization to a group of people in one particular place: *a highly centralized system of government* ▸ **cen·tral·iza·tion, -isa·tion** /ˌsentrəlaɪˈzeɪʃn; *NAmE* -ləˈz-/ *noun* [U]: *the centralization of political power*

ˌcentral ˈlocking *noun* [U] a system for locking a car in which all the doors can be locked or opened at the same time

ˌcentral ˈnervous system *noun* (*anatomy*) the part of the system of nerves in the body that consists of the brain and the SPINAL CORD ➲ see also NERVOUS SYSTEM

ˌcentral ˈprocessing unit *noun* (*computing*) (*abbr.* CPU) the part of a computer that controls all the other parts of the system

ˌcentral reserˈvation (*BrE*) (*NAmE* **me·dian**, **ˈmedian strip**) *noun* a narrow strip of land that separates the two sides of a major road such as a MOTORWAY or INTERSTATE

ˌCentral ˈStandard Time *noun* [U] (*abbr.* CST) the time used in winter in the central US and Canada, which is six hours earlier than GMT

ˈCentral time *noun* [U] the time at the line of LONGITUDE 90°W, which is the standard time in the central US and Canada

centre 🔑 (*especially US* **cen·ter**) /ˈsentə(r)/ *noun, verb*

■ ***noun***

▸ MIDDLE **1** 🔑 [C] the middle point or part of sth: *the centre of a circle* ◇ *a long table in the centre of the room* ◇ *chocolates with soft centres* ➲ VISUAL VOCAB page V58

▸ TOWN/CITY **2** 🔑 [C] (*especially BrE*) (*NAmE* usually **downtown** [usually sing.]) the main part of a town or city where there are a lot of shops/stores and offices: *in the* ***town/city centre*** ◇ *the centre of town* ◇ *a town-centre car park* **3** 🔑 [C] a place or an area where a lot of people live; a place where a lot of business or cultural activity takes place: *major urban/industrial centres* ◇ *a centre of population* ◇ *Small towns in South India serve as economic and cultural centres for the surrounding villages.*

▸ BUILDING **4** 🔑 [C] a building or place used for a particular purpose or activity: *a* ***shopping/sports/leisure/community centre*** ◇ *the Centre for Policy Studies*

▸ OF EXCELLENCE **5** [C] **~ of excellence** a place where a particular kind of work is done extremely well

▸ OF ATTENTION **6** [C, usually sing.] the point towards which people direct their attention: *Children like to be the* ***centre of attention.*** ◇ *The prime minister is* ***at the centre of*** *a political row over leaked Cabinet documents.*

▸ -CENTRED **7** (in adjectives) having the thing mentioned as the most important feature or centre of attention: *a child-centred approach to teaching* ➲ see also SELF-CENTRED

▸ IN POLITICS **8** (usually **the centre**) [sing.] a MODERATE (= middle) political position or party, between the extremes of LEFT-WING and RIGHT-WING parties: *a party of the centre*

▸ IN SPORT **9** [C] (in some team sports) a player or position in the middle of the pitch/field, court, etc. **IDM** see FRONT *n.*, LEFT *adv.*

■ ***verb*** **~ sth** to move sth so that it is in the centre of sth else: *Carefully centre the photograph on the page and stick it in place.*

PHR V **ˈcentre around/on/round/upon sb/sth | ˈcentre sth around/on/round/upon sb/sth** to be or make sb/sth become the person or thing around which most activity, etc. takes place: *State occasions always centred around the king.* ◇ *Discussions were centred on developments in Eastern Europe.* **ˈcentre sth in...** [usually passive] to make somewhere the place where an activity or event takes place: *Most of the fighting was centred in the north of the capital.*

ˌcentre ˈback (*especially US* **ˌcenter ˈback**) (also **ˌcentre ˈhalf** *especially US* **ˌcenter ˈhalf**) *noun* (in football (SOCCER) and some other sports) a player or position in the middle of the back line of players

centre·board (*especially US* **cen·ter·board**) /ˈsentəbɔːd; *NAmE* ˈsentərbɔːrd/ *noun* a board that can be passed through a hole in the bottom of a sailing boat to keep it steady when sailing

cen·tred (*especially US* **cen·tered**) /ˈsentəd; *NAmE* -ərd/ *adj.* (*especially NAmE*) calm, sensible and emotionally in control: *My family helps to keep me centred.* ➲ see also CENTRE (7)

centre·fold (*especially US* **cen·ter·fold**) /ˈsentəfəʊld; *NAmE* -tərfoʊld/ *noun* **1** a large picture, often of a young woman with few or no clothes on, folded to form the middle pages of a magazine **2** a person whose picture is the centrefold of a magazine

ˌcentre ˈforward (*especially US* **ˌcenter ˈforward**) *noun* (in football (SOCCER) and some other sports) a player or position in the middle of the front line of players

ˌcentre ˈhalf (*especially US* **ˌcenter ˈhalf**) *noun* = CENTRE BACK

ˌcentre-ˈleft (*especially US* **ˌcenter-ˈleft**) (*BrE* also **ˌleft-of-ˈcentre** *US* also **ˌleft-of-ˈcenter**) *adj.* (*politics*) supporting both CAPITALISM and gradual social change: *a centre-left coalition government* ▸ **ˌcentre-ˈleft** (*especially US* **ˌcenter-ˈleft**) *noun* [sing.]: *Most of the centre-left will give their support.*

ˌcentre of ˈgravity *noun* (*pl.* **centres of gravity**) the point in an object at which its weight is considered to act

centre·piece (*especially US* **cen·ter·piece**) /ˈsentəpiːs; *NAmE* -tərp-/ *noun* **1** [sing.] the most important item: *This treaty is the centrepiece of the government's foreign policy.* **2** a decoration for the centre of a table

ˌcentre-ˈright (*especially US* **ˌcenter-ˈright**) (also **ˌright-of-ˈcentre** *especially US* **ˌright-of-ˈcenter**) *adj.* (*politics*) supporting CAPITALISM and accepting some social change: *Europe's centre-right parties* ▸ **ˌcentre-ˈright** (*BrE*) (*US* **ˌcenter-ˈright**) *noun* [sing.]: *a politician of the centre-right*

ˌcentre ˈspread (*especially US* **ˌcenter ˈspread**) *noun* the two facing middle pages of a newspaper or magazine

ˌcentre ˈstage (*especially US* **ˌcenter ˈstage**) *noun* [U] an important position where sb/sth can easily get people's attention: *Education is* ***taking centre stage*** *in the government's plans.* ◇ *This region continues to* ***occupy centre stage*** *in world affairs.* ▸ **ˌcentre ˈstage** *adv.*: *The minister said, 'We are putting full employment centre stage'.*

-centric /ˈsentrɪk/ *suffix* **1** having a particular centre: *geocentric* **2** (often *disapproving*) based on a particular way of thinking: *Eurocentric* ◇ *ethnocentric*

cen·tri·fu·gal /ˌsentrɪˈfjuːgl; senˈtrɪfjəgl/ *adj.* (*technical*) moving or tending to move away from a centre

ˌcentriˌfugal ˈforce (also **cenˈtrifugal force**) *noun* (*physics*) a force that appears to cause an object travelling around a centre to fly away from the centre and off its CIRCULAR path

cen·tri·fuge /ˈsentrɪfjuːdʒ/ *noun* a machine with a part that spins around to separate substances, for example liquids from solids, by forcing the heavier substance to the outer edge

cen·tri·pet·al /sen'trɪpɪtl; ˌsentrɪ'pi:tl/ *adj.* (*technical*) moving or tending to move towards a centre

cen·trist /'sentrɪst/ *noun* a person with political views that are not extreme SYN **moderate** ▸ **cen·trist** *adj.*

C

cen·tur·ion /sen'tjʊəriən; *NAmE* -'tʃʊr-/ *noun* (in ancient Rome) an army officer who commanded 100 soldiers

cen·tury 0→ /'sentʃəri/ *noun* (*pl.* -ies)
1 0→ a period of 100 years **2** 0→ (*abbr.* c, cent.) any of the periods of 100 years before or after the birth of Christ: *the 20th century* (= AD 1901–2000 or 1900–1999) ◇ *eighteenth-century writers* **3** (in CRICKET) a score of 100 RUNS by one player IDM see TURN *n.*

CEO /ˌsi: i: 'əʊ; *NAmE* 'oʊ/ *abbr.* chief executive officer (the person with the highest rank in a business company)

cep /sep/ *noun* a type of MUSHROOM which many people consider to be one of the best to eat

ceph·al·ic /sɪ'fælɪk; *BrE* also ke'fælɪk/ *adj.* (*anatomy*) in or related to the head

ceph·alo·pod /'sefələpɒd; *NAmE* -pɑ:d/ *noun* (*biology*) a type of MOLLUSC with a combined head and body and large eyes. Cephalopods have arms and/or TENTACLES (= long thin parts like arms), which may have SUCKERS (= round parts that suck) on them. OCTOPUS and SQUID are cephalopods. ➲ VISUAL VOCAB page V11

cer·am·ic /sə'ræmɪk/ *noun* **1** [C, usually pl.] a pot or other object made of CLAY that has been made permanently hard by heat: *an exhibition of ceramics by Picasso* **2 ce·ramics** [U] the art of making and decorating ceramics ▸ **cer·am·ic** *adj.*: *ceramic tiles*

cer·eal /'sɪəriəl; *NAmE* 'sɪr-/ *noun* **1** [C] one of various types of grass that produce grains that can be eaten or are used to make flour or bread. WHEAT, BARLEY and RYE are all cereals: *cereal crops* ➲ VISUAL VOCAB page V28 **2** [U] the grain produced by cereal crops **3** [C, U] food made from the grain of cereals, often eaten for breakfast with milk: *breakfast cereals* ◇ *a bowl of cereal*

ce·re·bel·lum /ˌserə'beləm/ *noun* (*pl.* **ce·re·bel·lums** or **cere·bella** /-'belə/) (*anatomy*) the part of the brain at the back of the head that controls the activity of the muscles

cere·bral /'serəbrəl; *NAmE* sə'ri:brəl/ *adj.* **1** relating to the brain: *a cerebral haemorrhage* **2** (*formal*) relating to the mind rather than the feelings SYN **intellectual**: *His poetry is very cerebral.*

ˌcerebral 'palsy *noun* [U] a medical condition usually caused by brain damage before or at birth that causes the loss of control of movement in the arms and legs

cere·brum /sə'ri:brəm; 'serəbrəm/ *noun* (*pl.* **ce·re·bra** /-brə/) (*anatomy*) the front part of the brain, responsible for thoughts, emotions and personality

cere·mo·nial /ˌserɪ'məʊniəl; *NAmE* -'moʊ-/ *adj.*, *noun*
■ ***adj.*** relating to or used in a ceremony: *ceremonial occasions* ◇ *a ceremonial sword* ▸ **cere·mo·ni·al·ly** /-niəli/ *adv.*
■ ***noun*** [U, C] the system of rules and traditions that states how things should be done at a ceremony or formal occasion: *The visit was conducted with all due ceremonial.*

cere·mo·ni·ous /ˌserə'məʊniəs; *NAmE* -'moʊ-/ *adj.* (*formal*) behaving or performed in an extremely formal way OPP **unceremonious** ▸ **cere·mo·ni·ous·ly** *adv.*

cere·mony 0→ /'serəməni; *NAmE* -moʊni/ *noun* (*pl.* -ies)
1 0→ [C] a public or religious occasion that includes a series of formal or traditional actions: *an awards/opening ceremony* ◇ *a wedding/marriage ceremony* ➲ COLLOCATIONS at MARRIAGE **2** [U] formal behaviour; traditional actions and words used on particular formal occasions
IDM **stand on 'ceremony** (*BrE*) to behave formally: *Please don't stand on ceremony* (= Please be natural and relaxed) *with me.* **without 'ceremony** in a very rough or informal way: *He found himself pushed without ceremony out of the house and the door slammed in his face.* ➲ see also MASTER OF CEREMONIES

cer·ise /sə'ri:z; sə'ri:s/ *adj.* pinkish-red in colour ▸ **cer·ise** *noun* [U]

cer·ium /'sɪəriəm; *NAmE* 'sɪr-/ *noun* [U] (*symb.* Ce) a chemical element. Cerium is a silver-white metal used in the production of glass and CERAMICS.

cert /sɜ:t; *NAmE* sɜ:rt/ *noun* (*BrE, informal*) a thing that is sure to happen or be successful SYN **certainty**: *That horse is a* **dead cert** *for* (= is sure to win) *the next race.*

cert. *abbr.* **1** CERTIFICATE **2** CERTIFIED

cer·tain 0→ /'sɜ:tn; *NAmE* 'sɜ:rtn/ *adj.*, *pron.*
■ ***adj.*** **1** 0→ that you can rely on to happen or to be true: *The climbers face certain death if the rescue today is unsuccessful.* ◇ **~ (that)...** *It is certain that they will agree.* ◇ **~ to do sth** *She looks certain to win an Oscar.* ◇ *They are certain to agree.* ◇ **~ of sth/of doing sth** *If you want to be certain of getting a ticket, book now.* ➲ SYNONYMS at SURE **2** 0→ firmly believing sth; having no doubts: **~ (that)...** *She wasn't certain (that) he had seen her.* ◇ **~ of/about sth** *Are you absolutely certain about this?* ◇ **~ who/where, etc...** *I'm not certain who was there.* ◇ ***To my certain knowledge*** *he was somewhere else at the time* (= I am sure about it). **3** 0→ used to mention a particular thing, person or group without giving any more details about it or them: *For certain personal reasons I shall not be able to attend.* ◇ *Certain people might disagree with this.* ◇ *They refused to release their hostages unless certain conditions were met.* **4** (*formal*) used with a person's name to show that the speaker does not know the person: *It was a certain Dr Davis who performed the operation.* **5** 0→ slight; noticeable, but difficult to describe: *That's true,* **to a certain extent**. ◇ *I felt there was a certain coldness in her manner.*
IDM **for 'certain** 0→ without doubt: *I can't say for certain when we'll arrive.* **make certain (that...)** 0→ to find out whether sth is definitely true: *I think there's a bus at 8 but you'd better call to make certain.* **make certain of sth/of doing sth** to do sth in order to be sure that sth else will happen: *You'll have to leave soon to make certain of getting there on time.* **of a certain 'age** if you talk about a person being **of a certain age**, you mean that they are no longer young but not yet old: *The show appeals to an audience of a certain age.*
■ ***pron.*** **certain of...** (*formal*) used for talking about some members of a group of people or things without giving their names: *Certain of those present were unwilling to discuss the matter further.*

Synonyms

certain

bound • sure • definite • guaranteed

These are all words describing sth that will definitely happen or is definitely true.

certain that you can rely on to happen or be true: *It's certain that they will agree.* ◇ *They are certain to agree.*

bound [not before noun] certain to happen, or to do or be sth. NOTE **Bound** is only used in the phrase *bound to do/be, etc.*: *There are bound to be changes when the new system is introduced.* ◇ *You've done so much work —you're bound to pass the exam.*

sure certain to happen or be true; that can be trusted on relied on: *She's sure to be picked for the team.* ◇ *It's sure to rain.*

definite (*rather informal*) certain to happen; that is not going to change: *Is it definite that he's leaving?*

guaranteed certain to have a particular result: *That kind of behaviour is guaranteed to make him angry.*

PATTERNS
- certain/sure **of** sth
- certain/bound/sure/guaranteed **to do sth**
- certain/definite **that...**
- **I couldn't say for** certain/sure/definite.

cer·tain·ly 0→ /'sɜ:tnli; *NAmE* 'sɜ:rtnli/ *adv.*
1 0→ without doubt SYN **definitely**: *Without treatment,*

she will almost certainly die. ◇ *Certainly, the early years are crucial to a child's development.* ◇ *I'm certainly never going there again.* ➲ note at SURELY ➲ LANGUAGE BANK at NEVERTHELESS **2** 🗝 (used in answer to questions) of course: *'May I see your passport, Mr Scott?' 'Certainly.'* ◇ *'Do you think all this money will change your life?' 'Certainly not.'*

cer·tainty /ˈsɜːtnti; *NAmE* ˈsɜːrtnti/ *noun* (*pl.* -ies) **1** [C] a thing that is certain: *political/moral certainties* ◇ *Her return to the team now seems a certainty.* **2** [U] the state of being certain: *There is no certainty that the president's removal would end the civil war.* ◇ *I can't say* **with** *any* **certainty** *where I'll be next week.*

cer·ti·fi·able /ˈsɜːtɪfaɪəbl; *NAmE* ˈsɜːrt-/ *adj.* **1** a person who is **certifiable** can or should be officially stated to be INSANE: (*informal*) *He's certifiable* (= he's crazy). **2** (*especially NAmE*) good enough to be officially accepted or recommended ▶ **cer·ti·fi·ably** *adv.*: *certifiably insane*

cer·tifi·cate 🗝 *noun, verb*

■ ***noun*** /səˈtɪfɪkət; *NAmE* sərˈt-/ (*abbr.* cert.) **1** 🗝 an official document that may be used to prove that the facts it states are true: *a* ***birth/marriage/death certificate*** **2** 🗝 an official document proving that you have completed a course of study or passed an exam; a qualification obtained after a course of study or an exam: *a Postgraduate Certificate in Education* (= a British qualification for teachers)

■ ***verb*** /səˈtɪfɪkeɪt; *NAmE* sərˈt-/ **~ sb** (**to do sth**) (*BrE*) to give sb an official document proving that they have successfully completed a training course, especially for a particular profession

cer·tifi·cated /səˈtɪfɪkeɪtɪd; *NAmE* sərˈt-/ *adj.* (*BrE*) having the certificate which shows that the necessary training for a particular job has been done

cer·ti·fi·ca·tion /ˌsɜːtɪfɪˈkeɪʃn; *NAmE* ˌsɜːrt-/ *noun* [U] (*technical*) **1** the act of CERTIFYING sth: *the medical certification of the cause of death* **2** the process of giving certificates for a course of education: *the certification of the exam modules*

ˌcertified ˈcheque (*BrE*) (*NAmE* **ˌcertified ˈcheck**) *noun* a cheque that a bank guarantees

ˌcertified ˈmail (*NAmE*) (*BrE* **reˌcorded deˈlivery**) *noun* [U] a method of sending a letter or package in which the person sending it gets an official note to say it has been posted and the person receiving it must sign a form when it is delivered ➲ compare REGISTERED MAIL

ˌcertified ˌpublic acˈcountant (*NAmE*) (*BrE* **ˌchartered acˈcountant**) *noun* a fully trained and qualified ACCOUNTANT

cer·tify /ˈsɜːtɪfaɪ; *NAmE* ˈsɜːrt-/ *verb* (**cer·ti·fies, cer·ti·fying, cer·ti·fied, cer·ti·fied**) **1** (*formal*) to state officially, especially in writing, that sth is true: **~ (that)...** *He handed her a piece of paper certifying (that) she was in good health.* ◇ *This* (= this document) *is to certify that...* ◇ **~ sb/sth + adj.** *He was certified dead on arrival.* ◇ **~ sb/sth (as) sth** *The accounts were certified (as) correct by the finance department.* ◇ **~ sb/sth to be/do sth** *The plants must be certified to be virus free.* **2** [usually passive] **~ sb (as sth)** to give sb an official document proving that they are qualified to work in a particular profession **3** [usually passive] **~ sb (+ adj.)** (*BrE, law*) to officially state that sb is mentally ill, so that they can be given medical treatment: *Patients must be certified before they can be admitted to the hospital.*

cer·ti·tude /ˈsɜːtɪtjuːd; *NAmE* ˈsɜːrtɪtuːd/ *noun* [U, C] (*formal*) a feeling of being certain; a thing about which you are certain: *'You will like Rome,' he said, with absolute certitude.* ◇ *the collapse of moral certitudes*

cer·ul·ean /sɪˈruːliən/ *adj.* (*literary*) deep blue in colour

ceru·men /sɪˈruːmən/ *noun* [U] (*technical*) a substance like WAX which is produced in the ear SYN **earwax**

cer·vical /ˈsɜːvɪkl; səˈvaɪkl; *NAmE* ˈsɜːrvɪkl/ *adj.* [only before noun] (*anatomy*) **1** connected with the cervix: *cervical cancer* **2** connected with the neck: *the cervical spine*

ˌcervical ˈsmear *noun* (*BrE*) = SMEAR TEST

cer·vix /ˈsɜːvɪks; *NAmE* ˈsɜːrv-/ *noun* (*pl.* **cer·vi·ces** /-vɪsiːz/ or **cer·vi·xes** /-vɪksɪz/) (*anatomy*) the narrow passage at the opening of a woman's WOMB

ce·sar·ean, ce·sar·ian (*US*) = CAESAREAN

ces·ium (*NAmE*) (*BrE* **cae·sium**) /ˈsiːziəm/ *noun* [U] (*symb.* Cs) a chemical element. Cesium is a soft silver-white metal that reacts strongly in water, used in PHOTOELECTRIC CELLS.

ces·sa·tion /seˈseɪʃn/ *noun* [U, C] (*formal*) the stopping of sth; a pause in sth: *Mexico called for an immediate cessation of hostilities.*

ces·sion /ˈseʃn/ *noun* [U, C] (*formal*) the act of giving up land or rights, especially to another country after a war ➲ see also CEDE

cess·pit /ˈsespɪt/ (also **cess·pool** /ˈsespuːl/) *noun* **1** a covered hole or container in the ground for collecting waste from a building, especially from the toilets **2** a place where dishonest or immoral people gather: *a cesspit of corruption*

CET /ˌsiː iː ˈtiː/ *abbr.* CENTRAL EUROPEAN TIME

cet·acean /sɪˈteɪʃn/ *adj., noun* (*biology*)

■ ***adj.*** (also **cet·aceous** /sɪˈteɪʃəs/) connected with the group of creatures that includes WHALES and DOLPHINS

■ ***noun*** a WHALE, DOLPHIN, or other sea creature that belongs to the same group ➲ VISUAL VOCAB page V10

cf. *abbr.* (in writing) compare

CFC /ˌsiː ef ˈsiː/ *noun* [C, U] the abbreviation for 'chlorofluorocarbon' (a type of gas used especially in AEROSOLS (= types of container that release liquid in the form of a spray). CFCs are harmful to the earth's OZONE LAYER.)

CFL /ˌsiː ef ˈel/ *abbr.* Canadian Football League (the organization of professional football teams in Canada)

CGI /ˌsiː dʒiː ˈaɪ/ *abbr.* computer-generated imagery: *The movie 'Dinosaur' combines CGI animation with live-action location shots.*

chaat /tʃɑːt/ *noun* [U] a S Asian dish consisting of fruit or vegetables with spices

Chab·lis /ˈʃæbliː; *NAmE* ʃæˈbliː/ *noun* [U, C] a type of dry white French wine

cha·cha /ˈtʃɑːtʃɑː/ *noun* (*IndE*) **1** an uncle **2** a male cousin of your parents **3** a male friend of your family

cha-cha /ˈtʃɑː tʃɑː/ (also **ˈcha-cha-cha**) *noun* a S American dance with small fast steps: *to* ***dance/do the cha-cha***

cha-ching /tʃəˈtʃɪŋ/ *exclamation* (*NAmE, informal*) = KA-CHING

chad /tʃæd/ *noun* the small piece that is removed when a hole is made in a piece of card, etc.

cha·dor /ˈtʃɑːdɔː(r)/ *noun* a large piece of cloth that covers a woman's head and upper body so that only the face can be seen, worn by some Muslim women

chafe /tʃeɪf/ *verb* **1** [I, T] if skin **chafes**, or if sth **chafes** it, it becomes sore because the thing is rubbing against it: *Her wrists chafed where the rope had been.* ◇ **~ sth** *The collar was far too tight and chafed her neck.* **2** [I] **~ (at/under sth)** (*formal*) to feel annoyed and impatient about sth, especially because it limits what you can do: *He soon chafed at the restrictions of his situation.*

chaff /tʃɑːf; *NAmE* tʃæf/ *noun, verb*

■ ***noun*** [U] **1** the outer covering of the seeds of grain such as WHEAT, which is separated from the grain before it is eaten **2** STRAW (= dried STEMS of WHEAT) and HAY (= dried grass) cut up as food for cows IDM see WHEAT

■ ***verb*** **~ sb** (*old-fashioned* or *formal*) to make jokes about sb in a friendly way SYN **tease**

chaf·finch /ˈtʃæfɪntʃ/ *noun* a small European bird of the FINCH family

ˈchafing dish *noun* a metal pan used for keeping food warm at the table

chag·rin /ˈʃæɡrɪn; *NAmE* ʃəˈɡrɪn/ *noun* [U] (*formal*) a feeling of being disappointed or annoyed ▶ **chag·rined** *adj.*

C

chai /tʃaɪ/ *noun* [U] (*IndE, informal*) tea

chain ⚷ /tʃeɪn/ *noun, verb*

■ ***noun***

▸ METAL RINGS **1** ⚷ [C, U] a series of connected metal rings, used for pulling or fastening things; a length of chain used for a particular purpose: *a short length of chain* ◇ *She wore a heavy gold chain around her neck.* ◇ *The mayor wore his chain of office.* ◇ *a bicycle chain* ◇ *The prisoners were kept* ***in chains*** (= with chains around their arms and legs, to prevent them from escaping). ➲ picture at ROPE ➲ VISUAL VOCAB pages V41, V53

▸ CONNECTED THINGS **2** ⚷ [C] a series of connected things or people: *to set in motion a* ***chain of events*** ◇ *a* ***chain of command*** (= a system in an organization by which instructions are passed from one person to another) ◇ ***mountain/island chains*** ◇ *Volunteers formed a* ***human chain*** *to rescue precious items from the burning house.* ➲ see also FOOD CHAIN

▸ OF SHOPS/HOTELS **3** ⚷ [C] a group of shops/stores or hotels owned by the same company: *a chain of supermarkets/a supermarket chain*

▸ RESTRICTION **4** [C, usually pl.] (*formal* or *literary*) a thing that restricts sb's freedom or ability to do sth: *the chains of fear/misery*

▸ IN HOUSE BUYING **5** [C, usually sing.] (*BrE*) a situation in which a number of people selling and buying houses must each complete the sale of their house before buying from the next person IDM see BALL *n.*, LINK *n.*, WEAK

■ ***verb*** ⚷ [often passive] to fasten sth with a chain; to fasten sb/sth to another person or thing with a chain, so that they do not escape or get stolen: **~ sb/sth** *The doors were always locked and chained.* ◇ **~ sb/sth up** *The dog was chained up for the night.* ◇ **~ sb/sth to sb/sth** *She chained her bicycle to the gate.* ◇ (*figurative*) *I've been chained to my desk all week* (= because there was so much work).

ˈchain gang *noun* a group of prisoners chained together and forced to work

ˈchain letter *noun* a letter sent to several people asking them to make copies of the letter and send them on to more people

ˌchain-ˌlink ˈfence *noun* a fence made of wire in a diamond pattern

ˈchain mail (also **mail**) *noun* [U] ARMOUR (= covering to protect the body when fighting) made of small metal rings linked together

ˌchain reˈaction *noun* **1** (*chemistry, physics*) a chemical or nuclear change that forms products which themselves cause more changes and new products **2** a series of events, each of which causes the next: *It set off a chain reaction in the international money markets.*

chain·saw /ˈtʃeɪnsɔː/ *noun* a tool made of a chain with sharp teeth set in it, that is driven by a motor and used for cutting wood

ˈchain-smoke *verb* [I, T] **~ (sth)** to smoke cigarettes continuously, lighting the next one from the one you have just smoked ▸ **ˈchain-smoker** *noun*

ˈchain store (*BrE* also **mul·tiple**, **ˌmultiple ˈstore**) *noun* a shop/store that is one of a series of similar shops/stores owned by the same company

chair ⚷ /tʃeə(r); *NAmE* tʃer/ *noun, verb*

■ ***noun*** **1** ⚷ [C] a piece of furniture for one person to sit on, with a back, a seat and four legs: *a table and chairs* ◇ *Sit on your chair!* ◇ *an old man asleep in a chair* (= an ARMCHAIR) ➲ VISUAL VOCAB pages V18,V19 ➲ see also ARMCHAIR, DECKCHAIR, EASY CHAIR, HIGH CHAIR, MUSICAL CHAIRS, ROCKING CHAIR, WHEELCHAIR **2 the chair** [sing.] the position of being in charge of a meeting or committee; the person who holds this position: *She takes the chair in all our meetings.* ◇ *Who is in the chair today?* ◇ *He was elected chair of the city council.* **3** [C] the position of being in charge of a department in a university: *He holds the chair of philosophy at Oxford.* **4 the chair** [sing.] (*US, informal*) = THE ELECTRIC CHAIR

■ ***verb*** **~ sth** to act as the chairman or chairwoman of a meeting, discussion, etc: *Who's chairing the meeting?*

chair·lift /ˈtʃeəlɪft; *NAmE* ˈtʃer-/ *noun* a series of chairs hanging from a moving cable, for carrying people up and down a mountain

chair·man ⚷ /ˈtʃeəmən; *NAmE* ˈtʃer-/ *noun* (*pl.* -men /-mən/)

1 ⚷ the person in charge of a meeting, who tells people when they can speak, etc. **2** ⚷ the person in charge of a committee, a company, etc: *the chairman of the board of governors* (= of a school) ◇ *The chairman of the company presented the annual report.* ➲ note at GENDER

chair·man·ship /ˈtʃeəmənʃɪp; *NAmE* ˈtʃer-/ *noun* **1** [C] the position of a chairman or chairwoman: *the chairmanship of the committee* **2** [U] the state of being a chairman or chairwoman: *under her skilful chairmanship*

chair·per·son /ˈtʃeəpɜːsn; *NAmE* ˈtʃerpɜːrsn/ *noun* (*pl.* -per·sons) a chairman or chairwoman ➲ see also CHAIR (2)

chair·woman ⚷ /ˈtʃeəwʊmən; *NAmE* ˈtʃer-/ *noun* (*pl.* -women /-wɪmɪn/)

a woman in charge of a meeting, a committee or an organization ➲ note at GENDER

chaise /ʃeɪz/ *noun* a CARRIAGE pulled by a horse or horses, used in the past

chaise longue /ˌʃeɪz ˈlɒŋ; *NAmE* ˈlɔːŋ/ *noun* (*pl.* chaises longues /ˌʃeɪz ˈlɒŋ; *NAmE* ˈlɔːŋ/) (from *French*) **1** a long low seat with a back and one arm, on which the person sitting can stretch out their legs **2** (*NAmE*) (also *informal* **chaise lounge**) a long chair with a back that can be vertical for sitting on or flat for lying on outdoors ➲ VISUAL VOCAB page V18

chakra /ˈtʃʌkrə/ *noun* (in YOGA) each of the main centres of spiritual power in the human body

cha·let /ˈʃæleɪ; *NAmE* ʃæˈleɪ/ *noun* **1** a wooden house with a roof that slopes steeply down over the sides, usually built in mountain areas, especially in Switzerland **2** (*BrE*) a small house or HUT, especially one used by people on holiday/vacation at the sea

chal·ice /ˈtʃælɪs/ *noun* a large cup for holding wine, especially one from which wine is drunk in the Christian COMMUNION service IDM see POISON *v.*

chalk /tʃɔːk/ *noun, verb*

■ ***noun*** **1** [U] a type of soft white stone: *the chalk cliffs of southern England* **2** [U, C] a substance similar to chalk made into white or coloured sticks for writing or drawing: *a* ***piece/stick of chalk*** ◇ *drawing diagrams with chalk on the blackboard* ◇ *a box of coloured chalks*

IDM **ˌchalk and ˈcheese** (*BrE*) if two people or things are like **chalk and cheese** or as different as **chalk and cheese**, they are completely different from each other ➲ more at LONG *adj.*

■ ***verb*** **~ sth (up) (on sth)** to write or draw sth with chalk: *She chalked (up) the day's menu on the board.*

PHR V **ˌchalk ˈup sth** (*informal*) to achieve or record a success, points in a game, etc: *The team chalked up their tenth win this season.* **ˌchalk sth ˈup to sth** (*NAmE, informal*) to consider that sth is caused by sth: *We can chalk that win up to a lot of luck.* IDM see EXPERIENCE *n.*

chalk·board /ˈtʃɔːkbɔːd; *NAmE* -bɔːrd/ *noun* (*especially NAmE*) = BLACKBOARD

chalky /ˈtʃɔːki/ *adj.* containing chalk or like chalk

chal·lenge ⚷ AW /ˈtʃælɪndʒ/ *noun, verb*

■ ***noun*** **1** ⚷ a new or difficult task that tests sb's ability and skill: *an* ***exciting/interesting challenge*** ◇ *The role will be the biggest challenge of his acting career.* ◇ *to* ***face a challenge*** (= to have to deal with one) ◇ *Destruction of the environment is one of the most* ***serious challenges*** *we face.* ◇ *Schools must* ***meet the challenge of*** *new technology* (= deal with it successfully). **2** ⚷ an invitation or a suggestion to sb that they should enter a competition, fight, etc: *to* ***accept/take up a challenge*** ◇ *to* ***mount a challenge*** **3** ⚷ **~ (to sth)** a statement or an action that shows that sb refuses to accept sth and questions whether it is right, legal, etc: *It was a direct challenge to the president's authority.* ◇ *Their legal challenge was unsuccessful.*

▪ ***verb*** **1** ~ **sth** to question whether a statement or an action is right, legal, etc; to refuse to accept sth SYN **dispute**: *The story was completely untrue and was successfully challenged in court.* ◊ *She does not like anyone challenging her authority.* ◊ *This discovery challenges traditional beliefs.* ➲ LANGUAGE BANK at ARGUE **2** to invite sb to enter a competition, fight, etc; to suggest strongly that sb should do sth (especially when you think that they might be unwilling to do it): **~ sb (to sth)** *Mike challenged me to a game of chess.* ◊ **~ sb to do sth** *The opposition leader challenged the prime minister to call an election.* **3** ~ **sb** to test sb's ability and skills, especially in an interesting way: *The job doesn't really challenge her.* **4** ~ **sb** to order sb to stop and say who they are or what they are doing: *We were challenged by police at the border.*

chal·lenged AW /ˈtʃælɪndʒd/ *adj.* (*especially NAmE*) (used with an adverb) a polite way of referring to sb who has a DISABILITY of some sort: *a competition for physically challenged athletes* ◊ (*humorous*) *I'm financially challenged at the moment* (= I have no money).

chal·len·ger AW /ˈtʃælɪndʒə(r)/ *noun* a person who competes with sb else in sport or in politics for an important position that the other person already holds: *the official challenger for the world championship title*

chal·len·ging AW /ˈtʃælɪndʒɪŋ/ *adj.* **1** difficult in an interesting way that tests your ability: *challenging work/questions/problems* ◊ *a challenging and rewarding career as a teacher* ➲ SYNONYMS at DIFFICULT **2** done in a way that invites people to disagree or argue with you, or shows that you disagree with them: *She gave him a challenging look. 'Are you really sure?' she demanded.*

cham·ber /ˈtʃeɪmbə(r)/ *noun*
1 [C] a hall in a public building that is used for formal meetings: *The members left the council chamber.* ◊ *the* ***Senate/House chamber*** ➲ see also CHAMBER OF COMMERCE **2** [C+sing./pl. v.] one of the parts of a parliament: *the* ***Lower/Upper Chamber*** (= in Britain, the House of Commons/House of Lords) ◊ *the Chamber of Deputies in the Italian parliament* ◊ *Under Senate rules, the chamber must vote on the bill by this Friday.* **3** [C] (in compounds) a room used for the particular purpose that is mentioned: *a burial chamber* ◊ *Divers transfer from the water to a decompression chamber.* ➲ see also GAS CHAMBER **4** [C] a space in the body, in a plant or in a machine, which is separated from the rest: *the chambers of the heart* ◊ *the rocket's combustion chamber* ◊ *the chamber of a gun* (= the part that holds the bullets) **5** [C] a space under the ground which is almost completely closed on all sides: *They found themselves in a vast underground chamber.* **6** [C] (*old use*) a bedroom or private room

cham·ber·lain /ˈtʃeɪmbəlɪn; *NAmE* -bərlɪn/ *noun* an official who managed the home and servants of a king, queen or important family in past centuries

cham·ber·maid /ˈtʃeɪmbəmeɪd; *NAmE* -bərm-/ *noun* a woman whose job is to clean bedrooms, usually in a hotel

ˈchamber music *noun* [U] CLASSICAL music written for a small group of instruments

ˌChamber of ˈCommerce *noun* a group of local business people who work together to help business and trade in a particular town

ˌchamber of ˈhorrors *noun* [sing.] a part of a museum displaying objects used to kill people in a cruel and painful way or scenes showing how they died

ˈchamber orchestra *noun* a small group of musicians who play CLASSICAL music together

ˈchamber pot (also *slang, offensive* **piss·pot**) *noun* a round container that people in the past had in the bedroom and used for URINATING in at night ➲ compare POTTY

cha·meleon /kəˈmiːliən/ *noun* **1** a small LIZARD (= a type of REPTILE) that can change colour according to its surroundings **2** (often *disapproving*) a person who changes their behaviour or opinions according to the situation

cham·fer /ˈtʃæmfə(r)/ *noun* (*technical*) a cut made along an edge or on a corner so that it slopes rather than being at 90°

cham·ois *noun* (*pl.* **cham·ois**) **1** /ˈʃæmwɑː; *NAmE* ˈʃæmi/ [C] an animal like a small DEER, that lives in the mountains of Europe and Asia **2** /ˈʃæmi/ (also **sham·my**) (*BrE* also **ˌchamois ˈleather**, **ˌshammy ˈleather**) [U, C] a type of soft leather, made from the skin of GOATS, sheep, etc; a piece of this, used especially for cleaning windows **3** /ˈʃæmi/ [U] (*NAmE*) a type of soft thick cotton cloth, used especially for making shirts

chamo·mile (*especially NAmE*) (also **camo·mile** especially in *BrE*) /ˈkæməmaɪl/ *noun* [U] a plant with a sweet smell and small white and yellow flowers. Its dried leaves and flowers are used to make tea, medicine, etc: *chamomile tea*

champ /tʃæmp/ *verb, noun*
▪ ***verb*** [I, T] ~ (**sth**) (especially of horses) to bite or eat sth noisily
IDM **ˌchamping at the ˈbit** (*informal*) impatient to do or start doing sth
▪ ***noun*** an informal way of referring to a champion, often used in newspapers: *Scottish champs celebrate victory!*

cham·pagne /ʃæmˈpeɪn/ *noun* [U, C] a French SPARKLING white wine (= one with bubbles) that is drunk on special occasions: *a glass of champagne*

ˌchampagne ˈsocialist *noun* (*BrE, disapproving*) a person who has SOCIALIST ideas but is rich or has social advantages

cham·pers /ˈʃæmpəz; *NAmE* -pərz/ *noun* [U] (*BrE, informal*) = CHAMPAGNE

cham·pion /ˈtʃæmpiən/ *noun, verb*
▪ ***noun*** **1** a person, team, etc. that has won a competition, especially in a sport: *the world basketball champions* ◊ *a* ***champion jockey/boxer/swimmer*** ◊ *the reigning champion* (= the person who is champion now) **2** ~ (**of sth**) a person who fights for, or speaks in support of, a group of people or a belief: *She was a champion of the poor all her life.*
▪ ***verb*** ~ **sth** to fight for or speak in support of a group of people or a belief: *He has always championed the cause of gay rights.*

cham·pion·ship /ˈtʃæmpiənʃɪp/ *noun* **1** (also **cham·pion·ships** [pl.]) a competition to find the best player or team in a particular sport: *the National Basketball Association Championship* ◊ *He won a silver medal at the European Championships.* **2** the position of being a champion: *They've held the championship for the past two years.*

chance /tʃɑːns; *NAmE* tʃæns/ *noun, verb, adj.*
▪ ***noun*** **1** [C, U] a possibility of sth happening, especially sth that you want: **~ of doing sth** *Is there any chance of getting tickets for tonight?* ◊ *She has only* ***a slim chance*** *of passing the exam.* ◊ **~ that...** *There's a* ***slight chance*** *that he'll be back in time.* ◊ *There is* ***no chance*** *that he will change his mind.* ◊ **~ of sth happening** *What chance is there of anybody being found alive?* ◊ **~ of sth** *Nowadays a premature baby* ***has a very good chance*** *of survival.* ◊ *The operation has a* ***fifty-fifty chance*** *of success.* ◊ *an* ***outside chance*** (= a very small one) ◊ *The chances are a million to one against being struck by lightning.* **2** [C] a suitable time or situation when you have the opportunity to do sth: *It was the chance she had been waiting for.* ◊ *Jeff deceived me once already—I won't give him* ***a second chance****.* ◊ *This is your* ***big chance*** (= opportunity for success). ◊ **~ of sth** *We won't* ***get another chance*** *of a holiday this year.* ◊ **~ to do sth** *Please* ***give me a chance*** *to explain.* ◊ *Tonight is your* ***last chance*** *to catch the play at your local theatre.* ◊ **~ for sb to do sth** *There will be a chance for parents to look around the school.* **3** [C] an unpleasant or dangerous possibility: *When installing electrical equipment don't* ***take any chances****. A mistake could kill.* **4** [U] the way that some things happen without any cause that you can see or understand: *I met her* ***by chance*** (= without planning to) *at the airport.* ◊ *Chess is not a* ***game of chance****.* ◊ *It was* ***pure chance*** *that we were both there.* ◊ *We'll plan everything very carefully and* ***leave nothing to chance****.* ➲ SYNONYMS at LUCK
IDM **as ˌchance would ˈhave it** happening in a way that

C

was lucky, although it was not planned: *As chance would have it, John was going to London too, so I went with him.* **be ˌin with a ˈchance (of doing sth)** (*BrE, informal*) to have the possibility of succeeding or achieving sth: *'Do you think we'll win?' 'I think we're in with a chance.'* ◇ *He's in with a good chance of passing the exam.* **by ˈany chance** used especially in questions, to ask whether sth is true, possible, etc.: *Are you in love with him, by any chance?* **the chances ˈare (that)...** (*informal*) it is likely that...: *The chances are you won't have to pay.* **ˈchance would be a fine thing** (*BrE, informal*) people say **chance would be a fine thing** to show that they would like to do or have the thing that sb has mentioned, but that they do not think that it is very likely **give sb/sth half a ˈchance** to give sb/sth some opportunity to do sth: *That dog will give you a nasty bite, given half a chance.* **ˈno chance** (*informal*) there is no possibility: *'Do you think he'll do it?' 'No chance.'* **on the ˈoff chance (that)** because of the possibility of sth happening, although it is unlikely: *I didn't think you'd be at home but I just called by on the off chance.* **stand a ˈchance (of doing sth)** to have the possibility of succeeding or achieving sth: *The driver didn't stand a chance of stopping in time.* **take a ˈchance (on sth)** to decide to do sth, knowing that it might be the wrong choice: *We took a chance on the weather and planned to have the party outside.* **take your ˈchances** to take a risk or to use the opportunities that you have and hope that things will happen in the way that you want: *He took his chances and jumped into the water.* ➲ more at CAT, DOG *n.*, EVEN *adj.*, EYE *n.*, FAT *adj.*, FIGHT *v.*, SNOWBALL *n.*, SPORTING

■ ***verb*** **1** [T] (*informal*) to risk sth, although you know the result may not be successful: **~ sth** *She was* ***chancing her luck*** *driving without a licence.* ◇ *'Take an umbrella.' 'No, I'll* ***chance it****'* (= take the risk that it may rain). ◇ **~ doing sth** *I stayed hidden; I couldn't chance coming out.* **2** *linking verb* (*formal*) to happen or to do sth by chance: **~ to do sth** *If I do chance to find out where she is, I'll inform you immediately.* ◇ *They chanced to be staying at the same hotel.* ◇ **it chanced (that)...** *It chanced (that) they were staying at the same hotel.*

IDM **ˌchance your ˈarm** (*BrE, informal*) to take a risk although you will probably fail

PHR V **ˈchance on/upon sb/sth** (*formal*) to find or meet sb/sth unexpectedly or by chance: *One day he chanced upon Emma's diary and began reading it.*

■ ***adj.*** [only before noun] not planned SYN **unplanned**: *a chance meeting/encounter*

chan·cel /ˈtʃɑːnsl; *NAmE* ˈtʃænsl/ *noun* the part of a church near the ALTAR, where the priests and the CHOIR (= singers) sit during services

chan·cel·lery /ˈtʃɑːnsələri; *NAmE* ˈtʃæn-/ *noun* (*pl.* **-ies**) **1** [C, usually sing.] the place where a chancellor has his or her office **2** [sing.+ sing./pl. v.] the staff in the department of a chancellor

chan·cel·lor /ˈtʃɑːnsələ(r); *NAmE* ˈtʃæns-/ (also **Chancellor**) *noun* (often used in a title) **1** the head of government in Germany or Austria: *Chancellor Adenauer* **2** (*BrE*) = CHANCELLOR OF THE EXCHEQUER: *MPs waited for the chancellor's announcement.* **3** the official head of a university in Britain. Chancellor is an HONORARY title. ➲ compare VICE CHANCELLOR **4** the head of some American universities **5** used in the titles of some senior state officials in Britain: *the Lord Chancellor* (= a senior law official)

ˌChancellor of the Exˈchequer *noun* (in Britain) the government minister who is responsible for financial affairs

chan·cer /ˈtʃɑːnsə(r); *NAmE* ˈtʃænsər/ *noun* (*BrE, informal*) a person who is always looking for opportunities to gain an advantage, even when they do not deserve to do so

chan·cery /ˈtʃɑːnsəri; *NAmE* ˈtʃæns-/ *noun* [sing.] **1 Chancery** (*law*) a division of the High Court in Britain **2** (*especially BrE*) an office where public records are kept **3** (also **ˈchancery court**) a court in the US that decides legal cases based on the principle of EQUITY **4** the offices where the official representative of a country works, in another country

chancy /ˈtʃɑːnsi; *NAmE* ˈtʃænsi/ *adj.* (*informal*) involving risks and UNCERTAINTY SYN **risky**

chan·de·lier /ˌʃændəˈlɪə(r); *NAmE* -ˈlɪr/ *noun* a large round frame with branches that hold lights or CANDLES. Chandeliers are decorated with many small pieces of glass and hang from the ceiling.

chand·ler /ˈtʃɑːndlə(r); *NAmE* ˈtʃænd-/ (also **ˈship's chandler**) *noun* a person or shop/store that sells equipment for ships

change 🔑 /tʃeɪndʒ/ *verb, noun*

■ ***verb***

▸ BECOME/MAKE DIFFERENT **1** 🔑 [I] to become different: *Rick hasn't changed. He looks exactly the same as he did at school.* ◇ *changing attitudes towards education* ◇ *Her life changed completely when she won the lottery.* **2** 🔑 [T] **~ sb/sth** to make sb/sth different: *Fame hasn't really changed him.* ◇ *Computers have changed the way people work.* **3** 🔑 [I, T] to pass or make sb/sth pass from one state or form into another: *Wait for the traffic lights to change.* ◇ **~ (from A) to/into B** *The lights changed from red to green.* ◇ *Caterpillars change into butterflies.* ◇ **~ sb/sth (from A) to/into B** *With a wave of her magic wand, she changed the frog into a handsome prince.* **4** 🔑 [T] **~ sth** to stop having one state, position or direction and start having another: *Leaves change colour in autumn.* ◇ *The wind has changed direction.* ◇ *Our ship changed course.*

▸ REPLACE **5** 🔑 [T] to replace one thing, person, service, etc. with sth new or different: **~ sb/sth** *I want to change my doctor.* ◇ *That back tyre needs changing.* ◇ **~ sb/sth (for sb/sth)** *We change our car every two years.* ◇ *We changed the car for a bigger one.* ◇ **~ sth (to sth)** *Marie changed her name when she got married.* ◇ *She changed her name to his.*

▸ EXCHANGE **6** 🔑 [T] (used with a plural object) to exchange positions, places, etc. with sb else, so that you have what they have, and they have what you have: **~ sth** *At half-time the teams change ends.* ◇ *Can we change seats?* ◇ **~ sth with sb** *Can I change seats with you?*

▸ CLOTHES **7** 🔑 [I, T] to put on different or clean clothes: *I went into the bedroom to change.* ◇ **~ into sth** *She changed into her swimsuit.* ◇ **~ out of sth** *You need to change out of those wet things.* ◇ **~ sth** (*especially NAmE*) *I didn't have time to* ***change clothes*** *before the party.* ◇ (*especially BrE*) *I didn't have time to* ***get changed*** *before the party* (= to put different clothes on).

▸ BABY **8** [T] **~ sb/sth** to put clean clothes or a clean NAPPY/DIAPER on a baby: *She can't even change a nappy.* ◇ *The baby needs changing.* ◇ *There are baby changing facilities in all our stores.*

▸ BED **9** [T] **~ sth** to put clean sheets, etc. on a bed: *to change the sheets* ◇ *Could you help me change the bed?*

▸ MONEY **10** 🔑 [T] to exchange money into the money of another country: **~ sth** *Where can I change my traveller's cheques?* ◇ **~ sth into sth** *to change dollars into yen* **11** 🔑 [T] to exchange money for the same amount in different coins or notes: **~ sth** *Can you change a £20 note?* ◇ **~ sth for/into sth** *to change a dollar bill for four quarters*

▸ GOODS **12** 🔑 [T] **~ sth (for sth)** (*BrE*) to exchange sth that you have bought for sth else, especially because there is sth wrong with it; to give a customer a new item because there is sth wrong with the one they have bought: *This shirt I bought's too small—I'll have to change it for a bigger one.* ◇ *Of course we'll change it for a larger size, Madam.*

▸ BUS/TRAIN/PLANE **13** 🔑 [I, T] to go from one bus, train, etc. to another in order to continue a journey: *Where do I have to change?* ◇ *Change at Reading (for London).* ◇ **~ sth** *I stopped in Moscow only to change planes.* ➲ see also UNCHANGING

IDM **change ˈhands** to pass to a different owner: *The house has changed hands several times.* **change horses in midˈstream** to change to a different or new activity while you are in the middle of sth else; to change from supporting one person or thing to another **change your/sb's ˈmind** 🔑 to change a decision or an opinion: *Nothing will make me change my mind.* **change your ˈtune** (*informal*) to express a different opinion or behave in a different way when your situation changes: *Wait until it happens to him —he'll soon change his tune.* **change your 'ways** to start to live or behave in a different way from before ➲ more at CHOP *v.*, LEOPARD, PLACE *n.*

PHR V **,change sth↔a'round/'round** 🔑 to move things or people into different positions: *You've changed all the furniture around.* **,change 'back (into sb/sth)** to return to a previous situation, form, etc. **,change 'back (into sth)** to take off your clothes and put on what you were wearing earlier: *She changed back into her work clothes.* **,change sth 'back (into sth)** to exchange an amount of money into the CURRENCY that it was in before: *You can change back unused dollars into pounds at the bank.* **,change 'down** (*BrE*) to start using a lower gear when you are driving a car, etc: *Change down into second.* **,change 'over (from sth) (to sth)** to change from one system or position to another: *The farm has changed over to organic methods.* ➲ related noun CHANGEOVER **,change 'up** (*BrE*) to start using a higher gear when driving a car, etc: *Change up into fifth.*

■ ***noun***

▸ DIFFERENCE **1** 🔑 [C, U] **~ (in/to sth)** the act or result of sth becoming different: *a change in the weather ◇ important changes to the tax system ◇ There was* ***no change*** *in the patient's condition overnight. ◇ She is someone who hates change. ◇ social/political/economic change*

▸ STH NEW AND INTERESTING **2** 🔑 **a change** [sing.] **~ (from sth)** the fact of a situation, a place or an experience being different from what is usual and therefore likely to be interesting, enjoyable, etc: *Finishing early was* ***a welcome change.*** *◇ Let's stay in tonight* ***for a change.*** *◇ Can you just listen* ***for a change?*** *◇ It* ***makes a change*** *to read some good news for once.*

▸ REPLACING STH **3** 🔑 [C] **~ (of sth)** | **~ (from sth to sth)** the process of replacing sth with sth new or different; a thing that is used to replace sth: *a change of address ◇ a change of government ◇ a change from agriculture to industry ◇ There will be a crew change when we land at Dubai. ◇* (*BrE*) *Let's get away for the weekend. A* ***change of scene*** (= time in a different place) *will do you good.*

▸ OF CLOTHES **4 ~ of clothes, etc.** [C] an extra set of clothes, etc: *She packed a change of clothes for the weekend. ◇ I keep a change of shoes in the car.*

▸ MONEY **5** 🔑 [U] the money that you get back when you have paid for sth giving more money than the amount it costs: *Don't forget your change! ◇ That's 40p change. ◇ The ticket machine gives change.* **6** 🔑 [U] coins rather than paper money: *Do you have any change for the phone? ◇ a dollar* ***in change*** (= coins that together are worth one dollar) *◇ I didn't have any* ***small change*** (= coins of low value) *to leave as a tip. ◇ He puts his* ***loose change*** *in a money box for the children. ◇ Could you give me* ***change for*** *a ten pound note* (= coins or notes that are worth this amount)? ➲ SYNONYMS at MONEY

▸ OF BUS/TRAIN/PLANE **7** [C] an occasion when you go from one bus, train or plane to another during a journey: *The journey involved three changes.*

IDM **a change for the 'better/'worse** a person, thing, situation, etc. that is better/worse than the previous or present one **a ,change of 'heart** if you have **a change of heart**, your attitude towards sth changes, usually making you feel more friendly, helpful, etc. **a ,change of 'mind** an act of changing what you think about a situation, etc. **get no change out of sb** (*BrE, informal*) to get no help or information from sb ➲ more at RING *v.*, WIND[1] *n.*

change·able /'tʃeɪndʒəbl/ *adj.* likely to change; often changing SYN **unpredictable**: *The weather is very changeable at this time of year.* ➲ compare UNCHANGEABLE ▸ **change·abil·ity** /,tʃeɪndʒə'bɪləti/ *noun* [U]

changed /tʃeɪndʒd/ *adj.* [only before noun] (of people or situations) very different from what they were before: *She's a* ***changed woman*** *since she got that job. ◇ This will not be possible in the changed economic climate.* OPP **unchanged**

change·less /'tʃeɪndʒləs/ *adj.* (*formal*) never changing

change·ling /'tʃeɪndʒlɪŋ/ *noun* (*literary*) a child who is believed to have been secretly left in exchange for another, especially (in stories) by FAIRIES

the ,change of 'life *noun* [sing.] (*informal*) = MENOPAUSE

change·over /'tʃeɪndʒəʊvə(r); *NAmE* -oʊv-/ *noun* a change from one system, or method of working to another SYN **switch**: *the changeover from a manual to a computerized system ◇ a changeover period*

'change purse *noun* (*NAmE*) a small bag made of leather, plastic, etc. for carrying coins ➲ VISUAL VOCAB page V52 ➲ compare PURSE

chan·ger /'tʃeɪndʒə(r)/ *noun* (often in compounds) **1** a piece of equipment that holds several discs, etc. and is able to switch between them: *The car comes with white leather seats and a 6-CD changer.* **2** a person or thing that changes sth, usually in order to improve it: *The whole experience was a life changer for me.*

'changing room *noun* (*especially BrE*) a room for changing clothes in, especially before playing sports ➲ compare LOCKER ROOM ➲ see also FITTING ROOM

chan·nel 🔑 AW /'tʃænl/ *noun, verb*

■ ***noun***

▸ ON TELEVISION/RADIO **1** 🔑 [C] a television station: *What's on Channel 4 tonight? ◇ a* ***movie/sports channel*** *◇ to* ***change/switch channels*** ➲ COLLOCATIONS at TELEVISION **2** 🔑 [C] a band of radio waves used for broadcasting television or radio programmes: ***terrestrial/satellite channels***

▸ FOR COMMUNICATING **3** 🔑 [C] (also **channels** [pl.]) a method or system that people use to get information, to communicate, or to send sth somewhere: *Complaints must be made* ***through the proper channels.*** *◇ The newsletter is a useful* ***channel of communication*** *between teacher and students. ◇ The company has worldwide distribution channels.*

▸ FOR IDEAS/FEELINGS **4** [C] a way of expressing ideas and feelings: *The campaign provided a channel for protest against the war. ◇ Music is a great channel for releasing your emotions.*

▸ WATER **5** [C] a passage that water can flow along, especially in the ground, on the bottom of a river, etc: *drainage channels in the rice fields* **6** [C] a deep passage of water in a river or near the coast that can be used as route for ships **7** [C] a passage of water that connects two areas of water, especially two seas: *the Bristol Channel* **8 the Channel** [sing.] the area of sea between England and France, also known as **the English Channel**: *the Channel Tunnel ◇ cross-Channel ferries ◇ news from* ***across the Channel*** (= from France)

■ ***verb*** (-ll-, *especially US* -l-)

▸ IDEAS/FEELINGS **1 ~ sth (into sth)** to direct money, feelings, ideas, etc. towards a particular thing or purpose: *He channels his aggression into sport.*

▸ MONEY/HELP **2 ~ sth (through sth)** to send money, help, etc. using a particular route: *Money for the project will be channelled through local government.*

▸ WATER/LIGHT **3 ~ sth** to carry or send water, light, etc. through a passage: *A sensor channels the light signal along an optical fibre.*

'channel-hop *verb* (-pp-) (also **'channel-surf**) [I] to repeatedly switch from one television channel to another

the 'Channel Islands *noun* [pl.] a group of islands near the north-western coast of France that belong to Britain but have their own parliaments and laws

chant /tʃɑːnt; *NAmE* tʃænt/ *noun, verb*

■ ***noun*** **1** [C] words or phrases that a group of people shout or sing again and again: *The crowd broke into chants of 'Out! Out!' ◇ football chants* **2** [C, U] a religious song or prayer or a way of singing, using only a few notes that are repeated many times: *a Buddhist chant* ➲ see also GREGORIAN CHANT

■ ***verb*** **1** [I, T] to sing or shout the same words or phrases many times: *A group of protesters, chanting and carrying placards, waited outside. ◇* **~ sth** *The crowd chanted their hero's name. ◇ 'Resign! Resign!' they chanted.* **2** [I, T] **~ (sth)** to sing or say a religious song or prayer using only a few notes that are repeated many times ▸ **chant·ing** *noun* [U]: *The chanting rose in volume.*

chant·er /ˈtʃɑːntə(r); *NAmE* ˈtʃæntər/ *noun* (*music*) the part of a set of BAGPIPES that is like a pipe with finger holes, on which the music is played

chan·ter·elle /ˈʃɑːntərel; ˌʃɑːntəˈrel/ *noun* a yellowish MUSHROOM that grows in woods and has a hollow part in the centre

chant·euse /ʃɑːnˈtɜːz/ *noun* (from *French*) a female singer of popular songs, especially in a NIGHTCLUB

chan·try /ˈtʃɑːntri; *NAmE* ˈtʃæntri/ *noun* (*pl.* -ies) (also ˌ**chantry ˈchapel**) a small church or part of a church paid for by sb, so that priests could say prayers for them there after their death

chanty *noun* (*pl.* -ies) (also **chantey**) (both *US*) /ˈʃænti/ (*BrE, CanE* **shanty**, ˈ**sea shanty**) a song that sailors traditionally used to sing while pulling ropes, etc.

Cha·nuk·kah, Cha·nu·kah = HANUKKAH

chaos /ˈkeɪɒs; *NAmE* ˈkeɪɑːs/ *noun* [U] a state of complete confusion and lack of order: *economic/political/domestic chaos* ◇ *Heavy snow has caused* ***total chaos*** *on the roads.* ◇ *The house was* ***in chaos*** *after the party.*

ˈ**chaos theory** *noun* [U] (*mathematics*) the study of a group of connected things that are very sensitive so that small changes in conditions affect them very much

cha·ot·ic /keɪˈɒtɪk; *NAmE* -ˈɑːtɪk/ *adj.* in a state of complete confusion and lack of order: *The traffic in the city is chaotic in the rush hour.* ▸ **cha·ot·ic·al·ly** /keɪˈɒtɪkli; *NAmE* -ˈɑːtɪk-/ *adv.*

chap /tʃæp/ *noun* (*BrE, informal*, becoming *old-fashioned*) used to talk about a man in a friendly way: *He isn't such a bad chap really.*

chap. *abbr.* (in writing) chapter

chap·ar·ral /ˌʃæpəˈræl/ *noun* [U] (*NAmE*) an area of dry land that is covered with small bushes

cha·patti (also **cha·pati**) /tʃəˈpæti; -ˈpɑːti/ *noun* a type of flat round S Asian bread

chapel /ˈtʃæpl/ *noun* **1** [C] a small building or room used for Christian worship in a school, prison, large private house, etc: *a college chapel* **2** [C] a separate part of a church or CATHEDRAL, with its own ALTAR, used for some services and private prayer **3** [C, U] the word for a church used in some Christian DENOMINATIONS, for example by Nonconformists in Britain: *a Methodist chapel* ◇ *a Mormon chapel* ◇ *She always went to chapel on Sundays.* **4** [C] a small building or room used for funeral services, especially at a CEMETERY or CREMATORIUM **6** [C+sing./pl. v.] (*BrE*) a branch of a TRADE/LABOR UNION in a newspaper office or printing house; the members of the branch

ˌ**chapel of ˈrest** *noun* (*BrE*) a room at an UNDERTAKER'S where dead bodies are kept before the funeral

chap·er·one (*BrE* also **chap·eron**) /ˈʃæpərəʊn; *NAmE* -oʊn/ *noun, verb*

■ ***noun*** **1** (in the past) an older woman who, on social occasions, took care of a young woman who was not married **2** a person who takes care of children in public, especially when they are working, for example as actors **3** (*NAmE*) a person, such as a parent or a teacher, who goes with a group of young people on a trip or to a dance to encourage good behaviour

■ ***verb* ~ sb** to act as a chaperone for sb, especially a woman

chap·kan /ˈtʃæpkən/ *noun* a long coat worn by men, especially in northern India and Pakistan

chap·lain /ˈtʃæplɪn/ *noun* a priest or other Christian minister who is responsible for the religious needs of people in a prison, hospital, etc. or in the armed forces ➲ compare PADRE, PRIEST

chap·lain·cy /ˈtʃæplɪnsi/ *noun* (*pl.* -ies) the position or work of a chaplain; the place where a chaplain works

chap·let /ˈtʃæplət/ *noun* a circle of leaves, flowers or JEWELS worn on the head

chapped /tʃæpt/ *adj.* (of the skin or lips) rough, dry and sore, especially because of wind or cold weather

chaps /tʃæps/ *noun* [pl.] leather coverings worn as protection over trousers/pants by COWBOYS, etc. when riding a horse: *a pair of chaps*

chap·ter 🔑 AW /ˈtʃæptə(r)/ *noun*

1 🔑 (*abbr.* **chap.**) [C] a separate section of a book, usually with a number or title: *I've just finished Chapter 3.* ◇ *in the* ***previous/next/last chapter*** ◇ *Have you read the chapter on the legal system?* **2** [C] a period of time in a person's life or in history: *a difficult chapter in our country's history* **3** [C+sing./pl. v.] all the priests of a CATHEDRAL or members of a religious community: *a meeting of the dean and chapter* **4** [C] (*especially NAmE*) a local branch of a society, club, etc: *the local chapter of the Rotary club*

IDM ˌ**chapter and ˈverse** the exact details of sth, especially the exact place where particular information may be found: *I can't give chapter and verse, but that's the rough outline of our legal position.* **a** ˌ**chapter of ˈaccidents** (*BrE*) a series of unfortunate events

ˌ**Chapter ˈ11** *noun* [U] (*law*) in the US, a section of the law dealing with BANKRUPTCY (= being unable to pay debts), that allows companies to stop paying their debts in the normal way while they try to find a solution to their financial problems: *The company has* ***filed for Chapter 11*** *bankruptcy protection.* ➲ compare ADMINISTRATION

ˌ**Chapter ˈ7** *noun* [U] (*law*) in the US, a section of the law dealing with BANKRUPTCY (= being unable to pay debts), that allows a court to take property belonging to a company or person which is then sold to pay their debts ➲ compare LIQUIDATION

ˈ**chapter house** *noun* a building where all the priests of a CATHEDRAL or members of a religious community meet

char /tʃɑː(r)/ *verb, noun*

■ ***verb*** (-rr-) **1** [I, T] **~ (sth)** to become black by burning; to make sth black by burning it ➲ see also CHARRED ➲ SYNONYMS at BURN **2** [I] (*old-fashioned, BrE*) to work as a cleaner in a house

■ ***noun*** (*old-fashioned, BrE*) **1** [C] = CHARWOMAN **2** [U] (*informal*) tea: *a cup of char*

chara·banc /ˈʃærəbæŋ/ *noun* (*old-fashioned, BrE*) an early type of bus, used in the past especially for pleasure trips

char·ac·ter 🔑 /ˈkærəktə(r)/ *noun*

▸ QUALITIES/FEATURES **1** 🔑 [C, usually sing.] all the qualities and features that make a person, groups of people, and places different from others: *to have a* ***strong/weak character*** ◇ ***character traits/defects*** ◇ *The book gives a fascinating insight into Mrs Obama's character.* ◇ *Generosity is part of the American character.* ◇ *The character of the neighbourhood hasn't changed at all.* **2** 🔑 [C, usually sing., U] the way that sth is, or a particular quality or feature that a thing, an event or a place has SYN **nature**: *the delicate character of the light in the evening* ◇ *buildings that are very simple* ***in character*** **3** 🔑 [U] (*approving*) strong personal qualities such as the ability to deal with difficult or dangerous situations: *Everyone admires her strength of character and determination.* ◇ *He showed great character returning to the sport after his accident.* ◇ *Adventure camps are considered to be* ***character-building*** (= meant to improve sb's strong qualities). **4** 🔑 [U] (usually *approving*) the interesting or unusual quality that a place or a person has: *The modern hotels here have no real character.* ◇ *a face with a lot of character*

▸ STRANGE/INTERESTING PERSON **5** [C] (*informal*) (used with an adjective) a person, particularly an unpleasant or strange one: *There were some really strange characters hanging around the bar.* **6** [C] (*informal*) an interesting or unusual person: *She's a character!*

▸ REPUTATION **7** [C, U] (*formal*) the opinion that people have of you, particularly of whether you can be trusted or relied on: *She was a victim of* ***character assassination*** (= an unfair attack on the good opinion people had of her). ◇ *a* ***slur/attack on his character*** ◇ *My teacher agreed to be a* ***character witness*** *for me in court.* ◇ *a* ***character reference*** (= a letter that a person who knows you well writes to an employer to tell them about your good qualities)

▸ IN BOOK/PLAY/MOVIE **8** [C] a person or an animal in a book, play or film/movie: *a **major/minor character** in the book* ◇ *cartoon characters* ➲ COLLOCATIONS at LITERATURE

▸ SYMBOL/LETTER **9** [C] a letter, sign, mark or symbol used in writing, printing or on computers: *Chinese characters* ◇ *a line 30 characters long* ➲ picture at IDEOGRAM

IDM ˌ**in ˈcharacter** | ˌ**out of ˈcharacter** typical/not typical of a person's character: *Her behaviour last night was completely out of character.* ˌ**in ˈcharacter (with sth)** in the same style as sth: *The new wing of the museum was not really in character with the rest of the building.*

ˈ**character actor** *noun* an actor who always takes the parts of interesting or unusual people

char·ac·ter·ful /ˈkærəktəfl; *NAmE* -tərfl/ *adj.* very interesting and unusual

char·ac·ter·is·tic /ˌkærəktəˈrɪstɪk/ *adj., noun*

■ ***adj.*** **~ (of sth/sb)** very typical of sth or of sb's character: *She spoke with characteristic enthusiasm.* OPP **uncharacteristic** ▸ **char·ac·ter·is·tic·al·ly** *adv.*: *Characteristically, Helen paid for everyone.*

■ ***noun*** **~ (of sth/sb)** a typical feature or quality that sth/sb has: *The need to communicate is a key characteristic of human society.* ◇ *The two groups of children have quite different characteristics.* ◇ *Personal characteristics, such as age and sex are taken into account.* ◇ *genetic characteristics*

char·ac·ter·iza·tion (*BrE* also **-isa·tion**) /ˌkærəktəraɪˈzeɪʃn/ *noun* [U, C] **1** the way that a writer makes characters in a book or play seem real **2** (*formal*) the way in which sb/sth is described or defined SYN **portrayal**: *This is an unfair characterization of the Prime Minister.*

char·ac·ter·ize (*BrE* also **-ise**) /ˈkærəktəraɪz/ *verb* (*formal*) **1 ~ sb/sth** to be typical of a person, place or thing: *the rolling hills that characterize this part of England* **2 ~ sb/sth** [often passive] to give sb/sth its typical or most noticeable qualities or features: *The city is characterized by tall modern buildings in steel and glass.* **3 ~ sb/sth (as sth)** to describe or show the qualities of sb/sth in a particular way: *activities that are characterized as 'male' or 'female' work*

char·ac·ter·less /ˈkærəktələs; *NAmE* -tərləs/ *adj.* having no interesting qualities

ˈ**character recognition** *noun* [U] the ability of a computer to read numbers or letters that are printed or written by hand

cha·rade /ʃəˈrɑːd; *NAmE* ʃəˈreɪd/ *noun* **1** [C] a situation in which people pretend that sth is true when it clearly is not SYN **pretence**: *Their whole marriage had been a charade—they had never loved each other.* **2 charades** [U] a game in which one player acts out the syllables of a word or title and the other players try to guess what it is: *Let's play charades.*

char·broil /ˈtʃɑːbrɔɪl; *NAmE* ˈtʃɑːr-/ *verb* **~ sth** to cook meat or other food over CHARCOAL

char·coal /ˈtʃɑːkəʊl; *NAmE* ˈtʃɑːrkoʊl/ *noun* [U] **1** a black substance made by burning wood slowly in an oven with little air. Charcoal is used as a fuel or for drawing: *charcoal grilled steaks* ◇ *a charcoal drawing* **2** (also ˌ**charcoal ˈgrey**) a very dark grey colour

chard /tʃɑːd; *NAmE* tʃɑːrd/ (also ˌ**Swiss ˈchard**) *noun* [U] a vegetable with large leaves and thick white, yellow or red STEMS

Char·don·nay /ˈʃɑːdəneɪ; *NAmE* ˈʃɑːrd-/ *noun* [U, C] a type of white wine, or the type of GRAPE from which it is made

charge /tʃɑːdʒ; *NAmE* tʃɑːrdʒ/ *noun, verb*

■ ***noun***

▸ MONEY **1** [C, U] **~ (for sth)** the amount of money that sb asks for goods and services: *We have to make a small charge for refreshments.* ◇ *admission charges* ◇ *Delivery is **free of charge**.* ➲ SYNONYMS at RATE **2** [C, U] (*NAmE, informal*) = ACCOUNT (3), CHARGE ACCOUNT, CREDIT ACCOUNT: *Would you like to put that on your charge?* ◇ *'Are you paying cash?' 'No, it'll be a charge.'*

▸ OF CRIME/STH WRONG **3** [C, U] an official claim made by the police that sb has committed a crime: *criminal charges* ◇ *a murder/an assault charge* ◇ *He will be sent back to England **to face a charge of*** (= to be on trial for) *armed robbery.* ◇ *They decided to **drop the charges** against the newspaper and settle out of court.* ◇ *After being questioned by the police, she was released **without charge**.* ➲ COLLOCATIONS at JUSTICE **4** [C] a statement accusing sb of doing sth wrong or bad SYN **allegation**: *She rejected the charge that the story was untrue.* ◇ *Be careful you don't **leave yourself open to charges** of political bias.*

▸ RESPONSIBILITY **5** [U] a position of having control over sb/sth; responsibility for sb/sth: *She has charge of the day-to-day running of the business.* ◇ *They left the au pair **in charge of** the children for a week.* ◇ *He **took charge of** the farm after his father's death.* ◇ *I'm leaving the school in your charge.* **6** [C] (*formal* or *humorous*) a person that you have responsibility for and care for

▸ ELECTRICITY **7** [C, U] the amount of electricity that is put into a battery or carried by a substance: *a **positive/negative charge***

▸ RUSH/ATTACK **8** [C] a sudden rush or violent attack, for example by soldiers, wild animals or players in some sports: *He led the charge down the field.*

▸ EXPLOSIVE **9** [C] the amount of EXPLOSIVE needed to fire a gun or make an explosion ➲ see also DEPTH CHARGE

▸ STRONG FEELING **10** [sing.] the power to cause strong feelings: *the emotional charge of the piano piece*

▸ TASK **11** [sing.] (*formal*) a task or duty: *His charge was to obtain specific information.*

IDM **bring/press/prefer ˈcharges against sb** (*law*) to accuse sb formally of a crime so that there can be a trial in court **get a ˈcharge out of sth** (*NAmE*) to get a strong feeling of excitement or pleasure from sth ➲ more at REVERSE *v.*

■ ***verb***

▸ MONEY **1** [T, I] to ask an amount of money for goods or a service: **~ sth for sth** *What did they charge for the repairs?* ◇ *The restaurant charged £20 for dinner.* ◇ **~ sb for sth** *We won't charge you for delivery.* ◇ **~ sth at sth** *Calls are charged at 36p per minute.* ◇ **~ sb sth (for sth)** *He only charged me half price.* ◇ **~ for sth** *Do you think museums should charge for admission?* ◇ **~ (sb) to do sth** *The bank doesn't charge to stop a payment.* **2** [T] to record the cost of sth as an amount that sb has to pay: **~ sth to sth** *They charge the calls to their credit-card account.* ◇ (*NAmE*) **~ sth** *Don't worry. I'll **charge it*** (= pay by credit card).

▸ WITH CRIME/STH WRONG **3** [T] to accuse sb formally of a crime so that there can be a trial in court: **~ sb** *Several people were arrested but nobody was charged.* ◇ **~ sb with sth/with doing sth** *He was charged with murder.* **4** [T] **~ sb (with sth/with doing sth)** (*formal*) to accuse sb publicly of doing sth wrong or bad: *Opposition MPs charged the minister with neglecting her duty.*

▸ RUSH/ATTACK **5** [I, T] to rush forward and attack sb/sth: *The bull put its head down and charged.* ◇ **~ (at) sb/sth** *We charged at the enemy.* **6** [I] **+ adv./prep.** to rush in a particular direction: *The children charged down the stairs.* ◇ *He came charging into my room and demanded to know what was going on.*

▸ WITH ELECTRICITY **7** [T] to pass electricity through sth so that it is stored there: **~ sth** *Before use, the battery must be charged.* ◇ **~ sth up** *The shaver can be charged up and used when travelling.*

▸ WITH RESPONSIBILITY/TASK **8** [T] (usually passive) (*formal*) to give sb a responsibility or task: **~ sb with sth** *The committee has been charged with the development of sport in the region.* ◇ **~ sb with doing sth** *The governing body is charged with managing the school within its budget.*

▸ WITH STRONG FEELING **9** [T] (usually passive) **~ sth (with sth)** (*literary*) to fill sb with an emotion: *The room was charged with hatred.* ◇ *a **highly charged** atmosphere*

▸ GLASS **10** [T] **~ sth** (*BrE, formal*) to fill a glass: *Please charge your glasses and drink a toast to the bride and groom!*

▸ GUN **11** [T] **~ sth** (*old use*) to load a gun

charge·able /ˈtʃɑːdʒəbl; *NAmE* ˈtʃɑːrdʒ-/ *adj.* **~ (to sb/sth) 1** (of a sum of money) that must be paid by sb: *Any* *expenses you may incur will be chargeable to the company.* **2** (of income or other money that you earn) that you must pay tax on: ***chargeable earnings/income***

ˈcharge account *noun* (*NAmE*) = ACCOUNT *n* (3)

C

ˈcharge capping *noun* [U] (*BrE*) the act of setting a limit on the amount of money that the local government of an area can charge people in order to pay for public services

ˈcharge card *noun* a small plastic card provided by a shop/store which you use to buy goods there, paying for them later ➲ see also CREDIT CARD

charged /tʃɑːdʒd; *NAmE* tʃɑːrdʒd/ *adj.* **~ (with sth)** full of or causing strong feelings or opinions: *a highly charged atmosphere* ◇ *a politically charged issue* ◇ *The dialogue is charged with menace.*

chargé d'af·faires /ˌʃɑːʒeɪ dæˈfeə(r); *NAmE* ˌʃɑːrʒeɪ dæˈfer/ *noun* (*pl.* **chargés d'af·faires** /ˌʃɑːʒeɪ dæˈfeə(r); *NAmE* ˌʃɑːrʒeɪ dæˈfer/) (from *French*) **1** an official who takes the place of an AMBASSADOR in a foreign country when he or she is away **2** an official below the rank of AMBASSADOR who acts as the senior representative of his or her country in a foreign country where there is no AMBASSADOR

charge·hand /ˈtʃɑːdʒhænd; *NAmE* ˈtʃɑːrdʒ-/ *noun* (*BrE*) a worker in charge of others on a particular job, but below the rank of a FOREMAN

ˈcharge nurse *noun* (*BrE*) a nurse, especially a man, who is in charge of a hospital WARD

char·ger /ˈtʃɑːdʒə(r); *NAmE* ˈtʃɑːrdʒ-/ *noun* **1** a piece of equipment for loading a battery with electricity **2** (*old use*) a horse that a soldier rode in battle in the past

ˈcharge sheet *noun* (*BrE*) a record kept in a police station of the names of people that the police have stated to be guilty of a crime (= that they have charged)

charge·sheet /ˈtʃɑːdʒʃiːt; *NAmE* ˈtʃɑːrdʒ-/ *verb* [T] **~ sb (for sth)** (*IndE*) to accuse sb formally of committing an offence and to ask for an official reply or defence

char·grill /ˈtʃɑːɡrɪl; *NAmE* ˈtʃɑːr-/ *verb* **~ sth** [usually passive] to cook meat, fish, or vegetables over a very high heat so that the outside is slightly burnt

char·iot /ˈtʃæriət/ *noun* an open vehicle with two wheels, pulled by horses, used in ancient times in battle and for racing

char·iot·eer /ˌtʃæriəˈtɪə(r); *NAmE* -ˈtɪr/ *noun* the driver of a chariot

cha·risma /kəˈrɪzmə/ *noun* [U] the powerful personal quality that some people have to attract and impress other people: *The President has great personal charisma.* ◇ *a lack of charisma*

cha·ris·mat·ic /ˌkærɪzˈmætɪk/ *adj., noun*
■ ***adj.*** **1** having charisma: *a charismatic leader* **OPP uncharismatic** **2** (of a Christian religious group) believing in special gifts from God; worshipping in a very enthusiastic way ▸ **cha·ris·mat·ic·al·ly** /-kli/ *adv.*
■ ***noun*** (often **Charismatic**) a charismatic Christian

char·it·able /ˈtʃærətəbl/ *adj.* **1** connected with a charity or charities: ***a charitable institution/foundation/trust*** ◇ *a **charitable donation/gift*** ◇ (*BrE*) *to have **charitable status*** (= to be an official charity) **2** helping people who are poor or in need: *His later years were devoted largely to **charitable work**.* **3** kind in your attitude to other people, especially when you are judging them: *Let's be charitable and assume she just made a mistake.* **OPP uncharitable** ▸ **char·it·ably** /-bli/ *adv.*: *Try to think about him a little more charitably.*

char·ity 🔑 /ˈtʃærəti/ *noun* (*pl.* -ies)
1 🔑 [C] an organization for helping people in need: *Many charities sent money to help the victims of the famine.* ◇ *The concert will raise money for local charities.* **2** 🔑 [U] the aim of giving money, food, help, etc. to people who are in need: *Most of the runners in the London Marathon are **raising money for charity**.* ◇ *Do you give much to charity?* ◇ *a charity concert* (= organized to get money for charity) ◇ *to **live on/off charity*** (= to live on money which other people give you because you are poor) **3** [U] (*formal*) kindness and sympathy towards other people, especially when you are judging them: *Her article showed no charity towards her former friends.*
IDM **charity begins at ˈhome** (*saying*) you should help and care for your own family, etc. before you start helping other people

ˈcharity shop (*BrE*) (*NAmE* **ˈthrift shop/store**) *noun* a shop/store that sells clothes and other goods given by people to raise money for a charity

char·lady /ˈtʃɑːleɪdi; *NAmE* ˈtʃɑːr-/ *noun* (*pl.* -ies) (*old-fashioned, BrE*) = CHARWOMAN

char·la·tan /ˈʃɑːlətən; *NAmE* ˈʃɑːrl-/ *noun* a person who claims to have knowledge or skills that they do not really have

charles·ton /ˈtʃɑːlstən; *NAmE* ˈtʃɑːrl-/ *noun* (usually **the charleston**) [sing.] a fast dance that was popular in the 1920s

char·ley horse /ˈtʃɑːli hɔːs; *NAmE* ˈtʃɑːrli hɔːrs/ *noun* [usually sing.] (*NAmE, informal*) = CRAMP: *Ow! I just got a charley horse in my leg.*

char·lie /ˈtʃɑːli; *NAmE* ˈtʃɑːrli/ *noun* (*old-fashioned, BrE, informal*) a silly person: *You must have felt a proper charlie!*

charm /tʃɑːm; *NAmE* tʃɑːrm/ *noun, verb*
■ ***noun*** **1** [U] the power of pleasing or attracting people: *a man of great charm* ◇ *The hotel is full of charm and character.* **2** [C] a feature or quality that is pleasing or attractive: *her physical charms* (= her beauty) **3** [C] a small object worn on a chain or BRACELET, that is believed to bring good luck: *a lucky charm* ◇ *a charm bracelet* ➲ **VISUAL VOCAB** page V53 **4** [C] an act or words believed to have magic power **SYN spell**
IDM **ˌwork like a ˈcharm** to be immediately and completely successful ➲ more at THIRD
■ ***verb*** **1** [T, I] **~ (sb)** to please or attract sb in order to make them like you or do what you want: *He was charmed by her beauty and wit.* ◇ *Her words had lost their power to charm.* **2** [T] **~ sb/sth** to control or protect sb/sth using magic, or as if using magic: *He has led **a charmed life*** (= he has been lucky even in dangerous or difficult situations).
PHR V **ˌcharm sth ˈout of sb** to obtain sth such as information, money, etc. from sb by using charm

ˌcharmed ˈcircle *noun* [sing.] a group of people who have special influence

charm·er /ˈtʃɑːmə(r); *NAmE* ˈtʃɑːrm-/ *noun* a person who acts in a way that makes them attractive to other people, sometimes using this to influence others ➲ see also SNAKE CHARMER

charm·ing /ˈtʃɑːmɪŋ; *NAmE* ˈtʃɑːrmɪŋ/ *adj.* **1** very pleasant or attractive: *The cottage is tiny, but it's charming.* ◇ *She's a charming person.* **2** (*ironic, informal*) used to show that you have a low opinion of sb's behaviour: *They left me to tidy it all up myself. Charming, wasn't it?* ▸ **charm·ing·ly** *adv.*

charm·less /ˈtʃɑːmləs; *NAmE* ˈtʃɑːrm-/ *adj.* (*formal*) not at all pleasant or interesting: *a charmless industrial town*

ˈcharm offensive *noun* a situation in which a person, for example a politician, is especially friendly and pleasant in order to get other people to like them and to support their opinions

ˈcharm school *noun* a school where young people are taught to behave in a polite way

char·nel house /ˈtʃɑːnl haʊs; *NAmE* ˈtʃɑːrnl/ *noun* a place used in the past for keeping dead human bodies or bones

charred /ˈtʃɑːd; *NAmE* tʃɑːrd/ *adj.* [usually before noun] burnt and black: *the charred remains of a burnt-out car*

chart 🔑 **AW** /tʃɑːt; *NAmE* tʃɑːrt/ *noun, verb*
■ ***noun*** **1** 🔑 [C] a page or sheet of information in the form of diagrams, lists of figures, etc: *a weather chart* ◇ *a sales chart* (= showing the level of a company's sales) ➲ **LANGUAGE BANK** at ILLUSTRATE ➲ **WRITING TUTOR** page WT16 ➲ see also BAR CHART, FLOW CHART, PIE CHART **2** [C] a detailed map of the sea: *a naval chart* **3 the**

charts [pl.] (*especially BrE*) a list, produced each week, of the songs or albums that have sold the most copies or been DOWNLOADED the most: *The album went straight into the charts at number 1.* ◇ *to top the charts* (= to be the song or album that has sold more copies than all the others)

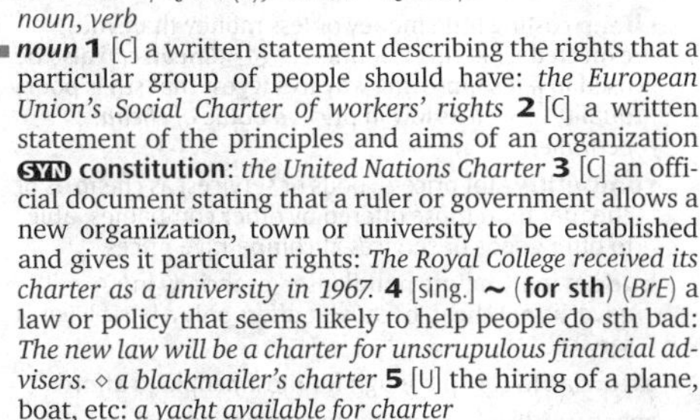

IDM ˌ**off the 'charts** (*informal, especially NAmE*) extremely high in level: *World demand for the product is off the charts.*

■ **verb 1** ~ **sth** to record or follow the progress or development of sb/sth: *The exhibition* ***charts the history of*** *the palace.* **2** ~ **sth** to plan a course of action: *She had carefully charted her route to the top of her profession.* **3** ~ **csth** to make a map of an area SYN **map**: *Cook charted the coast of New Zealand in 1768.*

char·ter /ˈtʃɑːtə(r); *NAmE* ˈtʃɑːrt-/ *noun, verb*

■ **noun 1** [C] a written statement describing the rights that a particular group of people should have: *the European Union's Social Charter of workers' rights* **2** [C] a written statement of the principles and aims of an organization SYN **constitution**: *the United Nations Charter* **3** [C] an official document stating that a ruler or government allows a new organization, town or university to be established and gives it particular rights: *The Royal College received its charter as a university in 1967.* **4** [sing.] ~ (**for sth**) (*BrE*) a law or policy that seems likely to help people do sth bad: *The new law will be a charter for unscrupulous financial advisers.* ◇ *a blackmailer's charter* **5** [U] the hiring of a plane, boat, etc: *a yacht available for charter*

■ **verb 1** ~ **sth** to hire/rent a plane, boat, etc. for your own use: *a chartered plane* **2** ~ **sth** to state officially that a new organization, town or university has been established and has special rights

char·tered /ˈtʃɑːtəd; *NAmE* ˈtʃɑːrtərd/ *adj.* [only before noun] **1** (*BrE*) qualified according to the rules of a professional organization that has a royal charter: *a* ***chartered accountant/surveyor/engineer*** **2** (of an aircraft, a ship or a boat) hired for a particular purpose: *a chartered plane*

ˌ**chartered acˈcountant** (*BrE*) (*US* ˌ**certified public acˈcountant**) *noun* a fully trained and qualified ACCOUNTANT

ˈ**charter flight** *noun* a flight in an aircraft in which all the seats are paid for by a travel company and then sold to their customers, usually at a lower cost than that of a SCHEDULED FLIGHT

ˌ**charter ˈmember** (*NAmE*) (*BrE* ˌ**founder ˈmember**) *noun* one of the first members of a society, an organization, etc, especially one who helped start it

char·treuse /ʃɑːˈtrɜːz; *NAmE* ʃɑːrˈtruːz/ *noun* [U] **1** a green or yellow LIQUEUR (= a strong sweet alcoholic drink) **2** a pale yellow or pale green colour

ˈ**chart-topping** *adj.* [only before noun] (of a CD, singer, etc.) having reached the highest position in the music CHARTS: *his latest chart-topping hit* ▸ ˈ**chart-topper** *noun*

char·woman /ˈtʃɑːwʊmən; *NAmE* ˈtʃɑːr-/ *noun* (*pl.* **-women** /-wɪmɪn/) (also **char**, **char·lady**) (all *BrE, old-fashioned*) a woman whose job is to clean a house, an office building, etc.

chary /ˈtʃeəri; *NAmE* ˈtʃeri/ *adj.* ~ **of sth/of doing sth** not willing to risk doing sth; fearing possible problems if you do sth SYN **wary**

chase 0‑w /tʃeɪs/ *verb, noun*

■ **verb**

▸ RUN/DRIVE AFTER **1** 0‑w [T, I] to run, drive, etc. after sb/sth in order to catch them: ~ **sb/sth** *My dog likes chasing rabbits.* ◇ *The kids* ***chased each other*** *around the kitchen table.* ◇ ~ **after sb/sth** *He chased after the burglar but couldn't catch him.*

▸ MONEY/WORK/SUCCESS **2** [T] ~ **sth** to try to obtain or achieve sth, for example money, work or success: *Too many people are chasing too few jobs nowadays.* ◇ *The team is chasing its first win in five games.*

▸ MAN/WOMAN **3** [I, T] (*informal*) to try to persuade sb to have a sexual relationship with you: ~ **after sb** *Kevin's been chasing after Joan for months.* ◇ ~ **sb** *Girls are always chasing him.*

▸ REMIND SB **4** [T] ~ **sb** (*informal*) to persuade sb to do sth that they should have done already: *I need to chase him about organizing the meeting.*

▸ RUSH **5** [I] + **adv./prep.** (*informal*) to rush or hurry somewhere: *I've been* ***chasing around*** *town all morning looking for a present for Sharon.*

▸ METAL **6** [T] ~ **sth** (*technical*) to cut patterns or designs on metal: *chased silver*

IDM **chase your (own) ˈtail** (*informal*) to be very busy but in fact achieve very little

PHR V ˌ**chase sb/sth↔aˈway, ˈoff, ˈout, etc.** 0‑w to force sb/sth to run away ˌ**chase sb↔ˈup** to contact sb in order to remind them to do sth that they should have done already: *We need to chase up all members who have not yet paid.* ˌ**chase sth↔ˈup** (*BrE*) (*NAmE* ˌ**chase sth↔ˈdown**) to find sth that is needed; to deal with sth that has been forgotten: *My job was to chase up late replies.*

■ **noun**

▸ RUNNING/DRIVING AFTER **1** 0‑w [C] (often used with *the*) an act of running or driving after sb/sth in order to catch them: *The thieves were caught by police after a short chase.* ◇ *a high-speed car chase* ◇ *We lost him in the narrow streets and had to* ***give up the chase*** (= stop chasing him). ◇ *to* ***take up the chase*** (= start chasing sb)

▸ FOR SUCCESS/MONEY/WORK **2** [sing.] a process of trying hard to get sth: *Three teams are involved in the chase for the championship.*

▸ IN SPORT **3 the chase** [sing.] hunting animals as a sport **4** [C] = STEEPLECHASE ➲ see also WILD GOOSE CHASE

IDM **cut to the ˈchase** (*informal*) to stop wasting time and start talking about the most important thing: *Right, let's cut to the chase. How much is it going to cost?* **give ˈchase** to run after sb/sth in order to catch them: *We gave chase along the footpath.*

chaser /ˈtʃeɪsə(r)/ *noun* **1** a drink that you have after another of a different kind, for example a stronger alcoholic drink after a weak one: *a beer with a whisky chaser* **2** a horse for STEEPLECHASE racing (= in which horses must jump over a series of fences)

Chas·id·ism /ˈxæsɪdɪzəm/ *noun* [U] = HASIDISM

chasm /ˈkæzəm/ *noun* **1** [C] (*literary*) a deep crack or opening in the ground **2** [sing.] ~ (**between A and B**) (*formal*) a very big difference between two people or groups, for example because they have different attitudes SYN **gulf**

chas·sis /ˈʃæsi/ *noun* (*pl.* **chas·sis** /-siz/) the frame that a vehicle is built on

chaste /tʃeɪst/ *adj.* **1** (*old-fashioned*) not having sex with anyone; only having sex with the person that you are married to: *to remain chaste* **2** (*formal*) not expressing sexual feelings: *a* ***chaste kiss*** *on the cheek* **3** (*formal*) simple and plain in style; not decorated: *the cool, chaste interior of the hall* ▸ **chaste·ly** *adv.*: *He kissed her chastely on the cheek.*

chas·ten /ˈtʃeɪsn/ *verb* [often passive] ~ **sb** (*formal*) to make sb feel sorry for sth they have done: *He felt* ***suitably chastened*** *and apologized.* ◇ *She gave them a chastening lecture.* ◇ *It was a* ***chastening experience***.

chas·tise /tʃæˈstaɪz/ *verb* **1** ~ **sb** (**for sth/for doing sth**) (*formal*) to criticize sb for doing sth wrong: *He chastised the team for their lack of commitment.* **2** ~ **sb** (*old-fashioned*) to punish sb physically SYN **beat** ▸ **chas·tise·ment** /tʃæˈstaɪzmənt; ˈtʃæstɪzmənt/ *noun* [U]

chas·tity /ˈtʃæstəti/ *noun* [U] the state of not having sex with anyone or only having sex with the person you are married to; being CHASTE: *vows of chastity* (= those taken by some priests)

ˈ**chastity belt** *noun* a device worn by some women in the past to prevent them from being able to have sex

C

C

chat 0-ᵣ /tʃæt/ *verb, noun*
■ *verb* (-tt-) **1** 0-ᵣ [I] to talk in a friendly informal way to sb: **~ (to/with sb)** *My kids spend hours chatting on the phone to their friends.* ◇ **~ away (to/with sb)** *Within minutes of being introduced they were chatting away like old friends.* ◇ **~ about sth/sb** *What were you chatting about?* **2** [I] **~ (away) (to/with sb) | ~ (about sth/sb)** to exchange messages with other people on the Internet, especially in a CHAT ROOM: *He's been on the computer all morning, chatting with his friends.*

PHR V ˌ**chat sb↔ˈup** (*BrE, informal*) to talk in a friendly way to sb you are sexually attracted to: *She went straight over and tried to chat him up.*

■ *noun* **1** 0-ᵣ [C] (*especially BrE*) a friendly informal conversation: *I just called in for a chat.* ◇ *I had a long chat with her.* ➲ SYNONYMS at DISCUSSION **2** [U] talking, especially informal conversation: *That's enough chat from me—on with the music!* ➲ SYNONYMS at DISCUSSION **3** [U, C] communication between people on the Internet: *chat software* ◇ *Internet chat services* ◇ *Fans are invited to an online chat.*

cha·teau (also **châ·teau**) /ˈʃætəʊ; *NAmE* ʃæˈtoʊ/ *noun* (*pl.* **cha·teaux**, **châ·teaux** or **cha·teaus**, **châ·teaus** /-təʊz; *NAmE* -ˈtoʊz/) (*from French*) a castle or large country house in France

chat·line /ˈtʃætlaɪn/ *noun* **1** a telephone service which allows a number of people who call in separately to have a conversation, especially for fun **2** a telephone service which people can call to talk to sb about sex in order to feel sexually excited

ˈ**chat room** *noun* an area on the Internet where people can communicate with each other, usually about one particular topic ➲ COLLOCATIONS at EMAIL

ˈ**chat show** (*BrE*) (also ˈ**talk show** *NAmE, BrE*) *noun* a television or radio programme in which famous people are asked questions and talk in an informal way about their work and opinions on various topics: *a chat-show host*

chat·tel /ˈtʃætl/ *noun* [C, U] (*law* or *old-fashioned*) something that belongs to you ➲ see also GOODS AND CHATTELS

chat·ter /ˈtʃætə(r)/ *verb, noun*
■ *verb* **1** [I] **~ (away/on) (to sb) (about sth)** to talk quickly and continuously, especially about things that are not important: *They chattered away happily for a while.* ◇ *The children chattered to each other excitedly about the next day's events.* **2** [I] (of teeth) to knock together continuously because you are cold or frightened **3** [I] (of birds or MONKEYS) to make a series of short high sounds

IDM **the ˈchattering classes** (*BrE, usually disapproving*) the people in society who like to give their opinions on political or social issues

■ *noun* [U] **1** continuous rapid talk about things that are not important: *Jane's constant chatter was beginning to annoy him.* ◇ *idle chatter* **2** a series of quick short high sounds that some animals make: *the chatter of monkeys* **3** a series of short sounds made by things knocking together: *the chatter of teeth*

chat·ter·box /ˈtʃætəbɒks; *NAmE* ˈtʃætərbɑːks/ *noun* (*informal*) a person who talks a lot, especially a child

chatty /ˈtʃæti/ *adj.* (**chat·tier**, **chat·ti·est**) (*informal, especially BrE*) **1** talking a lot in a friendly way: *You're very chatty today, Alice.* **2** having a friendly informal style: *a chatty letter*

ˈ**chat-up** *noun* [C, U] an occasion when a person is talking to sb in a way that shows they are interested in them sexually: *Is that your best* ***chat-up line****?*

chauf·feur /ˈʃəʊfə(r); *NAmE* ʃoʊˈfɜːr/ *noun, verb*
■ *noun* a person whose job is to drive a car, especially for sb rich or important
■ *verb* **~ sb** to drive sb in a car, usually as your job: *He was chauffeured to all his meetings.* ◇ *a chauffeured limousine*

chau·vin·ism /ˈʃəʊvɪnɪzəm; *NAmE* ˈʃoʊ-/ *noun* [U] (*disapproving*) **1** an aggressive and unreasonable belief that your own country is better than all others **2** = MALE CHAUVINISM

chau·vin·ist /ˈʃəʊvɪnɪst; *NAmE* ˈʃoʊ-/ *noun* **1** = MALE CHAUVINIST **2** a person who has an aggressive and unreasonable belief that their own country is better than all others ▸ **chau·vin·is·tic** /ˌʃəʊvɪˈnɪstɪk; *NAmE* ˌʃoʊ-/ (also *less frequent* **chau·vin·ist**) *adj.* **chau·vin·is·tic·al·ly** /-kli/ *adv.*

chav /tʃæv/ *noun* (*BrE, slang*) a young person, often without a high level of education, who follows a particular fashion

ChB /ˌsiː eɪtʃ ˈbiː/ *abbr.* (*BrE*) Bachelor of Surgery

Synonyms

cheap

competitive • budget • affordable • reasonable • inexpensive

These words all describe a product or service that costs little money or less money than you expected.

cheap costing little money or less money than you expected; charging low prices. NOTE **Cheap** can also be used in a disapproving way to suggest that sth is poor quality as well as low in price: *a bottle of cheap perfume.*

competitive (of prices, goods or services) as cheap as or cheaper than those offered by other companies; able to offer goods or services at competitive prices.

budget [only before noun] (used especially in advertising) cheap because it offers only a basic level of service.

affordable cheap enough for most people to afford.

reasonable (of prices) not too expensive.

inexpensive (*rather formal*) cheap. NOTE **Inexpensive** is often used to mean that sth is good value for its price. It is sometimes used instead of **cheap**, because **cheap** can suggest that sth is poor quality.

PATTERNS
- cheap/competitive/budget/affordable/reasonable **prices/fares/rates**
- cheap/competitive/budget/affordable/inexpensive **products/services**

cheap 0-ᵣ /tʃiːp/ *adj., adv.*
■ *adj.* (**cheap·er**, **cheap·est**)
▸ LOW PRICE **1** 0-ᵣ costing little money or less money than you expected SYN **inexpensive**: *cheap fares* ◇ *Personal computers are cheap and getting cheaper.* ◇ *Cycling is a cheap way to get around.* ◇ *The printer isn't exactly cheap at £200.* ◇ *immigrant workers, used as a source of* ***cheap labour*** (= workers who are paid very little, especially unfairly) ➲ see also DIRT CHEAP OPP **expensive** **2** 0-ᵣ charging low prices: *a cheap restaurant/hotel* ◇ (*BrE*) *We found a* ***cheap and cheerful*** *cafe* (= one that is simple and charges low prices but is pleasant). OPP **expensive**
▸ POOR QUALITY **3** 0-ᵣ (*disapproving*) low in price and quality: *cheap perfume/jewellery/shoes* ◇ (*BrE*) *a* ***cheap and nasty*** *bottle of wine*
▸ UNKIND **4** unpleasant or unkind and rather obvious: *I was tired of his cheap jokes at my expense.*
▸ LOW STATUS **5** (*disapproving*) having a low status and therefore not deserving respect: *He's just a cheap crook.* ◇ *His treatment of her made her* ***feel cheap*** (= ashamed, because she had lost her respect for herself).
▸ NOT GENEROUS **6** (*NAmE*) (*BrE* **mean**) (*informal, disapproving*) not liking to spend money: *Don't be so cheap!*
▸ **cheap·ness** *noun* [U]

IDM **cheap at the ˈprice** (also **cheap at ˈtwice the price**) (*BrE* also **cheap at ˈhalf the price**) so good or useful that the cost does not seem too much **on the ˈcheap** spending less money than you usually need to spend to do sth: *a guide to decorating your house on the cheap* ➲ more at LIFE

■ *adv.* (*comparative* **cheap·er**, no *superlative*) (*informal*) for a low price: *I got this dress cheap in a sale.*

IDM **be ˌgoing ˈcheap** to be offered for sale at a lower price than usual **sth does not come ˈcheap** something is expensive: *Violins like this don't come cheap.*

cheap·en /ˈtʃiːpən/ *verb* **1 ~ sb/yourself** to make sb lose respect for himself or herself **SYN degrade**: *She never cheapened herself by lowering her standards.* **2 ~ sth** to make sth lower in price: *to cheapen the cost of raw materials* **3 ~ sth** to make sth appear to have less value: *The movie was accused of cheapening human life.*

cheap·ly /ˈtʃiːpli/ *adv.* without spending or costing much money: *I'm sure I could buy this more cheaply somewhere else.* ◇ *a cheaply made movie*

cheapo /ˈtʃiːpəʊ; NAmE -poʊ/ *adj.* [only before noun] (*informal, disapproving*) cheap and often of poor quality

cheap·skate /ˈtʃiːpskeɪt/ *noun* (*informal, disapproving*) a person who does not like to spend money

cheat /tʃiːt/ *verb, noun*

■ *verb* **1** [T] **~ sb/sth** to trick sb or make them believe sth which is not true: *She is accused of attempting to cheat the taxman.* ◇ *Many people **feel cheated** by the government's refusal to hold a referendum.* ◇ *He **cheated his way** into the job.* **2** [I] **~ (at sth)** to act in a dishonest way in order to gain an advantage, especially in a game, a competition, an exam, etc: *He cheats at cards.* ◇ *You're not allowed to look at the answers—**that's cheating**.* **3** [I] **~ (on sb)** (of sb who is married or who has a regular sexual partner) to have a secret sexual relationship with sb else

IDM **cheat ˈdeath** (often used in newspapers) to survive in a situation where you could have died

PHR V **ˈcheat sb (ˈout) of sth** to prevent sb from having sth, especially in a way that is not honest or fair: *They cheated him out of his share of the profits.*

■ *noun* (*especially BrE*) **1** (also **cheat·er** especially in *NAmE*) [C] a person who cheats, especially in a game: *You little cheat!* **2** [sing.] something that seems unfair or dishonest, for example a way of doing sth with less effort than it usually needs: *It's really a cheat, but you can use ready-made pastry if you want.* **3** [C] (*computing*) a program you can use to move immediately to the next stage of a computer game without needing to play the game: *There's a cheat you can use to get to the next level.*

> **Synonyms**
>
> **cheat**
>
> **fool • deceive • betray • take in • trick • con**
>
> These words all mean to make sb believe sth that is not true, especially in order to get what you want.
>
> **cheat** to make sb believe sth that is not true, in order to get money or sth else from them: *She is accused of attempting to cheat the taxman.* ◇ *He cheated his way into the job.* **NOTE** **Cheat** also means to act in a dishonest way in order to gain an advantage, especially in a game, competition or exam: *You're not allowed to look at the answers— that's cheating.*
>
> **fool** to make sb believe sth that is not true, especially in order to laugh at them or to get what you want: *Just don't be fooled into investing any money with them.*
>
> **deceive** to make sb believe sth that is not true, especially sb who trusts you, in order to get what you want: *She deceived him into handing over all his savings.*
>
> **betray** to hurt sb who trusts you, especially by deceiving them or not being loyal to them: *She felt betrayed when she found out the truth about him.*
>
> **take sb in** [often passive] to deceive sb, usually in order to get what you want: *I was taken in by her story.*
>
> **trick** to deceive sb, especially in a clever way, in order to get what you want.
>
> **con** (*informal*) to deceive sb, especially in order to get money from them or get them to do sth for you: *They had been conned out of £100 000.*
>
> **WHICH WORD?**
>
> Many of these words involve making sb believe sth that is not true, but some of them are more disapproving than others. **Deceive** is probably the worst because people typically deceive friends, relations and others who know and trust them. People may *feel cheated/betrayed* by sb in authority who they trusted to look after their interests. If sb **takes you in**, they may do it by acting a part and using words and charm effectively. If sb **cheats/fools/tricks/cons** you, they may get sth from you and make you feel stupid. However, sb might **fool** you just as a joke; and to **trick** sb is sometimes seen as a clever thing to do, if the person being tricked is seen as a bad person who deserves it.
>
> **PATTERNS**
>
> - to cheat/fool/trick/con sb **out of** sth
> - to cheat/fool/deceive/betray/trick/con sb **into doing** sth
> - to **feel** cheated/fooled/deceived/betrayed/tricked/conned
> - to fool/deceive **yourself**
> - to cheat/trick/con **your way** into sth

ˈcheat sheet *noun* (*informal*) a set of notes to help you remember important information, especially one taken secretly into an exam room

check /tʃek/ *verb, noun, exclamation*

■ *verb*

▸ EXAMINE **1** [T] **~ sth (for sth)** to examine sth to see if it is correct, safe or acceptable: *Check the container for cracks or leaks.* ◇ *She gave me the minutes of the meeting to read and check.* ◇ *Check the oil and water before setting off.* ◇ *Check your work before handing it in.*

▸ MAKE SURE **2** [I, T] to find out if sth/sb is present, correct or true or if sth is how you think it is: *'Is Mary in the office?' 'Just a moment. I'll go and check.'* ◇ **~ sth** *Hang on—I just need to check my email.* ◇ **~ (that)**... *Go and check (that) I've locked the windows.* ◇ **~ (with sb) (what/whether, etc...)** *You'd better check with Jane what time she's expecting us tonight.* ➲ see also CROSS-CHECK, DOUBLE-CHECK

▸ CONTROL **3** [T] **~ sth** to control sth; to stop sth from increasing or getting worse: *The government is determined to check the growth of public spending.* **4** [T] to stop yourself from saying or doing sth or from showing a particular emotion: **~ sth** *to check your anger/laughter/tears* ◇ **~ yourself** *She wanted to tell him the whole truth but she checked herself—it wasn't the right moment.*

▸ COATS/BAGS/CASES **5** [T] **~ sth** (*NAmE*) to leave coats, bags, etc. in an official place (called a CHECKROOM) while you are visiting a club, restaurant, etc: *Do you want to check your coats?* **6** [T] **~ sth** (*NAmE*) to leave bags or cases with an official so that they can be put on a plane or train

▸ MAKE MARK **7** [T] **~ sth** (*NAmE*) (*BrE* **tick**) to put a mark (✓) next to an item on a list, an answer, etc: *Check the box next to the right answer.*

PHR V **ˌcheck ˈin (at...)** to go to a desk in a hotel, an airport, etc. and tell an official there that you have arrived: *Please check in at least an hour before departure.* ◇ *We've checked in at the hotel.* ➲ related noun CHECK-IN **ˌcheck sth↔ˈin** to leave bags or cases with an official to be put on a plane or train: *We checked in our luggage and went through to the departure lounge.* ➲ related noun CHECK-IN **ˈcheck into...** to arrive at a hotel or private hospital to begin your stay there: *He checked into a top London clinic yesterday for an operation on his knee.* **ˌcheck sb/sth↔ˈoff** (*NAmE*) (*BrE* **ˌtick sb/sth ˈoff**) to put a mark (✓) beside a name or an item on a list to show that sth has been dealt with: *Check the names off as the guests arrive.* **ˈcheck on sb/sth** to make sure that there is nothing wrong with sb/sth: *I'll just go and check on the children.* **ˌcheck ˈout** to be found to be true or acceptable after being examined: *The local police found her story didn't check out.* **ˌcheck ˈout (of...)** to pay your bill and leave a hotel, etc: *Guests should check out of their rooms by noon.* ➲ related noun CHECKOUT (2) **ˌcheck sb/sth↔ˈout** **1** to find out if sth is correct, or if sb is acceptable: *The police are checking out his alibi.* ◇ *We'll have to check him out before we employ him.* **2**

(*informal*) to look at or examine a person or thing that seems interesting or attractive: *Check out the prices at our new store!* ◇ *Hey, check out that car!* ˌ**check sth↔ˈout** to borrow sth from an official place, for example a book from a library: *The book has been checked out in your name.* ˌ**check ˈover/ˈthrough↔sth** 🔑 to examine sth carefully to make sure that it is correct or acceptable: *Check over your work for mistakes.* ˌ**check ˈup on sb** 🔑 to make sure that sb is doing what they should be doing: *My parents are always checking up on me.* ˌ**check ˈup on sth** to find out if sth is true or correct: *I need to check up on a few things before I can decide.*

Synonyms

check

examine • inspect • go over sth

These words all mean to look closely to make sure that everything is correct, in good condition, or acceptable.

check to look at sth closely to make sure that everything is correct, in good condition, safe or satisfactory: *Check your work before handing it in.*

examine to look at sb/sth closely to see if there is anything wrong or to find the cause of a problem: *The goods were examined for damage on arrival.*

inspect to look at sb/sth closely to make sure that everything is satisfactory; to officially visit a school, factory, etc. in order to check that rules are being obeyed and that standards are acceptable: *Make sure you inspect the goods before signing for them.* ◇ *The Tourist Board inspects all recommended hotels at least once a year.*

CHECK, EXAMINE OR INSPECT?

All these words can be used when you are looking for possible problems, but only **check** is used for mistakes: ~~*Examine/Inspect your work before handing it in.*~~ Only **examine** is used when looking for the cause of a problem: ~~*The doctor checked/inspected her but could find nothing wrong.*~~ **Examine** is used more often about a professional person: *The surveyor examined the walls for signs of damp.* **Inspect** is used more often about an official: *Public health officials were called in to inspect the restaurant.*

go over sth to check sth carefully for mistakes, damage or anything dangerous: *Go over your work for spelling mistakes before you hand it in.*

PATTERNS

- to check/examine/inspect/go over (sth) **for** sth
- to check/examine/inspect/go over sth **to see if/whether...**
- to check/examine/inspect/go over sth **carefully/thoroughly**

▪ ***noun***

▸ EXAMINATION **1** 🔑 [C] **~ (for/on sth)** an act of making sure that sth is safe, correct or in good condition by examining it: *Could you give the tyres a check?* ◇ *a health check* ◇ *The drugs were found in their car during a routine check by police.* ◇ *a check for spelling mistakes* ◇ *I'll just have a quick check to see if the letter's arrived yet.* ◇ *It is vital to **keep a check on** your speed* (= look at it regularly in order to control it). ➲ see also REALITY CHECK

▸ INVESTIGATION **2** 🔑 [C] **~ (on sb/sth)** an investigation to find out more information about sth: *The police **ran a check** on the registration number of the car.* ◇ *Was any check made on Mr Morris when he applied for the post?*

▸ CONTROL **3** [C] **~ (on/to sth)** (*formal*) something that delays the progress of sth else or stops it from getting worse: *A cold spring will provide a natural check on the number of insects.* **4 checks** [pl.] (*formal*) rules that are designed to control the amount of power, especially political power, that one person or group has ➲ see also CHECKS AND BALANCES

▸ PATTERN **5** [C, U] a pattern of squares, usually of two colours: *Do you prefer checks or stripes?* ◇ *a check shirt/suit* ◇ *a yellow and red check skirt* ➲ see also CHECKED

▸ MONEY **6** [C] (*US*) = CHEQUE **7** [C] (*NAmE*) = BILL: *Can I have the check, please?* ➲ SYNONYMS at BILL

▸ FOR COATS/BAGS **8** [C] (*NAmE*) **coat ~** a place in a club, restaurant, etc. where you can leave your coat or bag **9** [C] (*NAmE*) a ticket that you get when you leave your coat, bag, etc. in, for example, a restaurant or theatre

▸ IN GAME **10** [U] (in CHESS) a position in which a player's king (= the most important piece) can be directly attacked by the other player's pieces: *There, you're in check.* ➲ see also CHECKMATE

▸ MARK **11** (also **ˈcheck mark**) (both *NAmE*) (*BrE* **tick**) [C] a mark (✓) put beside a sum or an item on a list, usually to show that it has been checked or done or is correct ➲ compare CROSS, X (4)

IDM **hold/keep sth in ˈcheck** to keep sth under control so that it does not spread or get worse ➲ more at RAIN CHECK

▪ ***exclamation*** used to show that you agree with sb or that sth on a list has been dealt with: *'Do you have your tickets?' 'Check.' 'Passport?' 'Check.'*

check·book *noun* (*US*) = CHEQUEBOOK

check·box /ˈtʃekbɒks; *NAmE* -bɑːks/ (*BrE* also **tick·box**) *noun* a small square on a computer screen that you click on with the mouse to choose whether a particular function is switched on or off

checked /tʃekt/ *adj.* having a pattern of squares, usually of two colours: *checked material* ➲ see also CHECK

check·er /ˈtʃekə(r)/ *noun* ➲ see also CHECKERS **1** (*especially US*) a person who works at the CHECKOUT in a supermarket **2** (in compounds) a computer program that you use to check sth, for example the spelling and grammar of sth you have written: *a **spelling/grammar/virus checker*** **3** a person who checks things: *a quality control checker*

check·er·board /ˈtʃekəbɔːd; *NAmE* ˈtʃekərbɔːrd/ (*NAmE*) (*BrE* **draught·board**) *noun* a board with black and white squares, used for playing DRAUGHTS/CHECKERS

check·ered *adj.* (*especially NAmE*) = CHEQUERED

check·ers /ˈtʃekəz; *NAmE* -ərz/ (*NAmE*) (*BrE* **draughts**) *noun* [U] a game for two players using 24 round pieces on a board marked with black and white squares

ˈ**check-in** *noun* **1** [C, U] the place where you go first when you arrive at an airport, to show your ticket, etc. **2** [U] the act of showing your ticket, etc. when you arrive at an airport: *Do you know your check-in time?* ◇ (*BrE*) *the check-in desk* ◇ (*NAmE*) *the check-in counter*

ˈ**checking account** (*US*) (*BrE* ˈ**current account**) (*CanE* ˈ**chequing account**) *noun* a type of bank account that you can take money out of at any time, and that provides you with a CHEQUEBOOK and CASH CARD ➲ compare DEPOSIT ACCOUNT

check·list /ˈtʃeklɪst/ *noun* a list of the things that you must remember to do, to take with you or to find out

check·mate /ˌtʃekˈmeɪt; ˈtʃekmeɪt/ (also **mate**) *noun* [U] **1** (in CHESS) a position in which one player cannot prevent his or her king (= the most important piece) being captured and therefore loses the game ➲ see also CHECK ➲ compare STALEMATE **2** a situation in which sb has been completely defeated ▸ **check·mate** (also **mate**) *verb*: **~ sb/sth** *His king had been checkmated.* ◇ *She hoped the plan would checkmate her opponents.*

check·out /ˈtʃekaʊt/ *noun* **1** [C] the place where you pay for the things that you are buying in a supermarket: *a **checkout assistant/operator*** **2** [U] the time when you leave a hotel at the end of your stay: *At checkout, your bill will be printed for you.*

check·point /ˈtʃekpɔɪnt/ *noun* a place, especially on a border between two countries, where people have to stop so their vehicles and documents can be checked

check·room /ˈtʃekruːm; -rʊm/ *noun* (*NAmE*) = CLOAKROOM

ˌchecks and ˈbalances *noun* [pl.] **1** influences in an organization or political system which help to keep it fair and stop a small group from keeping all the power **2** (in the US) the principle of government by which the President, Congress and the Supreme Court each have some control over the others ➲ compare SEPARATION OF POWERS

check·sum /ˈtʃeksʌm/ *noun* (*computing*) the total of the numbers in a piece of DIGITAL data, used to check that the data is correct

ˈcheck-up *noun* an examination of sth, especially a medical one to make sure that you are healthy: *to* ***go for/to have a check-up*** ◇ *a* ***medical/dental/routine/thorough check-up***

Ched·dar /ˈtʃedə(r)/ (also **ˌCheddar ˈcheese**) *noun* [U] a type of hard yellow cheese

cheek 🔑 /tʃiːk/ *noun, verb*

■ ***noun*** **1** 🔑 [C] either side of the face below the eyes: ***chubby/rosy/pink cheeks*** ◇ *He kissed her on both cheeks.* ◇ *Couples were dancing* ***cheek to cheek.*** ➲ COLLOCATIONS at PHYSICAL ➲ VISUAL VOCAB page V48 **2 -cheeked** (in adjectives) having the type of cheeks mentioned: ***chubby-cheeked/rosy-cheeked/hollow-cheeked*** **3** [C] (*informal*) either of the BUTTOCKS **4** [U, sing.] (*BrE*) talk or behaviour that people think is annoying, rude or lacking in respect SYN **nerve**: *What a cheek!* ◇ *He* ***had the cheek*** *to ask his ex-girlfriend to babysit for them.* ◇ *I think they've* ***got a cheek*** *making you pay to park the car.*

IDM **ˌcheek by ˈjowl** (**with sb/sth**) very close to sb/sth **turn the other ˈcheek** to make a deliberate decision to remain calm and not to act in an aggressive way when sb has hurt you or made you angry ➲ more at ROSE *n.*, TONGUE *n.*

■ ***verb*** **~ sb** (*BrE, informal*) to speak to sb in a rude way that shows a lack of respect

cheek·bone /ˈtʃiːkbəʊn; *NAmE* -boʊn/ *noun* the bone below the eye ➲ VISUAL VOCAB page V48

cheeky /ˈtʃiːki/ *adj.* (**cheek·ier, cheeki·est**) (*BrE, informal*) rude in an amusing or an annoying way: *You cheeky monkey!* ◇ *a cheeky grin* ◇ *You're getting far too cheeky!* ➲ SYNONYMS at RUDE ▸ **cheek·ily** *adv.* **cheeki·ness** *noun* [U]

cheep /tʃiːp/ *verb* [I] (of young birds) to make short high sounds ▸ **cheep** *noun*

cheer /tʃɪə(r); *NAmE* tʃɪr/ *noun, verb*

■ ***noun*** ➲ see also CHEERS **1** [C] a shout of joy, support or praise: *A great* ***cheer went up*** *from the crowd.* ◇ *cheers of encouragement* ◇ ***Three cheers for*** *the winners!* (= used when you are asking a group of people to cheer three times, in order to CONGRATULATE sb, etc.) OPP **boo 2** [C] (*NAmE*) a special song or poem used by CHEERLEADERS **3** [U] (*formal* or *literary*) an atmosphere of happiness

■ ***verb*** **1** [I, T] to shout loudly, to show support or praise for sb, or to give them encouragement: *We all cheered as the team came on to the field.* ◇ *Cheering crowds greeted their arrival.* ◇ **~ sb** *The crowd cheered the President as he drove slowly by.* ➲ SYNONYMS at SHOUT OPP **boo 2** [T] **~ sb** [usually passive] to give hope, comfort or encouragement to sb: *She was cheered by the news from home.* ▸ **cheer·ing** *noun* [U]: *He came on stage amid clapping and cheering.* **cheer·ing** *adj.*: *The results of the test were very cheering.*

PHR V **ˌcheer sb↔ˈon** to give shouts of encouragement to sb in a race, competition, etc. **ˌcheer ˈup** | **ˌcheer sb/sth↔ˈup** to become more cheerful; to make sb/sth more cheerful: *Oh, come on—cheer up!* ◇ *Give Mary a call; she needs cheering up.* ◇ *Bright curtains can cheer up a dull room.*

cheer·ful 🔑 /ˈtʃɪəfl; *NAmE* ˈtʃɪrfl/ *adj.*

1 🔑 happy, and showing it by the way that you behave: *You're not your usual cheerful self today.* ◇ *a cheerful, hard-working employee* ◇ *a cheerful smile/voice* **2** 🔑 giving you a feeling of happiness: *a bright, cheerful restaurant* ◇ *walls painted in cheerful* (= light and bright) *colours* ◇ *a chatty, cheerful letter* ▸ **cheer·ful·ly** 🔑 /-fəli/ *adv.*: *to* ***laugh/nod/whistle cheerfully*** ◇ *I could cheerfully have killed him when he said that* (= I would have liked to). ◇ *She cheerfully admitted that she had no experience at all* (= she wasn't afraid to do so). **cheer·ful·ness** *noun* [U]

cheerio /ˌtʃɪəriˈəʊ; *NAmE* ˌtʃɪriˈoʊ/ *exclamation* (*BrE, informal*) goodbye: *Cheerio! I'll see you later.*

cheer·lead·er /ˈtʃɪəliːdə(r); *NAmE* ˈtʃɪrl-/ *noun* **1** (in the US) one of the members of a group of young people (usually women) wearing special uniforms, who encourage the crowd to CHEER for their team at a sports event **2** a person who supports a particular politician, idea, or way of doing sth ▸ **cheer·leading** /ˈtʃɪəliːdɪŋ/ *noun* [U]: *a* ***cheerleading squad/team*** ◇ *the President's continued cheerleading for the 'strong dollar'*

cheer·less /ˈtʃɪələs; *NAmE* ˈtʃɪrl-/ *adj.* (*formal*) (of a place, etc.) without warmth or colour so it makes you feel depressed SYN **gloomy**: *a dark and cheerless room*

cheers /tʃɪəz; *NAmE* tʃɪrz/ *exclamation* **1** a word that people say to each other as they lift up their glasses to drink **2** (*BrE, informal*) thank you: *'Have another biscuit.' 'Cheers.'* **3** (*BrE, informal*) goodbye: *Cheers then. See you later.*

cheery /ˈtʃɪəri; *NAmE* ˈtʃɪri/ *adj.* (**cheer·ier, cheeri·est**) (*informal*) (of a person or their behaviour) happy and cheerful: *a* ***cheery remark/smile/wave*** ◇ *He left with a cheery 'See you again soon'.* ▸ **cheer·ily** *adv.*

cheese 🔑 /tʃiːz/ *noun*

1 🔑 [U, C] a type of food made from milk that can be either soft or hard and is usually white or yellow in colour; a particular type of this food: *Cheddar cheese* ◇ *goat's cheese* (= made from the milk of a GOAT) ◇ *a* ***cheese sandwich/salad*** ◇ *a* ***chunk/piece/slice of cheese*** ◇ *a selection of French cheeses* ◇ *a cheese knife* (= a knife with a special curved blade with two points on the end, used for cutting and picking up pieces of cheese) ➲ VISUAL VOCAB page V19 ➲ see also AMERICAN CHEESE, BLUE CHEESE, CAULIFLOWER CHEESE, COTTAGE CHEESE, CREAM CHEESE, MACARONI CHEESE **2 cheese!** what you ask sb to say before you take their photograph IDM see BIG *adj.*, CHALK *n.*, HARD *adj.*

cheese·board /ˈtʃiːzbɔːd; *NAmE* -bɔːrd/ *noun* **1** a board that is used to cut cheese on ➲ VISUAL VOCAB page V19 **2** a variety of cheeses that are served at the end of a meal ➲ VISUAL VOCAB page V19

cheese·bur·ger /ˈtʃiːzbɜːɡə(r); *NAmE* -bɜːrɡ-/ *noun* a HAMBURGER with a slice of cheese on top of the meat

cheese·cake /ˈtʃiːzkeɪk/ *noun* [C, U] a cold DESSERT (= a sweet dish) made from a soft mixture of CREAM CHEESE, sugar, eggs, etc. on a base of cake or crushed biscuits/cookies, sometimes with fruit on top: *a strawberry cheesecake* ◇ *Is there any cheesecake left?*

cheese·cloth /ˈtʃiːzklɒθ; *NAmE* -klɔːθ/ *noun* [U] a type of loose cotton cloth used especially for making shirts

ˌcheesed ˈoff *adj.* [not before noun] **~ (with/about sb/sth)** (*BrE, informal*) annoyed or bored

ˈcheese-paring *adj.* (*disapproving*) not liking to spend money SYN **mean** ▸ **ˈcheese-paring** *noun* [U]

ˌcheese ˈstraw *noun* (*BrE*) a stick of PASTRY with cheese in it, eaten as a SNACK

cheesy /ˈtʃiːzi/ *adj.* (**chees·ier, cheesi·est**) **1** (*informal*) not very good or original, and without style, in a way that is embarrassing but amusing: *a cheesy horror movie* **2** (*informal*) too emotional or romantic, in a way that is embarrassing: *a cheesy love song* **3** (of a smile) done in an exaggerated and probably not sincere way: *She had a* ***cheesy grin*** *on her face.* **4** smelling or tasting of cheese

chee·tah /ˈtʃiːtə/ *noun* a wild animal of the cat family, with black spots, that runs very fast

chef /ʃef/ *noun* a professional cook, especially the most senior cook in a restaurant, hotel, etc.

chef-d'oeuvre /ˌʃeɪ ˈdɜːvrə; *NAmE* also ˈduːvrə/ *noun* (*pl.* **chefs-d'oeuvre** /ˌʃeɪ ˈdɜːvrə; *NAmE* also ˈduːvrə/) (from

C

French, formal) a very good piece of work, especially the best work by a particular artist, writer, etc. **SYN masterpiece**

ˌchef's 'salad (also **ˌchef 'salad**) *noun* (*NAmE*) a large salad consisting of LETTUCE, tomato and other vegetables with slices of cheese and meat such as chicken or HAM on top

ˌChelsea 'bun *noun* (*BrE*) a small round cake containing dried fruit

ˌChelsea 'tractor *noun* (*BrE, informal, disapproving*) a large vehicle such as an SUV that is designed to be used in the country but is used in towns and cities instead of a normal car: *the environmental cost of driving a Chelsea tractor*

chem·ical O-w AW /'kemɪkl/ *adj., noun*
■ **adj. 1** O-w connected with chemistry: *a chemical element* ◇ *the chemical industry* **2** O-w produced by or using processes which involve changes to atoms or MOLECULES: ***chemical reactions/processes*** ▸ **chem·ic·al·ly** AW /-kli/ *adv.*: *The raw sewage is chemically treated.*
■ ***noun*** O-w a substance obtained by or used in a chemical process

ˌchemical engi'neering *noun* [U] the study of the design and use of machines in industrial chemical processes ▸ **ˌchemical engi'neer** *noun*

ˌchemical 'warfare *noun* [U] the use of poisonous gases and chemicals as weapons in a war

ˌchemical 'weapon *noun* a weapon that uses poisonous gases and chemicals to kill and injure people ➲ compare BIOLOGICAL WEAPON

che·mise /ʃə'mi:z/ *noun* a piece of women's underwear or a NIGHTDRESS

chem·ist O-w /'kemɪst/ *noun*
1 (also **dis'pensing chemist**) (both *BrE*) (*NAmE* **druggist**) a person whose job is to prepare and sell medicines, and who works in a shop ➲ compare PHARMACIST **2** O-w **chemist's** (*pl.* **chem·ists**) (*BrE*) a shop/store that sells medicines and usually also soap, make-up, etc: *You can obtain the product from all good chemists.* ◇ *Take this prescription to the chemist's.* ◇ *I'll get it at the chemist's.* ◇ *a chemist's/chemist shop* ➲ see also DRUGSTORE ➲ compare PHARMACY **3** O-w a scientist who studies chemistry: *a research chemist*

chem·is·try O-w /'kemɪstri/ *noun* [U]
1 O-w the scientific study of the structure of substances, how they react when combined or in contact with one another, and how they behave under different conditions: *a degree in chemistry* ◇ *the university's chemistry department* ◇ ***inorganic/organic chemistry*** ➲ see also BIOCHEMISTRY **2** (*technical*) the chemical structure and behaviour of a particular substance: *the chemistry of copper* ◇ *The patient's blood chemistry was monitored regularly.* **3** the relationship between two people, usually a strong sexual attraction: *sexual chemistry* ◇ *The chemistry just wasn't right.*

chemo /'ki:məʊ; *NAmE* -moʊ/ *noun* [U] (*informal*) = CHEMOTHERAPY

chemo·recep·tor /'ki:məʊrɪseptə(r); *NAmE* 'ki:moʊ-/ *noun* (*biology*) a cell or sense organ that is sensitive to chemical STIMULI, making a response possible

chemo·ther·apy /ˌki:məʊ'θerəpi; *NAmE* -moʊ-/ (also *informal* **chemo**) *noun* [U] the treatment of disease, especially cancer, with the use of chemical substances ➲ compare RADIATION, RADIOTHERAPY

che·nille /ʃə'ni:l/ *noun* [U] a type of thick, soft thread; cloth made from this: *a chenille sweater*

cheong·sam /tʃɒŋ'sæm; *NAmE* 'tʃɑ:ŋsæm/ *noun* (from *Chinese*) a straight, tightly fitting silk dress with a high neck and short sleeves and an opening at the bottom on each side, worn by women from China and Indonesia

cheque O-w (*BrE*) (*US* **check**) /tʃek/ *noun*
a printed form that you can write on and sign as a way of paying for sth instead of using money: *a cheque for £50* ◇ *to write a cheque* ◇ *to make a cheque out to sb* ◇ *to pay by cheque* ◇ *to cash a cheque* (= to get or give money for a cheque) ➲ COLLOCATIONS at FINANCE ➲ picture at MONEY ➲ see also BLANK CHEQUE, TRAVELLER'S CHEQUE

cheque·book (*BrE*) (*US* **check·book**) /'tʃekbʊk/ *noun* a book of printed cheques ➲ picture at MONEY

ˌchequebook 'journalism *noun* [U] (*BrE, disapproving*) the practice of journalists paying people large amounts of money to give them personal or private information for a newspaper story

'cheque card (also **ˌcheque guaran'tee card**) *noun* (both *BrE*) a card that you must show when you pay by cheque to prove that the bank you have an account with will pay the money on the cheque ➲ compare CASH CARD

che·quered (*BrE*) (also **check·ered** *NAmE, BrE*) /'tʃekəd; *NAmE* -kərd/ *adj.* **1 ~ past/history/career** a person's past, etc. that contains both successful and not successful periods **2** having a pattern of squares of different colours

the ˌchequered 'flag (*BrE*) (also **check·ered flag** *NAmE, BrE*) *noun* a flag with black and white squares that is waved when a driver has finished a motor race

'chequing account *noun* (*CanE*) = CURRENT ACCOUNT

cher·ish /'tʃerɪʃ/ *verb* (*formal*) **1 ~ sb/sth** to love sb/sth very much and want to protect them or it: *Children need to be cherished.* ◇ *her **most cherished possession*** **2 ~ sth** to keep an idea, a hope or a pleasant feeling in your mind for a long time: ***Cherish the memory** of those days in Paris.*

Chero·kee /'tʃerəki:/ *noun* (*pl.* **Chero·kee** or **Chero·kees**) a member of a Native American people, many of whom now live in the US states of Oklahoma and North Carolina

che·root /ʃə'ru:t/ *noun* a type of CIGAR with two open ends

cherry /'tʃeri/ *noun, adj.*
■ ***noun*** (*pl.* **-ies**) **1** [C] a small soft round fruit with shiny red or black skin and a large seed inside ➲ VISUAL VOCAB page V26 **2** (also **'cherry tree**) [C] a tree on which cherries grow, or a similar tree, grown for its flowers: *cherry blossom* ◇ *a winter-flowering cherry* **3** (also **cherry·wood** /'tʃeriwʊd/) [U] the wood of the cherry tree **4** (also **ˌcherry 'red**) [U] a bright red colour IDM see BITE *n.*
■ ***adj.*** (also **ˌcherry 'red**) bright red in colour: *cherry lips*

'cherry-pick *verb* [T, I] **~ (sb/sth)** to choose the best people or things from a group and leave those which are not so good

'cherry picker *noun* **1** a type of tall CRANE which lifts people up so that they can work in very high places **2** a person who picks CHERRIES

'cherry tomato *noun* a type of very small tomato

cherub /'tʃerəb/ *noun* **1** (*pl.* **cher·ubs** or **cher·ubim** /-bɪm/) (in art) a type of ANGEL, shown as a small, fat, usually male, child with wings ➲ compare SERAPH **2** (*pl.* **cher·ubs**) (*informal*) a pretty child; a child who behaves well ▸ **cher·ub·ic** /tʃə'ru:bɪk/ *adj.*: (*formal*) *a cherubic face* (= looking round and innocent, like a small child's)

cher·vil /'tʃɜ:vɪl; *NAmE* 'tʃɜ:rvɪl/ *noun* [U] a plant with leaves that are used in cooking as a HERB

chess /tʃes/ *noun* [U] a game for two people played on a board marked with black and white squares on which each playing piece (representing a king, queen, castle, etc.) is moved according to special rules. The aim is to put the other player's king in a position from which it cannot escape (= to CHECKMATE it). ➲ VISUAL VOCAB page V33

chess·board /'tʃesbɔ:d; *NAmE* -bɔ:rd/ *noun* a board with 64 black and white squares that chess is played on ➲ VISUAL VOCAB page V33

chess·man /'tʃesmæn/ *noun* (*pl.* **-men** /-men/) any of the 32 pieces used in the game of chess

chest O-w /tʃest/ *noun*
1 O-w the top part of the front of the body, between the neck and the stomach: *The bullet hit him in the chest.* ◇

She gasped for breath, her chest heaving. ◊ *a chest infection* ◊ *chest pains* ◊ *a hairy chest* ➲ COLLOCATIONS at PHYSICAL ➲ VISUAL VOCAB page V48 **2 -chested** (in adjectives) having the type of chest mentioned: *flat-chested* ◊ *broad-chested* **3** a large strong box, usually made of wood, used for storing things in and/or moving them from one place to another: *a medicine chest* ◊ *a treasure chest* ➲ see also HOPE CHEST, TEA CHEST, WAR CHEST

IDM **,get sth off your 'chest** to talk about sth that has been worrying you for a long time so that you feel less anxious ➲ more at CARD *n.*

ches·ter·field /ˈtʃestəfiːld; *NAmE* ˈtʃestərf-/ *noun* **1** a type of SOFA that has arms and a back that are all the same height **2** (*CanE*) any type of SOFA

chest·nut /ˈtʃesnʌt/ *noun, adj.*

■ ***noun* 1** (also **'chestnut tree**) [C] a large tree with spreading branches, that produces smooth brown nuts inside cases which are covered with SPIKES. There are several types of chestnut tree. ➲ see also HORSE CHESTNUT **2** [C] a smooth brown nut of a chestnut tree, some types of which can be eaten: *roast chestnuts* ➲ VISUAL VOCAB page V28 ➲ see also WATER CHESTNUT ➲ compare CONKER **3** [U] a deep reddish-brown colour **4** [C] a horse of a reddish-brown colour **5 old chestnut** [C] (*informal*) an old joke or story that has been told so many times that it is no longer amusing or interesting

■ ***adj.*** reddish-brown in colour

,chest of 'drawers *noun* (*pl.* **chests of drawers**) (*NAmE* also **bur·eau, dresser**) a piece of furniture with drawers for keeping clothes in ➲ VISUAL VOCAB page V20

chesty /ˈtʃesti/ *adj.* (*informal, especially BrE*) suffering from or showing signs of chest disease

chev·ron /ˈʃevrən/ *noun* **1** a line or pattern in the shape of a V **2** a piece of cloth in the shape of a V which soldiers and police officers wear on their uniforms to show their rank

chew 🔑 /tʃuː/ *verb, noun*

■ ***verb* 1** 🔑 [I, T] to bite food into small pieces in your mouth with your teeth to make it easier to swallow: **~ (at/on/through sth)** *After the operation you may find it difficult to chew and swallow.* ◊ **~ sth (up)** *teeth designed for chewing meat* ◊ *He is always chewing gum.* **2** [I, T] to bite sth continuously, for example because you are nervous or to taste it: **~ on sth** *Rosa chewed on her lip and stared at the floor.* ◊ *The dog was chewing on a bone.* ◊ **~ sth** *to chew your nails*

IDM **,chew the 'fat** (*informal*) to have a long friendly talk with sb about sth ➲ more at BITE *v.*

PHR V **,chew sb 'out** (*NAmE, informal*) to tell sb angrily that you do not approve of their actions: *He got chewed out by the boss for lying.* **,chew sth↔'over** to think about or discuss sth slowly and carefully

■ ***noun* 1** an act of chewing sth **2** a type of sweet/candy that you chew **3** a piece of TOBACCO that you chew

'chewing gum (also **gum**) *noun* [U] a sweet/candy that you chew but do not swallow

'chewing-stick *noun* a stick made from the STEM or root of particular plants that you chew at one end and then use to clean your teeth (used in some parts of Africa and Asia)

chewy /ˈtʃuːi/ *adj.* (**chew·ier, chewi·est**) (of food) needing to be chewed a lot before it can be swallowed

Chey·enne /ʃaɪˈen/ *noun* (*pl.* **Chey·enne** or **Chey·ennes**) a member of a Native American people, many of whom now live in the US states of Oklahoma and Montana

chez /ʃeɪ/ *prep.* (*from French*) at the home of: *I spent a pleasant evening chez the Stewarts.*

chi /kaɪ/ *noun* the 22nd letter of the Greek alphabet (Χ, χ)

Chi·anti /kiˈænti/ *noun* [U, C] a dry red wine from the region of Tuscany in Italy

chiaro·scuro /kiˌɑːrəˈskʊərəʊ; *NAmE* -ˈskʊroʊ/ *noun* [U] (*art*) the way light and shade are shown; the contrast between light and shade

chi·as·mus /kaɪˈæzməs; *NAmE* kɪˈæz-/ *noun* [U, C] (*pl.* **chi·as·mi** /kaɪˈæzmi; kɪˈæz-/) (*technical*) a technique used in writing or in speeches, in which words, ideas, etc. are repeated in reverse order

chic /ʃiːk/ *adj.* very fashionable and elegant SYN **stylish**: *She is always so chic, so elegant.* ◊ *a chic new restaurant* ▸ **chic** *noun* [U]: *a perfectly dressed woman with an air of chic that was unmistakably French*

chi·ca /ˈtʃiːkə/ *noun* (*US, from Spanish, informal*) a girl or young woman

Chi·cana /tʃɪˈkɑːnə; ʃɪ-; -ˈkeɪn-; *NAmE* tʃɪˈkɑːnə; ʃɪ-/ *noun* (*especially US, from Spanish*) a girl or woman living in the US whose family came from Mexico ➲ compare CHICANO, HISPANIC, LATINO

chi·cane /ʃɪˈkeɪn/ *noun* (*BrE*) a sharp double bend, either on a track where cars race, or on an ordinary road to stop vehicles from going too fast

chi·can·ery /ʃɪˈkeɪnəri/ *noun* [U] (*formal*) the use of complicated plans and clever talk in order to trick people

Chi·cano /tʃɪˈkɑːnəʊ; ʃɪ-; *NAmE* -noʊ; *BrE* also -ˈkeɪn-/ *noun* (*pl.* **-os**) (*especially US, from Spanish*) a person living in the US whose family came from Mexico ➲ compare CHICANA, HISPANIC, LATINO

chi·chi /ˈʃiːʃiː/ *adj.* used to describe a style of decoration that contains too many details and lacks taste

chick /tʃɪk/ *noun* **1** a baby bird, especially a baby chicken **2** (*old-fashioned*, sometimes *offensive*) a way of referring to a young woman

chicka·dee /ˈtʃɪkədiː; ˌtʃɪkəˈdiː/ *noun* a small N American bird of the TIT family. There are many types of chickadee.

chick·en 🔑 /ˈtʃɪkɪn/ *noun, verb, adj.*

■ ***noun* 1** 🔑 [C] a large bird that is often kept for its eggs or meat: *They keep chickens in the back yard.* ◊ *free-range chickens* ➲ compare COCK, HEN ➲ VISUAL VOCAB page V10 **2** 🔑 [U] meat from a chicken: ***fried/roast chicken*** ◊ ***chicken stock/soup*** ◊ ***chicken breasts/livers/thighs*** ◊ *chicken and chips* ➲ see also SPRING CHICKEN

IDM **a ,chicken-and-'egg situation, problem, etc.** a situation in which it is difficult to tell which one of two things was the cause of the other **play 'chicken** to play a game in which people do sth dangerous for as long as they can to show how brave they are. The person who stops first has lost the game. ➲ more at COUNT *v.*, HEADLESS, HOME *adv.*

■ ***verb***

PHR V **,chicken 'out (of sth/of doing sth)** (*informal*) to decide not to do sth because you are afraid

■ ***adj.*** [not before noun] (*informal*) not brave; afraid to do sth SYN **cowardly**

'chicken feed *noun* [U] (*informal*) an amount of money that is not large enough to be important

'chicken flu *noun* [U] = BIRD FLU

chick·en·pox /ˈtʃɪkɪnpɒks; *NAmE* -pɑːks/ *noun* [U] a disease, especially of children, that causes a slight fever and many spots on the skin: *to* ***catch/get/have chickenpox***

'chicken run *noun* an area surrounded by a fence in which chickens are kept

chick·en·shit /ˈtʃɪkɪnʃɪt/ *noun, adj.*

■ ***noun*** [U] (*NAmE, slang*) nonsense

■ ***adj.*** (*NAmE, slang*) (of a person) not brave SYN **cowardly**

'chicken wire *noun* [U] thin wire made into sheets like nets with a pattern of shapes with six sides

'chick flick *noun* (*informal*) a film/movie that is intended especially for women

'chick lit *noun* [U] (*informal*) novels that are intended especially for women, often with a young, single woman as the main character

chick·pea /ˈtʃɪk piː/ *noun* (*especially BrE*) (*NAmE* usually **gar·banzo, gar'banzo bean**) a hard round seed, like a light brown PEA, that is cooked and eaten as a vegetable ➲ VISUAL VOCAB page V27

'chickpea flour *noun* = GRAM FLOUR

chick·weed /ˈtʃɪkwiːd/ *noun* [U] a small plant with white flowers that often grows as a WEED over a wide area

chi·co /ˈtʃiːkəʊ; NAmE -koʊ/ *noun* (*pl.* **-os**) (*US, from Spanish, informal*) a boy or young man

chic·ory /ˈtʃɪkəri/ *noun* [U] **1** (*BrE*) (*NAmE* **en·dive**) [C, U] a small pale green plant with bitter leaves that are eaten raw or cooked as a vegetable. The root can be dried and used with or instead of coffee. **2** (*NAmE*) (*BrE* **en·dive**) (*NAmE* also ˌ**curly** ˈ**endive, fri·sée**) a plant with green curly leaves that are eaten raw as a vegetable

chide /tʃaɪd/ *verb* (*formal*) to criticize or blame sb because they have done sth wrong SYN **rebuke**: **~ sb/yourself** (**for sth/for doing sth**) *She chided herself for being so impatient with the children.* ◇ **~ (sb) + speech** *'Isn't that a bit selfish?' he chided.*

chief 0-π /tʃiːf/ *adj., noun*
■ *adj.* [only before noun] **1** 0-π most important: *the chief cause/problem/reason* ◇ *one of the President's chief rivals* ➲ SYNONYMS at MAIN **2** 0-π (often **Chief**) highest in rank: *the Chief Education Officer* ◇ *the chief financial officer of the company* ◇ *Detective Chief Inspector Williams* **3 -in-ˈchief** (in nouns) of the highest rank: *commander-in-chief* ➲ see also CHIEFLY
■ *noun* **1** 0-π a person with a high rank or the highest rank in a company or an organization: ***army/industry/police chiefs*** **2** (often as a title) a leader or ruler of a people or community: *Chief Buthelezi* ◇ *Chief Crazy Horse*
IDM **too many ˌchiefs and not enough ˈIndians** (*BrE, informal*) used to describe a situation in which there are too many people telling other people what to do, and not enough people to do the work

ˌ**chief ˈconstable** *noun* (in Britain) a senior police officer who is in charge of the police force in a particular area: *Chief Constable Brian Turner*

ˌ**chief eˈxecutive** *noun* **1** the person with the highest rank in a company or an organization **2 Chief Executive** the President of the US

ˌ**chief eˈxecutive officer** *noun* (*abbr.* **CEO**) the person in a company who has the most power and authority

ˌ**chief inˈspector** *noun* (in Britain) a police officer above the rank of an INSPECTOR

ˌ**chief ˈjustice** (also **Chief Justice**) *noun* the most important judge in a court, especially the US Supreme Court

chief·ly /ˈtʃiːfli/ *adv.* not completely, but as a most important part SYN **primarily, mainly**: *We are chiefly concerned with improving educational standards.* ◇ *He's travelled widely, chiefly in Africa and Asia.*

ˌ**chief of ˈstaff** *noun* (*pl.* ˌ**chiefs of ˈstaff**) an officer of very high rank, responsible for advising the person who commands each of the armed forces ➲ see also JOINT CHIEFS OF STAFF

ˌ**chief superinˈtendent** *noun* (in Britain) a police officer above the rank of SUPERINTENDENT

chief·tain /ˈtʃiːftən/ *noun* the leader of a people or a CLAN in Scotland

chif·fon /ˈʃɪfɒn; NAmE ʃɪˈfɑːn/ *noun* [U] a type of fine transparent cloth made from silk or NYLON, used especially for making clothes ➲ VISUAL VOCAB page V53

chig·ger /ˈtʃɪɡə(r)/ (also **jig·ger**) *noun* a small FLEA that lives in tropical regions and lays eggs under a person's or animal's skin, causing painful areas on the skin

chi·gnon /ˈʃiːnjɒn; NAmE -jɑːn/ *noun* (from *French*) a style for women's hair in which the hair is pulled back and twisted into a smooth knot at the back ➲ VISUAL VOCAB page V49

chi·hua·hua /tʃɪˈwɑːwə; NAmE -ˈwɑːwɑː/ *noun* a very small dog with smooth hair

chi·kun·gun·ya /ˌtʃɪkənˈɡʌnjə/ *noun* [U] a disease similar to DENGUE caused by a virus, found in E Africa and parts of Asia and carried by MOSQUITOES

chil·blain /ˈtʃɪlbleɪn/ *noun* [usually pl.] a painful red swelling on the hands or feet that is caused by cold or bad CIRCULATION of the blood

child 0-π /tʃaɪld/ *noun* (*pl.* **chil·dren** /ˈtʃɪldrən/)
1 0-π a young human who is not yet an adult: *a child of three/a three-year-old child* ◇ *men, women and children* ◇ *an unborn child* ◇ *not suitable for young children* ◇ *I lived in London as a child.* ◇ *a child star* ➲ see also BRAINCHILD, LATCHKEY CHILD, POSTER CHILD, SCHOOLCHILD **2** 0-π a son or daughter of any age: *They have three grown-up children.* ◇ *a support group for adult children of alcoholics* ◇ *They can't* ***have children.*** ➲ see also GODCHILD, GRANDCHILD, LOVE CHILD, ONLY CHILD, STEPCHILD ➲ compare KID **3** a person who is strongly influenced by the ideas and attitudes of a particular time or person: *a child of the 90s* **4** (*disapproving*) an adult who behaves like a child and is not MATURE or responsible
IDM **be with ˈchild** (*old-fashioned*) to be pregnant **be ˈchild's play** (*informal*) to be very easy to do, so not even a child would find it difficult

Collocations

Children

Having a baby/child

- **want** a baby/a child/kids
- **start** a family
- **conceive/be expecting/be going to have** a baby/child
- **miss** your period
- **become/get/ be/find out that you are** pregnant
- **have** a baby/a child/kids/a son/a daughter/twins/a family
- **have** a normal/a difficult/an unwanted pregnancy; an easy/a difficult/a home birth
- **be in/go into/induce** labour (*especially US*) labor
- **have/suffer/cause** a miscarriage
- **give** birth to a child/baby/daughter/son/twins

Parenting

- **bring up**/(*especially NAmE*) **raise** a child/family
- **care for**/(*especially BrE*) **look after** a baby/child/kid
- **change** (*BrE*) a nappy/(*NAmE*) a diaper/a baby
- **feed/breastfeed/bottle-feed** a baby
- **be entitled to/go on** maternity/paternity leave
- **go back/return to work** after maternity leave
- **need/find/get** a babysitter/good quality affordable childcare
- **balance/combine work and** childcare/child-rearing/family life
- **educate/teach/home-school** a child/kid
- **punish/discipline/spoil** a child/kid
- **adopt** a baby/child/kid
- **offer a baby for/put a baby up for** adoption
- (*especially BrE*) **foster** a child/kid
- **be placed with/be raised by** foster parents

ˈ**child abuse** *noun* [U] the crime of harming a child in a physical, sexual or emotional way: *victims of child abuse*

child·bear·ing /ˈtʃaɪldbeərɪŋ; NAmE -ber-/ *noun* [U] the process of giving birth to children: *women* ***of childbearing age***

ˌ**child ˈbenefit** *noun* [U] (in Britain) money that the government regularly pays to parents of children up to a particular age

child·birth /ˈtʃaɪldbɜːθ; NAmE -bɜːrθ/ *noun* [U] the process of giving birth to a baby: *pregnancy and childbirth* ◇ *His wife died* ***in childbirth.***

child·care /ˈtʃaɪldkeə(r); NAmE -ker/ *noun* [U] the care of children, especially while parents are at work: *childcare facilities for working parents* ➲ COLLOCATIONS at CHILD

child·hood /ˈtʃaɪldhʊd/ *noun* [U, C] the period of sb's life when they are a child: *childhood, adolescence and adulthood* ◇ *in early childhood* ◇ ***childhood memories/experiences*** ◇ *She had a happy childhood.* ◇ *childhood cancer* ➲ COLLOCATIONS at AGE

IDM **a/sb's second ˈchildhood** a time in the life of an adult person when they behave like a child again

child·ish /ˈtʃaɪldɪʃ/ *adj.* **1** connected with or typical of a child: *childish handwriting* **2** (*disapproving*) (of an adult) behaving in a stupid or silly way SYN **immature**: *Don't be so childish!* OPP **mature** ➲ compare CHILDLIKE ▸ **child·ish·ly** *adv.*: *to behave childishly* **child·ish·ness** *noun* [U]

child·less /ˈtʃaɪldləs/ *adj.* having no children: *a **childless couple/marriage***

child·like /ˈtʃaɪldlaɪk/ *adj.* (usually *approving*) having the qualities that children usually have, especially INNOCENCE: ***childlike enthusiasm/simplicity/delight*** ➲ compare CHILDISH

child·mind·er /ˈtʃaɪldmaɪndə(r)/ *noun* (*BrE*) a person who is paid to care for children while their parents are at work. A childminder usually does this in his or her own home. ➲ see also BABYSITTER

child·proof /ˈtʃaɪldpruːf/ *adj.* designed so that young children cannot open, use, or damage it: *childproof containers for medicines*

ˈchild restraint *noun* a belt, or small seat with a belt, that is used in a car to control and protect a child

ˈchild seat *noun* = CAR SEAT

chili /ˈtʃɪli/ (*NAmE*) **1** [C] = CHILLI **2** [U] = CHILLI CON CARNE

chill /tʃɪl/ *noun, verb, adj.*

■ ***noun*** **1** [sing.] a feeling of being cold: *There's a chill in the air this morning.* ◇ *A small fire was burning to **take the chill off** the room.* **2** [C] an illness caused by being cold and wet, causing fever and SHIVERING (= shaking of the body) **3** [sing.] a feeling of fear: *a **chill of fear/apprehension*** ◇ *His words **sent a chill down her spine**.*

■ ***verb*** **1** [T, usually passive] **~ sb** to make sb very cold: *They were chilled by the icy wind.* ◇ *Let's go home, I'm **chilled to the bone*** (= very cold). **2** [I, T] when food or a drink **chills** or when sb **chills** it, it is made very cold but it does not freeze: *Let the pudding chill for an hour until set.* ◇ **~ sth** *This wine is best served chilled.* ◇ *chilled foods* (= for example in a supermarket) **3** [T] **~ sb/sth** (*literary*) to frighten sb: *His words chilled her.* ◇ *What he saw **chilled his blood/chilled him to the bone**.* **4** [I] (also ˌ**chill ˈout**) (*informal*) = CHILL OUT: *We went home and chilled in front of the TV.* ◇ *Just chill, Mum, everything's going to be OK.*

PHR V ˌ**chill ˈout** (*informal*) to spend time relaxing; to relax and stop feeling angry or nervous about sth: *They sometimes meet up to chill out and watch a movie.* ◇ *Sit down and chill out!*

■ ***adj.*** (*formal*) (especially of weather and the wind) cold, in an unpleasant way: *the chill grey dawn* ◇ *a chill wind*

chill·ax /tʃɪˈlæks/ *verb* [I] (*slang*) to relax and stop feeling angry or nervous about sth: *Chillax, dude—I'm on your team.*

ˌ**chilled-ˈout** (also **chilled**) *adj.* (*informal*) very relaxed: *a chilled-out atmosphere* ◇ *He felt totally chilled.*

ˈ**chill factor** *noun* the extent to which the wind makes the air feel colder; a number which represents this

chilli (*BrE*) (*NAmE* **chili**) /ˈtʃɪli/ *noun* (*pl.* **chil·lies**, *NAmE* **chilies**) **1** (*NAmE* also ˈ**chili pepper**) [C, U] the small green or red fruit of a type of pepper plant that is used in cooking to give a hot taste to food, often dried or made into powder, also called chilli or **chilli powder** ➲ VISUAL VOCAB page V27 **2** [U] = CHILLI CON CARNE

chilli con carne /ˌtʃɪli kɒn ˈkɑːni; *NAmE* kɑːn ˈkɑːrni/ (*especially BrE*) (*BrE* also **chilli**) (*NAmE* also **chili**) *noun* [U] a hot spicy Mexican dish made with meat, BEANS and chillies

chill·ing /ˈtʃɪlɪŋ/ *adj.* frightening, usually because it is connected with sth violent or cruel: *a chilling story* ◇ *The film evokes chilling reminders of the war.*

chill·out /ˈtʃɪlaʊt/ *noun* [U] a style of electronic music that is not fast or lively and is intended to make you relaxed and calm

chilly /ˈtʃɪli/ *adj.* (**chill·ier, chilli·est**) **1** (especially of the weather or a place, but also of people) too cold to be comfortable: *It's chilly today.* ◇ *I was feeling chilly.* ➲ SYNONYMS at COLD **2** not friendly: *The visitors got a chilly reception.* ▸ **chil·li·ness** *noun* [U]

chime /tʃaɪm/ *verb, noun*

■ ***verb*** [I, T] (of a bell or a clock) to ring; to show the time by making a ringing sound: *I heard the clock chime.* ◇ *Eight o'clock had already chimed.* ◇ **~ sth** *The clock chimed midday.*

PHR V ˌ**chime ˈin (with sth)** to join or interrupt a conversation: *He kept chiming in with his own opinions.* ◇ **+ speech** *'And me!' she chimed in.* **chime (in) with sth** (of plans, ideas, etc.) to agree with sth; to be similar to sth: *His opinions chimed in with the mood of the nation.*

■ ***noun*** a ringing sound, especially one that is made by a bell: *door chimes* ➲ see also WIND CHIMES

chi·mera (also **chi·maera**) /kaɪˈmɪərə; *NAmE* -ˈmɪrə/ *noun* **1** (in ancient Greek stories) a creature with a LION's head, a GOAT's body and a snake's tail, that can breathe out fire **2** (*formal*) an impossible idea or hope

chim·ney /ˈtʃɪmni/ *noun* **1** a structure through which smoke or steam is carried up away from a fire, etc. and through the roof of a building; the part of this that is above the roof: *He threw a bit of paper onto the fire and it flew up the chimney.* ◇ *the factory chimneys of an industrial landscape* ➲ VISUAL VOCAB page V15 **2** (*technical*) a narrow opening in an area of rock that a person can climb up

ˈ**chim·ney breast** *noun* (*BrE*) the wall around the bottom part of a chimney, above a FIREPLACE

ˈ**chim·ney piece** *noun* (*BrE*) a brick or stone structure that is built over a FIREPLACE

ˈ**chim·ney pot** *noun* (*BrE*) a short wide pipe that is placed on top of a chimney ➲ VISUAL VOCAB page V15

ˈ**chim·ney stack** *noun* (*BrE*) **1** the part of the chimney that is above the roof of a building **2** (*NAmE* **smokestack**) a very tall chimney, especially one in a factory

ˈ**chimney sweep** (also **sweep**) *noun* a person whose job is to clean the inside of chimneys

chim·pan·zee /ˌtʃɪmpænˈziː/ (also *informal* **chimp**) *noun* a small intelligent African APE (= an animal like a large MONKEY without a tail) ➲ VISUAL VOCAB page V10

chin 🔑 /tʃɪn/ *noun*

the part of the face below the mouth and above the neck ➲ COLLOCATIONS at PHYSICAL ➲ VISUAL VOCAB page V48 ➲ see also DOUBLE CHIN

IDM **(keep your) ˈchin up** (*informal*) used to tell sb to try to stay cheerful even though they are in a difficult or unpleasant situation: *Chin up! Only two exams left.* **take sth on the ˈchin** (*informal*) **1** to accept a difficult or unpleasant situation without complaining, trying to make excuses, etc. **2** (*NAmE*) to be damaged or badly affected by something ➲ more at CHUCK *v.*

china /ˈtʃaɪnə/ *noun* [U] **1** white CLAY which is baked and used for making delicate cups, plates, etc: *a china vase* ➲ see also BONE CHINA **2** cups, plates, etc. that are made of china: *She got out the best china.* IDM see BULL, TEA

ˌ**china-ˈblue** *adj.* pale greyish-blue in colour ▸ ˌ**china ˈblue** *noun* [U]

ˌ**china ˈclay** *noun* [U] = KAOLIN

China·town /ˈtʃaɪnətaʊn/ *noun* [U, C] the area of a city where many Chinese people live and there are Chinese shops/stores and restaurants

chin·chilla /tʃɪnˈtʃɪlə/ *noun* **1** [C] an animal like a RABBIT with soft silver-grey fur. Chinchillas are often kept on farms for their fur. **2** [U] the skin and fur of the chinchilla, used for making expensive coats, etc.

Chi·nese /ˌtʃaɪˈniːz/ *adj., noun* (*pl.* **Chi·nese**)

■ ***adj.*** from or connected with China

■ ***noun*** **1** [C] a person from China, or whose family was originally from China **2** [U] the language of China

ˌ**Chinese ˈcabbage** *noun* [U] (*BrE* also ˌ**Chinese ˈleaves** [pl.], ˌ**Chinese ˈleaf** [U]) a type of vegetable that is eaten cooked or in salads. There are two types of Chinese

C

cabbage, one with long light-green leaves and thick white STEMS which is similar to LETTUCE and one with darker green leaves and thicker white STEMS. The first type is usually called 'Chinese leaves' in British English and the second type is called 'pak choi' (*BrE*) or 'bok choy' (*NAmE*).

C

ˌChinese ˈchequers (*BrE*) (*NAmE* **ˌChinese ˈcheckers**) *noun* [U] a game for two to six players who try to move the playing pieces from one corner to the opposite corner of the board, which is shaped like a star ➲ VISUAL VOCAB page V33

ˌChinese ˈlantern *noun* **1** a lamp that is inside a paper case, with a handle to carry it **2** a plant with white flowers and round orange fruits inside a material like paper

ˌChinese ˈwhispers *noun* [U] (*BrE*) the situation when information is passed from one person to another and gets slightly changed each time

Ching·lish /ˈtʃɪŋglɪʃ/ *noun* [U] (*informal*) language which is a mixture of ENGLISH and CHINESE, especially a type of English that includes many Chinese words and/or follows Chinese grammar rules

Chink /tʃɪŋk/ *noun* (*taboo, slang*) a very offensive word for a Chinese person

chink /tʃɪŋk/ *noun, verb*

■ ***noun*** **1** a narrow opening in sth, especially one that lets light through: *a chink in the curtains* **2 ~ of light** a small area of light shining through a narrow opening **3** [usually sing.] the light ringing sound that is made when glass objects or coins touch: *the chink of glasses*

IDM **a chink in sb's ˈarmour** a weak point in sb's argument, character, etc, that can be used in an attack

■ ***verb*** [I, T] when glasses, coins or other glass or metal objects **chink** or when you **chink** them, they make a light ringing sound SYN **clink**: *the sound of bottles chinking* ◇ **~ sth** *We chinked glasses and drank to each other's health.*

chin·less /ˈtʃɪnləs/ *adj.* (of a man) having a very small chin (often thought of as a sign of a weak character)

IDM **a chinless ˈwonder** (*BrE, humorous, disapproving*) a young, upper-class man who is weak and stupid

chi·nois·erie /ʃinˈwɑːzəri/ *noun* [U] (*art*) the use of Chinese images, designs and techniques in Western art, furniture and ARCHITECTURE

chi·nook /tʃɪˈnuːk; ʃɪ-/ *noun* **1** (also **chiˌnook ˈwind**) a warm dry wind that blows down the east side of the Rocky Mountains at the end of winter **2** (also **chiˌnook ˈsalmon**) a large N Pacific SALMON which is eaten as food

chinos /ˈtʃiːnəʊz; *NAmE* -noʊz/ *noun* [pl.] informal trousers/pants made from strong cotton: *a pair of chinos*

chintz /tʃɪnts/ *noun* [U, C] a type of shiny cotton cloth with a printed design, especially of flowers, used for making curtains, covering furniture, etc.

chintzy /ˈtʃɪntsi/ *adj.* **1** (*BrE*) covered in or decorated with chintz **2** (*NAmE, informal*) cheap and not attractive **3** (*NAmE, humorous*) not willing to spend money SYN **cheap, stingy**

ˈchin-up *noun* (*especially NAmE*) = PULL-UP

chin·wag /ˈtʃɪnwæg/ *noun* [sing.] (*BrE, informal*) a friendly, informal conversation with sb that you know well SYN **chat**

chips (*BrE*)
(*also* **French fries** *NAmE, BrE*)

crisps (*BrE*)
chips (*NAmE*)

chip 0-π /tʃɪp/ *noun, verb*

■ ***noun*** **1** 0-π the place from which a small piece of wood, glass, etc. has broken from an object: *This mug has a chip in it.* ➲ picture at BROKEN **2** 0-π a small piece of wood, glass, etc. that has broken or been broken off an object: *chips of wood* ◇ *chocolate chip cookies* (= biscuits containing small pieces of chocolate) **3** 0-π (*BrE*) (also **ˌFrench ˈfry, fry** *NAmE, BrE*) [usually pl.] a long thin piece of potato fried in oil or fat: *All main courses are served with chips or baked potato.* ➲ see also FISH AND CHIPS **4** (also **poˈtato chip**) (both *NAmE*) (*BrE* **crisp, poˌtato ˈcrisp**) a thin round slice of potato that is fried until hard then dried and eaten cold. Chips are sold in bags and have many different flavours. **5** = TORTILLA CHIP **6** = MICROCHIP: *chip technology* ➲ see also V-CHIP **7** a small flat piece of plastic used to represent a particular amount of money in some types of gambling: (*figurative*) *The release of prisoners was used as a* ***bargaining chip***. **8** (also **ˈchip shot**) (in GOLF, football (SOCCER), etc.) an act of hitting or kicking a ball high in the air so that it lands within a short distance ➲ see also BLUE-CHIP

IDM **a ˌchip off the old ˈblock** (*informal*) a person who is very similar to their mother or father in the way that they look or behave **have a ˈchip on your shoulder** (**about sth**) (*informal*) to be sensitive about sth that happened in the past and become easily offended if it is mentioned because you think that you were treated unfairly **have had your ˈchips** (*BrE, informal*) to be in a situation in which you are certain to be defeated or killed **when the chips are ˈdown** (*informal*) used to refer to a difficult situation in which you are forced to decide what is important to you: *I'm not sure what I'll do when the chips are down.* ➲ more at CASH *v.*

■ ***verb*** (-pp-) **1** [T, I] **~ (sth)** to damage sth by breaking a small piece off it; to become damaged in this way: *a badly chipped saucer* ◇ *She chipped one of her front teeth.* ◇ *These plates chip easily.* ➲ picture at BROKEN **2** [T] **~ sth + adv./prep.** to cut or break small pieces off sth with a tool: *Chip away the damaged area.* ◇ *The fossils had been chipped out of the rock.* **3** [T, I] **~ (sth)** (especially in GOLF and football (SOCCER)) to hit or kick the ball so that it goes high in the air and then lands within a short distance **4** [T] **~ potatoes** (*BrE*) to cut potatoes into long thin pieces and fry them in deep oil **5** [T] **~ sth** to put a MICROCHIP under the skin of a dog or other animal so that it can be identified if it is lost or stolen

PHR V **ˌchip aˈway at sth** to keep breaking small pieces off sth: *He was chipping away at the stone.* ◇ (*figurative*) *They chipped away at the power of the government* (= gradually made it weaker). **ˌchip ˈin** (**with sth**) (*informal*) **1** to join in or interrupt a conversation; to add sth to a conversation or discussion: *Pete and Anne chipped in with suggestions.* ◇ **+ speech** *'That's different,' she chipped in.* **2** (also **ˌchip ˈin sth**) to give some money so that a group of people can buy sth together SYN **contribute**: *If everyone chips in we'll be able to buy her a really nice present.* ◇ *We each chipped in (with) £5.* **ˌchip ˈoff** | **ˌchip sth↔ˈoff** to damage sth by breaking a small piece off it; to be damaged in this way: *He chipped off a piece of his tooth.* ◇ *The paint had chipped off.*

ˌchip and ˈPIN (also **chip and pin**) *noun* [U] a system of paying for sth with a credit card or DEBIT CARD in which the card has information stored on it in the form of a MICROCHIP and you prove your identity by typing a number (your PIN) rather than by signing your name: *Chip and PIN is designed to combat credit card fraud.*

chip·board /ˈtʃɪpbɔːd; *NAmE* -bɔːrd/ *noun* [U] a type of board that is used for building, made of small pieces of wood that are pressed together and stuck with glue

ˈchip card *noun* a plastic card on which information is stored in the form of a MICROCHIP: *Chip cards will be the money of the future.*

chip·munk /ˈtʃɪpmʌŋk/ *noun* a small N American animal of the SQUIRREL family, with light and dark marks on its back

chipo·lata /ˌtʃɪpəˈlɑːtə/ *noun* (*especially BrE*) a small thin SAUSAGE

chip·per /ˈtʃɪpə(r)/ *adj., noun*

■ ***adj.*** (*informal*) cheerful and lively

■ ***noun*** **1** a machine which cuts wood into very small pieces **2** a device which cuts potatoes into chips/fries **3** (*ScotE, IrishE, informal*) a chip shop

chip·pings /ˈtʃɪpɪŋz/ *noun* [pl.] (*BrE*) small pieces of stone or wood

chippy /ˈtʃɪpi/ *noun, adj.*
■ ***noun*** (also **chip·pie**) (*pl.* -ies) (*BrE, informal*) **1** = CHIP SHOP **2** = CARPENTER
■ ***adj.*** (*informal*) (of a person) getting annoyed or offended easily

ˈ**chip shop** (also *informal* **chip·py**, **chip·pie**) *noun* (in Britain) a shop that cooks and sells fish and chips and other fried food for people to take home and eat

ˈ**chip shot** *noun* = CHIP (8)

chiro·mancy /ˈkaɪrəʊmænsi; *NAmE* ˈkaɪroʊ-/ *noun* [U] the practice of telling what will happen in the future by looking at the lines on sb's PALMS SYN **palmistry** ▸ **chiro·man·cer** /ˈkaɪrəʊmænsə(r); *NAmE* ˈkaɪroʊ-/ *noun*

chir·opo·dist /kɪˈrɒpədɪst; *NAmE* kɪˈrɑːp-/ (*especially BrE*) (*NAmE* usually **po·dia·trist**) *noun* a person whose job is the care and treatment of people's feet

chir·opody /kɪˈrɒpədi; *NAmE* kɪˈrɑːp-/ (*especially BrE*) (*NAmE* usually **po·dia·try**) *noun* [U] the work of a chiropodist

chiro·prac·tic /ˌkaɪərəʊˈpræktɪk; *NAmE* -roʊ-/ *noun* [U] the medical profession which involves treating some diseases and physical problems by pressing and moving the bones in a person's SPINE or joints; the work of a chiropractor

chiro·prac·tor /ˈkaɪərəʊpræktə(r); *NAmE* -roʊ-/ *noun* a person whose job involves treating some diseases and physical problems by pressing and moving the bones in a person's SPINE or joints ➲ compare OSTEOPATH

chirp /tʃɜːp; *NAmE* tʃɜːrp/ (also **chir·rup**) *verb* **1** [I] (of small birds and some insects) to make short high sounds **2** [I, T] to speak in a lively and cheerful way ▸ **chirp** (also **chir·rup**) *noun*

chirpy /ˈtʃɜːpi; *NAmE* ˈtʃɜːrpi/ *adj.* (*informal*) lively and cheerful; in a good mood ▸ **chirp·ily** *adv.* **chirpi·ness** *noun* [U]

chir·rup /ˈtʃɪrəp/ *verb, noun* = CHIRP

chisel /ˈtʃɪzl/ *noun, verb*
■ ***noun*** a tool with a sharp flat edge at the end, used for shaping wood, stone or metal ➲ VISUAL VOCAB pages V17, V35
■ ***verb*** (-ll-, *especially US* -l-) **1** [T, I] ~ (**sth**) (+ **adv./prep.**) to cut or shape wood or stone with a chisel: *A name was chiselled into the stone.* ◇ *She was chiselling some marble.* **2** [T] ~ **sb** (**out of sth**) (*informal, especially NAmE*) to get money or some advantage from sb by cheating them: *They chiseled him out of hundreds of dollars.* ▸ **chisel·ler** (*especially US* **chisel·er**) /ˈtʃɪzlə(r)/ *noun*

chis·elled (*BrE*) (*especially US* **chis·eled**) /ˈtʃɪzld/ *adj.* (of a person's face) having clear strong features

chi-square test /ˌkaɪ ˈskweə test; *NAmE* ˈskwer/ *noun* (*statistics*) a calculation that is used to test how well a set of data fits the results that were expected according to a theory

chit /tʃɪt/ *noun* (*BrE*) **1** a short written note, signed by sb, showing an amount of money that is owed, or giving sb permission to do sth **2** (*old-fashioned, disapproving*) a young woman or girl, especially one who is thought to have no respect for older people

ˈ**chit-chat** *noun* [U] (*informal*) conversation about things that are not important SYN **chat**

chit·ter·lings /ˈtʃɪtəlɪŋz; *NAmE* ˈtʃɪtər-/ *noun* [pl.] pig's INTESTINES, eaten as food

chiv·al·rous /ˈʃɪvlrəs/ *adj.* (of men) polite, kind and behaving with honour, especially towards women SYN **gallant** ▸ **chiv·al·rous·ly** *adv.*

chiv·alry /ˈʃɪvəlri/ *noun* [U] **1** polite and kind behaviour that shows a sense of honour, especially by men towards women **2** (in the Middle Ages) the religious and moral system of behaviour which the perfect KNIGHT was expected to follow

chives /tʃaɪvz/ *noun* [pl.] the long thin leaves of a plant with purple flowers. Chives taste like onions and are used to give flavour to food. ➲ VISUAL VOCAB page V28 ▸ **chive** *adj.* [only before noun]: *a chive and garlic dressing*

chivvy /ˈtʃɪvi/ *verb* (**chiv·vies, chivvy·ing, chiv·vied, chiv·vied**) ~ **sb** (**into sth/along**) | ~ **sb to do sth** (*BrE*) to try and make sb hurry or do sth quickly, especially when they do not want to do it: *He chivvied them into the car.*

chla·mydia /kləˈmɪdiə/ *noun* [U] (*medical*) a disease caused by bacteria, which is caught by having sex with an infected person

chlor·ide /ˈklɔːraɪd/ *noun* [U, C] (*chemistry*) a COMPOUND of CHLORINE and another chemical element ➲ see also SODIUM CHLORIDE

chlor·in·ate /ˈklɔːrɪneɪt/ *verb* ~ **sth** to put chlorine in sth, especially water ▸ **chlor·in·ation** /ˌklɔːrɪˈneɪʃn/ *noun* [U]: *a chlorination plant*

chlor·ine /ˈklɔːriːn/ *noun* [U] (*symb.* **Cl**) a chemical element. Chlorine is a poisonous greenish gas with a strong smell. It is often used in swimming pools to keep the water clean.

chloro·fluoro·car·bon /ˌklɔːrəʊˈflʊərəʊkɑːbən; *NAmE* ˌklɔːroʊˈflʊroʊkɑːrbən/ *noun* (*chemistry*) a CFC; a COMPOUND containing CARBON FLUORINE and CHLORINE that is harmful to the OZONE LAYER

chloro·form /ˈklɒrəfɔːm; *NAmE* ˈklɔːrəfɔːrm/ *noun* [U] (*symb.* $CHCl_3$) a clear liquid used in the past in medicine, etc. to make people unconscious, for example before an operation

chloro·phyll /ˈklɒrəfɪl; *NAmE* ˈklɔːr-/ *noun* [U] the green substance in plants that absorbs light from the sun to help them grow ➲ see also PHOTOSYNTHESIS

chloro·plast /ˈklɒrəplɑːst; *NAmE* ˈklɔːrəplæst/ *noun* (*biology*) the structure in plant cells that contains CHLOROPHYLL and in which PHOTOSYNTHESIS takes place

choc /tʃɒk; *NAmE* tʃɑːk/ *noun* (*BrE, informal*) a chocolate: *a box of chocs*

choca·hol·ic = CHOCOHOLIC

choccy /ˈtʃɒki; *NAmE* ˈtʃɑːki/ *noun* (*pl.* -ies) [U, C] (*BrE, informal*) chocolate; a sweet/candy made of chocolate: *a box of choccies*

ˈ**choc ice** *noun* (*BrE*) a small block of ice cream covered with chocolate

chock-a-block /ˌtʃɒk ə ˈblɒk; *NAmE* ˌtʃɑːk ə ˈblɑːk/ (also **chocka** /ˈtʃɒkə; *NAmE* ˈtʃɑːkə/) *adj.* [not before noun] ~ (**with sth/sb**) (*BrE, informal*) very full of things or people pressed close together: *The shelves were chock-a-block with ornaments.* ◇ *It was chock-a-block in town today* (= full of people).

chock-full /ˌtʃɒk ˈfʊl; *NAmE* ˌtʃɑːk/ *adj.* [not before noun] ~ (**of sth/sb**) (*informal*) completely full

choco·hol·ic (also **choca·hol·ic**) /ˌtʃɒkəˈhɒlɪk; *NAmE* ˌtʃɑːkəˈhɑːlɪk; -ˈhɔːlɪk/ *noun* (*informal*) a person who likes chocolate very much and eats a lot of it

choc·olate O→ /ˈtʃɒklət; *NAmE* ˈtʃɑːk-; ˈtʃɔːk-/ *noun* **1** O→ [U] a hard brown sweet food made from COCOA BEANS, used in cooking to add flavour to cakes, etc. or eaten as a sweet/candy: ***a bar/piece of chocolate*** ◇ *a chocolate cake* ◇ *a chocolate factory* ➲ see also MILK CHOCOLATE, PLAIN CHOCOLATE **2** O→ [C] a sweet/candy that is made of or covered with chocolate: *a box of chocolates* **3** [U, C] (*BrE*) = HOT CHOCOLATE: *a mug of drinking chocolate* ➲ compare COCOA **4** [U] a dark brown colour

ˈ**chocolate-box** *adj.* [only before noun] (*BrE*) (especially of places) very pretty, but in a way that does not seem real: *a chocolate-box village*

choice O→ /tʃɔɪs/ *noun, adj.*
■ ***noun*** **1** O→ [C] ~ (**between A and B**) an act of choosing between two or more possibilities; something that you can choose: *women forced to make a choice between family and career* ◇ *We are faced with a difficult choice.* ◇ *We aim to help students make more informed career choices.* ◇ *There is a wide range of choices open to you.* ➲ SYNONYMS at OPTION **2** O→ [U, sing.] the right to choose or the possibility of choosing: *If I had the choice, I would stop working tomor-*

row. ◇ He **had no choice** but to leave (= this was the only thing he could do). ◇ *She's going to do it. She doesn't have* **much choice**, *really, does she?* ◇ *This government is committed to extending parental choice in education.* **3** ⊶ [C] a person or thing that is chosen: *She's the obvious choice for the job.* ◇ *Hawaii remains a popular choice for winter vacation travel.* ◇ *This colour wasn't my first choice.* ◇ *She wouldn't be my choice as manager.* **4** ⊶ [sing., U] the number or range of different things from which to choose: *The menu has a good choice of desserts.* ◇ *There wasn't* **much choice** *of colour.* ➲ see also HOBSON'S CHOICE, MULTIPLE-CHOICE

IDM **by 'choice** because you have chosen: *I wouldn't go there by choice.* **of 'choice (for sb/sth)** (used after a noun) that is chosen by a particular group of people or for a particular purpose: *It's the software of choice for business use.* **of your 'choice** that you choose yourself: *First prize will be a meal for two at the restaurant of your choice.* ➲ more at PAY *v.*, SPOILT

■ ***adj.*** (**choicer, choicest**) [only before noun] **1** (especially of food) of very good quality **2** (*NAmE*) (of meat) of very good, but not the highest, quality **3** **~ words/phrases** carefully chosen words or phrases: *She summed up the situation in a few choice phrases.* ◇ (*humorous*) *He used some pretty choice* (= rude or offensive) *language.*

Synonyms

choice

favourite • preference • selection • pick

These are all words for a person or thing that is chosen, or that is liked more than others.

choice a person or thing that is chosen: *She's the obvious choice for the job.*

favourite/favorite a person or thing that you like more than the others of the same type: *Which one's your favourite?*

preference a thing that is liked better or best: *Tastes and preferences vary from individual to individual.*

FAVOURITE OR PREFERENCE?

Your **favourites** are the things you like best, and that you have, do, listen to, etc. often; your **preferences** are the things that you would rather have or do if you can choose.

selection a number of people or things that have been chosen from a larger group: *A selection of reader's comments are published below.*

pick (*rather informal, especially NAmE*) a person or thing that is chosen: *She was his pick for best actress.*

PATTERNS

- sb's choice/favourite/pick **for** sth
- sb's choice/selection/pick **as** sth
- an **obvious** choice/favourite/selection
- a(n) **excellent/good/popular/fine** choice/selection

choir /ˈkwaɪə(r)/ *noun* **1** [C+sing./pl. v.] a group of people who sing together, for example in church services or public performances: *She sings in the school choir.* ➲ COLLOCATIONS at MUSIC **2** [C] the part of a church where the choir sits during services

choir·boy /ˈkwaɪəbɔɪ; *NAmE* ˈkwaɪərbɔɪ/, **choir·girl** /ˈkwaɪəgɜːl; *NAmE* ˈkwaɪərgɜːrl/ *noun* a boy or girl who sings in the choir of a church ➲ see also CHORISTER

choir·mas·ter /ˈkwaɪəmɑːstə(r); *NAmE* ˈkwaɪərmæstər/ *noun* a person who trains a CHOIR to sing

choke /tʃəʊk; *NAmE* tʃoʊk/ *verb, noun*

■ ***verb*** **1** [I, T] to be unable to breathe because the passage to your lungs is blocked or you cannot get enough air; to make sb unable to breathe: *She almost* **choked to death** *in the thick fumes.* ◇ **~ on sth** *He was choking on a piece of toast.* ◇ **~ sb** *Very small toys can choke a baby.* **2** [T] **~ sb** to make sb stop breathing by squeezing their throat SYN **strangle**: *He may have been choked or poisoned.* **3** [I, T] to be unable to speak normally especially because of strong emotion; to make sb feel too emotional to speak normally: **~ (with sth)** *His voice was choking with rage.* ◇ **~ sth** *Despair choked her words.* ◇ *'I can't bear it,' he said in a choked voice.* ➲ see also CHOKED **4** [T] to block or fill a passage, space, etc. so that movement is difficult: **~ sth (with sth)** *The pond was choked with rotten leaves.* ◇ **~ sth up (with sth)** *The roads are choked up with traffic.* **5** [I] (*NAmE, informal*) to fail at sth, for example because you are nervous

PHR V **ˌchoke sth↔ˈback** to try hard to prevent your feelings from showing: *to* **choke back tears/anger/sobs** **ˌchoke sth↔ˈdown** to swallow sth with difficulty **ˌchoke sth↔ˈoff 1** to prevent or limit sth: *High prices have choked off demand.* **2** to interrupt sth; to stop sth: *Her screams were suddenly choked off.* **ˌchoke ˈout | choke out sth** to say sth with great difficulty because you feel a strong emotion: *He choked out a reply.* ◇ **+ speech** *'I hate you!' she choked out.* **ˌchoke ˈup** (*NAmE*) to find it difficult to speak, because of the strong emotion that you are feeling: *She choked up when she began to talk about her mother.*

■ ***noun*** **1** a device that controls the amount of air flowing into the engine of a vehicle **2** an act or the sound of choking

choked /tʃəʊkt; *NAmE* tʃoʊkt/ *adj.* [not before noun] **~ up (about sth)** (*BrE* also, *informal*) **~ (about sth)** upset or angry about sth, so that you find it difficult to speak

choker /ˈtʃəʊkə(r); *NAmE* ˈtʃoʊ-/ *noun* a piece of jewellery or narrow band of cloth worn closely around the neck

chola /ˈtʃəʊlə; *NAmE* ˈtʃoʊlə/ *noun* (from *Spanish*) a woman from Latin America who has both Spanish and Native American ANCESTORS ➲ compare CHOLO

chol·era /ˈkɒlərə; *NAmE* ˈkɑːl-/ *noun* [U] a disease caught from infected water that causes severe DIARRHOEA and VOMITING and often causes death

chol·er·ic /ˈkɒlərɪk; *NAmE* ˈkɑːl-/ *adj.* (*formal*) easily made angry SYN **bad-tempered**

chol·es·terol /kəˈlestərɒl; *NAmE* -rɔːl/ *noun* [U] a substance found in blood, fat and most TISSUES of the body. Too much cholesterol can cause heart disease. ➲ COLLOCATIONS at DIET

cholo /ˈtʃəʊləʊ; *NAmE* ˈtʃoʊloʊ/ *noun* (*pl.* **-os**) a person from Latin America who has both Spanish and Native American ANCESTORS ➲ compare CHOLA

chomp /tʃɒmp; *NAmE* tʃɑːmp; tʃɔːmp/ *verb* [I, T] to eat or bite food noisily SYN **munch**: **~ (away) (on/through sth)** *She was chomping away on a bagel.* ◇ **~ sth** *He* **chomped his way** *through two hot dogs.*

choo-choo /ˈtʃuːtʃuː/ *noun* (*pl.* **choo-choos**) a child's word for a train

chook /tʃʊk/ *noun* (*AustralE, NZE, informal*) **1** a chicken **2** an offensive word for an older woman

choose ⊶ /tʃuːz/ *verb* (**chose** /tʃəʊz; *NAmE* tʃoʊz/, **chosen** /ˈtʃəʊzn; *NAmE* ˈtʃoʊzn/)

1 ⊶ [I, T] to decide which thing or person you want out of the ones that are available: *You choose, I can't decide.* ◇ *There are plenty of restaurants to choose from.* ◇ **~ between A and/or B** *She had to choose between staying in the UK or going home.* ◇ **~ sth** *Sarah chose her words carefully.* ◇ *This site has been chosen for the new school.* ◇ **~ A from B** *We have to choose a new manager from a shortlist of five candidates.* ◇ **~ sb/sth as/for sth** *He chose banking as a career.* ◇ *We chose Phil McSweeney as/for chairperson.* ◇ **~ whether, wat, etc...** *You'll have to choose whether to buy it or not.* ◇ **~ to do sth** *We chose to go by train.* ◇ **~ sb to be/do sth** *We chose Phil McSweeney to be chairperson.* **2** ⊶ [I, T] to prefer or decide to do sth: *Employees can retire at 60 if they choose.* ◇ **~ to do sth** *Many people choose not to marry.* ➲ see also CHOICE *n.*

IDM **there is nothing/not much/little to choose between A and B** there is very little difference between two or more things or people ➲ more at PICK *v.*

chooser /ˈtʃuːzə(r)/ *noun* IDM see BEGGAR *n.*

C

Synonyms

choose

select • pick • decide • opt • go for

These words all mean to decide which thing or person you want out of the ones that are available.

choose to decide which thing or person you want out of the ones that are available: *You choose—I can't decide.*

select [often passive] to choose sb/sth, usually carefully, from a group of people or things: *He was selected for the team.* ◇ *a randomly selected sample of 23 schools*

pick (*rather informal*) to choose sb/sth from a group of people or things: *She picked the best cake for herself.*

CHOOSE, SELECT OR PICK?

Choose is the most general of these words and the only one that can be used without an object. When you **select** sth, you choose it carefully, unless you actually say that it is *selected randomly/at random*. **Pick** is a more informal word and often a less careful action, used especially when the choice being made is not very important.

decide to choose between two or more possibilities: *We're still trying to* ***decide on*** *a venue.*

opt to choose to take or not to take a particular course of action: *After graduating she opted for a career in music.* ◇ *After a lot of thought, I* ***opted against*** *buying a motorbike.*

go for sth (*rather informal*) to choose sth: *I think I'll go for the fruit salad.*

PATTERNS

- to choose/select/pick/decide **between** A and/or B
- to choose/select/pick A **from** B
- to opt/go **for** sb/sth
- to choose/decide/opt **to do sth**
- to choose/select/pick sb/sth **carefully/at random**
- **randomly** chosen/selected/picked

choosy /ˈtʃuːzi/ *adj.* (**choos·ier**, **choosi·est**) (*informal*) careful in choosing; difficult to please **SYN** **fussy**, **picky**: *I'm very choosy about my clothes.*

chop 0-ᴡ /tʃɒp; *NAmE* tʃɑːp/ *verb*, *noun*
■ ***verb*** (-pp-) **1** 0-ᴡ to cut sth into pieces with a sharp tool such as a knife: **~ sth** *He was chopping logs for firewood.* ◇ *Add the finely chopped onions.* ◇ **~ sth** (**up**) (**into sth**) *Chop the carrots up into small pieces.* ◇ (*figurative*) *The country was chopped up into small administrative areas.* ➲ COLLOCATIONS at COOKING ➲ VISUAL VOCAB page V25 **2** [usually passive] **~ sth** (**from sth**) (**to sth**) (*informal*) to reduce sth by a large amount; to stop sth **SYN** **cut**: *The share price was chopped from 50 pence to 20 pence.* **3 ~ sb/sth** to hit sb/sth with a short downward stroke or blow
IDM ˌ**chop and** ˈ**change** (*BrE*, *informal*) to keep changing your mind or what you are doing
PHR V ˈ**chop** (**away**) **at sth** to aim blows at sth with a heavy sharp tool such as an AXE ˌ**chop sth**↔ˈ**down** 0-ᴡ to make sth, such as a tree, fall by cutting it at the base with a sharp tool ˌ**chop sth**↔ˈ**off** (**sth**) 0-ᴡ to remove sth by cutting it with a sharp tool: *He chopped a branch off the tree.* ◇ (*informal*) *Anne Boleyn had her head chopped off.*
■ ***noun*** **1** [C] a thick slice of meat with a bone attached to it, especially from a pig or sheep: *a* ***pork/lamb chop*** **2** [C] an act of cutting sth with a quick downward movement using an AXE or a knife **3** [C] an act of hitting sb/sth with the side of your hand in a quick downward movement: *a karate chop* **4 chops** [pl.] (*informal*) the part of a person's or an animal's face around the mouth: *The dog sat licking its chops.*
IDM **get/be given the** ˈ**chop** (*BrE*, *informal*) **1** (of a person) to be dismissed from a job: *The whole department has been given the chop.* **2** (of a plan, project, etc.) to be stopped or ended: *Three more schemes have got the chop.* **be for the** ˈ**chop** (*BrE*, *informal*) **1** (of a person) to be likely to be dismissed from a job: *Who's next for the chop?* **2** (of a plan, project, etc.) to be likely to be stopped or ended **not much** ˈ**chop** (*AustralE*, *NZE*, *informal*) not very good or useful

ˌ**chop-**ˈ**chop** *exclamation* (*BrE*, *informal*) hurry up!: *Chop-chop! We haven't got all day!* **ORIGIN** From pidgin English based on a Chinese word for 'quick'.

chop·per /ˈtʃɒpə(r); *NAmE* ˈtʃɑːp-/ *noun* **1** [C] (*informal*) = HELICOPTER **2** [C] a large heavy knife or small AXE **3** [C] (*NAmE*) a type of motorcycle with a very long piece of metal connecting the front wheel to the HANDLEBARS **4 choppers** [pl.] (*informal*) teeth

ˈ**chopping board** (*BrE*) (*NAmE* ˈ**cutting board**) *noun* a board made of wood or plastic used for cutting meat or vegetables on ➲ VISUAL VOCAB page V23

choppy /ˈtʃɒpi; *NAmE* ˈtʃɑːpi/ *adj.* (**chop·pier**, **chop·pi·est**) **1** (of the sea, etc.) with a lot of small waves; not calm: *choppy waters* **2** (*NAmE*, *disapproving*) (of a style of writing) containing a lot of short sentences and changing topics too often

chop·stick /ˈtʃɒpstɪk; *NAmE* ˈtʃɑːp-/ *noun* [usually pl.] either of a pair of thin sticks that are used for eating with, especially in some Asian countries ➲ VISUAL VOCAB page V19 ➲ picture at STICK

chop suey /ˌtʃɒp ˈsuːi; *NAmE* ˌtʃɑːp/ *noun* [U] a Chinese-style dish of small pieces of meat fried with vegetables and served with rice

choral /ˈkɔːrəl/ *adj.* connected with, written for or sung by a CHOIR (= a group of singers): *choral music*

chor·ale /kɒˈrɑːl; *NAmE* kəˈræl; -ˈrɑːl/ *noun* **1** a piece of church music sung by a group of singers **2** (*especially NAmE*) a group of singers; a CHOIR

chord /kɔːd; *NAmE* kɔːrd/ *noun* **1** (*music*) two or more notes played together **2** (*mathematics*) a straight line that joins two points on a curve ➲ VISUAL VOCAB page V58 ➲ see also VOCAL CORDS
IDM **strike/touch a** ˈ**chord** (**with sb**) to say or do sth that makes people feel sympathy or enthusiasm: *The speaker had obviously struck a chord with his audience.*

chore /tʃɔː(r)/ *noun* **1** a task that you do regularly: *doing the* ***household/domestic chores*** ➲ SYNONYMS at TASK **2** an unpleasant or boring task: *Shopping's a real chore for me.*

cho·rea /kəˈriə/ *noun* [U] (*medical*) a condition in which parts of the body make quick sudden movements that cannot be controlled

choreo·graph /ˈkɒriəgrɑːf; -græf; *NAmE* ˈkɔːriəgræf/ *verb* **~ sth** to design and arrange the steps and movements for dancers in a BALLET or a show: (*figurative*) *There was some carefully choreographed flag-waving as the President drove by.*

chore·og·raphy /ˌkɒriˈɒgrəfi; *NAmE* ˌkɔːriˈɑːg-/ *noun* [U] the art of designing and arranging the steps and movements in dances, especially in BALLET; the steps and movements in a particular ballet or show ▸ **chore·og·raph·er** /ˌkɒriˈɒgrəfə(r); *NAmE* ˌkɔːriˈɑːg-/ *noun* **choreo·graph·ic** /ˌkɒriəˈgræfɪk; *NAmE* ˌkɔːriə-/ *adj.*

chor·ic /ˈkɔːrɪk; *BrE* also ˈkɒrɪk/ *adj.* (*technical*) relating to a CHORUS that is spoken in a play, etc.

chor·is·ter /ˈkɒrɪstə(r); *NAmE* ˈkɔːr-; ˈkɑːr-/ *noun* a person, especially a boy, who sings in the CHOIR of a church

chor·izo /tʃəˈriːzəʊ; *NAmE* -zoʊ/ *noun* [U, C] (*pl.* **-os**) (from *Spanish*) a spicy Spanish or Latin American SAUSAGE

chor·tle /ˈtʃɔːtl; *NAmE* ˈtʃɔːrtl/ *verb* [I, T] to laugh loudly with pleasure or because you are amused: *Gill chortled with delight.* ▸ **chor·tle** *noun*

chorus /ˈkɔːrəs/ *noun*, *verb*
■ ***noun*** **1** [C] part of a song that is sung after each VERSE **SYN** **refrain**: *Everyone joined in the chorus.* **2** [C] a piece of music, usually part of a larger work, that is written for a CHOIR (= a group of singers): *the Hallelujah Chorus* **3** [C+sing./pl. v.] (often in names) a large group of singers **SYN** **choir**: *the Bath Festival Chorus* **4** [C+sing./pl. v.] a group of performers who sing and dance in a musical show: *the chorus line* (= a line of singers and dancers performing together) **5 a ~ of sth** [sing.] the sound of a lot of

people expressing approval or disapproval at the same time: *a **chorus of praise/complaint*** ◇ *a chorus of voices calling for her resignation* ➲ see also DAWN CHORUS **6** [sing.+ sing./pl. v.] (in ancient Greek drama) a group of performers who comment together on the events of the play **7** [sing.] (especially in 16th century drama) an actor who speaks the opening and closing words of the play

C

IDM **in chorus** all together SYN **in unison**: *'Thank you,' they said in chorus.*

■ ***verb*** **~ sth** to sing or say sth all together: *'Hello, Paul,' they chorused.*

'chorus girl *noun* a girl or young woman who is a member of the chorus in a musical show, etc.

chose *past tense* of CHOOSE

chosen *past part.* of CHOOSE

chough /tʃʌf/ *noun* a bird of the CROW family, with blue-black feathers and red legs

choux pastry /ˌʃuː 'peɪstri/ *noun* [U] a type of very light PASTRY made with eggs

chow /tʃaʊ/ *noun* **1** [U] (*slang*) food **2** (also **'chow chow**) [C] a dog with long thick hair, a curled tail and a blue-black tongue, originally from China

chow·der /'tʃaʊdə(r)/ *noun* [U] a thick soup made with fish and vegetables: *clam chowder* ➲ see also BISQUE

chowk /tʃaʊk/ *noun* (*IndE*) an open area with a market at a place where two roads meet in a city: *Chandni Chowk*

chow mein /ˌtʃaʊ 'meɪn/ *noun* [U] a Chinese-style dish of fried NOODLES served with small pieces of meat and vegetables: *chicken chow mein*

Chrimbo (also **Crimbo**) /'krɪmbəʊ; *NAmE* -boʊ/ *noun* [U] (*BrE, informal*) Christmas

Chris·sake /'kraɪseɪk/ (also **Chris·sakes** /-seɪks/) *noun* [U] (*taboo, informal*)

IDM **for 'Chrissake** a swear word that many people find offensive, used to show that you are angry, annoyed or surprised: *For Chrissake, listen!*

Christ /kraɪst/ (also **Jesus**, **Jesus 'Christ**) *noun, exclamation*

■ ***noun*** the man that Christians believe is the son of God and on whose teachings the Christian religion is based

■ ***exclamation*** (*taboo, informal*) a swear word that many people find offensive, used to show that you are angry, annoyed or surprised: *Christ! Look at the time—I'm late!*

chris·ten /'krɪsn/ *verb* **1** to give a name to a baby at his or her baptism to welcome him or her into the Christian Church: **~ sb + noun** *The child was christened Mary.* ◇ **~ sb** *Did you have your children christened?* **2 ~ sb/sth** (+ **noun**) to give a name to sb/sth: *This area has been christened 'Britain's last wilderness'.* ◇ *They christened the boat 'Oceania'.* **3 ~ sth** (*informal*) to use sth for the first time

Chris·ten·dom /'krɪsndəm/ *noun* [U] (*old-fashioned*) all the Christian people and countries of the world

chris·ten·ing /'krɪsnɪŋ/ *noun* a Christian ceremony in which a baby is officially named and welcomed into the Christian Church ➲ compare BAPTISM

Chris·tian /'krɪstʃən/ *adj., noun*

■ ***adj.*** **1** based on or believing the teachings of Jesus Christ: *the **Christian Church/faith/religion*** ◇ *She had a Christian upbringing.* ◇ *a Christian country* **2** connected with Christians: *the Christian sector of the city* **3** (also **christian**) showing the qualities that are thought of as typical of a Christian; good and kind

■ ***noun*** a person who believes in the teachings of Jesus Christ or has been BAPTIZED in a Christian church: *Only 10% of the population are now practising Christians.*

the 'Christian era *noun* [sing.] the period of time that begins with the birth of Christ

Chris·tian·ity /ˌkrɪsti'ænəti/ *noun* [U] the religion that is based on the teachings of Jesus Christ and the belief that he was the son of God

'Christian name *noun* (*BrE*) (in Western countries) a name given to sb when they are born or when they are CHRISTENED; a personal name, not a family name: *We're all on Christian name terms here.*

ˌChristian 'Science *noun* [U] the beliefs of a religious group called the Church of Christ, Scientist, which include the belief that the physical world is not real and that you can cure illness only by prayer ▶ **ˌChristian 'Scientist** *noun*

Christ·mas /'krɪsməs/ *noun* [U, C] **1** (also **ˌChristmas 'Day**) 25 December, the day when Christians celebrate the birth of Christ: ***Christmas dinner/presents*** ➲ see also BOXING DAY **2** (also **Christ·mas·time**) the period that includes Christmas Day and the days close to it: *the **Christmas holidays/vacation*** ◇ *Are you spending Christmas with your family?* ◇ *Happy Christmas!* ◇ *Merry Christmas and a Happy New Year!* ➲ see also WHITE CHRISTMAS

'Christmas box *noun* (*BrE, old-fashioned*) a small gift, usually of money, given at Christmas to sb who provides a service during the year, for example a POSTMAN

'Christmas cake *noun* [C, U] a fruit cake covered with MARZIPAN and ICING, traditionally eaten in Britain and some other countries at Christmas

'Christmas card *noun* a card with a picture on it that you send to friends and relatives at Christmas with your good wishes

ˌChristmas 'carol *noun* = CAROL

ˌChristmas 'cracker *noun* = CRACKER

ˌChristmas 'Eve *noun* [U, C] the day before Christmas Day, 24 December; the evening of this day

ˌChristmas 'pudding *noun* [C, U] a hot PUDDING (= a sweet dish) like a dark fruit cake, traditionally eaten in Britain at Christmas

ˌChristmas 'stocking (also **stock·ing**) *noun* a long sock which children leave out when they go to bed on Christmas Eve so that it can be filled with presents

Christ·massy /'krɪsməsi/ *adj.* (*informal*) typical of Christmas: *We put up the decorations and the tree and started to feel Christmassy at last.*

Christ·mas·time /'krɪsməstaɪm/ *noun* [U, C] = CHRISTMAS (2)

'Christmas tree *noun* an EVERGREEN tree, or an artificial tree that looks similar, that people cover with decorations and coloured lights and have in their homes or outside at Christmas

chroma /'krəʊmə; *NAmE* 'kroʊmə/ *noun* [U] (*technical*) the degree to which a colour is pure or strong, or the fact that it is pure or strong

chro·mat·ic /krə'mætɪk/ *adj.* (*music*) of the **chromatic scale**, a series of musical notes that rise and fall in SEMITONES/HALF TONES ➲ compare DIATONIC

chro·ma·tog·raphy /ˌkrəʊmə'tɒgrəfi; *NAmE* ˌkroʊmə'tɑːg-/ *noun* [U] (*chemistry*) the separation of a mixture by passing it through a material through which some parts of the mixture travel further than others ▶ **chro·ma·to·graph·ic** /krəʊˌmætə'græfɪk; *NAmE* ˌkroʊ-/ *adj.*

chrome /krəʊm; *NAmE* kroʊm/ *noun* [U] a hard shiny metal used especially as a covering which protects another metal; chromium or an ALLOY of chromium and other metals

ˌchrome 'steel (also **ˌchromium 'steel**) *noun* [U] a hard steel containing CHROMIUM that is used for making tools

chro·mium /'krəʊmiəm; *NAmE* 'kroʊ-/ *noun* [U] (*symb.* Cr) a chemical element. Chromium is a hard grey metal that shines brightly when polished and is often used to cover other metals in order to prevent them from RUSTING: *chromium-plated steel*

ˌchromium 'steel *noun* [U] = CHROME STEEL

chromo·some /'krəʊməsəʊm; *NAmE* 'kroʊməsoʊm/ *noun* (*biology*) one of the very small structures like threads in the NUCLEI (= central parts) of animal and plant cells, that carry the GENES ➲ see also SEX CHROMOSOME, X CHROMOSOME, Y CHROMOSOME ▶ **chromo·somal**

/ˌkrəʊməˈsəʊməl; *NAmE* ˌkroʊməˈsoʊməl/ *adj.*: *chromosomal abnormalities*

chron·ic /ˈkrɒnɪk; *NAmE* ˈkrɑːn-/ *adj.* **1** (especially of a disease) lasting for a long time; difficult to cure or get rid of: *chronic bronchitis/arthritis/asthma* ◇ *the country's chronic unemployment problem* ◇ *a chronic shortage of housing in rural areas* OPP **acute 2** having had a disease for a long time: *a* ***chronic alcoholic/depressive*** **3** (*BrE, informal*) very bad: *The film was just chronic.* ▸ **chron·ic·al·ly** /ˈkrɒnɪkli; *NAmE* ˈkrɑːn-/ *adv.*: *a hospital for the chronically ill*

ˌ**chronic faˈtigue syndrome** (*BrE* also **ME, my·al·gic en·ceph·alo·my·eli·tis**) *noun* [U] an illness that makes people feel extremely weak and tired and that can last a long time

chron·icle /ˈkrɒnɪkl; *NAmE* ˈkrɑːn-/ *noun, verb*

▪ ***noun*** a written record of events in the order in which they happened: *the Anglo-Saxon Chronicle* ◇ *Her latest novel is a chronicle of life in a Devon village.*

▪ ***verb*** **~ sth** (*formal*) to record events in the order in which they happened: *Her achievements are chronicled in a new biography out this week.* ▸ **chron·ic·ler** /ˈkrɒnɪklə(r); *NAmE* ˈkrɑːn-/ *noun*

chrono- /ˈkrɒnəʊ; *NAmE* ˈkrɑːnoʊ/ *combining form* (in nouns, adjectives and adverbs) connected with time: *chronological*

chrono·graph /ˈkrɒnəgrɑːf; *NAmE* ˈkrɑːnəgræf/ *noun* **1** a device for recording time extremely accurately **2** a STOPWATCH

chrono·logic·al /ˌkrɒnəˈlɒdʒɪkl; *NAmE* ˌkrɑːnəˈlɑːdʒ-/ *adj.* **1** (of a number of events) arranged in the order in which they happened: *The facts should be presented* ***in chronological order.*** **2 ~ age** (*formal*) the number of years a person has lived as opposed to their level of physical, mental or emotional development ➲ compare MENTAL AGE ▸ **chrono·logic·al·ly** /-kli/ *adv.*

chron·ology /krəˈnɒlədʒi; *NAmE* -ˈnɑːl-/ *noun* (*pl.* -ies) [U, C] the order in which a series of events happened; a list of these events in order: *Historians seem to have confused the chronology of these events.* ◇ *a chronology of Mozart's life*

chron·om·eter /krəˈnɒmɪtə(r); *NAmE* -ˈnɑːm-/ *noun* a very accurate clock, especially one used at sea

chrys·alis /ˈkrɪsəlɪs/ *noun* (also **chrys·alid**) the form of an insect, especially a BUTTERFLY or MOTH, while it is changing into an adult inside a hard case, also called a chrysalis ➲ VISUAL VOCAB page V11 ➲ compare PUPA

chrys·an·the·mum /krɪˈsænθəməm; -ˈzæn-/ *noun* a large, brightly coloured garden flower that is shaped like a ball and made up of many long narrow PETALS ➲ VISUAL VOCAB page V9

chub /tʃʌb/ *noun* (*pl.* **chub**) a FRESHWATER fish with a thick body

chubby /ˈtʃʌbi/ *adj.* (**chub·bier, chub·bi·est**) slightly fat in a way that people usually find attractive: ***chubby cheeks/fingers/hands*** ▸ **chub·bi·ness** *noun* [U]

chuck /tʃʌk/ *verb, noun*

▪ ***verb*** **1** (*informal, especially BrE*) to throw sth carelessly or without much thought: **~ sth** (**+ adv./prep.**) *He chucked the paper in a drawer.* ◇ **~ sb sth** *Chuck me the newspaper, would you?* ➲ SYNONYMS at THROW **2** (*informal*) to give up or stop doing sth: **~ sth** *You haven't chucked your job!* ◇ **~ sth in/up** *I'm going to* ***chuck it all in*** (= give up my job) *and go abroad.* **3 ~ sb** (*BrE, informal*) to leave your boyfriend or girlfriend and stop having a relationship with him or her: *Has he chucked her?* **4 ~ sth** (*informal*) to throw sth away: *That's no good—just chuck it.*

IDM **chuck sb under the chin** (*old-fashioned, BrE*) to touch sb gently under the chin in a friendly way **it's ˈchucking it down** (*BrE, informal*) it's raining heavily

PHR V ˌ**chuck sth↔aˈway** | ˌ**chuck sth↔ˈout** (*informal*) to throw sth away: *Those old clothes can be chucked out.* ˌ**chuck sb ˈoff** (**sth**) | ˌ**chuck sb ˈout** (**of sth**) (*informal*) to force sb to leave a place or a job: *They got chucked off the bus.* ◇ *You can't just chuck him out.*

▪ ***noun*** **1** [C] a part of a tool such as a DRILL that can be adjusted to hold sth tightly ➲ VISUAL VOCAB page V17 **2** [sing.] (*NEngE, informal*) a friendly way of addressing sb: *What's up with you, chuck?* **3** (also ˌ**chuck ˈsteak**) [U] meat from the shoulder of a cow

ˌ**chucker ˈout** *noun* (*BrE, informal*) a person employed to make people leave a social event if they have not been invited or if they cause trouble

C

chuckle /ˈtʃʌkl/ *verb* [I] **~** (**at/about sth**) to laugh quietly: *She chuckled at the memory.* ▸ **chuckle** *noun*: *She gave a chuckle of delight.*

chuffed /tʃʌft/ *adj.* [not before noun] **~** (**about sth**) (*BrE, informal*) very pleased

chuff·ing /ˈtʃʌfɪŋ/ *adj.* (*NEngE, slang*) a mild swear word that some people use when they are annoyed, to avoid saying 'fucking': *The whole chuffing world's gone mad.*

chug /tʃʌg/ *verb, noun*

▪ ***verb*** (-gg-) **1** [I] (**+ adv./prep.**) to move making the sound of an engine running slowly: *The boat chugged down the river.* **2** [T] **~ sth** (*NAmE, slang*) to drink all of sth quickly without stopping

▪ ***noun*** the sound made by a chugging engine

chukka /ˈtʃʌkə/ *noun* one of the periods of 7½ minutes into which a game of POLO is divided

chum /tʃʌm/ *noun* (*old-fashioned, informal*) a friend: *an old school chum*

chummy /ˈtʃʌmi/ *adj.* (*old-fashioned, informal*) very friendly ▸ **chum·mily** *adv.* **chum·mi·ness** *noun* [U]

chump /tʃʌmp/ *noun* (*old-fashioned, informal*) a stupid person: *Don't be such a chump!*

chun·der /ˈtʃʌndə(r)/ *verb* [I] (*BrE, informal*) to VOMIT ▸ **chun·der** *noun* [U]

chunk /tʃʌŋk/ *noun* **1** a thick solid piece that has been cut or broken off sth: *a chunk of cheese/masonry* **2** (*informal*) a fairly large amount of sth: *I've already written a fair chunk of the article.* **3** (*linguistics*) a phrase or group of words which can be learnt as a unit by sb who is learning a language. Examples of chunks are 'Can I have the bill, please?' and 'Pleased to meet you'. IDM see BLOW *v.*

chunk·ing /ˈtʃʌŋkɪŋ/ *noun* [U] (*linguistics*) the use of chunks (3) in language

chunky /ˈtʃʌŋki/ *adj.* (**chunki·er, chunki·est**) **1** thick and heavy: *a chunky gold bracelet* ◇ (*BrE*) *a chunky sweater* **2** having a short strong body: *a squat chunky man* **3** (of food) containing thick pieces: *chunky marmalade*

chun·ter /ˈtʃʌntə(r)/ *verb* [I] **~** (**on**) (**about sth**) (*BrE, informal*) to talk or complain about sth in a way that other people think is boring or annoying SYN **witter**

church 0-w /tʃɜːtʃ; *NAmE* tʃɜːrtʃ/ *noun*
1 0-w [C] a building where Christians go to worship: *a church tower* ◇ *The procession moved into the church.* ◇ *church services* **2** 0-w [U] a service or services in a church: *How often do you* ***go to church?*** ◇ (*BrE*) *They're* ***at church*** (= attending a church service). ◇ (*NAmE*) *They're* ***in church.*** ◇ *Church is at 9 o'clock.* ➲ COLLOCATIONS at RELIGION ➲ note at SCHOOL **3** 0-w **Church** [C] a particular group of Christians: *the Anglican Church* ◇ *the Catholic Church* ◇ *the Free Churches* ➲ see also DENOMINATION **4** 0-w (**the**) **Church** [sing.] the ministers of the Christian religion; the institution of the Christian religion: *The Church has a duty to condemn violence.* ◇ *the conflict between Church and State* ◇ *to go into the Church* (= to become a Christian minister) IDM see BROAD *adj.*

church·goer /ˈtʃɜːtʃgəʊə(r); *NAmE* ˈtʃɜːrtʃgoʊər/ *noun* a person who goes to church services regularly ▸ **church·going** *noun* [U]

church·man /ˈtʃɜːtʃmən; *NAmE* ˈtʃɜːrtʃ-/, **church·woman** /ˈtʃɜːtʃwʊmən; *NAmE* ˈtʃɜːrtʃ-/ *noun* (*pl.* -men /-mən/, -women /-wɪmɪn/) = CLERGYMAN, CLERGYWOMAN

the ˌ**Church of ˈEngland** *noun* (*abbr.* CE, C of E) [sing.] the official Church in England, whose leader is the Queen or King

the ˌChurch of ˈScotland *noun* [sing.] the official (Presbyterian) Church in Scotland

church·war·den /ˌtʃɜːtʃˈwɔːdn; *NAmE* ˌtʃɜːrtʃˈwɔːrdn/ *noun* (in the Anglican Church) a person who is chosen by the members of a church to take care of church property and money

churchy /ˈtʃɜːtʃi; *NAmE* ˈtʃɜːr-/ *adj.* (**church·ier, churchi·est**) (*disapproving*) (of a person) religious in a way that involves going to church, PRAYING, etc. a lot, but often not accepting other people's views

church·yard /ˈtʃɜːtʃjɑːd; *NAmE* ˈtʃɜːrtʃjɑːrd/ *noun* an area of land around a church, often used for burying people in ➲ compare CEMETERY, GRAVEYARD

churi·dar /ˈtʃʊridɑː(r)/ *noun* tight trousers worn with a KAMEEZ OR KURTA

churl /tʃɜːl; *NAmE* tʃɜːrl/ *noun* (*old-fashioned*) a rude unpleasant person

churl·ish /ˈtʃɜːlɪʃ; *NAmE* ˈtʃɜːrlɪʃ/ *adj.* (*formal*) rude or bad-tempered: *It would be churlish to refuse such a generous offer.* ▶ **churl·ish·ly** *adv.* **churl·ish·ness** *noun* [U]

churn /tʃɜːn; *NAmE* tʃɜːrn/ *verb, noun*
■ ***verb*** **1** [I, T] if water, mud, etc. **churns**, or if sth **churns it** (**up**), it moves or is moved around violently: **~ (up)** *The water churned beneath the huge ship.* ◇ **~ sth (up)** *Vast crowds had churned the field into a sea of mud.* **2** [I, T] **~ (sth)** if your stomach **churns** or if sth **churns** your stomach, you feel a strong, unpleasant feeling of worry, disgust or fear: *My stomach churned as the names were read out.* **3** [I, T] **~ (sb) (up)** to feel or to make sb feel upset or emotionally confused: *Conflicting emotions churned inside him.* **4** [T] **~ sth** to turn and stir milk in a special container in order to make butter
PHR V **ˌchurn sth↔ˈout** (*informal*, often *disapproving*) to produce sth quickly and in large amounts
■ ***noun*** **1** a machine in which milk or cream is shaken to make butter **2** (*BrE*) a large metal container in which milk was carried from a farm in the past

ˈchurn rate *noun* (*business*) the number of people who stop using a product and change to another or who leave the company they work for and go to another

chute /ʃuːt/ *noun* **1** a tube or passage down which people or things can slide: *a **water chute*** (= at a swimming pool) ◇ *a **laundry/rubbish/garbage chute*** (= from the upper floors of a high building) **2** (*informal*) = PARACHUTE

ˌChutes and ˈLadders™ *noun* [U] (*US*) a children's game played on a special board with pictures of chutes and ladders on it. Players move their pieces up the ladders to go forward and down the chutes to go back. ➲ see also SNAKES AND LADDERS

chut·ney /ˈtʃʌtni/ *noun* [U] a cold thick sauce made from fruit, sugar, spices, and VINEGAR, eaten with cold meat, cheese, etc.

chutz·pah /ˈxʊtspə; ˈhʊ-/ *noun* [U] (often *approving*) behaviour, or a person's attitude, that is rude or shocking but so confident that people may feel forced to admire it SYN **nerve**

Ci *abbr.* CURIE(s)

CIA /ˌsiː aɪ ˈeɪ/ *abbr.* Central Intelligence Agency (a department of the US government which collects information about other countries, often secretly)

cia·batta /tʃəˈbætə; -ˈbɑːtə/ *noun* [U, C] (from *Italian*) a type of Italian bread made in a long flat shape; a SANDWICH made with this type of bread

ciao /tʃaʊ/ *exclamation* (from *Italian, informal*) goodbye

ci·cada /sɪˈkɑːdə; *NAmE* sɪˈkeɪdə/ *noun* a large insect with transparent wings, common in hot countries. The male makes a continuous high sound after dark by making two MEMBRANES (= pieces of thin skin) on its body VIBRATE (= move very fast).

CID /ˌsiː aɪ ˈdiː/ *abbr.* Criminal Investigation Department (the department of the British police force that is responsible for solving crimes)

-cide *combining form* (in nouns) **1** the act of killing: *suicide* ◇ *genocide* **2** a person or thing that kills: *insecticide* ▶ **-cidal** (in adjectives): *homicidal*

cider /ˈsaɪdə(r)/ *noun* **1** (*BrE*) (*NAmE* **ˈhard cider**) [U, C] an alcoholic drink made from the juice of apples: ***dry/sweet cider*** ◇ *cider apples* ◇ *a cider press* (= for squeezing the juice from apples) **2** (*NAmE*) [U, C] a drink made from the juice of apples that does not contain alcohol **3** [C] a glass of cider ➲ compare PERRY

cigar /sɪˈɡɑː(r)/ *noun* a roll of dried TOBACCO leaves that people smoke, like a cigarette but bigger and without paper around it: *cigar smoke* IDM see CLOSE *adj.*

cig·ar·ette 0→ /ˌsɪɡəˈret; *NAmE* ˈsɪɡəret/ *noun* a thin tube of paper filled with TOBACCO, for smoking: ***a packet/pack of cigarettes*** ◇ *to light a cigarette*

cigaˈrette end (*BrE*) (also **cigaˈrette butt** *NAmE, BrE*) *noun* the part of a cigarette that is left when sb has finished smoking it

cigaˈrette holder *noun* a narrow tube for holding a cigarette in while you are smoking

cigaˈrette lighter *noun* = LIGHTER

cigaˈrette paper *noun* a thin piece of paper in which people roll TOBACCO to make their own cigarettes

cig·ar·illo /ˌsɪɡəˈrɪləʊ; *NAmE* -loʊ/ *noun* (*pl.* **-os**) a small CIGAR

ciggy /ˈsɪɡi/ *noun* (*pl.* **-ies**) (*informal*) a cigarette

ci·lan·tro /sɪˈlæntrəʊ; *NAmE* -troʊ/ *noun* [U] (*NAmE*) the leaves of the CORIANDER plant, used in cooking as a HERB ➲ VISUAL VOCAB page V28

cil·iary muscle /ˈsɪliəri mʌsl/ *noun* (*anatomy*) a muscle in the eye that controls how much the LENS curves ➲ VISUAL VOCAB page V48

C.-in-C. /ˌsiː ɪn ˈsiː/ *abbr.* COMMANDER-IN-CHIEF

cinch /sɪntʃ/ *noun, verb*
■ ***noun*** [sing.] (*informal*) **1** something that is very easy SYN **doddle**: *The first question is a cinch.* **2** (*especially NAmE*) a thing that is certain to happen; a person who is certain to do sth: *He's a cinch to win the race.*
■ ***verb*** **1 ~ sth** (*especially NAmE*) to fasten sth tightly around your waist; to be fastened around sb's waist **2 ~ sth** (*NAmE*) to fasten a GIRTH around a horse **3 ~ sth** (*NAmE, informal*) to make sth certain

cin·der /ˈsɪndə(r)/ *noun* [usually pl.] a small piece of ASH or partly burnt coal, wood, etc. that is no longer burning but may still be hot: *a cinder track* (= a track for runners made with finely crushed cinders) IDM see BURN *v.*

ˈcinder block (*NAmE*) (*BrE* **ˈbreeze block**) *noun* a light building block, made of sand, coal ASHES and CEMENT

Cin·der·ella /ˌsɪndəˈrelə/ *noun* [usually sing.] a person or thing that has been ignored and deserves to receive more attention: *For years radio has been the Cinderella of the media world.* ORIGIN From the European fairy tale about a beautiful girl, **Cinderella**, who was treated in a cruel way by her two ugly sisters. She had to do all the work and received no reward or thanks until she met and married Prince Charming.

cine /ˈsɪni/ *adj.* [only before noun] (*BrE*) connected with films/movies and the film/movie industry: ***a cine camera/film/photographer***

cine·aste (also **cine·ast**) /ˈsɪniæst/ *noun* (from *French*) a person who knows a lot about films/movies and is very enthusiastic about them

cin·ema 0→ /ˈsɪnəmə/ *noun*
1 0→ (*BrE*) (*NAmE* **ˈmovie theater, theater**) [C] a building in which films/movies are shown: *the local cinema* ➲ VISUAL VOCAB page V3 **2** 0→ **the cinema** [sing.] (*BrE*) (*NAmE* **the movies**) when you go to **the cinema** or to **the movies**, you go to a cinema/movie theater to see a film/movie: *I used to go to the cinema every week.* **3** 0→ [U, sing.] (*especially BrE*) (*NAmE* usually **the movies**) films/

movies as an art or an industry: *one of the great successes of British cinema*

Collocations

Cinema/the movies

Watching

- **go to/take sb to (see)** a film/movie
- **go to/sit in** (*BrE*) the cinema/(*NAmE*) the (movie) theater
- **rent** a film/movie/DVD
- **download** a film/movie/video
- **burn/copy/rip** a DVD
- **see/watch** a film/movie/DVD/video/preview/trailer

Showing

- **show/screen** a film/movie
- **promote/distribute/review** a film/movie
- (*BrE*) **be on at** the cinema
- **be released on/come out on/be out on** DVD
- **captivate/delight/grip/thrill** the audience
- **do well/badly** at the box office
- **get a lot of/live up to the** hype

Film-making

- **write/co-write** a film/movie/script/screenplay
- **direct/produce/make/shoot/edit** a film/movie/sequel/video
- **make** a romantic comedy/a thriller/an action movie
- **do/work on** a sequel/remake
- **film/shoot** the opening scene/an action sequence/footage (of sth)
- **compose/create/do/write** the soundtrack
- **cut/edit (out)** a scene/sequence

Acting

- **have/get/do** an audition
- **get/have/play** a leading/starring/supporting role
- **play** a character/James Bond/the bad guy
- **act in/appear in/star in** a film/movie/remake
- **do/perform/attempt** a stunt
- **work in/make it big in** Hollywood
- **forge/carve/make/pursue** a career in Hollywood

Describing films

- the camera **pulls back/pans over sth/zooms in (on sth)**
- the camera **focuses on sth/lingers on sth**
- **shoot sb/show sb** in extreme close-up
- **use** odd/unusual camera angles
- **be filmed/shot** on location/in a studio
- **be set/take place** in London/in the '60s
- **have** a happy ending/plot twist

'cinema-goer *noun* (*BrE*) = FILM-GOER

Cinema·Scope™ /'sɪnəməskəʊp; *NAmE* -skoʊp/ *noun* a method of showing films/movies which makes the picture on the screen very wide

cine·mat·ic /ˌsɪnə'mætɪk/ *adj.* (*technical*) connected with films/movies and how they are made: ***cinematic effects/techniques***

cine·ma·tog·raphy /ˌsɪnəmə'tɒɡrəfi; *NAmE* -'tɑːɡ-/ *noun* [U] (*technical*) the art or process of making films/movies ▸ **cine·ma·tog·raph·er** /ˌsɪnəmə'tɒɡrəfə(r); *NAmE* -'tɑːɡ-/ *noun* **cine·ma·tog·raph·ic** /ˌsɪnəmætə'ɡræfɪk/ *adj.*

cine·phile /'sɪnifaɪl/ *noun* a person who is very interested in films/movies

cinna·bar /'sɪnəbɑː(r)/ *noun* [U] **1** a bright red mineral that is sometimes used to give colour to things **2** the bright red colour of cinnabar

cin·na·mon /'sɪnəmən/ *noun* [U] the inner BARK of a SE Asian tree, used in cooking as a spice, especially to give flavour to sweet foods ⊃ VISUAL VOCAB page V28

ci·pher (also **cy·pher**) /'saɪfə(r)/ *noun* **1** [U, C] a secret way of writing, especially one in which a set of letters or symbols is used to represent others SYN **code**: *a message in cipher* ⊃ see also DECIPHER **2** [C] (*formal, disapproving*) a person or thing of no importance **3** (*BrE*) the first letters of sb's name combined in a design and used to mark things

C

circa /'sɜːkə; *NAmE* 'sɜːrkə/ *prep.* (from *Latin*) (*abbr.* c) (used with dates) about: *born circa 150 BC*

cir·ca·dian /sɜː'keɪdiən; *NAmE* sɜːr'k-/ *adj.* [only before noun] (*technical*) connected with the changes in the bodies of people or animals over each period of 24 hours

cir·cle 🔑 /'sɜːkl; *NAmE* 'sɜːrkl/ *noun, verb*

▪ ***noun*** **1** 🔑 a completely round flat shape: *Cut out two circles of paper.* ⊃ VISUAL VOCAB page V58 ⊃ see also SEMICIRCLE **2** 🔑 the line that forms the edge of a circle: *Draw a circle.* ◇ *She walked the horse round* ***in a circle.*** ⊃ see also ANTARCTIC CIRCLE, ARCTIC CIRCLE, TURNING CIRCLE **3** 🔑 a thing or a group of people or things shaped like a circle: *a circle of trees/chairs* ◇ *The children stood in a circle.* ⊃ see also CORN CIRCLE, CROP CIRCLE **4** (*BrE*) (also **balcony** *NAmE, BrE*) an upper floor of a theatre or cinema/movie theater where the seats are arranged in curved rows: *We had seats in the circle.* ⊃ see also DRESS CIRCLE **5** a group of people who are connected because they have the same interests, jobs, etc: *the family circle* ◇ *She's well known in theatrical circles.* ◇ *a large* ***circle of friends*** ⊃ see also CHARMED CIRCLE, INNER CIRCLE, VICIOUS CIRCLE

IDM **come, turn, etc. full 'circle** to return to the situation in which you started, after a series of events or experiences **go round in 'circles** to work hard at sth or discuss sth without making any progress **run round in 'circles** (*informal*) to be busy doing sth without achieving anything important or making progress

▪ ***verb*** **1** [I, T] to move in a circle, especially in the air: **~ (around) (above/over sb/sth)** *Seagulls circled around above his head.* ◇ **~ sth** *The plane circled the airport to burn up excess fuel.* **2** [T] **~ sth** to draw a circle around sth: *Spelling mistakes are circled in red ink.*

IDM **circle the 'wagons** (*NAmE*) to join together with people who have the same ideas and beliefs as you, and avoid contact with those who do not, who may threaten or attack you: *When your way of life is threatened you have to circle the wagons and defend yourself.* ORIGIN From the practice of arranging a WAGON TRAIN in a circle to defend against attack.

circ·let /'sɜːklət; *NAmE* 'sɜːrk-/ *noun* a round band made of PRECIOUS METAL, flowers, etc, worn around the head for decoration

cir·cuit /'sɜːkɪt; *NAmE* 'sɜːrkɪt/ *noun* **1** a line, route, or journey around a place: *The race ended with eight laps of a city centre circuit.* ◇ *The earth takes a year to make a circuit of* (= go around) *the sun.* **2** the complete path of wires and equipment along which an electric current flows: *an electrical circuit* ◇ *a circuit diagram* (= one showing all the connections in the different parts of the circuit) ⊃ see also INTEGRATED CIRCUIT, PRINTED CIRCUIT, SHORT CIRCUIT **3** (in sport) a series of games or matches in which the same players regularly take part: *the women's tennis circuit* **4** a track for cars or motorcycles to race around **5** a series of places or events of a particular kind at which the same people appear or take part: *the* ***lecture/cabaret circuit*** ⊃ see also CLOSED-CIRCUIT TELEVISION **6** a regular journey made by a judge to hear court cases in each of the courts of law in a particular area: *a circuit court/judge*

'circuit board *noun* a board that holds electrical circuits inside a piece of electrical equipment

'circuit-breaker *noun* a device that can automatically stop an electric current if it becomes dangerous

cir·cu·it·ous /sə'kjuːɪtəs; *NAmE* sər'k-/ *adj.* (*formal*) (of a route or journey) long and not direct SYN **roundabout** ▸ **cir·cu·it·ous·ly** *adv.*

cir·cuit·ry /'sɜːkɪtri; *NAmE* 'sɜːrk-/ *noun* [U] a system of electrical CIRCUITS or the equipment that forms this

'circuit training *noun* [U] a type of training in sport in which different exercises are each done for a short time

C

cir·cu·lar /'sɜːkjələ(r); *NAmE* 'sɜːrk-/ *adj.*, *noun*

▪ ***adj.*** **1** shaped like a circle; round: *a circular building* **2** moving around in a circle: *a circular tour of the city* **3** (of an argument or a theory) using an idea or a statement to prove sth which is then used to prove the idea or statement at the beginning **4** (of a letter) sent to a large number of people ▸ **cir·cu·lar·ity** /ˌsɜːkjə'lærəti; *NAmE* ˌsɜːrk-/ *noun* [U]: *There is a dangerous circularity about this argument.*

▪ ***noun*** a printed letter, notice or advertisement that is sent to a large number of people at the same time

ˌcircular 'saw (*NAmE* also **'buzz saw**) *noun* a SAW in the form of a metal disc that turns quickly, driven by a motor, and is used for cutting wood, etc.

cir·cu·late /'sɜːkjəleɪt; *NAmE* 'sɜːrk-/ *verb* **1** [I, T] when a liquid, gas, or air **circulates** or **is circulated**, it moves continuously around a place or system: *The condition prevents the blood from circulating freely.* ◇ **~ sth** *Cooled air is circulated throughout the building.* **2** [I, T] **~ (sth)** if a story, an idea, information, etc. **circulates** or if you **circulate** it, it spreads or it is passed from one person to another: *Rumours began to circulate about his financial problems.* **3** [T] **~ sth (to sb)** to send goods or information to all the people in a group: *The document will be circulated to all members.* **4** [I] to move around a group, especially at a party, talking to different people

cir·cu·la·tion /ˌsɜːkjə'leɪʃn; *NAmE* ˌsɜːrk-/ *noun* **1** [U] the movement of blood around the body: *Regular exercise will improve blood circulation.* ◇ *to have* ***good/bad circulation*** **2** [U] the passing or spreading of sth from one person or place to another: *the* ***circulation of money/information/ideas*** ◇ *A number of forged tickets are* ***in circulation.*** ◇ *The coins were* ***taken out of circulation.*** ◇ *Copies of the magazine were* ***withdrawn from circulation.*** **3** [U] the fact that sb takes part in social activities at a particular time: *Anne has been ill but now she's back* ***in circulation.*** ◇ *I was* ***out of circulation*** *for months after the baby was born.* **4** [C, usually sing.] the usual number of copies of a newspaper or magazine that are sold each day, week, etc: *a daily circulation of more than one million* **5** [U, C] the movement of sth (for example air, water, gas, etc.) around an area or inside a system or machine

cir·cu·la·tory /ˌsɜːkjə'leɪtəri; *NAmE* 'sɜːrkjələtɔːri/ *adj.* relating to the circulation of the blood

cir·cum·cise /'sɜːkəmsaɪz; *NAmE* 'sɜːrk-/ *verb* **1 ~ sb** to remove the FORESKIN of a boy or man for religious or medical reasons **2 ~ sb** to cut off part of the sex organs of a girl or woman

cir·cum·ci·sion /ˌsɜːkəm'sɪʒn; *NAmE* ˌsɜːrk-/ *noun* [U, C] the act of circumcising sb; the religious ceremony when sb, especially a baby, is circumcised

cir·cum·fer·ence /sə'kʌmfərəns; *NAmE* sər'k-/ *noun* [C, U] a line that goes around a circle or any other curved shape; the length of this line: *the circumference of the earth* ◇ *The earth is almost 25 000 miles* ***in circumference.*** ➲ VISUAL VOCAB page V58 ➲ compare PERIMETER

cir·cum·flex /'sɜːkəmfleks; *NAmE* 'sɜːrk-/ (also **ˌcircumflex 'accent**) *noun* the mark placed over a vowel in some languages to show how it should be pronounced, as over the *o* in *rôle* ➲ compare ACUTE ACCENT, GRAVE², TILDE, UMLAUT

cir·cum·lo·cu·tion /ˌsɜːkəmlə'kjuːʃn; *NAmE* ˌsɜːrk-/ *noun* [U, C] (*formal*) using more words than are necessary, instead of speaking or writing in a clear, direct way ▸ **cir·cum·lo·cu·tory** /ˌsɜːkəm'lɒkjʊtəri; ˌsɜːkəmlə'kjuːtəri; *NAmE* ˌsɜːrkəm'lɑːkjətɔːri/ *adj.*

cir·cum·navi·gate /ˌsɜːkəm'nævɪgeɪt; *NAmE* ˌsɜːrk-/ *verb* **~ sth** (*formal*) to sail all the way around sth, especially all the way around the world ▸ **cir·cum·navi·ga·tion** /ˌsɜːkəmˌnævɪ'geɪʃn; *NAmE* ˌsɜːrk-/ *noun* [U]

cir·cum·scribe /'sɜːkəmskraɪb; *NAmE* 'sɜːrk-/ *verb* **1** [often passive] **~ sth** (*formal*) to limit sb/sth's freedom, rights, power, etc. SYN **restrict**: *The power of the monarchy was circumscribed by the new law.* **2 ~ sth** (*technical*) to draw a circle around another shape ▸ **cir·cum·scrip·tion** /ˌsɜːkəm'skrɪpʃn; *NAmE* ˌsɜːrk-/ *noun* [U]

cir·cum·spect /'sɜːkəmspekt; *NAmE* 'sɜːrk-/ *adj.* (*formal*) thinking very carefully about sth before doing it, because there may be risks involved SYN **cautious** ▸ **cir·cum·spec·tion** /ˌsɜːkəm'spekʃn; *NAmE* ˌsɜːrk-/ *noun* [U] **cir·cum·spect·ly** *adv.*

cir·cum·stance 0-ᴡ AW /'sɜːkəmstəns; -stɑːns; -stæns; *NAmE* 'sɜːrkəmstæns/ *noun*

1 0-ᴡ [C, usually pl.] the conditions and facts that are connected with and affect a situation, an event or an action: *The company reserves the right to cancel this agreement in certain circumstances.* ◇ *changing social and political circumstances* ◇ *I know I can trust her in any circumstance.* ◇ *Police said there were no* ***suspicious circumstances*** *surrounding the boy's death.* ◇ *The ship sank in mysterious circumstances.* ◇ *She never discovered the true circumstances of her birth.* ➲ SYNONYMS at SITUATION **2** 0-ᴡ **circumstances** [pl.] the conditions of a person's life, especially the money they have: *Grants are awarded according to your* ***financial circumstances.*** ◇ ***family/domestic/personal circumstances*** **3** [U] (*formal*) situations and events that affect and influence your life and that are not in your control: *a* ***victim of circumstance*** (= a person who has suffered because of a situation that they cannot control) ◇ *He had to leave the country through* ***force of circumstance*** (= events made it necessary).

IDM **in/under the 'circumstances** used before or after a statement to show that you have thought about the conditions that affect a situation before making a decision or a statement: *Under the circumstances, it seemed better not to tell him about the accident.* ◇ *She did the job very well in the circumstances.* **in/under no circumstances** used to emphasize that sth should never happen or be allowed: *Under no circumstances should you lend Paul any money.* ◇ *Don't open the door, in any circumstances.* ➲ more at POMP, REDUCE

cir·cum·stan·tial /ˌsɜːkəm'stænʃl; *NAmE* ˌsɜːrk-/ *adj.* **1** (*law*) containing information and details that strongly suggest that sth is true but do not prove it: *circumstantial evidence* ◇ *The case against him was largely circumstantial.* **2** (*formal*) connected with particular circumstances: *Their problems were circumstantial rather than personal.*

cir·cum·vent /ˌsɜːkəm'vent; *NAmE* ˌsɜːrk-/ *verb* (*formal*) **1 ~ sth** to find a way of avoiding a difficulty or a rule: *They found a way of circumventing the law.* **2 ~ sth** to go or travel around sth that is blocking your way ▸ **cir·cum·ven·tion** /ˌsɜːkəm'venʃn; *NAmE* ˌsɜːrk-/ *noun* [U]

cir·cus /'sɜːkəs; *NAmE* 'sɜːrkəs/ *noun* **1** [C] a group of entertainers, sometimes with trained animals, who perform skilful or amusing acts in a show that travels around to different places **2 the circus** [sing.] a show performed by circus entertainers, usually in a large tent called a BIG TOP: *We took the children to the circus.* **3** [sing.] (*informal, disapproving*) a group of people or an event that attracts a lot of attention: *A media circus surrounded the royal couple wherever they went.* ◇ *the American electoral circus* **4** [C] (*BrE*) (used in some place names) a round open area in a town where several streets meet: *Piccadilly Circus* **5** [C] (in ancient Rome) a place like a big round outdoor theatre for public games, races, etc.

cirque /sɜːk; *NAmE* sɜːrk/ *noun* (*geology*) = CORRIE

cir·rho·sis /sə'rəʊsɪs; *NAmE* -'roʊ-/ *noun* [U] a serious disease of the LIVER, caused especially by drinking too much alcohol

cir·rus /'sɪrəs/ *noun* [U] (*technical*) a type of light cloud that forms high in the sky

CIS /ˌsiː aɪ 'es/ *abbr.* Commonwealth of Independent States (a group of independent countries that were part of the Soviet Union until 1991)

cissy (*BrE*) = SISSY

cis·tern /ˈsɪstən; *NAmE* -tərn/ *noun* (*BrE*) a container in which water is stored in a building, especially one in the roof or connected to a toilet ➲ VISUAL VOCAB page V21

cita·del /ˈsɪtədəl; -del/ *noun* (in the past) a castle on high ground in or near a city where people could go when the city was being attacked: (*figurative*) *citadels of private economic power*

cit·ation AW /saɪˈteɪʃn/ *noun* (*formal*) **1** [C] words or lines taken from a book or a speech SYN **quotation** **2** [C] an official statement about sth special that sb has done, especially about acts of courage in a war: *a citation for bravery* **3** [U] an act of citing or being cited: *Space does not permit the citation of the examples.* **4** [C] (*NAmE*) = SUMMONS: *The judge issued a contempt citation against the woman for violating a previous court order.*

cite AW /saɪt/ *verb* (*formal*) **1** **~ sth (as sth)** to mention sth as a reason or an example, or in order to support what you are saying: *He cited his heavy workload as the reason for his breakdown.* ➲ SYNONYMS at MENTION **2** **~ sth** to speak or write the exact words from a book, an author, etc. SYN **quote** **3** **~ sb (for sth)** (*law*) to order sb to appear in court; to name sb officially in a legal case: *She was cited in the divorce proceedings.* **4** **~ sb (for sth)** to mention sb officially or publicly because they deserve special praise: *He was cited for bravery.*

citi·fied /ˈsɪtɪfaɪd/ *adj.* (usually *disapproving*) characteristic of a city: *his citified surroundings*

citi·zen 0‑w /ˈsɪtɪzn/ *noun*
1 0‑w a person who has the legal right to belong to a particular country: *She's Italian by birth but is now an Australian citizen.* ◇ *British citizens living in other parts of the European Union* **2** 0‑w a person who lives in a particular place: *the citizens of Budapest* ◇ *When you're old, people treat you like a* ***second-class citizen***. ➲ see also SENIOR CITIZEN ➲ compare SUBJECT (6)

ˌcitizen ˈjournalism *noun* [U] reports and pictures of events recorded by ordinary people and shown on the Internet: *citizen journalism websites* ▶ **ˌcitizen ˈjournalist** *noun*

citi·zen·ry /ˈsɪtɪzənri/ *noun* [sing.+ sing./pl. v.] (*formal*) (less *formal* in *NAmE*) all the citizens of a particular town, country, etc.

ˌcitizen's ˈarrest *noun* an arrest made by a member of the public, not by the police

ˈCitizens' Band *noun* [U] = CB

citi·zen·ship /ˈsɪtɪzənʃɪp/ *noun* [U] **1** the legal right to belong to a particular country: *French citizenship* ◇ *You can apply for citizenship after five years' residency.* ➲ COLLOCATIONS at RACE **2** the state of being a citizen and accepting the responsibilities of it: *an education that prepares young people for citizenship*

cit·ric /ˈsɪtrɪk/ *adj.* relating to fruit such as lemons, oranges and LIMES: *a citric flavour*

cit·ric acid /ˌsɪtrɪk ˈæsɪd/ *noun* [U] a weak acid found in the juice of lemons and other sour fruits

cit·ron /ˈsɪtrən/ *noun* [C, U] a yellow fruit like a large lemon

cit·ron·ella /ˌsɪtrəˈnelə/ *noun* [U] a type of grass from which an oil used in PERFUMES and soap is obtained

cit·rus /ˈsɪtrəs/ *noun* [U] fruit belonging to the group of fruit that includes oranges, lemons, LIMES and GRAPEFRUIT: ***citrus fruit/trees/growers*** ◇ *fabric in bright citrus shades* (= orange, yellow or green) ➲ VISUAL VOCAB page V26

city 0‑w /ˈsɪti/ *noun* (*pl.* **-ies**)
1 0‑w [C] a large and important town: *the city centre* ◇ *one of the world's most beautiful cities* ◇ *a major city* ◇ *the country's* ***capital city*** ◇ *Mexico City* ➲ COLLOCATIONS at TOWN ➲ VISUAL VOCAB pages V2, V3 ➲ see also INNER CITY **2** [C] (*BrE*) a town that has been given special rights by a king or queen, usually one that has a CATHEDRAL: *the city of York* **3** [C] (*NAmE*) a town that has been given special rights by the state government **4** 0‑w [sing.+ sing./pl. v.] all the people who live in a city: *The city turned out to welcome the victorious team home.* **5** **the City** [sing.] (*BrE*) Britain's financial and business centre, in the oldest part of London: *a City stockbroker* ◇ *What is the City's reaction to the cut in interest rates?* **6** [U] (*informal*) used after other nouns to say that a place is full of a particular thing: *It's not exactly fun city here is it?* IDM see FREEDOM

the ˌCity and ˈGuilds Institute *noun* [sing.] (in Britain) an organization that gives qualifications in technical subjects and practical skills

ˈcity desk *noun* **1** (*BrE*) the department of a newspaper that deals with financial news **2** (*NAmE*) the department of a newspaper that deals with local news

ˈcity editor *noun* **1** (*BrE*) a journalist who is responsible for financial news in a newspaper or magazine **2** (*NAmE*) a journalist who is responsible for local news in a newspaper or magazine

ˌcity ˈfather *noun* [usually pl.] a person with experience of governing a city

ˌcity ˈgent *noun* (*BrE, informal*) a business person, especially a man who works in the financial area of London

ˌcity ˈhall *noun* [C, U] (*NAmE*) the local government of a city and the offices it uses

city·scape /ˈsɪtiskeɪp/ *noun* the appearance of a city or urban area, especially in a picture; a picture of a city

ˌcity ˈslicker *noun* (*informal*, often *disapproving*) a person who behaves in a way that is typical of people who live in big cities

ˌcity ˈstate *noun* (especially in the past) an independent state consisting of a city and the area around it (for example, Athens in ancient times)

civet /ˈsɪvɪt/ *noun* **1** [C] a wild animal like a cat, that lives in central Africa and Asia **2** [U] a substance with a strong smell, obtained from a civet, and used in making PERFUME

civic /ˈsɪvɪk/ *adj.* [usually before noun] **1** officially connected with a town or city: ***civic buildings/leaders*** **2** connected with the people who live in a town or city: *a sense of* ***civic pride*** (= pride that people feel for their town or city) ◇ ***civic duties/responsibilities***

ˌcivic ˈcentre *noun* **1** (*BrE*) the area where the public buildings are, in a town **2** **civic center** (*NAmE*) a large building where public entertainments and meetings are held: *Atlanta Civic Center*

ˌcivic ˈholiday *noun* (*CanE*) a holiday that is taken on the first Monday in August in all of Canada apart from Quebec, Alberta and Prince Edward Island

civ·ics /ˈsɪvɪks/ *noun* [U] (*especially NAmE*) the school subject which studies the way government works and deals with the rights and duties that you have as a citizen and a member of a particular society

civil 0‑w AW /ˈsɪvl/ *adj.*
1 0‑w [only before noun] connected with the people who live in a country: *civil unrest* (= that is caused by groups of people within a country) ➲ see also CIVIL WAR **2** 0‑w [only before noun] connected with the state rather than with religion or with the armed forces: *a civil marriage ceremony* **3** [only before noun] involving personal legal matters and not criminal law: *a civil court* ➲ compare CRIMINAL ➲ see also CIVIL LAW **4** polite in a formal way but possibly not friendly OPP **uncivil** ▶ **civ·il·ly** /ˈsɪvəli/ *adv.*: *She greeted him civilly but with no sign of affection.*

ˌcivil deˈfence (*especially US* **ˌcivil deˈfense**) *noun* [U] the organization and training of ordinary people to protect themselves from attack during a war or, in the US, from natural disasters such as HURRICANES

ˌcivil disoˈbedience *noun* [U] refusal by a large group of people to obey particular laws or pay taxes, usually as a form of peaceful political protest

ˌcivil engiˈneering *noun* [U] the design, building and repair of roads, bridges, CANALS, etc; the study of this as a subject ▶ **ˌcivil engiˈneer** *noun*

ci·vil·ian /səˈvɪliən/ *noun* a person who is not a member of the armed forces or the police ➲ COLLOCATIONS at WAR

▸ **ci·vil·ian** *adj.* [usually before noun]: *He left the army and returned to civilian life.* ➲ compare MILITARY

ci·vil·ity /sə'vɪləti/ *noun* (*formal*) **1** [U] polite behaviour: *Staff members are trained to treat customers with civility at all times.* **2 civilities** [pl.] remarks that are said only in order to be polite

C

civ·il·iza·tion (*BrE* also **-isa·tion**) /ˌsɪvəlaɪ'zeɪʃn; *NAmE* -lə'z-/ *noun* **1** [U] a state of human society that is very developed and organized: *the technology of modern civilization* ◇ *The Victorians regarded the railways as bringing progress and civilization.* **2** [U, C] a society, its culture and its way of life during a particular period of time or in a particular part of the world: *the civilizations of ancient Greece and Rome* ◇ *diseases that are common in Western civilization* **3** [U] all the people in the world and the societies they live in, considered as a whole: *Environmental damage threatens the whole of civilization.* **4** [U] (often *humorous*) a place that offers you the comfortable way of life of a modern society: *It's good to be back in civilization after two weeks in a tent!*

civ·il·ize (*BrE* also **-ise**) /'sɪvəlaɪz/ *verb* **~ sb/sth** to educate and improve a person or a society; to make sb's behaviour or manners better: *The girls in a class tend to have a civilizing influence on the boys.*

civ·il·ized (*BrE* also **-ised**) /'sɪvəlaɪzd/ *adj.* **1** well-organized socially with a very developed culture and way of life: *the civilized world* ◇ *rising crime in our so-called civilized societies* ◇ *civilized peoples* **2** having laws and customs that are fair and morally acceptable: *No civilized country should allow such terrible injustices.* **3** having or showing polite and reasonable behaviour: *We couldn't even have a civilized conversation any more.* **4** typical of a comfortable and pleasant way of life: *Breakfast on the terrace —how civilized!* OPP **uncivilized**

ˌcivil 'law *noun* [U] law that deals with the rights of private citizens rather than with crime

ˌcivil 'liberty *noun* [C, usually pl., U] the right of people to be free to say or do what they want while respecting others and staying within the law

the 'Civil List *noun* [sing.] a sum of money that is given to the British royal family each year by Parliament

ˌcivil 'marriage *noun* a marriage with no religious ceremony

ˌcivil 'partnership *noun* a relationship between two people of the same sex, recognized as having the same legal status as a marriage between a man and a woman

ˌcivil 'rights *noun* [pl.] the rights that every person in a society has, for example to be treated equally, to be able to vote, work, etc. whatever their sex, race or religion: *the civil rights leader Martin Luther King*

the ˌcivil 'rights movement *noun* [sing.] (in the US) the campaign in the 1950s and 1960s to change the laws so that African Americans have the same rights as others ➲ COLLOCATIONS at RACE

ˌcivil 'servant *noun* a person who works in the civil service

the ˌcivil 'service *noun* [sing.] the government departments in a country, except the armed forces, and the people who work for them

ˌcivil 'war *noun* **1** [C, U] a war between groups of people in the same country: *the Spanish Civil War* ◇ *30 years of bitter civil war* ➲ COLLOCATIONS at WAR **2 the Civil War** the war fought in the US between the northern and the southern states in the years 1861 to 1865

civ·vies /'sɪviz/ *noun* [pl.] (*slang*) (used by people in the armed forces) ordinary clothes, not military uniform

Civvy Street /'sɪvi striːt/ *noun* [U] (*old-fashioned, BrE, slang*) ordinary life outside the armed forces

CJD /ˌsiː dʒeɪ 'diː/ *abbr.* CREUTZFELDT-JAKOB DISEASE ➲ see also NEW VARIANT CJD

cl *abbr.* (*pl.* **cl** or **cls**) CENTILITRE: *75cl*

clack /klæk/ *verb* [I] if two hard objects **clack**, they make a short loud sound when they hit each other: *Her heels clacked on the marble floor.* ▸ **clack** *noun* [sing.]: *the clack of high heels on the floor* ◇ *the clack of her knitting needles*

clad /klæd/ *adj.* (usually *formal*) **1 ~ (in sth)** (often used after an adverb or in compounds) wearing a particular type of clothing SYN **dressed**: *She was clad in blue velvet.* ◇ ***warmly/scantily clad*** ◇ *leather-clad motorcyclists* **2 -clad** (in compounds) covered in a particular thing: *snow-clad hills*

clad·ding /'klædɪŋ/ *noun* [U] a covering of a hard material, used as protection

Synonyms

claim

allegation • assertion

These are all words for a statement that sth is true, although it has not been proved.

claim a statement that sth is true, although it has not been proved.

allegation (*rather formal*) a public statement that is made without giving proof, accusing sb of doing sth that is wrong or illegal.

assertion (*rather formal*) a statement of sth that you strongly believe to be true, although it has not been proved.

CLAIM OR ASSERTION?

When the point in doubt is a matter of opinion, not fact, use **assertion**: ~~She made sweeping claims about the role of women in society.~~ When you are talking about a matter of fact you can use either word; an **assertion** may be slightly stronger than a **claim** and it is a more formal word.

PATTERNS

- a(n) claim/allegation/assertion **that...**
- a(n) claim/allegation/assertion **about/of** sth
- **false/unfounded/conflicting** claims/allegations/assertions
- to **make/deny** a(n) claim/allegation/assertion
- to **withdraw** a(n) claim/allegation

claim 🔑 /kleɪm/ *verb, noun*

■ ***verb***

▸ SAY STH IS TRUE **1** 🔑 [T] to say that sth is true although it has not been proved and other people may not believe it: **~ (that)...** *He claims (that) he was not given a fair hearing.* ◇ **~ (sb/sth) to be/do sth** *I don't claim to be an expert.* ◇ **~ sth** *Scientists are claiming a major breakthrough in the fight against cancer.* ◇ **it is claimed that...** *It was claimed that some doctors were working 80 hours a week.* ➲ LANGUAGE BANK at ARGUE

▸ DEMAND LEGAL RIGHT **2** 🔑 [T] **~ sth** to demand or ask for sth because you believe it is your legal right to own or to have it: *A lot of lost property is never claimed.* ◇ *He claimed political asylum.*

▸ MONEY **3** 🔑 [T, I] to ask for money from the government or a company because you have a right to it: **~ sth** *He's not entitled to claim unemployment benefit.* ◇ **~ sth from sth** *She claimed damages from the company for the injury she had suffered.* ◇ *You could have claimed the cost of the hotel room from your insurance.* ◇ **~ (on sth) (for sth)** *You can claim on your insurance for that coat you left on the train.*

▸ ATTENTION/THOUGHT **4** [T] **~ sth** to get or take sb's attention: *A most unwelcome event claimed his attention.*

▸ GAIN/WIN **5** [T] **~ sth** to gain, win or achieve sth: *She has finally claimed a place on the team.*

▸ CAUSE DEATH **6** [T] **~ sth** (of a disaster, an accident, etc.) to cause sb's death: *The car crash claimed three lives.*

PHR V **ˌclaim sth↔'back** to ask or demand to have sth returned because you have a right to it: *You can claim back the tax on your purchases.*

■ ***noun***

▸ SAYING STH IS TRUE **1** 🔑 [C] **~ (that...)** a statement that sth is true although it has not been proved and other people

may not agree with or believe it: *The singer has denied the magazine's claim that she is leaving the band.*
▸ LEGAL RIGHT **2** 0‑ᴛ [C, U] **~ (on/to sth)** a right that sb believes they have to sth, especially property, land, etc: *They had no claim on the land.* ◇ *She has more claim to the book's success than anybody* (= she deserves to be praised for it).
▸ FOR MONEY **3** 0‑ᴛ [C] **~ (for sth)** a request for a sum of money that you believe you have a right to, especially from a company, the government, etc: *You can* ***make a claim*** *on your insurance policy.* ◇ *to* ***put in a claim*** *for an allowance* ◇ *a claim for £2 000* ◇ *Make sure your claims for expenses are submitted by the end of the month.* ◇ *a three per cent* ***pay claim*** ◇ *Complete a* ***claim form*** (= an official document which you must use in order to request money from an organization).
IDM ˌ**claim to** ˈ**fame** (often *humorous*) one thing that makes a person or place important or interesting: *His main claim to fame is that he went to school with the Prime Minister.* **have a claim on sb** to have the right to demand time, attention, etc. from sb **lay claim to sth** to state that you have a right to own sth **make no claim** used when you are saying that you cannot do sth: *I make no claim to understand modern art.* ➲ more at STAKE *v.*

claim·ant /ˈkleɪmənt/ *noun* **1** a person who claims sth because they believe they have a right to it **2** (*BrE*) a person who is receiving money from the state because they are unemployed, etc.

clair·voy·ance /kleəˈvɔɪəns; *NAmE* klerˈv-/ *noun* [U] the power that some people are believed to have to be able to see future events or to communicate with people who are dead or far away ▸ **clair·voy·ant** /kleəˈvɔɪənt; *NAmE* klerˈv-/ *noun*: *to consult a clairvoyant* **clair·voy·ant** *adj.*

clam /klæm/
■ ***noun*** a SHELLFISH that can be eaten. It has a shell in two parts that can open and close: ***clam chowder/soup*** ➲ picture at SHELLFISH
■ ***verb*** (-mm-)
PHR V ˌ**clam** ˈ**up (on sb)** (*informal*) to refuse to speak, especially when sb asks you about sth

clam·bake /ˈklæmbeɪk/ *noun* (*NAmE*) an outdoor party, especially for eating clams and other SEAFOOD

clam·ber /ˈklæmbə(r)/ *verb* [I] **+ adv./prep.** to climb or move with difficulty or a lot of effort, using your hands and feet SYN **scramble**: *The children clambered up the steep bank.*

clammy /ˈklæmi/ *adj.* (**clam·mier**, **clam·mi·est**) damp in an unpleasant way: *His skin felt cold and clammy.* ◇ *clammy hands*

clam·our (*especially US* **clamor**) /ˈklæmə(r)/ *verb, noun*
■ ***verb*** **1** [I, T] (*formal*) to demand sth loudly: **~ (for sth)** *People began to clamour for his resignation.* ◇ **~ to do sth** *Everyone was clamouring to know how much they would get.* ◇ **+ speech** *'Play with us!' the children clamoured.* **2** [I] (of many people) to shout loudly, especially in a confused way
■ ***noun*** [sing., U] (*formal*) **1** a loud noise especially one that is made by a lot of people or animals: *the clamour of the market* **2 ~ (for sth)** a demand for sth made by a lot of people: *The clamour for her resignation grew louder.* ▸ **clam·or·ous** /ˈklæmərəs/ *adj.*

clamp /klæmp/ *verb, noun*
■ ***verb*** **1** [T] to hold sth tightly, or fasten two things together, with a clamp: **~ A to B** *Clamp one end of the plank to the edge of the table.* ◇ **~ A and B (together)** *Clamp the two halves together until the glue dries.* **2** [T, I] to hold or fasten sth very tightly so that it does not move; to be held tightly: **~ sth + adv./prep.** *He had a cigar clamped between his teeth.* ◇ *She clamped a pair of headphones over her ears.* ◇ **+ adv./prep.** *Her lips clamped tightly together.* ◇ **~ (sth) + adj.** *He clamped his mouth shut.* **3** [T, often passive] **~ sth/sb** (*BrE*) to fix a clamp to a car's wheel so that the car cannot be driven away
PHR V ˌ**clamp** ˈ**down (on sb/sth)** to take strict action in order to prevent sth, especially crime: *a campaign by police to clamp down on street crime* ➲ related noun CLAMPDOWN ˈ**clamp sth on sb** (*especially NAmE*) to force sb to accept sth such as a restriction or law: *The army* ***clamped a curfew on*** *the city.*
■ ***noun*** **1** a tool for holding things tightly together, usually by means of a screw ➲ VISUAL VOCAB page V57 **2** (*also* ˈ**wheel clamp**) (both *BrE*) (*US* ˌ**Denver** ˈ**boot**, **boot**) a device that is attached to the wheel of a car that has been parked illegally, so that it cannot be driven away

clamp·down /ˈklæmpdaʊn/ *noun* [usually sing.] sudden action that is taken in order to stop an illegal activity: *a clampdown on drinking and driving*

clam·shell /ˈklæmʃel/ *adj.* [only before noun] having a lid or other part that opens and shuts like the shell of a CLAM: *a* ***clamshell phone*** ▸ **clam·shell** *noun*

clan /klæn/ *noun* [C+sing./pl. v.] **1** a group of families who are related to each other, especially in Scotland: *the Macleod clan* ◇ *clan warfare* **2** (*informal*, sometimes *humorous*) a very large family, or a group of people who are connected because of a particular thing: *one of a growing clan of stars who have left Hollywood*

clan·des·tine /klænˈdestɪn; ˈklændəstaɪn/ *adj.* (*formal*) done secretly or kept secret: *a* ***clandestine meeting/relationship***

clang /klæŋ/ *verb* [I, T] to make a loud ringing sound like that of metal being hit; to cause sth to make this sound SYN **clank**: *Bells were clanging in the tower.* ◇ **+ adj.** *The gates* ***clanged shut****.* ◇ **~ sth + adv./prep.** *The trams clanged their way along the streets.* ◇ *He clanged a spoon against a glass.* ▸ **clang** (*also* **clang·ing**) *noun* [usually sing.]

clang·er /ˈklæŋə(r)/ *noun* (*BrE, informal*) an obvious and embarrassing mistake: *Mentioning her ex-husband was a bit of a clanger.* ◇ *He was always* ***dropping clangers*** (= making embarrassing mistakes or remarks).

clang·our (*especially US* **clangor**) /ˈklæŋgə(r)/ *noun* (*formal*) a continuous loud crashing or ringing sound ▸ **clang·or·ous** /ˈklæŋgərəs/ *adj.*

clank /klæŋk/ *verb* [I, T] to make a loud sound like pieces of metal hitting each other; to cause sth to make this sound: *clanking chains* ◇ **+ adj.** *I heard a door clank shut.* ◇ **~ sth** *The guard clanked his heavy ring of keys.* ▸ **clank** (*also* **clank·ing**) *noun* [usually sing.]

clan·nish /ˈklænɪʃ/ *adj.* (often *disapproving*) (of members of a group) not showing interest in people who are not in the group

clans·man /ˈklænzmən/ *noun* (*pl.* **-men** /-mən/) a member of a CLAN

clap 0‑ᴛ /klæp/ *verb, noun*
■ ***verb*** (-pp-) **1** 0‑ᴛ [I, T] to hit your open hands together several times to show that you approve of or have enjoyed sth: *The audience cheered and clapped.* ◇ **~ sb/sth** *Everyone clapped us when we went up to get our prize.* **2** 0‑ᴛ [I, T] to hit your open hands together: *Everyone clapped in time to the music.* ◇ **~ your hands** *She clapped her hands in delight.* ◇ *He clapped his hands for silence.* **3** [T] **~ sb on the back/shoulder** to lightly hit sb with your open hand, usually in a friendly way **4** [T] **~ sth + adv./prep.** to put sth/sb somewhere quickly and suddenly: *'Oh dear!' she cried,* ***clapping a hand*** *over her mouth.* ◇ *to* ***clap sb in irons/jail/prison*** ▸ **clap·ping** *noun* [U]: *I could hear the sound of clapping from the other room.* IDM see EYE *n.*
■ ***noun*** **1** 0‑ᴛ [sing.] an act of clapping the hands; the sound this makes: *Give him a clap!* (= to praise sb at the end of a performance) **2** [C] a sudden loud noise: *a clap of thunder* **3** (*also* **the clap**) [U] (*informal*) a disease of the sexual organs, caught by having sex with an infected person SYN **gonorrhoea**

clap·board /ˈklæpbɔːd; *NAmE* ˈklæbərd/ *noun* [U] (*especially NAmE*) = WEATHERBOARD

Clap·ham omni·bus /ˌklæpəm ˈɒmnɪbəs; *NAmE* ˈɑːmnɪbəs/ *noun* (*BrE*)
IDM **the man on the** ˌ**Clapham** ˈ**omnibus** (*BrE, informal*) an ordinary person who is typical of many others: *Can you persuade the man on the Clapham omnibus that it is useful?*

ˌclapped ˈout *adj.* (*BrE, informal*) (of a car or machine) old and in bad condition: *The van's totally clapped out.* ◇ *a clapped-out old Mini*

clap·per /ˈklæpə(r)/ *noun* the piece of metal inside a bell that hits the sides and makes the bell ring IDM **like the ˈclappers** (*BrE, informal*) extremely fast: *to **run/ride/drive like the clappers***

clap·per·board /ˈklæpəbɔːd; *NAmE* ˈklæpərbɔːrd/ *noun* a device that is used when making films/movies. It consists of two connected boards that are hit together at the start of a scene, and its purpose is to help to match the pictures with the sound.

clap·trap /ˈklæptræp/ *noun* [U] (*informal*) stupid talk that has no value

claque /klæk/ *noun* a group of people who are paid to clap or BOO a performer or public speaker

claret /ˈklærət/ *noun* **1** [U, C] a dry red wine, especially from the Bordeaux area of France. There are several types of claret. **2** [U] a dark red colour

clar·ify AW /ˈklærəfaɪ/ *verb* (**clari·fies, clari·fy·ing, clari·fied, clari·fied**) **1** (*formal*) to make sth clearer or easier to understand: **~ sth** *to **clarify a situation/problem/issue*** ◇ *I hope this **clarifies my position**.* ◇ **~ what/how, etc…** *She asked him to clarify what he meant.* ➲ LANGUAGE BANK at DEFINE **2 ~ sth** to make sth, especially butter, pure by heating it: *clarified butter* ▸ **clari·fi·ca·tion** AW /ˌklærəfɪˈkeɪʃn/ *noun* [U, C]: *I am **seeking clarification of** the regulations.*

clari·net /ˌklærəˈnet/ *noun* a musical instrument of the WOODWIND group. It is shaped like a pipe and has a REED and a MOUTHPIECE at the top that you blow into. ➲ VISUAL VOCAB page V30

cla·ri·net·tist (*NAmE* **cla·ri·net·ist**) /ˌklærəˈnetɪst/ *noun* a person who plays the clarinet

clar·ion call /ˈklæriən kɔːl/ *noun* [sing.] (*formal*) a clear message or request for people to do sth

clar·ity AW /ˈklærəti/ *noun* [U] **1** the quality of being expressed clearly: *a lack of clarity in the law* **2** the ability to think about or understand sth clearly: ***clarity of thought/purpose/vision*** **3** if a picture, substance or sound has **clarity**, you can see or hear it very clearly, or see through it easily: *the clarity of sound on a CD*

clash /klæʃ/ *noun, verb*

■ ***noun***

▸ FIGHT **1 ~ (with sb)** | **~ (between A and B)** a short fight between two groups of people: *Clashes broke out between police and demonstrators.* ➲ SYNONYMS at FIGHT

▸ ARGUMENT **2 ~ (with sb) (over sth)** | **~ (between A and B) (over sth)** an argument between two people or groups of people who have different beliefs and ideas SYN **conflict**: *a head-on clash between the two leaders over education policy*

▸ DIFFERENCE **3** the difference that exists between two things that are opposed to each other SYN **conflict**: *a **clash of interests/opinions/cultures*** ◇ *a **personality clash** with the boss*

▸ OF TWO EVENTS **4** a situation in which two events happen at the same time so that you cannot go to or see them both: *a clash in the timetable/schedule*

▸ OF COLOURS **5** the situation when two colours, designs, etc. look ugly when they are put together

▸ LOUD NOISE **6** a loud noise made by two metal objects being hit together: *a **clash of cymbals/swords***

▸ IN SPORT **7** (used in newspapers, about sports) an occasion when two teams or players compete against each other: *Bayern's clash with Roma in the Champions League.*

■ ***verb***

▸ FIGHT/COMPETE **1** [I] **~ (with sb)** to come together and fight or compete in a contest: *The two sets of supporters clashed outside the stadium.* ◇ *The two teams clash in tomorrow's final.*

▸ ARGUE **2** [I] **~ (with sb) (over/on sth)** to argue or disagree seriously with sb about sth, and to show this in public: *The leaders and members clashed on the issue.* ◇ *The leaders clashed with party members on the issue.*

▸ BE DIFFERENT **3** [I] **~ (with sth)** (of beliefs, ideas or personalities) to be very different and opposed to each other: *His left-wing views clashed with his father's politics.* ◇ *His views and his father's clashed.* ◇ *They have clashing personalities.*

▸ OF TWO EVENTS **4** [I] **~ (with sth)** (of events) to happen at the same time so that you cannot go to or see them both: *Unfortunately your party clashes with a wedding I'm going to.* ◇ *There are two good movies on TV tonight, but they clash.*

▸ OF COLOURS **5** [I] **~ (with sth)** (of colours, patterns or styles) to look ugly when put together: *The wallpaper clashes with the carpet.* ◇ *The wallpaper and the carpet clash.*

▸ MAKE LOUD NOISE **6** [I, T] to hit together and make a loud ringing noise; to make two metal objects do this: **~ (together)** *The long blades clashed together.* ◇ **~ sth (together)** *She clashed the cymbals.*

clasp /klɑːsp; *NAmE* klæsp/ *verb, noun*

■ ***verb*** **1 ~ sth** to hold sth tightly in your hand: *He leaned forward, his **hands clasped** tightly together.* ◇ *They clasped hands* (= held each other's hands). ◇ *I stood there, clasping the door handle.* ➲ SYNONYMS at HOLD **2 ~ sb/sth** to hold sb/sth tightly with your arms around them: *She clasped the children in her arms.* ◇ *He **clasped** her **to him**.* **3 ~ sth (+ adv./prep.)** to fasten sth with a clasp: *She clasped the bracelet around her wrist.*

■ ***noun*** **1** [C] a device that fastens sth, such as a bag or the ends of a belt or a piece of jewellery: *the clasp of a necklace/handbag* ➲ VISUAL VOCAB page V53 **2** [sing.] a tight hold with your hand or in your arms: *He took her hand in his firm warm clasp.*

class 0-w /klɑːs; *NAmE* klæs/ *noun, verb, adj.*

■ ***noun***

▸ IN EDUCATION **1** 0-w [C+sing./pl. v.] a group of students who are taught together: *We were in the same class at school.* ◇ *She is the youngest in her class.* ◇ *He came **top of the class**.* ◇ *The whole class was/were told to stay behind after school.* **2** 0-w [C, U] an occasion when a group of students meets to be taught SYN **lesson**: *I was late for a class.* ◇ *See me after class.* ◇ *She works hard **in class*** (= during the class). ◇ *I have a history class at 9 o'clock.* ➲ COLLOCATIONS at EDUCATION **3** 0-w [C] (also **classes** [pl.]) a series of classes on a particular subject SYN **course**: *I've been **taking classes** in pottery.* ◇ *Are you still doing your French evening class?* **4** [C+sing./pl. v.] (*especially NAmE*) a group of students who finish their studies at school, college or university in a particular year: *the class of 2008*

▸ IN SOCIETY **5** 0-w [C+sing./pl. v.] one of the groups of people in a society that are thought of as being at the same social or economic level: *the **working/middle/upper class*** ◇ *The party tries to appeal to all classes of society.* ◇ *the professional classes* **6** 0-w [U] the way that people are divided into different social and economic groups: *differences of class, race or gender* ◇ *the class system* ◇ *a society in which class is more important than ability*

▸ GROUP OF PEOPLE/ANIMALS **7** 0-w [C] a group of people, animals or things that have similar characteristics or qualities: *It was good accommodation for a hotel of this class.* ◇ *different classes of drugs* ◇ *Dickens was **in a different class** from* (= was much better than) *most of his contemporaries.* ◇ *As a jazz singer she's **in a class of her own*** (= better than most others). ➲ see also FIRST-CLASS, HIGH-CLASS, LOW-CLASS, SECOND-CLASS

▸ SKILL/STYLE **8** 0-w [U] an elegant quality or a high level of skill that is impressive: *She **has class** all right—she looks like a model.* ◇ *There's a real touch of class about this team.*

▸ IN TRAIN/PLANE **9** 0-w [C] (especially in compounds) each of several different levels of comfort that are available to travellers in a plane, etc: *He always travels business class.* ◇ *The first-class compartment is situated at the front of the train.* ➲ see also BUSINESS CLASS, ECONOMY CLASS SYNDROME, FIRST CLASS, SECOND-CLASS, THIRD-CLASS, TOURIST CLASS

▸ OF UNIVERSITY DEGREE **10** [C] (especially in compounds) one of the levels of achievement in a British university degree exam: *a **first-/second-/third-class** degree*

▸ BIOLOGY **11** [C] a group into which animals, plants, etc. that have similar characteristics are divided, below a

PHYLUM ➲ compare FAMILY, GENUS, SPECIES **IDM** see CHATTER *v.*

■ ***verb*** [often passive] **~ sb/sth (as sth)**

▸ PUT INTO GROUP to think or decide that sb/sth is a particular type of person or thing **SYN** **classify**: *Immigrant workers were classed as aliens.*

■ ***adj.*** [only before noun] (*informal*)

▸ WITH SKILL/STYLE very good: *a* ***class player/performer*** ◇ *She's a real* ***class act.***

ˌclass ˈaction *noun* (*NAmE*) a type of LAWSUIT that is started by a group of people who have the same problem

ˈclass-conscious *adj.* very aware of belonging to a particular social class and of the differences between social classes ▸ **ˈclass-conscious·ness** *noun* [U]

clas·sic 🔑 **AW** /ˈklæsɪk/ *adj., noun*

■ ***adj.*** [usually before noun] **1** 🔑 accepted or deserving to be accepted as one of the best or most important of its kind: *a classic novel/study/goal* **2** 🔑 (also **clas·sic·al**) with all the features you would expect to find; very typical: *a* ***classic example*** *of poor communication* ◇ *She displayed the classic symptoms of depression.* ◇ *I made the classic mistake of clapping in a pause in the music!* **3** 🔑 elegant, but simple and traditional in style or design; not affected by changes in fashion: *a classic grey suit* ◇ *classic design* ◇ ***classic cars*** (= cars which are no longer made, but which are still popular) **4** (*informal*) people say **That's classic!** when they find sth very amusing, when they think sb has been very stupid or when sth annoying, but not surprising, happens: *She's not going to help? Oh, that's classic!*

■ ***noun*** **1** 🔑 [C] a book, film/movie or song which is well known and considered to be of very high quality, setting standards for other books, etc: *English classics such as 'Alice in Wonderland'* ◇ *The novel may become a modern classic.* **2** 🔑 [C] a thing that is an excellent example of its kind: *That match was a classic.* **3** **Classics** [U] the study of ancient Greek and Roman culture, especially their languages and literature: *a degree in Classics*

Synonyms

classic / classical

These adjectives are frequently used with the following nouns:

classic ~	classical ~
example	music
case	ballet
novel	architecture
work	scholar
car	period

- **Classic** describes something that is accepted as being of very high quality and one of the best of its kind: *a classic movie/work*. It is also used to describe a typical example of something: *a classic example/mistake*, or something elegant but simple and traditional: *classic design*.
- **Classical** describes a form of traditional Western music and other things that are traditional in style: *a classical composer* ◇ *a classical theory*. It is also used to talk about things that are connected with the culture of Ancient Greece and Rome: *a classical scholar* ◇ *classical mythology*.

clas·sic·al **AW** /ˈklæsɪkl/ *adj.* [usually before noun] **1** widely accepted and used for a long time; traditional in style or idea: *the classical economics of Smith and Ricardo* ◇ *the classical theory of unemployment* ◇ *classical and modern ballet* **2** connected with or influenced by the culture of ancient Greece and Rome: *classical studies* ◇ *a classical scholar* (= an expert in Latin and Greek) **3** (of music) written in a Western musical tradition, usually using an established form (for example a SYMPHONY) and not played on electronic instruments. Classical music is generally considered to be serious and to have a lasting value: *He plays classical music, as well as pop and jazz.* ◇ *a* ***classical composer/violinist*** ➲ COLLOCATIONS at MUSIC **4** = CLASSIC: *These are classical examples of food allergy.* **5** (of a language) ancient in its form and no longer used in a spoken form: *classical Arabic* **6** simple and attractive: *the classical elegance of the design* ▸ **clas·sic·al·ly** /ˈklæsɪkli/ *adv.*: *Her face is classically beautiful.* ◇ *a* ***classically trained*** *singer*

clas·si·cism /ˈklæsɪsɪzəm/ *noun* [U] **1** a style of art and literature that is simple and elegant and is based on the styles of ancient Greece and Rome. Classicism was popular in Europe in the 18th century. **2** a style or form that has simple, natural qualities and pleasing combinations of parts

clas·si·cist /ˈklæsɪsɪst/ *noun* **1** a person who studies ancient Greek or Latin **2** a person who follows classicism in art or literature

clas·si·fi·able /ˈklæsɪfaɪəbl/ *adj.* that you can or should CLASSIFY: *The information was not easily classifiable.* ◇ *top-secret or classifiable information*

clas·si·fi·ca·tion /ˌklæsɪfɪˈkeɪʃn/ *noun* **1** [U] the act or process of putting people or things into a group or class (= of CLASSIFYING them): *a style of music that defies classification* (= is like no other) **2** [C] a group, class, division, etc. into which sb or sth is put **3** [U] (*biology*) the act of putting animals, plants, etc. into groups, classes or divisions according to their characteristics **4** [C] (*technical*) a system of arranging books, tapes, magazines, etc. in a library into groups according to their subject

clas·si·fied /ˈklæsɪfaɪd/ *adj.* [usually before noun] **1** (of information) officially secret and available only to particular people: ***classified information/documents/material*** **OPP** **unclassified** **2** with information arranged in groups according to subjects: *a classified catalogue* **3** **classifieds** *noun* [pl.] = CLASSIFIED ADVERTISEMENTS

ˌclassified adˈvertisements (also **ˌclassified ˈads**, **ˈclassifieds**) (*BrE* also **ˈsmall ads**) (*NAmE* also **ˈwant ads**) *noun* [pl.] the section in a newspaper with small advertisements arranged in groups according to their subject, that are placed by people or small companies who want to buy or sell sth, find or offer a job, etc.

clas·si·fier /ˈklæsɪfaɪə(r)/ *noun* (*grammar*) an AFFIX or word which shows that a word belongs to a group of words with similar meanings. For example the prefix 'un' is a classifier that shows the word is negative.

clas·sify /ˈklæsɪfaɪ/ *verb* (**clas·si·fies, clas·si·fy·ing, clas·si·fied, clas·si·fied**) **1** **~ sth** to arrange sth in groups according to features that they have in common: *The books in the library* ***are classified according to*** *subject.* ◇ *Patients* ***are classified into*** *three categories.* **2** **~ sb/sth as sth** to decide which type or group sb/sth belongs to: *Only eleven of these accidents were classified as major.*

class·less /ˈklɑːsləs; *NAmE* ˈklæs-/ *adj.* **1** (*approving*) with no divisions into social classes: *Will Britain ever become a classless society?* **2** not clearly belonging to a particular social class: *a classless accent* ▸ **class·less·ness** *noun* [U]

class·mate /ˈklɑːsmeɪt; *NAmE* ˈklæs-/ *noun* a person who is or was in the same class as you at school or college

class·room 🔑 /ˈklɑːsruːm; -rʊm; *NAmE* ˈklæs-/ *noun* a room where a class of children or students is taught: *classroom activities* ◇ *the use of computers in the classroom* ➲ VISUAL VOCAB page V57

ˌclass ˈstruggle (also **ˌclass ˈwar**) *noun* [U, sing.] (*politics*) opposition between the different social classes in society, especially that described in Marxist theory

classy /ˈklɑːsi; *NAmE* ˈklæsi/ *adj.* (**class·ier, classi·est**) (*informal*) of high quality; expensive and/or fashionable: *a classy player* ◇ *a classy hotel/restaurant*

clat·ter /ˈklætə(r)/ *verb* **1** [I] if hard objects **clatter**, they knock together and make a loud noise: *He dropped the knife and it clattered on the stone floor.* ◇ *Her cup clattered in the saucer.* **2** [I] **+ adv./prep.** to move making a loud noise like hard objects knocking together: *The cart clat-*

tered over the cobbles. ◇ *She heard him clattering around downstairs.* ▸ **clat·ter** (also **clat·ter·ing**) *noun* [sing.]: *the clatter of horses' hoofs*

clause AW /klɔːz/ *noun* **1** (*grammar*) a group of words that includes a subject and a verb, and forms a sentence or part of a sentence: *In the sentence 'They often go to Italy because they love the food', 'They often go to Italy' is the main clause and 'because they love the food' is a subordinate clause.* **2** an item in a legal document that says that a particular thing must or must not be done

C

claus·tro·pho·bia /ˌklɔːstrəˈfəʊbiə; *NAmE* -ˈfoʊ-/ *noun* [U] an extreme fear of being in a small confined place; the unpleasant feeling that a person gets in a situation which restricts them: *to suffer from claustrophobia* ◇ *She felt she had to escape from the claustrophobia of family life.* ➲ compare AGORAPHOBIA

claus·tro·pho·bic /ˌklɔːstrəˈfəʊbɪk; *NAmE* -ˈfoʊ-/ *adj.* giving you claustrophobia; suffering from claustrophobia: *the claustrophobic atmosphere of the room* ◇ *to feel claustrophobic* ▸ **claus·tro·pho·bic** *noun*

clave /kleɪv; ˈklɑːveɪ/ *noun* **1** one of a pair of wooden sticks that are hit together to make a sound **2** a rhythm that forms the basis of Latin music

clavi·chord /ˈklævɪkɔːd; *NAmE* -kɔːrd/ *noun* an early type of musical instrument, like a piano with a very soft tone

clav·icle /ˈklævɪkl/ *noun* (*anatomy*) the COLLARBONE ➲ VISUAL VOCAB page V48

claw /klɔː/ *noun, verb*

■ ***noun*** **1** one of the sharp curved nails on the end of an animal's or a bird's foot ➲ VISUAL VOCAB page V10 **2** a long, sharp curved part of the body of some types of SHELLFISH, used for catching and holding things: *the claws of a crab* ➲ picture at SHELLFISH ➲ VISUAL VOCAB page V11 **3** part of a tool or machine, like a claw, used for holding, pulling or lifting things ➲ VISUAL VOCAB page V17 ➲ see also CLAW HAMMER

IDM **get your claws into sb 1** (*disapproving*) if a woman **gets her claws** into a man, she tries hard to make him marry her or to have a relationship with her **2** to criticize sb severely: *Wait until the media gets its claws into her.* ➲ more at RED *adj.*

■ ***verb*** [I, T] to scratch or tear sb/sth with claws or with your nails: **~ at sb/sth** *The cat was clawing at the leg of the chair.* ◇ **~ sb/sth** *She had clawed Stephen across the face.* ◇ (*figurative*) *His hands clawed the air.*

IDM **claw your way back, into sth, out of sth, to sth, etc.** to gradually achieve sth or move somewhere by using a lot of determination and effort: *She clawed her way to the top of her profession.* ◇ *Slowly, he clawed his way out from under the collapsed building.*

PHR V ˌ**claw sth↔ˈback 1** to get sth back that you have lost, usually by using a lot of effort **2** (of a government) to get back money that has been paid to people, usually by taxing them ➲ related noun CLAWBACK

claw·back /ˈklɔːbæk/ *noun* (*BrE, business*) the act of getting money back from people it has been paid to; the money that is paid back

ˈ**claw hammer** *noun* a hammer with one split, curved side that is used for pulling out nails

clay /kleɪ/ *noun* [U] a type of heavy, sticky earth that becomes hard when it is baked and is used to make things such as pots and bricks ➲ SYNONYMS at SOIL IDM see FOOT *n.*

ˈ**clay court** *noun* a TENNIS COURT that has a surface made of clay

clayey /kleɪi/ *adj.* containing clay; like clay: *clayey soil*

clay·more /ˈkleɪmɔː(r)/ *noun* a large SWORD with a broad blade with two sharp edges that was used in Scotland in the past

ˌ**clay ˈpigeon shooting** (*BrE*) (*NAmE* ˈ**skeet shooting**) *noun* a sport in which a disc of baked clay (called a **clay pigeon**) is thrown into the air for people to shoot at

clean 0‑w /kliːn/ *adj., verb, adv., noun*

■ ***adj.*** (clean·er, clean·est)

▸ NOT DIRTY **1** 0‑w not dirty: *Are your hands clean?* ◇ *to **wipe sth clean*** ◇ *The hotel was **spotlessly*** (= extremely) ***clean***. ◇ (*BrE*) *It is your responsibility to **keep** the room **clean and tidy***. ◇ (*NAmE*) ***Keep** your room **neat and clean***. ◇ *I can't find a clean shirt* (= one I haven't worn since it was washed). **2** 0‑w having a clean appearance and clean surroundings: *Cats are very clean animals.*

▸ NOT HARMFUL **3** 0‑w free from harmful or unpleasant substances: *clean drinking water* ◇ *clean air* ◇ *cleaner cars* (= not producing so many harmful substances)

▸ PAPER **4** 0‑w [usually before noun] with nothing written on it: *a clean sheet of paper*

▸ NOT OFFENSIVE **5** 0‑w not offensive or referring to sex; not doing anything that is considered immoral or bad: *The entertainment was **good clean fun** for the whole family.* ◇ *Keep the jokes clean please!* ◇ *The sport has a very clean image.*

▸ NOT ILLEGAL **6** 0‑w not showing or having any record of doing sth that is against the law: *a **clean driving licence/driver's license*** ◇ *a clean police record* **7** (*informal*) not owning or carrying anything illegal such as drugs or weapons: *The police searched her but she was clean.*

▸ FAIR **8** played or done in a fair way and within the rules: *It was a tough but clean game.*

▸ SMOOTH/SIMPLE **9** having a smooth edge, surface or shape; simple and regular: *A sharp knife makes a clean cut.* ◇ *a modern design with clean lines and a bright appearance*

▸ ACCURATE **10** done in a skilful and accurate way: *The plane made a clean take-off.*

▸ TASTE/SMELL **11** tasting, smelling or looking pleasant and fresh: *The wine has a clean taste and a lovely golden colour.* ➲ compare UNCLEAN

IDM **as clean as a ˈwhistle** (*informal*) very clean **a clean bill of ˈhealth** a report that says sb is healthy or that sth is in good condition **a clean ˈbreak 1** a complete separation from a person, an organization, a way of life, etc: *She wanted to make a clean break with the past.* **2** a break in a bone in one place **a clean ˈsheet/ˈslate** a record of your work or behaviour that does not show any mistakes or bad things that you have done: *No government operates with a completely clean sheet.* ◇ *They kept a clean sheet in the match* (= no goals were scored against them). **make a clean ˈbreast of sth** to tell the truth about sth so that you no longer feel guilty **make a clean sweep (of sth) 1** to remove all the people or things from an organization that are thought to be unnecessary or need changing **2** to win all the prizes or parts of a game or competition; to win an election completely: *China made a clean sweep of the medals in the gymnastics events.* ◇ *The opinion poll suggests a clean sweep for the Democrats.* ➲ more at NOSE *n.*, WIPE *v.*

■ ***verb*** **1** 0‑w [T, I] **~ (sth)** to make sth free from dirt or dust by washing or rubbing it: *to clean the windows/bath/floor* ◇ *to clean a wound* ◇ *Have you **cleaned your teeth**?* ◇ *The villa is cleaned twice a week.* ◇ *I spent all day cooking and cleaning.* ➲ see also DRY-CLEAN, SPRING-CLEAN **2** [I] to become clean: *This oven cleans easily* (= is easy to clean). **3** [T] **~ sth** = DRY-CLEAN: *This coat is filthy. I'll **have it cleaned**.* **4** [T] **~ sth** to remove the inside parts of a fish, chicken, etc. before you cook it

IDM **clean ˈhouse** (*NAmE*) **1** to remove people or things that are not necessary or wanted: *The new manager said he wanted to clean house.* **2** to make your house clean **clean up your ˈact** (*informal*) to start behaving in a moral or responsible way: *He cleaned up his act and came off drugs.*

PHR V ˌ**clean sth↔ˈdown** to clean sth thoroughly: *All the equipment should be cleaned down regularly.* ˈ**clean sth off/from sth** | ˌ**clean sth↔ˈoff** to remove sth from sth by brushing, rubbing, etc: *I cleaned the mud off my shoes.* ˌ**clean sth↔ˈout** to clean the inside of sth thoroughly: *I must clean the fish tank out.* ˌ**clean sb ˈout** (*informal*) to use all of sb's money: *Paying for all those drinks has cleaned me out.* ˌ**clean sb/sth ˈout** (*informal*) to steal everything from a person or place: *The burglars totally cleaned her out.* ˌ**clean ˈup** (*informal*) to win or make a lot of money: *This film should clean up at the box offices.* ˌ**clean (yourself) ˈup** 0‑w (*informal*) to make yourself clean, usually by washing: *I need to change and clean up.* ◇ *Go and clean yourself* up. ◇ *You'd better* ***get cleaned up****.* ➲ related noun CLEAN-UP ˌ**clean ˈup** | ˌ**clean sth↔ˈup** to remove dirt, etc. from somewhere: *He always expected other people to* ***clean up after*** *him* (= when he had made the place dirty or untidy). ◇ *Who's going to clean up this mess?* ◇ *to clean up beaches after an oil spillage* ➲ related noun CLEAN-UP ˌ**clean sth↔ˈup** to remove crime and immoral behaviour from a place or an activity: *The new mayor is determined to clean up the city.* ◇ *Soccer needs to* ***clean up its image****.* ➲ related noun CLEAN-UP

■ ***adv.*** (*informal*) used to emphasize that an action takes place completely: *The thief got clean away.* ◇ *I clean forgot about calling him.*

IDM **come clean (with sb) (about sth)** to admit and explain sth that you have kept as a secret: *Isn't it time the government came clean about their plans for education?*

■ ***noun*** [sing.] the act or process of cleaning sth: *The house needed a good clean.*

Synonyms

clean

wash • rinse • cleanse • dry-clean

These words all mean to remove dirt from sth, especially by using water and/or soap.

clean to remove dirt or dust from sth, especially by using water or chemicals: *The villa is cleaned twice a week.* ◇ *Have you cleaned your teeth?* ◇ *This coat is filthy. I'll have it cleaned* (= dry-cleaned).

wash to remove dirt from sth using water and usually soap: *He quickly washed his hands and face.* ◇ *These jeans need washing.*

rinse to remove dirt, etc. from sth using clean water only, not soap; to remove the soap from sth with clean water after washing it: *Make sure you rinse all the soap out.*

cleanse to clean your skin or a wound.

dry-clean to clean clothes using chemicals instead of water.

PATTERNS
- to clean/wash/rinse/cleanse sth **in/with** sth
- to clean/wash/rinse sth **from** sth
- to clean/wash/cleanse a **wound**
- to clean/wash the **car/floor**
- to wash/rinse your **hair**
- to **have sth** cleaned/washed/dry-cleaned

ˌ**clean and ˈjerk** *noun* an exercise in WEIGHTLIFTING in which a bar with weights is lifted to the shoulder, and then raised above the head

ˌ**clean-ˈcut** *adj.* (especially of a young man) looking neat and clean and therefore socially acceptable: *Simon's clean-cut good looks*

clean·er /ˈkliːnə(r)/ *noun* **1** a person whose job is to clean other people's houses or offices, etc: *an office cleaner* **2** a machine or substance that is used for cleaning: *a vacuum cleaner* ◇ *a bottle of kitchen cleaner* **3 cleaner's** (*pl.* cleaners) (also ˌ**dry-ˈcleaner's**) a shop/store where clothes, curtains, etc. are cleaned, especially with chemicals: *Can you pick up my suit from the cleaner's?*

IDM **take sb to the ˈcleaners** (*informal*) **1** to steal all of sb's money, etc, or to get it using a trick **2** to defeat sb completely: *Our team got taken to the cleaners.*

clean·ing /ˈkliːnɪŋ/ *noun* [U] the work of making the inside of a house, etc. clean: *They pay someone to* ***do the cleaning****.* ➲ VISUAL VOCAB page V17

ˈ**cleaning lady** (also ˈ**cleaning woman**) *noun* a woman whose job is to clean the rooms and furniture in an office, a house, etc.

ˌ**clean-ˈlimbed** *adj.* (of a person) thin and with a good shape: *a clean-limbed model*

clean·li·ness /ˈklenlinəs/ *noun* [U] the state of being clean or the habit of keeping things clean: *Some people are obsessive about cleanliness.*

ˌ**clean-ˈliving** *adj.* (of a person) living a healthy life, by not drinking alcohol, not having sex with a lot of different people, etc.

clean·ly /ˈkliːnli/ *adv.* **1** easily and smoothly in one movement: *The boat moved cleanly through the water.* **2** in a clean way: *fuel that burns cleanly*

cleanse /klenz/ *verb* **1** [T, I] **~ (sth)** to clean your skin or a wound: *a cleansing cream* ➲ SYNONYMS at CLEAN **2** [T] **~ sb (of/from sth)** (*literary*) to take away sb's guilty feelings or SIN ➲ see also ETHNIC CLEANSING

cleans·er /ˈklenzə(r)/ *noun* **1** a liquid or cream for cleaning your face, especially for removing make-up **2** a substance that contains chemicals and is used for cleaning things

ˌ**clean-ˈshaven** *adj.* a man who is **clean-shaven** does not have a beard or MOUSTACHE (= hair that has been allowed to grow on the face)

ˈ**clean-up** *noun* [usually sing.] the process of removing dirt, pollution, or things that are considered bad or immoral from a place: *the clean-up of the river* ◇ *a clean-up campaign*

clear 0-w /klɪə(r); *NAmE* klɪr/ *adj., verb, adv., noun*

■ **adj.** (**clear·er, clear·est**)

WORD FAMILY
clear *adj.* (≠ unclear)
clearly *adv.*
clarity *noun*
clarify *verb*

▸ WITHOUT CONFUSION/DOUBT **1** 0-w easy to understand and not causing any confusion: *She gave me clear and precise directions.* ◇ *Are these instructions clear enough?* ◇ *You'll do as you're told, is that clear?* ◇ *This behaviour must stop—do I* ***make myself clear*** (= express myself clearly so there is no doubt about what I mean)? ◇ *I hope I* ***made it clear*** *to him that he was no longer welcome here.* **2** 0-w obvious and leaving no doubt at all: *This is a clear case of fraud.* ◇ *She won the election by a clear majority.* ◇ *His height gives him a clear advantage.* ◇ **~ (to sb) (that)...** ***It was*** *quite* ***clear*** *to me* ***that*** *she was lying.* ◇ **~ what, how, whether, etc...** *It is not clear what they want us to do.* ➲ LANGUAGE BANK at EVIDENCE, IMPERSONAL **3** 0-w having or feeling no doubt or confusion: **~ about/on sth** *Are you clear about the arrangements for tomorrow?* ◇ *My memory is not clear on that point.* ◇ **~ what, how, whether, etc...** *I'm still not clear what the job involves.* ◇ *We need a* ***clear understanding*** *of the problems involved.* ➲ SYNONYMS at SURE

▸ MIND **4** 0-w thinking in a sensible and logical way, especially in a difficult situation: *a clear thinker* ◇ *You'll need to* ***keep a clear head*** *for your interview.*

▸ EASY TO SEE/HEAR **5** 0-w easy to see or hear: *The photo wasn't very clear.* ◇ *The voice on the phone was clear and strong.* ◇ *She was in Australia but I could hear her voice* ***as clear as a bell.***

▸ TRANSPARENT **6** 0-w that you can see through: *The water was so clear we could see the bottom of the lake.* ◇ *clear glass* ◇ *a clear colourless liquid*

▸ SKY/WEATHER **7** 0-w without cloud or MIST: *a clear blue sky* ◇ *On a clear day you can see France.*

▸ SKIN **8** without spots or marks: *clear skin* ◇ *a clear complexion*

▸ EYES **9** bright and lively

▸ NOT BLOCKED **10 ~ (of sth)** free from things that are blocking the way or covering the surface of sth: *The road was clear and I ran over.* ◇ *All exits must be kept clear of baggage.* ◇ *You won't get a clear view of the stage from here.* ◇ *I always leave a clear desk at the end of the day.*

▸ CONSCIENCE **11** if you have a **clear** CONSCIENCE or your CONSCIENCE is **clear**, you do not feel guilty

▸ FREE FROM STH BAD **12 ~ of sth** free from sth that is unpleasant: *They were still not clear of all suspicion.* ◇ *We are finally clear of debt.*

▸ NOT TOUCHING/NEAR **13** [not before noun] **~ (of sb/sth)** not touching sth; a distance away from sth: *The plane climbed*

until it was clear of the clouds. ◇ Make sure you park your car clear of the entrance.
▸ PERIOD OF TIME **14** [only before noun] whole or complete: *Allow three clear days for the letter to arrive.*
▸ SUM OF MONEY **15** [only before noun] remaining when taxes, costs, etc. have been taken away SYN **net**: *They had made a clear profit of £2 000.*
▸ PHONETICS **16** (of a speech sound) produced with the central part of the tongue close to the top of the mouth. In many accents of English, clear /l/ is used before a vowel, as in *leave.* OPP **dark**

IDM **be clear 'sailing** (*US*) = BE PLAIN SAILING at PLAIN *adj.* **(as) clear as 'day** easy to see or understand **(as) clear as 'mud** (*informal, humorous*) not clear at all; not easy to understand: *Oh well, that's all as clear as mud, then.* ➲ more at FIELD *n.*, HEAD *n.*, LOUD *adv.*

Synonyms

clear

obvious • apparent • evident • plain

These words all describe sth that is easy to see or understand and leaves no doubts or confusion.

clear easy to see or understand and leaving no doubts: *It was quite clear to me that she was lying.*

obvious easy to see or understand: *It's obvious from what he said that something is wrong.*

apparent [not usually before noun] (*rather formal*) easy to see or understand: *It was apparent from her face that she was really upset.*

evident (*rather formal*) easy to see or understand: *The orchestra played with evident enjoyment.*

plain easy to see or understand: *He **made it** very **plain** that he wanted us to leave.*

WHICH WORD?

These words all have almost exactly the same meaning. There are slight differences in register and patterns of use. If you *make sth clear/plain*, you do so deliberately because you want people to understand sth; if you *make sth obvious*, you usually do it without meaning to: ~~*I hope I make myself obvious.*~~ ◇ ~~*Try not to make it so clear/plain.*~~ In the expressions *clear majority, for obvious reasons, for no apparent reason* and *plain to see*, none of the other words can be used instead. You can have *a clear/an obvious/a plain case of sth* but not: ~~*an evident case of sth*~~.

PATTERNS

- clear/obvious/apparent/evident/plain **to** sb/sth
- clear/obvious/apparent/evident/plain **that/what/who/how/where/why...**
- to **seem/become/make sth** clear/obvious/apparent/evident/plain
- **perfectly/quite/very** clear/obvious/apparent/evident/plain

■ *verb*
▸ REMOVE STH/SB **1** [T] to remove sth that is not wanted or needed from a place: **~ sth/sb** *I had cleared my desk before I left.* ◇ *It was several hours before the road was cleared after the accident.* ◇ *It's your turn to **clear the table*** (= to take away the dirty plates, etc. after a meal). ◇ *She **cleared a space** on the sofa for him to sit down.* ◇ **~ A (of B)** *I cleared my desk of papers.* ◇ *The streets had been cleared of snow.* ◇ **~ B (from/off A)** *Clear all those papers off the desk.* ◇ *The remains of the snow had been cleared from the streets.* ➲ see also CLEAR AWAY **2** [T] **~ sth** to make people leave a place: *After the bomb warning, police cleared the streets.*
▸ NOT BE BLOCKED **3** [I] to move freely again; to no longer be blocked: *The traffic took a long time to clear after the accident.* ◇ *The boy's lungs cleared and he began to breathe more easily.*
▸ OF LIQUID **4** [I] when a liquid **clears**, it becomes transparent and you can see through it: *The muddy water slowly cleared.*
▸ OF SMOKE, ETC. **5** [I] **~ (away)** when smoke, FOG, etc. **clears**, it disappears so that it is easier to see things: *The mist will clear by mid-morning.*
▸ OF SKY/WEATHER **6** [I] when the sky or the weather **clears**, it becomes brighter and free of cloud or rain: *The sky cleared after the storm.* ◇ *The rain is clearing slowly.*
▸ YOUR HEAD/MIND **7** [I, T] if your head or mind **clears**, or you **clear** it, you become free of thoughts that worry or confuse you or the effects of alcohol, a blow, etc. and you are able to think clearly: *As her mind cleared, she remembered what had happened.* ◇ **~ sth** *I went for a walk to clear my head.*
▸ OF FACE/EXPRESSION **8** [I] if your face or expression **clears**, you stop looking angry or worried
▸ PROVE SB INNOCENT **9** [T] **~ sb (of sth)** to prove that sb is innocent: *She was cleared of all charges against her.* ◇ *Throughout his years in prison, he fought to **clear his name**.*
▸ GIVE OFFICIAL PERMISSION **10** [T] to give or get official approval for sth to be done: **~ sth** *His appointment had been cleared by the board.* ◇ **~ sth with sb/sth** *I'll have to **clear it** with the manager.* **11** [T] **~ sth** to give official permission for a person, a ship, a plane or goods to leave or enter a place: *The plane had been cleared for take-off.* ◇ *to clear goods through customs* **12** [T] **~ sb** to decide officially, after finding out information about sb, that they can be given special work or allowed to see secret papers: *She hasn't been cleared by security.*
▸ MONEY **13** [I, T] **~ (sth)** if a cheque that you pay into your bank account **clears**, or a bank **clears** it, the money is available for you to use: *Cheques usually take three working days to clear.* **14** [T] **~ sth** to gain or earn a sum of money as profit: *She cleared £1 000 on the deal.* **15** [T] **~ sth** if you **clear** a debt or a loan, you pay all the money back
▸ GET OVER/PAST **16** [T] **~ sth** to jump over or get past sth without touching it: *The horse cleared the fence easily.* ◇ *The car only just cleared* (= avoided hitting) *the gatepost.*
▸ IN SPORT **17** [T, I] **~ (sth)** (in football (SOCCER) and some other sports) if you **clear** a ball, or a ball **clears**, it is kicked or hit away from the area near your own goal

IDM **clear the 'air** to improve a difficult or TENSE situation by talking about worries, doubts, etc. **clear the 'decks** (*informal*) to prepare for an activity, event, etc. by removing anything that is not essential to it **clear your 'throat** to cough so that you can speak clearly **clear the way (for sth/for sth to happen)** to remove things that are stopping the progress or movement of sth: *The ruling could clear the way for extradition proceedings.* ➲ more at COAST *n.*, COBWEB

PHR V **,clear a'way | ,clear sth↔a'way** to remove sth because it is not wanted or needed, or in order to leave a clear space: *He cleared away and made coffee.* ◇ *It's time your toys were cleared away.* **,clear 'off** (*informal*) to go or run away: *He cleared off when he heard the police siren.* ◇ *You've no right to be here. Clear off!* **,clear 'out (of...)** (*informal*) to leave a place quickly: *He cleared out with all the money and left her with the kids.* **,clear 'out | ,clear sth↔'out** to make sth empty and clean by removing things or throwing things away: *to clear out a drawer/room* ◇ *We cleared out all our old clothes.* ◇ *I found the letters when I was clearing out after my father died.* ➲ related noun CLEAR-OUT **,clear 'up 1** (of the weather) to become fine or bright: *I hope it clears up this afternoon.* **2** (of an illness, infection, etc.) to disappear: *Has your rash cleared up yet?* **,clear 'up | ,clear sth↔'up** to make sth clean and neat: *It's time to clear up.* ◇ *I'm fed up with **clearing up after you**!* ◇ *Clear up your own mess!* **,clear sth↔'up** to solve or explain sth: *to **clear up a mystery/difficulty/misunderstanding***

■ *adv.*
▸ NOT NEAR/TOUCHING **1** **~ (of sth)** away from sth; not near or touching sth: *Stand clear of the train doors.* ◇ *He injured his arm as he jumped clear of the car.* ◇ *By lap two Walker was two metres clear of the rest of the runners.*
▸ ALL THE WAY **2** (*especially NAmE*) all the way to sth that is far away: *She could see clear down the highway into the town.*

IDM **keep/stay/steer clear (of sb/sth)** to avoid a person or thing because it may cause problems ➲ more at WAY *n.*

■ ***noun***
IDM **in the 'clear** (*informal*) no longer in danger or thought to be guilty of sth: *It seems that the original suspect is in the clear.*

clear·ance /ˈklɪərəns; *NAmE* ˈklɪr-/ *noun* **1** [C, U] the removal of things that are not wanted: *forest clearances* ◇ *slum clearance* (= the removal of houses that are in very bad condition in an area of a town) ◇ *a clearance sale* (= in a shop/store, when goods are sold cheaply to get rid of them quickly) **2** [U, C] the amount of space or distance that is needed between two objects so that they do not touch each other: *There is not much clearance for vehicles passing under this bridge.* ◇ *a clearance of one metre* **3** [U, C] official permission that is given to sb before they can work somewhere, have particular information, or do sth they want to do: *I'm waiting for clearance from headquarters.* ◇ *All employees at the submarine base require security clearance.* **4** [U] official permission for a person or vehicle to enter or leave an airport or a country: *The pilot was waiting for clearance for take-off.* **5** [U, C] the process of a cheque being paid by a bank **6** [C] a **clearance** in football (SOCCER) and some other sports is when a player kicks or hits the ball away from the goal of his or her own team

ˌclear-ˈcut *adj.* definite and easy to see or identify: *There is no clear-cut answer to this question.*

ˌclear-ˈheaded *adj.* able to think in a clear and sensible way, especially in a difficult situation

clear·ing /ˈklɪərɪŋ; *NAmE* ˈklɪrɪŋ/ *noun* **1** [C] an open space in a forest where there are no trees SYN **glade** ➲ VISUAL VOCAB page V4 **2** [U] (in Britain) the system used by universities to find students for the places on their courses that have not been filled shortly before the beginning of the academic year: *She got into university through clearing.* ◇ *You can apply for a place through the clearing system.* ◇ *The university has a limited number of clearing places this year.*

ˈclearing bank *noun* (in Britain) a bank that uses a clearing house when dealing with other banks

ˈclearing house *noun* **1** a central office that banks use in order to pay each other money and exchange cheques, etc. **2** an organization that collects and exchanges information on behalf of people or other organizations

clear·ly 0➔ /ˈklɪəli; *NAmE* ˈklɪrli/ *adv.*
1 0➔ in a way that is easy to see or hear: *Please speak clearly after the tone.* **2** 0➔ in a way that is sensible and easy to understand: *She explained everything very clearly.* **3** 0➔ used to emphasize that what you are saying is obvious and true SYN **obviously**: *Clearly, this will cost a lot more than we realized.*

clear·ness /ˈklɪənəs; *NAmE* ˈklɪrnəs/ *noun* [U] (much less frequent than *clarity*) the state of being clear

ˈclear-out *noun* [usually sing.] (*informal, especially BrE*) a process of getting rid of things or people that you no longer want: *have a clear-out*

ˌclear-ˈsighted *adj.* understanding or thinking clearly; able to make good decisions and judgements

ˈclear-up *noun* (*BrE*) the process of removing rubbish and tidying things: *a massive clear-up operation*

clear·way /ˈklɪəweɪ; *NAmE* ˈklɪrweɪ/ *noun* (in Britain) a road on which vehicles must not stop

cleat /kliːt/ *noun* **1** [C] a small wooden or metal bar fastened to sth, on which ropes may be fastened by winding **2** [C] a piece of rubber on the bottom of a shoe, etc. to stop it from slipping ➲ VISUAL VOCAB page V53 **3 cleats** [pl.] (*NAmE*) shoes with cleats, often worn for playing sports ➲ VISUAL VOCAB page V53 ➲ compare FOOTBALL BOOT, SPIKE (2), STUD (3)

cleav·age /ˈkliːvɪdʒ/ *noun* **1** [C, U] the space between a woman's breasts that can be seen above a dress that does not completely cover them **2** [C] (*formal*) a difference or division between people or groups

cleave /kliːv/ *verb* (**cleaved, cleaved** HELP Less commonly, **cleft** /kleft/ and **clove** /kləʊv/ /kloʊv/ are used for the past tense, and **cleft** and **cloven** /ˈkləʊvn/ /ˈkloʊv-/ for the past participle.) **1** [T] **~ sth** (*old-fashioned* or *literary*) to split or cut sth in two using sth sharp and heavy: *She cleaved his skull (in two) with an axe.* ◇ (*figurative*) *His skin was cleft with deep lines.* **2** [I, T] (*old-fashioned* or *literary*) to move quickly through sth: **~ through sth** *a ship cleaving through the water* ◇ **~ sth** *The huge boat cleaved the darkness.* **3** [I] **~ to sth/sb** (*literary*) to stick close to sth/sb: *Her tongue clove to the roof of her mouth.* **4** (**cleaved, cleaved**) [I] **~ to sth** (*formal*) to continue to believe in or be loyal to sth: *to* ***cleave to a belief/idea*** IDM see CLEFT

cleav·er /ˈkliːvə(r)/ *noun* a heavy knife with a broad blade, used for cutting large pieces of meat ➲ VISUAL VOCAB page V23

clef /klef/ *noun* (*music*) a symbol at the beginning of a line of printed music (called a STAVE OR STAFF) that shows the PITCH of the notes on it: *the* ***treble/bass clef*** ➲ picture at MUSIC

cleft /kleft/ *noun, adj.* ➲ see also CLEAVE *v.*
■ ***noun*** a natural opening or crack, for example in the ground or in rock, or in a person's chin: *a cleft in the rocks*
■ ***adj.***
IDM **be (caught) in a cleft 'stick** to be in a difficult situation when any action you take will have bad results

ˌcleft ˈlip *noun* a condition in which sb is born with their upper lip split

ˌcleft ˈpalate *noun* a condition in which sb is born with the roof of their mouth split, making them unable to speak clearly

ˌcleft ˈsentence *noun* (*grammar*) a sentence that begins with 'it' or 'that' and has a following clause, for example, 'it is you that I love', or 'that is my mother you're insulting'

cle·ma·tis /ˈklemətɪs; kləˈmeɪtɪs/ *noun* [C, U] a climbing plant with large white, purple or pink flowers

clem·ency /ˈklemənsi/ *noun* [U] (*formal*) kindness shown to sb when they are being punished; willingness not to punish sb so severely SYN **mercy**: *a plea for clemency*

clem·ent /ˈklemənt/ *adj.* (*formal*) **1** (especially of weather) mild and pleasant OPP **inclement 2** showing kindness and MERCY to sb who is being punished

clem·en·tine /ˈkleməntiːn/ *noun* a fruit like a small orange

clench /klentʃ/ *verb* **1** [T, I] **~ (sth)** when you **clench** your hands, teeth, etc, or when they **clench**, you press or squeeze them together tightly, usually showing that you are angry, determined or upset: *He* ***clenched his fists*** *in anger.* ◇ *Through* ***clenched teeth*** *she told him to leave.* ◇ *His fists clenched slowly until his knuckles were white.* **2** [T] **~ sth (in/between sth)** to hold sth tightly and firmly: *Her pen was clenched between her teeth.*

clere·story /ˈklɪəstɔːri; *NAmE* ˈklɪrs-/ *noun* (*pl.* **-ies**) (*architecture*) the upper part of a wall in a large church, with a row of windows in it, above the level of the lower roofs

clergy /ˈklɜːdʒi; *NAmE* ˈklɜːrdʒi/ (often **the clergy**) *noun* [pl.] the priests or ministers of a religion, especially of the Christian Church: *All the local clergy were asked to attend the ceremony.* ◇ *The new proposals affect both clergy and laity.* ➲ COLLOCATIONS at RELIGION ➲ compare LAITY

cler·gy·man /ˈklɜːdʒimən; *NAmE* ˈklɜːrdʒ-/ (also **church·man**) *noun* (*pl.* **-men** /-mən/) a male priest or minister in the Christian Church ➲ compare PRIEST

cler·gy·wo·man /ˈklɜːdʒiwʊmən; *NAmE* ˈklɜːrdʒ-/ *noun* (*pl.* **-women** /-wɪmɪn/) a female priest or minister in the Christian Church

cler·ic /ˈklerɪk/ *noun* **1** (*old-fashioned* or *formal*) a member of the clergy **2** a religious leader in any religion: *Muslim clerics*

cler·ic·al /ˈklerɪkl/ *adj.* **1** connected with office work: ***clerical workers/staff/assistants*** ◇ *a clerical error* (= one made in copying or calculating sth) **2** connected with the CLERGY (= priests): *a* ***clerical collar*** (= one that fastens at the back, worn by some priests)

clerk 0-w /klɑːk; *NAmE* klɜːrk/ *noun, verb*
■ *noun* **1** 0-w a person whose job is to keep the records or accounts in an office, shop/store etc: *an office clerk* ➲ see also FILING CLERK **2** 0-w an official in charge of the records of a council, court, etc: *the Town Clerk* ◇ *the Clerk of the Court* ➲ see also CLERK OF WORKS, COUNTY CLERK, PARISH CLERK **3** 0-w (*NAmE*) = SALES CLERK: *The clerk at the counter gave me too little change.* **4** (also ˈ**desk clerk**) (both *NAmE*) a person whose job is dealing with people arriving at or leaving a hotel SYN **receptionist**
■ *verb* [I] (*NAmE*) to work as a clerk: *a clerking job*

ˌ**clerk of ˈworks** *noun* (*BrE*) a person whose job is to be in charge of repairs to buildings or of building works, for an organization or institution

clever 0-w /ˈklevə(r)/ *adj.* (**clever·er, clever·est**)
HELP You can also use **more clever** and **most clever**.
1 0-w (*especially BrE*) quick at learning and understanding things SYN **intelligent**: *a clever child* ◇ *Clever girl!* ◇ *How clever of you to work it out!* ◇ *He's* ***too clever by half****, if you ask me* (= it annoys me or makes me suspicious). ➲ SYNONYMS at INTELLIGENT **2** 0-w **~ (at sth)** (*especially BrE*) skilful: *She's clever at getting what she wants.* ◇ *He's clever with his hands.* **3** 0-w showing intelligence or skill, for example in the design of an object, in an idea or sb's actions: *a clever little gadget* ◇ *What a clever idea!* ◇ *That* (= what you just did) *wasn't very clever, was it?* (= it wasn't sensible) **4** (*BrE, informal, disapproving*) quick with words in a way that annoys people or does not show respect: *Don't you get clever with me!* ▸ **clev·er·ly** *adv.* **clev·er·ness** *noun* [U] IDM see BOX *v.*

ˈ**clever Dick** (also ˈ**clever clogs**) *noun* (both *BrE, informal, disapproving*) a person who thinks they are always right or that they know everything

cli·ché (also **cliche**) /ˈkliːʃeɪ; *NAmE* kliːˈʃeɪ/ *noun* (*disapproving*) **1** [C] a phrase or an idea that has been used so often that it no longer has much meaning and is not interesting: *She trotted out the old cliché that 'a trouble shared is a trouble halved.'* **2** [U] the use of clichés in writing or speaking ▸ **cli·chéd** *adj.*: *a clichéd view of upper-class life*

click 0-w /klɪk/ *verb, noun*
■ *verb* **1** 0-w [I, T] to make or cause sth to make a short sharp sound: (**+ adv./prep.**) *The cameras clicked away.* ◇ *The bolt clicked into place.* ◇ **+ adj.** *The door* ***clicked shut****.* ◇ **~ sth** *He* ***clicked his fingers*** *at the waiter.* ◇ *Polly* ***clicked her tongue*** *in annoyance.* **2** 0-w [T, I] to choose a particular function or item on a computer screen, etc, by pressing one of the buttons on a mouse or TOUCH PAD: **~ sth** *Click the OK button to start.* ◇ **~ (on sth)** *I clicked on the link to the next page of the website.* ◇ *To run a window, just double-click on the icon.* ➲ see also DOUBLE-CLICK **3** [I] (*informal*) to suddenly become clear or understood: *Suddenly* ***it clicked****—we'd been talking about different people.* ◇ *It all* ***clicked into place****.* **4** [I] (*informal*) to become friends with sb at once; to become popular with sb: *We met at a party and clicked immediately.* ◇ **~ with sb** *He's never really clicked with his students.* **5** [I] (*informal*) to work well together: *The team don't seem to have clicked yet.*
PHR V ˌ**click ˈthrough (to sth)** to visit a website by clicking on an electronic link or advertisement on another web page
■ *noun* **1** 0-w a short sharp sound: *The door closed with a click.* **2** 0-w the act of pressing the button on a computer mouse or TOUCH PAD **3** (*phonetics*) a speech sound made by pressing the tongue against the top of the mouth or the part of the mouth behind the upper front teeth, then releasing it quickly, causing air to be sucked in. Clicks are found especially in southern African languages: *click languages* **4** = KLICK

click·able /ˈklɪkəbl/ *adj.* (*computing*) if text or an image is **clickable**, you can click on it with the mouse or TOUCH PAD in order to make sth happen

click·stream /ˈklɪkstriːm/ *noun* a record of all the websites a person visits when spending time on the Internet

cli·ent 0-w /ˈklaɪənt/ *noun*
1 0-w a person who uses the services or advice of a professional person or organization: *a lawyer with many famous clients* ◇ *to act on behalf of a client* ◇ *Social workers must always consider the best interests of their clients.* **2** (*computing*) a computer that is linked to a SERVER

cli·en·tele /ˌkliːənˈtel; *NAmE* ˌklaɪənˈtel/ *noun* [sing.+ sing./pl. v.] all the customers or clients of a shop/store, restaurant, organization, etc: *an international clientele*

ˌ**client-ˈserver** *adj.* [only before noun] (*computing*) (of a computer system) in which a central SERVER provides data to a number of computers connected together in a network ➲ see also PEER-TO-PEER

ˌ**client ˈstate** *noun* a country which depends on a larger and more powerful country for support and protection

cliff /klɪf/ *noun* a high area of rock with a very steep side, often at the edge of the sea or ocean: *the* ***cliff edge/top*** ◇ *the chalk cliffs of southern England* ◇ *a castle perched high on the cliffs above the river* ➲ VISUAL VOCAB page V5

cliff·hang·er /ˈklɪfhæŋə(r)/ *noun* a situation in a story, film/movie, competition, etc. that is very exciting because you cannot guess what will happen next, or you do not find out immediately what happens next: *The first part of the serial ended with a real cliffhanger.* ▸ **cliff·hang·ing** *adj.*

cliff·top /ˈklɪftɒp; *NAmE* -tɑːp/ *noun* the area of land at the top of a cliff ➲ VISUAL VOCAB page V5

cli·mac·tic /klaɪˈmæktɪk/ *adj.* (*formal*) (of an event or a point in time) very exciting, most important

cli·mate 0-w /ˈklaɪmət/ *noun*
1 0-w [C, U] the regular pattern of weather conditions of a particular place: *a* ***mild/temperate/warm/wet climate*** ◇ *the harsh climate of the Arctic regions* **2** 0-w [C] an area with particular weather conditions: *They wanted to move to a warmer climate.* **3** 0-w [C] a general attitude or feeling; an atmosphere or a situation which exists in a particular place: *the present political climate* ◇ *the current* ***climate of opinion*** (= what people generally are thinking about a particular issue) ◇ *a* ***climate of suspicion/violence*** ◇ *We need to create a climate in which business can prosper.*

ˈ**climate change** *noun* [U] changes in the earth's weather, including changes in temperature, wind patterns and RAINFALL, especially the increase in the temperature of the earth's atmosphere that is caused by the increase of particular gases, especially CARBON DIOXIDE: *the threat of global climate change* ➲ COLLOCATIONS at ENVIRONMENT ➲ compare GLOBAL WARMING

cli·mat·ic /klaɪˈmætɪk/ *adj.* [only before noun] connected with the climate of a particular area: ***climatic changes/conditions*** ▸ **cli·mat·ic·al·ly** /-kli/ *adv.*

cli·mat·ology /ˌklaɪməˈtɒlədʒi; *NAmE* -ˈtɑːl-/ *noun* [U] the scientific study of climate ▸ **cli·ma·to·logic·al** /ˌklaɪmətəˈlɒdʒɪkl; *NAmE* -ˈlɑːdʒ-/ *adj.* **cli·mat·olo·gist** /ˌklaɪməˈtɒlədʒɪst; *NAmE* -ˈtɑːl-/ *noun*

cli·max /ˈklaɪmæks/ *noun, verb*
■ *noun* **1** the most exciting or important event or point in time: *to* ***come to/reach a climax*** ◇ *the climax of his political career* **2** the most exciting part of a play, piece of music, etc. that usually happens near the end **3** the highest point of sexual pleasure SYN **orgasm** ➲ compare ANTI-CLIMAX
■ *verb* **1** [I, T] to come to or form the best, most exciting, or most important point in sth: **~ with/in sth** *The festival will climax on Sunday with a gala concert.* ◇ **~ sth** (*especially NAmE*) *The sensational verdict climaxed a six-month trial.* **2** [I] to have an ORGASM

climb 0-w /klaɪm/ *verb, noun*
■ *verb*
▸ GO UP **1** 0-w [T, I] **~ (up) (sth)** to go up sth towards the top: *to climb a mountain/hill/tree/wall* ◇ *She climbed up the stairs.* ◇ *The car slowly climbed the hill.* ◇ *As they climbed higher, the air became cooler.*
▸ GO THROUGH/DOWN/OVER **2** 0-w [I] **+ adv./prep.** to move somewhere, especially with difficulty or effort: *I climbed through the window.* ◇ *Sue climbed into bed.* ◇ *Can you climb down?* ◇ *The boys climbed over the wall.*
▸ MOUNTAIN/ROCK, ETC. **3** 0-w **go climbing** to go up moun-

tains or climb rocks as a hobby or sport: *He likes to go climbing most weekends.*

▸ AIRCRAFT/SUN, ETC. **4** 🔑 [I] to go higher in the sky: *The plane climbed to 33 000 feet.*

▸ SLOPE UP **5** 🔑 [I] to slope upwards: *From here the path climbs steeply to the summit.*

▸ OF PLANTS **6** [I] to grow up a wall or frame: *a climbing rose*

▸ INCREASE **7** 🔑 [I] (of temperature, a country's money, etc.) to increase in value or amount: *The dollar has been climbing all week.* ◇ *The paper's circulation continues to climb.*

▸ IMPROVE POSITION/STATUS **8** [I] **~ (to sth)** to move to a higher position or social rank by your own effort: *In a few years he had climbed to the top of his profession.* ◇ *The team has now climbed to fourth in the league.* IDM see BANDWAGON

PHR V ˌ**climb ˈdown (over sth)** to admit that you have made a mistake or that you were wrong ➲ related noun CLIMBDOWN

■ ***noun***

▸ MOUNTAIN/STEPS **1** an act of climbing up a mountain, rock or large number of steps; a period of time spent climbing: *an exhausting climb* ◇ *It's an hour's climb to the summit.* **2** a mountain or rock which people climb up for sport: *Titan's Wall is the mountain's hardest rock climb.*

▸ INCREASE **3** [usually sing.] an increase in value or amount: *the dollar's climb against the euro*

▸ TO A HIGHER POSITION OR STATUS **4** [usually sing.] progress to a higher status, standard or position: *a rapid climb to stardom* ◇ *the long slow climb out of the recession*

climb·down /ˈklaɪmdaʊn/ *noun* (*BrE*) an act of admitting that you were wrong, or of changing your position in an argument: *The Chancellor was forced into a humiliating climbdown on his economic policies.*

climb·er /ˈklaɪmə(r)/ *noun* **1** a person who climbs (especially mountains) or an animal that climbs: *climbers and hill walkers* ◇ *Monkeys are efficient climbers.* **2** a climbing plant ➲ VISUAL VOCAB page V16 ➲ see also SOCIAL CLIMBER

climb·ing 🔑 /ˈklaɪmɪŋ/ *noun* [U] the sport or activity of climbing rocks or mountains: *to **go climbing*** ◇ *a climbing accident*

ˈ**climbing frame** (*BrE*) (*NAmE* ˈ**jungle gym**) *noun* a structure made of metal bars joined together for children to climb and play on ➲ picture at FRAME ➲ VISUAL VOCAB page V32

ˈ**climbing wall** *noun* a wall with parts to hold onto, usually inside a building, for people to practise climbing on

clime /klaɪm/ *noun* [usually pl.] (*literary* or *humorous*) a country with a particular kind of climate: *I'm heading for sunnier climes next month.*

clinch /klɪntʃ/ *verb, noun*

■ ***verb*** (*informal*) **1 ~ sth** to succeed in achieving or winning sth: *to **clinch an argument/a deal/a victory*** **2 ~ sth** to provide the answer to sth; to settle sth that was not certain: *'I'll pay your airfare.' 'Okay, **that clinches it**—I'll come with you.'* ◇ *a clinching argument*

■ ***noun*** **1** (*informal*) a position in which two lovers hold each other tightly SYN **embrace** **2** a position in a fight in which two opponents hold each other tightly

clinch·er /ˈklɪntʃə(r)/ *noun* [usually sing.] (*informal*) a fact, a remark or an event that settles an argument, a decision or a competition

cline /klaɪn/ *noun* a series of similar items in which each is almost the same as the ones next to it, but the last is very different from the first SYN **continuum**

cling /klɪŋ/ *verb* (**clung, clung** /klʌŋ/) **1** [I] to hold on tightly to sb/sth: **~ to sb/sth** *survivors clinging to a raft* ◇ **~ on to sb/sth** *She clung on to her baby.* ◇ **~ on** *Cling on tight!* ◇ **~ together** *They clung together, shivering with cold.* ➲ SYNONYMS at HOLD **2** [I] to stick to sth: *a dress that clings* (= fits closely and shows the shape of your body) ◇ **~ to sth** *The wet shirt clung to his chest.* ◇ *The smell of smoke still clung to her clothes.* **3** [I] **~ (to sb)** (usually *disapproving*) to stay close to sb, especially because you need them emotionally: *After her mother's death, Sara clung to her aunt more than ever.*

PHR V ˈ**cling to sth** | ˌ**cling ˈon to sth** to be unwilling to get rid of sth, or stop doing sth: *Throughout the trial she had clung to the belief that he was innocent.* ◇ *He had one last hope to cling on to.* ◇ *She managed to cling on to life for another couple of years.*

ˈ**cling film** (*BrE*) (*NAmE* ˈ**plastic wrap, Saˈran Wrap™**) *noun* [U] a thin transparent plastic material that sticks to a surface and to itself, used especially for wrapping food

cling·ing /ˈklɪŋɪŋ/ (also **clingy** /ˈklɪŋi/) *adj.* **1** (of clothes or material) sticking to the body and showing its shape **2** (usually *disapproving*) needing another person too much: *a clinging child*

clin·ic /ˈklɪnɪk/ *noun* **1** a building or part of a hospital where people can go for special medical treatment or advice: *the local family planning clinic* **2** (*especially BrE*) a period of time during which doctors give special medical treatment or advice: *The antenatal clinic is on Wednesdays.* **3** (*especially BrE*) a private hospital or one that treats health problems of a particular kind: *He is being treated at the London clinic.* ◇ *a rehabilitation clinic for alcoholics* **4** (*NAmE*) a building where visiting patients can get medical treatment; a building shared by a group of doctors who work together **5** an occasion in a hospital when medical students learn by watching a specialist examine and treat patients **6** an occasion at which a professional person, especially a SPORTSMAN or SPORTSWOMAN gives advice and training: *a coaching clinic for young tennis players*

clin·ic·al /ˈklɪnɪkl/ *adj.* **1** [only before noun] relating to the examination and treatment of patients and their illnesses: *clinical research* (= done on patients, not just considering theory) ◇ *clinical training* (= the part of a doctor's training done in a hospital) ◇ *clinical trials of a drug* **2** (*disapproving*) cold and calm and without feeling or sympathy: *He watched her suffering with clinical detachment.* **3** (*disapproving*) (of a room, building, etc.) very plain; without decoration ▸ **clin·ic·al·ly** /-kli/ *adv.*: *clinically dead* (= judged to be dead from the condition of the body) ◇ *clinically depressed*

clin·ician /klɪˈnɪʃn/ *noun* a doctor, PSYCHOLOGIST, etc. who has direct contact with patients

clink /klɪŋk/ *verb, noun*

■ ***verb*** [I, T] to make or cause sth to make a sharp ringing sound, like that of glasses being hit against each other SYN **chink**: *clinking coins* ◇ **~ sth** *They clinked glasses and drank to each other's health.*

■ ***noun*** [sing.] **1** (also **clink·ing**) a sharp ringing sound like the sound made by glasses being hit against each other **2** (*old-fashioned, slang*) prison

clink·er /ˈklɪŋkə(r)/ *noun* **1** [U, C] the hard rough substance left after coal has burnt at a high temperature; a piece of this substance **2** [sing.] (*NAmE*) a wrong musical note: *The singer hit a clinker.*

clip /klɪp/ *noun, verb*

■ ***noun*** **1** [C] (often in compounds) a small metal or plastic object used for holding things together or in place: *a hair clip* ◇ *toe clips on a bicycle* ➲ VISUAL VOCAB page V56 ➲ see also BICYCLE CLIP, BULLDOG CLIP, PAPER CLIP **2** [C] a piece of jewellery that fastens to your clothes: *a diamond clip* **3** [sing.] the act of cutting sth to make it shorter: *He gave the hedge a clip.* **4** [C] a short part of a film/movie that is shown separately: *Here is a clip from her latest movie.* **5** [C] (*BrE, informal*) a quick hit with your hand: *She gave him **a clip round the ear** for being cheeky.* **6** [C] a set of bullets in a metal container that is placed in or attached to a gun for firing

IDM **at a fast, good, steady, etc. ˈclip** (*especially NAmE*) quickly

■ ***verb*** (**-pp-**) **1** [T, I] to fasten sth to sth else with a clip; to be fastened with a clip: **~ sth + adv./prep.** *He **clipped** the microphone (**on**) **to** his collar.* ◇ ***Clip** the pages **together**.* ◇ **+ adv./prep.** *Do those earrings clip on?* **2** [T] to cut sth with scissors or SHEARS, in order to make it shorter or neater; to remove sth from somewhere by cutting it off: **~ sth** *to clip a hedge* ◇ **~ sth from sth/off (sth)** *He clipped off a length of wire.* **3** [T] to hit the edge or side of sth: **~ sth** *The car clipped the kerb as it turned.* ◇ **~ sth + adv./prep.** *She* *clipped the ball into the net.* **4** [T] **~ sth** (**out of/from sth**) to cut sth out of sth else using scissors: *to clip a coupon (out of the paper)*

IDM **clip sb's 'wings** to restrict a person's freedom or power

PHR V **,clip sth 'off sth** (*informal*) to reduce the time that it takes to do sth by a particular length of time: *She clipped two seconds off her previous best time.*

'clip art *noun* [U] (*computing*) pictures and symbols that are stored in computer programs or on websites for computer users to copy and add to their own documents

clip·board /'klɪpbɔːd; *NAmE* -bɔːrd/ *noun* **1** a small board with a clip at the top for holding papers, used by sb who wants to write while standing or moving around ➲ VISUAL VOCAB page V56 **2** (*computing*) a place where information from a computer file is stored for a time until it is added to another file

clip-clop /'klɪp klɒp; *NAmE* klɑːp/ *noun* a sound like the sound of a horse's HOOFS on a hard surface

'clip joint *noun* (*informal, disapproving*) a NIGHTCLUB which charges prices that are too high

'clip-on *adj.* [only before noun] fastened to sth with a CLIP: *clip-on earrings* ➲ VISUAL VOCAB page V53

clipped /klɪpt/ *adj.* (of a person's way of speaking) clear and fast but not very friendly: *his clipped military tones*

clip·per /'klɪpə(r)/ *noun* **1 clippers** [pl.] a tool for cutting small pieces off things: *a pair of clippers* ➲ see also NAIL CLIPPERS **2** a fast sailing ship, used in the past

clip·ping /'klɪpɪŋ/ *noun* **1** [usually pl.] a piece cut off sth: ***hedge/nail clippings*** **2** (*especially NAmE*) (also **'press clipping** *BrE, NAmE*) (*BrE* also **cut·ting**, **'press cutting**) an article or a story that you cut from a newspaper or magazine and keep

clique /kliːk/ *noun* [C+sing./pl. v.] (often *disapproving*) a small group of people who spend their time together and do not allow others to join them

cliquey /'kliːki/ (also **cliqu·ish** /'kliːkɪʃ/) *adj.* (*disapproving*) tending to form a clique; controlled by cliques: *He found the school very cliquey and elitist.*

clit·oris /'klɪtərɪs/ *noun* the small sensitive organ just above the opening of a woman's VAGINA which becomes larger when she is sexually excited ▸ **clit·or·al** /'klɪtərəl/ *adj.* [only before noun]

Cllr *abbr.* (*BrE*) (used before names in writing) COUNCILLOR: *Cllr Michael Booth*

cloak /kləʊk; *NAmE* kloʊk/ *noun, verb*

■ ***noun*** **1** [C] a type of coat that has no sleeves, fastens at the neck and hangs loosely from the shoulders, worn especially in the past **2** [sing.] (*literary*) a thing that hides or covers sb/sth: *They left under the cloak of darkness.*

■ ***verb*** **~ sth** (**in sth**) [often passive] (*literary*) to cover or hide sth: *The hills were cloaked in thick mist.* ◇ *The meeting was **cloaked in mystery**.* ▸ **cloaked** *adj.*: *a tall cloaked figure* (= a person wearing a cloak)

,cloak-and-'dagger *adj.* [only before noun] **cloak-and-dagger** activities are secret and mysterious, sometimes in a way that people think is unnecessary or ridiculous

cloak·room /'kləʊkruːm; -rʊm; *NAmE* 'kloʊk-/ *noun* **1** (*especially BrE*) (*NAmE* usually **check·room**, **'coat check**, **coat·room**) a room in a public building where people can leave coats, bags, etc. for a time **2** (*BrE*) a room that contains a toilet or toilets ➲ note at TOILET

clob·ber /'klɒbə(r); *NAmE* 'klɑːb-/ *verb, noun*

■ ***verb*** (*informal*) **1 ~ sb** to hit sb very hard **2** [often passive] **~ sb/sth** to affect sb badly or to punish them, especially by making them lose money: *The paper got clobbered with libel damages of half a million pounds.* **3** [usually passive] **~ sb/sth** to defeat sb completely: *We got clobbered in the game on Saturday.*

■ ***noun*** [U] (*BrE, informal*) a person's clothes or equipment SYN **stuff**

cloche /klɒʃ; *NAmE* kloʊʃ/ *noun* **1** (also **,cloche 'hat**) a woman's hat, shaped like a bell, and fitting close to the head, worn especially in the 1920s **2** a glass or plastic cover placed over young plants to protect them from cold weather ➲ VISUAL VOCAB page V16

clocks and watches

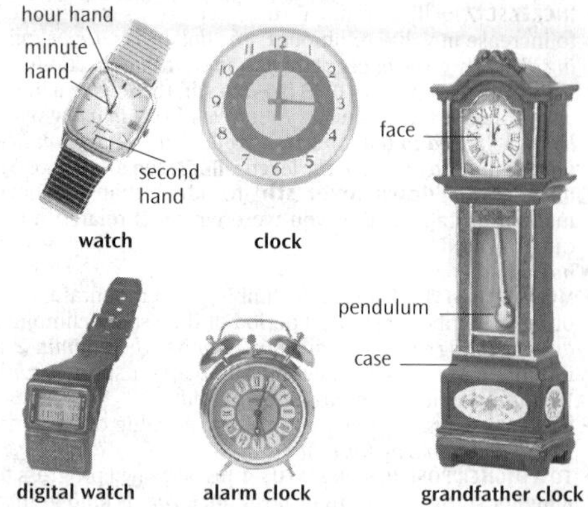

clock 🔑 /klɒk; *NAmE* klɑːk/ *noun, verb*

■ ***noun*** **1** 🔑 [C] an instrument for measuring and showing time, in a room or on the wall of a building (not worn or carried like a watch): *It was ten past six by the kitchen clock.* ◇ *The **clock struck** twelve/midnight.* ◇ *The **clock is fast/slow**.* ◇ *The clock has stopped.* ◇ *the **clock face*** (= the front part of a clock with the numbers on) ◇ *The **hands of the clock** crept slowly around.* ◇ *Ellen heard the loud **ticking of the clock** in the hall.* ➲ see also ALARM CLOCK, BIOLOGICAL CLOCK, BODY CLOCK, CARRIAGE CLOCK, CUCKOO CLOCK, GRANDFATHER CLOCK, O'CLOCK, TIME CLOCK **2 the clock** [sing.] (*informal*) = MILOMETER: *a used car with 20 000 miles on the clock*

IDM **against the 'clock** if you do sth **against the clock**, you do it fast in order to finish before a particular time **around/round the 'clock** all day and all night without stopping **put the clocks forward/back** (*BrE*) (*NAmE* **set/move the clocks ahead/back**) to change the time shown by clocks, usually by one hour, when the time changes officially, for example at the beginning and end of summer **put/turn the 'clock back 1** to return to a situation that existed in the past; to remember a past age: *I wish we could turn the clock back two years and give the marriage another chance.* **2** (*disapproving*) to return to old-fashioned methods or ideas: *The new censorship law will turn the clock back 50 years.* **run down/out the 'clock** (*US*) if a sports team tries to **run down/out the clock** at the end of a game, it stops trying to score and just tries to keep hold of the ball to stop the other team from scoring ➲ compare TIME-WASTING **the clocks go forward/back** the time changes officially, for example at the beginning and end of summer ➲ more at BEAT *v.*, RACE *n.*, STOP *v.*, WATCH *v.*

■ ***verb*** **1 ~ sth** to reach a particular time or speed: *He clocked 10.09 seconds in the 100 metres final.* **2** to measure the speed at which sb/sth is travelling: **~ sb doing sth** *The police clocked her doing over 100 miles an hour.* ◇ **~ sb/sth** (**at sth**) *Wind gusts at 80 m.p.h. were clocked at Rapid City.* **3 ~ sb** | **~ that…** | **~ what/where, etc…** (*BrE, informal*) to notice or recognize sb: *I clocked her in the driving mirror.* **4 ~ sth** (*BrE, informal*) to illegally reduce the number of miles shown on a vehicle's MILOMETER (= instrument that measures the number of miles it has travelled) in order to make the vehicle appear to have travelled fewer miles than it really has

PHR V **,clock 'in/'on** (*BrE*) (*NAmE* **,punch 'in**) to record the time at which you arrive at work, especially by putting a card into a machine **,clock 'out/'off** (*BrE*) (*NAmE* **,punch 'out**) to record the time at which you leave work, especially by putting a card into a machine **,clock 'up sth** to reach a particular amount or number: *On the trip we clocked up* over 1800 miles. ◇ *He has clocked up more than 25 years on the committee.*

clock·er /ˈklɒkə(r); *NAmE* ˈklɑːk-/ *noun (informal)* **1** (*BrE*) a person who illegally changes a car's MILOMETER so that the car seems to have travelled fewer miles than it really has **2** (*NAmE*) a person who sells illegal drugs, especially COCAINE or CRACK

ˌclock ˈradio *noun* a clock combined with a radio that can be set to come on at a particular time in order to wake sb up ➲ VISUAL VOCAB page V20

ˈclock speed *noun* [U] (*computing*) the speed at which a computer operates: *This machine has a clock speed of 1.6GHz.*

ˈclock tower *noun* a tall tower, usually part of another building, with a clock at the top ➲ VISUAL VOCAB page V2

ˈclock-watcher *noun* (*disapproving*) a worker who is always checking the time to make sure that they do not work longer than they need to

clock·wise /ˈklɒkwaɪz; *NAmE* ˈklɑːk-/ *adv., adj.* moving around in the same direction as the hands of a clock: *Turn the key clockwise.* ◇ *a clockwise direction* OPP **anticlockwise, counterclockwise**

clock·work /ˈklɒkwɜːk; *NAmE* ˈklɑːkwɜːrk/ *noun* [U] machinery with wheels and SPRINGS like that inside a clock: *clockwork toys* (= toys that you wind up with a key)
IDM **go/run like ˈclockwork** to happen according to plan; to happen without difficulties or problems ➲ more at REGULAR *adj.*

clod /klɒd; *NAmE* klɑːd/ *noun* **1** [usually pl.] a lump of earth or CLAY **2** (*informal*) a stupid person

clod·hop·per /ˈklɒdhɒpə(r); *NAmE* ˈklɑːdhɑːp-/ *noun* (*informal*) **1** [usually pl.] a large heavy shoe **2** (*disapproving*) an awkward or CLUMSY person

clog /klɒg; *NAmE* klɑːg; klɔːg/ *verb, noun*
■ *verb* (-gg-) [T, often passive, I] to block sth or to become blocked: **~ sth (up) (with sth)** *The narrow streets were clogged with traffic.* ◇ *Tears clogged her throat.* ◇ **~ (up) (with sth)** *Within a few years the pipes began to clog up.*
■ *noun* a shoe that is completely made of wood or one that has a thick wooden SOLE and a leather top ➲ VISUAL VOCAB page V52 IDM see POP *v.*

ˈclog dance *noun* a dance that is performed by people wearing clogs

clois·ter /ˈklɔɪstə(r)/ *noun* **1** [C, usually pl.] a covered passage with ARCHES around a square garden, usually forming part of a CATHEDRAL, CONVENT or MONASTERY ➲ VISUAL VOCAB page V12 **2** [sing.] life in a CONVENT or MONASTERY

clois·tered /ˈklɔɪstəd; *NAmE* -tərd/ *adj.* (*formal*) protected from the problems and dangers of normal life: *a cloistered life* ◇ *the cloistered world of the university*

clone /kləʊn; *NAmE* kloʊn/ *noun, verb*
■ *noun* **1** (*biology*) a plant or an animal that is produced naturally or artificially from the cells of another plant or animal and is therefore exactly the same as it **2** (*sometimes disapproving*) a person or thing that seems to be an exact copy of another **3** (*computing*) a computer designed to work in exactly the same way as another, usually one made by a different company and more expensive
■ *verb* **1 ~ sth** to produce an exact copy of an animal or a plant from its cells: *A team from the UK were the first to successfully clone an animal.* ◇ *Dolly, the cloned sheep* **2 ~ sth** to illegally make an electronic copy of stored information from a person's credit card or mobile/cell phone so that you can make payments or phone calls but the owner of the card or phone receives the bill

clonk /klɒŋk; *NAmE* klɑːŋk/ *noun* (*BrE, informal*) a short loud sound of heavy things hitting each other ▸ **clonk** *verb* [I, T] **~ (sth)**

close¹ 0→ /kləʊz; *NAmE* kloʊz/ *verb, noun* ➲ see also CLOSE²
■ *verb*
▸ WINDOW/DOOR, ETC. **1** 0→ [T, I] **~ (sth)** to put sth into a position so that it covers an opening; to get into this position SYN **shut**: *Would anyone mind if I closed the window?* ◇ *She closed the gate behind her.* ◇ *It's dark now—let's close the curtains.* ◇ *I closed my eyes against the bright light.* ◇ *The doors open and close automatically.* OPP **open**
▸ BOOK/UMBRELLA, ETC. **2** 0→ [T] **~ sth (up)** to move the parts of sth together so that it is no longer open SYN **shut**: *to close a book/an umbrella* OPP **open**
▸ SHOP/STORE/BUSINESS, ETC. **3** 0→ [T, often passive, I] to make the work of a shop/store, etc. stop for a period of time; to not be open for people to use: **~ sth (for sth)** *The museum has been closed for renovation.* ◇ **~ sth (to sb/sth)** *The road was closed to traffic for two days.* ◇ **~ (for sth)** *What time does the bank close?* ◇ *We close for lunch between twelve and two.* OPP **open** **4** 0→ [T, I] **~ (sth)** (also **ˌclose ˈdown, ˌclose sth↔ˈdown**) if a company, shop/store, etc. **closes**, or if you **close** it, it stops operating as a business: *The club was closed by the police.* ◇ *The hospital closed at the end of last year.* ◇ *The play closed after just three nights.* OPP **open**
▸ END **5** 0→ [T, I] to end or make sth end: *The meeting will close at 10.00 p.m.* ◇ *The offer closes at the end of the week.* ◇ **~ sth** *to close a meeting/debate* ◇ *to close a case/an investigation* ◇ *to close an account* (= to stop keeping money in a bank account) ◇ *The subject is now closed* (= we will not discuss it again). OPP **open**
▸ FINANCE **6** [I] **~ (at sth)** to be worth a particular amount at the end of the day's business: *Shares in the company closed at 265p.* ◇ *closing prices*
▸ DISTANCE/DIFFERENCE **7** [T, I] **~ (sth)** to make the distance or difference between two people or things smaller; to become smaller or narrower: *These measures are aimed at* ***closing the gap*** *between rich and poor.* ◇ *The gap between the two top teams is closing all the time.*
▸ HOLD FIRMLY **8** [T, I] **~ (sth) about/around/over sb/sth** to hold sth/sb firmly: *She closed her hand over his.* ◇ *Her hand closed over his.*
IDM **close the book on sth** to stop doing sth because you no longer believe you will be successful or will find a solution: *The police have closed the book on the case* (= they have stopped trying to solve it). **close its doors** (of a business, etc.) to stop trading: *The factory closed its doors for the last time in 2009.* **close your ˈmind to sth** to refuse to think about sth as a possibility **close ˈranks 1** if a group of people **close ranks**, they work closely together to defend themselves, especially when they are being criticized: *It's not unusual for the police to close ranks when one of their officers is being investigated.* **2** if soldiers **close ranks**, they move closer together in order to defend themselves ➲ more at DOOR, EAR, EYE *n.*
PHR V **ˌclose ˈdown** (*BrE*) when a radio or television station **closes down**, it stops broadcasting at the end of the day ➲ related noun CLOSE-DOWN **ˌclose ˈdown | ˌclose sth↔ˈdown** = CLOSE¹(4): *All the steelworks around here were closed down in the 1980s.* ➲ related noun CLOSE-DOWN OPP **open up** **ˌclose ˈin 1** when the days **close in**, they become gradually shorter during the autumn/fall **2** if the weather **closes in**, it gets worse **3** when the night **closes in**, it gets darker: *They huddled around the fire as the night closed in.* **ˌclose ˈin (on sb/sth)** to move nearer to sb/sth, especially in order to attack them: *The lions closed in on their prey.* **ˌclose sth↔ˈoff** to separate sth from other parts so that people cannot use it: *The entrance to the train station was closed off following the explosion.* **ˌclose ˈout sth** (*NAmE*) **1** to sell goods very cheaply in order to get rid of them quickly ➲ related noun CLOSEOUT **2** to finish or settle sth: *A rock concert closed out the festivities.* **ˌclose ˈover sb/sth** to surround and cover sb/sth: *The water closed over his head.* **ˌclose ˈup 1** when a wound **closes up**, it heals **2** to hide your thoughts or emotions: *She closed up when I asked about her family.* **ˌclose ˈup | ˌclose sth↔ˈup 1** to shut and lock sth such as a shop/store or a building, especially for a short period of time: *Why don't we close up and go out for lunch?* ◇ *Can the last one out close up the office?* OPP **open up** **2** to come closer together; to bring people or things closer together: *Traffic was heavy and cars were closing up behind each other.* **3** to become

narrower and less open: *Every time he tried to speak, his throat closed up with fear.* OPP **open up**

■ ***noun*** [sing.] (*formal*) the end of a period of time or an activity: *at the close of the 17th century* ◇ *His life was* ***drawing to a close****.* ◇ *Can we* ***bring*** *this meeting* ***to a close****?*

C

Which Word?

close / shut

You can **close** and **shut** doors, windows, your eyes, mouth, etc.

- **Shut** can suggest more noise and is often found in phrases such as *slammed shut, banged shut, snapped shut.*
- **Shut** is also usually used for containers such as boxes, suitcases, etc.
- To talk about the time when shops, offices, etc. are not open, use **close** or **shut**: *What time do the banks close/shut?* ◇ *A strike has shut the factory.* You can also use **closed** or **shut** (*NAmE* usually **closed**): *The store is closed/shut today.* Especially in *NAmE*, **shut** can sound less polite.
- **Closed** is used in front of a noun, but **shut** is not: *a closed window.*
- We usually use **closed** about roads, airports, etc: *The road is closed because of the snow.*
- **Close** is also used in formal English to talk about ending a meeting or conversation.

close[2] 🔑 /kləʊs; *NAmE* kloʊs/ *adj., adv., noun* ➲ see also CLOSE[1]

■ ***adj.*** (closer, clos·est)

▸ NEAR **1** 🔑 [not usually before noun] **~ (to sb/sth)** | **~ (together)** near in space or time: *Our new house is close to the school.* ◇ *I had no idea the beach was so close.* ◇ *The two buildings are* ***close together****.* ◇ *This is the closest we can get to the beach by car.* ◇ *We all have to work* ***in close proximity*** (= near each other). ◇ *The President was shot* ***at close range*** (= from a short distance away). ◇ *The children are close to each other in age.* ◇ *Their birthdays are very* ***close together****.* ➲ note at NEAR

▸ ALMOST/LIKELY **2** 🔑 [not before noun] **~ to sth** | **~ to doing sth** almost in a particular state; likely to do sth soon: *He was close to tears.* ◇ *The new library is close to completion.* ◇ *She knew she was close to death.* ◇ *We are close to signing the agreement.*

▸ RELATIONSHIP **3** 🔑 **~ (to sb)** knowing sb very well and liking them very much: *Jo is a very* ***close friend****.* ◇ *She is very close to her father.* ◇ *She and her father are very close.* ◇ *We're a very close family.* **4** 🔑 near in family relationship: *close relatives, such as your mother and father, and brothers and sisters* OPP **distant** **5** 🔑 very involved in the work or activities of sb else, usually seeing and talking to them regularly: *He is one of the prime minister's closest advisers.* ◇ *The college has close links with many other institutions.* ◇ *She has kept in* ***close contact*** *with the victims' families.* ◇ *We keep in* ***close touch*** *with the police.*

▸ CAREFUL **6** 🔑 [only before noun] careful and thorough: *Take a* ***close look*** *at this photograph.* ◇ ***On closer examination*** *the painting proved to be a fake.* ◇ *Pay* ***close attention*** *to what I am telling you.*

▸ SIMILAR **7** 🔑 **~ (to sth)** very similar to sth else or to an amount: *There's a close resemblance* (= they look very similar). ◇ *His feeling for her was close to hatred.* ◇ *The total was close to 20% of the workforce.* ◇ *We tried to match the colours, but this is the closest we could get.*

▸ COMPETITION/ELECTION, ETC. **8** 🔑 won by only a small amount or distance: *a* ***close contest/match/election*** ◇ *It was a very* ***close finish****.* ◇ *I think it's going to be close.* ◇ *Our team came a* ***close second*** (= nearly won). ◇ *The game was closer than the score suggests.* ◇ *The result is going to be* ***too close to call*** (= either side may win).

▸ ALMOST BAD RESULT **9** used to describe sth, usually a dangerous or unpleasant situation, that nearly happens: *Phew! That was close—that car nearly hit us.* ◇ *We caught the bus in the end but it was close* (= we nearly missed it).

▸ WITHOUT SPACE **10** with little or no space in between: *over 1 000 pages of close print* ◇ *The soldiers advanced in close formation.*

▸ CUT SHORT **11** cut very short, near to the skin: *a* ***close haircut/shave***

▸ GUARDED **12** [only before noun] carefully guarded: *The donor's identity is a* ***close secret****.* ◇ *She was kept under* ***close arrest****.*

▸ WEATHER/ROOM **13** warm in an uncomfortable way because there does not seem to be enough fresh air SYN **stuffy**

▸ PRIVATE **14** [not before noun] **~ (about sth)** not willing to give personal information about yourself: *He was close about his past.*

▸ MEAN **15** [not before noun] (*BrE*) not liking to spend money: *She's always been very close with her money.*

▸ PHONETICS **16** (also **high**) (of a vowel) produced with the mouth in a relatively closed position ➲ compare OPEN

▶ **close·ly** 🔑 *adv.*: *I sat and watched everyone very closely* (= carefully). ◇ *He walked into the room, closely followed by the rest of the family.* ◇ *a closely contested election* ◇ *She closely resembled her mother at the same age.* ◇ *The two events are closely connected.* **close·ness** *noun* [U]

IDM **at/from ˌclose ˈquarters** very near: *fighting at close quarters* **close, but no ciˈgar** (*informal, especially NAmE*) used to tell sb that their attempt or guess was almost but not quite successful **a ˌclose ˈcall/ˈshave** (*informal*) a situation in which you only just manage to avoid an accident, etc. **a close ˈthing** a situation in which success or failure is equally possible: *We got him out in the end, but it was a close thing.* **close to ˈhome** if a remark or topic of discussion is **close to home**, it is accurate or connected with you in a way that makes you uncomfortable or embarrassed: *Her remarks about me were embarrassingly close to home.* **keep a close ˈeye/ˈwatch on sb/sth** to watch sb/sth carefully: *Over the next few months we will keep a close eye on sales.* ➲ more at HAND *n.*, HEART

■ ***adv.*** (closer, clos·est) near; not far away: *They sat* ***close together****.* ◇ *Don't* ***come*** *too* ***close****!* ◇ *She* ***held*** *Tom* ***close*** *and pressed her cheek to his.* ◇ *I couldn't* ***get close*** *enough to see.* ◇ *A second police car followed* ***close behind****.*

IDM **close at ˈhand** near; in a place where sb/sth can be reached easily: *There are good cafes and a restaurant close at hand.* **close ˈby (sb/sth)** at a short distance (from sb/sth): *Our friends live close by.* ◇ *The route passes close by the town.* **close on** | **close to** almost; nearly: *She is close on sixty.* ◇ *It is close on midnight.* ◇ *a profit close to £200 million* **a close run ˈthing** a situation in which sb only just wins or loses, for example in a competition or an election **close ˈto** | **close ˈup** in a position very near to sth: *The picture looks very different when you see it close to.* **close up to sb/sth** very near in space to sb/sth: *She snuggled close up to him.* **come close (to sth/to doing sth)** to almost reach or do sth: *He'd come close to death.* ◇ *We didn't win but we came close.* **run sb/sth ˈclose** (*BrE*) to be nearly as good, fast, successful, etc. as sb/sth else: *Germany ran Argentina very close in the final.* ➲ more at CARD *n.*, MARK *n.*, SAIL *v.*

■ ***noun*** **1** (*BrE*) (especially in street names) a street that is closed at one end: *Brookside Close* **2** the grounds and buildings that surround and belong to a CATHEDRAL

close-cropped /ˌkləʊs ˈkrɒpt; *NAmE* ˌkloʊs ˈkrɑːpt/ *adj.* (of hair, grass, etc.) cut very short

closed 🔑 /kləʊzd; *NAmE* kloʊzd/ *adj.*

1 🔑 [not before noun] shut: *Keep the door closed.* **2** 🔑 [not before noun] shut, especially of a shop/store or public building that is not open for a period of time: *The museum is closed on Mondays.* ◇ *This road is closed to traffic.* **3** 🔑 not willing to accept outside influences or new ideas: *a closed society* ◇ *He has a closed mind.* **4** [usually before noun] limited to a particular group of people; not open to everyone: *a closed membership* OPP **open** ➲ note at CLOSE[1]

IDM **behind closed ˈdoors** without the public being allowed to attend or know what is happening; in private **a closed ˈbook (to sb)** a subject or person that you know nothing about

ˌclosed-ˈcaptioned *adj.* (*NAmE*) (of a TV programme) having CAPTIONS that can only be read if you have a special machine (= a DECODER)

ˌclosed-ˌcircuit ˈtelevision *noun* [U] (*abbr.* CCTV) a television system that works within a limited area, for example a public building, to protect it from crime

close-down /ˈkləʊz daʊn; *NAmE* ˈkloʊz/ *noun* [U, sing.] the stopping of work, especially permanently, in an office, a factory, etc.

ˈclosed season *noun* [sing.] = CLOSE SEASON

ˌclosed ˈshop *noun* a factory, business, etc. in which employees must all be members of a particular TRADE/LABOR UNION

ˈclosed syllable *noun* (*phonetics*) a syllable which ends with a consonant, for example *sit*

close-fitting /ˌkləʊs ˈfɪtɪŋ; *NAmE* ˌkloʊs/ *adj.* (of clothes) fitting tightly, showing the shape of the body

close harmony /ˌkləʊs ˈhɑːməni; *NAmE* ˌkloʊs ˈhɑːrməni/ *noun* [U] (*music*) a style of singing in HARMONY in which the different notes are close together

close-knit /ˌkləʊs ˈnɪt; *NAmE* ˌkloʊs/ (also *less frequent* **ˌclosely-ˈknit**) *adj.* (of a group of people) having strong relationships with each other and taking a close, friendly interest in each other's activities and problems: *the close-knit community of a small village*

close-mouthed /ˌkləʊs ˈmaʊðd; *NAmE* ˌkloʊs/ *adj.* [not usually before noun] not willing to say much about sth because you want to keep a secret

close·out /ˈkləʊzaʊt; *NAmE* ˈkloʊz-/ *noun* (*NAmE*) an occasion when goods are sold cheaply in order to get rid of them quickly

close-range /ˌkləʊs ˈreɪndʒ; *NAmE* ˌkloʊs/ *adj.* [only before noun] at or from a short distance: *The close-range shot was blocked by the goalkeeper.*

close-run /ˌkləʊs ˈrʌn; *NAmE* ˌkloʊs/ *adj.* [usually before noun] (of a race or competition) won by a very small amount or distance: *The election was a close-run thing.*

close season /ˈkləʊz siːzn; *NAmE* ˈkloʊz/ *noun* [sing.] (*BrE*) **1** (also **ˈclosed season** *NAmE, BrE*) the time of year when it is illegal to kill particular kinds of animal, bird and fish because they are breeding OPP **open season** **2** (*NAmE* **ˈoff season**) (in sport) the time during the summer when teams do not play important games

close-set /ˌkləʊs ˈset; *NAmE* ˌkloʊs/ *adj.* very close together: *close-set eyes*

closet 0-w /ˈklɒzɪt; *NAmE* ˈklɑːzət/ *noun, adj., verb*

■ ***noun*** 0-w (*especially NAmE*) a small room or a space in a wall with a door that reaches the floor, used for storing things: *a walk-in closet* ➲ VISUAL VOCAB page V20 ➲ compare CUPBOARD, WARDROBE ➲ see also WATER CLOSET

IDM **come out of the ˈcloset** to admit sth openly that you kept secret before, especially because of shame or embarrassment: *Homosexuals in public life are now coming out of the closet.* ➲ see also COME OUT (10) IDM see SKELETON

■ ***adj.*** [only before noun] used to describe people who want to keep some fact about themselves secret: *closet gays* ◇ *I suspect he's a closet fascist.*

■ ***verb*** **~ sb/yourself + adv./prep.** to put sb in a room away from other people, especially so that they can talk privately with sb, or so that they can be alone: *He was closeted with the President for much of the day.* ◇ *She had closeted herself away in her room.*

close-up /ˈkləʊs ʌp; *NAmE* ˈkloʊs/ *noun* [C, U] a photograph, or picture in a film/movie, taken very close to sb/sth so that it shows a lot of detail: *a close-up of a human eye* ◇ *It was strange to see her own face* ***in close-up*** *on the screen.* ◇ *close-up pictures of the planet*

clos·ing /ˈkləʊzɪŋ; *NAmE* ˈkloʊzɪŋ/ *adj., noun*

■ ***adj.*** [only before noun] coming at the end of a speech, a period of time or an activity: *his closing remarks* ◇ *the closing stages of the game* OPP **opening**

■ ***noun*** [U] the act of shutting sth such as a factory, hospital, school, etc. permanently: *the closing of the local school* OPP **opening**

ˈclosing date *noun* the last date by which sth must be done, such as applying for a job or entering a competition

ˈclosing time *noun* [C, U] the time when a pub, shop/store, bar, etc. ends business for the day and people have to leave

clos·ure /ˈkləʊʒə(r); *NAmE* ˈkloʊ-/ *noun* **1** [C, U] the situation when a factory, school, hospital, etc. shuts permanently: *factory closures* ◇ *The hospital has been threatened with closure.* **2** [C, U] the temporary closing of a road or bridge **3** [U] the feeling that a difficult or an unpleasant experience has come to an end or been dealt with in an acceptable way: *The conviction of their son's murderer helped to give them a sense of closure.*

clot /klɒt; *NAmE* klɑːt/ *noun, verb*

■ ***noun*** **1** = BLOOD CLOT: *They removed a clot from his brain.* **2** (*old-fashioned, BrE, informal*) a stupid person

■ ***verb*** (-tt-) [I, T] **~ (sth)** when blood or cream **clots** or when sth **clots** it, it forms thick lumps or clots: *a drug that stops blood from clotting during operations* ◇ *the blood clotting agent, Factor 8*

cloth 0-w /klɒθ; *NAmE* klɔːθ/ *noun* (*pl.* **cloths** /klɒθs; *NAmE* klɔːðz/)

1 0-w [U] material made by WEAVING or knitting cotton, wool, silk, etc: ***woollen/cotton cloth*** ◇ *bandages made from strips of cloth* ◇ *the* ***cloth industry/trade*** ◇ *a cloth bag* ➲ note at FABRIC **2** 0-w [C] (often in compounds) a piece of cloth, often used for a special purpose, especially cleaning things or covering a table: *Wipe the surface with a damp cloth.* ➲ see also DISHCLOTH, DROP CLOTH, FLOORCLOTH, TABLECLOTH **3 the cloth** [sing.] (*literary*) used to refer to Christian priests as a group: *a man of the cloth*

IDM see COAT *n.*

ˌcloth ˈcap (also **ˌflat ˈcap**) (both *BrE*) *noun* a soft cap, normally made of wool, traditionally a symbol of working

Synonyms

clothes

clothing • garment • dress • wear • gear

These are all words for the things that you wear, such as shirts, jackets, dresses and trousers.

clothes [pl.] the things that you wear, such as shirts, jackets, dresses and trousers.

clothing [U] (*rather formal*) clothes, especially a particular type of clothes: *warm clothing*

CLOTHES OR CLOTHING?

Clothing is more formal than **clothes** and is used especially to mean 'a particular type of clothes'. There is no singular form of **clothes** or **clothing**: *a piece/an item/an article of clothing* is used to talk about one thing that you wear such as a dress or shirt.

garment (*formal*) a piece of clothing: *He was wearing a strange shapeless garment.* NOTE **Garment** should only be used in formal or literary contexts; in everyday contexts use *a piece of clothing.*

dress [U] clothes, especially when worn in a particular style or for a particular occasion: *We were allowed to wear casual dress on Fridays.*

wear [U] (usually in compounds) clothes for a particular purpose or occasion, especially when it is being sold in shops/stores: *the children's wear department*

gear [U] (*informal*) clothes: *Her friends were all wearing the latest gear* (= fashionable clothes).

PATTERNS

- **casual** clothes/clothing/dress/wear/gear
- **evening/formal** clothes/dress/wear
- **designer/sports** clothes/clothing/garments/wear/gear
- **children's/men's/women's** clothes/clothing/garments/wear
- to **have on/be in/wear** ...clothes/garments/dress/gear

C

men: *The party has shed its cloth cap image* (= it is not just a working-class party any more). ➲ VISUAL VOCAB page V53

clothe /kləʊð; *NAmE* kloʊð/ *verb* **1 ~ sb/yourself (in sth)** (*formal*) to dress sb/yourself: *They clothe their children in the latest fashions.* ◇ (*figurative*) *Climbing plants clothed the courtyard walls.* **2 ~ sb** to provide clothes for sb to wear: *the costs of feeding and clothing a family*

ˈ**cloth-eared** *adj.* (*BrE, informal, disapproving*) (of a person) unable to hear or understand things clearly

clothed /kləʊðd; *NAmE* kloʊðd/ *adj.* [not usually before noun] **~ (in sth)** dressed in a particular way: *a man clothed in black* ◇ *She jumped* ***fully clothed*** *into the water.* ◇ (*figurative*) *The valley was clothed in trees and shrubs.*

clothes 0-ᴡ /kləʊðz; kləʊz; *NAmE* kloʊðz; kloʊz/ *noun* [pl.] the things that you wear, such as trousers/pants, dresses and jackets: *I bought some new clothes for the trip.* ◇ *to* ***put on/take off your clothes*** ◇ *Bring* ***a change of clothes*** *with you.* ◇ *She has no* ***clothes sense*** (= she does not know what clothes look attractive). ➲ COLLOCATIONS at FASHION ➲ VISUAL VOCAB pages V50, V51 IDM see EMPEROR

ˈ**clothes hanger** *noun* = HANGER

ˈ**clothes horse** *noun* **1** (*BrE*) a wooden or plastic folding frame that you put clothes on to dry after you have washed them **2** (*disapproving*) a person, especially a woman, who is too interested in fashionable clothes

ˈ**clothes line** (*BrE*) (also **line** *NAmE, BrE*) (*BrE* also ˈ**washing line**) *noun* a piece of thin rope or wire, attached to posts, that you hang clothes on to dry outside after you have washed them

ˈ**clothes peg** (*BrE*) (*NAmE* ˈ**clothes·pin**) *noun* = PEG (3) ➲ picture at PEG

clo·thier /ˈkləʊðiə(r); *NAmE* ˈkloʊ-/ *noun* (*formal*) a person or company that makes or sells clothes or cloth

cloth·ing 0-ᴡ /ˈkləʊðɪŋ; *NAmE* ˈkloʊðɪŋ/ *noun* [U] clothes, especially a particular type of clothes: *protective clothing* ◇ *the high cost of food and clothing* ◇ *an* ***item/article of clothing*** ➲ SYNONYMS at CLOTHES IDM see WOLF *n.*

ˌ**clot·ted** ˈ**cream** *noun* [U] a very thick type of cream made by slowly heating milk, made and eaten especially in Britain: *scones and jam with clotted cream*

ˈ**clotting factor** *noun* [C, U] (*biology*) any of the substances in the blood which help it to CLOT (= become thick and form lumps)

cloud 0-ᴡ /klaʊd/ *noun, verb*

■ ***noun*** **1** 0-ᴡ [C, U] a grey or white mass made of very small drops of water, that floats in the sky: *The sun went behind a cloud.* ◇ *The plane was flying in cloud most of the way.* ➲ COLLOCATIONS at WEATHER ➲ see also STORM CLOUD, THUNDERCLOUD **2** 0-ᴡ [C] a large mass of sth in the air, for example dust or smoke, or a number of insects flying all together **3** [C] something that makes you feel sad or anxious: *Her father's illness* ***cast a cloud over*** *her wedding day.* ◇ *The only dark* ***cloud on the horizon*** *was that they might have to move house.* ◇ *He still has* ***a cloud*** *of suspicion* ***hanging over him.***

IDM **every cloud has a silver ˈlining** (*saying*) every sad or difficult situation has a positive side **on cloud ˈnine** (*old-fashioned, informal*) extremely happy **under a ˈcloud** if sb is **under a cloud**, other people think that they have done sth wrong and are suspicious of them ➲ more at HEAD *n.*

■ ***verb*** **1** [T] **~ sth** if sth **clouds** your judgement, memory, etc, it makes it difficult for you to understand or remember sth clearly: *Doubts were beginning to cloud my mind.* ◇ *His judgement was clouded by jealousy.* **2** [I, T] (*formal*) (of sb's face) to show sadness, fear, anger, etc; to make sb look sad, afraid, angry, etc: **~ (over)** *Her face clouded over with anger.* ◇ **~ sth** *Suspicion clouded his face.* **3** [T] **~ the issue** to make sth you are discussing or considering less clear, especially by introducing subjects that are not connected with it **4** [I] **~ (over)** (of the sky) to fill with clouds: *It was beginning to cloud over.* **5** [T] **~ sth** to make sth less pleasant or enjoyable: *His last years were clouded by financial worries.* **6** [I, T] if glass, water, etc. **clouds**, or if sth **clouds** it, it becomes less transparent: **~ (with sth)** *Her eyes clouded with tears.* ◇ **~ sth** *Steam had clouded the mirror.*

cloud·burst /ˈklaʊdbɜːst; *NAmE* -bɜːrst/ *noun* a sudden very heavy fall of rain

ˈ**cloud computing** *noun* [U] a way of using computers in which data and software are stored mainly on a central computer, to which users have access over the Internet

ˌ**cloud** ˈ**cuckoo land** (*BrE*) (*NAmE* **cloud·land**, ˈ**la-la land**) *noun* [U] (*informal, disapproving*) if you say that sb is living **in cloud cuckoo land**, you mean that they do not understand what a situation is really like, but think it is much better than it is

ˈ**cloud forest** *noun* [C, U] a forest in tropical or SUBTROPICAL parts of the world that usually has thick cloud at the level of the tops of the trees ➲ compare RAINFOREST

cloud·less /ˈklaʊdləs/ *adj.* clear; with no clouds: *a cloudless sky*

cloudy /ˈklaʊdi/ *adj.* (**cloud·ier, cloudi·est**) **1** (of the sky or the weather) covered with clouds; with a lot of clouds OPP **clear**: *a grey, cloudy day* **2** (of liquids) not clear or transparent ▸ **cloudi·ness** *noun* [U]

clout /klaʊt/ *noun, verb*

■ ***noun*** **1** [U] power and influence: ***political/financial clout*** ◇ *I knew his opinion carried a lot of clout with them.* **2** [C, usually sing.] (*informal*) a blow with the hand or a hard object

■ ***verb*** **~ sb** (*informal*) to hit sb hard, especially with your hand

clove /kləʊv; *NAmE* kloʊv/ *noun* **1** [C, U] the dried flower of a tropical tree, used in cooking as a spice, especially to give flavour to sweet foods. Cloves look like small nails. ➲ VISUAL VOCAB page V28 **2** [C] **a garlic ~ | a ~ of garlic** one of the small separate sections of a BULB (= the round underground part) of GARLIC ➲ VISUAL VOCAB page V27 ➲ see also CLEAVE *v.*

ˌ**cloven** ˈ**hoof** *noun* the foot of an animal such as a cow, a sheep, or a GOAT, that is divided into two parts

clo·ver /ˈkləʊvə(r); *NAmE* ˈkloʊ-/ *noun* [U] a small wild plant that usually has three leaves on each STEM and purple, pink or white flowers that are shaped like balls: *a four-leaf clover* (= one with four leaves instead of three, thought to bring good luck)

IDM **be/live in clover** (*informal*) to have enough money to be able to live a very comfortable life

clover·leaf /ˈkləʊvəliːf; *NAmE* ˈkloʊvər-/ *noun* (*NAmE*) a place where a number of main roads meet at different levels, with curved sections that form the pattern of a four-leaf clover

clown /klaʊn/ *noun, verb*

■ ***noun*** **1** an entertainer who wears funny clothes and a large red nose and does silly things to make people laugh: (*figurative*) *Robert was always the class clown* (= he did silly things to make the other students laugh). **2** (*disapproving*) a person that you disapprove of because they act in a stupid way: *What do those clowns in the government think they are doing?*

■ ***verb*** [I] **~ (around)** (often *disapproving*) to behave in a silly way, especially in order to make other people laugh

clown·ish /ˈklaʊnɪʃ/ *adj.* like a clown; silly

cloy /klɔɪ/ [I] (of sth pleasant or sweet) to start to become slightly disgusting or annoying, because there is too much of it: *After a while, the rich sauce begins to cloy.*

cloy·ing /ˈklɔɪɪŋ/ *adj.* (*formal*) **1** (of food, a smell, etc.) so sweet that it is unpleasant **2** using emotion in a very obvious way, so that the result is unpleasant: *the cloying sentimentality of her novels* ▸ **cloy·ing·ly** *adv.*

cloze test /ˈkləʊz test; *NAmE* ˈkloʊz/ *noun* a type of test in which you have to put suitable words in spaces in a text where words have been left out

club 0-ᴡ /klʌb/ *noun, verb*

■ ***noun***

▸ FOR ACTIVITY/SPORT **1** 0-ᴡ [C+sing./pl. v.] (especially in compounds) a group of people who meet together regularly, for a particular activity, sport, etc: *a golf/tennis, etc. club* ◇ *a chess/film/movie, etc. club* ◇ *to join/belong to a club* ◇ *The club has/have voted to admit new members.* ➲ see also FAN CLUB, YOUTH CLUB **2** [C] the building or rooms that a particular club uses: *We had lunch at the golf club.* ◇ *the club bar* ➲ see also COUNTRY CLUB, HEALTH CLUB **3** [C+sing./pl. v.] (*BrE*) a professional sports organization that includes the players, managers, owners and members: *Manchester United Football Club*

▸ MUSIC/DANCING **4** [C] a place where people, especially young people, go and listen to music, dance, etc: *a jazz club* ◇ *the club scene in Newcastle* ➲ see also CLUBBING, NIGHTCLUB, STRIP CLUB

▸ SOCIAL **5** [C+sing./pl. v.] (especially in Britain) an organization and a place where people, usually men only, can meet together socially or stay: *He's a member of several London clubs.*

▸ SELLING BOOKS/CDS **6** [C] an organization that sells books, CDs, etc. cheaply to its members: *a music club* ➲ see also BOOK CLUB

▸ WEAPON **7** [C] a heavy stick with one end thicker than the other, that is used as a weapon ➲ see also BILLY CLUB

▸ IN GOLF **8** [C] = GOLF CLUB

▸ IN CARD GAMES **9 clubs** [pl., U] one of the four sets of cards (called SUITS) in a PACK/DECK of cards. The clubs have a black design shaped like three black leaves on a short STEM: *the five/queen/ace of clubs* ➲ VISUAL VOCAB page V32 **10** [C] one card from the SUIT called clubs: *I played a club.*

IDM **be in the club** (*BrE, informal*) to be pregnant ➲ more at JOIN *v.*

■ *verb* (-bb-) **1** [T] **~ sb/sth** to hit a person or an animal with a heavy stick or similar object: *The victim was* ***clubbed to death*** *with a baseball bat.* **2** [I] **go clubbing** (*BrE, informal*) to spend time dancing and drinking in NIGHTCLUBS

PHR V ˌ**club to'gether** (*BrE*) if two or more people **club together**, they each give an amount of money and the total is used to pay for sth: *We clubbed together to buy them a new television.*

club·bing /'klʌbɪŋ/ *noun* [U] the activity of going to NIGHTCLUBS regularly: *They* ***go clubbing*** *most weekends.* ▸ **club·ber** *noun*: *The venue was packed with 3 000 clubbers.*

ˈ**club car** *noun* (*NAmE*) a coach/car on a train with comfortable chairs and tables, where you can buy sth to eat or drink

ˈ**club class** *noun* [U] (*BrE*) = BUSINESS CLASS

ˌ**club 'foot** *noun* [C, U] a foot that has been DEFORMED (= badly shaped) since birth ▸ ˌ**club-'footed** *adj.*

club·house /'klʌbhaʊs/ *noun* the building used by a club, especially a sports club

club·land /'klʌblænd/ *noun* [U] (*BrE*) popular NIGHTCLUBS in general and the people who go to them; an area of a town where there are a lot of NIGHTCLUBS: *modern clubland* ◇ *London's clubland*

ˌ**club 'sandwich** *noun* a SANDWICH consisting of three slices of bread with two layers of food between them

cluck /klʌk/ *verb, noun*

■ *verb* **1** [I] when a chicken **clucks**, it makes a series of short low sounds **2** [I] to make a short low sound with your tongue to show that you feel sorry for sb or that you disapprove of sth: *The teacher clucked sympathetically at the child's story.*

■ *noun* the low, short sounds that a chicken makes: (*figurative*) *a* ***cluck of impatience/annoyance***

clucky /'klʌki/ *adj.* (*AustralE, NZE, informal*) **1** (of a HEN) sitting or ready to sit on eggs SYN **broody 2** (of a woman) wanting to have a baby SYN **broody**

clue /klu:/ *noun, verb*

■ *noun* **1 ~ (to sth)** an object, a piece of evidence or some information that helps the police solve a crime: *The police think the videotape may hold some vital clues to the identity of the killer.* **2 ~ (to sth)** a fact or a piece of evidence that helps you discover the answer to a problem: *Diet may hold the clue to the causes of migraine.* **3** some words or a piece of information that helps you find the answers to a CROSSWORD, a game or a question: *'You'll never guess who I saw today!' 'Give me a clue.'*

IDM **not have a 'clue** (*informal*) **1** to know nothing about sth or about how to do sth: *I don't have a clue where she lives.* **2** (*disapproving*) to be very stupid: *Don't ask him to do it—he doesn't have a clue!*

■ *verb*

PHR V ˌ**clue sb 'in (on sth)** (*informal*) to give sb the most recent information about sth: *He's just clued me in on the latest developments.*

ˌ**clued-'up** (*BrE*) (*NAmE* ˌ**clued-'in**) *adj.* **~ (on sth)** (*informal*) knowing a lot about sth; having a lot of information about sth

clue·less /'klu:ləs/ *adj.* (*informal, disapproving*) very stupid; not able to understand or to do sth: *He's completely clueless about computers.*

clump /klʌmp/ *noun, verb*

■ *noun* **1** a small group of things or people very close together, especially trees or plants; a bunch of sth such as grass or hair: *a* ***clump of trees/bushes*** **2** the sound made by sb putting their feet down very heavily

■ *verb* **1** [I] **+ adv./prep.** (*especially BrE*) to put your feet down noisily and heavily as you walk: *The children clumped down the stairs.* **2** [I, T] **~ (together)** | **~ A and B (together)** to come together or be brought together to form a tight group: *Galaxies tend to clump together in clusters.*

clumpy /klʌmpi/ *adj.* (*BrE*) (of shoes and boots) big, thick and heavy

clumsy /'klʌmzi/ *adj.* (**clum·sier**, **clum·si·est**) **1** (of people and animals) moving or doing things in a very awkward way: *I spilt your coffee. Sorry—that was clumsy of me.* ◇ *His clumsy fingers couldn't untie the knot.* **2** (of actions and statements) done without skill or in a way that offends people: *She made* ***a clumsy attempt*** *to apologize.* **3** (of objects) difficult to move or use easily; not well designed **4** (of processes) awkward; too complicated to understand or use easily: *The complaints procedure is clumsy and time-consuming.* ▸ **clum·si·ly** /-ɪli/ *adv.* **clum·si·ness** *noun* [U]

clung *past tense, past part.* of CLING

clunk /klʌŋk/ *noun* a dull sound made by two heavy objects hitting each other ▸ **clunk** *verb* [I]

clunk·er /'klʌŋkə(r)/ *noun* (*NAmE, informal*) **1** an old car in bad condition **2** a serious mistake

clunky /'klʌŋki/ *adj.* (*informal, especially NAmE*) heavy and awkward: *clunky leather shoes* ◇ (*figurative*) *The movie is ruined by wooden acting and clunky dialogue.*

clus·ter /'klʌstə(r)/ *noun, verb*

■ *noun* **1** a group of things of the same type that grow or appear close together: *a cluster of stars* ◇ *The plant bears its flowers in clusters.* ◇ *a leukaemia cluster* (= an area where there are more cases of the disease than you would expect) **2** a group of people, animals or things close together: *a cluster of spectators* ◇ *a little cluster of houses* **3** (*phonetics*) a group of consonants which come together in a word or phrase, for example /str/ at the beginning of *string*: *a consonant cluster*

■ *verb* [I] to come together in a small group or groups: **~ together** *The children clustered together in the corner of the room.* ◇ **~ around/round sb/sth** *The doctors* ***clustered*** *anxiously* ***around*** *his bed.*

ˈ**cluster bomb** *noun* a type of bomb that throws out smaller bombs when it explodes

clutch /klʌtʃ/ *verb, noun*

■ *verb* **1** [T, I] to hold sb/sth tightly SYN **grip**: **~ sth (+ adv./prep.)** *He clutched the child to him.* ◇ *She stood there, the flowers still clutched in her hand.* ◇ **+ adv./prep.** *I clutched on to the chair for support* ➲ SYNONYMS at HOLD **2** [T, I] to take hold of sth suddenly, because you are afraid or in pain: **~ sth** *He gasped and clutched his stomach.* ◇ **~ at sb/sth** (*figurative*) *Fear clutched at her heart.* IDM see STRAW ➲ SYNONYMS at HOLD

C

PHR V 'clutch/'catch at sth/sb to try to quickly get hold of sth/sb SYN grab at
■ *noun* **1** [C] the PEDAL in a car or other vehicle that you press with your foot so that you can change gear: *Put your foot on the clutch.* ➲ COLLOCATIONS at DRIVING ➲ VISUAL VOCAB page V42 **2** [C] a device in a machine that connects and DISCONNECTS working parts, especially the engine and the gears: *The car needs a new clutch.* **3 a ~ of sth** [sing.] (*BrE*) a group of people, animals or things: *He's won a whole clutch of awards.* **4 clutches** [pl.] (*informal*) power or control: *He managed to escape **from** their **clutches**.* ◇ *Now that she had him **in** her **clutches**, she wasn't going to let go.* **5** [C, usually sing.] a tight hold on sb/sth SYN **grip**: (*figurative*) *She felt the sudden clutch of fear.* **6** [C] a group of eggs that a bird lays at one time; the young birds that come out of a group of eggs at the same time **7** [C] (*NAmE*) = CLUTCH BAG

'clutch bag (*NAmE* also **clutch**) *noun* a small, flat bag that women carry in their hands, especially on formal occasions ➲ VISUAL VOCAB page V52

clut·ter /ˈklʌtə(r)/ *verb, noun*
■ *verb* **~ sth (up) (with sth/sb)** to fill a place with too many things, so that it is untidy: *Don't clutter the page with too many diagrams.* ◇ *I don't want all these files cluttering up my desk.* ◇ (*figurative*) *Try not to clutter your head with trivia.*
■ *noun* [U, sing.] (*disapproving*) a lot of things in an untidy state, especially things that are not necessary or are not being used; a state of confusion SYN **mess**: *There's always so much clutter on your desk!* ◇ *There was a clutter of bottles and tubes on the shelf.*

clut·tered /ˈklʌtəd; *NAmE* -tərd/ *adj.* **~ (up) (with sb/sth)** covered with, or full of, a lot of things or people, in a way that is untidy: *a **cluttered room/desk*** ◇ (*figurative*) *a cluttered mind* OPP **uncluttered**

CM *abbr.* COMMAND MODULE

cm *abbr.* (*pl.* **cm** or **cms**) CENTIMETRE

CND /ˌsiː en ˈdiː/ *abbr.* Campaign for Nuclear Disarmament (a British organization whose aim is to persuade countries to get rid of their nuclear weapons)

CNN /ˌsiː en ˈen/ *abbr.* Cable News Network (an American broadcasting company that sends television news programmes all over the world)

CO /ˌsiː ˈəʊ; *NAmE* ˈoʊ/ *abbr.* Commanding Officer (an officer who commands a group of soldiers, sailors, etc.)

Co. /kəʊ; *NAmE* koʊ/ *abbr.* **1** (*business*) company: *Pitt, Briggs & Co.* **2** (in writing) county **3 and co.** (*BrE, informal*) and other members of a group of people: *Were Jane and co. at the party?*

co- /kəʊ; *NAmE* koʊ/ *prefix* (used in adjectives, adverbs, nouns and verbs) together with: *co-produced* ◇ *cooperatively* ◇ *co-author* ◇ *coexist*

c/o /ˌsiː ˈəʊ; *NAmE* ˈoʊ/ *abbr.* (used on letters to a person staying at sb else's house) care of: *Mr P Brown, c/o Ms M Jones*

coach 0-π /kəʊtʃ; *NAmE* koʊtʃ/ *noun, verb*
■ *noun* **1** 0-π [C] a person who trains a person or team in sport: *a **basketball/football/tennis, etc. coach*** ◇ *Italy's national coach* **2** [C] (*BrE*) a person who gives private lessons to sb, often to prepare them for an exam: *a maths coach* **3** [C] = LIFE COACH **4** 0-π [C] (*BrE*) a comfortable bus for carrying passengers over long distances: *They went to Italy on a **coach tour**.* ◇ *Travel is **by coach** overnight to Berlin.* ◇ *a **coach station*** (= where coaches start and end their journey) ◇ *a coach party* (= a group of people travelling together on a coach) ➲ VISUAL VOCAB page V46 **5** 0-π [C] (*BrE*) = CARRIAGE: *a railway coach* **6** [C] a large closed vehicle with four wheels, pulled by horses, used in the past for carrying passengers ➲ see also STAGECOACH **7** [U] (*NAmE*) the cheapest seats in a plane: *to fly coach* ◇ ***coach fares/passengers/seats*** IDM see DRIVE *v.*
■ *verb* **1** to train sb to play a sport, to do a job better, or to improve a skill: **~ sb (in/for sth)** *Her father coached her for the Olympics.* ◇ **~ sb (to do sth)** *She has coached hundreds of young singers.* ◇ **~ sth** *He coaches basketball and soccer.* **2 ~ sb (in/for sth)** (*especially BrE*) to give a student extra teaching in a particular subject especially so that they will pass an exam **3 ~ sb (in/on sth)** | **~ sb (to do sth)** to give sb special instructions for what they should do or say in a particular situation: *They believed the witnesses had been coached on what to say.*

'coach house *noun* a building where CARRIAGES pulled by horses are or were kept

coach·ing /ˈkəʊtʃɪŋ; *NAmE* ˈkoʊtʃ-/ *noun* [U] **1** the process of training sb to play a sport, to do a job better or to improve a skill: *a coaching session* **2** (*especially BrE*) the process of giving a student extra teaching in a particular subject

'coaching inn *noun* in the past, an INN along a route used by horses, at which horses could be changed

coach·load /ˈkəʊtʃləʊd; *NAmE* ˈkoʊtʃloʊd/ *noun* (*BrE*) a group of people travelling together in a coach: *Tourists were arriving **by the coachload**.*

coach·man /ˈkəʊtʃmən; *NAmE* ˈkoʊtʃ-/ *noun* (*pl.* **-men** /-mən/) (in the past) a man who drove a COACH pulled by horses

coach·work /ˈkəʊtʃwɜːk; *NAmE* ˈkoʊtʃwɜːrk/ *noun* [U] (*BrE*) the metal outer part of a road or railway/railroad vehicle

co·agu·late /kəʊˈæɡjuleɪt; *NAmE* koʊ-/ *verb* [I, T] **~ (sth)** if a liquid **coagulates** or sth **coagulates** it, it becomes thick and partly solid SYN **congeal**: *Blood began to coagulate around the edges of the wound.* ▶ **co·agu·la·tion** /kəʊˌæɡjuˈleɪʃn; *NAmE* koʊ-/ *noun* [U]

coal 0-π /kəʊl; *NAmE* koʊl/ *noun*
1 0-π [U] a hard black mineral that is found below the ground and burnt to produce heat: *I put more coal on the fire.* ◇ *a lump of coal* ◇ *a coal fire* ◇ *a coal mine* ◇ *the coal industry* **2** [C] a piece of coal, especially one that is burning: *A hot coal fell out of the fire and burnt the carpet.*
IDM **carry, take, etc. coals to 'Newcastle** (*BrE*) to take goods to a place where there are already plenty of them; to supply sth where it is not needed ORIGIN Newcastle-upon-Tyne, in the north of England, was once an important coal-mining centre. ➲ more at HAUL *v.*, RAKE *v.*

ˌcoal-'black *adj.* very dark in colour: *coal-black eyes*

co·alesce /ˌkəʊəˈles; *NAmE* ˌkoʊə-/ *verb* [I] **~ (into/with sth)** (*formal*) to come together to form one larger group, substance, etc. SYN **amalgamate**: *The puddles had coalesced into a small stream.* ▶ **co·ales·cence** /ˌkəʊəˈlesns; *NAmE* ˌkoʊə-/ *noun* [U]

coal·face /ˈkəʊlfeɪs; *NAmE* ˈkoʊl-/ (also **face**) *noun* the place deep inside a mine where the coal is cut out of the rock
IDM **at the 'coalface** (*BrE*) where the real work is done, not just where people talk about it: *Many of the best ideas come from doctors at the coalface.*

coal·field /ˈkəʊlfiːld; *NAmE* ˈkoʊl-/ *noun* a large area where there is a lot of coal under the ground

ˌcoal-'fired *adj.* using coal as fuel: *a coal-fired power station*

'coal gas *noun* [U] a mixture of gases produced from coal, that can be used for electricity and heating

coal·house /ˈkəʊlhaʊs; *NAmE* ˈkoʊl-/ *noun* a small building for storing coal, especially in sb's garden in the past

co·ali·tion /ˌkəʊəˈlɪʃn; *NAmE* ˌkoʊə-/ *noun* **1** [C+sing./pl. v.] a government formed by two or more political parties working together: *to form a coalition* ◇ *a two-party coalition* ◇ *a coalition government* **2** [C+sing./pl. v.] a group formed by people from several different groups, especially political ones, agreeing to work together for a particular purpose: *a coalition of environmental and consumer groups* **3** [U] the act of two or more groups joining together: *They didn't rule out coalition with the Social Democrats.*

coal·man /ˈkəʊlmən; *NAmE* ˈkoʊl-/ *noun* (*pl.* **-men** /-mən/) a man whose job is to deliver coal to people's houses

'coal mine (also **pit**) *noun* a place underground where coal is dug

ˈ**coal miner** *noun* a person whose job is digging coal in a coal mine

ˈ**coal scuttle** (also **scuttle**) *noun* a container with a handle, used for carrying coal and usually kept beside the FIREPLACE ➲ VISUAL VOCAB page V18

ˈ**coal tar** *noun* [U] a thick black sticky substance produced when gas is made from coal

coarse /kɔːs; *NAmE* kɔːrs/ *adj.* (**coars·er, coars·est**) **1** (of skin or cloth) rough: *coarse hands/linen* OPP **smooth, soft** **2** consisting of relatively large pieces: *coarse sand/salt/hair* OPP **fine** **3** rude and offensive, especially about sex SYN **vulgar**: ***coarse manners/laughter*** ▶ **coarse·ly** *adv.*: *coarsely chopped onions* (= cut into large pieces) ◇ *He laughed coarsely at her.* **coarse·ness** *noun* [U]

ˌ**coarse** ˈ**fish** *noun* (*pl.* **coarse fish**) (*BrE*) any fish, except SALMON and TROUT, that lives in rivers and lakes rather than in the sea

ˌ**coarse** ˈ**fishing** *noun* [U] (*BrE*) the sport of catching coarse fish: *to go coarse fishing*

coars·en /ˈkɔːsn; *NAmE* ˈkɔːrsn/ *verb* **1** [I, T] to become or make sth become thicker and/or rougher: *Her hair gradually coarsened as she grew older.* ◇ **~ sth** *His features had been coarsened by the weather.* **2** to become or make sb become less polite and often offensive in the way they behave: [T, I] **~ (sb)** *The six long years in prison had coarsened him.*

Synonyms

coast

beach • seaside • coastline • sand • seashore

These are all words for the land beside or near to the sea, a river or a lake.

coast the land beside or near to the sea or ocean: *a town on the south coast of England* ◇ *The coast road is closed due to bad weather.* NOTE It is nearly always **the coast**, except when it is uncountable: *That's a pretty stretch of coast.*

beach an area of sand, or small stones, beside the sea or a lake: *She took the kids to the beach for the day.* ◇ *sandy beaches*

seaside (*especially BrE*) an area that is by the sea, especially one where people go for a day or a holiday: *a trip to the seaside* NOTE It is always **the seaside**, except when it is used before a noun: *a seaside resort.* **The seaside** is British English; in American English **seaside** is only used before a noun.

coastline the land along a coast, especially when you are thinking of its shape or appearance: *California's rugged coastline*

sand a large area of sand on a beach: *We went for a walk along the sand.* ◇ *a resort with miles of golden sands*

the seashore the land along the edge of the sea or ocean, usually where there is sand and rocks: *He liked to look for shells on the seashore.*

BEACH OR SEASHORE?

Beach is usually used to talk about a sandy area next to the sea where people lie in the sun or play, for example when they are on holiday/vacation. **Seashore** is used more to talk about the area by the sea in terms of things such as waves, sea shells, rocks, etc, especially where people walk for pleasure.

PATTERNS

- **along** the coast/beach/coastline/seashore
- **on** the coast/beach/coastline/sands/seashore
- **at** the coast/beach/seaside/seashore
- **by** the coast/seaside/seashore
- a(n) **rocky/unspoiled** coast/beach/coastline
- to **go to** the coast/beach/seaside/seashore

coast 0➡ /kəʊst; *NAmE* koʊst/ *noun, verb*
■ ***noun*** 0➡ [C, U] the land beside or near to the sea or ocean: *a town on the south coast of England* ◇ *islands off the west coast of Ireland* ◇ *a trip to the coast* ◇ *We walked along the coast for five miles.* ◇ *the Welsh coast* ◇ *a pretty stretch of coast* ◇ *the coast road* ➲ VISUAL VOCAB pages V4, V5
IDM **the** ˌ**coast is** ˈ**clear** (*informal*) there is no danger of being seen or caught: *As soon as the coast was clear he climbed in through the window.*
■ ***verb*** **1** [I] (**+ adv./prep.**) (of a car or a bicycle) to move, especially down a hill, without using any power: *The car coasted along until it stopped.* ◇ *She took her feet off the pedals and coasted downhill.* **2** [I] (**+ adv./prep.**) (of a vehicle) to move quickly and smoothly, without using much power: *The plane coasted down the runway.* **3** [I] **~ (through/to sth)** to be successful at sth without having to try hard: *He coasted through his final exams.* **4** [I] **~ (along)** (*disapproving*) to put very little effort into sth: *You're just coasting—it's time to work hard now.* **5** [I] (of a ship) to stay close to land while sailing around the coast

coast·al /ˈkəʊstl; *NAmE* ˈkoʊstl/ *adj.* [usually before noun] of or near a coast: ***coastal waters/resorts/scenery*** ◇ *a **coastal path*** (= one that follows the line of the coast) ➲ VISUAL VOCAB page V4 ➲ compare INLAND

coast·eer·ing /ˌkəʊstˈɪərɪŋ; *NAmE* ˌkoʊstˈɪrɪŋ/ *noun* [U] the sport of following a route around a coast by climbing, jumping off CLIFFS and swimming

coast·er /ˈkəʊstə(r); *NAmE* ˈkoʊst-/ *noun* **1** a small flat object which you put under a glass to protect the top of a table ➲ VISUAL VOCAB page V18 **2** a ship that sails from port to port along a coast ➲ see also ROLLER COASTER

coast·guard /ˈkəʊstgɑːd; *NAmE* ˈkoʊstgɑːrd/ *noun* **1** (usually **the coastguard**) [sing.] an official organization (in the US a branch of the armed forces) whose job is to watch the sea near a coast in order to help ships and people in trouble, and to stop people from breaking the law: *The coastguard was alerted.* ◇ *They radioed Dover Coastguard.* ◇ *a coastguard station* **2** [C] (*especially BrE*) (*US* usually **coast·guards·man** /ˈkəʊstgɑːdzmən; *NAmE* ˈkoʊstgɑːrd-/ *pl.* **-men** /-mən/) a member of this organization

coast·line /ˈkəʊstlaɪn; *NAmE* ˈkoʊst-/ *noun* the land along a coast, especially when you are thinking of its shape or appearance: *a **rugged/rocky/beautiful coastline*** ◇ *to protect the coastline from oil spillage* ➲ SYNONYMS at COAST

coat 0➡ /kəʊt; *NAmE* koʊt/ *noun, verb*
■ ***noun*** **1** 0➡ a piece of outdoor clothing that is worn over other clothes to keep warm or dry. Coats have sleeves and may be long or short: *a fur/leather coat* ◇ *a long winter coat* ◇ *to **put on/take off your coat*** ➲ VISUAL VOCAB page V50 ➲ see also DUFFEL COAT, GREATCOAT, HOUSECOAT, OVERCOAT, PETTICOAT, RAINCOAT, TRENCH COAT **2** (*NAmE*) (*old-fashioned* in *BrE*) a jacket that is worn as part of a suit ➲ see also FROCK COAT, MORNING COAT, TAILCOAT, WAISTCOAT **3** 0➡ the fur, hair or wool that covers an animal's body: *a dog with a **smooth/shaggy coat*** ➲ VISUAL VOCAB page V10 **4** 0➡ a layer of paint or some other substance that covers a surface: *to give the walls a second coat of paint* ➲ see also TOPCOAT, UNDERCOAT
IDM ˌ**cut your** ˈ**coat ac**ˌ**cording to your** ˈ**cloth** (*saying*) to do only what you have enough money to do and no more
■ ***verb*** [often passive] **~ sth (with/in sth)** to cover sth with a layer of a substance: *cookies thickly coated with chocolate* ◇ *A film of dust coated the table.* ➲ see also SUGAR-COATED

ˈ**coat check** *noun* (*NAmE*) = CLOAKROOM

ˈ**coat hanger** *noun* = HANGER

coati /kəʊˈɑːti; *NAmE* koʊ-/ (also **co·ati·mundi** /kəʊˌɑːtiˈmʌndi; *NAmE* koʊ-/) *noun* a small animal with a long nose and a long tail with lines across it, which lives mainly in Central and S America

coat·ing /ˈkəʊtɪŋ; *NAmE* ˈkoʊt-/ *noun* a thin layer of a substance covering a surface: *a thin coating of chocolate* ◇ *magnetic coating on a floppy disk*

ˌcoat of ˈarms *noun* (*pl.* **coats of arms**) (also **arms**) a design or a SHIELD that is a special symbol of a family, city or other organization: *the royal coat of arms*

coat·room /ˈkəʊtruːm; -rʊm; *NAmE* ˈkoʊt-/ *noun* (*NAmE*) = CLOAKROOM (1)

C

ˈcoat stand *noun* a stand with hooks for hanging coats and hats on

ˈcoat-tails *noun* [pl.]

IDM **on sb's coat-tails** using the success and influence of another person to help yourself become successful: *She got where she is today on her brother's coat-tails.*

ˌco-ˈauthor *noun* a person who writes a book or an article with sb else ▶ **ˌco-ˈauthor** *verb* [T] **~ sth** **ˌco-ˈauthor·ship** *noun* [U]

coax /kəʊks; *NAmE* koʊks/ *verb* to persuade sb to do sth by talking to them in a kind and gentle way SYN **cajole**: **~ sb/sth (into doing sth)** *She coaxed the horse into coming a little closer.* ◇ **~ sb/sth (into/out of sth)** *He was coaxed out of retirement to help the failing company.* ◇ **~ sb/sth (+ adv./prep.)** *She had to coax the car along.* ◇ **~ (sb/sth) + speech** *'Nearly there,' she coaxed.*

PHR V **coax sth out of/from sb** to gently persuade sb to do sth or give you sth: *The director coaxed a brilliant performance out of the cast.*

coax·ing /ˈkəʊksɪŋ; *NAmE* ˈkoʊ-/ *noun* [U] gentle attempts to persuade sb to do sth or to get a machine to start: *No amount of coaxing will make me change my mind.* ▶ **coax·ing** *adj.* **coax·ing·ly** *adv.*

cob /kɒb; *NAmE* kɑːb/ *noun* **1** = CORNCOB: *corn on the cob* **2** a strong horse with short legs **3** (*BrE*) a round LOAF of bread: *a crusty cob*

co·balt /ˈkəʊbɔːlt; *NAmE* ˈkoʊ-/ *noun* [U] **1** (*symb.* **Co**) a chemical element. Cobalt is a hard silver-white metal, often mixed with other metals and used to give a deep blue-green colour to glass. **2** (also **ˌcobalt ˈblue**) a deep blue-green colour

cob·ber /ˈkɒbə(r); *NAmE* ˈkɑːb-/ *noun* (*AustralE, NZE, informal*) (used especially by a man addressing another man) a friend

cob·ble /ˈkɒbl; *NAmE* ˈkɑːbl/ *verb* **~ sth** (*old-fashioned*) to make or repair shoes

PHR V **ˌcobble sth↔toˈgether** to produce sth quickly and without great care or effort, so that it can be used but is not perfect: *The essay was cobbled together from some old notes.*

cob·bled /ˈkɒbld; *NAmE* ˈkɑːbld/ *adj.* (of streets and roads) having a surface that is made of COBBLES

cob·bler /ˈkɒblə(r); *NAmE* ˈkɑːb-/ *noun* **1** [C] a type of fruit or meat PIE with a thick bread-like layer on top: *peach cobbler* **2** [C] (*old-fashioned*) a person who repairs shoes ➲ compare SHOEMAKER **3** [U] **cobblers** (*BrE, informal*) nonsense: *He said it was all a load of cobblers.*

cob·bles /ˈkɒblz; *NAmE* ˈkɑːblz/ (also **cobble·stones**) *noun* [pl.] small stones used to make the surfaces of roads, especially in the past

cobble·stones /ˈkɒblstəʊnz; *NAmE* ˈkɑːblstoʊnz/ *noun* [pl.] = COBBLES ▶ **cobble·stone** *adj.*

COBOL /ˈkəʊbɒl; *NAmE* ˈkoʊbɔːl/ *noun* [U] an early computer language used in business programs

cobra /ˈkəʊbrə; *NAmE* ˈkoʊ-/ *noun* a poisonous snake that can spread the skin at the back of its neck to make itself look bigger. Cobras live in Asia and Africa. ➲ VISUAL VOCAB page V11

cob·web /ˈkɒbweb; *NAmE* ˈkɑːb-/ *noun* a fine net of threads made by a spider to catch insects; a single thread of this net (usually used when it is old and covered with dirt): *Thick cobwebs hung in the dusty corners.* ◇ *He brushed a cobweb out of his hair.* ➲ see also WEB, SPIDER'S WEB ▶ **cob·webbed** /ˈkɒbwebd; *NAmE* ˈkɑːb-/ *adj.*: *cobwebbed corners*

IDM **blow/clear the ˈcobwebs away** to help sb start sth in a fresh, lively state of mind: *A brisk walk should blow the cobwebs away.*

coca /ˈkəʊkə; *NAmE* ˈkoʊ-/ *noun* [U] a tropical bush whose leaves are used to make the drug COCAINE

Coca-Cola™ /ˌkəʊkə ˈkəʊlə; *NAmE* ˌkoʊkə ˈkoʊlə/ (also *informal* **Coke™**) *noun* **1** [U, C] a popular type of COLA drink **2** [C] a glass, bottle or can of Coca-Cola

co·caine /kəʊˈkeɪn; *NAmE* koʊ-/ (also *informal* **coke**) *noun* [U] a powerful drug that some people take illegally for pleasure and can become ADDICTED to. Doctors sometimes use it as an ANAESTHETIC.

coc·cyx /ˈkɒksɪks; *NAmE* ˈkɑːk-/ *noun* (*pl.* **coc·cyxes** or **coc·cy·ges** /ˈkɒksɪdʒiːz; *NAmE* ˈkɑːk-/) (*anatomy*) the small bone at the bottom of the SPINE SYN **tailbone** ➲ VISUAL VOCAB page V48

coch·in·eal /ˌkɒtʃɪˈniːl; *NAmE* ˈkɑːtʃəniːl/ *noun* [U] a bright red substance used to give colour to food

coch·lea /ˈkɒkliə; *NAmE* ˈkoʊk-; ˈkɑːk-/ *noun* (*pl.* **coch·leae** /-klii:/) (*anatomy*) a small curved tube inside the ear, which contains a small part that sends nerve signals to the brain when sounds cause it to VIBRATE

cock /kɒk; *NAmE* kɑːk/ *noun, verb*

■ *noun* **1** (*BrE*) (also **roost·er** *NAmE, BrE*) [C] an adult male chicken: *The cock crowed.* ➲ compare HEN **2** [C] (especially in compounds) a male of any other bird: *a cock pheasant* ➲ see also PEACOCK **3** [C] (*taboo, slang*) a PENIS **4** [C] = STOPCOCK ➲ see also BALLCOCK **5** [sing.] (*old-fashioned, BrE, slang*) used as a friendly form of address between men ➲ see also HALF-COCK

■ *verb* **1 ~ sth** to raise a part of your body so that it is vertical or at an angle: *The dog cocked its leg by every tree on our route* (= in order to URINATE). ◇ *He cocked an inquisitive eyebrow at her.* ◇ *She cocked her head to one side and looked at me.* ◇ *The dog stood listening, its ears cocked.* **2 ~ a gun/pistol/rifle** to raise the HAMMER on a gun so that it is ready to fire

IDM **cock an ear/eye at sth/sb** to look at or listen to sb/sth carefully and with a lot of attention **cock a snook at sb/sth** (*BrE*) to say or do sth that clearly shows you do not respect sb/sth: *to cock a snook at authority*

PHR V **ˌcock sth↔ˈup** (*BrE, slang*) to ruin sth by doing it badly, or by making a careless or stupid mistake SYN **bungle**: *I really cocked that exam up!* ◇ *She cocked up all the arrangements for the party.* ➲ related noun COCK-UP

cock·ade /kɒˈkeɪd; *NAmE* kɑː-/ *noun* a decorated BADGE or an arrangement of RIBBONS, feathers, etc. that is worn in a hat to show military rank, membership of a political party, etc.

cock-a-doodle-doo /ˌkɒk ə ˌduːdl ˈduː; *NAmE* ˌkɑːk/ *noun* the word for the sound that a COCK/ROOSTER makes

ˌcock-a-ˈhoop *adj.* [not usually before noun] **~ (about/at/over sth)** (*informal*) very pleased and excited, especially about achieving sth

cock-a-leekie /ˌkɒk ə ˈliːki; *NAmE* ˌkɑːk/ (also **ˌcock-a-leekie ˈsoup**) *noun* [U] a type of Scottish soup, made with chicken and LEEKS (= long vegetables that taste like onions)

cock·ama·mie (also **cock·ama·my**) /ˈkɒkəmeɪmi; *NAmE* ˈkɑːk-/ *adj.* (*NAmE, informal*) (of an idea, a story, etc.) silly; not to be believed

ˌcock and ˈbull story *noun* a story that is unlikely to be true but is used as an explanation or excuse

cocka·tiel /ˌkɒkəˈtiːl; *NAmE* ˌkɑːk-/ *noun* an Australian PARROT with a grey body and a yellow and orange face

cocka·too /ˌkɒkəˈtuː; *NAmE* ˈkɑːkətuː/ *noun* (*pl.* **-oos**) an Australian bird of the PARROT family, with a large row of feathers (called a CREST) standing up on its head

cock·cha·fer /ˈkɒktʃeɪfə(r); *NAmE* ˈkɑːk-/ (also **ˈMay bug**) *noun* a large brown insect that flies and makes a loud noise in early evening in summer

cock·crow /ˈkɒkkrəʊ; *NAmE* ˈkɑːkkroʊ/ *noun* [U] (*literary*) the time of the day when it is becoming light SYN **dawn**

ˌcocked ˈhat *noun* IDM see KNOCK *v.*

cock·er /'kɒkə(r); *NAmE* 'kɑːk-/ (also ˌ**cocker 'spaniel**) *noun* a small SPANIEL (= type of dog) with soft hair

cock·erel /'kɒkərəl; *NAmE* 'kɑːk-/ *noun* a young male chicken

cock·eyed /'kɒkaɪd; *NAmE* 'kɑːk-/ *adj.* (*informal*) **1** not level or straight SYN **crooked**: *Doesn't that picture look cockeyed to you?* **2** not practical; not likely to succeed: *a cockeyed scheme to make people use less water*

cock·fight /'kɒkfaɪt; *NAmE* 'kɑːk-/ *noun* a fight between two adult male chickens, watched as a sport and illegal in many countries ▶ **cock·fight·ing** *noun* [U]

cockle /'kɒkl; *NAmE* 'kɑːkl/ *noun* a small SHELLFISH that can be eaten IDM see WARM *v.*

cockle·shell /'kɒklʃel; *NAmE* 'kɑːkl-/ *noun* **1** the shell of a cockle **2** a small light boat

cock·ney /'kɒkni; *NAmE* 'kɑːkni/ *noun* **1** [C] a person from the East End of London **2** [U] the way of speaking that is typical of cockneys: *a cockney accent*

cock·pit /'kɒkpɪt; *NAmE* 'kɑːk-/ *noun* the area in a plane, boat or racing car where the pilot or driver sits ➲ VISUAL VOCAB page V45, page V43

cock·roach /'kɒkrəʊtʃ; *NAmE* 'kɑːkroʊtʃ/ (also *NAmE informal* **roach**) *noun* a large brown insect with wings, that lives in houses, especially where there is dirt

cock·sucker /'kɒksʌkə(r); *NAmE* 'kɑːk-/ *noun* (*taboo, slang*) an offensive word used to insult sb, usually a man

cock·sure /ˌkɒk'ʃʊə(r); -'ʃɔː(r); *NAmE* ˌkɑːk'ʃʊr/ *adj.* (*old-fashioned, informal*) confident in a way that is annoying to other people and that they might find offensive

cock·tail /'kɒkteɪl; *NAmE* 'kɑːk-/ *noun* **1** [C] a drink usually made from a mixture of one or more SPIRITS (= strong alcoholic drinks) and fruit juice. It can also be made without alcohol: *a* ***cocktail bar/cabinet/lounge*** **2** [C, U] a dish of small pieces of food, usually served cold: *a prawn/shrimp cocktail* ◇ *fruit cocktail* **3** [C] a mixture of different substances, usually ones that do not mix together well: *a lethal cocktail of drugs* ➲ see also MOLOTOV COCKTAIL

'cocktail dress *noun* a dress that is suitable for formal social occasions

'cocktail party *noun* a formal social occasion, usually in the early evening, when people drink COCKTAILS or other alcoholic drinks

'cocktail stick *noun* (*BrE*) a small, sharp piece of wood on which small pieces of food are placed, for guests to eat at parties

'cock-teaser (also **'cock-tease**, **'prick-teaser**, **'prick-tease**) *noun* (*taboo, slang*) an offensive word used to describe a woman who makes a man think she will have sex with him when she will not

'cock-up *noun* (*BrE, informal*) a mistake that spoils people's arrangements; sth that has been spoilt because it was badly organized: *There's been a bit of a cock-up over the travel arrangements.*

cocky /'kɒki; *NAmE* 'kɑːki/ *adj.* (**cock·ier**, **cocki·est**) (*informal*) too confident about yourself in a way that annoys other people ▶ **cocki·ness** *noun* [U]

cocoa /'kəʊkəʊ; *NAmE* 'koʊkoʊ/ *noun* **1** [U] dark brown powder made from the crushed seeds (called **cocoa beans**) of a tropical tree **2** [U] a hot drink made by mixing cocoa powder with milk and/or water and usually sugar: *a mug of cocoa* **3** [C] a cup of cocoa ➲ compare CHOCOLATE, DRINKING CHOCOLATE

'cocoa butter *noun* [U] fat that is obtained from cocoa BEANS and used in making chocolate and COSMETICS

co·co·nut /'kəʊkənʌt; *NAmE* 'koʊ-/ *noun* **1** [C] the large nut of a tropical tree called a **coconut palm**. It grows inside a hard shell and contains a soft white substance that can be eaten and juice that can be drunk. ➲ VISUAL VOCAB page V26 **2** [U] the soft white substance inside a coconut, used in cooking: *desiccated coconut* ◇ *coconut biscuits/cookies* ◇ *coconut oil*

'coconut butter *noun* [U] a solid substance inside COCONUTS that is used to make soap, CANDLES, etc.

ˌ**coconut 'matting** *noun* [U] (*BrE*) a material used to cover floors that is made from the hair inside the outer shell of coconuts

'coconut shy *noun* (*pl.* **coconut shies**) (*BrE*) an outdoor entertainment in which people try to knock coconuts off stands by throwing balls at them

co·coon /kə'kuːn/ *noun, verb*

■ ***noun*** **1** a covering of silk threads that some insects make to protect themselves before they become adults **2** a soft covering that wraps all around a person or thing and forms a protection: (*figurative*) *the cocoon of a caring family*

■ ***verb*** [usually passive] **~ sb/sth (in sth)** to protect sb/sth by surrounding them or it completely with sth: *We were warm and safe, cocooned in our sleeping bags.*

co·coon·ing /kə'kuːnɪŋ/ *noun* [U] the habit of spending more of your free time at home and less time going out and doing things with other people

coco·yam /'kəʊkəʊjæm; *NAmE* 'koʊkoʊ-/ *noun* [C, U] (*WAfrE*) a plant whose roots can be cooked and eaten or made into flour: *roasted cocoyam* ➲ see also FUFU

cod /kɒd; *NAmE* kɑːd/ *noun, adj.*

■ ***noun*** [C, U] (*pl.* **cod**) a large sea fish with white flesh that is used for food: *fishing for cod* ◇ *cod fillets*

■ ***adj.*** [only before noun] (*BrE, informal*) not genuine or real: *a cod American accent* ◇ *cod psychology*

COD /ˌsiː əʊ 'diː; *NAmE* oʊ/ *abbr.* cash on delivery or (in American English) collect on delivery (payment for goods will be made when the goods are delivered)

coda /'kəʊdə; *NAmE* 'koʊdə/ *noun* the final passage of a piece of music: (*figurative*) *The final two months were a miserable coda to the President's first period in office.*

cod·dle /'kɒdl; *NAmE* 'kɑːdl/ *verb* **1 ~ sb** (often *disapproving*) to treat sb with too much care and attention ➲ compare MOLLYCODDLE **2 ~ sth** to cook eggs in water slightly below boiling point

code 0-ᴡ AW /kəʊd; *NAmE* koʊd/ *noun, verb*

■ ***noun*** **1** 0-ᴡ [C, U] (often in compounds) a system of words, letters, numbers or symbols that represent a message or record information secretly or in a shorter form: *to* ***break/crack a code*** (= to understand and read the message) ◇ *It's written* ***in code.*** ◇ *Tap your* ***code number*** *into the machine.* ◇ *In the event of the machine not operating correctly, an* ***error code*** *will appear.* ➲ see also AREA CODE, BARCODE, MORSE CODE, POSTCODE, SORT CODE, ZIP CODE **2** 0-ᴡ [C] = DIALLING CODE: *There are three codes for London.* **3** [U] (*computing*) a system of computer programming instructions ➲ see also MACHINE CODE, SOURCE CODE **4** [C] a set of moral principles or rules of behaviour that are generally accepted by society or a social group: *a strict code of conduct* **5** [C] a system of laws or written rules that state how people in an institution or a country should behave: *the penal code* ➲ see also DRESS CODE, HIGHWAY CODE

■ ***verb*** **1 ~ sth** to write or print words, letters, numbers, etc. on sth so that you know what it is, what group it belongs to, etc: *Each order is coded separately.* **2 ~ sth** to put a message into code so that it can only be understood by a few people **3 ~ sth** (*computing*) to write a computer program by putting one system of numbers, words and symbols into another system SYN **encode**

coded /'kəʊdɪd; *NAmE* 'koʊ-/ *adj.* **1** [only before noun] a **coded** message or **coded** information is written or sent using a special system of words, letters, numbers, etc. that can only be understood by a few other people or by a computer: *a coded warning of a bomb at the airport* **2** expressed in an indirect way: *There was coded criticism of the government from some party members.*

co·deine /'kəʊdiːn; *NAmE* 'koʊ-/ *noun* [U] a drug used to reduce pain

C

ˈcode name *noun* a name used for a person or thing in order to keep the real name secret ▶ **ˈcode-named** *adj.* [not before noun]: *a drug investigation, code-named Snoopy*

ˌcode of ˈpractice *noun* (*pl.* **codes of practice**) a set of standards that members of a particular profession agree to follow in their work

co·depend·ency /ˌkəʊdɪˈpendənsi; *NAmE* koʊ-/ *noun* [U] (*psychology*) a situation in which two people have a close relationship in which they rely too much on each other emotionally, especially when one person is caring for the other one ▶ **co·depend·ent** *adj., noun*

CODESA /kəʊˈdesə; *NAmE* koʊ-/ *abbr.* Convention for a Democratic South Africa (in the past, the group of politicians who discussed how South Africa would become a DEMOCRACY)

ˈcode-sharing *noun* [U] (*technical*) an agreement between two or more AIRLINES to carry each other's passengers and use their own set of letters and numbers for flights provided by another airline

ˈcode switching *noun* [U] (*linguistics*) the practice of changing between languages when you are speaking

codex /ˈkəʊdeks; *NAmE* ˈkoʊ-/ *noun* (*pl.* **co·di·ces** /ˈkəʊdɪsiːz; ˈkɒd-; *NAmE* ˈkoʊ-; ˈkɑːd-/ or **codexes**) **1** an ancient text in the form of a book **2** an official list of medicines or chemicals

cod·ger /ˈkɒdʒə(r); *NAmE* ˈkɑːdʒ-/ *noun* (*informal*) **old ~** an informal way of referring to an old man that shows that you do not respect him

co·di·cil /ˈkəʊdɪsɪl; *NAmE* ˈkɑːdəsl/ *noun* (*law*) an instruction that is added later to a WILL, usually to change a part of it

co·dify /ˈkəʊdɪfaɪ; *NAmE* ˈkɑːd-/ *verb* (**co·di·fies, co·di·fy·ing, co·di·fied, co·di·fied**) **~ sth** (*technical*) to arrange laws, rules, etc. into a system ▶ **co·difi·ca·tion** /ˌkəʊdɪfɪˈkeɪʃn; *NAmE* ˌkɑːd-/ *noun* [U]

ˌcod liver ˈoil *noun* [U] a thick yellow oil from the LIVER of COD (= a type of fish), containing a lot of VITAMINS A and D and often given as a medicine

cod·piece /ˈkɒdpiːs; *NAmE* ˈkɑːd-/ *noun* a piece of cloth, especially a decorative one, attached to a man's lower clothing and covering his GENITALS, worn in Europe in the 15th and 16th centuries

cods·wal·lop /ˈkɒdzwɒləp; *NAmE* ˈkɑːdzwɑːləp/ *noun* [U] (*old-fashioned, BrE, informal*) nonsense: *I've never heard such a load of old codswallop in my life.*

coed /ˌkəʊˈed; *NAmE* ˌkoʊ-/ *noun* (*old-fashioned, NAmE*) a female student at a co-educational school or college

ˌco-eduˈcation·al (also *informal* **coed**) *adj.* (of a school or an EDUCATIONAL system) where girls and boys are taught together ▶ **ˌco-eduˈcation** *noun* [U]

co·ef·fi·cient /ˌkəʊɪˈfɪʃnt; *NAmE* ˌkoʊ-/ *noun* **1** (*mathematics*) a number which is placed before another quantity and which multiplies it, for example 3 in the quantity 3x **2** (*physics*) a number that measures a particular property (= characteristic) of a substance: *the coefficient of friction*

coela·canth /ˈsiːləkænθ/ *noun* a large fish found mainly in the seas near Madagascar. It was thought to be EXTINCT until one was discovered in 1938.

coel·iac disease (*BrE*) (*NAmE* **celiac disease**) /ˈsiːliæk dɪziːz/ *noun* [U] a disease in which sb cannot DIGEST food (= break it down in their body) because their body is very sensitive to GLUTEN (= a substance that is found in flour, especially WHEAT flour)

co·erce /kəʊˈɜːs; *NAmE* koʊˈɜːrs/ *verb* **~ sb** (**into sth/into doing sth**) | **~ sb** (**to do sth**) (*formal*) to force sb to do sth by using threats: *They were coerced into negotiating a settlement.*

co·er·cion /kəʊˈɜːʃn; *NAmE* koʊˈɜːrʒn/ *noun* [U] (*formal*) the action of making sb do sth that they do not want to do, using force or threatening to use force: *He claimed he had only acted under coercion.*

co·er·cive /kəʊˈɜːsɪv; *NAmE* koʊˈɜːrsɪv/ *adj.* (*formal*) using force or the threat of force: ***coercive measures/powers***

co·eval /kəʊˈiːvl; *NAmE* koʊ-/ *adj.* (*formal*) **~** (**with sth**) (of two or more things) having the same age or date of origin: *The industry is coeval with the construction of the first railways.*

co·ex·ist /ˌkəʊɪɡˈzɪst; *NAmE* ˌkoʊ-/ *verb* [I] **~** (**with sb/sth**) (*formal*) to exist together in the same place or at the same time, especially in a peaceful way: *The illness frequently coexists with other chronic diseases.* ◇ *English speakers now coexist peacefully with their Spanish-speaking neighbours.* ◇ *Different traditions coexist successfully side by side.*

co·ex·ist·ence /ˌkəʊɪɡˈzɪstəns; *NAmE* ˌkoʊ-/ *noun* [U] the state of being together in the same place at the same time: *to live in **uneasy/peaceful coexistence** within one nation*

C of E /ˌsiː əv ˈiː/ *abbr.* Church of England ➲ see also CE

cof·fee 0‑m /ˈkɒfi; *NAmE* ˈkɔːf-; ˈkɑːf-/ *noun*
1 0‑m [U, C] the ROASTED seeds (called **coffee beans**) of a tropical bush; a powder made from them: ***decaffeinated/instant coffee*** ◇ ***ground/real coffee*** ◇ *a jar of coffee* ◇ *a blend of Brazilian and Colombian coffees* ◇ *coffee ice cream*
2 0‑m [U] a hot drink made from coffee powder and boiling water. It may be drunk with milk and/or sugar added: ***black/white coffee*** (= without/with milk) ◇ *Tea or coffee?* ◇ *I'll just make the coffee.* ◇ *Let's talk over coffee* (= while drinking coffee). **3** 0‑m [C] a cup of coffee: *Two strong black coffees, please.* **4** [U] the colour of coffee mixed with milk; light brown **IDM** see WAKE *v.*

ˈcoffee bar *noun* **1** (*BrE*) (also **ˈcoffee shop** *NAmE, BrE*) a place, sometimes in a store, train station, etc, where you can buy coffee, tea, other drinks without alcohol and sometimes simple meals **2** (*NAmE*) a small restaurant that sells special sorts of coffee and cakes

ˈcoffee break *noun* a short period of rest when you stop working and drink coffee: *to have a coffee break*

ˈcoffee cake *noun* (*NAmE*) a small cake with melted sugar on top that people eat with coffee

ˈcoffee house *noun* **1** a restaurant serving coffee, etc, especially one of a type popular in Britain in the 18th century or one in a city in Central Europe: *the coffee houses of Vienna* **2** (*NAmE*) a restaurant serving coffee, etc. where people go to listen to music, poetry, etc.

ˈcoffee machine *noun* **1** = COFFEE MAKER **2** a machine that you put coins in to get a cup of coffee

ˈcoffee maker (also **ˈcoffee machine**) *noun* a small machine for making cups of coffee ➲ VISUAL VOCAB page V22

ˈcoffee morning *noun* (*BrE*) a social event held in the morning, often at a person's house, where money is usually given to help a charity

ˈcoffee shop *noun* a small restaurant, often in a store, hotel, etc, where coffee, tea, other drinks without alcohol and simple food are served

ˈcoffee table *noun* a small low table for putting magazines, cups, etc. on, usually in front of a SOFA ➲ VISUAL VOCAB page V18

ˈcoffee-table book *noun* a large expensive book containing many pictures or photographs, that is designed for people to look through rather than to read carefully

cof·fer /ˈkɒfə(r); *NAmE* ˈkɔːf-; ˈkɑːf-/ *noun* **1** [C] a large strong box, used in the past for storing money or valuable objects **2** (also **coffers** [pl.]) a way of referring to the money that a government, an organization, etc. has available to spend: *The nation's coffers are empty.*

cof·fin /ˈkɒfɪn; *NAmE* ˈkɔːfɪn; ˈkɑːfɪn/ (*especially BrE*) (*NAmE* usually **cas·ket**) *noun* a box in which a dead body is buried or CREMATED **IDM** see NAIL *n.*

cog /kɒɡ; *NAmE* kɑːɡ/ *noun* **1** one of a series of teeth on the edge of a wheel that fit between the teeth on the next wheel and cause it to move ➲ picture at COGWHEEL **2** = COGWHEEL
IDM **a cog in the maˈchine/ˈwheel** (*informal*) a person who is a small part of a large organization

co·gent /ˈkəʊdʒənt; *NAmE* ˈkoʊ-/ *adj.* (*formal*) strongly and clearly expressed in a way that influences what people believe SYN **convincing**: *She put forward some cogent reasons for abandoning the plan.* ▸ **co·gency** /ˈkəʊdʒənsi; *NAmE* ˈkoʊ-/ *noun* [U] **co·gent·ly** *adv.*

cogi·tate /ˈkɒdʒɪteɪt; *NAmE* ˈkɑːdʒ-/ *verb* [I] ~ (**about/on sth**) (*formal*) to think carefully about sth ▸ **cogi·ta·tion** /ˌkɒdʒɪˈteɪʃn; *NAmE* ˌkɑːdʒ-/ *noun* [U, C]

co·gnac /ˈkɒnjæk; *NAmE* ˈkoʊn-/ *noun* **1** [U, C] a type of fine BRANDY made in western France **2** [C] a glass of cognac

cog·nate /ˈkɒgneɪt; *NAmE* ˈkɑːg-/ *adj., noun*
■ ***adj.*** **1** (*linguistics*) having the same origin as another word or language: *'Haus' in German is cognate with 'house' in English.* ◇ *German and Dutch are cognate languages.* **2** (*formal*) related in some way and therefore similar: *a cognate development*
■ ***noun*** (*linguistics*) a word that has the same origin as another: *'Haus' and 'house' are cognates.*

cog·ni·tion /kɒgˈnɪʃn; *NAmE* kɑːg-/ *noun* [U] (*psychology*) the process by which knowledge and understanding is developed in the mind

cog·ni·tive /ˈkɒgnətɪv; *NAmE* ˈkɑːg-/ *adj.* [usually before noun] connected with mental processes of understanding: *a child's cognitive development* ◇ *cognitive psychology*

cog·ni·zance (*BrE* also **-i·sance**) /ˈkɒgnɪzəns; *NAmE* ˈkɑːg-/ *noun* [U] (*formal*) knowledge or understanding of sth ▸ **cog·ni·zant, -i·sant** *adj.* [not before noun]: *cognizant of the importance of the case*
IDM **take cognizance of sth** (*law*) to understand or consider sth; to take notice of sth

co·gnos·centi /ˌkɒnjəˈʃenti; *NAmE* ˌkɑːn-/ *noun* [pl.] **the cognoscenti** (from *Italian, formal*) people with a lot of knowledge about a particular subject

cogwheel

cog·wheel /ˈkɒgwiːl; *NAmE* ˈkɑːg-/ (also **cog**) *noun* a wheel with a series of teeth on the edge that fit between the teeth on the next wheel and cause it to move

co·habit /kəʊˈhæbɪt; *NAmE* koʊ-/ *verb* [I] ~ (**with sb**) (*formal*) (usually of a man and a woman) to live together and have a sexual relationship without being married ▸ **co·hab·it·ation** /ˌkəʊˌhæbɪˈteɪʃn; *NAmE* ˌkoʊ-/ *noun* [U]

co·here /kəʊˈhɪə(r); *NAmE* koʊˈhɪr/ *verb* (*formal*) **1** [I] ~ (**with sth**) (of different ideas, arguments, sentences, etc.) to have a clear logical connection so that together they make a whole: *This view does not cohere with their other beliefs.* **2** [I] (of people) to work closely together: *It can be difficult to get a group of people to cohere.*

co·her·ence AW /kəʊˈhɪərəns; *NAmE* koʊˈhɪr-/ *noun* [U] (*formal*) the situation in which all the parts of sth fit together well: *The points you make are fine, but the whole essay lacks coherence.* OPP **incoherence**

co·her·ent AW /kəʊˈhɪərənt; *NAmE* koʊˈhɪr-/ *adj.* **1** (of ideas, thoughts, arguments, etc.) logical and well organized; easy to understand and clear: ***a coherent narrative/account/explanation*** ◇ *a coherent policy for the transport system* **2** (of a person) able to talk and express yourself clearly: *She only became coherent again two hours after the attack.* OPP **incoherent** ▸ **co·her·ent·ly** AW *adv.*

co·he·sion /kəʊˈhiːʒn; *NAmE* koʊ-/ *noun* [U] **1** (*formal*) the act or state of keeping together SYN **unity**: *the cohesion of the nuclear family* ◇ ***social/political/economic cohesion*** **2** (*physics, chemistry*) the force causing MOLECULES of the same substance to stick together

co·he·sive /kəʊˈhiːsɪv; *NAmE* koʊ-/ *adj.* (*formal*) **1** forming a united whole: *a cohesive group* **2** causing people or things to become united: *the cohesive power of shared suffering* ◇ *well-structured sentences illustrating the use of cohesive markers such as 'nevertheless' and 'however'* ▸ **co·he·sive·ness** *noun* [U]

co·hort /ˈkəʊhɔːt; *NAmE* ˈkoʊhɔːrt/ *noun* [C+sing./pl. v.] **1** (*technical*) a group of people who share a common feature or aspect of behaviour: *the 1999 birth cohort* (= all those born in 1999) **2** (*disapproving*) a member of a group of people who support another person: *Robinson and his cohorts were soon ejected from the hall.*

C

coif·fure /kwɑːˈfjʊə(r); *NAmE* -ˈfjʊr/ *noun* (from *French, formal* or *humorous*) the way in which a person's hair is arranged SYN **hairstyle**

coil /kɔɪl/ *verb, noun*
■ ***verb*** [I, T] to wind into a series of circles; to make sth do this: ~ **up** *The snake coiled up, ready to strike.* ◇ ~ **round, around, etc. sth** *Mist coiled around the tops of the hills.* ◇ ~ **sth** (+ **adv./prep.**) *to coil a rope into a loop* ◇ *Her hair was coiled on top of her head.* ◇ *a coiled spring* ➲ picture at KNOT
■ ***noun*** **1** a series of circles formed by winding up a length of rope, wire, etc: *a coil of wire* **2** one circle of rope, wire, etc. in a series: *Shake the rope and let the coils unwind.* ◇ *a snake's coils* **3** a length of wire, wound into circles, that can carry electricity **4** = IUD

coin 0-w /kɔɪn/ *noun, verb*
■ ***noun*** **1** 0-w [C] a small flat piece of metal used as money: *a euro coin* ➲ picture at MONEY **2** [U] money made of metal: *notes and coin* IDM see SIDE *n.*, TWO
■ ***verb*** **1** ~ **sth** to invent a new word or phrase that other people then begin to use: *The term 'cardboard city' was coined to describe communities of homeless people living in cardboard boxes.* **2** ~ **sth** to make coins out of metal
IDM **be ˈcoining it (in)** | **be ˌcoining ˈmoney** (*BrE, informal*) to earn a lot of money quickly or easily SYN **rake in** **to coin a ˈphrase** **1** used to introduce a well-known expression that you have changed slightly in order to be funny **2** used to show that you are aware that you are using an expression that is not new: *Oh well, no news is good news, to coin a phrase.*

coin·age /ˈkɔɪnɪdʒ/ *noun* **1** [U] the coins used in a particular place or at a particular time; coins of a particular type: *Roman coinage* ◇ ***gold/silver/bronze coinage*** **2** [U] the system of money used in a particular country: *decimal coinage* **3** [C, U] a word or phrase that has been invented recently; the process of inventing a word or phrase: *new coinages*

ˈcoin box *noun* (*BrE, old-fashioned*) a public telephone that you put coins in to operate

co·in·cide AW /ˌkəʊɪnˈsaɪd; *NAmE* ˌkoʊ-/ *verb* **1** [I] (of two or more events) to take place at the same time: *It's a pity our trips to New York don't coincide.* ◇ ~ **with sth** *The strike was timed to coincide with the party conference.* **2** [I] (*formal*) (of ideas, opinions, etc.) to be the same or very similar: *The interests of employers and employees do not always coincide.* ◇ ~ **with sth** *Her story coincided exactly with her brother's.* **3** [I] (*formal*) (of objects or places) to meet; to share the same space: *At this point the two paths coincide briefly.* ◇ ~ **with sth** *The present position of the house coincides with that of an earlier dwelling.*

co·in·ci·dence AW /kəʊˈɪnsɪdəns; *NAmE* koʊ-/ *noun* **1** [C, U] the fact of two things happening at the same time by chance, in a surprising way: ***a strange/an extraordinary/a remarkable coincidence*** ◇ ***What a coincidence!*** *I wasn't expecting to see you here.* ◇ *It's* ***not a coincidence that*** *none of the directors are women* (= it did not happen by chance). ◇ ***By*** (***sheer***) ***coincidence****, I met the person we'd been discussing the next day.* ➲ SYNONYMS at LUCK **2** [sing.] (*formal*) the fact of things being present at the same time: *the coincidence of inflation and unemployment* **3** [sing.] (*formal*) the fact of two or more opinions, etc. being the same: *a coincidence of interests between the two partners*

co·in·ci·dent AW /kəʊˈɪnsɪdənt; *NAmE* koʊ-/ *adj.* ~ (**with sth**) (*formal*) happening in the same place or at the same time

co·in·ci·dent·al AW /kəʊˌɪnsɪˈdentl; *NAmE* koʊ-/ *adj.* [not usually before noun] happening by chance; not planned: *I suppose your presence here today is not* ***entirely***

coincidental. ◇ *It's **purely coincidental that** we both chose to call our daughters Emma.* ▸ **co·in·ci·den·tal·ly** /-təli/ *adv.*: *Coincidentally, they had both studied in Paris.*

coir /ˈkɔɪə(r)/ *noun* [U] rough material made from the shells of COCONUTS, used for making ropes, for covering floors, etc.

co·itus /ˈkɔɪtəs; ˈkəʊɪtəs; *NAmE* ˈkoʊ-/ *noun* [U] (*medical* or *formal*) = SEXUAL INTERCOURSE

coitus interruptus /ˌkɔɪtəs ɪntəˈrʌptəs; ˌkəʊɪtəs; *NAmE* ˌkoʊ-/ *noun* [U] an act of SEXUAL INTERCOURSE in which the man removes his PENIS from the woman's body before he EJACULATES, in order to prevent the woman from becoming pregnant

Coke™ /kəʊk; *NAmE* koʊk/ *noun* [C, U] (*informal*) = COCA-COLA: *Can I have a Diet Coke?*

coke /kəʊk; *NAmE* koʊk/ *noun* [U] **1** (*informal*) = COCAINE **2** a black substance that is produced from coal and burnt to provide heat

Col. *abbr.* (in writing) COLONEL: *Col. Stewart*

col /kɒl; *NAmE* kɑːl/ *noun* (*technical*) a low point between two higher points in a mountain range SYN **pass**

col. *abbr.* (in writing) COLUMN

cola /ˈkəʊlə; *NAmE* ˈkoʊlə/ *noun* **1** [U, C] a sweet brown, FIZZY drink (= with bubbles) that does not contain alcohol. Its flavour comes from the seeds of a W African tree and other substances. **2** [C] a glass, can or bottle of cola ➲ see also COCA-COLA, COKE

col·an·der /ˈkʌləndə(r); *NAmE* ˈkɑːl-/ *noun* a metal or plastic bowl with a lot of small holes in it, used for DRAINING water from vegetables, etc. after washing or cooking ➲ VISUAL VOCAB page V23

ˈcola nut (also **ˈkola nut**) *noun* the seed of the cola tree, that can be chewed or made into a drink

cold 0‑w /kəʊld; *NAmE* koʊld/ *adj., noun, adv.*

■ ***adj.*** (cold·er, cold·est)

▸ LOW TEMPERATURE **1** 0‑w having a lower than usual temperature; having a temperature lower than the human body: *I'm cold. Turn the heating up.* ◇ *to **feel/look cold*** ◇ *cold hands and feet* ◇ *a cold room/house* ◇ *hot and cold water in every room* ◇ *Isn't it cold today?* ◇ ***It's freezing cold.*** ◇ *to **get/turn colder*** ◇ ***bitterly cold** weather* ◇ *the coldest May on record* ◇ (*BrE*) *The water has gone cold.*

▸ FOOD/DRINK **2** 0‑w not heated; cooled after being cooked: *a cold drink* ◇ *Hot and cold food is available in the cafeteria.* ◇ *cold chicken for lunch*

▸ UNFRIENDLY **3** 0‑w (of a person) without emotion; unfriendly: *to give sb a **cold look/stare/welcome*** ◇ *Her manner was **cold and distant**.* ◇ *He was staring at her with **cold eyes**.*

▸ LIGHT/COLOURS **4** 0‑w seeming to lack warmth, in an unpleasant way: *clear cold light* ◇ *cold grey skies*

▸ ROUTE **5** not easy to find: *The police followed the robbers to the airport but then the **trail went cold**.*

▸ IN GAMES **6** used in children's games to say that the person playing is not close to finding a person or thing, or to guessing the correct answer

▸ UNCONSCIOUS **7 out ~** [not before noun] (*informal*) unconscious: *He was knocked out cold in the second round.*

▸ FACTS **8 the ~ facts/truth** facts with nothing added to make them more interesting or pleasant ➲ see also COLDLY, COLDNESS

IDM **a cold ˈfish** a person who seems unfriendly and without strong emotions **get/have cold ˈfeet** (*informal*) to suddenly become nervous about doing sth that you had planned to do: *He was going to ask her but he got cold feet and said nothing.* **give sb the cold ˈshoulder** (*informal*) to treat sb in an unfriendly way ➲ see also COLD-SHOULDER **in cold ˈblood** acting in a way that is deliberately cruel; with no pity: *to kill sb in cold blood* **in the cold light of day** when you have had time to think calmly about sth; in the morning when things are clearer: *These things always look different in the cold light of day.* **leave sb ˈcold** to fail to affect or interest sb: *Most modern art leaves me cold.* **pour/throw cold ˈwater on sth** to give reasons for not being in favour of sth; to criticize sth ➲ more at BLOOD, BLOW *v.*, HOT *adj.*

■ ***noun***

▸ LOW TEMPERATURE **1** 0‑w [U] a lack of heat or warmth; a low temperature, especially in the atmosphere: *He shivered with cold.* ◇ *Don't stand outside **in the cold**.* ◇ *She doesn't seem to **feel the cold**.* ◇ *You'll **catch your death of cold*** (= used to warn sb they could become ill if they do not keep warm in cold weather).

▸ ILLNESS **2** 0‑w [C] (also *less frequent* **the ˌcommon ˈcold**) a common illness that affects the nose and/or throat, making you cough, SNEEZE, etc: *I've got a cold.* ◇ *a **bad/heavy/slight cold*** ◇ *to **catch a cold*** ➲ COLLOCATIONS at ILL

IDM **come in from the ˈcold** to become accepted or included in a group, etc. after a period of being outside it **leave sb ˌout in the ˈcold** to not include sb in a group or an activity ➲ more at CATCH *v.*

■ ***adv.*** **1** (*NAmE*) suddenly and completely: *His final request stopped her cold.* **2** without preparing: *I can't just walk in there cold and give a speech.*

Synonyms

cold

cool • freezing • chilly • lukewarm • tepid

These words all describe sb/sth that has a low temperature.

cold having a temperature that is lower than usual or lower than the human body; (of food or drink) not heated; cooled after being cooked: *I'm cold. Turn the heating up.* ◇ *Outside it was bitterly cold.* ◇ *a cold wind* ◇ *hot and cold water* ◇ *It's cold chicken for lunch.*

cool (*often approving*) fairly cold, especially in a pleasant way: *a long cool drink* ◇ *We found a cool place to sit.*

freezing extremely cold; having a temperature below 0° Celsius: *It's absolutely freezing outside.* ◇ *I'm freezing!*

chilly (*rather informal*) too cold to be comfortable: *Bring a coat. It might turn chilly later.*

lukewarm (*often disapproving*) slightly warm, sometimes in an unpleasant way: *Her coffee was now lukewarm.*

tepid (*often disapproving*) slightly warm, sometimes in an unpleasant way: *a jug of tepid water*

LUKEWARM OR TEPID?

There is really no difference in meaning or use between these words.

PATTERNS

- to **feel/get** cold/cool/chilly
- cold/cool/freezing/chilly **air/weather**
- a cold/cool/freezing/chilly **wind**
- cold/cool/freezing/lukewarm/tepid **water**
- a cold/cool/lukewarm/tepid **shower/bath**
- cold/lukewarm/tepid **tea/coffee/food**
- a cold/cool **drink**
- **It's** cold/chilly/freezing **outside.**

ˌcold-ˈblooded *adj.* **1** (of people and their actions) showing no feelings or pity for other people: *a cold-blooded killer* **2** (*biology*) (of animals, for example fish or snakes) having a body temperature that depends on the temperature of the surrounding air or water ➲ compare WARM-BLOODED ▸ **ˌcold-ˈblooded·ly** *adv.*

ˌcold-ˈcalling *noun* [U] the practice of telephoning sb that you do not know, in order to sell them sth ▸ **ˌcold ˈcall** *noun*

ˌcold ˈcash (*NAmE*) (*BrE* **ˌhard ˈcash**) *noun* [U] money, especially in the form of coins and notes, that you can spend

ˌcold ˈcomfort *noun* [U] the fact that sth that would normally be good does not make you happy because the whole situation is bad: *A small drop in the inflation rate was cold comfort for the millions without a job.*

ˈcold cream *noun* [U] a thick white cream that people use for cleaning their face or making their skin soft

ˈcold cuts *noun* [pl.] (*especially NAmE*) slices of cooked meat that are served cold

ˈcold frame (also **frame**) *noun* a small wooden or metal frame covered with glass that you grow seeds or small plants in to protect them from cold weather ➲ picture at FRAME ➲ VISUAL VOCAB page V16

ˌcold ˈfusion *noun* [U] (*physics*) NUCLEAR FUSION that takes place at or near room temperature

ˌcold-ˈhearted *adj.* not showing any love or sympathy for other people; unkind ➲ compare WARM-HEARTED

coldie /ˈkəʊldi; *NAmE* ˈkoʊl-/ *noun* (*AustralE, informal*) a cold can or bottle of beer

cold·ly 🔑 /ˈkəʊldli; *NAmE* ˈkoʊld-/ *adv.* without any emotion or warm feelings; in an unfriendly way

cold·ness /ˈkəʊldnəs; *NAmE* ˈkoʊld-/ *noun* [U] **1** the lack of warm feelings; unfriendly behaviour: *She was hurt by the coldness in his voice.* **2** the state of being cold: *the icy coldness of the water* OPP **warmth**

ˌcold-ˈshoulder *verb* **~ sb** to treat sb in an unfriendly way ➲ see also GIVE SB THE COLD SHOULDER at COLD *adj.*

ˈcold snap *noun* (*informal*) a sudden short period of very cold weather

ˈcold sore (*NAmE* also **ˈfever blister**) *noun* a small painful spot on the lips or inside the mouth that is caused by a virus

ˈcold spell *noun* a period when the weather is colder than usual

ˌcold ˈstorage *noun* [U] a place where food, etc. can be kept fresh or frozen until it is needed; the storing of sth in such a place: (*figurative*) *I've had to* **put** *my plans* **into cold storage** (= I've decided not to carry them out immediately but to keep them for later).

ˈcold store *noun* a room where food, etc. can be kept at a low temperature in order to keep it in good condition

ˌcold ˈsweat *noun* [usually sing.] a state when you have sweat on your face or body but still feel cold, usually because you are very frightened or anxious: *to break out into a cold sweat* ◇ *I woke up in a cold sweat about the interview.*

ˌcold ˈturkey *noun* [U] the unpleasant state that drug ADDICTS experience when they suddenly stop taking a drug; a way of treating drug ADDICTS that makes them experience this state ▶ **ˌcold ˈturkey** *adv.*: *I quit smoking cold turkey.*

ˌcold ˈwar *noun* [sing., U] (often **Cold War**) a very unfriendly relationship between two countries who are not actually fighting each other, usually used about the situation between the US and the Soviet Union after the Second World War

cole·slaw /ˈkəʊlslɔː; *NAmE* ˈkoʊl-/ *noun* [U] pieces of raw CABBAGE, carrot, onion, etc, mixed with MAYONNAISE and eaten with meat or salads

coley /ˈkəʊli; *NAmE* ˈkoʊli/ *noun* [C, U] (*pl.* **coley** or **coleys**) a N Atlantic fish that is used for food

colic /ˈkɒlɪk; *NAmE* ˈkɑːlɪk/ *noun* [U] severe pain in the stomach and BOWELS, suffered especially by babies ▶ **col·icky** *adj.*

col·itis /kəˈlaɪtɪs/ *noun* [U] (*medical*) a disease that causes pain and swelling in the COLON (= part of the BOWELS)

col·lab·or·ate /kəˈlæbəreɪt/ *verb* **1** [I] to work together with sb in order to produce or achieve sth: *Researchers around the world are collaborating to develop a new vaccine.* ◇ **~ (with sb) (on sth)** *We have collaborated on many projects over the years.* ◇ **~ (with sb) (in sth/in doing sth)** *She agreed to collaborate with him in writing her biography.* **2** [I] **~ (with sb)** (*disapproving*) to help the enemy who has taken control of your country during a war

col·lab·or·ation /kəˌlæbəˈreɪʃn/ *noun* **1** [U, C] the act of working with another person or group of people to create or produce sth: *It was a collaboration that produced extremely useful results.* ◇ **~ (with sb) (on sth)** *She wrote the book* **in collaboration** *with one of her students.* ◇ *The government worked in close collaboration with teachers on the new curriculum.* ◇ **~ (between A and B)** *collaboration between the teachers and the government* **2** [C] a piece of work produced by two or more people or groups of people working together **3** [U] (*disapproving*) the act of helping the enemy during a war when they have taken control of your country

col·lab·ora·tive /kəˈlæbərətɪv; *NAmE* -reɪtɪv/ *adj.* [only before noun] (*formal*) involving, or done by, several people or groups of people working together: ***collaborative projects/studies/research*** ◇ *a* ***collaborative effort/venture*** ▶ **col·lab·ora·tive·ly** *adv.*

col·lab·or·ator /kəˈlæbəreɪtə(r)/ *noun* **1** a person who works with another person to create or produce sth such as a book **2** (*disapproving*) a person who helps the enemy in a war, when they have taken control of the person's country

col·lage /ˈkɒlɑːʒ; *NAmE* kəˈlɑːʒ/ *noun* **1** [U, C] the art of making a picture by sticking pieces of coloured paper, cloth, or photographs onto a surface; a picture that you make by doing this **2** [C] a collection of things, which may be similar or different: *an interesting collage of 1960s songs*

col·lagen /ˈkɒlədʒən; *NAmE* ˈkɑːl-/ *noun* [U] a PROTEIN found in skin and bone, sometimes INJECTED into the body, especially the face, to improve its appearance: *collagen injections*

col·lapse 🔑 AW /kəˈlæps/ *verb, noun*

■ ***verb***

▸ OF BUILDING **1** 🔑 [I] to fall down or fall in suddenly, often after breaking apart SYN **give way**: *The roof collapsed under the weight of snow.*

▸ OF SICK PERSON **2** 🔑 [I] to fall down (and usually become unconscious), especially because you are very ill/sick: *He collapsed in the street and died two hours later.*

▸ RELAX **3** [I] (*informal*) to sit or lie down and relax, especially after working hard: *When I get home I like to collapse on the sofa and listen to music.*

▸ FAIL **4** 🔑 [I] to fail suddenly or completely SYN **break down**: *Talks between management and unions have collapsed.* ◇ *All opposition to the plan has collapsed.*

▸ OF PRICES/CURRENCIES **5** 🔑 [I] to decrease suddenly in amount or value: *Share prices collapsed after news of poor trading figures.*

▸ FOLD **6** [I, T] **~ (sth)** to fold sth into a shape that uses less space; to be able to be folded in this way SYN **fold up**: *The table collapses for easy storage.*

▸ MEDICAL **7** [I, T] **~ (sth)** if a lung or BLOOD VESSEL **collapses** or **is collapsed**, it falls in and becomes flat and empty

▶ **col·lapsed** AW *adj.*: *collapsed buildings* ◇ *a collapsed investment bank* ◇ *a collapsed lung*

■ ***noun***

▸ FAILURE **1** 🔑 [C, usually sing., U] a sudden failure of sth, such as an institution, a business or a course of action: *the collapse of law and order in the area* ◇ *The peace talks were* ***on the verge of collapse.***

▸ OF BUILDING **2** 🔑 [U] the action of a building suddenly falling: *The walls were strengthened to protect them from collapse.*

▸ ILLNESS **3** 🔑 [U, C, usually sing.] a medical condition when a person suddenly becomes very ill/sick, or when sb falls because they are ill/sick or weak: *a state of* ***mental/nervous collapse*** ◇ *She was taken to hospital after her collapse at work.*

▸ OF PRICES/CURRENCIES **4** 🔑 [C, usually sing.] a sudden fall in value: *the collapse of share prices/the dollar/the market*

col·laps·ible AW /kəˈlæpsəbl/ *adj.* that can be folded flat or made into a smaller shape that uses less space: *a* ***collapsible chair/boat/bicycle***

col·lar /ˈkɒlə(r); *NAmE* ˈkɑːl-/ *noun, verb*

■ ***noun*** **1** the part around the neck of a shirt, jacket or coat that usually folds down: *a coat with a fur collar* ◇ *I turned up my collar against the wind* (= to keep warm). ◇ *He always wears* ***a collar and tie*** *for work.* ➲ VISUAL VOCAB page V51 ➲ see also BLUE-COLLAR, DOG COLLAR, WHITE-COLLAR, WING COLLAR **2** a band of leather or plastic put around the neck of an animal, especially a dog: *a* ***collar and lead/ leash*** **3** (*technical*) a band made of a strong material that is put round sth, such as a pipe or a piece of machinery, to make it stronger or to join two parts together IDM see HOT *adj.*

C

■ ***verb*** (*informal*) **1 ~ sb** to capture sb and hold them tightly so that they cannot escape from you: *Police collared the culprit as he was leaving the premises.* **2 ~ sb** to stop sb in order to talk to them: *I was collared in the street by a woman doing a survey.*

col·lar·bone /ˈkɒləbəʊn; *NAmE* ˈkɑːlərboʊn/ *noun* either of the two bones that go from the base of the neck to the shoulders SYN **clavicle** ⊃ VISUAL VOCAB page V48

col·lard greens /ˈkɒlɑːd griːnz; *NAmE* ˈkɑːlərd/ *noun* [pl.] (*NAmE*) = KALE

col·lar·less /ˈkɒləlәs; *NAmE* ˈkɑːlərləs/ *adj.* with no collar: *a collarless shirt*

col·late /kəˈleɪt/ *verb* **1 ~ sth** to collect information together from different sources in order to examine and compare it: *to* ***collate data/information/figures*** **2 ~ sth** to collect pieces of paper or the pages of a book, etc. and arrange them in the correct order ▸ **col·la·tion** /kəˈleɪʃn/ *noun* [U]: *the collation of information*

col·lat·eral /kəˈlætərəl/ *noun, adj.*

■ ***noun*** [U] (*finance*) property or sth valuable that you promise to give to sb if you cannot pay back money that you borrow

■ ***adj.*** (*formal*) connected with sth else, but in addition to it and less important: *collateral benefits* ◇ *The government denied that there had been any* ***collateral damage*** (= injury to ordinary people or buildings) *during the bombing raid.*

col·league 🔑 AW /ˈkɒliːg; *NAmE* ˈkɑː-/ *noun* a person that you work with, especially in a profession or a business: *a colleague of mine from the office* ◇ *We were friends and colleagues for more than 20 years.* ◇ *the Prime Minister and his Cabinet colleagues*

col·lect 🔑 /kəˈlekt/ *verb, adj., adv.*

■ ***verb***

▸ BRING TOGETHER **1** 🔑 [T] to bring things together from different people or places SYN **gather**: **~ sth** *to* ***collect data/evidence/information*** ◇ *We're collecting signatures for a petition.* ◇ **~ sth from sb/sth** *Samples were collected from over 200 patients.*

▸ AS HOBBY **2** 🔑 [T] **~ sth** to buy or find things of a particular type and keep them as a hobby: *to* ***collect stamps/postcards, etc.*** ⊃ see also STAMP COLLECTING ⊃ VISUAL VOCAB page V35

▸ OF PEOPLE **3** [I] to come together in one place to form a larger group SYN **gather**: *A crowd began to collect in front of the embassy.*

▸ INCREASE IN AMOUNT **4** 🔑 [I, T] to gradually increase in amount in a place; to gradually obtain more and more of sth in a place SYN **accumulate**: *Dirt had collected in the corners of the room.* ◇ **~ sth** *We seem to have collected an enormous number of boxes* (= without intending to). ◇ *That guitar's been sitting* ***collecting dust*** (= not being used) *for years now.*

▸ TAKE AWAY **5** 🔑 [T] to go somewhere in order to take sb/sth away: **~ sth** (**from...**) *What day do they collect the rubbish/garbage?* ◇ *The package is waiting to be collected.* ◇ (*BrE*) **~ sb** (**from...**) *She's gone to collect her son from school.*

▸ MONEY **6** 🔑 [I, T] to ask people to give you money for a particular purpose: **~** (**for sth**) *We're collecting for local charities.* ◇ **~ sth** (**for sth**) *We collected over £300 for the appeal.* **7** [T] **~ sth** to obtain the money, etc. that sb owes, for example by going to their house to get it: *to* ***collect rent/debts/tax***

▸ RECEIVE/WIN **8** [T, I] **~** (**sth**) to receive sth; to win sth: *She collected £25 000 in compensation.* ◇ *to collect a prize/a medal*

IDM **collect yourself/your thoughts 1** to try to control your emotions and become calm: *I'm fine—I just need a minute to collect myself.* **2** to prepare yourself mentally for sth: *She paused to collect her thoughts before entering the interview room.*

PHR V **col,lect sth↔'up** to bring together things that are no longer being used: *Would somebody collect up all the dirty glasses?*

■ ***adj.*** (*NAmE*) (of a telephone call) paid for by the person who receives the call: *to make a collect call* ⊃ see also REVERSE *v.* (7) ▸ **col·lect** *adv.*: *to call sb collect*

Synonyms

collect

gather • accumulate • amass

These words all mean to get more of sth over a period of time, or to increase in quantity over a period of time.

collect to bring things or information together from different people or places; to gradually increase in amount in a place: *We've been collecting data from various sources.* ◇ *Dirt had collected in the corners of the room.* NOTE People sometimes **collect** things of a particular type as a hobby: *to collect stamps.*

gather to bring things together that have been spread around; to collect information from different sources: *I waited while he* ***gathered up*** *his papers.* ◇ *Detectives have spent months gathering evidence.*

COLLECT OR GATHER?

Both **collect** and **gather** can be used in the same way to talk about bringing together data, information or evidence. When talking about things, **gather** is used with words like *things, belongings* or *papers* when the things are spread around within a short distance. **Collect** is used for getting examples of sth from different people or places that are physically separated.

accumulate (*rather formal*) to gradually get more and more of sth over a period of time; to gradually increase in number or quantity over a period of time : *I seem to have accumulated a lot of books.* ◇ *Debts began to accumulate.*

amass (*rather formal*) to collect sth in large quantities, especially money, debts or information: *He amassed a fortune from silver mining.*

PATTERNS

- to collect/gather/accumulate/amass **data/evidence/information**
- to accumulate/amass **a fortune/debts**
- **dirt/dust/debris** collects/accumulates
- to **gradually/slowly** collect/gather/accumulate (sth)

col·lect·able (also **col·lect·ible**) /kəˈlektəbl/ *adj.* worth collecting because it is beautiful or may become valuable ▸ **col·lect·able** (also **col·lect·ible**) *noun* [usually pl.]

col·lect·ed /kəˈlektɪd/ *adj.* **1** [not before noun] very calm and in control of yourself: *She always stays* ***cool, calm and collected*** *in a crisis.* **2 ~ works, papers, poems, etc.** all the books, etc. written by one author, published in one book or in a set

col·lec·tion 🔑 /kəˈlekʃn/ *noun*

▸ GROUP OF OBJECTS/PEOPLE **1** 🔑 [C] a group of objects, often of the same sort, that have been collected: *a* ***stamp/coin, etc. collection*** ◇ *The painting comes from his private collection.* **2** [C] a group of objects or people: *There was a collection of books and shoes on the floor.* ◇ *There is always a strange collection of runners in the London Marathon.*

▸ TAKING AWAY/BRINGING TOGETHER **3** 🔑 [C, U] an act of taking sth away from a place; an act of bringing things together into one place: ***refuse/garbage collection*** ◇ *The last collection from this postbox is at 5.15.* ◇ *Your suit will be ready for collection on Tuesday.* ◇ *The first stage in research is data collection.* ⊃ compare PICKUP

▸ POEMS/STORIES/MUSIC **4** [C] a group of poems, stories or pieces of music published together as one book or disc: *a collection of stories by women writers*

▸ MONEY **5** [C] an act of collecting money to help a charity or during a church service; the money collected: *a house-to-*

house collection for Cancer Research ◇ *The total collection last week amounted to £250.*

▸ NEW CLOTHES **6** [C] a range of new clothes or items for the home that are designed, made and offered for sale, often for a particular season: *Armani's stunning new autumn collection* ➲ COLLOCATIONS at FASHION

col·lect·ive /kəˈlektɪv/ *adj., noun*

■ ***adj.*** [usually before noun] **1** done or shared by all members of a group of people; involving a whole group or society: ***collective leadership/decision-making/responsibility*** ◇ *collective memory* (= things that a group of people or a community know or remember, that are often passed from parents to children) **2** used to refer to all members of a group: *The collective name for mast, boom and sails on a boat is the 'rig'.* ▸ **col·lect·ive·ly** *adv.*: *the collectively agreed rate* ◇ *We have had a successful year, both collectively and individually.* ◇ *rain, snow and hail, collectively known as 'precipitation'* (= as a group)

■ ***noun*** a group of people who own a business or a farm and run it together; the business that they run: *an independent collective making films for television*

colˌlective ˈbargaining *noun* [U] discussions between a TRADE/LABOR UNION and an employer about the pay and working conditions of the union members

colˌlective ˈfarm *noun* a large farm, or a group of farms, owned by the government and run by a group of people

colˌlective ˈnoun *noun* (*grammar*) a singular noun, such as *committee* or *team*, that refers to a group of people, animals or things and, in British English, can be used with either a singular or a plural verb. In American English it must be used with a singular verb.

colˌlective unˈconscious *noun* [sing.] (*psychology*) the part of the unconscious mind that is thought to be shared with other humans because it is passed from generation to generation

col·lect·iv·ism /kəˈlektɪvɪzəm/ *noun* [U] the political system in which all farms, businesses and industries are owned by the government or by all the people ▸ **col·lect·iv·ist** *adj.*

col·lect·iv·ize (*BrE* also **-ise**) /kəˈlektɪvaɪz/ *verb* [often passive] **~ sth** to join several private farms, industries, etc. together so that they are controlled by the community or by the government ▸ **col·lect·iv·iza·tion, -isa·tion** /kəˌlektɪvaɪˈzeɪʃn; *NAmE* -vəˈz-/ *noun* [U]

col·lect·or /kəˈlektə(r)/ *noun* **1** (especially in compounds) a person who collects things, either as a hobby or as a job: *a stamp collector* ◇ ***ticket/tax/debt collectors*** **2** the chief officer of a district in some S Asian countries

col·lect·or·ate /kəˈlektərət/ *noun* **1** (in some S Asian countries) the area under the authority of a COLLECTOR **2** the office in which a COLLECTOR is based

colˈlector's item *noun* a thing that is valued because it is very old or rare, or because it has some special interest

col·leen /kɒˈliːn; *NAmE* kɑːˈl-/ *noun* **1** (*IrishE*) a girl or young woman **2** (*old-fashioned* or *humorous*) a girl or young woman from Ireland

col·lege 🔑 /ˈkɒlɪdʒ; *NAmE* ˈkɑːl-/ *noun* **1** 🔑 [C, U] (often in names) (in Britain) a place where students go to study or to receive training after they have left school: *a college of further education* (= providing education and training for people over 16) ◇ *a secretarial college* ◇ *the Royal College of Art* ◇ *a* ***college course/library/student*** ◇ *She's* ***at college.*** ➲ see also COMMUNITY COLLEGE (1), SIXTH-FORM COLLEGE **2** 🔑 [C, U] (often in names) (in the US) a university where students can study for a degree after they have left school: *Carleton College* ◇ *a* ***college campus/student*** ◇ *a private college* ◇ *He got interested in politics when he was* ***in college.*** ◇ *She's away* ***at college*** *in California.* ◇ *He's hoping to* ***go to college*** *next year.* ➲ COLLOCATIONS at EDUCATION ➲ see also COMMUNITY COLLEGE (2) **3** [C, U] (*CanE*) a place where you can study for higher or more specialist qualifications after you finish high school **4** [C, U] one of the separate institutions that some British universities, such as Oxford and Cambridge, are divided into: *King's College, Cambridge* ◇ *a tour of Oxford colleges* ◇ *Most students live in college.* **5** (in the US) one of the main divisions of some large universities: *The history department is part of the College of Arts and Sciences.* **6** [C+sing./pl. v.] the teachers and/or students of a college **7** [C] (especially in names, in Britain and some other countries) a SECONDARY SCHOOL, especially one where you must pay: *Eton College* **8** [C] (usually in names) an organized group of professional people with special interests, duties or powers: *the Royal College of Physicians* ◇ *the American College of Cardiology* ➲ see also ELECTORAL COLLEGE

British / American

college / university

- In both *BrE* and *NAmE* a **college** is a place where you can go to study after you leave secondary school. In Britain you can go to a **college** to study or to receive training in a particular skill. In the US you can study for your first degree at a **college**. A **university** offers more advanced degrees in addition to first degrees.
- In *NAmE* **college** is often used to mean a **university**, especially when talking about people who are studying for their first degree. **The** is not used when you are talking about someone studying there: *My son has gone away to college.* ◇ *'Where did you go to college?' 'Ohio State University.'*
- In *BrE* you can say: *My daughter is at university.* In *NAmE* you cannot use **university** or **college** in this way. You use it with **a** or **the** to mean a particular university or college: *I didn't want to go to a large university.*

col·le·gi·ate /kəˈliːdʒiət/ *adj.* **1** relating to a college or its students: *collegiate life* **2** (*BrE*) divided into a number of colleges: *a collegiate university*

colˌlegiate ˈinstitute *noun* (in some parts of Canada) a public high school

col·lide /kəˈlaɪd/ *verb* **1** [I] if two people, vehicles, etc. **collide**, they crash into each other; if a person, vehicle, etc. **collides** with another, or with sth that is not moving, they crash into it: *The car and the van collided head-on in thick fog.* ◇ **~ with sth/sb** *The car collided head-on with the van.* ◇ *As he fell, his head collided with the table.* ➲ SYNONYMS at CRASH **2** [I] **~ (with sb) (over sth)** (*formal*) (of people, their opinions, etc.) to disagree strongly: *They regularly collide over policy decisions.* ➲ see also COLLISION

col·lider /kəˈlaɪdə(r)/ *noun* (*physics*) a machine for making two streams of PARTICLES move at high speed and crash into each other

col·lie /ˈkɒli; *NAmE* ˈkɑːli/ *noun* a dog of which there are several types. Those with long pointed noses and long thick hair are popular as pets. Smaller collies with shorter hair are often trained to help control sheep on a farm.

col·lier /ˈkɒliə(r); *NAmE* ˈkɑːl-/ *noun* **1** (*old-fashioned, especially BrE*) = COAL MINER **2** a ship that carries coal

col·liery /ˈkɒliəri; *NAmE* ˈkɑːl-/ *noun* (*pl.* **-ies**) (*BrE*) a coal mine with its buildings and equipment

col·li·gate /ˈkɒlɪgeɪt; *NAmE* ˈkɑːl-/ *verb* [I, T] **~ (with sth)** | **~ sth (with sth)** **1** (*formal*) if two ideas, facts, etc. **colligate**, or **are colligated**, they are linked together by a single explanation or theory **2** (*linguistics*) if two words **colligate**, or **are colligated**, they occur together and are linked by grammar

col·li·sion /kəˈlɪʒn/ *noun* [C, U] **~ (with sb/sth)** | **~ (between/of A and B)** **1** an accident in which two vehicles or people crash into each other: *a collision between two trains* ◇ *Stewart was injured in a collision with another player.* ◇ *a* ***head-on collision*** (= between two vehicles that are moving towards each other) ◇ *a mid-air collision* (= between two aircraft while they are flying) ◇ *His car was* ***in collision with*** *a motorbike.* **2** (*formal*) a strong disagreement between two people or between opposing ideas, opinions, etc; the meeting of two things that are very different: *a collision between two opposing points of view* ◇ *In his work we see the collision of two different traditions.*

C

IDM **be on a col'lision course (with sb/sth) 1** to be in a situation which is almost certain to cause a disagreement or argument: *I was on a collision course with my boss over the sales figures.* **2** to be moving in a direction in which it is likely that you will crash into sb/sth: *A giant iceberg was on a collision course with the ship.*

col·lo·cate /ˈkɒləkeɪt; *NAmE* ˈkɑːl-/ *verb* [I] (*linguistics*) **~ (with sth)** (of words) to be often used together in a language: *'Bitter' collocates with 'tears' but 'sour' does not.* ◇ *'Bitter' and 'tears' collocate.* ▶ **col·lo·cate** /ˈkɒləkət; *NAmE* ˈkɑːl-/ *noun*: *'Bitter' and 'tears' are collocates.*

col·lo·ca·tion /ˌkɒləˈkeɪʃn; *NAmE* ˌkɑːl-/ *noun* (*linguistics*) **1** [C] a combination of words in a language, that happens very often and more frequently than would happen by chance: *'Resounding success' and 'crying shame' are English collocations.* **2** [U] the fact of two or more words often being used together, in a way that happens more frequently than would happen by chance: *Advanced students need to be aware of the importance of collocation.*

col·lo·quial /kəˈləʊkwiəl; *NAmE* -ˈloʊ-/ *adj.* (of words and language) used in conversation but not in formal speechorwriting SYN **informal** ▶ **col·lo·qui·al·ly** /-kwiəli/ *adv.*

col·lo·qui·al·ism /kəˈləʊkwiəlɪzəm; *NAmE* -ˈloʊ-/ *noun* a word or phrase that is used in conversation but not in formal speech or writing

col·lo·quium /kəˈləʊkwiəm; *NAmE* -ˈloʊ-/ *noun* (*pl.* **col·lo·quia** /kəˈləʊkwiə; *NAmE* -ˈloʊ-/) a formal academic SEMINAR or conference

col·lo·quy /ˈkɒləkwi; *NAmE* ˈkɑːl-/ *noun* (*pl.* **-ies**) (*formal*) a conversation

col·lude /kəˈluːd/ *verb* [I] (*formal, disapproving*) to work together secretly or illegally in order to trick other people: **~ (with sb) (in sth/in doing sth)** *Several people had colluded in the murder.* ◇ **~ (with sb) (to do sth)** *They colluded with terrorists to overthrow the government.*

col·lu·sion /kəˈluːʒn/ *noun* [U] (*formal, disapproving*) secret agreement especially in order to do sth dishonest or to trick people: *The police were corrupt and were operating* ***in collusion with*** *the drug dealers.* ◇ *There was collusion between the two witnesses* (= they gave the same false evidence). ▶ **col·lu·sive** /kəˈluːsɪv/ *adj.*

colly·wob·bles /ˈkɒliwɒblz; *NAmE* ˈkɑːliwɑː-/ *noun* [pl.] (*old-fashioned, BrE, informal*) **1** a nervous feeling of fear and worry **2** a pain in the stomach

colo·bus /ˈkɒləbəs; *NAmE* ˈkɑːl-/ (also **ˈcolobus monkey**) *noun* a small African MONKEY with a long tail, that eats leaves

co·logne /kəˈləʊn; *NAmE* kəˈloʊn/ (also **eau de cologne**) *noun* [U] a type of light PERFUME

colon /ˈkəʊlən; *NAmE* ˈkoʊ-/ *noun* **1** the mark (:) used to introduce a list, a summary, an explanation, etc. or before reporting what sb has said ➲ compare SEMICOLON **2** (*anatomy*) the main part of the large INTESTINE (= part of the BOWELS) ➲ VISUAL VOCAB page V48

col·onel /ˈkɜːnl; *NAmE* ˈkɜːrnl/ *noun* (*abbr.* **Col.**) an officer of high rank in the army, the MARINES, or the US AIR FORCE: *Colonel Jim Edge*

ˌColonel ˈBlimp *noun* = BLIMP

co·lo·nial /kəˈləʊniəl; *NAmE* -ˈloʊ-/ *adj., noun*

■ ***adj.*** **1** connected with or belonging to a country that controls another country: *a colonial power* ◇ *Tunisia achieved independence from French colonial rule in 1956.* ◇ *Western colonial attitudes* ➲ see also COLONY **2** (often **Colonial**) typical of or connected with the US at the time when it was still a British COLONY: *life in colonial times*

■ ***noun*** a person who lives in a COLONY and who comes from the country that controls it: *British colonials in India*

co·lo·ni·al·ism /kəˈləʊniəlɪzəm; *NAmE* -ˈloʊ-/ *noun* [U] the practice by which a powerful country controls another country or other countries: *European colonialism* ▶ **co·lo·ni·al·ist** *adj., noun*: *colonialist laws*

co·lo·nic /kəˈlɒnɪk; *NAmE* -ˈlɑːn-/ *adj.* (*anatomy*) connected with the COLON (= part of the BOWELS): ***colonic irrigation*** (= the process of washing out the COLON with water)

col·on·ist /ˈkɒlənɪst; *NAmE* ˈkɑːl-/ *noun* a person who settles in an area that has become a COLONY

col·on·ize (*BrE* also **-ise**) /ˈkɒlənaɪz; *NAmE* ˈkɑː-/ *verb* **1 ~ sth** to take control of an area or a country that is not your own, especially using force, and send people from your own country to live there: *The area was colonized by the Vikings.* **2 ~ sth** (*biology*) (of animals or plants) to live or grow in large numbers in a particular area: *The slopes are colonized by flowering plants.* ◇ *Bats had colonized the ruins.* ▶ **col·on·iza·tion, -isa·tion** /ˌkɒlənaɪˈzeɪʃn; *NAmE* ˌkɑːlənəˈz-/ *noun* [U]: *the colonization of the 'New World'* ◇ *plant colonization* **col·on·izer, -iser** *noun*

col·on·nade /ˌkɒləˈneɪd; *NAmE* ˌkɑːl-/ *noun* a row of stone columns with equal spaces between them, usually supporting a roof ➲ VISUAL VOCAB page V12 ▶ **col·on·naded** /ˌkɒləˈneɪdɪd; *NAmE* ˌkɑːl-/ *adj.*

col·ony /ˈkɒləni; *NAmE* ˈkɑːl-/ *noun* (*pl.* **-ies**) **1** [C] a country or an area that is governed by people from another, more powerful, country: *former British colonies* **2** [sing.+ sing./pl. v.] a group of people who go to live permanently in a colony **3** [C+sing./pl. v.] a group of people from the same place or with the same work or interests who live in a particular city or country or who live together: *the American colony in Paris* ◇ *an artists' colony* **4** [C] (*IndE*) a small town set up by an employer or an organization for its workers **5** [C+sing./pl. v.] (*biology*) a group of plants or animals that live together or grow in the same place: *a colony of ants* ◇ *a bird colony*

color (*especially US*) = COLOUR HELP You will find most words formed with **color** at the spelling **colour**.

col·or·ant (*especially US*) = COLOURANT

col·or·ation (*BrE* also **col·our·ation**) /ˌkʌləˈreɪʃn/ *noun* [U] (*technical*) the natural colours and patterns on a plant or an animal

col·ora·tura /ˌkɒlərəˈtʊərə; *NAmE* ˌkʌlərəˈtʊrə/ *noun* [U] (*music*) complicated passages for a singer, for example in OPERA: *a coloratura soprano* (= one who often sings coloratura passages)

ˈcolor bar (*especially US*) = COLOUR BAR

ˈcolor-blind (*especially US*) = COLOUR-BLIND

ˈcolor code (*especially US*) = COLOUR CODE

col·ored (*especially US*) = COLOURED

color·fast (*especially US*) = COLOUR FAST

col·or·ful (*especially US*) = COLOURFUL

ˈcolor guard *noun* (*US*) a small group of people who carry official flags in a ceremony

col·or·ing (*especially US*) = COLOURING

col·or·ist, col·or·istic (*especially US*) = COLOURIST, COLOURISTIC

col·or·ize (*BrE* also **col·our·ize**) /ˈkʌləraɪz/ *verb* **~ sth** (*technical*) to add colour to a black and white film/movie, using a computer process

col·or·less (*especially US*) = COLOURLESS

ˈcolor line (also **ˈcolor bar**) (both *US*) (*BrE* **ˈcolour bar**) *noun* [usually sing.] a social system which does not allow black people the same rights as white people

ˈcolor scheme (*especially US*) = COLOUR SCHEME

ˈcolor separation (*especially US*) = COLOUR SEPARATION

col·os·sal /kəˈlɒsl; *NAmE* kəˈlɑːsl/ *adj.* extremely large: *a colossal statue* ◇ *The singer earns a colossal amount of money.*

col·os·sus /kəˈlɒsəs; *NAmE* -ˈlɑːs-/ *noun* **1** [sing.] (*formal*) a person or thing that is extremely important or large in size **2** [C] (*pl.* **co·lossi** /kəˈlɒsaɪ; *NAmE* -ˈlɑːs-/) an extremely large statue

col·os·tomy /kəˈlɒstəmi; *NAmE* kəˈlɑːs-/ *noun* (*pl.* **-ies**) (*medical*) an operation in which part of a person's COLON (= the lower part of the BOWELS) is removed and an opening is made in the ABDOMEN through which the person can get rid of waste matter from the body

col·os·trum /kəˈlɒstrəm; *NAmE* -ˈlɑːs-/ *noun* [U] the substance produced in the breasts of a new mother, which has a lot of ANTIBODIES which help her baby to resist disease

Synonyms

colour

shade • hue • tint • tinge

These words all describe the appearance of things, resulting from the way in which they reflect light.

colour/color the appearance that things have, resulting from the way in which they reflect light. Red, green and blue are colours: *What's your favourite colour?* ◇ *bright/dark/light colours*

shade a particular form of a colour, especially when describing how light or dark it is. Sky blue is a shade of blue.

hue (*literary* or *technical*) a colour or a particular shade of a colour: *His face took on an unhealthy, whitish hue.*

tint a shade or small amount of a particular colour; a faint colour covering a surface: *leaves with red and gold autumn tints*

tinge a small amount of a colour: *There was a pink tinge to the sky.*

TINT OR TINGE?

You can say: *a reddish tint/tinge* or: *a tinge of red* but not: ~~*a tint of red*~~. **Tint** is often used in the plural, but **tinge** is almost always singular.

PATTERNS

- a **warm/rich** colour/shade/hue/tint
- a **bright/vivid/vibrant/dark/deep** colour/shade/hue
- a **pale/pastel/soft/subtle/delicate** colour/shade/hue
- a **light/strong/neutral/natural** colour/shade

col·our 🔑 (*especially US* **color**) /ˈkʌlə(r)/ *noun, verb*

■ *noun*

▸ RED, GREEN, ETC. **1** 🔑 [C, U] the appearance that things have that results from the way in which they reflect light. Red, orange and green are colours: *What's your favourite colour?* ◇ ***bright/dark/light colours*** ◇ *available in 12 different colours* ◇ *the colour of the sky* ◇ *Her hair is a reddish-brown colour.* ◇ *Foods which go through a factory process lose much of their colour, flavour and texture.* ◇ *The garden was a mass of colour.* **2** 🔑 [U] (usually before another noun) the use of all the colours, not only black and white: *a colour TV* ◇ ***colour photography/printing*** ◇ *a full-colour brochure* ◇ *Do you dream **in colour**?*

▸ OF SKIN **3** 🔑 [U, C] the colour of a person's skin, when it shows the race they belong to: *discrimination on the grounds of race, colour or religion* ◇ (*especially NAmE*) ***a person/man/woman of colour*** (= who is not white)

▸ OF FACE **4** [U] a red or pink colour in sb's face, especially when it shows that they look healthy or that they are embarrassed: *The fresh air brought colour to their cheeks.* ◇ *Colour flooded her face when she thought of what had happened.* ◇ *His face was drained of colour* (= he looked pale and ill).

▸ SUBSTANCE **5** [C, U] a substance that is used to give colour to sth: *a semi-permanent hair colour that lasts six to eight washes* ➲ see also WATERCOLOUR

▸ INTERESTING DETAILS **6** [U] interesting and exciting details or qualities: *The old town is full of colour and attractions.* ◇ *Her acting added warmth and colour to the production.* ◇ *to **add/give/lend colour** to sth* (= make it brighter, more interesting, etc.) ➲ see also LOCAL COLOUR

▸ OF TEAM/COUNTRY, ETC. **7 colours** [pl.] the particular colours that are used on clothes, flags, etc. to represent a team, school, political party or country: *Red and white are the team colours.* ◇ *Spain's national colours* ◇ (*figurative*) *There are people of different political colours on the committee.* **8 colours** [pl.] (*especially BrE*) a flag, BADGE, etc. that represents a team, country, ship, etc: *Most buildings had a flagpole with the national colours flying.* ◇ *sailing under the French colours*

IDM **see the colour of sb's ˈmoney** (*informal*) to make sure that sb has enough money to pay for sth ➲ more at FLYING *adj.*, LEND *n.*, NAIL *v.*, TRUE *adj.* ➲ see also OFF COLOUR

■ *verb*

▸ PUT COLOUR ON STH **1** 🔑 [I, T] to put colour on sth using paint, coloured pencils, etc: *The children love to draw and colour.* ◇ *a colouring book* (= with pictures that you can add colour to) ◇ **~ sth** *How long have you been colouring* (=DYEING) *your hair?* ◇ **~ sth + adj.** *He drew a monster and coloured it green.*

▸ OF FACE **2** [I] **~ (at sth)** (of a person or their face) to become red with embarrassment SYN **blush**: *She coloured at his remarks.*

▸ AFFECT **3** [T] **~ sth** to affect sth, especially in a negative way: *This incident coloured her whole life.* ◇ *Don't let your judgement be coloured by personal feelings.*

PHR V **ˌcolour sth↔ˈin** to put colour inside a particular area, shape, etc. using coloured pencils, CRAYONS, etc: *I'll draw a tree and you can colour it in.*

col·our·ant /ˈkʌlərənt/ (*especially US* **col·or·ant**) *noun* a substance that is used to put colour in sth, especially a person's hair

col·our·ation (*BrE*) = COLORATION

ˈcolour bar (*especially US* **ˈcolor bar, color line**) *noun* [usually sing.] a social system which does not allow black people the same rights as white people

ˈcolour-blind (*especially US* **ˈcolor-blind**) *adj.* **1** unable to see the difference between some colours, especially red and green **2** treating people with different coloured skin in exactly the same way ▸ **ˈcolour-blindness** (*especially US* **ˈcolor-blindness**) *noun* [U]

ˈcolour code (*especially US* **ˈcolor code**) *noun* a system of marking things with different colours so that you can easily identify them ▸ **ˈcolour-coded** (*especially US* **ˈcolor-coded**) *adj.*: *The files have labels that are colour-coded according to subject.*

col·oured 🔑 (*especially US* **col·ored**) /ˈkʌləd; *NAmE* -ərd/ *adj., noun*

■ *adj.* **1** 🔑 (often in compounds) having a particular colour or different colours: *brightly coloured balloons* ◇ *coloured lights* ◇ *She was wearing a cream-coloured suit.* **2** (*old-fashioned* or *offensive*) (of a person) from a race that does not have white skin **3 Coloured** (in South Africa) having parents who are of different races

■ *noun* **1** (*old-fashioned* or *offensive*) a person who does not have white skin **2 Coloured** (in South Africa) a person whose parents are of different races

ˈcolour fast (*especially US* **ˈcolor-fast**) *adj.* cloth that is **colour fast** will not lose colour when it is washed

col·our·ful (*especially US* **col·or·ful**) /ˈkʌləfl; *NAmE* -ərfl/ *adj.* **1** full of bright colours or having a lot of different colours: *colourful shop windows* ◇ *The male birds are more colourful than the females.* **2** interesting or exciting; full of variety, sometimes in a way that is slightly shocking: *a **colourful history/past/career*** ◇ *one of the book's most colourful characters*

col·our·ing (*especially US* **col·or·ing**) /ˈkʌlərɪŋ/ *noun* **1** [U, C] a substance that is used to give a particular colour to food: *red **food colouring*** **2** [U] the colour of a person's skin, eyes and hair: *Blue suited her fair colouring.* **3** [U] the colours that exist in sth, especially a plant or an animal: *insects with vivid yellow and black colouring*

C

col·our·ist (*especially US* **col·or·ist**) /ˈkʌlərɪst/ *noun* a person who uses colour, especially an artist or a hairdresser

col·our·istic (also **col·or·istic**) /ˌkʌləˈrɪstɪk/ *adj.* (*technical*) showing or relating to a special use of colour: *colouristic effects*

col·our·ize (*BrE*) = COLORIZE

col·our·less (*especially US* **col·or·less**) /ˈkʌlələs; *NAmE* -lərl-/ *adj.* **1** without colour or very pale: *a colourless liquid like water* ◇ *colourless lips* **2** not interesting SYN **dull**: *a colourless personality*

ˈcolour scheme (*especially US* **ˈcolor scheme**) *noun* the way in which colours are arranged, especially in the furniture and decoration of a room

ˈcolour separation (*especially US* **ˈcolor separation**) *noun* (*technical*) **1** [C] one of four images of sth made using only the colours CYAN, MAGENTA, yellow, or black. The four images containing these colours are then used together to print an image in full colour. **2** [U] the process that is used to do this

ˈcolour supplement *noun* (*BrE*) a magazine printed in colour and forming an extra part of a newspaper, particularly on Saturdays or Sundays

col·our·way /ˈkʌləweɪ; *NAmE* -lərw-/ *noun* (*BrE*) a colour or combination of colours which a piece of clothing, etc. is available in: *The designs are available in two colourways: red/grey or blue/grey.*

colt /kəʊlt; *NAmE* koʊlt/ *noun* **1** a young male horse up to the age of four or five ➲ compare FILLY, STALLION **2** (*BrE*) a member of a sports team consisting of young players **3 Colt™** a type of small gun

colt·ish /ˈkəʊltɪʃ; *NAmE* ˈkoʊlt-/ *adj.* (of a person) moving with a lot of energy but in an awkward way

col·um·bine /ˈkɒləmbaɪn; *NAmE* ˈkɑːl-/ *noun* **1** [C, U] a garden plant with delicate leaves and pointed blue flowers that hang down **2 Col·um·bine** [sing.] a female character in traditional Italian theatre

Col·um·bus Day /kəˈlʌmbəs deɪ/ *noun* [U, C] a national holiday in the US on the second Monday in October when people celebrate the arrival of Christopher Columbus in America in 1492

col·umn 0‑ /ˈkɒləm; *NAmE* ˈkɑːləm/ *noun*
1 0‑ a tall, solid, vertical post, usually round and made of stone, which supports or decorates a building or stands alone as a MONUMENT: *The temple is supported by marble columns.* ◇ *Nelson's Column in London* ➲ VISUAL VOCAB page V12 **2** 0‑ a thing shaped like a column: *a column of smoke* (= smoke rising straight up) ➲ see also SPINAL COLUMN, STEERING COLUMN **3** 0‑ (*abbr.* **col.**) one of the vertical sections into which the printed page of a book, newspaper, etc. is divided: *a column of text* ◇ *a dictionary with two columns per page* ◇ *Put a mark in the appropriate column.* ◇ *Their divorce filled a lot of* **column inches** *in the national papers* (= got a lot of attention). **4** 0‑ a part of a newspaper or magazine which appears regularly and deals with a particular subject or is written by a particular writer: *the gossip/financial column* ◇ *I always read her column in the local paper.* ➲ see also AGONY COLUMN, PERSONAL COLUMN **5** 0‑ a series of numbers or words arranged one under the other down a page: *to add up a column of figures* **6** a long, moving line of people or vehicles: *a long column of troops and tanks* ➲ see also FIFTH COLUMN

col·um·nist /ˈkɒləmnɪst; *NAmE* ˈkɑːl-/ *noun* a journalist who writes regular articles for a newspaper or magazine

coma /ˈkəʊmə; *NAmE* ˈkoʊmə/ *noun* a deep unconscious state, usually lasting a long time and caused by serious illness or injury: *to* **go into/be in a coma**

Com·an·che /kəˈmæntʃi/ *noun* (*pl.* **Com·an·che** or **Com·an·ches**) a member of a Native American people, many of whom live in the US state of Oklahoma

co·ma·tose /ˈkəʊmətəʊs; *NAmE* ˈkoʊmətoʊs/ *adj.* **1** (*medical*) deeply unconscious; in a coma **2** (*humorous*) extremely tired and lacking in energy; sleeping deeply

comb /kəʊm; *NAmE* koʊm/ *noun, verb*
■ *noun* **1** [C] a flat piece of plastic or metal with a row of thin teeth along one side, used for making your hair neat; a smaller version of this worn by women in their hair to hold it in place or as a decoration ➲ VISUAL VOCAB page V21 **2** [C, usually sing.] the act of using a comb on your hair: *Your hair needs a good comb.* **3** [C, U] = HONEYCOMB **4** [C] the soft, red piece of flesh on the head of a male chicken IDM see FINE-TOOTH COMB *adj.*
■ *verb* **1** [T] **~ sth** to pull a comb through your hair in order to make it neat: *Don't forget to comb your hair!* ◇ *Her hair was neatly combed back.* **2** [T, I] to search sth carefully in order to find sb/sth SYN **scour**: **~ sth** *I combed the shops looking for something to wear.* ◇ **~ sth for sb/sth** *The police combed the area for clues.* ◇ **~ through sth** (**for sb/sth**) *They combed through the files for evidence of fraud.* **3** [T] **~ sth** (*technical*) to make wool, cotton, etc. clean and straight using a special comb so that it can be used to make cloth
PHR V **ˌcomb sth↔ˈout** to pull a comb through hair in order to make it neat or to remove knots from it

com·bat /ˈkɒmbæt; *NAmE* ˈkɑːm-/ *noun, verb*
■ *noun* [U, C] fighting or a fight, especially during a time of war: *He was killed* **in combat**. ◇ ***armed/unarmed combat*** (= with/without weapons) ◇ *combat troops* ◇ *combat boots* ➲ see also SINGLE COMBAT
■ *verb* (-t- or -tt-) **1 ~ sth** to stop sth unpleasant or harmful from happening or from getting worse: *measures to* ***combat crime/inflation/unemployment/disease*** **2 ~ sb** (*formal*) to fight against an enemy

com·bat·ant /ˈkɒmbətənt; *NAmE* ˈkɑːm-/ *noun* a person or group involved in fighting in a war or battle ➲ compare NON-COMBATANT

ˈcombat fatigue (also **ˈbattle fatigue**) *noun* [U] mental problems caused by being in a war for a long period of time

ˈcombat fatigues (also **ˈbattle fatigues**) *noun* [pl.] clothes that soldiers wear for fighting that are covered in brown and green marks to make them difficult to see

com·bat·ive /ˈkɒmbətɪv; *NAmE* kəmˈbætɪv/ *adj.* ready and willing to fight or argue: *in a* ***combative mood/spirit***

com·bats /ˈkɒmbæts; *NAmE* ˈkɑːm-/ (also **ˈcombat trousers**) *noun* [pl.] (*BrE*) = CARGO PANTS

combi = KOMBI

com·bin·ation 0‑ /ˌkɒmbɪˈneɪʃn; *NAmE* ˌkɑːm-/ *noun*
1 0‑ [C] two or more things joined or mixed together to form a single unit: *His treatment was a combination of surgery, radiation and drugs.* ◇ *What an unusual combination of flavours!* ◇ *Technology and good management. That's a* ***winning combination*** (= one that will certainly be successful). **2** 0‑ [U] the act of joining or mixing together two or more things to form a single unit: *The firm is working on a new product* **in combination with** *several overseas partners.* ◇ *These paints can be used individually or* **in combination**. **3** [C] a series of numbers or letters used to open a combination lock: *I can't remember the combination.* **4 combinations** (*BrE*) [pl.] a piece of underwear covering the body and legs, worn in the past

combiˈnation lock *noun* a type of lock which can only be opened by using a particular series of numbers or letters

com·bine 0‑ *verb, noun*
■ *verb* /kəmˈbaɪn/ **1** 0‑ [I, T] to come together to form a single thing or group; to join two or more things or groups together to form a single one: *Hydrogen and oxygen combine to form water.* ◇ **~ with sth** *Hydrogen combines with oxygen to form water.* ◇ **~ to do sth** *Several factors had combined to ruin our plans.* ◇ **~ sth** *Combine all the ingredients in a bowl.* ◇ **~ sth with sth** *Combine the eggs with a little flour.* ◇ **~ A and B** (**together**) *Combine the eggs and the flour.* ◇ *The German team scored a* ***combined total*** *of 652 points.* **2** 0‑ [T] to have two or more different features or characteristics; to put two or more different things, features or

qualities together: **~ sth** *We are still looking for someone who combines all the necessary qualities.* ◇ **~ A and/with B** *The hotel combines comfort with convenience.* ◇ *This model combines a telephone and fax machine.* ◇ *They have successfully combined the old with the new in this room.* ◇ *a kitchen and dining-room combined* **3** [T] **~ A and/with B** to do two or more things at the same time: *The trip will combine business with pleasure.* ◇ *She has successfully combined a career and bringing up a family.* **4** [I, T] to come together in order to work or act together; to put two things or groups together so that they work or act together: *They combined against a common enemy.* ◇ **~ sth (with sth)** *the combined effects of the two drugs* ◇ *You should try to combine exercise with a healthy diet.* ◇ *It took the* ***combined efforts*** *of both the press and the public to bring about a change in the law.* IDM see FORCE *n.*

■ ***noun*** /ˈkɒmbaɪn; *NAmE* ˈkɑːm-/ **1** (*BrE* also **ˌcombine ˈharvester**) a large farm machine which cuts a crop and separates the grains from the rest of the plant **2** a group of people or organizations acting together in business

comˈbining form *noun* (*grammar*) a form of a word that can combine with another word or another combining form to make a new word, for example *techno-* and *-phobe* in *technophobe*

combo /ˈkɒmbəʊ; *NAmE* ˈkɑːmboʊ/ *noun* (*pl.* -os) **1** a small band that plays JAZZ or dance music **2** (*informal, especially NAmE*) a number of different things combined together, especially different types of food: *I'll have the steak and chicken combo platter.*

com·bust /kəmˈbʌst/ *verb* [I, T] **~ (sth)** to start to burn; to start to burn sth

com·bust·ible /kəmˈbʌstəbl/ *adj.* able to begin burning easily SYN **flammable**: ***combustible material/gases***

com·bus·tion /kəmˈbʌstʃən/ *noun* [U] **1** the process of burning **2** (*technical*) a chemical process in which substances combine with the OXYGEN in the air to produce heat and light

comˈbustion chamber *noun* a space in which combustion takes place, for example in an engine

come /kʌm/ *verb, prep., exclamation, noun*

■ ***verb*** (came /keɪm/, come)

▸ TO A PLACE **1** [I] to move to or towards a person or place: (**+ adv./prep.**) *He came into the room and shut the door.* ◇ *She comes to work by bus.* ◇ *My son is coming home soon.* ◇ *Come here!* ◇ *Come and see us soon!* ◇ ***Here comes*** *Jo!* (= Jo is coming) ◇ *There's a storm coming.* ◇ **~ to do sth** *They're coming to stay for a week.* HELP In spoken English **come** can be used with **and** plus another verb, instead of with **to** and the infinitive, to show purpose or to tell sb what to do: *When did she last come and see you?* ◇ *Come and have your dinner.* The **and** is sometimes left out, especially in *NAmE*: ***Come have*** *your dinner.* **2** [I] **~ (to...)** to arrive at or reach a place: *They continued until they came to a river.* ◇ *What time did you come* (= to my house)? ◇ *Spring came late this year.* ◇ *Your breakfast is coming soon.* ◇ *Have any letters come for me?* ◇ *Help came at last.* ◇ *The CD* ***comes complete*** *with all the words of the songs.* ◇ *The time has come* (= now is the moment) *to act.* **3** [I] to arrive somewhere in order to do sth or get sth: **~ for sth** *I've come for my book.* ◇ **~ about sth** *I've come about my book.* ◇ **~ to do sth** *I've come to get my book.* ◇ **~ doing sth** *He came looking for me.* **4** [I] to move or travel, especially with sb else, to a particular place or in order to be present at an event: *I've only come for an hour.* ◇ *Thanks for coming* (= to my house, party, etc.). ◇ **~ (to sth) (with sb)** *Are you coming to the club with us tonight?* ◇ **~ doing sth** *Why don't you come skating tonight?*

▸ RUNNING/HURRYING ETC. **5** [I] **~ doing sth (+ adv.prep.)** to move in a particular way or while doing sth else: *The children came running into the room.*

▸ TRAVEL **6** [I] **+ noun** to travel a particular distance: *We've come 50 miles this morning.* ◇ (*figurative*) *The company has* ***come a long way*** (= made lot of progress) *in the last 5 years.*

▸ HAPPEN **7** [I] to happen: *The agreement came after several hours of negotiations.* ◇ *The rains came too late to do any good.* ◇ **~ as sth** *Her death came as a terrible shock to us.* ◇ *His resignation came as no surprise.* **8** [T] **~ to do sth** used in questions to talk about how or why sth happened: *How did he come to break his leg?* ◇ *How do you come to be so late?* ➲ see also HOW COME?

▸ TO A POSITION/STATE **9** [I] **+ adv./prep.** (not used in the progressive tenses) to have a particular position: *That comes a long way down my list of priorities.* ◇ *His family comes first* (= is the most important thing in his life). ◇ *She came second* (= received the second highest score) *in the exam.* **10** [I] **~ to/into sth** used in many expressions to show that sth has reached a particular state: *At last winter* ***came to an end.*** ◇ *He* ***came to power*** *in 2006.* ◇ *When will they* ***come to a decision****?* ◇ *The trees are coming into leaf.* **11** [I] (not used in the progressive tenses) (of goods, products, etc.) to be available or to exist in a particular way: **~ in sth** *This dress comes in black and red.* ◇ **+ adj.** (*informal*) *New cars don't* ***come cheap*** (= they are expensive). **12** [I, T] to become: **+ adj.** *The buttons had come undone.* ◇ *The handle came loose.* ◇ *Everything will* ***come right*** *in the end.* ◇ **~ to do sth** *This design came to be known as the Oriental style.* **13** [T] **~ to do sth** to reach a point where you realize, understand or believe sth: *In time she came to love him.* ◇ *She had come to see the problem in a new light.* ◇ *I've come to expect this kind of behaviour from him.*

▸ SEX **14** [I] (*slang*) to have an ORGASM

IDM Most idioms containing **come** are at the entries for the nouns or adjectives in the idioms, for example **come a cropper** is at **cropper**. **be as ˌclever, ˌstupid, etc. as they ˈcome** (*informal*) to be very clever, stupid, etc. **ˌcome aˈgain?** (*informal*) used to ask sb to repeat sth: *'She's an entomologist.' 'Come again?' 'An entomologist—she studies insects.'* **ˌcome and ˈgo 1** to arrive and leave; to move freely: *They had a party next door—we heard people* ***coming and going*** *all night.* **2** to be present for a short time and then go away: *The pain in my leg comes and goes.* **come ˈeasily, ˈnaturally, etc. to sb** (of an activity, a skill, etc.) to be easy, natural, etc. for sb to do: *Acting comes naturally to her.* **ˌcome over (all) ˈfaint, ˈdizzy, ˈgiddy, etc.** (*old-fashioned, BrE, informal*) to suddenly feel ill/sick or faint **come to ˈnothing | not ˈcome to anything** to be unsuccessful; to have no successful result: *How sad that all his hard work should come to nothing.* ◇ *Her plans didn't come to anything.* **come to ˈthat | if it comes to ˈthat** (*informal, especially BrE*) used to introduce sth extra that is connected with what has just been said: *I don't really trust him—nor his wife, come to that.* **ˌcome what ˈmay** despite any problems or difficulties you may have: *He promised to support her come what may.* **how come (...)?** used to say you do not understand how sth can happen and would like an explanation: *If she spent five years in Paris, how come her French is so bad?* **not ˈcome to much** to not be important or successful **to ˈcome** (used after a noun) in the future: *They may well regret the decision* ***in years to come.*** ◇ *This will be a problem* ***for some time to come*** (= for a period of time in the future). **when it comes to sth/to doing sth** when it is a question of sth: *When it comes to getting things done, he's useless.* **where sb is ˈcoming from** (*informal*) somebody's ideas, beliefs, personality, etc. that makes them say what they have said: *I see where you're coming from* (= I understand what you mean).

PHR V **ˌcome aˈbout (that...)** to happen: *Can you tell me how the accident came about?*

ˌcome aˈcross (also **ˌcome ˈover**) **1** to be understood: *He spoke for a long time but his meaning didn't really come across.* **2** to make a particular impression: *She comes across well in interviews.* ◇ *He came over as a sympathetic person.*

ˈcome across sb/sth [no passive] to meet or find sb/sth by chance: *I came across children sleeping under bridges.* ◇ *She came across some old photographs in a drawer.* **ˌcome aˈcross (with sth)** [no passive] to provide or supply sth when you need it: *I hoped she'd come across with some more information.*

ˌcome ˈafter sb [no passive] to chase or follow sb

ˌcome aˈlong 1 to arrive; to appear: *When the right opportunity comes along, she'll take it.* **2** to go somewhere with sb: *I'm glad you came along.* **3** (*informal*) to improve or develop in the way that you want **SYN** **progress**: *Your French has come along a lot recently.* **4** used in orders to tell sb to hurry, or to try harder: *Come along! We're late.* ◇ *Come along! It's easy!*

C

ˌ**come aˈpart** to break into pieces: *The book just came apart in my hands.* ◇ (*figurative*) *My whole life had* ***come apart at the seams.***

ˌ**come aˈround/ˈround 1** 0‑ (also ˌ**come ˈto**) to become conscious again: *Your mother hasn't yet come round from the anaesthetic.* **2** (of a date or a regular event) to happen again: *My birthday seems to come around quicker every year.* ˌ**come aˈround/ˈround (to...)** 0‑ to come to a place, especially sb's house, to visit for a short time: *Do come around and see us some time.* ˌ**come aˈround/ˈround (to sth)** to change your mood or your opinion: *He'll never come round to our way of thinking.*

ˈ**come at sb** [no passive] to move towards sb as though you are going to attack them: *She came at me with a knife.* ◇ (*figurative*) *The noise came at us from all sides.* ˈ**come at sth** to think about a problem, question, etc. in a particular way **SYN** **approach**: *We're getting nowhere—let's come at it from another angle.*

ˌ**come aˈway (from sth)** to become separated from sth: *The plaster had started to come away from the wall.* ˌ**come aˈway with sth** [no passive] to leave a place with a particular feeling or impression: *We came away with the impression that all was not well with their marriage.*

ˌ**come ˈback 1** to return: *You came back* (= came home) *very late last night.* ◇ *The colour was coming back to her cheeks.* ◇ (*figurative*) *United came back from being two goals down to win 3–2.* ➲ SYNONYMS at RETURN **2** to become popular or successful again: *Long hair for men seems to be coming back in.* ➲ related noun COMEBACK (2) ˌ**come ˈback (at sb) (with sth)** to reply to sb angrily or with force: *She came back at the speaker with some sharp questions.* ➲ related noun COMEBACK (3) ˌ**come ˈback (to sb)** to return to sb's memory: *It's all coming back to me now.* ◇ *Once you've been in France a few days, your French will soon come back.* ˌ**come ˈback to sth** [no passive] to return to a subject, an idea, etc: *Let's come back to the point at issue.* ◇ *It all comes back to a question of money.*

ˈ**come before sb/sth** [no passive] (*formal*) to be presented to sb/sth for discussion or a decision: *The case comes before the court next week.*

ˌ**come beˈtween sb and sb** [no passive] to damage a relationship between two people: *I'd hate anything to come between us.*

ˌ**come ˈby** (*NAmE*) to make a short visit to a place, in order to see sb: *She came by the house.* ˈ**come by sth 1** to manage to get sth: *Jobs are hard to come by these days.* **2** to receive sth: *How did you come by that scratch on your cheek?*

ˌ**come ˈdown 1** to break and fall to the ground: *The ceiling came down with a terrific crash.* **2** (of rain, snow, etc.) to fall: *The rain came down in torrents.* **3** (of an aircraft) to land or fall from the sky: *We were forced to come down in a field.* **4** 0‑ if a price, a temperature, a rate, etc. **comes down**, it gets lower: *The price of gas is coming down.* ◇ *Gas is coming down in price.* **5** to decide and say publicly that you support or oppose sb: *The committee came down in support of his application.* **6** 0‑ to reach as far down as a particular point: *Her hair comes down to her waist.* ˌ**come ˈdown (from...)** (*BrE, formal*) to leave a university, especially Oxford or Cambridge, at the end of a term or after finishing your studies **OPP** **come up (to...)** ˌ**come ˈdown (from...) (to...)** to come from one place to another, usually from the north of a country to the south, or from a larger place to a smaller one ˌ**come ˈdown on sb** [no passive] (*informal*) to criticize sb severely or punish sb: *Don't come down too hard on her.* ◇ *The courts are coming down heavily on young offenders.* ˌ**come ˈdown (to sb)** to have come from a long time in the past: *The name has come down from the last century.* ˌ**come ˈdown to sth** [no passive] to be able to be explained by a single important point: *What* ***it comes down to*** *is, either I get more money or I leave.* ˌ**come ˈdown with sth** [no passive] to get an illness that is not very serious: *I think I'm coming down with flu.*

ˌ**come ˈforward** to offer your help, services, etc: *Several people came forward with information.* ◇ *Police have asked witnesses of the accident to come forward.*

ˈ**come from...** 0‑ (not used in the progressive tenses) to have as your place of birth or the place where you live: *She comes from London.* ◇ *Where do you come from?* ˈ**come from sth 1** 0‑ to start in a particular place or be produced from a particular thing: *Much of our butter comes from New Zealand.* ◇ *This wool comes from goats, not sheep.* ◇ *This poem comes from his new book.* ◇ *Where does her attitude come from?* ◇ *Where's that smell coming from?* ◇ *He comes from a family of actors.* ◇ *'She doesn't try hard enough.' 'That's rich,* ***coming from you*** (= you do not try hard either).*'* **2** = COME OF STH

ˌ**come ˈin 1** when the TIDE **comes in**, it moves towards the land **OPP** **go out 2** to finish a race in a particular position: *My horse came in last.* **3** to become fashionable: *Long hair for men came in in the sixties.* **OPP** **go out 4** to become available: *We're still waiting for copies of the book to come in.* **5** to have a part in sth: *I understand the plan perfectly, but I can't see where I come in.* **6** 0‑ to arrive somewhere; to be received: *The train is coming in now.* ◇ *News is coming in of a serious plane crash in France.* ◇ *She has over a thousand pounds a month coming in from her investments.* **7** to take part in a discussion: *Would you like to come in at this point, Susan?* **8** (of a law or rule) to be introduced; to begin to be used ˌ**come ˈin for sth** [no passive] to receive sth, especially sth unpleasant: *The government's economic policies have come in for a lot of criticism.* ˌ**come ˈin (on sth)** to become involved in sth: *If you want to come in on the deal, you need to decide now.*

ˌ**come ˈinto sth** [no passive] **1** to be left money by sb who has died: *She came into a fortune when her uncle died.* **2** to be important in a particular situation: *I've worked very hard to pass this exam—luck doesn't come into it.*

ˈ**come of/from sth** to be the result of sth: *I made a few enquiries, but nothing* ***came of it*** *in the end.* ◇ **~ doing sth** *That comes of eating too much!*

ˌ**come ˈoff 1** 0‑ to be able to be removed: *Does this hood come off?* ◇ *That mark won't come off.* **2** (*informal*) to take place; to happen: *Did the trip to Rome ever come off?* **3** (*informal*) (of a plan, etc.) to be successful; to have the intended effect or result: *They had wanted it to be a surprise but the plan didn't come off.* **4 ~ well, badly, etc.** (*informal*) to be successful/not successful in a fight, contest, etc: *I thought they came off very well in the debate.*

ˌ**come ˈoff (sth) 1** to fall from sth: *to come off your bicycle/horse* **2** 0‑ to become separated from sth: *When I tried to lift the jug, the handle came off in my hand.* ◇ *A button had come off my coat.* ˌ**come ˈoff it** (*informal*) used to disagree with sb rudely: *Come off it! We don't have a chance.* ˌ**come ˈoff sth** [no passive] to stop taking medicine, a drug, alcohol, etc: *I've tried to get him to come off the tranquillizers.*

ˌ**come ˈon 1** (of an actor) to walk onto the stage **2** (of a player) to join a team during a game: *Owen came on for Brown ten minutes before the end of the game.* **3** 0‑ (*informal*) to improve or develop in the way you want: *The project is coming on fine.* **4** 0‑ used in orders to tell sb to hurry or to try harder: *Come on! We don't have much time.* ◇ *Come on! Try once more.* **5** 0‑ used to show that you know what sb has said is not correct: *Oh, come on—you know that isn't true!* **6** (usually used in the progressive tenses) (of an illness or a mood) to begin: *I can feel a cold coming on.* ◇ *I think there's rain coming on.* ◇ **~ to do sth** *It came on to rain.* **7** (of a TV programme, etc.) to start: *What time does the news come on?* **8** 0‑ to begin to operate: *Set the oven to come on at six.* ◇ *When does the heating come on?* ˈ**come on/upon sb/sth** [no passive] (*formal*) to meet or find sb/sth by chance ˌ**come ˈon to sb** (*informal*) to behave in a way that shows sb that you want to have a sexual relationship with them ➲ related noun COME-ON ˌ**come ˈon to sth** [no passive] to start talking about a subject: *I'd like to come on to that question later.*

ˌ**come ˈout 1** 0‑ when the sun, moon or stars **come out**, they appear: *The rain stopped and the sun came out.* **2** (of flowers) to open: *The daffodils came out early this year.* **3** 0‑ to be produced or published: *When is her new novel* *coming out?* **4** (of news, the truth, etc.) to become known: *The full story came out at the trial.* ◇ **it comes out that...** *It came out that he'd been telling lies.* **5** if a photograph **comes out**, it is a clear picture when it is developed and printed: *The photos from our trip didn't come out.* **6** to be shown clearly: *Her best qualities come out in a crisis.* **7** when words **come out**, they are spoken: *I tried to say 'I love you,' but the words wouldn't come out.* **8** to say publicly whether you agree or disagree with sth: *He came out against the plan.* ◇ *In her speech, the senator came out in favour of a change in the law.* **9** (*BrE*) to stop work and go on strike **10** to no longer hide the fact that you are HOMOSEXUAL **11** (of a young UPPER-CLASS girl, especially in the past) to be formally introduced into society ˌ**come 'out (of sth)** **1** (of an object) to be removed from a place where it is fixed: *This nail won't come out.* **2** (of dirt, a mark, etc.) to be removed from sth by washing or cleaning: *These ink stains won't come out of my dress.* ◇ *Will the colour come out* (= become faint or disappear) *if I wash it?* ˌ**come 'out at sth** [no passive] to add up to a particular cost or sum: *The total bill comes out at £500.* ˌ**come 'out in sth** [no passive] (of a person) to become covered in spots, etc. on the skin: *Hot weather makes her come out in a rash.* ˌ**come 'out of yourself** to relax and become more confident and friendly with other people: *It was when she started drama classes that she really came out of herself.* ˌ**come 'out of sth** [no passive] to develop from sth: *The book came out of his experiences in India.* ◇ *Rock music came out of the blues.* ˌ**come 'out with sth** [no passive] to say sth, especially sth surprising or rude: *He came out with a stream of abuse.* ◇ *She sometimes comes out with the most extraordinary remarks.*

ˌ**come 'over** **1** (*BrE, informal*) to suddenly feel sth: **+ adj.** *to come over funny/dizzy/faint* ◇ *I come over all shy whenever I see her.* **2** = COME ACROSS: *He came over well in the interview.* ˌ**come 'over (to...)** to come to a place, especially sb's house, to visit for a short time ˌ**come 'over (to...) (from...)** to travel from one place to another, usually over a long distance: *Why don't you come over to England in the summer?* ◇ *Her grandparents came over from Ireland during the famine.* ˌ**come 'over (to sth)** to change from one side, opinion, etc. to another ˌ**come 'over sb** [no passive] to affect sb: *A fit of dizziness came over her.* ◇ ***I can't think what came over me*** (= I do not know what caused me to behave in that way).

ˌ**come 'round** | ˌ**come 'round (to sth)** (*BrE*) = COME AROUND

ˌ**come 'through** (of news or a message) to arrive by telephone, radio, etc. or through an official organization: *A message is just coming through.* ˌ**come 'through (sth)** to get better after a serious illness or to avoid serious injury SYN **survive**: *With such a weak heart she was lucky to come through the operation.* ˌ**come 'through (with sth)** to successfully do or complete sth that you have promised to do: *We were worried she wouldn't be able to handle it, but she came through in the end.* ◇ *The bank finally came through with the money.*

ˌ**come 'to** = COME AROUND (1) ˌ**come to your'self** (*old-fashioned*) to return to your normal state **'come to sb** [no passive] (of an idea) to enter your mind: *The idea came to me in the bath.* ◇ **~ that...** *It suddenly came to her that she had been wrong all along.* **'come to sth** [no passive] **1** to add up to sth: *The bill came to $30.* ◇ *I never expected those few items to come to so much.* **2** to reach a particular situation, especially a bad one: *The doctors will operate if necessary—but it may not come to that.* ◇ *Who'd have thought things would come to this* (= become so bad)?

ˌ**come to'gether** if two or more different people or things **come together**, they form a united group: *Three colleges have come together to create a new university.* ◇ *Bits and pieces of things he'd read and heard were coming together, and he began to understand.*

'come under sth [no passive] **1** to be included in a particular group: *What heading does this come under?* **2** to be a person that others are attacking or criticizing: *The head teacher came under a lot of criticism from the parents.* **3** to be controlled or influenced by sth: *All her students came under her spell.*

ˌ**come 'up** **1** (of plants) to appear above the soil: *The daffodils are just beginning to come up.* **2** (of the sun) to rise: *We watched the sun come up.* **3** to happen: *I'm afraid something urgent has come up.* ◇ *We'll let you know if any vacancies come up.* **4** to be mentioned or discussed: *The subject came up in conversation.* ◇ *The question is bound to come up at the meeting.* **5** (of an event or a time) to be going to happen very soon: *Her birthday is coming up soon.* **6** to be dealt with by a court: *Her divorce case comes up next month.* **7** if your number, name, ticket, etc. **comes up** in a betting game, it is chosen and you win sth **8** (*informal*) (usually used in the progressive tenses) to arrive; to be ready soon: *'Is lunch ready?' 'Coming up!'* ˌ**come 'up (to ...)** (*BrE, formal*) to arrive at a university, especially Oxford or Cambridge, at the beginning of a term or in order to begin your studies OPP **come down (from...)** ˌ**come 'up (to...) (from...)** to come from one place to another, especially from the south of a country to the north or from a smaller place to a larger one: *Why don't you come up to Scotland for a few days?* ˌ**come 'up (to sb)** to move towards sb, in order to talk to them: *He came up to me and asked me the way to the station.* ˌ**come 'up against sb/sth** [no passive] to be faced with or opposed by sb/sth: *We expect to come up against a lot of opposition to the plan.* ˌ**come 'up for sth** [no passive] **1** to be considered for a job, an important position, etc: *She comes up for re-election next year.* **2** to be reaching the time when sth must be done: *His contract is coming up for renewal.* ˌ**come 'up to sth** [no passive] **1** to reach as far as a particular point: *The water came up to my neck.* **2** to reach an acceptable level or standard: *His performance didn't really come up to his usual high standard.* ◇ *Their trip to France didn't come up to expectations.* ˌ**come 'up with sth** [no passive] to find or produce an answer, a sum of money, etc: *She came up with a new idea for increasing sales.* ◇ *How soon can you come up with the money?*

'come upon sb/sth = COME ON SB/STH

■ ***prep.*** (*old-fashioned, informal*) when the time mentioned comes: *They would have been married forty years come this June.*

■ ***exclamation*** (*old-fashioned*) used when encouraging sb to be sensible or reasonable, or when showing slight disapproval: *Oh come now, things aren't as bad as all that.* ◇ *Come, come, Miss Jones, you know perfectly well what I mean.*

■ ***noun*** [U] (*slang*) SEMEN

come·back /'kʌmbæk/ *noun* **1** [usually sing.] if a person in public life makes a **comeback**, they start doing sth again which they had stopped doing, or they become popular again: *an ageing pop star trying to stage a comeback* **2** if a thing makes a **comeback**, it becomes popular and fashionable or successful again **3** (*informal*) a quick reply to a critical remark SYN **retort** **4** a way of holding sb responsible for sth wrong which has been done to you: *You agreed to the contract, so now you have no comeback.*

com·edian /kə'mi:diən/ *noun* an entertainer who makes people laugh by telling jokes or funny stories

com·edi·enne /kəˌmi:di'en/ *noun* (*old-fashioned*) a female entertainer who makes people laugh by telling jokes or funny stories

come·down /'kʌmdaʊn/ *noun* [usually sing.] (*informal*) a situation in which a person is not as important as before, or does not get as much respect from other people

com·edy /'kɒmədi; *NAmE* 'kɑ:m-/ *noun* (*pl.* -ies) **1** [C, U] a play or film/movie that is intended to be funny, usually with a happy ending; plays and films/movies of this type: *a romantic comedy* ⇨ compare TRAGEDY: *slapstick comedy* ⇨ see also BLACK *adj.* (9), SITUATION COMEDY **2** [U] an amusing aspect of sth SYN **humour**: *He didn't appreciate the comedy of the situation.*

ˌ**comedy of 'manners** *noun* an amusing play, film/movie, or book that shows the silly behaviour of a particular group of people

C

ˌ**come-ˈhither** *adj.* [only before noun] (of sb's expression) appearing to be trying to attract sb sexually: *a come-hither look*

come·ly /ˈkʌmli/ *adj.* (*literary*) (especially of a woman) pleasant to look at SYN **attractive**

ˈ**come-on** *noun* [usually sing.] (*informal*) an object or action which is intended to attract sb or to persuade them to do sth: *She was definitely giving him the come-on* (= trying to attract him sexually).

comer /ˈkʌmə(r)/ *noun* **1 all comers** [pl.] anyone who is interested in, or comes forward for, sth, especially a competition: *The event is open to all comers.* **2** (with adjectives) a person who arrives somewhere ➲ see also LATECOMER, NEWCOMER **3** (*NAmE, informal*) a person who is likely to be successful

com·est·ible /kəˈmestɪbl/ *adj., noun* (*formal*)
- *adj.* that can be eaten SYN **edible**
- *noun* [usually pl.] an item of food

comet /ˈkɒmɪt; *NAmE* ˈkɑːmət/ *noun* a mass of ice and dust that moves around the sun and looks like a bright star with a tail

come·up·pance /kʌmˈʌpəns/ *noun* [sing.] (*informal*) a punishment for sth bad that you have done, that other people feel you really deserve: *I was glad to see that the bad guy* **got his comeuppance** *at the end of the movie.*

com·fit /ˈkʌmfɪt/ *noun* (*old-fashioned*) a sweet/candy consisting of a nut, seed or fruit covered with sugar

com·fort 0‑ /ˈkʌmfət; *NAmE* -fərt/ *noun, verb*

> **WORD FAMILY**
> **comfort** *noun, verb*
> **comfortable** *adj.* (≠ uncomfortable)
> **comfortably** *adv.* (≠ uncomfortably)
> **comforting** *adj.*

- *noun* **1** 0‑ [U] the state of being physically relaxed and free from pain; the state of having a pleasant life, with everything that you need: *These tennis shoes are designed* **for comfort** *and performance.* ◇ *With DVD, you can watch the latest movies* **in the comfort of** *your own home.* ◇ *The hotel offers a high standard of comfort and service.* ◇ *They had enough money to live* **in comfort** *in their old age.* **2** 0‑ [U] a feeling of not suffering or worrying so much; a feeling of being less unhappy SYN **consolation**: *to* **take/draw comfort** *from sb's words* ◇ *I tried to offer a few words* **of comfort**. ◇ *The sound of gunfire was* **too close for comfort**. ◇ **If it's any comfort** *to you, I'm in the same situation.* ◇ *His words were* **of little comfort** *in the circumstances.* ◇ **comfort food** (= food that makes you feel better) **3** 0‑ [sing.] a person or thing that helps you when you are suffering, worried or unhappy: *The children have* **been a great comfort to** *me through all of this.* ◇ *It's a comfort to know that she is safe.* ➲ see also COLD COMFORT **4** 0‑ [C, usually pl.] a thing that makes your life easier or more comfortable: *The hotel has all modern comforts/every modern comfort.* ◇ *material comforts* (= money and possessions) ➲ see also CREATURE COMFORTS
- *verb* to make sb who is worried or unhappy feel better by being kind and sympathetic towards them: **~ sb** *The victim's widow was today being comforted by family and friends.* ◇ *She comforted herself with the thought that it would soon be spring.* ◇ **it comforts sb to do sth** *It comforted her to feel his arms around her.*

com·fort·able 0‑ /ˈkʌmftəbl; *BrE* also -fət-; *NAmE* also -fərt-/ *adj.*
- CLOTHES/FURNITURE **1** 0‑ (of clothes, furniture, etc.) making you feel physically relaxed; pleasant to wear, sit on, etc: *It's such a comfortable bed.* ◇ *These new shoes are not very comfortable.* ◇ *a warm comfortable house* OPP **uncomfortable**
- PHYSICALLY RELAXED **2** 0‑ feeling physically relaxed in a pleasant way; warm enough, without pain, etc: *Are you comfortable?* ◇ *She shifted into a more comfortable position on the chair.* ◇ *Please* **make yourself comfortable** *while I get some coffee.* ◇ *The patient is comfortable* (= not in pain) *after his operation.* OPP **uncomfortable**
- CONFIDENT **3** 0‑ confident and not worried or afraid: *He's more comfortable with computers than with people.* OPP **uncomfortable**
- HAVING MONEY **4** 0‑ having enough money to buy what you want without worrying about the cost: *They're not millionaires, but they're certainly very comfortable.* ➲ SYNONYMS at RICH
- VICTORY **5** quite large; allowing you to win easily: *The party won with a comfortable majority.* ◇ *a comfortable 2–0 win*

com·fort·ably 0‑ /ˈkʌmftəbli; *BrE* also -fət-; *NAmE* also -fərt-/ *adv.*
1 0‑ in a comfortable way: *All the rooms were comfortably furnished.* ◇ *If you're all sitting comfortably, then I'll begin.* **2** with no problem SYN **easily**: *He can comfortably afford the extra expense.* ◇ *They are comfortably ahead in the opinion polls.*
IDM ˌ**comfortably ˈoff** having enough money to buy what you want without worrying too much about the cost

com·fort·er /ˈkʌmfətə(r); *NAmE* -fərt-/ *noun* **1** a person or thing that makes you feel calmer or less worried **2** (*NAmE*) a type of thick cover for a bed ➲ compare QUILT

com·fort·ing /ˈkʌmfətɪŋ; *NAmE* -fərt-/ *adj.* making you feel calmer and less worried or unhappy: *her comforting words* ◇ *It's comforting to know that you'll be there.* ▸ **com·fort·ing·ly** *adv.*

com·fort·less /ˈkʌmfətləs; *NAmE* -fərt-/ *adj.* (*formal*) without anything to make a place more comfortable

ˈ**comfort ˌstation** *noun* (*NAmE*) a room with a toilet in a public place, for example for people who are travelling

ˈ**comfort zone** *noun* **1** (sometimes *disapproving*) a place or situation in which you feel safe or comfortable, especially when you choose to stay in this situation instead of trying to work harder or achieve more: *Stepping outside your comfort zone and trying new things can be a great experience.* ◇ *We cannot afford to have anyone operating in a comfort zone.* **2** (*approving*) (especially in sport) a state in which you feel confident and are performing at your best: *I knew if I could find my comfort zone I would be difficult to beat.*

com·frey /ˈkʌmfri/ *noun* [U, C] a plant with large leaves covered with small hairs and small bell-shaped flowers

comfy /ˈkʌmfi/ *adj.* (**com·fier**, **com·fi·est**) (*informal*) comfortable: *a comfy armchair/bed* HELP **more comfy** is also common as a comparative.

comic /ˈkɒmɪk; *NAmE* ˈkɑːmɪk/ *adj., noun*
- *adj.* **1** amusing and making you laugh: *a comic monologue/story* ◇ *The play is both comic and tragic.* ◇ *She can always be relied on to provide* **comic relief** (= sth to make you laugh) *at a boring party.* ➲ SYNONYMS at FUNNY **2** [only before noun] connected with comedy (= entertainment that is funny and that makes people laugh): *a comic opera* ◇ *a comic actor*
- *noun* **1** an entertainer who makes people laugh by telling jokes or funny stories SYN **comedian** **2** (*NAmE* also ˈ**comic book**) a magazine, especially for children, that tells stories through pictures **3 the comics** [pl.] (*NAmE*) the section of a newspaper that contains COMIC STRIPS

com·ic·al /ˈkɒmɪkl; *NAmE* ˈkɑːm-/ *adj.* funny or amusing because of being strange or unusual ▸ **com·ic·al·ly** /-kli/ *adv.*

ˈ**comic strip** (also **car·toon**) (*BrE* also ˌ**strip carˈtoon**) (*NAmE* also **strip**) *noun* a series of drawings inside boxes that tell a story and are often printed in newspapers

com·ing /ˈkʌmɪŋ/ *noun, adj.*
- *noun* [sing.] **the ~ of sth** the time when sth new begins: *With the coming of modern technology, many jobs were lost.*
IDM ˌ**comings and ˈgoings** (*informal*) the movement of people arriving at and leaving a particular place: *It's hard to keep track of the children's comings and goings.*
- *adj.* [only before noun] happening soon; next: *in the coming months* ◇ *This coming Sunday is her birthday.*

ˌ**coming of ˈage** *noun* [sing.] the time when a person reaches the age at which they have an adult's legal rights and responsibilities

comma /ˈkɒmə; *NAmE* ˈkɑːmə/ *noun* the mark (,) used to separate the items in a list or to show where there is a slight pause in a sentence ➲ see also INVERTED COMMAS

com·mand /kəˈmɑːnd; *NAmE* kəˈmænd/ *noun, verb*

■ ***noun***

▸ ORDER **1** [C] an order given to a person or an animal: *Begin when I give the command.* ◇ *You must obey the captain's commands.*

▸ FOR COMPUTER **2** [C] an instruction given to a computer

▸ CONTROL **3** [U] control and authority over a situation or a group of people: *He has 1 200 men under his command.* ◇ *He **has command** of 1 200 men.* ◇ *The police arrived and **took command of** the situation.* ◇ *For the first time in years, she felt **in command of** her life.* ◇ *He looked relaxed and totally **in command of himself**.* ◇ *Who is **in command** here?* ➲ see also SECOND IN COMMAND

▸ IN ARMY **4 Command** [C] a part of an army, AIR FORCE, etc. that is organized and controlled separately; a group of officers who give orders: *Bomber Command*

▸ KNOWLEDGE **5** [U, sing.] **~ (of sth)** your knowledge of sth; your ability to do or use sth, especially a language: *Applicants will be expected to have (a) good command of English.*

IDM **at your comˈmand** if you have a skill or an amount of sth **at your command**, you are able to use it well and completely **be at sb's comˈmand** (*formal*) to be ready to obey sb: *I'm at your command—what would you like me to do?* ➲ more at WISH *n.*

■ ***verb***

▸ ORDER **1** [T] (of sb in a position of authority) to tell sb to do sth SYN **order**: **~ sb to do sth** *He commanded his men to retreat.* ◇ **~ sth** *She commanded the release of the prisoners.* ◇ **+ speech** *'Come here!' he commanded (them).* ◇ **~ that...** (*formal*) *The commission intervened and commanded that work on the building cease.* ◇ (*BrE* also) *The commission commanded that work on the building should cease.*

▸ IN ARMY **2** [T, I] **~ (sb/sth)** to be in charge of a group of people in the army, navy, etc: *The troops were commanded by General Haig.*

▸ DESERVE AND GET **3** [T, no passive] (not used in the progressive tenses) **~ sth** to deserve and get sth because of the special qualities you have: *to command sympathy/support* ◇ *She was able to command the respect of the class.* ◇ *The headlines commanded her attention.* ◇ *As a top lawyer, he can expect to command a six-figure salary.*

▸ VIEW **4** [T, no passive] (not used in the progressive tenses) **~ sth** (*formal*) to be in a position from where you can see or control sth: *The hotel commands a fine view of the valley.*

▸ CONTROL **5** [T, no passive] (not used in the progressive tenses) **~ sth** (*formal*) to have control of sth; to have sth available for use: *The party was no longer able to command a majority in Parliament.* ◇ *the power and finances commanded by the police*

com·mand·ant /ˈkɒməndænt; *NAmE* ˈkɑːm-/ *noun* the officer in charge of a particular military group or institution

comˌmand eˈconomy *noun* = PLANNED ECONOMY

com·man·deer /ˌkɒmənˈdɪə(r); *NAmE* ˌkɑːmənˈdɪr/ *verb* **~ sth** to take control of a building, a vehicle, etc. for military purposes during a war, or by force for your own use SYN **requisition**

com·mand·er /kəˈmɑːndə(r); *NAmE* -ˈmæn-/ *noun* **1** a person who is in charge of sth, especially an officer in charge of a particular group of soldiers or a military operation: *military/allied/field/flight commanders* ◇ *the commander of the expedition* **2** (*abbr.* **Cdr**) an officer of fairly high rank in the British or American navy **3** (*abbr.* **Cdr**) (in Britain) a London police officer of high rank

comˌmander-in-ˈchief (*abbr.* **C.-in-C.**) *noun* (*pl.* **commanders-in-chief**) the officer who commands all the armed forces of a country or all its forces in a particular area

com·mand·ing /kəˈmɑːndɪŋ; *NAmE* -ˈmæn-/ *adj.* **1** [only before noun] in a position of authority that allows you to give formal orders: *Who is your commanding officer?* **2** [usually before noun] if you are in a **commanding position** or have a **commanding lead**, you are likely to win a race or competition **3** [usually before noun] powerful and making people admire and obey you: *a **commanding figure/presence/voice*** **4** [only before noun] if a building is in a **commanding position** or has a **commanding view**, you can see the area around very well from it: *The castle occupies a commanding position on a hill.*

com·mand·ment /kəˈmɑːndmənt; *NAmE* -ˈmæn-/ *noun* a law given by God, especially any of **the Ten Commandments** given to the Jews in the Bible ➲ COLLOCATIONS at RELIGION

comˈmand module *noun* (*abbr.* **CM**) the part of a SPACECRAFT that remains after the rest has separated from it, where the controls and the people that operate them are located

com·mando /kəˈmɑːndəʊ; *NAmE* kəˈmændoʊ/ *noun* (*pl.* **-os**) a soldier or a group of soldiers who are trained to make quick attacks in enemy areas

IDM **go comˈmando** (*informal, humorous*) to not wear underwear under your clothes

comˌmand perˈformance *noun* [usually sing.] a special performance, for example at a theatre, that is given for a head of state

com·media dell'arte /kɒˌmeɪdɪə del ˈɑːteɪ; *NAmE* kəˌmeɪdɪə del ˈɑːrteɪ/ *noun* [U] (from *Italian*) traditional Italian theatre in which the same characters appeared in different plays

com·mem·or·ate /kəˈmeməreɪt/ *verb* **~ sth/sb** to remind people of an important person or event from the past with a special action or object; to exist to remind people of a person or an event from the past: *A series of movies will be shown to commemorate the 30th anniversary of his death.* ◇ *A plaque commemorates the battle.*

com·mem·or·ation /kəˌmeməˈreɪʃn/ *noun* [U, C] an action, or a ceremony, etc. that makes people remember and show respect for an important person or event in the past: *a commemoration service* ◇ *a statue **in commemoration of** a national hero*

com·mem·ora·tive /kəˈmemərətɪv; *NAmE* -əreɪt-/ *adj.* intended to help people remember and respect an important person or event in the past: *commemorative stamps*

com·mence AW /kəˈmens/ *verb* [I, T] (*formal*) to begin to happen; to begin sth: *The meeting is scheduled to commence at noon.* ◇ *I will be on leave during the week commencing 15 February.* ◇ **~ with sth** *The day commenced with a welcome from the principal.* ◇ **~ sth** *She commenced her medical career in 1956.* ◇ **~ doing sth** *We commence building next week.* ◇ **~ to do sth** *Operators commenced to build pipelines in 1862.* ➲ SYNONYMS at START

com·mence·ment AW /kəˈmensmənt/ *noun* [U, C, usually sing.] **1** (*formal*) beginning: *the commencement of the financial year* **2** (*NAmE*) a ceremony at which students receive their academic degrees or DIPLOMAS SYN **graduation**

com·mend /kəˈmend/ *verb* **1 ~ sb (for sth/for doing sth)** | **~ sb (on sth/on doing sth)** to praise sb/sth, especially publicly: *She was commended on her handling of the situation.* ◇ *His designs were **highly commended** by the judges* (= they did not get a prize but they were especially praised). **2 ~ sb/sth (to sb)** (*formal*) to recommend sb/sth to sb: *She is an excellent worker and I commend her to you without reservation.* ◇ *The movie **has little to commend it*** (= it has few good qualities). **3 ~ itself to sb** (*formal*) if sth **commends** itself to sb, they approve of it: *His outspoken behaviour did not commend itself to his colleagues.* **4 ~ sb/sth to sb** (*formal*) to give sb/sth to sb in order to be taken care of: *We commend her soul to God.*

com·mend·able /kəˈmendəbl/ *adj.* (*formal*) deserving praise and approval: *commendable honesty* ▸ **com·mend·ably** /-əbli/ *adv.*

com·men·da·tion /ˌkɒmenˈdeɪʃn; *NAmE* ˌkɑːm-/ *noun* **1** [U] (*formal*) praise; approval **2** [C] **~ (for sth)** an award or official statement giving public praise for sb/sth: *a commendation for bravery*

C

com·men·sal /kə'mensl/ *adj.* (*biology*) living on another animal or plant and getting food from the situation, but doing no harm: *commensal organisms* ▶ **com·men·sal·ism** /kə'menslɪzəm/ *noun* [U]

com·men·sur·ate /kə'menʃərət/ *adj.* **~ (with sth)** (*formal*) matching sth in size, importance, quality, etc: *Salary will be commensurate with experience.* OPP **incommensurate** ▶ **com·men·sur·ate·ly** *adv.*

com·ment 0-ᴡ AW /'kɒment; *NAmE* 'kɑːm-/ *noun, verb*

■ ***noun*** **1** 0-ᴡ [C, U] **~ (about/on sth)** something that you say or write which gives an opinion on or explains sb/sth: *Have you any comment to make about the cause of the disaster?* ◇ *She* ***made*** *helpful* ***comments*** *on my work.* ◇ *The director was not available for comment.* ◇ *He handed me the document without comment.* ◇ (*especially BrE*) *What she said was* ***fair comment*** (= a reasonable criticism). ➲ SYNONYMS at STATEMENT **2** [sing., U] criticism that shows the faults of sth: *The results are a clear comment on government education policy.* ◇ *There was a lot of comment about his behaviour.*

IDM ˌ**no** ˈ**comment** (said in reply to a question, usually from a journalist) I have nothing to say about that: *'Will you resign, sir?' 'No comment!'*

■ ***verb*** 0-ᴡ [I, T] **~ (on/upon sth)** to express an opinion about sth: *I don't feel I can comment on their decision.* ◇ *He refused to comment until after the trial.* ◇ **~ that...** *A spokesperson commented that levels of carbon dioxide were very high.* ◇ **+ speech** *'Not his best performance,' she commented to the woman sitting next to her.*

Synonyms

comment

note • remark • observe

These words all mean to say or write a fact or opinion.

comment to express an opinion or give facts about sth: *He refused to comment until after the trial.*

note (*rather formal*) to mention sth because it is important or interesting: *He noted in passing that the company's record on safety issues was not good.*

remark to say or write what you have noticed about a situation: *Critics remarked that the play was not original.*

observe (*formal*) to say or write what you have noticed about a situation: *She observed that it was getting late.*

COMMENT, REMARK OR OBSERVE?

If you **comment on** sth you say sth about it; if you **remark on** sth or **observe** sth, you say sth about it that you have noticed: there is often not much difference between the three. However, while you can *refuse to comment* (without *on*), you cannot 'refuse to remark' or 'refuse to observe' (without *on*): ~~*He refused to remark/observe until after the trial.*~~

PATTERNS

- to comment/note/remark/observe **that...**
- to comment on/note/remark/observe **how...**
- to comment/remark **on** sth
- to comment/remark/observe **to** sb
- **'It's long,'** he commented/noted/remarked/observed.

com·men·tary AW /'kɒməntri; *NAmE* 'kɑːmənteri/ *noun* (*pl.* -ies) **~ (on sth)** **1** [C, U] a spoken description of an event that is given while it is happening, especially on the radio or television: *a sports commentary* ◇ *Our reporters will give* ***a running commentary*** (= a continuous one) *on the election results as they are announced.* ◇ *He kept up* ***a running commentary*** *on everyone who came in or went out.* **2** [C] a written explanation or discussion of sth such as a book or a play: *a critical commentary on the final speech of the play* **3** [C, U] a criticism or discussion of sth: *The petty quarrels were a sad commentary on the state of the government.* ◇ *political commentary*

com·men·tate /'kɒmənteɪt; *NAmE* 'kɑːm-/ *verb* [I] **~ (on sth)** to give a spoken description of an event as it happens, especially on television or radio: *Who will be commentating on the game?*

com·men·ta·tor AW /'kɒmənteɪtə(r); *NAmE* 'kɑːm-/ *noun* **~ (on sth)** **1** a person who is an expert on a particular subject and talks or writes about it on television or radio, or in a newspaper: *a political commentator* **2** a person who describes an event while it is happening, especially on television or radio: *a* ***television/sports commentator***

com·merce /'kɒmɜːs; *NAmE* 'kɑːmɜːrs/ *noun* [U] trade, especially between countries; the buying and selling of goods and services: *leaders of industry and commerce* ➲ see also CHAMBER OF COMMERCE

com·mer·cial 0-ᴡ /kə'mɜːʃl; *NAmE* kə'mɜːrʃl/ *adj., noun*

■ ***adj.*** **1** 0-ᴡ [usually before noun] connected with the buying and selling of goods and services: *the commercial heart of the city* ◇ *a commercial vehicle* (= one that is used for carrying goods or passengers who pay) ➲ SYNONYMS at ECONOMIC **2** 0-ᴡ [only before noun] making or intended to make a profit: *The movie was not a commercial success* (= did not make money). ◇ *commercial baby foods* ◇ *the first commercial flights across the Atlantic* ➲ SYNONYMS at SUCCESSFUL **3** (*disapproving*) more concerned with profit and being popular than with quality: *Their more recent music is far too commercial.* **4** (of television or radio) paid for by the money charged for broadcasting advertisements: *a commercial radio station/TV channel* ▶ **com·mer·cial·ly** /-ʃəli/ *adv.*: *commercially produced/grown/developed* ◇ *The product is not yet commercially available.* ◇ *His invention was not commercially successful.*

■ ***noun*** an advertisement on the radio or on television ➲ SYNONYMS at ADVERTISEMENT ➲ COLLOCATIONS at TELEVISION

com·mer·cial·ism /kə'mɜːʃəlɪzəm; *NAmE* -'mɜːrʃl-/ *noun* [U] (*disapproving*) the fact of being more interested in making money than in the value or quality of things

com·mer·cial·ize (*BrE* also **-ise**) /kə'mɜːʃəlaɪz; *NAmE* -'mɜːrʃl-/ *verb* [often passive] **~ sth** to use sth to try to make a profit, especially in a way that other people do not approve of: *Their music has become very commercialized in recent years.* ▶ **com·mer·cial·iza·tion, -isa·tion** /kəˌmɜːʃəlaɪ'zeɪʃn; *NAmE* -ˌmɜːrʃlə'z-/ *noun* [U]

comˌmercial ˈtraveller *noun* (*old-fashioned, BrE*) = SALES REPRESENTATIVE

com·mie /'kɒmi; *NAmE* 'kɑːmi/ *noun* (*especially NAmE*) an insulting way of referring to sb that you think has ideas similar to those of COMMUNISTS or SOCIALISTS, or who is a member of a COMMUNIST or SOCIALIST party

com·mingle /kə'mɪŋgl/ *verb* [I, T] (*formal* or *technical*) to mix two or more things together or to be mixed, when it is impossible for the things to be separated afterwards: **~ (with sth)** *The fluid must be prevented from commingling with other fluids.* ◇ **~ sth (with sth)** (*finance*) *Campaign funds must not be commingled with other money.*

com·mis·er·ate /kə'mɪzəreɪt/ *verb* [I, T] **~ (with sb) (on/about/for/over sth)** | **+ speech** to show sb sympathy when they are upset or disappointed about sth: *She commiserated with the losers on their defeat.*

com·mis·er·ation /kəˌmɪzə'reɪʃn/ *noun* [U, C] (*formal*) an expression of sympathy for sb who has had sth unpleasant happen to them, especially not winning a competition: *I offered him my commiseration.* ◇ *Commiserations to the losing team!*

com·mis·sar /ˌkɒmɪ'sɑː(r); *NAmE* ˌkɑːm-/ *noun* an officer of the Communist Party, especially in the past in the Soviet Union

com·mis·sar·iat /ˌkɒmɪ'seəriət; *NAmE* ˌkɑːmɪ'ser-/ *noun* **1** a department of the army that is responsible for food supplies **2** a government department in the Soviet Union before 1946

com·mis·sary /'kɒmɪsəri; *NAmE* 'kɑːmɪseri/ *noun* (*pl.* -ies) (*NAmE*) **1** a shop/store that sells food, etc. in a military base, a prison, etc. **2** a restaurant for people working in a large organization, especially a film studio

com·mis·sion 0-w AW /kəˈmɪʃn/ *noun, verb*

■ *noun*

▸ OFFICIAL GROUP **1** 0-w (often **Commission**) [C] an official group of people who have been given responsibility to control sth, or to find out about sth, usually for the government: *the European Commission* ◇ (*BrE*) *The government has set up a* ***commission of inquiry*** *into the disturbances at the prison.* ◇ *a commission on human rights*

▸ MONEY **2** 0-w [U, C] an amount of money that is paid to sb for selling goods and which increases with the amount of goods that are sold: *You get a 10% commission on everything you sell.* ◇ *He earned £2 000 in commission last month.* ◇ *In this job you work* ***on commission*** (= are paid according to the amount you sell). **3** 0-w [U] an amount of money that is charged by a bank, etc. for providing a particular service: *1% commission is charged for cashing traveller's cheques.*

▸ FOR ART/MUSIC, ETC. **4** 0-w [C] a formal request to sb to design or make a piece of work such as a building or a painting

▸ IN ARMED FORCES **5** [C] an officer's position in the armed forces

▸ OF CRIME **6** [U] (*formal*) the act of doing sth wrong or illegal: *the commission of a crime*

IDM **in/out of comˈmission** available/not available to be used: *Several of the airline's planes are temporarily out of commission and undergoing safety checks.*

■ *verb*

▸ PIECE OF ART/MUSIC, ETC. **1** 0-w to officially ask sb to write, make or create sth or to do a task for you: **~ sb to do sth** *She has been commissioned to write a new national anthem.* ◇ **~ sth** *Publishers have commissioned a French translation of the book.*

▸ IN ARMED FORCES **2** [usually passive] to choose sb as an officer in one of the armed forces: **~ sb** *She was commissioned in 2007.* ◇ **~ sb (as) sth** *He has just been commissioned (as a) pilot officer.*

com·mis·sion·aire /kəˌmɪʃəˈneə(r); *NAmE* -ˈner/ *noun* (*BrE*, becoming *old-fashioned*) a person in uniform whose job is to stand at the entrance to a hotel, etc. and open the door for visitors, find them taxis, etc. ➲ see also DOORMAN

comˌmissioned ˈofficer *noun* an officer in the armed forces who has a higher rank, such as a captain or a GENERAL ➲ compare NON-COMMISSIONED OFFICER

com·mis·sion·er AW /kəˈmɪʃənə(r)/ *noun* **1** (usually **Commissioner**) a member of a COMMISSION (= an official group of people who are responsible for controlling sth or finding out about sth): *the Church Commissioners* (= the group of people responsible for controlling the financial affairs of the Church of England) ◇ *European Commissioners* **2** (also **poˈlice commissioner** especially in *NAmE*) the head of a particular police force in some countries **3** the head of a government department in some countries: *the* ***agriculture/health, etc. commissioner*** ◇ *Commissioner Rhodes was unavailable for comment.* ➲ see also HIGH COMMISSIONER **4** (in the US) an official chosen by a sports association to control it: *the baseball commissioner*

comˌmissioner for ˈoaths *noun* (*BrE*) a lawyer who has official authority to be present when sb makes a formal promise that a written statement that they will use as evidence in court is true

the Comˌmission on Civil ˈRights *noun* [sing.] (in the US) a government organization that works for equal rights for all Americans

com·mit 0-w AW /kəˈmɪt/ *verb* (-tt-)

▸ CRIME **1** 0-w [T] **~ a crime, etc.** to do sth wrong or illegal: *to* ***commit murder/adultery*** ◇ *Most crimes are committed by young men.* ◇ *appalling crimes committed against innocent children*

▸ SUICIDE **2** 0-w [T] **~ suicide** to kill yourself deliberately

▸ PROMISE/SAY DEFINITELY **3** 0-w [T, often passive] to promise sincerely that you will definitely do sth, keep to an agreement or arrangement, etc: **~ sb/yourself (to sth/to doing sth)** *The President is committed to reforming health care.* ◇ *Borrowers should think carefully before committing themselves to taking out a loan.* ◇ **~ sb/yourself to do sth** *Both sides committed themselves to settle the dispute peacefully.* **4** [T] **~ yourself (to sth)** to give an opinion or make a decision openly so that it is then difficult to change it: *You don't have to commit yourself now, just think about it.* ➲ see also NON-COMMITTAL

▸ BE LOYAL **5** [I] **~ (to sb/sth)** to be completely loyal to one person, organization, etc. or give all your time and effort to your work, an activity, etc: *Why are so many men scared to commit?* (= say they will be loyal to one person) ➲ see also COMMITTED

▸ MONEY/TIME **6** [T] **~ sth** to spend money or time on sth/sb: *The council has committed large amounts of money to housing projects.*

▸ TO HOSPITAL/PRISON **7** [T, often passive] **~ sb to sth** to order sb to be sent to a hospital, prison, etc: *She was committed to a psychiatric hospital.*

▸ SB FOR TRIAL **8** [T] **~ sb** to send sb for trial in court

▸ STH TO MEMORY **9** [T] **~ sth to memory** to learn sth well enough to remember it exactly: *She committed the instructions to memory.*

▸ STH TO PAPER/WRITING **10** [T] **~ sth to paper/writing** to write sth down

com·mit·ment 0-w AW /kəˈmɪtmənt/ *noun* **1** 0-w [C, U] a promise to do sth or to behave in a particular way; a promise to support sb/sth; the fact of committing yourself: **~ (to sb/sth)** *She doesn't want to* ***make a*** *big emotional* ***commitment*** *to Steve at the moment.* ◇ *the government's commitment to public services* ◇ **~ to do/doing sth** *The company's commitment to providing quality at a reasonable price has been vital to its success.* **2** 0-w [U] **~ (to sb/sth)** the willingness to work hard and give your energy and time to a job or an activity: *A career as an actor requires one hundred per cent commitment.* **3** 0-w [C] a thing that you have promised or agreed to do, or that you have to do: *He's busy for the next month with filming commitments.* ◇ *Women very often have to juggle work with their family commitments.* **4** [U, C] **~ (of sth) (to sth)** agreeing to use money, time or people in order to achieve sth: *the commitment of resources to education* ◇ *Achieving success at this level requires a commitment of time and energy.*

com·mit·tal /kəˈmɪtl/ *noun* [U] (*technical*) the official process of sending sb to prison or to a mental hospital: *He was released on bail pending committal proceedings.*

com·mit·ted AW /kəˈmɪtɪd/ *adj.* (*approving*) willing to work hard and give your time and energy to sth; believing strongly in sth: *a committed member of the team* ◇ *They are committed socialists.* OPP **uncommitted**

com·mit·tee 0-w /kəˈmɪti/ *noun* [C+sing./pl. v.] a group of people who are chosen, usually by a larger group, to make decisions or to deal with a particular subject: *She's on the management committee.* ◇ *The committee has/have decided to close the restaurant.* ◇ *a committee member/a member of the committee* ◇ *a committee meeting*

com·mode /kəˈməʊd; *NAmE* kəˈmoʊd/ *noun* **1** a piece of furniture that looks like a chair but has a toilet under the seat **2** a piece of furniture, especially an old or ANTIQUE one, with drawers for storing things in

com·modi·ous /kəˈməʊdiəs; *NAmE* -ˈmoʊ-/ *adj.* (*formal*) having a lot of space

com·mod·ity AW /kəˈmɒdəti; *NAmE* -ˈmɑːd-/ *noun* (*pl.* -ies) **1** (*economics*) a product or a raw material that can be bought and sold: *rice, flour and other basic commodities* ◇ *a drop in commodity prices* ◇ *Crude oil is the world's most important commodity.* ➲ SYNONYMS at PRODUCT **2** (*formal*) a thing that is useful or has a useful quality: *Water is a precious commodity that is often taken for granted in the West.*

com·mo·dore /ˈkɒmədɔː(r); *NAmE* ˈkɑːm-/ *noun* (*abbr.* Cdre) an officer of high rank in the navy: *Commodore John Barry*

com·mon 0-ᵚ /ˈkɒmən; *NAmE* ˈkɑːmən/ *adj., noun*
■ *adj.* (com·mon·er, com·mon·est) HELP **more common** and **most common** are more frequent **1** 0-ᵚ happening often; existing in large numbers or in many places: *Jackson is a common English name.* ◇ *Breast cancer is the most common form of cancer among women in this country.* ◇ *Some birds which were once* ***a common sight*** *are now becoming rare.* ◇ *a common spelling mistake* OPP **uncommon** **2** 0-ᵚ [usually before noun] **~ (to sb/sth)** shared by or belonging to two or more people or by the people in a group: *They share a common interest in photography.* ◇ *basic features which are common to all human languages* ◇ *We are working together for a common purpose.* ◇ *common ownership of the land* ◇ *This decision was taken for the* ***common good*** (= the advantage of everyone). ◇ *It is,* ***by common consent****, Scotland's prettiest coast* (= everyone agrees that it is). **3** 0-ᵚ [only before noun] ordinary; not unusual or special: *the common garden frog* ◇ *Shakespeare's work was popular among* ***the common people*** *in his day.* ◇ *In most people's eyes she was nothing more than a* ***common criminal.*** ◇ *You'd think he'd have the* ***common courtesy*** *to apologize* (= this would be the polite behaviour that people would expect). ◇ *It's only* ***common decency*** *to let her know what's happening* (= people would expect it). **4** (*BrE, disapproving*) typical of sb from a low social class and not having good manners: *She thought he was very common and uneducated.*
IDM **ˌcommon or ˈgarden** (*BrE*) (*NAmE* **ˈgarden-variety**) (*informal*) ordinary; with no special features **the ˌcommon ˈtouch** the ability of a powerful or famous person to talk to and understand ordinary people **make common ˈcause with sb** (*formal*) to be united with sb about sth that you both agree on, believe in or wish to achieve ➲ more at KNOWLEDGE
■ *noun* **1** [C] an area of open land in a town or village that anyone may use: *We went for a walk on the common.* ◇ *Wimbledon Common* **2 commons** [sing.] (*US*) a large room where students can eat in a school, college, etc: *The commons is next to the gym.* ➲ see also COMMONS
IDM **have sth in common (with sb)** 0-ᵚ (of people) to have the same interests, ideas, etc. as sb else: *Tim and I have nothing in common./I have nothing in common with Tim.* **have sth in common (with sth)** 0-ᵚ (of things, places, etc.) to have the same features, characteristics, etc: *The two cultures have a lot in common.* **in common** (*technical*) by everyone in a group: *They hold the property as tenants in common.* **in common with sb/sth** (*formal*) in the same way as sb/sth: *Britain, in common with many other industrialized countries, has experienced major changes over the last 100 years.*

the ˌcommon ˈcold *noun* [sing.] = COLD *n* (2)

ˌcommon deˈnominator *noun* **1** (*mathematics*) a number that can be divided exactly by all the numbers below the line in a set of FRACTIONS ➲ compare DENOMINATOR **2** an idea, attitude or experience that is shared by all the members of a group ➲ see also LOWEST COMMON DENOMINATOR

com·mon·er /ˈkɒmənə(r); *NAmE* ˈkɑːm-/ *noun* a person who does not come from a royal or NOBLE family ➲ compare ARISTOCRAT

ˌCommon ˈEra *noun* [sing.] (*abbr.* CE) the period since the birth of Christ when the Christian CALENDAR starts counting years: *1890 CE*

ˌcommon ˈground *noun* [U] opinions, interests and aims that you share with sb, although you may not agree with them about other things: *Despite our disagreements, we have been able to find some common ground.*

com·mon·hold /ˈkɒmənhəʊld; *NAmE* ˈkɑːmənhoʊld/ *noun* [U] (*BrE, law*) a system in which each person owns their flat/apartment in a building but the building and shared areas are owned by everyone together

ˈcommon land *noun* [U] (*BrE*) land that belongs to or may be used by the local community

ˌcommon ˈlaw *noun* [U] (in England) a system of laws that have been developed from customs and from decisions made by judges, not created by Parliament ➲ compare CASE LAW, STATUTE LAW

ˌcommon-law ˈhusband, ˌcommon-law ˈwife *noun* a person that a woman or man has lived with for a long time and who is recognized as a husband or wife, without a formal marriage ceremony

com·mon·ly 0-ᵚ /ˈkɒmənli; *NAmE* ˈkɑːm-/ *adv.* usually; very often; by most people: *Christopher is commonly known as Kit.* ◇ *commonly held opinions* ◇ *This is one of the most commonly used methods.*

ˌcommon ˈmarket *noun* **1** [C, usually sing.] a group of countries that have agreed on low taxes on goods traded between countries in the group, and higher fixed taxes on goods imported from countries outside the group **2 the Common Market** [sing.] a former name of the European Union

ˌcommon ˈnoun *noun* (*grammar*) a word such as *table, cat,* or *sea*, that refers to an object or a thing but is not the name of a particular person, place or thing ➲ compare ABSTRACT NOUN, PROPER NOUN

com·mon·place /ˈkɒmənpleɪs; *NAmE* ˈkɑːm-/ *adj., noun*
■ *adj.* done very often, or existing in many places, and therefore not unusual: *Computers are now commonplace in primary classrooms.*
■ *noun* (*formal*) **1** [usually sing.] an event, etc. that happens very often and is not unusual **2** a remark, etc. that is not new or interesting

ˈcommonplace book *noun* (especially in the past) a book into which you copy parts of other books, poems, etc. and add your own comments

ˌcommon ˈrat *noun* = BROWN RAT

ˈcommon room *noun* (*especially BrE*) a room used by the teachers or students of a school, college, etc. when they are not teaching or studying

Com·mons /ˈkɒmənz; *NAmE* ˈkɑːm-/ *noun* **the Commons** [pl.] = THE HOUSE OF COMMONS ➲ compare THE LORDS

ˌcommon ˈsense *noun* [U] the ability to think about things in a practical way and make sensible decisions: *For goodness' sake, just use your common sense!* ◇ *a common-sense approach to a problem*

com·mon·wealth /ˈkɒmənwelθ; *NAmE* ˈkɑːm-/ *noun* [sing.] **1 the Commonwealth** an organization consisting of the United Kingdom and other countries, including most of the countries that used to be part of the British Empire: *a member of the Commonwealth* ◇ *Commonwealth countries* **2** (usually **the Commonwealth**) used in the official names of, and to refer to, some states of the US (Kentucky, Massachusetts, Pennsylvania and Virginia): *the Commonwealth of Virginia* ◇ *The city and the Commonwealth have lost a great leader.* **3** (*NAmE*) an independent country that is strongly connected to the US: *Puerto Rico remains a US commonwealth, not a state.* **4** (usually **Commonwealth**) used in the names of some groups of countries or states that have chosen to be politically linked with each other: *the Commonwealth of Independent States (CIS)*

com·mo·tion /kəˈməʊʃn; *NAmE* -ˈmoʊ-/ *noun* [C, usually sing., U] sudden noisy confusion or excitement: *I heard a commotion and went to see what was happening.* ◇ *The crowd waiting outside was causing a commotion.*

com·mu·nal /kəˈmjuːnl; *BrE* also ˈkɒmjənl/ *adj.* **1** shared by, or for the use of, a number of people, especially people who live together SYN **shared**: *a* ***communal kitchen/garden, etc.*** ◇ *As a student he tried communal living for a few years.* **2** involving different groups of people in a community: *communal violence between religious groups* ▸ **com·mu·nal·ly** *adv.*: *The property was owned communally.*

com·mu·nal·ism /kəˈmjuːnəlɪzəm; ˈkɒmjənəl-; *NAmE* ˈkɑːm-/ *noun* [U] **1** the fact of living together and sharing possessions and responsibilities **2** (*IndE*) a strong sense of belonging to a particular, especially religious, community, which can lead to extreme behaviour or violence towards others

com·mune *noun, verb*

▪ ***noun*** /ˈkɒmjuːn; *NAmE* ˈkɑːm-/ [C+sing./pl. v.] **1** a group of people who live together and share responsibilities, possessions, etc: *a 1970s hippy commune* **2** the smallest division of local government in France and some other countries

▪ ***verb*** /kəˈmjuːn/

PHR V **comˈmune with sb/sth** (*formal*) to share your emotions and feelings with sb/sth without speaking: *He spent much of this time* ***communing with nature.***

com·mu·nic·able AW /kəˈmjuːnɪkəbl/ *adj.* (*formal*) that sb can pass on to other people or communicate to sb else: *communicable diseases*

com·mu·ni·cant /kəˈmjuːnɪkənt/ *noun* a person who receives COMMUNION in a Christian church service

com·mu·ni·cate 0‒ AW /kəˈmjuːnɪkeɪt/ *verb*

▸ EXCHANGE INFORMATION **1** 0‒ [I, T] to exchange information, news, ideas, etc. with sb: *We only communicate by email.* ◇ *They communicated in sign language.* ◇ **~ with sb/sth** *Dolphins use sound to communicate with each other.* ◇ **~ sth (to sb)** *to communicate information/a message to sb* ➲ SYNONYMS at TALK

▸ SHARE IDEAS/FEELINGS **2** 0‒ [I, T] to make your ideas, feelings, thoughts, etc. known to other people so that they understand them: *Candidates must be able to communicate effectively.* ◇ **~ sth (to sb)** *He was eager to communicate his ideas to the group.* ◇ *Her nervousness was communicating itself to the children.* ◇ **~ how/what, etc...** *They failed to communicate what was happening and why.* **3** 0‒ [I] **~ (with sb)** to have a good relationship because you are able to understand and talk about your own and other people's thoughts, feelings, etc: *The novel is about a family who can't communicate with each other.*

▸ DISEASE **4** [T, usually passive] **~ sth** to pass a disease from one person, animal, etc. to another: *The disease is communicated through dirty drinking water.*

▸ OF TWO ROOMS **5** [I] if two rooms **communicate**, they are next to each other and you can get from one to the other: *a* ***communicating door*** (= one that connects two rooms)

com·mu·ni·ca·tion 0‒ AW /kəˌmjuːnɪˈkeɪʃn/ *noun*

1 0‒ [U] the activity or process of expressing ideas and feelings or of giving people information: *Speech is the fastest method of communication between people.* ◇ *All channels of communication need to be kept open.* ◇ *Doctors do not always have good* ***communication skills.*** ◇ *non-verbal communication* ◇ *We are in regular communication by email.* **2** 0‒ [U] (also **communications** [pl.]) methods of sending information, especially telephones, radio, computers, etc. or roads and railways: ***communication systems/links/technology*** ◇ *The new airport will improve communications between the islands.* ◇ *Snow has prevented communication with the outside world for three days.* **3** [C] (*formal*) a message, letter or telephone call: *a communication from the leader of the party*

com·mu·ni·ca·tive AW /kəˈmjuːnɪkətɪv; *NAmE* -keɪtɪv/ *adj.* **1** willing to talk and give information to other people: *I don't find him very communicative.* OPP **uncommunicative** **2** connected with the ability to communicate in a language, especially a foreign language: *communicative skills*

the comˈmunicative approach *noun* [sing.] (also **comˌmunicative ˈlanguage teaching** [U]) a method of teaching a foreign language which stresses the importance of learning to communicate information and ideas in the language

comˌmunicative ˈcompetence *noun* [U] (*linguistics*) a person's ability to communicate information and ideas in a foreign language

com·mu·ni·ca·tor /kəˈmjuːnɪkeɪtə(r)/ *noun* a person who communicates sth to others: *an effective/skilled/successful communicator* ◇ *a poor communicator* ➲ SYNONYMS at SPEAKER

com·mu·nion /kəˈmjuːniən/ *noun* **1** (also **Communion, ˌHoly Comˈmunion**) [U] a ceremony in the Christian Church during which people eat bread and drink wine in memory of the last meal that Christ had with his DISCIPLES: *to go to Communion* (= attend church for this celebration) ◇ *to* ***take/receive communion*** (= receive the bread and wine) ➲ see also EUCHARIST, MASS **2** [U] **~ (with sb/sth)** (*formal*) the state of sharing or exchanging thoughts and feelings; the feeling of being part of sth: *poets living in communion with nature* **3** [C] (*technical*) a group of people with the same religious beliefs: *the Anglican communion*

com·mu·ni·qué /kəˈmjuːnɪkeɪ; *NAmE* kəˌmjuːnəˈkeɪ/ *noun* an official statement or report, especially to newspapers

com·mun·ism /ˈkɒmjunɪzəm; *NAmE* ˈkɑːm-/ *noun* [U] **1** a political movement that believes in an economic system in which the state controls the means of producing everything on behalf of the people. It aims to create a society in which everyone is treated equally. **2 Communism** the system of government by a ruling Communist Party, such as in the former Soviet Union ➲ compare CAPITALISM

com·mun·ist /ˈkɒmjənɪst; *NAmE* ˈkɑːm-/ *noun* **1** a person who believes in or supports communism **2 Communist** a member of a Communist Party ▸ **com·mun·ist** (also **Communist**) *adj.*: *communist ideology* ◇ *a Communist country/government/leader*

the ˈCommunist Party *noun* a political party that supports COMMUNISM or rules in a COMMUNIST country

com·mu·nity 0‒ AW /kəˈmjuːnəti/ *noun* (*pl.* -ies) **1** 0‒ [sing.] all the people who live in a particular area, country, etc. when talked about as a group: *The* ***local community*** *was shocked by the murders.* ◇ *health workers based in the community* (= working with people in a local area) ◇ ***the international community*** (= the countries of the world as a group) ◇ *good community relations with the police* ◇ (*NAmE*) ***community parks/libraries*** (= paid for by the local town/city) **2** 0‒ [C+sing./pl. v.] a group of people who share the same religion, race, job, etc: *the Polish community in London* ◇ *ethnic communities* ◇ *the farming community* **3** 0‒ [U] the feeling of sharing things and belonging to a group in the place where you live: *There is a strong sense of community in this town.* ◇ *community spirit* ➲ COLLOCATIONS at TOWN **4** [C] (*biology*) a group of plants and animals growing or living in the same place or environment

comˌmunity ˈcare (also **ˌcare in the comˈmunity**) *noun* [U] (*BrE*) medical and other care for people who need help over a long period, which allows them to live at home rather than in a hospital

comˈmunity centre (*BrE*) (*NAmE* **comˈmunity center**) *noun* a place where people from the same area can meet for social events or sports or to take classes

comˈmunity college *noun* **1** (also **comˈmunity school**) (in Britain) a SECONDARY SCHOOL that is open to adults from the local community as well as to its own students **2** (in the US) a college that is mainly for students from the local community and that offers programmes that are two years long, including programmes in practical skills.

comˌmunity ˈlanguage learning *noun* [U] a method of teaching a foreign language that uses small groups and other ways of reducing students' anxiety

comˌmunity ˈproperty *noun* [U] (*NAmE, law*) property that is considered to belong equally to a married couple

comˌmunity ˈservice *noun* [U] work helping people in the local community that sb does without being paid, either because they want to, or because they have been ordered to by a court as a punishment

com·mut·able /kəˈmjuːtəbl/ *adj.* **1** (of a place or a distance) close enough or short enough to make travelling to

C

work every day a possibility **2** (*law*) a **commutable** punishment can be made less severe **3** (*formal*) able to be changed

com·mu·ta·tion /ˌkɒmjuˈteɪʃn; *NAmE* ˌkɑːm-/ *noun* [C, U] **1** (*law*) the act of making a punishment less severe: *a commutation of the death sentence to life imprisonment* **2** (*finance*) the act of replacing one method of payment with another; a payment that is replaced with another

com·mu·ta·tive /kəˈmjuːtətɪv/ *adj.* (*mathematics*) (of a calculation) giving the same result whatever the order in which the quantities are shown

com·mu·ta·tor /ˈkɒmjuteɪtə(r); *NAmE* ˈkɑːm-/ *noun* (*physics*) **1** a device that connects a motor to the electricity supply **2** a device for changing the direction in which electricity flows

com·mute /kəˈmjuːt/ *verb, noun*

■ ***verb*** **1** [I, T] to travel regularly by bus, train, car, etc. between your place of work and your home: **~ (from A) (to B)** *She commutes from Oxford to London every day.* ◇ **~ between A and B** *He spent that year commuting between New York and Chicago.* ◇ *I live **within commuting distance of** Dublin.* ◇ **~ sth** *People are prepared to commute long distances if they are desperate for work.* **2** [T] **~ sth (to sth)** (*law*) to replace one punishment with another that is less severe **3** [T] **~ sth (for/into sth)** (*finance*) to exchange one form of payment, for sth else

■ ***noun*** the journey that a person makes when they commute to work: *a two-hour commute into downtown Washington* ◇ *I have only a short commute to work.*

com·muter /kəˈmjuːtə(r)/ *noun* a person who travels into a city to work each day, usually from quite far away: (*BrE*) *the **commuter belt*** (= the area around a city where people live and from which they travel to work in the city)

comp /kɒmp; *NAmE* kɑːmp/ *noun* (*informal*) **1** [C] (*BrE*) = COMPREHENSIVE *n.*: *Her children go to the local comp.* **2** [C] (*BrE*) = COMPETITION **3** [C] (*NAmE*) a COMPLIMENTARY ticket, meal, etc. (= one that you do not have to pay for) **4** [U] (*NAmE*) = COMPENSATION: ***comp time*** (= time off work given for working extra hours)

com·pact *adj., noun, verb*

■ ***adj.*** /kəmˈpækt; ˈkɒmpækt; *NAmE* ˈkɑːm-/ **1** smaller than is usual for things of the same kind: *a compact camera* **2** using or filling only a small amount of space: *The kitchen was compact but well equipped.* **3** closely and firmly packed together: *a compact mass of earth* **4** (of a person or an animal) small and strong: *He had a compact and muscular body.* ▸ **com·pact·ly** *adv.* **com·pact·ness** *noun* [U]

■ ***noun*** /ˈkɒmpækt; *NAmE* ˈkɑːm-/ **1** (*NAmE*) a small car ➲ compare SUBCOMPACT **2** a small flat box with a mirror, containing powder that women use on their faces ➲ VISUAL VOCAB page V49 **3** (*formal*) a formal agreement between two or more people or countries

■ ***verb*** /kəmˈpækt/ [usually passive] **~ sth** to press sth together firmly: *a layer of compacted snow*

ˌcompact ˈdisc *noun* = CD

com·padre /kɒmˈpɑːdreɪ; *NAmE* kəm-/ *noun* (*NAmE*, *informal*, from *Spanish*) used as a friendly way of addressing sb

com·pan·ion /kəmˈpæniən/ *noun* **1** a person or an animal that travels with you or spends a lot of time with you: *travelling companions* ◇ (*figurative*) *Fear was the hostages' constant companion.* **2** a person who has similar tastes, interests, etc. to your own and whose company you enjoy: *She was a charming dinner companion.* ◇ *His younger brother is not much of a companion for him.* ◇ *They're drinking companions* (= they go out drinking together). **3** a person who shares in your work, pleasures, sadness, etc: *We became companions in misfortune.* **4** a person, usually a woman, employed to live with and help sb, especially sb old or ill/sick **5** one of a pair of things that go together or can be used together: *A companion volume is soon to be published.* **6** used in book titles to describe a book giving useful facts and information on a particular subject: *A Companion to French Literature* ➲ see also BOON COMPANION

com·pan·ion·able /kəmˈpæniənəbl/ *adj.* friendly ▸ **com·pan·ion·ably** /-əbli/ *adv.*

com·pan·ion·ship /kəmˈpæniənʃɪp/ *noun* [U] the pleasant feeling that you have when you have a friendly relationship with sb and are not alone: *They meet at the club for companionship and advice.* ◇ *She had only her cat for companionship.*

com·pan·ion·way /kəmˈpæniənweɪ/ *noun* (*technical*) a set of stairs on a ship

com·pany 0-★ /ˈkʌmpəni/ *noun* (*pl.* -ies)

▸ BUSINESS **1** 0-★ [C+sing./pl. v.] (*abbr.* Co.) (often in names) a business organization that makes money by producing or selling goods or services: *the largest computer company in the world* ◇ *the National Bus Company* ◇ *She joined the company in 2009.* ◇ *Company profits were 5% lower than last year.* ➲ COLLOCATIONS at BUSINESS

▸ THEATRE/DANCE **2** 0-★ (often in names) [C+sing./pl. v.] a group of people who work or perform together: *a **theatre/dance, etc. company*** ◇ *the Royal Shakespeare Company*

▸ BEING WITH SB **3** 0-★ [U] the fact of being with sb else and not alone: *I enjoy Jo's company* (= I enjoy being with her). ◇ *She enjoys her own company* (= being by herself) *when she is travelling.* ◇ *The children are very **good company*** (= pleasant to be with) *at this age.* ◇ *a pleasant evening in the company of friends* ◇ *He's coming with me **for company**.*

▸ GUESTS **4** [U] (*formal*) guests in your house: *I didn't realize you **had company**.*

▸ GROUP OF PEOPLE **5** [U] (*formal*) a group of people together: *She told the assembled company what had happened.* ◇ *It is bad manners to whisper **in company*** (= in a group of people).

▸ SOLDIERS **6** [C+sing./pl. v.] a group of soldiers that is part of a BATTALION

IDM **the ˈcompany sb keeps** the people that sb spends time with: *Judging by the company he kept, Mark must have been a wealthy man.* **get into/keep bad ˈcompany** to be friends with people that others disapprove of **in company with sb/sth** (*formal*) together with or at the same time as sb/sth: *She arrived in company with the ship's captain.* ◇ *The US dollar went through a difficult time, in company with the oil market.* **in good ˈcompany** if you say that sb is **in good company**, you mean that they should not worry about a mistake, etc. because sb else, especially sb more important, has done the same thing **keep sb ˈcompany** to stay with sb so that they are not alone: *I'll keep you company while you're waiting.* **two's ˈcompany (, three's a ˈcrowd)** (*saying*) used to suggest that it is better to be in a group of only two people than have a third person with you as well ➲ more at PART *v.*, PRESENT *adj.*

company ˈcar *noun* a car which is provided by the company that you work for

com·par·able /ˈkɒmpərəbl; *NAmE* ˈkɑːm-/ *adj.* **~ (to/with sb/sth)** similar to sb/sth else and able to be compared: *A comparable house in the south of the city would cost twice as much.* ◇ *The situation in the US is not directly comparable to that in the UK.* ◇ *Inflation is now at a rate comparable with that in other European countries.* ▸ **com·par·abil·ity** /ˌkɒmpərəˈbɪləti; *NAmE* ˌkɑːm-/ *noun* [U]: *Each group will have the same set of questions, in order to ensure comparability.*

com·para·tive /kəmˈpærətɪv/ *adj., noun*

■ ***adj.*** **1** connected with studying things to find out how similar or different they are: *a comparative study of the educational systems of two countries* ◇ *comparative linguistics* **2** measured or judged by how similar or different it is to sth else SYN **relative**: *Then he was living in comparative comfort* (= compared with others or with his own life at a previous time). ◇ *The company is a comparative newcomer to the software market* (= other companies have been in business much longer). **3** (*grammar*) relating to adjectives or adverbs that express more in amount, degree or quality, for example *better, worse, slower* and *more difficult* ➲ compare SUPERLATIVE

■ ***noun*** (*grammar*) the form of an adjective or adverb that expresses more in amount, degree or quality: *'Better' is the comparative of 'good' and 'more difficult' is the comparative of 'difficult'.* ➲ compare SUPERLATIVE

com·para·tive·ly /kəm'pærətɪvli/ *adv.* as compared to sth/sb else SYN **relatively**: *The unit is comparatively easy to install and cheap to operate.* ◇ *He died comparatively young* (= at a younger age than most people die). ◇ *comparatively few/low/rare/recent*

com·pare /kəm'peə(r); *NAmE* -'per/ *verb, noun*

■ ***verb*** **1** (*abbr.* cf., cp.) [T] to examine people or things to see how they are similar and how they are different: **~ A and B** *It is interesting to compare their situation and ours.* ◇ *We compared the two reports carefully.* ◇ **~ A with/to B** *We carefully compared the first report with the second.* ◇ *My own problems seem insignificant* ***compared with*** *other people's.* ◇ *I've had some difficulties, but they were* ***nothing compared to*** *yours* (= they were not nearly as bad as yours). ◇ *Standards in health care have improved enormously compared to 40 years ago.* ➲ LANGUAGE BANK at CONTRAST, ILLUSTRATE **2** [I] **~ with sb/sth** to be similar to sb/sth else, either better or worse: *This school compares with the best in the country* (= it is as good as them). ◇ *This house doesn't compare with our previous one* (= it is not as good). ◇ *Their prices* ***compare favourably*** *with those of their competitors.* **3** [T] **~ A to B** to show or state that sb/sth is similar to sb/sth else: *The critics compared his work to that of Martin Amis.*

IDM **compare 'notes (with sb)** if two or more people **compare notes**, they each say what they think about the same event, situation, etc. **you can't compare ˌapples and 'oranges** (*NAmE*) it is impossible to say that one thing is better than another if the two are completely different: *They are both great but you can't compare apples and oranges.*

■ ***noun***

IDM **beyond/without com'pare** (*literary*) better than anything else of the same kind

com·pari·son /kəm'pærɪsn/ *noun*

1 [U] **~ (with sb/sth)** the process of comparing two or more people or things: *Comparison with other oil-producing countries is extremely interesting.* ◇ *I enclose the two plans* ***for comparison.*** ◇ *The education system* ***bears/stands no comparison with*** (= is not as good as) *that in many Asian countries.* **2** [C] an occasion when two or more people or things are compared: **~ of A and B** *a comparison of the rail systems in Britain and France* ◇ **~ of A with B** *a comparison of men's salaries with those of women* ◇ **~ between A and B** *comparisons between Britain and the rest of Europe* ◇ **~ of A to B** *a comparison of the brain to a computer* (= showing what is similar) ◇ **~ (with sth)** *It is difficult to* ***make a comparison*** *with her previous book—they are completely different.* ◇ *You can* ***draw comparisons*** *with the situation in Ireland* (= say how the two situations are similar). ➲ LANGUAGE BANK at SIMILARLY ➲ WRITING TUTOR page WT6

IDM **by comparison** used especially at the beginning of a sentence when the next thing that is mentioned is compared with sth in the previous sentence: *By comparison, expenditure on education increased last year.* **by/in comparison (with sb/sth)** when compared with sb/sth: *The second half of the game was dull by comparison with the first.* ◇ *The tallest buildings in London are small in comparison with New York's skyscrapers.* **there's no com'parison** used to emphasize the difference between two people or things that are being compared: *In terms of price there's no comparison* (= one thing is much more expensive than the other). ➲ more at PALE *v.*

com·part·ment /kəm'pɑːtmənt; *NAmE* -'pɑːrt-/ *noun* **1** one of the separate sections which a coach/car on a train is divided into **2** one of the separate sections that sth such as a piece of furniture or equipment has for keeping things in: *The desk has a secret compartment.* ◇ *There is a handy storage compartment beneath the oven.* ➲ see also GLOVE COMPARTMENT

com·part·men·tal·ize (*BrE* also **-ise**) /ˌkɒmpɑːt'mentəlaɪz; *NAmE* kəmˌpɑːrt-/ *verb* **~ sth (into sth)** to divide sth into separate sections, especially so that one thing does not affect the other: *Life today is rigidly compartmentalized into work and leisure.*

com·pass /'kʌmpəs/ *noun* **1** (also **magˌnetic 'compass**) [C] an instrument for finding direction, with a needle that always points to the north: *a map and compass* ◇ *the* ***points of the compass*** (= N, S, E, W, etc.) ➲ VISUAL VOCAB page V34 **2** [C] (also **compasses** [pl.]) an instrument with two long thin parts joined together at the top, used for drawing circles and measuring distances on a map: *a pair of compasses* **3** [sing.] (*formal*) a range or an extent, especially of what can be achieved in a particular situation: *the compass of a singer's voice* (= the range from the lowest to the highest note that he or she can sing)

compasses

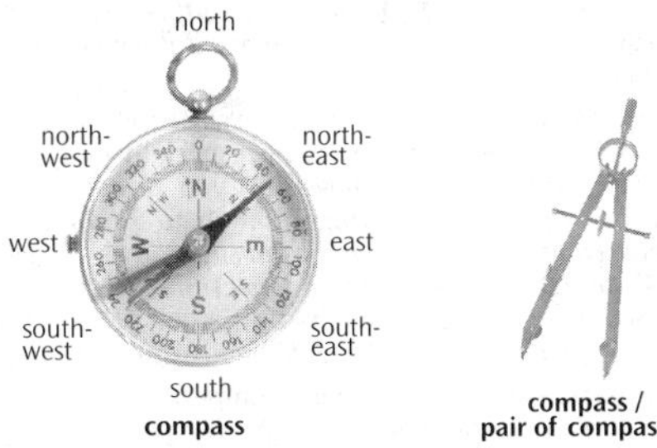

com·pas·sion /kəm'pæʃn/ *noun* [U] **~ (for sb)** a strong feeling of sympathy for people who are suffering and a desire to help them: *to* ***feel/show compassion***

com·pas·sion·ate /kəm'pæʃənət/ *adj.* feeling or showing sympathy for people who are suffering: *He was allowed to go home on compassionate grounds* (= because he was suffering). ▶ **com·pas·sion·ate·ly** *adv.*

comˌpassionate 'leave *noun* [U] (*BrE*) time that you are allowed to be away from work because sb in your family is ill/sick or has died

com·pati·bil·ity AW /kəmˌpætə'bɪləti/ *noun* [U] **~ (with sb/sth)** | **~ (between A and B)** **1** the ability of people or things to live or exist together without problems **2** the ability of machines, especially computers, and computer programs to be used together

com·pat·ible AW /kəm'pætəbl/ *adj.* **1 ~ (with sth)** (of machines, especially computers) able to be used together: *compatible software* ◇ *The new system will be compatible with existing equipment.* **2 ~ (with sth)** (of ideas, methods or things) able to exist or be used together without causing problems: *Are measures to protect the environment compatible with economic growth?* ◇ *compatible blood groups* **3 ~ (with sb)** if two people are **compatible**, they can have a good relationship because they have similar ideas, interests, etc. OPP **incompatible** ▶ **com·pat·ibly** /-əbli/ *adv.*

com·pat·riot /kəm'pætriət; *NAmE* -'peɪt-/ *noun* a person who was born in, or is a citizen of, the same country as sb else SYN **countryman**: *He played against one of his compatriots in the semi-final.*

com·pel /kəm'pel/ *verb* (-ll-) (*formal*) **1** to force sb to do sth; to make sth necessary: **~ sb to do sth** *The law can compel fathers to make regular payments for their children.* ◇ *I* ***feel compelled to*** *write and tell you how much I enjoyed your book.* ◇ **~ sth** *Last year ill health compelled his retirement.* **2 ~ sth** (not used in the progressive tenses) to cause a particular reaction: *He spoke with an authority that compelled the attention of the whole crowd.* ➲ see also COMPULSION

com·pel·ling /kəm'pelɪŋ/ *adj.* **1** that makes you pay attention to it because it is so interesting and exciting: *Her latest book makes compelling reading.* ➲ SYNONYMS at INTERESTING **2** so strong that you must do sth about it: *a* ***compelling need/desire*** **3** that makes you think it is true: *There is no compelling reason to believe him.* ◇ *compelling evidence* ▶ **com·pel·ling·ly** *adv.*: *compellingly attractive*

com·pen·dious /kəm'pendiəs/ *adj.* (*formal*) containing all the necessary facts about sth: *a compendious description*

C

com·pen·dium /kəm'pendiəm/ *noun* (*pl.* **com·pen·dia** /-diə/ or **com·pen·diums**) a collection of facts, drawings and photographs on a particular subject, especially in a book

com·pen·sate AW /'kɒmpenseɪt; *NAmE* 'kɑːm-/ *verb* **1** [I] **~ (for sth)** to provide sth good to balance or reduce the bad effects of damage, loss, etc. SYN **make up for**: *Nothing can compensate for the loss of a loved one.* **2** [T] **~ sb (for sth)** to pay sb money because they have suffered some damage, loss, injury, etc: *Her lawyers say she should be compensated for the suffering she had been caused.* ▸ **com·pen·sa·tory** AW /ˌkɒmpen'seɪtəri; *NAmE* kəm'pensətɔːri/ *adj.*: *He received a compensatory payment of $20 000.*

com·pen·sa·tion AW /ˌkɒmpen'seɪʃn; *NAmE* ˌkɑːm-/ *noun* **1** [U, C] **~ (for sth)** something, especially money, that sb gives you because they have hurt you, or damaged sth that you own; the act of giving this to sb: *to* ***claim/award/receive compensation*** ◇ *to pay compensation for injuries at work* ◇ *to receive £10 000* ***in compensation.*** **2** [C, usually pl.] **~ (for sth)** things that make a bad situation better: *I wish I were young again, but getting older has its compensations.*

com·père /'kɒmpeə(r); *NAmE* 'kɑːmper/ *noun, verb*
■ ***noun*** (*BrE*) a person who introduces the people who perform in a television programme, show in a theatre, etc. SYN **emcee**: *to act as (a) compère*
■ ***verb*** [T, I] **~ (sth)** (*BrE*) to act as a compère for a show

com·pete 0-w /kəm'piːt/ *verb* **1** 0-w [I, T] to try to be more successful or better than sb else who is trying to do the same as you: **~ (with/against sb) (for sth)** *Several companies are competing for the contract.* ◇ *We can't compete with them on price.* ◇ *Young children will usually compete for their mother's attention.* ◇ *Small traders cannot compete in the face of cheap foreign imports.* ◇ **~ to do sth** *There are too many magazines competing to attract readers.* **2** 0-w [I] **~ (in sth) (against sb)** to take part in a contest or game: *He's hoping to compete in the London marathon.*

com·pe·tence /'kɒmpɪtəns; *NAmE* 'kɑːm-/ *noun* **1** (also *less frequent* **com·pe·ten·cy**) [U, C] **~ (in sth)** | **~ (in doing sth)** the ability to do sth well: *to gain a high level of competence in English* ◇ *professional/technical competence* OPP **incompetence 2** [U] (*law*) the power that a court, an organization or a person has to deal with sth: *The judge has to act within the competence of the court.* ◇ *outside sb's area of competence* **3** [C] (also *less frequent* **com·pe·ten·cy**) (*technical*) a skill that you need in a particular job or for a particular task: *The syllabus lists the knowledge and competences required at this level.*

com·pe·tency /'kɒmpɪtənsi; *NAmE* 'kɑːm-/ *noun* (*pl.* -ies) = COMPETENCE

com·pe·tent /'kɒmpɪtənt; *NAmE* 'kɑːm-/ *adj.* **~ (to do sth) 1** having enough skill or knowledge to do sth well or to the necessary standard: *Make sure the firm is competent to carry out the work.* ◇ *He's very competent in his work.* OPP **incompetent 2** of a good standard but not very good **3** having the power to decide sth: *The case was referred to a competent authority.* ▸ **com·pe·tent·ly** *adv.*: *to perform competently*

com·pe·ti·tion 0-w /ˌkɒmpə'tɪʃn; *NAmE* ˌkɑːm-/ *noun* **1** 0-w [U] **~ (between/with sb) (for sth)** a situation in which people or organizations compete with each other for sth that not everyone can have: *There is now intense competition between schools to attract students.* ◇ *We are* ***in competition with*** *four other companies for the contract.* ◇ *We won the contract in the face of* ***stiff competition.*** **2** 0-w [C] an event in which people compete with each other to find out who is the best at sth: *a* ***music/photo, etc. competition*** ◇ *to* ***enter/win/lose a competition*** **3 the competition** [sing.+ sing./pl. v.] the people who are competing against sb: *We'll be able to assess the competition at the conference.*

com·peti·tive 0-w /kəm'petətɪv/ *adj.* **1** 0-w used to describe a situation in which people or organizations compete against each other: ***competitive games/sports*** ◇ *Graduates have to fight for jobs in a* ***highly competitive*** *market.* **2** 0-w **~ (with sb/sth)** as good as or better than others: *a shop selling clothes at competitive prices* (= as low as any other shop) ◇ *We need to work harder to remain competitive with other companies.* ◇ *to gain a* ***competitive advantage*** *over rival companies* ➲ SYNONYMS at CHEAP **3** 0-w (of a person) trying very hard to be better than others: *You have to be highly competitive to do well in sport these days.* OPP **uncompetitive** ▸ **com·peti·tive·ly** *adv.*: *competitively priced goods* **com·peti·tive·ness** *noun*: *the competitiveness of British industry*

com·peti·tor /kəm'petɪtə(r)/ *noun* **1** a person or an organization that competes against others, especially in business: *our* ***main/major competitor*** **2** a person who takes part in a competition: *Over 200 competitors entered the race.*

com·pil·ation AW /ˌkɒmpɪ'leɪʃn; *NAmE* ˌkɑːm-/ *noun* **1** [C] a collection of items, especially pieces of music or writing, taken from different places and put together: *Her latest CD is a compilation of all her best singles.* ◇ *a compilation album* **2** [U] the process of compiling sth: *the compilation of a dictionary*

com·pile AW /kəm'paɪl/ *verb* **1 ~ sth** to produce a book, list, report, etc. by bringing together different items, articles, songs, etc: *We are trying to compile a list of suitable people for the job.* ◇ *The album was compiled from live recordings from last year's tour.* **2 ~ sth** (*computing*) to translate instructions from one computer language into another so that a particular computer can understand them

com·piler /kəm'paɪlə(r)/ *noun* **1** a person who compiles sth **2** (*computing*) a program that translates instructions from one computer language into another for a computer to understand

Synonyms

complain

protest • object • grumble • moan • whine

These words all mean to say that you are annoyed, unhappy or not satisfied about sb/sth.

complain to say that you are annoyed, unhappy or not satisfied about sb/sth: *I'm going to complain to the manager about this.*

protest to say or do sth to show that you disagree with or disapprove of sth, especially publicly; to give sth as a reason for protesting: *Students took to the streets to* ***protest against*** *the decision.*

object to say that you disagree with or disapprove of sth; to give sth as a reason for objecting: *If nobody objects, we'll postpone the meeting till next week.* ◇ *He objected that the police had arrested him without sufficient evidence.*

grumble (*rather informal, disapproving*) to complain about sb/sth in a bad-tempered way: *They kept grumbling that they were cold.*

moan (*BrE, rather informal, disapproving*) to complain about sb/sth in an annoying way: *What are you moaning on about now?*

whine (*rather informal, disapproving*) to complain in an annoying, crying voice: *Stop whining!* ◇ *'I want to go home,' whined Toby.* NOTE **Whine** is often used to talk about the way that young children complain.

PATTERNS
- to complain/protest/grumble/moan/whine **about** sth
- to complain/protest/grumble/moan **at** sth
- to complain/protest/object/grumble/moan/whine **to** sb
- to complain/protest/object/grumble/moan/whine **that...**

com·pla·cency /kəm'pleɪsnsi/ *noun* [U] (usually *disapproving*) a feeling of satisfaction with yourself or with a situation, so that you do not think any change is necessary; the state of being complacent: *Despite signs of an improvement in the economy, there is no room for complacency.*

com·pla·cent /kəm'pleɪsnt/ *adj.* ~ **(about sb/sth)** (usually *disapproving*) too satisfied with yourself or with a situation, so that you do not feel that any change is necessary; showing or feeling complacency: *a dangerously complacent attitude to the increase in unemployment* ◇ *We must not become complacent about progress.* ▸ **com·pla·cent·ly** *adv.*

com·plain 0-ᴡ /kəm'pleɪn/ *verb* [I, T] to say that you are annoyed, unhappy or not satisfied about sb/sth: ~ **(to sb)** **(about/of sth)** *I'm going to complain to the manager about this.* ◇ *The defendant complained of intimidation during the investigation.* ◇ *She never complains, but she's obviously exhausted.* ◇ (*informal*) *'How are you?' 'Oh, I can't complain* (= I'm all right).' ◇ ~ **(that)...** *He* ***complained bitterly*** *that he had been unfairly treated.* ◇ **+ speech** *'It's not fair,' she complained.*
PHR V **com'plain of sth** to say that you feel ill/sick or are suffering from a pain: *She left early, complaining of a headache.*

com·plain·ant *noun* (*BrE, law*) = PLAINTIFF

com·plaint 0-ᴡ /kəm'pleɪnt/ *noun* **1** 0-ᴡ [C] a reason for not being satisfied; a statement that sb makes saying that they are not satisfied: ~ **(about sb/sth)** *The most common complaint is about poor service.* ◇ *We received a number of complaints from customers about the lack of parking facilities.* ◇ *I'd like to* ***make a complaint*** *about the noise.* ◇ ~ **(against sb/sth)** *I believe you have a complaint against one of our nurses.* ◇ ~ **(that...)** *a* ***complaint that*** *he had been unfairly treated* ◇ *a* ***formal complaint*** ◇ (*formal*) *to* ***file/lodge*** (= make) ***a complaint*** ➲ WRITING TUTOR page WT24 **2** 0-ᴡ [U] the act of complaining: *I can see no* ***grounds for complaint.*** ◇ *a letter of complaint* **3** [C] an illness, especially one that is not serious, and often one that affects a particular part of the body: *a skin complaint*

com·plai·sant /kəm'pleɪzənt/ *adj.* (*old-fashioned*) ready to accept other people's actions and opinions and to do what other people want ▸ **com·plai·sance** /kəm'pleɪzəns/ *noun* [U]

com·plect·ed /kəm'plektɪd/ *adj.* (*NAmE, informal*) (used with adjectives) with skin and a COMPLEXION of the type mentioned: ***fair/dark complected***

com·ple·ment AW *verb, noun*
■ ***verb*** /'kɒmplɪment; *NAmE* 'kɑːm-/ ~ **sth** to add to sth in a way that improves it or makes it more attractive: *The excellent menu is complemented by a good wine list.* ◇ *The team needs players who* ***complement each other.*** ➲ note at COMPLIMENT
■ ***noun*** /'kɒmplɪmənt; *NAmE* 'kɑːm-/ **1** ~ **(to sth)** a thing that adds new qualities to sth in a way that improves it or makes it more attractive **2** the complete number or quantity needed or allowed: *We've taken our full complement of trainees this year.* **3** (*grammar*) a word or phrase, especially an adjective or a noun, that is used after linking verbs such as *be* and *become*, and describes the subject of the verb. In some descriptions of grammar it is used to refer to any word or phrase which is GOVERNED by a verb and usually comes after the verb in a sentence: *In the sentences 'I'm angry' and 'He became a politician', 'angry' and 'politician' are complements.*

com·ple·men·tary AW /ˌkɒmplɪ'mentri; *NAmE* ˌkɑːm-/ *adj.* ~ **(to sth)** two people or things that are **complementary** are different but together form a useful or attractive combination of skills, qualities or physical features: *The school's approach must be complementary to that of the parents.* ➲ note at COMPLIMENT

ˌcomplementary 'angle *noun* (*geometry*) either of two angles which together make 90° ➲ compare SUPPLEMENTARY ANGLE

ˌcomplementary 'colour (*especially US* **ˌcomplementary 'color**) *noun* (*technical*) **1** a colour that, when mixed with another colour, gives black or white **2** a colour that gives the greatest contrast when combined with a particular colour: *The designer has chosen the complementary colours blue and orange.*

ˌcomplementary 'medicine *noun* [U] (*BrE*) medical treatment that is not part of the usual scientific treatment used in Western countries, for example ACUPUNCTURE

com·ple·men·ta·tion /ˌkɒmplɪmen'teɪʃn; *NAmE* ˌkɑːm-/ *noun* [U] **1** the fact of complementing sth **2** (*grammar*) the complements of a verb in a clause

com·ple·men·tizer (*BrE* also **-iser**) /'kɒmplɪməntaɪzə(r); *NAmE* 'kɑːm-/ *noun* (*grammar*) a word or part of a word that shows a clause is being used as a complement

com·plete 0-ᴡ /kəm'pliːt/ *adj., verb*
■ ***adj.*** **1** 0-ᴡ [usually before noun] used when you are emphasizing sth, to mean 'to the greatest degree possible' SYN **total**: *We were in complete agreement.* ◇ *a complete change* ◇ *in complete silence* ◇ *a complete stranger* ◇ *It came as a complete surprise.* ◇ *I felt a complete idiot.* **2** 0-ᴡ including all the parts, etc. that are necessary; whole: *I've collected the complete set.* ◇ *a complete guide to events in Oxford* ◇ *the* ***complete works*** *of Tolstoy* ◇ *You will receive payment for each complete day that you work.* OPP **incomplete** **3** ~ **with sth** [not before noun] including sth as an extra part or feature: *The furniture comes complete with tools and instructions for assembly.* ◇ *The book, complete with CD, costs £35.* **4** 0-ᴡ [not before noun] finished: *Work on the office building will be complete at the end of the year.* OPP **incomplete** ▸ **com·plete·ness** *noun* [U]: *the accuracy and completeness of the information* ◇ *For the sake of completeness, all names are given in full.*
■ ***verb*** **1** 0-ᴡ [often passive] ~ **sth** to finish making or doing sth: *She's just completed a master's degree in Law.* ◇ *The project should be completed within a year.* **2** 0-ᴡ ~ **sth** to write all the information you are asked for on a form SYN **fill in/out**: *2 000 shoppers completed our questionnaire.* **3** 0-ᴡ ~ **sth** to make sth whole or perfect: *I only need one more card to complete the set.*

com·plete·ly 0-ᴡ /kəm'pliːtli/ *adv.* (used to emphasize the following word or phrase) in every way possible SYN **totally**: *completely different* ◇ *completely and utterly broke* ◇ *I've completely forgotten her name.* ◇ *The explosion completely destroyed the building.*

com·ple·tion /kəm'pliːʃn/ *noun* **1** [U] the act or process of finishing sth; the state of being finished and complete: *the completion of the new hospital building* ◇ *Satisfactory completion of the course does not ensure you a job.* ◇ *The project is* ***due for completion*** *in the spring.* ◇ *The road is* ***nearing completion*** (= it is nearly finished). ◇ *the date of completion/the completion date* **2** [U, C] (*BrE*) the formal act of completing the sale of property, for example the sale of a house

com·plex 0-ᴡ AW *adj., noun*
■ ***adj.*** /'kɒmpleks; *NAmE* kəm'pleks; 'kɑːm-/ **1** 0-ᴡ made of many different things or parts that are connected; difficult to understand SYN **complicated**: *complex machinery* ◇ *the complex structure of the human brain* ◇ *a complex argument/problem/subject* **2** (*grammar*) (of a word or sentence) containing one main part (= the ROOT of a word or MAIN CLAUSE of a sentence) and one or more other parts (called AFFIXES or SUBORDINATE CLAUSES) ➲ compare COMPOUND *adj.*
■ ***noun*** /'kɒmpleks; *NAmE* 'kɑːm-/ **1** a group of buildings of a similar type together in one place: *a sports complex* ◇ *an industrial complex* (= a site with many factories) ➲ SYNONYMS at BUILDING **2** a group of things that are connected: *This is just one of a whole complex of issues.* **3** (especially in compounds) a mental state that is not normal: *to suffer from a guilt complex* ➲ see also INFERIORITY COMPLEX, OEDIPUS COMPLEX, PERSECUTION COMPLEX **4** if sb has a **complex** about sth, they are worried about it in way that is not normal

com·plex·ion /kəm'plekʃn/ *noun* **1** the natural colour and condition of the skin on a person's face: *a pale/bad* *complexion* ➲ COLLOCATIONS at PHYSICAL **2** [usually sing.] the general character of sth: *a move which changed the political complexion of the country*

IDM **put a new/different com'plexion on sth** to change the way that a situation appears

C

com·plex·ity AW /kəm'pleksəti/ *noun* **1** [U] the state of being formed of many parts; the state of being difficult to understand: *the increasing complexity of modern telecommunication systems* ◇ *I was astonished by the size and complexity of the problem.* **2 complexities** [pl.] the features of a problem or situation that are difficult to understand: *the complexities of the system*

ˌcomplex 'number *noun* (*mathematics*) a number containing both a REAL NUMBER and an IMAGINARY NUMBER

com·pli·ance /kəm'plaɪəns/ *noun* [U] ~ (**with sth**) the practice of obeying rules or requests made by people in authority: *procedures that must be followed to ensure full compliance with the law* ◇ *Safety measures were carried out* ***in compliance with*** *paragraph 6 of the building regulations.* OPP **non-compliance** ➲ see also COMPLY

com·pli·ant /kəm'plaɪənt/ *adj.* **1** (usually *disapproving*) too willing to agree with other people or to obey rules: *By then, Henry seemed less compliant with his wife's wishes than he had six months before.* ◇ *We should not be producing compliant students who do not dare to criticize.* **2** in agreement with a set of rules: *This site is HTML compliant.* ➲ see also COMPLY

com·pli·cate 0-m /'kɒmplɪkeɪt; *NAmE* 'kɑːm-/ *verb* **~ sth** to make sth more difficult to do, understand or deal with: *I do not wish to complicate the task more than is necessary.* ◇ ***To complicate matters*** *further, there will be no transport available till 8 o'clock.* ◇ *The issue* ***is complicated by the fact that*** *a vital document is missing.*

com·pli·cated 0-m /'kɒmplɪkeɪtɪd; *NAmE* 'kɑːm-/ *adj.* made of many different things or parts that are connected; difficult to understand SYN **complex**: *a complicated system* ◇ *The instructions look very complicated.* ◇ *It's all very complicated—but I'll try and explain.*

com·pli·ca·tion /ˌkɒmplɪ'keɪʃn; *NAmE* ˌkɑːm-/ *noun* **1** [C, U] a thing that makes a situation more complicated or difficult: *The bad weather added a further complication to our journey.* **2** [C, usually pl.] (*medical*) a new problem or illness that makes treatment of a previous one more complicated or difficult: *She developed complications after the surgery.*

com·pli·cit /kəm'plɪsɪt/ *adj.* ~ (**in/with sb/sth**) involved with other people in sth wrong or illegal: *Several officers were complicit in the cover-up.*

com·pli·city /kəm'plɪsəti/ *noun* [U] ~ (**in sth**) (*formal*) the act of taking part with another person in a crime SYN **collusion**: *to be guilty of complicity in the murder* ◇ *evident complicity between the two brothers*

com·pli·ment *noun, verb*

- ***noun*** /'kɒmplɪmənt; *NAmE* 'kɑːm-/ **1** [C] a remark that expresses praise or admiration of sb: ***to pay sb a compliment*** (= to praise them for sth) ◇ *'You understand the problem because you're so much older.' 'I'll* ***take that as a compliment!'*** ◇ *It's a* ***great compliment*** *to be asked to do the job.* ◇ *to* ***return the compliment*** (= to treat sb in the same way as they have treated you) **2 compliments** [pl.] (*formal*) polite words or good wishes, especially when used to express praise and admiration: *My compliments to the chef!* ◇ (*BrE*) *Compliments of the season!* (= for Christmas or the New Year) ◇ *Please accept these flowers* ***with the compliments of*** (= as a gift from) *the manager.* IDM see BACKHANDED
- ***verb*** /'kɒmplɪment; *NAmE* 'kɑːm-/ **~ sb** (**on sth**) to tell sb that you like or admire sth they have done, their appearance, etc: *She complimented him on his excellent German.*

Which Word?

compliment / complement

- These words have similar spellings but completely different meanings. If you **compliment** someone, you say something very nice to them: *She complimented me on my English.* If one thing **complements** another, the two things work or look better because they are together: *The different flavours complement each other perfectly.*
- The adjectives are also often confused. **Complimentary**: *She made some very complimentary remarks about my English.* It can also mean 'free': *There was a complimentary basket of fruit in our room.* **Complementary**: *The team members have different but complementary skills.*

com·pli·men·tary /ˌkɒmplɪ'mentri; *NAmE* ˌkɑːm-/ *adj.* **1** given free: *complimentary tickets for the show* **2 ~** (**about sth**) expressing admiration, praise, etc: *a complimentary remark* ◇ *She was extremely complimentary about his work.* OPP **uncomplimentary** ➲ note at COMPLIMENT

'compliments slip *noun* (*BrE*) a small piece of paper printed with the name of a company, that is sent out together with information, goods, etc.

com·ply /kəm'plaɪ/ *verb* (**com·plies, com·ply·ing, com·plied, com·plied**) [I] **~** (**with sth**) to obey a rule, an order, etc: *They refused to comply with the UN resolution.* ➲ see also COMPLIANCE

compo /'kɒmpəʊ; *NAmE* 'kɑːmpoʊ/ *noun* [U] (*AustralE, NZE, informal*) money that is paid to a worker if he/she gets injured at work SYN **compensation**

com·pon·ent AW /kəm'pəʊnənt; *NAmE* -'poʊ-/ *noun* one of several parts of which sth is made: *the components of a machine* ◇ *the car component industry* ◇ ***Key components*** *of the government's plan are...* ◇ *Trust is a* ***vital component*** *in any relationship.* ▶ **com·pon·ent** *adj.* [only before noun]: *Break the problem down into its* ***component parts.***

com·pon·en·tial an·aly·sis /kɒmpəˌnenʃl ə'næləsɪs; *NAmE* kɑːm-/ *noun* [U] (*linguistics*) the study of meaning by analysing the different parts of words

com·port /kəm'pɔːt; *NAmE* -'pɔːrt/ *verb* **~ yourself + adv./prep.** (*formal*) to behave in a particular way: *She always comports herself with great dignity.*

com·port·ment /kəm'pɔːtmənt; *NAmE* -'pɔːrt-/ *noun* [U] (*formal*) the way in which sb/sth behaves: *She won admiration for her comportment during the trial.*

com·pose /kəm'pəʊz; *NAmE* -'poʊz/ *verb* **1** [T] (not used in the progressive tenses) **~ sth** (*formal*) to combine together to form a whole SYN **make up**: *Ten men compose the committee.* ➲ see also COMPOSED **2** [T, I] **~** (**sth**) to write music: *Mozart composed his last opera shortly before he died.* **3** [T] **~ a letter/speech/poem** to write a letter, etc. usually with a lot of care and thought: *She composed a letter of protest.* **4** [T, no passive] (*formal*) to manage to control your feelings or expression: **~ yourself** *Emma frowned, making an effort to compose herself.* ◇ **~ sth** *I was so confused that I could hardly compose my thoughts.* ➲ see also COMPOSURE

com·posed /kəm'pəʊzd; *NAmE* -'poʊzd/ *adj.* **1 be composed of sth** (*formal*) to be made or formed from several parts, things or people: *The committee is composed mainly of lawyers.* ➲ SYNONYMS at CONSIST OF **2** [not usually before noun] calm and in control of your feelings: *She seemed outwardly composed.*

com·poser /kəm'pəʊzə(r); *NAmE* -'poʊz-/ *noun* a person who writes music, especially CLASSICAL music

com·pos·ite /'kɒmpəzɪt; *NAmE* kəm'pɑːzət/ *adj., noun*

- ***adj.*** [only before noun] made of different parts or materials: *a composite picture* (= one made from several pictures)
- ***noun*** **1** something made by putting together different parts or materials: *The document was a composite of information from various sources.* **2** (also **com'posite sketch**)

(both *US*) (*BrE* **Iden·ti·kit™**) a set of drawings of different features that can be put together to form the face of a person, especially sb wanted by the police, using descriptions given by people who saw the person; a picture made in this way

com·pos·ition /ˌkɒmpəˈzɪʃn; *NAmE* ˌkɑːm-/ *noun* **1** [U] the different parts which sth is made of; the way in which the different parts are organized: *the chemical composition of the soil* ◇ *the composition of the board of directors* ➲ SYNONYMS at STRUCTURE **2** [C] (*formal*) a piece of music or art, or a poem: *one of Beethoven's finest compositions* **3** [U] the act of COMPOSING sth: *pieces performed in the order of their composition* **4** [U] the art of writing music: *to study composition* **5** [C] a short text that is written as a school exercise; a short essay **6** [U] (*art*) the arrangement of people or objects in a painting or photograph

com·posi·tor /kəmˈpɒzɪtə(r); *NAmE* -ˈpɑːz-/ *noun* a person who arranges text on a page before printing

com·pos men·tis /ˌkɒmpəs ˈmentɪs; *NAmE* ˌkɑːm-/ *adj.* [not before noun] (from *Latin*, *formal* or *humorous*) having full control of your mind OPP **non compos mentis**

com·post /ˈkɒmpɒst; *NAmE* ˈkɑːmpoʊst/ *noun, verb*

▪ ***noun*** [U, C] a mixture of decayed plants, food, etc. that can be added to soil to help plants grow: ***potting compost*** (= a mixture of soil and compost that you can buy to grow new plants in) ➲ VISUAL VOCAB page V7

▪ ***verb*** **1 ~ sth** to make sth into compost **2 ~ sth** to put compost on or in sth

ˈcompost bin *noun* a container in the garden where leaves, plants, etc. are put, to make compost ➲ VISUAL VOCAB pages V7, V16

ˈcompost heap (*especially BrE*) (*NAmE* usually **ˈcompost pile**) *noun* a place in the garden where leaves, plants, etc. are piled, to make compost

com·pos·ure /kəmˈpəʊʒə(r); *NAmE* -ˈpoʊ-/ *noun* [U] the state of being calm and in control of your feelings or behaviour: *to* ***keep/lose/recover/regain your composure***

com·pote /ˈkɒmpɒt; *NAmE* ˈkɑːmpoʊt/ *noun* [C, U] a cold DESSERT (= a sweet dish) made of fruit that has been cooked slowly with sugar

com·pound AW *noun, adj., verb*

▪ ***noun*** /ˈkɒmpaʊnd; *NAmE* ˈkɑːm-/ **1** a thing consisting of two or more separate things combined together **2** (*chemistry*) a substance formed by a chemical reaction of two or more elements in fixed amounts relative to each other: *Common salt is a compound of sodium and chlorine.* ➲ compare ELEMENT, MIXTURE **3** (*grammar*) a noun, an adjective or a verb made of two or more words or parts of words, written as one or more words, or joined by a hyphen. *Travel agent*, *dark-haired* and *bathroom* are all compounds. **4** an area surrounded by a fence or wall in which a factory or other group of buildings stands: *a prison compound*

▪ ***adj.*** /ˈkɒmpaʊnd; *NAmE* ˈkɑːm-/ [only before noun] (*technical*) formed of two or more parts: *a compound adjective, such as fair-skinned* ◇ *A compound sentence contains two or more clauses.*

▪ ***verb*** /kəmˈpaʊnd/ **1** [often passive] **~ sth** to make sth bad become even worse by causing further damage or problems: *The problems were compounded by severe food shortages.* **2 be compounded of/from sth** (*formal*) to be formed from sth: *The DNA molecule is compounded from many smaller molecules.* **3** [often passive] **~ sth (with sth)** (*formal* or *technical*) to mix sth together: *liquid soaps compounded with disinfectant* **4 ~ sth** (*finance*) to pay or charge interest on an amount of money that includes any interest already earned or charged

ˌcompound ˈeye *noun* (*biology*) an eye like that of most insects, made up of several parts that work separately

ˌcompound ˈfracture *noun* an injury in which a bone in the body is broken and part of the bone comes through the skin ➲ compare SIMPLE FRACTURE

ˌcompound ˈinterest *noun* [U] interest that is paid both on the original amount of money saved and on the interest that has been added to it ➲ compare SIMPLE INTEREST

com·pre·hend /ˌkɒmprɪˈhend; *NAmE* ˌkɑːm-/ *verb* [I, T] (often used in negative sentences) (*formal*) to understand sth fully: *He stood staring at the dead body, unable to comprehend.* ◇ **~ sth** *The infinite distances of space are too great for the human mind to comprehend.* ◇ **~ how/why, etc...** *She could not comprehend how someone would risk people's lives in that way.* ◇ **~ that...** *He simply could not comprehend that she could be guilty.* ➲ SYNONYMS at UNDERSTAND

com·pre·hen·sible /ˌkɒmprɪˈhensəbl; *NAmE* ˌkɑːm-/ *adj.* **~ (to sb)** (*formal*) that can be understood by sb: ***easily/readily comprehensible*** *to the average reader* OPP **incomprehensible** ▸ **com·pre·hen·sib·il·ity** /ˌkɒmprɪˌhensəˈbɪləti; *NAmE* ˌkɑːm-/ *noun* [U]

com·pre·hen·sion /ˌkɒmprɪˈhenʃn; *NAmE* ˌkɑːm-/ *noun* **1** [U] the ability to understand: *speech and comprehension* ◇ *His behaviour was completely* ***beyond comprehension*** (= impossible to understand). ◇ *She had no comprehension of what was involved.* **2** [U, C] an exercise that trains students to understand a language: *listening comprehension* ◇ *a reading comprehension*

com·pre·hen·sive AW /ˌkɒmprɪˈhensɪv; *NAmE* ˌkɑːm-/ *adj., noun*

▪ ***adj.*** **1** including all, or almost all, the items, details, facts, information, etc, that may be concerned SYN **complete, full**: *a comprehensive list of addresses* ◇ *a comprehensive study* ◇ *comprehensive insurance* (= covering all risks) **2** (*BrE*) (of education) designed for students of all abilities in the same school ▸ **com·pre·hen·sive·ness** *noun* [U]

▪ ***noun*** (also **compreˈhensive school**) (also *informal* **comp**) (in Britain) a SECONDARY SCHOOL for young people of all levels of ability

com·pre·hen·sive·ly AW /ˌkɒmprɪˈhensɪvli; *NAmE* ˌkɑːm-/ *adv.* completely; thoroughly: *They were comprehensively beaten in the final.*

com·press *verb, noun*

▪ ***verb*** /kəmˈpres/ **1** [T, I] to press or squeeze sth together or into a smaller space; to be pressed or squeezed in this way: **~ sth (into sth)** *compressed air/gas* ◇ **~ (into sth)** *Her lips compressed into a thin line.* **2** [T] **~ sth (into sth)** to reduce sth and fit it into a smaller space or amount of time SYN **condense**: *The main arguments were compressed into one chapter.* **3** [T] **~ sth** (*computing*) to make computer files, etc. smaller so that they use less space on a disk, etc. OPP **decompress** ▸ **com·pres·sion** /kəmˈpreʃn/ *noun* [U]: *the compression of air* ◇ *data compression*

▪ ***noun*** /ˈkɒmpres; *NAmE* ˈkɑːm-/ a cloth that is pressed onto a part of the body to stop the loss of blood, reduce pain, etc.

com·pres·sor /kəmˈpresə(r)/ *noun* a machine that compresses air or other gases

com·prise AW /kəmˈpraɪz/ *verb* (not used in the progressive tenses) (*formal*) **1** (also **be comprised of**) **~ sth** to have sb/sth as parts or members SYN **consist of**: *The collection comprises 327 paintings.* ◇ *The committee is comprised of representatives from both the public and private sectors.* **2 ~ sth** to be the parts or members that form sth SYN **make sth up**: *Older people comprise a large proportion of those living in poverty.* ➲ SYNONYMS at CONSIST OF ➲ LANGUAGE BANK at PROPORTION

com·prom·ise /ˈkɒmprəmaɪz; *NAmE* ˈkɑːm-/ *noun, verb*

▪ ***noun*** **1** [C] an agreement made between two people or groups in which each side gives up some of the things they want so that both sides are happy at the end: *After lengthy talks the two sides finally* ***reached a compromise***. ◇ *In any relationship, you have to* ***make compromises***. ◇ *a* ***compromise solution/agreement/candidate*** **2** [C] **~ (between A and B)** a solution to a problem in which two or more things cannot exist together as they are, in which each thing is reduced or changed slightly so that they can exist together: *This model represents the best compromise between price and quality.* **3** [U] the act of reaching a compromise: *Compromise is an inevitable part of life.* ◇ *There is no prospect of compromise in sight.*

▪ ***verb*** **1** [I] to give up some of your demands after a disagreement with sb, in order to reach an agreement: *Neither side is prepared to compromise.* ◇ **~ (with sb) (on sth)** *After much argument, the judges finally compromised on* (= agreed to give the prize to) *the 18-year old pianist.* ◇ *They were unwilling to compromise with the terrorists.* **2** [T, I] to do sth that is against your principles or does not reach standards that you have set: **~ sth** *I refuse to compromise my principles.* ◇ **~ (on sth)** *We are not prepared to compromise on safety standards.* **3** [T] **~ sb/sth/yourself** to bring sb/sth/yourself into danger or under suspicion, especially by acting in a way that is not very sensible: *She had already compromised herself by accepting his invitation.* ◇ *Defeat at this stage would* **compromise their chances** (= reduce their chances) *of reaching the finals of the competition.*

com·prom·is·ing /ˈkɒmprəmaɪzɪŋ; *NAmE* ˈkɑːm-/ *adj.* if sth is **compromising**, it shows or tells people sth that you want to keep secret, because it is wrong or embarrassing: *compromising photos* ◇ *They were discovered together in a* **compromising situation**.

comp·trol·ler /kənˈtrəʊlə(r); *NAmE* -ˈtroʊ-/ *noun* = CONTROLLER (3)

com·pul·sion /kəmˈpʌlʃn/ *noun* **1** [U, C] (*formal*) strong pressure that makes sb do sth that they do not want to do: **~ (to do sth)** *You are under no compulsion to pay immediately.* ◇ **~ (on sb) to do sth** *There are no compulsions on students to attend classes.* **2** [C] **~ (to do sth)** a strong desire to do sth, especially sth that is wrong, silly or dangerous SYN **urge**: *He felt a great compulsion to tell her everything.* ➲ see also COMPEL

com·pul·sive /kəmˈpʌlsɪv/ *adj.* **1** (of behaviour) that is difficult to stop or control: ***compulsive eating/spending/gambling*** **2** (of people) not being able to control their behaviour: *a* ***compulsive drinker/gambler/liar*** **3** that makes you pay attention to it because it is so interesting and exciting: *The programme made compulsive viewing.* ▸ **com·pul·sive·ly** *adv.*: *She watched him compulsively.* ◇ *a compulsively readable book*

com·pul·sory /kəmˈpʌlsəri/ *adj.* that must be done because of a law or a rule SYN **mandatory**: ***It is compulsory for*** *all motorcyclists to wear helmets.* ◇ *English is a* ***compulsory subject*** *at this level.* ◇ ***compulsory education/schooling*** ◇ *compulsory redundancies* OPP **voluntary** ▸ **com·pul·sor·ily** /kəmˈpʌlsərəli/ *adv.*: *Over 600 workers were made compulsorily redundant.*

comˌpulsory ˈpurchase *noun* [U, C] (*BrE*) an occasion when sb is officially ordered to sell land or property to the government or other authority: *a compulsory purchase order*

com·punc·tion /kəmˈpʌŋkʃn/ *noun* [U] (also [C] in *NAmE*) **~ (about doing sth)** (*formal*) a guilty feeling about doing sth: *She felt no compunction about leaving her job.* ◇ *He had lied to her without compunction.* ◇ (*US*) *She has no compunctions about rejecting the plan.*

com·pu·ta·tion AW /ˌkɒmpjuˈteɪʃn; *NAmE* ˌkɑːm-/ *noun* [C, U] (*formal*) an act or the process of calculating sth: *All the statistical computations were performed by the new software system.* ◇ *an error in the computation*

com·pu·ta·tion·al AW /ˌkɒmpjuˈteɪʃənl; *NAmE* ˌkɑːm-/ *adj.* [usually before noun] using or connected with computers: *computational methods* ◇ *a computational approach*

compuˌtational linˈguistics *noun* [U] the study of language and speech using computers

com·pute AW /kəmˈpjuːt/ *verb* **~ sth** (*formal*) to calculate sth: *The losses were computed at £5 million.* ▸ **com·put·able** AW *adj.*

com·puter O-w AW /kəmˈpjuːtə(r)/ *noun* an electronic machine that can store, organize and find information, do calculations and control other machines: *a personal computer* ◇ *Our sales information is processed by computer.* ◇ *a computer program* ◇ ***computer software/hardware/graphics*** ◇ *a computer error* ◇ *computer-aided design* ➲ VISUAL VOCAB page V54 ➲ see also DESKTOP COMPUTER, MICROCOMPUTER, PERSONAL COMPUTER, SUPERCOMPUTER

comˈputer game *noun* a game played on a computer

com·pu·ter·ize (*BrE* also **-ise**) /kəmˈpjuːtəraɪz/ *verb* **1 ~ sth** to provide a computer or computers to do the work of sth: *The factory has been fully computerized.* **2 ~ sth** to store information on a computer: *computerized databases* ◇ *The firm has computerized its records.* ▸ **com·pu·ter·iza·tion, -isa·tion** /kəmˌpjuːtəraɪˈzeɪʃn; *NAmE* -rəˈz-/ *noun* [U]

comˌputer-ˈliterate (also **com·puter·ate**) *adj.* able to use computers well ▸ **comˌputer ˈliteracy** *noun* [U]

comˌputer ˈscience *noun* [U] the study of computers and how they can be used: *a degree in computer science* ▸ **comˌputer ˈscientist** *noun*

com·put·ing AW /kəmˈpjuːtɪŋ/ *noun* [U] the fact of using computers: *to work in computing* ◇ *to study computing* ◇ ***educational/network/scientific computing*** ◇ ***computing power/services/skills/systems*** ➲ VISUAL VOCAB pages V54, V55

com·rade /ˈkɒmreɪd; *NAmE* ˈkɑːmræd/ *noun* **1** a person who is a member of the same COMMUNIST or SOCIALIST political party as the person speaking **2** (*BrE* also ˌ**comrade-in-ˈarms**) (*old-fashioned*) a friend or other person that you work with, especially as soldiers during a war: *They were old army comrades.* ▸ **com·rade·ly** /ˈkɒmreɪdli; *NAmE* ˈkɑːmrædli/ *adj.* **com·rade·ship** /ˈkɒmreɪdʃɪp; *NAmE* ˈkɑːmræd-/ *noun* [U]: (*formal*) *There was a sense of comradeship between them.*

Con. *abbr.* (in British politics) CONSERVATIVE

con /kɒn; *NAmE* kɑːn/ *noun, verb*

■ ***noun*** (*informal*) **1** [sing.] (also *BrE formal* ˈ**confidence trick**) (also *NAmE formal* ˈ**confidence game**) a trick; an act of cheating sb: *The so-called bargain was just a big con!* ◇ (*BrE*) *a con trick* ◇ (*NAmE*) *a con game* ◇ *He's a real* ***con artist*** (= a person who regularly cheats others). ➲ see also CON MAN, MOD CONS **2** [C] = CONVICT IDM see PRO *n.*

■ ***verb*** (-nn-) (*informal*) to trick sb, especially in order to get money from them or persuade them to do sth for you: **~ sb (into doing sth)** *I was conned into buying a useless car.* ◇ **~ sb (out of sth)** *They had been conned out of £100 000.* ◇ **~ your way into sth** *He conned his way into the job using false references.* ➲ SYNONYMS at CHEAT

con·ation /kəˈneɪʃn/ *noun* [U] (*philosophy, psychology*) a mental process that makes you want to do sth or decide to do sth ▸ **cona·tive** /ˈkɒnətɪv; *NAmE* ˈkɑːn-/ *adj.*

con·cat·en·ation /kənˌkætəˈneɪʃn/ *noun* (*formal*) a series of things or events that are linked together: *a strange* ***concatenation of events***

con·cave /kɒnˈkeɪv; *NAmE* kɑːnˈk-; ˈkɑːn-/ *adj.* (of an outline or a surface) curving in: *a* ***concave lens/mirror*** OPP **convex**

con·cav·ity /ˌkɒnˈkævəti; *NAmE* kɑːn-/ *noun* (*pl.* -ies) (*technical*) **1** [U] the quality of being concave (= curving in) **2** [C] a shape or place that curves in

con·ceal /kənˈsiːl/ *verb* (*formal*) to hide sb/sth: **~ sb/sth** *The paintings were concealed beneath a thick layer of plaster.* ◇ *Tim could barely conceal his disappointment.* ◇ *She sat down to* ***conceal the fact that*** *she was trembling.* ◇ **~ sb/sth from sb/sth** *For a long time his death was concealed from her.* ➲ SYNONYMS at HIDE ➲ see also ILL-CONCEALED

con·ceal·er /kənˈsiːlə(r)/ *noun* [U, C] a skin-coloured cream or powder used to cover spots or marks on the skin or dark circles under the eyes ➲ VISUAL VOCAB page V49

con·ceal·ment /kənˈsiːlmənt/ *noun* [U] (*formal*) the act of hiding sth; the state of being hidden: *the concealment of crime* ◇ *Many animals rely on concealment for protection.*

con·cede /kənˈsiːd/ *verb* **1** [T] to admit that sth is true, logical, etc: **+ speech** *'Not bad,' she conceded grudgingly.* ◇ **~ (that)...** *He was forced to concede (that) there might be difficulties.* ◇ **~ sth** *I had to concede the logic of this.* ◇ **~ sth to sb** *He reluctantly* ***conceded the point*** *to me.* ◇ **~ sb sth** *He reluctantly conceded me the point.* ◇ **it is conceded that...** ***It must be conceded that*** *different judges have different approaches to these cases.* ➲ SYNONYMS at ADMIT **2** [T] to give sth away, especially unwillingly; to allow sb to have sth: **~ sth (to sb)** *The President was obliged to concede power to* the army. ◇ England conceded a goal immediately after half-time. ◇ ~ **sb sth** *Women were only conceded full voting rights in the 1950s.* **3** [I, T] ~ (**defeat**) to admit that you have lost a game, an election, etc: *After losing this decisive battle, the general was forced to concede.* ◇ *Injury forced Hicks to concede defeat.* ➲ see also CONCESSION

con·ceit /kən'siːt/ *noun* **1** [U] (*disapproving*) too much pride in yourself and what you do **2** [C] (*formal*) an artistic effect or device, especially one that is very clever or tries to be very clever but does not succeed: *The ill-advised conceit of the guardian angel dooms the film from the start.* **3** (*technical*) a clever expression in writing or speech that involves a comparison between two things SYN **metaphor**: *The idea of the wind singing is a romantic conceit.*

con·ceit·ed /kən'siːtɪd/ *adj.* (*disapproving*) having too much pride in yourself and what you do: *a very conceited person* ◇ *It's very conceited of you to assume that your work is always the best.* ▸ **con·ceit·ed·ly** *adv.*

con·ceiv·able AW /kən'siːvəbl/ *adj.* that you can imagine or believe SYN **pos·sible**: *It is conceivable that I'll see her tomorrow.* ◇ *a beautiful city with buildings of every conceivable age and style* OPP **inconceivable** ▸ **con·ceiv·ably** AW /-əbli/ *adv.*: *The disease could conceivably be transferred to humans.*

con·ceive AW /kən'siːv/ *verb* **1** [T] (*formal*) to form an idea, a plan, etc. in your mind; to imagine sth: ~ **sth** *He conceived the idea of transforming the old power station into an arts centre.* ◇ ~ **of sth** (**as sth**) *God is often conceived of as male.* ◇ ~ (**that**)... *I cannot conceive* (= I do not believe) (*that*) *he would wish to harm us.* ◇ ~ **what/how, etc...** *I cannot conceive what it must be like.* **2** [I, T] when a woman **conceives** or **conceives a child**, she becomes pregnant: *She is unable to conceive.* ◇ ~ **sth** *Their first child was conceived on their wedding night.* ➲ see also CONCEPTION

> **WORD FAMILY**
> **conceive** *verb*
> **conceivable** *adj.* (≠ inconceivable)
> **conceivably** *adv.*
> **concept** *noun*
> **conception** *noun*
> **conceptual** *adj.*

con·cen·trate 🔑 AW /'kɒnsntreɪt; *NAmE* 'kɑːn-/ *verb, noun*

■ *verb* **1** 🔑 [I, T] to give all your attention to sth and not think about anything else: ~ (**on sth/on doing sth**) *I can't concentrate with all that noise going on.* ◇ ~ **sth** *Nothing* **concentrates the mind** *better than the knowledge that you could die tomorrow* (= it makes you think very clearly). ◇ ~ **sth** (**on sth/on doing sth**) *I decided to* **concentrate** *all* **my efforts** *on finding somewhere to live.* **2** [T] ~ **sth + adv./prep.** to bring sth together in one place: *Power is largely concentrated in the hands of a small elite.* ◇ *We need to concentrate resources on the most run-down areas.* ◇ *Fighting was concentrated around the towns to the north.* **3** [T] ~ **sth** (*technical*) to increase the strength of a substance by reducing its volume, for example by boiling it SYN **reduce**

PHR V **'concentrate on sth** 🔑 to spend more time doing one particular thing than others: *In this lecture I shall concentrate on the early years of Charles's reign.*

■ *noun* [C, U] a substance that is made stronger because water or other substances have been removed: *mineral concentrates found at the bottom of rivers* ◇ *jams made with fruit juice concentrate*

con·cen·trated AW /'kɒnsntreɪtɪd; *NAmE* 'kɑːn-/ *adj.* **1** showing determination to do sth: *He made a concentrated effort to finish the work on time.* **2** (of a substance) made stronger because water or other substances have been removed: *concentrated orange juice* ◇ *a concentrated solution of salt in water* **3** if sth exists or happens in a **concentrated** way, there is a lot of it in one place or at one time: *concentrated gunfire*

con·cen·tra·tion 🔑 AW /ˌkɒnsn'treɪʃn; *NAmE* ˌkɑːn-/ *noun* **1** 🔑 [U] the ability to direct all your effort and attention on one thing, without thinking of other things: *This book requires a great deal of concentration.* ◇ *Tiredness affects your powers of concentration.* **2** [U] ~ (**on sth**) the process of people directing effort and attention on a particular thing: *a need for greater concentration on environmental issues* **3** [C] ~ (**of sth**) a lot of sth in one place: *a concentration of industry in the north of the country* **4** [C, U] the amount of a substance in a liquid or in another substance: *glucose concentrations in the blood*

C

concen'tration camp *noun* a type of prison, often consisting of a number of buildings inside a fence, where political prisoners, etc. are kept in extremely bad conditions: *a Nazi concentration camp*

con·cen·tric /kən'sentrɪk/ *adj.* (*geometry*) (of circles) having the same centre: *concentric rings*

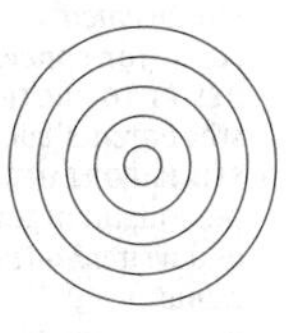

con·cept 🔑 AW /'kɒnsept; *NAmE* 'kɑːn-/ *noun* an idea or a principle that is connected with sth ABSTRACT: ~ (**of sth**) *the concept of social class* ◇ *concepts such as 'civilization' and 'government'* ◇ *He can't grasp the basic concepts of mathematics.* ◇ ~ (**that...**) *the concept that everyone should have equality of opportunity*

'concept album *noun* a collection of pieces of popular music, all having the same theme and recorded on one CD, etc.

con·cep·tion AW /kən'sepʃn/ *noun* **1** [U] the process of forming an idea or a plan: *The plan was brilliant in its conception but failed because of lack of money.* **2** [C, U] ~ (**of sth**) | ~ (**that...**) an understanding or a belief of what sth is or what sth should be: *Marx's conception of social justice* ◇ *He has* **no conception of** *how difficult life is if you're unemployed.* **3** [U, C] the process of an egg being FERTILIZED inside a woman's body so that she becomes pregnant: *the moment of conception* ➲ see also CONCEIVE

con·cep·tual AW /kən'septʃuəl/ *adj.* (*formal*) related to or based on ideas: *a conceptual framework within which children's needs are assessed* ◇ *a conceptual model* ▸ **con·cep·tu·al·ly** AW *adv.*: *conceptually similar/distinct*

conˌceptual 'art *noun* [U] art in which the idea which the work of art represents is considered to be the most important thing about it

con·cep·tual·ism /kən'septʃuəlɪzəm/ *noun* [U] (*philosophy*) the theory that general ideas such as 'beauty' and 'red' exist only as ideas in the mind ▸ **con·cep·tual·ist** /kən'septʃuəlɪst/ *noun*

con·cep·tu·al·ize (*BrE* also **-ise**) AW /kən'septʃuəlaɪz/ *verb* ~ **sth** (**as sth**) (*formal*) to form an idea of sth in your mind

con·cern 🔑 /kən'sɜːn; *NAmE* -'sɜːrn/ *verb, noun*

■ *verb*

▸ AFFECT/INVOLVE **1** 🔑 [often passive] ~ **sb/sth** to affect sb/sth; to involve sb/sth: *Don't interfere in what doesn't concern you.* ◇ *The loss was a tragedy for* **all concerned** (= all those affected by it). ◇ *Where our children's education is concerned, no compromise is acceptable.* ◇ *The individuals concerned have some explaining to do.* ◇ **To whom it may concern** ... (= used for example, at the beginning of a public notice or of a job reference about sb's character and ability) ◇ *Everyone who* **was** *directly* **concerned in** (= had some responsibility for) *the incident has now resigned.*

▸ BE ABOUT **2** 🔑 ~ **sth** (also **be concerned with sth**) to be about sth: *The story concerns the prince's efforts to rescue Pamina.* ◇ *The book is primarily concerned with Soviet-American relations during the Cold War.* ◇ *This chapter concerns itself with the historical background.* ◇ *One major difference between these computers* **concerns the way** *in which they store information.*

▸ WORRY SB **3** 🔑 to worry sb: ~ **sb** *What concerns me is our lack of preparation for the change.* ◇ ~ **sb that...** *It concerns me that you no longer seem to care.* ➲ see also CONCERNED

▸ TAKE AN INTEREST **4** ~ **yourself with/about sth** to take an interest in sth: *He didn't concern himself with the details.*

▸ CONSIDER IMPORTANT **5** **be concerned to do sth** (*formal*) to think it is important to do sth: *She was concerned* *to write about situations that everybody could identify with.* IDM see FAR *adv.*

■ ***noun***

▸ WORRY **1** [U, C] a feeling of worry, especially one that is shared by many people: **~ (about sth/sb)** *There is growing concern about violence on television.* ◇ *In the meeting, voters raised concerns about health care.* ◇ **~ (for sth/sb)** *She hasn't been seen for four days and there is concern for her safety.* ◇ **~ (over sth/sb)** *The report expressed concern over continuing high unemployment.* ◇ **~ (that...)** *There is widespread concern that new houses will be built on protected land.* ◇ *Stress at work is* ***a matter of concern to*** *staff and management.* ◇ *The President's health was giving serious* ***cause for concern.*** ➲ compare UNCONCERN

▸ DESIRE TO PROTECT **2** [U] a desire to protect and help sb/sth: *parents' concern for their children*

▸ STH IMPORTANT **3** [C] something that is important to a person, an organization, etc: *What are your main concerns as a writer?* ◇ *The government's primary concern is to reduce crime.*

▸ RESPONSIBILITY **4** [C, usually sing.] (*formal*) something that is your responsibility or that you have a right to know about: *This matter is their concern.* ◇ *How much money I make is none of your concern.*

▸ COMPANY **5** [C] a company or business SYN **firm**: *a major publishing concern* IDM see GOING *adj.*

con·cerned /kən'sɜːnd; *NAmE* -'sɜːrnd/ *adj.* **1** worried and feeling concern about sth: *Concerned parents held a meeting.* ◇ **~ about/for sth** *The President is deeply concerned about this issue.* ◇ **~ for sth** *He didn't seem in the least concerned for her safety.* ◇ **~ (that)...** *She was concerned that she might miss the turning and get lost.* ➲ SYNONYMS at WORRIED **2** **~ (about/with sth)** interested in sth: *They were more concerned with how the other women had dressed than with what the speaker was saying.* OPP **unconcerned** ➲ LANGUAGE BANK at ABOUT IDM see FAR *adv.*

con·cern·ing /kən'sɜːnɪŋ; *NAmE* -'sɜːrn-/ *prep.* (*formal*) about sth; involving sb/sth: *He asked several questions concerning the future of the company.* ◇ *All cases concerning children are dealt with in a special children's court.*

con·cert /'kɒnsət; *NAmE* 'kɑːnsərt/ *noun* a public performance of music: *a concert of music by Bach* ◇ *a* ***classical/rock/pop concert*** ◇ *They're* ***in concert*** *at Wembley Arena.* ◇ *a* ***concert hall/pianist*** ➲ COLLOCATIONS at MUSIC

IDM **in concert with sb/sth** (*formal*) working together with sb/sth

con·cer·tante /ˌkɒntʃə'tænteɪ; -ti; *NAmE* ˌkɑːn-/ *adj.* [only before noun] (*music*) (from *Italian*) related to a piece of music which contains an important part for a SOLO singer or player and which is similar to a CONCERTO in character

'concert band *noun* a large group of people who play wind instruments together, and who perform in a concert hall ➲ compare MILITARY BAND

con·cert·ed /kən'sɜːtɪd; *NAmE* -'sɜːrt-/ *adj.* [only before noun] done in a planned and determined way, especially by more than one person, government, country, etc: ***a concerted approach/attack/campaign*** ◇ *She has begun to* ***make a concerted effort to*** *find a job.*

con·cert·goer /'kɒnsətgəʊə(r); *NAmE* 'kɑːnsərtgoʊər/ *noun* a person who regularly goes to concerts, especially of CLASSICAL music

ˌconcert 'grand *noun* a piano of the largest size, used especially for concerts

con·cer·tina /ˌkɒnsə'tiːnə; *NAmE* ˌkɑːnsər't-/ *noun, verb*

■ ***noun*** a musical instrument like a small ACCORDION, that you hold in both hands. You press the ends together and pull them apart to produce sounds. ➲ picture at ACCORDION

■ ***verb*** (**con·cer·tina·ing**, **con·cer·tinaed**, **con·cer·tinaed**) [I] (*BrE*) to fold up like a concertina: *The truck crashed into the tree and concertinaed.*

con·cert·mas·ter /'kɒnsətmɑːstə(r); *NAmE* 'kɑːnsərtmæs-/ (*especially NAmE*) (*BrE* also **lead·er**) *noun* the most important VIOLIN player in an ORCHESTRA

con·certo /kən'tʃɜːtəʊ; *NAmE* -'tʃɜːrtoʊ/ *noun* (*pl.* **-os**) a piece of music for one or more SOLO instruments playing with an ORCHESTRA: *a piano concerto* ◇ *a concerto for flute and harp*

con·ces·sion /kən'seʃn/ *noun* **1** [C, U] something that you allow or do, or allow sb to have, in order to end an argument or to make a situation less difficult: *The firm will be forced to* ***make concessions*** *if it wants to avoid a strike.* ◇ *to win a concession from sb* ◇ ***a major/an important concession*** ◇ *She* ***made no concession*** *to his age; she expected him to work as hard as she did.* ➲ see also CONCEDE **2** [U] the act of giving sth or allowing sth; the act of CONCEDING: *the concession of university status to some colleges* ◇ (*especially NAmE*) *McCain's concession speech* (= when he admitted that he had lost the election) **3** [C, usually pl.] (*BrE*) a reduction in an amount of money that has to be paid; a ticket that is sold at a reduced price to a particular group of people: *tax concessions* ◇ *Tickets are £3; there is a £1 concession for students.* ◇ *Adults £2.50, concessions £2, family £5* **4** [C] a right or an advantage that is given to a group of people, an organization, etc, especially by a government or an employer: *The Bolivian government has granted logging concessions covering 22 million hectares.* **5** [C] the right to sell sth in a particular place; the place where you sell it, sometimes an area which is part of a larger building or store: *the burger concessions at the stadium*

con·ces·sion·aire /kənˌseʃə'neə(r); *NAmE* -'ner/ *noun* (*especially BrE*) a person or a business that has been given a concession to sell sth

con·ces·sion·ary /kən'seʃənəri; *NAmE* -neri/ *adj.* [usually before noun] (*BrE*) costing less money for people in particular situations; given as a CONCESSION (3): ***concessionary rates/fares/travel***

con·ces·sive /kən'sesɪv/ *adj.* (*grammar*) (of a preposition or conjunction) used at the beginning of a clause to say that the action of the main clause is in fact true or possible, despite the situation. 'Despite' and 'although' are concessive words.

conch /kɒntʃ; *NAmE* kɑːntʃ/ *noun* the shell of a sea creature which is also called a conch

con·chie (also **con·chy**) /'kɒntʃi; *NAmE* 'kɑːn-/ *noun* (*pl.* **-ies**) (*BrE, informal, old-fashioned*) a CONSCIENTIOUS OBJECTOR

conc·ierge /'kɒnsieəʒ; *NAmE* kɔːn'sjerʒ; kɑːn'sjerʒ/ *noun* (from *French*) **1** a person, especially in France, who takes care of a building containing flats/apartments and checks people entering and leaving the building **2** (*especially NAmE*) a person in a hotel whose job is to help guests by giving them information, arranging theatre tickets, etc.

con·cili·ate /kən'sɪlieɪt/ *verb* **~ sb** (*formal*) to make sb less angry or more friendly, especially by being kind and pleasant or by giving them sth SYN **pacify** ▸ **con·cili·ation** /kənˌsɪli'eɪʃn/ *noun* [U]: *A conciliation service helps to settle disputes between employers and workers.*

con·cili·ator /kən'sɪlieɪtə(r)/ *noun* a person or an organization that tries to make angry people calm so that they can discuss or solve their problems successfully

con·cili·atory /kən'sɪliətəri; *NAmE* -tɔːri/ *adj.* having the intention or effect of making angry people calm: ***a conciliatory approach/attitude/gesture/move***

con·cise /kən'saɪs/ *adj.* **1** giving only the information that is necessary and important, using few words: *a concise summary* ◇ *clear concise instructions* **2** [only before noun] (of a book) shorter than the original book, on which it was based: *a concise dictionary* ▸ **con·cise·ly** *adv.* **con·cise·ness** (also *less frequent* **con·ci·sion** /kən'sɪʒn/) *noun* [U]

con·clave /'kɒŋkleɪv; *NAmE* 'kɑːŋ-/ *noun* (*formal*) a meeting to discuss sth in private; the people at this meeting

con·clude 0‑ⁿ AW /kən'klu:d/ *verb*
1 0‑ⁿ [T] (not used in the progressive tenses) to decide or believe sth as a result of what you have heard or seen: **~ sth (from sth)** *What do you conclude from that?* ◇ **~ (that)** ... *The report concluded (that) the cheapest option was to close the laboratory.* ◇ **~ from sth that...** *He concluded from their remarks that they were not in favour of the plan.* ◇ **it is concluded that...** *It was concluded that the level of change necessary would be low.* ◇ **+ speech** *'So it should be safe to continue,' he concluded.* ➲ LANGUAGE BANK at CONCLUSION **2** 0‑ⁿ [I, T] (*formal*) to come to an end; to bring sth to an end: *Let me make just a few concluding remarks.* ◇ **~ with sth** *The programme concluded with Stravinsky's 'Rite of Spring'.* ◇ **~ by doing sth** *He concluded by wishing everyone a safe trip home.* ◇ **~ sth (with sth)** *The commission concluded its investigation last month.* ◇ **+ speech** *'Anyway, she should be back soon,' he concluded.* **3** [T] **~ sth (with sb)** (*formal*) to arrange and settle an agreement with sb formally and finally: *They concluded a treaty with Turkey.* ◇ *A trade agreement was concluded between the two countries.*

con·clu·sion 0‑ⁿ AW /kən'klu:ʒn/ *noun*
1 0‑ⁿ [C] something that you decide when you have thought about all the information connected with the situation: *I've* ***come to the conclusion*** *that he's not the right person for the job.* ◇ *It took the jury some time to* ***reach the conclusion*** *that she was guilty.* ◇ *New evidence might* ***lead to the conclusion*** *that we are wrong.* ◇ *We can safely* ***draw some conclusions*** *from our discussion.* ➲ COLLOCATIONS at SCIENTIFIC **2** 0‑ⁿ [C, usually sing.] the end of sth such as a speech or a piece of writing: *The conclusion of the book was disappointing.* ◇ ***In conclusion*** (= finally), *I would like to thank...* ◇ *If we took this argument to its* ***logical conclusion*** *...* **3** [U] the formal and final arrangement of sth official SYN **completion**: *the successful conclusion of a trade treaty*
IDM **jump/leap to con'clusions | jump/leap to the con'clusion that...** to make a decision about sb/sth too quickly, before you know or have thought about all the facts: *There I go again—jumping to conclusions.* ➲ more at FOREGONE

Language Bank

conclusion

Summing up an argument

- **In conclusion**, the study has provided useful insights into the issues relating to people's perception of crime.
- Based on this study, **it can be concluded that** the introduction of new street lighting did not reduce reported crime.
- **To sum up**, no evidence can be found to support the view that improved street lighting reduces reported crime.
- The available evidence clearly **leads to the conclusion that** the media do have an influence on the public perception of crime.
- **The main conclusion to be drawn from** this study is that public perception of crime is significantly influenced by crime news reporting.
- **This study has shown that** people's fear of crime is out of all proportion to crime itself.
- Fear of crime is out of all proportion to the actual level of crime, and the reasons for this **can be summarized as follows**. First...
- **Overall/In general**, women are more likely than men to feel insecure walking alone after dark.

➲ Language Banks at EMPHASIS, FIRST, GENERALLY

con·clu·sive AW /kən'klu:sɪv/ *adj.* proving sth, and allowing no doubt or confusion: ***conclusive evidence/proof/results*** OPP **inconclusive** ▸ **con·clu·sive·ly** AW *adv.*: *to prove sth conclusively*

con·coct /kən'kɒkt; *NAmE* -'kɑ:kt/ *verb* **1 ~ sth** to make sth, especially food or drink, by mixing different things: *The soup was concocted from up to a dozen different kinds of fish.* **2 ~ sth** to invent a story, an excuse, etc. SYN **cook up, make up**: *She concocted some elaborate story to explain her absence.*

con·coc·tion /kən'kɒkʃn; *NAmE* -'kɑ:kʃn/ *noun* a strange or unusual mixture of things, especially drinks or medicines: *a concoction of cream and rum*

C

con·comi·tant /kən'kɒmɪtənt; *NAmE* -'kɑ:m-/ *adj., noun*
■ ***adj.*** (*formal*) happening at the same time as sth else, especially because one thing is related to or causes the other
■ ***noun*** (*formal*) a thing that happens at the same time as sth else

con·cord /'kɒŋkɔ:d; *NAmE* 'kɑ:ŋkɔ:rd/ *noun* [U] **1 ~ (with sb)** (*formal*) peace and agreement SYN **harmony**: *living in concord with neighbouring states* OPP **discord** **2** [U] **~ (with sth)** (*grammar*) (of words in a phrase) the fact of having the same NUMBER, GENDER or PERSON SYN **agreement**

con·cord·ance /kən'kɔ:dəns; *NAmE* -'kɔ:rd-/ *noun* **1** [C] an alphabetical list of the words used in a book, etc. showing where and how often they are used: *a Bible concordance* **2** [C] a list produced by a computer that shows all the examples of an individual word in a book, etc. **3** [U] (*technical*) the state of being similar to sth or CONSISTENT with it: *There is reasonable concordance between the two sets of results.*

con·cordat /kən'kɔ:dæt; *NAmE* -'kɔ:rd-; *BrE* also kɒn-/ *noun* an agreement, especially between the Roman Catholic Church and the state

con·course /'kɒŋkɔ:s; *NAmE* 'kɑ:ŋkɔ:rs/ *noun* a large, open part of a public building, especially an airport or a train station: *the station concourse*

con·crete 0‑ⁿ /'kɒŋkri:t; *NAmE* 'kɑ:ŋ-/ *adj., noun, verb*
■ ***adj.*** **1** 0‑ⁿ made of concrete: *a concrete floor* **2** 0‑ⁿ based on facts, not on ideas or guesses: ***concrete evidence/proposals/proof*** ◇ *'It's only a suspicion,' she said, 'nothing concrete.'* ◇ *It is easier to think* ***in concrete terms*** *rather than in the abstract.* ➲ compare ABSTRACT (1) **3** a **concrete** object is one that you can see and feel ▸ **con·crete·ly** *adv.*
■ ***noun*** 0‑ⁿ [U] building material that is made by mixing together CEMENT, sand, small stones and water: *a slab of concrete*
■ ***verb*** **~ sth (over)** to cover sth with concrete: *The garden had been concreted over.*

ˌconcrete 'jungle *noun* [usually sing.] a way of describing a city or an area that is unpleasant because it has many large modern buildings and no trees or parks

'concrete mixer *noun* = CEMENT MIXER

ˌconcrete 'poetry *noun* [U] poetry in which the meaning or effect is communicated partly by using patterns of words or letters that are visible on the page

con·cu·bine /'kɒŋkjubaɪn; *NAmE* 'kɑ:ŋ-/ *noun* (especially in some societies in the past) a woman who lives with a man, often in addition to his wife or wives, but who is less important than they are

con·cu·pis·cence /kən'kju:pɪsns/ *noun* [U] (*formal, often disapproving*) strong sexual desire SYN **lust**

con·cur /kən'kɜ:(r)/ *verb* (-rr-) [I, T] **~ (with sb) (in sth) | ~ (with sth) | ~ (that...) | (+ speech)** (*formal*) to agree: *Historians have concurred with each other in this view.* ◇ *The coroner concurred with this assessment.*

con·cur·rence /kən'kʌrəns; *NAmE* -'kɜ:r-/ *noun* (*formal*) **1** [U, sing.] agreement: *The doctor may seek the concurrence of a relative before carrying out the procedure.* **2** [sing.] an example of two or more things happening at the same time: *an unfortunate concurrence of events*

con·cur·rent AW /kən'kʌrənt; *NAmE* -'kɜ:r-/ *adj.* **~ (with sth)** existing or happening at the same time: *He was imprisoned for two concurrent terms of 30 months and 18 months.* ▸ **con·cur·rent·ly** AW *adv.*: *The prison sentences will run concurrently.*

C

con·cuss /kən'kʌs/ *verb* **~ sb** to hit sb on the head, making them become unconscious or confused for a short time ▸ **con·cussed** *adj.*: *She was concussed after the fall.*

con·cus·sion /kən'kʌʃn/ *noun* [U] (This word is only [C] in *NAmE*.) a temporary loss of CONSCIOUSNESS caused by a blow to the head; the effects of a severe blow to the head such as confusion and temporary loss of physical and mental abilities: (*BrE*) *He was taken to hospital with concussion.* ◇ (*NAmE*) *He was taken to the hospital with a concussion.*

con·demn /kən'dem/ *verb*
▸ EXPRESS DISAPPROVAL **1 ~ sb/sth** (**for/as sth**) to express very strong disapproval of sb/sth, usually for moral reasons: *The government issued a statement condemning the killings.* ◇ *The editor of the newspaper was condemned as lacking integrity.*
▸ SB TO PUNISHMENT **2** [usually passive] to say what sb's punishment will be SYN **sentence**: **~ sb** (**to sth**) *He was condemned to death for murder and later hanged.* ◇ **~ sb to do sth** *She was condemned to hang for killing her husband.*
▸ SB TO DIFFICULT SITUATION **3** [usually passive] **~ sb to sth** to force sb to accept a difficult or unpleasant situation SYN **doom**: *He was condemned to a life of hardship.* ◇ *They were condemned to spend every holiday on a rainy campsite.*
▸ STH DANGEROUS **4** [usually passive] **~ sth** (**as sth**) to say officially that sth is not safe enough to be used: *a condemned building* ◇ *The meat was condemned as unfit to eat.*
▸ SHOW GUILT **5 ~ sb** to show or suggest that sb is guilty of sth: *She is condemned out of her own mouth* (= her own words show that she is guilty).

con·dem·na·tion /ˌkɒndem'neɪʃn; *NAmE* ˌkɑːn-/ *noun* [U, C] **~** (**of sb/sth**) an expression of very strong disapproval: *There was widespread condemnation of the invasion.*

conˌdemned 'cell *noun* (*BrE*) a prison cell where a person who is going to be punished by death is kept

con·den·sa·tion /ˌkɒnden'seɪʃn; *NAmE* ˌkɑːn-/ *noun* **1** [U] drops of water that form on a cold surface when warm water VAPOUR becomes cool **2** [U] the process of a gas changing to a liquid **3** [C, usually sing., U] (*formal*) the process of making a book, etc. shorter by taking out anything that is not necessary

con·dense /kən'dens/ *verb* **1** [I, T] to change from a gas into a liquid; to make a gas change into a liquid: **~** (**into sth**) *Steam condenses into water when it cools.* ◇ **~ sth** (**into sth**) *The steam was condensed rapidly by injecting cold water into the cylinder.* **2** [I, T] **~** (**sth**) if a liquid **condenses** or you **condense** it, it becomes thicker and stronger because it has lost some of its water SYN **reduce**: *Condense the soup by boiling it for several minutes.* **3** [T] **~ sth** (**into sth**) to put sth such as a piece of writing into fewer words; to put a lot of information into a small space: *The article was condensed into just two pages.* ◇ *The author has condensed a great deal of material into just 100 pages.*

conˌdensed 'milk *noun* [U] a type of thick sweet milk that is sold in cans

con·dens·er /kən'densə(r)/ *noun* **1** a device that cools gas in order to change it into a liquid **2** a device that receives or stores electricity, especially in a car engine

con·des·cend /ˌkɒndɪ'send; *NAmE* ˌkɑːn-/ *verb* **1** [T] **~ to do sth** (often *disapproving*) to do sth that you think it is below your social or professional position to do SYN **deign**: *We had to wait almost an hour before he condescended to see us.* **2** [I] **~ to sb** to behave towards sb as though you are more important and more intelligent than they are: *When giving a talk, be careful not to condescend to your audience.* ▸ **con·des·cen·sion** /ˌkɒndɪ'senʃn; *NAmE* ˌkɑːn-/ *noun* [U]: *Her smile was a mixture of pity and condescension.*

con·des·cend·ing /ˌkɒndɪ'sendɪŋ; *NAmE* ˌkɑːn-/ *adj.* behaving as though you are more important and more intelligent than other people: *He has a condescending attitude towards women.* ▸ **con·des·cend·ing·ly** *adv.*

con·dign /kən'daɪn/ *adj.* (*formal*) (of a punishment) appropriate to the crime

con·di·ment /'kɒndɪmənt; *NAmE* 'kɑːn-/ *noun* [usually pl.] **1** (*BrE*) a substance such as salt or pepper that is used to give flavour to food **2** (*especially NAmE*) a sauce, etc. that is used to give flavour to food, or that is eaten with food

Synonyms

condition / state

The following adjectives are frequently used with these nouns:

~ condition	~ state
good	present
excellent	current
physical	mental
poor	solid
human	no
perfect	emotional
no	physical
better	natural

- **State** is a more general word than **condition** and is used for the condition that something is in at a particular time. It can be used without an adjective: *the present state of medical knowledge* ◇ *We're worried about his mental state.* ◇ *What a state this room is in* (= very bad).
- **Condition** is used with an adjective and refers especially to the appearance, quality or working order of somebody or something: *The car is in excellent condition.*

con·di·tion 0-w /kən'dɪʃn/ *noun, verb*

■ ***noun***
▸ STATE OF STH **1** 0-w [U, sing.] the state that sth is in: *to be* ***in bad/good/excellent condition*** ◇ *a used car in perfect condition*
▸ MEDICAL **2** 0-w [U, sing.] the state of sb's health or how fit they are: *He is overweight and* ***out of condition*** (= not physically fit). ◇ *You are* ***in no condition*** (= too ill/sick, etc.) *to go anywhere.* ◇ *The motorcyclist was in a* ***critical condition*** *in hospital last night.* **3** 0-w [C] an illness or a medical problem that you have for a long time because it is not possible to cure it: *a medical condition* ◇ *He suffers from a serious* ***heart condition.*** ➲ SYNONYMS at DISEASE
▸ CIRCUMSTANCES **4** 0-w **conditions** [pl.] the circumstances or situation in which people live, work or do things: ***living/housing/working conditions*** ◇ *changing economic conditions* ◇ *neglected children living* ***under*** *the most appalling* ***conditions*** ◇ *a strike to improve* ***pay and conditions*** ➲ SYNONYMS at SITUATION **5** 0-w **conditions** [pl.] the physical situation that affects how sth happens: *The plants grow best in cool, damp conditions.* ◇ ***freezing/icy/humid, etc. conditions*** ◇ *Conditions are ideal* (= the weather is very good) *for sailing today.* ◇ *treacherous* ***driving conditions***
▸ RULE **6** 0-w [C] a rule or decision that you must agree to, sometimes forming part of a contract or an official agreement: *the* ***terms and conditions*** *of employment* ◇ *The offer is* ***subject to certain conditions.*** ◇ *They agreed to lend us the car* ***on condition that*** (= only if) *we returned it before the weekend.* ◇ *They will give us the money* ***on one condition***—*that we pay it back within six months.* ◇ (*especially NAmE*) *They agreed* ***under the condition that*** *the matter be dealt with promptly.* ◇ *Congress can* ***impose strict conditions*** *on the bank.* ◇ *They have agreed to the ceasefire provided their* ***conditions are met.***
▸ NECESSARY SITUATION **7** 0-w [C] a situation that must exist in order for sth else to happen: *a necessary condition for economic growth* ◇ *A good training programme is one of the conditions for successful industry.*
▸ STATE OF GROUP **8** [sing.] (*formal*) the state of a particular group of people because of their situation in life, their problems, etc: *He spoke angrily about the condition of the*

urban poor. ◇ *Work is basic to* ***the human condition*** (= the fact of being alive).

IDM **on 'no condition** (*US* also **under 'no condition**) (*formal*) not in any situation; never: *You must on no condition tell them what happened.* ➲ more at MINT *n.*

■ ***verb*** **1** [usually passive] to train sb/sth to behave in a particular way or to become used to a particular situation: **~ sb/sth (to sth)** *the difference between inborn and* ***conditioned reflexes*** (= reactions that are learned/not natural) ◇ *Patients can become conditioned to particular forms of treatment.* ◇ **~ sb/sth to do sth** *The rats had been conditioned to ring a bell when they wanted food.* **2 ~ sb/sth** to have an important effect on sb/sth; to influence the way that sth happens: *Gender roles are often conditioned by cultural factors.* **3 ~ sth** to keep sth such as your hair or skin healthy: *a shampoo that cleans and conditions hair* ◇ *a polish for conditioning leather*

con·di·tion·al /kən'dɪʃənl/ *adj., noun*

■ ***adj.*** **1 ~ (on/upon sth)** depending on sth: ***conditional approval/acceptance*** ◇ *Payment is conditional upon delivery of the goods* (= if the goods are not delivered the money will not be paid) ◇ *He was found guilty and given a* ***conditional discharge*** (= allowed to go free on particular conditions). ◇ *a conditional offer* (= that depends on particular conditions being met) OPP **unconditional** **2** [only before noun] (*grammar*) expressing sth that must happen or be true if another thing is to happen or be true: *a* ***conditional sentence/clause*** ▸ **con·di·tion·al·ly** /-ʃənəli/ *adv.*: *The offer was made conditionally.*

■ ***noun*** (*grammar*) **1** [C] a sentence or clause that begins with *if* or *unless* and expresses a condition **2 the conditional** [sing.] the form of a verb that expresses a conditional action, for example *should* in *If I should die...*: *the* ***present/past/perfect conditional*** ◇ *the* ***first/second/third conditional***

con·di·tion·er /kən'dɪʃənə(r)/ *noun* [C, U] **1** a liquid that makes hair soft and shiny after washing: *shampoo and conditioner* **2** a liquid, used after washing clothes, that makes them softer: *fabric conditioner*

con·di·tion·ing /kən'dɪʃənɪŋ/ *noun* [U] the training or experience that an animal or a person has that makes them behave in a particular way in a particular situation: *Is personality the result of conditioning from parents and society, or are we born with it?* ➲ see also AIR CONDITIONING

condo /'kɒndəʊ; *NAmE* 'kɑːndoʊ/ *noun* (*pl.* -os) (*NAmE, informal*) = CONDOMINIUM

con·dol·ence /kən'dəʊləns; *NAmE* -'doʊ-/ *noun* [C, usually pl., U] sympathy that you feel for sb when a person in their family or that they know well has died; an expression of this sympathy: *to* ***give/offer/express*** *your* ***condolences*** ◇ *Our condolences go to his wife and family.* ◇ *a letter of condolence*

con·dom /'kɒndɒm; *NAmE* 'kɑːndəm/ *noun* **1** (*BrE* also **sheath**) (also *NAmE formal* or *technical* **prophy·lac·tic**) a thin rubber covering that a man wears over his PENIS during sex to stop a woman from becoming pregnant or to protect against disease **2 female condom** a thin rubber device that a woman wears inside her VAGINA during sex to prevent herself from becoming pregnant

con·do·min·ium /ˌkɒndə'mɪniəm; *NAmE* ˌkɑːn-/ (also *informal* **condo**) *noun* (*especially NAmE*) an apartment building or group of houses in which each flat/apartment/house is owned by the person living in it but the shared areas are owned by everyone together; a flat/apartment/house in such a building or group of houses

con·done /kən'dəʊn; *NAmE* -'doʊn/ *verb* **~ sth | ~ (sb) doing sth** to accept behaviour that is morally wrong or to treat it as if it were not serious: *Terrorism can never be condoned.*

con·dor /'kɒndɔː(r); *NAmE* 'kɑːn-/ *noun* a large bird of the VULTURE family, that lives mainly in S America

con·du·cive /kən'djuːsɪv; *NAmE* -'duːs-/ *adj.* **~ to sth** making it easy, possible or likely for sth to happen: *Chairs in rows are not as conducive to discussion as chairs arranged in a circle.*

con·duct 🔑 AW *verb, noun*

■ ***verb*** /kən'dʌkt/ **1** 🔑 [T] **~ sth** (*formal*) to organize and/or do a particular activity: *to* ***conduct an experiment/an inquiry/a survey*** ◇ *The negotiations have been conducted in a positive manner.* **2** 🔑 [T, I] **~ (sth)** to direct a group of people who are singing or playing music: *a concert by the Philharmonic Orchestra, conducted by Sir Colin Davis* **3** [T] **~ sb/sth + adv./prep.** (*formal*) to lead or guide sb through or around a place: *a* ***conducted tour*** *of Athens* (= one with a guide, giving information about it) ◇ *The guide conducted us around the ruins of the ancient city.* **4** [T] **~ yourself + adv./prep.** (*formal*) to behave in a particular way: *He conducted himself far better than expected.* **5** [T] **~ sth** (*technical*) (of a substance) to allow heat or electricity to pass along or through it: *Copper conducts electricity well.*

■ ***noun*** /'kɒndʌkt; *NAmE* 'kɑːn-/ [U] (*formal*) **1** 🔑 a person's behaviour in a particular place or in a particular situation: *The sport has a strict code of conduct.* **2 ~ of sth** the way in which a business or an activity is organized and managed: *There was growing criticism of the government's conduct of the war.* ➲ see also SAFE CONDUCT

con·duct·ance /kən'dʌktəns/ *noun* [U] (*physics*) the degree to which an object allows electricity or heat to pass through it

con·duc·tion /kən'dʌkʃn/ *noun* [U] (*physics*) the process by which heat or electricity passes through a material

con·duct·ive /kən'dʌktɪv/ *adj.* (*physics*) able to CONDUCT electricity, heat, etc. ▸ **con·duct·iv·ity** /ˌkɒndʌk'tɪvəti; *NAmE* ˌkɑːn-/ *noun* [U]

conˌductive edu'cation *noun* [U] a treatment for people with CEREBRAL PALSY that was developed in Hungary and that involves special physical exercises and learning methods

con·duct·or /kən'dʌktə(r)/ *noun* **1** a person who stands in front of an ORCHESTRA, a group of singers etc, and directs their performance, especially sb who does this as a profession **2** (*BrE* also **guard**) a person who is in charge of a train and travels with it, but does not drive it **3** (*BrE*) a person whose job is to collect money from passengers on a bus or check their tickets: *a bus conductor* **4** (*physics*) a substance that allows electricity or heat to pass along it or through it: *Wood is a poor conductor.* ➲ see also LIGHTNING CONDUCTOR

con·duc·tress /kən'dʌktrəs/ *noun* (*BrE, old-fashioned*) a woman who collects money from passengers on a bus or checks their tickets

con·duit /'kɒndjuɪt; *NAmE* 'kɑːnduɪt/ *noun* **1** (*technical*) a pipe, channel or tube which liquid, gas or electrical wire can pass through **2** (*formal*) a person, an organization or a country that is used to pass things or information to other people or places: *The organization had acted as a conduit for money from the arms industry.*

cone /kəʊn; *NAmE* koʊn/ *noun, verb*

■ ***noun*** **1** a solid or hollow object with a round flat base and sides that slope up to a point ➲ VISUAL VOCAB page V58 ➲ see also CONIC, CONICAL **2** a solid or hollow object that is shaped like a cone: *a paper cone full of popcorn* ◇ *the cone of a volcano* ➲ see also NOSE CONE **3** (also **'traffic cone**) a plastic object shaped like a cone and often red and white, or yellow, in colour, used on roads to show where vehicles are not allowed to go, for example while repairs are being done **4** (also *old-fashioned* **cornet**) a piece of thin crisp biscuit shaped like a cone, which you can put ice cream in to eat it **5** the hard dry fruit of a PINE or FIR tree: *a pine cone* ➲ VISUAL VOCAB page V8 ➲ see also FIR CONE

■ ***verb***

PHR V **ˌcone sth↔'off** to close a road or part of a road by putting a line of cones across it

con·fab /'kɒnfæb; *NAmE* 'kɑːn-/ *noun* (*informal*) **1** an informal private discussion or conversation **2** (*NAmE*) a meeting or conference of the members of a profession or group: *the annual movie confab in Cannes*

con·fabu·la·tion /kənˌfæbjə'leɪʃn/ *noun* [C, U] (*formal*) **1** a story that sb has invented in their mind; the act of inventing a story in your mind **2** a conversation; the activity of having a conversation

con·fec·tion /kən'fekʃn/ *noun* **1** (*formal*) a cake or other sweet food that looks very attractive **2** a thing such as a building or piece of clothing, that is made in a skilful or complicated way

con·fec·tion·er /kən'fekʃənə(r)/ *noun* a person or a business that makes or sells cakes and sweets/candy

con'fectioner's sugar (also **'powdered sugar**) (both *US*) (*BrE* **'icing sugar**) *noun* [U] fine white powder made from sugar, that is mixed with water to make icing

con·fec·tion·ery /kən'fekʃənəri; *NAmE* -ʃəneri/ *noun* [U] sweets/candy, chocolate, etc.

con·fed·er·acy /kən'fedərəsi/ *noun* **1** [C] a union of states, groups of people or political parties with the same aim **2 the Confederacy** [sing.] = THE CONFEDERATE STATES

con·fed·er·ate /kən'fedərət/ *noun, adj.*

- ***noun*** a person who helps sb, especially to do sth illegal or secret SYN **accomplice**
- ***adj.*** belonging to a confederacy

the Con,federate 'States *noun* [pl.] (also **the Confederacy**) the eleven southern states of the US which left the United States in 1860-1, starting the American Civil War

con·fed·er·ation /kən,fedə'reɪʃn/ *noun* **1** an organization consisting of countries, businesses, etc. that have joined together in order to help each other: *the Confederation of British Industry* **2 Confederation** (in Canada) the joining together of PROVINCES and TERRITORIES forming Canada, which began 1 July, 1867

con·fer AW /kən'fɜː(r)/ *verb* (-rr-) (*formal*) **1** [I] **~ (with sb) (on/about sth)** to discuss sth with sb, in order to exchange opinions or get advice: *He wanted to confer with his colleagues before reaching a decision.* **2** [T] **~ sth (on/upon sb)** to give sb an award, a university degree or a particular honour or right: *An honorary degree was conferred on him by Oxford University in 2009.*

con·fer·ence 0‑ AW /'kɒnfərəns; *NAmE* 'kɑːn-/ *noun*

1 0‑ a large official meeting, usually lasting for a few days, at which people with the same work or interests come together to discuss their views: *The hotel is used for exhibitions, conferences and social events.* ◇ *a* ***conference room/centre/hall*** ◇ *She is attending a three-day conference on AIDS education.* ◇ *The conference will be held in Glasgow.* ◇ *delegates to the Labour Party's annual conference* **2** 0‑ a meeting at which people have formal discussions: *Ministers from all four countries involved will meet at the* ***conference table*** *this week.* ◇ *He was* ***in conference*** *with his lawyers all day.* ➲ see also PRESS CONFERENCE **3** (*especially NAmE*) a group of sports teams that play against each other in a league: *Southeast Conference football champions*

'conference call *noun* a telephone call in which three or more people take part

con·fer·en·cing /'kɒnfərənsɪŋ; *NAmE* 'kɑːn-/ *noun* the activity of organizing or taking part in meetings, especially when people are in different places and use telephones, computers, or video to communicate: *video conferencing*

con·fer·ment /kən'fɜːmənt; *NAmE* -'fɜːrm-/ *noun* [U, C] (*formal*) the action of giving sb an award, a university degree or a particular honour or right

con·fess /kən'fes/ *verb* **1** [I, T] to admit, especially formally or to the police, that you have done sth wrong or illegal: *After hours of questioning, the suspect confessed.* ◇ **~ to sth/to doing sth** *She confessed to the murder.* ◇ **~ (that)...** *He confessed that he had stolen the money.* ◇ **~ sth** *We persuaded her to confess her crime.* **2** [I, T] to admit sth that you feel ashamed or embarrassed about: **~ sth** *She was reluctant to confess her ignorance.* ◇ **~ to sth/to doing sth** *I* ***must confess*** *to knowing nothing about computers.* ◇ **~ (that)...** *I confess (that) I know nothing about computers.* ◇ **+ speech** *'I know nothing about them,' he confessed.* ◇ **~ yourself + adj.** (*formal*) *I confess myself bewildered by their explanation.* ➲ see also SELF-CONFESSED ➲ SYNONYMS at ADMIT **3** [I, T] **~ (sth) (to sb)** (especially in the Roman Catholic Church) to tell God or a priest about the bad things you have done so that you can say that you are sorry and be forgiven **4** [T] **~ sb** (of a priest) to hear sb confess their SINS (= the bad things they have done)

con·fes·sion /kən'feʃn/ *noun* **1** [C, U] a statement that a person makes, admitting that they are guilty of a crime; the act of making such a statement: *After hours of questioning by police, she made a full confession.* **2** [C, U] a statement admitting sth that you are ashamed or embarrassed about; the act of making such a statement SYN **admission**: *I've a confession to make—I lied about my age.* **3** [U, C] (especially in the Roman Catholic Church) a private statement to a priest about the bad things that you have done: *to go to confession* ◇ *to hear sb's confession* **4** [C] (*formal*) a statement of your religious beliefs, principles, etc: *a confession of faith*

con·fes·sion·al /kən'feʃənl/ *noun* a private place in a church where a priest listens to people making confessions

con·fes·sor /kən'fesə(r)/ *noun* a Roman Catholic priest who listens to sb's CONFESSION (3)

con·fetti /kən'feti/ *noun* [U] small pieces of coloured paper that people often throw at weddings over people who have just been married, or (in the US) at other special events

con·fi·dant (*feminine also* con·fi·dante) /'kɒnfɪdænt; ,kɒnfɪ'dɑːnt; *NAmE* 'kɑːnfɪdænt/ *noun* a person that you trust and who you talk to about private or secret things: *a* ***close/trusted confidant*** *of the President*

con·fide /kən'faɪd/ *verb* to tell sb secrets and personal information that you do not want other people to know: **~ sth (to sb)** *She confided all her secrets to her best friend.* ◇ **~ (to sb) that...** *He confided to me that he had applied for another job.* ◇ **+ speech** *'It was a lie,' he confided.*

PHR V **con'fide in sb** to tell sb secrets and personal information because you feel you can trust them: *It is important to have someone you can confide in.*

con·fi·dence 0‑ /'kɒnfɪdəns; *NAmE* 'kɑːn-/ *noun*

- BELIEF IN OTHERS **1** 0‑ [U] **~ (in sb/sth)** the feeling that you can trust, believe in and be sure about the abilities or good qualities of sb/sth: *The players all* ***have confidence in*** *their manager.* ◇ *A fall in unemployment will help to restore consumer confidence.* ◇ *a lack of confidence in the government* ◇ *The new contracts have undermined the confidence of employees.* ◇ *She has every confidence in her students' abilities.* ➲ see also VOTE OF CONFIDENCE, VOTE OF NO CONFIDENCE
- BELIEF IN YOURSELF **2** 0‑ [U] a belief in your own ability to do things and be successful: *He answered the questions* ***with confidence****.* ◇ *People often* ***lose confidence*** *when they are criticized.* ◇ *He* ***gained confidence*** *when he went to college.* ◇ *She suffers from a* ***lack of confidence****.* ◇ *While girls* ***lack confidence****, boys often overestimate their abilities.* ◇ *I didn't have any confidence in myself at school.*
- FEELING CERTAIN **3** 0‑ [U] the feeling that you are certain about sth: *They could not say* ***with confidence*** *that he would be able to walk again after the accident.* ◇ *He expressed his* ***confidence that*** *they would win.*
- TRUST **4** [U] a feeling of trust that sb will keep information private: *Eva told me about their relationship* ***in confidence****.* ◇ *This is in the* ***strictest confidence****.* ◇ *It took a long time to gain her confidence* (= make her feel she could trust me).
- A SECRET **5** [C] (*formal*) a secret that you tell sb: *The girls exchanged confidences.* ◇ *I could never forgive Mike for betraying a confidence.*

IDM **be in sb's confidence** to be trusted with sb's secrets: *He is said to be very much in the President's confidence.* **take sb into your confidence** to tell sb secrets and personal information about yourself: *She took me into her confidence and told me about the problems she was facing.*

'confidence trick (*BrE*) (*NAmE* **'confidence game**) *noun* (*formal*) = CON

'confidence trickster *noun* (*BrE, formal*) a person who tricks others into giving him or her money, etc.

C

con·fi·dent 0‑w /ˈkɒnfɪdənt; *NAmE* ˈkɑːn-/ *adj.* **1** 0‑w feeling sure about your own ability to do things and be successful: *She was in a relaxed, confident mood.* ◇ *The teacher wants the children to feel confident about asking questions when they don't understand.* ➲ see also SELF-CONFIDENT **2** 0‑w feeling certain that sth will happen in the way that you want or expect: **~ of sth/doing sth** *The team feels confident of winning.* ◇ **~ that...** *I'm confident that you will get the job.* ➲ SYNONYMS at SURE ▸ **con·fi·dent·ly** 0‑w *adv.*

con·fi·den·tial /ˌkɒnfɪˈdenʃl; *NAmE* ˌkɑːn-/ *adj.* **1** meant to be kept secret and not told to or shared with other people: ***confidential information/documents*** ◇ *Your medical records are **strictly confidential*** (= completely secret). **2** (of a way of speaking) showing that what you are saying is private or secret: *He spoke in a confidential tone, his voice low.* **3** [only before noun] trusted with private or secret information: *a confidential secretary* ▸ **con·fi·den·tial·ly** /-ʃəli/ *adv.*: *She told me confidentially that she is going to retire early.*

con·fi·den·tial·ity /ˌkɒnfɪˌdenʃiˈæləti; *NAmE* ˌkɑːn-/ *noun* [U] a situation in which you expect sb to keep information secret: *They signed a confidentiality agreement.* ◇ *All letters will be treated with complete confidentiality.*

con·fid·ing /kənˈfaɪdɪŋ/ *adj.* [usually before noun] showing trust; showing that you want to tell sb a secret: *a confiding relationship* ▸ **con·fid·ing·ly** *adv.*

con·fig·ur·ation /kənˌfɪɡəˈreɪʃn; *NAmE* -ˌfɪɡjəˈr-/ *noun* **1** (*formal* or *technical*) an arrangement of the parts of sth or a group of things; the form or shape that this arrangement produces **2** (*computing*) the equipment and programs that form a computer system and the way that these are set up to run

con·fig·ure /kənˈfɪɡə(r); *NAmE* -ˈfɪɡjər/ *verb* [usually passive] **~ sth** (*technical*) to arrange sth in a particular way, especially computer equipment; to make equipment or software work in the way that the user prefers

con·fine 0‑w AW /kənˈfaɪn/ *verb* **1** 0‑w **~ sb/sth to sth** [often passive] to keep sb/sth inside the limits of a particular activity, subject, area, etc. SYN **restrict**: *The work will not be confined to the Glasgow area.* ◇ *I will **confine myself** to looking at the period from 1900 to 1916.* **2** 0‑w **~ sb/sth** (**in sth**) [usually passive] to keep a person or an animal in a small or closed space: *Keep the dog confined in a suitable travelling cage.* ◇ *Here the river is confined in a narrow channel.* ◇ *The soldiers concerned were **confined to barracks*** (= had to stay in the BARRACKS, as a punishment). **3 be confined to bed, a wheelchair, etc.** to have to stay in bed, in a WHEELCHAIR, etc: *She was confined to bed with the flu.* ◇ *He was confined to a wheelchair after the accident.*

con·fined 0‑w AW /kənˈfaɪnd/ *adj.* [usually before noun] (of a space or an area) small and surrounded by walls or sides: *It is cruel to keep animals in confined spaces.*

con·fine·ment /kənˈfaɪnmənt/ *noun* **1** [U] the state of being forced to stay in a closed space, prison, etc, the act of putting sb there: *her confinement to a wheelchair* ◇ *years of confinement as a political prisoner* ➲ see also SOLITARY CONFINEMENT **2** [U, C] (*formal* or *old-fashioned*) the time when a woman gives birth to a baby: *the expected date of confinement* ◇ *a **hospital/home confinement***

con·fines /ˈkɒnfaɪnz; *NAmE* ˈkɑːn-/ *noun* [pl.] (*formal*) limits or borders: *It is beyond the confines of human knowledge.* ◇ *the confines of family life*

con·firm 0‑w AW /kənˈfɜːm; *NAmE* -ˈfɜːrm/ *verb* **1** 0‑w to state or show that sth is definitely true or correct, especially by providing evidence: **~ sth** *Rumours of job losses were later confirmed* ◇ *His guilty expression confirmed my suspicions.* ◇ *Please write to confirm your reservation* (= say that it is definite). ◇ **~ (that)...** *Has everyone confirmed (that) they're coming?* ◇ **~ what/when, etc...** *Can you confirm what happened?* ◇ **it is confirmed that...** *It has been confirmed that the meeting will take place next week.* **2** 0‑w **~ sth** | **~ sb** (**in sth**) to make sb feel or believe sth even more strongly: *The walk in the mountains confirmed his fear of heights.* **3** 0‑w to make a position, an agreement, etc. more definite or official; to establish sb/sth firmly: **~ sth** *After a six-month probationary period, her position was confirmed.* ◇ **~ sb as sth** *He was confirmed as captain for the rest of the season.* ◇ **~ sb in sth** *I'm very happy to confirm you in your post.* **4** [usually passive] **~ sb** to make sb a full member of the Christian Church: *She was baptized when she was a month old and confirmed when she was thirteen.*

con·firm·ation AW /ˌkɒnfəˈmeɪʃn; *NAmE* ˌkɑːnfərˈm-/ *noun* [U, C] **1** a statement, letter, etc. that shows that sth is true, correct or definite: *I'm still waiting for confirmation of the test results.* **2** a ceremony at which a person becomes a full member of the Christian Church **3** a Jewish ceremony similar to a BAR MITZVAH or BAT MITZVAH but usually for young people over the age of 16

con·firmed /kənˈfɜːmd; *NAmE* -ˈfɜːrmd/ *adj.* [only before noun] having a particular habit or way of life and not likely to change: *a **confirmed bachelor*** (= a man who is not likely to get married, often used in newspapers to refer to a HOMOSEXUAL man)

con·fis·cate /ˈkɒnfɪskeɪt; *NAmE* ˈkɑːn-/ *verb* **~ sth** to officially take sth away from sb, especially as a punishment: *Their land was confiscated after the war.* ◇ *The teacher threatened to confiscate their phones if they kept using them in class.* ▸ **con·fis·ca·tion** /ˌkɒnfɪˈskeɪʃn; *NAmE* ˌkɑːn-/ *noun* [U, C]

con·flag·ra·tion /ˌkɒnfləˈɡreɪʃn; *NAmE* ˌkɑːn-/ *noun* (*formal*) a very large fire that destroys a lot of land or buildings

con·flate /kənˈfleɪt/ *verb* **~ A and/with B** (*formal*) to put two or more things together to make one new thing ▸ **con·fla·tion** /kənˈfleɪʃn/ *noun* [U, C]

con·flict 0‑w AW *noun, verb*

■ ***noun*** /ˈkɒnflɪkt; *NAmE* ˈkɑːn-/ [C, U] **~ (between A and B)** | **~ (over sth)** **1** 0‑w a situation in which people, groups or countries are involved in a serious disagreement or argument: *a conflict between two cultures* ◇ *The violence was the result of political and ethnic conflicts.* ◇ *She found herself **in conflict with** her parents over her future career.* ◇ *John often **comes into conflict** with his boss.* ◇ *The government has done nothing to **resolve the conflict** over nurses' pay.* **2** 0‑w a violent situation or period of fighting between two countries: ***armed/military conflict*** ➲ COLLOCATIONS at WAR **3** 0‑w a situation in which there are opposing ideas, opinions, feelings or wishes; a situation in which it is difficult to choose: *The story tells of a classic conflict between love and duty.* ◇ *Her diary was a record of her inner conflict.* ◇ *Many of these ideas appear to be **in conflict with** each other.*

IDM **conflict of ˈinterest(s)** a situation in which sb has two jobs, aims, roles, etc. and cannot treat both of them equally and fairly at the same time: *There was a conflict of interest between his business dealings and his political activities.*

■ ***verb*** 0‑w /kənˈflɪkt/ [I] **~ (with sth)** if two ideas, beliefs, stories, etc. **conflict**, it is not possible for them to exist together or for them both to be true SYN **clash**: ***conflicting emotions/interests/loyalties*** ◇ *These results conflict with earlier findings.* ◇ *Reports conflicted on how much of the aid was reaching the famine victims.*

con·flict·ed /kənˈflɪktɪd/ *adj.* (*especially NAmE*) confused about what to do or choose because you have strong but opposing feelings

con·flu·ence /ˈkɒnfluəns; *NAmE* ˈkɑːn-/ *noun* [usually sing.] **1** (*technical*) the place where two rivers flow together and become one **2** (*formal*) the fact of two or more things becoming one: *a confluence of social factors*

con·form AW /kənˈfɔːm; *NAmE* -ˈfɔːrm/ *verb* **1** [I] to behave and think in the same way as most other people in a group or society: *There is considerable pressure on teenagers to conform.* ◇ **~ to sth** *He refused to conform to the local customs.* **2** [I] **~ to/with sth** to obey a rule, law, etc. SYN **comply**: *The building does not conform with safety regulations.* **3** [I] **~ to sth** to agree with or match sth: *It did not conform to the usual stereotype of an industrial city.*

C

con·form·able AW /kən'fɔːməbl; NAmE -'fɔːrm-/ *adj.* **~ to/with sth** (*formal*) similar in form or nature to sth; in agreement with sth SYN **consistent**: *What happens in cases where common law is not conformable to the constitution?* ▸ **con·form·abil·ity** AW /kən,fɔːmə'bɪləti; NAmE -'fɔːrm-/ *noun* [U]

con·form·ance AW /kən'fɔːməns; NAmE -'fɔːrm-/ *noun* [U] **~ (to/with sth)** (*formal*) the fact of following the rules or standards of sth: *You need to ensure conformance to strict quality guidelines.* SYN **conformity**

con·form·ation AW /,kɒnfɔː'meɪʃn; NAmE ,kɑːnfɔːr'm-/ *noun* [U, C] (*formal*) the way in which sth is formed; the structure of sth, especially an animal

con·form·ist AW /kən'fɔːmɪst; NAmE -'fɔːrm-/ *noun* (often *disapproving*) a person who behaves and thinks in the same way as most other people and who does not want to be different ▸ **con·form·ist** *adj.* ➲ see also NONCONFORMIST

con·form·ity AW /kən'fɔːməti; NAmE -'fɔːrm-/ *noun* [U] **~ (to/with sth)** (*formal*) behaviour or actions that follow the accepted rules of society

IDM **in con'formity with sth** following the rules of sth; conforming to sth: *regulations that are in conformity with European law*

con·found /kən'faʊnd/ *verb* (*formal*) **1 ~ sb** to confuse and surprise sb SYN **baffle**: *The sudden rise in share prices has confounded economists.* **2 ~ sb/sth** to prove sb/sth wrong: *to confound expectations* ◇ *She confounded her critics and proved she could do the job.* **3 ~ sb** (*old-fashioned*) to defeat an enemy

IDM **con'found it/you!** (*old-fashioned*) used to show that you are angry about sth/with sb

con·found·ed /kən'faʊndɪd/ *adj.* [only before noun] (*old-fashioned*) used when describing sth to show that you are annoyed

con·fra·ter·nity /,kɒnfrə'tɜːnɪti; NAmE ,kɑːn-/ *noun* (*pl.* -ies) (*formal*) a group of people who join together especially for a religious purpose or to help other people

con·front 0→ /kən'frʌnt/ *verb*
1 0→ **~ sb/sth** (of problems or a difficult situation) to appear and need to be dealt with by sb: *the economic problems confronting the country* ◇ *The government found itself confronted by massive opposition.* **2** 0→ **~ sth** to deal with a problem or difficult situation SYN **face up to**: *She knew that she had to confront her fears.* **3** 0→ **~ sb** to face sb so that they cannot avoid seeing and hearing you, especially in an unfriendly or dangerous situation: *This was the first time he had confronted an armed robber.* **4** 0→ **~ sb with sb/sth** to make sb face or deal with an unpleasant or difficult person or situation: *He confronted her with a choice between her career or their relationship.* **5 be confronted with sth** to have sth in front of you that you have to deal with or react to: *Most people when confronted with a horse will pat it.*

con·fron·ta·tion /,kɒnfrʌn'teɪʃn; NAmE ,kɑːnfrən-/ *noun* [U, C] **~ (with sb)** | **~ (between A and B)** a situation in which there is an angry disagreement between people or groups who have different opinions: *She wanted to avoid another confrontation with her father.* ◇ *confrontation between employers and unions*

con·fron·ta·tion·al /,kɒnfrʌn'teɪʃnl; NAmE ,kɑːnfrən-/ *adj.* tending to deal with people in an aggressive way that is likely to cause arguments, rather than discussing things with them

Con·fu·cian /kən'fjuːʃən/ *adj.* [usually before noun] based on or believing the teachings of the Chinese PHILOSOPHER Confucius ▸ **Con·fu·cian** *noun* **Con·fu·cian·ism** *noun* [U]

con·fus·able /kən'fjuːzəbl/ *adj.* if two things are **confusable**, it is easy to confuse them: *'Historic' and 'historical' are easily confusable.* ◇ *The various types of owl are easily confusable with one another.* ▸ **con·fus·able** *noun*: *confusables such as 'principle' and 'principal'*

con·fuse 0→ /kən'fjuːz/ *verb*
1 0→ **~ sb** to make sb unable to think clearly or understand sth: *They confused me with conflicting accounts of what happened.* **2** 0→ **~ A and/with B** to think wrongly that sb/sth is sb/sth else SYN **mix up**: *People often confuse me and my twin sister.* ◇ *Be careful not to confuse quantity with quality.* **3** 0→ **~ sth** to make a subject more difficult to understand: *His comments only served to confuse the issue further.*

con·fused 0→ /kən'fjuːzd/ *adj.*
1 0→ unable to think clearly or to understand what is happening or what sb is saying: *People are confused about all the different labels on food these days.* ◇ *He was depressed and in a confused state of mind.* ◇ *I'm confused—say all that again.* **2** 0→ not clear or easy to understand: *The children gave a confused account of what had happened.* ▸ **con·fused·ly** /-ədli/ *adv.*

con·fus·ing 0→ /kən'fjuːzɪŋ/ *adj.*
difficult to understand; not clear: *The instructions on the box are very confusing.* ◇ *a very confusing experience* ▸ **con·fus·ing·ly** *adv.*

con·fu·sion 0→ /kən'fjuːʒn/ *noun*
1 0→ [U, C] **~ (about/over sth)** | **~ (as to sth)** a state of not being certain about what is happening, what you should do, what sth means, etc: *There is some confusion about what the correct procedure should be.* ◇ *a confusion as to what to do next* **2** 0→ [U, C] **~ (between A and B)** the fact of making a mistake about who sb is or what sth is: *To avoid confusion, please write the children's names clearly on all their school clothes.* ◇ *confusion between letters of the alphabet like 'o' or 'a'* **3** 0→ [U] a feeling of embarrassment when you do not understand sth and are not sure what to do in a situation: *He looked at me* ***in confusion*** *and did not answer the question.* **4** 0→ [U] a confused situation in which people do not know what action to take: *Fighting had broken out and all was chaos and confusion.* ◇ *Her unexpected arrival threw us into total confusion.*

con·fute /kən'fjuːt/ *verb* **~ sb/sth** (*formal*) to prove a person or an argument to be wrong

conga /'kɒŋgə; NAmE 'kɑːŋgə/ *noun* **1** a fast dance in which the dancers follow a leader in a long winding line, with each person holding on to the person in front; a piece of music for this dance **2** (also **'conga drum**) a tall narrow drum that you play with your hands ➲ VISUAL VOCAB page V30

con·geal /kən'dʒiːl/ *verb* [I] (of blood, fat, etc.) to become thick or solid: *congealed blood* ◇ *The cold remains of supper had congealed on the plate.* ◇ (*figurative*) *The bitterness and tears had congealed into hatred.*

con·gen·ial /kən'dʒiːniəl/ *adj.* (*formal*) **1** (of a person) pleasant to spend time with because their interests and character are similar to your own: *a congenial colleague* **2 ~ (to sb)** (of a place, job, etc.) pleasant because it suits your character: *a congenial working environment* **3 ~ (to sth)** (*formal*) suitable for sth: *a situation that was congenial to the expression of nationalist opinions*

con·geni·tal /kən'dʒenɪtl/ *adj.* **1** (of a disease or medical condition) existing since or before birth: *congenital abnormalities* **2** [only before noun] existing as part of a person's character and not likely to change: *a congenital inability to tell the truth* **3** [only before noun] (of a person) born with a particular illness: (*figurative*) *a congenital liar* (= one who will not change) ▸ **con·geni·tal·ly** /-təli/ *adv.*

con·ger /'kɒŋgə(r); NAmE 'kɑːŋ-/ (also **,conger 'eel**) *noun* a large EEL (= a long thin fish) that lives in the sea

con·gest·ed /kən'dʒestɪd/ *adj.* **1 ~ (with sth)** crowded; full of traffic: *congested city streets* ◇ *Many of Europe's airports are heavily congested.* **2** (*medical*) (of a part of the body) blocked with blood or MUCUS

con·ges·tion /kən'dʒestʃən/ *noun* [U] **1** the state of being crowded and full of traffic: *traffic congestion and pollution* ➲ COLLOCATIONS at TOWN **2** (*medical*) the state of part of the body being blocked with blood or MUCUS: *congestion of the lungs* ◇ *medicine to relieve nasal congestion*

con'gestion charge *noun* (*BrE*) an amount of money that people have to pay for driving their cars into the centre of some cities as a way of stopping the city centre from becoming too full of traffic ▶ con'gestion charging *noun* [U]

con·glom·er·ate /kən'glɒmərət; *NAmE* -'glɑːm-/ *noun* **1** [C] (*business*) a large company formed by joining together different firms: *a media conglomerate* **2** [sing.] (*formal*) a number of things or parts that are put together to form a whole **3** [U] (*geology*) a type of rock made of small stones held together by dried CLAY

con·glom·er·ation /kən,glɒmə'reɪʃn; *NAmE* -,glɑːm-/ *noun* **1** [C, usually sing.] **a ~ (of sth)** (*formal*) a mixture of different things that are found all together: *a conglomeration of buildings of different sizes and styles* **2** [U] the process of forming a conglomerate or the state of being a conglomerate

con·grats /kən'græts/ *noun* [pl.] (*informal*) = CONGRATULATIONS

con·gratu·late /kən'grætʃuleɪt/ *verb* **1** ⊶ **~ sb (on sth)** to tell sb that you are pleased about their success or achievements: *I congratulated them all on their results.* ◇ *The authors are to be congratulated on producing such a clear and authoritative work.* **2 ~ yourself (on sth)** to feel pleased and proud because you have achieved sth or been successful at sth: *You can congratulate yourself on having done an excellent job.*

con·gratu·la·tion ⊶ /kən,grætʃu'leɪʃn/ *noun* **1** ⊶ **congratulations** [pl.] a message congratulating sb (= saying that you are happy about their good luck or success): *to* ***offer/send*** *your* ***congratulations*** *to sb* **2** ⊶ **Congratulations!** used when you want to congratulate sb: *'We're getting married!' 'Congratulations!'* ◇ *Congratulations on your exam results!* **3** ⊶ [U] the act of congratulating sb: *a letter of congratulation*

con·gratu·la·tory /kən,grætʃu'leɪtəri; *NAmE* kən'grætʃələtɔːri/ *adj.* expressing congratulations: *a congratulatory message*

con·gre·gate /'kɒŋgrɪgeɪt; *NAmE* 'kɑːŋ-/ *verb* [I] to come together in a group: *Young people often congregate in the main square in the evenings.*

con·gre·ga·tion /,kɒŋgrɪ'geɪʃn; *NAmE* ,kɑːŋ-/ *noun* [C+sing./pl. v.] **1** a group of people who are gathered together in a church to worship God, not including the priest and CHOIR: *The congregation stood to sing the hymn.* ➲ COLLOCATIONS at RELIGION **2** the group of people who belong to a particular church and go there regularly to worship ▶ **con·gre·ga·tion·al** /-ʃənl/ *adj.*

Con·gre·ga·tion·al·ism /,kɒŋgrɪ'geɪʃnəlɪzəm; *NAmE* ,kɑːŋ-/ *noun* [U] a type of Christianity in which the congregation of each church is responsible for its own affairs ▶ **Con·gre·ga·tion·al** *adj.* **Con·gre·ga·tion·al·ist** *noun*

con·gress ⊶ /'kɒŋgres; *NAmE* 'kɑːŋgrəs/ *noun* **1** ⊶ [C] a large formal meeting or series of meetings where representatives from different groups discuss ideas, make decisions, etc: *an international congress of trades unions* **2** ⊶ [C+sing./pl. v.] **Congress** (in the US and some other countries) the name of the group of people who are elected to make laws, in the US consisting of the Senate and the HOUSE OF REPRESENTATIVES: *Congress will vote on the proposals tomorrow.* ➲ COLLOCATIONS at POLITICS **3** [C+sing./pl. v.] used in the names of political parties in some countries: *the African National Congress*

con·gres·sion·al /kən'greʃənl/ *adj.* [only before noun] related to or belonging to a congress or the Congress in the US: *a* ***congressional committee/bill*** ◇ *the midterm Congressional elections*

con·gress·man /'kɒŋgresmən; *NAmE* 'kɑːŋgrəs-/, **con·gress·woman** /'kɒŋgreswʊmən; *NAmE* 'kɑːŋgrəs-/ *noun* (often **Congressman, Congresswoman**) (*pl.* -men /-mən/, -women /-wɪmɪn/) (also **con·gress·person** /-pɜːsn; *NAmE* -pɜːrsn/) a member of Congress in the US, especially the House of Representatives

con·gru·ent /'kɒŋgruənt; *NAmE* 'kɑːŋ-/ *adj.* **1** (*geometry*) having the same size and shape: *congruent triangles* **2 ~ (with sth)** (*formal*) suitable for sth; appropriate in a particular situation ▶ **con·gru·ence** /'kɒŋgruəns; *NAmE* 'kɑːŋ-/ *noun* [U]

conic /'kɒnɪk; *NAmE* 'kɑːnɪk/ *adj., noun* (*geometry*)
■ ***adj.*** of or related to a CONE
■ ***noun*** = CONIC SECTION

con·ic·al /'kɒnɪkl; *NAmE* 'kɑːn-/ *adj.* shaped like a CONE

,conic 'section (also **conic**) *noun* (*geometry*) a shape formed when a flat surface meets a CONE with a round base ➲ VISUAL VOCAB page V58

con·ifer /'kɒnɪfə(r); 'kəʊn-; *NAmE* 'kɑːn-; 'koʊn-/ *noun* any tree that produces hard dry fruit called CONES. Most conifers are EVERGREEN (= have leaves that stay on the tree all year). ➲ VISUAL VOCAB page V4 ▶ **con·ifer·ous** /kə'nɪfərəs/ *adj.*: ***coniferous trees/forests***

con·jec·ture /kən'dʒektʃə(r)/ *noun, verb*
■ ***noun*** (*formal*) **1** [C] an opinion or idea that is not based on definite knowledge and is formed by guessing SYN **guess**: *The truth of his conjecture was confirmed by the newspaper report.* **2** [U] the forming of an opinion or idea that is not based on definite knowledge: *What was going through the killer's mind is a matter for conjecture.* ➲ see also GUESSWORK ▶ **con·jec·tural** /kən'dʒektʃərəl/ *adj.*
■ ***verb*** [I, T] (*formal*) to form an opinion about sth even though you do not have much information on it SYN **guess**: **~ (about sth)** *We can only conjecture about what was in the killer's mind.* ◇ **~ what/how, etc...** *We can only conjecture what was in the killer's mind* ◇ **~ that...** *He conjectured that the population might double in ten years.* ◇ **~ sth** *She conjectured the existence of a completely new species.* ◇ **~ sth to do sth** *The remains are conjectured to be thousands of years old.*

con·join /kən'dʒɔɪn/ *verb* [I, T] **~ (sth)** (*formal*) to join together; to join two or more things together

con,joined 'twin *noun* (*technical*) (also **,Siamese 'twin**) one of two people who are born with their bodies joined together in some way, sometimes sharing the same organs

con·joint /kən'dʒɔɪnt/ *adj.* [usually before noun] (*formal*) combining all or both the people or things involved ▶ **con·joint·ly** *adv.*

con·ju·gal /'kɒndʒəgl; *NAmE* 'kɑːn-/ *adj.* [only before noun] (*formal*) connected with marriage and the sexual relationship between a husband and wife: *conjugal love*

,conjugal 'rights *noun* [pl.] the rights that a husband and wife each has in a marriage, especially the right to have sex with their partner

con·ju·gate /'kɒndʒəgeɪt; *NAmE* 'kɑːn-/ *verb* (*grammar*) **1** [T] **~ sth** to give the different forms of a verb, as they vary according to NUMBER, PERSON, tense, etc. **2** [I] (of a verb) to have different forms, showing NUMBER, PERSON, tense, etc: *How does this verb conjugate?* ➲ compare DECLINE

con·ju·ga·tion /,kɒndʒu'geɪʃn; *NAmE* ,kɑːndʒə-/ *noun* (*grammar*) **1** [C, U] the way in which a verb conjugates: *a verb with an irregular conjugation* **2** [C] a group of verbs that conjugate in the same way: *Latin verbs of the second conjugation*

con·junc·tion /kən'dʒʌŋkʃn/ *noun* **1** [C] (*grammar*) a word that joins words, phrases or sentences, for example 'and', 'but', 'or' **2** [C] (*formal*) a combination of events, etc, that causes a particular result: *The conjunction of low inflation and low unemployment came as a very pleasant surprise.* **3** [C, U] (*astronomy*) the fact of stars, planets, etc. passing close together as seen from the earth
IDM **in con'junction with** (*formal*) together with: *The police are working in conjunction with tax officers on the investigation.* ◇ *The system is designed to be used in conjunction with a word processing program.*

con·junc·tiv·itis /kən,dʒʌŋktɪ'vaɪtɪs/ *noun* [U] an infectious eye disease that causes pain and swelling in part of the eye

con·jure /'kʌndʒə(r)/ *verb* [I, T] to do clever tricks such as making things seem to appear or disappear as if by magic: *Her grandfather taught her to conjure.* ◇ **~ sth + adv./prep.**

C

He could conjure coins from behind people's ears. IDM see NAME *n.*

PHR V ˌconjure sth↔ˈup **1** to make sth appear as a picture in your mind SYN **evoke**: *That smell always conjures up memories of holidays in France.* **2** to make sb/sth appear by using special magic words **conjure sth from/out of sth** to create sth or make sth appear in a surprising or unexpected way: *He conjured a delicious meal out of a few leftovers.*

con·jur·ing /ˈkʌndʒərɪŋ/ *noun* [U] entertainment in the form of magic tricks, especially ones which seem to make things appear or disappear: *a conjuring trick*

con·juror (also **con·jurer**) /ˈkʌndʒərə(r)/ *noun* a person who performs conjuring tricks

conk /kɒŋk; *NAmE* kɑːŋk; kɔːŋk/ *verb, noun*

■ ***verb*** **~ sb** (*informal, especially NAmE*) to hit sb hard on their head

PHR V ˌconk ˈout (*informal*) **1** (of a machine, etc.) to stop working: *The car conked out halfway up the hill.* **2** (of a person) to go to sleep

■ ***noun*** (*BrE, informal*) a person's nose

conk·er /ˈkɒŋkə(r); *NAmE* ˈkɑːŋ-/ *noun* (*informal, especially BrE*) **1** [C] the smooth shiny brown nut of the HORSE CHESTNUT tree ⇨ VISUAL VOCAB page V8 ⇨ compare CHESTNUT, HORSE CHESTNUT **2 conkers** [U] a children's game played with conkers on strings, in which two players take turns to try to hit and break each other's conker

ˈ**con man** *noun* (*informal*) a man who tricks others into giving him money, etc.

con·nect 🔑 /kəˈnekt/ *verb*

▸ JOIN **1** 🔑 [T, I] **~ (A to/with/and B)** to join together two or more things; to be joined together: *The towns are connected by train and bus services.* ◇ *The canal was built to connect Sheffield with the Humber estuary.* ◇ *a connecting door* (= one that connects two rooms) ◇ *The rooms on this floor connect.*

▸ ELECTRICITY/GAS/WATER **2** 🔑 [T] **~ sth (to sth)** to join sth to the main supply of electricity, gas, water, etc. or to another piece of equipment: *First connect the printer to the computer.* ◇ *We're waiting for the telephone to be connected.* OPP **disconnect**

▸ INTERNET **3** 🔑 [I, T] **~ (sb) (to sth)** to join a computer to the Internet or a computer network: *Click 'Continue' to connect to the Internet.* OPP **disconnect**

▸ LINK **4** 🔑 [T] **~ sb/sth (with sb/sth)** to notice or make a link between people, things, events, etc. SYN **associate**: *There was nothing to connect him with the crime.* ◇ *I was surprised to hear them mentioned together: I had never connected them before.*

▸ OF TRAIN/BUS/PLANE **5** [I] **~ (with sth)** to arrive just before another one leaves so that passengers can change from one to the other: *His flight to Amsterdam connects with an afternoon flight to New York.* ◇ *There's a connecting flight at noon.*

▸ TELEPHONE LINES **6** [T] **~ sb** to join telephone lines so that people can speak to each other SYN **put through**: *Hold on please, I'm trying to connect you.* OPP **disconnect**

▸ FORM RELATIONSHIP **7** [I] **~ (with sb)** (*especially NAmE*) to form a good relationship with sb so that you like and understand each other: *They met a couple of times but they didn't really connect.*

▸ HIT **8** [I] (*especially NAmE*) **~ (with sb/sth)** (*informal*) to hit sb/sth: *The blow connected and she felt a surge of pain.*

PHR V **conˌnect sth↔ˈup (to sth)** | **conˌnect ˈup (to sth)** to join sth to a supply of electricity, gas, etc. or to another piece of equipment; to be joined in this way: *She connected up the two computers.* OPP **disconnect**

con·nect·ed 🔑 /kəˈnektɪd/ *adj.*
~ (with sb/sth) (of two or more things or people) having a link between them: *market prices and other connected matters* ◇ *They are connected by marriage.* ◇ *jobs connected with the environment* ◇ *The two issues are* ***closely connected.*** OPP **unconnected** ⇨ see also WELL CONNECTED

con·nect·ed·ness /kəˈnektɪdnəs/ *noun* [U] **~ (to/with sb/sth)** a feeling that you have a link with sb/sth or are part of a group: *the benefits of helping students feel a sense of connectedness to their school*

con·nec·tion 🔑 (*BrE* also *old-fashioned* **con·nex·ion**) /kəˈnekʃn/ *noun*

▸ LINK **1** 🔑 [C] something that connects two facts, ideas, etc. SYN **link**: **~ (between A and B)** *Scientists have established a connection between cholesterol levels and heart disease.* ◇ **~ (with sth)** *a* ***direct/close/strong connection*** *with sth* ◇ *How did you* ***make the connection*** (= realize that there was a connection between two facts that did not seem to be related)?

▸ BEING CONNECTED **2** 🔑 [U, C] **~ (to sth)** the act of connecting or the state of being connected: *Connection to the gas supply was delayed for three days.* ◇ *I'm having problems with my Internet connection.*

▸ IN ELECTRICAL SYSTEM **3** 🔑 [C] a point, especially in an electrical system, where two parts connect: *A faulty connection caused the machine to stop.*

▸ TRAIN/BUS/PLANE **4** 🔑 [C] a train, bus or plane at a station or an airport that a passenger can take soon after getting off another in order to continue their journey: *We arrived in good time for the connection to Paris.* **5** [C, usually pl.] a means of travelling to another place: *There are good bus and train connections between the resort and major cities.*

▸ PERSON/ORGANIZATION **6** [C, usually pl.] a person or an organization that you know and that can help or advise you in your social or professional life SYN **contact**: *One of my business connections gave them my name.*

▸ DISTANT RELATIVES **7 connections** [pl.] people who are your relatives, but not members of your close family: *She is British but also has German connections.*

IDM **in connection with sb/sth** 🔑 for reasons connected with sb/sth: *A man has been arrested in connection with the murder of the teenager.* ◇ *I am writing to you in connection with your recent job application.* **in this/that connection** (*formal*) for reasons connected with sth recently mentioned

con·nect·ive /kəˈnektɪv/ *adj., noun*

■ ***adj.*** (*medical*) that connects things: *connective tissue*

■ ***noun*** (*grammar*) a word that connects two parts of a sentence: *Don't overuse a causal connective like 'because'.*

con·nec·tiv·ity /ˌkɒnekˈtɪvəti; *NAmE* ˌkɑːn-/ *noun* [U] (*technical*) the state of being connected or the degree to which two things are connected: *ISDN connectivity allows computers to communicate over a network.*

con·nec·tor /kəˈnektə(r)/ *noun* a thing that links two or more things together: *a cable connector*

con·ning tower /ˈkɒnɪŋ taʊə(r); *NAmE* ˈkɑːnɪŋ/ *noun* a raised structure on a SUBMARINE containing the PERISCOPE

con·nip·tion /kəˈnɪpʃn/ (also **conˈniption fit**) *noun* (*old-fashioned, NAmE*) a sudden attack of anger or fear: *He had a conniption when he heard the news.*

con·niv·ance /kəˈnaɪvəns/ *noun* [U] (*disapproving*) help in doing sth wrong; the failure to stop sth wrong from happening: *The crime was committed with the connivance of a police officer.*

con·nive /kəˈnaɪv/ *verb* (*formal, disapproving*) **1** [I] **~ at/in sth** to seem to allow sth wrong to happen: *She knew that if she said nothing she would be conniving in an injustice.* **2** [I] **~ (with sb) (to do sth)** to work together with sb to do sth wrong or illegal SYN **conspire**: *The government was accused of having connived with the security forces to permit murder.*

con·niv·ing /kəˈnaɪvɪŋ/ *adj.* (*disapproving*) behaving in a way that secretly hurts others or deliberately fails to prevent others from being hurt

con·nois·seur /ˌkɒnəˈsɜː(r); *NAmE* ˌkɑːnəˈsɜːr; -ˈsʊr/ *noun* an expert on matters involving the judgement of beauty, quality or skill in art, food or music: *a connoisseur of Italian painting* ◇ *a wine connoisseur*

con·no·ta·tion /ˌkɒnəˈteɪʃn; *NAmE* ˌkɑːn-/ *noun* an idea suggested by a word in addition to its main meaning: *The* *word 'professional' has connotations of skill and excellence.* ◇ *negative connotations* ➲ compare DENOTATION

con·note /kəˈnəʊt; *NAmE* kəˈnoʊt/ *verb* **~ sth** (*formal*) (of a word) to suggest a feeling, an idea, etc. as well as the main meaning ➲ compare DENOTE

con·nub·ial /kəˈnjuːbiəl; *NAmE* -ˈnuː-/ *adj.* (*literary*) related to marriage, or the relationship between husband and wife

con·quer /ˈkɒŋkə(r); *NAmE* ˈkɑːŋ-/ *verb* **1 ~ sb/sth** to take control of a country or city and its people by force: *The Normans conquered England in 1066.* ◇ ***conquered peoples/races/territories*** **2 ~ sb** to defeat sb, especially in a competition, race, etc: *The world champion conquered yet another challenger last night.* **3 ~ sth** to succeed in dealing with or controlling sth: *The only way to conquer a fear is to face it.* ◇ *Mount Everest was conquered* (= successfully climbed) *in 1953.* **4 ~ sth** to become very popular or successful in a place: *The band is now setting out to conquer the world.*

con·queror /ˈkɒŋkərə(r); *NAmE* ˈkɑːŋ-/ *noun* a person who conquers: *William the Conqueror* (= King William I of England)

con·quest /ˈkɒŋkwest; *NAmE* ˈkɑːŋ-/ *noun* **1** [sing., U] the act of taking control of a country, city, etc. by force: *the Norman Conquest* (= of England in 1066) **2** [C] an area of land taken by force: *the Spanish conquests in South America* **3** [C] (usually *humorous*) a person that sb has persuaded to love them or to have sex with them: *I'm just one of his many conquests.* **4** [U] the act of gaining control over sth that is difficult or dangerous: *the conquest of inflation*

con·quis·ta·dor /kɒnˈkwɪstədɔː(r); -ˈkɪst-; *NAmE* kɑːn-/ *noun* (*pl.* **con·quis·ta·dores** /kɒnˌkwɪstəˈdɔːreɪz; -ˌkɪstə-; *NAmE* kɑːn-/ or **con·quis·ta·dors**) (from *Spanish*) one of the Spanish people who took control of Mexico and Peru by force in the 16th century

con·san·guin·ity /ˌkɒnsæŋˈɡwɪnəti; *NAmE* ˌkɑːn-/ *noun* [U] (*formal*) relationship by birth in the same family

con·science /ˈkɒnʃəns; *NAmE* ˈkɑːn-/ *noun* **1** [C, U] the part of your mind that tells you whether your actions are right or wrong: *to have a* ***clear/guilty conscience*** (= to feel that you have done right/wrong) ◇ *This is a* ***matter of*** *individual* ***conscience*** (= everyone must make their own judgement about it). ◇ *He won't let it trouble his conscience.* ➲ see also SOCIAL CONSCIENCE **2** [U, C] a guilty feeling about sth you have done or failed to do: *She was seized by a sudden pang of conscience.* ◇ *I have a terrible conscience about it.* **3** [U] the fact of behaving in a way that you feel is right even though this may cause problems: *freedom of conscience* (= the freedom to do what you believe to be right) ◇ *Emilia is the voice of conscience in the play.* ➲ see also PRISONER OF CONSCIENCE
IDM **in (all/good) conscience** (*formal*) believing your actions to be fair SYN **honestly**: *We cannot in all conscience refuse to help.* **on your ˈconscience** making you feel guilty for doing or failing to do sth: *I'll write and apologize. I've had it on my conscience for weeks.* ➲ more at PRICK *v.*

ˈconscience-stricken *adj.* feeling guilty about sth you have done or failed to do

con·scien·tious /ˌkɒnʃiˈenʃəs; *NAmE* ˌkɑːn-/ *adj.* taking care to do things carefully and correctly: *a conscientious student/teacher/worker* ▶ **con·scien·tious·ly** *adv.*: *She performed all her duties conscientiously.* **con·scien·tious·ness** *noun* [U]

ˌconscientious obˈjector *noun* a person who refuses to serve in the armed forces for moral reasons ➲ compare DRAFT DODGER, PACIFIST

con·scien·tize (*BrE* also **-ise**) /ˈkɒnʃəntaɪz; *NAmE* ˈkɑːn-/ *verb* **~ sb/yourself** (*SAfrE*) to make sb/yourself aware of important social or political issues: *People need to be conscientized about their rights.*

con·scious 🔑 /ˈkɒnʃəs; *NAmE* ˈkɑːn-/ *adj.*
1 🔑 [not before noun] aware of sth; noticing sth: **~ of sth** *She's very conscious of the problems involved.* ◇ **~ of doing sth** *He became acutely conscious of having failed his parents.* ◇ **~ that…** *I was vaguely conscious that I was being watched.* OPP **unconscious** ➲ see also SELF-CONSCIOUS **2** 🔑 able to use your senses and mental powers to understand what is happening: *A patient who is not fully conscious should never be left alone.* OPP **unconscious 3** 🔑 (of actions, feelings, etc.) deliberate or controlled: *to make a* ***conscious decision*** ◇ *I made a* ***conscious effort*** *to get there on time.* ◇ *a conscious act of cruelty* OPP **unconscious** ➲ compare SUBCONSCIOUS **4** 🔑 being particularly interested in sth: *environmentally conscious* ◇ *They have become increasingly health-conscious.* ▶ **con·scious·ly** *adv.*: *Consciously or unconsciously, you made a choice.*

con·scious·ness /ˈkɒnʃəsnəs; *NAmE* ˈkɑːn-/ *noun* [U] **1** the state of being able to use your senses and mental powers to understand what is happening: *I can't remember any more—I must have* ***lost consciousness.*** ◇ *She did not* ***regain consciousness*** *and died the next day.* **2** the state of being aware of sth SYN **awareness**: *his consciousness of the challenge facing him* ◇ ***class-consciousness*** (=consciousness of different classes in society) **3** the ideas and opinions of a person or group: *her newly-developed political consciousness* ➲ see also STREAM OF CONSCIOUSNESS

ˈconsciousness-raising *noun* [U] the process of making people aware of important social and political issues

con·script *verb, noun*
■ ***verb*** /kənˈskrɪpt/ (*especially BrE*) (*NAmE* usually **draft**) [usually passive] **~ sb (into sth)** to make sb join the armed forces SYN **call up**: *He was conscripted into the army in 1939.*
■ ***noun*** /ˈkɒnskrɪpt; *NAmE* ˈkɑːn-/ (*especially BrE*) (*US* usually **draft·ee**) a person who has been conscripted to join the armed forces: *young army conscripts* ◇ ***conscript soldiers/armies*** ➲ compare VOLUNTEER

con·scrip·tion /kənˈskrɪpʃn/ *noun* [U] (*especially BrE*) (*US* usually **the draft**) the practice of ordering people by law to serve in the armed forces SYN **call-up**

con·se·crate /ˈkɒnsɪkreɪt; *NAmE* ˈkɑːn-/ *verb* **1 ~ sth** to state officially in a religious ceremony that sth is holy and can be used for religious purposes: *The church was consecrated in 1853.* ◇ *consecrated ground* **2 ~ sth** (in Christian belief) to make bread and wine into the body and blood of Christ **3 ~ sb (as) (sth)** to state officially in a religious ceremony that sb is now a priest, etc: *He was consecrated (as) bishop last year.* **4 ~ sth/sb/yourself to sth** (*formal*) to give sth/sb/yourself to a special purpose, especially a religious one ▶ **con·se·cra·tion** /ˌkɒnsɪˈkreɪʃn; *NAmE* ˌkɑːn-/ *noun* [C, U]: *the consecration of a church/bishop*

con·secu·tive /kənˈsekjətɪv/ *adj.* [usually before noun] following one after another in a series, without interruption: *She was absent for nine consecutive days.* ◇ *He is beginning his fourth consecutive term of office.* ▶ **con·secu·tive·ly** *adv.*

con·sen·su·al /kənˈsenʃuəl/ *adj.* (*formal*) **1** which people in general agree with: *a consensual approach* **2** (of an activity) which the people taking part have agreed to: *consensual sex*

con·sen·sus AW /kənˈsensəs/ *noun* [sing., U] an opinion that all members of a group agree with: **~ (about/on sth)** *She is skilled at achieving consensus on sensitive issues.* ◇ *There is a growing* ***consensus of opinion*** *on this issue.* ◇ *an attempt to* ***reach a consensus*** ◇ **~ (among sb) (about/on sth)** *There is a general consensus among teachers about the need for greater security in schools.* ◇ **~ (that…)** *There seems to be a consensus that the plan should be rejected.*

con·sent AW /kənˈsent/ *noun, verb*
■ ***noun*** **1** [U] **~ (to sth)** permission to do sth, especially given by sb in authority: *Children under 16 cannot* ***give consent*** *to medical treatment.* ◇ *The written consent of a parent is required.* ◇ *to* ***refuse/withhold*** *your* ***consent*** ◇ *He is charged with taking a car* ***without*** *the owner's* ***consent.*** ➲ see also AGE OF CONSENT **2** [U] agreement about sth: *She was chosen as leader* ***by common consent*** (= everyone agreed to the choice). ◇ ***By mutual consent*** *they didn't go out* (= they both agreed not to). **3** [C] an official document giving permission for sth
■ ***verb*** [I] (rather *formal*) to agree to sth or give your permis-

sion for sth: *When she told them what she intended they readily consented.* ◇ **~ to sth** *He reluctantly consented to his daughter's marriage.* ◇ **~ to do sth** *She finally consented to answer our questions.* ➲ SYNONYMS at AGREE

C

con,senting 'adult *noun* a person who is considered old enough, by law, to decide whether they should agree to have sex; a person who has agreed to have sex

con·se·quence 🗝 AW /ˈkɒnsɪkwəns; *NAmE* ˈkɑːnsəkwens/ *noun*
1 🗝 [C] **~ (of sth) (for sb/sth)** a result of sth that has happened: *This decision could have* **serious consequences** *for the industry.* ◇ *Two hundred people lost their jobs* **as a** *direct* **consequence** *of the merger.* ◇ *He drove too fast with tragic consequences.* ◇ *to* **suffer/face/take the consequences** *of your actions* ➲ SYNONYMS at RESULT ➲ LANGUAGE BANK at CONSEQUENTLY **2** [U] (*formal*) importance: *Don't worry. It's* **of no consequence.**
IDM **in consequence (of sth)** (*formal*) as a result of sth: *The child was born deformed in consequence of an injury to its mother.*

con·se·quent AW /ˈkɒnsɪkwənt; *NAmE* ˈkɑːnsəkwənt/ *adj.* (*formal*) happening as a result of sth SYN **resultant**: *the lowering of taxes and the consequent increase in spending* ◇ **~ on/upon sth** *the responsibilities consequent upon the arrival of a new child*

con·se·quen·tial /ˌkɒnsɪˈkwenʃl; *NAmE* ˌkɑːnsəˈk-/ *adj.* (*formal*) **1** happening as a result or an effect of sth SYN **resultant**: *retirement and the consequential reduction in income* **2** important; that will have important results: *The report discusses a number of consequential matters that are yet to be decided.* OPP **inconsequential** ▸ **con·se·quen·tial·ly** /-ʃəli/ *adv.*

con·se·quent·ly AW /ˈkɒnsɪkwəntli; *NAmE* ˈkɑːnsəkwentli/ *adv.* as a result; therefore: *This poses a threat to agriculture and the food chain, and consequently to human health.*

Language Bank

consequently
Describing the effect of something

- **One consequence of** changes in diet over recent years has been a dramatic increase in cases of childhood obesity.
- Many parents today do not have time to cook healthy meals for their children. **Consequently/As a consequence**, many children grow up eating too much junk food.
- Many children spend their free time watching TV instead of playing outside. **As a result**, more and more of them are becoming overweight.
- Last year junk food was banned in schools. **The effect of this** has been to create a black market in the playground, with pupils bringing sweets from home to sell to other pupils.

➲ note at EFFECT
➲ Language Banks at BECAUSE OF, CAUSE, THEREFORE

con·ser·vancy /kənˈsɜːvənsi; *NAmE* -ˈsɜːrv-/ *noun* **1 Conservancy** [sing.+ sing./pl. v.] a group of officials who control the use of a port, a river, an area of land, etc: *the Thames Conservancy* ◇ *Texas Nature Conservancy* **2** [U] (*formal*) the protection of the natural environment SYN **conservation**: *nature conservancy*

con·ser·va·tion /ˌkɒnsəˈveɪʃn; *NAmE* ˌkɑːnsərˈv-/ *noun* [U] **1** the protection of the natural environment SYN **conservancy**: *to be interested in wildlife conservation* ➲ LANGUAGE BANK at IMPERSONAL **2** the official protection of buildings that have historical or artistic importance **3** the act of preventing sth from being lost, wasted, damaged or destroyed: *to encourage the* **conservation of water/fuel** ◇ *energy conservation* ➲ see also CONSERVE

conser'vation area *noun* (in the UK) an area where the natural environment or the buildings are protected by law from being damaged or changed

con·ser·va·tion·ist /ˌkɒnsəˈveɪʃənɪst; *NAmE* ˌkɑːnsərˈv-/ *noun* a person who takes an active part in the protection of the environment: *a meeting of local conservationists*

con·ser·va·tism /kənˈsɜːvətɪzəm; *NAmE* -ˈsɜːrv-/ *noun* [U] **1** the tendency to resist great or sudden change: *the innate conservatism of older people* **2** (also **Conservatism**) the political belief that society should change as little as possible: *an examination of the political theories of conservatism and liberalism* **3** (usually **Conservatism**) the principles of the Conservative Party in British politics

con·ser·va·tive 🗝 /kənˈsɜːvətɪv; *NAmE* -ˈsɜːrv-/ *adj., noun*
■ ***adj.* 1** 🗝 opposed to great or sudden social change; showing that you prefer traditional styles and values: *the conservative views of his parents* ◇ *Her style of dress was never conservative.* **2** (usually **Conservative**) connected with the British Conservative Party: *Conservative members/supporters* **3** 🗝 (of an estimate) lower than what is probably the real amount or number: ***At a conservative estimate****, he'll be earning £50 000.* ▸ **con·ser·va·tive·ly** *adv.*
■ ***noun* 1** (usually **Conservative**) (*abbr.* Con.) a member or supporter of the British Conservative Party **2** a conservative person

the Con'servative Party *noun* [sing.+ sing./pl. v.] one of the main British political parties, on the political right, which especially believes in FREE ENTERPRISE and that industry should be privately owned

con·ser·va·toire /kənˈsɜːvətwɑː(r); *NAmE* -ˈsɜːrv-/ (*BrE*) (*NAmE* **con·ser·va·tory**) *noun* a school or college at which people are trained in music and theatre

con·ser·va·tor /kənˈsɜːvətə(r); *NAmE* -ˈsɜːrv-/ *noun* a person who is responsible for repairing and preserving works of art, buildings and other things of cultural interest

con·ser·va·tory /kənˈsɜːvətri; *NAmE* -ˈsɜːrvətɔːri/ *noun* (*pl.* -ies) **1** (*BrE*) a room with glass walls and a glass roof that is built on the side of a house. Conservatories are used for sitting in to enjoy the sun, and to protect plants from cold weather. ➲ VISUAL VOCAB page V16 **2** (*NAmE*) (*BrE* **con·ser·va·toire**) a school or college at which people are trained in music and theatre

con·serve *verb, noun*
■ ***verb*** /kənˈsɜːv; *NAmE* -ˈsɜːrv/ **1 ~ sth** to use as little of sth as possible so that it lasts a long time: *Help to conserve energy by insulating your home.* **2 ~ sth** to protect sth and prevent it from being changed or destroyed: *new laws to conserve wildlife in the area* ➲ see also CONSERVATION
■ ***noun*** /ˈkɒnsɜːv; *NAmE* ˈkɑːnsɜːrv/ [C, U] jam containing large or whole pieces of fruit

con·sider 🗝 /kənˈsɪdə(r)/ *verb*
1 🗝 [I, T] to think about sth carefully, especially in order to make a decision: *I'd like some time to consider.* ◇ **~ sth** *She considered her options.* ◇ *a* **carefully considered** *response* ◇ *The company is being actively considered as a potential partner* (= it is thought possible that it could become one). ◇ **~ doing sth** *We're considering buying a new car.* ◇ **~ how/what, etc...** *We need to consider how the law might be reformed.* ◇ *He was considering what to do next.* ➲ LANGUAGE BANK at ABOUT **2** 🗝 [T] to think of sb/sth in a particular way: **~ sb/sth + noun | ~ sb/sth (to be) sth | ~ sb/sth (as) sth** *He considers himself an expert on the subject.* ◇ *This award is considered (to be) a great honour.* ◇ *These workers are considered (as) a high-risk group.* ◇ **~ sb/sth + adj. | ~ sb/sth (to be) sth** ***Consider yourself lucky*** *you weren't fired.* ◇ *Who do you consider (to be) responsible for the accident?* ◇ **~ sb/sth to do sth** *He's generally considered to have the finest tenor voice in the country.* ◇ **~ (that)...** *She considers that it is too early to form a definite conclusion.* ◇ **it is considered that...** *It is considered that the proposed development would create much-needed jobs.* ➲ SYNONYMS at REGARD **3** 🗝 [T] **~ sb/sth** to think about sth, especially the feelings of other people, and be influenced by it when making a decision, etc: *You should consider other people before you act.* **4** [T] **~ sb/sth** (*formal*) to look carefully at sb/sth: *He stood there, considering the painting.*

IDM **all things con'sidered** thinking carefully about all the facts, especially the problems or difficulties, of a situation: *She's had a lot of problems since her husband died but she seems quite cheerful, all things considered.* **your con,sidered o'pinion** your opinion that is the result of careful thought

con·sid·er·able 0-π AW /kən'sɪdərəbl/ *adj.* (rather *formal*) great in amount, size, importance, etc. SYN **significant**: *The project wasted a considerable amount of time and money.* ◇ *Damage to the building was considerable.*

con·sid·er·ably 0-π AW /kən'sɪdərəbli/ *adv.* (*formal*) much; a lot SYN **significantly**: *The need for sleep varies considerably from person to person.*

con·sid·er·ate /kən'sɪdərət/ *adj.* always thinking of other people's wishes and feelings; careful not to hurt or upset others SYN **thoughtful**: *She is always polite and considerate towards her employees.* ◇ *It was very considerate of him to wait.* OPP **inconsiderate** ▸ **con·sid·er·ate·ly** *adv.*

con·sid·er·ation 0-π /kən,sɪdə'reɪʃn/ *noun* **1** 0-π [U, C] (*formal*) the act of thinking carefully about sth: *Careful consideration should be given to issues of health and safety.* ◇ *The proposals are currently* ***under consideration*** (= being discussed). ◇ *After a few moments' consideration, he began to speak.* ◇ *a consideration of the legal issues involved* **2** 0-π [C] something that must be thought about when you are planning or deciding sth: ***economic/commercial/environmental/practical considerations*** ◇ *Time is another important consideration.* **3** 0-π [U] ~ (**for sb/sth**) the quality of being sensitive towards others and thinking about their wishes and feelings: *They showed no consideration whatsoever for my feelings.* ◇ *Journalists stayed away from the funeral* ***out of consideration for*** *the bereaved family.* **4** [C] (*formal*) a reward or payment for a service
IDM **in consideration of sth** (*formal*) as payment for sth: *a small sum in consideration of your services* **take sth into consideration** 0-π to think about and include a particular thing or fact when you are forming an opinion or making a decision: *The candidates' experience and qualifications will be taken into consideration when the decision is made.* ◇ *Taking everything into consideration, the event was a great success.* ⊃ more at MATURE *adj.*

con·sider·ing /kən'sɪdərɪŋ/ *prep., conj., adv.* used to show that you are thinking about a particular fact, and are influenced by it, when you make a statement about sth: *She's very active, considering her age.* ◇ *Considering he's only just started, he knows quite a lot about it.* ◇ (*informal*) *You've done very well, considering* (= in the difficult circumstances).

con·sign /kən'saɪn/ *verb* (*formal*) **1** ~ **sb/sth to sth** to put sb/sth somewhere in order to get rid of them/it: *I consigned her letter to the wastebasket.* ◇ *What I didn't want was to see my mother consigned to an old people's home.* **2** ~ **sb/sth to sth** to put sb/sth in an unpleasant situation: *The decision to close the factory has* ***consigned*** *6 000 people* ***to the scrapheap.*** ◇ *A car accident consigned him to a wheelchair for the rest of his life.* **3** ~ **sth to sb** to give or send sth to sb

con·sign·ment /kən'saɪnmənt/ *noun* **1** [C] a quantity of goods that are sent or delivered somewhere: *a consignment of medicines* **2** [U] the act of sending or delivering sb/sth

con'signment store *noun* (*NAmE*) a shop/store where people take their old clothes, etc. to be sold to sb else. The consignment store keeps part of the money after an item is sold and gives the other part to the person who brought it in.

con·sist 0-π AW /kən'sɪst/ *verb* (not used in the progressive tenses)
PHR V **con'sist in sth** (*formal*) to have sth as the main or only part or feature: *The beauty of the city consists in its magnificent buildings.* ◇ ~ **doing sth** *True education does not consist in simply being taught facts.* **con'sist of sb/sth** 0-π to be formed from the things or people mentioned: *The committee consists of ten members.* ◇ *Their diet consisted largely of vegetables.* ◇ ~ **doing sth** *Most of the fieldwork consisted of making tape recordings.*

Synonyms

consist of sb/sth

comprise • make up sth • constitute • be composed of sb/sth

These words all mean to be formed from the things or people mentioned, or to be the parts that form sth.

consist of sb/sth to be formed from the things, people or activities mentioned: *Their diet consists largely of vegetables.*

comprise (*rather formal*) to be formed from the things or people mentioned: *The collection comprises 327 paintings.* NOTE **Comprise** can also be used to refer to the parts or members of sth: *Older people comprise a large proportion of those living in poverty.* However, this is less frequent.

make up sth (*rather informal*) to be the parts or people that form sth: *Women make up 56% of the student numbers.*

constitute to be the parts or people that form sth: *People under the age of 40 constitute the majority of the labour force.*

be composed of sb/sth (*rather formal*) to be formed from the things or people mentioned: *Around 15% of our diet is composed of protein.*

WHICH WORD?

Consist of sb/sth is the most general of these words and the only one that can be used for activities with the *-ing* form of a verb: *My work at that time just consisted of typing letters.* The other main difference is between those verbs that take the whole as the subject and the parts as the object: *The group consists of/comprises/is made up of/is composed of ten people.* and those that take the parts as the subject and the whole as the object: *Ten people make up/constitute/comprise the group.* It is not correct to use 'comprises of' or 'is composed by/from'.

con·sist·ency AW /kən'sɪstənsi/ *noun* (*pl.* -ies) **1** [U] (*approving*) the quality of always behaving in the same way or of having the same opinions, standard, etc; the quality of being consistent: *She has played with great consistency all season.* ◇ *We need to ensure the consistency of service to our customers.* OPP **inconsistency** **2** [C, U] the **consistency** of a mixture or a liquid substance is how thick, smooth, etc. it is: *Beat the ingredients together to a creamy consistency.* ◇ *The cement should have the consistency of wet sand.*

con·sist·ent AW /kən'sɪstənt/ *adj.* **1** (*approving*) always behaving in the same way, or having the same opinions, standards, etc: *She's not very consistent in the way she treats her children.* ◇ *He has been Milan's most consistent* (= most consistently good) *player this season.* ◇ *We must be consistent in applying the rules.* ◇ *a consistent approach to the problem* **2** happening in the same way and continuing for a period of time: *the party's consistent failure to come up with any new policies* ◇ *a pattern of consistent growth in the economy* **3** ~ **with sth** in agreement with sth; not CONTRADICTING sth: *The results are entirely consistent with our earlier research.* ◇ *injuries consistent with a fall from an upper storey* (= similar to those such a fall would have caused) **4** (of an argument or a set of ideas) having different parts that all agree with each other: *a well-thought-out and consistent argument* OPP **inconsistent** ▸ **con·sist·ent·ly** AW *adv.*: *Her work has been of a consistently high standard.* ◇ *We have argued consistently for a change in the law.*

con·sola·tion /,kɒnsə'leɪʃn; *NAmE* ,kɑːn-/ *noun* [U, C] a thing or person that makes you feel better when you are unhappy or disappointed **SYN comfort**: *a few words of consolation* ◇ *If it's any consolation, she didn't get the job, either.* ◇ *The children were a great consolation to him when his wife died.*

C

conso'lation prize *noun* a small prize given to sb who has not won a competition

con·sola·tory /kən'sɒlətəri; *NAmE* kən'soʊlətɔːri; -'sɑːlə-/ *adj.* (*formal*) intended to make sb who is unhappy or disappointed feel better

con·sole[1] /kən'səʊl; *NAmE* -'soʊl/ *verb* to give comfort or sympathy to sb who is unhappy or disappointed **SYN comfort**: **~ sb/yourself** *Nothing could console him when his wife died.* ◇ *She put a consoling arm around his shoulders.* ◇ **~ sb/yourself with sth** *Console yourself with the thought that you did your best.* ◇ **~ sb/yourself that...** *I didn't like lying but I consoled myself that it was for a good cause.* ◇ **~ sb + speech** *'Never mind,' Anne consoled her.*

con·sole[2] /'kɒnsəʊl; *NAmE* 'kɑːnsoʊl/ *noun* a flat surface which contains all the controls and switches for a machine, a piece of electronic equipment, etc.

con·soli·date /kən'sɒlɪdeɪt; *NAmE* -'sɑːl-/ *verb* **1** [T, I] **~ (sth)** to make a position of power or success stronger so that it is more likely to continue: *With this new movie he has* ***consolidated*** *his* ***position*** *as the country's leading director.* ◇ *Italy consolidated their lead with a second goal.* **2** [T, I] **~ (sth)** (*technical*) to join things together into one; to be joined into one: *All the debts have been consolidated.* ◇ *consolidated accounts* ◇ *The two companies consolidated for greater efficiency.* ▶ **con·soli·da·tion** /kən,sɒlɪ'deɪʃn; *NAmE* -,sɑːl-/ *noun* [U]: *the consolidation of power* ◇ *the consolidation of Japan's banking industry*

con·sommé /kən'sɒmeɪ; *NAmE* ,kɑːnsə'meɪ/ *noun* [U] a clear soup made with the juices from meat

con·son·ance /'kɒnsənəns; *NAmE* 'kɑːn-/ *noun* **1** [U] **~ (with sth)** (*formal*) agreement: *a policy that is popular because of its consonance with traditional party doctrine* **2** [U, C] (*music*) a combination of musical notes that sound pleasing together **OPP dissonance**

con·son·ant /'kɒnsənənt; *NAmE* 'kɑːn-/ *noun, adj.*
■ ***noun*** **1** (*phonetics*) a speech sound made by completely or partly stopping the flow of air being breathed out through the mouth **2** a letter of the alphabet that represents a consonant sound, for example 'b', 'c', 'd', 'f', etc. ⊃ compare VOWEL
■ ***adj.*** **~ with sth** (*formal*) agreeing with or being the same as sth else

con·son·ant·al /,kɒnsə'næntl; *NAmE* ,kɑːn-/ *adj.* (*phonetics*) relating to or consisting of a consonant or consonants ⊃ compare VOCALIC

con·sort *noun, verb*
■ ***noun*** /'kɒnsɔːt; *NAmE* 'kɑːnsɔːrt/ **1** the husband or wife of a ruler: *the prince consort* (= the queen's husband) **2** a group of old-fashioned musical instruments, or a group of musicians who play music from several centuries ago
■ ***verb*** /kən'sɔːt; *NAmE* -'sɔːrt/ [I] **~ with sb** (*formal*) to spend time with sb that other people do not approve of: *He is known to have consorted with prostitutes.*

con·sor·tium /kən'sɔːtiəm; *NAmE* -'sɔːrt-/ *noun* (*pl.* **con·sor·tiums** or **con·sor·tia** /-tiə; *BrE* also -'sɔːʃə; *NAmE* also -'sɔːrʃə/) a group of people, countries, companies, etc. who are working together on a particular project: *the Anglo-French consortium that built the Channel Tunnel*

con·spicu·ous /kən'spɪkjuəs/ *adj.* easy to see or notice; likely to attract attention: *Mary's red hair always made her conspicuous at school.* ◇ *I felt very conspicuous in my new car.* ◇ *The advertisements were all posted in a conspicuous place.* ◇ *The event was a conspicuous success* (= a very great one). **OPP inconspicuous** ▶ **con·spicu·ous·ly** *adv.*: *Women were conspicuously absent from* (= there were surprisingly few women on) *the planning committee.* **con·spicu·ous·ness** *noun* [U]
IDM con,spicuous by your 'absence not present in a situation or place, when it is obvious that you should be there: *When it came to cleaning up afterwards, Anne was conspicuous by her absence.*

con,spicuous con'sumption *noun* [U] the buying of expensive goods in order to impress people and show them how rich you are

con·spir·acy /kən'spɪrəsi/ *noun* [C, U] (*pl.* **-ies**) a secret plan by a group of people to do sth harmful or illegal: **~ (to do sth)** *a conspiracy to overthrow the government* ◇ **~ (against sb/sth)** *conspiracies against the president* ◇ **~ (to sth)** *They were charged with conspiracy to murder.* ◇ *a* ***conspiracy of silence*** (= an agreement not to talk publicly about sth which should be made public) ◇ *a* ***conspiracy theory*** (= the belief that a secret conspiracy is responsible for a particular event)

con·spir·ator /kən'spɪrətə(r)/ *noun* a person who is involved in a conspiracy

con·spira·tor·ial /kən,spɪrə'tɔːriəl/ *adj.* **1** connected with, or like, a conspiracy **2** (of a person's behaviour) suggesting that a secret is being shared: *'I know you understand,' he said and gave a conspiratorial wink.* ▶ **con·spira·tori·al·ly** *adv.*

con·spire /kən'spaɪə(r)/ *verb* (*formal*) **1** [I] to secretly plan with other people to do sth illegal or harmful: **~ (with sb) (against sb)** *They were accused of conspiring against the king.* ◇ **~ (together) (to do sth)** *They deny conspiring together to smuggle drugs.* ◇ **~ (with sb) (to do sth)** *She admitted conspiring with her lover to murder her husband.* **2** [I] (of events) to seem to work together to make sth bad happen: **~ against sb/sth** ***Circumstances had conspired against*** *them.* ◇ **~ to do sth** *Everything conspired to make her life a misery.*

con·stable /'kʌnstəbl; *NAmE* 'kɑːn-/ *noun* **1** (*BrE*) (used especially when talking to a police officer of the lowest rank) = POLICE CONSTABLE: *Have you finished your report, Constable?* ⊃ see also CHIEF CONSTABLE **2** (in the US) a peace officer with some of the powers of a police officer, typically in a small town

con·stabu·lary /kən'stæbjələri; *NAmE* -leri/ *noun* [C+sing./pl. v.] (*pl.* **-ies**) (in Britain) the police force of a particular area or town

con·stancy **AW** /'kɒnstənsi; *NAmE* 'kɑːn-/ *noun* [U] (*formal*) **1** the quality of staying the same and not changing **2** (*approving*) the quality of being faithful **SYN fidelity**: *He admired her courage and constancy.*

con·stant 🔑 **AW** /'kɒnstənt; *NAmE* 'kɑːn-/ *adj., noun*
■ ***adj.*** **1** 🔑 [usually before noun] happening all the time or repeatedly: *constant interruptions* ◇ *a constant stream of visitors all day* ◇ *Babies need constant attention.* ◇ *This entrance is in constant use.* **2** 🔑 that does not change **SYN fixed**: *travelling at a constant speed of 50 m.p.h.*
■ ***noun*** (*technical*) a number or quantity that does not vary **OPP variable**

con·stant·ly 🔑 **AW** /'kɒnstəntli; *NAmE* 'kɑːn-/ *adv.* all the time; repeatedly: *Fashion is constantly changing.* ◇ *Heat the sauce, stirring constantly.*

con·sta·tive /'kɒnstətɪv; *NAmE* 'kɑːn-, kən'steɪtɪv/ *adj.* (*grammar*) stating that sth is real or true ⊃ see also PERFORMATIVE

con·stel·la·tion /,kɒnstə'leɪʃn; *NAmE* ,kɑːn-/ *noun* **1** a group of stars that forms a shape in the sky and has a name **2** (*formal*) a group of related ideas, things or people: *a constellation of Hollywood talent*

con·ster·na·tion /,kɒnstə'neɪʃn; *NAmE* ,kɑːnstər'n-/ *noun* [U] (*formal*) a worried, sad feeling after you have received an unpleasant surprise **SYN dismay**: *The announcement of her retirement caused consternation among tennis fans.*

con·sti·pated /'kɒnstɪpeɪtɪd; *NAmE* 'kɑːn-/ *adj.* unable to get rid of waste material from the BOWELS easily

con·sti·pa·tion /,kɒnstɪ'peɪʃn; *NAmE* ,kɑːn-/ *noun* [U] the condition of being unable to get rid of waste material from the BOWELS easily (= being constipated)

con·stitu·ency AW /kən'stɪtjuənsi; NAmE -tʃu-/ (pl. -ies) *noun* **1** (*especially BrE*) [C] a district that elects its own representative to parliament: *Unemployment is high in her constituency.* ◇ *He owns a house in his Darlington constituency.* **2** [C+sing./pl. v.] the people who live in and vote in a particular district: *constituency opinion* **3** [C+sing./pl. v.] a particular group of people in society who are likely to support a person, an idea or a product

con·stitu·ent AW /kən'stɪtjuənt; NAmE -tʃu-/ *noun, adj.*
- ***noun*** **1** a person who lives, and can vote in a constituency: *She has the full support of her constituents.* **2** one of the parts of sth that combine to form the whole
- ***adj.*** [only before noun] (*formal*) forming or helping to make a whole: *to break something up into its **constituent parts/elements***

con͵stituent as'sembly *noun* [C+sing./pl. v.] a group of elected representatives with the power to make or change a country's CONSTITUTION

con·sti·tute AW /'kɒnstɪtjuːt; NAmE 'kɑːnstətuːt/ *verb* (*formal*) **1** *linking verb* + **noun** (not used in the progressive tenses) to be considered to be sth: *Does such an activity constitute a criminal offence?* ◇ *The increase in racial tension constitutes a threat to our society.* **2** *linking verb* + **noun** (not used in the progressive tenses) to be the parts that together form sth SYN **make up**: *Female workers constitute the majority of the labour force.* ➲ note at COMPRISE ➲ SYNONYMS at CONSIST OF **3** [T, usually passive] **~ sth** to form a group legally or officially SYN **establish, set up**: *The committee was constituted in 1974 by an Act of Parliament.*

con·sti·tu·tion AW /͵kɒnstɪ'tjuːʃn; NAmE ͵kɑːnstə'tuːʃn/ *noun* **1** [C] the system of laws and basic principles that a state, a country or an organization is governed by: *your right to vote under the constitution* ◇ *According to the constitution...* ◇ *to propose a new amendment to the Constitution* ◇ *the South African Constitution* **2** [C] the condition of a person's body and how healthy it is: *to have a **healthy/strong/weak constitution*** **3** [U, C] (*formal*) the way sth is formed or organized SYN **structure**: *the genetic constitution of cells* **4** [U] (*formal*) the act of forming sth SYN **establishment, setting up**: *He recommended the constitution of a review committee.*

con·sti·tu·tion·al AW /͵kɒnstɪ'tjuːʃənl; NAmE ͵kɑːnstə'tuː-/ *adj., noun*
- ***adj.*** **1** [only before noun] connected with the constitution of a country or an organization: ***constitutional government/reform*** ◇ *a constitutional amendment* **2** allowed or limited by the constitution of a country or an organization: *They can't pass this law. It's not constitutional.* ◇ ***constitutional rights*** ◇ *a **constitutional monarchy*** (= a country with a king or queen whose power is controlled by a set of laws and basic principles) OPP **unconstitutional** **3** [usually before noun] related to the body's ability to stay healthy, be strong and fight illness: *constitutional remedies* ▸ **con·sti·tu·tion·al·ly** AW /-ʃənəli/ *adv.*: *constitutionally guaranteed rights* ◇ *He was much weakened constitutionally by the disease.*
- ***noun*** (*old-fashioned* or *humorous*) a short walk that people take because it is good for their health

Cons͵titutional 'Court *noun* [sing.] in South Africa, the highest court dealing with cases related to the constitution

con·sti·tu·tion·al·ism /͵kɒnstɪ'tjuːʃənəlɪzəm; NAmE ͵kɑːnstə'tuː-/ *noun* [U] a belief in constitutional government

con·sti·tu·tion·al·ity /͵kɒnstɪ͵tjuːʃə'næləti; NAmE ͵kɑːnstə͵tuː-/ *noun* [U] (*technical*) the fact that sth is acceptable according to a CONSTITUTION: *They questioned the constitutionality of the law.*

con·sti·tu·tive AW /͵kɒnstɪ'tjuːtɪv; NAmE ͵kɑːnstə'tuːtɪv/ *adj.* (*formal*) **~ (of sth)** forming a part, often an essential part, of sth: *Memory is constitutive of identity.*

con·strain AW /kən'streɪn/ *verb* (*formal*) **1** [usually passive] **~ sb to do sth** to force sb to do sth or behave in a particular way: *The evidence was so compelling that he **felt constrained to** accept it.* **2** [often passive] to restrict or limit sb/sth: **~ sth** *Research has been constrained by a lack of funds.* ◇ **~ sb (from doing sth)** *She felt constrained from continuing by the threat of losing her job.* ➲ see also UNCONSTRAINED

con·strained /kən'streɪnd/ *adj.* (*formal*) not natural; forced or too controlled: *constrained emotions*

con·straint AW /kən'streɪnt/ *noun* **1** [C] a thing that limits or restricts sth, or your freedom to do sth SYN **restriction**: ***constraints of time/money/space*** ◇ ***financial/economic/legal/political constraints*** ◇ **~ on sth** *This decision will impose serious constraints on all schools.* ➲ SYNONYMS at LIMIT **2** [U] strict control over the way that you behave or are allowed to behave: *At last we could relax and talk without constraint.*

con·strict /kən'strɪkt/ *verb* **1** [I, T] to become tighter or narrower; to make sth tighter or narrower: *Her **throat constricted** and she swallowed hard.* ◇ **~ sth** *a drug that constricts the blood vessels.* **2** **~ sb** to limit or restrict what sb is able to do: *Film-makers of the time were constricted by the censors.* ◇ *constricting rules and regulations* ▸ **con·strict·ed** *adj.*: *Her throat felt dry and constricted.* ◇ *a constricted vision of the world* **con·stric·tion** /kən'strɪkʃn/ *noun* [U, C]: *a feeling of constriction in the chest* ◇ *political constrictions*

con·struct 0‑w AW *verb, noun*
- ***verb*** /kən'strʌkt/ **1** 0‑w [often passive] to build or make sth such as a road, building or machine: **~ sth** *When was the bridge constructed?* ◇ **~ sth from/out of/of sth** *They constructed a shelter out of fallen branches.* ➲ SYNONYMS at BUILD **2** 0‑w **~ sth** to form sth by putting different things together SYN **put together**: *You must learn how to construct a logical argument.* ◇ *to construct a theory* ◇ *a well-constructed novel* **3** **~ sth** (*geometry*) to draw a line or shape according to the rules of mathematics: *to construct a triangle*
- ***noun*** /'kɒnstrʌkt; NAmE 'kɑːn-/ (*formal*) **1** an idea or a belief that is based on various pieces of evidence which are not always true: *a contrast between lived reality and the construct held in the mind* **2** (*linguistics*) a group of words that form a phrase **3** a thing that is built or made

con·struc·tion 0‑w AW /kən'strʌkʃn/ *noun*
- ▸ OF ROADS/BUILDINGS **1** 0‑w [U] the process or method of building or making sth, especially roads, buildings, bridges, etc: *the construction industry* ◇ *road construction* ◇ *Work has begun on the construction of the new airport.* ◇ *Our new offices are still **under construction*** (= being built). ◇ *the construction of a new database* **2** 0‑w [U] the way that sth has been built or made: *strong in construction* ◇ *ships of steel construction* ➲ SYNONYMS at STRUCTURE
- ▸ BUILDING/STRUCTURE **3** [C] (*formal*) a thing that has been built or made: *The summer house was a simple wooden construction.*
- ▸ GRAMMAR **4** [C] the way in which words are used together and arranged to form a sentence, phrase, etc: *grammatical constructions*
- ▸ OF THEORY, ETC. **5** [U, C] the creating of sth from ideas, opinions and knowledge: *the construction of a new theory*
- ▸ MEANING **6** [C] (*formal*) the way in which words, actions, statements, etc. are understood by sb SYN **interpretation**: *What construction do you put on this letter* (= what do you think it means)?

con·struc·tion·al /kən'strʌkʃənl/ *adj.* connected with the making or building of things

con'struction paper *noun* [U] (*NAmE*) thick coloured paper that people cut out to make designs, models, etc.

con'struction site *noun* (*especially NAmE*) = BUILDING SITE

con·struct·ive AW /kən'strʌktɪv/ *adj.* having a useful and helpful effect rather than being negative or with no purpose: ***constructive criticism/suggestions/advice*** ◇ *His work involved helping hyperactive children to use their energy in a constructive way.* ◇ *The government is encouraging all parties to play a constructive role in the reform process.* ➲ compare DESTRUCTIVE ▸ **con·struct·ive·ly** *adv.*

C

con,structive dis'missal *noun* [U] (*BrE, law*) a situation in which you are forced to leave your job because it is changed in a way that makes it impossible for you to continue doing it

con·struct·or /kən'strʌktə(r)/ *noun* a person or company that builds things, especially cars or aircraft

con·strue /kən'stru:/ *verb* [usually passive] (*formal*) to understand the meaning of a word, a sentence, or an action in a particular way SYN **interpret**: **~ sth** *He considered how the remark was to be construed.* ◇ **~ sth as sth** *Her words could hardly be construed as an apology.*

con·sul /'kɒnsl; *NAmE* 'kɑ:nsl/ *noun* a government official who is the representative of his or her country in a foreign city: *the British consul in Miami* ▸ **con·su·lar** /'kɒnsjələ(r); *NAmE* 'kɑ:nsəl-/ *adj.*: *consular officials*

con·sul·ate /'kɒnsjələt; *NAmE* 'kɑ:nsəl-/ *noun* the building where a consul works ➲ compare EMBASSY

con·sult O-w AW /kən'sʌlt/ *verb*
1 O-w [T, I] to go to sb for information or advice: **~ sb** *If the pain continues, consult your doctor.* ◇ **~ sb about sth** *Have you consulted your lawyer about this?* ◇ *a consulting engineer* (= one who has expert knowledge and gives advice) ◇ (*NAmE*) **~ with sb** (**about/on sth**) *Consult with your physician about possible treatments.* **2** O-w [T, I] to discuss sth with sb to get their permission for sth, or to help you make a decision: **~ sb** *You shouldn't have done it without consulting me.* ◇ **~ sb about/on sth** *I expect to be consulted about major issues.* ◇ **~ with sb** (**about/on sth**) *I need to consult with my colleagues on the proposals.* ➲ SYNONYMS at TALK **3** O-w [T] **~ sth** to look in or at sth to get information SYN **refer to**: *He consulted the manual.*

con·sult·ancy AW /kən'sʌltənsi/ *noun* (*pl.* -ies) **1** [C] a company that gives expert advice on a particular subject to other companies or organizations: *a* ***management/design/computer, etc. consultancy*** **2** [U] expert advice that a company or person is paid to provide on a particular subject: *consultancy fees*

con·sult·ant AW /kən'sʌltənt/ *noun* **1** a person who knows a lot about a particular subject and is employed to give advice about it to other people: *a firm of management consultants* ◇ **~ on sth** *the President's consultant on economic affairs* **2** (*BrE*) a hospital doctor of the highest rank who is a specialist in a particular area of medicine: *a consultant in obstetrics* ◇ *a consultant surgeon* ➲ compare REGISTRAR

con·sult·ation AW /,kɒnsl'teɪʃn; *NAmE* ,kɑ:n-/ *noun*
1 [U] the act of discussing sth with sb or with a group of people before making a decision about it: *a* ***consultation document/paper/period/process*** ◇ *acting* ***in consultation with*** *all the departments involved* ◇ *The decision was taken after close consultation with local residents.* ➲ SYNONYMS at DISCUSSION **2** [C] a formal meeting to discuss sth: *extensive consultations between the two countries* ➲ SYNONYMS at DISCUSSION **3** [C] a meeting with an expert, especially a doctor, to get advice or treatment ➲ SYNONYMS at INTERVIEW **4** [U] the act of looking for information in a book, etc: *There is a large collection of texts available for consultation on-screen.*

con·sulta·tive AW /kən'sʌltətɪv/ *adj.* giving advice or making suggestions SYN **advisory**: *a* ***consultative committee/body/document***

con'sulting room *noun* a room where a doctor talks to and examines patients

con·sum·able /kən'sju:məbl; *NAmE* -'su:m-/ *adj., noun* (*business*)
■ ***adj.*** intended to be bought, used and then replaced: *consumable electronic goods*
■ ***noun*** **con·sum·ables** [pl.] goods that are intended to be used fairly quickly and then replaced: *computer consumables such as CD-Rs and printer cartridges*

con·sume AW /kən'sju:m; *NAmE* -'su:m/ *verb* (*formal*)
1 **~ sth** to use sth, especially fuel, energy or time: *The electricity industry consumes large amounts of fossil fuels.* **2** **~ sth** to eat or drink sth: *Before he died he had consumed a large quantity of alcohol.* **3** **~ sb** (**with sth**) [usually passive] to fill sb with a strong feeling: *Carolyn was consumed with guilt.* ◇ *Rage consumed him.* **4** **~ sth** (of fire) to completely destroy sth: *The hotel was quickly consumed by fire.* ➲ see also ALL-CONSUMING, CONSUMING, CONSUMPTION, TIME-CONSUMING

con·sumer O-w AW /kən'sju:mə(r); *NAmE* -'su:-/ *noun*
a person who buys goods or uses services: ***consumer demand/choice/rights*** ◇ *Health-conscious consumers want more information about the food they buy.* ◇ *a* ***consumer society*** (= one where buying and selling is considered to be very important) ◇ *Tax cuts will boost* ***consumer confidence*** *after the recession.* ➲ compare PRODUCER

con,sumer 'durables (*BrE*) (*NAmE* **'durable goods**) *noun* [pl.] (*business*) goods which are expected to last for a long time after they have been bought, such as cars, televisions, etc.

con'sumer goods *noun* [pl.] goods such as food, clothing, etc. bought by individual customers ➲ compare CAPITAL GOODS

con·sumer·ism /kən'sju:mərɪzəm; *NAmE* -'su:-/ *noun* [U] (sometimes *disapproving*) the buying and using of goods and services; the belief that it is good for a society or an individual person to buy and use a large quantity of goods and services ▸ **con·sumer·ist** *adj.*: *consumerist values*

con,sumer 'price index (*BrE* also **con,sumer 'prices index**) *noun* [sing.] (*abbr.* **CPI**) a list of the prices of some ordinary goods and services which shows how much these prices change each month ➲ see also RETAIL PRICE INDEX

con·sum·ing /kən'sju:mɪŋ; *NAmE* -'su:-/ *adj.* [only before noun] (of a feeling, an interest, etc.) so strong or important that it takes up all your time and energy: *Basketball is his* ***consuming passion***. ➲ see also ALL-CONSUMING, TIME-CONSUMING

con·sum·mate[1] /kən'sʌmət; 'kɒnsəmət; *NAmE* 'kɑ:n-/ *adj.* [usually before noun] (*formal*) extremely skilled; perfect: *She was a consummate performer.* ◇ *He played the shot with consummate skill.* ◇ (*disapproving*) *a consummate liar* ▸ **con·sum·mate·ly** *adv.*

con·sum·mate[2] /'kɒnsəmeɪt; *NAmE* 'kɑ:n-/ *verb* (*formal*) **1** **~ sth** to make a marriage or a relationship complete by having sex: *The marriage lasted only a week and was never consummated.* **2** **~ sth** to make sth complete or perfect

con·sum·ma·tion /,kɒnsə'meɪʃn; *NAmE* ,kɑ:n-/ *noun* [C, U] **1** the act of making a marriage or relationship complete by having sex **2** the fact of making sth complete or perfect: *The paintings are the consummation of his life's work.*

con·sump·tion AW /kən'sʌmpʃn/ *noun* [U] **1** the act of using energy, food or materials; the amount used: *the production of fuel for* ***domestic consumption*** (= to be used in the country where it is produced) ◇ *Gas and oil consumption always increases in cold weather.* ◇ *The meat was declared unfit for* ***human consumption***. ◇ *He was advised to reduce his alcohol consumption.* ◇ *Her speech to party members was not intended for* ***public consumption*** (= to be heard by the public). ➲ see also CONSUME **2** the act of buying and using products: *Consumption rather than saving has become the central feature of contemporary societies.* ➲ see also CONSPICUOUS CONSUMPTION, CONSUME **3** (*old-fashioned*) a serious infectious disease of the lungs SYN **tuberculosis**

con·sump·tive /kən'sʌmptɪv/ *noun* (*old-fashioned*) a person who suffers from consumption (= a disease of the lungs) ▸ **con·sump·tive** *adj.*

cont. (also **contd**) *abbr.* continued: *cont. on p74*

con·tact O-w AW /'kɒntækt; *NAmE* 'kɑ:n-/ *noun, verb*
■ ***noun***
▸ ACT OF COMMUNICATING **1** O-w [U] **~** (**with sb**) | **~** (**between A and B**) the act of communicating with sb, especially regularly: *I don't have much contact with my uncle.* ◇ *There is little contact between the two organizations.* ◇ *Have you kept* ***in contact with*** *any of your friends from college* (= do

you still see them or speak or write to them)? ◇ *She's* **lost contact with** (= no longer sees or writes to) *her son.* ◇ *I finally* **made contact with** (= succeeded in speaking to or meeting) *her in Paris.* ◇ *The organization* **put me in contact with** *other people in a similar position* (= gave me their addresses or telephone numbers). ◇ *two people avoiding* **eye contact** (= avoiding looking directly at each other) ◇ *Here's my* **contact number** (= temporary telephone number) *while I'm away.* ◇ *I'll give you my* **contact details** (= telephone number, email address, etc.).

▸ TOUCHING SB/STH **2** [U] the state of touching sth: *His fingers were briefly* **in contact with** *the ball.* ◇ *This substance should not* **come into contact with** *food.* ◇ *a fear of physical contact* ◇ *This pesticide kills insects* **on contact** (= as soon as it touches them).

▸ MEETING SB/STH **3** [U] the state of meeting sb or having to deal with sth: *In her job she often* **comes into contact with** (= meets) *lawyers.* ◇ *Children should be* **brought into contact with** *poetry at an early age.*

▸ RELATIONSHIP **4** [C, usually pl.] an occasion on which you meet or communicate with sb; a relationship with sb: *We have good contacts with the local community.* ◇ *The company has maintained trade contacts with India.*

▸ PERSON **5** [C] a person that you know, especially sb who can be helpful to you in your work: **social/personal contacts** ◇ *I've made some useful contacts in journalism.*

▸ ELECTRICAL **6** [C] an electrical connection: *The switches close the contacts and complete the circuit.*

▸ FOR EYES **7 contacts** [pl.] (*informal*) = CONTACT LENSES ➲ see also CONTACT LENS

▸ MEDICAL **8** [C] a person who may be infectious because he or she has recently been near to sb with a CONTAGIOUS disease IDM see POINT *n.*

■ ***verb*** **~ sb** to communicate with sb, for example by telephone or letter: *I've been trying to contact you all day.* ▸ **con·tact·able** AW *adj.*: *I'll be contactable on this number:...*

ˈcontact lens (also *informal* **con·tact, lens**) *noun* [usually pl.] a small round piece of thin plastic that you put on your eye to help you see better: *to* **wear contact lenses**

ˈcontact sport *noun* a sport in which players have physical contact with each other OPP **non-contact sport**

con·ta·gion /kənˈteɪdʒən/ *noun* **1** [U] the spreading of a disease by people touching each other: *There is no risk of contagion.* **2** [C] (*old use*) a disease that can be spread by people touching each other. **3** [C] (*formal*) something bad that spreads quickly by being passed from person to person ➲ compare INFECTION

con·ta·gious /kənˈteɪdʒəs/ *adj.* **1** a **contagious** disease spreads by people touching each other: *Scarlet fever is highly contagious.* ◇ (*figurative*) *His enthusiasm was contagious* (= spread quickly to other people). ◇ *a contagious laugh* **2** [not usually before noun] if a person is **contagious**, they have a disease that can be spread to other people by touch ➲ compare INFECTIOUS ▸ **con·ta·gious·ly** *adv.*

con·tain /kənˈteɪn/ *verb* (not used in the progressive tenses)
1 **~ sth** if sth **contains** sth else, it has that thing inside it or as part of it: *This drink doesn't contain any alcohol.* ◇ *Her statement contained one or two inaccuracies.* ◇ *a brown envelope containing dollar bills* ◇ *The bottle contains* (= can hold) *two litres.* **2** to keep your feelings under control SYN **restrain**: **~ sth** *She was unable to contain her excitement.* ◇ **~ yourself** *I was so furious I just couldn't* **contain myself** (= I had to express my feelings). **3** **~ sth** to prevent sth harmful from spreading or getting worse: *to contain an epidemic* ◇ *Government forces have failed to contain the rebellion.*

con·tain·er /kənˈteɪnə(r)/ *noun*
1 a box, bottle, etc. in which sth can be stored or transported: *Food will last longer if kept in an airtight container.* **2** a large metal or wooden box of a standard size in which goods are packed so that they can easily be lifted onto a ship, train, etc. to be transported: *a container ship* (= one designed to transport such containers) ➲ VISUAL VOCAB page V44

con·tain·er·ized /kənˈteɪnəraɪzd/ *adj.* packed and transported in CONTAINERS (2): *containerized cargo* ▸ **con·tain·er·iz·ation** /kən,teɪnəraɪˈzeɪʃn/ *noun* [U]

con·tain·ment /kənˈteɪnmənt/ *noun* [U] (*formal*) **1** the act of keeping sth under control so that it cannot spread in a harmful way: *the containment of the epidemic* **2** the act of keeping another country's power within limits so that it does not become too powerful: *a policy of containment*

C

con·tam·in·ant /kənˈtæmɪnənt/ *noun* (*technical*) a substance that makes sth IMPURE: *Filters do not remove all contaminants from water.*

con·tam·in·ate /kənˈtæmɪneɪt/ *verb* **1** **~ sth (with sth)** to make a substance or place dirty or no longer pure by adding a substance that is dangerous or carries disease SYN **adulterate**: *The drinking water has become contaminated with lead.* ◇ **contaminated blood/food/soil** **2** **~ sth** (*formal*) to influence people's ideas or attitudes in a bad way: *They were accused of contaminating the minds of our young people.* ➲ see also UNCONTAMINATED ▸ **con·tam·in·ation** /kən,tæmɪˈneɪʃn/ *noun* [U]: *radioactive contamination* ➲ see also CROSS-CONTAMINATION

contd *abbr.* = CONT.

con·tem·plate /ˈkɒntəmpleɪt; *NAmE* ˈkɑːn-/ *verb* **1** [T] to think about whether you should do sth, or how you should do sth SYN **consider, think about/of**: **~ sth** *You're too young to be contemplating retirement.* ◇ **~ doing sth** *I have never contemplated living abroad.* ◇ **~ how/what, etc ...** *He continued while she contemplated how to answer.* **2** [T] to think carefully about and accept the possibility of sth happening: **~ sth** *The thought of war is too awful to contemplate.* ◇ **~ how/what, etc...** *I can't contemplate what it would be like to be alone.* ◇ **~ that...** *She contemplated that things might get even worse.* **3** [T, I] **~ (sth)** (*formal*) to think deeply about sth for a long time: *to contemplate your future* ◇ *She lay in bed, contemplating.* **4** [T] **~ sb/sth** (*formal*) to look at sb/sth in a careful way for a long time SYN **stare at**: *She contemplated him in silence.*

con·tem·pla·tion /,kɒntəmˈpleɪʃn; *NAmE* ,kɑːn-/ *noun* [U] (*formal*) **1** the act of thinking deeply about sth: *He sat there deep in contemplation.* ◇ *a few moments of quiet contemplation* ◇ *a life of prayer and contemplation* **2** the act of looking at sth in a calm and careful way: *She turned from her contemplation of the photograph.*
IDM **in contemˈplation** (*formal*) being considered: *By 1613 even more desperate measures were in contemplation.*

con·tem·pla·tive /kənˈtemplətɪv/ *adj.*
■ (*formal*) **1** thinking quietly and seriously about sth: *She was in contemplative mood.* **2** spending time thinking deeply about religious matters: *the contemplative life* (= life in a religious community)

con·tem·por·an·eous /kən,tempəˈreɪniəs/ *adj.* **~ (with sb/sth)** (*formal*) happening or existing at the same time SYN **contemporary**: *How do we know that the signature is contemporaneous with the document?* ◇ **contemporaneous events/accounts** ▸ **con·tem·por·an·eous·ly** *adv.*

con·tem·por·ary AW /kənˈtemprəri; *NAmE* -pəreri/ *adj., noun*
■ ***adj.*** **1** **~ (with sb/sth)** belonging to the same time: *We have no contemporary account of the battle* (= written near the time that it happened). ◇ *He was contemporary with the dramatist Congreve.* **2** belonging to the present time SYN **modern**: *life in contemporary Britain* ◇ **contemporary fiction/music/dance**
■ ***noun*** (*pl.* **-ies**) a person who lives or lived at the same time as sb else, especially sb who is about the same age: *She and I were contemporaries at college.* ◇ *He was a contemporary of Freud and may have known him.*

con·tempt /kənˈtempt/ *noun* [U, sing.] **1** the feeling that sb/sth is without value and deserves no respect at all: *She looked at him* **with contempt**. ◇ *I shall treat that suggestion with the contempt it deserves.* ◇ *His treatment of his children is* **beneath contempt** (= so unacceptable that it is not even worth feeling contempt for). ◇ *Politicians seem to be gener-*

ally **held in contempt** by ordinary people. ◇ **~ for sb/sth** *They had shown a contempt for the values she thought important.* **2 ~ for sth** a lack of worry or fear about rules, danger, etc: *The firefighters showed a contempt for their own safety.* ◇ *His remarks betray a staggering contempt for the truth* (= are completely false). **3** = CONTEMPT OF COURT: *He could be jailed for two years for contempt.* ◇ *She was held **in contempt** for refusing to testify.* IDM see FAMILIARITY

con·tempt·ible /kənˈtemptəbl/ *adj.* (*formal*) not deserving any respect at all SYN **despicable**: *contemptible behaviour*

conˌtempt of ˈcourt (also **con·tempt**) *noun* [U] the crime of refusing to obey an order made by a court; not showing respect for a court or judge: *Any person who disregards this order will be in contempt of court.*

con·temp·tu·ous /kənˈtemptʃuəs/ *adj.* feeling or showing that you have no respect for sb/sth SYN **scornful**: *She gave him a contemptuous look.* ◇ **~ of sb/sth** *He was contemptuous of everything I did.* ▸ **con·temp·tu·ous·ly** *adv.*: *to laugh contemptuously*

con·tend /kənˈtend/ *verb* **1** [T] **~ that...** (*formal*) to say that sth is true, especially in an argument SYN **maintain**: *I would contend that the minister's thinking is flawed on this point.* **2** [I] **~ (for sth)** to compete against sb in order to gain sth: *Three armed groups were contending for power.*

PHR V **conˈtend with sth/sb** to have to deal with a problem or with a difficult situation or person: *Nurses often have to contend with violent or drunken patients.*

con·tend·er /kənˈtendə(r)/ *noun* a person who takes part in a competition or tries to win sth: *a contender for a gold medal in the Olympics* ◇ *a **leading/serious/strong contender** for the party leadership*

con·tent[1] 🔑 /ˈkɒntent; *NAmE* ˈkɑːn-/ *noun* ➲ see also CONTENT[2]
1 🔑 **contents** [pl.] the things that are contained in sth: *He tipped the contents of the bag onto the table.* ◇ *Fire has caused severe damage to the contents of the building.* ◇ *She hadn't read the letter and so was unaware of its contents.* **2** 🔑 **contents** [pl.] the different sections that are contained in a book: *a table of contents* (= the list at the front of a book) ◇ *a contents page* **3** 🔑 [sing.] the subject matter of a book, speech, programme, etc: *Your tone of voice is as important as the content of what you have to say.* ◇ *The content of the course depends on what the students would like to study.* ◇ *Her poetry has a good deal of political content.* **4** 🔑 [sing.] (following a noun) the amount of a substance that is contained in sth else: *food with a high fat content* ◇ *the alcohol content of a drink* **5** [U] (*computing*) the information or other material contained on a website or CD-ROM: *online content providers*

con·tent[2] /kənˈtent/ *adj., verb, noun* ➲ see also CONTENT[1]
■ *adj.* [not before noun] **1 ~ (with sth)** happy and satisfied with what you have: *Not content with stealing my boyfriend* (= not thinking that this was enough), *she has turned all my friends against me.* ◇ *He seemed more content, less bitter.* ◇ *He had to be content with third place.* ➲ SYNONYMS at HAPPY **2 ~ to do sth** willing to do sth: *I was content to wait.* ➲ compare CONTENTED
■ *verb* **1 ~ yourself with sth** to accept and be satisfied with sth and not try to have or do sth better: *Martina contented herself with a bowl of soup.* **2 ~ sb** (*formal*) to make sb feel happy or satisfied: *My apology seemed to content him.*
■ *noun* = CONTENTMENT IDM see HEART

con·tent·ed /kənˈtentɪd/ *adj.* [usually before noun] showing or feeling happiness or satisfaction, especially because your life is good: *a contented smile* ◇ *He was a contented man.* ➲ compare CONTENT[2] *adj.* OPP **discontented** ➲ SYNONYMS at HAPPY ▸ **con·tent·ed·ly** *adv.*: *She smiled contentedly.*

con·ten·tion /kənˈtenʃn/ *noun* (*formal*) **1** [U] angry disagreement between people SYN **dispute**: *One area of contention is the availability of nursery care.* ◇ *a point of contention* **2** [C] **~ (that...)** a belief or an opinion that you express, especially in an argument: *It is our client's contention that the fire was an accident.* ◇ *I would reject that contention.*

IDM **in conˈtention (for sth)** with a chance of winning sth: *Only three teams are now in contention for the title.* **out of conˈtention (for sth)** without a chance of winning sth ➲ more at BONE *n.*

con·ten·tious /kənˈtenʃəs/ *adj.* (*formal*) **1** likely to cause disagreement between people: *a **contentious issue/topic/subject*** ◇ *Both views are highly contentious.* OPP **uncontentious 2** liking to argue; involving a lot of arguing: *a contentious meeting*

con·tent·ment /kənˈtentmənt/ (also *less frequent* **content**) *noun* [U] a feeling of happiness or satisfaction: *He has found contentment at last.* ◇ *a sigh of contentment* ➲ compare DISCONTENT ➲ SYNONYMS at SATISFACTION

ˈcontent word *noun* (*linguistics*) a noun, verb, adjective or adverb whose main function is to express meaning ➲ compare FUNCTION WORD

con·test 🔑 *noun, verb*
■ *noun* /ˈkɒntest; *NAmE* ˈkɑːn-/ **1** 🔑 a competition in which people try to win sth: *a singing contest* ◇ *a talent contest* ◇ *to **enter/win/lose a contest*** ➲ see also BEAUTY CONTEST **2** 🔑 **~ (for sth)** a struggle to gain control or power: *a contest for the leadership of the party*
IDM **be ˌno ˈcontest** used to say that one side in a competition is so much stronger or better than the other that it is sure to win easily
■ *verb* /kənˈtest/ **1 ~ sth** to take part in a competition, election, etc. and try to win it: *Three candidates contested the leadership.* ◇ *a **hotly/fiercely/keenly contested** game* (= one in which the players try very hard to win and the scores are close) **2 ~ sth** to formally oppose a decision or statement because you think it is wrong: *to contest a will* (= try to show that it was not correctly made in law) ◇ *The divorce was not contested.*

con·test·ant /kənˈtestənt/ *noun* a person who takes part in a contest: *Please welcome our next contestant.*

con·text 🔑 AW /ˈkɒntekst; *NAmE* ˈkɑːn-/ *noun* [C, U] **1** 🔑 the situation in which sth happens and that helps you to understand it: *This speech needs to be set **in the context of** Britain in the 1960s.* ◇ *His decision can only be understood **in context**.* **2** 🔑 the words that come just before and after a word, phrase or statement and help you to understand its meaning: *You should be able to guess the meaning of the word from the context.* ◇ *This quotation has been taken **out of context*** (= repeated without giving the circumstances in which it was said).

con·text·ual AW /kənˈtekstʃuəl/ *adj.* (*formal*) connected with a particular context: *contextual information* ◇ *contextual clues to the meaning* ▸ **con·text·ual·ly** *adv.*

con·text·ual·ize (*BrE* also **-ise**) AW /kənˈtekstʃuəlaɪz/ *verb* **~ sth** (*formal*) to consider sth in relation to the situation in which it happens or exists ▸ **con·text·ual·iza·tion, -isa·tion** /kənˌtekstʃuəlaɪˈzeɪʃn/ *noun* [U]

con·tigu·ous /kənˈtɪgjuəs/ *adj.* (*formal* or *technical*) touching or next to sth: *The countries are contiguous.* ◇ **~ with/to sth** *The bruising was not contiguous to the wound.* ▸ **con·tigu·ity** /ˌkɒntɪˈgjuːəti; *NAmE* ˌkɑːn-/ *noun* [U]

con·tin·ence /ˈkɒntɪnəns; *NAmE* ˈkɑːn-/ *noun* [U] **1** (*formal*) the control of your feelings, especially your desire to have sex **2** the ability to control the BLADDER and BOWELS OPP **incontinence** ▸ **con·tin·ent** /ˈkɒntɪnənt; *NAmE* ˈkɑːn-/ *adj.* OPP **incontinent**

con·tin·ent 🔑 /ˈkɒntɪnənt; *NAmE* ˈkɑːn-/ *noun* **1** 🔑 [C] one of the large land masses of the earth such as Europe, Asia or Africa: *the continent of Africa* ◇ *the African continent* **2 the Continent** [sing.] (*BrE*) the main part of the continent of Europe, not including Britain or Ireland: *We're going to spend a weekend on the Continent.*

con·tin·en·tal /ˌkɒntɪˈnentl; *NAmE* ˌkɑːn-/ *adj., noun*
■ *adj.* **1** (also **Continental**) [only before noun] (*BrE*) of or in the continent of Europe, not including Britain and Ireland: *a popular continental holiday resort* ◇ *Britain's continental neighbours* **2** (*BrE*) following the customs of countries in

western and southern Europe: *a continental lifestyle* ◇ *The shutters and the balconies make the street look almost continental.* **3** [only before noun] connected with the main part of the N American continent: *Prices are often higher in Hawaii than in the continental United States.* **4** forming part of, or typical of, any of the seven main land masses of the earth: *continental Antarctica/Asia/Europe* ◇ *to study continental geography*

■ ***noun*** (*BrE*, *old-fashioned*, often *disapproving*) a person who lives in the continent of Europe: *The continentals have never understood our preference for warm beer.*

ˌcontinental ˈbreakfast *noun* a light breakfast, usually consisting of coffee and bread rolls with butter and jam ➲ compare ENGLISH BREAKFAST

ˌcontinental ˈclimate *noun* a fairly dry pattern of weather with very hot summers and very cold winters, that is typical of the central regions of the US, Canada and Russia, for example

ˌcontinental ˈdrift *noun* [U] (*geology*) the slow movement of the continents towards and away from each other during the history of the earth ➲ see also PLATE TECTONICS

ˌcontinental ˈquilt *noun* (*BrE*) = DUVET

ˌcontinental ˈshelf *noun* [usually sing.] (*geology*) the area of land on the edge of a continent that slopes into the ocean

ˌcontinental ˈslope *noun* [sing.] (*geology*) the steep surface that goes down from the outer edge of the continental shelf to the ocean floor

con·tin·gency /kənˈtɪndʒənsi/ *noun* (*pl.* -ies) an event that may or may not happen SYN **possibility**: *We must consider all possible contingencies.* ◇ *to make* ***contingency plans*** (= plans for what to do if a particular event happens or does not happen) ◇ *a* ***contingency fund*** (= to pay for sth that might happen in the future)

conˈtingency fee *noun* (in the US) an amount of money that is paid to a lawyer only if the person he or she is advising wins in court

con·tin·gent /kənˈtɪndʒənt/ *noun, adj.*

■ ***noun*** [C+sing./pl. v.] **1** a group of people at a meeting or an event who have sth in common, especially the place they come from, that is not shared by other people at the event: *The largest contingent was from the United States.* ◇ *A strong contingent of local residents were there to block the proposal.* **2** a group of soldiers that are part of a larger force: *the French contingent in the UN peacekeeping force*

■ ***adj.*** **1** **~ (on/upon sth)** (*formal*) depending on sth that may or may not happen: *All payments are contingent upon satisfactory completion dates.* **2** **~ worker/work/job** (*business*) a person, or work done by a person, who does not have a permanent contract with a company: *the spread of contingent work throughout the economy* ▶ **con·tin·gent·ly** *adv.*

con·tin·ual /kənˈtɪnjuəl/ *adj.* [only before noun] **1** repeated many times in a way that is annoying: ***continual complaints/interruptions*** **2** continuing without interruption SYN **continuous**: *He was in a continual process of rewriting his material.* ◇ *We lived in continual fear of being discovered.* ◇ *Her daughter was a continual source of delight to her.* ➲ note at CONTINUOUS ▶ **con·tinu·al·ly** /-juəli/ *adv.*: *They argue continually about money.* ◇ *the need to adapt to new and continually changing circumstances* ◇ *New products are continually being developed.*

con·tinu·ance /kənˈtɪnjuəns/ *noun* **1** [U] (*formal*) the state of continuing to exist or function: *We can no longer support the President's continuance in office.* **2** [C] (*NAmE*, *law*) a decision that a court case should be heard later: *The judge refused his motion for a continuance.*

con·tinu·ant /kənˈtɪnjuənt/ *noun* (*phonetics*) a consonant that is pronounced with the breath passing through the throat, so that the sound can be continued. /f/, /l/ and /m/ are examples of continuants. ▶ **con·tinu·ant** *adj.* [only before noun]: *continuant consonants*

con·tinu·ation /kənˌtɪnjuˈeɪʃn/ *noun* **1** [U, sing.] an act or the state of continuing: *They are anxious to ensure the continuation of the economic reform programme.* ◇ **~ in sth** *This year saw a continuation in the upward trend in sales.* **2** [C] something that continues or follows sth else: *Her new book is a continuation of her autobiography.* **3** [C] something that is joined on to sth else and forms a part of it: *There are plans to build a continuation of the bypass next year.*

con·tinue 🔑 /kənˈtɪnjuː/ *verb* **1** 🔑 [I, T] to keep existing or happening without stopping: *The exhibition continues until 25 July.* ◇ *The trial is expected to continue for three months.* ◇ **~ to do sth** *The rain continued to fall all afternoon.* ◇ **~ doing sth** *The rain continued falling all afternoon.* **2** 🔑 [I, T] to keep doing sth without stopping: **~ doing sth** *She wanted to continue working until she was 60.* ◇ **~ to do sth** *He continued to ignore everything I was saying.* ◇ **~ (with sth)** *Are you going to continue with the project?* ◇ **~ sth** *The board of inquiry is continuing its investigations.* **3** 🔑 [I] (+ **adv./prep.**) to go or move further in the same direction: *The path continued over rough, rocky ground.* ◇ *He continued on his way.* **4** 🔑 [I] **~ (as sth)** to remain in a particular job or condition: *I want you to continue as project manager.* ◇ *She will continue in her present job until a replacement can be found.* **5** 🔑 [I, T] to start or start sth again after stopping for a time SYN **resume**: *The story continues in our next issue.* ◇ **~ sth** *The story will be continued in our next issue.* **6** 🔑 [I, T] to start speaking again after stopping: *Please continue—I didn't mean to interrupt.* ◇ **+ speech** *'In fact,' he continued, 'I'd like to congratulate you.'*

con·tinued /kənˈtɪnjuːd/ (also **con·tinu·ing** /kənˈtɪnjuɪŋ/) *adj.* [only before noun] existing in the same state without change or interruption: *We are grateful for your* ***continued/continuing support.*** ◇ *continued interest* ◇ *continuing involvement*

conˌtinuing eduˈcation *noun* [U] = ADULT EDUCATION

con·tinu·ity /ˌkɒntɪˈnjuːəti; *NAmE* ˌkɑːntəˈnuː-/ *noun* (*pl.* -ies) **1** [U] the fact of not stopping or not changing: *to* ***ensure/provide/maintain continuity*** *of fuel supplies* OPP **discontinuity** **2** [U, C] a logical connection between the parts of sth, or between two things: *The novel fails to achieve narrative continuity.* ◇ *There are obvious continuities between diet and health.* OPP **discontinuity** **3** [U] (*technical*) the organization of a film/movie or television programme, especially making sure that people's clothes, objects, etc. are the same from one scene to the next

con·tinuo /kənˈtɪnjuəʊ; *NAmE* -juoʊ/ *noun* [U] (*music*) (from *Italian*) a musical part played to accompany another instrument, in which a line of low notes is shown with figures to represent the higher notes to be played above them: *a trio for two violins and continuo*

con·tinu·ous 🔑 /kənˈtɪnjuəs/ *adj.* **1** 🔑 happening or existing for a period of time without interruption: *She was in continuous employment until the age of sixty-five.* ◇ *The rain has been continuous since this morning.* **2** 🔑 spreading in a line or over an area without any spaces: *a continuous line of traffic* **3** 🔑 (*informal*) repeated many times SYN **continual**: *For four days the town suffered continuous attacks.* HELP **Continual** is much more frequent in this meaning. **4** (*grammar*) = PROGRESSIVE: *the continuous tenses* ▶ **con·tinu·ous·ly** 🔑 *adv.*: *He has lived and worked in France almost continuously since 1990.*

conˌtinuous asˈsessment *noun* [U] (*BrE*) a system of giving a student a final mark/grade based on work done during a course of study rather than on one exam

con·tinuum /kənˈtɪnjuəm/ *noun* (*pl.* **con·tinua** /-juə/) a series of similar items in which each is almost the same as the ones next to it but the last is very different from the first SYN **cline**: *It is impossible to say at what point along the continuum a dialect becomes a separate language.*

con·tort /kənˈtɔːt; *NAmE* -ˈtɔːrt/ *verb* [I, T] to become twisted or make sth twisted out of its natural or normal shape: *His face contorted with anger.* ◇ **~ sth** *Her mouth was contorted in a snarl.* ▶ **con·tort·ed** *adj.*: ***contorted limbs/bodies*** ◇ (*figurative*) *It was a contorted version of the truth.*

C

Synonyms

continuous / continual

These adjectives are frequently used with the following nouns:

continuous ~	continual ~
process	change
employment	problems
flow	updating
line	questions
speech	pain
supply	fear

- **Continuous** describes something that continues without stopping.
- **Continual** usually describes an action that is repeated again and again.
- The difference between these two words is now disappearing. In particular, **continual** can also mean the same as **continuous** and is used especially about undesirable things: *Life was a continual struggle for them.* However, **continuous** is much more frequent in this sense.

con·tor·tion /kən'tɔːʃn; *NAmE* -'tɔːrʃn/ *noun* **1** [U] the state of the face or body being twisted out of its natural shape: *Their bodies had suffered contortion as a result of malnutrition.* **2** [C] a movement which twists the body out of its natural shape: *His facial contortions amused the audience of schoolchildren.* ◇ (*figurative*) *We had to go through all the usual contortions* (= a difficult series of actions) *to get a ticket.*

con·tor·tion·ist /kən'tɔːʃənɪst; *NAmE* -'tɔːrʃ-/ *noun* a performer who does contortions of their body to entertain others

con·tour /'kɒntʊə(r); *NAmE* 'kɑːntʊr/ *noun* **1** the outer edges of sth; the outline of its shape or form: *The road follows the natural contours of the coastline.* ◇ *She traced the contours of his face with her finger.* **2** (also '**contour line**) a line on a map that joins points that are the same height above sea level: *a contour map* (= a map that includes these lines)

con·toured /'kɒntʊəd; *NAmE* 'kɑːntʊrd/ *adj.* **1** with a specially designed outline that makes sth attractive or comfortable: *It is smoothly contoured to look like a racing car.* **2** having or showing contours (2): ***contoured hills/maps***

contra- /'kɒntrə; *NAmE* 'kɑːntrə/ *combining form* **1** (in nouns, verbs and adjectives) against; opposite: *contraflow* ◇ *contradict* **2** (in nouns) (*music*) having a PITCH an OCTAVE below: *a contrabassoon*

con·tra·band /'kɒntrəbænd; *NAmE* 'kɑːn-/ *noun* [U] goods that are illegally taken into or out of a country: *contraband goods* ◇ *to smuggle contraband*

con·tra·cep·tion /ˌkɒntrə'sepʃn; *NAmE* ˌkɑːn-/ *noun* [U] the practice of preventing a woman from becoming pregnant; the methods of doing this SYN **birth control**: *to give advice about contraception*

con·tra·cep·tive /ˌkɒntrə'septɪv; *NAmE* ˌkɑːn-/ *noun* a drug, device or practice used to prevent a woman becoming pregnant: *oral contraceptives* ▶ **con·tra·cep·tive** *adj.* [only before noun]: *a contraceptive pill* ◇ *contraceptive advice/precautions/methods*

con·tract 0-w AW *noun, verb*

■ ***noun*** /'kɒntrækt; *NAmE* 'kɑːn-/ **1** 0-w an official written agreement: *a contract of employment* ◇ *a research contract* ◇ **~ with sb** *to **enter into/make/sign a contract** with the supplier* ◇ **~ between A and B** *These clauses form part of the contract between buyer and seller.* ◇ **~ for sth** *a contract for the supply of vehicles* ◇ **~ to do sth** *to **win/be awarded a contract** to build a new school* ◇ *a **contract worker*** (= one employed on a contract for a fixed period of time) ◇ *I was **on a** three-year **contract** that expired last week.* ◇ ***Under the terms of the contract** the job should have been finished yesterday.* ◇ *She is **under contract to*** (= has a contract to work for) *a major American computer firm.* ◇ *The offer has been accepted, **subject to contract*** (= the agreement is not official until the contract is signed). ◇ *They were sued for **breach of contract*** (= not keeping to a contract). **2 ~ (on sb)** (*informal*) an agreement to kill sb for money: *to take out a contract on sb*

■ ***verb*** /kən'trækt/ **1** 0-w [I, T] to become less or smaller; to make sth become less or smaller: *Glass contracts as it cools.* ◇ *a contracting market* ◇ *The heart muscles contract to expel the blood.* ◇ **~ sth** *The exercise consists of stretching and contracting the leg muscles.* ◇ **~ sth to sth** *'I will' and 'I shall' are usually contracted to 'I'll'* (= made shorter). OPP **expand** **2** [T] **~ sth** (*formal* or *medical*) to get an illness: *to contract AIDS/a virus/a disease* **3** [T] to make a legal agreement with sb for them to work for you or provide you with a service: **~ sb to do sth** *The player is contracted to play until August.* ◇ **~ sb (to sth)** *Several computer engineers have been contracted to the finance department.* **4** [I] **~ to do sth** to make a legal agreement to work for sb or provide them with a service: *She has contracted to work 20 hours a week.* **5** [T] **~ a marriage/an alliance (with sb)** (*formal*) to formally agree to marry sb/form an ALLIANCE with sb

PHR V **conˌtract 'in (to sth)** (*BrE*) to formally agree that you will take part in sth **conˌtract 'out (of sth)** (*BrE*) to formally agree that you will not take part in sth: *Many employees contracted out of the pension plan.* **conˌtract sth↔'out (to sb)** to arrange for work to be done by another company rather than your own

ˌcontract 'bridge *noun* [U] the standard form of the card game BRIDGE, in which points are given only for sets of cards that are BID and won

con·tract·ile /kən'træktaɪl/ *adj.* (*biology*) (of living TISSUE, organs, etc.) able to contract or, of an opening or tube, become narrower

con·trac·tion /kən'trækʃn/ *noun* **1** [U] the process of becoming smaller: *the expansion and contraction of the metal* ◇ *The sudden contraction of the markets left them with a lot of unwanted stock.* OPP **expansion** **2** [C, U] a sudden and painful contracting of muscles, especially of the muscles around a woman's WOMB that happen when she is giving birth to a child: *The contractions started coming every five minutes.* **3** [C] (*linguistics*) a short form of a word: *'He's' may be a contraction of 'he is' or 'he has'.*

con·tract·or AW /kən'træktə(r)/ *noun* a person or company that has a contract to do work or provide goods or services for another company: *a **building/haulage, etc. contractor*** ◇ *to employ an outside contractor*

con·tract·ual /kən'træktʃuəl/ *adj.* connected with the conditions of a legal written agreement; agreed in a contract ▶ **con·trac·tu·al·ly** *adv.*

con·tra·dict AW /ˌkɒntrə'dɪkt; *NAmE* ˌkɑːn-/ *verb* **1** to say that sth that sb else has said is wrong, and that the opposite is true: **~ sth** *All evening her husband contradicted everything she said.* ◇ **~ sb/yourself** *You've just **contradicted yourself*** (= said the opposite of what you said before). ◇ **~ (sb) + speech** *'No, it's not,' she contradicted (him).* **2 ~ sth | ~ each other** (of statements or pieces of evidence) to be so different from each other that one of them must be wrong: *The two stories contradict each other.* ➲ LANGUAGE BANK at EVIDENCE

con·tra·dic·tion AW /ˌkɒntrə'dɪkʃn; *NAmE* ˌkɑːn-/ *noun* **1** [C, U] **~ (between A and B)** a lack of agreement between facts, opinions, actions, etc: *There is a contradiction between the two sets of figures.* ◇ *His public speeches are **in direct contradiction to** his personal lifestyle.* ◇ *How can we resolve this apparent contradiction?* **2** [U, C] the act of saying that sth that sb else has said is wrong or not true; an example of this: *I think I can say, **without fear of contradiction**, that...* ◇ *Now you say you both left at ten—that's a contradiction of your last statement.*

IDM **a ˌcontradiction in 'terms** a statement containing two words that contradict each other's meaning: *A 'nomad settlement' is a contradiction in terms.*

con·tra·dict·ory AW /ˌkɒntrəˈdɪktəri; *NAmE* ˌkɑːn-/ *adj.* containing or showing a contradiction SYN **conflicting**: *We are faced with two apparently contradictory statements.* ◇ *The advice I received was often contradictory.*

con·tra·dis·tinc·tion /ˌkɒntrədɪˈstɪŋkʃn; *NAmE* ˌkɑːn-/ *noun*
IDM **in contradistinction to sth/sb** (*formal*) in contrast with sth/sb

con·tra·flow /ˈkɒntrəfləʊ; *NAmE* ˈkɑːntrəfloʊ/ *noun* (*BrE*) a system that is used when one half of a large road is closed for repairs, and the traffic going in both directions has to use the other half: *A contraflow system is in operation on this section of the motorway.*

con·tra·indi·cate /ˌkɒntrəˈɪndɪkeɪt; *NAmE* ˌkɑːn-/ *verb* **~ sth** (*medical*) if a drug or treatment is **contraindicated**, there is a medical reason why it should not be used in a particular situation: *This drug is contraindicated in patients with asthma.*

con·tra·indi·ca·tion /ˌkɒntrəˌɪndɪˈkeɪʃn; *NAmE* ˌkɑːn-/ *noun* (*medical*) a possible reason for not giving sb a particular drug or medical treatment

con·tralto /kənˈtræltəʊ; *NAmE* -toʊ/ *noun* (*pl.* -os) = ALTO

con·trap·tion /kənˈtræpʃn/ *noun* a machine or piece of equipment that looks strange: *She showed us a strange contraption that looked like a satellite dish.*

con·tra·pun·tal /ˌkɒntrəˈpʌntl; *NAmE* ˌkɑːn-/ *adj.* (*music*) having two or more tunes played together to form a whole ➲ see also COUNTERPOINT

con·trari·wise /kənˈtreəriwaɪz; *NAmE* -ˈtrer-/ *adv.* (*formal*) **1** used at the beginning of a sentence or clause to introduce a contrast **2** in the opposite way: *It worked contrariwise—first you dialled the number, then you put the money in.*

con·trary[1] AW /ˈkɒntrəri; *NAmE* ˈkɑːntreri/ *adj., noun* ➲ see also CONTRARY[2]
■ *adj.* **1 ~ to sth** different from sth; against sth: ***Contrary to popular belief****, many cats dislike milk.* ◇ *The government has decided that the publication of the report would be 'contrary to the public interest'.* **2** [only before noun] completely different in nature or direction SYN **opposite**: ***contrary advice/opinions/arguments*** ◇ *The contrary view is that prison provides an excellent education—in crime.*
■ *noun* **the contrary** [sing.] the opposite fact, event or situation: *In the end the contrary was proved true: he was innocent and she was guilty.*
IDM **on the ˈcontrary** used to introduce a statement that says the opposite of the last one: *'It must have been terrible.' 'On the contrary, I enjoyed every minute.'* **ˌquite the ˈcontrary** used to emphasize that the opposite of what has been said is true: *I don't find him funny at all. Quite the contrary.* **to the ˈcontrary** showing or proving the opposite: *Show me some evidence to the contrary* (= proving that sth is not true). ◇ *I will expect to see you on Sunday unless I hear anything to the contrary* (= that you are not coming).

con·trary[2] AW /kənˈtreəri; *NAmE* -ˈtreri/ *adj.* (*formal, disapproving*) (usually of children) behaving badly; choosing to do or say the opposite of what is expected: *She was such a contrary child—it was impossible to please her.* ➲ see also CONTRARY[1] ▶ **con·trar·ily** AW *adv.* **con·trari·ness** *noun* [U]

con·trast 🔑 AW *noun, verb*
■ *noun* /ˈkɒntrɑːst; *NAmE* ˈkɑːntræst/ **1** 🔑 [C, U] a difference between two or more people or things that you can see clearly when they are compared or put close together; the fact of comparing two or more things in order to show the differences between them: **~ (between A and B)** *There is an obvious contrast between the cultures of East and West.* ◇ **~ (to sb/sth)** *The company lost $7 million this quarter **in contrast to** a profit of $6.2 million a year earlier.* ◇ *The situation when we arrived was in **marked contrast** to the news reports.* ◇ *The poverty of her childhood **stands in** total **contrast to** her life in Hollywood.* ◇ **~ (with sb/sth)** *to show a **sharp/stark/striking contrast** with sth* ◇ **~ (in sth)** *A wool jacket complements the silk trousers and provides an interesting contrast in texture.* ◇ *When you look at their new system, ours seems very old-fashioned **by contrast**.* ◇ **~ (of sth)** *Careful contrast of the two plans shows some important differences.* **2** [C, usually sing.] **~ (to sb/sth)** a person or thing that is clearly different from sb/sth else: *The work you did today is quite a contrast to* (= very much better/worse than) *what you did last week.* **3** [U] differences in colour or in light and dark, used in photographs and paintings to create a special effect: *The artist's use of contrast is masterly.* **4** [U] the amount of difference between light and dark in a photograph or the picture on a television screen: *Use this button to adjust the contrast.*
■ *verb* /kənˈtrɑːst; *NAmE* -ˈtræst/ **1** 🔑 [T] **~ (A and/with B)** to compare two things in order to show the differences between them: *It is interesting to contrast the British legal system with the American one.* ◇ *The poem contrasts youth and age.* **2** 🔑 [I] **~ (with sth)** to show a clear difference when close together or when compared: *Her actions **contrasted sharply** with her promises.* ◇ *Her actions and her promises contrasted sharply.*

Language Bank

contrast

Highlighting differences

- This survey **highlights a number of differences in** the way that teenage boys and girls in the UK spend their free time.
- **One of the main differences between** the girls **and** the boys who took part in the research was the way in which they use the Internet.
- **Unlike** the girls, who use the Internet mainly to keep in touch with friends, the boys questioned in this survey tend to use the Internet for playing computer games.
- The girls **differ from** the boys **in that** they tend to spend more time keeping in touch with friends on the telephone or on social networking websites.
- **Compared to** the boys, the girls spend much more time chatting to friends on the telephone.
- On average the girls spend four hours a week chatting to friends on the phone. **In contrast**, very few of the boys spend more than five minutes a day talking to their friends in this way.
- The boys prefer competitive sports and computer games, **whereas/while** the girls seem to enjoy more cooperative activities, such as shopping with friends.
- When the girls go shopping, they mainly buy clothes and cosmetics. The boys, **on the other hand**, tend to purchase computer games or gadgets.

➲ Language Banks at GENERALLY, ILLUSTRATE, PROPORTION, SIMILARLY, SURPRISING

con·trast·ing 🔑 AW /kənˈtrɑːstɪŋ; *NAmE* -ˈtræs-/ *adj.* [usually before noun]
very different in style, colour or attitude: *bright, contrasting colours* ◇ *The book explores contrasting views of the poet's early work.*

con·trast·ive AW /kənˈtrɑːstɪv; *NAmE* -ˈtræst-/ *adj.* (*linguistics*) showing the differences between languages: *a contrastive analysis of British and Australian English*

con·tra·vene /ˌkɒntrəˈviːn; *NAmE* ˌkɑːn-/ *verb* **~ sth** (*formal*) to do sth that is not allowed by a law or rule SYN **infringe**: *The company was found guilty of contravening safety regulations.* ▶ **con·tra·ven·tion** /ˌkɒntrəˈvenʃn; *NAmE* ˌkɑːn-/ *noun* [U, C] SYN **infringement**: *These actions are **in contravention of** European law.*

con·tre·temps /ˈkɒntrətɒ̃; *NAmE* ˈkɑːntrətɑ̃ː; ˈkɔːntrətɑ̃ː/ *noun* (*pl.* **con·tre·temps**) (from *French, formal* or *humorous*) an unfortunate event or embarrassing disagreement with another person

con·trib·ute 🔑 AW /kənˈtrɪbjuːt; *BrE* also ˈkɒntrɪbjuːt/ *verb*
1 🔑 [T, I] to give sth, especially money or goods, to help

C

sb/sth: **~ sth (to/towards sth)** *We contributed £5 000 to the earthquake fund.* ◇ **~ (to/towards sth)** *Would you like to contribute to our collection?* ◇ *Do you wish to contribute?* **2** 🔑 [I] **~ (to sth)** to be one of the causes of sth: *Medical negligence was said to have contributed to her death.* ◇ *Human error may have been a* ***contributing factor.*** ➲ LANGUAGE BANK at CAUSE **3** 🔑 [I, T] to increase, improve or add to sth: **~ to sth** *Immigrants have contributed to British culture in many ways.* ◇ **~ sth to sth** *This book contributes little to our understanding of the subject.* **4** 🔑 [T, I] to write things for a newspaper, magazine, or a radio or television programme; to speak during a meeting or conversation, especially to give your opinion: **~ sth (to sth)** *She contributed a number of articles to the magazine.* ◇ **~ (to sth)** *He contributes regularly to the magazine 'New Scientist'.* ◇ *We hope everyone will contribute to the discussion.*

con·tri·bu·tion 🔑 AW /ˌkɒntrɪˈbjuːʃn; *NAmE* ˌkɑːn-/ *noun* **1** 🔑 [C] a sum of money that is given to a person or an organization in order to help pay for sth SYN **donation** : **~ (to sth)** *to* ***make a contribution*** *to charity* ◇ *a substantial contribution* ◇ *All contributions will be gratefully received.* ◇ **~ (toward(s) sth/doing sth)** *valuable contributions towards the upkeep of the cathedral* **2** 🔑 [C] **~ (to sth)** a sum of money that you pay regularly to your employer or the government in order to pay for benefits such as health insurance, a pension, etc: *monthly contributions to the pension scheme* ➲ SYNONYMS at PAYMENT **3** 🔑 [C, usually sing.] an action or a service that helps to cause or increase sth: **~ (to sth)** *He* ***made a*** *very positive* ***contribution*** *to the success of the project.* ◇ *the car's contribution to the greenhouse effect* ◇ **~ (toward(s) sth/doing sth)** *These measures would make a valuable contribution towards reducing industrial accidents.* **4** 🔑 [C] **~ (to sth)** an item that forms part of a book, magazine, broadcast, discussion, etc: *an important contribution to the debate* ◇ *All contributions for the May issue must be received by Friday.* **5** [U] **~ (to sth)** the act of giving sth, especially money, to help a person or an organization: *We rely entirely on voluntary contribution.*

con·tribu·tor AW /kənˈtrɪbjətə(r)/ *noun* **1 ~ (to sth)** a person who writes articles for a magazine or a book, or who talks on a radio or television programme or at a meeting **2 ~ (to sth)** a person or thing that provides money to help pay for sth, or support sth: *Older people are important contributors to the economy.* **3 ~ (to sth)** something that helps to cause sth: *Sulphur dioxide is a pollutant and a major contributor to acid rain.*

con·tribu·tory /kənˈtrɪbjətəri; *NAmE* -tɔːri/ *adj.* [usually before noun] **1** helping to cause sth: *Alcohol is a* ***contributory factor*** *in 10% of all road accidents.* **2** involving payments from the people who will benefit: *a* ***contributory*** *pension* ***scheme/plan*** (= paid for by both employers and employees) OPP **non-contributory**

con·trite /kənˈtraɪt; *BrE* also ˈkɒntraɪt/ *adj.* (*formal*) very sorry for sth bad that you have done ▸ **con·trite·ly** *adv.* **con·tri·tion** /kənˈtrɪʃn/ *noun* [U]: *a look of contrition*

con·triv·ance /kənˈtraɪvəns/ *noun* (*formal*) **1** [C, U] (usually *disapproving*) something that sb has done or written that does not seem natural; the fact of seeming artificial: *The film is spoilt by unrealistic contrivances of plot.* ◇ *The story is told with a complete absence of contrivance.* **2** [C] a clever or complicated device or tool made for a particular purpose **3** [C, U] a clever plan or trick; the act of using a clever plan or trick: *an ingenious contrivance to get her to sign the document without reading it*

con·trive /kənˈtraɪv/ *verb* (*formal*) **1 ~ to do sth** to manage to do sth despite difficulties: *She contrived to spend a couple of hours with him every Sunday evening.* **2 ~ sth** to succeed in making sth happen despite difficulties: *I decided to contrive a meeting between the two of them.* **3 ~ sth** to think of or make sth, for example a plan or a machine, in a clever way: *They contrived a plan to defraud the company.*

con·trived /kənˈtraɪvd/ *adj.* (*disapproving*) planned in advance and not natural or genuine; written or arranged in a way that is not natural or realistic: *a contrived situation* ◇ *The book's happy ending seemed contrived.*

con·trol 🔑 /kənˈtrəʊl; *NAmE* -ˈtroʊl/ *noun, verb*

■ ***noun***

▸ POWER **1** 🔑 [U] **~ (of/over sb/sth)** the power to make decisions about how a country, an area, an organization, etc. is run: *The party is expecting to* ***gain control of*** *the council in the next election.* ◇ *The Democrats will probably* ***lose control of*** *Congress.* ◇ *A military junta* ***took control of the country.*** ◇ *The city is* ***in the control of*** *enemy forces.* ◇ *The city is* ***under enemy control.*** **2** 🔑 [U] **~ (of/over sb/sth)** the ability to make sb/sth do what you want: *The teacher* ***had no control*** *over the children.* ◇ *She struggled to* ***keep control of*** *her voice.* ◇ *She* ***lost control*** *of her car on the ice.* ◇ *He got so angry he* ***lost control*** (= shouted and said or did things he would not normally do). ◇ *Owing to* ***circumstances beyond our control,*** *the flight to Rome has been cancelled.* ◇ *The coach made the team work hard on ball control* (= in a ball game). ➲ see also SELF-CONTROL

▸ LIMITING/MANAGING **3** 🔑 [U, C] **~ (of/on sth)** (often in compounds) the act of restricting, limiting or managing sth; a method of doing this: *traffic control* ◇ *talks on arms control* ◇ *government controls on trade and industry* ◇ *A new advance has been made in the control of malaria.* ◇ *Price controls on food were ended.* ◇ *a pest control officer* ➲ see also BIRTH CONTROL, QUALITY CONTROL ➲ SYNONYMS at LIMIT

▸ IN MACHINE **4** 🔑 [C, usually pl.] the switches and buttons, etc. that you use to operate a machine or a vehicle: *the controls of an aircraft* ◇ *the control panel* ◇ *the volume control of a CD player* ◇ *The co-pilot was* ***at the controls*** *when the plane landed.* ➲ see also REMOTE CONTROL

▸ IN EXPERIMENT **5** [C] (*technical*) a person, thing or group used as a standard of comparison for checking the results of a scientific experiment; an experiment whose result is known, used for checking working methods: *One group was treated with the new drug, and the* ***control group*** *was given a sugar pill.*

▸ PLACE **6** [sing.] a place where orders are given or where checks are made; the people who work in this place: *air traffic control* ◇ *We went through passport control and into the departure lounge.* ◇ *This is Mission Control calling the space shuttle Discovery.*

▸ ON COMPUTER **7** [U] (also **conˈtrol key** [sing.]) (on a computer keyboard) a key that you press when you want to perform a particular operation

IDM **be in control (of sth) 1** 🔑 to direct or manage an organization, an area or a situation: *He's reached retiring age, but he's still firmly in control.* ◇ *There has been some violence after the match, but the police are now in control of the situation.* **2** 🔑 to be able to organize your life well and keep calm: *In spite of all her family problems, she's really in control.* **be/get/run/etc. out of conˈtrol** 🔑 to be or become impossible to manage or to control: *The children are completely out of control since their father left.* ◇ *A truck ran out of control on the hill.* **be under conˈtrol** 🔑 to be being dealt with successfully: *Don't worry—everything's under control!* **bring/get/keep sth under conˈtrol** 🔑 to succeed in dealing with sth so that it does not cause any damage or hurt anyone: *It took two hours to bring the fire under control.* ◇ *Please keep your dog under control!*

■ ***verb*** (-ll-)

▸ HAVE POWER **1** 🔑 **~ sb/sth** to have power over a person, company, country, etc. so that you are able to decide what they must do or how it is run: *By the age of 21 he controlled the company.* ◇ *The whole territory is now controlled by the army.* ◇ *Can't you control your children?*

▸ LIMIT/MANAGE **2** 🔑 to limit sth or make it happen in a particular way: **~ sth** *government attempts to control immigration* ◇ *Many biological processes are controlled by hormones.* ◇ **~ what/how, etc...** *Parents should control what their kids watch on television.* **3** 🔑 **~ sth** to stop sth from spreading or getting worse: *Firefighters are still trying to control the blaze.* ◇ *She was given drugs to control the pain.*

▸ MACHINE **4** 🔑 **~ sth** to make sth, such as a machine or system, work in the way that you want it to: *This knob controls*

the volume. ◇ *The traffic lights are controlled by a central computer.*
▸ STAY CALM **5** to manage to make yourself remain calm, even though you are upset or angry: **~ yourself** *I was so furious I couldn't control myself and I hit him.* ◇ **~ sth** *He was finding it difficult to control his feelings.*

con'trol freak *noun* (*informal, disapproving*) a person who always wants to be in control of their own and others' lives, and to organize how things are done

con·trol·lable /kən'trəʊləbl; *NAmE* -'troʊ-/ *adj.* that can be controlled

con·trolled /kən'trəʊld; *NAmE* -'troʊld/ *adj.*
1 done or arranged in a very careful way: *a controlled explosion* ◇ *a controlled environment* **2** limited, or managed by law or by rules: *controlled airspace* **3 -controlled** (in compounds) managed by a particular group, or in a particular way: *a British-controlled company* ◇ *computer-controlled systems* **4** remaining calm and not getting angry or upset: *She remained quiet and controlled.* ➲ compare UNCONTROLLED

con,trolled e'conomy *noun* (*economics*) a type of economic system in which a government controls its country's industries and decides what goods should be produced and in what amounts

con,trolled 'substance *noun* (*technical*) an illegal drug: *to be arrested for possession of a controlled substance*

con·trol·ler /kən'trəʊlə(r); *NAmE* -'troʊ-/ *noun* **1** a person who manages or directs sth, especially a large organization or part of an organization ➲ see also AIR TRAFFIC CONTROLLER **2** (*technical*) a device that controls or REGULATES a machine or part of a machine: *a temperature controller* **3** (also **comp·trol·ler**) a person who is in charge of the financial accounts of a business company

con,trolling 'interest *noun* [usually sing.] the fact of owning enough shares in a company to be able to make decisions about what the company should do

con'trol tower *noun* a building at an airport from which the movements of aircraft are controlled

con·tro·ver·sial AW /,kɒntrə'vɜːʃl; *NAmE* ,kɑːntrə'vɜːrʃl/ *adj.* causing a lot of angry public discussion and disagreement: *a **highly controversial** topic* ◇ *a controversial plan to build a new road* ◇ *Winston Churchill and Richard Nixon were both controversial figures.* OPP **non-controversial, uncontroversial** ▸ **con·tro·ver·sial·ly** AW /-ʃəli/ *adv.*

con·tro·versy AW /'kɒntrəvɜːsi; *NAmE* 'kɑːntrəvɜːrsi; *BrE* also kən'trɒvəsi/ *noun* [U, C] (*pl.* -ies) **~ (over/about/surrounding sb/sth)** public discussion and argument about sth that many people strongly disagree about, disapprove of, or are shocked by: *to **arouse/cause controversy*** ◇ *a bitter **controversy over/about** the site of the new airport* ◇ *the controversy surrounding his latest movie* ◇ *The President resigned amid considerable controversy.*

con·tro·vert /,kɒntrə'vɜːt; *NAmE* 'kɑːntrəvɜːrt/ *verb* **~ sth** (*formal*) to say or prove that sth is not true SYN **refute** ➲ see also INCONTROVERTIBLE

con·tu·ma·cious /,kɒntju'meɪʃəs; *NAmE* ,kɑːntu-/ *adj.* (*old use* or *law*) lacking respect for authority

con·tu·sion /kən'tjuːʒn; *NAmE* -'tuː-/ *noun* [C, U] (*medical*) an injury to part of the body that does not break the skin SYN **bruise**

con·un·drum /kə'nʌndrəm/ *noun* **1** a confusing problem or question that is very difficult to solve **2** a question, usually involving a trick with words, that you ask for fun SYN **riddle**

con·ur·ba·tion /,kɒnɜː'beɪʃn; *NAmE* ,kɑːnɜːr'b-/ *noun* (*formal*) a large area where towns have grown and joined together, often around a city

con·va·lesce /,kɒnvə'les; *NAmE* ,kɑːn-/ *verb* [I] (*formal*) to spend time getting your health and strength back after an illness SYN **recuperate**: *She is convalescing at home after her operation.*

con·va·les·cence /,kɒnvə'lesns; *NAmE* ,kɑːn-/ *noun* [sing., U] a period of time when you get well again after an illness or a medical operation; the process of getting well: *You need four to six weeks' convalescence.*

con·va·les·cent /,kɒnvə'lesnt; *NAmE* ,kɑːn-/ *adj.* connected with convalescence; in the process of convalescence: *a convalescent home* (= a type of hospital where people go to get well after an illness) ◇ *a convalescent child* ▸ **con·va·les·cent** *noun*: *I treated him as a convalescent, not as a sick man.*

con·vec·tion /kən'vekʃn/ *noun* [U] (*technical*) the process in which heat moves through a gas or a liquid as the hotter part rises and the cooler, heavier part sinks

con·vect·or /kən'vektə(r)/ (also **con,vector 'heater**) *noun* a device for heating the air in a room using convection

con·vene AW /kən'viːn/ *verb* (*formal*) **1** [T] **~ sth** to arrange for people to come together for a formal meeting: *to convene a meeting* ◇ *A Board of Inquiry was convened immediately after the accident.* **2** [I] to come together for a formal meeting: *The committee will convene at 11.30 next Thursday.*

con·vener (also **con·venor**) /kən'viːnə(r)/ *noun* **1** a person who arranges meetings of groups or committees **2** (*BrE*) a senior official of a TRADE/LABOR UNION at a factory or other place of work

con·veni·ence /kən'viːniəns/ *noun* **1** [U] the quality of being useful, easy or suitable for sb: *We have provided seats **for the convenience** of our customers.* ◇ ***For** (**the sake of**) **convenience**, the two groups have been treated as one in this report.* ◇ *In this resort you can enjoy all the **comfort and convenience** of modern tourism.* ➲ compare INCONVENIENCE ➲ see also FLAG OF CONVENIENCE, MARRIAGE OF CONVENIENCE **2** [C] something that is useful and can make things easier or quicker to do, or more comfortable: *It was a great convenience to have the school so near.* ◇ *The house had all the modern conveniences* (= central heating, etc.) *that were unusual at that time.* ➲ see also PUBLIC CONVENIENCE
IDM **at sb's con'venience** (*formal*) at a time or a place which is suitable for sb: *Can you telephone me at your convenience to arrange a meeting?* ➲ more at EARLY *adj.*

con'venience food *noun* [C, U] food that you buy frozen or in a box or can, that you can prepare and cook very quickly and easily

con'venience store *noun* (*especially NAmE*) a shop/store that sells food, newspapers, etc. and often stays open 24 hours a day

con·veni·ent /kən'viːniənt/ *adj.*
1 **~ (for sb/sth)** useful, easy or quick to do; not causing problems: *It is very convenient to pay by credit card.* ◇ *You'll find these meals quick and convenient to prepare.* ◇ *Fruit is a convenient source of vitamins and energy.* ◇ *A bicycle is often more convenient than a car in towns.* ◇ *I can't see him now—it isn't convenient.* ◇ *I'll call back at a more convenient time.* ◇ (*disapproving*) *He used his wife's birthday as a convenient excuse for not going to the meeting.* **2** near to a particular place; easy to get to: (*BrE*) **~ (for sth)** *The house is very convenient for several schools.* ◇ (*NAmE*) **~ (to sth)** *The hotel is convenient to downtown.* OPP **inconvenient** ▸ **con·veni·ent·ly** *adv.*: *The report can be conveniently divided into three main sections.* ◇ *The hotel is conveniently situated close to the beach.* ◇ *She conveniently forgot to mention that her husband would be at the party, too* (= because it suited her not to say).

con·venor = CONVENER

con·vent /'kɒnvənt; *NAmE* 'kɑːnvent; -vənt/ *noun* **1** a building in which NUNS (= members of a female religious community) live together ➲ COLLOCATIONS at RELIGION **2** (also **'convent school**) a school run by NUNS

con·ven·tion AW /kən'venʃn/ *noun*
1 [C, U] the way in which sth is done that most people in a society expect and consider to be polite or the right way to do it: *social conventions* ◇ ***By convention** the deputy leader was always a woman.* ◇ *She is a young woman who enjoys*

flouting conventions. **2** [C] a large meeting of the members of a profession, a political party, etc. SYN **conference**: *to hold a convention* ◇ *the Democratic Party Convention* (= to elect a candidate for president) **3** [C] an official agreement between countries or leaders: *the Geneva convention* ◇ *the United Nations convention on the rights of the child* **4** [C, U] a traditional method or style in literature, art or the theatre: *the conventions of Greek tragedy*

con·ven·tion·al AW /kən'venʃənl/ *adj.* **1** (often *disapproving*) tending to follow what is done or considered acceptable by society in general; normal and ordinary, and perhaps not very interesting: ***conventional behaviour/morality*** ◇ *She's very conventional in her views.* OPP **unconventional** **2** [usually before noun] following what is traditional or the way sth has been done for a long time: ***conventional methods/approaches*** ◇ ***conventional medicine*** ◇ *It's not a hotel, in the conventional sense, but rather a whole village turned into a hotel.* ◇ *You can use a microwave or cook it in a conventional oven.* OPP **unconventional** **3** [usually before noun] (especially of weapons) not nuclear: ***conventional forces/weapons*** ◇ *a conventional power station* (= using oil or coal as fuel, rather than nuclear power) ▸ **con·ven·tion·al·ity** /kən,venʃə'næləti/ *noun* [U] **con·ven·tion·al·ly** AW /-ʃənəli/ *adv.*: *conventionally dressed* ◇ *conventionally grown food* (= grown according to conventional methods) IDM see WISDOM

con·ven·tion·eer /kən,venʃə'nɪə(r); *NAmE* -'nɪr/ *noun* (*NAmE*) a person who is attending a convention

con·verge /kən'vɜːdʒ; *NAmE* -'vɜːrdʒ/ *verb* **1** [I] **~ (on...)** (of people or vehicles) to move towards a place from different directions and meet: *Thousands of supporters converged on London for the rally.* **2** [I] (of two or more lines, paths, etc.) to move towards each other and meet at a point: *There was a signpost where the two paths converged.* **3** [I] if ideas, policies, aims, etc. **converge**, they become very similar or the same OPP **diverge** ▸ **con·ver·gent** /-dʒənt/ *adj.*: ***convergent lines/opinions*** **con·ver·gence** *noun* [U]

con·ver·sant /kən'vɜːsnt; *NAmE* -'vɜːrs-/ *adj.* **~ with sth** (*formal*) knowing about sth; familiar with sth: *You need to become fully conversant with the company's procedures.*

con·ver·sa·tion /,kɒnvə'seɪʃn; *NAmE* ,kɑːnvər's-/ *noun* [C, U] **~ (with sb) (about sth)** an informal talk involving a small group of people or only two; the activity of talking in this way: *a telephone conversation* ◇ *I had a long conversation with her the other day.* ◇ *The main* ***topic of conversation*** *was the likely outcome of the election.* ◇ *Don was* ***deep in conversation*** *with the girl on his right.* ◇ (*BrE*) *to* ***get into conversation*** *with sb* ◇ (*NAmE*) *to* ***get into a conversation*** *with sb* ◇ *The conversation turned to gardening.* ◇ *I tried to* ***make conversation*** (= to speak in order to appear polite). ➲ SYNONYMS at DISCUSSION

con·ver·sa·tion·al /,kɒnvə'seɪʃənl; *NAmE* ,kɑːnvər's-/ *adj.* **1** not formal; as used in conversation SYN **colloquial**: *a casual and conversational tone* ◇ *I learnt conversational Spanish at evening classes.* **2** [only before noun] connected with conversation: *Men have a more direct conversational style.* ▸ **con·ver·sa·tion·al·ly** *adv.*: *'Have you been here long?' he asked conversationally.*

con·ver·sa·tion·al·ist /,kɒnvə'seɪʃənəlɪst; *NAmE* ,kɑːnvər's-/ *noun* a person who is good at talking to others, especially in an informal way

conver'sation piece *noun* **1** an object that is talked about a lot because it is unusual **2** (*art*) a type of painting in which a group of people are shown in the countryside or in a home

conver'sation stopper *noun* (*informal*) an unexpected or shocking remark, which people do not know how to reply to

con·verse¹ /kən'vɜːs; *NAmE* -'vɜːrs/ *verb* [I] **~ (with sb)** (*formal*) to have a conversation with sb

con·verse² AW /'kɒnvɜːs; *NAmE* 'kɑːnvɜːrs/ *noun* **the converse** [sing.] (*formal*) the opposite or reverse of a fact or statement: *Building new roads increases traffic and the converse is equally true: reducing the number and size of roads means less traffic.* ▸ **con·verse** *adj.*: *the converse effect*

con·verse·ly AW /'kɒnvɜːsli; *NAmE* 'kɑːnvɜːrs-/ *adv.* (*formal*) in a way that is the opposite or reverse of sth: *You can add the fluid to the powder, or, conversely, the powder to the fluid.*

con·ver·sion AW /kən'vɜːʃn; *NAmE* -'vɜːrʒn; -ʃn/ *noun* **1** [U, C] **~ (from sth) (into/to sth)** the act or process of changing sth from one form, use or system to another: *the conversion of farm buildings into family homes* ◇ *No conversion from analogue to digital data is needed.* ◇ *a metric conversion table* (= showing how to change METRIC amounts into or out of another system) ◇ *a firm which specializes in house conversions* (= turning large houses into several smaller flats/apartments) **2** [U, C] **~ (from sth) (to sth)** the process or experience of changing your religion or beliefs: *the conversion of the Anglo-Saxons by Christian missionaries* ◇ *his conversion from Judaism to Christianity* **3** [C] (in RUGBY and AMERICAN FOOTBALL) a way of scoring extra points after scoring a TRY or a TOUCHDOWN **4** [C] **barn/loft ~** a building or room that has been changed so that it can be used for a different purpose, especially for living in

con'version van (also '**van conversion**) *noun* (*US*) a vehicle in which the back part behind the driver has been arranged as a living space

con·vert AW *verb, noun*

■ ***verb*** /kən'vɜːt; *NAmE* -'vɜːrt/ **1** [T, I] to change or make sth change from one form, purpose, system, etc. to another: **~ sth (into sth)** *The hotel is going to be converted into a nursing home.* ◇ *What rate will I get if I convert my dollars into euros?* ◇ **~ (from sth) (into/to sth)** *We've converted from oil to gas central heating.* **2** [I] **~ into/to sth** to be able to be changed from one form, purpose, or system to another: *a sofa that converts into a bed* **3** [I, T] to change or make sb change their religion or beliefs: **~ (from sth) (to sth)** *He converted from Christianity to Islam.* ◇ **~ sb (from sth) (to sth)** *She was soon converted to the socialist cause.* **4** [I, T] to change an opinion, a habit, etc: **~ (from sth) to sth** *I've converted to organic food.* ◇ **~ sb (from sth) (to sth)** *I didn't use to like opera but my husband has converted me.* **5** [T] **~ sth** (in RUGBY and AMERICAN FOOTBALL) to score extra points after a TRY or a TOUCHDOWN IDM see PREACH

■ ***noun*** /'kɒnvɜːt; *NAmE* 'kɑːnvɜːrt/ **~ (from sth) (to sth)** a person who has changed their religion, beliefs or opinions: *a convert to Islam* ◇ *converts from other faiths* ◇ *a* ***convert to the cause***

con·vert·er (also **con·ver·tor**) /kən'vɜːtə(r); *NAmE* -'vɜːrt-/ *noun* **1** a person or thing that converts sth: *a catalytic converter* **2** (*physics*) a device for converting ALTERNATING CURRENT into DIRECT CURRENT or the other way around **3** (*physics*) a device for converting a radio signal from one FREQUENCY to another

con·vert·ible AW /kən'vɜːtəbl; *NAmE* -'vɜːrt-/ *adj., noun*

■ ***adj.*** that can be changed to a different form or use: *a convertible sofa* (= one that can be used as a bed) ◇ *convertible currencies* (= ones that can be exchanged for those of other countries) ◇ **~ into/to sth** *The bonds are convertible into ordinary shares.* ▸ **con·vert·ibil·ity** /kən,vɜːtə'bɪləti; *NAmE* -,vɜːrt-/ *noun* [U]

■ ***noun*** a car with a roof that can be folded down or taken off ➲ VISUAL VOCAB page V42

con·vex /'kɒnveks; *NAmE* 'kɑːn-/ *adj.* (of an outline or a surface) curving out: *a* ***convex lens/mirror*** OPP **concave** ▸ **con·vex·ity** /kɒn'veksəti; *NAmE* kɑːn'v-/ *noun* [U]

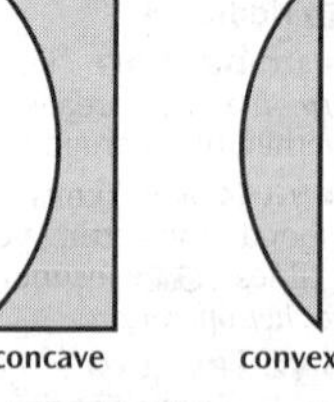

C

con·vey /kən'veɪ/ *verb* **1** to make ideas, feelings, etc. known to sb SYN **communicate**: **~ sth** *Colours like red convey a sense of energy and strength.* ◇ **~ sth to sb** (*formal*) *Please convey my apologies to your wife.* ◇ **~ how, what, etc ...** *He tried desperately to convey how urgent the situation was.* ◇ **~ that...** *She did not wish to convey that they were all at fault.* **2 ~ sb/sth** (**from...**) (**to...**) (*formal*) to take, carry or transport sb/sth from one place to another: *Pipes convey hot water from the boiler to the radiators.*

con·vey·ance /kən'veɪəns/ *noun* **1** [U] (*formal*) the process of taking sb/sth from one place to another: *the conveyance of goods by rail* **2** [C] (*formal*) a vehicle: *horse-drawn conveyances* **3** [C] (*law*) a legal document that moves property from one owner to another

con·vey·an·cer /kən'veɪənsə(r)/ *noun* a lawyer who is an expert in conveyancing

con·vey·an·cing /kən'veɪənsɪŋ/ *noun* [U] (*law*) the branch of law concerned with moving property from one owner to another

con·vey·or /kən'veɪə(r)/ *noun* **1** = CONVEYOR BELT **2** (also **con·vey·er**) (*formal*) a person or thing that carries sth or makes sth known

con'veyor belt (also **con·vey·or**) *noun* a continuous moving band used for transporting goods from one part of a building to another, for example products in a factory or suitcases in an airport

con·vict *verb, noun*

■ ***verb*** /kən'vɪkt/ [often passive] **~ sb** (**of sth**) to decide and state officially in court that sb is guilty of a crime: *a convicted murderer* ◇ *He was convicted of fraud.* ➲ COLLOCATIONS at JUSTICE OPP **acquit**

■ ***noun*** /'kɒnvɪkt; *NAmE* 'kɑːn-/ (also *informal* **con**) a person who has been found guilty of a crime and sent to prison: *an escaped convict*

con·vic·tion /kən'vɪkʃn/ *noun* **1** [C, U] **~** (**for sth**) the act of finding sb guilty of a crime in court; the fact of having been found guilty: *She has six previous convictions for theft.* ◇ *He plans to appeal against his conviction.* ◇ *an offence which carries, on conviction, a sentence of not more than five years' imprisonment* OPP **acquittal** ➲ COLLOCATIONS at JUSTICE **2** [C, U] **~** (**that...**) a strong opinion or belief: *strong* ***political/moral convictions*** ◇ *She was motivated by deep religious conviction.* ◇ *a conviction that all would be well in the end* **3** [U] the feeling or appearance of believing sth strongly and of being sure about it: *'Not true!' she said with conviction.* ◇ *He said he agreed but his voice lacked conviction.* ◇ *The leader's speech in defence of the policy didn't* ***carry much conviction.*** IDM see COURAGE

con·vince 0-π AW /kən'vɪns/ *verb* **1** 0-π to make sb/yourself believe that sth is true: **~ sb/yourself** (**of sth**) *You'll need to convince them of your enthusiasm for the job.* ◇ **~ sb/yourself** (**that**)**...** *I'd convinced myself (that) I was right.* **2** 0-π **~ sb to do sth** to persuade sb to do sth: *I've been trying to convince him to see a doctor.* ➲ note at PERSUADE

con·vinced AW /kən'vɪnst/ *adj.* **1** [not before noun] completely sure about sth: *Sam nodded but he didn't look convinced.* ◇ **~ of sth** *I am convinced of her innocence.* ◇ **~ that...** *I am convinced that she is innocent.* OPP **unconvinced** ➲ SYNONYMS at SURE **2** [only before noun] believing strongly in a particular religion or set of political ideas: *a convinced Christian*

con·vin·cing AW /kən'vɪnsɪŋ/ *adj.* that makes sb believe that sth is true: *a* ***convincing argument/explanation/case*** ◇ *She sounded very convincing to me* (= I believed what she said). ◇ *a* ***convincing victory/win*** (= an easy one) OPP **unconvincing** ▸ **con·vin·cing·ly** AW *adv.*: *Her case was convincingly argued.* ◇ *They won convincingly.*

con·viv·ial /kən'vɪviəl/ *adj.* cheerful and friendly in atmosphere or character SYN **sociable**: *a convivial evening/atmosphere* ◇ *convivial company* ▸ **con·vivi·al·ity** /kənˌvɪvi'æləti/ *noun* [U]

con·vo·ca·tion /ˌkɒnvə'keɪʃn; *NAmE* ˌkɑːn-/ *noun* (*formal*) **1** [C] a large formal meeting, especially of Church officials or members of a university **2** [U] the act of calling together a convocation **3** [C] (*NAmE*) a ceremony held in a university or college when students receive their degrees

con·voke /kən'vəʊk; *NAmE* -'voʊk/ *verb* **~ sb/sth** (*formal*) to gather together a group of people for a formal meeting SYN **convene**

con·vo·luted /'kɒnvəluːtɪd; *NAmE* 'kɑːn-/ *adj.* **1** extremely complicated and difficult to follow: *a* ***convoluted argument/explanation*** ◇ *a book with a convoluted plot* **2** (*formal*) having many twists or curves: *a convoluted coastline*

con·vo·lu·tion /ˌkɒnvə'luːʃn; *NAmE* ˌkɑːn-/ *noun* [usually pl.] (*formal*) **1** a thing that is very complicated and difficult to follow: *the bizarre convolutions of the story* **2** a twist or curve, especially one of many: *the convolutions of the brain*

con·vol·vu·lus /kən'vɒlvjələs; *NAmE* -'vɑːlv-/ *noun* [C, U] a wild plant with TRIANGULAR leaves and flowers that are shaped like TRUMPETS. It climbs up walls, fences, etc. and twists itself around other plants.

con·voy /'kɒnvɔɪ; *NAmE* 'kɑːn-/ *noun* a group of vehicles or ships travelling together, especially when soldiers or other vehicles travel with them for protection: *a* ***convoy of trucks/lorries/freighters*** ◇ *A United Nations* ***aid convoy*** *loaded with food and medicine finally got through to the besieged town.*

IDM **in 'convoy** (of travelling vehicles) as a group; together: *We drove in convoy because I didn't know the route.*

con·vulse /kən'vʌls/ *verb* **1** [T, I] **~** (**sb**) (**with sth**) (rather *formal*) to cause a sudden shaking movement in sb's body; to make this movement: *A violent shiver convulsed him.* ◇ *His whole body convulsed.* **2** [T] **be convulsed with laughter, anger, etc.** to be laughing so much, so angry, etc. that you cannot control your movements

con·vul·sion /kən'vʌlʃn/ *noun* [usually pl.] (rather *formal*) **1** a sudden shaking movement of the body that cannot be controlled: *The child went into convulsions.* SYN **fit** **2** a sudden important change that happens to a country or an organization SYN **upheaval**

con·vul·sive /kən'vʌlsɪv/ *adj.* (of movements or actions) sudden and impossible to control: *a* ***convulsive movement/attack/fit*** ◇ *Her breath came in convulsive gasps.* ▸ **con·vul·sive·ly** *adv.*: *weeping convulsively*

coo /kuː/ *verb, exclamation*

■ ***verb*** (**coo·ing, cooed, cooed**) **1** [I] when a DOVE or a PIGEON **coos**, it makes a soft low sound **2** [I, T] (**+ speech**) to say sth in a soft quiet voice, especially to sb you love IDM see BILL *v.* ▸ **coo** *noun*

■ ***exclamation*** (*BrE, informal*) used to show that you are surprised: *Coo, look at him!*

ˌco-oc'cur *verb* [I] to occur together or at the same time: *The words 'heavy' and 'rain' co-occur frequently.* ▸ **co-oc'currence** *noun* [U]

cooee /'kuːiː/ *exclamation* (*old-fashioned, BrE, informal*) used as a way of attracting sb's attention

IDM **within 'cooee** (**of**) (*AustralE, NZE*) not far (from): *There's loads of cheap accommodation within cooee of the airport.*

cook 0-π /kʊk/ *verb, noun*

■ ***verb*** **1** 0-π [I, T] to prepare food by heating it, for example by boiling, baking or frying it: *Where did you learn to cook?* ◇ **~ sth** *What's the best way to cook trout?* ◇ *Who's going to cook supper?* ◇ *He cooked lunch for me.* ◇ **~ sb sth** *He cooked me lunch.* ➲ COLLOCATIONS at COOKING ➲ VISUAL VOCAB pages V24, V25 **2** 0-π [I] (of food) to be prepared by boiling, baking, frying, etc: *While the pasta is cooking, prepare the sauce.* **3** [I] **be cooking** (*informal*) to be planned secretly: *Everyone is being very secretive—there's something cooking.*

IDM **be cooking with 'gas** (*NAmE, informal*) to be doing sth very well and successfully **ˌcook the 'books** (*informal*) to change facts or figures dishonestly or illegally: *His accountant had been cooking the books for years.* **cook sb's 'goose** (*informal*) to ruin sb's chances of success

PHR V ˌ**cook sth↔ˈup** (*informal*) to invent sth, especially in order to trick sb **SYN** **concoct**: *to cook up a story*

■ ***noun*** a person who cooks food or whose job is cooking: *John is a very good cook* (= he cooks well). ◇ *Who was the cook* (= who cooked the food)? ◇ *She was employed as a cook in a hotel.* ➲ compare CHEF

IDM **too many cooks spoil the ˈbroth** (*saying*) if too many people are involved in doing sth, it will not be done well

cook·book /ˈkʊkbʊk/ (*BrE* also ˈ**cookery book**) *noun* a book that gives instructions on cooking and how to cook individual dishes

ˈ**cook-chill** *adj.* [only before noun] (*BrE*) food prepared by the **cook-chill** method is cooked, kept at a low temperature and then heated again

cook·er /ˈkʊkə(r)/ (*BrE*) (*NAmE* **range**) (also **stove** *NAmE, BrE*) *noun* a large piece of equipment for cooking food, containing an oven and gas or electric rings on top: *a gas cooker* ◇ *an electric cooker* ➲ see also PRESSURE COOKER

cook·ery /ˈkʊkəri/ *noun* [U] (*especially BrE*) the art or activity of preparing and cooking food: *a cookery course* ◇ *Italian cookery*

ˈ**cookery book** *noun* (*BrE*) = COOKBOOK

cook·house /ˈkʊkhaʊs/ *noun* an outdoor kitchen, for example in a military camp

cookie /ˈkʊki/ *noun* (*pl.* -ies)
1 (*especially NAmE*) a small flat sweet cake for one person, usually baked until crisp: *chocolate chip cookies* ◇ *a cookie jar* ➲ compare BISCUIT, CRACKER ➲ see also FORTUNE COOKIE **2** **smart/tough ~** (*NAmE, informal*) a smart/tough person **3** (*computing*) a computer file with information in it that is sent to the central SERVER each time a particular person uses a NETWORK or the Internet ➲ COLLOCATIONS at EMAIL **IDM** see WAY *n.*

ˈ**cookie cutter** *noun, adj.*
■ ***noun*** (*NAmE*) an object used for cutting biscuits in a particular shape
■ ***adj.*** ˈ**cookie-cutter** [only before noun] (*NAmE, disapproving*) having no special characteristics; not original in any way: *Handmade goods appeal to those who are tired of cookie-cutter products.*

ˈ**cookie jar** *noun* (*NAmE*) a container for biscuits
IDM **get caught/found with your hand in the** ˈ**cookie jar** (*informal*) to be discovered when doing sth that is illegal or dishonest

ˈ**cookie sheet** (*NAmE*) (*BrE* ˈ**baking sheet**, ˈ**baking tray**) *noun* a small sheet of metal used for baking food on

cook·ing /ˈkʊkɪŋ/ *noun, adj.*
■ ***noun*** [U] **1** the process of preparing food: *My husband does all the cooking.* ◇ *a book on Indian cooking* ➲ VISUAL VOCAB pages V24, V25 **2** food that has been prepared in a particular way: *The restaurant offers traditional home cooking* (= food similar to that cooked at home). ◇ *They serve good French cooking.*
■ ***adj.*** suitable for cooking rather than eating raw or drinking: *cooking sherry*

ˈ**cooking apple** *noun* (*BrE*) any type of apple that is suitable for cooking, rather than eating raw ➲ compare EATING APPLE

ˈ**cooking gas** (*US*) (*BrE* **Calor gas™**) *noun* [U] a type of gas stored as a liquid under pressure in metal containers and used for heating and cooking in places where there is no gas supply

cook·out /ˈkʊkaʊt/ *noun* (*NAmE, informal*) a meal or party when food is cooked over an open fire outdoors, for example at a beach ➲ compare BARBECUE

cook·shop /ˈkʊkʃɒp; *NAmE* -ʃɑːp/ *noun* (*BrE*) a shop/store where equipment for cooking with is sold

cook·ware /ˈkʊkweə(r); *NAmE* -wer/ *noun* [U] pots and containers used in cooking

Collocations

Cooking

Preparing

- **prepare** a dish/a meal/a menu/dinner/the fish
- **weigh out** 100g/4oz of sugar/the ingredients
- **wash/rinse** the lettuce/spinach/watercress
- **chop/slice/dice** the carrots/onions/potatoes
- **peel** the carrots/onion/potatoes/garlic/orange
- **grate** a carrot/the cheese/some nutmeg
- **remove/discard** the bones/seeds/skin
- **blend/combine/mix (together)** the flour and water/all the ingredients
- **beat/whisk** the cream/eggs/egg whites
- **knead/shape/roll (out)** the dough

Cooking

- **heat** the oil in a frying pan
- **preheat/heat** the oven/(*BrE*) the grill/(*NAmE*) the broiler
- **bring to** (*BrE*) the boil/(*NAmE*) a boil
- **stir** constantly/gently with a wooden spoon
- **reduce** the heat
- **simmer** gently for 20 minutes/until reduced by half
- **melt** the butter/chocolate/cheese/sugar
- **brown** the meat for 8-20 minutes
- **drain** the pasta/the water from the pot/in a colander
- **mash** the potatoes/banana/avocado

Ways of cooking

- **cook** food/fish/meat/rice/pasta/a Persian dish
- **bake** (a loaf of) bread/a cake/(*especially NAmE*) cookies/(*BrE*) biscuits/a pie/potatoes/fish/scones/muffins
- **boil** cabbage/potatoes/an egg/water
- **fry/deep-fry/stir-fry** the chicken/vegetables
- **grill** meat/steak/chicken/sausages/a hot dog
- **roast** potatoes/peppers/meat/chicken/lamb
- **sauté** garlic/mushrooms/onions/potatoes/vegetables
- **steam** rice/vegetables/spinach/asparagus/dumplings
- **toast** bread/nuts
- **microwave** food/popcorn/(*BrE*) a ready meal

Serving

- **serve** in a glass/on a bed of rice/with potatoes
- **arrange** the slices on a plate/in a layer
- **carve** the meat/lamb/chicken/turkey
- **dress/toss** a salad
- **dress with/drizzle with** olive oil/vinaigrette
- **top with** a slice of lemon/a scoop of ice cream/whipped cream/syrup
- **garnish with** a sprig of parsley/fresh basil leaves/lemon wedges/a slice of lime/a twist of orange
- **sprinkle with** salt/sugar/herbs/parsley/freshly ground black pepper

cool /kuːl/ *adj., verb, noun*
■ ***adj.*** (cool·er, cool·est)
▸ FAIRLY COLD **1** fairly cold; not hot or warm: *a cool breeze/drink/climate* ◇ *Cooler weather is forecast for the weekend.* ◇ *Let's sit in the shade and keep cool.* ◇ *Store lemons in a cool dry place.* ➲ SYNONYMS at COLD
▸ COLOURS **2** making you feel pleasantly cool: *a room painted in cool greens and blues*
▸ CALM **3** calm; not excited, angry or emotional: *Keep cool!* ◇ *She tried to remain* ***cool, calm and collected*** (= calm). ◇ *He has a* ***cool head*** (= he stays calm in an emergency).
▸ NOT FRIENDLY/ENTHUSIASTIC **4** not friendly, interested or enthusiastic: *She was decidedly cool about the proposal.* ◇ *They gave the Prime Minister* ***a cool reception***.
▸ APPROVING **5** (*informal*) used to show that you admire or approve of sth because it is fashionable, attractive and

often different: *You look pretty cool with that new haircut.* ◇ *It's a cool movie.* ➲ SYNONYMS at GREAT **6** (*informal*) people say **Cool!** or **That's cool** to show that they approve of sth or agree to a suggestion: *'We're meeting Jake for lunch and we can go on the yacht in the afternoon.' 'Cool!'* ◇ *'Can you come at 10.30 tomorrow?' 'That's cool'.* ◇ *I was surprised that she got the job, but* ***I'm cool with it*** (= it's not a problem for me).
▸ CONFIDENT **7** (*informal*) calm and confident in a way that lacks respect for other people, but makes people admire you as well as disapprove: *She just took his keys and walked out with them, cool as you please.*
▸ MONEY **8** [only before noun] (*informal*) used about a sum of money to emphasize how large it is: *The car cost a cool thirty thousand.* ➲ see also COOLLY, COOLNESS
IDM **(as) ˌcool as a ˈcucumber** very calm and controlled, especially in a difficult situation **play it ˈcool** (*informal*) to deal with a situation in a calm way and not show what you are really feeling ➲ more at LONG *adj.*
■ ***verb***
▸ BECOME COLDER **1** [I, T] to become or to make sb/sth become cool or cooler: *Glass contracts as it cools.* ◇ **~ sth** *The cylinder is cooled by a jet of water.*
▸ BECOME CALMER **2** [I] to become calmer, less excited or less enthusiastic: *I think we should wait until tempers have cooled.* ◇ *Relations between them have definitely cooled* (= they are not as friendly with each other as they were).
IDM **ˈcool it!** (*informal*) used to tell sb to be calmer and less excited or angry **ˌcool your ˈheels** (*informal*) to have to wait for sb/sth
PHR V **ˌcool ˈdown/ˈoff 1** to become cool or cooler: *We cooled off with a swim in the lake.* **2** to become calm, less excited or less enthusiastic: *I think you should wait until she's cooled down a little.* **ˌcool sb↔ˈdown/ˈoff 1** to make sb feel cooler: *Drink plenty of cold water to cool yourself down.* **2** to make sb calm, less excited or less enthusiastic: *A few hours in a police cell should cool him off.* **ˌcool sth↔ˈdown/ˈoff** to make sth cool or cooler **ˌcool ˈout** (*informal*) to relax and become calm after a period of activity or stress: *It's a wonderful place to cool out with a glass of beer.* ◇ *It sounds like he needs some time to cool out.*
■ ***noun*** **the cool** [sing.] cool air or a cool place: *the cool of the evening*
IDM **keep your cool** (*informal*) to remain calm in a difficult situation **lose your cool** (*informal*) to become angry or excited

coola·bah *noun* = COOLIBAH

cool·ant /ˈkuːlənt/ *noun* [C, U] a liquid that is used for cooling an engine, a nuclear REACTOR, etc.

ˈcool bag, **ˈcool box** *noun* (*BrE*) a bag or box which keeps food or drinks cold and which can be used for a PICNIC ➲ see also COOLER

cool·drink /ˈkuːldrɪŋk/ *noun* (*SAfrE*) = SOFT DRINK

cool·er /ˈkuːlə(r)/ *noun* **1** [C] a container or machine which cools things, especially drinks, or keeps them cold: *the office water cooler* ◇ (*especially NAmE*) *They took a cooler full of drinks to the beach.* ➲ VISUAL VOCAB page V56 **2** [C] (*NAmE*) a drink with ice and usually wine in it: *a wine cooler*

ˌcool-ˈheaded *adj.* calm; not showing excitement or nerves: *a cool-headed assessment of the situation*

coo·li·bah /ˈkuːlɪbɑː/ (also **coola·bah**) *noun* an Australian tree that produces a strong hard wood

coolie /ˈkuːli/ *noun* (*old-fashioned, taboo*) an offensive word for a worker in Eastern countries with no special skills or training

ˌcooling-ˈoff period *noun* **1** a period of time during which two sides in a disagreement try to reach an agreement before taking further action, for example by going on strike **2** a period of time after sb has agreed to buy sth, such as an insurance plan, during which they can change their mind

ˈcooling tower *noun* a large high round building used in industry for cooling water before it is used again

cool·ly /ˈkuːlli/ *adv.* **1** in a way that is not friendly or enthusiastic: *'We're just good friends,' she said coolly.* ◇ *He received my suggestion coolly.* **2** in a calm way

cool·ness /ˈkuːlnəs/ *noun* [U] the quality of being cool: *the delicious coolness of the water* ◇ *I admire her coolness under pressure.* ◇ *I noticed a certain coolness* (= lack of friendly feeling) *between them.*

coon /kuːn/ *noun* (*taboo, slang*) a very offensive word for a black person

coop /kuːp/ *noun, verb*
■ ***noun*** a CAGE for chickens, etc. IDM see FLY *v.*
■ ***verb***
PHR V **ˌcoop sb/sth ˈup** [usually passive] to keep a person or an animal inside a building or in a small space

ˈco-op *noun* (*informal*) a COOPERATIVE shop/store, society or business: *a housing co-op*

coop·er /ˈkuːpə(r)/ *noun* a person who makes BARRELS

co·oper·ate AW (*BrE* also **co-operate**) /kəʊˈɒpəreɪt; *NAmE* koʊˈɑːp-/ *verb* **1** [I] **~ (with sb) (in/on sth)** to work together with sb else in order to achieve sth: *The two groups agreed to cooperate with each other.* ◇ *They had co-operated closely in the planning of the project.* **2** [I] **~ (with sb) (in/on sth)** to be helpful by doing what sb asks you to do: *Their captors told them they would be killed unless they cooperated.*

co·oper·ation AW (*BrE* also **co-operation**) /kəʊˌɒpəˈreɪʃn; *NAmE* koʊˌɑːp-/ *noun* [U] **1** the fact of doing sth together or of working together towards a shared aim: **~ (with sb) (in doing sth)** *a report produced by the government in cooperation with the chemical industry* ◇ **~ (between A and B)** *We would like to see closer cooperation between parents and schools.* **2 ~ (in doing sth)** willingness to be helpful and do as you are asked: *We would be grateful for your cooperation in clearing the hall as quickly as possible.*

co·opera·tive AW (*BrE* also **co-operative**) /kəʊˈɒpərətɪv; *NAmE* koʊˈɑːp-/ *adj., noun*
■ ***adj.*** **1** [usually before noun] involving doing sth together or working together with others towards a shared aim: *Cooperative activity is essential to effective community work.* **2** helpful by doing what you are asked to do: *Employees will generally be more cooperative if their views are taken seriously.* OPP **uncooperative 3** [usually before noun] (*business*) owned and run by the people involved, with the profits shared by them: *a cooperative farm* ▶ **co·opera·tive·ly** AW (*BrE* also **co-operatively**) *adv.*
■ ***noun*** a cooperative business or other organization: *agricultural cooperatives in India* ◇ *The factory is now a workers' cooperative.*

ˌco-ˈopt *verb* **1 ~ sb (onto/into sth)** to make sb a member of a group, committee, etc. by the agreement of all the other members: *She was co-opted onto the board.* **2 ~ sb (onto/into sth)** to include sb in sth, often when they do not want to be part of it

co·ord·in·ate AW (*BrE* also **co-ordinate**) *verb, noun*
■ ***verb*** /kəʊˈɔːdɪneɪt; *NAmE* koʊˈɔːrd-/ **1** [T] **~ sth** to organize the different parts of an activity and the people involved in it so that it works well: *They appointed a new manager to coordinate the work of the team.* ◇ *We need to develop a co-ordinated approach to the problem.* **2** [T] **~ sth** to make the different parts of your body work well together ➲ see also UNCOORDINATED **3** [I, T] **~ (sth) (with sth)** (rather *formal*) if you **coordinate** clothes, furniture, etc. or if they **coordinate**, they look nice together: *This shade coordinates with a wide range of other colours.* ▶ **co·ord·in·ator** (*BrE* also **co-ordinator**) *noun*: *The campaign needs an effective co-ordinator.*
■ ***noun*** /kəʊˈɔːdɪnət; *NAmE* koʊˈɔːrd-/ **1** [C] either of two numbers or letters used to fix the position of a point on a map or GRAPH: *the x, y coordinates of any point on a line* **2 coordinates** [pl.] (used in shops/stores etc.) pieces of clothing that can be worn together because, for example, the colours look good together

coordinate clause /kəʊˌɔːdmət ˈklɔːz; *NAmE* koʊˌɔːrd-/ *noun* (*grammar*) each of two or more parts of a sentence, often joined by *and*, *or*, *but*, etc, that make separate statements that each have an equal importance ➲ compare SUBORDINATE CLAUSE

C

coˌordinating conˈjunction *noun* (*grammar*) a word such as *or*, *and* or *but*, that connects clauses or sentences of equal importance ➲ compare SUBORDINATING CONJUNCTION

co·ord·in·ation AW (*BrE* also **co-ordination**) /kəʊˌɔːdɪˈneɪʃn; *NAmE* koʊˌɔːrd-/ *noun* [U] **1** the act of making parts of sth, groups of people, etc. work together in an efficient and organized way: *a need for greater coordination between departments* ◇ *a lack of coordination in conservation policy* ◇ *a pamphlet produced by the government* ***in coordination with*** (= working together with) *the Sports Council* ◇ *advice on colour coordination* (= choosing colours that look nice together, for example in clothes or furniture) **2** the ability to control your movements well: *You need good hand-eye coordination to play ball games.*

coot /kuːt/ *noun* **1** a black bird with a white FOREHEAD and beak that lives on or near water **2 old ~** (*NAmE*, *informal*) a stupid person IDM see BALD

cop /kɒp; *NAmE* kɑːp/ *noun*, *verb*

■ ***noun*** (*informal*) a police officer: *Somebody call the cops!* ◇ *children playing* ***cops and robbers*** ◇ *a TV cop show*

IDM **not much ˈcop** (*BrE*, *slang*) not very good: *He's not much cop as a singer.* ➲ more at FAIR *adj.*

■ ***verb*** (-pp-) (*informal*) **1 ~ sth** to receive or suffer sth unpleasant: *He copped all the hassle after the accident.* **2 ~ sth** to notice sth: ***Cop a load of this!*** (= Listen to this)

IDM **cop hold of sth** (*BrE*, *informal*) to take hold of sth **cop a ˈplea** (*NAmE*, *informal*) to admit in court to being guilty of a small crime in the hope of receiving less severe punishment for a more serious crime ➲ compare PLEA-BARGAINING **ˈcop it** (*BrE*, *slang*) **1** to be punished **2** to be killed

PHR V **ˌcop ˈoff (with sb)** (*BrE*, *slang*) to start a sexual or romantic experience with sb: *Who did he cop off with at the party?* **ˌcop ˈout (of sth)** (*informal*) to avoid or stop doing sth that you should do because you are afraid, lazy, etc: *You're not going to cop out at the last minute, are you?* ➲ related noun COP-OUT

cope 0-w /kəʊp; *NAmE* koʊp/ *verb*, *noun*

■ ***verb*** 0-w [I] to deal successfully with sth difficult SYN **manage**: *I got to the stage where I wasn't coping any more.* ◇ **~ with sth** *He wasn't able to cope with the stresses and strains of the job.* ◇ *Desert plants are adapted to cope with extreme heat.*

■ ***noun*** a long loose piece of clothing worn by priests on special occasions

copier /ˈkɒpiə(r); *NAmE* ˈkɑːp-/ *noun* (*especially NAmE*) = PHOTOCOPIER

ˈco-pilot *noun* a second pilot who helps the main pilot in an aircraft

cop·ing /ˈkəʊpɪŋ; *NAmE* ˈkoʊpɪŋ/ *noun* (*architecture*) the top row of bricks or stones, usually sloping, on a wall

co·pi·ous /ˈkəʊpiəs; *NAmE* ˈkoʊ-/ *adj.* in large amounts SYN **abundant**: *copious* (= large) *amounts of water* ◇ *I took copious notes.* ◇ *She supports her theory with copious evidence.* ▶ **co·pi·ous·ly** *adv.*: *bleeding copiously*

ˈcop-out *noun* (*informal*, *disapproving*) a way of avoiding doing sth that you should do, or an excuse for not doing it: *Not turning up was just a cop-out.*

cop·per /ˈkɒpə(r); *NAmE* ˈkɑːp-/ *noun* **1** [U] (*symb.* Cu) a chemical element. Copper is a soft reddish-brown metal used for making electric wires, pipes and coins: *a copper mine* ◇ *copper pipes* ◇ *copper-coloured hair* **2 coppers** [pl.] (*BrE*) brown coins that do not have much value: *I only paid a few coppers for it.* **3** [C] (*BrE*, *informal*) a police officer

ˌcopper ˈbeech *noun* a tall type of BEECH tree with smooth BARK and reddish-brown leaves

ˌcopper-ˈbottomed *adj.* (*BrE*) that you can trust or rely on completely: *a copper-bottomed guarantee*

cop·per·head /ˈkɒpəhed; *NAmE* ˈkɑːpər-/ *noun* one of several types of poisonous snake that are a brownish colour

cop·per·plate /ˈkɒpəpleɪt; *NAmE* ˈkɑːpər-/ *noun* [U] a neat old-fashioned way of writing with sloping letters joined together

cop·pery /ˈkɒpəri; *NAmE* ˈkɑːp-/ *adj.* similar to or having the colour of COPPER: *coppery hair*

cop·pice /ˈkɒpɪs; *NAmE* ˈkɑːp-/ *verb*, *noun*

■ ***verb*** [T, I] **~ (sth)** (*technical*) to cut back young trees in order to make them grow faster

■ ***noun*** = COPSE

copra /ˈkɒprə; *NAmE* ˈkɑːprə/ *noun* [U] the dried white flesh of COCONUTS

copse /kɒps; *NAmE* kɑːps/ (also **cop·pice**) *noun* a small area of trees or bushes growing together ➲ VISUAL VOCAB page V2

ˈcop shop *noun* (*informal*) a police station

cop·ter /ˈkɒptə(r); *NAmE* ˈkɑːp-/ *noun* (*informal*) = HELICOPTER

cop·ula /ˈkɒpjələ; *NAmE* ˈkɑːp-/ *noun* (*grammar*) = LINKING VERB

copu·late /ˈkɒpjuleɪt; *NAmE* ˈkɑːp-/ *verb* [I] **~ (with sb/sth)** (*technical*) to have sex ▶ **copu·la·tion** /ˌkɒpjuˈleɪʃn; *NAmE* ˌkɑːp-/ *noun* [U]

copy 0-w /ˈkɒpi; *NAmE* ˈkɑːpi/ *noun*, *verb*

■ ***noun*** (*pl.* -ies) **1** 0-w [C] **~ (of sth)** a thing that is made to be the same as sth else, especially a document or a work of art: *I will send you a copy of the report.* ◇ *The thieves replaced the original painting with a copy.* ◇ *You should* ***make a copy*** *of the disk as a backup.* ➲ see also HARD COPY **2** 0-w [C] a single example of a book, newspaper, etc. of which many have been made: *a copy of 'The Times'* ◇ *The book sold 20 000 copies within two weeks.* ➲ see also BACK COPY **3** [U] written material that is to be printed in a newspaper, magazine, etc; news or information that can be used in a newspaper article or advertisement: *The subeditors prepare the reporters' copy for the paper and write the headlines.* ◇ *This will make great copy for the advertisement.* **4** [C] = PHOTOCOPY: *Could I have ten copies of this page, please?* **5** [C] (*IndE*) a book used by students for writing exercises, etc. in

■ ***verb*** (**cop·ies**, **copy·ing**, **cop·ied**, **cop·ied**) **1** 0-w [T] **~ sth** to make sth that is exactly like sth else: *They copied the designs from those on Greek vases.* ◇ *Everything in the computer's memory can be copied onto DVDs.* **2** 0-w [T] to write sth exactly as it is written somewhere else: **~ sth (from sth) (into/onto sth)** *She copied the phone number into her address book.* ◇ **~ sth (down/out)** *I copied out several poems.* **3** 0-w [T] **~ sb/sth** to behave or do sth in the same way as sb else SYN **imitate**: *She copies everything her sister does.* ◇ *Their tactics have been copied by other terrorist organizations.* **4** 0-w [I] **~ (from/off sb)** to cheat in an exam, school work, etc. by writing what sb else has written and pretending it is your own work **5** [T] **~ sth** (*especially NAmE*) = PHOTOCOPY

PHR V **ˌcopy sb ˈin (on sth)** to send sb a copy of a letter, email message, etc. that you are sending to sb else: *Can you copy me in on your report?*

copy·book /ˈkɒpibʊk; *NAmE* ˈkɑːp-/ *noun*, *adj.*

■ ***noun*** a book, used in the past by children in school, containing examples of writing which school students had to copy IDM see BLOT *v.*

■ ***adj.*** [only before noun] (*BrE*) done exactly how it should be done: *It was a copybook operation by the police.*

copy·cat /ˈkɒpikæt; *NAmE* ˈkɑːp-/ *noun*, *adj.*

■ ***noun*** (*informal*, *disapproving*) used especially by children about and to a person who copies what sb else does because they have no ideas of their own

■ ***adj.*** [only before noun] (of crimes) similar to and seen as copying an earlier well-known crime

ˈcopy editor *noun* a person whose job is to correct and prepare a text for printing ▶ **ˈcopy-edit** *verb* [T, I]

copy·ist /ˈkɒpiɪst; *NAmE* ˈkɑːp-/ *noun* a person who makes copies of written documents or works of art

copy·right /ˈkɒpiraɪt; *NAmE* ˈkɑːp-/ *noun, adj., verb*
■ ***noun*** [U, C] **~ (in/on sth)** if a person or an organization holds the **copyright** on a piece of writing, music, etc, they are the only people who have the legal right to publish, broadcast, perform it, etc, and other people must ask their permission to use it or any part of it: *Who owns the copyright on this song?* ◇ *Copyright expires seventy years after the death of the author.* ◇ *They were sued for* ***breach/infringement*** *of copyright.*
■ ***adj.*** (*abbr.* ©) protected by copyright; not allowed to be copied without permission: *copyright material*
■ ***verb*** **~ sth** to get the copyright for sth

ˈ**copyright library** *noun* in the UK and Ireland, a library that must receive a copy of every book that is published in the country

ˈ**copy typist** *noun* (*BrE*) a person whose job is to type things that they copy from written documents

copy·writer /ˈkɒpiraɪtə(r); *NAmE* ˈkɑːp-/ *noun* a person whose job is to write the words for advertising material

coq au vin /ˌkɒk əʊ ˈvæ̃; *NAmE* ˌkoʊk oʊ; ˌkɑːk/ *noun* [U] (from *French*) a dish of chicken cooked in wine

co·quet·ry /ˈkɒkɪtri; *NAmE* ˈkoʊk-/ *noun* [U] (*literary*) behaviour that is typical of a coquette

co·quette /kɒˈket; *NAmE* koʊˈket/ *noun* (*literary, often disapproving*) a woman who behaves in a way that is intended to attract men SYN **flirt** ▸ **co·quet·tish** /kɒˈketɪʃ; *NAmE* koʊˈk-/ *adj.*: *a coquettish smile* **co·quet·tish·ly** *adv.*

cor /kɔː(r)/ (also ˌ**cor ˈbli·mey**) *exclamation* (*BrE, informal*) used when you are surprised, pleased or impressed by sth: *Cor! Look at that!*

cor·acle /ˈkɒrəkl; *NAmE* ˈkɔːr-; ˈkɑːr-/ *noun* a small round boat with a wooden frame, used in Wales and Ireland

coral /ˈkɒrəl; *NAmE* ˈkɔːrəl; ˈkɑːrəl/ *noun, adj.*
■ ***noun*** **1** [U] a hard substance that is red, pink or white in colour, and that forms on the bottom of the sea from the bones of very small creatures. Coral is often used in jewellery: ***coral reefs/islands*** ◇ *a coral necklace* **2** [C] a creature that produces coral
■ ***adj.*** pink or red in colour, like coral: *coral lipstick*

cor ang·lais /ˌkɔːr ˈɒŋgleɪ; *NAmE* ɔːŋˈgleɪ/ *noun* (*pl.* **cors anglais** /ˌkɔːr ˈɒŋgleɪ; *NAmE* ɔːŋˈgleɪ/) (*especially BrE*) (also ˌ**English ˈhorn** especially in *NAmE*) a musical instrument of the WOODWIND group, like an OBOE but larger and playing lower notes

cor·bel /ˈkɔːbl; *NAmE* ˈkɔːrbl/ *noun* (*architecture*) a piece of stone or wood that sticks out from a wall to support sth, for example an ARCH

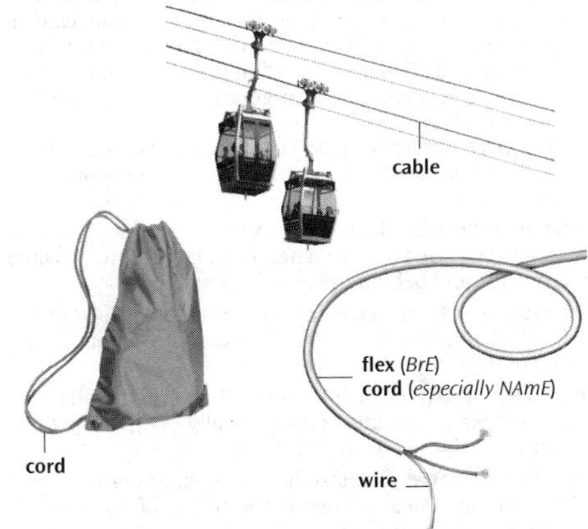

cord /kɔːd; *NAmE* kɔːrd/ *noun* **1** [U, C] strong thick string or thin rope; a piece of this: *a* ***piece/length of cord*** ◇ *picture cord* (= used for hanging pictures) ◇ *a silk bag tied with a gold cord* **2** (*especially NAmE*) (*BrE* also **flex**) [C, U] a piece of wire that is covered with plastic, used for carrying electricity to a piece of equipment: *an electrical cord* ◇ *telephone cord* ➲ see also CORDLESS **3** [U] = CORDUROY: *a cord jacket* **4 cords** (also *old-fashioned* **corduroys**) [pl.] trousers/pants made of CORDUROY: *a pair of cords* ➲ see also SPINAL CORD, UMBILICAL CORD, VOCAL CORDS

cord·ed /ˈkɔːdɪd; *NAmE* ˈkɔːrd-/ *adj.* **1** (of cloth) having raised lines SYN **ribbed** **2** (of a muscle) TENSE and standing out so that it looks like a piece of cord **3** that has a cord attached: *a corded phone* OPP **cordless**

cor·dial /ˈkɔːdiəl; *NAmE* ˈkɔːrdʒəl/ *adj., noun*
■ ***adj.*** (*formal*) pleasant and friendly: *a* ***cordial atmosphere/meeting/relationship*** ▸ **cor·di·al·ity** /ˌkɔːdiˈæləti; *NAmE* ˌkɔːrdʒi-/ *noun* [U]: *I was greeted with a show of cordiality.*
■ ***noun*** **1** (*BrE*) [U, C] a sweet drink that does not contain alcohol, made from fruit juice. It is drunk with water added: *blackcurrant cordial* **2** [U, C] (*NAmE*) = LIQUEUR **3** [C] a glass of cordial

cor·di·al·ly /ˈkɔːdiəli; *NAmE* ˈkɔːrdʒəli/ *adv.* (*formal*) **1** in a pleasant and friendly manner: *You are cordially invited to a celebration for Mr Michael Brown on his retirement.* **2** (used with verbs showing dislike) very much: *They cordially detest each other.*

cord·ite /ˈkɔːdaɪt; *NAmE* ˈkɔːrd-/ *noun* [U] an EXPLOSIVE used in bullets, bombs, etc.

cord·less /ˈkɔːdləs; *NAmE* ˈkɔːrd-/ *adj.* (of a telephone or an electrical tool) not connected to its power supply by wires: *a* ***cordless phone/drill*** OPP **corded**

cor·don /ˈkɔːdn; *NAmE* ˈkɔːrdn/ *noun, verb*
■ ***noun*** a line or ring of police officers, soldiers, etc. guarding sth or stopping people from entering or leaving a place: *Demonstrators broke through the police cordon.*
■ ***verb***
PHR V ˌ**cordon sth**↔ˈ**off** to stop people from getting into an area by surrounding it with police, soldiers, etc: *Police cordoned off the area until the bomb was made safe.*

cor·don bleu /ˌkɔːdɒ̃ ˈblɜː; *NAmE* ˌkɔːrdɔ̃ː/ *adj.* [usually before noun] (from *French*) of the highest standard of skill in cooking: *a cordon bleu chef* ◇ *cordon bleu cuisine*

cor·du·roy /ˈkɔːdərɔɪ; *NAmE* ˈkɔːrd-/ *noun* **1** (also **cord**) [U] a type of strong soft cotton cloth with a pattern of raised parallel lines on it, used for making clothes: *a corduroy jacket* **2 cor·du·roys** [pl.] (*old-fashioned*) = CORDS

core 🔑 AW /kɔː(r)/ *noun, adj., verb*
■ ***noun*** **1** 🔑 the hard central part of a fruit such as an apple, that contains the seeds ➲ VISUAL VOCAB page V26 **2** 🔑 the central part of an object: *the earth's core* ◇ *the core of a nuclear reactor* **3** 🔑 the most important or central part of sth: *the core of the argument* ◇ *Concern for the environment is* ***at the core*** *of our policies.* **4** a small group of people who take part in a particular activity: *He gathered a small core of advisers around him.* ➲ see also HARD CORE
IDM **to the ˈcore** so that the whole of a thing or a person is affected: *She was shaken to the core by the news.* ◇ *He's a politician to the core* (= in all his attitudes and actions).
■ ***adj.*** **1** most important; main or essential: *core subjects* (= subjects that all the students have to study) *such as English and mathematics* ◇ *the core curriculum* ◇ *We need to concentrate on our* ***core business.*** ◇ *The use of new technology is core to our strategy.* **2 ~ beliefs, values, principles, etc.** the most important or central beliefs, etc. of a person or group: *The party is losing touch with its core values.* **3** used to describe the most important members of a group: *The team is built around a core group of players.*
■ ***verb*** **~ sth** to take out the core of a fruit

co·referen·tial /ˌkəʊrefəˈrenʃl; *NAmE* ˌkoʊ-/ *adj.* (*linguistics*) if two words or expressions are **coreferential**, they refer to the same thing. For example, in the sentence 'I had a camera but I lost it', 'a camera' and 'it' are coreferential.

ˌ**co-reˈspond·ent** *noun* (*law*) a person who is said to have committed ADULTERY with the husband or wife of sb who is trying to get divorced

corgi /ˈkɔːgi; *NAmE* ˈkɔːrgi/ *noun* a small dog with short legs and a pointed nose

C

cori·an·der /ˌkɒriˈændə(r); *NAmE* ˌkɔːr-/ *noun* [U] a plant whose leaves are used in cooking as a HERB and whose seeds are used in cooking as a spice ➲ compare CILANTRO ➲ VISUAL VOCAB page V28

Cor·inth·ian /kəˈrɪnθiən/ *adj.* [usually before noun] (*architecture*) used to describe a style of ARCHITECTURE in ancient Greece that has thin columns with decorations of leaves at the top: ***Corinthian columns/capitals***

cork /kɔːk; *NAmE* kɔːrk/ *noun, verb*
■ ***noun* 1** [U] a light, soft material that is the thick BARK of a type of Mediterranean OAK tree: *a cork mat* ◇ *cork tiles* **2** [C] a small round object made of cork or plastic, that is used for closing bottles, especially wine bottles. ➲ VISUAL VOCAB page V29 ➲ SYNONYMS at LID
■ ***verb* ~ sth** to close a bottle with a cork OPP **uncork**

cork·age /ˈkɔːkɪdʒ; *NAmE* ˈkɔːrk-/ *noun* [U] the money that a restaurant charges if you want to drink wine there that you have bought somewhere else

corked /kɔːkt; *NAmE* kɔːrkt/ *adj.* (of wine) with a bad taste because the cork has decayed

cork·er /ˈkɔːkə(r); *NAmE* ˈkɔːrk-/ *noun* [usually sing.] (*old-fashioned, BrE, informal*) a person or thing that is extremely good, beautiful or amusing

cork·screw /ˈkɔːkskruː; *NAmE* ˈkɔːrk-/ *noun, verb*
■ ***noun*** a tool for pulling CORKS from bottles. Most corkscrews have a handle and a long twisted piece of metal for pushing into the cork. ➲ VISUAL VOCAB page V23
■ ***verb*** [I] (+ **adv./prep**) to move in a particular direction while turning in circles

corm /kɔːm; *NAmE* kɔːrm/ *noun* the small round underground part of some plants, from which the new plant grows every year

cor·mor·ant /ˈkɔːmərənt; *NAmE* ˈkɔːrm-/ *noun* a large black bird with a long neck that lives near the sea or other areas of water

corn /kɔːn; *NAmE* kɔːrn/ *noun* **1** (*BrE*) [U] any plant that is grown for its grain, such as WHEAT; the grain of these plants: *a field of corn* ◇ ***ears/sheaves of corn*** ◇ *corn-fed chicken* ➲ COLLOCATIONS at FARMING **2** (*NAmE*) (*BrE* **maize**) [U] a tall plant grown for its large yellow grains that are used for making flour or eaten as a vegetable; the grains of this plant ➲ VISUAL VOCAB page V28 ➲ see also CORNCOB, CORN ON THE COB **3** (*NAmE*) (*BrE* **sweet-corn**) [U] the yellow seeds of a type of corn (MAIZE) plant, also called corn, which grow on thick STEMS and are cooked and eaten as a vegetable ➲ VISUAL VOCAB page V27 **4** [C] a small area of hard skin on the foot, especially the toe, that is sometimes painful

ˌcorn ˈbeef *noun* [U] = CORNED BEEF

the ˈCorn Belt *noun* the US states of the Midwest where MAIZE/CORN is an important crop

corn·bread /ˈkɔːnbred; *NAmE* ˈkɔːrn-/ *noun* [U] a kind of flat bread made with MAIZE (CORN) flour

ˈcorn chip *noun* (*NAmE*) a thin, crisp piece of food made from crushed corn (MAIZE) that has been fried

ˈcorn circle *noun* = CROP CIRCLE

corn·cob /ˈkɔːnkɒb; *NAmE* ˈkɔːrnkɑːb/ (*especially BrE*) (also **cob** *NAmE, BrE*) *noun* the long hard part of the MAIZE (CORN) plant that the rows of yellow grains grow on

cor·nea /ˈkɔːniə; *NAmE* ˈkɔːrniə/ *noun* (*anatomy*) the transparent layer which covers and protects the outer part of the eye ➲ VISUAL VOCAB page V48 ▶ **cor·neal** /ˈkɔːniəl; *NAmE* ˈkɔːrn-/ *adj.* [only before noun]: *a corneal transplant*

corned beef /ˌkɔːnd ˈbiːf; *NAmE* ˌkɔːrnd/ (also ˌ**corn ˈbeef**) *noun* [U] beef that has been cooked and preserved using salt, often sold in cans

cor·ne·lian /kɔːˈniːliən; *NAmE* kɔːrˈn-/ *noun* = CARNELIAN

cor·ner 0‒ /ˈkɔːnə(r); *NAmE* ˈkɔːrn-/ *noun, verb*
■ ***noun***
▸ OF BUILDING/OBJECT/SHAPE **1** 0‒ a part of sth where two or more sides, lines or edges join: *the four corners of a square* ◇ *Write your address in the top right-hand corner of the letter.* ◇ *I hit my knee on the corner of the table.* ◇ *A smile lifted the corner of his mouth.* ◇ *a speck of dirt in the corner of her eye*
▸ -CORNERED **2** (in adjectives) with the number of corners mentioned; involving the number of groups mentioned: *a three-cornered hat* ◇ *a three-cornered fight*
▸ OF ROOM/BOX **3** 0‒ the place inside a room or a box where two sides join; the area around this place: *There was a television in the far corner of the room.* ◇ *a* ***corner table/seat/cupboard***
▸ OF ROADS **4** 0‒ a place where two streets join: *There was a group of youths standing on the* ***street corner.*** ◇ *Turn right at the corner of Sunset and Crescent Heights Boulevards.* ◇ *There's a hotel* ***on/at the corner*** *of my street.* ◇ *The wind hit him as he* ***turned the corner.*** **5** 0‒ a sharp bend in a road: *The car was taking the corners too fast.*
▸ AREA/REGION **6** a region or an area of a place (sometimes used for one that is far away or difficult to reach): *She lives in a quiet corner of rural Yorkshire.* ◇ *Students come here* ***from the four corners*** *of the world.* ◇ *He knew every corner of the old town.*
▸ DIFFICULT SITUATION **7** [usually sing.] a difficult situation: *to* ***back/drive/force sb into a corner*** ◇ *They had got her in a corner, and there wasn't much she could do about it.* ◇ *He was used to talking his way out of* ***tight corners.***
▸ IN SPORT **8** (in sports such as football (SOCCER) and HOCKEY) a free kick or hit that you take from the corner of your opponent's end of the field: *to take a corner* ◇ *The referee awarded a corner.* ➲ see also CORNER KICK **9** (in boxing and WRESTLING) any of the four corners of a RING; the supporters who help in the corner

IDM **(just) around/round the ˈcorner** very near: *Her house is just around the corner.* ◇ (*figurative*) *There were good times around the corner* (= they would soon come). **cut ˈcorners** (*disapproving*) to do sth in the easiest, cheapest or quickest way, often by ignoring rules or leaving sth out **cut the ˈcorner** (also **cut off the ˈcorner** especially in *BrE*) to go across the corner of an area and not around the sides of it, because it is quicker **see sth out of the corner of your ˈeye** to see sth by accident or not very clearly because you see it from the side of your eye and are not looking straight at it: *Out of the corner of her eye, she saw him coming closer.* **turn the ˈcorner** to pass a very important point in an illness or a difficult situation and begin to improve ➲ more at FIGHT *v.*, TIGHT

■ ***verb***
▸ TRAP SB **1** [T, often passive] **~ sb/sth** to get a person or an animal into a place or situation from which they cannot escape: *The man was finally cornered by police in a garage.* ◇ *If cornered, the snake will defend itself.* **2** [T] **~ sb** to go towards sb in a determined way, because you want to speak to them: *I found myself cornered by her on the stairs.*
▸ THE MARKET **3** [T] **~ the market (in sth)** to get control of the trade in a particular type of goods: *They've cornered the market in silver.*
▸ OF VEHICLE/DRIVER **4** [I] (*BrE*) to go around a corner: *The car has excellent cornering* (= it is easy to steer around corners).

cor·ner·back /ˈkɔːnəbæk; *NAmE* ˈkɔːrnər-/ *noun* (in AMERICAN FOOTBALL) a defending player whose position is outside and behind the LINEBACKERS

ˈcorner kick (also **cor·ner**) *noun* (in football (SOCCER)) a free kick that you take from the corner of your opponent's end of the field

ˈcorner shop *noun* (*BrE*) a small shop that sells food, newspapers, cigarettes, etc, especially one near people's houses

cor·ner·stone /ˈkɔːnəstəʊn; *NAmE* ˈkɔːrnərstoʊn/ *noun* **1** (*especially NAmE*) a stone at the corner of the base of a building, often laid in a special ceremony **2** the most important part of sth that the rest depends on: *This study is the cornerstone of the whole research programme.*

cor·net /ˈkɔːnɪt; *NAmE* ˈkɔːrnɪt/ *noun* **1** a BRASS musical instrument like a small TRUMPET **2** (*BrE, old-fashioned*) = CONE (4): *an ice-cream cornet*

cor·netto /kɔːˈnetəʊ; *NAmE* kɔːrˈnetoʊ/ *noun* (*pl.* **cor·netti**) (from *Italian*) an early musical instrument consisting of a curved tube with holes in that you cover with your fingers while blowing into the end

'corn exchange *noun* (*BrE*) a building where grain used to be bought and sold

corn·field /'kɔːnfiːld; *NAmE* 'kɔːrn-/ *noun* a field in which CORN is grown

corn·flakes /'kɔːnfleɪks; *NAmE* 'kɔːrn-/ *noun* [pl.] small crisp yellow pieces of crushed MAIZE (CORN), usually eaten with milk and sugar for breakfast

corn·flour /'kɔːnflaʊə(r); *NAmE* 'kɔːrn-/ (*BrE*) (*NAmE* **corn·starch**) *noun* [U] fine white flour made from MAIZE (CORN), used especially for making sauces thicker

corn·flower /'kɔːnflaʊə(r); *NAmE* 'kɔːrn-/ *noun* a small wild plant with blue flowers

cor·nice /'kɔːnɪs; *NAmE* 'kɔːrnɪs/ *noun* (*architecture*) a decorative border around the top of the walls in a room or on the outside walls of a building

Corn·ish /'kɔːnɪʃ; *NAmE* 'kɔːrnɪʃ/ *noun, adj.*

- ***noun*** [U] the Celtic language that was spoken in Cornwall in England. Nobody now uses Cornish as a first language.
- ***adj.*** connected with Cornwall, or its people, language or culture

,Cornish 'Cream *noun* [U] CLOTTED CREAM (= a very thick type of cream) from Cornwall

Cornish pasty /,kɔːnɪʃ 'pæsti; *NAmE* ,kɔːrnɪʃ/ *noun* (*BrE*) a small PIE in the shape of a half circle, containing meat and vegetables

corn·meal /'kɔːnmiːl; *NAmE* 'kɔːrn-/ *noun* [U] flour made from MAIZE (CORN)

,corn on the 'cob *noun* [U] MAIZE (CORN) that is cooked with all the grains still attached to the inner part and eaten as a vegetable ➲ VISUAL VOCAB page V27

'corn pone (also **pone**) (both *US*) *noun* [U] a type of bread made from CORN (MAIZE) and water

corn·rows /'kɔːnrəʊz; *NAmE* 'kɔːrnroʊz/ *noun* [pl.] a HAIRSTYLE worn especially by black women, in which the hair is put into lines of PLAITS along the head ➲ VISUAL VOCAB page V49

corn·starch /'kɔːnstɑːtʃ; *NAmE* 'kɔːrnstɑːrtʃ/ (*NAmE*) (*BrE* **corn·flour**) *noun* [U] fine white flour made from CORN (MAIZE), used especially for making sauces thicker

,corn 'syrup *noun* [U] a thick sweet liquid made from CORN (MAIZE) and used in cooking

cor·nu·co·pia /,kɔːnju'kəʊpiə; *NAmE* ,kɔːrnju'koʊpiə/ *noun* **1** (also **,horn of 'plenty**) a decorative object shaped like an animal's horn, shown in art as full of fruit and flowers **2** (*formal*) something that is or contains a large supply of good things: *The book is a cornucopia of good ideas.*

corny /'kɔːni; *NAmE* 'kɔːrni/ *adj.* (**corn·ier, corni·est**) (*informal*) not original; used too often to be interesting or to sound sincere: *a **corny joke/song*** ◇ *I know it sounds corny, but it really was love at first sight!*

cor·olla /kə'rɒlə; *NAmE* -'rɑːlə; -'roʊlə/ *noun* (*biology*) the ring of PETALS around the central part of a flower

cor·ol·lary /kə'rɒləri; *NAmE* 'kɔːrəleri; 'kɑːr-/ *noun* (*pl.* -ies) **~ (of/to sth)** (*formal* or *technical*) a situation, an argument or a fact that is the natural and direct result of another one

cor·ona /kə'rəʊnə; *NAmE* -'roʊ-/ *noun* (*pl.* **co·ro·nae** /-niː/) (*astronomy*) (also *informal* **halo**) a ring of light seen around the sun or moon, especially during an ECLIPSE

cor·on·ary /'kɒrənri; *NAmE* 'kɔːrəneri; 'kɑːrəneri/ *adj.* (*medical*) connected with the heart, particularly the ARTERIES that take blood to the heart: *coronary (heart) disease* ◇ *a coronary patient* (= sb suffering from coronary disease)

,coronary 'artery *noun* (*anatomy*) either of the two ARTERIES that supply blood to the heart

,coronary throm'bosis (also *informal* **cor·on·ary**) *noun* [C, U] (*medical*) a blocking of the flow of blood by a blood CLOT in an ARTERY supplying blood to the heart ➲ compare HEART ATTACK

cor·on·ation /,kɒrə'neɪʃn; *NAmE* ,kɔːr-; ,kɑːr-/ *noun* a ceremony at which a crown is formally placed on the head of a new king or queen

cor·on·er /'kɒrənə(r); *NAmE* 'kɔːr-; 'kɑːr-/ *noun* an official whose job is to discover the cause of any sudden, violent or suspicious death by holding an INQUEST

C

cor·onet /'kɒrənet; *NAmE* ,kɔːrə'net; ,kɑːr-/ *noun* **1** a small crown worn on formal occasions by princes, princesses, lords, etc. **2** a round decoration for the head, especially one made of flowers

Corp. *abbr.* CORPORATION

cor·pora *pl.* of CORPUS

cor·poral /'kɔːpərəl; *NAmE* 'kɔːrp-/ *noun* (*abbr.* **Cpl**) a member of one of the lower ranks in the army, the MARINES or the British AIR FORCE: *Corporal Smith*

,corporal 'punishment *noun* [U] the physical punishment of people, especially by hitting them

cor·por·ate **AW** /'kɔːpərət; *NAmE* 'kɔːrp-/ *adj.* [only before noun] **1** connected with a corporation: ***corporate finance/planning/strategy*** ◇ ***corporate identity*** (= the image of a company, that all its members share) ◇ ***corporate hospitality*** (= when companies entertain customers to help develop good business relationships) **2** (*technical*) forming a CORPORATION: *The BBC is a **corporate body**.* ◇ *The law applies to both individuals and corporate bodies.* **3** involving or shared by all the members of a group: *corporate responsibility*

,corporate 'raider *noun* (*business*) a person or company that regularly buys large numbers of shares in other companies against their wishes, either to control them or to sell them again for a large profit

cor·por·ation **AW** /,kɔːpə'reɪʃn; *NAmE* ,kɔːrp-/ *noun* **1** (*abbr.* **Corp.**) a large business company: *multinational corporations* ◇ *the Chrysler corporation* **2** an organization or a group of organizations that is recognized by law as a single unit: *urban development corporations* **3** (*BrE*) a group of people elected to govern a large town or city and provide public services

,corpo'ration tax *noun* [U] (*BrE*) a tax that companies pay on their profits

cor·por·at·ism /'kɔːpərətɪzəm; *NAmE* 'kɔːrp-/ *noun* [U] the control of a country, etc. by large groups, especially businesses

cor·por·at·or /'kɔːpəreɪtə(r); *NAmE* 'kɔːrp-/ *noun* (*IndE*) an elected member of the government of a town or city

cor·por·eal /kɔː'pɔːriəl; *NAmE* kɔːr'p-/ *adj.* (*formal*) **1** that can be touched; physical rather than spiritual: *his corporeal presence* **2** of or for the body: *corporeal needs*

corps /kɔː(r)/ *noun* (*pl.* **corps** /kɔːz; *NAmE* kɔːrz/) [C+sing./pl. v.] **1** a large unit of an army, consisting of two or more DIVISIONS: *the commander of the third army corps* **2** one of the groups of an army with a special responsibility: *the Royal Army Medical Corps* **3** a group of people involved in a particular job or activity: *a corps of trained and experienced doctors* ➲ see also DIPLOMATIC CORPS, PRESS CORPS

corps de bal·let /,kɔː də 'bæleɪ; *NAmE* ,kɔːr də bæ'leɪ/ *noun* [C+sing./pl. v.] (from *French*) dancers in a BALLET company who dance together as a group

corpse /kɔːps; *NAmE* kɔːrps/ *noun*

- ***noun*** a dead body, especially of a human

cor·pu·lent /'kɔːpjələnt; *NAmE* 'kɔːrp-/ *adj.* (*formal*) (of a person) fat. People say 'corpulent' to avoid saying 'fat'. ▸ **cor·pu·lence** *noun* [U]

cor·pus /'kɔːpəs; *NAmE* 'kɔːrpəs/ *noun* (*pl.* **cor·pora** /'kɔːpərə; *NAmE* 'kɔːrp-/ or **cor·puses** /-sɪz/) (*technical*) a collection of written or spoken texts: *a corpus of 100 million words of spoken English* ◇ *the whole corpus of Renaissance poetry* ➲ see also HABEAS CORPUS

cor·puscle /ˈkɔːpʌsl; *NAmE* ˈkɔːrp-/ *noun* (*anatomy*) any of the red or white cells found in blood: ***red/white corpuscles***

cor·ral /kəˈrɑːl; *NAmE* -ˈræl/ *noun, verb*

- ***noun*** (in N America) a fenced area for horses, cows etc. on a farm or RANCH: *They drove the ponies into a corral.*
- ***verb*** (-ll-, *US* also -l-) **1 ~ sth** to force horses or cows into a corral **2 ~ sb** to gather a group of people together and keep them in a particular place

cor·rect 0-ᴡ /kəˈrekt/ *adj., verb*

- ***adj.*** **1** 0-ᴡ accurate or true, without any mistakes SYN **right**: *Do you have the correct time?* ◇ *the correct answer* ◇ *Please check that these details are correct.* ◇ *'Are you in charge here?' 'That's correct.'* ◇ *Am I correct in saying that you know a lot about wine?* OPP **incorrect** ➲ SYNONYMS at TRUE **2** 0-ᴡ right and suitable, so that sth is done as it should be done: *Do you know the correct way to shut the machine down?* ◇ *I think you've made the correct decision.* ➲ SYNONYMS at RIGHT **3** taking care to speak or behave in a way that follows the accepted standards or rules: *a correct young lady* ◇ *He is always very correct in his speech.* OPP **incorrect** ➲ see also POLITICALLY CORRECT ▸ **cor·rect·ly** 0-ᴡ *adv.*: *Have you spelled it correctly?* ◇ *They reasoned, correctly, that she was away for the weekend.* ◇ *He was looking correctly grave.* **cor·rect·ness** *noun* [U]: *The correctness of this decision may be doubted.* ➲ see also POLITICAL CORRECTNESS IDM see PRESENT *adj.*
- ***verb*** **1** 0-ᴡ **~ sth** to make sth right or accurate, for example by changing it or removing mistakes: *Read through your work and correct any mistakes that you find.* ◇ *Their eyesight can be corrected in just a few minutes by the use of a laser.* ◇ *They issued a statement correcting the one they had made earlier.* **2** 0-ᴡ **~ sth** (of a teacher) to mark the mistakes in a piece of work (and sometimes give a mark/grade to the work): *I spent all evening correcting essays.* **3** to tell sb that they have made a mistake: **~ sb** *Correct me if I'm wrong, but isn't this last year's brochure?* ◇ *Yes, you're right—I* ***stand corrected*** (= I accept that I made a mistake). ◇ **~ (sb) + speech** *'It's Yates, not Wates,' she corrected him.*

cor·rec·tion /kəˈrekʃn/ *noun, exclamation*

- ***noun*** **1** [C] a change that makes sth more accurate than it was before: *I've made a few small corrections to your report.* ◇ *The paper had to publish a correction to the story.* **2** [U] the act or process of correcting sth: *There are some programming errors that need correction.* **3** [U] (*old-fashioned*) punishment: *the correction of young offenders*
- ***exclamation*** (*informal*) used when you want to correct sth that you have just said: *I don't know. Correction—I do know, but I'm not going to tell you.*

cor·rec·tion·al /kəˈrekʃənl/ *adj.* [only before noun] (*especially NAmE*) concerned with improving the behaviour of criminals, usually by punishing them: *a* ***correctional center/institution/facility*** (= a prison)

corˈrection fluid *noun* [U] a white liquid that you use to cover mistakes that you make when you are writing or typing, and that you can write on top of ➲ VISUAL VOCAB page V56 ➲ see also TIPPEX, WITEOUT

cor·rect·ive /kəˈrektɪv/ *adj., noun*

- ***adj.*** (*formal*) designed to make sth right that was wrong before: *We need to take* ***corrective action*** *to halt this country's decline.* ◇ ***corrective measures*** ◇ ***corrective surgery/glasses***
- ***noun*** **~ (to sth)** (*formal*) something that helps to give a more accurate or fairer view of sb/sth: *I should like to add a corrective to what I have written previously.*

cor·rel·ate /ˈkɒrəleɪt; *NAmE* ˈkɔːr-; ˈkɑːr-/ *verb* (*formal*) **1** [I] if two or more facts, figures, etc. **correlate** or if a fact, figure, etc. **correlates** with another, the facts are closely connected and affect or depend on each other: *The figures do not seem to correlate.* ◇ **~ with sth** *A high-fat diet correlates with a greater risk of heart disease.* **2** [T] **~ sth** to show that there is a close connection between two or more facts, figures, etc: *Researchers are trying to correlate the two sets of figures.* ▸ **cor·rel·ate** /ˈkɒrələt; *NAmE* ˈkɔːr-; ˈkɑːr-/ *noun*

cor·rel·ation /ˌkɒrəˈleɪʃn; *NAmE* ˌkɔːr-/ *noun* [C, U] a connection between two things in which one thing changes as the other does: **~ (between A and B)** *There is a direct correlation between exposure to sun and skin cancer.* ◇ **~ (of A with B)** *the correlation of social power with wealth*

cor·rela·tive /kəˈrelətɪv/ *noun* (*formal*) a fact or an idea that is closely related to or depends on another fact or idea ▸ **cor·rela·tive** *adj.*

cor·res·pond AW /ˌkɒrəˈspɒnd; *NAmE* ˌkɔːrəˈspɑːnd; ˌkɑː-/ *verb* **1** [I] to be the same as or match sth SYN **agree, tally**: *Your account and hers do not correspond.* ◇ **~ with sth** *Your account of events does not correspond with hers.* ◇ **~ to sth** *The written record of the conversation doesn't correspond to* (= is different from) *what was actually said.* **2** [I] **~ (to sth)** to be similar to or the same as sth else SYN **equivalent**: *The British job of Lecturer corresponds roughly to the US Associate Professor.* **3** [I] **~ (with sb)** (*formal*) to write letters to sb and receive letters from them

cor·res·pond·ence AW /ˌkɒrəˈspɒndəns; *NAmE* ˌkɔːrəˈspɑːn-; ˌkɑː-/ *noun* (*formal*) **1** [U] **~ (with sb)** the letters a person sends and receives: ***personal/private correspondence*** ◇ *The editor welcomes correspondence from readers on any subject.* ◇ *the* ***correspondence column/page*** (= in a newspaper) **2** [U, C] **~ (with sb)** the activity of writing letters: *I refused to enter into any correspondence* (= to exchange letters) *with him about it.* ◇ *We have been* ***in correspondence*** *for months.* ◇ *We kept up a correspondence for many years.* **3** [C, U] **~ (between A and B)** a connection between two things; the fact of two things being similar: *There is a close correspondence between the two extracts.*

correˈspondence course *noun* a course of study that you do at home, using books and exercises sent to you by post/mail or by email

cor·res·pond·ent /ˌkɒrəˈspɒndənt; *NAmE* ˌkɔːrəˈspɑːn-; ˌkɑː-/ *noun* **1** a person who reports news from a particular country or on a particular subject for a newspaper or a television or radio station: *the BBC's political correspondent* ◇ *a* ***foreign/war/sports, etc. correspondent*** ◇ *our Delhi correspondent* **2** (used with an adjective) a person who writes letters to another person: *She's a poor correspondent* (= she does not write regularly).

cor·res·pond·ing AW /ˌkɒrəˈspɒndɪŋ; *NAmE* ˌkɔːrəˈspɑːn-; ˌkɑː-/ *adj.* matching or connected with sth that you have just mentioned SYN **equivalent**: *A change in the money supply brings a corresponding change in expenditure.* ◇ *Profits have risen by 15 per cent compared with the corresponding period last year.* ◇ *The Redskins lost to the Cowboys in the corresponding game last year.* ◇ **~ to sth** *Give each picture a number corresponding to its position on the page.* ▸ **cor·res·pond·ing·ly** AW *adv.*: *a period of high demand and correspondingly high prices*

corresˈponding angles (also **ˈF angles**) *noun* (*geometry*) equal angles formed on the same side of a line that crosses two parallel lines ➲ VISUAL VOCAB page V58 ➲ compare ALTERNATE ANGLES

cor·ri·dor /ˈkɒrɪdɔː(r); *NAmE* ˈkɔːr-; ˈkɑːr-/ *noun* **1** (*NAmE* also **hall·way**) a long narrow passage in a building, with doors that open into rooms on either side: *His room is along the corridor.* ➲ VISUAL VOCAB page V57 **2** a passage on a train **3** a long narrow strip of land belonging to one country that passes through the land of another country; a part of the sky over a country that planes, for example from another country, can fly through ➲ see also AIR CORRIDOR **4** a long narrow strip of land that follows the course of an important road or river: *the electronics industry in the M4 corridor*

IDM **the corridors of ˈpower** (sometimes *humorous*) the higher levels of government, where important decisions are made

cor·rie /ˈkɒri; *NAmE* ˈkɔːri; ˈkɑːri/ (also **cirque, cwm**) *noun* (*geology*) a round hollow area in the side of a mountain

cor·rob·or·ate /kəˈrɒbəreɪt; *NAmE* -ˈrɑːb-/ [I, T, often passive] **~ (sth)** (*formal*) to provide evidence or information that supports a statement, theory, etc. SYN **confirm**: *The evidence was corroborated by two independent witnesses.* ◇ *corroborating evidence* ▶ **cor·rob·or·ation** /kəˌrɒbəˈreɪʃn; *NAmE* -ˌrɑːbə-/ *noun* [U]

cor·rob·ora·tive /kəˈrɒbərətɪv; *NAmE* kəˈrɑːbəreɪtɪv/ *adj.* (*formal*) [usually before noun] giving support to a statement or theory: *Is there any* ***corroborative evidence*** *for this theory?*

cor·rode /kəˈrəʊd; *NAmE* kəˈroʊd/ *verb* [T, I] **~ (sth)** to destroy sth slowly, especially by chemical action; to be destroyed in this way: *Acid corrodes metal.* ◇ (*figurative*) *Corruption corrodes public confidence in a political system.* ◇ *The copper pipework has corroded in places.* ▶ **cor·ro·sion** /kəˈrəʊʒn; *NAmE* -ˈroʊ-/ *noun* [U]: *Look for signs of corrosion.* ◇ *Clean off any corrosion before applying the paint.* ➲ VISUAL VOCAB page V6

cor·ro·sive /kəˈrəʊsɪv; *NAmE* -ˈroʊ-/ *adj.* **1** tending to destroy sth slowly by chemical action: *the corrosive effects of salt water* ◇ *corrosive acid* **2** (*formal*) tending to damage sth gradually: *Unemployment is having a corrosive effect on our economy.*

cor·ru·gated /ˈkɒrəgeɪtɪd; *NAmE* ˈkɔːr-; ˈkɑːr-/ *adj.* shaped into a series of regular folds that look like waves: *a* ***corrugated iron*** *roof* ◇ *corrugated cardboard*

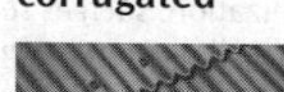
corrugated

corrugated iron roof

cor·rupt /kəˈrʌpt/ *adj., verb*

■ ***adj.*** **1** (of people) willing to use their power to do dishonest or illegal things in return for money or to get an advantage: *a corrupt regime* ◇ *corrupt officials accepting bribes* **2** (of behaviour) dishonest or immoral: *corrupt practices* ◇ *The whole system is inefficient and corrupt.* **3** (*computing*) containing changes or faults, and no longer in the original state: *corrupt software* ◇ *The text on the disk seems to be corrupt.* ▶ **cor·rupt·ly** *adv.*

■ ***verb*** **1** [T] **~ sb** to have a bad effect on sb and make them behave in an immoral or dishonest way: *He was corrupted by power and ambition.* ◇ *the corrupting effects of great wealth* **2** [T, often passive] **~ sth** to change the original form of sth, so that it is damaged or spoiled in some way: *a corrupted form of Buddhism* **3** [T, I] **~ (sth)** (*computing*) to cause mistakes to appear in a computer file, etc. with the result that the information in it is no longer correct: *The program has somehow corrupted the system files.* ◇ *corrupted data* ◇ *The disk will corrupt if it is overloaded.*

cor·rupt·ible /kəˈrʌptəbl/ *adj.* that can be corrupted OPP **incorruptible**

cor·rup·tion /kəˈrʌpʃn/ *noun* **1** [U] dishonest or illegal behaviour, especially of people in authority: *allegations of* ***bribery and corruption*** ◇ *The new district attorney has promised to fight police corruption.* ➲ COLLOCATIONS at CRIME **2** [U] the act or effect of making sb change from moral to immoral standards of behaviour: *He claimed that sex and violence on TV led to the corruption of young people.* **3** [C, usually sing.] the form of a word or phrase that has become changed from its original form in some way: *The word 'holiday' is a corruption of 'holy day'.*

cor·sage /kɔːˈsɑːʒ; *NAmE* kɔːrˈsɑːʒ/ *noun* a small bunch of flowers that is worn on a woman's dress, for example at a wedding

cor·set /ˈkɔːsɪt; *NAmE* ˈkɔːrsɪt/ *noun* a piece of women's underwear, fitting the body tightly, worn especially in the past to make the waist look smaller

cor·tège (also **cor·tege** especially in *US*) /kɔːˈteʒ; -ˈteɪʒ; *NAmE* kɔːrˈteʒ/ *noun* a line of cars or people moving along slowly at a funeral SYN **funeral procession**

cor·tex /ˈkɔːteks; *NAmE* ˈkɔːrt-/ *noun* (*pl.* **cor·ti·ces** /ˈkɔːtɪsiːz; *NAmE* ˈkɔːrt-/) (*anatomy*) the outer layer of an organ in the body, especially the brain: *the* ***cerebral/renal cortex*** (= around the brain/KIDNEY) ▶ **cor·tic·al** /ˈkɔːtɪkl; *NAmE* ˈkɔːrt-/ *adj.*

cor·ti·sone /ˈkɔːtɪzəʊn; -səʊn; *NAmE* ˈkɔːrtəsoʊn; -zoʊn/ *noun* [U] (*medical*) a HORMONE used in the treatment of diseases such as ARTHRITIS, to reduce swelling

cor·us·cate /ˈkɒrəskeɪt; *NAmE* ˈkɔːr-; ˈkɑːr-/ *verb* (*literary*) **1** [I] (of light) to flash **2** [I] (of a person) to be full of life, enthusiasm or humour ▶ **cor·us·cat·ing** /ˈkɒrəskeɪtɪŋ; *NAmE* ˈkɔːr-/ *adj.*: *coruscating wit* **cor·us·cat·ing·ly** *adv.*: *coruscatingly brilliant*

cor·vette /kɔːˈvet; *NAmE* kɔːrˈvet/ *noun* a small fast ship used in war to protect other ships from attack

cos[1] (also **'cos, 'cause, coz**) /kəz; *BrE* also kɒz/ *conj.* (*BrE, informal*) because: *I can't see her at all, cos it's too dark.*

cos[2] *abbr.* (in writing) COSINE

COSATU /kəʊˈsɑːtuː; *NAmE* ˈkoʊ-/ *abbr.* the Congress of South African Trade Unions (= a political organization in South Africa that represents many unions)

cosh /kɒʃ; *NAmE* kɑːʃ/ *noun, verb*

■ ***noun*** (*especially BrE*) a short thick heavy stick, for example a piece of metal or solid rubber, that is used as a weapon IDM **under the 'cosh** (*BrE, informal*) experiencing a lot of pressure: *Our side was under the cosh for most of the second half.*

■ ***verb*** **~ sb** (*especially BrE*) to hit sb hard with a cosh or sth similar

ˌco-'signatory *noun* one of two or more people who sign a formal document: ***co-signatories of/to*** *the treaty*

co·sine /ˈkəʊsaɪn; *NAmE* ˈkoʊ-/ *noun* (*abbr.* **cos**) (*mathematics*) the RATIO of the length of the side next to an ACUTE ANGLE in a RIGHT-ANGLED triangle to the length of the longest side (= the HYPOTENUSE) ➲ compare SINE, TANGENT

cos lettuce /ˌkɒs ˈletɪs; ˌkɒz; *NAmE* ˌkɑːs; ˌkɔːs/ (*BrE*) (*NAmE* **ro·maine**) *noun* [C, U] a type of LETTUCE with long crisp leaves

cos·met·ic /kɒzˈmetɪk; *NAmE* kɑːz-/ *noun, adj.*

■ ***noun*** [usually pl.] a substance that you put on your face or body to make it more attractive: *the cosmetics industry* ◇ *a cosmetic company* ◇ *cosmetic products* ➲ COLLOCATIONS at FASHION

■ ***adj.*** **1** improving only the outside appearance of sth and not its basic character: *These reforms are not merely cosmetic.* ◇ *She dismissed the plan as a cosmetic exercise to win votes.* **2** connected with medical treatment that is intended to improve a person's appearance: *cosmetic surgery* ◇ *cosmetic dental work* ▶ **cos·met·ic·al·ly** /-kli/ *adv.*

cos·mic /ˈkɒzmɪk; *NAmE* ˈkɑːz-/ *adj.* [usually before noun] **1** connected with the whole universe: *Do you believe in a cosmic plan?* **2** very great and important: *This was disaster on a cosmic scale.*

ˌcosmic 'dust *noun* [U] (*astronomy*) very small pieces of matter floating in space

ˌcosmic 'rays *noun* [pl.] RAYS that reach the earth from outer space

cos·mol·ogy /kɒzˈmɒlədʒi; *NAmE* kɑːzˈmɑːl-/ *noun* [U] the scientific study of the universe and its origin and development ▶ **cosmo·logic·al** /ˌkɒzməˈlɒdʒɪkl; *NAmE* ˌkɑːzməˈlɑːdʒ-/ *adj.* **cos·molo·gist** /kɒzˈmɒlədʒɪst; *NAmE* kɑːzˈmɑːl-/ *noun*

cosmo·naut /ˈkɒzmənɔːt; *NAmE* ˈkɑːz-/ *noun* an ASTRONAUT from the former Soviet Union

cosmo·pol·itan /ˌkɒzməˈpɒlɪtən; *NAmE* ˌkɑːzməˈpɑːl-/ *adj., noun*

■ ***adj.*** (*approving*) **1** containing people of different types or from different countries, and influenced by their culture: *a* ***cosmopolitan city/resort*** ◇ *The club has a cosmopolitan atmosphere.* **2** having or showing a wide experience of people and things from many different countries: *people with a truly cosmopolitan outlook* ◇ *cosmopolitan young people*

■ ***noun*** a person who has experience of many different parts of the world: *She's a real cosmopolitan.*

C

cos·mos /ˈkɒzmɒs; *NAmE* ˈkɑːzmoʊs; -məs/ **the cosmos** *noun* [sing.] the universe, especially when it is thought of as an ordered system: *the structure of the cosmos* ◇ *our place in the cosmos*

cos·set /ˈkɒsɪt; *NAmE* ˈkɑːs-/ *verb* **~ sb** (often *disapproving*) to treat sb with a lot of care and give them a lot of attention, sometimes too much SYN **pamper**

cost 🔑 /kɒst; *NAmE* kɔːst/ *noun, verb*

■ ***noun*** **1** 🔑 [C, U] the amount of money that you need in order to buy, make or do sth: *the* ***high/low cost*** *of housing* ◇ *A new computer system has been installed* ***at a cost of*** *£80 000.* ◇ *The plan had to be abandoned on grounds of cost.* ◇ *We did not even make enough money to* ***cover the cost*** *of the food.* ◇ *Consumers will have to* ***bear the*** *full* ***cost*** *of these pay increases.* ◇ *The total cost to you* (= the amount you have to pay) *is £3 000.* ➲ SYNONYMS at PRICE **2** 🔑 **costs** [pl.] the total amount of money that needs to be spent by a business: *The use of cheap labour helped to keep costs down.* ◇ *to* ***cut/reduce costs*** ◇ ***running/operating/labour costs*** ◇ *We have had to raise our prices because of rising costs.* ➲ COLLOCATIONS at BUSINESS **3** 🔑 [U, sing.] the effort, loss or damage that is involved in order to do or achieve sth: *the terrible cost of the war in death and suffering* ◇ *the environmental cost of nuclear power* ◇ *She saved him from the fire but* ***at the cost of*** *her own life* (= she died). ◇ *He worked non-stop for three months,* ***at*** *considerable* ***cost to*** *his health.* ◇ *I felt a need to please people, whatever* ***the cost in*** *time and energy.* **4 costs** (*NAmE* also ˈ**court costs**) [pl.] the sum of money that sb is ordered to pay for lawyers, etc. in a legal case: *He was ordered to pay £2 000 costs.*

IDM **at ˈall cost/costs** whatever is needed to achieve sth: *You must stop the press from finding out at all costs.* **at ˈany cost** under any circumstances: *He is determined to win at any cost.* **at ˈcost** for only the amount of money that is needed to make or get sth, without any profit being added on: *goods sold at cost* **know/learn/find sth to your ˈcost** to know sth because of sth unpleasant that has happened to you: *He's a ruthless businessman, as I know to my cost.* ➲ more at COUNT *v.*

■ ***verb*** (cost, cost) HELP In sense 4 **costed** is used for the past tense and past participle. **1** 🔑 if sth **costs** a particular amount of money, you need to pay that amount in order to buy, make or do it: **~ sth** *How much did it cost?* ◇ *I didn't get it because it cost too much.* ◇ *Tickets cost ten dollars each.* ◇ *Calls to the helpline cost 38p per minute.* ◇ *Don't use too much of it—it* ***cost a lot of money.*** ◇ *All these reforms will* ***cost money*** (= be expensive). ◇ *Good food need not* ***cost a fortune*** (= cost a lot of money). ◇ **~ sb sth** *The meal cost us about £40.* ◇ *This is costing the taxpayer £10 billion a year.* ◇ **~ sth to do sth** *The hospital will cost an estimated £2 million to build.* ◇ *It costs a fortune to fly first class.* **2** 🔑 to cause the loss of sth: **~ sb sth** *That one mistake almost cost him his life.* ◇ *A late penalty cost United the game* (= meant that they did not win the game). ◇ **~ sth** *The closure of the factory is likely to cost 1 000 jobs.* **3 ~ sb sth** to involve you in making an effort or doing sth unpleasant: *The accident cost me a visit to the doctor.* ◇ *Financial worries cost her many sleepless nights.* **4** (**costed, costed**) [usually passive] to estimate how much money will be needed for sth or the price that should be charged for sth: **~ sth** *The project needs to be costed in detail.* ◇ *Their accountants have costed the project at $8.1 million.* ◇ **~ sth out** *Have you costed out these proposals yet?* ➲ see also COSTING

IDM **cost sb ˈdear** to make sb suffer a lot: *That one mistake has cost him dear over the years.* **it will ˈcost you** (*informal*) used to say that sth will be expensive: *There is a de luxe model available, but it'll cost you.* ➲ more at ARM *n.*

ˈ**cost accounting** *noun* [U] (*business*) the process of recording and analysing the costs involved in running a business

cos·tal /ˈkɒstl; *NAmE* ˈkɑːstl/ *adj.* (*anatomy*) connected with the RIBS

ˈ**co-star** *noun, verb*

■ ***noun*** one of two or more famous actors who appear together in a film/movie or play

Synonyms

costs

spending • expenditure • expenses • overheads • outlay

These are all words for money spent by a government, an organization or a person.

costs the total amount of money that needs to be spent by a business: *labour/production costs* ◇ *rising costs*

spending the amount of money that is spent, especially by a government or an organization: *public spending* ◇ *More spending on health was promised.*

expenditure (*rather formal*) an amount of money spent by a government, an organization or a person: *expenditure on education*

expenses money that has to be spent by a person or an organization; money that you spend while you are working which your employer will pay back to you later: *legal expenses* ◇ *travel expenses*

overhead(s) the regular costs of running a business or organization, such as rent, electricity and wages: *High overheads mean small profit margins.*

outlay the money that you have to spend in order to start a new business or project, or in order to save yourself money or time later: *The best equipment is costly but is well worth the outlay.*

PATTERNS

- spending/expenditure/outlay **on** sth
- **high/low** costs/spending/expenditure/expenses/overheads
- **total** costs/spending/expenditure/expenses/overheads/outlay
- **capital** costs/spending/expenditure/expenses/outlay
- **household** costs/spending/expenditure/expenses
- **government/public/education/health** costs/spending/expenditure
- to **increase/reduce** costs/spending/expenditure/expenses/overheads/the outlay

■ ***verb*** (-rr-) **1** [I] **~ (with sb)** to appear as one of the main actors with sb in a play or film/movie: *a new movie in which Russell Crowe co-stars with Cate Blanchett* **2** [T] **~ sb** (of a film/movie or play) to have two or more famous actors acting in it: *a new movie co-starring Russell Crowe and Cate Blanchett*

ˈ**cost-benefit** *noun* [U] (*economics*) the relationship between the cost of doing sth and the value of the benefit that results from it: *cost-benefit analysis*

ˈ**cost-cutting** *noun* [U] the reduction of the amount of money spent on sth, especially because of financial difficulty: *Deliveries of mail could be delayed because of cost-cutting.* ◇ *a* ***cost-cutting exercise/measure/programme***

ˌ**cost-efˈfective** *adj.* giving the best possible profit or benefits in comparison with the money that is spent ▸ ˌ**cost-efˈfect·ive·ness** *noun* [U]

cos·ter·mon·ger /ˈkɒstəmʌŋɡə(r); *NAmE* ˈkɑːstərm-/ *noun* (*BrE*) (in the past) a person who sold fruit and vegetables in the street

cost·ing /ˈkɒstɪŋ; *NAmE* ˈkɔːst-/ *noun* an estimate of how much money will be needed for sth: *Here is a detailed costing of our proposals.* ◇ *You'd better do some costings.*

cost·ly /ˈkɒstli; *NAmE* ˈkɔːst-/ *adj.* (**cost·lier, cost·li·est**) HELP You can also use **more costly** and **most costly**. **1** costing a lot of money, especially more than you want to pay SYN **expensive**: *Buying new furniture may prove too costly.* ➲ SYNONYMS at EXPENSIVE **2** causing problems or the loss of sth SYN **expensive**: *a* ***costly mistake/failure*** ◇ *Mining can be costly in terms of lives* (= too many people can die). ▸ **cost·li·ness** *noun* [U]

the ˌcost of ˈliving *noun* [sing.] the amount of money that people need to pay for food, clothing and somewhere to live: *a steady rise in the cost of living* ◇ *the high cost of living in London*

ˌcost ˈprice *noun* [U] the cost of producing sth or the price at which it is sold without profit: *Copies of the CD can be purchased at cost price.* ➲ compare SELLING PRICE

cos·tume /ˈkɒstjuːm; *NAmE* ˈkɑːstuːm/ *noun* **1** [C, U] the clothes worn by people from a particular place or during a particular historical period ➲ see also NATIONAL COSTUME **2** [C, U] the clothes worn by actors in a play or film/movie, or worn by sb to make them look like sth else: *The actors were still in costume and make-up.* ◇ *She has four costume changes during the play.* ◇ *He went to the party in a giant chicken costume.* ◇ *a costume designer* **3** [C] (*BrE, informal*) = SWIMMING COSTUME

cos·tumed /ˈkɒstjuːmd; *NAmE* ˈkɑːstuːmd/ *adj.* [usually before noun] wearing a costume

ˈcostume drama *noun* [C, U] a play or film/movie set in the past

ˈcostume jewellery *noun* [U] large heavy jewellery that can look expensive but is made with cheap materials

ˈcostume party *noun* (*NAmE*) a party where all the guests wear special clothes, in order to look like a different person, an animal, etc.

cos·tu·mier /kɒsˈtjuːmiə(r); *NAmE* kɑːsˈtuːmieɪ/ (*BrE*) (*NAmE* **ˈcos·tu·mer**) *noun* a person or company that makes COSTUMES or has COSTUMES to hire, especially for the theatre: *a firm of theatrical costumiers*

cosy (*BrE*) (*NAmE* **cozy**) /ˈkəʊzi; *NAmE* ˈkoʊzi/ *adj., verb*

■ ***adj.*** (**cosi·er, cosi·est, cozi·er, cozi·est**) **1** warm, comfortable and safe, especially because of being small or confined SYN **snug**: *a cosy little room* ◇ *a cosy feeling* ◇ *I felt warm and cosy sitting by the fire.* **2** friendly and private: *a cosy chat with a friend* **3** (often *disapproving*) easy and convenient, but not always honest or right: *The firm has a cosy relationship with the Ministry of Defence.* ◇ *The danger is that things get too cosy.* ▶ **cosi·ly** (*BrE*) (*NAmE* **cozi·ly**) *adv.*: *sitting cosily by the fire* **cosi·ness** (*BrE*) (*NAmE* **cozi·ness**) *noun* [U]: *the warmth and cosiness of the kitchen*

■ ***verb*** (**cosies, cosy·ing, cosied, cosied**)

PHR V **ˌcosy ˈup to sb** (*BrE*) (*NAmE* **ˌcozy ˈup to sb**) (*informal*) to act in a friendly way towards sb, especially sb who will be useful to you

cot /kɒt; *NAmE* kɑːt/ *noun* **1** (*BrE*) (*NAmE* **crib**) a small bed with high sides for a baby or young child: *a travel cot* (= one that can be moved around easily, used when travelling) ➲ VISUAL VOCAB page V20 ➲ see also CARRYCOT **2** (*NAmE*) (*BrE* **ˌcamp ˈbed**) a light narrow bed that you can fold up and carry easily ➲ VISUAL VOCAB page V20

ˈcot death (*BrE*) (*NAmE* **ˈcrib death**) *noun* [U, C] the sudden death while sleeping of a baby that appears to be healthy

co·terie /ˈkəʊtəri; *NAmE* ˈkoʊ-/ *noun* [C+sing./pl. v.] (*formal*, often *disapproving*) a small group of people who have the same interests and do things together but do not like to include others

co·ter·min·ous /kəʊˈtɜːmɪnəs; *NAmE* koʊˈtɜːrm-/ *adj.* [not usually before noun] (*formal*) **1** ~ (**with sth**) (of countries or areas) sharing a border **2** ~ (**with sth**) (of things or ideas) having so much in common that they are almost the same as each other

cot·tage 0-w /ˈkɒtɪdʒ; *NAmE* ˈkɑːt-/ *noun* a small house, especially in the country: *a charming country cottage with roses around the door* ◇ (*BrE*) *a holiday cottage* ➲ VISUAL VOCAB page V14

ˌcottage ˈcheese *noun* [U] soft white cheese with small lumps in it

ˌcottage ˈhospital *noun* (*BrE*) a small hospital in a country area

ˌcot·tage ˈin·dus·try *noun* a small business in which the work is done by people in their homes: *Weaving and knitting are traditional cottage industries.*

ˌcottage ˈloaf *noun* (*BrE*) a LOAF of bread consisting of a large round piece with a smaller round piece on top

ˌcottage ˈpie *noun* [C, U] = SHEPHERD'S PIE

cot·tager /ˈkɒtɪdʒə(r); *NAmE* ˈkɑːt-/ *noun* (*BrE*) (especially in the past) a person who lives in a small house or cottage in the country

cot·ta·ging /ˈkɒtɪdʒɪŋ; *NAmE* ˈkɑːt-/ *noun* [U] (*BrE, slang*) the practice of HOMOSEXUAL men looking for sexual partners in a public toilet/bathroom

cot·ton 0-w /ˈkɒtn; *NAmE* ˈkɑːtn/ *noun, verb*

■ ***noun*** [U] **1** 0-w a plant grown in warm countries for the soft white hairs around its seeds that are used to make cloth and thread: ***cotton fields/plants*** ◇ *bales of cotton* **2** 0-w the cloth made from the cotton plant: *The sheets are 100% pure cotton.* ◇ *a cotton shirt/skirt* ◇ *printed cotton cloth* ◇ *the cotton industry* ◇ *a cotton mill* **3** (*especially BrE*) thread that is used for sewing: *sewing cotton* ◇ *a cotton reel* ➲ VISUAL VOCAB page V35 **4** (*NAmE*) (*US* also **abˌsorbent ˈcotton**) (*BrE* **ˌcotton ˈwool**) a soft mass of white material that is used for cleaning the skin or a wound: *Use a cotton ball to apply the lotion.*

■ ***verb***

PHR V **ˌcotton ˈon** (**to sth**) (*informal*) to begin to understand or realize sth without being told: *I suddenly cottoned on to what he was doing.* **ˈcotton** (**up**) **to sb/sth** (*NAmE, informal*) to make an attempt to be friendly to sb

the ˈCotton Belt *noun* the states in the southern US where cotton was the main crop

ˌcotton ˈbud (*BrE*) (also **Q-tip™** *NAmE, BrE*) *noun* a small stick with COTTON WOOL at each end, used for cleaning inside the ears, etc.

ˌcotton ˈcandy (*NAmE*) (*BrE* **candy·floss**) *noun* [U] a type of sweet/candy in the form of a mass of sticky threads made from melted sugar and served on a stick, especially at FAIRGROUNDS

ˈcotton gin (also **gin**) *noun* a machine for separating the seeds of a cotton plant from the cotton

cotton·mouth /ˈkɒtnmaʊθ; *NAmE* ˈkɑːtn-/ (also **ˌcottonmouth ˈmoccasin, ˌwater ˈmoccasin**) *noun* a poisonous snake which lives near water in the US

cot·ton·wood /ˈkɒtnwʊd; *NAmE* ˈkɑːtn-/ (also **ˈcottonwood tree**) *noun* a type of N American POPLAR tree, with seeds that are covered in hairs that look like white cotton

ˌcotton ˈwool (*BrE*) (*US* **abˌsorbent ˈcotton**) *noun* [U] a soft mass of white material that is used for cleaning the skin or a wound: *cotton wool balls*

couch /kaʊtʃ/ *noun, verb*

■ ***noun*** **1** a long comfortable seat for two or more people to sit on SYN **settee, sofa** ➲ VISUAL VOCAB page V18 **2** a long piece of furniture like a bed, especially in a doctor's office: *on the psychiatrist's couch*

■ ***verb*** [usually passive] **~ sth** (**in sth**) (*formal*) to say or write words in a particular style or manner: *The letter was deliberately **couched in** very vague **terms**.*

couch·ette /kuːˈʃet/ *noun* a narrow bed on a train, that folds down from the wall

ˈcouch potato *noun* (*informal, disapproving*) a person who spends a lot of time sitting and watching television

cou·gar /ˈkuːgə(r)/ *noun* (*especially NAmE*) = PUMA

cough 0-w /kɒf; *NAmE* kɔːf/ *verb, noun*

■ ***verb*** **1** 0-w [I] to force out air suddenly and noisily through your throat, for example when you have a cold: *I couldn't stop coughing.* ◇ *to **cough nervously/politely/discreetly*** **2** [T] **~ sth** (**up**) to force sth out of your throat or lungs by coughing: *Sometimes she coughed (up) blood.* **3** [I] (of an engine) to make a sudden unpleasant noise

PHR V **ˌcough ˈup** | **ˌcough sth↔ˈup** (*informal*) to give sth, especially money, unwillingly: *Steve finally coughed up the money he owed us.*

■ ***noun*** **1** 0-w an act or a sound of coughing: *She gave a little cough to attract my attention.* **2** 0-w an illness or infection that makes you cough often: *to have a **dry/persistent/hacking cough*** ◇ *My cold's better, but I can't seem to shake off this cough.* ➲ see also WHOOPING COUGH

cough·ing /ˈkɒfɪŋ; *NAmE* ˈkɔːfɪŋ/ *noun* [U] the action of coughing: *Another fit of coughing seized him.*

ˈ**cough mixture** (*BrE*) (also ˈ**cough syrup**, ˈ**cough medicine** *BrE, NAmE*) *noun* [U] liquid medicine that you take for a cough

C

could /kəd; *strong form* kʊd/ *modal verb* (*negative* **could not**, *short form* **couldn't** /ˈkʊdnt/) **1** used as the past tense of 'can': *She said that she couldn't come.* ◇ *I couldn't hear what they were saying.* ◇ *Sorry, I couldn't get any more.* ➲ note at CAN¹ **2** used to ask if you can do sth: *Could I use your phone, please?* ◇ *Could we stop by next week?* **3** used to politely ask sb to do sth for you: *Could you babysit for us on Friday?* **4** used to show that sth is or might be possible: *I could do it now, if you like.* ◇ *Don't worry—they could have just forgotten to call.* ◇ *You couldn't have left it on the bus, could you?* ◇ *'Have some more cake.' 'Oh, I couldn't, thank you* (= I'm too full).' **5** used to suggest sth: *We could write a letter to the director.* ◇ *You could always try his home number.* **6** used to show that you are annoyed that sb did not do sth: *They could have let me know they were going to be late!* **7** (*informal*) used to emphasize how strongly you want to express your feelings: *I'm so fed up I could scream!* ➲ note at MODAL

IDM **could do with sth** (*informal*) used to say that you need or would like to have sth: *I could do with a drink!* ◇ *Her hair could have done with a wash.*

cou·lis /ˈkuːli; *NAmE* kuːˈliː/ *noun* (*pl.* **cou·lis**) (from *French*) a thin fruit sauce

cou·lomb /ˈkuːlɒm; *NAmE* -lɑːm; -lɔːm/ *noun* (*abbr.* C) (*physics*) a unit for measuring electric charge

coun·cil /ˈkaʊnsl/ *noun* [C+sing./pl. v.] **1** a group of people who are elected to govern an area such as a city or county: *a **city/county/borough/district council*** ◇ *She's on the local council.* ◇ *a **council member/meeting*** **2** (*BrE*) the organization that provides services in a city or county, for example education, houses, libraries, etc: ***council workers/services*** **3** a group of people chosen to give advice, make rules, do research, provide money, etc: *the Medical Research Council* ◇ *In Britain, the Arts Council gives grants to theatres.* **4** (*formal*) (especially in the past) a formal meeting to discuss what action to take in a particular situation: *The King held a council at Nottingham from 14 to 19 October 1330.* ➲ see also PRIVY COUNCIL

ˈ**council chamber** *noun* (*BrE*) a large room in which a council meets

ˈ**council estate** *noun* (*BrE*) a large group of houses built by a local council

ˈ**council house**, ˈ**council flat** *noun* (*BrE*) a house or flat rented from the local council

coun·cil·lor (*NAmE* also **coun·cil·or**) /ˈkaʊnsələ(r)/ *noun* (*abbr.* Cllr) a member of a council: *Councillor Ann Jones* ◇ *Talk to your local councillor about the problem.* ➲ see also COUNCILMAN, COUNCILWOMAN

coun·cil·man /ˈkaʊnslmən/ *noun* (*pl.* **-men** /-mən/) (*US*) = COUNCILLOR

ˌ**council of ˈwar** *noun* (*pl.* **councils of war**) (*BrE*) a meeting to discuss how to deal with an urgent and difficult situation

ˈ**council tax** *noun* (often **the council tax**) [sing., U] (in Britain) a tax charged by local councils, based on the value of a person's home

coun·cil·woman /ˈkaʊnslwʊmən/ *noun* (*pl.* **-women** /-wɪmɪn/) (*US*) = COUNCILLOR

coun·sel /ˈkaʊnsl/ *noun, verb*

■ ***noun*** [U, C] **1** (*formal*) advice, especially given by older people or experts; a piece of advice: *Listen to the counsel of your elders.* ◇ *In the end, wiser counsels prevailed.* **2** (*law*) a lawyer or group of lawyers representing sb in court: *to be represented by counsel* ◇ *the **counsel for the defence/prosecution*** ◇ ***defence/prosecuting counsel*** ◇ *The court then heard counsel for the dead woman's father.* ➲ COLLOCATIONS at JUSTICE ➲ see also KING'S/QUEEN'S COUNSEL ➲ note at LAWYER

IDM **a counsel of desˈpair** (*formal*) advice not to try to do sth because it is too difficult **a counsel of perˈfection** (*formal*) advice that is good but that is difficult or impossible to follow **keep your own ˈcounsel** (*formal*) to keep your opinions, plans, etc. secret

■ ***verb*** (-ll-, *especially US* -l-) **1** ~ **sb** to listen to and give support or professional advice to sb who needs help: *Therapists were brought in to counsel the bereaved.* **2** (*formal*) to advise sb to do sth: ~ **sth** *Most experts counsel caution in such cases.* ◇ ~ **sb to do sth** *He counselled them to give up the plan.*

coun·sel·ling (*especially US* **coun·sel·ing**) /ˈkaʊnsəlɪŋ/ *noun* [U] professional advice about a problem: *marriage guidance counselling* ◇ *a student counselling service*

coun·sel·lor (*especially US* **coun·sel·or**) /ˈkaʊnsələ(r)/ *noun* **1** a person who has been trained to advise people with problems, especially personal problems: *a marriage guidance counsellor* **2** (*NAmE, IrishE*) a lawyer **3** (*NAmE*) a person who is in charge of young people at a summer camp

count /kaʊnt/ *verb, noun*

■ ***verb***

▸ SAY NUMBERS **1** [I] to say numbers in the correct order: *Billy can't count yet.* ◇ ~ **to/up to sth** *She can count up to 10 in Italian.* ◇ ~ (**from sth**) **to/up to sth** *to count from 1 to 10*

▸ FIND TOTAL **2** [T, I] to calculate the total number of people, things, etc. in a particular group: ~ **sth** (**up**) *The diet is based on counting calories.* ◇ ~ (**up**) **how many...** *She began to count up how many guests they had to invite.* ◇ ~ **from...** *There are 12 weeks to go, counting from today.*

▸ INCLUDE **3** [T] ~ **sb/sth** to include sb/sth when you calculate a total: *We have invited 50 people, **not counting** the children.*

▸ MATTER **4** [I] (not used in the progressive tenses) to be important SYN **matter**: *Every point in this game counts.* ◇ ***It's the thought that counts*** (= used about a small but kind action or gift). ◇ ~ **for sth** *The fact that she had apologized counted for nothing with him.*

▸ ACCEPT OFFICIALLY **5** [I, T] to be officially accepted; to accept sth officially: *Don't go over that line or your throw won't count.* ◇ ~ **sth** *Applications received after 1 July will not be counted.*

▸ CONSIDER **6** [I, T] ~ **as sb/sth** | ~ **sb/sth** (**as**) **sb/sth** to consider sb/sth in a particular way; to be considered in a particular way: ~ (**sb/sth**) **as sb/sth** *For tax purposes that money counts/is counted as income.* ◇ ~ **sb/sth/yourself + adv./prep.** *I count him among my closest friends.* ◇ ~ **sb/sth/yourself + adj.** ***I count myself lucky** to have known him.* ◇ ~ **sb/sth/yourself + noun** *She counts herself one of the lucky ones.*

IDM **be able to count sb/sth on** (**the fingers of**) **one ˈhand** used to say that the total number of sb/sth is very small **...and ˈcounting** used to say that a total is continuing to increase: *The movie's ticket sales add up to $39 million, and counting.* **count your ˈblessings** to be grateful for the good things in your life **don't count your ˈchickens** (**before they are ˈhatched**) (*saying*) you should not be too confident that sth will be successful, because sth may still go wrong **count the cost** (**of sth**) to feel the bad effects of a mistake, an accident, etc: *The town is now counting the cost of its failure to provide adequate flood protection.* **count ˈsheep** to imagine that sheep are jumping over a fence and to count them, as a way of getting to sleep **stand up and be ˈcounted** to say publicly that you support sb or you agree with sth **who's ˈcounting?** (*informal*) used to say that you do not care how many times sth happens

PHR V ˌ**count aˈgainst sb** | ˌ**count sth aˈgainst sb** to be considered or to consider sth to be a disadvantage in sb: *For that job her lack of experience may count against her.* ˌ**count ˈdown** (**to sth**) to think about a future event with pleasure or excitement and count the minutes, days, etc. until it happens: *She's already counting down to the big day.* ➲ related noun COUNTDOWN ˌ**count sb ˈin** to include sb in an activity: *I hear you're organizing a trip to the game next week? Count me in!* ˈ**count on sb/sth** to trust sb to do sth or to be sure that sth will happen **SYN bank on sth:** *'I'm sure he'll help.' '**Don't count on it.**'* ◇ **~ sb/sth to do sth** *I'm counting on you to help me.* ◇ **~ doing sth** *Few people can count on having a job for life.* ◇ **~ sb/sth doing sth** *We can't count on this warm weather lasting.* ➲ SYNONYMS at TRUST **ˌcount sb/sth↔ˈout** to count things one after the other as you put them somewhere: *She counted out $70 in $10 bills.* **ˌcount sb ˈout** to not include sb in an activity: *If you're going out tonight you'll have to count me out.* **ˌcount toˈwards/toˈward sth** to be included as part of sth that you hope to achieve in the future: *Students gain college credits which count towards their degree.*

■ ***noun***

▸ TOTAL **1** [usually sing.] an act of counting to find the total number of sth; the total number that you find: *The bus driver did a quick count of the empty seats.* ◇ *If the election result is close, there will be a second count.* ◇ *The body count* (= the total number of people who have died) *stands at 24.* ➲ see also HEADCOUNT

▸ SAYING NUMBERS **2** [usually sing.] an act of saying numbers in order beginning with 1: *Raise your leg and hold for a count of ten.* ◇ *He was knocked to the ground and stayed down for a count of eight* (= in boxing).

▸ MEASUREMENT **3** [usually sing.] (*technical*) a measurement of the amount of sth contained in a particular substance or area: *a raised white blood cell count* ➲ see also BLOOD COUNT, POLLEN COUNT

▸ CRIME **4** (*law*) a crime that sb is accused of committing: *They were found guilty on all counts.* ◇ *She appeared in court on three counts of fraud.*

▸ IN DISCUSSION/ARGUMENT **5** [usually pl.] a point made during a discussion or an argument: *I disagree with you on both counts.*

▸ RANK/TITLE **6** (in some European countries) a NOBLEMAN of high rank, similar to an EARL in Britain: *Count Tolstoy* ➲ see also COUNTESS

IDM **at the last ˈcount** according to the latest information about the numbers of sth: *She'd applied for 30 jobs at the last count.* **keep (a) count (of sth)** to remember or keep a record of numbers or amounts of sth over a period of time: *Keep a count of your calorie intake for one week.* **lose count (of sth)** to forget the total of sth before you have finished counting it: *I lost count and had to start again.* ◇ *She had lost count of the number of times she'd told him to be careful* (= she could not remember because there were so many). **ˌout for the ˈcount** (*BrE*) (*NAmE* **ˌdown for the ˈcount**) **1** (of a BOXER) unable to get up again within ten seconds after being knocked down **2** in a deep sleep

count·able /ˈkaʊntəbl/ *adj.* (*grammar*) a noun that is **countable** can be used in the plural or with *a* or *an*, for example *table, cat* and *idea* **OPP uncountable**

count·down /ˈkaʊntdaʊn/ *noun* **~ (to sth) 1** [sing., U] the action of counting seconds backwards to zero, for example before a SPACECRAFT is launched **2** [sing.] the period of time just before sth important happens: *the countdown to the wedding*

coun·ten·ance /ˈkaʊntənəns/ *noun, verb*

■ ***noun*** (*formal* or *literary*) a person's face or their expression

■ ***verb*** **~ sth | ~ (sb) doing sth** (*formal*) to support sth or agree to sth happening **SYN consent to**: *The committee refused to countenance his proposals.*

coun·ter 🔑 /ˈkaʊntə(r)/ *noun, verb, adv.*

■ ***noun*** **1** 🔑 a long flat surface over which goods are sold or business is done in a shop/store, bank, etc: *I asked the woman **behind the counter** if they had any postcards.* **2** (also **counter·top**) (both *NAmE*) (*BrE* **work·top**, **ˈwork surface**) a flat surface in a kitchen for preparing food on ➲ VISUAL VOCAB page V22 **3** a small disc used for playing or scoring in some board games ➲ VISUAL VOCAB page V33 ➲ see also BARGAINING COUNTER **4** (especially in compounds) an electronic device for counting sth: *The needle on the rev counter soared.* ➲ VISUAL VOCAB page V42 ➲ see also GEIGER COUNTER ➲ compare BEAN COUNTER **5** [usually sing.] **~ (to sb/sth)** (*formal*) a response to sb/sth that opposes their ideas, position, etc: *The employers' association was seen as a counter to union power.*

IDM **over the ˈcounter** goods, especially medicines, for sale **over the counter** can be bought without a PRESCRIPTION (= written permission from a doctor to buy a medicine) or special licence: *These tablets are available over the counter.* ➲ see also OVER-THE-COUNTER **under the ˈcounter** goods that are bought or sold **under the counter** are sold secretly and sometimes illegally

■ ***verb*** **1** [T, I] **~ (sb/sth) (with sth)** to reply to sb by trying to prove that what they said is not true: **~ sb/sth** *Such arguments are not easily countered.* ◇ **~ that...** *I tried to argue but he countered that the plans were not yet finished.* ◇ **~ (sb) + speech** *'But I was standing right here!' he countered.* ◇ **~ with sth** *Butler has countered with a lawsuit against the firm.* **2** [T] **~ sth** to do sth to reduce or prevent the bad effects of sth **SYN counteract**: *Businesses would like to see new laws to counter late payments of debts.*

■ ***adv.*** **~ to sth** in the opposite direction to sth; in opposition to sth: *The government's plans **run counter** to agreed European policy on this issue.*

counter- /ˈkaʊntə(r)/ *combining form* (in nouns, verbs, adjectives and adverbs) **1** against; opposite: *counterterrorism* ◇ *counter-argument* **2** CORRESPONDING: *counterpart*

coun·ter·act /ˌkaʊntərˈækt/ *verb* **~ sth** to do sth to reduce or prevent the bad or harmful effects of sth **SYN counter**: *These exercises aim to counteract the effects of stress and tension.*

ˈcounter-attack *noun, verb*

■ ***noun*** an attack made in response to the attack of an enemy or opponent in war, sport or an argument

■ ***verb*** [I, T] **~ (sb)** to make an attack in response to the attack of an enemy or opponent in war, sport or an argument **SYN retaliate**

coun·ter·bal·ance *verb, noun*

■ ***verb*** /ˌkaʊntəˈbæləns; *NAmE* ˌkaʊntərˈb-/ **~ sth** (*formal*) to have an equal but opposite effect to sth else **SYN offset**: *Parents' natural desire to protect their children should be counterbalanced by the child's need for independence.*

■ ***noun*** /ˈkaʊntəbæləns; *NAmE* ˈkaʊntərb-/ (also **coun·ter·weight**) [usually sing.] **~ (to sth)** a thing that has an equal but opposite effect to sth else and can be used to limit the bad effects of sth: *The accused's right to silence was a vital counterbalance to the powers of the police.*

coun·ter·blast /ˈkaʊntəblɑːst; *NAmE* ˈkaʊntərblæst/ *noun* **~ (to sth)** a very strong spoken or written reply to sth that has been said or written

coun·ter·claim /ˈkaʊntəkleɪm; *NAmE* -tərk-/ *noun* a claim made in reply to another claim and different from it

coun·ter·clock·wise /ˌkaʊntəˈklɒkwaɪz; *NAmE* -tərˈklɑːk-/ (*NAmE*) (*BrE* **anti·clock·wise**) *adv., adj.* in the opposite direction to the movement of the hands of a clock **OPP clockwise**

coun·ter·cul·ture /ˈkaʊntəkʌltʃə(r); *NAmE* -tərk-/ *noun* [C, U] a way of life and set of ideas that are opposed to those accepted by most of society; a group of people who share such a way of life and such ideas

ˌcounter-ˈespion·age *noun* [U] secret action taken by a country to prevent an enemy country from finding out its secrets

coun·ter·fac·tual /ˌkaʊntəˈfæktʃuəl; *NAmE* -tər-/ *adj.* (*formal*) connected with what did not happen or what is not the case: *counterfactual questions such as 'What if the President had not been assassinated?'* ◇ *an interesting exercise in counterfactual history* ▸ **coun·ter·fac·tual** *noun*: *'What if' questions involving counterfactuals are familiar in historical speculations.*

coun·ter·feit /ˈkaʊntəfɪt; *NAmE* -tərf-/ *adj., verb*

■ ***adj.*** (*formal*) (of money and goods for sale) made to look exactly like sth in order to trick people into thinking that they are getting the real thing **SYN fake**: *counterfeit watches* ◇ *Are you aware these notes are counterfeit?* **OPP genuine** ▸ **coun·ter·feit** *noun* ➲ compare FORGERY

■ ***verb*** **~ sth** (*formal*) to make an exact copy of sth in order to trick people into thinking that it is the real thing ➲ compare FORGE ▸ **coun·ter·feit·ing** *noun* [U]

C

coun·ter·feit·er /ˈkaʊntəfɪtə(r); *NAmE* -tərf-/ *noun* a person who counterfeits money or goods ➲ compare FORGER

coun·ter·foil /ˈkaʊntəfɔɪl; *NAmE* -tərfɔɪl/ *noun* (*BrE*) the part of a cheque, ticket, etc. that you keep when you give the other part to sb else SYN **stub**

ˌcounter-inˈsurgency *noun* [U] action taken against a group of people who are trying to take control of a country by force

ˌcounter-inˈtelli·gence *noun* [U] secret action taken by a country to prevent an enemy country from finding out its secrets, for example by giving them false information; the department of a government, etc. that is responsible for this

ˌcounter-inˈtuitive *adj.* the opposite of what you would expect or what seems to be obvious: *These results seem counter-intuitive.* ▶ **ˌcounter-inˈtuitive·ly** *adv.*

coun·ter·mand /ˌkaʊntəˈmɑːnd; *NAmE* ˈkaʊntərmænd/ *verb* **~ sth** (*formal*) to cancel an order that has been given, especially by giving a different order

coun·ter·meas·ure /ˈkaʊntəmeʒə(r); *NAmE* -tərm-/ *noun* a course of action taken to protect against sth that is considered bad or dangerous

coun·ter·of·fen·sive /ˈkaʊntərəfensɪv/ *noun* an attack made in order to defend against enemy attacks

coun·ter·pane /ˈkaʊntəpeɪn; *NAmE* -tərp-/ *noun* (*old-fashioned, BrE*) = BEDSPREAD

coun·ter·part /ˈkaʊntəpɑːt; *NAmE* -tərpɑːrt/ *noun* a person or thing that has the same position or function as sb/sth else in a different place or situation SYN **opposite number**: *The Foreign Minister held talks with his Chinese counterpart.* ◇ *The women's shoe, like its male counterpart, is specifically designed for the serious tennis player.*

coun·ter·point /ˈkaʊntəpɔɪnt; *NAmE* -tərp-/ *noun, verb*
- *noun* **1** [U] (*music*) the combination of two or more tunes played together to form a single piece of music SYN **polyphony**: *The two melodies are played in counterpoint.* ➲ see also CONTRAPUNTAL **2** [C] **~ (to sth)** (*music*) a tune played in combination with another one **3** [U, C] (*formal*) a pleasing or interesting contrast: *This work is in austere counterpoint to that of Gaudi.*
- *verb* **~ sth (with/against sth)** (*formal*) to contrast sth with sth else; to form a contrast with sth

coun·ter·pro·duct·ive /ˌkaʊntəprəˈdʌktɪv; *NAmE* -tərp-/ *adj.* [not usually before noun] having the opposite effect to the one which was intended ➲ compare PRODUCTIVE

ˌcounter-ˌrevoˈlu·tion *noun* [C, U] opposition to or violent action against a government that came to power as a result of a revolution, in order to destroy and replace it

ˌcounter-ˌrevoˈlu·tion·ary *noun* a person involved in a counter-revolution ▶ **ˌcounter-ˌrevoˈlu·tion·ary** *adj.*

coun·ter·sign /ˈkaʊntəsaɪn; *NAmE* -tərs-/ *verb* **~ sth** (*technical*) to sign a document that has already been signed by another person, especially in order to show that it is valid

coun·ter·tenor /ˌkaʊntəˈtenə(r); *NAmE* ˌkaʊntər-/ *noun* a man who is trained to sing with a very high voice; a male ALTO ➲ compare ALTO

counter·terror·ism /ˌkaʊntəˈterərɪzəm; *NAmE* ˌkaʊntər-/ *noun* [U] action taken to prevent the activities of political groups who use violence to try to achieve their aims ▶ **counter·terror·ist** /ˌkaʊntəˈterərɪst; *NAmE* ˌkaʊntər-/ *adj.*

coun·ter·top /ˈkaʊntətɒp; *NAmE* ˈkaʊntərtɑːp/ *noun* (*NAmE*) = COUNTER

coun·ter·vail·ing /ˈkaʊntəveɪlɪŋ; *NAmE* -tərv-/ *adj.* [only before noun] (*formal*) having an equal but opposite effect

coun·ter·weight /ˈkaʊntəweɪt; *NAmE* -tərw-/ *noun* [usually sing.] = COUNTERBALANCE

count·ess /ˈkaʊntəs; -es/ *noun* **1** a woman who has the rank of a COUNT or an EARL **2** the wife of a COUNT or an EARL: *the Earl and Countess of Rosebery*

count·less /ˈkaʊntləs/ *adj.* [usually before noun] very many; too many to be counted or mentioned: *I've warned her countless times.* ◇ *The new treatment could save Emma's life and the lives of countless others.* ➲ compare UNCOUNTABLE

ˈcount noun *noun* (*grammar*) a countable noun OPP **uncount noun**

coun·tri·fied /ˈkʌntrifaɪd/ *adj.* (often *disapproving*) like the countryside or the people who live there

Synonyms

country

landscape • countryside • terrain • land • scenery

These are all words for areas away from towns and cities, with fields, woods and farms.

country (often **the country**) an area that is away from towns and cities, especially one with particular natural features: *She lives in the country.* ◇ *an area of wooded country*

landscape everything that you can see when you look across a large area of land, especially in the country: *This pattern of woods and fields is typical of the English landscape.*

countryside land outside towns and cities, with fields, woods and farms. NOTE **Countryside** is usually used when you are talking about the beauty or peacefulness of a country area: *a little village in the French countryside.*

terrain (*formal*) land. NOTE **Terrain** is used when you are describing the natural features of an area, for example if it is rough, flat, etc: *The truck bumped its way over the rough terrain.*

land (usually **the land**) the countryside; the way people live in the country as opposed to in towns and cities: *Many younger people are leaving the land to find work in the cities.*

scenery the natural features of an area, such as mountains, valleys, rivers and forests, especially when these are attractive to look at: *We stopped on the mountain pass to admire the scenery.*

PATTERNS
- **mountainous/mountain/wild/rugged** country/landscape/countryside/terrain/scenery
- **beautiful/glorious/dramatic** country/landscape/countryside/scenery
- **open** country/landscape/countryside/terrain/land
- **rolling** country/landscape/countryside
- to **protect** the landscape/countryside/land

coun·try 0‑w /ˈkʌntri/ *noun* (*pl.* -ies)
1 0‑w [C] an area of land that has or used to have its own government and laws: *European countries* ◇ *leading industrial countries* ◇ *She didn't know what life in a* ***foreign country*** *would be like.* ◇ *It's good to meet people from* ***different parts of the country.*** **2** 0‑w [U] (often following an adjective) an area of land, especially with particular physical features, suitable for a particular purpose or connected with a particular person or people: ***open/wooded, etc. country*** ◇ *superb* ***walking country*** ◇ *Explore Thomas Hardy country.* ➲ see also BACKCOUNTRY **3** 0‑w **the country** [sing.] the people of a country; the nation as a whole: *They have the support of most of the country.* ◇ *The rich benefited from the reforms, not the* ***country as a whole.*** ➲ see also MOTHER COUNTRY, THE OLD COUNTRY, UP-COUNTRY **4** 0‑w **the country** [sing.] any area outside towns and cities, with fields, woods, farms, etc: *to live* ***in the country*** ◇ *We spent a pleasant day in the country.* ◇ *a country lane*

➲ COLLOCATIONS at TOWN **5** [U] = COUNTRY AND WESTERN: *pop, folk and country*

IDM **across 'country** directly across fields, etc; not by a main road: *riding across country* ➲ see also CROSS-COUNTRY **go to the 'country** (*BrE*) (of a government) to hold an election to choose a new parliament ➲ more at FREE *adj.*

Which Word?

country / state

- **Country** is the most usual, neutral word for a geographical area that has or used to have its own government.
- **State** emphasizes the political organization of an area under an independent government. Especially in *BrE*, it can also mean the government: *the member states of the EU* ◇ *The state provides free education.* In *NAmE* **the state** usually refers to one of the 50 states of the US, not to the government of the country as a whole.

ˌcountry and 'western (*abbr.* C & W) (also **'country music, country**) *noun* [U] a type of music in the style of the traditional music of the southern and western US: *a country and western singer*

ˌcountry 'bumpkin (also **bump·kin**) *noun* (*disapproving*) a person from the countryside who seems stupid

'country club *noun* a club in the country, or on the edge of a town, where people can play sports and go to social events

ˌcountry 'cousin *noun* a person from the country who does not know much about life in the city, and who dresses or behaves in a way that shows this

ˌcountry 'dance *noun* (*BrE*) a type of traditional dance, especially one in which couples dance in long lines or circles ▸ **ˌcountry 'dancing** *noun* [U]

ˌcountry 'house *noun* (*BrE*) a large house in the country, especially one that belongs or used to belong to a rich important family

coun·try·made /ˈkʌntrimeɪd/ *adj.* (*IndE*) not made by a professional person: *a countrymade pistol*

coun·try·man /ˈkʌntrimən/ *noun* (*pl.* **-men** /-mən/) **1** a person born in or living in the same country as sb else SYN **compatriot**: *The champion looks set to play his* ***fellow countryman*** *in the final.* **2** a man living or born in the country, not in the town

ˌcountry 'mile *noun* (becoming *old-fashioned, especially BrE*) a long distance: *He won the race by a country mile.*

'country music *noun* [U] = COUNTRY AND WESTERN

ˌcountry 'seat *noun* (*BrE*) = SEAT (7)

coun·try·side 0‑ᴡ /ˈkʌntrisaɪd/ *noun* [U] land outside towns and cities, with fields, woods, etc: *The surrounding countryside is windswept and rocky.* ◇ *magnificent views over open countryside* ◇ *Everyone should enjoy the right of access to the countryside.* ➲ SYNONYMS at COUNTRY ➲ COLLOCATIONS at TOWN ➲ VISUAL VOCAB pages V2, V3

coun·try·wide /ˌkʌntriˈwaɪd/ *adj.* over the whole of a country SYN **nationwide**: *a countrywide mail-order service* ▸ **coun·try·wide** *adv.*: *The film will be released in London in March and countrywide in May.*

coun·try·woman /ˈkʌntriwʊmən/ *noun* (*pl.* **-women** /-wɪmɪn/) **1** a woman living or born in the country, not the town **2** a woman born or living in the same country as sb else

county 0‑ᴡ /ˈkaʊnti/ *noun, adj.*

■ ***noun*** 0‑ᴡ (*pl.* **-ies**) (*abbr.* **Co.**) an area of Britain, Ireland or the US that has its own government: *the southern counties* ◇ *county boundaries* ◇ *Orange County* ➲ see also THE HOME COUNTIES

■ ***adj.*** (*BrE*, usually *disapproving*) typical of English upper-class people

ˌcounty 'clerk *noun* (in the US) an elected county official who is responsible for elections and who keeps records of who owns buildings in the county, etc.

ˌcounty 'council *noun* [C+sing./pl. v.] (in Britain) a group of people elected to the local government of a county: *a member of Lancashire County Council* ▸ **ˌcounty 'councillor** *noun*

ˌcounty 'court *noun* a local court. In Britain county courts only deal with private disagreements but in the US they also deal with criminal cases. ➲ compare CROWN COURT

ˌcounty 'town (*BrE*) (*NAmE* **ˌcounty 'seat**) *noun* the main town of a county, where its government is

coun·ty·wide /ˌkaʊntiˈwaɪd/ *adj.* over the whole of a county ▸ **coun·ty·wide** *adv.*

coup /kuː/ *noun* (*pl.* **coups** /kuːz/) **1** (also **coup d'état**) a sudden change of government that is illegal and often violent: *He seized power in a military coup in 2008.* ◇ *to* ***stage/mount a coup*** ◇ *an attempted coup* ◇ ***a failed/an abortive coup*** ◇ *She lost her position in a boardroom coup* (= a sudden change of power among senior managers in a company). **2** the fact of achieving sth that was difficult to do: *Getting this contract has been quite a coup for us.*

coup de grâce /ˌkuː də ˈɡrɑːs/ *noun* [sing.] (from *French*, *formal*) **1** an action or event that finally ends sth that has been getting weaker or worse: *My disastrous exam results dealt the coup de grâce to my university career.* **2** a hit or shot that finally kills a person or an animal, especially to put an end to their suffering SYN **death blow**

coup d'état /ˌkuː deɪˈtɑː/ *noun* (*pl.* **coups d'état** /ˌkuː deɪˈtɑː/) = COUP

coup de théâtre /ˌkuː də teɪˈɑːtrə/ *noun* (*pl.* **coups de théâtre** /ˌkuː də teɪˈɑːtrə/) (from *French*) **1** something very dramatic and surprising that happens, especially in a play **2** a play, show, etc. which is very successful

coupé /ˈkuːpeɪ; *NAmE* kuːˈpeɪ/ (*NAmE* also **coupe** /kuːp/) *noun* a car with two doors and usually a sloping back

couple 0‑ᴡ AW /ˈkʌpl/ *noun, verb*

■ ***noun*** HELP In *BrE* a plural verb is usually used in all 3 senses. **1** 0‑ᴡ [sing.+ sing./pl. v.] **~ (of sth)** two people or things: *I saw a couple of men get out.* **2** 0‑ᴡ [sing.+ sing./pl. v.] **~ (of sth)** a small number of people or things SYN **a few**: *a couple of minutes* ◇ *We went there a couple of years ago.* ◇ *I've seen her a couple of times before.* ◇ *I'll be with you in a minute. There are a couple of things I have to do first.* ◇ *There are a couple more files to read first.* ◇ *We can do it in the* ***next couple of*** *weeks.* ◇ *The* ***last couple of*** *years have been difficult.* **3** 0‑ᴡ [C+sing./pl. v.] two people who are seen together, especially if they are married or in a romantic or sexual relationship: *married couples* ◇ *a young/an elderly couple* ◇ *Several couples were on the dance floor.* ◇ *The couple was/were married in 2006.* ➲ COLLOCATIONS at MARRIAGE IDM see SHAKE *n.* ▸ **a couple** 0‑ᴡ *pron.*: *Do you need any more glasses? I've got a couple I can lend you.* **couple** *det.*: (*NAmE*) *It's only a couple blocks away.*

■ ***verb*** **1** [T, usually passive] to join together two parts of sth, for example two vehicles or pieces of equipment: **~ A and B together** *The two train cars had been coupled together.* ◇ **~ A (to B)** *CDTV uses a CD-ROM system that is coupled to a powerful computer.* **2** [I] (*formal*) (of two people or animals) to have sex

PHR V **'couple sb/sth with sb/sth** [usually passive] to link one thing, situation, etc. to another SYN **combine with**: *Overproduction, coupled with falling sales, has led to huge losses for the company.*

coup·let /ˈkʌplət/ *noun* two lines of poetry of equal length one after the other: *a poem written in rhyming couplets* ➲ see also HEROIC COUPLET

coup·ling AW /ˈkʌplɪŋ/ *noun* **1** [usually sing.] an action of joining or combining two things: *a coupling of Mozart's Prague Symphony and Schubert's Unfinished Symphony* (= for example, on the same CD) **2** (*formal*) an act of having

C

sex: *illicit couplings* **3** (*technical*) a thing that joins together two parts of sth, two vehicles or two pieces of equipment

cou·pon /ˈkuːpɒn; *NAmE* -pɑːn; ˈkjuː-/ *noun* **1** a small piece of printed paper that you can exchange for sth or that gives you the right to buy sth at a cheaper price than normal: *money-off coupons* ◇ *clothing coupons* ◇ *an international reply coupon* **2** a printed form, often cut out from a newspaper, that is used to enter a competition, order goods, etc: *Fill in and return the attached coupon.*

cour·age 0-m /ˈkʌrɪdʒ; *NAmE* ˈkɜːr-/ *noun* [U] the ability to do sth dangerous, or to face pain or opposition, without showing fear SYN **bravery**: *He showed great courage and determination.* ◇ *I haven't yet* ***plucked up the courage*** *to ask her.* ◇ ***moral/physical courage*** ◇ *courage in the face of danger* ➲ see also DUTCH COURAGE
IDM **have/lack the courage of your conˈvictions** to be/not be brave enough to do what you feel to be right **take courage (from sth)** to begin to feel happier and more confident because of sth **take your ˌcourage in both ˈhands** to make yourself do sth that you are afraid of: *Taking her courage in both hands, she opened the door and walked in.* ➲ more at SCREW *v.*

cour·age·ous /kəˈreɪdʒəs/ *adj.* showing courage SYN **brave**: *a very courageous decision* ◇ *I hope people will be courageous enough to speak out against this injustice.* OPP **cowardly** ▸ **cour·age·ous·ly** *adv.*

cour·gette /kʊəˈʒet; kɔːˈʒet; *NAmE* kʊrˈʒet/ (*BrE*) (*NAmE* **zuc·chini**) *noun* a long vegetable with dark green skin and white flesh ➲ VISUAL VOCAB page V27

cour·ier /ˈkʊriə(r)/ *noun* **1** a person or company whose job is to take packages or important papers somewhere: *We sent the documents by courier.* **2** (*BrE*) a person who is employed by a travel company to give advice and help to a group of tourists on holiday ▸ **cour·ier** *verb*: **~ sth** *Courier that letter—it needs to get there today* (= send it by courier).

course 0-m /kɔːs; *NAmE* kɔːrs/ *noun, verb*
■ *noun*
▸ EDUCATION **1** 0-m [C] **~ (in/on sth)** a series of lessons or lectures on a particular subject: *a* ***French/chemistry, etc. course*** ◇ *to* ***take/do a course*** *in art and design* ◇ *to* ***go on a*** *management training* ***course*** ◇ *The college* ***runs*** *specialist language* ***courses.*** ➲ COLLOCATIONS at EDUCATION ➲ see also CORRESPONDENCE COURSE, CRASH *adj.*, FOUNDATION COURSE, INDUCTION COURSE, REFRESHER COURSE, SANDWICH COURSE **2** 0-m [C] (*especially BrE*) a period of study at a college or university that leads to an exam or a qualification: *a degree course* ◇ *a two-year postgraduate course leading to a master's degree* ➲ compare PROGRAMME *n.* (5)
▸ DIRECTION **3** [U, C, usually sing.] a direction or route followed by a ship or an aircraft: *The plane was* ***on/off course*** (= going/not going in the right direction). ◇ *He radioed the pilot to* ***change course.*** ◇ *They* ***set a course*** *for the islands.* **4** [C, usually sing.] the general direction in which sb's ideas or actions are moving: *The president appears likely to* ***change course*** *on some key issues.* ◇ *Politicians are often obliged to steer a course between incompatible interests.*
▸ ACTION **5** (also **ˌcourse of ˈaction**) [C] a way of acting in or dealing with a particular situation: *There are various courses open to us.* ◇ *What course of action would you recommend?* ◇ *The wisest course would be to say nothing.*
▸ DEVELOPMENT **6** [sing.] **~ of sth** the way sth develops or should develop: *an event that changed the* ***course of history*** ◇ *The unexpected* ***course of events*** *aroused considerable alarm.*
▸ PART OF MEAL **7** [C] any of the separate parts of a meal: *a four-course dinner* ◇ *The main course was roast duck.* ➲ COLLOCATIONS at RESTAURANT
▸ FOR GOLF **8** [C] = GOLF COURSE: *He set a new course record.*
▸ FOR RACES **9** 0-m [C] an area of land or water where races are held: *She was overtaken on the last stretch of the course.* ➲ see also ASSAULT COURSE, RACECOURSE

British / American

course / program

- In *BrE* **course** is used for a series of lessons or lectures on a particular subject: *a physics course* ◇ *a course of ten lectures.* In *NAmE* you would say: *a physics course/program* ◇ *a program of ten lectures.*
- In *NAmE* a **course** is usually an individual unit that forms part of a longer period of study: *I have to take a physics course/class.* This is called a **module** in Britain, especially in a college or university.
- In *BrE* **course** can also mean a period of study at a college or university: *a two-year college course.* In *NAmE* you would say: *a two-year college program.*

▸ OF RIVER **10** [C, usually sing.] the direction a river moves in: *The path follows the course of the river.*
▸ MEDICAL TREATMENT **11** [C] **~ (of sth)** a series of medical treatments, pills, etc: *to prescribe a course of antibiotics*
▸ IN WALL **12** [C] a continuous layer of bricks, stone, etc. in a wall: *A new damp-proof course could cost £1 000 or more.*
IDM **in course of sth** (*formal*) going through a particular process: *The new textbook is in course of preparation.* **in/over the course of...** (used with expressions for periods of time) during: *He's seen many changes in the course of his long life.* ◇ *The company faces major challenges over the course of the next few years.* **in the course of ˈtime** when enough time has passed SYN **eventually**: *It is possible that in the course of time a cure for cancer will be found.* **in the ordinary, normal, etc. course of events, things, etc.** as things usually happen SYN **normally**: *In the normal course of things we would not treat her disappearance as suspicious.* **of course 1** 0-m (also **course**) (*informal*) used to emphasize that what you are saying is true or correct: *'Don't you like my mother?' 'Of course I do!'* ◇ *'Will you be there?' 'Course I will.'* **2** 0-m (also **course**) (*informal*) used as a polite way of giving sb permission to do sth: *'Can I come, too?' 'Course you can.'* ◇ *'Can I have one of those pens?' 'Of course—help yourself.'* **3** 0-m (*informal*) used as a polite way of agreeing with what sb has just said: *'I did all I could to help.' 'Of course,' he murmured gently.* **4** 0-m used to show that what you are saying is not surprising or is generally known or accepted: *Ben, of course, was the last to arrive.* ◇ *Of course, there are other ways of doing this.* ➲ LANGUAGE BANK at NEVERTHELESS **of ˈcourse not** 0-m (also ˈ**course not**) used to emphasize that you are saying 'no': *'Are you going?' 'Of course not.'* ◇ *'Do you mind?' 'No, of course not.'* **on ˈcourse for sth/to do sth** likely to achieve or do sth because you have already started to do it: *The American economy is on course for higher inflation*

More About

of course

- **Of course** is often used to show that what you are saying is not surprising or is generally known or accepted. For this reason, and because it can be difficult to get the right intonation, you may not sound polite if you use **of course** or **of course not** when you answer a request for information or permission. It can be safer to use a different word or phrase.
- *'Is this the right room for the English class?' 'Yes, it is.'* ◇ ~~*'Of course.'*~~ or ~~*'Of course it is.'*~~
- *'Can I borrow your dictionary?' 'Certainly.' (formal)* ◇ *'Sure.' (informal)*
- *'Do you mind if I borrow your dictionary?' 'Not at all.'* ◇ *'Go ahead.' (informal).*
- If you say **of course/of course not** it may sound as though you think the answer to the question is obvious and that the person should not ask. In the same way, **of course** should not be used as a reply to a statement of fact or when someone expresses an opinion: *'It's a lovely day.' 'It certainly is.'/ 'Yes it is.'* ◇ ~~*'Of course it is.'*~~ ◇ *'I think you'll enjoy that play.' 'I'm sure I will.'/ 'Yes, it sounds really good.'* ◇ ~~*'Of course.'*~~

than Britain by the end of the year. **run/take its ˈcourse** to develop in the usual way and come to the usual end: *When her tears had run their course, she felt calmer and more in control.* ◇ *With minor ailments the best thing is often to let nature take its course.* ➲ more at COLLISION, DUE *adj.*, HORSE *n.*, MATTER *n.*, MIDDLE *adj.*, PAR, PERVERT *v.*, STAY *v.*
■ ***verb*** [I] **+ adv./prep.** (*literary*) (of liquid) to move or flow quickly

course·book /ˈkɔːsbʊk; *NAmE* ˈkɔːrs-/ *noun* (*BrE*) a book for studying from, used regularly in class

ˌcourse of ˈaction *noun* (*pl.* ˌcourses of ˈaction) = COURSE (5)

course·ware /ˈkɔːsweə(r); *NAmE* ˈkɔːrswer/ *noun* [U] (*computing*) computer programs that are designed to be used to teach a subject

course·work /ˈkɔːswɜːk; *NAmE* ˈkɔːrswɜːrk/ *noun* [U] work that students do during a course of study, not in exams, that is included in their final mark/grade: *Coursework accounts for 40% of the final marks.*

cours·ing /ˈkɔːsɪŋ; *NAmE* ˈkɔːr-/ *noun* [U] the sport of hunting animals with dogs, using sight rather than smell: *hare coursing*

court 🔑 /kɔːt; *NAmE* kɔːrt/ *noun, verb*
■ ***noun***
▸ LAW **1** 🔑 [C, U] the place where legal trials take place and where crimes, etc. are judged: *the* ***civil/criminal courts*** ◇ *Her lawyer made a statement outside the court.* ◇ *She will appear* ***in court*** *tomorrow.* ◇ *They* ***took*** *their landlord* ***to court*** *for breaking the contract.* ◇ *The case took five years to* ***come to court*** (= to be heard by the court). ◇ *There wasn't enough evidence to* ***bring the case to court*** (= start a trial). ◇ *He won the* ***court case*** *and was awarded damages.* ◇ *She can't pay her tax and is facing* ***court action****.* ◇ *The case was* ***settled out of court*** (= a decision was reached without a trial). ➲ COLLOCATIONS at JUSTICE ➲ note at SCHOOL ➲ see also COURTHOUSE, COURTROOM **2** 🔑 **the court** [sing.] the people in a court, especially those who make the decisions, such as the judge and JURY: *Please tell the court what happened.* ➲ see also CONTEMPT OF COURT, COUNTY COURT, CROWN COURT, HIGH COURT, JUVENILE COURT, SUPREME COURT
▸ FOR SPORT **3** [C] a place where games such as TENNIS are played: *a* ***tennis/squash/badminton court*** ◇ *He won after only 52 minutes* ***on court****.* ➲ VISUAL VOCAB pages V36, V37 ➲ see also CLAY COURT, GRASS COURT
▸ KINGS/QUEENS **4** [C, U] the official place where kings and queens live: *the court of Queen Victoria* **5 the court** [sing.] the king or queen, their family, and the people who work for them and/or give advice to them
▸ BUILDINGS **6** [C] = COURTYARD **7** (*abbr.* Ct) [C] used in the names of blocks of flats or apartment buildings, or of some short streets; (in Britain) used in the name of some large houses **8** [C] a large open section of a building, often with a glass roof: *the food court at the shopping mall*
IDM **hold ˈcourt (with sb)** to entertain people by telling them interesting or funny things **rule/throw sth out of ˈcourt** to say that sth is completely wrong or not worth considering, especially in a trial: *The charges were thrown out of court.* ◇ *Well that's my theory ruled out of court.* ➲ more at BALL *n.*, LAUGH *v.*, PAY *v.*
■ ***verb***
▸ TRY TO PLEASE **1** [T] **~ sb** to try to please sb in order to get sth you want, especially the support of a person, an organization, etc. SYN **cultivate**: *Both candidates have spent the last month courting the media.*
▸ TRY TO GET **2** [T] **~ sth** (*formal*) to try to obtain sth: *He has never courted popularity.*
▸ INVITE STH BAD **3** [T] **~ sth** (*formal*) to do sth that might result in sth unpleasant happening: *to* ***court danger/death/disaster*** ◇ *As a politician he has often courted controversy.*
▸ HAVE RELATIONSHIP **4** [T] **~ sb** (*old-fashioned*) if a man **courts** a woman, he spends time with her and tries to make her love him, so that they can get married **5 be courting** [I] (*old-fashioned*) (of a man and a woman) to have a romantic relationship before getting married: *At that time they had been courting for several years.* ➲ see also COURTSHIP

Which Word?

court / law court / court of law

- All these words can be used to refer to a place where legal trials take place. **Court** and (*formal*) **court of law** usually refer to the actual room where cases are judged. **Courtroom** is also used for this. **Law court** (*BrE*) is more often used to refer to the building: *The prison is opposite the law court.* **Courthouse** is used for this in *NAmE*.

ˈcourt card (*BrE*) (also **ˈface card** *NAmE, BrE*) *noun* a PLAYING CARD with a picture of a king, queen or JACK on it ➲ VISUAL VOCAB page V32

ˈcourt costs *noun* [pl.] (*NAmE*) = COSTS at COST *n.*

cour·te·ous /ˈkɜːtiəs; *NAmE* ˈkɜːrt-/ *adj.* polite, especially in a way that shows respect: *a courteous young man* ◇ *The hotel staff are friendly and courteous.* OPP **discourteous** ▸ **cour·te·ous·ly** *adv.*

cour·tesan /ˌkɔːtɪˈzæn; *NAmE* ˈkɔːrtɪzn/ *noun* (in the past) a PROSTITUTE, especially one with rich customers

cour·tesy /ˈkɜːtəsi; *NAmE* ˈkɜːrt-/ *noun, adj.*
■ ***noun*** (*pl.* -ies) **1** [U] polite behaviour that shows respect for other people SYN **politeness**: *I was treated with the utmost courtesy by the staff.* ◇ *It's only* ***common courtesy*** *to tell the neighbours that we'll be having a party* (= the sort of behaviour that people would expect). **2** [C, usually pl.] (*formal*) a polite thing that you say or do when you meet people in formal situations: *an exchange of courtesies before the meeting*
IDM **courtesy of sb/sth 1** (also **by courtesy of sb/sth**) with the official permission of sb/sth and as a favour: *The pictures have been reproduced by courtesy of the British Museum.* **2** given as a prize or provided free by a person or an organization: *Win a weekend in Rome, courtesy of Fiat.* **3** as the result of a particular thing or situation: *Viewers can see the stadium from the air, courtesy of a camera fastened to the plane.* **do sb the courtesy of doing sth** to be polite by doing the thing that is mentioned: *Please do me the courtesy of listening to what I'm saying.* **have the courtesy to do sth** to know when you should do sth in order to be polite: *You think he'd at least have the courtesy to call to say he'd be late.*
■ ***adj.*** [only before noun] (of a bus, car, etc.) provided free, at no cost to the person using it: *A* ***courtesy bus*** *operates between the hotel and the town centre.* ◇ *The dealer will provide you with a* ***courtesy car*** *while your vehicle is being repaired.*

ˈcourtesy call *noun* **1** (also **ˈcourtesy visit**) a formal or official visit, usually by one important person to another, just to be polite, not to discuss important business **2** a telephone call from a company to one of its customers, for example to see if they are satisfied with the company's service.

ˈcourtesy light *noun* a small light inside a car which is automatically switched on when sb opens the door

ˈcourtesy title *noun* a title that sb is allowed to use but which has no legal status

court·house /ˈkɔːthaʊs; *NAmE* ˈkɔːrt-/ *noun* **1** (*especially NAmE*) a building containing courts of law ➲ note at COURT **2** (in the US) a building containing the offices of a county government

court·ier /ˈkɔːtiə(r); *NAmE* ˈkɔːrt-/ *noun* (especially in the past) a person who is part of the COURT of a king or queen

court·ly /ˈkɔːtli; *NAmE* ˈkɔːrt-/ *adj.* (*formal* or *literary*) extremely polite and full of respect, especially in an old-fashioned way

ˌcourtly ˈlove *noun* [U] a tradition in literature, especially in Medieval times, involving the faithful love of a KNIGHT for his married LADY, with whom he can never have a relationship

C

ˌcourt ˈmartial *noun* [C, U] (*pl.* **courts martial**) a military court that deals with members of the armed forces who break military law; a trial at such a court: *He was convicted at a court martial.* ◇ *All the men now face court martial.*

ˌcourt-ˈmar·tial *verb* (-ll-, *US* -l-) [often passive] **~ sb** to hold a trial of sb in a military court: *He was court-martialled for desertion.*

ˌcourt of apˈpeal *noun* **1** (*pl.* **courts of appeal**) a court that people can go to in order to try and change decisions that have been made by a lower court ➲ see also APPELLATE COURT **2** **ˌCourt of Apˈpeal** [sing.] (*BrE*) the highest court in Britain (apart from the Supreme Court), that can change decisions made by a lower court **3** **ˌCourt of Apˈpeals** [C] (*US*) one of the courts in the US that can change decisions made by a lower court

ˌcourt of ˈclaims *noun* (*US*) a court in the US that hears claims made against the government

ˌcourt of inˈquiry (also **ˌcourt of enˈquiry**) *noun* (*pl.* **courts of inquiry/enquiry**) (*BrE*) a special official group of people that investigates a particular problem

ˌcourt of ˈlaw *noun* (*pl.* **courts of law**) (*formal*) (also **law court**) a room or building where legal cases are judged ➲ note at COURT

ˌCourt of ˈSession *noun* in Scotland, the highest court that deals with CIVIL cases (= not criminal cases)

ˌcourt ˈorder *noun* a decision that is made in court about what must happen in a particular situation

court·room /ˈkɔːtruːm; -rʊm; *NAmE* ˈkɔːrt-/ *noun* a room in which trials or other legal cases are held ➲ note at COURT

court·ship /ˈkɔːtʃɪp; *NAmE* ˈkɔːrt-/ *noun* **1** [C, U] (*old-fashioned*) the time when two people have a romantic relationship before they get married; the process of developing this relationship: *They married after a short courtship.* ◇ *Mr Elton's courtship of Harriet* **2** [U] the special way animals behave in order to attract a mate for producing young animals: *courtship displays* **3** **~ (of sb/sth)** (*formal*) the process or act of attracting a business partner, etc: *the company's courtship by the government*

ˈcourt shoe (*BrE*) (*NAmE* **pump**) *noun* a woman's formal shoe that is plain and does not cover the top part of the foot ➲ VISUAL VOCAB page V52

ˌcourt ˈtennis (*NAmE*) (*BrE* **ˈreal tennis**) (*AustralE* **ˈroyal tennis**) *noun* [U] an old form of tennis played inside a building with a hard ball

court·yard /ˈkɔːtjɑːd; *NAmE* ˈkɔːrtjɑːrd/ (also **court**) *noun* an open space that is partly or completely surrounded by buildings and is usually part of a castle, a large house, etc: *the* ***central/inner courtyard***

cous·cous /ˈkʊskʊs; ˈkuːskuːs/ *noun* [U] a type of N African food made from crushed WHEAT; a dish of meat and/or vegetables with couscous

cousin 🗝 /ˈkʌzn/ *noun*
1 🗝 (also **ˌfirst ˈcousin**) a child of your aunt or uncle: *She's my cousin.* ◇ *We're cousins.* ➲ see also COUNTRY COUSIN, SECOND COUSIN **2** 🗝 a person who is in your wider family but who is not closely related to you: *He's a distant cousin of mine.* **3** [usually pl.] a way of describing people from another country who are similar in some way to people in your own country: *our American cousins* **4** [usually pl.] a way of describing things that are similar or related in some way: *Asian elephants are smaller than their African cousins.*

ˈcousin brother *noun* (*IndE, informal*) a male cousin of your own generation

ˈcousin sister *noun* (*IndE, informal*) a female cousin of your own generation

cou·ture /kuˈtjʊə(r); *NAmE* -ˈtʊr/ *noun* [U] (from *French*) the design and production of expensive and fashionable clothes; these clothes: *a couture evening dress* ➲ see also HAUTE COUTURE

cou·tur·ier /kuˈtjʊərieɪ; *NAmE* -ˈtʊr-/ *noun* (from *French*) a person who designs, makes and sells expensive, fashionable clothes, especially for women SYN **fashion designer**

co·va·lent /ˌkəʊˈveɪlənt; *NAmE* ˌkoʊ-/ *adj.* (*chemistry*) (of a chemical BOND) sharing a pair of ELECTRONS ➲ compare IONIC

cove /kəʊv; *NAmE* koʊv/ *noun* **1** a small bay (= an area of sea that is partly surrounded by land): *a secluded cove* ➲ VISUAL VOCAB page V5 **2** (*old-fashioned, BrE, informal*) a man

coven /ˈkʌvn/ *noun* a group or meeting of WITCHES

cov·en·ant /ˈkʌvənənt/ *noun* a promise to sb, or a legal agreement, especially one to pay a regular amount of money to sb/sth: *God's covenant with Abraham* ◇ *a covenant to a charity* ▸ **cov·en·ant** *verb*: **~ sth** *All profits are covenanted to medical charities.*

Cov·en·try /ˈkʌvəntri; *BrE* also ˈkɒv-; *NAmE* also ˈkɑːv-/ *noun*
IDM **send sb to ˈCoventry** (*BrE*) to refuse to speak to sb, as a way of punishing them for sth that they have done

cover 🗝 /ˈkʌvə(r)/ *verb, noun*
■ *verb*
▸ HIDE/PROTECT **1** 🗝 [T] **~ sth (with sth)** to place sth over or in front of sth in order to hide or protect it: *Cover the chicken loosely with foil.* ◇ *She covered her face with her hands.* ◇ (*figurative*) *He laughed to cover* (= hide) *his nervousness.* ➲ SYNONYMS at HIDE
▸ SPREAD OVER SURFACE **2** 🗝 [T] **~ sth** to lie or spread over the surface of sth: *Snow covered the ground.* ◇ *Much of the country is covered by forest.* **3** 🗝 [T] to put or spread a layer of liquid, dust, etc. on sb/sth: **~ sb/sth in sth** *The players were soon covered in mud.* ◇ **~ sb/sth with sth** *The wind blew in from the desert and covered everything with sand.*
▸ INCLUDE **4** 🗝 [T] **~ sth** to include sth; to deal with sth: *The survey covers all aspects of the business.* ◇ *The lectures* ***covered*** *a lot of* ***ground*** (= a lot of material, subjects, etc.). ◇ *the sales team covering the northern part of the country* (= selling to people in that area) ◇ *Do the rules cover* (= do they apply to) *a case like this?*
▸ MONEY **5** 🗝 [T] **~ sth** to be or provide enough money for sth: *$100 should cover your expenses.* ◇ *Your parents will have to cover your tuition fees.* ◇ *The show barely* ***covered its costs.***
▸ DISTANCE/AREA **6** [T] **~ sth** to travel the distance mentioned: *By sunset we had covered thirty miles.* ◇ *They walked for a long time and* ***covered*** *a good deal of* ***ground.*** **7** [T] **~ sth** to spread over the area mentioned: *The reserve covers an area of some 1 140 square kilometres.*
▸ REPORT NEWS **8** [T] **~ sth** to report on an event for television, a newspaper, etc; to show an event on television: *She's covering the party's annual conference.* ◇ *The BBC will cover all the major games of the tournament.*
▸ FOR SB **9** [I] **~ for sb** to do sb's work or duties while they are away: *I'm covering for Jane while she's on leave.* **10** [I] **~ for sb** to invent a lie or an excuse that will stop sb from getting into trouble: *I have to go out for a minute—will you cover for me if anyone asks where I am?*
▸ WITH INSURANCE **11** [T] to protect sb against loss, injury, etc. by insurance: **~ sb/sth (against/for sth)** *Are you fully covered for fire and theft?* ◇ **~ sb/sth to do sth** *Does this policy cover my husband to drive?*
▸ AGAINST BLAME **12** [T] **~ yourself (against sth)** to take action in order to protect yourself against being blamed for sth: *One reason doctors take temperatures is to cover themselves against negligence claims.*
▸ WITH GUN **13** [T] **~ sb** to protect sb by threatening to shoot at anyone who tries to attack them: *Cover me while I move forward.* **14** [T] **~ sb/sth** to aim a gun at a place or person so that nobody can escape or shoot: *The police covered the exits to the building.* ◇ *Don't move—we've* ***got you covered!***
▸ SONG **15** [T] **~ sth** to record a new version of a song that was originally recorded by another band or singer: *They've covered an old Rolling Stones number.*

IDM **cover all the 'bases** to consider and deal with all the things that could happen or could be needed when you are arranging sth **cover your 'back** (*informal*) (*NAmE* also **cover your 'ass**, *taboo, slang*) to realize that you may be blamed or criticized for sth later and take action to avoid this: *Get everything in writing in order to cover your back.* **cover your 'tracks** to try and hide what you have done, because you do not want other people to find out about it: *He had attempted to cover his tracks by making her death appear like suicide.* ➲ more at MULTITUDE

PHR V **,cover sth↔'in** to put a covering or roof over an open space **,cover sth↔'over** to cover sth completely so that it cannot be seen **SYN** **conceal**: *The Roman remains are now covered over by office buildings.* **,cover 'up** | **,cover yourself 'up** to put on more clothes **,cover sth↔'up** 🔑 **1** to cover sth completely so that it cannot be seen: *He covered up the body with a sheet.* **2** 🔑 (*disapproving*) to try to stop people from knowing the truth about a mistake, a crime, etc. ➲ related noun COVER-UP

■ ***noun***

▸ PROTECTION/SHELTER **1** 🔑 [C] a thing that is put over or on another thing, usually to protect it or to decorate it: *a cushion cover* ◇ *a plastic waterproof cover for the stroller* ➲ **VISUAL VOCAB** page V57 ➲ see also DUST COVER, LOOSE COVER **2** [U] a place that provides shelter from bad weather or protection from an attack: *Everyone ran* ***for cover*** *when it started to rain.* ◇ *The climbers* ***took cover*** *from the storm in a cave.* ◇ *After the explosion the street was full of people* ***running for cover.***

▸ OF BOOK **3** 🔑 [C] the outside of a book or a magazine: *the* ***front/back cover*** ◇ *Her face was* ***on the cover*** (= the front cover) *of every magazine.* ◇ *He always reads the paper* ***from cover to cover*** (= everything in it).

▸ INSURANCE **4** (*BrE*) (*NAmE* **cov·er·age**) [U] ~ (**against sth**) protection that an insurance company provides by promising to pay you money if a particular event happens: *accident cover* ◇ *cover against accidental damage*

▸ WITH WEAPONS **5** [U] support and protection that is provided when sb is attacking or in danger of being attacked: *The ships needed air cover* (= protection by military planes) *once they reached enemy waters.*

▸ TREES/PLANTS **6** [U] trees and plants that grow on an area of land: *The total forest cover of the earth is decreasing.*

▸ CLOUD/SNOW **7** [U] the fact of the sky being covered with cloud or the ground with snow: *Fog and low cloud cover are expected this afternoon.* ◇ *In this area there is snow cover for six months of the year.*

▸ ON BED **8 the covers** [pl.] the sheets, BLANKETS, etc. on a bed: *She threw back the covers and leapt out of bed.*

▸ SONG **9** [C] = COVER VERSION

▸ HIDING STH **10** [C, usually sing.] ~ (**for sth**) activities or behaviour that seem honest or true but that hide sb's real identity or feelings, or that hide sth illegal: *His work as a civil servant was a cover for his activities as a spy.* ◇ *Her overconfident attitude was a cover for her nervousness.* ◇ *It would only take one phone call to* ***blow their cover*** (= make known their true identities and what they were really doing).

▸ FOR SB'S WORK **11** [U] the fact of sb doing another person's job when they are away or when there are not enough staff: *It's the manager's job to organize cover for staff who are absent.* ◇ *Ambulance drivers provided only emergency cover during the dispute.*

IDM **break 'cover** to leave a place that you have been hiding in, usually at a high speed **under 'cover 1** pretending to be sb else in order to do sth secretly: *a police officer working under cover* **2** under a structure that gives protection from the weather **under (the) cover of sth** hidden or protected by sth: *Later, under cover of darkness, they crept into the house.* **under separate 'cover** (*business*) in a separate envelope: *The information you requested is being forwarded to you under separate cover.* ➲ more at JUDGE *v.*

cov·er·age /ˈkʌvərɪdʒ/ *noun* [U] **1** the reporting of news and sport in newspapers and on the radio and television: ***media/newspaper/press coverage*** ◇ *tonight's* ***live coverage*** *of the hockey game* **2** the range or quality of information that is included in a book or course of study, on television, etc: *magazines with extensive coverage of diet and health topics* **3** the amount of sth that sth provides; the amount or way that sth covers an area: *Immunization coverage against fatal diseases has increased to 99% in some countries.* **4** (*NAmE*) (*BrE* **cover**) protection that an insurance company provides by promising to pay you money if a particular event happens: *insurance coverage* ◇ *Medicaid health coverage for low-income families*

cov·er·alls /ˈkʌvərɔːlz/ (*NAmE*) (*BrE* **overalls**) *noun* [pl.] a loose piece of clothing like a shirt and trousers/pants in one piece, made of heavy cloth and usually worn over other clothing by workers doing dirty work ➲ picture at OVERALL

'cover charge *noun* [usually sing.] an amount of money that you pay in some restaurants or clubs in addition to the cost of the food and drink

covered 🔑 /ˈkʌvəd; *NAmE* -vərd/ *adj.*
1 🔑 [not before noun] ~ **in/with sth** having a layer or amount of sth on it: *His face was covered in blood.* ◇ *The walls were covered with pictures.* **2** 🔑 having a roof over it: *a covered area of the stadium with seats*

,covered 'wagon *noun* a large wooden vehicle with a curved roof made of cloth, that is pulled by horses, used especially in the past in N America by people travelling across the land to the west

'cover girl *noun* a young woman whose photograph is on the front of a magazine

cov·er·ing 🔑 /ˈkʌvərɪŋ/ *noun*
1 🔑 a layer of sth that covers sth else: *a thick covering of snow on the ground* **2** 🔑 a layer of material such as carpet or WALLPAPER, used to cover, decorate and protect floors, walls, etc: ***floor/wall coverings*** **3** 🔑 a piece of material that covers sth: *He pulled the plastic covering off the dead body.*

,covering 'letter (*BrE*) (*NAmE* **'cover letter**) *noun* a letter containing extra information that you send with sth ➲ **WRITING TUTOR** page WT32

cov·er·let /ˈkʌvələt; *NAmE* -vərl-/ *noun* (*old-fashioned*) a type of BEDSPREAD to cover a bed

'cover story *noun* **1** the main story in a magazine, that goes with the picture shown on the front cover **2** a story that is invented in order to hide sth, especially a person's identity or their reasons for doing sth

cov·ert *adj., noun*
■ ***adj.*** /ˈkʌvət; ˈkəʊvɜːt; *NAmE* ˈkoʊvɜːrt/ (*formal*) secret or hidden, making it difficult to notice: ***covert operations/surveillance*** ◇ *He stole a covert glance at her across the table.* ➲ compare OVERT ▸ **cov·ert·ly** *adv.*: *She watched him covertly in the mirror.*
■ ***noun*** /ˈkʌvət; *NAmE* -vərt/ an area of thick low bushes and trees where animals can hide

'cover-up *noun* [usually sing.] action that is taken to hide a mistake or illegal activity from the public: *Government sources denied there had been a deliberate cover-up.*

'cover version (also **cover**) *noun* a new recording of an old song by a different band or singer

covet /ˈkʌvət/ *verb* ~ **sth** (*formal*) to want sth very much, especially sth that belongs to sb else: *He had long coveted the chance to work with a famous musician.* ◇ *They are this year's winners of the coveted trophy* (= that everyone would like to win).

cov·et·ous /ˈkʌvətəs/ *adj.* (*formal*) having a strong desire for the things that other people have ▸ **cov·et·ous·ness** *noun* [U]

cow 🔑 /kaʊ/ *noun, verb*
■ ***noun*** **1** 🔑 a large animal kept on farms to produce milk or beef: *cow's milk* ◇ *a herd of dairy cows* (= cows kept for their milk) ➲ compare BULL, CALF, HEIFER ➲ see also CATTLE **2** the female of the ELEPHANT, WHALE and some other large animals ➲ compare BULL **3** (*slang, disapproving*) an offensive word for a woman: *You stupid cow!* **4** (*AustralE, NZE*) an unpleasant person, thing or situation ➲ see also CASH COW, SACRED COW

IDM **have a 'cow** (*NAmE, informal*) to become very angry or anxious about sth: *Don't have a cow—it's no big deal.* **till the 'cows come home** (*informal*) for a very long time; for ever

■ ***verb*** [usually passive] **~ sb** to frighten sb in order to make them obey you SYN **intimidate**: *She was easily cowed by people in authority.*

C

cow·ard /'kaʊəd; *NAmE* -ərd/ *noun* (*disapproving*) a person who is not brave or who does not have the courage to do things that other people do not think are especially difficult: *You coward! What are you afraid of?* ◇ *I'm a real coward when it comes to going to the dentist.* ▶ **cow·ard·ly** *adj.*: *a cowardly attack on a defenceless man*

cow·ard·ice /'kaʊədɪs; *NAmE* -ərd-/ *noun* [U] fear or lack of courage OPP **bravery, courage**

cow·bell /'kaʊbel/ *noun* a bell that is put around a cow's neck so that the cow can easily be found

cow·boy /'kaʊbɔɪ/ *noun* **1** a man who rides a horse and whose job is to take care of CATTLE in the western parts of the US: *cowboy boots* ➲ VISUAL VOCAB page V52 **2** a man like this as a character in a film/movie about the American West: *children playing a game of* ***cowboys and Indians*** **3** (*BrE, informal, disapproving*) a dishonest person in business, especially sb who produces work of bad quality or charges too high a price

'cowboy hat *noun* a hat with a wide BRIM, worn by American cowboys ➲ VISUAL VOCAB page V53

cow·catch·er /'kaʊkætʃə(r)/ *noun* (*NAmE*) a pointed metal structure at the front of a train that is used for pushing things off the track

'cow chip *noun* (*US*) a very hard COWPAT

cowed /kaʊd/ *adj.* made to feel afraid and that you are not as good as sb else ➲ see also COW *v.*

cower /'kaʊə(r)/ *verb* [I] to bend low and/or move backwards because you are frightened: *A gun went off and people cowered behind walls and under tables.*

cow·girl /'kaʊgɜːl; *NAmE* -gɜːrl/ *noun* a female COWBOY in the American West

cow·hand /'kaʊhænd/ *noun* a person whose job is taking care of cows

cow·hide /'kaʊhaɪd/ *noun* [U] strong leather made from the skin of a cow

cowl /kaʊl/ *noun* **1** a large loose covering for the head, worn especially by MONKS **2** a cover for a CHIMNEY, etc, usually made of metal. Cowls often turn with the wind and are designed to improve the flow of air or smoke.

cow·lick /'kaʊlɪk/ *noun* a piece of hair that grows in a different direction from the rest of your hair and is difficult to make lie flat ➲ VISUAL VOCAB page V49

cowl·ing /'kaʊlɪŋ/ *noun* (*technical*) a metal cover for an engine, especially on an aircraft ➲ VISUAL VOCAB page V43

'cowl neck *noun* a COLLAR on a woman's sweater that hangs in several folds

'co-worker *noun* a person that sb works with, doing the same kind of job SYN **colleague**

'cow parsley *noun* [U] a European wild plant with a lot of very small white flowers that look like LACE

cow·pat /'kaʊpæt/ (*BrE*) *noun* a round flat piece of solid waste from a cow

cow·pea /'kaʊpiː/ *noun* a type of BEAN that is white with a black spot and is grown for food: *Cowpeas are an important crop in many African countries.*

cow·poke /'kaʊpəʊk; *NAmE* -poʊk/ *noun* (*NAmE, old-fashioned* or *humorous*) = COWBOY

cow·rie /'kaʊri/ *noun* a small shiny shell that was used as money in the past in parts of Africa and Asia

cow·shed /'kaʊʃed/ *noun* (*BrE*) a farm building in which cows are kept

cow·slip /'kaʊslɪp/ *noun* a small wild plant with yellow flowers with a sweet smell

cox /kɒks; *NAmE* kɑːks/ *noun, verb*

■ ***noun*** (also **cox·swain**) the person who controls the direction of a ROWING BOAT while other people are ROWING

■ ***verb*** [T, I] **~ (sth)** to control the direction of a ROWING BOAT while other people are ROWING; to act as a cox

cox·swain /'kɒksn; *NAmE* 'kɑːksn/ *noun* **1** the person who is in charge of a LIFEBOAT and who controls its direction **2** = COX

coy /kɔɪ/ *adj.* **1** shy or pretending to be shy and innocent, especially about love or sex, and sometimes in order to make people more interested in you: *She gave me a coy smile.* **2 ~ (about sth)** not willing to give information about sth, or answer questions that tell people too much about you SYN **reticent**: *She was a little coy about how much her dress cost.* ▶ **coyly** *adv.* **coy·ness** *noun* [U]

coy·ote /kaɪ'əʊti; *NAmE* -'oʊti; *BrE* also kɔɪ-; *NAmE* also 'kaɪoʊt/ (also **'prairie wolf**) *noun* a N American wild animal of the dog family

coy·pu /'kɔɪpuː/ *noun* a large S American animal, like a BEAVER, that lives near water

coz *conj.* = COS[1]

cozy (*NAmE*) (*BrE* **cosy**) /'kəʊzi; *NAmE* 'koʊzi/ *adj., verb*

■ ***adj.*** (**cozi·er, cozi·est, cosi·er, cosi·est**) **1** warm, comfortable and safe, especially because of being small or confined SYN **snug**: *a cozy little room* ◇ *a cozy feeling* ◇ *I felt warm and cozy sitting by the fire.* **2** friendly and private: *a cozy chat with a friend* **3** (often *disapproving*) easy and convenient, but not always honest or right: *The firm has a cozy relationship with the Department of Defense.* ◇ *The danger is that things get too cozy.* ▶ **cozi·ly** (*NAmE*) (*BrE* **cosi·ly**) *adv.*: *sitting cozily by the fire* **cozi·ness** (*NAmE*) (*BrE* **cosi·ness**) *noun* [U]: *the warmth and coziness of the kitchen*

■ ***verb*** (**cozies, cozy·ing, cozied, cozied**)

PHR V **,cozy 'up to sb** (*NAmE*) (*BrE* **,cosy 'up to sb**) (*informal*) to act in a friendly way towards sb, especially sb who will be useful to you

cp. *abbr.* (in writing) compare

CPE /,siː piː 'iː/ *noun* [U] the abbreviation for 'Certificate of Proficiency in English' (a British test, set by the University of Cambridge, that measures a person's ability to speak and write English at a very advanced level)

CPI /,siː piː 'aɪ/ *abbr.* CONSUMER PRICE INDEX

Cpl (*BrE*) (*NAmE* **Cpl.**) *abbr.* (in writing) CORPORAL

CPR /,siː piː 'ɑː(r)/ *noun* [U] the abbreviation for 'cardiopulmonary resuscitation' (breathing air into the mouth of an unconscious person and pressing on their chest to keep them alive by sending air around their body)

CPU /,siː piː 'juː/ *abbr.* (*computing*) central processing unit (the part of a computer that controls all the other parts of the system)

crab /kræb/ *noun* **1** [C] a sea creature with a hard shell, eight legs and two PINCERS (= curved and pointed arms for catching and holding things). Crabs move sideways on land. ➲ VISUAL VOCAB page V11 ➲ see also HERMIT CRAB **2** [U] meat from a crab, used for food: *dressed crab* **3 crabs** (*informal*) the condition caused by having LICE (called **crab lice**) in the hair around the GENITALS

'crab apple *noun* a tree that produces fruit like small hard sour apples, also called crab apples

crabbed /'kræbɪd; kræbd/ *adj.* **1** (*literary*) (of sb's writing) small and difficult to read **2** (*old-fashioned*) = CRABBY

crabby /'kræbi/ *adj.* (*informal*) (of people) bad-tempered and unpleasant

crab·grass /'kræbgrɑːs; *NAmE* -græs/ *noun* [U] (*especially NAmE*) a type of grass that grows where it is not wanted, spreads quickly and is hard to get rid of

'crab stick *noun* a small pink stick made from pressed pieces of fish that have been flavoured to taste like CRAB

crab·wise /'kræbwaɪz/ *adv.* (of a movement) in a sideways direction, like a CRAB

crack 🔑 /kræk/ *verb, noun, adj.*

■ ***verb***

▸ BREAK **1** 🔑 [I, T] to break without dividing into separate parts; to break sth in this way: *The ice cracked as I stepped onto it.* ◇ **~ sth** *He has cracked a bone in his arm.* ◇ *Her lips*

were dry and cracked. **2** [I, T] to break open or into pieces; to break sth in this way: **+ adv./prep.** *A chunk of the cliff had cracked off in a storm.* ◇ (*figurative*) *His face cracked into a smile.* ◇ **~ sth** *to crack a nut* ◇ **~ sth + adv./prep.** *She cracked an egg into the pan.*
▸ HIT **3** [T] **~ sth/sb (on/against sth)** to hit sth/sb with a short hard blow: *I cracked my head on the low ceiling.* ◇ *He cracked me on the head with a ruler.*
▸ MAKE SOUND **4** [I, T] to make a sharp sound; to make sth do this: *A shot cracked across the ridge.* [no passive]: **~ sth** *He* ***cracked his whip*** *and galloped away.*
▸ OF VOICE **5** [I] if your voice **cracks**, it changes in depth, volume, etc. suddenly and in a way that you cannot control: *In a voice cracking with emotion, he told us of his son's death.*
▸ UNDER PRESSURE **6** [I] to no longer be able to function normally because of pressure: *Things are terrible at work and people are cracking under the strain.* ◇ *They questioned him for days before he cracked.* ◇ *The old institutions are cracking.*
▸ FIND SOLUTION **7** [T] **~ sth** to find the solution to a problem, etc; to find the way to do sth difficult: *to crack the enemy's code* ◇ (*informal*) *After a year in this job I think* ***I've got it cracked!***
▸ STOP SB/STH **8** [T] **~ sth** to find a way of stopping or defeating a criminal or an enemy: *Police have cracked a major drugs ring.*
▸ OPEN BOTTLE **9** [T] **~ (open) a bottle** (*informal*) to open a bottle, especially of wine, and drink it
▸ A JOKE **10** [T] **~ a joke** (*informal*) to tell a joke
IDM **get 'cracking** (*informal*) to begin immediately and work quickly SYN **get going**: *There's a lot to be done, so let's get cracking.* **not all, everything, etc. sb's cracked 'up to be** (*informal*) not as good as people say: *He's not nearly such a good writer as he's cracked up to be.* **crack the 'whip** to use your authority or power to make sb work very hard, usually by treating them in a strict way ➲ more at NUT *n.*, SLEDGEHAMMER
PHR V **ˌcrack 'down (on sb/sth)** to try harder to prevent an illegal activity and deal more severely with those who are caught doing it: *Police are cracking down on drug dealers.* ➲ related noun CRACKDOWN **ˌcrack 'on (with sth)** (*BrE, informal*) to work hard at sth so that you finish it quickly; to pass or continue quickly: *If we crack on with the painting we should finish it today.* ◇ *Time was cracking on and we were nowhere near finished.* **ˌcrack 'up** (*informal*) **1** to become ill, either physically or mentally, because of pressure: *You'll crack up if you carry on working like this.* **2** to start laughing a lot: *He walked in and everyone just cracked up.* **ˌcrack sb 'up** (*informal*) to make sb laugh a lot: *Gill's so funny, she just cracks me up.*
■ ***noun***
▸ BREAK **1** [C] **~ (in sth)** a line on the surface of sth where it has broken but not split into separate parts: *This cup has a crack in it.* ◇ *Cracks began to appear in the walls.* ◇ (*figurative*) *The cracks* (= faults) *in the government's economic policy are already beginning to show.* ➲ picture at BROKEN
▸ NARROW OPENING **2** [C] a narrow space or opening: *She peeped through the crack in the curtains.* ◇ *The door opened a crack* (= a small amount).
▸ SOUND **3** [C] a sudden loud noise: *a crack of thunder* ◇ *the sharp crack of a rifle shot*
▸ HIT **4** [C] **~ (on sth)** a sharp blow that can be heard: *She fell over and got a nasty crack on the head.*
▸ ATTEMPT **5** [C] **~ (at sth)** | **~ (at doing sth)** (*informal*) an occasion when you try to do sth SYN **attempt**: *She hopes to have another crack at the world record this year.*
▸ DRUG **6** (also **ˌcrack co'caine**) [U] a powerful, illegal drug that is a form of COCAINE: *a crack addict*
▸ JOKE **7** [C] (*informal*) a joke, especially a critical one: *He made a very unfair crack about her looks.*
▸ CONVERSATION **8** (also **craic**) [U, sing.] (*IrishE, informal*) a good time; friendly, enjoyable talk: *Where's the crack tonight?* ◇ *He's a person who enjoys a drink and a bit of crack.*
IDM **at the crack of 'dawn** (*informal*) very early in the morning ➲ more at FAIR *adj.*
■ ***adj.*** [only before noun] expert and highly trained; excellent at sth: *crack troops* ◇ *He's a crack shot* (= accurate and skilled at shooting).

crack·brained /'krækbreɪnd/ *adj.* (*informal*) crazy and unlikely to succeed: *a crackbrained idea*

crack·down /'krækdaʊn/ *noun* **~ (on sb/sth)** severe action taken to restrict the activities of criminals or of people opposed to the government or sb in authority: *a military crackdown on student protesters* ◇ *a crackdown on crime*

C

cracked /krækt/ *adj.*
1 damaged with lines in its surface but not completely broken: *a cracked mirror/mug* ◇ *He suffered cracked ribs and bruising.* ◇ *She passed her tongue over her cracked lips and tried to speak.* ➲ picture at BROKEN **2** (of sb's voice) sounding rough with sudden changes in how loud or high it is, because the person is upset: *'I'm just fine,' she said in a cracked voice.* **3** [not before noun] (*informal*) crazy: *I think he must be cracked, don't you?*

crack·er /'krækə(r)/ *noun*
1 a thin dry biscuit that is often salty and usually eaten with cheese ➲ see also CREAM CRACKER, GRAHAM CRACKER **2** (also **ˌChristmas 'cracker**) a tube of coloured paper that makes a loud EXPLOSIVE sound when it is pulled open by two people. Crackers usually contain a paper hat, a small present and a joke, and are used in Britain at Christmas parties and meals: *Who wants to pull this cracker with me?* ➲ see also FIRECRACKER **3** (*BrE, informal*) something that you think is very good, funny, etc: *It was a cracker of a goal.* ◇ *I've got a joke for you. It's a real cracker!* **4** (*NAmE, slang*) an offensive word for a poor white person with little education from the southern US **5** (*informal*) a person who illegally finds a way of looking at or stealing information on sb else's computer system **6** (*old-fashioned, BrE, informal*) an attractive woman

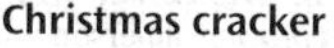
Christmas cracker

crack·er·jack /'krækədʒæk; *NAmE* -kərdʒæk/ *noun* (*NAmE, informal*) an excellent person or thing ▸ **crack·er·jack** *adj.*

crack·ers /'krækəz; *NAmE* -kərz/ *adj.* [not before noun] (*BrE, informal*) crazy: *That noise is driving me crackers.*

crack·head /'krækhed/ *noun* (*slang*) a person who uses the illegal drug CRACK

'crack house *noun* a place where people sell CRACK (= a type of illegal drug)

crack·ing /'krækɪŋ/ *noun, adj.*
■ ***noun*** [U] **1** lines on a surface where it is damaged or beginning to break: *All planes are being inspected for possible cracking and corrosion.* **2** the sound of sth cracking: *the cracking of thunder/twigs*
■ ***adj.*** [usually before noun] (*BrE, informal*) excellent: *That was a cracking goal.* ◇ *She's in cracking form at the moment.* ◇ *We set off* ***at a cracking pace*** (= very quickly). ▸ **crack·ing** *adv.*: *a cracking good* (= extremely good) *dinner*

crackle /'krækl/ *verb, noun*
■ ***verb*** [I] to make short sharp sounds like sth that is burning in a fire: *A log fire crackled in the hearth.* ◇ *The radio crackled into life.* ◇ (*figurative*) *The atmosphere crackled with tension.*
■ ***noun*** [U, C] a series of short sharp sounds: *the distant crackle of machine-gun fire* ▸ **crack·ly** /'krækli/ *adj.*: *She picked up the phone and heard a crackly voice saying: 'Sue here.'*

crack·ling /'kræklɪŋ/ *noun* **1** [U, sing.] a series of sharp sounds: *He could hear the crackling of burning trees.* **2** [U] (*BrE*) (*US* **crack·lings** [pl.]) the hard skin of PORK (= meat from a pig) that has been cooked in the oven

crack·pot /'krækpɒt; *NAmE* -pɑːt/ *noun* (*informal*) a person with strange or crazy ideas ▸ **crack·pot** *adj.* [only before noun]: ***crackpot ideas/theories***

-cracy *combining form* (in nouns) the government or rule of: *democracy* ◇ *bureaucracy*

C

cra·dle /ˈkreɪdl/ *noun, verb*
▪ *noun* **1** a small bed for a baby which can be pushed gently from side to side: *She rocked the baby to sleep in its cradle.* ➲ VISUAL VOCAB page V20 **2** [usually sing.] **~ of sth** the place where sth important began: *Greece, the cradle of Western civilization* **3** (*BrE*) a small platform that can be moved up and down the outside of a high building, used by people cleaning windows, etc. **4** the part of a telephone on which the RECEIVER rests
IDM **from the ˌcradle to the ˈgrave** a way of referring to the whole of a person's life, from birth until death ➲ more at ROB
▪ *verb* **~ sb/sth** to hold sb/sth gently in your arms or hands: *The old man cradled the tiny baby in his arms.*

ˈcradle cap *noun* [U] a skin condition that causes dry rough yellow areas on top of a baby's head

ˈcradle-snatcher (*BrE*) (*NAmE* **ˈcradle-robber**) *noun* (*disapproving*) a person who has a sexual relationship with a much younger person ▸ **ˈcradle-snatch** (*BrE*) (*NAmE* **ˈcradle-rob**) *verb* [I]

craft 🔑 /krɑːft; *NAmE* kræft/ *noun, verb*
▪ *noun* **1** 🔑 [C, U] an activity involving a special skill at making things with your hands: *traditional crafts like basket-weaving* ◇ *a* ***craft fair/workshop*** ◇ *Craft, Design and Technology* (= a subject in some British schools) ➲ see also ARTS AND CRAFTS **2** 🔑 [sing.] all the skills needed for a particular activity: *chefs who learned their craft in top hotels* ◇ *the writer's craft* **3** [U] (*formal, disapproving*) skill in making people believe what you want them to believe: *He knew how to win by craft and diplomacy what he could not gain by force.* **4** [C] (*pl.* **craft**) (*formal*) a boat or ship: *Hundreds of small craft bobbed around the liner as it steamed into the harbour.* ◇ *a* ***landing/pleasure craft*** **5** [C] (*pl.* **craft**) an aircraft or SPACECRAFT
▪ *verb* [usually passive] **~ sth** to make sth using special skills, especially with your hands SYN **fashion**: *All the furniture is crafted from natural materials.* ◇ *a carefully crafted speech* ➲ see also HANDCRAFTED

ˈcraft knife *noun* (*BrE*) a very sharp knife used for cutting paper or thin pieces of wood

crafts·man /ˈkrɑːftsmən; *NAmE* ˈkræf-/ (also **crafts·person**) *noun* (*pl.* **-men** /-mən/) a skilled person, especially one who makes beautiful things by hand: *rugs handmade by local craftsmen* ◇ *It is clearly the work of a master craftsman.* ➲ see also CRAFTSWOMAN

crafts·man·ship /ˈkrɑːftsmənʃɪp; *NAmE* ˈkræf-/ *noun* [U] **1** the level of skill shown by sb in making sth beautiful with their hands: *The whole house is a monument to her craftsmanship.* **2** the quality of design and work shown by sth that has been made by hand: *the superb craftsmanship of the carvings*

crafts·person /ˈkrɑːftspɜːsn; *NAmE* ˈkræftspɜːrsn/ *noun* (*pl.* **-people** /-piːpl/) = CRAFTSMAN

crafts·woman /ˈkrɑːftswʊmən; *NAmE* ˈkræf-/ *noun* (*pl.* **-women** /-wɪmɪn/) a skilled woman, especially one who makes beautiful things by hand ➲ note at GENDER

craft·work /ˈkrɑːftwɜːk; *NAmE* ˈkræftwɜːrk/ *noun* [U] work done by a CRAFTSMAN

crafty /ˈkrɑːfti; *NAmE* ˈkræfti/ *adj.* (**craft·ier, crafti·est**) (usually *disapproving*) clever at getting what you want, especially by indirect or dishonest methods SYN **cunning, wily**: *He's a crafty old devil.* ◇ *one of the party's craftiest political strategists* ▸ **craft·ily** *adv.* **crafti·ness** *noun* [U]

crag /kræg/ *noun* a high steep rough mass of rock: *a castle set on a crag above the village*

craggy /ˈkrægi/ *adj.* **1** having many crags: *a craggy coastline* **2** (usually *approving*) (of a man's face) having strong features and deep lines

craic *noun* = CRACK (8)

cram /kræm/ *verb* (**-mm-**) **1** [T, I] to push or force sb/sth into a small space; to move into a small space with the result that it is full: **~ sb/sth into/onto sth** *He crammed eight people into his car.* ◇ **~ sth in** *I could never cram in all that she does in a day.* ◇ **~ sth + adv./prep.** *I managed to cram down a few mouthfuls of food.* ◇ **~ sth** *Supporters crammed the streets.* ◇ **~ sth full** *I bought a large basket and crammed it full of presents.* ◇ **~ into/onto sth** *We all managed to cram into his car.* **2** [I] **~ (for sth)** (*NAmE, informal* or rather *old-fashioned, BrE*) to learn a lot of things in a short time, in preparation for an exam SYN **swot**: *He's been cramming for his exams all week.*

crammed /kræmd/ *adj.* **1 ~ (with sb/sth)** full of things or people SYN **packed**: *All the shelves were crammed with books.* ◇ *The room was* ***crammed full*** *of people.* ◇ *The article was* ***crammed full*** *of ideas.* **2** [not before noun] **~ (with sb/sth)** if people are **crammed** into a place, there is not much room for them in it SYN **packed**: *We were crammed four to an office.*

cram·mer /ˈkræmə(r)/ *noun* (*BrE*) a school or book that prepares people quickly for exams

cramp /kræmp/ *noun, verb*
▪ *noun* **1** [U, C] (*NAmE* also **ˈcharley horse**) a sudden pain that you get when the muscles in a particular part of your body contract, usually caused by cold or too much exercise: (*BrE*) *to get cramp in your leg* ◇ (*NAmE*) *to get a cramp in your leg* ➲ see also WRITER'S CRAMP **2 cramps** [pl.] severe pain in the stomach
▪ *verb* **~ sth** to prevent the development or progress of sb/sth SYN **restrict**: *Tighter trade restrictions might cramp economic growth.*
IDM **cramp sb's ˈstyle** (*informal*) to stop sb from behaving in the way they want to

cramped /kræmpt/ *adj.* **1** a **cramped** room, etc. does not have enough space for the people in it: *working in cramped conditions* **2** (of people) not having room to move freely **3** (of sb's writing) with small letters close together and therefore difficult to read

cram·pon /ˈkræmpɒn; *NAmE* -pɑːn/ *noun* [usually pl.] a metal plate with pointed pieces of metal underneath, worn on sb's shoes when they are walking or climbing on ice and snow

cran·berry /ˈkrænbəri; *NAmE* -beri/ *noun* (*pl.* **-ies**) a small sour red BERRY that grows on a small bush and is used in cooking: *cranberry sauce*

crane /kreɪn/ *noun, verb*
▪ *noun* **1** a tall machine with a long arm, used to lift and move building materials and other heavy objects ➲ VISUAL VOCAB pages V2, V47 **2** a large bird with long legs and a long neck ➲ see also BLUE CRANE
▪ *verb* [I, T] to lean or stretch over sth in order to see sth better; to stretch your neck: (**+ adv./prep.**) *People were craning out of the windows and waving.* ◇ **~ sth** *She* ***craned her neck*** *to get a better view of the stage.*

ˈcrane fly (also *informal* **ˌdaddy-ˈlong-legs**) *noun* a flying insect with very long legs

cra·nium /ˈkreɪniəm/ *noun* (*pl.* **cra·ni·ums** or **cra·nia** /ˈkreɪniə/) (*anatomy*) the bone structure that forms the head and surrounds and protects the brain SYN **skull** ➲ VISUAL VOCAB page V48 ▸ **cra·nial** /ˈkreɪniəl/ *adj.* [only before noun]: *cranial nerves/injuries*

crank /kræŋk/ *noun, verb*
▪ *noun* **1** (*disapproving*) a person with ideas that other people find strange SYN **eccentric**: *Vegetarians are no longer dismissed as cranks.* **2** (*NAmE*) a person who easily gets angry or annoyed **3** a bar and handle in the shape of an L that you pull or turn to produce movement in a machine, etc. ➲ VISUAL VOCAB page V41
▪ *verb* **~ sth (up)** to make sth turn or move by using a crank: *to crank an engine* ◇ (*figurative*) *He has a limited time to crank the reforms into action.*
PHR V **ˌcrank sth↔ˈout** (*informal*) to produce a lot of sth quickly, especially things of low quality SYN **turn out** **ˌcrank sth↔ˈup** (*informal*) **1** to make a machine, etc. work or work at a higher level **2** to make music, etc. louder SYN **turn up**: *Crank up the volume!*

crank·shaft /ˈkræŋkʃɑːft; *NAmE* -ʃæft/ *noun* (*technical*) a long piece of metal in a vehicle that connects the engine to the wheels and helps turn the engine's power into movement

cranky /ˈkræŋki/ *adj.* (*informal*) **1** (*BrE*) strange SYN **eccentric**: *cranky ideas/schemes* **2** (*especially NAmE*) bad-tempered: *The kids were getting tired and a little cranky.*

cranny /ˈkræni/ *noun* (*pl.* **-ies**) a very small hole or opening, especially in a wall IDM see NOOK

crap /kræp/ *noun, adj., verb*

■ ***noun*** (*taboo, slang*) **1** [U] nonsense: *He's so full of crap.* ◇ *Let's* **cut the crap** *and get down to business.* ◇ (*BrE*) *You're talking a* **load of crap!** ◇ (*NAmE*) *What a* **bunch of crap!** **2** [U] something of bad quality: *This work is complete crap.* ◇ (*BrE*) *Her latest film is a* **load of crap.** ◇ (*NAmE*) *Her latest movie is a* **bunch of crap.** HELP More acceptable words are **rubbish, garbage, trash** or **junk**. **3** [U] criticism or unfair treatment: *I'm not going to take this crap any more.* **4** [U] solid waste matter from the BOWELS SYN **excrement** **5** [sing.] an act of emptying solid waste matter from the BOWELS: *to have a crap* IDM see BUG *v.*

■ ***adj.*** (*BrE, taboo, slang*) bad; of very bad quality: *a crap band* ◇ *The concert was crap.* ▶ **crap** *adv.*: *The team played crap yesterday.*

■ ***verb*** (**-pp-**) [I] (*taboo, slang*) to empty solid waste from the BOWELS SYN **defecate** HELP A more polite way of expressing this is 'to go to the toilet/lavatory' (*BrE*), 'to go to the bathroom' (*NAmE*), or 'to go'. A more formal expression is 'to empty the bowels'.

crappy /ˈkræpi/ *adj.* (**crap·pier, crap·pi·est**) [usually before noun] (*slang*) of very bad quality: *a crappy novel*

craps /kræps/ *noun* [U] (*NAmE*) a gambling game played with two DICE: *to* **shoot craps** (= play this game) ▶ **crap** *adj.* [only before noun]: *a crap game*

crap·shoot /ˈkræpʃuːt/ *noun* (*NAmE*) **1** a game of CRAPS **2** (*informal*) a situation whose success or result is based on luck rather than on effort or careful organization

crash 🔑 /kræʃ/ *noun, verb, adj.*

■ ***noun***

▸ VEHICLE ACCIDENT **1** 🔑 (*NAmE* also **wreck**) an accident in which a vehicle hits sth, for example another vehicle, usually causing damage and often injuring or killing the passengers: *A girl was killed yesterday in a crash involving a stolen car.* ◇ *a* **car/plane crash** ➲ COLLOCATIONS at DRIVING

▸ LOUD NOISE **2** 🔑 [usually sing.] a sudden loud noise made, for example, by sth falling or breaking: *The tree fell with a great crash.* ◇ *The first distant crash of thunder shook the air.*

▸ IN FINANCE/BUSINESS **3** 🔑 a sudden serious fall in the price or value of sth; the occasion when a business, etc. fails SYN **collapse**: *the 1987 stock market crash*

▸ COMPUTING **4** 🔑 a sudden failure of a machine or system, especially of a computer or computer system

■ ***verb***

▸ OF VEHICLE **1** 🔑 [I, T] if a vehicle **crashes** or the driver **crashes** it, it hits an object or another vehicle, causing damage: *I was terrified that the plane would crash.* ◇ *We're going to crash, aren't we?* ◇ **~ into sth** *A truck went out of control and crashed into the back of a bus.* ◇ **~ sth (into sth)** *He crashed his car into a wall.*

▸ HIT HARD/LOUD NOISE **2** 🔑 [I, T] to hit sth hard while moving, causing noise and/or damage; to make sth hit sb/sth in this way: **+ adv./prep.** *A brick crashed through the window.* ◇ *With a sweep of his hand he sent the glasses crashing to the floor.* ◇ **+ adj.** *The door crashed open.* ◇ **~ sth + adj.** *She stormed out of the room and crashed the door shut behind her.* **3** 🔑 [I] to make a loud noise: *Thunder crashed overhead.*

▸ IN FINANCE/BUSINESS **4** 🔑 [I] (of prices, a business, shares, etc.) to lose value or fail suddenly and quickly: *Share prices crashed to an all-time low yesterday.* ◇ *The company crashed with debts of £50 million.*

▸ COMPUTING **5** 🔑 [I, T] **~ (sth)** if a computer **crashes** or you **crash** a computer, it stops working suddenly: *Files can be lost if the system suddenly crashes.*

▸ PARTY **6** [T] **~ sth** (*informal*) = GATECRASH

▸ IN SPORT **7** [I] (**+ adv./prep**) (*especially BrE*) to lose very badly in a sports game: *The team crashed to their worst defeat this season.*

▸ SLEEP **8** [I] **~ (out)** (*informal*) to fall asleep; to sleep somewhere you do not usually sleep: *I was so tired I crashed out on the sofa.* ◇ *I've come to crash on your floor for a couple of nights.*

▸ MEDICAL **9** [I] if sb **crashes**, their heart stops beating

IDM **a crashing ˈbore** (*old-fashioned, BrE*) a very boring person

PHR V **ˌcrash ˈout (of sth)** (*sport*) (*BrE*) to lose a game with the result that you have to stop playing in a competition: *They crashed out of the World Cup after a 2-1 defeat to Brazil.*

■ ***adj.*** [only before noun] involving hard work or a lot of effort over a short period of time in order to achieve quick results: *a crash course in computer programming* ◇ *a crash diet*

Synonyms

crash

slam • collide • smash • wreck

These are all words that can be used when sth, especially a vehicle, hits sth else very hard and is damaged or destroyed.

crash (*rather informal*) to hit an object or another vehicle, causing damage; to make a vehicle do this: *I was terrified that the plane would crash.*

slam (sth) into/against sb/sth to crash into sth with a lot of force; to make sth do this: *The car skidded and slammed into a tree.*

collide (*rather formal*) (of two vehicles or people) to crash into each other; (of a vehicle or person) to crash into sb/sth else: *The car and the van collided head-on in thick fog.*

smash (*rather informal*) to crash into sth with a lot of force; to make sth do this; to crash a car: *Ramraiders smashed a stolen car through the shop window.*

CRASH, SLAM OR SMASH?

Crash is used especially to talk about vehicles and can be used without a preposition: *We're going to crash, aren't we?* In this meaning **slam** and **smash** always take a preposition: ~~*We're going to slam/smash, aren't we?*~~ They are used for a much wider range of things than just vehicles. **Crash** can also be used for other things, if used with a preposition: *He crashed down the telephone receiver.*

wreck to crash a vehicle and damage it so badly that it is not worth repairing

PATTERNS

- **two vehicles** crash/collide
- **two vehicles** crash/slam/smash **into each other**
- to crash/smash/wreck a **car**

ˈcrash barrier (*BrE*) (*NAmE* **ˈguard rail**) *noun* a strong low fence or wall at the side of a road or between the two halves of a major road such as a MOTORWAY or INTERSTATE

ˈcrash helmet *noun* a hat made of very strong material and worn when riding a motorcycle to protect the head ➲ VISUAL VOCAB page V53

ˈcrash-land *verb* [I, T] **~ (sth)** if a plane **crash-lands** or a pilot **crash-lands** it, the pilot lands it roughly in an emergency, usually because it is damaged and cannot land normally ▶ **ˌcrash ˈlanding** *noun*: *to make a crash landing*

ˈcrash-test *verb* **~ sth** to deliberately crash a new vehicle under controlled conditions in order to test how it reacts or to improve its safety ▶ **ˈcrash test** *noun*

ˌcrash-test ˈdummy *noun* a model of a person used in crash tests to see what would happen to a driver or passenger in a real crash

crass /kræs/ *adj.* very stupid and showing no sympathy or understanding SYN **insensitive**: *the crass questions all dis-*

abled people get asked ◇ *an act of crass* (= great) *stupidity* ▶ **crass·ly** *adv.* **crass·ness** *noun* [U]

-crat *combining form* (in nouns) a member or supporter of a particular type of government or system: *democrat* ◇ *bureaucrat* ▶ **-cratic** (in adjectives): *aristocratic*

crate /kreɪt/ *noun, verb*
■ *noun* **1** a large wooden container for transporting goods: *a crate of bananas* **2** a container made of plastic or metal divided into small sections, for transporting or storing bottles: *a beer crate* **3** the amount of sth contained in a crate: *They drank two crates of beer.*
■ *verb* **~ sth (up)** to pack sth in a crate

crater /ˈkreɪtə(r)/ *noun* **1** a large hole in the top of a VOLCANO **2** a large hole in the ground caused by the explosion of a bomb or by sth large hitting it: *a meteorite crater*

cra·vat /krəˈvæt/ (*NAmE* also **ascot**) *noun* a short wide strip of silk, etc. worn by men around the neck, folded inside the COLLAR of a shirt

crave /kreɪv/ *verb* **1** [T, I] **~ (for) sth | ~ to do sth** to have a very strong desire for sth SYN **long for**: *She has always craved excitement.* **2** [T] **~ sth** (*BrE, old use*) to ask for sth seriously: *I must crave your pardon.*

cra·ven /ˈkreɪvn/ *adj.* (*formal, disapproving*) lacking courage SYN **cowardly** OPP **brave** ▶ **craven·ly** *adv.*

crav·ing /ˈkreɪvɪŋ/ *noun* a strong desire for sth: **~ (for sth)** *a craving for chocolate* ◇ **~ (to do sth)** *a desperate craving to be loved*

craw /krɔː/ *noun* the part of a bird's throat where food is kept IDM see STICK *v.*

craw·fish /ˈkrɔːfɪʃ/ *noun* (*especially NAmE*) = CRAYFISH

crawl /krɔːl/ *verb, noun*
■ *verb* **1** [I] (**+ adv./prep.**) to move forward on your hands and knees, with your body close to the ground: *Our baby is just starting to crawl.* ◇ *A man was crawling away from the burning wreckage.* **2** [I] (**+ adv./prep.**) when an insect **crawls**, it moves forward on its legs: *There's a spider crawling up your leg.* **3** [I] (**+ adv./prep.**) to move forward very slowly: *The traffic was crawling along.* ◇ *The weeks crawled by.* **4** [I] **~ (to sb)** (*informal, disapproving*) to be too friendly or helpful to sb in authority, in a way that is not sincere, especially in order to get an advantage from them: *She's always crawling to the boss.* IDM see SKIN *n.*, WOODWORK
PHR V **be ˈcrawling with sth** (*informal*) to be full of or completely covered with people, insects or animals, in a way that is unpleasant: *The place was crawling with journalists.* ◇ *Her hair was crawling with lice.*
■ *noun* **1** [sing.] a very slow speed: *The traffic slowed to a crawl.* ➲ see also PUB CRAWL **2** (often **the crawl**) [sing., U] a fast swimming stroke that you do lying on your front moving one arm over your head, and then the other, while kicking with your feet: *a swimmer doing the crawl* ➲ VISUAL VOCAB page V37

crawl·er /ˈkrɔːlə(r)/ *noun* (*informal*) **1** (*BrE, disapproving*) a person who tries to get sb's favour by praising them, doing what will please them, etc. **2** a thing or person that crawls, such as a vehicle, an insect or a baby ➲ see also KERB-CRAWLER

cray·fish /ˈkreɪfɪʃ/ (*especially BrE*) (also **craw·fish** *NAmE, BrE*) *noun* [C, U] (*pl.* **cray·fish, craw·fish**) an animal like a small LOBSTER, that lives in rivers and lakes and can be eaten, or one like a large lobster, that lives in the sea and can be eaten

crayon /ˈkreɪən/ *noun* a coloured pencil or stick of soft coloured CHALK or WAX, used for drawing ▶ **crayon** *verb* [I, T] **~ (sth)**

craze /kreɪz/ *noun* **~ (for sth)** an enthusiastic interest in sth that is shared by many people but that usually does not last very long; a thing that people have a craze for SYN **fad**: *the latest fitness craze to sweep the country*

crazed /kreɪzd/ *adj.* **~ (with sth)** (*formal*) full of strong feelings and lacking control: ***crazed with fear/grief/jealousy*** ◇ *a **crazed killer** roaming the streets*

crazy 0‑w /ˈkreɪzi/ *adj., noun*
■ *adj.* (**cra·zier, crazi·est**) (*informal*) **1** 0‑w (*especially NAmE*) not sensible; stupid: *Are you crazy? We could get killed doing that.* ◇ *She must be crazy to lend him money.* ◇ *He drove like an idiot, passing in the craziest places.* ◇ *What a crazy idea!* ◇ *I know it sounds crazy but it just might work.* **2** 0‑w very angry: *That noise is **driving me crazy**.* ◇ *Marie says he **went crazy**, and smashed the room up.* **3** 0‑w **~ (about sth)** (often in compounds) very enthusiastic or excited about sth: *Rick is crazy about football.* ◇ *He's football-crazy.* ◇ *I'm not crazy about Chinese food* (= I don't like it very much). ◇ *The crowd **went crazy** when the band came on stage.* ◇ *You're so beautiful you're **driving me crazy**.* **4** 0‑w **~ about sb** liking sb very much; in love with sb: *I've been crazy about him since the first time I saw him.* **5** 0‑w (*especially NAmE*) mentally ill; INSANE: *She's crazy—she ought to be locked up.* ➲ SYNONYMS at MAD ▶ **crazi·ly** *adv.* **cra·zi·ness** *noun* [U]
IDM **like ˈcrazy/ˈmad** (*informal*) very fast, hard, much, etc: *We worked like crazy to get it done on time.*
■ *noun* (*pl.* **-ies**) (*informal, especially NAmE*) a crazy person

ˈcrazy golf *noun* [U] (*BrE*) = MINIGOLF

ˌcrazy ˈpaving *noun* [U] (*BrE*) pieces of stone of different shapes and sizes, fitted together on the ground to make a path or PATIO

ˌcrazy ˈquilt *noun* (*NAmE*) a type of QUILT in which small pieces of cloth of different shape, colour, design and size are sewn together ➲ compare PATCHWORK

CRE /ˌsiː ɑːr ˈiː/ *abbr.* Commission for Racial Equality (a government organization in Britain that protects the rights of people of all races)

creak /kriːk/ *verb, noun*
■ *verb* [I] to make the sound that a door sometimes makes when you open it or that a wooden floor sometimes makes when you step on it: *She heard a floorboard creak upstairs.* ◇ *a creaking **bed/gate/stair*** ◇ *The table creaked and groaned under the weight.* ◇ **+ adj.** *The door creaked open.*
IDM **ˌcreak under the ˈstrain** if a system or service **creaks under the strain**, it cannot deal effectively with all the things it is expected to do or provide
■ *noun* [C] (also **creak·ing** [U, C]) a sound, for example that sometimes made by a door when it opens or shuts, or by a wooden floor when you step on it: *the creak/creaking of the door* ◇ *Distant creaks and groans echoed eerily along the dark corridors.*

creaky /ˈkriːki/ *adj.* **1** making creaks: *a creaky old chair* **2** old and not in good condition: *the country's creaky legal machinery*

cream 0‑w /kriːm/ *noun, adj., verb*
■ *noun* **1** 0‑w [U] the thick pale yellowish-white FATTY liquid that rises to the top of milk, used in cooking or as a type of sauce to put on fruit, etc: *strawberries and cream* ◇ *Would you like milk or cream in your coffee?* ◇ ***fresh/whipped cream*** ◇ (*BrE*) *cream cakes* (= containing cream) ◇ (*BrE*) ***double/single cream*** (= thick/thin cream) ➲ see also CLOTTED CREAM, ICE CREAM, SALAD CREAM, SOUR CREAM, WHIPPING CREAM **2** [C] (in compounds) a sweet/candy that has a soft substance like cream inside: *a **chocolate/peppermint cream*** **3** 0‑w [U, C] a soft substance or thick liquid used on your skin to protect it or make it feel soft; a similar substance used for cleaning things: *hand/moisturizing cream* ◇ *antiseptic cream* ◇ *a cream cleaner* ➲ see also COLD CREAM, FACE CREAM, SHAVING CREAM **4** 0‑w [U] a pale yellowish-white colour **5 the ~ of sth** the best people or things in a particular group: *the cream of New York society* ◇ ***the cream of the crop*** *of this season's movies* IDM see CAT
■ *adj.* 0‑w pale yellowish-white in colour: *a cream linen suit*
■ *verb* **1 ~ sth (together)** to mix things together into a soft smooth mixture: *Cream the butter and sugar together.* **2 ~ sb** (*NAmE, informal*) to completely defeat sb: *We got creamed in the first round.*
PHR V **ˌcream sb/sth↔ˈoff** to take sth away, usually the best people or things or an amount of money, in order to get an advantage for yourself: *The best students were creamed off by the grammar schools.*

ˌcream ˈcheese *noun* [U, C] soft white cheese containing a lot of cream

ˌcream ˈcracker *noun* (*BrE*) a dry biscuit, often eaten with cheese

cream·er /ˈkriːmə(r)/ *noun* **1** [U] a liquid or powder that you can put in coffee, etc. instead of cream or milk: *non-dairy creamer* **2** [C] (*NAmE*) a small container for holding and pouring cream

cream·ery /ˈkriːməri/ *noun* (*pl.* **-ies**) a place where milk and cream are made into butter and cheese

ˌcream ˈpuff *noun* (*NAmE*) **1** = PROFITEROLE **2** (*slang, disapproving*) a person who is not strong or brave SYN **wimp**

ˌcream ˈsoda *noun* [U, C] (*especially NAmE*) a FIZZY drink (= one with bubbles) that tastes of VANILLA

ˌcream ˈtea *noun* (*BrE*) a special meal eaten in the afternoon, consisting of tea with SCONES, jam and thick cream

creamy /ˈkriːmi/ *adj.* (**cream·ier, creami·est**) **1** thick and smooth like cream; containing a lot of cream: *a* ***creamy*** *sauce/soup* **2** pale yellowish-white in colour: *creamy skin*

crease /kriːs/ *noun, verb*

■ ***noun*** **1** an untidy line that is made in cloth or paper when it is pressed or crushed: *She smoothed the creases out of her skirt.* ◇ *a shirt made of crease-resistant material* **2** a neat line that you make in sth, for example when you fold it: *trousers with a sharp crease in the legs* ➲ VISUAL VOCAB page V50 **3** a line in the skin, especially on the face: *creases around the eyes* **4** (in CRICKET) a white line on the ground near each WICKET that marks the position of the BOWLER and the BATSMAN

■ ***verb*** **1** [T, I] **~ (sth)** to make lines on cloth or paper by folding or crushing it; to develop lines in this way: *Pack your suit carefully so that you don't crease it.* **2** [T, I] **~ (sth)** to make lines in the skin; to develop lines in the skin: *A frown creased her forehead.* ◇ *Her face creased into a smile.* ▸ **creased** *adj.*: *I can't wear this blouse. It's creased.*

PHR V **ˌcrease ˈup** | **ˌcrease sb ˈup** (*BrE, informal*) to start laughing or make sb start laughing SYN **crack (sb) up**: *Ed creased up laughing.* ◇ *Her jokes really creased me up.*

cre·ate 0‑w AW /kriˈeɪt/ *verb*

1 0‑w **~ sth** to make sth happen or exist: *Scientists disagree about how the universe was created.* ◇ *The main purpose of industry is to create wealth.* ◇ *The government plans to create more jobs for young people.* ◇ *Create a new directory and put all your files into it.* ◇ *Try this new dish, created by our head chef.* ➲ SYNONYMS at MAKE **2** 0‑w **~ sth** to produce a particular feeling or impression: *The company is trying to create a young energetic image.* ◇ *The announcement only succeeded in creating confusion.* ◇ *They've painted it red to create a feeling of warmth.* **3** to give sb a particular rank or title: **~ sth** *The government has created eight new peers.* ◇ **~ sth + noun** *He was created a baronet in 1715.*

cre·ation AW /kriˈeɪʃn/ *noun* **1** [U] the act or process of making sth that is new, or of causing sth to exist that did not exist before: *the process of database creation* ◇ *wealth creation* ◇ *He had been with the company since its creation in 1989.* ➲ see also JOB CREATION **2** [C] (*often humorous*) a thing that sb has made, especially sth that shows ability or imagination: *a literary creation* ◇ *The cake was a delicious creation of sponge, cream and fruit.* **3** (usually **the Creation**) [sing.] the making of the world, especially by God as described in the Bible **4** (often **Creation**) [U] the world and all the living things in it

cre·ation·ism /kriˈeɪʃnɪzəm/ *noun* [U] the belief that the universe was made by God exactly as described in the Bible ▸ **cre·ation·ist** *adj., noun*

creˈation science *noun* [U] science that tries to find proof that God created the world

cre·ative AW /kriˈeɪtɪv/ *adj., noun*

■ ***adj.*** **1** [only before noun] involving the use of skill and the imagination to produce sth new or a work of art: *a course on* ***creative writing*** (= writing stories, plays and poems) ◇ *the creative and performing arts* ◇ ***creative thinking*** (= thinking about problems in a new way or thinking of new ideas) ◇ *the company's creative team* ◇ *the creative process* **2** having the skill and ability to produce sth new, especially a work of art; showing this ability: *She's very creative—she writes poetry and paints.* ◇ *Do you have any ideas? You're the creative one.* ▸ **cre·ative·ly** AW *adv.* **cre·ativ·ity** AW /ˌkriːeɪˈtɪvəti/ *noun* [U]: *Creativity and originality are more important than technical skill.*

■ ***noun*** **1** [C] a person who is creative: *The exhibition features the paintings of local creatives.* **2** [U] creative ideas or material: *We need to produce better creative if we want to attract big clients.*

creˌative acˈcounting *noun* [U] (*disapproving*) a way of doing or presenting the accounts of a business that might not show what the true situation really is

cre·ator AW /kriˈeɪtə(r)/ *noun* **1** [C] a person who has made or invented a particular thing: *Walt Disney, the creator of Mickey Mouse* **2** **the Creator** [sing.] God

crea·ture 0‑w /ˈkriːtʃə(r)/ *noun*

1 0‑w a living thing, real or imaginary, that can move around, such as an animal: *The dormouse is a shy, nocturnal creature.* ◇ *respect for all* ***living creatures*** ◇ *strange creatures from outer space* **2** (especially following an adjective) a person, considered in a particular way: *You pathetic creature!* ◇ *She was an exotic creature with long red hair and brilliant green eyes.* ◇ *He always goes to bed at ten—he's* ***a creature of habit*** (= he likes to do the same things at the same time every day).

IDM **a/the creature of sb** | **sb's creature** (*formal, disapproving*) a person or thing that depends completely on sb else and is controlled by them

ˌcreature ˈcomforts *noun* [pl.] all the things that make life, or a particular place, comfortable, such as good food, comfortable furniture or modern equipment

crèche (also **creche**) /kreʃ/ *noun* **1** (*BrE*) a place where babies and small children are taken care of while their parents are working, studying, shopping, etc. ➲ compare DAY NURSERY **2** (*NAmE*) (*BrE* **crib**) a model of the scene of Jesus Christ's birth, placed in churches and homes at Christmas

cred /kred/ *noun* [U] = STREET CRED

cre·dence /ˈkriːdns/ *noun* [U] (*formal*) **1** a quality that an idea or a story has that makes you believe it is true: *Historical evidence* ***lends credence to*** *his theory.* **2** belief in sth as true: *They could* ***give no credence*** *to the findings of the survey.* ◇ *Alternative medicine has been* ***gaining credence*** (= becoming more widely accepted) *recently.*

cre·den·tial /krəˈdenʃl/ *verb* **~ sb** (*NAmE*) to provide sb with credentials

cre·den·tials /krəˈdenʃlz/ *noun* [pl.] **1 ~ (as/for sth)** the qualities, training or experience that make you suitable to do sth: *He has all the credentials for the job.* ◇ *She will first have to establish her leadership credentials.* **2** documents such as letters that prove that you are who you claim to be, and can therefore be trusted

cred·ibil·ity /ˌkredəˈbɪləti/ *noun* [U] the quality that sb/sth has that makes people believe or trust them: *to* ***gain/lack/lose credibility*** ◇ *The prosecution did its best to* ***undermine the credibility*** *of the witness.* ◇ *Newspapers were talking of a* ***credibility gap*** *between what he said and what he did.* ➲ see also STREET CRED

cred·ible /ˈkredəbl/ *adj.* **1** that can be believed or trusted SYN **convincing**: *a* ***credible explanation/witness*** ◇ *It is just not credible that she would cheat.* **2** that can be accepted, because it seems possible that it could be successful SYN **viable**: *Community service is seen as the only credible alternative to imprisonment.* ▸ **cred·ibly** /-əbli/ *adv.*: *We can credibly describe the band's latest album as their best yet.*

credit 0‑w AW /ˈkredɪt/ *noun, verb*

■ ***noun***

▸ BUY NOW–PAY LATER **1** 0‑w [U] an arrangement that you make, with a shop/store for example, to pay later for sth you buy: *to* ***get/refuse credit*** ◇ *We bought the dishwasher* ***on credit.*** ◇ *to offer* ***interest-free credit*** (= allow sb to pay later, without any extra charge) ◇ *a credit agreement* ◇

C

credit facilities/terms ◇ *Your* **credit limit** *is now £2 000.* ◇ *He's a bad* **credit risk** (= he is unlikely to pay the money later). ➲ compare HIRE PURCHASE
▸ MONEY BORROWED **2** 🗝 [U, C] money that you borrow from a bank; a loan: *The bank refused further credit to the company.* ➲ COLLOCATIONS at FINANCE **3** [U] the status of being trusted to pay back money to sb who lends it to you: *Her credit isn't good anywhere now.*
▸ MONEY IN BANK **4** 🗝 [U] if you or your bank account are **in credit**, there is money in the account **5** [C, U] a sum of money paid into a bank account; a record of the payment: *a credit of £50* ◇ *You'll be paid by direct credit into your bank account.* OPP **debit**
▸ MONEY BACK **6** [C, U] (*technical*) a payment that sb has a right to for a particular reason: *a tax credit*
▸ PRAISE **7** 🗝 [U] **~ (for sth)** praise or approval because you are responsible for sth good that has happened: *He's a player who rarely seems to get the credit he deserves.* ◇ *I can't take all the credit for the show's success—it was a team effort.* ◇ *We did all the work and she gets all the credit!* ◇ *Credit will be given in the exam for good spelling and grammar.* ◇ *At least give him credit for trying* (= praise him because he tried, even if he did not succeed). ➲ compare BLAME, DISCREDIT **8** [sing.] **~ to sb/sth** a person or thing whose qualities or achievements are praised and who therefore earns respect for sb/sth else: *She is a credit to the school.*
▸ ON MOVIE/TV PROGRAMME **9** [C, usually pl.] the act of mentioning sb who worked on a project such as a film/movie or a television programme: *She was given a programme credit for her work on the costumes for the play.* ◇ **The credits** (= the list of all the people involved) *seemed to last almost as long as the film!*
▸ UNIT OF STUDY **10** [C] a unit of study at a college or university (in the US, also at a school); the fact of having successfully completed a unit of study: *My math class is worth three credits.*
IDM **do sb credit | do credit to sb/sth** if sth **does credit** to a person or an organization, they deserve to be praised for it: *Your honesty does you great credit.* **have sth to your credit** to have achieved sth: *He's only 30, and he already has four novels to his credit.* **on the 'credit side** used to introduce the good points about sb/sth, especially after the bad points have been mentioned **to sb's credit** making sb deserve praise or respect: *To his credit, Jack never told anyone exactly what had happened.*
■ *verb*
▸ PUT MONEY IN BANK **1** to add an amount of money to sb's bank account: **~ A (with B)** *Your account has been credited with $50 000.* ◇ **~ B (to A)** *$50 000 has been credited to your account.* OPP **debit**
▸ WITH ACHIEVEMENT **2** [usually passive] to believe or say that sb is responsible for doing sth, especially sth good: **~ sb** *All the contributors are credited on the title page.* ◇ **~ A with B** *The company is credited with inventing the industrial robot.* ◇ **~ B to A** *The invention of the industrial robot is credited to the company.*
▸ WITH QUALITY **3 ~ A with B** to believe that sb/sth has a particular good quality or feature: *I credited you with a little more sense.* **4** [usually passive] **~ sb/sth as sth** to believe that sb/sth is of a particular type or quality: *The cheetah is generally credited as the world's fastest animal.*
▸ BELIEVE **5 ~ sth | ~ what, how, etc... | ~ that...** (*BrE*) (used mainly in questions and negative sentences) to believe sth, especially sth surprising or unexpected: *He's been promoted—would you credit it?*

cred·it·able /'kredɪtəbl/ *adj.* (*formal*) **1** of a quite good standard and deserving praise or approval SYN **praiseworthy**: *It was a very creditable result for the team.* **2** morally good SYN **admirable**: *There was nothing very creditable in what he did.* ▸ **cred·it·ably** /'kredɪtəbli/ *adv.*

'credit account *noun* (*BrE*) = ACCOUNT (3)

'credit card 🗝 *noun*
a small plastic card that you can use to buy goods and services and pay for them later: *All major credit cards are accepted at our hotels.* ➲ picture at MONEY ➲ see also CHARGE CARD, CHEQUE CARD, DEBIT CARD, STORE CARD

'credit crunch *noun* [usually sing.] (*economics*) an economic condition in which it suddenly becomes difficult and expensive to borrow money

'credit note *noun* (*BrE*) a letter that a shop/store gives you when you have returned sth and that allows you to have goods of the same value in exchange

cred·it·or AW /'kredɪtə(r)/ *noun* a person, company, etc. that sb owes money to ➲ compare DEBTOR

'credit rating *noun* a judgement made by a bank, etc. about how likely sb is to pay back money that they borrow, and how safe it is to lend money to them

'credit transfer *noun* (*BrE*) the process of sending money from one person's bank account to another's

'credit union *noun* an organization that lends money to its members at low rates of interest

credit·worthy /'kredɪtwɜːði; *NAmE* -wɜːrði/ *adj.* able to be trusted to pay back money that is owed; safe to lend money to ▸ **credit·worthi·ness** *noun* [U]

credo /'kriːdəʊ; 'kreɪdəʊ; *NAmE* -doʊ/ *noun* (*pl.* **-os**) (*formal*) a set of beliefs SYN **creed**

cre·du·lity /krɪ'djuːləti; *NAmE* -'duː-/ *noun* [U] (*formal*) the ability or willingness to believe that sth is real or true: *The plot of the novel stretches credulity to the limit* (= it is almost impossible to believe).

credu·lous /'kredjələs; *NAmE* -dʒə-/ *adj.* (*formal*) too ready to believe things and therefore easy to trick SYN **gullibility** ➲ compare INCREDULOUS

Cree /kriː/ *noun* (*pl.* **Cree** or **Crees**) a member of a Native American people, many of whom live in central Canada

creed /kriːd/ *noun* **1** a set of principles or religious beliefs: *people of all races, colours and creeds* ◇ *What is his political creed?* **2 the Creed** [sing.] a statement of Christian belief that is spoken as part of some church services

Creek /kriːk/ *noun* (*pl.* **Creek** or **Creeks**) a member of a Native American people, many of whom now live in the US state of Oklahoma

creek /kriːk/ *noun* **1** (*BrE*) a narrow area of water where the sea flows into the land SYN **inlet 2** (*NAmE, AustralE, NZE*) a small river or stream
IDM **up the 'creek (without a 'paddle)** (*informal*) in a difficult or bad situation: *I was really up the creek without my car.*

creel /kriːl/ *noun* a BASKET for holding fish that have just been caught

creep /kriːp/ *verb, noun*
■ *verb* (**crept, crept** /krept/) HELP In the phrasal verb **creep sb out, creeped** is used for the past simple and past participle. **1** [I] **(+ adv./prep.)** (of people or animals) to move slowly, quietly and carefully, because you do not want to be seen or heard: *I crept up the stairs, trying not to wake my parents.* **2** [I] **(+ adv./prep.)** (*NAmE*) to move with your body close to the ground; to move slowly on your hands and knees SYN **crawl 3** [I] **(+ adv./prep.)** to move or develop very slowly: *Her arms crept around his neck.* ◇ *A slight feeling of suspicion crept over me.* **4** [I] **(+ adv./prep.)** (of plants) to grow along the ground or up walls using long STEMS or roots ➲ see also CREEPER **5** [I] **~ (to sb)** (*BrE, informal, disapproving*) to be too friendly or helpful to sb in authority in a way that is not sincere, especially in order to get an advantage from them IDM see FLESH *n.*
PHR V **,creep 'in/'into sth** to begin to happen or affect sth: *As she became more tired, errors began to creep into her work.* **,creep sb 'out (creeped, creeped)** (*NAmE, informal*) to make sb feel afraid, uncomfortable or disgusted: *He said the empty streets creeped him out.* **,creep 'up** to gradually increase in amount, price, etc: *House prices are creeping up again.* **,creep 'up on sb 1** to move slowly nearer to sb, usually from behind, without being seen or heard: *Don't creep up on me like that!* **2** to begin to affect sb, especially before they realize it: *Tiredness can easily creep up on you while you're driving.*
■ *noun* **1** [C] (*informal*) a person that you dislike very much and find very unpleasant: *He's a nasty little creep!* **2** [C]

(*BrE, informal*) a person who is not sincere but tries to win your approval by being nice to you **3** [U] (in compounds) (often *disapproving*) the development of a project beyond the goal that was originally agreed: *The World Bank has been accused of **mission creep** when seeking to address these concerns.* ◇ *The inclusion of health data on identity cards was condemned as **function creep**.*

IDM **give sb the 'creeps** (*informal*) to make sb feel nervous and slightly frightened, especially because sb/sth is unpleasant or strange

creep·er /'kri:pə(r)/ *noun* a plant that grows along the ground, up walls, etc, often winding itself around other plants ➲ see also VIRGINIA CREEPER

creep·ing /'kri:pɪŋ/ *adj.* [only before noun] (of sth bad) happening or moving gradually and not easily noticed: *creeping inflation*

creepy /'kri:pi/ *adj.* (**creep·ier**, **creepi·est**) (*informal*) **1** causing an unpleasant feeling of fear or slight horror SYN **scary**: *a creepy ghost story* ◇ *It's kind of creepy down in the cellar!* **2** strange in a way that makes you feel nervous: *What a creepy coincidence.* SYN **spooky**

creepy-crawly /ˌkri:pi 'krɔ:li/ *noun* (*pl.* **-ies**) (*informal*) an insect, a WORM, etc. when you think of it as unpleasant

cre·mains /krɪ'meɪnz/ *noun* [pl.] (*NAmE*) the powder that is left after a dead person's body has been CREMATED (= burned) SYN **ashes**

cre·mate /krə'meɪt/ *verb* [often passive] **~ sb/sth** to burn a dead body, especially as part of a funeral ceremony

cre·ma·tion /krə'meɪʃn/ *noun* **1** [U] the act of cremating sb **2** [C] a funeral at which the dead person is cremated

crema·tor·ium /ˌkremə'tɔ:riəm/ *noun* (*pl.* **crema·toria** /-'tɔ:riə/ or **crema·tor·iums**) (*NAmE* also **crema·tory** /'kri:mətɔ:ri; 'krem-/ *pl.* **-ies**) a building in which the bodies of dead people are burned

crème brûlée /ˌkrem bru:'leɪ/ *noun* [C, U] (*pl.* **crèmes brûlées** /ˌkrem bru:'leɪ/) (from *French*) a cold DESSERT (= a sweet dish) made from cream, with burnt sugar on top

crème caramel /ˌkrem 'kærəmel/ *noun* [C, U] (*pl.* **crèmes caramels** /ˌkrem 'kærəmel/) (*BrE*, from *French*) (*NAmE* **flan**) a cold DESSERT (= a sweet dish) made from milk, eggs and sugar

crème de la crème /ˌkrem də lɑ: 'krem/ *noun* [sing.] (from *French*, *formal* or *humorous*) the best people or things of their kind: *This school takes only the crème de la crème.*

crème de menthe /ˌkrem də 'mɒnθ; *NAmE* 'menθ/ *noun* [U, C] (*pl.* **crèmes de menthe** /ˌkrem də 'mɒnθ; *NAmE* 'menθ/) (from *French*) a strong sweet alcoholic drink made with MINT

crème fraiche /ˌkrem 'freʃ/ *noun* [U] (from *French*) thick cream with a slightly sour taste

cren·el·lated (*US* also **cren·el·ated**) /'krenəleɪtɪd/ *adj.* (*technical*) (of a tower, castle, etc.) having BATTLEMENTS

Cre·ole /'kri:əʊl; *NAmE* -oʊl/ (also **creole**) *noun* **1** [C] a person of mixed European and African race, especially one who lives in the West Indies **2** [C] a person whose ANCESTORS were among the first Europeans who settled in the West Indies or S America, or one of the French or Spanish people who settled in the southern states of the US: *Creole cookery* **3** [U] a language formed when a mixture of a European language with a local language (especially an African language spoken by SLAVES in the West Indies) is spoken as a first language ➲ compare PIDGIN

cre·ol·ize (*BrE* also **-ise**) /'kri:əlaɪz; *BrE* also 'krɪə-/ *verb* **~ sth** (*linguistics*) to change a language by combining it with a language from another place: *Creolized forms of Latin were spoken in various parts of Europe.* ▸ **cre·ol·iza·tion, -isa·tion** /ˌkri:əlaɪ'zeɪʃn; *BrE* also 'krɪəlaɪzeɪʃn/ *noun* [U, C]

creo·sote /'kri:əsəʊt; *NAmE* -soʊt/ *noun, verb*

■ ***noun*** [U] a thick brown liquid that is made from COAL TAR, used to preserve wood

■ ***verb* ~ sth** to paint or preserve sth with creosote

crêpe (also **crepe**) /kreɪp/ *noun* **1** [U] a type of light thin cloth, made especially from cotton or silk, with a surface that is covered in lines and folds: *a black crêpe dress* ◇ *a crêpe bandage* **2** [U] a type of strong rubber with a rough surface, used for making the SOLES of shoes: *crêpe-soled shoes* **3** [C] a thin PANCAKE

'crêpe paper *noun* [U] a type of thin brightly coloured paper that stretches and has a surface covered in lines and folds, used especially for making decorations

crept *past tense, past part.* of CREEP

cre·pus·cul·ar /krɪ'pʌskjələ(r)/ *adj.* (*literary*) related to the period of the evening when the sun has just gone down but there is still some light in the sky

cres·cendo /krə'ʃendəʊ; *NAmE* -doʊ/ *noun* (*pl.* **-os**) [C, U] **1** (*music*) a gradual increase in how loudly a piece of music is played or sung OPP **diminuendo** **2** a gradual increase in noise; the loudest point of a period of continuous noise SYN **swell**: *Voices rose in a crescendo and drowned him out.* ◇ (*figurative*) *The advertising campaign reached a crescendo just before Christmas.*

cres·cent /'kresnt; *BrE* also 'kreznt/ *noun* **1** [C] a curved shape that is wide in the middle and pointed at each end: *a crescent moon* **2** [C] (often used in street names) a curved street with a row of houses on it: *I live at 7 Park Crescent.* **3 the Crescent** [sing.] the curved shape that is used as a symbol of Islam ➲ see also THE RED CRESCENT

cress /kres/ *noun* [U] a small plant with thin STEMS and very small leaves, often eaten in salads and SANDWICHES ➲ see also WATERCRESS

crest /krest/ *noun, verb*

■ ***noun*** **1** [usually sing.] **~ (of sth)** the top part of a hill or wave: *surfers riding the crest of the wave* ➲ VISUAL VOCAB page V4 **2** a design used as the symbol of a particular family, organization, etc, especially one that has a long history: *the university crest* **3** a group of feathers that stand up on top of a bird's head ➲ VISUAL VOCAB page V10

IDM **the crest of a/the 'wave** a situation in which sb is very successful, happy, etc. ➲ more at RIDE *v.*

■ ***verb*** **1** [T] **~ sth** (*formal*) to reach the top of a hill, mountain or wave: *He slowed the pace as they crested the ridge.* **2** [I] (*NAmE*) (of a flood, wave, etc.) to reach its highest level before it falls again: (*figurative*) *The level of debt crested at a massive $290 billion in 2009.*

crest·ed /'krestɪd/ *adj.* **1** marked with a crest: *crested notepaper* **2** used especially in names of birds or animals which have a crest: *crested newts*

crest·fall·en /'krestfɔ:lən/ *adj.* sad and disappointed because you have failed and you did not expect to

Cret·aceous /krɪ'teɪʃəs/ *adj.* (*geology*) of the PERIOD between around 146 to 65 million years ago, when dinosaurs lived (until they died out); of the rocks formed during this time ▸ **the Cret·aceous** *noun* [sing.]

cre·tin /'kretɪn; *NAmE* 'kri:tn/ *noun* (*informal, offensive*) a very stupid person: *Why did you do that, you cretin?* ▸ **cret·in·ous** /'kretɪnəs; *NAmE* 'kri:tnəs/ *adj.*

Creutzfeldt-Jakob disease /ˌkrɔɪtsfelt 'jækɒb dɪzi:z; *NAmE* 'jækɔ:b/ *noun* [U] (*abbr.* **CJD**) a brain disease that causes gradual loss of control of the mind and body and, finally, death. It is believed to be caused by PRIONS and is linked to BSE in cows.

cre·vasse /krə'væs/ *noun* a deep open crack, especially in ice, for example in a GLACIER

crev·ice /'krevɪs/ *noun* a narrow crack in a rock or wall

crew /kru:/ *noun, verb*

■ ***noun*** **1** [C+sing./pl. v.] all the people working on a ship, plane, etc: *None of the passengers and crew were injured.* ◇ *crew members* ➲ see also AIRCREW, CABIN CREW, FLIGHT CREW **2** [C+sing./pl. v.] all the people working on a ship, plane etc. except the officers who are in charge: *the officers and crew* **3** [C+sing./pl. v.] a group of people with special skills working together: *a **film/camera crew*** ◇ *an ambulance crew* ➲ see also GROUND CREW **4** [sing.] (usually *disapproving*) a group of people: *The people she invited were a pretty **motley crew*** (= a strange mix of types of people).

5 [C+sing./pl. v.] a team of people who ROW boats in races: *a member of the Cambridge crew* **6** [U] (*NAmE*) the sport of ROWING with other people in a boat: *I'm thinking of going out for crew this semester* (= joining the ROWING team).
■ ***verb*** [T, I] to be part of a crew, especially on a ship: **~ (sth)** *Normally the boat is crewed by five people.* ◇ **~ (for sb)** *I crewed for him on his yacht last summer.*

C

'crew cut *noun* a HAIRSTYLE for men in which the hair is cut very short ➲ VISUAL VOCAB page V49 ▸ **'crew-cut** *adj.*: *crew-cut teenagers*

crew·man /'kru:mən/ *noun* (*pl.* -men /-mən/) a member of a CREW, usually a man

ˌcrew 'neck *noun* a round neck on a sweater, etc. ➲ VISUAL VOCAB page V51

crib /krɪb/ *noun, verb*
■ ***noun*** **1** (*NAmE*) (*BrE* **cot**) a small bed with high sides for a baby or young child ➲ VISUAL VOCAB page V20 **2** a long open box that horses and cows can eat from SYN **manger** **3** (*BrE*) (*NAmE* **crèche**) a model of the scene of Jesus Christ's birth, placed in churches and homes at Christmas **4** (*informal*) written information such as answers to questions, often used dishonestly by students in tests: *a crib sheet* **5** = CRIBBAGE **6** (*NAmE, informal*) the house, flat/apartment, etc. where sb lives
■ ***verb*** (-bb-) [I, T] **~ (sth) (from sb)** (*old-fashioned*) to dishonestly copy work from another student or from a book

crib·bage /'krɪbɪdʒ/ (also **crib**) *noun* [U] a card game in which players score points by collecting different combinations of cards. The score is kept by putting small PEGS in holes in a board.

'crib death (*NAmE*) (*BrE* **'cot death**) *noun* [U, C] the sudden death while sleeping of a baby that appears to be healthy

crick /krɪk/ (*NAmE* also **kink**) *noun* [usually sing.] a sudden painful stiff feeling in the muscles of your neck or back ▸ **crick** *verb*: **~ sth** *I suffered a cricked neck during a game of tennis.*

cricket /'krɪkɪt/ *noun* **1** [U] a game played on grass by two teams of 11 players. Players score points (called RUNS) by hitting the ball with a wooden BAT and running between two sets of vertical wooden sticks, called STUMPS: *a **cricket match/team/club/ball*** ➲ VISUAL VOCAB page V36 **2** [C] a small brown jumping insect that makes a loud high sound by rubbing its wings together: *the chirping of crickets*
IDM **not 'cricket** (*old-fashioned, BrE, informal*) unfair; not HONOURABLE

crick·et·er /'krɪkɪtə(r)/ *noun* a cricket player

cricket·ing /'krɪkɪtɪŋ/ *adj.* [only before noun] playing cricket; connected with cricket: *cricketing nations* ◇ *a cricketing jersey*

cri de cœur /ˌkri: də 'kɜ:(r)/ *noun* (*pl.* **cris de cœur** /ˌkri: də 'kɜ:(r)/) (from *French*) an act of asking for sth, or protesting, in a way that shows you care deeply about sth

cried *past tense, past part.* of CRY

crier /'kraɪə(r)/ *noun* = TOWN CRIER

cri·key /'kraɪki/ *exclamation* (*BrE, old-fashioned, informal*) used to show that sb is surprised or annoyed: *Crikey, is that the time?*

Crimbo = CHRIMBO

crime O‑w /kraɪm/ *noun*
1 O‑w [U] activities that involve breaking the law: *an increase in violent crime* ◇ *the fight against crime* ◇ *Stores spend more and more on **crime prevention** every year.* ◇ ***petty/serious crime*** ◇ *the connection between drugs and **organized crime*** ◇ *He **turned to crime** when he dropped out of school.* ◇ *The **crime rate** is rising.* ◇ ***crime fiction/novels*** (= stories about crime) ◇ ***crime figures/statistics*** ◇ *She's a **crime writer*** (= she writes stories about crime). ➲ COLLOCATIONS at JUSTICE **2** O‑w [C] **~ (against sb)** an illegal act or activity that can be punished by law: *to **commit a crime*** (= do sth illegal) ◇ *The massacre was a **crime against humanity**.* ➲ see also WAR CRIME **3 a crime** [sing.] (*informal*) an act that you think is immoral or is a big mistake: *It's a crime to waste so much money.*

Collocations

Crime

Committing a crime

- **commit** a crime/a murder/a violent assault/a brutal killing/an armed robbery/fraud
- **be involved in** terrorism/a suspected arson attack/people smuggling/human trafficking
- **engage/participate in** criminal activity/illegal practices/acts of mindless vandalism
- **steal** sb's wallet/purse/(*BrE*) mobile phone/(*NAmE*) cell phone
- **rob** a bank/a person/a tourist
- **break into**/(*BrE*) **burgle**/(*NAmE*) **burglarize** a house/a home/an apartment
- **hijack** a plane/ship/bus
- **smuggle** drugs/weapons/arms/immigrants
- **launder** drug money (through sth)
- **forge** documents/certificates/passports
- **take/accept/pay sb/offer (sb)** a bribe
- **run** a phishing/an email/an Internet scam

Fighting crime

- **combat/fight** crime/terrorism/corruption/drug trafficking
- **prevent/stop** credit-card fraud/child abuse/software piracy
- **deter/stop** criminals/burglars/thieves/shoplifters/vandals
- **reduce/tackle/crack down on** knife/gun/violent/street crime; (*especially BrE*) antisocial behaviour
- **foil** a bank raid/a terrorist plot
- **help/support/protect** the victims of crime

Investigating crime

- **report** a crime/a theft/a rape/an attack/(*especially BrE*) an incident to the police
- **witness** the crime/attack/murder/incident
- **investigate** a murder/(*especially NAmE*) a homicide/a burglary/a robbery/the alleged incident
- **conduct/launch/pursue** an investigation (into...); (*especially BrE*) a police/murder inquiry
- **investigate/reopen** a criminal/murder case
- **examine/investigate/find fingerprints at** the crime scene/the scene of crime
- **collect/gather** forensic evidence
- **uncover** new evidence/a fraud/a scam/a plot/a conspiracy/political corruption/a cache of weapons
- **describe/identify** a suspect/the culprit/the perpetrator/the assailant/the attacker
- **question/interrogate** a suspect/witness
- **solve/crack** the case

➲ more collocations at JUSTICE

'crime wave *noun* [sing.] a situation in which there is a sudden increase in the number of crimes that are committed

crim·inal O‑w /'krɪmɪnl/ *adj., noun*
■ ***adj.*** **1** O‑w [usually before noun] (rather *formal* or *law*) connected with or involving crime: ***criminal offences/behaviour*** ◇ ***criminal damage*** (= the crime of damaging sb's property deliberately) ◇ ***criminal negligence*** (= the illegal act of sb failing to do sth that they should do, with the result that sb else is harmed) **2** O‑w [only before noun] connected to the laws that deal with crime: *criminal law* ◇ *the criminal justice system* ◇ *a criminal lawyer* ◇ *to bring criminal charges against sb* ➲ compare CIVIL **3** morally wrong: *This is a criminal waste of resources.*
■ ***noun*** O‑w a person who commits a crime: *Society does not*

know how to deal with **hardened criminals** (= people who regularly commit crimes and are not sorry for what they do). ◇ (*especially NAmE*) *a* ***career criminal*** ➲ COLLOCATIONS at CRIME

crim·in·al·ity /ˌkrɪmɪˈnæləti/ *noun* [U] the fact of people being involved in crime; criminal acts

crim·in·al·ize (*BrE* also **-ise**) /ˈkrɪmɪnəlaɪz/ *verb* **1 ~ sth** to make sth illegal by passing a new law: *The use of opium was not criminalized until fairly recently.* **2 ~ sb** to treat sb as a criminal ▸ **crim·in·al·iza·tion, -isa·tion** /ˌkrɪmɪnəlaɪˈzeɪʃn; *NAmE* -ləˈz-/ *noun* [U]

crim·in·al·ly /ˈkrɪmɪnəli/ *adv.* according to the laws that deal with crime: *criminally insane*

ˌcriminal ˈrecord *noun* = RECORD (6)

crim·in·ology /ˌkrɪmɪˈnɒlədʒi; *NAmE* -ˈnɑːl-/ *noun* [U] the scientific study of crime and criminals ▸ **crim·ino·logic·al** /ˌkrɪmɪnəˈlɒdʒɪkl; *NAmE* -ˈlɑːdʒ-/ *adj.* **crim·in·olo·gist** /-dʒɪst/ *noun*

crimp /krɪmp/ *verb, noun*
■ ***verb*** **1 ~ sth** to make curls in sb's hair by pressing it with a heated tool **2 ~ sth** to press cloth or paper into small folds **3 ~ sth** (*NAmE, informal*) to restrict the growth or development of sth
■ ***noun***
IDM **put a ˈcrimp in/on sth** (*NAmE, informal*) to have a bad or negative effect on sth

Crim·plene™ /ˈkrɪmpliːn/ *noun* [U] an artificial material used for making clothes, that does not get lines on it when it is folded or crushed

crim·son /ˈkrɪmzn/ *adj.* dark red in colour: *She went crimson* (= her face became very red because she was embarrassed). ▸ **crim·son** *noun* [U]

cringe /krɪndʒ/ *verb* **1** [I] to move back and/or away from sb because you are afraid SYN **cower**: *a child cringing in terror* **2** [I] to feel very embarrassed and uncomfortable about sth: *I cringe when I think of the poems I wrote then.*

cringe·worthy /ˈkrɪndʒwɜːði; *NAmE* -wɜːrði/ (also **ˈcringe-making**) *adj.* (both *BrE, informal*) making you feel embarrassed or uncomfortable: *It was a cringeworthy performance from start to finish.*

crin·kle /ˈkrɪŋkl/ *verb, noun*
■ ***verb*** [I, T] to become covered with or to form a lot of thin folds or lines, especially in skin, cloth or paper: *He smiled, his* ***eyes crinkling****.* ◇ *Her face crinkled up in a smile.* ◇ **~ sth** *The binding had faded and the pages were crinkled.*
■ ***noun*** a very thin fold or line made on paper, cloth or skin

crin·kly /ˈkrɪŋkli/ *adj.* **1** having a lot of thin folds or lines: *crinkly silver foil* **2** (of hair) having a lot of small curls or waves

crin·ol·ine /ˈkrɪnəlɪn/ *noun* a frame that was worn under a skirt by some women in the past in order to give the skirt a very round full shape

cripes /kraɪps/ *exclamation* (*BrE, old-fashioned, informal*) used to show that sb is surprised or annoyed

crip·ple /ˈkrɪpl/ *verb, noun*
■ ***verb*** **1** [usually passive] **~ sb** to damage sb's body so that they are no longer able to walk or move normally SYN **disable**: *He was crippled by polio as a child.* ◇ *to be crippled with arthritis* **2** [usually passive] **~ sb/sth** to seriously damage or harm sb/sth: *The pilot tried to land his crippled plane.* ▸ **crip·pling** *adj.*: *a crippling disease* ◇ *crippling debts*
■ ***noun*** (*old-fashioned* or *offensive*) a person who is unable to walk or move normally because of a disease or injury: (*figurative*) *He's an emotional cripple* (= he cannot express his feelings). HELP People now use **disabled person** instead of 'cripple'.

cri·sis 🔑 /ˈkraɪsɪs/ *noun* [C, U] (*pl.* **cri·ses** /-siːz/)
1 🔑 a time of great danger, difficulty or confusion when problems must be solved or important decisions must be made: *a* ***political/financial crisis*** ◇ *the government's latest* ***economic crisis*** ◇ *The business is still* ***in crisis*** *but it has survived the worst of the recession.* ◇ *The Labour Party was facing an* ***identity crisis****.* ◇ *an expert in* ***crisis management*** ◇ *We provide help to families in crisis situations.* ◇ *In times of crisis I know which friends I can turn to.* ◇ *The party was suffering a* ***crisis of confidence*** *among its supporters* (= they did not trust it any longer). ➲ see also MIDLIFE CRISIS **2** 🔑 a time when a problem, a bad situation or an illness is at its worst point: *Their marriage has reached crisis point.* ◇ *The fever has passed its crisis.* ➲ see also CRITICAL

C

crisp 🔑 /krɪsp/ *adj., noun, verb*
■ ***adj.*** (**crisp·er, crisp·est**) (usually *approving*) **1** 🔑 (of food) (also **crispy**) pleasantly hard and dry: *Bake until the pastry is golden and crisp.* **2** 🔑 (of fruit and vegetables) (also **crispy**) firm and fresh: *a* ***crisp apple/lettuce*** **3** (of paper or cloth) fresh and clean; new and slightly stiff without any folds in it: *a crisp new $5 bill* ◇ *a crisp white shirt* **4** (of the air or the weather) pleasantly dry and cold: *a crisp winter morning* ◇ *The air was crisp and clear and the sky was blue.* **5** (of snow, leaves, etc.) firm or dry and making a pleasant noise when crushed: *deep, crisp snow* **6** (of sounds, images, etc.) pleasantly clear and sharp: *The recording sounds very crisp, considering its age.* **7** (sometimes *disapproving*) (of a person's way of speaking) quick and confident in a way that suggests that the person is busy or is not being friendly: *Her answer was crisp, and she gave no details.* ▸ **crisp·ly** *adv.*: *crisply fried potatoes* ◇ *'Take a seat,' she said crisply.* **crisp·ness** *noun* [U]: *The salad had lost its crispness.*
■ ***noun*** **1** (also **poˌtato ˈcrisp**) (both *BrE*) (*NAmE* **chip, poˈtato chip**) a thin round slice of potato that is fried until hard then dried and eaten cold. Crisps are sold in bags and have many different flavours. ➲ picture at CHIP **2** (*NAmE*) (*BrE* **crum·ble**) [U, C] a DESSERT (= a sweet dish) made from fruit that is covered with a rough mixture of flour, butter and sugar, cooked in the oven and usually served hot: *apple crisp* IDM see BURN *v.*
■ ***verb*** [I, T] **~ (sth)** to become or make sth crisp

crisp·bread /ˈkrɪspbred/ *noun* [C, U] a thin crisp biscuit made of WHEAT or RYE, often eaten with cheese or instead of bread

crispy /ˈkrɪspi/ *adj.* (*approving*) = CRISP: *crispy batter*

criss-cross /ˈkrɪs krɒs; *NAmE* krɔːs/ *adj., verb*
■ ***adj.*** [usually before noun] with many straight lines that cross each other: *a criss-cross pattern* ▸ **criss-cross** *noun* [sing.]: *a criss-cross of streets*
■ ***verb*** [T, I] **~ (sth)** | **~ sth (with sth)** to make a pattern on sth with many straight lines that cross each other: *The city is criss-crossed with canals.*

cri·ter·ion 🔑 AW /kraɪˈtɪəriən; *NAmE* -ˈtɪr-/ *noun* (*pl.* **cri·teria** /-riə/)
a standard or principle by which sth is judged, or with the help of which a decision is made: *The main criterion is value for money.* ◇ *What criteria are used for assessing a student's ability?*

crit·ic /ˈkrɪtɪk/ *noun* **1** a person who expresses opinions about the good and bad qualities of books, music, etc: *a* ***music/theatre/literary, etc. critic*** ◇ *The critics loved the movie.* **2** a person who expresses disapproval of sb/sth and talks about their bad qualities, especially publicly: *She is one of the ruling party's most outspoken critics.* ◇ *a critic of private health care*

crit·ic·al 🔑 /ˈkrɪtɪkl/ *adj.*
▸ EXPRESSING DISAPPROVAL **1** 🔑 expressing disapproval of sb/sth and saying what you think is bad about them: *a* ***critical comment/report*** ◇ *The supervisor is always very critical.* ◇ **~ of sb/sth** *Tom's parents were highly critical of the school.*
▸ IMPORTANT **2** 🔑 extremely important because a future situation will be affected by it SYN **crucial**: *a critical factor in the election campaign* ◇ *Reducing levels of carbon dioxide in the atmosphere is* ***of critical importance****.* ◇ *Your decision is* ***critical to*** *our future.* ➲ SYNONYMS at ESSENTIAL
▸ SERIOUS/DANGEROUS **3** 🔑 serious, uncertain and possibly dangerous: *The first 24 hours after the operation are the most critical.* ◇ *a critical moment in our country's history* ◇ *One of the victims of the fire remains* ***in a critical condition****.* ➲ see also CRISIS

▸ MAKING CAREFUL JUDGEMENTS **4** involving making fair, careful judgements about the good and bad qualities of sb/sth: *Students are encouraged to develop critical thinking instead of accepting opinions without questioning them.*
▸ OF ART/MUSIC/BOOKS, ETC. **5** [only before noun] according to the judgement of critics of art, music, literature, etc: *the film director's greatest critical success* ◇ *In her day she never received the* ***critical acclaim*** (= praise from the critics) *she deserved.*
▸ **crit·ic·al·ly** /-ɪkli/ *adv.*: *She spoke critically of her father.* ◇ *He is* ***critically ill*** *in intensive care.* ◇ *I looked at myself critically in the mirror.*

ˌcritical ˈmass *noun* (*physics*) the smallest amount of a substance that is needed for a nuclear CHAIN REACTION to take place

ˌcritical ˈpath *noun* [sing.] (*technical*) the order of work that should be followed to complete a project as fast and as cheaply as possible

ˌcritical ˈtheory *noun* [U] a way of thinking about and examining culture and literature by considering the social, historical, and IDEOLOGICAL forces that affect it and make it the way it is

criti·cism /ˈkrɪtɪsɪzəm/ *noun*
1 [U, C] the act of expressing disapproval of sb/sth and opinions about their faults or bad qualities; a statement showing disapproval: *The plan has attracted criticism from consumer groups.* ◇ *People in public life must always be* ***open to criticism*** (= willing to accept being criticized). ◇ *Ben is very sensitive, he just can't* ***take criticism.*** ◇ *to offer sb* ***constructive criticism*** (= that is meant to be helpful) ◇ *I didn't mean it as a criticism.* ◇ ***criticisms levelled at*** (= aimed at) *journalists* ◇ **~ of sb/sth** *There was* ***widespread criticism*** *of the government's handling of the disaster.* ◇ **~ that...** *My only criticism of the house is that it is on a main road.* OPP **praise** **2** [U] the work or activity of making fair, careful judgements about the good and bad qualities of sb/sth, especially books, music, etc: *literary criticism*

criti·cize (*BrE* also **-ise**) /ˈkrɪtɪsaɪz/ *verb*
1 [I, T] to say that you disapprove of sb/sth; to say what you do not like or think is wrong about sb/sth: *All you ever do is criticize!* ◇ **~ sb/sth** *The decision was criticized by environmental groups.* ◇ **~ sb/sth for sth** *The government has been criticized for not taking the problem seriously.* OPP **praise** **2** [T] **~ sth** (*BrE*) to judge the good and bad qualities of sth: *We were taught how to criticize poems.*

cri·tique /krɪˈtiːk/ *noun, verb*
■ ***noun*** a piece of written criticism of a set of ideas, a work of art, etc: *a feminist critique of Freud's theories*
■ ***verb*** **~ sth** to write or give your opinion of, or reaction to, a set of ideas, a work of art, etc: *Her job involves critiquing designs by fashion students.*

crit·ter /ˈkrɪtə(r)/ *noun* (*NAmE, informal*) a living creature: *wild critters*

croak /krəʊk; *NAmE* kroʊk/ *verb, noun*
■ ***verb*** **1** [I] to make a rough low sound, like the sound a FROG makes **2** [I, T] to speak or say sth with a rough low voice: *I had a sore throat and could only croak.* ◇ **~ sth** *He managed to croak a greeting.* ◇ **+ speech** *'I'm fine,' she croaked.* **3** [I] (*slang*) to die
■ ***noun*** a rough low sound made in the throat, like the sound made by a FROG

croaky /ˈkrəʊki; *NAmE* ˈkroʊ-/ *adj.* (*informal*) (of sb's voice) deep and rough, especially because of a sore throat

croc /krɒk; *NAmE* krɑːk/ *noun* (*informal*) = CROCODILE

cro·chet /ˈkrəʊʃeɪ; *NAmE* kroʊˈʃeɪ/ *noun, verb*
■ ***noun*** [U] a way of making clothes, etc. from wool or cotton using a special thick needle with a hook at the end to make a pattern of connected threads ➲ VISUAL VOCAB page V35
■ ***verb*** (**cro·chet·ing, cro·cheted**) [T, I] **~ (sth)** to make sth using crochet: *a crocheted shawl*

crock /krɒk; *NAmE* krɑːk/ *noun* **1** **crocks** [pl.] (*old-fashioned*) cups, plates, dishes, etc. **2** [C] (*old use*) a large pot made of baked CLAY **3** [C] (*BrE, informal*) an old person **4** [C] (*BrE, informal*) an old car in bad condition
IDM **a ˌcrock of ˈshit** (*taboo, slang, especially NAmE*) something that is not true ➲ more at GOLD *n.*

crocked /krɒkt; *NAmE* krɑːkt/ *adj.* [not before noun] (*NAmE, slang*) drunk

crock·ery /ˈkrɒkəri; *NAmE* ˈkrɑːk-/ *noun* [U] **1** (*especially BrE*) plates, cups, dishes, etc. **2** (*NAmE*) dishes, etc. that you use in the oven

croco·dile /ˈkrɒkədaɪl; *NAmE* ˈkrɑːk-/ (also *informal* **croc**) *noun* **1** [C] a large REPTILE with a long tail, hard skin and very big JAWS. Crocodiles live in rivers and lakes in hot countries. **2** [U] crocodile skin made into leather: *crocodile shoes* **3** [C] (*BrE*) a long line of people, especially children, walking in pairs
IDM **ˈcrocodile tears** if sb SHEDS (= cries) **crocodile tears**, they pretend to be sad about sth, but they are not really sad at all

ˈcrocodile clip (*especially BrE*) (also **ˈalligator clip** *especially NAmE*) *noun* an object with sharp teeth used for holding things together, that is held closed by a spring and that you squeeze to open: *Use the crocodile clips to attach the cables to the battery.*

cro·cus /ˈkrəʊkəs; *NAmE* ˈkroʊ-/ *noun* a small yellow, purple or white flower that appears in early spring

croft /krɒft; *NAmE* krɔːft/ *noun* (*BrE*) a small farm or the house on it, especially in Scotland

croft·er /ˈkrɒftə(r); *NAmE* ˈkrɔːft-/ *noun* (*BrE*) a person who rents or owns a small family farm, especially in Scotland

Crohn's disease /ˈkrəʊnz dɪziːz; *NAmE* ˈkroʊnz/ *noun* [U] a disease affecting the lower INTESTINES, in which they develop many sore areas. The disease lasts for many years and is difficult to cure.

crois·sant /ˈkrwæsɒ̃; *NAmE* krwɑːˈsɑ̃ː; krəˈsɑːnt/ *noun* (from *French*) a small sweet roll with a curved shape, eaten especially at breakfast

crone /krəʊn; *NAmE* kroʊn/ *noun* (*literary*) an ugly old woman

crony /ˈkrəʊni; *NAmE* ˈkroʊni/ *noun* [usually pl.] (*pl.* **-ies**) (often *disapproving*) a person that sb spends a lot of time with: *He was playing cards with his cronies.*

cro·ny·ism /ˈkrəʊniɪzəm; *NAmE* ˈkroʊ-/ *noun* [U] (*disapproving*) the situation in which people in power give jobs to their friends

crook /krʊk/ *noun, verb, adj.*
■ ***noun*** **1** (*informal*) a dishonest person SYN **criminal**: *That salesman is a real crook.* **2** **~ of your arm/elbow** the place where your arm bends at the elbow **3** a long stick with a hook at one end, used especially in the past by SHEPHERDS for catching sheep IDM see HOOK *n.*
■ ***verb*** **~ sth** to bend your finger or arm
■ ***adj.*** [not usually before noun] (*AustralE, NZE, informal*) ill/sick

crooked /ˈkrʊkɪd/ *adj.* **1** not in a straight line; bent or twisted: *a crooked nose/smile* ◇ *a village of crooked streets* ◇ *Your glasses are on crooked.* OPP **straight** **2** dishonest: *a crooked businessman/deal* **3** **~ (on sb)** (*AustralE, informal*) annoyed: *It's not you I'm* ***crooked on,*** *it's him.*
▸ **crook·ed·ly** *adv.*

croon /kruːn/ *verb* [T, I] **~ (sth)** to sing sth quietly and gently: *She gently crooned a lullaby.*

croon·er /ˈkruːnə(r)/ *noun* (*old-fashioned*) a male singer who sings slow romantic songs

crop /krɒp; *NAmE* krɑːp/ *noun, verb*
■ ***noun***
▸ PLANTS FOR FOOD **1** [C] a plant that is grown in large quantities, especially as food: *Sugar is an important crop on the island.* ◇ ***crop rotation/production/yield*** ◇ *The crops are regularly sprayed with pesticides.* ➲ COLLOCATIONS at FARMING ➲ VISUAL VOCAB page V2 ➲ see also CASH CROP, CATCH CROP **2** [C] the amount of grain, fruit, etc. that is grown in one season SYN **harvest**: *a fall in this year's coffee crop* ◇ *We are looking forward to a* ***bumper crop*** (= a very large one).

▸ GROUP OF PEOPLE **3** [sing.] **a ~ of sth** a group of people who do sth at the same time; a number of things that happen at the same time: *the current crop of trainees* ◇ *She is really* ***the cream of the crop*** (= the best in her group). ◇ *a* ***crop of*** *disasters/injuries*
▸ WHIP **4** [C] a short WHIP used by horse riders: *a riding crop*
▸ HAIR **5** [C] a very short HAIRSTYLE **6** [sing.] **a ~ of dark, fair, etc. hair/curls** hair that is short and thick: *He had a thick crop of black curly hair.*
▸ OF BIRD **7** (*technical*) a part of a bird's throat shaped like a bag where food is stored before it passes into the stomach
■ *verb* (-pp-)
▸ HAIR **1** [T] **~ sth (+ adj.)** to cut sb's hair very short: *closely cropped hair* ➲ VISUAL VOCAB page V49
▸ PHOTOGRAPH **2** [T] **~ sth** (*technical*) to cut off part of a photograph or picture
▸ OF ANIMALS **3** [T] **~ sth** to bite off and eat the tops of plants, especially grass
▸ PLANTS **4** [I] (of plants) to produce a crop: *The potatoes cropped well this year.* **5** [T] **~ sth** to use land to grow crops: *The river valley is intensively cropped.*
PHR V **ˌcrop ˈup** to appear or happen, especially when it is not expected SYN **come up**: *His name just cropped up in conversation.* ◇ *I'll be late—something's cropped up at home.*

ˈcrop circle (also **ˈcorn circle**) *noun* a round area in a field of crops that has suddenly become flat. Some people say that crop circles were made by creatures from outer space.

ˈcrop dusting *noun* [U] the practice of spraying crops with chemicals such as PESTICIDES from a plane

crop·per /ˈkrɒpə(r); *NAmE* ˈkrɑːp-/ *noun*
IDM **come a ˈcropper** (*BrE, informal*) **1** (of a person) to fall over **2** to have a failure or near disaster: *We nearly came a cropper in the second half of the game.*

ˌcrop ˈtop *noun* a woman's informal piece of clothing for the upper body, cut short so that the stomach can be seen

cro·quet /ˈkrəʊkeɪ; *NAmE* kroʊˈkeɪ/ *noun* [U] a game played on grass in which players use wooden hammers (called MALLETS) to knock wooden balls through a series of HOOPS (= curved wires)

cro·quette /krəʊˈket; *NAmE* kroʊ-/ *noun* a small amount of MASHED potato, fish, etc, shaped into a ball or tube, covered with BREADCRUMBS and fried

crore /krɔː(r)/ *noun* (*IndE*) ten million; one hundred LAKHS

cro·sier (also **croz·ier**) /ˈkrəʊziə(r); *NAmE* ˈkroʊʒər/ *noun* a long stick, usually curved at one end, carried by a BISHOP (= a Christian priest of high rank) at religious ceremonies

cross 0‒ /krɒs; *NAmE* krɔːs/ *noun, verb, adj.*
■ *noun*
▸ MARK ON PAPER **1** 0‒ [C] a mark or an object formed by two lines crossing each other (X or +); the mark (X) is often used on paper to show sth: *I've put a cross on the map to show where the hotel is.* ◇ *Put a tick if the answer is correct and a cross if it's wrong.* ◇ *Sign your name on the form where I've put a cross.* ◇ *Those who could not write signed with a cross.* ➲ see also NOUGHTS AND CROSSES ➲ compare TICK
▸ FOR PUNISHMENT **2** [C] a long vertical piece of wood with a shorter piece across it near the top. In the past people were hung on crosses and left to die as a punishment.
▸ CHRISTIAN SYMBOL **3 the Cross** [sing.] the cross that Jesus Christ died on, used as a symbol of Christianity **4** 0‒ [C] an object, a design, a piece of jewellery, etc. in the shape of a cross, used as a symbol of Christianity: *She wore a small gold cross on a chain around her neck.*
▸ MEDAL **5** (usually **Cross**) [C] a small decoration in the shape of a cross that is given to sb as an honour for doing sth very brave
▸ MIXTURE **6** [C, usually sing.] **~ (between A and B)** a mixture of two different things, breeds of animal, etc: *The play was a cross between a farce and a tragedy.* ◇ *A mule is a cross between a horse and a donkey.* ➲ see also HYBRID
▸ IN SPORT **7** [C] (in football (SOCCER) or HOCKEY) a kick or hit of the ball across the field rather than up or down it ➲ see also THE RED CROSS
IDM **have a (heavy) ˈcross to bear** to have a difficult problem that makes you worried or unhappy but that you have to deal with: *We all have our crosses to bear.*
■ *verb*
▸ GO/PUT ACROSS **1** 0‒ [I, T] to go across; to pass or stretch from one side to the other: **~ (over)** *I waved and she crossed over* (= crossed the road towards me). ◇ **~ (over) (from...) (to/into...)** *We crossed from Dover to Calais.* ◇ **~ sth** *to* ***cross a/the road*** ◇ *to* ***cross the sea/mountains*** ◇ *to cross France by train* ◇ *The bridge crosses the River Dee.* ◇ *A look of annoyance* ***crossed her face.*** ◇ *They crossed the finishing line together* (= in a race). ◇ **~ over sth** *He crossed over the road and joined me.* **2** 0‒ [I] to pass across each other: *The roads cross just outside the town.* ◇ *The straps cross over at the back and are tied at the waist.* ◇ *Our letters must have crossed in the mail* (= each was sent before the other was received). ◇ *We seem to have a* ***crossed line*** (= a telephone call that interrupts another call because of a wrong connection). **3** 0‒ [T] **~ sth** to put or place sth across or over sth else: *to* ***cross your arms/legs*** (= place one arm or leg over the other) ◇ *She sat with her legs crossed.* ◇ *a flag with a design of two crossed keys*
▸ OPPOSE **4** [T] **~ sb** to oppose sb or speak against them or their plans or wishes: *She's really nice until you cross her.* ◇ (*literary*) *He had been* ***crossed in love*** (= the person he loved was not faithful to him).
▸ MIX ANIMALS/PLANTS **5** [T] **~ A with B | ~ A and B** to make two different types of animal breed together; to mix two types of plant to form a new one: *A mule is the product of a horse crossed with a donkey.* ◇ (*figurative*) *He behaved like an army officer crossed with a professor.*
▸ IN SPORT **6** [I] (in football (SOCCER) or HOCKEY) to kick or pass a ball sideways across the field
▸ DRAW LINE **7** [T] **~ sth** to draw a line across sth: *to cross your t's* (= the letters in writing) ◇ (*BrE*) *to cross a cheque* (= to draw two lines across it so that it can only be paid through a bank account)
▸ MAKE CHRISTIAN SYMBOL **8** [T] **~ yourself** to make the sign of the cross (= the Christian symbol) on your chest
IDM **cross that bridge when you ˈcome to it** to worry about a problem when it actually happens and not before **cross your ˈfingers** to hope that your plans will be successful (sometimes putting one finger across another as a sign of hoping for good luck): *I'm crossing my fingers that my proposal will be accepted.* ◇ *Keep your fingers crossed!* **cross my ˈheart (and hope to die)** (*informal*) used to emphasize that you are telling the truth or will do what you promise: *I saw him do it—cross my heart.* **cross your ˈmind** (of thoughts, etc.) to come into your mind SYN **occur to sb**: *It never crossed my mind that she might lose* (= I was sure that she would win). **ˌcross sb's ˌpalm with ˈsilver** to give sb money so that they will do you a favour, especially tell your FORTUNE **ˌcross sb's ˈpath | people's ˌpaths ˈcross** if sb **crosses sb's path** or **their paths cross**, they meet by chance: *I hope I never cross her path again.* ◇ *Our paths were to cross again many years later.* **cross ˈswords (with sb)** to fight or argue with sb ➲ more at DOT *v.*, WIRE *n.*
PHR V **ˌcross sb/sth↔ˈoff | ˌcross sb/sth ˈoff sth** to draw a line through a person's name or an item on a list because they/it is no longer required or involved: *We can cross his name off; he's not coming.* **ˌcross sth↔ˈout/ˈthrough** 0‒ to draw a line through a word, usually because it is wrong **ˌcross ˈover (to/into sth)** to move or change from one type of culture, music, political party, etc. to another: *a cult movie that has crossed over to mass appeal* ➲ related noun CROSSOVER
■ *adj.* (**cross·er, cross·est**) **~ (with sb)** (*especially BrE*) annoyed or quite angry: *I was cross with him for being late.* ◇ *Please don't* ***get cross.*** *Let me explain.* ➲ SYNONYMS at ANGRY ▸ **cross·ly** *adv.*: *'Well what did you expect?' she said crossly.*

cross- /krɒs; *NAmE* krɔːs/ *combining form* (in nouns, verbs, adjectives and adverbs) involving movement or action from one thing to another or between two things: *cross-Channel ferries* ◇ *cross-fertilize* ◇ *crossfire*

C

cross·bar /ˈkrɒsbɑː(r); *NAmE* ˈkrɔːs-/ *noun* **1** the bar joining the two vertical posts of a goal ➲ VISUAL VOCAB page V36 **2** the bar between the seat and the HANDLEBARS of a man's bicycle ➲ VISUAL VOCAB page V41

ˈ**cross-bencher** *noun* (*BrE*) a member of the British House of Lords who does not belong to a particular political party ▸ ˈ**cross benches** *noun* [pl.]: *members who sit on the cross benches*

cross·bones /ˈkrɒsbəʊnz; *NAmE* ˈkrɔːsboʊnz/ *noun* [pl.] ➲ SKULL AND CROSSBONES

ˈ**cross-border** *adj.* [only before noun] involving activity across a border between two countries: *a cross-border raid by guerrillas*

cross·bow /ˈkrɒsbəʊ; *NAmE* ˈkrɔːsboʊ/ *noun* a weapon which consists of a BOW²(1) that is fixed onto a larger piece of wood, and that shoots short heavy arrows (called BOLTS) ➲ picture at BOLT

ˈ**cross-breed** *verb, noun*
- *verb* [T, I] **~ (sth)** to make an animal or a plant breed with a different breed; to breed with an animal or a plant of a different breed: *cross-bred sheep* ▸ ˌ**cross-ˈbreeding** *noun* [U]
- *noun* an animal or a plant that is a result of cross-breeding ➲ compare HYBRID

ˌ**cross-ˈcheck** *verb* to make sure that information, figures etc. are correct by using a different method or system to check them: **~ sth** *Cross-check your answers with a calculator.* ◇ **~ sth against sth** *Baggage should be cross-checked against the names of individual passengers.* ▸ ˈ**cross-check** *noun*

ˌ**cross-contam·iˈn·ation** *noun* [U] the process by which harmful bacteria spread from one substance to another

ˌ**cross-ˈcountry** *adj., adv., noun*
- *adj.* [usually before noun], *adv.* **1** across fields or open country rather than on roads or a track: *cross-country running* ◇ *We rode cross-country.* **2** from one part of a country to the other, especially not using main roads or routes: *cross-country train journeys*
- *noun* **1** **the cross-country** [sing.] a cross-country running or SKIING race **2** [U] the sport of running or SKIING across country ➲ compare DOWNHILL *n.*

ˌ**cross-country ˈskiing** (also **lang·lauf**) *noun* [U] the sport of SKIING across the countryside, rather than down mountains ➲ VISUAL VOCAB page V39

ˌ**cross-ˈcultural** *adj.* involving or containing ideas from two or more different countries or cultures

ˈ**cross-current** *noun* **1** a current of water in a river or in the sea that flows across the main current **2** [usually pl.] (*formal*) a set of beliefs or ideas that are different from others, especially from those that most people hold

ˌ**cross-curˈricu·lar** *adj.* (*BrE*) affecting or connected with different parts of the school CURRICULUM

ˌ**cross-ˈdressing** *noun* [U] the practice of wearing clothes usually worn by a person of the opposite sex, especially for sexual pleasure SYN **transvestism** ▸ ˌ**cross-ˈdresser** *noun*

ˌ**cross-eˈxamine** *verb* **~ sb** to question sb carefully and in a lot of detail about answers that they have already given, especially in court: *The witness was cross-examined for over two hours.* ➲ COLLOCATIONS at JUSTICE ▸ ˌ**cross-eˌxamiˈn·ation** *noun* [U, C]: *He broke down* ***under cross-examination*** (= while he was being cross-examined) *and admitted his part in the assault.*

ˌ**cross-ˈeyed** *adj.* having one or both eyes looking towards the nose

ˌ**cross-ˈfertil·ize** (*BrE* also **-ise**) *verb* **1 ~ sth** (*biology*) to FERTILIZE a plant using POLLEN from a different plant of the same SPECIES **2 ~ sth** to help sth develop in a useful or positive way by mixing ideas from a different area: *The study of psychology has recently been widely cross-fertilized by new discoveries in genetics.* ▸ ˌ**cross-ˌfertil·iˈza·tion, -isa·tion** *noun* [U, sing.]

cross·fire /ˈkrɒsfaɪə(r); *NAmE* ˈkrɔːs-/ *noun* [U] the firing of guns from two or more directions at the same time, so that the bullets cross: *The doctor was killed in crossfire as he went to help the wounded.* ◇ (*figurative*) *When two industrial giants clash, small companies can get* ***caught in the crossfire*** (= become involved and suffer as a result).

ˈ**cross-hatch** *verb* **~ sth** (*technical*) to mark or colour sth with two sets of parallel lines crossing each other ▸ ˈ**cross-hatching** *noun* [U]

ˈ**cross head** *noun* a screw with a cross shape in the top

ˈ**cross-infection** *noun* [U] (*medical*) an occasion when sb passes an infection to sb who has a different infection

cross·ing /ˈkrɒsɪŋ; *NAmE* ˈkrɔːs-/ *noun* **1** a place where you can safely cross a road, a river, etc, or from one country to another: *The child was killed when a car failed to stop at the crossing.* ◇ *The next crossing point is a long way downstream.* ◇ *He was arrested by guards at the border crossing.* ➲ see also LEVEL CROSSING, PEDESTRIAN CROSSING, PELICAN CROSSING, ZEBRA CROSSING **2** a place where two lines, two roads or two tracks cross SYN **intersection** **3** a journey across a sea or a wide river: *a three-hour ferry crossing* ◇ *a rough crossing from Dover to Calais* ◇ *the first Atlantic crossing* **4** an act of going from one side to another: *attempted crossings of the border*

cross-legged /ˌkrɒs ˈlegd; -ˈlegɪd; *NAmE* ˌkrɔːs/ *adv.* sitting on the floor with your legs pulled up in front of you and with one leg or foot over the other ▸ **cross-legged** *adj.*: *the cross-legged figure of the Hindu god*

cross·over /ˈkrɒsəʊvə(r); *NAmE* ˈkrɔːsoʊ-/ *noun* the process or result of changing from one area of activity or style of doing sth to another: *The album was an exciting jazz-pop crossover.*

cross·piece /ˈkrɒspiːs; *NAmE* ˈkrɔːs-/ *noun* (*technical*) a piece of a structure or a tool that lies or is fixed across another piece

ˌ**cross-ˈplatform** *adj.* (of a computer program or an electronic device) that can be used with different types of computers or programs

ˌ**cross-ˈpollin·ate** *verb* **~ sth** (*biology*) to move POLLEN from a flower or plant onto another flower or plant so that it produces seeds ▸ ˌ**cross-polliˈn·ation** *noun* [U]

ˌ**cross-proˈmotion** *noun* [C, U] (*business*) a set of advertisements or other activities that are designed to help a company sell two different products, or to help two companies sell their products or services together

ˌ**cross ˈpurposes** *noun* [pl.] if two people are **at cross purposes**, they do not understand each other because they are talking about or aiming at different things, without realizing it: *I think we're talking at cross purposes; that's not what I meant at all.*

ˌ**cross-ˈquestion** *verb* **~ sb** to question sb thoroughly and often in a way that seems aggressive

ˌ**cross-reˈfer** *verb* (-rr-) [T, I] **~ (sth) to sth** to refer to another text or part of a text, especially to give more information about sth: *The entry for 'polygraph' is cross-referred to the entry for 'lie detector'.*

ˌ**cross ˈreference** *noun* **~ (to sth)** a note that tells a reader to look in another part of a book or file for further information

cross·roads /ˈkrɒsrəʊdz; *NAmE* ˈkrɔːsroʊdz/ *noun* (*pl.* **cross·roads**) a place where two roads meet and cross each other: *At the next crossroads, turn right.* ◇ (*figurative*) *He has reached a career crossroads* (= he must decide which way to go next in his career). ➲ see also INTERSECTION, JUNCTION

IDM **at a/the ˈcrossroads** at an important point in sb's life or development

ˈ**cross section** *noun* **1** [C, U] what you see when you cut through the middle of sth so that you can see the different layers it is made of; a drawing of this view: *a diagram representing a cross section of the human eye* ◇ *the human eye* ***in cross section*** **2** [C, usually sing.] a group of people or things that are typical of a larger group: *a representative cross section of society*

ˌcross-ˈselling *noun* [U] (*business*) the activity of selling a different extra product to a customer who is already buying a product from a company

ˈcross street *noun* (*NAmE*) a street that crosses another street

cross·talk /ˈkrɒstɔːk; *NAmE* ˈkrɔːs-/ *noun* [U] (*technical*) a situation in which a communications system is picking up the wrong signals

cross·town /ˌkrɒsˈtaʊn; *NAmE* ˌkrɔːs-/ *adj.* (*NAmE*) going from one side of a town or city to the other: *a crosstown bus*

ˈcross-trainer *noun* **1** a piece of exercise equipment that you use standing up, with parts that you push up and down with your feet and parts that you hold onto and push with your arms **2** a type of sports shoe that can be worn for more than one kind of sport

ˈcross-training *noun* [U] the activity of training in sports other than your main sport in order to make yourself fitter and able to do your main sport better

cross·walk /ˈkrɒswɔːk; *NAmE* ˈkrɔːs-/ (*NAmE*) (*BrE* **peˌdestrian ˈcrossing**) *noun* a part of a road where vehicles must stop to allow people to cross ➲ see also ZEBRA CROSSING

cross·wind /ˈkrɒswɪnd; *NAmE* ˈkrɔːs-/ *noun* a wind that is blowing across the direction that you are moving in

cross·wise /ˈkrɒswaɪz; *NAmE* ˈkrɔːs-/ *adv.* **1** across, especially from one corner to the opposite one: *Cut the fabric crosswise.* **2** in the form of a cross

cross·word /ˈkrɒswɜːd; *NAmE* ˈkrɔːswɜːrd/ (also ˈ**crossword puzzle**) *noun* a game in which you have to fit words across and downwards into spaces with numbers in a square diagram. You find the words by solving CLUES: *to* ***do a/the crossword*** ◇ *I've finished the crossword apart from 3 across and 10 down.* ➲ VISUAL VOCAB page V33

crotch /krɒtʃ; *NAmE* krɑːtʃ/ (also **crutch**) *noun* **1** the part of the body where the legs join at the top, including the area around the GENITALS **2** the part of a pair of trousers/pants, etc. that covers the crotch: *There's a hole in the crotch.*

crot·chet /ˈkrɒtʃɪt; *NAmE* ˈkrɑːtʃ-/ (*BrE*) (*NAmE* ˈ**quarter note**) *noun* (*music*) a note that lasts half as long as a MINIM/HALF NOTE ➲ picture at MUSIC

crot·chety /ˈkrɒtʃəti; *NAmE* ˈkrɑːtʃ-/ *adj.* (*informal*) bad-tempered; easily made angry: *He was tired and crotchety.*

crotch·less /ˈkrɒtʃləs; *NAmE* ˈkrɑːtʃ-/ *adj.* (of underwear) having a hole at the CROTCH

crouch /kraʊtʃ/ *verb, noun*

■ ***verb*** [I] (+ **adv./prep.**) to put your body close to the ground by bending your legs under you SYN **squat**: *He* ***crouched down*** *beside her.* ◇ *Doyle crouched behind a hedge.* ▸ **crouched** *adj.*: *She sat crouched in a corner.*

PHR V ˈ**crouch over sb/sth** to bend over sb/sth so that you are very close to them or it: *He crouched over the papers on his desk.*

■ ***noun*** [sing.] a crouching position: *She dropped to a crouch.*

croup /kruːp/ *noun* [U] a disease of children that makes them cough a lot and have difficulty breathing

croup·ier /ˈkruːpieɪ; *NAmE* also -piər/ *noun* a person whose job is to be in charge of a gambling table and collect and pay out money, give out cards, etc.

crou·ton /ˈkruːtɒn; *NAmE* -tɑːn/ *noun* a small piece of cold crisp fried bread served in soup or as part of a salad

Crow /krəʊ; *NAmE* kroʊ/ *noun* (*pl.* **Crow** or **Crows**) a member of a Native American people, many of whom live in the US state of Montana

crow /krəʊ; *NAmE* kroʊ/ *noun, verb*

■ ***noun*** **1** a large bird, completely or mostly black, with a rough unpleasant cry **2** a sound like that of a COCK/ROOSTER crowing: *She gave a little crow of triumph.*

IDM **as the ˈcrow flies** in a straight line: *The villages are no more than a mile apart as the crow flies.* ➲ more at EAT, STONE *v.*

■ ***verb*** **1** [I] (of a COCK/ROOSTER) to make repeated loud high sounds, especially early in the morning **2** [I, T] (*disapproving*) to talk too proudly about sth you have achieved, especially when sb else has been unsuccessful SYN **boast, gloat**: **~ (about/over sth)** *He won't stop crowing about his victory.* ◇ **+ speech** *'I've won, I've won!' she crowed.* ◇ **~ that ...** *He crowed that they had sold out in one day.* **3** [I] (*BrE*) (of a baby) to make happy sounds

C

crow·bar /ˈkrəʊbɑː(r); *NAmE* ˈkroʊ-/ *noun* a straight iron bar, usually with a curved end, used for forcing open boxes and moving heavy objects

crowd 0-π /kraʊd/ *noun, verb*

■ ***noun*** **1** 0-π [C+sing./pl. v.] a large number of people gathered together in a public place, for example in the streets or at a sports game: *He pushed his way through the crowd.* ◇ *A small crowd had gathered outside the church.* ◇ *Police had to break up the crowd.* ◇ *Crowds of people poured into the street.* ◇ *I want to get there early to avoid the crowds.* ◇ *The match attracted a capacity crowd of 80 000.* ◇ *The crowd cheered the winning hit.* ◇ *crowd control* ◇ *crowd trouble* ◇ *A whole crowd of us are going to the ball* (= a lot of us). ◇ *He left the hotel surrounded by crowds of journalists.* **2** [C+sing./pl. v.] (*informal*, often *disapproving*) a particular group of people: *Bob introduced her to some of the usual crowd* (= people who often meet each other). ◇ *the bright young theatrical crowd* **3 the crowd** [sing.] (sometimes *disapproving*) ordinary people, not special or unusual in any way: *We all like to think we* ***stand out from the crowd*** (= are different from and better than other people). ◇ *He prefers to be* ***one of the crowd***. ◇ *She's quite happy to* ***follow the crowd***.

■ ***verb*** **1 ~ sth** to fill a place so there is little room to move: *Thousands of people crowded the narrow streets.* **2 ~ sth** to fill your mind so that you can think of nothing else: *Memories crowded his mind.* **3 ~ sb** (*informal*) to stand very close to sb so that they feel uncomfortable or nervous

PHR V ˌ**crowd aˈround/ˈround (sb/sth)** to gather in large numbers around sb/sth: *We all crowded around the stove to keep warm.* ◇ *Photographers were crowding around outside.* ˌ**crowd ˈin (on sb)** | ˌ**crowd ˈinto sth** (of thoughts, questions etc.) to fill your mind so that you can think of nothing else: *Too many uncomfortable thoughts were crowding in on her.* ◇ *Memories came crowding into her mind.* ˌ**crowd ˈinto/ˈonto sth** | ˌ**crowd ˈin** to move in large numbers into a small space: *We all crowded into her office to sing 'Happy Birthday'.* ˌ**crowd sb/sth ˈinto/ˈonto sth** | ˌ**crowd sb/sth ˈin** to put many people or things into a small space: *Guests were crowded into the few remaining rooms.* ˌ**crowd sb/sth ˈout** to fill a place so that other people or things are kept out

crowd·ed 0-π /ˈkraʊdɪd/ *adj.* **~ (with sth) 1** 0-π having a lot of people or too many people: *crowded streets* ◇ *a crowded bar* ◇ *In the spring the place is crowded with skiers.* ◇ *London was very crowded.* ➲ compare UNCROWDED **2** 0-π full of sth: *a room crowded with books* ◇ *We have a very crowded schedule.*

ˈ**crowd-pleaser** *noun* (*informal*) a person or performance that always pleases an audience

ˈ**crowd-puller** *noun* (*informal*) a person or thing that always attracts a large audience

crown 0-π /kraʊn/ *noun, verb*

■ ***noun***

▸ OF KING/QUEEN **1** 0-π [C] an object in the shape of a circle, usually made of gold and PRECIOUS STONES, that a king or queen wears on his or her head on official occasions **2 the Crown** [sing.] the government of a country, thought of as being represented by a king or queen: *land owned by the Crown* ◇ *a Minister of the Crown* ◇ *Who's appearing for the Crown* (= bringing a criminal charge against sb on behalf of the state) *in this case?* **3 the crown** [sing.] the position or power of a king or queen: *She refused the crown* (= refused to become queen). ◇ *his claim to the French crown*

▸ OF FLOWERS/LEAVES **4** [C] a circle of flowers, leaves, etc. that is worn on sb's head, sometimes as a sign of victory

C

▸ IN SPORTS COMPETITION **5** [C, usually sing.] (*informal*) the position of winning a sports competition: *She is determined to retain her Wimbledon crown.*
▸ OF HEAD/HAT **6** (usually **the crown**) [sing.] the top part of the head or a hat ➲ VISUAL VOCAB page V48, page V52
▸ HIGHEST PART **7** (usually **the crown**) [sing.] the highest part of sth: *the crown of a hill*
▸ ON TOOTH **8** [C] an artificial cover for a damaged tooth
▸ SHAPE **9** [C] anything in the shape of a crown, especially as a decoration or a BADGE
▸ MONEY **10** [C] a unit of money in several European countries: *Czech crowns* **11** [C] an old British coin worth five SHILLINGS (= now 25p) IDM see JEWEL

■ *verb*
▸ KING/QUEEN **1** to put a crown on the head of a new king or queen as a sign of royal power: **~ sb** *Queen Elizabeth was crowned in 1953.* ◇ **~ sb + noun** *The prince was soon to be crowned King of England.*
▸ COVER TOP **2** [usually passive] **~ sth (with sth)** to form or cover the top of sth: *His head was crowned with a mop of brown curls.*
▸ MAKE COMPLETE **3** [often passive] **~ sth (with sth)** to make sth complete or perfect, especially by adding an achievement, a success, etc: *The award of the Nobel Prize has crowned a glorious career in physics.* ◇ *Their efforts were finally crowned with success.*
▸ HIT ON HEAD **4 ~ sb** (*old-fashioned, informal*) to hit sb on the head
▸ TOOTH **5 ~ sth** to put an artificial cover on a tooth SYN **cap**: *I've had one of my teeth crowned.*

IDM **to crown it 'all** (*BrE, informal*) used to say that sth is the final and worst event in a series of unpleasant or annoying events: *It was cold and raining, and, to crown it all, we had to walk home.*

ˌCrown 'Colony *noun* a COLONY ruled directly by the British government

ˌCrown 'Court *noun* (in England and Wales) a court which deals with criminal cases, with a judge and JURY ➲ compare COUNTY COURT

crown·ing /ˈkraʊnɪŋ/ *adj.* [only before noun] making sth perfect or complete: *The cathedral is the* ***crowning glory*** *of the city.* ◇ *His 'Beethoven' sculpture is seen as the crowning achievement of his career.*

ˌcrown 'jewels *noun* [pl.] the crown and other objects worn or carried by a king or queen on formal occasions

ˌCrown 'prince *noun* (in some countries) a prince who will become king when the present king or queen dies

ˌCrown prin'cess *noun* **1** the wife of a Crown prince **2** (in some countries) a princess who will become queen when the present king or queen dies

ˌCrown 'prosecutor *noun* in England and Wales, a lawyer who works for the state

'crow's feet *noun* [pl.] lines in the skin around the outer corner of a person's eye

'crow's nest *noun* a platform at the top of a ship's MAST (= the post that supports the sails) from which sb can see a long way and watch for land, danger, etc.

croz·ier = CROSIER

cru·cial 0→ AW /ˈkruːʃl/ *adj.* extremely important, because it will affect other things SYN **critical, essential**: *a* ***crucial factor/issue/decision*** ◇ *topics of crucial importance* ◇ *The next few weeks are going to be crucial.* ◇ **~ to/for sth** *Winning this contract is crucial to the success of the company.* ◇ **~ that...** ***It is crucial that*** *we get this right.* ◇ *Parents* ***play a crucial role*** *in preparing their child for school.* ◇ *He wasn't there* ***at the crucial moment*** (= when he was needed most). ➲ SYNONYMS at ESSENTIAL ➲ LANGUAGE BANK at EMPHASIS, VITAL ▸ **cru·cial·ly** AW /-ʃəli/ *adv.*: *crucially important*

cru·cible /ˈkruːsɪbl/ *noun* **1** a pot in which substances are heated to high temperatures, metals are melted, etc. ➲ VISUAL VOCAB page V57 **2** (*formal* or *literary*) a place or situation in which people or ideas are tested severely, often creating sth new or exciting in the process

cru·ci·fix /ˈkruːsəfɪks/ *noun* a model of a cross with a figure of Jesus Christ on it, as a symbol of the Christian religion

cru·ci·fix·ion /ˌkruːsəˈfɪkʃn/ *noun* (sometimes **Crucifixion**) **1** [C, U] the act of killing sb by fastening them to a cross: *the Crucifixion* (= of Jesus) **2** [C] a painting or other work of art representing the crucifixion of Jesus Christ

cru·ci·form /ˈkruːsɪfɔːm; *NAmE* -fɔːrm/ *adj.* (*technical*) (especially of buildings) in the shape of a cross

cru·cify /ˈkruːsɪfaɪ/ *verb* (**cru·ci·fies, cru·ci·fy·ing, cru·ci·fied, cru·ci·fied**) **1 ~ sb** to kill sb as a punishment by fastening them to a wooden cross **2 ~ sb** (*informal*) to criticize or punish sb very severely: *The prime minister was crucified in the press for his handling of the affair.*

crud /krʌd/ *noun* [U] (*informal*) any dirty or unpleasant substance

cruddy /ˈkrʌdi/ *adj.* (**crud·dier, crud·di·est**) (*informal, especially NAmE*) bad, dirty or of low quality: *We got really cruddy service in that restaurant last time.*

crude /kruːd/ *adj., noun*
■ *adj.* (**cruder, cru·dest**) **1** simple and not very accurate but giving a general idea of sth: ***In crude terms****, the causes of mental illness seem to be of three main kinds.* **2** (of objects or works of art) simply made, not showing much skill or attention to detail: *a crude drawing of a face* **3** (of people or the way they behave) offensive or rude, especially about sex SYN **vulgar**: ***crude jokes/language*** **4** [usually before noun] (of oil and other natural substances) in its natural state, before it has been treated with chemicals: ***crude oil/metal*** ▸ **crude·ly** *adv.*: *a crudely drawn ship* ◇ *To put it crudely, the poor are going without food so that the rich can drive cars.* **crude·ness** *noun* [U]
■ *noun* (also ˌ**crude 'oil**) [U] oil in its natural state, before it has been treated with chemicals: *50 000 barrels of crude*

cru·di·tés /ˈkruːdɪteɪ; *NAmE* ˌkruːdɪˈteɪ/ *noun* [pl.] (from *French*) pieces of raw vegetables that are eaten at the beginning of a meal

cru·dity /ˈkruːdəti/ *noun* [U, C] (*pl.* **-ies**) the fact of being CRUDE; an example of sth CRUDE: *Despite the crudity of their methods and equipment, the experiment was a considerable success.* ◇ *the novel's structural crudities* ◇ *The crudity of her language shocked him.*

cruel 0→ /ˈkruːəl/ *adj.* (**cruel·ler, cruel·lest**)
1 0→ **~ (to sb/sth)** having a desire to cause pain and suffering: *a cruel dictator* ◇ *I can't stand people who are cruel to animals.* ◇ *Her eyes were cruel and hard.* ◇ *Sometimes you have to* ***be cruel to be kind*** (= make sb suffer because it will be good for them later). OPP **kind** **2** 0→ causing pain or suffering: *a* ***cruel punishment/joke*** ◇ *Her father's death was a* ***cruel blow.*** ▸ **cruel·ly** /ˈkruːəli/ *adv.*: *The dog had been cruelly treated.* ◇ *I was cruelly deceived.*

cruelty /ˈkruːəlti/ *noun* (*pl.* **-ies**) **1** [U] **~ (to sb/sth)** behaviour that causes pain or suffering to others, especially deliberately: *cruelty to animals* ◇ *The deliberate cruelty of his words cut her like a knife.* OPP **kindness** **2** [C, usually pl.] a cruel action **3** [C, U] something that happens that seems unfair: *the cruelties of life*

cruet /ˈkruːɪt/ *noun* a small container, or set of containers, for salt, pepper, oil, etc. for use on the table at meals

cruise /kruːz/ *noun, verb*
■ *noun* a journey by sea, visiting different places, especially as a holiday/vacation: *I'd love to go on a round-the-world cruise.* ◇ *a luxury cruise ship* ➲ COLLOCATIONS at TRAVEL
■ *verb* **1** [I, T] to travel in a ship or boat visiting different places, especially as a holiday/vacation: (**+ adv./prep.**) *They cruised down the Nile.* ◇ **~ sth** *We spent two weeks cruising the Bahamas.* **2** [I] (**+ adv./prep.**) (of a car, plane, etc.) to travel at a steady speed: *a light aircraft cruising at 4 000 feet* ◇ *a cruising speed of 50 miles an hour* **3** [I, T] (of a car, etc. or its driver) to drive along slowly, especially when you are looking at or for sth: **+ adv./prep.** *She cruised around the block looking for a parking space.* ◇ **~ sth** *Taxis cruised the streets, looking for fares.* **4** [I] **+ adv./prep.** to win or achieve sth easily: *The home team*

cruised to victory. **5** [I, T] **~ (sth)** (*slang*) to go around in public places looking for a sexual partner

'cruise control *noun* [U] a device in a vehicle that allows it to stay at the speed that the driver has chosen

,cruise 'missile *noun* a large weapon with a WARHEAD that flies close to the ground and is guided by its own computer to an exact place

cruiser /'kru:zə(r)/ *noun* **1** a large fast ship used in war **2** (also **'cabin cruiser**) a boat with a motor and room for people to sleep, used for pleasure trips ➲ VISUAL VOCAB page V44 **3** (*NAmE*) a police car

crumb /krʌm/ *noun* **1** a very small piece of food, especially of bread or cake, that has fallen off a larger piece: *She stood up and brushed the crumbs from her sweater.* **2** a small piece or amount: *a few crumbs of useful information* ◇ *The government's only* ***crumb of comfort*** *is that their opponents are as confused as they are.*

crum·ble /'krʌmbl/ *verb, noun*

■ ***verb*** **1** [I, T] to break or break sth into very small pieces: *Rice flour makes the cake less likely to crumble.* ◇ **~ sth** *Crumble the cheese over the salad.* **2** [I] if a building or piece of land **is crumbling**, parts of it are breaking off: *buildings crumbling into dust* ◇ *crumbling stonework* ◇ *The cliff is gradually crumbling away.* **3** [I] to begin to fail or get weaker or to come to an end: *a crumbling business/relationship* ◇ **~ away** *All his hopes began to crumble away.* ◇ **~ into/to sth** *The empire finally crumbled into dust.* IDM see WAY *n.*

■ ***noun*** (*BrE*) (*NAmE* **crisp**) [U, C] a DESSERT (= a sweet dish) made from fruit that is covered with a rough mixture of flour, butter and sugar, cooked in the oven and usually served hot: *apple crumble and custard*

crum·bly /'krʌmbli/ *adj.* that easily breaks into very small pieces: *crumbly soil/cheese*

crumbs /krʌmz/ *exclamation* (*old-fashioned, BrE, informal*) used to show that you are surprised: *Oh crumbs! Is that the time?*

crummy /'krʌmi/ *adj.* (*informal*) of very bad quality: *Most of his songs are pretty crummy.*

crum·pet /'krʌmpɪt/ *noun* (*BrE*) **1** [C] a small flat round cake with small holes in the top, eaten hot with butter **2** [U] (*slang*) an offensive way of referring to people who are sexually attractive, usually women

crum·ple /'krʌmpl/ *verb* **1** [T, I] **~ (sth) (up) (into sth)** to crush sth into folds; to become crushed into folds: *She crumpled the letter up into a ball and threw it on the fire.* ◇ *This material crumples very easily.* ➲ picture at SQUEEZE **2** [I] **~ (up)** if your face **crumples**, you look sad and disappointed, as if you might cry **3** [I] **~ (up)** to fall down in an uncontrolled way because you are injured, unconscious, drunk, etc. SYN **collapse**: *He crumpled up in agony.* ▶ **crump·led** *adj.*: ***crumpled clothes/papers*** ◇ *A crumpled figure lay motionless in the doorway.*

'crumple zone *noun* the part of a car that is designed to crumple easily if there is an accident, to protect the people in the car

crunch /krʌntʃ/ *noun, verb, adj.*

■ ***noun*** **1** [C, usually sing.] a noise like the sound of sth firm being crushed: *the crunch of feet on snow* ◇ *The car drew up with a crunch of gravel.* **2 the crunch** [sing.] (*informal*) an important and often unpleasant situation or piece of information: ***The crunch came*** *when she returned from America.* ◇ *He always says he'll help but* ***when it comes to the crunch*** (= when it is time for action) *he does nothing.* ◇ *The crunch is that we can't afford to go abroad this year.* **3** [C, usually sing.] (*especially NAmE*) a situation in which there is suddenly not enough of sth, especially money: *a* ***budget/energy/housing crunch*** **4** [C] = SIT-UP

■ ***verb*** **1** [T, I] **~ (on) sth** to crush sth noisily between your teeth when you are eating: *She crunched her apple noisily.* **2** [I, T] **~ (sth)** to make or cause sth to make a noise like sth hard being crushed SYN **scrunch**: *The snow crunched under our feet.* **3** [I] **+ adv./prep.** to move over a surface, making a loud crushing noise: *I crunched across the gravel to the front door.* **4** [T] **~ sth** (*computing*) to deal with large amounts of data very quickly ➲ see also NUMBER CRUNCHING

PHR V **,crunch sth↔'up** to crush sth completely: *He crunched up the empty pack and threw it out of the window.*

■ ***adj.*** [only before noun] (*informal*) a **crunch** meeting, sports game, etc. is very important and may be the last chance to succeed: *Sunday's crunch game with Leeds*

crunchy /'krʌntʃi/ *adj.* (*approving*) (especially of food) firm and crisp and making a sharp sound when you bite or crush it: *a crunchy salad*

cru·sade /kru:'seɪd/ *noun, verb*

■ ***noun*** **1 ~ (for/against sth)** | **~ (to do sth)** a long and determined effort to achieve sth that you believe to be right or to stop sth that you believe to be wrong SYN **campaign**: *to lead a crusade against crime* ◇ *a moral crusade* **2** (sometimes **Crusade**) any of the wars fought in Palestine by European Christian countries against the Muslims in the Middle Ages

■ ***verb*** [I] to make a long and determined effort to achieve sth that you believe to be right or to stop sth you believe to be wrong SYN **campaign**

cru·sader /kru:'seɪdə(r)/ *noun* a person who takes part in a crusade: *moral crusaders*

crush 🔑 /krʌʃ/ *verb, noun*

■ ***verb*** **1** 🔑 [T] **~ sb/sth** to press or squeeze sth so hard that it is damaged or injured, or loses its shape: *The car was completely crushed under the truck.* ◇ *They crush the olives with a heavy wooden press.* ◇ *Several people were* ***crushed to death*** *in the accident.* **2** 🔑 [T] **~ sb/sth + adv./prep.** to push or press sb/sth into a small space: *Over twenty prisoners were crushed into a small dark cell.* **3** 🔑 [T] **~ sth** to break sth into small pieces or into a powder by pressing hard: *Add two cloves of crushed garlic.* ➲ picture at SQUEEZE **4** [T, I] **~ (sth)** to become or make sth full of folds or lines **5** [T] **~ sb** to use violent methods to defeat people who are opposing you SYN **put down, quash**: *The army was sent in to crush the rebellion.* **6 ~ sb** to destroy sb's confidence or happiness: *She felt completely crushed by the teacher's criticism.*

■ ***noun*** **1** [C, usually sing.] a crowd of people pressed close together in a small space: *a big crush in the theatre bar* ◇ *I couldn't find a way through the crush.* **2** [C] **~ (on sb)** a strong feeling of love, that usually does not last very long, that a young person has for sb older: *a schoolgirl crush* ◇ *I had a huge crush on her.* **3** [U] a drink made from fruit juice

'crush barrier *noun* (*BrE*) a temporary metal fence used for keeping back a crowd

crush·er /'krʌʃə(r)/ *noun* (often in compounds) a machine or tool for crushing sth: *a garlic crusher* ➲ VISUAL VOCAB page V23

crush·ing /'krʌʃɪŋ/ *adj.* [usually before noun] used to emphasize how bad or severe sth is: *a* ***crushing defeat*** *in the election* ◇ *The shipyard has been dealt another* ***crushing blow*** *with the failure to win this contract.* ▶ **crush·ing·ly** *adv.*

crust /krʌst/ *noun* **1** [C, U] the hard outer surface of bread: *sandwiches with the crusts cut off* **2** [C, usually sing.] a layer of PASTRY, especially on top of a PIE: *Bake until the crust is golden.* **3** [C, U] a hard layer or surface, especially above or around sth soft or liquid: *a thin crust of ice* ◇ *the earth's crust* ➲ see also THE UPPER CRUST IDM see EARN

crust·acean /krʌ'steɪʃn/ *noun* (*technical*) any creature with a soft body that is divided into sections, and a hard outer shell. Most crustaceans live in water. CRABS, LOBSTERS and SHRIMPS are all crustaceans. ➲ VISUAL VOCAB page V11 ➲ compare SHELLFISH

crust·ed /'krʌstɪd/ *adj.* [not usually before noun] **~ (with sth)** having a hard layer or covering of sth

crusty /'krʌsti/ *adj., noun*

■ ***adj.*** (**crust·ier, crusti·est**) **1** (of food) having a hard outer layer: *fresh crusty bread* **2** (*informal*) (especially of older people) bad-tempered; easily irritated: *a crusty old man*

■ ***noun*** (also **crustie**) (*pl.* **-ies**) (*BrE, informal*) a person who usually has no permanent home, has a dirty or untidy appearance, and rejects the way that most people live in Western society

crutch /krʌtʃ/ *noun* **1** one of two long sticks that you put under your arms to help you walk after you have injured your leg or foot: *After the accident I spent six months* ***on crutches.*** **2** (usually *disapproving*) a person or thing that gives you help or support but often makes you depend on them too much **3** = CROTCH

crux /krʌks/ *noun* [sing.] **the ~ (of sth)** the most important or difficult part of a problem or an issue SYN **nub**: *Now we come to* ***the crux of the matter.***

Vocabulary Building

Cry

To **cry** is the most general word for producing tears when you are unhappy or hurt, or when you are extremely happy.

- To **sob** means to cry noisily, taking sudden, sharp breaths.
- To **wail** means to cry in a loud high voice.
- To **whimper** means to cry making low, weak noises.
- To **weep** (*literary* or *formal*) means to cry quietly for a long time.

All these verbs can be used like 'say': *'I don't want you to go,' she cried/wailed/sobbed.*

- To **be in tears** means to be crying.
- To **burst into tears** means to suddenly begin to cry.
- To **cry your eyes out** means to cry a lot or for a long time, because you are very sad.

cry 🔑 /kraɪ/ *verb, noun*

■ ***verb*** **(cries, cry·ing, cried, cried) 1** 🔑 [I, T] to produce tears from your eyes because you are unhappy or hurt: *It's all right. Don't cry.* ◇ *I just couldn't stop crying.* ◇ **~ for sb/sth** *The baby was crying for* (= because it wanted) *its mother.* ◇ **~ about/over sth** *There's nothing to cry about.* ◇ **~ with sth** *He felt like crying with rage.* ◇ **+ speech** *'Waaa!' she cried.* ◇ *I found him* ***crying his eyes out*** (= crying very much). ◇ *That night she* ***cried herself to sleep.*** **2** 🔑 [I, T] to shout loudly: **~ for sth** *She ran to the window and cried for help.* ◇ **+ speech** *'You're safe!' Tom cried in delight.* ➲ SYNONYMS at SHOUT **3** [I] (of a bird or an animal) to make a loud unpleasant noise: *Seagulls followed the boat, crying loudly.*

IDM **,cry 'foul** (*informal*) to complain that sb else has done sth wrong or unfair **cry over spilt 'milk** (*BrE*) (*US* **cry over spilled 'milk**) to waste time worrying about sth that has happened that you cannot do anything about: *As the saying goes —****it's no use crying over spilt milk.*** **cry 'wolf** to call for help when you do not need it, with the result that when you do need it people do not believe you **for ,crying out 'loud** (*informal*) used to show you are angry or surprised: *For crying out loud! Why did you have to do that?* ➲ more at LAUGH *v.*, SHOULDER *n.*

PHR V **,cry 'off** (*BrE, informal*) to say that you cannot do sth that you promised to do: *She said she was coming to the party, but cried off at the last moment.* **,cry 'out** to make a loud sound without words because you are hurt, afraid, surprised, etc: *She tried to stop herself from crying out.* ◇ *to* ***cry out in fear/alarm/pain*** **,cry 'out/,cry 'out sth** 🔑 to shout sth loudly: *She cried out for help.* ◇ *She cried out his name.* ◇ **+ speech** *'Help!' he cried out.* ➲ SYNONYMS at CALL **,cry 'out for sth** (usually used in the progressive tenses) to need sth very much: *The company is crying out for fresh new talent.*

■ ***noun*** (*pl.* **cries**) **1** 🔑 [C] a loud sound without words that expresses a strong feeling: *to* ***give a cry of anguish/despair/relief/surprise/terror, etc.*** **2** 🔑 [C] a loud shout: *With a cry of 'Stop thief!' he ran after the boy.* ◇ *Her answer was greeted with cries of outrage.* **3** 🔑 [C] the sound made by a bird or an animal: *the cry of gulls circling overhead* **4** 🔑 [sing.] an action or a period of crying: *I felt a lot better after a good long cry.* **5** 🔑 [C] **~ (for sth)** an urgent demand or request for sth: *Her suicide attempt was really a* ***cry for help.*** **6** [C] (especially in compounds) a word or phrase that expresses a group's beliefs and calls people to action: *a battle cry*

IDM **in full 'cry** talking or shouting loudly and in an enthusiastic way: *The Leeds supporters were in full cry.* ➲ more at FAR *adj.*, HUE

cry·baby /'kraɪbeɪbi/ *noun* (*pl.* -ies) (*informal, disapproving*) a person, especially a child, who cries too often or without good reason: *Don't be such a crybaby.*

cry·ing /'kraɪɪŋ/ *adj., noun*

■ ***adj.*** [only before noun]

IDM **be a crying 'shame** (*informal*) used to emphasize that you think sth is extremely bad or shocking: *It's a crying shame to waste all that food.* **a crying 'need (for sth)** a great and urgent need for sth

■ ***noun*** [U] the sound or act of crying: *the crying of terrified children*

cryo·gen·ic /,kraɪə'dʒenɪk/ *adj.* (*physics*) involving the use of very low temperatures: *a cryogenic storage system*

cryo·gen·ics /,kraɪə'dʒenɪks/ *noun* [U] (*physics*) the scientific study of the production and effects of very low temperatures ➲ compare CRYONICS

cry·on·ics /kraɪ'ɒnɪks; *NAmE* -ɑːn-/ *noun* [U] (*medical*) the process of freezing a body at the moment of its death with the hope that it will be brought back to life at some future time ➲ compare CRYOGENICS

crypt /krɪpt/ *noun* a room under the floor of a church, used especially in the past as a place for burying people

cryp·tic /'krɪptɪk/ *adj.* with a meaning that is hidden or not easily understood SYN **mysterious**: *a* ***cryptic message/remark/smile*** ◇ *a cryptic crossword clue* ▶ **cryp·tic·al·ly** /-kli/ *adv.*: *'Yes and no,' she replied cryptically.*

crypto- /'krɪptəʊ; *NAmE* -toʊ/ *combining form* (in nouns) secret: *a crypto-communist*

crypt·og·raphy /krɪp'tɒgrəfi; *NAmE* -'tɑːg-/ *noun* [U] the art of writing or solving codes

crypto·spor·id·ium /,krɪptəʊspə'rɪdiəm; *NAmE* ,krɪptoʊ-/ *noun* a PARASITE found in water that causes infections inside the body

crys·tal /'krɪstl/ *noun* **1** [C] a small piece of a substance with many even sides, that is formed naturally when the substance becomes solid: ***ice/salt crystals*** **2** [U, C] a clear mineral, such as QUARTZ, used in making jewellery and decorative objects: *a pair of crystal earrings* **3** [U] glass of very high quality: *a* ***crystal chandelier/vase*** **4** [C] (*NAmE*) a piece of glass or plastic that covers the face of a watch ➲ see also LIQUID CRYSTAL DISPLAY **5** = METH

,crystal 'ball *noun* a clear glass ball used by people who claim they can predict what will happen in the future by looking into it: *Without a crystal ball, it's impossible to say where we'll be next year.*

,crystal 'clear *adj.* **1** (of glass, water, etc.) completely clear and bright **2** very easy to understand; completely obvious: *I want to make my meaning crystal clear.*

crys·tal·line /'krɪstəlaɪn/ *adj.* **1** (*technical*) made of or similar to CRYSTALS: ***crystalline structure/rocks*** **2** (*formal*) very clear SYN **transparent**: *water of crystalline purity*

crys·tal·lize (*BrE* also **-ise**) /'krɪstəlaɪz/ *verb* **1** [I, T] (of thoughts, plans, beliefs, etc.) to become clear and fixed; to make thoughts, beliefs, etc. clear and fixed: *Our ideas began to crystallize into a definite plan.* ◇ **~ sth** *The final chapter crystallizes all the main issues.* **2** [I, T] **~ (sth)** (*technical*) to form or make sth form into CRYSTALS: *The salt crystallizes as the water evaporates.* ▶ **crys·tal·lization, -isa·tion** /,krɪstəlaɪ'zeɪʃn; *NAmE* -lə'z-/ *noun* [U, sing.]

crys·tal·lized (*BrE* also **-ised**) /'krɪstəlaɪzd/ *adj.* (especially of fruit) preserved in and covered with sugar

crystal·log·raphy /,krɪstə'lɒgrəfi; *NAmE* -'lɑːg-/ *noun* [U] the branch of science that deals with CRYSTALS ▶ **crystal·log·raph·er** /,krɪstə'lɒgrəfə(r); *NAmE* -'lɑːg-/ *noun*

crystal meth *noun* = METH

'crystal set (also **,crystal 'radio**) *noun* a simple early radio which was listened to wearing HEADPHONES

the CSA /,si: es 'eɪ/ *abbr.* the Child Support Agency (a government organization in Britain that decides how much money a parent who does not live with a child must contribute to support the child)

'C-section *noun* (*NAmE*) = CAESAREAN

CS gas /,si: es 'gæs/ *noun* [U] a gas that stings the eyes, producing tears and making it difficult to breathe. CS gas is sometimes used to control crowds. ➲ see also TEAR GAS

CST /,si: es 'ti:/ *abbr.* CENTRAL STANDARD TIME

Ct (also **Ct.** especially in *NAmE*) *abbr.* (used in written addresses) COURT: *30 Willow Ct*

ct (also **ct.** especially in *NAmE*) *abbr.* **1** (in writing) CARAT: *an 18ct gold ring* **2** (in writing) CENT(S): *50 cts*

CTC /,si: ti: 'si:/ *noun* (in the UK) the abbreviation for 'City Technology College' (a school in a town or city that teaches technology, science and mathematics to young people between the ages of 11 and 18)

CT scan /,si: 'ti: skæn/ *noun* = CAT SCAN

cu. *abbr.* (in writing) CUBIC: *a volume of 2 cu. m* (= 2 cubic metres)

cub /kʌb/ *noun* **1** [C] a young BEAR, LION, FOX, etc: *a lioness guarding her cubs* **2 the Cubs** (*BrE*) (*US* **the 'Cub Scouts**) [pl.] a branch of the SCOUT ASSOCIATION for boys between the ages of eight and ten or eleven: *to join the Cubs* **3 Cub** (also **'Cub Scout**) [C] a member of the Cubs ➲ compare BROWNIE

Cuban /'kju:bən/ *adj., noun*
- **adj.** from or connected with Cuba
- **noun** a person from Cuba

cub·by·hole /'kʌbihəʊl; *NAmE* -hoʊl/ *noun* **1** a small room or a small space: *My office is a cubbyhole in the basement.* **2** (*SAfrE*) a small space or shelf facing the front seats of a car where you can keep papers, maps, etc. ➲ compare GLOVE COMPARTMENT

cube /kju:b/ *noun, verb*
- **noun 1** a solid or hollow figure with six equal square sides ➲ VISUAL VOCAB page V58 **2** a piece of sth, especially food, with six sides: *Cut the meat into cubes.* ➲ see also ICE CUBE, STOCK CUBE, SUGAR CUBE **3** (*mathematics*) the number that you get when you multiply a number by itself twice: *The cube of 5 (5^3) is 125 ($5 \times 5 \times 5$).*
- **verb 1** [usually passive] **~ sth** (*mathematics*) to multiply a number by itself twice: *10 cubed is 1 000.* **2 ~ sth** to cut food into cubes SYN **dice**

,cube 'root *noun* (*mathematics*) a number which, when multiplied by itself twice, produces a particular number: *The cube root of 64 ($\sqrt[3]{64}$) is 4.* ➲ compare SQUARE ROOT

cubic /'kju:bɪk/ *adj.* **1** (*abbr.* **cu**) [only before noun] used to show that a measurement is the volume of sth, that is the height multiplied by the length and the width: ***cubic centimetres/inches/metres*** **2** measured or expressed in cubic units: *the cubic capacity of a car's engine* **3** having the shape of a cube: *a cubic figure*

cu·bicle /'kju:bɪkl/ *noun* a small room that is made by separating off part of a larger room: *a shower cubicle* ◇ (*BrE*) *a changing cubicle* (= for example at a public swimming pool) ◇ (*especially NAmE*) *an office cubicle*

cu·bism /'kju:bɪzəm/ (also **Cubism**) *noun* [U] a style and movement in early 20th century art in which objects and people are represented as GEOMETRIC shapes, often shown from many different angles at the same time ▸ **cu·bist** (also **Cubist**) *noun*: *The exhibition includes works by the Cubists.* **cu·bist** (also **Cubist**) *adj.* [usually before noun]: *cubist paintings*

cubit /'kju:bɪt/ *noun* an ancient measurement of length, about 45 cm or the length from the elbow to the end of the fingers

cu·boid /'kju:bɔɪd/ *noun, adj.*
- **noun** (*geometry*) a solid object which has six RECTANGULAR sides at RIGHT ANGLES to each other
- **adj.** shaped approximately like a CUBE

,cub re'porter *noun* a young newspaper REPORTER without much experience

cuck·old /'kʌkəʊld; *NAmE* -oʊld/ *noun, verb*
- **noun** (*old use, disapproving*) a man whose wife has sex with another man
- **verb** (*old use*) **1 ~ sb** (of a man) to make another man a cuckold by having sex with his wife **2 ~ sb** (of a woman) to make her husband a cuckold by having sex with another man

cuckoo /'kʊku:/ *noun, adj.*
- **noun** (*pl.* **-oos**) a bird with a call that sounds like its name. Cuckoos leave their eggs in the nests of other birds. ➲ see also CLOUD CUCKOO LAND
- **adj.** [not before noun] (*old-fashioned, informal*) crazy

'cuckoo clock *noun* a clock that has a small toy bird inside that comes out every hour and marks the hours with a sound like that of a cuckoo

cu·cum·ber /'kju:kʌmbə(r)/ *noun* [C, U] a long vegetable with dark green skin and light green flesh, that is usually eaten raw ➲ VISUAL VOCAB page V27 ➲ see also SEA CUCUMBER IDM see COOL *adj.*

cud /kʌd/ *noun* [U] the food that cows and similar animals bring back from the stomach into the mouth to chew again: *cows chewing the cud*

cud·dle /'kʌdl/ *verb, noun*
- **verb** [I, T] to hold sb/sth close in your arms to show love or affection SYN **hug**: *A couple of teenagers were kissing and cuddling on the doorstep.* ◇ **~ sth** (**+ adj.**) *The little boy cuddled the teddy bear close.*

PHR V **,cuddle 'up (to/against sb/sth)** | **,cuddle 'up (together)** to sit or lie very close to sb/sth: *She cuddled up against him.* ◇ *We cuddled up together under the blanket.*
- **noun** [usually sing.] the action of holding sb close in your arms to show love or affection SYN **hug**: *to give sb a cuddle*

cud·dly /'kʌdli/ *adj.* (*informal*) (**cud·dlier, cud·dli·est**) **1** (*approving*) if a person is **cuddly**, they make you want to cuddle them **2** [only before noun] (of a child's toy) soft and designed to be cuddled: *a cuddly rabbit*

cudgel /'kʌdʒl/ *noun, verb*
- **noun** a short thick stick that is used as a weapon

IDM **take up (the) cudgels on behalf of sb/sth** (*old-fashioned*) to defend or support sb/sth strongly
- **verb** (*BrE*) (**-ll-**, *especially US* **-l-**) **~ sb** to hit sb with a cudgel

IDM **cudgel your 'brains** (*old-fashioned, BrE*) to think very hard

cue /kju:/ *noun, verb*
- **noun 1** an action or event that is a signal for sb to do sth: **~ (for sth)** *Jon's arrival was a cue for more champagne.* ◇ **~ (to do sth)** *I think that's my cue to explain why I'm here.* **2** a few words or an action in a play that is a signal for another actor to do sth: *She stood in the wings and waited for her cue to go on.* **3** a long wooden stick with a leather tip, used for hitting the ball in the games of BILLIARDS, POOL and SNOOKER ➲ VISUAL VOCAB page V34

IDM **(right) on cue** at exactly the moment you expect or that is appropriate: *'Where is that boy?' As if on cue, Simon appeared in the doorway.* **take your 'cue from sb/sth** to copy what sb else does as an example of how to behave or what to do: *Investors are taking their cue from the big banks and selling dollars.*
- **verb** (**cue·ing, cued, cued**) **~ sb** to give sb a signal so they know when to start doing sth: *Can you cue me when you want me to begin speaking?*

'cue ball *noun* the ball that is hit with the cue in games such as BILLIARDS and SNOOKER ➲ VISUAL VOCAB page V34

'cue card *noun* a large card held up behind a television camera so that it can be read by actors or television PRESENTERS but cannot be seen on television

cuff /kʌf/ *noun, verb*
- **noun 1** [C] the end of a coat or shirt sleeve at the wrist: *a collar and cuffs of white lace* ➲ VISUAL VOCAB page V51 **2 cuffs** [pl.] (*informal*) = HANDCUFFS **3** (*NAmE*) (*BrE* **'turn-**

up) [C] the bottom of the leg of a pair of trousers/pants that has been folded over on the outside **4** [C] a light hit with an open hand: *to give sb a friendly cuff*

IDM ˌ**off the ˈcuff** (of speaking, remarks, etc.) without previous thought or preparation: *I'm just speaking off the cuff here—I haven't seen the results yet.* ◇ *an off-the-cuff remark*

C

■ ***verb*** **~ sb** to hit sb quickly and lightly with your hand, especially in a way that is not serious: *She cuffed him lightly around his head.*

cuff·link /ˈkʌflɪŋk/ *noun* [usually pl.] one of a pair of small decorative objects used for fastening shirt cuffs together: *a pair of gold cufflinks* ➲ VISUAL VOCAB page V53

cuis·ine /kwɪˈziːn/ *noun* [U, C] (from *French*) **1** a style of cooking: *Italian cuisine* **2** the food served in a restaurant (usually an expensive one): *The hotel restaurant is noted for its excellent cuisine.* ➲ see also HAUTE CUISINE, NOUVELLE CUISINE

cul-de-sac /ˈkʌl də sæk/ *noun* (*pl.* **cul-de-sacs** or **culs-de-sac**) (from *French*) a street that is closed at one end

cu·lin·ary /ˈkʌlɪnəri; *NAmE* -neri/ *adj.* [only before noun] (*formal*) connected with cooking or food: *culinary skills* ◇ *Savour the culinary delights of Mexico.*

cull /kʌl/ *verb, noun*

■ ***verb*** **~ sth** to kill a particular number of animals of a group in order to prevent the group from getting too large

PHR V ˈ**cull sth from sth** to choose or collect sth from a source or several different sources: *an exhibition of paintings culled from regional art galleries*

■ ***noun*** the act of killing some animals (usually the weakest ones) of a group in order to prevent the group from getting too large: *the annual seal cull*

cul·min·ate /ˈkʌlmɪneɪt/ *verb* [I] **~ (in/with sth)** (*formal*) to end with a particular result, or at a particular point: *a gun battle which culminated in the death of two police officers* ◇ *Months of hard work culminated in success.* ◇ *Their summer tour will culminate at a spectacular concert in London.*

cul·min·ation /ˌkʌlmɪˈneɪʃn/ *noun* [sing.] (*formal*) the highest point or end of sth, usually happening after a long time: *The reforms marked the successful culmination of a long campaign.*

cu·lottes /kjuːˈlɒts; *NAmE* kuːˈlɑːts/ *noun* [pl.] women's wide short trousers/pants that are made to look like a skirt: *a pair of culottes*

culp·able /ˈkʌlpəbl/ *adj.* (*formal*) responsible and deserving blame for having done sth wrong ▸ **culp·abil·ity** /ˌkʌlpəˈbɪləti/ *noun* [U] **culp·ably** /ˈkʌlpəbli/ *adv.*

ˌ**culpable ˈhomicide** *noun* [U] (*law*) in some countries, the crime of killing sb illegally but not deliberately ➲ compare JUSTIFIABLE HOMICIDE

cul·prit /ˈkʌlprɪt/ *noun* **1** a person who has done sth wrong or against the law: *The police quickly identified the real culprits.* **2** a person or thing responsible for causing a problem: *The main culprit in the current crisis seems to be modern farming techniques.*

cult /kʌlt/ *noun, adj.*

■ ***noun*** **1** [usually sing.] **~ (of sth)** a way of life, an attitude, an idea, etc. that has become very popular: *the cult of physical fitness* ◇ *An extraordinary* ***personality cult*** *had been created around the leader.* **2** a small group of people who have extreme religious beliefs and who are not part of any established religion: *Their son ran away from home and joined a cult.* **3** (*formal*) a system of religious beliefs and practices: *the Chinese cult of ancestor worship*

■ ***adj.*** [only before noun] very popular with a particular group of people; treating sb/sth as a cult figure, etc: *a* ***cult movie/book*** ◇ *The singer has become a* ***cult figure*** *in America.* ◇ *The cartoon has achieved* ***cult status.*** ◇ *The TV series has a* ***cult following*** *among young people.*

cul·tiv·able /ˈkʌltɪvəbl/ *adj.* (of land) that can be used to grow crops

cul·ti·var /ˈkʌltɪvɑː(r)/ *noun* (*technical*) a type of plant that has been deliberately developed to have particular features

cul·ti·vate /ˈkʌltɪveɪt/ *verb* (*formal*) **1 ~ sth** to prepare and use land for growing plants or crops: *The land around here has never been cultivated.* **2 ~ sth** to grow plants or crops SYN **grow**: *The people cultivate mainly rice and beans.* **3 ~ sb/sth** (sometimes *disapproving*) to try to get sb's friendship or support: *He purposely tried to cultivate good relations with the press.* ◇ *It helps if you go out of your way to cultivate the local people.* **4 ~ sth** to develop an attitude, a way of talking or behaving, etc: *She cultivated an air of sophistication.*

cul·ti·vated /ˈkʌltɪveɪtɪd/ *adj.* **1** (of people) having a high level of education and showing good manners SYN **cultured** **2** (of land) used to grow crops: *cultivated fields* **3** (of plants that are also wild) grown on a farm, etc. in order to be sold: *cultivated mushrooms* OPP **wild**

cul·ti·va·tion /ˌkʌltɪˈveɪʃn/ *noun* [U] **1** the preparation and use of land for growing plants or crops: *fertile land that is* ***under cultivation*** (= being CULTIVATED) ◇ ***rice/wheat, etc. cultivation*** ➲ see also SHIFTING CULTIVATION **2** the deliberate development of a particular relationship, quality or skill: *the cultivation of a good relationship with local firms*

cul·ti·va·tor /ˈkʌltɪveɪtə(r)/ *noun* **1** a person who CULTIVATES (= grows crops on) the land **2** a machine for breaking up soil and destroying WEEDS (= plants growing where they are not wanted)

cul·tural 🔑 AW /ˈkʌltʃərəl/ *adj.* [usually before noun] **1** 🔑 connected with the culture of a particular society or group, its customs, beliefs, etc: *cultural differences between the two communities* ◇ *economic, social and cultural factors* **2** 🔑 connected with art, literature, music, etc: *a cultural event* ◇ *Europe's cultural heritage* ◇ *The orchestra is very important for the cultural life of the city.* ▸ **cul·tur·al·ly** AW /-rəli/ *adv.*

cul·ture 🔑 AW /ˈkʌltʃə(r)/ *noun, verb*

■ ***noun***

▸ WAY OF LIFE **1** 🔑 [U] the customs and beliefs, art, way of life and social organization of a particular country or group: ***European/Islamic/African/American, etc. culture*** ◇ *working-class culture* **2** 🔑 [C] a country, group, etc. with its own beliefs, etc: *The children are taught to respect different cultures.* ◇ *the effect of technology on traditional cultures*

▸ ART/MUSIC/LITERATURE **3** 🔑 [U] art, music, literature, etc, thought of as a group: *Venice is a beautiful city full of culture and history.* ◇ ***popular culture*** (= that is enjoyed by a lot of people) ◇ *the Minister for Culture*

▸ BELIEFS/ATTITUDES **4** 🔑 [C, U] the beliefs and attitudes about sth that people in a particular group or organization share: *The political cultures of the United States and Europe are very different.* ◇ *A culture of failure exists in some schools.* ◇ *company culture* ◇ *We are living in a consumer culture.*

▸ GROWING/BREEDING **5** [U] (*technical*) the growing of plants or breeding of particular animals in order to get a particular substance or crop from them: *the culture of silkworms* (= for silk)

▸ CELLS/BACTERIA **6** [C] (*biology, medical*) a group of cells or bacteria, especially one taken from a person or an animal and grown for medical or scientific study, or to produce food; the process of obtaining and growing these cells: *a culture of cells from the tumour* ◇ *Yogurt is made from active cultures.* ◇ *to do/take a throat culture*

■ ***verb*** **~ sth** (*biology, medical*) to grow a group of cells or bacteria for medical or scientific study

cul·tured AW /ˈkʌltʃəd; *NAmE* -tʃərd/ *adj.* **1** (of people) well educated and able to understand and enjoy art, literature, etc. SYN **cultivated** OPP **uncultured** **2** (of cells or bacteria) grown for medical or scientific study **3** (of PEARLS) grown artificially

ˈ**culture shock** *noun* [C, U] a feeling of confusion and anxiety that sb may feel when they live in or visit another country

'culture vulture *noun* (*humorous*) a person who is very interested in serious art, music, literature, etc.

cul·vert /'kʌlvət; *NAmE* -vərt/ *noun* a tunnel that carries a river or a pipe for water under a road

cum /kʌm/ *prep.* (used for linking two nouns) and; as well as: *a bedroom-cum-study*

cum·ber·some /'kʌmbəsəm; *NAmE* -bərs-/ *adj.* **1** large and heavy; difficult to carry SYN **bulky**: *cumbersome machinery* **2** slow and complicated: *cumbersome legal procedures* **3** (of words or phrases) long or complicated: *The organization changed its cumbersome title to something easier to remember.*

cumin /'kʌmɪn/ *noun* [U] the dried seeds of the cumin plant, used in cooking as a spice: *cumin seeds* ➲ VISUAL VOCAB page V28

cum laude /ˌkʊm 'lɔːdi; 'laʊdeɪ/ *adv., adj.* (from *Latin*) (in the US) at the third of the three highest levels of achievement that students can reach when they finish their studies at college: *He graduated cum laude.* ➲ compare MAGNA CUM LAUDE, SUMMA CUM LAUDE

cum·mer·bund /'kʌməbʌnd; *NAmE* -mərb-/ *noun* a wide band of silk, etc. worn around the waist, especially under a DINNER JACKET

cu·mu·la·tive /'kjuːmjələtɪv; *NAmE* -leɪtɪv/ *adj.* **1** having a result that increases in strength or importance each time more of sth is added: *the **cumulative effect** of human activity on the world environment* **2** including all the amounts that have been added previously: *the monthly sales figures and the cumulative total for the past six months* ▸ **cu·mu·la·tive·ly** *adv.*

cu·mu·lo·nim·bus /ˌkjuːmələʊ'nɪmbəs; *NAmE* -loʊ-/ *noun* [U] (*technical*) a high mass of thick cloud with a flat base, often seen during THUNDERSTORMS

cu·mu·lus /'kjuːmjələs/ *noun* [U] (*technical*) a type of thick white cloud

cu·nei·form /'kjuːnɪfɔːm; *NAmE* -fɔːrm/ *noun* [U] an ancient system of writing used in Persia and Assyria

cun·ni·lin·gus /ˌkʌnɪ'lɪŋgəs/ *noun* [U] the act of touching a woman's sex organs with the mouth and tongue in order to give sexual pleasure

cun·ning /'kʌnɪŋ/ *adj., noun*

▪ ***adj.*** **1** (*disapproving*) able to get what you want in a clever way, especially by tricking or cheating sb SYN **crafty, wily**: *a cunning liar* ◇ *He was as cunning as a fox.* **2** clever and skilful SYN **ingenious**: *It was a cunning piece of detective work.* ▸ **cun·ning·ly** *adv.*: *The microphone was cunningly concealed in the bookcase.*

▪ ***noun*** [U] the ability to achieve sth by tricking or cheating other people in a clever way SYN **craftiness**: *It took energy and cunning just to survive.* ◇ *She used low cunning* (= dishonest behaviour) *to get what she wanted.*

cunt /kʌnt/ *noun* (*taboo, slang*) **1** a woman's VAGINA and outer sexual organs **2** a very offensive word used to insult sb and to show anger or dislike: *You stupid cunt!*

cup 🔑 /kʌp/ *noun, verb*

▪ ***noun*** **1** 🔑 [C] a small container shaped like a bowl, usually with a handle, used for drinking tea, coffee, etc: *a teacup* ◇ *a coffee cup* ◇ *a cup and saucer* ◇ *a paper cup* ➲ VISUAL VOCAB page V19 **2** 🔑 [C] the contents of a cup: *She drank the whole cup.* ◇ *Would you like a cup of tea?* **3** 🔑 [C] a unit for measuring quantity used in cooking in the US; a metal or plastic container used to measure this quantity: *two cups of flour and half a cup of butter* **4** 🔑 [C] a thing shaped like a cup: *an egg cup* **5** 🔑 [C] a gold or silver cup on a STEM, often with two handles, that is given as a prize in a competition: *She's won several cups for skating.* ◇ *He lifted the cup for the fifth time this year* (= it was the fifth time he had won). ➲ picture at MEDAL **6** 🔑 [sing.] (usually **Cup**) a sports competition in which a cup is given as a prize: *the World Cup* **7** [C] one of the two parts of a BRA that cover the breast: *a C cup* **8** [C, U] a drink made from wine mixed with, for example, fruit juice **9** [C] (*NAmE*) (in GOLF) a hollow in the ground that you must get the ball into **10** [C] (*NAmE*) a piece of plastic that a man wears over his sex organs to protect them while he is playing a sport

IDM **in your 'cups** (*old-fashioned*) having drunk too much alcohol: *He gets very maudlin when he's in his cups.* **not sb's cup of 'tea** (*informal*) not what sb likes or is interested in: *An evening at the opera isn't everyone's cup of tea.* ◇ *He's nice enough but not really my cup of tea.* ➲ more at SLIP *n.*

▪ ***verb*** (-pp-) **1 ~ your hand(s) (around/over sth)** to make your hands into the shape of a bowl: *She held the bird gently in cupped hands.* **2 ~ sth (in your hands)** to hold sth, making your hands into a round shape: *He cupped her face in his hands and kissed her.*

cup·board 🔑 /'kʌbəd; *NAmE* -bərd/ *noun* **1** 🔑 a piece of furniture with doors and shelves used for storing dishes, food, clothes, etc: *kitchen cupboards* **2** 🔑 (*BrE*) (*NAmE* **closet**) a space in a wall with a door that reaches the ground, used for storing things: *built-in cupboards* ➲ see also AIRING CUPBOARD, BROOM CUPBOARD

IDM **the ˌcupboard is 'bare** (*BrE*) used to say that there is no money for sth: *They are seeking more funds but the cupboard is bare.* ORIGIN This expression refers to a children's nursery rhyme about Old Mother Hubbard, who had nothing in her cupboard to feed her dog. **'cupboard love** (*BrE*) affection that sb, especially a child, shows towards sb else in order to get sth ➲ more at SKELETON

cup·cake *noun* /'kʌpkeɪk/ (*especially NAmE*) (*BrE* also **'fairy cake**) *noun* a small cake, baked in a paper container shaped like a cup and often with ICING on top

'cup final (also **Cup Final**) *noun* (*BrE*) (especially in football (SOCCER)) the last match in a series of matches in a competition that gives a cup as a prize to the winners: *cup final tickets* ◇ *the FA Cup Final*

cup·ful /'kʌpfʊl/ *noun* the amount that a cup will hold: *3 cupfuls of water* ➲ see also CUP

Cupid /'kjuːpɪd/ *noun* **1** the Roman god of love who is shown as a beautiful baby boy with wings, carrying a BOW and arrow **2 cupid** [C] a picture or statue of a baby boy who looks like Cupid

IDM **play 'Cupid** to try to start a romantic relationship between two people

cu·pid·ity /kjuː'pɪdəti/ *noun* [U] (*formal*) a strong desire for more wealth, possessions, power, etc. than a person needs SYN **greed**

cu·pola /'kjuːpələ/ *noun* a round part on top of a building (like a small DOME) ➲ VISUAL VOCAB page V12

cuppa /'kʌpə/ *noun* (*BrE, informal*) a cup of tea: *Do you fancy a cuppa?*

cup·ping /'kʌpɪŋ/ *noun* [U] a way of treating pain by putting special cups on the skin and heating them so that the flow of blood to the skin increases

'cup tie *noun* (*BrE*) (especially in football (SOCCER)) a match between two teams in a competition that gives a cup as a prize to the winner

cur /kɜː(r)/ *noun* (*old-fashioned, disapproving*) an aggressive dog, especially a MONGREL

cur·able /'kjʊərəbl; *NAmE* 'kjʊr-/ *adj.* (of an illness) that can be cured: *Most skin cancers are curable if treated early.* OPP **incurable**

cura·çao /ˌkjʊərə'saʊ; -'seɪəʊ; *NAmE* ˌkjuːrə'soʊ; -'saʊ/ *noun* [U, C] a strong alcoholic drink made from the skin of bitter oranges

cur·acy /'kjʊərəsi; *NAmE* 'kjʊr-/ *noun* (*pl.* -ies) the position of a curate; the time that sb is a curate

cur·ate[1] ➲ see also CURATE[2] /'kjʊərət; *NAmE* 'kjʊrət/ *noun* (in the Anglican Church) an assistant to a VICAR (= a priest, who is in charge of the church or churches in a particular area)

IDM **the/a ˌcurate's 'egg** (*BrE*) something that has some good parts and some bad ones

cur·ate[2] /kjʊə'reɪt; *NAmE* kjʊ'r-/ *verb* **~ sth** to select, organize and look after the objects or works of art in a museum or art gallery, etc.

cura·tive /'kjʊərətɪv; *NAmE* 'kjʊr-/ *adj.* (*formal*) able to cure illness SYN **healing**: *the curative properties of herbs* ➲ compare PREVENTIVE

cur·ator /kjʊəˈreɪtə(r); *NAmE* kjʊˈr-/ *noun* a person whose job is to be in charge of the objects or works of art in a museum or art gallery, etc.

curb /kɜːb; *NAmE* kɜːrb/ *verb, noun*
▪ *verb* **~ sth** to control or limit sth, especially sth bad SYN **check**: *He needs to learn to curb his temper.* ◇ *A range of policies have been introduced aimed at curbing inflation.*
▪ *noun* **1** **~ (on sth)** something that controls and puts limits on sth: *curbs on government spending* **2** (*NAmE*) (*BrE* **kerb**) the edge of the raised path at the side of a road, usually made of long pieces of stone: *The bus mounted the curb* (= went onto the SIDEWALK/PAVEMENT) *and hit a tree.* ➲ VISUAL VOCAB page V3

curb·side (*NAmE*) (*BrE* **kerb·side**) /ˈkɜːbsaɪd; *NAmE* ˈkɜːrb-/ *noun* [U] the side of the street or path near the curb/kerb

curb·stone (*NAmE*) (*BrE* **kerb·stone**) /ˈkɜːbstəʊn; *NAmE* ˈkɜːrb-/ *noun* a block of stone or concrete in a curb/kerb

curd /kɜːd; *NAmE* kɜːrd/ *noun* [U] (also **curds** [pl.]) a thick soft substance that is formed when milk turns sour

ˈ**curd cheese** *noun* [U, C] (*BrE*) a type of soft cheese ➲ compare QUARK

cur·dle /ˈkɜːdl; *NAmE* ˈkɜːrdl/ *verb* **1** [I, T] **~ (sth)** when a liquid, especially milk, **curdles** or sth **curdles** it, it separates into solid and liquid parts **2** [I, T] **~ (sth)** if sth **curdles** your blood or makes your blood **curdle**, it makes you extremely frightened or shocked ➲ see also BLOOD-CURDLING

cure /kjʊə(r); *NAmE* kjʊr/ *verb, noun*
▪ *verb* **1** **~ sb (of sth)** to make a person or an animal healthy again after an illness: *Will you be able to cure him, Doctor?* ➲ COLLOCATIONS at ILL **2** **~ sth** to make an illness go away: *TB is a serious illness, but it can be cured.* **3** **~ sth** to deal with a problem successfully: *I finally managed to cure the rattling noise in my car.* **4** **~ sb of sth** to stop sb from behaving in a particular way, especially a way that is bad or annoying **5** **~ sth** to treat food or TOBACCO with smoke, salt, etc. in order to preserve it IDM see KILL *v.*
▪ *noun* **1** **~ (for sth)** a medicine or medical treatment that cures an illness: *the search for a cure for cancer* ◇ *There is no known cure but the illness can be treated.* **2** the act of curing sb of an illness or the process of being cured: *Doctors cannot effect a cure if the disease has spread too far.* ◇ *The cure took six weeks.* **3** **~ (for sth)** something that will solve a problem, improve a bad situation, etc: *a cure for poverty* IDM see PREVENTION

ˈ**cure-all** *noun* something that people believe can cure any problem or any disease SYN **panacea**

cur·few /ˈkɜːfjuː; *NAmE* ˈkɜːrf-/ *noun* [C, U] **1** a law which says that people must not go outside after a particular time at night until the morning; the time after which nobody must go outside: *The army imposed a dusk-to-dawn curfew.* ◇ *You must get home before curfew.* ➲ COLLOCATIONS at WAR **2** (*NAmE*) a time when children must be home in the evening: *I have a 10 o'clock curfew.*

curie /ˈkjʊəri; *NAmE* ˈkjʊri/ *noun* (*abbr.* Ci) (*physics*) a unit for measuring RADIOACTIVITY

curio /ˈkjʊəriəʊ; *NAmE* ˈkjʊrioʊ/ *noun* (*pl.* -os) a small object that is rare or unusual, often sth that people collect

curi·os·ity /ˌkjʊəriˈɒsəti; *NAmE* ˌkjʊriˈɑːs-/ *noun* (*pl.* -ies) **1** [U, sing.] **~ (about sth)** | **~ (to do sth)** a strong desire to know about sth: *Children show curiosity about everything.* ◇ *a certain curiosity to see what would happen next* ◇ *The letter wasn't addressed to me but I opened it* **out of curiosity**. ◇ *His answer did not* **satisfy my curiosity** *at all.* ◇ *Sophie's* **curiosity was aroused** *by the mysterious phone call.* ◇ *intellectual curiosity* ◇ *'Why do you ask?' 'Oh, just* **idle curiosity**' (= no particular reason). **2** [C] an unusual and interesting thing: *The museum is full of historical curiosities.*
IDM **curiosity killed the ˈcat** (*saying*) used to tell sb not to ask questions or try to find out about things that do not concern them

curi·ous /ˈkjʊəriəs; *NAmE* ˈkjʊr-/ *adj.* **1** **~ (about sth)** | **~ (to do sth)** having a strong desire to know about sth SYN **inquisitive**: *They were very curious about the people who lived upstairs.* ◇ *I was curious to find out what she had said.* ◇ *Everyone was* **curious as to** *why Mark was leaving.* ◇ *He is such a curious boy, always asking questions.* **2** **~ (that...)** strange and unusual: *There was a curious mixture of people in the audience.* ◇ *It was a curious feeling, as though we were floating on air.* ◇ ***It was curious that*** *she didn't tell anyone.* ▸ **curi·ous·ly** *adv.*: *'Are you really an artist?' Sara asked curiously.* ◇ *His clothes were curiously old-fashioned.* ◇ *Curiously enough, a year later exactly the same thing happened again.*

cur·ium /ˈkjʊəriəm; *NAmE* ˈkjʊr-/ *noun* [U] (*symb.* **Cm**) a chemical element. Curium is a RADIOACTIVE metal produced artificially from PLUTONIUM.

curl /kɜːl; *NAmE* kɜːrl/ *verb, noun*
▪ *verb* **1** [I, T] **~ (sth)** to form or make sth form into a curl or curls: *His hair curls naturally.* **2** [I, T] to form or make sth form into a curved shape: **(+ adv./prep.)** *The cat curled into a ball and went to sleep.* ◇ **~ sth (+ adv./prep.)** *She curled her legs up under her.* **3** [I, T] to move while forming into a twisted or curved shape; to make sth do this: **(+ adv./prep.)** *The smoke curled steadily upwards.* ◇ **~ sth (+ adv./prep.)** *He turned and curled the ball around the goalkeeper.* **4** [T, I] **~ (sth)** if you **curl** your lip or your lip **curls**, you move your lip upwards and sideways to show that you think sb/sth is stupid or that you are better than they are IDM see TOE *n.*
PHR V ˌ**curl ˈup** | **be ˌcurled ˈup** to lie or sit with your back curved and your arms and legs bent close to your body: *She curled up and closed her eyes.* ➲ picture at CURVED ˌ**curl ˈup** | ˌ**curl sb ˈup** (*BrE, informal*) to become or make sb become very embarrassed ˌ**curl ˈup** | ˌ**curl sth↔ˈup** to form or make sth form into a tightly curled shape: *The paper started to shrivel and curl up in the heat.*
▪ *noun* **1** [C] a small bunch of hair that forms a curved or round shape: *Her hair was a mass of curls.* ◇ *The baby had dark eyes and dark curls.* **2** [C, U] the tendency of hair to form curls: *His hair had a natural curl.* **3** [C] a thing that forms a curved or round shape: *a curl of smoke* ◇ *Decorate the cake with curls of chocolate.* ◇ *a contemptuous curl of the lip* (= an expression showing disapproval)

curl·er /ˈkɜːlə(r); *NAmE* ˈkɜːrl-/ *noun* [usually pl.] a small plastic or metal tube which you can wrap wet hair around in order to make it curl SYN **roller**

cur·lew /ˈkɜːljuː; *NAmE* ˈkɜːrl-/ *noun* a bird with a long thin beak that curves downwards, that lives near water

cur·li·cue /ˈkɜːlɪkjuː; *NAmE* ˈkɜːrl-/ *noun* (*technical*) a decorative curl or twist in writing or in a design

curl·ing /ˈkɜːlɪŋ; *NAmE* ˈkɜːrlɪŋ/ *noun* [U] a game played on ice, in which players slide heavy flat stones towards a mark

ˈ**curling iron** (*NAmE*) (*BrE* **tongs**, ˈ**curling tongs**) *noun* a tool that is heated and used for curling hair

ˈ**curling tongs** *noun* [pl.] (*BrE*) = CURLING IRON

curly /ˈkɜːli; *NAmE* ˈkɜːrli/ *adj.* (**curl·ier**, **curli·est**) having a lot of curls or a curved shape: *short curly hair* ◇ *a dog with a curly tail* ➲ picture at CURVED ➲ VISUAL VOCAB page V49 OPP **straight**

ˌ**curly ˈendive** *noun* [C, U] = CHICORY (2)

cur·mudg·eon /kɜːˈmʌdʒən; *NAmE* kɜːrˈm-/ *noun* (*old-fashioned*) a bad-tempered person, often an old one ▸ **cur·mudg·eon·ly** *adj.*

cur·rant /ˈkʌrənt; *NAmE* ˈkɜːr-/ *noun* **1** a small dried GRAPE, used in cakes, etc: *a currant bun* **2** (usually in compounds) a small black, red or white BERRY that grows in bunches on bushes: *blackcurrants* ◇ *currant bushes*

cur·rency AW /ˈkʌrənsi; *NAmE* ˈkɜːr-/ *noun* (*pl.* -ies) **1** [C, U] the system of money that a country uses: *trading in foreign currencies* ◇ *a single European currency* ◇ *You'll need some cash in* **local currency** *but you can also use your credit card.* ➲ see also HARD CURRENCY **2** [U] the fact that sth is used or accepted by a lot of people: *The term 'post-industrial' now has* **wide currency**. ◇ *The qualification has* **gained currency** *all over the world.*

cur·rent 0-w /ˈkʌrənt; *NAmE* ˈkɜːr-/ *adj., noun*
■ ***adj.*** **1** 0-w [only before noun] happening now; of the present time: *current prices* ◇ *a budget for the current year* ◇ *your current employer* ➲ note at ACTUAL **2** 0-w being used by or accepted by most people: *words that are no longer current*
■ ***noun*** **1** 0-w the movement of water in the sea or a river; the movement of air in a particular direction: *He swam to the shore against a* ***strong current***. ◇ *Birds use warm air currents to help their flight.* **2** 0-w the flow of electricity through a wire, etc: *a 15 amp electrical current* ➲ see also AC, DC **3** the fact of particular ideas, opinions or feelings being present in a group of people: *Ministers are worried by this current of anti-government feeling.*

ˈ**current account** (*BrE*) (*US* ˈ**checking account** *CanE* ˈ**chequing account**) *noun* a type of bank account that you can take money out of at any time, and that provides you with a CHEQUEBOOK and CASH CARD ➲ compare DEPOSIT ACCOUNT

ˌ**current afˈfairs** *noun* [pl.] events of political or social importance that are happening now

cur·rent·ly 0-w /ˈkʌrəntli; *NAmE* ˈkɜːr-/ *adv.* at the present time: *The hourly charge is currently £35.* ◇ *Currently, over 500 students are enrolled on the course.* ◇ *All the options are* ***currently available***. ◇ *This matter is currently being discussed.*

cur·ricu·lar /kəˈrɪkjələ(r)/ *adj.* connected with the curriculum of a school, etc. ➲ see also EXTRA-CURRICULAR

cur·ricu·lum /kəˈrɪkjələm/ *noun* (*pl.* **cur·ric·ula** /-lə/ or **cur·ricu·lums**) the subjects that are included in a course of study or taught in a school, college, etc: *the school curriculum* ◇ (*BrE*) *Spanish is on the curriculum.* ◇ (*NAmE*) *Spanish is in the curriculum.* ➲ COLLOCATIONS at EDUCATION ➲ compare SYLLABUS

cur·ricu·lum vitae /kəˌrɪkjələm ˈviːtaɪ/ (*abbr.* **CV**) *noun* **1** (*BrE*) (*NAmE* **ré·sumé**) a written record of your education and the jobs you have done, that you send when you are applying for a job: *Applications with a full curriculum vitae and two references should reach the Principal by June 12th.* **2** (also **vita**) (*US*) a record of a university/college teacher's education and where they have worked, also including a list of books and articles that they have published and courses that they have taught, used when they are applying for a job

cur·ried /ˈkʌrid; *NAmE* ˈkɜːr-/ *adj.* [only before noun] cooked with hot spices: ***curried chicken/beef/eggs, etc.***

curry /ˈkʌri; *NAmE* ˈkɜːri/ *noun, verb*
■ ***noun*** [C, U] a S Asian dish of meat, vegetables, etc. cooked with hot spices, often served with rice: *a chicken curry* ◇ *Would you like some more curry?*
■ ***verb*** (**cur·ries, curry·ing, cur·ried, cur·ried**) **~ sth** to make curry out of meat or vegetables
IDM **curry ˈfavour (with sb)** (*disapproving*) to try to get sb to like or support you by praising or helping them a lot

ˈ**curry powder** *noun* [U] a powder made from a mixture of spices, used to give a hot flavour to food, especially curry

curse /kɜːs; *NAmE* kɜːrs/ *noun, verb*
■ ***noun*** **1** (also *old-fashioned, informal* **cuss**) [C] a rude or offensive word or phrase that some people use when they are very angry **SYN** **oath, swear word**: *He muttered a curse at the other driver.* **2** [C] a word or phrase that has a magic power to make sth bad happen: *The family thought that they were* ***under a curse***. ➲ compare HEX **3** [C] something that causes harm or evil: *the curse of drug addiction* ◇ *Noise is a curse of modern city life.* **4 the curse** [sing.] (*old-fashioned, informal*) = MENSTRUATION
■ ***verb*** **1** [I] to swear: *He hit his head as he stood up and cursed loudly.* **2** [T] to say rude things to sb or think rude things about sb/sth: **~ sb/sth/yourself** *She cursed her bad luck.* ◇ **~ sb/sth/yourself for sth** *He cursed himself for his stupidity.* **3** [T] **~ sb/sth** to use a magic word or phrase against sb in order to harm them: *Legend has it that the whole village had been cursed by a witch.* ➲ compare HEX
PHR V **be ˈcursed with sth** to continuously suffer from or be affected by sth bad: *She seems cursed with bad luck.*

cursed *adj.* **1** /kɜːst; *NAmE* kɜːrst/ having a curse (2) on it; suffering from a curse (2): *The necklace was cursed.* ◇ *The whole family seemed cursed.* **2** /ˈkɜːsɪd; *NAmE* ˈkɜːrsɪd/ [only before noun] (*old-fashioned*) unpleasant; annoying

cur·sive /ˈkɜːsɪv; *NAmE* ˈkɜːrs-/ *adj.* (*technical*) (of HANDWRITING) with the letters joined together

cur·sor /ˈkɜːsə(r); *NAmE* ˈkɜːrs-/ *noun* a small mark on a computer screen that can be moved and that shows the position on the screen where, for example, text will be added ➲ VISUAL VOCAB page V55

curs·ory /ˈkɜːsəri; *NAmE* ˈkɜːrs-/ *adj.* (often *disapproving*) done quickly and without giving enough attention to details **SYN** **brief, perfunctory**: *a* ***cursory glance/examination/inspection*** ▸ **cur·sor·ily** /ˈkɜːsərəli; *NAmE* ˈkɜːrs-/ *adv.*

curt /kɜːt; *NAmE* kɜːrt/ *adj.* (of a person's manner or behaviour) appearing rude because very few words are used, or because sth is done in a very quick way **SYN** **abrupt, brusque**: *a curt reply* ◇ *a curt nod* ◇ *His tone was curt and unfriendly.* ▸ **curt·ly** *adv.* **curt·ness** *noun* [U]

cur·tail /kɜːˈteɪl; *NAmE* kɜːrˈt-/ *verb* **~ sth** (*formal*) to limit sth or make it last for a shorter time: *Spending on books has been severely curtailed.* ◇ *The lecture was curtailed by the fire alarm going off.* ▸ **cur·tail·ment** *noun* [U]: *the curtailment of civil liberties*

cur·tain 0-w /ˈkɜːtn; *NAmE* ˈkɜːrtn/ *noun, verb*
■ ***noun*** **1** 0-w [C] a piece of cloth that is hung to cover a window ➲ VISUAL VOCAB page V18: *to* ***draw/pull/close the curtains*** (= to pull them across the window so they cover it) ◇ *to* ***draw/draw back/pull back the curtains*** (= to open them, so that the window is no longer covered) ◇ *It was ten in the morning but the curtains were still drawn* (= closed). ◇ *a pair of curtains* ➲ see also DRAPE **2** [C] (*NAmE*) (*BrE* ˌ**net ˈcurtain**) a very thin piece of cloth that you hang at a window, which allows light to enter but stops people outside from being able to see inside **3** 0-w [C] a piece of cloth that is hung up as a screen in a room or around a bed, for example: *a shower curtain* ➲ see also THE IRON CURTAIN **4** 0-w [sing.] a piece of thick, heavy cloth that hangs in front of the stage in the theatre: *The audience was waiting for the curtain to rise* (= for the play to begin). ◇ *There was tremendous applause when the curtain came down* (= the play ended). ◇ *We left just before the* ***final curtain***. ◇ (*figurative*) *The curtain has fallen on her long and distinguished career* (= her career has ended). ◇ (*figurative*) *It's time to face the* ***final curtain*** (= the end; death). **5** [C, usually sing.] a thing that covers, hides or protects sth: *a* ***curtain of rain/smoke*** ◇ *She pushed back the curtain of brown hair from her eyes.*
IDM **be ˈcurtains (for sb)** (*informal*) to be a situation without hope or that you cannot escape from: *When I saw he had a gun, I thought it was curtains for me.* **bring down the ˈcurtain on sth | bring the ˈcurtain down on sth** to finish or mark the end of sth: *His sudden decision to retire brought down the curtain on a distinguished career.*
■ ***verb*** **~ sth** to provide curtains for a window or a room
PHR V ˌ**curtain sth↔ˈoff** to separate an area of a room with a curtain or curtains

ˈ**curtain call** *noun* the time in the theatre when the actors come to the front of the stage at the end of a play to receive the APPLAUSE of the audience

ˈ**curtain-raiser** *noun* **1 ~ (to sth)** a small event that prepares for a more important one **2 ~ (to sth)** a short performance before the main performance in a theatre, etc.

curtsy (also **curt·sey**) /ˈkɜːtsi; *NAmE* ˈkɜːrtsi/ *noun* (*pl.* **-ies** or **-eys**) a formal sign made by a woman in a dance or to say hello or goodbye to an important person, by bending her knees with one foot in front of the other ▸ **curtsy** *verb* (**curt·sies, curt·sy·ing, curt·sied, curt·sied**) (also **curt·sey**) [I]: **~ (to sb)** *She curtsied to the Queen.*

curv·aceous /kɜːˈveɪʃəs; *NAmE* kɜːrˈv-/ *adj.* (*informal*) used in newspapers, etc. to describe a woman whose body has attractive curves

C

C

curv·ature /ˈkɜːvətʃə(r); *NAmE* ˈkɜːrv-/ *noun* [U] (*technical*) the state of being curved; the amount that sth is curved: *the curvature of the earth* ◇ *curvature of the spine*

curve 🔑 /kɜːv; *NAmE* kɜːrv/ *noun, verb*

■ ***noun* 1** 🔑 a line or surface that bends gradually; a smooth bend: *the delicate curve of her ear* ◇ *a pattern of straight lines and curves* ◇ (*especially NAmE*) *a curve in the road* ◇ (*especially NAmE*) *The driver lost control on a curve and the vehicle hit a tree.* ◇ *to plot a curve on a graph* ◇ (*technical*) *the unemployment-income curve* (= a line on a GRAPH showing the relationship between the number of unemployed people and national income) ➲ see also LEARNING CURVE **2** (also ˈ**curve ball**) (*NAmE*) (in BASEBALL) a ball that moves in a curve when it is thrown to the BATTER: (*figurative*) *One of the journalists* ***threw*** *the senator* ***a curve*** (= surprised him by asking a difficult question).

IDM **ahead of/behind the ˈcurve** (*especially NAmE, business*) in advance of or behind a particular trend: *Our expert advice will help you stay ahead of the curve.* ◇ *We've fallen behind the curve when it comes to developing new digital products.*

■ ***verb*** 🔑 [I, T] **~ (sth)** (**+ adv./prep.**) to move or make sth move in the shape of a curve; to be in the shape of a curve: *The road curved around the bay.* ◇ *The ball curved through the air.* ◇ *His lips curved in a smile.*

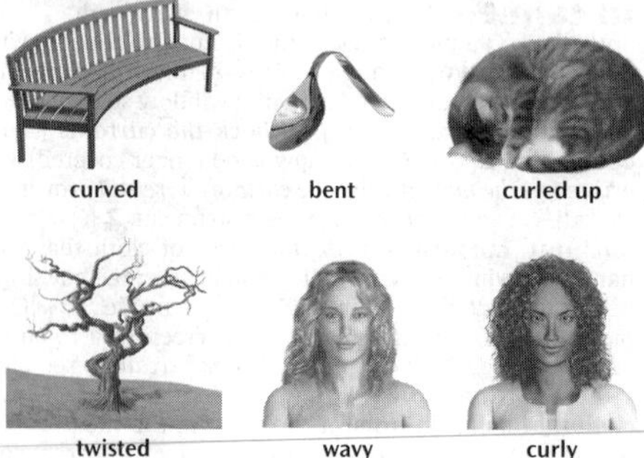

curved | bent | curled up
twisted | wavy | curly

curved 🔑 /kɜːvd; *NAmE* kɜːrvd/ *adj.* having a round shape: *a curved path/roof/blade*

curvi·lin·ear /ˌkɜːvɪˈlɪniə(r); *NAmE* ˌkɜːrv-/ *adj.* (*formal*) consisting of a curved line or lines

curvy /ˈkɜːvi; *NAmE* ˈkɜːrvi/ *adj.* (*informal*) having curves: *a curvy body* ◇ *curvy lines*

cush·ion /ˈkʊʃn/ *noun, verb*

■ ***noun* 1** (*NAmE* also **pil·low**) a cloth bag filled with soft material or feathers that is used, for example, to make a seat more comfortable: *matching curtains and cushions* ◇ *a floor cushion* (= a large cushion that you put on the floor to sit on) ◇ *a pile of scatter cushions* (= small cushions, often in bright colours, that you put on chairs, etc.) ◇ (*figurative*) *a cushion of moss on a rock* ➲ VISUAL VOCAB page V18 **2** a layer of sth between two surfaces that keeps them apart: *A hovercraft rides on a cushion of air.* **3** [usually sing.] **~ (against sth)** something that protects you against sth unpleasant that might happen: *His savings were a comfortable cushion against financial problems.* ◇ *The team built up a safe cushion of two goals in the first half.* **4** (in the game of BILLIARDS, etc.) the soft inside edge along each side of the table, that the balls BOUNCE off ➲ VISUAL VOCAB page V34

■ ***verb* 1 ~ sth** to make the effect of a fall or hit less severe: *My fall was cushioned by the deep snow.* **2 ~ sb/sth** (**against/from sth**) to protect sb/sth from being hurt or damaged or from the unpleasant effects of sth: *The south of the country has been cushioned from the worst effects of the recession.* ◇ *He broke the news of my brother's death to me, making no effort to* ***cushion the blow*** (= make the news less shocking). **3** [usually passive] **~ sth** to make sth soft with a cushion

cushy /ˈkʊʃi/ *adj.* (**cush·ier, cushi·est**) (*informal*, often *disapproving*) very easy and pleasant; needing little or no effort: *a cushy job*

IDM **a cushy ˈnumber** (*BrE*) an easy job; a pleasant situation that other people would like

cusp /kʌsp/ *noun* **1** (*technical*) a pointed end where two curves meet: *the cusp of a leaf* **2** the time when one sign of the ZODIAC ends and the next begins: *I was born* ***on the cusp*** *between Virgo and Libra.* ◇ (*figurative*) *He was on the cusp between small acting roles and moderate fame.*

cuss /kʌs/ *verb, noun*

■ ***verb*** [I, T] **~ (sb/sth)** (*old-fashioned, informal*) to swear at sb: *My dad used to come home drunk, shouting and cussing.*

■ ***noun*** (*old-fashioned, informal*) **1** used with a negative adjective to describe a person: *He's an awkward cuss.* **2** = CURSE: *cuss words*

cussed /ˈkʌsɪd/ *adj.* (*old-fashioned, informal*) (of people) not willing to be helpful SYN **stubborn** ▸ **cuss·ed·ly** *adv.* **cuss·ed·ness** *noun* [U]

cus·tard /ˈkʌstəd; *NAmE* -tərd/ *noun* **1** [U] (*especially BrE*) (*NAmE* usually ˌ**custard ˈsauce**) a sweet yellow sauce made from milk, sugar, eggs and flour, usually served hot with cooked fruit, PUDDINGS, etc: *apple pie and custard* **2** [C, U] a mixture of eggs, milk and sugar baked until it is firm

ˌ**custard ˈpie** *noun* a flat PIE filled with sth soft and wet that looks like custard, that performers throw at each other to make people laugh

cus·to·dial /kʌˈstəʊdiəl; *NAmE* -ˈstoʊ-/ *adj.* [usually before noun] (*law*) **1** involving sending sb to prison: *The judge gave him a* ***custodial sentence*** (= sent him to prison). **2** connected with the right or duty of taking care of sb; having CUSTODY: *The mother is usually the custodial parent after a divorce.* OPP **non-custodial**

cus·to·dian /kʌˈstəʊdiən; *NAmE* -ˈstoʊ-/ *noun* **1** a person who takes responsibility for taking care of or protecting sth: *the museum's custodians* ◇ *a self-appointed custodian of public morals* **2** (*NAmE*) (*BrE* **care·taker**) (*NAmE* also, *ScotE* **jani·tor**) a person whose job is to take care of a building such as a school or a block of flats or an apartment building

cus·tody /ˈkʌstədi/ *noun* [U] **1** the legal right or duty to take care of or keep sb/sth; the act of taking care of sth/sb: *Who will* ***have custody*** *of the children?* ◇ *The divorce court awarded custody to the child's mother.* ◇ *The parents were locked in a bitter battle for custody.* ◇ *The bank provides* ***safe custody*** *for valuables.* ◇ *The castle is now* ***in the custody of*** *the state.* ➲ COLLOCATIONS at MARRIAGE **2** the state of being in prison, especially while waiting for trial: *After the riot, 32 people were taken into* ***police custody***. ◇ (*BrE*) *He was* ***remanded in custody***, *charged with the murder of a policeman.* ➲ see also YOUTH CUSTODY

cus·tom 🔑 /ˈkʌstəm/ *noun, adj.*

■ ***noun*** ➲ see also CUSTOMS **1** 🔑 [C, U] **~ (of doing sth)** an accepted way of behaving or of doing things in a society or a community: *an* ***old/ancient custom*** ◇ *the custom of giving presents at Christmas* ◇ *It's a* ***local custom***. ◇ ***It is the custom*** *in that country for women to marry young.* **2** [sing.] (*formal* or *literary*) the way a person always behaves SYN **habit, practice**: *It was her custom to rise early.* ◇ *As was his custom, he knocked three times.* **3** [U] (*BrE, formal*) (also **business** *NAmE, BrE*) the fact of a person or people buying goods or services at a shop/store or business: *Thank you for your custom. Please call again.* ◇ *We've lost a lot of custom since prices went up.*

■ ***adj.*** [only before noun] (*especially NAmE*) = CUSTOM-BUILT, CUSTOM-MADE: *a custom motorcycle*

cus·tom·ary /ˈkʌstəməri; *NAmE* -meri/ *adj.* **1** if sth is **customary**, it is what people usually do in a particular place or situation SYN **usual**: *Is it customary to tip hairdressers in this country?* **2** typical of a particular person SYN **habitual**: *She arranged everything with her customary efficiency.* ▸ **cus·tom·ar·ily** /ˈkʌstəmərəli; *NAmE* ˌkʌstəˈmerəli/ *adv.*

ˌ**custom-ˈbuilt** (also **custom** especially in *NAmE*) *adj.* designed and built for a particular person

cus·tom·er O‑ /ˈkʌstəmə(r)/ *noun* **1** O‑ a person or an organization that buys sth from a shop/store or business: *one of the shop's* ***best/biggest customers*** ◇ *They know me—I'm a* ***regular customer.*** ◇ *the* ***customer service*** *department* ◇ *The firm has excellent customer relations.* ⊃ COLLOCATIONS at SHOPPING **2** (*old-fashioned, informal*) used after an adjective to describe a particular type of person: *an awkward customer*

ˈ**customer base** *noun* [usually sing.] (*business*) all the people who buy or use a particular product or service: *We need to appeal to a wider customer base.*

ˈ**customer-facing** *adj.* [only before noun] (*business*) dealing directly with customers or used by customers: *customer-facing operations such as call centres* ◇ *customer-facing software applications*

cus·tom·ize (*BrE* also **-ise**) /ˈkʌstəmaɪz/ *verb* **~ sth** to make or change sth to suit the needs of the owner: *You can customize the software in several ways.* ▶ **cus·tom·ized** *adj.*: *a customized car*

ˌ**custom-ˈmade** (also **cus·tom** especially in *NAmE*) *adj.* designed and made for a particular person ⊃ see also BESPOKE

cus·toms O‑ /ˈkʌstəmz/ *noun* [pl.] **1** O‑ (usually **Customs**) (*BrE* also **Customs and Excise**) (*US* also **US Customs Service**) the government department that collects taxes on goods bought and sold and on goods brought into the country, and that checks what is brought in: *The Customs have seized large quantities of smuggled heroin.* ◇ *a customs officer* HELP *NAmE* uses a singular verb with **customs** in this meaning. **2** O‑ the place at a port or an airport where your bags are checked as you come into a country: *to go through customs and passport control* **3** O‑ the taxes that must be paid to the government when goods are brought in from other countries: *to pay customs on sth* ◇ ***customs duty/duties*** ⊃ SYNONYMS at TAX ⊃ compare EXCISE

ˈ**customs union** *noun* a group of states that agree to have the same taxes on imported goods

cut O‑ /kʌt/ *verb, noun*

■ ***verb*** (**cut·ting, cut, cut**)

▸ WOUND/HOLE **1** O‑ [T, I] to make an opening or a wound in sth, especially with a sharp tool such as a knife or scissors: **~ sth** *She cut her finger on a piece of glass.* ◇ **~ yourself** *He cut himself* (= his face) *shaving.* ◇ **~ sth + adj.** *She had fallen and* ***cut*** *her head* ***open.*** ◇ **~ through sth** *You need a powerful saw to cut through metal.* ◇ (*figurative*) *The canoe cut through the water.*

▸ REMOVE WITH KNIFE **2** O‑ [T] to remove sth or a part of sth, using a knife, etc: **~ sth (from sth)** *He cut four thick slices from the loaf.* ◇ *a bunch of cut flowers* ◇ **~ sb sth** *I cut them all a piece of birthday cake.* ◇ **~ sth for sb** *I cut a piece of birthday cake for them all.* **3** [T] **~ sth (in sth)** to make or form sth by removing material with a knife, etc: *The climbers cut steps in the ice.* ◇ *Workmen* ***cut a hole*** *in the pipe.*

▸ DIVIDE **4** O‑ [T] to divide sth into two or more pieces with a knife, etc: **~ sth** *Don't cut the string, untie the knots.* ◇ **~ sth in/into sth** *He cut the loaf into thick slices.* ◇ *The bus was cut in two by the train.* ◇ *Now cut the tomatoes in half.*

▸ HAIR/NAILS/GRASS, ETC. **5** O‑ [T] to make sth shorter by cutting: **~ sth** *to* ***cut your hair/nails*** ◇ *to* ***cut the grass/lawn/hedge*** ◇ **~ sth + adj.** *He's* ***had his hair cut*** *really short.*

▸ RELEASE **6** [T] to allow sb to escape from somewhere by cutting the rope, object, etc. that is holding them: **~ sb (from sth)** *The injured driver had to be cut from the wreckage.* ◇ **~ sb + adj.** *Two survivors were* ***cut free*** *after being trapped for twenty minutes.*

▸ CLOTHING **7** [T, usually passive] **~ sth + adj.** to design and make a piece of clothing in a particular way: *The swimsuit was cut high in the leg.*

▸ ABLE TO CUT/BE CUT **8** O‑ [I] to be capable of cutting: *This knife won't cut.* **9** [I] to be capable of being cut: *Sandstone cuts easily.*

▸ REDUCE **10** O‑ [T] to reduce sth by removing a part of it: **~ sth** *to* ***cut prices/taxes/spending/production*** ◇ *Buyers will bargain hard to* ***cut the cost of*** *the house they want.* ◇ **~ sth by...** *His salary has been cut by ten per cent.* ◇ **~ sth (from...) (to...)** *Could you cut your essay from 5 000 to 3 000 words?*

▸ REMOVE **11** O‑ [T] **~ sth (from sth)** to remove sth from sth: *This scene was cut from the final version of the movie.*

▸ COMPUTING **12** [I, T] **~ (sth)** to DELETE (= remove) part of a text on a computer screen in order to place it somewhere else: *You can* ***cut and paste*** *between different programs.*

▸ STOP **13** [T] **~ sth** (*informal*) used to tell sb to stop doing sth: *Cut the chatter and get on with your work!*

▸ END **14** [T] **~ sth** to completely end a relationship or all communication with sb SYN **sever**: *She has cut all ties with her family.*

▸ IN MOVIE/TV **15** [T] **~ sth** to prepare a film/movie or tape by removing parts of it or putting them in a different order SYN **edit** ⊃ see also DIRECTOR'S CUT **16** [I] (usually used in orders) to stop filming or recording: *The director shouted 'Cut!'* **17** [I] **~ (from sth) to sth** (in films/movies, radio or television) to move quickly from one scene to another: *The scene cuts from the bedroom to the street.*

▸ MISS CLASS **18** [T] **~ sth** (*informal, especially NAmE*) to stay away from a class that you should go to: *He's always* ***cutting class.***

▸ UPSET **19** [T] **~ sb** to hurt sb emotionally: *His cruel remarks cut her deeply.*

▸ IN CARD GAMES **20** [I, T] **~ (sth)** to lift and turn up a PACK/DECK of PLAYING CARDS in order to decide who is to play first, etc: *Let's cut for dealer.*

▸ GEOMETRY **21** [T] **~ sth** (of a line) to cross another line: *The line cuts the circle at two points.*

▸ A TOOTH **22** [T] **~ a tooth** to have a new tooth beginning to appear through the GUM: *When did she cut her first tooth?*

▸ A DISC, ETC. **23** [T] **~ a disc, etc.** to make a recording of music on a record, CD, etc: *The Beatles cut their first disc in 1962.*

▸ DRUG **24** [T] **~ sth (with sth)** to mix an illegal drug such as HEROIN with another substance

IDM Most idioms containing **cut** are at the entries for the nouns and adjectives in the idioms, for example **cut your losses** is at **loss**. **cut and ˈrun** (*BrE, informal*) to make a quick or sudden escape (**not**) ˈ**cut it** (*informal*) to (not) be as good as is expected or needed: *He won't cut it as a professional singer.*

PHR V ˌ**cut aˈcross sth 1** to affect or be true for different groups that usually remain separate: *Opinion on this issue cuts across traditional political boundaries.* **2** (also ˌ**cut ˈthrough sth**) to go across sth in order to make your route shorter: *I usually cut across the park on my way home.*

ˌ**cut sth↔aˈway (from sth)** to remove sth from sth by cutting: *They cut away all the dead branches from the tree.*

ˌ**cut sth↔ˈback 1** O‑ (also ˌ**cut ˈback (on sth)**) to reduce sth: *If we don't sell more we'll have to cut back production.* ◇ *to cut back on spending* ⊃ related noun CUTBACK **2** to make a bush, etc. smaller by cutting branches off SYN **prune**: *to cut back a rose bush*

ˌ**cut sb↔ˈdown** (*formal*) to kill sb: *He was cut down by an assassin's bullet.* ˌ**cut sth↔ˈdown** O‑ to make sth fall down by cutting it at the base: *to cut down a tree* ˌ**cut sth↔ˈdown (to...)** | ˌ**cut ˈdown (on sth)** O‑ to reduce the size, amount or number of sth: *We need to cut the article down to 1 000 words.* ◇ *The doctor told him to cut down on his drinking.* ◇ *I won't have a cigarette, thanks—I'm trying to cut down* (= smoke fewer).

ˌ**cut ˈin 1** if a motor or an engine **cuts in**, it starts working: *Emergency generators cut in.* **2** (*NAmE*) (*BrE* ˌ**push ˈin**) to go in front of other people who are waiting ˌ**cut ˈin (on sb/sth) 1** to interrupt sb when they are speaking SYN **butt in**: *She kept cutting in on our conversation.* ◇ **+ speech** *'Forget it!' she cut in.* **2** (of a vehicle or its driver) to move suddenly in front of another vehicle, leaving little space between the two vehicles ˌ**cut sb ˈin (on sth)** (*informal*) to give sb a share of the profit in a business or an activity

ˌ**cut sb↔ˈoff 1** [often passive] to interrupt sb who is speaking on the telephone by breaking the connection: *We were cut off in the middle of our conversation.* **2** to refuse to let sb receive any of your property after you die SYN **disinherit**: *He* ***cut*** *his son* ***off without a penny.*** ˌ**cut sb/sth↔ˈoff 1** to

C

interrupt sb and stop them from speaking: *My explanation was cut off by loud protests.* **2** [often passive] to stop the supply of sth to sb: *Our water supply has been cut off.* ◇ *They were cut off for not paying their phone bill.* **ˌcut sth↔ˈoff 1** (also **ˌcut sth ˈoff sth**) to remove sth from sth larger by cutting: *He had his finger cut off in an accident at work.* ◇ (*figurative*) *The winner cut ten seconds off* (= ran the distance ten seconds faster than) *the world record.* ➲ see also CUT-OFF **2** to block or get in the way of sth: *They cut off the enemy's retreat.* ◇ *The new factory cuts off our view of the hills.* **ˌcut sb/sth ˈoff (from sb/sth)** [often passive] to prevent sb/sth from leaving or reaching a place or communicating with people outside a place: *The army was cut off from its base.* ◇ *She feels very cut off living in the country.* ◇ *He* ***cut himself off*** *from all human contact.* **ˌcut ˈout** if a motor or an engine **cuts out**, it suddenly stops working ➲ related noun CUT-OUT **ˌcut sb↔ˈout (of sth)** to not allow sb to be involved in sth: *Don't cut your parents out of your lives.* ◇ *Furious, his mother cut him out of her will* (= refused to let him receive any of her property after she died). **ˌcut sth↔ˈout 1** to make sth by cutting: *She cut the dress out of some old material.* ◇ (*figurative*) *He's cut out a niche for himself* (= found a suitable job) *in journalism.* ➲ related noun CUT-OUT **2** to leave sth out of a piece of writing, etc. SYN **omit**: *I would cut out the bit about working as a waitress.* **3** (*informal*) used to tell sb to stop doing or saying sth annoying: *I'm sick of you two arguing —just* ***cut it out!*** **4** to block sth, especially light: *Tall trees cut out the sunlight.* **ˌcut sth↔ˈout (of sth) 1** to remove sth from sth larger by cutting, usually with scissors: *I cut this article out of the newspaper.* **2** to stop doing, using or eating sth: *I've been advised to cut sugar out of my diet.* **be ˌcut ˈout for sth | be ˌcut ˈout to be sth** (*informal*) to have the qualities and abilities needed for sth: *He's not cut out for teaching.* ◇ *He's not cut out to be a teacher.* **ˌcut ˈthrough sth 1** = CUT ACROSS STH **2** (also **ˌcut sth ˈthrough sth**) to make a path or passage through sth by cutting: *They used a machete to cut through the bush.* ◇ *The prisoners* ***cut their way through*** *the barbed wire.* **ˌcut ˈup** (*NAmE, informal*) to behave in a noisy and silly way **ˌcut sb↔ˈup** (*informal*) **1** to injure sb badly by cutting or hitting them: *He was very badly cut up in the fight.* **2** [usually passive] to upset sb emotionally: *She was pretty cut up about them leaving.* **ˌcut sb/sth↔ˈup** (*BrE*) to suddenly drive in front of another vehicle in a dangerous way **ˌcut sth↔ˈup** to divide sth into small pieces with a knife, etc: *He cut up the meat on his plate.*

■ ***noun***

▸ WOUND **1** a wound caused by sth sharp: *cuts and bruises on the face* ◇ *Blood poured from the deep cut on his arm.*

▸ HOLE **2** a hole or an opening in sth, made with sth sharp: *Using sharp scissors, make a small cut in the material.*

▸ REDUCTION **3** ~ **(in sth)** a reduction in amount, size, supply, etc: ***price/tax/job cuts*** ◇ *They had to take a 20% cut in pay.* ◇ *They announced cuts in public spending.* ➲ see also POWER CUT, SHORT CUT

▸ OF HAIR **4** [usually sing.] an act of cutting sb's hair; the style in which it is cut: *Your hair could do with a cut* (= it is too long). ◇ *a cut and blow-dry* ➲ see also BUZZ CUT

▸ OF CLOTHING **5** [usually sing.] the shape and style that a piece of clothing has because of the way the cloth is cut: *the elegant cut of her dress*

▸ SHARE OF MONEY **6** a share in sth, especially money: *They were rewarded with a cut of 5% from the profits.*

▸ OF MOVIE/PLAY, ETC. **7** ~ **(in sth)** an act of removing part of a film/movie, play, piece of writing, etc: *The director objected to the cuts ordered by the censor.* ◇ *She made some cuts before handing over the finished novel.*

▸ MEAT **8** a piece of meat cut from an animal: *a lean cut of pork* ◇ *cheap cuts of stewing lamb* ➲ see also COLD CUTS

IDM **a cut above sb/sth** better than sb/sth: *His latest novel is a* ***cut above the rest.*** **the ˌcut and ˈthrust (of sth)** (*BrE*) the lively or aggressive way that sth is done: *the cut and thrust of political debate*

Synonyms

cut

slash • cut sth back • scale sth back • rationalize • downsize

These words all mean to reduce the amount or size of sth, especially of an amount of money or a business.

cut to reduce sth, especially an amount of money that is demanded, spent, earned, etc. or the size of a business: *The President has promised to cut taxes significantly.* ◇ *Buyers will bargain hard to cut the cost of the house they want.* ◇ *His salary has been cut by ten per cent.* ◇ *Could you cut your essay from 5 000 to 3 000 words?*

slash [often passive] (*rather informal*) (often used in newspapers) to reduce sth by a large amount: *The workforce has been slashed by half.*

cut sth back/cut back on sth to reduce sth, especially an amount of money or business: *We had to cut back production.*

scale sth back (*especially NAmE* or *business*) to reduce sth, especially an amount of money or business: *The IMF has scaled back its growth forecasts for the next decade.*

rationalize (*BrE, business*) to make changes to a business or system, in order to make it more efficient, especially by spending less money.

downsize (*business*) to make a company or organization smaller by reducing the number of jobs in it, in order to reduce costs. NOTE **Downsize** is often used by people who want to avoid saying more obvious words like 'dismiss' or 'make redundant' because they sound too negative.

PATTERNS

- to cut/slash/cut back on/scale back/rationalize **spending/production**
- to cut/slash/cut back on **jobs**
- to cut/slash/downsize **the workforce**
- to cut/slash/rationalize **the cost** of sth
- to cut/slash **prices/taxes/the budget**
- to cut sth/slash sth/cut sth back **drastically**

ˌcut and ˈdried *adj.* [not usually before noun] decided in a way that cannot be changed or argued about: *The inquiry is by no means cut and dried.*

cu·ta·ne·ous /kjuˈteɪniəs/ *adj.* (*anatomy*) connected with the skin

cut·away /ˈkʌtəweɪ/ *adj., noun*

■ ***adj.*** [only before noun] (of a model or diagram) with some outside parts left out, in order to show what the inside looks like: *a cutaway picture of the inside of a nuclear reactor*

■ ***noun*** **1** (*especially NAmE*) ~ **(to sb/sth)** (on television, in a film/movie, etc.) a picture that shows sth different from the main thing that is being shown: *There was a cutaway to Jackson's guest on the podium.* **2** a model or diagram with some outside parts left out, in order to show what the inside looks like **3** (*NAmE*) (*BrE* **ˈmorning coat**) a black or grey jacket for men, short at the front and very long at the back, worn as part of morning dress

cut·back /ˈkʌtbæk/ *noun* [usually pl.] ~ **(in sth)** a reduction in sth: *cutbacks in public spending* ◇ *staff cutbacks*

ˌcut-ˈdown *adj.* [only before noun] reduced in length, size or range: *a cut-down version of the program*

cute /kjuːt/ *adj.* (**cuter, cutest**) **1** pretty and attractive: *a cute little baby* ◇ (*BrE*) *an unbearably cute picture of two kittens* (= it seems SENTIMENTAL) **2** (*informal, especially NAmE*) sexually attractive: *Check out those cute guys over there!* **3** (*informal, especially NAmE*) clever, sometimes in an annoying way because a person is trying to get an advantage for himself or herself: *She had a really cute idea.* ◇ *Don't get cute with me!* ▸ **cute·ly** *adv.*: *to smile cutely* **cute·ness** *noun* [U]

cutesy /ˈkjuːtsi/ *adj.* (*informal*) too pretty or attractive in a way that is annoying or not realistic

ˌ**cut ˈglass** *noun* [U] glass with patterns cut in it: *a cut-glass vase*

cut·icle /ˈkjuːtɪkl/ *noun* an area of hard skin at the base of the nails on the fingers and toes ➲ VISUAL VOCAB page V48

cutie /ˈkjuːti/ *noun* (*informal*) a person who is attractive or kind: *He's a real cutie.*

cut·lass /ˈkʌtləs/ *noun* a short SWORD with a curved blade that was used as a weapon by sailors and PIRATES in the past

cut·lery /ˈkʌtləri/ *noun* [U] **1** (*especially BrE*) (*NAmE* usually **flat·ware**, **sil·ver·ware**) knives, forks and spoons, used for eating and serving food ➲ VISUAL VOCAB page V19 **2** (*NAmE*) knives, etc. that are sharp

cut·let /ˈkʌtlət/ *noun* **1** a thick slice of meat, especially LAMB or PORK (= meat from a pig), that is cooked and served with the bone still attached **2** (in compounds) finely chopped pieces of meat, fish, vegetables, etc. that are pressed together into a flat piece, covered with BREADCRUMBS and cooked: *nut cutlets*

ˈ**cut-off** *noun, adj.*
- *noun* **1** a point or limit when you stop sth: *The government announced a cut-off in overseas aid.* ◇ *Is there a cut-off point between childhood and adulthood?* **2** **cut-offs** [pl.] cut-off trousers/pants: *wearing frayed cut-offs*
- *adj.* [only before noun] (of trousers/pants) made shorter by cutting off part of the legs: *cut-off jeans*

ˈ**cut-out** *noun* **1** a shape cut out of paper, wood, etc: *a cardboard cut-out* **2** a piece of safety equipment that stops an electric current from flowing through sth: *A cut-out stops the kettle boiling dry.*

ˌ**cut-ˈprice** *adj.* [only before noun] (*especially BrE*) (*NAmE* usually ˌ**cut-ˈrate**) **1** sold at a reduced price: ***cut-price goods/fares*** **2** selling goods at a reduced price: ***a cut-price store/supermarket***

cut·ter /ˈkʌtə(r)/ *noun* **1** (usually in compounds) a person or thing that cuts: *a pastry cutter* **2** **cutters** [pl.] (usually in compounds) a tool for cutting: *a pair of wire cutters* **3** a small fast ship **4** a ship's boat, used for travelling between the ship and land

ˈ**cut-throat** *adj.* [usually before noun] (of an activity) in which people compete with each other in aggressive and unfair ways: *the cut-throat world of politics*

ˌ**cut-throat ˈrazor** *noun* a RAZOR (= a tool used for shaving) with a long sharp blade ➲ compare SAFETY RAZOR

cut·ting /ˈkʌtɪŋ/ *noun, adj.*
- *noun* **1** (also ˈ**press cutting**) (both *BrE*) (also **clip·ping**, ˈ**press clipping** *NAmE, BrE*) an article or a story that you cut from a newspaper or magazine and keep: ***newspaper/press cuttings*** **2** a piece cut off a plant that will be used to grow a new plant **3** (*BrE*) a narrow open passage that is dug through high ground for a road, railway/railroad or CANAL
- *adj.* [usually before noun] **1** unkind and likely to hurt sb's feelings SYN **biting**: *a cutting remark* **2** (of winds) cold in a sharp and unpleasant way SYN **biting**

ˈ**cutting board** (*NAmE*) (*BrE* ˈ**chopping board**) *noun* a board made of wood or plastic used for cutting meat or vegetables on

ˌ**cutting ˈedge** *noun* [sing.] **1** **the ~ (of sth)** the newest, most advanced stage in the development of sth: *working **at the cutting edge** of computer technology* ➲ compare BLEEDING EDGE **2** an aspect of sth that gives it an advantage: *We're relying on him to give the team a cutting edge.*

ˈ**cutting grass** *noun* = GRASSCUTTER

ˈ**cutting room** *noun* a room in which the different parts of a film/movie are cut and put into order

cuttle·fish /ˈkʌtlfɪʃ/ *noun* (*pl.* **cuttle·fish**) a sea creature with eight arms, two TENTACLES (= long thin parts like arms) and a wide flat shell inside its body, that produces a black substance like ink when it is attacked

cutup /ˈkʌtʌp/ *noun* (*NAmE, informal*) a person who behaves in a silly way in order to attract attention and make people laugh

CV /ˌsiː ˈviː/ (*BrE*) (*NAmE* **résumé**) *noun* the abbreviation for 'curriculum vitae' (a written record of your education and the jobs you have done, that you send when you are applying for a job): *Send a full CV with your job application.* ➲ COLLOCATIONS at JOB ➲ WRITING TUTOR page WT30

cwm /kʊm/ *noun* (*geology*) = CORRIE

ˈ**C-word** *noun* (*informal*, sometimes *offensive*) used to replace a word beginning with C that you do not want to say, for example the offensive swear word 'cunt', or 'cancer': *An employee who uses the C-word to a colleague will be suspended.* ◇ *I hate it when people refer to cancer as the C-word.* ➲ compare F-WORD

cwt *abbr.* (*pl.* **cwt**) (in writing) HUNDREDWEIGHT

cwtch /kʊtʃ/ *verb* [I, T] **~ (sb)** (*WelshE*) to be held close in sb's arms in a loving way; to hold sb in this way: *Cwtch up to your mam!* ▸ **cwtch** *noun*

-cy, -acy *suffix* (in nouns) **1** the state or quality of: *infancy* ◇ *accuracy* **2** the status or position of: *chaplaincy*

cyan /ˈsaɪən/ *noun* [U] (*technical*) a greenish-blue colour, used in printing

cy·an·ide /ˈsaɪənaɪd/ *noun* [U] a highly poisonous chemical

cyber- /ˈsaɪbə(r)/ *combining form* (in nouns and adjectives) connected with electronic communication networks, especially the Internet: *cybernetics* ◇ *cybercafe*

cyber·cafe /ˈsaɪbəkæfeɪ; *NAmE* ˈsaɪbər-/ *noun* a CAFE with computers on which customers can use the Internet, send emails, etc.

cyber·crime /ˈsaɪbəkraɪm; *NAmE* ˈsaɪbər-/ *noun* [U, C] crime that is committed using the Internet, for example by stealing sb's personal or bank details or infecting their computer with a virus

cyber·naut /ˈsaɪbənɔːt; *NAmE* ˈsaɪbərnɔːt/ *noun* (*computing*) **1** a person who wears special devices in order to experience VIRTUAL REALITY **2** a person who uses the Internet

cy·ber·net·ics /ˌsaɪbəˈnetɪks; *NAmE* -bərˈn-/ *noun* [U] the scientific study of communication and control, especially concerned with comparing human and animal brains with machines and electronic devices ▸ **cy·ber·net·ic** *adj.*

cyber·punk /ˈsaɪbəpʌŋk; *NAmE* -bərp-/ *noun* [U] stories set in an imaginary future world controlled by technology and computers

cyber·sex /ˈsaɪbəseks; *NAmE* ˈsaɪbər-/ *noun* [U] communication between people using the Internet which makes them sexually excited

cyber·space /ˈsaɪbəspeɪs; *NAmE* -bərs-/ *noun* [U] the imaginary place where electronic messages, etc. exist while they are being sent between computers

cyber·squat·ting /ˈsaɪbəskwɒtɪŋ; *NAmE* ˈsaɪbərskwɑːtɪŋ/ *noun* [U] the illegal activity of buying and officially recording an address on the Internet that is the name of an existing company or a well-known person, with the intention of selling it to the owner in order to make money ▸ **cyber·squat·ter** *noun*

cy·borg /ˈsaɪbɔːg; *NAmE* -bɔːrg/ *noun* (in SCIENCE FICTION stories) a creature that is part human, part machine

cyc·la·men /ˈsɪkləmən; *NAmE* ˈsaɪk-/ *noun* (*pl.* **cyc·la·men** or **cyc·la·mens**) a plant with pink, purple or white flowers that grow on long STEMS pointing downwards, often grown indoors

cycle 🔑 AW /ˈsaɪkl/ *noun, verb*
- *noun* **1** 🔑 a bicycle or motorcycle: *We went for a cycle ride on Sunday.* ◇ *a **cycle route/track*** ➲ see also BIKE **2** 🔑 the fact of a series of events being repeated many times, always in the same order: *the cycle of the seasons* ➲ see also LIFE CYCLE **3** a complete set or series, for example of

movements in a machine: *eight cycles per second* ◇ *the rinse cycle* (= in a washing machine)

■ ***verb*** 🔑 [I] (**+adv./prep.**) (*especially BrE*) to ride a bicycle; to travel by bicycle: *I usually cycle home through the park.* ➲ compare BICYCLE, BIKE

C

'cycle lane (*BrE*) (*NAmE* **'bicycle lane**, *informal* **'bike lane**) *noun* a part of a road that only bicycles are allowed to use ➲ VISUAL VOCAB page V3

'cycle-rickshaw *noun* a vehicle like a bicycle with three wheels, with a covered seat for passengers behind the driver, used especially in some Asian countries

cyc·lic AW /'saɪklɪk; 'sɪk-/ (also **cyc·lic·al** /'saɪklɪkl; 'sɪk-/) *adj.* [usually before noun] repeated many times and always happening in the same order: *the cyclic processes of nature* ◇ *Economic activity often follows a cyclical pattern.* ▸ **cyc·lic·al·ly** *adv.*: *events that occur cyclically*

cyc·ling 🔑 /'saɪklɪŋ/ *noun* [U] the sport or activity of riding a bicycle: *to go cycling* ◇ *Cycling is Europe's second most popular sport.* ◇ *cycling shorts* ➲ VISUAL VOCAB page V39

cyc·list /'saɪklɪst/ *noun* a person who rides a bicycle ➲ compare BICYCLIST

cyclo-cross /'saɪkləʊ krɒs; *NAmE* 'saɪkloʊ krɔːs/ *noun* [U] the sport of racing bicycles over rough ground, which in places is too difficult to ride on so you have to carry your bicycle and run

cyc·lone /'saɪkləʊn; *NAmE* -kloʊn/ *noun* a violent tropical storm in which strong winds move in a circle ➲ compare HURRICANE, TYPHOON ▸ **cyc·lon·ic** /saɪ'klɒnɪk; *NAmE* -'klɑːn-/ *adj.*

Cy·clops /'saɪklɒps; *NAmE* -klɑːps/ *noun* (in ancient Greek stories) a giant with only one eye in the middle of his face

cyclo·tron /'saɪkləʊtrɒn; *NAmE* 'saɪkloʊtrɑːn/ *noun* (*physics*) a machine which makes atoms or ELECTRONS move more quickly, using electrical and MAGNETIC FIELDS

cyg·net /'sɪgnət/ *noun* a young SWAN (= a large white bird with a long neck that lives on or near water)

cy·lin·der /'sɪlɪndə(r)/ *noun* **1** a solid or hollow figure with round ends and long straight sides ➲ VISUAL VOCAB page V58 **2** an object shaped like a cylinder, especially one used as a container: *a* ***gas/oxygen cylinder*** ➲ VISUAL VOCAB page V57 **3** the hollow tube in an engine, shaped like a cylinder, inside which the PISTON moves: *a six-cylinder engine*

IDM **working/firing on all 'cylinders** (*informal*) using all your energy to do sth; working as well as possible

cy·lin·dric·al /sə'lɪndrɪkl/ *adj.* shaped like a cylinder: *huge cylindrical gas tanks*

cym·bal /'sɪmbl/ *noun* a musical instrument in the form of a round metal plate. It is hit with a stick, or two cymbals are hit against each other: *a* ***clash/crash of cymbals*** ➲ VISUAL VOCAB page V30

Cymru /'kʌmri/ *noun* the name for 'Wales' in the Welsh language ➲ see also PLAID CYMRU

cynic /'sɪnɪk/ *noun* **1** a person who believes that people only do things to help themselves, rather than for good or sincere reasons **2** a person who does not believe that sth good will happen or that sth is important: *Cynics will say that there is not the slightest chance of success.* ▸ **cyni·cism** /'sɪnɪsɪzəm/ *noun* [U]: *In a world full of cynicism she was the one person I felt I could trust.*

cyn·ic·al /'sɪnɪkl/ *adj.* **1** believing that people only do things to help themselves rather than for good or honest reasons: *Do you have to be so cynical about everything?* ◇ *a cynical view/smile* **2** not believing that sth good will happen or that sth is important: *I'm a bit cynical about the benefits of the plan.* **3** not caring that sth might hurt other people, if there is some advantage for you: *a cynical disregard for the safety of others* ◇ *a deliberate and cynical foul* ▸ **cyn·ic·al·ly** /-kli/ *adv.*

cyn·o·sure /'sɪnəzjʊə(r); 'saɪn-; -ʃʊə(r); *NAmE* 'saɪnəʃʊr; 'sɪn-/ *noun* [sing.] (*formal*) a person or thing that is the centre of attention: *Ruth was the cynosure of all eyes.*

cy·pher = CIPHER

cy·press /'saɪprəs/ *noun* a tall straight EVERGREEN tree

Cy·ril·lic /sə'rɪlɪk/ *adj.* the **Cyrillic** alphabet is used to write Russian, Bulgarian and some other European languages ▸ **Cy·ril·lic** *noun* [U]

cyst /sɪst/ *noun* a GROWTH containing liquid that forms in or on a person's or an animal's body and may need to be removed

cys·tic fi·bro·sis /ˌsɪstɪk faɪ'brəʊsɪs; *NAmE* -'broʊ-/ *noun* [U] a serious medical condition that some people are born with, in which GLANDS in the lungs and other organs do not work correctly. It often leads to infections and can result in early death.

cyst·itis /sɪ'staɪtɪs/ *noun* [U] an infection of the BLADDER, especially in women, that causes frequent, painful URINATION

cy·tol·o·gy /saɪ'tɒlədʒi; *NAmE* -'tɑːl-/ *noun* [U] the scientific study of the structure and function of cells from living things

cyto·megalo·virus /ˌsaɪtəʊ'megələʊvaɪrəs; *NAmE* ˌsaɪtoʊ'megəloʊ-/ *noun* (*medical*) a virus that usually causes mild infections, but that can be serious for people with AIDS or for new babies

cy·to·plasm /'saɪtəʊplæzəm; *NAmE* -toʊ-/ *noun* [U] (*biology*) all the living material in a cell, not including the NUCLEUS ▸ **cy·to·plas·mic** /ˌsaɪtəʊ'plæzmɪk; *NAmE* -toʊ-/ *adj.* ➲ compare PROTOPLASM

czar, czar·ina, czar·ism, czar·ist = TSAR, TSARINA, TSARISM, TSARIST

Dd

D /diː/ *noun, abbr., symbol*

■ ***noun*** (also **d**) [C, U] (*pl.* **Ds, D's, d's** /diːz/) **1** the fourth letter of the English alphabet: *'Dog' begins with (a) D/'D'.* **2 D** (*music*) the second note in the SCALE OF C MAJOR **3 D** the fourth highest mark/grade that a student can get for a piece of work, showing that it is not very good: *He got (a) D/'D' in/for Geography.* ➲ see also D-DAY

■ ***abbr.*** (also **D.** especially in *NAmE*) (in politics in the US) DEMOCRAT; DEMOCRATIC

■ ***symbol*** the number 500 in ROMAN NUMERALS

d. *abbr.* **1** (in writing) died: *Emily Clifton, d. 1865* **2 d** (in the system of money used in the past in Britain) a PENNY

-d *suffix* ➲ -ED

DA (*BrE*) (*US* **D.A.**) /ˌdiː ˈeɪ/ *abbr.* DISTRICT ATTORNEY

dab /dæb/ *verb, noun*

■ ***verb*** (**-bb-**) **1** to touch sth lightly, usually several times: **~ sth** *She dabbed her eyes and blew her nose.* ◇ **~ at sth** *He dabbed at the cut with his handkerchief.* **2 ~ sth + adv./prep.** to put sth on a surface with quick light movements: *She dabbed a little perfume behind her ears.*

■ ***noun*** **1** a small amount of a liquid, cream or powder that is put on a surface in a quick gentle movement: *She put a dab of perfume behind her ears.* **2** an act of gently touching or pressing sth without rubbing: *He gave the cut a quick dab with a towel.* **3** a small flat fish **4** (*WelshE*) a person or thing: *He's in hospital again.* ***Poor dab.***

dab·ble /ˈdæbl/ *verb* **1** [I] **~ (in/with sth)** to take part in a sport, an activity, etc. but not very seriously: *He dabbles in local politics.* **2** [T] **~ sth (in sth)** to move your hands, feet, etc. around in water: *She dabbled her toes in the stream.*

ˌdab ˈhand *noun* (*BrE, informal*) a person who is very good at doing sth or using sth: *He's a dab hand at cooking spaghetti.* ◇ *She's a dab hand with a paintbrush.*

dacha /ˈdætʃə/ *noun* a Russian country house

dachs·hund /ˈdæksnd; *NAmE* ˈdɑːkshʊnd/ (also *BrE informal* **ˈsausage dog**) *noun* a small dog with a long body, long ears and very short legs

dac·oit /dəˈkɔɪt/ *noun* (*IndE*) a member of a group of armed thieves

dac·tyl /ˈdæktɪl/ *noun* (*technical*) a unit of sound in poetry consisting of one strong or long syllable followed by two weak or short syllables

dad 🔑 /dæd/ *noun* (*informal*)
(often used as a name) father: *That's my dad over there.* ◇ *Do you live with your mum or your dad?* ◇ *Is it OK if I borrow the car, Dad?*

Dada /ˈdɑːdɑː/ *noun* [U] an early 20th century movement in art, literature, music and film which made fun of social and artistic conventions ▸ **Dada·ism** /ˈdɑːdɑːɪzəm/ *noun* [U] **Dada·ist** /ˈdɑːdɑːɪst/ *noun*

daddy /ˈdædi/ *noun* (*pl.* **-ies**) used especially by and to young children, and often as a name, to mean 'father': *What does your daddy look like?* ◇ *Daddy, where are you?* ◇ *Come to Daddy.*

ˌdaddy-ˈlong-legs *noun* (*pl.* **daddy-long-legs**) (*informal*) **1** = CRANE FLY **2** (*NAmE*) a small creature like a spider with very long legs

dado /ˈdeɪdəʊ; *NAmE* -doʊ/ *noun* (*pl.* **-os**, *NAmE* **-oes**) the lower part of the wall of a room when it is a different colour or material from the top part

ˈdado rail *noun* a raised line around the wall of a room, that separates the dado from the upper part of the wall

dae·mon /ˈdiːmən/ *noun* a creature in stories from ancient Greece that is half man and half god

daf·fo·dil /ˈdæfədɪl/ *noun* a tall yellow spring flower shaped like a TRUMPET. It is a national symbol of Wales. ➲ VISUAL VOCAB page V9

daffy /ˈdæfi/ *adj.* (**daf·fier, daf·fi·est**) (*informal*) silly

daft /dɑːft; *NAmE* dæft/ *adj.* (**daft·er, daft·est**) (*BrE, informal*) silly, often in a way that is amusing: *Don't be so daft!* ◇ *She's not as daft as she looks.* ◇ *What a daft thing to say!* ▸ **daft·ness** *noun* [U]

IDM **ˌdaft as a ˈbrush** (*BrE, informal*) very silly

dag /dæg/ *noun* (*informal*) **1** (*AustralE, NZE*) a person who is strange or different in an amusing way **2** (*AustralE*) a person who is not fashionable **3** (*AustralE, NZE*) a dirty piece of wool that hangs down from a sheep's bottom

dagga /ˈdæxə/ *noun* [U] (*SAfrE*) = MARIJUANA: *She was arrested for smoking dagga.*

dag·ger /ˈdægə(r)/ *noun* a short pointed knife that is used as a weapon ➲ picture at SWORD ➲ see also CLOAK-AND-DAGGER

IDM **at daggers ˈdrawn** (*BrE*) if two people are **at daggers drawn**, they are very angry with each other **look ˈdaggers at sb** to look at sb in a very angry way

daggy /ˈdægi/ *adj.* (*AustralE, informal*) **1** not fashionable: *a daggy restaurant* **2** untidy or dirty

dago /ˈdeɪgəʊ; *NAmE* -goʊ/ *noun* (*pl.* **-os** or **-oes**) (*taboo, slang*) a very offensive word for a person from Italy, Spain or Portugal

da·guerre·otype (also **da·guerro·type**) /dəˈgerətaɪp/ *noun* a photograph taken using an early process that used a silver plate and MERCURY gas

dah·lia /ˈdeɪliə; *NAmE* ˈdæliə/ *noun* a large brightly coloured garden flower, often shaped like a ball

dai·kon /ˈdaɪkɒn; *NAmE* -kɑːn/ *noun* [U, C] = MOOLI

the Dáil /dɔɪl/ *noun* [sing.+ sing./pl. v.] one of the parts of the parliament of the Republic of Ireland, whose members are elected by the people

daily 🔑 /ˈdeɪli/ *adj., adv., noun*

■ ***adj.*** [only before noun] **1** 🔑 happening, done or produced every day: *a daily routine/visit/newspaper* ◇ *events affecting the* ***daily lives*** *of millions of people* ◇ *Invoices are signed* ***on a daily basis.*** **2** 🔑 connected with one day's work: *They charge a daily rate.*

IDM **your daily ˈbread** the basic things that you need to live, especially food

■ ***adv.*** every day: *The machines are inspected twice daily.*

■ ***noun*** (*pl.* **-ies**) **1** a newspaper published every day except Sunday: *The story was in all the dailies.* **2** (also **ˌdaily ˈhelp**) (*old-fashioned, BrE*) a person employed to come to sb's house each day to clean it and do other jobs

dainty /ˈdeɪnti/ *adj.* (**dain·tier, dain·ti·est**) **1** (of people and things) small and delicate in a way that people find attractive SYN **delicate**: *dainty feet* ◇ *a dainty porcelain cup* **2** (of movements) careful, often in a way that suggests good manners SYN **delicate**: *She took a dainty little bite of the apple.* ▸ **dain·tily** *adv.*: *She blew her nose as daintily as possible.* **dain·ti·ness** *noun* [U]

dai·quiri /ˈdaɪkɪri; ˈdæk-/ *noun* an alcoholic drink made from RUM mixed with fruit juice, sugar, etc.

dairy /ˈdeəri; *NAmE* ˈderi/ *noun, adj.*

■ ***noun*** (*pl.* **-ies**) **1** [C] a place on a farm where milk is kept and where butter and cheese are made **2** [C] a company that sells milk, eggs, cheese and other milk products **3** [C] (*NZE*) a small local shop: *I went to buy a paper at the corner dairy.* **4** [U] milk, eggs, cheese and other milk products: *The doctor told me to eat less red meat and dairy.*

■ ***adj.*** [only before noun] **1** made from milk: ***dairy products/produce*** **2** connected with the production of milk rather than meat: *the dairy industry* ◇ ***dairy cattle/farmers*** ◇ ***a dairy cow/farm***

dairy·maid /ˈdeərimeɪd; *NAmE* ˈderi-/ *noun* (*old-fashioned*) a woman who works in a dairy (1)

dairy·man /ˈdeərimən; *NAmE* ˈderi-/ *noun* (*pl.* **-men** /-mən/) **1** a man who works in a dairy (1) **2** a man who owns or manages a dairy (2) and sells the products

dais /ˈdeɪɪs/ *noun* a stage, especially at one end of a room, on which people stand to make speeches to an audience

daisy /ˈdeɪzi/ *noun* (*pl.* **-ies**) a small wild flower with white PETALS around a yellow centre; a taller plant with similar but larger flowers IDM see PUSH *v.* ➲ see also MICHAELMAS DAISY ➲ VISUAL VOCAB page V9

ˈ**daisy chain** *noun* a string of daisies tied together to wear around the neck, etc.

ˈ**daisy cutter** *noun* **1** (in CRICKET or BASEBALL) a ball hit or thrown to roll or BOUNCE low along the ground **2** a very powerful bomb dropped from an aircraft that explodes close to the ground and causes a lot of destruction over a large area

ˈ**daisy wheel** *noun* a small disc, used in some printers and TYPEWRITERS, with metal letters around the edge which print onto paper: *a daisy wheel printer*

daks /dæks/ *noun* [pl.] (*AustralE, NZE, informal*) trousers/pants

dal = DHAL

dala-dala /ˈdælə dælə/ *noun* (in Tanzania) a small bus used as a taxi

the Dalai Lama /ˌdælaɪ ˈlɑːmə/ *noun* [sing.] the leader of Tibetan Buddhism and, in former times, the ruler of Tibet

dale /deɪl/ *noun* (*literary* or *dialect*) a valley, especially in northern England: *the Yorkshire Dales*

Dalit /ˈdʌlɪt/ *noun* (in the traditional Indian CASTE system) a member of the caste that is considered the lowest and that has the fewest advantages: *the Dalits' struggle for social and economic rights*

dal·li·ance /ˈdæliəns/ *noun* [U, C] (*old-fashioned* or *humorous*) **1** the behaviour of sb who is dallying with sb/sth: *It turned out to be his last dalliance with the education system.* **2** a sexual relationship that is not serious

dally /ˈdæli/ *verb* (**dal·lies, dally·ing, dal·lied, dal·lied**) [I] (*old-fashioned*) to do sth too slowly; to take too much time making a decision
PHR V ˈ**dally with sb/sth** (*old-fashioned*) to treat sb/sth in a way that is not serious enough ➲ see also DILLY-DALLY

Dal·ma·tian /dælˈmeɪʃn/ *noun* a large dog that has short white hair with black spots

dam /dæm/ *noun, verb*
■ *noun* **1** a barrier that is built across a river in order to stop the water from flowing, used especially to make a RESERVOIR (= a lake for storing water) or to produce electricity **2** (*technical*) the mother of some animals, especially horses ➲ compare SIRE **3** = DENTAL DAM
■ *verb* (**-mm-**) **~ sth (up)** to build a dam across a river, especially in order to make an artificial lake for use as a water supply, etc.

dam·age 🔑 /ˈdæmɪdʒ/ *noun, verb*
■ *noun* **1** 🔑 [U] **~ (to sth)** physical harm caused to sth which makes it less attractive, useful or valuable: ***serious/severe/extensive/permanent/minor damage*** ◇ ***brain/liver etc. damage*** ◇ ***fire/smoke/bomb/storm damage*** ◇ *The earthquake caused damage to property estimated at $6 million.* ◇ *The storm didn't **do** much **damage**.* ◇ *Let's take a look at the damage.* ◇ *I insist on paying for the damage.* ◇ *Make sure you insure your camera against loss or damage.* **2** 🔑 [U] **~ (to sb/sth)** harmful effects on sb/sth: *emotional damage resulting from divorce* ◇ *damage to a person's reputation* ◇ *This could cause serious damage to the country's economy.* ◇ *I'm going—I've done enough damage here already.* **3 damages** [pl.] an amount of money that a court decides should be paid to sb by the person, company, etc. that has caused them harm or injury: *He was ordered to pay damages totalling £30 000.* ◇ *They intend to sue for damages.* ◇ *Ann was awarded £6 000 (in) damages.*
IDM **what's the ˈdamage?** (*informal*) a way of asking how much sth costs
■ *verb* 🔑 **~ sth/sb** to harm or spoil sth/sb: *The fire badly damaged the town hall.* ◇ *Several vehicles were damaged in the crash.* ◇ *Smoking seriously damages your health.* ◇ *The allegations are likely to damage his political career.* ◇ *emotionally damaged children* ➲ COLLOCATIONS at INJURY

Synonyms

damage

hurt • harm • impair

These words all mean to have a bad effect on sb/sth.

damage to cause physical harm to sth, making it less attractive, useful or valuable; to have a bad effect on sb/sth's life, health, happiness or chances of success: *The fire badly damaged the town hall.* ◇ *emotionally damaged children*

hurt (*rather informal*) to have a bad effect on sb/sth's life, health, happiness or chances of success: *Hard work never hurt anyone.*

harm to have a bad effect on sb/sth's life, health, happiness or chances of success: *Pollution can harm marine life.*

DAMAGE, HURT OR HARM?

Hurt is slightly less formal than **damage** or **harm**, especially when it is used in negative statements: *It won't hurt him to have to wait a bit.* ◇ ~~*It won't damage/harm him to have to wait a bit.*~~ **Harm** is also often used to talk about ways in which things in the natural world such as *wildlife* and the *environment* are affected by human activity.

impair (*rather formal*) to damage sb's health, abilities or chances: *Even one drink can impair driving performance.*

PATTERNS
- to damage/hurt/harm/impair sb's **chances**
- to damage/hurt/harm sb's **interests/reputation**
- to damage/harm/impair sb's **health**
- to **seriously/greatly** damage/hurt/harm/impair sb/sth
- to **badly/severely** damage/hurt/impair sb/sth

ˌ**damage limiˈtation** (also ˌ**damage conˈtrol** especially in *NAmE*) *noun* [U] the process of trying to limit the amount of damage that is caused by sth

dam·aging /ˈdæmɪdʒɪŋ/ *adj.* causing damage; having a bad effect on sb/sth: ***damaging consequences/effects*** ◇ **~ to sb/sth** *Lead is potentially damaging to children's health.*

Da·mas·cus /dəˈmæskəs/ *noun*
IDM **the road to Daˈmascus** an experience that results in a great change in a person's attitudes or beliefs: *Spending a night in jail was his road to Damascus.* ORIGIN From the story in the Bible in which St Paul hears the voice of God on the road to Damascus and becomes a Christian.

dam·ask /ˈdæməsk/ *noun* [U] a type of thick cloth, usually made from silk or LINEN, with a pattern that is visible on both sides: *a damask tablecloth*

dame /deɪm/ *noun* **1 Dame** (in Britain) a title given to a woman as a special honour because of the work she has done: *Dame Maggie Smith* **2** (*old-fashioned, NAmE, informal*) a woman **3** = PANTOMIME DAME

damn /dæm/ *exclamation, adj., verb, adv., noun*
■ *exclamation* (also *old-fashioned* **dam·mit** /ˈdæmɪt/, ˈ**damn it**) (*informal*) a swear word that people use to show that they are annoyed, disappointed, etc.: *Oh damn! I forgot he was coming.*
■ *adj.* (also **damned**) [only before noun] (*informal*) **1** a swear word that people use to show that they are annoyed with sb/sth: *Where's that damn book!* ◇ *The damned thing won't start!* ◇ *It's none of your damn business!* ◇ *He's a damn nuisance!* **2** a swear word that people use to emphasize what they are saying: *What a damn shame!* IDM see THING
■ *verb* **1 ~ sb/sth** (*informal*) used when swearing at sb/sth to show that you are angry: *Damn you! I'm not going to let you bully me.* ◇ *Damn this machine! Why won't it work?* **2 ~ sb** (of God) to decide that sb must suffer in hell **3 ~ sb/sth** to criticize sb/sth very strongly: *The film was damned by the critics for its mindless violence.*
IDM **damn the consequences, expense, etc.** (*informal*)

used to say that you are going to do sth even though you know it may be expensive, have bad results, etc.: *Let's celebrate and damn the expense!* **damn sb/sth with faint ˈpraise** to praise sb/sth only a little, in order to show that you do not really like them/it **I'll be damned!** (*old-fashioned, informal*) used to show that you are very surprised about sth **I'm damned if…** (*informal*) used to show that you refuse to do sth or do not know sth: *I'm damned if I'll apologize!* ◇ *I'm damned if I know who he is.* ➲ more at NEAR *adv.*

■ ***adv.*** (also **damned**) (*informal*) **1** a swear word that people use to show that they are annoyed with sb/sth: *Don't be so damn silly!* ◇ *What a damn stupid question!* ◇ *You* ***know damn well*** (= you know very well) *what I mean!* ◇ *I'll damn well leave tonight* (= I am determined to). **2** a swear word that people use to emphasize what they are saying: *damn good* ◇ *We got out pretty damned fast!* ◇ *I'm damn sure she had no idea.*

IDM **damn ˈall** (*BrE*) nothing: *I know damn all about computers.*

■ ***noun***

IDM **not care/give a ˈdamn (about sb/sth)** (*informal*) to not care at all about sb/sth

dam·nable /ˈdæmnəbl/ *adj.* (*old-fashioned*) bad or annoying ▸ **dam·nably** /ˈdæmnəbli/ *adv.*

dam·na·tion /dæmˈneɪʃn/ *noun* [U] the state of being in hell; the act of sending sb to hell: *eternal damnation*

damned /dæmd/ *adj., adv., noun*

■ ***adj., adv.*** = DAMN

■ ***noun* the damned** [pl.] people who are forced to live in hell after they die

damned·est /ˈdæmdɪst/ *noun, adj.* (*informal*)

IDM **the damnedest…** (*especially NAmE*) the most surprising…: *It's the damnedest thing I ever saw.* **do/try your ˈdamnedest (to do sth)** to try as hard as you can (to do sth): *She did her damnedest to get it done on time.*

damn·ing /ˈdæmɪŋ/ *adj.* critical of sb/sth; suggesting that sb is guilty: ***damning criticism/evidence*** ◇ *a* ***damning conclusion/report*** ◇ *Her report is expected to deliver a damning indictment of education standards.*

Damo·cles /ˈdæməkliːz/ *noun* IDM see SWORD

damp 🔑 /dæmp/ *adj., noun, verb*

■ ***adj.*** 🔑 (**damp·er**, **damp·est**) slightly wet, often in a way that is unpleasant: *The cottage was cold and damp.* ◇ *It feels damp in here.* ◇ *damp clothes* ◇ *Wipe the surface with a damp cloth.* ➲ SYNONYMS at WET ▸ **damp·ly** *adv.*: *The blouse clung damply to her skin.*

IDM **a damp ˈsquib** (*BrE, informal*) an event that is disappointing because it is not as exciting or impressive as expected

■ ***noun*** [U] (*BrE*) the state of being damp; areas on a wall, etc. that are damp: *The old house smells of damp.* ◇ *Those marks above the window look like damp to me.*

■ ***verb* ~ sth** = DAMPEN: *She damped a towel and wrapped it round his leg.*

PHR V ˌ**damp ˈdown sth** to make an emotion or a feeling less strong ˌ**damp sth↔ˈdown** to make a fire burn more slowly or stop burning

ˈ**damp course** (also ˈ**damp-proof course**) *noun* (both *BrE*) a layer of material near the bottom of a wall that is used to stop damp rising from the ground

damp·en /ˈdæmpən/ *verb* **1** (also *less frequent* **damp**) **~ sth** to make sth slightly wet: *Perspiration dampened her face and neck.* ◇ *He dampened his hair to make it lie flat.* **2 ~ sth** to make sth such as a feeling or a reaction less strong: *None of the setbacks could* ***dampen his enthusiasm*** *for the project.* ◇ *She wasn't going to let anything* ***dampen her spirits*** *today.*

damp·er /ˈdæmpə(r)/ *noun* **1** a piece of metal that can be moved to allow more or less air into a fire so that the fire burns more or less strongly **2** a device in a piano that is used to reduce the level of the sound produced

IDM **put a ˈdamper on sth** (*BrE* also **put a ˈdampener on sth**) (*informal*) to make sth less enjoyable, successful, etc.

damp·ness /ˈdæmpnəs/ *noun* [U] the fact or state of being damp: *To avoid dampness, air the room regularly.*

ˈ**damp-proof course** *noun* = DAMP COURSE

dam·sel /ˈdæmzl/ *noun* (*old use*) a young woman who is not married

IDM **a ˌdamsel in diˈstress** (*humorous*) a woman who needs help

dam·sel·fly /ˈdæmzlflaɪ/ *noun* (*pl.* **-ies**) an insect with a long thin body and two pairs of wings

dam·son /ˈdæmzn/ *noun* a small purple fruit, like a PLUM: *a damson tree*

dan /dæn/ *noun* **1** one of the levels in KARATE or JUDO **2** a person who has reached a particular level in KARATE or JUDO

dance 🔑 /dɑːns; *NAmE* dæns/ *noun, verb*

■ ***noun*** **1** 🔑 [C] a series of movements and steps that are usually performed to music; a particular example of these movements and steps: *a* ***dance class/routine*** ◇ *Find a partner and practise these new* ***dance steps.*** ◇ *Do you know any other Latin American dances?* ◇ *The next dance will be a waltz.* ➲ see also RAIN DANCE **2** 🔑 [U] the art of dancing, especially for entertainment: *an evening of drama, music and dance* ◇ ***modern/classical dance*** ◇ *a* ***dance company/troupe*** **3** 🔑 [C] an act of dancing: *Let's have a dance.* ◇ *He did a little dance of triumph.* **4** 🔑 [C] a social event at which people dance: *We hold a dance every year to raise money for charity.* **5** 🔑 [C] a piece of music for dancing to: *The band finished with a few slow dances.* IDM see LEAD[1] *v.*, SONG

■ ***verb*** **1** 🔑 [I] to move your body to the sound and rhythm of music: *Do you want to dance?* ◇ *He asked me to dance.* ◇ *They stayed up all night singing and dancing.* ◇ *They danced to the music of a string quartet.* ◇ *Ruth danced all evening with Richard.* ◇ *Ruth and Richard danced together all evening.* **2** 🔑 [T] **~ sth** to do a particular type of dance: *to dance the tango* ◇ *to dance a waltz* **3** [I] to move in a lively way: *The children danced around her.* ◇ *The sun shone on the sea and the waves danced and sparkled.* ◇ *The words danced before her tired eyes.*

IDM ˌ**dance atˈtendance on sb** (*BrE, formal*) to be with sb and do things to help and please them ˌ**dance the ˈnight away** to dance for the whole evening or night **dance to sb's ˈtune** (*BrE*) to do whatever sb tells you to

ˈ**dance band** *noun* a group of musicians who play music at dances

ˈ**dance floor** *noun* an area where people can dance in a hotel, restaurant, etc.

ˈ**dance hall** *noun* a large public room where people pay to go and dance (more common in the past than now) ➲ compare BALLROOM

dan·cer 🔑 /ˈdɑːnsə(r); *NAmE* ˈdæn-/ *noun* a person who dances or whose job is dancing: *She's a fantastic dancer.* ◇ *He's a dancer with the Royal Ballet.*

dan·cing 🔑 /ˈdɑːnsɪŋ; *NAmE* ˈdæn-/ *noun* [U] moving your body to music: *dancing classes* ◇ *There was music and dancing till two in the morning.* ➲ see also COUNTRY DANCING, LAP DANCING, POLE DANCING, TABLE DANCING

ˌ**D and ˈC** *abbr.* DILATATION AND CURETTAGE

dan·delion /ˈdændɪlaɪən/ *noun* a small wild plant with a bright yellow flower that becomes a soft white ball of seeds called a **dandelion clock** ➲ VISUAL VOCAB page V9

dan·di·fied /ˈdændɪfaɪd/ *adj.* (*old-fashioned, disapproving*) (of a man) caring a lot about his clothes and appearance

dan·dle /ˈdændl/ *verb* **~ sb** (*old-fashioned*) to play with a baby or young child by moving them up and down on your knee

dan·druff /ˈdændrʌf/ *noun* [U] very small pieces of dead skin, seen as a white dust in a person's hair

dandy /ˈdændi/ *noun, adj.*

■ ***noun*** (*pl.* **-ies**) (*old-fashioned*) a man who cares a lot about his clothes and appearance

■ ***adj.*** (*old-fashioned, especially NAmE*) very good

dang /dæŋ/ *adj., exclamation* (*NAmE, informal*) a mild swear word, used instead of DAMN: *It's just dang stupid!*

dan·ger 0-ᴡ /ˈdeɪndʒə(r)/ *noun*
1 0-ᴡ [U] **~ (of sth)** the possibility of sth happening that will injure, harm or kill sb, or damage or destroy sth: *Danger! Keep Out!* ◇ *Children's lives are* ***in danger*** *every time they cross this road.* ◇ *Doctors said she is now* ***out of danger*** (= not likely to die). **2** 0-ᴡ [C, U] the possibility of sth bad or unpleasant happening: *There is no danger of a bush fire now.* ◇ **~ of sth** *The building is* ***in danger of*** *collapsing.* ◇ *How many factory workers are* ***in danger of*** *losing their jobs?* ◇ *'Nicky won't find out, will she?' 'Oh, no, there's no danger of that.'* ◇ **~ that...** *There is a danger that the political disorder of the past will return.* **3** 0-ᴡ [C] **~ (to sb/sth)** a person or thing that may cause damage, or harm sb: *Smoking is a serious danger to health.* ◇ *Police said the man was a danger to the public.* ◇ *the hidden dangers in your home* ➲ see also ENDANGER
IDM **be on/off the ˈdanger list** (*BrE*) to be so ill/sick that you may die; to no longer be very ill/sick

ˈdanger money (*BrE*) (*US* **ˈhazard pay, ˈdanger pay**) *noun* [U] extra pay for doing work that is dangerous

dan·ger·ous 0-ᴡ /ˈdeɪndʒərəs/ *adj.*
likely to injure or harm sb, or to damage or destroy sth: *a dangerous road/illness/sport* ◇ *dangerous levels of carbon monoxide* ◇ *The prisoners who escaped are violent and dangerous.* ◇ *The situation is* ***highly dangerous.*** ◇ (*BrE*) *a conviction for dangerous driving* ◇ **~ for sb** *The traffic here is very dangerous for children.* ◇ **~ for sb to do sth** *It would be dangerous for you to stay here.* ▸ **dan·ger·ous·ly** *adv.*: *She was standing dangerously close to the fire.* ◇ *His father is dangerously ill* (= so ill that he might die). ◇ *Mel enjoys living dangerously* (= doing things that involve risk or danger).
IDM **dangerous ˈground** a situation or subject that is likely to make sb angry, or that involves risk: *We'd be* ***on dangerous ground*** *if we asked about race or religion.*

dan·gle /ˈdæŋgl/ *verb* **1** [I] (**+adv./prep.**) to hang or swing freely: *Gold charms dangled from her bracelet.* ◇ *A single light bulb dangled from the ceiling.* ◇ *He sat on the edge with his legs dangling over the side.* **2** [T] **~ sth** to hold sth so that it hangs or swings freely: *She dangled her car keys nervously as she spoke.* ▸ **dan·gly** /ˈdæŋgli/ *adj.*: *a pair of dangly earrings* ➲ VISUAL VOCAB page V53
IDM **keep/leave sb ˈdangling** (*informal*) to keep sb in an uncertain state by not telling them sth that they want to know: *She kept him dangling for a week before making her decision.*
PHR V **ˌdangle sth beˈfore/in ˈfront of sb** to offer sb sth good in order to persuade them to do sth

ˌdangling parˈticiple *noun* (*grammar*) a participle that relates to a noun that is not mentioned HELP 'Dangling participles' are not considered correct. In the sentence 'While walking home, my phone rang', 'walking' is a dangling participle. A correct form of the sentence would be 'While I was walking home, my phone rang'.

Dan·ish /ˈdeɪnɪʃ/ *adj., noun*
■ ***adj.*** from or connected with Denmark
■ ***noun*** **1** [U] the language of Denmark **2** [C] = DANISH PASTRY

ˌDanish ˈblue *noun* [U] a type of soft cheese with blue parts in it and a strong flavour

ˌDanish ˈpastry (*especially BrE*) (also **Dan·ish** *NAmE, BrE*) *noun* a sweet cake made of light PASTRY, often containing apple, nuts, etc. and/or covered with ICING

dank /dæŋk/ *adj.* (especially of a place) damp, cold and unpleasant: *a dark dank cave* ▸ **dank·ness** *noun* [U]

dap·per /ˈdæpə(r)/ *adj.* (of a man) small with a neat appearance and nice clothes

dap·pled /ˈdæpld/ *adj.* marked with spots of colour, or shade: *the cool dappled light under the trees*

dapple grey (*BrE*) (*NAmE* **dapple gray**) /ˌdæpl ˈgreɪ/ *adj.* (of a horse) grey or white with darker round marks ▸ **dapple grey** *noun*

Darby and Joan /ˌdɑːbi ən ˈdʒəʊn; *NAmE* ˌdɑːrbi ən ˈdʒoʊn/ *noun* [pl.] (*BrE*) a way of referring to an old couple who are happily married

dare 0-ᴡ /deə(r); *NAmE* der/ *verb, noun*
■ ***verb*** **1** 0-ᴡ (not usually used in the progressive tenses) to be brave enough to do sth: *She said it as loudly as she dared.* ◇ **~ (to) do sth** *He didn't dare (to) say what he thought.* ◇ *They daren't ask for any more money.* ◇ (*literary*) *She dared not breathe a word of it to anybody.* ◇ *There was something,* ***dare I say it,*** *a little unusual about him.* **2** [T] to persuade sb to do sth dangerous, difficult or embarrassing so that they can show that they are not afraid: **~ sb** *Go on! Take it! I dare you.* ◇ **~ sb to do sth** *Some of the older boys had dared him to do it.* ➲ note at MODAL
IDM **don't you dare!** (*informal*) used to tell sb strongly not to do sth: *'I'll tell her about it.' 'Don't you dare!'* ◇ *Don't you dare say anything to anybody.* **how ˈdare you, etc.** used to show that you are angry about sth that sb has done: *How dare you talk to me like that?* ◇ *How dare she imply that I was lying?* **I dare say** (also **I daresay** especially in *BrE*) used when you are saying that sth is probable: *I dare say you know about it already.*
■ ***noun*** [usually sing.] something dangerous, difficult or embarrassing that you try to persuade sb to do, to see if they will do it: (*BrE*) *He climbed onto the roof* ***for a dare.*** ◇ (*NAmE*) *She learned to fly* ***on a dare.***

Grammar Point

dare

- **Dare** (sense 1) usually forms negatives and questions like an ordinary verb and is followed by an infinitive with *to*. It is most common in the negative: *I didn't dare to ask.* ◇ *He won't dare to break his promise.* ◇ *You told him? How did you dare?* ◇ *I hardly dared to hope she'd remember me.* In positive sentences a phrase like **not be afraid** is often used instead: *She wasn't afraid* (= she dared) *to tell him the truth.*
- It can also be used like a modal verb especially in present tense negative forms in *BrE*, and is followed by an infinitive without *to*: *I daren't tell her the truth.*
- In spoken English, the forms of the ordinary verb are often used with an infinitive without *to*: *Don't you dare tell her what I said!* ◇ *I didn't dare look at him.*

dare·devil /ˈdeədevl; *NAmE* ˈderd-/ *noun* a person who enjoys doing dangerous things, in a way that other people may think is stupid: *a reckless daredevil* ▸ **dare·devil** *adj.* [only before noun]: *Don't try any daredevil stunts.*

dar·ing /ˈdeərɪŋ; *NAmE* ˈder-/ *adj., noun*
■ ***adj.*** brave; willing to do dangerous or unusual things; involving danger or taking risks: *a daring walk in space* ◇ *There are plenty of activities at the resort for the less daring.* ◇ *The gallery was known for putting on daring exhibitions.* ◇ *a daring strapless dress in black silk* ▸ **dar·ing·ly** *adv.*
■ ***noun*** [U] courage and the willingness to take risks: *the skill and daring of the mountain climbers*

dark 0-ᴡ /dɑːk; *NAmE* dɑːrk/ *adj., noun*
■ ***adj.*** (**dark·er, dark·est**)
▸ WITH LITTLE LIGHT **1** 0-ᴡ with no or very little light, especially because it is night: *a dark room/street/forest* ◇ *What time does it* ***get dark*** *in summer?* ◇ *It was dark outside and I couldn't see much.* OPP **light**
▸ COLOURS **2** 0-ᴡ not light; closer in shade to black than to white: ***dark blue/green/red, etc.*** ◇ *Darker colours are more practical and don't show stains.* OPP **light, pale** **3** 0-ᴡ having a colour that is close to black: *a dark suit* ◇ *dark-coloured wood* ◇ *The dark clouds in the sky meant that a storm was coming.*
▸ HAIR/SKIN/EYES **4** 0-ᴡ brown or black in colour: *Sue has long dark hair.* ◇ *Even if you have dark skin, you still need protection from the sun.* **5** 0-ᴡ (of a person) having dark hair, eyes, etc: *a dark handsome stranger* OPP **fair**

▸ MYSTERIOUS **6** mysterious; hidden and not known about: *There are no dark secrets in our family.*
▸ EVIL **7** evil or frightening: *There was a darker side to his nature.* ◇ *the dark forces of the imagination*
▸ WITHOUT HOPE **8** unpleasant and without any hope that sth good will happen: *the darkest days of Fascism* ◇ *The film is a dark vision of the future.*
▸ PHONETICS **9** (of a speech sound) produced with the back part of the tongue close to the back of the mouth. In many accents of English, dark /l/ is used after a vowel, as in *ball*. OPP **clear**
IDM **a dark 'horse 1** (*BrE*) a person who does not tell other people much about their life, and who surprises other people by having interesting qualities **2** a person taking part in a race, etc. who surprises everyone by winning **keep sth 'dark** (*BrE, informal*) to keep sth secret and not tell people about it
■ ***noun***
▸ NO LIGHT **1** **the dark** [sing.] the lack of light in a place, especially because it is night: *All the lights went out and we were left* ***in the dark.*** ◇ *Are the children afraid of the dark?* ◇ *animals that can see in the dark*
▸ COLOUR **2** [U] an amount of sth that is dark in colour: *patterns of light and dark*
IDM **after/before dark** after/before the sun goes down and it is night: *Try to get home before dark.* ◇ *Don't go out alone after dark.* **in the 'dark (about sth)** knowing nothing about sth: *Workers were kept in the dark about the plans to sell the company.* ◇ *She arrived at the meeting as much in the dark as everyone else.* **a shot/stab in the 'dark** a guess; sth you do without knowing what the result will be: *The figure he came up with was really just a shot in the dark.* ➲ more at LEAP *n.*

the 'dark ages *noun* [pl.] **1 the Dark Ages** the period of European history between the end of the Roman Empire and the 10th century AD **2** (often *humorous*) a period of history or a time when sth was not developed or modern: *Back in the dark ages of computing, in about 1980, they started a software company.*

'dark chocolate (*BrE* also **'plain chocolate**) *noun* [U] dark brown chocolate with a slightly bitter taste, made without milk being added ➲ compare MILK CHOCOLATE

dark·en /'dɑːkən; *NAmE* 'dɑːrk-/ *verb* **1** [I, T] to become dark; to make sth dark: *The sky began to darken as the storm approached.* ◇ **~ sth** *We walked quickly through the darkened streets.* ◇ *a darkened room* **2** [I, T] to become unhappy or angry; to make sb unhappy or angry: *Her mood darkened at the news.* ◇ *Luke's face darkened* (= he looked angry). ◇ **~ sth** *It was a tragedy that darkened his later life.*
IDM **never darken my 'door again** (*old-fashioned, humorous*) used to tell sb never to come to your home again

ˌdark 'glasses *noun* [pl.] glasses that have dark-coloured LENSES ➲ see also SUNGLASSES

darkie /'dɑːki; *NAmE* 'dɑːrki/ *noun* (*taboo, old-fashioned*) a very offensive word for a black person

dark·ling /'dɑːklɪŋ; *NAmE* 'dɑːrk-/ *adj.* (*literary*) becoming dark or connected with the dark: *the darkling sky*

dark·ly /'dɑːkli; *NAmE* 'dɑːrk-/ *adv.* **1** in a threatening or unpleasant way: *He hinted darkly that all was not well.* **2** showing a dark colour: *Her eyes burned darkly.*

ˌdark 'matter *noun* [U] (*astronomy*) according to some theories, material which exists in space that does not produce any light

dark·ness /'dɑːknəs; *NAmE* 'dɑːrk-/ *noun* [U] **1** the state of being dark, without any light: *After a few minutes our eyes got used to the darkness.* ◇ *The house was plunged into* ***total darkness*** *when the electricity was cut off.* ◇ *The sun went down and* ***darkness fell*** (= it became night). ◇ *There is an extra hour of darkness on winter mornings.* ◇ *Parking is not allowed during the* ***hours of darkness.*** ◇ *Her face was* ***in darkness.*** ◇ *They managed to escape* ***under cover of darkness.*** **2** the quality or state of being dark in colour: *It depends on the darkness of your skin.* **3** (*literary*) evil: *the forces of darkness*

dark·room /'dɑːkruːm; -rʊm; *NAmE* 'dɑːrk-/ *noun* a room that can be made completely dark, where you can take film out of a camera and develop photographs

ˌdark 'star *noun* (*astronomy*) an object in space similar to a star, that produces no light or very little light

dar·ling /'dɑːlɪŋ; *NAmE* 'dɑːrlɪŋ/ *noun, adj.*
■ ***noun*** **1** (*informal*) a way of addressing sb that you love: *What's the matter, darling?* **2** a person who is very friendly and kind: *You are a darling, Hugo.* **3 the ~ of sb/sth** a person who is especially liked and very popular: *She is the darling of the newspapers and can do no wrong.*
■ ***adj.*** [only before noun] (*informal*) much loved; very attractive, special, etc: *My darling daughter.* ◇ *'Darling Henry,' the letter began.*

darm·stadt·ium /'dɑːmʃtætiəm; *NAmE* 'dɑːrm-/ *noun* [U] (*symb.* **Ds**) a chemical element. Darmstadtium is a RADIOACTIVE element that is produced artificially.

darn /dɑːn; *NAmE* dɑːrn/ *verb, noun, adj., adv.*
■ ***verb*** [T, I] **~ (sth)** to repair a hole in a piece of clothing by sewing STITCHES across the hole: *to darn socks*
IDM **'darn it!** (*informal, especially NAmE*) used as a mild swear word to show that you are angry or annoyed about sth, to avoid saying 'damn': *Darn it! I've lost my keys!* **I'll be 'darned!** (*informal, especially NAmE*) used to show that you are surprised about sth
■ ***noun*** a place on a piece of clothing that has been repaired by darning
■ ***adj.*** (also **darned**) (*informal*) used as a mild swear word, to emphasize sth: *Why don't you switch the darn thing off and listen to me!*
■ ***adv.*** (also **darned**) (*informal*) used as a mild swear word, instead of saying DAMN, to mean 'extremely' or 'very': *You had a darn good try.* ◇ *It's darn cold tonight.*

darned /dɑːnd; *NAmE* dɑːrnd/ *adj., adv.* = DARN: *That's a darned good idea!* ▸ **darned·est** *adj.*

dart /dɑːt; *NAmE* dɑːrt/ *noun, verb*
■ ***noun*** **1** [C] a small pointed object, sometimes with feathers to help it fly, that is shot as a weapon or thrown in the game of darts: *a poisoned dart* ➲ VISUAL VOCAB page V34 **2 darts** [U] a game in which darts are thrown at a round board marked with numbers for scoring. Darts is often played in British pubs: *a darts match* ➲ VISUAL VOCAB page V34 **3** [sing.] a sudden quick movement SYN **dash**: *She* ***made a dart for*** *the door.* **4** [sing.] (*literary*) a sudden feeling of a strong emotion: *Nina felt a sudden dart of panic.* **5** [C] a pointed fold that is sewn in a piece of clothing to make it fit better
■ ***verb*** **1** [I] **+ adv./prep.** to move suddenly and quickly in a particular direction: *A dog darted across the road in front of me.* ◇ *Her eyes darted around the room, looking for Greg.* **2** [T] to look at sb suddenly and quickly **~ a glance/look (at sb)**: *He darted an impatient look at Vicky.* ◇ **~ sb a glance/look** *He darted Vicky an impatient look.*

dart·board /'dɑːtbɔːd; *NAmE* 'dɑːrtbɔːrd/ *noun* a round board used in the game of darts ➲ VISUAL VOCAB page V34

Dar·win·ism /'dɑːwɪnɪzəm; *NAmE* 'dɑːr-/ *noun* [U] (*biology*) the theory that living things EVOLVE by NATURAL SELECTION, developed by Charles Darwin in the 19th century ▸ **Dar·win·ian** /dɑː'wɪniən; *NAmE* dɑːr-/ *adj.*: *Darwinian ideas*

dash /dæʃ/ *noun, verb*
■ ***noun***
▸ STH DONE QUICKLY **1** [sing.] **a ~ (for sth)** an act of going somewhere suddenly and/or quickly: *When the doors opened, there was a* ***mad dash*** *for seats.* ◇ *a 60-mile dash to safety* ◇ *He jumped off the bus and* ***made a dash for*** *the nearest bar.* ◇ *We waited for the police to leave then* ***made a dash for it*** (= left quickly in order to escape). **2** [sing.] an act of doing sth quickly because you do not have enough time: *a last-minute dash to buy presents*
▸ SMALL AMOUNT **3** [C, usually sing.] **~ (of sth)** a small amount of sth that is added to sth else: *Add a dash of lemon juice.* ◇ *The rug adds a dash of colour to the room.* ➲ compare SPLASH
▸ SYMBOL **4** [C] the mark (—) used to separate parts of a sentence, often instead of a colon or in pairs instead of brackets/parentheses ➲ compare HYPHEN

▸ RACE **5** [C, usually sing.] (*especially NAmE*) a race in which the people taking part run very fast over a short distance **SYN** **sprint**: *the 100-meter dash*
▸ WAY OF BEHAVING **6** [U] (*old-fashioned, approving*) a way of behaving that combines style, enthusiasm and confidence
▸ PART OF CAR **7** [C] (*informal*) = DASHBOARD ➲ see also PEBBLE-DASH
IDM **cut a 'dash** (*BrE*) to look attractive in a particular set of clothes, especially in a way that makes other people notice you: *He cut quite a dash in his uniform.*
■ *verb*
▸ GO QUICKLY **1** [I] to go somewhere very quickly **SYN** **rush**: *I must dash* (= leave quickly), *I'm late.* ◇ **+ adv./prep.** *She dashed off to keep an appointment.* ◇ *He dashed along the platform and jumped on the train.*
▸ THROW/BEAT **2** [T, I] to throw sth or make sth fall violently onto a hard surface; to beat against a surface: **~ sth + adv./prep.** *The boat was dashed repeatedly against the rocks.* ◇ **+ adv./prep.** *The waves were dashing against the harbour wall.*
IDM **dash sb's 'hopes** to destroy sb's hopes by making what they were hoping for impossible **dash (it)!** | **dash it all!** (*old-fashioned, BrE*) used to show that you are annoyed about sth
PHR V **ˌdash sth↔'off** to write or draw sth very quickly: *I dashed off a note to my brother.*

dash·board /'dæʃbɔːd; *NAmE* -bɔːrd/ (also **fa·scia**) (also *informal* **dash** especially in *NAmE*) *noun* the part of a car in front of the driver that has instruments and controls in it ➲ VISUAL VOCAB page V42

dash·ed /dæʃt/ *adj.* [only before noun] (*BrE, old-fashioned, informal*) used as a mild swear word by some people to emphasize sth or to show they are annoyed

dash·iki /'dɑːʃɪki/ *noun* a loose shirt or longer piece of clothing worn by men in W Africa, often made from cloth with brightly coloured patterns

dash·ing /'dæʃɪŋ/ *adj.* (*old-fashioned*) **1** (usually of a man) attractive, confident and elegant: *a dashing young officer* ◇ *his dashing good looks* **2** (of a thing) attractive and fashionable: *his dashing red waistcoat*

das·tard·ly /'dæstədli; *NAmE* -tərd-/ *adj.* (*old-fashioned*) evil and cruel: *My first part was Captain O'Hagarty, a dastardly villain in a children's play.*

DAT /dæt/ *abbr.* DIGITAL AUDIOTAPE

data 0‑‑ **AW** /'deɪtə; *BrE* also 'dɑːtə; *NAmE* also 'dætə/ *noun* (used as a plural noun in technical English, when the singular is *datum*)
1 0‑‑ [U, pl.] facts or information, especially when examined and used to find out things or to make decisions: *This data was collected from 69 countries.* ◇ *the analysis/interpretation of the data* ◇ *raw data* (= that has not been analysed) ◇ *demographical/historical/personal data* ◇ (*technical*) *These data show that most cancers are detected as a result of clinical follow-up.* ➲ COLLOCATIONS at SCIENTIFIC **2** 0‑‑ [U] information that is stored by a computer: *data retrieval* (= ways of storing or finding information on a computer)

data·bank /'deɪtəbæŋk; *NAmE* also 'dætə-/ *noun* a large amount of data on a particular subject that is stored in a computer

data·base /'deɪtəbeɪs; *NAmE* also 'dætə-/ *noun* an organized set of data that is stored in a computer and can be looked at and used in various ways

ˌdatabase 'management system *noun* (*abbr.* DBMS) (*computing*) a system for organizing and managing a large amount of data

dat·able /'deɪtəbl/ *adj.* that can be dated to a particular time: *pottery that is datable to the second century*

'data capture *noun* [U] the action or process of collecting data, especially using computers

'data mining *noun* [U] (*computing*) looking at large amounts of information that has been collected on a computer and using it to provide new information

ˌdata 'processing *noun* [U] (*computing*) a series of actions that a computer performs on data to produce an output

'data projector (also **projector**) *noun* a piece of equipment that takes data and images from a computer and shows them on a wall or large screen ➲ compare OVERHEAD PROJECTOR, PROJECTOR, SLIDE PROJECTOR ➲ VISUAL VOCAB page V56

ˌdata pro'tection *noun* [U] legal restrictions that keep information stored on computers private and that control who can read it or use it

'data set *noun* (*computing*) a collection of data which is treated as a single unit by a computer

'data warehouse *noun* a large amount of data which comes from different parts of a business and which is stored together

date 0‑‑ /deɪt/ *noun, verb*
■ *noun*
▸ PARTICULAR DAY **1** 0‑‑ [C] a particular day of the month, sometimes in a particular year, given in numbers and words: *'What's the date today?' 'The 10th.'* ◇ *Write* **today's date** *at the top of the page.* ◇ *We need to* **fix a date** *for the next meeting.* ◇ *They haven't* **set a date** *for the wedding yet.* ◇ *I can't come on that date.* ◇ *Please give your name, address and* **date of birth**. ◇ (*especially NAmE*) *name, address and* **birth date** ◇ *There's no date on this letter.* ➲ see also BEST-BEFORE DATE, CLOSING DATE, SELL-BY DATE
▸ PAST TIME/FUTURE **2** 0‑‑ [sing., U] a time in the past or future that is not a particular day: *The details can be added* **at a later date**. ◇ *The work will be carried out* **at a future date**. ◇ *a building of late Roman date*
▸ ARRANGEMENT TO MEET **3** 0‑‑ [C] (*BrE*) an arrangement to meet sb at a particular time: *Call me next week and we'll try and* **make a date**.
▸ ROMANTIC MEETING **4** 0‑‑ [C] a meeting that you have arranged with a boyfriend or girlfriend or with sb who might become a boyfriend or girlfriend: *I've got a date with Lucy tomorrow night.* ◇ *Paul's not coming. He's got a* **hot date** (= an exciting one). ➲ COLLOCATIONS at MARRIAGE ➲ see also BLIND DATE, DOUBLE DATE **5** [C] (*especially NAmE*) a boyfriend or girlfriend with whom you have arranged a date: *My date is meeting me at seven.*
▸ FRUIT **6** [C] a sweet sticky brown fruit that grows on a tree called a **date palm**, common in N Africa and W Asia
IDM **to 'date** until now: *To date, we have received over 200 replies.* ◇ *The exhibition contains some of his best work to date.* ➲ see also OUT OF DATE, UP TO DATE
■ *verb*
▸ WRITE DATE **1** 0‑‑ [T] **~ sth** to write or print the date on sth: *Thank you for your letter dated 24th March.*
▸ FIND AGE **2** 0‑‑ [T] **~ sth (at/to sth)** to say when sth old existed or was made: *The skeleton has been dated at about 2 000 BC.*
▸ OF CLOTHES/WORDS **3** [I] to become old-fashioned: *She designs classic clothes which do not date.*
▸ PERSON **4** [T] **~ sb** if sth **dates** you, it shows that you are fairly old or older than the people you are with: *I was at the Woodstock festival—that dates me, doesn't it?*
▸ HAVE RELATIONSHIP **5** [T, I] **~ (sb)** (*especially NAmE*) to have a romantic relationship with sb: *She's been dating Ron for several months.*
PHR V **ˌdate 'back (to...)** | **'date from...** 0‑‑ to have existed since a particular time in the past or for the length of time mentioned: *The college dates back to medieval times.* ◇ *The custom dates back hundreds of years.* ◇ *a law dating from the 17th century*

date·book /'deɪtbʊk/ (*NAmE*) (*BrE* **diary**) *noun* a book with spaces for each day of the year in which you can write down things you have to do in the future ➲ VISUAL VOCAB page V56

dated /'deɪtɪd/ *adj.* old-fashioned; belonging to a time in the past ➲ compare UNDATED

'Date Line *noun* = INTERNATIONAL DATE LINE

'date rape *noun* [U] the crime of RAPING sb, committed by a person he or she has gone out with on a DATE

'dating agency (also **'dating service**) *noun* a business or an organization that arranges meetings between single people who want to begin a romantic relationship: *He met his wife through a* ***computer dating agency.***

dat·ive /ˈdeɪtɪv/ *noun* (*grammar*) (in some languages) the form of a noun, a pronoun or an adjective when it is the INDIRECT OBJECT of a verb or is connected with the INDIRECT OBJECT: *In the sentence, 'I sent her a postcard', the word 'her' is* ***in the dative.*** ➲ compare ABLATIVE, ACCUSATIVE, GENITIVE, LOCATIVE, NOMINATIVE, VOCATIVE ▸ **dat·ive** *adj.*

datum /ˈdeɪtəm/ *noun* (*pl.* **data**) (*technical*) a fact or piece of information ➲ see also DATA

daub /dɔːb/ *verb, noun*

■ ***verb*** **~ A on, etc. B | ~ B with A | + adv./prep.** to spread a substance such as paint, mud, etc. thickly and/or carelessly onto sth: *The walls of the building were daubed with red paint.*

■ ***noun*** **1** [U] a mixture of CLAY, etc. that was used in the past for making walls: *walls made of* ***wattle and daub*** **2** [C] a small amount of a substance such as paint that has been spread carelessly: *a daub of lipstick* **3** [C] a badly painted picture

daugh·ter 🔑 /ˈdɔːtə(r)/ *noun*

1 🔑 a person's female child: *We have two sons and a daughter.* ◇ *They have three grown-up daughters.* ◇ *She's the daughter of an Oxford professor.* ➲ COLLOCATIONS at CHILD ➲ see also GOD-DAUGHTER, GRANDDAUGHTER, STEPDAUGHTER **2** (*literary*) a woman who belongs to a particular place or country, etc: *one of the town's most famous daughters*

ˈdaughter-in-law *noun* (*pl.* **daughters-in-law**) the wife of your son ➲ compare SON-IN-LAW

daunt /dɔːnt/ *verb* [usually passive] **~ sb** to make sb feel nervous and less confident about doing sth SYN **intimidate**: *She was a brave woman but she felt daunted by the task ahead.* ▸ **daunt·ing** *adj.* SYN **intimidating**: *She has the* ***daunting task*** *of cooking for 20 people every day.* ◇ *Starting a new job can be a* ***daunting prospect.*** **daunt·ing·ly** *adv.*

IDM **nothing ˈdaunted** (*BrE, formal*) confident about sth difficult you have to do: *Nothing daunted, the people set about rebuilding their homes.*

daunt·less /ˈdɔːntləs/ *adj.* (*literary*) not easily frightened or stopped from doing sth difficult SYN **resolute**

dau·phin /ˈdəʊfæ̃; -fæn; *NAmE* ˈdoʊ-/ *noun* (*old use*) the oldest son of the king of France

David and Goliath /ˌdeɪvɪd ənd ɡəˈlaɪəθ/ *adj.* used to describe a situation in which a small or weak person or organization tries to defeat another much larger or stronger opponent: *The match looks like being a David and Goliath contest.* ORIGIN From the Bible story in which Goliath, a giant, is killed by the boy David with a stone.

daw·dle /ˈdɔːdl/ *verb* [I] to take a long time to do sth or go somewhere: *Stop dawdling! We're going to be late!* ◇ **+ adv./prep.** *They dawdled along by the river, laughing and talking.*

dawn /dɔːn/ *noun, verb*

■ ***noun*** **1** [U, C] the time of day when light first appears SYN **daybreak, sunrise**: *They start work* ***at dawn.*** ◇ *It's almost dawn.* ◇ *We arrived in Sydney as* ***dawn broke*** (= as the first light could be seen). ◇ *I woke up just before dawn.* ◇ *summer's early dawns* ◇ *He works* ***from dawn till dusk*** (= from morning till night). ➲ compare DUSK **2** [sing.] **~ (of sth)** the beginning or first signs of sth: *the* ***dawn of civilization/time/history*** ◇ *Peace marked a new dawn in the country's history.* IDM see BREAK *n.*, CRACK *n.*

■ ***verb*** **1** [I] (of a day or a period of time) to begin: *The following morning dawned bright and warm.* ◇ *A new technological age had dawned.* **2** [I] to become obvious or easy to understand: *Slowly the awful truth dawned.* IDM see LIGHT *n.*

PHR V **ˈdawn on sb** [no passive] if sth **dawns on you**, you begin to realize it for the first time: **it dawns on sb that...** *Suddenly it dawned on me that they couldn't possibly have met before.*

the ˌdawn ˈchorus *noun* [sing.] (*BrE*) the sound of birds singing very early in the morning

day 🔑 /deɪ/ *noun*

1 🔑 [C] a period of 24 hours: *I saw Tom three days ago.* ◇ *'What day is it today?' 'Monday.'* ◇ *We're going away* ***in a few days/in a few days' time.*** ◇ *They left* ***the day before yesterday*** (= two days ago). ◇ *We're meeting* ***the day after tomorrow*** (= in two days). ◇ *New Year's Day* ◇ *Take the medicine three times* ***a day.*** ◇ *We can't go there today. You can go* ***another day.*** ➲ see also FIELD DAY, OFF DAY, RED-LETTER DAY, SPORTS DAY **2** 🔑 [U] the time between when it becomes light in the morning and when it becomes dark in the evening: *The sun was shining* ***all day.*** ◇ *I could sit and watch the river* ***all day long.*** ◇ *He works at night and sleeps* ***during the day.*** ◇ *Nocturnal animals sleep* ***by day*** *and hunt by night.* **3** 🔑 [C, usually sing.] the hours of the day when you are awake, working, etc: *a seven-hour* ***working day*** ◇ *It's been* ***a long day*** (= I've been very busy). ◇ *Did you have a good day?* ◇ *She didn't do a full* ***day's work.*** ◇ *I took a half day off yesterday.* ◇ (*NAmE*) *Have a nice day!* ➲ see also WORKDAY **4** 🔑 [C, usually pl.] a particular period of time or history: *in Queen Victoria's day* ◇ *the* ***early days*** *of computers* ◇ *Most women stayed at home* ***in those days.*** ◇ (*informal*) *in the* ***old days*** (= in the past) ➲ see also GLORY DAYS, HEYDAY, NOWADAYS, THE PRESENT DAY HELP There are many other compounds ending in **day**. You will find them at their place in the alphabet.

IDM **all in a day's ˈwork** part of your normal working life and not unusual **any day (now)** (*informal*) very soon: *The letter should arrive any day now.* **carry/win the ˈday** (*formal*) to be successful against sb/sth: *Despite strong opposition, the ruling party carried the day.* **day after ˈday** 🔑 each day repeatedly (used especially when sth is boring or annoying): *She hates doing the same work day after day.* **day by ˈday** all the time; a little at a time and gradually: *Day by day his condition improved.* **day ˈin, day ˈout** every day for a long period of time **a day of ˈreckoning** the time when sb will have to deal with the result of sth that they have done wrong, or be punished for sth bad that they have done **sb's/sth's days are ˈnumbered** a person or thing will not continue to live, exist or be successful for much longer: *His days as leader of the party are numbered.* **from day ˈone** (*informal*) from the beginning: *It's never worked from day one.* **from day to ˈday 1** with no thoughts or plans for the future: *They live from day to day, looking after their sick daughter.* **2** if a situation changes **from day to day**, it changes often: *A baby's need for food can vary from day to day.* **from ˌone day to the ˈnext** if a situation changes **from one day to the next**, it is uncertain and not likely to stay the same each day: *I never know what to expect from one day to the next.* **have had your ˈday** to no longer be successful, powerful, etc: *She's had her day as a supermodel.* **have seen/known better ˈdays** (*humorous*) to be in poor condition: *Our car has seen better days!* **if he's, she's, etc. a ˈday** (*informal*) (used when talking about sb's age) at least: *He must be 70 if he's a day!* **in sb's ˈday 1** during the part of sb's life when they were most successful, famous, etc: *She was a great dancer in her day.* **2** when sb was young: *In my day, there were plenty of jobs when you left school.* **in ˈthis day and age** now, in the modern world **it's not sb's ˈday** (*informal*) used when several unfortunate or unpleasant things happen on the same day: *My car broke down and then I locked myself out—it's just not my day!* **make sb's ˈday** to make sb feel very happy on a particular day: *The phone call from Mike really made my day.* **make a day of it** (*informal*) to make a particular enjoyable activity last for a whole day instead of only part of it **not have all ˈday** to not have much time: *Come on! We don't have all day!* **of sb's ˈday** during a particular period of time when sb lived: *the best player of his day* ◇ *Bessie Smith was the Madonna of her day.* **of the ˈday** that is served on a particular day in a restaurant: *soup of the day* **ˈone day** 🔑 at some time in the future, or on a particular day in the past: *One day, I want to leave the city and move to the country.* ◇ *One day, he walked out of the house with a small bag and never came back.* **ˈone of these days** before a long time has passed: *One of these days you'll come back and ask me to forgive you.* **one of**

those 'days (*informal*) a day when there are a lot of mistakes and a lot of things go wrong: *It's been one of those days!* **'some day** at an unknown time in the future: *Some day I'll be famous.* **take it/things one ˌday at a 'time** (*informal*) to not think about what will happen in the future: *I don't know if he'll get better. We're just taking it one day at a time.* **'that'll be the day** (*informal, ironic*) used when you are saying that sth is very unlikely to happen: *Paul? Apologize? That'll be the day!* **'these days** 🔑 (*informal*) used to talk about the present, especially when you are comparing it with the past: *These days kids grow up so quickly.* **'those were the days** (*informal*) used to suggest that a time in the past was happier or better than now **to the 'day** exactly: *It's been three years to the day since we met.* **to this 'day** even now, when a lot of time has passed: *To this day, I still don't understand why he did it.* ➲ more at BACK *adv.*, BORN, BREAK *n.*, CALL *v.*, CLEAR *adj.*, COLD *adj.*, DEED, DOG *n.*, EARLY *adj.*, END *n.*, END *v.*, EVIL, FORTH, GIVE *v.*, LATE *adv.*, LIVE¹, LIVELONG, NICE, NINE, NIGHT, OLD, ORDER *n.*, OTHER *adj.*, PASS *v.*, PLAIN *adj.*, RAINY, ROME, SALAD, SAVE *v.*, TIME *n.*

'day boy *noun* (*BrE*) a boy DAY PUPIL

day·break /ˈdeɪbreɪk/ *noun* [U] the time of day when light first appears SYN **dawn**: *We left before daybreak.*

'day care *noun* [U] care for small children, or for old or sick people, away from home, during the day: *Day care is provided by the company she works for.* ◇ *a day care centre*

'day centre *noun* (*BrE*) a place that provides care for old or sick people during the day

day·dream /ˈdeɪdriːm/ *noun* pleasant thoughts that make you forget about the present: *She stared out of the window, lost in a daydream.* ▶ **day·dream** *verb* [I]: ~ (**about sb/sth**) *I would spend hours daydreaming about a house of my own.*

'day girl *noun* (*BrE*) a girl DAY PUPIL

Day-Glo™ /ˈdeɪ gləʊ; *NAmE* gloʊ/ *adj.* having a very bright orange, yellow, green or pink colour: *Day-Glo cycling shorts*

'day job *noun* [sing.] the paid work that sb normally does IDM **don't give up the 'day job** (*informal, humorous*) used to tell sb that they should continue doing what they are used to, rather than trying sth new which they are likely to fail at: *So you want to be a writer? Well my advice is, don't give up the day job.*

day·light /ˈdeɪlaɪt/ *noun* [U] the light that comes from the sun during the day: *They emerged from the church into the bright daylight.* ◇ *The street looks very different* **in daylight**. ◇ *They left* **before daylight** (= before the sun had risen).
IDM **ˌdaylight 'robbery** (*informal*) the fact of sb charging too much money for sth: *You wouldn't believe some of the prices they charge; it's daylight robbery.* ➲ more at BROAD *adj.*

day·lights /ˈdeɪlaɪts/ *noun* [pl.]
IDM **beat/knock the (living) 'daylights out of sb** (*informal*) to hit sb very hard several times and hurt them very much **frighten/scare the (living) 'daylights out of sb** (*informal*) to frighten sb very much

ˌdaylight 'saving time (*abbr.* DST) (also **'daylight time**) (both *NAmE*) (*BrE* **'summer time**) *noun* [U] the period during which in some countries the clocks are put forward one hour, so that it is light for an extra hour in the evening

day·long /ˈdeɪlɒŋ; *NAmE* -lɔːŋ/ *adj.* [only before noun] (*especially NAmE*) lasting for a whole day: *a daylong meeting*

'day nursery (also **nursery**) (both *BrE*) (*NAmE* **'day care center**) *noun* a place where small children are cared for while their parents are at work ➲ compare CRÈCHE, NURSERY SCHOOL

ˌday 'off *noun* (*pl.* **days off**) a day on which you do not have to work: *Most weeks, Sunday is my only day off.* ◇ *Why not take a few days off?*

the ˌDay of 'Judgement *noun* [sing.] = JUDGEMENT DAY

ˌday 'out *noun* (*pl.* **days out**) a trip or visit somewhere for a day: *We had a day out in the country.* ➲ SYNONYMS at TRIP

'day pupil (*BrE*) (also **'day student** *NAmE, BrE*) *noun* a school student who goes to a BOARDING SCHOOL but lives at home

ˌday re'lease *noun* (*BrE*) [U] a system of allowing employees days off work for education: *time off for study on day release* ◇ *a day release course*

ˌday re'turn *noun* (*BrE*) a ticket at a reduced price for a journey to a place and back again on the same day

'day room *noun* a room in a hospital or other institution where people can sit, relax, watch television, etc. during the day

'day school *noun* **1** (*old-fashioned*) a private school with students who live at home and only go to school during the day ➲ compare BOARDING SCHOOL **2** (*BrE*) a course of education lasting one day, at which a particular topic is discussed: *a day school at Leeds University on women in Victorian times*

'day student (*especially NAmE*) (*BrE* also **'day pupil**) *noun* a school student who goes to a BOARDING SCHOOL but lives at home

day·time /ˈdeɪtaɪm/ *noun* [U] the period during the day between the time when it gets light and the time when it gets dark: *You don't often see this bird* **in (the) daytime**. ◇ *The park is open* **during (the) daytime**. ◇ *Daytime temperatures never fell below 30°C.* ◇ *Please give your name and daytime phone number.*

ˌday-to-'day *adj.* [only before noun] **1** planning for only one day at a time: *I have organized the cleaning* **on a day-to-day basis**, *until our usual cleaner returns.* **2** involving the usual events or tasks of each day: *She has been looking after the* **day-to-day running** *of the school.*

'day trading *noun* [U] (*finance*) buying and selling shares very quickly on the same day using the Internet in order to make a profit from small price changes ▶ **'day trader** *noun*

'day trip *noun* a trip or visit completed in one day: *a day trip to France* ▶ **'day tripper** *noun* (*BrE*)

day·wear /ˈdeɪweə(r); *NAmE* -wer/ *noun* [U] clothes for wearing every day, for example for working or shopping, not for special occasions

daze /deɪz/ *noun*
IDM **in a daze** in a confused state: *I've been in a complete daze since hearing the news.*

dazed /deɪzd/ *adj.* unable to think clearly, especially because of a shock or because you have been hit on the head: *Survivors waited for the rescue boats, dazed and frightened.* ◇ *Jimmy was still dazed by the blow to his head.*

daz·zle /ˈdæzl/ *verb, noun*
■ ***verb*** [often passive] **1** [T, I] ~ (**sb**) if a strong light **dazzles** you, it is so bright that you cannot see for a short time SYN **blind**: *He was momentarily dazzled by the strong sunlight.* **2** [T] ~ **sb** to impress sb a lot with your beauty, skill, etc: *He was dazzled by the warmth of her smile.* ▶ **daz·zling** *adj.* SYN **brilliant**: *a dazzling display of oriental dance* **daz·zlingly** *adv.*: *She was dazzlingly beautiful.*
■ ***noun*** [U, sing.] **1** the quality that bright light has that stops you from seeing clearly **2** a thing or quality that impresses you but may prevent you from understanding or thinking clearly

d.b.a. /ˌdiː biː ˈeɪ/ *abbr.* (*US*) doing business as: *Philip Smith, d.b.a. Phil's Signs*

DBMS /ˌdiː biː em ˈes/ *abbr.* DATABASE MANAGEMENT SYSTEM

DC /ˌdiː ˈsiː/ *abbr.* **1** DIRECT CURRENT ➲ compare ALTERNATING CURRENT **2** District of Columbia in the US: *Washington, DC*

DCMS /ˌdiː siː em ˈes/ *abbr.* (in Britain) Department for Culture, Media, and Sport

'D-Day *noun* [U] a date on which sth important is expected to happen ORIGIN From the name given to 6 June 1944, the day on which the British, US and other armies landed on the beaches of northern France in the Second World War.

DDT /ˌdiː diː ˈtiː/ *noun* [U] a chemical used, especially in the past, for killing insects that harm crops

de- /diː/ *prefix* (in verbs and related nouns, adjectives and adverbs) **1** the opposite of: *decentralization* **2** removing sth: *to defrost the refrigerator* (= remove layers of ice from it)

dea·con /ˈdiːkən/ *noun* **1** (in the Roman Catholic, Anglican and Orthodox Churches) a religious leader just below the rank of a priest **2** (in some Nonconformist Churches) a person who is not a member of the CLERGY, but who helps a minister with church business affairs

dea·con·ess /ˌdiːkəˈnes; *NAmE* ˈdiːkənəs/ *noun* (in some Christian Churches) a woman who has duties that are similar to those of a deacon

de·activ·ate /ˌdiːˈæktɪveɪt/ *verb* **~ sth** to make sth such as a device or chemical process stop working: *Do you know how to deactivate the alarm?*

dead 🔑 /ded/ *adj., noun, adv.*

■ ***adj.***

▸ NOT ALIVE **1** 🔑 no longer alive: *My mother's dead; she died in 1987.* ◇ *a dead person/animal* ◇ *dead leaves/wood/skin* ◇ *He was shot dead by a gunman outside his home.* ◇ *Catherine's* ***dead body*** *lay peacefully on the bed.* ◇ *He* ***dropped dead*** (= died suddenly) *last week.* ◇ *The poor child looks* ***more dead than alive.*** ◇ (*figurative*) *In ten years he'll be* ***dead and buried*** *as a politician.*

▸ IDEA/BELIEF/PLAN **2** 🔑 [not before noun] no longer believed in or aimed for: *Many believe the peace plan is dead.* ◇ *Unfortunately racism is not yet dead.* ◇ *Though the idea may be dead, it is far from being buried* (= people still talk about it, even though there is nothing new to say).

▸ NOT USED **3** 🔑 belonging to the past; no longer practised or fashionable: *Is the Western a dead art form?* ◇ *a dead language* (= one that is no longer spoken, for example Latin)

▸ FINISHED **4** (*informal*) finished; not able to be used any more: *dead matches* ◇ *There were two dead bottles of wine on the table.*

▸ MACHINE **5** 🔑 (of machines or equipment) not working because of a lack of power: *a dead battery* ◇ *The hard disk is dead.* ◇ *Suddenly the phone* ***went dead.***

▸ PLACE **6** (*informal, disapproving*) very quiet, without activity or interest: *There were no theatres, no cinemas, no coffee bars. It was dead as anything.*

▸ BUSINESS **7** (*informal, disapproving*) without activity; with nobody buying or selling anything: *'The market is absolutely dead this morning,' said one foreign exchange trader.* ◇ *Winter is traditionally the dead season for the housing market.*

▸ TIRED **8** [not usually before noun] (*informal*) extremely tired; not well: ***half dead*** *with cold and hunger* ◇ *She felt* ***dead on her feet*** *and didn't have the energy to question them further.*

▸ WITHOUT FEELING **9** [not before noun] (of a part of the body) unable to feel because of cold, etc. SYN **numb**: *My left arm had* ***gone dead.*** **10 ~ to sth** unable to feel or understand emotions SYN **insensitive**: *He was dead to all feelings of pity.* **11** (especially of sb's voice, eyes or face) showing no emotion SYN **expressionless**: *She said, 'I'm sorry, too,' in a quiet, dead voice.* ◇ *His usually dead grey eyes were sparkling.*

▸ COMPLETE/EXACT **12** [only before noun] complete or exact: *a* ***dead silence/calm*** ◇ *the* ***dead centre*** *of the target* ◇ *The car gave a sudden jerk and came to a* ***dead stop.*** ◇ (*BrE*) *This horse is a* ***dead cert*** *for* (= will certainly win) *the race tomorrow.* ◇ *She crumpled to the floor* ***in a dead faint*** (= completely unconscious).

▸ NEVER ALIVE **13** never having been alive: *dead matter* (= for example rock) ◇ *a dead planet* (= one with no life on it)

▸ IN SPORT **14** outside the playing area

IDM **be a dead ˈringer for sb** (*informal*) to look very like sb: *She's a dead ringer for a girl I used to know.* (as) **ˌdead as a/the ˈdodo** (*BrE, informal*) completely dead; no longer interesting or valid (as) **ˌdead as a ˈdoornail** (*informal*) completely dead **a ˌdead ˈduck** (*informal*) a plan, an event, etc. that has failed or is certain to fail and that is therefore not worth discussing **be dead and ˈgone** (*informal*) to be dead: *You'll be sorry you said that when I'm dead and gone.* **the dead hand of sth** an influence that controls or restricts sth: *We need to free business from the dead hand of bureaucracy.* **ˌdead in the ˈwater** a person or plan that is **dead in the water** has failed and has little hope of succeeding in the future: *His leadership campaign is dead in the water.* **dead ˈmeat** (*informal*) in serious trouble: *If anyone finds out, you're dead meat.* **ˌdead on arˈrival** (*abbr.* DOA) **1** (of an accident victim or other patient) already dead when arriving at hospital: *She was pronounced dead on arrival.* **2** (*NAmE, informal*) very unlikely to be successful; not working when it is delivered: *The bill was dead on arrival in the Senate.* ◇ *The software was DOA.* **ˌdead to the ˈworld** fast asleep **over ˌmy dead ˈbody** (*informal*) used to show you are strongly opposed to sth: *She moves into our home over my dead body.* **sb wouldn't be seen/caught ˈdead...** (*informal*) used to say that you would not like to wear particular clothes, or to be in a particular situation: *She wouldn't be seen dead in a hat.* ◇ *He wouldn't be caught dead going to a club with his mother.* ➲ more at FLOG, KNOCK *v.*

■ ***noun*** **the dead 1** [pl.] people who have died: *The dead and wounded in that one attack amounted to 6 000.* **2** [sing.] the state of being dead: *Christians believe that God raised Jesus from the dead.* ◇ (*figurative*) *In nine years he has brought his party back from the dead almost to the brink of power.*

IDM **in the ˌdead of ˈnight** (*BrE* also **at ˌdead of ˈnight**) in the quietest part of the night: *I crept out of bed in the dead of night and sneaked downstairs.* **in the ˌdead of ˈwinter** in the coldest part of winter

■ ***adv.*** (*informal*)

▸ COMPLETELY **1** completely; exactly: *You're dead right!* ◇ (*BrE*) *a dead straight road* ◇ (*BrE*) *The train was dead on time.* ◇ *He's dead against the idea.* ◇ *The sight made him* ***stop dead in his tracks*** (= stop suddenly). ◇ *She's* ***dead set on*** *getting* (= determined to get) *this new job.*

▸ VERY **2** (*BrE, informal*) very; extremely: *The instructions are dead easy to follow.* ◇ *You were dead lucky to get that job.* ◇ *I was dead scared.*

IDM **cut sb ˈdead** (*BrE*) to pretend not to have seen sb; to refuse to say hello to sb: *She saw me, recognized me and cut me dead.* ➲ more at RIGHT *n.*

ˌdead ˈbeat (also **beat**) *adj.* [not before noun] (*informal*) very tired: *You look dead beat.*

dead·beat /ˈdedbiːt/ *noun* (*informal*) **1** (*especially NAmE*) a lazy person; a person with no job and no money, who is not part of normal society **2** (*NAmE*) a person or company that tries to avoid paying their debts **3** (also **ˌdeadbeat ˈdad**) (*NAmE*) a father who does not live with his children and does not pay their mother any money to take care of them

dead·bolt /ˈdedbəʊlt; *NAmE* -boʊlt/ (*especially NAmE*) (*BrE* also **dead·lock**) *noun* a type of lock on a door that needs a key to open or close it

dead·en /ˈdedn/ *verb* **~ sth** to make sth such as a sound, a feeling, etc. less strong SYN **dull**: *He was given drugs to deaden the pain.* ▸ **dead·en·ing** *adj.* [only before noun]: *the deadening effect of alcohol on your reactions*

ˌdead ˈend *noun* **1** a road, passage, etc. that is closed at one end: *The first street we tried turned out to be a dead end.* **2** a point at which you can make no further progress in what you are doing: *We had come to a dead end in our research.* ◇ *He's in a* ***dead-end job*** *in the local factory* (= one with low wages and no hope of promotion). ◇ *These negotiations are a* ***dead-end street*** (= they have reached a point where no further progress is possible).

dead·head /ˈdedhed/ *verb* **~ sth** (*BrE*) to remove dead flowers from a plant

ˌdead ˈheat *noun* **1** (*especially BrE*) a result in a race when two of those taking part finish at exactly the same time **2** (*NAmE*) a situation during a race or competition, etc. when two or more people are at the same level: *The two candidates are* ***in a dead heat*** *in the polls.*

D

ˌ**dead ˈletter** *noun* **1** [usually sing.] a law or an agreement that still exists but that is ignored **2** (*especially NAmE*) a letter that cannot be delivered to an address or to the person who sent it

dead·line /ˈdedlaɪn/ *noun* **~** (**for sth**) a point in time by which sth must be done: *I prefer to* ***work to a deadline.*** ◇ *The deadline for applications is 30 April.* ◇ *the January 15 deadline set by the United Nations*

dead·lock /ˈdedlɒk; *NAmE* -lɑːk/ *noun* **1** [sing., U] a complete failure to reach agreement or settle an argument SYN **stalemate**: *European agriculture ministers failed to* ***break the deadlock*** *over farm subsidies.* ◇ (*BrE*) *The strike appeared to have reached deadlock.* ◇ (*NAmE, BrE*) *The strike has reached a deadlock.* **2** (*BrE*) (also **dead·bolt** *NAmE, BrE*) [C] a type of lock on a door that needs a key to open or close it ▶ **dead·locked** *adj.* [not before noun]: *Despite months of discussion the negotiations remained deadlocked.*

ˌ**dead ˈloss** *noun* [usually sing.] (*BrE, informal*) a person or thing that is not helpful or useful: *He may be a very talented designer, but as a manager he's a dead loss.*

dead·ly /ˈdedli/ *adj., adv.*

■ *adj.* (**dead·lier, dead·li·est**) HELP **More deadly** and **deadliest** are the usual forms. You can also use **most deadly**. **1** causing or likely to cause death SYN **lethal**: *a* ***deadly weapon/disease*** ◇ ***deadly poison*** ◇ *The cobra is one of the world's deadliest snakes.* ◇ *The terrorists have chosen to play a deadly game with the civilian population.* **2** [only before noun] extreme; complete: *I'm* ***in deadly earnest.*** ◇ *We sat* ***in deadly silence.*** ◇ *They are* ***deadly enemies*** (= are full of hatred for each other). **3** extremely effective, so that no defence is possible: *His aim is deadly* (= so accurate that he can kill easily). ◇ *It was the deadly striker's 11th goal of the season.* **4** (*informal*) very boring: *The lecture was absolutely deadly.*

■ *adv.* **1** (*informal*) extremely: ***deadly serious/dull*** **2** = DEATHLY: ***deadly pale/cold***

dead·ly night·shade /ˌdedli ˈnaɪtʃeɪd/ (also **bella·donna**) *noun* [U] a very poisonous plant with purple flowers and black BERRIES

ˌ**deadly ˈsin** *noun* one of the seven actions for which you can go to hell, in Christian tradition: *Greed is one of the* ***seven deadly sins.***

dead·pan /ˈdedpæn/ *adj.* without any expression or emotion; often pretending to be serious when you are joking: *deadpan humour*

dead·weight /ˌdedˈweɪt/ *noun* [usually sing.] **1** a thing that is very heavy and difficult to lift or move **2** a person or thing that makes it difficult for sth to succeed or change

ˌ**dead ˈwood** *noun* [U] people or things that have become useless or unnecessary in an organization

ˈ**dead zone** *noun* **1** a place or a period of time in which nothing happens: *The town is a cultural dead zone.* **2** an area which separates two places, groups of people, etc: *The UN is trying to maintain a dead zone between the warring groups.* **3** a place where a mobile/cell phone does not work because no signal can be received **4** (*biology*) an area of water in which animals cannot live because there is not enough OXYGEN

deaf 0‑ /def/ *adj.* (**deaf·er, deaf·est**)
1 0‑ unable to hear anything or unable to hear very well: *to* ***become/go deaf*** ◇ *She was born deaf.* ➲ see also STONE DEAF, TONE-DEAF **2 the deaf** *noun* [pl.] people who cannot hear: *television subtitles for the deaf and hard of hearing* **3** [not before noun] **~ to sth** not willing to listen or pay attention to sth: *He was deaf to my requests for help.* ▶ **deaf·ness** *noun* [U]

IDM (**as**) ˌ**deaf as a ˈpost** (*informal*) very deaf **fall on deaf ˈears** to be ignored or not noticed by other people: *Her advice fell on deaf ears.* **turn a deaf ˈear** (**to sb/sth**) to ignore or refuse to listen to sb/sth: *He turned a deaf ear to the rumours.*

deaf·en /ˈdefn/ *verb* [usually passive] **1 ~ sb** to make sb unable to hear the sounds around them because there is too much noise: *The noise of the siren was deafening her.* **2 ~ sb** to make sb deaf

deaf·en·ing /ˈdefnɪŋ/ *adj.* very loud: *deafening applause* ◇ *The noise of the machine was deafening.* ◇ *The government's response to the report has been a* ***deafening silence*** (= it was very noticeable that nothing was said or done). ▶ **deaf·en·ing·ly** *adv.*

ˌ**deaf ˈmute** *noun* (sometimes *offensive*) a person who is unable to hear or speak

deal 0‑ /diːl/ *verb, noun*

■ *verb* (**dealt, dealt** /delt/)

▸ CARDS **1** [I, T] to give cards to each player in a game of cards: *Whose turn is it to deal?* ◇ **~ (sth) (out) (to sb)** *Start by dealing out ten cards to each player.* ◇ **~ sb sth** *He dealt me two aces.*

▸ DRUGS **2** [I, T] **~ (sth)** to buy and sell illegal drugs: *You can often see people dealing openly on the streets.*

IDM **deal sb/sth a ˈblow | deal a ˈblow to sb/sth** (*formal*) **1** to be very shocking or harmful to sb/sth: *Her sudden death dealt a blow to the whole country.* **2** to hit sb/sth ➲ more at WHEEL *v.*

PHR V ˈ**deal in sth 1** 0‑ to buy and sell a particular product SYN **trade in**: *The company deals in computer software.* **2** to accept sth as a basis for your decisions, attitudes or actions: *We don't deal in rumours or guesswork.* ˌ**deal sb ˈin** (*informal, especially NAmE*) to include sb in an activity: *That sounds great. Deal me in!* ˌ**deal sth↔ˈout 1** to share sth out among a group of people SYN **distribute**: *The profits were dealt out among the investors.* **2** to say what punishment sb should have: *Many judges deal out harsher sentences to men than to women.* ˈ**deal with sb** 0‑ to take appropriate action in a particular situation or according to who you are talking to, managing, etc. SYN **handle**: *She is used to dealing with all kinds of people in her job.* ˈ**deal with sb/sth** 0‑ to do business with a person, a company or an organization ˈ**deal with sth 1** 0‑ to solve a problem, perform a task, etc: *to deal with enquiries/issues/complaints* ◇ *Have you dealt with these letters yet?* ◇ *He's good at dealing with pressure.* **2** 0‑ to be about sth: *Her poems often deal with the subject of death.* ➲ LANGUAGE BANK at ABOUT

■ *noun*

▸ A LOT **1** 0‑ [sing.] **a good/great ~** much; a lot: *They spent a great deal of money.* ◇ *It took a great deal of time.* ◇ *I'm feeling a good deal better.* ◇ *We see them a great deal* (= often).

▸ BUSINESS AGREEMENT **2** 0‑ [C] an agreement, especially in business, on particular conditions for buying or doing sth: *to* ***make/sign/conclude/close a deal*** (*with sb*) ◇ (*informal*) *Did you* ***cut a deal*** (= make one)? ◇ ***We did a deal*** *with the management on overtime.* ◇ *They were hoping for a better pay deal.* ◇ ***A deal was struck*** *after lengthy negotiations.* ◇ ***The deal fell through*** (= no agreement was reached). ◇ *I got a* ***good deal*** *on the car* (= bought it cheaply). ◇ ***It's a deal!*** (= I agree to your terms) ◇ *Listen.* ***This is the deal*** (= this is what we have agreed and are going to do). ➲ COLLOCATIONS at BUSINESS ➲ see also PACKAGE

▸ TREATMENT **3** [C, usually sing.] the way that sb/sth is treated: *If elected, the party has promised a* ***new deal*** (= better and fairer treatment) *for teachers.* ◇ *They knew they'd been given a* ***raw/rough deal*** (= been treated unfairly). ◇ *We tried to ensure that everyone got a* ***fair deal.*** ◇ *It was a* ***square deal*** *for everyone.*

▸ IN CARD GAMES **4** [C, usually sing.] the action of giving out cards to the players: *It's your deal.*

▸ WOOD **5** [U] (*especially BrE*) the soft pale wood of FIR or PINE trees, especially when it is cut into boards for making things: *a deal table*

IDM **what's the ˈdeal?** (*informal*) what is happening in the present situation?: *What's the deal? Do you want to go out or not?* ➲ more at BIG *adj.*, DONE *adj.*, STRIKE *v.*

ˈ**deal-breaker** *noun* (*especially NAmE*) something that causes sb to reject a deal in politics or business: *The candidate's support for the war is the deal-breaker* (= people will not vote for the candidate because of it).

deal·er /ˈdiːlə(r)/ *noun* **1** a person whose business is buying and selling a particular product: *an art/antique dealer* ◇ **~ in sth** *He's a dealer in second-hand cars.* ➲ see also

WHEELER-DEALER **2** a person who sells illegal drugs **3** the person who gives out the cards in a card game

deal·er·ship /ˈdiːləʃɪp; *NAmE* -lərʃ-/ *noun* a business that buys and sells products, especially cars, for a particular company; the position of being a dealer who can buy and sell sth: *a Ford dealership*

deal·ing /ˈdiːlɪŋ/ *noun* **1 dealings** [pl.] business activities; the relations that you have with sb in business: *Have you **had** any previous **dealings with** this company?* ◇ *I knew nothing of his business dealings.* ◇ *She has always been very polite in her dealings with me.* **2** [U] a way of doing business with sb: *a reputation for **fair/honest dealing*** **3** [U, C] buying and selling: *drug dealing* ◇ *dealings in shares*

dealt *past tense, past part.* of DEAL

dean /diːn/ *noun* **1** (in the Anglican Church) a priest of high rank who is in charge of the other priests in a CATHEDRAL **2** (also ˌ**rural** ˈ**dean**) (*BrE*) a priest who is in charge of the priests of several churches in an area **3** a person in a university who is in charge of a department of studies **4** (in a college or university, especially at Oxford or Cambridge) a person who is responsible for the discipline of students **5** (*NAmE*) = DOYEN

dean·ery /ˈdiːnəri/ *noun* (*pl.* -ies) **1** a group of PARISHES controlled by a dean (2) **2** the office or house of a dean (1,2)

ˌ**dean's** ˈ**list** *noun* (in the US) a list that is published every year of the best students in a college or university

dear 0→ /dɪə(r); *NAmE* dɪr/ *adj., exclamation, noun, adv.*

■ ***adj.*** (**dear·er**, **dear·est**) **1** 0→ loved by or important to sb: *He's one of my dearest friends.* ◇ **~ to sb** *Her daughter is very dear to her.* **2** 0→ **Dear** used at the beginning of a letter before the name or title of the person that you are writing to: *Dear Sir or Madam* ◇ *Dear Mrs Jones* **3** [not usually before noun] (*BrE*) expensive; costing a lot of money: *Everything's so dear now, isn't it?* OPP **cheap**

IDM **dear old/little...** (*BrE*) used to describe sb in a way that shows affection: *Dear old Sue! I knew she'd help.* ◇ *Their baby's a dear little thing.* **hold sb/sth** ˈ**dear** (*formal*) to care very much for sb/sth; to value sb/sth highly: *He had destroyed everything we held dear.* ➲ more at HEART, LIFE, NEAR *adj.*

■ ***exclamation*** used in expressions that show that you are surprised, upset, annoyed or worried: ***Oh dear!*** *I think I've lost my purse!* ◇ ***Oh dear!*** *What a shame.* ◇ ***Dear me!*** *What a mess!* ◇ ***Dear oh dear!*** *What are you going to do now?*

■ ***noun*** **1** (*BrE, informal*) a kind person: *Isn't he a dear?* ◇ ***Be a dear and*** *fetch me my coat.* **2** used when speaking to sb you love: *Would you like a drink, dear?* ◇ *Come here, my dear.* **3** used when speaking to sb in a friendly way, for example by an older person to a young person or a child: *What's your name, dear?* ➲ compare DUCK

■ ***adv.*** (*BrE*) at a high price: *to buy cheap and sell dear*

IDM see COST *v.*

dear·est /ˈdɪərɪst; *NAmE* ˈdɪr-/ *adj., noun*

■ ***adj.*** (*old-fashioned*) **1** used when writing to sb you love: *'Dearest Nina', the letter began.* **2** [usually before noun] that you feel deeply: *It was her **dearest wish** to have a family.*

■ ***noun*** (*old-fashioned*) used when speaking to sb you love: *Come (my) dearest, let's go home.* IDM see NEAR *n.*

dearie /ˈdɪəri; *NAmE* ˈdɪri/ *noun* (*old-fashioned, BrE, informal*) used to address sb in a friendly way: *Sit down, dearie.*

dear·ly /ˈdɪəli; *NAmE* ˈdɪrli/ *adv.* **1** very much: *She loves him dearly.* ◇ *I would **dearly like/love** to know what he was thinking.* ◇ ***dearly beloved*** (= used by a minister at a Christian church service to address people) **2** in a way that causes a lot of suffering or damage, or that costs a lot of money: *Success has **cost him dearly**.* ◇ *She **paid dearly** for her mistake.*

dearth /dɜːθ; *NAmE* dɜːrθ/ *noun* [sing.] **~** (**of sth**) a lack of sth; the fact of there not being enough of sth SYN **scarcity**: *There was a dearth of reliable information on the subject.*

death 0→ /deθ/ *noun*

1 0→ [C] the fact of sb dying or being killed: *a **sudden/violent/peaceful, etc. death*** ◇ *the anniversary of his wife's death* ◇ *an increase in deaths from cancer* ◇ *He died a slow and painful death.* **2** 0→ [U] the end of life; the state of being dead: *Two children were burnt **to death** in the fire* (= they died as a result of the fire). ◇ *He's drinking himself **to death*** (= so that it will kill him). ◇ *Police are trying to establish the **cause of death**.* ◇ *Do you believe in **life after death**?* ◇ *a **death camp*** (= a place where prisoners are killed, usually in a war) ◇ *He was **sentenced to death*** (= to be EXECUTED). **3** 0→ [U] **~ of sth** the permanent end or destruction of sth: *the death of all my plans* ◇ *the death of fascism* **4** (also **Death**) [U] (*literary*) the power that destroys life, imagined as human in form: *Death is often shown in paintings as a human skeleton.* ➲ see also SUDDEN DEATH

IDM **at death's** ˈ**door** (often *humorous*) so ill/sick that you may die **be the** ˈ**death of sb** (*informal*) to worry or upset sb very much: *Those kids will be the death of me.* ˌ**do sth to** ˈ**death** to do or perform sth so often that people become tired of seeing or hearing it: *That joke's been done to death.* **frighten/scare sb to** ˈ**death** to frighten sb very much **look/feel like death warmed** ˈ**up** (*BrE*) (*NAmE* **like death warmed** ˈ**over**) (*informal*) to look or feel very ill/sick or tired **put sb to death** to kill sb as a punishment SYN **execute**: *The prisoner will be put to death at dawn.* **to death** extremely; very much: *to be bored to death* ◇ *I'm **sick to death** of your endless criticism.* **to the death** until sb is dead: *a fight to the death* ➲ more at CATCH *v.*, CHEAT *v.*, DICE *v.*, DIE *v.*, FATE, FIGHT *v.*, FLOG, GRIM, KISS *n.*, LIFE, MATTER *n.*

death·bed /ˈdeθbed/ *noun* [usually sing.] the bed in which sb is dying or dies: *a **deathbed confession/conversion*** ◇ *He told me the truth **on his deathbed*** (= as he lay dying). ◇ *She **was on her deathbed*** (= going to die very soon). ◇ (*humorous*) *You'd have to be practically on your deathbed before the doctor would come and see you!*

ˈ**death blow** *noun* an event that destroys or puts an end to sth: *They thought the arrival of television would **deal a death blow** to mass cinema audiences.*

ˈ**death certificate** *noun* an official document, signed by a doctor, that states the cause and time of sb's death

ˈ**death duty** *noun* [usually pl.] (*old-fashioned, BrE*) = INHERITANCE TAX

ˈ**death knell** (also **knell**) *noun* [sing.] an event that means that the end or destruction of sth will come soon

death·less /ˈdeθləs/ *adj.* never dying or forgotten SYN **immortal**: (*ironic*) *written in his usual deathless prose* (= very bad)

death·ly /ˈdeθli/ (also *less frequent* **dead·ly**) *adv.* like a dead person; suggesting death: *Her face was deathly pale.* ◇ *The house was deathly still.* ▸ **death·ly** *adj.*: *A **deathly hush** fell over the room as he walked in.*

ˈ**death mask** *noun* a model of the face of a person who has just died, made by pressing a soft substance over their face and removing it when it becomes hard

the ˈ**death penalty** *noun* [sing.] the punishment of being killed that is used in some countries for very serious crimes: *the **abolition/return of the death penalty*** ◇ *The two men are **facing the death penalty**.* ➲ COLLOCATIONS at JUSTICE

ˈ**death rate** *noun* **1** the number of deaths every year for every 1 000 people in the population of a place: *a **high/low death rate*** **2** the number of deaths every year from a particular disease or in a particular group: *Death rates from heart disease have risen considerably in recent years.*

ˈ**death rattle** *noun* [sing.] a sound sometimes heard in the throat of a dying person

ˌ**death** ˈ**row** *noun* [U] the cells in a prison for prisoners who are waiting to be killed as punishment for a serious crime: *prisoners **on death row*** ➲ COLLOCATIONS at JUSTICE

ˈ**death sentence** *noun* the legal punishment of being killed for a serious crime: *to **be given/to receive the death sentence** for murder*

ˈ**death's head** *noun* a human SKULL (= the bone structure of the head) used as a symbol of death

D

D

ˈ**death squad** *noun* a group of people who are ordered by a government to kill other people, especially the government's political opponents

ˈ**death throes** *noun* [pl.] **1** the final stages of sth just before it comes to an end: *The regime is now in its death throes.* **2** violent pains and movements at the moment of death

ˈ**death toll** *noun* the number of people killed in an accident, a war, a disaster, etc.

death·trap /ˈdeθtræp/ *noun* (*informal*) a building, vehicle, etc. that is dangerous and could cause sb's death: *The cars blocking the exits could turn this place into a deathtrap.*

ˈ**death warrant** *noun* an official document stating that sb should receive the punishment of being killed for a crime that they have committed: *The President* ***signed the death warrant.*** ◇ *If you pay the ransom, you may be signing your son's death warrant.* ◇ (*figurative*) *By withdrawing the funding, the government signed the project's death warrant.*

ˌ**death-watch ˈbeetle** *noun* a small insect that eats into old wood, making sounds like a watch TICKING

ˈ**death wish** *noun* [sing.] a desire to die, often that sb is not aware of

deb /deb/ *noun* (*informal*) = DEBUTANTE

de·bacle /deɪˈbɑːkl; dɪˈb-/ *noun* an event or a situation that is a complete failure and causes embarrassment

debar /dɪˈbɑː(r)/ *verb* (-rr-) [usually passive] **~ sb** (**from sth/from doing sth**) (*formal*) to officially prevent sb from doing sth, joining sth, etc: *He was debarred from holding public office.*

de·base /dɪˈbeɪs/ *verb* **~ sb/sth** to make sb/sth less valuable or respected SYN **devalue**: *Sport is being debased by commercial sponsorship.* ▸ **de·base·ment** *noun* [U]

de·bat·able AW /dɪˈbeɪtəbl/ *adj.* not certain because people can have different ideas and opinions about the thing being discussed SYN **arguable**, **questionable**: *a debatable point* ◇ ***It is highly debatable whether*** *conditions have improved for low-income families.*

de·bate 0-π AW /dɪˈbeɪt/ *noun, verb*

▪ ***noun*** [C, U] **~ (on/about/over sth) 1** 0-π a formal discussion of an issue at a public meeting or in a parliament. In a debate two or more speakers express opposing views and then there is often a vote on the issue: *a debate on abortion* ◇ *The minister opened the debate* (= was the first to speak). ◇ *The motion* ***under debate*** (= being discussed) *was put to a vote.* ◇ *After a long debate, Congress approved the proposal.* ➲ SYNONYMS at DISCUSSION ➲ COLLOCATIONS at POLITICS **2** 0-π an argument or discussion expressing different opinions: *a* ***heated/wide-ranging/lively debate*** ◇ *the current debate about tax* ◇ *There had been much debate on the issue of childcare.* ◇ *Whether he deserves what has happened to him is* ***open to debate/a matter for debate*** (= cannot be certain or decided yet). ◇ *The theatre's future is a subject of considerable debate.*

▪ ***verb*** **1** 0-π [T, I] to discuss sth, especially formally, before making a decision or finding a solution SYN **discuss**: **~ (sth)** *Politicians will be debating the bill later this week.* ◇ *The question of the origin of the universe is still* ***hotly debated*** (= strongly argued about) *by scientists.* ◇ **~ whether, what, etc...** *The committee will debate whether to lower the age of club membership to 16.* ➲ SYNONYMS at TALK **2** [I, T] to think carefully about sth before making a decision: **~ (with yourself)** *She debated with herself for a while, and then picked up the phone.* ◇ **~ whether, what, etc...** *We're debating whether or not to go skiing this winter.* ◇ **~ doing sth** *For a moment he debated going after her.* ▸ **de·bat·ing** *noun* [U]: *a debating society at a school*

de·bater /dɪˈbeɪtə(r)/ *noun* a person who is involved in a debate

de·bauched /dɪˈbɔːtʃt/ *adj.* a **debauched** person is immoral in their sexual behaviour, drinks a lot of alcohol, takes drugs, etc. SYN **depraved**, **dissolute**

de·bauch·ery /dɪˈbɔːtʃəri/ *noun* [U] immoral behaviour involving sex, alcohol or drugs

de·ben·ture /dɪˈbentʃə(r)/ *noun* (*BrE, finance*) an official document that is given by a company, showing it has borrowed money from a person and stating the interest payments that it will make to them

de·bili·tate /dɪˈbɪlɪteɪt/ *verb* (*formal*) **1 ~ sb/sth** to make sb's body or mind weaker: *a debilitating disease* **2 ~ sth** to make a country, an organization, etc. weaker: *Prolonged strike action debilitated the industry.*

de·bil·ity /dɪˈbɪləti/ *noun* [U, C] (*pl.* -ies) (*formal*) physical weakness, especially as a result of illness

debit /ˈdebɪt/ *noun, verb*

▪ ***noun*** **1** a written note in a bank account or other financial record of a sum of money owed or spent: *on the debit side of an account* ◇ (*figurative*) *On the debit side* (= a negative result will be that) *the new shopping centre will increase traffic problems.* **2** a sum of money taken from a bank account OPP **credit** *n.* ➲ see also DIRECT DEBIT

▪ ***verb*** **~ sth** when a bank **debits** an account, it takes money from it: *The money will be debited from your account each month.* OPP **credit** ➲ COLLOCATIONS at FINANCE

ˈ**debit card** *noun* a plastic card that can be used to take money directly from your bank account when you pay for sth ➲ compare CREDIT CARD

de·bon·air /ˌdebəˈneə(r); *NAmE* -ˈner/ *adj.* (*old-fashioned*) (usually of men) fashionable and confident

de·brief /ˌdiːˈbriːf/ *verb* **~ sb** (**on sth**) to ask sb questions officially, in order to get information about the task that they have just completed: *He was taken to a US airbase to be debriefed on the mission.* ➲ compare BRIEF ▸ **de·brief·ing** *noun* [U, C]: *a debriefing session*

deb·ris /ˈdebriː; ˈdeɪ-; *NAmE* dəˈbriː/ *noun* [U] **1** pieces of wood, metal, brick, etc. that are left after sth has been destroyed: *Emergency teams are still clearing the debris from the plane crash.* **2** (*formal*) pieces of material that are not wanted and rubbish/garbage that are left somewhere: *Clear away leaves and other garden debris from the pond.*

debt 0-π /det/ *noun*

1 0-π [C] a sum of money that sb owes: *I need to* ***pay off*** *all my* ***debts*** *before I leave the country.* ◇ *an outstanding debt of £300* ◇ *He had* ***run up*** *credit card* ***debts*** *of thousands of dollars.* ➲ COLLOCATIONS at FINANCE **2** 0-π [U] the situation of owing money, especially when you cannot pay: *He died heavily* ***in debt.*** ◇ *The club is £4 million* ***in debt.*** ◇ *We were poor but we never* ***got into debt.*** ◇ *It's hard to stay* ***out of debt*** *when you are a student.* ◇ *a country's foreign debt burden* ➲ see also BAD DEBT **3** [C, usually sing.] the fact that you should feel grateful to sb because they have helped you or been kind to you: *to* ***owe a debt of gratitude to sb*** ◇ *I would like to acknowledge my debt to my teachers.*

IDM **be in sb's ˈdebt** (*formal*) to feel grateful to sb for their help, kindness, etc.

debt·or /ˈdetə(r)/ *noun* a person, a country or an organization that owes money OPP **creditor**

debug /ˌdiːˈbʌɡ/ *verb* (-gg-) **~ sth** (*computing*) to look for and remove the faults in a computer program

de·bug·ger /ˌdiːˈbʌɡə(r)/ *noun* a computer program that helps to find and correct mistakes in other programs

de·bunk /ˌdiːˈbʌŋk/ *verb* **~ sth** to show that an idea, a belief, etc. is false; to show that sth is not as good as people think it is: *His theories have been debunked by recent research.*

debut (also **début**) /ˈdeɪbjuː; ˈdebjuː; *NAmE* deɪˈbjuː/ *noun, verb*

▪ ***noun*** the first public appearance of a performer or sports player: *He will* ***make his debut*** *for the first team this week.* ◇ *the band's debut album*

▪ ***verb*** **1** [I] (of a performer or show) to make a first public appearance: *The ballet will debut next month in New York.* **2** [T] **~ sth** (*especially NAmE, business*) to present a new product or advertising campaign to the market: *They will debut the products at the trade show.*

debu·tante /'debjutɑːnt/ (also *informal* **deb**) *noun* a young, rich or UPPER-CLASS woman who is going to fashionable social events for the first time

deca- /'dekə/ *combining form* (in nouns) ten; having ten: *decathlon* ➲ compare DECI-

dec·ade 🔑 AW /'dekeɪd; dɪ'keɪd/ *noun* a period of ten years, especially a continuous period, such as 1910–1919 or 2000–2009

deca·dence /'dekədəns/ *noun* [U] (*disapproving*) behaviour, attitudes, etc. which show a fall in standards, especially moral ones, and an interest in pleasure and enjoyment rather than more serious things: *the decadence of modern Western society*

deca·dent /'dekədənt/ *adj.* (*disapproving*) having or showing low standards, especially moral ones, and an interest only in pleasure and enjoyment rather than serious things: *the decadent rich* ◇ *a* ***decadent lifestyle/society***

Decaf™ (also **decaff**) (both *BrE*) (*NAmE* **decaf**) /'diːkæf/ *noun* [U, C] (*informal*) decaffeinated coffee: (*BrE*) *Regular coffee or Decaf?* ◇ *I'll have a decaff, please.*

de·caf·fein·ated /ˌdiː'kæfɪneɪtɪd/ *adj.* (of coffee or tea) with most or all of the CAFFEINE removed ▸ **de·caf·fein·ated** *noun* [U, C]

decal /'diːkæl/ *noun* (*NAmE*) = TRANSFER (5)

deca·litre (*US* **deca·liter**, **deka·liter**) /'dekəliːtə(r)/ *noun* a unit for measuring volume, equal to 10 litres

deca·metre (*US* **deca·meter**, **deka·meter**) /'dekəmiːtə(r)/ *noun* a unit for measuring length, equal to 10 metres

de·camp /dɪ'kæmp/ *verb* [I] ~ **(from...)** **(to...)** to leave a place suddenly, often secretly

de·cant /dɪ'kænt/ *verb* ~ **sth** **(into sth)** to pour liquid, especially wine, from one container into another

de·cant·er /dɪ'kæntə(r)/ *noun* a glass bottle, often decorated, that wine and other alcoholic drinks are poured into from an ordinary bottle before serving

de·capi·tate /dɪ'kæpɪteɪt/ *verb* ~ **sb/sth** to cut off sb's head SYN **behead**: *His decapitated body was found floating in a canal.* ▸ **de·capi·ta·tion** /dɪˌkæpɪ'teɪʃn/ *noun* [U, C]

deca·syl·lable /'dekəsɪləbl/ *noun* (*technical*) a line of poetry with ten syllables ▸ **deca·syl·lab·ic** /ˌdekəsɪ'læbɪk/ *adj.*: *a decasyllabic line*

dec·ath·lete /dɪ'kæθliːt/ *noun* a person who competes in a decathlon

dec·ath·lon /dɪ'kæθlən/ *noun* a sporting event in which people compete in ten different sports ➲ compare BIATHLON, HEPTATHLON, PENTATHLON, TETRATHLON, TRIATHLON

decay 🔑 /dɪ'keɪ/ *noun, verb*

■ ***noun*** [U] **1** 🔑 the process or result of being destroyed by natural causes or by not being cared for (= of decaying): *tooth decay* ◇ *The landlord had let the building* ***fall into decay***. ◇ *The smell of death and decay hung over the town.* **2** 🔑 the gradual destruction of a society, an institution, a system, etc: ***economic/moral/urban decay*** ◇ *the decay of the old industries*

■ ***verb*** **1** 🔑 [I, T] ~ **(sth)** to be destroyed gradually by natural processes; to destroy sth in this way SYN **rot**: *decaying leaves/teeth/food* **2** 🔑 [I] if a building or an area **decays**, its condition slowly becomes worse: *decaying inner city areas* **3** [I] to become less powerful and lose influence over people, society, etc: *decaying standards of morality*

de·cease /dɪ'siːs/ *noun* [U] (*law* or *formal*) the death of a person

de·ceased /dɪ'siːst/ *adj.* (*law* or *formal*) **1** dead: *her deceased parents* **2** **the deceased** *noun* (*pl.* **the deceased**) a person who has died, especially recently

de·ceit /dɪ'siːt/ *noun* [U, C] dishonest behaviour that is intended to make sb believe sth that is not true; an example of this behaviour SYN **deception**: *He was accused of lies and deceit.* ◇ *Everyone was involved in this web of deceit.* ◇ *Their marriage was an illusion and a deceit.*

de·ceit·ful /dɪ'siːtfl/ *adj.* (*formal*) behaving in a dishonest way by telling lies and making people believe things that are not true SYN **dishonest** ▸ **de·ceit·ful·ly** /-fəli/ *adv.* **de·ceit·ful·ness** *noun* [U]

de·ceive /dɪ'siːv/ *verb* **1** [T] to make sb believe sth that is not true: ~ **sb** *Her husband had been deceiving her for years.* ◇ ~ **sb into doing sth** *She deceived him into handing over all his savings.* ➲ SYNONYMS at CHEAT **2** [T] ~ **yourself** **(that...)** to refuse to admit to yourself that sth unpleasant is true: *You're deceiving yourself if you think he'll change his mind.* **3** [T, I] ~ **(sb)** to make sb have a wrong idea about sb/sth SYN **mislead**: *Unless my eyes deceive me, that's his wife.* ➲ see also DECEPTIVE ▸ **de·ceiver** *noun* IDM see FLATTER

de·cel·er·ate /ˌdiː'seləreɪt/ *verb* (*formal*) **1** [I, T] ~ **(sth)** to reduce the speed at which a vehicle is travelling **2** [I, T] ~ **(sth)** to become or make sth become slower SYN **slow down**: *Economic growth decelerated sharply in June.* OPP **accelerate** ▸ **de·cel·er·ation** /ˌdiːseləˈreɪʃn/ *noun* [U]

De·cem·ber 🔑 /dɪ'sembə(r)/ *noun* [U, C] (*abbr.* Dec.) the 12th and last month of the year HELP To see how **December** is used, look at the examples at **April**.

de·cency /'diːsnsi/ *noun* **1** [U] honest, polite behaviour that follows accepted moral standards and shows respect for others: *Her behaviour showed a total lack of* ***common decency***. ◇ *Have you no* ***sense of decency***? ◇ *He might* ***have had the decency to*** *apologize.* **2** **the decencies** [pl.] (*formal*) standards of behaviour in society that people think are acceptable: *the basic decencies of civilized society*

de·cent /'diːsnt/ *adj.* **1** of a good enough standard or quality: (*informal*) *a decent meal/job/place to live* ◇ *I need a decent night's sleep.* **2** (of people or behaviour) honest and fair; treating people with respect: *ordinary, decent, hard-working people* ◇ *Everyone said he was a decent sort of guy.* **3** acceptable to people in a particular situation: *a decent burial* ◇ *That dress isn't decent.* ◇ *She ought to have waited for a decent interval before getting married again.* **4** (*informal*) wearing enough clothes to allow sb to see you: *I can't go to the door—I'm not decent.* ➲ compare INDECENT ▸ **de·cent·ly** *adv.*

IDM **to do the decent 'thing** to do what people or society expect, especially in a difficult situation: *He did the decent thing and resigned.*

de·cen·tral·ize (*BrE* also **-ise**) /ˌdiː'sentrəlaɪz/ *verb* [T, I] ~ **(sth)** to give some of the power of a central government, organization, etc. to smaller parts or organizations around the country: *decentralized authority/administration* OPP **centralize** ▸ **de·cen·tral·iza·tion, -isa·tion** /ˌdiːˌsentrəlaɪ'zeɪʃn; *NAmE* -lə'z-/ *noun* [U, sing.]

de·cep·tion /dɪ'sepʃn/ *noun* **1** [U] the act of deliberately making sb believe sth that is not true (= of DECEIVING them) SYN **deceit**: *a drama full of lies and deception* ◇ *He was accused of obtaining property by deception.* **2** [C] a trick intended to make sb believe sth that is not true SYN **deceit**: *The whole episode had been a cruel deception.*

de·cep·tive /dɪ'septɪv/ *adj.* likely to make you believe sth that is not true SYN **misleading**: *a deceptive advertisement* ◇ *Appearances can often be deceptive* (= things are not always what they seem to be). ◇ *the deceptive simplicity of her writing style* (= it seems simple but is not really) ▸ **de·cep·tive·ly** *adv.*: *a deceptively simple idea*

deci- /'desɪ-/ *combining form* (in nouns; often used in units of measurement) one tenth: *decilitre* ➲ compare DECA-

deci·bel /'desɪbel/ *noun* a unit for measuring how loud a sound is

de·cide 🔑 /dɪ'saɪd/ *verb*

1 🔑 [I, T] to think carefully about the different possibilities that are available and choose one of them: *It's up to you to decide.* ◇ ~ **between A and B** *It was difficult to decide between the two candidates.* ◇ ~ **against sth** *They decided against taking legal action.* ◇ ~ **what, whether, etc...** *I can't decide what to wear.* ◇ ~ **(that)...** *She decided (that) she

D

wanted to live in France. ◇ **~ to do sth** *We've decided not to go away after all.* ◇ **~ sth** *We might be hiring more people but nothing has been decided yet.* ◇ **it is decided (that)...** *It was decided (that) the school should purchase new software.*

WORD FAMILY
decide *verb*
decision *noun* (≠ indecision)
decisive *adj.* (≠ indecisive)
undecided *adj.*

D

➲ SYNONYMS at CHOOSE **2** [T, I] (*law*) to make an official or legal judgement: **~ sth** *The case will be decided by a jury.* ◇ **~ for/in favour of sb** | **~ in sb's favour** *The Appeal Court decided in their favour.* ◇ **~ against sb** *It is always possible that the judge may decide against you.* **3** [T, I] to affect the result of sth: **~ (sth)** *A mixture of skill and good luck decided the outcome of the game.* ◇ **~ if, whether, etc...** *A number of factors decide whether a movie will be successful or not.* **4** [T] to be the reason why sb does sth: *For most customers, price is **the deciding factor**.* ◇ **~ sb (to do sth)** *They offered me free accommodation for a year, and that decided me.*

PHR V **de'cide on/upon sth** 🔑 to choose sth from a number of possibilities: *We're still trying to decide on a venue.*

de·cided /dɪˈsaɪdɪd/ *adj.* **1** [only before noun] obvious and definite: *His height was a decided advantage in the job.* **2** (*especially BrE*) having very strong opinions: *She was a very decided young woman, eager to do some good in the world.* ◇ *The child is very decided about what she wants and doesn't want.* ➲ compare UNDECIDED

de·cided·ly /dɪˈsaɪdɪdli/ *adv.* **1** (used with an adjective or adverb) definitely and in an obvious way: *Amy was looking decidedly worried.* **2** (*BrE*) in a way that shows that you are sure and determined about sth: *'I won't go,' she said decidedly.*

de·cider /dɪˈsaɪdə(r)/ *noun* [usually sing.] the game, race, etc. that will decide who the winner is in a competition

de·cidu·ous /dɪˈsɪdʒuəs; -dju-/ *adj.* (of a tree, bush etc.) that loses its leaves every year ➲ compare EVERGREEN ➲ VISUAL VOCAB page V8

decile /ˈdesaɪl; *NAmE* also ˈdesl/ *noun* (*statistics*) one of ten equal groups into which a collection of things or people can be divided according to the DISTRIBUTION of a particular VARIABLE: *families in the top decile of income* (= the 10% of families with the highest income)

deci·litre (*especially US* **deci·liter**) /ˈdesɪliːtə(r)/ *noun* a unit for measuring liquids. There are 10 decilitres in a litre.

deci·mal /ˈdesɪml/ *adj., noun*

▪ ***adj.*** based on or counted in tens or tenths: *the decimal system*

▪ ***noun*** (also ˌ**decimal** ˈ**fraction**) a FRACTION (= a number less than one) that is shown as a dot or point followed by the number of tenths, HUNDREDTHS, etc: *The decimal 0.61 stands for 61 hundredths.* ➲ compare VULGAR FRACTION

deci·mal·ize (*BrE* also **-ise**) /ˈdesɪməlaɪz/ *verb* **1 ~ sth** to change a system of coins or weights and measurements to a decimal system **2 ~ sth** to express an amount using the decimal system instead of the system it is already expressed in: *The question asks you to decimalize the fraction 7/8.* ▸ **deci·mal·iza·tion, -isa·tion** /ˌdesɪməlaɪˈzeɪʃn; *NAmE* -ləˈz-/ *noun* [U]

ˌ**decimal** ˈ**place** *noun* the position of a number after a decimal point: *The figure is **accurate to two decimal places**.*

ˌ**decimal** ˈ**point** *noun* a dot or point used to separate the whole number from the tenths, HUNDREDTHS, etc. of a decimal, for example in 0.61

deci·mate /ˈdesɪmeɪt/ *verb* **1** [usually passive] **~ sth** to kill large numbers of animals, plants or people in a particular area: *The rabbit population was decimated by the disease.* **2 ~ sth** (*informal*) to severely damage sth or make sth weaker: *Cheap imports decimated the British cycle industry.* ▸ **deci·ma·tion** /ˌdesɪˈmeɪʃn/ *noun* [U]

deci·metre (*especially US* **deci·meter**) /ˈdesɪmiːtə(r)/ *noun* a unit for measuring length. There are 10 decimetres in a metre.

de·cipher /dɪˈsaɪfə(r)/ *verb* **~ sth** to succeed in finding the meaning of sth that is difficult to read or understand: *to decipher a code* ◇ *Can anyone decipher his handwriting?* ➲ see also INDECIPHERABLE

de·ci·sion 🔑 /dɪˈsɪʒn/ *noun*
1 🔑 [C] **~ (on/about sth)** | **~ (to do sth)** a choice or judgement that you make after thinking and talking about what is the best thing to do: *to **make a decision*** (= to decide) ◇ (*BrE*) *to **take a decision*** (= to decide) ◇ *We need a decision on this by next week.* ◇ *Who **took the decision** to go ahead with the project?* ◇ *He is really bad at **making decisions**.* ◇ *We finally **reached a decision*** (= decided after some difficulty). ◇ *We must **come to a decision** about what to do next by tomorrow.* ◇ *a big* (= an important) *decision* ◇ *The final decision is yours.* ◇ *It's a difficult decision for any doctor.* ◇ *The editor's decision is final.* ◇ *Mary is the decision-maker in the house.* **2** (also **de·cisive·ness**) [U] the ability to decide sth clearly and quickly: *This is not a job for someone who lacks decision.* **OPP** **indecision** **3** [U] the process of deciding sth: *The moment of decision had arrived.*

de'cision-making *noun* [U] the process of deciding about sth important, especially in a group of people or in an organization ▸ **de'cision-maker** *noun*

de·cisive /dɪˈsaɪsɪv/ *adj.* **1** very important for the final result of a particular situation: *a **decisive factor/victory/battle*** ◇ *She has **played a decisive role** in the peace negotiations.* ◇ *a **decisive step*** (= an important action that will change a situation) *towards a cleaner environment* ➲ SYNONYMS at ESSENTIAL **2** able to decide sth quickly and with confidence: *decisive management* ◇ *The government must take **decisive action** on gun control.* **OPP** **indecisive** ▸ **de·cisive·ly** *adv.*

de·cisive·ness /dɪˈsaɪsɪvnəs/ *noun* [U] = DECISION (2)

deck /dek/ *noun, verb*

▪ ***noun*** **1** the top outside floor of a ship or boat: *I was the only person **on deck** at that time of night.* ◇ *As the storm began, everyone disappeared **below deck(s)**.* **2** one of the floors of a ship or a bus: *the **upper/lower/main deck** of a ship* ◇ *We sat on the top deck of the bus.* ◇ *My cabin is on deck C.* ➲ see also DOUBLE-DECKER, FLIGHT DECK, SINGLE-DECKER **3** (also ˌ**deck of** ˈ**cards**) (both *especially NAmE*) (*BrE* also **pack**) a complete set of 52 PLAYING CARDS ➲ VISUAL VOCAB page V32 **4** a wooden floor that is built outside the back of a house where you can sit and relax ➲ VISUAL VOCAB page V16 **5** a part of a SOUND SYSTEM that records and/or plays sounds on a disc or tape: *a **cassette/tape deck*** **IDM** see CLEAR *v.*, HAND *n.*, HIT *v.*

▪ ***verb*** **1** [often passive] **~ sb/sth (out) (in/with sth)** to decorate sb/sth with sth: *The room was decked out in flowers and balloons.* **2 ~ sb** (*informal*) to hit sb very hard so that they fall to the ground

deck·chair /ˈdektʃeə(r); *NAmE* -tʃer/ *noun* a folding chair with a seat made from a long strip of material on a wooden or metal frame, used for example on a beach ➲ VISUAL VOCAB page V16

deck·hand /ˈdekhænd/ *noun* a worker on a ship who does work that is not skilled

deck·ing /ˈdekɪŋ/ *noun* [U] wood used to build a floor (called a DECK) in the garden/yard next to or near a house

ˈ**deck shoe** *noun* a flat shoe made of strong cloth or soft leather, with a soft SOLE which does not slip

de·claim /dɪˈkleɪm/ *verb* [T, I] **~ (against) sth** | **~ that...** | **+ speech** (*formal*) to say sth loudly; to speak loudly and with force about sth you feel strongly about, especially in public: *She declaimed the famous opening speech of the play.* ◇ *He declaimed against the evils of alcohol.*

dec·lam·ation /ˌdekləˈmeɪʃn/ *noun* (*formal*) **1** [U] the act of speaking or of expressing sth to an audience in a formal way **2** [C] a speech or piece of writing that strongly expresses feelings and opinions

de·clama·tory /dɪˈklæmətəri; *NAmE* -tɔːri/ *adj.* (*formal*) expressing feelings or opinions in a strong way in a speech or a piece of writing

dec·lar·ation /ˌdekləˈreɪʃn/ *noun* **1** [C, U] an official or formal statement, especially about the plans of a government or an organization; the act of making such a statement: *to* ***issue/sign a declaration*** ◇ *the declaration of war* ◇ *the Declaration of Independence* (= of the United States) **2** [C] a written or spoken statement, especially about what people feel or believe: *a* ***declaration of love/faith/guilt*** ➲ SYNONYMS at STATEMENT **3** [C] an official written statement giving information: *a declaration of income* ◇ *customs declarations* (= giving details of goods that have been brought into a country)

the Decla,ration of Inde'pendence *noun* [sing.] the document which stated that the thirteen British COLONIES in America were independent of Britain. It was adopted on July 4, 1776.

de·clara·tive /dɪˈklærətɪv/ *adj.* (*grammar*) (of a sentence) in the form of a simple statement

Synonyms

declare

state • indicate • announce

These words all mean to say sth, usually firmly and clearly and often in public.

declare (*rather formal*) to say sth officially or publicly; to state sth firmly and clearly: *to declare war* ◇ *The painting was declared to be a forgery.*

state (*rather formal*) to formally write or say sth, especially in a careful and clear way: *He has already stated his intention to run for election.*

indicate (*rather formal*) to state sth, sometimes in a way that is slightly indirect: *During our meeting, he indicated his willingness to cooperate.*

announce to tell people officially about a decision or plans; to give information about sth in a public place, especially through a loudspeaker; to say sth in a loud and/or serious way: *They haven't formally announced their engagement yet.* ◇ *Has our flight been announced yet?*

DECLARE OR ANNOUNCE?

Declare is used more often for giving judgements; **announce** is used more often for giving facts: ~~*The painting was announced to be a forgery.*~~ ◇ ~~*They haven't formally declared their engagement yet.*~~

PATTERNS

- to declare/state/indicate/announce **that...**
- to declare/state sb/sth **to be** sth
- to declare/state/indicate/announce **your intention** to do sth
- to declare/state/announce sth **formally/publicly/officially**
- to declare/state/announce sth **firmly/confidently**

de·clare 🔑 /dɪˈkleə(r); *NAmE* dɪˈkler/ *verb* **1** 🔑 [T] to say sth officially or publicly: **~ sth** *The government has declared a state of emergency.* ◇ *Germany* ***declared war on*** *France on 1 August 1914.* ◇ *The government has* ***declared war on*** (= officially stated its intention to stop) *illiteracy.* ◇ **~ that...** *The court declared that strike action was illegal.* ◇ **~ sth + noun** *The area has been declared a national park.* ◇ **~ sth to be sth** *The painting was declared to be a forgery.* ◇ **~ sth + adj.** *The contract was declared void.* ◇ *I declare this bridge open.* **2** 🔑 [T] to state sth firmly and clearly: **+ speech** *'I'll do it!' Tom declared.* ◇ **~ that...** *He declared that he was in love with her.* ◇ **~ sth** *Few people dared to declare their opposition to the regime.* ◇ **~ yourself + adj./noun** *She declared herself extremely hurt by his lack of support.* **3** 🔑 [T] **~ sth** to tell the tax authorities how much money you have earned: *All income must be declared.* **4** 🔑 [T] **~ sth** to tell customs officers (= at the border of a country) that you are carrying goods on which you should pay tax: *Do you have anything to declare?* **5** [I] (in CRICKET) to decide to end your INNINGS (= the period during which your team is BATTING) before all your players have BATTED

PHR V **de,clare a'gainst sb/sth** (*BrE, formal*) to say publicly that you do not support sb/sth **de'clare for sb/sth** (*BrE, formal*) to say publicly that you support sb/sth

de·clared /dɪˈkleəd; *NAmE* -ˈklerd/ *adj.* [only before noun] stated in an open way so that people know about it SYN **professed**: *the government's declared intention to reduce crime*

de·clas·sify /ˌdiːˈklæsɪfaɪ/ *verb* (**de·clas·si·fies, de·clas·si·fy·ing, de·clas·si·fied, de·clas·si·fied**) **~ sth** to state officially that secret government information is no longer secret: *declassified* ***information/documents*** OPP **classify** ▸ **de·clas·si·fi·ca·tion** /ˌdiːˌklæsɪfɪˈkeɪʃn/ *noun* [U]

de·clen·sion /dɪˈklenʃn/ *noun* (*grammar*) **1** [C] a set of nouns, adjectives or pronouns that change in the same way to show CASE, number and GENDER **2** [U] the way in which some sets of nouns, adjectives and pronouns change their form or endings to show CASE, number or GENDER

de·cline 🔑 AW /dɪˈklaɪn/ *noun, verb*

■ ***noun*** 🔑 [C, usually sing., U] **~ (in sth)** | **~ (of sth)** a continuous decrease in the number, value, quality, etc. of sth: *a* ***rapid/sharp/gradual decline*** ◇ ***urban/economic decline*** ◇ *The company reported a small decline in its profits.* ◇ *An increase in cars has resulted in the decline of public transport.* ◇ *The town* ***fell into*** *(****a****)* ***decline*** (= started to be less busy, important, etc.) *after the mine closed.* ◇ *Industry in Britain has been* ***in decline*** *since the 1970s.*

■ ***verb*** **1** 🔑 [I] (rather *formal*) to become smaller, fewer, weaker, etc: *Support for the party continues to decline.* ◇ *The number of tourists to the resort declined by 10% last year.* ◇ *Her health was declining rapidly.* **2** [I, T] (*formal*) to refuse politely to accept or to do sth SYN **refuse**: *I offered to give them a lift but they declined.* ◇ **~ sth** *to* ***decline an offer/invitation*** ◇ **~ to do sth** *Their spokesman declined to comment on the allegations.* **3** [I, T] **~ (sth)** (*grammar*) if a noun, an adjective or a pronoun **declines**, it has different forms according to whether it is the subject or the object of a verb, whether it is in the singular or plural, etc. When you **decline** a noun, etc, you list these forms. ➲ compare CONJUGATE

IDM **sb's declining 'years** (*literary*) the last years of sb's life

declutter (also **de-clutter**) /diːˈklʌtə(r)/ *verb* [I, T] to remove things that you do not use so that you have more space and can easily find things when you need them: *Moving is a good opportunity to declutter.* ◇ **~ sth** *a 7-step plan to help you declutter your home*

de·code /ˌdiːˈkəʊd; *NAmE* -ˈkoʊd/ *verb* **1** **~ sth** to find the meaning of sth, especially sth that has been written in code SYN **decipher** **2** **~ sth** to receive an electronic signal and change it into pictures that can be shown on a television screen: *decoding equipment* **3** **~ sth** (*linguistics*) to understand the meaning of sth in a foreign language ➲ compare ENCODE

de·coder /ˌdiːˈkəʊdə(r); *NAmE* -ˈkoʊ-/ *noun* a device that changes an electronic signal into a form that people can understand, such as sound and pictures: *a* ***satellite/video decoder***

dé·col·le·tage /ˌdeɪkɒlˈtɑːʒ; *NAmE* -kɑːləˈt-/ (also **dé·col·leté** /deɪˈkɒlteɪ; *NAmE* ˌdeɪkɑːlˈteɪ/) *noun* (from *French*) the top edge of a woman's dress, etc. that is designed to be very low in order to show her shoulders and the top part of her breasts ▸ **dé·col·leté** *adj.*

de·col·on·iza·tion (*BrE* also **-isa·tion**) /diːˌkɒlənaɪˈzeɪʃn; *NAmE* -ˌkɑːlənəˈz-/ *noun* [U] the process of a COLONY or COLONIES becoming independent

de·com·mis·sion /ˌdiːkəˈmɪʃn/ *verb* **~ sth** to officially stop using weapons, a nuclear power station, etc.

de·com·pose /ˌdiːkəmˈpəʊz; *NAmE* -ˈpoʊz/ *verb* **1** [I, T] to be destroyed gradually by natural chemical processes SYN **decay, rot**: *a decomposing corpse* ◇ *As the waste materials decompose, they produce methane gas.* ◇ **~ sth** *a decomposed body* **2** [T, I] **~ (sth) (into sth)** (*technical*) to divide sth into smaller parts; to divide into smaller parts ▸ **de·com·pos·ition** /ˌdiːkɒmpəˈzɪʃn; *NAmE* -kɑːm-/ *noun* [U]: *the decomposition of organic waste*

de·com·press /ˌdiːkəmˈpres/ *verb* **1** [I, T] **~ (sth)** to have the air pressure in sth reduced to a normal level or to reduce it to its normal level **2** [T] **~ sth** (*computing*) to return files, etc. to their original size after they have been COMPRESSED OPP **compress**

D

de·com·pres·sion /ˌdiːkəmˈpreʃn/ *noun* [U] **1** a reduction in air pressure; the act of reducing the pressure of the air: *a* ***decompression chamber*** (= a piece of equipment that DIVERS sit in so that they can return slowly to normal air pressure after being deep in the sea) ◇ ***decompression sickness*** (= severe pain and difficulty in breathing experienced by DIVERS who come back to the surface of deep water too quickly) ➲ see also BENDS **2** (*technical*) the act or process of allowing sth that has been compressed (= made smaller) to fill the space that it originally took up

de·com·pres·sor /ˌdiːkəmˈpresə(r)/ *noun* (*BrE*) **1** (*technical*) a device for reducing pressure in a vehicle's engine **2** (*computing*) a computer program which returns files, etc. to their original size after they have been COMPRESSED

de·con·gest·ant /ˌdiːkənˈdʒestənt/ *noun* a medicine that helps sb with a cold to breathe more easily: *a nasal decongestant*

de·con·se·crate /ˌdiːˈkɒnsɪkreɪt; *NAmE* -ˈkɑːn-/ *verb* **~ sth** (*religion*) to stop using sth, especially a building, for a religious purpose: *a deconsecrated church* ▸ **de·con·se·cra·tion** *noun* [U]

de·con·struct /ˌdiːkənˈstrʌkt/ *verb* **~ sth** (*technical*) (in literature and philosophy) to analyse a text in order to show that there is no fixed meaning within the text but that the meaning is created each time in the act of reading

de·con·struc·tion /ˌdiːkənˈstrʌkʃn/ *noun* [U] (*technical*) (in literature and philosophy) a theory that states that it is impossible for a text to have one fixed meaning, and emphasizes the role of the reader in the production of meaning ➲ compare STRUCTURALISM ▸ **de·con·struc·tion·ist** *noun, adj.*: *a deconstructionist critic/approach*

de·con·tam·in·ate /ˌdiːkənˈtæmɪneɪt/ *verb* **~ sth** to remove harmful substances from a place or thing: *the process of decontaminating areas exposed to radioactivity* ▸ **de·con·tam·in·ation** /ˌdiːkənˌtæmɪˈneɪʃn/ *noun* [U]

de·con·trol /ˌdiːkənˈtrəʊl; *NAmE* -ˈtroʊl/ *verb* (-ll-) **~ sth** (*formal, especially NAmE*) if a government **decontrols** sth, it removes legal controls from it SYN **deregulate** ▸ **de·con·trol** *noun* [U]

decor /ˈdeɪkɔː(r); *NAmE* deɪˈkɔːr/ *noun* [U, C, usually sing.] the style in which the inside of a building is decorated: *interior decor* ◇ *the restaurant's elegant new decor*

dec·or·ate 0‑w /ˈdekəreɪt/ *verb*
1 0‑w [T] **~ sth (with sth)** to make sth look more attractive by putting things on it: *They decorated the room with flowers and balloons.* ◇ *The cake was decorated to look like a car.* **2** 0‑w [I, T] (*especially BrE*) to put paint, WALLPAPER, etc. on the walls and ceilings of a room or house: *I hate decorating.* ◇ *He has his own painting and decorating business.* ◇ **~ sth** *We need to decorate the sitting room.* ◇ *The sitting room needs decorating.* **3** 0‑w [T] **~ sth** to be placed on sth in order to make it look more attractive SYN **adorn**: *Photographs of actors decorated the walls of the restaurant.* **4** [T, usually passive] **~ sb (for sth)** to give sb a MEDAL as a sign of respect for sth they have done

dec·or·ation 0‑w /ˌdekəˈreɪʃn/ *noun*
1 0‑w [C, usually pl.] a thing that makes sth look more attractive on special occasions: *Christmas decorations* ◇ *a table decoration* **2** 0‑w [U, C] a pattern, etc. that is added to sth and that stops it from being plain: *the elaborate decoration on the carved wooden door* **3** 0‑w [U] the style in which sth is decorated: *a Chinese theme in the interior decoration* **4** [U] (*BrE*) the act or process of decorating sth such as the inside of a house by painting it, etc. **5** [C] a MEDAL that is given to sb as an honour

Collocations

Decorating and home improvement

Houses
- **refurbish/renovate/**(*BrE*) **do up** a building/a house
- **convert** a building/house/room into homes/offices/ (*especially NAmE*) apartments/(*BrE*) flats
- **extend/enlarge** a house/building/room/kitchen
- **build** (*BrE*) an extension (to the back/rear of a house)/ (*NAmE*) an addition (on/to sth)/(*BrE*) a conservatory
- **knock down/demolish** a house/home/building/wall
- **knock out/through** the wall separating two rooms

Decoration
- **furnish/paint/**(*especially BrE*) **decorate** a home/house/ apartment/flat/room
- **be decorated** in bright colours/(*especially US*) colors/in a traditional style/with flowers/with paintings
- **paint/plaster** the walls/ceiling
- **hang/put up/strip off/remove** the wallpaper
- **install/replace/remove** the bathroom fixtures/(*BrE*) fittings
- **build/put up** shelves
- **lay** wooden flooring/timber decking/floor tiles/a carpet/a patio
- **put up/hang/take down** a picture/painting/poster/ curtain

DIY/home improvement
- **do** (*BrE*) DIY/carpentry/the plumbing/the wiring
- **make** home improvements
- **add/install** central heating/underfloor heating/ insulation
- **fit/install** double-glazing/a smoke alarm
- **insulate** your house/your home/the walls/the pipes/ the tanks/(*especially BrE*) the loft
- **fix/repair** a roof/a leak/a pipe/the plumbing/a leaking (*especially BrE*) tap/(*NAmE usually*) faucet
- **block/clog (up)/unblock/unclog** a pipe/sink
- **make/drill/fill** a hole
- **hammer (in)/pull out/remove** a nail
- **tighten/untighten/loosen/remove** a screw
- **saw/cut/treat/stain/varnish/paint** wood

dec·ora·tive 0‑w /ˈdekərətɪv; *NAmE* ˈdekəreɪtɪv/ *adj.* (of an object or a building) decorated in a way that makes it attractive; intended to look attractive or pretty: *The mirror is functional yet decorative.* ◇ *purely decorative arches*

ˌdecorative ˈarts *noun* [pl.] artistic activities which produce objects which are useful and beautiful at the same time

dec·or·ator /ˈdekəreɪtə(r)/ *noun* a person whose job is painting and decorating houses

dec·or·ous /ˈdekərəs/ *adj.* (*formal*) polite and appropriate in a particular social situation; not shocking SYN **proper**: *a decorous kiss* ▸ **dec·or·ous·ly** *adv.*

de·corum /dɪˈkɔːrəm/ *noun* [U] (*formal*) polite behaviour that is appropriate in a social situation SYN **propriety**

dé·coup·age /ˌdeɪkuːˈpɑːʒ/ *noun* [U] (*art*) the art of decorating furniture or other objects by cutting out pictures or designs on paper and sticking them onto the surface

de·couple /diːˈkʌpl/ *verb* **~ sth (from sth)** (*formal*) to end the connection or relationship between two things

decoy /ˈdiːkɔɪ/ *noun* [C] **1** an animal or a bird, or a model of one, that attracts other animals or birds, especially so that they can be shot by people who are hunting them **2** a thing or a person that is used to trick sb into doing what you want them to do, going where you want them to go, etc. ▸ **decoy** /dɪˈkɔɪ/ *verb* **~ sth**

de·crease 0-π *verb, noun*

■ ***verb*** 0-π /dɪˈkriːs/ [I, T] (rather *formal*) to become or make sth become smaller in size, number, etc: **~ (from sth) (to sth)** *The number of new students decreased from 210 to 160 this year.* ◇ *a decreasing population* ◇ **~ by sth** *The price of wheat has decreased by 5%.* ◇ **~ in sth** *This species of bird is decreasing in numbers every year.* ◇ **~ sth** *People should decrease the amount of fat they eat.* OPP **increase**

■ ***noun*** 0-π /ˈdiːkriːs/ [C, U] the process of reducing sth or the amount that sth is reduced by SYN **reduction**: **~ (in sth)** *There has been some decrease in military spending this year.* ◇ **~ (of sth)** *a decrease of nearly 6% in the number of visitors to the museum* OPP **increase**

de·cree /dɪˈkriː/ *noun, verb*

■ ***noun*** **1** [C, U] an official order from a ruler or a government that becomes the law: *to* ***issue/sign a decree*** ◇ *a leader who rules* ***by decree*** (= not in a DEMOCRATIC way) **2** [C] a decision that is made in court

■ ***verb*** (**de·cree·ing**, **de·creed**, **de·creed**) [T, I] to decide, judge or order sth officially: **~ (sth)** *The government decreed a state of emergency.* ◇ **~ what, how, etc...** *We cannot decree what the committee should do.* ◇ **it is decreed that...** *It was decreed that the following day would be a holiday.*

deˌcree ˈabsolute *noun* [sing.] (*BrE, law*) an order from a court that finally ends a marriage, making the two people divorced: *The period between the decree nisi and the decree absolute was six weeks.*

decree nisi /dɪˌkriː ˈnaɪsaɪ/ *noun* [sing.] (*BrE, law*) an order from a court that a marriage will end after a fixed amount of time unless there is a good reason why it should not

de·crepit /dɪˈkrepɪt/ *adj.* (of a thing or person) very old and not in good condition or health

de·crepi·tude /dɪˈkrepɪtjuːd; *NAmE* -tuːd/ *noun* [U] (*formal*) the state of being old and in poor condition or health

de·crim·in·al·ize (*BrE* also **-ise**) /diːˈkrɪmɪnəlaɪz/ *verb* **~ sth** to change the law so that sth is no longer illegal: *There are moves to decriminalize some soft drugs.* OPP **criminalize** ▸ **de·crim·in·al·iza·tion**, **-isa·tion** /diːˌkrɪmɪnəlaɪˈzeɪʃn; *NAmE* -ləˈz-/ *noun* [U]

decry /dɪˈkraɪ/ *verb* (**de·cries**, **de·cry·ing**, **de·cried**, **de·cried**) **~ sb/sth (as sth)** (*formal*) to strongly criticize sb/sth, especially publicly SYN **condemn**: *The measures were decried as useless.*

de·crypt /diːˈkrɪpt/ *verb* **~ sth** (*computing*) to change information that is in code into ordinary language so that it can be understood by anyone OPP **encrypt** ▸ **de·cryp·tion** /diːˈkrɪpʃn/ *noun* [U] OPP **encryption**

dedi·cate /ˈdedɪkeɪt/ *verb* **1** to give a lot of your time and effort to a particular activity or purpose because you think it is important SYN **devote**: **~ yourself/sth to sth** *She dedicates herself to her work.* ◇ **~ yourself/sth to doing sth** *He dedicated his life to helping the poor.* **2** **~ sth to sb** to say at the beginning of a book, a piece of music or a performance that you are doing it for sb, as a way of thanking them or showing respect: *This book is dedicated to my parents.* **3** to hold an official ceremony to say that a building or an object has a special purpose or is special to the memory of a particular person: **~ sth** *The chapel was dedicated in 1880.* ◇ **~ sth to sb/sth** *A memorial stone was dedicated to those who were killed in the war.*

dedi·cated /ˈdedɪkeɪtɪd/ *adj.* **1** working hard at sth because it is very important to you SYN **committed**: *a dedicated teacher* ◇ **~ to sth** *She is dedicated to her job.* **2** [only before noun] designed to do only one particular type of work; used for one particular purpose only: *Software is exported through a dedicated satellite link.*

ded·ica·tion /ˌdedɪˈkeɪʃn/ *noun* **1** [U] **~ (to sth)** (*approving*) the hard work and effort that sb puts into an activity or purpose because they think it is important SYN **commitment**: *hard work and dedication* **2** [C] a ceremony that is held to show that a building or an object has a special purpose or is special to the memory of a particular person **3** [C] the words that are used at the beginning of a book, piece of music, a performance, etc. to offer it to sb as a sign of thanks or respect

de·duce AW /dɪˈdjuːs; *NAmE* dɪˈduːs/ *verb* (*formal*) to form an opinion about sth based on the information or evidence that is available SYN **infer**: **~ sth (from sth)** *We can deduce a lot from what people choose to buy.* ◇ **~ (from sth) that, what, how, etc...** *Can we deduce from your silence that you do not approve?* ➲ see also DEDUCTION ▸ **de·du·cible** /dɪˈdjuːsəbl; *NAmE* -ˈduːs-/ *adj.*

de·duct /dɪˈdʌkt/ *verb* [often passive] to take away money, points, etc. from a total amount SYN **subtract**: **~ sth** *Ten points will be deducted for a wrong answer.* ◇ **~ sth from sth** *The cost of your uniform will be deducted from your wages.*

de·duct·ible /dɪˈdʌktəbl/ *adj., noun*

■ ***adj.*** that can be taken away from an amount of money you earn, from tax, etc: *These costs are deductible from profits.* ◇ *tax-deductible expenses* (= that you do not have to pay tax on)

■ ***noun*** (*NAmE*) (*BrE* **ex·cess**) the part of an insurance claim that a person has to pay while the insurance company pays the rest: *a policy with a very high deductible*

de·duc·tion AW /dɪˈdʌkʃn/ *noun* **1** [U, C] the process of using information you have in order to understand a particular situation or to find the answer to a problem: *He arrived at the solution by a simple process of deduction.* ◇ *If my deductions are correct, I can tell you who the killer was.* ➲ compare INDUCTION (3) ➲ see also DEDUCE **2** [U, C] the process of taking an amount of sth, especially money, away from a total; the amount that is taken away: *deductions from your pay for tax, etc.* ◇ *tax deductions*

de·duct·ive /dɪˈdʌktɪv/ *adj.* [usually before noun] using knowledge about things that are generally true in order to think about and understand particular situations or problems: ***deductive logic/reasoning*** ➲ compare INDUCTIVE

deed /diːd/ *noun* **1** (*formal, literary*) a thing that sb does that is usually very good or very bad SYN **act**: *a* ***brave/charitable/evil/good deed*** ◇ *a tale of heroic deeds* **2** (often plural in BrE) a legal document that you sign, especially one that proves that you own a house or a building: *the deeds of the house* ➲ COLLOCATIONS at HOUSE ➲ see also TITLE DEED

IDM ▸ **your good deed for the ˈday** a helpful, kind thing that you do

ˌdeed of ˈcovenant *noun* (*BrE*) an agreement to pay a regular amount of money to sb/sth, especially a charity, that means that they also receive the tax that would have to be paid on this money: *Signing a deed of covenant makes £1 worth £1.33.*

ˈdeed poll *noun* [U, sing.] (*BrE*) a legal document signed by only one person, especially in order to change their name: *Smith changed his name* ***by deed poll*** *to Jervis-Smith.*

dee·jay /ˈdiːdʒeɪ/ *noun, verb*

■ ***noun*** (*informal*) = DISC JOCKEY

■ ***verb*** [I] to perform as a DISC JOCKEY, especially in a club

deem /diːm/ *verb* **~ sth + noun/adj.** | **~ sth to be sth** | **~ (that)...** (*formal*) (not usually used in the progressive tenses) to have a particular opinion about sth SYN **consider**: *The evening was deemed a great success.* ◇ *She* ***deemed it*** *prudent not to say anything.* ◇ *They would take any action* ***deemed necessary***.

deep 0-π /diːp/ *adj., adv., noun*

> **WORD FAMILY**
> **deep** *adj., adv.*
> **deeply** *adv.*
> **deepen** *verb*
> **depth** *noun*

■ ***adj.*** (**deep·er**, **deep·est**)

▸ TOP TO BOTTOM **1** 0-π having a large distance from the top or surface to the bottom: *a deep hole/well/river* ◇ *deep water/snow* OPP **shallow**

▸ FRONT TO BACK **2** 0-π having a large distance from the front edge to the furthest point inside: *a deep cut/wound* ◇ *a deep space* OPP **shallow**

▸ MEASUREMENT **3** 0-π used to describe or ask about the depth of sth: *The water is only a few inches deep.* ◇ *How deep is the wound?*

D

▸ -DEEP **4** (in adjectives) as far up or down as the point mentioned: *The water was only waist-deep so I walked ashore.* **5** (in adjectives) in the number of rows mentioned, one behind the other: *They were standing three-deep at the bar.*
▸ BREATH/SIGH **6** [usually before noun] taking in or giving out a lot of air: *She took a deep breath.* ◇ *He gave a deep sigh.*
▸ SOUNDS **7** low: *I heard his deep warm voice filling the room.* ◇ *a **deep roar/groan***
▸ COLOURS **8** strong and dark: *a rich deep red* OPP **pale**
▸ SLEEP **9** a person in a **deep** sleep is difficult to wake: *to be in a **deep sleep/trance/coma*** OPP **light**
▸ SERIOUS **10** extreme or serious: *He's **in deep trouble**.* ◇ *a deep economic recession* ◇ *The affair had exposed deep divisions within the party.* ◇ *a place of great power and of deep significance*
▸ EMOTIONS **11** strongly felt SYN **sincere**: *deep respect* ◇ *a deep sense of loss*
▸ KNOWLEDGE **12** showing great knowledge or understanding: *a deep understanding*
▸ DIFFICULT TO UNDERSTAND **13** difficult to understand SYN **profound**: *This discussion's getting too deep for me.* ◇ *He pondered, as if over some deep philosophical point.*
▸ INVOLVED **14** **~ in sth** fully involved in an activity or a state: *to be **deep in thought/conversation*** ◇ *He is often so deep in his books that he forgets to eat.* ◇ *The firm ended up **deep in debt**.*
▸ PERSON **15** if a person is **deep**, they hide their real feelings and opinions: *She's always been a deep one, trusting no one.*
▸ IN SPORT **16** to or from a position far down or across the field: *a deep ball from Beckham* ➲ see also DEPTH

IDM **go off the 'deep end** (*informal*) to suddenly become very angry or emotional **in deep 'water(s)** (*informal*) in trouble or difficulty **jump/be thrown in at the 'deep end** (*informal*) to start or be made to start a new and difficult activity that you are not prepared for: *Junior hospital doctors are thrown in at the deep end in their first jobs.* ➲ more at DEVIL, SHIT *n.*

■ ***adv.*** (**deep·er, deep·est**) **~ (below, into, under, etc.)** a long way below the surface of sth or a long way inside or into sth: *Dig deeper!* ◇ *The miners were trapped deep underground.* ◇ *whales that feed deep beneath the waves* ◇ *He gazed deep into her eyes.* ◇ *They sat and talked **deep into the night*** (= until very late). ◇ *deep in the forest* ◇ *He stood with his hands deep in his pockets.*

IDM **deep 'down 1** if you know sth **deep down**, you know your true feelings about sth, although you may not admit them to yourself: *Deep down I still loved him.* **2** if sth is true **deep down**, it is really like that, although it may not be obvious to people: *He seems confident but deep down he's quite insecure.* **go/run 'deep** (of emotions, beliefs, etc.) to be felt in a strong way, especially for a long time: *Dignity and pride run deep in this community.* ➲ more at DIG *v.*, STILL

■ ***noun*** [sing.] **the deep** (*literary*) the sea

Which Word?

deep / deeply

- The adverbs **deep** and **deeply** can both mean 'a long way down or into something'. **Deep** can only mean this and is more common than **deeply** in this sense. It is usually followed by a word like *into* or *below*: *We decided to go deeper into the jungle.*
- **Deeply** usually means 'very much': *deeply in love* ◇ *deeply shocked.* You can use **deep down** (but not **deeply**) to talk about a person's real nature: *She can seem stern, but deep down she's a very kind person.* ◇ ~~*She can seem stern, but deeply she's a very kind person.*~~

,deep-'dyed *adj.* (*NAmE*) having a particular characteristic or opinion very strongly: *a deep-dyed socialist*

deep·en /'di:pən/ *verb* **1** [I, T] **~ (sth) (into sth)** if an emotion or a feeling **deepens**, or if sth **deepens** it, it becomes stronger: *Their friendship soon deepened into love.* **2** [I, T] **~ (sth)** to become worse; to make sth worse: *Warships were sent in as the crisis deepened.* ◇ *a deepening economic recession* **3** [I, T] to become deeper; to make sth deeper: *The water deepened gradually.* ◇ *His frown deepened.* ◇ **~ sth** *There were plans to deepen a stretch of the river.* **4** [T] **~ sth** to improve your knowledge or understanding of sth: *an opportunity for students to deepen their understanding of different cultures* **5** [I, T] **~ (sth)** if colour or light **deepens** or if sth **deepens** it, it becomes darker: *deepening shadows* **6** [I, T] **~ (sth) (to sth)** if a sound or voice **deepens** or if you **deepen** it, it becomes lower or you make it lower: *His voice deepened to a growl.* **7** [I] if your breathing **deepens**, you breathe more deeply than usual

,deep 'freeze (*BrE*) (*US* **Deep·freeze™**, **,deep 'freezer**) *noun* = FREEZER

,deep-'frozen *adj.* preserved at an extremely low temperature

,deep-'fry *verb* [usually passive] **~ sth** to cook food in oil that covers it completely: *deep-fried chicken pieces*

deep·ly /'di:pli/ *adv.*
1 very; very much: *She is deeply religious.* ◇ *They were deeply disturbed by the accident.* ◇ *Opinion is **deeply divided** on this issue.* ◇ ***deeply rooted** customs/ideas* ◇ ***deeply held** beliefs/convictions/views* (= that sb feels very strongly) **2** used with some verbs to show that sth is done in a very complete way: *to **breathe/sigh/exhale deeply*** (= using all of the air in your lungs) ◇ ***sleep deeply*** (= in a way that makes it difficult for you to wake up) ◇ *to **think deeply*** (= about all the aspects of sth) **3** to a depth that is quite a long way from the surface of sth: *to drill deeply into the wood* ➲ note at DEEP

,deep-'rooted, **,deep-'seated** *adj.* [usually before noun] (of feelings and beliefs) very fixed and strong; difficult to change or to destroy: *a deep-rooted desire* ◇ *The country's political divisions are deep-seated.*

'deep-sea (also *less frequent* **'deep-water**) *adj.* [only before noun] of or in the deeper parts of the sea: *a deep-sea diver* ◇ ***deep-sea fishing/diving***

,deep-'set *adj.* (*formal*) eyes that are **deep-set** seem to be quite far back in a person's face

,deep-'six *verb* [usually passive] **~ sth** (*NAmE, informal*) to decide not to do or use sth that you had planned to do or use: *Plans to build a new mall were deep-sixed after protests from local residents.*

the ,Deep 'South *noun* [sing.] the southern states of the US, especially Georgia, Alabama, Mississippi, Louisiana and South Carolina

'deep structure (also **'D-structure**) *noun* (*grammar*) the basic relationships between the different parts of a sentence, which show how we think when we are using language ➲ compare SURFACE STRUCTURE

,deep vein throm'bosis *noun* [U, C] (*abbr.* **DVT**) (*medical*) a serious condition caused by a blood CLOT (= a thick mass of blood) forming in a VEIN: *Passengers on long-haul flights are being warned about the risks of deep vein thrombosis.*

deer /dɪə(r); *NAmE* dɪr/ *noun* (*pl.* **deer**) an animal with long legs, that eats grass, leaves, etc. and can run fast. Most male deer have ANTLERS (= horns shaped like branches). There are many types of deer: *a herd of deer* ◇ *a deer park* ➲ see also FALLOW DEER, RED DEER, REINDEER, ROE DEER, DOE, FAWN, STAG

deer·stalk·er /'dɪəstɔ:kə(r); *NAmE* 'dɪrs-/ *noun* a cap with two PEAKS, one in front and one behind, and two pieces of cloth which are usually tied together on top but can be folded down to cover the ears

def /def/ *adj.* (*slang*) excellent: *a def band*

de·face /dɪ'feɪs/ *verb* **~ sth** to damage the appearance of sth especially by drawing or writing on it ▸ **de·face·ment** *noun* [U]

de facto /,deɪ 'fæktəʊ; *NAmE* -toʊ/ *adj.* [usually before noun] (from *Latin, formal*) existing as a fact although it may not be legally accepted as existing: *The general took de facto control of the country.* ▸ **de facto** *adv.*: *He continued to rule the country de facto.* ➲ compare DE JURE

defae·cate, defae·ca·tion (*BrE*) = DEFECATE, DEFECATION

def·am·ation /ˌdefəˈmeɪʃn/ *noun* [U, C] (*formal*) the act of damaging sb's reputation by saying or writing bad or false things about them: *The company sued for defamation.*

de·fama·tory /dɪˈfæmətri; *NAmE* -tɔːri/ *adj.* (*formal*) (of speech or writing) intended to harm sb by saying or writing bad or false things about them

de·fame /dɪˈfeɪm/ *verb* **~ sb/sth** (*formal*) to harm sb by saying or writing bad or false things about them

de·fault /dɪˈfɔːlt; ˈdiːfɔːlt/ *noun, verb*
■ ***noun*** **1** [U, C] failure to do sth that must be done by law, especially paying a debt: *The company is in default on the loan.* ◇ *Mortgage defaults have risen in the last year.* **2** [U, C, usually sing.] (*computing*) what happens or appears if you do not make any other choice or change: *The default option is to save your work every five minutes.* ◇ *On this screen, 256 colours is the default.*
IDM **by deˈfault** **1** a game or competition can be won **by default** if there are no other people, teams, etc. taking part **2** if sth happens **by default**, it happens because you have not made any other decision or choices which would make things happen in a different way **in deˈfault of sth** (*formal*) because of a lack of sth: *They accepted what he had said **in default of** any evidence to disprove it.*
■ ***verb*** **1** [I] **~ (on sth)** to fail to do sth that you legally have to do, especially by not paying a debt: *to default on a loan/debt* ◇ *defaulting borrowers/tenants* **2** [I] **~ (to sth)** (*computing*) to happen when you do not make any other choice or change ▸ **de·fault·er** *noun*: *mortgage defaulters*

de·feat 🔑 /dɪˈfiːt/ *verb, noun*
■ ***verb*** **1** 🔑 **~ sb/sth** to win against sb in a war, competition, sports game, etc. SYN **beat**: *He defeated the champion in three sets.* ◇ *a defeated army* **2** 🔑 **~ sth** to stop sth from being successful: *The motion was defeated by 19 votes.* ◇ *Staying late at the office to discuss shorter working hours rather **defeats the object of the exercise!*** **3** **~ sb** (*formal*) if sth **defeats** you, you cannot understand it: *The instruction manual completely defeated me.*
■ ***noun*** **1** 🔑 [U, C] failure to win or to be successful: *The party faces defeat in the election.* ◇ *a **narrow/heavy defeat*** ◇ *The world champion has only had two defeats in 20 fights.* ◇ *They finally had to **admit defeat*** (= stop trying to be successful). **2** 🔑 [C, usually sing.] the act of winning a victory over sb/sth: *the defeat of fascism*

de·feat·ist /dɪˈfiːtɪst/ *adj.* expecting not to succeed, and showing it in a particular situation: *a **defeatist attitude/view*** ▸ **de·feat·ist** *noun*: *He is a pessimist and a defeatist.* **de·feat·ism** *noun* [U]

defe·cate (*BrE* also **defae·cate**) /ˈdefəkeɪt; ˈdiː-/ *verb* [I] (*formal*) to get rid of solid waste from your body through your BOWELS ▸ **defe·ca·tion** (*BrE* also **defae·ca·tion**) /ˌdefəˈkeɪʃn; ˌdiː-/ *noun* [U]

de·fect *noun, verb*
■ ***noun*** /ˈdiːfekt; dɪˈfekt/ a fault in sth or in the way it has been made which means that it is not perfect: *a speech defect* ◇ *a defect in the glass*
■ ***verb*** /dɪˈfekt/ [I] **~ (from sth) (to sth)** to leave a political party, country, etc. to join another that is considered to be an enemy ▸ **de·fec·tion** /dɪˈfekʃn/ *noun* [U, C]: **~ (from sth) (to sth)** *There have been several defections from the ruling party.* **de·fect·or** *noun*

de·fect·ive /dɪˈfektɪv/ *adj.* having a fault or faults; not perfect or complete SYN **faulty**: *defective goods* ◇ *Her hearing was found to be slightly defective.* ▸ **de·fect·ive·ly** *adv.* **de·fect·ive·ness** *noun* [U]

de·fence 🔑 (*especially US* **de·fense**) /dɪˈfens/ *noun*
▸ PROTECTION AGAINST ATTACK **1** 🔑 [U] the act of protecting sb/sth from attack, criticism, etc: *soldiers who died **in defence of** their country* ◇ *When her brother was criticized she **leapt to his defence**.* ◇ *What points can be raised in defence of this argument?* ◇ *I have to say **in her defence** that she knew nothing about it beforehand.* ➲ see also SELF-DEFENCE **2** 🔑 [C, U] **~ (against sth)** something that provides protection against attack from enemies, the weather, illness, etc: *The town walls were built as a defence against enemy attacks.* ◇ *The harbour's sea defences are in poor condition.* ◇ *The body has natural **defence mechanisms** to protect it from disease.* ◇ *Humour is a more effective defence than violence.* **3** 🔑 [U] the organization of the people and systems that are used by a government to protect a country from attack: *(BrE) the Ministry of Defence* ◇ *(NAmE) the Department of Defense* ◇ *Further cuts in defence spending are being considered.*
▸ SUPPORT **4** [C] something that is said or written in order to support sth: *a defence of Marxism*
▸ LAW **5** [C] what is said in court to prove that a person did not commit a crime; the act of presenting this argument in court: *Her defence was that she was somewhere completely different at the time of the crime.* ◇ *He wanted to conduct his own defence.* **6 the defence** [sing.+ sing./pl. v.] the lawyer or lawyers whose job is to prove in court that a person did not commit a crime ➲ compare PROSECUTION
▸ IN SPORT **7** [sing., U] the players who must prevent the other team from scoring; the position of these players on the sports field: *Welford cut through the defence to score the winning goal.* ◇ *(BrE) She plays **in defence**.* ◇ *(NAmE) He plays **on defense**.* ➲ compare ATTACK, OFFENSE **8** [C] a contest, game, etc. in which the previous winner or winners compete in order to try to win again: *Barcelona's defence of the Champions League title*

de·fence·less (*especially US* **de·fense·less**) /dɪˈfensləs/ *adj.* weak; not able to protect yourself; having no protection: *defenceless children* ◇ *The village is defenceless against attack.* ▸ **de·fence·less·ness** (*especially US* **de·fense·less·ness**) *noun* [U]

de·fend 🔑 /dɪˈfend/ *verb*
▸ PROTECT AGAINST ATTACK **1** 🔑 [T, I] to protect sb/sth from attack: **~ sb/yourself/sth** *Troops have been sent to defend the borders.* ◇ **~ sb/yourself/sth from/against sb/sth** *All our officers are trained to defend themselves against knife attacks.* ◇ **~ against sb/sth** *It is impossible to defend against an all-out attack.*
▸ SUPPORT **2** 🔑 [T] to say or write sth in support of sb/sth that has been criticized: **~ sth** *How can you defend such behaviour?* ◇ **~ sb/yourself/sth from/against sb/sth** *Politicians are skilled at defending themselves against their critics.*
▸ IN SPORT **3** [I, T] **~ (sth)** (in sports) to protect your own goal to stop your opponents from scoring OPP **attack**
▸ IN COMPETITIONS **4** [T] **~ sth** to take part in a competition that you won the last time and try to win it again: *He is **defending champion**.* ◇ *She will be **defending her title** at next month's championships.* ◇ *(politics) He intends to defend his seat in the next election.*
▸ LAW **5** [T, I] **~ (sb/yourself)** to act as a lawyer for sb who has been charged with a crime: *He has employed one of the UK's top lawyers to defend him.* ➲ compare PROSECUTE

de·fend·ant /dɪˈfendənt/ *noun* the person in a trial who is accused of committing a crime, or who is being sued by another person ➲ COLLOCATIONS at JUSTICE ➲ compare ACCUSED, PLAINTIFF

de·fend·er /dɪˈfendə(r)/ *noun* **1** a player who must stop the other team from scoring in games such as football (SOCCER), HOCKEY, etc. **2** a person who defends and believes in protecting sth: *a passionate defender of human rights*

de·fense (*especially US*) = DEFENCE

de·fens·ible /dɪˈfensəbl/ *adj.* **1** able to be supported by reasons or arguments that show that it is right or should be allowed: *Is abortion morally defensible?* OPP **indefensible** **2** (of a place) able to be defended from an attack

de·fen·sive /dɪˈfensɪv/ *adj., noun*
■ ***adj.*** **1** protecting sb/sth against attack: *a defensive measure* ◇ *Troops took up a defensive position around the town.* ➲ compare OFFENSIVE **2** behaving in a way that shows that you feel that people are criticizing you: *Don't ask him about his plans—he just gets defensive.* **3** (*sport*) connected with trying to prevent the other team or player from scoring points or goals: *defensive play* ➲ compare OFFENSIVE ▸ **de·fen·sive·ly** *adv.* **de·fen·sive·ness** *noun* [U]

■ *noun*
IDM **on/onto the deˈfensive** acting in a way that shows that you expect to be attacked or criticized; having to defend yourself: *Their questions about the money put her on the defensive.* ◇ *Warnings of an enemy attack forced the troops onto the defensive.*

deˌfensive ˈmedicine *noun* [U] (*especially NAmE*) medical treatment that involves more tests, operations, etc. than a person really needs because a doctor is worried that a claim or complaint may be made against them in court if they make a mistake in the treatment they give

defer /dɪˈfɜː(r)/ *verb* (-rr-) ~ (**doing**) **sth** (*formal*) to delay sth until a later time SYN **put off**: *The department deferred the decision for six months.* ◇ *She had applied for deferred admission to college.* ▶ **de·fer·ment, de·fer·ral** /dɪˈfɜːrəl/ *noun* [U, C]
PHR V **deˈfer to sb/sth** (*formal*) to agree to accept what sb has decided or what they think about sb/sth because you respect him or her: *We will defer to whatever the committee decides.*

def·er·ence /ˈdefərəns/ *noun* [U] behaviour that shows that you respect sb/sth: *The women wore veils* **in deference to** *the customs of the country.* ◇ *The flags were lowered* **out of deference to** *the bereaved family.* ▶ **def·er·en·tial** /ˌdefəˈrenʃl/ *adj.* **def·er·en·tial·ly** /-ʃəli/ *adv.*

de·fi·ance /dɪˈfaɪəns/ *noun* [U] open refusal to obey sb/sth: *a* **look/an act/a gesture of defiance** ◇ *Nuclear testing was resumed* **in defiance of** *an international ban.*

deˈfiance campaign *noun* (in South Africa in the past, especially in the period after 1952) a series of activities in which black people refused to obey laws that were not fair

de·fi·ant /dɪˈfaɪənt/ *adj.* openly refusing to obey sb/sth, sometimes in an aggressive way: *a defiant teenager* ◇ *The terrorists sent a defiant message to the government.* ▶ **de·fi·ant·ly** *adv.*

de·fib·ril·la·tion /ˌdiːfɪbrɪˈleɪʃn/ *noun* [U] (*medical*) the use of a controlled electric shock from a defibrillator to return the heart to its natural rhythm

de·fib·ril·la·tor /diːˈfɪbrɪleɪtə(r)/ *noun* (*medical*) a piece of equipment used to control the movements of the heart muscles by giving the heart a controlled electric shock

de·fi·ciency /dɪˈfɪʃnsi/ *noun* (*pl.* -ies) (*formal*) **1** [U, C] ~ (**in/of sth**) the state of not having, or not having enough of, sth that is essential SYN **shortage**: *Vitamin deficiency in the diet can cause illness.* ◇ *a deficiency of Vitamin B* **2** [C] ~ (**in/of sth**) a fault or a weakness in sth/sb that makes it or them less successful: *deficiencies in the computer system*

de·fi·cient /dɪˈfɪʃnt/ *adj.* (*formal*) **1** ~ (**in sth**) not having enough of sth, especially sth that is essential: *a diet that is deficient in vitamin A* **2** not good enough: *Deaf people are sometimes treated as being mentally deficient.*

def·icit /ˈdefɪsɪt/ *noun* **1** (*economics*) the amount by which money spent or owed is greater than money earned in a particular period of time: *a* **budget/trade deficit** ◇ *The trade balance has been* **in deficit** *for the past five years.* ➲ COLLOCATIONS at INTERNATIONAL ➲ compare SURPLUS **2** (*formal*) the amount by which sth, especially an amount of money, is too small or smaller than sth else: *There's a deficit of $3 million in the total needed to complete the project.* ◇ *The team has to come back from a 2–0 deficit in the first half.*

de·fied *past tense, past part.* of DEFY

de·file¹ /dɪˈfaɪl/ *verb* ~ **sth** (*formal* or *literary*) to make sth dirty or no longer pure, especially sth that people consider important or holy: *Many victims of burglary feel their homes have been defiled.* ◇ *The altar had been defiled by vandals.* ▶ **de·file·ment** *noun* [U, C]

de·file² /dɪˈfaɪl; ˈdiːfaɪl/ *noun* (*formal*) a narrow way through mountains

de·fine 🔑 AW /dɪˈfaɪn/ *verb*
1 🔑 to say or explain what the meaning of a word or phrase is: ~ **sth** *The term 'mental illness' is difficult to define.* ◇ ~ **sth as sth** *Life imprisonment is defined as 60 years under state law.* **2** 🔑 to describe or show sth accurately: ~ **sth** *We need to define the task ahead very clearly.* ◇ *The difficulty of a problem was* **defined in terms of** *how long it took to complete.* ◇ ~ **what, how, etc...** *It is difficult to define what makes him so popular.* **3** ~ **sth** to show clearly a line, shape or edge: *The mountain was* **sharply defined** *against the sky.* ▶ **de·fin·able** AW *adj.*

Language Bank

define
Defining terms

- **It is important to clarify what is meant by** climate change.
- Climate change **can/may be defined as** 'the long-term fluctuations in temperature, precipitation, wind and other aspects of the earth's climate'.
- **A generally accepted definition of** global warming **is** the gradual increase in the overall temperature of the earth's atmosphere due to the greenhouse effect.
- The greenhouse effect **is defined** by the author **as** the process by which heat from the sun is trapped in the earth's atmosphere, causing the temperature of the earth to rise.
- The author **uses the term** climate change **to refer to** any significant change in measures of climate lasting for an extended period.
- **The term** 'carbon footprint' **refers to** the amount of carbon dioxide released into the atmosphere as a result of the activities of an individual or organization.
- Scientists suggest that increased carbon dioxide in the atmosphere will result in an increase in global temperatures, and **the term** 'global warming' **is used** to describe this phenomenon.

➲ Language Bank at FIRST

deˌfined ˈbenefit *noun* a fixed amount of money that will be paid by a PENSION PLAN, especially when this amount is based on your salary at the end of your working life and the number of years you worked

deˌfined contriˈbution *noun* fixed payments that are made to a PENSION PLAN, where the amount that will be paid out can change

de·fin·ing /dɪˈfaɪnɪŋ/ *adj.* = RESTRICTIVE (2)

deˈfining vocabulary *noun* a set of carefully chosen words used to write the explanations in some dictionaries

def·in·ite 🔑 AW /ˈdefɪnət/ *adj., noun*
■ *adj.* **1** 🔑 ~ (**that...**) sure or certain; unlikely to change: *Can you give me a definite answer by tomorrow?* ◇ *Is it definite that he's leaving?* ◇ *I've heard rumours, but nothing definite.* ◇ *a definite offer of a job* ◇ *I'm not sure—I can find out* **for definite** *if you like.* ◇ *That's definite then, is it?* ◇ *They have very definite ideas on how to bring up children.* ➲ SYNONYMS at CERTAIN **2** 🔑 easily or clearly seen or understood; obvious SYN **clear**: *The look on her face was a definite sign that something was wrong.* ◇ *There was a definite feeling that things were getting worse.* **3** [not before noun] ~ (**about something**) | ~ (**that...**) (of a person) sure that sth is true or that sth is going to happen and stating it to other people: *I'm definite about this.*
■ *noun* [sing.] (*informal*) sth that you are certain about or that you know will happen; sb who is sure to do sth: *'We're moving our office to Glasgow.' 'That's a definite, is it?'* ◇ *'Is Sarah coming to the party?' 'Yes, she's a definite.'*

ˌdefinite ˈarticle *noun* (*grammar*) the word *the* in English, or a similar word in another language ➲ compare INDEFINITE ARTICLE

def·in·ite·ly 🔑 AW /ˈdefɪnətli/ *adv.*
1 🔑 (*informal*) a way of emphasizing that sth is true and that there is no doubt about it: *I definitely remember sending the letter.* ◇ *'Was it what you expected?' 'Yes, definitely.'* ◇ *'Do you plan to have children?' 'Definitely not!'* ◇ *Some old people want help; others most definitely do not.* **2** 🔑 in a

way that is certain or that shows that you are certain: *The date of the move has not been definitely decided yet* (= it may change). ◇ *Please say definitely whether you will be coming or not.*

def·in·ition 0‑m AW /ˌdefɪˈnɪʃn/ *noun* **1** 0‑m [C, U] an explanation of the meaning of a word or phrase, especially in a dictionary; the act of stating the meanings of words and phrases: *clear simple definitions* ◇ *Neighbours* ***by definition*** *live close by* (= this is what being a neighbour means). ➲ LANGUAGE BANK at DEFINE **2** 0‑m [C] what an idea, etc. means: *What's your definition of happiness?* **3** [U] the quality of being clear and easy to see: *The definition of the digital TV pictures is excellent.*

de·fini·tive AW /dɪˈfɪnətɪv/ *adj.* **1** final; not able to be changed: *a* ***definitive agreement/answer/statement*** ◇ *The* ***definitive version*** *of the text is ready to be published.* **2** [usually before noun] considered to be the best of its kind and almost impossible to improve: *the definitive biography of Einstein* ▶ **de·fini·tive·ly** *adv.*

de·flate *verb* **1** /dɪˈfleɪt; ˌdiː-/ [T, I] **~ (sth)** to let air or gas out of a tyre, BALLOON, etc; to become smaller because of air or gas coming out **2** /dɪˈfleɪt/ [T, often passive] **~ sb/sth** to make sb feel less confident; to make sb/sth feel or seem less important: *All the criticism had left her feeling totally deflated.* **3** /ˌdiːˈfleɪt/ [T] **~ sth** (*economics*) to reduce the amount of money being used in a country so that prices fall or stay steady ➲ compare INFLATE (3), REFLATE

de·fla·tion /ˌdiːˈfleɪʃn/ *noun* [U] **1** (*economics*) a reduction in the amount of money in a country's economy so that prices fall or remain the same ➲ COLLOCATIONS at ECONOMY **2** the action of air being removed from sth OPP **inflation** ▶ **de·fla·tion·ary** /ˌdiːˈfleɪʃənri; *NAmE* -neri/ *adj.*: *deflationary policies*

de·flect /dɪˈflekt/ *verb* **1** [I, T] to change direction or make sth change direction, especially after hitting sth: *The ball deflected off Reid's body into the goal.* ◇ **~ sth** *He raised his arm to try to deflect the blow.* **2** [T] **~ sth** to succeed in preventing sth from being directed towards you SYN **divert**: *All attempts to* ***deflect attention*** *from his private life have failed.* ◇ *She sought to* ***deflect criticism*** *by blaming her family.* **3** [T] **~ sb (from sth)** to prevent sb from doing sth that they are determined to do: *The government will not be deflected from its commitments.*

de·flec·tion /dɪˈflekʃn/ *noun* [U, C, usually sing.] a sudden change in the direction that sth is moving in, usually after it has hit sth; the act of causing sth to change direction: *the angle of deflection* ◇ *the deflection of the missile away from its target* ◇ *The goal was scored with a deflection off the goalkeeper.*

de·flower /ˌdiːˈflaʊə(r)/ *verb* **~ sb** (*old-fashioned, literary*) to have sex with a woman who has not had sex before

defog /ˌdiːˈfɒg; *NAmE* -ˈfɔːg; -ˈfɑːg/ *verb* (-gg-) [T, I] **~ (sth)** (*NAmE*) (*BrE* **de·mist**) to remove the CONDENSATION from a car's windows so that you can see clearly

de·fo·liant /ˌdiːˈfəʊliənt; *NAmE* -ˈfoʊ-/ *noun* [C, U] a chemical that removes the leaves from plants, sometimes used as a weapon in war

de·foli·ate /ˌdiːˈfəʊlieɪt; *NAmE* -ˈfoʊ-/ *verb* **~ sth** (*technical*) to destroy the leaves of trees or plants, especially with chemicals ▶ **de·foli·ation** /ˌdiːˌfəʊliˈeɪʃn; *NAmE* -ˌfoʊ-/ *noun* [U]

de·for·est /ˌdiːˈfɒrɪst; *NAmE* -ˈfɔːr-; -ˈfɑːr-/ (also **dis·af·for·est**) *verb* [usually passive] **~ sth** to cut down and destroy all the trees in a place: *Two thirds of the region has been deforested in the past decade.*

de·for·est·ation /ˌdiːˌfɒrɪˈsteɪʃn; *NAmE* -ˌfɔːr-; -ˌfɑːr-/ *noun* [U] the act of cutting down or burning the trees in an area ➲ COLLOCATIONS at ENVIRONMENT ➲ VISUAL VOCAB page V6 ➲ compare AFFORESTATION, REFORESTATION

de·form /dɪˈfɔːm; *NAmE* -ˈfɔːrm/ *verb* **~ sth** to change or spoil the usual or natural shape of sth: *The disease had deformed his spine.*

de·form·ation /ˌdiːfɔːˈmeɪʃn; *NAmE* -fɔːrˈm-/ *noun* **1** [U] the process or result of changing and spoiling the normal shape of sth **2** [C] a change in the normal shape of sth as a result of injury or illness: *a deformation of the spine*

de·formed /dɪˈfɔːmd; *NAmE* -ˈfɔːrmd/ *adj.* (of a person or a part of the body) having a shape that is not normal because it has grown wrongly: *She was born with deformed hands.*

de·form·ity /dɪˈfɔːməti; *NAmE* -ˈfɔːrm-/ *noun* (*pl.* -ies) [C, U] a condition in which a part of the body is not the normal shape because of injury, illness or because it has grown wrongly SYN **malformation**: *Drugs taken during pregnancy may cause physical deformity in babies.*

D

DEFRA /ˈdefrə/ *abbr.* (in Britain) Department for Environment, Food and Rural Affairs

de·frag·ment /ˌdiːfrægˈment/ (also *informal* **de·frag** /ˌdiːˈfræg/) *verb* **~ sth** (*computing*) to organize the files on a computer so that information relating to each file is stored in the same area, so the computer works faster

de·fraud /dɪˈfrɔːd/ *verb* [I, T] to get money illegally from a person or an organization by tricking them: *All three men were charged with conspiracy to defraud.* ◇ **~ sb (of sth)** *They were accused of defrauding the company of $14 000.*

de·fray /dɪˈfreɪ/ *verb* **~ costs/expenses** (*formal*) to give sb back the money that they have spent on sth

de·frock /ˌdiːˈfrɒk; *NAmE* -ˈfrɑːk/ *verb* [usually passive] **~ sb** to officially remove a priest from his or her job, because he or she has done sth wrong: *a defrocked priest*

de·frost /ˌdiːˈfrɒst; *NAmE* -ˈfrɔːst/ *verb* **1** [I, T] to become or make sth warmer, especially food, so that it is no longer frozen: *It will take about four hours to defrost.* ◇ **~ sth** *Make sure you defrost the chicken completely before cooking.* **2** [T, I] **~ (sth)** when you **defrost** a fridge/refrigerator or FREEZER, or when it **defrosts**, you remove the ice from it ➲ compare DE-ICE, MELT, THAW, UNFREEZE **3** [T] **~ sth** (*NAmE*) to remove ice from the surface of a car's windows ▶ **de·frost·er** *noun*

deft /deft/ *adj.* **1** (of a person's movements) skilful and quick: ***deft hands/fingers/footwork*** ◇ *He finished off the painting with a few deft strokes of the brush.* **2** skilful: *her deft command of the language* ▶ **deft·ly** *adv.*: *I threw her a towel which she deftly caught.* ◇ *They deftly avoided answering my questions.* **deft·ness** *noun* [U]

de·funct /dɪˈfʌŋkt/ *adj.* (*formal*) no longer existing, operating or being used

de·fuse /ˌdiːˈfjuːz/ *verb* **1 ~ sth** to stop a possibly dangerous or difficult situation from developing, especially by making people less angry or nervous: *Local police are trying to defuse racial tension in the community.* **2 ~ sth** to remove the FUSE from a bomb so that it cannot explode

defy /dɪˈfaɪ/ *verb* (**de·fies**, **defy·ing**, **de·fied**, **de·fied**) **1 ~ sb/sth** to refuse to obey or show respect for sb in authority, a law, a rule, etc: *I wouldn't have dared to defy my teachers.* ◇ *Hundreds of people today defied the ban on political gatherings.* **2 ~ belief, explanation, description, etc.** to be impossible or almost impossible to believe, explain, describe, etc: *a political move that defies explanation* ◇ *The beauty of the scene defies description.* **3 ~ sth** to successfully resist sth to a very unusual degree: *The baby boy* ***defied all the odds*** *and survived* (= stayed alive when it seemed certain that he would die).

> **WORD FAMILY**
> **defy** *verb*
> **defiance** *noun*
> **defiant** *adj.*

IDM **I defy you/anyone to do sth** used to say that sb should try to do sth, as a way of emphasizing that you think it is impossible to do it: *I defy anyone not to cry at the end of the film.*

deg. *abbr.* DEGREE(S): *26 deg. C*

de·gen·er·ate *verb, adj., noun*

■ ***verb*** /dɪˈdʒenəreɪt/ [I] to become worse, for example by becoming lower in quality or weaker SYN **deteriorate**: *Her health degenerated quickly.* ◇ **~ into sth** *The march degenerated into a riot.*

■ ***adj.*** /dɪˈdʒenərət/ **1** having moral standards that have fallen to a level that is very low and unacceptable to most people: *a degenerate popular culture* **2** (*technical*) having

returned to a simple structure; lacking sth that is usually present ▶ **de·gen·er·acy** /dɪˈdʒenərəsi/ *noun* [U]
■ ***noun*** /dɪˈdʒenerət/ a person whose behaviour shows moral standards that have fallen to a very low level

de·gen·er·ation /dɪˌdʒenəˈreɪʃn/ *noun* [U] the process of becoming worse or less acceptable in quality or condition: *social/moral degeneration* ◇ *Intensive farming in the area has caused severe degeneration of the land.*

D

de·gen·era·tive /dɪˈdʒenərətɪv/ *adj.* (*technical*) (of an illness) getting or likely to get worse as time passes: *degenerative diseases such as arthritis*

de·grad·able /dɪˈgreɪdəbl/ *adj.* (*especially NAmE, technical*) that can be changed to a simpler form ➲ see also BIODEGRADABLE

deg·rad·ation /ˌdegrəˈdeɪʃn/ *noun* [U] **1** a situation in which sb has lost all SELF-RESPECT and the respect of other people: *the degradation of being sent to prison* **2** (*technical*) the process of sth being damaged or made worse: *environmental degradation*

de·grade /dɪˈgreɪd/ *verb* **1** [T] **~ sb** to show or treat sb in a way that makes them seem not worth any respect or not worth taking seriously: *This poster is offensive and degrades women.* **2** [I, T] **~ (sth)** (*technical*) to change or make sth change to a simpler chemical form **3** [T] **~ sth** (*technical*) to make sth become worse, especially in quality

de·grad·ing /dɪˈgreɪdɪŋ/ *adj.* treating sb as if they have no value, so that they lose their SELF-RESPECT and the respect of other people: *the inhuman and degrading treatment of prisoners*

de·grease /ˌdiːˈgriːs/ *verb* **~ sth** to remove GREASE or oil from sth

de·gree 0→ /dɪˈgriː/ *noun*
1 0→ [C] a unit for measuring angles: *an angle of ninety degrees (90°)* **2** 0→ [C] (*abbr.* **deg.**) a unit for measuring temperature: *Water freezes at 32 degrees Fahrenheit (32°F) or zero/nought degrees Celsius (0°C).* **3** 0→ [C, U] the amount or level of sth: *Her job demands a high degree of skill.* ◇ *I agree with you* ***to a certain degree.*** ◇ *To what degree can parents be held responsible for a child's behaviour?* ◇ *Most pop music is influenced, to a greater or lesser degree, by the blues.* **4** 0→ [C] the qualification obtained by students who successfully complete a university or college course: *My brother has a master's degree from Harvard.* ◇ *She has a degree in Biochemistry from Queen's University.* ◇ *a four-year degree course* ➲ COLLOCATIONS at EDUCATION **5** [C] (*BrE*) a university or college course, normally lasting three years or more: *I'm hoping to do a chemistry degree.* **6** [C] a level in a scale of how serious sth is: *murder in the first degree* (= of the most serious kind) ◇ *first-degree murder* ◇ *third-degree* (= very serious) *burns*
IDM▶ **by deˈgrees** slowly and gradually: *By degrees their friendship grew into love.* ➲ more at NTH

de·hu·man·ize (*BrE* also **-ise**) /ˌdiːˈhjuːmənaɪz/ *verb* **~ sb** to make sb lose their human qualities such as kindness, pity, etc: *the dehumanizing effects of poverty and squalor* ▶ **de·hu·man·iza·tion, -isa·tion** /diːˌhjuːmənaɪˈzeɪʃn; *NAmE* -nəˈz-/ *noun* [U]

de·hu·midi·fier /ˌdiːhjuːˈmɪdɪfaɪə(r)/ *noun* an electrical machine for removing water from the air ➲ see also HUMIDIFIER

de·hy·drate /diːˈhaɪdreɪt; ˌdiːhaɪˈdreɪt/ *verb* **1** [T, usually passive] **~ sth** to remove the water from sth, especially food, in order to preserve it **2** [I, T] to lose too much water from your body; to make a person's body lose too much water: *Runners can dehydrate very quickly in this heat.* ◇ **~ sb** *the dehydrating effects of alcohol* ▶ **de·hy·dra·tion** /ˌdiːhaɪˈdreɪʃn/ *noun* [U]: *to suffer from dehydration* **de·hy·drated** /ˌdiːhaɪˈdreɪtɪd/ *adj.*: *Drink lots of water to avoid becoming dehydrated.*

de-ice /ˌdiː ˈaɪs/ *verb* **~ sth** to remove the ice from sth ➲ compare DEFROST, MELT, THAW, UNFREEZE

de-icer /ˌdiː ˈaɪsə(r)/ *noun* [C, U] a substance that is put on a surface to remove ice or to stop it from forming

deic·tic /ˈdaɪktɪk; ˈdeɪktɪk/ *adj.* (*linguistics*) relating to a word or expression whose meaning depends on who says it, where they are, who they are talking to, etc, for example 'you', 'me', 'here', 'next week'.

deify /ˈdeɪɪfaɪ; ˈdiːɪfaɪ/ *verb* (**dei·fies, dei·fy·ing, dei·fied, dei·fied**) **~ sb** (*formal*) to treat or worship sb as a god ▶ **dei·fi·ca·tion** /ˌdeɪɪfɪˈkeɪʃn; ˌdiːɪfɪˈkeɪʃn/ *noun* [U]: *the deification of medieval kings*

deign /deɪn/ *verb* **~ to do sth** (*disapproving*) to do sth in a way that shows you think you are too important to do it SYN **condescend**: *She just grunted, not deigning to look up from the page.*

deism /ˈdeɪɪzəm; ˈdiːɪz-/ *noun* [U] belief in God, especially a God that created the universe but does not take part in it ▶ **deist** /ˈdeɪɪst; ˈdiːɪst/ *noun* **de·is·tic** /deɪˈɪstɪk; diːˈɪ-/ *adj.*

deity /ˈdeɪəti; ˈdiːəti/ *noun* (*pl.* **-ies**) **1** [C] a god or GODDESS: *Greek/Roman/Hindu deities* **2 the Deity** [sing.] (*formal*) God

deixis /ˈdeɪksɪs; ˈdaɪksɪs/ *noun* [U] (*linguistics*) the function or use of DEICTIC words or expressions (= ones whose meaning depends on where, when or by whom they are used)

déjà vu /ˌdeɪʒɑː ˈvuː/ *noun* [U] (from *French*) the feeling that you have previously experienced sth which is happening to you now: *I had a strong sense of déjà vu as I entered the room.*

de·ject·ed /dɪˈdʒektɪd/ *adj.* unhappy and disappointed SYN **despondent**: *She looked so dejected when she lost the game.* ▶ **de·ject·ed·ly** *adv.*

de·jec·tion /dɪˈdʒekʃn/ *noun* [U] a feeling of unhappiness and disappointment

de jure /ˌdeɪ ˈdʒʊəri; *NAmE* ˈdʒʊri/ *adj., adv.* (from *Latin, law*) according to the law: *He held power de jure and de facto* (= both according to the law and in reality). ➲ compare DE FACTO

deka·liter /ˈdekəliːtə(r)/ *noun* (*US*) = DECALITRE

deka·meter /ˈdekəmiːtə(r)/ *noun* (*US*) = DECAMETRE

dekko /ˈdekəʊ; *NAmE* -koʊ/ *noun*
IDM▶ **have a dekko (at sth)** (*old-fashioned, BrE, slang*) to look (at sth) ORIGIN From the Hindi word for 'look!', used by the British army in India in the past.

delay 0→ /dɪˈleɪ/ *noun, verb*
■ ***noun*** **1** 0→ [C] a period of time when sb/sth has to wait because of a problem that makes sth slow or late: *Commuters will face long delays on the roads today.* ◇ *We apologize for the delay in answering your letter.* ◇ *a delay of two hours/a two-hour delay* ➲ COLLOCATIONS at TRAVEL **2** 0→ [C, U] a situation in which sth does not happen when it should; the act of delaying: *There's no time for delay.* ◇ *Report it to the police* ***without delay*** (= immediately).
■ ***verb*** **1** 0→ [I, T] to not do sth until a later time or to make sth happen at a later time SYN **defer**: *Don't delay—call us today!* ◇ **~ sth** *The judge will delay his verdict until he receives medical reports on the offender.* ◇ *She's suffering a* ***delayed reaction*** (= a reaction that did not happen immediately) *to the shock.* ◇ **~ doing sth** *He delayed telling her the news, waiting for the right moment.* **2** 0→ [T] **~ sb** to make sb late or force them to do sth more slowly SYN **hold up**: *Thousands of commuters were delayed for over an hour.* ◇ *The government is accused of using* ***delaying tactics*** (= deliberately doing sth to delay a process, decision, etc.).

de·lect·able /dɪˈlektəbl/ *adj.* **1** (of food and drink) extremely pleasant to taste, smell or look at SYN **delicious**: *the delectable smell of freshly baked bread* **2** (*humorous*) (of a person) very attractive: *his delectable body*

de·lect·ation /ˌdiːlekˈteɪʃn/ *noun* [U] (*formal* or *humorous*) enjoyment or entertainment SYN **delight**

dele·gate *noun, verb*
■ ***noun*** /ˈdelɪgət/ a person who is chosen or elected to represent the views of a group of people and vote and make decisions for them: *The conference was attended by delegates from 56 countries.*

a miracle that Socrates lasted as long as he did; it is rather a shock that Jesus could preach even for three years, given his absolute Selflessness.

Young men and women may come again to understand that Self at its best is a protection, and only a protection, for the life of Soul, and that when the moment comes for Soul to exert itself—Whitman's moment came in 1854 and 1855 when he wrote and published the stunning poems—Self must stand aside. It's said that when Wallace Stevens stepped into the room wearing his three-piece suit and his insurance man's frown, the temperature dropped twenty degrees. How much strength of Self was necessary to defend the Soul who wrote "Sunday Morning" and *Notes toward a Supreme Fiction?* Clearly a great deal. It is always dangerous to invoke Self to protect Soul, as Whitman and Stevens did. Self, given freedom, can consume Soul, or counterfeit it. But in a world as greedy and violent as this one, Self's tough guidance and protection may be a necessity.

The young who wish a better world will also see that what appear to be tensions among the ideals are only apparent. Is the warrior the exclusive inverse of the man or woman of compassion? To everything there is a season. There will always be a time when we need defense from our enemies, our real enemies, and then Hector is the figure we will not be able to do without. Compassion may be our central ideal in the time of peace, but peace is not forever.

There are seasons too for the individual. She may find herself at one time an aspiring thinker, at another a fighter, at a third a creator. And she will judge herself not only on the feeling of fullness that these ideals create within but also on what she contributes to other people by virtue of engaging her ideals. Hope will replace desire and for a while she will feel free. She may at times feel consumed by Self. There will be a family to feed and protect, aging parents to tend; there will be the push and toss of daily life—the "pulling and hauling" as Whitman calls it. But in every act of

courage or compassion or true th
her begin to swell, and she'll feel
piness. She'll feel intimations of
begin, as well as she can, to mov
will be the resurrection of her Sou

Bibliography

1. The Hero

Adkins, A. W. H. *Merit and Responsibility: A Study in Greek Values*. Oxford: Clarendon, 1960.

Amory, A. "The Gates of Horn and Ivory." *Yale Classical Studies* 20 (1966): 3–51.

Bassett, S. E. "Achilles' Treatment of Hector's Body." *Transactions and Proceedings of the American Philological Association* 64 (1933): 41–65.

———. *The Poetry of Homer*. Berkeley: University of California Press, 1938.

Bowra, Sir Maurice. *Tradition and Design in the Iliad*. Oxford: Clarendon, 1930.

Campbell, J. K. "Honour and the Devil." *Honour and Shame*. Ed. J. G. Peristiany. Chicago: University of Chicago Press, 1966. 139–170.

Carpenter, Rhys. *Folk Tale, Fiction and Saga in the Homeric Epics*. Berkeley: University of California Press, 1958.

Dietrich, B. C. *Death, Fate and the Gods*. University of London Classical Studies III. London: Athlone Press, 1965.

Dodds, E. R. *The Greeks and the Irrational*. Berkeley: University of California Press, 1951.

Edwards, Mark W. *Homer: Poet of The Iliad*. Baltimore: Johns Hopkins University Press, 1987.

Else, G. *Aristotle's "Poetics": The Argument*. Cambridge, MA: Harvard University Press, 1957.

Emerson, Ralph Waldo. *Society and Solitude.* Boston: James R. Osgood, 1871.

Finley, M. I. *The World of Odysseus.* New York: Viking, 1954.

Griffin, Jasper. *Homer on Life and Death.* Oxford: Clarendon, 1980.

Homer. *The Iliad.* Trans. Robert Fagles. New York: Penguin, 1998.

Horkheimer, Max, and Theodor W. Adorno. *Dialectic of Enlightenment.* Trans. John Cumming. New York: Continuum, 1994.

Jaynes, Julian. *The Origins of Consciousness in the Breakdown of the Bicameral Mind.* Boston: Houghton Mifflin, 1976.

Jones, J. *On Aristotle and Greek Tragedy.* New York: Oxford University Press, 1962.

Kirk, G. S. *The Songs of Homer.* Cambridge: Cambridge University Press, 1962.

Knox, Bernard, ed. *The Norton Book of Classical Literature.* New York: Norton, 1993.

Lukacs, Georg. *The Theory of the Novel.* Cambridge, MA: MIT Press, 1974.

MacIntyre, Alasdair. *After Virtue: A Study in Moral Theory.* Notre Dame, IN: University of Notre Dame Press, 1981.

Murray, G. *The Rise of the Greek Epic.* 3rd ed. Oxford: Clarendon, 1924.

Nagy, Gregory. *The Best of the Achaeans: Concepts of the Hero in Archaic Greek Poetry.* Baltimore: Johns Hopkins University Press, 1979.

Nietzsche, Friedrich. *Early Greek Philosophy and other Essays.* New York: Macmillan, 1911.

———. *Thus Spoke Zarathustra.* Trans. Walter Kaufmann. New York: Viking Press, 1971.

Page, Denis L. *History and the Homeric Iliad.* Berkeley: University of California Press, 1959.

Redfield, James M. *Nature and Culture in the Iliad.* Chicago: University of Chicago Press, 1975.

Scott, John A. *The Unity of Homer.* Berkeley: University of California Press, 1921.

Segal, C. "The Theme of the Mutilation of the Corpse in the *Iliad.*" *Mnemosyne,* suppl. 17, 1971.

Shay, Jonathan. *Achilles in Vietnam: Combat Trauma and the Undoing of Character.* New York: Simon and Schuster, 1995.

Snell, Bruno. *The Discovery of the Mind.* Trans. T. G. Rosenmeyer. Cambridge, MA: Harvard University Press, 1953.

Steiner, George. *Language and Silence: Essays on Language, Literature, and the Inhuman.* New York: Atheneum, 1967.

Steiner, George, and Robert Fagles, eds. *Homer: A Collection of Critical Essays.* Englewood Cliffs, NJ: Prentice-Hall, 1962.

Wade-Gery, H. T. *The Poet of the Iliad.* Cambridge: Cambridge University Press, 1952.

Weil, Simone. "*The Iliad,* Poem of Force." *The Simone Weil Reader.* New York: McKay, 1977.

Whitman, C. H. *Homer and the Homeric Tradition.* Cambridge, MA: Harvard University Press, 1958.

Williams, Bernard. *Shame and Necessity.* Berkeley: University of California Press, 2008.

2. The Saint

Alter, Robert, and Frank Kermode, eds. *The Literary Guide to the Bible.* London: Grafton, 1987.

Armstrong, Karen. *Buddha.* New York: Penguin, 2004.

——. *The Great Transformation: The Beginning of Our Religious Traditions.* New York: Knopf, 2006.

Baker, D. L. *Two Testaments, One Bible.* Leicester, U.K.: Inter-Varsity Press, 1976.

Barker, Margaret. *The Older Testament: The Survival of Themes from the Ancient Royal Cult in Sectarian Judaism and Early Christianity.* London: SPCK, 1987.

Blake, William. *Complete Poetry and Prose of William Blake.* Ed. David Erdman, with commentary by Harold Bloom. 2nd ed. Berkeley: University of California Press, 1982.

Bloom, Harold. *Jesus and Yahweh: The Names Divine.* New York: Riverhead, 2005.

Bodhi, Bhikkhu. *In the Buddha's Words: An Anthology of Discourses from the Pali Canon.* Boston: Wisdom Publications, 2005.

Bottero, Jean. *The Birth of God: The Bible and the Historian.* Trans. Kees W. Bolle. University Park: Pennsylvania State University Press, 2000.

Brockington, John. *The Sanskrit Epics.* Leiden: Brill, 1998.

Campbell, Joseph. *The Hero with a Thousand Faces.* Princeton, NJ: Princeton University Press, 1949.

———. *Transformations of Myth through Time.* New York: Perennial Library, 1990.

Chakravarti, Sures Chandra. *The Philosophy of the Upanishads.* Calcutta: University of Calcutta, 1935.

Chang, K. C. *Art, Myth and Ritual: The Path to Political Authority in Ancient China.* Cambridge, MA: Harvard University Press, 1983.

Chaudhuri, Nirad C. *Hinduism: A Religion to Live By.* New Delhi: B. I. Publications, 1979.

Ching, Julia. *Mysticism and Kingship in China: The Heart of Chinese Wisdom.* Cambridge: Cambridge University Press, 1997.

Collins, Steven. *Selfless Persons: Imagery and Thought in Theravada Buddhism.* Cambridge: Cambridge University Press, 1982.

Confucius. *The Analects.* New York: Penguin, 1979.

Conze, Edward. *Buddhism: Its Essence and Development.* Oxford: Bruno Cassirer, 1951.

———. *Buddhist Meditation.* London: Allen and Unwin, 1956.

———. *A Short History of Buddhism.* Oxford: Allen and Unwin, 1980.

Crossan, John Dominic. *The Birth of Christianity: Discovering What Happened in the Years Immediately after the Execution of Jesus.* New York: HarperOne, 1998.

Dawson, Raymond. *Confucius.* Oxford: Oxford University Press, 1981.

Douglas, Mary. *Purity and Danger.* London: Praeger, 1966.

Dutt, Sukumar. *Buddha and Five After-Centuries.* London: Luzac, 1957.

Edwardes, Michael. *In the Blowing Out of a Flame: The World of the Buddha and the World of Man.* London: Allen and Unwin, 1976.

Eisenstadt, S. N., ed. *The Origins and Diversity of Axial Age Civilizations.* Albany: State University of New York Press, 1986.

Eliade, Mircea. *Patterns in Comparative Religion.* Trans. Rosemary Sheed. London: Sheed and Ward, 1958.

———. *The Sacred and the Profane.* Trans. Willard R. Trask. New York: Harcourt, Brace, 1959.

Erdosy, G. *Urbanization in Early Historic India.* Oxford: British Archaeological Reports, 1988.

Fingarette, Herbert. *Confucius: The Secular as Sacred.* New York: Harper and Row, 1972.

Flood, Gavin. *An Introduction to Hinduism.* Cambridge: Cambridge University Press, 1996.

Frawley, David. *Gods, Sages and Kings: Vedic Secrets of Ancient Civilization.* Salt Lake City: Passage, 1991.

Friedman, Richard Eliott. *Who Wrote the Bible?* New York: Harper and Row, 1987.

Frye, Northrop. *Fearful Symmetry: A Study of William Blake.* Princeton, NJ: Princeton University Press, 1947.

Fung Yu-Lan. *A Short History of Chinese Philosophy.* Ed. and trans. Derk Bodde. New York: Free Press, 1976.

Ghosh, A. *The City in Early Historical India.* Simla: Indian Institute for Advance Study, 1973.

Gide, André. *Journals 1889–1949.* New York: Knopf, 1956.

Girard, René. *Violence and the Sacred.* Trans. Patrick Gregory. Baltimore: Johns Hopkins University Press, 1977.

Gombrich, Richard F. *Buddhist Precept and Practice: Traditional Buddhism in the Rural Highlands of Ceylon.* London: Kegan Paul International, 1995.

Gonda, Jan. *Change and Continuity in Indian Religion.* The Hague: Mouton, 1965.

Granet, Michael. *Chinese Civilization.* Trans. Kathleen Innes and Mabel Brailsford. London: Barnes and Noble, 1951.

——. *The Religion of the Chinese People.* Trans. and ed. Maurice Freedman. Oxford: Blackwell, 1975.

Harnack, Adolf von. *Marcion: The Gospel of the Alien God.* Durham, NC: Labyrinth, 1924.

Hiltebeitel, Alf. *The Ritual of Battle: Krishna in the Mahabharata.* Ithaca, NY: Cornell University Press, 1976.

Hopkins, E. Washington. *The Great Epic of India.* New York: C. Scribner's Sons, 1902.

Hopkins, Thomas J. *The Hindu Religious Tradition.* Belmont, CA: Wadsworth, 1971.

Ivanhoe, Philip J. *Confucian Moral Self-Cultivation.* 2nd ed. Indianapolis: Hackett, 2000.

——. *Ethics in the Confucian Tradition.* 2nd ed. Indianapolis: Hackett, 2002.

Jenkins, Philip. *Laying Down the Sword: Why We Can't Ignore the Bible's Violent Verses.* New York: HarperCollins, 2011.

Keith, Arthur Berriedale. *The Religion and Philosophy of the Veda and Upanishads.* Cambridge, MA: Harvard University Press, 1925.

Kermode, Frank. *The Genesis of Secrecy: On the Interpretation of Narrative.* Cambridge, MA: Harvard University Press, 1990.

King, Winston L. *Buddhism and Christianity.* Philadelphia: Westminster, 1962.

Ling, Trevor. *The Buddha: Buddhist Civilization in India and Ceylon.* London: Temple Smith, 1973.

Loewe, Michael, and Edward L. Shaughnessy, eds. *The Cambridge History of Ancient China.* Cambridge: Cambridge University Press, 1996.

Lopez, Donald S. *Buddhism.* London: Allen Lane, 2001.

———, ed. *Buddhist Scriptures.* New York: Penguin, 2004.

McArthur, Meher. *Confucius.* London: Quercus, 2010.

Miles, Jack. *Christ: A Crisis in the Life of God.* New York: Vintage, 2002.

———. *God: A Biography.* New York: Vintage, 1996.

Miller, Barbara Stoler, trans. *The Bhagavad-Gita: Krishna's Counsel in Time of War.* New York: Bantam Classics, 1986.

Mote, Frederick F. *Intellectual Foundations of China.* New York: McGraw-Hill, 1988.

Nanamoli, Bhikku, trans. and ed. *The Life of the Buddha, According to the Pali Canon.* Kandy, Sri Lanka: Buddhist Publication Society, 1972.

Narain, A. K., ed. *Studies in the History of Buddhism.* Delhi: B. R. Publishing, 1980.

The New Oxford Annotated Bible. Ed. Bruce M. Metzger and Roland E. Murphy. New York: Oxford University Press, 1989.

Oldenberg, Hermann. *Buddha: His Life, His Doctrine, His Order.* Trans. William Hoey. London: Williams and Norgate, 1882.

Rahula, Walpola. *What the Buddha Taught.* 2nd ed. Oxford: Fraser, 1959.

Santayana, George. *Interpretations of Poetry and Religion.* Cambridge, MA: MIT Press, 1989.

Skilton, Andrew. *A Concise History of Buddhism.* Birmingham, U.K.: Windhorse Publications, 1994.

Slater, Robert Larson. *Paradox and Nirvana.* Chicago: University of Chicago Press, 1951.

Smart, Ninian. *The Religious Experience of Mankind.* New York: Scribner, 1983.

Smith, D. Howard. *Chinese Religions.* London: Weidenfeld and Nicolson, 1968.

———. *Confucius.* London: Temple Smith, 1973.

Smith, Huston. *The World's Religions.* San Francisco: HarperSanFrancisco, 1991.

Smith, Mark S. *The Early History of God: Yahweh and the Other Deities in Ancient Israel.* New York: Harper and Row, 1990.

Tarnas, Richard. *The Passion of the Western Mind: Understanding the Ideas That Have Shaped Our World View.* New York: Ballantine, 1991.

Thomas, Edward J. *The Life of Buddha as Legend and History.* London: Routledge and Kegan Paul, 1969.

Thompson, Thomas L. *The Bible in History: How Writers Create a Past.* London: Jonathan Cape, 1999.

Tolstoy, Leo. *The Kingdom of God Is Within You.* Mineola, NY: Dover, 2006.

Vermes, Geza. *Jesus the Jew: A Historian's Reading of the Bible.* London: Collins, 1973.

Vetter, Tilmann. *The Ideas and Meditative Practices of Early Buddhism.* Leiden: Brill, 1988.

Yoder, John H. *The Politics of Jesus.* Grand Rapids, MI: William B. Eerdman, 1972.

Zaehner, R. S. *Hinduism.* London: Oxford University Press, 1962.

3. The Thinker

Allen, Gay Wilson. *Waldo Emerson: A Biography.* New York: Viking, 1981.

Bloom, Allan, ed. and trans. *The Republic of Plato.* New York: Basic Books, 1968.

Bloom, Harold. *Figures of Capable Imagination.* New York: Continuum, 1976.

Chamberlain, Leslie. *Nietzsche in Turin: An Intimate Biography.* New York: Picador, 1996.

Derrida, Jacques. "Plato's Pharmacy." *Dissemination.* Trans. Barbara Johnson, Chicago: University of Chicago Press, 1981. 61–171.

Dodds, E. R. *The Greeks and the Irrational.* Berkeley: University of California Press, 1951.

Dover, K. J. *Greek Homosexuality.* Cambridge, MA: Harvard University Press, 1989.

——. *Greek Popular Morality in the Time of Plato and Aristotle.* Oxford: Blackwell, 1974.

Ellison, Julie. *Emerson's Romantic Style.* Princeton, NJ: Princeton University Press, 1984.

Emerson, Ralph Waldo. *Essays and Lectures.* New York: Library of America, 1983.

Foucault, Michel. *L'Usage des plaisirs.* Paris: Gallimard, 1984.

Hamilton, Edith, and Huntington Cairns, eds. *The Collected Dialogues of Plato.* New York: Pantheon, 1961.

Havelock, Eric. *Preface to Plato.* Cambridge, MA: Harvard University Press, 1963.

Kaufmann, Walter. *Nietzsche: Philosopher, Psychologist, Antichrist.* Princeton, NJ: Princeton University Press, 1974.

Lear, Jonathan. *Open Minded: Working out the Logic of the Soul.* Cambridge, MA: Harvard University Press, 1998.

Murdoch, Iris. *The Fire and the Sun: Why Plato Banished the Artists.* Oxford: Clarendon, 1977.

Nehamas, Alexander. *Nietzsche: Life as Literature.* Cambridge, MA: Harvard University Press, 1987.

Nietzsche, Friedrich. *The Birth of Tragedy and the Genealogy of Morals.* Trans. Francis Golffing. New York: Doubleday, 1956.

Nussbaum, Martha. *The Fragility of Goodness: Luck and Ethics in Greek Tragedy and Philosophy.* Cambridge: Cambridge University Press, 1986.

Packer, B. L. *Emerson's Fall: A New Interpretation of the Major Essays.* New York: Continuum, 1982.

Paglia, Camille. *Sexual Personae: Art and Decadence from Nefertiti to Emily Dickinson.* New Haven, CT: Yale University Press, 1990.

Plato. *The Last Days of Socrates.* New York: Penguin, 2003.

Poirier, Richard. *The Renewal of Literature: Emersonian Reflections.* New Haven, CT: Yale University Press, 1988.

Richardson, Robert. *Emerson: The Mind on Fire.* Berkeley: University of California Press, 1986.

Rorty, Richard. *Contingency, Irony, and Solidarity.* Cambridge: Cambridge University Press, 1989.

Ross, W. D. *Plato's Theory of Ideas.* Oxford: Clarendon, 1951.

Ryle, Gilbert. *Plato's Progress.* Cambridge: Cambridge University Press, 1966.

Schopenhauer, Arthur. *The World as Will and Representation.* Trans. E. F. J. Payne. 2 vols. New York: Dover, 1966.

Snell, Bruno. *The Discovery of the Mind in Greek Philosophy and Literature.* New York: Dover, 1982.

Strauss, Leo. *Persecution and the Art of Writing.* Glencoe, IL: Free Press, 1952.

Thoreau, Henry David. *Walden and Civil Disobedience.* New York: Penguin, 1983.

Vlastos, Gregory. *Platonic Studies.* Princeton, NJ: Princeton University Press, 1981.

Whicher, Stephen E. *Freedom and Fate: An Inner Life of Ralph Waldo Emerson.* New York: A. S. Barnes, 1961.

4. Shakespeare and the Early Modern Self

Auden, W. H. *Lectures on Shakespeare.* Ed. Arthur C. Kirsch. Princeton, NJ: Princeton University Press, 2000.

Barber, C. L. *Shakespeare's Festive Comedy.* Princeton, NJ: Princeton University Press, 1959.

Barish, Jonas A. *The Antitheatrical Prejudice.* Berkeley: University of California Press, 1981.

Barton, Anne. *Essays, Mainly Shakespearian.* Cambridge: Cambridge University Press, 1994.

Bate, Jonathan, and Russell Jackson. *Shakespeare: An Illustrated Stage History.* Oxford: Oxford University Press, 1996.

Bloom, Harold. *Shakespeare: The Invention of the Human.* New York: Riverhead, 1999.

Bradley, A. C. *Shakespearean Tragedy.* Reprint. New York: St. Martin's, 1967.

Cavell, Stanley. *Disowning Knowledge in Six Plays of Shakespeare.* Cambridge: Cambridge University Press, 1987.

Crewe, Jonathan. *Trials of Authorship: Anterior Forms and Poetic Reconstruction from Wyatt to Shakespeare.* Berkeley: University of California Press, 1990.

Dollimore, Jonathan, and Alan Sinfield. *Political Shakespeare.* Ithaca, NY: Cornell University Press, 1985.

Engle, Lars. *Shakespearean Pragmatism: Market of His Time.* Chicago: University of Chicago Press, 1993.

Felperin, Howard. *Shakespearean Romance.* Princeton, NJ: Princeton University Press, 1972.

Fineman, Joel. *Shakespeare's Perjured Eye: The Invention of Poetic Subjectivity in the Sonnets.* Berkeley: University of California Press, 1986.

Frye, Northrop. *A Natural Perspective: The Development of Shakespearean Comedy and Romance.* New York: Columbia University Press, 1965.

——. *Fools of Time: Studies in Shakespearean Tragedy.* Toronto: University of Toronto Press, 1967.

Frye, Roland M. *Shakespeare and Christian Doctrine.* Princeton, NJ: Princeton University Press, 1963.

Garber, Marjorie, ed. *Cannibals, Witches, Divorce: Estranging the Renaissance.* Baltimore: Johns Hopkins University Press, 1987.

Goddard, Harold C. *The Meaning of Shakespeare.* 2 vols. Chicago: University of Chicago Press, 1951.

Granville-Barker, Harley. *Prefaces to Shakespeare.* Rev. ed. 4 vols. Princeton, NJ: Princeton University Press, 1946–1947.

Greenblatt, Stephen. *Learning to Curse: Essays in Early Modern Culture.* London: Routledge, 1990.

——, ed. *The Norton Shakespeare.* New York: Norton, 1997.

——. *Renaissance Self-Fashioning: From More to Shakespeare.* Chicago: University of Chicago Press, 1980.

——. *Shakespearean Negotiations.* Oxford: Oxford University Press, 1988.

Hauser, Arnold. *The Social History of Art.* 4 vols. London: Routledge, 1999.

Hazlitt, William. *Characters of Shakespeare's Plays.* New York: Dutton, 1910.

Honan, Park. *Shakespeare: A Life.* Oxford: Oxford University Press, 1998.

Hunter, G. K. *English Drama, 1586–1642: The Age of Shakespeare.* Oxford: Oxford University Press, 1997.

Hyman, Stanley Edgar. *Iago: Some Approaches to the Illusion of His Motivation.* New York: Atheneum, 1970.

Jardine, Lisa. *Still Harping on Daughters: Women and Drama in the Age of Shakespeare.* 1983. 2nd ed. New York: Columbia University Press, 1989.

Johnson, Samuel. *The Works of Samuel Johnson.* Ed. Arthur Sherbo. New Haven, CT: Yale University Press, 1968.

Kahn, Coppélia. *Roman Shakespeare: Warriors, Wounds, and Women.* London: Routledge, 1997.

Kantorowicz, Ernst. *The King's Two Bodies.* Princeton, NJ: Princeton University Press, 1957.

Kinney, Arthur. *Humanist Poetics.* Amherst: University of Massachusetts Press, 1986.

Knight, G. Wilson. *The Wheel of Fire: Interpretation of Shakespeare's Tragedy.* Rev. ed. New York: Barnes and Noble, 1965.

Kott, Jan. *Shakespeare Our Contemporary.* Trans. Boleslaw Taborski. New York: Norton, 1964.

Levin, Harry. *The Myth of the Golden Age in the Renaissance.* Bloomington: Indiana University Press, 1969.

Lewalski, Barbara. *Writing Women in Jacobean England.* Cambridge, MA: Harvard University Press, 1993.

Lovejoy, Arthur O. *The Great Chain of Being: A Study of the History of an Idea.* Cambridge, MA: Harvard University Press, 1936.

Mack, Maynard. *Everybody's Shakespeare.* Lincoln: University of Nebraska Press, 1993.

——. *King Lear in Our Time.* Berkeley: University of California Press, 1965.

Maus, Katharine E. *Inwardness and Theater in the English Renaissance.* Chicago: University of Chicago Press, 1995.

Montrose, Louis Adrian. "'Shaping Fantasies': Figurations of Gender and Power in Elizabethan Culture." *Representations* 2 (1983): 61–94.

——. "The Elizabethan Subject and the Spenserian Text." *Literary Theory / Renaissance Texts.* Ed. Patricia Parker and David Quint. Baltimore: Johns Hopkins University Press, 1986.

——. *The Purpose of Playing: Shakespeare and the Cultural Politics of the Elizabethan Theatre.* Chicago: University of Chicago Press, 1996.

Mullaney, Steven. *The Place of the Stage: License, Play, and Power in Renaissance England.* Chicago: University of Chicago Press, 1988.

Orgel, Stephen. *The Illusion of Power: Political Theater in the English Renaissance.* Berkeley: University of California Press, 1975.

——. *Impersonations: The Performance of Gender in Shakespeare's England.* Cambridge: Cambridge University Press, 1996.

Parker, Patricia. *Literary Fat Ladies: Rhetoric, Gender, Property.* London: Methuen, 1987.

——. *Shakespeare from the Margins: Language, Culture, Context.* Chicago: University of Chicago Press, 1996.

Parker, Patricia, and Geoffrey Hartman, eds. *Shakespeare and the Question of Theory.* London: Methuen, 1985.

Plutarch. *Plutarch's Lives.* Vol. 2. New York: Modern Library, 2001.

Quinones, Ricardo J. *The Renaissance Discovery of Time.* Cambridge, MA: Harvard University Press, 1972.

Rossiter, A. P. *Angel with Horns, and Other Shakespearean Lectures.* Ed. Graham Storey. London: Longmans Green, 1961.

Santayana, George. *Interpretations of Poetry and Religion.* Cambridge, MA: MIT Press, 1989.

Schopenhauer, Arthur. *Parerga and Paralipomena.* Vol. 2. Oxford: Clarendon, 2010.

Shakespeare, William. *The Riverside Shakespeare.* Ed. G. Blakemore Evans. Boston: Houghton Mifflin, 1997.

Shuger, Debora Kuller. *Habits of Thought in the English Renaissance: Religion, Politics, and the Dominant Culture.* Berkeley: University of California Press, 1990.

Skura, Meredith. *Shakespeare the Actor and the Purposes of Playing.* Chicago: University of Chicago Press, 1993.

Stone, Lawrence. *The Crisis of the Aristocracy, 1558–1641.* Oxford: Oxford University Press, 1965.

Taylor, Gary. *Reinventing Shakespeare: A Cultural History, from the Restoration to the Present.* London: Weidenfeld and Nicolson, 1989.

Tolstoy, Leo. *Last Steps: The Late Writings of Leo Tolstoy.* New York: Penguin, 2009.

5. The Poet

Abrams, M. H., ed. *English Romantic Poets: Modern Essays in Criticism.* New York: Oxford University Press, 1960.

———. *The Mirror and the Lamp: Romantic Theory and the Critical Tradition.* New York: Oxford University Press, 1953.

———. *Natural Supernaturalism: Tradition and Revolution in Romantic Literature.* New York: Norton, 1971.

———, ed. *Wordsworth: A Collection of Critical Essays.* Englewood Cliffs, NJ: Prentice-Hall, 1972.

Ackroyd, Peter. *Blake: A Biography.* New York: Knopf, 1996.

Adams, Hazard. *William Blake: A Reading of the Shorter Poems.* Seattle: University of Washington Press, 1963.

Arnold, Matthew. *Essays in Criticism: Second Series.* London: Macmillan, 1935.

Bate, Walter Jackson. *Coleridge.* New York: Macmillan, 1968.

———. *From Classic to Romantic: Premises of Taste in Eighteenth-Century England.* Cambridge, MA: Harvard University Press, 1949.

———. *John Keats.* Cambridge, MA: Harvard University Press, 1963.

———. *Negative Capability: The Intuitive Approach in Keats.* Cambridge, MA: Harvard University Press, 1939.

Beer, John B. *Coleridge, the Visionary.* London: Chatto and Windus, 1959.

Bentley, G. E. *William Blake in the Desolate Market.* Montreal: McGill–Queen's University Press, 2014.

Bewell, Alan. *Wordsworth and the Enlightenment: Nature, Man, and Society in the Experimental Poetry.* New Haven, CT: Yale University Press, 1989.

Blake, William. *Complete Poetry and Prose of William Blake.* Ed. David Erdman, with commentary by Harold Bloom. 2nd ed. Berkeley: University of California Press, 1982.

Bloom, Harold. *Blake's Apocalypse: A Study in Poetic Argument.* Garden City, NY: Doubleday, 1965.

———. *The Ringers in the Tower: Studies in Romantic Tradition.* Chicago: University of Chicago Press, 1971.

———, ed. *Romanticism and Consciousness: Essays in Criticism.* New York: Norton, 1970.

———. *Shelley's Mythmaking.* Ithaca, NY: Cornell University Press, 1969.

———. *The Visionary Company: A Reading of English Romantic Poetry.* Rev. and enlarged ed. Ithaca, NY: Cornell University Press, 1971.

Bloom, Harold, and Lionel Trilling, eds. *Romantic Poetry and Prose.* New York: Oxford University Press, 1973.

Bradley, A. C. *Oxford Lectures on Poetry.* London: Macmillan, 1909.

Bush, Douglas. *Mythology and the Romantic Tradition in English Poetry.* Cambridge, MA: Harvard University Press, 1937.

Butler, Marilyn. *Romantics, Rebels and Reactionaries: English Literature and Its Background, 1760–1830.* New York: Oxford University Press, 1982.

Cobban, Alfred. *Edmund Burke and the Revolt against the Eighteenth Century.* 2nd ed. London: Allen and Unwin, 1960.

Coburn, Kathleen, ed. *Coleridge: A Collection of Critical Essays.* Englewood Cliffs, NJ: Prentice-Hall, 1967.

Damon, S. Foster. *A Blake Dictionary: The Ideas and Symbols of William Blake.* New York: Dutton, 1971.

——. *William Blake: His Philosophy and Symbols.* New York: Peter Smith, 1947.

Damrosch, Leopold. *Symbol and Truth in Blake's Myth.* Princeton, NJ: Princeton University Press, 1982.

Dickstein, Morris. *Keats and His Poetry: A Study in Development.* Chicago: University of Chicago Press, 1971.

Erdman, David V. *Blake, Prophet against Empire: A Poet's Interpretation of the History of His Own Times.* Princeton, NJ: Princeton University Press, 1954.

Erdman, David V., and John Ernest Grant. *Blake's Visionary Forms Dramatic.* Princeton, NJ: Princeton University Press, 1970.

Ferber, Michael. *The Social Vision of William Blake.* Princeton, NJ: Princeton University Press, 1985.

Ferry, David. *The Limits of Mortality: An Essay on Wordsworth's Major Poems.* Middletown, CT: Wesleyan University Press, 1959.

Fogle, Richard Harter. *Romantic Poets and Prose Writers.* Northbrook, IL: AHM Publishing, 1967.

Frye, Northrop, ed. *Blake: A Collection of Critical Essays.* Englewood Cliffs, NJ: Prentice-Hall, 1966.

——. *Fearful Symmetry: A Study of William Blake.* Boston: Beacon, 1962.

Gilchrist, Alexander. *Life of William Blake.* London: Macmillan, 1863.

Hartman, Geoffrey. *Beyond Formalism: Literary Essays, 1958–1970.* New Haven, CT: Yale University Press, 1970.

——. *The Fate of Reading, and Other Essays.* Chicago: University of Chicago Press, 1975.

——. *New Perspectives on Coleridge and Wordsworth: Selected Papers from the English Institute.* New York: Columbia University Press, 1972.

——. *Wordsworth's Poetry, 1787–1814.* New Haven, CT: Yale University Press, 1964.

House, Humphry. *Coleridge.* London: Hart/Davis, 1967.

Jack, Ian. *English Literature, 1815–1832.* New York: Oxford University Press, 1963.

Jones, John. *The Egotistical Sublime: A History of Wordsworth's Imagination.* London: Chatto and Windus, 1953.

Kermode, Frank. *Romantic Image.* London: Routledge and Paul, 1957.

Knight, George Wilson. *The Burning Oracle: Studies in the Poetry of Action.* London: Oxford University Press, 1939.

Levinson, Marjorie. *Wordsworth's Great Period Poems: Four Essays*. Cambridge: Cambridge University Press, 1986.

Lowes, John Livingston. *The Road to Xanadu: A Study in the Ways of the Imagination*. Boston: Houghton Mifflin, 1927.

Makdisi, Saree. *William Blake and the Impossible History of the 1790s*. Chicago: University of Chicago Press, 2003.

Marchand, Leslie Alexis. *Byron: A Biography*. 3 vols. New York: Knopf, 1957.

McGann, Jerome J. *Fiery Dust: Byron's Poetic Development*. Chicago: University of Chicago Press, 1968.

———. *The Romantic Ideology: A Critical Investigation*. Chicago: University of Chicago Press, 1985.

Murry, John Middleton. *Keats*. 4th ed. New York: Noonday, 1955.

———. *Keats and Shakespeare: A Study of Keats' Poetic Life from 1816 to 1820*. London: Milford–Oxford University Press, 1926.

Paglia, Camille. *Break, Blow, Burn: Camille Paglia Reads Forty-Three of the World's Best Poems*. New York: Vintage, 2006.

Percival, Milton Oswin. *William Blake's Circle of Destiny*. New York: Octagon Books, 1977.

Pulos, C. E. *The Deep Truth: A Study of Shelley's Skepticism*. Lincoln: University of Nebraska Press, 1954.

Quinney, Laura. *William Blake on Self and Soul*. Cambridge. MA: Harvard University Press, 2009.

Richards, I. A. *Coleridge on Imagination*. New York: Norton, 1950.

Ross, Marlon. *The Contours of Masculine Desire: Romanticism and the Rise of Women's Poetry*. New York: Oxford University Press, 1989.

Schorer, Mark. *William Blake: The Politics of Vision*. New York: Henry Holt, 1946.

Shelley, Percy Bysshe. *The Poems of Shelley*. Oxford: Oxford University Press, 1961.

Wasserman, Earl R. *The Finer Tone: Keats' Major Poems*. Baltimore: Johns Hopkins University Press, 1953.

———. *Shelley: A Critical Reading*. Baltimore: Johns Hopkins University Press, 1971.

White, Newman Ivey. *Shelley*. 2 vols. New York: Knopf, 1940.

Williams, Raymond. *Culture and Society, 1780–1950*. New York: Columbia University Press, 1960.

Wilson, Milton Thomas. *Shelley's Later Poetry: A Study of His Prophetic Imagination.* New York: Columbia University Press, 1959.

Woodring, Carl. *Politics in English Romantic Poetry.* Cambridge, MA: Harvard University Press, 1970.

——. *Wordsworth.* Boston: Houghton Mifflin, 1965.

6. Freud and the Ideal Self

Behling, Katja. *Martha Freud: A Biography.* Trans. R. D. V. Glasgow. Cambridge: Polity, 2005.

Bowie, Malcolm. *Lacan.* Cambridge, MA: Harvard University Press, 1991.

Brabant, Eva, Ernst Falzeder, and Patrizia Giampieri-Deutsch, eds. *The Correspondence of Sigmund Freud and Sándor Ferenczi.* Vol. 1, 1908–1914. Trans. Peter Hoffer. Cambridge, MA: Belknap Press of Harvard University Press, 1993.

Breger, Louis. *Sigmund Freud: Darkness in the Midst of Vision.* New York: John Wiley and Sons, 2000.

Brod, Max. *Franz Kafka: A Biography.* New York: Schocken, 1947.

Brome, Vincent. *Ernest Jones: A Biography.* New York: Norton, 1983.

Burke, Kenneth. *The Philosophy of Literary Form.* Berkeley: University of California Press, 1974.

Clark, Ronald W. *Freud, the Man and His Cause.* London: Jonathan Cape, 1980.

Edmundson, Mark. *The Death of Sigmund Freud.* New York: Bloomsbury, 2007.

——. *Towards Reading Freud: Self-Creation in Milton, Wordsworth, Emerson, and Sigmund Freud.* Princeton, NJ: Princeton University Press, 1990.

Engelman, Edmund. *Berggasse 19: Sigmund Freud's Home and Offices, Vienna 1938.* Chicago: University of Chicago Press, 1976.

Fine, Reuben. *A History of Psychoanalysis.* New York: Columbia University Press, 1979.

Freud, Ernst L. *Letters of Sigmund Freud.* Trans. Tania and James Stern. New York: Basic Books, 1960.

Freud, Ernst L., ed. *The Letters of Sigmund Freud and Arnold Zweig.* Trans. Elaine Robson-Scott and William D. Robson-Scott. New York: Harcourt, Brace and World, 1970.

Freud, Ernst L., Lucie Freud, and Ilse Grubrich-Simitis, eds. *Sigmund Freud: His Life in Pictures and Words.* Trans. Christine Trollope. New York: Harcourt Brace Jovanovich, 1978.

Freud, Ernst L., and Heinrich Meng. *Psychoanalysis and Faith: The Letters of Sigmund Freud and Oskar Pfister.* Trans. Eric Mosbacher. London: Hogarth, 1963.

Freud, Martin. *Sigmund Freud, Man and Father.* New York: Jason Aronson, 1983.

Freud, Sigmund. *The Standard Edition of the Complete Psychological Works of Sigmund Freud.* Trans. James Strachey et al. 24 vols. London: Hogarth, 1953.

Gay, Peter. *Freud: A Life for Our Time.* New York: Norton, 1971.

H. D. [Hilda Doolittle]. *Tribute to Freud.* New York: Pantheon, 1956.

Jones, Ernest. *The Life and Work of Sigmund Freud.* 3 vols. New York: Basic Books, 1957.

Lear, Jonathan. *Love and Its Place in Nature: A Philosophical Interpretation of Freudian Psychoanalysis.* New York: Farrar, Straus and Giroux, 1991.

Masson, Jeffrey, M., ed. and trans. *The Complete Letters of Sigmund Freud to Wilhelm Fliess, 1887–1904.* Cambridge, MA: Harvard University Press, 1985.

McGuire, William, ed. *The Freud/Jung Letters: The Correspondence between Sigmund Freud and C. G. Jung.* Trans. Ralph Manheim and R. F. C. Hull. Princeton, NJ: Princeton University Press, 1974.

McGuire, William, and R. F. C. Hull, eds. *C. G. Jung Speaking.* Princeton, NJ: Princeton University Press, 1977.

Miller, Jonathan, ed. *Freud: The Man, His World, His Influence.* Boston: Little, Brown, 1972.

Molnar, Michael, ed. and trans. *The Diary of Sigmund Freud, 1929–1939: A Record of the Final Decade.* New York: Charles Scribner's Sons, 1992.

Paskauskas, R. Andrew, ed. *The Complete Correspondence of Sigmund Freud and Ernest Jones, 1908–1939.* Cambridge, MA: Harvard University Press, 1993.

Pfeiffer, Ernst, ed. *Sigmund Freud and Lou Andreas-Salomé: Letters.* Trans. William D. Robson-Scott and Elaine Robson-Scott. New York: Norton, 1985.

Phillips, Adam. *Darwin's Worms.* London: Faber and Faber, 1999.

———. *Terrors and Experts.* London: Faber and Faber, 1995.

Rieff, Philip. *Freud: The Mind of the Moralist.* Chicago: University of Chicago Press, 1959.

Roazen, Paul. *Freud and His Followers.* New York: Knopf, 1975.

Rosenzweig, Saul. *The Historic Expedition to America: Freud, Jung and Hall the King-Maker.* St. Louis: Rana House, 1994.

Said, Edward W. *Freud and the Non-European.* London: Verso, 2003.

Schorske, Carl E. *Fin-de-Siècle Vienna: Politics and Culture.* New York: Random House, 1981.

Schur, Max. *Freud: Living and Dying.* New York: International Universities Press, 1972.

Strachey, James, et al., eds. *The Standard Edition of the Complete Psychological Works of Sigmund Freud.* 24 vols. London: Hogarth, 1953–1974.

Unwerth, Matthew von. *Freud's Requiem: Mourning, Memory, and the Invisible History of a Summer Walk.* New York: Riverhead, 2005.

Van den Berg, Jan Hendrich. *The Changing Nature of Man: Introduction to a Historical Psychology.* Trans. H. F. Croes. New York: Delta, 1961.

Acknowledgments

This book took some time to write and in the process accrued multiple debts.

I am grateful, first, to the many students at the University of Virginia who enrolled in Literary Ideals. The course became this book—and it did so with their generous and high-spirited help.

Great gratitude to the two friends who read the manuscript cover to cover and provided perceptive commentary and suggestions: Lars Engle and David Mikics.

Thanks to those who read individual chapters and, based on learned expertise, offered their advice. On Confucius, I am indebted to my brother-in-law, the distinguished Sinologist Kirk Denton; on the New Testament, I profited from the comments of Stephen Cushman and Charles Mathewes. Karen Lang offered thoughts on Gautama based on a lifetime study of Buddhism. On Shakespeare, I am indebted to a careful reading by Gordon Braden.

Three anonymous readers for Harvard University Press posed tough questions and offered excellent advice. I thank them all.

Errors that might occur here owe nothing to these fine and generous helpers, but only to me.

Thanks to the colleges and universities that invited me to give talks based on the material in this book. I am grateful to the College of William & Mary (Cloud Lecture), Syracuse University, the University of Alabama (Phi Beta Kappa Lecture), Amherst College, North Carolina Lutheran College, Longwood University, Luther College, Liberty University, Elmhurst College, the Ohio State University, the University of Houston (Houston Lecture), the University of Nebraska (Knoll Lecture), and the Institute for Advanced Studies in Culture at the University of Virginia.

I am especially grateful to David Clemens, who invited me to Monterey Bay Community College to talk about ideals, and who has been a potent supporter of this project from the start.

Thanks to those who read sections of the book or discussed its overall direction with me, in particular Peter Devine, Alex Star, and Michael Pollan. Thanks to my colleagues in the English Department at the University of Virginia: it would be hard to imagine a more amiable, accomplished, and accepting group. Thanks to John Casteen, who appointed me to a university professorship, and Terry Sullivan, who now oversees the appointment. The time and resources that came with that position have helped make this and numerous other projects possible.

I'm most grateful to Lindsay Waters at Harvard University Press, an editor who is more than an editor, and to his assistant, Amanda Peery. Thanks too to Susan Campbell, my generous copyeditor; Melody Negron for giving so much valuable help in the production of the book; and Christian Howard for helping me to prepare the manuscript.

Finally: gratitude and love abounding to my family—Liz and Willie and Matthew.

This book is dedicated foremost to my mother, who loved my brother and sister and me, no matter what we did or did not do.

Index

Achilles, 2–4; pride, 20–23; restitution, 28–30, 44; and Patroclus, 37–40; killing of Hector, 40–43; encounter with Priam, 45–47; compared to Buddha, 54, 56–57; compared to Socrates, 115–116, 118; in *Troilus and Cressida*, 170–172

Agamemnon, 20–23, 28–30, 44

Andromache, 32–33, 35, 47

Arendt, Hannah, 112

Aristotle, 154, 224

Arnold, Matthew, 253

Astyanax, 31–33, 35, 74

Blake, William, 187–188; Romantic love, 14, 199–201, 211–212; forgiveness, 78; *Songs of Innocence and Experience*, 188–190, 193–197, 206; Selfhood, 189–191, 216; erotic love, 191–193; religion, 196–198; *Milton*, 201–204; Urizen, 204–207

Bloom, Harold, 10, 137–138, 185

Buddha, 51–54; compared to Achilles, 54, 56–57; truth, 56; teaching, 58–61; Soul, 62; Universal Being, 237. *See also* Freud, Sigmund: compared to Jesus, Buddha, and Confucius

Caesar, Julius, 141, 165–167, 180–181, 183

Cervantes, Miguel de, 11, 155, 184

Chaucer, Geoffrey, 140–141

Christ. *See* Jesus

Coleridge, Samuel Taylor, 187, 199, 209

Confucius, 62–63; teaching, 63–65; ideal of the gentleman, 66–67. *See also* Buddha: Universal Being; Freud, Sigmund: compared to Jesus, Buddha, and Confucius

Coriolanus, 167–168, 173

Crane, Hart, 186, 199, 209, 215

Darwin, Charles, 109, 213, 222

David (King in Biblical Old Testament), 68–69

Derrida, Jacques, 132, 234

Descartes, René, 137

Dickens, Charles, 183–184

Eliot, T. S., 82, 230

Emerson, Ralph Waldo: creative reading, 107–108; nature, 108–110; as spiritual friend of Henry David Thoreau, 111–112; thinking as an intellectual endeavor, 111–112, 118, 133–134

Foucault, Michel, 131

Freud, Sigmund, 219–221; and Shakespearean drama, 12–13, 165; Self, 14, 221–222; Eros, 186, 205–206,

Freud, Sigmund *(continued)* 230–234, 242; psychoanalysis, 203–204, 243–245; dreams, 212; nature, 213; *The Ego and the Id*, 222–224; talking cure, 224–226; *Civilization and Its Discontents*, 228; unity of being, 234–236; compared to Jesus, Buddha, and Confucius, 236–237; *Moses and Monotheism*, 238; Death Drive, 240–241; and Kant, 242
Frye, Northrop, 35, 77, 80, 90, 206–207

Gautama. *See* Buddha
Gide, André, 88
Ginsberg, Allen, 199, 207, 215
Goethe, Johann Wolfgang von, 176, 179

Hamlet, 12, 141, 174–175, 180
Hauser, Arnold, 11, 153–154
Hector, 3–4; as hero, 30–31; as father, 32–33, 35; killing of Patroclus, 38–40; death of, 40–43; burial of, 47; in *Troilius and Cressida*, 171–172
Heidegger, Martin, 103
Homer: *The Iliad*, 2, 21–23, 28, 38, 48, 51; Homeric heroes, 4, 23–24; critiqued by Plato, 4–5, 123–125, 239; *The Odyssey*, 38

Iago: inverse of Othello, 145–146, 148–149; perspectivism, 147; Shakespeare as Iago figure, 151–152. *See also* Shakespeare, William: dramatic characters

James, Henry, Sr., 111
Jesus: compassion, 7–10, 67–68, 72–74, 87–88; and Old Testament tradition, 71–72, 88, 98; Gospels, 75, 86–87; performing miracles, 75, 77; and William Blake, 78, 196–198; forgiveness, 78–79; and children, 81–82, 195–196; and women, 82–83; and Romans, 83–85; retributive God, 88–92, 94; crucifixion, 93; and American Christianity, 255–256. *See also* Buddha: Universal Being; Freud, Sigmund: compared to Jesus, Buddha, and Confucius
Jonson, Ben, 140
Jung, Carl Gustav, 226–227

Kant, Immanuel, 105, 242
Keats, John: on Shakespeare, 95, 138–139, 152; negative capability, 11, 206–207; Romantic poet, 199, 215; "Ode to Psyche," 208

Lacan, Jacques, 60, 242
Lawrence, D. H., 199
Lukacs, Georg, 25

Macbeth: as warrior, 156–157, 161; masculinity, 158–161; *Macbeth*, 161; and nihilism, 163–164. *See also* Shakespeare, William: dramatic characters
Mann, Thomas, 176
Marlowe, Christopher, 140, 176
Marx, Karl, 36, 178, 226–227
Milton, John, 69, 105, 243. *See also* Blake, William: *Milton*

Nietzsche, Friedrich, 9, 23, 28, 49–50, 78; *The Birth of Tragedy*, 104, 141; *The Genealogy of Morals*, 104, 146; and Schopenhauer, 104–105, 112; and Kant, 105; *The Genealogy of Knowledge*, 110; contra Plato, 126; "perspectival" seeing, 145; and Romanticism, 185–186. *See also* Emerson, Ralph Waldo: thinking as an intellectual endeavor

Odysseus, 5, 29, 36, 38
Othello: *Othello*, 141, 151; as hero, 144–145; inverse of Iago, 145–146, 148–149; and doubt, 148–150, 155; death of, 152–153. *See also* Shakespeare, William: dramatic characters

Plato: critique of Homer, 4–5, 123–125, 239; *The Republic*, 5, 122–124; philosophic Truth, 5–6, 127, 129; ideal

of the thinker, 102–103; mistrust of writing, 106; and women, 112; need for positive enlightenment, 118–119; allegory of the cave, 119–122; and Nietzsche, 126; *The Symposium*, 191, 200
Plutarch, 165–168, 173
Priam, 32, 41, 45–47

Santayana, George, 178–179
Saul (King in Biblical Old Testament), 68, 70–71
Schopenhauer, Arthur, 8, 107, 110–111, 118, 149–150. *See also* Nietzsche, Friedrich: and Schopenhauer
Shakespeare, William: anti-idealism, 10–12; *The Merchant of Venice*, 11, 78, 179–180; *Hamlet*, 12, 141, 174–175, 180; dramatic characters, 137–138, 149–150, 173–174, 175; personal values, 138–140; Homeric values, 140; *Troilus and Cressida*, 140, 168–169, 171–172; *Titus Andronicus*, 141–144; *Othello*, 141, 151; *The Tempest*, 141, 176; *Julius Caesar*, 141, 183; as Iago figure, 151–152; and women, 155–156, 164; *Macbeth*, 161; *Romeo and Juliet*, 169, 177; literary style, 172; academic interpretations of, 172–173; and religious figures, 176–177; Catholicism, 178–179; and Romanticism, 186–187. *See also* Freud, Sigmund: and Shakespearean drama; Keats, John: on Shakespeare
Shelley, Percy; Romantic poet, 13, 199, 215; erotic love, 186; *Prometheus Unbound*, 206–207, 209–210, 231
Socrates, 110, 113–115; in *The Republic*, 5, 122–124; ideal of the thinker, 102–103; compared to Achilles, 115–116, 118; death of, 117–118; allegory of the cave, 119–122; candor, 127–129; in *The Symposium*, 191, 200

Thoreau, Henry David, 10; the thinking man, 103–104; *Walden*, 104; friend of Emerson, 111–112
Tolstoy, Leo, 177–178

Virgil, 143

Whitman, Walt, 14, 199–200, 215, 257–258
Wordsworth, William, 189, 199, 201, 206, 208, 215

Yahweh: loving God, 7; beyond human conception, 24–25; warrior God, 69–70, 93; retributive God, 88–92, 94; and American Christianity, 255–256. *See also* Jesus: and Old Testament tradition

■ *verb* /ˈdelɪgeɪt/ **1** [I, T] to give part of your work, power or authority to sb in a lower position than you: *Some managers find it difficult to delegate.* ◇ **~ (sth) (to sb)** *The job had to be delegated to an assistant.* **2** [T] **~ sb to do sth** [usually passive] to choose sb to do sth: *I've been delegated to organize the Christmas party.*

dele·ga·tion /ˌdelɪˈgeɪʃn/ *noun* **1** [C+sing./pl. v.] a group of people who represent the views of an organization, a country, etc: *the Dutch delegation to the United Nations* ◇ *a delegation of teachers* ➲ COLLOCATIONS at INTERNATIONAL **2** [U] the process of giving sb work or responsibilities that would usually be yours: *delegation of authority/decision-making*

de·lete /dɪˈliːt/ *verb* **~ sth (from sth)** to remove sth that has been written or printed, or that has been stored on a computer: *Your name has been deleted from the list.* ◇ *This command deletes files from the directory.* ◇ (*BrE*) *Mr/Mrs/Ms* (***delete as appropriate***) ➲ COLLOCATIONS at EMAIL ▸ **de·le·tion** /dɪˈliːʃn/ *noun* [U, C]: *He made several deletions to the manuscript.*

dele·teri·ous /ˌdeləˈtɪəriəs; *NAmE* -ˈtɪr-/ *adj.* (*formal*) harmful and damaging

deli /ˈdeli/ *noun* = DELICATESSEN

de·lib·er·ate 0-π *adj., verb*

■ *adj.* /dɪˈlɪbərət/ **1** 0-π done on purpose rather than by accident SYN **intentional, planned**: *a deliberate act of vandalism* ◇ *The speech was a deliberate attempt to embarrass the government.* OPP **unintentional** **2** (of a movement or an action) done slowly and carefully: *She spoke in a slow and deliberate way.*

■ *verb* /dɪˈlɪbəreɪt/ [I, T] (*formal*) to think very carefully about sth, usually before making a decision: *The jury deliberated for five days before finding him guilty.* ◇ **~ (on) whether, what, etc...** *They deliberated (on) whether to continue with the talks.*

de·lib·er·ate·ly 0-π /dɪˈlɪbərətli/ *adv.*
1 0-π done in a way that was planned, not by chance SYN **intentionally, on purpose**: *She's been deliberately ignoring him all day.* **2** slowly and carefully: *He packed up his possessions slowly and deliberately.*

de·lib·er·ation /dɪˌlɪbəˈreɪʃn/ *noun* (*formal*) **1** [U, C, usually pl.] the process of carefully considering or discussing sth: *After ten hours of deliberation, the jury returned a verdict of 'not guilty'.* ◇ *The deliberations of the committee are completely confidential.* **2** [U] the quality of being slow and careful in what you say or do: *She signed her name with great deliberation.*

deli·cacy /ˈdelɪkəsi/ *noun* (*pl.* -ies) **1** [U] the quality of being, or appearing to be, easy to damage or break: *the delicacy of the fabric* **2** [U] the quality of being done carefully and gently: *the delicacy of his touch* **3** [U] very careful behaviour in a difficult situation so that nobody is offended SYN **tact**: *She handled the situation with great sensitivity and delicacy.* **4** [U] the fact that a situation is difficult and sb may be easily offended: *I need to talk to you about a matter of some delicacy.* **5** [C] a type of food considered to be very special in a particular place SYN **speciality**: *local delicacies*

deli·cate 0-π /ˈdelɪkət/ *adj.*
1 0-π easily damaged or broken SYN **fragile**: *delicate china teacups* ◇ *The eye is one of the most delicate organs of the body.* ◇ *the delicate ecological balance of the rainforest* ◇ *Babies have very delicate skin.* ◇ *a cool wash cycle for delicate fabrics* **2** 0-π (of a person) not strong and easily becoming ill/sick: *a* ***delicate child/constitution*** **3** 0-π small and having a beautiful shape or appearance: *his delicate hands* **4** 0-π made or formed in a very careful and detailed way: *the delicate mechanisms of a clock* **5** 0-π showing or needing skilful, careful or sensitive treatment: *I admired your delicate handling of the situation.* ◇ *a delicate problem* ◇ *The delicate surgical operation took five hours.* **6** 0-π (of colours, flavours and smells) light and pleasant; not strong SYN **subtle**: *a* ***delicate fragrance/flavour*** ◇ *a river scene painted in delicate watercolours* ▸ **deli·cate·ly** *adv.*: *He stepped delicately over the broken glass.* ◇ *delicately balanced flavours*

deli·ca·tes·sen /ˌdelɪkəˈtesn/ (also **deli**) *noun* a shop/store or part of one that sells cooked meats and cheeses, and special or unusual foods that come from other countries

de·li·cious /dɪˈlɪʃəs/ *adj.* **1** having a very pleasant taste or smell: *Who cooked this? It's delicious.* **2** (*literary*) extremely pleasant or enjoyable: *the delicious coolness of the breeze* ▸ **de·li·cious·ly** *adv.*: *deliciously creamy soup*

de·light 0-π /dɪˈlaɪt/ *noun, verb*

■ *noun* **1** 0-π [U] a feeling of great pleasure SYN **joy**: *a feeling of* ***sheer/pure delight*** ◇ *The children squealed* ***with delight*** *when they saw the puppy.* ◇ *She won the game easily,* ***to the delight of*** *all her fans.* ◇ *He* ***takes (great) delight in*** (= enjoys) *proving others wrong.* ➲ SYNONYMS at PLEASURE **2** [C] something that gives you great pleasure SYN **joy**: *This guitar is a delight to play.* ◇ *the delights of living in the country*

■ *verb* 0-π **~ sb** to give sb a lot of pleasure and enjoyment: *This news will delight his fans all over the world.*

PHR V **deˈlight in sth/doing sth** [no passive] to enjoy doing sth very much, especially sth that makes other people feel embarrassed, uncomfortable, etc.

de·light·ed 0-π /dɪˈlaɪtɪd/ *adj.*
very pleased: *a delighted smile* ◇ **~ to do sth** *I'd be absolutely delighted to come.* ◇ **~ that...** *I was delighted that you could stay.* ◇ **~ by/at sth** *She was delighted by/at the news of the wedding.* ◇ **~ with sth** *I was delighted with my presents.* ➲ SYNONYMS at GLAD ▸ **de·light·ed·ly** *adv.*

de·light·ful /dɪˈlaɪtfl/ *adj.* very pleasant SYN **charming**: *a delightful book/restaurant/town* ◇ *a delightful child* ➲ SYNONYMS at WONDERFUL ▸ **de·light·ful·ly** /dɪˈlaɪtfəli/ *adv.*

de·limit /diˈlɪmɪt/ *verb* **~ sth** (*formal*) to decide what the limits of sth are

de·lin·eate /dɪˈlɪnieɪt/ *verb* **~ sth** (*formal*) to describe, draw or explain sth in detail: *Our objectives need to be precisely delineated.* ◇ *The ship's route is clearly delineated on the map.* ▸ **de·lin·ea·tion** /dɪˌlɪniˈeɪʃn/ *noun* [U, C]

de·lin·quency /dɪˈlɪŋkwənsi/ *noun* [U, C] (*pl.* -ies) bad or criminal behaviour, usually of young people: *an increase in juvenile delinquency*

de·lin·quent /dɪˈlɪŋkwənt/ *adj.* **1** (especially of young people or their behaviour) showing a tendency to commit crimes: *delinquent teenagers* **2** (*NAmE, finance*) having failed to pay money that is owed: *a delinquent borrower* **3** (*NAmE, finance*) (of a sum of money) not having been paid in time: *a delinquent loan* ▸ **de·lin·quent** *noun* ➲ see also JUVENILE DELINQUENT

deli·quesce /ˌdelɪˈkwes/ *verb* (*formal*) **1** [I] to become liquid as a result of decaying **2** [I] (*chemistry*) to become liquid as a result of absorbing water from the air ▸ **deli·ques·cence** /ˌdelɪˈkwesns/ *noun* [U]

de·li·ri·ous /dɪˈlɪriəs; *BrE* also -ˈlɪəriəs/ *adj.* **1** in an excited state and not able to think or speak clearly, usually because of fever: *He became delirious and couldn't recognize people.* **2** extremely excited and happy: *The crowds were delirious with joy.* ▸ **de·li·ri·ous·ly** *adv.*

de·lir·ium /dɪˈlɪriəm; *BrE* also -ˈlɪəriəm/ *noun* [U] a mental state where sb becomes delirious, usually because of illness: *fits of delirium*

delirium tremens /dɪˌlɪriəm ˈtriːmenz; *BrE* also -ˌlɪəriəm/ *noun* [U] (*medical*) = DTs

de·liver 0-π /dɪˈlɪvə(r)/ *verb*

▸ TAKE GOODS/LETTERS **1** 0-π [T, I] to take goods, letters, etc. to the person or people they have been sent to; to take sb somewhere: **~ sth** *Do you have your milk delivered?* ◇ **~ (sth) to sb/sth** *Leaflets have been delivered to every household.* ◇ **~ (to sb/sth)** *We promise to deliver within 48 hours.*

▸ GIVE SPEECH **2** 0-π [T] **~ sth** to give a speech, talk, etc. or other official statement: *She is due to deliver a lecture on genetic engineering.* ◇ *He delivered his lines confidently.* ◇ *The jury finally delivered its verdict.*

▸ KEEP PROMISE **3** [I, T] to do what you promised to do or what you are expected to do; to produce or provide what people expect you to: *He has promised to finish the job by June and I am sure he will deliver.* ◇ **~ on sth** *She always delivers on her promises.* ◇ **~ sth** *If you can't deliver improved sales figures, you're fired.* ◇ *The team delivered a stunning victory last night.*

▸ GIVE TO SB'S CONTROL **4** [T] **~ sb/sth (up/over) (to sb)** (*formal*) to give sb/sth to sb else so that they are under this person's control: *They delivered their prisoner over to the invading army.*

▸ BABY **5** [T] **~ a baby** to help a woman to give birth to a baby: *The baby was delivered by Caesarean section.* **6** [T] **be delivered of a baby** (*formal*) to give birth to a baby: *She was delivered of a healthy boy.*

▸ THROW **7** [T] **~ sth** to throw or aim sth: *He **delivered the blow*** (= hit sb hard) *with all his force.*

▸ RESCUE **8** [T] **~ sb (from sth)** (*old use*) to rescue sb from sth bad SYN **save** IDM see GOODS, SIGN *v.*

D

de·liver·able /dɪˈlɪvərəbl/ *noun* [usually pl.] a product that a company promises to have ready for a customer: *computer software deliverables*

de·liv·er·ance /dɪˈlɪvərəns/ *noun* [U] **~ (from sth)** (*formal*) the state of being rescued from danger, evil or pain

de·liv·ery 0-w /dɪˈlɪvəri/ *noun* (*pl.* -ies)
1 0-w [U, C] the act of taking goods, letters, etc. to the people they have been sent to: *a delivery van* ◇ *Please pay for goods **on delivery*** (= when you receive them). ◇ *Allow 28 days **for delivery**.* ◇ *Is there a **postal/mail delivery** on Saturdays?* ◇ (*formal*) *When can you **take delivery of*** (= be available to receive) *the car?* ◇ (*figurative*) *the delivery of public services* **2** [C, U] the process of giving birth to a baby: *an **easy/difficult delivery*** ◇ *a **delivery room/ward*** (= in a hospital, etc.) **3** [sing.] the way in which sb speaks, sings a song, etc. in public: *The beautiful poetry was ruined by her poor delivery.* **4** [C] a ball that is thrown, especially in CRICKET or BASEBALL: *a fast delivery* IDM see CASH *n.*

dell /del/ *noun* (*literary*) a small valley with trees growing in or around it

de·louse /ˌdiːˈlaʊs/ *verb* **~ sb/sth** to remove LICE (= small insects) from sb's hair or from an animal's coat

Del·phic /ˈdelfɪk/ *adj.* **1** relating to the ancient Greek ORACLE at Delphi (= the place where people went to ask the gods for advice or information about the future) **2** (often **delphic**) (*formal*) with a meaning that is deliberately hidden or difficult to understand: *a delphic utterance*

del·phin·ium /delˈfɪniəm/ *noun* a tall garden plant with blue or white flowers growing up its STEM

DELTA /ˈdeltə/ *noun* [U] the abbreviation for 'Diploma in English Language Teaching to Adults' (a British qualification from the University of Cambridge for experienced teachers of English as a foreign language)

delta /ˈdeltə/ *noun* **1** the fourth letter of the Greek alphabet (Δ, δ) **2** an area of land, shaped like a triangle, where a river has split into several smaller rivers before entering the sea: *the Nile Delta*

del·toids /ˈdeltɔɪdz/ (also *informal* **delts** /delts/) *noun* [pl.] (*anatomy*) the thick triangle-shaped muscles that cover the shoulder joints

de·lude /dɪˈluːd/ *verb* to make sb believe sth that is not true SYN **deceive**: **~ sb** *You poor deluded creature.* ◇ **~ yourself** *He's deluding himself if he thinks it's going to be easy.* ◇ **~ sb/yourself into doing sth** *Don't be deluded into thinking that we are out of danger yet.* ◇ **~ yourself that...** *She had been deluding herself that he loved her.* ➲ see also DELUSION

del·uge /ˈdeljuːdʒ/ *noun, verb*
■ ***noun*** [usually sing.] **1** a sudden very heavy fall of rain SYN **flood** **2** a large number of things that happen or arrive at the same time: *a **deluge of calls/complaints/letters***
■ ***verb*** **1 ~ sb/sth (with sth)** [usually passive] to send or give sb/sth a large number of things at the same time SYN **flood, inundate**: *We have been deluged with applications for the job.* **2** [often passive] **~ sth** (*formal*) to flood a place with water: *The campsite was deluged by a flash flood.*

de·lu·sion /dɪˈluːʒn/ *noun* **1** [C] a false belief or opinion about yourself or your situation: *the delusions of the mentally ill* ◇ *Don't go getting **delusions of grandeur*** (= a belief that you are more important than you actually are). **2** [U] the act of believing or making yourself believe sth that is not true

de·lu·sive /dɪˈluːsɪv/ (also **de·lu·sory** /dɪˈluːsəri; -zəri/) *adj.* (*formal*) not real or true SYN **deceptive**

de luxe (also **de·luxe**) /ˌdə ˈlʌks; ˈlʊks/ *adj.* [usually before noun] of a higher quality and more expensive than usual SYN **luxury**: *a de luxe hotel*

delve /delv/ *verb* [I] **+ adv./prep.** to search for sth inside a bag, container, etc. SYN **dig**: *She delved in her handbag for a pen.*
PHR V **ˌdelve ˈinto sth** to try hard to find out more information about sth: *She had started to delve into her father's distant past.*

Dem. *abbr.* (in politics in the US) DEMOCRAT; DEMOCRATIC

dema·gogue /ˈdeməgɒg; *NAmE* -gɑːg/ *noun* (*disapproving*) a political leader who tries to win support by using arguments based on emotion rather than reason ▸ **dema·gog·ic** /ˌdeməˈgɒgɪk; *NAmE* -ˈgɑːg-/ *adj.* **dema·gogy** /ˈdeməgɒgi; *NAmE* -gɑːgi/ *noun* [U]

Synonyms

demand

require • expect • insist • ask

These words all mean to say that sb should do or have sth.

demand to ask for sth very firmly; to say very firmly that sb should have or do sth: *She demanded an immediate explanation.*

require [often passive] (*rather formal*) to make sb do or have sth, especially because it is necessary according to a law or set of rules or standards: *All candidates will be required to take a short test.*

expect to demand that sb should do, have or be sth, especially because it is their duty or responsibility: *I expect to be paid promptly for the work.*

insist to demand that sth happens or that sb agrees to do sth: *I didn't want to go but he insisted.* ◇ *We **insist on** the highest standards at all times.*

ask to expect or demand sth: *You're asking too much of him.*

DEMAND, EXPECT OR ASK?

Ask is not as strong as **demand** or **expect**, both of which can be more like a command.

PATTERNS

- to demand/require/expect/ask sth **of/from** sb
- to demand/require/expect/insist/ask **that...**
- to require/expect/ask sb **to do sth**
- to demand/require/expect/ask **a lot/too much/a great deal**
- **to be too much** to expect/ask

de·mand 0-w /dɪˈmɑːnd; *NAmE* dɪˈmænd/ *noun, verb*
■ ***noun*** **1** 0-w [C] **~ (for sth/that...)** a very firm request for sth; sth that sb needs: *a demand for higher pay* ◇ *demands that the law on gun ownership should be changed* ◇ *firms attempting to **meet/satisfy** their customers' **demands*** (= to give them what they are asking for) **2** 0-w **demands** [pl.] **~ (of sth)** | **~ (on sb)** things that sb/sth makes you do, especially things that are difficult, make you tired, worried, etc: *the demands of children/work* ◇ *Flying **makes** enormous **demands** on pilots.* **3** 0-w [U, C] **~ (for sth/sb)** the desire or need of customers for goods or services which

they want to buy or use: *to meet the demand for a product* ◇ *There's an increased demand for organic produce these days.* ◇ *Demand is exceeding supply.* ➲ COLLOCATIONS at ECONOMY

IDM **by popular de'mand** because a lot of people have asked for sth: *By popular demand, the play will run for another week.* **in de'mand** 🗝 wanted by a lot of people: *Good secretaries are always in demand.* **on de'mand** done or happening whenever sb asks: *Feed the baby on demand.* ◇ *on-demand printing of books* ➲ see also SUPPLY AND DEMAND

■ ***verb*** **1** 🗝 to ask for sth very firmly: **~ sth** *She demanded an immediate explanation.* ◇ **~ that...** *The UN has demanded that all troops be withdrawn.* ◇ (*BrE* also) *They are demanding that all troops should be withdrawn.* ◇ **~ to do sth** *I demand to see the manager.* ◇ **+ speech** *'Who the hell are you?' he demanded angrily.* ➲ SYNONYMS at ASK **2** 🗝 **~ sth** to need sth in order to be done successfully: *This sport demands both speed and strength.*

de·mand·ing /dɪˈmɑːndɪŋ; *NAmE* -ˈmæn-/ *adj.* **1** (of a piece of work) needing a lot of skill, patience, effort, etc: *The work is physically demanding.* ➲ SYNONYMS at DIFFICULT **2** (of a person) expecting a lot of work or attention from others; not easily satisfied: *a demanding boss/child* **OPP** **undemanding**

de·mar·cate /ˈdiːmɑːkeɪt; *NAmE* -mɑːrk-/ *verb* **~ sth** (*formal*) to mark or establish the limits of sth: *Plots of land have been demarcated by barbed wire.*

de·mar·ca·tion /ˌdiːmɑːˈkeɪʃn; *NAmE* -mɑːrˈk-/ *noun* [U, C] a border or line that separates two things, such as types of work, groups of people or areas of land: *It was hard to draw clear lines of demarcation between work and leisure.* ◇ *social demarcations*

de·mean /dɪˈmiːn/ *verb* **1 ~ yourself** to do sth that makes people have less respect for you: *I wouldn't demean myself by asking for charity.* **2 ~ sb/sth** to make people have less respect for sb/sth **SYN** **degrade**: *Such images demean women.*

de·mean·ing /dɪˈmiːnɪŋ/ *adj.* putting sb in a position that does not give them the respect that they should have **SYN** **humiliating**: *He found it demeaning to work for his former employee.*

de·mean·our (*especially US* **de·meanor**) /dɪˈmiːnə(r)/ *noun* [U] (*formal*) the way that sb looks or behaves: *He maintained a professional demeanour throughout.*

de·men·ted /dɪˈmentɪd/ *adj.* **1** (*especially BrE*) behaving in a crazy way because you are extremely upset or worried: *I've been nearly demented with worry about you.* **2** (*old-fashioned* or *medical*) having a mental illness ▸ **de·men·ted·ly** *adv.*

de·men·tia /dɪˈmenʃə/ *noun* [U] (*medical*) a serious mental DISORDER caused by brain disease or injury, that affects the ability to think, remember and behave normally ➲ see also SENILE DEMENTIA

dem·er·ara sugar /ˌdeməreərə ˈʃʊgə(r); *NAmE* -rerə/ *noun* [U] (*BrE*) a type of rough brown sugar

de·merge /ˌdiːˈmɜːdʒ; *NAmE* -ˈmɜːrdʒ/ *verb* [T, I] **~ (sth)** (*BrE, business*) to separate a company into smaller companies, usually into the companies that had previously been joined together; to be split in this way

de·mer·ger /ˌdiːˈmɜːdʒə(r); *NAmE* -ˈmɜːrdʒ-/ *noun* [C, U] (*BrE, business*) the act of separating a company from a larger company, especially when they had previously been joined together

de·merit /diːˈmerɪt/ *noun* (*formal*) **1** [usually pl.] a fault in sth or a disadvantage of sth: *the merits and demerits of the scheme* **2** (*NAmE*) a mark on sb's school record showing that they have done sth wrong: *You'll get three demerits if you're caught smoking on school grounds.*

de·mesne /dəˈmeɪn/ *noun* **1** (in the past) land attached to a MANOR (= large house) that was kept by the owners for their own use **2** (*old use*) a region or large area of land

demi- /ˈdemi/ *prefix* (in nouns) half; partly: *demigod*

demi·god /ˈdemigɒd; *NAmE* -gɑːd/ *noun* **1** a minor god, or a BEING that is partly a god and partly human **2** a ruler or other person who is treated like a god

demi·john /ˈdemidʒɒn; *NAmE* -dʒɑːn/ *noun* a very large bottle with a narrow opening at the top, for holding and transporting water, wine, etc.

de·mili·tar·ize (*BrE* also **-ise**) /ˌdiːˈmɪlɪtəraɪz/ *verb* [usually passive] **~ sth** to remove military forces from an area: *a* ***demilitarized zone*** **OPP** **militarize** ▸ **de·mili·tar·iza·tion, -isa·tion** /ˌdiːˌmɪlɪtəraɪˈzeɪʃn; *NAmE* -rəˈz-/ *noun* [U]

demi-monde /ˌdemi ˈmɒnd; *NAmE* ˈmɑːnd/ *noun* [sing.] (from *French*) people whose behaviour or beliefs prevent them from being fully accepted as part of the main group in society

de·mise /dɪˈmaɪz/ *noun* [sing.] **1** the end or failure of an institution, an idea, a company, etc. **2** (*formal* or *humorous*) death: *his* ***imminent/sudden/sad demise***

de·mist /ˌdiːˈmɪst/ (*BrE*) (*NAmE* **de·fog**) *verb* **~ sth** to remove the CONDENSATION from a car's windows so that you can see clearly

de·mist·er /ˌdiːˈmɪstə(r)/ *noun* a device, spray, etc. that removes CONDENSATION, especially from the windows of a car

demi·urge /ˈdemiɜːdʒ; *NAmE* -ɜːrdʒ/ *noun* (*literary*) **1** a BEING that is responsible for creating the world **2** a BEING that controls the part of the world which is not spiritual

demo /ˈdeməʊ; *NAmE* -moʊ/ *noun, verb*

■ ***noun*** (*pl.* -os) (*informal*) **1** (*especially BrE*) = DEMONSTRATION (1): *They all went on the demo.* **2** = DEMONSTRATION (2): ***I'll give you a demo.*** **3** a record or tape with an example of sb's music on it: *a demo tape*

■ ***verb*** **~ sth** to use sth, especially a piece of software, to show sb or to see for yourself how it works: *He demoed the new program he had just created.* ◇ *Can I demo the software before I buy it?*

demo- *prefix* (in nouns, adjectives and adverbs) connected with people or population: *democracy* ◇ *democratic*

demob /ˌdiːˈmɒb; *NAmE* -ˈmɑːb/ *verb* (-bb-) [usually passive] **~ sb** (*BrE, informal*) = DEMOBILIZE: *He was demobbed in 1946.* ▸ **demob** *noun* [U] (*BrE*)

de·mo·bil·ize (*BrE* also **-ise**) /dɪˈməʊbəlaɪz; *NAmE* -ˈmoʊ-/ (also *BrE informal* **demob**) *verb* **~ sb** to release sb from military service, especially at the end of a war ➲ compare MOBILIZE ▸ **de·mo·bil·iza·tion, -isa·tion** /dɪˌməʊbəlaɪˈzeɪʃn; *NAmE* -ˌmoʊbələˈz-/ *noun* [U]

dem·oc·racy /dɪˈmɒkrəsi; *NAmE* -ˈmɑːk-/ *noun* (*pl.* -ies) **1** [U] a system of government in which all the people of a country can vote to elect their representatives: *parliamentary democracy* ◇ *the principles of democracy* **2** [C] a country which has this system of government: *Western democracies* ◇ *I thought we were supposed to be living in a democracy.* **3** [U] fair and equal treatment of everyone in an organization, etc, and their right to take part in making decisions: *the fight for justice and democracy*

demo·crat /ˈdeməkræt/ *noun* **1** a person who believes in or supports democracy **2** **Democrat** (*abbr.* **D, Dem.**) a member or supporter of the Democratic Party of the US ➲ compare REPUBLICAN

demo·crat·ic /ˌdeməˈkrætɪk/ *adj.* **1** (of a country, state, system, etc.) controlled by representatives who are elected by the people of a country; connected with this system: *a democratic country* ◇ *a democratic system* ◇ *democratic government* **2** based on the principle that all members have an equal right to be involved in running an organization, etc: *democratic participation* ◇ *a democratic decision* **3** based on the principle that all members of society are equal rather than divided by money or social class: *a democratic society* ◇ *democratic reforms* **4** **Democratic** (*abbr.* **Dem., D**) connected with the Democratic Party in the US: *the Democratic senator from Oregon* ▸ **demo·crat·ic·al·ly** /-kli/ *adv.*: *a democratically elected government* ◇ *democratically controlled* ◇ *The decision was taken democratically.*

D

the Demo'cratic Party *noun* [sing.] one of the two main political parties in the US, usually considered to be in favour of social reform ➲ compare THE REPUBLICAN PARTY

dem·oc·ra·tize (*BrE* also **-ise**) /dɪˈmɒkrətaɪz; *NAmE* -ˈmɑːk-/ *verb* **~ sth** (*formal*) to make a country or an institution more democratic ▶ **dem·oc·ra·tiza·tion, -isa·tion** /dɪˌmɒkrətaɪˈzeɪʃn; *NAmE* -ˌmɑːkrətəˈz-/ *noun* [U]

demo·graph·ic /ˌdeməˈɡræfɪk/ *noun, adj.*
- ***noun* 1 demographics** [pl.] (*statistics*) data relating to the population and different groups within it: *the demographics of radio listeners* **2** [sing.] (*business*) a group of customers who are of a similar age, the same sex, etc: *The products are designed to appeal to a young demographic.* ◇ *the 18–30 demographic*
- ***adj.*** relating to the population and different groups within it: ***demographic changes/trends/factors*** ▶ **demo·graph·ic·al·ly** *adv.*

demo·graph·ics /ˌdeməˈɡræfɪks/ *noun* [pl.] (*statistics*) data relating to the population and different groups within it: *the demographics of radio listeners*

dem·og·raphy /dɪˈmɒɡrəfi; *NAmE* -ˈmɑːɡ-/ *noun* [U] the changing number of births, deaths, diseases, etc. in a community over a period of time; the scientific study of these changes: *the social demography of Africa* ▶ **dem·og·raph·er** /dɪˈmɒɡrəfə(r); *NAmE* -ˈmɑːɡ-/ *noun*

de·mol·ish /dɪˈmɒlɪʃ; *NAmE* -ˈmɑːl-/ *verb* **1 ~ sth** to pull or knock down a building: *The factory is due to be demolished next year.* **2 ~ sth** to destroy sth accidentally: *The car had skidded across the road and demolished part of the wall.* **3 ~ sth** to show that an idea or theory is completely wrong: *A recent book has demolished this theory.* **4 ~ sb/sth** to defeat sb easily and completely: *They demolished New Zealand 44–6 in the final.* **5 ~ sth** (*BrE, informal*) to eat sth very quickly: *The children demolished their burgers and chips.* ▶ **demo·li·tion** /ˌdeməˈlɪʃn/ *noun* [U, C]: *The whole row of houses is scheduled for demolition.* ◇ *His speech did a very effective* ***demolition job*** *on the government's proposals.*

ˌdemolition ˈderby (*NAmE*) (*BrE* **ˈstock-car racing**) *noun* [C] a type of race in which the competing cars are allowed to hit each other

demon /ˈdiːmən/ *noun* **1** an evil spirit: *demons torturing the sinners in Hell* **2** (*informal*) a person who does sth very well or with a lot of energy: *He skis like a demon.* **3** something that causes a person to worry and makes them unhappy: *the demons of jealousy*

IDM **the demon ˈdrink** (*BrE, humorous*) alcoholic drink

de·mon·ic /diˈmɒnɪk; *NAmE* -ˈmɑːn-/ *adj.* connected with, or like, a demon: *demonic forces* ◇ *a demonic appearance*

de·mon·ize (*BrE* also **-ise**) /ˈdiːmənaɪz/ *verb* **~ sb/sth** to describe sb/sth in a way that is intended to make other people think of them or it as evil or dangerous: *He was demonized by the right-wing press.* ▶ **de·mon·iza·tion, -isa·tion** /ˌdiːmənaɪˈzeɪʃn/ *noun* [U]

dem·on·strable AW /dɪˈmɒnstrəbl; *NAmE* -ˈmɑːn-; *BrE* also ˈdemənstrəbl/ *adj.* (*formal*) that can be shown or proved: *a demonstrable need* ▶ **dem·on·strably** AW /-bli/ *adv.*: *demonstrably unfair*

dem·on·strate 0-w AW /ˈdemənstreɪt/ *verb*
1 0-w [T] to show sth clearly by giving proof or evidence: **~ that...** *These results demonstrate convincingly that our campaign is working.* ◇ **~ sth** (**to sb**) *Let me demonstrate to you some of the difficulties we are facing.* ◇ **~ how, what, etc ...** *His sudden departure had demonstrated how unreliable he was.* ◇ **~ sb/sth to be sth** *The theories were demonstrated to be false.* ◇ **it is demonstrated that...** *It has been demonstrated that this drug is effective.* ➲ LANGUAGE BANK at EVIDENCE **2** [T] **~ sth** to show by your actions that you have a particular quality, feeling or opinion SYN **display**: *You need to demonstrate more self-control.* ◇ *We want to demonstrate our commitment to human rights.* **3** 0-w [T] to show and explain how sth works or how to do sth: **~ sth** (**to sb**) *Her job involves demonstrating new educational software.* ◇ **~** (**to sb**) **how, what, etc...** *Let me demonstrate to you how it works.* **4** 0-w [I] to take part in a public meeting or march, usually as a protest or to show support for sth SYN **protest**: **~** (**against sth**) *students demonstrating against the war* ◇ **~** (**in favour/support of sth**) *They are demonstrating in favour of free higher education.*

de·mon·stra·tion AW /ˌdemənˈstreɪʃn/ *noun* **1** (also *informal* **demo** especially in *BrE*) [C] **~** (**against sb/sth**) a public meeting or march at which people show that they are protesting against or supporting sb/sth: ***to take part in/go on a demonstration*** ◇ *to* ***hold/stage a demonstration*** ◇ ***mass demonstrations*** *in support of the exiled leader* ◇ *anti-government demonstrations* ◇ *a* ***peaceful/violent demonstration*** ➲ compare MARCH **2** (also *informal* **demo**) [C, U] an act of showing or explaining how sth works or is done: *We were given a brief demonstration of the computer's functions.* ◇ *a practical demonstration* ◇ *We provide demonstration of videoconferencing over the Internet.* **3** [C, U] an act of giving proof or evidence for sth: *a demonstration of the connection between the two sets of figures* ◇ *a demonstration of how something that seems simple can turn out to be very complicated* **4** [C] an act of showing a feeling or an opinion: *a public demonstration of affection* ◇ *a demonstration of support for the reforms*

de·mon·stra·tive AW /dɪˈmɒnstrətɪv; *NAmE* -ˈmɑːn-/ *adj., noun*
- ***adj.* 1** showing feelings openly, especially feelings of affection: *Some people are more demonstrative than others.* ◇ *a demonstrative greeting* **2** (*grammar*) used to identify the person or thing that is being referred to: *'This' and 'that' are demonstrative pronouns.* ▶ **de·mon·stra·tive·ly** AW *adv.*
- ***noun*** (*grammar*) a demonstrative pronoun or determiner

dem·on·stra·tor AW /ˈdemənstreɪtə(r)/ *noun* **1** a person who takes part in a public meeting or march in order to protest against sb/sth or to show support for sb/sth **2** a person whose job is to show or explain how sth works or is done

de·mor·al·ize (*BrE* also **-ise**) /dɪˈmɒrəlaɪz; *NAmE* -ˈmɔːr-/ *verb* [usually passive] **~ sb** to make sb lose confidence or hope SYN **dishearten**: *Constant criticism is enough to demoralize anybody.* ▶ **de·mor·al·ized, -ised** *adj.*: *The workers here seem very demoralized.* **de·mor·al·iz·ing, -is·ing** *adj.*: *the demoralizing effects of unemployment* **de·mor·al·iza·tion, -isa·tion** /dɪˌmɒrəlaɪˈzeɪʃn; *NAmE* -ˌmɔːrələˈz-/ *noun* [U]

de·mote /ˌdiːˈməʊt; *NAmE* -ˈmoʊt/ *verb* [often passive] **~ sb** (**from sth**) (**to sth**) to move sb to a lower position or rank, often as a punishment OPP **promote** ▶ **de·mo·tion** /ˌdiːˈməʊʃn; *NAmE* -ˈmoʊ-/ *noun* [C, U]

dem·ot·ic /dɪˈmɒtɪk; *NAmE* -ˈmɑːt-/ *adj.* (*formal*) used by or typical of ordinary people

de·mo·tiv·ate /ˌdiːˈməʊtɪveɪt; *NAmE* -ˈmoʊ-/ *verb* **~ sb** to make sb feel that it is not worth making an effort: *Failure can demotivate students.* ▶ **de·mo·tiv·at·ing** *adj.* **de·mo·tiv·ated** *adj.* **de·mo·tiv·ation** /ˌdiːməʊtɪˈveɪʃn; *NAmE* -moʊ-/ *noun* [U]

demur /dɪˈmɜː(r)/ *verb, noun*
- ***verb*** (-rr-) [I] (**+ speech**) (*formal*) to say that you do not agree with sth or that you refuse to do sth: *At first she demurred, but then finally agreed.*
- ***noun***

IDM **without deˈmur** (*formal*) without objecting or hesitating: *They accepted without demur.*

de·mure /dɪˈmjʊə(r); *NAmE* dɪˈmjʊr/ *adj.* **1** (of a woman or a girl) behaving in a way that does not attract attention to herself or her body; quiet and serious SYN **modest**: *a demure young lady* **2** suggesting that a woman or girl is demure SYN **modest**: *a demure smile* ◇ *a demure navy blouse with a white collar* ▶ **de·mure·ly** *adv.*

de·mys·tify /ˌdiːˈmɪstɪfaɪ/ *verb* (**de·mys·ti·fies, de·mys·ti·fy·ing, de·mys·ti·fied, de·mys·ti·fied**) **~ sth** to make sth easier to understand and less complicated by explaining it in a clear and simple way ▶ **de·mys·ti·fi·ca·tion** /ˌdiːˌmɪstɪfɪˈkeɪʃn/ *noun* [U]

stop taking or using it): ***drug/alcohol dependence*** **3 ~ of A and B** (*technical*) the fact of one thing being affected by another: *the close dependence of soil and landforms*

de·pend·ency /dɪˈpendənsi/ *noun* (*pl.* -ies) **1** [U] **~ (on/upon sb/sth)** the state of relying on sb/sth for sth, especially when this is not normal or necessary: *financial dependency* ◇ *Their aim is to reduce people's dependency on the welfare state.* ◇ *the* ***dependency culture*** (= a way of life in which people depend too much on money from the government) ➲ compare CODEPENDENCY **2** [C] a country, an area, etc. that is controlled by another country **3** = DEPENDENCE (2)

de·pend·ent /dɪˈpendənt/ *adj.*, *noun*

■ ***adj.*** **1** needing sb/sth in order to survive or be successful: *a woman with several dependent children* ◇ **~ on/upon sb/sth** *You can't be dependent on your parents all your life.* ◇ **~ on/upon sb/sth for sth** *The festival is heavily dependent on sponsorship for its success.* **2 ~ on/upon sth** ADDICTED to sth (= unable to stop taking or using it): *to be dependent on drugs* **3 ~ on/upon sth** (*formal*) affected or decided by sth: *A child's development is dependent on many factors.* ◇ *The price is dependent on how many extras you choose.*

■ ***noun*** (*especially NAmE*) = DEPENDANT

deˌpendent ˈclause *noun* (*grammar*) = SUBORDINATE CLAUSE

deˌpendent ˈvariable *noun* (*mathematics*) a VARIABLE whose value depends on another variable

de·per·son·al·ize (*BrE* also **-ise**) /diːˈpɜːsənəlaɪz; *NAmE* -ˈpɜːrs-/ *verb* **~ sth** [often passive] to make sth less personal so that it does not seem as if humans with feelings and personality are involved

de·pict /dɪˈpɪkt/ *verb* (rather *formal*) **1** to show an image of sb/sth in a picture: **~ sb/sth (as sb/sth)** *a painting depicting the Virgin and Child* ◇ **~ sb/sth doing sth** *The artist had depicted her lying on a bed.* **2** to describe sth in words, or give an impression of sth in words or with a picture: **~ sb/sth** *The novel depicts French society in the 1930s.* ◇ **~ sb/sth as sb/sth** *The advertisements depict smoking as glamorous and attractive.* ▸ **de·pic·tion** /dɪˈpɪkʃn/ *noun* [U, C]: *They object to the movie's depiction of gay people.*

de·pila·tor /ˈdepɪleɪtə(r); *NAmE* dɪˈpɪlətɔːr/ *noun* a device which removes hair from your body by pulling it out

de·pila·tory /dɪˈpɪlətri; *NAmE* -tɔːri/ *noun* (*pl.* -ies) a substance used for removing body hair ▸ **de·pila·tory** *adj.* [only before noun]: *depilatory creams*

de·plane /diːˈpleɪn/ *verb* [I] (*NAmE*) to get off a plane **SYN disembark**

de·plete /dɪˈpliːt/ *verb* [usually passive] **~ sth** (*formal*) to reduce sth by a large amount so that there is not enough left: *Food supplies were severely depleted.* ▸ **de·ple·tion** /dɪˈpliːʃn/ *noun* [U]: *ozone depletion* ◇ *the depletion of fish stocks*

de·plor·able /dɪˈplɔːrəbl/ *adj.* (*formal*) very bad and unacceptable, often in a way that shocks people **SYN appalling**: *a deplorable incident* ◇ *They were living in the most deplorable conditions.* ◇ *The acting was deplorable.* ▸ **de·plor·ably** /-əbli/ *adv.*: *They behaved deplorably.* ◇ ***deplorably high/low/bad***

de·plore /dɪˈplɔː(r)/ *verb* **~ sth** (*formal*) to strongly disapprove of sth and criticize it, especially publicly: *Like everyone else, I deplore and condemn this killing.*

de·ploy /dɪˈplɔɪ/ *verb* **1 ~ sb/sth** (*technical*) to move soldiers or weapons into a position where they are ready for military action: *2000 troops were deployed in the area.* ◇ *At least 5 000 missiles were deployed along the border.* **2 ~ sth** (*formal*) to use sth effectively: *to* ***deploy arguments/resources*** ▸ **de·ploy·ment** *noun* [U, C]

de·popu·late /ˌdiːˈpɒpjuleɪt; *NAmE* -ˈpɑːp-/ *verb* [usually passive] **~ sth** to reduce the number of people living in a place: *Whole stretches of land were laid waste and depopulated.* ▸ **de·popu·la·tion** /ˌdiːˌpɒpjuˈleɪʃn; *NAmE* -ˌpɑːp-/ *noun* [U]

de·port /dɪˈpɔːt; *NAmE* dɪˈpɔːrt/ *verb* **~ sb** to force sb to leave a country, usually because they have broken the law or because they have no legal right to be there ▸ **de·port·ation** /ˌdiːpɔːˈteɪʃn; *NAmE* -pɔːrˈt-/ *noun* [C, U]: *Several of the asylum seekers now face deportation.* ◇ *a deportation order*

de·port·ee /ˌdiːpɔːˈtiː; *NAmE* -pɔːr-/ *noun* a person who has been DEPORTED or is going to be deported

de·port·ment /dɪˈpɔːtmənt; *NAmE* -ˈpɔːrt-/ *noun* [U] (*formal*) **1** (*BrE*) the way in which a person stands and moves: *lessons for young ladies in deportment and etiquette* **2** (*old-fashioned, especially NAmE*) the way in which a person behaves

de·pose /dɪˈpəʊz; *NAmE* dɪˈpoʊz/ *verb* **~ sb** to remove sb, especially a ruler, from power: *The president was deposed in a military coup.*

de·posit 🔑 /dɪˈpɒzɪt; *NAmE* -ˈpɑːz-/ *noun*, *verb*

■ ***noun***

▸ MONEY **1** 🔑 [usually sing.] **a ~ (on sth)** a sum of money that is given as the first part of a larger payment **SYN down payment**: *They normally ask you to pay $100 (as a) deposit.* ◇ (*BrE*) *We've put down a 5% deposit on the house.* ➲ SYNONYMS at PAYMENT ➲ COLLOCATIONS at HOUSE **2** 🔑 [usually sing.] a sum of money that is paid by sb when they rent sth and that is returned to them if they do not lose or damage the thing they are renting: *to pay a deposit* **3** a sum of money that is paid into a bank account: *Deposits can be made at any branch.* **OPP withdrawal** ➲ COLLOCATIONS at FINANCE **4** (in the British political system) the amount of money that a candidate in an election to Parliament has to pay, and that is returned if he/she gets enough votes: *All the other candidates* ***lost their deposits.***

▸ SUBSTANCE **5** a layer of a substance that has formed naturally underground: ***mineral/gold/coal deposits*** **6** a layer of a substance that has been left somewhere, especially by a river, flood, etc, or is found at the bottom of a liquid: *The rain left a deposit of mud on the windows.* ◇ *fatty deposits in the arteries of the heart*

■ ***verb***

▸ PUT DOWN **1 ~ sb/sth + adv./prep.** to put or lay sb/sth down in a particular place: *She deposited a pile of books on my desk.* ◇ (*informal*) *I was whisked off in a taxi and deposited outside the hotel.*

▸ LEAVE SUBSTANCE **2 ~ sth** (especially of a river or a liquid) to leave a layer of sth on the surface of sth, especially gradually and over a period of time: *Sand was deposited which hardened into sandstone.*

▸ MONEY **3** 🔑 **~ sth** to put money into a bank account: *Millions were deposited in Swiss bank accounts.* **4** 🔑 **~ sth** to pay a sum of money as the first part of a larger payment; to pay a sum of money that you will get back if you return in good condition sth that you have rented

▸ PUT IN SAFE PLACE **5 ~ sth (in sth) | ~ sth (with sb/sth)** to put sth valuable or important in a place where it will be safe: *Guests may deposit their valuables in the hotel safe.*

deˈposit account *noun* (*BrE*) a type of account at a bank or BUILDING SOCIETY that pays interest on money that is left in it ➲ compare CURRENT ACCOUNT

de·pos·ition /ˌdepəˈzɪʃn/ *noun* **1** [U, C] (*technical*) the natural process of leaving a layer of a substance on rocks or soil; a substance left in this way: ***marine/river deposition*** **2** [U, C] the act of removing sb, especially a ruler, from power: *the deposition of the King* **3** [C] (*law*) a formal statement, taken from sb and used in court

de·pos·it·or /dɪˈpɒzɪtə(r); *NAmE* -ˈpɑːz-/ *noun* a person who puts money in a bank account

de·posi·tory /dɪˈpɒzɪtri; *NAmE* dɪˈpɑːzətɔːri/ *noun* (*pl.* -ies) a place where things can be stored

depot /ˈdepəʊ; *NAmE* ˈdiːpoʊ/ *noun* **1** a place where large amounts of food, goods or equipment are stored: *an arms depot* **2** (*BrE*) a place where buses or other vehicles are kept and repaired **3** (*NAmE*) a small station where trains or buses stop

D

de·prave /dɪˈpreɪv/ *verb* **~ sb** (*formal*) to make sb morally bad SYN **corrupt**: *In my view this book would deprave young children.*

de·praved /dɪˈpreɪvd/ *adj.* (*formal*) morally bad SYN **wicked, evil**: *This is the work of a depraved mind.*

de·prav·ity /dɪˈprævəti/ *noun* [U] (*formal*) the state of being morally bad SYN **wickedness**: *a life of depravity*

D

dep·re·cate /ˈdeprəkeɪt/ *verb* **~ sth** (*formal*) to feel and express strong disapproval of sth ▸ **dep·re·cat·ing** (also *less frequent* **dep·re·ca·tory** /ˌdeprəˈkeɪtəri; *NAmE* ˈdeprɪkətɔːri/) *adj.*: *a deprecating comment* **dep·re·cat·ing·ly** *adv.*

de·pre·ci·ate /dɪˈpriːʃieɪt/ *verb* **1** [I] to become less valuable over a period of time: *New cars start to depreciate as soon as they are on the road.* ◇ *Shares continued to depreciate on the stock markets today.* OPP **appreciate 2** [T] **~ sth** (*business*) to reduce the value, as stated in the company's accounts, of a particular ASSET over a particular period of time: *The bank depreciates PCs over a period of five years.* **3** [T] **~ sth** (*formal*) to make sth seem unimportant or of no value: *I had no intention of depreciating your contribution.* ▸ **de·pre·ci·ation** /dɪˌpriːʃiˈeɪʃn/ *noun* [U]: *currency depreciation* ◇ *the depreciation of fixed assets*

dep·re·da·tion /ˌdeprəˈdeɪʃn/ *noun* [usually pl.] (*formal*) acts that cause damage to people's property, lives, etc.

de·press 0‑w AW /dɪˈpres/ *verb* **1** 0‑w to make sb sad and without enthusiasm or hope: **~ sb** *Wet weather always depresses me.* ◇ **it depresses sb to do sth** *It depresses me to see so many young girls smoking.* **2 ~ sth** to make trade, business, etc. less active: *The recession has depressed the housing market.* **3 ~ sth** to make the value of prices or wages lower: *to* ***depress wages/prices*** **4 ~ sth** (*formal*) to press or push sth down, especially part of a machine: *to depress the clutch pedal* (= when driving).

de·pres·sant /dɪˈpresnt/ *noun* (*medical*) a drug which slows the rate of the body's functions

de·pressed 0‑w AW /dɪˈprest/ *adj.* **1** 0‑w very sad and without hope: *She felt very depressed about the future.* **2** 0‑w suffering from the medical condition of DEPRESSION **3** (of a place or an industry) without enough economic activity or jobs for people: *an attempt to bring jobs to depressed areas* **4** having a lower amount or level than usual: *depressed prices*

de·press·ing 0‑w AW /dɪˈpresɪŋ/ *adj.* making you feel very sad and without enthusiasm: *a* ***depressing sight/thought/experience*** ◇ *Looking for a job these days can be very depressing.* ▸ **de·press·ing·ly** *adv.*: *a depressingly familiar experience*

de·pres·sion AW /dɪˈpreʃn/ *noun* **1** [U] a medical condition in which a person feels very sad and anxious and often has physical SYMPTOMS such as being unable to sleep, etc: *clinical depression* ◇ *She suffered from severe depression after losing her job.* ➲ see also POST-NATAL DEPRESSION, POST-PARTUM DEPRESSION **2** [U, C] the state of feeling very sad and without hope: *There was a feeling of gloom and depression in the office when the news of the job cuts was announced.* **3** [C, U] a period when there is little economic activity and many people are poor or without jobs: *The country was in the grip of (an) economic depression.* ◇ *the great Depression of the 1930s* **4** [C] (*formal*) a part of a surface that is lower than the parts around it SYN **hollow**: *Rainwater collects in shallow depressions on the ground.* **5** [C] (*technical*) a weather condition in which the pressure of the air becomes lower, often causing rain ➲ compare ANTICYCLONE

de·pres·sive /dɪˈpresɪv/ *adj., noun*
- ***adj.*** connected with the medical condition of depression: *depressive illness*
- ***noun*** a person who is suffering from the medical condition of depression ➲ see also MANIC-DEPRESSIVE

de·pres·sor /dɪˈpresə(r)/ *noun* = TONGUE DEPRESSOR

de·priv·ation /ˌdeprɪˈveɪʃn/ *noun* [U] the fact of not having sth that you need, like enough food, money or a home; the process that causes this: *neglected children suffering from social deprivation* ◇ *sleep deprivation* ◇ *the deprivation of war* (= the suffering caused by not having enough of some things)

de·prive /dɪˈpraɪv/ *verb*
PHR V **deˈprive sb/sth of sth** to prevent sb from having or doing sth, especially sth important: *They were imprisoned and deprived of their basic rights.* ◇ *Why should you* ***deprive yourself*** *of such simple pleasures?*

de·prived /dɪˈpraɪvd/ *adj.* without enough food, education, and all the things that are necessary for people to live a happy and comfortable life: *a* ***deprived childhood/background/area*** ◇ ***economically/emotionally/socially deprived*** ➲ SYNONYMS at POOR

Dept (also **Dept.** especially in *NAmE*) *abbr.* (in writing) department

depth 0‑w /depθ/ *noun*
▸ MEASUREMENT **1** 0‑w [C, U] the distance from the top or surface to the bottom of sth: *What's the depth of the water here?* ◇ *Water was found* ***at a depth of*** *30 metres.* ◇ *They dug down* ***to a depth of*** *two metres.* ◇ *Many dolphins can dive to depths of 200 metres.* ◇ *The oil well extended several hundreds of feet* ***in depth.*** ◇ *the depth of a cut/wound/crack* **2** 0‑w [C, U] the distance from the front to the back of sth: *The depth of the shelves is 30 centimetres.*
▸ OF FEELINGS **3** 0‑w [U] the strength and power of feelings: *the depth of her love*
▸ OF KNOWLEDGE **4** 0‑w [U] (*approving*) the quality of knowing or understanding a lot of details about sth; the ability to provide and explain these details: *a writer of great wisdom and depth* ◇ *a job that doesn't require any great* ***depth of knowledge*** ◇ *His ideas lack depth.*
▸ DEEPEST PART **5** 0‑w [C, usually pl.] the deepest, most extreme or serious part of sth: *the* ***depths of the ocean*** ◇ *to live* ***in the depths of the country*** (= a long way from a town) ◇ *in the* ***depths of winter*** (= when it is coldest) ◇ *She was* ***in the depths of despair*** ◇ *He gazed into the depths of her eyes.* ◇ *Her paintings reveal* ***hidden depths*** (= unknown and interesting things about her character).
▸ OF COLOUR **6** [U] the strength of a colour: *Strong light will affect the depth of colour of your carpets and curtains.*
▸ PICTURE/PHOTOGRAPH **7** [U] (*technical*) the quality in a work of art or a photograph which makes it appear not to be flat ➲ see also DEEP
IDM **ˌin ˈdepth** 0‑w in a detailed and thorough way: *I haven't looked at the report in depth yet.* ◇ *an in-depth study* **be out of your ˈdepth 1** (*BrE*) to be in water that is too deep to stand in with your head above water **2** to be unable to understand sth because it is too difficult; to be in a situation that you cannot control: *He felt totally out of his depth in his new job.* ➲ more at PLUMB *v.*

ˈdepth charge *noun* a bomb that is set to explode underwater, used to destroy SUBMARINES

ˌdepth of ˈfield (also **ˌdepth of ˈfocus**) *noun* (*technical*) the distance between the nearest and the furthest objects that a camera can produce a clear image of at the same time

depu·ta·tion /ˌdepjuˈteɪʃn/ *noun* [C+sing./pl. v.] a small group of people who are asked or allowed to act or speak for others

de·pute /dɪˈpjuːt/ *verb* **~ sb to do sth** [often passive] (*formal*) to give sb else the authority to represent you or do sth for you SYN **delegate**: *He was deputed to put our views to the committee.*

depu·tize (*BrE* also **-ise**) /ˈdepjutaɪz/ *verb* [I] **~ (for sb)** to do sth that sb in a higher position than you would usually do: *Ms Green has asked me to deputize for her at the meeting.*

dep·uty /ˈdepjuti/ *noun* (*pl.* -ies) **1** a person who is the next most important person below a business manager, a head of a school, a political leader, etc. and who does the person's job when he or she is away: *I'm acting as deputy till the manager returns.* ◇ *the deputy head of a school* **2** the name for a member of parliament in some countries **3** (in the US) a police officer who helps the SHERIFF of an area

de·racin·ate /ˌdiːˈræsɪneɪt/ *verb* **~ sb** (*formal*) to force sb to leave the place or situation in which they feel comfortable ▶ **de·racin·ated** /ˌdiːˈræsɪneɪtɪd/ *adj.*

de·rail /dɪˈreɪl/ *verb* [I, T] (of a train) to leave the track; to make a train do this: *The train derailed and plunged into the river.* ◇ **~ sth** (*figurative*) *This latest incident could derail the peace process.* ▶ **de·rail·ment** *noun* [C, U]

de·rail·leur /dɪˈreɪljə(r)/ *noun* (*technical*) a type of gear on a bicycle that works by lifting the chain from one gear wheel to another larger or smaller one

de·ranged /dɪˈreɪndʒd/ *adj.* unable to behave and think normally, especially because of mental illness: *mentally deranged* ◇ *a deranged attacker* ▶ **de·range·ment** *noun* [U]: *He seemed to be on the verge of total derangement.*

derby /ˈdɑːbi; *NAmE* ˈdɜːrbi/ *noun* (*pl.* -ies) **1** (*NAmE*) = BOWLER (2) **2** (*BrE*) a sports competition between teams from the same area or town: *a* ***local derby*** *between the two North London sides* ◇ *a derby match* **3** a race or sports competition: *a motorcycle derby* ⊃ see also DEMOLITION DERBY **4 Derby** used in the name of several horse races which happen every year: *the Epsom Derby* ◇ *the Kentucky Derby*

de·regu·late AW /ˌdiːˈregjuleɪt/ *verb* [often passive] **~ sth** to free a trade, a business activity, etc. from rules and controls SYN **decontrol**: *deregulated financial markets* ▶ **de·regu·la·tion** AW /ˌdiːˌregjuˈleɪʃn/ *noun* [U] **de·regu·la·tory** /ˌdiːˈregjələtəri; *NAmE* -tɔːri/ *adj.* [only before noun]: *deregulatory reforms*

dere·lict /ˈderəlɪkt/ *adj.*, *noun*

■ ***adj.*** (especially of land or buildings) not used or cared for and in bad condition: ***derelict land/buildings/sites***

■ ***noun*** (*formal*) a person without a home, a job or property SYN **vagrant**: *derelicts living on the streets*

dere·lic·tion /ˌderəˈlɪkʃn/ *noun* (*formal*) **1** [U] the state of being derelict: ***industrial/urban dereliction*** ◇ *a house in a state of dereliction* **2** [U, sing.] **~ of duty** (*formal* or *law*) the fact of deliberately not doing what you ought to do, especially when it is part of your job: *The police officers were found guilty of serious* ***dereliction of duty***.

de·ride /dɪˈraɪd/ *verb* [often passive] **~ sb/sth** (**as sth**) | **+ speech** (*formal*) to treat sb/sth as ridiculous and not worth considering seriously SYN **mock**: *His views were derided as old-fashioned.*

de ri·gueur /ˌdə rɪˈɡɜː(r)/ *adj.* [not before noun] (from *French*) considered necessary if you wish to be accepted socially: *Evening dress is de rigueur at the casino.*

de·ri·sion /dɪˈrɪʒn/ *noun* [U] a strong feeling that sb/sth is ridiculous and not worth considering seriously, shown by laughing in an unkind way or by making unkind remarks SYN **scorn**: *Her speech was greeted with howls of derision.* ◇ *He became an object of universal derision.*

de·ri·sive /dɪˈraɪsɪv/ (also *less frequent* **de·ri·sory**) *adj.* unkind and showing that you think sb/sth is ridiculous: *She gave a short, derisive laugh.* ▶ **de·ri·sive·ly** *adv.*

de·ri·sory /dɪˈraɪsəri/ *adj.* (*formal*) **1** too small or of too little value to be considered seriously SYN **laughable**: *They offered us a derisory £10 a week.* **2** = DERISIVE

der·iv·ation AW /ˌderɪˈveɪʃn/ *noun* [U, C] the origin or development of sth, especially a word: *a word of Greek derivation*

de·riva·tive AW /dɪˈrɪvətɪv/ *noun, adj.*

■ ***noun*** a word or thing that has been developed or produced from another word or thing: *'Happiness' is a derivative of 'happy'.* ◇ *Crack is a highly potent and addictive derivative of cocaine.*

■ ***adj.*** (usually *disapproving*) copied from sth else; not having new or original ideas: *a* ***derivative design/style***

de·rive 0-w AW /dɪˈraɪv/ *verb*

PHR V **deˈrive from sth** | **be deˈrived from sth** 0-w to come or develop from sth: *The word 'politics' is derived from a Greek word meaning 'city'.* **deˈrive sth from sth** **1** (*formal*) to get sth from sth: *He derived great pleasure from painting.* **2** (*technical*) to obtain a substance from sth: *The new drug is derived from fish oil.*

derma·titis /ˌdɜːməˈtaɪtɪs; *NAmE* ˌdɜːrm-/ *noun* [U] (*medical*) a skin condition in which the skin becomes red, swollen and sore

derma·tolo·gist /ˌdɜːməˈtɒlədʒɪst; *NAmE* ˌdɜːrməˈtɑːl-/ *noun* a doctor who studies and treats skin diseases

derma·tol·ogy /ˌdɜːməˈtɒlədʒi; *NAmE* ˌdɜːrməˈtɑːl-/ *noun* [U] the scientific study of skin diseases ▶ **derma·to·logi·cal** /ˌdɜːmətəˈlɒdʒɪkl; *NAmE* ˌdɜːrmətəˈlɑːdʒ-/ *adj.*

der·mis /ˈdɜːmɪs; *NAmE* ˈdɜːr-/ *noun* [U] (*biology*) the skin

dero·gate /ˈderəɡeɪt/ *verb* **~ sth** (*formal*) to state that sth or sb is without worth

PHR V **ˈderogate from sth** to ignore a responsibility or duty

dero·ga·tion /ˌderəˈɡeɪʃn/ *noun* [U, C] (*formal*) **1** an occasion when a rule or law is allowed to be ignored **2** words or actions which show that sb or sth is considered to have no worth

de·roga·tory /dɪˈrɒɡətri; *NAmE* dɪˈrɑːɡətɔːri/ *adj.* (*formal*) showing a critical attitude towards sb SYN **insulting**: ***derogatory remarks/comments***

der·rick /ˈderɪk/ *noun* **1** a tall machine used for moving or lifting heavy weights, especially on a ship; a type of CRANE **2** a tall structure over an OIL WELL for holding the DRILL (= the machine that makes the hole in the ground for getting the oil out)

derring-do /ˌderɪŋ ˈduː/ *noun* [U] (*old-fashioned, humorous*) brave actions, like those in adventure stories

der·vish /ˈdɜːvɪʃ; *NAmE* ˈdɜːrvɪʃ/ *noun* a member of a Muslim religious group whose members make a promise to stay poor and live without comforts or pleasures. They perform a fast lively dance as part of their worship: *He threw himself around the stage like a whirling dervish.*

de·sal·in·ation /ˌdiːˌsælɪˈneɪʃn/ *noun* [U] the process of removing salt from sea water: *a desalination plant*

de·scale /ˌdiːˈskeɪl/ *verb* **~ sth** (*BrE*) to remove the SCALE (= the hard white material left on pipes, etc. by water when it is heated) from sth

des·cant /ˈdeskænt/ *noun* (*music*) a tune that is sung or played at the same time as, and usually higher than, the main tune

ˌdescant reˈcorder (*BrE*) (*NAmE* **soˌprano reˈcorder**) *noun* (*music*) the most common size of RECORDER (= a musical instrument in the shape of a pipe that you blow into), with a high range of notes

des·cend /dɪˈsend/ *verb* **1** [I, T] (*formal*) to come or go down from a higher to a lower level: *The plane began to descend.* ◇ *The results, ranked* ***in descending order*** (= from the highest to the lowest) *are as follows....* ◇ **~ sth** *She descended the stairs slowly.* OPP **ascend** **2** [I] (*formal*) (of a hill, etc.) to slope downwards: *At this point the path descends steeply.* OPP **ascend** **3** [I] (*literary*) (of night, DARKNESS, a mood, etc.) to arrive and begin to affect sb/sth SYN **fall**: *Night descends quickly in the tropics.* ◇ **~ on/upon sb/sth** *Calm descended on the crowd.*

PHR V **be desˈcended from sb** to be related to sb who lived a long time ago: *He claims to be descended from a Spanish prince.* **desˈcend into sth** [no passive] (*formal*) to gradually get into a bad state: *The country was descending into chaos.* **desˈcend on/upon sb/sth** to visit sb/sth in large numbers, sometimes unexpectedly: *Hundreds of football fans descended on the city.* **desˈcend to sth** [no passive] to do sth that makes people stop respecting you: *They descended to the level of personal insults.*

des·cend·ant /dɪˈsendənt/ *noun* **1** a person's **descendants** are their children, their children's children, and all the people who live after them who are related to them: *He was an O'Conor and a* ***direct descendant*** *of the last High King of Ireland.* ◇ *Many of them are descendants of the original settlers.* **2** something that has developed from sth similar in the past

des·cent /dɪˈsent/ *noun* (*formal*) **1** [C, usually sing.] an action of coming or going down: *The plane began its descent to Heathrow.* ◇ (*figurative*) *the country's swift descent into anarchy* OPP **ascent 2** [C] a slope going downwards: *There is a gradual descent to the sea.* OPP **ascent 3** [U] a person's family origins SYN **ancestry**: *to be of Scottish descent* ◇ **~ from sb** *He traces his line of descent from the Stuart kings.*

D

de·scribe 🔑 /dɪˈskraɪb/ *verb*
1 🔑 to say what sb/sth is like: **~ sb/sth (to/for sb)** *Can you describe him to me?* ◇ **~ sb/sth as sth** *The man was described as tall and dark, and aged about 20.* ◇ *Jim was described by his colleagues as 'unusual'.* ◇ **~ how, what, etc...** *Describe how you did it.* ◇ **~ (sb/sth) doing sth** *Several people described seeing strange lights in the sky.* **2 ~ sth** (*formal* or *technical*) to make a movement which has a particular shape; to form a particular shape: *The shark described a circle around the shoal of fish.* ▸ **de·scrib·able** *adj.*

de·scrip·tion 🔑 /dɪˈskrɪpʃn/ *noun*
1 🔑 [C, U] **~ (of sb/sth)** a piece of writing or speech that says what sb/sth is like; the act of writing or saying in words what sb/sth is like: *to give a* ***detailed/full description*** *of the procedure* ◇ *a* ***brief/general description*** *of the software* ◇ *Police have issued a description of the gunman.* ◇ *'Scared stiff' is an apt description of how I felt at that moment.* ◇ *a personal pain that goes* ***beyond description*** (= is too great to express in words) ◇ *the novelist's powers of description* **2** [C] **of some, all, every, etc. ~** of some, etc. type: *boats of every description / all descriptions* ◇ *Their money came from trade of some description.* ◇ *medals, coins and things of that description*
IDM **answer/fit a description (of sb/sth)** to be like a particular person or thing: *A child answering the description of the missing boy was found safe and well in London yesterday.* ➲ more at BEGGAR *v.*

de·scrip·tive /dɪˈskrɪptɪv/ *adj.* **1** saying what sb/sth is like; describing sth: *the descriptive passages in the novel* ◇ *The term I used was meant to be purely descriptive* (= not judging). **2** (*linguistics*) saying how language is actually used, without giving rules for how it should be used OPP **prescriptive**

de·scrip·tor /dɪˈskrɪptə(r)/ *noun* (*linguistics*) a word or expression used to describe or identify sth

des·cry /dɪˈskraɪ/ *verb* (**des·cries, des·cry·ing, des·cried, des·cried**) **~ sb/sth** (*literary*) to suddenly see sb/sth

dese·crate /ˈdesɪkreɪt/ *verb* **~ sth** to damage a holy thing or place or treat it without respect: *desecrated graves* ▸ **dese·cra·tion** /ˌdesɪˈkreɪʃn/ *noun* [U]: *the desecration of a cemetery* ◇ (*figurative*) *the desecration of the countryside by new roads*

de·seg·re·gate /ˌdiːˈsegrɪgeɪt/ *verb* **~ sth** to end the policy of SEGREGATION in a place in which people of different races are kept separate in public places, etc. ▸ **de·seg·re·ga·tion** /ˌdiːˌsegrɪˈgeɪʃn/ *noun* [U]

de·select /ˌdiːsɪˈlekt/ *verb* **1 ~ sb** if the local branch of a political party in Britain **deselects** the existing Member of Parliament, it does not choose him or her as a candidate at the next election **2 ~ sth** (*computing*) to remove sth from the list of possible choices on a computer menu ▸ **de·selec·tion** *noun* [U]

de·sen·si·tize (*BrE* also **-ise**) /ˌdiːˈsensətaɪz/ *verb* [usually passive] **1 ~ sb/sth (to sth)** to make sb/sth less aware of sth, especially a problem or sth bad, by making them become used to it: *People are increasingly becoming desensitized to violence on television.* **2 ~ sb/sth** (*technical*) to treat sb/sth so that they will stop being sensitive to physical or chemical changes, or to a particular substance ▸ **de·sen·si·tiza·tion, -isa·tion** /ˌdiːˌsensətaɪˈzeɪʃn; *NAmE* -təˈz-/ *noun* [U]

des·ert 🔑 *noun, verb*
■ ***noun*** 🔑 /ˈdezət; *NAmE* ˈdezərt/ ➲ see also DESERTS [C, U] a large area of land that has very little water and very few plants growing on it. Many deserts are covered by sand: *the Sahara Desert* ◇ *Somalia is mostly desert.* ◇ *burning desert sands* ◇ (*figurative*) *a cultural desert* (= a place without any culture)
■ ***verb*** /dɪˈzɜːt; *NAmE* dɪˈzɜːrt/ **1** 🔑 [T] **~ sb** to leave sb without help or support SYN **abandon**: *She was deserted by her husband.* **2** 🔑 [T, often passive] **~ sth** to go away from a place and leave it empty SYN **abandon**: *The villages had been deserted.* ◇ *The owl seems to have deserted its nest.* **3** 🔑 [I, T] **~ (sth)** to leave the armed forces without permission: *Large numbers of soldiers deserted as defeat became inevitable.* **4** [T] **~ sth (for sth)** to stop using, buying or supporting sth: *Why did you desert teaching for politics?* **5** [T] **~ sb** if a particular quality **deserts** you, it is not there when you need it: *Her courage seemed to desert her for a moment.* ▸ **de·ser·tion** /dɪˈzɜːʃn; *NAmE* -ˈzɜːr-/ *noun* [U, C]: *She felt betrayed by her husband's desertion.* ◇ *The army was badly affected by desertions.* IDM see SINK *v.*

ˈ**desert boot** *noun* a SUEDE boot that just covers the ankle

des·ert·ed 🔑 /dɪˈzɜːtɪd; *NAmE* -ˈzɜːrt-/ *adj.*
1 🔑 (of a place) with no people in it: *deserted streets* **2** 🔑 left by a person or people who do not intend to return SYN **abandoned**: *a deserted village* ◇ *deserted wives*

de·sert·er /dɪˈzɜːtə(r); *NAmE* -ˈzɜːrt-/ *noun* a person who leaves the army, navy, etc. without permission (=DESERTS)

desert·ifi·ca·tion /dɪˌzɜːtɪfɪˈkeɪʃn; *NAmE* -ˌzɜːrt-/ *noun* [U] (*technical*) the process of becoming or making sth a desert

ˌ**desert** ˈ**island** *noun* a tropical island where no people live

des·erts /dɪˈzɜːts; *NAmE* dɪˈzɜːrts/ *noun* [pl.]
IDM **sb's (just) deserts** what sb deserves, especially when it is sth bad: *The family of the victim said that the killer had* ***got his just deserts*** *when he was jailed for life.*

de·serve 🔑 /dɪˈzɜːv; *NAmE* dɪˈzɜːrv/ *verb* (not used in the progressive tenses)
if sb/sth **deserves** sth, it is right that they should have it, because of the way they have behaved or because of what they are: **~ sth** *You deserve a rest after all that hard work.* ◇ *The report deserves careful consideration.* ◇ *One player in particular deserves a mention.* ◇ *What have I done to deserve this?* ◇ **~ to do sth** *They didn't deserve to win.* ◇ *He deserves to be locked up for ever for what he did.* ◇ **~ doing sth** *Several other points deserve mentioning.*
IDM **sb deˌserves a ˈmedal** (*informal*) used to say that you admire sb because they have done sth difficult or unpleasant **ˌget what you deˈserve | deˌserve all/everything you ˈget** (*informal*) used to say that you think sb has earned the bad things that happen to them ➲ more at TURN *n.*

de·served·ly /dɪˈzɜːvɪdli; *NAmE* -ˈzɜːrv-/ *adv.* in the way that is deserved; correctly: *The restaurant is deservedly popular.* ◇ *He has just been chosen for the top job, and* ***deservedly so.***

de·serv·ing /dɪˈzɜːvɪŋ; *NAmE* -ˈzɜːrv-/ *adj.* **~ (of sth)** (*formal*) that deserves help, praise, a reward, etc: *to give money to a deserving cause* ◇ *This family is one of the most deserving cases.* ◇ *an issue deserving of attention* OPP **undeserving**

dés·ha·billé /ˌdezæbiːˈjeɪ/ (also **dis·ha·bille** /ˌdɪsəˈbiːl; -ˈbiː/) *noun* [U] (*formal* or *humorous*) the state of wearing no clothes or very few clothes: *in a state of déshabillé*

des·ic·cated /ˈdesɪkeɪtɪd/ *adj.* **1** (of food) dried in order to preserve it: *desiccated coconut* **2** (*technical*) completely dry: *treeless and desiccated soil*

des·ic·ca·tion /ˌdesɪˈkeɪʃn/ *noun* [U] (*technical*) the process of becoming completely dry

de·sid·er·atum /dɪˌzɪdəˈrɑːtəm; -ˈreɪtəm/ *noun* (*pl.* **desiderata** /-ɑːtə; -eɪtə/) (from *Latin*, *formal*) a thing that is wanted or needed

de·sign 🔑 AW /dɪˈzaɪn/ *noun, verb*
■ ***noun***
▸ ARRANGEMENT **1** 🔑 [U, C] the general arrangement of the different parts of sth that is made, such as a building, book, machine, etc: *The basic design of the car is very simi-*

lar to that of earlier models. ◇ *special new design features* ◇ *The magazine will appear in a new design from next month.*
▸ DRAWING/PLAN/MODEL **2** [U] the art or process of deciding how sth will look, work, etc. by drawing plans, making models, etc: *a course in art and design* ◇ *a design studio* ◇ *computer-aided design* ◇ *the design and development of new products* ➲ see also INTERIOR DESIGN **3** [C] **~ (for sth)** a drawing or plan from which sth may be made: *designs for aircraft* ◇ *new and original designs*
▸ PATTERN **4** [C] an arrangement of lines and shapes as a decoration SYN **pattern**: ***floral/abstract/geometric designs*** ◇ *The tiles come in a huge range of colours and designs.*
▸ INTENTION **5** [U, C] a plan or an intention: *It happened—whether **by accident or design**—that the two of them were left alone after all the others had gone.* ◇ *It is all part of his **grand design**.*
IDM **have designs on sb** (*formal* or *humorous*) to want to start a sexual relationship with sb **have designs on sth** (*formal*) to be planning to get sth for yourself, often in a way that other people do not approve of: *Rumours spread that the Duke had designs on the crown* (= wanted to make himself king).
■ ***verb***
▸ DRAW PLANS **1** to decide how sth will look, work, etc, especially by drawing plans or making models: **~ sth** *to design a car/a dress/an office* ◇ *a badly designed kitchen* ◇ **~ sth for sb/sth** *They asked me to design a poster for the campaign.* ◇ **~ sb sth** *Could you design us a poster?*
▸ PLAN STH **2** **~ sth** to think of and plan a system, a way of doing sth, etc: *We need to design a new syllabus for the third year.*
▸ FOR SPECIAL PURPOSE **3** [usually passive] to make, plan or intend sth for a particular purpose or use: **~ sth (for sth)** *The method is specifically designed for use in small groups.* ◇ **~ sth (as sth)** *This course is primarily designed as an introduction to the subject.* ◇ **~ sth to do sth** *The programme is designed to help people who have been out of work for a long time.*

des·ig·nate *verb, adj.*
■ ***verb*** /ˈdezɪgneɪt/ [often passive] (*formal*) **1** to say officially that sb/sth has a particular character or name; to describe sb/sth in a particular way: **~ sb/sth (as) sth** *This area has been designated (as) a National Park.* ◇ **~ sb/sth (as being/having sth)** *Several pupils were designated as having moderate or severe learning difficulties.* ◇ *a designated nature reserve* ◇ *designated seats for the elderly* **2** to choose or name sb for a particular job or position: **~ sb/sth** *The director is allowed to designate his/her successor.* ◇ **~ sb (as) sth** *Who has she designated (as) her deputy?* ◇ **~ sb to do sth** *the man designated to succeed the president* **3** **~ sth (by sth)** to show sth using a particular mark or sign: *The different types are designated by the letters A, B and C.*
■ ***adj.*** /ˈdezɪgneɪt; -nət/ [after noun] (*formal*) chosen to do a job but not yet having officially started it: *an interview with the director designate*

ˌdesignated ˈdriver *noun* (*informal*) the person who agrees to drive and not drink alcohol when people go to a party, a bar, etc.

ˌdesignated ˈhitter *noun* (in BASEBALL) a player who is named at the start of the game as the person who will hit the ball in place of the PITCHER

des·ig·na·tion /ˌdezɪgˈneɪʃn/ *noun* (*formal*) **1** [U] **~ (as sth)** the action of choosing a person or thing for a particular purpose, or of giving them or it a particular status: *The district is under consideration for designation as a conservation area.* **2** [C] a name, title or description: *Her official designation is Financial Controller.*

de·sign·er AW /dɪˈzaɪnə(r)/ *noun, adj.*
■ ***noun*** a person whose job is to decide how things such as clothes, furniture, tools, etc. will look or work by making drawings, plans or patterns: *a **fashion/jewellery, etc. designer*** ◇ *an industrial designer*
■ ***adj.*** [only before noun] made by a famous designer; expensive and having a famous brand name: *designer jeans* ◇ *designer labels* ◇ *designer water* ◇ *He had a trendy haircut, an earring and **designer stubble*** (= a short beard, grown for two or three days and thought to look fashionable). ➲ COLLOCATIONS at FASHION

deˌsigner ˈbaby *noun* (used especially in newspapers) a baby that is born from an EMBRYO which was selected from a number of embryos produced using IVF, for example because the parents want a baby that can provide cells to treat a brother's or sister's medical condition

deˌsigner ˈdrug *noun* a drug produced artificially, usually one that is illegal

de·sir·able /dɪˈzaɪərəbl/ *adj.* **1** (*formal*) that you would like to have or do; worth having or doing: *She chatted for a few minutes about the qualities she considered **desirable in** a secretary.* ◇ *Such measures are desirable, if not essential.* ◇ *The house has many desirable features.* ◇ *highly desirable* ◇ **~ that** (*BrE*) *It is **desirable that** interest rates should be reduced.* ◇ (*NAmE*) *It is **desirable that** interest rates be reduced.* ◇ **~ (for sb) (to do sth)** ***It is** no longer **desirable for** adult children to live with their parents.* OPP **undesirable** **2** (of a person) causing other people to feel sexual desire ▸ **de·sir·abil·ity** /dɪˌzaɪərəˈbɪləti/ *noun* [U]: (*formal*) *No one questions the desirability of cheaper fares.*

de·sire /dɪˈzaɪə(r)/ *noun, verb*
■ ***noun*** **1** [C, U] a strong wish to have or do sth: *enough money to satisfy all your desires* ◇ **~ for sth** *a strong desire for power* ◇ **~ to do sth** *She felt an overwhelming desire to return home.* ◇ (*formal*) *I have no desire* (= I do not want) *to discuss the matter further.* ◇ (*formal*) *He has expressed a desire to see you.* **2** [U, C] **~ (for sb)** a strong wish to have sex with sb: *She felt a surge of love and desire for him.* **3** [C, usually sing.] a person or thing that is wished for: *When she agreed to marry him he felt he had achieved **his heart's desire**.*
■ ***verb*** (not used in the progressive tenses) **1** (*formal*) to want sth; to wish for sth: **~ sth** *We all desire health and happiness.* ◇ *The house had everything you could desire.* ◇ *The medicine did not achieve **the desired effect**.* ◇ **~ (sb/sth) to do sth** *Fewer people desire to live in the north of the country.* **2** **~ sb** to be sexually attracted to sb: *He still desired her.*
IDM **leave a lot, much, something, etc. to be deˈsired** to be bad or unacceptable

de·sir·ous /dɪˈzaɪərəs/ *adj.* [not before noun] **~ (of sth / of doing sth)** | **~ (to do sth)** (*formal*) having a wish for sth; wanting sth: *At that point Franco was desirous of prolonging the war.*

de·sist /dɪˈzɪst; dɪˈsɪst/ *verb* [I] **~ (from sth/from doing sth)** (*formal*) to stop doing sth: *They agreed to desist from the bombing campaign.*

desk /desk/ *noun*
1 a piece of furniture like a table, usually with drawers in it, that you sit at to read, write, work, etc: *He used to be a pilot but now he has **a desk job**.* ➲ VISUAL VOCAB page V56 **2** a place where you can get information or be served at an airport, a hotel, etc: *the check-in desk* ◇ *the reception desk* ➲ see also CASH DESK, FRONT DESK **3** an office at a newspaper, television company, etc. that deals with a particular subject: *the sports desk* ➲ see also CITY DESK, NEWS DESK

ˈdesk clerk *noun* (*NAmE*) = CLERK

de·skill /diːˈskɪl/ *verb* **~ sth** (*technical*) to reduce the amount of skill that is needed to do a particular job ▸ **de·skill·ing** *noun* [U]

desk·top /ˈdesktɒp; *NAmE* -tɑːp/ *noun* **1** the top of a desk **2** a screen on a computer which shows the ICONS of the programs that can be used ➲ VISUAL VOCAB page V55 **3** = DESKTOP COMPUTER

ˌdesktop comˈputer (also **desk·top**) *noun* a computer with a keyboard, screen and main processing unit, that fits on a desk ➲ compare LAPTOP, NOTEBOOK

ˌdesktop ˈpublishing *noun* [U] (*abbr.* DTP) the use of a small computer and a printer to produce a small book, a magazine or other printed material

deso·late *adj., verb*
■ ***adj.*** /ˈdesələt/ **1** (of a place) empty and without people,

making you feel sad or frightened: *a bleak and desolate landscape* **2** very lonely and unhappy SYN **forlorn**
■ ***verb*** /'desəleɪt/ [usually passive] **~ sb** (*literary*) to make sb feel sad and without hope: *She had been desolated by the death of her friend.*

deso·la·tion /ˌdesə'leɪʃn/ *noun* [U] (*formal*) **1** the feeling of being very lonely and unhappy **2** the state of a place that is ruined or destroyed and offers no joy or hope to people: *a scene of utter desolation*

D

des·pair /dɪ'speə(r); *NAmE* dɪ'sper/ *noun, verb*
■ ***noun*** [U] the feeling of having lost all hope: *She uttered a cry of despair.* ◇ *A deep sense of despair overwhelmed him.* ◇ *He gave up the struggle **in despair**.* ◇ *One harsh word would send her into **the depths of despair**.* ◇ *Eventually, **driven to despair**, he threw himself under a train.* ➲ see also DESPERATE
IDM **be the despair of sb** to make sb worried or unhappy, because they cannot help: *My handwriting was the despair of my teachers.* ➲ more at COUNSEL *n.*
■ ***verb*** [I] to stop having any hope that a situation will change or improve: *Don't despair! We'll think of a way out of this.* ◇ **~ of sth/sb** *I despair of him; he can't keep a job for more than six months.* ◇ **~ of doing sth** *They'd almost despaired of ever having children.*

des·pair·ing /dɪ'speərɪŋ; *NAmE* -'sper-/ *adj.* showing or feeling the loss of all hope: *a **despairing cry/look/sigh*** ◇ *With every day that passed he became ever more despairing.* ▸ **des·pair·ing·ly** *adv.*: *She looked despairingly at the mess.*

des·patch (*BrE*) = DISPATCH

des·per·ado /ˌdespə'rɑːdəʊ; *NAmE* -doʊ/ *noun* (*pl.* **-oes** or **-os**) (*old-fashioned*) a man who does dangerous and criminal things without caring about himself or other people

des·per·ate 🔑 /'despərət/ *adj.*
1 🔑 feeling or showing that you have little hope and are ready to do anything without worrying about danger to yourself or others: *The prisoners grew increasingly desperate.* ◇ *Stores are getting desperate after two years of poor sales.* ◇ *Somewhere out there was a desperate man, cold, hungry, hunted.* ◇ *I heard sounds of a desperate struggle in the next room.* **2** 🔑 [usually before noun] (of an action) giving little hope of success; tried when everything else has failed: *a **desperate bid** for freedom* ◇ *She clung to the edge **in a desperate attempt** to save herself.* ◇ *His increasing financial difficulties forced him to take **desperate measures**.* ◇ *Doctors were fighting a **desperate battle** to save the little girl's life.* **3** 🔑 [not usually before noun] needing or wanting sth very much: **~ (for sth)** *He was so desperate for a job he would have done anything.* ◇ (*informal*) *I'm desperate for a cigarette.* ◇ **~ (to do sth)** *I was absolutely desperate to see her.* **4** 🔑 (of a situation) extremely serious or dangerous: *The children are **in desperate need** of love and attention.* ◇ *They face a desperate shortage of clean water.* ▸ **des·per·ate·ly** 🔑 *adv.*: ***desperately ill/unhappy/lonely*** ◇ *He took a deep breath, desperately trying to keep calm.* ◇ *They desperately wanted a child.* ◇ *She looked desperately around for a weapon.*

des·per·ation /ˌdespə'reɪʃn/ *noun* [U] the state of being desperate: ***In desperation**, she called Louise and asked for her help.* ◇ *There was a note of desperation in his voice.* ◇ *an act of sheer desperation*

de·spic·able /dɪ'spɪkəbl; *rarely* 'despɪkəbl/ *adj.* (*formal*) very unpleasant or evil: *a **despicable act/crime*** ◇ *I hate you! You're despicable.*

des·pise /dɪ'spaɪz/ *verb* **~ sb/sth** (not used in the progressive tenses) to dislike and have no respect for sb/sth: *She despised gossip in any form.* ◇ *He despised himself for being so cowardly.* ➲ SYNONYMS at HATE

des·pite 🔑 AW /dɪ'spaɪt/ *prep.*
1 🔑 used to show that sth happened or is true although sth else might have happened to prevent it SYN **in spite of**: *Her voice was shaking despite all her efforts to control it.* ◇ *Despite applying for hundreds of jobs, he is still out of work.* ◇ *She was good at physics **despite the fact that** she found it boring.* ➲ LANGUAGE BANK at HOWEVER **2 despite yourself** used to show that sb did not intend to do the thing mentioned SYN **in spite of**: *He had to laugh despite himself.*

de·spoil /dɪ'spɔɪl/ *verb* **~ sth (of sth)** (*literary*) to steal sth valuable from a place; to make a place less attractive by damaging or destroying it SYN **plunder**

des·pond /dɪ'spɒnd; *NAmE* -'spɑːnd/ *noun* [U] ➲ SLOUGH OF DESPOND

des·pond·ent /dɪ'spɒndənt; *NAmE* -'spɑːn-/ *adj.* **~ (about sth)** | (*especially NAmE*) **~ (over sth)** sad, without much hope SYN **dejected**: *She was becoming increasingly despondent about the way things were going.* ▸ **des·pond·ency** /dɪ'spɒndənsi; *NAmE* -'spɑːn-/ *noun* [U]: *a mood of despondency* ◇ *Life's not all gloom and despondency.* **des·pond·ent·ly** *adv.*

des·pot /'despɒt; *NAmE* 'despɑːt/ *noun* a ruler with great power, especially one who uses it in a cruel way: *an enlightened despot* (= one who tries to use his/her power in a good way) ▸ **des·pot·ic** /dɪ'spɒtɪk; *NAmE* -'spɑːt-/ *adj.*: ***despotic power/rule***

des·pot·ism /'despətɪzəm/ *noun* [U] the rule of a despot

des res /ˌdez 'rez/ *noun* [usually sing.] (*BrE*, *humorous*) an attractive house, especially a large one (from the words 'desirable residence')

des·sert /dɪ'zɜːt; *NAmE* dɪ'zɜːrt/ *noun* [U, C] sweet food eaten at the end of a meal: *What's **for dessert**?* ◇ *a rich chocolate dessert* ◇ *a dessert wine* ◇ (*BrE*) *the dessert trolley* (= a table on wheels from which you choose your dessert in a restaurant) ➲ COLLOCATIONS at RESTAURANT ➲ compare AFTERS, PUDDING, SWEET

des·sert·spoon /dɪ'zɜːtspuːn; *NAmE* -'zɜːrt-/ *noun* **1** a spoon of medium size ➲ VISUAL VOCAB page V19 **2** (also **des·sert·spoon·ful** /-fʊl/) the amount a dessertspoon can hold

de·sta·bil·ize (*BrE* also **-ise**) /ˌdiː'steɪbəlaɪz/ *verb* **~ sth** to make a system, country, government, etc. become less firmly established or successful: *Terrorist attacks were threatening to destabilize the government.* ◇ *The news had a destabilizing effect on the stock market.* ➲ compare STABILIZE ▸ **de·sta·bil·iza·tion, -isa·tion** /ˌdiːˌsteɪbəlaɪ'zeɪʃn; *NAmE* -lə'z-/ *noun* [U]

des·tin·ation /ˌdestɪ'neɪʃn/ *noun, adj.*
■ ***noun*** a place to which sb/sth is going or being sent: *popular **holiday destinations** like the Bahamas* ◇ *to **arrive at/reach your destination*** ◇ *Our luggage was checked all the way through to our **final destination**.*
■ ***adj.*** **~ hotel/store/restaurant, etc.** a hotel, store, etc. that people will make a special trip to visit

des·tined /'destɪnd/ *adj.* (*formal*) **1** having a future which has been decided or planned at an earlier time, especially by FATE: **~ for sth** *He was destined for a military career, like his father before him.* ◇ **~ to do sth** *We seem destined never to meet.* **2 ~ for...** on the way to or intended for a place SYN **bound for**: *goods destined for Poland*

des·tiny /'destəni/ *noun* (*pl.* **-ies**) **1** [C] what happens to sb or what will happen to them in the future, especially things that they cannot change or avoid: *the destinies of nations* ◇ *He wants to be in control of his own destiny.* **2** [U] the power believed to control events SYN **fate**: *I believe there's some force guiding us—call it God, destiny or fate.* ➲ SYNONYMS at LUCK

des·ti·tute /'destɪtjuːt; *NAmE* -tuːt/ *adj.* **1** without money, food and the other things necessary for life: *When he died, his family was left completely destitute.* **2 the destitute** *noun* [pl.] people who are destitute **3 ~ of sth** (*formal*) lacking sth: *They seem destitute of ordinary human feelings.* ▸ **des·ti·tu·tion** /ˌdestɪ'tjuːʃn; *NAmE* -'tuːʃn/ *noun* [U]: *homelessness and destitution*

de·stock /ˌdiː'stɒk; *NAmE* -'stɑːk/ *verb* [I, T] **~ (sth)** (*BrE*, *business*) to reduce the amount of goods in a shop/store, the amount of materials kept available for making sth in a factory, etc.

de-stress /ˌdiː ˈstres/ *verb* [I, T] **~ (sb/yourself)** to relax after working hard or experiencing stress; to reduce the amount of stress that you experience: *De-stress yourself with a relaxing bath.*

des·troy /dɪˈstrɔɪ/ *verb*
1 **~ sth/sb** to damage sth so badly that it no longer exists, works, etc: *The building was completely destroyed by fire.* ◇ *They've destroyed all the evidence.* ◇ *Heat gradually destroys vitamin C.* ◇ *You have destroyed my hopes of happiness.* ◇ *Failure was slowly destroying him* (= making him less and less confident and happy). **2** **~ sth** to kill an animal deliberately, usually because it is sick or not wanted: *The injured horse had to be destroyed.* ➲ see also SOUL-DESTROYING

WORD FAMILY
destroy *verb*
destroyer *noun*
destruction *noun*
destructive *adj.*
indestructible *adj.*

des·troy·er /dɪˈstrɔɪə(r)/ *noun* **1** a small fast ship used in war, for example to protect larger ships **2** a person or thing that destroys: *Sugar is the destroyer of healthy teeth.*

de·struc·tion /dɪˈstrʌkʃn/ *noun* [U] the act of destroying sth; the process of being destroyed: *the destruction of the rainforests* ◇ *weapons of mass destruction* ◇ *a tidal wave bringing* ***death and destruction*** *in its wake* ◇ *The central argument is that capitalism* ***sows the seeds of its own destruction*** (= creates the forces that destroy it).

de·struc·tive /dɪˈstrʌktɪv/ *adj.* causing destruction or damage: *the destructive power of modern weapons* ◇ *the destructive effects of anxiety* ➲ compare CONSTRUCTIVE ▸ **de·struc·tive·ly** *adv.* **de·struc·tive·ness** *noun* [U]

des·ul·tory /ˈdesəltri; *NAmE* -tɔːri/ *adj.* (*formal*) going from one thing to another, without a definite plan and without enthusiasm: *I wandered about in a desultory fashion.* ◇ *a desultory conversation* ▸ **des·ul·tor·ily** *adv.*

Det *abbr.* (*BrE*) (in writing) DETECTIVE: *Det Insp* (= Inspector) *Cox*

de·tach /dɪˈtætʃ/ *verb* **1** [T, I] to remove sth from sth larger; to become separated from sth: **~ sth** *Detach the coupon and return it as soon as possible* ◇ **~ sth from sth** *One of the panels had become detached from the main structure.* ◇ **~ (from sth)** *The skis should detach from the boot if you fall.* ➲ compare ATTACH **2** [T] **~ yourself (from sb/sth)** (*formal*) to leave or separate yourself from sb/sth: *She detached herself from his embrace.* ◇ (*figurative*) *I tried to detach myself from the reality of these terrible events.* **3** [T] **~ sb/sth** (*technical*) to send a group of soldiers, etc. away from the main group, especially to do special duties

de·tach·able /dɪˈtætʃəbl/ *adj.* that can be taken off **SYN removable**: *a coat with a detachable hood*

de·tached /dɪˈtætʃt/ *adj.* **1** (of a house) not joined to another house on either side ➲ VISUAL VOCAB page V15 ➲ compare SEMI-DETACHED **2** showing a lack of feeling **SYN indifferent**: *She wanted him to stop being so cool, so detached, so cynical.* **3** (*approving*) not influenced by other people or by your own feelings **SYN impartial**: *a detached observer*

de·tach·ment /dɪˈtætʃmənt/ *noun* **1** [U] the state of not being involved in sth in an emotional or personal way: *He answered with an air of detachment.* ◇ *She felt a sense of detachment from what was going on.* **OPP involvement** **2** [U] (*approving*) the state of not being influenced by other people or by your own feelings: *In judging these issues a degree of critical detachment is required.* **3** [C] a group of soldiers, ships, etc. sent away from a larger group, especially to do special duties: *a detachment of artillery* **4** [U] the act of detaching sth; the process of being detached from sth: *to suffer detachment of the retina*

de·tail /ˈdiːteɪl; *US* also dɪˈteɪl/ *noun, verb*
■ *noun*
▸ FACTS/INFORMATION **1** [C] a small individual fact or item; a less important fact or item: *an expedition planned down to the last detail* ◇ *He stood still, absorbing every detail of the street.* ◇ *Tell me the main points now; leave* ***the details*** *till later.* **2** [U] the small facts or features of sth, when you consider them all together: *This issue will be discussed* ***in*** *more* ***detail*** *in the next chapter.* ◇ *The research has been carried out with scrupulous* ***attention to detail.*** ◇ *He had* ***an eye for detail*** (= noticed and remembered small details). ◇ *The fine detail of the plan has yet to be worked out.* **3** **details** [pl.] information about sth: *Please supply the following details: name, age and sex.* ◇ *Further details and booking forms are available on request.* ◇ *They didn't give any details about the game.* ◇ *'We had a terrible time—' 'Oh, spare me the details* (= don't tell me any more).'
▸ SMALL PARTS **4** [C, U] a small part of a picture or painting; the smaller or less important parts of a picture, pattern, etc. when you consider them all together: *This is a detail from the 1844 Turner painting.* ◇ *a huge picture with a lot of detail in it*
▸ SOLDIERS **5** [C] a group of soldiers given special duties
IDM **go into ˈdetail(s)** to explain sth fully: *I can't go into details now; it would take too long.*
■ *verb*
▸ GIVE FACTS/INFORMATION **1** **~ sth** to give a list of facts or all the available information about sth: *The brochure details all the hotels in the area and their facilities.*
▸ ORDER SOLDIER **2** [often passive] **~ sb (to do sth)** to give an official order to sb, especially a soldier, to do a particular task: *Several of the men were detailed to form a search party.*
▸ CLEAN CAR **3** **~ sth** (*NAmE*) to clean a car extremely thoroughly: *He got work for a while detailing cars.*

de·tailed /ˈdiːteɪld; *NAmE* also dɪˈteɪld/ *adj.* giving many details and a lot of information; paying great attention to details: *a* ***detailed description/analysis/study*** ◇ *He gave me* ***detailed instructions*** *on how to get there.*

de·tail·ing /ˈdiːteɪlɪŋ; *NAmE* also dɪˈteɪlɪŋ/ *noun* [U] small details put on a building, piece of clothing, etc, especially for decoration

de·tain /dɪˈteɪn/ *verb* **1** **~ sb** to keep sb in an official place, such as a police station, a prison or a hospital, and prevent them from leaving: *One man has been detained for questioning.* **2** **~ sb** (*formal*) to delay sb or prevent them from going somewhere: *I'm sorry—he'll be late; he's been detained at a meeting.* ➲ see also DETENTION

de·tain·ee /ˌdiːteɪˈniː/ *noun* a person who is kept in prison, usually because of his or her political opinions

de·tect **AW** /dɪˈtekt/ *verb* **~ sth** to discover or notice sth, especially sth that is not easy to see, hear, etc: *The tests are designed to detect the disease early.* ◇ *an instrument that can detect small amounts of radiation* ◇ *Do I detect a note of criticism?* ➲ SYNONYMS at NOTICE ▸ **de·tect·able** **AW** *adj.*: *The noise is barely detectable by the human ear.* **OPP undetectable**

de·tec·tion **AW** /dɪˈtekʃn/ *noun* [U] the process of detecting sth; the fact of being detected: *crime prevention and detection* ◇ *Last year the detection rate for car theft was just 13%.* ◇ *Many problems, however, escape detection.* ◇ *Early detection of cancers is vitally important.*

de·tect·ive **AW** /dɪˈtektɪv/ *noun* (*abbr.* **Det**) **1** a person, especially a police officer, whose job is to examine crimes and catch criminals: *Detective Inspector (Roger) Brown* ◇ *detectives from the anti-terrorist squad* ◇ *a* ***detective story/novel*** ➲ see also STORE DETECTIVE **2** a person employed by sb to find out information about sb/sth ➲ see also PRIVATE DETECTIVE

de·tect·or **AW** /dɪˈtektə(r)/ *noun* a piece of equipment for discovering the presence of sth, such as metal, smoke, EXPLOSIVES or changes in pressure or temperature: *a smoke detector*

dé·tente (also **de·tente** especially in *NAmE*) /ˌdeɪˈtɑːnt/ *noun* [U] (from *French, formal*) an improvement in the relationship between two or more countries which have been unfriendly towards each other in the past

de·ten·tion /dɪˈtenʃn/ *noun* **1** [U] the state of being kept in a place, especially a prison, and prevented from leaving: *a sentence of 12 months' detention in a young offender insti-*

D

tution ◇ *police powers of arrest and detention* ◇ *allegations of torture and detention without trial* ◇ *a detention camp* **2** [U, C] the punishment of being kept at school for a time after other students have gone home: *They can't give me (a) detention for this.* ➲ see also DETAIN

de'tention centre (*BrE*) (*NAmE* **de'tention center**) *noun* **1** a place where young people who have committed offences are kept in detention **2** a place where people are kept in detention, especially people who have entered a country illegally

deter /dɪ'tɜː(r)/ *verb* (-rr-) [T, I] **~ (sb)** (**from sth/from doing sth**) to make sb decide not to do sth or continue doing sth, especially by making them understand the difficulties and unpleasant results of their actions: *I told him I wasn't interested, but he wasn't deterred.* ◇ *The high price of the service could deter people from seeking advice.* ➲ see also DETERRENT

de·ter·gent /dɪ'tɜːdʒənt; *NAmE* -'tɜːrdʒ-/ *noun* [U, C] a liquid or powder that helps remove dirt, for example from clothes or dishes

de·teri·or·ate /dɪ'tɪəriəreɪt; *NAmE* -'tɪr-/ *verb* [I] to become worse: *Her health deteriorated rapidly, and she died shortly afterwards.* ◇ *deteriorating weather conditions* ◇ **~ into sth** *The discussion quickly deteriorated into an angry argument.* ▸ **de·teri·or·ation** /dɪˌtɪəriə'reɪʃn; *NAmE* -ˌtɪr-/ *noun* [U, C]: *a serious deterioration in relations between the two countries*

de·ter·min·able /dɪ'tɜːmɪnəbl; *NAmE* -'tɜːrm-/ *adj.* (*formal*) that can be found out or calculated: *During the third month of pregnancy the sex of the child becomes determinable.*

de·ter·min·ant /dɪ'tɜːmɪnənt; *NAmE* -'tɜːrm-/ *noun* (*formal*) a thing that decides whether or how sth happens

de·ter·min·ate /dɪ'tɜːmɪnət; *NAmE* -'tɜːrm-/ *adj.* (*formal*) fixed and definite: *a sentence with a determinate meaning* **OPP indeterminate**

de·ter·min·ation 0-w /dɪˌtɜːmɪ'neɪʃn; *NAmE* -ˌtɜːrm-/ *noun*
1 0-w [U] the quality that makes you continue trying to do sth even when this is difficult: ***fierce/grim/dogged determination*** ◇ *He fought the illness with courage and determination.* ◇ *They had survived by sheer determination.* ◇ **~ to do sth** *I admire her determination to get it right.* **2** [U] (*formal*) the process of deciding sth officially: *factors influencing the determination of future policy* **3** [U, C] (*technical*) the act of finding out or calculating sth: *Both methods rely on the accurate determination of the pressure of the gas.*

de·ter·mine 0-w /dɪ'tɜːmɪn; *NAmE* -'tɜːrm-/ *verb* (*formal*)
1 0-w [T] to discover the facts about sth; to calculate sth exactly **SYN establish**: **~ sth** *An inquiry was set up to determine the cause of the accident.* ◇ **~ what, whether, etc...** *We set out to determine exactly what happened that night.* ◇ **it is determined that...** *It was determined that she had died of natural causes.* **2** [T] **~ sth** | **~ what, whether, etc...** to make sth happen in a particular way or be of a particular type: *Age and experience will be **determining factors** in our choice of candidate.* ◇ *Upbringing plays an important part in determining a person's character.* **3** [T] to officially decide and/or arrange sth: **~ sth** *A date for the meeting has yet to be determined.* ◇ **~ (that)...** *The court determined (that) the defendant should pay the legal costs.* **4** [T, I] **~ to do sth** | **~ (that)...** | **~ on sth** to decide definitely to do sth: *They determined to start early.*

de·ter·mined 0-w /dɪ'tɜːmɪnd; *NAmE* -'tɜːrm-/ *adj.*
1 0-w [not before noun] **~ (to do sth)** if you are **determined** to do sth, you have made a firm decision to do it and you will not let anyone prevent you: *I'm determined to succeed.* **2** 0-w showing a person's determination to do sth: *a determined effort to stop smoking* ◇ *The proposal had been dropped in the face of determined opposition.* **IDM** see BOUND *adj.* ▸ **de·ter·mined·ly** *adv.*

de·ter·miner /dɪ'tɜːmɪnə(r); *NAmE* -'tɜːrm-/ *noun* (*grammar*) (abbreviation *det.* in this dictionary) a word such as *the, some, my*, etc. that comes before a noun to show how the noun is being used

de·ter·min·ism /dɪ'tɜːmɪnɪzəm; *NAmE* -'tɜːrm-/ *noun* [U] (*philosophy*) the belief that people are not free to choose what they are like or how they behave, because these things are decided by their surroundings and other things over which they have no control ▸ **de·ter·min·is·tic** /dɪˌtɜːmɪ'nɪstɪk; *NAmE* -ˌtɜːrm-/ *adj.*

de·ter·rent /dɪ'terənt; *NAmE* -'tɜːr-/ *noun* **~ (to sb/sth)** a thing that makes sb less likely to do sth (= that deters them): *Hopefully his punishment will act as a deterrent to others.* ◇ *the country's **nuclear deterrents*** (= nuclear weapons that are intended to stop an enemy from attacking) ▸ **de·ter·rence** /dɪ'terəns; *NAmE* -'tɜːr-/ *noun* [U] (*formal*) **de·ter·rent** *adj.*: *a deterrent effect*

de·test /dɪ'test/ *verb* (not used in the progressive tenses) **~ sb/sth** | **~ doing sth** to hate sb/sth very much **SYN loathe**: *They detested each other on sight.* ➲ SYNONYMS at HATE ▸ **de·test·ation** /ˌdiːte'steɪʃn/ *noun* [U]

de·test·able /dɪ'testəbl/ *adj.* that deserves to be hated: *All terrorist crime is detestable, whoever the victims.*

de·throne /ˌdiː'θrəʊn; *NAmE* -'θroʊn/ *verb* **~ sb** to remove a king or queen from power; to remove sb from a position of authority or power

det·on·ate /'detəneɪt/ *verb* [I, T] **~ (sth)** to explode, or to make a bomb or other device explode: *Two other bombs failed to detonate.* ➲ SYNONYMS at EXPLODE

det·on·ation /ˌdetə'neɪʃn/ *noun* [C, U] an explosion; the action of making sth explode

det·on·ator /'detəneɪtə(r)/ *noun* a device for making sth, especially a bomb, explode

de·tour /'diːtʊə(r); *NAmE* -tʊr/ *noun, verb*
▪ ***noun*** **1** a longer route that you take in order to avoid a problem or to visit a place: *We had to make a detour around the flooded fields.* ◇ *It's well worth making a detour to see the village.* **2** (*NAmE*) (*BrE* **di·ver·sion**) a road or route that is used when the usual one is closed
▪ ***verb*** [I, T] (*NAmE*) **~ (sb/sth)** (**to...**) to take a longer route in order to avoid a problem or to visit a place; to make sb/sth take a longer route: *The President detoured to Chicago for a special meeting.*

detox /'diːtɒks; *NAmE* -tɑːks/ *noun* [U] (*informal*) **1** the process of removing harmful substances from your body by only eating and drinking particular things **2** = DETOXIFICATION: *a detox clinic* ◇ *He's gone into detox.*

de·toxi·fi·ca·tion /diːˌtɒksɪfɪ'keɪʃn; *NAmE* -ˌtɑːks-/ (also *informal* **detox**) *noun* [U] treatment given to people to help them stop drinking alcohol or taking drugs: *a detoxification unit*

de·tox·ify /ˌdiː'tɒksɪfaɪ; *NAmE* -'tɑːks-/ *verb* (**de·toxi·fies, de·toxi·fy·ing, de·toxi·fied, de·toxi·fied**) **1 ~ sth** to remove harmful substances or poisons from sth **2 ~ sb** to treat sb in order to help them stop drinking too much alcohol or taking drugs

de·tract /dɪ'trækt/ *verb*
PHR V de'tract from sth | **de'tract sth from sth** (not used in the progressive tenses) to make sth seem less good or enjoyable **SYN take away from**: *He was determined not to let anything detract from his enjoyment of the trip.*

de·tract·or /dɪ'træktə(r)/ *noun* [usually pl.] (especially *formal*) a person who tries to make sb/sth seem less good or valuable by criticizing it

de·train /ˌdiː'treɪn/ *verb* [I, T] **~ (sb)** (*formal*) to leave a train or make sb leave a train

det·ri·ment /'detrɪmənt/ *noun* [U, C, usually sing.] (*formal*) the act of causing harm or damage; sth that causes harm or damage
IDM to the detriment of sb/sth | **to sb/sth's detriment** resulting in harm or damage to sb/sth: *He was engrossed in his job to the detriment of his health.* **without detriment (to sb/sth)** not resulting in harm or damage to sb/sth

det·ri·ment·al /ˌdetrɪˈmentl/ *adj.* **~ (to sb/sth)** (*formal*) harmful SYN **damaging**: *the sun's* ***detrimental effect*** *on skin* ◇ *The policy will be detrimental to the peace process.* ▸ **det·ri·men·tal·ly** /-təli/ *adv.*

de·tritus /dɪˈtraɪtəs/ *noun* [U] **1** (*technical*) natural waste material that is left after sth has been used or broken up: *organic detritus from fish and plants* **2** (*formal*) any kind of rubbish/garbage that is left after an event or when sth has been used SYN **debris**: *the detritus of everyday life*

de trop /ˌdə ˈtrəʊ; *NAmE* ˈtroʊ/ *adj.* [not before noun] (from *French, formal*) not wanted, especially in a social situation with other people

deuce /djuːs; *NAmE* duːs/ *noun* **1** [U, C] (in TENNIS) the situation when both players have 40 as a score, after which one player must win two points one after the other in order to win the game **2** [C] (*NAmE*) a PLAYING CARD with two PIPS on it: *the deuce of clubs* **3 the deuce** [sing.] (*old-fashioned, informal*) used in questions to show that you are annoyed: *What the deuce is he doing?*

deuced /djuːst; *NAmE* also duːst/ *adj.* [only before noun] (*old use*) used for emphasizing feelings, especially anger, disappointment or surprise: *The man's a deuced fool!* ▸ **deuced** *adv.*: *It's deuced awkward.*

deur·me·kaar /ˌdjɜːməˈkɑː(r); *NAmE* ˌdjɜːrm-/ *adj.* (*SAfrE, informal*) in a confused state

deus ex machina /ˌdeɪʊs eks ˈmækɪnə/ *noun* [sing.] (*literary*) an unexpected power or event that saves a situation that seems without hope, especially in a play or novel

deu·ter·ium /djuːˈtɪəriəm; *NAmE* -ˈtɪr-; duːˈt-/ *noun* [U] (*symb.* D) (*chemistry*) an ISOTOPE (= a different form) of HYDROGEN with twice the mass of the usual isotope

Deutsch·mark /ˈdɔɪtʃmɑːk; *NAmE* -mɑːrk/ (also **mark**) *noun* (*abbr.* **DM**) the former unit of money in Germany (replaced in 2002 by the euro)

de·value /ˌdiːˈvæljuː/ *verb* **1** [I, T] **~ (sth) (against sth)** (*finance*) to reduce the value of the money of one country when it is exchanged for the money of another country OPP **revalue 2** [T] **~ sth** to give a lower value to sth, making it seem less important than it really is: *Work in the home is often ignored and devalued.* ▸ **de·valu·ation** /ˌdiːˌvæljuˈeɪʃn/ *noun* [C, U]: *There has been a further small devaluation against the dollar.*

Deva·nag·ari /ˌdeɪvəˈnɑːɡəri; ˌdev-/ *noun* [U] the alphabet used to write Sanskrit, Hindi and some other Indian languages

dev·as·tate /ˈdevəsteɪt/ *verb* **1 ~ sth** to completely destroy a place or an area: *The bomb devastated much of the old part of the city.* **2** [often passive] **~ sb** to make sb feel very shocked and sad

dev·as·tated /ˈdevəsteɪtɪd/ *adj.* extremely upset and shocked: *His family is absolutely devastated.*

dev·as·tat·ing /ˈdevəsteɪtɪŋ/ *adj.* **1** causing a lot of damage and destruction SYN **disastrous**: *a* ***devastating explosion/fire/cyclone*** ◇ *Oil spills are having a* ***devastating effect*** *on coral reefs in the ocean.* ◇ *He received devastating injuries in the accident.* ◇ *It will be a* ***devastating blow*** *to the local community if the factory closes.* **2** extremely shocking to a person: *the devastating news that her father was dead* **3** impressive and powerful: *his devastating performance in the 100 metres* ◇ *Her smile was devastating.* ◇ *a devastating attack on the President's economic record* ▸ **dev·as·tat·ing·ly** *adv.*: *a devastatingly handsome man*

dev·as·ta·tion /ˌdevəˈsteɪʃn/ *noun* [U] great destruction or damage, especially over a wide area: *The bomb caused widespread devastation.*

de·velop 0‑‑ /dɪˈveləp/ *verb*

▸ GROW BIGGER/STRONGER **1** 0‑‑ [I, T] to gradually grow or become bigger, more advanced, stronger, etc; to make sth do this: *The child is developing normally.* ◇ **~ (from sth) (into sth)** *The place has rapidly developed from a small fishing community into a thriving tourist resort.* ◇ **~ sth (from sth) (into sth)** *She developed the company from nothing.*

▸ NEW IDEA/PRODUCT **2** 0‑‑ [T] **~ sth** to think of or produce a new idea, product, etc. and make it successful: *The company develops and markets new software.* ➲ SYNONYMS at MAKE

▸ DISEASE/PROBLEM **3** 0‑‑ [I, T] **~ (sth)** to begin to have sth such as a disease or a problem; to start to affect sb/sth: *Her son developed asthma when he was two.* ◇ *The car developed engine trouble and we had to stop.*

▸ HAPPEN/CHANGE **4** 0‑‑ [I] to start to happen or change, especially in a bad way: *A crisis was rapidly developing in the Gulf.* ◇ *We need more time to see how things develop before we take action.*

▸ BECOME BETTER **5** 0‑‑ [T, I] **~ (sth)** to start to have a skill, ability, quality, etc. that becomes better and stronger; to become better and stronger: *He's developed a real flair for management.* ◇ *Their relationship has developed over a number of years.*

▸ BUILD HOUSES **6** 0‑‑ [T] **~ sth** to build new houses, factories, etc. on an area of land, especially land that was not being used effectively before: *The site is being developed by a French company.*

▸ IDEA/STORY **7** [T] **~ sth** to make an idea, a story, etc. clearer by explaining it further SYN **elaborate on**: *She develops the theme more fully in her later books.*

▸ PHOTOGRAPHS **8** [T] **~ sth** to treat film which has been used to take photographs with chemicals so that the pictures can be seen: *I had the film developed yesterday.*

de·veloped /dɪˈveləpt/ *adj.* **1** (of a country, society, etc.) having many industries and a complicated economic system: *financial aid to less developed countries* ◇ *The average citizen in the* ***developed world*** *uses over 155kg of paper per year.* ➲ compare UNDERDEVELOPED **2** in an advanced state: *children with highly developed problem-solving skills* ➲ see also WELL DEVELOPED

de·vel·op·er /dɪˈveləpə(r)/ *noun* **1** [C] a person or company that buys land or buildings in order to build new houses, shops/stores, etc, or to improve the old ones, and makes a profit from doing this: *property developers* **2** [C] a person or a company that designs and creates new products: *a software developer* **3** [U] a chemical substance that is used for developing photographs from a film

de·vel·op·ing /dɪˈveləpɪŋ/ *adj.* [only before noun] (of a country, society, etc.) poor, and trying to make its industry and economic system more advanced: ***developing countries/nations/economies*** ➲ compare UNDERDEVELOPED

de·vel·op·ment 0‑‑ /dɪˈveləpmənt/ *noun*

▸ GROWTH **1** 0‑‑ [U] the gradual growth of sth so that it becomes more advanced, stronger, etc: *a baby's development in the womb* ◇ *the development of basic skills such as literacy and numeracy* ◇ *career development*

▸ NEW PRODUCT **2** 0‑‑ [U, C] the process of producing or creating sth new or more advanced; a new or advanced product: *the development of vaccines against tropical diseases* ◇ *developments in aviation technology* ◇ *This piece of equipment is an exciting new development.* ➲ see also RESEARCH AND DEVELOPMENT

▸ NEW EVENT **3** 0‑‑ [C] a new event or stage that is likely to affect what happens in a continuing situation: *the latest developments in the war* ◇ *Are there further developments in the investigation?*

▸ NEW BUILDINGS **4** 0‑‑ [C] a piece of land with new buildings on it: *a* ***commercial/business/housing development*** ➲ see also RIBBON DEVELOPMENT **5** 0‑‑ [U] the process of using an area of land, especially to make a profit by building on it, etc: *He bought the land for development.*

de·vel·op·men·tal /dɪˌveləpˈmentl/ *adj.* **1** in a state of developing or being developed: *The product is still at a developmental stage.* **2** connected with the development of sb/sth: *developmental psychology* ▸ **de·vel·op·men·tal·ly** *adv.*

deˈvelopment area *noun* (*BrE*) an area where new industries are encouraged in order to create jobs

de·vi·ant /ˈdiːviənt/ *adj.* different from what most people consider to be normal and acceptable: ***deviant behaviour/sexuality*** ▸ **de·vi·ant** *noun*: *sexual deviants* **de·vi·ance**

D

/-viəns/, **de·vi·ancy** /ˈdiːviənsi/ *noun* [U]: *a study of social deviance and crime*

de·vi·ate AW /ˈdiːvieɪt/ *verb* [I] ~ (**from sth**) to be different from sth; to do sth in a different way from what is usual or expected: *The bus had to deviate from its usual route because of a road closure.* ◇ *He never deviated from his original plan.*

D

de·vi·ation AW /ˌdiːviˈeɪʃn/ *noun* **1** [U, C] ~ (**from sth**) the act of moving away from what is normal or acceptable; a difference from what is expected or acceptable: *deviation from the previously accepted norms* ◇ *sexual deviation* ◇ *a deviation from the plan* **2** [C] ~ (**from sth**) (*technical*) the amount by which a single measurement is different from the average: *a compass deviation of 5°* (= from true north) ➲ see also STANDARD DEVIATION

de·vice 🔑 AW /dɪˈvaɪs/ *noun* **1** 🔑 an object or a piece of equipment that has been designed to do a particular job: *a water-saving device* ◇ *electrical labour-saving devices around the home* **2** a bomb or weapon that will explode: *A powerful device exploded outside the station.* ◇ *the world's first atomic device* **3** a method of doing sth that produces a particular result or effect: *Sending advertising by email is very successful as a marketing device.* **4** a plan or trick that is used to get sth that sb wants: *The report was a device used to hide rather than reveal problems.*
IDM **leave sb to their own deˈvices** to leave sb alone to do as they wish, and not tell them what to do

devil /ˈdevl/ *noun* **1 the Devil** (in the Christian, Jewish and Muslim religions) the most powerful evil BEING SYN **Satan** **2** an evil spirit: *They believed she was possessed by devils.* **3** (*informal*) a person who behaves badly, especially a child: *a naughty little devil* **4** (*informal*) used to talk about sb and to emphasize an opinion that you have of them: *I miss the old devil, now that he's gone.* ◇ *She's off to Greece for a month—lucky devil!*
IDM **be a ˈdevil** (*BrE*) people say **Be a devil!** to encourage sb to do sth that they are not sure about doing: *Go on, be a devil, buy both of them.* **better the ˌdevil you ˈknow (than the ˌdevil you ˈdon't)** (*saying*) used to say that it is easier and wiser to stay in a bad situation that you know and can deal with rather than change to a new situation which may be much worse **between the ˌdevil and the ˌdeep blue ˈsea** in a difficult situation where there are two equally unpleasant or unacceptable choices **the ˈdevil** (*old-fashioned*) very difficult or unpleasant: *These berries are the devil to pick because they're so small.* **the ˌdevil looks after his ˈown** (*saying*) bad people often seem to have good luck **the devil makes work for idle ˈhands** (*saying*) people who do not have enough to do often start to do wrong: *She blamed the crimes on the local jobless teenagers. 'The devil makes work for idle hands,' she would say.* **a ˈdevil of a job/time** (*old-fashioned*) a very difficult or unpleasant job or time: *I've had a devil of a job finding you.* **go to the ˈdevil!** (*old-fashioned, informal*) used, in an unfriendly way, to tell sb to go away **like the ˈdevil** (*old-fashioned, informal*) very hard, fast, etc: *We ran like the devil.* **speak/talk of the ˈdevil** (*informal*) people say **speak/talk of the devil** when sb they have been talking about appears unexpectedly: *Well, speak of the devil—here's Alice now!* **what, where, who, why, etc. the ˈdevil …** (*old-fashioned*) used in questions to show that you are annoyed or surprised: *What the devil do you think you're doing?* ➲ more at NEED *n.*, PAY *v.*, SELL *v.*

devil·ish /ˈdevəlɪʃ/ *adj.* **1** cruel or evil: *a devilish conspiracy* **2** morally bad, but in a way that people find attractive: *He was handsome, with a devilish charm.*

devil·ish·ly /ˈdevəlɪʃli/ *adv.* (*old-fashioned*) extremely; very: *a devilishly hot day*

dev·illed (*BrE*) (*US* **dev·iled**) /ˈdevld/ *adj.* cooked in a thick liquid containing hot spices

ˌdevil-may-ˈcare *adj.* [usually before noun] cheerful and not worrying about the future

dev·il·ment /ˈdevlmənt/ (also **dev·il·ry** /ˈdevlri/) *noun* (*formal*) wild behaviour that causes trouble SYN **mischief**

ˌdevil's ˈadvocate *noun* a person who expresses an opinion that they do not really hold in order to encourage a discussion about a subject: *Often the interviewer will need to **play devil's advocate** in order to get a discussion going.*

de·vi·ous /ˈdiːviəs/ *adj.* **1** behaving in a dishonest or indirect way, or tricking people, in order to get sth SYN **deceitful, underhand**: *a devious politician* ◇ *He got rich by devious means.* **2** ~ **route/path** a route or path that is not straight but has many changes in direction; not direct: *a devious route from the airport* ▶ **de·vi·ous·ly** *adv.* **de·vi·ous·ness** *noun* [U]

de·vise /dɪˈvaɪz/ *verb* ~ **sth** to invent sth new or a new way of doing sth SYN **think up**: *A new system has been devised to control traffic in the city.*

de·voice /ˌdiːˈvɔɪs/ *verb* ~ **sth** (*phonetics*) to make a speech sound, usually a consonant, VOICELESS

de·void /dɪˈvɔɪd/ *adj.* ~ **of sth** completely lacking in sth: *The letter was devoid of warmth and feeling.*

de·vo·lu·tion /ˌdiːvəˈluːʃn; *NAmE* ˌdev-/ *noun* [U] the act of giving power from a central authority or government to an authority or a government in a local region

de·volve /dɪˈvɒlv; *NAmE* -ˈvɑːlv/ *verb*
PHR V **deˈvolve on/upon sb/sth** (*formal*) **1** if property, money, etc. **devolves on/upon** you, you receive it after sb else dies **2** if a duty, responsibility, etc. **devolves on/upon** you, it is given to you by sb at a higher level of authority **deˈvolve sth to/on/upon sb** to give a duty, responsibility, power, etc. to sb who has less authority than you: *The central government devolved most tax-raising powers to the regional authorities.*

de·volved /dɪˈvɒlvd; *NAmE* -ˈvɑːlvd/ *adj.* if power or authority is **devolved**, it has been passed to sb who has less power: *devolved responsibility* ◇ *a system of devolved government*

de·vote 🔑 AW /dɪˈvəʊt; *NAmE* dɪˈvoʊt/ *verb*
PHR V **deˈvote yourself to sb/sth** 🔑 to give most of your time, energy, attention, etc. to sb/sth: *She devoted herself to her career.* **deˈvote sth to sth** 🔑 to give an amount of time, attention, etc. to sth: *I could only devote two hours a day to the work.*

de·voted 🔑 /dɪˈvəʊtɪd; *NAmE* -ˈvoʊt-/ *adj.* ~ **(to sb/sth)** having great love for sb/sth and being loyal to them: *They are devoted to their children.* ◇ *a devoted son/friend/fan* ➲ SYNONYMS at LOVE ▶ **de·voted·ly** *adv.*

de·votee /ˌdevəˈtiː/ *noun* **1** ~ (**of sb/sth**) a person who admires and is very enthusiastic about sb/sth: *a devotee of science fiction* **2** ~ (**of sb/sth**) a very religious person who belongs to a particular group: *devotees of Krishna*

de·vo·tion AW /dɪˈvəʊʃn; *NAmE* -ˈvoʊ-/ *noun* **1** [U, sing.] ~ (**to sb/sth**) great love, care and support for sb/sth: *His devotion to his wife and family is touching.* **2** [U, sing.] ~ (**to sb/sth**) the action of spending a lot of time or energy on sth SYN **dedication**: *her **devotion to duty*** ◇ *Her devotion to the job left her with very little free time.* **3 devotions** [pl.] prayers and other religious practices

de·vo·tion·al /dɪˈvəʊʃənl; *NAmE* -ˈvoʊ-/ *adj.* (of music, etc.) connected with or used in religious services

de·vour /dɪˈvaʊə(r)/ *verb* **1** ~ **sth** to eat all of sth quickly, especially because you are very hungry SYN **gobble up** **2** to read or look at sth with great interest and enthusiasm: *She devoured everything she could lay her hands on: books, magazines and newspapers.* **3** ~ **sb/th** (*formal*) to destroy sb/sth SYN **engulf**: *Flames devoured the house.*
IDM **be devoured by sth** to be filled with a strong emotion that seems to control you: *She was devoured by envy and hatred.*

de·vout /dɪˈvaʊt/ *adj.* (of a person) believing strongly in a particular religion and obeying its laws and practices: *a devout Christian/Muslim* ▶ **de·vout·ly** *adv.*: *a devoutly Catholic region* ◇ *She devoutly* (= very strongly) *hoped he was telling the truth.*

dew /dju:; *NAmE* du:/ *noun* [U] the very small drops of water that form on the ground, etc. during the night: *The grass was wet with early morning dew.*

dew·berry /'dju:bəri; *NAmE* 'du:beri; 'dju:-/ *noun* (*pl.* -ies) a small soft black or blue-black fruit like a BLACKBERRY, or the bush that it grows on

dew·drop /'dju:drɒp; *NAmE* 'du:drɑ:p/ *noun* a small drop of dew or other liquid

Dewey decimal classification /ˌdju:i 'desɪml klæsɪfɪkeɪʃn; *NAmE* also ˌdu:i/ (also **'Dewey system**) *noun* [sing.] an international system for arranging books in a library

'dew point *noun* [sing.] (*technical*) the temperature at which air can hold no more water. Below this temperature the water comes out of the air in the form of drops.

dewy /'dju:i; *NAmE* du:i/ *adj.* wet with DEW

ˌdewy-'eyed *adj.* (*disapproving*) showing emotion about sth, perhaps with a few tears in the eyes SYN **sentimental**

dex·ter·ity /dek'sterəti/ *noun* [U] skill in using your hands or your mind: *You need manual dexterity to be good at video games.* ◇ ***mental/verbal dexterity***

dex·ter·ous (also **dex·trous**) /'dekstrəs/ *adj.* (*formal*) skilful with your hands; skilfully done ▸ **dex·ter·ous·ly** (also **dex·trous·ly**) *adv.*

dex·trose /'dekstrəʊz; -əʊs; *NAmE* -oʊz; -oʊs/ *noun* [U] (*chemistry*) a form of GLUCOSE (= a type of natural sugar)

DFID /ˌdi: ef aɪ 'di:/ *abbr.* (in Britain) Department for International Development

dhal (also **dal**) /dɑ:l/ *noun* [U] a S Asian dish made from LENTILS or other PULSES (= seeds from certain plants)

dhania /'dɑ:niə/ *noun* [U] (*EAfrE, IndE, SAfrE*) the leaves or seeds of the CORIANDER plant, used to flavour food

dhan·sak /'dʌnsɑ:k; 'dænsæk/ *noun* an Indian meat or vegetable dish cooked with LENTILS and CORIANDER

dharma /'dɑ:mə; *NAmE* 'dɑ:r-/ *noun* [U] (in Indian religion) truth or law that affects the whole universe

dharna /'dɜ:nə; -nɑ:; *NAmE* 'dɜ:rn-/ *noun* (*IndE*) **1** an act of lying flat on the floor with your face down as an act of worship in a TEMPLE **2** a form of protest in which a group of people refuse to leave a factory, public place, etc.

dhoti /'dəʊti; *NAmE* 'doʊti/ *noun* a long piece of cloth worn by Hindu men. It is sometimes tied round the waist, with the lower part passed between the legs and put into the cloth at the back, so that the knees are usually covered.

dhow /daʊ/ *noun* an Arab ship with one large sail in the shape of a triangle

dhurrie (also **durrie**) /'dʌri/ *noun* a heavy cotton RUG (= small carpet) from S Asia

DI /ˌdi: 'aɪ/ *abbr.* Detective Inspector (a British police officer of middle rank): *DI Ross*

di- /daɪ/ *combining form* (*chemistry*) (in nouns that are names of chemical COMPOUNDS) containing two atoms or groups of the type mentioned: *carbon dioxide*

dia·betes /ˌdaɪə'bi:ti:z/ *noun* [U] a medical condition which makes the patient produce a lot of URINE and feel very thirsty. There are several types of diabetes.

dia·bet·ic /ˌdaɪə'betɪk/ *adj., noun*
■ ***adj.*** **1** having or connected with diabetes: *She's diabetic.* ◇ *a diabetic patient* ◇ *diabetic complications* **2** suitable for or used by sb who has diabetes: *a diabetic diet*
■ ***noun*** a person who suffers from DIABETES

dia·bol·ical /ˌdaɪə'bɒlɪkl; *NAmE* -'bɑ:l-/ *adj.* **1** (*informal, especially BrE*) extremely bad or annoying SYN **terrible**: *The traffic was diabolical.* **2** (also *less frequent* **dia·bol·ic** /ˌdaɪə'bɒlɪk; *NAmE* -'bɑ:l-/) morally bad and evil; like a DEVIL ▸ **dia·bol·ic·al·ly** /-kli/ *adv.*

dia·chron·ic /ˌdaɪə'krɒnɪk; *NAmE* -'krɑ:n-/ *adj.* (*technical*) relating to the way sth, especially a language, has developed over time ➲ compare SYNCHRONIC

dia·crit·ic /ˌdaɪə'krɪtɪk/ *noun* (*linguistics*) a mark such as an accent, placed over, under or through a letter in some languages, to show that the letter should be pronounced in a different way from the same letter without a mark ▸ **dia·crit·ic·al** /-'krɪtɪkl/ *adj.*: *diacritical marks*

dia·dem /'daɪədem/ *noun* a crown, worn especially as a sign of royal power

di·aer·esis (*BrE*) (*US* **di·er·esis**) /daɪ'erəsɪs/ (*pl.* di·aer·eses, di·er·eses /-si:z/) *noun* (*technical*) the mark placed over a vowel to show that it is pronounced separately, as in *naïve*

D

diag·nose /'daɪəgnəʊz; ˌdaɪəg'nəʊz; *NAmE* -'noʊs/ *verb* [T, I] to say exactly what an illness or the cause of a problem is: **~ (sth)** *The test is used to diagnose a variety of diseases.* ◇ **~ sth as sth** *The illness was diagnosed as cancer.* ◇ **~ sb with sth** *He has recently been diagnosed with angina.* ◇ **~ sb (as) sth** *He was diagnosed (as) a diabetic when he was 64.* ◇ **~ sb + adj./noun** *He was diagnosed (a) diabetic.* ➲ COLLOCATIONS at ILL

diag·no·sis /ˌdaɪəg'nəʊsɪs; *NAmE* -'noʊ-/ *noun* [C, U] (*pl.* diag·noses /-si:z/) **~ (of sth)** the act of discovering or identifying the exact cause of an illness or a problem: *diagnosis of lung cancer* ◇ *They are waiting for the doctor's diagnosis.* ◇ *An accurate* ***diagnosis was made*** *after a series of tests.*

diag·nos·tic /ˌdaɪəg'nɒstɪk; *NAmE* -'nɑ:s-/ *adj., noun*
■ ***adj.*** [usually before noun] (*technical*) connected with identifying sth, especially an illness: *to carry out* ***diagnostic assessments/tests*** ◇ *specific conditions which are diagnostic of AIDS*
■ ***noun*** (*computing*) **1** (also **ˌdiag'nostic program**) [C] a program used for identifying a computer fault **2** [C] a message on a computer screen giving information about a fault **3 diagnostics** [U] the practice or methods of diagnosis

di·ag·onal /daɪ'ægənl/ *adj., noun*
■ ***adj.*** (of a straight line) at an angle; joining two opposite sides of sth at an angle: *diagonal stripes* ➲ VISUAL VOCAB page V58 ▸ **di·ag·onal·ly** /-nəli/ *adv.*: *Walk diagonally across the field to the far corner and then turn left.*
■ ***noun*** a straight line that joins two opposite sides of sth at an angle; a straight line that is at an angle

dia·gram 0‑w /'daɪəgræm/ *noun* a simple drawing using lines to explain where sth is, how sth works, etc: *a diagram of the wiring system* ◇ *The results are shown in diagram 2.* ▸ **dia·gram·mat·ic** /ˌdaɪəgrə'mætɪk/ *adj.* **dia·gram·mat·ic·al·ly** /-kli/ *adv.*

dial /'daɪəl/ *noun, verb*
■ ***noun*** **1** the face of a clock or watch, or a similar control on a machine, piece of equipment or vehicle that shows a measurement of time, amount, speed, temperature, etc: *an alarm clock with a luminous dial* ◇ *Check the tyre pressure on the dial.* ➲ see also SUNDIAL **2** the round control on a radio, cooker/stove, etc. that you turn in order to adjust sth, for example to choose a particular station or to choose a particular temperature **3** the round part on some older telephones, with holes for the fingers, that you move around to call a particular number
■ ***verb*** (-ll-, *NAmE* -l-) [T, I] **~ (sth)** to use a telephone by pushing buttons or turning the dial to call a number: *He dialled the number and waited.* ◇ *Dial 0033 for France.* ➲ COLLOCATIONS at PHONE

dia·lect /'daɪəlekt/ *noun* [C, U] the form of a language that is spoken in one area with grammar, words and pronunciation that may be different from other forms of the same language: *the Yorkshire dialect* ➲ compare ACCENT, IDIOLECT ▸ **dia·lect·al** /ˌdaɪə'lektl/ *adj.*

dia·lect·ic /ˌdaɪə'lektɪk/ *noun* [sing.] (also *less frequent* **dia·lect·ics** [U]) **1** (*philosophy*) a method of discovering the truth of ideas by discussion and logical argument and by considering ideas that are opposed to each other **2** (*formal*) the way in which two aspects of a situation affect each other ▸ **dia·lect·ic·al** /-kl/ *adj.*

diaˌlectical ma'terialism *noun* [U] (*philosophy*) the Marxist theory that all change results from opposing social forces, which come into conflict because of material needs

dial·ler (*BrE*) (*NAmE* **dial·er**) /ˈdaɪələ(r)/ *noun* a computer program or piece of equipment which calls telephone numbers automatically

ˈ**dialling code** (also **code**) *noun* (*BrE*) the numbers that are used for a particular town, area or country, in front of an individual telephone number: *international dialling codes* ➲ compare AREA CODE

D

ˈ**dialling tone** (*BrE*) (*NAmE* ˈ**dial tone**) *noun* the sound that you hear when you pick up a telephone that means you can make a call

ˈ**dialog box** (*BrE* also ˈ**dialogue box**) *noun* a box that appears on a computer screen asking the user to choose what they want to do next ➲ VISUAL VOCAB page V55

dia·logue (*NAmE* also **dia·log**) /ˈdaɪəlɒɡ; *NAmE* -lɑːɡ; -lɔːɡ/ *noun* [C, U] **1** conversations in a book, play, or film/movie: *The novel has long descriptions and not much dialogue.* ◇ *dialogues for language learners* ➲ SYNONYMS at DISCUSSION **2** a formal discussion between two groups or countries, especially when they are trying to solve a problem, end a disagreement, etc: *The President told waiting reporters there had been a constructive dialogue.* ➲ compare MONOLOGUE

ˈ**dial-up** *adj.* [only before noun] using a telephone line and a MODEM to connect your computer to the Internet

dia·ly·sis /ˌdaɪˈæləsɪs/ *noun* [U] (*technical*) a process for separating substances from a liquid, especially for taking waste substances out of the blood of people with damaged KIDNEYS: ***kidney/renal dialysis*** ◇ *a dialysis machine*

dia·manté /ˌdiːəˈmɒnteɪ; *NAmE* ˌdiːəmɑːnˈteɪ/ *adj.* decorated with glass that is cut to look like diamonds: *diamanté earrings*

dia·man·tine /ˌdaɪəˈmæntiːn/ *adj.* (*technical*) **1** made from, or looking like, diamonds **2** very hard or strong

diam·eter /daɪˈæmɪtə(r)/ *noun* **1** a straight line going from one side of a circle or any other round object to the other side, passing through the centre: *the diameter of a tree trunk* ◇ *The dome is 42.3 metres* ***in diameter.*** ➲ VISUAL VOCAB page V58 ➲ compare RADIUS **2** (*technical*) a measurement of the power of an instrument to MAGNIFY sth: *a lens magnifying 300 diameters* (= making sth look 300 times larger than it really is)

dia·met·ric·al /ˌdaɪəˈmetrɪkl/ *adj.* [usually before noun] **1** used to emphasize that people or things are completely different: *He's the* ***diametrical opposite*** *of his brother.* **2** relating to the DIAMETER of sth

dia·met·ric·al·ly /ˌdaɪəˈmetrɪkli/ *adv.* **~ opposed/opposite** completely different: *We hold diametrically opposed views.*

dia·mond 🔑 /ˈdaɪəmənd/ *noun*
1 🔑 [U, C] a clear PRECIOUS STONE of pure CARBON, the hardest substance known. Diamonds are used in jewellery and also in industry, especially for cutting glass: *a ring with a diamond in it* ◇ *a* ***diamond ring/necklace*** ◇ *She was wearing her diamonds* (= jewellery with diamonds in it). ◇ *The lights shone like diamonds.* ➲ see also ROUGH DIAMOND **2** 🔑 [C] a shape with four straight sides of equal length and with angles that are not RIGHT ANGLES **3 diamonds** [pl., U] one of the four SUITS (= sets) in a PACK/DECK of cards. The cards are marked with red diamond shapes: *the ten of diamonds* ➲ VISUAL VOCAB page V32 **4** [C] a card of this SUIT: *You must play a diamond if you have one.* **5** [C] (in BASEBALL) the space inside the lines that connect the four BASES; also used to mean the whole BASEBALL field

ˌ**dia·mond in the** ˈ**rough** (*NAmE*) (*BrE* ˌ**rough** ˈ**diamond**) *noun* a person who has many good qualities even though they do not seem to be very polite, educated, etc.

ˌ**dia·mond** ˈ**ju·bi·lee** *noun* [usually sing.] the 60th anniversary of an important event, especially of sb becoming king/queen; a celebration of this event ➲ compare GOLDEN JUBILEE, SILVER JUBILEE

ˌ**dia·mond** ˈ**wed·ding** (*BrE*) (*NAmE* ˌ**dia·mond an·ni·ver·sary**) (also ˌ**dia·mond** ˈ**wed·ding an·ni·ver·sary** *NAmE, BrE*) *noun* the 60th anniversary of a wedding ➲ compare GOLDEN WEDDING, RUBY WEDDING, SILVER WEDDING

dia·mor·phine /ˌdaɪəˈmɔːfiːn; *NAmE* -ˈmɔːrf-/ *noun* [U] a powerful drug that is made from OPIUM and used to reduce pain

di·aper /ˈdaɪəpə(r); *NAmE* ˈdaɪpər/ (*NAmE*) (*BrE* **nappy**) *noun* a piece of soft cloth or other thick material that is folded around a baby's bottom and between its legs to absorb and hold its body waste: *a diaper rash*

di·aph·an·ous /daɪˈæfənəs/ *adj.* (*formal*) (of cloth) so light and fine that you can almost see through it

dia·phragm /ˈdaɪəfræm/ *noun* **1** (*anatomy*) the layer of muscle between the lungs and the stomach, used especially to control breathing **2** (*BrE* also **cap**) a rubber or plastic device that a woman places inside her VAGINA before having sex to prevent SPERM from entering the WOMB and making her pregnant **3** any thin piece of material used to separate the parts of a machine, etc. **4** (*technical*) a thin disc used to turn electronic signals into sound and sound into electronic signals in telephones, LOUDSPEAKERS, etc.

diar·ist /ˈdaɪərɪst/ *noun* a person who writes a diary, especially one that is later published: *Samuel Pepys, the famous 17th century diarist*

diar·rhoea (*BrE*) (*NAmE* **diar·rhea**) /ˌdaɪəˈrɪə; *NAmE* -ˈriːə/ (also *informal* **the runs**) *noun* [U] an illness in which waste matter is emptied from the BOWELS much more frequently than normal, and in liquid form: *Symptoms include diarrhoea and vomiting.*

diary 🔑 /ˈdaɪəri/ *noun* (*pl.* -ies)
1 🔑 (*BrE*) (*NAmE* **date·book**) a book with spaces for each day of the year in which you can write down things you have to do in the future ➲ VISUAL VOCAB page V56: *a desk diary* ◇ *I'll make a note of our next meeting in my diary.* **2** 🔑 a book in which you can write down the experiences you have each day, your private thoughts, etc: *Do you* ***keep a diary*** (= write one regularly)? ➲ see also JOURNAL, VIDEO DIARY ➲ note at AGENDA

dias·pora /daɪˈæspərə/ *noun* [sing.] (*formal*) **1 the diaspora** the movement of the Jewish people away from their own country to live and work in other countries **2** the movement of people from any nation or group away from their own country

di·atom·ic /ˌdaɪəˈtɒmɪk; *NAmE* -ˈtɑːmɪk/ *adj.* (*chemistry*) consisting of two atoms

dia·ton·ic /ˌdaɪəˈtɒnɪk; *NAmE* -ˈtɑːn-/ *adj.* (*music*) using only the notes of the appropriate MAJOR OR MINOR SCALE ➲ compare CHROMATIC

dia·tribe /ˈdaɪətraɪb/ *noun* **~ (against sb/sth)** (*formal*) a long and angry speech or piece of writing attacking and criticizing sb/sth: *He launched a bitter diatribe against the younger generation.*

di·aze·pam /daɪˈæzəpæm/ *noun* [U] (*medical*) a drug that is used to make people feel less anxious and more relaxed

dibs /dɪbz/
IDM **dibs on...** (*NAmE*) (*BrE* **bags (I)...**) used to claim sth as yours before sb else can claim it

dice /daɪs/ *noun, verb*
▪ ***noun*** (*pl.* **dice**) **1** (also **die** especially in *NAmE*) [C] a small CUBE of wood, plastic, etc, with a different number of spots on each of its sides, used in games of chance: *a pair of dice* ◇ *to* ***roll/throw/shake the dice*** **2** [U] a game played with dice: *We played dice all night.* ➲ VISUAL VOCAB page V33
IDM **no** ˈ**dice** (*informal, especially NAmE*) used to show that you refuse to do sth, or that sth cannot be done: *'Did you get that job?' 'No dice.'* ➲ more at LOAD *v.*
▪ ***verb*** **~ sth** to cut meat, vegetables, etc. into small square pieces: *diced carrots* ➲ VISUAL VOCAB page V25
IDM **dice with death** (*informal*) to risk your life by doing sth that you know is dangerous

dicey /ˈdaɪsi/ *adj.* (*informal*) uncertain and dangerous
SYN **risky**

di·chot·omy /daɪˈkɒtəmi; *NAmE* -ˈkɑːt-/ *noun* [usually sing.] (*pl.* -ies) **~ (between A and B)** (*formal*) the separation that exists between two groups or things that are completely opposite to and different from each other

dick /dɪk/ *noun* (*taboo, slang*) **1** a man's PENIS **2** = DICKHEAD ➲ see also CLEVER DICK

dick·ens /ˈdɪkɪnz/ *noun* **the dickens** (*old-fashioned, informal*) **1** used in questions instead of 'devil' to show that you are annoyed or surprised: *Where the dickens did he go?* **2** (*NAmE*) used when you are saying how attractive, etc. sb is: *cute as the dickens*

Dick·ens·ian /dɪˈkenziən/ *adj.* connected with or typical of the novels of Charles Dickens, which often describe social problems and bad social conditions: *a Dickensian slum*

dicker /ˈdɪkə(r)/ *verb* [I] **~ (with sb) (over sth)** (*especially NAmE*) to argue about or discuss sth with sb, especially in order to agree on a price SYN **bargain**

dick·head /ˈdɪkhed/ (also **dick**) *noun* (*taboo, slang*) a very rude way of referring to sb, especially a man, that you think is stupid SYN **idiot**

dicky /ˈdɪki/ *adj., noun*

▪ ***adj.*** (*old-fashioned, BrE, informal*) not healthy; not working correctly: *a dicky heart*

▪ ***noun*** (also **dickey**) (*pl.* **dickies** or **dickeys**) (*IndE*) the BOOT/TRUNK of a car

ˈ**dicky bird** *noun* (*BrE*) (used by or when speaking to young children) a bird

IDM **not say, hear, etc. a dicky bird** (*BrE, informal*) to say, hear, etc. nothing: *He won't say a dicky bird, but we think he knows who did it.* ORIGIN This idiom is from rhyming slang, in which 'dicky bird' stands for 'word'.

di·coty·ledon /ˌdaɪkɒtɪˈliːdən; *NAmE* -kɑːt-/ (also **dicot** /ˈdaɪkɒt; *NAmE* -kɑːt/) *noun* (*biology*) a plant whose seeds form EMBRYOS that produce two leaves ➲ compare MONOCOTYLEDON

Dicta·phone™ /ˈdɪktəfəʊn; *NAmE* -foʊn/ *noun* a small machine used to record people speaking, so that their words can be played back later and written down

dic·tate *verb, noun*

▪ ***verb*** /dɪkˈteɪt; *NAmE* ˈdɪkteɪt/ **1** [T, I] **~ (sth) (to sb)** to say words for sb else to write down: *He dictated a letter to his secretary.* **2** [T] to tell sb what to do, especially in an annoying way: **~ sth (to sb)** *They are in no position to **dictate terms*** (= tell other people what to do). ◇ **~ how, what, etc .../that...** *What right do they have to dictate how we live our lives?* **3** [T, I] to control or influence how sth happens SYN **determine**: **~ (sth)** *When we take our vacations is very much dictated by Greg's work schedule.* ◇ **~ where, what, etc...** *It's generally your job that dictates where you live now.* ◇ **~ that...** *The social conventions of the day dictated that she should remain at home with her parents.*

PHR V **dicˈtate to sb** [often passive] to give orders to sb, often in a rude or aggressive way: *She refused to be dictated to by anyone.*

▪ ***noun*** /ˈdɪkteɪt/ [usually pl.] (*formal*) an order or a rule that you must obey: *to follow the dictates of fashion*

dic·ta·tion /dɪkˈteɪʃn/ *noun* **1** [U] the act of speaking or reading so that sb can write down the words **2** [C, U] a test in which students write down what is being read to them, especially in language lessons

dic·ta·tor /dɪkˈteɪtə(r); *NAmE* ˈdɪkteɪtər/ *noun* (*disapproving*) **1** a ruler who has complete power over a country, especially one who has gained it using military force **2** a person who behaves as if they have complete power over other people, and tells them what to do

dic·ta·tor·ial /ˌdɪktəˈtɔːriəl/ *adj.* (*disapproving*) **1** connected with or controlled by a dictator: *a dictatorial ruler* ◇ *a dictatorial regime* **2** using power in an unreasonable way by telling people what to do and not listening to their views or wishes: *dictatorial behaviour* ▶ **dic·ta·tori·al·ly** /-əli/ *adv.*

dic·ta·tor·ship /ˌdɪkˈteɪtəʃɪp; *NAmE* -tərʃ-/ *noun* **1** [C, U] government by a dictator ➲ COLLOCATIONS at POLITICS **2** [C] a country that is ruled by a dictator

dic·tion /ˈdɪkʃn/ *noun* [U] **1** the way that sb pronounces words: *clear diction* **2** (*technical*) the choice and use of words in literature

dic·tion·ary 🔑 /ˈdɪkʃənri; *NAmE* -neri/ *noun* (*pl.* -ies)

1 🔑 a book that gives a list of the words of a language in alphabetical order and explains what they mean, or gives a word for them in a foreign language: *a Spanish-English dictionary* **2** a book that explains the words that are used in a particular subject: *a dictionary of mathematics* **3** a list of words in electronic form, for example stored in a computer's SPELLCHECKER

dic·tum /ˈdɪktəm/ *noun* (*pl.* **dicta** /-tə/ or **dic·tums**) (*formal*) a statement that expresses sth that people believe is always true or should be followed

did /dɪd/ ➲ DO

di·dac·tic /daɪˈdæktɪk/ *adj.* (*formal*) **1** designed to teach people sth, especially a moral lesson: *didactic art* **2** (*usually disapproving*) telling people things rather than letting them find out for themselves ▶ **di·dac·tic·al·ly** /-kli/ *adv.*

did·dle /ˈdɪdl/ *verb* **~ sb (out of sth)** (*BrE, informal*) to get money or some advantage from sb by cheating them SYN **cheat**

diddly /ˈdɪdli/ (also ˌ**diddly-ˈsquat**) *noun* (*NAmE, informal*) (used in negative sentences) not anything; nothing: *She doesn't know diddly about it.*

did·dums /ˈdɪdəmz/ *exclamation, noun* (*BrE, informal*)

▪ ***exclamation*** used for showing sympathy, especially in a way which is not sincere

▪ ***noun*** used when addressing sb to show sympathy, especially when you are not being sincere: *Is Diddums OK?*

diddy /ˈdɪdi/ *adj.* (*BrE, informal*) very small: *a diddy little camera*

didg·eri·doo /ˌdɪdʒəriˈduː/ *noun* (*pl.* -oos) an Australian musical instrument consisting of a long wooden tube which you blow through to produce a variety of deep sounds

didi /ˈdiːdiː/ *noun* (*IndE*) **1** an older sister: *Didi taught me how to read.* **2** used after the name of an older female cousin of the same generation **3** used when speaking to an older female who is not related to you, as a title showing respect: *Didi, could you help me with this bag?*

didn't /ˈdɪdnt/ *short form* did not

die 🔑 /daɪ/ *verb, noun*

▪ ***verb*** (**dies, dying, died, died**) **1** 🔑 [I, T] to stop living: *Her husband died suddenly last week.* ◇ *That plant's died.* ◇ **~ of/from sth** *to die of/from cancer* ◇ **~ for sth** *He died for his beliefs.* ◇ *I'll never forget it **to my dying day*** (= until I die). ◇ (*informal*) ***I nearly died** when I saw him there* (= it was very embarrassing). ◇ **~ sth** *to **die a violent/painful/natural, etc. death*** ◇ **+ adj.** *She died young.* ◇ *At least they died happy.* ◇ **+ noun** *He died a poor man.* **2** 🔑 [I] to stop existing; to disappear: *The old customs are dying.* ◇ *His secret died with him* (= he never told anyone). ◇ *The words died on my lips* (= I stopped speaking). **3** [I] (of a machine) to stop working: *The engine spluttered and died.* ◇ *My car just **died on me**.*

IDM **be ˈdying for sth/to do sth** 🔑 (*informal*) to want sth or want to do sth very much: *I'm dying for a glass of water.* ◇ *I'm dying to know what happened.* **die a/the ˈdeath** (*BrE, informal*) to fail completely: *The play got terrible reviews and quickly died a death.* **die in your ˈbed** to die because you are old or ill/sick **die ˈlaughing** to find sth extremely funny: *I nearly died laughing when she said that.* **old ˌhabits, ˌtraditions, etc. die ˈhard** used to say that things change very slowly **to ˈdie for** (*informal*) if you think sth is **to die for**, you really want it, and would do anything to get it: *She was wearing a dress to die for.* ➲ more at CROSS *v.*, FLY *n.*, SAY *v.*

PHR V ˌ**die aˈway** 🔑 to become gradually weaker or fainter and finally disappear: *The sound of their laughter died away.* ˌ**die ˈback** if a plant **dies back**, it loses its leaves but remains alive ˌ**die ˈdown** to become gradually less strong, loud, noticeable, etc: *The flames finally died down.* ◇ *When the applause had died down, she began her speech.* ˌ**die ˈoff** to die one after the other until there are none left ˌ**die ˈout** 🗝 to stop existing: *This species has nearly died out because its habitat is being destroyed.*

■ ***noun*** **1** a block of metal with a special shape, or with a pattern cut into it, that is used for shaping other pieces of metal such as coins, or for making patterns on paper or leather **2** (*especially NAmE*) = DICE

IDM **the die is cast** (*saying*) used to say that an event has happened or a decision has been made that cannot be changed

ˈ**die-cast** *adj.* (of a metal object) made by pouring liquid metal into a MOULD and allowing it to cool

die·hard /ˈdaɪhɑːd; *NAmE* -hɑːrd/ *adj.* strongly opposing change and new ideas: *diehard supporters of the exiled king* ▸ **die·hard** *noun*: *A few diehards are trying to stop the reforms.*

diesel /ˈdiːzl/ *noun* **1** (also ˈ**diesel fuel**, ˈ**diesel oil**) [U] a type of heavy oil used as a fuel instead of petrol/gas: *a* ***diesel engine*** (= one that burns diesel) ◇ ***diesel cars/locomotives/trains*** ➲ compare PETROL **2** [C] a vehicle that uses diesel fuel: *Our new car is a diesel.*

diet 🗝 /ˈdaɪət/ *noun, verb*

■ ***noun*** **1** 🗝 [C, U] the food that you eat and drink regularly: *to have a* ***healthy, balanced diet*** ◇ *the Japanese diet of rice, vegetables and fish* ◇ *to receive advice on diet* **2** 🗝 [C] a limited variety or amount of food that you eat for medical reasons or because you want to lose weight; a time when you only eat this limited variety or amount: *a* ***low-fat, salt-free diet*** ◇ ***diet drinks*** (= with fewer CALORIES than normal) ◇ *I decided to* ***go on a diet*** (= to lose weight) *before my holiday.* **3** [sing.] **a ~ of sth** (*disapproving*) a large amount of a restricted range of activities: *Children today are brought up on a diet of television cartoons and soap operas.* ▸ **diet·ary** /ˈdaɪətəri; *NAmE* -teri/ *adj.* [usually before noun]: ***dietary advice/changes/habits*** ◇ *dietary fibre*

■ ***verb*** [I] to eat less food or only food of a particular type in order to lose weight SYN **be on a diet**: *She's always dieting but she never seems to lose any weight.*

diet·er /ˈdaɪətə(r)/ *noun* a person who is trying to lose weight on a diet

diet·et·ics /ˌdaɪəˈtetɪks/ *noun* [U] the scientific study of diet and healthy eating ▸ **diet·et·ic** *adj.*: *dietetic advice*

diet·itian (also **diet·ician**) /ˌdaɪəˈtɪʃn/ *noun* a person whose job is to advise people on what kind of food they should eat to keep healthy

dif·fer /ˈdɪfə(r)/ *verb* **1** [I] to be different from sb/sth: *They hold differing views.* ◇ **A ~s from B** *French differs from English in this respect.* ◇ **A and B ~ (from each other)** *French and English differ in this respect.* ◇ **~ between A and B** *Ideas on childcare may differ considerably between the parents.* ➲ LANGUAGE BANK at CONTRAST **2** [I] to disagree with sb: **~ (with sb) (about/on/over sth)** *I have to differ with you on that.* ◇ **~ (as to sth)** *Medical opinion differs as to how to treat the disease.* IDM see AGREE, BEG

dif·fer·ence 🗝 /ˈdɪfrəns/ *noun*

1 🗝 [C, U] **~ (between A and B)** | **~ (in sth)** the way in which two people or things are not like each other; the way in which sb/sth has changed: *There are no significant differences between the education systems of the two countries.* ◇ *He was studying the complex similarities and differences between humans and animals.* ◇ *There's no difference in the results.* ◇ *I can never* ***tell the difference*** (= distinguish) *between the twins* ◇ *She noticed a* ***marked difference*** *in the children on her second visit.* ◇ *There's* ***a world of difference*** *between liking someone and loving them.* ◇ ***What a difference!*** *You look great with your hair like that.* OPP **similarity** ➲ LANGUAGE BANK at CONTRAST **2** 🗝 [sing., U] **~ (in sth) (between A and B)** the amount that sth is greater or smaller than sth else: *There's not much difference in price between the two computers.* ◇ *There's an age difference of six years between the boys* (= one is six years older than the other). ◇ *I'll lend you £500 and you'll have to find the difference* (= the rest of the money that you need). ◇ *We measured the difference in temperature.* **3** [C] a disagreement between people: *We* ***have our differences****, but she's still my sister.* ◇ *Why don't you* ***settle your differences*** *and be friends again?* ◇ *There was* ***a difference of opinion*** *over who had won.*

IDM **make a, no, some, etc. difference (to/in sb/sth)** 🗝 to have an effect/no effect on sb/sth: *The rain didn't make much difference to the game.* ◇ *Your age shouldn't make any difference to whether you get the job or not.* ◇ *Changing schools made a* ***big difference*** *to my life.* ◇ *What difference will it make if he knows or not?* ◇ *I don't think it makes* ***a lot of difference*** *what colour it is* (= it is not important). ◇ *'Shall we go on Friday or Saturday?' 'It makes no difference (to me).'* **make all the ˈdifference (to sb/sth)** to have an important effect on sb/sth; to make sb feel better: *A few kind words at the right time make all the difference.* **same ˈdifference** (*informal*) used to say that you think the

Collocations

Diet and exercise

Weight

- **put on/gain/lose** weight/a few kilos/a few pounds
- **watch/control/struggle with** your weight
- **be/become** seriously overweight/underweight
- **be/become** clinically/morbidly obese
- **achieve/facilitate/promote/stimulate** weight loss
- **slim down to** 70 kilos/(*BrE*) 11 stone/(*especially NAmE*) 160 pounds
- **combat/prevent/tackle/treat** obesity
- **develop/have/suffer from/struggle with/recover from** anorexia/bulimia/an eating disorder
- **be on/go on/follow** a crash/strict diet
- **have/suffer from** a negative/poor body image
- **have/develop** a positive/healthy body image

Healthy eating

- **eat** a balanced diet/healthily/sensibly
- **get/provide/receive** adequate/proper nutrition
- **contain/get/provide** essential nutrients/vitamins/minerals
- **be high/low in** calories/fat/fibre/(*especially US*) fiber/protein/vitamin D/Omega-3 fatty acids
- **contain (no)/use/be full of/be free from** additives/chemical preservatives/artificial sweeteners
- **avoid/cut down on/cut out** alcohol/caffeine/fatty foods
- **stop/give up/**(*especially NAmE*) **quit** smoking

Exercise

- (*BrE*) **take** regular exercise
- **do** moderate/strenuous/vigorous exercise
- **play** football/hockey/tennis
- **go** cycling/jogging/running
- **go to/visit/**(*especially NAmE*) **hit/work out at** the gym
- **strengthen/tone/train** your stomach muscles
- **contract/relax/stretch/use/work** your lower-body muscles
- **build (up)/gain** muscle
- **improve/increase** your stamina/energy levels/physical fitness
- **burn/consume/expend** calories

Staying healthy

- **be/get/keep/stay** healthy/in shape/(*especially BrE*) fit
- **lower** your cholesterol/blood pressure
- **boost/stimulate/strengthen** your immune system
- **prevent/reduce the risk of** heart disease/high blood pressure/diabetes/osteoporosis
- **reduce/relieve/manage/combat** stress
- **enhance/promote** relaxation/physical and mental well-being

differences between two things are not important: *'That's not a xylophone, it's a glockenspiel.' 'Same difference.'* **with a 'difference** (*informal*) (after nouns) used to show that sth is interesting or unusual: *The traditional backpack with a difference—it's waterproof.* ➲ more at BURY, SINK *v.*, SPLIT *v.*, WORLD

dif·fer·ent 🔑 /ˈdɪfrənt/ *adj.*
1 🔑 **~ (from/to/than sb/sth)** not the same as sb/sth; not like sb/sth else: *American English is significantly different from British English.* ◇ (*BrE*) *It's very different to what I'm used to.* ◇ (*NAmE*) *He saw he was no different than anybody else.* ◇ *It's different now than it was a year ago.* ◇ *People often give very different accounts of the same event.* ◇ *My son's terribly untidy; my daughter's* ***no different.*** OPP **similar 2** 🔑 [only before noun] separate and individual: *She offered us five different kinds of cake.* ◇ *The programme was about customs in different parts of the country.* ◇ *They are sold in many different colours.* ◇ *I looked it up in three different dictionaries.* **3** [not usually before noun] (*informal*) unusual; not like other people or things: *'Did you enjoy the play?' 'Well, it was certainly different!'* ▶ **dif·fer·ent·ly** 🔑 *adv.*: *Boys and girls may behave differently.* ◇ *The male bird has a differently shaped head.*
IDM **a different kettle of fish** (*informal*) a completely different situation or person from the one previously mentioned ➲ more at COMPLEXION, KNOW *v.*, MATTER *n.*, MARCH, PULL *v.*, SING *v.*, TELL

British / American

different from / to / than

- **Different from** is the most common structure in both *BrE* and *NAmE*. **Different to** is also used in *BrE*: *Paul's very different from/to his brother.* ◇ *This visit is very different from/to last time.*
- In *NAmE* people also say **different than**: *Your trains are different than ours.* ◇ *You look different than before.*
- Before a clause you can also use **different from** (and **different than** in *NAmE*): *She looked different from what I'd expected.* ◇ *She looked different than (what) I'd expected.*

dif·fer·en·tial /ˌdɪfəˈrenʃl/ *noun, adj.*
■ *noun* **1 ~ (between A and B)** a difference in the amount, value or size of sth, especially the difference in rates of pay for people doing different work in the same industry or profession: ***wage/pay/income differentials*** **2** (also **ˌdifferential ˈgear**) a gear that makes it possible for a vehicle's back wheels to turn at different speeds when going around corners
■ *adj.* [only before noun] (*formal*) showing or depending on a difference; not equal: *the differential treatment of prisoners based on sex and social class* ◇ *differential rates of pay*

ˌdifferential ˈcalculus *noun* [U] (*mathematics*) a type of mathematics that deals with quantities that change in time. It is used to calculate a quantity at a particular moment ➲ compare INTEGRAL CALCULUS

diffeˌrential eˈquation *noun* (*mathematics*) an EQUATION that involves FUNCTIONS (= quantities that can vary) and their rates of change

dif·fer·en·ti·ate AW /ˌdɪfəˈrenʃieɪt/ *verb* **1** [I, T] to recognize or show that two things are not the same SYN **distinguish**: **~ (between) A and B** *It's difficult to differentiate between the two varieties.* ◇ **~ A (from B)** *I can't differentiate one variety from another.* **2** [T] **~ sth (from sth)** to be the particular thing that shows that things or people are not the same SYN **distinguish**: *The male's yellow beak differentiates it from the female.* **3** [I] **~ between A and B** to treat people or things in a different way, especially in an unfair way SYN **discriminate** ▶ **dif·fer·en·ti·ation** AW /ˌdɪfəˌrenʃiˈeɪʃn/ *noun* [U]

dif·fi·cult 🔑 /ˈdɪfɪkəlt/ *adj.*
1 🔑 **~ (for sb) (to do sth)** not easy; needing effort or skill to do or to understand: *a difficult problem/task/exam* ◇ ***It's difficult*** *for them to get here much before seven.* ◇ *It's really difficult to read your writing.* ◇ *Your writing is really difficult to read.* ◇ *She* ***finds it*** *very* ***difficult*** *to get up early.* **2** 🔑 full of problems; causing a lot of trouble: *to be in a* ***difficult position/situation*** ◇ *My boss is* ***making life*** *very* ***difficult*** *for me.* ◇ *13 is a difficult age.* **3** 🔑 (of people) not easy to please; not helpful SYN **awkward**: *a difficult child/customer/boss* ◇ *Don't pay any attention to her—she's just being difficult.* IDM see JOB, LIFE

D

Synonyms

difficult

hard • challenging • demanding • taxing

These words all describe sth that is not easy and requires a lot of effort or skill to do.

difficult not easy; needing effort or skill to do or understand: *The exam questions were quite difficult.* ◇ *It is difficult for young people to find jobs around here.*

hard not easy; needing effort or skill to do or understand: *I always found languages quite hard at school.* ◇ *It was one of the hardest things I ever did.*

DIFFICULT OR HARD?

Hard is slightly less formal than **difficult**. It is used particularly in the structure *hard to believe/say/find/take, etc.*, although **difficult** can also be used in any of these examples.

challenging (*approving*) difficult in an interesting way that tests your ability.

demanding difficult to do or deal with and needing a lot of effort, skill or patience: *It is a technically demanding piece of music to play.*

taxing (often used in negative statements) difficult to do and needing a lot of mental or physical effort: *This shouldn't be too taxing for you.*

PATTERNS

- difficult/hard/challenging/demanding/taxing **for** sb
- difficult/hard **to do sth**
- **physically** difficult/hard/challenging/demanding/taxing
- **technically** difficult/challenging/demanding
- **mentally/intellectually** challenging/demanding/taxing

dif·fi·culty 🔑 /ˈdɪfɪkəlti/ *noun* (*pl.* -ies)
1 🔑 [C, usually pl., U] a problem; a thing or situation that causes problems: *the difficulties of English syntax* ◇ *children with severe learning difficulties* ◇ *We've* ***run into difficulties/difficulty*** *with the new project.* ◇ *He* ***got into difficulties*** *while swimming and had to be rescued.* ◇ *The bank is* ***in difficulty/difficulties.*** ◇ *It was a time fraught with difficulties and frustration.* **2** 🔑 [U] the state or quality of being hard to do or to understand; the effort that sth involves: *I had considerable difficulty (in) persuading her to leave.* ◇ *I had no difficulty (in) making myself understood.* ◇ *The changes were made with surprisingly little difficulty.* ◇ *He spoke slowly and with great difficulty.* ◇ *We found the house* ***without difficulty.*** ◇ *They discussed the difficulty of studying abroad.* HELP You cannot say 'have difficulty to do sth': ~~*I had difficulty to persuade her to leave.*~~ **3** 🔑 [U] how hard sth is: *varying levels of difficulty* ◇ *questions of increasing difficulty*

dif·fi·dent /ˈdɪfɪdənt/ *adj.* **~ (about sth)** not having much confidence in yourself; not wanting to talk about yourself SYN **shy**: *a* ***diffident manner/smile*** ◇ *He was modest and diffident about his own success.* ▶ **dif·fi·dence** /-dəns/ *noun* [U]: *She overcame her natural diffidence and spoke with great frankness.* **dif·fi·dent·ly** *adv.*

dif·fract /dɪˈfrækt/ *verb* **~ sth** (*physics*) to break up a stream of light into a series of dark and light bands or into the different colours of the SPECTRUM ▶ **dif·frac·tion** /dɪˈfrækʃn/ *noun* [U]

dif·fuse *adj., verb*
■ ***adj.*** /dɪˈfjuːs/ **1** spread over a wide area: *diffuse light* ◇ *a diffuse community* **2** not clear or easy to understand; using a lot of words: *a diffuse style of writing* ▶ **dif·fuse·ly** *adv.* **dif·fuse·ness** *noun* [U]
■ ***verb*** /dɪˈfjuːz/ **1** [T, I] **~ (sth)** (*formal*) to spread sth or become spread widely in all directions: *The problem is how to diffuse power without creating anarchy.* ◇ *Technologies diffuse rapidly.* **2** [I, T] **~ (sth)** (*technical*) if a gas or liquid **diffuses** or **is diffused** in a substance, it becomes slowly mixed with that substance **3** [T] **~ sth** (*formal*) to make light shine less brightly by spreading it in many directions: *The moon was fuller than the night before, but the light was diffused by cloud.* ▶ **dif·fu·sion** /dɪˈfjuːʒn/ *noun* [U]

dif·fu·ser /dɪˈfjuːzə(r)/ *noun* **1** a device used in photography to avoid dark shadows or areas which are too bright **2** a part that is attached to a HAIRDRYER to spread the hot air around the head and dry the hair more gently

dig 0-w /dɪɡ/ *verb, noun*
■ ***verb*** (**dig·ging, dug, dug** /dʌɡ/) **1** 0-w [I, T] to make a hole in the ground or to move soil from one place to another using your hands, a tool or a machine: **~ (for sth)** *to dig for coal/gold/Roman remains* ◇ *They dug deeper and deeper but still found nothing.* ◇ *I think I'll* ***do some digging*** *in the garden.* ◇ **~ sth** *to* ***dig a ditch/grave/hole/tunnel*** ◇ (*BrE*) *I've been digging the garden.* **2** [T] **~ sth** to remove sth from the ground with a tool: *I'll dig some potatoes for lunch.* **3** [I] (+ **adv./prep.**) to search in sth in order to find an object in sth: *I dug around in my bag for a pen.* **4** [T] **~ sth** (*old-fashioned, slang*) to approve of or like sth very much
IDM ▶ **dig ˈdeep (into sth)** **1** to search thoroughly for information: *You'll need to dig deep into the records to find the figures you want.* **2** to try hard to provide the money, equipment, etc. that is needed: *We're asking you to dig deep for the earthquake victims.* **dig your ˈheels/ˈtoes in** to refuse to do sth or to change your mind about sth: *They dug in their heels and would not lower the price.* **dig (deep) in/into your pocket(s), savings, etc.** to spend a lot of your own money on sth **dig sb in the ˈribs** to push your finger or your elbow into sb's side, especially to attract their attention **dig yourself into a ˈhole** to get yourself into a bad situation that will be very difficult to get out of **dig your own ˈgrave | dig a ˈgrave for yourself** to do sth that will have very harmful results for you
PHR V ▶ **ˌdig ˈin** (*informal*) **1** used to tell sb to start to eat: *Help yourselves, everybody! Dig in!* **2** to wait, or deal with a difficult situation, with great patience: *There is nothing we can do except dig in and wait.* **ˌdig sth↔ˈin** **1** to mix soil with another substance by digging the two substances together: *The manure should be well dug in.* **2** to push sth into sth else: *He dug his fork into the steak.* **ˌdig yourself ˈin** (of soldiers) to protect yourself against an attack by making a safe place in the ground **ˌdig ˈinto sth** **1** (*informal*) to start to eat food with enthusiasm: *She dug into her bowl of pasta.* **2** to push or rub against your body in a painful or uncomfortable way: *His fingers dug painfully into my arm.* **3** to find out information by searching or asking questions: *Will you dig a little into his past and see what you find?* **ˌdig sth ˈinto sth** **1** to mix soil with another substance by digging the two substances together **2** to push or press sth into sth else: *She dug her hands deeper into her pockets.* **ˌdig sb/sth↔ˈout (of sth)** **1** to remove sb/sth from somewhere by digging the ground around them or it: *More than a dozen people were dug out of the avalanche alive.* **2** to find sth that has been hidden or forgotten for a long time: *I went to the attic and dug out Grandad's medals.* **ˌdig sth↔ˈover** to prepare ground by digging the soil to remove stones, etc. **ˌdig sth↔ˈup** **1** to break the ground into small pieces before planting seeds, building sth, etc: *They are digging up the football field to lay a new surface.* **2** to remove sth from the ground by digging: *An old Roman vase was dug up here last month.* **3** to discover information about sb/sth SYN **unearth**: *Tabloid newspapers love to dig up scandal.*
■ ***noun*** ➲ see also DIGS **1** a small push with your finger or elbow: *She gave him* ***a dig in the ribs.*** **2 ~ (at sb/sth)** a remark that is intended to annoy or upset sb: *He kept making sly little digs at me.* ◇ *to* ***have a dig at sb/sth*** **3** an occasion when an organized group of people dig in the ground to discover old buildings or objects, in order to find out more about their history SYN **excavation**: *to go on a dig* ◇ *an archaeological dig*

the dig·er·ati /ˌdɪdʒəˈrɑːti/ *noun* [pl.] (*humorous*) people who are very good at using computers or who use computers a lot ➲ compare LITERATI

di·gest *verb, noun*
■ ***verb*** /daɪˈdʒest; dɪ-/ **1** [T, I] **~ (sth)** when you **digest** food, or it **digests**, it is changed into substances that your body can use: *Humans cannot digest plants such as grass.* ◇ *You should allow a little time after a meal for the food to digest.* **2** [T] **~ sth** to think about sth so that you fully understand it: *He paused, waiting for her to digest the information.*
■ ***noun*** /ˈdaɪdʒest/ a short report containing the most important facts of a longer report or piece of writing; a collection of short reports: *a monthly news digest*

di·gest·ible /daɪˈdʒestəbl; dɪ-/ *adj.* easy to digest; pleasant to eat or easy to understand OPP **indigestible**

di·ges·tion /daɪˈdʒestʃən; dɪ-/ *noun* **1** [U] the process of digesting food ➲ compare INDIGESTION **2** [C, usually sing.] the ability to digest food: *to have a* ***good/poor digestion***

di·gest·ive /daɪˈdʒestɪv; dɪ-/ *adj.* [only before noun] connected with the digestion of food: *the* ***digestive system/tract*** ◇ *digestive problems*

diˈgestive biscuit (also **digestive**) *noun* (*BrE*) a round sweet biscuit made from WHOLEMEAL flour, sometimes covered with chocolate: *a packet of chocolate digestives*

diˈgestive system *noun* the series of organs inside the body that digest food

dig·ger /ˈdɪɡə(r)/ *noun* **1** a large machine that is used for digging up the ground **2** a person or an animal that digs ➲ see also GOLD-DIGGER **3** (*AustralE, NZE, old-fashioned, informal*) a man

digit /ˈdɪdʒɪt/ *noun* **1** any of the numbers from 0 to 9: *The number 57306 contains five digits.* ◇ *a four-digit number* **2** (*anatomy*) a finger, thumb or toe

digit·al /ˈdɪdʒɪtl/ *adj., noun*
■ ***adj.*** **1** using a system of receiving and sending information as a series of the numbers one and zero, showing that an electronic signal is there or is not there: *a digital camera* ◇ *digital terrestrial and digital satellite broadcasting* **2** (of clocks, watches, etc.) showing information by using figures, rather than with HANDS that point to numbers: *a* ***digital clock/watch*** ➲ picture at CLOCK ➲ compare ANALOGUE ▶ **digit·al·ly** /-təli/ *adv.*: *digitally remastered tapes*
■ ***noun*** [U] digital television: *How long have you had digital?* ◇ *With digital you can choose the camera angle you want.*

digi·talis /ˌdɪdʒɪˈteɪlɪs; *NAmE* also -ˈtælɪs/ *noun* [U] (*medical*) a drug made from the FOXGLOVE plant, that helps the heart muscle to work

digit·al·ize (*BrE* also **-ise**) /ˈdɪdʒɪtəlaɪz/ *verb* **~ sth** = DIGITIZE

ˌdigital reˈcording *noun* [C, U] a recording in which sounds or pictures are represented by a series of numbers showing that an electronic signal is there or is not there; the process of making a recording in this way

ˌdigital ˈsignature *noun* (*computing*) a way of secretly adding sb's name to an electronic message or document to prove the identity of the person who is sending it and show that the data has not been changed at all

ˌdigital ˈtelevision *noun* **1** [U] the system of broadcasting television using digital signals **2** [C] a television set that can receive digital signals

digit·ize (*BrE* also **-ise**) /ˈdɪdʒɪtaɪz/ (also **digit·al·ize**) *verb* **~ sth** to change data into a DIGITAL form that can be easily read and processed by a computer: *a digitized map*

di·glos·sia /daɪˈɡlɒsiə; *NAmE* -ˈɡlɔːs-; -ˈɡlɑːs-/ *noun* [U] (*linguistics*) a situation in which two languages or two forms of a language are used under different conditions in a community ▶ **di·glos·sic** *adj.*

dig·ni·fied /ˈdɪɡnɪfaɪd/ *adj.* calm and serious and deserving respect: *a dignified person/manner/voice* ◇ *Throughout his trial he maintained a dignified silence.* OPP **undignified**

dig·nify /ˈdɪɡnɪfaɪ/ *verb* (**dig·ni·fies**, **dig·ni·fy·ing**, **dig·ni·fied**) (*formal*) **1** ~ **sb/sth** to make sb/sth seem impressive: *The mayor was there to dignify the celebrations.* **2** ~ **sth** to make sth appear important when it is not really: *I'm not going to dignify his comments by reacting to them.*

dig·ni·tary /ˈdɪɡnɪtəri; *NAmE* -teri/ *noun* (*pl.* **-ies**) a person who has an important official position SYN **VIP**

dig·nity /ˈdɪɡnəti/ *noun* [U] **1** a calm and serious manner that deserves respect: *She accepted the criticism with quiet dignity.* **2** the fact of being given honour and respect by people: *the dignity of work* ◇ *The terminally ill should be allowed to die with dignity.* **3** a sense of your own importance and value: *It's difficult to preserve your dignity when you have no job and no home.*
IDM **be͵neath your ˈdignity** below what you see as your own importance or worth **͵stand on your ˈdignity** (*formal*) to demand to be treated with the respect that you think that you deserve

di·graph /ˈdaɪɡrɑːf; *NAmE* -ɡræf/ *noun* a combination of two letters representing one sound, for example 'ph' and 'sh' in English

di·gress /daɪˈɡres/ *verb* [I] (*formal*) to start to talk about sth that is not connected with the main point of what you are saying ▸ **di·gres·sion** /daɪˈɡreʃn/ *noun* [C, U]: *After several digressions, he finally got to the point.*

digs /dɪɡz/ *noun* [pl.] (*old-fashioned, informal*) a room or rooms that you rent to live in SYN **lodgings**

dike *noun* = DYKE

dik·tat /ˈdɪktæt; *NAmE* dɪkˈtæt/ *noun* [C, U] (*disapproving*) an order given by a government, for example, that people must obey: *an EU diktat from Brussels* ◇ *government by diktat*

di·lapi·dated /dɪˈlæpɪdeɪtɪd/ *adj.* (of furniture and buildings) old and in very bad condition SYN **ramshackle** ▸ **di·lapi·da·tion** /dɪ͵læpɪˈdeɪʃn/ *noun* [U]: *in a state of dilapidation*

dila·ta·tion /͵daɪləˈteɪʃn; ͵dɪlə-; *BrE* also ͵daɪleɪ-/ *noun* [U] (*medical*) the process of becoming wider (= of becoming dilated), or the action of making sth become wider

dila͵tation and curetˈtage (also **D and C**) *noun* (*medical*) an operation in which the CERVIX is opened and material is removed from the UTERUS, for example after a MISCARRIAGE

di·late /daɪˈleɪt/ *verb* [I, T] to become or to make sth larger, wider or more open: *Her eyes dilated with fear.* ◇ ~ **sth** *dilated pupils/nostrils* ◇ *Red wine can help to dilate blood vessels.* OPP **contract** ▸ **dila·tion** /daɪˈleɪʃn/ *noun* [U, C]

dila·tory /ˈdɪlətəri; *NAmE* -tɔːri/ *adj.* ~ (**in doing sth**) (*formal*) not acting quickly enough; causing delay: *The government has been dilatory in dealing with the problem of unemployment.*

dildo /ˈdɪldəʊ; *NAmE* -doʊ/ *noun* (*pl.* **dildos** or **dildoes**) an object shaped like a PENIS that is used for sexual pleasure

di·lemma /dɪˈlemə; daɪ-/ *noun* a situation which makes problems, often one in which you have to make a very difficult choice between things of equal importance SYN **predicament**: *to face a dilemma* ◇ *to be in a dilemma*
IDM see HORN

dil·et·tante /͵dɪləˈtænti/ *noun* (*pl.* **dil·et·tanti** /-tiː/ or **dil·et·tan·tes**) (*disapproving*) a person who does or studies sth but is not serious about it and does not have much knowledge ▸ **di·let·tante** *adj.*: *a dilettante artist*

dili·gence /ˈdɪlɪdʒəns/ *noun* [U] (*formal*) careful and thorough work or effort: *She shows great diligence in her schoolwork.*

dili·gent /ˈdɪlɪdʒənt/ *adj.* (*formal*) showing care and effort in your work or duties: *a* ***diligent student/worker*** ▸ **dili·gent·ly** *adv.*

dill /dɪl/ *noun* [U] a plant with yellow flowers whose leaves and seeds have a strong taste and are used in cooking as a HERB. Dill is often added to vegetables kept in VINEGAR: *dill pickles* ➲ VISUAL VOCAB page V28

dilly-dally /ˈdɪli dæli/ *verb* (**dilly-dallies**, **dilly-dallying**, **dilly-dallied**, **dilly-dallied**) [I] (*old-fashioned, informal*) to take too long to do sth, go somewhere or make a decision SYN **dawdle**

di·lute *verb, adj.* /daɪˈluːt; *BrE* also -ˈljuːt/
■ ***verb*** **1** ~ **sth** (**with sth**) to make a liquid weaker by adding water or another liquid to it SYN **water down**: *The paint can be diluted with water to make a lighter shade.* **2** ~ **sth** to make sth weaker or less effective SYN **water down**: *Large classes dilute the quality of education that children receive.* ▸ **di·lu·tion** /daɪˈluːʃn; *BrE* also -ˈljuːʃn/ *noun* [U]: *the dilution of sewage* ◇ *This is a serious dilution of their election promises.*
■ ***adj.*** (also **di·luted**) (of a liquid) made weaker by adding water or another substance: *a* ***dilute acid/solution***

dim /dɪm/ *adj., verb*
■ ***adj.*** (**dim·mer**, **dim·mest**)
▸ LIGHT **1** not bright: *the dim glow of the fire in the grate* ◇ *This light is too dim to read by.*
▸ PLACE **2** where you cannot see well because there is not much light: *a dim room/street*
▸ SHAPE **3** that you cannot see well because there is not much light: *the dim outline of a house in the moonlight* ◇ *I could see a dim shape in the doorway.*
▸ EYES **4** not able to see well: *His eyesight is getting dim.*
▸ MEMORIES **5** that you cannot remember or imagine clearly SYN **vague**: *dim memories* ◇ *She had a dim recollection of the visit.* ◇ (*humorous*) *in the* ***dim and distant*** *past*
▸ PERSON **6** (*informal, especially BrE*) not intelligent: *He's very dim.*
▸ SITUATION **7** not giving any reason to have hope; not good: *Her future career prospects look dim.*
▸ **dim·ness** *noun* [U]: *It took a while for his eyes to adjust to the dimness.* ➲ see also DIMLY
IDM **take a dim view of sb/sth** to disapprove of sb/sth; to not have a good opinion of sb/sth: *She took a dim view of my suggestion.*
■ ***verb*** (**-mm-**)
▸ LIGHT **1** [I, T] ~ (**sth**) if a light **dims** or if you **dim** it, it becomes or you make it less bright: *The lights in the theatre dimmed as the curtain rose.*
▸ FEELING/QUALITY **2** [I, T] ~ (**sth**) if a feeling or quality **dims**, or if sth **dims** it, it becomes less strong: *Her passion for dancing never dimmed over the years.*

dime /daɪm/ *noun* a coin of the US and Canada worth ten cents
IDM **a ͵dime a ˈdozen** (*NAmE*) (*BrE* **͵two/͵ten a ˈpenny**) very common and therefore not valuable

ˈdime novel *noun* (*NAmE, old-fashioned*) a cheap popular novel, usually an exciting adventure or romantic story

di·men·sion AW /daɪˈmenʃn; dɪ-/ *noun* **1** a measurement in space, for example the height, width or length of sth: *We measured the dimensions of the kitchen.* ◇ *computer design tools that work in three dimensions* ➲ see also THE FOURTH DIMENSION **2** [usually pl.] the size and extent of a situation: *a problem of considerable dimensions* **3** an aspect, or way of looking at or thinking about sth: *Her job added a new dimension to her life.* ◇ *the social dimension of unemployment*

-dimensional AW /daɪˈmenʃənl; dɪ-/ *combining form* (in adjectives) having the number of dimensions mentioned: *a multidimensional model* ➲ see also MULTIDIMENSIONAL, THREE-DIMENSIONAL, TWO-DIMENSIONAL

ˈdime store *noun* (*old-fashioned, NAmE*) = FIVE-AND-DIME

di·min·ish AW /dɪˈmɪnɪʃ/ *verb* **1** [I, T] ~ (**sth**) to become or to make sth become smaller, weaker, etc. SYN **decrease**: *The world's resources are rapidly diminishing.* ◇ *His influence has diminished with time.* ◇ *Our efforts were producing* ***diminishing returns*** (= we achieved less although we spent more time or money). **2** [T] ~ **sb/sth** to make sb/sth seem less important than they really are

SYN belittle: *I don't wish to diminish the importance of their contribution.*

di,minished responsi'bility *noun* [U] (*BrE, law*) a state in which a person who is accused of a crime is not considered to be responsible for their actions, because they are mentally ill: *He was found not guilty of murder on the grounds of diminished responsibility.*

di·minu·endo /dɪˌmɪnju'endəʊ; *NAmE* -doʊ/ *noun* (*pl.* -os) [C, U] (*music*) a gradual decrease in how loudly a piece of music is played or sung OPP **crescendo**

dim·in·ution AW /ˌdɪmɪ'nju:ʃn; *NAmE* -'nu:ʃn/ *noun* **~ (of/in sth)** (*formal*) **1** [U] the act of reducing sth or of being reduced: *the diminution of political power* **2** [C, usually sing.] a reduction; an amount reduced: *a diminution in population growth*

di·minu·tive /dɪ'mɪnjətɪv/ *adj., noun*

■ ***adj.*** (*formal*) very small: *She was a diminutive figure beside her husband.*

■ ***noun*** **1** a word or an ending of a word that shows that sb/sth is small, for example *piglet* (= a young pig), *kitchenette* (= a small kitchen) **2** a short informal form of a word, especially a name: *'Nick' is a common diminutive of 'Nicholas'.*

dimly /'dɪmli/ *adv.* not very brightly or clearly: *a dimly lit room* ◇ *I was* ***dimly aware*** (= only just aware) *of the sound of a car in the distance.* ◇ *I did remember, but only dimly.*

'dim·mer switch (also **dim·mer**) *noun* **1** a switch that allows you to make an electric light brighter or less bright **2** (*NAmE*) (*BrE* **'dip switch**) a switch that allows you to make the front lights on a car point downwards

dimple /'dɪmpl/ *verb, noun*

■ ***verb*** [I] to make a hollow place appear on each of your cheeks, especially by smiling

■ ***noun*** **1** a small hollow place in the skin, especially in the cheek or chin: *She had a dimple which appeared when she smiled.* **2** any small hollow place in a surface: *a pane of glass with a dimple pattern* ▶ **dimpled** /'dɪmpld/ *adj.*: *a dimpled chin*

dim sum /ˌdɪm 'sʌm/ (also **dim sim** /ˌdɪm 'sɪm/) *noun* [U] (from *Chinese*) a Chinese dish or meal consisting of small pieces of food wrapped in sheets of DOUGH

ˌdim-'witted *adj.* (*informal*) stupid: *a dim-witted child* ▶ **dim·wit** *noun*

din /dɪn/ *noun* [sing.] a loud, unpleasant noise that lasts for a long time SYN **racket**: *The children were making an awful din.*

dinar /'di:nɑ:(r)/ *noun* a unit of money in Serbia and various countries in the Middle East and N Africa

din-dins /'dɪndɪnz/ (*BrE*) (*NAmE* **din-din** /'dɪndɪn/) *noun* [U] (*humorous*) (used when talking to a baby or a pet) food

dine /daɪn/ *verb* [I] (*formal*) to eat dinner: *We dined with my parents at a restaurant in town.* ➲ COLLOCATIONS at RESTAURANT

PHR V **'dine on sth** (*formal*) to have a particular type of food for dinner **ˌdine 'out** to eat dinner in a restaurant or sb else's home **ˌdine 'out on sth** (*informal*) to tell other people about sth that has happened to you, in order to make them interested in you IDM see WINE *v.*

diner /'daɪnə(r)/ *noun* **1** a person eating a meal, especially in a restaurant: *a restaurant capable of seating 100 diners* **2** (*especially NAmE*) a small, usually cheap, restaurant: *a roadside diner*

din·ero /dɪ'neərəʊ; *NAmE* dɪ'neroʊ/ *noun* [U] (*informal, especially NAmE*, from *Spanish*) money

din·ette /daɪ'net/ *noun* (*especially NAmE*) a small room or part of a room for eating meals

ding /dɪŋ/ *noun, verb*

■ ***noun*** **1** (*NAmE*) a blow, especially one that causes slight damage to a car, etc: *I got a ding in my rear fender.* **2** used to represent the sound made by a bell: *The lift came to a halt with a loud 'ding'.*

■ ***verb*** **1** [I] to make a sound like a bell: *The computer just dings when I press a key.* **2** [T] **~ sth** (*NAmE*) to cause slight damage to a car, etc: *I dinged my passenger door.* **3** [T] **~ sb** (*NAmE*) to hit sb: (*figurative*) *My department got dinged by the budget cuts.*

ding·bat /'dɪŋbæt/ *noun* (*NAmE, slang*) a stupid person

ding-dong /'dɪŋ dɒŋ; *NAmE* dɔ:ŋ/ *noun* **1** [U] used to represent the sound made by a bell: *I rang the doorbell. Ding-dong! No answer.* **2** (*BrE, informal*) an argument or fight: *They were having a real ding-dong on the doorstep.*

dinghy /'dɪŋi; 'dɪŋgi/ *noun* (*pl.* -ies) **1** a small open boat that you sail or ROW: *a sailing dinghy* ➲ VISUAL VOCAB page V44 ➲ compare YACHT **2** = RUBBER DINGHY

dingo /'dɪŋgəʊ; *NAmE* -goʊ/ *noun* (*pl.* -oes) a wild Australian dog

dingy /'dɪndʒi/ *adj.* (**din·gier, din·gi·est**) dark and dirty: *a dingy room/hotel* ◇ *dingy curtains/clothes* ▶ **din·gi·ness** *noun* [U]

'dining car (*BrE* also **'restaurant car**) *noun* a coach/car on a train in which meals are served

'dining room *noun* a room that is used mainly for eating meals in ➲ VISUAL VOCAB page V19

'dining table *noun* a table for having meals on ➲ compare DINNER TABLE ➲ VISUAL VOCAB page V19

dink /dɪŋk/ *noun* (also **'drop shot**) (in TENNIS) a soft hit that makes the ball land on the ground without BOUNCING much ▶ **dink** *verb* **~ sth**

din·kum /'dɪŋkəm/ *adj.* (*AustralE, NZE, informal*) (of an article or a person) real or genuine: *If you're dinkum, I'll help you.* ➲ see also FAIR DINKUM

dinky /'dɪŋki/ *adj.* (*informal*) **1** (*BrE, approving*) small and neat in an attractive way: *What a dinky little hat!* **2** (*NAmE, disapproving*) too small: *I grew up in a dinky little town that didn't even have a movie theater.*

din·ner 0-w /'dɪnə(r)/ *noun*

1 0-w [U, C] the main meal of the day, eaten either in the middle of the day or in the evening: *It's time for dinner.* ◇ *When do you* ***have dinner***? ◇ *What time do you serve dinner?* ◇ *Let's invite them to dinner tomorrow.* ◇ *What shall we have* ***for dinner*** *tonight?* ◇ *It's your turn to cook dinner.* ◇ *She didn't eat much dinner.* ◇ *I never eat a big dinner.* ◇ *Christmas dinner* ◇ *a three-course dinner* ◇ *I'd like to take you out* ***to dinner*** *tonight.* ◇ (*BrE*) ***school dinners*** (= meals provided at school in the middle of the day) ➲ COLLOCATIONS at RESTAURANT ➲ note at MEAL **2** 0-w [C] a large formal social gathering at which dinner is eaten: *The club's annual dinner will be held on 3 June.* ➲ see also DINNER PARTY

IDM **ˌdone like a 'dinner** (*AustralE, NZE, informal*) completely defeated ➲ more at DOG *n.*

'dinner dance *noun* a social event in the evening that includes a formal meal and dancing

'dinner jacket (*BrE*) (also **tux·edo** *NAmE, BrE*) *noun* a black or white jacket worn with a BOW TIE at formal occasions in the evening ➲ compare TAILS *n.* (6)

'dinner lady (*BrE*) (*US* **'lunch lady**) *noun* a woman whose job is to serve meals to children in schools

'dinner party *noun* a social event at which a small group of people eat dinner at sb's house

'dinner service *noun* a set of matching plates, dishes, etc. for serving a meal

'dinner suit (*BrE*) (also **tux·edo** *NAmE, BrE*) *noun* a DINNER JACKET and trousers/pants, worn with a BOW TIE at formal occasions in the evening

'dinner table *noun* (often **the dinner table**) [usually sing.] the table at which people are eating dinner; an occasion when people are eating together: *conversation at the dinner table* ➲ compare DINING TABLE

'dinner theater *noun* (*NAmE*) a restaurant where you see a play after your meal

'dinner time *noun* the time at which dinner is normally eaten

din·ner·ware /'dɪnəweə(r); *NAmE* 'dɪnərwer/ *noun* [U] (*NAmE*) plates, dishes, etc. used for serving a meal

dino·saur /'daɪnəsɔː(r)/ *noun* **1** an animal that lived millions of years ago but is now EXTINCT (= it no longer exists). There were many types of dinosaur, some of which were very large. **2** (*disapproving*) a person or thing that is old-fashioned and cannot change in the changing conditions of modern life

dint /dɪnt/ *noun*
IDM **by dint of sth/of doing sth** (*formal*) by means of sth: *He succeeded by dint of hard work.*

dio·cese /'daɪəsɪs/ *noun* (*pl.* **dio·ceses** /'daɪəsiːz/) (in the Christian Church) a district for which a BISHOP is responsible ▶ **dio·cesan** /daɪ'ɒsɪsn; *NAmE* -'ɑːs-/ *adj.*

diode /'daɪəʊd; *NAmE* -oʊd/ *noun* (*technical*) an electronic device in which the electric current passes in one direction only, for example a SILICON CHIP

Dio·nys·iac /ˌdaɪə'nɪziæk/ (also **Dio·nys·ian**) /ˌdaɪə'nɪziən/ *adj.* (*formal*) **1** relating to the ancient Greek god Dionysus **2** relating to the physical senses and the emotions, especially when they are expressed without control ➲ compare APOLLONIAN

di·optre (*especially US* **di·opter**) /daɪ'ɒptə(r); *NAmE* -'ɑːp-/ *noun* (*physics*) a unit for measuring the power of a LENS to REFRACT light (= make it change direction)

di·op·trics /daɪ'ɒptrɪks; *NAmE* -'ɑːp-/ *noun* [U] (*physics*) the scientific study of REFRACTION (= the way light changes direction when it goes through glass, etc.) ▶ **di·op·tric** /daɪ'ɒptrɪk; *NAmE* -'ɑːp-/ *adj.*

dio·rama /ˌdaɪə'rɑːmə; *NAmE* also -'ræmə/ *noun* a model representing a scene with figures, especially in a museum

di·ox·ide /daɪ'ɒksaɪd; *NAmE* -'ɑːks-/ *noun* [U, C] (*chemistry*) a substance formed by combining two atoms of OXYGEN and one atom of another chemical element ➲ see also CARBON DIOXIDE

di·oxin /daɪ'ɒksɪn; *NAmE* -'ɑːks-/ *noun* a chemical used in industry and farming. Most dioxins are poisonous.

dip /dɪp/ *verb, noun*
■ ***verb*** (-pp-) **1** [T] to put sth quickly into a liquid and take it out again: **~ sth (into sth)** *He dipped the brush into the paint.* ◇ **~ sth (in)** *Dip your hand in to see how hot the water is.* ◇ *The fruit had been dipped in chocolate.* **2** [I, T] to go downwards or to a lower level; to make sth do this SYN **fall**: **(+ adv./prep.)** *The sun dipped below the horizon.* ◇ *Sales for this quarter have dipped from 38.7 million to 33 million.* ◇ *The road dipped suddenly as we approached the town.* ◇ **~ sth (+ adv./prep.)** *The plane dipped its wings.* **3** [T] **~ sth** (*BrE*) if you **dip** your HEADLIGHTS when driving a car at night, you make the light from them point down so that other drivers do not have the light in their eyes **4** [T] **~ sth** when farmers **dip** animals, especially sheep, they put them in a bath of a liquid containing chemicals in order to kill insects, etc.
IDM **dip into your 'pocket** (*informal*) to spend some of your own money on sth **dip a 'toe in/into sth | dip a 'toe in/into the water** (*informal*) to start doing sth very carefully to see if it will be successful or not
PHR V **ˌdip 'into sth 1** to put your hand into a container to take sth out: *She dipped into her purse and took out some coins.* **2** to read or watch only parts of sth: *I have only had time to dip into the report.* **3** to take an amount from money that you have saved: *We took out a loan for the car because we didn't want to dip into our savings.*
■ ***noun*** **1** [C] (*informal*) a quick swim: *Let's* ***go for a dip*** *before breakfast.* **2** [C] a decrease in the amount or success of sth, usually for only a short period SYN **fall**: *a sharp* ***dip in*** *profits* **3** [C] a place where a surface suddenly drops to a lower level and then rises again: *a dip in the road* ◇ *Puddles had formed in the dips.* **4** [C, U] a thick mixture into which pieces of food are dipped before being eaten **5** [U, C] a liquid containing a chemical into which sheep and other animals can be dipped in order to kill insects on them **6** [sing.] **~ into sth** a quick look at sth: *A brief dip into history serves to confirm this view.* **7** [C, usually sing.] a quick movement of sth down and up: *He gave a dip of his head.* ➲ see also LUCKY DIP

diph·theria /dɪf'θɪəriə; *NAmE* -'θɪriə; dɪp-/ *noun* [U] a serious infectious disease of the throat that causes difficulty in breathing

diph·thong /'dɪfθɒŋ; 'dɪp-; *NAmE* -θɑːŋ; -θɔːŋ/ *noun* (*phonetics*) a combination of two vowel sounds or vowel letters, for example the sounds /aɪ/ in *pipe* /paɪp/ or the letters *ou* in *doubt* ➲ compare MONOPHTHONG, TRIPHTHONG ▶ **diph·thong·al** /dɪf'θɒŋgl; dɪp-; *NAmE* -'θɑːŋgl; -'θɔːŋgl/ *adj.*

dip·lod·ocus /dɪ'plɒdəkəs; ˌdɪplə'dəʊkəs; *NAmE* -'plɑːd-; -'doʊk-/ *noun* a very large DINOSAUR with a long thin neck and tail

dip·loid /'dɪplɔɪd/ *adj.* (*biology*) (of a cell) containing two complete sets of CHROMOSOMES, one from each parent ➲ compare HAPLOID

dip·loma /dɪ'pləʊmə; *NAmE* -'ploʊ-/ *noun* **1** (*BrE*) a course of study at a college or university: *a two-year diploma course* ◇ *She is taking a diploma in management studies.* **2** a document showing that you have completed a course of study or part of your education: *a High School diploma*

dip·lo·macy /dɪ'pləʊməsi; *NAmE* -'ploʊ-/ *noun* [U] **1** the activity of managing relations between different countries; the skill in doing this: *international diplomacy* ◇ *Diplomacy is better than war.* ➲ COLLOCATIONS at INTERNATIONAL **2** skill in dealing with people in difficult situations without upsetting or offending them SYN **tact** ➲ see also SHUTTLE DIPLOMACY

dip·lo·mat /'dɪpləmæt/ *noun* **1** (also *old-fashioned* **dip·lo·ma·tist**) a person whose job is to represent his or her country in a foreign country, for example, in an EMBASSY **2** a person who is skilled at dealing with other people

dip·lo·mat·ic /ˌdɪplə'mætɪk/ *adj.* **1** connected with managing relations between countries (=DIPLOMACY): *a diplomatic crisis* ◇ *Attempts are being made to settle the dispute by diplomatic means.* ◇ *to* ***break off/establish/restore diplomatic relations*** *with a country* **2** having or showing skill in dealing with people in difficult situations SYN **tactful**: *a diplomatic answer* ▶ **dip·lo·mat·ic·al·ly** /-kli/ *adv.*: *The country remained diplomatically isolated.* ◇ *'Why don't we take a break for coffee?' she suggested diplomatically.*

ˌdiploˌmatic 'bag (*BrE*) (*US* **ˌdiploˌmatic 'pouch**) *noun* a container that is used for sending official letters and documents between a government and its representatives in another country and that cannot be opened by customs officers

ˌdiplo'matic corps *noun* (usually **the diplomatic corps**) [C+sing./pl. v.] (*pl.* **diplomatic corps**) all the DIPLOMATS who work in a particular city or country

ˌdiploˌmatic im'munity *noun* [U] special rights given to diplomats working in a foreign country which mean they cannot be arrested, taxed, etc. in that country

the Diplo'matic Service (*especially BrE*) (*NAmE* usually **the 'Foreign Service**) *noun* [sing.] the government department concerned with representing a country in foreign countries

dip·lo·ma·tist /dɪ'pləʊmətɪst; *NAmE* -'ploʊ-/ *noun* (*old-fashioned*) = DIPLOMAT

di·pole /'daɪpəʊl; *NAmE* -poʊl/ *noun* (*physics*) a pair of separated POLES, one positive and one negative

dip·per /'dɪpə(r)/ *noun* a bird that lives near rivers ➲ see also BIG DIPPER

dippy /'dɪpi/ *adj.* (*informal*) stupid; crazy

dipso·maniac /ˌdɪpsə'meɪniæk/ *noun* a person who has a strong desire for alcoholic drink that they cannot control SYN **alcoholic**

dip·stick /'dɪpstɪk/ *noun* **1** a long straight piece of metal used for measuring the amount of liquid in a container, especially the amount of oil in an engine **2** (*informal*) a stupid person

D

'dip switch (*BrE*) (*NAmE* **'dim·mer switch**) *noun* a switch that allows you to make the front lights on a car point downwards

dip·tych /'dɪptɪk/ *noun* (*technical*) a painting, especially a religious one, with two wooden panels that can be closed like a book

dire /'daɪə(r)/ *adj.* (**direr**, **dir·est**) **1** [usually before noun] (*formal*) very serious: *living in dire poverty* ◇ ***dire warnings/threats*** ◇ *Such action may have* ***dire consequences.*** ◇ *We're* ***in dire need of*** *your help.* ◇ *The firm is* ***in dire straits*** (= in a very difficult situation) *and may go bankrupt.* **2** (*BrE, informal*) very bad: *The acting was dire.*

D

dir·ect 0‑‑ /də'rekt; dɪ-; daɪ-/ *adj., verb, adv.*

■ ***adj.***

▸ NOBODY/NOTHING IN BETWEEN **1** 0‑‑ [usually before noun] happening or done without involving other people, actions, etc. in between: *They are in direct contact with the hijackers.* ◇ *His death was a direct result of your action.* ◇ *We are looking for somebody with direct experience of this type of work.* ◇ *This information has* ***a direct bearing on*** (= it is closely connected with) *the case.* OPP **indirect**

▸ JOURNEY/ROUTE **2** 0‑‑ going in the straightest line between two places without stopping or changing direction: *the most* ***direct route/course*** ◇ *a* ***direct flight*** (= a flight that does not stop) ◇ *There's a* ***direct train*** *to Leeds* (= it may stop at other stations but you do not have to change trains). ◇ *a* ***direct hit*** (= a hit that is accurate and does not touch sth else first) OPP **indirect**

▸ HEAT/LIGHT **3** 0‑‑ [only before noun] with nothing between sth and the source of the heat or light: *Protect your child from direct sunlight by using a sunscreen.*

▸ SAYING WHAT YOU MEAN **4** 0‑‑ saying exactly what you mean in a way that nobody can pretend not to understand: *a* ***direct answer/question*** ◇ *You'll have to get used to his direct manner.* OPP **indirect** ⊃ SYNONYMS at HONEST

▸ EXACT **5** [only before noun] exact: *That's the* ***direct opposite*** *of what you told me yesterday.* ◇ *a* ***direct quote*** (= one using a person's exact words)

▸ RELATIONSHIP **6** [only before noun] related through parents and children rather than brothers, sisters, aunts, etc: *a direct descendant of the country's first president* OPP **indirect**

■ ***verb***

▸ AIM **1** 0‑‑ [T] to aim sth in a particular direction or at a particular person: **~ sth at sth/sb** *The machine directs a powerful beam at the affected part of the body.* ◇ *Was that remark directed at me?* ◇ **~ sth to/towards sth/sb** *There are three main issues that we need to direct our attention to.* ◇ **~ sth against sth/sb** *Most of his anger was directed against himself.*

▸ CONTROL **2** 0‑‑ [T] **~ sb/sth** to control or be in charge of sb/sth: *A new manager has been appointed to direct the project.* ◇ *He was asked to take command and* ***direct operations.***

▸ MOVIE/PLAY/MUSIC **3** 0‑‑ [I, T] to be in charge of actors in a play, or a film/movie, or musicians in an ORCHESTRA, etc: *She prefers to act rather than direct.* ◇ **~ sb/sth** *The movie was directed by Steven Spielberg.* ◇ *She now directs a large choir.* ⊃ COLLOCATIONS at CINEMA

▸ SHOW THE WAY **4** 0‑‑ [T] **~ sb (to…)** to tell or show sb how to get to somewhere or where to go: *Could you direct me to the station?* ◇ *A police officer was directing the traffic.* ⊃ SYNONYMS at TAKE

▸ GIVE ORDER **5** [T] (*formal*) to give an official order SYN **order**: **~ sb to do sth** *The police officers had been directed to search the building.* ◇ **~ that…** *The judge directed that the mother be given custody of the children.* ◇ (*BrE* also) *The judge directed that the mother should be given custody of the children.* ⊃ SYNONYMS at ORDER

▸ LETTER/COMMENT **6** [T] **~ sth to…** (*formal*) to send a letter, etc. to a particular place or to a particular person: *Direct any complaints to the Customer Services department.*

■ ***adv.***

▸ JOURNEY/ROUTE **1** without stopping or changing direction: *We flew direct to Hong Kong.* ◇ *The 10.40 goes direct to Leeds.*

▸ NOBODY IN BETWEEN **2** without involving other people: *I prefer to deal with him direct.*

di,rect 'access *noun* [U] (*computing*) the ability to get data immediately from any part of a computer file

di,rect 'action *noun* [U, C] the use of strikes, protests, etc. instead of discussion in order to get what you want

di,rect 'current *noun* [C, U] (*abbr.* **DC**) an electric current that flows in one direction only ⊃ compare ALTERNATING CURRENT

di,rect 'debit *noun* [U, C] (*BrE*) an instruction to your bank to allow sb else to take an amount of money from your account on a particular date, especially to pay bills: *We pay all our bills* ***by direct debit.*** ⊃ compare STANDING ORDER

di,rect de'posit *noun* [U] (*NAmE*) the system of paying sb's wages straight into their bank account

dir·ec·tion 0‑‑ /də'rekʃn; dɪ-; daɪ-/ *noun*

▸ WHERE TO **1** 0‑‑ [C, U] the general position a person or thing moves or points towards: *Tom went off* ***in the direction of*** *home.* ◇ *She glanced* ***in his direction.*** ◇ *The aircraft was flying in a northerly direction.* ◇ *The road was blocked in both directions.* ◇ *They hit a truck coming in* ***the opposite direction.*** ◇ *Has the wind* ***changed direction?*** ◇ *When the police arrived, the crowd scattered* ***in all directions.*** ◇ *I lost all* ***sense of direction*** (= I didn't know which way to go).

▸ DEVELOPMENT **2** 0‑‑ [C, U] the general way in which a person or thing develops: *The exhibition provides evidence of several new directions in her work.* ◇ *I am very unhappy with the direction the club is taking.* ◇ *It's only a small improvement, but at least it's* ***a step in the right direction.***

▸ WHERE FROM **3** [C] the general position a person or thing comes or develops from: *Support came from an unexpected direction.* ◇ *Let us approach the subject from a different direction.*

▸ PURPOSE **4** 0‑‑ [U] a purpose; an aim: *We are looking for somebody with a clear* ***sense of direction.*** ◇ *Once again her life felt lacking in direction.*

▸ INSTRUCTIONS **5** 0‑‑ [C, usually pl.] instructions about how to do sth, where to go, etc: *Let's stop and ask for directions.* ◇ *Simple directions for assembling the model are printed on the box.*

▸ CONTROL **6** 0‑‑ [U] the art of managing or guiding sb/sth: *All work was produced by the students* ***under the direction of*** *John Williams.*

▸ FILM/MOVIE **7** [U] the instructions given by sb directing a film/movie: *There is some clever direction and the film is very well shot.* IDM see PULL *v.*

dir·ec·tion·al /də'rekʃənl; dɪ-; daɪ-/ *adj.* (*technical*) **1** producing or receiving signals, sound, etc. better in one particular direction: *a* ***directional microphone/aerial*** **2** connected with the direction in which sth is moving: *directional stability*

dir·ec·tion·less /də'rekʃnləs; dɪ-; daɪ-/ *adj.* (*formal*) without a direction or purpose

dir·ect·ive /də'rektɪv; dɪ-; daɪ-/ *noun, adj.*

■ ***noun*** an official instruction: *The EU has issued a new set of directives on pollution.*

■ ***adj.*** (*formal*) giving instructions: *They are seeking a central, directive role in national energy policy.*

dir·ect·ly 0‑‑ /də'rektli; dɪ-; daɪ-/ *adv., conj.*

■ ***adv.*** **1** 0‑‑ in a direct line or manner: *He drove her directly to her hotel.* ◇ *She looked directly at us.* ◇ *He's directly responsible to the boss.* ◇ *We have not been directly affected by the cuts.* OPP **indirectly** **2** 0‑‑ exactly in a particular position: ***directly opposite/below/ahead*** ◇ *They remain directly opposed to these new plans.* **3** immediately: *She left directly after the show.* **4** (*old-fashioned, BrE*) soon SYN **shortly**: *Tell them I'll be there directly.*

■ ***conj.*** (*BrE*) as soon as: *I went home directly I had finished work.*

di,rect 'mail *noun* [U] advertisements that are sent to people through the post/mail

di,rect 'marketing *noun* [U] the business of selling products or services directly to customers who order by mail or by telephone instead of going to a shop/store

the di'rect method *noun* [sing.] a way of teaching a foreign language using only that language and not treating the study of grammar as the most important thing

dir·ect·ness /dəˈrektnəs; dɪ-; daɪ-/ *noun* [U] the quality of being simple and clear, so that it is impossible not to understand: *'What's that?' she asked with her usual directness.*

di,rect 'object *noun* (*grammar*) a noun, noun phrase or pronoun that refers to a person or thing that is directly affected by the action of a verb: *In 'I met him in town', the word 'him' is the direct object.* ➲ compare INDIRECT OBJECT

dir·ect·or 🔑 /dəˈrektə(r); dɪ-; daɪ-/ *noun* **1** 🔑 one of a group of senior managers who run a company: *the* ***managing director*** ◇ *an* ***executive/non-executive director*** ◇ *He's on* ***the board of directors.*** **2** 🔑 a person who is in charge of a particular activity or department in a company, a college, etc: *the musical director* ◇ *a regional director* ◇ *the director of education* **3** 🔑 a person in charge of a film/movie or play who tells the actors and staff what to do ➲ compare PRODUCER

dir·ect·or·ate /dəˈrektərət; dɪ-; daɪ-/ *noun* **1** a section of a government department in charge of one particular activity: *the environmental directorate* **2** the group of directors who run a company SYN **board of directors**

di,rector 'general *noun* (*especially BrE*) the head of a large organization, especially a public organization: *the director general of the BBC*

dir·ect·or·ial /ˌdaɪrekˈtɔːriəl/ *adj.* [only before noun] connected with the position or work of a director, especially of a director of films/movies: *The film marks her directorial debut.*

Di,rector of ,Public Prose'cutions *noun* (*abbr.* **DPP**) (in England and Wales) a public official whose job is to decide whether people who are suspected of a crime should be brought to trial

di'rector's chair *noun* a folding wooden chair with crossed legs, a seat and back made of cloth, and sides on which you can rest your arms ➲ VISUAL VOCAB page V18

di'rector's cut *noun* a version of a film/movie, usually released some time after the original is first shown, that is exactly how the director wanted it to be

dir·ect·or·ship /dəˈrektəʃɪp; dɪ-; daɪ-; *NAmE* -tərʃ-/ *noun* the position of a company director; the period during which this is held

dir·ec·tory /dəˈrektəri; dɪ-; daɪ-/ *noun* (*pl.* -ies) **1** a book containing lists of information, usually in alphabetical order, for example people's telephone numbers or the names and addresses of businesses in a particular area: *a* ***telephone/trade directory*** ◇ *a directory of European Trade Associations* **2** a file containing a group of other files or programs in a computer

di,rectory en'quiries (*BrE*) (*NAmE* **di,rectory as'sistance** or *informal* **in·for·ma·tion**) *noun* [U+sing./pl. v.] a telephone service that you can use to find out a person's telephone number

di,rect 'rule *noun* [U] government of a region by a central government, when that region has had its own government in the past

di,rect 'speech *noun* [U] (*grammar*) a speaker's actual words; the use of these in writing: *Only direct speech should go inside inverted commas.* ➲ compare INDIRECT SPEECH, REPORTED SPEECH

di,rect 'tax *noun* (*technical*) a tax which is collected directly from the person who pays it, for example income tax ➲ compare INDIRECT TAX ▸ **di,rect tax'ation** *noun* [U]

dirge /dɜːdʒ; *NAmE* dɜːrdʒ/ *noun* **1** a song sung in the past at a funeral or for a dead person **2** (*informal, disapproving*) any song or piece of music that is too slow and sad

diri·gible /ˈdɪrɪdʒəbl/ *adj., noun*
■ ***adj.*** (*formal*) able to be guided or steered: *a dirigible balloon*
■ ***noun*** an AIRSHIP

dirk /dɜːk; *NAmE* dɜːrk/ *noun* a long heavy pointed knife that was used as a weapon in Scotland in the past

dirndl /ˈdɜːndl; *NAmE* ˈdɜːrndl/ *noun* (from *German*) a very full wide skirt, pulled in tightly at the waist; a dress with a skirt like this and a closely fitting top

dirt 🔑 /dɜːt; *NAmE* dɜːrt/ *noun* [U]
1 🔑 any substance that makes sth dirty, for example dust, soil or mud: *His clothes were covered in dirt.* ◇ *First remove any grease or dirt from the surface.* **2** 🔑 (*especially NAmE*) loose earth or soil: *He picked up a handful of dirt and threw it at them.* ◇ *Pack the dirt firmly round the plants.* ◇ *They lived in a shack with a dirt floor.* ➲ SYNONYMS at SOIL **3** (*informal*) unpleasant or harmful information about sb that could be used to damage their reputation, career, etc: *Do you have any dirt on the new guy?* **4** (*informal*) = EXCREMENT: *dog dirt* IDM see DISH *v.*, TREAT *v.*

'dirt bike *noun* a motorcycle designed for rough ground, especially for competitions ➲ VISUAL VOCAB page V41

,dirt 'cheap *adj., adv.* (*informal*) very cheap: *It was dirt cheap.* ◇ *I got it dirt cheap.*

'dirt farmer *noun* (*NAmE*) a farmer who has poor land and does not make much money, and who does not pay anyone else to work on the farm

,dirt 'poor *adj.* (*NAmE, informal*) extremely poor

'dirt road (*NAmE* also **'dirt track**) *noun* a rough road in the country that is made from hard earth

'dirt track *noun* **1** (*NAmE*) = DIRT ROAD **2** a track made of CINDERS, soil, etc. used for motorcycle racing: *a dirt-track race*

Synonyms

dirty

dusty • filthy • muddy • soiled • grubby • stained

These words all describe sb/sth that is not clean.

dirty not clean; covered with dust, soil, mud, oil, etc: *If your hands are dirty, go and wash them.*

dusty full of dust; covered with dust: *There were shelves full of dusty books.*

filthy very dirty and unpleasant: *It's absolutely filthy in here.*

muddy full of or covered in mud: *Don't you come in here with those muddy boots on!*

soiled (*rather formal*) dirty, especially with waste from the body: *soiled nappies/diapers*

grubby (*rather informal*) rather dirty, usually because it has not been washed: *He hoped she wouldn't notice his grubby shirt cuffs.*

stained (often in compounds) covered with stains; marked with a stain (= a dirty mark that is difficult to remove): *a pair of paint-stained jeans*

PATTERNS
- dirty/dusty/filthy/muddy/soiled/grubby/stained **clothes**
- dirty/dusty/filthy/grubby **hands**
- a dirty/dusty/filthy **room**
- to **get** dirty/dusty/filthy/muddy/stained

dirty 🔑 /ˈdɜːti; *NAmE* ˈdɜːrti/ *adj., verb, adv.*
■ ***adj.*** (**dirt·ier, dirti·est**)
▸ NOT CLEAN **1** 🔑 not clean: *dirty hands/clothes* ◇ *a dirty mark* ◇ *Try not to get too dirty!* ◇ *I always get given the dirty jobs* (= jobs that make you become dirty).
▸ OFFENSIVE **2** 🔑 [usually before noun] connected with sex in an offensive way: *a* ***dirty joke/book*** ◇ *He's got a* ***dirty mind*** (= he often thinks about sex).
▸ UNPLEASANT/DISHONEST **3** [usually before noun] (*informal*) unpleasant or dishonest: *a dirty lie* ◇ *She's a dirty player.* ◇ *He's a great man for doing the dirty jobs* (= jobs which are unpleasant because they involve being dishonest or mean to people).

D

▸ COLOURS **4** [only before noun] dull: *a dirty brown carpet*
▸ DRUGS **5** (*NAmE, slang*) using illegal drugs
IDM **be a dirty 'word** to be a subject or an idea that people think is bad or immoral: *Profit is not a dirty word around here.* **(do sb's) 'dirty work** (to do) the unpleasant or dishonest jobs that sb else does not want to do **do the 'dirty on sb** (*BrE, informal*) to cheat sb who trusts you; to treat sb badly or unfairly: *I'd never do the dirty on my friends.* **,down and 'dirty** (*NAmE, informal*) **1** behaving in an unfair or aggressive way, especially because you want to win: *The candidate again got down and dirty with his rival.* **2** rude and shocking: *The singer got down and dirty at the club last night and made headlines again.* **give sb a dirty 'look** to look at sb in a way that shows you are annoyed with them ➲ more at HAND *n.*, WASH *v.*
■ *verb* **(dirt·ies, dirty·ing, dirt·ied, dirt·ied) ~ sth** to make sth dirty
■ *adv.*
IDM **dirty great/big** (*BrE, informal*) used to emphasize how large sth is: *When I turned round he was pointing a dirty great gun at me.* **play 'dirty** (*informal*) to behave or play a game in an unfair way ➲ more at TALK *v.*

'dirty bomb *noun* a bomb which contains RADIOACTIVE material

,dirty old 'man *noun* (*informal*) an older man whose interest in sex or in sexually attractive young people is considered to be offensive or not natural for sb of his age

,dirty 'trick *noun* **1** [usually pl.] dishonest, secret and often illegal activity by a political group or other organization that is intended to harm the reputation or success of an opponent: *a dirty tricks campaign* **2** an unpleasant and dishonest act: *What a dirty trick to play!*

,dirty week'end *noun* (*BrE, humorous*) a weekend spent away with a sexual partner, often in secret

dis (also **diss**) /dɪs/ *verb* (-ss-) **~ sb** (*informal, especially NAmE*) to show a lack of respect for sb, especially by saying insulting things to them

dis- /dɪs/ *prefix* (in adjectives, adverbs, nouns and verbs) not; the opposite of: *dishonest* ◇ *disagreeably* ◇ *disadvantage* ◇ *disappear*

dis·abil·ity /,dɪsə'bɪləti/ *noun* (*pl.* -ies) **1** [C] a physical or mental condition that means you cannot use a part of your body completely or easily, or that you cannot learn easily: *a* ***physical/mental disability*** ◇ *people with severe learning disabilities* **2** [U] the state of not being able to use a part of your body completely or easily; the state of not being able to learn easily: *He qualifies for help on the grounds of disability.* ➲ note at DISABLED

dis·able /dɪs'eɪbl/ *verb* **1 ~ sb** to injure or affect sb permanently so that, for example, they cannot walk or cannot use a part of their body: *He was disabled in a car accident.* ◇ *a disabling condition* **2 ~ sth** to make sth unable to work so that it cannot be used: *The burglars gained entry to the building after disabling the alarm.*

dis·abled 🔑 /dɪs'eɪbld/ *adj.*
1 🔑 unable to use a part of your body completely or easily because of a physical condition, illness, injury, etc; unable to learn easily: ***physically/mentally disabled*** ◇ *severely disabled* ◇ *He was born disabled.* ◇ *facilities for disabled people* **2 the disabled** *noun* [pl.] people who are disabled: *caring for the sick, elderly and disabled*

dis·able·ment /dɪs'eɪblmənt/ *noun* [U] (*formal*) the state of being disabled or the process of becoming disabled: *The insurance policy covers sudden death or disablement.*

dis·abuse /,dɪsə'bju:z/ *verb* **~ sb (of sth)** (*formal*) to tell sb that what they think is true is, in fact, not true

dis·ad·van·tage 🔑 /,dɪsəd'vɑ:ntɪdʒ; *NAmE* -'væn-/ *noun* [C, U]
something that causes problems and tends to stop sb/sth from succeeding or making progress: *a* ***serious/severe/considerable disadvantage*** ◇ **~ (of sth)** *One* ***major disadvantage*** *of the area is the lack of public transport.* ◇ **~ (to sth)** *There are disadvantages to the plan.* ◇ *What's the* ***main disadvantage?*** ◇ *I was* ***at a disadvantage*** *compared to the younger members of the team.* ◇ *The fact that he didn't speak a foreign language* ***put him at a*** *distinct* ***disadvantage.*** ◇ *I hope my lack of experience won't* ***be to my disadvantage.*** ◇ *The advantages of the scheme far* ***outweighed the disadvantages.*** ◇ *Many children in the class suffered severe social and economic disadvantage.* OPP **advantage** ▸ **dis·ad·van·tage** *verb* **~ sb/sth**

Which Word?

disabled / handicapped

- **Disabled** is the most generally accepted term to refer to people with a permanent illness or injury that makes it difficult for them to use part of their body completely or easily. **Handicapped** is slightly old-fashioned and many people now think it is offensive. People also now prefer to use the word **disability** rather than **handicap**. The expression **disabled people** is often preferred to **the disabled** because it sounds more personal.
- **Disabled** and **disability** can be used with other words to talk about a mental condition: *mentally disabled* ◇ *learning disabilities.*
- If somebody's ability to hear, speak or see has been damaged but not destroyed completely, they have **impaired hearing/speech/sight** (or **vision**). They can be described as **visually/hearing impaired** or **partially sighted**: *The museum has special facilities for blind and partially sighted visitors.*

dis·ad·van·taged /,dɪsəd'vɑ:ntɪdʒd; *NAmE* -'væn-/ *adj.* **1** not having the things, such as education, or enough money, that people need in order to succeed in life SYN **deprived**: ***disadvantaged groups/children*** ◇ *a severely disadvantaged area* OPP **advantaged** ➲ SYNONYMS at POOR **2 the disadvantaged** *noun* [pl.] people who are disadvantaged

dis·ad·van·ta·geous /,dɪsædvæn'teɪdʒəs/ *adj.* **~ (to/for sb)** (*formal*) causing sb to be in a worse situation compared to other people: *The deal will not be disadvantageous to your company.* OPP **advantageous**

dis·af·fect·ed /,dɪsə'fektɪd/ *adj.* no longer satisfied with your situation, organization, belief etc. and therefore not loyal to it: *Some disaffected members left to form a new party.* ▸ **dis·af·fec·tion** /,dɪsə'fekʃn/ *noun* [U]: *There are signs of growing disaffection amongst voters.*

dis·af·fili·ate /,dɪsə'fɪlieɪt/ *verb* [I, T] **~ (sth) (from sth)** to end the link between a group, a company or an organization and a larger one: *The local club has disaffiliated from the National Athletic Association.* ▸ **dis·af·fili·ation** /,dɪsəf-ɪli'eɪʃn/ *noun* [U]

dis·agree 🔑 /,dɪsə'gri:/ *verb*
1 🔑 [I] if two people **disagree** or one person **disagrees** with another about sth, they have a different opinion about it: *Even friends disagree sometimes.* ◇ *No, I disagree. I don't think it would be the right thing to do.* ◇ **~ (with sb) (about/on/over sth)** *He disagreed with his parents on most things.* ◇ *Some people disagree with this argument.* ◇ **~ that ...** *Few would disagree that students learn best when they are interested in the topic.* **2** 🔑 [I] if statements or reports **disagree**, they give different information OPP **agree**
PHR V **disa'gree with sb** if sth, especially food, **disagrees** with you, it has a bad effect on you and makes you feel ill/sick **disa'gree with sth/with doing sth** 🔑 to believe that sth is bad or wrong; to disapprove of sth: *I disagree with violent protests.*

dis·agree·able /,dɪsə'gri:əbl/ *adj.* (*formal*) **1** not nice or enjoyable SYN **unpleasant**: *a disagreeable smell/experience/job* **2** (of a person) rude and unfriendly SYN **unpleasant**: *a disagreeable bad-tempered man* OPP **agreeable** ▸ **dis·agree·ably** /-əbli/ *adv.*

dis·agree·ment 🔑 /,dɪsə'gri:mənt/ *noun*
1 🔑 [U, C] a situation where people have different opinions about sth and often argue: **~ (about/on/over/as to sth)** *Disagreement arose about exactly how to plan the show.*

◇ *disagreement on the method to be used* ◇ *There is considerable disagreement over the safety of the treatment.* ◇ **~ (between A and B)** *It was a source of disagreement between the two states.* ◇ **~ (among...)** *There is disagreement among archaeologists as to the age of the sculpture.* ◇ **~ (with sb)** *They have had several disagreements with their neighbours.* **OPP agreement 2** [U, C] **~ between A and B** a difference between two things that should be the same: *The comparison shows considerable disagreement between theory and practice.*

dis·allow /ˌdɪsəˈlaʊ/ *verb* **~ sth** [often passive] (*formal*) to officially refuse to accept sth because it is not valid: *to **disallow a claim/an appeal*** ◇ *The second goal was disallowed.* ➲ compare ALLOW (6)

dis·am·bigu·ate /ˌdɪsæmˈbɪgjueɪt/ *verb* **~ sth** (*technical*) to show clearly the difference between two or more words, phrases, etc. which are similar in meaning

dis·ap·pear 🔑 /ˌdɪsəˈpɪə(r); *NAmE* -ˈpɪr/ *verb* **1** 🔑 [I] **(+ adv./prep.)** to become impossible to see **SYN vanish**: *The plane disappeared behind a cloud.* ◇ *Lisa watched until the train **disappeared from view**.* **2** 🔑 [I] to stop existing **SYN vanish**: *Her nervousness quickly disappeared once she was on stage.* ◇ *The problem won't just disappear.* ◇ *Our countryside is disappearing at an alarming rate.* **3** 🔑 [I] to be lost or impossible to find **SYN vanish**: *I can never find a pen in this house. They disappear as soon as I buy them.* ◇ **~ from sth** *The child disappeared from his home some time after four.* ▶ **dis·ap·pear·ance** /-ˈpɪərəns; *NAmE* -ˈpɪr-/ *noun* [U, C]: *the disappearance of many species of plants and animals from our planet* ◇ *Police are investigating the disappearance of a young woman.* **IDM** see ACT *n.*, FACE *n.*

dis·ap·point 🔑 /ˌdɪsəˈpɔɪnt/ *verb* **1** 🔑 [T, I] **~ (sb) | (it disappoints sb that...)** to make sb feel sad because sth that they hope for or expect to happen does not happen or is not as good as they hoped: *Her decision to cancel the concert is bound to disappoint her fans.* ◇ *I hate to disappoint you, but I'm just not interested.* ◇ *The movie had disappointed her* (= it wasn't as good as she had expected). ◇ *His latest novel does not disappoint.* **2** [T] **~ sth** to prevent sth that sb hopes for from becoming a reality: *The new government had soon disappointed the hopes of many of its supporters.*

dis·ap·point·ed 🔑 /ˌdɪsəˈpɔɪntɪd/ *adj.* upset because sth you hoped for has not happened or been as good, successful, etc. as you expected: **~ (at/by sth)** *They were **bitterly disappointed** at the result of the game.* ◇ *I was disappointed by the quality of the wine.* ◇ **~ (in/with sb/sth)** *I'm disappointed in you—I really thought I could trust you!* ◇ *I was very disappointed with myself.* ◇ **~ (to see, hear, etc.)** *He was disappointed to see she wasn't at the party.* ◇ **~ (that...)** *I'm disappointed (that) it was sold out.* ◇ **~ (not) to be...** *She was disappointed not to be chosen.*

dis·ap·point·ing 🔑 /ˌdɪsəˈpɔɪntɪŋ/ *adj.* not as good, successful, etc. as you had hoped; making you feel disappointed: *a disappointing result/performance* ◇ *The outcome of the court case was disappointing for the family involved.* ▶ **dis·ap·point·ing·ly** *adv.*: *The room was disappointingly small.*

dis·ap·point·ment 🔑 /ˌdɪsəˈpɔɪntmənt/ *noun* **1** 🔑 [U] sadness because sth has not happened or been as good, successful, etc. as you expected or hoped: *Book early for the show to avoid disappointment.* ◇ ***To our great disappointment**, it rained every day of the trip.* ◇ *He found it difficult to hide his disappointment when she didn't arrive.* **2** 🔑 [C] a person or thing that is disappointing: *a **bitter/major disappointment*** ◇ *That new restaurant was a big disappointment.* ◇ **~ to sb** *I always felt I was a disappointment to my father.*

dis·ap·pro·ba·tion /ˌdɪsˌæprəˈbeɪʃn/ *noun* [U] (*formal*) disapproval of sb/sth that you think is morally wrong

dis·ap·proval 🔑 /ˌdɪsəˈpruːvl/ *noun* [U] **~ (of sb/sth)** a feeling that you do not like an idea, an action or sb's behaviour because you think it is bad, not suitable or going to have a bad effect on sb else: *disapproval of his methods* ◇ *to show/express disapproval* ◇ *He shook his head **in disapproval**.* ◇ *She looked at my clothes **with disapproval**.* **OPP approval**

dis·ap·prove 🔑 /ˌdɪsəˈpruːv/ *verb* [I, T] to think that sb/sth is not good or suitable; to not approve of sb/sth: *She wants to be an actress, but her parents disapprove.* ◇ **~ of sb/sth** *He **strongly disapproved** of the changes that had been made.* ◇ **~ sth** (*NAmE*) *A solid majority disapproves the way the president is handling the controversy.* **OPP approve**

dis·ap·prov·ing 🔑 /ˌdɪsəˈpruːvɪŋ/ *adj.* showing that you do not approve of sb/sth: *a **disapproving glance/tone/look*** **OPP approving** ▶ **dis·ap·prov·ing·ly** *adv.*: *He looked disapprovingly at the row of empty wine bottles.*

dis·arm /dɪsˈɑːm; *NAmE* -ˈɑːrm/ *verb* **1** [T] **~ sb** to take a weapon or weapons away from sb: *Most of the rebels were captured and disarmed.* **2** [I] (of a country or a group of people) to reduce the size of an army or to give up some or all weapons, especially nuclear weapons **3** [T] **~ sb** to make sb feel less angry or critical: *He disarmed her immediately by apologizing profusely.* ➲ compare ARM

dis·arma·ment /dɪsˈɑːməmənt; *NAmE* -ˈɑːrm-/ *noun* [U] the fact of a country reducing the size of its armed forces or the number of weapons, especially nuclear weapons, that it has: *nuclear disarmament* ◇ *disarmament talks* ➲ compare ARMAMENT

dis·arm·ing /dɪsˈɑːmɪŋ; *NAmE* -ˈɑːrm-/ *adj.* making people feel less angry or suspicious than they were before: *a disarming smile* ▶ **dis·arm·ing·ly** *adv.*: *disarmingly frank*

dis·ar·range /ˌdɪsəˈreɪndʒ/ *verb* [usually passive] **~ sth** (*formal*) to make sth untidy

dis·array /ˌdɪsəˈreɪ/ *noun* [U] a state of confusion and lack of organization in a situation or a place: *The peace talks broke up **in disarray**.* ◇ *Our plans were **thrown into disarray** by her arrival.*

dis·as·sem·ble /ˌdɪsəˈsembl/ *verb* **1** [T] **~ sth** to take apart a machine or structure so that it is in separate pieces: *We had to completely disassemble the engine to find the problem.* **OPP assemble 2** [T] **~ sth** (*computing*) to translate sth from computer code into a language that can be read by humans **3** [I] (*formal*) (of a group of people) to move apart and go away in different directions: *The concert ended and the crowd disassembled.*

dis·as·sem·bler /ˌdɪsəˈsemblə(r)/ *noun* (*computing*) a program used to disassemble computer code

dis·as·so·ci·ate /ˌdɪsəˈsəʊʃieɪt; -ˈsəʊs-; *NAmE* -ˈsoʊ-/ *verb* = DISSOCIATE

dis·as·ter 🔑 /dɪˈzɑːstə(r); *NAmE* -ˈzæs-/ *noun* **1** 🔑 [C] an unexpected event, such as a very bad accident, a flood or a fire, that kills a lot of people or causes a lot of damage **SYN catastrophe**: *an **air disaster*** ◇ *environmental disasters* ◇ *Thousands died in the disaster.* ◇ *a **natural disaster*** (= one that is caused by nature) **2** 🔑 [C, U] a very bad situation that causes problems: *Losing your job doesn't have to be such a disaster.* ◇ ***Disaster struck** when the wheel came off.* ◇ *financial disaster* ◇ *Letting her organize the party is a **recipe for disaster*** (= something that is likely to go badly wrong). **3** 🔑 [C, U] (*informal*) a complete failure: *As a teacher, he's a disaster.* ◇ *The play's first night was a total disaster.* **IDM** see WAIT *v.*

diˈsaster area *noun* **1** a place where a disaster has happened and which needs special help **2** (*informal*) a place or situation that has a lot of problems, is a failure, or is badly organized

dis·as·trous /dɪˈzɑːstrəs; *NAmE* -ˈzæs-/ *adj.* very bad, harmful or unsuccessful **SYN catastrophic, devastating**: *a disastrous harvest/fire/result* ◇ *Lowering interest rates could have disastrous consequences for the economy.* ▶ **dis·as·trous·ly** *adv.*: *How could everything go so disastrously wrong?*

dis·avow /ˌdɪsəˈvaʊ/ *verb* **~ sth** (*formal*) to state publicly that you have no knowledge of sth or that you are not responsible for sth/sb: *They disavowed claims of a split in the party.* ▸ **dis·avowal** /-ˈvaʊəl/ *noun* [C, U]

dis·band /dɪsˈbænd/ *verb* [T, I] **~ (sb/sth)** to stop sb/sth from operating as a group; to separate or no longer operate as a group: *They set about disbanding the terrorist groups.* ◇ *The committee formally disbanded in August.* ▸ **dis·band·ment** *noun* [U]

D

dis·bar /dɪsˈbɑː(r)/ *verb* (-rr-) [usually passive] **~ sb (from sth/from doing sth)** to stop a lawyer from working in the legal profession, especially because he or she has done sth illegal

dis·be·lief /ˌdɪsbɪˈliːf/ *noun* [U] the feeling of not being able to believe sth: *He stared at me **in disbelief**.* ◇ *To enjoy the movie you have to **suspend your disbelief*** (= pretend to believe sth, even if it seems very unlikely). ➲ compare BELIEF (3), UNBELIEF

dis·be·lieve /ˌdɪsbɪˈliːv/ *verb* [T, I] (not used in the progressive tenses) **~ (sth)** (*formal*) to not believe that sth is true or that sb is telling the truth: *Why should I disbelieve her story?* ▸ **dis·be·liev·ing** *adj.*: *a **disbelieving look/smile/laugh*** **dis·be·liev·ing·ly** *adv.*

PHR V **disbeˈlieve in sth** to not believe that sth exists

dis·burse /dɪsˈbɜːs; *NAmE* -ˈbɜːrs/ *verb* **~ sth** (*formal*) to pay money to sb from a large amount that has been collected for a purpose ▸ **dis·burse·ment** *noun* [U, C]: *the disbursement of funds* ◇ *aid disbursements*

disc 0‑ (also **disk** especially in *NAmE*) /dɪsk/ *noun* **1** 0‑ a thin flat round object: *He wears an identity disc around his neck.* **2** 0‑ = CD: *This recording is available on-line or **on disc**.* **3** 0‑ (*BrE*) a disk for a computer **4** (*old-fashioned*) = RECORD (2) **5** a structure made of CARTILAGE between the bones of the back: *He's been off work with a **slipped disc*** (= one that has moved from its correct position, causing pain).

dis·card *verb, noun*

■ ***verb*** /dɪsˈkɑːd; *NAmE* -ˈkɑːrd/ **1** [T] (*formal*) to get rid of sth that you no longer want or need: **~ sb/sth** *The room was littered with discarded newspapers.* ◇ *He had discarded his jacket because of the heat.* ◇ (*figurative*) *She could now discard all thought of promotion.* ◇ **~ sb/sth as sth** *10% of the data was discarded as unreliable* **2** [T, I] **~ (sth)** (in card games) to get rid of a card that you do not want

■ ***noun*** /ˈdɪskɑːd; *NAmE* -kɑːrd/ a person or thing that is not wanted or thrown away, especially a card in a card game

ˈ**disc brake** *noun* [usually pl.] a BRAKE that works by two surfaces pressing onto a disc in the centre of a wheel

dis·cern /dɪˈsɜːn; *NAmE* -ˈsɜːrn/ *verb* (not used in the progressive tenses) (*formal*) **1** to know, recognize or understand sth, especially sth that is not obvious SYN **detect**: **~ sth** *It is possible to discern a number of different techniques in her work.* ◇ *He discerned a certain coldness in their welcome.* ◇ **~ how, whether, etc...** *It is often difficult to discern how widespread public support is.* ◇ **~ that...** *I quickly discerned that something was wrong.* **2 ~ sth** to see or hear sth, but not very clearly SYN **make out**: *We could just discern the house in the distance.* ▸ **dis·cern·ible** *adj.* (*formal*) SYN **perceptible**: *There is often no discernible difference between rival brands.* ◇ *His face was barely discernible in the gloom.*

dis·cern·ing /dɪˈsɜːnɪŋ; *NAmE* -ˈsɜːrn-/ *adj.* (*approving*) able to show good judgement about the quality of sb/sth

dis·cern·ment /dɪˈsɜːnmənt; *NAmE* -ˈsɜːrn-/ *noun* [U] (*formal, approving*) the ability to show good judgement about the quality of sb/sth SYN **discrimination**: *He shows great discernment in his choice of friends.*

dis·charge *verb, noun*

■ ***verb*** /dɪsˈtʃɑːdʒ; *NAmE* -ˈtʃɑːrdʒ/ (*formal*)

▸ FROM HOSPITAL/JOB **1** [T, usually passive] **~ sb (from sth)** to give sb official permission to leave a place or job; to make sb leave a job: *Patients were being discharged from the hospital too early.* ◇ *She had discharged herself against medical advice.* ◇ *He was discharged from the army following his injury.* ◇ *She was discharged from the police force for bad conduct.*

▸ FROM PRISON/COURT **2** [T, often passive] **~ sb** to allow sb to leave prison or court: *He was **conditionally discharged** after admitting the theft.*

▸ GAS/LIQUID **3** [I, T] when a gas or a liquid **discharges** or **is discharged**, or sb **discharges** it, it flows somewhere: **~ (into sth)** *The river is diverted through the power station before discharging into the sea.* ◇ **~ sth (into sth)** *The factory was fined for discharging chemicals into the river.*

▸ FORCE/POWER **4** [T, I] **~ (sth)** (*technical*) to release force or power: *Lightning is caused by clouds discharging electricity.*

▸ DUTY **5** [T] **~ sth** to do everything that is necessary to perform and complete a particular duty: *to **discharge your duties/responsibilities/obligations*** ◇ *to **discharge a debt*** (= to pay it)

▸ GUN **6** [T] **~ sth** to fire a gun, etc.

■ ***noun*** /ˈdɪstʃɑːdʒ; *NAmE* -tʃɑːrdʒ/ (*formal*)

▸ OF LIQUID/GAS **1** [U, C] the action of releasing a substance such as a liquid or gas; a substance that comes out from inside somewhere: *a ban on the discharge of toxic waste* ◇ *thunder and lightning caused by electrical discharges* ◇ ***nasal/vaginal discharge*** (= from the nose/VAGINA)

▸ FROM HOSPITAL/JOB **2** [U, C] **~ (from sth)** the act of officially allowing sb, or of telling sb, to leave somewhere, especially sb in a hospital or the army

▸ OF DUTY **3** [U] the act of performing a task or a duty or of paying money that is owed: *the **discharge of debts/obligations***

dis·ciple /dɪˈsaɪpl/ *noun* **1** a person who believes in and follows the teachings of a religious or political leader SYN **follower**: *a disciple of the economist John Maynard Keynes* **2** (according to the Bible) one of the people who followed Jesus Christ and his teachings when he was living on earth, especially one of the twelve APOSTLES

dis·cip·lin·ar·ian /ˌdɪsəplɪˈneəriən; *NAmE* -ˈner-/ *noun* a person who believes in using rules and punishments for controlling people: *She's a very strict disciplinarian.*

dis·cip·lin·ary /ˈdɪsəplɪnəri; ˌdɪsəˈplɪnəri; *NAmE* ˈdɪsəpləneri/ *adj.* connected with the punishment of people who break rules: *a disciplinary hearing* (= to decide if sb has done sth wrong) ◇ *The company will be taking **disciplinary action** against him.*

dis·cip·line 0‑ /ˈdɪsəplɪn/ *noun, verb*

■ ***noun*** **1** 0‑ [U] the practice of training people to obey rules and orders and punishing them if they do not; the controlled behaviour or situation that results from this training: *The school has a reputation for high standards of discipline.* ◇ *Strict discipline is imposed on army recruits.* ◇ *She keeps good discipline in class.* **2** [C] a method of training your mind or body or of controlling your behaviour; an area of activity where this is necessary: *Yoga is a good discipline for learning to relax.* **3** [U] the ability to control your behaviour or the way you live, work, etc: *He'll never get anywhere working for himself—he's got no discipline.* ➲ see also SELF-DISCIPLINE **4** [C] (*formal*) an area of knowledge; a subject that people study or are taught, especially in a university

■ ***verb*** **1 ~ sb (for sth)** to punish sb for sth they have done: *The officers were disciplined for using racist language.* **2 ~ sb** to train sb, especially a child, to obey particular rules and control the way they behave: *a guide to the best ways of disciplining your child* **3** to control the way you behave and make yourself do things that you believe you should do: **~ yourself** *Dieting is a matter of disciplining yourself.* ◇ **~ yourself to do sth** *He disciplined himself to exercise at least three times a week.* ▸ **dis·cip·lined** *adj.*: *a disciplined army/team* ◇ *a disciplined approach to work*

ˈ**disc jockey** *noun* (*abbr.* **DJ**) (also *informal* **dee·jay**) a person whose job is to introduce and play recorded popular music, on radio or television or at a club

dis·claim /dɪsˈkleɪm/ *verb* (*formal*) **1 ~ sth** to state publicly that you have no knowledge of sth, or that you are not responsible for sth SYN **deny**: *She disclaimed any knowledge of her husband's whereabouts.* ◇ *The rebels disclaimed all responsibility for the explosion.* **2 ~ sth** to give up your right to sth, such as property or a title SYN **renounce**

D

dis·claim·er /dɪsˈkleɪmə(r)/ *noun* **1** (*formal*) a statement in which sb says that they are not connected with or responsible for sth, or that they do not have any knowledge of it **2** (*law*) a statement in which a person says officially that they do not claim the right to do sth

dis·close /dɪsˈkləʊz; *NAmE* -ˈkloʊz/ *verb* (*formal*) **1** to give sb information about sth, especially sth that was previously secret SYN **reveal**: **~ sth (to sb)** *The spokesman refused to disclose details of the takeover to the press.* ◇ **~ that...** *The report discloses that human error was to blame for the accident.* ◇ **it is disclosed that...** *It was disclosed that two women were being interviewed by the police.* ◇ **~ what, whether, etc...** *I cannot disclose what we discussed.* **2 ~ sth** to allow sth that was hidden to be seen SYN **reveal**: *The door swung open, disclosing a long dark passage.*

dis·clo·sure /dɪsˈkləʊʒə(r); *NAmE* -ˈkloʊ-/ *noun* (*formal*) **1** [U] the act of making sth known or public that was previously secret or private SYN **revelation**: *the newspaper's disclosure of defence secrets* **2** [C] information or a fact that is made known or public that was previously secret or private SYN **revelation**: *startling disclosures about his private life*

disco /ˈdɪskəʊ; *NAmE* ˈdɪskoʊ/ (*pl.* -os) *noun* **1** (also *old-fashioned* **disco·theque**) a club or party where people dance to recorded pop music: ***disco music/dancing*** ◇ *the youth club disco* **2** the lights and sound equipment for such an event

disc·og·raphy /dɪsˈkɒɡrəfi; *NAmE* -ˈkɑːɡ-/ *noun* (*pl.* **disc·og·raph·ies**) **1** [C] all of the music that has been performed, written or collected by a particular person; a list of this music **2** [U] the study of musical recordings or collections

dis·col·or·ation (*BrE* also **dis·col·our·ation**) /ˌdɪsˌkʌləˈreɪʃn/ *noun* **1** [U] the process of becoming discoloured: *discoloration caused by the sun* **2** [C] a place where sth has become discoloured

dis·col·our (*especially US* **dis·color**) /dɪsˈkʌlə(r)/ *verb* [I, T] to change colour, or to make the colour of sth change, in a way that makes it look less attractive: *Plastic tends to discolour with age.* ◇ **~ sth** *The pipes were beginning to rust, discolouring the water.*

dis·comfit /dɪsˈkʌmfɪt/ *verb* [often passive] **~ sb** (*literary*) to make sb feel confused or embarrassed ▸ **dis·com·fit·ure** /dɪsˈkʌmfɪtʃə(r)/ *noun* [U]: *He was clearly taking delight in her discomfiture.*

dis·com·fort /dɪsˈkʌmfət; *NAmE* -fərt/ *noun, verb*

■ ***noun*** (*formal*) **1** [U] a feeling of slight pain or of being physically uncomfortable: *You will experience some minor discomfort during the treatment.* ◇ *abdominal discomfort* **2** [U] a feeling of worry or embarrassment SYN **unease**: *John's presence caused her considerable discomfort.* **3** [C] something that makes you feel uncomfortable or causes you a slight feeling of pain

■ ***verb*** [often passive] **~ sb** (*formal*) to make sb feel anxious or embarrassed

dis·com·pose /ˌdɪskəmˈpəʊz; *NAmE* -ˈpoʊz/ *verb* **~ sb** (*formal*) to disturb sb and make them feel anxious SYN **disconcert, disturb** ▸ **dis·com·pos·ure** /ˌdɪskəmˈpəʊʒə(r); *NAmE* -ˈpoʊ-/ *noun* [U]

dis·con·cert /ˌdɪskənˈsɜːt; *NAmE* -ˈsɜːrt/ *verb* **~ sb** to make sb feel anxious, confused or embarrassed SYN **disturb**: *His answer rather disconcerted her.* ▸ **dis·con·cert·ed** *adj.*: *I was disconcerted to find that everyone else already knew it.* **dis·con·cert·ing** *adj.*: *She had the disconcerting habit of saying exactly what she thought.* **dis·con·cert·ing·ly** *adv.*

dis·con·nect /ˌdɪskəˈnekt/ *verb* **1** [T] **~ sth (from sth)** to remove a piece of equipment from a supply of gas, water or electricity: *First, disconnect the boiler from the water mains.* **2** [T] **~ sb/sth** [usually passive] to officially stop the supply of telephone lines, water, electricity or gas to a building: *You may be disconnected if you do not pay the bill.* **3** [T] **~ sth (from sth)** to separate sth from sth: *The ski had become disconnected from the boot.* **4** [T] **~ sb** [usually passive] to break the contact between two people who are talking on the telephone: *We were suddenly disconnected.* **5** [T, I, often passive] to end a connection to the Internet: **~ sb (from sth)** *I keep getting disconnected when I'm online.* ◇ **~ (from sth)** *My computer crashes every time I disconnect from the Internet.* OPP **connect** ▸ **dis·con·nec·tion** *noun* [U, C]

dis·con·nect·ed /ˌdɪskəˈnektɪd/ *adj.* **1** not related to or connected with the things or people around: ***disconnected images/thoughts/ideas*** ◇ *I felt disconnected from the world around me.* **2** (of speech or writing) with the parts not connected in a logical order SYN **disjointed, incoherent**

dis·con·so·late /dɪsˈkɒnsələt; *NAmE* -ˈkɑːn-/ *adj.* (*formal*) very unhappy and disappointed SYN **dejected** ▸ **dis·con·so·late·ly** *adv.*

dis·con·tent /ˌdɪskənˈtent/ (also **dis·con·tent·ment** /ˌdɪskənˈtentmənt/) *noun* [U, C] **~ (at/over/with sth)** a feeling of being unhappy because you are not satisfied with a particular situation; sth that makes you have this feeling SYN **dissatisfaction**: *There is widespread discontent among the staff at the proposed changes to pay and conditions.* ⊃ compare CONTENTMENT

dis·con·tent·ed /ˌdɪskənˈtentɪd/ *adj.* **~ (with sth)** unhappy because you are not satisfied with your situation SYN **dissatisfied** OPP **contented** ▸ **dis·con·tent·ed·ly** *adv.*

dis·con·tinue /ˌdɪskənˈtɪnjuː/ *verb* (*formal*) **1 ~ (doing) sth** to stop doing, using or providing sth, especially sth that you have been doing, using or providing regularly: *It was decided to discontinue the treatment after three months.* **2** [usually passive] **~ sth** to stop making a product: *a sale of discontinued china*

dis·con·tinu·ity /ˌdɪsˌkɒntɪˈnjuːəti; *NAmE* -ˌkɑːntəˈnuː-/ *noun* (*pl.* -ies) (*formal*) **1** [U] the state of not being continuous: *discontinuity in the children's education* **2** [C] a break or change in a continuous process: *Changes in government led to discontinuities in policy.* OPP **continuity**

dis·con·tinu·ous /ˌdɪskənˈtɪnjuəs/ *adj.* (*formal*) not continuous; stopping and starting again SYN **intermittent**

dis·cord /ˈdɪskɔːd; *NAmE* -kɔːrd/ *noun* **1** [U] (*formal*) disagreement; arguing: ***marital/family discord*** ◇ *A note of discord surfaced during the proceedings.* OPP **concord** ⊃ compare HARMONY **2** [C, U] (*music*) a combination of musical notes that do not sound pleasant together

dis·cord·ant /dɪsˈkɔːdənt; *NAmE* -ˈkɔːrd-/ *adj.* **1** [usually before noun] (*formal*) not in agreement; combining with other things in a way that is strange or unpleasant: *discordant views* **2** (of sounds) not sounding pleasant together OPP **harmonious**

disco·theque /ˈdɪskətek/ *noun* (*old-fashioned*) = DISCO

dis·count 🔑 *noun, verb*

■ ***noun*** 🔑 /ˈdɪskaʊnt/ [C, U] an amount of money that is taken off the usual cost of sth SYN **reduction**: *to **get/give/offer a discount*** ◇ ***discount rates/prices*** ◇ **~ (on/off sth)** *They're offering a 10% discount on all sofas this month.* ◇ *They were selling everything **at a discount*** (= at reduced prices). ◇ *a **discount shop*** (= one that regularly sells goods at reduced prices) ◇ *Do you give any discount?* ⊃ COLLOCATIONS at SHOPPING

■ ***verb*** /dɪsˈkaʊnt; *NAmE* also ˈdɪskaʊnt/ **1** (*formal*) to think or say that sth is not important or not true SYN **dismiss**: **~ sth** *We cannot **discount the possibility of** further strikes.* ◇ **~ sth as sth** *The news reports were being discounted as propaganda.* **2 ~ sth** to take an amount of money off the usual cost of sth; to sell sth at a discount SYN **reduce**: ***discounted prices/fares***

dis·counter /ˈdɪskaʊntə(r)/ (also ˈ**discount store**) *noun* a shop/store that sells things very cheaply, often in large quantities or from a limited range of goods

ˈ**discount rate** *noun* (*finance*) **1** the minimum rate of interest that banks in the US and some other countries must pay when they borrow money from other banks **2** the amount that the price of a BILL OF EXCHANGE is re-

D

duced by when it is bought before it reaches its full value **3** the rate at which an investment increases in value each year

dis·cour·age /dɪs'kʌrɪdʒ; *NAmE* -'kɜːr-/ *verb* **1** to try to prevent sth or to prevent sb from doing sth, especially by making it difficult to do or by showing that you do not approve of it: **~ (doing) sth** *a campaign to discourage smoking among teenagers* ◇ **~ sb** *I leave a light on when I'm out to discourage burglars.* ◇ **~ sb from doing sth** *His parents tried to discourage him from being an actor.* **2** to make sb feel less confident or enthusiastic about doing sth SYN **dishearten**: **~ sb** *Don't be discouraged by the first failure—try again!* ◇ **~ sb from doing sth** *The weather discouraged people from attending.* OPP **encourage** ▸ **dis·cour·aged** *adj.* [not usually before noun] SYN **disheartened**: *Learners can feel very discouraged if an exercise is too difficult.* **dis·cour·aging** *adj.*: *a* ***discouraging experience/response/result*** **dis·cour·aging·ly** *adv.*

dis·cour·age·ment /dɪs'kʌrɪdʒmənt; *NAmE* -'kɜːr-/ *noun* **1** [U] a feeling that you no longer have the confidence or enthusiasm to do sth: *an atmosphere of discouragement and despair* **2** [U] the action of trying to stop sth: *the government's discouragement of political protest* **3** [C] a thing that discourages sb from doing sth: *Despite all these discouragements, she refused to give up.*

dis·course *noun, verb*

■ ***noun*** /'dɪskɔːs; *NAmE* -kɔːrs/ **1** [C, U] (*formal*) a long and serious treatment or discussion of a subject in speech or writing: *a discourse on issues of gender and sexuality* ◇ *He was hoping for some lively political discourse at the meeting.* **2** [U] (*linguistics*) the use of language in speech and writing in order to produce meaning; language that is studied, usually in order to see how the different parts of a text are connected: ***spoken/written discourse*** ◇ *discourse analysis*

■ ***verb*** /dɪs'kɔːs; *NAmE* -'kɔːrs/

PHR V **dis'course on/upon sth** (*formal*) to talk or give a long speech about sth that you know a lot about

'discourse marker *noun* (*grammar*) a word or phrase that organizes spoken language into different parts, for example 'Well...' or 'On the other hand...'

dis·cour·teous /dɪs'kɜːtiəs; *NAmE* -'kɜːrt-/ *adj.* (*formal*) having bad manners and not showing respect for other people SYN **impolite** OPP **courteous** ➲ SYNONYMS at RUDE

dis·cour·tesy /dɪs'kɜːtəsi; *NAmE* -'kɜːrt-/ *noun* [U, C] (*pl.* -ies) (*formal*) behaviour or an action that is not polite

dis·cover 🔑 /dɪ'skʌvə(r)/ *verb*
1 🔑 **~ sth** to be the first person to become aware that a particular place or thing exists: *Cook is credited with discovering Hawaii.* ◇ *Scientists around the world are working to discover a cure for AIDS.* **2** 🔑 to find sb/sth that was hidden or that you did not expect to find: **~ sb/sth** *Police discovered a large stash of drugs while searching the house.* ◇ *We discovered this beach while we were sailing around the island.* ◇ **~ sb/sth doing sth** *He was discovered hiding in a shed.* ◇ **~ sb/sth + adj.** *She was discovered dead at her home in Leeds.* **3** 🔑 to find out about sth; to find some information about sth: **~ sth** *I've just discovered hang-gliding!* ◇ **~ (that)...** *It was a shock to discover (that) he couldn't read.* ◇ **~ why, how, etc...** *We never did discover why she gave up her job.* ◇ **it is discovered that...** *It was later discovered that the diaries were a fraud.* ◇ **sb/sth is discovered to be/have ...** *He was later discovered to be seriously ill.* **4** [often passive] **~ sb** to be the first person to realize that sb is very good at singing, acting, etc. and help them to become successful and famous: *The singer was discovered while still at school.* ▸ **dis·cov·er·er** *noun*: *the discoverer of penicillin*

dis·cov·ery 🔑 /dɪ'skʌvəri/ *noun* (*pl.* -ies)
1 🔑 [C, U] an act or the process of finding sb/sth, or learning about sth that was not known about before: **~ (of sth)** *the discovery of antibiotics in the 20th century* ◇ *The discovery of a child's body in the river has shocked the community.* ◇ *the discovery of new talent in the art world* ◇ *Researchers in this field have* ***made*** *some important new* ***discoveries.*** ◇ *He saw life as a voyage of discovery.* ◇ **~ (that...)** *She was shocked by the discovery that he had been unfaithful.* **2** 🔑 [C] a thing, fact or person that is found or learned about for the first time: *The drug is not a new discovery—it's been known about for years.*

dis·credit /dɪs'kredɪt/ *verb, noun*

■ ***verb*** **1 ~ sb/sth** to make people stop respecting sb/sth: *The photos were deliberately taken to discredit the President.* ◇ *a discredited* ***government/policy*** **2 ~ sth** to make people stop believing that sth is true; to make sth appear unlikely to be true: *These theories are now largely discredited among linguists.*

■ ***noun*** [U] (*formal*) damage to sb's reputation; loss of respect: *Violent football fans* ***bring discredit on*** *the teams they support.* ◇ *Britain,* ***to its discredit,*** *did not speak out against these atrocities.* ➲ compare CREDIT *n.* (7)

dis·cred·it·able /dɪs'kredɪtəbl/ *adj.* (*formal*) bad and unacceptable; causing people to lose respect

dis·creet /dɪ'skriːt/ *adj.* careful in what you say or do, in order to keep sth secret or to avoid causing embarrassment or difficulty for sb SYN **tactful**: *He was always very discreet about his love affairs.* ◇ *You ought to make a few discreet enquiries before you sign anything.* ▸ **dis·creet·ly** *adv.*: *She coughed discreetly to announce her presence.*

> **WORD FAMILY**
> **discreet** *adj.* (≠ indiscreet)
> **discretion** *noun* (≠ indiscretion)

dis·crep·ancy /dɪs'krepənsi/ *noun* (*pl.* -ies) [C, U] a difference between two or more things that should be the same: **~ (in sth)** *wide discrepancies in prices quoted for the work* ◇ **~ (between A and B)** *What are the reasons for the discrepancy between girls' and boys' performance in school?*

dis·crete AW /dɪ'skriːt/ *adj.* (*formal* or *technical*) independent of other things of the same type SYN **separate**: *The organisms can be divided into discrete categories.* ▸ **dis·crete·ly** AW *adv.* **dis·crete·ness** *noun* [U]

dis·cre·tion AW /dɪ'skreʃn/ *noun* [U] **1** the freedom or power to decide what should be done in a particular situation: *I'll leave it up to you to* ***use your discretion.*** ◇ *How much to tell terminally ill patients is* ***left to the discretion of*** *the doctor.* **2** care in what you say or do, in order to keep sth secret or to avoid causing embarrassment to or difficulty for sb; the quality of being DISCREET: *This is confidential, but I know that I can rely on your discretion.* ➲ compare INDISCRETION

IDM **at sb's di'scretion** according to what sb decides or wishes to do: *Bail is granted at the discretion of the court.* ◇ *There is no service charge and tipping is at your discretion.* **di,scretion is the ,better part of 'valour** (*saying*) you should avoid danger and not take unnecessary risks

dis·cre·tion·ary AW /dɪ'skreʃənəri; *NAmE* -neri/ *adj.* [usually before noun] (*formal*) decided according to the judgement of a person in authority about what is necessary in each particular situation; not decided by rules: *You may be eligible for a discretionary grant for your university course.*

dis·crim·in·ate AW /dɪ'skrɪmɪneɪt/ *verb* **1** [I, T] to recognize that there is a difference between people or things; to show a difference between people or things SYN **differentiate, distinguish**: **~ (between A and B)** *The computer program was unable to discriminate between letters and numbers.* ◇ **~ sth** *When do babies learn to discriminate voices?* ◇ **~ A from B** *A number of features discriminate this species from others.* **2** [I] to treat one person or group worse/better than another in an unfair way: **~ (against sb)** | **~ (in favour of sb)** *practices that discriminate against women and in favour of men* ◇ **~ (on the grounds of sth)** *It is illegal to discriminate on grounds of race, sex or religion.*

dis·crim·in·at·ing /dɪ'skrɪmɪneɪtɪŋ/ *adj.* (*approving*) able to judge the good quality of sth SYN **discerning**: *a* ***discriminating audience/customer***

dis·crim·in·ation AW /dɪ,skrɪmɪ'neɪʃn/ *noun* **1** [U] the practice of treating sb or a particular group in society less fairly than others: ***age/racial/sex/sexual discrimination*** (= because of sb's age, race or sex) ◇ **~ against sb**

discrimination against the elderly ◇ **~ in favour of sb** *discrimination in favour of the young* ◇ **~ on the grounds of sth** *discrimination on the grounds of race, gender, or sexual orientation* ➲ COLLOCATIONS at RACE ➲ see also POSITIVE DISCRIMINATION **2** [U] (*approving*) the ability to judge what is good, true, etc. SYN **discernment**: *He showed great discrimination in his choice of friends.* **3** (*formal*) [U, C] the ability to recognize a difference between one thing and another; a difference that is recognized: *to learn discrimination between right and wrong* ◇ *fine discriminations*

dis·crim·in·atory /dɪˈskrɪmɪnətəri; *NAmE* dɪˈskrɪmɪnətɔːri/ *adj.* unfair; treating sb or one group of people worse than others: ***discriminatory practices/rules/measures*** ◇ ***sexually/racially discriminatory** laws*

dis·cur·sive /dɪsˈkɜːsɪv; *NAmE* -ˈkɜːrs-/ *adj.* (*formal*) (of a style of writing or speaking) moving from one point to another without any strict structure: *the discursive style of the novel*

dis·cus /ˈdɪskəs/ *noun* **1** [C] a heavy flat round object thrown in a sporting event **2 the discus** [sing.] the event or sport of throwing a discus as far as possible ➲ VISUAL VOCAB page V38

Synonyms

discussion

conversation • dialogue • talk • debate • consultation • chat • gossip

These are all words for an occasion when people talk about sth.

discussion a detailed conversation about sth that is considered to be important: *Discussions are still taking place between the two leaders.*

conversation a talk, usually a private or informal one, involving two people or a small group; the activity of talking in this way: *a telephone conversation*

dialogue conversations in a book, play or film: *The novel has long descriptions and not much dialogue.* A **dialogue** is also a formal discussion between two groups, especially when they are trying to solve a problem or end a dispute: *The President told waiting reporters there had been a constructive dialogue.*

talk a conversation or discussion, often one about a problem or sth important for the people involved: *I had a long talk with my boss about my career prospects.*

debate a formal discussion of an issue at a public meeting or in a parliament. In a debate two or more speakers express opposing views and then there is often a vote on the issue: *a debate on prison reform*

consultation a formal discussion between groups of people before a decision is made about sth: *There have been extensive consultations between the two countries.*

chat a friendly informal conversation; informal talking. NOTE The countable use of **chat** is especially British English: *I just called in for a chat about the kids.*

gossip a conversation about other people and their private lives: *We had a good gossip about the boss.*

PATTERNS

- a discussion/conversation/dialogue/talk/debate/consultation/chat/gossip **about** sth
- a discussion/conversation/dialogue/debate/consultation **on** sth
- **in (close)** discussion/conversation/dialogue/debate/consultation **with** sb
- to **have** a discussion/conversation/dialogue/talk/debate/consultation/chat/gossip **with** sb
- to **hold** a discussion/conversation/debate/consultation

dis·cuss 🔑 /dɪˈskʌs/ *verb* **1** 🔑 to talk about sth with sb, especially in order to decide sth: **~ sth with sb** *Have you discussed the problem with anyone?* ◇ **~ sth** *I'm not prepared to discuss this on the phone.* ◇ **~ when, what, etc...** *We need to discuss when we should go.* ◇ **~ (sb/sth) doing sth** *We briefly discussed buying a second car.* HELP You cannot say 'discuss about sth': ~~*I discussed about my problem with my parents.*~~ Look also at **discussion.** ➲ SYNONYMS at TALK **2** 🔑 **~ sth | ~ what, how, etc ...** to write or talk about sth in detail, showing the different ideas and opinions about it: *This topic will be discussed at greater length in the next chapter.* ➲ LANGUAGE BANK at ABOUT ➲ note at EXAMINE

dis·cus·sion 🔑 /dɪˈskʌʃn/ *noun* [U, C] **1** 🔑 the process of discussing sb/sth; a conversation about sb/sth: *a **topic/subject for discussion*** ◇ *After considerable discussion, they decided to accept our offer.* ◇ *The plans have been **under discussion*** (= being talked about) *for a year now.* ◇ *Discussions are still taking place between the two leaders.* ◇ **~ (with sb) (about/on sb/sth)** *We **had a discussion** with them about the differences between Britain and the US.* **2** 🔑 **~ (of sth)** a speech or a piece of writing that discusses many different aspects of a subject: *Her article is a discussion of the methods used in research.*

dis·dain /dɪsˈdeɪn/ *noun, verb*

■ ***noun*** [U, sing.] the feeling that sb/sth is not good enough to deserve your respect or attention SYN **contempt**: *to treat sb **with disdain*** ◇ **~ for sb/sth** *a disdain for the law*

■ ***verb*** (*formal*) **1 ~ sb/sth** to think that sb/sth is not good enough to deserve your respect: *She disdained his offer of help.* **2 ~ to do sth** to refuse to do sth because you think

Synonyms

disease

illness • disorder • infection • condition • ailment • bug

These are all words for a medical problem.

disease a medical problem affecting humans, animals or plants, often caused by infection: *He suffers from a rare blood disease.*

illness a medical problem, or a period of suffering from one: *She died after a long illness.*

DISEASE OR ILLNESS?

Disease is used to talk about more severe physical medical problems, especially those that affect the organs. **Illness** is used to talk about both more severe and more minor medical problems, and those that affect mental health: ~~*heart/kidney/liver illness*~~ ◇ ~~*mental disease*~~. **Disease** is not used about a period of illness: ~~*she died after a long disease*~~

disorder (*rather formal*) an illness that causes a part of the body to stop functioning correctly: *a rare disorder of the liver.* NOTE A **disorder** is generally not infectious. **Disorder** is used most frequently with words relating to mental problems, for example *psychiatric, personality, mental* and *eating*. When it is used to talk about physical problems, it is most often used with *blood, bowel* and *kidney*, and these are commonly *serious, severe* or *rare*.

infection an illness that is caused by bacteria or a virus and that affects one part of the body: *a throat infection*

condition a medical problem that you have for a long time because it is not possible to cure it: *a heart condition*

ailment (*rather formal*) an illness that is not very serious: *childhood ailments*

bug (*informal*) an infectious illness that is usually fairly mild: *a nasty flu bug*

PATTERNS

- to **have/suffer from** a(n) disease/illness/disorder/infection/condition/ailment/bug
- to **catch/contract/get/pick up** a(n) disease/illness/infection/bug

that you are too important to do it: *He disdained to turn to his son for advice.*

dis·dain·ful /dɪsˈdeɪnfl/ *adj.* **~ (of sb/sth)** showing disdain **SYN contemptuous, dismissive**: *She's always been disdainful of people who haven't been to college.* ▸ **dis·dain·ful·ly** /-fəli/ *adv.*

D

dis·ease 0⊸ /dɪˈziːz/ *noun* [U, C] **1** 0⊸ an illness affecting humans, animals or plants, often caused by infection: ***heart/liver/kidney, etc. disease*** ◇ *health measures to prevent the* ***spread of disease*** ◇ *an* ***infectious/contagious disease*** (= one that can be passed to sb very easily) ◇ *It is not known what causes the disease.* ◇ *protection against sexually transmitted diseases* ◇ *He suffers from a rare blood disease.* ➲ COLLOCATIONS at ILL **2** [C] (*formal*) something that is very wrong with people's attitudes, way of life or with society: *Greed is a disease of modern society.*

dis·eased /dɪˈziːzd/ *adj.* suffering from a disease: *diseased tissue* ◇ *the diseased social system*

dis·em·bark /ˌdɪsɪmˈbɑːk; *NAmE* -ˈbɑːrk/ *verb* [I] **~ (from sth)** (*formal*) to leave a vehicle, especially a ship or an aircraft, at the end of a journey **OPP embark** ▸ **dis·em·bark·ation** /ˌdɪsˌembɑːˈkeɪʃn; *NAmE* -bɑːrˈk-/ *noun* [U]

dis·em·bod·ied /ˌdɪsɪmˈbɒdid; *NAmE* -ˈbɑːdid/ *adj.* [usually before noun] **1** (of sounds) coming from a person or place that cannot be seen or identified: *a disembodied voice* **2** separated from the body: *disembodied spirits*

dis·em·bowel /ˌdɪsɪmˈbaʊəl/ *verb* (-ll-, *especially US* -l-) **~ sb/sth** to take the stomach, BOWELS and other organs out of a person or animal

dis·en·chant·ed /ˌdɪsɪnˈtʃɑːntɪd; *NAmE* -ˈtʃænt-/ *adj.* **~ (with sb/sth)** no longer feeling enthusiasm for sb/sth; not believing sth is good or worth doing **SYN disillusioned**: *He was becoming disenchanted with his job as a lawyer.* ▸ **dis·en·chant·ment** *noun* [U]: *a growing* ***sense/feeling of disenchantment*** *with his job*

dis·en·fran·chise /ˌdɪsɪnˈfræntʃaɪz/ *verb* **~ sb** to take away sb's rights, especially their right to vote **OPP enfranchise**

dis·en·gage /ˌdɪsɪnˈɡeɪdʒ/ *verb* **1** [T, I] (*formal*) to free sb/sth from the person or thing that is holding them or it; to become free: **~ yourself (from sb/sth)** *She gently disengaged herself from her sleeping son.* ◇ (*figurative*) *They wished to disengage themselves from these policies.* ◇ **~ (sth/sb) (from sth/sb)** *to disengage the clutch* (= when driving a car) ◇ *We saw the booster rockets disengage and fall into the sea.* **2** [I, T] **~ (sth)** (*technical*) if an army **disengages** or sb **disengages** it, it stops fighting and moves away ➲ compare ENGAGE ▸ **dis·en·gage·ment** *noun* [U]

dis·en·tan·gle /ˌdɪsɪnˈtæŋɡl/ *verb* **1 ~ sth (from sth)** to separate different arguments, ideas, etc. that have become confused: *It's not easy to disentangle the truth from the official statistics.* **2 ~ sth/sb (from sth)** to free sb/sth from sth that has become wrapped or twisted around it or them: *He tried to disentangle his fingers from her hair.* ◇ (*figurative*) *She has just disentangled herself from a painful relationship.* **3 ~ sth** to get rid of the twists and knots in sth: *He was sitting on the deck disentangling a coil of rope.* ➲ compare ENTANGLE

dis·equi·lib·rium /ˌdɪsˌiːkwɪˈlɪbriəm; ˌdɪsˌek-/ *noun* [U] (*formal* or *technical*) a loss or lack of balance in a situation

dis·es·tab·lish **AW** /ˌdɪsɪˈstæblɪʃ/ *verb* **~ sth** (*formal*) to end the official status of a national Church: *a campaign to disestablish the Church of England* ▸ **dis·es·tab·lish·ment** **AW** *noun* [U]

dis·favour (*especially US* **dis·favor**) /dɪsˈfeɪvə(r)/ *noun* [U] (*formal*) the feeling that you do not like or approve of sb/sth

dis·fig·ure /dɪsˈfɪɡə(r); *NAmE* -ɡjər/ *verb* **~ sb/sth** to spoil the appearance of a person, thing or place: *Her face was disfigured by a long red scar.* ▸ **dis·fig·ure·ment** *noun* [U, C]: *He suffered permanent disfigurement in the fire.*

dis·gorge /dɪsˈɡɔːdʒ; *NAmE* -ˈɡɔːrdʒ/ *verb* (*formal*) **1 ~ sth** to pour sth out in large quantities: *The pipe disgorges sewage into the sea.* **2 ~ sb/sth** if a vehicle or building **disgorges** people, they come out of it in large numbers: *The bus disgorged a crowd of noisy children.*

dis·grace /dɪsˈɡreɪs/ *noun, verb*

■ ***noun*** **1** [U] the loss of other people's respect and approval because of the bad way sb has behaved **SYN shame**: *Her behaviour has* ***brought disgrace on*** *her family.* ◇ *The swimmer was sent home from the Olympics* ***in disgrace***. ◇ *There is no disgrace in being poor.* ◇ *Sam was* ***in disgrace*** *with his parents.* **2** [sing.] **a ~ (to sb/sth)** a person or thing that is so bad that people connected with them or it feel or should feel ashamed: *Your homework is an absolute disgrace.* ◇ *That sort of behaviour is* ***a disgrace to*** *the legal profession.* ◇ *The state of our roads is a national disgrace.* ◇ ***It's a disgrace that*** (= it is very wrong that) *they are paid so little.*

■ ***verb*** **1** to behave badly in a way that makes you or other people feel ashamed: **~ yourself** *I disgraced myself by drinking far too much.* ◇ **~ sb/sth** *He had disgraced the family name.* **2 be disgraced** to lose the respect of people, usually so that you lose a position of power: *He was publicly disgraced and sent into exile.* ◇ *a disgraced politician/leader*

dis·grace·ful /dɪsˈɡreɪsfl/ *adj.* very bad or unacceptable; that people should feel ashamed about: *His behaviour was absolutely disgraceful!* ◇ *It's disgraceful that none of the family tried to help her.* ◇ *a disgraceful waste of money* ▸ **dis·grace·ful·ly** /-fəli/ *adv.*

dis·grun·tled /dɪsˈɡrʌntld/ *adj.* annoyed or disappointed because sth has happened to upset you: *disgruntled employees* ◇ **~ at sb/sth** *I left feeling disgruntled at the way I'd been treated.*

dis·guise /dɪsˈɡaɪz/ *verb, noun*

■ ***verb*** **1** to change your appearance so that people cannot recognize you: **~ sb** *The hijackers were heavily disguised.* ◇ **~ sb as sb/sth** *They got in disguised as security guards.* ◇ **~ yourself (as sb/sth)** *She disguised herself as a boy.* **2 ~ sth** to hide sth or change it, so that it cannot be recognized **SYN conceal**: *She made no attempt to disguise her surprise.* ◇ *It was a* ***thinly disguised*** *attack on the President.* ◇ *She couldn't* ***disguise the fact that*** *she felt uncomfortable.* ➲ SYNONYMS at HIDE

■ ***noun*** **1** [C, U] a thing that you wear or use to change your appearance so that people do not recognize you: *She wore glasses and a wig as a disguise.* ◇ *The star travelled* ***in disguise*** (= wearing a disguise). ◇ (*figurative*) *A vote for the Liberal Democrats is just a Labour vote* ***in disguise***. **2** [U] the art of changing your appearance so that people do not recognize you: *He is a master of disguise.* **IDM** see BLESSING

dis·gust 0⊸ /dɪsˈɡʌst/ *noun, verb*

■ ***noun*** 0⊸ [U] a strong feeling of dislike or disapproval for sb/sth that you feel is unacceptable, or for sth that looks, smells, etc. unpleasant: **~ (at/with sth)** *She expressed her disgust at the programme by writing a letter of complaint.* ◇ **~ (for sb)** *I can only feel disgust for these criminals.* ◇ *The idea fills me* ***with disgust***. ◇ *He walked away* ***in disgust***. ◇ *Much* ***to my disgust***, *they refused to help.* ◇ *She wrinkled her nose* ***in disgust*** *at the smell.*

■ ***verb*** 0⊸ **~ sb** if sth **disgusts** you, it makes you feel shocked and almost ill/sick because it is so unpleasant: *The level of violence in the film really disgusted me.*

dis·gust·ed 0⊸ /dɪsˈɡʌstɪd/ *adj.* feeling or showing disgust: **~ (at/by sb/sth)** *I was disgusted at/by the sight.* ◇ **~ (with sb/sth/yourself)** *I was disgusted with myself for eating so much.* ◇ **~ (to see, hear, etc...)** *He was disgusted to see such awful living conditions.* ▸ **dis·gust·ed·ly** *adv.*: *'This champagne is warm!', he said disgustedly.*

dis·gust·ing 0⊸ /dɪsˈɡʌstɪŋ/ *adj.* **1** 0⊸ extremely unpleasant **SYN revolting**: *The kitchen was in a disgusting state when she left.* ◇ *What a disgusting smell!* **2** 0⊸ unacceptable and shocking **SYN despicable, outrageous**: *I think it's disgusting that they're closing the* *local hospital.* ◇ *His language is disgusting* (= he uses a lot of offensive words).

Synonyms

disgusting

foul • revolting • repulsive • offensive • gross

These words all describe sth, especially a smell, taste or habit, that is extremely unpleasant and often makes you feel slightly ill.

disgusting extremely unpleasant and making you feel slightly ill: *What a disgusting smell!*

foul dirty, and tasting or smelling bad: *She could smell his foul breath.*

revolting extremely unpleasant and making you feel slightly ill: *The stew looked revolting.*

DISGUSTING OR REVOLTING?

Both of these words are used to describe things that smell and taste unpleasant, unpleasant personal habits and people who have them. There is no real difference in meaning, but **disgusting** is more frequent, especially in spoken English.

repulsive (*rather formal*) extremely unpleasant in a way that offends you or makes you feel slightly ill. NOTE **Repulsive** usually describes people, their behaviour or habits, which you may find offensive for physical or moral reasons.

offensive (*formal*) (especially of smells) extremely unpleasant.

gross (*informal*) (of a smell, taste or personal habit) extremely unpleasant.

PATTERNS

- disgusting/repulsive/offensive **to** sb
- to **find sb/sth** disgusting/revolting/repulsive/offensive
- to **smell/taste** disgusting/foul/gross
- a(n) disgusting/foul/revolting/offensive/gross **smell**
- a disgusting/revolting/gross **habit**
- disgusting/offensive/gross **behaviour**
- a disgusting/revolting/repulsive **man/woman/person**

dis·gust·ing·ly /dɪs'gʌstɪŋli/ *adv.* **1** (sometimes *humorous*) extremely (in a way that other people feel jealous of): *He looked disgustingly healthy when he got back from the Bahamas.* **2** in a disgusting way: *disgustingly dirty*

dish 0‑w /dɪʃ/ *noun, verb*

■ ***noun* 1** 0‑w [C] a flat shallow container for cooking food in or serving it from: *a glass dish* ◇ *an ovenproof dish* ◇ *a baking/serving dish* ◇ *They helped themselves from a large dish of pasta.* ➲ VISUAL VOCAB page V19 **2** 0‑w **the dishes** [pl.] the plates, bowls, cups, etc. that have been used for a meal and need to be washed: *I'll **do the dishes*** (= wash them). **3** 0‑w [C] food prepared in a particular way as part of a meal: *a vegetarian/fish dish* ◇ *This makes an excellent hot **main dish**.* ◇ *I can recommend the chef's **dish of the day**.* ➲ see also SIDE DISH **4** [C] any object that is shaped like a dish or bowl: *a soap dish* ➲ VISUAL VOCAB page V21 ➲ see also SATELLITE DISH **5** [C] (*informal*) a sexually attractive person: *What a dish!*

■ ***verb***

IDM ˌ**dish the** ˈ**dirt** (**on sb**) (*informal*) to tell people unkind or unpleasant things about sb, especially about their private life ˌ**dish it** ˈ**out** (*disapproving*) to criticize other people: *He enjoys dishing it out, but he really can't take it* (= cannot accept criticism from other people).

PHR V ˌ**dish sth**↔ˈ**out 1** (*informal*) to give sth, often to a lot of people or in large amounts: *Students dished out leaflets to passers-by.* ◇ *She's always dishing out advice, even when you don't want it.* **2** to serve food onto plates for a meal: *Can you dish out the potatoes, please?* ˌ**dish** ˈ**up** | ˌ**dish sth**↔ˈ**up** to serve food onto plates for a meal ˌ**dish** ˈ**up sth** to offer sth to sb, especially sth that is not very good

dis·ha·bille /ˌdɪsəˈbiːl; -ˈbiː/ *adj.* = DÉSHABILLÉ

dis·har·mony /dɪsˈhɑːməni; *NAmE* -ˈhɑːrm-/ *noun* [U] (*formal*) a lack of agreement about important things, which causes bad feelings between people or groups of people: ***marital/racial/social disharmony*** OPP **harmony**

dish·cloth /ˈdɪʃklɒθ; *NAmE* -klɔːθ/ (*NAmE* usually **dish-rag**) *noun* a cloth for washing dishes ➲ VISUAL VOCAB page V22

dis·heart·en /dɪsˈhɑːtn; *NAmE* -ˈhɑːrtn/ *verb* **~ sb** to make sb lose hope or confidence SYN **discourage**: *Don't let this defeat dishearten you.* ▶ **dis·heart·ened** *adj.*: *a disheartened team* **dis·heart·en·ing** /-ˈhɑːtnɪŋ; *NAmE* -ˈhɑːrt-/ *adj.*: *a disheartening experience*

dish·ev·elled /dɪˈʃevld/ (*especially BrE*) (*NAmE* usually **dish·ev·eled**) *adj.* (of hair, clothes or sb's general appearance) very untidy SYN **unkempt**: *He looked tired and dishevelled.*

dis·hon·est 0‑w /dɪsˈɒnɪst; *NAmE* -ˈɑːn-/ *adj.* not honest; intending to trick people: *Beware of dishonest traders in the tourist areas.* ◇ *I don't like him, and it would be dishonest of me to pretend otherwise.* OPP **honest** ▶ **dis·hon·est·ly** 0‑w *adv.* **dis·hon·esty** *noun* [U]

dis·hon·our (*especially US* **dis·honor**) /dɪsˈɒnə(r); *NAmE* -ˈɑːn-/ *noun, verb*

■ ***noun*** [U] (*formal*) a loss of honour or respect because you have done sth immoral or unacceptable

■ ***verb*** (*formal*) **1 ~ sb/sth** to make sb/sth lose the respect of other people: *You have dishonoured the name of the school.* **2 ~ sth** to refuse to keep an agreement or promise: *He had dishonoured nearly all of his election pledges.* OPP **honour**

dis·hon·our·able (*especially US* **dis·hon·or·able**) /dɪsˈɒnərəbl; *NAmE* -ˈɑːn-/ *adj.* not deserving respect; immoral or unacceptable: *It would have been dishonourable of her not to keep her promise.* ◇ *He was given a **dishonourable discharge*** (= an order to leave the army for unacceptable behaviour). OPP **honourable** ▶ **dis·hon·our·ably** /-nərəbli/ *adv.*

dish·pan /ˈdɪʃpæn/ *noun* (*NAmE*) a bowl for washing plates, etc. in

dish·rag /ˈdɪʃræg/ *noun* (*NAmE*) = DISHCLOTH

dish·towel /ˈdɪʃtaʊəl/ (*NAmE*) (*BrE* ˈ**tea towel**, ˈ**tea cloth**) *noun* a small towel used for drying cups, plates, knives, etc. after they have been washed ➲ VISUAL VOCAB page V22

dish·wash·er /ˈdɪʃwɒʃə(r); *NAmE* -wɔːʃ-; -wɑːʃ-/ *noun* **1** a machine for washing plates, cups, etc: *to **load/stack the dishwasher*** ➲ VISUAL VOCAB page V22 **2** a person whose job is to wash plates, etc, for example in a restaurant

dish·water /ˈdɪʃwɔːtə(r)/ *noun* [U] water that sb has used to wash dirty plates, etc. IDM see DULL *adj.*

dishy /ˈdɪʃi/ *adj.* (**dish·ier**, **dishi·est**) (*old-fashioned, informal, especially BrE*) (of a person) physically attractive

dis·il·lu·sion /ˌdɪsɪˈluːʒn/ *verb* **~ sb** to destroy sb's belief in or good opinion of sb/sth: *I hate to disillusion you, but not everyone is as honest as you.* ▶ **dis·il·lu·sion** *noun* [U] = DISILLUSIONMENT

dis·il·lu·sioned /ˌdɪsɪˈluːʒnd/ *adj.* **~** (**by/with sb/sth**) disappointed because the person you admired or the idea you believed to be good and true now seems without value SYN **disenchanted**: *I soon became disillusioned with the job.*

dis·il·lu·sion·ment /ˌdɪsɪˈluːʒnmənt/ (also **dis·il·lu·sion**) *noun* [U, sing.] **~** (**with sth**) the state of being disillusioned SYN **disenchantment**: *There is widespread disillusionment with the present government.*

dis·in·cen·tive /ˌdɪsɪnˈsentɪv/ *noun* [C] a thing that makes sb less willing to do sth OPP **incentive**

dis·in·clin·ation /ˌdɪsˌɪnklɪˈneɪʃn/ *noun* [sing., U] (*formal*) a lack of willingness to do sth; a lack of enthusiasm for sth: *There was a general disinclination to return to the office after lunch.*

dis·in·clined /ˌdɪsɪnˈklaɪnd/ *adj.* [not before noun] **~ (to do sth)** (*formal*) not willing SYN **reluctant**: *He was strongly disinclined to believe anything that she said.*

dis·in·fect /ˌdɪsɪnˈfekt/ *verb* **1 ~ sth** to clean sth using a substance that kills bacteria: *to disinfect a surface/room/wound* **2 ~ sth** to run a computer program to get rid of a computer virus ▶ **dis·in·fec·tion** *noun* [U]

D

dis·in·fect·ant /ˌdɪsɪnˈfektənt/ *noun* [U, C] a substance that disinfects: *a strong smell of disinfectant*

dis·in·for·ma·tion /ˌdɪsˌɪnfəˈmeɪʃn; *NAmE* -fərˈm-/ *noun* [U] false information that is given deliberately, especially by government organizations

dis·in·genu·ous /ˌdɪsɪnˈdʒenjuəs/ *adj.* [not usually before noun] (*formal*) not sincere, especially when you pretend to know less about sth than you really do: *It would be disingenuous of me to claim I had never seen it.* ➲ compare INGENUOUS ▶ **dis·in·genu·ous·ly** *adv.*

dis·in·herit /ˌdɪsɪnˈherɪt/ *verb* **~ sb** to prevent sb, especially your son or daughter, from receiving your money or property after your death ➲ compare INHERIT (1)

dis·in·hibit /ˌdɪsɪnˈhɪbɪt/ *verb* **~ sb** (*formal*) to help sb to stop feeling shy so that they can relax and show their feelings ▶ **dis·in·hib·ition** /ˌdɪsɪnhɪˈbɪʃn/ *noun* [U]

dis·in·te·grate /dɪsˈɪntɪɡreɪt/ *verb* **1** [I] to break into small parts or pieces and be destroyed: *The plane disintegrated as it fell into the sea.* **2** [I] to become much less strong or united and be gradually destroyed SYN **fall apart**: *The authority of the central government was rapidly disintegrating.* ▶ **dis·in·te·gra·tion** /dɪsˌɪntɪˈɡreɪʃn/ *noun* [U]: *the gradual disintegration of traditional values*

dis·in·ter /ˌdɪsɪnˈtɜː(r)/ *verb* (-rr-) (*formal*) **1 ~ sth** to dig up sth, especially a dead body, from the ground OPP **inter** **2 ~ sth (from sth)** to find sth that has been hidden or lost for a long time

dis·in·ter·est /dɪsˈɪntrəst; -trest/ *noun* [U] **1 ~ (in sth)** lack of interest: *His total disinterest in money puzzled his family.* **2** the fact of not being involved in sth

dis·in·ter·est·ed /dɪsˈɪntrəstɪd; -trestɪd/ *adj.* **1** not influenced by personal feelings, or by the chance of getting some advantage for yourself SYN **impartial, objective, unbiased**: *a* ***disinterested onlooker/spectator*** ◇ *Her advice appeared to be disinterested.* **2** (*informal*) not interested ➲ note at INTERESTED ▶ **dis·in·ter·est·ed·ly** *adv.*

dis·in·vest /ˌdɪsɪnˈvest/ *verb* [I] **~ (from sth)** (*business*) to stop investing money in a company, industry or country; to reduce the amount of money invested

dis·in·vest·ment /ˌdɪsɪnˈvestmənt/ *noun* [U] (*finance*) the process of reducing the amount of money that you have invested in a particular company, industry, etc.

dis·joint·ed /dɪsˈdʒɔɪntɪd/ *adj.* not communicated or described in a clear or logical way; not connected SYN **disconnected, incoherent**

dis·junc·tion /dɪsˈdʒʌŋkʃn/ (also *less frequent* **dis·junc·ture** /dɪsˈdʒʌŋktʃə(r)/) *noun* **~ (between A and B)** (*formal*) a difference between two things that you would expect to be in agreement with each other

disk 🔑 /dɪsk/ *noun*
1 🔑 (*especially NAmE*) = DISC: *Red blood cells are roughly the shape of a disk.* **2** 🔑 (also **magˌnetic ˈdisk**) (*computing*) a device for storing information on a computer, with a MAGNETIC surface that records information received in electronic form ➲ see also FLOPPY DISK, HARD DISK

ˈdisk drive *noun* a device that passes data between a disk and the memory of a computer or from one disk or computer to another ➲ VISUAL VOCAB page V54

disk·ette /dɪsˈket/ *noun* = FLOPPY DISK

dis·like 🔑 /dɪsˈlaɪk/ *verb, noun*
■ ***verb*** 🔑 (rather *formal*) to not like sb/sth: **~ sb/sth** *Why do you dislike him so much?* ◇ *He* ***disliked it*** *when she behaved badly in front of his mother.* ◇ **~ doing sth** *I dislike being away from my family.* ◇ ***Much as she disliked*** *going to funerals* (= although she did not like it at all), *she knew she had to be there.* ◇ **~ sb/sth doing sth** *He disliked her staying away from home.* ➲ SYNONYMS at HATE OPP **like**
■ ***noun*** **1** 🔑 [U, sing.] **~ (of/for sb/sth)** a feeling of not liking sb/sth: *He did not try to hide his dislike of his boss.* ◇ *She* ***took an instant dislike to*** *the house and the neighbourhood.* **2** 🔑 [C, usually pl.] a thing that you do not like: *I've told you all my* ***likes and dislikes.***

dis·locate /ˈdɪsləkeɪt; *NAmE* -loʊk-; dɪsˈloʊ-/ *verb* **1 ~ sth** to put a bone out of its normal position in a joint: *He dislocated his shoulder in the accident.* ◇ *a dislocated finger* ➲ COLLOCATIONS at INJURY **2 ~ sth** to stop a system, plan etc. from working or continuing in the normal way SYN **disrupt** ▶ **dis·loca·tion** /ˌdɪsləˈkeɪʃn; *NAmE* -loʊ-/ *noun* [C, U]: *a dislocation of the shoulder* ◇ *These policies could cause severe economic and social dislocation.*

dis·lodge /dɪsˈlɒdʒ; *NAmE* -ˈlɑːdʒ/ *verb* (*formal*) **1 ~ sth (from sth)** to force or knock sth out of its position: *The wind dislodged one or two tiles from the roof.* **2 ~ sb (from sth)** to force sb to leave a place, position or job: *The rebels have so far failed to dislodge the President.*

dis·loyal /dɪsˈlɔɪəl/ *adj.* **~ (to sb/sth)** not loyal or faithful to your friends, family, country, etc: *He was accused of being disloyal to the government.* ▶ **dis·loy·alty** /-ˈlɔɪəlti/ *noun* [U]

dis·mal /ˈdɪzməl/ *adj.* **1** causing or showing sadness SYN **gloomy, miserable**: *dismal conditions/surroundings/weather* **2** (*informal*) not skilful or successful; of very low quality: *The singer gave a dismal performance of some old songs.* ◇ *Their recent attempt to increase sales has been a* ***dismal failure.*** ▶ **dis·mal·ly** /-məli/ *adv.*: *I tried not to laugh but failed dismally* (= was completely unsuccessful).

dis·man·tle /dɪsˈmæntl/ *verb* **1 ~ sth** to take apart a machine or structure so that it is in separate pieces: *I had to dismantle the engine in order to repair it.* ◇ *The steel mill was dismantled piece by piece.* **2 ~ sth** to end an organization or system gradually in an organized way: *The government was in the process of dismantling the state-owned industries.* ▶ **dis·mant·ling** *noun* [U]

dis·may /dɪsˈmeɪ/ *noun, verb*
■ ***noun*** [U] a worried, sad feeling after you have received an unpleasant surprise: *She could not hide her dismay at the result.* ◇ *He looked at her* ***in dismay.*** ◇ ***To her dismay,*** *her name was not on the list.* ◇ *The news has been greeted* ***with dismay*** *by local business leaders.*
■ ***verb*** **~ sb** to make sb feel shocked and disappointed: *Their reaction dismayed him.* ▶ **dis·mayed** *adj.*: **~ (at/by sth)** *He was dismayed at the change in his old friend.* ◇ *The suggestion was greeted by a dismayed silence.* ◇ **~ (to find, hear, see, etc...)** *They were dismayed to find that the ferry had already left.*

dis·mem·ber /dɪsˈmembə(r)/ *verb* **1 ~ sth** to cut or tear the dead body of a person or an animal into pieces **2 ~ sth** (*formal*) to divide a country, an organization, etc. into smaller parts ▶ **dis·mem·ber·ment** *noun* [U]

dis·miss 🔑 /dɪsˈmɪs/ *verb*
1 🔑 to decide that sb/sth is not important and not worth thinking or talking about SYN **wave aside**: **~ sb/sth** *I think we can safely dismiss their objections.* ◇ **~ sb/sth as sth** *Vegetarians are no longer dismissed as cranks.* ◇ *He dismissed the opinion polls as worthless.* ◇ *The suggestion should not be* ***dismissed out of hand*** (= without thinking about it). **2** 🔑 to put thoughts or feelings out of your mind: **~ sth** *Dismissing her fears, she climbed higher.* ◇ **~ sb/sth from sth** *He dismissed her from his mind.* **3** 🔑 **~ sb (from sth)** to officially remove sb from their job SYN **fire, sack**: *She claims she was unfairly dismissed from her post.* **4 ~ sb** to send sb away or allow them to leave: *At 12 o'clock the class was dismissed.* **5 ~ sth** (*law*) to say that a trial or legal case should not continue, usually because there is not enough evidence: *The case was dismissed.* **6 ~ sb** (in CRICKET) to end the INNINGS of a player or team

dis·missal /dɪsˈmɪsl/ *noun* **1** [U, C] the act of dismissing sb from their job; an example of this: *He still hopes to win his claim against* ***unfair dismissal.*** ◇ *The dismissals followed the resignation of the chairman.* **2** [U] the failure to consider sth as important: *Her casual dismissal of the* *threats seemed irresponsible.* **3** [U, C] (*law*) the act of not allowing a trial or legal case to continue, usually because there is not enough evidence: *the dismissal of the appeal* **4** [U, C] the act of sending sb away or allowing them to leave **5** [U, C] (in CRICKET) the end of the INNINGS of a player or team

dis·mis·sive /dɪsˈmɪsɪv/ *adj.* **~ (of sb/sth)** showing that you do not believe a person or thing to be important or worth considering SYN **disdainful**: *a **dismissive gesture/tone*** ▶ **dis·mis·sive·ly** *adv.*: *to **shrug/wave dismissively***

dis·mount /dɪsˈmaʊnt/ *verb* [I] **~ (from sth)** (*formal*) to get off a horse, bicycle or motorcycle OPP **mount**

dis·obedi·ence /ˌdɪsəˈbiːdiəns/ *noun* [U] failure or refusal to obey ➲ see also CIVIL DISOBEDIENCE OPP **obedience**

dis·obedi·ent /ˌdɪsəˈbiːdiənt/ *adj.* failing or refusing to obey: *a disobedient child* OPP **obedient**

dis·obey /ˌdɪsəˈbeɪ/ *verb* [T, I] **~ (sb/sth)** to refuse to do what a person, law, order, etc. tells you to do; to refuse to obey: *He was punished for disobeying orders.* OPP **obey**

dis·obli·ging /ˌdɪsəˈblaɪdʒɪŋ/ *adj.* deliberately not helpful: *a disobliging manner*

dis·order /dɪsˈɔːdə(r); *NAmE* -ˈɔːrd-/ *noun* **1** [U] (*formal*) an untidy state; a lack of order or organization: *His financial affairs were **in complete disorder**.* ◇ *The room was in a state of disorder.* OPP **order** **2** [U] (*formal*) violent behaviour of large groups of people: *an outbreak of rioting and **public disorder*** ➲ compare ORDER (3) **3** [C, U] (*medical*) an illness that causes a part of the body to stop functioning correctly: *a **blood/bowel, etc. disorder*** ◇ ***eating disorders*** ◇ *He was suffering from some form of psychiatric disorder.* ➲ SYNONYMS at DISEASE

dis·ordered /dɪsˈɔːdəd; *NAmE* -ˈɔːrdərd/ *adj.* **1** showing a lack of order or control: *disordered hair* ◇ *a disordered state* OPP **ordered** **2** (*technical*) suffering from a mental or physical disorder: *emotionally disordered children*

dis·or·der·ly /dɪsˈɔːdəli; *NAmE* -ˈɔːrdərli/ *adj.* [usually before noun] (*formal*) **1** (of people or behaviour) showing lack of control; publicly violent or noisy: *disorderly conduct* ◇ *They were arrested for being **drunk and disorderly**.* **2** untidy: *newspapers in a disorderly pile by the door* OPP **orderly**

disˌorderly ˈhouse *noun* (*law*) (*old use*) a BROTHEL (= place where people pay to have sex)

dis·or·gan·ized (*BrE* also **-ised**) /dɪsˈɔːɡənaɪzd; *NAmE* -ˈɔːrɡ-/ (also *less frequent* **un·or·gan·ized, -ised**) *adj.* badly planned; not able to plan or organize well: *It was a hectic disorganized weekend.* ◇ *She's so disorganized.* ➲ compare ORGANIZED ▶ **dis·or·gan·iza·tion, -isa·tion** /dɪsˌɔːɡənaɪˈzeɪʃn; *NAmE* -ˌɔːrɡənəˈz-/ *noun* [U]

dis·orien·tate /dɪsˈɔːrienteɪt/ (*BrE*) (also **dis·orient** /dɪsˈɔːrient/ *NAmE, BrE*) *verb* **1 ~ sb** to make sb unable to recognize where they are or where they should go: *The darkness had disorientated him.* **2 ~ sb** to make sb feel confused: *Ex-soldiers can be disorientated by the transition to civilian life.* ➲ compare ORIENT ▶ **dis·orien·tated** (also **dis·orient·ed**) *adj.*: *She felt shocked and totally disorientated.* **dis·orien·ta·tion** /dɪsˌɔːriənˈteɪʃn/ *noun* [U]

dis·own /dɪsˈəʊn; *NAmE* -ˈoʊn/ *verb* **~ sb/sth** to decide that you no longer want to be connected with or responsible for sb/sth: *Her family disowned her for marrying a foreigner.*

dis·par·age /dɪˈspærɪdʒ/ *verb* **~ sb/sth** (*formal*) to suggest that sb/sth is not important or valuable SYN **belittle**: *I don't mean to disparage your achievements.* ▶ **dis·par·age·ment** *noun* [U] **dis·para·ging** *adj.*: *disparaging remarks* **dis·para·ging·ly** *adv.*: *He spoke disparagingly of his colleagues.*

dis·par·ate /ˈdɪspərət/ *adj.* (*formal*) **1** made up of parts or people that are very different from each other: *a disparate group of individuals* **2** (of two or more things) so different from each other that they cannot be compared or cannot work together

dis·par·ity /dɪˈspærəti/ *noun* [U, C] (*pl.* **-ies**) (*formal*) a difference, especially one connected with unfair treatment: *the wide disparity between rich and poor*

dis·pas·sion·ate /dɪsˈpæʃənət/ *adj.* (*approving*) not influenced by emotion SYN **impartial**: *taking a calm, dispassionate view of the situation* ◇ *a dispassionate observer* ▶ **dis·pas·sion·ate·ly** *adv.*

D

dis·patch (*BrE* also **des·patch**) /dɪˈspætʃ/ *verb, noun*

■ ***verb*** **1 ~ sb/sth (to…)** (*formal*) to send sb/sth somewhere, especially for a special purpose: *Troops have been dispatched to the area.* ◇ *A courier was dispatched to collect the documents.* **2 ~ sth (to sb/sth)** (*formal*) to send a letter, package or message somewhere: *Goods are dispatched within 24 hours of your order reaching us.* **3 ~ sb/sth** (*formal*) to deal or finish with sb/sth quickly and completely: *He dispatched the younger player in straight sets.* **4 ~ sb/sth** (*old-fashioned*) to kill a person or an animal

■ ***noun*** **1** [U] (*formal*) the act of sending sb/sth somewhere: *More food supplies are ready for immediate dispatch.* **2** [C] a message or report sent quickly from one military officer to another or between government officials **3** [C] a report sent to a newspaper by a journalist who is working in a foreign country: *dispatches from the war zone*

IDM **with diˈspatch** (*formal*) quickly and efficiently

diˈspatch box (also **deˈspatch box**) (both *BrE*) *noun* **1** [C] a container for carrying official documents **2 the Dispatch Box** [sing.] a box on a table in the centre of the House of Commons in the British parliament, which ministers stand next to when they speak

dis·patch·er /dɪˈspætʃə(r)/ *noun* **1** (*NAmE*) a person whose job is to see that trains, buses, planes, etc. leave on time **2** a person whose job is to send emergency vehicles to where they are needed

diˈspatch rider (also **deˈspatch rider**) *noun* (both *BrE*) a person whose job is to carry messages or packages by motorcycle

dis·pel /dɪˈspel/ *verb* (**-ll-**) **~ sth** to make sth, especially a feeling or belief, go away or disappear: *His speech dispelled any fears about his health.*

dis·pens·able /dɪˈspensəbl/ *adj.* [not usually before noun] not necessary; that can be got rid of: *They looked on music and art lessons as dispensable.* OPP **essential, indispensable**

dis·pens·ary /dɪˈspensəri/ *noun* (*pl.* **-ies**) **1** a place in a hospital, shop/store, etc. where medicines are prepared for patients **2** (*old-fashioned*) a place where patients are treated, especially one run by a charity

dis·pen·sa·tion /ˌdɪspenˈseɪʃn/ *noun* **1** [C, U] special permission, especially from a religious leader, to do sth that is not usually allowed or legal: *She needed a special dispensation to remarry.* ◇ *The sport's ruling body gave him dispensation to compete in national competitions.* **2** [U] (*formal*) the act or process of providing sth, especially by sb in authority: *the dispensation of justice* **3** [C] (*technical*) a political or religious system that operates in a country at a particular time

dis·pense /dɪˈspens/ *verb* **1 ~ sth (to sb)** (*formal*) to give out sth to people: *The machine dispenses a range of drinks and snacks.* **2 ~ sth (to sb)** (*formal*) to provide sth, especially a service, for people: *The organization dispenses free health care to the poor.* ◇ *to **dispense justice/advice*** **3 ~ sth** to prepare medicine and give it to people, as a job: *to dispense a prescription* ◇ (*BrE*) *to dispense medicine* ◇ (*BrE*) *a dispensing chemist*

PHR V **diˈspense with sb/sth** to stop using sb/sth because you no longer need them or it SYN **do away with**: *Debit cards dispense with the need for cash altogether.* ◇ *I think we can **dispense with the formalities*** (= speak openly and naturally to each other).

dis·pens·er /dɪˈspensə(r)/ *noun* a machine or container holding money, drinks, paper towels, etc. that you can obtain quickly, for example by pulling a handle or pressing buttons: *a soap dispenser* ➲ VISUAL VOCAB pages V21, V56 ➲ see also CASH DISPENSER

dis'pensing chemist *noun* (*BrE*) = CHEMIST (1)

dis·pers·al /dɪ'spɜːsl; *NAmE* dɪ'spɜːrsl/ *noun* [U, C] (*formal*) the process of sending sb/sth in different directions; the process of spreading sth over a wide area: *police trained in crowd dispersal* ◇ *the dispersal of seeds*

D

dis·perse /dɪ'spɜːs; *NAmE* dɪ'spɜːrs/ *verb* **1** [I, T] to move apart and go away in different directions; to make sb/sth do this: *The fog began to disperse.* ◇ *The* ***crowd dispersed*** *quickly.* ◇ **~ sb/sth** *Police dispersed the protesters with tear gas.* **2** [T, I] **~ (sth)** to spread or to make sth spread over a wide area SYN **scatter**: *The seeds are dispersed by the wind.*

dis·per·sion /dɪ'spɜːʃn; *NAmE* dɪ'spɜːrʒn/ *noun* [U] (*technical*) the process by which people or things are spread over a wide area

dis·pirited /dɪ'spɪrɪtɪd/ *adj.* having no hope or enthusiasm: *She looked tired and dispirited.* ➲ compare SPIRITED

dis·pir·it·ing /dɪ'spɪrɪtɪŋ/ *adj.* making sb lose their hope or enthusiasm: *a* ***dispiriting experience/failure***

dis·place AW /dɪs'pleɪs/ *verb* [often passive] (*formal*) **1 ~ sb/sth** to take the place of sb/sth SYN **replace**: *Gradually factory workers have been displaced by machines.* ◇ (*technical*) *The ship displaces 58 000 tonnes* (= as a way of measuring its size). **2 ~ sb** to force people to move away from their home to another place: *Around 10 000 people have been displaced by the fighting.* **3 ~ sth** to move sth from its usual position: *Check for roof tiles that have been displaced by the wind.* **4 ~ sb** (*especially NAmE*) to remove sb from a job or position: *displaced workers*

di,splaced 'person *noun* (*pl.* di,splaced 'persons) (*technical*) a REFUGEE

dis·place·ment AW /dɪs'pleɪsmənt/ *noun* [U] **1** (*formal*) the act of displacing sb/sth; the process of being displaced: *the largest displacement of civilian population since World War Two* **2** [C] (*physics*) the amount of a liquid moved out of place by sth floating or put in it, especially a ship floating in water: *a ship with a displacement of 10 000 tonnes*

dis'placement activity *noun* **1** [U] things that you do in order to avoid doing what you are supposed to be doing **2** (*biology, psychology*) [U, C] behaviour in animals or humans that seems to have no connection with the situation in which it is performed, resulting from two conflicting urges

dis·play 🔑 AW /dɪ'spleɪ/ *verb, noun*

▪ ***verb*** **1** 🔑 [T] **~ sth (to sb)** to put sth in a place where people can see it easily; to show sth to people SYN **exhibit**: *The exhibition gives local artists an opportunity to display their work.* ◇ *She displayed her bruises for all to see.* **2** 🔑 [T] **~ sth** to show signs of sth, especially a quality or feeling: *I have rarely seen her display any sign of emotion.* ◇ *These statistics display a definite trend.* **3** 🔑 [T] **~ sth** (of a computer, etc.) to show information: *The screen will display the username in the top right-hand corner.* ◇ *This column displays the title of the mail message.* **4** [I] (*technical*) (of male birds and animals) to show a special pattern of behaviour that is intended to attract a female bird or animal

▪ ***noun*** **1** 🔑 an arrangement of things in a public place to inform or entertain people or advertise sth for sale: *a beautiful floral display outside the Town Hall* ◇ *a window display* ◇ *a display cabinet* **2** 🔑 an act of performing a skill or of showing sth happening, in order to entertain: *a firework display* ◇ *a breathtaking display of aerobatics* **3** an occasion when you show a particular quality, feeling or ability by the way that you behave: *a display of affection/strength/wealth* **4** the words, pictures, etc. shown on a computer screen: *a high resolution colour display* ➲ see also LIQUID CRYSTAL DISPLAY, VDU

IDM **on di'splay** 🔑 put in a place where people can look at it SYN **on show**: *Designs for the new sports hall are on display in the library.* ◇ *to put sth on* ***temporary/permanent display***

dis'play bin (*BrE* also **'dump bin**) *noun* a box in a shop/store for displaying goods, especially goods whose prices have been reduced

dis·please /dɪs'pliːz/ *verb* **~ sb** (*formal*) to make sb feel upset, annoyed or not satisfied OPP **please** ▸ **dis·pleased** *adj.*: **~ (with sb/sth)** *Are you displeased with my work?* ◇ **~ (at sth)** *She was not displeased at the effect she was having on the young man.* **dis·pleas·ing** *adj.*: **~ (to sb/sth)** *His remarks were clearly not displeasing to her.*

dis·pleas·ure /dɪs'pleʒə(r)/ *noun* [U] **~ (at/with sb/sth)** (*formal*) the feeling of being upset and annoyed SYN **annoyance**: *She made no attempt to hide her displeasure at the prospect.* ➲ compare PLEASURE

dis·port /dɪ'spɔːt; *NAmE* dɪ'spɔːrt/ *verb* **~ yourself** (*old-fashioned* or *humorous*) to enjoy yourself by doing sth active

dis·pos·able AW /dɪ'spəʊzəbl; *NAmE* -'spoʊ-/ *adj.* [usually before noun] **1** made to be thrown away after use: *disposable gloves/razors* ◇ (*BrE*) *disposable nappies* ◇ (*NAmE*) *disposable diapers* **2** (*finance*) available for use: ***disposable assets/capital/resources*** ◇ *a person's* ***disposable income*** (= money they are free to spend after paying taxes, etc.)

dis·pos·ables /dɪ'spəʊzəblz; *NAmE* -'spoʊ-/ *noun* [pl.] items such as NAPPIES/DIAPERS and CONTACT LENSES that are designed to be thrown away after use

dis·posal AW /dɪ'spəʊzl; *NAmE* -'spoʊ-/ *noun* **1** [U] the act of getting rid of sth: *a bomb disposal squad* ◇ *sewage disposal systems* ◇ *the disposal of nuclear waste* **2** [C] (*business*) the sale of part of a business, property, etc. **3** [C] (*NAmE*) = WASTE-DISPOSAL UNIT

IDM **at your/sb's disposal** available for use as you prefer/sb prefers: *He will have a car at his disposal for the whole month.* ◇ *Well, I'm at your disposal* (= I am ready to help you in any way I can).

dis·pose AW /dɪ'spəʊz; *NAmE* dɪ'spoʊz/ *verb* (*formal*) **1 ~ sth/sb + adv./prep.** to arrange things or people in a particular way or position **2 ~ sb to/toward(s) sth** | **~ sb to do sth** to make sb behave in a particular way: *a drug that disposes the patient towards sleep*

PHR V **di'spose of sb/sth** **1** to get rid of sb/sth that you do not want or cannot keep: *the difficulties of disposing of nuclear waste* ◇ *to dispose of stolen property* **2** to deal with a problem, question or threat successfully: *That seems to have disposed of most of their arguments.* **3** to defeat or kill sb: *It took her a mere 20 minutes to dispose of her opponent.*

dis·posed AW /dɪ'spəʊzd; *NAmE* dɪ'spoʊzd/ *adj.* [not before noun] (*formal*) **1 ~ (to do sth)** willing or prepared to do sth: *I'm not disposed to argue.* ◇ *You're most welcome to join us if you feel so disposed.* **2** (following an adverb) **~ to/towards sb/sth** having a good/bad opinion of a person or thing: *She seems favourably disposed to the move.* ➲ see also ILL-DISPOSED, WELL DISPOSED

dis·pos·ition /,dɪspə'zɪʃn/ *noun* **1** [C, usually sing.] (*formal*) the natural qualities of a person's character SYN **temperament**: *to have a cheerful disposition* ◇ *people of a nervous disposition* **2** [C, usually sing.] **~ to/towards sth** | **~ to do sth** (*formal*) a tendency to behave in a particular way: *to* ***have/show a disposition*** *towards violence* **3** [C, usually sing.] (*formal*) the way sth is placed or arranged SYN **arrangement** **4** [C, U] (*law*) a formal act of giving property or money to sb

dis·pos·sess /,dɪspə'zes/ *verb* [usually passive] **~ sb (of sth)** (*formal*) to take sb's property, land or house away from them ▸ **dis·pos·ses·sion** /,dɪspə'zeʃn/ *noun* [U]

the dis·pos·sessed /,dɪspə'zest/ *noun* [pl.] people who have had property taken away from them

dis·pro·por·tion AW /,dɪsprə'pɔːʃn; *NAmE* -'pɔːrʃn/ *noun* [U, C] (*formal*) the state of two things not being at an equally high or low level; an example of this: **~ (between A and B)** *the disproportion between the extra responsibilities and the small salary increase* ◇ **~ (of A to B)** *a profession with a high disproportion of male to female employees*

dis·pro·por·tion·ate AW /,dɪsprə'pɔːʃənət; *NAmE* -'pɔːrʃ-/ *adj.* **~ (to sth)** too large or too small when compared with sth else: *The area contains a disproportionate number of young middle-class families.* ➲ compare PRO-

PORTIONATE ▶ **dis·pro·por·tion·ately** AW *adv.*: *The lower-paid spend a disproportionately large amount of their earnings on food.*

dis·prove /ˌdɪsˈpruːv/ *verb* **~ sth** to show that sth is wrong or false: *The theory has now been disproved.* OPP **prove**

dis·put·able /dɪˈspjuːtəbl/ *adj.* (*formal*) that can or should be questioned or argued about ➲ compare INDISPUTABLE

dis·pu·ta·tion /ˌdɪspjuˈteɪʃn/ *noun* [C, U] (*formal*) a discussion about sth that people cannot agree on

dis·pute *noun, verb*

■ ***noun*** /dɪˈspjuːt; ˈdɪspjuːt/ [C, U] an argument or a disagreement between two people, groups or countries; discussion about a subject where there is disagreement: **~ (between A and B)** *a dispute between the two countries about the border* ◇ **~ (over/about sth)** *the latest dispute over fishing rights* ◇ ***industrial/pay disputes*** ◇ *The union is* ***in dispute with*** *management over working hours.* ◇ *The cause of the accident was still* ***in dispute*** (= being argued about). ◇ *The matter was settled* ***beyond dispute*** *by the court judgment* (= it could no longer be argued about). ◇ *His theories are* ***open to dispute*** (= can be disagreed with).

■ ***verb*** /dɪˈspjuːt/ **1** [T] to question whether sth is true and valid: **~ sth** *These figures have been disputed.* ◇ *to* ***dispute a decision/claim*** ◇ *The family wanted to dispute the will.* ◇ **~ that...** *No one is disputing that there is a problem.* ◇ **~ whether, how, etc... | it is disputed whether, how, etc ...** *It is disputed whether the law applies in this case.* **2** [T, I] **~ (sth)** to argue or disagree strongly with sb about sth, especially about who owns sth: *disputed territory* ◇ *The issue remains* ***hotly disputed.*** **3** [T] **~ sth** to fight to get control of sth or to win sth: *On the last lap three runners were disputing the lead.*

dis·qual·ify /dɪsˈkwɒlɪfaɪ; *NAmE* -ˈkwɑːl-/ *verb* (**dis·quali·fies, dis·quali·fy·ing, dis·quali·fied, dis·quali·fied**) to prevent sb from doing sth because they have broken a rule or are not suitable SYN **bar**: **~ sb (from sth)** *He was disqualified from the competition for using drugs.* ◇ **~ sb (from doing sth)** (*BrE*) *You could be disqualified from driving for up to three years.* ◇ **~ sb (for sth)** *A heart condition disqualified him for military service.* ▶ **dis·quali·fi·ca·tion** /dɪsˌkwɒlɪfɪˈkeɪʃn; *NAmE* -ˌkwɑːl-/ *noun* [C, U]: *Any form of cheating means automatic disqualification.*

dis·quiet /dɪsˈkwaɪət/ *noun* [U] **~ (about/over sth)** (*formal*) feelings of worry and unhappiness about sth SYN **unease**: *There is considerable public disquiet about the safety of the new trains.*

dis·quiet·ing /dɪsˈkwaɪətɪŋ/ *adj.* (*formal*) causing worry and unhappiness

dis·quisi·tion /ˌdɪskwɪˈzɪʃn/ *noun* (*formal*) a long complicated speech or written report on a particular subject

dis·re·gard /ˌdɪsrɪˈɡɑːd; *NAmE* -ˈɡɑːrd/ *verb, noun*

■ ***verb*** **~ sth** (*formal*) to not consider sth; to treat sth as unimportant SYN **ignore**: *The board completely disregarded my recommendations.* ◇ *Safety rules were disregarded.*

■ ***noun*** [U] **~ (for/of sb/sth)** (*formal*) the act of treating sb/sth as unimportant and not caring about them/it: *She shows a total disregard for other people's feelings.*

dis·re·pair /ˌdɪsrɪˈpeə(r); *NAmE* -ˈper/ *noun* [U] a building, road, etc. that is in a state of **disrepair** has not been taken care of and is broken or in bad condition: *The station quickly* ***fell into disrepair*** *after it was closed.*

dis·rep·ut·able /dɪsˈrepjətəbl/ *adj.* that people consider to be dishonest and bad: *She spent the evening with her disreputable brother Stefan.* ◇ *a disreputable area of the city* OPP **respectable** ➲ compare REPUTABLE

dis·re·pute /ˌdɪsrɪˈpjuːt/ *noun* [U] (*formal*) the fact that sb/sth loses the respect of other people: *The players' behaviour on the field is likely to* ***bring*** *the game* ***into disrepute.***

dis·res·pect /ˌdɪsrɪˈspekt/ *noun, verb*

■ ***noun*** [U, C] **~ (for/to sb/sth)** a lack of respect for sb/sth: *disrespect for the law/the dead* ◇ ***No disrespect intended*** *sir. It was just a joke.* ▶ **dis·res·pect·ful** /-fl/ *adj.* **~ (to sb/sth)** **dis·res·pect·ful·ly** /-fəli/ *adv.*

■ ***verb*** **~ sb/sth** (*informal*) to speak about or treat sb/sth without respect: *They were accused of disrespecting the country's flag.* HELP Some people consider that it is not correct to use **disrespect** as a verb, and that you should use the noun instead, especially in formal and written English: *They were accused of treating the country's flag with disrespect.*

dis·robe /dɪsˈrəʊb; *NAmE* -ˈroʊb/ *verb* [I, T] **~ (sb)** (*formal* or *humorous*) to take off your or sb else's clothes; to take off clothes worn for an official ceremony: *She went behind the screen to disrobe.*

dis·rupt /dɪsˈrʌpt/ *verb* **~ sth** to make it difficult for sth to continue in the normal way: *Demonstrators succeeded in disrupting the meeting.* ◇ *Bus services will be disrupted tomorrow because of the bridge closure.* ▶ **dis·rup·tion** /dɪsˈrʌpʃn/ *noun* [U, C]: *We aim to help you move house with minimum disruption to yourself.* ◇ *disruptions to rail services* ◇ *The strike caused serious disruptions.*

dis·rup·tive /dɪsˈrʌptɪv/ *adj.* causing problems, noise, etc. so that sth cannot continue normally: *She had a disruptive influence on the rest of the class.*

diss = DIS

dis·sat·is·fac·tion /ˌdɪsˌsætɪsˈfækʃn/ *noun* [U] **~ (with/at sb/sth)** a feeling that you are not pleased and satisfied: *Many people have expressed their dissatisfaction with the arrangement.* OPP **satisfaction**

dis·sat·is·fied /dɪsˈsætɪsfaɪd; dɪˈsæt-/ *adj.* not happy or satisfied with sb/sth: *dissatisfied customers* ◇ **~ with sb/sth** *If you are dissatisfied with our service, please write to the manager.* OPP **satisfied** ➲ compare UNSATISFIED

dis·sect /dɪˈsekt; daɪ-/ *verb* **1 ~ sth** to cut up a dead person, animal or plant in order to study it **2 ~ sth** to study sth closely and/or discuss it in great detail: *Her latest novel was dissected by the critics.* **3 ~ sth** to divide sth into smaller pieces, areas, etc: *The city is dissected by a network of old canals.* ▶ **dis·sec·tion** /dɪˈsekʃn; daɪ-/ *noun* [U, C]: *anatomical dissection* ◇ *Your enjoyment of a novel can suffer from too much analysis and dissection.*

dis·sem·ble /dɪˈsembl/ *verb* [I, T] **~ (sth)** (*formal*) to hide your real feelings or intentions, often by pretending to have different ones: *She was a very honest person who was incapable of dissembling.*

dis·sem·in·ate /dɪˈsemɪneɪt/ *verb* **~ sth** (*formal*) to spread information, knowledge, etc. so that it reaches many people: *Their findings have been* ***widely disseminated.*** ▶ **dis·sem·in·ation** /dɪˌsemɪˈneɪʃn/ *noun* [U]

dis·sen·sion /dɪˈsenʃn/ *noun* [U] (*formal*) disagreement between people or within a group: *dissension within the government*

dis·sent /dɪˈsent/ *noun, verb*

■ ***noun*** (*formal*) **1** [U] the fact of having or expressing opinions that are different from those that are officially accepted: ***political/religious dissent*** **2** [C] (*NAmE*) a judge's statement giving reasons why he or she disagrees with a decision made by the other judges in a court case

■ ***verb*** [I] **~ (from sth)** (*formal*) to have or express opinions that are different from those that are officially accepted: *Only two ministers dissented from the official view.* ▶ **dis·sent·ing** *adj.*: ***dissenting groups/voices/views/opinion***

dis·sent·er /dɪˈsentə(r)/ *noun* a person who does not agree with opinions that are officially or generally accepted

dis·ser·ta·tion /ˌdɪsəˈteɪʃn; *NAmE* -sərˈt-/ *noun* **~ (on sth)** a long piece of writing on a particular subject, especially one written for a university degree ➲ WRITING TUTOR page WT10

dis·ser·vice /dɪsˈsɜːvɪs; dɪˈsɜː-; *NAmE* -ˈsɜːrv-/ *noun* [sing.] IDM **do sb a disˈservice** to do sth that harms sb and the opinion that other people have of them

dis·si·dent /ˈdɪsɪdənt/ *noun* a person who strongly disagrees with and criticizes their government, especially in a country where this kind of action is dangerous ▸ **dis·si·dence** /ˈdɪsɪdəns/ *noun* [U] **dis·si·dent** *adj.*

dis·simi·lar AW /dɪˈsɪmɪlə(r)/ *adj.* ~ (**from/to sb/sth**) (*formal*) not the same: *These wines are* **not dissimilar** (= are similar). OPP **similar** ▸ **dis·simi·lar·ity** /ˌdɪsɪmɪˈlærəti/ *noun* [C, U]

dis·simu·late /dɪˈsɪmjuleɪt/ *verb* [T, I] ~ (**sth**) (*formal*) to hide your real feelings or intentions, often by pretending to have different ones SYN **dissemble** ▸ **dis·simu·la·tion** /dɪˌsɪmjuˈleɪʃn/ *noun* [U]

D

dis·si·pate /ˈdɪsɪpeɪt/ *verb* (*formal*) **1** [I, T] to gradually become or make sth become weaker until it disappears: *Eventually, his anger dissipated.* ◇ ~ **sth** *Her laughter soon dissipated the tension in the air.* **2** [T] ~ **sth** to waste sth, such as time or money, especially by not planning the best way of using it SYN **squander**

dis·si·pated /ˈdɪsɪpeɪtɪd/ *adj.* (*disapproving*) enjoying activities that are harmful such as drinking too much alcohol

dis·si·pa·tion /ˌdɪsɪˈpeɪʃn/ *noun* [U] (*formal*) **1** the process of disappearing or of making sth disappear: *the dissipation of energy in the form of heat* **2** the act of wasting money or spending money until there is none left: *concerns about the dissipation of the country's wealth* **3** (*disapproving*) behaviour which is enjoyable but has a harmful effect on you

dis·so·ci·ate /dɪˈsəʊʃieɪt; -ˈsəʊs-; *NAmE* -ˈsoʊ-/ *verb* **1** (also **dis·as·so·ci·ate**) ~ **yourself/sb from sb/sth** to say or do sth to show that you are not connected with or do not support sb/sth; to make it clear that sth is not connected with a particular plan, action, etc: *He tried to dissociate himself from the party's more extreme views.* ◇ *They were determined to dissociate the UN from any agreement to impose sanctions.* **2** ~ **sb/sth** (**from sth**) (*formal*) to think of two people or things as separate and not connected with each other: *She tried to dissociate the two events in her mind.* OPP **associate** ▸ **dis·so·ci·ation** /dɪˌsəʊʃiˈeɪʃn; -ˌsəʊs-; *NAmE* -ˌsoʊ-/ *noun* [U]

dis·sol·ute /ˈdɪsəluːt/ *adj.* (*formal, disapproving*) enjoying immoral activities and not caring about behaving in a morally acceptable way

dis·sol·ution /ˌdɪsəˈluːʃn/ *noun* [U] ~ (**of sth**) (*formal*) **1** the act of officially ending a marriage, a business agreement or a parliament **2** the process in which sth gradually disappears: *the dissolution of barriers of class and race* **3** the act of breaking up an organization, etc.

dis·solve 🔑 /dɪˈzɒlv; *NAmE* -ˈzɑːlv/ *verb* **1** 🔑 [I] ~ (**in sth**) (of a solid) to mix with a liquid and become part of it: *Salt dissolves in water.* ◇ *Heat gently until the sugar dissolves.* **2** 🔑 [T] ~ **sth** (**in sth**) to make a solid become part of a liquid: *Dissolve the tablet in water.* **3** [T] ~ **sth** to officially end a marriage, business agreement or parliament: *Their marriage was dissolved in 1999.* ◇ *The election was announced and parliament was dissolved.* **4** [I, T] to disappear; to make sth disappear: *When the ambulance had gone, the crowd dissolved.* ◇ ~ **sth** *His calm response dissolved her anger.* **5** [I] ~ **into laughter, tears, etc.** to suddenly start laughing, crying, etc: *When the teacher looked up, the children dissolved into giggles.* ◇ *Every time she heard his name, she dissolved into tears.* **6** [T, I] to remove or destroy sth, especially by a chemical process; to be destroyed in this way: ~ **sth** (**away**) *a new detergent that dissolves stains* ◇ ~ (**away**) *All the original calcium had dissolved away.*

dis·son·ance /ˈdɪsənəns/ *noun* **1** [C, U] (*music*) a combination of musical notes that do not sound pleasant together OPP **consonance** **2** [U] (*formal*) lack of agreement ▸ **dis·son·ant** /ˈdɪsənənt/ *adj.*: ***dissonant voices/notes***

dis·suade /dɪˈsweɪd/ *verb* ~ **sb** (**from sth/from doing sth**) to persuade sb not to do sth: *I tried to dissuade him from giving up his job.* ◇ *They were going to set off in the fog, but were dissuaded.*

dis·taff /ˈdɪstɑːf; *NAmE* ˈdɪstæf/ *noun* a stick that was used in the past for holding wool when it was spun by hand
IDM **on the distaff side** (*old-fashioned*) on the woman's side of the family

dis·tal /ˈdɪstl/ *adj.* (*anatomy*) located away from the centre of the body or at the far end of sth: *the distal end of the tibia*

dis·tance 🔑 /ˈdɪstəns/ *noun, verb*
▪ ***noun*** **1** 🔑 [C, U] the amount of space between two places or things: *a* ***short/long distance*** ◇ *the distance of the earth from the sun* ◇ ***a distance of*** *200 kilometres* ◇ *What's the distance between New York City and Boston/from New York City to Boston?* ◇ *In the US, distance is measured in miles.* ◇ *The beach is* ***within walking distance*** *of my house* (= you can walk there easily). ◇ *Paul has to drive very long distances as part of his job.* ◇ *Our parents live some* ***distance away*** (= quite far away). ➲ see also LONG-DISTANCE, MIDDLE DISTANCE, OUTDISTANCE **2** 🔑 [U] being far away in space or in time: *Distance is no problem on the Internet.* **3** 🔑 [sing.] a point that is a particular amount of space away from sth else: *You'll never get the ball in from that distance.* **4** [C, usually sing., U] a difference or lack of a connection between two things: *The distance between fashion and art remains as great as ever.* ◇ *The government is keen to* ***put some distance between*** *itself and these events* (= show that there is no connection between them). ◇ (*BrE*) *Eddie is,* ***by some distance*** (= by a great amount), *the funniest character in the show.* **5** [U, C] a situation in which there is a lack of friendly feelings or of a close relationship between two people or groups of people: *The coldness and distance in her voice took me by surprise.*
IDM **at/from a ˈdistance** from a place or time that is not near; from far away: *She had loved him at a distance for years.* **go the** (**full**) **ˈdistance** to continue playing in a competition or sports contest until the end: *Nobody thought he would last 15 rounds, but he went the full distance.* **in/into the ˈdistance** 🔑 far away but still able to be seen or heard: *We saw lights in the distance.* ◇ *Alice stood staring into the distance.* **keep sb at a ˈdistance** to refuse to be friendly with sb; to not let sb be friendly towards you **keep your ˈdistance** (**from sb/sth**) **1** to make sure you are not too near sb/sth **2** to avoid getting too friendly or involved with a person, group, etc: *She was warned to keep her distance from Charles if she didn't want to get hurt.* ➲ more at SHOUTING, SPIT *v.*, STRIKE *v.*
▪ ***verb*** ~ **yourself/sb/sth** (**from sb/sth**) to become, or to make sb/sth become, less involved or connected with sb/sth: *When he retired, he tried to distance himself from politics.* ◇ *It's not always easy for nurses to distance themselves emotionally.*

ˈdistance learning *noun* [U] a system of education in which people study at home with the help of special Internet sites and television and radio programmes, and send or email work to their teachers

dis·tant /ˈdɪstənt/ *adj.* **1** far away in space or time: *the distant sound of music* ◇ *distant stars/planets* ◇ *The time we spent together is now a distant memory.* ◇ (*formal*) *The airport was about 20 kilometres distant.* ◇ *a star 30 000 light years distant from the Earth* ◇ (*figurative*) *Peace was just a distant hope* (= not very likely). **2** ~ (**from sth**) not like sth else SYN **remote**: *Their life seemed utterly distant from his own.* **3** [only before noun] (of a person) related to you but not closely: *a* ***distant cousin/aunt/relative*** **4** not friendly; not wanting a close relationship with sb: *Pat sounded very cold and distant on the phone.* **5** not paying attention to sth but thinking about sth completely different: *There was a distant look in her eyes; her mind was obviously on something else.* ▸ **dis·tant·ly** *adv.*: *Somewhere, distantly, he could hear the sound of the sea.* ◇ *We're distantly related.* ◇ *Holly smiled distantly.*
IDM **the** (**ˌdim and**) **ˌdistant ˈpast** a long time ago: *stories from the distant past* **in the not too ˌdistant ˈfuture** not a long time in the future but fairly soon

dis·taste /dɪsˈteɪst/ *noun* [U, sing.] a feeling that sb/sth is unpleasant or offensive: *He looked around the filthy room in distaste.* ◇ ~ **for sb/sth** *a distaste for politics of any sort*

dis·taste·ful /dɪsˈteɪstfl/ *adj.* (*formal*) unpleasant or offensive

dis·tem·per /dɪˈstempə(r)/ *noun* [U] **1** an infectious disease of animals, especially cats and dogs, that causes fever and coughing **2** (*BrE*) a type of paint that is mixed with water and used on walls

dis·tend /dɪˈstend/ *verb* [I, T] **~ (sth)** (*formal* or *medical*) to swell or make sth swell because of pressure from inside: *starving children with huge distended bellies* ▶ **dis·ten·sion** /dɪˈstenʃn/ *noun* [U]: *distension of the stomach*

dis·til (*NAmE* also **dis·till**) /dɪˈstɪl/ *verb* (-ll-) **1 ~ sth (from sth)** to make a liquid pure by heating it until it becomes a gas, then cooling it and collecting the drops of liquid that form: *to distil fresh water from sea water* ◇ *distilled water* **2 ~ sth** to make sth such as a strong alcoholic drink in this way: *The factory distils and bottles whisky.* **3 ~ sth (from/into sth)** (*formal*) to get the essential meaning or ideas from thoughts, information, experiences, etc: *The notes I made on my travels were distilled into a book.* ▶ **dis·til·la·tion** /ˌdɪstɪˈleɪʃn/ *noun* [C, U]: *the distillation process*

dis·til·late /ˈdɪstɪleɪt/ *noun* [U, C] (*technical*) a substance which is formed by distilling a liquid

dis·til·ler /dɪˈstɪlə(r)/ *noun* a person or company that produces SPIRITS (= strong alcoholic drinks) such as WHISKY by distilling them

dis·til·lery /dɪˈstɪləri/ *noun* (*pl.* -ies) a factory where strong alcoholic drink is made by the process of distilling

dis·tinct AW /dɪˈstɪŋkt/ *adj.* **1** easily or clearly heard, seen, felt, etc: *There was a distinct smell of gas.* ◇ *His voice was quiet but every word was distinct.* **2** clearly different or of a different kind: *The results of the survey fell into two distinct groups.* ◇ **~ from sth** *Jamaican reggae music is quite distinct from North American jazz or blues.* ◇ *rural areas, **as distinct from** major cities* **3** [only before noun] used to emphasize that you think an idea or situation definitely exists and is important SYN **definite**: *Being tall gave Tony a distinct advantage.* ◇ *I had the distinct impression I was being watched.* ◇ *A strike is now a distinct possibility.* ▶ **dis·tinct·ly** AW *adv.*: *I distinctly heard someone calling me.* ◇ *a distinctly Australian accent* ◇ *He could remember everything very distinctly.* **dis·tinct·ness** *noun* [U]

dis·tinc·tion AW /dɪˈstɪŋkʃn/ *noun* **1** [C] **~ (between A and B)** a clear difference or contrast especially between people or things that are similar or related: *distinctions between traditional and modern societies* ◇ *Philosophers did not use to **make a distinction** between arts and science.* ◇ *We need to **draw a distinction** between the two events.* **2** [U] the quality of being excellent or important: *a writer of distinction* **3** [sing.] the quality of being sth that is special: *She **had the distinction of** being the first woman to fly the Atlantic.* **4** [U] **~ (between A and B)** the separation of people or things into different groups: *The new law **makes no distinction** between adults and children* (= treats them equally). ◇ *All groups are entitled to this money **without distinction**.* **5** [C, U] a special mark/grade or award that is given to sb, especially a student, for excellent work: *Naomi got a distinction in maths.* ◇ *He graduated **with distinction**.*

dis·tinct·ive AW /dɪˈstɪŋktɪv/ *adj.* having a quality or characteristic that makes sth different and easily noticed SYN **characteristic**: *clothes with a distinctive style* ◇ *The male bird has distinctive white markings on its head.* ▶ **dis·tinct·ive·ly** AW *adv.*: *a distinctively nutty flavour*

dis·tin·guish 🔑 /dɪˈstɪŋgwɪʃ/ *verb*
1 🔑 [I, T] to recognize the difference between two people or things SYN **differentiate**: **~ between A and B** *At what age are children able to distinguish between right and wrong?* ◇ **~ A from B** *It was hard to distinguish one twin from the other.* ◇ **~ A and B** *Sometimes reality and fantasy are hard to distinguish.* **2** 🔑 [T] (not used in the progressive tenses) **~ A (from B)** to be a characteristic that makes two people, animals or things different: *What was it that distinguished her from her classmates?* ◇ *The male bird is distinguished from the female by its red beak.* ◇ *Does your cat have any distinguishing marks?* **3** [T] (not used in the progressive tenses) **~ sth** to be able to see or hear sth SYN **differentiate, make out**: *I could not distinguish her words, but she sounded agitated.* **4** [T] **~ yourself (as sth)** to do sth so well that people notice and admire you: *She has already distinguished herself as an athlete.* ▶ **dis·tin·guish·able** /dɪˈstɪŋgwɪʃəbl/ *adj.*: **~ (from sb/sth)** *The male bird is easily distinguishable from the female.* ◇ *The coast was barely distinguishable in the mist.*

dis·tin·guished /dɪˈstɪŋgwɪʃt/ *adj.* **1** very successful and admired by other people: *a distinguished career in medicine* **2** having an appearance that makes sb look important or that makes people admire or respect them: *I think grey hair makes you look very distinguished.*

dis·tort AW /dɪˈstɔːt; *NAmE* dɪˈstɔːrt/ *verb* **1 ~ sth** to change the shape, appearance or sound of sth so that it is strange or not clear: *a fairground mirror that distorts your shape* ◇ *The loudspeaker seemed to distort his voice.* **2 ~ sth** to twist or change facts, ideas, etc. so that they are no longer correct or true: *Newspapers are often guilty of distorting the truth.* ◇ *The article gave a distorted picture of his childhood.* ▶ **dis·tort·ion** AW /dɪˈstɔːʃn; *NAmE* dɪˈstɔːrʃn/ *noun* [C, U]: *modern alloys that are resistant to wear and distortion* ◇ *a distortion of the facts*

dis·tract /dɪˈstrækt/ *verb* **~ sb/sth (from sth)** to take sb's attention away from what they are trying to do SYN **divert**: *You're distracting me from my work.* ◇ *Don't talk to her—she's very easily distracted.* ◇ *It was another attempt to **distract attention** from the truth.* ▶ **dis·tract·ing** *adj.*: *distracting thoughts* ◇ *a distracting noise*

dis·tract·ed /dɪˈstræktɪd/ *adj.* **~ (by sb/sth)** unable to pay attention to sb/sth because you are worried or thinking about sth else ▶ **dis·tract·ed·ly** *adv.*

dis·trac·tion /dɪˈstrækʃn/ *noun* **1** [C, U] a thing that takes your attention away from what you are doing or thinking about: *I find it hard to work at home because there are too many distractions.* ◇ *cinema audiences looking for distraction* **2** [C] an activity that amuses or entertains you
IDM **to diˈstraction** so that you become upset, excited or angry, and not able to think clearly: *The children are **driving me to distraction** today.*

dis·trac·tor /dɪˈstræktə(r)/ *noun* **1** a person or thing that takes your attention away from what you should be doing **2** one of the wrong answers in a MULTIPLE-CHOICE test

dis·traught /dɪˈstrɔːt/ *adj.* extremely upset and anxious so that you cannot think clearly

dis·tress /dɪˈstres/ *noun, verb*
■ ***noun*** [U] **1** a feeling of great worry or unhappiness; great suffering: *The newspaper article caused the actor considerable distress.* ◇ *She was obviously **in distress** after the attack.* ◇ *deep emotional distress* **2** suffering and problems caused by not having enough money, food, etc. SYN **hardship**: ***economic/financial distress*** **3** a situation in which a ship, plane, etc. is in danger or difficulty and needs help: ***a distress signal*** (= a message asking for help) ◇ *It is a rule of the sea to help another boat **in distress**.* IDM see DAMSEL
■ ***verb*** to make sb feel very worried or unhappy: **~ sb** *It was clear that the letter had deeply distressed her.* ◇ **~ yourself** *Don't distress yourself* (= don't worry).

dis·tressed /dɪˈstrest/ *adj.* **1** upset and anxious: *He was too distressed and confused to answer their questions.* **2** suffering pain; in a poor physical condition: *When the baby was born, it was blue and distressed.* **3** (of a piece of clothing or furniture) made to look older and more worn than it really is: *a distressed leather jacket* **4** (*formal* or *business*) having problems caused by lack of money: *They buy up financially distressed companies.* ◇ *The charity helps kids in distressed situations.*

dis·tress·ing /dɪˈstresɪŋ/ *adj.* making you feel extremely upset, especially because of sb's suffering ▶ **dis·tress·ing·ly** *adv.*

dis·trib·ute 🔑 AW /dɪˈstrɪbjuːt; ˈdɪstrɪbjuːt/ *verb*
1 🔑 to give things to a large number of people; to share sth between a number of people: **~ sth** *The newspaper is distributed free.* ◇ **~ sth to sb/sth** *The organization distributed food to the earthquake victims.* ◇ **~ sth among sb/sth** *The money was distributed among schools in the area.* **2** 🔑 **~ sth** to send goods to shops/stores and businesses so that they can be sold: *Who distributes our products in the*

D

UK? **3** [often passive] **~ sth** to spread sth, or different parts of sth, over an area: *Make sure that your weight is evenly distributed.*

dis·tri·bu·tion AW /ˌdɪstrɪˈbjuːʃn/ *noun* **1** [U, C] the way that sth is shared or exists over a particular area or among a particular group of people: *the unfair distribution of wealth* ◇ *The map shows the distribution of this species across the world.* ◇ *They studied the geographical distribution of the disease.* **2** [U] the act of giving or delivering sth to a number of people: *the distribution of food and medicines to the flood victims* ◇ *He was arrested on drug distribution charges.* **3** [U] (*business*) the system of transporting and delivering goods: *distribution costs* ◇ *worldwide distribution systems* ◇ *marketing, sales and distribution* ▸ **dis·tri·bu·tion·al** AW /-ʃənl/ *adj.*

distriˈbution board *noun* (*BrE, physics*) a board that contains the connections for several electrical CIRCUITS

dis·tribu·tive AW /dɪˈstrɪbjətɪv/ *adj.* [usually before noun] (*business*) connected with distribution of goods

dis·tribu·tor AW /dɪˈstrɪbjətə(r)/ *noun* **1** a person or company that supplies goods to shops/stores, etc: *Japan's largest software distributor* **2** a device in an engine that sends electric current to the SPARK PLUGS

dis·trict /ˈdɪstrɪkt/ *noun* **1** an area of a country or town, especially one that has particular features: *the City of London's financial district* **2** one of the areas which a country, town or state is divided into for purposes of organization, with official BOUNDARIES (= borders): *a* ***tax/postal district*** ◇ *a school district* ◇ *congressional districts* ◇ *district councils*

ˌdistrict aˈttorney *noun* (*abbr.* DA) (in the US) a lawyer who is responsible for bringing criminal charges against sb in a particular area or state

ˌdistrict ˈcourt *noun* (in the US) a court that deals with cases in a particular area

ˌdistrict ˈnurse *noun* (in Britain) a nurse who visits patients in their homes

dis·trust /dɪsˈtrʌst/ *noun, verb*
- ***noun*** [U, sing.] a feeling of not being able to trust sb/sth: *They looked at each other with distrust.* ◇ **~ of sb/sth** *He has a deep distrust of all modern technology.* ▸ **dis·trust·ful** /-fl/ *adj.*: *distrustful of authority*
- ***verb*** **~ sb/sth** to feel that you cannot trust or believe sb/sth: *She distrusted his motives for wanting to see her again.* ➲ compare MISTRUST

Which Word?

distrust / mistrust

- There is very little difference between these two words, but **distrust** is more common and perhaps slightly stronger. If you are sure that someone is acting dishonestly or cannot be relied on, you are more likely to say that you **distrust** them. If you are expressing doubts and suspicions, on the other hand, you would probably use **mistrust**.

dis·turb /dɪˈstɜːb; *NAmE* -ˈstɜːrb/ *verb* **1** **~ sb/sth** to interrupt sb when they are trying to work, sleep, etc: *I'm sorry to disturb you, but can I talk to you for a moment?* ◇ *If you get up early, try not to disturb everyone else.* ◇ ***Do not disturb*** (= a sign placed on the outside of the door of a hotel room, office, etc.) ◇ *She awoke early after a disturbed night.* **2** **~ sth** to move sth or change its position: *Don't disturb the papers on my desk.* **3** to make sb worry: **~ sb** *The letter shocked and disturbed me.* ◇ **it disturbs sb to do sth** *It disturbed her to realize that she was alone.*

dis·turb·ance /dɪˈstɜːbəns; *NAmE* -ˈstɜːrb-/ *noun* **1** [U, C, usually sing.] actions that make you stop what you are doing, or that upset the normal state that sth is in; the act of disturbing sb/sth or the fact of being disturbed: *The building work is creating constant noise, dust and disturbance.* ◇ *a disturbance in the usual pattern of events* ◇ *the disturbance of the local wildlife by tourists* **2** [C] a situation in which people behave violently in a public place: *serious disturbances in the streets* ◇ *He was charged with causing a disturbance after the game.* **3** [U, C] a state in which sb's mind or a function of the body is upset and not working normally: *emotional disturbance*

dis·turbed /dɪˈstɜːbd; *NAmE* -ˈstɜːrbd/ *adj.* **1** mentally ill, especially because of very unhappy or shocking experiences: *a special school for emotionally disturbed children* ➲ note at MENTALLY ILL **2** unhappy and full of bad or shocking experiences: *The killer had a disturbed family background.* **3** very anxious and unhappy about sth: *I was deeply disturbed and depressed by the news.* ➲ compare UNDISTURBED

dis·turb·ing /dɪˈstɜːbɪŋ; *NAmE* -ˈstɜːrb-/ *adj.* making you feel anxious and upset or shocked: *a disturbing piece of news* ▸ **dis·turb·ing·ly** *adv.*

dis·unite /ˌdɪsjuˈnaɪt/ *verb* [usually passive] **~ sb/sth** (*formal*) to make a group of people unable to agree with each other or work together: *a disunited political party*

dis·unity /dɪsˈjuːnəti/ *noun* [U] (*formal*) a lack of agreement between people: *disunity within the Conservative party* OPP **unity**

dis·use /dɪsˈjuːs/ *noun* [U] a situation in which sth is no longer being used: *The factory* ***fell into disuse*** *twenty years ago.*

dis·used /ˌdɪsˈjuːzd/ *adj.* [usually before noun] no longer used: *a disused station* ➲ compare UNUSED

ditch /dɪtʃ/ *noun, verb*
- ***noun*** a long channel dug at the side of a field or road, to hold or take away water ➲ VISUAL VOCAB page V2
- ***verb*** **1** [T] **~ sth/sb** (*informal*) to get rid of sth/sb because you no longer want or need it/them: *The new road building programme has been ditched.* ◇ *He ditched his girlfriend.* **2** [T, I] **~ (sth)** if a pilot **ditches** an aircraft, or if it **ditches**, it lands in the sea in an emergency **3** [T] **~ school** (*NAmE, informal*) to stay away from school without permission

ditch·water /ˈdɪtʃwɔːtə(r)/ *noun* [U] IDM see DULL *adv.*

dither /ˈdɪðə(r)/ *verb, noun*
- ***verb*** [I] to hesitate about what to do because you are unable to decide: *Stop dithering and get on with it.* ◇ **~ over sth** *She was dithering over what to wear.*
- ***noun*** [sing.] (*informal*) **1** a state of not being able to decide what you should do: *I'm* ***in a dither*** *about who to invite.* **2** a state of excitement or worry: *Don't get yourself* ***in a dither*** *over everything.*

di·tran·si·tive /daɪˈtrænsətɪv; -ˈtrænz-/ *adj.* (*grammar*) (of verbs) used with two objects. In the sentence 'I gave her the book', for example, the verb 'give' is ditransitive and 'her' and 'the books' are both objects.

ditsy = DITZY

ditto /ˈdɪtəʊ; *NAmE* -toʊ/ *noun, adv.*
- ***noun*** (*abbr.* do.) (*symb.* ") used, especially in a list, underneath a particular word or phrase, to show that it is repeated and to avoid having to write it again
- ***adv.*** (*informal*) used instead of a particular word or phrase, to avoid repeating it: *The waiters were rude and unhelpful, the manager ditto.*

ditty /ˈdɪti/ *noun* (*pl.* **-ies**) (often *humorous*) a short simple song

ditzy (also **ditsy**) /ˈdɪtsi/ *adj.* (*informal, especially NAmE*) (usually of a woman) silly; not able to be trusted to remember things or to think in an organized way

di·ur·et·ic /ˌdaɪjuˈretɪk/ *noun* (*medical*) a substance that causes an increase in the flow of URINE ▸ **di·ur·et·ic** *adj.*: ***diuretic drugs/effects***

di·ur·nal /daɪˈɜːnl; *NAmE* -ˈɜːrnl/ *adj.* **1** (*biology*) (of animals) active during the day OPP **nocturnal** **2** (*astronomy*) taking one day: *the diurnal rotation of the earth*

Div. *abbr.* (in writing) DIVISION: *League Div. 1* (= in football/SOCCER)

diva /ˈdiːvə/ *noun* a famous woman singer, especially an OPERA singer

Di·vali = DIWALI

divan /dɪˈvæn; *NAmE* ˈdaɪvæn/ *noun* **1** (also **diˌvan ˈbed**) (both *BrE*) a bed with a thick base and a MATTRESS ➲ VISUAL VOCAB page V20 **2** a long low soft seat without a back or arms

dive /daɪv/ *verb, noun*

■ ***verb*** (**dived, dived**, *NAmE* also **dove** /dəʊv; *NAmE* doʊv/, **dived**)

▸ JUMP INTO WATER **1** [I] **~ (from/off sth) (into sth)** | **~ (in)** to jump into water with your head and arms going in first: *We dived into the river to cool off.*

▸ UNDERWATER **2** (usually **go diving**) [I] to swim underwater wearing breathing equipment, collecting or looking at things: *to dive for pearls* ◇ *The main purpose of his holiday to Greece was to go diving.* ➲ see also DIVING **3** [I] to go to a deeper level underwater: *The whale dived as the harpoon struck it.*

▸ OF BIRDS/AIRCRAFT **4** [I] to go steeply down through the air: *The seagulls soared then dived.* ➲ see also NOSEDIVE

▸ OF PRICES **5** [I] to fall suddenly SYN **plunge**: *The share price dived from 49p to an all-time low of 40p.*

▸ MOVE/JUMP/FALL **6** [I] (*informal*) to move or jump quickly in a particular direction, especially to avoid sth, to try to catch a ball, etc: **~ for sth** *We heard an explosion and* ***dived for cover*** (= got into a place where we would be protected). ◇ *The goalie dived for the ball, but missed it.* ◇ **+ adv./prep.** *It started to rain so we dived into the nearest cafe.* **7** [I] (in football (SOCCER), HOCKEY, etc.) to fall deliberately when sb TACKLES you, so that the REFEREE awards a FOUL

PHR V **ˈdive into sth** (*informal*) to put your hand quickly into sth such as a bag or pocket: *She dived into her bag and took out a couple of coins.*

■ ***noun***

▸ JUMP INTO WATER **1** a jump into deep water with your head first and your arms in front of you: *a spectacular high dive* (= from high above the water)

▸ UNDERWATER **2** an act of going underwater and swimming there with special equipment: *a dive to a depth of 18 metres*

▸ OF BIRDS/AIRCRAFT **3** an act of suddenly flying downwards

▸ BAR/CLUB **4** (*informal*) a bar, music club, etc. that is cheap, and perhaps dark or dirty

▸ FALL **5** (*BrE*) (in football (SOCCER), HOCKEY, etc.) a deliberate fall that a player makes when sb TACKLES them, so that the REFEREE awards a FOUL

IDM **make a ˈdive (for sth)** to suddenly move or jump forward to do sth or reach sb/sth: *The goalkeeper made a dive for the ball.* **take a ˈdive** (*informal*) to suddenly get worse: *Profits really took a dive last year.*

ˈdive-bomb *verb* **~ sb/sth** (of an aircraft, a bird, etc.) to dive steeply through the air and attack sb/sth

diver /ˈdaɪvə(r)/ *noun* **1** a person who works underwater, usually with special equipment: *a deep-sea diver* ➲ compare FROGMAN **2** a person who jumps into the water with their head first and their arms in front of them

di·verge /daɪˈvɜːdʒ; *NAmE* -ˈvɜːrdʒ/ *verb* (*formal*) **1** [I] to separate and go in different directions: *The parallel lines appear to diverge.* ◇ *We went through school and college together, but then our paths diverged.* ◇ **~ from sth** *The coastal road diverges from the freeway just north of Santa Monica.* ◇ *Many species have diverged from a single ancestor.* **2** [I] **~ (from sth)** (*formal*) (of opinions, views, etc.) to be different: *Opinions diverge greatly on this issue.* **3** [I] **~ from sth** to be or become different from what is expected, planned, etc: *to diverge from the norm* ◇ *He diverged from established procedure.* OPP **converge** ▸ **di·ver·gence** /daɪˈvɜːdʒəns; *NAmE* -ˈvɜːrdʒ-/ *noun* [C, U]: *a wide divergence of opinion* **di·ver·gent** /-dʒənt/ *adj.*: ***divergent paths/opinions***

divers /ˈdaɪvəz; *NAmE* -vərz/ *adj.* [only before noun] (*old use*) of many different kinds

di·verse AW /daɪˈvɜːs; *NAmE* -ˈvɜːrs/ *adj.* very different from each other and of various kinds: *people from diverse cultures* ◇ *My interests are very diverse.*

di·ver·sify AW /daɪˈvɜːsɪfaɪ; *NAmE* -ˈvɜːrs-/ *verb* (**di·ver·si·fies, di·ver·si·fy·ing, di·ver·si·fied, di·ver·si·fied**) **1** [I, T] **~ (sth) (into sth)** (especially of a business or company) to develop a wider range of products, interests, skills, etc. in order to be more successful or reduce risk SYN **branch out**: *Farmers are being encouraged to diversify into new crops.* **2** [I, T] to change or to make sth change so that there is greater variety: *Patterns of family life are diversifying.* ◇ **~ sth** *The culture has been diversified with the arrival of immigrants.* ▸ **di·ver·si·fi·ca·tion** AW /daɪˌvɜːsɪfɪˈkeɪʃn; *NAmE* -ˌvɜːrs-/ *noun* [U]

di·ver·sion /daɪˈvɜːʃn; *NAmE* -ˈvɜːrʒn/ *noun* **1** [C, U] the act of changing the direction that sb/sth is following, or what sth is used for: *a river diversion project* ◇ *We made a short diversion to go and look at the castle.* ◇ *the diversion of funds from the public to the private sector of industry* **2** [C] something that takes your attention away from sb/sth while sth else is happening: *For the government, the war was a welcome diversion from the country's economic problems.* ◇ *A smoke bomb* ***created a diversion*** *while the robbery took place.* **3** [C] (*BrE*) (*NAmE* **de·tour**) a road or route that is used when the usual one is closed: *Diversions will be signposted.* **4** [C] (*formal*) an activity that is done for pleasure, especially because it takes your attention away from sth else SYN **distraction**: *The party will make a pleasant diversion.* ◇ *The city is full of diversions.*

di·ver·sion·ary /daɪˈvɜːʃənəri; *NAmE* -ˈvɜːrʒəneri/ *adj.* intended to take sb's attention away from sth

di·ver·sity AW /daɪˈvɜːsəti; *NAmE* -ˈvɜːrs-/ *noun* **1** [U, C, usually sing.] a range of many people or things that are very different from each other SYN **variety**: *the biological diversity of the rainforests* ◇ *a* ***great/wide/rich diversity*** *of opinion* **2** [U] the quality or fact of including a range of many people or things: *There is a need for greater diversity and choice in education.* ➲ COLLOCATIONS at RACE

di·vert /daɪˈvɜːt; *NAmE* -ˈvɜːrt/ *verb* **~ sb/sth (from sth) (to sth) 1** to make sb/sth change direction: *Northbound traffic will have to be diverted onto minor roads.* **2 ~ sth** to use money, materials, etc. for a different purpose from their original purpose **3 ~ sth** to take sb's thoughts or attention away from sth SYN **distract**: *The war diverted people's attention away from the economic situation.* **4 ~ sb** (*formal*) to entertain people: *Children are easily diverted.*

di·vert·ing /daɪˈvɜːtɪŋ; *NAmE* -ˈvɜːrt-/ *adj.* (*formal*) entertaining and amusing

di·vest /daɪˈvest/ *verb* (*formal*) **1 ~ sb/yourself of sth** to remove clothes: *He divested himself of his jacket.* **2 ~ yourself of sth** to get rid of sth: *The company is divesting itself of some of its assets.* **3 ~ sb/sth of sth** to take sth away from sb/sth: *After her illness she was divested of much of her responsibility.*

di·vest·ment /daɪˈvestmənt/ *noun* [U, C] (*finance*) the act of selling the shares you have bought in a company or of taking money away from where you have invested it

div·ide 0‑w /dɪˈvaɪd/ *verb, noun*

■ ***verb***

> **WORD FAMILY**
> **divide** *verb, noun*
> **division** *noun*
> **divisive** *adj.*

▸ SEPARATE **1** 0‑w [I, T] to separate or make sth separate into parts SYN **split up**: **~ (up) (into sth)** *The cells began to divide rapidly.* ◇ **~ sth (up) (into sth)** *A sentence can be divided up into meaningful segments.* **2** 0‑w [T] to separate sth into parts and give a share to each of a number of different people, etc. SYN **share (out)**: **~ sth (up/out)** *Jack divided up the rest of the cash.* ◇ **~ sth (up/out) between/among sb** *We divided the work between us.* **3** 0‑w [T] **~ sth (between A and B)** to use different parts of your time, energy, etc. for different activities, etc: *He divides his energies between politics and business.* **4** 0‑w [T] **~ A from B** (*formal*) to separate two people or things: *Can it ever be right to divide a mother from her child?* **5** [T] **~ sth (off)** | **~ A from B** to be the real or imaginary line or barrier that separates two people or things SYN **separate (off)**: *A fence divides off the western side of the grounds.* **6** 0‑w [I] (of a road) to separ-

ate into two parts that lead in different directions: *Where the path divides, keep right.*
▸ CAUSE DISAGREEMENT **7** [T] **~ sb/sth** to make two or more people disagree SYN **split**: *The issue has divided the government.*
▸ MATHEMATICS **8** [T, I] **~ (sth) by sth** to find out how many times one number is contained in another: *30 divided by 6 is 5* (30 ÷ 6 = 5). **9** [I, T] **~ (sth) into sth** to be able to be multiplied to give another number: *5 divides into 30 6 times.*

D

IDM **di,vide and 'rule** to keep control over people by making them disagree with and fight each other, therefore not giving them the chance to unite and oppose you together: *a policy of divide and rule* ⊃ more at MIDDLE *n.*

■ ***noun*** [usually sing.]
▸ DIFFERENCE **1** a difference between two groups of people that separates them from each other: *the* ***North/South divide*** ◇ **~ between A and B** *the divide between Catholics and Protestants in Northern Ireland*
▸ BETWEEN RIVERS **2** (*especially NAmE*) a line of high land that separates two systems of rivers SYN **watershed** IDM see BRIDGE *v.*

div·ided /dɪˈvaɪdɪd/ *adj.* (of a group or an organization) split by disagreements or different opinions: *The government is divided on this issue.* ◇ *a deeply divided society* ◇ *The regime is profoundly* ***divided against itself.***

di,vided 'highway (*NAmE*) (*BrE* **,dual 'carriageway**) *noun* a road with a strip of land in the middle that divides the lines of traffic moving in opposite directions

divi·dend /ˈdɪvɪdend/ *noun* **1** an amount of the profits that a company pays to people who own shares in the company: *dividend payments of 50 cents a share* **2** (*BrE*) a money prize that is given to winners in the FOOTBALL POOLS IDM see PAY *v.*

div·ider /dɪˈvaɪdə(r)/ *noun* **1** [C] a thing that divides sth: *a room divider* (= a screen or door that divides a room into two parts) **2 dividers** [pl.] an instrument made of two long thin metal parts joined together at the top, used for measuring lines and angles: *a pair of dividers*

di'viding line *noun* [usually sing.] **1** something that marks the separation between two things or ideas: *There is no clear dividing line between what is good and what is bad.* **2** a place that separates two areas: *The river was chosen as a dividing line between the two districts.*

div·in·ation /ˌdɪvɪˈneɪʃn/ *noun* [U] the act of finding out and saying what will happen in the future

di·vine /dɪˈvaɪn/ *adj., verb*
■ ***adj.*** **1** [usually before noun] coming from or connected with God or a god: ***divine law/love/will*** ◇ ***divine intervention*** (= help from God to change a situation) **2** (*old-fashioned*) wonderful; beautiful ▸ **div·ine·ly** *adv.*
■ ***verb*** **1** [T] **~ what, whether, etc… | ~ sth** (*formal*) to find out sth by guessing: *She could divine what he was thinking just by looking at him.* **2** [T, I] **~ (sth)** to search for underground water using a stick in the shape of a Y, called a **divining rod**

di,vine 'right *noun* [U, sing.] **1** (in the past) the belief that the right of a king or queen to rule comes directly from God rather than from the agreement of the people **2** a right that sb thinks they have to do sth, without needing to ask anyone else: *No player has a divine right to be in this team.*

div·ing /ˈdaɪvɪŋ/ *noun* [U] **1** the sport or activity of diving into water with your head and arms first: *a diving competition* **2** the activity of swimming underwater using special breathing equipment: *I'd love to* ***go diving*** *in the Aegean.* ◇ *a diving suit* ⊃ see also SKIN-DIVING

'diving bell *noun* a container that has a supply of air and that is open at the bottom, in which a person can be carried down to the deep ocean

'diving board *noun* a board at the side of or above a swimming pool from which people can jump or DIVE into the water

div·in·ity /dɪˈvɪnəti/ *noun* (*pl.* **-ies**) **1** [U] the quality of being a god or like God: *the divinity of Christ* **2** [C] a god or GODDESS: *Roman/Greek/Egyptian divinities* **3** [U] the study of the nature of God and religious belief SYN **theology**: *a doctor of Divinity*

div·is·ible /dɪˈvɪzəbl/ *adj.* [not before noun] **~ (by sth)** that can be divided, usually with nothing remaining: *8 is divisible by 2 and 4, but not by 3.* OPP **indivisible**

div·ision /dɪˈvɪʒn/ *noun*
▸ INTO SEPARATE PARTS **1** [U, sing.] the process or result of dividing into separate parts; the process or result of dividing sth or sharing it out: *cell division* ◇ **~ of sth** *a fair division of time and resources* ◇ **~ of sth between A and B** *the division of labour between the sexes* ◇ **~ (of sth) into sth** *the division of the population into age groups*
▸ MATHEMATICS **2** [U] the process of dividing one number by another: *the division sign* (÷) ⊃ compare MULTIPLICATION ⊃ see also LONG DIVISION
▸ DISAGREEMENT/DIFFERENCE **3** [C, U] a disagreement or difference in opinion, way of life, etc, especially between members of a society or an organization: **~ (in/within sth)** *There are* ***deep divisions*** *in the party over the war.* ◇ *the work of healing the divisions within society* ◇ **~ (between A and B)** *divisions between rich and poor* ◇ ***social/class divisions***
▸ PART OF ORGANIZATION **4** [C+sing./pl. v.] (*abbr.* **Div.**) a large and important unit or section of an organization: *the company's sales division*
▸ IN SPORT **5** [C+sing./pl. v.] (*abbr.* **Div.**) (in Britain) one of the group of teams that a sport competition is divided into, especially in football (SOCCER): *the* ***first division/division one*** ◇ *a first-division team*
▸ PART OF ARMY **6** [C+sing./pl. v.] (*abbr.* **Div.**) a unit of an army, consisting of several BRIGADES or REGIMENTS: *the Guards Armoured Division*
▸ BORDER **7** [C] a line that divides sth: *A hedge forms the division between their land and ours.*
▸ IN PARLIAMENT **8** [C] (*technical*) the separation of members of the British parliament into groups to vote for or against sth: *The Bill was read without a division.*

div·ision·al /dɪˈvɪʒənl/ *adj.* [only before noun] belonging to or connected with a DIVISION (= a section of the army or department of an organization): *the* ***divisional commander/headquarters***

di'vision bell *noun* a bell which is rung in the British parliament when it is time for a DIVISION (8)

di'vision lobby *noun* one of the two halls in the British parliament to which members go when there is a DIVISION (8)

div·isive /dɪˈvaɪsɪv/ *adj.* (*disapproving*) causing people to be split into groups that disagree with or oppose each other: *He believes that unemployment is socially divisive.* ⊃ see also DIVIDE ▸ **div·isive·ly** *adv.* **div·isive·ness** *noun* [U]

div·isor /dɪˈvaɪzə(r)/ *noun* (*mathematics*) a number by which another number is divided

di·vorce /dɪˈvɔːs; *NAmE* dɪˈvɔːrs/ *noun, verb*
■ ***noun*** **1** [U, C] the legal ending of a marriage: *The marriage* ***ended in divorce*** *in 1996.* ◇ *an increase in the* ***divorce rate*** (= the number of divorces in a year) ◇ *They have agreed to* ***get a divorce.*** ◇ ***Divorce proceedings*** (= the legal process of divorce) *started today.* ⊃ COLLOCATIONS at MARRIAGE ⊃ compare SEPARATION **2** [C, usually sing.] (*formal*) **~ (between A and B)** a separation; the ending of a relationship between two things: *the divorce between religion and science*
■ ***verb*** **1** [T, I] **~ (sb)** to end your marriage to sb legally: *They're* ***getting divorced.*** ◇ *She's divorcing her husband.* ◇ *I'd heard they're divorcing.* **2** [T, often passive] **~ sb/sth from sth** (*formal*) to separate a person, an idea, a subject, etc. from sth; to keep two things separate: *They believed that art should be divorced from politics.* ◇ *When he was depressed, he felt utterly divorced from reality.*

di·vorcé /dɪˌvɔːˈseɪ; *NAmE* dɪˌvɔːrˈseɪ/ *noun* (*NAmE*) a man whose marriage has been legally ended

di·vorced /dɪˈvɔːst; *NAmE* -ˈvɔːrst/ *adj.* **1** no longer married: *Many divorced men remarry and have second families.* ◇ *My parents are divorced.* ◇ *Are they going to* **get divorced**? ➲ COLLOCATIONS at MARRIAGE **2 ~ from sth** (*formal*) appearing not to be affected by sth; separate from sth: *He seems completely divorced from reality.*

di·vor·cee /dɪˌvɔːˈsiː; *NAmE* dɪˌvɔːrˈseɪ/ *noun* (*BrE*) a person whose marriage has been legally ended, especially a woman

di·vorcée /dɪˌvɔːˈseɪ; *NAmE* dɪˌvɔːrˈseɪ/ *noun* (*NAmE*) a woman whose marriage has been legally ended

divot /ˈdɪvət/ *noun* a piece of grass and earth that is dug out by accident, for example by a CLUB when sb is playing GOLF

di·vulge /daɪˈvʌldʒ/ *verb* **~ sth (to sb)** | **~ what, whether, etc...** (*formal*) to give sb information that is supposed to be secret SYN **reveal**: *Police refused to divulge the identity of the suspect.*

divvy /ˈdɪvi/ *verb* (**div·vies, divvy·ing, div·vied, div·vied**) PHR V **ˌdivvy sth↔ˈup** (*informal*) to divide sth, especially money into two or more parts

Di·wali (also **Di·vali**) /diːˈwɑːli/ *noun* [U] a Hindu festival that is held in the autumn/fall, celebrated by lighting CANDLES and CLAY lamps, and with FIREWORKS

Dix·ie /ˈdɪksi/ *noun* [U] an informal name for the south-eastern states of the US

Dixie·land /ˈdɪksilænd/ *noun* [U] a type of traditional JAZZ ➲ see also TRAD

DIY /ˌdiː aɪ ˈwaɪ/ *noun* [U] (*BrE*) the abbreviation for 'do-it-yourself' (the activity of making, repairing or decorating things in the home yourself, instead of paying sb to do it): *a DIY store* ➲ COLLOCATIONS at DECORATE ➲ VISUAL VOCAB page V17

di·zyg·ot·ic twin /ˌdaɪzaɪˌɡɒtɪk ˈtwɪn; *NAmE* -ˌɡɑːtɪk/ (also **di·zyg·ous twin** /daɪˌzaɪɡəs ˈtwɪn/) *adj.* (*technical*) = FRATERNAL TWIN ➲ compare MONOZYGOTIC TWIN

dizzy /ˈdɪzi/ *adj.* (**diz·ziest, diz·zi·est**) **1** feeling as if everything is spinning around you and that you are not able to balance SYN **giddy**: *Climbing so high made me* **feel dizzy**. ◇ *I suffer from* **dizzy spells** (= short periods when I am dizzy). **2** making you feel dizzy; making you feel that a situation is changing very fast SYN **giddy**: *the dizzy descent from the summit* ◇ *the dizzy pace of life in Hong Kong* **3** (*informal, especially NAmE*) silly or stupid SYN **giddy**: *a dizzy blonde* ▶ **diz·zily** *adv.* **diz·zi·ness** *noun* [U]
IDM **the dizzy ˈheights (of sth)** (*informal*) an important or impressive position: *She dreamed of reaching the dizzy heights of stardom.*

dizzy·ing /ˈdɪziɪŋ/ *adj.* making you feel dizzy: *The car drove past at a dizzying speed.*

DJ /ˈdiː dʒeɪ/ *noun, verb*
■ ***noun*** **1** the abbreviation for DISC JOCKEY **2** (*BrE*) the abbreviation for DINNER JACKET
■ ***verb*** (**DJ's, DJ'ing, DJ'd, DJ'd**) [I] to perform as a DISC JOCKEY, especially in a club

djib·bah (also **djib·ba**) /ˈdʒɪbə/ *noun* = JIBBA

djinn /dʒɪn/ *noun* (in Arabian stories) a spirit with magic powers SYN **genie**

DLitt (*NAmE* **D.Litt**) /ˌdiː ˈlɪt/ *noun* the abbreviation for 'Doctor of Letters' (a university degree at the highest level, awarded for a long record of academic research, or as an HONORARY degree to recognize sb's contribution to society)

DMA /ˌdiː em ˈeɪ/ *noun* [U] the abbreviation for 'direct memory access' (a system that allows a device attached to a computer to take data from the computer's memory without using the CENTRAL PROCESSING UNIT)

DMs /ˌdiː ˈemz/ *noun* (*informal*) = DR MARTENS

DNA /ˌdiː en ˈeɪ/ *noun* [U] (*chemistry*) deoxyribonucleic acid (the chemical in the cells of animals and plants that carries GENETIC information and is a type of NUCLEIC ACID): *a DNA test*

ˌDNA ˈfingerprinting *noun* [U] = GENETIC FINGERPRINTING

do[1] /də; du; *strong form* duː/ *verb, auxiliary verb, noun* ➲ IRREGULAR VERBS ➲ see also DO[2]
■ ***verb***
▸ ACTION **1** [T] **~ sth** used to refer to actions that you do not mention by name or do not know about: *What are you doing this evening?* ◇ *We will do what we can to help.* ◇ *Are you doing anything tomorrow evening?* ◇ *The company ought to do something about the poor service.* ◇ *What have you done to your hair?* ◇ *There's* **nothing to do** (= no means of passing the time in an enjoyable way) *in this place.* ◇ *There's* **nothing we can do** *about it* (= we can't change the situation). ◇ ***What can I do for you*** (= how can I help)?
▸ BEHAVE **2** [I] to act or behave in the way mentioned: **~ as...** *Do as you're told!* ◇ *They are free to do as they please.* ◇ **+ adv./prep.** *You* **would do well to** (= I advise you to) *consider all the options before buying.*
▸ SUCCEED/PROGRESS **3** [I] **+ adv./prep.** used to ask or talk about the success or progress of sb/sth: *How is the business doing?* ◇ *She* **did well** *out of* (= made a big profit from) *the deal.* ◇ *He's* **doing very well** *at school* (= his work is good). ◇ *Both mother and baby are* **doing well** (= after the birth of the baby). ◇ (*informal*) **How are you doing** (= how are you)?
▸ TASK/ACTIVITY **4** [T] **~ sth** to work at or perform an activity or a task: *I'm doing some research on the subject.* ◇ *I have a number of things to do today.* ◇ *I do aerobics once a week.* ◇ *Let's do* (= meet for) *lunch.* ◇ (*informal*) *Sorry. I don't do funny* (= I can't be funny). **5** [T] **~ sth** used with nouns to talk about tasks such as cleaning, washing, arranging, etc.: *to do* (= wash) *the dishes* ◇ *to do* (= arrange) *the flowers* ◇ *I like the way you've done your hair.* **6** [T] to perform the activity or task mentioned **~ the ironing, cooking, shopping, etc.**: *I like listening to the radio when I'm doing the ironing.* ◇ **~ some, a little, etc. acting, writing, etc.** *She did a lot of acting when she was at college.*
▸ JOB **7** [T] **~ sth** (usually used in questions) to work at sth as a job: ***What do you do*** (= what is your job)? ◇ *What does she want to do when she leaves school?* ◇ *What did she* ***do for a living***? ◇ *What's Tom doing these days?*
▸ STUDY **8** [T] **~ sth** to learn or study sth: *I'm doing physics, biology and chemistry.* ◇ *Have you done any* (= studied anything by) *Keats?*
▸ SOLVE **9** [T] **~ sth** to find the answer to sth; to solve sth: *I can't do this sum.* ◇ *Are you good at doing crosswords?*
▸ MAKE **10** [T] to produce or make sth: **~ sth** ***to do a drawing/painting/sketch*** ◇ *Does this pub do* (= provide) *lunches?* ◇ *Who's doing* (= organizing and preparing) *the food for the wedding reception?* ◇ **~ sth for sb** *I'll do a copy for you.* ◇ **~ sb sth** *I'll do you a copy.* ➲ note at MAKE
▸ PERFORM **11** [T] **~ sth** to perform or produce a play, an OPERA, etc: *The local dramatic society is doing 'Hamlet' next month.*
▸ COPY SB **12** [T] **~ sb/sth** to copy sb's behaviour or the way sb speaks, sings, etc, especially in order to make people laugh: *He does a great Elvis Presley.* ◇ *Can you do a Welsh accent?*
▸ FINISH **13** [I, T] to finish sth **have/be done**: *Sit there and wait till I've done.* ◇ **have/be done doing sth** *I've done talking—let's get started.* ◇ **get sth done** *Did you get your article done in time?*
▸ TRAVEL **14** [T] **~ sth** to travel a particular distance: *How many miles did you do during your tour?* ◇ *My car does 40 miles to the gallon* (= uses one gallon of petrol/gas to travel 40 miles). **15** [T] **~ sth** to complete a journey/trip: *We did the round trip in two hours.*
▸ SPEED **16** [T] **~ sth** to travel at or reach a particular speed: *The car was doing 90 miles an hour.*
▸ VISIT **17** [T] **~ sth** (*informal*) to visit a place as a tourist: *We did Tokyo in three days.*
▸ SPEND TIME **18** [T] **~ sth** to spend a period of time doing sth: *She did a year at college, but then dropped out.* ◇ *He did six years* (= in prison) *for armed robbery.*
▸ DEAL WITH **19** [T] **~ sb/sth** to deal with or attend to sb/sth: *The hairdresser said she could do me* (= cut my hair) *at three.*
▸ BE SUITABLE/ENOUGH **20** [I, T] to be suitable or be enough

D

for sb/sth: *'Can you lend me some money?' 'Sure—**will $20 do?**'* ◇ **~ for sb/sth** *These shoes **won't do** for the party.* ◇ **~ as sth** *The box will **do fine as** a table.* ◇ **~ sb** (**+ adv./prep.**) (*especially BrE*) *This room **will do me** nicely, thank you* (= it has everything I need).
▸ COOK **21** [T] **~ sth** to cook sth: *How would you like your steak done?*
▸ CHEAT **22** [T, usually passive] **~ sb** (*BrE, informal*) to cheat sb: *This isn't a genuine antique—you've been done.*
▸ PUNISH **23** [T] **~ sb** (**for sth**) (*BrE, informal*) to punish sb: *They did him for tax evasion.* ◇ *She **got done** for speeding.*
▸ STEAL **24** [T] **~ sth** (*informal*) to steal from a place: *The gang did a warehouse and a supermarket.*
▸ TAKE DRUGS **25** [T] **~ sth** (*informal*) to take an illegal drug: *He doesn't smoke, drink or **do drugs**.*
▸ HAVE SEX **26** [T] **~ it** (*slang*) to have sex

IDM Most idioms containing **do** are at the entries for the nouns and adjectives in the idioms, for example **do a bunk** is at **bunk**. **be/have to do with sb/sth** to be about or connected with sb/sth: *'What do you want to see me about?' 'It's to do with that letter you sent me.'* **have (got) something, nothing, a lot, etc. to do with sb/sth** used to talk about how much sb/sth is connected with sb/sth: *Her job has something to do with computers.* ◇ *'How much do you earn?' 'What's it got to do with you?'* ◇ *Hard work has a lot to do with* (= is an important reason for) *her success.* ◇ *We don't have very much to do with our neighbours* (= we do not speak to them very often). ◇ *I'd have nothing to do with him, if I were you.* **it won't 'do** (*especially BrE*) used to say that a situation is not acceptable and should be changed or improved: *This is the third time you've been late this week; it simply won't do.* **not 'do anything/a lot/much for sb** (*informal*) used to say that sth does not make sb look attractive: *That hairstyle doesn't do anything for her.* **ˌnothing 'doing** (*informal*) used to refuse a request: *'Can you lend me ten dollars?' 'Nothing doing!'* **no you 'don't** (*informal*) used to show that you intend to stop sb from doing sth that they were going to do: *Sharon went to get into the taxi. 'Oh no you don't,' said Steve.* **that 'does it** (*informal*) used to show that you will not accept sth any longer: *That does it, I'm off. I'm not having you swear at me like that.* **that's 'done it** (*informal*) used to say that an accident, a mistake, etc. has spoiled or ruined sth: *That's done it. You've completely broken it this time.* **that will 'do** used to order sb to stop doing or saying sth: *That'll do, children—you're getting far too noisy.* **what do you do for sth?** used to ask how sb manages to obtain the thing mentioned: *What do you do for entertainment out here?* **what is sb/sth doing...?** used to ask why sb/sth is in the place mentioned: *What are these shoes doing on my desk?*

PHR V **ˌdo aˈway with sb/yourself** (*informal*) to kill sb/yourself **ˌdo aˈway with sth** (*informal*) to stop doing or having sth; to make sth end SYN **abolish**: *He thinks it's time we did away with the monarchy.* **ˌdo sb/sth 'down** (*BrE, informal*) to criticize sb/sth unfairly **'do for sb/sth** [usually passive] (*informal*) to ruin, destroy or kill sb/sth: *Without that contract, we're done for.* **ˌdo sb/yourself 'in** (*informal*) **1** to kill sb/yourself **2** [usually passive] to make sb very tired: *Come and sit down—you look done in.* **ˌdo sth↔'in** (*informal*) to injure a part of the body: *He did his back in lifting heavy furniture.* **ˌdo sb 'out of sth** (*informal*) to unfairly prevent sb from having what they ought to have: *She was done out of her promotion.* **ˌdo sb 'over** (*informal, especially BrE*) to attack and beat sb severely: *He was done over by a gang of thugs.* **ˌdo sth↔'over 1** to clean or decorate sth again: *The paintwork will need doing over soon.* **2** (*NAmE*) to do sth again: *She insisted that everything be done over.* **3** (*BrE, informal*) to enter a building by force and steal things: *He got home to find that his flat had been done over.* **ˌdo 'up** to be fastened: *The skirt does up at the back.* **ˌdo sth↔'up 1** to fasten a coat, skirt, etc: *He never bothers to do his jacket up.* OPP **undo 2** to make sth into a package SYN **wrap**: *She was carrying a package done up in brown paper.* **3** (*BrE*) to repair and decorate a house, etc: *He makes money by buying old houses and doing them up.* **ˌdo yourself 'up** (*informal*) to make yourself more attractive by putting on MAKE-UP, attractive clothes, etc. **'do sth with sb/sth** (used in negative sentences and questions with *what*): *I don't know what to do with* (= how to use) *all the food that's left over.* ◇ *What have you done with* (= where have you put) *my umbrella?* ◇ *What have you been doing with yourselves* (= how have you been passing the time)? ➲ see also CAN'T BE DOING WITH at CAN[1], COULD DO WITH at COULD **ˌdo withˈout (sb/sth)** to manage without sb/sth: *She **can't do without** a secretary.* ◇ *If they can't get it to us in time, we'll just have to do without.* ◇ **~ doing sth** (*ironic*) *I **could have done without** being* (= I wish I had not been) *woken up at three in the morning.*

■ ***auxiliary verb*** (**does** /dʌz/, **did** /dɪd/, **done** /dʌn/) **1** used before a full verb to form negative sentences and questions: *I don't like fish.* ◇ *They didn't go to Paris.* ◇ *Don't forget to write.* ◇ *Does she speak French?* **2** used to make QUESTION TAGS (= short questions at the end of statements): *You live in New York, don't you?* ◇ *She doesn't work here, does she?* **3** used to avoid repeating a full verb: *He plays better than he did a year ago.* ◇ *She works harder than he does.* ◇ *'Who won?' 'I did.'* ◇ *'I love peaches.' '**So do I.**'* ◇ *'I don't want to go back.' '**Neither do I.**'* **4** used when no other auxiliary verb is present, to emphasize what you are saying: *He does look tired.* ◇ *She did at least write to say thank you.* ◇ (*BrE*) *Do shut up!* **5** used to change the order of the subject and verb when an adverb is moved to the front: *Not only does she speak Spanish, she's also good with computers.*

■ ***noun*** /duː/ (*pl.* **dos** or **do's** /duːz/) (*BrE, informal*) a party; a social event: *Are you having a big do for your birthday?*

IDM **dos and don'ts** (also **do's and don'ts**) (*informal*) rules that you should follow: *Here are some dos and don'ts for exercise during pregnancy.* ➲ more at FAIR *adj.*

Vocabulary Building

Household jobs: do or make?

- To talk about jobs in the home you can use such phrases as **wash the dishes**, **clean the kitchen floor**, **set the table**, etc. In conversation the verb **do** is often used instead: *Let me do the dishes.* ◇ *Michael said he would do the kitchen floor.* ◇ *It's your turn to do the table.* **Do** is often used with nouns ending *-ing*: *to do the shopping/cleaning/ironing/vacuuming.*
- The verb **make** is used especially in the phrase **make the beds** and when you are talking about preparing or cooking food: *He makes a great lasagne.* ◇ *I'll make breakfast while you're having a shower.* You can also say **get**, **get ready** and, especially in *NAmE*, **fix** for preparing meals: *Can you get dinner while I put the kids to bed?* ◇ *Sit down — I'll fix supper for you.*

do² /dəʊ; *NAmE* doʊ/ *noun* = DOH ➲ see also DO[1]

do. *abbr.* DITTO

DOA /ˌdiː əʊ ˈeɪ; *NAmE* -oʊ-/ *abbr.* = DEAD ON ARRIVAL at DEAD *adj.*

do·able /ˈduːəbl/ *adj.* (*informal*) **1** [not usually before noun] able to be done: *It's not doable by Friday.* ➲ compare FEASIBLE **2** (*BrE*) sexually attractive

D.O.B. *abbr.* date of birth

dob /dɒb; *NAmE* dɑːb/ *verb* (**-bb-**) (*BrE, informal*)
PHR V **ˌdob sb 'in (to sb) for sth/for doing sth** to tell sb about sth that another person has done wrong: *Sue dobbed me in to the teacher.*

Dobermann (pinscher) (also **Doberman (pinscher)** especially in *NAmE*) /ˌdəʊbəmən (ˈpɪnʃə(r)); *NAmE* ˌdoʊbərmən/ *noun* a large dog with short dark hair, often used for guarding buildings

doc /dɒk; *NAmE* dɑːk/ *noun* (*informal, especially NAmE*) a way of addressing or talking about a doctor

do·cent /ˈdəʊsnt; *NAmE* ˈdoʊ-/ *noun* (*NAmE*) **1** a teacher at some universities who is not a regular member of the department **2** a person whose job is to show tourists around a museum, etc. and talk to them about it

do·cile /ˈdəʊsaɪl; *NAmE* ˈdɑːsl/ *adj.* quiet and easy to control: *a docile child/horse* ▸ **do·cile·ly** /-saɪlli; *NAmE* -səli/ *adv.* **do·cil·ity** /dəʊˈsɪləti; *NAmE* dɑːˈs-/ *noun* [U]

dock /dɒk; *NAmE* dɑːk/ *noun, verb*

■ ***noun*** **1** [C] a part of a port where ships are repaired, or where goods are put onto or taken off them: *dock workers* ◇ *The ship was* ***in dock****.* ⊃ see also DRY DOCK **2 docks** [pl.] a group of docks in a port and the buildings around them that are used for repairing ships, storing goods, etc. **3** [C] (*NAmE*) = JETTY **4** [C] (*NAmE*) a raised platform for loading vehicles or trains **5** [C] the part of a court where the person who has been accused of a crime stands or sits during a trial: *He's been* ***in the dock*** (= on trial for a crime) *several times already.* ⊃ COLLOCATIONS at JUSTICE **6** [U] a wild plant of northern Europe with large thick leaves that can be rubbed on skin that has been stung by NETTLES to make it less painful: *dock leaves*

■ ***verb*** **1** [I, T] **~ (sth)** if a ship **docks** or you **dock** a ship, it sails into a HARBOUR and stays there: *The ferry is expected to dock at 6.* **2** [I, T] **~ (sth)** if two SPACECRAFT **dock**, or **are docked**, they are joined together in space: *Next year, a technology module will be docked on the space station.* **3** [T] to take away part of sb's wages, etc: **~ sth** *If you're late, your wages will be docked.* ◇ **~ sth from/off sth** *They've docked 15% off my pay for this week.* **4** [T] **~ sth** (*computing*) to connect a computer to a DOCKING STATION OPP **undock** **5** [T] **~ sth** to cut an animal's tail short

dock·er /ˈdɒkə(r); *NAmE* ˈdɑːk-/ *noun* a person whose job is moving goods on and off ships

Dock·ers™ /ˈdɒkəz; *NAmE* ˈdɑːkərz/ *noun* [pl.] a US make of trousers/pants made of cotton

docket /ˈdɒkɪt; *NAmE* ˈdɑːk-/ *noun* **1** (*business*) a document or label that shows what is in a package, which goods have been delivered, which jobs have been done, etc. **2** (*NAmE*) (also ˈ**docket sheet**) a list of cases to be dealt with in a particular court **3** (*NAmE*) a list of items to be discussed at a meeting

ˈ**docking station** *noun* (*computing*) a device to which a LAPTOP computer can be connected so that it can be used like a DESKTOP computer

dock·land /ˈdɒklænd; *NAmE* ˈdɑːk-/ *noun* [U] (also **docklands** [pl.]) (*BrE*) the district near DOCKS (= the place where ships are loaded and unloaded in a port): *plans to further redevelop Bristol's docklands*

dock·side /ˈdɒksaɪd; *NAmE* ˈdɑːk-/ *noun* [sing.] the area around the DOCKS (= the place where ships are loaded and unloaded) in a port

dock·yard /ˈdɒkjɑːd; *NAmE* ˈdɑːkjɑːrd/ *noun* an area with DOCKS (= the place where ships are loaded and unloaded in a port) and equipment for building and repairing ships

ˌ**Doc ˈMartens** *noun* (*informal*) = DR MARTENS

doc·tor 0‑w /ˈdɒktə(r); *NAmE* ˈdɑːk-/ *noun, verb*

■ ***noun*** (*abbr.* Dr) **1** 0‑w a person who has been trained in medical science, whose job is to treat people who are ill/sick or injured: *You'd better* ***see a doctor*** *about that cough.* ◇ *Doctor Staples* (= as a title/form of address) **2** 0‑w **doctor's** a place where a doctor sees patients: *an appointment at the doctor's* **3** 0‑w a person who has received the highest university degree: *a Doctor of Philosophy/Law* ◇ *Doctor Franks* (= as a title/form of address) **4** (*especially NAmE*) used as a title or form of address for a dentist

IDM **just what the doctor ˈordered** (*humorous*) exactly what sb wants or needs

■ ***verb*** **1 ~ sth** to change sth in order to trick sb SYN **falsify**: *He was accused of doctoring the figures.* **2 ~ sth** to add sth harmful to food or drink: *The wine had been doctored.* **3 ~ sth** (*informal*) to remove part of the sex organs of an animal SYN **neuter**

doc·tor·al /ˈdɒktərəl; *NAmE* ˈdɑːk-/ *adj.* [only before noun] connected with a doctorate: (*BrE*) *a doctoral thesis* ◇ (*NAmE*) *a doctoral dissertation*

doc·tor·ate /ˈdɒktərət; *NAmE* ˈdɑːk-/ *noun* the highest university degree: *She's studying for her doctorate.*

doc·trin·aire /ˌdɒktrɪˈneə(r); *NAmE* ˌdɑːktrəˈner/ *adj.* (*disapproving*) strictly following a theory in all circumstances, even if there are practical problems or disagreement: *a doctrinaire communist* ◇ ***doctrinaire attitudes/beliefs/policies***

doc·tri·nal /dɒkˈtraɪnl; *NAmE* ˈdɑːktrənl/ *adj.* (*formal*) relating to a doctrine or doctrines: *the doctrinal position of the English church* ◇ (*disapproving*) *a rigidly doctrinal approach* ▸ **doc·tri·nal·ly** *adv.*

doc·trine /ˈdɒktrɪn; *NAmE* ˈdɑːk-/ *noun* **1** [C, U] a belief or set of beliefs held and taught by a Church, a political party, etc: *the doctrine of parliamentary sovereignty* ◇ *Christian doctrine* **2 Doctrine** [C] (*US*) a statement of government policy: *the Monroe Doctrine*

D

docu·drama /ˈdɒkjudrɑːmə; *NAmE* ˈdɑːk-/ *noun* a film/movie, usually made for television, in which real events are shown in the form of a story

docu·ment 0‑w AW *noun, verb*

■ ***noun*** /ˈdɒkjumənt; *NAmE* ˈdɑːk-/ **1** 0‑w an official paper or book that gives information about sth, or that can be used as evidence or proof of sth: *legal documents* ◇ *travel documents* ◇ *Copies of the relevant documents must be filed at court.* ◇ *One of the documents leaked to the press was a memorandum written by the head of the security police.* **2** 0‑w a computer file that contains text that has a name that identifies it: *Save the document before closing.* ⊃ VISUAL VOCAB page V55

■ ***verb*** /ˈdɒkjument; *NAmE* ˈdɑːk-/ **1 ~ sth** to record the details of sth: *Causes of the disease have been well documented.* **2 ~ sth** to prove or support sth with documents: *documented evidence*

docu·men·tary /ˌdɒkjuˈmentri; *NAmE* ˌdɑːk-/ *noun, adj.*

■ ***noun*** (*pl.* -ies) a film or a radio or television programme giving facts about sth: *a television documentary about/on the future of nuclear power* ⊃ COLLOCATIONS at TELEVISION

■ ***adj.*** [only before noun] **1** consisting of documents: ***documentary evidence/sources/material*** **2** giving a record of or report on the facts about sth, especially by using pictures, recordings, etc. of people involved: *a documentary film about the war*

docu·men·ta·tion AW /ˌdɒkjumenˈteɪʃn; *NAmE* ˌdɑːk-/ *noun* [U] **1** the documents that are required for sth, or that give evidence or proof of sth: *I couldn't enter the country because I didn't have all the necessary documentation.* **2** the act of recording sth in a document; the state of being recorded in a document: *the documentation of an agreement*

ˈ**document case** *noun* a soft flat case without a handle, usually made from leather, plastic, etc, and used for holding and carrying documents

docu·soap /ˈdɒkjusəʊp; *NAmE* ˈdɑːkjusoʊp/ *noun* (*BrE*) a television programme about the lives of real people, presented as entertainment ⊃ see also SOAP OPERA

DOD /ˌdiː əʊ ˈdiː; *NAmE* oʊ/ *abbr.* Department of Defense (the government department in the US that is responsible for defence)

dod·der·ing /ˈdɒdərɪŋ; *NAmE* ˈdɑːd-/ (*BrE* also **doddery** /ˈdɒdəri; *NAmE* ˈdɑːd-/) *adj.* weak, slow and not able to walk in a steady way, especially because you are old

dod·dle /ˈdɒdl; *NAmE* ˈdɑːdl/ *noun* [sing.] (*BrE, informal*) a task or an activity that is very easy SYN **cinch**: *The first year of the course was an absolute doddle.* ◇ *The machine is a doddle to set up and use.*

do·deca·he·dron /ˌdəʊdekəˈhiːdrən; -ˈhed-; *NAmE* ˌdoʊ-/ *noun* (*geometry*) a solid figure with twelve flat sides

do·deca·phon·ic /ˌdəʊdekəˈfɒnɪk; *NAmE* ˌdoʊdekəˈfɑːnɪk/ *adj.* (*music*) = TWELVE-NOTE

dodge /dɒdʒ; *NAmE* dɑːdʒ/ *verb, noun*

■ ***verb*** **1** [T, I] to move quickly and suddenly to one side in order to avoid sb/sth: **~ sth** *He ran across the road, dodging the traffic.* ◇ **(+ adv./prep.)** *The girl dodged behind a tree to hide from the other children.* **2** [T] (rather *informal*) to avoid doing sth, especially in a dishonest way: **~ sth** *He dodged his military service.* ◇ **~ doing sth** *She tried to dodge paying her taxes.*

D

■ *noun* (*informal*) a clever and dishonest trick, played in order to avoid sth: *a tax dodge* ◇ *When it comes to getting off work, he knows all the dodges.*

dodge·ball /ˈdɒdʒbɔːl; *NAmE* ˈdɑːdʒ-/ *noun* [U] (*NAmE*) a game in which teams of players form circles and try to hit other teams with a large ball

dodgem /ˈdɒdʒəm; *NAmE* ˈdɑːdʒəm/ *noun* (*BrE*) **1 the dodgems** [pl.] a ride at a FUNFAIR in which people drive small electric cars around a track, trying to chase and hit the other cars: *The kids wanted to go on the dodgems.* **2** (also ˈ**dodgem car**) (also ˈ**bumper car** *NAmE, BrE*) one of the small electric cars that you drive in the dodgems

dodger /ˈdɒdʒə(r); *NAmE* ˈdɑːdʒ-/ *noun* (*informal*) a person who dishonestly avoids doing sth: *tax dodgers* ◇ *a crack-down on fare dodgers on trains* ➲ see also DRAFT DODGER

dodgy /ˈdɒdʒi; *NAmE* ˈdɑːdʒi/ *adj.* (*BrE, informal*) (**dodgi·er, dodgi·est**) **1** seeming or likely to be dishonest SYN **suspicious**: *He made a lot of money, using some very dodgy methods.* ◇ *I don't want to get involved in anything dodgy.* **2** not working well; not in good condition: *I can't play—I've got a dodgy knee.* ◇ *The marriage had been distinctly dodgy for a long time.* **3** involving risk, danger or difficulty: *If you get into any dodgy situations, call me.*

dodo /ˈdəʊdəʊ; *NAmE* ˈdoʊdoʊ/ *noun* (*pl.* **-os**) **1** a large bird that could not fly and that is now EXTINCT (= no longer exists) **2** (*NAmE*) a stupid person IDM see DEAD *adj.*

DOE /ˌdiː əʊ ˈiː; *NAmE* oʊ/ *abbr.* Department of Energy (the US government department that plans and controls the development of the country's sources of energy)

doe /dəʊ; *NAmE* doʊ/ *noun* a female DEER, RABBIT or HARE ➲ compare BUCK, HIND, STAG

doer /ˈduːə(r)/ *noun* (*approving*) a person who does things rather than thinking or talking about them: *We need fewer organizers and more doers.*

does /dʌz/ ➲ DO

doesn't /ˈdʌznt/ *short form* does not

doff /dɒf; *NAmE* dɑːf; dɔːf/ *verb, adj.*

■ *verb* **~ sth** (*old-fashioned*) to take off your hat, especially to show respect for sb/sth

■ *adj.* (*SAfrE, informal*) stupid

dog 0-w /dɒg; *NAmE* dɔːg/ *noun, verb*

■ *noun* **1** 0-w [C] an animal with four legs and a tail, often kept as a pet or trained for work, for example hunting or guarding buildings. There are many types of dog, some of which are wild: *I took the dog for a walk.* ◇ *I could hear a dog barking.* ◇ *dog food* ◇ *guard dogs* ◇ *a dog and her puppies* ➲ see also GUIDE DOG, GUN DOG, HEARING DOG, LAPDOG, PRAIRIE DOG, SHEEPDOG, SNIFFER DOG, TRACKER DOG **2** [C] a male dog, FOX or WOLF ➲ compare BITCH **3 the dogs** [pl.] (*BrE, informal*) GREYHOUND racing **4** [C] (*informal, especially NAmE*) a thing of low quality; a failure: *Her last movie was an absolute dog.* **5** [C] (*informal*) an offensive way of describing a woman who is not considered attractive **6** [C] (*informal, disapproving*) used, especially after an adjective, to describe a man who has done sth bad: *You dirty dog!* ➲ see also HOT DOG, SHAGGY-DOG STORY, TOP DOG, WATCHDOG

IDM **a ˌdog and ˈpony show** (*NAmE, informal, disapproving*) an event that is planned only in order to impress people so that they will support or buy sth **(a case of) ˌdog eat ˈdog** a situation in business, politics, etc. where there is a lot of competition and people are willing to harm each other in order to succeed: *I'm afraid in this line of work it's a case of dog eat dog.* ◇ *We're operating in a dog-eat-dog world.* **a ˌdog in the ˈmanger** a person who stops other people from enjoying what he or she cannot use or does not want **a dog's ˈbreakfast/ˈdinner** (*BrE, informal*) a thing that has been done badly SYN **mess**: *He's made a real dog's breakfast of these accounts.* **a ˈdog's life** an unhappy life, full of problems or unfair treatment **every dog has his/its ˈday** (*saying*) everyone has good luck or success at some point in their life **give a dog a bad ˈname** (*saying*) when a person already has a bad reputation, it is difficult to change it because others will continue to blame or suspect him/her **go to the ˈdogs** (*NAmE* also **go to hell in a ˈhandbasket**) (*informal*) to get into a very bad state: *This firm's gone to the dogs since the new management took over.* **not have a ˈdog's chance** to have no chance at all: *He hasn't a dog's chance of passing the exam.* **why keep a ˌdog and bark yourˈself?** (*informal, saying*) if sb can do a task for you, there is no point in doing it yourself ➲ more at HAIR, RAIN *v.*, SICK *adj.*, SLEEP *v.*, TAIL *n.*, TEACH

■ *verb* (**-gg-**) **1 ~ sb/sth** (of a problem or bad luck) to cause you trouble for a long time: *He had been dogged by bad health all his life.* **2 ~ sb/sth** to follow sb closely: *She had the impression that someone was dogging her steps.*

ˈ**dog biscuit** *noun* a small hard biscuit fed to dogs

dog·box /ˈdɒgbɒks; *NAmE* ˈdɔːgbɑːks/ *noun*

IDM **be in the ˈdogbox** (*SAfrE*) = BE IN THE DOGHOUSE

dog·catch·er /ˈdɒgkætʃə(r); *NAmE* ˈdɔːg-/ (*NAmE*, becoming *old-fashioned*) (*NAmE formal* ˌ**animal conˈtrol officer** *BrE* ˈ**dog warden**) *noun* a person whose job is to catch dogs and cats that are walking freely in the streets and do not seem to have a home

ˈ**dog collar** *noun* **1** a COLLAR for a dog **2** (*informal*) a stiff white COLLAR fastened at the back and worn by some Christian priests

ˈ**dog days** *noun* [pl.] the hottest period of the year

ˈ**dog-eared** *adj.* (of a book) used so much that the corners of many of the pages are turned down

ˌ**dog-ˈend** *noun* (*BrE, informal*) the end of a cigarette that has been smoked

dog·fight /ˈdɒgfaɪt; *NAmE* ˈdɔːg-/ *noun* **1** a fight between aircraft in which they fly around close to each other **2** a struggle between two people or groups in order to win sth **3 dog fight** a fight between dogs, especially one that is arranged illegally, for entertainment ▸ **dog·fight·ing** *noun* [U]

dog·fish /ˈdɒgfɪʃ; *NAmE* ˈdɔːg-/ *noun* (*pl.* **dog·fish**) a small SHARK (= an aggressive sea fish with very sharp teeth)

dog·ged /ˈdɒgɪd; *NAmE* ˈdɔːg-/ *adj.* [usually before noun] (*approving*) showing determination; not giving up easily SYN **tenacious**: *dogged determination/persistence* ◇ *their dogged defence of the city* ▸ **dog·ged·ly** *adv.* SYN **tenaciously dog·ged·ness** *noun* [U] SYN **tenacity**

dog·gerel /ˈdɒgərəl; *NAmE* ˈdɔːg-; ˈdɑːg-/ *noun* [U] poetry that is badly written or ridiculous, sometimes because the writer has not intended it to be serious

doggo /ˈdɒgəʊ; *NAmE* ˈdɔːgoʊ/ *adv.* **lie ~** (*old-fashioned, informal*) to lie still and quiet, so that other people will not notice you

dog·gone /ˈdɒgɒn; *NAmE* ˈdɔːggɔːn/ *adj.* [only before noun], *adv., exclamation* (*NAmE, informal*) used to show that you are annoyed or surprised: *Where's the doggone key?* ◇ *Don't drive so doggone fast.* ◇ *Well, doggone it!*

doggy /ˈdɒgi; *NAmE* ˈdɔːgi/ *noun, adj.*

■ *noun* (also **dog·gie**) (*pl.* **-ies**) (*informal*) a child's word for a dog

■ *adj.* [only before noun] of or like a dog: *a doggy smell*

ˈ**doggy bag** (also ˈ**doggie bag**) *noun* (*informal*) a bag for taking home any food that is left after a meal in a restaurant

ˈ**doggy-paddle** *noun* = DOG-PADDLE

ˈ**dog handler** *noun* a police officer who works with a trained dog

dog·house /ˈdɒghaʊs; *NAmE* ˈdɔːg-/ (*NAmE*) (*BrE* **kennel**) *noun* a small shelter for a dog to sleep in

IDM **be in the doghouse** (*informal, NAmE, BrE*) if you are **in the doghouse**, sb is annoyed with you because of sth that you have done

dogie /ˈdəʊgi; *NAmE* ˈdoʊgi/ *noun* (*NAmE*) a young cow that has lost its mother

ˈ**dog-leg** *noun* a sharp bend, especially in a road or on a GOLF COURSE

dogma /ˈdɒɡmə; *NAmE* ˈdɔːɡmə/ *noun* [U, C] (often *disapproving*) a belief or set of beliefs held by a group or organization, which others are expected to accept without argument: ***political/religious/party dogma*** ◇ *one of the central dogmas of the Church*

dog·mat·ic /dɒɡˈmætɪk; *NAmE* dɔːɡ-/ *adj.* (*disapproving*) being certain that your beliefs are right and that others should accept them, without paying attention to evidence or other opinions: *a* ***dogmatic approach*** ◇ *There is a danger of becoming too dogmatic about teaching methods.* ▸ **dog·mat·ic·al·ly** /-kli/ *adv.*

dog·ma·tism /ˈdɒɡmətɪzəm; *NAmE* ˈdɔːɡ-/ *noun* [U] (*disapproving*) behaviour and attitudes that are dogmatic

ˌdo-ˈgooder *noun* (*informal, disapproving*) a person who tries to help other people but who does it in a way that is annoying

ˈdog-paddle (also **ˈdoggy-paddle**) *noun* [U] a simple swimming stroke, with short quick movements like those of a dog in the water

dogs·body /ˈdɒɡzbɒdi; *NAmE* ˈdɔːɡzbɑːdi/ *noun* (*pl.* -ies) (*BrE, informal*) a person who does all the boring jobs that nobody else wants to do, and who is treated as being less important than other people

dog·sled /ˈdɒɡsled; *NAmE* ˈdɔːɡ-/ *noun* (*NAmE*) a SLEDGE (= a vehicle that slides over snow) pulled by dogs, used especially in Canada and Alaska

ˈdog tag *noun* (*NAmE, slang*) a small piece of metal that US soldiers wear round their necks with their name and number on it

ˌdog-ˈtired *adj.* [not usually before noun] (*informal*) very tired SYN **exhausted**

ˈdog warden (*BrE*) (*NAmE* becoming *old-fashioned* **dog-catch·er**, *formal* **animal control officer**) *noun* a person whose job is to catch dogs and cats that are walking freely in the streets and do not seem to have a home

dog·wood /ˈdɒɡwʊd; *NAmE* ˈdɔːɡ-/ *noun* [U, C] a bush or small tree with red or pink BERRIES and red STEMS, that grows in northern regions; the hard wood of this tree

DoH *abbr.* (in Britain) Department of Health

d'oh /dəʊ; *NAmE* doʊ/ *exclamation* (*informal*) used when you have just said or done sth that you know is stupid: *D'oh! That was the biggest mistake ever.* ORIGIN Used by Homer Simpson in *The Simpsons* television series.

doh (also **do**) /dəʊ; *NAmE* doʊ/ *noun* (*music*) the 1st and 8th note of a MAJOR SCALE

DOI /ˌdiː əʊ ˈaɪ; *NAmE* oʊ/ *abbr.* **1** (*computing*) digital object identifier (a series of numbers and letters that identifies a particular text or document published in electronic form on the Internet) **2** Department of the Interior (the US government department responsible for protecting the country's environment)

doily /ˈdɔɪli/ *noun* (*pl.* -ies) **1** a small circle of paper or cloth with a pattern of very small holes in it, that you put on a plate under a cake or SANDWICHES **2** (*NAmE*) a small decorative MAT that you put on top of a piece of furniture

doing /ˈduːɪŋ/ *noun* [C, usually pl., U] a thing done or caused by sb: *I've been hearing a lot about your doings recently.* ◇ *I promise you this was none of my doing* (= I didn't do it).

IDM **take some ˈdoing | take a lot of ˈdoing** to be hard work; to be difficult: *Getting it finished by tomorrow will take some doing.*

ˌdo-it-yourˈself *noun* [U] (*especially BrE*) = DIY: *The materials you need are available from any good do-it-yourself store.*

dojo /ˈdəʊdʒəʊ; *NAmE* ˈdoʊdʒoʊ/ *noun* (*pl.* -os) (from *Japanese*) a hall or school where JUDO or other similar MARTIAL ARTS (= fighting sports) are practised

Dolby™ /ˈdɒlbi; ˈdəʊlbi; *NAmE* ˈdɔːlbi; ˈdoʊlbi/ *noun* [U] a system for reducing background noise in sound recordings

dol·drums /ˈdɒldrəmz; *NAmE* ˈdoʊl-/ *noun* [pl.] (usually **the doldrums**) **1** the state of feeling sad or depressed: *He's been* ***in the doldrums*** *ever since she left him.* **2** a lack of activity or improvement: *The bond market normally revives after the summer doldrums.* ◇ *Despite these measures, the economy remains* ***in the doldrums.*** ORIGIN From the place in the ocean near the equator where there are sudden periods of calm. A sailing ship caught in this area can be stuck there because of a lack of wind.

dole /dəʊl; *NAmE* doʊl/ *noun, verb*

■ ***noun*** [sing.] (usually **the dole**) (*BrE, informal*) money paid by the state to unemployed people: *He's been* ***on the dole*** (= without a job) *for a year.* ◇ *The government is changing the rules for claiming dole.* ◇ *lengthening dole queues* ◇ *We could all be* ***in the dole queue*** *on Monday* (= have lost our jobs). ➲ COLLOCATIONS at UNEMPLOYMENT

■ ***verb***

PHR V **ˌdole sth↔ˈout (to sb)** (*informal*) to give out an amount of food, money, etc. to a number of people in a group

dole·ful /ˈdəʊlfl; *NAmE* ˈdoʊlfl/ *adj.* very sad SYN **mournful**: *a* ***doleful expression/face/song*** ◇ *a doleful looking man* ▸ **dole·ful·ly** /-fəli/ *adv.*

doll /dɒl; *NAmE* dɑːl/ *noun, verb*

■ ***noun*** **1** a child's toy in the shape of a person, especially a baby or a child: *a rag doll* (= one made out of cloth) **2** (*old-fashioned, informal, especially NAmE*) a word used to describe a pretty or attractive woman, now often considered offensive: *She's quite a doll.*

■ ***verb***

PHR V **ˌdoll sb/yourself ˈup** (*informal*) to make sb/yourself look attractive for a party, etc, with fashionable clothes: *Are you* ***getting dolled up*** *for the party?*

dol·lar 0→ /ˈdɒlə(r); *NAmE* ˈdɑːl-/ *noun*

1 0→ [C] (*symb.* $) the unit of money in the US, Canada, Australia and several other countries: *You will be paid in American dollars.* ➲ compare BUCK ➲ see also TOP DOLLAR **2** 0→ [C] a BANKNOTE or coin worth one dollar: *Do you have a dollar?* ◇ *a dollar bill* **3 the dollar** [sing.] (*finance*) the value of the US dollar compared with the value of the money of other countries: *The dollar closed two cents down.*

IDM see BET *v.*, MILLION

dol·lar·ize (*BrE* also **-ise**) /ˈdɒləraɪz; *NAmE* ˈdɑːl-/ *verb* [T, I] **~ (sth)** (of a country) to start using the US dollar as its own CURRENCY ▸ **dol·lar·iza·tion, -isa·tion** /ˌdɒləraɪˈzeɪʃn; *NAmE* ˌdɑːl-/ *noun* [U]

doll·house /ˈdɒlhaʊs; *NAmE* ˈdɑːl-/ (*NAmE*) (*BrE* **ˈdoll's house**) *noun* a toy house with small furniture and sometimes DOLLS in it for children to play with ➲ VISUAL VOCAB page V32

dol·lop /ˈdɒləp; *NAmE* ˈdɑːləp/ *noun* (*informal*) **1** a lump of soft food, often dropped from a spoon: *a dollop of whipped cream* **2** an amount of sth: *A dollop of romance now and then is good for everybody.*

ˈdoll's house (*BrE*) (*NAmE* **doll·house**) *noun* a toy house with small furniture and sometimes DOLLS in it for children to play with ➲ VISUAL VOCAB page V32

dolly /ˈdɒli; *NAmE* ˈdɑːli; ˈdɔːli/ *noun* (*pl.* -ies) **1** a child's word for a DOLL **2** (*especially NAmE*) a low platform on wheels for moving heavy objects

ˈdolly bird *noun* (*old-fashioned, BrE, informal*) a way of referring to a young woman who is considered attractive but not very intelligent

dol·men /ˈdɒlmen; *NAmE* ˈdoʊl-/ *noun* a pair or group of vertical stones with a large flat stone on top, built in ancient times to mark a place where sb was buried

dol·or·ous /ˈdɒlərəs; *NAmE* ˈdoʊl-/ *adj.* [usually before noun] (*literary*) feeling or showing great sadness

dol·phin /ˈdɒlfɪn; *NAmE* ˈdɑːl-/ *noun* a sea animal (a MAMMAL) that looks like a large fish with a pointed mouth. Dolphins are very intelligent and often friendly towards humans. There are several types of dolphin: *a school of dolphins* ➲ compare PORPOISE

dol·phin·arium /ˌdɒlfɪˈneəriəm; *NAmE* ˌdɑːlfɪˈneriəm/ *noun* (*pl.* **dol·phin·ariums** or **dol·phin·aria** /-riə/) a build-

D

ing with a pool where people can go to see dolphins, especially ones who have been trained to do tricks

dolt /dəʊlt; *NAmE* doʊlt/ *noun* (*disapproving*) a stupid person SYN **idiot** ▶ **dolt·ish** *adj.*

-dom *suffix* (in nouns) **1** the condition or state of: *freedom* ◇ *martyrdom* **2** the rank of; an area ruled by: *kingdom* **3** the group of: *officialdom*

D

do·main AW /dəˈmeɪn; dəʊ-; *NAmE* doʊ-/ *noun* **1** an area of knowledge or activity; especially one that sb is responsible for: *The care of older people is being placed firmly within the domain of the family.* ◇ *Physics used to be very much a male domain.* ➲ see also PUBLIC DOMAIN **2** lands owned or ruled by a particular person, government, etc, especially in the past: *The Spice Islands were within the Spanish domains.* **3** (*computing*) a set of websites on the Internet which end with the same group of letters, for example '.com', '.org' **4** (*mathematics*) the range of possible values of a particular VARIABLE

doˈmain name *noun* (*computing*) a name which identifies a website or group of websites on the Internet

dome /dəʊm; *NAmE* doʊm/ *noun* **1** a round roof with a CIRCULAR base: *the dome of St Paul's Cathedral* ➲ VISUAL VOCAB pages V2, V12 **2** a thing or a building shaped like a dome: *his bald dome of a head* **3** (*NAmE*) (in names) a sports STADIUM whose roof is shaped like a dome: *the Houston Astrodome*

domed /dəʊmd; *NAmE* doʊmd/ *adj.* [usually before noun] having or shaped like a dome: *a* ***domed forehead/ceiling***

do·mes·tic 0➛ AW /dəˈmestɪk/ *adj., noun*

■ ***adj.*** **1** 0➛ [usually before noun] of or inside a particular country; not foreign or international: ***domestic affairs/politics*** ◇ ***domestic flights*** (= to and from places within a country) ◇ *Output consists of both exports and sales on the domestic market.* OPP **foreign** **2** 0➛ [only before noun] used in the home; connected with the home or family: *domestic appliances* ◇ *domestic chores* ◇ *the growing problem of* ***domestic violence*** (= violence between members of the same family) ◇ ***domestic service*** (= the work of a servant in a large house) **3** liking home life; enjoying or good at cooking, cleaning the house, etc: *I'm not a very domestic sort of person.* **4** 0➛ (of animals) kept on farms or as pets; not wild ▶ **do·mes·tic·al·ly** AW /-kli/ *adv.*: *domestically produced goods*

■ ***noun*** **1** (also ˌ**domestic ˈhelp**, ˌ**domestic ˈworker**) a servant who works in sb's house, doing the cleaning and other jobs **2** (*BrE, informal*) a fight between two members of the same family: *The police were called to sort out a domestic.*

do·mes·ti·cate AW /dəˈmestɪkeɪt/ *verb* **1** ~ **sth** to make a wild animal used to living with or working for humans **2** ~ **sth** to grow plants or crops for human use SYN **cultivate** **3** ~ **sb** (often *humorous*) to make sb good at cooking, caring for a house, etc; to make sb enjoy home life: *Some men are very hard to domesticate.* ▶ **do·mes·ti·cated** AW *adj.*: *domesticated animals* ◇ *They've become a lot more domesticated since they got married.* **do·mes·ti·ca·tion** /dəˌmestɪˈkeɪʃn/ *noun* [U]: *the domestication of cattle*

do·mes·ti·city /ˌdəʊmeˈstɪsəti; ˌdɒm-; *NAmE* ˌdoʊ-; ˌdɑːm-/ *noun* [U] home or family life: *an atmosphere of happy domesticity*

doˌmestic ˈscience *noun* (*old-fashioned, BrE*) = HOME ECONOMICS

ˈ**dome tent** *noun* a tent which forms the shape of a dome ➲ compare FRAME TENT, RIDGE TENT

domi·cile /ˈdɒmɪsaɪl; *NAmE* ˈdɑːm-; ˈdoʊm-/ *noun* (*formal* or *law*) the place where sb lives, especially when it is stated for official or legal purposes

domi·ciled /ˈdɒmɪsaɪld; *NAmE* ˈdɑːm-; ˈdoʊm-/ *adj.* [not before noun] (*formal* or *law*) living in a particular place: *to be domiciled in the United Kingdom*

domi·cil·iary /ˌdɒmɪˈsɪliəri; *NAmE* ˌdɑːməˈsɪlieri; ˌdoʊ-/ *adj.* [only before noun] (*formal*) in sb's home: *a* ***domiciliary visit*** (= for example, by a doctor) ◇ ***domiciliary care/services/treatment***

dom·in·ant AW /ˈdɒmɪnənt; *NAmE* ˈdɑːm-/ *adj.* **1** more important, powerful or noticeable than other things: *The firm has achieved a dominant position in the world market.* ◇ *The dominant feature of the room was the large fireplace.* **2** (*biology*) a **dominant** GENE causes a person to have a particular physical characteristic, for example brown eyes, even if only one of their parents has passed on this GENE ➲ compare RECESSIVE ▶ **dom·in·ance** AW /ˈdɒmɪnəns; *NAmE* ˈdɑː-/ *noun* [U]: *to achieve/assert dominance over sb* ◇ *political/economic dominance*

dom·in·ate 0➛ AW /ˈdɒmɪneɪt; *NAmE* ˈdɑːm-/ *verb* **1** 0➛ [T, I] ~ **(sb/sth)** to control or have a lot of influence over sb/sth, especially in an unpleasant way: *As a child he was dominated by his father.* ◇ *He tended to dominate the conversation.* ◇ *She always says a lot in meetings, but she doesn't dominate.* **2** 0➛ [T] ~ **sth** to be the most important or noticeable feature of sth: *The train crash dominated the news.* **3** [T] ~ **sth** to be the largest, highest or most obvious thing in a place: *The cathedral dominates the city.* **4** [T, I] ~ **(sth)** (*sport*) to play much better than your opponent in a game: *Arsenal dominated the first half of the match.* ▶ **dom·in·ation** AW /ˌdɒmɪˈneɪʃn; *NAmE* ˌdɑː-/ *noun* [U]: *political domination* ◇ *companies fighting for domination of the software market*

dom·in·atrix /ˌdɒmɪˈneɪtrɪks; *NAmE* ˌdɑːm-/ *noun* (*pl.* **dom·in·atri·ces** /ˌdɒmɪˈneɪtrɪsiːz; *NAmE* ˌdɑːm-/, **dom·in·atrixes**) a woman who controls a man during sex, often using violence to give sexual pleasure

dom·in·eer·ing /ˌdɒmɪˈnɪərɪŋ; *NAmE* ˌdɑːməˈnɪr-/ *adj.* (*disapproving*) trying to control other people without considering their opinions or feelings: *a cold and domineering father* ◇ *a domineering manner*

Do·min·ic·an /dəˈmɪnɪkən/ *noun* a member of a Christian group of MONKS or NUNS following the rules of St Dominic ▶ **Do·min·ic·an** *adj.*

do·min·ion /dəˈmɪniən/ *noun* **1** [U] ~ **(over sb/sth)** (*literary*) authority to rule; control: *Man has dominion over the natural world.* ◇ *Soon the whole country was under his sole dominion.* **2** [C] (*formal*) an area controlled by one ruler: *the vast dominions of the Roman Empire* **3** (often **Dominion**) [C] (in the past) any of the countries of the British Commonwealth that had their own government ➲ compare COLONY, PROTECTORATE

dom·ino /ˈdɒmɪnəʊ; *NAmE* ˈdɑːmənoʊ/ *noun* (*pl.* **-oes**) **1** [C] a small flat block, often made of wood, marked on one side with two groups of dots representing numbers, used for playing games ➲ VISUAL VOCAB page V33 **2 dominoes** [U] a game played with a set of dominoes, in which players take turns to put them onto a table

ˈ**domino effect** *noun* [usually sing.] a situation in which one event causes a series of similar events to happen one after the other

dom·pas /ˈdɒmpʌs; *NAmE* ˈdɔːm-/ *noun* (*SAfrE, informal, disapproving*) (in South Africa in the past) the official document that black people had to carry with them to prove their identity and where they could live or work

don /dɒn; *NAmE* dɑːn/ *noun, verb*

■ ***noun*** **1** (*BrE*) a teacher at a university, especially Oxford or Cambridge ➲ see also DONNISH **2** (*informal*) the leader of a group of criminals involved with the Mafia

■ ***verb*** (-nn-) ~ **sth** (*formal*) to put clothes, etc. on: *He donned his jacket and went out.*

do·nate /dəʊˈneɪt; *NAmE* ˈdoʊneɪt/ *verb* **1** ~ **sth (to sb/sth)** to give money, food, clothes, etc. to sb/sth, especially a charity: *He donated thousands of pounds to charity.* **2** ~ **sth (to sb/sth)** to allow doctors to remove blood or a body organ in order to help sb who needs it: *All donated blood is tested for HIV and other infections.*

do·na·tion /dəʊˈneɪʃn; *NAmE* doʊ-/ *noun* [C, U] something that is given to a person or an organization such as a charity, in order to help them; the act of giving sth in this way: ~ **(to sb/sth)** *to* ***make a donation*** *to charity* ◇ *a* ***gen-***

erous/large/small **donation** ◇ **~ (of…)** *a donation of £200/a £200 donation* ◇ *The work of the charity is funded by voluntary donations.* ◇ ***organ donation*** (= allowing doctors to use an organ from your body after your death in order to save a sick person's life)

done /dʌn/ *adj., exclamation* ➲ see also DO *v.*

■ ***adj.*** [not before noun] **1** finished; completed: *When you're done, perhaps I can say something.* ◇ **~ with** *I'll be glad when this job is* ***over and done with.*** **2** (of food) cooked enough: *The meat isn't quite done yet.* **3** (*BrE*) socially acceptable, especially among people who have a strict set of social rules: *At school, it simply wasn't done to show that you cared for anything except cricket.*

IDM **be 'done for** (*informal*) to be in a very bad situation; to be certain to fail: *Unless we start making some sales, we're done for.* ◇ *When he pointed the gun at me, I thought I was done for* (= about to die). **be/get 'done for sth/for doing sth** (*BrE, informal*) to be caught and punished for doing sth illegal but not too serious: *I got done for speeding on my way back.* **be done 'in** (*informal*) to be extremely tired SYN **be exhausted** **be the ˌdone 'thing** (*BrE*) to be socially acceptable behaviour **be/have 'done with sth** to have finished dealing with sb, or doing or using sth: *If you've done with that magazine, can I have a look at it?* **a ˌdone 'deal** an agreement or a plan that has been finally completed or agreed: *The merger is by no means a done deal yet.* **done and 'dusted** (*BrE, informal*) completely finished: *That's my article for the magazine done and dusted.* **have 'done with it** (*BrE*) to do sth unpleasant as quickly as possible, so that it is finished: *Why not tell her you're quitting and have done with it?* ➲ more at EASY *adv.*, HARD *adv.*, SOON

■ ***exclamation*** used to show that you accept an offer: *'I'll give you £800 for it.' 'Done!'*

doner kebab /ˌdɒnə kɪ'bæb; *NAmE* ˌdoʊnər/ *noun* (*BrE*) thin slices of cooked meat, usually served with PITTA bread ➲ see also KEBAB

donga /'dɒŋgə; *NAmE* 'dɑːŋgə; 'dɔːŋgə/ *noun* (*SAfrE*) a deep channel in the ground that is formed by the action of water: *The car slid into a donga at the side of the road.*

don·gle /'dɒŋgl; *NAmE* 'dɑːŋgl; 'dɔːŋgl/ *noun* (*computing*) **1** a cable that is used to attach a computer to a telephone system or to another computer **2** a device or code that is needed in order to use protected software

Don Juan /ˌdɒn 'dʒʊən; ˌdɒn 'hwɑːn; *NAmE* ˌdɑːn/ *noun* (*informal*) a man who has sex with a lot of women ORIGIN From the name of a character from Spanish legend who was skilled at persuading women to have sex with him.

don·key /'dɒŋki; *NAmE* 'dɔːŋ-; 'dɑːŋ-/ *noun* an animal of the horse family, with short legs and long ears. People ride donkeys or use them to carry heavy loads.

IDM **'donkey's years** (*BrE, informal*) a very long time: *We've known each other for donkey's years.* ➲ more at TALK *v.*

'donkey jacket *noun* (*BrE*) a thick short coat, usually dark blue, worn especially by people working outside

'donkey work *noun* [U] (*informal*) the hard boring part of a job or task

don·nish /'dɒnɪʃ; *NAmE* 'dɑːn-/ *adj.* (*BrE*) (usually of a man) serious and concerned with academic rather than practical matters: *He has a somewhat donnish air about him.*

donor /'dəʊnə(r); *NAmE* 'doʊ-/ *noun* **1** a person or an organization that makes a gift of money, clothes, food, etc. to a charity, etc: *international aid donors* (= countries which give money, etc. to help other countries) ◇ *She is one of the charity's main donors.* **2** a person who gives blood or a part of his or her body to be used by doctors in medical treatment: *a blood donor* ◇ *The heart transplant will take place as soon as a suitable donor can be found.* ◇ *donor organs* ◇ *a donor card* (= a card that you carry giving permission for doctors to use parts of your body after your death)

don't /dəʊnt; *NAmE* doʊnt/ *short form* do not

ˌdon't-'know *noun* a person who does not have a strong opinion about a question which they are asked in an OPINION POLL: *A quarter of all the people surveyed were don't-knows.*

donut *noun* (*especially NAmE*) = DOUGHNUT

doo·dah /'duːdɑː/ (*BrE*) (*NAmE* **doo·dad** /'duːdæd/) *noun* (*informal*) a small object whose name you have forgotten or do not know

doo·dle /'duːdl/ *verb* [I] to draw lines, shapes, etc, especially when you are bored or thinking about sth else: *I often doodle when I'm on the phone.* ▶ **doo·dle** *noun*

doo·fus /'duːfəs/ *noun* (*NAmE, informal*) a stupid person

doo·hickey /'duːhɪki/ *noun* (*NAmE, informal*) a small object whose name you have forgotten or do not know, especially part of a machine

doo·lal·ly /duː'læli/ *adj.* [not before noun] (*BrE, informal*) crazy: *The poor chap's gone doolally.*

doom /duːm/ *noun, verb*

■ ***noun*** [U] death or destruction; any terrible event that you cannot avoid: *to* ***meet your doom*** ◇ *She had* ***a sense of impending doom*** (= felt that sth very bad was going to happen).

IDM **ˌdoom and 'gloom** | **ˌgloom and 'doom** a general feeling of having lost all hope, and of PESSIMISM (= expecting things to go badly): *Despite the obvious setbacks, it is not all doom and gloom for the England team.* **ˌprophet of 'doom** | **'doom merchant** a person who predicts that things will go very badly: *The prophets of doom who said television would kill off the book were wrong.*

■ ***verb*** [usually passive] **~ sb/sth (to sth)** | **~ sb/sth to do sth** to make sb/sth certain to fail, suffer, die, etc: *The plan was* ***doomed to failure.*** ◇ *The marriage was* ***doomed from the start.***

'doom-laden *adj.* [usually before noun] predicting or leading to death or destruction: *doom-laden economic forecasts*

doom·sayer /'duːmseɪə(r)/ (*especially NAmE*) (*BrE* also **doom·ster** /'duːmstə(r)/) *noun* a person who says that sth very bad is going to happen

dooms·day /'duːmzdeɪ/ *noun* [sing.] the last day of the world when Christians believe that everyone will be judged by God

IDM **till 'doomsday** (*informal*) a very long time; for ever: *This job's going to take me till doomsday.*

doomy /'duːmi/ *adj.* (**doom·ier**, **doomi·est**) suggesting disaster and unhappiness: *doomy predictions* ◇ *Their new album is their doomiest.*

Doona™ /'duːnə/ *noun* (*AustralE*) a large cloth bag that is filled with feathers or other soft material and that you have on top of you in bed to keep yourself warm SYN **duvet**

door 🔑 /dɔː(r)/ *noun*

1 🔑 [C] a piece of wood, glass, etc. that is opened and closed so that people can get in and out of a room, building, car, etc; a similar thing in a cupboard/closet: *a* ***knock on the door*** ◇ *to* ***open/shut/close/slam/lock/bolt*** *the door* ◇ *to* ***answer the door*** (= to go and open it because sb has knocked on it or rung the bell) ◇ *the* ***front/back door*** (= at the entrance at the front/back of a building) ◇ *the bedroom door* ◇ *the door frame* ◇ *a four-door saloon car* ◇ *the fridge door* ◇ *Shut the door!* ◇ *Close the door behind you, please.* ◇ *The door closed behind him.* ➲ VISUAL VOCAB pages V22, V42 ➲ see also BACK-DOOR, FIRE DOOR, FRENCH DOOR, OPEN-DOOR, REVOLVING DOOR, SLIDING DOOR, STABLE DOOR, STAGE DOOR, SWING DOOR, TRAPDOOR **2** 🔑 [C] the space when a door is open: *Marc appeared through a door at the far end of the room.* ◇ (*informal*) *She's just arrived—she's just* ***come in the door.*** ◇ (*informal*) *He walked* ***out the door.*** **3** 🔑 [C] the area close to the entrance of a building: *There's somebody* ***at the door*** (= at the front door of a house). ◇ *'Can I help you?' asked the man at the door.* ➲ see also DOORWAY **4** [C] a house, room, etc. that is a particular number of houses, rooms, etc. away from another: *the family that lives three doors up from us* ◇ *Our other branch is just a few doors down the road.* ➲ see also NEXT DOOR **5** [U] (*BrE*) the amount of money made by selling tickets for an event SYN **gate**: *50% of the door will go to the Red Cross.*

IDM **be on the door** to work at the entrance to a theatre, club, etc, for example collecting tickets from people as they enter **close/shut the 'door on sth** to make it unlikely that sth will happen: *She was careful not to close the door on the possibility of further talks.* **(from) ˌdoor to 'door** from building to building: *The journey takes about an hour door to door.* ◇ *a door-to-door salesman* **(open) the door to sth** (to provide) the means of getting or reaching sth; (to create) the opportunity for sth: *The agreement will open the door to increased international trade.* ◇ *Our courses are the door to success in English.* **lay sth at sb's 'door** (*formal*) to say that sb is responsible for sth that has gone wrong **leave the door 'open (for sth)** to make sure that there is still the possibility of doing sth **out of 'doors** not inside a building: *You should spend more time out of doors in the fresh air.* **shut/slam the door in sb's face 1** to shut a door hard when sb is trying to come in **2** to refuse to talk to sb or meet them, in a rude way **to sb's door** directly to sb's house: *We promise to deliver to your door within 48 hours of you ordering.* ➲ more at BACK *adj.*, BARN, BEAT *v.*, CLOSE[1] *v.*, CLOSED, DARKEN, DEATH, FOOT *n.*, OPEN *v.*, SHOW *v.*, STABLE DOOR *n.*, WOLF *n.*

door·bell /ˈdɔːbel; *NAmE* ˈdɔːrbel/ *noun* a bell with a button outside a house that you push to let the people inside know that you are there: *to ring the doorbell*

ˌdo-or-ˈdie *adj.* having or needing great determination: *a do-or-die attitude*

ˈdoor furniture *noun* [U] (*BrE, technical*) the handles, KNOCKERS, etc. on a door

door·keeper /ˈdɔːkiːpə(r); *NAmE* ˈdɔːrk-/ *noun* a person who guards the entrance to a large building, especially to check on people going in

door·knob /ˈdɔːnɒb; *NAmE* ˈdɔːrnɑːb/ *noun* a type of round handle for a door, that you turn in order to open the door

ˈdoor knocker *noun* = KNOCKER

door·man /ˈdɔːmən; *NAmE* ˈdɔːrmən/ *noun* (*pl.* -men /-mən/) a man, often in uniform, whose job is to stand at the entrance to a large building such as a hotel or a theatre, and open the door for visitors, find them taxis, etc. ➲ compare PORTER (3)

door·mat /ˈdɔːmæt; *NAmE* ˈdɔːrmæt/ *noun* **1** a small piece of strong material near a door that people can clean their shoes on **2** (*informal*) a person who allows other people to treat them badly but usually does not complain

door·nail /ˈdɔːneɪl; *NAmE* ˈdɔːrn-/ *noun* IDM see DEAD *adj.*

door·step /ˈdɔːstep; *NAmE* ˈdɔːrs-/ *noun, verb*
■ *noun* **1** a step outside a door of a building, or the area that is very close to the door: *The police turned up on their doorstep at 3 o'clock this morning.* ➲ VISUAL VOCAB page V15 **2** (*BrE, informal*) a thick piece of bread, usually one that is made into a SANDWICH
IDM **on the/your 'doorstep** very close to where a person lives: *The nightlife is great with bars and clubs right on the doorstep.*
■ *verb* (-pp-) [T, I] **~ (sb)** (*BrE*) when a journalist **doorsteps** sb, he or she goes to the person's house to try to speak to them, even if they do not want to say anything

door·stop /ˈdɔːstɒp; *NAmE* ˈdɔːrstɑːp/ *noun* a thing that is used to stop a door from closing or to prevent it from hitting and damaging a wall when it is opened

door·way /ˈdɔːweɪ; *NAmE* ˈdɔːrweɪ/ *noun* an opening into a building or a room, where the door is: *She stood* ***in the doorway*** *for a moment before going in.* ◇ *homeless people sleeping in shop doorways*

doo·zy (also **doo·zie**) /ˈduːzi/ *noun* (*pl.* -ies) (*NAmE, informal*) something that is very special or unusual

dop /dɒp; *NAmE* dɑːp/ *noun, verb* (*SAfrE, informal*)
■ *noun* an alcoholic drink: *Let's* ***have a dop.***
■ *verb* (-pp-) **1** [I, T] **~ (sth)** to drink alcohol, especially in large amounts: *They lay around dopping all day.* **2** [T] **~ sth** (*slang*) to not pass a test or an exam; to not be successful in completing a period of study at a school, university, etc: *I dopped my first year at varsity.*

dopa·mine /ˈdəʊpəmiːn; *NAmE* ˈdoʊ-/ *noun* [U] a chemical produced by nerve cells which has an effect on other cells

dope /dəʊp; *NAmE* doʊp/ *noun, verb*
■ *noun* **1** [U] (*informal*) a drug that is taken illegally for pleasure, especially CANNABIS or, in the US, HEROIN **2** [U] a drug that is taken by a person or given to an animal to affect their performance in a race or sport: *The athlete failed a* ***dope test*** (= a medical test showed that he had taken such drugs). **3** [C] (*informal*) a stupid person SYN **idiot 4** [U] **the ~ (on sb/sth)** (*informal*) information on sb/sth, especially details that are not generally known: *Give me the dope on the new boss.*
■ *verb* **1 ~ sb/sth** to give a drug to a person or an animal in order to affect their performance in a race or sport **2 ~ sb/sth** to give sb a drug, often in their food or drink, in order to make them unconscious; to put a drug in food, etc: *Thieves doped a guard dog and stole $10 000 worth of goods.* ◇ *The wine was doped.* **3** [usually passive] **~ sb (up)** (*informal*) if sb is **doped** or **doped up**, they cannot think clearly or act normally because they are under the influence of drugs

dopey /ˈdəʊpi; *NAmE* ˈdoʊpi/ *adj.* (*informal*) (**dopi·er, dopi·est**) **1** rather stupid: *a dopey grin* **2** not fully awake or thinking clearly, sometimes because you have taken a drug: *I felt dopey and drowsy after the operation.*

dop·pel·gän·ger /ˈdɒplgæŋə(r); -geŋ-; *NAmE* ˈdɑːpl-/ *noun* (from *German*) a person's **doppelgänger** is another person who looks exactly like them

the Dop·pler effect /ˈdɒplər ɪfekt; *NAmE* ˈdɑːp-/ *noun* [sing.] (*physics*) the way that sound waves, light waves, etc. change according to the direction that the source is moving in with relation to the person who is observing

ˈDoppler shift *noun* (*physics*) the change in sound, colour, etc. caused by the Doppler effect

Dorian Gray /ˌdɔːriən ˈɡreɪ/ *noun* [usually sing.] a person who continues to look young and beautiful, even though they are growing older or behaving in an immoral way: *He's a real Dorian Gray, apparently untouched by the ageing process.* ORIGIN From the story by Oscar Wilde, *The Picture of Dorian Gray*, in which Dorian Gray is a beautiful young man who behaves in an immoral way. He secretly keeps a painting of himself, which gradually changes, making him look older and more evil in it. Dorian himself continues to look young and beautiful.

Doric /ˈdɒrɪk; *NAmE* ˈdɔːrɪk; ˈdɑːrɪk/ *adj.* [usually before noun] (*architecture*) used to describe the oldest style of ARCHITECTURE in ancient Greece that has thick plain columns and no decoration at the top: *a Doric column/temple*

dork /dɔːk; *NAmE* dɔːrk/ *noun* (*informal*) a stupid or boring person that other people laugh at ▶ **dorky** *adj.*

dorm /dɔːm; *NAmE* dɔːrm/ *noun* (*informal*) = DORMITORY

dor·mant /ˈdɔːmənt; *NAmE* ˈdɔːrm-/ *adj.* not active or growing now but able to become active or to grow in the future SYN **inactive**: *a dormant volcano* ◇ *During the winter the seeds* ***lie dormant*** *in the soil.* OPP **active** ▶ **dor·mancy** /ˈdɔːmənsi; *NAmE* ˈdɔːrm-/ *noun* [U]

ˌdormer ˈwindow (also **dormer**) *noun* a vertical window in a room that is built into a sloping roof ➲ VISUAL VOCAB page V15

dor·mi·tory /ˈdɔːmətri; *NAmE* ˈdɔːrmətɔːri/ *noun* (*pl.* -ies) (also *informal* **dorm**) **1** a room for several people to sleep in, especially in a school or other institution **2** (*NAmE*) (*BrE* **ˌhall of ˈresidence, hall**) a building for university or college students to live in

ˈdormitory town (*BrE*) (*NAmE* **ˈbedroom community, ˈbedroom suburb**) *noun* a town that people live in and from where they travel to work in a bigger town or city

dor·mouse /ˈdɔːmaʊs; *NAmE* ˈdɔːrm-/ *noun* (*pl.* **dor·mice** /-maɪs/) a small animal like a mouse, with a tail covered in fur

dorp /dɔːp; *NAmE* dɔːrp/ *noun* (*SAfrE, informal*) a small town or village in the country

dor·sal /ˈdɔːsl; *NAmE* ˈdɔːrsl/ *adj.* [only before noun] (*technical*) on or connected with the back of a fish or an animal: *a shark's dorsal fin* ➲ VISUAL VOCAB page V10

dory /ˈdɔːri/ *noun* (*pl.* -ies) a narrow fish that has a deep body and that can open its mouth very wide

DOS /dɒs; *NAmE* dɔːs/ *abbr.* (*computing*) disk operating system

dosa /ˈdəʊsə; *NAmE* ˈdoʊ-/ *noun* a southern Indian PANCAKE made with rice flour

dos·age /ˈdəʊsɪdʒ; *NAmE* ˈdoʊ-/ *noun* [usually sing.] an amount of sth, usually a medicine or a drug, that is taken regularly over a particular period of time: *a* ***high/low dosage*** ◇ *to* ***increase/reduce the dosage*** ◇ *Do not exceed the* ***recommended dosage.***

dos and don'ts ➲ DO[1] *n.*

dose /dəʊs; *NAmE* doʊs/ *noun, verb*

■ ***noun*** **1** an amount of a medicine or a drug that is taken once, or regularly over a period of time: *a* ***high/low/lethal dose*** ◇ *Repeat the dose after 12 hours if necessary.* **2** (*informal*) an amount of sth: *A dose of flu kept me off work.* ◇ *Workers at the nuclear plant were exposed to high doses of radiation.* ◇ *I can cope with her* ***in small doses*** (= for short amounts of time).

IDM **like a dose of 'salts** (*old-fashioned, BrE, informal*) very fast and easily ➲ more at MEDICINE

■ ***verb*** **~ sb/yourself (up) (with sth)** to give sb/yourself a medicine or drug: *She dosed herself up with vitamin pills.* ◇ *He was heavily dosed with painkillers.*

dosh /dɒʃ; *NAmE* dɑːʃ/ *noun* [U] (*BrE, slang*) money

doss /dɒs; *NAmE* dɑːs/ *verb, noun*

■ ***verb*** (*BrE, slang*) **1** [I] **~ (down)** to sleep somewhere, especially somewhere uncomfortable or without a real bed: *You can doss down on my floor.* **2** [I] **~ (about/around)** to spend your time not doing very much: *We were just dossing about in lessons today.*

■ ***noun*** (*BrE*) something that does not need much effort

doss·er /ˈdɒsə(r); *NAmE* ˈdɑːs-/ *noun* (*BrE*) **1** a person who has no permanent home and who lives and sleeps on the streets or in cheap HOSTELS **2** (*informal*) a person who is very lazy

doss·house /ˈdɒshaʊs; *NAmE* ˈdɑːs-/ (*BrE*) (*NAmE* **flophouse**) *noun* (*informal*) a cheap place to stay for people who have no home

dos·sier /ˈdɒsieɪ; *NAmE* ˈdɔːs-; ˈdɑːs-/ *noun* (*formal*) a collection of documents that contain information about a person, an event or a subject SYN **file**: *to* ***assemble/compile a dossier*** ◇ **~ on sb/sth** *We have a dossier on him.*

dot 🔑 /dɒt; *NAmE* dɑːt/ *noun, verb*

■ ***noun*** **1** 🔑 a small round mark, especially one that is printed: *There are dots above the letters i and j.* ◇ *Text and graphics are printed at 300 dots per inch.* ◇ *The helicopters appeared as two black dots on the horizon.* ➲ SYNONYMS at PATCH **2** 🔑 (*computing*) a symbol like a full stop/period used to separate parts of a DOMAIN NAME, a URL or an email address

IDM **on the 'dot** (*informal*) exactly on time or at the exact time mentioned: *The taxi showed up on the dot.* ◇ *Breakfast is served at 8 on the dot.* ➲ more at YEAR

■ ***verb*** (-tt-) **1 ~ sth** to put a dot above or next to a letter or word: *Why do you never dot your i's?* **2** [usually passive] **~ sth** to spread things or people over an area; to be spread over an area: *The countryside was* ***dotted with*** *small villages.* ◇ *Small villages dot the countryside.* ◇ *There are lots of Italian restaurants* ***dotted around*** *London.* **3** to put very small amounts of sth in a number of places on a surface: **~ A on/over B** *Dot the cream all over your face.* ◇ **~ B with A** *Dot your face with the cream.*

IDM **dot your ˌi's and cross your 't's** to pay attention to the small details when you are finishing a task

dot·age /ˈdəʊtɪdʒ; *NAmE* ˈdoʊ-/ *noun*

IDM **be in your dotage** to be old and not always able to think clearly

dot-com (also **dot·com**) /ˌdɒt ˈkɒm; *NAmE* ˌdɑːt ˈkɑːm/ *noun* a company that sells goods and services on the Internet, especially one whose address ends '.com': *The weaker dot-coms have collapsed.* ◇ *a dot-com millionaire*

dote /dəʊt; *NAmE* doʊt/ *verb*

PHR V **'dote on/upon sb** to feel and show great love for sb, ignoring their faults: *He dotes on his children.* ➲ SYNONYMS at LOVE

dot·ing /ˈdəʊtɪŋ; *NAmE* ˈdoʊtɪŋ/ *adj.* [only before noun] showing a lot of love for sb, often ignoring their faults

ˌdot 'matrix printer *noun* a machine that prints letters, numbers, etc. formed from very small dots

dot·ted /ˈdɒtɪd; *NAmE* ˈdɑːt-/ *adj.* **1** covered in dots **2** [only before noun] (*music*) (of a musical note) followed by a dot to show that it is one and a half times the length of the same note without the dot

ˌdot·ted 'line *noun* a line made of dots: *Country boundaries are shown on this map as dotted lines.* ◇ *Fold along the dotted line.* ◇ *Write your name on the dotted line.* ➲ VISUAL VOCAB page V58 IDM see SIGN *v.*

dotty /ˈdɒti; *NAmE* ˈdɑːti/ *adj.* (**dot·tier, dot·ti·est**) (*old-fashioned, BrE, informal*) **1** slightly crazy or silly SYN **eccentric** **2 ~ about sb/sth** having romantic feelings for sb; being enthusiastic about sth

double 🔑 /ˈdʌbl/ *adj., det., adv., noun, verb*

■ ***adj.*** [usually before noun]

▸ TWICE AS MUCH/MANY **1** 🔑 twice as much or as many as usual: *a double helping* ◇ *two double whiskies*

▸ WITH TWO PARTS **2** 🔑 having or made of two things or parts that are equal or similar: *double doors* ◇ *a double-page advertisement* ◇ *'Otter' is spelt with a double t.* ◇ *My extension is two four double 0 (2400).*

▸ FOR TWO PEOPLE **3** 🔑 made for two people or things: *a* ***double bed/room*** ➲ VISUAL VOCAB page V20 ➲ compare SINGLE *adj.* (4)

▸ COMBINING TWO THINGS **4** 🔑 combining two things or qualities: *a* ***double meaning/purpose/aim*** ◇ *It has the double advantage of being both easy and cheap.*

■ ***det.*** 🔑

▸ TWICE AS MUCH/MANY twice as much or as many as: *His income is double hers.* ◇ *He earns double what she does.* ◇ *We need double the amount we already have.*

■ ***adv.*** 🔑

▸ IN TWO PARTS in twos or in two parts: *I thought I was* ***seeing double*** (= seeing two of sth). ◇ *Fold the blanket double.* ◇ *I had to* ***bend double*** *to get under the table.*

■ ***noun***

▸ TWICE AS MUCH/MANY **1** 🔑 [U] twice the number or amount: *He gets paid double for doing the same job I do.*

▸ ALCOHOLIC DRINK **2** [C] a glass of strong alcoholic drink containing twice the usual amount: *Two Scotches, please —and make those doubles, will you?*

▸ PERSON/THING **3** [C] a person or thing that looks exactly like another: *She's the double of her mother.* **4** [C] an actor who replaces another actor in a film/movie to do dangerous or other special things ➲ see also BODY DOUBLE

▸ BEDROOM **5** [C] = DOUBLE ROOM: *Is that a single or a double you want?* ➲ compare SINGLE *n.* (3)

▸ IN SPORT **6 doubles** [U+sing./pl. v.] a game, especially of TENNIS, in which one pair plays another: *mixed doubles* (= in which each pair consists of a man and a woman) ➲ compare SINGLES *n.* (5) **7 the double** [sing.] the fact of winning two important competitions or beating the same player or team twice, in the same season or year

IDM **at the 'double** (*BrE*) (*NAmE* **on the 'double**) (*informal*) quickly; hurrying **ˌdouble or 'quits** (*BrE*) (*NAmE* **ˌdouble or 'nothing**) (in gambling) a risk in which you could win twice the amount you pay, or you could lose all your money

■ ***verb***

▸ BECOME TWICE AS MUCH/MANY **1** 🔑 [I, T] to become, or make sth become, twice as much or as many: *Membership almost doubled in two years.* ◇ **~ sth** *Double all the quantities in the recipe to make enough for eight people.*

▸ FOLD **2** [T] **~ sth** (**over**) to bend or fold sth so that there are two layers: *She doubled the blanket and put it under his head.*
▸ IN BASEBALL **3** [I] to hit the ball far enough for you to get to second BASE: *He doubled to left field.*
PHR V **ˈdouble as sth** | **ˌdouble ˈup as sth** to have another use or function as well as the main one: *The kitchen doubles as a dining room.* **ˌdouble ˈback** to turn back and go in the direction you have come from **ˌdouble ˈup** (**on sth/with sb**) (*informal*) to form a pair in order to do sth or to share sth: *We'll have to double up on books; there aren't enough to go around.* ◇ *They only have one room left: you'll have to double up with Peter.* **ˌdouble ˈup/ˈover** | **ˌdouble sb ˈup/ˈover** to bend or to make your body bend over quickly, for example because you are in pain: *Jo doubled up with laughter.* ◇ *I was doubled over with pain.*

Synonyms

double / dual

These adjectives are frequently used with the following nouns:

double ~	dual ~
bed	purpose
doors	function
figures	role
standards	approach
thickness	citizenship

- **Dual** describes something that has two parts, uses or aspects.
- **Double** can be used with a similar meaning, but when it is used to describe something that has two parts, the two parts are usually the same or very similar.
- **Double**, but not **dual**, can describe something that is made for two people or things, or is twice as big as usual.

ˈdouble act *noun* two people who work together, usually to entertain an audience

ˌdouble-ˈaction *adj.* [usually before noun] **1** working in two ways: *double-action tablets* **2** (of a gun) needing two separate actions for preparing to fire and firing

ˌdouble ˈagent *noun* a person who is a SPY for a particular country, and also for another country which is an enemy of the first one

ˌdouble ˈbar *noun* (*music*) a pair of vertical lines at the end of a piece of music

ˌdouble-ˈbarrelled (*especially US* **ˌdouble-ˈbarreled**) *adj.* [usually before noun] **1** (of a gun) having two BARRELS (= places where the bullets come out) **2** (*BrE*) (of a family name) having two parts, sometimes joined by a hyphen, for example 'Day-Lewis' **3** (of a plan, etc.) having two parts, and therefore likely to be effective

ˌdouble ˈbass (also **bass**) *noun* the largest musical instrument in the VIOLIN family, that plays very low notes ➲ VISUAL VOCAB page V30

ˌdouble ˈbill (*NAmE* also **ˌdouble ˈfeature**) *noun* two films/movies, television programmes, etc. that are shown one after the other

ˌdouble ˈbind *noun* [usually sing.] a situation in which it is difficult to choose what to do because whatever you choose will have negative results

ˌdouble-ˈblind *adj.* [only before noun] (of a test) conducted so that neither the organizer nor any other people involved know any information which might influence the results: *A randomized double-blind study was carried out to test the drug's effectiveness.*

ˌdouble ˈbluff *noun* a way of trying to trick sb by telling them the truth while hoping that they think you are lying

ˌdouble-ˈbook *verb* [often passive] **~ sth** to promise the same room, seat, table, etc. to two different people at the same time ➲ compare OVERBOOK ▸ **ˌdouble-ˈbooking** *noun* [C, U]

ˌdouble-ˈbreast·ed *adj.* a **double-breasted** jacket or coat has two front parts so that one part covers the other when the buttons are done up, and two rows of buttons can be seen ➲ compare SINGLE-BREASTED

ˌdouble-ˈcheck *verb* [T, I] **~ (sth)** | **~ (that)...** to check sth for a second time or with great care: *I'll double-check the figures.* ▸ **ˌdouble-ˈcheck** *noun*

ˌdouble ˈchin *noun* a fold of fat under a person's chin, that looks like another chin

ˌdouble-ˈclick *verb* [I, T] **~ (on) sth** (*computing*) to choose a particular function or item on a computer screen, etc. by pressing one of the buttons on a mouse twice quickly

ˌdouble ˈcream *noun* [U] (*BrE*) thick cream which contains a lot of fat and can be mixed so that it is no longer liquid ➲ compare SINGLE CREAM

ˌdouble-ˈcross *verb* **~ sb** to cheat or trick sb who trusts you (usually in connection with sth illegal or dishonest): *He double-crossed the rest of the gang and disappeared with all the money.* ▸ **ˌdouble-ˈcross** *noun* [usually sing.]

ˌdouble ˈdate *noun* an occasion when two couples go out together on a DATE ▸ **ˌdouble-ˈdate** *verb* [I]

ˌdouble-ˈdealer *noun* (*informal*) a dishonest person who cheats other people ▸ **ˌdouble-ˈdealing** *noun* [U]

ˌdouble-ˈdecker *noun* **1** a bus with two floors, one on top of the other ➲ VISUAL VOCAB page V46 ➲ compare SINGLE-DECKER **2** (*NAmE*) a SANDWICH made from three pieces of bread with two layers of food between them

ˌdouble-ˈdensity *adj.* (*computing*) (of a computer disk) able to hold twice the amount of data as other older disks of the same size

ˌdouble ˈdigits *noun* [pl.] (*NAmE*) = DOUBLE FIGURES ▸ **ˌdouble-ˈdigit** *adj.* (*NAmE*) = DOUBLE-FIGURE

ˌdouble ˈDutch *noun* [U] (*BrE, informal*) speech or writing that is impossible to understand, and that seems to be nonsense

ˌdouble-ˈedged *adj.* **1** (of a knife, etc.) having two cutting edges **2** (of a remark, comment, etc.) having two possible meanings SYN **ambiguous** **3** having two different parts or uses, often parts that contrast with each other: *the double-edged quality of life in a small town—security and boredom*
IDM **be a double-edged ˈsword/ˈweapon** to be sth that has both advantages and disadvantages

double en·ten·dre /ˌduːbl ɒ̃ˈtɒ̃drə; *NAmE* ɑ̃ːˈtɑ̃ːdrə/ *noun* (from *French*) a word or phrase that can be understood in two different ways, one of which usually refers to sex

ˌdouble-entry ˈbookkeeping *noun* [U] (*business*) a system of keeping financial records in which each piece of business is recorded as a CREDIT in one account and a DEBIT in another

ˌdouble ˈfault *noun* (in TENNIS) the loss of a point caused by a player not SERVING correctly twice ▸ **ˌdouble-ˈfault** *verb* [I]

ˌdouble ˈfeature *noun* (*NAmE*) = DOUBLE BILL

ˌdouble ˈfigures (*especially BrE*) (*NAmE* usually **ˌdouble ˈdigits**) *noun* [pl.] used to describe a number that is not less than 10 and not more than 99: *Inflation is* ***in double figures.*** ▸ **ˌdouble-ˈfigure** (*especially BrE*) (*NAmE* usually **ˌdouble-ˈdigit**) *adj.* [only before noun]: *a double-figure pay rise*

ˌdouble ˈglazing *noun* [U] (*especially BrE*) windows that have two layers of glass with a space between them, designed to make the room warmer and to reduce noise ➲ COLLOCATIONS at DECORATE ▸ **ˌdouble-ˈglaze** *verb* **~ sth** **ˌdouble-ˈglazed** *adj.*: *double-glazed windows*

ˌdouble-ˈheader *noun* (*NAmE*) (in BASEBALL) two games that are played on the same day, traditionally on a Sunday, and usually by the same two teams

ˌ**double ˈhelix** *noun* (*biology*) the structure of DNA, consisting of two connected long thin pieces that form a SPIRAL shape

ˌ**double ˈjeopardy** *noun* [U] (in US law) the fact of taking sb to court twice for the same crime, or punishing sb twice for the same reason. This is not allowed under the Fifth AMENDMENT of the US CONSTITUTION.

ˌ**double-ˈjointed** *adj.* having joints in your fingers, arms, etc. that allow you to bend them both backwards and forwards

ˌ**double ˈlife** *noun* a life of a person who leads two different lives which are kept separate from each other, usually because one of them involves secret, often illegal or immoral, activities: *to **live/lead a double life***

ˌ**double ˈnegative** *noun* (*grammar*) a negative statement containing two negative words. 'I didn't say nothing' is a double negative because it contains two negative words, 'n't' and 'nothing'. This use is not considered correct in standard English.

ˌ**double-ˈpark** *verb* [T, I, usually passive] **~ (sth)** to park a car or other vehicle beside one that is already parked in a street: *A car stood double-parked almost in the middle of the road.* ◇ *I'll have to rush—I'm double-parked.*

ˌ**double ˈplay** *noun* (*NAmE*) (in BASEBALL) a situation in which two players are put out (= made to finish their attempt at scoring a RUN)

ˌ**double ˈquick** *adv.* (*BrE*, *informal*) very quickly ▶ ˌ**double-ˈquick** *adj.* [only before noun]: *The TV was repaired in **double-quick time**.*

ˌ**double ˈrhyme** *noun* [U] (in poetry) a pair of words which have two parts ending with the same sounds, for example 'reading' and 'speeding'

ˌ**double ˈroom** (also **double**) *noun* a bedroom for two people

double·speak /ˈdʌblspiːk/ (also ˈ**double·talk**) *noun* [U] language that is intended to make people believe sth which is not true, or that can be understood in two different ways

ˌ**double ˈstandard** *noun* a rule or moral principle that is unfair because it is used in one situation, but not in another, or because it treats one group of people in a way that is different from the treatment of another

doub·let /ˈdʌblət/ *noun* a short, tightly fitting jacket worn by men from the 14th to the 17th century: *dressed in **doublet and hose***

ˌ**double ˈtake** *noun* if you **do a double take**, you wait for a moment before you react to sth that has happened, because it is very surprising

double·talk /ˈdʌbltɔːk/ *noun* [U] = DOUBLESPEAK

double·think /ˈdʌblθɪŋk/ *noun* [U] the act of holding two opposite opinions or beliefs at the same time; the ability to do this

ˌ**double ˈtime** *noun* [U] twice sb's normal pay, that they earn for working at times which are not normal working hours

ˌ**double ˈvision** *noun* [U] if you have **double vision**, you can see two things where there is actually only one

doub·loon /dʌˈbluːn/ *noun* (in the past) a Spanish gold coin

doubly /ˈdʌbli/ *adv.* (used before adjectives) **1** more than usual: ***doubly difficult/hard/important*** ◇ *I made doubly sure I locked all the doors when I went out.* **2** in two ways; for two reasons: *I was doubly attracted to the house—by its size and its location.*

doubt 🔑 /daʊt/ *noun, verb*

■ ***noun*** 🔑 [U, C] a feeling of being uncertain about sth or not believing sth: *a feeling of doubt and uncertainty* ◇ **~ (about sth)** ***There is some doubt** about the best way to do it.* ◇ *The article **raised doubts** about how effective the new drug really was.* ◇ **~ (that...)** ***There is no doubt** at all that we did the right thing.* ◇ **~ (as to sth)** *If you are **in any doubt as to whether** you should be doing these exercises, consult your doctor.* ◇ *New evidence has **cast doubt on** the guilt of the man jailed for the crime.* ◇ *She knew **without a shadow of a doubt** that he was lying to her.* ◇ *Whether he will continue to be successful in future is **open to doubt**.* ➲ LANGUAGE BANK at IMPERSONAL

IDM **beyond (any) ˈdoubt** in a way that shows that sth is completely certain: *The research showed beyond doubt that smoking contributes to heart disease.* ◇ (*law*) *The prosecution was able to establish **beyond reasonable doubt** that the woman had been lying.* **be in ˈdoubt** 🔑 to be uncertain: *The success of the system is not in doubt.* **have your ˈdoubts (about sth)** to have reasons why you are not certain about whether sth is good or whether sth good will happen: *I've had my doubts about his work since he joined the firm.* ◇ *It may be all right. Personally, I have my doubts.* **if in ˈdoubt** used to give advice to sb who cannot decide what to do: *If in doubt, wear black.* ˌ**no ˈdoubt** **1** 🔑 used when you are saying that sth is probable: *No doubt she'll call us when she gets there.* **2** 🔑 used when you are saying that sth is certainly true: *He's made some great movies. There's **no doubt about it**.* **without/beyond ˈdoubt** 🔑 used when you are giving your opinion and emphasizing the point that you are making: *This meeting has been, without doubt, one of the most useful we have had so far.* ➲ more at BENEFIT *n.*

■ ***verb*** **1** 🔑 to feel uncertain about sth; to feel that sth is not true, will probably not happen, etc: **~ sth** *There seems no reason to doubt her story.* ◇ *'Do you think England will win?'—'**I doubt it**.'* ◇ **~ (that)...** *I never doubted (that) she would come.* ◇ **~ whether, if, etc...** ***I doubt whether/if** the new one will be any better.* **2** **~ sb/sth** to not trust sb/sth; to not believe sb: *I had no reason to doubt him.* ▶ **doubt·er** *noun*

doubt·ful /ˈdaʊtfl/ *adj.* **1** (of a person) not sure; uncertain and feeling doubt **SYN** **dubious**: **~ (about sth)** *Rose was doubtful about the whole idea.* ◇ **~ (about doing sth)** *He was doubtful about accepting extra work.* **2** unlikely; not probable: **~ (if...)** *It's doubtful if this painting is a Picasso.* ◇ **~ (that...)** *With her injuries it's doubtful that she'll ever walk again.* ◇ **~ (whether...)** *It's doubtful whether the car will last another year.* ◇ **~ (for sth)** *He is injured and is doubtful for the game tomorrow* (= unlikely to play). **3** [not usually before noun] (of a thing) uncertain and likely to get worse: *At the beginning of the war things were looking very doubtful.* **4** [only before noun] of low value; probably not genuine or of a quality that you can rely on **SYN** **dubious**: *This wine is of doubtful quality.* ▶ **doubt·ful·ly** /-fəli/ *adv.*

doubt·ing Thomas /ˌdaʊtɪŋ ˈtɒməs; *NAmE* ˈtɑːm-/ *noun* [sing.] (*old-fashioned*) a person who is unlikely to believe sth until they see proof of it **ORIGIN** From St Thomas in the Bible, who did not believe that Jesus Christ had risen from the dead until he saw and touched his wounds.

doubt·less /ˈdaʊtləs/ *adv.* (also *less frequent* **doubt·less·ly**) almost certainly **SYN** **without doubt**: *He would doubtless disapprove of what Kelly was doing.*

douche /duːʃ/ *noun* a method of washing inside a woman's VAGINA using a stream of water ▶ **douche** *verb* [I, T] **~ (sth)**

dough /dəʊ; *NAmE* doʊ/ *noun* **1** [U, sing.] a mixture of flour, water, etc. that is made into bread and PASTRY: *Knead the dough on a floured surface.* **2** [U] (*old-fashioned, slang*) money

dough·nut (also **donut** especially in *NAmE*) /ˈdəʊnʌt; *NAmE* ˈdoʊ-/ *noun* a small cake made of fried dough, usually in the shape of a ring, or round and filled with jam/jelly, fruit, cream, etc.

doughty /ˈdaʊti/ *adj.* (*old-fashioned*) brave and strong

doula /ˈduːlə/ *noun* (*NAmE*) a woman whose role is to provide emotional support to a woman who is giving birth ➲ compare MIDWIFE

dour /ˈdaʊə(r); *BrE* also dʊə(r); *NAmE* also dʊr/ *adj.* **1** (of a person) giving the impression of being unfriendly and severe **2** (of a thing, a place, or a situation) not pleasant; with no features that make it lively or interesting: *The city, drab and dour by day, is transformed at night.* ◇ *The game*

D

proved to be a dour struggle, with both men determined to win. ▶ **dour·ly** *adv.*

douse (also **dowse**) /daʊs/ *verb* **1** **~ sth** (**with sth**) to stop a fire from burning by pouring water over it; to put out a light **2** **~ sb/sth** (**in/with sth**) to pour a lot of liquid over sb/sth; to SOAK sb/sth in liquid: *The car was doused in petrol and set alight.*

D

dove[1] /dʌv/ *noun* **1** a bird of the PIGEON family. The white dove is often used as a symbol of peace: *A dove cooed softly.* ◇ *He wore a dove-grey suit.* ➲ see also TURTLE DOVE **2** a person, especially a politician, who prefers peace and discussion to war OPP **hawk**

dove[2] /dəʊv; *NAmE* doʊv/ (*NAmE*) *past tense of* DIVE

dove·cote /ˈdʌvkɒt; ˈdʌvkəʊt; *NAmE* -kɑːt; -koʊt/ (also **dove·cot** /ˈdʌvkɒt; *NAmE* -kɑːt/) *noun* a small building for DOVES or PIGEONS to live in

dove·tail /ˈdʌvteɪl/ *verb, noun*

■ ***verb*** [I, T] (*formal*) **~** (**sth**) (**with/into sth**) if two things **dovetail** or if one thing **dovetails** with another, they fit together well: *My plans dovetailed nicely with hers.*

■ ***noun*** (also ˌ**dovetail ˈjoint**) a joint for fixing two pieces of wood together

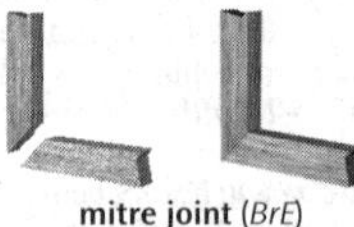

dovetail joint

mitre joint (*BrE*)
miter joint (*NAmE*)

dov·ish /ˈdʌvɪʃ/ *adj.* preferring to use peaceful discussion rather than military action in order to solve a political problem OPP **hawkish**

dow·ager /ˈdaʊədʒə(r)/ *noun* **1** a woman of high social rank who has a title from her dead husband: *the dowager Duchess of Norfolk* **2** (*informal*) an impressive, usually rich, old woman

dowdy /ˈdaʊdi/ *adj.* (**dow·dier**, **dow·di·est**) **1** (of a woman) not attractive or fashionable **2** (of a thing) dull or boring and not attractive SYN **drab**: *a dowdy dress*

dow·el /ˈdaʊəl/ (also ˈ**dowel rod**) *noun* a small piece of wood, plastic, etc. in the shape of a CYLINDER, used to fix larger pieces of wood, plastic, etc. together

dowel·ling (*BrE*) (*US* **dowel·ing**) /ˈdaʊəlɪŋ/ *noun* [U] short pieces of wooden, metal or plastic ROD that are used for holding parts of sth together

the Dow Jones Index /ˌdaʊ ˈdʒəʊnz ɪndeks; *NAmE* ˈdʒoʊnz/ (also ˌ**Dow ˈJones average, the ˈDow**) *noun* [sing.] a list of the share prices of 30 US industrial companies that can be used to compare the prices to previous levels

down 🔑 /daʊn/ *adv., prep., verb, adj., noun*

■ ***adv.*** HELP For the special uses of **down** in phrasal verbs, look at the entries for the verbs. For example **climb down** is in the phrasal verb section at **climb**. **1** 🔑 to or at a lower place or position: *She jumped down off the chair.* ◇ *He looked down at her.* ◇ *We watched as the sun went down.* ◇ *She bent down to pick up her glove.* ◇ *Mary's not down yet* (= she is still upstairs). ◇ *The baby can't keep any food down* (= in her body). **2** 🔑 from a standing or vertical position to a sitting or horizontal one: *Please sit down.* ◇ *He had to go and lie down for a while.* **3** 🔑 at a lower level or rate: *Prices have gone down recently.* ◇ *We're already two goals down* (= the other team has two goals more). ➲ LANGUAGE BANK at FALL **4** 🔑 used to show that the amount or strength of sth is lower, or that there is less activity: *Turn the music down!* ◇ *The class settled down and she began the lesson.* **5** (in a CROSSWORD) reading from top to bottom, not from side to side: *I can't do 3 down.* **6** 🔑 to or in the south of a country: *They flew down to Texas.* ◇ *Houses are more expensive down south.* **7** 🔑 on paper; on a list: *Did you get that down?* ◇ *I always write everything down.* ◇ *Have you got me down for the trip?* **8** used to show the limits in a range or an order: *Everyone will be there, from the Principal down.* **9** having lost the amount of money mentioned: *At the end of the day we were £20 down.* **10** if you pay an amount of money **down**, you pay that to start with, and the rest later **11** (*informal*) used to say how far you have got in a list of things you have to do: *Well, I've seen six apartments so far. That's six down and four to go!* **12** (*informal*) to or at a local place such as a shop/store, pub, etc: *I'm just going down to the post office.* ◇ *I saw him down at the shops.* HELP In informal British English, **to** and **at** are often left out after **down** in this sense: *He's gone down the shops.*

IDM **be down to sb** (*informal*) to be the responsibility of sb: *It's down to you to check the door.* **be down to sb/sth** to be caused by a particular person or thing: *She claimed her problems were down to the media.* **be down to sth** to have only a little money left: *I'm down to my last dollar.* **be/go down with sth** to have or catch an illness **down through sth** (*formal*) during a long period of time: *Down through the years this town has seen many changes.* **down to the last, smallest, final, etc. sth** including every small part or detail of sth: *She organized everything down to the last detail.* **down ˈunder** (*informal*) to or in Australia and/or New Zealand **down with sb/sth** used to say that you are opposed to sth, or to a person: *The crowds chanted 'Down with NATO!'* ➲ more at MAN *n.*

■ ***prep.*** **1** 🔑 from a high or higher point on sth to a lower one: *The stone rolled down the hill.* ◇ *Tears ran down her face.* ◇ *Her hair hung down her back to her waist.* **2** 🔑 along; towards the direction in which you are facing: *He lives just down the street.* ◇ *Go down the road till you reach the traffic lights.* ◇ *There's a bridge a mile down the river from here.* **3** all through a period of time: *an exhibition of costumes down the ages* (= from all periods of history)

■ ***verb*** (*informal*) **1** **~ sth** to finish a drink or eat sth quickly: *We downed our coffees and left.* **2** **~ sb/sth** to force sb/sth down to the ground: *to down a plane*

IDM ˌ**down ˈtools** (*BrE*) (of workers) to stop work; to go on strike

■ ***adj.*** [not before noun] **1** (*informal*) sad or depressed: *I feel a bit down today.* **2** (of a computer or computer system) not working: *The system was down all morning.* ➲ see also DOWNTIME IDM see HIT *v.*, KICK *v.*, LUCK *n.*, MOUTH *n.*

■ ***noun*** ➲ see also DOWNS **1** [U] the very fine soft feathers of a bird: *duck down* **2** [U] fine soft hair ➲ see also DOWNY **3** [C] (in AMERICAN FOOTBALL) one of a series of four chances to carry the ball forward ten yards that a team is allowed. These series continue until the team loses the ball or fails to go forward ten yards in four downs.

IDM **have a ˈdown on sb/sth** (*BrE, informal*) to have a bad opinion of a person or thing ➲ more at UP *n.*

ˌ**down and ˈout** *adj.* (of a person) **1** without money, a home or a job, and living on the streets: *a novel about being down and out in London* **2** certain to be defeated

ˈ**down-and-out** *noun* a person without money, a home or a job, who lives on the streets

ˌ**down at ˈheel** *adj.* looking less attractive and fashionable than before, usually because of a lack of money: *The town has become very down at heel.* ◇ *a down-at-heel hotel*

down·beat /ˈdaʊnbiːt/ *adj.* (*informal*) **1** dull or depressing; not having much hope for the future: *The overall mood of the meeting was downbeat.* OPP **upbeat** **2** not showing strong feelings or enthusiasm

down·cast /ˈdaʊnkɑːst; *NAmE* -kæst/ *adj.* **1** (of eyes) looking down: *Eyes downcast, she continued eating.* **2** (of a person or an expression) sad or depressed SYN **dejected**: *A group of downcast men stood waiting for food.*

down·draught (*BrE*) (*NAmE* **down·draft**) /ˈdaʊndrɑːft; *NAmE* -dræft/ *noun* a downward movement of air, for example down a CHIMNEY

down·er /ˈdaʊnə(r)/ *noun* (*informal*) **1** [usually pl.] a drug, especially a BARBITURATE, that relaxes you or makes you want to sleep ➲ compare UPPER **2** an experience that makes you feel sad or depressed: *Not getting the promotion was a real downer.* ◇ *He's really **on a downer*** (= very depressed).

down·fall /ˈdaʊnfɔːl/ *noun* [sing.] the loss of a person's money, power, social position, etc; the thing that causes this: *The sex scandal finally led to his downfall.* ◇ *Greed was her downfall.*

down·grade /ˌdaʊnˈɡreɪd/ *verb* **1 ~ sb/sth** (**from sth**) (**to sth**) to move sb/sth down to a lower rank or level: *She's been downgraded from principal to vice-principal.* **2 ~ sth/sb** to make sth/sb seem less important or valuable than it/they really are ➲ compare UPGRADE ▸ **down·grad·ing** *noun* [U, C]: *a downgrading of diplomatic relations*

down·heart·ed /ˌdaʊnˈhɑːtɪd; *NAmE* -ˈhɑːrtɪd/ *adj.* [not before noun] feeling depressed or sad: *We're disappointed by these results but we're not downhearted.*

down·hill *adv., adj., noun*

■ ***adv.*** /ˌdaʊnˈhɪl/ towards the bottom of a hill; in a direction that goes down: *to* ***run/walk/cycle downhill*** **OPP uphill**

IDM ˌ**go down**ˈ**hill** to get worse in quality, health, etc. **SYN deteriorate**: *Their marriage went downhill after the first child was born.*

■ ***adj.*** /ˌdaʊnˈhɪl/ going or sloping towards the bottom of a hill: *a downhill path* **OPP uphill**

IDM be (all) downhill | be ˌ**downhill all the** ˈ**way** (*informal*) **1** to be easy compared to what came before: *It's all downhill from here. We'll soon be finished.* **2** to become worse or less successful: *It's been all downhill for his career since then, with four defeats in five games.* ◇ *I started work as a journalist and it was downhill all the way for my health.*

■ ***noun*** /ˈdaʊnhɪl/ [U] the type of SKIING in which you go directly down a mountain; a race in which people SKI down a mountain ➲ VISUAL VOCAB page V39 ➲ compare CROSS-COUNTRY

ˌ**down-**ˈ**home** *adj.* (*NAmE*) used to describe a person or thing that reminds you of a simple way of life, typical of the country, not the town

Down·ing Street /ˈdaʊnɪŋ striːt/ *noun* [sing.] (not used with *the*) a way of referring to the British prime minister and government, taken from the name of the street where the prime minister lives: *Downing Street issued a statement late last night.*

down·light·er /ˈdaʊnlaɪtə(r)/ (also **down·light** /ˈdaʊnlaɪt/) *noun* a light on a wall which shines downwards ➲ compare UPLIGHTER

down·link /ˈdaʊnlɪŋk/ *noun* a communications link by which information is received from space or from an aircraft ▸ **down·link** *verb*: **~ sth** *Any organization can downlink the program without charge.*

down·load *verb, noun*

■ ***verb*** /ˌdaʊnˈləʊd; *NAmE* -ˈloʊd/ **~ sth** (*computing*) to move data to a smaller computer system from a larger one **OPP upload** ➲ COLLOCATIONS at EMAIL ➲ compare LOAD

■ ***noun*** /ˈdaʊnləʊd; *NAmE* -loʊd/ (*computing*) data which is downloaded from another computer system ▸ **down·load·able** /ˌdaʊnˈləʊdəbl; *NAmE* -ˈloʊd-/ *adj.*

down·low /ˈdaʊnləʊ; *NAmE* -loʊ/ *noun, adj.*

■ ***noun* the downlow** [sing.] (*informal*) **~ on** (**sb/sth**) the true facts about sb/sth, especially those considered most important to know **SYN low-down**: *the website that gives you the downlow on the best movies*

IDM on the ˈ**downlow** secretly; not wanting other people to discover what you are doing

■ ***adj.*** [only before noun] (*slang*) used to refer to a man who appears to be HETEROSEXUAL, but secretly has sex with men

down·mark·et /ˌdaʊnˈmɑːkɪt; *NAmE* -ˈmɑːrkɪt/ (*BrE*) (*NAmE* **down·scale**) *adj.* (*disapproving*) cheap and of poor quality: *The company wants to break away from its downmarket image.* **OPP upmarket** ▸ **down·mark·et** *adv.*: *To get more viewers the TV station was forced to* ***go downmarket.***

down·most /ˈdaʊnməʊst; *NAmE* -moʊst/ *adj.* (*especially BrE*) nearest to the ground or lower level ▸ **down·most** *adv.*

ˌ**down** ˈ**payment** *noun* a sum of money that is given as the first part of a larger payment: *We are saving for a down payment on a house.* ➲ COLLOCATIONS at HOUSE

down·pipe /ˈdaʊnpaɪp/ (*BrE*) (*US* ˈ**fall-pipe**) *noun* a pipe for carrying water from a roof down to the ground or to a DRAIN

down·play /ˌdaʊnˈpleɪ/ *verb* **~ sth** to make people think that sth is less important than it really is **SYN play down**: *The coach is downplaying the team's poor performance.*

down·pour /ˈdaʊnpɔː(r)/ *noun* [usually sing.] a heavy fall of rain that often starts suddenly

down·right /ˈdaʊnraɪt/ *adj.* [only before noun] used as a way of emphasizing sth negative or unpleasant: *There was suspicion and even downright hatred between them.* ▸ **down·right** *adv.*: *She couldn't think of anything to say that wasn't downright rude.* ◇ *It's not just stupid—it's downright dangerous.*

down·river /ˌdaʊnˈrɪvə(r)/ *adv.* = DOWNSTREAM

downs /daʊnz/ *noun* **the downs** [pl.] an area of open land with low hills, especially in southern England

down·scale /ˌdaʊnˈskeɪl/ (*NAmE*) (*BrE* **down·mark·et**) *adj.* (*disapproving*) cheap and of poor quality **OPP upscale** ▸ **down·scale** *adv.*

down·shift /ˈdaʊnʃɪft/ *verb* **1** [I] (*NAmE*) to change to a lower gear in a vehicle **2** [I] to change to a job or style of life where you may earn less but which puts less pressure on you and involves less stress ➲ COLLOCATIONS at TOWN ▸ **down·shift** *noun* [C, U] **down·shift·er** *noun*

down·side /ˈdaʊnsaɪd/ *noun* [sing.] the disadvantages or less positive aspects of sth **OPP upside**

down·size /ˈdaʊnsaɪz/ *verb* [I, T] **~** (**sth**) (*business*) to reduce the number of people who work in a company, business, etc. in order to reduce costs ➲ SYNONYMS at CUT ▸ **down·siz·ing** *noun* [U]

down·spout /ˈdaʊnspaʊt/ *noun* (*NAmE*) = DRAINPIPE

ˈ**Down's syndrome** (*NAmE* usually ˈ**Down syndrome**) *noun* [U] a medical condition, caused by a fault with one CHROMOSOME, in which a person is born with particular physical characteristics and a mental ability that is below average

down·stage /ˈdaʊnsteɪdʒ/ *adv.* towards the front of the stage in a theatre ▸ **down·stage** *adj.* **OPP upstage**

down·stairs 0‑ /ˌdaʊnˈsteəz; *NAmE* -ˈsterz/ *adv., noun*

■ ***adv.*** 0‑ down the stairs; on or to a floor or a house or building lower than the one you are on, especially the one at ground level: *She rushed downstairs and burst into the kitchen.* ◇ *Wait downstairs in the hall.* **OPP upstairs** ▸ **down·stairs** 0‑ *adj.* [only before noun]: *a downstairs bathroom*

■ ***noun*** 0‑ [sing.] the lower floor of a house or building, especially the one at ground level: *We're painting the downstairs.* **OPP upstairs**

down·stream /ˌdaʊnˈstriːm/ *adv., adj.*

■ (also *less frequent* **down·river**) ***adv.*** **~** (**of/from sth**) in the direction in which a river flows: *to* ***drift/float downstream*** ◇ *downstream of/from the bridge* **OPP upstream**

■ ***adj.*** **1** (also *less frequent* **down·river**) in a position along a river which is nearer the sea: *downstream areas* **OPP upstream** **2** happening as a consequence of sth that has happened earlier: *downstream effects*

down·swing /ˈdaʊnswɪŋ/ *noun* [usually sing.] **1 ~** (**in sth**) a situation in which sth gets worse or decreases over a period of time: *the current downswing in the airline industry* ◇ *He is on a career downswing.* **OPP upswing** **2** (in GOLF) the downward movement of a CLUB when a player is about to hit the ball

ˈ**Down syndrome** *noun* [U] (*NAmE*) = DOWN'S SYNDROME

down·tick /ˈdaʊntɪk/ *noun* [C, usually sing.] (*NAmE, economics*) a small decrease in the level or value of sth, especially in the price of shares: *The shares were bought* ***on a downtick.*** **OPP uptick**

down·time /ˈdaʊntaɪm/ *noun* [U] **1** the time during which a machine, especially a computer, is not working ➲ compare UPTIME **2** (*especially NAmE*) the time when sb stops working and is able to relax: *Everyone needs a little downtime.*

D

D

ˌ**down to ˈearth** *adj.* (*approving*) sensible and practical, in a way that is helpful and friendly

down·town /ˌdaʊnˈtaʊn/ *adv.* (*especially NAmE*) in or towards the centre of a city, especially its main business area: *to go/work downtown* ➲ COLLOCATIONS at TOWN ➲ compare MIDTOWN, TOWN CENTRE, UPTOWN ▸ ˈ**down·town** *adj.*: *a downtown store* ˈ**down·town** *noun* [U]: *a hotel in the heart of downtown*

down·trend /ˈdaʊntrend/ *noun* [sing.] a situation in which business activity or performance decreases or becomes worse over a period of time OPP **uptrend**

down·trod·den /ˈdaʊntrɒdn; *NAmE* -trɑːdn/ *adj.* **downtrodden** people are treated so badly by the people with authority and power that they no longer have the energy or ability to fight back

down·turn /ˈdaʊntɜːn; *NAmE* -tɜːrn/ *noun* [usually sing.] **~ (in sth)** a fall in the amount of business that is done; a time when the economy becomes weaker: *a* ***downturn in sales/trade/business*** ◇ *the economic downturn of 2008/2009* OPP **upturn**

down·ward 0‑ /ˈdaʊnwəd; *NAmE* -wərd/ *adj.* [usually before noun]
moving or pointing towards a lower level: *the downward slope of a hill* ◇ *the downward trend in inflation* ◇ *She was trapped in a* ***downward spiral*** *of personal unhappiness.* OPP **upward** ▸ **down·ward·ly** *adv.*

down·wards 0‑ /ˈdaʊnwədz; *NAmE* -wərdz/ (also **down·ward** especially in *NAmE*) *adv.*
towards the ground or towards a lower level: *She was lying* ***face downwards*** *on the grass.* ◇ *The garden sloped gently downwards to the river.* ◇ *It was a policy welcomed by world leaders from the US president downwards.* OPP **upwards** ➲ LANGUAGE BANK at FALL

down·wind /ˌdaʊnˈwɪnd/ *adv.* in the direction in which the wind is blowing: *sailing downwind* ◇ **~ of sth** *Warnings were issued to people living downwind of the fire to stay indoors.* OPP **upwind** ▸ **down·wind** *adj.*

downy /ˈdaʊni/ *adj.* covered in sth very soft, especially hair or feathers ➲ see also DOWN *n.*

dowry /ˈdaʊri/ *noun* (*pl.* -ies) **1** money and/or property that, in some societies, a wife or her family must pay to her husband when they get married **2** money and/or property that, in some societies, a husband must pay to his wife's family when they get married

dowse /daʊz/ *verb* **1** [I] to look for underground water or minerals by using a special stick or long piece of metal that moves when it comes near water, etc. **2** = DOUSE ▸ **dow·ser** *noun*

ˈ**dowsing rod** *noun* a stick used when dowsing for water or minerals underground

doxy /ˈdɒksi; *NAmE* ˈdɑːksi/ *noun* (*pl.* -ies) (*old use*) **1** a woman who is sb's lover **2** a PROSTITUTE

doyen /ˈdɔɪən/ (*NAmE* usually **dean**) *noun* the most respected or most experienced member of a group or profession: *Richard Dawkins, the doyen of evolutionary biologists*

doy·enne /dɔɪˈen/ *noun* the most respected or most experienced woman member of a group or profession: *Martha Graham, the doyenne of American modern dance*

doz. *abbr.* (in writing) DOZEN: *2 doz. eggs*

doze /dəʊz; *NAmE* doʊz/ *verb, noun*
▪ ***verb*** [I] to sleep lightly for a short time ➲ SYNONYMS at SLEEP
PHR V ˌ**doze** ˈ**off** to go to sleep, especially during the day: *She dozed off in front of the fire.*
▪ ***noun*** [sing.] a short period of sleep, usually during the day: *I had a doze on the train.*

dozen 0‑ /ˈdʌzn/ *noun, det.* (*pl.* **dozen**)
1 0‑ [C] (*abbr.* **doz.**) a group of twelve of the same thing: *Give me a dozen, please.* ◇ *two dozen eggs* ◇ *three dozen red roses* ➲ see also BAKER'S DOZEN **2** 0‑ [C] a group of approximately twelve people or things: *several dozen/a few dozen people* ◇ *The company employs no more than* ***a couple of dozen*** *people.* ◇ *Only about* ***half a dozen*** *people turned up.* ◇ *There was only space for a* ***half-dozen*** *tables.* **3** 0‑ **dozens** [pl.] (*informal*) a lot of people or things: *They arrived* ***in dozens*** (= in large numbers). ◇ **~ of sth** *I've been there dozens of times.* IDM see DIME, NINETEEN, SIX

dozy /ˈdəʊzi; *NAmE* ˈdoʊzi/ *adj.* (*informal*) **1** not looking or feeling awake **2** (*BrE*) stupid; not intelligent

DPhil /ˌdiː ˈfɪl/ *noun* (*BrE*) the abbreviation for 'Doctor of Philosophy': *to* ***be/have/do a DPhil*** ◇ *James Mendelssohn DPhil*

dpi /ˌdiː piː ˈaɪ/ *abbr.* (*computing*) dots per inch (a measure of how clear the images produced by a printer, SCANNER, etc. are)

DPP /ˌdiː piː ˈpiː/ *abbr.* (in England and Wales) DIRECTOR OF PUBLIC PROSECUTIONS

Dr (*BrE*) (also **Dr.** *NAmE, BrE*) *abbr.* **1** (in writing) Doctor: *Dr (Jane) Walker* **2** (in street names) DRIVE

drab /dræb/ *adj.* (**drab·ber**, **drab·best**) without interest or colour; dull and boring: *a cold drab little office* ◇ *drab women, dressed in browns and greys* ▸ **drab·ness** *noun* [U]

drabs /dræbz/ *noun* IDM see DRIBS

drachma /ˈdrækmə/ *noun* (*pl.* **drachmas** or **drachmae** /ˈdrækmiː/) the former unit of money in Greece (replaced in 2002 by the euro)

dra·co·nian /drəˈkəʊniən; *NAmE* -ˈkoʊ-/ *adj.* (*formal*) (of a law, punishment, etc.) extremely cruel and severe ORIGIN From **Draco**, a legislator in ancient Athens who gave severe punishments for crimes, especially the punishment of being killed.

Drac·ula /ˈdrækjələ/ *noun* a character in many horror films who is a VAMPIRE. Vampires appear at night and suck the blood of their victims. ORIGIN From the novel *Dracula* by Bram Stoker.

draft 0‑ AW /drɑːft; *NAmE* dræft/ *noun, adj., verb*
▪ ***noun*** **1** 0‑ [C] a rough written version of sth that is not yet in its final form: *I've made a* ***rough draft*** *of the letter.* ◇ *This is only the first draft of my speech.* ◇ *the* ***final draft*** (= the final version) ◇ *The legislation is still in* ***draft form.*** ◇ *a* ***draft constitution/treaty/agreement*** **2** [C] (*finance*) a written order to a bank to pay money to sb: *Payment must be made* ***by bank draft*** *drawn on a UK bank.* **3 the draft** [sing.] (*especially US*) = CONSCRIPTION **4** [sing.] (*NAmE*) a system in which professional teams in some sports choose players each year from among college students **5** [C] (*NAmE*) = DRAUGHT: *Can you shut the door? There's a draft in here.*
▪ ***adj.*** (*NAmE*) = DRAUGHT
▪ ***verb*** (also **draught** especially in *BrE*) **1** 0‑ **~ sth** to write the first rough version of sth such as a letter, speech or book: *to* ***draft a constitution/contract/bill*** ◇ *I'll draft a letter for you.* **2 ~ sb + adv./prep.** to choose people and send them somewhere for a special task: *Extra police are being drafted in to control the crowds.* **3** [usually passive] **~ sb** (*NAmE*) = CONSCRIPT: *They were drafted into the army.*

ˈ**draft dodger** *noun* (*NAmE, disapproving*) a person who illegally tries to avoid doing military service ➲ compare CONSCIENTIOUS OBJECTOR

draft·ee /ˌdrɑːfˈtiː; *NAmE* ˌdræfˈtiː/ *noun* (*US*) = CONSCRIPT

draft·er /ˈdrɑːftə(r); *NAmE* ˈdræftər/ *noun* **1** a person who prepares a rough version of a plan, document, etc. **2** (*NAmE*) = DRAFTSMAN (2)

drafts·man /ˈdrɑːftsmən; *NAmE* ˈdræftsmən/, **drafts·woman** /ˈdrɑːftswʊmən; *NAmE* ˈdræftswʊmən/ *noun* (*pl.* **-men** /-mən/, **-women** /-wɪmɪn/) **1** (*NAmE*) = DRAUGHTSMAN, DRAUGHTSWOMAN **2** (*NAmE* also **draft·er**) a person who writes official or legal documents: *the draftsmen of the constitution*

drafts·man·ship (*NAmE*) = DRAUGHTSMANSHIP

drafts·pers·on /ˈdrɑːftspɜːsn; *NAmE* ˈdræftspɜːrsn/ *noun* (*NAmE*) = DRAUGHTSPERSON (1)

drafty /ˈdræfti/ (*NAmE*) = DRAUGHTY

drag 0-ᴛ /dræɡ/ *verb, noun*

■ *verb* (-gg-)

▸ PULL **1** 0-ᴛ [T] (+ **adv.prep.**) to pull sb/sth along with effort and difficulty: *I dragged the chair over to the window.* ◊ *They dragged her from her bed.* ➲ SYNONYMS at PULL

▸ MOVE SLOWLY **2** [T, I] to move yourself slowly and with effort: **~ yourself + adv./prep.** *I managed to drag myself out of bed.* ◊ **+ adv./prep.** *She always drags behind when we walk anywhere.*

▸ PERSUADE SB TO GO **3** [T] **~ sb/yourself + adv./prep.** to persuade sb to come or go somewhere they do not really want to come or go to: *I'm sorry to drag you all this way in the heat.* ◊ *The party was so good I couldn't drag myself away.*

▸ OF TIME **4** [I] (of time or an event) to pass very slowly: *Time dragged terribly.* ◊ *The meeting really dragged.* ➲ see also DRAG ON

▸ TOUCH GROUND **5** [I, T] to move, or make sth move, partly touching the ground: *This dress is too long—it drags on the ground when I walk.* ◊ **~ sth** *He was dragging his coat in the mud.*

▸ SEARCH RIVER **6** [T] **~ sth** (**for sb/sth**) to search the bottom of a river, lake, etc. with nets or hooks: *They dragged the canal for the murder weapon.*

▸ COMPUTING **7** [T] **~ sth + adv./prep.** to move some text, an ICON, etc. across the screen of a computer using the mouse

IDM **drag your 'feet/'heels** to be deliberately slow in doing sth or in making a decision ➲ more at BOOTSTRAP

PHR V **,drag 'by** (of time) to pass very slowly: *The last few weeks of the summer really dragged by.* **,drag sb↔'down** to make sb feel weak or unhappy **,drag sb/sth↔'down** (**to sth**) to bring sb/sth to a lower social or economic level, a lower standard of behaviour, etc: *If he fails, he'll drag us all down with him.* **,drag sth/sb 'into sth** | **,drag sth/sb↔'in** **1** to start to talk about sth/sb that has nothing to do with what is being discussed: *Do you have to drag politics into everything?* **2** to try to get sb who is not connected with a situation involved in it: *Don't drag the children into our argument.* **,drag 'on** (*disapproving*) to go on for too long: *The dispute has dragged on for months.* **,drag sth↔'out** to make sth last longer than necessary SYN **prolong**: *Let's not drag out this discussion—we need to reach a decision.* **,drag sth 'out of sb** to make sb say sth they do not want to say: *We dragged a confession out of him.* **,drag sth↔'up** to mention an unpleasant story, fact, etc. that people do not want to remember or talk about: *Why do you have to keep dragging up my divorce?*

■ *noun*

▸ BORING PERSON/THING **1** [sing.] (*informal*) a boring person or thing; sth that is annoying: *He's such a drag.* ◊ *Walking's a drag—let's drive there.* ◊ *Having to work late every day is a drag.*

▸ SB/STH STOPPING PROGRESS **2** [sing.] **a ~ on sb/sth** (*informal*) a person or thing that makes progress difficult: *He came to be seen as a drag on his own party's prospects.*

▸ ON CIGARETTE **3** [C] (*informal*) an act of breathing in smoke from a cigarette, etc. SYN **draw**: *She took a long drag on her cigarette.*

▸ WOMEN'S CLOTHES **4** [U] (*informal*) clothes that are usually worn by the opposite sex (usually women's clothes worn by men): *He performed in drag.* ◊ *a* **drag queen** (= a man who dresses in women's clothes, usually in order to entertain people)

▸ PHYSICS **5** [U] the force of the air that acts against the movement of an aircraft or other vehicle ➲ compare LIFT ➲ see also MAIN DRAG

,drag-and-'drop *adj.* (*computing*) relating to the moving of ICONS, etc. on a screen using the mouse

dra·gée /'drɑːʒeɪ; *NAmE* drɑː'ʒeɪ/ *noun* **1** a sweet with a hard covering **2** a very small silver or gold-coloured ball, used for decorating cakes

drag·net /'dræɡnet/ *noun* **1** a net which is pulled through water to catch fish, or along the ground to catch animals **2** a thorough search, especially for a criminal

dragon /'dræɡən/ *noun* **1** (in stories) a large aggressive animal with wings and a long tail, that can breathe out fire **2** (*disapproving, especially BrE*) a woman who behaves in an aggressive and frightening way

'dragon boat *noun* a long narrow boat of traditional Chinese design that is used for racing and that is moved through the water by a lot of people using PADDLES. It is decorated to look like a dragon.

dragon·fly /'dræɡənflaɪ/ *noun* (*pl.* -ies) an insect with a long thin body, often brightly coloured, and two pairs of large transparent wings. Dragonflies are often seen over water. ➲ VISUAL VOCAB page V11

drag·oon /drə'ɡuːn/ *noun, verb*

■ *noun* a soldier in the past who rode a horse and carried a gun

■ *verb*

PHR V **dra'goon sb into sth/into doing sth** (*formal*) to force or persuade sb to do sth that they do not want to do SYN **coerce**

'drag race *noun* a race between specially adapted cars over a short distance ▸ **'drag racing** *noun* [U]

drag·ster /'dræɡstə(r)/ *noun* a car that is used in a drag race

drain /dreɪn/ *verb, noun*

■ *verb* **1** [T, I] **~** (**sth**) to make sth empty or dry by removing all the liquid from it; to become empty or dry in this way: *Drain and rinse the pasta.* ◊ *The marshes have been drained.* ◊ *You will need to drain the central heating system before you replace the radiator.* ◊ *The swimming pool drains very slowly.* ◊ *Leave the dishes to drain.* ➲ COLLOCATIONS at COOKING **2** [T, I] to make liquid flow away from sth; to flow away: **~ sth** (**from/out of sth**) *We had to drain the oil out of the engine.* ◊ **~ sth away/off** *Drain off the excess fat from the meat.* ◊ **~ away/off** *She pulled out the plug and the water drained away.* ◊ (*figurative*) *My anger slowly drained away.* ◊ **~ into sth** *The river drains into a lake.* ◊ **~ from/out of sth** *All the colour drained from his face when I told him the news* ◊ **~ of sth** *His face drained of colour.* **3** [T] **~ sth** to empty a cup or glass by drinking everything in it: *In one gulp, he drained the glass.* ◊ *She quickly drained the last of her drink.* **4** [T] to make sb/sth weaker, poorer, etc. by using up their/its strength, money, etc: **~ sb/sth** *My mother's hospital expenses were slowly draining my income.* ◊ *an exhausting and draining experience* ◊ **~ sb/sth of sth** *I felt drained of energy.*

■ *noun* **1** [C] a pipe that carries away dirty water or other liquid waste: *We had to call in a plumber to unblock the drain.* ◊ *The drains* (= the system of pipes) *date from the beginning of the century.* **2** [C] (*BrE*) (*US* **grate**, **'sewer grate**) a frame of metal bars over the opening to a drain in the ground **3** (*US*) (*BrE* **plug·hole**) [C] a hole in a bath/BATHTUB, SINK, etc. where the water flows away and into which a plug fits ➲ VISUAL VOCAB page V21 **4** [sing.] **a ~ on sb/sth** a thing that uses a lot of the time, money, etc. that could be used for sth else: *Military spending is a huge drain on the country's resources.* ➲ see also BRAIN DRAIN

IDM (**go**) **down the 'drain** (*BrE* also (**go**) **down the 'plug-hole**) (*informal*) (to be) wasted; (to get) very much worse: *It's just money down the drain, you know.* ◊ *Safety standards have gone down the drain.* ➲ more at LAUGH *v.*

drain·age /'dreɪnɪdʒ/ *noun* [U] **1** the process by which water or liquid waste is drained from an area: *a* ***drainage system/channel/ditch*** ◊ *The area has good natural drainage.* **2** a system of drains

drained /dreɪnd/ *adj.* [not usually before noun] very tired and without energy: *She suddenly felt totally drained.* ◊ *The experience left her* ***emotionally drained.***

'draining board (*BrE*) (*NAmE* **'drain·board**) *noun* the area next to a kitchen SINK where cups, plates, etc. are put for the water to run off, after they have been washed ➲ VISUAL VOCAB page V22

drain·pipe /'dreɪnpaɪp/ *noun* **1** (*NAmE* also **down·spout**) a pipe that carries RAINWATER from the roof of a building to a DRAIN ➲ VISUAL VOCAB page V15 ➲ picture at PIPE **2** a pipe that carries dirty water or other liquid waste away from a building

drake /dreɪk/ *noun* a male DUCK ➲ see also DUCKS AND DRAKES

D

dram /dræm/ *noun* (*especially ScotE*) a small amount of an alcoholic drink, especially WHISKY

drama 🔑 AW /ˈdrɑːmə/ *noun*
1 🔑 [C] a play for the theatre, television or radio: *a **costume/historical, etc. drama*** **2** 🔑 [U] plays considered as a form of literature: ***classical/Elizabethan/modern, etc. drama*** ◇ *a drama critic* ◇ *drama school* ◇ *a drama student* ◇ *I studied English and Drama at college.* **3** 🔑 [C] an exciting event: *A powerful human drama was unfolding before our eyes.* **4** [U] the fact of being exciting: *You couldn't help being thrilled by the drama of the situation.*
IDM **make a drama out of sth** to make a small problem or event seem more important or serious than it really is

ˈ**drama queen** *noun* (*informal, disapproving*) a person who behaves as if a small problem or event is more important or serious than it really is

dra·mat·ic 🔑 AW /drəˈmætɪk/ *adj.*
1 🔑 (of a change, an event, etc.) sudden, very great and often surprising: *a **dramatic increase/fall/change/improvement*** ◇ ***dramatic results/developments/news*** ◇ *The announcement had a **dramatic effect** on house prices.* **2** 🔑 exciting and impressive: *a dramatic victory* ◇ *They watched dramatic pictures of the police raid on TV.* ➲ SYNONYMS at EXCITING **3** 🔑 [usually before noun] connected with the theatre or plays: *a local dramatic society* **4** 🔑 exaggerated in order to create a special effect and attract people's attention: *He flung out his arms in a **dramatic gesture**.* ◇ *Don't be so dramatic!* ▸ **dra·mat·ic·al·ly** 🔑 AW /-kli/ *adv.*: *Prices have fallen dramatically.* ◇ *Events could have developed in a dramatically different way.* ◇ *'At last!' she cried dramatically.*

draˌmatic ˈirony *noun* [U] a situation in a play when a character's words carry an extra meaning to the audience because they know more than the character, especially about what is going to happen

dra·mat·ics /drəˈmætɪks/ *noun* [pl.] behaviour that does not seem sincere because it is exaggerated or too emotional ➲ see also AMATEUR DRAMATICS

drama·tis per·sonae /ˌdræmətɪs pɜːˈsəʊnaɪ; *NAmE* pɜːrˈsoʊ-/ *noun* [pl.] (from *Latin, formal*) all the characters in a play in the theatre

drama·tist AW /ˈdræmətɪst/ *noun* a person who writes plays for the theatre, television or radio SYN **playwright**: *a TV dramatist*

drama·tize (*BrE* also **-ise**) AW /ˈdræmətaɪz/ *verb* **1** [T] **~ sth** to present a book, an event, etc. as a play or a film/movie **2** [T, I] **~ (sth)** to make sth seem more exciting or important than it really is: *Don't worry too much about what she said—she tends to dramatize things.* ▸ **drama·tiza·tion, -isa·tion** AW /ˌdræmətaɪˈzeɪʃn; -təˈz-/ *noun* [U, C]: *a television dramatization of the trial*

drama·turgy /ˈdræmətɜːdʒi; *NAmE* -tɜːrdʒi/ *noun* [U] (*formal*) the study or activity of writing dramatic texts

dram·edy /ˈdrɑːmədi; *NAmE* ˈdræm-/ *noun* (*pl.* -ies) (*NAmE*) a television programme that is intended to be both humorous and serious

drank *past tense* of DRINK

drape /dreɪp/ *verb, noun*
■ *verb* **1 ~ sth around/over/across, etc. sth** to hang clothes, materials, etc. loosely on sb/sth: *She had a shawl draped around her shoulders.* ◇ *He draped his coat over the back of the chair.* ◇ *She draped a cover over the old sofa.* **2 ~ sb/sth in/with sth** to cover or decorate sb/sth with material: *walls draped in ivy* **3 ~ sth around/round/over, etc. sth** to allow part of your body to rest on sth in a relaxed way: *His arm was draped casually around her shoulders.*
■ *noun* (*especially NAmE*) (*NAmE* also **dra·pery**) [usually pl.] a long thick curtain: *blue velvet drapes*

draper /ˈdreɪpə(r)/ *noun* (*old-fashioned, BrE*) **1** a person who owns or manages a shop that sells cloth, curtains, etc. **2 draper's** (*pl.* **drapers**) a shop/store that sells cloth, curtains, etc.

dra·pery /ˈdreɪpəri/ *noun* (*pl.* -ies) **1** [U] (also **dra·per·ies** [pl.]) cloth or clothing hanging in loose folds: *a cradle swathed in draperies and blue ribbon* **2** [C, usually pl.] (*NAmE*) = DRAPE **3** [U] (*old-fashioned*) cloth and materials for sewing sold by a draper ➲ compare DRY GOODS

dras·tic /ˈdræstɪk; *BrE* also ˈdrɑːs-/ *adj.* extreme in a way that has a sudden, serious or violent effect on sth: ***drastic measures/changes*** ◇ *The government is threatening to **take drastic action**.* ◇ *a drastic shortage of food* ◇ *Talk to me before you do anything drastic.* ▸ **dras·tic·al·ly** /-kli/ *adv.*: *Output has been drastically reduced.* ◇ *Things have started to go drastically wrong.*

drat /dræt/ *exclamation* (*old-fashioned, informal*) used to show that you are annoyed: *Drat! I forgot my key.* ▸ **drat·ted** *adj.* [only before noun]: (*old-fashioned, BrE, informal*) *This dratted pen won't work.*

draught /drɑːft/ (*BrE*) (*NAmE* **draft**) *noun, adj., verb*
■ ***noun*** **1** [C] a flow of cool air in a room or other confined space: *There's a draught in here.* ◇ *A cold draught of air blew in from the open window.* ◇ *I was sitting **in a draught**.* **2** [C] (*formal*) one continuous action of swallowing liquid; the amount swallowed: *He took a deep draught of his beer.* **3** [C] (*old use* or *literary*) medicine in a liquid form: *a sleeping draught* (= one that makes you sleep) **4 draughts** (*BrE*) (*NAmE* **check·ers**) [U] a game for two players using 24 round pieces on a board marked with black and white squares **5** [C] (*BrE*) (*NAmE* **check·er**) one of the round pieces used in a game of draughts
IDM **on ˈdraught** (*BrE*) (of beer) taken from a large container (= a BARREL): *This beer is not available on draught* (= it is available only in bottles or cans).
■ ***adj.*** **1** [usually before noun] served from a large container (= a BARREL) rather than in a bottle: *draught beer* **2** [only before noun] used for pulling heavy loads: *a draught horse*
■ ***verb*** (*especially BrE*) = DRAFT

draught·board /ˈdrɑːftbɔːd; *NAmE* ˈdræftbɔːrd/ (*BrE*) (*NAmE* ˈ**check·er·board**) *noun* a board with black and white squares, used for playing DRAUGHTS/CHECKERS

ˈ**draught excluder** (*BrE*) (*NAmE* ˈ**weather strip**) *noun* [C, U] a piece of material that helps to prevent cold air coming through a door, window, etc.

draughts·man /ˈdrɑːftsmən/ (*BrE*) (*NAmE* **drafts·man**) *noun* (*pl.* **-men** /-mən/) **1** a person whose job is to draw detailed plans of machinery, buildings, etc. **2** a person who draws: *He's a poor draughtsman.* ➲ see also DRAUGHTSWOMAN, DRAUGHTSPERSON

draughts·man·ship (*BrE*) (*NAmE* **drafts·man·ship**) /ˈdrɑːftsmənʃɪp; *NAmE* ˈdræfts-/ *noun* [U] the ability to draw well: *You have to admire her superb draughtsmanship.*

draughts·person /ˈdrɑːftspɜːsn/ (*BrE*) (*NAmE* **drafts·person**) *noun* a draughtsman or a draughtswoman

draughts·woman /ˈdrɑːftswʊmən/ (*BrE*) (*NAmE* **drafts·woman** /ˈdræfts-/) *noun* (*pl.* **-women** /-wɪmɪn/) **1** a woman whose job is to draw detailed plans of machinery, buildings, etc. ➲ note at GENDER **2** a woman who draws ➲ see also DRAUGHTSMAN

draughty /ˈdrɑːfti/ (*BrE*) (*NAmE* **drafty**) *adj.* (**draught·ier, draughti·est**) (of a room, etc.) uncomfortable because cold air is blowing through: *a draughty room/corridor*

Dra·vid·ian /drəˈvɪdiən/ *adj.* connected with a group of languages spoken in southern India and in Sri Lanka, or with the people who speak these languages

draw 🔑 /drɔː/ *verb, noun*
■ ***verb*** (**drew** /druː/, **drawn** /drɔːn/)
▸ MAKE PICTURES **1** 🔑 [I, T] to make pictures, or a picture of sth, with a pencil, pen or CHALK (but not paint): *You draw beautifully.* ◇ **~ sth** *to **draw a picture/diagram/graph*** ◇ *She drew a house.* ◇ *He drew a circle in the sand with a stick.* ◇ (*figurative*) *The report drew a grim picture of inefficiency and corruption.* ➲ COLLOCATIONS at ART
▸ PULL **2** 🔑 [T] **~ sth/sb + adv./prep.** to move sth/sb by pulling it or them gently: *He drew the cork out of the bottle.* ◇ *I drew my chair up closer to the fire.* ◇ *She drew me onto the balcony.* ◇ *I tried to **draw him aside*** (= for example where I could talk to him privately). ◇ (*figurative*) *My eyes were drawn to the man in the corner.* ➲ SYNONYMS at PULL **3** [T] **~ sth** (of horses, etc.) to pull a vehicle such as a CARRIAGE:

The Queen's coach was drawn by six horses. ◇ *a horse-drawn carriage*

‣ CURTAINS **4** [T] **~ sth** to open or close curtains, etc: *The blinds were drawn.* ◇ *It was getting dark so I switched on the light and drew the curtains.* ◇ *She drew back the curtains and let the sunlight in.*

‣ MOVE **5** [I] **+ adv./prep.** to move in the direction mentioned: *The train drew into the station.* ◇ *The train drew in.* ◇ *The figures in the distance seemed to be drawing closer.* ◇ *Their car* **drew alongside** *ours.* ◇ (*figurative*) *Her retirement is drawing near.* ◇ (*figurative*) *The meeting was* **drawing to a close**.

‣ WEAPON **6** [T, I] **~ (sth) (on sb)** to take out a weapon, such as a gun or a SWORD, in order to attack sb: *She drew a revolver on me.* ◇ *He came towards them with his sword drawn.*

‣ ATTRACT **7** [T] to attract or interest sb: **~ sb** *The movie is drawing large audiences.* ◇ *The course draws students from all over the country.* ◇ **~ sb to sth** *Her screams drew passers-by to the scene.*

‣ GET REACTION **8** [T] to produce a reaction or response: **~ sth** *The plan has drawn a lot of criticism.* ◇ **~ sth from sb** *The announcement drew loud applause from the audience.*

‣ MAKE SB TALK **9** [T] **~ sb (about/on sth)** [often passive] to make sb say more about sth: *Spielberg refused to be drawn on his next movie.*

‣ CONCLUSION **10** [T] **~ sth (from sth)** to have a particular idea after you have studied sth or thought about it: *What conclusions did you draw from the report?* ◇ *We can draw some lessons for the future from this accident.*

‣ COMPARISON **11** [T] **~ sth** to express a comparison or a contrast: *to* ***draw an analogy/a comparison/a parallel/ a distinction*** *between two events*

‣ CHOOSE **12** [I, T] to decide sth by picking cards, tickets or numbers by chance: *We drew for partners.* ◇ **~ sth** *They had to* **draw lots** *to decide who would go.* ◇ *He drew the winning ticket.* ◇ *Names were drawn from a hat for the last few places.* ◇ *Italy has been drawn against Spain in the first round.* ◇ **~ sb/sth to do sth** *Italy has been drawn to play Spain.*

‣ GAME **13** [I, T] to finish a game without either team winning: *England and France drew.* ◇ *England and France drew 3–3.* ◇ **~ with/against sb** *England drew with/against France.* ◇ **~ sth** *England drew their game against France.*

‣ MONEY **14** [T] to take money or payments from a bank account or post office SYN **withdraw**: **~ sth out (of sth)** *I drew out £200.* ◇ *Can I draw $80 out of my account?* ◇ **~ sth (from sth)** *She went to the post office to draw her pension.* ◇ **~ sth on sth** *The cheque was drawn on his personal account.*

‣ LIQUID/GAS **15** [T] **~ sth (+adv./prep.)** to take or pull liquid or gas from somewhere: *to draw water from a well* ◇ *The device draws gas along the pipe.*

‣ SMOKE/AIR **16** [I, T] to breathe in smoke or air: **~ at/on sth** *He drew thoughtfully on his pipe.* ◇ **~ sth in** *She breathed deeply, drawing in the fresh mountain air.*

IDM **draw a 'blank** to get no response or result: *So far, the police investigation has drawn a blank.* **draw 'blood** to make sb BLEED **draw 'breath** (*BrE*) (*US* **draw a 'breath**) **1** to stop doing sth and rest: *She talks all the time and hardly stops to draw breath.* **2** (*literary*) to live; to be alive: *He was as kind a man as ever drew breath.* **draw sb's 'fire** to make sb direct their anger, criticism, etc. at you, so that others do not have to face it **draw a 'line under sth** (*BrE*) to say that sth is finished and not worth discussing any more **draw the 'line (at sth/at doing sth)** to refuse to do sth; to set a limit: *I don't mind helping, but I draw the line at doing everything myself.* ◇ *We would have liked to invite all our relatives, but you have to draw the line somewhere.* **draw the 'line (between sth and sth)** to distinguish between two closely related ideas: *Where do you draw the line between genius and madness?* **ˌdraw the short 'straw** (*BrE*) (*NAmE* **get the ˌshort end of the 'stick**) to be the person in a group who is chosen or forced to perform an unpleasant duty or task: *I drew the short straw and had to clean the toilets.* **ˌdraw 'straws (for sth)** to decide on sb to do or have sth, by choosing pieces of paper, etc: *We drew straws for who went first.* ➲ more at BATTLE *n.*, BEAD *n.*, DAGGER, HEIGHT, HORN, LOT *n.*, SIDE *n.*

PHR V **ˌdraw 'back** to move away from sb/sth: *He came close but she drew back.* **ˌdraw 'back (from sth/from doing sth)** to choose not to take action, especially because you feel nervous: *We drew back from taking our neighbours to court.* **ˌdraw sth↔'down** | **ˌdraw 'down** (*especially NAmE*) to reduce a supply of sth that has been created over a period of time; to be reduced: *There are many life events that can unexpectedly draw down savings.* ◇ *If we don't cut costs our reserves will draw down.* ➲ related noun DRAWDOWN **ˌdraw sth↔'down (from sth)** | **ˌdraw 'down on sth** (*especially NAmE*) (*BrE* usually **draw**) (*finance*) to take money from a fund that a bank, etc. has made available: *The company has already drawn down €600 million of its €725 million credit line.* ◇ *They can draw down on the loan at any time.* ➲ related noun DRAWDOWN **'draw sth from sb/sth** to take or obtain sth from a particular source: *to* ***draw support/comfort/strength*** *from your family* ◇ *She drew her inspiration from her childhood experiences.* **ˌdraw 'in** to become dark earlier in the evening as winter gets nearer: *The nights/days are drawing in.* **'draw sb into sth/into doing sth** | **ˌdraw sb↔'in** to involve sb or make sb take part in sth, although they may not want to take part at first: *youngsters drawn into a life of crime* ◇ *The book starts slowly, but it gradually draws you in.* **ˌdraw sth↔'off** to remove some liquid from a larger supply: *The doctor drew off some fluid to relieve the pressure.* **ˌdraw 'on** if a time or a season **draws on**, it passes: *Night was drawing on.* **'draw on/upon sth** to use a supply of sth that is available to you: *I'll have to draw on my savings.* ◇ *The novelist draws heavily on her personal experiences.* **ˌdraw 'out** to become lighter in the evening as summer gets nearer: *The* ***days/evenings*** *are drawing out.* **ˌdraw sb↔'out** to encourage sb to talk or express themselves freely **ˌdraw sth↔'out** to make sth last longer than usual or necessary: *She drew the interview out to over an hour.* ➲ see also LONG-DRAWN-OUT **ˌdraw 'up** if a vehicle **draws up**, it arrives and stops: *The cab drew up outside the house.* **ˌdraw sth↔'up** to make or write sth that needs careful thought or planning: *to draw up a contract/list*

■ ***noun***

‣ CHOOSING **1** (*US* also **draw·ing**) [usually sing.] **~ (for sth)** the act of choosing sth, for example the winner of a prize or the teams who play each other in a competition, usually by taking pieces of paper, etc. out of a container without being able to see what is written on them: *the draw for the second round of the Champions League* ◇ *The draw for the raffle takes place on Saturday.*

‣ SPORTS/GAMES **2** (*especially BrE*) a game in which both teams or players finish with the same number of points: *The match ended in a two-all draw.* ◇ *He managed to hold Smith to a draw* (= to stop him from winning when he seemed likely to do so). ➲ compare TIE *n.* (5) **3** (*NAmE* usually **draw·ing**) a competition in which the winners are chosen in a draw: *a prize draw* ➲ compare LOTTERY **4** (*BrE*) a sports match for which the teams or players are chosen in a draw: *Liverpool have an away draw against Manchester United.* **5** [usually sing.] a set of matches for which the teams or players are chosen in a draw: *There are only two seeded players left in the top half of the draw.*

‣ ATTRACTION **6** a person, a thing or an event that attracts a lot of people SYN **attraction**: *She is currently one of the biggest draws on the Irish music scene.*

‣ SMOKE **7** an act of breathing in the smoke from a cigarette SYN **drag**

IDM **be quick/fast on the 'draw 1** (*informal*) to be quick to understand or react in a new situation: *You can't fool him— he's always quick on the draw.* **2** to be quick at pulling out a gun in order to shoot it ➲ more at LUCK *n.*

draw·back /ˈdrɔːbæk/ *noun* **~ (of/to sth)** | **~ (of/to doing sth)** a disadvantage or problem that makes sth a less attractive idea SYN **disadvantage, snag**: *The main drawback to it is the cost.* ◇ *This is the one major drawback of the new system.*

draw·bridge /ˈdrɔːbrɪdʒ/ *noun* a bridge that can be pulled up, for example to stop people from entering a castle or to allow ships to pass under it

draw·down /ˈdrɔːdaʊn/ *noun* [C, U] ~ (**on sth**) **1** the act of reducing a supply of sth that has been created over a period of time; the amount used: *The cold winter has led to a larger-than-expected drawdown on oil stocks.* **2** (*finance*) the act of using money that is available to you; the amount used: *a drawdown of cash from the company's reserves*

D

drawer 0-ʷ *noun*
1 0-ʷ /drɔː(r)/ a part of a piece of furniture such as a desk, used for keeping things in. It is shaped like a box and has a handle on the front for pulling it out: *in the* ***top/middle/bottom drawer*** *of the desk* ➲ VISUAL VOCAB pages V19, V20, V22 ➲ see also CHEST OF DRAWERS, TOP DRAWER **2** /ˈdrɔːə(r)/ (*formal*) a person who writes a cheque

drawers /drɔːz; *NAmE* drɔːrz/ *noun* [pl.] (*old-fashioned*) KNICKERS or UNDERPANTS, especially ones that cover the upper parts of the legs

draw·ing 0-ʷ /ˈdrɔːɪŋ/ *noun*
1 0-ʷ [C] a picture made using a pencil or pen rather than paint: *a* ***pencil/charcoal drawing*** ◇ *a drawing of a yacht* ◇ *He* ***did/made a drawing*** *of the old farmhouse.* ➲ SYNONYMS at PICTURE ➲ COLLOCATIONS at ART **2** 0-ʷ [U] the art or skill of making pictures, plans, etc. using a pen or pencil: *I'm not very good at drawing.* ◇ *technical drawing* **3** (*NAmE*) = DRAW (1, 3)

ˈ**drawing board** *noun* a large flat board used for holding a piece of paper while a drawing or plan is being made
IDM (**go**) **back to the ˈdrawing board** to start thinking about a new way of doing sth after a previous plan or idea has failed **on the ˈdrawing board** being prepared or considered: *It's just one of several projects on the drawing board.*

ˈ**drawing pin** (*BrE*) (*NAmE* **thumb·tack**, **tack**) *noun* a short pin with a large round flat head, used especially for fastening paper to a board or wall ➲ VISUAL VOCAB page V56

ˈ**drawing power** (*NAmE*) (*BrE* ˈ**pulling power**) *noun* [U] the ability of sb/sth to attract people

ˈ**drawing room** *noun* (*formal* or *old-fashioned*) a room in a large house in which people relax and guests are entertained ➲ compare LIVING ROOM

drawl /drɔːl/ *verb* [T, I] + **speech** | ~ (**sth**) to speak or say sth slowly with vowel sounds that are longer than usual: *'Hi there!' she drawled lazily.* ◇ *He had a smooth drawling voice.* ▶ **drawl** *noun* [sing.]: *She spoke in a slow southern drawl.*

drawn /drɔːn/ *adj.* (of a person or their face) looking pale and thin because the person is ill/sick, tired or worried ➲ see also DRAW *v.*

ˌ**drawn-ˈout** *adj.* = LONG-DRAWN-OUT

draw·string /ˈdrɔːstrɪŋ/ *noun* a piece of string sewn inside the material at the top of a bag, pair of trousers/pants, etc. that can be pulled tighter in order to make the opening smaller: *They fasten with a drawstring.* ➲ VISUAL VOCAB page V51

dray /dreɪ/ *noun* a low flat vehicle pulled by horses and used in the past for carrying heavy loads, especially BARRELS of beer

dread /dred/ *verb, noun*
■ *verb* to be very afraid of sth; to fear that sth bad is going to happen: ~ **sth** *This was the moment he had been dreading.* ◇ ~ **doing sth** *I dread being sick.* ◇ ~ **sb doing sth** *She dreads her husband finding out.* ◇ ~ **to do sth** ***I dread to think*** *what would happen if there really was a fire here.* ◇ ~ **that** *... I both hoped and dreaded that he would come.*
■ *noun* [U, C, usually sing.] a feeling of great fear about sth that might or will happen in the future; a thing that causes this feeling: *The prospect of growing old* ***fills me with dread.*** ◇ *She has an irrational dread of hospitals.* ◇ *The committee members* ***live in dread of*** (= are always worried about) *anything that may cause a scandal.* ◇ *My greatest dread is that my parents will find out.*

dread·ed /ˈdredɪd/ (also *formal* **dread**) *adj.* [only before noun] causing fear: *The dreaded moment had finally arrived.* ◇ (*humorous*) *Did I hear the dreaded word 'homework'?*

dread·ful /ˈdredfl/ *adj.* (*especially BrE*) **1** very bad or unpleasant: *What dreadful weather!* ◇ *What a dreadful thing to say!* ◇ *It's dreadful the way they treat their staff.* ◇ *How dreadful!* ◇ *Jane* ***looked dreadful*** (= looked ill or tired). ➲ SYNONYMS at TERRIBLE **2** [only before noun] used to emphasize how bad sth is SYN **terrible**: *She's making a dreadful mess of things.* ◇ *I'm afraid there's been a dreadful mistake.* **3** [usually before noun] causing fear or suffering SYN **terrible**: *a dreadful accident* ◇ *They suffered dreadful injuries.*

dread·ful·ly /ˈdredfəli/ *adv.* (*especially BrE*) **1** extremely; very much: *I'm dreadfully sorry.* ◇ *I miss you dreadfully.* **2** very badly: *They suffered dreadfully during the war.*

dread·locks /ˈdredlɒks; *NAmE* -lɑːks/ (also *informal* **dreads** /dredz/) *noun* [pl.] hair that is twisted into long thick pieces that hang down from the head, worn especially by RASTAFARIANS ➲ VISUAL VOCAB page V49

dread·nought /ˈdrednɔːt/ *noun* a type of ship used in war in the early 20th century

dream 0-ʷ /driːm/ *noun, verb*
■ *noun* **1** 0-ʷ [C] a series of images, events and feelings that happen in your mind while you are asleep: *I had a vivid dream about my old school.* ◇ *I thought someone came into the bedroom, but it was just a dream.* ◇ *'Goodnight. Sweet dreams.'* ➲ compare NIGHTMARE ➲ see also WET DREAM **2** 0-ʷ [C] a wish to have or be sth, especially one that seems difficult to achieve: *Her lifelong dream was to be a famous writer.* ◇ *He wanted to be rich but it was an impossible dream.* ◇ *If I win, it will be a* ***dream come true.*** ◇ *She tried to turn her dream of running her own business into reality.* ◇ *a* ***dream car/house/job, etc.*** ◇ *I've finally found the man* ***of my dreams.*** ◇ *a chance to* ***fulfil a*** *childhood* ***dream*** ◇ *It was the end of all my hopes and dreams.* ➲ see also PIPE DREAM **3** 0-ʷ [sing.] a state of mind or a situation in which things do not seem real or part of normal life: *She walked around* ***in a dream*** *all day.* ➲ see also DAYDREAM **4** [sing.] (*informal*) a beautiful or wonderful person or thing: *That meal was an absolute dream.*
IDM **go/work like a ˈdream 1** to work very well: *My new car goes like a dream.* **2** to happen without problems, in the way that you had planned **in your ˈdreams** (*informal*) used to tell sb that sth they are hoping for is not likely to happen: *'I'll be a manager before I'm 30.' 'In your dreams.'* **like a bad ˈdream** (of a situation) so unpleasant that you cannot believe it is true: *In broad daylight the events of the night before seemed like a bad dream.* ➲ more at WILD *adj.*
■ *verb* (**dreamt**, **dreamt** /dremt/) or (**dreamed**, **dreamed**) **1** 0-ʷ [I, T] to experience a series of images, events and feelings in your mind while you are asleep: *Did I talk in my sleep? I must have been dreaming.* ◇ ~ **of/about sb/sth** *I dreamt about you last night.* ◇ ~ **sth** *Did it really happen or did I just dream it?* ◇ ~ (**that**)... *I dreamt (that) I got the job.* **2** 0-ʷ [I, T] to imagine and think about sth that you would like to happen: ~ **of/about sth** *She dreams of running her own business.* ◇ *It was the kind of trip most of us only dream about.* ◇ ~ **of/about doing sth** (*informal*) *I* ***wouldn't dream of*** *going without you* (= I would never go without you). ◇ ~ **sth** *Who'd have dreamt it? They're getting married.* ◇ ~ (**that**)... *I* ***never dreamt*** *(that) I'd actually get the job.*
PHR V ˌ**dream sth aˈway** to waste time just thinking about things you would like to do without actually doing anything ˌ**dream ˈon** (*informal*) you say **dream on** to tell sb that an idea is not practical or likely to happen ˌ**dream sth↔ˈup** (*informal*) to have an idea, especially a very unusual or silly one SYN **think up**: *Trust you to dream up a crazy idea like this!*

dream·boat /ˈdriːmbəʊt; *NAmE* -boʊt/ *noun* (*old-fashioned, informal*) a man who is very attractive

dream·catch·er /ˈdriːmkætʃə(r)/ *noun* a ring containing a decorated net, originally made by Native Americans, and thought to give its owner good dreams

dream·er /ˈdriːmə(r)/ *noun* **1** (sometimes *disapproving*) a person who has ideas or plans that are not practical or realistic **2** (usually *disapproving*) a person who does not pay attention to what is happening around them, but thinks about other things instead **3** a person who dreams: *Dreamers do not always remember their dreams.*

dreamcatcher

dream·land /ˈdriːmlænd/ *noun* [U] (*especially BrE, disapproving*) a pleasant but not very realistic situation that only exists in your mind: *You must be living in dreamland if you think he'll change his mind.*

dream·less /ˈdriːmləs/ *adj.* (of sleep) without dreams; deep and peaceful

dream·like /ˈdriːmlaɪk/ *adj.* as if existing or happening in a dream

ˈdream team *noun* the best possible combination of people for a particular competition or activity

ˈdream ticket *noun* [sing.] (used especially in newspapers about candidates for an election) a combination of people who, together, are considered to be the best

Dream·time /ˈdriːmtaɪm/ *noun* [U] = ALCHERINGA

dream·world /ˈdriːmwɜːld; *NAmE* -wɜːrld/ *noun* a world that is not like the real world; a person's idea of reality that is not realistic: *If he thinks it's easy to get a job, he's* ***living in a dreamworld.***

dreamy /ˈdriːmi/ *adj.* (**dream·ier, dreami·est**) **1** looking as though you are thinking about other things and not paying attention to what is happening around you: *She had a dreamy look in her eyes.* **2** (of a person or an idea) having a lot of imagination, but not very realistic: *Paul was dreamy and not very practical.* **3** as if you are in a dream or asleep: *He moved in the dreamy way of a man in a state of shock.* **4** (*informal*) pleasant and gentle; that makes you feel relaxed: *a slow, dreamy melody* **5** (*informal*) beautiful; wonderful: *What's he like? I bet he's really dreamy.* ▸ **dream·ily** /-ɪli/ *adv.* **dreami·ness** *noun* [U]

dreary /ˈdrɪəri; *NAmE* ˈdrɪri/ *adj.* (**drear·ier, dreari·est**) that makes you feel sad; dull and not interesting SYN **dull**: *a dreary winter's day* ◇ *a* ***dreary film*** ◇ *a long and dreary journey on the train* ▸ **drear·ily** /ˈdrɪərəli; *NAmE* ˈdrɪr-/ *adv.* **dreari·ness** *noun* [U]

dreck /drek/ *noun* [U] (*slang, especially NAmE*) something that you think is of very bad quality: *The movie is utter dreck.*

dredge /dredʒ/ *verb* **1** [T, I] **~ (sth) (for sth)** to remove mud, stones, etc. from the bottom of a river, CANAL, etc. using a boat or special machine, to make it deeper or to search for sth: *They're dredging the harbour so that larger ships can use it.* ◇ *They dredge the bay for gravel.* **2** [T] **~ sth (up) (from sth)** to bring sth up from the bottom of a river, etc. using a boat or special machine: *waste dredged (up) from the seabed* **3** [T] **~ sth in/with sth** to cover food lightly with sugar, flour, etc: *Dredge the top of the cake with icing sugar.*

PHR V **ˌdredge sth↔ˈup** **1** (usually *disapproving*) to mention sth that has been forgotten, especially sth unpleasant or embarrassing: *The papers keep trying to dredge up details of his past love life.* **2** to manage to remember sth, especially sth that happened a long time ago: *Now she was dredging up memories from the depths of her mind.*

dredger /ˈdredʒə(r)/ *noun* a boat or machine that is used to clear mud, etc. from the bottom of a river, or to make the river wider

dregs /dregz/ *noun* [pl.] **1** the last drops of a liquid, mixed with little pieces of solid material that are left in the bottom of a container: *coffee dregs* **2** the worst and most useless parts of sth: *the dregs of society* **3** (*literary*) the last parts of sth: *the last dregs of daylight*

dreich /driːx/ *adj.* (*ScotE*) dull and depressing: *dreich weather on the Scottish coast*

drench /drentʃ/ *verb* [often passive] to make sb/sth completely wet SYN **soak**: **~ sb/sth** *We were caught in the storm and got drenched to the skin.* ◇ **~ sb/sth in/with sth** *His face was drenched with sweat.* ◇ (*figurative*) *She drenched herself in perfume.* ➲ SYNONYMS at WET

dress 🔑 /dres/ *noun, verb*

■ ***noun***

▸ CLOTHES **1** 🔑 [C] a piece of women's clothing that is made in one piece and covers the body down to the legs, sometimes reaching to below the knees, or to the ankles: *a long white dress* ◇ *a wedding dress* ➲ VISUAL VOCAB page V50 ➲ see also COCKTAIL DRESS, EVENING DRESS, SUNDRESS **2** 🔑 [U] clothes for either men or women: *to wear* ***casual/formal dress*** ◇ *He has no* ***dress sense*** (= no idea of how to dress well). ➲ see also EVENING DRESS, FANCY DRESS, HEADDRESS, MORNING DRESS

■ ***verb***

▸ CLOTHES **1** 🔑 [I, T] to put clothes on yourself/sb: **~ (in sth)** *I dressed quickly.* ◇ **~ sb (in sth)** *She dressed the children in their best clothes.* ◇ *Get up and* ***get dressed!*** OPP **undress** ➲ COLLOCATIONS at FASHION **2** 🔑 [I, T] to wear a particular type or style of clothes: *to* ***dress well/badly/fashionably/comfortably*** ◇ **~ for/in/as sth** *You should dress for cold weather today.* ◇ *She always dressed entirely in black.* ◇ **~ sb (for/in/as sth)** *He was dressed as a woman* (= he was wearing women's clothes). ➲ SYNONYMS at CLOTHES ➲ COLLOCATIONS at FASHION **3** [I] to put on formal clothes: *Do they expect us to dress for dinner?* **4** [T] **~ sb** to provide clothes for sb: *He dresses many of Hollywood's most famous young stars.*

▸ WOUND **5** [T] **~ sth** to clean, treat and cover a wound: *The nurse will dress that cut for you.*

▸ FOOD **6** [T] **~ sth** to prepare food for cooking or eating: *to* ***dress a salad*** (= put oil or VINEGAR, etc. on it) ◇ *to* ***dress a chicken*** (= take out the parts you cannot eat)

▸ DECORATE **7** [T] **~ sth** (*formal*) to decorate or arrange sth: *to dress a shop window* (= arrange a display of clothes or goods in it)

▸ STONE/WOOD/LEATHER **8** [T] **~ sth** to prepare a material such as stone, wood, leather, etc. for use IDM see MUTTON, PART *n.*

PHR V **ˌdress ˈdown** to wear clothes that are more informal than those you usually wear, for example in an office **ˌdress sb ˈdown** to criticize or be angry with sb because they have done sth wrong ➲ related noun DRESSING-DOWN **ˌdress ˈup** 🔑 to wear clothes that are more formal than those you usually wear **ˌdress ˈup | ˌdress sb ˈup** 🔑 to put on special clothes, especially to pretend to be sb/sth different: *Kids love dressing up.* ◇ *The boys were all dressed up as pirates.* ◇ (*BrE*) *dressing-up clothes* ◇ (*NAmE*) *dress-up clothes* **ˌdress sth ˈup** to present sth in a way that makes it seem better or different: *However much you try to dress it up, office work is not glamorous.*

dress·age /ˈdresɑːʒ/ *noun* [U] a set of controlled movements that a rider trains a horse to perform; a competition in which these movements are performed

ˌdress ˈcircle (*especially BrE*) (*NAmE* usually **ˌfirst ˈbalcony**) *noun* the first level of seats above the ground floor in a theatre

ˈdress code *noun* rules about what clothes people should wear at work: *The company has a strict dress code—all male employees are expected to wear suits.*

dressed 🔑 /drest/ *adj.* [not before noun]

1 🔑 wearing clothes and not naked or wearing clothes for sleeping: *Hurry up and* ***get dressed.*** ◇ *fully dressed* ◇ *I can't go to the door—I'm not dressed yet.* **2** 🔑 wearing clothes of a particular type: *smartly dressed* ◇ **~ in...** *The bride was dressed in white.* ◇ *He was casually dressed in jeans and a T-shirt.*

IDM **dressed to ˈkill** (*informal*) wearing the kind of clothes that will make people notice and admire you **dressed (up) to the ˈnines** (*informal*) wearing very elegant or formal clothes ➲ more at MUTTON

dress·er /ˈdresə(r)/ *noun* **1** (also **ˌWelsh ˈdresser**) (*BrE*) a large piece of wooden furniture with shelves in the top part and cupboards below, used for displaying and storing cups, plates, etc. **2** (*NAmE*) = CHEST OF DRAWERS **3** (used with an adjective) a person who dresses in the way mentioned: *a snappy dresser* **4** (in a theatre) a person whose job is to take care of an actor's clothes for a play and help him/her to get dressed

dress·ing /ˈdresɪŋ/ *noun* **1** (also ˈ**salad dressing**) [C, U] a thin sauce used to add flavour to salads, usually made from oil, VINEGAR, salt, pepper, etc. ➲ see also FRENCH DRESSING **2** [U] (*NAmE*) = STUFFING (1) **3** [C] a piece of soft material placed over a wound in order to protect it **4** [U] the act of putting on clothes: *Many of our patients need help with dressing.* ➲ see also CROSS-DRESSING, POWER DRESSING, WINDOW DRESSING

D

ˌ**dressing-ˈdown** *noun* [sing.] (*old-fashioned, informal*) an occasion when sb speaks angrily to a person because they have done sth wrong

ˈ**dressing gown** (*BrE*) (*NAmE* **bath·robe, robe**) *noun* a long loose piece of clothing, usually with a belt, worn indoors over night clothes, for example when you first get out of bed ➲ VISUAL VOCAB page V51

ˈ**dressing room** *noun* **1** a room for changing your clothes in, especially one for actors or, in British English, for sports players **2** a small room next to a bedroom in some large houses, in which clothes are kept and people get dressed **3** (*NAmE*) = FITTING ROOM

ˈ**dressing table** (*NAmE* also **van·ity**, ˈ**vanity table**) *noun* a piece of bedroom furniture like a table with drawers and a mirror on top ➲ VISUAL VOCAB page V20

dress·maker /ˈdresmeɪkə(r)/ *noun* a person who makes women's clothes, especially as a job ▶ **dress·mak·ing** *noun* [U]

ˌ**dress reˈhearsal** *noun* the final practice of a play in the theatre, using the clothes and lights that will be used for the real performance: (*figurative*) *The earlier protests had just been dress rehearsals for full-scale revolution.*

ˈ**dress shirt** *noun* **1** a white shirt worn on formal occasions with a BOW TIE and suit **2** (*NAmE*) a smart shirt with long sleeves, which can be worn with a tie

ˈ**dress uniform** *noun* [U] a uniform that army, navy, etc. officers wear for formal occasions and ceremonies

dressy /ˈdresi/ *adj.* (**dress·ier, dressi·est**) **1** (of clothes) elegant and formal **2** (of people) liking to wear elegant or fashionable clothes

drew *past tense* of DRAW

drey /dreɪ/ *noun* the home of a SQUIRREL

drib·ble /ˈdrɪbl/ *verb, noun*

■ *verb* **1** [I, T] **~ (sth)** to let SALIVA or another liquid come out of your mouth and run down your chin SYN **drool** **2** [I] **+ adv./prep.** to fall in small drops or in a thin stream: *Melted wax dribbled down the side of the candle.* **3** [T] **~ sth (into/over/onto sth)** to pour sth slowly, in drops or a thin stream SYN **drizzle, trickle**: *Dribble a little olive oil over the salad.* **4** [T, I] **~ (sth) (+ adv./prep.)** (in football (SOCCER) and some other sports) to move the ball along with several short kicks, hits or BOUNCES: *She dribbled the ball the length of the field.* ◇ *He dribbled past two defenders and scored a magnificent goal.*

■ *noun* **1** [C] a very small amount of liquid, in a thin stream: *a dribble of blood* ◇ *Add just a dribble of oil.* **2** [U] (*especially BrE*) SALIVA (= liquid) from a person's mouth: *There was dribble all down the baby's front.* **3** [C] the act of dribbling the ball in a sport

dribs /drɪbz/ *noun* [pl.]

IDM **in ˌdribs and ˈdrabs** (*informal*) in small amounts or numbers over a period of time: *She paid me in dribs and drabs, not all at once.*

dried *past tense, past part.* of DRY

ˌ**dried ˈfruit** *noun* [U, C] fruit (for example, CURRANTS or RAISINS) that has been dried to be used in cooking or eaten on its own

drier = DRYER ➲ see also DRY *adj.*

dri·est ➲ DRY *adj.*

drift /drɪft/ *noun, verb*

■ *noun*

▸ SLOW MOVEMENT **1** [sing., U] a slow steady movement from one place to another; a gradual change or development from one situation to another, especially to sth bad: *a population drift away from rural areas* ◇ *attempts to halt the drift towards war*

▸ OF SHIP **2** [U] the movement of a ship or plane away from its direction because of currents or wind

▸ OF SEA/AIR **3** [U, C] the movement of the sea or air SYN **current**: *the general direction of drift on the east coast* ◇ *He knew the hidden drifts in that part of the river.*

▸ OF SNOW **4** [C] a large pile of sth, especially snow, made by the wind: *The road was blocked by deep drifts of snow.* ➲ see also SNOWDRIFT

▸ OF FLOWERS **5** [C] a large mass of sth, especially flowers: *Plant daffodils in informal drifts.*

▸ MEANING **6** [sing.] the general meaning of what sb says or writes SYN **gist**: *Do you* ***catch my drift?*** ◇ *My German isn't very good, but I* ***got the drift*** *of what she said.* ➲ see also CONTINENTAL DRIFT

■ *verb*

▸ MOVE SLOWLY **1** [I] (**+ adv./prep.**) to move along smoothly and slowly in water or air: *Clouds drifted across the sky.* ◇ *The empty boat drifted out to sea.* **2** [I] **+ adv./prep.** to move or go somewhere slowly: *The crowd drifted away from the scene of the accident.* ◇ *Her gaze drifted around the room.*

▸ WITHOUT PURPOSE **3** [I] (**+ adv./prep.**) to happen or change, or to do sth without a particular plan or purpose: *I didn't intend to be a teacher—I just drifted into it.* ◇ *He hasn't decided what to do yet—he's just drifting.* ◇ *The conversation drifted onto politics.*

▸ INTO STATE/SITUATION **4** [I] **~ in/into sth** to go from one situation or state to another without realizing it: *Finally she drifted into sleep.* ◇ *The injured man tried to speak but soon drifted into unconsciousness.*

▸ OF SNOW/SAND **5** [I] to be blown into large piles by the wind: *drifting sand* ◇ *Some roads are closed because of drifting.*

▸ FLOAT **6** [T] **+ adv./prep.** to make sth float somewhere: *The logs are drifted downstream to the mill.*

PHR V ˌ**drift aˈpart** to become less friendly or close to sb: *As children we were very close, but as we grew up we just drifted apart.* ˌ**drift ˈoff (to sleep)** to fall asleep: *I didn't hear the storm. I must have drifted off by then.*

drift·er /ˈdrɪftə(r)/ *noun* (*disapproving*) a person who moves from one job or place to another with no real purpose

ˈ**drift net** *noun* a very large net used by fishing boats. The net has weights at the bottom and FLOATS at the top and is allowed to hang in the sea.

drift·wood /ˈdrɪftwʊd/ *noun* [U] wood that the sea carries up onto land, or that floats on the water

drill /drɪl/ *noun, verb*

■ *noun* **1** [C] a tool or machine with a pointed end for making holes: *an electric drill* ◇ *a pneumatic drill* ◇ *a hand drill* ◇ *a dentist's drill* ◇ *a drill bit* (= the pointed part at the end of the drill) ➲ VISUAL VOCAB page V17 **2** [C, U] a way of learning sth by means of repeated exercises **3** [C, U] a practice of what to do in an emergency, for example if there is a fire: *a fire drill* **4** [U] military training in marching, the use of weapons, etc: *rifle drill* **5 the drill** [sing.] (*old-fashioned, BrE*) the correct or usual way to do sth SYN **procedure**: *What's the drill for claiming expenses?* **6** [U] a type of strong cotton cloth **7** [C] a machine for planting seeds in rows

■ *verb* **1** [T, I] to make a hole in sth, using a drill: **~ sth** *Drill a series of holes in the frame.* ◇ **~ (for sth)** *They're* ***drilling for oil*** *off the Irish coast.* ◇ **~ (through sth)** *He drilled through the wall by mistake.* **2** [T] to teach sb to do sth by making them repeat it a lot of times: **~ sb to do sth** *The children were drilled to leave the classroom quickly when the fire bell rang.* ◇ **~ sb** *a well-drilled team* ◇ **~ sb in sth** *Recruits are drilled in basic techniques over the five-day course.* **3** [T] **~ sb** to train soldiers to perform military actions

PHR V ˌ**drill ˈdown** (*computing* or *business*) to go to deeper levels of an organized set of data in order to find more detail, especially on a computer or a website: *Navigation is good and there's a display to show how far you've drilled* *down.* ˈ**drill sth into sb** to make sb remember or learn sth by repeating it often: *It was drilled into us at an early age never to drop litter.*

drily (also **dryly**) /ˈdraɪli/ *adv.* ➲ see also DRY **1** if sb speaks **drily**, they are being humorous, but not in an obvious way: *'That's a lovely purple suit you're wearing,' she said drily.* **2** in a way that shows no emotion: *He smiled drily and leaned back in his chair.* **3** in a way that shows that there is no liquid present: *She coughed drily.* ◇ *He swallowed drily and nodded.*

drink 🔑 /drɪŋk/ *noun, verb*

■ ***noun*** **1** 🔑 [C, U] a liquid for drinking; an amount of a liquid that you drink: *Can I **have a drink**?* ◇ *soft drinks* (= cold drinks without alcohol) ◇ *a drink of water* ◇ *food and drink* ◇ *She took a drink from the glass and then put it down.* **2** 🔑 [C, U] alcohol or an alcoholic drink; sth that you drink on a social occasion: *They went **for a drink**.* ◇ *The drinks are on me* (= I'll pay for them). ◇ *I need **a stiff drink*** (= a very strong drink). ◇ (*BrE*) *He's got **a drink problem**.* ◇ (*NAmE*) *He has a **drinking problem**.* ◇ (*humorous*) *The children are enough to **drive me to drink**.* ◇ (*BrE*) *They came home **the worse for drink*** (= drunk). ◇ *She **took to drink*** (= often drank too much alcohol) *after her marriage broke up.* **3 drinks** [pl.] (*BrE*) a social occasion where you have alcoholic drinks: *Would you like to come for drinks on Sunday?* ◇ *a drinks party* IDM see DEMON, MEAT

■ ***verb*** (**drank** /dræŋk/, **drunk** /drʌŋk/) **1** 🔑 [T, I] **~ (sth)** to take liquid into your mouth and swallow it: *What would you like to drink?* ◇ *In hot weather, drink plenty of water.* ◇ *I don't drink coffee.* ◇ *He was drinking straight from the bottle.* **2** 🔑 [I, T] to drink alcohol, especially when it is done regularly: *He doesn't drink.* ◇ *Don't **drink and drive*** (= drive a car after drinking alcohol). ◇ *She's been drinking heavily since she lost her job.* ◇ **~ sth** *I drank far too much last night.* ◇ **~ yourself + adj.** *He had drunk himself unconscious on vodka.* ➲ see also DRUNK

IDM **drink sb's ˈhealth** (*BrE*) to wish sb good health as you lift your glass, and then drink from it **drink like a ˈfish** to drink a lot of alcohol regularly ˌ**drink sb under the ˈtable** (*informal*) to drink more alcohol than sb else without becoming as drunk as they are ➲ more at EAT, HORSE *n.*

PHR V ˌ**drink sth↔ˈin** to look at or listen to sth with great interest and enjoyment: *We just stood there drinking in the scenery.* ˈ**drink to sb/sth** to wish sb good luck, health or success as you lift your glass and then drink from it SYN **toast**: *All raise your glasses and drink to Katie and Tom!* ˌ**drink ˈup** | ˌ**drink (sth)↔ˈup** to drink all of sth: *Drink up and let's go.* ◇ *Come on, drink up your juice.*

drink·able /ˈdrɪŋkəbl/ *adj.* **1** clean and safe to drink **2** pleasant to drink: *a very drinkable wine*

ˌ**drink-ˈdriver** (*BrE*) (also ˌ**drunk ˈdriver** *NAmE, BrE*) *noun* a person who drives a vehicle after drinking too much alcohol

ˌ**drink-ˈdriving** (also ˌ**drunken ˈdriving**) (both *BrE*) (also ˈ**drunk driving** *NAmE, BrE*) *noun* [U] driving a vehicle after drinking too much alcohol

drink·er /ˈdrɪŋkə(r)/ *noun* **1** a person who drinks alcohol regularly, especially sb who drinks too much: *a **heavy/moderate drinker*** **2** (after a noun) a person who regularly drinks the particular drink mentioned: *a coffee drinker*

drink·ing /ˈdrɪŋkɪŋ/ *noun* [U] the act of drinking alcohol: *Drinking is not advised during pregnancy.* ◇ *There are tough penalties for drinking and driving.*

ˈ**drinking box** *noun* (*CanE*) a small cardboard box of juice, etc. that has a drinking straw with it that can be pushed through a small hole in the top

ˈ**drinking chocolate** *noun* [U] (*BrE*) a sweet chocolate powder or a hot drink made from this powder mixed with hot milk and/or water ➲ compare COCOA

ˈ**drinking fountain** (*especially BrE*) (*NAmE* usually ˈ**water fountain**) *noun* a device that supplies water for drinking in public places

ˈ**drinking straw** *noun* = STRAW

ˌ**drinking-ˈup time** *noun* [U] (*BrE*) in Britain, the time between when a pub stops serving drinks and when it closes, when people are allowed to finish drinks that they bought earlier

ˈ**drinking water** *noun* [U] water that is safe for drinking

drip /drɪp/ *verb, noun*

■ ***verb*** (-pp-) **1** [I] (**+ adv./prep.**) (of liquid) to fall in small drops: *She was hot and sweat dripped into her eyes.* ◇ *Water was dripping down the walls.* **2** [I, T] to produce drops of liquid: *The tap was dripping.* ◇ **+ adv./prep.** *Her hair dripped down her back.* ◇ **~ sth** (**+adv./prep.**) *Be careful, you're dripping paint everywhere!* **3** [I, T] to contain or hold a lot of sth: **~ with sth** *The trees were dripping with fruit.* ◇ **~ sth** *His voice dripped sarcasm.*

■ ***noun*** **1** [sing.] the sound or action of small drops of liquid falling continuously: *The silence was broken only by the steady drip, drip of water from the roof.* **2** [C] a small drop of liquid that falls from sth: *We put a bucket under the hole in the roof to catch the drips.* **3** (*NAmE* also **IV**) [C] (*medical*) a piece of equipment that passes liquid food, medicine or blood very slowly through a tube into a patient's VEIN: *She's been put **on a drip**.* **4** [C] (*informal*, becoming *old-fashioned*) a boring or stupid person with a weak personality SYN **wimp**: *Don't be such a drip—come and join in the fun!*

ˌ**drip-ˈdry** *adj.* made of a type of cloth that will dry quickly without CREASES when you hang it up wet

ˈ**drip-feed** *verb* (**drip-fed, drip-fed**) **~ sb/sth** to give sb sth in separate small amounts ▶ ˈ**drip feed** *noun* [U, C]: *the steady drip feed of leaked documents in the papers*

drip·ping /ˈdrɪpɪŋ/ *adj., noun*

■ ***adj.*** **~ (with sth)** very wet: *Her face was dripping with sweat.* ◇ *His clothes were still **dripping wet**.* ◇ (*figurative*) *His wife came in, dripping with diamonds.*

■ ***noun*** [U] fat that comes out of meat when it is cooked, often kept for frying other food in

drip·py /ˈdrɪpi/ *adj.* (**drip·pier, drip·pi·est**) (*informal*) **1** boring, stupid and weak or SENTIMENTAL: *her drippy boyfriend* **2** in a liquid state, and likely to fall in drops: *drippy paint* ◇ *a drippy nose* (= with drops of liquid falling from it) ▶ **drip·pily** *adv.* **drip·pi·ness** *noun* [U]

drive 🔑 /draɪv/ *verb, noun*

■ ***verb*** (**drove** /drəʊv; *NAmE* droʊv/, **driven** /ˈdrɪvn/)

▸ VEHICLE **1** 🔑 [I, T] to operate a vehicle so that it goes in a particular direction: *Can you drive?* ◇ *Don't drive so fast!* ◇ *I drove to work this morning.* ◇ *Shall we drive* (= go there by car) *or go by train?* ◇ **~ sth** *He drives a taxi* (= that is his job). ➲ COLLOCATIONS at DRIVING **2** 🔑 [T] **~ sb** (**+ adv./prep.**) to take sb somewhere in a car, taxi, etc: *Could you drive me home?* ➲ SYNONYMS at TAKE **3** 🔑 [T] **~ sth** to own or use a particular type of vehicle: *What car do you drive?*

▸ MACHINE **4** 🔑 [T, usually passive] **~ sth** to provide the power that makes a machine work: *a steam-driven locomotive*

▸ MAKE SB DO STH **5** 🔑 [T] **~ sb** (**+ adv./prep.**) to force sb to act in a particular way: *The urge to survive drove them on.* ◇ *You're driving yourself too hard.* **6** 🔑 [T] to make sb very angry, crazy, etc. or to make them do sth extreme: **~ sb + adj.** *to **drive sb crazy/mad/insane*** ◇ **~ sb to do sth** *Hunger drove her to steal.* ◇ **~ sb to sth** *Those kids are driving me to despair.* ◇ (*humorous*) *It's enough to **drive you to drink*** (= to make you start drinking too much alcohol).

▸ MAKE SB/STH MOVE **7** [T] **~ sb/sth + adv./prep.** to force sb/sth to move in a particular direction: *to drive sheep into a field* ◇ *The enemy was driven back.*

▸ CAUSE STH TO MAKE PROGRESS **8** [T] **~ sth** to influence sth or cause it to make progress: *This is the main factor driving investment in the area.*

▸ HIT/PUSH **9** [T] **~ sth + adv./prep.** to force sth to go in a particular direction or into a particular position by pushing it, hitting it, etc: *to drive a nail into a piece of wood*

▸ MAKE A HOLE **10** [T] **~ sth + adv./prep.** to make an opening in or through sth by using force: *They drove a tunnel through the solid rock.*

▸ IN SPORT **11** [T, I] **~ (sth)** (**+ adv./prep.**) to hit a ball with force, sending it forward: *to drive the ball into the rough* (= in GOLF)

▸ WIND/WATER **12** [T] **~ sth** (**+ adv./prep.**) to carry sth along:

D

Huge waves drove the yacht onto the rocks. **13** [I] (**+ adv./prep.**) to fall or move rapidly and with great force: *The waves drove against the shore.*

IDM **drive a coach and 'horses through sth** to spoil sth, for example a plan **drive sth 'home (to sb)** to make sb understand or accept sth by saying it often, loudly, angrily, etc: *You will really need to drive your point home.* **what sb is 'driving at** (*informal*) the thing sb is trying to say: *I wish I knew what they were driving at.* ➲ more at GROUND *n.*, HARD *adj.*, NEED *n.*, SNOW *n.*

PHR V **ˌdrive aˈway | ˌdrive sb/sth aˈway** 🗝 to leave in a vehicle; to take sb away in a vehicle: *We heard him drive away.* ◇ *Someone drove the car away in the night.* **ˌdrive sb aˈway** 🗝 to make sb not want to stay or not want to go somewhere: *Her constant nagging drove him away.* ◇ *Terrorist threats are driving away tourists.* **ˌdrive ˈoff 1** 🗝 (of a driver, car, etc.) to leave: *The robbers drove off in a stolen vehicle.* **2** (in GOLF) to hit the ball to begin a game **ˌdrive sb/sth↔ˈoff** to force sb/sth to go back or away: *The defenders drove off each attack.* **ˌdrive ˈon** to continue driving: *Don't stop—drive on!* **ˌdrive sb/sth↔ˈout (of sth)** to make sb/sth disappear or stop doing sth: *New fashions drive out old ones.* **ˌdrive sth↔ˈup/ˈdown** to make sth such as prices rise or fall quickly

■ ***noun***

▸ IN/OF VEHICLE **1** 🗝 [C] a journey in a car or other vehicle: *Let's **go for a drive**.* ◇ *It's a three-hour drive to London.* **2** [C, U] the equipment in a vehicle that takes power from the engine to the wheels: *the drive shaft* ◇ *a car with four-wheel drive* ◇ *a **left-/right-hand drive** car* (= a car where the driver and the controls are on the left/right)

▸ OUTSIDE HOUSE **3** (also **drive·way**) [C] a wide hard path or a private road that leads from the street to a house: *There were two cars parked **in/on** the drive.* ➲ VISUAL VOCAB page V15

▸ EFFORT **4** [C] an organized effort by a group of people to achieve sth: *a **recruitment/export/economy drive*** ◇ **~ for sth** *a drive for greater efficiency* ◇ **~ to do sth** *the government's drive to reduce energy consumption* ➲ SYNONYMS at CAMPAIGN

▸ DESIRE/ENERGY **5** [C, U] a strong desire or need in people: *a strong sexual drive* **6** [U] (*approving*) a strong desire to do things and achieve sth; great energy: *He'll do very well—he has tremendous drive.*

▸ IN SPORT **7** [C] a long hard hit or kick: *She has a strong forehand drive* (= in TENNIS). ◇ *He scored with a brilliant 25-yard drive.*

▸ COMPUTING **8** [C] the part of a computer that reads and stores information on disks or tapes: *a 750GB hard drive* ◇ *a CD drive* ➲ VISUAL VOCAB page V54 ➲ see also DISK DRIVE

▸ GAMES **9** [C] (*BrE*) a social occasion when a lot of people compete in a game such as WHIST or BINGO

▸ ANIMALS/ENEMY **10** [C] an act of chasing animals or the enemy and making them go into a smaller area, especially in order to kill or capture them

▸ ROAD **11 Drive** (*abbr.* **Dr**) used in the names of roads: *21 Island Heights Drive*

'drive bay *noun* (*computing*) a space inside a computer for a DISK DRIVE

'drive-by *adj.* (*NAmE*) [only before noun] a **drive-by** shooting, etc. is done from a moving car: *a drive-by killing* ▸ **'drive-by** *noun*

'drive-in *noun* a place where you can watch films/movies, eat, etc. without leaving your car: *We stopped at a drive-in for a hamburger.* ◇ *drive-in movies*

drivel /ˈdrɪvl/ *noun, verb*

■ ***noun*** [U] (*informal, disapproving*) silly nonsense: *How can you watch that drivel on TV?*

■ ***verb*** (-ll-, *US* -l-) [I] **~ (on) (about sth)** (usually used in the progressive tenses) to keep talking about silly or unimportant things

driven /ˈdrɪvn/ *adj.* **1** (of a person) determined to succeed, and working very hard to do so **2 -driven** (in compounds) influenced or caused by a particular thing: *a market-driven economy* ◇ *a character-driven movie* ➲ see also DRIVE, DROVE, DRIVEN *v.*

Collocations

Driving

Having a car

- **have/own/**(*BrE*) **run** a car
- **ride** a motorcycle/motorbike
- **drive/prefer/use** an automatic/a manual/(*NAmE, informal*) a stick shift
- **have/get** your car **serviced/fixed/repaired**
- **buy/sell** a used car/(*especially BrE*) a second-hand car
- **take/pass/fail** a (*BrE*) driving test/(*both NAmE*) driver's test/road test
- **get/obtain/have/lose/carry** a/your (*BrE*) driving licence/(*NAmE*) driver's license

Driving

- **put on/fasten/**(*NAmE*) **buckle/wear/undo** your seat belt/safety belt
- **put/turn/leave** the key in the ignition
- **start** the car/engine
- (*BrE*) **change/**(*NAmE*) **shift/put sth into** gear
- **press/put your foot on** the brake pedal/clutch/accelerator
- **release** the clutch/(*especially BrE*) the handbrake/(*both NAmE*) the emergency brake/the parking brake
- **drive/park/reverse** the car
- (*BrE*) **indicate** left/right
- (*especially NAmE*) **signal** that you are turning left/right
- **take/miss** (*BrE*) the turning/(*especially NAmE*) the turn
- **apply/hit/slam on** the brake(s)
- **beep/honk/**(*especially BrE*) **toot/**(*BrE*) **sound** your horn

Problems and accidents

- a car **skids/crashes (into sth)/collides (with sth)**
- **swerve to avoid** an oncoming car/a pedestrian
- **crash/lose control of** the car
- **have/be in/be killed in/survive** a car crash/a car accident/(*NAmE*) a car wreck/a hit-and-run
- **be run over/knocked down by** a car/bus/truck
- **dent/hit** (*BrE*) the bonnet/(*NAmE*) the hood
- **break/crack/shatter** (*BrE*) the windscreen/(*NAmE*) the windshield
- **blow/**(*especially BrE*) **burst/puncture** (*BrE*) a tyre/(*NAmE*) a tire
- **get/have** (*BrE*) a flat tyre/a flat tire/a puncture
- **inflate/change/fit/replace/check** a tyre/tire

Traffic and driving regulations

- **be caught in/get stuck in/sit in** a traffic jam
- **cause** congestion/tailbacks/traffic jams/gridlock
- **experience/face** lengthy delays
- **beat/avoid** the traffic/the rush hour
- **break/observe/**(*NAmE*) **drive** the speed limit
- **be caught on** (*BrE*) a speed camera
- **stop sb for/pull sb over for/**(*BrE, informal*) **be done for** speeding
- (*both informal*) **run/**(*BrE*) **jump** a red light/the lights
- **be arrested for/charged with** (*BrE*) drink-driving/(*both US*) driving under the influence (DUI)/driving while intoxicated (DWI)
- **be banned/**(*BrE*) **disqualified** from driving

driver 🗝 /ˈdraɪvə(r)/ *noun*
1 🗝 a person who drives a vehicle: *a **bus/train/ambulance/taxi driver*** ◇ *She climbed into the driver's seat.* ◇ (*BrE*) *a **learner driver*** (= one who has not yet passed a driving test) ◇ (*NAmE*) *a **student driver*** ◇ *The car comes equipped with a driver's airbag.* ➲ see also BACK-SEAT DRIVER **2** (in GOLF) a CLUB with a wooden head **3** (*com-*

puting) software that controls the sending of data between a computer and a piece of equipment that is attached to it, such as a printer **4** one of the main things that influence sth or cause it to make progress: *Housing is a key driver of the economy.* IDM see SEAT *n.*

ˈdriver's license (*NAmE*) (*BrE* **ˈdriving licence**) *noun* an official document that shows that you are qualified to drive

ˈdriver's test *noun* (*NAmE*) = DRIVING TEST

drive·shaft /ˈdraɪvʃɑːft; *NAmE* -ʃæft/ *noun* a long thin part of a machine that turns round and round and sends power from the engine to another part of the machine

ˈdrive-through (also **ˈdrive-thru**) *noun* (*NAmE*) a restaurant, bank, etc. where you can be served without having to get out of your car

ˈdrive time *noun* [U] a time during the day when many people are driving their cars, for example to or from work ▸ **ˈdrive-time** *adj.*: *a drive-time radio show*

drive·way /ˈdraɪvweɪ/ *noun* = DRIVE (3): *There was a car parked* ***in/on*** *the driveway.*

driv·ing 0→ /ˈdraɪvɪŋ/ *noun, adj.*

■ ***noun*** 0→ [U] the way that sb drives a vehicle; the act of driving: *dangerous driving* ◇ *driving lessons* IDM see SEAT *n.*

■ ***adj.*** [only before noun] **1** strong and powerful; having a strong influence in making sth happen: *Who was* ***the driving force*** (= the person with the strongest influence) *in the band?* **2** (of rain, snow, etc.) falling very fast and at an angle

ˈdriving licence (*BrE*) (*NAmE* **ˈdriver's license**) *noun* an official document that shows that you are qualified to drive

ˈdriving range *noun* a place where people can practise hitting GOLF balls

ˈdriving school *noun* a business that gives people lessons in how to drive a car, etc.

ˈdriving test (*NAmE* also **ˈdriver's test**, **ˈroad test**) *noun* a test that must be passed before you are qualified to drive a car, etc.

ˌdriving under the ˈinfluence *noun* [U] (*abbr.* DUI) (*US*) (in some states in the US) the crime of driving a vehicle after drinking too much alcohol. It is a less serious crime than 'driving while intoxicated'.

ˌdriving while inˈtoxicated *noun* [U] (*abbr.* DWI) (*US*) the crime of driving a vehicle after drinking too much alcohol

driz·zle /ˈdrɪzl/ *verb, noun*

■ ***verb*** **1** [I] when **it is drizzling**, it is raining lightly **2** [T] **~ sth** (**over sth**) to pour a small amount of liquid over the surface of sth SYN **dribble**

■ ***noun*** [U, sing.] light fine rain ▸ **driz·zly** /ˈdrɪzli/ *adj.*: *a dull, drizzly morning*

DRM /ˌdiː ɑːr ˈem/ *abbr.* (*computing*) digital rights management (actions and devices that are used by the owners of software or information to prevent people from copying it from the Internet)

Dr Mar·tens™ /ˌdɒktə ˈmɑːtɪnz; *NAmE* ˌdɑːktər ˈmɑːrtnz/ (also *informal* **Doc Martens**, **DMs**) *noun* [pl.] a type of comfortable heavy boot or shoe with LACES

drogue /drəʊg; *NAmE* droʊg/ *noun* a small PARACHUTE, used to pull a larger one from its bag

droit de seigneur /ˌdrwʌ də senˈjɜː(r)/ *noun* [U] (from *French*) the right of a lord to have sex with a woman of lower social rank on her wedding night, said to exist in the Middle Ages

droll /drəʊl; *NAmE* droʊl/ *adj.* (*old-fashioned* or *ironic*) amusing, but not in a way that you expect

drom·ed·ary /ˈdrɒmədəri; *NAmE* ˈdrɑːməderi/ *noun* (*pl.* -ies) an animal of the CAMEL family, with only one HUMP, that lives in desert countries

drone /drəʊn; *NAmE* droʊn/ *noun, verb*

■ ***noun*** **1** [usually sing.] a continuous low noise: *the distant drone of traffic* **2** [usually sing.] a continuous low sound made by some musical instruments, for example the BAGPIPES, over which other notes are played or sung; the part of the instrument that makes this noise **3** a male BEE that does not work ➲ compare QUEEN BEE, WORKER **4** a person who is lazy and gives nothing to society while others work **5** an aircraft without a pilot, controlled from the ground

■ ***verb*** [I] to make a continuous low noise: *A plane was droning in the distance.* ◇ *a droning voice*

PHR V **ˌdrone ˈon** (**about sth**) to talk for a long time in a boring way

drongo /ˈdrɒŋgəʊ; *NAmE* ˈdrɑːŋgoʊ/ *noun* (*pl.* -os or -oes) **1** a shiny black bird with a long tail **2** (*AustralE, NZE, slang*) a stupid person

drool /druːl/ *verb* **1** [I] to let SALIVA (= liquid) come out of your mouth SYN **dribble**: *The dog was* ***drooling at the mouth.*** **2** [I] **~ (over sb/sth)** (*disapproving*) to show in a silly or exaggerated way that you want or admire sb/sth very much: *teenagers drooling over photos of movie stars*

droop /druːp/ *verb* **1** [I] to bend, hang or move downwards, especially because of being weak or tired: *She was so tired, her eyelids were beginning to droop.* **2** [I] to become sad or depressed: *Our spirits drooped when we heard the news.* ▸ **droop** *noun* [sing.]: *the slight droop of her mouth* **droopy** *adj.*: *a droopy moustache*

drop 0→ /drɒp; *NAmE* drɑːp/ *verb, noun*

■ ***verb*** (-pp-)

▸ FALL **1** 0→ [I, T] to fall or allow sth to fall by accident: *The climber slipped and dropped to his death.* ◇ **~ sth** *Be careful not to drop that plate.* **2** 0→ [I, T] to fall or make sth fall deliberately: **+ adv./prep.** *He staggered in and dropped into a chair.* ◇ **~ sth (+ adv./prep.)** *Medical supplies are being dropped into the stricken area.* ◇ (*BrE*) *He dropped his trousers* (= undid them and let them fall). ◇ (*NAmE*) *He dropped his pants.* **3** [I] (*informal*) to fall down or be no longer able to stand because you are extremely tired: *I feel* ***ready to drop.*** ◇ *She expects everyone to work till they drop.*

▸ BECOME WEAKER/LESS **4** 0→ [I, T] to become or make sth weaker, lower or less SYN **fall**: *The temperature has dropped considerably.* ◇ *At last the wind dropped.* ◇ *His* ***voice dropped*** *to a whisper.* ◇ *The Dutch team have dropped to fifth place.* ◇ *The price of shares dropped by 14p.* ◇ *Shares* ***dropped in price*** *by 14p.* ◇ **~ sth** *She* ***dropped her voice*** *dramatically.* ◇ *You must drop your speed in built-up areas.* ➲ LANGUAGE BANK at FALL

▸ EYES **5** [I, T] **your eyes/gaze ~** | **~ your eyes/gaze** (*formal*) to look down: *Her eyes dropped to her lap.*

▸ SLOPE DOWNWARDS **6** [I] **~ (away)** (**from sth**) to slope steeply downwards: *In front of them the valley dropped sharply away from the road.*

▸ DELIVER/SEND **7** [T] to stop so that sb can get out of a car, etc; to deliver sth on the way to somewhere else: **~ sb/sth** *Can you drop me near the bank?* ◇ **~ sb/sth off** *You left your jacket, but I can drop it off on my way to work tomorrow.* **8** [T] **~ sb a line/note** to send a short letter to sb: *Drop me a line when you get there.*

▸ LEAVE OUT **9** [T] **~ sb/sth** (**from sth**) to leave sb/sth out by accident or deliberately: *She's been dropped from the team because of injury.* ◇ *He spoke with a cockney accent and* ***dropped his aitches*** (= did not pronounce the letter 'h' at the start of words).

▸ FRIENDS **10** [T] **~ sb** to stop seeing sb socially: *She's dropped most of her old friends.*

▸ STOP **11** [T] **~ sth** to stop doing or discussing sth; to not continue with sth: *I dropped German* (= stopped studying it) *when I was 14.* ◇ ***Drop everything*** *and come at once!* ◇ *Look, can we just* ***drop it*** (= stop talking about it)? ◇ *I think we'd better* ***drop the subject.*** ◇ *Let's drop the formalities—please call me Mike.* ◇ *The police decided to drop the charges against her.*

▸ HINT **12** [T] **~ a hint** to say or do sth in order to show sb, in an indirect way, what you are thinking

▸ IN KNITTING **13** [T] **~ a stitch** to let a STITCH go off the needle

IDM **drop the ˈball** (*NAmE, informal*) to make a mistake and spoil sth that you are responsible for **drop a ˈbrick/ˈclanger** (*BrE, informal*) to say sth that offends or embar-

D

rasses sb, although you did not intend to **drop 'dead 1** (*informal*) to die suddenly and unexpectedly **2** (*informal*) used to tell sb, rudely, to stop annoying you, INTERFERING, etc. ➲ see also DROP-DEAD **drop sb 'in it** (*BrE, informal*) to put sb in an embarrassing situation, especially by telling a secret that you should not have told **drop 'names** to mention famous people you know or have met in order to impress others ➲ related noun NAME-DROPPING **,drop your 'bundle** (*AustralE, NZE, informal*) to suddenly not be able to think clearly; to act in a stupid way because you have lost control over yourself **let sb/sth 'drop 1** to do or say nothing more about sb/sth: *I suggest we let the matter drop.* **2** to mention sb/sth in a conversation, by accident or as if by accident: *He* ***let it drop that*** *the Prime Minister was a close friend of his.* ➲ more at BOTTOM *n.*, FLY *n.*, HEAR, JAW *n.*, LAP *n.*, PENNY

PHR V **,drop a'way** to become weaker or less: *She could feel the tension drop away.* **,drop 'back/be'hind | ,drop be'hind sb** to move or fall into position behind sb else: *We cannot afford to drop behind our competitors.* **,drop 'by/'in/'round | ,drop 'in on sb | ,drop 'into sth** to pay an informal visit to a person or a place: *Drop by sometime.* ◇ *I thought I'd drop in on you while I was passing.* ◇ *Sorry we're late—we dropped into the pub on the way.* **,drop 'off** (*BrE, informal*) **1** to fall into a light sleep SYN **fall asleep**: *I dropped off and missed the end of the film.* **2** to become fewer or less: *Traffic in the town has dropped off since the bypass opened.* **,drop 'out** (**of sth**) **1** 🔑 to no longer take part in or be part of sth: *He has dropped out of active politics.* ◇ *a word that has dropped out of the language* **2** 🔑 to leave school, college, etc. without finishing your studies: *She started a degree but dropped out after only a year.* ➲ related noun DROPOUT (1) **3** to reject the ideas and ways of behaving that are accepted by the rest of society ➲ related noun DROPOUT (2)

■ ***noun***

▸ OF LIQUID **1** 🔑 [C] a very small amount of liquid that forms a round shape: *drops of rain* ◇ *a drop of blood* ➲ see also RAINDROP, TEARDROP **2** 🔑 [C, usually sing.] a small quantity of a liquid: *Could I have a drop more milk in my coffee, please?* ◇ *I haven't touched a drop* (= drunk any alcohol) *all evening.*

▸ FALL **3** 🔑 [C, usually sing.] **~ (in sth)** a fall or reduction in the amount, level or number of sth: *a* ***drop in prices/temperature, etc.*** ◇ *a* ***dramatic/sharp drop*** *in profits* ◇ *a five per cent drop* ➲ LANGUAGE BANK at FALL

▸ DISTANCE **4** [sing.] a distance down from a high point to a lower point: *There was a sheer drop of fifty metres to the rocks below.* ◇ *a twenty-foot drop*

▸ MEDICINE **5 drops** [pl.] a liquid medicine that you put one drop at a time into your eyes, ears or nose: *eye drops*

▸ DELIVERING **6** [C] the act of delivering sb/sth in a vehicle or by plane; the act of dropping sth: *Aid agencies are organizing food drops to civilians in the war zone.* ◇ *a parachute drop*

▸ SWEET/CANDY **7** [C] a small round sweet/candy of the type mentioned: *fruit drops* ◇ *cough drops* (= sweets/candy to help a cough)

IDM **at the ,drop of a 'hat** immediately; without hesitating: *The company can't expect me to move my home and family at the drop of a hat.* **a ,drop in the 'ocean** (*BrE*) (*NAmE* **a ,drop in the 'bucket**) an amount of sth that is too small or unimportant to make any real difference to a situation

'drop cloth (*NAmE*) (*BrE* **'dust sheet**) *noun* a large sheet that is used to protect floors, furniture, etc. from dust or paint

,drop-'dead *adv.* (*informal*) used before an adjective to emphasize that sb/sth is attractive in a very noticeable way: *a drop-dead gorgeous Hollywood star*

,drop-down 'menu *noun* (*computing*) a menu that appears on a computer screen when you choose it, and that stays there until you choose one of the functions on it ➲ VISUAL VOCAB page V55

'drop goal *noun* (in RUGBY) a goal scored by dropping the ball onto the ground and kicking it over the CROSSBAR as it BOUNCES

,drop 'handlebars *noun* [pl.] low curved handles on a bicycle

'drop-in *adj.* [only before noun] able to be visited without arranging a fixed time first: *a drop-in centre*

'drop kick *noun* (in RUGBY) a kick made by dropping the ball onto the ground and kicking it as it BOUNCES ▸ **'drop-kick** *verb* **~ sth**

drop·let /'drɒplət; *NAmE* 'drɑːp-/ *noun* a small drop of a liquid

drop·out /'drɒpaʊt; *NAmE* 'drɑːp-/ *noun* **1** a person who leaves school or college before they have finished their studies: *college dropouts* ◇ *a university with a high dropout rate* **2** a person who rejects the ideas and ways of behaving that are accepted by the rest of society

drop·per /'drɒpə(r); *NAmE* 'drɑːp-/ *noun* a short glass tube with a hollow rubber end used for measuring medicine or other liquids in drops ➲ VISUAL VOCAB page V57

drop·pings /'drɒpɪŋz; *NAmE* 'drɑːp-/ *noun* the solid waste matter of birds and animals (usually small animals)

'drop shot *noun* = DINK

dropsy /'drɒpsi; *NAmE* 'drɑːpsi/ *noun* [U] (*old-fashioned*) = OEDEMA

'drop zone *noun* the area in which sb/sth should land after being dropped from an aircraft

dros·oph·ila /drɒ'sɒfɪlə; *NAmE* drə'sɑːfɪlə/ (*pl.* **dros·oph·ila**) *noun* a small fly that feeds on fruit and is often used in scientific research

dross /drɒs; *NAmE* drɔːs; drɑːs/ *noun* [U] **1** (*especially BrE*) something of very low quality; the least valuable part of sth: *mass-produced dross* **2** (*technical*) a waste substance, especially that separated from a metal when it is melted

drought /draʊt/ *noun* [U, C] a long period of time when there is little or no rain: *two years of severe drought* ◇ *one of the worst droughts on record*

drove /drəʊv; *NAmE* droʊv/ *noun* [usually pl.] a large number of people or animals, often moving or doing sth as a group: *droves of tourists* ◇ *People were leaving the countryside* ***in droves*** *to look for work in the cities.* ➲ see also DRIVE *v.*

drover /'drəʊvə(r); *NAmE* 'droʊv-/ *noun* a person who moves groups of cows or sheep from one place to another, especially to market

drown /draʊn/ *verb* **1** [I, T] to die because you have been underwater too long and you cannot breathe; to kill sb in this way: *Two children drowned after falling into the river.* ◇ *He had attempted to rescue the drowning man.* ◇ **~ sb/sth/yourself** *She tried to drown herself.* ◇ *He was drowned at sea.* ◇ *They had drowned the unwanted kittens.* **2** [T] **~ sth** (**in sth**) to make sth very wet; to completely cover sth in water or another liquid SYN **drench**: *The fruit was drowned in cream.* **3** [T] **~ sb/sth** (**out**) (of a sound) to be louder than other sounds so that you cannot hear them: *She turned up the radio to drown out the noise from next door.* ▸ **drown·ing** *noun* [U, C]: *death by drowning* ◇ *Alcohol plays a part in an estimated 30% of drownings.*

IDM **drown your 'fears/'loneliness/'sorrows, etc.** (especially *humorous*) to get drunk in order to forget your problems

drowse /draʊz/ *verb* [I] to be in a light sleep or almost asleep

drowsy /'draʊzi/ *adj.* (**drows·ier**, **drowsi·est**) **1** tired and almost asleep SYN **sleepy**: *The tablets may make you feel drowsy.* **2** making you feel relaxed and tired: *a drowsy afternoon in the sunshine* ▸ **drows·ily** /-ɪli/ *adv.* **drow·si·ness** *noun* [U]: *The drugs tend to cause drowsiness.*

drub·bing /'drʌbɪŋ/ *noun* (*informal*) (in a sport) a situation where one team easily beats another: *We* ***gave them a drubbing*** *in the match on Saturday.*

drudge /drʌdʒ/ *noun* a person who has to do long hard boring jobs

drudg·ery /'drʌdʒəri/ *noun* [U] hard boring work

drug 0-m /drʌɡ/ *noun, verb*
■ ***noun*** **1** 0-m an illegal substance that some people smoke, INJECT, etc. for the physical and mental effects it has: *He does not smoke or* ***take drugs****.* ◇ *teenagers experimenting with drugs* ◇ *I found out Steve was* ***on drugs*** (= regularly used drugs). ◇ *drug and alcohol abuse* ◇ *a* ***hard*** (= very harmful) ***drug*** *such as heroin* ◇ *a* ***soft drug*** (= one that is not considered very harmful) ◇ *Drugs have been seized with a street value of two million dollars.* ◇ *She was a* ***drug addict*** (= could not stop using drugs). ◇ *He was charged with* ***pushing drugs*** (= selling them). ◇ (*informal*) *I don't* ***do drugs*** (= use them). ◇ *drug rehabilitation* **2** 0-m a substance used as a medicine or used in a medicine: *prescribed drugs* ◇ *The doctor put me on a course of pain-killing drugs.* ◇ *drug companies* ◇ *The drug has some bad side effects.* ⊃ COLLOCATIONS at ILL ⊃ see also DESIGNER DRUG
■ ***verb*** (-gg-) **1 ~ sb/sth** to give a person or an animal a drug, especially to make them unconscious, or to affect their performance in a race or competition: *He was drugged and bundled into the back of the car.* ◇ *It's illegal to drug horses before a race.* **2 ~ sth** to add a drug to sb's food or drink to make them unconscious or SLEEPY: *Her drink must have been drugged.*
IDM **be drugged up to the 'eyeballs** to have taken or been given a lot of drugs

'drug dealer *noun* a person who sells illegal drugs

drug·gie (*BrE* also **drug·gy**) /'drʌɡi/ *noun* (*pl.* -ies) (*informal*) a person who takes illegal drugs regularly

drug·ging /'drʌɡɪŋ/ *noun* [U] the act of taking a drug, especially an illegal one: *They were feeling the effects of drinking and drugging all night.*

drug·gist /'drʌɡɪst/ *noun* (*NAmE*) **1** (also **chem·ist, dis'pensing chemist** both *BrE*) a person whose job is to prepare and sell medicines, and who works in a shop **2** = PHARMACIST (1)

drug·gy /'drʌɡi/ *adj., noun*
■ ***adj.*** (**drug·gier, drug·gi·est**) (*informal*) using or involving illegal drugs
■ ***noun*** (*BrE*) = DRUGGIE

'drug peddler *noun* = PEDDLER

drug·store 0-m /'drʌɡstɔː(r)/ *noun* (*NAmE*) a shop/store that sells medicines and also other types of goods, for example COSMETICS ⊃ compare PHARMACY ⊃ see also CHEMIST (2)

Druid /'druːɪd/ *noun* a priest of an ancient Celtic religion

drum 0-m /drʌm/ *noun, verb*
■ ***noun*** **1** 0-m a musical instrument made of a hollow round frame with plastic or skin stretched tightly across one or both ends. You play it by hitting it with sticks or with your hands: *a bass drum* ◇ *Tony Cox on drums* ◇ *to play the drums* ◇ *a regular drum beat* ⊃ VISUAL VOCAB page V30 **2** a large container for oil or chemicals, shaped like a CYLINDER: *a 50 gallon drum* ◇ *an oil drum* **3** a thing shaped like a drum, especially part of a machine: *The mixture flows to a revolving drum where the water is filtered out.*
IDM **beat/bang the 'drum (for sb/sth)** (*especially BrE*) to speak with enthusiasm in support of sb/sth ⊃ more at MARCH
■ ***verb*** (-mm-) **1** [I] to play a drum **2** [T, I] **~ (sth) on sth** to make a sound by hitting a surface again and again: *Impatiently, he* ***drummed his fingers*** *on the table.*
IDM **'drum sth into sb's head** = DRUM STH INTO SB
PHR V **'drum sth into sb** to make sb remember sth by repeating it a lot of times: *We had it drummed into us that we should never talk to strangers.* **,drum sb 'out (of sth)** [usually passive] to force sb to leave an organization as a punishment for doing sth wrong **,drum sth↔'up** to try hard to get support or business: *He had flown to the north of the country to drum up support for the campaign.*

,drum and 'bass (also **,drum 'n' 'bass**) *noun* [U] a type of electronic dance music developed in Britain in the early 1990s, which has a fast drum beat and a strong slower BASS beat

drum·beat /'drʌmbiːt/ *noun* the sound that a beat on a drum makes

'drum kit *noun* a set of drums ⊃ VISUAL VOCAB page V30

drum·lin /'drʌmlɪn/ *noun* (*geology*) a very small hill formed by the movement of a GLACIER (= a large moving mass of ice)

'drum machine *noun* an electronic musical instrument that produces the sound of drums

,drum 'major *noun* the leader of a marching band of musicians, especially in the army

,drum majo'rette (*especially BrE*) (*NAmE* usually **ma·jor·ette**) *noun* a girl in special brightly coloured clothes who walks in front of a marching band, spinning, throwing and catching a long stick (called a BATON)

drum·mer /'drʌmə(r)/ *noun* a person who plays a drum or drums IDM see MARCH

drum·ming /'drʌmɪŋ/ *noun* [U, sing.] **1** the act of playing a drum; the sound of a drum being played **2** a continuous sound or feeling like the beats of a drum: *the steady drumming of the rain on the tin roof*

,drum 'n' 'bass *noun* = DRUM AND BASS

drum·stick /'drʌmstɪk/ *noun* **1** a stick used for playing a drum ⊃ VISUAL VOCAB page V30 **2** the lower part of the leg of a chicken or other bird that is cooked and eaten as food: *a* ***chicken/turkey drumstick***

drunk 0-m /drʌŋk/ *adj., noun* ⊃ see also DRINK *v.*
■ ***adj.*** **1** 0-m [not usually before noun] having drunk so much alcohol that it is impossible to think or speak clearly: *She was too drunk to remember anything about the party.* ◇ *His only way of dealing with his problems was to go out and* ***get drunk****.* ◇ *They got drunk on vodka.* ◇ *Police arrested him for being* ***drunk and disorderly*** (= violent or noisy in a public place because of being drunk). OPP **sober** **2 ~ with sth** (*formal*) in a great state of excitement because of a particular emotion or situation: *drunk with success*
IDM **(as) drunk as a 'lord** (*BrE*) (*NAmE* **(as) drunk as a 'skunk**) (*informal*) very drunk ⊃ more at BLIND *adv.*, ROARING
■ ***noun*** a person who is drunk or who often gets drunk

drunk·ard /'drʌŋkəd; *NAmE* -ərd/ *noun* (*old-fashioned*) a person who gets drunk very often SYN **alcoholic**

,drunk 'driver (*especially NAmE*) (*BrE* also **,drink-'driver**) *noun* a person who drives a vehicle after drinking too much alcohol

'drunk driving (*especially NAmE*) (*BrE* also **,drink-'driving, ,drunken 'driving**) *noun* [U] driving a vehicle after drinking too much alcohol

drunk·en /'drʌŋkən/ *adj.* [only before noun] **1** drunk or often getting drunk: *a drunken driver* ◇ *She was often beaten by her drunken husband.* **2** showing the effects of too much alcohol; involving people who are drunk: *He came home to find her in a drunken stupor.* ◇ *a drunken brawl* ► **drunk·en·ly** *adv.*: *He staggered drunkenly to his feet.* **drunk·en·ness** *noun* [U]

,drunken 'driving *noun* [U] (*BrE*) = DRINK-DRIVING

'drunk tank *noun* (*informal, humorous, especially NAmE*) a place where people are put by the police because they are drunk: *He spent the night in the drunk tank.*

dry 0-m /draɪ/ *adj., verb*
■ ***adj.*** (**drier, dri·est**)
► NOT WET **1** 0-m not wet, damp or sticky; without water or MOISTURE: *Is my shirt dry yet?* ◇ *Store onions in a cool dry place.* ◇ *I'm afraid this cake has turned out very dry.* ◇ *Her mouth felt* ***as dry as a bone*** (= completely dry). ◇ *When the paint is completely dry, apply another coat.* ◇ *It was high summer and the rivers were dry* (= had no water in them). ⊃ see also BONE DRY OPP **wet**
► LITTLE RAIN **2** 0-m with very little rain: *weeks of hot* ***dry weather*** ◇ *the* ***dry season*** ◇ *I hope it* ***stays dry*** *for our picnic.* ◇ *Rattlesnakes occur in the warmer, drier parts of North America.* OPP **wet**
► SKIN/HAIR **3** without the natural oils that makes it soft and healthy: *a shampoo for dry hair*
► COUGH **4** that does not produce any PHLEGM (= the thick

D

liquid that forms in the nose and throat): *a dry hacking cough*
▸ BREAD **5** eaten on its own without any butter, jam, etc: *Breakfast consisted of dry bread and a cup of tea.*
▸ WINE **6** not sweet: *a crisp dry white wine* ◇ *a dry sherry* **OPP sweet**
▸ HUMOUR **7** (*approving*) very clever and expressed in a quiet way that is not obvious; often using IRONY: *He was a man of few words with a delightful dry sense of humour.*
▸ WITHOUT EMOTION **8** not showing emotion: *a dry voice*
▸ BORING **9** not interesting: *Government reports tend to make dry reading.*
▸ WITHOUT ALCOHOL **10** without alcohol; where it is illegal to buy, sell or drink alcohol: *We had a dry wedding* (= no alcoholic drinks were served). ◇ *a dry county/state*
▸ THIRSTY **11** (*informal, especially BrE*) thirsty; that makes you thirsty: *I'm a bit dry.* ◇ *This is dry work.*
▸ **dryly** *adv.* = DRILY **dry·ness** *noun* [U]
IDM **milk/suck sb/sth 'dry** to get from sb/sth all the money, help, information, etc. they have, usually giving nothing in return **not a dry eye in the 'house** (*humorous*) used to say that everyone was very emotional about sth: *There wasn't a dry eye in the house when they announced their engagement.* **run 'dry** to stop supplying water; to be all used so that none is left: *The wells in most villages in the region have run dry.* ◇ *Vaccine supplies started to run dry as the flu outbreak reached epidemic proportions.* ➲ more at BLEED, HIGH *adj.*, HOME *adv.*, POWDER *n.*, SQUEEZE *v.*
■ *verb* (dries, dry·ing, dried, dried) [I, T] to become dry; to make sth dry: *Be careful. The paint hasn't dried yet.* ◇ *You wash the dishes and I'll dry.* ◇ **~ sth** *Use this towel to dry your hands.* ◇ *dry your hair* ◇ *to* **dry your eyes/tears** (= stop crying)
PHR V **,dry 'off | ,dry sb/sth↔'off** to become dry or make sth dry: *We went swimming and then lay in the sun to dry off.* ◇ *We dried our boots off by the fire.* **,dry 'out | ,dry sb↔'out** (*informal*) to stop drinking alcohol after you have continuously been drinking too much; to cure sb of drinking too much alcohol: *He went to an expensive clinic to dry out.* **,dry 'out | ,dry sth↔'out** to become or to allow sth to become dry, in a way that is not wanted: *Water the plant regularly, never letting the soil dry out.* ◇ *Hot sun and cold winds can soon dry out your skin.* **,dry 'up 1** (of rivers, lakes, etc.) to become completely dry: *During the drought the river dried up.* **2** if a supply of sth **dries up**, there is gradually less of it until there is none left: *As she got older, offers of modelling work began to dry up.* **3** to suddenly stop talking because you do not know what to say next **,dry 'up | ,dry sth↔'up** (*BrE*) to dry dishes with a towel after you have washed them: *I'll wash and you can dry up.*

dryad /'draɪæd/ *noun* (in stories) a female spirit who lives in a tree

,dry 'cell *noun* the type of cell in a dry battery which contains chemicals only in solid form

,dry-'clean (also **clean**) *verb* **~ sth** to clean clothes using chemicals instead of water: *This garment must be dry-cleaned only.* ➲ SYNONYMS at CLEAN ▸ **,dry-'cleaning** *noun* [U]

,dry-'cleaner's *noun* = CLEANER

,dry 'dock *noun* [C, U] an area in a port from which the water can be removed, used for building or repairing ships

dryer (also **drier**) /'draɪə(r)/ *noun* (especially in compounds) a machine for drying sth: *a hairdryer* ➲ see also SPIN DRYER, TUMBLE DRYER

,dry-'eyed *adj.* [not before noun] not crying: *She remained dry-eyed throughout the trial.*

'dry farming *noun* [U] = DRY-LAND FARMING

'dry goods *noun* [pl.] **1** (*BrE*) types of food that are solid and dry, such as tea, coffee and flour **2** (*old-fashioned, NAmE*) cloth and things that are made out of cloth, such as clothes and sheets: *a dry goods store* ➲ compare DRAPERY

,dry 'ice *noun* [U] solid CARBON DIOXIDE used for keeping food, etc. cold or for producing special effects in the theatre

,dry 'land *noun* [U] land, rather than sea **SYN terra firma**: *It was a great relief to be back* **on dry land** *after such a rough crossing.*

dryly = DRILY

,dry 'milk (*US*) (*BrE* **'milk powder, ,powdered 'milk**) *noun* [U] dried milk in the form of a powder

,dry-'roasted *adj.* cooked in an oven without adding oil or fat: *dry-roasted peanuts*

,dry 'rot *noun* [U] **1** wood that has decayed and turned to powder **2** any FUNGUS that causes this decay

,dry 'run *noun* [usually sing.] a complete practice of a performance or way of doing sth, before the real one **SYN dummy run**

'dry slope (also **'dry-ski slope**) *noun* a steep slope with a special surface for practising SKIING

dry·stone wall /,draɪstəʊn 'wɔːl; *NAmE* -stoʊn/ *noun* (*BrE*) (*NAmE* **'dry wall**) a stone wall built without MORTAR (= a substance used in building to hold bricks or stones together) between the stones

dry·suit /'draɪsuːt; *BrE* also -sjuːt/ *noun* a piece of clothing that fits the whole body closely and keeps water out, worn by people swimming underwater or sailing ➲ compare WETSUIT

'dry wall *noun* [U] (*NAmE*) **1** = PLASTERBOARD **2** (*BrE* **dry·stone wall**) a stone wall built without MORTAR (= a substance used in building to hold bricks or stones together) between the stones

DSL /,diː es 'el/ *abbr.* (*computing*) digital subscriber line (a way of sending electronic data at high speed along ordinary telephone lines, used for supplying the Internet to homes, businesses, etc.)

DST /,diː es 'tiː/ *abbr.* DAYLIGHT SAVING TIME

DT /,diː 'tiː/ *noun* [U] (*BrE*) the abbreviation for design and technology (a school subject in which students learn about the role of technology in modern life and also design and make things for themselves)

DTI /,diː tiː 'aɪ/ *abbr.* (in Britain) Department of Trade and Industry

DTP /,diː tiː 'piː/ *abbr.* DESKTOP PUBLISHING

DTs (*BrE*) (*US* **D.T.'s**) /,diː 'tiːz/ *noun* [pl.] the abbreviation for 'delirium tremens' (a physical condition in which people who drink too much alcohol feel their body shaking and imagine that they are seeing things that are not really there)

dual /'djuːəl; *NAmE* 'duːəl/ *adj.* [only before noun] having two parts or aspects: *his dual role as composer and conductor* ◇ *She has* **dual nationality** (= is a citizen of two different countries). ◇ *The piece of furniture serves a dual purpose as a cupboard and as a table.* ➲ SYNONYMS at DOUBLE ➲ see also DUAL-PURPOSE

,dual 'carriageway (*BrE*) (*NAmE* **di,vided 'highway**) *noun* a road with a strip of land in the middle that divides the lines of traffic moving in opposite directions

,dual con'trols *noun* [pl.] two sets of instruments for controlling a vehicle or aircraft, so that a teacher, for example, can take control from the driver ▸ **,dual con'trol** *adj.*: *a dual-control vehicle*

dual·ism /'djuːəlɪzəm; *NAmE* 'duː-/ *noun* [U] **1** (*philosophy*) the theory that there are two opposite principles in everything, for example good and evil **2** (*formal*) the state of having two parts ▸ **dual·ist, dual·ist·ic** *adj.* **dual·ist** *noun*

dual·ity /djuː'æləti; *NAmE* duː-/ *noun* [U, C] (*pl.* -ies) (*formal*) the state of having two parts or aspects

,dual-'purpose *adj.* that can be used for two different purposes: *a dual-purpose vehicle* (= for carrying passengers or goods)

dub /dʌb/ *verb, noun*
■ *verb* (-bb-) **1 ~ sb + noun** to give sb/sth a particular name, often in a humorous or critical way: *The Belgian actor*

Jean–Claude Van Damme has been dubbed 'Muscles from Brussels'. **2 ~ sth** (**into sth**) to replace the original speech in a film/movie or television programme with words in another language: *an American movie dubbed into Italian* ➲ compare SUBTITLE **3 ~ sth** (*especially BrE*) to make a piece of music by mixing sounds from different recordings
▪ ***noun*** [U] a type of West Indian music or poetry with a strong beat

du·bi·ety /ˌdjuːˈbaɪəti; *NAmE* ˌduː-/ *noun* [U] (*formal*) the fact of being uncertain

du·bi·ous /ˈdjuːbiəs; *NAmE* ˈduː-/ *adj.* **1** [not usually before noun] **~ (about sth)/(about doing sth)** (of a person) not certain and slightly suspicious about sth; not knowing whether sth is good or bad **SYN doubtful**: *I was rather dubious about the whole idea.* **2** (*disapproving*) probably not honest **SYN suspicious**: *They indulged in some highly dubious business practices to obtain their current position in the market.* **3** that you cannot be sure about; that is probably not good: *They consider the plan to be of dubious benefit to most families.* ◇ (*ironic*) *She had the dubious honour of being the last woman to be hanged in England* (= it was not an honour at all). ▸ **du·bi·ous·ly** *adv.*

ˌDublin Bay ˈprawn *noun* = LANGOUSTINE

dub·nium /ˈdʌbniəm; *NAmE* ˈduːb-/ *noun* [U] (*symb.* **Db**) a RADIOACTIVE chemical element. Dubnium is produced when atoms COLLIDE (= crash into each other).

ducal /ˈdjuːkl; *NAmE* ˈduːkl/ *adj.* [only before noun] of or belonging to a DUKE

ducat /ˈdʌkət/ *noun* (in the past) a gold coin used in many European countries

duch·ess /ˈdʌtʃəs/ *noun* **1** the wife of a DUKE: *the Duchess of York* **2** a woman who has the rank of a DUKE

duchy /ˈdʌtʃi/ *noun* (*pl.* **-ies**) (also **duke·dom**) an area of land that is owned and controlled by a DUKE OR DUCHESS

duck /dʌk/ *noun, verb*
▪ ***noun* 1** (*pl.* **ducks** or **duck**) [C] a common bird that lives on or near water and has short legs, WEBBED feet (= feet with thin pieces of skin between the toes) and a wide beak. There are many types of duck, some of which are kept for their meat or eggs: *wild ducks* ◇ *duck eggs* ➲ VISUAL VOCAB page V10 **2** [C] a female duck ➲ compare DRAKE **3** [U] meat from a duck: *roast duck with orange sauce* **4** (also **duckie, ducks, ducky**) [C, usually sing.] (*BrE, informal*) a friendly way of addressing sb: *Anything else, duck?* ➲ compare DEAR, LOVE **5 a duck** [sing.] (in CRICKET) a BATSMAN'S score of zero: *He was out for a duck.* ➲ see also LAME DUCK, SITTING DUCK
IDM get/have (all) your ˌducks in a ˈrow (*especially NAmE*) to have made all the preparations needed to do sth; to be well organized (**take to sth**) **like a ˌduck to ˈwater** (to become used to sth) very easily, without any problems or fears: *She has taken to teaching like a duck to water.* ➲ more at DEAD *adj.*, WATER *n.*
▪ ***verb* 1** [I, T] to move your head or body downwards to avoid being hit or seen: *He had to duck as he came through the door.* ◇ **~ (down) (behind/under sth)** *We ducked down behind the wall so they wouldn't see us.* ◇ *He just managed to* ***duck out of sight.*** ◇ **~ sth** *She ducked her head and got into the car.* **2** [T] **~ sth** to avoid sth by moving your head or body out of the way **SYN dodge**: *He ducked the first few blows then started to fight back.* **3** [I] **+ adv./prep.** to move somewhere quickly, especially in order to avoid being seen: *She ducked into the adjoining room as we came in.* **4** [I, T] (rather *informal*) to avoid a difficult or unpleasant duty or responsibility: **~ out of sth** *It's his turn to cook dinner, but I bet he'll try to duck out of it.* ◇ **~ sth** *The government is ducking the issue.* **5** (*NAmE* also **dunk**) [T] **~ sb** to push sb underwater and hold them there for a short time: *The kids were ducking each other in the pool.*

ˌduck-billed ˈplatypus *noun* = PLATYPUS

duck·boards /ˈdʌkbɔːdz; *NAmE* -bɔːrdz/ *noun* [pl.] long narrow wooden boards used to make a path over wet ground

duck·ling /ˈdʌklɪŋ/ *noun* [C, U] a young duck; the meat of a young duck ➲ see also UGLY DUCKLING

ˌducks and ˈdrakes *noun* [U] (*BrE*) a game in which you make flat stones BOUNCE across the surface of water

ˌduck ˈsoup *noun* [U] (*NAmE, informal*) a problem that is easy to deal with, or an opponent who is easy to defeat

duck·weed /ˈdʌkwiːd/ *noun* [U] a very small plant that grows on the surface of still water

ducky /ˈdʌki/
▪ ***noun*** (*BrE, informal*) = DUCK (4)
▪ ***adj.*** (**duck·ier, ducki·est**) (*NAmE, old-fashioned* or *humorous*) very pleasant: *Everything is just ducky.*

duct /dʌkt/ *noun* **1** a pipe or tube carrying liquid, gas, electric or telephone wires, etc: *a heating/ventilation duct* **2** a tube in the body or in plants through which liquid passes: *the bile duct*

duc·tile /ˈdʌktaɪl/ *adj.* (*technical*) (of a metal) that can be made into a thin wire

duct·ing /ˈdʌktɪŋ/ *noun* [U] **1** a system of ducts **2** material in the form of a duct or ducts: *a short piece of ducting*

ˈduct tape *noun* [U] (*NAmE*) very strong cloth tape that is sticky on one side, often used for repairing things or covering holes in pipes

dud /dʌd/ *noun, adj.*
▪ ***noun* 1** [C] (*informal*) a thing that is useless, especially because it does not work correctly: *Two of the fireworks in the box were duds.* **2 duds** [pl.] (*slang*) clothes
▪ ***adj.*** [only before noun] useless; that does not work correctly: *a dud battery* ◇ *a dud cheque* (= written by sb who has not enough money in their bank account)

dude /duːd; djuːd/ *noun* (*slang, especially NAmE*) a man: *He's a real cool dude.* ◇ *Hey, dude, what's up?*

ˈdude ranch *noun* an American RANCH (= a large farm) where people can go on holiday/vacation and do the sort of activities that COWBOYS do **ORIGIN** From an old meaning of the word *dude*, a man from the city who wears fashionable clothes.

dudgeon /ˈdʌdʒən/ *noun* **IDM** see HIGH *adj.*

due 🔑 /djuː; *NAmE* duː/ *adj., noun, adv.*
▪ ***adj.***
▸ CAUSED BY **1** 🔑 [not before noun] **~ to sth/sb** caused by sb/sth; because of sb/sth: *The team's success was largely due to her efforts.* ◇ *Most of the problems were due to human error.* ◇ *The project had to be abandoned due to a lack of government funding.* ➲ LANGUAGE BANK at BECAUSE OF **HELP** Some people think that it is more correct to use **owing to** to mean 'because of' after a verb or at the beginning of a clause, as **due** is an adjective.
▸ EXPECTED **2** 🔑 [not before noun] arranged or expected: *When's the baby due?* ◇ *The next train is due in five minutes.* ◇ (*especially NAmE*) *My essay's due next Friday* (= it has to be given to the teacher by then). ◇ **~ to do sth** *Rose is due to start school in January.* ◇ **~ for sth** *The band's first album is due for release later this month.*
▸ OWED **3** 🔑 [not usually before noun] when a sum of money is **due**, it must be paid immediately: *Payment is due on 1 October.* **4** [not before noun] **~ (to sb)** owed to sb as a debt, because it is their right or because they have done sth to deserve it: *Have they been paid the money that is due to them?* ◇ *Our thanks are due to the whole team.* **5** [not before noun] owed sth; deserving sth: **~ sth** *I'm still due 15 days' leave.* ◇ **~ for sth** *She's due for promotion soon.*
▸ SUITABLE/RIGHT **6** [only before noun] (*formal*) that is suitable or right in the circumstances: *After due consideration, we have decided to appoint Mr Davis to the job.* ◇ *to make due allowance for sth* ◇ (*BrE*) *He was charged with driving without* **due care and attention**. ➲ compare UNDUE
IDM in ˌdue ˈcourse at the right time and not before: *Your request will be dealt with in due course.* ➲ more at RESPECT *n.*
▪ ***noun* 1 your/sb's ~** [U] a thing that should be given to sb by right: *He received a large reward, which was no more than his due* (= than what he deserved). ◇ *She's a slow worker, but* ***to give her her due*** (= to be fair to her), *she*

does try very hard. **2 dues** [pl.] charges, for example to be a member of a club: *to pay your dues*

■ ***adv.*** **~ north/south/east/west** exactly; in a straight line: *to sail due east* ◇ *The village lies five miles due north of York.*

ˌdue ˈdate *noun* [usually sing.] the date on or by which sth, especially a sum of money, is owed or expected

duel /ˈdjuːəl; *NAmE* ˈduːəl/ *noun* **1** a formal fight with weapons between two people, used in the past to settle a disagreement, especially over a matter of honour: *to* ***fight/win a duel*** ◇ *to* ***challenge sb to a duel*** **2** a competition or struggle between two people or groups: *a verbal duel* ▸ **duel** *verb* (-ll-, *US* -l-) [I]: *The two men duelled to the death.*

du·el·ling (*US* **du·el·ing**) /ˈdjuːəlɪŋ; *NAmE* ˈduːəlɪŋ/ *noun* [U] the practice of fighting duels

ˌdue ˈprocess of law (also **ˌdue ˈprocess**) *noun* [U] (*law*) (in the US) the right of a citizen to be treated fairly, especially the right to a fair trial

duet /djuˈet; *NAmE* duˈet/ (also *less frequent* **duo**) *noun* a piece of music for two players or singers: *a piano duet* ➲ compare SOLO, TRIO

duff /dʌf/ *adj., noun, verb*

■ ***adj.*** (*BrE, informal*) useless; that does not work as it should: *He sold me a duff radio.*

■ ***noun*** (*NAmE, informal*) a person's bottom

IDM **up the ˈduff** (*BrE, slang*) pregnant: *He got her up the duff.*

■ ***verb***

PHR V **ˌduff sb↔ˈup** (*BrE, informal*) to hit or kick sb severely SYN **beat up**

duf·fel bag (also **duf·fle bag**) /ˈdʌfl bæɡ/ *noun* **1** (*BrE*) a bag made out of cloth, shaped like a tube and closed by a string around the top. It is usually carried over the shoulder. **2** (*NAmE*) (*BrE* **hold·all**) a large bag made of strong cloth or soft leather, used when you are travelling for carrying clothes, etc. ➲ VISUAL VOCAB page V52

duf·fel coat (also **duf·fle coat**) /ˈdʌfl kəʊt; *NAmE* koʊt/ *noun* a heavy coat made of wool, that usually has a HOOD and is fastened with TOGGLES

duf·fer /ˈdʌfə(r)/ *noun* (*BrE, informal*) a person who is stupid or unable to do anything well

dug *past tense, past part.* of DIG

du·gong /ˈduːɡɒŋ; ˈdjuː-; *NAmE* ˈduːɡɑːŋ; -ɡɔːŋ/ *noun* a large sea animal with thick greyish skin, which lives mainly in the Indian Ocean and eats plants

dug·out /ˈdʌɡaʊt/ *noun* **1** a rough shelter made by digging a hole in the ground and covering it, used by soldiers **2** a shelter by the side of a football (SOCCER) or BASEBALL field where a team's manager, etc. can sit and watch the game **3** (also **ˌdugout caˈnoe**) a CANOE (= a type of light narrow boat) made by cutting out the inside of a tree TRUNK

DUI /ˌdiː juː ˈaɪ/ *abbr.* (*NAmE*) = DRIVING UNDER THE INFLUENCE

du jour /duː ˈʒʊə(r); *NAmE* duː ˈʒʊr/ *adj.* [after noun] (*informal, humorous*) very popular or important now: *This age group is the target group du jour.* ◇ *Facebook is the Internet phenomenon du jour.* ORIGIN From French, meaning 'of the day'.

duke /djuːk; *NAmE* duːk/ *noun* **1** a NOBLEMAN of the highest rank: *the Duke of Edinburgh* **2** (in some parts of Europe, especially in the past) a male ruler of a small independent state ➲ see also ARCHDUKE, DUCHESS, DUCHY, GRAND DUKE

duke·dom /ˈdjuːkdəm; *NAmE* ˈduːk-/ *noun* **1** the rank or position of a duke **2** = DUCHY

dulce /ˈdʌlseɪ/ *noun* [C, U] (*US*) a sweet food or drink, especially a sweet or jam

dul·cet /ˈdʌlsɪt/ *adj.* [only before noun] (*humorous* or *ironic*) sounding sweet and pleasant: *I thought I recognized your* ***dulcet tones*** (= the sound of your voice).

dul·ci·mer /ˈdʌlsɪmə(r)/ *noun* **1** a musical instrument that you play by hitting the metal strings with two HAMMERS **2** a musical instrument with strings, popular in American traditional music, that you lay on your knee and play with your fingers

dull 🔑 /dʌl/ *adj., verb*

■ ***adj.*** (**dull·er**, **dull·est**)

▸ BORING **1** 🔑 not interesting or exciting SYN **dreary**: *Life in a small town could be deadly dull.* ◇ *The first half of the game was pretty dull.* ◇ *There's* ***never a dull moment*** *when John's around.* ➲ SYNONYMS at BORING

▸ LIGHT/COLOURS **2** 🔑 not bright or shiny: *a dull grey colour* ◇ *dull, lifeless hair* ◇ *Her eyes were dull.*

▸ WEATHER **3** 🔑 not bright, with a lot of clouds SYN **overcast**: *It was a dull, grey day.*

▸ SOUNDS **4** not clear or loud: *The gates shut behind him with a dull thud.*

▸ PAIN **5** not very severe, but continuous: *a* ***dull ache/pain***

▸ PERSON **6** slow in understanding SYN **stupid**: *a dull pupil*

▸ TRADE **7** (*especially NAmE*) not busy; slow: *Don't sell into a dull market.*

▸ **dull·ness** *noun* [U] **dully** /ˈdʌlli/ *adv.*: *'I suppose so,' she said dully.* ◇ *His leg ached dully.*

IDM **(as) dull as ˈditchwater** (*BrE*) (*US* **(as) dull as ˈdishwater**) extremely boring ➲ more at WORK *n.*

■ ***verb***

▸ PAIN **1** [T, I] **~ (sth)** (of pain or an emotion) to become or be made weaker or less severe: *The tablets they gave him dulled the pain for a while.*

▸ PERSON **2** [T] **~ sb** to make a person slower or less lively: *He felt dulled and stupid with sleep.*

▸ COLOURS/SOUNDS **3** [I, T] to become or to make sth less bright, clean or sharp: *His eyes dulled and he slumped to the ground.* ◇ **~ sth** *The endless rain seemed to dull all sound.*

dull·ard /ˈdʌlɑːd; *NAmE* -lɑːrd/ *noun* (*old-fashioned*) a stupid person with no imagination

dulls·ville /ˈdʌlzvɪl/ *noun* [U] (*NAmE, informal*) a place or situation which is extremely boring

ˌdull-ˈwitted *adj.* (*old-fashioned*) not understanding quickly or easily SYN **stupid**

duly /ˈdjuːli; *NAmE* ˈduːli/ *adv.* **1** (*formal*) in the correct or expected manner: *The document was duly signed by the inspector.* **2** at the expected and correct time: *They duly arrived at 9.30 in spite of torrential rain.* ➲ compare UNDULY

dumb /dʌm/ *adj., verb*

■ ***adj.*** (**dumb·er**, **dumb·est**) **1** (*old-fashioned, sometimes offensive*) unable to speak: *She was born* ***deaf and dumb.*** HELP **Dumb** used in this meaning is old-fashioned and can be offensive. It is better to use **speech-impaired** instead. **2** temporarily not speaking or refusing to speak: *We were all* ***struck dumb*** *with amazement.* ◇ *We sat there in dumb silence.* **3** (*informal, especially NAmE*) stupid: *That was a pretty dumb thing to do.* ◇ *If the police question you,* ***act dumb*** (= pretend you do not know anything). ◇ *In her early movies she played a* ***dumb blonde.*** ▸ **dumb·ly** *adv.*: *'Are you all right?' Laura nodded dumbly.* **dumb·ness** *noun* [U]

■ ***verb***

PHR V **ˌdumb ˈdown** | **ˌdumb sth↔ˈdown** (*disapproving*) to make sth less accurate or EDUCATIONAL, and of worse quality, by trying to make it easier for people to understand ▸ **ˌdumbing ˈdown** *noun* [U]

ˌdumb ˈanimal *noun* [usually pl.] (*BrE*) an animal, especially when seen as deserving pity

ˈdumb-ass *adj.* [only before noun] (*NAmE, taboo, slang*) stupid

ˈdumb-bell *noun* **1** a short bar with a weight at each end, used for making the arm and shoulder muscles stronger ➲ VISUAL VOCAB page V35 **2** (*NAmE, informal*) a stupid person

dumb·found /dʌmˈfaʊnd/ *verb* **~ sb** to surprise or shock sb so much that they are unable to speak: *His reply dumbfounded me.*

dumb·found·ed /dʌmˈfaʊndɪd/ (also *less frequent* **dumb·struck** /ˈdʌmstrʌk/) *adj.* unable to speak because of surprise: *The news left her dumbfounded.*

dumbo /ˈdʌmbəʊ; *NAmE* -boʊ/ *noun* (*pl.* -oes) (*informal*) a stupid person

ˌ**dumb ˈwaiter** *noun* a small lift/elevator for carrying food and plates from one floor to another in a restaurant

dum·dum /ˈdʌmdʌm/ (also ˌ**dumdum ˈbullet**) *noun* a bullet that spreads out and breaks into many pieces when it hits sb **ORIGIN** It is named after the factory at Dumdum near Calcutta in India, where such bullets were originally made. They are now illegal.

dummy /ˈdʌmi/ *noun, adj., verb*

▪ ***noun*** (*pl.* -ies) **1** [C] a model of a person, used especially when making clothes or for showing them in a shop window: *a tailor's dummy* ➲ see also MANNEQUIN (2) **2** [C] a thing that seems to be real but is only a copy of the real thing **3** [C] (*NAmE, informal*) a stupid person: *Don't just stand there, you dummy.* **4** [C] (in some sports) an occasion when you pretend to make a particular move and then do not do so **5** [C] (*BrE*) (*NAmE* **paci·fier**) a specially shaped rubber or plastic object for a baby to suck **6** [U] (in card games, especially BRIDGE) the cards which are placed facing upwards on the table and which can be seen by all the players

▪ ***adj.*** [only before noun] made to look real, although it is actually a copy which does not work **SYN** **replica**: *a dummy bomb*

▪ ***verb*** [T, I] (in football (SOCCER)) to pretend to make a particular move in order to confuse your opponent: **~ sth** *She dummied a shot that brought the goalie to her knees.* ◇ **+ adv./prep.** *He dummied past five defenders, then shot at the near post.*

ˌ**dummy ˈrun** *noun* (*BrE*) a practice attack, performance, etc. before the real one **SYN** **dry run**

dump 0ᴿ /dʌmp/ *verb, noun*

▪ ***verb***

▸ GET RID OF **1** 0ᴿ **~ sth** to get rid of sth you do not want, especially in a place which is not suitable: *Too much toxic waste is being dumped at sea.* ◇ *The dead body was just dumped by the roadside.* **2 ~ sb/sth** (**on sb**) (*informal*) to get rid of sb/sth or leave them for sb else to deal with: *He's got no right to keep dumping his problems on me.* **3 ~ sth** (*business*) to get rid of goods by selling them at a very low price, often in another country

▸ PUT DOWN **4 ~ sth** to put sth down in a careless or untidy way: *Just dump your stuff over there—we'll sort it out later.*

▸ END RELATIONSHIP **5 ~ sb** (*informal*) to end a romantic relationship with sb: *Did you hear he's dumped his girlfriend?*

▸ COMPUTING **6 ~ sth** to copy information and move it somewhere to store it **IDM** see LAP *n.*

PHR V ˈ**dump on sb** (*informal, especially NAmE*) to criticize sb severely or treat them badly

▪ ***noun*** ➲ see also DUMPS

▸ FOR WASTE **1** 0ᴿ a place where waste or rubbish/garbage is taken and left: (*BrE*) *a* ***rubbish dump*** ◇ (*NAmE*) *a* ***garbage dump*** ◇ *the municipal dump* ◇ *a toxic/nuclear* ***waste dump*** **2** (also ˈ**mine dump**) (*SAfrE*) a hill that is formed when waste sand from the production of gold is piled in one place over a period of time

▸ DIRTY PLACE **3** (*informal, disapproving*) a dirty or unpleasant place: *How can you live in this dump?*

▸ FOR WEAPONS **4** a temporary store for military supplies: *an ammunition dump*

▸ COMPUTING **5** an act of copying data stored in a computer; a copy or list of the contents of this data ➲ see also SCREEN DUMP

▸ WASTE FROM BODY **6** [C] (*slang*) an act of passing waste matter from the body through the BOWELS: *to have a dump*

ˈ**dump bin** (*BrE*) (also **disˈplay bin** *US, BrE*) *noun* a box in a shop/store for displaying goods, especially goods whose prices have been reduced

dump·er /ˈdʌmpə(r)/ *noun* (*especially NAmE*) a person who throws away dangerous or harmful things, especially in the wrong place

ˈ**dumper truck** (*BrE*) (*NAmE* ˈ**dump truck**) *noun* a vehicle for carrying earth, stones, etc. in a container which can be lifted up for the load to fall out ➲ VISUAL VOCAB page V47

dump·ing /ˈdʌmpɪŋ/ *noun* [U] the act or practice of dumping sth, especially dangerous substances: *a ban on the dumping of radioactive waste at sea*

ˈ**dumping ground** *noun* [usually sing.] a place where sth that is not wanted is dumped

dump·ling /ˈdʌmplɪŋ/ *noun* **1** a small ball of DOUGH (= a mixture of flour, fat and water) that is cooked and served with meat dishes: *chicken with herb dumplings* **2** a small ball of PASTRY, often with fruit in it, eaten as a DESSERT: *apple dumplings*

dumps /dʌmps/ *noun* [pl.]

IDM **down in the ˈdumps** (*informal*) feeling unhappy **SYN** **depressed**

Dump·ster™ /ˈdʌmpstə(r)/ (*NAmE*) (*BrE* **skip**) *noun* a large open container for putting old bricks, rubbish/garbage, etc. in. The Dumpster is then loaded on a lorry/truck and taken away.

ˈ**dump truck** (*NAmE*) (*BrE* ˈ**dumper truck**) *noun* a vehicle for carrying earth, stones, etc. in a container which can be lifted up for the load to fall out ➲ VISUAL VOCAB page V47

dumpy /ˈdʌmpi/ *adj.* (especially of a person) short and fat

dun /dʌn/ *adj.* greyish-brown in colour ▸ **dun** *noun* [U]

dunce /dʌns/ *noun* (*old-fashioned*) a person, especially a child at school, who is stupid or slow to learn

ˌ**dunce's ˈcap** (*BrE*) (*NAmE* ˈ**dunce cap**) *noun* a pointed hat that was sometimes given in the past to a child in a class at school who was slow to learn

Dun·dee cake /dʌnˈdi: keɪk/ *noun* [C, U] a fruit cake, usually decorated with ALMONDS (= a type of nut)

dun·der·head /ˈdʌndəhed; *NAmE* ˈdʌndər-/ *noun* (*informal*) a silly or stupid person

dune /dju:n; *NAmE* du:n/ (also ˈ**sand dune**) *noun* a small hill of sand formed by the wind, near the sea or in a desert ➲ VISUAL VOCAB page V4

ˈ**dune buggy** *noun* = BEACH BUGGY

dung /dʌŋ/ *noun* [U] solid waste from animals, especially from large ones **SYN** **manure**: *cow dung*

dun·garees /ˌdʌŋgəˈri:z/ *noun* [pl.] **1** (*BrE*) (*NAmE* **overalls**, ˈ**bib overalls**) a piece of clothing that consists of trousers/pants with an extra piece of cloth covering the chest, held up by strips of cloth over the shoulders: *a pair of dungarees* ◇ *His dungarees were covered in grease.* ➲ picture at OVERALL **2** (*NAmE*) heavy cotton trousers/pants for working in

dun·geon /ˈdʌndʒən/ *noun* a dark underground room used as a prison, especially in a castle

dung·heap /ˈdʌŋhi:p/ (also **dung·hill** /ˈdʌŋhɪl/) *noun* a large pile of dung, especially on a farm

dunk /dʌŋk/ *verb* **1** [T] **~ sth** (**in/into sth**) to put food quickly into liquid before eating it: *She sat reading a magazine, dunking cookies in her coffee.* **2** [T] **~ sb/sth** (*especially NAmE*) to push sb underwater for a short time, as a joke; to put sth into water: *The camera survived being dunked in the river.* **3** [I, T] **~** (**sth**) (in BASKETBALL) to jump very high and put the ball through the BASKET with great force from above

dunno /dəˈnəʊ; *NAmE* dəˈnoʊ/ (*non-standard*) a way of writing the informal spoken form of 'I don't know'

dunny /ˈdʌni/ *noun* (*pl.* -ies) (*AustralE, NZE, informal*) a toilet

dunt /dʌnt/ *verb* **~ sth** (**+ adv./prep.**) (*ScotE*) to hit or knock sb or sth ▸ **dunt** *noun*

duo /ˈdju:əʊ; *NAmE* ˈdu:oʊ/ *noun* (*pl.* -os) **1** two people who perform together or are often seen or thought of together: *the comedy duo Laurel and Hardy* ➲ compare TRIO **2** = DUET

duo·de·num /ˌdju:əˈdi:nəm; *NAmE* ˌdu:ə-/ *noun* (*pl.* **duo·de·nums** or **duo·dena** /-ˈdi:nə/) (*anatomy*) the first part of the small INTESTINE, next to the stomach ➲ VISUAL VOCAB page V48 ➲ compare ILEUM, JEJUNUM ▶ **duo·denal** /ˌdjuːəˈdiːnl; *NAmE* ˌduːə-/ *adj.*: *a duodenal ulcer*

du·op·oly /djuːˈɒpəli; *NAmE* duːˈɑː-/ *noun* (*pl.* -ies) (*business*) **1** a right to trade in a particular product or service, held by only two companies or organizations **2** a group of two companies or organizations who hold a duopoly ➲ compare MONOPOLY

D

the DUP /ˌdiː juː ˈpiː/ *abbr.* the Democratic Unionist Party (a political party in Northern Ireland that wants it to remain a part of the United Kingdom)

du·patta /dʊˈpʌtə/ *noun* a long piece of material worn around the head and neck by women in S Asia, usually with a SALWAR or GHAGRA

dupe /djuːp; *NAmE* duːp/ *verb, noun*
■ ***verb*** to trick or cheat sb: **~ sb** *They soon realized they had been duped.* ◇ **~ sb into doing sth** *He was duped into giving them his credit card.*
■ ***noun*** (*formal*) a person who is tricked or cheated

du·plex /ˈdjuːpleks; *NAmE* ˈduː-/ *noun* (*especially NAmE*) **1** a building divided into two separate homes ➲ VISUAL VOCAB page V14 **2** a flat/apartment with rooms on two floors

du·pli·cate *verb, adj., noun*
■ ***verb*** /ˈdjuːplɪkeɪt; *NAmE* ˈduː-/ **1** [often passive] **~ sth** to make an exact copy of sth: *a duplicated form* **2 ~ sth** to do sth again, especially when it is unnecessary: *There's no point in duplicating work already done.* ▶ **du·pli·ca·tion** /ˌdjuːplɪˈkeɪʃn; *NAmE* ˌduː-/ *noun* [U, C]
■ ***adj.*** /ˈdjuːplɪkət; *NAmE* ˈduː-/ [only before noun] exactly like sth else; made as a copy of sth else: *a duplicate invoice*
■ ***noun*** /ˈdjuːplɪkət; *NAmE* ˈduː-/ one of two or more things that are the same in every detail SYN **copy**: *Is this a duplicate or the original?*
IDM **in duplicate** (of documents, etc.) as two copies that are exactly the same in every detail: *to prepare a contract in duplicate* ➲ compare TRIPLICATE

du·pli·city /djuːˈplɪsəti; *NAmE* duː-/ *noun* [U] (*formal*) dishonest behaviour that is intended to make sb believe sth which is not true SYN **deceit** ▶ **du·pli·ci·tous** /djuːˈplɪsɪtəs; *NAmE* duː-/ *adj.*

dur·able /ˈdjʊərəbl; *NAmE* ˈdʊr-/ *adj.* likely to last for a long time without breaking or getting weaker: *durable plastics* ◇ *negotiations for a durable peace* ▶ **dur·abil·ity** /ˌdjʊərəˈbɪləti; *NAmE* ˌdʊr-/ *noun* [U]: *the durability of gold* ➲ see also CONSUMER DURABLES

ˌdurable ˈgoods (*NAmE*) (*BrE* **conˌsumer ˈdurables**) *noun* [pl.] (*business*) goods which are expected to last for a long time after they have been bought, such as cars, televisions, etc.

dur·ation AW /djuˈreɪʃn; *NAmE* du-/ *noun* [U] (*formal*) the length of time that sth lasts or continues: *The school was used as a hospital for the duration of the war.* ◇ *a contract of three years' duration*
IDM **for the duration** (*informal*) until the end of a particular situation

dura·tive /ˈdjʊərətɪv; *NAmE* ˈdʊr-/ *adj.* (*grammar*) (of a verb tense, a word, etc.) describing an action that continues for some time

dur·ess /djuˈres; *NAmE* du-/ *noun* [U] (*formal*) threats or force that are used to make sb do sth: *He signed the confession* ***under duress***.

Durex™ /ˈdjʊəreks; *NAmE* ˈdjʊr-/ *noun* (*pl.* **Durex**) (*BrE*) a CONDOM

dur·ian /ˈdʊəriən; *NAmE* ˈdʊr-/ *noun* a large tropical fruit with a strong unpleasant smell but a sweet flavour ➲ VISUAL VOCAB page V26

dur·ing 0-w /ˈdjʊərɪŋ; *NAmE* ˈdʊr-/ *prep.*
1 0-w all through a period of time: *during the 1990s* ◇ *There are extra flights to Colorado during the winter.* ◇ *Please remain seated during the performance.* **2** 0-w at some point in a period of time: *He was taken to the hospital during the night.* ◇ *I only saw her once during my stay in Rome.*
HELP **During** is used to say when something happens; **for** answers the question 'how long?': *I stayed in London for a week.* ◇ ~~*I stayed in London during a week.*~~

durrie *noun* = DHURRIE

durum /ˈdjʊərəm; *NAmE* ˈdʊrəm/ (also **ˌdurum ˈwheat**) *noun* [U] a type of hard WHEAT, used to make PASTA

dusk /dʌsk/ *noun* [U] the time of day when the light has almost gone, but it is not yet dark SYN **twilight**: *The street lights go on* ***at dusk***. ➲ compare DAWN

dusky /ˈdʌski/ *adj.* (*literary*) not very bright; dark or soft in colour: *the dusky light inside the cave* ◇ *dusky pink*

dust 0-w /dʌst/ *noun, verb*
■ ***noun*** **1** 0-w [U] a fine powder that consists of very small pieces of sand, earth, etc: *A cloud of dust rose as the truck drove off.* ◇ *The workers wear masks to avoid inhaling the dust.* ➲ see also COSMIC DUST ➲ SYNONYMS at SOIL **2** 0-w the fine powder of dirt that forms in buildings, on furniture, floors, etc: *The books were all covered with dust.* ◇ *There wasn't a* ***speck of dust*** *anywhere in the room.* ◇ *That guitar's been sitting* ***gathering dust*** (= not being used) *for years now.* **3** a fine powder that consists of very small pieces of a particular substance: ***coal/gold dust*** ➲ see also DUSTY
IDM **leave sb in the ˈdust** (*NAmE*) to leave sb far behind **let the dust settle** | **wait for the dust to settle** to wait for a situation to become clear or certain ➲ more at BITE *v.*
■ ***verb*** **1** 0-w [I, T] to clean furniture, a room, etc. by removing dust from surfaces with a cloth: *I broke the vase while I was dusting.* ◇ **~ sth** *Could you dust the sitting room?* **2** [T] **~ sth** (**+ adv./prep.**) to remove dirt from sb/sth/yourself with your hands or a brush: *She dusted some ash from her sleeve.* **3** [T] **~ sth** (**with sth**) to cover sth with fine powder: *Dust the cake with sugar.* IDM see DONE
PHR V **ˌdust sb/sth↔ˈdown** (*especially BrE*) to remove dust, dirt, etc. from sb/sth: *Mel stood up and dusted herself down.* **ˌdust sb/sth↔ˈoff** to remove dust, dirt, etc. from sb/sth: (*figurative*) *For the concert, he dusted off some of his old hits.*

dust·ball /ˈdʌstbɔːl/ *noun* (*NAmE*) a mass of dust and small pieces of thread, hair, material, etc. ➲ compare DUST BUNNY

dust·bin /ˈdʌstbɪn/ (*BrE*) (*NAmE* **ˈgarbage can**, **ˈtrash can**) *noun* a large container with a lid, used for putting rubbish/garbage in, usually kept outside the house ➲ VISUAL VOCAB page V17 ➲ note at RUBBISH

ˈdust bowl *noun* an area of land that has been turned into desert by lack of rain or too much farming

ˈdust bunny *noun* (*NAmE, informal*) a DUSTBALL

dust·cart /ˈdʌstkɑːt; *NAmE* -kɑːrt/ (*BrE*) (*NAmE* **ˈgarbage truck**) *noun* a vehicle for collecting rubbish/garbage from outside houses, etc.

ˈdust cover *noun* **1** = DUST JACKET **2** a hard or soft plastic cover on a piece of equipment, etc. that protects it when it is not being used

ˈdust devil *noun* a small column of dust over land, caused by the wind

dust·er /ˈdʌstə(r)/ *noun* **1** a cloth for removing dust from furniture ➲ VISUAL VOCAB page V17 **2** (*old-fashioned, NAmE*) a piece of clothing that you wear over your other clothes when you are cleaning the house, etc. **3** (*NAmE*) a long coat that was worn by COWBOYS

ˈdust jacket (also **ˈdust cover**) *noun* a paper cover on a book that protects it but that can be removed

dust·man /ˈdʌstmən/ *noun* (*pl.* **-men** /-mən/) (also *informal* **bin·man**, *formal* **ˈrefuse collector**) (all *BrE*) (*NAmE* **ˈgarbage man**) a person whose job is to remove waste from outside houses, etc. ➲ note at RUBBISH

ˈdust mite (also **ˈhouse dust mite**) *noun* a very small creature that lives in houses and can cause ALLERGIES

dust·pan /ˈdʌstpæn/ *noun* a small flat container with a handle into which dust is brushed from the floor ➲ VISUAL VOCAB page V17

ˈdust sheet (*BrE*) (*NAmE* **ˈdrop cloth**) *noun* a large sheet that is used to protect floors, furniture, etc. from dust or paint

ˈdust storm *noun* a storm that carries clouds of dust in the wind over a wide area

ˈdust-up *noun* (*BrE, informal*) an argument or fight

dusty /ˈdʌsti/ *adj.* (**dust·ier, dusti·est**) **1** full of dust; covered with dust: *a dusty road* ◇ *piles of dusty books* ➲ SYNONYMS at DIRTY **2** (of a colour) not bright; dull: *dusty pink*

Dutch /dʌtʃ/ *adj.* of or connected with the Netherlands, its people or its language
IDM **go Dutch (with sb)** to share the cost of sth with sb

ˌDutch ˈauction *noun* a sale in which the price of an item is reduced until sb offers to buy it

ˌDutch ˈbarn *noun* (*BrE*) a farm building without walls that has a roof supported on poles, and is used for storing HAY (= dried grass), etc.

ˌDutch ˈcourage *noun* [U] (*BrE, informal*) the false courage or confidence that a person gets from drinking alcohol

ˌDutch ˈdoor (*NAmE*) (*BrE* **ˌstable ˈdoor**) *noun* a door which is divided into two parts so that the top part can be left open while the bottom part is kept shut

ˌDutch ˈelm disease *noun* [U] a disease that kills ELM trees

duti·ful /ˈdjuːtɪfl; *NAmE* ˈduː-/ *adj.* doing everything that you are expected to do; willing to obey and to show respect SYN **obedient**: *a dutiful daughter/son/wife* ▸ **duti·ful·ly** /-fəli/ *adv.*

duty 0-ᴡ /ˈdjuːti; *NAmE* ˈduːti/ *noun* (*pl.* -ies)
1 0-ᴡ [C, U] something that you feel you have to do because it is your moral or legal responsibility: *It is my duty to report it to the police.* ◇ *Local councillors* ***have a duty to*** *serve the community.* ◇ *I don't want you to visit me simply out of* ***a sense of duty.*** ◇ *your duties as a parent* ◇ *to* ***do your duty*** *for your country* **2** 0-ᴡ [U] the work that is your job: ***Report for duty*** *at 8 a.m.* ➲ see also NIGHT DUTY **3** 0-ᴡ **duties** [pl.] tasks that are part of your job: *I spend a lot of my time on administrative duties.* ◇ *Your duties will include setting up a new computer system.* ➲ see also HEAVY-DUTY ➲ SYNONYMS at TASK **4** 0-ᴡ [C, U] a tax that you pay on things that you buy, especially those that you bring into a country: ***customs/excise/import duties*** ◇ **~ on sth** *duty on wine and beer* ➲ SYNONYMS at TAX ➲ see also DEATH DUTY, STAMP DUTY
IDM **on/off duty** 0-ᴡ (of nurses, police officers, etc.) working/not working at a particular time: *Who's on duty today?* ◇ *What time do you go off duty?* ➲ see also OFF-DUTY ➲ more at BOUNDEN, LINE *n.*

ˌduty-ˈbound *adj.* [not before noun] (*formal*) having to do sth because it is your duty: *I felt duty-bound to help him.*

ˌduty-ˈfree *adj.* (of goods) that you can bring into a country without paying tax on them: *duty-free cigarettes* ▸ **ˌduty-ˈfree** *adv.* **ˌduty-ˈfree** *noun*: (*BrE, informal*) *We bought a load of duty-frees* (= duty-free goods) *at the airport.*

ˌduty-ˈfree shop (also **ˌduty-ˈfree**) *noun* a shop/store in an airport or on a ship, etc. that sells goods such as cigarettes, alcohol, PERFUME, etc. without tax on them

ˈduty officer *noun* the officer, for example in the police, army, etc, who is on duty at a particular time in a particular place

duvet /ˈduːveɪ; *NAmE* also duːˈveɪ/ (also **ˌcontinental ˈquilt, quilt**) *noun* (all *BrE*) a large cloth bag that is filled with feathers or other soft material and that you have on top of you in bed to keep yourself warm: *a* ***duvet cover*** (= a cover that you can wash, that you put over a duvet) ➲ VISUAL VOCAB page V20

ˈduvet day *noun* (*BrE, informal*) a day when you stay at home instead of going to work because you feel tired and want to rest but are not ill ➲ compare PERSONAL DAY

DVD 0-ᴡ /ˌdiː viː ˈdiː/ *noun*
a disk on which large amounts of information, especially photographs and video, can be stored, for use on a computer or **DVD player** (the abbreviation for 'digital videodisc' or 'digital versatile disc'): *a DVD-ROM drive* ◇ *Is it available* ***on DVD*** *yet?* ➲ COLLOCATIONS at CINEMA ➲ VISUAL VOCAB page V54

DVD-A /ˌdiː viː diː ˈeɪ/ *noun* a type of DVD that stores sound of very high quality (the abbreviation for 'digital versatile disc audio')

ˌDVˈD burn·er (also **ˌDVˈD writer**) *noun* a piece of equipment used for recording from a computer onto a DVD

DVD-R /ˌdiː viː diː ˈɑː(r)/ *noun* a type of DVD that you can use only once to record data (the abbreviation for 'digital versatile disc recordable')

DVD-ROM /ˌdiː viː diː ˈrɒm; *NAmE* ˈrɑːm/ *noun* a type of DVD that allows you to store data but not to record it (the abbreviation for 'digital versatile disc read-only memory')

DVD-RW /ˌdiː viː diː ɑː ˈdʌbljuː; *NAmE* ɑːr/ *noun* a type of DVD that you can use many times to record data (the abbreviation for 'digital versatile disc rewritable')

DVR /ˌdiː viː ˈɑː(r)/ *noun* a device that records video onto a hard disk or other memory device, using digital technology (the abbreviation for 'digital video recorder') SYN **PVR**

DVT /ˌdiː viː ˈtiː/ *abbr.* DEEP VEIN THROMBOSIS

dwaal /dwɑːl/ *noun* (*SAfrE*) a confused or very relaxed state of mind: *I was in a complete dwaal.*

dwarf /dwɔːf; *NAmE* dwɔːrf/ *noun, adj., verb*
■ ***noun*** (*pl.* **dwarfs** or **dwarves** /dwɔːvz; *NAmE* dwɔːrvz/) **1** (in stories) a creature like a small man, who has magic powers and who is usually described as living and working under the ground, especially working with metal **2** (sometimes *offensive*) an extremely small person, who will never grow to a normal size because of a physical problem; a person suffering from DWARFISM HELP There is no other word that is generally considered more acceptable.
■ ***adj.*** [only before noun] (of a plant or an animal) much smaller than the normal size: *dwarf conifers*
■ ***verb*** **~ sth** to make sth seem small or unimportant compared with sth else: *The old houses were dwarfed by the huge new tower blocks.*

dwarf·ism /ˈdwɔːfɪzəm; *NAmE* ˈdwɔːrf-/ *noun* the medical condition of being a dwarf. People who suffer from this condition are very short and often have short arms and legs.

ˌdwarf ˈplanet *noun* a round object in space that goes around the sun but is not as large as a planet and does not clear other objects from its path: *the dwarf planets Pluto, Ceres, Eris, Makemake and Haumea* ➲ compare PLUTOID

dweeb /dwiːb/ *noun* (*slang, especially NAmE*) a person, especially a boy or a man, who does not have good social skills and is not fashionable

dwell /dwel/ *verb* (**dwelt, dwelt** or **dwelled, dwelled**) [I] **+ adv./prep.** (*formal* or *literary*) to live somewhere: *For ten years she dwelled among the nomads of North America.*
PHR V **ˈdwell on/upon sth** **1** to think or talk a lot about sth, especially sth it would be better to forget: *So you made a mistake, but there's no need to dwell on it.* **2** to look at sth for a long time

dwell·er /ˈdwelə(r)/ *noun* (especially in compounds) a person or an animal that lives in the particular place that is mentioned: *apartment dwellers*

dwell·ing /ˈdwelɪŋ/ *noun* (*formal*) a house, flat/apartment, etc. where a person lives: *The development will consist of 66 dwellings and a number of offices.*

ˈdwelling house *noun* (*BrE, law*) a house that people live in, not one that is used as an office, etc.

ˈdwelling place *noun* (*old-fashioned*) the place where sb lives

DWI /ˌdiː dʌbljuː ˈaɪ/ *abbr.* (*US*) DRIVING WHILE INTOXICATED

dwin·dle /ˈdwɪndl/ *verb* [I] to become gradually less or smaller: *dwindling audiences* ◇ **~ (away) (to sth)** *Support for the party has dwindled away to nothing.* ◇ **~ (from sth) (to sth)** *Membership of the club has dwindled from 70 to 20.*

DWP /ˌdiː dʌbljuː ˈpiː/ *abbr.* (in Britain) Department for Work and Pensions

dyad /ˈdaɪæd/ *noun* **1** (*technical*) something that consists of two parts: *the mother-child dyad* **2** (*mathematics*) an OPERATOR which is the combination of two VECTORS ▸ **dyad·ic** /daɪˈædɪk/ *adj.*

dye /daɪ/ *verb, noun*
■ *verb* (**dyes, dye·ing, dyed, dyed**) to change the colour of sth, especially by using a special liquid or substance: **~ sth** *to dye fabric* ◇ **~ sth + adj.** *She dyed her hair blonde.* ➲ see also TIE-DYE
■ *noun* [C, U] a substance that is used to change the colour of things such as cloth or hair: *black dye* ◇ *hair dye* ◇ ***natural/chemical/vegetable dyes***

ˌdyed in the ˈwool *adj.* [usually before noun] (usually *disapproving*) having strong beliefs or opinions that are never going to change: *dyed-in-the-wool traditionalists* ORIGIN From the idea that wool which was dyed in its raw state gave a more even and lasting colour.

dying 0-w /ˈdaɪɪŋ/ *adj.*
1 0-w [only before noun] connected with or happening at the time of sb's death: *I will remember it* ***to my dying day.*** ◇ *her* ***dying wishes/words*** **2 the dying** *noun* [pl.] people who are dying: *doctors who care for the dying* IDM see BREATH ➲ see also DIE *v.*

dyke (also **dike**) /daɪk/ *noun* **1** a long thick wall that is built to stop water flooding onto a low area of land, especially from the sea **2** (*especially BrE*) a channel that carries water away from the land SYN **ditch** **3** (*taboo, slang*) a word for a LESBIAN, that is usually offensive

dy·nam·ic AW /daɪˈnæmɪk/ *noun, adj.*
■ *noun* **1 dynamics** [pl.] the way in which people or things behave and react to each other in a particular situation: *the dynamics of political change* ◇ ***group dynamics*** (= the way in which members of a group react to each other) **2 dynamics** [U] the science of the forces involved in movement: *fluid dynamics* ➲ compare STATICS **3** [sing.] (*formal*) a force that produces change, action or effects **4 dynamics** [pl.] (*music*) changes in volume in music
■ *adj.* **1** (*approving*) (of a person) having a lot of energy and a strong personality: *a dynamic leader* **2** (of a process) always changing and making progress OPP **static** **3** (*physics*) (of a force or power) producing movement OPP **static** **4** (*linguistics*) (of verbs) describing an action rather than a state. **Dynamic** verbs (for example *eat, grow, knock, die*) can be used in the progressive tenses. ➲ compare STATIVE ▸ **dy·nam·ic·al·ly** AW /-kli/ *adv.*

dyna·mism /ˈdaɪnəmɪzəm/ *noun* [U] energy and enthusiasm to make new things happen or to make things succeed

dyna·mite /ˈdaɪnəmaɪt/ *noun, verb*
■ *noun* [U] **1** a powerful EXPLOSIVE: *a stick of dynamite* **2** a thing that is likely to cause a violent reaction or a lot of trouble: *The abortion issue is political dynamite.* **3** (*informal, approving*) an extremely impressive or exciting person or thing: *Their new album is dynamite.*
■ *verb* **~ sth** to destroy or damage sth using dynamite

dy·namo /ˈdaɪnəməʊ; *NAmE* -moʊ/ *noun* (*pl.* -os) **1** a device for turning MECHANICAL energy (= energy from movement) into electricity; a GENERATOR **2** (*informal*) a person with a lot of energy: *the team's midfield dynamo* ◇ *She's a* ***human dynamo.***

dyn·asty /ˈdɪnəsti; *NAmE* ˈdaɪ-/ *noun* (*pl.* -ies) **1** a series of rulers of a country who all belong to the same family: *the Nehru-Gandhi dynasty* **2** a period of years during which members of a particular family rule a country ▸ **dyn·as·tic** /dɪˈnæstɪk; *NAmE* daɪ-/ *adj.* [usually before noun]: *dynastic history*

dys·en·tery /ˈdɪsəntri; *NAmE* -teri/ *noun* [U] an infection of the BOWELS that causes severe DIARRHOEA with loss of blood

dys·func·tion /dɪsˈfʌŋkʃn/ *noun* [U, C] **1** (*medical*) the fact of a part of the body not working normally: *He's suffering from sexual dysfunction caused by depression.* **2** the situation when the relationships within a society, family, etc. are not working normally: *a tale of loneliness and family dysfunction*

dys·func·tion·al /dɪsˈfʌŋkʃənl/ *adj.* (*technical*) not working normally or properly: *children from dysfunctional families*

dys·lexia /dɪsˈleksiə/ *noun* [U] a slight DISORDER of the brain that causes difficulty in reading and spelling, for example, but does not affect intelligence ▸ **dys·lex·ic** /dɪsˈleksɪk/ *adj.*: *He's dyslexic.* **dys·lex·ic** *noun*: *writing courses for dyslexics*

dys·mor·phia /dɪsˈmɔːfiə; *NAmE* -ˈmɔːrf-/ *noun* [U] (*medical*) a condition in which a part of the body grows larger than normal ▸ **dys·morph·ic** /dɪsˈmɔːfɪk; *NAmE* -ˈmɔːrf-/ *adj.*

dys·pep·sia /dɪsˈpepsiə; *NAmE* dɪsˈpepʃə/ *noun* [U] (*medical*) pain caused by difficulty in DIGESTING food SYN **indigestion**

dys·pep·tic /dɪsˈpeptɪk/ *adj.* **1** (*medical*) connected with or suffering from dyspepsia **2** (*formal*) bad-tempered

dys·phoria /dɪsˈfɔːriə/ *noun* [U] (*medical*) a state of worry or general unhappiness ➲ compare EUPHORIA ▸ **dys·phor·ic** /dɪsˈfɒrɪk; *NAmE* -ˈfɔːr-/ *adj.*

dys·prax·ia /dɪsˈpræksiə/ *noun* [U] a condition of the brain which causes children to have difficulties, for example with physical movement, with writing neatly, and with organizing themselves

dys·pro·sium /dɪsˈprəʊziəm; *NAmE* -ˈproʊ-/ *noun* [U] (*symb.* Dy) a chemical element. Dysprosium is a soft silver-white metal used in nuclear research.

dys·to·pia /dɪsˈtəʊpiə; *NAmE* -ˈtoʊ-/ *noun* an imaginary place or state in which everything is extremely bad or unpleasant ➲ compare UTOPIA ▸ **dys·to·pian** /dɪsˈtəʊpiən; *NAmE* -ˈtoʊ-/ (also **dys·top·ic** /dɪsˈtɒpɪk; *NAmE* -ˈtɑːp-/) *adj.*

dys·trophy ➲ MUSCULAR DYSTROPHY

Ee

E /iː/ *noun, abbr.*

■ ***noun*** (also **e**) [C, U] (*pl.* Es, E's, e's /iːz/) **1** the fifth letter in the English alphabet: *'Egg' begins with (an) E/'E'.* **2 E** (*music*) the third note in the SCALE of C MAJOR **3 E** the fifth highest mark/grade that a student can get for a piece of work, showing that it is very bad: *He got an **E in/for** French.* ➲ see also E-NUMBER

■ ***abbr.*** **1** East; Eastern: *E Asia* **2** (*slang*) the drug ECSTASY: *She had taken an E.*

e- /iː/ *combining form* (in nouns and verbs) connected with the use of electronic communication, especially the Internet, for sending information, doing business, etc: *e-commerce* ◇ *e-business* ➲ see also E-FIT, EMAIL

each 🔑 /iːtʃ/ *det., pron.*
used to refer to every one of two or more people or things, when you are thinking about them separately: *Each answer is worth 20 points.* ◇ *Each of the answers is worth 20 points.* ◇ *The answers are worth 20 points each.* ◇ *'Red or blue?' 'I'll take one of each, please.'* ◇ *We each have our own car.* ◇ *There aren't enough books for everyone to have one each.* ◇ *They lost $40 each.* ◇ *Each day that passed he grew more and more desperate.*

Grammar Point

each / every

- **Each** is used in front of a singular noun and is followed by a singular verb: *Each student has been given his or her own email address.* The use of *his* or *her* sometimes sounds slightly formal and it is becoming more common to use the plural pronoun *their*: *Each student has been given their own email address.*
- When **each** is used after a plural subject, it has a plural verb: *They each have their own email address.*
- **Every** is always followed by a singular verb: *Every student in the class is capable of passing the exam.*
- **Each of**, **each one of** and **every one of** are followed by a plural noun or pronoun, but the verb is usually singular: *Each (one) of the houses was slightly different.* ◇ *I bought a dozen eggs and every one of them was bad.* A plural verb is more informal.

each 'other 🔑 *pron.*
used as the object of a verb or preposition to show that each member of a group does sth to or for the other members: *Don and Susie really loved each other* (= he loved her and she loved him). ◇ *They looked at each other and laughed.* ◇ *We can wear each other's clothes.*

ˌeach 'way *adv., adj.* (*BrE*) if you bet money **each way** on a race, you win if your horse, etc. comes first, second or third in the race: *She put £5 each way on the favourite.* ◇ *an each-way bet*

eager /ˈiːɡə(r)/ *adj.* very interested and excited by sth that is going to happen or about sth that you want to do **SYN keen**: *eager crowds outside the stadium* ◇ **~ for sth** *She is eager for* (= wants very much to get) *her parents' approval.* ◇ **~ to do sth** *Everyone in the class seemed eager to learn.* ◇ *They're **eager to please*** (= wanting to be helpful). ▶ **eager·ly** *adv.*: *the band's eagerly awaited new CD* **eager·ness** *noun* [U, sing.]: *I couldn't hide my eagerness to get back home.*

ˌeager 'beaver *noun* (*informal*) an enthusiastic person who works very hard

eagle /ˈiːɡl/ *noun* **1** a large BIRD OF PREY (= a bird that kills other creatures for food) with a sharp curved beak and very good sight: *eagles soaring overhead* ➲ see also BALD EAGLE, GOLDEN EAGLE **2** (in GOLF) a score of two strokes less than the standard score for a hole (= two under PAR) ➲ compare BIRDIE, BOGEY

ˌeagle 'eye *noun* [usually sing.] if sb has an **eagle eye**, they watch things carefully and are good at noticing things: *Nothing escaped our teacher's eagle eye.* ▶ **ˌeagle-'eyed** *adj.* **SYN hawk-eyed**: *An eagle-eyed tourist found the suspicious package.*

eag·let /ˈiːɡlət/ *noun* a young eagle

EAL /ˌiː eɪ ˈel/ *abbr.* (in the UK and Ireland) English as an additional language (refers to the teaching of English in schools to children whose first language is not English) ➲ compare EFL, ESL, ESOL

EAP /ˌiː eɪ ˈpiː/ *abbr.* ENGLISH FOR ACADEMIC PURPOSES

ear 🔑 /ɪə(r); *NAmE* ɪr/ *noun*
1 🔑 [C] either of the organs on the sides of the head that you hear with: *an ear infection* ◇ *the **inner/outer ear*** ◇ *She whispered something in his ear.* ◇ *He put his hands over his ears.* ◇ *She's had her ears pierced.* ◇ *The elephant flapped its ears.* ◇ *He was always there with a sympathetic ear* (= a willingness to listen to people). ➲ **VISUAL VOCAB** page V48 ➲ see also CAULIFLOWER EAR, GLUE EAR, MIDDLE EAR **2 -eared** (in adjectives) having the type of ears mentioned: *a long-eared owl* **3** [sing.] an ability to recognize and copy sounds well: *You need a good ear to master the piano.* **4** [C] the top part of a grain plant, such as WHEAT, that contains the seeds: *ears of corn* ➲ **VISUAL VOCAB** page V28

IDM be all 'ears (*informal*) to be waiting with interest to hear what sb has to say: *'Do you know what he said?' 'Go on—I'm all ears.'* **be out on your 'ear** (*informal*) to be forced to leave (a job, etc.) **be up to your ears in sth** to have a lot of sth to deal with: *We're up to our ears in work.* **sth comes to/reaches sb's 'ears** somebody hears about sth, especially when other people already know about it: *News of his affair eventually reached her ears.* **sb's 'ears are burning** a person thinks that other people are talking about them, especially in an unkind way: *'I bumped into your ex-wife last night.' 'I thought I could feel my ears burning!'* **sb's 'ears are flapping** (*BrE, informal*) a person is trying to listen to sb else's conversation **go in 'one ear and out the 'other** (*informal*) (of information, etc.) to be forgotten quickly: *Everything I tell them just goes in one ear and out the other.* **have sth coming out of your 'ears** (*informal*) to have a lot of sth, especially more than you need **have sb's ear | have the ear of sb** to be able to give sb advice, influence them, etc. because they trust you: *He had the ear of the monarch.* **keep/have your ear to the 'ground** to make sure that you always find out about the most recent developments in a particular situation **play (sth) by 'ear** to play music by remembering how it sounds rather than by reading it **play it by 'ear** (*informal*) to decide how to deal with a situation as it develops rather than by having a plan to follow: *I don't know what they'll want when they arrive—we'll have to play it by ear.* **shut/close your 'ears to sth** to refuse to listen to sth: *She decided to shut her ears to all the rumours.* **smile/grin/beam from ear to 'ear** to be smiling, etc. a lot because you are very pleased about sth **with half an 'ear** without giving your full attention to what is being said, etc. ➲ more at BELIEVE, BEND *v.*, BOX *n.*, BOX *v.*, COCK *v.*, DEAF *adj.*, EASY *adj.*, FEEL *v.*, FLEA, LEND, MUSIC, OPEN *adj.*, PIG *n.*, PRICK *v.*, RING *v.*, SILK, THICK *adj.*, WALL *n.*, WET *adj.*, WORD *n.*

ear·ache /ˈɪəreɪk; *NAmE* ˈɪr-/ *noun* [U, C] pain inside the ear: *to have (an) earache*

ear·bash·ing /ˈɪəbæʃɪŋ; *NAmE* ˈɪr-/ *noun* [sing.] (*BrE, informal*) an occasion where sb criticizes a person in an angry way

ear·bud /ˈɪəbʌd; *NAmE* ˈɪr-/ *noun* [usually pl.] a very small HEADPHONE that is worn inside the ear ➲ **VISUAL VOCAB** page V54

'ear drops *noun* [pl.] liquid medicine that can be put into the ears

ear·drum /ˈɪədrʌm; *NAmE* ˈɪr-/ *noun* the piece of thin tightly stretched skin inside the ear which is moved by sound waves, making you able to hear: *a perforated eardrum*

ear·ful /ˈɪəfʊl; *NAmE* ˈɪrfʊl/ *noun* [sing.] (*informal*) if sb gives you an **earful**, they tell you for a long time how angry they are about sth

ear·hole /ˈɪəhəʊl; *NAmE* ˈɪrhoʊl/ *noun* (*informal*) the outer opening of the ear

earl /ɜːl; *NAmE* ɜːrl/ *noun* a NOBLEMAN of high rank: *the Earl of Essex* ➲ see also COUNTESS

ˌEarl ˈGrey *noun* [U] a type of tea flavoured with BERGAMOT

E

earli·est /ˈɜːliɪst; *NAmE* ˈɜːrl-/ *noun* [sing.] **the earliest** the time before which sth cannot happen: *The earliest we can finish is next Friday.* ◇ *We can't finish before next Friday **at the earliest**.*

ˈear lobe (also **lobe**) *noun* the soft part at the bottom of the ear ➲ VISUAL VOCAB page V48

early 🔑 /ˈɜːli; *NAmE* ˈɜːrli/ *adj., adv.*

■ ***adj.*** (earl·ier, earli·est) **1** 🔑 near the beginning of a period of time, an event etc: *the early morning* ◇ *my earliest memories* ◇ *The project is still in the early stages.* ◇ *the early 1990s* ◇ *in **the early days of** space exploration* (= when it was just beginning) ◇ *The earliest possible date I can make it is the third.* ◇ *He's in his early twenties.* ◇ *Mozart's early works* (= those written at the beginning of his career) ◇ *Early booking is essential, as space is limited.* **2** 🔑 arriving, or done before the usual, expected or planned time: *You're early! I wasn't expecting you till seven.* ◇ *The bus was ten minutes early.* ◇ *an early breakfast* ◇ *Let's **make an early start** tomorrow.* ◇ *She's an **early riser*** (= she gets up early in the morning). ◇ *He learnt to play the piano at an **early age**.* ◇ *early potatoes* (= that are ready to eat at the beginning of the season) OPP **late** ▸ **earli·ness** *noun* [U]

IDM **an ˈearly bird** (*humorous*) a person who gets up, arrives, etc. very early **at your earliest conˈvenience** (*business*) as soon as possible: *Please telephone at your earliest convenience.* **the ˌearly bird catches the ˈworm** (*saying*) the person who takes the opportunity to do sth before other people will have an advantage over them **it's early ˈdays (yet)** (*BrE*) used to say that it is too soon to be sure how a situation will develop ➲ more at BRIGHT *adj.*, HOUR, NIGHT

■ ***adv.*** (earl·ier, earli·est) **1** 🔑 near the beginning of a period of time, an event, a piece of work, etc: ***early in the week/year/season/morning*** ◇ *The best rooms go to those who book earliest.* ◇ *We arrived early the next day.* ◇ *He started writing music as early as 1989.* OPP **late 2** 🔑 before the usual, expected or planned time: *The bus came five minutes early.* ◇ *I woke up early this morning.* ◇ *The baby arrived earlier than expected.* OPP **late 3** 🔑 **earlier** before the present time or the time mentioned: *As I mentioned earlier ...* ◇ *a week earlier* ◇ *She had seen him earlier in the day.* OPP **later**

IDM **early ˈon** 🔑 at an early stage of a situation, relationship, period of time, etc: *I knew quite early on that I wanted to marry her.*

ˌearly ˈclosing *noun* [U] (*BrE*) the practice of closing shops on a particular afternoon every week (now no longer very common)

ˌearly ˈwarning *noun* [U, sing.] a thing that tells you in advance that sth serious or dangerous is going to happen: *an early warning of heart disease* ◇ *an early warning system* (= of enemy attack)

ear·mark /ˈɪəmɑːk; *NAmE* ˈɪrmɑːrk/ *verb, noun*

■ ***verb*** [usually passive] to decide that sth will be used for a particular purpose, or to state that sth will happen to sb/sth in the future: **~ sb/sth (for sb/sth)** *The money had been earmarked for spending on new school buildings.* ◇ *The factory has been earmarked for closure.* ◇ **~ sb/sth (as sb/sth)** *She was earmarked early as a possible champion.*

■ ***noun*** [usually pl.] (*NAmE*) a feature or quality that is typical of sb/sth: *The incident has all the earmarks of a terrorist attack.*

ear·muffs /ˈɪəmʌfs; *NAmE* ˈɪrmʌfs/ *noun* [pl.] a pair of coverings for the ears connected by a band across the top of the head, and worn to protect the ears, especially from cold: *a pair of earmuffs*

earn 🔑 /ɜːn; *NAmE* ɜːrn/ *verb*

1 🔑 [T, I] to get money for work that you do: **~ (sth)** *He earns about $40 000 a year.* ◇ *She **earned a living** as a part-time secretary.* ◇ *She must **earn a fortune*** (= earn a lot of money). ◇ *All the children are earning now.* ◇ **~ sb sth** *His victory in the tournament earned him $50 000.* ➲ COLLOCATIONS at FINANCE **2** 🔑 [T] **~ sth** to get money as profit or interest on money you lend, have in a bank, etc: *Your money would earn more in a high-interest account.* **3** 🔑 [T] to get sth that you deserve, usually because of sth good you have done or because of the good qualities you have: **~ sth** *He earned a reputation as an expert on tax law.* ◇ *As a teacher, she had earned the respect of her students.* ◇ *I need a rest. I think I've earned it, don't you?* ◇ *She's having a well-earned rest this week.* ◇ **~ sb sth** *His outstanding ability earned him a place on the team.*

IDM **ˌearn a/your ˈcrust** (*BrE, informal*) to earn enough money to live on **ˌearn your ˈkeep 1** to do useful or helpful things in return for being allowed to live or stay somewhere **2** to be worth the amount of time or money that is being spent: *He felt he no longer deserved such a high salary. He just wasn't earning his keep.* ➲ more at SPUR *n.*

ˌearned ˈrun *noun* (in BASEBALL) a RUN scored without the help of errors by the opposing team

earn·er /ˈɜːnə(r); *NAmE* ˈɜːrn-/ *noun* **1** a person who earns money for a job that they do: ***high/low earners*** ➲ see also WAGE EARNER **2** an activity or a business that makes a profit: *Tourism is the country's biggest foreign currency earner.* ◇ (*BrE, informal*) *Her new business has turned out to be a **nice little earner**.*

earn·est /ˈɜːnɪst; *NAmE* ˈɜːrn-/ *adj.* very serious and sincere: *an earnest young man* ◇ *Despite her earnest efforts, she could not find a job.* ▸ **earn·est·ly** *adv.* **earn·est·ness** *noun* [U]

IDM **in ˈearnest 1** more seriously and with more force or effort than before: *The work on the house will **begin in earnest** on Monday.* **2** very serious and sincere about what you are saying and about your intentions; in a way that shows that you are serious: *You may laugh but I'm in **deadly earnest**.* ◇ *I could tell she spoke in earnest.*

earn·ings /ˈɜːnɪŋz; *NAmE* ˈɜːrn-/ *noun* [pl.] **1** the money that you earn for the work that you do: *a rise in average earnings* ◇ *compensation for loss of earnings caused by the accident* ➲ SYNONYMS at INCOME **2** the profit that a company makes: *earnings per share* ◇ *export earnings* ➲ COLLOCATIONS at BUSINESS

ˌearnings-reˈlated *adj.* (*BrE*) (of payments, etc.) connected to and changing according to the amount of money that you earn: *an earnings-related pension scheme*

ear·phones /ˈɪəfəʊnz; *NAmE* ˈɪrfoʊnz/ *noun* [pl.] = HEADPHONES

ear·piece /ˈɪəpiːs; *NAmE* ˈɪrpiːs/ *noun* the part of a telephone or piece of electrical equipment that you hold next to or put into your ear so that you can listen

ˈear-piercing *adj., noun*

■ ***adj.*** [only before noun] very high, loud and unpleasant: *an ear-piercing scream*

■ ***noun*** [U] the practice of making small holes in sb's ears so jewellery can be put in them

ear·plug /ˈɪəplʌɡ; *NAmE* ˈɪrp-/ *noun* [usually pl.] a piece of soft material that you put into your ear to keep out noise or water

ear·ring /ˈɪərɪŋ; *NAmE* ˈɪrɪŋ/ *noun* a piece of jewellery that you fasten in or on your ear: *a pair of earrings* ➲ VISUAL VOCAB page V53

ear·set /ˈɪəset; *NAmE* ˈɪrset/ *noun* a piece of equipment that fits into your ear and has a MICROPHONE attached to it. It is connected to a telephone and allows you to use the telephone without using your hands.

ear·shot /ˈɪəʃɒt; *NAmE* ˈɪrʃɑːt/ *noun*

IDM **out of ˈearshot (of sb/sth)** too far away to hear sb/sth or to be heard: *We waited until Ted was safely out of earshot before discussing it.* **within ˈearshot (of sb/sth)** near enough to hear sb/sth or to be heard: *As she came within earshot of the group, she heard her name mentioned.*

'ear-splitting *adj.* extremely loud

earth /ɜːθ; *NAmE* ɜːrθ/ *noun, verb*

▪ ***noun* 1** (also **Earth**), **the Earth** [U, sing.] the world; the planet that we live on: *the* ***planet Earth*** ◇ *the history of* ***life on earth*** ◇ *the earth's ozone layer* ◇ *The earth revolves around the sun.* ◇ *I must be the happiest person* ***on earth!*** **2** [U, sing.] land; the hard surface of the world that is not the sea or the sky; the ground: *After a week at sea, it was good to feel the earth beneath our feet again.* ◇ *You could feel the earth shake as the truck came closer.* ➲ SYNONYMS at FLOOR **3** [U] the substance that plants grow in: *a* ***clod/lump/mound of earth*** ➲ SYNONYMS at SOIL **4** [C] the hole where an animal, especially a FOX, lives **5** (*BrE*) (*NAmE* **ground**) [C, usually sing.] a wire that connects an electric CIRCUIT with the ground and makes it safe

IDM **charge, cost, pay, etc. the 'earth** (*BrE, informal*) to charge, etc. a lot of money **come back/down to 'earth (with a 'bang/'bump)** | **bring sb (back) down to 'earth (with a 'bang/'bump)** (*informal*) to return, or to make sb return, to a normal way of thinking or behaving after a time when they have been very excited, not very practical, etc. ➲ see also DOWN TO EARTH **go to 'earth/'ground** (*BrE*) to hide, especially to escape from sb who is chasing you **how, why, where, who, etc. on 'earth** (*informal*) used to emphasize the question you are asking when you are surprised or angry or cannot think of an obvious answer: *What on earth are you doing?* ◇ *How on earth can she afford that?* **be, feel, look, taste, etc. like nothing on 'earth** (*informal*) to be, feel, look, taste, etc. very bad **on 'earth** used after negative nouns or pronouns to emphasize what you are saying: *Nothing on earth would persuade me to go with him.* **run sb/sth to 'earth/'ground** (*BrE*) to find sb/sth after looking hard for a long time ➲ more at END *n.*, FACE *n.*, MOVE *v.*, PROMISE *v.*, SALT *n.*, WIPE *v.*

▪ ***verb*** (*BrE*) (*NAmE* **ground**) [usually passive] **~ sth** to make electrical equipment safe by connecting it to the ground with a wire

earth·bound /'ɜːθbaʊnd; *NAmE* 'ɜːrθ-/ *adj.* **1** unable to leave the surface of the earth: *birds and their earthbound predators* **2** (*literary*) not spiritual or having much imagination

earth·en /'ɜːθn; *NAmE* 'ɜːrθn/ *adj.* [only before noun] **1** (of floors or walls) made of earth **2** (of objects) made of baked CLAY: *earthen pots*

earth·en·ware /'ɜːθnweə(r); *NAmE* 'ɜːrθnwer/ *adj.* made of very hard baked CLAY: *an earthenware bowl* ▸ **earth·en·ware** *noun* [U]

earth·ling /'ɜːθlɪŋ; *NAmE* 'ɜːrθ-/ *noun* (in SCIENCE FICTION stories) a word used by creatures from other planets to refer to a person living on the earth

earth·ly /'ɜːθli; *NAmE* 'ɜːrθ-/ *adj.* [usually before noun] **1** (*literary*) connected with life on earth and not with any spiritual life: *the sorrows of this earthly life* **2** (often used in questions and negatives for emphasis) possible: *There's* ***no earthly reason*** *why you shouldn't go.* ◇ *What earthly difference is my opinion going to make?* ◇ *He didn't have an earthly chance of getting the job.*

'earth mother *noun* **1** (also **Earth Mother**) a GODDESS who represents the earth as the source of life; a GODDESS of FERTILITY **2** (*informal*) a woman who seems very suited to being a mother

'earth mover *noun* a vehicle or machine that digs up large quantities of soil

earth·quake /'ɜːθkweɪk; *NAmE* 'ɜːrθ-/ (also *informal* **quake**) *noun* a sudden, violent shaking of the earth's surface

'earth science *noun* [C, U] a science concerned with studying the earth or part of it. Geography and GEOLOGY are both earth sciences. ➲ compare LIFE SCIENCES, NATURAL SCIENCE

'earth-shatter·ing *adj.* having a very great effect and of great importance: *an earth-shattering discovery*

earth·work /'ɜːθwɜːk; *NAmE* 'ɜːrθwɜːrk/ *noun* [usually pl.] a large bank of earth that was built long ago in the past and used as a defence

earth·worm /'ɜːθwɜːm; *NAmE* 'ɜːrθwɜːrm/ *noun* a common long thin WORM that lives in soil

earthy /'ɜːθi; *NAmE* 'ɜːrθi/ *adj.* (**earth·ier**, **earthi·est**) **1** concerned with the body, sex, etc. in an open and direct way that some people find rude or embarrassing: *an earthy sense of humour* **2** of or like earth or soil: *earthy colours* ▸ **earthi·ness** *noun* [U]

'ear trumpet *noun* a device shaped like a TRUMPET, used in the past by people who could not hear well

ear·wax /'ɪəwæks; *NAmE* 'ɪrwæks/ *noun* [U] the yellow substance produced inside the ear to protect it

ear·wig /'ɪəwɪɡ; *NAmE* 'ɪrwɪɡ/ *noun* a small brown insect with a long body and two curved pointed parts called PINCERS that stick out at the back end of its body

ease /iːz/ *noun, verb*

▪ ***noun*** [U] **1** lack of difficulty: *He passed the exam* ***with ease.*** ◇ *The ease with which she learns languages is astonishing.* ◇ *This computer is popular for its good design and* ***ease of use.*** ◇ *All important points are numbered* ***for ease of*** *reference* (= so that you can find them easily). **2** the state of feeling relaxed or comfortable without worries, problems or pain: *In his retirement, he lived a life of ease.*

IDM **(stand) at 'ease** used as a command to soldiers to tell them to stand with their feet apart and their hands behind their backs ➲ compare ATTENTION *n.* (5) **at (your) 'ease** relaxed and confident and not nervous or embarrassed: *I never feel completely at ease with him.* **put sb at (their) 'ease** to make sb feel relaxed and confident, not nervous or embarrassed ➲ more at ILL *adj.*, MIND *n.*

▪ ***verb* 1** [I, T] to become or to make sth less unpleasant, painful, severe, etc. SYN **alleviate**: *The pain immediately eased.* ◇ **~ sth** *This should help ease the pain.* ◇ *The plan should ease traffic congestion in the town.* ◇ *It would* ***ease my mind*** (= make me less worried) *to know that she was settled.* **2** [I, T] to move, or to move sb/sth, slowly and carefully: **+ adv./prep.** *He eased slowly forwards.* ◇ **~ sb/sth + adv./prep.** *She eased herself into a chair.* ◇ *He eased off* (= took off) *his shoes.* **3** [T] **~ sth** to make sth easier: *Ramps have been built to ease access for the disabled.* **4** [T, I] **~ (sth)** to make sth or to become less tight and more relaxed SYN **relax**: *Ease your grip on the wheel a little.* **5** [I, T] **~ (sth)** to become or make sth lower in price or value SYN **reduce**: *Share prices eased back from yesterday's levels.*

PHR V **'ease into sth** | **'ease yourself/sb into sth** to become or help sb to become familiar with sth new, especially a new job **ˌease 'off** | **ˌease 'off sth** to become or make sth become less strong, unpleasant, etc: *We waited until the traffic had eased off.* ◇ *Ease off the training a few days before the race.* **ˌease sb↔'out (of sth)** to force sb to leave a job or position of authority, especially by making it difficult or unpleasant for them over a period of time **ˌease 'up** **1** to reduce the speed at which you are travelling **2** to become less strong, unpleasant, etc.

ease·ful /'iːzfl/ *adj.* (*literary*) that provides comfort or peace

easel /'iːzl/ *noun* a wooden frame to hold a picture while it is being painted ➲ VISUAL VOCAB page V35

ease·ment /'iːzmənt/ *noun* [U] **1** (*law*) the right to cross or use sb's land for a particular purpose **2** (*literary*) a state or feeling of peace or happiness

eas·ily /'iːzəli/ *adv.*

1 without problems or difficulty: *I can easily finish it tonight.* ◇ *The museum is easily accessible by car.* **2** very probably; very likely: *Are you sure you locked the gate? You could easily have forgotten.* ◇ *The situation might* ***all too easily*** *have become a disaster.* **3 ~ the best, nicest, etc.** without doubt; definitely: *It's easily the best play I've seen this year.* **4** quickly; more quickly than is usual: *I get bored easily.* ◇ *He's easily distracted.*

east 0→ /iːst/ *noun, adj., adv.*

■ **noun** [U, sing.] (*abbr.* E) **1** 0→ (usually **the east**) the direction that you look towards to see the sun rise; one of the four main points of the COMPASS: *Which way is east?* ◇ *A gale was blowing from the east.* ◇ *a town **to the east of*** (= further east than) *Chicago* ➲ picture at COMPASS ➲ compare NORTH, SOUTH, WEST **2** 0→ (also **East**) the eastern part of a country, region or city: *I was born in the East, but now live in San Francisco.* **3** 0→ **the East** the countries of Asia, especially China, Japan and India **4 the East** (in the past) the Communist countries of Central and Eastern Europe: *East-West relations*

■ **adj.** [only before noun] **1** 0→ (also **East**) (*abbr.* E) in or towards the east: *East Africa* ◇ *They live on the east coast.* **2** 0→ an **east wind** blows from the east ➲ compare EASTERLY

■ **adv.** 0→ towards the east: *The house faces east.*

east·bound /ˈiːstbaʊnd/ *adj.* travelling or leading towards the east: *eastbound traffic* ◇ *the eastbound carriageway of the motorway*

ˌEast Coast ˈFever *noun* [U] a disease that cows in Africa can get by being bitten by a TICK (= a small insect), and which can kill them

the ˌEast ˈEnd *noun* an area of East London traditionally connected with working people ▸ **ˌEast ˈEnder** *noun*: *He's a real East Ender.*

Easter /ˈiːstə(r)/ *noun* **1** [U, C] (also **ˌEaster ˈDay, ˌEaster ˈSunday**) (in the Christian religion) a Sunday in March or April when Christians remember the death of Christ and his return to life **2** (also **East·er·time**) the period that includes Easter Day and the days close to it: *the Easter holidays/vacation*

ˈEaster egg *noun* **1** an egg made of chocolate that is given as a present and eaten at Easter **2** an egg with a shell that is painted and decorated at Easter

east·er·ly /ˈiːstəli; *NAmE* -ərli/ *adj., noun*

■ **adj.** [only before noun] **1** in or towards the east: *travelling in an easterly direction* **2** [usually before noun] (of winds) blowing from the east: *a cold easterly wind* ➲ compare EAST

■ **noun** (*pl.* -ies) a wind that blows from the east

east·ern 0→ /ˈiːstən; *NAmE* -ərn/ *adj.*

1 0→ (also **Eastern**) (*abbr.* E) [only before noun] located in the east or facing east: *eastern Spain* ◇ *Eastern Europe* ◇ *the eastern slopes of the mountain* **2** 0→ (usually **Eastern**) connected with the part of the world that is to the east of Europe: *Eastern cookery*

ˌEastern ˈDaylight Time *noun* [U] (*abbr.* EDT) the time used in the summer in the eastern US and Canada, which is four hours earlier than GMT

east·ern·er /ˈiːstənə(r); *NAmE* ˈiːstərnər/ *noun* a person who comes from or lives in the eastern part of a country, especially the US

east·ern·most /ˈiːstənməʊst; *NAmE* -ərnmoʊst/ *adj.* furthest east: *the easternmost city in Europe*

the ˌEastern ˌOrthodox ˈChurch *noun* = THE ORTHODOX CHURCH

ˌEastern ˈStandard Time *noun* [U] (*abbr.* EST) (also **Eastern time**) the time used in the winter in the eastern US and Canada, which is five hours earlier than GMT

ˈEastern time *noun* [U] the standard time in the eastern US and parts of Canada

East·er·time /ˈiːstətaɪm; *NAmE* ˈiːstərt-/ *noun* [U, C] = EASTER

ˌEast ˈIndian *noun* a person whose family originally came from the Indian SUBCONTINENT ▸ **ˌEast ˈIndian** *adj.*

ˌeast-north-ˈeast *noun* [sing.] (*abbr.* ENE) the direction at an equal distance between east and north-east ▸ **ˌeast-north-ˈeast** *adv.*

ˌeast-south-ˈeast *noun* [sing.] (*abbr.* ESE) the direction at an equal distance between east and south-east ▸ **ˌeast-south-ˈeast** *adv.*

east·wards /ˈiːstwədz; *NAmE* -wərdz/ (also **east·ward**) *adv.* towards the east: *to **go/look/turn eastwards*** ▸ **east·ward** *adj.*: *in an eastward direction*

easy 0→ /ˈiːzi/ *adj., adv.*

■ **adj.** (eas·ier, easi·est) **1** 0→ not difficult; done or obtained without a lot of effort or problems: *an easy exam/job* ◇ *He didn't **make it easy** for me to leave.* ◇ *Their house isn't the easiest place to get to.* ◇ *vegetables that are easy to grow* ◇ *Several schools are **within easy reach*** (= not far away). ◇ *It can't be easy for her, on her own with the children.* ◇ *It's easy for you to tell me to keep calm, but you're not in my position.* OPP **hard** **2** 0→ comfortable, relaxed and not worried: *I'll agree to anything for **an easy life**.* ◇ *I don't feel easy about letting the kids go out alone.* OPP **uneasy** **3** [only before noun] open to attack; not able to defend yourself: *She's an easy target for their criticisms.* ◇ *The baby fish are easy prey for birds.* **4** [only before noun] pleasant and friendly SYN **easy-going**: *He had a very easy manner.* OPP **awkward** **5** [not usually before noun] (*informal, disapproving*) (of women) willing to have sex with many different people ➲ see also EASILY ▸ **easi·ness** *noun* [U]

IDM **as ˌeasy as ˈanything/as ˈpie/as ABˈC/as falling off a ˈlog** (*informal*) very easy or very easily **ˌeasy ˈmoney** money that you get without having to work very hard for it **ˌeasy on the ˈear/ˈeye** (*informal*) pleasant to listen to or look at **have an easy ˈtime (of it)** (*BrE*) to have no difficulties or problems **I'm ˈeasy** (*BrE, informal*) used to say that you do not have a strong opinion when sb has offered you a choice: *'Do you want to watch this or the news?' 'Oh, I'm easy. It's up to you.'* **of easy ˈvirtue** (*old-fashioned*) (of a woman) willing to have sex with anyone **on ˈeasy street** enjoying a comfortable way of life with plenty of money **take the easy way ˈout** to end a difficult situation by choosing the simplest solution even if it is not the best one ➲ more at FREE *adj.*, OPTION, REACH *n.*, RIDE *n.*, TOUCH *n.*

■ **adv.** (eas·ier, easi·est) used to tell sb to be careful when doing sth: *Easy with that chair—one of its legs is loose.*

IDM **breathe/rest ˈeasy** to relax and stop worrying: *You can rest easy—I'm not going to tell anyone.* **be ˌeasier ˌsaid than ˈdone** (*saying*) to be much more difficult to do than to talk about: *'Why don't you get yourself a job?' 'That's easier said than done.'* **ˌeasy ˈcome, ˌeasy ˈgo** (*saying*) used to mean that sb does not care very much about money or possessions especially if they spend it or lose sth **ˌeasy ˈdoes it** (*informal*) used to tell sb to do sth, or move sth, slowly and carefully **go ˈeasy on sb** (*informal*) used to tell sb to treat a person in a gentle way and not to be too angry or severe: *Go easy on her—she's having a really hard time at the moment.* **go ˈeasy on/with sth** (*informal*) used to tell sb not to use too much of sth: *Go easy on the sugar.* **not come ˈeasy (to sb)** to be difficult for sb to do: *Talking about my problems doesn't come easy to me.* **ˌstand ˈeasy** used as a command to soldiers who are already standing AT EASE to tell them that they can stand in an even more relaxed way **ˌtake it ˈeasy** (*informal*) used to tell sb not to be worried or angry: *Take it easy! Don't panic.* **ˌtake it/things ˈeasy** to relax and avoid working too hard or doing too much: *The doctor told me to take it easy for a few weeks.*

ˈeasy-care *adj.* (of clothes or cloth) not needing to be ironed after washing

ˌeasy ˈchair *noun* a large comfortable chair: *to sit in an easy chair*

ˌeasy-ˈgoing *adj.* relaxed and happy to accept things without worrying or getting angry

ˌeasy ˈlistening *noun* [U] music that is pleasant and relaxing but that some people think is not very interesting

easy-peasy /ˌiːzi ˈpiːzi/ *adj.* (*BrE, informal*) (used especially by children) very easy

eat 0→ /iːt/ *verb* (ate /et; eɪt; *NAmE* eɪt/, eaten /ˈiːtn/)

1 0→ [I, T] to put food in your mouth, chew it and swallow it: *I was too nervous to eat.* ◇ *She doesn't eat sensibly* (= doesn't eat food that is good for her). ◇ **~ sth** *I don't eat meat.* ◇ *Would you like something to eat?* ◇ *I couldn't eat another thing* (= I have had enough food). ➲ COLLOCATIONS at DIET **2** 0→ [I] to have a meal: *Where shall we eat tonight?* ◇ *We ate at a pizzeria in town.*

IDM ˌ**eat sb aˈlive** (*informal*) **1** to criticize or punish sb severely because you are extremely angry with them **2** to defeat sb completely in an argument, a competition, etc: *The defence lawyers are going to eat you alive tomorrow.* **3** [usually passive] (of insects, etc.) to bite sb many times: *I was being eaten alive by mosquitoes.* ˌ**eat, drink and be ˈmerry** (*saying*) said to encourage sb to enjoy life now, while they can, and not to think of the future **eat your ˈheart out!** (*informal*) used to compare two things and say that one of them is better: *Look at him dance! Eat your heart out, Fred Astaire* (= he dances even better than Fred Astaire). **eat your ˈheart out (for sb/sth)** (*especially BrE*) to feel very unhappy, especially because you want sb/sth you cannot have **eat humble ˈpie** (*BrE*) (*NAmE* **eat ˈcrow**) to say and show that you are sorry for a mistake that you made **ORIGIN** From a pun on the old word **umbles**, meaning 'offal', which was considered to be food for poor people. **eat like a ˈhorse** (*informal*) to eat a lot: *She may be thin, but she eats like a horse.* **eat out of your/sb's ˈhand** to trust sb and be willing to do what they say: *She'll have them eating out of her hand in no time.* **eat sb out of ˌhouse and ˈhome** (*informal*, often *humorous*) to eat a lot of sb else's food **eat your ˈwords** to admit that what you said was wrong **I could eat a ˈhorse** (*informal*) used to say that you are very hungry **I'll eat my ˈhat** (*informal*) used to say that you think sth is very unlikely to happen: *If she's here on time, I'll eat my hat!* **what's eating him, etc?** (*informal*) used to ask what sb is annoyed or worried about ➲ more at CAKE *n.*, DOG *n.*

PHR V ˌ**eat sth↔aˈway** to reduce or destroy sth gradually **SYN** **erode**: *The coastline is being eaten away year by year.* ˌ**eat aˈway at sth/sb 1** to reduce or destroy sth gradually: *Woodworm had eaten away at the door frame.* ◇ *His constant criticism ate away at her self-confidence.* **2** to worry sb over a period of time ˈ**eat into sth 1** to use up a part of sth, especially sb's money or time: *Those repair bills have really eaten into my savings.* **2** to destroy or damage the surface of sth: *Rust had eaten into the metal.* ˌ**eat ˈout** 🗝 to have a meal in a restaurant, etc. rather than at home: *Do you feel like eating out tonight?* ˌ**eat ˈup** | ˌ**eat sth↔ˈup** 🗝 to eat all of sth: *Eat up! We've got to go out soon.* ◇ *Come on. Eat up your potatoes.* ˌ**eat sb ˈup** [usually passive] to fill sb with a particular emotion so that they cannot think of anything else: *She was eaten up by regrets.* ˌ**eat sth↔ˈup** to use sth in large quantities: *Legal costs had eaten up all the savings she had.*

eat·able /ˈiːtəbl/ *adj.* good enough to be eaten ➲ see also EDIBLE

eater /ˈiːtə(r)/ *noun* (usually after an adjective or a noun) a person or an animal that eats a particular thing or in a particular way: *We're not great meat eaters.* ◇ *He's a big eater* (= he eats a lot).

eat·ery /ˈiːtəri/ (*pl.* -ies) *noun* (*informal*, *especially NAmE*) a restaurant or other place that serves food

ˈ**eat-in** *adj.* [only before noun] (of a kitchen) big enough for eating in as well as cooking in

eat·ing /ˈiːtɪŋ/ *noun* [U] the act of eating sth: *healthy eating* **IDM** see PROOF

ˈ**eating apple** *noun* (*BrE*) any type of apple that can be eaten raw ➲ compare COOKING APPLE

ˈ**eating disorder** *noun* an emotional DISORDER that causes eating habits that are not normal, for example ANOREXIA

eats /iːts/ *noun* [pl.] (*informal*) food, especially at a party

eau de cologne /ˌəʊ də kəˈləʊn; *NAmE* ˌoʊ də kəˈloʊn/ *noun* [U] = COLOGNE

eau de toilette /ˌəʊ də twɑːˈlet; *NAmE* ˌoʊ/ *noun* [C, U] PERFUME that contains a lot of water and does not smell very strong

eaves /iːvz/ *noun* [pl.] the lower edges of a roof that stick out over the walls: *birds nesting under the eaves* ➲ VISUAL VOCAB page V15

eaves·drop /ˈiːvzdrɒp; *NAmE* -drɑːp/ *verb* (-pp-) [I] **~ (on sb/sth)** to listen secretly to what other people are saying: *We caught him eavesdropping outside the window.* ▶ **eaves·drop·per** *noun*

eaves·trough /ˈiːvztrɒf; *NAmE* -trɔːf; -trɑːf/ *noun* (*CanE*) = GUTTER (1)

eBay™ /ˈiːbeɪ/ *noun* [U] a website on the Internet where people can AUCTION goods (= sell them to the person who offers the most money for them): *He buys rare baseball cards on eBay.* ▶ **eBay** *verb* **~ sth**

ebb /eb/ *noun, verb*

■ ***noun*** **the ebb** [usually sing.] the period of time when the sea flows away from the land: *the ebb tide*

IDM **the ˌebb and ˈflow (of sth/sb)** the repeated, often regular, movement from one state to another; the repeated change in level, numbers or amount: *the ebb and flow of the seasons* ◇ *She sat in silence enjoying the ebb and flow of conversation.* ➲ more at LOW *adj.*

■ ***verb*** **1** [I] (*formal*) (of the TIDE in the sea) to move away from the land **SYN** **go out** **OPP** **flow 2** [I] **~ (away)** to become gradually weaker or less **SYN** **decrease**: *The pain was ebbing.* ◇ *As night fell, our enthusiasm began to ebb away.*

Ebola fever /iːˈbəʊlə fiːvə(r); əˈbəʊlə; *NAmE* -ˈboʊ-; fiːvər/ *noun* [U] a very serious disease, caused by a virus, which causes internal parts of the body to lose blood and usually ends in death

Eb·on·ics /eˈbɒnɪks; *NAmE* -ˈbɑːn-/ *noun* [U] a type of English spoken by many African Americans that has been considered by some people to be a separate language

ebony /ˈebəni/ *noun, adj.*

■ ***noun*** [U] the hard black wood of various tropical trees: *an ebony carving*

■ ***adj.*** black in colour: *ebony skin*

ˈ**e-book** *noun* a book that is displayed on a computer screen or on an electronic device that is held in the hand, instead of being printed on paper

ebul·li·ent /ɪˈbʌliənt; -ˈbʊl-/ *adj.* (*formal*) full of confidence, energy and good humour: *The Prime Minister was in ebullient mood.* ▶ **ebul·li·ence** /-əns/ *noun* [U] **ebul·li·ent·ly** *adv.*

ˈ**e-cash** *noun* [U] a system for sending and receiving payments using the Internet

ec·cen·tric /ɪkˈsentrɪk/ *adj.* considered by other people to be strange or unusual: *eccentric behaviour/clothes* ◇ *an eccentric aunt* ▶ **ec·cen·tric** *noun*: *Most people considered him a harmless eccentric.* **ec·cen·tric·al·ly** /-kli/ *adv.*

ec·cen·tri·city /ˌeksenˈtrɪsəti/ (*pl.* -ies) *noun* **1** [U] behaviour that people think is strange or unusual; the quality of being unusual and different from other people: *As a teacher, she had a reputation for eccentricity.* ◇ *Arthur was noted for the eccentricity of his clothes.* **2** [C, usually pl.] an unusual act or habit: *We all have our little eccentricities.*

Ec·cles cake /ˈeklz keɪk/ *noun* a small flat cake made from PASTRY with RAISINS inside

ec·cle·si·as·tic /ɪˌkliːziˈæstɪk/ *noun* (*formal*) a priest or minister in the Christian Church

ec·cle·si·as·tic·al /ɪˌkliːziˈæstɪkl/ *adj.* [usually before noun] connected with the Christian Church

ECG /ˌiː siː ˈdʒiː/ (*NAmE* also **EKG**) *noun* the abbreviation for 'electrocardiogram' (a medical test that measures and records electrical activity of the heart)

ech·elon /ˈeʃəlɒn; *NAmE* -lɑːn/ *noun* **1** [usually pl.] a rank or position of authority in an organization or a society: *the* ***lower/upper/top/higher echelons*** *of the Civil Service* **2** an arrangement of soldiers, planes, etc. in which each one is behind and to the side of the one in front

ech·idna /ɪˈkɪdnə/ (also ˌ**spiny ˈanteater**) *noun* an Australasian animal which has a long nose, sharp CLAWS on its feet, and sharp SPINES on its body, and which eats insects

ech·in·acea /ˌekɪˈneɪsiə; -ʃə/ *noun* [U, C] a plant similar to a DAISY, that is thought to help the body heal itself and fight infection

E

echo /ˈekəʊ; *NAmE* ˈekoʊ/ *noun, verb*
■ ***noun*** (*pl.* -oes) **1** the reflecting of sound off a wall or inside a confined space so that a noise appears to be repeated; a sound that is reflected back in this way: *There was an echo on the phone and I couldn't hear clearly.* ◇ *The hills sent back a faint echo.* ◇ *the echo of footsteps running down the corridor* **2** the fact of an idea, event, etc. being like another and reminding you of it; sth that reminds you of sth else: *Yesterday's crash has grim echoes of previous disasters.* **3** an opinion or attitude that agrees with or repeats one already expressed or thought: *His words were an echo of what she had heard many times before.* ◇ *The speech* ***found an echo*** *in the hearts of many of the audience* (= they agreed with it).
■ ***verb*** (**echoes, echo·ing, echoed, echoed**) **1** [I] if a sound **echoes**, it is reflected off a wall, the side of a mountain, etc. so that you can hear it again SYN **reverberate**: *Her footsteps echoed in the empty room.* ◇ *The gunshot echoed through the forest.* **2** [I, T] to send back and repeat a sound; to be full of a sound SYN **reverberate**: *The whole house echoed.* ◇ **~ to/with sth** *The street echoed with the cries of children.* ◇ **~ sth** (**back**) *The valley echoed back his voice.* **3** [T] **~ sth** to repeat an idea or opinion because you agree with it: *This is a view echoed by many on the right of the party.* **4** [T] **+ speech** | **~ sth** to repeat what sb else has just said, especially because you find it surprising: *'He's gone!' Viv echoed.*

echo·loca·tion /ˌekəʊləʊˈkeɪʃn; *NAmE* ˌekoʊloʊ-/ *noun* [U] the use of reflected sound waves for finding things, especially by creatures such as DOLPHINS and BATS

echt /ext/ *adj.* (from *German*) genuine and typical ▸ **echt** *adv.*: *echt Viennese cream cakes*

eclair /ɪˈkleə(r); *NAmE* ɪˈkler/ *noun* a long thin cake for one person, made of light PASTRY, filled with cream and usually with chocolate on top

eclamp·sia /ɪˈklæmpsiə/ *noun* [U] a condition in which a pregnant woman has high blood pressure and CONVULSIONS, which can be dangerous to the woman and the baby ➲ compare PRE-ECLAMPSIA

eclec·tic /ɪˈklektɪk/ *adj.* (*formal*) not following one style or set of ideas but choosing from or using a wide variety: *She has very eclectic tastes in literature.* ▸ **eclec·tic·al·ly** /-tɪkli/ *adv.* **eclec·ti·cism** /ɪˈklektɪsɪzəm/ *noun* [U]

eclipse /ɪˈklɪps/ *noun, verb*
■ ***noun*** **1** [C] an occasion when the moon passes between the earth and the sun so that you cannot see all or part of the sun for a time; an occasion when the earth passes between the moon and the sun so that you cannot see all or part of the moon for a time: *an* ***eclipse of the sun/moon*** ◇ *a* ***total/partial eclipse*** **2** [sing., U] a loss of importance, power, etc. especially because sb/sth else has become more important, powerful, etc: *The election result marked the eclipse of the right wing.* ◇ *Her work was* ***in eclipse*** *for most of the 20th century.*
■ ***verb*** **1** [often passive] **~ sth** (of the moon, the earth, etc.) to cause an eclipse **2 ~ sb/sth** to make sb/sth seem dull or unimportant by comparison SYN **outshine, overshadow**: *Though a talented player, he was completely eclipsed by his brother.*

eco- /ˈiːkəʊ; *NAmE* ˈiːkoʊ/ *combining form* (in nouns, adjectives and adverbs) connected with the environment: *eco-friendly* ◇ *eco-warriors* (= people who protest about damage to the environment) ◇ *eco-terrorism* (= the use of force or violent action in order to protest about damage to the environment)

eco·cide /ˈiːkəʊsaɪd; *NAmE* ˈiːkoʊ-/ *noun* [U] the destruction of the natural environment, especially when this is deliberate

ˌeco-ˈfriend·ly *adj.* not harmful to the environment: *eco-friendly products*

E. coli /ˌiː ˈkəʊlaɪ; *NAmE* -ˈkoʊ-/ *noun* [U] a type of bacteria that lives inside humans and some animals, some forms of which can cause FOOD POISONING

eco·logic·al /ˌiːkəˈlɒdʒɪkl; *NAmE* -ˈlɑːdʒ-/ *adj.* **1** connected with the relation of plants and living creatures to each other and to their environment: *We risk upsetting the ecological balance of the area.* ◇ *an ecological disaster* (= one that alters the whole balance of ecology in an area) **2** interested in and concerned about the ecology of a place: *the ecological movement* ▸ **eco·logic·al·ly** /-kli/ *adv.*: *The system is both practical and* ***ecologically sound.***

ecoˌlogical ˈfootprint *noun* a measure of the amount of the earth's resources used by a person or a population that lives in a particular way: *the ecological footprint of the average Canadian*

ecolo·gist /iˈkɒlədʒɪst; *NAmE* iˈkɑːl-/ *noun* **1** a scientist who studies ecology **2** a person who is interested in ecology and believes the environment should be protected

ecol·ogy /iˈkɒlədʒi; *NAmE* iˈkɑːl-/ *noun* [U] the relation of plants and living creatures to each other and to their environment; the study of this: ***plant/animal/human ecology*** ◇ *the ecology movement* ◇ *Oil pollution could damage the* ***fragile ecology*** *of the coral reefs.*

eco·nom·ic 🔑 AW /ˌiːkəˈnɒmɪk; ˌekə-; *NAmE* -ˈnɑːm-/ *adj.*
1 🔑 [only before noun] connected with the trade, industry and development of wealth of a country, an area or a society: *social, economic and political issues* ◇ ***economic growth/cooperation/development/reform*** ◇ *the government's economic policy* ◇ *economic history* ◇ *the current economic climate* **2** 🔑 (of a process, a business or an activity) producing enough profit to continue SYN **profitable** OPP **uneconomic** ➲ SYNONYMS at SUCCESSFUL

Synonyms

economic

financial • commercial • monetary • budgetary

These words all describe activities or situations that are connected with the use of money, especially by a business or country.

economic connected with the trade, industry and development of wealth of a country, an area or a society: *This book deals with the social, economic and political issues of the period.*

financial connected with money and finance: *She had got into financial difficulties.* ◇ *Tokyo is a major financial centre.*

commercial connected with the buying and selling of goods and services.

monetary (*formal* or *finance*) connected with money, especially all the money in a country: *closer European monetary union*

budgetary (*finance*) connected with a budget (= the money available or a plan of how it will be spent).

PATTERNS
- economic/financial/commercial/monetary/budgetary **affairs/decisions**
- the economic/financial/commercial/budgetary **climate**
- the economic/financial/commercial **side** of sth
- an economic/financial/commercial **centre**

eco·nom·ic·al AW /ˌiːkəˈnɒmɪkl; ˌekə-; *NAmE* -ˈnɑːm-/ *adj.* **1** providing good service or value in relation to the amount of time or money spent: *an economical car to run* (= one that does not use too much petrol/gas) ◇ *It would be more economical to buy the bigger size.* OPP **uneconomical** **2** using no more of sth than is necessary: *an economical use of space* ◇ *an economical prose style* (= one that uses no unnecessary words) OPP **uneconomical** **3** not spending more money than necessary SYN **frugal**: *He was economical in all areas of his life.*
IDM **economical with the ˈtruth** a way of saying that sb has left out some important facts, when you do not want to say that they are lying

eco·nom·ic·al·ly AW /ˌiːkəˈnɒmɪkli; ˌekə-; *NAmE* -ˈnɑːm-/ *adv.* **1** in a way connected with the trade, industry and development of wealth of a country, an area or a society: *The factory is no longer economically viable.* ◇ *Economically, the centre of Spain has lost its dominant role.* ◇ *the* ***economically active/inactive*** *population* (= those who are employed/unemployed) **2** in a way that provides good service or value in relation to the amount of time or money spent: *I'll do the job as economically as possible.* **3** in a way that uses no more of sth than is necessary: *The design is intended to use space as economically as possible.* ◇ *She writes elegantly and economically.*

Which Word?

economic / economical

- **Economic** means 'connected with the economy of a country or an area, or with the money that a society or an individual has': *the government's economic policy* ◇ *the economic aspects of having children.*

➲ see also ECONOMY 1

- **Economical** means 'spending money or using something in a careful way that avoids waste': *It is usually economical to buy washing powder in large quantities.*

➲ see also ECONOMY 3

ˌeconomic ˈmigrant *noun* a person who moves from their own country to a new country in order to find work or have a better standard of living: *They claimed they were political refugees and not economic migrants.*

eco·nom·ics AW /ˌiːkəˈnɒmɪks; ˌekə-; *NAmE* -ˈnɑːm-/ *noun* **1** [U] the study of how a society organizes its money, trade and industry: *He studied politics and economics at Yale.* ◇ *Keynesian/Marxist economics* ➲ see also HOME ECONOMICS **2** [pl., U] the way in which money influences, or is organized within an area of business or society: *The economics of the project are very encouraging.*

econo·mist AW /ɪˈkɒnəmɪst; *NAmE* ɪˈkɑːn-/ *noun* a person who studies or writes about economics

econo·mize (*BrE* also **-ise**) /ɪˈkɒnəmaɪz; *NAmE* ɪˈkɑːn-/ *verb* [I] **~ (on sth)** to use less money, time, etc. than you normally use: *Old people often try to economize on heating, thus endangering their health.* ➲ SYNONYMS at SAVE

econ·omy 0-ᴡ AW /ɪˈkɒnəmi; *NAmE* ɪˈkɑːn-/ *noun* (*pl.* -ies)

1 0-ᴡ (often **the economy**) [C] the relationship between production, trade and the supply of money in a particular country or region: *The economy is in recession.* ◇ *the world economy* ◇ *a market economy* (= one in which the price is fixed according to both cost and demand) **2** 0-ᴡ [C] a country, when you are thinking about its economic system: *Ireland was one of the fastest-growing economies in Western Europe in the 1990s.* **3** 0-ᴡ [C, U] the use of the time, money, etc. that is available in a way that avoids waste: *We need to make substantial economies.* ◇ *It's a* ***false economy*** *to buy cheap clothes* (= it seems cheaper but it is not really since they do not last very long). ◇ *She writes with a great economy of words* (= using only the necessary words). ◇ (*BrE*) *We're on an* ***economy drive*** *at home* (= trying to avoid waste and spend as little money as possible). ◇ *Buy the large* ***economy pack*** (= the one that gives you better value for money). ◇ *to fly* ***economy*** (***class***) (= by the cheapest class of air travel) ◇ *an economy fare* (= the cheapest)

eˈconomy class syndrome *noun* [U] (*BrE*) the fact of a person suffering from DEEP VEIN THROMBOSIS after they have travelled on a plane. This condition is thought to be more common among people who travel in the cheapest seats because they do not have space to move their legs much.

eco·sys·tem /ˈiːkəʊsɪstəm; *NAmE* ˈiːkoʊ-/ *noun* all the plants and living creatures in a particular area considered in relation to their physical environment ➲ COLLOCATIONS at ENVIRONMENT

eco·ter·ror·ism /ˈiːkəʊterərɪzəm; *NAmE* ˈiːkoʊ-/ *noun* [U] **1** violent activities which are done in order to draw attention to issues relating to the environment **2** deliberate damage to the environment, done in order to draw attention to a political issue ▸ **eco·ter·ror·ist** *noun*

Collocations

The economy

Managing the economy

- **handle/run/manage** the economy
- **boost** investment/spending/employment/growth
- **stimulate** demand/the economy/industry
- **cut/reduce** investment/spending/borrowing
- **reduce/curb/control/keep down** inflation
- **create/fuel** growth/demand/a boom/a bubble
- **encourage/foster/promote/stimulate/stifle** innovation/competition
- **encourage/work with/compete with** the private sector
- **increase/boost/promote** US/agricultural exports
- **ban/restrict/block** cheap/foreign imports
- the economy **grows/expands/shrinks/contracts/slows (down)/recovers/improves/is booming**
- **enjoy** an economic/housing/property boom

Economic problems

- **push up/drive up** prices/costs/inflation
- **damage/hurt/destroy** industry/the economy
- **cause/lead to/go into/avoid/escape** recession
- **experience/suffer** a recession/downturn
- **fight/combat** inflation/deflation/unemployment
- **cause/create** inflation/poverty/unemployment
- **create/burst** a housing/stock market bubble
- **cause/trigger** a stock market crash/the collapse of the banking system
- **face/be plunged into** a financial/an economic crisis
- **be caught in/experience** cycles of boom and bust

Public finance

- **cut/reduce/slash/increase/double** the defence/(*especially US*) defense/education/aid budget
- **increase/boost/slash/cut** public spending
- **increase/put up/raise/cut/lower/reduce** taxes
- **raise/cut/lower/reduce** interest rates
- **ease/loosen/tighten** monetary policy
- **balance** the (state/federal) budget
- **achieve/maintain** a balanced budget
- **run** a ($4 trillion) budget deficit/surplus

➲ more collocations at POLITICS, VOTING

eco·tour·ism /ˈiːkəʊtʊərɪzəm; -tɔːr-; *NAmE* ˈiːkoʊtʊr-/ *noun* [U] organized holidays/vacations that are designed so that the tourists damage the environment as little as possible, especially when some of the money they pay is used to protect the local environment and animals ▸ **eco·tour·ist** /ˈiːkəʊtʊərɪst; -tɔːr-; *NAmE* ˈiːkoʊtʊr-/ *noun*

eco·type /ˈiːkəʊtaɪp; *NAmE* ˈiːkoʊ-/ *noun* (*biology*) the type or race of a plant or animal that has adapted to live in particular local conditions

ecru /ˈeɪkruː; ˈekruː/ *noun* a light brown or cream colour

ec·stasy /ˈekstəsi/ *noun* (*pl.* **-ies**) **1** [U, C] a feeling or state of very great happiness SYN **bliss** **2** **Ecstasy** [U] (*abbr.* E) an illegal drug, taken especially by young people at parties, clubs, etc.

ec·stat·ic /ɪkˈstætɪk/ *adj.* very happy, excited and enthusiastic; feeling or showing great enthusiasm SYN **delighted**: *Sally was ecstatic about her new job.* ◇ *ecstatic applause/praise/reviews* ➲ SYNONYMS at EXCITED ▸ **ec·stat·ic·al·ly** /-kli/ *adv.*

-ec·tomy *combining form* (in nouns) a medical operation in which part of the body is removed: *appendectomy* (= removal of the APPENDIX)

E

E

ec·top·ic /ek'tɒpɪk; *NAmE* -'tɑːp-/ *adj.* (*medical*) in an **ectopic** PREGNANCY, the baby starts to develop outside the mother's WOMB

ecto·plasm /'ektəʊplæzəm; *NAmE* 'ektoʊ-/ *noun* [U] **1** (*biology*) (*old-fashioned*) the outer layer of the jelly-like substance inside cells ➲ compare ENDOPLASM **2** a substance which is said to come from the body of sb who is communicating with the spirit of a dead person, allowing the spirit to have a form

ecu·men·ic·al /ˌiːkjuː'menɪkl; ˌekjuː-/ *adj.* involving or uniting members of different branches of the Christian Church

ecu·men·ism /ɪ'kjuːmənɪzəm/ *noun* [U] the principle or aim of uniting different branches of the Christian Church

ec·zema /'eksɪmə; *NAmE* ɪɡ'ziːmə/ *noun* [U] a skin condition in which areas of skin become red, rough and ITCHY

-ed, -d *suffix* **1** (in adjectives) having; having the characteristics of: *talented* ◇ *bearded* ◇ *diseased* **2** (makes the past tense and past participle of regular verbs): *hated* ◇ *walked* ◇ *loved*

ed. (also **Ed.**) *abbr.* EDITED (BY), EDITION, EDITOR: *'Eighteenth Century Women Poets', Ed. Lonsdale* ◇ *7th ed.*

Edam /'iːdæm/ *noun* [U, C] a type of round yellow Dutch cheese that is covered with red WAX

eddy /'edi/ *noun, verb*
- **noun** (*pl.* -ies) a movement of air, dust or water in a circle
- **verb** (**ed·dies, eddy·ing, ed·died, ed·died**) [I] (of air, dust, water, etc.) to move around in a circle SYN **swirl**: *The waves swirled and eddied around the rocks.*

edema (*NAmE*) (*BrE* **oe·dema**) /ɪ'diːmə/ *noun* [U] (*medical*) a condition in which liquid collects in the spaces inside the body and makes it swell

Eden /'iːdn/ (also **the ˌGarden of 'Eden**) *noun* [sing.] (in the Bible) the beautiful garden where Adam and Eve, the first humans, lived before they did sth God had told them not to and were sent away, often seen as a place of happiness and INNOCENCE

edge 0-w /edʒ/ *noun, verb*
- **noun 1** 0-w [C] the outside limit of an object, a surface or an area; the part furthest from the centre: *He stood* ***on the edge of*** *the cliff.* ◇ *a big house* ***on/at the edge of town*** ◇ *Don't put that glass so near the edge of the table.* ◇ *I sat down at the water's edge.* ◇ *Stand the coin on its edge.* ➲ see also LEADING EDGE **2** 0-w [C] the sharp part of a blade, knife or SWORD that is used for cutting: *Be careful—it has a sharp edge.* ➲ VISUAL VOCAB page V23 ➲ see also KNIFE-EDGE **3** (usually **the edge**) [sing.] the point at which sth, especially sth bad, may begin to happen SYN **brink, verge**: *They had brought the country to the edge of disaster.* ➲ see also CUTTING EDGE **4** [sing.] a slight advantage over sb/sth: *The company needs to improve its* ***competitive edge***. ◇ **~ on/over sb/sth** *They have the edge on us.* **5** [sing.] a strong, often exciting, quality: *Her show now has a hard political edge to it.* **6** [sing.] a sharp tone of voice, often showing anger: *He did his best to remain calm, but there was a distinct edge to his voice.* **7 -edged** (in adjectives) having the type of edge or edges mentioned: *a lace-edged handkerchief* ➲ see also GILT-EDGED

IDM **be on 'edge** to be nervous, excited or bad-tempered ➲ SYNONYMS at NERVOUS **on the edge of your 'seat** very excited and giving your full attention to sth: *The game had the crowd on the edge of their seats.* **take the 'edge off sth** to make sth less strong, less bad, etc: *The sandwich took the edge off my appetite.* ➲ more at FRAY *v.*, RAZOR, ROUGH *adj.*, TEETER, TOOTH

- **verb 1** [I, T] to move or to move sth slowly and carefully in a particular direction: **+ adv./prep.** *She edged a little closer to me.* ◇ *I edged nervously past the dog.* ◇ **~ sth + adv./prep.** *Emily edged her chair forward.* **2** [T, usually passive] **~ sth (with/in sth)** to put sth around the edge of sth: *The handkerchief is edged with lace.* **3** [I] **+ adv./prep.** to increase or decrease slightly: *Prices edged up 2% in the year to December.*

PHR V **ˌedge sb/sth↔'out (of sth)** to move sb from their position or job gradually, especially when they are not fully aware of what is happening: *She was edged out of the company by the new director.*

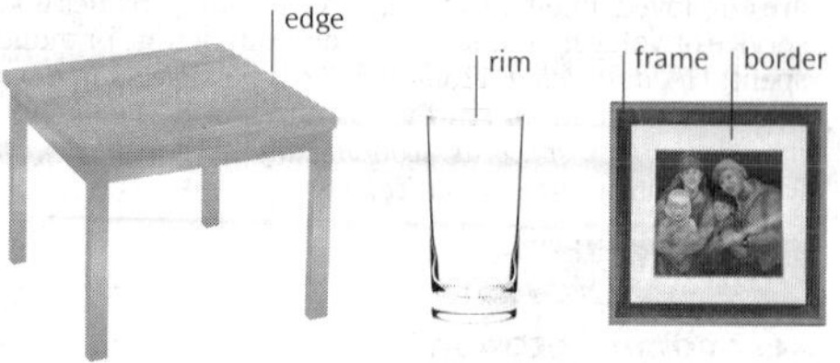

ˌedge 'city *noun* (*NAmE*) a large area of buildings on the edge of a city, usually near a main road

edge·ways /'edʒweɪz/ (*BrE*) (*NAmE* **edge·wise** /-waɪz/) *adv.* with the edge upwards or forwards; on one side: *You'll only get the desk through the door if you turn it edgeways.* IDM see WORD *n.*

edging /'edʒɪŋ/ *noun* [U, C] something that forms the border or edge of sth, added to make it more attractive, etc.

edgy /'edʒi/ *adj.* (*informal*) (**edgi·er, edgi·est**) **1** nervous, especially about what might happen: *She's been very edgy lately.* ◇ *After the recent unrest there is an edgy calm in the capital.* **2** (of a film/movie, book, piece of music, etc.) having a sharp exciting quality: *a clever, edgy film* ▶ **edgi·ly** *adv.*: *'I'm not sure I can make it tomorrow,' he said edgily.* **edgi·ness** *noun* [U, sing.]

EDI /ˌiː diː 'aɪ/ *noun* [U] (*computing*) the abbreviation for 'electronic data interchange' (a system that is used in business for sending information between different companies' computer systems)

ed·ible /'edəbl/ *adj.* fit or suitable to be eaten; not poisonous: *The food at the hotel was barely edible.* ◇ *edible fungi/snails/flowers*

edict /'iːdɪkt/ *noun* [U, C] (*formal*) an official order or statement given by sb in authority SYN **decree**

edi·fi·ca·tion /ˌedɪfɪ'keɪʃn/ *noun* [U] (*formal* or *humorous*) the improvement of sb's mind or character: *The books were intended for the edification of the masses.*

edi·fice /'edɪfɪs/ *noun* (*formal*) a large impressive building: *an imposing edifice* ◇ (*figurative*) *Their new manifesto hardly threatens to bring the* ***whole edifice of*** *capitalism crashing down.* ◇ (*figurative*) *an edifice of lies*

edify /'edɪfaɪ/ *verb* (**edi·fies, edify·ing, edi·fied, edi·fied**) [I, T] **~ sb** (*formal*) to improve people's minds or characters by teaching them about sth

edify·ing /'edɪfaɪɪŋ/ *adj.* (*formal* or *humorous*) likely to improve your mind or your character

edit AW /'edɪt/ *verb* **1** [T, I] **~ (sth)** to prepare a piece of writing, a book, etc. to be published by correcting the mistakes, making improvements to it, etc: *I know that this draft text will need to be edited.* ◇ *This is the edited version of my speech* (= some parts have been taken out). **2** [T] **~ sth** to prepare a book to be published by collecting together and arranging pieces of writing by one or more authors: *He's editing a book of essays by Isaiah Berlin.* **3** [T, I] **~ (sth)** (*computing*) to make changes to text or data on screen: *You can download the file and edit it on your computer.* **4** [T] **~ sth** when sb **edits** a film/movie, television programme, etc. they take what has been filmed or recorded and decide which parts to include and in which order: *They're showing the* ***edited highlights*** *of last month's game.* ➲ COLLOCATIONS at CINEMA **5** [T] **~ sth** to be responsible for planning and publishing a newspaper, magazine, etc. (= to be the EDITOR): *She used to edit a women's magazine.* ▶ **edit** *noun*: *I had time to do a quick edit of my essay before handing it in.*

PHR V **ˌedit sth↔'out (of sth)** to remove words, phrases or scenes from a book, programme, etc. before it is published or shown SYN **cut out**: *They edited out references to her father in the interview.*

edit·able /ˈedɪtəbl/ *adj.* (*computing*) (of text or software) that can be EDITED by the user: *an editable document*

edi·tion 🔑 AW /ɪˈdɪʃn/ *noun* **1** 🔑 the form in which a book is published: *a* ***paperback/hardback edition*** ◇ *She collects* ***first editions*** *of Victorian novels.* ◇ *the electronic edition of 'The Guardian'* **2** 🔑 a particular newspaper or magazine, or radio or television programme, especially one in a regular series: *Tonight's edition of 'Panorama' looks at unemployment.* **3** 🔑 (*abbr.* **ed.**) the total number of copies of a book, newspaper or magazine, etc. published at one time: *The dictionary is now in its eighth edition.* ◇ *The article appeared in the evening edition of 'The Mercury'.* ➲ see also LIMITED EDITION ➲ compare IMPRESSION (7)

edi·tor 🔑 AW /ˈedɪtə(r)/ *noun* **1** 🔑 a person who is in charge of a newspaper, magazine, etc, or part of one, and who decides what should be included: *the editor of the Washington Post* ◇ *the* ***sports/financial/fashion, etc. editor*** **2** 🔑 a person who prepares a book to be published, for example by checking and correcting the text, making improvements, etc. ➲ see also COPY EDITOR, SUBEDITOR **3** a person who prepares a film/movie, radio or television programme for being shown or broadcast by deciding what to include, and what order it should be in **4** a person who works as a journalist for radio or television reporting on a particular area of news: *our economics editor* **5** a person who chooses texts written by one or by several writers and prepares them to be published in a book: *She's the editor of a new collection of ghost stories.* **6** (*computing*) a program that allows you to change stored text or data ▸ **edit·or·ship** *noun* [U]: *the editorship of 'The Times'*

edi·tor·ial AW /ˌedɪˈtɔːriəl/ *adj., noun*
■ ***adj.*** [usually before noun] connected with the task of preparing sth such as a newspaper, a book or a television or radio programme, to be published or broadcast: *the magazine's editorial staff* ◇ *an editorial decision*
■ ***noun*** (*BrE* also **lead·er**, **ˌleading ˈarticle**) an important article in a newspaper, that expresses the editor's opinion about an item of news or an issue; in the US also a comment on radio or television that expresses the opinion of the STATION or network

edi·tor·ial·ize (*BrE* also **-ise**) /ˌedɪˈtɔːriəlaɪz/ *verb* **1** [I] to express your opinions rather than just reporting the news or giving the facts: *He accused the BBC of editorializing in its handling of the story.* **2** [I] (*NAmE*) to express an opinion in an editorial: *Yesterday the Washington Post editorialized on this subject.*

ˈedit suite *noun* a room containing electronic equipment for EDITING material recorded on video

EDT /ˌiː diː ˈtiː/ *abbr.* EASTERN DAYLIGHT TIME

edu·cate 🔑 /ˈedʒukeɪt/ *verb* **1** 🔑 [often passive] **~ sb** to teach sb over a period of time at a school, university, etc: *She was educated in the US.* ◇ *He was educated at his local comprehensive school and then at Oxford.* **2** 🔑 to teach sb about sth or how to do sth: **~ sb (in/on sth)** *Children need to be educated on the dangers of drug-taking.* ◇ **~ sb to do sth** *The campaign is intended to educate the public to respect the environment.*

edu·cated 🔑 /ˈedʒukeɪtɪd/ *adj.* **1** 🔑 **-educated** having had the kind of education mentioned; having been to the school, college or university mentioned: *privately educated children* ◇ *a British-educated lawyer* ◇ *He's a Princeton-educated Texan.* **2** 🔑 having had a high standard of education; showing a high standard of education: *an educated and articulate person* ◇ *the educated elite* ◇ *He spoke in an educated voice.*
IDM **an ˌeducated ˈguess** a guess that is based on some degree of knowledge, and is therefore likely to be correct

edu·ca·tion 🔑 /ˌedʒuˈkeɪʃn/ *noun* **1** 🔑 [U, sing.] a process of teaching, training and learning, especially in schools or colleges, to improve knowledge and develop skills: *primary/elementary education* ◇ *secondary education* ◇ *further/higher/post-secondary education* ◇ *students in full-time education* ◇ *adult education classes* ◇ *a college/university education* ◇ *the state education system* ◇ *a man of little education* ◇ *She completed her formal education in 1995.* **2** 🔑 [U, sing.] a particular kind of teaching or training: *health education* **3** 🔑 (also **Education**) [U] the institutions or people involved in teaching and training: *the Education Department* ◇ *the Department of Health, Education and Welfare* ◇ *There should be closer links between education and industry.* **4** 🔑 (usually **Education**) [U] the subject of study that deals with how to teach: *a College of Education* ◇ *a Bachelor of Education degree* ◇ *She's an education major.* **5** [sing.] (often *humorous*) an interesting experience that teaches you sth: *The rock concert was quite an education for my parents!*

Collocations

Education

Learning

- **acquire/get/lack** (an) education/training/(*BrE*) (some) qualifications
- **receive/provide sb with** training/tuition
- **develop/design/plan** a curriculum/(*especially BrE*) course/(*NAmE*) program/syllabus
- **give/go to/attend** a class/lesson/lecture/seminar
- **hold/run/conduct** a class/seminar/workshop
- **sign up for/take** a course/classes/lessons

School

- **go to/start** preschool/kindergarten/nursery school
- **be in the first, second, etc.** (*NAmE*) grade/(*especially BrE*) year (at school)
- **study/take/drop** history/chemistry/German, etc.
- (*BrE*) **leave/finish/drop out of**/(*NAmE*) **quit** school
- (*NAmE*) **graduate** high school/college

Problems at school

- **be the victim/target of** bullying
- (*BrE*) **play truant from**/(*both BrE, informal*) **bunk off/skive off** school (= not go to school when you should)
- (*both especially NAmE*) **skip/cut** class/school
- (*BrE*) **cheat** in/(*NAmE*) cheat on an exam/a test
- **get/be given** a detention (for doing sth)
- **be expelled from/be suspended from** school

Work and exams

- **do** your homework/(*BrE*) revision/a project on sth
- **work on/write/do/submit** an essay/a dissertation/a thesis/an assignment/(*NAmE*) a paper
- **finish/complete** your dissertation/thesis/studies/coursework
- **hand in**/(*NAmE*) **turn in** your homework/essay/assignment/paper
- **study/prepare**/(*BrE*) **revise**/(*NAmE*) **review**/(*NAmE, informal*) **cram** for a test/an exam
- **take**/(*both BrE*) **do/sit** a test/an exam
- (*especially BrE*) **mark**/(*especially NAmE*) **grade** homework/a test
- (*BrE*) **do well in**/(*NAmE*) **do well on**/(*informal, especially NAmE*) **ace** a test/an exam
- **pass/fail**/(*informal, especially NAmE*) **flunk** a test/an exam/a class/a course/a subject

University

- **apply to/get into/go to/start** college/(*BrE*) university
- **leave/graduate from** law school/college/(*BrE*) university (with a degree in computer science)
- **study for/take**/(*BrE*) **do/complete** a law degree/a degree in physics
- (*both NAmE*) **major/minor** in biology/philosophy
- **earn/receive/be awarded/get/have/hold** a master's degree/a bachelor's degree/a PhD in economics

E

edu·ca·tion·al /ˌedʒuˈkeɪʃənl/ *adj.* connected with education; providing education: *children with special educational needs* ◇ *an educational psychologist* ◇ *an educational visit* ◇ ***educational games/toys*** (= that teach you sth as well as amusing you) ◇ *Watching television can be very educational.* ▶ **edu·ca·tion·al·ly** /-ʃənəli/ *adv.*: *Children living in inner-city areas may be educationally disadvantaged.* ◇ *(old-fashioned) educationally subnormal*

edu·ca·tion·al·ist /ˌedʒuˈkeɪʃənəlɪst/ (also **edu·ca·tion·ist** /ˌedʒuˈkeɪʃənɪst/) *noun* a specialist in theories and methods of teaching

edu·ca·tive /ˈedjukətɪv/ *adj.* (*formal*) that teaches sth: *the educative role of the community*

edu·ca·tor /ˈedʒukeɪtə(r)/ *noun* (*formal*) **1** a person whose job is to teach or educate people: *adult educators* (= who teach adults) **2** (*especially NAmE*) a person who is an expert in the theories and methods of education ➲ see also EDUCATIONALIST

edu·tain·ment /ˌedjuˈteɪnmənt/ *noun* [U] products such as books, television programmes and especially computer software that both educate and entertain

Ed·ward·ian /edˈwɔːdiən; *NAmE* -ˈwɔːrd-/ *adj.* from the time of the British king Edward VII (1901–1910): *an Edwardian terraced house* ▶ **Ed·ward·ian** *noun*

-ee *suffix* (in nouns) **1** a person affected by an action: *employee* ➲ compare -ER, -OR **2** a person described as or concerned with: *absentee* ◇ *refugee*

EEG /ˌiː iː ˈdʒiː/ *noun* the abbreviation for 'electroencephalogram' (a medical test that measures and records electrical activity in the brain)

eejit /ˈiːdʒɪt/ *noun* (*informal, IrishE, ScotE, disapproving*) a way of saying IDIOT which represents the way it is pronounced by some people

eek /iːk/ *exclamation* used to express fear or surprise: *Eek! It moved!*

eel /iːl/ *noun* [C, U] a long thin sea or FRESHWATER fish that looks like a snake. There are several types of eel, some of which are used for food: *jellied eels*

e'en /iːn/ *adv.* (*literary*) = EVEN

e'er /eə(r); *NAmE* er/ *adv.* (*literary*) = EVER

-eer *suffix* **1** (in nouns) a person concerned with: *auctioneer* ◇ *mountaineer* **2** (in verbs) (often *disapproving*) to be concerned with: *profiteer* ◇ *commandeer*

eerie /ˈɪəri; *NAmE* ˈɪri/ *adj.* strange, mysterious and frightening SYN **uncanny**: *an eerie yellow light* ◇ *I found the silence underwater really eerie.* ▶ **eer·ily** /ˈɪərəli; *NAmE* ˈɪr-/ *adv.* **eeri·ness** *noun* [U]

eff /ef/ *verb*

IDM **eff and ˈblind** (*BrE, informal*) to use swear words: *There was a lot of effing and blinding going on.*

PHR V **ˌeff ˈoff** (*taboo, BrE*) a rude way of telling sb to go away, used instead of 'fuck off' ➲ see also EFFING

ef·face /ɪˈfeɪs/ *verb* **~ sth** (*formal*) to make sth disappear; to remove sth ➲ see also SELF-EFFACING

ef·fect 0⁻ /ɪˈfekt/ *noun, verb*

■ ***noun*** **1** 0⁻ [C, U] **~ (on sb/sth)** a change that sb/sth causes in sb/sth else; a result: *the effect of heat on metal* ◇ ***dramatic/long-term effects*** ◇ *to learn to distinguish between* ***cause and effect*** ◇ *the beneficial effects of exercise* ◇ *Modern farming methods can have an* ***adverse effect*** *on the environment.* ◇ *Her criticisms* ***had the effect of*** *discouraging him completely.* ◇ *Despite her ordeal, she seems to have suffered no* ***ill effects***. ◇ *I can certainly* ***feel the effects of*** *too many late nights.* ◇ *'I'm feeling really depressed.' 'The winter here has that effect sometimes.'* ◇ *I tried to persuade him, but with little or no effect.* ➲ LANGUAGE BANK at CONSEQUENTLY ➲ note at AFFECT ➲ see also GREENHOUSE EFFECT, KNOCK-ON, SIDE EFFECT **2** 0⁻ [C, U] a particular look, sound or impression that sb, such as an artist or a writer, wants to create: *The overall effect of the painting is overwhelming.* ◇ *The stage lighting gives the effect of a moonlit scene.* ◇ *Add a scarf for a casual effect.* ◇ *He only behaves like that* ***for effect*** (= in order to impress people). ➲ see also SPECIAL EFFECTS, SOUND EFFECT **3 effects** [pl.] (*formal*) your personal possessions SYN **belongings**: *The insurance policy covers all baggage and personal effects.*

IDM **bring/put sth into efˈfect** 0⁻ to cause sth to come into use: *The recommendations will soon be put into effect.* **come into efˈfect** 0⁻ to come into use; to begin to apply: *New controls come into effect next month.* **in efˈfect 1** used when you are stating what the facts of a situation are: *In effect, the two systems are identical.* ◇ *His wife had, in effect, run the government for the past six months.* **2** (of a law or rule) in use: *These laws are in effect in twenty states.* **take efˈfect 1** to start to produce the results that are intended: *The aspirins soon take effect.* **2** to come into use; to begin to apply: *The new law takes effect from tomorrow.* **to the efˈfect that... | to this/that efˈfect** used to show that you are giving the general meaning of what sb has said or written rather than the exact words: *He left a note to the effect that he would not be coming back.* ◇ *She told me to get out—or* ***words to that effect***. **to good, great, dramatic, etc. efˈfect** producing a good, successful, dramatic, etc. result or impression **to no efˈfect** not producing the result you intend or hope for: *We warned them, but to no effect.* **with immediate effect | with effect from...** (*formal*) starting now; starting from...: *The government has cut interest rates with effect from the beginning of next month.*

■ ***verb*** **~ sth** (*formal*) to make sth happen: *to* ***effect a cure/change/recovery*** ➲ note at AFFECT

ef·fect·ive 0⁻ /ɪˈfektɪv/ *adj.*

1 0⁻ producing the result that is wanted or intended; producing a successful result: *Long prison sentences can be a very effective deterrent for offenders.* ◇ *Aspirin is a simple but highly effective treatment.* ◇ *drugs that are effective against cancer* ◇ *I admire the effective use of colour in her paintings.* OPP **ineffective** ➲ see also COST-EFFECTIVE **2** [only before noun] in reality, although not officially intended: *the effective, if not the actual, leader of the party* ◇ *He has now taken effective control of the country.* **3** (*formal*) (of laws and rules) coming into use: *The new speed limit on this road becomes effective from 1 June.* ▶ **ef·fect·ive·ness** (also *less frequent* **ef·fect·iv·ity** /ɪˌfekˈtɪvɪti/) *noun* [U]: *to check the effectiveness of the security system*

ef·fect·ive·ly 0⁻ /ɪˈfektɪvli/ *adv.*

1 0⁻ in a way that produces the intended result or a successful result: *The company must reduce costs to compete effectively.* ◇ *You dealt with the situation very effectively.* OPP **ineffectively 2** used when you are saying what the facts of a situation are: *He was very polite but effectively he was telling me that I had no chance of getting the job.*

ef·fect·or /ɪˈfektə(r)/ *noun* (*biology*) an organ or a cell in the body that is made to react by sth outside the body

ef·fec·tual /ɪˈfektʃuəl/ *adj.* (*formal*) (of things, not people) producing the result that was intended SYN **effective**: *an effectual remedy* ➲ compare INEFFECTUAL ▶ **ef·fec·tual·ly** *adv.*

ef·fec·tu·ate /ɪˈfektʃueɪt/ *verb* **~ sth** (*formal*) to make sth happen SYN **cause**

ef·fem·in·ate /ɪˈfemɪnət/ *adj.* (*disapproving*) (of a man or a boy) looking, behaving or sounding like a woman or a girl ▶ **ef·fem·in·acy** /ɪˈfemɪnəsi/ *noun* [U]

ef·fer·ves·cent /ˌefəˈvesnt; *NAmE* ˌefərˈv-/ *adj.* **1** (*approving*) (of people and their behaviour) excited, enthusiastic and full of energy SYN **bubbly 2** (of a liquid) having or producing small bubbles of gas SYN **fizzy** ▶ **ef·fer·ves·cence** /ˌefəˈvesns; *NAmE* ˌefərˈv-/ *noun* [U]

ef·fete /ɪˈfiːt/ *adj.* (*disapproving*) **1** weak; without the power that it once had **2** (of a man) without strength; looking or behaving like a woman

ef·fi·ca·cious /ˌefɪˈkeɪʃəs/ *adj.* (*formal*) (of things, not of people) producing the result that was wanted or intended SYN **effective**: *They hope the new drug will prove especially efficacious in the relief of pain.*

ef·fi·cacy /ˈefɪkəsi/ *noun* [U] (*formal*) the ability of sth, especially a drug or a medical treatment, to produce the results that are wanted SYN **effectiveness**

ef·fi·ciency /ɪˈfɪʃnsi/ *noun* **1** [U] the quality of doing sth well with no waste of time or money: *improvements in efficiency at the factory* ◇ *I was impressed by the efficiency with which she handled the crisis.* **2 efficiencies** [pl.] ways of wasting less time and money or of saving time or money: *We are looking at our business to see where savings and efficiencies can be made.* **3** [U] (*technical*) the relationship between the amount of energy that goes into a machine or an engine, and the amount that it produces **4** [C] = EFFICIENCY APARTMENT

efˈficiency apartment (also **efˈficiency unit, ef·fi·ciency**) *noun* (*NAmE*) a small flat/apartment with one main room for living, cooking and sleeping in and a separate bathroom

ef·fi·cient 🔑 /ɪˈfɪʃnt/ *adj.* doing sth well and thoroughly with no waste of time, money, or energy: *an efficient secretary* ◇ *efficient heating equipment* ◇ *the efficient use of energy* ◇ *As we get older, our bodies become less efficient at burning up calories.* ◇ *fuel-efficient cars* (= that do not use much fuel) **OPP inefficient** ▸ **ef·fi·cient·ly** 🔑 *adv.*: *a very efficiently organized event*

ef·figy /ˈefɪdʒi/ *noun* (*pl.* -ies) **1** a statue of a famous person, a SAINT or a god: *stone effigies in the church* **2** a model of a person that makes them look ugly: *The demonstrators burned a crude effigy of the president.*

eff·ing (also **f-ing**) /ˈefɪŋ/ *adj.* [only before noun] (*taboo, slang*) a swear word that many people find offensive that is used to emphasize a comment or an angry statement; used instead of saying 'fucking'

ef·flor·es·cence /ˌefləˈresns/ *noun* [U, C] **1** (*formal*) the most developed stage of sth **2** (*chemistry*) the powder which appears on the surface of bricks, rocks, etc. when water EVAPORATES

ef·flu·ent /ˈefluənt/ *noun* [U, C] (*formal*) liquid waste, especially chemicals produced by factories, or SEWAGE

ef·fort 🔑 /ˈefət; *NAmE* ˈefərt/ *noun*
1 🔑 [U, C] the physical or mental energy that you need to do sth; sth that takes a lot of energy: *You should* ***put*** *more* ***effort into*** *your work.* ◇ *A lot of effort has gone into making this event a success.* ◇ *It's a long climb to the top, but well worth the effort.* ◇ *Getting up this morning was quite an effort* (= it was difficult). ◇ (*BrE*) ***With*** (***an***) ***effort*** (= with difficulty) *she managed to stop herself laughing.* **2** 🔑 [C] an attempt to do sth especially when it is difficult to do: *a* ***determined/real/special effort*** ◇ *to* ***make an effort*** ◇ *I didn't really feel like going out, but I am glad I* ***made the effort.*** ◇ **~** (**to do sth**) *The company has laid off 150 workers* ***in an effort to*** *save money.* ◇ *The local clubs are* ***making every effort*** *to interest more young people.* ◇ *We need to make a* ***concerted effort*** *to finish on time.* ◇ *I spent hours cleaning the house, but there isn't much to show* ***for all my efforts.*** ◇ *With an* ***effort of will*** *he resisted the temptation.* ◇ *The project was a* ***joint/group*** *effort.* **3** [C] (usually after a noun) a particular activity that a group of people organize in order to achieve sth: *the Russian space effort* ◇ *the United Nations' peacekeeping effort* **4** [C] the result of an attempt to do sth: *I'm afraid this essay is a poor effort.*
IDM see BEND *v.*

ef·fort·less /ˈefətləs; *NAmE* ˈefərt-/ *adj.* needing little or no effort, so that it seems easy: *She dances with effortless grace.* ◇ *He made playing the guitar look effortless.* ▸ **ef·fort·less·ly** *adv.* **ef·fort·less·ness** *noun* [U]

ef·front·ery /ɪˈfrʌntəri/ *noun* [U] (*formal*) behaviour that is confident and very rude, without any feeling of shame **SYN nerve**

ef·ful·gent /ɪˈfʌldʒənt/ *adj.* (*literary*) shining brightly ▸ **ef·ful·gence** /ɪˈfʌldʒəns/ *noun* [U]

ef·fu·sion /ɪˈfjuːʒn/ *noun* [C, U] **1** (*technical*) something, especially a liquid, that flows out of sb/sth; the act of flowing out **2** (*formal*) the expression of feelings in an exaggerated way; feelings that are expressed in this way

ef·fu·sive /ɪˈfjuːsɪv/ *adj.* showing much or too much emotion: *an effusive welcome* ◇ *He was effusive in his praise.* ▸ **ef·fu·sive·ly** *adv.*

E-fit™ /ˈiːfɪt/ *noun* (*BrE*) a picture of a person who is wanted by the police, made using a computer program that puts together and makes changes to pictures of different features of faces, based on information that is given by sb who has seen the person ➲ compare IDENTIKIT, PHOTO-FIT

EFL /ˌiː ef ˈel/ *abbr.* (*BrE*) English as a foreign language (refers to the teaching of English to people for whom it is not the first language) ➲ compare EAL, EAP, ESL, ESOL

ˈe-friend *noun* = E-PAL

EFTA /ˈeftə/ *abbr.* European Free Trade Association (an economic association of some European countries)

e.g. 🔑 /ˌiː ˈdʒiː/ *abbr.* for example (from Latin 'exempli gratia'): *popular pets, e.g. cats and dogs*

Language Bank

e.g.

Giving examples

- The website has a variety of interactive exercises (**e.g.** matching games, crosswords and quizzes).
- The website has a variety of interactive exercises, **including** matching games, crosswords and quizzes.
- Web 2.0 technologies, **such as** wikis, blogs and social networking sites, have changed the way that people use the Internet.
- Many websites now allow users to contribute information. **A good example of this is** the 'wiki', a type of website that anyone can edit.
- Wikis vary in how open they are. **For example**, some wikis allow anybody to edit content, while others only allow registered users to do this.
- Wikis vary in how open they are. Some wikis, **for example/for instance**, allow anybody to edit content, while others only allow registered users to do this.
- More and more people read their news on the Internet. **To take one example,** over 14 million people now read the online version of 'The Oxford Herald'.
- Online newspapers are now more popular than paper ones. 'The Oxford Herald' **is a case in point**. Its print circulation has fallen in recent years, while its website attracts millions of users every month.

➲ note at EXAMPLE
➲ Language Banks at ADDITION, ARGUE, EVIDENCE, ILLUSTRATE

egali·tar·ian /iˌɡælɪˈteəriən; *NAmE* -ˈter-/ *adj.* based on, or holding, the belief that everyone is equal and should have the same rights and opportunities ▸ **egali·tar·ian** *noun*: *He described himself as 'an egalitarian'.* **egali·tar·ian·ism** /-ɪzəm/ *noun* [U]

egg 🔑 /eɡ/ *noun, verb*
■ ***noun*** **1** 🔑 [C] a small OVAL object with a thin hard shell produced by a female bird and containing a young bird; a similar object produced by a female fish, insect, etc: *The female sits on the eggs until they hatch.* ◇ *The fish lay thousands of eggs at one time.* ◇ *crocodile eggs* ➲ **COLLOCATIONS** at LIFE ➲ **VISUAL VOCAB** pages V10, V11 **2** 🔑 [C, U] a bird's egg, especially one from a chicken, that is eaten as food: *a* ***boiled egg*** ◇ *bacon and eggs* ◇ ***fried/poached/scrambled eggs*** ◇ *Bind the mixture together with a little beaten egg.* ◇ *You've got some egg on your shirt.* ◇ ***egg yolks/whites*** ◇ *egg noodles* ◇ *ducks'/quails' eggs* ◇ *a chocolate egg* (= made from chocolate in the shape of an egg) ➲ see also EASTER EGG, SCOTCH EGG **3** 🔑 [C] (in women and female animals) a cell that combines with a SPERM to create a baby or young animal **SYN ovum**: *The male sperm fertilizes the female egg.* ◇ *an egg donor* ➲ see also NEST EGG
IDM **a ˈgood egg** (*old-fashioned, informal*) a person who you can rely on to behave well **have ˈegg on/all over your**

face (*informal*) to be made to look stupid: *They were left with egg on their faces when only ten people showed up.* **put all your eggs in one 'basket** to rely on one particular course of action for success rather than giving yourself several different possibilities ➲ more at CHICKEN *n.*, CURATE, KILL *v.*, OMELETTE, SURE *adv.*, TEACH

■ *verb*

PHR V **,egg sb↔'on** (*informal*) to encourage sb to do sth, especially sth that they should not do: *He hit the other boy again and again as his friends egged him on.*

E

,egg-and-'spoon race *noun* (*BrE*) a race, usually run by children, in which those taking part have to hold an egg balanced in a spoon

'egg cup *noun* a small cup for holding a boiled egg ➲ VISUAL VOCAB page V19

egg·head /'eghed/ *noun* (*informal, disapproving* or *humorous*) a person who is very intelligent and is only interested in studying

egg·nog /'egnɒg; *NAmE* -nɑ:g; -nɔ:g/ (*BrE* also **'egg flip**) *noun* [U, C] an alcoholic drink made by mixing beer, wine, etc. with eggs and milk

egg·plant /'egplɑ:nt; *NAmE* -plænt/ (*NAmE*) (*BrE* **au·ber·gine**) *noun* [C, U] a vegetable with shiny dark purple skin and soft white flesh ➲ VISUAL VOCAB page V27

,egg 'roll *noun* (*NAmE*) a type of SPRING ROLL in which the PASTRY is made with eggs

egg·shell /'egʃel/ *noun* **1** [C, U] the hard thin outside of an egg **2** [U] (*BrE*) a type of paint that is smooth but not shiny when it dries

'egg timer *noun* a device that you use to measure the time needed to boil an egg

ego /'i:gəʊ; 'egəʊ; *NAmE* 'i:goʊ/ *noun* (*pl.* -os) **1** your sense of your own value and importance: *He has the biggest ego of anyone I've ever met.* ◇ *Winning the prize really* **boosted her ego.** **2** (*psychology*) the part of the mind that is responsible for your sense of who you are (= your identity) ➲ compare SUPEREGO ➲ see also ALTER EGO ➲ compare ID

ego·cen·tric /,egəʊ'sentrɪk; ,i:g-; *NAmE* ,i:goʊ-/ *adj.* thinking only about yourself and not about what other people need or want **SYN** **selfish**

ego·ism /'egəʊɪzəm; 'i:g-; *NAmE* -goʊ-/ (also **egot·ism** /'egətɪzəm; 'i:g-/) *noun* [U] (*disapproving*) the fact of thinking that you are better or more important than anyone else ▸ **ego·is·tic** /,egəʊ'ɪstɪk; ,i:g-; *NAmE* -goʊ-/ (also **egot·is·tic·al** /,egə'tɪstɪkl; ,i:gə-/, **egot·is·tic** /,egə'tɪstɪk; ,i:gə-/) *adj.* **egot·is·tic·al·ly** /-kli/ *adv.*

ego·ist /'egəʊɪst; 'i:g-; *NAmE* 'i:goʊ-/ (also **egot·ist** /'egətɪst; 'i:gə-/) *noun* (*disapproving*) a person who thinks that he or she is better than other people and who thinks and talks too much about himself or herself

ego·mania /,egəʊ'meɪniə; ,i:gəʊ-; *NAmE* ,i:goʊ-/ *noun* [U] a mental condition in which sb is interested in themselves or concerned about themselves in a way that is not normal ▸ **ego·maniac** /,egəʊ'meɪniæk; ,i:gəʊ-; *NAmE* ,i:goʊ-/ *noun* **ego·ma·ni·acal** /,egəʊmə'naɪəkl; ,i:gəʊ-; *NAmE* ,i:goʊ-/ *adj.*

'ego-surfing *noun* [U] (often *humorous*) the activity of searching the Internet to find places where your own name has been mentioned

'ego trip *noun* (usually *disapproving*) an activity that sb does because it makes them feel good and important

egre·gious /ɪ'gri:dʒiəs/ *adj.* (*formal*) extremely bad

e·gress /'i:gres/ *noun* [U] (*formal*) the act of leaving a place ➲ compare ACCESS, INGRESS

egret /'i:grət/ *noun* a bird of the HERON family, with long legs and long white tail feathers

Egypt·ology /,i:dʒɪp'tɒlədʒi; *NAmE* -'tɑ:l-/ *noun* [U] the study of the language, history and culture of ancient Egypt ▸ **Egyp·tolo·gist** /,i:dʒɪp'tɒlədʒɪst; *NAmE* -'tɑ:l-/ *noun*

eh /eɪ/ *exclamation* (*BrE*) (*NAmE* usually **huh**) **1** the sound that people make when they want sb to repeat sth: *'I'm not hungry.' 'Eh?' 'I said I'm not hungry.'* **2** the sound that people make when they want sb to agree or reply: *So what do you think, eh?* **3** the sound people make when they are surprised: *Another new dress, eh!*

Eid (also **Id**) /i:d/ *noun* one of the two main Muslim festivals, either **Eid ul-Fitr** /,i:d ʊl 'fɪtrə/ at the end of Ramadan, or **Eid ul-Adha** /,i:d ʊl 'ɑ:də/ which celebrates the end of the PILGRIMAGE to Mecca and Abraham's SACRIFICE of a sheep

ei·der·down /'aɪdədaʊn; *NAmE* -dərd-/ *noun* (*BrE*) a thick, warm cover for a bed, filled with feathers or other soft material, and usually placed on top of a sheet and BLANKETS

eider duck /'aɪdə dʌk; *NAmE* 'aɪdər/ *noun* a large DUCK with soft feathers, that lives in northern countries

eight 🔑 /eɪt/

1 🔑 *number* 8 **HELP** There are examples of how to use numbers at the entry for **five.** **2** *noun* a team of eight people who ROW a long narrow boat in races; the boat they row ➲ see also FIGURE OF EIGHT

eight·een 🔑 /,eɪ'ti:n/ *number*

18 ▸ **eight·eenth** 🔑 /,eɪ'ti:nθ/ *ordinal number, noun* **HELP** There are examples of how to use ordinal numbers at the entry for **fifth.**

eighth 🔑 /eɪtθ/ *ordinal number, noun*

■ ***ordinal number*** 🔑 8th **HELP** There are examples of how to use ordinal numbers at the entry for **fifth.**

■ ***noun*** 🔑 each of eight equal parts of sth

'eighth note (*NAmE*) (*BrE* **qua·ver**) *noun* (*music*) a note that lasts half as long as a CROTCHET/QUARTER NOTE ➲ picture at MUSIC

eighty 🔑 /'eɪti/

1 🔑 *number* 80 **2** *noun* **the eight·ies** [pl.] numbers, years or temperatures from 80 to 89 ▸ **eight·ieth** 🔑 /'eɪtiəθ/ *ordinal number, noun* **HELP** There are examples of how to use ordinal numbers at the entry for **fifth.**

IDM **in your eighties** between the ages of 80 and 89

eina /'eɪnɑ:/ *exclamation* (*SAfrE*) used to express sudden pain: *Eina! That was sore!*

ein·stein·ium /aɪn'staɪniəm/ *noun* [U] (*symb.* **Es**) a chemical element. Einsteinium is a RADIOACTIVE element produced artificially from PLUTONIUM and other elements.

ei·stedd·fod /aɪ'steðvɒd; *NAmE* -vɑ:d/ *noun* (*WelshE*) a type of festival, held in Wales, in which there are singing, music and poetry competitions

ei·ther 🔑 /'aɪðə(r); 'i:ðə(r)/ *det., pron., adv.*

■ ***det., pron.*** **1** 🔑 one or the other of two; it does not matter which: *You can park on either side of the street.* ◇ *You can keep one of the photos. Either of them—whichever you like.* ◇ *There are two types of qualification—either is acceptable.* ➲ note at NEITHER **2** 🔑 each of two: *The offices on either side were empty.* ◇ *There's a door at either end of the corridor.*

■ ***adv.*** **1** 🔑 used after negative phrases to state that a feeling or situation is similar to one already mentioned: *Pete can't go and I can't either.* ◇ (*NAmE, informal*) *'I don't like it.' 'Me either.'* (= Neither do I). **2** 🔑 used to add extra information to a statement: *I know a good Italian restaurant. It's not far from here, either.* **3** 🔑 **either... or...** used to show a choice of two things: *Well, I think she's either Czech or Slovak.* ◇ *I'm going to buy either a camera or a DVD player with the money.* ◇ *Either he could not come or he did not want to.* ➲ note at NEITHER ➲ compare OR

ejacu·late /i'dʒækjuleɪt/ *verb* **1** [I, T] **~ (sth)** when a man or a male animal **ejaculates**, SEMEN comes out through the PENIS **2 + speech** (*old-fashioned*) to say or shout sth suddenly **SYN** **exclaim**

ejacu·la·tion /i,dʒækju'leɪʃn/ *noun* **1** [C, U] the act of ejaculating; the moment when SPERM comes out of a man's PENIS: *premature ejaculation* **2** [C] (*formal*) a sudden shout or sound that you make when you are angry or surprised **SYN** **exclamation**

eject /i'dʒekt/ *verb* **1** [T] **~ sb (from sth)** (*formal*) to force sb to leave a place **SYN** **throw out**: *Police ejected a number* *of violent protesters from the hall.* **2** [T] **~ sth** (**from sth**) to push sth out suddenly and with a lot of force: *Used cartridges are ejected from the gun after firing.* **3** [I] (of a pilot) to escape from an aircraft that is going to crash, sometimes using an EJECTOR SEAT **4** [T, I] **~** (**sth**) when you **eject** a tape, disk, etc., or when it **ejects**, it comes out of the machine after you have pressed a button ▶ **ejec·tion** /iˈdʒekʃn/ *noun* [U, C]

eject·or seat /iˈdʒektə siːt; *NAmE* -tər/ (*US* also **ejection seat**) *noun* a seat that allows a pilot to be thrown out of an aircraft in an emergency

eke /iːk/ *verb*

PHR V ˌ**eke sth↔ˈout 1** to make a small supply of sth such as food or money last longer by using only small amounts of it: *She managed to eke out her student loan till the end of the year.* **2 ~ a living, etc.** to manage to live with very little money

EKG /ˌiː keɪ ˈdʒiː/ *abbr.* (*NAmE*) = ECG

elab·or·ate *adj., verb*

■ ***adj.*** /ɪˈlæbərət/ [usually before noun] very complicated and detailed; carefully prepared and organized: *elaborate designs* ◇ *She had prepared a very elaborate meal.* ◇ *an elaborate computer system* ▶ **elab·or·ate·ly** *adv.*: *an elaborately decorated room* **elab·or·ate·ness** *noun* [U]

■ ***verb*** /ɪˈlæbəreɪt/ **1** [I, T] to explain or describe sth in a more detailed way: **~** (**on/upon sth**) *He said he was resigning but did not elaborate on his reasons.* ◇ **~ sth** *She went on to elaborate her argument.* **2** [T] **~ sth** to develop a plan, an idea, etc. and make it complicated or detailed: *In his plays he takes simple traditional tales and elaborates them.* ▶ **elab·or·ation** /ɪˌlæbəˈreɪʃn/ *noun* [U, C]: *The importance of the plan needs no further elaboration.*

elan /eɪˈlɒ̃; eɪˈlæn; *NAmE* eɪˈlɑ̃ː/ *noun* [U] (from *French, literary*) great enthusiasm and energy, style and confidence

eland /ˈiːlənd/ *noun* (*pl.* **eland** or **elands**) a large African ANTELOPE with curled horns

elapse /ɪˈlæps/ *verb* [I] (not usually used in the progressive tenses) (*formal*) if a period of time **elapses**, it passes SYN **go by**: *Many years elapsed before they met again.*

eˌlapsed ˈtime *noun* [U] (*technical*) used to describe the time that passes between the start and end of a project or a computer operation, in contrast to the actual time needed to do a particular task which is part of the project

elas·tic /ɪˈlæstɪk/ *noun, adj.*

■ ***noun*** [U] material made with rubber, that can stretch and then return to its original size: *This skirt needs some new elastic in the waist.*

■ ***adj.*** **1** made with elastic: *an elastic headband* **2** able to stretch and return to its original size and shape: *elastic materials* **3** that can change or be changed: *Our plans are fairly elastic.*

elas·ti·cated /ɪˈlæstɪkeɪtɪd/ (*BrE*) (*NAmE* **elas·ti·cized** /ɪˈlæstɪsaɪzd/) *adj.* (of clothing, or part of a piece of clothing) made using elastic material that can stretch: *a skirt with an elasticated waist*

eˌlastic ˈband *noun* (*BrE*) = RUBBER BAND ➲ VISUAL VOCAB page V56

elas·ti·city /ˌiːlæˈstɪsəti; ˌelæ-; ɪˌlæ-/ *noun* [U] the quality that sth has of being able to stretch and return to its original size and shape (= of being elastic)

elas·tin /ɪˈlæstɪn/ *noun* [U] (*biology*) a natural substance that stretches easily, found in the skin, the heart and other body TISSUES

elasto·mer /ɪˈlæstəmə(r)/ *noun* (*chemistry*) a natural or artificial chemical that behaves like rubber

elated /iˈleɪtɪd/ *adj.* **~** (**at/by sth**) very happy and excited because of sth good that has happened, or will happen: *They were elated at the result.* ◇ *I was elated by the prospect of the new job ahead.* ➲ SYNONYMS at EXCITED

ela·tion /iˈleɪʃn/ *noun* [U] a feeling of great happiness and excitement

elbow 🔑 /ˈelbəʊ; *NAmE* -boʊ/ *noun, verb*

■ ***noun*** **1** 🔑 the joint between the upper and lower parts of the arm where it bends in the middle: *She jabbed him with her elbow.* ◇ *He's fractured his elbow.* ➲ VISUAL VOCAB page V48 **2** 🔑 the part of a piece of clothing that covers the elbow: *The jacket was worn at the elbows.* **3** a part of a pipe, CHIMNEY, etc. where it bends at a sharp angle

IDM **get the ˈelbow** (*BrE, informal*) to be told by sb that they no longer want to have a relationship with you; to be told to go away **give sb the ˈelbow** (*BrE, informal*) to tell sb that you no longer want to have a relationship with them; to tell sb to go away ➲ more at KNOW *v.*, POWER *n.*, RUB *v.*

■ ***verb*** **~ sb/sth** (**+adv./prep.**) to push sb with your elbow, usually in order to get past them: *She elbowed me out of the way to get to the front of the line.* ◇ *He* ***elbowed his way*** *through the crowd.*

ˈelbow grease *noun* [U] (*informal*) the effort used in physical work, especially in cleaning or polishing sth

ˈelbow room *noun* [U] (*informal*) enough space to move or walk in

elder /ˈeldə(r)/ *adj., noun*

■ ***adj.*** **1** [only before noun] (of people, especially two members of the same family) older: *my elder brother* ◇ *his elder sister* **2 the elder** used without a noun immediately after it to show who is the older of two people: *the elder of their two sons* **3 the elder** (*formal*) used before or after sb's name to show that they are the older of two people who have the same name: *the elder Pitt* ◇ *Pitt the elder* ➲ note at OLD ➲ compare THE YOUNGER at YOUNG *adj.* (6)

■ ***noun*** **1 elders** [pl.] people of greater age, experience and authority: *Children have no respect for their elders nowadays.* ◇ *the village elders* (= the old and respected people of the village) **2 my, etc. elder** [sing.] (*formal*) a person older than me, etc: *He is her elder by several years.* **3** [C] an official in some Christian churches **4** [C] a small tree with white flowers with a sweet smell (**elderflowers**) and bunches of small black BERRIES (**elderberries**)

IDM **your ˌelders and ˈbetters** people who are older and wiser than you and whom you should respect

ˈelder abuse *noun* [U] the crime of harming or stealing from an old person, committed by sb who is trusted to care for or help them

elder·berry /ˈeldəberi; *NAmE* ˈeldərb-/ *noun* (*pl.* **-ies**) a small black BERRY that grows in bunches on an elder tree

elder·care /ˈeldəkeə(r); *NAmE* ˈeldərker/ *noun* [U] (*especially NAmE*) help for old people, especially services such as special homes and medical care: *nursing homes and other eldercare facilities*

elder·flower /ˈeldəflaʊə(r); *NAmE* ˈeldərf-/ *noun* the flower of the elder tree, used to make wines and other drinks

eld·er·ly 🔑 /ˈeldəli; *NAmE* -ərli/ *adj.*

1 🔑 (of people) used as a polite word for 'old': *an elderly couple* ◇ *elderly relatives* ➲ SYNONYMS at OLD **2 the elderly** *noun* [pl.] people who are old

ˌelder ˈstatesman *noun* **1** an old and respected politician or former politician whose advice is still valued because of his or her long experience **2** any experienced and respected person whose advice or work is valued: *an elder statesman of golf*

eld·est /ˈeldɪst/ *adj.* **1** (of people, especially of three or more members of the same family) oldest: *Tom is my eldest son.* **2 the eldest** used without a noun immediately after it to show who is the oldest of three or more people: *the eldest of their three children* ➲ note at OLD

eld·ritch /ˈeldrɪtʃ/ *adj.* [usually before noun] (*literary*) strange and frightening: *an eldritch screech*

elect 🔑 /ɪˈlekt/ *verb, adj.*

■ ***verb*** **1** 🔑 to choose sb to do a particular job by voting for them: **~ sb/sth** *an* ***elected assembly/leader/representative*** ◇ *the newly elected government* ◇ **~ sb to sth** *She became the first black woman to be elected to the Senate.* ◇ **~ sb** (**as**) **sth** | **~ sb + noun** *He was elected (as) MP for Oxford East.* ➲ COLLOCATIONS at VOTE **2 ~ to do sth** (*formal*) to choose to do sth: *Increasing numbers of people elect to work from home nowadays.*

■ ***adj.*** **1** used after nouns to show that sb has been chosen for a job, but is not yet doing that job: *the president elect* **2 the elect** *noun* [pl.] (*religion*) people who have been chosen to be saved from punishment after death

elec·tion 0‑ᴡ /ɪˈlekʃn/ *noun*
1 0‑ᴡ [U, C] the process of choosing a person or a group of people for a position, especially a political position, by voting: ***election campaigns/results*** ◇ *to* ***win/lose an election*** ◇ *to* ***fight an election*** ◇ *to* ***vote in an election*** ◇ *In America, presidential* ***elections are held*** *every four years.* ◇ *The prime minister is about to* ***call*** (= announce) ***an election.*** ◇ (*especially BrE*) *How many candidates are* ***standing for election?*** ◇ (*especially NAmE*) *to* ***run for election*** ➲ COLLOCATIONS at VOTE **2** 0‑ᴡ [U] the fact of having been chosen by election: **~ (as sth)** *We welcome his election as president.* ◇ **~ (to sth)** *a year after her election to the committee* ➲ see also BY-ELECTION, GENERAL ELECTION

Synonyms

election

vote • poll • referendum • ballot

These are all words for an event in which people choose a representative or decide sth by voting.

election an occasion on which people officially choose a political representative or government by voting: *Who did you vote for in the last election?*

vote an occasion on which a group of people vote for sb/sth: *They took a vote on who should go first.*

poll (*journalism*) the process of voting in an election: *They suffered a defeat* ***at the polls.***

referendum an occasion on which all the adults in a country can vote on a particular issue

ballot the system of voting by marking an election paper, especially in secret; an occasion on which a vote is held: *The leader will be chosen by secret ballot.* NOTE **Ballot** is usually used about a vote within an organization rather than an occasion on which the public vote.

PATTERNS
- a **national/local** election/vote/poll/referendum/ballot
- to **have/hold/conduct** a(n) election/vote/poll/referendum/ballot

elec·tion·eer·ing /ɪˌlekʃəˈnɪərɪŋ; *NAmE* -ˈnɪr-/ *noun* [U] the activity of making speeches and visiting people to try to persuade them to vote for a particular politician or political party in an election

elect·ive /ɪˈlektɪv/ *adj., noun*
■ ***adj.*** [usually before noun] (*formal*) **1** using or chosen by election: *an elective democracy* ◇ *an elective assembly* ◇ *an elective member* ◇ *He had never held elective office* (= a position which is filled by election). **2** having the power to elect: *an elective body* **3** (of medical treatment) that you choose to have; that is not urgent SYN **optional**: *elective surgery* **4** (of a course or subject) that a student can choose SYN **optional**
■ ***noun*** (*especially NAmE*) a course or subject at a college or school which a student can choose to do

elect·or /ɪˈlektə(r)/ *noun* a person who has the right to vote in an election

elect·or·al /ɪˈlektərəl/ *adj.* [only before noun] connected with elections: ***electoral systems/reforms*** ▶ **elect·or·al·ly** /-rəli/ *adv.*: *an electorally effective campaign*

eˌlectoral ˈcollege *noun* **1 the Electoral College** (in the US) a group of people who come together to elect the President and Vice-President, based on the votes of people in each state **2** (*BrE*) a group of people who are chosen to represent the members of a political party, etc. in the election of a leader

eˌlectoral ˈregister (also **eˌlectoral ˈroll**) *noun* (in Britain) the official list of people who have the right to vote in a particular area

elect·or·ate /ɪˈlektərət/ *noun* [C+sing./pl. v.] **1** the people in a country or an area who have the right to vote, thought of as a group: *Only 60% of the electorate voted in the last election.* ➲ COLLOCATIONS at VOTE **2** (*AustralE, NZE*) = CONSTITUENCY (1)

elec·tric 0‑ᴡ /ɪˈlektrɪk/ *adj., noun*
■ ***adj.*** **1** 0‑ᴡ [usually before noun] connected with electricity; using, produced by or producing electricity: *an electric motor* ◇ *an* ***electric light/guitar, etc.*** ◇ *an* ***electric current/charge*** ◇ *an electric generator* ◇ *an* ***electric plug/socket/switch*** (= that carries electricity) ➲ see also ELECTRIC SHOCK, ELECTRICAL STORM **2** full of excitement; making people excited SYN **electrifying**: *The atmosphere was electric.*
■ ***noun*** [U] (*informal*) used to refer to the supply of electricity to a building: *The electric will be off tomorrow.* ◇ *I've paid the electric* (= the bill for the supply of electricity).

Synonyms

electric / electrical

These adjectives are frequently used with the following nouns:

electric ~	electrical ~
light	equipment
guitar	wiring
drill	signal
chair	engineer
shock	shock

- **Electric** is usually used to describe something that uses or produces electricity. You use **electrical** with more general nouns such as *equipment* and *wiring* and things that are concerned with electricity: *an electrical fault*. However, the distinction is not always so clear now: *an electric/electrical company* ◇ *an electric/electrical current* ◇ *an electric/electrical shock.*

elec·tric·al 0‑ᴡ /ɪˈlektrɪkl/ *adj.*
connected with electricity; using or producing electricity: *an electrical fault in the engine* ◇ ***electrical equipment/appliances*** ◇ ***electrical power/energy*** ▶ **elec·tric·al·ly** /-kli/ *adv.*: *a car with electrically operated windows* ◇ *electrically charged particles*

eˌlectrical engiˈneering *noun* [U] the design and building of machines and systems that use or produce electricity; the study of this subject ▶ **eˌlectrical engiˈneer** *noun*

eˌlectrical ˈstorm (*BrE* also **eˌlectric ˈstorm**) *noun* a violent storm in which electricity is produced in the atmosphere

eˌlectric ˈblanket *noun* a BLANKET for a bed that is heated by electricity passing through the wires inside it (usually used under the bottom sheet of the bed)

eˌlectric ˈblue *noun* [U] a bright or METALLIC blue colour

eˌlectric ˈchair (usually **the electric chair**) (also *informal* **the chair**) *noun* [sing.] (especially in the US) a chair in which criminals are killed by passing a powerful electric current through their bodies; the method of EXECUTION which uses this chair: *He was sent to the electric chair.* ◇ *They face death by the electric chair.*

eˌlectric ˈfence *noun* a wire fence through which an electric current can be passed

elec·tri·cian /ɪˌlekˈtrɪʃn/ *noun* a person whose job is to connect, repair, etc. electrical equipment

elec·tri·city 0‑ᴡ /ɪˌlekˈtrɪsəti/ *noun*
1 0‑ᴡ [U] a form of energy from charged ELEMENTARY PARTICLES, usually supplied as electric current through cables, wires, etc. for lighting, heating, driving machines,

etc: *a waste of electricity* ◇ *The electricity is off* (= there is no electric power supply). **2** [U, sing.] a feeling of great emotion, excitement, etc.

e͵lectric 'razor *noun* = SHAVER

elec·trics /ɪ'lektrɪks/ *noun* [pl.] (*BrE, informal*) the system of electrical wires in a house, car or machine: *There's a problem with the electrics.*

e͵lectric 'shock (also **shock**) *noun* a sudden painful feeling that you get when electricity passes through your body

elec·tri·fi·ca·tion /ɪ͵lektrɪfɪ'keɪʃn/ *noun* [U] the process of changing sth so that it works by electricity

elec·trify /ɪ'lektrɪfaɪ/ *verb* (**elec·tri·fies**, **elec·tri·fy·ing**, **elec·tri·fied**, **elec·tri·fied**) **1** [usually passive] **~ sth** to make sth work by using electricity; to pass an electrical current through sth: *The railway line was electrified in the 1950s.* ◇ *He had all the fences around his home electrified.* **2 ~ sb** to make sb feel very excited and enthusiastic about sth: *Her performance electrified the audience.*

elec·tri·fy·ing /ɪ'lektrɪfaɪɪŋ/ *adj.* very exciting: *The dancers gave an electrifying performance.*

elec·tro- /ɪ'lektrəʊ; *NAmE* -troʊ/ *combining form* (in nouns, adjectives, verbs and adverbs) connected with electricity: *electromagnetism*

elec·tro·car·dio·gram /ɪ͵lektrəʊ'kɑːdiəʊgræm; *NAmE* ɪ͵lektroʊ'kɑːrdioʊ-/ *noun* = ECG

elec·tro·con·vul·sive therapy /ɪ͵lektrəʊkən'vʌlsɪv θerəpi; *NAmE* -troʊ-/ (also **e'lec·tro·shock ther·apy**) *noun* [U] a medical treatment of mental illness that passes electricity through the patient's brain

elec·tro·cute /ɪ'lektrəkjuːt/ *verb* [usually passive] **~ sb** to injure or kill sb by passing electricity through their body: *The boy was electrocuted when he wandered onto a railway track.* ◇ *He was electrocuted in Virginia in 2006* (= punished by being killed in the electric chair). ▸ **elec·tro·cu·tion** /ɪ͵lektrə'kjuːʃn/ *noun* [U]: *Six people were drowned; five died from electrocution.* ◇ *He was sentenced to death by electrocution.*

elec·trode /ɪ'lektrəʊd; *NAmE* -troʊd/ *noun* either of two points (or TERMINALS) by which an electric current enters or leaves a battery or other electrical device ➲ see also ANODE, CATHODE

elec·tro·dynam·ics /ɪ͵lektrəʊdaɪ'næmɪks; *NAmE* -troʊ-/ *noun* [U] (*physics*) the study of the way that electric currents and MAGNETIC FIELDS affect each other

elec·tro·enceph·alo·gram /ɪ͵lektrəʊɪn'sefələgræm; -'kefələ-; *NAmE* -troʊɪn'sef-/ *noun* = EEG

elec·troly·sis /ɪ͵lek'trɒləsɪs; *NAmE* -'trɑːl-/ *noun* [U] **1** the destruction of the roots of hairs by means of an electric current, as a beauty treatment **2** (*chemistry*) the separation of a liquid (or electrolyte) into its chemical parts by passing an electric current through it

elec·tro·lyte /ɪ'lektrəlaɪt/ *noun* (*chemistry*) a liquid that an electric current can pass through, especially in an electric cell or battery ▸ **elec·tro·ly·tic** /ɪ͵lektrə'lɪtɪk/ *adj.*

elec·tro·mag·net /ɪ'lektrəʊmægnət; *NAmE* -troʊ-/ *noun* (*physics*) a piece of metal which becomes MAGNETIC when electricity is passed through it

elec·tro·mag·net·ic /ɪ͵lektrəʊmæg'netɪk; *NAmE* -troʊ-/ *adj.* (*physics*) having both electrical and MAGNETIC characteristics (or PROPERTIES): *an* ***electromagnetic wave/field***

elec·tro·mag·net·ism /ɪ͵lektrəʊ'mægnətɪzəm; *NAmE* -troʊ-/ *noun* [U] (*physics*) the production of a MAGNETIC FIELD by means of an electric current, or of an electric current by means of a MAGNETIC FIELD

elec·tron /ɪ'lektrɒn; *NAmE* -trɑːn/ *noun* (*physics*) a very small piece of matter (= a substance) with a negative electric charge, found in all atoms ➲ see also NEUTRON, PROTON

elec·tron·ic 🔑 /ɪ͵lek'trɒnɪk; *NAmE* -'trɑːnɪk/ *adj.* [usually before noun]
1 🔑 (of a device) having or using many small parts, such as MICROCHIPS, that control and direct a small electric current: *an electronic calculator* ◇ *electronic music* ◇ *This dictionary is available in electronic form.* **2** 🔑 concerned with electronic equipment: *an electronic engineer*

elec·tron·ic·al·ly /ɪ͵lek'trɒnɪkli; *NAmE* -'trɑːn-/ *adv.* in an electronic way, or using a device that works in an electronic way: *to process data electronically* (= using a computer)

͵electronic 'mail *noun* [U] (*formal*) = EMAIL

͵electronic 'organizer *noun* a very small computer which can be carried around, used for storing information such as addresses and important dates

͵electronic 'publishing *noun* [U] the business of publishing books in a form that can be read on a computer, for example as CD-ROMs

elec·tron·ics /ɪ͵lek'trɒnɪks; *NAmE* -'trɑːn-/ *noun* **1** [U] the branch of science and technology that studies electric currents in electronic equipment **2** [U] the use of electronic technology, especially in developing new equipment: *the electronics industry* **3 electronics** [pl.] the electronic CIRCUITS and COMPONENTS (= parts) used in electronic equipment: *a fault in the electronics*

elec͵tronic 'tagging *noun* [U] the system of attaching an electronic device to a person so that the police, etc. know where the person is

e͵lectron 'microscope *noun* a very powerful MICROSCOPE that uses ELECTRONS instead of light

elec·tro·plate /ɪ'lektrəpleɪt/ *verb* [usually passive] **~ sth** to cover sth with a thin layer of metal using ELECTROLYSIS

elec·tro·shock ther·apy /ɪ'lektrəʊʃɒk θerəpi; *NAmE* -troʊʃɑːk/ *noun* = ELECTROCONVULSIVE THERAPY

elec·tro·stat·ic /ɪ͵lektrəʊ'stætɪk; *NAmE* -troʊ-/ *adj.* (*physics*) used to talk about electric charges that are not moving, rather than electric currents

ele·gant 🔑 /'elɪgənt/ *adj.*
1 🔑 (of people or their behaviour) attractive and showing a good sense of style SYN **stylish**: *She was tall and elegant.* **2** 🔑 (of clothes, places and things) attractive and designed well SYN **stylish**: *an elegant dress* ◇ *an elegant room/restaurant* **3** (of a plan or an idea) clever but simple: *an elegant solution to the problem* ▸ **ele·gance** /'elɪgəns/ *noun* [U]: *She dresses with casual elegance.* ◇ *His writing combines elegance and wit.* **ele·gant·ly** *adv.*: *elegantly dressed* ◇ *elegantly furnished*

ele·giac /͵elɪ'dʒaɪək/ *adj.* (*formal* or *literary*) expressing sadness, especially about the past or people who have died

elegy /'elədʒi/ *noun* (*pl.* **-ies**) a poem or song that expresses sadness, especially for sb who has died

elem·ent 🔑 AW /'elɪmənt/ *noun*
▸ PART/AMOUNT **1** 🔑 [C] **~ (in/of sth)** a necessary or typical part of sth: *Cost was* ***a key element*** *in our decision.* ◇ *The story has all the elements of a soap opera.* ◇ *Customer relations is an important element of the job.* **2** 🔑 [C, usually sing.] **~ of surprise, risk, truth, etc.** a small amount of a quality or feeling: *We need to preserve the element of surprise.* ◇ *There appears to be an element of truth in his story.*
▸ GROUP OF PEOPLE **3** [C, usually pl.] a group of people who form a part of a larger group or society: ***moderate/radical elements*** *within the party* ◇ *unruly elements in the school*
▸ CHEMISTRY **4** 🔑 [C] a simple chemical substance that consists of atoms of only one type and cannot be split by chemical means into a simpler substance. Gold, OXYGEN and CARBON are all elements. ➲ compare COMPOUND
▸ EARTH/AIR/FIRE/WATER **5** [C] one of the four substances: earth, air, fire and water, which people used to believe everything else was made of
▸ WEATHER **6 the elements** [pl.] the weather, especially bad weather: *Are we going to brave the elements and go for a walk?* ◇ *to be exposed to the elements*
▸ BASIC PRINCIPLES **7 elements** [pl.] the basic principles of a subject that you have to learn first SYN **basics**: *He taught me the elements of map-reading.*

E

▸ ENVIRONMENT **8** [C, usually sing.] a natural or suitable environment, especially for an animal: *Water is a fish's natural element.*

▸ ELECTRICAL PART **9** [C] the part of a piece of electrical equipment that gives out heat: *The kettle needs a new element.*

IDM **in your 'element** doing what you are good at and enjoy: *She's really in her element at parties.* **out of your 'element** in a situation that you are not used to and that makes you feel uncomfortable

elem·en·tal /ˌelɪ'mentl/ *adj.* [usually before noun] (*formal*) **1** wild and powerful; like the forces of nature: *the elemental fury of the storm* **2** basic and important: *an elemental truth*

elem·en·tary /ˌelɪ'mentri/ *adj.* **1** in or connected with the first stages of a course of study: *an elementary English course* ◇ *a book for elementary students* ◇ *at an elementary level* ➲ compare PRIMARY, SECONDARY **2** of the most basic kind: *the elementary laws of economics* ◇ *an elementary mistake* **3** very simple and easy: *elementary questions*

ˌelementary 'particle *noun* (*physics*) any of the different types of very small pieces of matter (= a substance) smaller than an atom

ˌele'mentary school (also *informal* **'grade school**) *noun* (in the US) a school for children between the ages of about 6 and 12

ele·phant /'elɪfənt/ *noun* a very large animal with thick grey skin, large ears, two curved outer teeth called TUSKS and a long nose called a TRUNK. There are two types of elephant, the African and the Asian: *herds of elephants/elephant herds* ◇ *a baby elephant* ➲ see also WHITE ELEPHANT

IDM **the ˌelephant in the 'room** a problem or question that everyone knows about but does not mention because it is easier not to discuss it: *The elephant in the room was the money that had to be paid in bribes.*

ele·phant·ia·sis /ˌelɪfən'taɪəsɪs/ *noun* [U] (*medical*) a condition in which part of the body swells and becomes very large because the LYMPHATIC system is blocked

ele·phant·ine /ˌelɪ'fæntaɪn; *NAmE* -tiːn/ *adj.* (*formal* or *humorous*) very large and CLUMSY; like an elephant

ele·vate /'elɪveɪt/ *verb* **1** (*formal*) to give sb/sth a higher position or rank, often more important than they deserve SYN **raise, promote**: **~ sb/sth (to sth)** *He elevated many of his friends to powerful positions within the government.* ◇ **~ sth (into sth)** *It was an attempt to elevate football to a subject worthy of serious study.* **2 ~ sth** (*technical* or *formal*) to lift sth up or put sth in a higher position: *It is important that the injured leg should be elevated.* **3 ~ sth** (*technical*) to make the level of sth increase: *Smoking often elevates blood pressure.* **4 ~ sth** (*formal*) to improve a person's mood, so that they feel happy: *The song never failed to elevate his spirits.*

ele·vated /'elɪveɪtɪd/ *adj.* [usually before noun] **1** high in rank: *an elevated status* **2** (*formal*) having a high moral or INTELLECTUAL level: *elevated language/sentiments/thoughts* **3** higher than the area around; above the level of the ground: *The house is in an elevated position, overlooking the town.* ◇ *an* ***elevated highway/railway/road*** (= one that runs on a bridge above the ground or street) **4** (*technical*) higher than normal: *elevated blood pressure*

ele·vat·ing /'elɪveɪtɪŋ/ *adj.* making people think about serious and interesting subjects: *Reading this essay was an elevating experience.*

ele·va·tion /ˌelɪ'veɪʃn/ *noun* **1** [U] (*formal*) the process of sb getting a higher or more important rank: *his elevation to the presidency* **2** [C, usually sing.] (*technical*) the height of a place, especially its height above sea level: *The city is at an elevation of 2 000 metres.* **3** [C] (*formal*) a piece of ground that is higher than the area around **4** [C] (*architecture*) one side of a building, or a drawing of this by an ARCHITECT: *the* ***front/rear/side elevation*** *of a house* ➲ compare PLAN *n.* (4) **5** [U, sing.] (*technical*) an increase in the level or amount of sth: *elevation of blood sugar levels*

ele·va·tor 🔑 /'elɪveɪtə(r)/ *noun* **1** 🔑 (*NAmE*) (*BrE* **lift**) a machine that carries people or goods up and down to different levels in a building or a mine: *It's on the fifth floor, so we'd better take the elevator.* **2** a place for storing large quantities of grain **3** a part in the tail of an aircraft that is moved to make it go up and down ➲ VISUAL VOCAB page V43

eleven 🔑 /ɪ'levn/ **1** 🔑 *number* 11 **2** *noun* a team of eleven players for football (SOCCER), CRICKET or HOCKEY: *She was chosen for the first eleven.* ▸ **elev·enth** 🔑 /ɪ'levnθ/ *ordinal number, noun* HELP There are examples of how to use ordinal numbers at the entry for **fifth**.

IDM **at the eˌleventh 'hour** at the last possible moment; just in time

eˌleven-'plus *noun* (usually **the eleven-plus**) [sing.] an exam that all children used to take in Britain at the age of eleven to decide which type of SECONDARY SCHOOL they should go to. It is still taken in a few areas.

elev·enses /ɪ'levnzɪz/ *noun* [U] (*old-fashioned, BrE, informal*) a very small meal, for example biscuits with tea or coffee, that people sometimes have at about eleven o'clock in the morning

ELF /elf/ *abbr.* (*linguistics*) English as a lingua franca

elf /elf/ *noun* (*pl.* **elves** /elvz/) (in stories) a creature like a small person with pointed ears, who has magic powers

elfin /'elfɪn/ *adj.* (of a person or their features) small and delicate: *an elfin face*

elicit /i'lɪsɪt/ *verb* **~ sth (from sb)** (*formal*) to get information or a reaction from sb, often with difficulty: *I could elicit no response from him.* ◇ *Her tears elicited great sympathy from her audience.* ▸ **elicit·ation** /iˌlɪsɪ'teɪʃn/ *noun* [U]

elide /i'laɪd/ *verb* **~ sth** (*phonetics*) to leave out the sound of part of a word when you are pronouncing it: *The 't' in 'often' may be elided.* ➲ see also ELISION

eli·gible /'elɪdʒəbl/ *adj.* **1** a person who is **eligible** for sth or to do sth, is able to have or do it because they have the right qualifications, are the right age, etc: **~ (for sth)** *Only those over 70 are eligible for the special payment.* ◇ **~ (to do sth)** *When are you eligible to vote in your country?* OPP **ineligible** **2** an **eligible** young man or woman is thought to be a good choice as a husband/wife, usually because they are rich or attractive ▸ **eli·gi·bil·ity** /ˌelɪdʒə'bɪləti/ *noun* [U]

elim·in·ate AW /ɪ'lɪmɪneɪt/ *verb* **1** to remove or get rid of sth/sb: **~ sth/sb** *Credit cards eliminate the need to carry a lot of cash.* ◇ **~ sth/sb from sth** *The police have eliminated two suspects from their investigation.* ◇ *This diet claims to eliminate toxins from the body.* **2 ~ sb (from sth)** [usually passive] to defeat a person or a team so that they no longer take part in a competition, etc. SYN **knock out**: *All the English teams were eliminated in the early stages of the competition.* **3 ~ sb** (*formal*) to kill sb, especially an enemy or opponent: *Most of the regime's left-wing opponents were eliminated.* ▸ **elim·in·ation** AW /ɪˌlɪmɪ'neɪʃn/ *noun* [U, C]: *the* ***elimination of disease/poverty/crime*** ◇ *There were three eliminations in the first round of the competition.* ◇ *the elimination of toxins from the body*

eˌlimi'nation reaction *noun* (*chemistry*) a chemical reaction which involves the separation of a substance from other substances ➲ compare ADDITION REACTION

eli·sion /ɪ'lɪʒn/ *noun* [U, C] (*phonetics*) the act of leaving out the sound of part of a word when you are pronouncing it, as in *we'll, don't* and *let's* ➲ see also ELIDE

elite /eɪ'liːt; ɪ'liːt/ *noun* [C+sing./pl. v.] a group of people in a society, etc. who are powerful and have a lot of influence, because they are rich, intelligent, etc: *a member of the* ***ruling/intellectual elite*** ◇ *Public opinion is influenced by the small elite who control the media.* ◇ *In these countries, only the elite can afford an education for their children.* ▸ **elite** *adj.* [only before noun]: *an elite group of senior officials* ◇ *an elite military academy*

elit·ism /eɪ'liːtɪzəm; ɪ-/ *noun* [U] (often *disapproving*) **1** a way of organizing a system, society, etc. so that only a few people (= an elite) have power or influence: *Many* *people believe that private education encourages elitism.* **2** the feeling of being better than other people that being part of an elite encourages ▸ **elit·ist** *adj.*: *an elitist model of society* ◇ *She accused him of being elitist.* **elit·ist** *noun*

elixir /ɪˈlɪksə(r); *BrE* also -sɪə(r)/ *noun* (*literary*) a magic liquid that is believed to cure illnesses or to make people live for ever: *the* ***elixir of life/youth***

Eliza·bethan /ɪˌlɪzəˈbiːθn/ *adj.* connected with the time when Queen Elizabeth I was queen of England (1558–1603) ▸ **Eliza·bethan** *noun*: *Shakespeare was an Elizabethan.*

elk /elk/ *noun* (*pl.* **elk** or **elks**) **1** (*BrE*) a large DEER that lives in the north of Europe, Asia and N America. In N America it is called a MOOSE. **2** (*NAmE*) = WAPITI **3 Elk** a member of the Benevolent and Protective Order of Elks, a US social organization that gives money to charity

elk (*BrE*)
moose (*NAmE*)

wapiti (*NAmE also* **elk**)

ell /el/ *noun* a unit used in the past for measuring cloth, equal to about 45 inches or 115 centimetres

el·lipse /ɪˈlɪps/ *noun* (*technical*) a regular OVAL shape, like a circle that has been squeezed on two sides ➲ VISUAL VOCAB page V58

el·lip·sis /ɪˈlɪpsɪs/ *noun* (*pl.* **el·lip·ses** /-siːz/) [C, U] **1** (*grammar*) the act of leaving out a word or words from a sentence deliberately, when the meaning can be understood without them **2** three dots (...) used to show that a word or words have been left out

el·lip·tic·al /ɪˈlɪptɪkl/ *adj.* **1** (*grammar*) with a word or words left out of a sentence deliberately: *an elliptical remark* (= one that suggests more than is actually said) **2** (also *less frequent* **el·lip·tic** /ɪˈlɪptɪk/) (*geometry*) connected with or in the form of an ELLIPSE ▸ **el·lip·tic·al·ly** /-kli/ *adv.*: *to speak/write elliptically*

Ellis Island /ˌelɪs ˈaɪlənd/ *noun* a small island near New York City that from 1892 to 1943 was the official place of entry for people coming to live in the US from other countries

elm /elm/ *noun* **1** [C, U] (also **ˈelm tree**) a tall tree with broad leaves: *a line of stately elms* ◇ *The hedgerows were planted with elm.* **2** [U] the hard wood of the elm tree

El Niño /ˌel ˈniːnjəʊ; *NAmE* -joʊ/ *noun* [U] a set of changes in the weather system near the coast of northern Peru and Ecuador that happens every few years, causing the surface of the Pacific Ocean there to become warmer and having severe effects on the weather in many parts of the world ➲ compare LA NIÑA

elo·cu·tion /ˌeləˈkjuːʃn/ *noun* [U] the ability to speak clearly and correctly, especially in public and pronouncing the words in a way that is considered to be socially acceptable

elong·ate /ˈiːlɒŋgeɪt; *NAmE* ɪˈlɔːŋ-; ɪˈlɑːŋ-/ *verb* [I, T] **~ (sth)** to become longer; to make sth longer SYN **lengthen** ▸ **elonga·tion** /ˌiːlɒŋˈgeɪʃn; *NAmE* ˌiːlɔːŋ-; ˌiːlɑːŋ-/ *noun* [U]: *the elongation of vowel sounds*

elong·ated /ˈiːlɒŋgeɪtɪd; *NAmE* ɪˈlɔːŋ-; ɪˈlɑːŋ-/ *adj.* long and thin, often in a way that is not normal: *Modigliani's women have strangely elongated faces.*

elope /ɪˈləʊp; *NAmE* ɪˈloʊp/ *verb* [I] **~ (with sb)** to run away with sb in order to marry them secretly ▸ **elope·ment** /ɪˈləʊpmənt; *NAmE* ɪˈloʊp-/ *noun* [C, U]

elo·quent /ˈeləkwənt/ *adj.* **1** able to use language and express your opinions well, especially when you are speaking in public: *an* ***eloquent speech/speaker*** **2** (of a look or movement) able to express a feeling: *His eyes were eloquent.* ▸ **elo·quence** /ˈeləkwəns/ *noun* [U]: *a speech of passionate eloquence* ◇ *the eloquence of his smile* **elo·quen·tly** *adv.*: *She spoke eloquently on the subject.* ◇ *His face expressed his grief more eloquently than any words.*

else 🔑 /els/ *adv.*
(used in questions or after *nothing, nobody, something, anything*, etc.) **1** 🔑 in addition to sth already mentioned: *What else did he say?* ◇ *I don't want anything else, thanks.* ◇ *I'm taking a few clothes and some books, not much else.* **2** 🔑 different: *Ask somebody else to help you.* ◇ *Haven't you got anything else to wear?* ◇ *Why didn't you come? Everybody else was there.* ◇ *Yes I did give it to her. What else could I do?*
IDM **or else 1** 🔑 if not SYN **otherwise**: *Hurry up or else you'll be late.* ◇ *They can't be coming or else they'd have called.* **2** 🔑 used to introduce the second of two possibilities: *He either forgot or else decided not to come.* **3** (*informal*) used to threaten or warn sb: *Just shut up, or else!*

else·where 🔑 /ˌelsˈweə(r); *NAmE* -ˈwer/ *adv.*
in, at or to another place: *The answer to the problem must be sought elsewhere.* ◇ *Our favourite restaurant was closed, so we had to go elsewhere.* ◇ *Elsewhere, the weather today has been fairly sunny.* ◇ *Prices are higher here than elsewhere.*

ELT /ˌiː el ˈtiː/ *abbr.* (*BrE*) English Language Teaching (the teaching of English to people for whom it is not the first language)

elu·ci·date /iˈluːsɪdeɪt/ *verb* [T, I] (*formal*) to make sth clearer by explaining it more fully SYN **explain**: **~ (sth)** *He elucidated a point of grammar.* ◇ *Let me elucidate.* ◇ **~ what, how, etc...** *I will try to elucidate what I think the problems are.* ▸ **elu·ci·da·tion** /iˌluːsɪˈdeɪʃn/ *noun* [U, C]: *Their objectives and methods require further elucidation.*

elude /iˈluːd/ *verb* **1 ~ sb/sth** to manage to avoid or escape from sb/sth, especially in a clever way: *The two men managed to elude the police for six weeks.* **2 ~ sb** if sth **eludes** you, you are not able to achieve it, or not able to remember or understand it: *He was extremely tired but sleep eluded him.* ◇ *They're a popular band but chart success has eluded them so far.* ◇ *Finally he remembered the tiny detail that had eluded him the night before.*

elu·sive /iˈluːsɪv/ *adj.* difficult to find, define, or achieve: *Eric, as elusive as ever, was nowhere to be found.* ◇ *the elusive concept of 'literature'* ◇ *A solution to the problem of toxic waste is* ***proving elusive***. ▸ **elu·sive·ly** *adv.* **elu·sive·ness** *noun* [U]

elver /ˈelvə(r)/ *noun* a young EEL

elves *pl.* of ELF

Elys·ian /ɪˈlɪziən; *NAmE* ɪˈliːʒən/ *adj.* (*literary*) relating to heaven or to a place of perfect happiness
IDM **the ˌElysian ˈFields** (in ancient Greek stories) a wonderful place where some people were taken by the gods after death

em- ➲ EN-

'em /əm/ *pron.* (*informal*) = THEM: *Don't let 'em get away.*

ema·ci·ated /ɪˈmeɪʃieɪtɪd; ɪˈmeɪs-/ *adj.* thin and weak, usually because of illness or lack of food ▸ **ema·ci·ation** /ɪˌmeɪsiˈeɪʃn/ *noun* [U]: *She was very thin, almost to the point of emaciation.*

email 🔑 (also **e-mail**) /ˈiːmeɪl/ *noun, verb*
■ ***noun*** **1** 🔑 (also *formal* **ˌelectronic ˈmail**) [U] a way of sending messages and data to other people by means of

computers connected together in a network: *to send a message by email* **2** [C, U] a message sent by email ➲ WRITING TUTOR page WT26

■ *verb* [T, I] to send a message to sb by email: **~ (sb)** *Patrick emailed me yesterday.* ◇ **~ sth (to sb)** *I'll email the documents to her.* ◇ **~ sb sth** *I'll email her the documents.*

Collocations

Email and the Internet

Email

- **receive/get/open** an email
- **write/send/answer/forward/delete** an email
- **check/read/access** your email
- **block/filter (out)** junk/spam/unsolicited email
- **exchange** email addresses
- **open/check** your inbox
- junk mail **fills/floods/clogs** your inbox
- **have/set up** an email account
- **open/send/contain** an attachment
- **sign up for/receive** email alerts

Connecting to the Internet

- **use/access/log onto** the Internet/the Web
- **go** online/on the Internet
- **have** a high-speed/dial-up/broadband/wireless (Internet) connection
- **access/connect to/locate** the server
- **use/open/close/launch** a/your web browser
- **browse/surf/search/scour** the Internet/the Web
- **send/contain/spread/detect** a (computer/email) virus
- **update** your anti-virus software
- **install/use/configure** a firewall
- **accept/enable/block/delete** cookies

Using the Internet

- **visit/check** a website/an Internet site/sb's blog
- **create/design/launch** a website/social networking site
- **start/write/post/read** a blog
- **update** your blog/a website
- **be in/meet sb in/go into/enter** an Internet chat room
- **download/upload** music/software/a song/a podcast/a file/a copy of sth
- **share** information/data/files
- **post** a comment/message on a website/an online message board/a web forum/an internet chat room
- **stream** video/audio/music/content over the Internet
- **join/participate in/visit/provide** a (web-based/web/online/Internet/discussion) forum
- **generate/increase/monitor** Internet traffic

em·an·ate /ˈeməneɪt/ *verb* **~ sth** (*formal*) to produce or show sth: *He emanates power and confidence.* ▸ **em·an·ation** /ˌeməˈneɪʃn/ *noun* [C, U]

PHR V **ˈemanate from sth** to come from sth or somewhere SYN **issue from**: *The sound of loud music emanated from the building.* ◇ *The proposal originally emanated from the UN.*

eman·ci·pate /ɪˈmænsɪpeɪt/ *verb* [often passive] **~ sb (from sth)** (*formal*) to free sb, especially from legal, political or social restrictions SYN **set free**: *Slaves were not emancipated until 1863 in the United States.* ▸ **eman·ci·pated** *adj.*: *Are women now fully emancipated* (= with the same rights and opportunities as men)? ◇ *an emancipated young woman* (= one with modern ideas about women's place in society) **eman·ci·pa·tion** /ɪˌmænsɪˈpeɪʃn/ *noun* [U]: *the emancipation of slaves*

emas·cu·late /iˈmæskjuleɪt/ *verb* [often passive] (*formal*) **1 ~ sb/sth** to make sb/sth less powerful or less effective **2 ~ sb** to make a man feel that he has lost his male role or qualities ▸ **emas·cu·la·tion** /iˌmæskjuˈleɪʃn/ *noun* [U]

em·balm /ɪmˈbɑːm/ *verb* **~ sth** to prevent a dead body from decaying by treating it with special substances to preserve it ▸ **em·balm·er** /ɪmˈbɑːmə(r)/ *noun*

em·bank·ment /ɪmˈbæŋkmənt/ *noun* **1** a wall of stone or earth made to keep water back or to carry a road or railway/railroad over low ground **2** a slope made of earth or stone that rises up from either side of a road or railway/railroad

em·bargo /ɪmˈbɑːɡəʊ; *NAmE* ɪmˈbɑːrɡoʊ/ *noun, verb*

■ *noun* (*pl.* -oes) an official order that bans trade with another country SYN **boycott**: *an* ***arms embargo*** ◇ **~ (on sth)** *an embargo on arms sales to certain countries* ◇ *a* ***trade embargo*** *against certain countries* ◇ *to* ***impose/enforce/lift an embargo*** ➲ COLLOCATIONS at INTERNATIONAL

■ *verb* (**em·bar·goes**, **em·bargo·ing**, **em·bar·goed**, **em·bar·goed**) **~ sth** to place an embargo on sth SYN **boycott**: *There have been calls to embargo all arms shipments to the region.*

em·bark /ɪmˈbɑːk; *NAmE* ɪmˈbɑːrk/ *verb* [I, T] (*formal*) to get onto a ship; to put sth onto a ship: *We stood on the pier and watched as they embarked.* ◇ **~ sb/sth** *They embarked the troops by night.* OPP **disembark** ▸ **em·bark·ation** /ˌembɑːˈkeɪʃn/ *noun* [U, C]: *Embarkation will be at 14:20 hours.*

PHR V **emˈbark on/upon sth** (*formal*) to start to do sth new or difficult: *She is about to embark on a diplomatic career.*

em·bar·rass /ɪmˈbærəs/ *verb*
1 to make sb feel shy, awkward or ashamed, especially in a social situation: **~ sb** *Her questions about my private life embarrassed me.* ◇ *I didn't want to embarrass him by kissing him in front of his friends.* ◇ **it embarrasses sb to do sth** *It embarrassed her to meet strange men in the corridor at night.* **2** **~ sb** to cause problems or difficulties for sb: *The speech was deliberately designed to embarrass the prime minister.*

em·bar·rassed /ɪmˈbærəst/ *adj.*
1 (of a person or their behaviour) shy, awkward or ashamed, especially in a social situation: *I've never felt so embarrassed in my life!* ◇ *Her remark was followed by an embarrassed silence.* ◇ **~ about sth** *She's embarrassed about her height.* ◇ **~ at sth** *He felt embarrassed at being the centre of attention.* ◇ **~ to do sth** *Some women are too embarrassed to consult their doctor about the problem.* ➲ note at ASHAMED **2 financially ~** (*informal*) not having any money; in a difficult financial situation

em·bar·rass·ing /ɪmˈbærəsɪŋ/ *adj.*
1 making you feel shy, awkward or ashamed: *an* ***embarrassing mistake/question/situation*** ◇ *It can be embarrassing for children to tell complete strangers about such incidents.* ◇ *It was so embarrassing having to sing in public.* **2** causing sb to look stupid, dishonest, etc: *The report is likely to prove highly embarrassing to the government.* ▸ **em·bar·rass·ing·ly** *adv.*: *The play was embarrassingly bad.*

em·bar·rass·ment /ɪmˈbærəsmənt/ *noun*
1 [U] shy, awkward or guilty feelings; a feeling of being embarrassed: *I nearly died of embarrassment when he said that.* ◇ *I'm glad you offered—it saved me the embarrassment of having to ask.* ◇ *Much* **to her embarrassment** *she realized that everybody had been listening to her singing.* **2** [C] **~ (to/for sb)** a situation which causes problems for sb: *Her resignation will be a severe embarrassment to the party.* **3** [C] **~ (to sb)** a person who causes problems for another person or other people and makes them feel embarrassed

IDM **an embarrassment of ˈriches** so many good things that it is difficult to choose just one

em·bassy /ˈembəsi/ *noun* (*pl.* -ies) **1** a group of officials led by an AMBASSADOR who represent their government in a foreign country: *embassy officials* ◇ *to inform the embassy of the situation* **2** the building in which an embassy works: *a demonstration outside the Russian Embassy* ➲ compare CONSULATE, HIGH COMMISSION

em·bat·tled /ɪmˈbætld/ *adj.* **1** surrounded by problems and difficulties: *the embattled party leader* **2** (of an army, a city, etc.) involved in war; surrounded by the enemy

embed (also **imbed**) /ɪmˈbed/ *verb* (**-dd-**) [usually passive] **1 ~ sth (in sth)** to fix sth firmly into a substance or solid object: *an operation to remove glass that was embedded in his leg* ◇ *The bullet embedded itself in the wall.* ◇ *(figurative) These attitudes are deeply embedded in our society* (= felt very strongly and difficult to change). **2 ~ sb** to send a journalist, photographer, etc. to an area where there is fighting, so that he or she can travel with the army and report what is happening: *embedded reporters in the war zone* **3 ~ sth** (*linguistics*) to place a sentence inside another sentence. In the sentence 'I'm aware that she knows', *she knows* is an embedded sentence.

em·bel·lish /ɪmˈbelɪʃ/ *verb* (*formal*) **1 ~ sth** to make sth more beautiful by adding decorations to it **SYN decorate** **2 ~ sth** to make a story more interesting by adding details that are not always true **SYN embroider** ▸ **em·bel·lish·ment** *noun* [U, C]: *Good pasta needs very little embellishment.* ◇ *a 16th century church with 18th century embellishments*

ember /ˈembə(r)/ *noun* [usually pl.] a piece of wood or coal that is not burning but is still red and hot after a fire has died

em·bez·zle /ɪmˈbezl/ *verb* [T, I] **~ (sth)** to steal money that you are responsible for or that belongs to your employer: *He was found guilty of embezzling $150 000 of public funds.* ▸ **em·bezzle·ment** *noun* [U]: *She was found guilty of embezzlement.* **em·bez·zler** /ɪmˈbezlə(r)/ *noun*

em·bit·ter /ɪmˈbɪtə(r)/ *verb* **~ sb** to make sb feel angry or disappointed about sth over a long period of time ▸ **em·bit·tered** *adj.*: *a sick and embittered old man* ◇ *an embittered laugh*

em·bla·zon /ɪmˈbleɪzn/ (also **blazon**) *verb* [usually passive] to decorate sth with a design, a symbol or words so that people will notice it easily: **~ A with B** *baseball caps emblazoned with the team's logo* ◇ **~ B on, across, etc. A** *The team's logo was emblazoned on the baseball caps.*

em·blem /ˈembləm/ *noun* **~ (of sth) 1** a design or picture that represents a country or an organization: *America's national emblem, the bald eagle* ◇ *the club emblem* **2** something that represents a perfect example or a principle: *The dove is an emblem of peace.*

em·blem·at·ic /ˌembləˈmætɪk/ *adj.* **~ (of sth)** (*formal*) **1** that represents or is a symbol of sth **SYN representative** **2** that is considered typical of a situation, an area of work, etc. **SYN typical**: *The violence is emblematic of what is happening in our inner cities.*

em·bodi·ment /ɪmˈbɒdimənt; *NAmE* -ˈbɑːd-/ *noun* [usually sing.] **~ of sth** (*formal*) a person or thing that represents or is a typical example of an idea or a quality **SYN epitome**: *He is the embodiment of the young successful businessman.*

em·body /ɪmˈbɒdi; *NAmE* ɪmˈbɑːdi/ *verb* (**em·bodies, em·body·ing, em·bodied, em·bodied**) **1** to express or represent an idea or a quality **SYN represent**: **~ sth** *a politician who embodied the hopes of black youth* ◇ **be embodied in sth** *the principles embodied in the Declaration of Human Rights* **2 ~ sth** (*formal*) to include or contain sth: *This model embodies many new features.*

em·bold·en /ɪmˈbəʊldən; *NAmE* -ˈboʊl-/ *verb* **1** [usually passive] (*formal*) to make sb feel braver or more confident: **~ sb** *Emboldened by the wine, he went over to introduce himself to her.* ◇ **~ sb to do sth** *With such a majority, the administration was emboldened to introduce radical new policies.* **2 ~ sth** (*technical*) to make a piece of text appear in BOLD print

em·bol·ism /ˈembəlɪzəm/ *noun* (*medical*) a condition in which a BLOOD CLOT or air bubble blocks an ARTERY in the body

em·bolus /ˈembələs/ *noun* (*pl.* **em·boli** /-laɪ; -liː/) (*medical*) a BLOOD CLOT, air bubble, or small object that causes an embolism

em·boss /ɪmˈbɒs; *NAmE* ɪmˈbɔːs; ɪmˈbɑːs/ *verb* [usually passive] to put a raised design or piece of writing on paper, leather, etc: **~ A with B** *stationery embossed with the hotel's name* ◇ **~ B on A** *The hotel's name was embossed on the stationery.* ▸ **em·bossed** *adj.*: *embossed stationery*

em·bouch·ure /ˌɒmbʊˈʃʊə(r); *NAmE* ˌɑːmbʊˈʃʊr/ *noun* (*music*) **1** the shape of the mouth when playing a WIND INSTRUMENT **2** the MOUTHPIECE of a FLUTE

em·brace /ɪmˈbreɪs/ *verb* **1** [I, T] (*formal*) to put your arms around sb as a sign of love or friendship **SYN hug**: *They embraced and promised to keep in touch.* ◇ **~ sb** *She embraced her son warmly.* **2 ~ sth** (*formal*) to accept an idea, a proposal, a set of beliefs, etc, especially when it is done with enthusiasm: *to embrace democracy/feminism/Islam* **3 ~ sth** (*formal*) to include sth: *The talks embraced a wide range of issues.* ▸ **em·brace** *noun* [C, U]: *He held her in a warm embrace.* ◇ *There were tears and embraces as they said goodbye.* ◇ *the country's eager embrace of modern technology*

E

em·bras·ure /ɪmˈbreɪʒə(r)/ *noun* (*architecture*) an opening in a wall for a door or window, wider on the inside than on the outside

em·bro·ca·tion /ˌembrəˈkeɪʃn/ *noun* [U] a liquid for rubbing on sore muscles to make them less painful, for example after too much exercise

em·broi·der /ɪmˈbrɔɪdə(r)/ *verb* **1** [T, I] to decorate cloth with a pattern of STITCHES usually using coloured thread: **~ A on B** *She embroidered flowers on the cushion covers.* ◇ **~ B with A** *She embroidered the cushion cover with flowers.* ◇ **~ (sth)** *an embroidered blouse* ◇ *She sat in the window, embroidering.* **2** [T] **~ sth** to make a story more interesting by adding details that are not always true **SYN embellish**

em·broi·dery /ɪmˈbrɔɪdəri/ *noun* **1** [U, C] patterns that are sewn onto cloth using threads of various colours; cloth that is decorated in this way: *a beautiful piece of embroidery* ◇ *Indian embroideries* **2** [U] the skill or activity of decorating cloth in this way ➲ **VISUAL VOCAB** page V35

em·broil /ɪmˈbrɔɪl/ *verb* [often passive] **~ sb/yourself (in sth)** (*formal*) to involve sb/yourself in an argument or a difficult situation: *He became embroiled in a dispute with his neighbours.* ◇ *I was reluctant to embroil myself in his problems.*

em·bryo /ˈembriəʊ; *NAmE* -brioʊ/ *noun* (*pl.* **-os**) a young animal or plant in the very early stages of development before birth, or before coming out of its egg or seed, especially a human egg in the first eight weeks after FERTILIZATION: *human embryos* ◇ *(figurative) the embryo of an idea* ◇ *an embryo politician* (= one who is not yet very experienced)

IDM **in embryo** existing but not yet fully developed: *The idea already existed in embryo in his earlier novels.*

em·bry·ology /ˌembriˈɒlədʒi; *NAmE* -ˈɑːl-/ *noun* [U] the scientific study of the development of embryos ▸ **em·bryo·logic·al** /ˌembriəˈlɒdʒɪkl; *NAmE* -ˈlɑːdʒ-/ *adj.* **em·bry·olo·gist** /ˌembriˈɒlədʒɪst; *NAmE* -ˈɑːl-/ *noun*

em·bry·on·ic /ˌembriˈɒnɪk; *NAmE* -ˈɑːnɪk/ *adj.* [usually before noun] **1** (*formal*) in an early stage of development: *The plan, as yet, only exists in embryonic form.* **2** (*technical*) of an embryo: *embryonic cells*

emcee /emˈsiː/ *noun* (*NAmE, informal*) **1** a person who introduces guests or entertainers at a formal occasion **SYN master of ceremonies** **2** an MC (3) at a club or party ▸ **emcee** *verb* [I, T] **~ (sth)**

emend /iˈmend/ *verb* **~ sth** (*formal*) to remove the mistakes in a piece of writing, especially before it is printed **SYN correct**

emend·ation /ˌiːmenˈdeɪʃn/ *noun* [C, U] (*formal*) a letter or word that has been changed or corrected in a text; the act of making changes to a text

em·er·ald /ˈemərəld/ *noun* **1** [C, U] a bright green PRECIOUS STONE: *an emerald ring* **2** (also ˌ**emerald** ˈ**green**) [U] a bright green colour ▸ **em·er·ald** (also ˌ**emerald** ˈ**green**) *adj.*

E

the ˌEmerald ˈIsle *noun* [sing.] (*literary*) a name for Ireland

emerge 🔑 AW /iˈmɜːdʒ; *NAmE* iˈmɜːrdʒ/ *verb* **1** 🔑 [I] to come out of a dark, confined or hidden place: **~ (from sth)** *The swimmer emerged from the lake.* ◇ *She finally emerged from her room at noon.* ◇ **~ (into sth)** *We emerged into bright sunlight.* **2** 🔑 [I, T] (of facts, ideas, etc.) to become known SYN **transpire**: *No new evidence emerged during the investigation.* ◇ **it emerges that...** *It emerged that the company was going to be sold.* **3** 🔑 [I] to start to exist; to appear or become known: *After the elections opposition groups began to emerge.* ◇ *the emerging markets of South Asia* ◇ **~ as sth** *He emerged as a key figure in the campaign* **4** [I] **~ (from sth)** to survive a difficult situation or experience: *She emerged from the scandal with her reputation intact.* ▶ **emer·gence** AW /-dʒəns/ *noun* [U]: *the island's emergence from the sea 3 000 years ago* ◇ *the emergence of new technologies*

emer·gency 🔑 /iˈmɜːdʒənsi; *NAmE* iˈmɜːrdʒ-/ *noun* (*pl.* **-ies**) [C, U] a sudden serious and dangerous event or situation which needs immediate action to deal with it: *The government has declared a* ***state of emergency*** *following the earthquake.* ◇ *This door should only be used* ***in an emergency***. ◇ *the emergency exit* (= to be used in an emergency) ◇ *The government had to take emergency action.* ◇ *The pilot made an emergency landing in a field.* ◇ *I always have some extra cash with me* ***for emergencies***. ◇ *The government has been granted* ***emergency powers*** (= to deal with an emergency).

eˈmergency brake *noun* (*NAmE*) **1** = HANDBRAKE ➲ VISUAL VOCAB page V42 **2** a BRAKE on a train that can be pulled in an emergency

eˈmergency room (*NAmE*) (*abbr.* ER) (*BrE* **ˌaccident and eˈmergency**) *noun* the part of a hospital where people who need urgent treatment are taken

eˈmergency services *noun* [pl.] (*BrE*) the public organizations that deal with emergencies: the police, fire, ambulance and COASTGUARD services ➲ compare FIRST RESPONDER

emer·gent AW /iˈmɜːdʒənt; *NAmE* iˈmɜːrdʒ-/ *adj.* [usually before noun] new and still developing: ***emergent nations/states***

emeri·tus /iˈmerɪtəs/ *adj.* (often **Emeritus**) used with a title to show that a person, usually a university teacher, keeps the title as an honour, although he or she has stopped working: *the Emeritus Professor of Biology* HELP In *NAmE* the form **Emerita** /iˈmerɪtə/ is used for women: *Professor Emerita Mary Judd*

emery /ˈeməri/ *noun* [U] a hard mineral used especially in powder form for polishing things and making them smooth

ˈemery board *noun* a small strip of wood or cardboard covered in emery, used for shaping your nails ➲ VISUAL VOCAB page V21

emet·ic /iˈmetɪk/ *noun* (*medical*) a substance that makes you VOMIT (= bring up food from the stomach) ▶ **emet·ic** *adj.*

emi·grant /ˈemɪɡrənt/ *noun* a person who leaves their country to live in another: *emigrant workers* ◇ *emigrants to Canada* ➲ compare IMMIGRANT

emi·grate /ˈemɪɡreɪt/ *verb* [I] **~ (from...) (to...)** to leave your own country to go and live permanently in another country ➲ compare IMMIGRATE ▶ **emi·gra·tion** /ˌemɪˈɡreɪʃn/ *noun* [U, C]: *the mass emigration of Jews from Eastern Europe* ➲ compare IMMIGRATION

émi·gré /ˈemɪɡreɪ/ *noun* (from *French*) a person who has left their own country, usually for political reasons SYN **exile**

emi·nence /ˈemɪnəns/ *noun* **1** [U] (*formal*) the quality of being famous and respected, especially in a profession: *a man of political eminence* **2** [C] **His/Your Eminence** a title used in speaking to or about a CARDINAL (= a priest of the highest rank in the Roman Catholic Church): *Their Eminences will see you now.* **3** [C] (*old-fashioned* or *formal*) an area of high ground

emi·nent /ˈemɪnənt/ *adj.* [usually before noun] **1** (of people) famous and respected, especially in a particular profession: *an eminent architect* **2** (of good qualities) unusual; excellent: *a man of eminent good sense*

ˌeminent doˈmain *noun* [U] (*NAmE, law*) the right to force sb to sell land or a building if it is needed by the government

emi·nent·ly /ˈemɪnəntli/ *adv.* (*formal*) (used to emphasize a positive quality) very; extremely: *She seems eminently suitable for the job.*

emir (also **amir**) /eˈmɪə(r); ˈeɪmɪə(r); *NAmE* eˈmɪr; eɪˈmɪr/ *noun* the title given to some Muslim rulers: *the Emir of Kuwait*

emir·ate /ˈemɪərət; ˈemɪrət; *NAmE* ˈemərət/ *noun* **1** the position of an emir **2** an area of land that is ruled over by an emir: *the United Arab Emirates* **3** the period of time that an emir rules

emis·sary /ˈemɪsəri; *NAmE* -seri/ *noun* (*pl.* **-ies**) (*formal*) a person who is sent to deliver an official message, especially from one country to another, or to perform a special task SYN **envoy**

emis·sion /iˈmɪʃn/ *noun* **1** [U] (*formal*) the production or sending out of light, heat, gas, etc: *the emission of carbon dioxide into the atmosphere* ◇ *emission controls* **2** [C] gas, etc. that is sent out into the air: *The government has pledged to clean up industrial emissions.* ➲ COLLOCATIONS at ENVIRONMENT

eˈmissions trading *noun* = CARBON TRADING

emit /iˈmɪt/ *verb* (**-tt-**) **~ sth** (*formal*) to send out sth such as light, heat, sound, gas, etc: *The metal container began to emit a clicking sound.* ◇ *Sulphur gases were emitted by the volcano.*

Em·men·tal (also **Em·men·thal**) /ˈeməntɑːl/ *noun* [U] a type of Swiss cheese, with holes in it

Emmy /ˈemi/ *noun* (*pl.* **-ies**) one of the awards given every year in the US for achievement in the making of television programmes

emo /ˈiːməʊ; *NAmE* ˈiːmoʊ/ *noun* (*pl.* **emos**) **1** [U] a style of rock music that developed from PUNK, but has more complicated musical arrangements and deals with more emotional subjects **2** [C] a person who likes emo music and often follows emo fashion, wearing tight jeans and having long black hair. Emos are typically supposed to be emotional and sensitive and full of ANGST.

emol·li·ent /iˈmɒliənt; *NAmE* iˈmɑːl-/ *adj., noun*
- ***adj.*** (*formal*) **1** making a person or situation calmer in the hope of keeping relations peaceful SYN **soothing**: *an emollient reply* **2** (*technical*) used for making your skin soft or less painful SYN **soothing**: *an emollient cream*
- ***noun*** [C, U] (*technical*) a liquid or cream that is used to make the skin soft

emolu·ment /ɪˈmɒljumənt; *NAmE* ɪˈmɑːl-/ *noun* [usually pl.] (*formal*) money paid to sb for work they have done, especially to sb who earns a lot of money

emote /ɪˈməʊt; *NAmE* ɪˈmoʊt/ *verb* [I] to show emotion in a very obvious way

emoti·con /ɪˈməʊtɪkɒn; *NAmE* ɪˈmoʊtɪkɑːn/ *noun* (*computing*) a short set of keyboard symbols that represents the expression on sb's face, used in email, etc. to show the feelings of the person sending the message. For example :-) represents a smiling face (when you look at it sideways).

emo·tion 🔑 /ɪˈməʊʃn; *NAmE* ɪˈmoʊʃn/ *noun* [C, U] a strong feeling such as love, fear or anger; the part of a person's character that consists of feelings: *He lost control of his emotions.* ◇ *They expressed mixed emotions at the news.* ◇ ***Emotions are running high*** (= people are feeling very excited, angry, etc.). ◇ *The decision was based on emotion rather than rational thought.* ◇ *She showed no emotion at the verdict.* ◇ *Mary was overcome with emotion.*

emo·tion·al 🔑 /ɪˈməʊʃənl; *NAmE* ɪˈmoʊ-/ *adj.* **1** 🔑 [usually before noun] connected with people's feelings

(= with the emotions): ***emotional problems/needs*** ◇ *emotional stress* ◇ *a child's emotional and intellectual development* ◇ *Mothers are often the ones who provide* ***emotional support*** *for the family.* **2** causing people to feel strong emotions SYN **emotive**: *emotional language* ◇ *abortion and other* ***emotional issues*** **3** (sometimes *disapproving*) showing strong emotions, sometimes in a way that other people think is unnecessary: *an* ***emotional outburst/response/reaction*** ◇ *They made an emotional appeal for help.* ◇ *He tends to* ***get emotional*** *on these occasions.* ▶ **emo·tion·al·ly** /-ʃənəli/ *adv.*: *emotionally disturbed children* ◇ *I try not to become emotionally involved.* ◇ *They have suffered physically and emotionally.* ◇ *an emotionally charged atmosphere*

e,motional in'telligence *noun* [U] the ability to understand your emotions and those of other people and to behave appropriately in different situations

emo·tion·less /ɪ'məʊʃənləs; *NAmE* ɪ'moʊ-/ *adj.* not showing any emotion: *an emotionless voice*

emo·tive /i'məʊtɪv; *NAmE* i'moʊ-/ *adj.* causing people to feel strong emotions SYN **emotional**: ***emotive language/words*** ◇ *Capital punishment is a highly* ***emotive issue.***

em·panel = IMPANEL

em·pa·thize (*BrE* also **-ise**) /'empəθaɪz/ *verb* [I] ~ (**with sb/sth**) to understand another person's feelings and experiences, especially because you have been in a similar situation

em·pathy /'empəθi/ *noun* [U] the ability to understand another person's feelings, experience, etc: ~ (**with sb/sth**) *the writer's imaginative empathy with his subject* ◇ ~ (**for sb/sth**) *empathy for other people's situations* ◇ ~ (**between A and B**) *The empathy between the two women was obvious.*

em·peror /'empərə(r)/ *noun* the ruler of an empire: *the Roman emperors* ◇ *the Emperor Napoleon* ➲ see also EMPRESS

IDM **the ,emperor has no 'clothes** used to describe a situation in which everybody suddenly realizes that they were mistaken in believing that sb/sth was very good, important, etc.: *Soon investors will realize that the emperor has no clothes and there will be a big sell-off in stocks.* ORIGIN From the story of *The Emperor's New Clothes* by Hans Christian Andersen, in which the emperor is tricked into thinking he is wearing beautiful new clothes and everyone pretends to admire them, until a little boy points out that he is naked.

> **Language Bank**
>
> **emphasis**
>
> Highlighting an important point
>
> - This case **emphasizes/highlights** the importance of honest communication between managers and employees.
> - Effective communication skills are **essential/crucial/vital**.
> - **It should be noted that** this study considers only verbal communication. Non-verbal communication is not dealt with here.
> - **It is important to remember that/An important point to remember is that** non-verbal communication plays a key role in getting your message across.
> - Communication is not only about the words you use but also your body language and, **especially/above all**, the effectiveness with which you listen.
> - I would like to **draw attention to** the role of listening in effective communication.
> - Choose your words carefully: **in particular**, avoid confusing and ambiguous language.
> - Finally, and perhaps **most importantly**, you must learn to listen as well as to speak.
>
> ➲ note at ESSENTIAL
> ➲ Language Bank at VITAL

em·phasis AW /'emfəsɪs/ *noun* (*pl.* **em·phases** /-si:z/) [U, C]
1 special importance that is given to sth SYN **stress**: ~ (**on/upon sth**) *The emphasis is very much on learning the spoken language.* ◇ *to* ***put/lay/place emphasis*** *on sth* ◇ *We provide all types of information,* ***with an emphasis on*** *legal advice.* ◇ *There has been* ***a shift of emphasis*** *from manufacturing to service industries.* ◇ *The course has a vocational emphasis.* ◇ *The examples we will look at have quite different emphases.* **2** the extra force given to a word or phrase when spoken, especially in order to show that it is important; a way of writing a word (for example drawing a line underneath it) to show that it is important SYN **stress**: *'I can assure you,' she added with emphasis, 'the figures are correct.'*

em·pha·size (*BrE* also **-ise**) AW /'emfəsaɪz/ *verb*
1 to give special importance to sth SYN **stress**: ~ **sth** *His speech emphasized the importance of attracting industry to the town.* ◇ ~ **that...** *She emphasized that their plan would mean sacrifices and hard work.* ◇ ~ **how, what, etc ...** *He emphasized how little was known about the disease.* ◇ **it must/should be emphasized that...** *It should be emphasized that this is only one possible explanation.* ◇ **+ speech** *'This must be our top priority,' he emphasized.* ➲ LANGUAGE BANK at EMPHASIS **2** ~ **sth** to make sth more noticeable: *She swept her hair back from her face to emphasize her high cheekbones.* **3** ~ **sth** to give extra force to a word or phrase when you are speaking, especially to show that it is important ➲ SYNONYMS at STRESS

em·phat·ic AW /ɪm'fætɪk/ *adj.* **1** an **emphatic** statement, answer, etc. is given with force to show that it is important: *an* ***emphatic denial/rejection*** **2** (of a person) making it very clear what you mean by speaking with force: *He was emphatic that he could not work with her.* **3** an **emphatic** victory, win, or defeat is one in which one team or player wins by a large amount ▶ **em·phat·ic·al·ly** AW /-kli/ *adv.*: *'Certainly not,' he replied emphatically.* ◇ *She is emphatically opposed to the proposals.* ◇ *He has always emphatically denied the allegations.* ◇ *The proposal was emphatically defeated.*

em·phy·se·ma /,emfɪ'si:mə/ *noun* [U] (*medical*) a condition that affects the lungs, making it difficult to breathe

em·pire /'empaɪə(r)/ *noun*
1 a group of countries or states that are controlled by one ruler or government: *the Roman empire* **2** a group of commercial organizations controlled by one person or company: *a business empire*

'empire-,building *noun* [U] (usually *disapproving*) the process of obtaining extra land, authority, etc. in order to increase your own power or position

'Empire line *noun* a style of women's dress with the WAISTLINE positioned just below the breasts and a low-cut neck

em·pir·ic·al AW /ɪm'pɪrɪkl/ *adj.* [usually before noun] (*formal*) based on experiments or experience rather than ideas or theories: ***empirical evidence/knowledge/research*** ◇ *an* ***empirical study*** OPP **theoretical** ▶ **em·pir·ic·al·ly** AW /-kli/ *adv.*: *Such claims need to be tested empirically.*

em·piri·cism AW /ɪm'pɪrɪsɪzəm/ *noun* [U] (*philosophy*) the use of experiments or experience as the basis for your ideas; the belief in these methods ▶ **em·piri·cist** /-sɪst/ *adj.*: *an empiricist theory* **em·piri·cist** *noun*: *the English empiricist, John Locke*

em·place·ment /ɪm'pleɪsmənt/ *noun* (*technical*) a position that has been specially prepared so that a large gun can be fired from it

em·ploy /ɪm'plɔɪ/ *verb, noun*
■ ***verb*** **1** to give sb a job to do for payment: ~ **sb** *How many people does the company employ?* ◇ ~ **sb as sth** *For the past three years he has been employed as a firefighter.* ◇ ~ **sb to do sth** *A number of people have been employed to deal with the backlog of work.* ➲ COLLOCATIONS at JOB ➲ see also SELF-EMPLOYED, UNEMPLOYED **2** ~ **sth** (*formal*) to use sth such as a skill, method, etc. for a

particular purpose: *He criticized the repressive methods employed by the country's government.* ◇ *The police had to employ force to enter the building.*

IDM **be employed in doing sth** if a person or their time is **employed in doing sth**, the person spends time doing that thing: *She was employed in making a list of all the jobs to be done.*

■ ***noun*** [U]

IDM **in sb's em'ploy | in the em'ploy of sb** (*formal*) working for sb; employed by sb

E

em·ploy·able /ɪm'plɔɪəbl/ *adj.* having the skills and qualifications that will make sb want to employ you

em·ploy·ee 🔑 /ɪm'plɔɪiː/ *noun* a person who is paid to work for sb: *The firm has over 500 employees.* ◇ *government employees* ◇ ***employee rights/relations***

em·ploy·er 🔑 /ɪm'plɔɪə(r)/ *noun* a person or company that pays people to work for them: *They're very good employers* (= they treat the people that work for them well). ◇ *one of the largest employers in the area*

em·ploy·ment 🔑 /ɪm'plɔɪmənt/ *noun* **1** 🔑 [U, C] work, especially when it is done to earn money; the state of being employed: *to be in* ***paid employment*** ◇ ***full-time/part-time employment*** ◇ ***conditions/terms of employment*** ◇ *Graduates are finding it more and more difficult to find employment.* ◇ *pensions from previous employments* ➲ SYNONYMS at WORK ➲ COLLOCATIONS at JOB, UNEMPLOYMENT **2** 🔑 [U] the situation in which people have work: *The government is aiming at* ***full employment***. ◇ *Changes in farming methods have badly affected employment in the area.* OPP **unemployment** **3** [U] the act of employing sb: *The law prevented the employment of children under ten in the cotton mills.* **4** [U] **~ (of sth)** (*formal*) the use of sth: *the employment of artillery in the capture of the town*

em'ployment agency *noun* a business that helps people to find work and employers to find workers

em,ployment tri'bunal (also **in,dustrial tri'bunal**) *noun* (*BrE*) a type of court that can decide on disagreements between employees and employers: *She took her case to an employment tribunal.*

em·por·ium /em'pɔːriəm/ *noun* (*pl.* **em·por·iums** or **em·poria** /-riə/) **1** (*old-fashioned*) a large shop/store **2** a shop/store that sells a particular type of goods: *an arts and crafts emporium*

em·power /ɪm'paʊə(r)/ *verb* [often passive] **1 ~ sb (to do sth)** (*formal*) to give sb the power or authority to do sth SYN **authorize**: *The courts were empowered to impose the death sentence for certain crimes.* **2 ~ sb (to do sth)** to give sb more control over their own life or the situation they are in: *The movement actively empowered women and gave them confidence in themselves.* ▸ **em·power·ment** *noun* [U]: *the empowerment of the individual*

emp·ress /'emprəs/ *noun* **1** a woman who is the ruler of an empire: *the Empress of Egypt* **2** the wife of an EMPEROR

emp·ties /'emptiz/ *noun* [pl.] empty bottles or glasses

emp·ti·ness /'emptinəs/ *noun* [U, sing.] **1** a feeling of being sad because nothing seems to have any value: *There was an aching emptiness in her heart.* **2** the fact that there is nothing or nobody in a place: *The silence and emptiness of the house did not scare her.* **3** (*formal*) a place that is empty: *He stared out at the vast emptiness that was the sea.*

empty 🔑 /'empti/ *adj., verb*

■ ***adj.*** (**emp·tier, emp·ti·est**) **1** 🔑 with no people or things inside: *an empty box/glass* ◇ *empty hands* (= not holding anything) ◇ *an empty plate* (= with no food on it) ◇ *The theatre was* ***half empty***. ◇ *an empty house/room/bus* ◇ *Is this an empty chair* (= a chair that nobody else is using)? ◇ *The house had been* ***standing empty*** (= without people living in it) *for some time.* ◇ *It's not good to drink alcohol* ***on an empty stomach*** (= without having eaten something). ◇ **~ of sth** (*formal*) *The room was empty of furniture.* **2** 🔑 [usually before noun] (of sth that sb says or does) with no meaning; not meaning what is said SYN **hollow**: *empty words* ◇ *an empty promise* ◇ *an empty gesture aimed at pleasing the crowds* **3** 🔑 (of a person, or a person's life) unhappy because life does not seem to have a purpose, usually after sth sad has happened: *Three months after his death, she still felt empty.* ◇ *My life seems empty without you.* **4 ~ of sth** without a quality that you would expect to be there: *words that were empty of meaning* ▸ **emp·ti·ly** *adv.*: *She stood staring emptily into space.*

■ ***verb*** (**emp·ties, empty·ing, emp·tied, emp·tied**) **1** 🔑 [T] to remove everything that is in a container, etc: **~ sth** *He emptied the ashtrays, washed the glasses and went to bed.* ◇ *He emptied his glass and asked for a refill.* ◇ **~ sth out** *I emptied out my pockets but could not find my keys.* ◇ **~ sth out of sth** *She emptied the water out of the vase.* ◇ **~ sth of sth** *The room had been emptied of all furniture.* ◇ (*figurative*) *She emptied her mind of all thoughts of home.* **2** 🔑 [I] to become empty: *The streets soon emptied when the rain started.* ◇ **~ out** *The tank empties out in five minutes.* **3** 🔑 [T] **~ sth (out)** to take out the contents of sth and put them somewhere else: *She emptied the contents of her bag onto the table.* ◇ *Many factories emptied their waste into the river.* **4** 🔑 [T] **~ sth** to make sure that everyone leaves a room, building, etc. SYN **evacuate**: *Police had instructions to empty the building because of a bomb threat.* **5** [I] to flow or move out from one place to another: **~ into/onto sth** *The Rhine empties into the North Sea.* ◇ **~ out into/onto sth** *Fans emptied out onto the streets after the concert.*

,empty-'handed *adj.* [not usually before noun] without getting what you wanted; without taking sth to sb: *The robbers fled empty-handed.* ◇ *She visited every Sunday and never arrived empty-handed.*

,empty-'headed *adj.* (*disapproving*) unable to think or behave in an intelligent way

the ,empty 'nest *noun* [sing.] the situation that parents are in when their children have grown up and left home

,empty 'nester *noun* [usually pl.] a parent whose children have grown up and left home

EMS /,iː em 'es/ *noun* **1** [U] the abbreviation for 'enhanced message service' (a system for sending pictures, music and long written messages from one mobile/cell phone to another) **2** [C] a message sent by EMS

EMU /,iː em 'juː/ *abbr.* Economic and Monetary Union (of the European Union)

emu /'iːmjuː/ *noun* a large Australian bird that can run fast but cannot fly

emu·late /'emjuleɪt/ *verb* **1 ~ sb/sth** (*formal*) to try to do sth as well as sb else because you admire them: *She hopes to emulate her sister's sporting achievements.* **2 ~ sth** (*computing*) (of a computer program, etc.) to work in the same way as another computer, etc. and perform the same tasks ▸ **emu·la·tion** /,emju'leɪʃn/ *noun* [U, C]

emu·la·tor /'emjuleɪtə(r)/ *noun* (*computing*) a device or piece of software that makes it possible to use programs, etc. on one type of computer even though they have been designed for a different type

emul·si·fier /ɪ'mʌlsɪfaɪə(r)/ *noun* (*chemistry*) a substance that is added to food to make the different substances in them combine to form a smooth mixture

emul·sify /ɪ'mʌlsɪfaɪ/ *verb* (**emul·si·fies, emul·si·fy·ing, emul·si·fied, emul·si·fied**) [I, T] **~ (sth)** (*technical*) if two liquids of different thicknesses **emulsify** or **are emulsified**, they combine to form a smooth mixture

emul·sion /ɪ'mʌlʃn/ *noun* [C, U] **1** any mixture of liquids that do not normally mix together, such as oil and water **2** (also **e'mulsion paint**) (*BrE*) a type of paint used on walls and ceilings that dries without leaving a shiny surface **3** (*technical*) a substance on the surface of PHOTOGRAPHIC film that makes it sensitive to light

en- /ɪn/ (also **em-** /ɪm/ before *b*, *m* or *p*) *prefix* (in verbs) **1** to put into the thing or condition mentioned: *encase* ◇ *endanger* ◇ *empower* **2** to cause to be: *enlarge* ◇ *embolden*

-en *suffix* **1** (in verbs) to make or become: *blacken* ◇ *sadden* **2** (in adjectives) made of; looking like: *wooden* ◇ *golden*

en·able 🔑 AW /ɪˈneɪbl/ *verb* **1** 🔑 **~ sb to do sth** to make it possible for sb to do sth SYN **allow**: *The software enables you to create your own DVDs.* ◇ *a new programme to enable older people to study at college* **2** 🔑 to make it possible for sth to happen or exist by creating the necessary conditions SYN **allow**: **~ sth to do sth** *Insulin enables the body to use and store sugar.* ◇ **~ sth** *a new train line to enable easier access to the stadium* ➲ LANGUAGE BANK at PROCESS

-enabled /ɪˈneɪbld/ *adj.* (in compound adjectives) (*computing*) that can be used with a particular system or technology, especially the Internet: *web-enabled phones*

eˈnabling act *noun* a law which allows a person or an organization to do sth, especially to make rules

enact /ɪˈnækt/ *verb* **1** [often passive] **~ sth** | **it is enacted that…** (*law*) to pass a law: *legislation enacted by parliament* **2** [often passive] **~ sth** (*formal*) to perform a play or act a part in a play: *scenes from history enacted by local residents* **3 be enacted** (*formal*) to take place SYN **be played out**: *They seemed unaware of the drama being enacted a few feet away from them.*

en·act·ment /ɪˈnæktmənt/ *noun* [U, C] (*law*) the process of a law becoming official; a law which has been made official

en·amel /ɪˈnæml/ *noun* **1** [U, C] a substance that is melted onto metal, pots, etc. and forms a hard shiny surface to protect or decorate them; an object made from enamel: *a chipped enamel bowl* ◇ *a handle inlaid with enamel* ◇ *an exhibition of enamels and jewellery* **2** [U] the hard white outer layer of a tooth **3** (also **eˌnamel ˈpaint**) [U, C] a type of paint that dries to leave a hard shiny surface

en·am·elled (*especially US* **en·am·eled**) /ɪˈnæmld/ *adj.* [usually before noun] covered or decorated with enamel.

en·am·oured (*especially US* **en·amored**) /ɪˈnæməd; *NAmE* -ərd/ *adj.* **1** (*formal*) (often in negative sentences) liking sth a lot: **~ of sth** *He was less than enamoured of the music.* ◇ **~ with sth** (*humorous*) *I'm not exactly enamoured with the idea of spending a whole day with them.* **2 ~ of/with sb** (*literary*) in love with sb

en bloc /ˌɒ̃ ˈblɒk; *NAmE* ˌɑ̃ː ˈblɑːk/ *adv.* (from *French*) as a group rather than separately: *There are reports of teachers resigning en bloc.*

enc. = ENCL.

en·camp /ɪnˈkæmp/ *verb* [I, T] (*formal*) if a group of people **encamp** or **are encamped** somewhere, they set up a camp or have set up a camp there

en·camp·ment /ɪnˈkæmpmənt/ *noun* a group of tents, HUTS, etc. where people live together, usually for only a short period of time: *a military encampment*

en·cap·su·late /ɪnˈkæpsjuleɪt/ *verb* **~ sth (in sth)** (*formal*) to express the most important parts of sth in a few words, a small space or a single object SYN **sum up**: *The poem encapsulates many of the central themes of her writing.* ▸ **en·cap·su·la·tion** *noun* [U, C]

en·case /ɪnˈkeɪs/ *verb* [often passive] **~ sth (in sth)** (*formal*) to surround or cover sth completely, especially to protect it: *The reactor is encased in concrete and steel.*

en·cash /ɪnˈkæʃ/ *verb* **~ sth** (*BrE, formal*) to exchange a cheque, etc. for money SYN **cash** ▸ **en·cash·ment** *noun* [U, C]

-ence ➲ -ANCE

en·ceph·al·itis /enˌsefəˈlaɪtəs; -ˌkefə-/ *noun* [U] (*medical*) a condition in which the brain becomes swollen, caused by an infection or ALLERGIC reaction

en·ceph·al·op·athy /enˌsefəˈlɒpəθi; -ˌkefə-; *NAmE* -ˈlɑːp-/ *noun* [U] (*medical*) a disease in which the functioning of the brain is affected by infection, BLOOD POISONING, etc. ➲ see also BSE

en·chant /ɪnˈtʃɑːnt; *NAmE* -ˈtʃænt/ *verb* **1 ~ sb** (*formal*) to attract sb strongly and make them feel very interested, excited, etc. SYN **delight** **2 ~ sb/sth** to place sb/sth under a magic SPELL (= magic words that have special powers) SYN **bewitch**

en·chant·ed /ɪnˈtʃɑːntɪd; *NAmE* -ˈtʃæntɪd/ *adj.* **1** placed under a SPELL (= magic words that have special powers): *an* ***enchanted forest/kingdom*** **2** (*formal*) filled with great pleasure SYN **delighted**: *He was enchanted to see her again after so long.*

en·chant·er /ɪnˈtʃɑːntə(r); *NAmE* -ˈtʃæn-/ *noun* (in stories) a man who has magic powers that he uses to control people

en·chant·ing /ɪnˈtʃɑːntɪŋ; *NAmE* -ˈtʃæntɪŋ/ *adj.* attractive and pleasing SYN **delightful**: *an enchanting view* ▸ **en·chant·ing·ly** *adv.*

en·chant·ment /ɪnˈtʃɑːntmənt; *NAmE* -ˈtʃænt-/ *noun* **1** [U] (*formal*) a feeling of great pleasure **2** [U] the state of being under a magic SPELL: *It was a place of deep mystery and enchantment.* **3** [C] (*literary*) = SPELL: *They had been turned to stone by an enchantment.*

en·chant·ress /ɪnˈtʃɑːntrəs; *NAmE* -ˈtʃæn-/ *noun* **1** (in stories) a woman who has magic powers that she uses to control people **2** (*literary*) a woman that men find very attractive and interesting

en·chil·ada /ˌentʃɪˈlɑːdə/ *noun* (from *Spanish*) a Mexican dish consisting of a TORTILLA filled with meat and covered with a spicy sauce

IDM **the whole enchilˈada** (*informal*) the whole thing; everything ➲ more at BIG *adj.*

en·cir·cle /ɪnˈsɜːkl; *NAmE* ɪnˈsɜːrkl/ *verb* **~ sb/sth** (*formal*) to surround sb/sth completely in a circle: *Jack's arms encircled her waist.* ◇ *The island is encircled by a coral reef.* ▸ **en·circle·ment** *noun* [U]

encl. (also **enc.**) *abbr.* (*business*) enclosed (used on business letters to show that another document is being sent in the same envelope)

en·clave /ˈenkleɪv/ *noun* an area of a country or city where the people have a different religion, culture or NATIONALITY from those who live in the country or city that surrounds it

en·close /ɪnˈkləʊz; *NAmE* ɪnˈkloʊz/ *verb* **1** [usually passive] **~ sth (in/with sth)** to build a wall, fence, etc. around sth: *The yard had been enclosed with iron railings.* ◇ *The land was enclosed in the seventeenth century* (= in Britain, when public land was made private property). ◇ (*figurative*) *All translated words should be enclosed in brackets.* **2 ~ sth** (especially of a wall, fence, etc.) to surround sth: *Low hedges enclosed the flower beds.* ◇ (*figurative*) *She felt his arms enclose her.* **3 ~ sth (with sth)** to put sth in the same envelope, package, etc. as sth else: *Please return the completed form, enclosing a recent photograph.*

en·closed /ɪnˈkləʊzd; *NAmE* ɪnˈkloʊzd/ *adj.* **1** with walls, etc. all around: *Do not use this substance in an enclosed space.* **2** (*abbr.* **encl.**) sent with a letter, etc: *Please complete the enclosed application form.* ◇ *Please* ***find enclosed*** *a cheque for £100.* **3** (of religious communities) having little contact with the outside world

en·clos·ure /ɪnˈkləʊʒə(r); *NAmE* -ˈkloʊ-/ *noun* **1** [C] a piece of land that is surrounded by a fence or wall and is used for a particular purpose: *a wildlife enclosure* **2** [U, C] the act of placing a fence or wall around a piece of land: *the enclosure of common land in the seventeenth century* **3** [C] something that is placed in an envelope with a letter

en·code /ɪnˈkəʊd; *NAmE* ɪnˈkoʊd/ *verb* **1 ~ sth** to change ordinary language into letters, symbols, etc. in order to send secret messages **2 ~ sth** (*computing*) to change information into a form that can be processed by a computer **3 ~ sth** (*linguistics*) to express the meaning of sth in a foreign language ➲ compare DECODE

en·co·mium /enˈkəʊmiəm; *NAmE* -ˈkoʊm-/ *noun* (*pl.* **en·co·miums** or **en·co·mia** /enˈkəʊmiə; *NAmE* -ˈkoʊm-/) (*formal*) a speech or piece of writing that praises sb or sth highly

en·com·pass /ɪnˈkʌmpəs/ *verb* (*formal*) **1 ~ sth** to include a large number or range of things: *The job encompasses a wide range of responsibilities.* ◇ *The group* *encompasses all ages.* **2 ~ sth** to surround or cover sth completely: *The fog soon encompassed the whole valley.*

en·core /ˈɒŋkɔː(r); *NAmE* ˈɑːŋ-/ *noun, exclamation*
■ ***noun*** an extra short performance given at the end of a concert or other performance; a request for this made by an audience calling out: *She played a Chopin waltz as an encore.* ◇ *The group got three encores.*
■ ***exclamation*** an audience calls out **encore!** at the end of a concert to ask the performer to play or sing another piece of music

E

en·coun·ter 🔑 AW /ɪnˈkaʊntə(r)/ *verb, noun*
■ ***verb*** **1** 🔑 **~ sth** to experience sth, especially sth unpleasant or difficult, while you are trying to do sth else SYN **meet with, run into**: *We encountered a number of difficulties in the first week.* ◇ *I had never encountered such resistance before.* **2** 🔑 **~ sb/sth** (*formal*) to meet sb, or discover or experience sth, especially sb/sth new, unusual or unexpected SYN **come across**: *She was the most remarkable woman he had ever encountered.*
■ ***noun*** **1** 🔑 a meeting, especially one that is sudden, unexpected or violent: **~ (with sb/sth)** *Three of them were killed in the subsequent encounter with the police.* ◇ **~ (between A and B)** *The story describes the extraordinary encounter between a man and a dolphin.* ◇ *a chance encounter* ◇ *I've had a number of* ***close encounters*** (= situations that could have been dangerous) *with bad drivers.* ◇ *It was his first sexual encounter* (= first experience of sex). **2** a sports match against a particular player or team: *She has beaten her opponent in all of their previous encounters.* **3** (*IndE*) an incident in which police shoot dead a suspected criminal

enˈcounter group *noun* a group of people who meet regularly in order to help each other with emotional and PSYCHOLOGICAL problems

en·cour·age 🔑 /ɪnˈkʌrɪdʒ; *NAmE* -ˈkɜːr-/ *verb*
1 🔑 to give sb support, courage or hope: **~ sb in sth** *My parents have always encouraged me in my choice of career.* ◇ **~ sb** *We were greatly encouraged by the positive response of the public.* **2** 🔑 **~ sb to do sth** | **~ doing sth** to persuade sb to do sth by making it easier for them and making them believe it is a good thing to do: *Banks actively encourage people to borrow money.* **3** 🔑 to make sth more likely to happen or develop: **~ sth (in sb/sth)** *They claim that some computer games encourage violent behaviour in young children.* ◇ **~ sb to do sth** *Music and lighting are used to encourage shoppers to buy more.* ◇ **~ doing sth** *Technology encourages multitasking.* OPP **discourage**
▶ **en·cour·aging** *adj.* [not usually before noun]: *This month's unemployment figures are not very encouraging.* ◇ *You could try being a little more encouraging!* **en·cour·aging·ly** *adv.*: *to smile encouragingly* ◇ *The attendance was encouragingly high.*

en·cour·age·ment 🔑 /ɪnˈkʌrɪdʒmənt; *NAmE* -ˈkɜːr-/ *noun* [U, C, usually sing.]
the act of encouraging sb to do sth; something that encourages sb: *a few words of encouragement* ◇ *He needs all the support and encouragement he can get.* ◇ *With a little encouragement from his parents he should do well.* ◇ **~ (to sb) (to do sth)** *She was given every encouragement to try something new.* ◇ *Her words were a great encouragement to them.* OPP **discouragement**

en·croach /ɪnˈkrəʊtʃ; *NAmE* ɪnˈkroʊtʃ/ *verb* (*formal*) **1** [I] **~ (on/upon sth)** (*disapproving*) to begin to affect or use up too much of sb's time, rights, personal life, etc: *I won't encroach on your time any longer.* ◇ *He never allows work to encroach upon his family life.* **2** [I] **~ (on/upon sth)** to slowly begin to cover more and more of an area: *The growing town soon encroached on the surrounding countryside.* ◇ *the encroaching tide* (= that is coming in) ▶ **en·croach·ment** *noun* [U, C]: **~ (on/upon sth)** *the regime's many encroachments on human rights*

en·crust·ation /ˌenkrʌˈsteɪʃn/ *noun* = INCRUSTATION

en·crust·ed /ɪnˈkrʌstɪd/ *adj.* **~ (with/in sth)** covered with a thin hard layer of sth; forming a thin hard layer on sth: *a crown encrusted with diamonds* ◇ *encrusted blood*

en·crypt /ɪnˈkrɪpt/ *verb* **~ sth** (*computing*) to put information into a special code, especially in order to prevent people from looking at it without authority OPP **decrypt**
▶ **en·cryp·tion** /ɪnˈkrɪpʃn/ *noun* [U] OPP **decryption**

en·cum·ber /ɪnˈkʌmbə(r)/ *verb* [usually passive] (*formal*) **1 ~ sb/sth (with sth)** to make it difficult for sb to do sth or for sth to happen: *The police operation was encumbered by crowds of reporters.* **2 ~ sb/sth (with sth)** to be large and/or heavy and make it difficult for sb to move: *The frogmen were encumbered by their diving equipment.*

en·cum·brance /ɪnˈkʌmbrəns/ *noun* (*formal*) a person or thing that prevents sb from moving easily or from doing what they want SYN **burden**: *I felt I was being an encumbrance to them.*

-ency ➲ -ANCY

en·cyc·lic·al /ɪnˈsɪklɪkl/ *noun* an official letter written by the Pope and sent to all Roman Catholic BISHOPS

en·cyc·lo·pe·dia (*BrE* also **-pae·dia**) /ɪnˌsaɪkləˈpiːdiə/ *noun* a book or set of books giving information about all areas of knowledge or about different areas of one particular subject, usually arranged in alphabetical order; a similar collection of information on a website or CD-ROM: *an* ***online encyclopedia***

en·cyclo·pe·dic (*BrE* also **-paedic**) /ɪnˌsaɪkləˈpiːdɪk/ *adj.* **1** connected with encyclopedias or the type of information found in them: *encyclopedic information* ◇ *an encyclopedic dictionary* **2** having a lot of information about a wide variety of subjects; containing complete information about a particular subject: *She has an encyclopedic knowledge of natural history.*

end 🔑 /end/ *noun, verb*
■ ***noun***
▸ FINAL PART **1** 🔑 the final part of a period of time, an event, an activity or a story: ***at the end of*** *the week* ◇ *We didn't leave until the* ***very end.*** ◇ *the end of the book* ◇ *We had to hear about the whole journey* ***from beginning to end.*** ◇ *It's the end of an era.*
▸ FURTHEST PART **2** 🔑 the part of an object or a place that is the furthest away from its centre: *Turn right at the end of the road.* ◇ *I joined the end of the queue.* ◇ *Go to the end of the line!* ◇ *You've got something on the end of your nose.* ◇ *Tie the ends of the string together.* ◇ *That's his wife sitting at* ***the far end*** *of the table.* ◇ *These two products are from opposite ends of the price range.* ◇ *We've travelled from one end of Mexico to the other.* ◇ *They live in the end house.* ➲ see also BIG END, DEAD END, EAST END, SPLIT ENDS, TAIL END
▸ FINISH **3** 🔑 a situation in which sth does not exist any more: *the end of all his dreams* ◇ *The meeting* ***came to an end*** (= finished). ◇ *The war was finally* ***at an end.*** ◇ *The coup* ***brought*** *his corrupt regime* ***to an end.*** ◇ *There's no* ***end in sight*** *to the present crisis.* ◇ *They have* ***called for an end to*** *violence.* ◇ *That was by no means the end of the matter.*
▸ AIM **4** an aim or a purpose: *They are prepared to use violence in pursuit of their ends.* ◇ *She is exploiting the current situation for her own ends.* ◇ ***With this end in view*** (= in order to achieve this) *they employed 50 new staff.* ◇ *We are willing to make any concessions necessary* ***to this end*** (= in order to achieve this). ➲ SYNONYMS at TARGET
▸ PART OF ACTIVITY **5** [usually sing.] a part of an activity with which sb is concerned, especially in business: *We need somebody to handle the marketing end of the business.* ◇ *Are there any problems at your end?* ◇ *I have kept my end of the bargain.*
▸ OF TELEPHONE LINE/JOURNEY **6** [usually sing.] either of two places connected by a telephone call, journey, etc: *I answered the phone but there was no one* ***at the other end.*** ◇ *Jean is going to meet me at* ***the other end.***
▸ OF SPORTS FIELD **7** one of the two halves of a sports field: *The teams changed ends at half-time.*
▸ PIECE LEFT **8** (*BrE*) a small piece that is left after sth has been used: *a cigarette end* ➲ see also FAG END, LOOSE END, ODDS AND ENDS
▸ DEATH **9** [usually sing.] a person's death. People say 'end' to avoid saying 'death': *She came to* ***an untimely end*** (= died young). ◇ *I was with him at the end* (= when he died). ◇ (*literary*) *He* ***met his end*** (= died) *at the Battle of Waterloo.*

IDM **at the ˌend of the ˈday** (*BrE, informal*) used to introduce the most important fact after everything has been considered: *At the end of the day, he'll still have to make his own decision.* **a bad/sticky ˈend** (*BrE*) something unpleasant that happens to sb, for example punishment or a violent death, usually because of their own actions: *He'll* ***come to a sticky end*** *one of these days if he carries on like that.* **be at the end of sth** to have almost nothing left of sth: *I'm at the end of my patience.* ◇ *They are at the end of their food supply.* **be at the ˌend of your ˈtether** (*BrE*) (*NAmE* **be at the ˌend of your ˈrope**) to feel that you cannot deal with a difficult situation any more because you are too tired, worried, etc. **be the ˈend** (*BrE, informal*) when you say that people or situations are **the end**, you mean that you are annoyed with them **an ˌend in itˈself** a thing that is itself important and not just a part of sth more important **the end justifies the ˈmeans** (*saying*) bad or unfair methods of doing sth are acceptable if the result of that action is good or positive **(reach) the end of the ˈline/ˈroad** (to reach) the point at which sth can no longer continue in the same way: *A defeat in the second round marked the end of the line for last year's champion.* **end of ˈstory** (*informal*) (*NAmE* also **end ˈof...**) used when you are stating that there is nothing more that can be said or done about sth **ˌend to ˈend** in a line, with the ends touching: *They arranged the tables end to end.* **get/have your ˈend away** (*BrE, slang*) to have sex **go to the ˌends of the ˈearth** to do everything possible, even if it is difficult, in order to get or achieve sth: *I'd go to the ends of the earth to see her again.* **in the ˈend** **1** 0-w after a long period of time or series of events: *He tried various jobs and in the end became an accountant.* **2** 0-w after everything has been considered: *You can try your best to impress the interviewers but in the end it's often just a question of luck.* **keep your ˈend up** (*BrE, informal*) to continue to be cheerful in a difficult situation **make (both) ends ˈmeet** to earn just enough money to be able to buy the things you need: *Many families struggle to make ends meet.* **no ˈend** (*informal*) very much: *It upset me no end to hear they'd split up.* **no ˈend of sth** (*informal*) a lot of sth: *We had no end of trouble getting them to agree.* **not the end of the ˈworld** (*informal*) not the worst thing that could happen to sb: *Failing one exam is not the end of the world.* **on ˈend** **1** in a vertical position: *It'll fit if you stand it on end.* **2** for the stated length of time, without stopping: *He would disappear for* ***weeks on end.*** **put an ˈend to yourself | put an ˈend to it all** to kill yourself ➲ more at BEGINNING, BITTER *adj.*, BURN *v.*, DEEP *adj.*, HAIR, HEAR, LIGHT *n.*, LOOSE END, MEANS, RECEIVE, ROUGH *adj.*, SHARP *adj.*, SHORT *n.*, THIN *adj.*, WIT, WRONG *adj.*

■ ***verb*** 0-w [I, T] to finish; to make sth finish: *The road ends here.* ◇ *How does the story end?* ◇ *The speaker ended by suggesting some topics for discussion.* ◇ **~ with sth** *Her note ended with the words: 'See you soon.'* ◇ **~ sth** *They decided to end their relationship.* ◇ **~ sth with sth** *They ended the play with a song.* ◇ **+ speech** *'And that was that,' she ended.*

IDM **a/the sth to end all sths** used to emphasize how large, important, exciting, etc. you think sth is: *The movie has a car chase to end all car chases.* **ˌend your ˈdays/ˈlife (in sth)** to spend the last part of your life in a particular state or place: *He ended his days in poverty.* **ˌend in ˈtears** (*BrE, informal*) if you say that sth will **end in tears**, you are warning sb that what they are doing will have an unhappy or unpleasant result **ˈend it all | ˌend your ˈlife** to kill yourself

PHR V **ˈend in sth** [no passive] **1** 0-w to have sth as an ending: *The word I'm thinking of ends in '-ous'.* **2** 0-w to have sth as a result: *Their long struggle ended in failure.* ◇ *The debate ended in uproar.* **ˌend ˈup** 0-w to find yourself in a place or situation that you did not intend or expect to be in: **~ doing sth** *I ended up doing all the work myself.* ◇ **+ adv./prep.** *If you go on like this you'll end up in prison.* ◇ **+ adj.** *If he carries on driving like that, he'll end up dead.*

en·dan·ger /ɪnˈdeɪndʒə(r)/ *verb* **~ sb/sth** to put sb/sth in a situation in which they could be harmed or damaged: *The health of our children is being endangered by exhaust fumes.* ◇ *That one mistake seriously endangered the future of the company.* ◇ *The sea turtle is an* ***endangered species*** (= it may soon no longer exist).

en·dear /ɪnˈdɪə(r); *NAmE* -ˈdɪr/ *verb*

PHR V **enˈdear sb/yourself to sb** to make sb/yourself popular: *Their policies on taxation didn't endear them to voters.* ◇ *She was a talented teacher who endeared herself to all who worked with her.*

en·dear·ing /ɪnˈdɪərɪŋ; *NAmE* -ˈdɪr-/ *adj.* causing people to feel affection SYN **lovable**: *an endearing habit* ▶ **en·dear·ing·ly** *adv.*

en·dear·ment /ɪnˈdɪəmənt; *NAmE* -ˈdɪrm-/ *noun* [C, U] a word or an expression that is used to show affection: *They were whispering endearments to each other.* ◇ *'Darling' is a term of endearment.*

en·deav·our (*especially US* **en·deavor**) /ɪnˈdevə(r)/ *noun, verb*

■ ***noun*** [U, C] (*formal*) an attempt to do sth, especially sth new or difficult: *Please make every endeavour to arrive on time.* ◇ *advances in the field of scientific endeavour* ◇ *The manager is expected to use his or her best endeavours to promote the artist's career.*

■ ***verb*** **~ to do sth** (*formal*) to try very hard to do sth SYN **strive**: *I will endeavour to do my best for my country.*

en·dem·ic /enˈdemɪk/ *adj.* regularly found in a particular place or among a particular group of people and difficult to get rid of: **~ (in...)** *Malaria is endemic in many hot countries.* ◇ *Corruption is endemic in the system.* ◇ **~ (among...)** *an attitude endemic among senior members of the profession* ◇ **~ (to...)** *species endemic to* (= only found in) *Madagascar* ◇ *the endemic problem of racism* ➲ compare PANDEMIC

end·game /ˈendgeɪm/ *noun* **1** the final stage of a game of CHESS **2** the final stage of a political process

end·ing 0-w /ˈendɪŋ/ *noun*

1 0-w the last part of a story, film/movie, etc: *His stories usually have a* ***happy ending***. OPP **opening** **2** 0-w the act of finishing sth; the last part of sth: *the anniversary of the ending of the Pacific War* ◇ *It was the perfect ending to the perfect day.* **3** 0-w the last part of a word, that is added to a main part: *verb endings* ◇ *a* ***masculine/feminine ending***

en·dive /ˈendaɪv; -dɪv/ *noun* [C, U] **1** (*BrE*) (*NAmE* **chic·ory**, **ˌcurly ˈendive**, **fri·sée** [U]) a plant with green curly leaves that are eaten raw as a vegetable **2** (*NAmE*) (*BrE* **chic·ory**) a small pale green plant with bitter leaves that are eaten raw or cooked as a vegetable. The root can be dried and used with or instead of coffee.

end·less /ˈendləs/ *adj.* **1** very large in size or amount and seeming to have no end SYN **limitless**: *endless patience* ◇ *endless opportunities for making money* ◇ *The possibilities are endless.* ◇ *an endless list of things to do* ◇ *We don't have an endless supply of money, you know.* **2** continuing for a long time and seeming to have no end: *an endless round of parties and visits* ◇ *The journey seemed endless.* ◇ *I've had enough of their endless arguing.* **3** (*technical*) (of a LOOP, etc.) having the ends joined together so it forms one piece: *an endless loop of tape* ▶ **end·less·ly** *adv.*: *She talks endlessly about her problems.* ◇ *an endlessly repeated pattern*

end·note /ˈendnəʊt; *NAmE* -noʊt/ *noun* a note printed at the end of a book or section of a book ➲ WRITING TUTOR page WT11

endo·crine /ˈendəʊkrɪn; -kraɪn; *NAmE* ˈendəkrɪn/ *adj.* (*biology*) connected with GLANDS that put HORMONES and other products directly into the blood: *the endocrine system* ➲ compare EXOCRINE

endo·crin·ology /ˌendəʊkrɪˈnɒlədʒi; *NAmE* ˌendoʊkrəˈnɑːl-/ *noun* [U] (*medical*) the part of medicine concerning the endocrine system and HORMONES ▶ **endo·crin·olo·gist** /-dʒɪst/ *noun*

en·dog·amy /enˈdɒgəmi; *NAmE* -ˈdɑːg-/ *noun* [U] (*technical*) the custom of marrying only people from your local community ➲ compare EXOGAMY

en·dogen·ous /enˈdɒdʒənəs; *NAmE* -ˈdɑːdʒ-/ *adj.* (*medical*) (of a disease or SYMPTOM) having no obvious cause ➲ compare EXOGENOUS

endo·plasm /ˈendəʊplæzəm; *NAmE* ˈendoʊ-/ *noun* [U] (*biology*) (*old-fashioned*) the more liquid inner layer of the jelly-like substance inside cells ⊃ compare ECTOPLASM

en·dor·phin /enˈdɔːfɪn; *NAmE* -ˈdɔːrf-/ *noun* (*biology*) a HORMONE produced in the brain that reduces the feeling of pain

en·dorse /ɪnˈdɔːs; *NAmE* ɪnˈdɔːrs/ *verb* **1 ~ sth** to say publicly that you support a person, statement or course of action: *I wholeheartedly endorse his remarks.* ◇ *Members of all parties endorsed a ban on land mines.* **2 ~ sth** to say in an advertisement that you use and like a particular product so that other people will want to buy it **3 ~ sth** to write your name on the back of a cheque so that it can be paid into a bank account **4** [usually passive] **~ sth** (*BrE*) to write details of a driving offence on sb's DRIVING LICENCE: *You risk having your licence endorsed.*

en·dorse·ment /ɪnˈdɔːsmənt; *NAmE* -ˈdɔːrs-/ *noun* [C, U] **1** a public statement or action showing that you support sb/sth: *The election victory is a clear endorsement of their policies.* ◇ *a letter of endorsement* **2** a statement made in an advertisement, usually by sb famous or important, saying that they use and like a particular product **3** (*BrE*) details of a driving offence written on sb's DRIVING LICENCE

en·do·scope /ˈendəskəʊp; *NAmE* -skoʊp/ *noun* an instrument used in medical operations which consists of a very small camera on a long thin tube which can be put into a person's body so that the parts inside can be seen

en·dos·co·py /enˈdɒskəpi; *NAmE* -ˈdɑːsk-/ *noun* [C, U] (*pl.* -ies) (*medical*) a medical operation in which an endoscope is put into a person's body so that the parts inside can be seen

endo·skel·eton /ˈendəʊskelɪtn; *NAmE* ˈendoʊ-/ *noun* (*anatomy*) the bones inside the body of an animal that give it shape and support ⊃ compare EXOSKELETON

endo·sperm /ˈendəʊspɜːm; *NAmE* ˈendoʊspɜːrm/ *noun* [U] (*biology*) the part of the plant seed that provides food for the EMBRYO

endo·ther·mic /ˌendəʊˈθɜːmɪk; *NAmE* ˌendoʊˈθɜːrmɪk/ *adj.* (*chemistry*) (of a chemical reaction) needing heat in order to take place ⊃ compare EXOTHERMIC

endow /ɪnˈdaʊ/ *verb* **~ sth** to give a large sum of money to a school, a college or another institution to provide it with an income

PHR V **be enˈdowed with sth** (*formal*) to naturally have a particular feature, quality, etc: *She was endowed with intelligence and wit.* ⊃ see also WELL ENDOWED **enˈdow sb/sth with sth** (*formal*) **1** to believe or imagine that sb/sth has a particular quality: *She had endowed Marcus with the qualities she wanted him to possess.* **2** to give sth to sb/sth: *to endow sb with a responsibility*

en·dow·ment /ɪnˈdaʊmənt/ *noun* (*formal*) **1** [C, U] money that is given to a school, a college or another institution to provide it with an income; the act of giving this money **2** [C, usually pl.] a quality or an ability that you are born with

enˈdowment mortgage *noun* (*BrE*) a type of MORTGAGE (= money borrowed to buy property) in which money is regularly paid into an endowment policy. At the end of a particular period of time this money is then used to pay back the money that was borrowed ⊃ compare REPAYMENT MORTGAGE

enˈdowment policy *noun* (*BrE*) a type of life insurance in which a person regularly pays money to an insurance company, and receives a sum of money from them at the end of a particular period of time

end·paper /ˈendpeɪpə(r)/ *noun* (*technical*) a blank or decorated page stuck inside the front or back cover of a book

ˈend product *noun* something that is produced by a particular activity or process

ˌend reˈsult *noun* [usually sing.] the final result of a particular activity or process

ˈend run *noun* (in AMERICAN FOOTBALL) an attempt by the person carrying the ball to run around the end of the line of defending players

en·dur·ance /ɪnˈdjʊərəns; *NAmE* -ˈdʊr-/ *noun* [U] the ability to continue doing sth painful or difficult for a long period of time without complaining: *He showed remarkable endurance throughout his illness.* ◇ *They were humiliated* ***beyond endurance****.* ◇ *This event tests both physical and mental endurance.* ◇ *powers of endurance* ◇ *The party turned out to be more of an* ***endurance test*** *than a pleasure.*

en·dure /ɪnˈdjʊə(r); *NAmE* -ˈdʊr/ *verb* (*formal*) **1** [T] to experience and deal with sth that is painful or unpleasant, especially without complaining **SYN** **bear**: **~ sth** *They had to endure a long wait before the case came to trial.* ◇ *She could not endure the thought of parting.* ◇ *The pain was almost too great to endure.* ◇ (*formal*) *a love that endures all things and never fails* ◇ **~ doing sth** *He can't endure being defeated.* ◇ **~ to do sth** *He can't endure to be defeated.* **2** [I] to continue to exist for a long time **SYN** **last**: *a success that will endure* ▸ **en·dur·able** /ɪnˈdjʊərəbl; *NAmE* -ˈdʊr-/ *adj.*: *I felt that life was no longer endurable.* **OPP** **unendurable**

en·dur·ing /ɪnˈdjʊərɪŋ; *NAmE* -ˈdʊr-/ *adj.* lasting for a long time: *enduring memories* ◇ *What is the reason for the game's enduring appeal?* ▸ **en·dur·ing·ly** *adv.*: *an enduringly popular style*

ˌend-ˈuser *noun* a person who actually uses a product rather than one who makes or sells it, especially a person who uses a product connected with computers

end·ways /ˈendweɪz/ (also **end·wise** /-waɪz/) *adv.* **1** (also ˌ**endways/ˌendwise ˈon**) (of an object) with one end facing up, forwards, or towards the person who is looking at it: *We turned the table endways to get it through the doors.* ◇ *The first picture was taken from the side of the building, and the second one endways on.* **2** with the end of one thing touching the end of another: *The stones are laid down endways to make a path.*

ˈend zone *noun* the area at the end of an AMERICAN FOOTBALL field into which the ball must be carried or passed in order to score points

enema /ˈenəmə/ *noun* a liquid that is put into a person's RECTUM (= the opening through which solid waste leaves the body) in order to clean out the BOWELS, especially before a medical operation; the act of cleaning out the bowels in this way

enemy 🔑 /ˈenəmi/ *noun* (*pl.* -ies) **1** 🔑 [C] a person who hates sb or who acts or speaks against sb/sth: *He has a lot of enemies in the company.* ◇ *After just one day, she had already* ***made an enemy of*** *her manager.* ◇ *It is rare to find a prominent politician with few* ***political enemies****.* ◇ *The state has a duty to protect its citizens against external enemies.* ◇ *Birds are the* ***natural enemies*** *of many insect pests* (= they kill them). ⊃ see also ENMITY **2** 🔑 **the enemy** [sing.+ sing./pl. v.] a country that you are fighting a war against; the soldiers, etc. of this country: *The enemy was/were forced to retreat.* ◇ ***enemy forces/aircraft/territory*** ◇ *behind* ***enemy lines*** (= the area controlled by the enemy) ⊃ COLLOCATIONS at WAR **3** 🔑 [C] **~ (of sth)** (*formal*) anything that harms sth or prevents it from being successful: *Poverty and ignorance are the enemies of progress.* **IDM** see WORST *adj.*

en·er·get·ic **AW** /ˌenəˈdʒetɪk; *NAmE* ˌenərˈdʒ-/ *adj.* having or needing a lot of energy and enthusiasm: *He knew I was energetic and dynamic and would get things done.* ◇ *an energetic supporter* ◇ *The heart responds well to energetic exercise.* ◇ *For the more energetic* (= people who prefer physical activities), *we offer windsurfing and diving.* ◇ *I think I'd prefer something a little less energetic.* ▸ **en·er·get·ic·al·ly** **AW** /-kli/ *adv.*

en·er·gize (*BrE* also **-ise**) /ˈenədʒaɪz; *NAmE* ˈenərdʒ-/ *verb* **1 ~ sb** to make sb enthusiastic about sth **2 ~ sb** to give sb more energy, strength, etc: *a refreshing and energizing fruit drink* **3 ~ sth** (*technical*) to supply power or energy to a machine, an atom, etc.

en·ergy 🔑 **AW** /ˈenədʒi; *NAmE* -ərdʒi/ *noun* **1** 🔑 [U] the ability to put effort and enthusiasm into an activity, work, etc: *It's a waste of time and energy.* ◇ *She's* *always* ***full of energy.*** ◇ ***nervous energy*** (= energy produced by feeling nervous) **2 energies** [pl.] the physical and mental effort that you use to do sth: *She put all her energies into her work.* ◇ ***creative/destructive energies*** **3** 0‐w [U] a source of power, such as fuel, used for driving machines, providing heat, etc: ***solar/nuclear energy*** ◇ *It is important to conserve energy.* ◇ *an energy crisis* (= for example when fuel is not freely available) ➲ COLLOCATIONS at ENVIRONMENT **4** [U] (*physics*) the ability of matter or RADIATION to work because of its mass, movement, electric charge, etc: ***kinetic/potential, etc. energy***

ener·vate /ˈenəveɪt; *NAmE* ˈenərv-/ *verb* **~ sb** (*formal*) to make sb feel weak and tired: *an enervating disease/climate* ▸ **en·er·va·tion** /ˌenəˈveɪʃn; *NAmE* ˌenərˈv-/ *noun* [U]

en·fant ter·rible /ˌɒfɒ teˈriːbl; *NAmE* ˌɑːfɑː/ *noun* (*pl.* **en·fants ter·ribles** /ˌɒfɒ teˈriːbl; *NAmE* ˌɑːfɑː/) (from *French*) a person who is young and successful and whose behaviour and ideas may be unusual and may shock or embarrass other people

en·fee·ble /ɪnˈfiːbl/ *verb* **~ sb/sth** (*formal*) to make sb/sth weak ▸ **en·fee·bled** *adj.*

en·fold /ɪnˈfəʊld; *NAmE* ɪnˈfoʊld/ *verb* (*literary*) **1 ~ sb/sth** (**in sth**) to hold sb in your arms in a way that shows affection SYN **embrace**: *She lay quietly, enfolded in his arms.* **2 ~ sb/sth** (**in sth**) to surround or cover sb/sth completely: *Darkness spread and enfolded him.*

en·force AW /ɪnˈfɔːs; *NAmE* ɪnˈfɔːrs/ *verb* **1 ~ sth** (**on/against sb/sth**) to make sure that people obey a particular law or rule: *It's the job of the police to enforce the law.* ◇ *The legislation will be difficult to enforce.* ◇ *United Nations troops enforced a ceasefire in the area.* **2 ~ sth** (**on sb**) to make sth happen or force sb to do sth: *You can't enforce cooperation between the players.* ▸ **en·force·able** /-əbl/ *adj.*: *A gambling debt is not legally enforceable.* **en·force·ment** AW *noun* [U]: *strict enforcement of regulations* ◇ ***law enforcement*** *officers*

en·forced AW /ɪnˈfɔːst; *NAmE* ɪnˈfɔːrst/ *adj.* that sb is forced to do or experience without being able to control it: *a period of enforced absence*

en·for·cer /ɪnˈfɔːsə(r); *NAmE* -fɔːrs-/ *noun* a person whose responsibility is to make sure that other people perform the actions they are supposed to, especially in a government

en·fran·chise /ɪnˈfræntʃaɪz/ *verb* [usually passive] **~ sb** (*formal*) to give sb the right to vote in an election OPP **disenfranchise** ▸ **en·fran·chise·ment** /ɪnˈfræntʃɪzmənt/ *noun* [U]

eng. *abbr.* (*BrE*) (in writing) engineer; engineering

en·gage 0‐w /ɪnˈgeɪdʒ/ *verb*
1 0‐w [T] **~ sth** (*formal*) to succeed in attracting and keeping sb's attention and interest: *It is a movie that engages both the mind and the eye.* **2** 0‐w [T] **~ sb** (**as sth**) | **~ sth** | **~ sb to do sth** (*formal*) to employ sb to do a particular job: *He is currently engaged as a consultant.* **3** [I] **~** (**with sth/sb**) to become involved with and try to understand sth/sb: *She has the ability to engage with young minds.* **4** [T, I] **~** (**sb**) (*formal*) to begin fighting with sb: *to engage the enemy* **5** [I, T] when a part of a machine **engages**, or when you **engage** it, it fits together with another part of the machine and the machine begins to work: *The cogwheels are not engaging.* ◇ **~ with sth** *One cogwheel engages with the next.* ◇ **~ sth** *Engage the clutch before selecting a gear.* OPP **disengage**
PHR V **enˈgage in sth** | **enˈgage sb in sth** (*formal*) to take part in sth; to make sb take part in sth: *Even in prison, he continued to engage in criminal activities.* ◇ *She tried desperately to* ***engage him in conversation.***

en·gaged 0‐w /ɪnˈgeɪdʒd/ *adj.*
1 0‐w (*formal*) busy doing sth: **~** (**in sth**) *They are engaged in talks with the Irish government.* ◇ *They were engaged in conversation.* ◇ **~** (**on sth**) *He is now engaged on his second novel.* ◇ *I can't come to dinner on Tuesday—I'm* ***otherwise engaged*** (= I have already arranged to do something else). **2** 0‐w having agreed to marry sb: *When did you* ***get engaged?*** ◇ *an engaged couple* ◇ **~ to sb** *She's engaged to Peter.* ◇ *They are engaged to be married* (= to each other). ➲ COLLOCATIONS at MARRIAGE **3** 0‐w (*BrE*) (*NAmE* **busy**) (of a telephone line) being used: *I couldn't get through—the line's engaged.* ◇ *I phoned earlier but you were engaged* (= using your phone). ◇ *the* ***engaged tone/signal*** ➲ COLLOCATIONS at PHONE **4** 0‐w (*BrE*) (of a public toilet/bathroom) being used OPP **vacant**

en·gage·ment /ɪnˈgeɪdʒmənt/ *noun*
▸ BEFORE MARRIAGE **1** [C] an agreement to marry sb; the period during which two people are engaged: *Their engagement was announced in the local paper.* ◇ **~** (**to sb**) *She has* ***broken off her engagement*** *to Charles.* ◇ *an engagement party* ◇ *a long/short engagement*
▸ ARRANGEMENT TO DO STH **2** [C] an arrangement to do sth at a particular time, especially sth official or sth connected with your job: *an* ***engagement book/diary*** ◇ *He has a number of social engagements next week.* ◇ *It was her first* ***official engagement.*** ◇ *I had to refuse because of a* ***prior engagement.***
▸ FIGHTING **3** [C, U] (*technical*) fighting between two armies, etc: *The general tried to avoid an engagement with the enemy.*
▸ BEING INVOLVED **4** [U] **~** (**with sb/sth**) (*formal*) being involved with sb/sth in an attempt to understand them/it: *Her views are based on years of engagement with the problems of the inner city.*
▸ EMPLOYMENT **5** [U, C] (*BrE*) an arrangement to employ sb; the process of employing sb: *The terms of engagement are to be agreed in writing.*

enˈgagement ring *noun* a ring that a man gives to a woman when they agree to get married

en·gaging /ɪnˈgeɪdʒɪŋ/ *adj.* interesting or pleasant in a way that attracts your attention: *an engaging smile* ▸ **en·ga·ging·ly** *adv.*

en·gen·der /ɪnˈdʒendə(r)/ *verb* **~ sth** (*formal*) to make a feeling or situation exist: *The issue engendered controversy.*

en·gine 0‐w /ˈendʒɪn/ *noun*
1 0‐w the part of a vehicle that produces power to make the vehicle move: *a* ***diesel/petrol engine*** ◇ *My car had to have a new engine.* ◇ *engine trouble* ◇ *I* ***switched/turned the engine off.*** ➲ VISUAL VOCAB page V41 ➲ see also INTERNAL-COMBUSTION ENGINE, JET ENGINE, TRACTION ENGINE **2** (also **loco·mo·tive**) a vehicle that pulls a train ➲ VISUAL VOCAB page V47 **3 -engined** (in adjectives) having the type or number of engines mentioned: *a twin-engined speedboat* ➲ see also FIRE ENGINE, SEARCH ENGINE

ˈengine driver (*BrE*, becoming *old-fashioned*) (*NAmE* **en·gin·eer**) *noun* a person whose job is driving a railway/railroad engine

en·gin·eer 0‐w /ˌendʒɪˈnɪə(r); *NAmE* -ˈnɪr/ *noun, verb*
▪ ***noun*** **1** 0‐w a person whose job involves designing and building engines, machines, roads, bridges, etc. ➲ see also CHEMICAL ENGINEER, CIVIL ENGINEER, ELECTRICAL ENGINEER, LIGHTING ENGINEER, MECHANICAL ENGINEER, SOFTWARE ENGINEER, SOUND ENGINEER **2** 0‐w a person who is trained to repair machines and electrical equipment: *They're sending an engineer to fix the phone.* **3** a person whose job is to control and repair engines, especially on a ship or an aircraft: *a flight engineer* ◇ *the chief engineer on a cruise liner* **4** (*NAmE*) (*BrE* **ˈengine driver**) a person whose job is driving a railway/railroad engine **5** a soldier trained to design and build military structures
▪ ***verb*** **1 ~ sth** (often *disapproving*) to arrange for sth to happen or take place, especially when this is done secretly in order to give yourself an advantage SYN **contrive**: *She engineered a further meeting with him.* **2** [usually passive] **~ sth** to design and build sth: *The car is beautifully engineered and a pleasure to drive.* **3 ~ sth** to change the GENETIC structure of sth SYN **genetically modify**: *genetically engineered crops*

en·gin·eer·ing 0‐w /ˌendʒɪˈnɪərɪŋ; *NAmE* -ˈnɪr-/ *noun* [U]
1 0‐w the activity of applying scientific knowledge to the design, building and control of machines, roads, bridges,

E

electrical equipment, etc: *The bridge is a triumph of modern engineering.* ➲ compare REVERSE ENGINEERING **2** 0-ᵣ (also ˌ**engineering ˈscience**) the study of engineering as a subject: *a degree in engineering* ➲ see also CHEMICAL ENGINEERING, CIVIL ENGINEERING, ELECTRICAL ENGINEERING, GENETIC ENGINEERING, MECHANICAL ENGINEERING, SOCIAL ENGINEERING

ˈ**engine room** *noun* **1** the part of a ship where the engines are **2** the part of an organization where most of the important activity takes place or important decisions are made

E

Eng·lish /ˈɪŋɡlɪʃ/ *noun, adj.*

▪ ***noun*** **1** [U, C] the language, originally of England, now spoken in many other countries and used as a language of international communication throughout the world: *She speaks good English.* ◇ *I need to improve my English.* ◇ *world Englishes* **2** [U] English language or literature as a subject of study: *a degree in English* ◇ *English is my best subject.* **3 the English** [pl.] the people of England (sometimes wrongly used to mean the British, including the Scots, the Welsh and the Northern Irish) IDM see PLAIN *adj.*

▪ ***adj.*** connected with England, its people or its language: *the English countryside* ◇ *an English man/woman* ◇ *typically English attitudes* ◇ *an English dictionary* ➲ note at BRITISH

ˌ**English ˈbreakfast** *noun* [C, U] a large breakfast, usually consisting of CEREAL (= food made from grain), cooked BACON and eggs, TOAST and tea or coffee ➲ compare CONTINENTAL BREAKFAST

ˌ**English for ˌAcademic ˈPurposes** (*abbr.* EAP) *noun* [U] the teaching of English for people who are using English for study, but whose first language is not English

ˌ**English ˈhorn** *noun* (*especially NAmE*) = COR ANGLAIS

Eng·lish·man /ˈɪŋɡlɪʃmən/ *noun* (*pl.* **-men** /-mən/) a man from England

IDM **an ˌEnglishman's ˌhome is his ˈcastle** (*BrE*) (*US* **a ˌman's ˌhome is his ˈcastle**) (*saying*) a person's home is a place where they can be private and safe and do as they like

ˌ**English ˈmuffin** (*NAmE*) (*BrE* **muf·fin**) *noun* a type of round flat bread roll, usually TOASTED and eaten hot with butter

ˌ**English ˈrose** *noun* an attractive girl with fair skin and an appearance that is thought to be typical of English people

Eng·lish·woman /ˈɪŋɡlɪʃwʊmən/ *noun* (*pl.* **-women** /-wɪmɪn/) a woman from England

en·gorge /ɪnˈɡɔːdʒ; *NAmE* ɪnˈɡɔːrdʒ/ *verb* **~ sth** (*technical*) to cause sth to become filled with blood or another liquid and to swell

en·grave /ɪnˈɡreɪv/ *verb* [often passive] to cut words or designs on wood, stone, metal, etc: **~ A (with B)** *The silver cup was engraved with his name.* ◇ **~ B on A** *His name was engraved on the silver cup.*

IDM **be engraved on/in your ˈheart, ˈmemory, ˈmind, etc.** to be sth that you will never forget because it affected you so strongly

en·graver /ɪnˈɡreɪvə(r)/ *noun* a person whose job is to cut words or designs on wood, stone, metal, etc.

en·grav·ing /ɪnˈɡreɪvɪŋ/ *noun* **1** [C] a picture made by cutting a design on a piece of metal and then printing the design on paper **2** [U] the art or process of cutting designs on wood, stone, metal, etc. ➲ COLLOCATIONS at ART

en·gross /ɪnˈɡrəʊs; *NAmE* ɪnˈɡroʊs/ *verb* **~ sb** if sth **engrosses** you, it is so interesting that you give it all your attention and time ▸ **en·gross·ing** /ɪnˈɡrəʊsɪŋ; *NAmE* -ˈɡroʊs-/ *adj.*: *an engrossing problem*

en·grossed /ɪnˈɡrəʊst; *NAmE* ɪnˈɡroʊst/ *adj.* **~ (in/with sth)** so interested or involved in sth that you give it all your attention: *She was engrossed in conversation.*

en·gulf /ɪnˈɡʌlf/ *verb* (*formal*) **1 ~ sb/sth** to surround or to cover sb/sth completely: *He was engulfed by a crowd of reporters.* ◇ *The vehicle was* **engulfed in flames**. **2 ~ sb/sth** to affect sb/sth very strongly: *Fear engulfed her.*

en·hance AW /ɪnˈhɑːns; *NAmE* -ˈhæns/ *verb* **~ sth** to increase or further improve the good quality, value or status of sb/sth: *This is an opportunity to enhance the reputation of the company.* ◇ *the skilled use of make-up to enhance your best features* ▸ **en·hanced** AW *adj.*: *enhanced efficiency* **en·hance·ment** AW *noun* [U, C]: *equipment for the enhancement of sound quality* ◇ *software enhancements*

en·hancer /ɪnˈhɑːnsə(r); *NAmE* -ˈhæns-/ *noun* (*technical*) a substance or device that is designed to improve sth: *flavour enhancers*

en·igma /ɪˈnɪɡmə/ *noun* a person, thing or situation that is mysterious and difficult to understand SYN **mystery, puzzle**

en·ig·mat·ic /ˌenɪɡˈmætɪk/ *adj.* mysterious and difficult to understand: *an enigmatic smile* ▸ **en·ig·mat·ic·al·ly** /-kli/ *adv.*: *'I might,' he said enigmatically.*

en·jambe·ment (also **en·jamb·ment**) /ɪnˈdʒæmbmənt/ *noun* [U, C] (from *French*, *technical*) the fact of a sentence continuing beyond the end of a line of poetry ➲ compare CAESURA

en·join /ɪnˈdʒɔɪn/ *verb* **1** [often passive] **~ sb to do sth** | **~ sth** (*formal*) to order or strongly advise sb to do sth; to say that a particular action or quality is necessary **2 ~ sb from doing sth** (*law*) to legally prevent sb from doing sth, for example with an INJUNCTION

enjoy 0-ᵣ /ɪnˈdʒɔɪ/ *verb*

1 0-ᵣ [T] to get pleasure from sth: **~ sth** *We thoroughly enjoyed our time in New York.* ◇ *Thanks for a great evening. I really* **enjoyed it**. ◇ **~ doing sth** *I enjoy playing tennis and squash.* **2** 0-ᵣ [T] **~ yourself** to be happy and get pleasure from what you are doing: *They all enjoyed themselves at the party.* **3** [T] **~ sth** (*formal*) to have sth good that is an advantage to you: *People in this country enjoy a high standard of living.* ◇ *He's always enjoyed good health.* **4** [I] **enjoy!** (*informal*) used to say that you hope sb gets pleasure from sth that you are giving them or recommending to them: *Here's that book I promised you. Enjoy!*

Grammar Point

enjoy

Note the following patterns:

- *I enjoyed myself at the party.* ◇ ~~*I enjoyed at the party.*~~
- *Thanks. I really enjoyed it.* ◇ ~~*Thanks. I really enjoyed.*~~
- *I enjoy playing basketball.* ◇ ~~*I enjoy to play basketball.*~~
- *I enjoy reading very much.* ◇ ~~*I enjoy very much reading.*~~
- *I hope you enjoy your trip.* ◇ ~~*I hope you enjoy with your trip.*~~

en·joy·able 0-ᵣ /ɪnˈdʒɔɪəbl/ *adj.* giving pleasure: *an enjoyable weekend/experience* ◇ ***highly/really/thoroughly/very enjoyable*** ▸ **en·joy·ably** /-əbli/ *adv.*: *The evening passed enjoyably.*

en·joy·ment 0-ᵣ /ɪnˈdʒɔɪmənt/ *noun*

1 0-ᵣ [U] the pleasure that you get from sth: *He spoiled my enjoyment of the game by talking all through it.* ◇ *The rules are there to ensure everyone's safety and enjoyment.* ◇ *Children seem to have lost their enjoyment in reading.* ◇ *I get a lot of enjoyment from my grandchildren.* ➲ SYNONYMS at FUN **2** [C] something that gives you pleasure: *Children like to share interests and enjoyments with their parents.* **3** [U] **~ of sth** (*formal*) the fact of having and using sth: *the enjoyment of equal rights*

en·large /ɪnˈlɑːdʒ; *NAmE* -ˈlɑːrdʒ/ *verb* **1** [T, I] **~ (sth)** to make sth bigger; to become bigger: *There are plans to enlarge the recreation area.* ◇ *Reading will enlarge your vocabulary.* **2** [T, usually passive] **~ sth** to make a bigger copy of a photograph or document: *We're going to have this picture enlarged.* ▸ **en·larged** *adj.*: *an enlarged heart*

PHR V **enˈlarge on/upon sth** (*formal*) to say or write more about sth that has been mentioned SYN **elaborate**

en·large·ment /ɪnˈlɑːdʒmənt; *NAmE* -ˈlɑːrdʒ-/ *noun* **1** [U, sing.] **~ (of sth)** the process or result of sth becoming or being made larger: *the enlargement of the company's overseas business activities* ◇ *There was widespread support for **EU enlargement*** (= the fact of more countries joining). **2** [C] something that has been made larger, especially a photograph: *If you like the picture I can send you an enlargement of it.* OPP **reduction**

en·lar·ger /ɪnˈlɑːdʒə(r); *NAmE* -ˈlɑːrdʒ-/ *noun* a piece of equipment for making photographs larger or smaller

en·light·en /ɪnˈlaɪtn/ *verb* **~ sb** (*formal*) to give sb information so that they understand sth better: *She didn't enlighten him about her background.* ▸ **en·light·en·ing** *adj.*: *It was a very enlightening interview.*

en·light·ened /ɪnˈlaɪtnd/ *adj.* [usually before noun] (*approving*) having or showing an understanding of people's needs, a situation, etc. that is not based on old-fashioned attitudes and PREJUDICE: ***enlightened opinions/attitudes/ideas***

en·light·en·ment /ɪnˈlaɪtnmənt/ *noun* **1** [U] knowledge about and understanding of sth; the process of understanding sth or making sb understand it: *The newspapers provided little enlightenment about the cause of the accident.* ◇ *spiritual enlightenment* ➲ COLLOCATIONS at RELIGION **2 the Enlightenment** [sing.] the period in the 18th century when many writers and scientists began to argue that science and reason were more important than religion and tradition

en·list /ɪnˈlɪst/ *verb* **1** [T] to persuade sb to help you or to join you in doing sth: **~ sth/sb (in sth)** *They hoped to **enlist the help of** the public in solving the crime.* ◇ **~ sb (as sth)** *We were enlisted as helpers.* ◇ **~ sb to do sth** *We were enlisted to help.* **2** [I, T] to join or to make sb join the armed forces SYN **call up, conscript, draft**: *They both enlisted in 1915.* ◇ **~ as sth** *to enlist as a soldier* ◇ **~ sb (in/into/for/as sth)** *He was enlisted into the US Navy.* ▸ **en·list·ment** *noun* [U]: *the enlistment of expert help* ◇ *his enlistment in the Royal Air Force*

en·list·ed /ɪnˈlɪstɪd/ *adj.* (*especially US*) (of a member of the army, etc.) having a rank that is below that of an officer: *enlisted men and women* ◇ *enlisted personnel*

en·liven /ɪnˈlaɪvn/ *verb* **~ sth** (*formal*) to make sth more interesting or more fun

en masse /ˌɒ̃ ˈmæs; *NAmE* ˌɑ̃ː/ *adv.* (from *French*) all together, and usually in large numbers

en·mesh /ɪnˈmeʃ/ *verb* [usually passive] **~ sb/sth (in sth)** (*formal*) to involve sb/sth in a bad situation that it is not easy to escape from

en·mity /ˈenməti/ *noun* [U, C] (*pl.* -ies) feelings of hatred towards sb: *personal enmities and political conflicts* ◇ *Her action earned her the enmity of two or three colleagues.* ◇ **~ between A and B** *the traditional problem of the enmity between Protestants and Catholics* ➲ see also ENEMY

en·noble /ɪˈnəʊbl; *NAmE* ɪˈnoʊbl/ *verb* (*formal*) **1** [usually passive] **~ sb** to make sb a member of the NOBILITY **2 ~ sb/sth** to give sb/sth a better moral character: *In a strange way she seemed ennobled by her grief.* ▸ **en·noble·ment** *noun* [U]

ennui /ɒnˈwiː; *NAmE* ɑːn-/ *noun* [U] (from *French, literary*) feelings of being bored and not satisfied because nothing interesting is happening

en·ol·ogy (*US*) (*BrE* **oen·ology**) /iːˈnɒlədʒi; *NAmE* -ˈnɑːl-/ *noun* [U] (*technical*) the study of wine

eno·phile (*US*) (*BrE* **oeno·phile**) /ˈiːnəfaɪl/ *noun* (*formal*) a person who knows a lot about wine

enor·mity AW /ɪˈnɔːməti; *NAmE* ɪˈnɔːrm-/ *noun* (*pl.* -ies) **1** [U] **the ~ of sth** (of a problem, etc.) the very great size, effect, etc. of sth; the fact of sth being very serious: *the enormity of the task* ◇ *People are still coming to terms with the enormity of the disaster.* ◇ *The full enormity of the crime has not yet been revealed.* **2** [C, usually pl.] (*formal*) a very serious crime: *the enormities of the Hitler regime*

enor·mous 0-w AW /ɪˈnɔːməs; *NAmE* ɪˈnɔːrməs/ *adj.* extremely large SYN **huge, immense**: *an enormous house/dog* ◇ *an **enormous amount** of time* ◇ *enormous interest* ◇ *The problems facing the President are enormous.*

enor·mous·ly AW /ɪˈnɔːməsli; *NAmE* ɪˈnɔːrm-/ *adv.* very; very much: ***enormously rich/powerful/grateful*** ◇ *The price of wine varies enormously depending on where it comes from.* ◇ *She was looking forward to the meeting enormously.*

enough 0-w /ɪˈnʌf/ *det., pron., adv.*

■ ***det.*** 0-w used before plural or uncountable nouns to mean 'as many or as much as sb needs or wants' SYN **sufficient**: *Have you made enough copies?* ◇ *Is there enough room for me?* ◇ *I didn't have enough clothes to last a week.* ◇ *Don't ask me to do it. I've got enough problems as it is.* ◇ (*old-fashioned*) *There was food enough for all.* HELP Although **enough** after a noun now sounds old-fashioned, **time enough** is still fairly common: *There'll be time enough to relax when you've finished your work.*

■ ***pron.*** 0-w as many or as much as sb needs or wants: *Six bottles should be enough.* ◇ *Have you had enough* (= to eat)? ◇ *If enough of you are interested, we'll organize a trip to the theatre.* ◇ *There was **nowhere near enough** for everybody.* ◇ *We've nearly run out of paper. Do you think there's enough for today?*

IDM **eˈnough already** (*informal, especially NAmE*) used to say that sth is annoying or boring and that you want it to stop **eˌnough is eˈnough** (*saying*) used when you think that sth should not continue any longer **eˌnough ˈsaid** used to say that you understand a situation and there is no need to say any more: *'He's a politician, remember.' 'Enough said.'* **have had eˈnough (of sth/sb)** used when sth/sb is annoying you and you no longer want to do, have or see it or them: *I've had enough of driving the kids around.*

■ ***adv.*** (used after verbs, adjectives and adverbs) **1** 0-w to the necessary degree: *I hadn't trained enough for the game.* ◇ *This house isn't big enough for us.* ◇ *She's old enough to decide for herself.* ◇ *We didn't leave early enough.* ◇ *Tell them it's just **not good enough**.* **2** 0-w to an acceptable degree, but not to a very great degree: *He seemed pleasant enough to me.* **3** 0-w to a degree that you do not wish to get any greater: *I hope my job's safe. Life is hard enough as it is.*

IDM **ˌcuriously, ˌfunnily, ˌoddly, ˌstrangely, etc. eˈnough** used to show that sth is surprising: *Funnily enough, I said the same thing myself only yesterday.* ➲ more at FAIR *adj.*, FAR *adv.*, LIKE *adv.*, MAN *n.*, NEAR *adv.*, RIGHT *adj.*, SURE *adv.*

en pas·sant /ˌɒ̃ ˈpæsɒ̃; *NAmE* ˌɑːn pɑːˈsɑːn/ *adv.* (from *French*) while talking about sth else and without giving much information: *He mentioned en passant that he was going away.*

en·quire (*especially BrE*) (also **inquire** *NAmE, BrE*) /ɪnˈkwaɪə(r)/ *verb* [I, T] (rather *formal*) to ask sb for some information: **~ (about sb/sth)** *I called the station to enquire about train times.* ◇ **~ (as to sb/sth)** *She enquired as to your whereabouts.* ◇ **~ why, where, etc...** *Might I enquire why you have not mentioned this until now?* ◇ **~ sth** *He enquired her name.* ◇ **+ speech** *'What is your name?' he enquired.* ➲ SYNONYMS at ASK HELP In British English people sometimes distinguish between **enquire** and **inquire**, using **enquire** for the general meaning of 'ask for information' and **inquire** for the more particular meaning of 'officially investigate': *I called to enquire about train times.* ◇ *A committee will inquire into the allegations.* However, you can use either spelling in either meaning. In American English **inquire** is usually used in both meanings.

PHR V **enˈquire after sb** (*formal*) to ask for information about sb, especially about their health or about what they are doing **enˈquire into sth** to find out more information about sth SYN **investigate**: *A committee was appointed to enquire into the allegations.* **enˈquire sth of sb** (*formal*) to ask sb sth: **(+ speech)** *'Will you be staying for lunch?' she enquired of Charles.*

en·quir·er (*especially BrE*) (also **in·quirer** *NAmE, BrE*) /ɪnˈkwaɪərə(r)/ *noun* (*formal*) a person who asks for information

E

en·quir·ing (also **in·quir·ing** especially in *NAmE*) /ɪn'kwaɪərɪŋ/ *adj.* [usually before noun] **1** showing an interest in learning new things: *a child with an enquiring mind* **2** asking for information: *an enquiring look* ▸ **en·quir·ing·ly** (also **in·quir·ing·ly** especially in *NAmE*) *adv.*

en·quiry 0-ᴛ (*especially BrE*) (also **in·quiry** *NAmE*, *BrE*) /ɪn'kwaɪəri; *NAmE* usually 'ɪnkwəri/ *noun* (*pl.* -ies) **1** 0-ᴛ [C] an official process to find out the cause of sth or to find out information about sth: *a* ***murder enquiry*** ◇ **~ into sth** *a* ***public enquiry*** *into the environmental effects of the proposed new road* ◇ *to* ***hold/order an enquiry*** *into the affair* ➲ COLLOCATIONS at CRIME **2** 0-ᴛ [C] a request for information about sb/sth; a question about sb/sth: *a telephone enquiry* ◇ **~** (**from sb**) (**about sb/sth**) *We received over 300 enquiries about the job.* ◇ *enquiries from prospective students* ◇ *I'll have to* ***make*** *a few* ***enquiries*** (= try to find out about it) *and get back to you.* ◇ (*BrE*) *Two men have been* ***helping police with their enquiries*** (= are being questioned about a crime, but have not been charged with it). **3** [U] the act of asking questions or collecting information about sb/sth: *scientific enquiry* ◇ *The police are following several* ***lines of enquiry.*** ◇ *a committee of enquiry* **4 enquiries** [pl.] (*BrE*) a place where you can get information: *Ask at enquiries to see if your bag has been handed in.* ➲ see also DIRECTORY ENQUIRIES HELP In British English people sometimes distinguish between **enquiry** and **inquiry**, using **enquiry** for the general meaning of 'a request for information' and **inquiry** for the more particular meaning of 'official investigation': *enquiries from prospective students* ◇ *a murder inquiry.* However, you can use either spelling in either meaning. In American English **inquiry** is usually used in both meanings.

en·rage /ɪn'reɪdʒ/ *verb* [usually passive] **~ sb** to make sb very angry SYN **infuriate**

en·rap·ture /ɪn'ræptʃə(r)/ *verb* [usually passive] **~ sb** (*formal*) to give sb great pleasure or joy SYN **enchant**

en·rap·tured /ɪn'ræptʃəd; *NAmE* -ərd/ *adj.* (*formal*) filled with great pleasure or joy SYN **enchanted**

en·rich /ɪn'rɪtʃ/ *verb* **1** to improve the quality of sth, often by adding sth to it: **~ sth** *The study of science has enriched all our lives.* ◇ **~ sth with sth** *Most breakfast cereals are enriched with vitamins.* **2 ~ sb/sth** to make sb/sth rich or richer: *a nation enriched by oil revenues* ◇ *He used his position to enrich himself.* ▸ **en·rich·ment** *noun* [U]

enrol /ɪn'rəʊl; *NAmE* ɪn'roʊl/ (*especially US* **en·roll**) *verb* (-ll-) [I, T] to arrange for yourself or for sb else to officially join a course, school, etc: *You need to enrol before the end of August.* ◇ (*BrE*) *to enrol on a course* ◇ (*NAmE*) *to enroll in a course* ◇ **~ sb** *The centre will soon be ready to enrol candidates for the new programme.* ➲ COLLOCATIONS at EDUCATION

en·rol·lee /ɪn,rəʊ'liː; *NAmE* ɪn,roʊ-/ *noun* (*NAmE*) a person who has officially joined a course, an organization, etc.

en·rol·ment (*especially US* **en·roll·ment**) /ɪn'rəʊlmənt; *NAmE* -'roʊl-/ *noun* [U, C] the act of officially joining a course, school, etc; the number of people who do this: *Enrolment is the first week of September.* ◇ *School enrolments are currently falling.*

en route /,ɒ̃ 'ruːt; ,ɒn; *NAmE* ,ɑ̃ː; ,ɑːn/ *adv.* (from *French*) on the way; while travelling from/to a particular place: *We stopped for a picnic en route.* ◇ **~** (**from...**) (**to...**) *The bus broke down en route from Boston to New York.* ◇ (*BrE*) **~** (**for ...**) *a plane en route for Heathrow*

en·sconce /ɪn'skɒns; *NAmE* -'skɑːns/ *verb* **be ensconced** (**+adv./prep.**) | **~ yourself** (**+adv./prep.**) (*formal*) if you **are ensconced** or **ensconce yourself** somewhere, you are made or make yourself comfortable and safe in that place or position

en·sem·ble /ɒn'sɒmbl; *NAmE* ɑːn'sɑːmbl/ *noun* **1** [C+sing./pl. v.] a small group of musicians, dancers or actors who perform together: *a* ***brass/wind/string, etc. ensemble*** ◇ *The ensemble is/are based in Lyons.* **2** [C, usually sing.] (*formal*) a number of things considered as a group **3** [C, usually sing.] a set of clothes that are worn together

en·shrine /ɪn'ʃraɪn/ *verb* [usually passive] **~ sth** (**in sth**) (*formal*) to make a law, right, etc. respected or official, especially by stating it in an important written document: *These rights are enshrined in the country's constitution.*

en·shroud /ɪn'ʃraʊd/ *verb* **~ sth** (*literary*) to cover or surround sth completely so that it cannot be seen or understood

en·sign /'ensən/ *noun* **1** a flag flown on a ship to show which country it belongs to: *the White Ensign* (= the flag of the British Navy) **2** an officer of low rank in the US navy: *Ensign Marshall*

en·slave /ɪn'sleɪv/ *verb* [usually passive] **1 ~ sb** to make sb a SLAVE **2 ~ sb/sth** (**to sth**) (*formal*) to make sb/sth completely depend on sth so that they cannot manage without it ▸ **en·slave·ment** *noun* [U]

en·snare /ɪn'sneə(r); *NAmE* ɪn'sner/ *verb* **~ sb/sth** (*formal*) to make sb/sth unable to escape from a difficult situation or from a person who wants to control them SYN **trap**: *young homeless people who become ensnared in a life of crime*

ensue /ɪn'sjuː; *NAmE* -'suː/ *verb* [I] (*formal*) to happen after or as a result of another event SYN **follow**: *An argument ensued.* ▸ **en·su·ing** *adj.*: *He had become separated from his parents in the ensuing panic.*

en suite /,ɒ̃ 'swiːt; *NAmE* ,ɑ̃ː/ *adj.*, *adv.* (*BrE*, from *French*) (of a bathroom) joined onto a bedroom and for use only by people in that bedroom: *Each bedroom in the hotel has a bathroom en suite/an en suite bathroom.* ◇ *an en suite bedroom* (= a bedroom with an en suite bathroom) ◇ *en suite facilities* ➲ VISUAL VOCAB page V20

en·sure 0-ᴛ AW (also **in·sure** especially in *NAmE*) /ɪn'ʃʊə(r); -'ʃɔː(r); *NAmE* ɪn'ʃʊr/ *verb* to make sure that sth happens or is definite: **~ sth** *The book ensured his success.* ◇ **~ sb sth** *Victory ensured them a place in the final.* ◇ **~** (**that**)... *Please ensure* (*that*) *all lights are switched off.*

ENT /,iː en 'tiː/ *abbr.* ear, nose and throat (as a department in a hospital)

-ent ➲ -ANT

en·tail /ɪn'teɪl/ *verb* to involve sth that cannot be avoided SYN **involve**: **~ sth** *The job entails a lot of hard work.* ◇ **be entailed in sth** *The girls learn exactly what is entailed in caring for a newborn baby.* ◇ **~** (**sb**) **doing sth** *It will entail driving a long distance every day.*

en·tan·gle /ɪn'tæŋgl/ *verb* [usually passive] **1 ~ sb/sth** (**in/with sth**) to make sb/sth become caught or twisted in sth: *The bird had* ***become entangled*** *in the wire netting.* **2** to involve sb in a difficult or complicated situation: **~ sb in sth** *He* ***became entangled*** *in a series of conflicts with the management.* ◇ **~ sb with sb** *She didn't want to* ***get entangled*** (= emotionally involved) *with him.*

en·tangle·ment /ɪn'tæŋglmənt/ *noun* **1** [C] a difficult or complicated relationship with another person or country **2** [U] the act of becoming entangled in sth; the state of being entangled: *Many dolphins die each year from entanglement in fishing nets.* **3 en·tangle·ments** [pl.] (*technical*) barriers made of BARBED WIRE, used to stop an enemy from getting close

en·tente /ɒn'tɒnt; *NAmE* ɑːn'tɑːnt/ *noun* [U, sing.] (from *French*) a friendly relationship between two countries: *the Franco-Russian entente*

en·tente cor·di·ale /,ɒntɒnt ,kɔːdi'ɑːl; *NAmE* ,ɑːntɑːnt ,kɔːrd-/ *noun* [U, sing.] (from *French*) a friendly relationship between two countries, especially between Britain and France

enter 0-ᴛ /'entə(r)/ *verb*

▸ COME/GO IN **1** 0-ᴛ [I, T] (not usually used in the passive) (*formal*) to come or go into sth: *Knock before you enter.* ◇ **~ sth** *Someone entered the room behind me.* ◇ *Where did the bullet enter the body?* ◇ (*figurative*) *A note of defiance entered her voice.* ◇ (*figurative*) *It never* ***entered my head*** (= I never thought) *that she would tell him about me.*

▸ JOIN INSTITUTION/START WORK **2** [T, no passive] **~ sth** (*formal*) to become a member of an institution; to start working in an organization or a profession: *to **enter a school/college/university** ◇ to **enter politics** ◇ to **enter Parliament*** (= become an MP) ◇ *to **enter the Church*** (= become a priest)

▸ BEGIN ACTIVITY **3** [T] **~ sth** to begin or become involved in an activity, a situation, etc: *to **enter a relationship/conflict/war** ◇ Several new firms have now entered the market. ◇ The investigation has entered a new phase. ◇ The strike is entering its fourth week.*

▸ EXAM/COMPETITION **4** [T, I] to put your name on the list for an exam, a race, a competition, etc; to do this for sb: **~ sth** *1 000 children entered the competition.* ◇ **~ sb/sth in sth** *Irish trainers have entered several horses in the race.* ◇ **~ sb/sth for sth** *How many students have been entered for the exam?* ◇ **~** (**for sth**) *Only four British players have entered for the championship.*

▸ WRITE INFORMATION **5** [T] to put names, numbers, details, etc. in a list, book or computer: **~ sth** (**in sth**) *Enter your name and occupation in the boxes* (= on a form). ◇ **~ sth** (**into sth**) *to enter data into a computer* ◇ **~ sth** (**on sth**) *to enter figures on a spreadsheet*

▸ SAY OFFICIALLY **6** [T] **~ sth** (*formal*) to say sth officially so that it can be recorded: *to **enter a plea** of not guilty* (= at the beginning of a court case) ◇ *to enter an offer* ➲ see also ENTRANCE, ENTRY **IDM** see FORCE *n.*, NAME *n.*

PHR V **'enter into sth** (*formal*) **1** to begin to discuss or deal with sth: *Let's not enter into details at this stage.* **2** to take an active part in sth: *They **entered into the spirit** of the occasion* (= began to enjoy and feel part of it). **3** [no passive] to form part of sth or have an influence on sth: *This possibility never entered into our calculations. ◇ Your personal feelings shouldn't enter into this at all.* **'enter into sth** (**with sb**) to begin sth or become involved in sth: *to enter into an agreement ◇ to enter into negotiations* **'enter on/upon sth** (*formal*) to start to do sth or become involved in it: *to enter on a new career*

en·ter·ic /en'terɪk/ *adj.* (*medical*) connected with the INTESTINES

en·ter·itis /ˌentə'raɪtəs/ *noun* [U] (*medical*) a painful infection in the INTESTINES that usually causes DIARRHOEA ➲ see also GASTROENTERITIS

en·ter·prise /'entəpraɪz; *NAmE* -tərp-/ *noun* **1** [C] a company or business: *an enterprise with a turnover of $26 billion ◇ **state-owned/public enterprises** ◇ small and medium-sized enterprises* **2** [C] a large project, especially one that is difficult **SYN** **venture**: *his latest business enterprise ◇ a **joint enterprise*** **3** [U] the development of businesses by the people of a country rather than by the government: *grants to encourage enterprise in the region ◇ an enterprise culture* (= in which people are encouraged to develop small businesses) ➲ see also FREE ENTERPRISE, PRIVATE ENTERPRISE **4** [U] (*approving*) the ability to think of new projects and make them successful **SYN** **initiative**: *a job in which enterprise is rewarded*

en·ter·pris·ing /'entəpraɪzɪŋ; *NAmE* -tərp-/ *adj.* (*approving*) having or showing the ability to think of new projects or new ways of doing things and make them successful

en·ter·tain /ˌentə'teɪn; *NAmE* -tər't-/ *verb* **1** [I, T] to invite people to eat or drink with you as your guests, especially in your home: *The job involves a lot of entertaining.* ◇ **~ sb** *Barbecues are a favourite way of entertaining friends.* **2** [T, I] **~** (**sb**) (**with sth**) to interest and amuse sb in order to please them: *He entertained us for hours with his stories and jokes. ◇ The aim of the series is both to entertain and inform.* **3** [T] (not used in the progressive tenses) **~ sth** (*formal*) to consider or allow yourself to think about an idea, a hope, a feeling, etc: *He had **entertained hopes** of a reconciliation. ◇ to **entertain a doubt/suspicion***

en·ter·tain·er /ˌentə'teɪnə(r); *NAmE* -tər't-/ *noun* a person whose job is amusing or interesting people, for example, by singing, telling jokes or dancing

en·ter·tain·ing /ˌentə'teɪnɪŋ; *NAmE* -tər't-/ *adj.* interesting and amusing: *an entertaining speech/evening ◇ I found the talk both informative and entertaining. ◇ She was always so funny and entertaining.* ➲ SYNONYMS at FUNNY ▸ **en·ter·tain·ing·ly** *adv.*

en·ter·tain·ment /ˌentə'teɪnmənt; *NAmE* -tər't-/ *noun* **1** [U, C] films/movies, music, etc. used to entertain people; an example of this: *radio, television and other forms of entertainment ◇ There will be **live entertainment** at the party. ◇ It was typical **family entertainment**. ◇ The entertainment was provided by a folk band. ◇ Local entertainments are listed in the newspaper. ◇ The show was good **entertainment value**.* **2** [U] the act of entertaining sb: *a budget for the entertainment of clients*

Synonyms

entertainment

fun • recreation • relaxation • play • pleasure • amusement

These are all words for things or activities used to entertain people when they are not working.

entertainment films, television, music, etc. used to entertain people: *There are three bars, with live entertainment seven nights a week.*

fun (*rather informal*) behaviour or activities that are not serious but come from a sense of enjoyment: *It wasn't serious—it was all done **in fun**. ◇ We didn't mean to hurt him. It was just **a bit of fun**. ◇ The lottery provides **harmless fun** for millions.*

recreation (*rather formal*) things people do for enjoyment when they are not working: *His only form of recreation is playing football.*

relaxation (*rather formal*) things people do to rest and enjoy themselves when they are not working; the ability to relax: *I go hill-walking for relaxation.*

RECREATION OR RELAXATION?

Both these words can be used for a wide range of activities, physical and mental, but **relaxation** is sometimes used for gentler activities than **recreation**: *I play the flute in a wind band for recreation. ◇ I listen to music for relaxation.*

play things that people, especially children, do for enjoyment rather than as work: *the happy sounds of children **at play***

pleasure the activity of enjoying yourself, especially in contrast to working: *Are you in Paris **for business or pleasure**?*

amusement the fact of being entertained by sth: *What do you do for amusement round here?*

PATTERNS

- to do sth **for** entertainment/fun/recreation/relaxation/pleasure/amusement
- to **provide** entertainment/fun/recreation/relaxation/amusement

en·thral (*BrE*) (*NAmE* **en·thrall**) /ɪn'θrɔːl/ *verb* (-ll-) [T, I, usually passive] **~** (**sb**) if sth **enthrals** you, it is so interesting, beautiful, etc. that you give it all your attention **SYN** **entrance**: *The child watched, enthralled by the bright moving images.* ▸ **en·thral·ling** *adj.*: *an enthralling performance*

en·throne /ɪn'θrəʊn; *NAmE* ɪn'θroʊn/ *verb* [usually passive] **~ sb** when a king, queen or important member of a Church is **enthroned**, they sit on a THRONE (= a special chair) in a ceremony to mark the beginning of their rule ▸ **en·throne·ment** *noun* [U, C]

en·thuse /ɪn'θjuːz; *NAmE* -'θuːz/ *verb* **1** [I, T] to talk in an enthusiastic and excited way about sth: **~** (**about/over sth/sb**) *The article enthused about the benefits that the new system would bring.* ◇ **+ speech** *'It's a wonderful idea', he* *enthused.* ◇ **~ that...** *The organizers enthused that it was their most successful event yet.* **2** [usually passive] **~ sb (with sth)** to make sb feel very interested and excited: *Everyone present was enthused by the idea.*

en·thu·si·asm 🔑 /ɪn'θju:ziæzəm; *NAmE* -'θu:-/ *noun*
1 🔑 [U] a strong feeling of excitement and interest in sth and a desire to become involved in it: **~ (for sth)** *I can't say I share your enthusiasm for the idea.* ◇ *He had a real enthusiasm for the work.* ◇ **~ (for doing sth)** *She never lost her enthusiasm for teaching.* ◇ *The news was greeted with a lack of enthusiasm by those at the meeting.* ◇ *'I don't mind,' she said, without much enthusiasm.* ◇ *full of enthusiasm* **2** [C] (*formal*) something that you are very interested in and spend a lot of time doing

E

en·thu·si·ast /ɪn'θju:ziæst; *NAmE* -'θu:-/ *noun* **1 ~ (for/of sth)** a person who is very interested in sth and spends a lot of time doing it: *a football enthusiast* ◇ *an enthusiast of jazz* **2 ~ (for/of sth)** a person who approves of sth and shows enthusiasm for it: *enthusiasts for a united Europe*

en·thu·si·ast·ic 🔑 /ɪn,θju:zi'æstɪk; *NAmE* -,θu:-/ *adj.*
feeling or showing a lot of excitement and interest about sb/sth: *an enthusiastic supporter* ◇ *an enthusiastic welcome* ◇ **~ about sb/sth** *You don't sound very enthusiastic about the idea.* ◇ **~ about doing sth** *She was even less enthusiastic about going to Spain.* ▶ **en·thu·si·as·tic·al·ly** 🔑 /-kli/ *adv.*

en·tice /ɪn'taɪs/ *verb* to persuade sb/sth to go somewhere or to do sth, usually by offering them sth SYN **persuade**: **~ sb/sth (+ adv./prep.)** *The bargain prices are expected to entice customers away from other stores.* ◇ *The animal refused to be enticed from its hole.* ◇ **~ sb into doing sth** *He was not enticed into parting with his cash.* ◇ **~ sb to do sth** *Try and entice the child to eat by offering small portions of their favourite food.* ▶ **en·tice·ment** *noun* [C, U]: *The party is offering low taxation as its main enticement.*

en·ticing /ɪn'taɪsɪŋ/ *adj.* something that is **enticing** is so attractive and interesting that you want to have it or know more about it: *The offer was too enticing to refuse.* ▶ **en·ticing·ly** *adv.*

en·tire 🔑 /ɪn'taɪə(r)/ *adj.* [only before noun]
(used when you are emphasizing that the whole of sth is involved) including everything, everyone or every part SYN **whole**: *The entire village was destroyed.* ◇ *I wasted an entire day on it.* ◇ *I have never in my entire life heard such nonsense!* ◇ *The disease threatens to wipe out the entire population.*

en·tire·ly 🔑 /ɪn'taɪəli; *NAmE* ɪn'taɪərli/ *adv.*
in every way possible; completely: *I entirely agree with you.* ◇ *I'm not entirely happy about the proposal.* ◇ *That's an entirely different matter.* ◇ *The audience was almost entirely female.*

en·tir·ety /ɪn'taɪərəti/ *noun* [sing.] (*formal*) **the ~ of sth** the whole of sth
IDM **in its/their en'tirety** as a whole, rather than in parts: *The poem is too long to quote in its entirety.*

en·title 🔑 /ɪn'taɪtl/ *verb*
1 🔑 [often passive] to give sb the right to have or to do sth: **~ sb to sth** *You will be entitled to your pension when you reach 65.* ◇ *Everyone's entitled to their own opinion.* ◇ **~ sb to do sth** *This ticket does not entitle you to travel first class.* **2** 🔑 [usually passive] **~ sth + noun** to give a title to a book, play, etc: *He read a poem entitled 'Salt'.*

en·title·ment /ɪn'taɪtlmənt/ *noun* (*formal*) **1** [U] **~ (to sth)** the official right to have or do sth: *This may affect your entitlement to compensation.* **2** [C] something that you have an official right to; the amount that you have the right to receive: *Your contributions will affect your pension entitlements.* **3** [C] (*NAmE*) a government system that provides financial support to a particular group of people: *a reform of entitlements* ◇ *Medicard, Medicare and other entitlement programs*

en·tity AW /'entəti/ *noun* (*pl.* -ies) (*formal*) something that exists separately from other things and has its own identity: *The unit has become part of a larger department and no longer exists as a **separate entity**.* ◇ *These countries can no longer be viewed as a **single entity**.*

en·tomb /ɪn'tu:m/ *verb* [usually passive] (*formal*) **1 ~ sb/sth (in sth)** to bury or completely cover sb/sth so that they cannot get out, be seen, etc. **2 ~ sb/sth (in sth)** to put a dead body in a TOMB

en·to·mol·ogy /,entə'mɒlədʒi; *NAmE* -'mɑ:l-/ *noun* [U] the scientific study of insects ▶ **en·to·mo·logic·al** /,entəmə'lɒdʒɪkl; *NAmE* -'lɑ:dʒ-/ *adj.* **en·to·molo·gist** /,entə'mɒlədʒɪst; *NAmE* -'mɑ:l-/ *noun*

en·tou·rage /'ɒntura:ʒ; *NAmE* 'ɑ:n-/ *noun* [C+sing./pl. v.] a group of people who travel with an important person

en·tr'acte /'ɒntrækt; 'ɒ̃t-; *NAmE* 'ɑ:ntrækt; ɑ:n'trækt/ *noun* (from *French*) **1** (*formal*) the time between the different parts of a play, show, etc. SYN **interval** **2** a short performance between the different parts of a play, show, etc.

en·trails /'entreɪlz/ *noun* [pl.] the organs inside the body of a person or an animal, especially their INTESTINES SYN **innards, insides**

en·trance¹ 🔑 /'entrəns/ *noun* ➲ see also ENTRANCE²
▸ DOOR/GATE **1** 🔑 [C] **~ (to sth)** a door, gate, passage, etc. used for entering a room, building or place: *the entrance to the museum/the museum entrance* ◇ *A lighthouse marks the entrance to the harbour.* ◇ *the **front/back/side entrance** of the house* ◇ *an **entrance hall/lobby*** ◇ *I'll meet you at the **main entrance**.* ➲ compare EXIT *n.* (1)
▸ GOING IN **2** [C, usually sing.] the act of entering a room, building or place, especially in a way that attracts the attention of other people: *His sudden entrance took everyone by surprise.* ◇ *A fanfare signalled the entrance of the king.* ◇ *She **made her entrance** after all the other guests had arrived.* ◇ *The hero **makes his entrance*** (= walks onto the stage) *in Scene 2.* **3** [U] **~ (to sth)** the right or opportunity to enter a building or place: *They were refused entrance to the exhibition.* ◇ *The police were unable to **gain entrance** to the house.* ◇ (*BrE*) *an **entrance fee*** (= money paid to go into a museum, etc.)
▸ BECOMING INVOLVED **4** [C] **~ (into sth)** the act of becoming involved in sth: *The company made a dramatic entrance into the export market.*
▸ TO CLUB/INSTITUTION **5** [U] permission to become a member of a club, society, university, etc: *a university entrance exam* ◇ *entrance requirements* ◇ **~ (to sth)** *Entrance to the golf club is by sponsorship only.* ➲ compare ENTRY

en·trance² /ɪn'trɑ:ns; *NAmE* -'træns/ *verb* [usually passive] **~ sb** (*formal*) to make sb feel great pleasure and admiration so that they give sb/sth all their attention SYN **enthral**: *He listened to her, entranced.* ➲ see also ENTRANCE¹ ▶ **en·tran·cing** *adj.*: *entrancing music*

'entrance hall *noun* (*especially BrE*) a large room inside the entrance of a large or public building

en·trant /'entrənt/ *noun* **1 ~ (to sth)** a person who has recently joined a profession, university, etc: *new women entrants to the police force* ◇ *university entrants* **2 ~ (to sth)** a person or an animal that enters a race or a competition; a person that enters an exam

en·trap /ɪn'træp/ *verb* (-pp-) [often passive] (*formal*) **1 ~ sb/sth** to put or catch sb/sth in a place or situation from which they cannot escape SYN **trap** **2 ~ sb (into doing sth)** to trick sb, and encourage them to do sth, especially to commit a crime, so that they can be arrested for it

en·trap·ment /ɪn'træpmənt/ *noun* [U] (*law*) the illegal act of tricking sb into committing a crime so that they can be arrested for it

en·treat /ɪn'tri:t/ *verb* (*formal*) to ask sb to do sth in a serious and often emotional way SYN **beg, implore**: **~ sb** *Please help me, I entreat you.* ◇ **~ sb to do sth** *She entreated him not to go.* ◇ **~ (sb) + speech** *'Please don't go,' she entreated (him).*

en·treaty /ɪn'tri:ti/ *noun* (*pl.* -ies) [C, U] (*formal*) a serious and often emotional request

en·trée /ˈɒntreɪ; *NAmE* ˈɑːn-/ *noun* (from *French*) **1** [C] (in a restaurant or at a formal meal) the main dish of the meal or a dish served before the main course **2** [U, C] **~ (into/to sth)** (*formal*) the right or ability to enter a social group or institution

en·trench (also **in·trench**) /ɪnˈtrentʃ/ *verb* [usually passive] **~ sth** (sometimes *disapproving*) to establish sth very firmly so that it is very difficult to change: *Sexism is* ***deeply entrenched*** *in our society.* ◇ ***entrenched attitudes/interests/opposition***

en·trench·ment /ɪnˈtrentʃmənt/ *noun* **1** [U] the fact of sth being firmly established **2** [C, usually pl.] a system of TRENCHES (= long narrow holes dug in the ground by soldiers to provide defence)

entre·pôt /ˈɒntrəpəʊ; *NAmE* ˈɑːntrəpoʊ/ *noun* (from *French*) a port or other place where goods are brought for import and export

entre·pre·neur /ˌɒntrəprəˈnɜː(r); *NAmE* ˌɑːn-/ *noun* a person who makes money by starting or running businesses, especially when this involves taking financial risks ▸ **en·tre·pre·neur·ial** /-ˈnɜːriəl/ *adj.*: *entrepreneurial skills* **entre·pre·neur·ship** *noun* [U]

en·tropy /ˈentrəpi/ *noun* [U] **1** (*technical*) a way of measuring the lack of order that exists in a system **2** (*physics*) (*symb.* S) a measurement of the energy that is present in a system or process but is not available to do work **3** a complete lack of order: *In the business world, entropy rules.* ▸ **en·trop·ic** /enˈtrɒpɪk; -ˈtrəʊp-; *NAmE* -ˈtrɑːp-/ *adj.* **en·trop·ical·ly** /-kli/ *adv.*

en·trust /ɪnˈtrʌst/ *verb* (*formal*) to make sb responsible for doing sth or taking care of sb: **~ A (to B)** *He entrusted the task to his nephew.* ◇ **~ B with A** *He entrusted his nephew with the task.*

entry 0▬ /ˈentri/ *noun* (*pl.* -ies)

▸ GOING IN **1** 0▬ [C, U] an act of going into or getting into a place: *She* ***made her entry*** *to the sound of thunderous applause.* ◇ *The children were surprised by the sudden entry of their teacher.* ◇ **~ (into sth)** *How did the thieves* ***gain entry*** *into the building?* **2** 0▬ [U] the right or opportunity to enter a place: **No Entry** (= for example, on a sign) ◇ **~ (to/into sth)** *Entry to the museum is free.* ◇ *to* ***be granted/refused entry*** *into the country*

▸ JOINING GROUP **3** 0▬ [U] **~ (into sth)** the right or opportunity to take part in sth or become a member of a group: *countries seeking entry into the European Union* ◇ *the entry of women into the workforce*

▸ IN COMPETITION **4** 0▬ [C] something that you do, write or make to take part in a competition, for example answering a set of questions: *There have been some impressive entries in the wildlife photography section* (= impressive photographs). ◇ *The closing date for entries is 31 March.* ◇ *The sender of the first correct entry drawn will win a weekend for two in Venice.* **5** [U] the act of taking part in a competition, race, etc: *Entry is open to anyone over the age of 18.* ◇ *an entry form* **6** [sing.] the total number of people who are taking part in a competition, race, etc: *There's a record entry for this year's marathon.*

▸ WRITTEN INFORMATION **7** 0▬ [C] an item, for example a piece of information, that is written or printed in a dictionary, an account book, a diary, etc: *an encyclopedia entry* ◇ **~ (in sth)** *There is no entry in his diary for that day.* **8** [U] the act of recording information in a computer, book, etc: *More keyboarding staff are required for data entry.*

▸ DOOR/GATE **9** (also **entry·way** /ˈentriweɪ/) (both *NAmE*) [C] a door, gate or passage where you enter a building; an entrance hall: *You can leave your umbrella in the entry.*

ˈ**entry-level** *adj.* [usually before noun] **1** (of a product) basic and suitable for new users who may later move on to a more advanced product: *an entry-level computer* **2** (of a job) at the lowest level in a company

Entry·phone™ /ˈentrifəʊn; *NAmE* -foʊn/ *noun* (*BrE*) a type of telephone on the wall next to the entrance to a building enabling a person inside the building to speak to a person outside before opening the door

en·twine /ɪnˈtwaɪn/ *verb* [usually passive] **1 ~ sth (with/in/around sth)** to twist or wind sth around sth else: *They strolled through the park, with arms entwined.* **2 be entwined (with sth)** to be very closely involved or connected with sth: *Her destiny was entwined with his.*

ˈ**E-number** *noun* (*BrE*) a number beginning with the letter E that is printed on packs and containers to show what artificial flavours and colours have been added to food and drink; an artificial flavour, colour, etc. added to food and drink: *This sauce is full of E-numbers.*

enu·mer·ate /ɪˈnjuːməreɪt; *NAmE* ɪˈnuː-/ *verb* **~ sth** (*formal*) to name things on a list one by one ▸ **enu·mer·ation** /ɪˌnjuːməˈreɪʃn; *NAmE* ɪˌnuː-/ *noun* [U, C]

enun·ci·ate /ɪˈnʌnsieɪt/ *verb* **1** [T, I] **~ (sth)** | **+ speech** to say or pronounce words clearly: *She enunciated each word slowly and carefully.* **2** [T] **~ sth** (*formal*) to express an idea clearly and exactly: *He enunciated his vision of the future.* ▸ **enun·ci·ation** /ɪˌnʌnsiˈeɪʃn/ *noun* [U]

en·ur·esis /ˌenjʊəˈriːsɪs; *NAmE* ˌenjʊˈriː-/ *noun* [U] (*medical*) URINATION (= letting waste liquid flow from the body) that is not under sb's control, especially in the case of a child who is asleep

en·velop /ɪnˈveləp/ *verb* **~ sb/sth (in sth)** (*formal*) to wrap sb/sth up or cover them or it completely: *She was enveloped in a huge white towel.* ◇ *Clouds enveloped the mountain tops.* ▸ **en·velop·ment** *noun* [U]

en·vel·ope 0▬ /ˈenvələʊp; ˈɒn-; *NAmE* ˈenvəloʊp; ˈɑːn-/ *noun*

1 0▬ a flat paper container used for sending letters in ➲ VISUAL VOCAB page V56: *writing paper and envelopes* ◇ *an* ***airmail/padded/prepaid envelope*** ➲ see also PAY ENVELOPE, SAE, SASE **2** a flat container made of plastic for keeping papers in IDM see PUSH *v.*

en·vi·able /ˈenviəbl/ *adj.* something that is **enviable** is the sort of thing that is good and that other people want to have too: *He is in the* ***enviable position*** *of having two job offers to choose from.* OPP **unenviable** ▸ **en·vi·ably** /-bli/ *adv.*: *an enviably mild climate*

en·vi·ous /ˈenviəs/ *adj.* **~ (of sb/sth)** wanting to be in the same situation as sb else; wanting sth that sb else has: *Everyone is so envious of her.* ◇ *They were envious of his success.* ◇ *He saw the envious look in the other boy's eyes.* ▸ **en·vi·ous·ly** *adv.*: *They look enviously at the success of their European counterparts.* ➲ see also ENVY

Synonyms

environment

setting • surroundings • background

These are all words for the type of place in which sb/sth exists or is situated.

environment the conditions in a place that affect the behaviour and development of sb/sth: *An unhappy* ***home environment*** *can affect children's behaviour.* ◇ *a pleasant* ***working environment***

setting a place or situation or a particular type, in which sth happens or exists: *The island provided an idyllic setting for the concert.*

surroundings everything that is around or near sb/sth: *The huts blend in perfectly with their surroundings.*

background the things or area behind or around the main objects or people that are in a place or picture: *The mountains in the background were capped with snow.*

PATTERNS

- **in** (a/an) environment/setting/surroundings
- (a/an) **new/unfamiliar** environment/setting/surroundings
- sb/sth's **immediate** environment/surroundings
- (a) **dramatic** setting/background

en·vir·on·ment 0▬ AW /ɪnˈvaɪrənmənt/ *noun* **1** 0▬ [C, U] the conditions that affect the behaviour and development of sb/sth; the physical conditions that sb/sth exists in: *a pleasant* ***working/learning environment*** ◇ *An unhappy* ***home environment*** *can affect a child's behaviour.* ◇ *They have created an environment in which productivity should flourish.* ◇ *the political environment* ◇ *tests carried out in a controlled environment* **2** 🔑 **the environment** [sing.] the natural world in which people, animals and plants live: *the Department of the Environment* ◇ *measures to protect the environment* ◇ *pollution of the environment* ◇ *damage to the environment* **3** [C] (*computing*) the complete structure within which a user, computer or program operates: *a desktop development environment*

Collocations

The environment

Environmental damage

- **cause/contribute to** climate change/global warming
- **produce** pollution/CO_2/greenhouse (gas) emissions
- **damage/destroy** the environment/a marine ecosystem/the ozone layer/coral reefs
- **degrade** ecosystems/habitats/the environment
- **harm** the environment/wildlife/marine life
- **threaten** natural habitats/coastal ecosystems/a species with extinction
- **deplete** natural resources/the ozone layer
- **pollute** rivers and lakes/waterways/the air/the atmosphere/the environment/oceans
- **contaminate** groundwater/the soil/food/crops
- **log** forests/rainforests/trees

Protecting the environment

- **address/combat/tackle** the threat/effects/impact of climate change
- **fight/take action on/reduce/stop** global warming
- **limit/curb/control** air/water/atmospheric/environmental pollution
- **cut/reduce** pollution/greenhouse gas emissions
- **offset** carbon/CO_2 emissions
- **reduce** (the size of) your carbon footprint
- **achieve/promote** sustainable development
- **preserve/conserve** biodiversity/natural resources
- **protect** endangered species/a coastal ecosystem
- **prevent/stop** soil erosion/overfishing/massive deforestation/damage to ecosystems
- **raise** awareness of environmental issues
- **save** the planet/the rainforests/an endangered species

Energy and resources

- **conserve/save/consume/waste** energy
- **manage/exploit/be rich in** natural resources
- **dump/dispose of** hazardous/toxic/nuclear waste
- **dispose of/throw away** litter/(*especially BrE*) rubbish/(*especially NAmE*) garbage/(*NAmE*) trash/sewage
- **use/be made from** recycled/recyclable/biodegradable material
- **recycle** bottles/packaging/paper/plastic/waste
- **promote/encourage** recycling/sustainable development/the use of renewable energy
- **develop/invest in/promote** renewable energy
- **reduce** your dependence/reliance on fossil fuels
- **get/obtain/generate/produce** electricity from wind, solar and wave power/renewable sources
- **build/develop** a (50-megawatt/offshore) wind farm
- **install/be fitted with/be powered by** solar panels

en·vir·on·men·tal 🔑 AW /ɪnˌvaɪrənˈmentl/ *adj.* [usually before noun] **1** 🔑 connected with the natural conditions in which people, animals and plants live; connected with the environment: *the environmental impact of pollution* ◇ ***environmental issues/problems*** ◇ *an* ***environmental group/movement*** (= that aims to improve or protect the natural environment) ◇ *environmental damage* **2** 🔑 connected with the conditions that affect the behaviour and development of sb/sth: *environmental influences* ◇ *an environmental health officer* ▸ **en·vir·on·men·tal·ly** AW /-təli/ *adv.*: *an environmentally sensitive area* (= one that is easily damaged or that contains rare animals, plants, etc.) ◇ *environmentally damaging*

en·vir·on·men·tal·ist AW /ɪnˌvaɪrənˈmentəlɪst/ *noun* a person who is concerned about the natural environment and wants to improve and protect it ▸ **en·vir·on·ment·al·ism** *noun* [U]

enˌvironmentally ˈfriendly (also **enˌvironment-ˈfriendly**) *adj.* (of products) not harming the environment: *environmentally friendly packaging*

en·vir·ons /ɪnˈvaɪrənz/ *noun* [pl.] (*formal*) the area surrounding a place: *Berlin and its environs* ◇ *people living in the immediate environs of a nuclear plant*

en·vis·age /ɪnˈvɪzɪdʒ/ (*especially BrE*) (*NAmE* usually **en·vis·ion**) *verb* to imagine what will happen in the future: **~ sth** *What level of profit do you envisage?* ◇ **~ (sb) doing sth** *I can't envisage her coping with this job.* ◇ **it is envisaged that...** *It is envisaged that the talks will take place in the spring.* ◇ **~ that...** *I envisage that the work will be completed next year.* ◇ **~ how, where, etc...** *It is difficult to envisage how people will react.* ➲ SYNONYMS at IMAGINE

en·vi·sion /ɪnˈvɪʒn/ *verb* **1 ~ sth** (*formal*) to imagine what a situation will be like in the future, especially a situation you intend to work towards: *They envision an equal society, free of poverty and disease.* ➲ SYNONYMS at IMAGINE **2** (*especially NAmE*) = ENVISAGE: *They didn't envision any problems with the new building.*

envoy /ˈenvɔɪ/ *noun* a person who represents a government or an organization and is sent as a representative to talk to other governments and organizations SYN **emissary**

envy /ˈenvi/ *noun, verb*

■ ***noun*** [U] the feeling of wanting to be in the same situation as sb else; the feeling of wanting sth that sb else has SYN **jealousy**: **~ (of sb)** *He couldn't conceal his envy of me.* ◇ **~ (at/of sth)** *She felt a pang of envy at the thought of his success.* ◇ *They looked* **with envy** *at her latest purchase.* ◇ *Her colleagues were* ***green with envy*** (= they had very strong feelings of envy).

IDM **be the envy of sb/sth** to be a person or thing that other people admire and that causes feelings of envy: *British television is the envy of the world.* ➲ see also ENVIABLE, ENVIOUS

■ ***verb*** (**en·vies, envy·ing, en·vied, en·vied**) **1** to wish you had the same qualities, possessions, opportunities, etc. as sb else: **~ sb** *He envied her—she seemed to have everything she could possibly want.* ◇ **~ sth** *She has always envied my success.* ◇ **~ sb sth** *I envied him his good looks.* ◇ **~ sb doing sth** *I envy you having such a close family.* **2** to be glad that you do not have to do what sb else has to do: **not ~ sb** *It's a difficult situation you're in. I don't envy you.* ◇ **not ~ sb sth** *I don't envy her that job.*

en·zyme /ˈenzaɪm/ *noun* (*biology*) a substance, produced by all living things, which helps a chemical change happen or happen more quickly, without being changed itself

eo·lian (*NAmE*) (*BrE* **ae·olian**) /iːˈəʊliən; *NAmE* iːˈoʊ-/ *adj.* (*technical*) connected with or caused by the action of the wind

eon (*especially NAmE*) (*BrE* usually **aeon**) /ˈiːən/ *noun* **1** (*formal*) an extremely long period of time; thousands of years **2** (*geology*) a major division of time, divided into ERAS: *eons of geological history*

ˈe-pal (also **ˈe-friend**) *noun* a person that you make friends with by sending emails, often sb you have never met

ep·aul·ette (*especially BrE*) (*NAmE* usually **ep·aulet**) /ˈepəlet/ *noun* a decoration on the shoulder of a coat, jacket, etc, especially when part of a military uniform

épée /ˈepeɪ; ˈepeɪ/ *noun* **1** [C] a SWORD used in the sport of FENCING **2** [U] (*NAmE*) the sport of FENCING with an épée

ephem·era /ɪˈfemərə/ *noun* [pl.] things that are important or used for only a short period of time: *a collection of postcards, tickets and other ephemera*

ephem·eral /ɪˈfemərəl/ *adj.* (*formal*) lasting or used for only a short period of time **SYN** **short-lived**

epic /ˈepɪk/ *noun, adj.*

■ ***noun*** **1** [C, U] a long poem about the actions of great men and women or about a nation's history; this style of poetry: *one of the great Hindu epics* ◇ *the creative genius of Greek epic* ➲ compare LYRIC **2** [C] a long film/movie or book that contains a lot of action, usually about a historical subject **3** [C] (sometimes *humorous*) a long and difficult job or activity that you think people should admire: *Their four-hour match on Centre Court was an epic.*

■ ***adj.*** [usually before noun] **1** having the features of an epic: *an epic poem* ➲ compare LYRIC **2** taking place over a long period of time and involving a lot of difficulties: *an **epic journey/struggle*** **3** very great and impressive: *a tragedy **of epic proportions***

epi·cene /ˈepɪsiːn/ *adj.* **1** (*formal*) having characteristics of both the male and female sex or of neither sex in particular: *epicene beauty* **2** (*grammar*) (of a word) having one form to represent male and female: *You can write **'s/he'** as an **epicene** pronoun when you are not referring to men or women in particular.*

epi·centre (*especially US* **epi·cen·ter**) /ˈepɪsentə(r)/ *noun* **1** the point on the earth's surface where the effects of an EARTHQUAKE are felt most strongly **2** (*formal*) the central point of sth

epi·cure /ˈepɪkjʊə(r); *NAmE* -kjʊr/ *noun* (*formal*) a person who enjoys food and drink of high quality and knows a lot about it

epi·cur·ean /ˌepɪkjʊəˈriːən; *NAmE* ˌepɪkjʊˈr-/ *adj.* (*formal*) devoted to pleasure and enjoying yourself ▸ **epi·cur·ean·ism** /ˌepɪkjʊəˈriːənɪzəm; *NAmE* ˌepɪkjʊˈriːən-/ *noun* [U]

epi·dem·ic /ˌepɪˈdemɪk/ *noun* **1** a large number of cases of a particular disease happening at the same time in a particular community: *the outbreak of a flu epidemic* ◇ *an epidemic of measles* **2** a sudden rapid increase in how often sth bad happens: *an epidemic of crime in the inner cities* ▸ **epi·dem·ic** *adj.*: *Car theft is now reaching **epidemic proportions**.* ➲ compare PANDEMIC

epi·demi·ology /ˌepɪˌdiːmiˈɒlədʒi; *NAmE* -ˈɑːl-/ *noun* [U] the scientific study of the spread and control of diseases ▸ **epi·demi·ologic·al** /ˌepɪˌdiːmiəˈlɒdʒɪkl; *NAmE* -ˈlɑːdʒ-/ *adj.* **epi·demi·olo·gist** /ˌepɪˌdiːmiˈɒlədʒɪst; *NAmE* -ˈɑːl-/ *noun*

epi·der·mis /ˌepɪˈdɜːmɪs; *NAmE* -ˈdɜːrm-/ *noun* [sing., U] (*anatomy*) the outer layer of the skin

epi·dural /ˌepɪˈdjʊərəl; *NAmE* usually -ˈdʊr-/ *noun* (*medical*) an ANAESTHETIC that is put into the lower part of the back so that no pain is felt below the waist: *Some mothers choose to have an epidural when giving birth.*

epi·glot·tis /ˌepɪˈɡlɒtɪs; *NAmE* -ˈɡlɑːtɪs/ *noun* (*anatomy*) a thin piece of TISSUE behind the tongue that prevents food or drink from entering the lungs

epi·gram /ˈepɪɡræm/ *noun* a short poem or phrase that expresses an idea in a clever or amusing way ▸ **epi·gram·mat·ic** /ˌepɪɡrəˈmætɪk/ *adj.*

epi·graph /ˈepɪɡrɑːf; *NAmE* -ɡræf/ *noun* a line of writing, short phrase, etc. on a building or statue, or as an introduction to part of a book

epi·lepsy /ˈepɪlepsi/ *noun* [U] a DISORDER of the nervous system that causes a person to become unconscious suddenly, often with violent movements of the body ▸ **epi·lep·tic** /ˌepɪˈleptɪk/ *adj.*: *an epileptic fit* **epi·lep·tic** *noun*: *Is she an epileptic?*

epi·logue /ˈepɪlɒɡ; *NAmE* -lɔːɡ; -lɑːɡ/ *noun* a speech, etc. at the end of a play, book, or film/movie that comments on or acts as a conclusion to what has happened ➲ compare PROLOGUE

Epiph·any /ɪˈpɪfəni/ *noun* a Christian festival, held on the 6 January, in memory of the time when the MAGI came to see the baby Jesus at Bethlehem

epis·cop·acy /ɪˈpɪskəpəsi/ *noun* [U] government of a church by BISHOPS

epis·cop·al /ɪˈpɪskəpl/ *adj.* **1** connected with a BISHOP or BISHOPS: *episcopal power* **2** (usually **Episcopal**) (also **Epis·co·pa·lian**) (of a Christian Church) that is governed by BISHOPS: *the Episcopal Church* (= the Anglican Church in Scotland and the US)

Epis·co·pa·lian /ɪˌpɪskəˈpeɪliən/ *noun* a member of the Episcopal Church

epis·co·pate /ɪˈpɪskəpət/ *noun* [usually sing.] (*religion*) **1 the episcopate** the BISHOPS of a particular church or area **2** the job of BISHOP or the period of time during which sb is bishop

episi·ot·omy /ɪˌpiːsiˈɒtəmi; *NAmE* -ˈɑːtəmi/ *noun* (*pl.* -ies) (*medical*) a cut that is sometimes made at the opening of a woman's VAGINA to make the birth of a baby easier or safer

epi·sode /ˈepɪsəʊd; *NAmE* -soʊd/ *noun* **1** an event, a situation, or a period of time in sb's life, a novel, etc. that is important or interesting in some way **SYN** **incident**: *I'd like to try and forget the whole episode.* ◇ *One of the funniest episodes in the book occurs in Chapter 6.* **2** one part of a story that is broadcast on television or radio in several parts

epi·sod·ic /ˌepɪˈsɒdɪk; *NAmE* -ˈsɑːd-/ *adj.* (*formal*) **1** happening occasionally and not at regular intervals **2** (of a story, etc.) containing or consisting of many separate and different events: *My memories of childhood are hazy and episodic.*

epi·stem·ic /ˌepɪˈstiːmɪk; -ˈstem-/ *adj.* (*formal*) relating to knowledge

epis·te·mol·ogy /ɪˌpɪstəˈmɒlədʒi; *NAmE* -ˈmɑːl-/ *noun* [U] the part of philosophy that deals with knowledge

epis·tle /ɪˈpɪsl/ *noun* **1 Epistle** any of the letters in the New Testament of the Bible, written by the first people who followed Christ: *the Epistles of St Paul* **2** (*formal* or *humorous*) a long, serious letter on an important subject

epis·tol·ary /ɪˈpɪstələri; *NAmE* -leri/ *adj.* (*formal*) written or expressed in the form of letters: *an epistolary novel*

epi·taph /ˈepɪtɑːf; *NAmE* -tæf/ *noun* **1** words that are written or said about a dead person, especially words on a GRAVESTONE **2 ~ (to sb/sth)** something which is left to remind people of a particular person, a period of time or an event: *These slums are an epitaph to the housing policy of the 1960s.*

epi·thet /ˈepɪθet/ *noun* **1** an adjective or phrase that is used to describe sb/sth's character or most important quality, especially in order to give praise or criticism: *The film is long and dramatic but does not quite earn the epithet 'epic'.* **2** (*especially NAmE*) an offensive word or phrase that is used about a person or group of people: *Racial epithets were scrawled on the walls.*

epit·ome /ɪˈpɪtəmi/ *noun* [sing.] **the ~ of sth** (*formal*) a perfect example of sth **SYN** **embodiment**: *He is the epitome of a modern young man.* ◇ *clothes that are the epitome of good taste*

epit·om·ize (*BrE* also **-ise**) /ɪˈpɪtəmaɪz/ *verb* **~ sth** to be a perfect example of sth: *The fighting qualities of the team are epitomized by the captain.* ◇ *These movies seem to epitomize the 1950s.*

epoch /ˈiːpɒk; *NAmE* ˈepək/ *noun* (*formal* or *literary*) **1** a period of time in history, especially one during which important events or changes happen **SYN** **era**: *The death of the emperor marked the end of an epoch in the country's history.* **2** (*geology*) a length of time which is a division of a PERIOD: *geological epochs*

ˈepoch-making *adj.* (*formal*) having a very important effect on people's lives and on history

E

ep·onym /ˈepənɪm/ *noun* (*technical*) a person or thing, or the name of a person or thing, from which a place, an invention, a discovery, etc. gets its name

epony·mous /ɪˈpɒnɪməs; *NAmE* ɪˈpɑːn-/ *adj.* [only before noun] the **eponymous** character of a book, play, film/movie, etc. is the one mentioned in the title SYN **titular**: *Don Quixote, eponymous hero of the great novel by Cervantes*

epoxy /ɪˈpɒksi; *NAmE* ɪˈpɑːksi/ *noun* [U, C] (*pl.* -ies) (also **eˌpoxy ˈresin**) a type of strong glue

E

ep·si·lon /ˈepsɪlɒn; epˈsaɪlɒn; *NAmE* ˈepsɪlɑːn/ *noun* the fifth letter of the Greek alphabet (Ε, ϵ)

Epsom salts /ˌepsəm ˈsɔːlts/ *noun* [pl.] a white powder that can be mixed with water and used as a medicine or LAXATIVE

equ·able /ˈekwəbl/ *adj.* (*formal*) **1** calm and not easily upset or annoyed: *an equable temperament* **2** (of weather) keeping a steady temperature with no sudden changes ▸ **equ·ably** /ˈekwəbli/ *adv.*

equal 0➔ /ˈiːkwəl/ *adj.*, *noun*, *verb*

■ ***adj.*** **1** 0➔ the same in size, quantity, value, etc. as sth else: *There is an equal number of boys and girls in the class.* ◇ *two pieces of wood equal in length/of equal length* ◇ **~ to sb/sth** *One unit of alcohol is equal to half a pint of beer.* HELP You can use **exactly**, **precisely**, **approximately**, etc. with **equal** in this meaning. **2** 0➔ having the same rights or being treated the same as other people, without differences such as race, religion or sex being considered: ***equal rights/pay*** ◇ *The company has an* ***equal opportunities*** *policy* (= gives the same chances of employment to everyone). ◇ *the desire for a more equal society* (= in which everyone has the same rights and chances) HELP You can use **more** with **equal** in this meaning. **3** **~ to sth** (*formal*) having the necessary strength, courage and ability to deal with sth successfully: *I hope that he proves equal to the challenge.* ➲ see also EQUALLY

IDM **on ˌequal ˈterms (with sb)** having the same advantages and disadvantages as sb else: *Can our industry compete on equal terms with its overseas rivals?* ➲ more at THING

■ ***noun*** 0➔ a person or thing of the same quality or with the same status, rights, etc. as another: *She treats the people who work for her as her equals.* ◇ *Our cars are the equal of those produced anywhere in the world.*

IDM **be without ˈequal | have no ˈequal** (*formal*) to be better than anything else or anyone else of the same type: *He is a player without equal.* **ˌsome (people, members, etc.) are more equal than ˈothers** (*saying*) although the members of a society, group, etc. appear to be equal, some, in fact, get better treatment than others ORIGIN This phrase is used by one of the pigs in the book 'Animal Farm' by George Orwell: 'All animals are equal but some animals are more equal than others.' ➲ more at FIRST *n.*

■ ***verb*** (-ll-, *US* -l-) **1** 0➔ *linking verb* **+ noun** to be the same in size, quantity, value, etc. as sth else: *2x plus y equals 7* (2x +y=7) ◇ *A metre equals 39.38 inches.* **2** 0➔ **~ sth** to be as good as sth else or do sth to the same standard as sb else: *This achievement is unlikely ever to be equalled.* ◇ *Her hatred of religion is equalled only by her loathing for politicians.* ◇ *With his last jump he equalled the world record.* **3** **~ sth** to lead to or result in sth: *Cooperation equals success.*

equal·ity /iˈkwɒləti; *NAmE* iˈkwɑː-/ *noun* [U] the fact of being equal in rights, status, advantages, etc: ***racial/social/sexual equality*** ◇ *equality of opportunity* ◇ *the principle of equality before the law* (= the law treats everyone the same) ◇ *Don't you believe in equality between men and women?* OPP **inequality** ➲ COLLOCATIONS at RACE

equal·ize (*BrE* also **-ise**) /ˈiːkwəlaɪz/ *verb* **1** [T] **~ sth** to make things equal in size, quantity, value, etc. in the whole of a place or group: *a policy to equalize the distribution of resources throughout the country* **2** [I] (*BrE*) (especially in football (SOCCER)) to score a goal that makes the score of both teams equal: *Rooney equalized early in the second half.* ▸ **equal·iza·tion, -isa·tion** /ˌiːkwəlaɪˈzeɪʃn; *NAmE* -ləˈz-/ *noun* [U]

equal·izer (*BrE* also **-iser**) /ˈiːkwəlaɪzər/ *noun* [usually sing.] (*BrE*) (especially in football (SOCCER)) a goal that makes the score of both teams equal: *Rooney scored the equalizer.*

equal·ly 0➔ /ˈiːkwəli/ *adv.*
1 0➔ to the same degree; in the same or in a similar way: *Diet and exercise are equally important.* ◇ *This job could be done* ***equally well*** *by a computer.* ◇ *We try to treat every member of staff equally.* **2** 0➔ in equal parts, amounts, etc: *The money was divided equally among her four children.* ◇ *They share the housework equally.* **3** used to introduce another phrase or idea that adds to and is as important as what you have just said: *I'm trying to do what is best, but equally I've got to consider the cost.*

ˈequals sign (also **ˈequal sign**) *noun* the symbol (=), used in mathematics

equa·nim·ity /ˌekwəˈnɪməti/ *noun* [U] (*formal*) a calm state of mind which means that you do not become angry or upset, especially in difficult situations: *She accepted the prospect of her operation* ***with equanimity***.

equate AW /iˈkweɪt/ *verb* **~ sth (with sth)** to think that sth is the same as sth else or is as important: *Some parents equate education with exam success.* ◇ *I don't see how you can equate the two things.*

PHR V **eˈquate to sth** to be equal to sth else: *A $5 000 raise equates to 25%.*

equa·tion AW /ɪˈkweɪʒn/ *noun* **1** [C] (*mathematics*) a statement showing that two amounts or values are equal, for example 2x + y = 54 **2** [U, sing.] the act of making sth equal or considering sth as equal (= of equating them): *The equation of wealth with happiness can be dangerous.* **3** [C, usually sing.] a problem or situation in which several things must be considered and dealt with: *When children* ***enter the equation***, *further tensions may arise within a marriage.*

equa·tor /ɪˈkweɪtə(r)/ (usually **the equator**) *noun* [sing.] an imaginary line around the earth at an equal distance from the North and South Poles

equa·tor·ial /ˌekwəˈtɔːriəl/ *adj.* near the equator or typical of a country that is near the equator: *equatorial rainforests* ◇ *an equatorial climate*

equerry /ɪˈkweri; ˈekwəri/ *noun* (*pl.* -ies) a male officer who acts as an assistant to a member of a royal family

eques·trian /ɪˈkwestriən/ *adj.* [usually before noun] connected with riding horses, especially as a sport: *equestrian events at the Olympic Games* ➲ VISUAL VOCAB page V38

eques·tri·an·ism /ɪˈkwestriənɪzəm/ *noun* [U] **1** the skill or sport of riding horses **2** an Olympic sport consisting of SHOWJUMPING, DRESSAGE and THREE-DAY EVENTING

equi- /ˈiːkwɪ-; ˈek-/ *combining form* (in nouns, adjectives and adverbs) equal; equally: *equidistant* ◇ *equilibrium*

equi·dis·tant /ˌiːkwɪˈdɪstənt; ˌek-/ *adj.* [not before noun] **~ (from sth)** (*formal*) equally far from two or more places: *All points on a circle are equidistant from the centre.*

equi·lat·eral tri·angle /ˌiːkwɪˌlætərəl ˈtraɪæŋgl/ *noun* (*geometry*) a triangle whose three sides are all the same length ➲ VISUAL VOCAB page V58

equi·lib·rium /ˌiːkwɪˈlɪbriəm; ˌek-/ *noun* [U, sing.] **1** a state of balance, especially between opposing forces or influences: *The point at which the solid and the liquid are* ***in equilibrium*** *is called the freezing point.* ◇ *Any disturbance to the body's state of equilibrium can produce stress.* ◇ *We have achieved an equilibrium in the economy.* **2** a calm state of mind and a balance of emotions: *He sat down to try and recover his equilibrium.*

equine /ˈekwaɪn; ˈiːk-; *NAmE* ˈiːk-/ *adj.* (*formal*) connected with horses; like a horse

equi·noc·tial /ˌiːkwɪˈnɒkʃl; ˌek-; *NAmE* -ˈnɑːk-/ *adj.* connected with an equinox

equi·nox /ˈiːkwɪnɒks; ˈek-; *NAmE* -nɑːks/ *noun* one of the two times in the year (around 20 March and 22 September) when the sun is above the EQUATOR and day and night are of equal length: *the **spring/autumn equinox***

equip AW /ɪˈkwɪp/ *verb* (-pp-) **1** to provide yourself/sb/sth with the things that are needed for a particular purpose or activity SYN **kit out**: **~ sth** *to be **fully/poorly equipped*** ◇ *She got a bank loan to rent and equip a small workshop.* ◇ **~ yourself/sb/sth (with sth) (for sth)** *He equipped himself with a street plan.* ◇ *The centre is **well equipped** for canoeing and mountaineering.* **2 ~ sb (for sth)** | **~ sb (to do sth)** to prepare sb for an activity or task, especially by teaching them what they need to know: *The course is designed to equip students for a career in nursing.*

equip·ment 0-w AW /ɪˈkwɪpmənt/ *noun* [U] **1** 0-w the things that are needed for a particular purpose or activity: *a useful **piece of equipment** for the kitchen* ◇ *office equipment* ◇ *new equipment for the sports club* ➲ VISUAL VOCAB page V57 **2** the process of providing a place or person with necessary things: *The equipment of the photographic studio was expensive.*

Synonyms

equipment

material • gear • kit • apparatus

These are all words for the things that you need for a particular purpose or activity.

equipment the things that are needed for a particular purpose or activity: *camping equipment* ◇ *a piece of equipment*

material things that are needed for a particular activity: *household cleaning materials* ◇ *teaching material*

EQUIPMENT OR MATERIAL?

Equipment is usually solid things, especially large ones. **Materials** may be liquids, powders or books, CDs, etc. containing information, as well as small solid items.

gear the equipment or clothes needed for a particular activity: *Skiing gear can be expensive.*

kit a set of tools or equipment that you use for a particular purpose: *a first-aid kit* ◇ *a tool kit*

apparatus the tools or other pieces of equipment that are needed for a particular activity or task: *breathing apparatus for firefighters* ◇ *laboratory apparatus* NOTE **Apparatus** is used especially for scientific, medical or technical purposes.

PATTERNS

- **electrical/electronic** equipment/gear/apparatus
- **sports** equipment/gear/kit
- **camping** equipment/gear
- **a piece of** equipment/apparatus

equi·poise /ˈiːkwɪpɔɪz; ˈek-/ *noun* [U] (*formal*) a state of balance

equit·able /ˈekwɪtəbl/ *adj.* (*formal*) fair and reasonable; treating everyone in an equal way SYN **fair** OPP **inequitable** ▶ **equit·ably** /-bli/ *adv.*

Equity /ˈekwəti/ *noun* [U] the TRADE/LABOR UNION for actors in the UK, the US and some other countries

equity /ˈekwəti/ *noun* **1** [U] (*finance*) the value of a company's shares; the value of a property after all charges and debts have been paid ➲ see also NEGATIVE EQUITY **2 equities** [pl.] (*finance*) shares in a company which do not pay a fixed amount of interest **3** [U] (*formal*) a situation in which everyone is treated equally SYN **fairness** OPP **inequity 4** [U] (*law*) (*especially BrE*) a system of natural justice allowing a fair judgement in a situation which is not covered by the existing laws

equiva·lent 0-w AW /ɪˈkwɪvələnt/ *adj.*, *noun*

■ ***adj.*** 0-w equal in value, amount, meaning, importance, etc: *250 grams or an equivalent amount in ounces* ◇ **~ to sth** *Eight kilometres is roughly equivalent to five miles.* ▶ **equiva·lence** AW /-ləns/ *noun* [U]: (*formal*) *There is no straightforward equivalence between economic progress and social well-being.*

■ ***noun*** 0-w a thing, amount, word, etc. that is equivalent to sth else: *Send €20 or the equivalent in your own currency.* ◇ **~ of/to sth** *Creutzfeldt-Jakob disease, the human equivalent of BSE* ◇ *Breathing such polluted air is the equivalent of* (= has the same effect as) *smoking ten cigarettes a day.* ◇ *The German 'Gymnasium' is the closest equivalent to the grammar school in England.*

equivo·cal /ɪˈkwɪvəkl/ *adj.* (*formal*) **1** (of words or statements) not having one clear or definite meaning or intention; able to be understood in more than one way SYN **ambiguous**: *She gave an equivocal answer, typical of a politician.* **2** (of actions or behaviour) difficult to understand or explain clearly or easily: *The experiments produced equivocal results.* ➲ see also UNEQUIVOCAL

equivo·cate /ɪˈkwɪvəkeɪt/ *verb* [I, T] (+ **speech**) (*formal*) to talk about sth in a way that is deliberately not clear in order to avoid or hide the truth

equivo·ca·tion /ɪˌkwɪvəˈkeɪʃn/ *noun* [C, U] (*formal*) a way of behaving or speaking that is not clear or definite and is intended to avoid or hide the truth

ER /ˌiː ˈɑː(r)/ *abbr.* EMERGENCY ROOM

er /ɜː(r)/ (also **erm**) *exclamation* (*BrE*) the sound that people make when they are deciding what to say next: *'Will you do it?' 'Er, yes, I suppose so.'*

-er *suffix* **1** (in nouns) a person or thing that: *lover* ◇ *computer* ➲ compare -EE, -OR **2** (in nouns) a person or thing that has the thing or quality mentioned: *three-wheeler* ◇ *foreigner* **3** (in nouns) a person concerned with: *astronomer* ◇ *philosopher* **4** (in nouns) a person belonging to: *New Yorker* **5** (makes comparative adjectives and adverbs): *wider* ◇ *bigger* ◇ *happier* ◇ *sooner* ➲ compare -EST

era /ˈɪərə; *NAmE* ˈɪrə; ˈerə/ *noun* **1** a period of time, usually in history, that is different from other periods because of particular characteristics or events: *the Victorian/modern/post-war era* ◇ *When she left the firm, it was the **end of an era*** (= things were different after that). **2** (*geology*) a length of time which is a division of an AEON

eradi·cate /ɪˈrædɪkeɪt/ *verb* to destroy or get rid of sth completely, especially sth bad SYN **wipe out**: **~ sth** *Diphtheria has been virtually eradicated in the United States.* ◇ **~ sth from sth** *We are determined to eradicate racism from our sport.* ▶ **eradi·ca·tion** /ɪˌrædɪˈkeɪʃn/ *noun* [U]

erase /ɪˈreɪz; *NAmE* ɪˈreɪs/ *verb* **1** to remove sth completely: **~ sth** *She tried to **erase the memory** of that evening.* ◇ **~ sth from sth** *All doubts were suddenly **erased from his mind**.* ◇ *You cannot erase injustice from the world.* **2 ~ sth** to make a mark or sth you have written disappear, for example by rubbing it, especially in order to correct it: *He had erased the wrong word.* ◇ *All the phone numbers had been erased.* **3 ~ sth** to remove a recording from a tape or information from a computer's memory: *Parts of the recording have been erased.*

eraser /ɪˈreɪzə(r); *NAmE* ɪˈreɪsər/ (*NAmE* or *formal*) (*BrE* also **rub·ber**) *noun* a small piece of rubber or a similar substance, used for removing pencil marks from paper; a piece of soft material used for removing CHALK marks from a BLACKBOARD ➲ VISUAL VOCAB page V56

eras·ure /ɪˈreɪʒə(r)/ *noun* [U] (*formal*) the act of removing or destroying sth: *the accidental erasure of important computer files*

er·bium /ˈɜːbiəm; *NAmE* ˈɜːrb-/ *noun* [U] (*symb.* Er) a chemical element. Erbium is a soft silver-white metal.

ere /eə(r); *NAmE* er/ *conj.*, *prep.* (*old use* or *literary*) before: *Ere long* (= soon) *they returned.*

erect /ɪˈrekt/ *adj.*, *verb*

■ ***adj.*** **1** (*formal*) in a vertical position SYN **straight**: *Stand with your arms by your side and your head erect.* **2** (of the PENIS or NIPPLES) larger than usual, stiff and standing up because of sexual excitement

■ ***verb*** (*formal*) **1 ~ sth** to build sth: *The church was erected in 1582.* ➲ SYNONYMS at BUILD **2 ~ sth** to put sth in position

E

and make it stand vertical SYN **put sth up**: *Police had to erect barriers to keep crowds back.* ◇ *to erect a tent* ➲ SYNONYMS at BUILD **3 ~ sth** to create or establish sth: *to erect trade barriers*

erect·ile /ɪ'rektaɪl; *NAmE* also ɪ'rektl/ *adj.* (*biology*) (of a part of the body) able to become stiff and stand up: *erectile tissue*

erec·tion /ɪ'rekʃn/ *noun* **1** [C] if a man has an **erection**, his PENIS is hard and stands up because he is sexually excited: *to* ***get/have an erection*** **2** [U] (*formal*) the act of building sth or putting it in a vertical position: *the erection of scaffolding around the building* **3** [C] (*formal*) a structure or building, especially a large one

E

erg /ɜ:g; *NAmE* ɜ:rg/ *noun* a unit of work or energy

erga·tive /'ɜ:gətɪv; *NAmE* 'ɜ:rg-/ *adj.* (*grammar*) (of verbs) able to be used in both a TRANSITIVE and an INTRANSITIVE way with the same meaning, where the object of the transitive verb is the same as the subject of the intransitive verb: *The verb 'grow' is ergative because you can say 'She grew flowers in her garden' or 'Flowers grew in her garden'.* ➲ compare CAUSATIVE, INCHOATIVE ▶ **er·ga·tive·ly** *adv.*

ergo /'ɜ:gəʊ; *NAmE* 'ɜ:rgoʊ/ *adv.* (from *Latin*, *formal* or *humorous*) therefore

er·go·nom·ic /ˌɜ:gə'nɒmɪk; *NAmE* ˌɜ:rgə'nɑ:m-/ *adj.* designed to improve people's working conditions and to help them work more efficiently: *ergonomic design* ▶ **er·go·nom·ic·al·ly** *adv.*: *The layout is hard to fault ergonomically.*

er·go·nom·ics /ˌɜ:gə'nɒmɪks; *NAmE* ˌɜ:rgə'nɑ:m-/ *noun* [U] the study of working conditions, especially the design of equipment and furniture, in order to help people work more efficiently

erm /ɜ:m/ *exclamation* (*BrE*) = ER: *'Shall we go?' 'Erm, yes, let's.'*

er·mine /'ɜ:mɪn; *NAmE* 'ɜ:rmɪn/ *noun* [U] the white winter fur of the STOAT, used especially to decorate the formal clothes of judges, kings, etc.

erode AW /ɪ'rəʊd; *NAmE* ɪ'roʊd/ *verb* [often passive] **1** [T, I] to gradually destroy the surface of sth through the action of wind, rain, etc; to be gradually destroyed in this way SYN **wear away**: **~ sth (away)** *The cliff face has been steadily eroded by the sea.* ◇ **~ (away)** *The rocks have eroded away over time.* **2** [T, I] **~ (sth)** to gradually destroy sth or make it weaker over a period of time; to be destroyed or made weaker in this way: *Her confidence has been slowly eroded by repeated failures.* ◇ *Mortgage payments have been eroded* (= decreased in value) *by inflation.* ▶ **ero·sion** AW /ɪ'rəʊʒn; *NAmE* ɪ'roʊʒn/ *noun* [U]: *the erosion of the coastline by the sea* ◇ *soil erosion* ◇ *the erosion of her confidence*

er·ogen·ous zone /ɪ'rɒdʒənəs zəʊn; *NAmE* ɪ'rɑ:dʒənəs zoʊn/ *noun* an area of the body that gives sexual pleasure when it is touched

Eros /'ɪərɒs; *NAmE* 'ɪrɑ:s; 'erɑ:s/ *noun* [U] (*formal*) sexual love or desire

erot·ic /ɪ'rɒtɪk; *NAmE* ɪ'rɑ:tɪk/ *adj.* showing or involving sexual desire and pleasure; intended to make sb feel sexual desire: *erotic art* ◇ *an erotic fantasy* ▶ **erot·ic·al·ly** /-kli/ *adv.*

erot·ica /ɪ'rɒtɪkə; *NAmE* ɪ'rɑ:t-/ *noun* [U] books, pictures, etc. that are intended to make sb feel sexual desire

eroti·cism /ɪ'rɒtɪsɪzəm; *NAmE* ɪ'rɑ:t-/ *noun* [U] the fact of expressing or describing sexual feelings and desire, especially in art, literature, etc.

err /ɜ:(r); *NAmE* er/ *verb* [I] (*old-fashioned, formal*) to make a mistake: *To err is human...*

IDM **err on the side of sth** to show too much of a good quality: *I thought it was better* ***to err on the side of caution*** (= to be too careful rather than take a risk).

er·rand /'erənd/ *noun* a job that you do for sb that involves going somewhere to take a message, to buy sth, deliver goods, etc: *He often* ***runs errands*** *for his grandmother.* ◇ *Her boss sent her* ***on an errand*** *into town.* ➲ see also FOOL'S ERRAND

er·rant /'erənt/ *adj.* [only before noun] (*formal* or *humorous*) **1** doing sth that is wrong; not behaving in an acceptable way **2** (of a husband or wife) not sexually faithful

er·rat·ic /ɪ'rætɪk/ *adj.*, *noun*

■ ***adj.*** (often *disapproving*) not happening at regular times; not following any plan or regular pattern; that you cannot rely on SYN **unpredictable**: *The electricity supply here is quite erratic.* ◇ *She had learnt to live with his sudden changes of mood and erratic behaviour.* ◇ *Mary is a gifted but erratic player* (= she does not always play well). ▶ **er·rat·ic·al·ly** /-kli/ *adv.*: *He was obviously upset and was driving erratically.*

■ ***noun*** (also **er,ratic 'block, er,ratic 'boulder**) (*geology*) a large rock that is different from the rock around and was left behind when a large mass of ice melted

er·ratum /e'rɑ:təm/ *noun* [usually pl.] (*pl.* **er·rata** /-tə/) (*technical*) a mistake in a book (shown in a list at the back or front)

er·ro·ne·ous AW /ɪ'rəʊniəs; *NAmE* ɪ'roʊ-/ *adj.* (*formal*) not correct; based on wrong information: ***erroneous conclusions/assumptions*** ▶ **er·ro·ne·ous·ly** AW *adv.*

error 0-π AW /'erə(r)/ *noun* [C, U] a mistake, especially one that causes problems or affects the result of sth: *No payments were made last week because of a computer error.* ◇ **~ in sth** *There are too many errors in your work.* ◇ **~ in doing sth** *I think you have made an error in calculating the total.* ◇ *A simple* ***error of judgement*** *meant that there was not enough food to go around.* ◇ *a* ***grave error*** (= a very serious mistake) ◇ *a* ***glaring error*** (= a mistake that is very obvious) ◇ *The delay was due to* ***human error*** (= a mistake made by a person rather than by a machine). ◇ *The computer system was switched off* ***in error*** (= by mistake). ◇ *There is no* ***room for error*** *in this job.* ➲ SYNONYMS at MISTAKE ➲ see also MARGIN OF ERROR

IDM **see, realize, etc. the ,error of your 'ways** (*formal* or *humorous*) to realize or admit that you have done sth wrong and decide to change your behaviour ➲ more at TRIAL *n.*

'error message *noun* (*computing*) a message that appears on a computer screen which tells you that you have done sth wrong or that the program cannot do what you want it to do

er·satz /'eəzæts; *NAmE* 'ersɑ:ts/ *adj.* artificial and not as good as the real thing or product: *ersatz coffee*

Erse /ɜ:s; *NAmE* ɜ:rs/ *noun* [U] (*old-fashioned*) the Scottish or Irish Gaelic language ➲ compare GAELIC, IRISH

erst·while /'ɜ:stwaɪl; *NAmE* 'ɜ:rst-/ *adj.* [only before noun] (*formal*) former; that until recently was the type of person or thing described but is not any more: *an erstwhile opponent* ◇ *His erstwhile friends turned against him.*

eru·dite /'erudaɪt/ *adj.* (*formal*) having or showing great knowledge that is gained from academic study SYN **learned**

eru·di·tion /ˌeru'dɪʃn/ *noun* [U] (*formal*) great academic knowledge

erupt /ɪ'rʌpt/ *verb* **1** [I, T] when a VOLCANO **erupts** or burning rocks, smoke, etc. **erupt** or **are erupted**, the burning rocks, etc. are thrown out from the volcano: *The volcano could erupt at any time.* ◇ **~ from sth** *Ash began to erupt from the crater.* ◇ **~ sth** *An immense volume of rocks and molten lava was erupted.* ➲ SYNONYMS at EXPLODE **2** [I] to start happening, suddenly and violently SYN **break out**: *Violence erupted outside the embassy gates.* ◇ **~ into sth** *The unrest erupted into revolution.* **3** [I, T] to suddenly express your feelings very strongly, especially by shouting loudly: *When Davis scored for the third time the crowd erupted.* ◇ **~ in/into sth** *My father just erupted into fury.* ◇ **+ speech** *'How dare you?' she erupted.* **4** [I] (of spots, etc.) to suddenly appear on your skin: *A rash had erupted all over his chest.* ▶ **erup·tion** /ɪ'rʌpʃn/ *noun* [C, U]: *a major volcanic eruption* ◇ *an eruption of violent protest* ◇ *skin rashes and eruptions*

erup·tive /ɪˈrʌptɪv/ *adj.* relating to or produced by the ERUPTION of a VOLCANO

-ery, -ry *suffix* (in nouns) **1** the group or class of: *greenery* ◇ *gadgetry* **2** the state or character of: *bravery* ◇ *rivalry* **3** the art or practice of: *cookery* ◇ *archery* **4** a place where sth is made, grows, lives, etc: *bakery* ◇ *orangery*

eryth·ro·cyte /ɪˈrɪθrəsaɪt/ *noun* (*biology*) = RED BLOOD CELL

es·cal·ate /ˈeskəleɪt/ *verb* [I, T] to become or make sth greater, worse, more serious, etc: **~ (into sth)** *The fighting escalated into a full-scale war.* ◇ *the* ***escalating costs*** *of health care* ◇ **~ sth (into sth)** *We do not want to escalate the war.* ▶ **es·cal·ation** /ˌeskəˈleɪʃn/ *noun* [C, U]: *an escalation in food prices* ◇ *further escalation of the conflict*

es·cal·ator /ˈeskəleɪtə(r)/ *noun* moving stairs that carry people between different floors of a large building

es·cal·ope /ˈeskəlɒp; eˈskæləp; *NAmE* ɪˈskɑːləp; ɪˈskæ-/ *noun* a thin slice of meat with no bones in it, often covered with BREADCRUMBS and fried: *escalopes of veal*

es·cap·ade /ˌeskəˈpeɪd; ˈeskəpeɪd/ *noun* an exciting adventure (often one that people think is dangerous or stupid): *Isabel's latest romantic escapade*

es·cape 🔑 /ɪˈskeɪp/ *verb, noun*

■ ***verb*** **1** 🔑 [I] to get away from a place where you have been kept as a prisoner or not allowed to leave: *Two prisoners have escaped.* ◇ **~ from sb/sth** *He escaped from prison this morning.* **2** 🔑 [I, T] to get away from an unpleasant or dangerous situation: **~ (from sth)** *She managed to escape from the burning car.* ◇ **~ (into sth)** (*figurative*) *As a child he would often escape into a dream world of his own.* ◇ **~ sth** *They were glad to have* ***escaped the clutches*** *of winter for another year.* **3** 🔑 [T, no passive] to avoid sth unpleasant or dangerous: **~ sth** *She was lucky to escape punishment.* ◇ *The pilot* ***escaped death*** *by seconds.* ◇ ***There was no escaping*** *the fact that he was overweight.* ◇ **~ doing sth** *He narrowly escaped being killed.* **4** 🔑 [I] to suffer no harm or less harm than you would expect: **~ (with sth)** *I was lucky to escape with minor injuries.* ◇ **+ adj.** *Both drivers* ***escaped unhurt.*** **5** [T, no passive] **~ sb/sth** to be forgotten or not noticed: *Her name escapes me* (= I can't remember it). ◇ *It might have* ***escaped your notice,*** *but I'm very busy at the moment.* **6** [I] (of gases, liquids, etc.) to get out of a container, especially through a hole or crack: *Put a lid on to prevent heat escaping.* ◇ *toxic waste escaping into the sea* **7** [T, I] **~ (sth)** (of a sound) to come out from your mouth without you intending it to: *A groan escaped her lips.*

■ ***noun*** **1** 🔑 [C, U] **~ (from sth)** the act or a method of escaping from a place or an unpleasant or dangerous situation: *an escape from a prisoner of war camp* ◇ *I had a* ***narrow escape*** (= I was lucky to have escaped). ◇ *There was no hope of escape from her disastrous marriage.* ◇ *He took an elaborate* ***escape route*** *from South Africa to Britain.* ◇ *As soon as he turned his back, she would* ***make her escape.*** ➲ see also FIRE ESCAPE **2** 🔑 [sing., U] a way of forgetting sth unpleasant or difficult for a short time: *For her, travel was an escape from the boredom of her everyday life.* **3** [C] the fact of a liquid, gas, etc. coming out of a pipe or container by accident; the amount that comes out: *an escape of gas* **4** [U] (also **eˈscape key** [C]) (*computing*) a button on a computer keyboard that you press to stop a particular operation or leave a program: *Press escape to get back to the menu.*

IDM **make ˌgood your eˈscape** (*formal*) to manage to escape completely ➲ more at BARN

esˈcape clause *noun* a part of a contract which states the conditions under which the contract may be broken

es·caped /ɪˈskeɪpt/ *adj.* [only before noun] having escaped from a place: *an escaped prisoner/lion*

es·capee /ɪˌskeɪˈpiː/ *noun* (*formal*) a person or an animal that has escaped from somewhere, especially sb who has escaped from prison

es·cap·ism /ɪˈskeɪpɪzəm/ *noun* [U] an activity, a form of entertainment, etc. that helps you avoid or forget unpleasant or boring things: *the pure escapism of adventure movies* ◇ *For John, books are a* ***form of escapism.*** ▶ **es·cap·ist** /-pɪst/ *adj.*

es·cap·olo·gist /ˌeskəˈpɒlədʒɪst; *NAmE* -ˈpɑːl-/ *noun* a performer who escapes from ropes, chains, boxes, etc.

es·carp·ment /ɪˈskɑːpmənt; *NAmE* ɪˈskɑːrp-/ *noun* a steep slope that separates an area of high ground from an area of lower ground

ES cell /ˌiː ˈes sel/ *noun* (*biology*) the abbreviation for 'embryonic stem cell' (a STEM CELL taken from an EMBRYO soon after it is formed)

eschat·ology /ˌeskəˈtɒlədʒi; *NAmE* -ˈtɑːl-/ *noun* [U] (*religion*) the part of THEOLOGY concerned with death and judgement ▶ **eschat·ologic·al** /eˌskætəˈlɒdʒɪkl; *NAmE* -ˈlɑːdʒ-/ *adj.*

es·chew /ɪsˈtʃuː/ *verb* **~ sth** (*formal*) to deliberately avoid or keep away from sth

es·cort *noun, verb*

■ ***noun*** /ˈeskɔːt; *NAmE* ˈeskɔːrt/ **1** [C, U] a person or group of people or vehicles that travels with sb/sth in order to protect or guard them: *Armed escorts are provided for visiting heads of state.* ◇ *Prisoners are taken to court* ***under police escort.*** **2** [C] (*formal* or *old-fashioned*) a person, especially a man, who takes sb to a particular social event **3** [C] a person, especially a woman, who is paid to go out socially with sb: *an* ***escort service/agency***

■ ***verb*** /ɪˈskɔːt; *NAmE* ɪˈskɔːrt/ **~ sb (+ adv./prep.)** to go with sb to protect or guard them or to show them the way: *The President arrived, escorted by twelve soldiers.* ➲ SYNONYMS at TAKE

es·cudo /eˈskuːdəʊ; *NAmE* -doʊ/ *noun* (*pl.* **-os**) the unit of money in Cape Verde, and formerly in Portugal (replaced in Portugal in 2002 by the euro)

es·cut·cheon /ɪˈskʌtʃn/ *noun* **1** a flat piece of metal around a KEYHOLE, door handle, or light switch **2** a SHIELD that has a COAT OF ARMS on it

-ese *suffix* **1** (in adjectives and nouns) of a country or city; a person who lives in a country or city; the language spoken there: *Chinese* ◇ *Viennese* **2** (in nouns) (often *disapproving*) the style or language of: *journalese* ◇ *officialese*

esker /ˈeskə(r)/ *noun* (*geology*) a long narrow area of small stones and earth that has been left by a large mass of ice that has melted

Es·kimo /ˈeskɪməʊ; *NAmE* -moʊ/ *noun* (*pl.* **Es·kimo** or **Es·kimos**) (sometimes *offensive*) a member of a race of people from northern Canada, and parts of Alaska, Greenland and Siberia. Some of these people prefer to use the name Inuit. ➲ compare INUIT

Esky™ /ˈeski/ *noun* (*pl.* **-ies**) (*AustralE*) a bag or box which keeps food or drinks cold and which can be used for a PICNIC

ESL /ˌiː es ˈel/ *abbr.* (in the US and Canada) English as a second language (refers to the teaching of English as a foreign language to people who are living in a country in which English is either the first or second language) ➲ compare EAL, EFL, ESOL

ESOL /ˈiːsɒl; *NAmE* -sɑːl/ *abbr.* (in the UK and Ireland) English for speakers of other languages (refers to the teaching of English as a foreign language to people who are living in a country in which English is either the first or second language) ➲ compare EAL, EFL, ESL

esopha·gus (*NAmE*) (*BrE* **oe·sopha·gus**) /iˈsɒfəgəs; *NAmE* iˈsɑː-/ *noun* (*pl.* **-pha·guses** or **-ph·agi** /-gaɪ/) (*anatomy*) the tube through which food passes from the mouth to the stomach **SYN** **gullet** ➲ VISUAL VOCAB page V48

eso·ter·ic /ˌesəˈterɪk; ˌiːsə-/ *adj.* (*formal*) likely to be understood or enjoyed by only a few people with a special knowledge or interest

ESP /ˌiː es ˈpiː/ *abbr.* **1** English for specific/special purposes (the teaching of English for scientific, technical, etc. purposes to people whose first language is not English) **2** extrasensory perception (the ability to know things without using the senses of sight, hearing, etc, for example to know what people are thinking or what will happen in the future)

esp. *abbr.* (in writing) especially

es·pa·drille /ˈespədrɪl/ *noun* a light shoe made of strong cloth with a SOLE made of rope ➲ VISUAL VOCAB page V52

es·pal·ier /ɪˈspæliə(r)/ *noun* **1** a tree or SHRUB that is grown flat along a wooden or wire frame on a wall **2** the frame that such a tree grows along

E

es·pe·cial /ɪˈspeʃl/ *adj.* [only before noun] (*BrE, formal*) greater or better than usual; special in some way or for a particular group: *a matter of especial importance* ◇ *The lecture will be of especial interest to history students.* ➲ compare SPECIAL *adj.* (5)

es·pe·cial·ly 🔑 /ɪˈspeʃəli/ *adv.* (*abbr.* esp.) **1** 🔑 more with one person, thing, etc. than with others, or more in particular circumstances than in others SYN **particularly**: *The car is quite small, especially if you have children.* ◇ *Teenagers are very fashion conscious, especially girls.* ◇ *I love Rome, especially in the spring.* ➲ LANGUAGE BANK at EMPHASIS **2** 🔑 for a particular purpose, person, etc: *I made it especially for you.* **3** very much; to a particular degree: *I wasn't feeling especially happy that day.* ◇ *'Do you like his novels?' 'Not especially.'*

Which Word?

especially / specially

- **Especially** usually means 'particularly': *She loves all sports, especially swimming..* It is not placed first in a sentence: *I especially like sweet things.* ~~*Especially I like sweet things.*~~
- **Specially** usually means 'for a particular purpose' and is often followed by a past participle, such as *designed, developed* or *made*: *a course specially designed to meet your needs* ◇ *She has her clothes specially made in Paris.*
- In *BrE*, **especially** and **specially** are often used in the same way and it can be hard to hear the difference when people speak. **Specially** is less formal: *I bought this especially/specially for you.* ◇ *It is especially/specially important to remember this.*
- The adjective for both **especially** and **specially** is usually **special**.

Es·per·anto /ˌespəˈræntəʊ; *NAmE* -toʊ/ *noun* [U] an artificial language invented in 1887 as a means of international communication, based on the main European languages but with easy grammar and pronunciation

es·pi·on·age /ˈespiənɑːʒ/ *noun* [U] the activity of secretly getting important political or military information about another country or of finding out another company's secrets by using SPIES SYN **spying**: *Some of the commercial activities were a cover for espionage.* ◇ *She may call it research; I call it industrial espionage.* ➲ see also COUNTER-ESPIONAGE

es·plan·ade /ˌespləˈneɪd/ *noun* a level area of open ground in a town for people to walk along, often by the sea or a river

es·pouse /ɪˈspaʊz/ *verb* **~ sth** (*formal*) to give your support to a belief, policy, etc: *They espoused the notion of equal opportunity for all in education.* ▶ **es·pousal** /ɪˈspaʊzl/ *noun* [U, sing.]: **~ of sth** *his recent espousal of populism*

es·presso /eˈspresəʊ; *NAmE* -soʊ/ *noun* (*pl.* -os) **1** [U] strong black coffee made by forcing steam or boiling water through ground coffee **2** [C] a cup of espresso

es·prit de corps /eˌspriː də ˈkɔː(r)/ *noun* [U] (from *French*) feelings of pride, care and support for each other, etc. that are shared by the members of a group

espy /eˈspaɪ/ *verb* (**espies, espy·ing, espied, espied**) **~ sb/sth** (*literary*) to see sb/sth suddenly SYN **catch sight of, spy**

Esq. *abbr.* **1** (*old-fashioned, especially BrE*) Esquire (a polite title written after a man's name, especially on an official letter addressed to him. If Esq. is used, Mr. is not then used): *Edward Smith, Esq.* **2** (*NAmE*) used as a title after the name of a male or female lawyer

Synonyms

essential

vital • crucial • critical • decisive • indispensable

These words all describe sb/sth that is extremely important and completely necessary because a particular situation or activity depends on them.

essential extremely important and completely necessary, because without it sth cannot exist, be made or be successful: *Experience is essential for this job.*

vital essential: *The police play a vital role in our society.*

ESSENTIAL OR VITAL?

These words have the same meaning but there can be a slight difference in tone. **Essential** is used to state a fact or opinion with authority. **Vital** is often used when there is some anxiety felt about sth, or a need to persuade sb that a fact or opinion is true, right or important. **Vital** is less often used in negative statements: *It was vital to show that he was not afraid.* ◇ ~~*Money is not vital to happiness.*~~

crucial extremely important because a particular situation or activity depends on it: *It is crucial that we get this right.*

critical extremely important because a particular situation or activity depends on it: *Your decision is critical to our future.*

CRUCIAL OR CRITICAL?

These words have the same meaning but there can be a slight difference in context. **Critical** is often used in technical matters of business or science; **crucial** is often used to talk about matters that may cause anxiety or other emotions.

decisive of the greatest importance in affecting the final result of a particular situation: *She has played a decisive role in the peace negotiations.*

indispensable essential; too important to be without: *Cars have become an indispensable part of our lives.*

PATTERNS

- essential/vital/crucial/critical/decisive/indispensable **for** sth
- essential/vital/crucial/critical/indispensable **to** sth
- essential/vital/crucial/critical **that...**
- essential/vital/crucial/critical **to do sth**
- a(n) essential/vital/crucial/critical/decisive/indispensable **part/factor**
- **of** vital/crucial/critical/decisive **importance**
- **absolutely** essential/vital/crucial/critical/decisive/indispensable

-esque *suffix* (in adjectives) in the style of: *statuesque* ◇ *Kafkaesque*

-ess *suffix* (in nouns) female: *lioness* ◇ *actress* ➲ note at GENDER

essay 🔑 *noun, verb*

■ *noun* /ˈeseɪ/ **1** 🔑 **~ (on sth)** a short piece of writing by a student as part of a course of study: *an essay on the causes of the First World War* ➲ WRITING TUTOR pages WT6-WT11 **2** 🔑 **~ (on sth)** a short piece of writing on a particular subject, written in order to be published **3 ~ (in sth)** (*formal*) an attempt to do sth: *His first essay in politics was a complete disaster.*

■ *verb* /eˈseɪ/ **~ sth** (*literary*) to try to do sth

es·say·ist /ˈeseɪɪst/ *noun* a person who writes essays to be published

es·sence /ˈesns/ *noun* **1** [U] **~ (of sth)** the most important quality or feature of sth, that makes it what it is: *His paint-*

ings capture the essence of France. ◇ ***In essence*** (= when you consider the most important points), *your situation isn't so different from mine.* **2** [U, C] a liquid taken from a plant, etc. that contains its smell and taste in a very strong form: *essence of rosewood* ◇ (*BrE*) ***coffee/vanilla/almond essence*** ➲ see also EXTRACT

IDM **of the 'essence** necessary and very important: *In this situation* ***time is of the essence*** (= we must do things as quickly as possible).

es·sen·tial 0-w /ɪ'senʃl/ *adj., noun*

■ ***adj.*** **1** 0-w completely necessary; extremely important in a particular situation or for a particular activity **SYN** **vital**: *an* ***essential part/ingredient/component*** *of sth* ◇ *essential services such as gas, water and electricity* ◇ *The museum is closed while essential repairs are being carried out.* ◇ *Even in small companies, computers are an essential tool.* ◇ **~ to sth** *Money is not essential to happiness.* ◇ **~ for sth** *Experience is essential for this job.* ◇ **it is essential to do sth** *It is essential to keep the two groups separate* ◇ **it is essential that...** *It is essential that you have some experience.* ➲ compare INESSENTIAL, NON-ESSENTIAL **OPP** **dispensable** ➲ LANGUAGE BANK at EMPHASIS, VITAL **2** 0-w [only before noun] connected with the most important aspect or basic nature of sb/sth **SYN** **fundamental**: *The essential difference between Sara and me is in our attitude to money.* ◇ *The essential character of the town has been destroyed by the new road.*

■ ***noun*** [usually pl.] **1** 0-w something that is needed in a particular situation or in order to do a particular thing: *I only had time to pack the* ***bare essentials*** (= the most necessary things). ◇ *The studio had all the essentials like heating and running water.* **2** 0-w an important basic fact or piece of knowledge about a subject: *the essentials of English grammar*

es·sen·tial·ly 0-w /ɪ'senʃəli/ *adv.*

when you think about the true, important or basic nature of sb/sth **SYN** **basically, fundamentally**: *There are three* ***essentially different*** *ways of tackling the problem.* ◇ *The pattern is* ***essentially the same*** *in all cases.* ◇ *Essentially, what we are suggesting is that the firm needs to change.* ◇ *He was, essentially, a teacher, not a manager.* ◇ *The article was essentially concerned with her relationship with her parents* (= it dealt with other things, but this was the most important).

es,sential 'oil *noun* an oil taken from a plant, used because of its strong smell for making PERFUME and in AROMATHERAPY

Essex girl /'esɪks gɜːl/ *noun* (*BrE, humorous, disapproving*) a name used especially in jokes to refer to a type of young woman who is not intelligent, dresses badly, talks in a loud and ugly way, and is very willing to have sex

EST /,iː es 'tiː/ *abbr.* EASTERN STANDARD TIME

-est *suffix* (makes superlative adjectives and adverbs): *widest* ◇ *biggest* ◇ *happiest* ◇ *soonest* ➲ compare -ER

es·tab·lish 0-w **AW** /ɪ'stæblɪʃ/ *verb*

1 0-w **~ sth** to start or create an organization, a system, etc. that is meant to last for a long time **SYN** **set up**: *The committee was established in 1912.* ◇ *The new treaty establishes a free trade zone.* **2** 0-w **~ sth** to start having a relationship, especially a formal one, with another person, group or country: *The school has established a successful relationship with the local community.* **3** 0-w **~ sb/sth/yourself (in sth) (as sth)** to hold a position for long enough or succeed in sth well enough to make people accept and respect you: *By then she was established as a star.* ◇ *He has just set up his own business but it will take him a while to* ***get established.*** **4** 0-w **~ sth** to make people accept a belief, claim, custom etc: *It was this campaign that established the paper's reputation.* ◇ *Traditions get established over time.* **5** 0-w to discover or prove the facts of a situation **SYN** **ascertain**: **~ sth** *Police are still trying to establish the cause of the accident.* ◇ **~ that...** *They have established that his injuries were caused by a fall.* ◇ **~ where, what, etc...** *We need to establish where she was at the time of the shooting.* ◇ **it is established that...** *It has since been established that the horse was drugged.*

es·tab·lished **AW** /ɪ'stæblɪʃt/ *adj.* [only before noun] **1** respected or given official status because it has existed or been used for a long time: *They are an established company with a good reputation.* ◇ *This unit is now an established part of the course.* ➲ see also WELL ESTABLISHED **2** (of a person) well known and respected in a job, etc. that they have been doing for a long time: *an established actor* **3** (of a Church or a religion) made official for a country

es·tab·lish·ment **AW** /ɪ'stæblɪʃmənt/ *noun* **1** [C] (*formal*) an organization, a large institution or a hotel: *an educational establishment* ◇ *a research establishment* ◇ *The hotel is a comfortable and well-run establishment.* **2** (usually **the Establishment**) [sing.+ sing./pl. v.] (often *disapproving*) the people in a society or a profession who have influence and power and who usually do not support change: *the* ***medical/military/political, etc. establishment*** ◇ *young people rebelling against the Establishment* **3** [U] the act of starting or creating sth that is meant to last for a long time: *The speaker announced the establishment of a new college.* ◇ *the establishment of diplomatic relations between the countries*

es·tate 0-w **AW** /ɪ'steɪt/ *noun*

1 0-w [C] a large area of land, usually in the country, that is owned by one person or family **2** 0-w [C] (*BrE*) an area of land with a lot of houses or factories of the same type on it: *She lives in a tower block on an estate in London.* ➲ see also COUNCIL ESTATE, HOUSING ESTATE, INDUSTRIAL ESTATE, TRADING ESTATE **3** (*law*) [C, U] all the money and property that a person owns, especially everything that is left when they die: *Her estate was left to her daughter.* **4** [C] (*BrE*) = ESTATE CAR

e'state agent (*BrE*) (*NAmE* **Real·tor™**, **'real estate agent**) *noun* a person whose job is to sell houses and land for people ➲ COLLOCATIONS at HOUSE

e'state car (also **estate**) (both *BrE*) (*NAmE* **'station wagon**) *noun* a car with a lot of space behind the back seats and a door at the back for loading large items ➲ VISUAL VOCAB page V42

e'state sale *noun* (*NAmE*) a sale of the possessions of a person who has died or is moving to another house

e'state tax *noun* [U] (*NAmE*) = INHERITANCE TAX

es·teem /ɪ'stiːm/ *noun, verb*

■ ***noun*** [U] (*formal*) great respect and admiration; a good opinion of sb: *She is* ***held in high esteem*** *by her colleagues.* ◇ *Please accept this small gift as a token of our esteem.* ➲ see also SELF-ESTEEM

■ ***verb*** (*formal*) (not used in the progressive tenses) **1** [usually passive] **~ sb/sth** to respect and admire sb/sth very much: *a* ***highly esteemed*** *scientist* **2** **~ sb/sth + noun** (*old-fashioned, formal*) to think of sb/sth in a particular way: *She was esteemed the perfect novelist.*

ester /'estə(r)/ *noun* (*chemistry*) a sweet-smelling substance that is formed from an ORGANIC acid and an alcohol

es·thete, es·thet·ic (*NAmE*) = AESTHETE, AESTHETIC

es·tim·able /'estɪməbl/ *adj.* (*old-fashioned* or *formal*) deserving respect and admiration

es·ti·mate 0-w **AW** *noun, verb*

■ ***noun*** /'estɪmət/ **1** 0-w a judgement that you make without having the exact details or figures about the size, amount, cost, etc. of sth: *I can give you a* ***rough estimate*** *of the amount of wood you will need.* ◇ *a* ***ballpark estimate*** (= an approximate estimate) ◇ *official government estimates of traffic growth over the next decade* ◇ *At least 5 000 people were killed, and that's a* ***conservative estimate*** (= the real figure will be higher). **2** 0-w a statement of how much a piece of work will probably cost

■ ***verb*** 0-w /'estɪmeɪt/ [often passive] to form an idea of the cost, size, value etc. of sth, but without calculating it exactly: **~ sth (at sth)** *The satellite will cost an estimated £400 million.* ◇ *Police estimate the crowd at 30 000.* ◇ **~ sth to do sth** *The deal is estimated to be worth around $1.5 million.* ◇ **~ (that)...** *We estimated (that) it would cost about €5 000.* ◇ **it is estimated (that)...** *It is estimated (that) the* *project will last four years.* ◇ **~ how many, large, etc...** *It is hard to estimate how many children suffer from dyslexia.*

es·ti·ma·tion AW /ˌestɪˈmeɪʃn/ *noun* (*formal*) **1** [sing.] a judgement or opinion about the value or quality of sb/sth: *Who is the best candidate* ***in your estimation****?* ◇ *Since he left his wife he's certainly* ***gone down in my estimation*** (= I have less respect for him). ◇ *She* ***went up in my estimation*** (= I have more respect for her) *when I discovered how much charity work she does.* **2** [C] a judgement about the levels or quantity of sth: *Estimations of our total world sales are around 50 million.*

E

es·tranged /ɪˈstreɪndʒd/ *adj.* (*formal*) **1** [usually before noun] no longer living with your husband or wife: *his estranged wife Emma* **2 ~ (from sb)** no longer friendly, loyal or in contact with sb: *He became estranged from his family after the argument.* **3 ~ (from sth)** no longer involved in or connected with sth, especially sth that used to be important to you: *She felt estranged from her former existence.*

es·trange·ment /ɪˈstreɪndʒmənt/ *noun* [U, C] (*formal*) the state of being estranged; a period of being estranged: **~ (from sb/sth)** *a period of estrangement from his wife* ◇ **~ (between A and B)** *The misunderstanding had caused a seven-year estrangement between them.*

es·tro·gen (*NAmE*) (*BrE* **oes·tro·gen**) /ˈiːstrədʒən; *NAmE* ˈes-/ *noun* [U] a HORMONE produced in women's OVARIES that causes them to develop the physical and sexual features that are characteristic of females and that causes them to prepare their body to have babies ➲ compare PROGESTERONE, TESTOSTERONE

es·trus (*NAmE*) (*BrE* **oes·trus**) /ˈiːstrəs; *NAmE* ˈestrəs/ *noun* [U] (*technical*) a period of time in which a female animal is ready to have sex

es·tu·ary /ˈestʃuəri; *NAmE* -eri/ (*pl.* -ies) *noun* the wide part of a river where it flows into the sea: *the Thames estuary* ➲ VISUAL VOCAB page V4

ˌEstuary ˈEnglish *noun* [U] a way of speaking which has features of standard English and of the type of English that is typical of London, used by many people in the south-east of England

ETA /ˌiː tiː ˈeɪ/ *abbr.* estimated time of arrival (the time at which an aircraft, a ship, etc. is expected to arrive) ➲ compare ETD

eta /ˈiːtə/ *noun* the 7th letter of the Greek alphabet (Η, η)

ˈe-tailing *noun* [U] the business of selling goods to the public over the Internet: *E-tailing in the US broke all records last year.* ▸ **ˈe-tailer** *noun*: *America's leading e-tailers*

et al. /ˌet ˈæl/ *abbr.* (used especially after names) and other people or things (from Latin 'et alii/alia'): *research by West et al., 1996*

etc. 0‑ /ˌet ˈsetərə; ˌɪt/ *abbr.* used after a list to show that there are other things that you could have mentioned (the abbreviation for 'et cetera'): *Remember to take some paper, a pen, etc.* ◇ *We talked about the contract, pay, etc.*

et cet·era /ˌet ˈsetərə; ˌɪt/ = ETC.

etch /etʃ/ *verb* **1** [T, I] to cut lines into a piece of glass, metal, etc. in order to make words or a picture: **~ (A) (in/into/on B)** *a glass tankard with his initials etched on it* ◇ **~ B (with A)** *a glass tankard etched with his initials* **2** [T, usually passive] (*literary*) if a feeling is **etched** on sb's face, or sb's face is **etched** with a feeling, that feeling can be seen very clearly: **~ A in/into/on B** *Tiredness was etched on his face.* ◇ **~ B with A** *His face was etched with tiredness.* **3** [T, usually passive] **~ sth (+ adv./prep.)** to make a strong clear mark or pattern on sth: *a mountain etched* (= having a clear outline) *against the sky*

IDM **be etched on your ˈheart/ˈmemory/ˈmind** if sth is **etched** on your memory, you remember it because it has made a strong impression on you

etch·ing /ˈetʃɪŋ/ *noun* [C, U] a picture that is printed from an etched piece of metal; the art of making these pictures

ETD /ˌiː tiː ˈdiː/ *abbr.* estimated time of departure (the time at which an aircraft, ship, etc. is expected to leave) ➲ compare ETA

eter·nal /ɪˈtɜːnl; *NAmE* ɪˈtɜːrnl/ *adj.* **1** without an end; existing or continuing forever: *the promise of eternal life in heaven* ◇ *She's an eternal optimist* (= she always expects that the best will happen). ◇ *eternal truths* (= ideas that are always true and never change) **2** [only before noun] (*disapproving*) happening often and seeming never to stop SYN **constant**: *I'm tired of your eternal arguments.* ▸ **eter·nal·ly** /ɪˈtɜːnəli; *NAmE* -ˈtɜːrn-/ *adv.*: *I'll be eternally grateful to you for this.* ◇ *women trying to look eternally young* IDM see HOPE *n.*

eˌternal ˈtriangle *noun* a situation where two people are in love with or having a sexual relationship with the same person

eˌternal ˈverity *noun* [usually pl.] (*formal*) an essential basic moral principle

eter·nity /ɪˈtɜːnəti; *NAmE* ɪˈtɜːrn-/ *noun* **1** [U] (*formal*) time without end, especially life continuing without end after death: *There will be rich and poor for all eternity.* ◇ *They believed that their souls would be condemned to burn in hell for eternity.* **2 an eternity** [sing.] (*informal*) a period of time that seems to be very long or to never end: *After what* ***seemed like an eternity*** *the nurse returned with the results of the test.*

eth /eð/ *noun* (*phonetics*) the letter ð that was used in Old English to represent the sounds /θ/ and /ð/ and later written as *th*. This letter is now used as a PHONETIC symbol for the sound /ð/, as in *this*.

eth·ane /ˈiːθeɪn/ *noun* [U] (*symb.* C_2H_6) (*chemistry*) a gas that has no colour or smell and that can burn. Ethane is found in natural gas and mineral oil.

etha·nol /ˈeθənɒl; *NAmE* -nɔːl; -nɑːl/ (also **ˌethyl ˈalcohol**) *noun* [U] (*chemistry*) the type of alcohol in alcoholic drinks, also used as a fuel or SOLVENT

eth·ene /ˈeθiːn/ *noun* [U] = ETHYLENE

ether /ˈiːθə(r)/ *noun* [U] **1** a clear liquid made from alcohol, used in industry as a SOLVENT and, in the past, in medicine to make people unconscious before an operation **2 the ether** (*old use* or *literary*) the upper part of the sky: *Her words disappeared into the ether.* **3 the ether** the air, when it is thought of as the place in which radio or electronic communication takes place

ether·eal /iˈθɪəriəl; *NAmE* iˈθɪr-/ *adj.* (*formal*) extremely delicate and light; seeming to belong to another, more spiritual, world: *ethereal music* ◇ *her ethereal beauty*

Ether·net /ˈiːθənet; *NAmE* ˈiːθərnet/ *noun* [sing.] (*computing*) a system for connecting a number of computer systems to form a network

ethic AW /ˈeθɪk/ *noun* **1 ethics** [pl.] moral principles that control or influence a person's behaviour: ***professional/business/medical ethics*** ◇ *to draw up a* ***code of ethics*** ◇ *He began to question the ethics of his position.* **2** [sing.] a system of moral principles or rules of behaviour: *a strongly defined work ethic* ◇ *the Protestant ethic* **3 ethics** [U] the branch of philosophy that deals with moral principles

eth·ic·al AW /ˈeθɪkl/ *adj.* **1** connected with beliefs and principles about what is right and wrong: ***ethical issues/standards/questions*** ◇ *the* ***ethical problems*** *of human embryo research* **2** morally correct or acceptable: *Is it ethical to promote cigarettes through advertising?* ◇ ***ethical investment*** (= investing money in businesses that are considered morally acceptable) ▸ **eth·ic·al·ly** AW /-kli/ *adv.*: *The committee judged that he had not behaved ethically.*

eth·nic AW /ˈeθnɪk/ *adj.*, *noun*

■ *adj.* **1** connected with or belonging to a nation, race or people that shares a cultural tradition: ***ethnic groups/communities*** ◇ ***ethnic strife/tensions/violence*** (= between people from different races or peoples) ◇ *ethnic Albanians living in Germany* **2** typical of a country or culture that is very different from modern Western culture and therefore interesting for people in Western countries: ***ethnic clothes/jewellery/cooking*** ▸ **eth·nic·al·ly** /-kli/ *adv.*: *an ethnically divided region*

■ ***noun*** (*especially NAmE*) a person from an ETHNIC MINORITY

ˌethnic 'cleansing *noun* [U] (used especially in news reports) the policy of forcing the people of a particular race or religion to leave an area or a country ➲ **COLLOCATIONS** at WAR

eth·ni·city AW /eθ'nɪsəti/ *noun* [U] (*technical*) the fact of belonging to a particular race: *Many factors are important, for example class, gender, age and ethnicity.*

ˌethnic mi'nority *noun* a group of people from a particular culture or of a particular race living in a country where the main group is of a different culture or race

ethno·cen·tric /ˌeθnəʊ'sentrɪk; *NAmE* ˌeθnoʊ-/ *adj.* based on the ideas and beliefs of one particular culture and using these to judge other cultures: *a white, ethnocentric school curriculum* ▸ **ethno·cen·trism** *noun* [U]

eth·nog·raph·er /eθ'nɒɡrəfə(r); *NAmE* -'nɑːɡ-/ *noun* a person who studies different races and cultures

eth·nog·raphy /eθ'nɒɡrəfi; *NAmE* -'nɑːɡ-/ *noun* [U] the scientific description of different races and cultures ▸ **ethno·graph·ic** /ˌeθnə'ɡræfɪk/ *adj.*: *ethnographic research*

eth·no·logy /eθ'nɒlədʒi; *NAmE* -'nɑːl-/ *noun* [U] the scientific study and comparison of human races ▸ **ethno·logic·al** /ˌeθnə'lɒdʒɪkl; *NAmE* -'lɑːdʒ-/ *adj.* **eth·nolo·gist** /eθ'nɒlədʒɪst; *NAmE* -'nɑːl-/ *noun*

ethos /'iːθɒs; *NAmE* 'iːθɑːs/ *noun* [sing.] (*formal*) the moral ideas and attitudes that belong to a particular group or society: *an ethos of public service*

ethyl /'eθɪl; 'iːθaɪl/ *adj.* [only before noun] (*chemistry*) containing the group of atoms C_2H_5, formed from ETHANE: *ethyl acetate*

ˌethyl 'alcohol *noun* [U] (*chemistry*) = ETHANOL

ethyl·ene /'eθɪliːn/ (also **eth·ene**) *noun* [U] (*symb.* C_2H_4) (*chemistry*) a gas which is present in coal, CRUDE OIL, and NATURAL GAS

eth·yne /'iːθaɪn; *NAmE* 'eθ-/ *noun* [U] (*symb.* C_2H_2) the chemical name for ACETYLENE

'e-ticket (*US* **'E-ticket™**) *noun* a ticket, for example a plane ticket, that you buy over the Internet and receive by email. Your purchase details are stored on computer so you do not need a paper ticket.

eti·ol·ated /'iːtiəleɪtɪd/ *adj.* **1** (*biology*) if a plant is **etiolated** it is pale because it does not receive enough light **2** (*formal*) lacking force and energy

eti·ology (*NAmE*) (*BrE* **aeti·ology**) /ˌiːti'ɒlədʒi; *NAmE* -'ɑːl-/ *noun* [U] (*medical*) the scientific study of the causes of disease

eti·quette /'etɪket; -kət/ *noun* [U] the formal rules of correct or polite behaviour in society or among members of a particular profession: *advice on etiquette* ◇ ***medical/legal/professional etiquette*** ➲ see also NETIQUETTE

Eton·ian /iː'təʊniən; *NAmE* -'toʊ-/ *noun* a person who is or was a student at the English private school Eton College

-ette *suffix* (in nouns) **1** small: *kitchenette* **2** female: *usherette*

étude /'eɪtjuːd; *NAmE* also -tuːd/ (from *French, especially NAmE*) (*BrE* also **study**) *noun* (*music*) a piece of music designed to give a player practice in technical skills

ety·mol·ogy /ˌetɪ'mɒlədʒi; *NAmE* -'mɑːl-/ *noun* (*pl.* **-ies**) **1** [U] the study of the origin and history of words and their meanings **2** [C] the origin and history of a particular word ▸ **etymo·logic·al** /ˌetɪmə'lɒdʒɪkl; *NAmE* -'lɑːdʒ-/ *adj.*: *an etymological dictionary*

EU /ˌiː 'juː/ *abbr.* EUROPEAN UNION

eu·ca·lyp·tus /ˌjuːkə'lɪptəs/ *noun* [C, U] (*pl.* **eu·ca·lyp·tuses** or **eu·ca·lyp·ti** /-taɪ/) (also **euca'lyptus tree**, **'gum tree**) a tall straight tree with leaves that produce an oil with a strong smell, that is used in medicine. There are several types of eucalyptus and they grow especially in Australasia. ➲ **VISUAL VOCAB** page V10

Eu·char·ist /'juːkərɪst/ *noun* [sing.] a ceremony in the Christian Church during which people eat bread and drink wine in memory of the last meal that Christ had with his DISCIPLES; the bread and wine taken at this ceremony ➲ see also COMMUNION, MASS

Eu·clid·ean geom·etry /juːˌklɪdiən dʒi'ɒmətri; *NAmE* -'ɑːm-/ *noun* [U] the system of GEOMETRY based on the work of Euclid

eu·gen·ics /juː'dʒenɪks/ *noun* [U] the study of methods to improve the mental and physical characteristics of the human race by choosing who may become parents ▸ **eu·gen·ic** *adj.* **eu·gen·ist** /juː'dʒiːnɪst/ (also **eu·geni·cist**) /juː'dʒenɪsɪst/ *noun*

eu·lo·gize (*BrE* also **-ise**) /'juːlədʒaɪz/ *verb* **~ sb/sth** (**as sth**) (*formal*) to praise sb/sth very highly: *He was eulogized as a hero.* ▸ **eu·lo·gis·tic** /ˌjuːlə'dʒɪstɪk/ *adj.*

eu·logy /'juːlədʒi/ *noun* [C, U] (*pl.* **-ies**) **1 ~ (of/to sb/sth)** a speech or piece of writing praising sb/sth very much: *a eulogy to marriage* **2 ~ (for/to sb)** (*especially NAmE*) a speech given at a funeral praising the person who has died

eu·nuch /'juːnək/ *noun* **1** a man who has been CASTRATED, especially one who guarded women in some Asian countries in the past **2** (*formal*) a person without power or influence: *a political eunuch*

eu·phem·ism /'juːfəmɪzəm/ *noun* **~ (for sth)** an indirect word or phrase that people often use to refer to sth embarrassing or unpleasant, sometimes to make it seem more acceptable than it really is: *'Pass away' is a euphemism for 'die'.* ◇ *'User fees' is just a politician's euphemism for taxes.* ▸ **eu·phem·is·tic** /ˌjuːfə'mɪstɪk/ *adj.*: *euphemistic language* **eu·phem·is·tic·al·ly** /ˌjuːfə'mɪstɪkli/ *adv.*: *The prison camps were euphemistically called 'retraining centres'.*

eu·pho·ni·ous /juː'fəʊniəs; *NAmE* -'foʊ-/ *adj.* (*formal*) (of a sound, word, etc.) pleasant to listen to ▸ **eu·pho·ny** /'juːfəni/ *noun* [U]

eu·pho·nium /juː'fəʊniəm; *NAmE* -'foʊ-/ *noun* a large BRASS musical instrument like a TUBA

eu·phoria /juː'fɔːriə/ *noun* [U] an extremely strong feeling of happiness and excitement that usually lasts only a short time ▸ **eu·phor·ic** /juː'fɒrɪk; *NAmE* -'fɔːr-/ *adj.*: *My euphoric mood could not last.* ➲ **SYNONYMS** at EXCITED

Eur·asian /ju'reɪʒn; -'reɪʃn/ *adj., noun*

■ ***adj.*** **1** of or connected with both Europe and Asia: *the Centre for Russian and Eurasian Studies* **2** having one Asian parent and one parent who is white or from Europe

■ ***noun*** a person with one Asian parent and one parent who is white or from Europe: *Singapore Eurasians*

eur·eka /ju'riːkə/ *exclamation* used to show pleasure at having found sth, especially the answer to a problem

eu'reka moment *noun* the moment when you suddenly understand sth important, have a great idea, or find the answer to a problem

eu·rhyth·mics (*BrE*) (*NAmE* **eu·ryth·mics**) /ju'rɪðmɪks/ *noun* [U] a form of exercise which combines physical movement with music and speech

Euro /'jʊərəʊ; *NAmE* 'jʊroʊ/ *adj.* (*informal*) (used especially in newspapers) connected with Europe, especially the European Union: *Euro rules*

euro 0‑ᵂ /'jʊərəʊ; *NAmE* 'jʊroʊ/ *noun* (*symb.* €) (*pl.* **euros** or **euro**) the unit of money of some countries of the European Union: *The price is given in dollars or euros.* ◇ *I paid five euros for it.* ◇ *10 million euro* ◇ *a 30-million-euro deal* ◇ *the value of **the euro** against the dollar*

Euro- /'jʊərəʊ; *NAmE* 'jʊroʊ/ *combining form* (in nouns and adjectives) connected with Europe or the European Union: *a Euro-MP* ◇ *Euro-elections*

Euro·crat /'jʊərəkræt; *NAmE* 'jʊr-/ *noun* (sometimes *disapproving*) an official of the European Union, especially a senior one

Euro·land /'jʊərəʊlænd; *NAmE* 'jʊroʊ-/ *noun* [U] = EUROZONE

E

Eur·ope /ˈjʊərəp; *NAmE* ˈjʊrəp/ *noun* [U] **1** the continent next to Asia in the east, the Atlantic Ocean in the west, and the Mediterranean Sea in the south: ***western/eastern/central Europe*** **2** the European Union: *countries wanting to join Europe* ◇ *He's very pro-Europe.* **3** (*BrE*) all of Europe except for Britain: *British holidaymakers in Europe*

Euro·pean /ˌjʊərəˈpiːən; *NAmE* ˌjʊr-/ *adj., noun*
■ ***adj.*** **1** of or connected with Europe: *European languages* **2** of or connected with the European Union: *European law* ◇ *our European partners*
■ ***noun*** **1** a person from Europe, or whose ANCESTORS came from Europe **2** (*BrE*) a person who supports the principles and aims of the European Union: *a good European*

the ˌEuropean Comˈmission *noun* [sing.] the group of people who are responsible for the work of the European Union and for suggesting new laws

Euro·pean·ize (*BrE* also **-ise**) /ˌjʊərəˈpiːənaɪz; *NAmE* ˌjʊr-/ *verb* **1 ~ sb/sth** to make sb/sth feel or seem European: *a Europeanized American* **2 ~ sth** to put sth under the control of the European Union ▶ **Euro·pean·iza·tion, -isa·tion** /ˌjʊərəpiːənaɪˈzeɪʃn; *NAmE* ˌjʊr-/ *noun* [U]

the ˌEuropean ˈParliament *noun* [sing.] the group of people who are elected in the countries of the European Union to make and change its laws

ˌEuropean ˈplan *noun* [sing.] (*NAmE*) a system of charging for a hotel room only, without meals ➲ compare BED AND BREAKFAST, HALF BOARD, FULL BOARD

the ˌEuropean ˈUnion *noun* [sing.] (*abbr.* EU) an economic and political organization, based in Brussels, that many European countries belong to

euro·pium /jʊərˈəʊpiəm; *NAmE* jʊrˈoʊ-/ *noun* [U] (*symb.* Eu) a chemical element. Europium is a silver-white metal used in colour television screens.

ˌEuro-ˈsceptic *noun* a person, especially a British politician, who is opposed to closer links with the European Union ▶ **ˌEuro-ˈsceptic** *adj.*

Euro·vision /ˈjʊərəvɪʒn; *NAmE* ˈjʊr-/ *noun* [sing.] an organization of European television companies that share news and programmes: *the Eurovision Song Contest*

the Euro·zone /ˈjʊərəʊzəʊn; *NAmE* ˈjʊroʊzoʊn/ *noun* [sing.] (also **Euro·land**) the countries in the European Union that use the euro as a unit of money

Eus·ta·chian tube /juːˈsteɪʃn tjuːb/ *noun* (*anatomy*) a narrow tube that joins the throat to the middle ear

eu·tha·nasia /ˌjuːθəˈneɪziə; *NAmE* -ˈneɪʒə/ *noun* [U] the practice (illegal in most countries) of killing without pain a person who is suffering from a disease that cannot be cured SYN **mercy killing**: *They argued in favour of legalizing* ***voluntary euthanasia*** (= people being able to ask for euthanasia themselves).

eu·than·ize (*BrE* also **-ise**) /ˈjuːθənaɪz/ *verb* **~ sb/sth** (*especially NAmE*) to kill a sick or injured animal or person by giving them drugs so that they die without pain SYN **put sth down, put sth to sleep**

eu·troph·ic /juːˈtrɒfɪk; *NAmE* -ˈtrɑːf-/ *adj.* (*technical*) (of a lake, river, etc.) containing too many food substances that encourage plants to grow, which then kill animal life by using too much OXYGEN from the water

eu·trophi·ca·tion /ˌjuːtrəfɪˈkeɪʃn/ *noun* [U] (*technical*) the process of too many plants growing on the surface of a river, lake, etc, often because chemicals that are used to help crops grow have been carried there by rain

evacu·ate /ɪˈvækjueɪt/ *verb* **1** [T] to move people from a place of danger to a safer place: **~ sth** *Police evacuated nearby buildings.* ◇ **~ sb (from...) (to...)** *Children were evacuated from London to escape the bombing.* **2** [T, I] **~ (sth)** to move out of a place because of danger, and leave the place empty: *Employees were urged to evacuate their offices immediately.* ◇ *Locals were told to evacuate.* **3** [T] **~ sth** (*formal*) to empty your BOWELS ▶ **evacu·ation** /ɪˌvækjuˈeɪʃn/ *noun* [U, C]: *the emergency evacuation of thousands of people after the earthquake*

evac·uee /ɪˌvækjuˈiː/ *noun* a person who is sent away from a place because it is dangerous, especially during a war

evade /ɪˈveɪd/ *verb* **1 ~ (doing) sth** to escape from sb/sth or avoid meeting sb: *For two weeks they evaded the press.* ◇ *He managed to* ***evade capture.*** **2 ~ (doing) sth** to find a way of not doing sth, especially sth that legally or morally you should do: *to evade payment of taxes* ◇ *She is trying to* ***evade all responsibility*** *for her behaviour.* **3** to avoid dealing with or talking about sth: **~ sth** *Come on, don't you think you're* ***evading the issue?*** ◇ **~ doing sth** *to evade answering a question* **4 ~ sb** (*formal*) to not come or happen to sb SYN **elude**: *The answer evaded him* (= he could not think of it). ➲ see also EVASION, EVASIVE

evalu·ate AW /ɪˈvæljueɪt/ *verb* to form an opinion of the amount, value or quality of sth after thinking about it carefully SYN **assess**: **~ sth** *Our research attempts to evaluate the effectiveness of the different drugs.* ◇ **~ how, whether, etc...** *We need to evaluate how well the policy is working.* ▶ **evalu·ation** AW /ɪˌvæljuˈeɪʃn/ *noun* [C, U]: *an evaluation of the health care system* **evalu·ative** AW /ɪˈvæljuətɪv/ *adj.*

evan·es·cent /ˌiːvəˈnesnt; *NAmE* usually ˌev-/ *adj.* (*literary*) disappearing quickly from sight or memory ▶ **evan·es·cence** *noun* [U]

evan·gel·ic·al /ˌiːvænˈdʒelɪkl/ *adj., noun*
■ ***adj.*** **1** of or belonging to a Christian group that emphasizes the authority of the Bible and the importance of people being saved through faith: *They're evangelical Christians.* **2** wanting very much to persuade people to accept your views and opinions: *He delivered his speech with evangelical fervour.* ▶ **evan·gel·ic·al·ism** *noun* [U]
■ ***noun*** a member of the evangelical branch of the Christian Church

evan·gel·ist /ɪˈvændʒəlɪst/ *noun* **1** a person who tries to persuade people to become Christians, especially by travelling around the country holding religious meetings or speaking on radio or television ➲ see also TELEVANGELIST **2 Evangelist** one of the four writers (Matthew, Mark, Luke, John) of the books called the GOSPELS in the Bible ▶ **evan·gel·ism** *noun* [U] **evan·gel·ist·ic** /ɪˌvændʒəˈlɪstɪk/ *adj.*: *an evangelistic meeting*

evan·gel·ize (*BrE* also **-ise**) /ɪˈvændʒəlaɪz/ *verb* **~ sb** to try to persuade people to become Christians

evap·or·ate /ɪˈvæpəreɪt/ *verb* **1** [I, T] if a liquid **evaporates** or if sth **evaporates** it, it changes into a gas, especially steam: *Heat until all the water has evaporated.* ◇ **~ sth** *The sun is constantly evaporating the earth's moisture.* **2** [I] to disappear, especially by gradually becoming less and less: *Her confidence had now completely evaporated.* ▶ **evap·or·ation** /ɪˌvæpəˈreɪʃn/ *noun* [U]

eˌvaporated ˈmilk *noun* [U] thick sweet milk sold in cans, often served with fruit instead of cream

eˈvaporating dish *noun* (*technical*) a dish in which scientists heat a liquid, so that it leaves a solid when it has disappeared ➲ VISUAL VOCAB page V57

eva·sion /ɪˈveɪʒn/ *noun* [C, U] **1** the act of avoiding sb or of avoiding sth that you are supposed to do: *His behaviour was an evasion of his responsibilities as a father.* ◇ *She's been charged with* ***tax evasion.*** **2** a statement that sb makes that avoids dealing with sth or talking about sth honestly and directly: *His speech was full of evasions and half-truths.* ➲ see also EVADE

eva·sive /ɪˈveɪsɪv/ *adj.* not willing to give clear answers to a question SYN **cagey**: ***evasive answers/comments/replies*** ◇ *Tessa was evasive about why she had not been at home that night.* ▶ **eva·sive·ly** *adv.*: *'I'm not sure,' she replied evasively.* **eva·sive·ness** *noun* [U]
IDM **take evasive action** to act in order to avoid danger or an unpleasant situation

eve /iːv/ *noun* **1** the day or evening before an event, especially a religious festival or holiday: *Christmas Eve* (= 24 December) ◇ *a New Year's Eve party* (= on 31 December) ◇ ***on the eve of*** *the election* **2** (*old use* or *literary*) evening

even 0→ /ˈiːvn/ *adv., adj., verb*
■ ***adv.*** **1** 0→ used to emphasize sth unexpected or surprising:

He never even opened the letter (= so he certainly didn't read it). ◇ *It was cold there even in summer* (= so it must have been very cold in winter). ◇ *Even a child can understand it* (= so adults certainly can). ◇ *She didn't even call to say she wasn't coming.* **2** used when you are comparing things, to make the comparison stronger: *You know even less about it than I do.* ◇ *She's even more intelligent than her sister.* **3** used to introduce a more exact description of sb/sth: *It's an unattractive building, ugly even.* ➲ note at ALTHOUGH

IDM **even as** (*formal*) just at the same time as sb does sth or as sth else happens: *Even as he shouted the warning the car skidded.* **even if/though** despite the fact or belief that; no matter whether: *I'll get there, even if I have to walk.* ◇ *I like her, even though she can be annoying at times.* ➲ note at ALTHOUGH ˌ**even ˈnow/ˈthen 1** despite what has/had happened: *I've shown him the photographs but even now he won't believe me.* ◇ *Even then she would not admit her mistake.* **2** (*formal*) at this or that exact moment: *The troops are even now preparing to march into the city.* ˌ**even ˈso** despite that: *There are a lot of spelling mistakes; even so, it's quite a good essay.* ➲ more at LESS *adv.*

■ *adj.*

▸ SMOOTH/LEVEL **1** smooth, level and flat: *You need an even surface to work on.* OPP **uneven**

▸ NOT CHANGING **2** not changing very much in amount, speed, etc: *an even temperature all year* ◇ *Children do not learn at an even pace.* OPP **uneven**

▸ EQUAL **3** (of an amount of sth) equal or the same for each person, team, place, etc: *Our scores are now even.* ◇ *the even distribution of food* OPP **uneven 4** (of two people or teams) equally balanced or of an equal standard: *an even contest* ◇ *The two players were pretty even.* OPP **uneven**

▸ NUMBERS **5** that can be divided exactly by two: *4, 6, 8, 10 are all* ***even numbers***. OPP **odd**

▸ SAME SIZE **6** equally spaced and the same size: *even features/teeth* OPP **uneven**

▸ CALM **7** calm; not changing or becoming upset: *She has a very even temperament.* ◇ *He spoke in a steady, even voice.* ▸ **even·ness** /ˈiːvənnəs/ *noun* [U]

IDM **be ˈeven** (*informal*) to no longer owe sb money or a favour **be/get ˈeven (with sb)** (*informal*) to cause sb the same amount of trouble or harm as they have caused you: *I'll get even with you for this, just you wait.* **break ˈeven** to complete a piece of business, etc. without either losing money or making a profit: *The company just about broke even last year.* **have an even ˈchance (of doing sth)** to be equally likely to do or not do sth: *She has more than an even chance of winning tomorrow.* **on an even ˈkeel** living, working or happening in a calm way, with no sudden changes, especially after a difficult time ➲ more at HONOUR *n.*

■ *verb*

IDM ˌ**even the ˈscore** to harm or punish sb who has harmed or cheated you in the past

PHR V ˌ**even ˈout** to become level or steady, usually after varying a lot: *House prices keep rising and falling but they should eventually even out.* ˌ**even sth↔ˈout** to spread things equally over a period of time or among a number of people: *He tried to even out the distribution of work among his employees.* ˌ**even sth↔ˈup** to make a situation or a competition more equal

ˌ**even-ˈhanded** *adj.* completely fair, especially when dealing with different groups of people

even·ing /ˈiːvnɪŋ/ *noun*

1 [C, U] the part of the day between the afternoon and the time you go to bed: *I'll see you tomorrow evening.* ◇ *Come over on Thursday evening.* ◇ *What do you usually do* ***in the evening***? ◇ *She's going to her sister's* ***for the evening***. ◇ *the long winter evenings* ◇ *the evening performance* ➲ see also GOOD EVENING **2** [C] an event of a particular type happening in the evening: *a musical evening at school* (= when music is performed) ▸ **even·ings** *adv.*: (*especially NAmE*) *He works evenings.* IDM see OTHER *adj.*

ˈ**evening class** *noun* a course of study for adults in the evening: *an evening class in car maintenance* ◇ *to* ***go to/attend evening classes***

ˈ**evening dress** *noun* **1** [U] elegant clothes worn for formal occasions in the evening: *Everyone was in evening dress.* **2** [C] a woman's long formal dress

ˌ**evening ˈprimrose** *noun* [C, U] a plant with yellow flowers that open in the evening, sometimes used as a medicine

the ˌ**evening ˈstar** *noun* [sing.] the planet Venus, when it is seen in the western sky after the sun has set

even·ly /ˈiːvnli/ *adv.* **1** in a smooth, regular or equal way: *Make sure the paint covers the surface evenly.* ◇ *She was fast asleep, breathing evenly.* ◇ ***evenly spaced*** *at four cm apart* **2** with equal amounts for each person or in each place: ***evenly distributed/divided*** ◇ *Incidence of the disease is fairly* ***evenly spread*** *across Europe.* ◇ *The two teams are very* ***evenly matched*** (= are equally likely to win). **3** calmly; without showing any emotion: *'I warned you not to phone me,' he said evenly.*

ˌ**even ˈmoney** *noun* (*BrE* also **evens** [pl.]) (in betting) ODDS that give an equal chance of winning or losing and that mean a person has the chance of winning the same amount of money that he or she has bet

even·song /ˈiːvnsɒŋ; *NAmE* -sɔːŋ; -sɑːŋ/ *noun* [U] the service of evening prayer in the Anglican Church ➲ compare MATINS, VESPERS

event /ɪˈvent/ *noun*

1 a thing that happens, especially sth important: *The election was the main event of 2008.* ◇ *In the light of later events the decision was proved right.* ◇ *The decisions we take now may influence* ***the course of events*** (= the way things happen) *in the future.* ◇ *Everyone was frightened by the strange* ***sequence of events***. ◇ ***In the normal course of events*** (= if things had happened as expected) *she would have gone with him.* **2** a planned public or social occasion: *a fund-raising event* ◇ *the social event of the year* **3** one of the races or competitions in a sports programme: *The 800 metres is the fourth event of the afternoon.* ➲ see also FIELD EVENT, TRACK EVENT

IDM **after the eˈvent** (*BrE*) after sth has happened: *Anyone can be wise after the event.* **in ˈany event | at ˈall events** used to emphasize or show that sth is true or will happen in spite of other circumstances SYN **in any case**: *I think she'll agree to do it but in any event, all she can say is 'no'.* **in the eˈvent** when the situation actually happened: *I got very nervous about the exam, but in the event, I needn't have worried; it was really easy.* **in the event of sth | in the event that sth happens** if sth happens: *In the event of an accident, call this number.* ◇ *Sheila will inherit everything in the event of his death.* **in ˈthat event** if that happens: *In that event, we will have to reconsider our offer.* ➲ more at HAPPY, WISE *adj.*

ˌ**even-ˈtempered** *adj.* not easily made angry or upset

event·ful /ɪˈventfl/ *adj.* full of things that happen, especially exciting, important or dangerous things: *an eventful day/life/journey*

even·tide /ˈiːvntaɪd/ *noun* [U] (*old use* or *literary*) evening

event·ing /ɪˈventɪŋ/ (also ˌ**three-day eˈventing**) *noun* [U] the sport of taking part in competitions riding horses. These are often held over three days and include riding across country, jumping and DRESSAGE.

even·tual AW /ɪˈventʃuəl/ *adj.* [only before noun] happening at the end of a period of time or of a process: *the eventual winner of the tournament* ◇ *It is impossible to predict what the eventual outcome will be.* ◇ *The village school may face eventual closure.*

even·tu·al·ity AW /ɪˌventʃuˈæləti/ *noun* (*pl.* -ies) (*formal*) something that may possibly happen, especially sth unpleasant: *We were prepared for* ***every eventuality***. ◇ *The money had been saved* ***for just such an eventuality***.

even·tu·al·ly AW /ɪˈventʃuəli/ *adv.* at the end of a period of time or a series of events: *Our flight eventually left five hours late.* ◇ *I'll get round to mending it eventually.* ◇ *She hopes to get a job on the local news-*

E

paper and eventually work for 'The Times'. HELP Use **finally** for the last in a list of things.

even·tu·ate /ɪ'ventʃueɪt/ *verb* [I] (*formal*) to happen as a result of sth

ever 0~ /'evə(r)/ *adv.*
1 0~ used in negative sentences and questions, or sentences with *if* to mean 'at any time': *Nothing ever happens here.* ◊ *Don't you ever get tired?* ◊ *If you're ever in Miami, come and see us.* ◊ *'Have you ever thought of changing your job?' 'No, never/No I haven't.'* ◊ *'Have you ever been to Rome?' 'Yes, I have, actually. Not long ago.'* ◊ *She* **hardly ever** (= almost never) *goes out.* ◊ *We see them very seldom,* **if ever**. ◊ (*informal*) *I'll* **never ever** *do that again!* **2** 0~ used for emphasis when you are comparing things: *It was raining harder than ever.* ◊ *It's my* **best ever** *score.* **3** (rather *formal*) all the time or every time; always: *Paul, ever the optimist, agreed to try again.* ◊ *She married the prince and they* **lived happily ever after**. ◊ *He said he would love her* **for ever** (**and ever**). ◊ *Their debts grew ever larger* (= kept increasing). ◊ *the ever-growing problem* ◊ *an ever-present danger* **4** used after *when, why*, etc. to show that you are surprised or shocked: *Why ever did you agree?*
IDM **all sb ever does is ...** used to emphasize that sb does the same thing very often, usually in an annoying way: *All he ever does is grumble about things.* **did you 'ever (...)!** (*old-fashioned, informal*) used to show that you are surprised or shocked: *Did you ever hear anything like it?* **ever since (...)** 0~ continuously since the time mentioned: *He's had a car ever since he was 18.* ◊ *I was bitten by a dog once and I've been afraid of them ever since.* **'ever so/'ever such a** (*informal, especially BrE*) very; really: *He looks ever so smart.* ◊ *She's ever such a nice woman.* ◊ *It's ever so easy.* **if ˌever there 'was (one)** (*informal*) used to emphasize that sth is certainly true: *That was a disaster if ever there was one!* **was/is/does, etc. sb 'ever!** (*informal, especially NAmE*) used to emphasize sth you are talking about: *'You must have been upset by that.' 'Was I ever!'* **yours 'ever/ever 'yours** sometimes used at the end of an informal letter, before you write your name

ever·green /'evəgriːn; *NAmE* 'evərg-/ *noun* a tree or bush that has green leaves all through the year ➲ VISUAL VOCAB page V8 ➲ compare CONIFER, DECIDUOUS ▸ **ever·green** *adj.*: *evergreen shrubs* ◊ (*figurative*) *a new production of Rossini's evergreen* (= always popular) *opera*

ever·last·ing /ˌevə'lɑːstɪŋ; *NAmE* ˌevər'læstɪŋ/ *adj.* **1** continuing for ever; never changing SYN **eternal**: *ever-lasting life/love* ◊ *an everlasting memory of her smile* ◊ **To his everlasting credit**, *he never told anyone what I'd done.* **2** (*disapproving*) continuing too long; repeated too often SYN **constant, interminable, never-ending**: *I'm tired of your everlasting complaints.* ▸ **ever·last·ing·ly** *adv.*

ever·more /ˌevə'mɔː(r); *NAmE* ˌevər'm-/ (also **for ever'more**) *adv.* (*literary*) always

every 0~ /'evri/ *det.*
1 0~ used with singular nouns to refer to all the members of a group of things or people: *She knows every student in the school.* ◊ *I could hear every word they said.* ◊ *We enjoyed every minute of our stay.* ◊ *Every day seemed the same to him.* ◊ **Every single** *time he calls, I'm out.* ◊ *I read* **every last** *article in the newspaper* (= all of them). ◊ *They were watching her every movement.* ◊ *Every one of their CDs has been a hit.* ➲ note at EACH **2** 0~ all possible: *We wish you every success.* ◊ *He had every reason to be angry.* **3** 0~ used to say how often sth happens or is done: *The buses go every 10 minutes.* ◊ *We had to stop every few miles.* ◊ *One in every three marriages ends in divorce.* ◊ *He has every third day off* (= he works for two days then has one day off then works for two days and so on). ◊ *We see each other* **every now and again**. ◊ **Every now and then** *he regretted his decision.*
IDM **every other** 0~ each ALTERNATE one (= the first, third, fifth, etc. one, but not the second, fourth, sixth, etc.): *They visit us every other week.*

every·body 0~ /'evribɒdi; *NAmE* -bɑːdi; -bʌdi/ *pron.* = EVERYONE: *Everybody knows Tom.* ◊ *Have you asked everybody?* ◊ *Didn't you like it?* **Everybody else** *did.*

every·day /'evrideɪ/ *adj.* [only before noun] used or happening every day or regularly; ordinary: *everyday objects* ◊ *The Internet has become part of* **everyday life**. ◊ *a small dictionary for everyday use*

Every·man /'evrimæn/ *noun* [sing.] an ordinary or typical person: *a story of Everyman*

every·one 0~ /'evriwʌn/ (also **every·body**) *pron.* every person; all people: *Everyone cheered and clapped.* ◊ *Everyone has a chance to win.* ◊ *Everyone brought their partner to the party.* ◊ (*formal*) *Everyone brought his or her partner to the party.* ◊ *The police questioned everyone in the room.* ◊ *The teacher commented on everyone's work.* ◊ **Everyone else** *was there.*

every·place /'evripleɪs/ *adv.* (*NAmE*) = EVERYWHERE

every·thing 0~ /'evriθɪŋ/ *pron.* (with a singular verb)
1 0~ all things: *Everything had gone.* ◊ *When we confronted him, he denied everything.* ◊ *Take this bag, and leave* **everything else** *to me.* ◊ *She seemed to* **have everything**—*looks, money, intelligence.* **2** 0~ the situation now; life generally: *Everything in the capital is now quiet.* ◊ *'How's everything with you?' 'Fine, thanks.'* **3** 0~ the most important thing: *Money isn't everything.* ◊ *My family* **means everything** *to me.*
IDM **and everything** (*informal*) and so on; and other similar things: *Have you got his name and address and everything?* ◊ *She told me about the baby and everything.*

every·where 0~ /'evriweə(r); *NAmE* -wer/ (*NAmE* also **every·place**) *adv., pron., conj.*
in, to or at every place; all places: *I've looked everywhere.* ◊ *He follows me everywhere.* ◊ *We'll have to eat here—***everywhere else** *is full.* ◊ *Everywhere we went was full of tourists.*

evict /ɪ'vɪkt/ *verb* **~ sb (from sth)** to force sb to leave a house or land, especially when you have the legal right to do so: *A number of tenants have been evicted for not paying the rent.* ▸ **evic·tion** /ɪ'vɪkʃn/ *noun* [U, C]: *to face eviction from your home*

Language Bank

evidence

Giving proof

- **There is clear evidence that** TV advertising influences what children buy.
- **It is clear** from numerous studies **that** TV advertising influences what children buy.
- Recent research **demonstrates** that TV advertising influences children's spending habits.
- Many parents think that TV advertising influences their children. This view **is supported by** the findings of a recent study, which **show** a clear link between television advertisements and children's spending habits.
- The findings also **reveal** that most children are unaware of the persuasive purpose of advertising.
- **There is little evidence that** children understand the persuasive intent of advertising.
- The results **contradict** claims that advertising is unrelated to children's spending habits.
- Manufacturers argue that it is difficult to **prove** that advertising alone influences what children buy.

➲ Language Banks at ARGUE, E.G., ILLUSTRATE

evi·dence 0~ AW /'evɪdəns/ *noun, verb*
■ ***noun*** **1** 0~ [U, C] the facts, signs or objects that make you believe that sth is true: **~ (of sth)** *There is convincing evidence of a link between exposure to sun and skin cancer.* ◊ *The room bore evidence of a struggle.* ◊ **~ (for sth)** *We found further scientific evidence for this theory.* ◊ **~ (that...)** *There is* **not a shred of evidence** *that the meeting actually took place.* ◊ **~ (to suggest, show, etc.)** *Have you any evidence to support this allegation?* ◊ **On the evidence of** *their recent*

matches, it is unlikely the Spanish team will win the cup. **2** 🔑 [U] the information that is used in court to try to prove sth: *I was asked to* ***give evidence*** (= to say what I knew, describe what I had seen, etc.) *at the trial.* ◇ *He was released when the judge ruled there was no evidence against him.* ➲ COLLOCATIONS at JUSTICE ➲ see also CIRCUMSTANTIAL
IDM **(be) in 'evidence** present and clearly seen: *The police were much in evidence at today's demonstration.* **turn King's/Queen's 'evidence** (*BrE*) (*US* **turn state's 'evidence**) to give information against other criminals in order to get a less severe punishment ➲ compare PLEA-BARGAINING ➲ more at BALANCE *n.*
■ *verb* [usually passive] **~ sth** (*formal*) to prove or show sth; to be evidence of sth SYN **testify to**: *The legal profession is still a largely male world,* ***as evidenced by*** *the small number of women judges.*

evi·dent AW /'evɪdənt/ *adj.* clear; easily seen SYN **obvious**: *The orchestra played with evident enjoyment.* ◇ **~ (to sb) (that...)** *It has now become evident to us that a mistake has been made.* ◇ **~ in/from sth** *The growing interest in history is clearly evident in the number of people visiting museums and country houses.* ➲ SYNONYMS at CLEAR ➲ see also SELF-EVIDENT

evi·den·tial AW /ˌevɪ'denʃl/ *adj.* [usually before noun] (*formal*) providing or connected with evidence: *The necessary evidential basis for her claim is lacking.*

evi·dent·ly AW /'evɪdəntli/ *adv.* **1** clearly; that can be seen or understood easily SYN **obviously**: *She walked slowly down the road, evidently in pain.* ◇ *'I'm afraid I couldn't finish the work last night.' 'Evidently not.'* **2** according to what people say SYN **apparently**: *Evidently, she had nothing to do with the whole affair.*

evil 🔑 /'iːvl; 'iːvɪl/ *adj., noun*
■ *adj.* **1** 🔑 (of people) enjoying harming others; morally bad and cruel: *an evil man* ◇ *an evil grin* **2** 🔑 having a harmful effect on people; morally bad: *evil deeds* ◇ *the evil effects of racism* **3** 🔑 connected with the DEVIL and with what is bad in the world: *evil spirits* **4** extremely unpleasant: *an evil smell*
IDM **the evil 'hour/'day/'moment** (often *humorous*) the time when you have to do sth difficult or unpleasant ➲ more at BREW *n.*, GENIUS *n.*
■ *noun* (*formal*) **1** 🔑 [U] a force that causes bad things to happen; morally bad behaviour: *the eternal struggle between good and evil* ◇ *the forces of evil* ◇ *You cannot pretend there's no evil in the world.* OPP **good** **2** 🔑 [C, usually pl.] a bad or harmful thing; the bad effect of sth: *the* ***evils of drugs/alcohol*** ◇ *social evils* IDM see LESSER, NECESSARY

'evil-doer *noun* (*formal*) a person who does very bad things

the ˌevil 'eye *noun* [sing.] the magic power to harm sb by looking at them

evil·ly /'iːvəli/ *adv.* in a morally bad or very unpleasant way: *to grin evilly* ◇ *to look evilly at sb*

evince /ɪ'vɪns/ *verb* **~ sth** (*formal*) to show clearly that you have a feeling or quality: *He evinced a strong desire to be reconciled with his family.*

evis·cer·ate /ɪ'vɪsəreɪt/ *verb* **~ sth** (*formal*) to remove the inner organs of a body SYN **disembowel**

evoca·tive /ɪ'vɒkətɪv; *NAmE* ɪ'vɑːk-/ *adj.* making you think of or remember a strong image or feeling, in a pleasant way: ***evocative smells/sounds/music*** ◇ **~ of sth** *Her new book is wonderfully evocative of village life.*

evoke /ɪ'vəʊk; *NAmE* ɪ'voʊk/ *verb* **~ sth** (*formal*) to bring a feeling, a memory or an image into your mind: *The music* ***evoked memories*** *of her youth.* ◇ *His case is unlikely to evoke public sympathy.* ► **evo·ca·tion** /ˌiːvəʊ'keɪʃn; *NAmE* ˌiːvoʊ-/ *noun* [C, U]: *a brilliant evocation of childhood in the 1940s*

evo·lu·tion AW /ˌiːvə'luːʃn; ˌev-/ *noun* [U] **1** (*biology*) the gradual development of plants, animals, etc. over many years as they adapt to changes in their environment: *the evolution of the human species* ◇ *Darwin's theory of evolution* **2** the gradual development of sth: *In politics Britain has preferred evolution to revolution* (= gradual development to sudden violent change).

evo·lu·tion·ary AW /ˌiːvə'luːʃənri; ˌev-; *NAmE* -neri/ *adj.* connected with evolution; connected with gradual development and change: *evolutionary theory* ◇ *evolutionary change* ► **evo·lu·tion·ar·ily** *adv.*

evo·lu·tion·ist AW /ˌiːvə'luːʃnɪst; ˌev-/ *noun, adj.*
■ *noun* a person who believes in the theories of EVOLUTION and NATURAL SELECTION
■ *adj.* relating to the theories of EVOLUTION and NATURAL SELECTION ► **evo·lu·tion·ism** /ˌiːvə'luːʃnɪzəm; ˌev-/ *noun*

E

evolve AW /i'vɒlv; *NAmE* i'vɑːlv/ *verb* **1** [I, T] to develop gradually, especially from a simple to a more complicated form; to develop sth in this way: **~ (from sth) (into sth)** *The idea evolved from a drawing I discovered in the attic.* ◇ *The company has evolved into a major chemical manufacturer.* ◇ **~ sth (from sth)** *Each school must evolve its own way of working.* **2** [I, T] (*biology*) (of plants, animals, etc.) to develop over time, often many generations, into forms that are better adapted to survive changes in their environment: **~ (from sth)** *The three species evolved from a single ancestor.* ◇ **~ sth** *The dolphin has evolved a highly developed jaw.*

ewe /juː/ *noun* a female sheep ➲ compare RAM

ewer /'juːə(r)/ *noun* a large JUG used in the past for carrying water

ex /eks/ *noun, prep.*
■ *noun* (*pl.* exes) (*informal*) a person's former wife, husband or partner: *The children are spending the weekend with my ex and his new wife.*
■ *prep.* (*BrE*) not including sth: *The price is £1 500 ex VAT.*

ex- 🔑 /eks/ *prefix* (in nouns)
former: *ex-wife* ◇ *ex-president*

ex·acer·bate /ɪg'zæsəbeɪt; *NAmE* ɪg'zæsərb-/ *verb* **~ sth** (*formal*) to make sth worse, especially a disease or problem SYN **aggravate**: *The symptoms may be exacerbated by certain drugs.* ► **ex·acer·ba·tion** *noun* [U, C]

exact 🔑 /ɪg'zækt/ *adj., verb*
■ *adj.* **1** 🔑 correct in every detail SYN **precise**: *She gave an exact description of the attacker.* ◇ ***an exact copy/replica*** *of the painting* ◇ *We need to know the exact time the incident occurred.* ◇ *What were his exact words?* ◇ *She's in her mid-thirties—thirty-six* ***to be exact***. ◇ *The colours were an exact match.* ◇ *He started to phone me at the exact moment I started to phone him* (= at the same time). ◇ *Her second husband was* ***the exact opposite*** *of her first* (= completely different). **2** 🔑 (of people) very accurate and careful about details SYN **meticulous, precise** **3** (of a science) using accurate measurements and following set rules SYN **precise**: *Assessing insurance risk can never be an exact science.* ► **exact·ness** *noun* [U]
■ *verb* (*formal*) **1** **~ sth (from sb)** to demand and get sth from sb: *She was determined to exact a promise from him.* **2** to make sth bad happen to sb: **~ sth** *He exacted* (= took) *a terrible revenge for their treatment of him.* ◇ **~ sth from sb** *Stress can exact a high price from workers* (= can affect them badly). ► **exac·tion** /ɪg'zækʃn/ *noun* [C, U] (*formal*)

exact·ing /ɪg'zæktɪŋ/ *adj.* needing or demanding a lot of effort and care about details SYN **demanding**: *exacting work* ◇ *products designed to meet the exacting standards of today's marketplace* ◇ *He was an exacting man to work for.*

exac·ti·tude /ɪg'zæktɪtjuːd; *NAmE* -tuːd/ *noun* [U] (*formal*) the quality of being very accurate and exact

exact·ly 🔑 /ɪg'zæktli/ *adv.*
1 🔑 used to emphasize that sth is correct in every way or in every detail SYN **precisely**: *I know exactly how she felt.* ◇ *Do exactly as I tell you.* ◇ *It happened almost exactly a year ago.* ◇ *It's exactly nine o'clock.* ◇ *You haven't changed at all—you still look* ***exactly the same***. ◇ *His words had* ***exactly the opposite*** *effect.* ◇ *Your answer is exactly right.* ◇ *It was a warm day, if not exactly hot.* **2** 🔑 (*informal*) used to ask for more information about sth: *Where exactly did you stay in France?* ◇ (*disapproving*) *Exactly what are you trying to tell*

me? **3** 🔑 used as a reply, agreeing with what sb has just said, or emphasizing that it is correct: *'You mean somebody in this room must be the murderer?' 'Exactly.'*
IDM **not exactly** (*informal*) **1** 🔑 used when you are saying the opposite of what you really mean: *He wasn't exactly pleased to see us—in fact he refused to open the door.* ◇ *It's not exactly beautiful, is it?* (= it's ugly) **2** 🔑 used when you are correcting sth that sb has said: *'So he told you you'd got the job?' 'Not exactly, but he said they were impressed with me.'*

E

ex·ag·ger·ate 🔑 /ɪɡˈzædʒəreɪt/ *verb* [I, T] to make sth seem larger, better, worse or more important than it really is: *The hotel was really filthy and I'm not exaggerating.* ◇ **~ sth** *He tends to exaggerate the difficulties.* ◇ *I'm sure he exaggerates his Irish accent* (= tries to sound more Irish than he really is). ◇ *Demand for the product has been greatly exaggerated.*

ex·ag·ger·ated 🔑 /ɪɡˈzædʒəreɪtɪd/ *adj.* **1** 🔑 made to seem larger, better, worse or more important than it really is or needs to be: *to make **greatly/grossly/wildly exaggerated** claims* ◇ *She has an exaggerated sense of her own importance.* **2** 🔑 (of an action) done in a way that makes people notice it: *He looked at me with exaggerated surprise.* ▸ **ex·ag·ger·ated·ly** *adv.*

ex·ag·ger·ation /ɪɡˌzædʒəˈreɪʃn/ *noun* [C, usually sing., U] a statement or description that makes sth seem larger, better, worse or more important than it really is; the act of making a statement like this: *a **slight/gross/wild exaggeration*** ◇ *It would be an exaggeration to say I knew her well—I only met her twice.* ◇ *It's no exaggeration to say that most students have never read a complete Shakespeare play.* ◇ *He told his story simply and without exaggeration.*

exalt /ɪɡˈzɔːlt/ *verb* (*formal*) **1 ~ sb (to sth)** to make sb rise to a higher rank or position, sometimes to one that they do not deserve **2 ~ sb/sth** to praise sb/sth very much

exalt·ation /ˌeɡzɔːlˈteɪʃn/ *noun* [U] (*formal*) **1** a feeling of very great joy or happiness **2** an act of raising sth/sb to a high position or rank: *the exaltation of emotion above logical reasoning*

exalt·ed /ɪɡˈzɔːltɪd/ *adj.* **1** (*formal* or *humorous*) of high rank, position or great importance: *She was the only woman to rise to such an exalted position.* ◇ *You're moving in very exalted circles!* **2** (*formal*) full of great joy and happiness: *I felt exalted and newly alive.*

exam 🔑 /ɪɡˈzæm/ (also *formal* **exam·in·ation**) *noun* **1** 🔑 a formal written, spoken or practical test, especially at school or college, to see how much you know about a subject, or what you can do: *to **take an exam*** ◇ *to **pass/fail an exam*** ◇ *an **exam paper*** ◇ *I got my **exam results** today.* ◇ *A lot of students suffer from **exam nerves**.* ◇ (*BrE*) *I hate **doing exams**.* ◇ (*BrE, formal*) *to **sit an exam*** ◇ (*BrE*) *to **mark an exam*** ◇ (*NAmE*) *to **grade an exam*** ◇ (*BrE*) *She did well **in her exams**.* ◇ (*NAmE*) *She did well **on her exams**.* ➲ COLLOCATIONS at EDUCATION **2** 🔑 (*NAmE*) a medical test of a particular part of the body: *an eye exam*

More About

exams

- **Exam** is the usual word for a written, spoken or practical test at school or college, especially an important one that you need to do in order to get a qualification. **Examination** is a very formal word. A **test** is something that students might be given in addition to, or sometimes instead of, regular exams, to see how much they have learned. A very short informal test is called a **quiz** in *NAmE*. **Quiz** in both *NAmE* and *BrE* also means a contest in which people try to answer questions: *a trivia quiz* ◇ *a quiz show.*

exam·in·ation 🔑 /ɪɡˌzæmɪˈneɪʃn/ *noun* **1** 🔑 [C] (*formal*) = EXAM: *to sit an examination in mathematics* ◇ *successful candidates in GCSE examinations* ◇ *Applicants are selected for jobs on the results of a competitive examination.* HELP Use: ***take/do/sit an examination*** not ~~*write an examination*~~. **2** 🔑 [U, C] the act of looking at or considering sth very carefully: *Careful examination of the ruins revealed an even earlier temple.* ◇ ***On closer examination** it was found that the signature was not genuine.* ◇ *Your proposals are still **under examination**.* ◇ *The issue needs **further examination**.* ◇ *The chapter concludes with a brief examination of some of the factors causing family break-up.* **3** 🔑 [C] a close look at sth/sb, especially to see if there is anything wrong or to find the cause of a problem: *a medical examination* ◇ *a post-mortem examination* ➲ see also CROSS-EXAMINATION

exam·ine 🔑 /ɪɡˈzæmɪn/ *verb* **1** 🔑 to consider or study an idea, a subject, etc. very carefully: **~ sth** *These ideas will be examined in more detail in Chapter 10.* ◇ **~ how, what, etc...** *It is necessary to examine how the proposals can be carried out.* ➲ LANGUAGE BANK at ABOUT **2** 🔑 to look at sb/sth closely, to see if there is anything wrong or to find the cause of a problem: **~ sb/sth** *The doctor examined her but could find nothing wrong.* ◇ **~ sth/sb for sth** *The goods were examined for damage on arrival.* ➲ SYNONYMS at CHECK **3 ~ sb (in/on sth)** (*formal*) to give sb a test to see how much they know about a subject or what they can do: *The students will be examined in all subjects at the end of term.* ◇ *You are only being examined on this semester's work.* **4 ~ sb** (*law*) to ask sb questions formally, especially in court ➲ see also CROSS-EXAMINE IDM see NEED *v.*

Synonyms

examine

analyse • review • study • discuss

These words all mean to think about, study or describe sb/sth carefully, especially in order to understand them, form an opinion of them or make a decision about them.

examine to think about, study or describe an idea, subject or piece of work very carefully: *These ideas will be examined in more detail in Chapter 10.*

analyse/analyze to examine the nature or structure of sth, especially by separating it into its parts, in order to understand or explain it: *The job involves gathering and analysing data.* ◇ *He tried to analyse his feelings.*

review to examine sth again, especially so that you can decide if it is necessary to make changes: *The government will review the situation later in the year.*

study to examine sb/sth in order to understand them or it: *We will study the report carefully before making a decision.*

EXAMINE OR STUDY?

You **examine** sth in order to understand it or to help other people understand it, for example by describing it in a book; you **study** sth in order to understand it yourself.

discuss to write or talk about sth in detail, showing the different ideas and opinions about it: *This topic will be discussed at greater length in the next chapter.*

PATTERNS

- to examine/analyse/review/study/discuss **what/how/whether...**
- to examine/analyse/review/study/discuss the **situation/evidence**
- to examine/analyse/review/study/discuss sth **carefully/critically/systematically/briefly**

exam·inee /ɪɡˌzæmɪˈniː/ *noun* a person who is being tested to see how much they know about a subject or what they can do; a person who is taking an exam

exam·in·er /ɪɡˈzæmɪnə(r)/ *noun* **1** a person who writes the questions for, or marks/grades, a test of knowledge or ability: *The papers are sent to **external examiners*** (= ones not connected with the students' school or college). **2** (*especially NAmE*) a person who has the official duty to check that things are being done correctly and according to the rules of an organization; a person who officially examines sth ➲ see also MEDICAL EXAMINER

ex·ample 🔑 /ɪɡˈzɑːmpl; *NAmE* -ˈzæmpl/ *noun* **1** 🔑 **~ (of sth)** something such as an object, a fact or a situation that shows, explains or supports what you say: *Can you give me an example of what you mean?* ◇ *This dictionary has many examples of how words are used.* ◇ *Just to give you an example of his generosity—he gave me his old car and wouldn't take any money for it.* ◇ *It is important to cite examples to support your argument.* ➲ LANGUAGE BANK at E.G. **2** 🔑 **~ (of sth)** a thing that is typical of or represents a particular group or set: *This is a good example of the artist's early work.* ◇ *It is a* ***perfect example*** *of a medieval castle.* ◇ *Japan is often quoted as the* ***prime example*** *of a modern industrial nation.* ◇ *It is a* ***classic example*** *of how not to design a new city centre.* **3** 🔑 a person or their behaviour that is thought to be a good model for others to copy: **~ (to sb)** *Her courage is an example to us all.* ◇ *He* ***sets an example*** *to the other students.* ◇ **~ (of sth)** *She is a* ***shining example*** *of what people with disabilities can achieve.* ◇ *He is a captain who leads* ***by example***. **4** a person's behaviour, either good or bad, that other people copy: *It would be a mistake to* ***follow his example***.
IDM **for example** 🔑 (*abbr.* **e.g.**) used to emphasize sth that explains or supports what you are saying; used to give an example of what you are saying: *There is a similar word in many languages, for example in French and Italian.* ◇ *The report is incomplete; it does not include sales in France, for example.* ◇ *It is possible to combine Computer Science with other subjects, for example Physics.* ➲ LANGUAGE BANK at E.G. **make an example of sb** to punish sb as a warning to others not to do the same thing

Synonyms

example

case • **instance** • **specimen** • **illustration**

These are all words for a thing or situation that is typical of a particular group or set, and is sometimes used to support an argument.

example something such as an object, a fact or a situation that shows, explains or supports what you say; a thing that is typical of or represents a particular group or set: *Can you give me an example of what you mean?*

case a particular situation or a situation of a particular type; a situation that relates to a particular person or thing: *In some cases people have had to wait several weeks for an appointment.*

instance (*rather formal*) a particular situation or a situation of a particular type: *The report highlights a number of instances of injustice.*

specimen an example of sth, especially an animal or plant: *The aquarium has some interesting specimens of unusual tropical fish.*

illustration (*rather formal*) a story, an event or an example that clearly shows the truth about sth: *The statistics are a clear illustration of the point I am trying to make.*

EXAMPLE OR ILLUSTRATION?

An **illustration** is often used to show that sth is true. An **example** is used to help to explain sth.

PATTERNS

- a(n) example/case/instance/specimen/illustration **of** sth
- **in** a particular case/instance
- **for** example/instance

ex·as·per·ate /ɪɡˈzæspəreɪt; *BrE* also -ˈzɑːsp-/ *verb* **~ sb** to annoy or irritate sb very much SYN **infuriate** ▶ **ex·as·per·ation** /ɪɡˌzæspəˈreɪʃn; *BrE* also -ˌzɑːsp-/ *noun* [U]: *He shook his head in exasperation.* ◇ *a groan/look/sigh of exasperation*

ex·as·per·ated /ɪɡˈzæspəreɪtɪd; *BrE* also -ˈzɑːsp-/ *adj.* extremely annoyed, especially if you cannot do anything to improve the situation SYN **infuriated**: *'Why won't you answer me?' he asked in an exasperated voice.* ◇ *She was becoming exasperated with all the questions they were asking.* ▶ **ex·as·per·ated·ly** *adv.*

ex·as·per·at·ing /ɪɡˈzæspəreɪtɪŋ; *BrE* also -ˈzɑːsp-/ *adj.* extremely annoying SYN **infuriating**

ex·cav·ate /ˈekskəveɪt/ *verb* **1** to dig in the ground to look for old buildings or objects that have been buried for a long time; to find sth by digging in this way: **~ sth** *The site has been excavated by archaeologists.* ◇ **~ sth from sth** *pottery and weapons excavated from the burial site* **2 ~ sth** (*formal*) to make a hole, etc. in the ground by digging: *The body was discovered when builders excavated the area.*

ex·cav·ation /ˌekskəˈveɪʃn/ *noun* **1** [C, U] the activity of digging in the ground to look for old buildings or objects that have been buried for a long time **2** [C, usually pl.] a place where people are digging to look for old buildings or objects: *The excavations are open to the public.* **3** [U] the act of digging, especially with a machine

ex·cav·ator /ˈekskəveɪtə(r)/ *noun* **1** a large machine that is used for digging and moving earth ➲ VISUAL VOCAB page V47 **2** a person who digs in the ground to look for old buildings and objects

ex·ceed AW /ɪkˈsiːd/ *verb* (*formal*) **1 ~ sth** to be greater than a particular number or amount: *The price will not exceed £100.* ◇ *His achievements have* ***exceeded expectations***. **2 ~ sth** to do more than the law or an order, etc. allows you to do: *She was exceeding the speed limit* (= driving faster than is allowed). ◇ *The officers had exceeded their authority.* ➲ see also EXCESS

ex·ceed·ing·ly /ɪkˈsiːdɪŋli/ *adv.* (*formal*, becoming *old-fashioned*) extremely; very; very much SYN **exceptionally**

excel /ɪkˈsel/ *verb* (-ll-) **1** [I] to be very good at doing sth: **~ (in/at sth)** *She has always excelled in foreign languages.* ◇ *As a child he excelled at music and art.* ◇ **~ (at doing sth)** *The team excels at turning defence into attack.* **2** [T] **~ yourself** (*BrE*) to do extremely well and even better than you usually do: *Rick's cooking was always good but this time he really excelled himself.*

Synonyms

excellent

outstanding • **perfect** • **superb**

These words all describe sth that is extremely good.

excellent extremely good. NOTE **Excellent** is used especially about standards of service or of sth that sb has worked to produce: *The rooms are excellent value at $20 a night.* ◇ *He speaks excellent English.* NOTE **Excellent** is also used to show that you are very pleased about sth or that you approve of sth: *You can all come? Excellent!*

outstanding extremely good. NOTE **Outstanding** is used especially about how well sb does sth or how good sb is at sth: *an outstanding achievement*

perfect extremely good. NOTE **Perfect** is used especially about conditions or how suitable sth is for a purpose: *Conditions were perfect for walking.* ◇ *She came up with the perfect excuse.*

superb (*informal*) extremely good or impressive: *The facilities at the hotel are superb.*

PATTERNS

- a(n) excellent/outstanding/perfect/superb **job/performance**
- a(n) excellent/outstanding/superb **achievement**
- **really/absolutely/quite** excellent/outstanding/perfect/superb

ex·cel·lence /ˈeksələns/ *noun* [U] the quality of being extremely good: *a reputation for academic excellence* ◇ **~ in sth** *The hospital is recognized as* ***a centre of excellence*** *in research and teaching.* ➲ see also PAR EXCELLENCE

Ex·cel·lency /ˈeksələnsi/ *noun* **His/Her/Your Excel·lency** (*pl.* -ies) a title used when talking to or about sb who has a very important official position, especially an AMBASSADOR: *Good evening, your Excellency.* ◇ *their Excellencies the French and Spanish Ambassadors*

E

ex·cel·lent 🔑 /ˈeksələnt/ *adj.* **1** 🔑 extremely good: *an excellent meal* ◇ *excellent service* ◇ *At $300 the bike is* ***excellent value.*** ◇ *She speaks excellent French.* ◇ (*informal*) *It was absolutely excellent.* **2** 🔑 used to show that you are very pleased about sth or that you approve of sth: *You can all come? Excellent!* ▸ **ex·cel·lent·ly** *adv.*

ex·cept 🔑 /ɪkˈsept/ *prep., conj., verb*

▪ ***prep.*** 🔑 (also **exˈcept for**) used before you mention the only thing or person about which a statement is not true **SYN** **apart from**: *We work every day except Sunday.* ◇ *They all came except Matt.* ◇ *I had nothing on except for my socks.* ➲ note at BESIDES

▪ ***conj.*** 🔑 **~ (that)...** used before you mention sth that makes a statement not completely true **SYN** **apart from the fact that**: *I didn't tell him anything except that I needed the money.* ◇ *Our dresses were the same except mine was red.*

▪ ***verb*** [usually passive] (*formal*) to not include sb/sth: **~ sb/sth** *The sanctions ban the sale of any products excepting medical supplies and food.* ◇ *Tours are arranged all year round (January excepted).* ◇ **~ sb/sth from sth** *Children under five are excepted from the survey.* **IDM** see PRESENT *adj.*

Language Bank

except

Making an exception

- She wrote all of the songs on the album **except for** the final track.
- **Apart from/aside from** the final track, all of the songs on the album were written by her.
- The songwriting — **with a few minor exceptions** — is of a very high quality.
- With only **one or two exceptions**, the songwriting is of a very high quality.
- The majority of the compositions are less than three minutes long, **with the notable exception of** the title track.
- **With the exception of** the title track, this album is a huge disappointment.
- Here is a list of all the band's CDs, **excluding** unofficial 'bootleg' recordings.

ex·cep·tion 🔑 /ɪkˈsepʃn/ *noun*

1 🔑 a person or thing that is not included in a general statement: *Most of the buildings in the town are modern, but the church is an exception.* ◇ *With very few exceptions, private schools get the best exam results.* ◇ *Nobody had much money at the time and I was* ***no exception.*** ➲ LANGUAGE BANK at EXCEPT **2** 🔑 a thing that does not follow a rule: *Good writing is unfortunately* ***the exception rather than the rule*** (= it is unusual). ◇ *There are always a lot of exceptions to grammar rules.*

IDM **the exception that proves the ˈrule** (*saying*) people say that sth is **the exception that proves the rule** when they are stating sth that seems to be different from the normal situation, but they mean that the normal situation remains true in general: *Most electronics companies have not done well this year, but ours is the exception that proves the rule.* **make an exˈception** 🔑 to allow sb not to follow the usual rule on one occasion: *Children are not usually allowed in, but I'm prepared to make an exception in this case.* **take exˈception to sth** to object strongly to sth; to be angry about sth: *I take great exception to the fact that you told my wife before you told me.* ◇ *No one could possibly take exception to his comments.* **with the exˈception of** 🔑 except; not including: *All his novels are set in Italy with the exception of his last.* ➲ LANGUAGE BANK at EXCEPT **without exˈception** 🔑 used to emphasize that the statement you are making is always true and everyone or everything is included: *All students without exception must take the English examination.*

ex·cep·tion·al /ɪkˈsepʃənl/ *adj.* **1** unusually good **SYN** **outstanding**: *At the age of five he showed exceptional talent as a musician.* ◇ *The quality of the recording is* ***quite exceptional.*** **2** very unusual: *This deadline will be extended only* ***in exceptional circumstances.*** **OPP** **unexceptional**

ex·cep·tion·al·ly /ɪkˈsepʃənəli/ *adv.* **1** used before an adjective or adverb to emphasize how strong or unusual the quality is: *The weather, even for January, was exceptionally cold.* ◇ *I thought Bill played exceptionally well.* **2** only in unusual circumstances: *Exceptionally, students may be accepted without formal qualifications.*

ex·cerpt /ˈeksɜːpt; *NAmE* -sɜːrpt/ *noun* **~ (from sth)** a short piece of writing, music, film, etc. taken from a longer whole ▸ **ex·cerpt** *verb*: **~ sth (from sth)** *The document was excerpted from an unidentified FBI file.*

ex·cess *noun, adj.*

▪ ***noun*** /ɪkˈses/ **1** [sing., U] more than is necessary, reasonable or acceptable: *You can throw away any excess.* ◇ **~ of sth** *Are you suffering from an excess of stress in your life?* ◇ *In an excess of enthusiasm I agreed to work late.* ◇ *He started drinking* ***to excess*** *after losing his job.* ◇ *The increase will not be* ***in excess of*** (= more than) *two per cent.* **2** [C, U] an amount by which sth is larger than sth else: *We cover costs up to £600 and then you pay the excess.* **3** [C, usually sing.] (*BrE*) (*NAmE* **de·duct·ible**) the part of an insurance claim that a person has to pay while the insurance company pays the rest: *There is an excess of £100 on each claim under this policy.* **4 excesses** [pl.] extreme behaviour that is unacceptable, illegal or immoral: *We need a free press to curb government excesses.*

▪ ***adj.*** /ˈekses/ [only before noun] in addition to an amount that is necessary, usual or legal: *Excess food is stored as fat.* ◇ *Driving with excess alcohol in the blood is a serious offence.*

ˌexcess ˈbaggage *noun* [U] bags, cases, etc. taken on to a plane that weigh more than the amount each passenger is allowed to carry without paying extra

ex·ces·sive /ɪkˈsesɪv/ *adj.* greater than what seems reasonable or appropriate: *They complained about the excessive noise coming from the upstairs flat.* ◇ *The amounts she borrowed were not excessive.* ◇ *Excessive drinking can lead to stomach disorders.* ▸ **ex·ces·sive·ly** *adv.*: *excessively high prices*

ex·change 🔑 /ɪksˈtʃeɪndʒ/ *noun, verb*

▪ ***noun***

▸ GIVING AND RECEIVING **1** 🔑 [C, U] an act of giving sth to sb or doing sth for sb and receiving sth in return: *The exchange of prisoners took place this morning.* ◇ *We need to promote an open exchange of ideas and information.* ◇ *an* ***exchange of glances/insults*** ◇ *an* ***exchange of fire*** (= between enemy soldiers) ◇ *I buy you lunch and you fix my computer. Is that a* ***fair exchange?*** ◇ *Would you like my old TV* ***in exchange for*** *this camera?* ◇ *I'll type your report if you'll babysit* ***in exchange.*** ➲ see also PART EXCHANGE

▸ CONVERSATION/ARGUMENT **2** [C] a conversation or an argument: *There was only time for a brief exchange.* ◇ *The Prime Minister was involved in a* ***heated exchange*** *with opposition MPs.*

▸ OF MONEY **3** 🔑 [U] the process of changing an amount of one CURRENCY (= the money used in one country) for an equal value of another: *currency exchange facilities* ◇ *Where can I find the best* ***exchange rate/rate of exchange?*** ➲ see also FOREIGN EXCHANGE

▸ BETWEEN TWO COUNTRIES **4** 🔑 [C] an arrangement when two people or groups from different countries visit each other's homes or do each other's jobs for a short time: *Our school does an exchange with a school in France.* ◇ *Nick* *went on the French exchange.* ◇ *trade and cultural exchanges with China*

▸ BUILDING **5** (often **Exchange**) [C] (in compounds) a building where business people met in the past to buy and sell a particular type of goods: *the old Corn Exchange* ➲ see also STOCK EXCHANGE

▸ TELEPHONE **6** [C] = TELEPHONE EXCHANGE

■ ***verb***

▸ GIVE AND RECEIVE **1** 🔑 to give sth to sb and at the same time receive the same type of thing from them: **~ sth** *to* ***exchange ideas/news/information*** ◇ *Juliet and David* ***exchanged glances*** (= they looked at each other). ◇ *Everyone in the group exchanged email addresses.* ◇ **~ sth with sb** *I shook hands and exchanged a few words with the manager.* ◇ *The two men* ***exchanged blows*** (= hit each other).

▸ MONEY/GOODS **2** 🔑 to give or return sth that you have and get sth different or better instead **SYN change**: **~ sth** *If it doesn't fit, take it back and the store will exchange it.* ◇ **~ A for B** *You can exchange your currency for dollars in the hotel.*

▸ CONTRACTS **3 ~ contracts** (*especially BrE*) to sign a contract with the person that you are buying sth from, especially a house or land **IDM** see WORD *n.*

ex·change·able /ɪks'tʃeɪndʒəbl/ *adj.* that can be exchanged: *These tokens are exchangeable for DVDs only.*

ex·chequer /ɪks'tʃekə(r)/ *noun* [sing.] **1** (often **the Exchequer**) (in Britain) the government department that controls public money **SYN treasury** ➲ see also CHANCELLOR OF THE EXCHEQUER **2** the public or national supply of money: *This resulted in a considerable loss to the exchequer.*

ex·cise[1] /'eksaɪz/ *noun* [U] a government tax on some goods made, sold or used within a country: *new excise duties on low-alcohol drinks* ◇ *a sharp increase in vehicle excise* ◇ *an excise officer* (= an official whose job is to collect excise) ➲ compare CUSTOMS

ex·cise[2] /ɪk'saɪz/ *verb* **~ sth (from sth)** (*formal*) to remove sth completely: *Certain passages were excised from the book.*

ex·ci·sion /ɪk'sɪʒn/ *noun* [U, C] (*formal* or *technical*) the act of removing sth completely from sth; the thing removed

ex·cit·able /ɪk'saɪtəbl/ *adj.* (of people or animals) likely to become easily excited: *a class of excitable ten-year-olds* ▸ **ex·cit·abil·ity** /ɪkˌsaɪtə'bɪləti/ *noun* [U]

Synonyms

excited

ecstatic • elated • euphoric • rapturous • exhilarated

These words all describe feeling or showing happiness and enthusiasm.

excited feeling or showing happiness and enthusiasm: *The kids were excited about the holiday.*

ecstatic very happy, excited and enthusiastic; showing this enthusiasm: *Sally was ecstatic about her new job.*

elated happy and excited because of sth good that has happened or will happen: *I was elated with the thrill of success.*

euphoric very happy and excited, but usually only for a short time: *My euphoric mood could not last.*

rapturous expressing extreme pleasure or enthusiasm: *He was greeted with rapturous applause.*

exhilarated happy and excited, especially after physical activity: *She felt exhilarated with the speed.*

PATTERNS

- to **feel** excited/elated/euphoric/exhilarated
- to be excited/ecstatic/elated/euphoric **at** sth
- to be excited/ecstatic/elated **about** sth
- to be excited/elated/exhilarated **by** sth
- to be ecstatic/elated/exhilarated **with** sth

ex·cite 🔑 /ɪk'saɪt/ *verb*
1 🔑 **~ sb** to make sb feel very pleased, interested or enthusiastic, especially about sth that is going to happen: *The prospect of a year in India greatly excited her.* **2** to make sb nervous or upset and unable to relax: **~ sb** *Try not to excite your baby too much before bedtime.* ◇ **~ yourself** *Don't excite yourself* (= keep calm). **3** to make sb feel a particular emotion or react in a particular way **SYN arouse**: **~ sth** *to* ***excite attention/criticism/curiosity*** ◇ *The news has certainly* ***excited comment*** (= made people talk about it). ◇ **~ sth in sb** *The European Parliament is not an institution which excites interest in voters.* **4 ~ sb** to make sb feel sexual desire **SYN arouse** **5 ~ sth** (*formal*) to make a part of the body or part of a physical system more active **SYN stimulate**

ex·cited 🔑 /ɪk'saɪtɪd/ *adj.*
1 🔑 feeling or showing happiness and enthusiasm: **~ (about sth)** *The children were excited about opening their presents.* ◇ **~ (at sth)** *I'm really excited at the prospect of working abroad.* ◇ **~ (by sth)** *Don't get too excited by the sight of your name in print.* ◇ **~ (to do sth)** *He was very excited to be asked to play for Wales.* ◇ *The new restaurant is* ***nothing to get excited about*** (= not particularly good). ◇ *An excited crowd of people gathered around her.* **2** nervous or upset and unable to relax: *Some horses become excited when they're in traffic.* **3** feeling sexual desire **SYN aroused** ▸ **ex·cited·ly** *adv.*: *She waved excitedly as the car approached.*

ex·cite·ment 🔑 /ɪk'saɪtmənt/ *noun*
1 🔑 [U] the state of feeling excited: *The news caused great excitement among her friends.* ◇ *to feel a* ***surge/thrill/shiver of excitement*** ◇ *He was flushed* ***with excitement*** *at the thought.* ◇ *The dog leapt and wagged its tail* ***in excitement.*** ◇ ***In her excitement*** *she dropped her glass.* **2** [C] (*formal*) something that you find exciting: *The new job was not without its excitements.*

ex·cit·ing 🔑 /ɪk'saɪtɪŋ/ *adj.*
causing great interest or excitement: *one of the most exciting developments in biology in recent years* ◇ *They waited and waited for something exciting to happen.* ◇ *an* ***exciting prospect/possibility*** ◇ *an* ***exciting story/discovery*** ▸ **ex·cit·ing·ly** *adv.*

Synonyms

exciting

dramatic • heady • thrilling • exhilarating

These words all describe an event, experience or feeling that causes excitement.

exciting causing great interest or excitement: *This is one of the most exciting developments in biology in recent years.*

dramatic (of events or scenes) exciting and impressive: *They watched dramatic pictures of the police raid on TV.*

heady having a strong effect on your senses; making you feel excited and hopeful: *the heady days of youth*

thrilling exciting and enjoyable: *Don't miss next week's thrilling episode!*

exhilarating very exciting and enjoyable: *My first parachute jump was an exhilarating experience.*

EXCITING, THRILLING OR EXHILARATING?

Exhilarating is the strongest of these words and **exciting** the least strong. **Exciting** is the most general and can be used to talk about any activity, experience, feeling or event that excites you. **Thrilling** is used especially for contests and stories where the ending is uncertain. **Exhilarating** is used especially for physical activities that involve speed and/or danger.

PATTERNS

- a(n) exciting/dramatic/heady/thrilling/exhilarating **experience/moment**
- a(n) exciting/dramatic/heady **atmosphere**
- a(n) exciting/dramatic/thrilling **finish/finale/victory/win**

ex·claim /ɪk'skleɪm/ *verb* [I, T] to say sth suddenly and loudly, especially because of strong emotion or pain: *She opened her eyes and exclaimed in delight at the scene.* ◇ **+ speech** *'It isn't fair!', he exclaimed angrily.* ◇ **~ that...** *She exclaimed that it was useless.* ➲ SYNONYMS at CALL

ex·clam·ation /ˌekskləˈmeɪʃn/ *noun* a short sound, word or phrase spoken suddenly to express an emotion. *Oh!, Look out!* and *Ow!* are exclamations: *He gave an exclamation of surprise.*

E

excla'mation mark (*especially BrE*) (*NAmE* usually **excla'mation point**) *noun* the mark (!) that is written after an exclamation

ex·clama·tory /ɪk'sklæmətri; ek-; *NAmE* -tɔːri/ *adj.* (*formal*) (of language) expressing surprise or strong feelings

ex·clude 0→ AW /ɪk'skluːd/ *verb*
1 0→ **~ sth (from sth)** to deliberately not include sth in what you are doing or considering: *The cost of borrowing has been excluded from the inflation figures.* ◇ *Try excluding fat from your diet.* ◇ *Buses run every hour, Sundays excluded.* OPP **include** **2** 0→ **~ sb/sth (from sth)** to prevent sb/sth from entering a place or taking part in sth: *Women are still excluded from some London clubs.* ◇ (*BrE*) *Concern is growing over the number of children excluded from school* (= not allowed to attend because of bad behaviour). ◇ *She felt excluded by the other girls* (= they did not let her join in what they were doing). **3 ~ sth** to decide that sth is not possible: *We should not* ***exclude the possibility*** *of negotiation.* ◇ *The police have excluded theft as a motive for the murder.* OPP **include**

ex·clud·ing 0→ AW /ɪk'skluːdɪŋ/ *prep.* not including: *Lunch costs £10 per person, excluding drinks.* ➲ LANGUAGE BANK at EXCEPT

ex·clu·sion AW /ɪk'skluːʒn/ *noun* **1** [U] **~ (of sb/sth) (from sth)** the act of preventing sb/sth from entering a place or taking part in sth: *He was disappointed with his exclusion from the England squad.* ◇ *Exclusion of air creates a vacuum in the bottle.* ◇ *Memories of the past filled her mind* ***to the exclusion of*** *all else.* **2** [C] a person or thing that is not included in sth: *Check the list of exclusions in the insurance policy.* **3** [U] **~ (of sth)** the act of deciding that sth is not possible: *the exclusion of robbery as a motive* **4** [U, C] (*BrE*) a situation in which a child is banned from attending school because of bad behaviour: *the exclusion of disruptive students from school* ◇ *Two exclusions from one school in the same week is unusual.* OPP **inclusion**

ex·clu·sion·ary AW /ɪk'skluːʒənri/ *adj.* (*formal*) designed to prevent a particular person or group of people from taking part in sth or doing sth

ex'clusion order *noun* (*BrE*) an official order not to go to a particular place: *The judge placed an exclusion order on him, banning him from city centre shops.*

ex'clusion zone *noun* an area where people are not allowed to enter because it is dangerous or is used for secret activities

ex·clu·sive AW /ɪk'skluːsɪv/ *adj., noun*
▪ ***adj.*** **1** only to be used by one particular person or group; only given to one particular person or group: *The hotel has exclusive access to the beach.* ◇ *exclusive rights to televise the World Cup* ◇ *His mother has told 'The Times' about his death in an exclusive interview* (= not given to any other newspaper). **2** (of a group, society, etc.) not very willing to allow new people to become members, especially if they are from a lower social class: *He belongs to an exclusive club.* **3** of a high quality and expensive and therefore not often bought or used by most people: *an exclusive hotel* ◇ *exclusive designer clothes* **4** not able to exist or be a true statement at the same time as sth else: *The two options are not* ***mutually exclusive*** (= you can have them both). **5 ~ of sb/sth** not including sb/sth: *The price is for accommodation only, exclusive of meals.* OPP **inclusive** ▸ **ex·clu·sive·ly** AW *adv.*: *a charity that relies almost exclusively on voluntary contributions* **ex·clu·sive·ness** *noun* [U]
▪ ***noun*** an item of news or a story about famous people that is published in only one newspaper or magazine

ex·clu·siv·ity /ˌeksklu:'sɪvəti/ (also **ex·clu·sive·ness** /ɪk'skluːsɪvnəs/) *noun* [U] the quality of being exclusive: *The resort still preserves a feeling of exclusivity.* ◇ *a designer whose clothes have not lost their exclusiveness*

ex·com·mu·ni·cate /ˌekskə'mjuːnɪkeɪt/ *verb* **~ sb (for sth)** to punish sb by officially stating that they can no longer be a member of a Christian Church, especially the Roman Catholic Church ▸ **ex·com·mu·ni·ca·tion** /ˌekskəˌmjuːnɪ'keɪʃn/ *noun* [U, C]

ex·cori·ate /ˌeks'kɔːrieɪt/ *verb* **1 ~ sth** (*medical*) to irritate a person's skin so that it starts to come off **2 ~ sb/sth** (*formal*) to criticize sb/sth severely ▸ **ex·cori·ation** *noun* [U, C]

ex·cre·ment /'ekskrɪmənt/ *noun* [U] (*formal*) solid waste matter that is passed from the body through the BOWELS SYN **faeces**: *the pollution of drinking water by untreated human excrement* ▸ **ex·cre·men·tal** *adj.*

ex·cres·cence /ɪk'skresns/ *noun* (*formal*) an ugly lump that has grown on a part of an animal's body or on a plant: (*figurative*) *The new office block is an excrescence* (= it is very ugly).

ex·creta /ɪk'skriːtə/ *noun* [U] (*formal*) solid and liquid waste matter passed from the body: *human excreta*

ex·crete /ɪk'skriːt/ *verb* [I] (*technical*) to pass solid or liquid waste matter from the body ▸ **ex·cre·tion** /ɪk'skriːʃn/ *noun* [U, C]

ex·cre·tory /ɪks'kriːtəri; *NAmE* 'ekskrətɔːri/ *adj.* (*biology*) connected with getting rid of waste matter from the body: *the excretory organs*

ex·cru·ci·at·ing /ɪk'skruːʃieɪtɪŋ/ *adj.* extremely painful or bad: *The pain in my back was excruciating.* ◇ *She groaned at the memory, suffering all over again the excruciating embarrassment of those moments.* ➲ SYNONYMS at PAINFUL ▸ **ex·cru·ci·at·ing·ly** *adv.*: *excruciatingly uncomfortable* ◇ ***excruciatingly painful/boring/embarrassing***

ex·cul·pate /'ekskʌlpeɪt/ *verb* **~ sb** (*formal*) to prove or state officially that sb is not guilty of sth ▸ **ex·cul·pa·tion** *noun* [U]

ex·cur·sion /ɪk'skɜːʃn; *NAmE* ɪk'skɜːrʒn/ *noun* **1** a short journey made for pleasure, especially one that has been organized for a group of people: *They've gone* ***on an excursion*** *to York.* ➲ SYNONYMS at TRIP **2 ~ into sth** (*formal*) a short period of trying a new or different activity: *After a brief excursion into drama, he concentrated on his main interest, which was poetry.*

ex·cus·able /ɪk'skjuːzəbl/ *adj.* [not usually before noun] that can be excused SYN **forgivable**: *Doing it once was just about excusable — doing it twice was certainly not.* OPP **inexcusable**

ex·cuse 0→ *noun, verb*
▪ ***noun*** /ɪk'skjuːs/ **1** 0→ a reason, either true or invented, that you give to explain or defend your behaviour: *Late again! What's your excuse this time?* ◇ **~ (for sth)** *There's* ***no excuse for*** *such behaviour.* ◇ **~ (for doing sth)** *His excuse for forgetting her birthday was that he had lost his diary.* ◇ *You don't have to* ***make excuses*** *for her* (= try to think of reasons for her behaviour). ◇ *It's late. I'm afraid I'll have to* ***make my excuses*** (= say I'm sorry, give my reasons and leave). ➲ SYNONYMS at REASON **2** 0→ a good reason that you give for doing sth that you want to do for other reasons: **~ (for sth/for doing sth)** *It's just an excuse for a party.* ◇ **~ (to do sth)** *It gave me an excuse to take the car.* **3** a very bad example of sth: *Why get involved with that pathetic excuse for a human being?* **4** (*NAmE*) a note written by a parent or doctor to explain why a student cannot go to school or sb cannot go to work
▪ ***verb*** /ɪk'skjuːz/ **1** 0→ to forgive sb for sth that they have done, for example not being polite or making a small mistake: **~ sth** *Please excuse the mess.* ◇ **~ sb** *You must excuse my father—he's not always that rude.* ◇ **~ sb for sth/for doing sth** *I hope you'll excuse me for being so late.* ◇ (*BrE*) *You* ***might be excused for*** *thinking that Ben is in charge* (= he is not, but it is an easy mistake to make). ◇ **~ sb doing sth** (*formal*) *Excuse my interrupting you.* **2** 0→ **~ sth | ~ sb/**

yourself (**for sth/for doing sth**) to make your or sb else's behaviour seem less offensive by finding reasons for it SYN **justify**: *Nothing can excuse such rudeness.* **3 ~ sb/yourself** (**from sth**) to allow sb to leave; to say in a polite way that you are leaving: *Now if you'll excuse me, I'm a very busy man.* ◇ *She excused herself and left the meeting early.* **4** [usually passive] **~ sb** (**from sth/from doing sth**) | **~ sb sth** to allow sb to not do sth that they should normally do: *She was excused from giving evidence because of her age.*

IDM **ex'cuse me 1** used to politely get sb's attention, especially sb you do not know: *Excuse me, is this the way to the station?* **2** used to politely ask sb to move so that you can get past them: *Excuse me, could you let me through?* **3** used to say that you are sorry for interrupting sb or behaving in a slightly rude way: *Guy sneezed loudly. 'Excuse me,' he said.* **4** used to disagree politely with sb: *Excuse me, but I don't think that's true.* **5** used to politely tell sb that you are going to leave or talk to sb else: *'Excuse me for a moment,' she said and left the room.* **6** (*especially NAmE*) used to say sorry for pushing sb or doing sth wrong: *Oh, excuse me. I didn't see you there.* **7 excuse me?** (*NAmE*) used when you did not hear what sb said and you want them to repeat it ➲ more at FRENCH *n.*

ˌex-di'rectory *adj.* (*BrE*) (of a person or telephone number) not listed in the public telephone book, at the request of the owner of the telephone. The telephone company will not give ex-directory numbers to people who ask for them: *an ex-directory number* ◇ *She's ex-directory.* ➲ see also UNLISTED

exeat /'eksiæt/ *noun* (*BrE*) permission from an institution such as a BOARDING SCHOOL to be away from it for a period of time

exec /ɪg'zek/ *noun* (*informal*) an executive in a business

exe·crable /'eksɪkrəbl/ *adj.* (*formal*) very bad SYN **terrible**

exe·cut·able /ɪg'zekjətəbl/ *adj.* (*computing*) (of a file or program) that can be run by a computer

exe·cute /'eksɪkju:t/ *verb* **1** [usually passive] **~ sb** (**for sth**) to kill sb, especially as a legal punishment: *He* **was executed** *for treason.* ◇ *The prisoners were executed by firing squad.* **2 ~ sth** (*formal*) to do a piece of work, perform a duty, put a plan into action, etc: *They drew up and executed a plan to reduce fuel consumption.* ◇ *The crime was very cleverly executed.* ◇ *Check that the computer has executed your commands.* **3 ~ sth** (*formal*) to successfully perform a skilful action or movement: *The pilot executed a perfect landing.* **4 ~ sth** (*formal*) to make or produce a work of art: *Picasso also executed several landscapes at Horta de San Juan.* **5 ~ sth** (*law*) to follow the instructions in a legal document; to make a document legally valid

exe·cu·tion /ˌeksɪ'kju:ʃn/ *noun* **1** [U, C] the act of killing sb, especially as a legal punishment: *He faced execution by hanging for murder.* ◇ *Over 200 executions were carried out last year.* **2** [U] (*formal*) the act of doing a piece of work, performing a duty, or putting a plan into action: *He had failed in the execution of his duty.* ◇ *The idea was good, but the execution was poor.* **3** [U] (*formal*) skill in performing or making sth, such as a piece of music or work of art: *Her execution of the piano piece was perfect.* **4** [U] (*law*) the act of following the instructions in a legal document, especially those in sb's WILL IDM see STAY *n.*

exe·cu·tion·er /ˌeksɪ'kju:ʃənə(r)/ *noun* a public official whose job is to execute criminals

ex·ecu·tive /ɪg'zekjətɪv/ *noun, adj.*

■ ***noun* 1** [C] a person who has an important job as a manager of a company or an organization: ***advertising/business/sales, etc. executives*** ◇ ***a chief/senior/top executive*** *in a computer firm* **2** [C+sing./pl. v.] a group of people who run a company or an organization: *The union's executive has/have yet to reach a decision.* **3 the executive** [sing.+ sing./pl. v.] the part of a government responsible for putting laws into effect ➲ compare JUDICIARY, LEGISLATURE

■ ***adj.*** [only before noun] **1** connected with managing a business or an organization, and with making plans and decisions: *She has an executive position in a finance company.* ◇ ***executive decisions/duties/jobs/positions*** ◇ *the executive dining room* **2** having the power to put important laws and decisions into effect: *executive authority* ◇ *an* ***executive board/body/committee/officer*** ◇ *Executive power is held by the president.* **3** expensive; for the use of sb who is considered important: *an* ***executive car/home*** ◇ *an* ***executive suite*** (= in a hotel) ◇ *an* ***executive lounge*** (= at an airport)

the e'xecutive branch *noun* [sing.] (in the US) the part of the government that is controlled by the President

eˌxecutive 'privilege *noun* [U] (in the US) the right of the President and the executive part of the government to keep official documents secret

ex·ecu·tor /ɪg'zekjətə(r)/ *noun* (*technical*) a person, bank, etc. that is chosen by sb who is making their WILL to follow the instructions in it

exe·gesis /ˌeksɪ'dʒi:sɪs/ *noun* [U, C] (*pl.* **exe·geses** /-si:z/) (*formal*) the detailed explanation of a piece of writing, especially religious writing

ex·em·plar /ɪg'zemplɑ:(r)/ *noun* (*formal*) a person or thing that is a good or typical example of sth SYN **model**

ex·em·plary /ɪg'zempləri/ *adj.* **1** providing a good example for people to copy: *Her behaviour was exemplary.* ◇ *a man of exemplary character* **2** [usually before noun] (*law* or *formal*) (of punishment) severe; used especially as a warning to others

ex·em·plify /ɪg'zemplɪfaɪ/ *verb* (**ex·em·pli·fies, ex·em·pli·fy·ing, ex·em·pli·fied, ex·em·pli·fied**) [often passive] (*formal*) **1 ~ sth** to be a typical example of sth: *Her early work is exemplified in her book, 'A Study of Children's Minds'.* ◇ *His food exemplifies Italian cooking at its best.* **2 ~ sth** to give an example in order to make sth clearer SYN **illustrate**: *She exemplified each of the points she was making with an amusing anecdote.* ▸ **ex·em·pli·fi·ca·tion** /ɪgˌzemplɪfɪ'keɪʃn/ *noun* [U, C]

ex·empt /ɪg'zempt/ *adj., verb*

■ ***adj.*** [not before noun] **~** (**from sth**) if sb/sth is **exempt** from sth, they are not affected by it, do not have to do it, pay it, etc: *The interest on the money is exempt from tax.* ◇ *Some students are exempt from certain exams.* ▸ **-exempt** (in compounds, forming adjectives): *tax-exempt donations to charity*

■ ***verb* ~ sb/sth** (**from sth/from doing sth**) (*formal*) to give or get sb's official permission not to do sth or not to pay sth they would normally have to do or pay: *His bad eyesight exempted him from military service.* ◇ *In 1983, charities were exempted from paying the tax.*

ex·emp·tion /ɪg'zempʃn/ *noun* **1** [U, C] **~** (**from sth**) official permission not to do sth or pay sth that you would normally have to do or pay: *She was given exemption from the final examination.* **2** [C] a part of your income that you do not have to pay tax on: *a tax exemption on money donated to charity*

ex·er·cise /'eksəsaɪz; *NAmE* -sərs-/ *noun, verb*

■ ***noun***

▸ ACTIVITY/MOVEMENTS **1** [U] physical or mental activity that you do to stay healthy or become stronger: *Swimming is good exercise.* ◇ *I don't* **get much exercise** *sitting in the office all day.* ◇ *The mind needs exercise as well as the body.* ◇ ***vigorous/gentle exercise*** ◇ (*BrE*) *to take exercise* ➲ COLLOCATIONS at DIET **2** [C] a set of movements or activities that you do to stay healthy or develop a skill: ***breathing/relaxation/stretching exercises*** ◇ *exercises for the piano* ◇ *Repeat the exercise ten times on each leg.*

▸ QUESTIONS **3** [C] a set of questions in a book that tests your knowledge or practises a skill: *grammar exercises* ◇ *Do exercise one for homework.*

▸ USE OF POWER/RIGHT/QUALITY **4** [U] **~ of sth** the use of power, a skill, a quality or a right to make sth happen: *the exercise of power by the government* ◇ *the exercise of discretion*

▸ FOR PARTICULAR RESULT **5** [C] an activity that is designed to achieve a particular result: *a communications exercise* ◇ *In the end it proved a pointless exercise.* ◇ **~ in sth** *an exercise in*

public relations ◇ *Staying calm was an exercise in self-control.*
▸ FOR SOLDIERS **6** [C, usually pl.] a set of activities for training soldiers: *military exercises*
▸ CEREMONIES **7 exercises** [pl.] (*NAmE*) ceremonies: *college graduation exercises*
■ *verb*
▸ USE POWER/RIGHT/QUALITY **1** [T] **~ sth** (*formal*) to use your power, rights or personal qualities in order to achieve sth: *When she appeared in court she exercised her right to remain silent.* ◇ *He was a man who exercised considerable influence over people.*
▸ DO PHYSICAL ACTIVITY **2** [I, T] to do sports or other physical activities in order to stay healthy or become stronger; to make an animal do this: *an hour's class of exercising to music* ◇ *How often do you exercise?* ◇ **~ sth** *Horses need to be exercised regularly.* **3** [T] **~ sth** to give a part of the body the movement and activity it needs to keep strong and healthy: *These movements will exercise your arms and shoulders.*
▸ BE ANXIOUS **4** [usually passive] **~ sb/sth (about sth)** (*formal*) if sb is **exercised** about sth, they are very anxious about it

'exercise ball (also **'Swiss ball™**) *noun* a large ball that you can sit on when doing exercises to make your muscles work in a different way

'exercise bike *noun* a bicycle that does not move forward but is used for getting exercise indoors ➲ VISUAL VOCAB page V35

'exercise book *noun* **1** (*BrE*) (*NAmE* **note·book**) a small book for students to write their work in ➲ VISUAL VOCAB page V57 **2** (*NAmE*) (*BrE* **work·book**) a book with exercises in it, often with spaces for students to write answers in, to help them practise what they have learnt

exert /ɪɡˈzɜːt; *NAmE* ɪɡˈzɜːrt/ *verb* **1 ~ sth** to use power or influence to affect sb/sth: *He exerted all his authority to make them accept the plan.* ◇ *The moon exerts a force on the earth that causes the tides.* **2 ~ yourself** to make a big physical or mental effort: *In order to be successful he would have to exert himself.*

ex·er·tion /ɪɡˈzɜːʃn; *NAmE* -ˈzɜːrʃ-/ *noun* **1** [U] (also **exer·tions** [pl.]) physical or mental effort; the act of making an effort: *She was hot and breathless from the exertion of cycling uphill.* ◇ *He needed to relax after the exertions of a busy day at work.* **2** [sing.] the use of power to make sth happen: *the* ***exertion of force/strength/authority***

exe·unt /ˈeksiʌnt/ *verb* [I] (from *Latin*) used in a play as a written instruction that tells two or more actors to leave the stage ➲ compare EXIT

ex·foli·ate /eksˈfəʊlieɪt; *NAmE* -ˈfoʊ-/ *verb* [I, T] **~ (sth)** to remove dead cells from the surface of skin in order to make it smoother ▸ **ex·foli·ation** *noun* [U]

ex gra·tia /ˌeks ˈɡreɪʃə/ *adj.* (from *Latin*) given or done as a gift or favour, not because there is a legal duty to do it: *ex gratia payments* ▸ **ex gra·tia** *adv.*: *The sum was paid ex gratia.*

ex·hale /eksˈheɪl/ *verb* [I, T] (*formal*) to breathe out the air or smoke, etc. in your lungs: *He sat back and exhaled deeply.* ◇ **~ sth** *She exhaled the smoke through her nose.* OPP **inhale** ▸ **ex·hal·ation** /ˌekshəˈleɪʃn/ *noun* [U, C]

ex·haust /ɪɡˈzɔːst/ *noun, verb*
■ *noun* **1** [U] waste gases that come out of a vehicle, an engine or a machine: *car* ***exhaust fumes/emissions*** **2** (also **ex'haust pipe**) (also **tail·pipe** especially in *NAmE*) [C] a pipe through which exhaust gases come out: *My car needs a new exhaust.* ➲ VISUAL VOCAB page V42
■ *verb* **1** to make sb feel very tired SYN **wear out**: **~ sb** *Even a short walk exhausted her.* ◇ **~ yourself** *There's no need to exhaust yourself clearing up—we'll do it.* **2 ~ sth** to use all of sth so that there is none left: *Within three days they had exhausted their supply of food.* ◇ *Don't give up until you have exhausted all the possibilities.* **3 ~ sth** to talk about or study a subject until there is nothing else to say about it: *I think we've exhausted that particular topic.*

ex·haust·ed /ɪɡˈzɔːstɪd/ *adj.* **1** very tired: *I'm exhausted!* ◇ *to feel* ***completely/utterly exhausted*** ◇ *The exhausted climbers were rescued by helicopter.* **2** completely used or finished: *You cannot grow crops on exhausted land.*

ex·haust·ing /ɪɡˈzɔːstɪŋ/ *adj.* making you feel very tired: *an exhausting day at work* ◇ *I find her exhausting—she never stops talking.*

ex·haus·tion /ɪɡˈzɔːstʃən/ *noun* [U] **1** the state of being very tired: *suffering from* ***physical/mental/nervous exhaustion*** ◇ *Her face was grey with exhaustion.* **2** (*formal*) the act of using sth until it is completely finished: *the exhaustion of natural resources*

ex·haust·ive /ɪɡˈzɔːstɪv/ *adj.* including everything possible; very thorough or complete: ***exhaustive research/tests*** ◇ *This list is not intended to be exhaustive.* ▸ **ex·haust·ive·ly** *adv.*: *Every product is exhaustively tested before being sold.*

ex'haust pipe *noun* = EXHAUST

ex·hibit AW /ɪɡˈzɪbɪt/ *verb, noun*
■ *verb* **1** [T, I] to show sth in a public place for people to enjoy or to give them information: **~ sth (at/in…)** *They will be exhibiting their new designs at the trade fairs.* ◇ **~ (at/in …)** *He exhibits regularly in local art galleries.* **2** [T] **~ sth** (*formal*) to show clearly that you have or feel a particular feeling, quality or ability SYN **display**: *The patient exhibited signs of fatigue and memory loss.*
■ *noun* **1** an object or a work of art put in a public place, for example a museum, so that people can see it **2** a thing that is used in court to prove that sb is guilty or not guilty: *The first exhibit was a knife which the prosecution claimed was the murder weapon.* **3** (*NAmE*) = EXHIBITION (1): *The new exhibit will tour a dozen US cities next year.*

ex·hib·ition AW /ˌeksɪˈbɪʃn/ *noun*
1 (*especially BrE*) (*NAmE* usually **ex·hibit**) [C] a collection of things, for example works of art, that are shown to the public: *Have you seen the Picasso exhibition?* ◇ *an exhibition of old photographs* ➲ COLLOCATIONS at ART **2** [U] **~ of sth** the act of showing sth, for example works of art, to the public: *She refused to allow the exhibition of her husband's work.* **3** [sing.] **an ~ of sth** (*formal*) the act of showing a skill, a feeling, or a kind of behaviour: *We were treated to an exhibition of the footballer's speed and skill.* ◇ *an appalling exhibition of bad manners* **4** [C] (*BrE*) an amount of money that is given as a prize to a student
IDM **make an exhi'bition of yourself** (*disapproving*) to behave in a bad or stupid way in public

ex·hib·ition·ism /ˌeksɪˈbɪʃənɪzəm/ *noun* [U] **1** (*disapproving*) behaviour that is intended to make people notice or admire you **2** (*psychology*) the mental condition that makes sb want to show their sexual organs in public

ex·hib·ition·ist /ˌeksɪˈbɪʃənɪst/ *noun* (usually *disapproving*) a person who likes to make other people notice him or her: *Children are natural exhibitionists.*

ex·hib·it·or /ɪɡˈzɪbɪtə(r)/ *noun* a person or a company that shows their work or products to the public

ex·hil·ar·ate /ɪɡˈzɪləreɪt/ *verb* **~ sb** to make sb feel very happy and excited: *Speed had always exhilarated him.* ▸ **ex·hil·ar·ated** *adj.*: *I felt exhilarated after a morning of skiing.* ➲ SYNONYMS at EXCITED **ex·hil·ar·ation** /ɪɡˌzɪləˈreɪʃn/ *noun* [U]: *the exhilaration of performing on stage*

ex·hil·ar·at·ing /ɪɡˈzɪləreɪtɪŋ/ *adj.* very exciting and enjoyable: *My first parachute jump was an exhilarating experience.* ➲ SYNONYMS at EXCITING

ex·hort /ɪɡˈzɔːt; *NAmE* ɪɡˈzɔːrt/ *verb* (*formal*) to try hard to persuade sb to do sth SYN **urge**: **~ sb to do sth** *The party leader exhorted his members to start preparing for government.* ◇ **~ sb to sth** *They had been exhorted to action.* ◇ **~ (sb) + speech** *'Come on!' he exhorted (them).* ▸ **ex·hort·ation** /ˌeɡzɔːˈteɪʃn; *NAmE* -zɔːrˈt-/ *noun* [C, U]

ex·hume /eksˈhjuːm; ɪɡˈzjuːm; *NAmE* ɪɡˈzuːm/ *verb* [usually passive] **~ sth** (*formal*) to remove a dead body from the ground especially in order to examine how the person died SYN **dig up** ▸ **ex·hum·ation** /ˌekshjuːˈmeɪʃn/ *noun* [U]

exi·gency /ˈeksɪdʒənsi; ɪɡˈzɪdʒ-/ *noun* [C, usually pl., U] (*pl.* -ies) (*formal*) an urgent need or demand that you must deal with SYN **demand**

ex·igu·ous /eɡˈzɪɡjuəs/ *adj.* (*formal*) very small in size or amount; hardly enough

exile /ˈeksaɪl; ˈeɡzaɪl/ *noun, verb*

■ ***noun* 1** [U, sing.] the state of being sent to live in another country that is not your own, especially for political reasons or as a punishment: *to be/live* ***in exile*** ◇ *to be forced/sent* ***into exile*** ◇ *to go* ***into exile*** ◇ *a place of exile* ◇ *He returned after 40 years of exile.* **2** [C] a person who chooses, or is forced to live away from his or her own country: *political exiles* ◇ *a* ***tax exile*** (= a rich person who moves to another country where taxes are lower)

■ ***verb*** [usually passive] **~ sb (from...)** to force sb to leave their country, especially for political reasons or as a punishment; to send sb into exile: *the party's exiled leaders*

exist 🔑 /ɪɡˈzɪst/ *verb*

1 🔑 [I] (not used in the progressive tenses) to be real; to be present in a place or situation: *Does life exist on other planets?* ◇ *The problem only exists in your head, Jane.* ◇ *Few of these monkeys still exist in the wild.* ◇ *On his retirement the post will* ***cease to exist.*** ◇ *The charity exists to support victims of crime.* **2** [I] **~ (on sth)** to live, especially in a difficult situation or with very little money: *We existed on a diet of rice.* ◇ *They can't exist on the money he's earning.*

ex·ist·ence 🔑 /ɪɡˈzɪstəns/ *noun*

1 🔑 [U] the state or fact of being real or living or of being present: *I was unaware of his existence until today.* ◇ *This is the oldest Hebrew manuscript* ***in existence.*** ◇ *Pakistan* ***came into existence*** *as an independent country in 1947.* ◇ *a crisis that threatens the industry's continued existence* **2** 🔑 [C] a way of living especially when this is difficult or boring: *The family endured a miserable existence in a cramped apartment.* ◇ *We led a poor but happy enough existence as children.* ◇ *They eke out a precarious existence* (= they have hardly enough money to live on). ◇ *The peasants depend on a good harvest for their* ***very existence*** (= in order to continue to live).

ex·ist·ent /ɪɡˈzɪstənt/ *adj., noun*

■ ***adj.*** (*formal*) existing; real: *creatures existent in nature* OPP **non-existent**

■ ***noun*** (*philosophy*) a thing that is real and exists: *The self is the only knowable existent.*

ex·ist·en·tial /ˌeɡzɪˈstenʃəl/ *adj.* [only before noun] **1** (*formal*) connected with human existence **2** (*philosophy*) connected with the theory of existentialism

ex·ist·en·tial·ism /ˌeɡzɪˈstenʃəlɪzəm/ *noun* [U] (*philosophy*) the theory that humans are free and responsible for their own actions in a world without meaning ▸ **ex·ist·en·tial·ist** /-ʃəlɪst/ *noun*: *Sartre was an existentialist.* **ex·ist·en·tial·ist** *adj.*: *existentialist theory*

ex·ist·ing /ɪɡˈzɪstɪŋ/ *adj.* [only before noun] found or used now: *New laws will soon replace existing legislation.*

exit 🔑 /ˈeksɪt; ˈeɡzɪt/ *noun, verb*

■ ***noun* 1** 🔑 a way out of a public building or vehicle: *Where's the exit?* ◇ *There is a* ***fire exit*** *on each floor of the building.* ◇ *The* ***emergency exit*** *is at the back of the bus.* ➲ compare ENTRANCE **2** 🔑 an act of leaving, especially of an actor from the stage: *The heroine* ***made her exit*** *to great applause.* ◇ *He made a quick exit to avoid meeting her.* ◇ *an* ***exit visa*** (= a stamp in a passport giving sb permission to leave a particular country) **3** 🔑 a place where vehicles can leave a road to join another road: *Leave the roundabout at the second exit.* ◇ *Take the exit for Brno.*

■ ***verb* 1** [I, T] (*formal*) to go out; to leave a building, stage, vehicle, etc: (**+ adv./prep.**) *The bullet entered her back and exited through her chest.* ◇ *We exited via a fire door.* ◇ **~ sth** *As the actors exited the stage the lights went on.* **2** [I, T] to finish using a computer program: **~ (from sth)** *To exit from this page, press the return key.* ◇ **~ sth** *I exited the database and switched off the computer.* **3** [I] **exit...** used in the instructions printed in a play to say that an actor must leave the stage ➲ compare EXEUNT

ˈ**exit exam** (also *formal* **exit examination**) *noun* (*especially NAmE*) an exam that you take at the end of the last year in school or at the end of a period of training: *a high school exit exam*

ˈ**exit poll** *noun* in an **exit poll** immediately after an election, people are asked how they voted, in order to predict the result of the election

ex libris /ˌeks ˈlɪbrɪs; ˈliːb-/ *adv.* written in the front of a book before the name of the person the book belongs to: *ex libris David Harries*

exo·crine /ˈeksəʊkraɪn; -krɪn; *NAmE* ˈeksəkrɪn; -kriːn/ *adj.* (*biology*) connected with GLANDS that do not put substances directly into the blood but export their product through tubes for use outside the body: *exocrine glands* ➲ compare ENDOCRINE

exo·dus /ˈeksədəs/ *noun* [sing.] **~ (from...) (to...)** (*formal* or *humorous*) a situation in which many people leave a place at the same time: *the* ***mass exodus*** *from Paris to the country in the summer*

ex of·fi·cio /ˌeks əˈfɪʃiəʊ; *NAmE* -ʃioʊ/ *adj.* (from *Latin, formal*) included or allowed because of your job, position or rank: *an ex officio member of the committee* ▸ **ex of·fi·cio** *adv.*

ex·og·amy /ekˈsɒɡəmi; *NAmE* -ˈsɑːɡ-/ *noun* [U] (*technical*) marriage outside your family or CASTE (= division of society) ➲ compare ENDOGAMY ▸ **ex·og·am·ous** /ekˈsɒɡəməs; *NAmE* -ˈsɑːɡ-/ *adj.*

ex·ogen·ous /ekˈsɒdʒənəs; ɪk-; *NAmE* ekˈsɑːdʒ-/ *adj.* (*medical*) (of a disease or SYMPTOM) having a cause that is outside the body ➲ compare ENDOGENOUS

ex·on·er·ate /ɪɡˈzɒnəreɪt; *NAmE* -ˈzɑːn-/ *verb* **~ sb (from sth)** (*formal*) to officially state that sb is not responsible for sth that they have been blamed for: *The police report exonerated Lewis from all charges of corruption.* ▸ **ex·on·er·ation** /ɪɡˌzɒnəˈreɪʃn; *NAmE* -ˌzɑːnə-/ *noun* [U]

ex·or·bi·tant /ɪɡˈzɔːbɪtənt; *NAmE* -ˈzɔːrb-/ *adj.* (*formal*) (of a price) much too high: ***exorbitant costs/fares/fees/prices/rents*** ▸ **ex·or·bi·tant·ly** *adv.*: *Prices are exorbitantly high in this shop.*

ex·or·cism /ˈeksɔːsɪzəm; *NAmE* -sɔːrs-/ *noun* [U, C] **1** the act of getting rid of an evil spirit from a place or a person's body by prayers or magic; a ceremony where this is done **2** (*formal*) the act of making yourself forget a bad experience or memory

ex·or·cist /ˈeksɔːsɪst; *NAmE* -sɔːrs-/ *noun* a person who makes evil spirits leave a place or a person's body by prayers or magic

ex·or·cize (*BrE* also **-ise**) /ˈeksɔːsaɪz; *NAmE* -sɔːrs-/ *verb* **1 ~ sth (from sb/sth)** to make an evil spirit leave a place or sb's body by special prayers or magic **2 ~ sth (from sth)** (*formal*) to remove sth that is bad or painful from your mind: *She had managed to exorcize these unhappy memories from her mind.*

exo·skel·eton /ˈeksəʊskelɪtn; *NAmE* ˈeksoʊ-/ *noun* (*biology*) a hard outer covering that protects the bodies of certain animals, such as insects ➲ compare ENDOSKELETON

exo·ther·mic /ˌeksəʊˈθɜːmɪk; *NAmE* ˌeksoʊˈθɜːrmɪk/ *adj.* (*chemistry*) (of a chemical reaction) producing heat ➲ compare ENDOTHERMIC

exot·ic /ɪɡˈzɒtɪk; *NAmE* ɪɡˈzɑːtɪk/ *adj.* from or in another country, especially a tropical one; seeming exciting and unusual because it is connected with foreign countries: *brightly-coloured* ***exotic flowers/plants/birds*** ◇ *She travels to all kinds of exotic locations all over the world.* ▸ **exot·ic·al·ly** /-kli/ *adv.*: *rainbows of exotically coloured blooms*

exot·ica /ɪɡˈzɒtɪkə; *NAmE* ɪɡˈzɑːt-/ *noun* [U] unusual and exciting things, especially from other countries

eˌxotic ˈdancer *noun* an entertainer who dances with very few clothes on, or who removes clothes while dancing

E

exoti·cism /ɪɡˈzɒtɪsɪzəm; *NAmE* ɪɡˈzɑːt-/ *noun* [U] (*formal*) the quality of being exciting and unusual that sth has because it is connected with foreign countries

ex·pand 🔑 AW /ɪkˈspænd/ *verb* **1** 🔑 [I, T] to become greater in size, number or importance; to make sth greater in size, number or importance: *Metals expand when they are heated.* ◇ *Student numbers are expanding rapidly.* ◇ *A child's vocabulary expands through reading.* ◇ *The waist expands to fit all sizes.* ◇ **~ sth** *In breathing the chest muscles expand the rib cage and allow air to be sucked into the lungs.* ◇ *The new system expanded the role of family doctors.* ◇ *There are no plans to expand the local airport.* OPP **contract 2** 🔑 [I, T] if a business **expands** or **is expanded**, new branches are opened, it makes more money, etc: *an expanding economy* (= with more businesses starting and growing) ◇ **~ sth** *We've expanded the business by opening two more stores.* **3** [I] to talk more; to add details to what you are saying: *I repeated the question and waited for her to expand.*
PHR V **exˈpand on/upon sth** to say more about sth and add some details: *Could you expand on that point, please?*

ex·pand·able /ɪkˈspændəbl/ *adj.* (*technical*) that can be expanded: *an expandable briefcase* ◇ **~ to sth** *The system has 1GB RAM, expandable to 4GB.*

ex·panse /ɪkˈspæns/ *noun* **~ (of sth)** a wide and open area of sth, especially land or water: *a* ***wide/vast expanse*** *of blue sky* ◇ *flat expanses of open farmland*

ex·pan·sion AW /ɪkˈspænʃn/ *noun* [U, C] an act of increasing or making sth increase in size, amount or importance: *a period of rapid economic expansion* ◇ *Despite the recession the company is confident of further expansion.* ◇ *The book is an expansion of a series of lectures given last year.*

ex·pan·sion·ary /ɪkˈspænʃənri/ *adj.* (*formal*) encouraging economic expansion: *This budget will have a net expansionary effect on the economy.*

exˈpansion card (also ˈ**add-in**) *noun* (*computing*) a CIRCUIT BOARD that can be put into a computer to give it more memory or make it able to do more things

ex·pan·sion·ism AW /ɪkˈspænʃənɪzəm/ *noun* [U] (sometimes *disapproving*) the belief in and process of increasing the size and importance of sth, especially in a country or a business: *the economic expansionism of America* ◇ ***military/territorial expansionism*** ▸ **ex·pan·sion·ist** /-ʃənɪst/ *adj.*: *expansionist policies* **ex·pan·sion·ist** *noun*: *He was a ruthless expansionist.*

ex·pan·sive AW /ɪkˈspænsɪv/ *adj.* **1** covering a large amount of space: *She opened her arms wide in an expansive gesture of welcome.* ◇ *landscape with expansive skies* **2** covering a large subject area, rather than trying to be exact and use few words: *We need to look at a more expansive definition of the term.* ◇ *The piece is written in his usual expansive style.* **3** friendly and willing to talk a lot: *She was clearly relaxed and in an expansive mood.* **4** (especially of a period of time) encouraging economic EXPANSION: *In the expansive 1990s bright graduates could advance rapidly.* ▸ **ex·pan·sive·ly** *adv.*: *He waved his arms expansively.* **ex·pan·sive·ness** *noun* [U]

ex·pati·ate /ɪkˈspeɪʃieɪt/ *verb*
PHR V **exˈpatiate on/upon sth** (*formal*) to write or speak in detail about a subject

ex·patri·ate /ˌeksˈpætriət; *NAmE* -ˈpeɪt-/ (also *informal* **expat** /ˌeksˈpæt/) *noun* a person living in a country that is not their own: *American expatriates in Paris* ▸ **ex·patri·ate** *adj.* [only before noun]: *expatriate Britons in Spain* ◇ *expatriate workers*

ex·pect 🔑 /ɪkˈspekt/ *verb* **1** 🔑 [T] to think or believe that sth will happen or that sb will do sth: **~ sth** *We are expecting a rise in food prices this month.* ◇ **~ sth from sb/sth** *Don't expect sympathy from me!* ◇ **~ sth of sb/sth** *That's not the sort of behaviour I expect of you!* ◇ **~ to do sth** *You can't expect to learn a foreign language in a few months.* ◇ *I looked back,* ***half expecting*** *to see someone following me.* ◇ **~ sb/sth to do sth** *House prices are expected to rise sharply.* ◇ *Do you really expect me to believe you?* ◇ **~ (that)...** *Many people were expecting (that) the peace talks would break down.* ◇ **it is expected that...** *It is expected that the report will suggest some major reforms.* **2** 🔑 [T] (often used in the progressive tenses) to be waiting for sb/sth to arrive, as this has been arranged: **~ sb/sth** *to expect a visit/call/letter from sb* ◇ *Are you expecting visitors?* ◇ *We were expecting him yesterday.* ◇ **~ sb to do sth** *We were expecting him to arrive yesterday.* **3** 🔑 to demand that sb will do sth because it is their duty or responsibility: **~ sth (from sb)** *Her parents expected high standards from her.* ◇ *He's still getting over his illness, so don't expect too much from him.* ◇ **~ sth (of sb)** *Are you clear what is expected of you?* ◇ **~ sb to do sth** *They expected all their children to be high achievers.* ◇ **~ to do sth** *I expect to be paid promptly for the work.* ➲ SYNONYMS at DEMAND **4** 🔑 [I, T] (*informal, especially BrE*) (not used in the progressive tenses) used when you think sth is probably true: *'Will you be late?'* ***'I expect so.'*** ◇ *'Are you going out tonight?'* ***'I don't expect so.'*** ◇ **~ (that...)** *'Who's eaten all the cake?' 'Tom, I expect/I expect it was Tom.'* HELP 'That' is nearly always left out. ➲ compare UNEXPECTED
IDM **be expecting a baby/child** 🔑 (*informal*) to be pregnant: *Ann's expecting a baby in June.* **be (only) to be exˈpected** to be likely to happen; to be quite normal: *A little tiredness after taking these drugs is to be expected.* **what (else) do you exˈpect?** (*informal*) used to tell sb not to be surprised by sth: *She swore at you? What do you expect when you treat her like that?*

Language Bank

expect

Discussing predictions

- The number of people using mobile phones to purchase goods and services is **expected/likely** to more than double by the end of 2015.
- Experts have **predicted/forecast** that the number of people using their mobile phones to pay for goods and services should exceed 190 million in 2015.
- This figure **is set to** reach 200 million by 2016.
- **By** 2015, 800 million mobile phone users worldwide **will** be participating in social networks via their phone.
- Sales of mobile phones in 2009 were lower **than expected**.
- The company's announcement of 1.26 billion handsets sold for the year is **in line with predictions**.

➲ Language Banks at FALL, ILLUSTRATE, INCREASE, PROPORTION

ex·pect·ancy /ɪkˈspektənsi/ *noun* [U] the state of expecting or hoping that sth, especially sth good or exciting, will happen: *There was* ***an air of expectancy*** *among the waiting crowd.* ➲ see also LIFE EXPECTANCY

ex·pect·ant /ɪkˈspektənt/ *adj.* **1** hoping for sth, especially sth good and exciting: *children with expectant faces waiting for the fireworks to begin* ◇ *A sudden roar came from the expectant crowd.* **2 ~ mother/father/parent** used to describe sb who is going to have a baby soon or become a father ▸ **ex·pect·ant·ly** *adv.*: *She looked at him expectantly.* ◇ *waiting expectantly*

ex·pect·ation 🔑 /ˌekspekˈteɪʃn/ *noun* **1** 🔑 [U, C] a belief that sth will happen because it is likely: **~ (of sth)** *We are confident in our expectation of a full recovery.* ◇ **~ (that...)** *There was a general expectation that he would win.* ◇ *The expectation is that property prices will rise.* ◇ *I applied for the post more in hope than expectation.* ◇ ***Contrary to expectations****, interest rates did not rise.* ◇ ***Against all expectations****, she was enjoying herself.* **2** 🔑 [C, usually pl., U] a hope that sth good will happen: *She went to college with great expectations.* ◇ *There was an air of expectation and great curiosity.* ◇ *The results exceeded our expectations.* ◇ *The numbers attending fell short of expectations.* ◇ *The event did not* ***live up to expectations****.* **3** 🔑 [C, usually pl.] a strong belief about the way sth should happen or how sb should behave: *Some parents have unrealistic expectations of their children.* ◇ *Unfortunately the new software has failed to* ***meet expectations.***

ˌexpectation of ˈlife *noun* [U] = LIFE EXPECTANCY

ex·pect·ed 0‑ /ɪkˈspektɪd/ *adj.* that you think will happen: *Double the expected number of people came to the meeting.* ◇ *this year's expected earnings* ➲ compare UNEXPECTED

ex·pec·tor·ant /ɪkˈspektərənt/ *noun* (*medical*) a cough medicine that helps you to get rid of thick liquid (=PHLEGM) from the lungs

ex·pec·tor·ate /ɪkˈspektəreɪt/ *verb* [I] (*formal*) to cough and make PHLEGM come up from your lungs into your mouth so you can SPIT it out ▶ **ex·pec·tor·ation** /ɪkˌspektəˈreɪʃn/ *noun* [U]

ex·pe·di·ent /ɪkˈspiːdiənt/ *noun, adj.*

■ ***noun*** an action that is useful or necessary for a particular purpose, but not always fair or right: *The disease was controlled* ***by the simple expedient of*** *not allowing anyone to leave the city.*

■ ***adj.*** [not usually before noun] (of an action) useful or necessary for a particular purpose, but not always fair or right: *The government has clearly decided that a cut in interest rates would be politically expedient.* **OPP inexpedient** ▶ **ex·pe·di·ency** /-ənsi/ *noun* [U]: *He acted out of expediency, not principle.* **ex·pe·di·ent·ly** *adv.*

ex·ped·ite /ˈekspədaɪt/ *verb* **~ sth** (*formal*) to make a process happen more quickly **SYN speed up**: *We have developed rapid order processing to expedite deliveries to customers.*

ex·ped·ition /ˌekspəˈdɪʃn/ *noun* **1** an organized journey with a particular purpose, especially to find out about a place that is not well known: *to* ***plan/lead/go on an expedition*** *to the North Pole* **2** the people who go on an expedition: *Three members of the Everest expedition were killed.* **3** (sometimes *humorous*) a short trip that you make when you want or need sth: *a shopping expedition* ➲ SYNONYMS at TRIP

ex·ped·ition·ary force /ˌekspəˈdɪʃənri fɔːs; *NAmE* -neri fɔːrs/ *noun* a group of soldiers who are sent to another country to fight in a war

ex·ped·itious /ˌekspəˈdɪʃəs/ *adj.* (*formal*) that works well without wasting time, money, etc. **SYN efficient** ▶ **ex·ped·itious·ly** *adv.*

expel /ɪkˈspel/ *verb* (-ll-) **1 ~ sb (from sth)** to officially make sb leave a school or an organization: *She was expelled from school at 15.* ◇ *Olympic athletes expelled for drug-taking* ➲ COLLOCATIONS at EDUCATION **2 ~ sb (from sth)** to force sb to leave a country: *Foreign journalists are being expelled.* **3 ~ sth (from sth)** (*technical*) to force air or water out of a part of the body or from a container: *to expel air from the lungs* ➲ see also EXPULSION

ex·pend /ɪkˈspend/ *verb* **~ sth (in/on sb) | ~ sth (in/on/doing sth)** (*formal*) to use or spend a lot of time, money, energy, etc: *She expended all her efforts on the care of home and children.*

ex·pend·able /ɪkˈspendəbl/ *adj.* (*formal*) if you consider people or things to be **expendable**, you think that you can get rid of them when they are no longer needed, or think it is acceptable if they are killed or destroyed **SYN dispensable**

ex·pend·iture /ɪkˈspendɪtʃə(r)/ *noun* [U, C] **1** the act of spending or using money; an amount of money spent: *a reduction in* ***public/government/military expenditure*** ◇ *plans to increase expenditure on health* ◇ *The budget provided for a total expenditure of £27 billion.* ➲ SYNONYMS at COSTS **2** the use of energy, time, materials, etc: *the expenditure of emotion* ◇ *This study represents a major expenditure of time and effort.* ➲ compare INCOME

ex·pense 0‑ /ɪkˈspens/ *noun*

1 0‑ [U] the money that you spend on sth: *The garden was transformed* ***at great expense.*** ◇ ***No expense was spared*** (= they spent as much money as was needed) *to make the party a success.* ◇ *He's arranged everything,* ***no expense spared.*** ◇ *She always travels first-class regardless of expense.* ◇ *The results are well worth the expense.* ➲ SYNONYMS at PRICE **2** 0‑ [C, usually sing.] something that makes you spend money: *Running a car is a big expense.* **3** 0‑ **expenses** [pl.] money spent in doing a particular job, or for a particular purpose: ***living/household/medical/legal, etc. expenses*** ◇ *Can I give you something towards expenses?* ◇ *financial help to meet the expenses of an emergency* ◇ *The payments he gets barely cover his expenses.* ➲ SYNONYMS at COSTS **4** 0‑ **expenses** [pl.] money that you spend while you are working and which your employer will pay back to you later: *You can claim back your* ***travelling/travel*** *expenses.* ◇ (*BrE*) *to take a client out for a meal* ***on expenses*** ◇ *an* ***all-expenses-paid*** *trip* ➲ SYNONYMS at COSTS

IDM at sb's expense **1** paid for by sb: *We were taken out for a meal at the company's expense.* **2** if you make a joke **at sb's expense**, you laugh at them and make them feel silly **at the expense of sb/sth** with loss or damage to sb/sth: *He built up the business at the expense of his health.* **go to the expense of sth/of doing sth | go to a lot of, etc. expense** to spend money on sth: *They went to all the expense of redecorating the house and then they moved.* **put sb to the expense of sth/of doing sth | put sb to a lot of, etc. expense** to make sb spend money on sth: *Their visit put us to a lot of expense.* ➲ more at OBJECT *n.*

exˈpense account *noun* an arrangement by which money spent by sb while they are at work is later paid back to them by their employer; a record of money spent in this way

ex·pen·sive 0‑ /ɪkˈspensɪv/ *adj.* costing a lot of money: *an expensive car/restaurant/holiday* ◇ *Art books are expensive to produce.* ◇ *I can't afford it, it's too expensive.* ◇ *Making the wrong decision could* ***prove expensive.*** ◇ *That dress was an* ***expensive mistake.*** **OPP inexpensive** ▶ **ex·pen·sive·ly** *adv.*: *expensively dressed/furnished* ◇ *There are other restaurants where you can eat less expensively.*

Synonyms

expensive

costly • overpriced • pricey

These word all describe sth that costs a lot of money.

- **expensive** costing a lot of money; charging high prices: *I can't afford it—it's just too expensive for me.* ◇ *an expensive restaurant*
- **costly** (*rather formal*) costing a lot of money, especially more than you want to pay: *You want to avoid costly legal proceedings if you can.*
- **overpriced** too expensive; costing more than it is worth: *ridiculously overpriced designer clothes*
- **pricey** (*informal*) expensive: *Houses in the village are now too pricey for local people to afford.*
- **dear** [not usually before noun] (*BrE*) expensive: *Everything's so dear now, isn't it?* **NOTE** This word is starting to become rather old-fashioned.

PATTERNS

- expensive/costly/overpriced/pricey **for** sb/sth
- expensive/costly **to do sth**
- **very/too/fairly/quite/pretty** expensive/costly/pricey

ex·peri·ence 0‑ /ɪkˈspɪəriəns; *NAmE* -ˈspɪr-/ *noun, verb*

■ ***noun*** **1** 0‑ [U] the knowledge and skill that you have gained through doing sth for a period of time; the process of gaining this: *to have over ten years' teaching experience* ◇ *Do you have any* ***previous experience*** *of this type of work?* ◇ *a doctor with* ***experience in*** *dealing with patients suffering from stress* ◇ *My lack of* ***practical experience*** *was a disadvantage.* ◇ *She didn't get paid much but it was all* ***good experience.*** ◇ *He gained valuable experience whilst working on the project.* ◇ *We all* ***learn by experience.*** ➲ see also WORK

EXPERIENCE **2** [U] the things that have happened to you that influence the way you think and behave: *Experience has taught me that life can be very unfair.* ◇ *It is important to try and* ***learn from experience.*** ◇ ***In my experience,*** *very few people really understand the problem.* ◇ *She knew* ***from past experience*** *that Ann would not give up easily.* ◇ *The book is based on* ***personal experience.*** ◇ ***direct/first-hand experience*** *of poverty* **3** [C] an event or activity that affects you in some way: *an enjoyable/exciting/unusual/unforgettable, etc. experience* ◇ **~ (of sth)** *It was her first experience of living alone.* ◇ *Living in Africa was very different from home and* ***quite an experience*** (= unusual for us). ◇ *I had a bad experience with fireworks once.* ◇ *He seems to have had some sort of religious experience.* **4 the … experience** [sing.] events or knowledge shared by all the members of a particular group in society, that influences the way they think and behave: *musical forms like jazz that emerged out of the Black American experience*

IDM **put sth down to ex'perience** (also **chalk sth up to ex'perience**) used to say that sb should think of a failure as being sth that they can learn from: *We lost a lot of money, but we just put it down to experience.*

■ ***verb*** **1** **~ sth** to have a particular situation affect you or happen to you: *The country experienced a foreign currency shortage for several months.* ◇ *Everyone experiences these problems at some time in their lives.* **2** **~ sth** to have and be aware of a particular emotion or physical feeling: *to experience pain/pleasure/unhappiness* ◇ *I experienced a moment of panic as I boarded the plane.*

ex·peri·enced /ɪk'spɪəriənst; *NAmE* -'spɪr-/ *adj.*
1 having knowledge or skill in a particular job or activity: *an experienced teacher* ◇ **~ in sth/in doing sth** *He's very experienced in looking after animals.* **2** having knowledge as a result of doing sth for a long time, or having had a lot of different experiences: *She's very young and not very experienced.* ◇ *an experienced traveller* (= sb who has travelled a lot) OPP **inexperienced**

ex·peri·en·tial /ɪkˌspɪəri'enʃl; *NAmE* -ˌspɪr-/ *adj.* (*formal* or *technical*) based on or involving experience: *experiential knowledge* ◇ *experiential learning methods*

ex·peri·ment /ɪk'sperɪmənt/ *noun, verb*

■ ***noun*** [C, U] **1** a scientific test that is done in order to study what happens and to gain new knowledge: *to* ***do/perform/conduct an experiment*** ◇ *proved* ***by experiment*** ◇ *laboratory experiments* ◇ *Many people do not like the idea of experiments on animals.* ➲ COLLOCATIONS at SCIENTIFIC **2** a new activity, idea or method that you try out to see what happens or what effect it has: *I've never cooked this before so it's an experiment.* ◇ **~ in sth** *the country's brief experiment in democracy*

■ ***verb*** **1** [I] **~ (on sb/sth)** | **~ (with sth)** to do a scientific experiment or experiments: *Some people feel that experimenting on animals is wrong.* **2** [I] **~ (on sb/sth)** | **~ (with sth)** to try or test new ideas, methods, etc. to find out what effect they have: *I experimented until I got the recipe just right.* ◇ *He wanted to experiment more with different textures in his paintings.* ▶ **ex·peri·ment·er** *noun*

ex·peri·men·tal /ɪkˌsperɪ'mentl/ *adj.* **1** based on new ideas, forms or methods that are used to find out what effect they have: *experimental teaching methods* ◇ ***experimental theatre/art/music*** ◇ *The equipment is still at the experimental stage.* **2** connected with scientific experiments: ***experimental conditions/data/evidence*** ▶ **ex·peri·men·tal·ly** /-təli/ *adv.*: *This theory can be confirmed experimentally.* ◇ *The new drug is being used experimentally on some patients.* ◇ *He moved his shoulder experimentally to see if it still hurt.*

ex·peri·men·ta·tion /ɪkˌsperɪmen'teɪʃn/ *noun* [U] (*formal*) the activity or process of experimenting: *experimentation with new teaching methods* ◇ *Many people object to experimentation on embryos.*

ex·pert AW /'ekspɜːt; *NAmE* -pɜːrt/ *noun, adj.*

■ ***noun*** a person with special knowledge, skill or training in sth: *a computer/medical expert* ◇ **~ (at/in/on sth)** *an expert in child psychology* ◇ *an expert on modern literature* ◇ **~ (at/in/on doing sth)** *He's an expert at getting his own way.* ◇ *Don't ask me—I'm no expert!*

■ ***adj.*** done with, having or involving great knowledge or skill: *to* ***seek expert advice/an expert opinion*** ◇ *an expert driver* ◇ *We need some expert help.* ◇ **~ (at/in sth)** *They are all expert in this field.* ◇ **~ (at/in doing sth)** *She's expert at making cheap but stylish clothes.* ➲ compare INEXPERT ▶ **ex·pert·ly** AW *adv.*: *The roads were icy but she stopped the car expertly.* ◇ *The music was expertly performed.*

ex·pert·ise AW /ˌekspɜː'tiːz; *NAmE* -pɜːr't-/ *noun* [U] expert knowledge or skill in a particular subject, activity or job: ***professional/scientific/technical, etc.*** *expertise* ◇ *We have the expertise to help you run your business.* ◇ **~ in sth/in doing sth** *They have considerable expertise in dealing with oil spills.*

ˌexpert 'system *noun* (*computing*) a computer system that can provide information and expert advice on a particular subject. The program asks users a series of questions about their problem and gives them advice based on its store of knowledge.

ex·pi·ate /'ekspieɪt/ *verb* **~ sth** (*formal*) to accept punishment for sth that you have done wrong in order to show that you are sorry: *He had a chance to confess and expiate his guilt.* ▶ **ex·pi·ation** /ˌekspi'eɪʃn/ *noun* [U, sing.]

ex·pir·ation /ˌekspə'reɪʃn/ *noun* [U] (*NAmE, formal*) = EXPIRY

expi'ration date *noun* (*NAmE*) (*BrE* **ex'piry date**) the date after which an official document, agreement, etc. is no longer valid, or after which sth should not be used or eaten: *Check the expiration date on your passport.* ◇ *The expiration date on this yogurt was November 20.*

ex·pire /ɪk'spaɪə(r)/ *verb* **1** [I] (of a document, an agreement, etc.) to be no longer valid because the period of time for which it could be used has ended SYN **run out**: *When does your driving licence expire?* **2** [I] (of a period of time, especially one during which sb holds a position of authority) to end: *His term of office expires at the end of June.* **3** [I] (*literary*) to die ➲ see also UNEXPIRED ▶ **ex·pired** *adj.*: *an expired passport*

ex·piry /ɪk'spaɪəri/ (*especially BrE*) (*NAmE* usually *formal* **ex·pir·ation**) *noun* [U] an ending of the period of time when an official document can be used, or when an agreement is valid: *the expiry of a fixed-term contract* ◇ *The licence can be renewed on expiry.*

ex'piry date (*BrE*) (*NAmE* **expi'ration date**) *noun* the date after which an official document, agreement, etc. is no longer valid, or after which sth should not be used or eaten: *Check the expiry date of your credit cards.*

ex·plain /ɪk'spleɪn/ *verb*

> **WORD FAMILY**
> **explain** *verb*
> **explanation** *noun*
> **explanatory** *adj.*
> **explicable** *adj.* (≠ inexplicable)

1 [T, I] to tell sb about sth in a way that makes it easy to understand: **~ (sth) (to sb)** *First, I'll explain the rules of the game.* ◇ *It was difficult to explain the problem to beginners.* ◇ *'Let me explain!' he added helpfully.* ◇ **~ that…** *I explained that an ambulance would be coming soon.* ◇ **~ who, how, etc…** *He explained who each person in the photo was.* ◇ **~ to sb who, how, etc…** *She explained to them what to do in an emergency.* ◇ **+ speech** *'It works like this,' she explained.* ◇ **it is explained that…** *It was explained that attendance was compulsory.* **2** [I, T] to give a reason, or be a reason, for sth: *She tried to explain but he wouldn't listen.* ◇ **~ that…** *Alex explained that his car had broken down.* ◇ **~ why, how, etc …** *Well, that doesn't explain why you didn't phone.* ◇ **~ sth (to sb)** *scientific findings that help explain the origins of the universe* ◇ *The government now has to explain its decision to the public.* ◇ (*informal*) *Oh well then, that* ***explains it*** (= I understand now why sth happened). HELP You cannot say 'explain me, him, her, etc.': *Can you explain the situation to me?* ◇ ~~*Can you explain me the situation?*~~ ◇ *I'll explain to you why I like it.* ◇ ~~*I'll explain you why I like it.*~~

IDM **ex'plain yourself 1** to give sb reasons for your behaviour, especially when they are angry or upset because

of it: *I really don't see why I should have to explain myself to you.* **2** to say what you mean in a clear way: *Could you explain yourself a little more—I didn't understand.*
PHR V **ex,plain sth↔a'way** to give reasons why sth is not your fault or why sth is not important

ex·plan·ation /ˌekspləˈneɪʃn/ *noun* **1** [C, U] a statement, fact, or situation that tells you why sth happened; a reason given for sth: *The most likely explanation is that his plane was delayed.* ◇ *to* ***offer/provide an explanation*** ◇ **~ (for sth)** *I can't think of any possible explanation for his absence.* ◇ **~ (for doing sth)** *She didn't* ***give an*** *adequate* ***explanation*** *for being late.* ◇ **~ (of sth)** *The book opens with an explanation of why some drugs are banned.* ◇ **~ (as to why...)** *an explanation as to why he had left early* ◇ *She left the room abruptly* ***without explanation.*** ◇ *'I had to see you,' he said, by way of explanation.* ➲ SYNONYMS at REASON **2** [C] a statement or piece of writing that tells you how sth works or makes sth easier to understand: *For a full explanation of how the machine works, turn to page 5.*

ex·plana·tory /ɪkˈsplænətri; *NAmE* -tɔːri/ *adj.* [usually before noun] giving the reasons for sth; intended to describe how sth works or to make sth easier to understand: *There are explanatory notes at the back of the book.* ➲ see also SELF-EXPLANATORY

ex·ple·tive /ɪkˈspliːtɪv; *NAmE* ˈeksplətɪv/ *noun* (*formal*) a word, especially a rude word, that you use when you are angry, or in pain SYN **swear word**

ex·plic·able /ɪkˈsplɪkəbl; ˈeksplɪkəbl/ *adj.* [not usually before noun] (*formal*) that can be explained or understood: *His behaviour is only explicable in terms of* (= because of) *his recent illness.* OPP **inexplicable**

ex·pli·cate /ˈeksplɪkeɪt/ *verb* **~ sth** (*formal*) to explain an idea or a work of literature in a lot of detail ▸ **ex·pli·ca·tion** /ˌekspIɪˈkeɪʃn/ *noun* [C, U]

ex·pli·cit AW /ɪkˈsplɪsɪt/ *adj.* **1** (of a statement or piece of writing) clear and easy to understand: *He gave me very explicit directions on how to get there.* **2** (of a person) saying sth clearly, exactly and openly SYN **frank**: *She was quite explicit about why she had left.* **3** said, done or shown in an open or direct way, so that you have no doubt about what is happening: *The reasons for the decision should be made explicit.* ◇ *She made some very explicit references to my personal life.* ◇ *a sexually explicit film* ➲ compare IMPLICIT ▸ **ex·pli·cit·ly** AW *adv.*: *The report states explicitly that the system was to blame.* ➲ compare IMPLICITLY **ex·pli·cit·ness** *noun* [U]: *He didn't like the degree of sexual explicitness in the film.*

ex·plode /ɪkˈspləʊd; *NAmE* ɪkˈsploʊd/ *verb*

▸ BURST VIOLENTLY **1** [I, T] to burst or make sth burst loudly and violently, causing damage SYN **blow up**: *Bombs were exploding all around the city.* ◇ **~ sth** *There was a huge bang as if someone had exploded a rocket outside.* ◇ *Bomb disposal experts exploded the device under controlled conditions.* ➲ compare IMPLODE

> **WORD FAMILY**
> **explode** *verb*
> **explosion** *noun*
> **explosive** *adj., noun*
> **unexploded** *adj.*

▸ GET ANGRY/DANGEROUS **2** [I, T] (of a person or situation) to suddenly become very angry or dangerous: **~ (with sth)** *Suddenly Charles exploded with rage.* ◇ **~ (into sth)** *The protest exploded into a riot.* ◇ **+ speech** *'Of course there's something wrong!' Jem exploded.*

▸ EXPRESS EMOTION **3** [I] **~ (into/with sth)** to suddenly express an emotion: *We all exploded into wild laughter.*

▸ MOVE SUDDENLY **4** [I] **~ (into sth)** to suddenly and quickly do sth; to move suddenly with a lot of force: *After ten minutes the game exploded into life.*

▸ MAKE LOUD NOISE **5** [I] to make a sudden very loud noise: *Thunder exploded overhead.*

▸ INCREASE QUICKLY **6** [I] to increase suddenly and very quickly in number: *the exploding world population*

▸ SHOW STH IS NOT TRUE **7** [T] **~ sth** to show that sth is not true, especially sth that people believe: *At last, a women's magazine to explode the myth that thin equals beautiful.*

> **Synonyms**
>
> **explode**
>
> **blow up • go off • burst • erupt • detonate**
>
> These are all words that can be used when sth bursts apart violently, causing damage or injury.
>
> **explode** to burst loudly and violently, causing damage; to make sth burst in this way: *The jet smashed into a hillside and exploded.* ◇ *The bomb was exploded under controlled conditions.*
>
> **blow (sth) up** to be destroyed by an explosion; to destroy sth by an explosion: *A police officer was killed when his car blew up.*
>
> **go off** (of a bomb) to explode; (of a gun) to be fired: *The bomb went off in a crowded street.* NOTE When used about guns, the choice of **go off** (instead of 'be fired') can suggest that the gun was fired by accident.
>
> **burst** to break open or apart, especially because of pressure from inside; to make sth break in this way: *That balloon's going to burst.*
>
> **erupt** (of a volcano) to throw out burning rocks and smoke; (of burning rocks and smoke) to be thrown out of a volcano.
>
> **detonate** (*rather formal*) (of a bomb) to explode; to make a bomb explode: *Two other bombs failed to detonate.*
>
> **PATTERNS**
> - a **bomb** explodes/blows up/goes off/bursts/detonates
> - a **car/plane/vehicle** explodes/blows up
> - a **firework/rocket** explodes/goes off

ex·ploded /ɪkˈspləʊdɪd; *NAmE* -ˈsploʊ-/ *adj.* (*technical*) (of a drawing or diagram) showing the parts of sth separately but also showing how they are connected to each other ➲ compare UNEXPLODED

ex·ploit AW *verb, noun*

■ ***verb*** /ɪkˈsplɔɪt/ **1 ~ sth** (*disapproving*) to treat a person or situation as an opportunity to gain an advantage for yourself: *He exploited his father's name to get himself a job.* ◇ *She realized that her youth and inexperience were being exploited.* **2 ~ sb** (*disapproving*) to treat sb unfairly by making them work and not giving them much in return: *What is being done to stop employers from exploiting young people?* **3 ~ sth** to use sth well in order to gain as much from it as possible: *She fully exploits the humour of her role in the play.* **4** to develop or use sth for business or industry: **~ sth** *No minerals have yet been exploited in Antarctica.* ◇ **~ sth for sth** *countries exploiting the rainforests for hardwood* ▸ **ex·ploit·er** *noun* [C]

■ ***noun*** /ˈeksplɔɪt/ [usually pl.] a brave, exciting or interesting act: *the daring exploits of Roman heroes*

ex·ploit·ation AW /ˌeksplɔɪˈteɪʃn/ *noun* [U] **1** (*disapproving*) a situation in which sb treats sb else in an unfair way, especially in order to make money from their work: *the exploitation of children* **2** the use of land, oil, minerals, etc: *commercial exploitation of the mineral resources in Antarctica* **3** (*disapproving*) the fact of using a situation in order to get an advantage for yourself: *exploitation of the situation for his own purposes*

ex·ploit·ative /ɪkˈsplɔɪtətɪv/ (*NAmE* also **ex·ploit·ive** /ɪkˈsplɔɪtɪv/) *adj.* treating sb unfairly in order to gain an advantage or to make money

ex·plor·ation /ˌekspləˈreɪʃn/ *noun* [C, U] **1** the act of travelling through a place in order to find out about it or look for sth in it: *the exploration of space* ◇ *oil exploration* (= searching for oil in the ground) **2** an examination of sth in order to find out about it: *the book's explorations of the human mind*

ex·plora·tory /ɪk'splɒrətri; *NAmE* ɪk'splɔːrətɔːri/ *adj.* done with the intention of examining sth in order to find out more about it: *exploratory surgery* ◇ *exploratory drilling for oil*

ex·plore ⊶ /ɪk'splɔː(r)/ *verb*
1 ⊶ [T, I] to travel to or around an area or a country in order to learn about it: **~ sth** (**for sth**) *The city is best explored on foot.* ◇ *They explored the land to the south of the Murray River.* ◇ **~** (**for sth**) *As soon as we arrived on the island we were eager to explore.* ◇ *companies exploring for* (= searching for) *oil* **2** ⊶ [T] **~ sth** to examine sth completely or carefully in order to find out more about it **SYN** **analyse**: *These ideas will be explored in more detail in chapter 7.* ➲ LANGUAGE BANK at ABOUT **3** [T] **~ sth** to feel sth with your hands or another part of the body: *She explored the sand with her toes.* ➲ see also UNEXPLORED

ex·plorer /ɪk'splɔːrə(r)/ *noun* a person who travels to unknown places in order to find out more about them

Ex'plorer Scout (*US*) (*BrE* **'Venture Scout**) *noun* a member of the senior branch of the SCOUT ASSOCIATION for young people between the ages of 15 or 16 and 20

ex·plo·sion ⊶ /ɪk'spləʊʒn; *NAmE* -'sploʊ-/ *noun*
1 ⊶ [C, U] the sudden violent bursting and loud noise of sth such as a bomb exploding; the act of deliberately causing sth to explode: *a* ***bomb/nuclear/gas explosion*** ◇ *There were two loud explosions and then the building burst into flames.* ◇ *Bomb Squad officers carried out a* ***controlled explosion*** *of the device.* ◇ *300 people were injured in the explosion.* **2** ⊶ [C] a large, sudden or rapid increase in the amount or number of sth: *a population explosion* ◇ *an explosion of interest in learning Japanese* **3** [C] (*formal*) a sudden, violent expression of emotion, especially anger **SYN** **outburst**

ex·plo·sive /ɪk'spləʊsɪv; -zɪv; *NAmE* -'sploʊ-/ *adj.*, *noun*
■ ***adj.*** **1** easily able or likely to explode: *an* ***explosive device*** (= a bomb) ◇ *an explosive mixture of chemicals* **2** likely to cause violence or strong feelings of anger or hatred: *a potentially explosive situation* **3** often having sudden violent or angry feelings: *an explosive temper* **4** increasing suddenly and rapidly: *the explosive growth of the export market* **5** (of a sound) sudden and loud ▶ **ex·plo·sive·ly** *adv.*
■ ***noun*** [C, U] a substance that is able or likely to cause an explosion: *plastic explosives* ◇ *The bomb was packed with several pounds of* ***high explosive***.

ex·po·nent /ɪk'spəʊnənt; *NAmE* -'spoʊ-/ *noun* **1** a person who supports an idea, theory, etc. and persuades others that it is good **SYN** **proponent**: *She was* ***a leading exponent*** *of free trade during her political career* **2** a person who is able to perform a particular activity with skill: *the most famous exponent of the art of mime* **3** (*mathematics*) a raised figure or symbol that shows how many times a quantity must be multiplied by itself, for example the figure 4 in a^4

ex·po·nen·tial /ˌekspə'nenʃl/ *adj.* **1** (*mathematics*) of or shown by an exponent: 2^4 *is an exponential expression.* ◇ *an* ***exponential curve/function*** **2** (*formal*) (of a rate of increase) becoming faster and faster: ***exponential growth/increase*** ▶ **ex·po·nen·ti·al·ly** /-ʃəli/ *adv.*: *to increase exponentially*

ex·port ⊶ **AW** *verb*, *noun*
■ ***verb*** /ɪk'spɔːt; *NAmE* ɪk'spɔːrt/ **1** ⊶ [T, I] **~** (**sth**) (**to sb**) to sell and send goods to another country: *The islands export sugar and fruit.* ◇ *90% of the engines are exported to Europe.* **2** [T] **~ sth** (**+ adv./prep.**) to introduce an idea or activity to another country or area: *American pop music has been exported around the world.* **3** [T] **~ sth** (*computing*) to send data to another program, changing its form so that the other program can read it **OPP** **import**
■ ***noun*** /'ekspɔːt; *NAmE* 'ekspɔːrt/ **1** ⊶ [U] the selling and transporting of goods to another country: *a ban on the export of live cattle* ◇ *Then the fruit is packaged* ***for export***. ◇ *export earnings* ◇ *an export licence* **2** ⊶ [C, usually pl.] a product that is sold to another country: *the country's major exports* ◇ *a fall in the value of exports* **OPP** **import** ➲ COLLOCATIONS at ECONOMY

ex·port·ation /ˌekspɔː'teɪʃn; *NAmE* ˌekspɔːr't-/ *noun* [U] the process of sending goods to another country for sale **OPP** **importation**

ex·port·er **AW** /ek'spɔːtə(r); *NAmE* ek'spɔːrt-/ *noun* a person, company or country that sells goods to another country: *the world's* ***largest/major/leading exporter*** *of cars* ◇ *The country is now a* ***net exporter*** *of fuel* (= it exports more than it imports). **OPP** **importer**

ex·pose ⊶ **AW** /ɪk'spəʊz; *NAmE* ɪk'spoʊz/ *verb*
▸ SHOW STH HIDDEN **1** ⊶ to show sth that is usually hidden **SYN** **reveal**: **~ sth** *He smiled suddenly, exposing a set of amazingly white teeth.* ◇ *Miles of sand are exposed at low tide.* ◇ *My job as a journalist is to expose the truth.* ◇ **~ sth to sb** *He did not want to expose his fears and insecurity to anyone.*
▸ SHOW TRUTH **2** ⊶ **~ sb/sth** (**as sth**) to tell the true facts about a person or a situation, and show them/it to be immoral, illegal, etc: *She was exposed as a liar and a fraud.* ◇ *He threatened to expose the racism that existed within the police force.*
▸ TO STH HARMFUL **3** ⊶ **~ sb/sth/yourself** (**to sth**) to put sb/sth in a place or situation where they are not protected from sth harmful or unpleasant: *to expose yourself to ridicule* ◇ *Do not expose babies to strong sunlight.*
▸ GIVE EXPERIENCE **4** **~ sb to sth** to let sb find out about sth by giving them experience of it or showing them what it is like: *We want to expose the kids to as much art and culture as possible.*
▸ FILM IN CAMERA **5** **~ sth** to allow light onto the film inside a camera when taking a photograph
▸ YOURSELF **6** **~ yourself** a man who **exposes** himself, shows his sexual organs in public in a way that is offensive to other people ➲ see also EXPOSURE

ex·posé /ek'spəʊzeɪ; *NAmE* ˌekspoʊ'zeɪ/ *noun* an account of the facts of a situation, especially when these are shocking or have deliberately been kept secret

ex·posed **AW** /ɪk'spəʊzd; *NAmE* ɪk'spoʊzd/ *adj.* **1** (of a place) not protected from the weather by trees, buildings or high ground **2** (of a person) not protected from attack or criticism: *She was left feeling exposed and vulnerable.* **3** (*finance*) likely to experience financial losses

ex·pos·ition /ˌekspə'zɪʃn/ *noun* (*formal*) **1** [C, U] a full explanation of a theory, plan, etc: *a clear and detailed exposition of their legal position* **2** [C] an event at which people, businesses, etc. show and sell their goods; a TRADE FAIR

ex·posi·tory /ɪk'spɒzətri; *NAmE* ɪk'spɑːzətɔːri/ *adj.* (*formal*) intended to explain or describe sth: *The film suffers from too much expository dialogue.*

ex·pos·tu·late /ɪk'spɒstʃuleɪt; *NAmE* ɪk'spɑːs-/ *verb* [I] (**+ speech**) (*formal*) to argue, disagree or protest about sth ▶ **ex·pos·tu·la·tion** /ɪkˌspɒstʃu'leɪʃn; *NAmE* ɪkˌspɑːs-/ *noun* [U, C]

ex·pos·ure **AW** /ɪk'spəʊʒə(r); *NAmE* -'spoʊ-/ *noun*
▸ TO STH HARMFUL **1** [U] **~** (**to sth**) the state of being in a place or situation where there is no protection from sth harmful or unpleasant: *prolonged exposure to harmful radiation* ◇ (*finance*) *the company's exposure on the foreign exchange markets* (= to the risk of making financial losses)
▸ SHOWING TRUTH **2** [U] the state of having the true facts about sb/sth told after they have been hidden because they are bad, immoral or illegal: *exposure as a liar and a fraud* ◇ *the exposure of illegal currency deals*
▸ ON TV/IN NEWSPAPERS, ETC. **3** [U] the fact of being discussed or mentioned on television, in newspapers, etc. **SYN** **publicity**: *Her new movie has had a lot of exposure in the media.*
▸ MEDICAL CONDITION **4** [U] a medical condition caused by being out in very cold weather for too long without protection: *Two climbers were brought in suffering from exposure.*
▸ FILM IN CAMERA **5** [C] a length of film in a camera that is used to take a photograph: *There are three exposures left on this roll of film.* **6** [C] the length of time for which light is

allowed to reach the film when taking a photograph: *I used a long exposure for this one.*
▸ SHOWING STH HIDDEN **7** [U] the act of showing sth that is usually hidden ➲ see also INDECENT EXPOSURE

ex·pound /ɪk'spaʊnd/ *verb* [T, I] (*formal*) to explain sth by talking about it in detail: **~ sth (to sb)** *He expounded his views on the subject to me at great length.* ◇ **~ on sth** *We listened as she expounded on the government's new policies.*

ex·press 🔑 /ɪk'spres/ *verb, adj., adv., noun*
■ ***verb*** **1** 🔑 to show or make known a feeling, an opinion, etc. by words, looks or actions: **~ sth** *Teachers have expressed concern about the changes.* ◇ *His views have been expressed in numerous speeches.* ◇ *to* **express fears/doubts/reservations** ◇ *to* **express interest/regret/surprise** ◇ **~ how, what, etc...** ***Words cannot express*** *how pleased I am.* ➲ see also UNEXPRESSED **2** 🔑 to speak, write or communicate in some other way what you think or feel: **~ yourself** *Teenagers often have difficulty expressing themselves.* ◇ **~ yourself + adv./prep.** *Perhaps I have not expressed myself very well.* ◇ *She expresses herself most fully in her paintings.* ◇ (*formal*) **~ yourself + adj.** *They expressed themselves delighted.* **3 ~ itself (+ adv./prep.)** (*formal*) (of a feeling) to become obvious in a particular way: *Their pleasure expressed itself in a burst of applause.* **4** (*mathematics*) to represent sth in a particular way, for example by symbols: **~ sth as sth** *The figures are expressed as percentages.* ◇ **~ sth in sth** *Educational expenditure is often expressed in terms of the amount spent per student.* **5 ~ sth (from sth)** to remove air or liquid from sth by pressing it: *Coconut milk is expressed from grated coconuts.* **6 ~ sth (to sb/sth)** (*NAmE*) to send sth by express post: *As soon as I receive payment I will express the book to you.*
■ ***adj.*** [only before noun] **1** 🔑 travelling very fast; operating very quickly: *an* ***express bus/coach/train*** ◇ *express delivery services* **2** 🔑 (of a letter, package, etc.) sent by express service: *express mail* **3** 🔑 (*NAmE*) (of a company that delivers packages) providing an express service: *an air express company* **4** (*formal*) (of a wish or an aim) clearly and openly stated SYN **definite**: *It was his* ***express wish*** *that you should have his gold watch after he died.* ◇ *I came here with the* ***express purpose*** *of speaking with the manager.*
■ ***adv.*** using a special fast service: *I'd like to send this express, please.*
■ ***noun*** **1** (also **ex'press train**) [C] a fast train that does not stop at many places: *the 8.27 express to Edinburgh* ◇ *the Trans-Siberian Express* **2** (also **ˌspecial de'livery**) [U] (*BrE*) a service for sending or transporting things quickly

ex·pres·sion 🔑 /ɪk'spreʃn/ *noun*
▸ SHOWING FEELINGS/IDEAS **1** 🔑 [U, C] things that people say, write or do in order to show their feelings, opinions and ideas: *an expression of support* ◇ *Expressions of sympathy flooded in from all over the country.* ◇ ***Freedom of expression*** (= freedom to say what you think) *is a basic human right.* ◇ (*formal*) *The poet's anger* ***finds expression in*** (= is shown in) *the last verse of the poem.* ◇ *Only in his dreams does he* ***give expression to*** *his fears.*
▸ ON FACE **2** 🔑 [C] a look on a person's face that shows their thoughts or feelings SYN **look**: *There was a worried expression on her face.* ◇ *an* ***expression of amazement/disbelief/horror*** ◇ *His expression changed from surprise to one of amusement.* ◇ *The expression in her eyes told me something was wrong.* ◇ *facial expressions*
▸ WORDS **3** 🔑 [C] a word or phrase: *an old-fashioned expression* ◇ (*informal*) *He's a pain in the butt,* ***if you'll pardon the expression.*** ➲ SYNONYMS at WORD
▸ IN MUSIC/ACTING **4** [U] a strong show of feeling when you are playing music, speaking, acting, etc: *Try to put a little more expression into it!*
▸ MATHEMATICS **5** [C] a group of signs that represent an idea or a quantity

ex·pres·sion·ism /ɪk'spreʃənɪzəm/ (also **Expressionism**) *noun* [U] a style and movement in early 20th century art, theatre, cinema and music that tries to express people's feelings and emotions rather than showing events or objects in a realistic way ▸ **ex·pres·sion·ist** /-ʃənɪst/ (also **Expressionist**) *noun, adj.*

ex·pres·sion·less /ɪk'spreʃənləs/ *adj.* not showing feelings, thoughts, etc: *an* ***expressionless face/tone/voice*** ➲ compare EXPRESSIVE

ex·pres·sive /ɪk'spresɪv/ *adj.* **1** showing or able to show your thoughts and feelings: *She has wonderfully expressive eyes.* ◇ *the expressive power of his music* ➲ compare EXPRESSIONLESS **2** [not before noun] **~ of sth** (*formal*) showing sth; existing as an expression of sth: *Every word and gesture is expressive of the artist's sincerity.* ▸ **ex·pres·sive·ly** *adv.* **ex·pres·sive·ness** *noun* [U]

E

ex'press lane *noun* (*NAmE*) **1** part of a road on which certain vehicles can travel faster because there is less traffic **2** a place in a shop/store where customers can pay without having to wait for a long time: *Customers with ten items or less can use the express lane.* ➲ compare CHECKOUT (1), TILL *n.* (2)

ex·press·ly /ɪk'spresli/ *adv.* (*formal*) **1** clearly; definitely: *She was expressly forbidden to touch my papers.* **2** for a special and deliberate purpose SYN **especially**: *The rule was introduced expressly for this purpose.*

ex·press·way /ɪk'spresweɪ/ *noun* (in the US) a wide road that allows traffic to travel fast through a city or other area where many people live

ex·pro·pri·ate /eks'prəʊprieɪt; *NAmE* -'proʊ-/ *verb* **1 ~ sth** (*formal* or *law*) (of a government or an authority) to officially take away private property from its owner for public use **2 ~ sth** (*formal*) to take sb's property and use it without permission ▸ **ex·pro·pri·ation** /ˌeksˌprəʊpri'eɪʃn; *NAmE* -ˌproʊ-/ *noun* [U]

ex·pul·sion /ɪk'spʌlʃn/ *noun* **1** [U, C] **~ (from...)** the act of forcing sb to leave a place; the act of EXPELLING sb: *These events led to the expulsion of senior diplomats from the country.* **2** [U, C] **~ (from...)** the act of sending sb away from a school or an organization, so that they can no longer belong to it; the act of EXPELLING sb: *The headteacher threatened the three girls with expulsion.* ◇ *The club faces expulsion from the football league.* **3** [U] **~ (from...)** (*formal*) the act of sending or driving a substance out of your body or a container

ex·punge /ɪk'spʌndʒ/ *verb* **~ sth (from sth)** (*formal*) to remove or get rid of sth, such as a name, piece of information or a memory, from a book or list, or from your mind SYN **erase**: *Details of his criminal activities were expunged from the file.* ◇ *What happened just before the accident was expunged from his memory.*

ex·pur·gate /'ekspəgeɪt; *NAmE* -pərg-/ *verb* **~ sth** [usually passive] (*formal*) to remove or leave out parts of a piece of writing or a conversation when printing or reporting it, because you think those parts could offend people

ex·quis·ite /ɪk'skwɪzɪt; 'ekskwɪzɪt/ *adj.* **1** extremely beautiful or carefully made: *exquisite craftsmanship* **2** (*formal*) (of a feeling) strongly felt SYN **acute**: ***exquisite pain/pleasure*** **3** (*formal*) delicate and sensitive: *The room was decorated in exquisite taste.* ◇ *an exquisite sense of timing* ▸ **ex·quis·ite·ly** *adv.*

ˌex-'service *adj.* (*BrE*) having previously been a member of the army, navy, etc: *ex-service personnel*

ˌex-'service·man, ˌex-'service·woman *noun* (*pl.* **-men** /-mən/, **-women** /-wɪmɪn/) (*BrE*) a person who used to be in the army, navy, etc.

ext. *abbr.* (used as part of a telephone number) EXTENSION: *Ext. 4299*

ex·tant /ek'stænt; 'ekstənt/ *adj.* (*formal*) (of sth very old) still in existence: *extant remains of the ancient wall*

ex·tem·pore /ek'stempəri/ *adj.* (*formal*) spoken or done without any previous thought or preparation SYN **impromptu** ▸ **ex·tem·pore** *adv.*

ex·tem·por·ize (*BrE* also **-ise**) /ɪk'stempəraɪz/ *verb* [I] (*formal*) to speak or perform without preparing or practising SYN **improvise** ▸ **ex·tem·por·iza·tion, -isa·tion** /ɪkˌstempəraɪ'zeɪʃn; *NAmE* -rə'z-/ *noun* [U]

ex·tend 0-w /ɪk'stend/ *verb*
▸ MAKE LONGER/LARGER/WIDER **1** 0-w [T] **~ sth** to make sth longer or larger: *to extend a fence/road/house* ◇ *There are plans to extend the no-smoking area.* **2** 0-w [T] **~ sth** to make sth last longer: *to* ***extend a deadline/visa*** ◇ *The show has been extended for another six weeks.* ◇ *Careful maintenance can* ***extend the life*** *of your car.* **3** 0-w [T] **~ sth** to make a business, an idea, an influence, etc. cover more areas or operate in more places: *The company plans to extend its operations into Europe.* ◇ *The school is extending the range of subjects taught.*
▸ INCLUDE **4** [I] **+ adv./prep.** to relate to or include sb/sth: *The offer does not extend to employees' partners.* ◇ *His willingness to help did not extend beyond making a few phone calls.*
▸ COVER AREA/TIME/DISTANCE **5** [I] **+ adv./prep.** to cover a particular area, distance or length of time: *Our land extends as far as the river.* ◇ *His writing career extended over a period of 40 years.* **6** [I] **+ adv./prep.** to make sth reach sth or stretch: *to extend a rope between two posts*
▸ PART OF BODY **7** [T] **~ sth** to stretch part of your body, especially an arm or a leg, away from yourself: *He extended his hand to* (= offered to shake hands with) *the new employee.* ◇ (*figurative*) *to* ***extend the hand of friendship*** *to* (= try to have good relations with) *another country*
▸ OFFER/GIVE **8** [T] (*formal*) to offer or give sth to sb: **~ sth to sb** *I'm sure you will join me in extending a very warm welcome to our visitors.* ◇ *to extend hospitality to overseas students* ◇ *The bank refused to extend credit to them* (= to lend them money). ◇ **~ sb sth** *to extend sb an invitation*
▸ USE EFFORT/ABILITY **9** [T, often passive] **~ sb/sth/yourself** to make sb/sth use all their effort, abilities, supplies, etc: *Jim didn't really have to extend himself in the exam.* ◇ *Hospitals were already fully extended because of the epidemic.* ➲ see also EXTENSION, EXTENSIVE

ex·tend·able (also **ex·tend·ible**) /ɪk'stendəbl/ *adj.* that can be made longer, or made valid for a longer time: *an extendable ladder* ◇ *The visa is for 14 days, extendable to one month.*

ex·tend·ed /ɪk'stendɪd/ *adj.* [only before noun] long or longer than usual or expected: *an extended lunch hour*

ex,tended 'family *noun* a family group with a close relationship among the members that includes not only parents and children but also uncles, aunts, grandparents, etc. ➲ compare NUCLEAR FAMILY

ex·ten·sion 0-w /ɪk'stenʃn/ *noun*
▸ INCREASING INFLUENCE **1** 0-w [U, C] **~ (of sth)** the act of increasing the area of activity, group of people, etc. that is affected by sth: *the extension of new technology into developing countries* ◇ *a gradual extension of the powers of central government* ◇ *The bank plans various extensions to its credit facilities.*
▸ OF BUILDING **2** 0-w [C] **~ (to sth)** (*BrE*) (*NAmE* **add·ition**) a new room or rooms that are added to a house ➲ **COLLOCATIONS** at DECORATE **3** 0-w [C] a new part that is added to a building: *a planned two-storey extension to the hospital*
▸ EXTRA TIME **4** 0-w [C] **~ (of sth)** an extra period of time allowed for sth: *He's been granted an extension of the contract for another year.* ◇ *a visa extension* ◇ (*BrE*) *The pub had an extension* (= was allowed to stay open longer) *on Christmas Eve.*
▸ TELEPHONE **5** 0-w [C] (*abbr.* **ext.**) an extra telephone line connected to a central telephone in a house or to a SWITCHBOARD in a large building. In a large building, each extension usually has its own number: *We have an extension in the bedroom.* ◇ *What's your extension number?* ◇ *Can I have extension 4332 please?*
▸ MAKING STH LONGER/LARGER **6** [U, C] the act of making sth longer or larger; the thing that is made longer and larger: *The extension of the subway will take several months.* ◇ *extensions to the original railway track* ◇ ***hair extensions*** (= pieces of artificial hair that are added to your hair to make it longer)
▸ COLLEGE/UNIVERSITY **7** [C] a part of a college or university that offers courses to students who are not studying FULL-TIME; a programme of study for these students: *La Salle Extension University* ◇ *extension courses*
▸ COMPUTING **8** the set of three letters that are placed after a dot at the end of the name of a file and that show what type of file it is
▸ ELECTRICAL **9** [C] (*BrE*) = EXTENSION LEAD
IDM **by ex'tension** (*formal*) taking the argument or situation one stage further: *The blame lies with the teachers and, by extension, with the Education Service.*

ex'tension agent *noun* (in the US) a person who works for a state university in a country area, and whose job is to give advice to farmers, do research into farming, etc.

ex'tension lead (also **extension**) (both *BrE*) (*NAmE* **ex'tension cord**) *noun* an extra length of electric wire, used when the wire on an electrical device is not long enough

ex·ten·sive 0-w /ɪk'stensɪv/ *adj.*
1 0-w covering a large area; great in amount: *The house has extensive grounds.* ◇ *The fire caused extensive damage.* ◇ *She suffered extensive injuries in the accident.* ◇ *Extensive repair work is being carried out.* ◇ *an extensive range of wines* **2** 0-w including or dealing with a wide range of information SYN **far-reaching**: *Extensive research has been done into this disease.* ◇ *His knowledge of music is extensive.* ▸ **ex·ten·sive·ly** *adv.*: *a spice used extensively in Eastern cooking* ◇ *She has travelled extensively.*

ex·ten·sor /ɪk'stensə(r); *NAmE* -sɔːr; *BrE* also ek's-/ (also **ex'tensor muscle**) *noun* (*anatomy*) a muscle that allows you to make part of your body straight or stretched out ➲ compare FLEXOR

ex·tent 0-w /ɪk'stent/ *noun* [sing., U]
1 0-w how large, important, serious, etc. sth is: *It is difficult to assess the* ***full extent*** *of the damage.* ◇ *She was exaggerating the* ***true extent*** *of the problem.* ◇ *I was amazed at the extent of his knowledge.* **2** the physical size of an area: *You can't see the* ***full extent*** *of the beach from here.*
IDM **to... extent** 0-w used to show how far sth is true or how great an effect it has: *To a* ***certain extent****, we are all responsible for this tragic situation.* ◇ *He had changed* ***to such an extent*** (= so much) *that I no longer recognized him.* ◇ ***To some extent*** *what she argues is true.* ◇ *The pollution of the forest has seriously affected plant life and,* ***to a lesser extent****, wildlife.* ◇ ***To what extent*** *is this true of all schools?* ◇ *The book discusses* ***the extent to which*** (= how much) *family life has changed over the past 50 years.*
➲ **LANGUAGE BANK** at GENERALLY

ex·tenu·at·ing /ɪk'stenjueɪtɪŋ/ *adj.* [only before noun] (*formal*) showing reasons why a wrong or illegal act, or a bad situation, should be judged less seriously or excused: *There were* ***extenuating circumstances*** *and the defendant did not receive a prison sentence.*

ex·ter·ior /ɪk'stɪəriə(r); *NAmE* -'stɪr-/ *noun, adj.*
■ ***noun*** **1** [C] the outside of sth, especially a building: *The exterior of the house needs painting.* OPP **interior** **2** [sing.] the way that sb appears or behaves, especially when this is very different from their real feelings or character: *Beneath his confident exterior, he was desperately nervous.*
■ ***adj.*** [usually before noun] on the outside of sth; done or happening outdoors: ***exterior walls/surfaces*** ◇ *The filming of the exterior scenes was done on the moors.* OPP **interior**

ex·ter·min·ate /ɪk'stɜːmɪneɪt; *NAmE* -'stɜːrm-/ *verb* **~ sb/sth** to kill all the members of a group of people or animals SYN **wipe out** ▸ **ex·ter·min·ation** /ɪk,stɜːmɪ'neɪʃn; *NAmE* -,stɜːrm-/ *noun* [U]

ex·tern /'ekstɜːn; *NAmE* -tɜːrn/ *noun* (*US*) a person who works in an institution but does not live there, especially a doctor or other worker in a hospital

ex·ter·nal AW /ɪk'stɜːnl; *NAmE* ɪk'stɜːrnl/ *adj.* **1** connected with or located on the outside of sth/sb: *the external walls of the building* ◇ *The lotion is* ***for external use*** *only* (= only for the skin and must not be swallowed). **2** happening or coming from outside a place, an organization, your particular situation, etc: *A combination of internal and external factors caused the company to close down.* ◇ *external pressures on the economy* ◇ *Many external influ-*

ences can affect your state of mind. **3** coming from or arranged by sb from outside a school, a university or an organization: (*BrE*) ***external examiners/assessors*** ◇ *An external auditor will verify the accounts.* **4** connected with foreign countries: *The government is committed to reducing the country's external debt.* ◇ *the Minister of State for External Affairs* **OPP internal** ▸ **ex·ter·nal·ly AW** /ɪk'stɜːnəli; *NAmE* -'stɜːrn-/ *adv.*: *The building has been restored externally and internally.* ◇ *The university has many externally funded research projects.*

ex,ternal 'ear *noun* (*anatomy*) the parts of the ear outside the EARDRUM

ex·ter·nal·ity AW /,ekstɜː'næləti; *NAmE* -stɜːr'n-/ *noun* **1** [C] (*economics*) a consequence of an industrial or commercial activity which affects other people or things without this being reflected in market prices: *Pollution is a negative externality that imposes a cost—reduced happiness—on the victims.* **2** [U] (*philosophy*) the fact of existing outside the person or thing that is aware of it: *man's externality to an indifferent natural world*

ex·ter·nal·ize (*BrE* also **-ise**) **AW** /ɪk'stɜːnəlaɪz; *NAmE* -'stɜːrn-/ *verb* **~ sth** (*formal*) to show what you are thinking and feeling by what you say or do ➲ compare INTERNALIZE ▸ **ex·ter·nal·iza·tion, -isa·tion AW** /ɪk,stɜːnəlaɪ'zeɪʃn; *NAmE* -,stɜːrn-/ *noun* [U]

ex·ter·nals /ɪk'stɜːnlz; *NAmE* -'stɜːrn-/ *noun* [pl.] (*formal*) the outer appearance of sth

ex·tinct /ɪk'stɪŋkt/ *adj.* **1** (of a type of plant, animal, etc.) no longer in existence: *an extinct species* ◇ *to become extinct* **2** (of a type of person, job or way of life) no longer in existence in society: *Servants are now almost extinct in modern society.* **3** (of a VOLCANO) no longer active **OPP active**

ex·tinc·tion /ɪk'stɪŋkʃn/ *noun* [U, C] a situation in which a plant, an animal, a way of life, etc. stops existing: *a tribe* ***threatened with extinction/in danger of extinction*** ◇ *The mountain gorilla is* ***on the verge of extinction.*** ◇ *We know of several mass extinctions in the earth's history.*

ex·tin·guish /ɪk'stɪŋgwɪʃ/ *verb* (*formal*) **1 ~ sth** to make a fire stop burning or a light stop shining **SYN put out**: *Firefighters tried to extinguish the flames.* ◇ *All lights had been extinguished.* **2 ~ sth** to destroy sth: *News of the bombing extinguished all hope of peace.*

ex·tin·guish·er *noun* = FIRE EXTINGUISHER

ex·tirp·ate /'ekstəpeɪt; *NAmE* -tərp-/ *verb* **~ sth** (*formal*) to destroy or get rid of sth that is bad or not wanted ▸ **ex·tir·pa·tion** /,ekstə'peɪʃn; *NAmE* -tər'p-/ *noun* [U]

extol /ɪk'stəʊl; *NAmE* ɪk'stoʊl/ *verb* (-ll-) (*formal*) to praise sb/sth very much: **~ sb/sth** *Doctors often* ***extol the virtues*** *of eating less fat.* ◇ **~ sb/sth as sth** *She was extolled as a genius.*

ex·tort /ɪk'stɔːt; *NAmE* ɪk'stɔːrt/ *verb* **~ sth** (**from sb**) to make sb give you sth by threatening them: *The gang extorted money from over 30 local businesses.* ▸ **ex·tor·tion** /ɪk'stɔːʃn; *NAmE* ɪk'stɔːrʃn/ *noun* [U, C]: *He was arrested and charged with extortion.*

ex·tor·tion·ate /ɪk'stɔːʃənət; *NAmE* -'stɔːrʃ-/ *adj.* (rather *informal, disapproving*) (of prices, etc.) much too high **SYN excessive, outrageous**: *They are offering loans at extortionate rates of interest.* ▸ **ex·tor·tion·ate·ly** *adv.*: *extortionately priced*

extra 🔑 /'ekstrə/ *adj., noun, adv.*

■ ***adj.*** 🔑 more than is usual, expected, or than exists already **SYN additional**: *Breakfast is provided at no extra charge.* ◇ *The conference is going to be a lot of extra work.* ◇ *an extra pint of milk* ◇ *The government has promised an extra £1 billion for health care.* ◇ *Take extra care on the roads this evening.* ➲ see also EXTRA TIME

■ ***noun*** **1** 🔑 a thing that is added to sth that is not usual, standard or necessary and that costs more: *The monthly fee is fixed and there are no* ***hidden extras*** (= unexpected costs). ◇ (*BrE*) *Metallic paint is* ***an optional extra*** (= a thing you can choose to have or not, but must pay more for if you have it). **2** a person who is employed to play a very small part in a film/movie, usually as a member of a crowd

■ ***adv.*** **1** 🔑 in addition; more than is usual, expected or exists already: *to* ***charge/pay/cost extra*** ◇ *I need to earn a bit extra this month.* ◇ *The rate for a room is £30, but breakfast is extra.* **2** 🔑 (with an adjective or adverb) more than usually: *You need to be extra careful not to make any mistakes.* ◇ *an extra large T-shirt* ◇ *She tried extra hard.*

extra- /'ekstrə/ *prefix* (in adjectives) **1** outside; beyond: *extramarital sex* ◇ *extraterrestrial beings* **2** (*informal*) very; more than usual: *extra-thin* ◇ *extra-special*

ex·tract AW *noun, verb*

■ ***noun*** /'ekstrækt/ **1** [C] **~ (from sth)** a short passage from a book, piece of music, etc. that gives you an idea of what the whole thing is like: *The following extract is taken from her new novel.* **2** [U, C] a substance that has been obtained from sth else using a particular process: *yeast extract* ◇ *face cream containing natural plant extracts* ◇ (*NAmE*) *vanilla extract* ➲ see also ESSENCE

■ ***verb*** /ɪk'strækt/ **1 ~ sth** (**from sb/sth**) to remove or obtain a substance from sth, for example by using an industrial or a chemical process: *a machine that extracts excess moisture from the air* ◇ *to extract essential oils from plants* **2 ~ sth** (**from sb/sth**) to obtain information, money, etc, often by taking it from sb who is unwilling to give it: *Journalists managed to extract all kinds of information about her private life.* **3 ~ sth** (**from sb/sth**) to choose information, etc. from a book, a computer, etc. to be used for a particular purpose: *This article is extracted from his new book.* **4 ~ sth** (**from sb/sth**) (*formal* or *technical*) to take or pull sth out, especially when this needs force or effort: *The dentist may decide that the wisdom teeth need to be extracted.* ◇ *He rifled through his briefcase and extracted a file.* **5 ~ sth** (**from sb/sth**) (*formal*) to get a particular feeling or quality from a situation **SYN derive**: *They are unlikely to extract much benefit from the trip.*

ex·trac·tion AW /ɪk'strækʃn/ *noun* **1** [U, C] the act or process of removing or obtaining sth from sth else: ***oil/mineral/coal, etc. extraction*** ◇ *the extraction of salt from the sea* **2** [U] **of... extraction** (*formal*) having a particular family origin: *an American of Hungarian extraction* **3** [C] (*technical*) the removal of a tooth

ex·tract·ive /ɪk'stræktɪv; ek-/ *adj.* (*technical*) relating to the process of removing or obtaining sth, especially minerals: *extractive industries*

ex·tract·or /ɪk'stræktə(r)/ *noun* **1** (also **ex'tractor fan**) a device that removes hot air, unpleasant smells, etc. from a room **2** a device or machine that removes sth from sth else: *a juice extractor*

,extra-cur'ricu·lar *adj.* [usually before noun] not part of the usual course of work or studies at a school or college: *She's involved in many* ***extra-curricular activities.***

extra·dite /'ekstrədaɪt/ *verb* **~ sb** (**to...**) (**from...**) to officially send back sb who has been accused or found guilty of a crime to the country where the crime was committed: *The British government attempted to extradite the suspects from Belgium.* ▸ **extra·di·tion** /,ekstrə'dɪʃn/ *noun* [U, C]: *the extradition of terrorist suspects* ◇ *an extradition treaty* ◇ *to start extradition proceedings*

extra·judi·cial /,ekstrədʒu'dɪʃl/ *adj.* happening outside the normal power of the law

extra·mar·it·al /,ekstrə'mærɪtl/ *adj.* happening outside marriage: *an extramarital affair*

extra·mural /,ekstrə'mjʊərəl; *NAmE* -'mjʊrəl/ *adj.* [usually before noun] **1** (*BrE*) arranged by a university, college, etc. for people who only study PART-TIME: ***extramural education/studies/departments*** ➲ see also EXTENSION (7) **2** (*formal*) happening or existing outside or separate from a place, an organization, etc: *The hospital provides extramural care to patients who do not need to be admitted.*

ex·tra·ne·ous /ɪk'streɪniəs/ *adj.* (*formal*) not directly connected with the particular situation you are in or the subject you are dealing with **SYN irrelevant**: *We do not want any extraneous information on the page.* ◇ **~ to sth** *We shall ignore factors extraneous to the problem.*

extra·or·din·aire /ɪk,strɔːdɪ'neə(r); *NAmE* ɪk,strɔːrdɪ'ner/ *adj.* (from *French, approving*, often *humorous*) used after nouns to say that sb is a good example of a particular kind of person: *Houdini, escape artist extraordinaire*

extra·or·din·ary 0-ᵂ /ɪk'strɔːdnri; *NAmE* ɪk'strɔːrdəneri/ *adj.*
1 0-ᵂ unexpected, surprising or strange **SYN incredible**: *It's extraordinary that he managed to sleep through the party.* ◇ *What an extraordinary thing to say!* **2** 0-ᵂ not normal or ordinary; greater or better than usual: *an extraordinary achievement* ◇ *She was a truly extraordinary woman.* ◇ *They went to extraordinary lengths to explain their behaviour.* ➲ compare ORDINARY **3** [only before noun] (*formal*) (of a meeting, etc.) arranged for a special purpose and happening in addition to what normally or regularly happens: *An extraordinary meeting was held to discuss the problem.* **4** (following nouns) (*technical*) (of an official) employed for a special purpose in addition to the usual staff: *an envoy extraordinary* ▶ **extra·or·din·ar·ily** /ɪk'strɔːdnrəli; *NAmE* ɪkˌstrɔːrdə'nerəli/ *adv.*: *He behaves extraordinarily for someone in his position.* ◇ *extraordinarily difficult* ◇ *She did extraordinarily well.*

exˌtraordinary renˈdition *noun* = RENDITION

ex·trapo·late /ɪk'stræpəleɪt/ *verb* [I, T] (*formal*) to estimate sth or form an opinion about sth, using the facts that you have now and that are valid for one situation and supposing that they will be valid for the new one: **~ (from/to sth)** *The figures were obtained by extrapolating from past trends.* ◇ **~ sth (from/to sth)** *We have extrapolated these results from research done in other countries.* ▶ **ex·trapo·la·tion** /ɪkˌstræpə'leɪʃn/ *noun* [U, C]: *Their age can be determined by extrapolation from their growth rate.*

extra·sens·ory perception /ˌekstrəˌsensəri pə'sepʃn; *NAmE* pər's-/ *noun* [U] = ESP

extra·solar /ˌekstrə'səʊlə(r); *NAmE* -'soʊlər/ *adj.* [usually before noun] (*technical*) (of a planet, etc.) located outside our SOLAR SYSTEM

extra·ter·res·trial /ˌekstrətə'restriəl/ *noun, adj.*
■ ***noun*** (in stories) a creature that comes from another planet; a creature that may exist on another planet
■ ***adj.*** connected with life existing outside the planet Earth: ***extraterrestrial beings/life***

extra·ter·ri·tor·ial /ˌekstrəterə'tɔːriəl/ *adj.* (of a law) valid outside the country where the law was made

ˌextra ˈtime (*BrE*) (*NAmE* **over·time**) *noun* [U] (*sport*) a set period of time that is added to the end of a sports game, etc, if there is no winner at the end of the normal period: *They won by a single goal after extra time.*

ex·trava·gance /ɪk'strævəgəns/ *noun* **1** [U] the act or habit of spending more money than you can afford or than is necessary **2** [C] something that you buy although it costs a lot of money, perhaps more than you can afford or than is necessary: *Going to the theatre is our only extravagance.* **3** [C, U] something that is impressive or noticeable because it is unusual or extreme: *the extravagance of Strauss's music*

ex·trava·gant /ɪk'strævəgənt/ *adj.* **1** spending a lot more money or using a lot more of sth than you can afford or than is necessary: *I felt very extravagant spending £100 on a dress.* ◇ *She's got very extravagant tastes.* ◇ *Residents were warned not to be* ***extravagant with*** *water, in view of the low rainfall this year.* **2** costing a lot more money than you can afford or is necessary: *an extravagant present* **3** (of ideas, speech or behaviour) very extreme or impressive but not reasonable or practical **SYN exaggerated**: *the* ***extravagant claims/promises*** *of politicians* ▶ **ex·trava·gant·ly** *adv.*: *extravagantly expensive* ◇ *extravagantly high hopes*

ex·trava·ganza /ɪkˌstrævə'gænzə/ *noun* a large, expensive and impressive entertainment

ex·tra·vert = EXTROVERT

ˌextra ˈvirgin *adj.* used to describe good quality oil obtained the first time that OLIVES are pressed: *extra virgin olive oil*

ex·treme 0-ᵂ /ɪk'striːm/ *adj., noun*
■ ***adj.*** **1** 0-ᵂ [usually before noun] very great in degree: *We are working under extreme pressure at the moment.* ◇ *people living in extreme poverty* ◇ *The heat in the desert was extreme.* **2** 0-ᵂ not ordinary or usual; serious or severe: *Children will be removed from their parents only* ***in extreme circumstances.*** ◇ *Don't go doing anything extreme like leaving the country.* ◇ *It was the most* ***extreme example*** *of cruelty to animals I had ever seen.* ◇ *extreme weather conditions* **3** 0-ᵂ (of people, political organizations, opinions, etc.) far from what most people consider to be normal, reasonable or acceptable: ***extreme left-wing/right-wing views*** **OPP moderate** **4** [only before noun] as far as possible from the centre, the beginning or in the direction mentioned: *Kerry is in the extreme west of Ireland.* ◇ *She sat on the extreme edge of her seat.*
■ ***noun*** **1** a feeling, situation, way of behaving, etc. that is as different as possible from another or is opposite to it: *extremes of love and hate* ◇ *He used to be very shy, but now he's gone to* ***the opposite extreme*** (= changed from one extreme kind of behaviour to another). **2** the greatest or highest degree of sth: *extremes of cold, wind or rain*
IDM **go, etc. to exˈtremes | take sth to exˈtremes** to act or be forced to act in a way that is far from normal or reasonable: *It's embarrassing the extremes he'll go to in order to impress his boss.* ◇ *Taken to extremes, this kind of behaviour can be dangerous.* **in the exˈtreme** (*formal*) to a great degree: *The journey would be dangerous in the extreme.*

exˈtreme fighting *noun* [U] = ULTIMATE FIGHTING

ex·treme·ly 0-ᵂ /ɪk'striːmli/ *adv.*
(usually with adjectives and adverbs) to a very high degree: *extremely important/useful/complicated* ◇ *She found it extremely difficult to get a job.*

exˌtreme ˈsports *noun* [pl.] sports that are extremely exciting to do and often dangerous, for example SKYDIVING and BUNGEE JUMPING ➲ **VISUAL VOCAB** page V40

exˌtreme ˈunction *noun* [U] (*religion*) (*old use*) in the Catholic Church, the ceremony of BLESSING sick or dying people: *He was given extreme unction.*

ex·tre·mis ➲ IN EXTREMIS

ex·trem·ism /ɪk'striːmɪzəm/ *noun* [U] political, religious, etc. ideas or actions that are extreme and not normal, reasonable or acceptable to most people: *political extremism*

ex·trem·ist /ɪk'striːmɪst/ *noun* (usually *disapproving*) a person whose opinions, especially about religion or politics, are extreme, and who may do things that are violent, illegal, etc. for what they believe: ***left-wing/right-wing/political/religious extremists*** ▶ **ex·trem·ist** *adj.* [usually before noun]: ***extremist attacks/groups/policies***

ex·trem·ity /ɪk'streməti/ *noun* (*pl.* -ies) **1** [C] the furthest point, end or limit of sth: *The lake is situated at the eastern extremity of the mountain range.* **2** [C, U] the degree to which a situation, a feeling, an action, etc. is extreme, difficult or unusual: *the extremities/extremity of pain* **3 extremities** [pl.] (*formal*) the parts of your body that are furthest from the centre, especially your hands and feet

ex·tri·cate /'ekstrɪkeɪt/ *verb* (*formal*) **1 ~ sb/sth/yourself (from sth)** to escape or enable sb to escape from a difficult situation: *He had managed to extricate himself from most of his official duties.* **2 ~ sb/sth/yourself (from sth)** to free sb/sth or yourself from a place where they/it or you are trapped: *They managed to extricate the pilot from the tangled control panel.*

ex·trin·sic /eks'trɪnsɪk; -zɪk/ *adj.* (*formal*) not belonging naturally to sb/sth; coming from or existing outside sb/sth rather than within them: *extrinsic factors* ➲ compare INTRINSIC

ex·tro·vert (also *less frequent* **ex·tra·vert**) /'ekstrəvɜːt; *NAmE* -vɜːrt/ *noun* a lively and confident person who enjoys being with other people **OPP introvert** ▶ **ex·tro·vert·ed** (*BrE* also **ex·tro·vert**) *adj.*

ex·trude /ɪk'struːd/ *verb* **1** [T, I] **~ (sth) (from sth)** (*formal*) to force or push sth out of sth; to be forced or pushed in this way: *Lava is extruded from the volcano.* **2** [T] **~ sth**

(*technical*) to shape metal or plastic by forcing it through a hole ▶ **ex·tru·sion** /ɪk'struːʒn/ *noun* [U]

ex·tru·sive /ɪk'struːsɪv/ *adj.* (*geology*) (of rock) that has been pushed out of the earth by a VOLCANO

ex·uber·ant /ɪg'zjuːbərənt; *NAmE* -'zuː-/ *adj.* **1** full of energy, excitement and happiness: *She gave an exuberant performance.* ◇ *an* ***exuberant personality/imagination*** ◇ *a picture painted in exuberant reds and yellows* **2** (of plants, etc.) strong and healthy; growing quickly and well ▶ **ex·uber·ance** /-rəns/ *noun* [U]: *We can excuse his behaviour as youthful exuberance.* **ex·uber·ant·ly** *adv.*

exude /ɪg'zjuːd; *NAmE* -'zuːd/ *verb* **1** [T, I] **~ (sth)** | **~ (from sb)** if you **exude** a particular feeling or quality, or it **exudes** from you, people can easily see that you have it: *She exuded confidence.* **2** [T, I] if sth **exudes** a liquid or smell, or a liquid or smell **exudes** from somewhere, the liquid, etc. comes out slowly: **~ sth** *The plant exudes a sticky fluid.* ◇ **~ (from sth)** *An awful smell exuded from the creature's body.*

exult /ɪg'zʌlt/ *verb* [I, T] (*formal*) to feel and show that you are very excited and happy because of sth that has happened: **~ (at/in sth)** *He leaned back, exulting at the success of his plan.* ◇ **+ speech** *'We won!' she exulted.*

ex·ult·ant /ɪg'zʌltənt/ *adj.* **~ (at sth)** (*formal*) feeling or showing great pride or happiness especially because of sth exciting that has happened SYN **triumphant** ▶ **ex·ult·ant·ly** *adv.*

ex·ult·ation /ˌegzʌl'teɪʃn/ *noun* [U] (*formal*) great pride or happiness, especially because of sth exciting that has happened

-ey ➲ -Y

eye 🔑 /aɪ/ *noun, verb*

■ ***noun***

▸ PART OF BODY **1** 🔑 [C] either of the two organs on the face that you see with: *The suspect has dark hair and green eyes.* ◇ *to* ***close/open*** *your* ***eyes*** ◇ *to* ***drop/lower*** *your* ***eyes*** (= to look down) ◇ *There were tears in his eyes.* ◇ *I have something in my eye.* ◇ *to make/avoid* ***eye contact*** *with sb* (= to look/avoid looking at them at the same time as they look at you) ◇ ***All eyes were on*** *him* (= everyone was looking at him) *as he walked on to the stage.* ➲ **COLLOCATIONS** at PHYSICAL ➲ **VISUAL VOCAB** page V48 ➲ see also BLACK EYE, COMPOUND EYE, LAZY EYE, SHUT-EYE **2** **-eyed** (in adjectives) having the type or number of eyes mentioned: *a blue-eyed blonde* ◇ *a one-eyed monster*

▸ ABILITY TO SEE **3** 🔑 [sing.] the ability to see: *A surgeon needs a good eye and a steady hand.* ➲ see also EAGLE EYE

▸ WAY OF SEEING **4** [C, usually sing.] a particular way of seeing sth: *He looked at the design* ***with the eye of*** *an engineer.* ◇ *She viewed the findings with a critical eye.* ◇ ***To my eye,*** *the windows seem out of proportion.*

▸ OF NEEDLE **5** [C] the hole in the end of a needle that you put the thread through

▸ ON CLOTHES **6** [C] a small thin piece of metal curved round, that a small hook fits into, used for fastening clothes: *It fastens with a* ***hook and eye.*** ➲ **VISUAL VOCAB** page V51

▸ OF STORM **7** [sing.] **a/the ~ of a/the storm, tornado, hurricane, etc.** a calm area at the centre of a storm, etc.

▸ ON POTATO **8** [C] a dark mark on a potato from which another plant will grow ➲ see also BULLSEYE, CATSEYE, THE EVIL EYE, FISHEYE LENS, RED-EYE

IDM **be all 'eyes** to be watching sb/sth carefully and with a lot of interest **before/in front of sb's (very) eyes** in sb's presence; in front of sb: *He had seen his life's work destroyed before his very eyes.* **be up to your eyes in sth** to have a lot of sth to deal with: *We're up to our eyes in work.* **cast/run an eye/your eyes over sth** to look at or examine sth quickly: *Could you just run your eyes over this report?* **clap/lay/set eyes on sb/sth** (*informal*) (usually used in negative sentences) to see sb/sth: *I haven't clapped eyes on them for weeks.* ◇ *I hope I never set eyes on this place again!* **an ˌeye for an 'eye (and a ˌtooth for a 'tooth)** (*saying*) used to say that you should punish sb by doing to them what they have done to you or to sb else **sb's eyes are bigger than their 'stomach** used to say that sb has been GREEDY by taking more food than they can eat **for sb's eyes 'only** to be seen only by a particular person: *I'll lend you the letters but they're for your eyes only.* **get your 'eye in** (*BrE*) (in ball games) to practise so that you are able to judge more clearly how fast and where the ball is going **have an eye for sth** to be able to judge if things look attractive, valuable, etc: *I've never had much of an eye for fashion.* ◇ *She has an eye for a bargain.* **have eyes in the back of your 'head** to be aware of everything that is happening around you, even things that seem difficult or impossible to see **have (got) eyes like a 'hawk** to be able to notice or see everything: *She's bound to notice that chipped glass. The woman has eyes like a hawk!* **have one eye/half an eye on sth** to look at or watch sth while doing sth else, especially in a secret way so that other people do not notice: *During his talk, most of the delegates had one eye on the clock.* **have your 'eye on sb 1** 🔑 to be watching sb carefully, especially to check that they do not do anything wrong **2** to be thinking about asking sb out, offering sb a job, etc. because you think they are attractive, good at their job, etc: *He's got his eye on the new girl in your class.* **have your 'eye on sth** to be thinking about buying sth **in the eyes of the 'law, 'world, etc.** according to the law, most people in the world, etc. **in 'sb's eyes** (*BrE* also **to 'sb's eyes**) in sb's opinion or according to the way that they see the situation: *She can do no wrong in her father's eyes.* **keep an eye on sb/sth** 🔑 to take care of sb/sth and make sure that they are not harmed, damaged, etc: *We've asked the neighbours to keep an eye on the house for us while we are away.* **keep an eye open/out (for sb/sth)** to look for sb/sth while you are doing other things: *Police have asked residents to keep an eye out for anything suspicious.* **keep your eye on the 'ball** to continue to give your attention to what is most important **keep your 'eyes peeled/skinned (for sb/sth)** to look carefully for sb/sth: *We kept our eyes peeled for any signs of life.* **look sb in the 'eye(s)/'face** (usually used in negative sentences and questions) to look straight at sb without feeling embarrassed or ashamed: *Can you look me in the eye and tell me you're not lying?* ◇ *I'll never be able to look her in the face again!* **make 'eyes at sb** | **give sb the 'eye** to look at sb in a way that shows that you find them sexually attractive: *He's definitely giving you the eye!* **ˌmy 'eye!** (*BrE, old-fashioned, informal*) used to show that you do not believe sb/sth: *'It's an antique.' 'An antique, my eye!'* **not see eye to 'eye with sb (on sth)** to not share the same views as sb about sth **not (be able to) take your 'eyes off sb/sth** to find sb/sth so interesting, attractive, etc. that you watch them all the time **one in the eye (for sb/sth)** (*informal*) a result, action, etc. that represents a defeat or disappointment for sb/sth: *The appointment of a woman was one in the eye for male domination.* **only have eyes for/have eyes only for sb** to be in love with only one particular person: *He's only ever had eyes for his wife.* **see, look at, etc. sth through sb's eyes** to think about or see sth the way that another person sees it: *Try looking at it through her eyes for a change.* **shut/close your eyes to sth** 🔑 to pretend that you have not noticed sth so that you do not have to deal with it **take your eye off the 'ball** to stop giving your attention to what is most important **under the (watchful) eye of sb** being watched carefully by sb: *The children played under the watchful eye of their father.* **what the eye doesn't 'see (the heart doesn't 'grieve over)** (*saying*) if a person does not know about sth that they would normally disapprove of, then it cannot hurt them: *What does it matter if I use his flat while he's away? What the eye doesn't see...!* **with an eye for/on/to the main chance** (*BrE*, usually *disapproving*) with the hope of using a particular situation in order to gain some advantage for yourself **with an eye to sth/to doing sth** with the intention of doing sth: *He bought the warehouse with an eye to converting it into a hotel.* **with your eyes 'open** fully aware of the possible problems or results of a particular course of action: *I went into this with my eyes open so I guess I only have myself to blame.* **with your eyes 'shut/'closed** having enough experience to be able to do sth easily: *I've made this trip so often, I could do it with my eyes shut.* ➲ more at APPLE, BAT *v.*, BEAUTY, BELIEVE, BIRD, BLIND

E

adj., BLINK *n.*, BLUE *adj.*, CATCH *v.*, CLOSE[2] *adj.*, COCK *v.*, CORNER *n.*, DRY *n.*, EASY *adj.*, FAR *adv.*, FEAST *v.*, HIT *v.*, MEET *v.*, MIND *n.*, NAKED, OPEN *adj.*, OPEN *v.*, PLEASE *v.*, PUBLIC *adj.*, PULL *v.*, ROVING, SIGHT *n.*, TWINKLING, WEATHER *n.*

■ ***verb*** (**eye·ing** or **eying**, **eyed**, **eyed**) **~ sb/sth (+ adv./prep.)** to look at sb/sth carefully, especially because you want sth or you are suspicious of sth: *to eye sb suspiciously* ◇ *He couldn't help eyeing the cakes hungrily.* ◇ *They eyed us with alarm.*

PHR V **,eye sb↔'up** (*informal*) to look at sb in a way that shows you have a special interest in them, especially a sexual interest

eye·ball /'aɪbɔːl/ *noun, verb*

■ ***noun*** the whole of the eye, including the part inside the head that cannot be seen ➲ VISUAL VOCAB page V48

IDM **,eyeball to 'eyeball (with sb)** very close to sb and looking at them, especially during an angry conversation, meeting, etc: *The protesters and police stood eyeball to eyeball.* ◇ *an eyeball-to-eyeball confrontation* **be up to your eyeballs in sth** to have a lot of sth to deal with: *They're up to their eyeballs in work.* ➲ more at DRUG *v.*

■ ***verb* ~ sb/sth** (*informal*) to look at sb/sth in a way that is very direct and not always polite or friendly

eye·bath /'aɪbɑːθ; *NAmE* -bæθ/ *noun* a small container that you put a liquid in to wash your eye with

eye·brow /'aɪbraʊ/ (also **brow**) *noun* [usually pl.] the line of hair above the eye ➲ COLLOCATIONS at PHYSICAL ➲ VISUAL VOCAB page V48

IDM **be up to your eyebrows in sth** to have a lot of sth to deal with: *He's in it* (= trouble) *up to his eyebrows.* ➲ more at RAISE *v.*

'eyebrow pencil *noun* a type of make-up in the form of a pencil, used for emphasizing or improving the shape of the EYEBROWS

'eye candy *noun* [U] (*informal*) a person or thing that is attractive but not intelligent or useful

'eye-catching *adj.* (of a thing) immediately noticeable because it is particularly interesting, bright or attractive: *an eye-catching advertisement*

eye·ful /'aɪfʊl/ *noun* **1** an amount of sth such as liquid or dust that has been thrown, or blown into your eye **2** (*informal*) a person or thing that is beautiful or interesting to look at

IDM **have/get an eyeful (of sth)** (*BrE, informal*) to look carefully at sth that is interesting or unusual

eye·glass /'aɪɡlɑːs; *NAmE* -ɡlæs/ *noun* **1** a LENS for one eye used to help you see more clearly with that eye **2 eyeglasses** (*NAmE*) = GLASSES

eye·lash /'aɪlæʃ/ (also **lash**) *noun* [usually pl.] one of the hairs growing on the edge of the EYELIDS: *false eyelashes* ◇ *She just* ***flutters her eyelashes*** *and the men come running!* ➲ COLLOCATIONS at PHYSICAL ➲ VISUAL VOCAB page V48

IDM see BAT *v.*

eye·let /'aɪlət/ *noun* a hole with a metal ring around it in a piece of cloth or leather, normally used for passing a rope or string through

'eye level *noun* [U] the height of a person's eyes: *Computer screens should be at eye level.* ◇ *an eye-level grill*

eye·lid /'aɪlɪd/ (also **lid**) *noun* either of the pieces of skin above and below the eye that cover it when you BLINK or close the eye ➲ VISUAL VOCAB page V48 IDM see BAT *v.*

eye·line /'aɪlaɪn/ *noun* the direction that sb is looking in

eye·liner /'aɪlaɪnə(r)/ (also **liner**) *noun* [U] a type of make-up, usually black, that is put around the edge of the eyes to make them more noticeable and attractive ➲ VISUAL VOCAB page V49

'eye-opener *noun* [usually sing.] an event, experience, etc. that is surprising and shows you sth that you did not already know: *Travelling around India was a real eye-opener for me.*

eye·patch /'aɪpætʃ/ *noun* a piece of material worn over one eye, usually because the eye is damaged

eye·piece /'aɪpiːs/ *noun* the piece of glass (= a LENS) at the end of a TELESCOPE or MICROSCOPE that you look through ➲ picture at BINOCULARS ➲ VISUAL VOCAB page V57

eye·shadow /'aɪʃædəʊ; *NAmE* -doʊ/ *noun* [C, U] a type of coloured make-up that is put on the skin above the eyes (= the EYELIDS) to make them look more attractive ➲ VISUAL VOCAB page V49

eye·sight /'aɪsaɪt/ *noun* [U] the ability to see: *to have* ***good/bad/poor eyesight*** ◇ *an eyesight test*

eye·sore /'aɪsɔː(r)/ *noun* a building, an object, etc. that is unpleasant to look at: *That old factory is a real eyesore!*

'eye strain *noun* [U] a condition of the eyes caused, for example, by a long period of reading or looking at a computer screen

'eye teeth *noun* [pl.]

IDM **give your eye teeth for sth/to do sth** (*BrE, informal*) used when you are saying that you want sth very much: *I'd give my eye teeth to own a car like that.*

eye·wall /'aɪwɔːl/ *noun* (*technical*) a thick ring of cloud around the EYE (= calm area at the centre) of a HURRICANE

eye·wash /'aɪwɒʃ; *NAmE* -wɔːʃ; -wɑːʃ/ *noun* [U] (*old-fashioned, informal*) words, promises, etc. that are not true or sincere

'eye-watering *adj.* (*informal, especially BrE*) so high or extreme that it is difficult or painful to think about it: *eye-watering fare increases* ▸ **eye-wateringly** *adv.*: *eye-wateringly high interest rates*

eye·wear /'aɪweə(r); *NAmE* -wer/ *noun* [U] (*formal*) things worn on the eyes such as glasses or CONTACT LENSES

eye·wit·ness /'aɪwɪtnəs/ *noun* a person who has seen a crime, accident, etc. and can describe it afterwards: *an eyewitness account of the suffering of the refugees* ➲ SYNONYMS at WITNESS ➲ see also WITNESS

eyrie (*especially BrE*) (*NAmE* usually **aerie**) /'ɪəri; 'eəri; 'aɪəri; *NAmE* 'ɪri; 'eri/ *noun* **1** a nest that is built high up among rocks by a BIRD OF PREY (= a bird that kills other creatures for food) such as an EAGLE **2** a room or building in a high place, especially one that is difficult to reach and from which sb can see what is happening below

'e-zine *noun* a magazine published in electronic form on the Internet

Ff

F /ef/ *noun, abbr.*
■ ***noun*** (also **f**) [C, U] (*pl.* **Fs, F's, f's** /efs/) **1** the 6th letter of the English alphabet: *'Fox' begins with (an) F/'F'.* **2 F** (*music*) the fourth note in the SCALE of C MAJOR **3** the 6th highest mark/grade that a student can get for a piece of work, showing that it is very bad and the student has failed: *He got* ***(an) F/'F' in/for*** *Chemistry.* ➲ see also F-WORD
■ ***abbr.*** **1** FAHRENHEIT: *Water freezes at 32°F.* **2** (*BrE*) (in academic titles) FELLOW of: *FRCM* (= Fellow of the Royal College of Music) **3** FARAD

f (*BrE*) (also **f.** *NAmE, BrE*) *abbr.* **1** female **2** (*grammar*) feminine **3** (*music*) loudly (from Italian 'forte')

F-1 visa /ˌef wʌn ˈviːzə/ *noun* a document that allows sb from another country to enter the US as a student

FA /ˌef ˈeɪ/ *noun* [sing.] **the FA** the abbreviation for 'Football Association' (the organization that controls the sport of football (SOCCER) in England and Wales)

fa = FAH

fab /fæb/ *adj.* (*BrE, informal*) extremely good

fable /ˈfeɪbl/ *noun* **1** [C, U] a traditional short story that teaches a moral lesson, especially one with animals as characters; these stories considered as a group: *Aesop's Fables* ◇ *a land rich in fable* **2** [U, C] a statement, or an account of sth, that is not true

fabled /ˈfeɪbld/ *adj.* (*literary* or *humorous*) famous and often talked about, but rarely seen SYN **legendary**: *a fabled monster* ◇ *For the first week he never actually saw the fabled Jack.*

Synonyms

fabric

cloth • material • textile

These are all words for woven or knitted cotton, silk, wool, etc, used for making things such as clothes and curtains, and for covering furniture.

fabric woven or knitted cotton, silk, wool, etc, used for making things such as clothes and curtains, and for covering furniture: *cotton fabric* ◇ *furnishing fabrics* NOTE **Fabric** is often fairly strong material, and is often used when talking about covering furniture or making curtains.

cloth fabric made by weaving or knitting cotton, wool, silk, etc: *His bandages had been made from strips of cloth.* NOTE **Cloth** is often fairly light material, especially in a form that has not been printed, treated, or prepared for use in any way. **Cloth** is frequently used in talking about buying and selling woven material.

material fabric used for making clothes, curtains, etc: *'What material is this dress made of?' 'Cotton.'* NOTE **Material** is a more general word than **fabric** or **cloth** as it has the related meaning of 'a substance that things can be made from'. It is not used when it might not be clear which type of material is meant: ~~*furnishing material*~~ ◇ ~~*the material industry*~~ ◇ ~~*a material manufacturer*~~

textile any type of fabric made by weaving or knitting: *He owns a factory producing a range of textiles.* ◇ *the textile industry* NOTE **Textile** is used mostly when talking about the business of making woven materials. The industry of making textiles is called **textiles**: *He got a job in textiles.*

PATTERNS

- **woven/cotton/woollen** fabric/cloth/material/textiles
- **synthetic** fabric/material/textiles
- **printed** fabric/cloth/textiles
- **furnishing/curtain/dress** fabric/material

fab·ric /ˈfæbrɪk/ *noun* **1** [U, C] material made by WEAVING wool, cotton, silk, etc. used for making clothes, curtains, etc. and for covering furniture: *cotton fabric* ◇ *furnishing fabrics* **2** [sing.] **the ~ (of sth)** (*formal*) the basic structure of a society, an organization, etc. that enables it to function successfully: *a trend which threatens the very* ***fabric of society*** ➲ SYNONYMS at STRUCTURE **3** [sing.] **the ~ (of sth)** the basic structure of a building, such as the walls, floor and roof

fab·ri·cate /ˈfæbrɪkeɪt/ *verb* [often passive] **1 ~ sth** to invent false information in order to trick people SYN **make up**: *The evidence was totally fabricated.* **2 ~ sth** (*technical*) to make or produce goods, equipment, etc. from various different materials SYN **manufacture** ▶ **fab·ri·ca·tion** /ˌfæbrɪˈkeɪʃn/ *noun* [C, U] (*formal*): *Her story was a complete fabrication from start to finish.*

fabu·list /ˈfæbjəlɪst/ *noun* (*formal*) a person who invents or tells stories

fabu·lous /ˈfæbjələs/ *adj.* **1** (*informal*) extremely good: *a fabulous performance* ◇ *Jana is a fabulous cook.* ➲ SYNONYMS at GREAT **2** (*formal*) very great: ***fabulous wealth/riches/beauty*** **3** [only before noun] (*literary*) appearing in FABLES: *fabulous beasts*

fabu·lous·ly /ˈfæbjələsli/ *adv.* (*formal*) extremely: ***fabulously wealthy/rich***

fa·cade /fəˈsɑːd/ *noun* **1** the front of a building **2** [usually sing.] the way that sb/sth appears to be, which is different from the way sb/sth really is: *She managed to maintain a facade of indifference.* ◇ *Squalor and poverty lay behind the city's glittering facade.*

face 🔑 /feɪs/ *noun, verb*
■ ***noun***
▸ FRONT OF HEAD **1** 🔑 the front part of the head between the FOREHEAD and the chin: *a pretty/round/freckled face* ◇ *He buried his face in his hands.* ◇ *You should have seen the look* ***on her face*** *when I told her!* ◇ *The expression on his face never changed.* ➲ VISUAL VOCAB page V48
▸ EXPRESSION **2** 🔑 an expression that is shown on sb's face: *a* ***sad/happy/smiling face*** ◇ *Her* ***face lit up*** (= showed happiness) *when she spoke of the past.* ◇ *His* ***face fell*** (= showed disappointment, sadness, etc.) *when he read the headlines.* ◇ *Sue's* ***face was a picture*** (= she looked very surprised, angry, etc.) *as she listened to her husband's speech.*
▸ -FACED **3** 🔑 (in adjectives) having the type of face or expression mentioned: *pale-faced* ◇ *grim-faced*
▸ PERSON **4** 🔑 (in compounds) used to refer to a person of the type mentioned: *She looked around for a* ***familiar face.*** ◇ *a well-known face on our television screens* ◇ *It's nice to see some* ***new faces*** *here this evening.* ◇ *I'm fed up of seeing the* ***same old faces*** *every time we go out!*
▸ SIDE/SURFACE **5** 🔑 a side or surface of sth: *the north face of the mountain* ◇ *The birds build their nests in the rock face.* ◇ *How many faces does a cube have?* ➲ see also COALFACE
▸ FRONT OF CLOCK **6** the front part of a clock or watch ➲ picture at CLOCK
▸ CHARACTER/ASPECT **7 ~ of sth** the particular character of sth: *the changing face of Britain* **8 ~ of sth** a particular aspect of sth: *the unacceptable face of capitalism* ➲ see also IN-YOUR-FACE, TYPEFACE, VOLTE-FACE

IDM **disappear/vanish off the face of the ˈearth** to disappear completely: *Keep looking—they can't just have vanished off the face of the earth.* **sb's face doesn't fit** used to say that sb will not get a particular job or position because they do not have the appearance, personality, etc. that the employer wants, even when this should not be important: *It doesn't matter how well qualified you are, if your face doesn't fit, you don't stand a chance.* **sb's face is like ˈthunder | sb has a face like ˈthunder** somebody looks very angry **ˌface to ˈface (with sb)** 🔑 close to and looking at sb: *The two have never met face to face before.* **ˌface to ˈface with sth** 🔑 in a situation where you have to accept that sth is true and deal with it: *She was at an early age brought face to face with the horrors of war.* **ˌface ˈup/**

'**down 1** (of a person) with your face and stomach facing upwards/downwards: *She lay face down on the bed.* **2** with the front part or surface facing upwards/downwards: *Place the card face up on the pile.* **have the 'face to do sth** (*BrE, informal*) to do sth that other people think is rude or shows a lack of respect without feeling embarrassed or ashamed **in sb's 'face** (*NAmE, informal*) annoying sb by criticizing them or telling them what to do all the time **in the face of 'sth 1** despite problems, difficulties, etc: *She showed great courage in the face of danger.* **2** as a result of sth: *He was unable to deny the charges in the face of new evidence.* **lose 'face** to be less respected or look stupid because of sth you have done SYN **be humiliated on the 'face of it** (*informal*) used to say that sth seems to be good, true, etc. but that this opinion may need to be changed when you know more about it: *On the face of it, it seems like a great deal.* **pull/make 'faces/a 'face (at sb)** to produce an expression on your face to show that you do not like sb/sth or in order to make sb laugh: *What are you pulling a face at now?* **put your 'face on** (*informal*) to put on MAKE-UP **set your face against sb/sth** (*especially BrE*) to be determined to oppose sb/sth: *Her father had set his face against the marriage.* **to sb's 'face** if you say sth **to sb's face**, you say it to them directly rather than to other people ➲ compare BEHIND SB'S BACK **'what's his/her face** (*informal*) used to refer to a person whose name you cannot remember: *Are you still working for what's her face?* ➲ more at BLOW *v.*, BLUE *adj.*, BRAVE *adj.*, DOOR *n.*, EGG *n.*, EYE *n.*, FEED *v.*, FLAT *adv.*, FLY *v.*, LAUGH *v.*, LONG *adj.*, NOSE *n.*, PLAIN *adj.*, PRETTY *adj.*, SAVE *v.*, SHOW *v.*, SHUT *v.*, SLAP *n.*, STARE *v.*, STRAIGHT *n.*, WIPE *v.*, WRITE

Vocabulary Building

Expressions on your face

- To **beam** is to have a big happy smile on your face.
- To **frown** is to make a serious, angry or worried expression by bringing your eyebrows closer together so that lines appear on your forehead.
- To **glare** or **glower** is to look in an angry, aggressive way.
- To **grimace** is to make an ugly expression with your face to show pain, disgust, etc.
- To **scowl** is to look at someone in an angry or annoyed way.
- To **smirk** is to smile in a silly or unpleasant way that shows that you are pleased with yourself, know something that other people do not know, etc.
- To **sneer** is to show that you have no respect for someone by turning your upper lip upwards.

These words can also be used as nouns: *She looked up with a puzzled frown.* ◇ *He gave me an icy glare.* ◇ *a grimace of pain*

■ ***verb***

▸ BE OPPOSITE **1** [T, I] to be opposite sb/sth; to have your face or front pointing towards sb/sth or in a particular direction: **~ sb/sth** *She turned and faced him.* ◇ *Most of the rooms face the sea.* ◇ **+ adv./prep.** *The terrace faces south.* ◇ *a north-facing wall* ◇ *Stand with your feet apart and your hands facing upwards.* ◇ *Which direction are you facing?*

▸ SB/STH DIFFICULT **2** [T] if you **face** a particular situation, or it **faces** you, you have to deal with it: **~ sth** *the problems faced by one-parent families* ◇ *The company is facing a financial crisis.* ◇ **be faced with sth** *She's faced with a difficult decision.* **3** [T] **~ sth** to accept that a difficult situation exists, although you would prefer not to: *It's not always easy to face the truth.* ◇ *She had to* ***face the fact that*** *her life had changed forever.* ◇ ***Face facts***—*she isn't coming back.* ◇ ***Let's face it,*** *we're not going to win.* **4** [T] if you **can't face** sth unpleasant, you feel unable or unwilling to deal with it: **~ sth** *I just can't face work today.* ◇ **~ doing sth** *I can't face seeing them.* **5** [T] **~ sb** to talk to or deal with sb, even though this is difficult or unpleasant: *How can I face Tom? He'll be so disappointed.*

▸ COVER SURFACE **6** [T, usually passive] **~ sth with sth** to cover a surface with another material: *a brick building faced with stone*

IDM **face the 'music** (*informal*) to accept and deal with criticism or punishment for sth you have done: *The others all ran off, leaving me to face the music.*

PHR V **,face sb↔'down** to oppose or beat sb by dealing with them directly and confidently **,face 'off** (*especially NAmE*) **1** to start a game such as ICE HOCKEY: *Both teams are ready to face off.* **2** to get ready to argue, fight or compete with sb: *The candidates are preparing to face off on TV tonight.* ➲ related noun FACE-OFF **,face 'up to sth** to accept and deal with sth that is difficult or unpleasant: *She had to face up to the fact that she would never walk again.*

Face·book™ /ˈfeɪsbʊk/ *noun* a SOCIAL NETWORKING website

'face card (*especially NAmE*) (*BrE* also **'court card**) *noun* a PLAYING CARD with a picture of a king, queen or JACK on it ➲ VISUAL VOCAB page V32

face·cloth /ˈfeɪsklɒθ; *NAmE* -klɔːθ/ *noun* (*BrE*) = FLANNEL

'face cream *noun* [U, C] a thick cream that you put on your face to clean the skin or keep it soft

face·less /ˈfeɪsləs/ *adj.* [usually before noun] (*disapproving*) having no noticeable characteristics or identity: *faceless bureaucrats* ◇ *faceless high-rise apartment blocks*

face·lift /ˈfeɪslɪft/ *noun* [usually sing.] **1** a medical operation in which the skin on a person's face is made tighter in order to make them look younger: *to have a facelift* **2** changes made to a building or place to make it look more attractive: *The town has recently been given a facelift.*

'face-off *noun* **1** (*informal, especially NAmE*) an argument or a fight: *a face-off between the presidential candidates* **2** the way of starting play in a game of ICE HOCKEY

'face pack *noun* (*BrE*) a substance that you put on your face and take off after a short period of time, used to clean your skin

'face powder *noun* powder that you put on your face to make it look less shiny

'face-saving *adj.* [only before noun] intended to protect sb's reputation and to avoid embarrassment: *a face-saving compromise*

facet /ˈfæsɪt/ *noun* **1 ~ (of sth)** a particular part or aspect of sth: *Now let's look at another facet of the problem.* **2** one of the flat sides of a JEWEL

'face time *noun* [U] (*NAmE, informal*) time that you spend talking face-to-face (= in person) to people you work with, rather than speaking on the phone or sending emails

fa·cetious /fəˈsiːʃəs/ *adj.* trying to appear amusing and intelligent at a time when other people do not think it is appropriate, and when it would be better to be serious SYN **flippant**: *a* ***facetious comment/remark*** ◇ *Stop being facetious; this is serious.* ▸ **fa·cetious·ly** *adv.* **fa·cetious·ness** *noun* [U]

,face-to-'face *adj.* involving people who are close together and looking at each other: *a face-to-face conversation* ◇ *I deal with customers on the phone and rarely meet them face-to-face.* ▸ **face-to-face** *adv.*: *He opened the door and* ***came face-to-face with*** *a burglar.* ◇ (*figurative*) *She was brought face-to-face with the horrors of war.*

,face 'value *noun* [U, sing.] the value of a stamp, coin, ticket, etc. that is shown on the front of it

IDM **take sth at face 'value** to believe that sth is what it appears to be, without questioning it: *Taken at face value, the figures look very encouraging.* ◇ *You shouldn't take anything she says at face value.*

fa·cia = FASCIA

fa·cial /ˈfeɪʃl/ *adj., noun*

■ ***adj.*** [usually before noun] connected with a person's face; on a person's face: *a facial expression* ◇ *facial hair* ▸ **fa·cial·ly** /ˈfeɪʃəli/ *adv.*: *Facially the two men were very different.*

■ ***noun*** a beauty treatment in which a person's face is

cleaned using creams, steam, etc. in order to improve the quality of the skin

fa·cile /ˈfæsaɪl; NAmE ˈfæsl/ *adj.* (*disapproving*) **1** produced without effort or careful thought SYN **glib**: *a facile **remark/generalization*** **2** [only before noun] (*formal*) obtained too easily and having little value: *a facile victory*

fa·cili·tate AW /fəˈsɪlɪteɪt/ *verb* **~ sth** (*formal*) to make an action or a process possible or easier: *The new trade agreement should facilitate more rapid economic growth.* ◇ *Structured teaching facilitates learning.* ► **fa·cili·ta·tion** AW /fəˌsɪlɪˈteɪʃn/ *noun* [U, sing.]

fa·cili·ta·tor AW /fəˈsɪlɪteɪtə(r)/ *noun* **1** a person who helps sb do sth more easily by discussing problems, giving advice, etc. rather than telling them what to do: *The teacher acts as a facilitator of learning.* **2** (*formal*) a thing that helps a process take place

fa·cil·ity 0-w AW /fəˈsɪləti/ *noun*
1 0-w **facilities** [pl.] buildings, services, equipment, etc. that are provided for a particular purpose: ***sports/leisure facilities*** ◇ *conference facilities* ◇ ***shopping/banking/cooking facilities*** ◇ *The hotel has special facilities for welcoming disabled people.* ◇ *All rooms have **private facilities*** (= a private bathroom). **2** [C] a special feature of a machine, service, etc. that makes it possible to do sth extra: *a bank account with an overdraft facility* ◇ *a facility for checking spelling* **3** [C] a place, usually including buildings, used for a particular purpose or activity: *the world's largest nuclear waste facility* ◇ *a new health care facility* **4** [sing., U] **~ (for sth)** a natural ability to learn or do sth easily: *She has a facility for languages.*

fa·cing /ˈfeɪsɪŋ/ *noun* **1** [C, U] a layer of brick, stone, etc. that covers the surface of a wall to make it look more attractive **2** [C, U] a layer of stiff material sewn around the inside of the neck, ARMHOLES, etc. of a piece of clothing to make them stronger **3 facings** [pl.] the COLLAR, CUFFS, etc. of a piece of clothing that are made in a different colour or material

fac·sim·ile /fækˈsɪməli/ *noun* **1** [C] an exact copy of sth: *a facsimile edition* ◇ *a manuscript reproduced **in facsimile*** **2** [C, U] (*formal*) = FAX: *a facsimile machine*

fact 0-w /fækt/ *noun*
1 0-w [sing.] **~ (that…)** used to refer to a particular situation that exists: *I could no longer ignore the fact that he was deeply unhappy.* ◇ ***Despite the fact that** she was wearing a seat belt, she was thrown sharply forward.* ◇ ***Due to the fact that** they did not read English, the prisoners were unaware of what they were signing.* ◇ *She was happy **apart from the fact that** she could not return home.* ◇ *Voluntary work was particularly important **in view of the fact that** women were often forced to give up paid work on marriage.* ◇ *How do you account for the fact that unemployment is still rising?* ◇ ***The fact remains** that we are still two teachers short.* ◇ *The mere fact of being poor makes such children criminals in the eyes of the police.* ➲ LANGUAGE BANK at HOWEVER **2** 0-w [C] a thing that is known to be true, especially when it can be proved: *Isn't it a fact that the firm is losing money?* ◇ (*informal*) *I haven't spoken to anyone in English for days **and that's a fact**.* ◇ *I **know for a fact*** (= I am certain) *that she's involved in something illegal.* ◇ *The judge instructed both lawyers to **stick to the facts** of the case.* ◇ *First, some basic facts about healthy eating!* ◇ *The report is based on **hard facts*** (= information that can be proved to be true). ◇ *If you're going to make accusations, you'd better **get your facts right*** (= make sure your information is correct). ◇ *It's about time you learnt to **face** (**the**) **facts*** (= accepted the truth about the situation). **3** 0-w [U] things that are true rather than things that have been invented: *The story is based on fact.* ◇ *It's important to distinguish fact from fiction.*
IDM **ˌafter the ˈfact** after sth has happened or been done, when it is too late to prevent it or change it: *On some vital decisions employees were only informed after the fact.* **the fact (of the matter) is (that)…** used to emphasize a statement, especially one that is the opposite of what has just been mentioned: *A new car would be wonderful but the fact of the matter is that we can't afford one.* **a ˌfact of ˈlife** a situation that cannot be changed, especially one that is unpleasant **ˌfacts and ˈfigures** accurate and detailed information: *I've asked to see all the facts and figures before I make a decision.* **the ˌfacts of ˈlife** the details about sex and about how babies are born, especially as told to children **the facts speak for themˈselves** it is not necessary to give any further explanation about sth because the information that is available already proves that it is true **in (actual) fact** **1** 0-w used to give extra details about sth that has just been mentioned: *I used to live in France; in fact, not far from where you're going.* **2** 0-w used to emphasize a statement, especially one that is the opposite of what has just been mentioned: *I thought the work would be difficult. In actual fact, it's very easy.* ➲ LANGUAGE BANK at HOWEVER **Is that a ˈfact?** (*informal*) used to reply to a statement that you find interesting or surprising, or that you do not believe: *'She says I'm one of the best students she's ever taught.' 'Is that a fact?'* ➲ more at MATTER *n.*, POINT *n.*

ˈfact-finding *adj.* [only before noun] done in order to find out information about a country, an organization, a situation, etc: *a **fact-finding mission/visit***

fac·tion /ˈfækʃn/ *noun* **1** [C] a small group of people within a larger one whose members have some different aims and beliefs to those of the larger group: *rival factions within the administration* ➲ COLLOCATIONS at POLITICS **2** [U] opposition, disagreement, etc. that exists between small groups of people within an organization or political party: *a party divided by faction and intrigue* **3** [U] films/movies, books, etc. that combine fact with FICTION (= imaginary events)

fac·tion·al /ˈfækʃənl/ *adj.* [only before noun] connected with the factions of an organization or political party: *factional conflict* ► **fac·tion·al·ism** *noun* [U]

fac·ti·tious /fækˈtɪʃəs/ *adj.* (*formal*) not genuine but created deliberately and made to appear to be true

fac·toid /ˈfæktɔɪd/ *noun* **1** something that is widely accepted as a fact, although it is probably not true **2** a small piece of interesting information, especially about sth that is not very important: *Here's a pop factoid for you.*

fac·tor 0-w AW /ˈfæktə(r)/ *noun, verb*
▪ ***noun*** **1** 0-w [C] one of several things that cause or influence sth: *economic factors* ◇ *The closure of the mine was the **single most important** factor in the town's decline.* ◇ *the **key/crucial/deciding factor*** ➲ LANGUAGE BANK at CAUSE **2** [C] (*mathematics*) a number that divides into another number exactly: *1, 2, 3, 4, 6 and 12 are the factors of 12.* **3** [C] the amount by which sth increases or decreases: *The real wage of the average worker has increased by a factor of over ten in the last 70 years.* **4** [C] a particular level on a scale of measurement: *a suntan lotion with a protection factor of 10* ◇ *The wind-chill factor will make it seem colder.* **5** [U] (*medical*) a substance in the blood that helps the CLOTTING process. There are several types of this substance: *Haemophiliacs have no factor 8 in their blood* IDM see FEEL-GOOD
▪ ***verb***
PHR V **ˌfactor sth↔ˈin** | **factor sth↔into sth** (*technical*) to include a particular fact or situation when you are thinking about or planning sth: *Remember to factor in staffing costs when you are planning the project.*

fac·tor VIII (also **factor 8**, **factor eight**) /ˌfæktər ˈeɪt/ *noun* [U] (*biology*) a substance in the blood that helps it to CLOT (= become thick)

fac·tor·ial /fækˈtɔːriəl/ *noun* (*mathematics*) the result when you multiply a whole number by all the numbers below it: *5! (= factorial 5) is 120 (= 5 × 4 × 3 × 2 × 1).*

fac·tor·ize (BrE also **-ise**) /ˈfæktəraɪz/ *verb* **~ sth** (*mathematics*) to express a number in terms of its FACTORS *n.* (2)

fac·tory 0-w /ˈfæktri; -təri/ *noun* (*pl.* -ies) a building or group of buildings where goods are made: *a car factory* ◇ *factory workers*

ˈfactory farm *noun* (BrE) a type of farm in which animals are kept inside in small spaces and are fed special food so that a large amount of meat, milk, etc. is produced as quickly and cheaply as possible ➲ compare BATTERY FARM ▶ 'factory farming noun [U]

Synonyms

factory

plant • mill • works • yard • workshop • foundry

These are all words for buildings or places where things are made or where industrial processes take place.

factory a building or group of buildings where goods are made: *a chocolate/cigarette/clothing factory*

plant a factory or place where power is produced or an industrial process takes place: *a nuclear power plant* ◇ *a manufacturing plant*

mill a factory that produces a particular type of material: *a cotton/paper/textile/woollen mill*

works (often in compounds) a place where things are made or an industrial process takes place: *a brickworks* ◇ *a steelworks* ◇ *Raw materials were carried to the works by barge.*

yard (usually in compounds) an area of land used for building sth: *a shipyard*

workshop a room or building in which things are made or repaired using tools or machinery: *a car repair workshop*

foundry a factory where metal or glass is melted and made into different shapes or objects: *an iron foundry*

PATTERNS

- a **car/chemical/munitions** factory/plant
- an **engineering** plant/works
- to **manage/run** a factory/plant/mill/works/yard/workshop/foundry
- to **work in/at** a factory/plant/mill/yard/workshop/foundry
- factory/mill/foundry **owners/managers/workers**

ˌfactory 'floor *noun* (often **the factory floor**) [sing.] the part of a factory where the goods are actually produced: *Jobs are at risk, not just* ***on the factory floor*** (= among the workers, rather than the managers) *but throughout the business.*

'factory ship *noun* a large ship used for catching fish, that has equipment for cleaning and freezing the fish on board

'factory shop (*BrE*) (also **'factory store**, **'factory outlet** *NAmE, BrE*) *noun* a shop/store in which goods are sold directly by the company that produces them at a cheaper price than normal

fac·to·tum /fæk'təʊtəm; *NAmE* -'toʊ-/ *noun* (*formal* or *humorous*) a person employed to do a wide variety of jobs for sb

'fact sheet *noun* a piece of paper or an electronic document giving information about a subject, especially (in Britain) one discussed on a radio or television programme

fac·tual /'fæktʃuəl/ *adj.* based on or containing facts: *a factual account of events* ◇ *factual information* ◇ *The essay contains a number of factual errors.* ▶ **fact·ual·ly** /-tʃuəli/ *adv.*: *factually correct*

fac·ulty /'fæklti/ *noun* (*pl.* -ies) **1** [C, usually pl.] any of the physical or mental abilities that a person is born with: *the faculty of sight* ◇ *She retained her mental faculties* (= the ability to think and understand) *until the day she died.* ◇ *to be* ***in full possession of your faculties*** (= be able to speak, hear, see, understand, etc.) **2** [sing.] **~ of/for (doing) sth** (*formal*) a particular ability for doing sth: *the faculty of understanding complex issues* ◇ *He had a faculty for seeing his own mistakes.* **3** [C] a department or group of related departments in a college or university: *the Faculty of Law* ◇ *the Arts Faculty* **4** [C+sing./pl. v.] all the teachers in a faculty of a college or university: *the Law School faculty* ◇ *a faculty meeting* ◇ *faculty members* **5** [C, U] (often **the faculty**) (*NAmE*) all the teachers of a particular university or college: *faculty members*

fad /fæd/ *noun* something that people are interested in for only a short period of time **SYN** **craze**: *the* ***latest/current fad*** ◇ *a fad for physical fitness* ◇ *Rap music proved to be more than just a* ***passing fad***.

faddy /'fædi/ *adj.* (*BrE, informal, disapproving*) liking some things and not others, especially food, in a way that other people think is unreasonable: *a faddy eater* ▶ **fad·di·ness** *noun* [U]

fade /feɪd/ *verb* **1** [I, T] to become or to make sth become paler or less bright: *The curtains had faded in the sun.* ◇ **~ from sth** *All colour had faded from the sky.* ◇ **~ sth** *The sun had faded the curtains.* ◇ *He was wearing faded blue jeans.* **2** [I] to disappear gradually: *Her smile faded.* ◇ **~ away** *Hopes of reaching an agreement seem to be fading away.* ◇ *The laughter faded away.* ◇ **~ to/into sth** *His voice faded to a whisper* (= gradually became quieter). ◇ *All other issues* ***fade into insignificance*** *compared with the struggle for survival.* **3** [I] if a sports player, team, actor, etc. **fades**, they stop playing or performing as well as they did before: *Black faded on the final bend.* **IDM** see WOODWORK

PHR V **ˌfade a'way** (of a person) to become very weak or ill/sick and die: *In the last weeks of her life she simply faded away.* **ˌfade 'in/'out** to become clearer or louder/less clear or quieter: *George saw the monitor black out and then a few words faded in.* **ˌfade sth 'in/'out** to make a picture or a sound clearer or louder/less clear or quieter: *Fade out the music at the end of the scene.*

'fade-out *noun* [U, C] (in cinema, broadcasting, etc.) the process of making a sound or an image gradually disappear; an occasion when this happens

fader /'feɪdə(r)/ *noun* (*technical*) a piece of equipment used to make sounds or images gradually appear or disappear

fae·ces (*BrE*) (*NAmE* **feces**) /'fiːsiːz/ *noun* [pl.] (*formal*) solid waste material that leaves the body through the ANUS **SYN** **excrement** ▶ **fae·cal** (*BrE*) (*NAmE* **fecal**) /'fiːkl/ *adj.* [only before noun]

faff /fæf/ *verb, noun* (*BrE, informal*)

■ ***verb***

PHR V **ˌfaff a'bout/a'round** to spend time doing things in a way that is not well organized and that does not achieve much: *Stop faffing about and get on with it!*

■ ***noun*** [U, sing.] a lot of activity that is not well organized and that may cause problems or be annoying: *There was the usual faff of finding somewhere to park the car.*

fag /fæg/ *noun* **1** [C] (*BrE, informal*) = CIGARETTE **2** (also **fag·got**) [C] (*NAmE, taboo, slang*) an offensive word for a male HOMOSEXUAL **3** [sing.] (*BrE, informal*) something that is boring and tiring to do: *It's too much of a fag to go out.* **4** [C] (*BrE*) (especially in the past) a boy at a PUBLIC SCHOOL who has to do jobs for an older boy

ˌfag 'end *noun* (*BrE, informal*) **1** [C] the last part of a cigarette that is left after it has been smoked **2** [sing.] **the ~ of sth** the last part of sth, especially when it is less important or interesting: *I only caught the fag end of their conversation.*

fagged /fægd/ (also **ˌfagged 'out**) *adj.* [not before noun] (*BrE, informal*) very tired **SYN** **exhausted**

IDM **I can't be 'fagged (to do sth)** used to say that you are too tired or bored to do sth

fag·got /'fægət/ *noun* **1** (*BrE*) a ball of finely chopped meat mixed with bread, baked or fried and eaten hot **2** (*NAmE*) = FAG (2) **3** a bunch of sticks tied together, used for burning on a fire

'fag hag *noun* (*slang, offensive*) a woman who likes to spend time with HOMOSEXUAL men

fah (also **fa**) /fɑː/ *noun* (*music*) the fourth note of a MAJOR SCALE

'fah-fee *noun* [U] (*SAfrE*) an illegal game in which you risk money on a particular number being chosen

Fahr·en·heit /'færənhaɪt/ *adj.* (*abbr.* F) of or using a scale of temperature in which water freezes at 32° and boils at 212°: *fifty degrees Fahrenheit* ▸ **Fahr·en·heit** *noun* [U]: *to give the temperature in Fahrenheit*

fail 🔑 /feɪl/ *verb, noun*

■ ***verb***

▸ NOT SUCCEED **1** 🔑 [I, T] to not be successful in achieving sth: *Many diets fail because they are boring.* ◇ *a failing school* ◇ **~ in sth** *I failed in my attempt to persuade her.* ◇ **~ to do sth** *She failed to get into art college.* ◇ *The song* ***can't fail*** *to be a hit* (= definitely will be a hit).

▸ NOT DO STH **2** 🔑 [I] to not do sth: **~ to do sth** *He failed to keep the appointment.* ◇ *She never fails to email every week.* ◇ ***I fail to see*** (= I don't understand) *why you won't even give it a try.* ◇ **~ in sth** *He felt he would be failing in his duty if he did not report it.*

▸ TEST/EXAM **3** 🔑 [T, I] to not pass a test or an exam; to decide that sb/sth has not passed a test or an exam: **~ (sth)** *He failed his driving test.* ◇ *She was disqualified after failing a drugs test.* ◇ *What will you do if you fail?* ◇ **~ sb** *The examiners failed over half the candidates.* OPP **pass**

▸ OF MACHINES/PARTS OF BODY **4** [I] to stop working: *The brakes on my bike failed half way down the hill.*

▸ OF HEALTH/SIGHT **5** [I] (especially in the progressive tenses) to become weak: *Her eyesight is failing.* ◇ *His last months in office were marred by failing health.*

▸ DISAPPOINT SB **6** [T] **~ sb** to disappoint sb; to be unable to help when needed: *When he lost his job, he felt he had failed his family.* ◇ *She tried to be brave, but her courage failed her.* ◇ (*figurative*) ***Words fail me*** (= I cannot express how I feel).

▸ NOT BE ENOUGH **7** [I] to not be enough when needed or expected: *The crops failed again last summer.* ◇ *The rains had failed and the rivers were dry.*

▸ OF COMPANY/BUSINESS **8** [I] to be unable to continue: *Several banks failed during the recession.*

IDM **if all else 'fails** used to suggest sth that sb can do if nothing else they have tried is successful: *If all else fails, you can always sell your motorbike.*

■ ***noun*** the result of an exam in which a person is not successful: *I got three passes and one fail.* OPP **pass**

IDM **without 'fail 1** when you tell sb to do sth **without fail**, you are telling them that they must do it: *I want you here by two o'clock without fail.* **2** always: *He emails every week without fail.*

failed /feɪld/ *adj.* [only before noun] not successful: *a failed writer* ◇ *a failed coup*

ˌfailed 'state *noun* a country in which the government is so weak that it has lost control of the structures of the state and other groups have more power

fail·ing /ˈfeɪlɪŋ/ *noun, prep.*

■ ***noun*** [usually pl.] a weakness or fault in sb/sth: *She is aware of her own failings.* ◇ *The inquiry acknowledges failings in the judicial system.*

■ ***prep.*** used to introduce a suggestion that could be considered if the one just mentioned is not possible: *Ask a friend to recommend a doctor or,* ***failing that****, ask for a list in your local library.*

'fail-safe *adj.* [usually before noun] (of machinery or equipment) designed to stop working if anything goes wrong: *a* ***fail-safe device/mechanism/system***

fail·ure 🔑 /ˈfeɪljə(r)/ *noun*

▸ NOT SUCCESSFUL **1** 🔑 [U] lack of success in doing or achieving sth: *The success or failure of the plan depends on you.* ◇ *The attempt was* ***doomed to failure****.* ◇ *All my efforts* ***ended in failure****.* ◇ *the problems of economic failure and increasing unemployment* ◇ *She is still coming to terms with the failure of her marriage.* OPP **success** **2** 🔑 [C] a person or thing that is not successful: *The whole thing was a complete failure.* ◇ *He was a failure as a teacher.* OPP **success**

▸ NOT DOING STH **3** 🔑 [U, C] **~ to do sth** an act of not doing sth, especially sth that you are expected to do: *the failure of the United Nations to maintain food supplies* ◇ *Failure to comply with the regulations will result in prosecution.*

▸ OF MACHINE/PART OF BODY **4** 🔑 [U, C] the state of not working correctly or as expected; an occasion when this happens: *patients suffering from* ***heart/kidney, etc. failure*** ◇ *A power failure plunged everything into darkness.* ◇ *The cause of the crash was given as engine failure.*

▸ OF BUSINESS **5** [C, U] **business ~** a situation in which a business has to close because it is not successful

▸ OF CROP/HARVEST **6** [U, C] **crop/harvest ~** a situation in which crops do not grow correctly and do not produce food

fain /feɪn/ *adv.* (*old use*) willingly or with pleasure: *I would fain do as you ask.*

faint 🔑 /feɪnt/ *adj., verb, noun*

■ ***adj.*** (**faint·er**, **faint·est**) **1** 🔑 that cannot be clearly seen, heard or smelt: *a* ***faint glow/glimmer/light*** ◇ *a faint smell of perfume* ◇ *We could hear their voices growing fainter as they walked down the road.* ◇ *His breathing became faint.* **2** 🔑 very small; possible but unlikely SYN **slight**: *There is still a faint hope that she may be cured.* ◇ *They don't have the faintest chance of winning.* **3** not enthusiastic: *a faint show of resistance* ◇ *a faint smile* **4** 🔑 [not before noun] feeling weak and tired and likely to become unconscious: *She suddenly felt faint.* ◇ *The walkers were faint from hunger.* ▸ **faint·ly** 🔑 *adv.*: *She smiled faintly.* ◇ *He looked faintly embarrassed.*

IDM **not have the 'faintest (idea)** (*informal*) to not know anything at all about sth: *I didn't have the faintest idea what you meant.* ⊃ more at DAMN *v.*

■ ***verb*** [I] to become unconscious when not enough blood is going to your brain, usually because of the heat, a shock, etc. SYN **pass out**: *to faint from hunger* ◇ *Suddenly the woman in front of me fainted.* ◇ (*informal*) *I almost fainted* (= I was very surprised) *when she told me.*

■ ***noun*** [sing.] the state of becoming unconscious: *He fell to the ground in a dead faint.*

ˌfaint-'hearted *adj., noun*

■ ***adj.*** lacking confidence and not brave; afraid of failing SYN **cowardly**

■ ***noun***

IDM **ˌnot for the ˌfaint-'hearted** not suitable for people who lack confidence or who get frightened easily: *The climb is* ***not for the faint-hearted*** (= is only for people who are brave).

faint·ness /ˈfeɪntnəs/ *noun* [U] the state of feeling weak and tired and likely to become unconscious

fair 🔑 /feə(r); *NAmE* fer/ *adj., adv., noun*

■ ***adj.*** (**fair·er**, **fair·est**)

▸ ACCEPTABLE/APPROPRIATE **1** 🔑 acceptable and appropriate in a particular situation: *a fair deal/wage/price/question* ◇ *The punishment was very fair.* ◇ **~ to sb (to do sth)** *Was it really fair to him to ask him to do all the work?* ◇ **~ on sb (to do sth)** *It's not fair on the students to keep changing the timetable.* ◇ **~ to do sth** ***It's only fair*** *to add that they were not told about the problem until the last minute.* ◇ *I think* ***it is fair to say that*** *they are pleased with this latest offer.* ◇ **~ that…** *It seems only fair that they should give us something in return.* ◇ ***To be fair****, she behaved better than we expected.* ◇ (*especially BrE*) *'You should really have asked me first.' 'Right, okay,* ***fair comment****.'* OPP **unfair**

▸ TREATING PEOPLE EQUALLY **2** 🔑 treating everyone equally and according to the rules or law: *She has always been scrupulously fair.* ◇ *demands for a fairer distribution of wealth* ◇ **~ (to sb)** *We have to be fair to both players.* ◇ *to receive a fair trial* ◇ *free and fair elections* ◇ ***It's not fair!*** *He always gets more than me.* ◇ *The new tax is fairer than the old system.* OPP **unfair**

▸ QUITE LARGE **3** 🔑 [only before noun] quite large in number, size or amount: *A fair number of people came a long.* ◇ *a fair-sized town* ◇ *We've still got* ***a fair bit*** (= quite a lot) *to do.*

▸ QUITE GOOD **4** (*especially BrE*) quite good: *There's* ***a fair chance*** *that we might win this time.* ◇ *It's a fair bet that they won't turn up.* ◇ *I have a fair idea of what happened.* ◇ *His knowledge of French is only fair.*

▸ HAIR/SKIN **5** 🔑 pale in colour: *a fair complexion* ◇ *She has long fair hair.* ◇ *All her children are fair* (= they all have fair hair). OPP **dark**

▸ WEATHER **6** 🔑 bright and not raining SYN **fine**: *a fair and breezy day* **7** (*literary*) (of winds) not too strong and blowing in the right direction: *They set sail with the first fair wind.*

▸ BEAUTIFUL **8** (*literary* or *old use*) beautiful: *a fair maiden*

IDM ˌ**all's ˌfair in ˌlove and ˈwar** (*saying*) in some situations any type of behaviour is acceptable to get what you want **be ˈfair!** (*informal*) used to tell sb to be reasonable in their judgement of sb/sth: *Be fair! She didn't know you were coming.* **by fair means or ˈfoul** using dishonest methods if honest ones do not work **a fair crack of the ˈwhip** (*BrE, informal*) a reasonable opportunity to show that you can do sth: *I felt we weren't given a fair crack of the whip.* **fair eˈnough** (*informal, especially BrE*) used to say that an idea or suggestion seems reasonable: *'We'll meet at 8.' 'Fair enough.'* ◇ *If you don't want to come, fair enough, but let Bill know.* **fair's ˈfair** (*informal*) (*BrE* also **fair ˈdos/ˈdo's**) used, especially as an exclamation, to say that you think that an action, decision, etc. is acceptable and appropriate because it means that everyone will be treated fairly: *Fair's fair—you can't expect them to cancel everything just because you can't make it.* **(give sb) a fair ˈhearing** (to allow sb) the opportunity to give their opinion of sth before deciding if they have done sth wrong, often in court: *I'll see that you get a fair hearing.* **(give sb/get) a fair ˈshake** (*NAmE, informal*) (to give sb/get) fair treatment that gives you the same chance as sb else **(more than) your fair share of sth** (more than) an amount of sth that is considered to be reasonable or acceptable: *He has more than his fair share of problems.* ◇ *I've had my fair share of success in the past.* **fair to ˈmiddling** (*old-fashioned*) not particularly good or bad **it's a fair ˈcop** (*BrE, informal, humorous*) used by sb who is caught doing sth wrong, to say that they admit that they are wrong

■ ***adv.*** according to the rules; in a way that is considered to be acceptable and appropriate: *Come on, you two, fight fair!* ◇ *They'll respect you as long as you* ***play fair*** (= behave honestly).

IDM **fair and ˈsquare | fairly and ˈsquarely** **1** honestly and according to the rules: *We won the election fair and square.* **2** (*BrE*) in a direct way that is easy to understand: *I told him fair and square to pack his bags.* **3** (*BrE*) exactly in the place you were aiming for: *I hit the target fair and square.* **set fair (to do sth/for sth)** (*BrE*) having the necessary qualities or conditions to succeed: *She seems set fair to win the championship.* ◇ *Conditions were set fair for stable economic development.* ➲ more at SAY *v.*

■ ***noun***

▸ ENTERTAINMENT **1** (*BrE* also **fun·fair**) (*NAmE* also **car·ni·val**) a type of entertainment in a field or park at which people can ride on large machines and play games to win prizes: *Let's take the kids to the fair.* ◇ *all the fun of the fair* **2** (*NAmE*) a type of entertainment in a field or park at which farm animals and products are shown and take part in competitions: *the* ***county/state fair*** **3** (*BrE*) = FÊTE

▸ BUSINESS **4** an event at which people, businesses, etc. show and sell their goods: *a world trade fair* ◇ *a craft/a book/an antique fair*

▸ ANIMAL MARKET **5** (*BrE*) (in the past) a market at which animals were sold: *a horse fair*

▸ JOBS **6 job/careers ~** an event at which people who are looking for jobs can get information about companies who might employ them

ˌ**fair ˈcopy** *noun* (*BrE*) a neat version of a piece of writing

ˌ**fair ˈdinkum** *adj., adv.* (*AustralE, NZE, informal*) **1** used to emphasize that sth is genuine or true, or to ask whether it is: *It's a fair dinkum Aussie wedding.* ◇ *'Burt's just told me he's packing up in a month.' 'Fair dinkum?'* **2** used to emphasize that behaviour is acceptable: *They were asking a lot for the car, but fair dinkum considering how new it is.*

the ˌfairer ˈsex *noun* = THE FAIR SEX

ˌ**fair ˈgame** *noun* [U] if a person or thing is said to be **fair game**, it is considered acceptable to play jokes on them, criticize them, etc: *The younger teachers were considered fair game by most of the kids.*

fair·ground /ˈfeəgraʊnd; *NAmE* ˈferg-/ *noun* **1** an outdoor area where a FAIR with entertainments is held **2** [usually pl.] (*NAmE*) a place where a FAIR showing farm animals, farm products, etc. is held: *the Ohio State Fairgrounds* **3** [usually pl.] (*NAmE*) a place where companies and businesses hold a FAIR to show their products: *the Milan trade fairgrounds*

ˌ**fair-ˈhaired** *adj.* with light or blonde hair

fair·ly 🔑 /ˈfeəli; *NAmE* ˈferli/ *adv.*
1 🔑 (before adjectives and adverbs) to some extent but not very: *a fairly easy book* ◇ *a fairly typical reaction* ◇ *I know him fairly well, but I wouldn't say we were really close friends.* ◇ *I go jogging fairly regularly.* ◇ *We'll have to leave fairly soon* (= before very long). ◇ *I'm fairly certain I can do the job.* ◇ *The report was fairly incomprehensible.* ◇ *I think you'll find it fairly difficult* (= you do not want to say that it is very difficult). ➲ note at QUITE **2** 🔑 in a fair and reasonable way; honestly: *He has always treated me very fairly.* ◇ *Her attitude could fairly be described as hostile.* **3** (*old-fashioned*) used to emphasize sth that you are saying: *The time fairly raced by.*

IDM **fairly and squarely** = FAIR AND SQUARE

ˌ**fair-ˈminded** *adj.* (of people) looking at and judging things in a fair and open way

fair·ness /ˈfeənəs; *NAmE* ˈfernəs/ *noun* [U] **1** the quality of treating people equally or in a way that is reasonable: *the fairness of the judicial system* **2** (of skin or hair) a pale colour: *A tan emphasized the fairness of her hair.*

IDM **in (all) fairness (to sb)** used to introduce a statement that defends sb who has just been criticized, or that explains another statement that may seem unreasonable: *In all fairness to him, he did try to stop her leaving.*

ˌ**fair ˈplay** *noun* [U] the fact of playing a game or acting honestly, fairly and according to the rules: *a player admired for his* ***sense of fair play*** ◇ *The task of the organization is to* ***ensure fair play*** *when food is distributed to the refugees.*

IDM **fair ˈplay to sb** (*BrE, informal*) used to express approval when sb has done sth that you think is right or reasonable

the ˌfair ˈsex (also **the ˌfairer ˈsex**) *noun* [sing.+ sing./pl. v.] (*old-fashioned*) women

ˌ**fair-ˈtrade** *adj.* involving trade which supports producers in developing countries by paying fair prices and making sure that workers have good working conditions and fair pay

fair·way /ˈfeəweɪ; *NAmE* ˈferweɪ/ *noun* (in GOLF) the long strip of short grass that you must hit the ball along before you get to the GREEN and the hole ➲ **VISUAL VOCAB** page V34 ➲ compare THE ROUGH

ˈ**fair-weather** *adj.* [only before noun] (*disapproving*) (of people) behaving in a particular way or doing a particular activity only when it is pleasant for them: ***a fair-weather friend*** (= sb who stops being a friend when you are in trouble)

fairy /ˈfeəri; *NAmE* ˈferi/ *noun* (*pl.* **-ies**) **1** (in stories) a creature like a small person, who has magic powers: ***a good/wicked fairy*** ➲ see also TOOTH FAIRY **2** (*slang, disapproving*) an offensive word for a HOMOSEXUAL man

ˈ**fairy cake** (*BrE*) (also **cup·cake** *NAmE, BrE*) *noun* a small cake, baked in a paper container shaped like a cup and often with ICING on top

ˌ**fairy ˈgodmother** *noun* a person who rescues you when you most need help

fairy·land /ˈfeərilænd; *NAmE* ˈferi-/ *noun* **1** [U] the home of FAIRIES **2** [sing.] a beautiful, special or unusual place: *The toyshop is a fairyland for young children.*

ˈ**fairy lights** *noun* [pl.] (*BrE*) small coloured electric lights used for decoration, especially on a tree at Christmas

ˈ**fairy tale** (also ˈ**fairy story**) *noun* **1** a story about magic or FAIRIES, usually for children **2** a story that sb tells that is not true; a lie: *Now tell me the truth: I don't want any more of your fairy stories.*

ˈ**fairy-tale** *adj.* typical of sth in a fairy tale: *a fairy-tale castle on an island* ◇ *a fairy-tale wedding in the cathedral*

fait ac·com·pli /ˌfeɪt əˈkɒmpliː; *NAmE* əˈkɑːm-/ *noun* [usually sing.] (*pl.* **faits ac·com·plis** /ˌfeɪz əˈkɒmpliː; *NAmE* əˈkɑːm-/) (*from French*) something that has already happened or been done and that you cannot change

faith 🗝 /feɪθ/ *noun*
1 🗝 [U] **~ (in sb/sth)** trust in sb's ability or knowledge; trust that sb/sth will do what has been promised: *I have great faith in you—I know you'll do well.* ◇ *We've* **lost faith in** *the government's promises.* ◇ *Her friend's kindness has* **restored her faith in** *human nature.* ◇ *He has* **blind faith** (= unreasonable trust) *in doctors' ability to find a cure.* **2** 🗝 [U, sing.] strong religious belief: *to lose your faith* ◇ *Faith is stronger than reason.* ➲ COLLOCATIONS at RELIGION **3** 🗝 [C] a particular religion: *the Christian faith* ◇ *The children are learning to understand people of different faiths.* **4** [U] **good ~** the intention to do sth right: *They handed over the weapons as a gesture of good faith.*
IDM **break/keep faith with sb** to break/keep a promise that you have made to sb; to stop/continue being loyal to sb **in bad ˈfaith** knowing that what you are doing is wrong **in good ˈfaith** believing that what you are doing is right; believing that sth is correct: *We printed the report in good faith but have now learnt that it was incorrect.* ➲ more at PIN *v.*

faith·ful 🗝 /ˈfeɪθfl/ *adj.*
1 🗝 staying with or supporting a particular person, organization or belief SYN **loyal**: *a* ***faithful servant/friend/dog*** ◇ *She was rewarded for her 40 years' faithful service with the company.* ◇ *I have been a faithful reader of your newspaper for many years.* ◇ **~ to sb/sth** *He* ***remained faithful*** *to the ideals of the party.* **2 the faithful** *noun* [pl.] people who believe in a religion; the loyal supporters of a political party: *The president will keep the support of the* ***party faithful.*** **3** 🗝 (of a wife, husband or partner) **~ (to sb)** not having a sexual relationship with anyone else OPP **unfaithful** **4** true and accurate; not changing anything: *a* ***faithful copy/account/description*** ◇ **~ to sth** *His translation manages to be faithful to the spirit of the original.* **5** [only before noun] able to be trusted; that you can rely on: *my faithful old car* ▸ **faith·ful·ness** *noun* [U]: *faithfulness to tradition* ◇ *She had doubts about his faithfulness.*

faith·ful·ly 🗝 /ˈfeɪθfəli/ *adv.*
1 🗝 accurately; carefully: *to follow instructions faithfully* ◇ *The events were faithfully recorded in her diary.* **2** 🗝 in a loyal way; in a way that you can rely on: *He had supported the local team faithfully for 30 years.* ◇ *She promised faithfully not to tell anyone my secret.*
IDM **Yours faithfully** 🗝 (*BrE*) used at the end of a formal letter before you sign your name, when you have addressed sb as 'Dear Sir/Dear Madam, etc.' and not by their name ➲ WRITING TUTOR page WT24

ˈfaith healing *noun* [U] a method of treating a sick person through the power of belief and prayer ▸ **ˈfaith healer** *noun*

faith·less /ˈfeɪθləs/ *adj.* (*formal*) not loyal; that you cannot rely on or trust: *a faithless friend*

ˈfaith school *noun* (*BrE*) a school especially for children of a particular religion: *He called for new faith schools to be created.* ➲ compare PAROCHIAL SCHOOL

fa·jitas /fəˈhiːtəs/ *noun* [pl.] (from *Spanish*) a Mexican dish of strips of meat and/or vegetables wrapped in a soft TORTILLA and often served with sour cream

fake /feɪk/ *adj., noun, verb*
■ ***adj.*** **1** (*disapproving*) not genuine; appearing to be sth it is not SYN **counterfeit**: *fake designer clothing* ◇ *a fake American accent* **2** made to look like sth else SYN **imitation**: *a jacket in fake fur* ◇ *Don't go out in the sun—get a fake tan from a bottle.* ➲ SYNONYMS at ARTIFICIAL
■ ***noun*** **1** an object such as a work of art, a coin or a piece of jewellery that is not genuine but has been made to look as if it is: *All the paintings proved to be fakes.* **2** a person who pretends to be what they are not in order to cheat people
■ ***verb*** **1** [T] **~ sth** to make sth false appear to be genuine, especially in order to cheat sb: *She faked her mother's signature on the document.* ◇ *He arranged the accident in order to fake his own death.* **2** [T, I] **~ (sth)** to pretend to have a particular feeling, illness, etc: *She's not really sick—she's just* ***faking it.*** ◇ *He faked a yawn.* ▸ **faker** *noun*

fakie /ˈfeɪki/ *noun* (*informal*) a movement backwards on a SKATEBOARD or SNOWBOARD

fakir (also **faquir**) /ˈfeɪkɪə(r); *NAmE* fəˈkɪr/ *noun* a Muslim (or somtimes a Hindu) who lives without possessions and survives by receiving food and money from other people

fala·fel (also **fela·fel**) /fəˈlæfl/ *noun* [U, C] (*pl.* **fala·fel** or **fala·fels**) a Middle Eastern dish consisting of small balls formed from crushed CHICKPEAS, usually eaten with flat bread; one of these balls

fal·con /ˈfɔːlkən; *NAmE* ˈfælkən/ *noun* a BIRD OF PREY (= a bird that kills other creatures for food) with long pointed wings

fal·con·er /ˈfɔːlkənə(r); *NAmE* ˈfælkənər/ *noun* a person who keeps and trains falcons, often for hunting

fal·con·ry /ˈfɔːlkənri; *NAmE* ˈfæl-/ *noun* [U] the art or sport of breeding falcons and training them to hunt other birds or animals

F

fall 🗝 /fɔːl/ *verb, noun*
■ ***verb*** (**fell** /fel/, **fall·en** /ˈfɔːlən/)
▸ DROP DOWN **1** 🗝 [I] to drop down from a higher level to a lower level: *September had come and the leaves were starting to fall.* ◇ *They were injured by falling rocks.* ◇ **+ adv./prep.** *Several of the books had fallen onto the floor.* ◇ *One of the kids fell into the river.* ◇ *The handle had fallen off the drawer.* ◇ *He fell 20 metres onto the rocks below.* ◇ *The rain was falling steadily.*
▸ STOP STANDING **2** 🗝 [I] to suddenly stop standing: *She slipped on the ice and fell.* ◇ **+ adv./prep.** *I* ***fell over*** *and cut my knee.* ◇ *The house looked as if it was about to fall down.* ➲ see also FALLEN
▸ OF HAIR/MATERIAL **3** 🗝 [I] **+ adv./prep.** to hang down: *Her hair fell over her shoulders in a mass of curls.*
▸ SLOPE DOWNWARDS **4** 🗝 [I] **~ (away/off)** to slope downwards: *The land falls away sharply towards the river.*
▸ DECREASE **5** 🗝 [I] to decrease in amount, number or strength: *Their profits have fallen by 30 per cent.* ◇ *Prices continued to fall on the stock market today.* ◇ *The temperature fell sharply in the night.* ◇ *falling birth rates* ◇ *Her voice fell to a whisper.* ◇ **+ noun** *Share prices fell 30p.* OPP **rise**
▸ BE DEFEATED **6** [I] to be defeated or captured: *The coup failed but the government fell shortly afterwards.* ◇ **~ to sb** *Troy finally fell to the Greeks.*
▸ DIE IN BATTLE **7** [I] (*literary*) to die in battle; to be shot: *a memorial to those who fell in the two world wars*
▸ BECOME **8** 🗝 [I] to pass into a particular state; to begin to be sth: **+ adj.** *He had fallen asleep on the sofa.* ◇ *The book fell open at a page of illustrations.* ◇ *The room had fallen silent.* ◇ *She fell ill soon after and did not recover.* ◇ **~ into sth** *I had fallen into conversation with a man on the train.* ◇ *The house had fallen into disrepair.* ◇ **+ noun** *She knew she must not fall prey to his charm.*
▸ HAPPEN/OCCUR **9** [I] (*literary*) to come quickly and suddenly SYN **descend**: *A sudden silence fell.* ◇ *Darkness falls quickly in the tropics.* ◇ **~ on sb/sth** *An expectant hush fell on the guests.* **10** [I] **+ adv./prep.** to happen or take place: *My birthday falls on a Monday this year.* **11** [I] **+ adv./prep.** to move in a particular direction or come in a particular position: *My eye fell on* (= I suddenly saw) *a curious object.* ◇ *Which syllable does the stress fall on?* ◇ *A shadow fell across her face.*
▸ BELONG TO GROUP **12** [I] **+ adv./prep.** to belong to a particular class, group or area of responsibility: *Out of over 400 staff there are just 7 that fall into this category.* ◇ *This case falls outside my jurisdiction.* ◇ *This falls under the heading of scientific research.*
IDM Idioms containing **fall** are at the entries for the nouns and adjectives in the idioms, for example **fall by the wayside** is at **wayside**.
PHR V **ˌfall aˈbout** (*BrE, informal*) to laugh a lot: **~ doing sth** *We all fell about laughing.*
ˌfall aˈpart **1** to be in very bad condition so that parts are breaking off: *My car is falling apart.* **2** to have so many problems that it is no longer possible to exist or function: *Their marriage finally fell apart.* ◇ *The deal fell apart when we failed to agree on a price.*
ˌfall aˈway to become gradually fewer or smaller; to disappear: *His supporters fell away as his popularity declined.* ◇

The market for their products fell away to almost nothing. ◇ *All our doubts fell away.* ◇ *The houses fell away as we left the city.*
ˌ**fall ˈback 1** to move or turn back **SYN retreat**: *The enemy fell back as our troops advanced.* **2** to decrease in value or amount ˌ**fall ˈback on sb/sth** [no passive] to go to sb for support; to have sth to use when you are in difficulty: *I have a little money in the bank to fall back on.* ◇ *She fell back on her usual excuse of having no time.* ➲ related noun FALLBACK
ˌ**fall beˈhind (sb/sth)** to fail to keep level with sb/sth: *She soon fell behind the leaders.* ˌ**fall beˈhind with sth** (also ˌ**fall beˈhind on sth** especially in *NAmE*) to not pay or do sth at the right time: *They had fallen behind on their mortgage repayments.* ◇ *He's fallen behind with his school work again.*
ˌ**fall ˈdown** to be shown to be not true or not good enough: *And that's where the theory falls down.* ➲ see also FALL *v.* (2)
ˈ**fall for sb** [no passive] (*informal*) to be strongly attracted to sb; to fall in love with sb: *They fell for each other instantly.*
ˈ**fall for sth** [no passive] (*informal*) to be tricked into believing sth that is not true: *I'm surprised you fell for that trick.*
ˌ**fall ˈin** if soldiers **fall in**, they form lines: *The sergeant ordered his men to fall in.* ˌ**fall ˈin with sb/sth** [no passive] (*BrE*) to agree to sth: *She fell in with my idea at once.*
ˈ**fall into sth** to be able to be divided into sth: *My talk falls naturally into three parts.*
ˌ**fall ˈoff** to decrease in quantity or quality: *Attendance at my lectures has fallen off considerably.* **OPP rise**
ˈ**fall on/upon sb/sth** [no passive] (*especially BrE*) **1** to attack or take hold of sb/sth with a lot of energy and enthusiasm: *They fell on him with sticks.* ◇ *The children fell on the food and ate it greedily.* **2** to be the responsibility of sb: *The full cost of the wedding fell on us.*
ˌ**fall ˈout 1** to become loose and drop: *His hair is falling out.* **2** if soldiers **fall out**, they leave their lines and move away ˌ**fall ˈout (with sb)** (*BrE*) to have an argument with sb so that you are no longer friendly with them
ˌ**fall ˈover** (*informal*) (of a computer or program) to stop working suddenly: *My spreadsheet keeps falling over.* ˌ**fall ˈover sb/sth** [no passive] to hit your foot against sth when you are walking and fall, or almost fall **SYN trip over**: *I rushed for the door and fell over the cat in the hallway.* ➲ see also FALL *v.* (2) ˌ**fall ˈover yourself to do sth** (*informal*) to try very hard or want very much to do sth: *He was falling over himself to be nice to me.*
ˌ**fall ˈthrough** to not be completed, or not happen: *Our plans fell through because of lack of money.*
ˈ**fall to sb** to become the duty or responsibility of sb: *With his partner away, all the work now fell to him.* ◇ **it falls to sb to do sth** *It fell to me to inform her of her son's death.* ˈ**fall to sth** (*literary*) to begin to do sth~ **doing sth**: *She fell to brooding about what had happened to her.*

■ ***noun***

▸ ACT OF FALLING **1** [C] an act of falling: *I had a bad fall and broke my arm.* ◇ *She was killed in a fall from a horse.*
▸ OF SNOW/ROCKS **2** [C] **~ (of sth)** an amount of snow, rocks, etc. that falls or has fallen: *a heavy fall of snow* ◇ *a rock fall*
▸ WAY STH FALLS/HAPPENS **3** [sing.] **~ of sth** the way in which sth falls or happens: *the fall of the dice* ◇ *the dark fall of her hair* (= the way her hair hangs down)
▸ OF WATER **4 falls** [pl.] (especially in names) a large amount of water falling down from a height **SYN waterfall**: *The falls upstream are full of salmon.* ◇ *Niagara Falls*
▸ AUTUMN **5** [C] (*NAmE*) = AUTUMN: *in the fall of 2009* ◇ *last fall* ◇ *fall weather*
▸ DECREASE **6** [C] **~ (in sth)** a decrease in size, number, rate or level: *a steep fall in profits* ◇ *a big fall in unemployment* **OPP rise**
▸ DEFEAT **7** [sing.] **~ (of sth)** a loss of political, economic, etc. power or success; the loss or defeat of a city, country, etc. in war: *the fall of the Roman Empire* ◇ *the **rise and fall** of British industry* ◇ *the fall of Berlin*
▸ LOSS OF RESPECT **8** [sing.] a situation in which a person, an organization, etc. loses the respect of other people because they have done sth wrong: *the TV preacher's spectacular **fall from grace***
▸ IN BIBLE **9 the Fall** [sing.] the occasion when Adam and Eve did not obey God and had to leave the Garden of Eden

IDM break sb's ˈfall to stop sb from falling onto sth hard: *Luckily, a bush broke his fall.* **take the ˈfall (for sb/sth)** (*informal, especially NAmE*) to accept responsibility or punishment for sth that you did not do, or did not do alone: *He took the fall for his boss and resigned.* ➲ more at PRIDE *n.*, RIDE *v.*

Language Bank

fall
Describing a decrease

- Car crime in Oxford **fell significantly** last year.
- Car crime **fell** by about a quarter over a 12-month period.
- The number of stolen vehicles **dropped** from 1 013 to 780, **a fall of** 26 per cent.
- According to this data, 780 vehicles were stolen, 26% **down** on the previous year.
- There was an 11% **drop** in reported thefts from motor vehicles, from 1 871 **to** 1 737.
- These figures show that, as far as car crime is concerned, **the main trend is downwards**.

➲ Language Banks at EXPECT, ILLUSTRATE, INCREASE, PROPORTION

fal·la·cious /fəˈleɪʃəs/ *adj.* (*formal*) wrong; based on a false idea: *a fallacious argument*
fal·lacy /ˈfæləsi/ *noun* (*pl.* -ies) **1** [C] a false idea that many people believe is true: ***It is a fallacy** to say that the camera never lies.* **2** [U, C] a false way of thinking about sth: *He detected the fallacy of her argument.* ➲ see also PATHETIC FALLACY
fall·back /ˈfɔːlbæk/ *noun* a plan or course of action that is ready to be used in an emergency if other things fail: *What's our fallback if they don't come up with the money?* ◇ *We need a **fallback position** if they won't do the job.*
fall·en /ˈfɔːlən/ *adj.* [only before noun] **1** lying on the ground, after falling: *a fallen tree* **2** (*formal*) (of a soldier) killed in a war ➲ see also FALL *v.*
ˌ**fallen ˈwoman** *noun* (*old-fashioned*) a way of describing a woman in the past who had a sexual relationship with sb who was not her husband
ˈ**fall guy** *noun* (*especially NAmE*) a person who is blamed or punished for sth wrong that another person has done **SYN scapegoat**
fall·ible /ˈfæləbl/ *adj.* able to make mistakes or be wrong: *Memory is selective and fallible.* ◇ *All human beings are fallible.* **OPP infallible** ▸ **fal·li·bil·ity** /ˌfæləˈbɪləti/ *noun* [U]: *human fallibility*
ˈ**falling-off** *noun* [sing.] (*BrE*) = FALL-OFF
ˌ**falling-ˈout** *noun* (*informal*) [sing.] a situation where people are no longer friends, caused by a disagreement or an argument: *Dave and I **had a falling-out**.*
ˌ**falling ˈstar** *noun* = SHOOTING STAR
ˈ**fall-off** (*BrE* also *less frequent* ˈ**falling-off**) *noun* [sing.] **~ (in sth)** a reduction in the number, amount or quality of sth: *a recent fall-off in sales*
Fal·lo·pian tube (also **fal·lo·pian tube**) /fəˌləʊpiən ˈtjuːb; *NAmE* fəˈloʊpiən tuːb/ *noun* (*anatomy*) one of the two tubes in the body of a woman or female animal along which eggs pass from the OVARIES to the UTERUS
fall·out /ˈfɔːlaʊt/ *noun* [U] **1** dangerous RADIOACTIVE dust that is in the air after a nuclear explosion **2** the bad results of a situation or an action
fal·low /ˈfæləʊ; *NAmE* -loʊ/ *adj.* **1** (of farm land) not used for growing crops, especially so that the quality of the land will improve: *Farmers are now paid to let their land **lie fallow**.* **2** (of a period of time) when nothing is created or

produced; not successful: *Contemporary dance is coming onto the arts scene again after a long fallow period.*

'fallow deer *noun* a small European DEER with white spots on its back

'fall-pipe (*US*) (*BrE* **down·pipe**) *noun* a pipe for carrying water from a roof down to the ground or to a DRAIN

false ⊶ /fɔːls/ *adj.*

▸ NOT TRUE **1** ⊶ wrong; not correct or true: *A whale is a fish. True or false?* ◇ *Predictions of an early improvement in the housing market proved false.* ◇ *She gave false information to the insurance company.* ◇ *He used a false name to get the job.*

▸ NOT NATURAL **2** ⊶ not natural SYN **artificial**: *false teeth/eyelashes* ◇ *a false beard* ➲ SYNONYMS at ARTIFICIAL

▸ NOT GENUINE **3** ⊶ not genuine, but made to look real to cheat people: *a false passport*

▸ NOT SINCERE **4** (of people's behaviour) not real or sincere: *false modesty* ◇ *She flashed him a false smile of congratulation.*

▸ WRONG/MISTAKEN **5** ⊶ [usually before noun] wrong or mistaken, because it is based on sth that is not true or correct: *a* ***false argument/assumption/belief*** ◇ *to give a* ***false impression*** *of wealth* ◇ *to lull sb into a* ***false sense of security*** (= make sb feel safe when they are really in danger) ◇ *They didn't want to raise any* ***false hopes****, but they believed her husband had escaped capture.* ◇ *Buying a cheap computer is a* ***false economy*** (= will not actually save you money).

▸ NOT FAITHFUL **6** (*literary*) (of people) not faithful: *a false lover*

▸ **false·ly** *adv.*: *to be falsely accused of sth* ◇ *She smiled falsely at his joke.*

IDM **by/under/on false pre'tences** by pretending to be sth that you are not, in order to gain some advantage for yourself: *She was accused of obtaining money under false pretences.* ➲ more at RING[2] *v.*

,false a'larm *noun* a warning about a danger that does not happen; a belief that sth bad is going to happen, when it is not: *The fire service was called out but it was a false alarm.*

,false be'ginner *noun* a person who has a basic knowledge of a language, but has started to study it again from the beginning

,false 'dawn *noun* [usually sing.] (*formal*) a situation in which you think that sth good is going to happen but it does not: *a false dawn for the economy*

,false 'friend *noun* **1** a person who seems to be your friend, but who is not loyal and cannot be trusted **2** a word in a foreign language that looks similar to a word in your own language, but has a different meaning: *The English word 'sensible' and the French word 'sensible' are false friends.*

false·hood /'fɔːlshʊd/ *noun* (*formal*) **1** [U] the state of not being true; the act of telling a lie: *to test the truth or falsehood of her claims* **2** [C] a statement that is not true SYN **lie**

,false im'prisonment *noun* [U] (*law*) the crime of illegally keeping sb as a prisoner somewhere

,false 'memory *noun* (*psychology*) a memory of sth that did not actually happen

,false 'move *noun* [usually sing.] an action that is not allowed or not recommended and that may cause a bad result: ***One false move*** *and the bomb might blow up.*

,false 'rib *noun* = FLOATING RIB

,false 'start *noun* **1** an attempt to begin sth that is not successful: *After a number of false starts, she finally found a job she liked.* **2** (*sport*) a situation when sb taking part in a race starts before the official signal has been given

,false 'teeth *noun* [pl.] a set of artificial teeth used by sb who has lost their natural teeth ➲ compare DENTURES

fal·setto /fɔːl'setəʊ; *NAmE* -toʊ/ *noun* (*pl.* -os) an unusually high voice, especially the voice that men use to sing very high notes

fal·sies /'fɔːlsiz/ *noun* [pl.] (*informal*) pieces of material used inside a BRA to make a woman's breasts seem larger

fals·ify /'fɔːlsɪfaɪ/ *verb* (**fal·si·fies, fal·si·fy·ing, fal·si·fied, fal·si·fied**) **~ sth** (*formal*) to change a written record or information so that it is no longer true ▸ **fal·si·fi·ca·tion** /,fɔːlsɪfɪ'keɪʃn/ *noun* [U, C]: *the deliberate falsification of the company's records*

fal·sity /'fɔːlsəti/ *noun* [U] the state of not being true or genuine OPP **truth**

Fal·staff·i·an /fɔːl'stɑːfiən; *NAmE* -'stæf-/ *adj.* (*literary*) fat, cheerful and eating and drinking a lot: *My uncle was a Falstaffian figure.* ORIGIN From Sir John Falstaff, a character in several plays by William Shakespeare.

fal·ter /'fɔːltə(r)/ *verb* **1** [I] to become weaker or less effective SYN **waver**: *The economy shows no signs of faltering.* ◇ *Her courage never faltered.* **2** [I, T] (**+ speech**) to speak in a way that shows that you are not confident: *His voice faltered as he began his speech.* **3** [I] to walk or behave in a way that shows that you are not confident: *She walked up to the platform without faltering.* ◇ *He never faltered in his commitment to the party.* ▸ **fal·ter·ing** /'fɔːltərɪŋ/ *adj.*: *the faltering peace talks* ◇ *the baby's first faltering steps*

F

fame ⊶ /feɪm/ *noun* [U] the state of being known and talked about by many people: *to* ***achieve/win*** *instant* ***fame*** ◇ *to* ***rise/shoot to fame*** *overnight* ◇ *Andrew Lloyd Webber of 'Evita' fame* (= famous for 'Evita') ◇ *The town's only* ***claim to fame*** *is that there was once a riot there.* ◇ *She went to Hollywood in search of* ***fame and fortune****.* ➲ see also FAMOUS

famed /feɪmd/ *adj.* **~** (**for sth**) very well known SYN **renowned**: *Las Vegas, famed for its casinos* ◇ *a famed poet and musician* ➲ see also FAMOUS

fa·mil·ial /fə'mɪliəl/ *adj.* [only before noun] (*formal*) **1** related to or typical of a family **2** (*medical*) (of diseases, conditions, etc.) affecting several members of a family: *familial left-handedness*

fa·mil·iar ⊶ /fə'mɪliə(r)/ *adj.*

1 ⊶ well known to you; often seen or heard and therefore easy to recognize: *to* ***look/sound/taste familiar*** ◇ *He's a familiar figure in the neighbourhood.* ◇ *Something about her voice was vaguely familiar.* ◇ **~ to sb** *The smell is very familiar to everyone who lives near a bakery.* ◇ *Violent attacks are becoming* ***all too familiar*** (= sadly familiar). OPP **unfamiliar** **2** ⊶ **~ with sth** knowing sth very well: *an area with which I had been familiar since childhood* ◇ *Are you familiar with the computer software they use?* OPP **unfamiliar** **3 ~** (**with sb**) (of a person's behaviour) very informal, sometimes in a way that is unpleasant: *You seem to be on very familiar terms with your tutor.* ◇ *After a few drinks her boss started getting too familiar for her liking.*

fa·mil·iar·ity /fə,mɪli'ærəti/ *noun* [U] **1 ~** (**with sth**) | **~** (**to sb**) the state of knowing sb/sth well; the state of recognizing sb/sth: *His familiarity with the language helped him enjoy his stay.* ◇ *When she saw the house, she had a feeling of familiarity.* **2** a friendly informal manner: *She addressed me with an easy familiarity that made me feel at home.*

IDM **familiarity breeds con'tempt** (*saying*) knowing sb/sth very well may cause you to lose admiration and respect for them/it

fa·mil·iar·ize (*BrE* also **-ise**) /fə'mɪliəraɪz/ *verb* **~ yourself/sb** (**with sth**) to learn about sth or teach sb about sth, so that you/they start to understand it SYN **acquaint**: *You'll need time to familiarize yourself with our procedures.* ▸ **fa·mil·iar·iza·tion, -isa·tion** /fə,mɪliəraɪ'zeɪʃn; *NAmE* -rə'z-/ *noun* [U]

fa·mil·iar·ly /fə'mɪliəli; *NAmE* -ərli/ *adv.* **1** in a friendly and informal manner, sometimes in a way that is too informal to be pleasant: *John Hunt, familiarly known to his friends as Jack* ◇ *He touched her cheek familiarly.* **2** in the way that is well known to people: *The elephant's nose or, more familiarly, trunk, is the most versatile organ in the animal kingdom.*

fam·ily ⊶ /'fæməli/ *noun, adj.*

■ ***noun*** (*pl.* -ies) **1** ⊶ [C+sing./pl. v.] a group consisting of one or two parents and their children: *the other members of my family* ◇ *Almost every family in the country owns a television.* ◇ *All my family enjoy skiing.* ◇ ***one-parent/single-***

parent families ◇ *a family of four* ◇ *families with young children* ➲ see also BLENDED FAMILY, NUCLEAR FAMILY **2** 🔑 [C+sing./pl. v., U] a group consisting of one or two parents, their children and close relations: *All our family came to Grandad's eightieth birthday party.* ◇ *The support of* ***family and friends*** *is vital.* ◇ *We've only told the* ***immediate family*** (= the closest relations). ◇ *the* ***Royal Family*** (= the children and close relations of the king or queen) ◇ *I always think of you as* ***one of the family.*** ◇ (*informal*) *She's family* (= she is a relation). ➲ see also EXTENDED FAMILY **3** 🔑 [C+sing./pl. v.] all the people who are related to each other, including those who are now dead: *Some families have farmed in this area for hundreds of years.* ◇ *This painting has* ***been in our family*** *for generations.* **4** 🔑 [C+sing./pl. v., U] a couple's or a person's children, especially young children: *They have a large family.* ◇ *I addressed it to Mr and Mrs Jones and family.* ◇ *Do they plan to* ***start a family*** (= have children)? ◇ *to* ***bring up/raise a family*** ➲ COLLOCATIONS at CHILD **5** 🔑 [C] a group of related animals and plants; a group of related things, especially languages: *Lions belong to the cat family.* ◇ *the Germanic family of languages*

F

IDM **(be/get) in the 'family way** (*old-fashioned, informal*) (to be/become) pregnant **run in the 'family** to be a common feature in a particular family: *Heart disease runs in the family.*

■ ***adj.*** [only before noun] **1** 🔑 connected with the family or a particular family: *family life* ◇ *your family background* **2** 🔑 owned by a family: *a family business* **3** 🔑 suitable for all members of a family, both adults and children: *a family show*

the 'Family Division *noun* [sing.] in the UK, the part of the High Court which deals with cases that affect families, for example when people get divorced or adopt a child

ˌfamily 'doctor *noun* (*informal, especially BrE*) = GENERAL PRACTITIONER

'family man *noun* a man who has a wife or partner and children; a man who enjoys being at home with his wife or partner and children: *I see he's become a family man.* ◇ *a devoted family man*

'family name *noun* the part of your name that shows which family you belong to ➲ compare SURNAME

ˌfamily 'planning *noun* [U] the process of controlling the number of children you have by using CONTRACEPTION

ˌfamily 'practitioner *noun* (*especially BrE*) = GENERAL PRACTITIONER

'family room *noun* **1** (*NAmE*) a room in a house where the family can relax, watch television, etc. **2** a room in a hotel for three or four people to sleep in, especially parents and children **3** (in Britain) a room in a pub where children are allowed to sit

ˌfamily 'tree *noun* a diagram that shows the relationship between members of a family over a long period of time: *How far back can you trace your family tree?*

fam·ine /ˈfæmɪn/ *noun* [C, U] a lack of food during a long period of time in a region: *a severe famine* ◇ *disasters such as floods and famine* ◇ *the threat of* ***widespread famine*** *in the area* ◇ *to raise money for* ***famine relief***

fam·ished /ˈfæmɪʃt/ *adj.* [not usually before noun] (*informal*, becoming *old-fashioned*) very hungry SYN **starving**: *When's lunch? I'm famished!*

fam·ous 🔑 /ˈfeɪməs/ *adj.*
known about by many people: *a famous artist/hotel* ◇ *the most famous lake in Italy* ◇ *One day, I'll be* ***rich and famous.*** ◇ **~ for sth** *He became internationally famous for his novels.* ◇ **~ as sth** *She was more famous as a writer than as a singer.* ➲ see also FAME, INFAMOUS, NOTORIOUS, WORLD-FAMOUS

IDM **ˌfamous ˌlast 'words** (*saying*) people sometimes say **Famous last words!** when they think sb is being too confident about sth that is going to happen: *'Everything's under control.' 'Famous last words!'* ORIGIN This phrase refers to a collection of quotations of the dying words of famous people.

fam·ous·ly /ˈfeɪməsli/ *adv.* in a way that is famous: *Some newspapers, most famously the New York Times, refuse to print the word Ms.*

IDM **get on/along 'famously** (*informal*, becoming *old-fashioned*) to have a very good relationship

fan 🔑 /fæn/ *noun, verb*

fans

■ ***noun*** **1** 🔑 a person who admires sb/sth or enjoys watching or listening to sb/sth very much: *movie fans* ◇ *crowds of football fans* ◇ *a big fan of Madonna* ◇ ***fan mail*** (= letters from fans to the person they admire) **2** 🔑 a machine with blades that go round to create a current of air: *to switch on the electric fan* ◇ *a fan heater* ➲ see also EXTRACTOR **3** a thing that you hold in your hand and wave to create a current of cool air IDM see SHIT *n.*

■ ***verb*** (-nn-) **1 ~ sb/sth/yourself** to make air blow onto sb/sth by waving a fan, your hand, etc: *He fanned himself with a newspaper to cool down.* **2 ~ sth** to make a fire burn more strongly by blowing on it: *Fanned by a westerly wind, the fire spread rapidly through the city.* **3 ~ sth** (*literary*) to make a feeling, an attitude, etc. stronger SYN **fuel**: *His reluctance to answer her questions simply fanned her curiosity.*

IDM **fan the 'flames (of sth)** to make a feeling such as anger, hatred, etc. worse: *His writings fanned the flames of racism.*

PHR V **ˌfan 'out | ˌfan sth↔'out** to spread out or spread sth out over an area: *The police fanned out to surround the house.* ◇ *The bird fanned out its tail feathers.*

fan·at·ic /fəˈnætɪk/ *noun* **1** (*informal*) a person who is extremely enthusiastic about sth SYN **enthusiast**: ***a fitness/crossword, etc. fanatic*** **2** (*disapproving*) a person who holds extreme or dangerous opinions SYN **extremist**: *religious fanatics* ▸ **fan·at·ic·al** /-kl/ *adj.*: *a fanatical supporter* ◇ *fanatical anti-royalists* ◇ *a fanatical interest in football* ◇ *She's fanatical about healthy eating.* **fan·at·ic·al·ly** /-kli/ *adv.*: *fanatically fit*

fan·ati·cism /fəˈnætɪsɪzəm/ *noun* [U] (*disapproving*) extreme beliefs or behaviour, especially in connection with religion or politics SYN **extremism**

'fan belt *noun* a belt that operates the machinery that cools a car engine

fan·boy /ˈfænbɔɪ/ *noun* (*informal*) a person, especially a boy or young man, who is extremely interested in sth such as a particular type of music or software: *a Nintendo fanboy* ◇ *Linux fanboys*

fan·ci·able /ˈfænsiəbl/ *adj.* (*BrE, informal*) sexually attractive

fan·cier /ˈfænsiə(r)/ *noun* (usually in compounds) (*especially BrE*) a person who has a special interest in sth, especially sb who keeps or breeds birds, animals or plants: *a pigeon fancier*

fan·ci·ful /ˈfænsɪfl/ *adj.* **1** (*disapproving*) based on imagination and not facts or reason **2** (of things) decorated in an unusual style that shows imagination: *a fanciful gold border* ▸ **fan·ci·ful·ly** /-fəli/ *adv.*

'fan club *noun* an organization that a person's fans belong to and that sends them information, etc. about that person

fancy 🔑 /ˈfænsi/ *verb, noun, adj.*

■ ***verb*** (fan·cies, fancy·ing, fan·cied, fan·cied) **1** 🔑 [T] (*BrE, informal*) to want sth or want to do sth SYN **feel like**: **~ sth** *Fancy a drink?* ◇ *She didn't fancy* (= did not like) *the idea of going home in the dark.* ◇ **~ doing sth** *Do you fancy going* *out this evening?* **2** [T] **~ sb** (*BrE, informal*) to be sexually attracted to sb: *I think she fancies me.* **3** [T] **~ yourself** (*BrE, informal, disapproving*) to think that you are very popular, attractive or intelligent: *He started to chat to me and I could tell that he really fancied himself.* **4** [T] (*BrE*) to like the idea of being sth or to believe, often wrongly, that you are sth: **~ yourself (as) sth** *She fancies herself (as) a serious actress.* **~ yourself + adv./prep.** **5** [I, T] **Fancy!** (*BrE, informal, becoming old-fashioned*) used to show that you are surprised or shocked by sth: *Fancy! She's never been in a plane before.* ◇ **~ doing sth** *Fancy meeting you here!* ◇ **~ sth** *'She remembered my name after all those years.' '**Fancy that!**'* **6** [T] (*BrE*) **~ sb/sth** to think that sb/sth will win or be successful at sth, especially in a race: *Which horse do you fancy in the next race?* ◇ *He's hoping to get the job but I don't **fancy his chances**.* **7** [T] **~ (that)...** (*literary*) to believe or imagine sth: *She fancied (that) she could hear footsteps.*

■ ***noun*** (*pl.* **-ies**) **1** [C, U] something that you imagine; your imagination SYN **fantasy**: *night-time fancies that disappear in the morning* ◇ *a child's wild **flights of fancy*** **2** [sing.] a feeling that you would like to have or to do sth SYN **whim**: *She said she wanted a dog but it was only a passing fancy.* **3** [C, usually pl.] (*BrE*) a small decorated cake

IDM **as/whenever, etc. the fancy 'takes you** as/whenever, etc. you feel like doing sth: *We bought a camper van so we could go away whenever the fancy took us.* **catch/take sb's 'fancy** to attract or please sb: *She looked through the hotel advertisements until one of them caught her fancy.* **take a 'fancy to sb/sth** (*especially BrE*) to start liking sb/sth, often without an obvious reason ➲ more at TICKLE *v.*

■ ***adj.*** (**fan·cier, fan·ci·est**) **1** unusually complicated, often in an unnecessary way; intended to impress other people: *a kitchen full of fancy gadgets* ◇ *They added a lot of fancy footwork to the dance.* ◇ *He's always using fancy legal words.* OPP **simple** **2** [only before noun] (especially of small things) with a lot of decorations or bright colours: *fancy goods* (= things sold as gifts or for decoration) ➲ compare PLAIN **3** (*sometimes disapproving*) expensive or connected with an expensive way of life: *fancy restaurants with fancy prices* ◇ *Don't come back with any fancy ideas.* **4** (*NAmE*) (of food) of high quality

,fancy 'dress *noun* [U] (*BrE*) clothes that you wear, especially at parties, to make you appear to be a different character: *guests **in fancy dress*** ◇ *a fancy-dress party* ➲ see also COSTUME, MASQUERADE

,fancy-'free *adj.* free to do what you like because you are not emotionally involved with anyone: *I was still **footloose and fancy-free*** (= free to enjoy myself) *in those days.*

'fancy man, 'fancy woman *noun* (*old-fashioned, informal, disapproving*) the man/woman with whom a person is having a romantic relationship, especially when one or both of them is married to sb else

fan·dango /fæn'dæŋgəʊ; *NAmE* -goʊ/ *noun* (*pl.* **fan·dan·goes** or **fan·dangos**) [C] a lively Spanish dance; a piece of music for this dance

fan·fare /'fænfeə(r); *NAmE* -fer/ *noun* **1** [C] a short loud piece of music that is played to celebrate sb/sth important arriving **2** [U, C] a large amount of activity and discussion on television, in newspapers, etc. to celebrate sb/sth: *The product was launched amid much fanfare worldwide.*

'fan fiction *noun* [U] a type of literature, usually written on the Internet, by people who admire a particular novel, film/movie, etc, with characters taken from these stories

fang /fæŋ/ *noun* [usually pl.] either of two long sharp teeth at the front of the mouths of some animals, such as a snake or dog ➲ VISUAL VOCAB page V11

'F angles *noun* [pl.] = CORRESPONDING ANGLES

fan·light /'fænlaɪt/ (*NAmE* also **tran·som**) *noun* a small window above a door or another window

Fanny /'fæni/ *noun* IDM see SWEET *adj.*

fanny /'fæni/ *noun* (*pl.* **-ies**) **1** (*BrE, taboo, slang*) the female sex organs **2** (*slang, especially NAmE*) a person's bottom

'fanny pack (*NAmE*) (*BrE* **bum·bag**) *noun* (*informal*) a small bag attached to a belt and worn around the waist, to keep money, etc. in ➲ VISUAL VOCAB page V52

fan·ta·sia /fæn'teɪziə/ *noun* a piece of music in a free form, often based on well-known tunes

fan·ta·size (*BrE* also **-ise**) /'fæntəsaɪz/ *verb* [I, T] **~ (about sth)** | **~ (that...)** to imagine that you are doing sth that you would like to do, or that sth that you would like to happen is happening, even though this is very unlikely: *He sometimes fantasized about winning the gold medal.* ▸ **fan·ta·sist** /'fæntəsɪst/ *noun*

fan·tas·tic /fæn'tæstɪk/ *adj.* **1** (*informal*) extremely good; excellent SYN **great, brilliant**: *a fantastic beach in Australia* ◇ *a fantastic achievement* ◇ *The weather was absolutely fantastic.* ◇ *You've got the job? Fantastic!* ➲ SYNONYMS at GREAT **2** (*informal*) very large; larger than you expected SYN **enormous, amazing**: *The response to our appeal was fantastic.* ◇ *The car costs a fantastic amount of money.* **3** (also *less frequent* **fan·tas·tic·al**) [usually before noun] strange and showing a lot of imagination SYN **weird**: *fantastic dreams of forests and jungles* **4** impossible to put into practice: *a **fantastic scheme/project*** ▸ **fan·tas·tic·al·ly** /fæn'tæstɪkli/ *adv.*: *fantastically successful* ◇ *a fantastically shaped piece of stone*

fan·tasy /'fæntəsi/ *noun* (*pl.* **-ies**) **1** [C] a pleasant situation that you imagine but that is unlikely to happen: *his childhood fantasies about becoming a famous football player* **2** [C] a product of your imagination: *Her books are usually escapist fantasies.* **3** [U] the act of imagining things; a person's imagination: *a work of fantasy* ◇ *Stop living in a **fantasy world**.*

,fantasy 'football *noun* [U] a competition in which you choose players to make your own imaginary team, and score points according to the performance of the real players

fan·zine /'fænziːn/ *noun* a magazine that is written and read by fans of a musician, sports team, etc.

fao *abbr.* (*BrE*) used in writing to mean 'for the attention of' (written on a document or letter to say who should deal with it) ➲ see also ATTN

FAQ /,ef eɪ 'kjuː/ *abbr.* used in writing to mean 'frequently asked questions'

fa·quir = FAKIR

far /fɑː(r)/ *adv., adj.*

■ ***adv.*** (**far·ther, far·thest** or **fur·ther, fur·thest**)

▸ DISTANCE **1** a long distance away: *We didn't go far.* ◇ *Have you come far?* ◇ *It's not far to the beach.* ◇ *There's not far to go now.* ◇ **~ (from, away, below, etc.)** *The restaurant is not far from here.* ◇ *countries as far apart as Japan and Brazil* ◇ *He looked down at the traffic far below.* ◇ *Far away in the distance, a train whistled.* ◇ *The farther north they went, the colder it became.* ◇ *a concert of music from **near and far*** HELP In positive sentences it is more usual to use **a long way**: *We went a long way.* ◇ *~~We went far.~~* ◇ *The restaurant is a long way from here.* **2** used when you are asking or talking about the distance between two places or the distance that has been travelled or is to be travelled: *How far is it to your house from here?* ◇ *How much further is it?* ◇ *We'll go by train **as far as** London, and then take a bus.* ◇ *We didn't go **as far as** the others.* ◇ *I'm not sure I can walk **so far**.*

▸ TIME **3** a long time from the present; for a large part of a particular period of time: **~ back** *The band made their first record as far back as 1990.* ◇ **~ ahead** *Let's try to plan further ahead.* ◇ **~ into sth** *We worked far into the night.*

▸ DEGREE **4** very much; to a great degree: *That's a far better idea.* ◇ *There are **far more** opportunities for young people than there used to be.* ◇ *It had been a success **far beyond** their expectations.* ◇ *He's fallen far behind in his work.* ◇ *She always gives us **far too much** homework.* **5** used when you are asking or talking about the degree to which sth is true or possible: *How far can we trust him?* ◇ *His parents supported him **as far as** they could.* ◇ *Plan your route in advance, using main roads **as far as possible**.*

▸ PROGRESS **6** used to talk about how much progress has been made in doing or achieving sth: *How far have you got*

F

with that report? ◇ *I read* ***as far as*** *the third chapter.* ➲ note at FARTHER

IDM **as far as the eye can/could 'see** to the HORIZON (= where the sky meets the land or sea): *The bleak moorland stretched on all sides as far as the eye could see.* **as far as I 'know | as far as I can re'member, 'see, 'tell, etc.** 🔑 used to say that you think you know, remember, understand, etc. sth but you cannot be completely sure, especially because you do not know all the facts: *As far as we knew, there was no cause for concern.* ◇ *As far as I can see, you've done nothing wrong.* ◇ *She lived in Chicago, as far as I can remember.* **as/so far as 'I am concerned** 🔑 used to give your personal opinion on sth: *As far as I am concerned, you can do what you like.* **as/so far as sb/sth is concerned | as/so far as sb/sth goes** 🔑 used to give facts or an opinion about a particular aspect of sth **as/so far as it 'goes** to a limited degree, usually less than is sufficient: *It's a good plan as far as it goes, but there are a lot of things they haven't thought of.* **by 'far** 🔑 (used with comparative or superlative adjectives or adverbs) by a great amount: *The last of these reasons is by far the most important.* ◇ *Amy is the smartest by far.* **carry/take sth too 'far** to continue doing sth beyond reasonable limits **far and a'way** (followed by comparative or superlative adjectives) by a very great amount: *She's far and away the best player.* **far and 'wide** over a large area: *They searched far and wide for the missing child.* **far be it from me to do sth (but...)** (*informal*) used when you are just about to disagree with sb or to criticize them and you would like them to think that you do not really want to do this: *Far be it from me to interfere in your affairs but I would like to give you just one piece of advice.* **far from sth/from doing sth** almost the opposite of sth or of what is expected: *It is far from clear* (= it is not clear) *what he intends to do.* ◇ *Computers, far from destroying jobs, can create employment.* **far 'from it** (*informal*) used to say that the opposite of what sb says is true: *'You're not angry then?' 'Far from it. I've never laughed so much in my life.'* **go 'far** (of people) to be very successful in the future: *She is very talented and should go far.* **go far enough** (used in questions and negative sentences) to achieve all that is wanted: *The new legislation is welcome but does not go far enough.* ◇ *Do these measures go far enough?* ◇ (*disapproving*) *Stop it now. The joke has gone far enough* (= it has continued too long). **go so/as far as to...** to be willing to go to extreme or surprising limits in dealing with sth: *I wouldn't go as far as to say that he's a liar* (= but I think he may be slightly dishonest). **go too 'far | go 'this/'that far** to behave in an extreme way that is not acceptable: *He's always been quite crude, but this time he's gone too far.* ◇ *I never thought she'd go this far.* **in so/as 'far as** to the degree that: *That's the truth, in so far as I know it.* **not far 'off/'out/'wrong** (*informal*) almost correct: *Your guess wasn't far out at all.* **not go 'far 1** (of money) to not be enough to buy a lot of things: *Five pounds doesn't go very far these days.* **2** (of a supply of sth) to not be enough for what is needed: *Four bottles of wine won't go far among twenty people.* **'so far | 'thus far** 🔑 until now; up to this point: *What do you think of the show so far?* ◇ *Detectives are so far at a loss to explain the reason for his death.* **,so 'far** 🔑 (*informal*) only to a limited degree: *I trust him only so far.* **,so far, so 'good** (*saying*) used to say that things have been successful until now and you hope that they will continue to be successful, but you know that the task, etc. is not finished yet ➲ more at AFIELD, FEW *adj.*, NEAR *adv.*

■ ***adj.*** (**far·ther, far·thest** or **fur·ther, fur·thest**) [only before noun]

▸ DISTANT **1** 🔑 at a greater distance away from you: *I saw her on the* ***far side*** *of the road.* ◇ *at the* ***far end*** *of the room* ◇ *They made for an empty table in the* ***far corner.*** **2** 🔑 at the furthest point in a particular direction: *the* ***far north*** *of Scotland* ◇ *Who is that on the* ***far left*** *of the photograph?* ◇ *She is on the* ***far right*** *of the party* (= holds extreme RIGHT-WING political views). **3** (*old-fashioned* or *literary*) a long distance away: *a far country*

IDM **a far cry from sth** a very different experience from sth **SYN** **remote**

Farad /ˈfærəd/ *noun* (*abbr.* F) (*physics*) a unit for measuring CAPACITANCE

far·away /ˈfɑːrəweɪ/ *adj.* [only before noun] **1** a long distance away **SYN** **distant**: *a war in a faraway country* **2 a ~ look/expression** an expression on your face that shows that your thoughts are far away from your present surroundings **SYN** **distant**

farce /fɑːs; *NAmE* fɑːrs/ *noun* **1** [C, U] a funny play for the theatre based on ridiculous and unlikely situations and events; this type of writing or performance: *a bedroom farce* (= a funny play about sex) **2** [C] a situation or an event that is so unfair or badly organized that it becomes ridiculous: *The trial was a complete farce.*

far·ci·cal /ˈfɑːsɪkl; *NAmE* ˈfɑːrs-/ *adj.* ridiculous and not worth taking seriously: *It was a farcical trial.* ◇ *a situation verging on the farcical*

fare /feə(r); *NAmE* fer/ *noun, verb*

■ ***noun*** **1** [C, U] the money that you pay to travel by bus, plane, taxi, etc: ***bus/taxi fares*** ◇ ***train/rail fares*** ◇ *Children travel (at) half fare.* ◇ *When do they start paying full fare?* ➲ see also AIRFARE, RETURN FARE ➲ note at RATE **2** [C] a passenger in a taxi: *The taxi driver picked up a fare at the station.* **3** [U] (*old-fashioned* or *formal*) food that is offered as a meal: *The restaurant provides good traditional fare.*

■ ***verb*** [I] **~ well, badly, better, etc.** to be successful/unsuccessful in a particular situation **SYN** **get on**: *The party fared very badly in the last election.*

the ,Far 'East *noun* China, Japan and other countries of E and SE Asia ➲ compare THE MIDDLE EAST ▸ **,Far 'Eastern** *adj.*

fare·well /ˌfeəˈwel; *NAmE* ˌferˈwel/ *noun, exclamation*

■ ***noun*** [C, U] the act of saying goodbye to sb: *She said her farewells and left.* ◇ *a* ***farewell party/drink, etc.***

■ ***exclamation*** (*old use* or *formal*) goodbye

■ ***verb*** **~ sb** (*AustralE*) to arrange a ceremony or party for sb because they are leaving: *The troops were farewelled at a ceremony in Darwin.*

,far-'fetched *adj.* very difficult to believe: *The whole story sounds very far-fetched.*

,far-'flung *adj.* [usually before noun] (*literary*) **1** a long distance away: *expeditions to the far-flung corners of the world* **2** spread over a wide area: *a newsletter that helps to keep all our far-flung graduates in touch*

,far 'gone *adj.* [not before noun] (*informal*) very ill/sick, crazy or drunk: *She was too far gone to understand anything we said to her.*

farm 🔑 /fɑːm; *NAmE* fɑːrm/ *noun, verb*

■ ***noun*** **1** 🔑 an area of land, and the buildings on it, used for growing crops and/or keeping animals: *a 200-hectare farm* ◇ *a* ***farm worker/labourer*** ◇ ***farm buildings/machinery*** ◇ *to* ***live/work on a farm*** ➲ COLLOCATIONS at FARMING ➲ VISUAL VOCAB page V2 **2** 🔑 the main house on a farm, where the farmer lives **3** (especially in compounds) a place where particular fish or animals are bred: *a trout/mink/pig farm* ➲ see also BATTERY FARM, COLLECTIVE FARM, DAIRY FARM, FACTORY FARM, FUNNY FARM, HEALTH FARM, TRUCK FARM, WIND FARM

■ ***verb*** [I, T] to use land for growing crops and/or keeping animals: *The family has farmed in Kent for over two hundred years.* ◇ **~ sth** *They farm dairy cattle.* ◇ *He farmed 200 acres of prime arable land.* ◇ *organically farmed produce*

IDM see BUY *v.*

PHR V **,farm sb↔'out (to sb)** (*BrE, disapproving*) to arrange for sb to be cared for by other people **,farm sb/sth↔'out to sb** to send out work for other people to do: *The company farms out a lot of work to freelancers.*

'farm belt *noun* (*US*) an area where there are a lot of farms

farm·er 🔑 /ˈfɑːmə(r); *NAmE* ˈfɑːrm-/ *noun* a person who owns or manages a farm

'farmers' market *noun* a place where farmers sell food directly to the public

farm·hand /ˈfɑːmhænd; *NAmE* ˈfɑːrm-/ (*NAmE* also **'field hand**) *noun* a person who works for a farmer

farm·house /ˈfɑːmhaʊs; *NAmE* ˈfɑːrm-/ *noun* the main house on a farm, where the farmer lives ➲ VISUAL VOCAB page V2

farm·ing 0→ /ˈfɑːmɪŋ; *NAmE* ˈfɑːrmɪŋ/ *noun* [U] the business of managing or working on a farm: *to take up farming* ◇ ***sheep/fish, etc. farming*** ◇ *organic farming* ◇ *modern farming methods* ◇ *a farming community*

Collocations

Farming

Growing food and raising animals

- **plant** trees/seeds/crops/vines/barley
- **grow/produce** corn/wheat/rice/fruit
- **plough**/(*NAmE*) **plow** land/a field
- **sow/harvest** seeds/crops/fields
- **spread** manure/fertilizer on sth
- **cultivate/irrigate/water/contaminate** crops/plants/fields/land
- **damage/destroy/lose** your crop
- **ripen/pick** fruit/berries/grapes
- **press/dry/ferment** grapes
- **grind/thresh** grain/corn/wheat
- **raise/rear/keep** chickens/poultry/cattle/pigs
- **raise/breed/feed/graze** livestock/cattle/sheep
- **kill/slaughter** livestock
- **preserve/smoke/cure/salt** meat

Modern farming

- **run** a fish farm/an organic dairy
- **engage in/be involved in** intensive (pig/fish) farming
- **use/apply** (chemical/organic) fertilizer/insecticides/pesticides
- **begin/do/conduct** field trials of GM (= genetically modified) crops
- **grow/develop** GM crops/seeds/plants/foods
- **fund/invest in** genetic engineering/research
- **improve/increase** crop yields
- **face/suffer from/alleviate** food shortages
- **label** food that contains GMOs (= genetically modified organisms)
- **eliminate/reduce** farm subsidies
- **oppose/be against** factory farming/GM food
- **promote/encourage/support** organic/sustainable farming

farm·land /ˈfɑːmlænd; *NAmE* ˈfɑːrm-/ *noun* [U, pl.] land that is used for farming: *250 acres of farmland* ◇ *the prosperous farmlands of Picardy*

farm·stead /ˈfɑːmsted; *NAmE* ˈfɑːrm-/ *noun* (*NAmE* or *formal*) a FARMHOUSE and the buildings near it

farm·yard /ˈfɑːmjɑːd; *NAmE* ˈfɑːrmjɑːrd/ *noun* an area that is surrounded by farm buildings ➲ VISUAL VOCAB page V2

ˈfar-off *adj.* [only before noun] **1** a long distance away SYN **distant, faraway, remote:** *a far-off land* **2** a long time ago SYN **distant:** *memories of those far-off days*

far·rago /fəˈrɑːɡəʊ; *NAmE* -ɡoʊ/ *noun* [usually sing.] (*pl.* -oes or -os) (*formal, disapproving*) a confused mixture of different things SYN **hotchpotch**

ˌfar-ˈreaching *adj.* likely to have a lot of influence or many effects: ***far-reaching consequences/implications*** ◇ ***far-reaching changes/reforms***

far·rier /ˈfæriə(r)/ *noun* a person whose job is making and fitting HORSESHOES for horses' feet

far·row /ˈfærəʊ; *NAmE* -roʊ/ *noun, verb*
- ***noun* 1** a group of baby pigs that are born together to the same mother SYN **litter 2** an act of giving birth to pigs
- ***verb*** [I] (of a female pig) to give birth

Farsi /ˈfɑːsiː; *NAmE* ˈfɑːrsiː/ *noun* [U] = PERSIAN

ˌfar-ˈsighted *adj.* **1** having or showing an understanding of the effects in the future of actions that you take now, and being able to plan for them: *the most far-sighted of politicians* ◇ *a far-sighted decision* **2** (*especially NAmE*) = LONG-SIGHTED ▸ **ˌfar-ˈsighted·ness** *noun* [U]

fart /fɑːt; *NAmE* fɑːrt/ *verb, noun*
- ***verb*** [I] (*taboo, slang*) to let air from the BOWELS come out through the ANUS, especially when it happens loudly HELP A more polite way of expressing this is 'to break wind'.

PHR V **ˌfart aˈround** (*BrE* also **ˌfart aˈbout**) (*taboo, slang*) to waste time by behaving in a silly way
- ***noun*** (*taboo, slang*) **1** an act of letting air from the BOWELS come out through the ANUS, especially when it happens loudly **2** an unpleasant, boring or stupid person

far·ther 0→ /ˈfɑːðə(r); *NAmE* ˈfɑːrð-/ *adv., adj.*
- ***adv.*** 0→ (comparative of *far*) at or to a greater distance in space or time: *farther north/south* ◇ ***farther along*** *the road* ◇ *I can't go* ***any farther.*** ◇ *As a family we grew* ***farther and farther*** *apart.* ◇ *We watched their ship moving gradually* ***farther away.*** ◇ *How much farther is it?* ◇ *They hadn't got any farther with the work* (= they had made no progress).
IDM see AFIELD
- ***adj.*** 0→ (comparative of *far*) at a greater distance in space, direction or time: *the farther shore of the lake*

Which Word?

farther / further / farthest / furthest

- These are the comparative and superlative forms of **far**.
- To talk about distance, use either **farther, farthest** or **further, furthest**. In *BrE*, **further, furthest** are the most common forms and in *NAmE*, **further** and **farthest**: *I have to travel further/farther to work now.*
- To talk about the degree or extent of something, **further/furthest** are usually preferred: *Let's consider this point further.*
- **Further**, but not **farther**, can also mean 'more' or 'additional': *Are there any further questions?* This sounds very formal in *NAmE*.

far·thest 0→ /ˈfɑːðɪst; *NAmE* ˈfɑːrð-/ (also **fur·thest**) *adv., adj.*
- ***adv.*** 0→ (superlative of *far*) at or to the greatest distance in space or time: *the house* ***farthest away*** *from the road* ◇ *a competition to see who could throw (the) farthest*
- ***adj.*** 0→ (superlative of *far*) at the greatest distance in space, direction or time: *the farthest point of the journey* ◇ *the part of the garden farthest from the house*

far·thing /ˈfɑːðɪŋ; *NAmE* ˈfɑːrðɪŋ/ *noun* in the past, a British coin worth one quarter of an old penny

far·thin·gale /ˈfɑːðɪŋɡeɪl; *NAmE* ˈfɑːr-/ *noun* in the past, a thick piece of material or set of large rings worn under a woman's skirt to give it a wide round shape

fa·scia /ˈfeɪʃə/ *noun* (*BrE*) **1** (also **facia**) = DASHBOARD **2** (also **ˈfascia board**) a board on the roof of a house, at the end of the RAFTERS **3** (also **facia**) a board above the entrance of a shop/store, with the name of the shop on it **4** (also **facia**) the hard cover on a mobile phone/cell phone

fas·cin·ate /ˈfæsɪneɪt/ *verb* [T, I] **~ (sb)** to attract or interest sb very much: *China has always fascinated me.* ◇ *It was a question that had fascinated him since he was a boy.* ◇ *The private lives of movie stars never fail to fascinate.*

fas·cin·ated /ˈfæsɪneɪtɪd/ *adj.* very interested: *The children watched, fascinated, as the picture began to appear.* ◇ **~ by sth** *I've always been fascinated by his ideas.* ◇ **~ to see, learn, etc.** *They were fascinated to see that it was similar to one they had at home.*

fas·cin·at·ing /ˈfæsɪneɪtɪŋ/ *adj.* extremely interesting and attractive: *a fascinating story/subject* ◇ *The results of* *the survey made fascinating reading.* ◇ *It's **fascinating to see** how different people approach the problem.* ◇ *I fail to see what women find so fascinating about him.* ➲ SYNONYMS at INTERESTING ▸ **fas·cin·at·ing·ly** *adv.*

fas·cin·ation /ˌfæsɪˈneɪʃn/ *noun* **1** [C, usually sing.] a very strong attraction, that makes sth very interesting: *Water **holds a fascination for** most children.* ◇ *The fascination of the game lies in trying to guess what your opponent is thinking.* **2** [U, sing.] the state of being very attracted to and interested in sb/sth: *The girls listened **in fascination** as the story unfolded.* ◇ **~ for/with sb/sth** *the public's enduring fascination with the Royal Family*

F

fas·cism (also **Fascism**) /ˈfæʃɪzəm/ *noun* [U] an extreme RIGHT-WING political system or attitude which is in favour of strong central government and which does not allow any opposition

fas·cist (also **Fascist**) /ˈfæʃɪst/ *noun* **1** a person who supports fascism **2** a way of referring to sb that you disapprove of because they have RIGHT-WING attitudes ▸ **fas·cist** *adj.*: *a fascist state* ◇ *fascist sympathies*

Collocations

Clothes and fashion

Clothes

- **be wearing** a new outfit/bright colours/fancy dress/fur/uniform
- **be (dressed) in** black/red/jeans and a T-shirt/your best suit/leather/silk/rags (= very old torn clothes)
- **be dressed for** work/school/dinner/a special occasion
- **be dressed as** a man/woman/clown/pirate
- **wear/dress in** casual/designer/second-hand clothes
- **wear** jewellery/(*especially US*) jewelry/accessories/a watch/glasses/contact lenses/perfume
- **have** a cowboy hat/red dress/blue suit **on**
- **put on/take off** your clothes/coat/shoes/helmet
- **pull on/pull off** your coat/gloves/socks
- **change into/get changed into** a pair of jeans/your pyjamas/(*especially US*) your pajamas

Appearance

- **change/enhance/improve** your appearance
- **create/get/have/give sth** a new/contemporary/retro look
- **brush/comb/shampoo/wash/blow-dry** your hair
- **have/get** a haircut/your hair cut/a new hairstyle
- **have/get** a piercing/your nose pierced
- **have/get** a tattoo/a tattoo done (on your arm)/a tattoo removed
- **have/get** a makeover/cosmetic surgery
- **use/wear/apply/put on** make-up/cosmetics

Fashion

- **follow/keep up with** (the) fashion/the latest fashions
- **spend/waste money on** designer clothes
- **be** fashionably/stylishly/well **dressed**
- **have** good/great/terrible/awful **taste** in clothes
- **update/revamp** your wardrobe
- **be in/come into/go out of** fashion
- **be (back/very much)** in vogue
- **create** a style/trend/vogue for sth
- **organize/put on** a fashion show
- **show/unveil** a designer's spring/summer collection
- **sashay/strut** down the catwalk/(*NAmE also*) runway
- **be on/do** a photo/fashion shoot

fash·ion 0━ /ˈfæʃn/ *noun, verb*
■ ***noun*** **1** 0━ [U, C] a popular style of clothes, hair, etc. at a particular time or place; the state of being popular: *dressed in the latest fashion* ◇ *the new season's fashions* ◇ *Long skirts have **come into fashion** again.* ◇ *Jeans are still **in fashion**.* ◇ *Some styles never **go out of fashion**.* **2** 0━ [C] a popular way of behaving, doing an activity, etc: *The fashion at the time was for teaching mainly the written language.* ◇ *Fashions in art and literature come and go.* **3** 0━ [U] the business of making or selling clothes in new and different styles: *a **fashion designer/magazine/show*** ◇ *the world of fashion* ◇ *the fashion industry*
IDM **after a ˈfashion** to some extent, but not very well: *I can play the piano, after a fashion.* **after the fashion of sb/sth** (*formal*) in the style of sb/sth: *The new library is very much after the fashion of Nash.* **in (a)... ˈfashion** (*formal*) in a particular way: *How could they behave in such a fashion?* ◇ *She was proved right, in dramatic fashion, when the whole department resigned.* **like it's going out of ˈfashion** (*informal*) used to emphasize that sb is doing sth or using sth a lot: *She's been spending money like it's going out of fashion.* ➲ see also PARROT-FASHION
■ ***verb*** to make or shape sth, especially with your hands: **~ A (from/out of B)** *She fashioned a pot from the clay.* ◇ **~ B (into A)** *She fashioned the clay into a pot.*

fash·ion·able 0━ /ˈfæʃnəbl/ *adj.*
1 0━ following a style that is popular at a particular time: *fashionable clothes/furniture/ideas* ◇ *It's becoming fashionable to have long hair again.* ◇ *Such thinking is fashionable among right-wing politicians.* **2** 0━ used or visited by people following a current fashion, especially by rich people: *a fashionable address/resort/restaurant* ◇ *She lives in a very fashionable part of London.* OPP **unfashionable** ➲ compare OLD-FASHIONED ▸ **fash·ion·ably** /-əbli/ *adv.*: *fashionably dressed* ◇ *His wife was blonde and fashionably thin.*

ˈfashion-conscious *adj.* aware of the latest fashions and wanting to follow them: *fashion-conscious teenagers*

ˈfashion designer *noun* a person who designs fashionable clothes

ˈfashion-forward *adj.* more modern than the current fashion: *We tend to be traditional rather than fashion-forward in our designs.*

fash·ion·ista /ˌfæʃnˈiːstə/ *noun* (used especially in newspapers) a fashion DESIGNER, or a person who is always dressed in a fashionable way

ˈfashion show *noun* an occasion where people can see new designs of clothes being worn by fashion models

ˈfashion statement *noun* something that you wear or own that is new or unusual and is meant to draw attention to you: *This shirt is great for anyone who wants to **make a fashion statement**.*

ˈfashion victim *noun* a person who always wears the newest fashions even if they do not suit him or her

fast 0━ /fɑːst; *NAmE* fæst/ *adj., adv., verb, noun*
■ ***adj.*** (**fast·er**, **fast·est**)
▸ QUICK **1** 0━ moving or able to move quickly: *a fast car/horse* ◇ *the world's fastest runner* **2** 0━ happening in a short time or without delay: *the fastest rate of increase for years* ◇ *a fast response time* **3** 0━ able to do sth quickly: *a fast learner*
▸ SURFACE **4** producing or allowing quick movement: *a **fast road/pitch*** ➲ see also FAST LANE
▸ WATCH/CLOCK **5** [not before noun] showing a time later than the true time: *I'm early—my watch must be fast.* ◇ *That clock's ten minutes fast.*
▸ PHOTOGRAPHIC FILM **6** (*technical*) very sensitive to light, and therefore useful when taking photographs in poor light or of sth that is moving very quickly
▸ FIRMLY FIXED **7** (of a boat, etc.) firmly fixed and safe: *He **made** the boat **fast**.*
▸ COLOURS IN CLOTHES **8** not likely to change or to come out when washed HELP There is no noun related to **fast**. Use **speed** in connection with vehicles, actions, etc; **quickness** is used about thinking.
IDM **fast and ˈfurious** (of films/movies, shows, etc.) full of rapid action and sudden changes: *In his latest movie, the action is fast and furious.* **a fast ˈtalker** a person who can talk very quickly and easily, but who cannot always be trusted **a fast ˈworker** (*informal*) a person who knows

how to get what they want quickly, especially when beginning a sexual relationship with sb ➲ more at BUCK *n.*, DRAW *n.*, HARD *adj.*, PULL *v.*

■ ***adv.*** (fast·er, fast·est)

▸ QUICKLY **1** 🔑 quickly: *Don't drive so fast!* ◇ *How fast were you going?* ◇ *I can't go any faster.* ◇ *The water was rising fast.* ◇ *Her heart beat faster.* ◇ (*formal*) *Night was fast approaching.* ◇ *a fast-flowing stream* ➲ note at QUICK **2** 🔑 in a short time; without delay: *Children grow up so fast these days.* ◇ *Britain is **fast becoming** a nation of fatties.* ◇ *The police said that they had reacted as fast as they could.*

▸ FIRMLY **3** 🔑 firmly; completely: *Within a few minutes she was **fast asleep*** (= sleeping deeply). ◇ *The boat was **stuck fast*** (= unable to move) *in the mud.* HELP There is no noun related to **fast**. Use **speed** in connection with vehicles, actions, etc; **quickness** is used about thinking.

IDM **as fast as your ˌlegs can ˈcarry you** as quickly as you can **hold ˈfast to sth** (*formal*) to continue to believe in an idea, etc. despite difficulties **play fast and ˈloose (with sb/sth)** (*old-fashioned*) to treat sb/sth in a way that shows that you feel no responsibility or respect for them **stand ˈfast/ˈfirm** to refuse to move back; to refuse to change your opinions ➲ more at THICK *adv.*

■ ***verb*** [I] to eat little or no food for a period of time, especially for religious or health reasons: *Muslims fast during Ramadan.*

■ ***noun*** a period during which you do not eat food, especially for religious or health reasons: *to go on a fast* ◇ *to break* (= end) *your fast*

Synonyms

fast / quick / rapid

These adjectives are frequently used with the following nouns:

fast ~	quick ~	rapid ~
car	glance	change
train	look	growth
bowler	reply	increase
pace	decision	decline
lane	way	progress

- **Fast** is used especially to describe a person or thing that moves or is able to move at great speed.
- **Quick** is more often used to describe something that is done in a short time or without delay.
- **Rapid**, **swift** and **speedy** are more formal words.
- **Rapid** is most commonly used to describe the speed at which something changes. It is not used to describe the speed at which something moves or is done: ~~*a rapid train*~~ ◇ ~~*We had a rapid coffee.*~~
- **Swift** usually describes something that happens or is done quickly and immediately: *a swift decision* ◇ *The government took swift action.*
- **Speedy** has a similar meaning: *a speedy recovery.* It is used less often to talk about the speed at which something moves: ~~*a speedy car.*~~
- For the use of **fast** and **quick** as adverbs, see the usage note at QUICK.

fast·ball /ˈfɑːstbɔːl; *NAmE* ˈfæst-/ *noun* **1** (in BASEBALL) a ball that is thrown at the PITCHER's fastest speed **2** = FAST-PITCH SOFTBALL

ˌfast ˈbowler (also **ˌpace ˈbowler**, **pace·man**) *noun* (in CRICKET) a person who BOWLS very fast

ˌfast ˈbreeder (also **ˌfast ˌbreeder reˈactor**) *noun* a REACTOR in a nuclear power station in which the reaction that produces energy is not made slower

fas·ten 🔑 /ˈfɑːsn; *NAmE* ˈfæsn/ *verb*
1 🔑 [T, I] to close or join together the two parts of sth; to become closed or joined together SYN **do up**: **~ sth** *Fasten your seatbelts, please.* ◇ **~ sth up** *He fastened up his coat and hurried out.* ◇ **~ (up)** *The dress fastens at the back.* OPP **unfasten** **2** 🔑 [T, I] **~ (sth)** to close sth firmly so that it will not open; to be closed in this way: *Fasten the gates securely so that they do not blow open.* ◇ *The window wouldn't fasten.* OPP **unfasten** **3** 🔑 [T] **~ sth + adv./prep.** to fix or place sth in a particular position, so that it will not move: *He fastened back the shutters.* **4** 🔑 [T] **~ A to B | ~ A and B (together)** to attach or tie one thing to another thing: *He fastened the papers together with a paper clip.* **5** [T, I] if you **fasten** your arms around sb, your teeth into sth, etc, or if your arms, teeth, etc. **fasten** around, into, etc. sb/sth, you hold the person/thing firmly with your arms, etc: **~ sth + adv./prep.** *The dog fastened its teeth in his leg.* ◇ **+ adv./prep.** *His hand fastened on her arm.* **6** [T, I] **~ (sth) (on sb/sth)** if you **fasten** your eyes on sb/sth or your eyes **fasten** on sb/sth, you look at them for a long time: *He fastened his gaze on her face.*

PHR V **ˈfasten on(to) sb/sth** to choose or follow sb/sth in a determined way SYN **latch on to sb/sth**

fas·ten·er /ˈfɑːsnə(r); *NAmE* ˈfæs-/ (also **fas·ten·ing**) *noun* a device, such as a button or a zip/zipper, used to close a piece of clothing; a device used to close a window, suitcase, etc. tightly ➲ VISUAL VOCAB page V51

fas·ten·ing /ˈfɑːsnɪŋ; *NAmE* ˈfæs-/ *noun* **1** = FASTENER **2** the place where sth, especially a piece of clothing, fastens; the way sth fastens: *The trousers have a fly fastening.*

ˌfast ˈfood *noun* [U] hot food, such as HAMBURGERS and chips/fries, that is served very quickly and can be taken away to be eaten in the street: *fast-food restaurants* ➲ compare SLOW FOOD

ˌfast-ˈforward *verb* **1** [T, I] **~ (sth)** to wind a tape or video forward without playing it **2** [I] **~ to sth | + adv./prep.** to move quickly forwards in time, especially to a later point in a story: *The action then fast-forwards to Ettore as a young man.* ▸ **ˌfast ˈforward** *noun* [U]: *Press fast forward to advance the tape.* ◇ *the fast-forward button*

fas·tidi·ous /fæˈstɪdiəs/ *adj.* **1** being careful that every detail of sth is correct SYN **meticulous**: *Everything was planned in fastidious detail.* ◇ *He was fastidious in his preparation for the big day.* **2** (sometimes *disapproving*) not liking things to be dirty or untidy: *She wasn't very fastidious about personal hygiene.* ▸ **fas·tidi·ous·ly** *adv.* **fas·tidi·ous·ness** *noun* [U]

ˈfast lane *noun* [sing.] the part of a major road such as a MOTORWAY or INTERSTATE where vehicles drive fastest

IDM **in the ˈfast lane** where things are most exciting and where a lot is happening: *He had a good job, plenty of money and he was enjoying **life in the fast lane**.*

fast·ness /ˈfɑːstnəs; *NAmE* ˈfæs-/ *noun* (*literary*) a place that is thought to be safe because it is difficult to get to or easy to defend SYN **stronghold**

ˈfast track *noun* [sing.] a quick way to achieve sth, for example a high position in a job ▸ **ˈfast-track** *adj.*: *the fast-track route to promotion* ◇ *fast-track graduates*

ˈfast-track *verb* **~ sb/sth** to make sb's progress in achieving sth, for example a high position in a job, quicker than usual

fat 🔑 /fæt/ *adj.*, *noun*

WORD FAMILY
fat *adj.*
fatty *adj.*
fatten *verb*
fattening *adj.*

■ ***adj.*** (fat·ter, fat·test) **1** 🔑 (of a person's or an animal's body) having too much flesh on it and weighing too much: *a big fat man/woman* ◇ *You'll **get fat** if you eat so much chocolate.* ◇ *He grew fatter and fatter.* ◇ *fat flabby legs* OPP **thin** **2** 🔑 thick or wide: *a fat volume on American history* **3** [only before noun] (*informal*) large in quantity; worth a lot of money: *a **fat sum/profit*** ◇ *He gave me a nice fat cheque.* ▸ **fat·ness** *noun* [U]: *Fatness tends to run in families.*

IDM **(a) fat ˈchance (of sth/doing sth)** (*informal*) used for saying that you do not believe sth is likely to happen: *'They might let us in without tickets.' 'Fat chance of that!'* **a fat lot of good, use, etc.** (*informal*) not at all good or useful: *Paul* *can't drive so he was a fat lot of use when I broke my arm.* **it's not ˌover until the fat lady ˈsings** (*saying*) used for saying that a situation may still change, for example that a contest, election, etc. is not finished yet, and sb still has a chance to win it

■ ***noun* 1** [U] a white or yellow substance in the bodies of animals and humans, stored under the skin: *excess body fat* ◇ *This ham has too much fat on it.* ➲ COLLOCATIONS at DIET **2** [C, U] a solid or liquid substance from animals or plants, treated so that it becomes pure for use in cooking: *Cook the meat in shallow fat.* **3** [C, U] animal and vegetable fats, when you are thinking of them as part of what a person eats: *You should cut down on fats and carbohydrates.* ◇ *foods which are* ***low in fat*** ◇ *reduced-fat margarines*
IDM see CHEW *v.*, LIVE[1]

F

Vocabulary Building

Saying that somebody is fat

- **Fat** is the most common and direct word, but it is not polite to say to someone that they are fat: *Does this dress make me look fat?* ◇ ~~*You're looking fat now.*~~
- **Overweight** is a more neutral word: *I'm a bit overweight.* It can also mean too fat, especially so that you are not fit.
- **Large** or **heavy** is less offensive than **fat**: *She's a rather large woman.* **Big** describes someone who is tall as well as fat: *Her sister is a big girl, isn't she?*
- **Plump** means slightly fat in an attractive way, often used to describe women.
- **Chubby** is used mainly to describe babies and children who are fat in a pleasant, healthy-looking way: *the baby's chubby cheeks*
- **Tubby** (*informal*) is used in a friendly way to describe people who are short and round, especially around the stomach.
- **Stocky** is a neutral word and means fairly short, broad and strong.
- **Stout** is often used to describe older people who have a round and heavy appearance: *a short stout man with a bald head*
- **Flabby** describes flesh that is fat and loose: *exercises to firm up flabby thighs*
- **Obese** is used by doctors to describe people who are so fat that they are unhealthy. It is also used in a general way to mean 'really fat'.

Note that although people talk a lot about their own size or weight, it is generally not considered polite to refer to a person's large size or their weight when you talk to them.
➲ note at THIN

fatal /ˈfeɪtl/ *adj.* **1** causing or ending in death: *a* ***fatal accident/blow/illness*** ◇ *a* ***potentially fatal*** *form of cancer* ◇ *If she gets ill again it could* ***prove fatal.*** ➲ compare MORTAL **2** causing disaster or failure: *a* ***fatal error/mistake*** ◇ *Any delay would be fatal.* ◇ *There was a* ***fatal flaw*** *in the plan.* ◇ *It'd be fatal to try and stop them now.* ▸ **fa·tal·ly** /-təli/ *adv.*: ***fatally injured/wounded*** ◇ *The plan was* ***fatally flawed*** *from the start.*

fa·tal·ism /ˈfeɪtəlɪzəm/ *noun* [U] the belief that events are decided by FATE and that you cannot control them; the fact of accepting that you cannot prevent sth from happening ▸ **fa·tal·ist** *noun*: *I'm a fatalist.*

fa·tal·is·tic /ˌfeɪtəˈlɪstɪk/ *adj.* showing a belief in FATE and feeling that you cannot control events or stop them from happening ▸ **fa·tal·is·tic·al·ly** /ˌfeɪtəˈlɪstɪkli/ *adv.*

fa·tal·ity /fəˈtæləti/ *noun* (*pl.* -ies) **1** [C] a death that is caused in an accident or a war, or by violence or disease: *Several people were injured, but there were no fatalities.* **2** [U] the fact that a particular disease will result in death: *to reduce the fatality of certain types of cancer* ◇ *Different forms of cancer have different fatality rates.* **3** [U] the belief or feeling that we have no control over what happens to us: *A sense of fatality gripped her.*

ˈfat camp *noun* [U, C] an organized holiday/vacation for fat children during which they are helped to lose weight

ˈfat cat *noun* (*informal, disapproving*) a person who earns, or who has, a lot of money (especially when compared to people who do not earn so much)

fate /feɪt/ *noun* **1** [C] the things, especially bad things, that will happen or have happened to sb/sth: ***The fate of*** *the three men is unknown.* ◇ *She sat outside, waiting to find out her fate.* ◇ *The court will* ***decide our fate/fates.*** ◇ *Each of the managers* ***suffered the same fate.*** ◇ *The government had* ***abandoned*** *the refugees* ***to their fate.*** ◇ *From that moment* ***our fate was sealed*** (= our future was decided). **2** [U] the power that is believed to control everything that happens and that cannot be stopped or changed: *Fate was kind to me that day.* ◇ *By a strange* ***twist of fate,*** *Andy and I were on the same plane.* ➲ SYNONYMS at LUCK
IDM **a fate worse than ˈdeath** (often *humorous*) a terrible thing that could happen ➲ more at TEMPT

fated /ˈfeɪtɪd/ *adj.* **1** ~ (**to do sth**) unable to escape a particular fate; certain to happen because everything is controlled by fate SYN **destined**: *We were fated never to meet again.* ◇ *He believes that everything in life is fated.* **2** = ILL-FATED

fate·ful /ˈfeɪtfl/ *adj.* [usually before noun] having an important, often very bad, effect on future events: *She looked back now to* ***that fateful day*** *in December.*

ˌfat-ˈfree *adj.* not containing any fat: *fat-free yogurt*

father /ˈfɑːðə(r)/ *noun, verb*
■ ***noun* 1** a male parent of a child or an animal; a person who is acting as the father to a child: *Ben's a wonderful father.* ◇ *You've been* ***like a father*** *to me.* ◇ *Our new boss is* ***a father of three*** (= he has three children). ◇ *He was a wonderful father to both his natural and adopted children.* ◇ (*old-fashioned*) *Father, I cannot lie to you.* ➲ see also GODFATHER, GRANDFATHER, STEPFATHER **2 fathers** [pl.] (*literary*) a person's ANCESTORS (= people who are related to you who lived in the past): *the land of our fathers* ➲ see also FOREFATHERS **3** ~ (**of sth**) the first man to introduce a new way of thinking about sth or of doing sth: *Henry Moore is considered to be the father of modern British sculpture.* ➲ see also FOUNDING FATHER **4 Father** used by Christians to refer to God: *Father, forgive us.* ◇ *God the Father* **5 Father** (*abbr.* Fr) the title of a priest, especially in the Roman Catholic Church and the Orthodox Church: *Father Dominic* ➲ see also HOLY FATHER
IDM **from ˌfather to ˈson** from one generation of a family to the next **like ˌfather, like ˈson** (*saying*) used to say that a son's character or behaviour is similar to that of his father ➲ more at OLD, WISH *n.*
■ ***verb* 1** ~ **sb** to become the father of a child by making a woman pregnant: *He claims to have fathered over 20 children.* **2** ~ **sth** to create new ideas or a new way of doing sth

ˌFather ˈChristmas *noun* (*BrE*) = SANTA CLAUS

ˈfather figure *noun* an older man that sb respects because he will advise and help them like a father

father·hood /ˈfɑːðəhʊd; *NAmE* -ðərhʊd/ *noun* [U] the state of being a father

ˈfather-in-law *noun* (*pl.* **fathers-in-law**) the father of your husband or wife ➲ compare MOTHER-IN-LAW

father·land /ˈfɑːðəlænd; *NAmE* -ðərlænd/ *noun* [usually sing.] (*old-fashioned*) (used especially about Germany) the country where a person, or their family, was born, especially when they feel very loyal towards it

father·less /ˈfɑːðələs; *NAmE* -ðərləs/ *adj.* [usually before noun] without a father, either because he has died or because he does not live with his children: ***fatherless children/families***

father·ly /ˈfɑːðəli; *NAmE* -ðərli/ *adj.* typical of a good father: *fatherly advice* ◇ *He keeps a fatherly eye on his players.*

ˈFather's Day *noun* a day when fathers receive cards and gifts from their children, usually the third Sunday in June

ˌFather ˈTime *noun* an imaginary figure who represents time and looks like an old man carrying a SCYTHE and an HOURGLASS

fathom /ˈfæðəm/ *verb, noun*
■ ***verb*** to understand or find an explanation for sth: **~ sb/sth (out)** *It is hard to fathom the pain felt at the death of a child.* ◇ **~ (out) what, where, etc…** *He couldn't fathom out what the man could possibly mean.*
■ ***noun*** a unit for measuring the depth of water, equal to 6 feet or 1.8 metres: *The ship sank in 20 fathoms.* ◇ (*figurative*) *She kept her feelings hidden fathoms deep.*

fa·tigue /fəˈtiːɡ/ *noun* **1** [U] a feeling of being extremely tired, usually because of hard work or exercise **SYN** **exhaustion, tiredness**: *physical and mental fatigue* ◇ *Driver fatigue was to blame for the accident.* ◇ *I was dropping with fatigue and could not keep my eyes open.* **2** [U] (usually after another noun) a feeling of not wanting to do a particular activity any longer because you have done too much of it: *battle fatigue* **3** [U] weakness in metal or wood caused by repeated bending or stretching: *The wing of the plane showed signs of* ***metal fatigue***. **4 fatigues** [pl.] loose clothes worn by soldiers **5 fatigues** [pl.] (*especially NAmE*) duties, such as cleaning and cooking, that soldiers have to do, especially as a punishment

fa·tigued /fəˈtiːɡd/ *adj.* [not usually before noun] (*formal*) very tired, both physically and mentally **SYN** **exhausted**

fa·tiguing /fəˈtiːɡɪŋ/ *adj.* (*formal*) very tiring, both physically and mentally **SYN** **exhausting**

fatso /ˈfætsəʊ; *NAmE* -soʊ/ *noun* (*pl.* -oes) = FATTY

fat·ten /ˈfætn/ *verb* [T, I] **~ (sb/sth) (up)** to make sb/sth fatter, especially an animal before killing it for food; to become fatter: *The piglets are taken from the sow to be fattened for market.* ◇ *She's very thin after her illness—but we'll soon fatten her up.*

fat·ten·ing /ˈfætnɪŋ/ *adj.* (of food) likely to make you fat: *fattening cakes*

fat·tism /ˈfætɪzəm/ *noun* [U] unfair treatment of people because of their large body size ▸ **fat·tist** *adj.*

fatty /ˈfæti/ *adj., noun*
■ ***adj.*** (**fat·tier, fat·ti·est**) containing a lot of fat; consisting of fat: *fatty foods* ◇ *fatty tissue*
■ ***noun*** (*pl.* -ies) (also **fatso**) (*informal, disapproving*) a fat person: *Britain is fast becoming a nation of fatties.*

ˌfatty ˈacid *noun* (*chemistry*) an acid that is found in fats and oils

fatu·ous /ˈfætʃuəs/ *adj.* (*formal*) stupid: *a fatuous comment/grin* ▸ **fatu·ous·ly** *adv.*

fatwa /ˈfætwɑː/ *noun* a decision or order made under Islamic law

fau·cet 0-w /ˈfɔːsɪt/ (*NAmE*) (*BrE* **tap**) *noun* a device that controls the flow of water from a pipe: *the* ***hot/cold faucet*** ◇ *to* ***turn a faucet on/off*** ➲ picture at PLUG ➲ VISUAL VOCAB pages V21, V22

fault 0-w /fɔːlt/ *noun, verb*
■ ***noun***
▸ RESPONSIBILITY **1** 0-w [U] the responsibility for sth wrong that has happened or been done: *Why should I say sorry when it's not* ***my fault***? ◇ *It's nobody's fault.* ◇ **~ (that…)** *It was* ***his fault*** *that we were late.* ◇ **~ (for doing sth)** *It's your* ***own fault*** *for being careless.* ◇ *Many people live in poverty* ***through no fault of their own***. ◇ *I think the owners are* ***at fault*** (= responsible) *for not warning us.*
▸ IN SB'S CHARACTER **2** 0-w [C] a bad or weak aspect of sb's character **SYN** **shortcoming**: *He's proud of his children and blind to their faults.* ◇ *I love her* ***for all her faults*** (= in spite of them).
▸ STH WRONG **3** 0-w [C] something that is wrong or not perfect; something that is wrong with a machine or system that stops it from working correctly **SYN** **defect**: *The book's virtues far outweigh its faults.* ◇ *The system,* ***for all its faults***, *is the best available at the moment.* ◇ *a major fault in the design* ◇ *a structural fault* ◇ *an electrical fault*
▸ IN TENNIS **4** [C] a mistake made when SERVING: *He has served a number of* ***double faults*** *in this set.*
▸ GEOLOGY **5** [C] a place where there is a break that is longer than usual in the layers of rock in the earth's CRUST: *the San Andreas fault* ◇ *a fault line*
IDM **to a ˈfault** used to say that sb has a lot, or even too much, of a particular good quality: *She is generous to a fault.* ➲ more at FIND *v.*
■ ***verb*** **~ sb/sth** (often used in negative sentences with *can* and *could*) to find a mistake or a weakness in sb/sth **SYN** **criticize**: *Her colleagues could not fault her dedication to the job.* ◇ *He had always been polite—she couldn't fault him on that.*

ˈfault-finding *noun* [U] the act of looking for faults in sb/sth

fault·less /ˈfɔːltləs/ *adj.* having no mistakes **SYN** **perfect**: *faultless English* ▸ **fault·less·ly** *adv.*

faulty /ˈfɔːlti/ *adj.* **1** not perfect; not working or made correctly **SYN** **defective**: *Ask for a refund if the goods are faulty.* ◇ *faulty workmanship* ◇ *an accident caused by a faulty signal* **2** (of a way of thinking) wrong or containing mistakes, often resulting in bad decisions: *faulty reasoning*

faun /fɔːn/ *noun* (in ancient Roman stories) a god of the woods, with a man's face and body and a GOAT's legs and horns

fauna /ˈfɔːnə/ *noun* [U, C] all the animals living in an area or in a particular period of history: *the local* ***flora and fauna*** (= plants and animals) ◇ (*technical*) *land and marine faunas*

Faust·ian /ˈfaʊstiən/ *adj.* (*formal*) **~ bargain/pact/agreement** an agreement in which sb agrees to do sth bad or dishonest, in return for money, success or power **ORIGIN** From **Faust**, who, according to the German legend, sold his soul to the Devil in return for many years of power and pleasure.

faute de mieux /ˌfəʊt də ˈmjɜː; *NAmE* ˌfoʊt/ *adv.* (from *French*) because there is nothing else that is better: *We were obliged, faute de mieux, to drink the local beverage.*

Fauve /fəʊv; *NAmE* foʊv/ *noun* a member of a group of French painters who were important in Fauvism

Fauv·ism /ˈfəʊvɪzəm; *NAmE* ˈfoʊv-/ *noun* [U] (*art*) a style of painting that uses bright colours and in which objects and people are represented in a non-realistic way. It was popular in Paris for a short period from 1905.

faux /fəʊ; *NAmE* foʊ/ *adj.* artificial, but intended to look or seem real: *The chairs were covered in faux animal skin.* ◇ *His accent was so faux.*

faux pas /ˌfəʊ ˈpɑː; *NAmE* ˌfoʊ/ *noun* (*pl.* **faux pas** /ˌfəʊ ˈpɑːz; *NAmE* ˌfoʊ/) (from *French*) an action or a remark that causes embarrassment because it is not socially correct

fava bean /ˈfɑːvə biːn/ (*NAmE*) (*BrE* **ˌbroad ˈbean**) *noun* a type of round, pale green BEAN. Several fava beans grow together inside a fat POD.

fave /feɪv/ *noun* (*informal*) a favourite person or thing: *That song is one of my faves.* ▸ **fave** *adj.*: *her fave TV show*

fa·vela /fæˈvelə/ *noun* (from *Portuguese*) a poor area in or near a Brazilian city, with many small houses that are close together and in bad condition ➲ compare SHANTY TOWN

fa·vour 0-w (*especially US* **favor**) /ˈfeɪvə(r)/ *noun, verb*
■ ***noun***
▸ HELP **1** 0-w [C] a thing that you do to help sb: *Could you* ***do me a favour*** *and pick up Sam from school today?* ◇ *Can I* ***ask a favour***? ◇ *I would never ask for any favours from her.* ◇ *I'm going* ***as a favour*** *to Ann, not because I want to.* ◇ *I'll ask Steve to take it. He* ***owes me a favour***. ◇ *Thanks for helping me out. I'll* ***return the favour*** (= help you because you have helped me) *some time.* ◇ ***Do yourself a favour*** (= help yourself) *and wear a helmet on the bike.*
▸ APPROVAL **2** 0-w [U] approval or support for sb/sth: *The suggestion to close the road has* ***found favour with*** (= been supported by) *local people.* ◇ *The programme has* ***lost favour*** *with viewers recently.* ◇ *an athlete who* ***fell from favour*** *after a drugs scandal* ◇ (*formal*) *The government* ***looks with favour upon*** (= approves of) *the report's recommendations.* ◇ *She's not* ***in favour with*** (= supported or

F

liked by) *the media just now.* ◇ *It seems Tim is* **back in favour** *with the boss* (= the boss likes him again).

▸ BETTER TREATMENT **3** [U] treatment that is generous to one person or group in a way that seems unfair to others SYN **bias**: *As an examiner, she showed no favour to any candidate.*

▸ PARTY GIFT **4 favors** [pl.] (*NAmE*) = PARTY FAVORS

▸ SEX **5 favours** [pl.] (*old-fashioned*) agreement to have sex with sb: *demands for sexual favours*

IDM ▸ **do sb no 'favours** to do sth that is not helpful to sb or that gives a bad impression of them: *You're not doing yourself any favours, working for nothing.* ◇ *The orchestra did Beethoven no favours.* **do me a 'favour!** (*informal*) used in reply to a question that you think is silly: *'Do you think they'll win?' 'Do me a favour! They haven't got a single decent player.'* **in favour (of sb/sth) 1** 🔑 if you are **in favour** of sb/sth, you support and agree with them/it: *He argued in favour of a strike.* ◇ *There were 247 votes in favour (of the motion) and 152 against.* ◇ *I'm* **all in favour of** (= completely support) *equal pay for equal work.* ◇ *Most of the 'don't knows' in the opinion polls* **came down in favour of** (= eventually chose to support) *the Democrats.* **2** in exchange for another thing (because the other thing is better or you want it more): *He abandoned teaching in favour of a career as a musician.* **in sb's favour 1** if sth is **in sb's favour**, it gives them an advantage or helps them: *The exchange rate is in our favour at the moment.* ◇ *She was willing to bend the rules in Mary's favour.* **2** a decision or judgement that is **in sb's favour** benefits that person or says that they were right ➲ more at CURRY *v.*, FEAR *n.*, STACKED

■ *verb*

▸ PREFER **1 ~ sth | ~ (sb) doing sth** to prefer one system, plan, way of doing sth, etc. to another: *Many countries favour a presidential system of government.*

▸ TREAT BETTER **2 ~ sb** to treat sb better than you treat other people, especially in an unfair way: *The treaty seems to favour the US.*

▸ HELP **3 ~ sth** to provide suitable conditions for a particular person, group, etc: *The warm climate favours many types of tropical plants.*

▸ LOOK LIKE PARENT **4 ~ sb** (*old-fashioned* or *NAmE*) to look like one of your parents or older relations: *She definitely favours her father.*

fa·vour·able (*especially US* **fa·vor·able**) /ˈfeɪvərəbl/ *adj.* **1** making people have a good opinion of sb/sth: *She* **made a favourable impression** *on his parents.* ◇ *The biography shows him in a favourable light.* **2** positive and showing your good opinion of sb/sth: *favourable comments* **3 ~ (to/for sb/sth)** good for sth and making it likely to be successful or have an advantage SYN **advantageous**: *The terms of the agreement are favourable to both sides.* ◇ *favourable economic conditions* **4** fairly good and not too expensive: *They offered me a loan on very* **favourable terms.** OPP **unfavourable** ▸ **fa·vour·abil·ity** (*especially US* **fa·vor·abil·ity**) /ˌfeɪvərəˈbɪləti/ *noun* [U] **fa·vour·ably** (*especially US* **fa·vor·ably**) /-əbli/ *adv.*: *He speaks very favourably of your work.* ◇ *These figures compare favourably with last year's.* ◇ *I was very favourably impressed with her work.*

fa·voured (*especially US* **favored**) /ˈfeɪvəd; *NAmE* -vərd/ *adj.* **1** treated in a special way or receiving special help or advantages in a way that may seem unfair: *a member of the President's favoured circle of advisers* **2** preferred by most people: *the favoured candidate* **3** (*formal*) particularly pleasant and worth having: *Their house is in a very favoured position near the park.*

fa·vour·ite 🔑 (*especially US* **fa·vor·ite**) /ˈfeɪvərɪt/ *adj., noun*

■ **adj.** 🔑 liked more than others of the same kind: *It's one of my favourite movies.* ◇ *Who is your favourite writer?* ◇ *January is my least favourite month.* ➲ SYNONYMS at CHOICE

IDM ▸ **sb's favourite 'son 1** a performer, politician, sports player, etc, who is popular where they were born **2** (in the US) a candidate for president who is supported by his or her own state in the first part of a campaign

■ **noun 1** 🔑 a person or thing that you like more than the others of the same type: *These biscuits are great favourites with the children.* ◇ *This song is a* **particular favourite** *of mine.* ◇ *The band played all my* **old favourites**. ◇ *Which one's your favourite?* ◇ *The programme has become a* **firm favourite** *with young people.* **2** 🔑 a person who is liked better by sb and receives better treatment than others: *She loved all her grandchildren but Ann was her favourite.* **3** the horse, runner, team, etc. that is expected to win: *The favourite came third.* ◇ **~ (for sth)** *Her horse is the* **hot favourite** *for the race.* ◇ **~ (to do sth)** *AC Milan, the* **hot favourites** *to win the Champions League* **4** the person who is expected by most people to get a particular job or position: **~ (for sth)** *She's the favourite for the job.* ◇ **~ (to do sth)** *She's the favourite to succeed him as leader.*

fa·vour·it·ism (*especially US* **fa·vor·it·ism**) /ˈfeɪvərɪtɪzəm/ *noun* [U] (*disapproving*) the act of unfairly treating one person better than others because you like them better: *The students accused the teacher of favouritism.*

fawn /fɔːn/ *adj., noun, verb*

■ **adj.** light yellowish-brown in colour: *a fawn coat*

■ **noun 1** [C] a DEER less than one year old **2** [U] a light yellowish-brown colour

■ **verb** [I] **~ (on/over sb)** (*disapproving*) to try to please sb by praising them or paying them too much attention

fax /fæks/ *noun, verb*

■ **noun** (also *formal* **fac·sim·ile**) **1** (also ˈ**fax machine**) [C] a machine that sends and receives documents in an electronic form along telephone wires and then prints them: *Do you have a fax?* **2** [U] a system for sending documents using a fax machine: *Can you send it to me* **by fax**? ◇ *What is your fax number?* **3** [C] a letter or message sent by fax: *Did you get my fax?* ◇ *You can send faxes by email from your computer.* ➲ COLLOCATIONS at PHONE

■ **verb** to send sb a document, message, etc. by fax: **~ sb sth** *Could you fax me the latest version?* ◇ **~ sth to sb** *Could you fax it to me?* ◇ **~ sth** *I faxed the list of hotels through to them.*

faze /feɪz/ *verb* **~ sb** [often passive] (*informal*) to make you feel confused or shocked, so that you do not know what to do SYN **disconcert**: *She wasn't fazed by his comments.* ◇ *He looked as if nothing could faze him.*

FBI /ˌef biː ˈaɪ/ *abbr.* Federal Bureau of Investigation (the police department in the US that is controlled by the national government and that is responsible for dealing with crimes that affect more than one state)

FC /ˌef ˈsiː/ *abbr.* (*BrE*) football club: *Liverpool FC*

FCE /ˌef siː ˈiː/ *noun* [U] the abbreviation for 'First Certificate in English' (a British test that measures a person's ability to speak and write English as a foreign language at an UPPER-INTERMEDIATE level): *When are you* **taking FCE**?

FCO /ˌef siː ˈəʊ; *NAmE* ˈoʊ/ *abbr.* FOREIGN AND COMMONWEALTH OFFICE

FDA /ˌef diː ˈeɪ/ *abbr.* Food and Drug Administration (the US government department that is responsible for making sure that food and drugs are safe to be sold)

FE /ˌef ˈiː/ *abbr.* (in Britain) FURTHER EDUCATION

fealty /ˈfiːəlti/ *noun* [U] (*old use*) a promise to be loyal to sb, especially a king or queen

fear 🔑 /fɪə(r); *NAmE* fɪr/ *noun, verb*

■ **noun** 🔑 [U, C] the bad feeling that you have when you are in danger, when sth bad might happen, or when a particular thing frightens you: *Her eyes showed no fear.* ◇ *The child was shaking* **with fear**. ◇ **~ (of sb/sth)** *(a)* **fear of the dark/spiders/flying, etc.** ◇ *We lived* **in constant fear of** *losing our jobs.* ◇ **~ (for sb/sth)** *her fears for her son's safety* ◇ *Alan spoke of his* **fears for the future**. ◇ **~ (that...)** *the fear that he had cancer* ◇ *The doctor's report confirmed our worst fears.*

IDM ▸ **for fear of sth/of doing sth | for fear (that)...** to avoid the danger of sth happening: *We spoke quietly for fear of waking the guards.* ◇ *I had to run away for fear (that) he might one day kill me.* **in ˌfear of your ˈlife** feeling frightened that you might be killed **ˌno ˈfear** (*BrE, informal*) used to say that you definitely do not want to do sth: *'Are you coming climbing?' 'No fear!'* **put the fear of ˈGod into sb** to make sb very frightened, especially in order to make them do sth **without fear or 'favour** (*formal*) in a fair way ➲ more at FOOL *n.*, STRIKE *v.*

■ ***verb*** **1** ⊶ [T] to be frightened of sb/sth or frightened of doing sth: **~ sb/sth** *All his employees fear him.* ◇ *to fear death/persecution/the unknown* ◇ *Don't worry, you have **nothing to fear from us**.* ◇ **~ to do sth** (*formal*) *She feared to tell him the truth.* ◇ **~ doing sth** (*formal*) *She feared going out at night.* **2** ⊶ [T, I] to feel that sth bad might have happened or might happen in the future: **~ sth** *She has been missing for three days now and police are beginning to **fear the worst*** (= think that she is dead). ◇ **~ sb/sth + adj.** *Hundreds of people are feared dead.* ◇ **be feared to be/have sth** *Women and children are feared to be among the victims.* ◇ **it is feared (that)...** *It is feared (that) he may have been kidnapped.* ◇ **~ (that)...** *She feared (that) he might be dead.* ◇ ***Never fear/Fear not*** (= Don't worry), *I shall return.* **3 I fear** [I] (*formal*) used to tell sb that you think that sth bad has happened or is true: *They are unlikely to get here on time, I fear.* ◇ *'He must be dead then?' '**I fear so**.'* ◇ *'She's not coming back?' '**I fear not**.'*

PHR V **'fear for sb/sth** to be worried about sb/sth: *We fear for his safety.* ◇ *He feared for his mother, left alone on the farm.*

Synonyms

fear

terror • panic • alarm • fright

These are all words for the bad feeling you have when you are afraid.

fear the bad feeling that you have when you are in danger, when sth bad might happen, or when a particular thing frightens you: *(a) fear of flying* ◇ *She showed no fear.*

terror a feeling of extreme fear: *Her eyes were wild with terror.*

panic a sudden feeling of great fear that cannot be controlled and prevents you from thinking clearly: *I had a sudden moment of panic.*

alarm fear or worry that sb feels when sth dangerous or unpleasant might happen: *The doctor said there was **no cause for alarm**.*

fright a feeling of fear, usually sudden: *She cried out in fright.*

FEAR OR FRIGHT?

Fright is a reaction to sth that has just happened or is happening now. Use **fear**, but not **fright**, to talk about things that always frighten you and things that may happen in the future: ~~*I have a fright of spiders.*~~ ◇ ~~*his fright of what might happen*~~

PATTERNS

- a fear/terror **of** sth
- **in** fear/terror/panic/alarm/fright
- fear/terror/panic/alarm **that...**
- to be **filled with** fear/terror/panic/alarm
- a **feeling of** fear/terror/panic/alarm

fear·ful /'fɪəfl; *NAmE* 'fɪrfl/ *adj.* **1** (*formal*) nervous and afraid: **~ (for sb)** *Parents are ever fearful for their children.* ◇ **~ (of sth/of doing sth)** *fearful of an attack* ◇ **~ (that...)** *She was fearful that she would fail.* **2** [only before noun] (*formal*) terrible and frightening **3** (*old-fashioned, informal*) extremely bad: *We made a fearful mess of the room.* ▸ **fear·ful·ly** /-fəli/ *adv.*: *We watched fearfully.* ◇ *fearfully* (= extremely) *expensive* **fear·ful·ness** *noun* [U]

fear·less /'fɪələs; *NAmE* 'fɪrləs/ *adj.* (*approving*) not afraid, in a way that people admire: *a fearless mountaineer* ▸ **fear·less·ly** *adv.* **fear·less·ness** *noun* [U]

fear·some /'fɪəsəm; *NAmE* 'fɪrsəm/ *adj.* (*formal*) making people feel very frightened

feas·ible /'fi:zəbl/ *adj.* that is possible and likely to be achieved SYN **practicable**: *a feasible plan/suggestion/idea* ◇ *It's just not feasible to manage the business on a part-time basis.* OPP **unfeasible** ▸ **feasi·bil·ity** /ˌfi:zə'bɪləti/ *noun* [U]: *a **feasibility study** on the proposed new airport* ◇ *I doubt the feasibility of the plan.*

feast /fi:st/ *noun, verb*

■ ***noun*** **1** a large or special meal, especially for a lot of people and to celebrate sth: *a wedding feast* **2** a day or period of time when there is a religious festival: *the feast of Christmas* ◇ *a feast day* **3** [usually sing.] a thing or an event that brings great pleasure: *a feast of colours* ◇ *The evening was a real feast for music lovers.*

■ ***verb*** [I] **~ (on sth)** to eat a large amount of food, with great enjoyment

IDM **feast your 'eyes (on sb/sth)** to look at sb/sth and get great pleasure

ˌFeast of 'Tabernacles *noun* [U] = SUCCOTH

ˌFeast of 'Weeks *noun* [U] = SHAVUOTH

feat /fi:t/ *noun* (*approving*) an action or a piece of work that needs skill, strength or courage: *The tunnel is a brilliant feat of engineering.* ◇ *to **perform/attempt/achieve** astonishing **feats*** ◇ *That was **no mean feat*** (= it was difficult to do).

fea·ther ⊶ /'feðə(r)/ *noun, verb*

■ ***noun*** ⊶ one of the many soft light parts covering a bird's body: *a peacock feather* ◇ *a feather pillow* (= one containing feathers) ➲ VISUAL VOCAB page V10

IDM **a 'feather in your cap** an action that you can be proud of ORIGIN This idiom comes from the Native American custom of giving a feather to sb who had been very brave in battle. ➲ more at BIRD, KNOCK *v.*, RUFFLE *v.*, SMOOTH *v.*

■ ***verb***

IDM **feather your (own) 'nest** to make yourself richer, especially by spending money on yourself that should be spent on sth else ➲ more at TAR *v.*

ˌfeather-'bed *verb* (-dd-) **~ sb/sth** (*BrE*) to make things easy for sb, especially by giving them money or good conditions of work

ˌfeather 'boa (also **boa**) *noun* a long thin piece of clothing like a SCARF, made of feathers and worn over the shoulders by women, especially in the past

'feather-brained *adj.* (*informal, disapproving*) very silly

ˌfeather 'duster *noun* a stick with feathers on the end of it that is used for cleaning ➲ VISUAL VOCAB page V17

fea·thered /'feðəd; *NAmE* -ðərd/ *adj.* covered with feathers or having feathers

fea·ther·weight /'feðəweɪt; *NAmE* 'feðərw-/ *noun* a BOXER weighing between 53.5 and 57 kilograms, heavier than a BANTAMWEIGHT

fea·thery /'feðəri/ *adj.* light and soft; like feathers

fea·ture ⊶ AW /'fi:tʃə(r)/ *noun, verb*

■ ***noun*** [C] **1** ⊶ something important, interesting or typical of a place or thing: *An interesting feature of the city is the old market.* ◇ *Teamwork is a **key feature** of the training programme.* ◇ *Which features do you look for when choosing a car?* ◇ *The software has no particular **distinguishing features**.* ◇ *geographical features* ➲ see also WATER FEATURE **2** ⊶ [usually pl.] a part of sb's face such as their nose, mouth and eyes: *his strong handsome features* ◇ *Her eyes are her most **striking feature**.* **3** ⊶ **~ (on sb/sth)** (in newspapers, on television, etc.) a special article or programme about sb/sth: *a special feature on education* **4** (*old-fashioned*) the main film/movie in a cinema programme

■ ***verb*** **1** ⊶ [T] to include a particular person or thing as a special feature: **~ sb/sth as sb/sth** *The film features Cary Grant as a professor.* ◇ **~ sb/sth** *The latest model features alloy wheels and an electronic alarm.* ◇ *Many of the hotels featured in the brochure offer special deals for weekend breaks.* **2** ⊶ [I] **~ (in sth)** to have an important part in sth: *Olive oil and garlic feature prominently in his recipes.*

'feature film *noun* a main film/movie with a story, rather than a DOCUMENTARY, etc.

ˈfeature-length *adj.* [usually before noun] of the same length as a typical film/movie

fea·ture·less /ˈfiːtʃələs; *NAmE* -tʃərl-/ *adj.* without any qualities or noticeable characteristics: *The countryside is flat and featureless.*

fe·brile /ˈfiːbraɪl; *NAmE* also ˈfeb-/ *adj.* **1** (*formal*) nervous, excited and very active: *a product of her febrile imagination* **2** (*medical*) (of an illness) caused by fever

Feb·ru·ary 🗝 /ˈfebruəri; *NAmE* -ueri/ *noun* [U, C] (*abbr.* **Feb.**)
the 2nd month of the year, between January and March HELP To see how **February** is used, look at the examples at **April**.

F

feces (*NAmE*) (*BrE* **fae·ces**) /ˈfiːsiːz/ *noun* [pl.] (*formal*) solid waste material that leaves the body through the ANUS SYN **excrement** ▸ **fecal** (*NAmE*) (*BrE* **fae·cal**) /ˈfiːkl/ *adj.* [only before noun]

feck·less /ˈfekləs/ *adj.* having a weak character; not behaving in a responsible way: *Her husband was a charming, but lazy and feckless man.* ▸ **feck·less·ness** *noun* [U]

fec·und /ˈfiːkənd; ˈfek-/ *adj.* (*formal*) **1** able to produce a lot of children, crops, etc. SYN **fertile** **2** producing new and useful things, especially ideas ▸ **fe·cund·ity** /fɪˈkʌndəti/ *noun* [U]

Fed /fed/ *noun* (*US, informal*) **1** [C] an officer of the FBI or another federal organization **2 the Fed** [sing.] = THE FEDERAL RESERVE

fed *past tense, past part.* of FEED

fed·eral 🗝 AW /ˈfedərəl/ *adj.*
1 🗝 having a system of government in which the individual states of a country have control over their own affairs, but are controlled by a central government for national decisions, etc: *a federal republic* **2** 🗝 (within a federal system, for example the US and Canada) connected with national government rather than the local government of an individual state: *a federal law* ◇ *state and federal income taxes* ▸ **fed·er·al·ly** *adv.*: *federally funded health care*

the ˌFederal ˌBureau of Investiˈgation *noun* [sing.] = FBI

fed·er·al·ist /ˈfedərəlɪst/ *noun* a supporter of a federal system of government ▸ **fed·er·al·ism** /ˈfedərəlɪzəm/ *noun* [U]: *European federalism* **fed·er·al·ist** *adj.*: *a federalist future in Europe*

the ˌFederal Reˈserve System (also **the Federal Reserve**) *noun* (*abbr.* the FRS) (also *informal* **the Fed**) [sing.] the organization that controls the supply of money in the US

fed·er·ate /ˈfedəreɪt/ *verb* [I] (*technical*) (of states, organizations, etc.) to unite under a central government or organization while keeping some local control

fed·er·ation AW /ˌfedəˈreɪʃn/ *noun* **1** [C] a country consisting of a group of individual states that have control over their own affairs but are controlled by a central government for national decisions, etc: *the Russian Federation* **2** [C] a group of clubs, TRADE/LABOR UNIONS, etc. that have joined together to form an organization: *the International Tennis Federation* **3** [U] the act of forming a federation: *Many MPs are against federation in Europe.*

fe·dora /fɪˈdɔːrə/ *noun* a low soft hat with a curled BRIM

ˌfed ˈup *adj.* [not before noun] (*informal*) bored or unhappy, especially with a situation that has continued for too long: *You look fed up. What's the matter?* ◇ **~ with sb/sth** *People are fed up with all these traffic jams.* ◇ *In the end, I just* **got** ***fed up with*** *his constant complaining.* ◇ *I wish he'd get a job. I'm* ***fed up with it*** (= with the situation). ◇ **~ with doing sth** *I'm fed up with waiting for her.* HELP Some people say 'fed up of sth' in informal British English, but this is not considered correct in standard English.

fee 🗝 AW /fiː/ *noun*
1 🗝 an amount of money that you pay for professional advice or services: *legal fees* ◇ *Does the bank* ***charge a fee*** *for setting up the account?* ◇ *fee-paying schools* (= that you have to pay to go to) ➲ SYNONYMS at RATE **2** 🗝 an amount of money that you pay to join an organization, or to do sth: *membership fees* ◇ *There is no* ***entrance fee*** *to the gallery.*

fee·ble /ˈfiːbl/ *adj.* (**fee·bler** /ˈfiːblə(r)/, **feeb·lest** /ˈfiːblɪst/) **1** very weak: *a feeble old man* ◇ *The heartbeat was feeble and irregular.* **2** not effective; not showing determination or energy: *a feeble argument/excuse/joke* ◇ *a feeble attempt to explain* ◇ *Don't be so feeble! Tell her you don't want to go.* ▸ **feeble·ness** *noun* [U] **feebly** /ˈfiːbli/ *adv.*

ˌfeeble-ˈminded *adj.* **1** (*old use, offensive*) having less than usual intelligence **2** weak and unable to make decisions

feed 🗝 /fiːd/ *verb, noun*
■ ***verb*** (**fed**, **fed** /fed/)
▸ GIVE/EAT FOOD **1** 🗝 [T] to give food to a person or an animal: **~ sb/sth/yourself** *Have you fed the cat yet?* ◇ *The baby can't feed itself yet* (= can't put food into its own mouth). ◇ **~ sb/sth (on) sth** *The cattle are fed (on) barley.* ◇ **~ sth to sb/sth** *The barley is fed to the cattle.* **2** 🗝 [I] (of a baby or an animal) to eat food: *Slugs and snails feed at night.* ➲ see also FEED ON/OFF STH **3** 🗝 [T] **~ sb** to provide food for a family or group of people: *They have a large family to feed.* ◇ *There's enough here to feed an army.*
▸ PLANT **4** 🗝 [T] **~ sth** to give a plant a special substance to make it grow: *Feed the plants once a week.*
▸ GIVE ADVICE/INFORMATION **5** [T] to give advice, information, etc. to sb/sth: **~ sb sth** *We are constantly fed gossip and speculation by the media.* ◇ **~ sth to sb** *Gossip and speculation are constantly fed to us by the media.*
▸ SUPPLY **6** [T] to supply sth to sb/sth: **~ A (with B)** *The electricity line is fed with power through an underground cable.* ◇ **~ B into A** *Power is fed into the electricity line through an underground cable.*
▸ PUT INTO MACHINE **7** [T] to put or push sth into or through a machine: **~ A (with B)** *He fed the meter with coins.* ◇ **~ B into A** *He fed coins into the meter.* ◇ **~ sth into/through sth** *The fabric is fed through the machine.*
▸ SATISFY NEED **8** [T] **~ sth** to satisfy a need, desire, etc. and keep it strong: *For drug addicts, the need to feed the addiction takes priority over everything else.*
IDM **ˌfeed your ˈface** (*informal*, usually *disapproving*) to eat a lot of food or too much food ➲ more at BITE *v.*
PHR V **ˌfeed ˈback (into/to sth)** to have an influence on the development of sth by reacting to it in some way: *What the audience tells me feeds back into my work.* **ˌfeed (sth) ↔ˈback (to sb)** to give information or opinions about sth, especially so that it can be improved: *Test results will be fed back to the schools.* **ˈfeed into sth** to have an influence on the development of sth: *The report's findings will feed into company policy.* **ˈfeed on/off sth** **1** (of an animal) to eat sth: *Butterflies feed on the flowers of garden plants.* **2** (often *disapproving*) to become stronger because of sth else: *Racism feeds on fear.* **ˌfeed ˈthrough (to sb/sth)** to reach sb/sth after going through a process or system: *It will take time for the higher rates to feed through to investors.* **ˌfeed sb↔ˈup** (*BrE*) to give a lot of food to sb to make them fatter or stronger
■ ***noun***
▸ MEAL FOR BABY/ANIMAL **1** [C] a meal of milk for a young baby; a meal for an animal: *her morning feed*
▸ FOR ANIMALS/PLANTS **2** [U, C] food for animals or plants: *winter feed for the horses*
▸ FOR MACHINE **3** [U] material supplied to a machine **4** [C] a pipe, device, etc. which supplies a machine with sth: *the cold feed to the water cylinder* ◇ *The printer has an automatic paper feed.*
▸ LARGE MEAL **5** [C] (*informal*) a large meal: *They needed a bath and a good feed.*
▸ TELEVISION PROGRAMMES **6** [U] (*NAmE*) television programmes that are sent from a central station to other stations in a network; the system of sending out these programmes: *network feed*

feed·back /ˈfiːdbæk/ *noun* [U] **1** advice, criticism or information about how good or useful sth or sb's work is: *I'd appreciate some feedback on my work.* ◇ *The teacher will* ***give you feedback*** *on the test.* ◇ *We need both positive and negative feedback from our customers.* **2** the unpleasant noise produced by electrical equipment such as an AMPLIFIER when some of the power returns to the system

feed·bag /ˈfi:dbæg/ (*NAmE*) (*BrE* **nose·bag**) *noun* a bag containing food for a horse, that you hang from its head

feed·er /ˈfi:də(r)/ *noun, adj.*

■ ***noun*** **1** (used with an adjective or a noun) an animal or plant that eats a particular thing or eats in a particular way: *plankton feeders* **2** a part of a machine that supplies sth to another part of the machine **3** a container filled with food for birds or animals

■ ***adj.*** [only before noun] **1** (of roads, rivers, etc.) leading to a bigger road, etc: *a **feeder road** to the motorway/freeway* **2** supplying goods, services, etc. to a large organization **3** (*NAmE*) (of animals on a farm) kept to be killed and used for meat

ˈfeeder school *noun* (*BrE*) a school from which most of the children go to a particular SECONDARY SCHOOL or college in the same area

feed·ing /ˈfi:dɪŋ/ *noun* [U] the act of giving food to a person, an animal or a plant: *breast/bottle feeding*

ˈfeeding bottle *noun* (*BrE*) a plastic bottle with a rubber top which a baby or young animal can suck milk through

ˈfeeding frenzy *noun* **1** an occasion when a group of SHARKS or other fish attack sth **2** a situation in which a lot of people compete with each other in an excited way because they want to get sth

the Feeding of the Five ˈThousand *noun* [sing.] a situation in which a lot of people need to be given food: *I made breakfast for all my son's friends—it was like the Feeding of the Five Thousand.* ORIGIN From the Bible story in which Jesus is said to have fed 5 000 people with five loaves of bread and two fish.

feed·stuff /ˈfi:dstʌf/ *noun* [U] (also **feedstuffs** [pl.]) food for farm animals, especially food that has been processed SYN **feed** ➲ compare FOODSTUFF

feel 🔑 /fi:l/ *verb, noun*

■ ***verb*** (**felt, felt** /felt/)

▸ WELL/SICK/HAPPY/SAD, ETC. **1** 🔑 *linking verb* to experience a particular feeling or emotion: **+ adj.** *The heat made him feel faint.* ◇ *She sounded more confident than she felt.* ◇ *I was feeling guilty.* ◇ *You'll feel better after a good night's sleep.* ◇ *She felt betrayed.* ◇ *I feel sorry for him.* ◇ **+ adv./prep.** *How are you feeling today?* ◇ *I know exactly how you feel* (= I feel sympathy for you). ◇ *Luckily I was feeling in a good mood.* ◇ **~ sth** *He seemed to feel no remorse at all.* ◇ **+ noun** *Standing there on stage I felt a complete idiot.* ◇ **~ like sth** *I felt like a complete idiot.*

▸ BE/BECOME AWARE **2** 🔑 [T] (not usually used in the progressive tenses) to notice or be aware of sth because it is touching you or having a physical effect on you SYN **sense**: **~ sth** *I could feel the warm sun on my back.* ◇ *She could not feel her legs.* ◇ *He felt a hand on his shoulder.* ◇ **~ sb/sth/yourself doing sth** *He felt a hand touching his shoulder.* ◇ *She could feel herself blushing.* ◇ **~ sb/sth/yourself do sth** *I felt something crawl up my arm.* ◇ *We felt the ground give way under our feet.* **3** 🔑 [T] (not usually used in the progressive tenses) **~ sth** to become aware of sth even though you cannot see it, hear it, etc. SYN **sense**: *Can you feel the tension in this room?*

▸ GIVE IMPRESSION **4** 🔑 *linking verb* (not used in the progressive tenses) to give you a particular feeling or impression: **+ adj.** *It felt strange to be back in my old school.* ◇ *My mouth felt completely dry.* ◇ **~ like sth** *The interview only took ten minutes, but it felt like hours.* ◇ *It **feels like rain*** (= seems likely to rain). ◇ **~ as if/though...** *Her head felt as if it would burst.* ◇ *It felt as though he had run a marathon.* ◇ *How does it feel to be alone all day?* HELP In spoken English people often use **like** instead of **as if** or **as though** in this meaning, especially in *NAmE*: *He felt like he'd run a marathon.* This is not considered correct in written *BrE*.

▸ TOUCH **5** 🔑 *linking verb* (not used in the progressive tenses) to have a particular physical quality which you become aware of by touching: **+ adj.** *The water feels warm.* ◇ *Its skin feels really smooth.* ◇ **~ like sth** *This wallet feels like leather.* **6** 🔑 [T] to deliberately move your fingers over sth in order to find out what it is like: **~ sth** *Can you feel the bump on my head?* ◇ *Try to tell what this is just by feeling it.* ◇ **~ how, what, etc...** *Feel how rough this is.*

▸ THINK/BELIEVE **7** 🔑 [T, I] (not usually used in the progressive tenses) to think or believe that sth is the case; to have a particular opinion or attitude: **~ (that)...** *We all felt (that) we were unlucky to lose.* ◇ *I felt (that) I had to apologize.* ◇ **~ it to be sth** *She felt it to be her duty to tell the police.* ◇ **~ it + noun** *She felt it her duty to tell the police.* ◇ **~ it + adj.** *I felt it advisable to do nothing.* ◇ **(+ adv./prep.)** *This is something I feel strongly about.* ◇ *This decision is, **I feel**, a huge mistake.* ➲ SYNONYMS at THINK

▸ BE STRONGLY AFFECTED **8** 🔑 [T] **~ sth** to experience the effects or results of sth, often strongly: *He feels the cold a lot.* ◇ *Cathy was really feeling the heat.* ◇ *She felt her mother's death very deeply.* ◇ *The effects of the recession are being felt everywhere.* ◇ *We all felt the force of her arguments.*

▸ SEARCH WITH HANDS **9** 🔑 [I] **~ (in sth/about/around, etc.)** **(for sth)** to search for sth with your hands, feet, etc: *He felt in his pockets for some money.* ◇ *I had to feel about in the dark for the light switch.*

IDM **ˌfeel your ˈage** to realize that you are getting old, especially compared with people you are with who are younger than you **feel your ˈears burning** to think or imagine that other people are talking about you **feel ˈfree (to do sth)** (*informal*) used to tell sb that they are allowed to do sth: *Feel free to ask questions if you don't understand.* ◇ *'Can I use your phone?' 'Feel free.'* **feel ˈgood** 🔑 to feel happy, confident, etc: *It makes me feel good to know my work is appreciated.* **feel (it) in your ˈbones (that...)** to be certain about sth even though you do not have any direct proof and cannot explain why you are certain: *I know I'm going to fail this exam—I can feel it in my bones.* **feel like sth/like doing sth** 🔑 (*informal*) to want to have or do sth: *I feel like a drink.* ◇ *We all felt like celebrating.* ◇ *We'll go for a walk if you feel like it.* **feel the ˈpinch** (*informal*) to not have enough money: *Lots of people who have lost their jobs are starting to feel the pinch.* **feel ˈsick** 🔑 (*especially BrE*) to feel as though you will VOMIT soon: *Mum! I feel sick.* **feel ˌsick to your ˈstomach** (*NAmE*) to feel as though you will VOMIT soon **feel your ˈway 1** to move along carefully, for example when it is dark, by touching walls, objects, etc. **2** to be careful about how you do things, usually because you are in a situation that you are not familiar with: *She was new in the job, still feeling her way.* **not feel yourˈself** to not feel healthy and well ➲ more at DEATH, FLATTER, HARD *adv.*, HONOUR *n.*, HONOUR *v.*, JELLY, MARK *n.*, MILLION, PRESENCE, SMALL *adj.*

PHR V **ˈfeel for sb** to have sympathy for sb: *I really felt for her when her husband died.* ◇ *I do feel for you, honestly.* **ˌfeel sb↔ˈup** (*informal*) to touch sb sexually, especially when they do not want you to SYN **grope** **ˌfeel ˈup to sth** to have the strength and energy to do or deal with sth: *Do we have to go to the party? I really don't feel up to it.* ◇ **~ doing sth** *After the accident she didn't feel up to driving.*

■ ***noun*** [sing.]

▸ TOUCH **1 the feel** the feeling you get when you touch sth or are touched: *You can tell it's silk by the feel.* ◇ *She loved the feel of the sun on her skin.* **2** an act of feeling or touching: *I had a feel of the material.*

▸ IMPRESSION **3** the impression that is created by a place, situation, etc; atmosphere: *It's a big city but it has the feel of a small town.* ◇ *The room has a comfortable feel to it.*

IDM **get the feel of sth/of doing sth** to become familiar with sth or with doing sth: *I haven't got the feel of the brakes in this car yet.* **have a feel for sth** to have an understanding of sth or be naturally good at doing it: *She has a real feel for languages.*

feel·er /ˈfi:lə(r)/ *noun* [usually pl.] either of the two long thin parts on the heads of some insects and of some animals that live in shells that they use to feel and touch things with SYN **antenna**

IDM **put out ˈfeelers** (*informal*) to try to find out what people think about a particular course of action before you do it

ˈfeel-good *adj.* making you feel happy and pleased about life: *a feel-good movie*

IDM the ˈfeel-good factor (*BrE*) (used especially in newspapers, etc.) the feeling of confidence in the future that is shared by many people

feel·ing 0→ /ˈfiːlɪŋ/ *noun*
▸ STH THAT YOU FEEL **1** 0→ [C] ~ (**of sth**) something that you feel through the mind or through the senses: *a **feeling of hunger/excitement/sadness, etc.*** ◇ *guilty feelings* ◇ *I've got a tight feeling in my stomach.* ◇ (*informal*) *'I really resent the way he treated me.' '**I know the feeling*** (= I know how you feel).' ◇ *'I'm going to miss you.' '**The feeling's mutual*** (= I feel exactly the same).'
▸ IDEA/BELIEF **2** 0→ [sing.] the idea or belief that a particular thing is true or a particular situation is likely to happen SYN **impression**: ~ (**of sth**) *He suddenly had the feeling of being followed.* ◇ ~ (**that...**) *I got the feeling that he didn't like me much.* ◇ *I had a nasty feeling that we were lost.*
▸ ATTITUDE/OPINION **3** 0→ [U, C] an attitude or opinion about sth: *The general feeling of the meeting was against the decision.* ◇ ~ (**about/on sth**) *I don't have any strong feelings about it one way or the other.* ◇ *She **had mixed feelings** about giving up her job.* ◇ *My own feeling is that we should buy the cheaper one.* ◇ *Public feeling is being ignored by the government.*
▸ EMOTIONS **4** 0→ **feelings** [pl.] a person's emotions rather than their thoughts or ideas: *He hates talking about his feelings.* ◇ *I didn't mean to **hurt your feelings*** (= offend you). **5** 0→ [U, C] strong emotion: *She spoke **with feeling** about the plight of the homeless.* ◇ ***Feelings are running high*** (= people are very angry or excited).
▸ UNDERSTANDING **6** 0→ [U] the ability to understand sb/sth or to do sth in a sensitive way: *He played the piano with great feeling.* ◇ ~ **for sb/sth** *She has a wonderful feeling for colour.*
▸ SYMPATHY/LOVE **7** [U, pl.] ~ (**for sb/sth**) sympathy or love for sb/sth: *You have no feeling for the sufferings of others.* ◇ *I still **have feelings** for her* (= feel attracted to her in a romantic way).
▸ PHYSICAL **8** 0→ [U] the ability to feel physically: *I've lost all feeling in my legs.*
▸ ATMOSPHERE **9** [sing.] the atmosphere of a place, situation, etc: *They have managed to recreate the feeling of the original theatre.*
IDM **bad/ill ˈfeeling** (also **bad/ill ˈfeelings** especially in *NAmE*) anger between people, especially after an argument or disagreement: *There was a lot of bad feeling between the two groups of students.* ➲ more at HARD *adj.*, SINK *v.*, SPARE

feel·ing·ly /ˈfiːlɪŋli/ *adv.* with strong emotion SYN **emotionally**: *He spoke feelingly about his dead father.*

feet *pl.* of FOOT

feign /feɪn/ *verb* ~ **sth** | ~ **to do sth** (*formal*) to pretend that you have a particular feeling or that you are ill/sick, tired, etc: *He survived the massacre by feigning death.* ◇ *'Who cares?' said Alex, feigning indifference.*

feint /feɪnt/ *noun, verb*
■ ***noun*** (especially in sport) a movement that is intended to make your opponent think you are going to do one thing when you are really going to do sth else
■ ***verb*** [I] (especially in sport) to confuse your opponent by making them think you are going to do one thing when you are really going to do sth else

feisty /ˈfaɪsti/ *adj.* (**feist·ier**, **feisti·est**) (*informal, approving*) (of people) strong, determined and not afraid of arguing with people

fela·fel = FALAFEL

feld·spar /ˈfeldspɑː(r)/ *noun* [U, C] a type of white or red rock

fe·lici·tous /fəˈlɪsɪtəs/ *adj.* (*formal* or *literary*) (especially of words) chosen well; very suitable; giving a good result SYN **apt**, **happy**: *a felicitous turn of phrase* ▸ **fe·lici·tous·ly** *adv.*

fe·li·city /fəˈlɪsəti/ *noun* (*pl.* **-ies**) (*formal* or *literary*) **1** [U] great happiness **2** [U] the quality of being well chosen or suitable **3** **felicities** [pl.] well-chosen or successful features, especially in a speech or piece of writing

fe·line /ˈfiːlaɪn/ *adj., noun*
■ ***adj.*** like a cat; connected with an animal of the cat family: *She walks with feline grace.*
■ ***noun*** (*formal*) a cat; an animal of the cat family

fell /fel/ *noun, verb, adj.* ➲ see also FALL
■ ***noun*** a hill or an area of hills in northern England
■ ***verb*** **1** ~ **sth** to cut down a tree **2** ~ **sb** (*literary*) to make sb fall to the ground: *He felled his opponent with a single blow.*
■ ***adj.*** (*literary*) very evil or violent
IDM **at/in one fell swoop** all at the same time; in a single action, especially a sudden or violent one

fella (also **fell·er**) /ˈfelə(r)/ *noun* (*informal*) **1** an informal way of referring to a man **2** an informal way of referring to sb's boyfriend: *Have you met her new fella?*

fel·late /fəˈleɪt; *NAmE* also ˈfeleɪt/ *verb* ~ **sb** (*formal*) to perform FELLATIO on a man

fel·la·tio /fəˈleɪʃiəʊ; *NAmE* -ʃioʊ/ *noun* [U] (*formal*) the practice of touching a man's PENIS with the tongue and lips to give sexual pleasure

fel·low 0→ /ˈfeləʊ; *NAmE* ˈfeloʊ/ *noun, adj.*
■ ***noun*** **1** 0→ (*informal*, becoming *old-fashioned*) a way of referring to a man or boy: *He's a nice old fellow.* ➲ see also FELLA **2** [usually pl.] a person that you work with or that is like you; a thing that is similar to the one mentioned: *She has a very good reputation among her fellows.* ◇ *Many caged birds live longer than their fellows in the wild.* **3** (*BrE*) a senior member of some colleges or universities: *a fellow of New College, Oxford* **4** a member of an academic or professional organization: *a fellow of the Royal College of Surgeons* **5** (*especially NAmE*) a GRADUATE student who holds a FELLOWSHIP: *a graduate fellow* ◇ *a teaching fellow*
■ ***adj.*** 0→ [only before noun] used to describe sb who is the same as you in some way, or in the same situation: ***fellow members/citizens/workers*** ◇ *my **fellow passengers** on the train*

ˌfellow ˈfeeling *noun* [U, C] a feeling of sympathy for sb because you have shared similar experiences

fel·low·ship /ˈfeləʊʃɪp; *NAmE* -loʊ-/ *noun* **1** [U] (*formal*) a feeling of friendship between people who do things together or share an interest **2** [C] an organized group of people who share an interest, aim or belief **3** [C] (*especially BrE*) the position of being a senior member of a college or university **4** [C] an award of money to a GRADUATE student to allow them to continue their studies or to do research **5** [C, U] the state of being a member of an academic or professional organization: *to be elected to fellowship of the British Academy*

ˌfellow-ˈtravel·ler *noun* **1** a person who is travelling to the same place as another person **2** a person who agrees with the aims of a political party, especially the Communist party, but is not a member of it

felon /ˈfelən/ *noun* (*especially NAmE, law*) a person who has committed a felony

fe·loni·ous /fəˈləʊniəs; *NAmE* -ˈloʊ-/ *adj.* (*formal*) relating to or involved in crime

fel·ony /ˈfeləni/ *noun* [C, U] (*pl.* **-ies**) (*US* or *old-fashioned, law*) the act of committing a serious crime such as murder or RAPE; a crime of this type: *a charge of felony* ➲ compare MISDEMEANOUR

felt /felt/ *noun* [U] a type of soft thick cloth made from wool or hair that has been pressed tightly together: *a felt hat* ➲ see also FEEL, FELT, FELT *v.*

ˌfelt-tip ˈpen (also **ˈfelt tip**, **ˌfelt-tipped ˈpen**) *noun* a pen that has a point made of felt

fe·male 0→ /ˈfiːmeɪl/ *adj., noun*
■ ***adj.*** **1** 0→ being a woman or a girl: *a female student/employee/artist* ◇ *Two of the candidates must be female.* **2** 0→ of the sex that can lay eggs or give birth to babies: *a female cat* **3** 0→ of women; typical of women; affecting women: *female characteristics* ◇ *the female role* ➲ compare FEMININE **4** (*biology*) (of plants and flowers) that can produce fruit **5** (*technical*) (of electrical equipment) having a hole that another part fits into: *a female plug* OPP **male**

F

■ *noun* **1** 🗝 an animal that can lay eggs or give birth to babies; a plant that can produce fruit **2** 🗝 (*formal*) a woman or a girl: *More females than males are employed in the factory.* **OPP** **male**

femi·nine /ˈfemənɪn/ *adj.*, *noun*

■ *adj.* **1** having the qualities or appearance considered to be typical of women; connected with women: *That dress makes you look very feminine.* ◇ *He had delicate, almost feminine, features.* ◇ *the traditional feminine role* ➲ compare FEMALE, MASCULINE **2** (*grammar*) belonging to a class of words that refer to female people or animals and often have a special form: *Some people prefer not to use the feminine form 'actress' and use the word 'actor' for both sexes.* **3** (*grammar*) (in some languages) belonging to a class of nouns, pronouns or adjectives that have feminine GENDER not MASCULINE or NEUTER: *The French word for 'table' is feminine.*

■ *noun* (*grammar*) **1 the feminine** [sing.] the feminine GENDER (= form of nouns, adjectives and pronouns) **2** [C] a feminine word or word form ➲ compare MASCULINE, NEUTER

femi·nin·ity /ˌfeməˈnɪnəti/ *noun* [U] the fact of being a woman; the qualities that are considered to be typical of women

femi·nism /ˈfemənɪzəm/ *noun* [U] the belief and aim that women should have the same rights and opportunities as men; the struggle to achieve this aim

femi·nist /ˈfemənɪst/ *noun* a person who supports the belief that women should have the same rights and opportunities as men ▸ **femi·nist** *adj.* [usually before noun]: *feminist demands/ideas/theories* ◇ *the feminist movement*

femi·nize (*BrE* also **-ise**) /ˈfemənaɪz/ *verb* **1 ~ sb** to make sb more like a woman **2 ~ sth** to make sth involve more women: *Offices became increasingly feminized during the 1960s.*

femme /fem/ *adj.* (sometimes *offensive*) (of a HOMOSEXUAL person) having qualities typical of a woman ➲ compare BUTCH

femme fa·tale /ˌfæm fəˈtɑːl; *NAmE* ˌfem fəˈtæl/ *noun* (*pl.* **femmes fa·tales** /ˌfæm fəˈtɑːl; -z; *NAmE* ˌfem fəˈtæl/) (from *French*) a very beautiful woman that men find sexually attractive but who brings them trouble or unhappiness

femto- /ˈfemtəʊ; *NAmE* -toʊ/ *combining form* (*technical*) (in units of measurement) 10^{-15}: *a femtosecond*

femur /ˈfiːmə(r)/ *noun* (*pl.* **fe·murs** or **fem·ora** /ˈfemərə/) (*anatomy*) the THIGH BONE ➲ VISUAL VOCAB page V48 ▸ **fem·oral** /ˈfemərəl/ *adj.* [only before noun]

fen /fen/ *noun* an area of low flat wet land, especially in the east of England

fence 🗝 /fens/ *noun*, *verb*

■ *noun* **1** 🗝 a structure made of wood or wire supported with posts that is put between two areas of land as a BOUNDARY, or around a garden/yard, field, etc. to keep animals in, or to keep people and animals out ➲ VISUAL VOCAB pages V2, V16 **2** a structure that horses must jump over in a race or a competition **3** (*informal*) a criminal who buys and sells stolen goods **IDM** see GRASS *n.*, MEND *v.*, SIDE *n.*, SIT

■ *verb* **1** [T] **~ sth** to surround or divide an area with a fence: *His property is fenced with barbed wire.* ➲ see also UNFENCED **2** [I] to take part in the sport of FENCING **3** [I] **~ (with sb)** to speak to sb in a clever way in order to gain an advantage in the conversation

PHR V ˌ**fence sb/sth↔ˈin** [often passive] **1** to surround sb/sth with a fence **2** to restrict sb's freedom **SYN** **hem sb in**: *She felt fenced in by domestic routine.* ˌ**fence sth↔ˈoff** [often passive] to divide one area from another with a fence

ˈ**fence-mending** *noun* [U] an attempt to improve relations between two people or groups and to try to find a solution to a disagreement between them

fen·cer /ˈfensə(r)/ *noun* a person who takes part in the sport of FENCING

fen·cing /ˈfensɪŋ/ *noun* [U] **1** the sport of fighting with long thin SWORDS ➲ VISUAL VOCAB page V39 **2** fences; wood, wire, or other material used for making fences: *The factory is surrounded by electric fencing.*

fend /fend/ *verb*

PHR V ˌ**fend for yourˈself** to take care of yourself without help from anyone else: *His parents agreed to pay the rent for his apartment but otherwise left him to fend for himself.* ˌ**fend sth/sb↔ˈoff** **1** to defend or protect yourself from sth/sb that is attacking you **SYN** **fight off**, **ward off**: *The police officer fended off the blows with his riot shield.* **2** to protect yourself from difficult questions, criticisms, etc, especially by avoiding them **SYN** **ward off**: *She managed to fend off questions about new tax increases.*

fend·er /ˈfendə(r)/ *noun* **1** (*NAmE*) (*BrE* **wing**) a part of a car that is above a wheel ➲ VISUAL VOCAB page V42 **2** (*NAmE*) (*BrE* **mud·guard**) a curved cover over a wheel of a bicycle **3** a frame around a FIREPLACE to prevent burning coal or wood from falling out **4** a soft solid object such as an old tyre or a piece of rope that is hung over the side of a boat so the boat is not damaged if it touches another boat, a wall, etc.

ˈ**fender bender** *noun* (*NAmE*, *informal*) a car accident in which there is not a lot of damage

feng shui /ˌfeŋ ˈʃuːi; ˌfʊŋ ˈʃweɪ/ *noun* [U] (from *Chinese*) a Chinese system for deciding the right position for a building and for placing objects inside a building in order to make people feel comfortable and happy

Fen·ian /ˈfiːniən/ *noun* **1** a member of an organization formed in the 1850s in the US and Ireland in order to end British rule in Ireland **2** (*informal*, *taboo*) (especially in Northern Ireland) an offensive word for a Catholic

fen·land /ˈfenlænd; -lənd/ *noun* [U, C] an area of low flat wet land in the east of England

fen·nel /ˈfenl/ *noun* [U] a vegetable that has a thick round STEM with a strong taste. The seeds and leaves are also used in cooking. ➲ VISUAL VOCAB page V27

fenu·greek /ˈfenjʊgriːk/ *noun* [U] a plant with hard yellow-brown seeds that are used in S Asian cooking as a spice

feral /ˈferəl/ *adj.* (of animals) living wild, especially after escaping from life as a pet or on a farm: *feral cats*

fe·ring·hee /fəˈrɪŋgi/ *noun* a word used in some Asian countries for any person with a white skin, especially a European or an American

fer·mata /fɜːˈmɑːtə; *NAmE* fɜːrˈm-/ *noun* (*music*) (*especially NAmE*) = PAUSE

fer·ment *verb*, *noun*

■ *verb* /fəˈment; *NAmE* fərˈm-/ [I, T] to experience a chemical change because of the action of YEAST or bacteria, often changing sugar to alcohol; to make sth change in this way: *Fruit juices ferment if they are kept for too long.* ◇ (*figurative*) *A blend of emotions fermented inside her.* ◇ **~ sth** *Red wine is fermented at a higher temperature than white.* ▸ **fer·men·ta·tion** /ˌfɜːmenˈteɪʃn; *NAmE* ˌfɜːrm-/ *noun* [U]

■ *noun* /ˈfɜːment; *NAmE* ˈfɜːrm-/ [U, sing.] (*formal*) a state of political or social excitement and confusion: *The country is in ferment.*

fer·mium /ˈfɜːmiəm; *NAmE* ˈfɜːrm-/ *noun* [U] (*symb.* **Fm**) a chemical element. Fermium is a very rare RADIOACTIVE metal.

fern /fɜːn; *NAmE* fɜːrn/ *noun* [C, U] a plant with large delicate leaves and no flowers that grows in wet areas or is grown in a pot. There are many types of fern. ➲ VISUAL VOCAB page V9 ▸ **ferny** *adj.*

fer·ocious /fəˈrəʊʃəs; *NAmE* -ˈroʊ-/ *adj.* very aggressive or violent; very strong **SYN** **savage**: *a ferocious beast/attack/storm* ◇ *a man driven by ferocious determination* ◇ *ferocious opposition to the plan* ▸ **fer·ocious·ly** *adv.*

fer·ocity /fəˈrɒsəti; *NAmE* fəˈrɑːs-/ *noun* [U] violence; aggressive behaviour: *The police were shocked by the ferocity of the attack.*

fer·ret /ˈferɪt/ *noun*, *verb*

■ *noun* a small aggressive animal with a long thin body, kept for chasing RABBITS from their holes, killing RATS, etc.

■ *verb* **1** [I] **~ (about/around) (for sth)** (*informal*) to search

F

for sth that is lost or hidden among a lot of things: *She opened the drawer and ferreted around for her keys.* **2** [I] to hunt RABBITS, RATS, etc. using ferrets

PHR V ˌ**ferret sb/sth**↔ˈ**out** (*informal*) to discover information or to find sb/sth by searching thoroughly, asking a lot of questions, etc.

Fer·ris wheel /ˈferɪs wiːl/ (*especially NAmE*) (*BrE* also ˌ**big ˈwheel**) *noun* a large wheel which stands in a vertical position at an AMUSEMENT PARK, with seats hanging at its edge for people to ride in

fer·rite /ˈferaɪt/ *noun* [U] **1** a chemical containing iron, used in electrical devices such as AERIALS/ANTENNAS **2** a form of pure iron that is found in steel which contains low amounts of CARBON

F

ferro·mag·net·ic /ˌferəʊmægˈnetɪk; *NAmE* ˌferoʊ-/ *adj.* (*physics*) having the kind of MAGNETISM which iron has

fer·rous /ˈferəs/ *adj.* [only before noun] (*technical*) containing iron; connected with iron

fer·rule /ˈferuːl; *NAmE* ˈferəl/ *noun* a piece of metal or rubber that covers the end of an umbrella or a stick to protect it

ferry /ˈferi/ *noun, verb*

▪ ***noun*** (*pl.* **-ies**) a boat or ship that carries people, vehicles and goods across a river or across a narrow part of the sea: *the cross-channel ferry service* ◇ *We caught the ferry at Ostend.* ◇ *the Dover-Calais ferry crossing* ◇ *the Staten Island ferry* ➲ **COLLOCATIONS** at TRAVEL ➲ **VISUAL VOCAB** page V44

▪ ***verb*** (**fer·ries**, **ferry·ing**, **fer·ried**, **fer·ried**) [T, I] **~ (sb/sth) (+ adv./prep.)** to carry people or goods in a boat or other vehicle from one place to another, often for a short distance and as a regular service: *He offered to ferry us across the river in his boat.* ◇ *The children need to be ferried to and from school.*

ˈ**ferry boat** *noun* a boat that is used as a ferry

ferry·man /ˈferimən/ *noun* (*pl.* **-men** /-mən/) a person in charge of a ferry across a river

fer·tile /ˈfɜːtaɪl; *NAmE* ˈfɜːrtl/ *adj.* **1** (of land or soil) that plants grow well in: *a fertile region* OPP **infertile** **2** (of people, animals or plants) that can produce babies, young animals, fruit or new plants: *The treatment has been tested on healthy fertile women under the age of 35.* OPP **infertile** **3** [usually before noun] that produces good results; that encourages activity: *a fertile partnership* ◇ *The region at the time was **fertile ground** for revolutionary movements* (= there were the necessary conditions for them to develop easily). **4** [usually before noun] (of a person's mind or imagination) that produces a lot of new ideas: *the product of a **fertile imagination*** ➲ compare STERILE

fer·til·ity /fəˈtɪləti; *NAmE* fərˈt-/ *noun* [U] the state of being fertile: *the fertility of the soil/land* ◇ *a god of fertility* ◇ *fertility treatment* (= medical help given to a person to help them have a baby) OPP **infertility**

fer·til·ize (*BrE* also **-ise**) /ˈfɜːtəlaɪz; *NAmE* ˈfɜːrt-/ *verb* **1 ~ sth** to put POLLEN into a plant so that a seed develops; to join SPERM with an egg so that a baby or young animal develops: *Flowers are often fertilized by bees as they gather nectar.* ◇ *a fertilized egg* **2 ~ sth** to add a substance to soil to make plants grow more successfully ▶ **fer·til·ization**, **-isa·tion** /ˌfɜːtəlaɪˈzeɪʃn; *NAmE* ˌfɜːrtələˈz-/ *noun* [U]: *Immediately after fertilization, the cells of the egg divide.* ◇ *the fertilization of soil with artificial chemicals*

fer·til·izer (*BrE* also **-iser**) /ˈfɜːtəlaɪzə(r); *NAmE* ˈfɜːrt-/ *noun* [C, U] a substance added to soil to make plants grow more successfully: ***artificial/chemical fertilizers*** ➲ **COLLOCATIONS** at FARMING

fer·vent /ˈfɜːvənt; *NAmE* ˈfɜːrv-/ *adj.* [usually before noun] having or showing very strong and sincere feelings about sth SYN **ardent**: *a **fervent admirer/believer/supporter*** ◇ *a **fervent belief/hope/desire*** ▶ **fer·vent·ly** *adv.*

fer·vid /ˈfɜːvɪd; *NAmE* ˈfɜːrvɪd/ *adj.* (*formal*) feeling sth too strongly; showing feelings that are too strong ▶ **fer·vid·ly** *adv.*

fer·vour (*especially US* **fer·vor**) /ˈfɜːvə(r); *NAmE* ˈfɜːrv-/ *noun* [U] very strong feelings about sth SYN **enthusiasm**: *She kissed him with unusual fervour.* ◇ *religious/patriotic fervour*

fess /fes/ *verb*

PHR V ˌ**fess ˈup** (*NAmE, informal*) to admit that you have done sth wrong SYN **own up**

-fest /fest/ *combining form* (in nouns) a festival or large meeting involving a particular activity or with a particular atmosphere: *a jazzfest* ◇ *a talkfest* (= a session involving long discussions) ◇ (usually *disapproving*) *a lovefest* (= an event in which people show too much affection for each other that may not be genuine)

fes·ter /ˈfestə(r)/ *verb* **1** [I] (of a wound or cut) to become badly infected: ***festering sores/wounds*** **2** [I] (of bad feelings or thoughts) to become much worse because you do not deal with them successfully

fes·ti·val 0-w /ˈfestɪvl/ *noun*

1 0-w a series of performances of music, plays, films/movies, etc, usually organized in the same place once a year; a series of public events connected with a particular activity or idea: *the Edinburgh festival* ◇ *the Cannes film festival* ◇ *a beer festival* ◇ *a rock festival* (= where bands perform, often outdoors and over a period of several days) **2** 0-w a day or period of the year when people stop working to celebrate a special event, often a religious one ➲ see also HARVEST FESTIVAL

fes·tive /ˈfestɪv/ *adj.* **1** typical of a special event or celebration: *a festive occasion* ◇ *The whole town is in **festive mood.*** **2** (*BrE*) connected with the period when people celebrate Christmas: *the **festive season/period*** ◇ *festive decorations*

fes·tiv·ity /feˈstɪvəti/ *noun* **1 festivities** [pl.] the activities that are organized to celebrate a special event **2** [U] the happiness and enjoyment that exist when people celebrate sth: *The wedding was an occasion of great festivity.* ◇ *an air of festivity*

fes·toon /feˈstuːn/ *verb, noun*

▪ ***verb*** [usually passive] **~ sb/sth (with sth)** to decorate sb/sth with flowers, coloured paper, etc, often as part of a celebration

▪ ***noun*** a chain of lights, coloured paper, flowers, etc, used to decorate sth

Fest·schrift /ˈfestʃrɪft/ *noun* (from *German*) a collection of articles published in honour of a SCHOLAR

feta cheese /ˌfetə ˈtʃiːz/ (also **feta**) *noun* [U] a type of Greek cheese made from sheep's milk

fetal (*especially NAmE*) (*BrE* usually **foe·tal**) /ˈfiːtl/ *adj.* [only before noun] connected with a fetus; typical of a fetus: *fetal abnormalities* ◇ *She lay curled up in a **fetal position.***

ˌ**fetal ˈalcohol syndrome** *noun* [U] (*medical*) a condition in which a child's mental and physical development are damaged because the mother drank too much alcohol while she was pregnant

fetch 0-w /fetʃ/ *verb*

1 0-w (*especially BrE*) to go to where sb/sth is and bring them/it back: **~ sb/sth** *to fetch help/a doctor* ◇ *The inhabitants have to walk a mile to fetch water.* ◇ *She's gone to fetch the kids from school.* ◇ **~ sb sth** *Could you fetch me my bag?* **2 ~ sth** to be sold for a particular price SYN **sell for**: *The painting is expected to fetch $10 000 at auction.*

IDM **fetch and ˈcarry (for sb)** to do a lot of little jobs for sb as if you were their servant

PHR V ˌ**fetch ˈup** (*informal, especially BrE*) to arrive somewhere without planning to: *And then, a few years later, he somehow fetched up in Rome.*

fetch·ing /ˈfetʃɪŋ/ *adj.* (*informal*) (especially of a person or their clothes) attractive ▶ **fetch·ing·ly** *adv.*

fete (also **fête**) /feɪt/ *noun, verb*

▪ ***noun*** **1** (also **fair**) (both *BrE*) (*NAmE* **car·ni·val**) an outdoor entertainment at which people can play games to win prizes, buy food and drink, etc, usually arranged to make money for a special purpose: *the **school/village/church fete*** **2** (*NAmE*) a special occasion held to celebrate sth: *a charity fete*

■ ***verb*** [usually passive] **~ sb** (*formal*) to welcome, praise or entertain sb publicly

fetid /ˈfetɪd/ (*BrE less frequent* **foe·tid**) *adj.* [usually before noun] (*formal*) smelling very unpleasant **SYN** **stinking**

fet·ish /ˈfetɪʃ/ *noun* **1** (usually *disapproving*) the fact that a person spends too much time doing or thinking about a particular thing: *She has a fetish about cleanliness.* ◇ *He makes a fetish of his work.* **2** the fact of getting sexual pleasure from a particular object: *to have a leather fetish* **3** an object that some people worship because they believe that it has magic powers ▸ **fet·ish·ism** *noun* [U]: *a magazine specializing in rubber fetishism* ◇ *the importance of animal fetishism in the history of Egypt* **fet·ish·ist** *noun*: *a leather fetishist* **fet·ish·is·tic** /ˌfetɪˈʃɪstɪk/ *adj.*

fet·ish·ize (*BrE* also **-ise**) /ˈfetɪʃaɪz/ *verb* **1 ~ sth** to spend too much time thinking about or doing sth **2 ~ sth** to get sexual pleasure from thinking about or looking at a particular thing

fet·lock /ˈfetlɒk; *NAmE* -lɑːk/ *noun* the part at the back of a horse's leg, just above its HOOF, where long hair grows

fet·ter /ˈfetə(r)/ *verb, noun*

■ ***verb*** [usually passive] **1 ~ sb** (*literary*) to restrict sb's freedom to do what they want **2 ~ sb** to put chains around a prisoner's feet **SYN** **shackle**

■ ***noun*** **1** [usually pl.] (*literary*) something that stops sb from doing what they want: *They were at last freed from the fetters of ignorance.* **2 fetters** [pl.] chains that are put around a prisoner's feet **SYN** **chains, shackles**

fet·tle /ˈfetl/ *noun*

IDM **in fine/good ˈfettle** (*old-fashioned, informal*) healthy; in good condition

fetus (*especially NAmE*) (*BrE* usually **foe·tus**) /ˈfiːtəs/ *noun* a young human or animal before it is born, especially a human more than eight weeks after FERTILIZATION

feud /fjuːd/ *noun, verb*

■ ***noun*** an angry and bitter argument between two people or groups of people that continues over a long period of time: **~ (between A and B)** *a long-running feud between the two artists* ◇ **~ (with sb)** *a feud with the neighbours* ◇ *a family feud* (= within a family or between two families) ◇ **~ (over sb/sth)** *a feud over money*

■ ***verb*** [I] **~ (with sb)** to have an angry and bitter argument with sb over a long period of time ▸ **feud·ing** *noun* [U]: *stories of bitter feuding between rival drug dealers*

feu·dal /ˈfjuːdl/ *adj.* [usually before noun] connected with or similar to feudalism: *the feudal system*

feu·dal·ism /ˈfjuːdəlɪzəm/ *noun* [U] the social system that existed during the Middle Ages in Europe in which people were given land and protection by a NOBLEMAN, and had to work and fight for him in return ▸ **feu·dal·ist·ic** /ˌfjuːdəˈlɪstɪk/ *adj.*

fever 🔑 /ˈfiːvə(r)/ *noun*

1 🔑 [C, U] a medical condition in which a person has a temperature that is higher than normal: *He has a high fever.* ◇ *Aspirin should help reduce the fever.* ➲ COLLOCATIONS at ILL ➲ compare TEMPERATURE **2** 🔑 [C, U] (*old-fashioned*) (used mainly in compounds) a particular type of disease in which sb has a high temperature: *She caught a fever on her travels in Africa, and died.* ➲ see also GLANDULAR FEVER, HAY FEVER, RHEUMATIC FEVER, SCARLET FEVER, YELLOW FEVER **3** [sing.] **~ (of sth)** a state of nervous excitement: *He waited for her arrival in a fever of impatience.* **4** [U] (especially in compounds) great interest or excitement about sth: *election fever*

ˈfever blister *noun* (*NAmE*) = COLD SORE

fe·vered /ˈfiːvəd; *NAmE* -vərd/ *adj.* [only before noun] **1** showing great excitement or worry: ***fevered excitement/speculation*** ◇ ***a fevered imagination/mind*** (= that imagines strange things) **2** suffering from a fever: *She mopped his* ***fevered brow.***

fever·few /ˈfiːvəfjuː; *NAmE* ˈfiːvər-/ *noun* [U] a plant of the DAISY family, sometimes used as a medicine

fe·ver·ish /ˈfiːvərɪʃ/ *adj.* **1** [usually before noun] showing strong feelings of excitement or worry, often with a lot of activity or quick movements: *The whole place was a scene of* ***feverish activity.*** ◇ *a state of feverish excitement* ◇ *feverish with longing* **2** suffering from a fever; caused by a fever: *She was aching and feverish.* ◇ *a feverish cold/dream* ▸ **fe·ver·ish·ly** *adv.*: *The team worked feverishly to the November deadline.* ◇ *Her mind raced feverishly.*

ˈfever pitch *noun* [U, C] a very high level of excitement or activity: *Speculation about his future had* ***reached fever pitch.*** ◇ *Excitement has been* ***at fever pitch*** *for days.*

few 🔑 /fjuː/ *det., adj., pron.*

■ ***det., adj.*** (fewer, few·est) **1** 🔑 used with plural nouns and a plural verb to mean 'not many': *Few people understand the difference.* ◇ *There seem to be fewer tourists around this year.* ◇ *Very few students learn Latin now.* **2** 🔑 (usually **a few**) used with plural nouns and a plural verb to mean 'a small number', 'some': *We've had a few replies.* ◇ *I need a few things from the store.* ◇ ***Quite a few*** *people are going to arrive early.* ◇ *I try to visit my parents* ***every few weeks.***

IDM **ˌfew and ˌfar beˈtween** not frequent; not happening often

■ ***pron.*** **1** 🔑 not many people, things or places: *Very few of his books are worth reading.* ◇ *You can pass with* ***as few as*** *25 points.* ◇ (*formal*) *Few will argue with this conclusion.* **2** 🔑 **a few** a small number of people, things or places; some: *I recognized a few of the other people.* ◇ *I've seen most of his movies. Only a few are as good as his first one.* ◇ *Could you give me a few more details?* **3** 🔑 **fewer** not as many as: *Fewer than 20 students passed all the exams.* ◇ *There are* ***no fewer than*** *100 different species in the area.* **HELP** Look at the note at **less**. **4 the few** used with a plural verb to mean 'a small group of people': *Real power belongs to the few.* ◇ *She was one of* ***the chosen few*** (= the small group with special rights).

IDM **quite a ˈfew** 🔑 (*BrE* also **a good ˈfew**) a fairly large number: *I've been there quite a few times.* **have ˈhad a few** (*informal*) to have had enough alcohol to make you drunk

fey /feɪ/ *adj.* (*literary*, sometimes *disapproving*) (usually of a person) sensitive and rather mysterious or strange; not acting in a very practical way

fez /fez/ *noun* (*pl.* **fezzes**) a round red hat with a flat top and a TASSEL but no BRIM, worn by men in some Muslim countries

ff *abbr.* (*music*) very loudly (from Italian 'fortissimo')

ff. *abbr.* written after the number of a page or line to mean 'and the following pages or lines': *See pp. 96 ff.*

fi·ancé /fiˈɒnseɪ; -ˈɑːns-; *NAmE* ˌfiːɑːnˈseɪ/ *noun* the man that a woman is engaged to: *Linda and her fiancé were there.* ➲ COLLOCATIONS at MARRIAGE

fi·an·cée /fiˈɒnseɪ; *NAmE* ˌfiːɑːnˈseɪ/ *noun* the woman that a man is engaged to: *Paul and his fiancée were there.* ➲ COLLOCATIONS at MARRIAGE

Fianna Fáil /fiˌænə ˈfɔɪl/ *noun* [sing.+ sing./pl. v.] one of the two main political parties in the Republic of Ireland, on the political left ➲ compare FINE GAEL

fi·asco /fiˈæskəʊ; *NAmE* fiˈæskoʊ/ *noun* (*pl.* **-os**, *NAmE* also **-oes**) (*informal*) something that does not succeed, often in a way that causes embarrassment **SYN** **disaster**: *What a fiasco!*

fiat /ˈfiːæt; ˈfaɪæt/ *noun* [C, U] (*formal*) an official order given by sb in authority **SYN** **decree**

fib /fɪb/ *noun, verb*

■ ***noun*** (*informal*) a statement that is not true; a lie about sth that is not important: *Stop* ***telling fibs.***

■ ***verb*** (**-bb-**) [I] (*informal*) to tell a lie, usually about sth that is not important: *Come on, don't fib! Where were you really last night?* ▸ **fib·ber** *noun*: *You fibber!*

Fi·bo·nacci ser·ies /ˌfɪbəˈnɑːtʃi sɪəriːz; *NAmE* sɪriːz/ *noun* (*mathematics*) a series of numbers in which each number is equal to the two numbers before it added together. Starting from 1, the series is 1,1,2,3,5,8,13, etc.

fibre (*especially US* **fiber**) /ˈfaɪbə(r)/ *noun* **1** [U] the part of food that helps to keep a person healthy by keeping the BOWELS working and moving other food quickly through

F

the body **SYN** **roughage**: ***dietary fibre*** ◇ *Dried fruits are especially* ***high in fibre.*** ◇ *a* ***high-/low-fibre diet*** **2** [C, U] a material such as cloth or rope that is made from a mass of natural or artificial threads: *nylon and other* ***man-made fibres*** **3** [C] one of the many thin threads that form body TISSUE, such as muscle, and natural materials, such as wood and cotton: ***cotton/wood/nerve/muscle fibres*** ◇ (*literary*) *She loved him with every fibre of her being.* ➲ see also MORAL FIBRE, OPTICAL FIBRE

fibre·board (*especially US* **fiber·board**) /ˈfaɪbəbɔːd; *NAmE* ˈfaɪbərbɔːrd/ *noun* [U] a building material made of wood or other plant fibres pressed together to form boards

fibre·glass (*especially US* **fiber-**) /ˈfaɪbəɡlɑːs; *NAmE* ˈfaɪbərɡlæs/ (*BrE* also ˌ**glass** ˈ**fibre**) (*US* also ˌ**glass** ˈ**fiber**) *noun* [U] a strong light material made from glass fibres and plastic, used for making boats, etc.

ˌ**fibre** ˈ**optics** (*especially US* ˌ**fiber** ˈ**optics**) *noun* [U] the use of thin fibres of glass, etc. for sending information in the form of light signals ▸ ˌ**fibre-**ˈ**optic** (*especially US* ˌ**fiber-**ˈ**optic**) *adj.*: *fibre-optic cables*

fi·brin /ˈfaɪbrɪn; ˈfɪb-/ *noun* [U] (*biology*) a PROTEIN that stops blood from flowing or being lost from a wound

fi·brino·gen /faɪˈbrɪnədʒən; fɪˈb-/ *noun* [U] (*biology*) a PROTEIN in the blood from which fibrin is produced

fibro /ˈfaɪbrəʊ; *NAmE* -oʊ/ *noun* (*pl.* **-os**) (*AustralE*) **1** [U] a mixture of sand, CEMENT, and plant FIBRES, used as a building material **2** [C] a house that is built mainly of such material

fi·broid /ˈfaɪbrɔɪd/ *noun* (*medical*) a mass of cells that form a lump, usually found in the wall of a woman's UTERUS

fi·broma /faɪˈbrəʊmə; *NAmE* -broʊ-/ *noun* (*medical*) a harmless lump that grows inside the body

fi·brous /ˈfaɪbrəs/ *adj.* [usually before noun] (*technical*) made of many fibres; looking like fibres: *fibrous tissue*

fib·ula /ˈfɪbjələ/ *noun* (*pl.* **fibu·lae** or **fibu·las**) (*anatomy*) the outer bone of the two bones in the lower part of the leg between the knee and the ankle ➲ VISUAL VOCAB page V48 ➲ see also TIBIA

fickle /ˈfɪkl/ *adj.* (*disapproving*) **1** changing often and suddenly: *The weather here is notoriously fickle.* ◇ *the fickle world of fashion* **2** (of a person) often changing their mind in an unreasonable way so that you cannot rely on them: *a fickle friend* ▸ **fickle·ness** *noun* [U]: *the fickleness of the English climate*

fic·tion /ˈfɪkʃn/ *noun* **1** [U] a type of literature that describes imaginary people and events, not real ones: *a work of popular fiction* ◇ *historical/romantic fiction* **OPP** **non-fiction** ➲ COLLOCATIONS at LITERATURE ➲ see also SCIENCE FICTION **2** [C, U] a thing that is invented or imagined and is not true: *For years he managed to keep up the fiction that he was not married.* **IDM** see TRUTH

fic·tion·al /ˈfɪkʃənl/ *adj.* not real or true; existing only in stories; connected with fiction: *fictional characters* ◇ *a fictional account of life on a desert island* ◇ *fictional techniques* **OPP** **real-life**

fic·tion·al·ize (*BrE* also **-ise**) /ˈfɪkʃənəlaɪz/ *verb* [usually passive] **~ sth** to write a book or make a film/movie about a true story, but changing some of the details, characters, etc: *a fictionalized account of his childhood*

fic·ti·tious /fɪkˈtɪʃəs/ *adj.* invented by sb rather than true: *All the places and characters in my novel are fictitious* (= they do not exist in real life).

fid·dle /ˈfɪdl/ *verb, noun*

■ ***verb*** **1** [I] **~ (with sth)** to keep touching or moving sth with your hands, especially because you are bored or nervous: *He was fiddling with his keys while he talked to me.* **2** [T] **~ sth** (*informal*) to change the details or figures of sth in order to try to get money dishonestly, or gain an advantage: *to fiddle the accounts* ◇ *She* ***fiddled the books*** (= changed a company's financial records) *while working as an accountant.* **3** [I] (*informal*) to play music on the VIOLIN **PHR V** ˌ**fiddle a**ˈ**bout/a**ˈ**round** to spend your time doing things that are not important ˌ**fiddle a**ˈ**bout/a**ˈ**round with sth** | ˈ**fiddle with sth** **1** to keep touching sth or making small changes to sth because you are not satisfied with it: *I've been fiddling about with this design for ages.* **2** to touch or move the parts of sth in order to try to change it or repair it: *Who's been fiddling with the TV again?*

■ ***noun*** (*informal*) **1** [C] = VIOLIN **2** [C] (*BrE*) something that is done dishonestly to get money **SYN** **fraud**: *an* ***insurance/tax, etc. fiddle*** **3** [sing.] (*BrE*) an act of moving sth or adjusting sth in order to make it work **4** [sing.] (*BrE*) something that is difficult to do

IDM **be on the** ˈ**fiddle** (*BrE*) to be doing sth dishonest to get money **play second** ˈ**fiddle (to sb/sth)** to be treated as less important than sb/sth; to have a less important position than sb/sth else ➲ more at FIT *adj.*

fid·dler /ˈfɪdlə(r)/ *noun* a person who plays the VIOLIN, especially to play FOLK MUSIC

fiddle·sticks /ˈfɪdlstɪks/ *exclamation* (*old-fashioned, informal*) used to say that you disagree with sb

fid·dling /ˈfɪdlɪŋ/ *adj.* [usually before noun] (*informal*) small, unimportant and often annoying

fid·dly /ˈfɪdli/ *adj.* (*BrE, informal*) (**fid·dlier, fid·dli·est**) difficult to do or use because small objects are involved: *Changing a fuse is one of those fiddly jobs I hate.*

fi·del·ity /fɪˈdeləti/ *noun* [U] **1** **~ (to sth)** (*formal*) the quality of being loyal to sb/sth: *fidelity to your principles* **2** **~ (to sb)** the quality of being faithful to your husband, wife or partner by not having a sexual relationship with anyone else: ***marital/sexual fidelity*** **OPP** **infidelity** **3** **~ (of sth) (to sth)** (*formal*) the quality of being accurate: *the fidelity of the translation to the original text* ➲ see also HIGH FIDELITY

fidget /ˈfɪdʒɪt/ *verb, noun*

■ ***verb*** [I] **~ (with sth)** to keep moving your body, your hands or your feet because you are nervous, bored, excited, etc: *Sit still and stop fidgeting!*

■ ***noun*** a person who is always fidgeting

fidgety /ˈfɪdʒɪti/ *adj.* (*informal*) (of a person) unable to remain still or quiet, usually because of being bored or nervous **SYN** **restless**

fidu·ciary /fɪˈdjuːʃəri; *NAmE* also fɪˈduːʃieri/ *adj., noun* (*law*)

■ ***adj.*** involving trust, especially in a situation where a person or company controls money or property belonging to others: *the company's fiduciary duty to its shareholders*

■ ***noun*** (*pl.* **-ies**) a person or company that is in a position of trust, especially when it involves controlling money or property belonging to others

fief /fiːf/ (also **fief·dom** /ˈfiːfdəm/) *noun* **1** (*law*) (*old use*) an area of land, especially a rented area for which the payment is work, not money **2** an area or a situation in which sb has control or influence: *She considers the office as her own private fiefdom.*

field 0‑w /fiːld/ *noun, verb*

■ ***noun***

▸ AREA OF LAND **1** 0‑w [C] an area of land in the country used for growing crops or keeping animals in, usually surrounded by a fence, etc: *People were working in the fields.* ◇ *a ploughed field* ◇ *a field of wheat* ◇ *We camped in a field near the village.* ➲ COLLOCATIONS at FARMING ➲ VISUAL VOCAB page V2 **2** [C] (usually in compounds) an area of land used for the purpose mentioned: *a landing field* ◇ *a medal for bravery in the field (of battle)* ➲ see also AIRFIELD, BATTLEFIELD, MINEFIELD **3** 0‑w [C] (usually in compounds) a large area of land covered with the thing mentioned; an area from which the thing mentioned is obtained: *ice fields* ◇ *gas fields* ➲ see also COALFIELD, GOLDFIELD, OILFIELD, SNOWFIELD

▸ SUBJECT/ACTIVITY **4** 0‑w [C] a particular subject or activity that sb works in or is interested in **SYN** **area**: *famous* ***in the field of*** *music* ◇ *All of them are experts in their chosen field.* ◇ *This discovery has opened up a whole new field of research.*

▸ PRACTICAL WORK **5** [C] (usually used as an adjective) the fact of people doing practical work or study, rather than working in a library or laboratory: *a **field study/investigation** ◇ **field research/methods** ◇ essential reading for those working **in the field*** ➲ see also FIELD TRIP, FIELDWORK

▸ IN SPORT **6** 🔑 (*BrE* also **pitch**) [C] (usually in compounds) an area of land used for playing a sport on: *a **baseball/rugby/football, etc. field** ◇ a sports field ◇ Today they **take the field*** (= go on to the field to play a game) *against county champions Essex.* ➲ see also PLAYING FIELD **7** (in CRICKET and BASEBALL) [sing.+ sing./pl. v.] the team that is trying to catch the ball rather than hit it **8** [sing.+ sing./pl. v.] all the people or animals competing in a particular sports event: *The field includes three world-record holders.*

▸ IN BUSINESS **9** [sing.+ sing./pl. v.] all the people or products competing in a particular area of business: *They **lead the field** in home entertainment systems.*

▸ PHYSICS **10** [C] (usually in compounds) an area within which the force mentioned has an effect: *the earth's gravitational field ◇ an electro-magnetic field*

▸ COMPUTING **11** [C] part of a record that is a separate item of data: *You will need to create separate fields for first name, surname and address.*

IDM **leave the field 'clear for sb | leave sb in possession of the 'field** to enable sb to be successful in a particular area of activity because other people or groups have given up competing with them **play the 'field** (*informal*) to have sexual relationships with a lot of different people

■ *verb*

▸ CANDIDATE/TEAM **1** [T] **~ sb/sth** to provide a candidate, speaker, team, etc. to represent you in an election, a competition, etc: *Each of the main parties fielded more than 300 candidates. ◇ England fielded a young side in the World Cup.*

▸ IN CRICKET/BASEBALL **2** [I] to be the person or the team that catches the ball and throws it back after sb has hit it: *He won the toss and chose to field first.* **3** [T] **~ sth** to catch the ball and throw it back: *He fielded the ball expertly.*

▸ QUESTIONS **4** [T] **~ sth** to receive and deal with questions or comments: *The BBC had to field more than 300 phone calls after last night's programme.*

'field day (*NAmE*) (*BrE* **'sports day**) *noun* a special day at school when there are no classes and children compete in sports events

IDM **have a 'field day** (*NAmE*, *BrE*) to be given the opportunity to do sth that you enjoy, especially sth that other people do not approve of: *The tabloid press had a field day with the latest government scandal.*

field·er /'fiːldə(r)/ *noun* (*BrE* also **fields·man**) (in CRICKET and BASEBALL) a member of the team that is trying to catch the ball rather than hit it

'field event *noun* [usually pl.] a sport done by ATHLETES that is not a race, for example jumping or throwing the JAVELIN ➲ VISUAL VOCAB page V38 ➲ compare TRACK EVENT

'field glasses *noun* [pl.] = BINOCULARS

'field goal *noun* **1** (in AMERICAN FOOTBALL or RUGBY) a goal scored by kicking the ball over the bar of the goal **2** (in BASKETBALL) a goal scored by throwing the ball through the net during normal play

'field hand *noun* (*NAmE*) = FARMHAND

'field hockey (*NAmE*) (*BrE* **hockey**) *noun* [U] a game played on a field by two teams of 11 players, with curved sticks and a small hard ball. Teams try to hit the ball into the other team's goal. ➲ VISUAL VOCAB page V36

'field hospital *noun* a temporary hospital near a BATTLEFIELD

'field house *noun* (*NAmE*) **1** a building at a sports field where people can change their clothes, have a shower, etc. **2** a building where sports events are held, with seats for people to watch

field·ing /'fiːldɪŋ/ *noun* [U] (in CRICKET and BASEBALL) the activity of catching and returning the ball

ˌfield 'marshal *noun* (*abbr.* FM) an officer of the highest rank in the British army: *Field Marshal Montgomery*

'field officer *noun* **1** a person in a company or other organization whose job involves practical work in a particular area or region **2** an officer of high rank in the army (= a MAJOR, LIEUTENANT COLONEL or COLONEL)

ˌfield of 'fire *noun* (*pl.* **fields of fire**) the area that you can hit when shooting from a particular position

ˌfield of 'vision (also **ˌfield of 'view** or *technical* **ˌvisual 'field**) *noun* (*pl.* **fields of vision/view, visual fields**) the total amount of space that you can see from a particular point without moving your head

fields·man /'fiːldzmən/ *noun* (*pl.* **-men** /-mən/) (*BrE*) = FIELDER

'field sports *noun* [pl.] (*BrE*) outdoor sports such as hunting, fishing and shooting

'field-test *verb* **~ sth** to test sth, such as a piece of equipment, in the place where it will be used ▸ **'field test** *noun*: *Laboratory and field tests have been conducted.*

'field trip *noun* a journey made by a group of people, often students, to study sth in its natural environment: *We went on a geology field trip.*

field·work /'fiːldwɜːk; *NAmE* -wɜːrk/ *noun* [U] research or study that is done in the real world rather than in a library or laboratory ▸ **field·worker** *noun*

fiend /fiːnd/ *noun* **1** a very cruel or unpleasant person **2** (*informal*) (used after another noun) a person who is very interested in the thing mentioned SYN **fanatic**: *a crossword fiend* **3** an evil spirit

fiend·ish /'fiːndɪʃ/ *adj.* [usually before noun] **1** cruel and unpleasant: *a fiendish act ◇ shrieks of fiendish laughter* **2** (*informal*) extremely clever and complicated, often in an unpleasant way: *a puzzle of fiendish complexity ◇ a fiendish plan* **3** (*informal*) extremely difficult: *a fiendish problem*

fiend·ish·ly /'fiːndɪʃli/ *adv.* (*informal*) very; extremely: ***fiendishly clever/complicated***

fierce /fɪəs; *NAmE* fɪrs/ *adj.* (**fier·cer**, **fier·cest**) **1** (especially of people or animals) angry and aggressive in a way that is frightening: *a fierce dog ◇ Two fierce eyes glared at them. ◇ He suddenly looked fierce. ◇ She spoke in a fierce whisper.* **2** (especially of actions or emotions) showing strong feelings or a lot of activity, often in a way that is violent: *fierce loyalty ◇ the scene of fierce fighting ◇ He launched a fierce attack on the Democrats. ◇ Competition from abroad became fiercer in the 1990s.* **3** (of weather conditions or temperatures) very strong in a way that could cause damage: *fierce wind ◇ the fierce heat of the flames* ▸ **fierce·ly** *adv.*: *'Let go of me,' she said fiercely. ◇ fiercely competitive ◇ The aircraft was burning fiercely.* **fierce·ness** *noun* [U]

IDM **something 'fierce** (*NAmE*, *informal*) very much; more than usual: *I sure do miss you something fierce!*

fiery /'faɪəri/ *adj.* [usually before noun] (**fier·ier**, **fieri·est**) **1** looking like fire; consisting of fire: *fiery red hair ◇ The sun was now sinking, a fiery ball of light in the west.* **2** quickly or easily becoming angry: *She has a **fiery temper**. ◇ a fiery young man* **3** showing strong emotions, especially anger SYN **passionate**: *a fiery look* **4** (of food or drink) causing a part of your body to feel as if it is burning: *a fiery Mexican dish*

fi·esta /fi'estə/ *noun* (from *Spanish*) a public event when people celebrate and are entertained with music and dancing, usually connected with a religious festival in countries where the people speak Spanish

FIFA /'fiːfə/ *abbr.* (from *French*) Fédération Internationale de Football Association (the international organization that controls the sport of football (SOCCER))

fife /faɪf/ *noun* a musical instrument like a small FLUTE that plays high notes and is used with drums in military music

fif·teen 🔑 /ˌfɪf'tiːn/ **1** 🔑 *number* 15 **2** *noun* a team of RUGBY UNION players: *He's in the first fifteen.* ▸ **fif·teenth** 🔑 /ˌfɪf'tiːnθ/ *ordinal number, noun* HELP There are examples of how to use ordinal numbers at the entry for **fifth**.

fifth 0‑m /fɪfθ/ *ordinal number, noun*
■ ***ordinal number*** 0‑m 5th: *Today is the fifth (of May).* ◇ *the fifth century BC* ◇ *It's her fifth birthday.* ◇ *My office is on the fifth floor.* ◇ *It's the fifth time that I've been to America.* ◇ *Her mother had just given birth to another child, her fifth.* ◇ *the world's fifth-largest oil exporter* ◇ *He finished fifth in the race.* ◇ *Edward V* (= Edward the Fifth)
■ ***noun*** 0‑m each of five equal parts of sth: *She cut the cake into fifths.* ◇ *He gave her a fifth of the total amount.*
IDM **take/plead the 'fifth** (*US*) to make use of the right to refuse to answer questions in court about a crime, because you may give information which will make it seem that you are guilty ORIGIN From the **Fifth Amendment** of the US Constitution, which guarantees this right.

F

ˌfifth 'column *noun* a group of people working secretly to help the enemy of the country or organization they are in ▸ **ˌfifth 'columnist** *noun*

ˌfifth gene'ration *adj.* (*computing*) relating to a type of computer that is starting to be developed which uses ARTIFICIAL INTELLIGENCE

fifth·ly /'fɪfθli/ *adv.* used to introduce the fifth of a list of points you want to make in a speech or piece of writing: *Fifthly, we need to consider the effect on the local population.*

fifty 0‑m /'fɪfti/
1 0‑m *number* 50 **2** *noun* **the fifties** [pl.] numbers, years or temperatures from 50 to 59: *She was born in the fifties.*
▸ **fif·ti·eth** 0‑m /'fɪftiəθ/ *ordinal number, noun* HELP There are examples of how to use ordinal numbers at the entry for **fifth**.
IDM **in your 'fifties** between the ages of 50 and 59: *He retired in his fifties.*

ˌfifty-'fifty *adj., adv.* (*informal*) divided equally between two people, groups or possibilities: *Costs are to be shared on **a fifty-fifty basis** between the government and local businesses.* ◇ *She has **a fifty-fifty chance** of winning* (= an equal chance of winning or losing). ◇ *Let's split this fifty-fifty.*

ˌfifty 'pence (also **ˌfifty pence 'piece, 50p** /ˌfɪfti 'piː/) *noun* a British coin worth 50 pence: *Put a fifty pence in the machine.* ◇ *Have you got a 50p?*

fig /fɪg/ *noun* a soft sweet fruit that is full of small seeds and often eaten dried: *a fig tree* ➲ VISUAL VOCAB page V26
IDM **not care/give a 'fig (for sb/sth)** (*old-fashioned, BrE, informal*) not to care at all about sth; to think that sth is not important

fig. *abbr.* **1** (in writing) FIGURE: *See fig. 3.* **2** (in writing) FIGURATIVE(LY)

fight 0‑m /faɪt/ *verb, noun*
■ ***verb*** (**fought, fought** /fɔːt/)
▸ IN WAR/BATTLE **1** 0‑m [I, T] to take part in a war or battle against an enemy: *soldiers trained to fight* ◇ *He fought in Vietnam.* ◇ **~ against sb** *My grandfather fought against the Fascists in Spain.* ◇ **~ sb/sth** *to **fight a war/battle*** ◇ *They gathered soldiers to fight the invading army.* ➲ COLLOCATIONS at WAR
▸ STRUGGLE/HIT **2** 0‑m [I, T] **~ (sb)** to struggle physically with sb: *My little brothers are always fighting.* ◇ *She'll **fight like a tiger** to protect her children.*
▸ IN CONTEST **3** 0‑m [T, I] to take part in a contest against sb: **~ sb/sth (for sth)** *to **fight an election/a campaign*** ◇ **~ for sth** *She's fighting for a place in the national team.*
▸ OPPOSE **4** 0‑m [T, I] **~ (sth)** to try hard to stop, deal with or oppose sth bad: *to **fight racism/corruption/poverty, etc.*** ◇ *Workers are fighting the decision to close the factory.* ◇ *The fire crews had problems fighting the blaze.* ◇ *We will fight for as long as it takes.*
▸ TRY TO GET/DO STH **5** [I, T] to try very hard to get sth or to achieve sth: **~ (for sth)** *He's still fighting for compensation after the accident.* ◇ **~ your way...** *She gradually fought her way to the top of the company.* ◇ **~ to do sth** *Doctors fought for more than six hours to save his life.* ➲ SYNONYMS at CAMPAIGN
▸ ARGUE **6** [I] **~ (with sb) (about/over sth)** to have an argument with sb about sth: *It's a trivial matter and not worth fighting about.*
▸ IN BOXING **7** [I, T] **~ (sb)** to take part in a BOXING match: *Doctors fear he may never fight again.*
▸ LAW **8** [T, I] to try to get what you want in court: **~ (sb) for sth** *He fought his wife for custody of the children.* ◇ **~ sth** *I'm determined to fight the case.*
▸ **fight·ing** 0‑m *noun* [U]: *Fighting broke out in three districts of the city last night.* ◇ *outbreaks of street fighting*
IDM **fight your/sb's 'corner** (*BrE*) to defend your/sb's position against other people **fight ˌfire with 'fire** to use similar methods in a fight or an argument to those your opponent is using **ˌfight for (your) 'life** to make a great effort to stay alive, especially when you are badly injured or seriously ill **a ˌfighting 'chance** a small chance of being successful if a great effort is made **fighting 'fit** extremely fit or healthy **fighting 'spirit** a feeling that you are ready to fight very hard for sth or to try sth difficult **fighting 'talk** comments or remarks that show that you are ready to fight very hard for sth: *What we want from the management is fighting talk.* **fight a ˌlosing 'battle** to try to do sth that you will probably never succeed in doing **fight 'shy of sth/of doing sth** to be unwilling to accept sth or do sth, and to try to avoid it: *Successive governments have fought shy of such measures.* **fight to the 'death/'finish** to fight until one of the two people or groups is dead, or until one person or group defeats the other **fight ˌtooth and 'nail** to fight in a very determined way for what you want: *The residents are fighting tooth and nail to stop the new development.* **fight your own battles** to be able to win an argument or get what you want without anyone's help: *I wouldn't get involved—he's old enough to fight his own battles.* ➲ more at LIVE[1]
PHR V **ˌfight 'back (against sb/sth)** to resist strongly or attack sb who has attacked you: *Don't let them bully you. Fight back!* ◇ *It is time to fight back against street crime.* **ˌfight sth↔'back/'down** to try hard not to do or show sth, especially not to show your feelings: *I was fighting back the tears.* ◇ *He fought down his disgust.* **ˌfight sb/sth↔'off** to resist sb/sth by fighting against them/it: *The jeweller was stabbed as he tried to fight the robbers off.* **ˌfight 'out sth | ˌfight it 'out** to fight or argue until an argument has been settled: *The conflict is still being fought out.* ◇ *They hadn't reached any agreement so we left them to fight it out.*

Synonyms

fight

clash • brawl • struggle • scuffle

These are all words for a situation in which people try to defeat each other using physical force.

fight a situation in which two or more people try to defeat each other using physical force: *He got into a fight with a man in the bar.*

clash (*journalism*) a short fight between two groups of people: *Clashes broke out between police and demonstrators.*

brawl a noisy and violent fight involving a group of people, usually in a public place: *a drunken brawl in a bar*

struggle a fight between two people or groups of people, especially when one of them is trying to escape, or to get sth from the other: *There were no signs of a struggle at the murder scene.*

scuffle a short and not very violent fight or struggle: *He was involved in a scuffle with a photographer.*

PATTERNS
- a fight/clash/brawl/struggle/scuffle **over** sth
- **in** a fight/brawl/struggle/scuffle
- a **violent** fight/clash/struggle
- to **be in/get into/be involved in** a fight/clash/brawl/scuffle
- a fight/clash/brawl/scuffle **breaks out**

■ ***noun***
▸ STRUGGLE **1** 0‑m [C] a struggle against sb/sth using physical

force: ~ (**with sb/sth**) *He got into a fight with a man in the bar.* ◇ *a* ***street/gang fight*** ◇ ~ (**between A and B**) *A* ***fight broke out*** *between rival groups of fans.* ◇ *a world title fight* (= fighting as a sport, especially BOXING)

▸ TRYING TO GET/DO STH **2** ⊶ [sing.] the work of trying to destroy, prevent or achieve sth: ~ (**against sth**) *the fight against crime* ◇ ~ (**for sth**) *a fight for survival* ◇ ~ (**to do sth**) *Workers won their fight to stop compulsory redundancies.*

▸ COMPETITION **3** [sing.] a competition or an act of competing, especially in a sport: *The team* ***put up a good fight*** (= they played well) *but were finally beaten.* ◇ *She now* ***has a fight on her hands*** (= will have to play very well) *to make it through to the next round.* ➲ SYNONYMS at CAMPAIGN

▸ ARGUMENT **4** ⊶ [C] ~ (**with sb**) (**over/about sth**) (*especially NAmE*) an argument about sth: *Did you have a fight with him?* ◇ *We had a fight over money.*

▸ BATTLE/WAR **5** [C] a battle, especially for a particular place or position: *In the fight for Lemburg, the Austrians were defeated.*

▸ DESIRE TO FIGHT **6** [U] the desire or ability to keep fighting for sth: *In spite of many defeats, they still had plenty of fight left in them.*

IDM **a fight to the ˈfinish** a sports competition, election, etc. between sides that are so equal in ability that they continue fighting very hard until the end ➲ more at PICK *v.*, SPOIL *v.*

fight·back /ˈfaɪtbæk/ *noun* [usually sing.] (*BrE*) an effort by a person, group or team to get back to a strong position that they have lost

fight·er /ˈfaɪtə(r)/ *noun* **1** (also ˈ**fighter plane**) a fast military plane designed to attack other aircraft: *a* ***jet fighter*** ◇ *a* ***fighter pilot*** ◇ *fighter bases* ➲ VISUAL VOCAB page V43 **2** a person who fights ➲ see also FIREFIGHTER, FREEDOM FIGHTER, PRIZEFIGHTER **3** (*approving*) a person who does not give up hope or admit that they are defeated

ˈfighter-bomber *noun* a military plane that can fight other planes in the air and also drop bombs

ˈfig leaf *noun* **1** a leaf of a FIG tree, traditionally used for covering the sex organs of naked bodies in paintings and on statues **2** a thing that is used to hide an embarrassing fact or situation

fig·ment /ˈfɪɡmənt/ *noun*

IDM **a figment of sb's imagiˈnation** something that sb has imagined and that does not really exist

fig·ura·tive /ˈfɪɡərətɪv; *NAmE* also ˈfɪɡjə-/ *adj.* [usually before noun] **1** (of language, words, phrases, etc.) used in a way that is different from the usual meaning, in order to create a particular mental picture. For example, 'He exploded with rage' shows a figurative use of the verb 'explode'. ➲ compare LITERAL, METAPHORICAL **2** (of paintings, art, etc.) showing people, animals and objects as they really look: *a figurative artist* ➲ compare ABSTRACT ▸ **fig·ura·tive·ly** *adv.*: *She is, figuratively speaking, holding a gun to his head.*

fig·ure ⊶ /ˈfɪɡə(r); *NAmE* ˈfɪɡjər/ *noun, verb*

■ ***noun***

▸ NUMBERS **1** ⊶ [C, usually pl.] a number representing a particular amount, especially one given in official information: *the latest* ***trade/sales/unemployment, etc. figures*** ◇ *By 2009, this figure had risen to 14 million.* ◇ *Experts put the real figure at closer to 75%.* **2** ⊶ [C] a symbol rather than a word representing one of the numbers between 0 and 9: *Write the figure '7' on the board.* ◇ *a six-figure salary* (= over 100 000 pounds or dollars) ◇ *His salary is now in six figures.* ➲ see also DOUBLE FIGURES, SINGLE FIGURES **3** ⊶ **figures** [pl.] (*informal*) the area of mathematics that deals with adding, multiplying, etc. numbers SYN **arithmetic**: *Are you any good at figures?* ◇ *I'm afraid I don't* ***have a head for figures*** (= I am not good at adding, etc.).

▸ PERSON **4** ⊶ [C] a person of the type mentioned: *a* ***leading figure*** *in the music industry* ◇ *a political figure* ◇ *a figure of authority* ➲ see also FATHER FIGURE, MOTHER FIGURE **5** ⊶ [C] the shape of a person seen from a distance or not clearly: *a tall figure in black*

▸ SHAPE OF BODY **6** ⊶ [C] the shape of the human body, especially a woman's body that is attractive: *She's always had a good figure.* ◇ *I'm watching my figure* (= trying not to get fat). ➲ COLLOCATIONS at PHYSICAL

▸ IN PAINTING/STORY **7** [C] a person or an animal in a drawing, painting, etc, or in a story: *The central figure in the painting is the artist's daughter.*

▸ STATUE **8** [C] a statue of a person or an animal: *a bronze figure of a horse*

▸ PICTURE/DIAGRAM **9** [C] (*abbr.* **fig.**) a picture, diagram, etc. in a book, that is referred to by a number: *The results are illustrated in figure 3 opposite.*

▸ GEOMETRY **10** [C] a particular shape formed by lines or surfaces: *a five-sided figure* ◇ *a solid figure*

▸ MOVEMENT ON ICE **11** [C] a pattern or series of movements performed on ice

IDM **be/become a figure of ˈfun** to be/become sb that other people laugh at **cut a... ˈfigure** (of a person) to have a particular appearance: *He cut a striking figure in his white dinner jacket.* **put a figure on sth** to say the exact price or number of sth ➲ more at FACT

■ ***verb***

▸ BE IMPORTANT **1** ⊶ [I] to be part of a process, situation, etc. especially an important part SYN **feature**: *My feelings about the matter didn't seem to figure at all.* ◇ ~ (**as sth**) (**in/on/among sth**) *Do I still figure in your plans?* ◇ *The question of the peace settlement is likely to* ***figure prominently*** *in the talks.* ◇ *It did not figure high on her list of priorities.*

▸ THINK/DECIDE **2** [T] (*informal*) to think or decide that sth will happen or is true: ~ (**that**)... *I figured* (*that*) *if I took the night train, I could be in Scotland by morning.* ◇ *We figured the sensible thing to do was to wait.* ◇ ~ **sth** *That's what I figured.* ◇ ~ **why, whether, etc...** *He tried to figure why she had come.*

▸ CALCULATE **3** [T] ~ **sth** (**at sth**) (*NAmE*) to calculate an amount or the cost of sth: *We figured the attendance at 150 000.*

IDM **go ˈfigure** (*NAmE, informal*) used to say that you do not understand the reason for sth, or that you do not want to give an explanation for sth because you think it is obvious: *People are more aware of the risks of smoking nowadays, but more young women are smoking than ever. Go figure!* **it/that figures** used to say that sth was expected or seems logical: *'John called in sick.' 'That figures, he wasn't feeling well yesterday.'* ◇ (*disapproving*) *'She was late again.' 'Yes, that figures.'*

PHR V **ˈfigure on sth** | **ˈfigure on** (**sb/sth**) **doing sth** to plan sth or to do sth; to expect sth (to happen) SYN **plan on**: *I hadn't figured on getting home so late.* **ˌfigure sb/sth↔ˈout 1** ⊶ to think about sb/sth until you understand them/it SYN **work out**: *We couldn't figure her out.* ◇ ~ **how, what, etc...** *I can't figure out how to do this.* **2** ⊶ to calculate an amount or the cost of sth SYN **work out**: ~ **how, what, etc...** *Have you figured out how much the trip will cost?*

fig·ured /ˈfɪɡəd; *NAmE* ˈfɪɡjərd/ *adj.* [only before noun] (*technical*) decorated with a small pattern: *figured pottery*

fig·ure·head /ˈfɪɡəhed; *NAmE* -ɡjərh-/ *noun* **1** a person who is in a high position in a country or an organization but who has no real power or authority **2** a large wooden statue, usually representing a woman, that used to be fixed to the front end of a ship

ˈfigure-hugging *adj.* [usually before noun] (of a piece of clothing) tight in an attractive way that shows the shape of a woman's body

ˌfigure of ˈeight (*BrE*) (*NAmE* **ˌfigure ˈeight**) *noun* (*pl.* **figures of eight, figure eights**) a pattern or movement that looks like the shape of the number 8

ˌfigure of ˈspeech *noun* (*pl.* **figures of speech**) a word or phrase used in a different way from its usual meaning in order to create a particular mental picture or effect

ˈfigure-skating *noun* [U] a type of ICE SKATING in which you cut patterns in the ice and do jumps and spins ➲ compare SPEED SKATING

fig·ur·ine /ˈfɪɡəriːn; *NAmE* ˌfɪɡjəˈriːn/ *noun* a small statue of a person or an animal used as a decorative object

F

fila·ment /ˈfɪləmənt/ *noun* **1** a thin wire in a LIGHT BULB that produces light when electricity is passed through it **2** (*technical*) a long thin piece of sth that looks like a thread: ***glass/metal filaments***

fil·bert /ˈfɪlbət; *NAmE* -bərt/ *noun* (*especially NAmE*) = HAZELNUT

filch /fɪltʃ/ *verb* **~ sth** (*informal*) to steal sth, especially sth small or not very valuable SYN **pinch**

file 0‑w AW /faɪl/ *noun, verb*

■ ***noun*** **1** 0‑w a box or folded piece of card for keeping loose papers together and in order: *a box file* ◇ *A stack of files awaited me on my desk.* ➲ VISUAL VOCAB page V56 **2** 0‑w a collection of information stored together in a computer, under a particular name: *to **access/copy/create/delete/download/save a file*** ◇ *Every file on the same disk must have a different name.* ➲ see also PDF **3** 0‑w a file and the information it contains, for example about a particular person or subject: *secret police files* ◇ *Your application will be kept **on file*** (= in a file, to be used later). ◇ **~ on sb** *to **have/open/keep a** confidential **file** on sb* ◇ *Police have re-opened the file* (= have started collecting information again) *on the missing girl.* **4** a metal tool with a rough surface for cutting or shaping hard substances or for making them smooth ➲ VISUAL VOCAB page V17 ➲ see also NAIL FILE **5** a line of people or things, one behind the other: *They set off **in file** behind the teacher.*

IDM **(in) single ˈfile** (also *old-fashioned* **(in) Indian file**) (in) one line, one behind the other: *They made their way in single file along the cliff path.*

■ ***verb*** **1** [T] to put and keep documents, etc. in a particular place and in a particular order so that you can find them easily; to put a document into a file: **~ sth (+ adv./prep.)** *The forms should be filed alphabetically.* ◇ *Please file it in my 'Research' file.* ◇ **~ sth away** *I filed the letters away in a drawer.* **2** [I, T] (*law*) to present sth so that it can be officially recorded and dealt with: **~ for sth** *to file for divorce* ◇ **~ sth** *to **file a claim/complaint/petition/lawsuit*** ◇ **~ to do sth** *He filed to divorce his wife.* **3** [T] **~ sth** (of a journalist) to send a report or a story to your employer **4** [I] + **adv./prep.** to walk in a line of people, one after the other, in a particular direction: *The doors of the museum opened and the visitors began to file in.* **5** [T] **~ sth (away/down, etc.)** to cut or shape sth or make sth smooth using a file: *to file your nails*

ˈfile cabinet (*NAmE*) (*BrE* **ˈfiling cabinet**) *noun* a piece of office furniture with deep drawers for storing files ➲ VISUAL VOCAB page V56

ˈfile clerk (*NAmE*) (*BrE* **ˈfiling clerk**) *noun* a person whose job is to FILE letters, etc. and do general office tasks

file·name /ˈfaɪlneɪm/ *noun* (*computing*) a name given to a computer file in order to identify it

ˈfile sharing *noun* [U] the practice of sharing computer files with other people over the Internet or another computer network: *Illegal music file-sharing sites have spread through the Net.*

filet *noun* (*NAmE*) = FILLET

fil·ial /ˈfɪliəl/ *adj.* [usually before noun] (*formal*) connected with the way children behave towards their parents: ***filial affection/duty***

fili·bus·ter /ˈfɪlɪbʌstə(r)/ *noun* (*especially NAmE*) a long speech made in a parliament in order to delay a vote ▸ **fili·bus·ter** *verb* [I]

fili·gree /ˈfɪlɪgriː/ *noun* [U] delicate decoration made from gold or silver wire

fil·ing /ˈfaɪlɪŋ/ *noun* **1** [U] the act of putting documents, letters, etc. into a file **2** [C] (*especially NAmE*) something that is placed in an official record: *a bankruptcy filing* **3 filings** [pl.] very small pieces of metal, made when a larger piece of metal is filed: *iron filings*

ˈfiling cabinet (*BrE*) (*NAmE* **ˈfile cabinet**) *noun* a piece of office furniture with deep drawers for storing files ➲ VISUAL VOCAB page V56

ˈfiling clerk (*BrE*) (*NAmE* **ˈfile clerk**) *noun* a person whose job is to FILE letters, etc. and do general office tasks

Fi·li·pino /ˌfɪlɪˈpiːnəʊ; *NAmE* -noʊ/ *noun, adj.*

■ ***noun*** (*pl.* -os) **1** [C] a person from the Philippines **2** [U] the language of the Philippines

■ ***adj.*** connected with the Philippines, its people or their language

fill 0‑w /fɪl/ *verb, noun*

■ ***verb***

▸ MAKE FULL **1** 0‑w [T, I] to make sth full of sth; to become full of sth: **~ sth** *Please fill this glass for me.* ◇ *to fill a vacuum/void* ◇ *The school is **filled to capacity**.* ◇ *Smoke filled the room.* ◇ *The wind filled the sails.* ◇ *A Disney film can always fill cinemas* (= attract a lot of people to see it). ◇ **~ sth with sth** *to fill a hole with earth/a bucket with water* ◇ **~ sth + adj.** *Fill a pan half full of water.* ◇ **~ (with sth)** *The room was filling quickly.* ◇ *Her eyes suddenly filled with tears.* ◇ *The sails filled with wind.*

▸ BLOCK HOLE **2** 0‑w [T] **~ sth (with sth)** to block a hole with a substance: *The crack in the wall had been filled with plaster.* ◇ *I need to have two teeth filled* (= to have FILLINGS put in them). ◇ (*figurative*) *The product has **filled a gap** in the market.*

▸ WITH FEELING **3** 0‑w [T] **~ sb (with sth)** to make sb have a strong feeling: *We were all filled with admiration for his achievements.*

▸ WITH SMELL/SOUND/LIGHT **4** 0‑w [T] **~ sth (with sth)** if a smell, sound or light **fills** a place, it is very strong, loud or bright and easy to notice

▸ -FILLED **5** (in adjectives) full of the thing mentioned: *a smoke-filled room* ◇ *a fun-filled day*

▸ A NEED **6** [T] **~ sth** to stop people from continuing to want or need sth: *More nurseries will be built to fill the need for high-quality child care.*

▸ JOB **7** [T] **~ sth** to do a job, have a role or position, etc: *He fills the post satisfactorily* (= performs his duties well). ◇ *The team needs someone to fill the role of manager very soon.* **8** [T] **~ sth** to appoint sb to a job: *The vacancy has already been filled.*

▸ TIME **9** [T] **~ sth (up)** to use up a particular period of time doing sth: *How do you fill your day now that you've retired?*

▸ WITH FOOD **10** [T] **~ sb/yourself (up) (with sth)** (*informal*) to make sb/yourself feel unable to eat any more: *The kids filled themselves with snacks.*

▸ AN ORDER **11** [T] **~ sth** if sb **fills** an order or a PRESCRIPTION, they give the customer what they have asked for ➲ see also UNFILLED

IDM **fill sb's shoes/boots** to do sb's job in an acceptable way when they are not there ➲ more at BILL *n.*

PHR V **ˌfill ˈin (for sb)** to do sb's job for a short time while they are not there **ˌfill sth↔ˈin 1** 0‑w (*BrE*) to complete a form, etc. by writing information on it: *to fill in an application form* ◇ *To order, fill in the coupon on p 54.* **2** 0‑w to fill sth completely: *The hole has been filled in.* **3** to spend time doing sth while waiting for sth more important: *He filled in the rest of the day watching television.* **4** to complete a drawing, etc. by covering the space inside the outline with colour **ˌfill sb ˈin (on sth)** to tell sb about sth that has happened **ˌfill ˈout** to become larger, rounder or fatter **ˌfill sth↔ˈout** 0‑w = FILL STH IN (1) **ˌfill ˈup (with sth)** | **ˌfill sth↔ˈup (with sth)** 0‑w to become completely full; to make sth completely full: *The ditches had filled up with mud.* ◇ *to fill up the tank with oil*

■ ***noun*** [sing.] **1 your ~ (of sth/sb)** as much of sth/sb as you are willing to accept: *I've had my fill of entertaining for one week.* **2 your ~ (of food/drink)** as much as you can eat/drink

fill·er /ˈfɪlə(r)/ *noun* **1** [U, C] a substance used to fill holes or cracks, especially in walls before painting them **2** [C] (*informal*) something that is not important but is used to complete sth else because nothing better is available: *The song was originally a filler on their first album.* ➲ see also STOCKING FILLER

ˈfiller cap *noun* a lid for covering the end of the pipe through which petrol/gas is put into a vehicle

fil·let /ˈfɪlɪt; *NAmE* fɪˈleɪ/ *noun, verb*

■ ***noun*** (*NAmE* also **filet**) [C, U] a piece of meat or fish that has no bones in it: *plaice fillets* ◇ *a fillet of cod* ◇ *fillet steak*

■ ***verb*** **~ sth** to remove the bones from a piece of fish or meat; to cut fish or meat into fillets

fill·ing /ˈfɪlɪŋ/ *noun, adj.*
■ ***noun*** **1** [C] a small amount of metal or other material used to fill a hole in a tooth: *I had to have two fillings at the dentist's today.* **2** [C, U] food put inside a SANDWICH, cake, PIE, etc: *a sponge cake with cream and jam filling* ◇ *a wide range of sandwich fillings* **3** [C, U] soft material used to fill CUSHIONS, PILLOWS, etc.
■ ***adj.*** (of food) making your stomach feel full: *This cake is very filling.*

ˈfilling station *noun* = GAS STATION, PETROL STATION

fil·lip /ˈfɪlɪp/ *noun* [sing.] **a ~ (to/for sth)** (*formal*) a thing or person that causes sth to improve suddenly SYN **boost**: *A drop in interest rates gave a welcome fillip to the housing market.*

ˈfill-up *noun* an occasion when a car is completely filled up with petrol/gas

filly /ˈfɪli/ *noun* (*pl.* **-ies**) a young female horse ➲ compare COLT, MARE

film 0‑ᵜ /fɪlm/ *noun, verb*
■ ***noun***
▸ MOVING PICTURES **1** 0‑ᵜ [C] (*especially BrE*) (*NAmE* usually **movie**) a series of moving pictures recorded with sound that tells a story, shown on television or at the cinema/movie theater: *Let's go to the cinema—**there's a good film on** this week.* ◇ *Let's stay in and **watch a film**.* ◇ *a **horror/documentary/feature film*** ◇ *a **silent film*** (= one recorded without sound) ◇ *an international **film festival*** ◇ *a **film crew/critic/director/producer*** ◇ *the **film version** of the novel* ◇ *to **make/shoot a film*** ➲ COLLOCATIONS at CINEMA **2** 0‑ᵜ [U] (*especially BrE*) (*NAmE* usually **the movies** [pl.]) (*BrE* also **the cin·ema**) the art or business of making films/movies: *to study film and photography* ◇ *the film industry* ➲ compare CINEMA **3** 0‑ᵜ [U] moving pictures of real events, shown for example on television SYN **footage**: *television news film of the riots* ◇ *The accident was captured/caught **on film**.*
▸ IN CAMERAS **4** 0‑ᵜ [U, C] thin plastic that is sensitive to light, used for taking photographs and making films/movies; a roll of this plastic, used in cameras: *a **roll of film*** ◇ *a 35mm film* ◇ *She put a new film in her camera.* ◇ *to **have a film developed***
▸ THIN LAYER **5** [C, usually sing.] **~ (of sth)** a thin layer of sth, usually on the surface of sth else SYN **coat, coating, layer**: *Everything was covered in a film of dust.* ➲ see also CLING FILM
■ ***verb*** 0‑ᵜ [I, T] to make a film/movie of a story or a real event: *They are filming in Moscow right now.* ◇ **~ sth** *The show was filmed on location in New York.* ◇ **~ sb/sth doing sth** *Two young boys were filmed stealing CDs on the security video.* ▸ **film·ing** *noun* [U]: *Filming was delayed because of bad weather.*

ˈfilm-goer (*especially BrE*) (*NAmE* usually **movie·goer**) (*BrE* also **ˈcinema-goer**) *noun* a person who goes to the cinema/movies, especially when they do it regularly

film·ic /ˈfɪlmɪk/ *adj.* [only before noun] (*formal*) connected with films/movies

ˈfilm-maker *noun* a person who makes films/movies ▸ **ˈfilm-making** *noun* [U]

film noir /ˌfɪlm ˈnwɑː(r)/ *noun* (from *French*) **1** [U] a style of making films/movies in which there are strong feelings of fear or evil; films/movies made in this style **2** [C] (*pl.* **films noirs** /ˌfɪlm ˈnwɑː(r)/) a film made in this style

film·og·raphy /ˌfɪlˈmɒɡrəfi; *NAmE* -ˈmɑːɡ-/ *noun* (*pl.* **-ies**) a list of films/movies made by a particular actor or director, or a list of films/movies that deal with a particular subject

ˈfilm star (*especially BrE*) (*NAmE* usually **ˈmovie star**) *noun* a male or female actor who is famous for being in films/movies

film·strip /ˈfɪlmstrɪp/ *noun* a series of images on a film, through which light is shone to show them on a screen

filmy /ˈfɪlmi/ *adj.* [usually before noun] thin and almost transparent SYN **sheer**: *a filmy cotton blouse*

Filo·fax™ /ˈfaɪləʊfæks; *NAmE* -loʊ-/ *noun* a small book with pages that can be added or removed easily, used for writing notes, addresses, etc. in ➲ see also PERSONAL ORGANIZER

filo pastry /ˈfiːləʊ ˌpeɪstri; *NAmE* ˈfiːloʊ/ (also **filo**) *noun* [U] a type of thin PASTRY, used in layers

filters

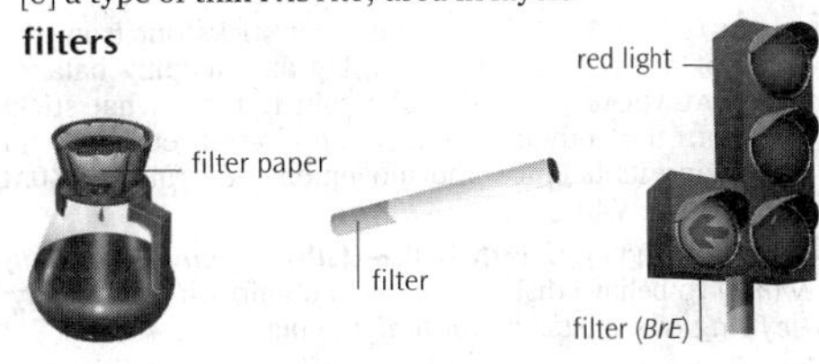

fil·ter /ˈfɪltə(r)/ *noun, verb*
■ ***noun*** **1** a device containing paper, sand, chemicals, etc. that a liquid or gas is passed through in order to remove any materials that are not wanted: *an **air/oil filter*** ◇ *a **coffee/water filter*** ◇ ***filter paper** for the coffee machine* ◇ *He smokes cigarettes without filters.* ➲ VISUAL VOCAB pages V22, V57 **2** a device that allows only particular types of light or sound to pass through it **3** (*computing*) a program that stops certain types of electronic information, email, etc. being sent to a computer **4** (*BrE*) a light on a set of TRAFFIC LIGHTS showing that traffic can turn left or right while traffic that wants to go straight ahead must wait
■ ***verb*** **1** [T] **~ sth** to pass liquid, light, etc. through a special device, especially to remove sth that is not wanted: *All drinking water must be filtered.* ◇ *Use a sun block that filters UVA effectively.* ◇ (*figurative*) *My secretary is very good at filtering my calls* (= making sure that calls that I do not want do not get through). ➲ see also FILTRATION **2** [T] **~ sth** to use a special program to check the content of emails or websites before they are sent to your computer **3** [I] **+ adv./prep.** (of people) to move slowly in a particular direction: *The doors opened and people started filtering through.* **4** [I] **+ adv./prep.** (of information, news, etc.) to slowly become known: *More details about the crash are filtering through.* **5** [I] **+ adv./prep.** (of light or sound) to come into a place slowly or in small amounts: *Sunlight filtered in through the curtains.* **6** [I] (*BrE*) (of traffic at traffic lights) to turn left at traffic lights while other vehicles wanting to go straight ahead or turn right must wait
PHR V **ˌfilter sth↔ˈout** **1** to remove sth that you do not want from a liquid, light, etc. by using a special device or substance: *to filter out dust particles/light/impurities* **2** to remove sb/sth that you do not want from a large number of people or things using a special system, device, etc: *The test is used to filter out candidates who may be unsuitable.* ◇ *The software filters out Internet sites whose content is not suitable for children.*

ˈfilter tip *noun* a filter at the end of a cigarette that removes some of the harmful substances from the smoke; a cigarette that has this filter

filth /fɪlθ/ *noun* [U] **1** any very dirty and unpleasant substance: *The floor was covered in grease and filth.* **2** words, magazines, etc. that are connected with sex and that are considered very rude and offensive: *How can you read such filth?* **3 the filth** [U] (*BrE, slang*) an offensive word for the police

filthy /ˈfɪlθi/ *adj., adv.*
■ ***adj.*** (**filth·ier, filthi·est**) **1** very dirty and unpleasant: *filthy rags/streets* ◇ *It's filthy in here!* ➲ SYNONYMS at DIRTY **2** very rude and offensive and usually connected with sex: ***filthy language/words*** ◇ *He's got a **filthy mind*** (= is always thinking about sex). **3** (*informal*) showing anger: *He was in a **filthy mood**.* ◇ *She has a **filthy temper**.* ◇ *Ann gave him a **filthy look**.* **4** (*BrE, informal*) (of the weather) cold and wet: *Isn't it a filthy day?* ▸ **filth·ily** *adv.* **filthi·ness** *noun* [U]
■ ***adv.*** (*informal*) **1 ~ dirty** extremely dirty **2 ~ rich** so rich

F

that you think the person is too rich and you find it offensive

fil·trate /ˈfɪltreɪt/ *noun* (*chemistry*) a liquid that has passed through a FILTER

fil·tra·tion /fɪlˈtreɪʃn/ *noun* [U] (*chemistry*) the process of FILTERING a liquid or gas

fin /fɪn/ *noun* **1** a thin flat part that sticks out from the body of a fish, used for swimming and keeping balance ➲ VISUAL VOCAB page V10 **2** a thin flat part that sticks out from the body of a vehicle, an aircraft, etc, used for improving its balance and movement: *tail fins* ➲ VISUAL VOCAB page V43

F

fin·agle /fɪˈneɪgl/ *verb* [T, I] ~ (**sth**) (*informal, especially NAmE*) to behave dishonestly or to obtain sth dishonestly: *He finagled some tickets for tonight's big game.*

final 0┳ AW /ˈfaɪnl/ *adj., noun*

■ *adj.* **1** 0┳ [only before noun] being or happening at the end of a series of events, actions, statements, etc: *his final act as party leader* ◇ *The referee blew the final whistle.* ◇ *The project is in its final stages.* ◇ *I'd like to return to the final point you made.* ➲ LANGUAGE BANK at PROCESS **2** 0┳ [only before noun] being the result of a particular process: *the final product* ◇ *No one could have predicted the final outcome.* **3** 0┳ that cannot be argued with or changed: *The judge's* ***decision is final.*** ◇ *Who has the* ***final say*** *around here?* ◇ *I'll give you $500 for it, and that's my* ***final offer!*** ◇ *I'm not coming,* ***and that's final!*** (= I will not change my mind) IDM see ANALYSIS, STRAW, WORD *n.*

■ *noun* **1** 0┳ [C] the last of a series of games or competitions in which the winner is decided: *She reached the final of the 100m hurdles.* ◇ *the 2010 World Cup Finals* (= the last few games in the competition) ◇ *The winner of each contest goes through to the* ***grand final.*** ➲ see also QUARTER-FINAL, SEMI-FINAL **2 finals** [pl.] (*BrE*) the last exams taken by university students at the end of their final year: *to* ***sit/take*** *your* ***finals*** **3** [C] (*NAmE*) an exam taken by school, university or college students at the end of a SEMESTER or QUARTER, usually in a topic that they will not study again

ˌfinal ˈclause *noun* (*grammar*) a clause that expresses purpose or intention, for example one that follows 'in order that' or 'so that'

fi·nale /fɪˈnɑːli; *NAmE* fɪˈnæli/ *noun* **1** the last part of a show or a piece of music: *the rousing finale of Beethoven's Ninth Symphony* ◇ *The festival ended with a* ***grand finale*** *in Hyde Park.* **2** ~ (**to sth**) (after an adjective) an ending to sth of the type mentioned: *a fitting finale to the day's events*

fi·nal·ist /ˈfaɪnəlɪst/ *noun* a person who takes part in the final of a game or competition: *an Olympic finalist*

fi·nal·ity AW /faɪˈnæləti/ *noun* [U] the quality of being final and impossible to change: *the finality of death* ◇ *There was a note of finality in his voice.*

fi·nal·ize (*BrE* also **-ise**) AW /ˈfaɪnəlaɪz/ *verb* ~ **sth** to complete the last part of a plan, trip, project, etc: *to* ***finalize*** *your* ***plans/arrangements*** ◇ *They met to finalize the terms of the treaty.* ▸ **fi·nal·iza·tion, -isa·tion** *noun* [U]

fi·nal·ly 0┳ AW /ˈfaɪnəli/ *adv.*
1 0┳ after a long time, especially when there has been some difficulty or delay SYN **eventually**: *The performance finally started half an hour late.* ◇ *I finally managed to get her attention.* ◇ *When they finally arrived it was well past midnight.* **2** 0┳ used to introduce the last in a list of things SYN **lastly**: *And finally, I would like to thank you all for coming here today.* ➲ LANGUAGE BANK at FIRST, PROCESS **3** 0┳ in a way that ends all discussion about sth: *The matter was not finally settled until later.*

fi·nance 0┳ AW /ˈfaɪnæns; faɪˈnæns; fəˈnæns/ *noun, verb*

■ *noun* **1** 0┳ (*especially BrE*) (*NAmE* usually **fi·nan·cing**) [U] ~ (**for sth**) money used to run a business, an activity or a project: *Finance for education comes from taxpayers.* **2** 0┳ [U] the activity of managing money, especially by a government or commercial organization: *the Minister of Finance* ◇ *the* ***finance director/department*** ◇ *a diploma in banking and finance* ◇ *the world of* ***high finance*** (= finance involving large companies or countries) **3** 0┳ **finances** [pl.] the money available to a person, an organization or a country; the way this money is managed: ***government/public/personal finances*** ◇ *It's about time you sorted out your finances.* ◇ *Moving house put a severe strain on our finances.*

■ *verb* 0┳ ~ **sth** to provide money for a project SYN **fund**: *The building project will be financed by the government.* ◇ *He took a job to finance his stay in Germany.*

Collocations

Finance

Income

- **earn** money/cash/(*informal*) a fortune
- **make** money/a fortune/(*informal*) a killing on the stock market
- **acquire/inherit/amass** wealth/a fortune
- **build up** funds/savings
- **get/receive/leave (sb)** an inheritance/a legacy
- **live on** a low wage/a fixed income/a pension
- **get/receive/draw/collect** a pension
- **depend/be dependent on** (*BrE*) benefits/(*NAmE*) welfare/social security

Expenditure

- **spend** money/your savings/(*informal*) a fortune on...
- **invest/put** your savings in...
- **throw away/waste/**(*informal*) **shell out** money on...
- **lose** your money/inheritance/pension
- **use up/**(*informal*) **wipe out** all your savings
- **pay (in)** cash
- **use/pay by** a credit/debit card
- **pay by/make out a/write sb a/accept** a (*BrE*) cheque/(*US*) check
- **change/exchange** money/currency (*BrE*) traveller's cheques/(*US*) traveler's checks
- **give/pay/leave (sb)** a deposit

Banks

- **have/hold/open/close/freeze** a bank account/an account
- **credit/debit/pay sth into/take money out of** your account
- **deposit** money/funds in your account
- **withdraw** money/cash/£30 from an ATM, etc.
- (*formal*) **make** a deposit/withdrawal
- **find/go to/use** (*especially NAmE*) an ATM/(*BrE*) a cash machine/dispenser
- **be** in credit/in debit/in the black/in the red/overdrawn

Personal finance

- **manage/handle/plan/run/**(*especially BrE*) **sort out** your finances
- **plan/manage/work out/stick to** a budget
- **offer/extend** credit (to sb)
- **arrange/take out** a loan/an overdraft
- **pay back/repay** money/a loan/a debt
- **pay for sth in** (*especially BrE*) instalments/(*NAmE usually*) installments

Financial difficulties

- **get into** debt/financial difficulties
- **be short of/**(*informal*) **be strapped for** cash
- **run out of/owe** money
- **face/get/**(*informal*) **be landed with** a bill for £...
- **can't afford** the cost of.../payments/rent
- **fall behind with/**(*especially NAmE*) **fall behind on** the mortgage/repayments/rent
- **incur/run up/accumulate** debts
- **tackle/reduce/settle** your debts

ˈfinance company (*BrE* also **ˈfinance house**) *noun* a company that lends money to people or businesses

fi·nan·cial 0-w AW /faɪˈnænʃl; fəˈnæ-/ *adj.* [usually before noun]
1 0-w connected with money and finance: *financial services* ◇ *to give financial advice* ◇ *to be in* ***financial difficulties*** ◇ *an independent* ***financial adviser*** ◇ *Tokyo and New York are major* ***financial centres.*** ➲ SYNONYMS at ECONOMIC **2** (*AustralE, NZE, informal*) having money ▸ **fi·nan·cial·ly** AW /-ʃəli/ *adv.*: *She is still* ***financially dependent*** *on her parents.* ◇ *Financially, I'm much better off than before.* ◇ *Such projects are not* ***financially viable*** *without government funding.*

fiˌnancial ˈaid *noun* [U] (*NAmE*) money that is given or lent to students at a university or college who cannot pay the full cost of their education: *to apply for financial aid*

the Fiˌnancial Times ˈindex *noun* = FTSE INDEX

fiˌnancial ˈyear (*BrE*) (*BrE* also **ˈtax year**) (*NAmE* **ˌfiscal ˈyear**) *noun* [usually sing.] a period of twelve months over which the accounts and taxes of a company or a person are calculated: *the current financial year*

fi·nan·cier AW /faɪˈnænsiə(r); fə-; *NAmE* ˌfɪnənˈsɪr/ *noun* a person who lends large amounts of money to businesses

fi·nan·cing /ˈfaɪnænsɪŋ; faɪˈnænsɪŋ; fəˈnænsɪŋ/ *noun* [U] (*NAmE*) = FINANCE: *The project will only go ahead if they can raise the necessary financing.*

finch /fɪntʃ/ *noun* (often in compounds) a small bird with a short beak. There are several types of finch. ➲ VISUAL VOCAB page V10 ➲ see also BULLFINCH, CHAFFINCH, GOLDFINCH

find 0-w /faɪnd/ *verb, noun*
▪ ***verb*** (**found, found** /faʊnd/)
▸ BY CHANCE **1** 0-w [T] to discover sb/sth unexpectedly or by chance: **~ sb/sth** *Look what I've found!* ◇ *We've found a great new restaurant near the office.* ◇ **~ sb/sth + adj.** *A whale was found washed up on the shore.*
▸ BY SEARCHING **2** 0-w [T] to get back sth/sb that was lost after searching for it/them: **~ sth for sb** *Can you find my bag for me?* ◇ **~ sb sth** *Can you find me my bag?* ◇ **~ sb/sth** *I wanted to talk to him but he was* ***nowhere to be found.*** ◇ **~ sb/sth + adj.** *The child was found safe and well.*
▸ BY STUDYING/THINKING **3** 0-w [T] to discover sth/sb by searching, studying or thinking carefully: **~ sth/sb** *scientists trying to find a cure for cancer* ◇ *I managed to find a solution to the problem.* ◇ *I'm having trouble finding anything new to say on this subject.* ◇ *Have they found anyone to replace her yet?* ◇ **~ sth for sb** *Can you find a hotel for me?* ◇ **~ sb sth** *Can you find me a hotel?*
▸ BY EXPERIENCE/TESTING **4** 0-w [T] to discover that sth is true after you have tried it, tested it or experienced it: **~ (that)** ... *I find (that) it pays to be honest.* ◇ *The report found that 30% of the firms studied had failed within a year.* ◇ **~ sb/sth + adj./noun** *We found the beds very comfortable.* ◇ **~ sb/sth to be/do sth** *They found him to be charming.* ◇ *Her blood was found to contain poison.* ◇ **it is found that...** ***It was found that*** *her blood contained poison.*
▸ HAVE OPINION/FEELING **5** 0-w [T] to have a particular feeling or opinion about sth: **~ sth + adj.** *You may find your illness hard to accept.* ◇ *You may* ***find it hard*** *to accept your illness.* ◇ *I find it amazing that they're still together.* ◇ **~ sth + noun** *She* ***finds it a strain*** *to meet new people.* ➲ SYNONYMS at REGARD
▸ HAVE/MAKE AVAILABLE **6** [T] **~ sth** to have sth available so that you can use it: *I keep meaning to write, but never seem to find (the) time.* ◇ *How are we going to find £5 000 for a car?*
▸ IN UNEXPECTED SITUATIONS **7** [T] to discover sb/sth/yourself doing sth or in a particular situation, especially when this is unexpected: **~ sb/sth/yourself + adv./prep.** *She woke up and found herself in a hospital bed.* ◇ **~ sb/sth/yourself + adj.** *We came home and found him asleep on the sofa.* ◇ **~ sb/sth/yourself doing sth** *I suddenly found myself running down the street.* ◇ **~ (that)...** *I was disappointed to find that they had left already.*
▸ REACH **8** [T] **~ sth** (of things) to arrive at sth naturally; to reach sth: *Water will always find its own level.* ◇ *Most of the money finds its way to the people who need it.* ◇ *The criticism found its mark* (= had the effect intended).
▸ EXIST/GROW **9** [T] **~ sth + adv./prep.** used to say that sth exists, grows, etc. somewhere: *These flowers are found only in Africa.* ◇ *You'll find this style of architecture all over the town.*
▸ IN COURT **10** [T, I] (*formal*) to make a particular decision in a court case: **~ sb + adj.** *The jury found him guilty.* ◇ *How do you find the accused?* ◇ **~ in sb's favour** *The court found in her favour.*
IDM **all ˈfound** (*old-fashioned, BrE*) with free food and accommodation in addition to your wages **find fault (with sb/sth)** to look for and discover mistakes in sb/sth; to complain about sb/sth **find your ˈfeet** to become able to act independently and with confidence: *I only recently joined the firm so I'm still finding my feet.* **find it in your heart/yourself to do sth** (*literary*) to be able or willing to do sth: *Can you find it in your heart to forgive her?* ◇ *He couldn't find it in himself to trust anyone again.* **find your ˈvoice/ˈtongue** to be able to speak or express your opinion **find your way (to...)** to discover the right route (to a place): *I hope you can find your way home.* **find your/its ˈway (to/into...)** to come to a place or a situation by chance or without intending to: *He eventually found his way into acting.* **take sb as you ˈfind them** to accept sb as they are without expecting them to behave in a special way or have special qualities ➲ more at BEARING, MATCH *n.*, NOWHERE
PHR V **ˈfind for/against sb** [no passive] (*law*) to make a decision in favour of/against sb in a court case: *The jury found for the defendant.* **ˌfind ˈout (about sth/sb)** | **ˌfind ˈout sth (about sth/sb)** 0-w to get some information about sth/sb by asking, reading, etc: *She'd been seeing the boy for a while, but didn't want her parents to find out.* ◇ *I haven't found anything out about him yet.* ◇ **~ what, when, etc...** *Can you find out what time the meeting starts?* ◇ **~ that...** *We found out later that we had been at the same school.* **ˌfind sb ˈout** to discover that sb has done sth wrong: *He had been cheating the taxman but it was years before he was found out.*
▪ ***noun*** a thing or person that has been found, especially one that is interesting, valuable or useful: *an important archaeological find* ◇ *Our new babysitter is* ***a real find.***

find·er /ˈfaɪndə(r)/ *noun* a person who finds sth ➲ see also VIEWFINDER
IDM **ˌfinders ˈkeepers** (*saying*) (often used by children) anyone who finds sth has a right to keep it

fin de siècle /ˌfæ̃ də ˈsjekl/ *adj.* (from *French*) typical of the end of the 19th century, especially of its art, literature and attitudes

find·ing /ˈfaɪndɪŋ/ *noun* **1** [usually pl.] information that is discovered as the result of research into sth: *The findings of the commission will be published today.* ➲ COLLOCATIONS at SCIENTIFIC **2** (*law*) a decision made by the judge or JURY in a court case

fine 0-w /faɪn/ *adj., adv., noun, verb*
▪ ***adj.*** (**finer, fin·est**)
▸ VERY GOOD **1** 0-w [usually before noun] of high quality; good: *a very fine performance* ◇ *fine clothes/wines/workmanship* ◇ *a particularly fine example of Saxon architecture* ◇ *Jim has made a fine job of the garden.* ◇ *people who enjoy the* ***finer things*** *in life* (= for example art, good food, etc.) ◇ *He tried to appeal to their* ***finer feelings*** (= feelings of duty, love, etc.). ◇ *It was his* ***finest hour*** (= most successful period) *as manager of the England team.*
▸ VERY WELL **2** 0-w (of a person) in good health: *'How are you?' 'Fine, thanks.'* ◇ *I was* ***feeling fine*** *when I got up this morning.* ➲ SYNONYMS at WELL
▸ ACCEPTABLE/GOOD ENOUGH **3** 0-w (also used as an exclamation) used to tell sb that an action, a suggestion or a decision is acceptable: *'I'll leave this here, OK?' 'Fine.'* ◇ *'Bob wants to know if he can come too.'* ***'That's fine by me.'***
4 0-w used to say you are satisfied with sth: *Don't worry. Your speech was fine.* ◇ *You go on without me.* ***I'll be fine.*** ◇

'Can I get you another drink?' 'No, thanks. ***I'm fine.'*** ◇ *(ironic) This is a* ***fine*** (= terrible) ***mess*** *we're in!* ◇ *(ironic)* ***You're a fine one to talk!*** (= you are not in a position to criticize, give advice, etc.)

▸ ATTRACTIVE **5** [usually before noun] pleasing to look at: *a fine view* ◇ *a fine-looking woman* ◇ *a fine figure of a man*

▸ DELICATE **6** [usually before noun] attractive and delicate: *fine bone china* ◇ *She has inherited her mother's fine features* (= a small nose, mouth, etc.).

▸ WEATHER **7** *(especially BrE)* bright and not raining: *a fine day/evening* ◇ *I hope it* ***stays fine*** *for the picnic.*

▸ VERY THIN **8** very thin or narrow: *fine blond hair* ◇ *a fine thread* ◇ *a brush with a fine tip*

▸ DETAIL/DISTINCTIONS **9** [usually before noun] difficult to see or describe SYN **subtle**: *You really need a magnifying glass to appreciate all the fine detail.* ◇ *There's no need to make such* ***fine distinctions.*** ◇ *There's* ***a fine line*** *between love and hate* (= it is easy for one to become the other).

▸ WITH SMALL GRAINS **10** made of very small grains: *fine sand* ◇ *Use a finer piece of sandpaper to finish.* OPP **coarse**

▸ PERSON **11** [only before noun] that you have a lot of respect for: *He was a fine man.*

▸ WORDS/SPEECHES **12** sounding important and impressive but unlikely to have any effect: *His speech was full of fine words which meant nothing.*

▸ METALS **13** *(technical)* containing only a particular ‑ ‑tal and no other substances that reduce the qual‑‑ ‑ ‑e gold

IDM **get sth down to a fine 'art** *(infor‑ ‑,)* to learn to do sth well and efficiently: *I spend so m‑ ‑n time travelling that I've got packing down to a fine a‑ .* **not to put too fine a 'point on it** used to emphasiz‑ sth that is expressed clearly and directly, especially ‑ ‑riticism: *Not to put too fine a point on it, I think yo‑ ‑re lying.* ➲ more at CHANCE *n.*, FETTLE, LINE *n.*

■ ***adv.*** *(informal)* in ‑ way that is acceptable or good enough: *Keep going lik‑ that—you're* ***doing fine.*** ◇ *Things were* ***going fine*** *un‑il you showed up.* ◇ *That arrangement* ***suits me fine.*** ◇ *(BrE) An omelette will* ***do me fine*** (= will be enough for me).

IDM **cut it/things 'fine** *(informal)* to leave yourself just enough time to do sth: *If we don't leave till after lunch we'll be cutting it very fine.*

■ ***noun*** a sum of money that must be paid as punishment for breaking a law or rule: *a parking fine* ◇ *Offenders will be liable to a* ***heavy fine*** (= one that costs a lot of money). ◇ *She has already paid over $2 000 in fines.* ➲ SYNONYMS at RATE ➲ COLLOCATIONS at JUSTICE

■ ***verb*** [often passive] to make sb pay money as an official punishment: **~ sb (for sth/for doing sth)** *She was fined for speeding.* ◇ **~ sb sth (for sth/for doing sth)** *The company was fined £20 000 for breaching safety regulations.*

fine 'art *noun* [U] (also **fine 'arts** [pl.]) forms of art, especially painting, drawing and SCULPTURE, that are created to be beautiful rather than useful

Fine Gael /ˌfiːnə ˈɡeɪl/ *noun* [sing.+ sing./pl. v.] the more conservative of the two main political parties in the Republic of Ireland ➲ compare FIANNA FÁIL

fine·ly /ˈfaɪnli/ *adv.* **1** into very small grains or pieces: *finely chopped herbs* **2** in a beautiful or impressive way: *a finely furnished room* **3** in a very delicate or exact way: *a finely tuned engine* ◇ *The match was finely balanced throughout.*

fine·ness /ˈfaɪnnəs/ *noun* [U] **1** the quality of being made of thin threads or lines very close together: *fineness of detail* **2** *(technical)* the quality of sth: *the fineness of the gold*

the ˌfine 'print *(NAmE)* *(BrE* **the ˌsmall 'print)** *noun* [U] the important details of an agreement or a legal document that are usually printed in small type and are therefore easy to miss

fin·ery /ˈfaɪnəri/ *noun* [U] *(formal)* brightly coloured and elegant clothes and jewellery, especially those that are worn for a special occasion

fi·nesse /fɪˈnes/ *noun, verb*

■ ***noun*** [U] great skill in dealing with people or situations, especially in a delicate way

■ ***verb*** *(especially NAmE)* **1 ~ sth** to deal with sth in a way that is clever but slightly dishonest: *to finesse a deal* **2 ~ sth** to do sth with a lot of skill or style

ˌfine-tooth 'comb (also **ˌfine-toothed 'comb**) *noun* a COMB in which the pointed parts are thin and very close together

IDM **go over/through sth with a fine-tooth/fine-toothed comb** to examine or search sth very carefully

ˌfine-'tune *verb* **~ sth** to make very sma‑ ‑ changes to sth so that it is as good as it can possibl‑ ‑e ▸ **ˌfine-'tuning** *noun* [U]: *The system is set up but it n‑ ‑ds some fine-tuning.*

f-ing /ˈefɪŋ/ *adj.* [only before noun ‑ ‑aboo, slang) = EFFING

fin·ger /ˈfɪŋɡə(r)/ *no‑ ‑, verb*

■ ***noun*** **1** one of the fo‑ ‑ ‑ong thin parts that stick out from the hand (or five ‑ ‑ the thumb is included): *She* ***ran her fingers*** *through ‑ ‑er hair.* ◇ *Hold the material between finger and thumb ‑ He was about to speak but she raised a finger to her li‑ .* ➲ COLLOCATIONS at PHYSICAL ➲ see also BUTTERFIN‑ ‑ERS, FOREFINGER, GREEN FINGERS, INDEX FINGER, ‑ITTLE FINGER, MIDDLE FINGER, RING FINGER **2 -fin‑ ‑ered** (in adjectives) having the type of fingers me‑ ‑ioned; having or using the number of fingers men‑ ‑ ‑ned: *long-fingered* ◇ *nimble-fingered* ◇ *a four-fingered chord* ➲ see also LIGHT-FINGERED **3** the part of a glove that covers the finger **4 ~ (of sth)** a long narrow piece of bread, cake, land, etc: *a finger of toast* ◇ *chocolate fingers* ➲ see also FISH FINGER

IDM **the ˌfinger of susˈpicion** if **the finger of suspicion** points or is pointed at sb, they are suspected of having committed a crime, being responsible for sth, etc. **get, pull, etc. your 'finger out** *(BrE, informal)* used to tell sb to start doing some work or making an effort: *You're going to have to pull your finger out if you want to pass this exam.* **give sb the 'finger** *(NAmE, informal)* to raise your middle finger in the air with the back part of your hand facing sb, done to be rude to sb or to show them that you are angry **have a finger in every 'pie** *(informal)* to be involved in a lot of different activities and have influence over them, especially when other people think that this is annoying **have, etc. your 'fingers in the till** *(BrE, informal)* to be stealing money from the place where you work **have/keep your finger on the 'pulse (of sth)** to always be aware of the most recent developments in a particular situation **lay a 'finger on sb** (usually used in negative sentences) to touch sb with the intention of hurting them physically: *I never laid a finger on her.* **not put your finger on sth** to not be able to identify what is wrong or different about a particular situation: *There was something odd about him but I couldn't put my finger on it.* **put/stick two 'fingers up at sb** *(BrE, informal)* to form the shape of a V with the two fingers nearest your thumb and raise your hand in the air with the back part of it facing sb, done to be rude to them or to show them that you are angry ➲ see also V-SIGN **work your fingers to the 'bone** to work very hard ➲ more at BURN *v.*, COUNT *v.*, CROSS *v.*, LIFT *v.*, POINT *v.*, SLIP *v.*, SNAP *v.*, STICKY, THUMB *n.*

■ ***verb*** **1 ~ sth** to touch or feel sth with your fingers: *Gary sat fingering his beard, saying nothing.* **2 ~ sb (for sth)** | **~ sb (as sth)** *(informal, especially NAmE)* to accuse sb of doing sth illegal and tell the police about it: *Who fingered him for the burglaries?*

finger·board /ˈfɪŋɡəbɔːd; *NAmE* ˈfɪŋɡərbɔːrd/ *noun* a flat strip on the neck of a musical instrument such as a GUITAR or VIOLIN, against which the strings are pressed to play different notes

'finger bowl *noun* a small bowl of water for washing your fingers during a meal

'finger food *noun* [U, C] pieces of food that you can easily eat with your fingers

fin·ger·ing /ˈfɪŋɡərɪŋ/ *noun* [U, C] the positions in which you put your fingers when playing a musical instrument

fin·ger·mark /ˈfɪŋɡəmɑːk; *NAmE* ˈfɪŋɡərmɑːrk/ *noun* [usually pl.] *(especially BrE)* a mark made by a finger, for example on a clean surface

fin·ger·nail /ˈfɪŋɡəneɪl; *NAmE* -ɡərn-/ *noun* the thin hard layer that covers the outer tip of each finger ➲ VISUAL VOCAB page V48

fin·ger·print /ˈfɪŋɡəprɪnt; *NAmE* -ɡərp-/ *noun* a mark made by the pattern of lines on the tip of a person's finger, often used by the police to identify criminals ➲ SYNONYMS at MARK ➲ see also GENETIC FINGERPRINT ▸ **fin·ger·print** *verb* **~ sb**

fin·ger·print·ing /ˈfɪŋɡəprɪntɪŋ; *NAmE* -ɡərp-/ *noun* [U] the practice of recording sb's fingerprints, often used by the police to identify criminals ➲ see also DNA FINGERPRINTING, GENETIC FINGERPRINTING

fin·ger·tip /ˈfɪŋɡətɪp; *NAmE* -ɡərt-/ *noun* [usually pl.] the end of the finger that is furthest from the hand
IDM **have sth at your ˈfingertips** to have the information, knowledge, etc. that is needed in a particular situation and be able to find it easily and use it quickly **to your ˈfingertips** (*BrE*) in every way: *She's a perfectionist to her fingertips.*

fin·ial /ˈfɪniəl/ *noun* **1** (*architecture*) a decorative part at the top of a roof, wall, etc. **2** a decorative part that fits on the end of a curtain pole ➲ VISUAL VOCAB page V18

fin·icky /ˈfɪnɪki/ *adj.* **1** (*disapproving*) too worried about what you eat, wear, etc; disliking many things SYN **fussy**: *a finicky eater* **2** needing great care and attention to detail SYN **fiddly**: *It's a very finicky job.*

fin·ish 🔑 /ˈfɪnɪʃ/ *verb, noun*
■ *verb* **1** 🔑 [T, I] to stop doing sth or making sth because it is complete: **~ (sth)** *Haven't you finished your homework yet?* ◇ *She finished law school last year.* ◇ *I thought you'd never finish!* ◇ *a beautifully finished piece of furniture* ◇ *He* **put the finishing touches** *to his painting* (= did the things that made it complete). ◇ **~ doing sth** *Be quiet! He hasn't finished speaking.* ◇ **+ speech** *'And that was all,' she finished.* **2** 🔑 [I, T] to come to an end; to bring sth to an end: *The play finished at 10.30.* ◇ **~ with sth** *The symphony finishes with a flourish.* ◇ **~ sth** *A cup of coffee finished the meal perfectly.* **3** 🔑 [T] **~ sth (off/up)** to eat, drink or use what remains of sth: *He finished off his drink with one large gulp.* ◇ *We might as well finish up the cake.* **4** 🔑 [I] to be in a particular state or position at the end of a race or a competition: **+ adj.** *She was delighted to finish second.* ◇ *The dollar finished the day slightly down.* ◇ **+ adv./prep.** *He finished 12 seconds outside the world record.* **5** [T] **~ sb (off)** (*informal*) to make sb so tired or impatient that they cannot do any more: *Climbing that hill really finished me off.* ◇ *A lecture from my parents now would just finish me.*
PHR V **ˌfinish sb/sth↔ˈoff** (*informal*) to destroy sb/sth, especially sb/sth that is badly injured or damaged: *The hunter moved in to finish the animal off.* **ˌfinish sth↔ˈoff** 🔑 to do the last part of sth; to make sth end by doing one last thing: *I need about an hour to finish off this report.* ◇ *They finished off the show with one of their most famous songs.* **ˌfinish ˈup...** (*BrE*) to be in a particular state or at a particular place after a series of events: **+ adj.** *If you're not careful, you could finish up seriously ill.* **ˈfinish with sb 1** (*BrE*) to end a relationship with sb: *She finished with her boyfriend last week.* **2** to stop dealing with a person: *He'll regret he ever said it once I've finished with him.* **ˈfinish with sth 1** to no longer need to use sth: *When you've finished with the book, can I see it?* **2** (*BrE, informal*) to stop doing sth: *I've finished with gambling.* **finish (up) with sth** to have sth at the end: *We had a five-course lunch and finished up with coffee and mints.* ◇ *To finish with, we'll listen to a few songs.*
■ *noun* **1** 🔑 [C, usually sing.] the last part or the end of sth: *a dramatic finish to the race* ◇ *It was* **a close finish**, *as they had predicted.* ◇ *They won in the end but it was a* **tight finish**. ◇ *The story was a lie* **from start to finish**. ◇ *I want to see the job through* **to the finish**. ➲ see also PHOTO FINISH **2** 🔑 [C, U] the last covering of paint, polish, etc. that is put onto the surface of sth; the condition of the surface: *a* **gloss/matt finish** ◇ *furniture available in a range of finishes* **3** [C, U] the final details that are added to sth to make it complete: *The bows will give a feminine finish to the curtains.* IDM see FIGHT *v.*

fin·ished 🔑 /ˈfɪnɪʃt/ *adj.*
1 🔑 [not before noun] no longer doing sth or dealing with sb/sth: *I won't be finished for another hour.* ◇ **~ with sb/sth** *I'm not finished with you yet.* **2** 🔑 [not before noun] no longer powerful, effective or able to continue: *If the newspapers find out, he's finished in politics.* ◇ *Their marriage was finished.* **3** 🔑 [usually before noun] fully completed, especially in a particular way: *the* **finished product/article** ◇ *a beautifully finished suit*

fin·ish·er /ˈfɪnɪʃə(r)/ *noun* a person or an animal that finishes a race, etc.

ˈfin·ish·ing line (*BrE*) (*NAmE* **ˈfinish line**) *noun* the line across a sports track, etc. that marks the end of a race: *The two horses crossed the finishing line together.*

ˈfin·ish·ing school *noun* a private school where young women from rich families are taught how to behave in fashionable society

fi·nite AW /ˈfaɪnaɪt/ *adj.* **1** having a definite limit or fixed size: *a finite number of possibilities* ◇ *The world's resources are finite.* OPP **infinite 2** (*grammar*) a **finite** verb form or clause shows a particular tense, PERSON and NUMBER: *'Am', 'is', 'are', 'was' and 'were' are the finite forms of 'be'; 'being', and 'been' are the non-finite forms.* OPP **non-finite**

fink /fɪŋk/ *noun* (*informal, especially NAmE*) an unpleasant person

fiord = FJORD

fir /fɜː(r)/ (also **ˈfir tree**) *noun* an EVERGREEN forest tree with leaves like needles ➲ VISUAL VOCAB page V8

ˈfir cone (*BrE*) (also **cone** *NAmE, BrE*) *noun* the hard fruit of the fir tree ➲ VISUAL VOCAB page V8

fire 🔑 /ˈfaɪə(r)/ *noun, verb*
■ *noun*
▸ STH BURNING **1** 🔑 [U] the flames, light and heat, and often smoke, that are produced when sth burns: *Most animals are afraid of fire.* **2** 🔑 [U, C] flames that are out of control and destroy buildings, trees, etc: *The car was now* **on fire**. ◇ *The warehouse has been badly damaged by fire.* ◇ *Several youths had* **set fire to** *the police car* (= had made it start burning). ◇ *A candle had* **set** *the curtains* **on fire**. ◇ *These thatched roofs frequently* **catch fire** (= start to burn). ◇ **forest fires** ◇ *Five people died in a house fire last night.* ◇ *A small fire had started in the kitchen.* ◇ **Fires** *were* **breaking out** *everywhere.* ◇ *It took two hours to* **put out the fire** (= stop it burning).
▸ FOR HEATING/COOKING **3** 🔑 [C] a pile of burning fuel, such as wood or coal, used for cooking food or heating a room: *to* **make/build a fire** ◇ *a* **log/coal fire** ◇ *Sam had* **lit a fire** *to welcome us home.* ◇ *Come and get warm by the fire.* ◇ *We sat in front of a* **roaring fire**. ➲ see also BONFIRE, CAMPFIRE **4** 🔑 [C] (*especially BrE*) a piece of equipment for heating a room: *a* **gas/electric fire** ◇ *Shall I put the fire on?* ➲ see also HEATER
▸ FROM GUNS **5** 🔑 [U] shots from guns: *a burst of machine-gun fire* ◇ *to* **return fire** (= to fire back at sb who is shooting at you) ◇ *The gunmen* **opened fire on** (= started shooting at) *the police.* ◇ *Their vehicle* **came under fire** (= was being shot at). ◇ *He ordered his men to* **hold their fire** (= not to shoot). ◇ *A young girl was* **in the line of fire** (= between the person shooting and what he/she was shooting at).
▸ ANGER/ENTHUSIASM **6** [U] very strong emotion, especially anger or enthusiasm: *Her eyes were full of fire.*
IDM **be/come under ˈfire** to be criticized severely for sth you have done: *The health minister has come under fire from all sides.* **hang/hold ˈfire** to delay or be delayed in taking action: *The project had hung fire for several years for lack of funds.* **on ˈfire** giving you a painful burning feeling: *He couldn't breathe. His chest was on fire.* **play with ˈfire** to act in a way that is not sensible and take dangerous risks ➲ more at BALL *n.*, BAPTISM, DRAW *v.*, FIGHT *v.*, FRYING PAN, HOUSE *n.*, IRON *n.*, SMOKE *n.*, WORLD
■ *verb*
▸ SHOOT **1** 🔑 [I, T] to shoot bullets from a gun: *The officer ordered his men to fire.* ◇ **~ on sb/sth** *Soldiers fired on the crowd.* ◇ **~ sth** *They ran away as soon as the first shot was fired.* ◇ **~ (sth) (into sth)** *He fired the gun into the air.* ◇

~ (sth) (at sb/sth) *Missiles were fired at the enemy.* ➲ COLLOCATIONS at WAR **2** [I, T] (of a gun) to shoot bullets out: *We heard the sound of guns firing.* ◇ **~ sth** *A starter's pistol fires only blanks.* **3** [T] **~ sth** to shoot an arrow: *She fired an arrow at the target.*
▸ FROM JOB **4** [T] **~ sb** to force sb to leave their job SYN **sack**: *We had to fire him for dishonesty.* ◇ *She got fired from her first job.* ◇ *He was responsible for* ***hiring and firing*** *staff.* ➲ COLLOCATIONS at UNEMPLOYMENT
▸ MAKE SB ENTHUSIASTIC **5** [T] **~ sb (with sth)** to make sb feel very excited about sth or interested in sth: *The talk had fired her with enthusiasm for the project.* ◇ *His imagination had been fired by the film.*
▸ OF ENGINE **6** [I] when an engine **fires**, an electrical SPARK is produced that makes the fuel burn and the engine start to work
▸ -FIRED **7** (in adjectives) using the fuel mentioned in order to operate: *gas-fired central heating*
▸ CLAY OBJECTS **8** [T] **~ sth** to heat a CLAY object to make it hard and strong: *to fire pottery* ◇ *to fire bricks in a kiln*
IDM **fire ˈquestions, ˈinsults, etc. at sb** to ask sb a lot of questions one after another or make a lot of comments very quickly: *The room was full of journalists, all firing questions at them.* ➲ more at CYLINDER
PHR V **ˌfire aˈway** (*informal*) used to tell sb to begin to speak or ask a question: *'I've got a few questions.' 'OK then, fire away.'* **ˌfire sth↔ˈoff 1** to shoot a bullet from a gun: *They fired off a volley of shots.* **2** to write or say sth to sb very quickly, often when you are angry: *He fired off a letter of complaint.* ◇ *She spent an hour firing off emails to all concerned.* **ˌfire sb↔ˈup** to make sb excited or interested in sth: *She's all fired up about her new job.* **ˌfire sth↔ˈup** (*informal*) to start a machine, piece of equipment, computer program, etc: *We need to fire up one of the generators.* ◇ *Let me fire up another window* (= on the computer screen).

ˈfire alarm *noun* a bell or other device that gives people warning of a fire in a building: *Who set off the fire alarm?*

fire·arm /ˈfaɪərɑːm; *NAmE* -ɑːrm/ *noun* (*formal*) a gun that can be carried: *The police were issued with firearms.*

fire·ball /ˈfaɪəbɔːl; *NAmE* ˈfaɪərb-/ *noun* a bright ball of fire, especially one at the centre of an explosion

fire·bomb /ˈfaɪəbɒm; *NAmE* ˈfaɪərbɑːm/ *noun* a bomb that makes a fire start burning after it explodes ▸ **fire·bomb** *verb* **~ sth**

fire·brand /ˈfaɪəbrænd; *NAmE* ˈfaɪərb-/ *noun* a person who is always encouraging other people to take strong political action, often causing trouble

fire·break /ˈfaɪəbreɪk; *NAmE* ˈfaɪərb-/ *noun* a thing that stops a fire from spreading, for example a special door or a strip of land in a forest that has been cleared of trees ➲ see also FIRE LINE

fire·brick /ˈfaɪəbrɪk; *NAmE* ˈfaɪər-/ *noun* [U, C] (*technical*) brick which is not destroyed by very strong heat; an individual block of this

ˈfire brigade (also **ˈfire service**) (both *BrE*) (*NAmE* **ˈfire department**) *noun* [C+sing./pl. v.] an organization of people who are trained and employed to put out fires and to rescue people from fires; the people who belong to this organization: *to call out the fire brigade* ◇ *The fire brigade were there in minutes.*

fire·bug /ˈfaɪəbʌɡ; *NAmE* ˈfaɪər-/ *noun* (*informal*) a person who deliberately starts fires

fire·crack·er /ˈfaɪəkrækə(r); *NAmE* ˈfaɪərk-/ *noun* a small FIREWORK that explodes with a loud noise

ˈfire de·part·ment (*NAmE*) (*BrE* **ˈfire brigade**, **ˈfire service**) *noun* [usually sing.] an organization of people who are trained and employed to put out fires and to rescue people from fires; the people who belong to this organization

ˈfire door *noun* a heavy door that is used to prevent a fire from spreading in a building

ˈfire drill (*BrE* also **ˈfire practice**) *noun* [C, U] a practice of what people must do in order to escape safely from a fire in a building

ˈfire-eater *noun* an entertainer who pretends to eat fire

ˈfire engine (*NAmE* also **ˈfire truck**) *noun* a special vehicle that carries equipment for fighting large fires

ˈfire es·cape *noun* metal stairs or a LADDER on the outside of a building, which people can use to escape from a fire ➲ VISUAL VOCAB page V14

ˈfire extinguisher (also **ex·tin·guish·er**) *noun* a metal container with water or chemicals inside for putting out small fires

fire·fight /ˈfaɪəfaɪt; *NAmE* ˈfaɪərf-/ *noun* (*technical*) a battle where guns are used, involving soldiers or the police

fire·fight·er /ˈfaɪəfaɪtə(r); *NAmE* ˈfaɪərf-/ *noun* a person whose job is to put out fires ➲ see also FIREMAN ▸ **fire·fight·ing** *noun* [U]: ***firefighting equipment/vehicles***

fire·fly /ˈfaɪəflaɪ; *NAmE* ˈfaɪərf-/ *noun* (*pl.* **-ies**) (*NAmE* also **ˈlightning bug**) a flying insect with a tail that shines in the dark

fire·guard /ˈfaɪəɡɑːd; *NAmE* ˈfaɪərɡɑːrd/ (*NAmE* also **ˈfire screen**) *noun* a metal frame that is put in front of a fire in a room to prevent people from burning themselves

ˈfire hose *noun* a long tube that is used for directing water onto fires

fire·house /ˈfaɪəhaʊs; *NAmE* ˈfaɪərh-/ *noun* (*US*) a FIRE STATION in a small town

ˈfire hydrant (also **hy·drant**) *noun* a pipe in the street through which water can be sent using a PUMP in order to put out fires or to clean the streets

fire·light /ˈfaɪəlaɪt; *NAmE* ˈfaɪərl-/ *noun* [U] the light that comes from a fire in a room

fire·light·er /ˈfaɪəlaɪtə(r); *NAmE* ˈfaɪərl-/ (*BrE*) (*NAmE* **ˈfire·start·er**) *noun* [C, U] a block of material that burns easily and is used to help start a coal or wood fire

ˈfire line *noun* (*NAmE*) a strip of land that has been cleared in order to stop a fire from spreading ➲ see also FIREBREAK

fire·man /ˈfaɪəmən; *NAmE* ˈfaɪərmən/ *noun* (*pl.* **-men** /-mən/) a person, usually a man, whose job is to put out fires ➲ see also FIREFIGHTER ➲ note at GENDER

fire·place /ˈfaɪəpleɪs; *NAmE* ˈfaɪərp-/ *noun* an open space for a fire in the wall of a room ➲ VISUAL VOCAB page V18

fire·power /ˈfaɪəpaʊə(r); *NAmE* ˈfaɪərp-/ *noun* [U] the number and size of guns that an army, a ship, etc. has available: (*figurative*) *The company has enormous financial firepower.*

ˈfire prac·tice *noun* [C, U] (*BrE*) = FIRE DRILL

fire·proof /ˈfaɪəpruːf; *NAmE* ˈfaɪərp-/ *adj.* able to resist great heat without burning or being badly damaged: *a fireproof door* ◇ *a fireproof dish* (= that can be heated in an oven)

ˈfire-raiser *noun* (*BrE*) a person who starts a fire deliberately SYN **arsonist** ▸ **ˈfire-raising** *noun* [U]

fire-retard·ant /ˈfaɪə rɪˌtɑːdənt; *NAmE* ˈfaɪər rɪˌtɑːrd-/ (also **ˈflame-retardant**) *adj.* [usually before noun] that makes a fire burn more slowly

ˈfire sale *noun* **1** a sale at low prices of things that a company or person owns, usually in order to pay debts: *The company was forced to have a fire sale of its assets.* **2** a sale of goods at low prices because they have been damaged by a fire or because they cannot be stored after a fire

ˈfire screen *noun* **1** (*NAmE*) = FIREGUARD **2** a screen, often decorative, that is put in front of an open fire in a room to protect people from the heat or from SPARKS, or to hide it when it is not lit

ˈfire ser·vice *noun* [usually sing.] (*BrE*) = FIRE BRIGADE

fire·side /ˈfaɪəsaɪd; *NAmE* ˈfaɪərs-/ *noun* [usually sing.] the part of a room beside the fire: *sitting* ***by the fireside***

ˈfire starter (*NAmE*) (*BrE* **fire·light·er**) *noun* a block of material that burns easily and is used to help start a coal or wood fire

fire·start·er /ˈfaɪəstɑːtə(r); *NAmE* ˈfaɪərstɑːrtər/ *noun* (*NAmE*) **1** a device that allows you to start a fire, usually by hitting a piece of FLINT (= a hard grey stone) against a piece of steel **2** (*BrE* **fire·light·er**) a block of material that burns easily and is used to help start a coal or wood fire **3** a person who commits the crime of deliberately setting fire to sth SYN **arsonist**

ˈ**fire station** *noun* a building for a FIRE BRIGADE or FIRE DEPARTMENT and its equipment

fire·storm /ˈfaɪəstɔːm; *NAmE* ˈfaɪərstɔːrm/ *noun* a very large fire, usually started by bombs, that is not under control and is made worse by the winds that it causes

ˈ**fire trap** *noun* a building that would be very dangerous if a fire started there, especially because it would be difficult for people to escape

ˈ**fire truck** *noun* (*NAmE*) = FIRE ENGINE

fire·wall /ˈfaɪəwɔːl; *NAmE* ˈfaɪərw-/ *noun* (*computing*) a part of a computer system that prevents people from getting at information without permission, but still allows them to receive information that is sent to them ➲ COLLOCATIONS at EMAIL

fire·water /ˈfaɪəwɔːtə(r); *NAmE* ˈfaɪər-/ *noun* [U] (*informal*) strong alcoholic drink

fire·wood /ˈfaɪəwʊd; *NAmE* ˈfaɪərwʊd/ *noun* [U] wood that has been cut into pieces to be used for burning in fires

fire·work /ˈfaɪəwɜːk; *NAmE* ˈfaɪərwɜːrk/ *noun* **1** [C] a small device containing powder that burns or explodes and produces bright coloured lights and loud noises, used especially at celebrations: (*BrE*) *to let off a few fireworks* ◇ (*NAmE*) *to set off a few fireworks* ◇ *a firework(s) display* **2** **fireworks** [pl.] a display of fireworks: *When do the fireworks start?* **3** **fireworks** [pl.] (*informal*) strong or angry words; exciting actions: *There'll be fireworks when he finds out!*

fir·ing /ˈfaɪərɪŋ/ *noun* **1** [U] the action of firing guns: *There was continuous firing throughout the night.* **2** [U, C] (*especially NAmE*) the action of forcing sb to leave their job: *teachers protesting against the firing of a colleague* ◇ *She's responsible for the hirings and firings.*

ˈ**firing line** *noun*
IDM **be in the** ˈ**firing line** (*BrE*) (*NAmE* **be on the** ˈ**firing line**) **1** to be in a position where you can be shot at **2** to be in a position where people can criticize or blame you: *The employment secretary found himself in the firing line over recent job cuts.*

ˈ**firing squad** *noun* [C+sing./pl. v., U] a group of soldiers who are ordered to shoot and kill sb who is found guilty of a crime: *He was executed by (a) firing squad.*

fir·kin /ˈfɜːkɪn; *NAmE* ˈfɜːrkɪn/ *noun* (*old use*) **1** a small BARREL (= a round container with flat ends), used mainly for liquids, butter or fish **2** a unit for measuring volume, equal to about 41 litres

firm 0‐w /fɜːm; *NAmE* fɜːrm/ *noun, adj., adv., verb*
■ ***noun*** 0‐w a business or company: *an engineering firm* ◇ *a firm of accountants* ➲ COLLOCATIONS at BUSINESS
■ ***adj.*** (**firm·er**, **firm·est**) **1** 0‐w fairly hard; not easy to press into a different shape: *a firm bed/mattress* ◇ *These peaches are still firm.* ◇ *Bake the cakes until they are firm to the touch.* **2** 0‐w not likely to change: *a* **firm believer** *in socialism* ◇ *a* **firm agreement/date/decision/offer/promise** ◇ **firm beliefs/conclusions/convictions/principles** ◇ *She is a* **firm favourite with** *the children.* ◇ *We have no* **firm evidence** *to support the case.* ◇ *They remained* **firm friends**. **3** 0‐w strongly fixed in place SYN **secure**: *Stand the fish tank on a firm base.* ◇ *No building can stand without firm foundations, and neither can a marriage.* **4** 0‐w (of sb's voice or hand movements) strong and steady: *'No,' she repeated, her voice firmer this time.* ◇ *With a* **firm grip** *on my hand, he pulled me away.* ◇ *Her handshake was cool and firm.* **5** (of sb's behaviour, position or understanding of sth) strong and in control: *to exercise* **firm control/discipline/leadership** ◇ *Parents must* **be firm with** *their children.* ◇ *The company now has a* **firm footing** *in the marketplace.* ◇ *This book will give your students a* **firm grasp of** *English grammar.* ◇ *We need to keep a* **firm grip** *on the situation.* **6** [usually before noun] **~ (against sth)** (of a country's money, etc.) not lower than another: *The euro remained firm against the dollar, but fell against the yen.* ➲ see also FIRMLY ▸ **firm·ness** *noun* [U]
IDM **be on firm** ˈ**ground** to be in a strong position in an argument, etc. because you know the facts: *Everyone agreed with me, so I knew I was on firm ground.* **a firm** ˈ**hand** strong control or discipline: *Those children need a firm hand to make them behave.* **take a firm** ˈ**line/**ˈ**stand (on/against sth)** to make your beliefs known and to try to make others follow them: *We need to take a firm line on tobacco advertising.* ◇ *They took a firm stand against drugs in the school.*
■ ***adv.***
IDM **hold** ˈ**firm (to sth)** (*formal*) to believe sth strongly and not change your mind: *She held firm to her principles.* **stand** ˈ**fast/**ˈ**firm** to refuse to move back; to refuse to change your opinions
■ ***verb*** **1** [T] **~ sth** to make sth become stronger or harder: *Firm the soil around the plant.* ◇ *This product claims to firm your body in six weeks.* **2** [I] **~ (to/at…)** (*finance*) (of shares, prices, etc.) to become steady or rise steadily: *Rank's shares firmed 3p to 696p.*
PHR V ˌ**firm** ˈ**up** to become harder or more solid: *Put the mixture somewhere cool to firm up.* ˌ**firm** ˈ**up sth** **1** to make arrangements more final and fixed: *The company has not yet firmed up its plans for expansion.* ◇ *The precise details still have to be firmed up.* **2** to make sth harder or more solid: *A few weeks of aerobics will firm up that flabby stomach.*

firma·ment /ˈfɜːməmənt; *NAmE* ˈfɜːrm-/ *noun* **the firmament** [sing.] (*old use* or *literary*) the sky: (*figurative*) *a rising star in the literary firmament*

firm·ly 0‐w /ˈfɜːmli; *NAmE* ˈfɜːrm-/ *adv.* in a strong or definite way: *'I can manage,' she said firmly.* ◇ *It is now firmly established as one of the leading brands in the country.* ◇ *Keep your eyes firmly fixed on the road ahead.*

firm·ware /ˈfɜːmweə(r); *NAmE* ˈfɜːrmwer/ *noun* [U] (*computing*) a type of computer software that is stored in such a way that it cannot be changed or lost

first 0‐w /fɜːst; *NAmE* fɜːrst/ *det., ordinal number, adv., noun*
■ ***det., ordinal number*** **1** 0‐w happening or coming before all other similar things or people; 1st: *his first wife* ◇ *It was the first time they had ever met.* ◇ *I didn't take the first bus.* ◇ *students in their first year at college* ◇ *your first impressions* ◇ *She resolved to do it at the first (*= earliest*) opportunity.* ◇ *King Edward I (*= pronounced 'King Edward the First'*)* ◇ *the first of May/May 1st* ◇ *His second book is better than his first.* **2** 0‐w the most important or best: *Your first duty is to your family.* ◇ *She won first prize in the competition.* ◇ *an issue of the first importance*
IDM Most idioms containing **first** are at the entries for the nouns and adjectives in the idioms, for example **on first acquaintance** is at **acquaintance**. **there's a first time for everything** (*saying, humorous*) the fact that sth has not happened before does not mean that it will never happen
■ ***adv.*** **1** 0‐w before anyone or anything else; at the beginning: *'Do you want a drink?' 'I'll finish my work first.'* ◇ *First I had to decide what to wear.* ◇ *Who* **came first** *in the race (*= who won*)?* ◇ *It plunged nose first into the river.* **2** 0‐w for the first time: *When did you first meet him?* **3** 0‐w used to introduce the first of a list of points you want to make in a speech or piece of writing SYN **firstly**: *This method has two advantages: first it is cheaper and second it is quicker.* ➲ LANGUAGE BANK at PROCESS **4** used to emphasize that you are determined not to do sth: *She swore that she wouldn't apologize—she'd die first!*
IDM **at** ˈ**first** at or in the beginning: *I didn't like the job much at first.* ◇ *At first I thought he was shy, but then I discovered he was just not interested in other people.* ◇ (*saying*) *If at first you don't succeed, try, try again.* ➲ note at FIRSTLY **come** ˈ**first** to be considered more important than anything else: *In any decision she makes, her family always comes first.* ˌ**first and** ˈ**foremost** more than anything else: *He does a*

little teaching, but first and foremost he's a writer. ˌ**first and ˈlast** in every way that is important; completely: *She regarded herself, first and last, as a musician.* ˌ**first ˈcome, ˌfirst ˈserved** (*saying*) people will be dealt with, seen, etc. strictly in the order in which they arrive: *Tickets are available on a first come, first served basis.* ˌ**first of ˈall 1** 🔑 before doing anything else; at the beginning: *First of all, let me ask you something.* ➲ LANGUAGE BANK at PROCESS **2** 🔑 as the most important thing: *The content of any article needs, first of all, to be relevant to the reader.* ➲ note at FIRSTLY ˌ**first ˈoff** (*informal, especially BrE*) before anything else: *First off, let's see how much it'll cost.* ˌ**first ˈup** (*BrE, informal*) to start with; before anything else ˌ**put sb/sth ˈfirst** to consider sb/sth to be more important than anyone/anything else: *She always puts her children first.* ➲ more at FOOT *n.*, HEAD *n.*, SAFETY

■ ***noun* 1** 🔑 **the first** [C] (*pl.* **the first**) the first person or thing mentioned; the first person or thing to do a particular thing: *I was the first in my family to go to college.* ◇ *Sheila and Jim were the first to arrive.* ◇ *I'd be* ***the first to admit*** (= I will most willingly admit) *I might be wrong.* ◇ ***The first I heard about*** *the wedding* (= the first time I became aware of it) *was when I saw it in the local paper.* **2** [C, usually sing.] an achievement, event, etc, never done or experienced before: *We went on a cruise, a first for both of us.* **3** (also ˌ**first ˈgear**) [U] the lowest gear on a car, bicycle, etc. that you use when you are moving slowly: *He stuck the car* ***in first*** *and revved.* **4** [C] ~ (**in sth**) the highest level of university degree at British universities: *She* ***got a first*** *in maths at Exeter.* ➲ compare SECOND, THIRD

IDM ˌ**first among ˈequals** the person or thing with the highest status in a group **from the** (**very**) **ˈfirst** from the beginning: *They were attracted to each other from the first.* **from ˌfirst to ˈlast** from beginning to end; during the whole time: *It's a fine performance that commands attention from first to last.*

Language Bank

first

Ordering your points

- This study has **the following** aims: **first**, to investigate how international students in the UK use humour; **second**, to examine how jokes can help to establish social relationships; and, **third**, to explore the role that humour plays in helping overseas students adjust to life in the UK.
- **Let us begin by** identifying some of the popular joke genres in the UK.
- **Next, let us turn to/Next, let us consider** the question of gender differences in the use of humour.
- **Finally/Lastly,** let us briefly examine the role of humour in defining a nation's culture.

➲ notes at FIRSTLY, LASTLY
➲ Language Banks at CONCLUSION, PROCESS

ˌ**first ˈaid** *noun* [U] simple medical treatment that is given to sb before a doctor comes or before the person can be taken to a hospital: *to give first aid* ◇ *a first-aid course*

ˌ**first ˈaider** *noun* (*BrE*) a person who is trained to give first aid

the ˌFirst Aˈmendment *noun* [sing.] the statement in the US Constitution that protects freedom of speech and religion and the right to meet in peaceful groups

ˌ**first ˈbalcony** *noun* (*NAmE*) = DRESS CIRCLE

ˌ**first ˈbase** *noun* (in BASEBALL) the first of the BASES that players must touch: *He didn't make it past first base.*

IDM **not get to first ˈbase** (**with sth/sb**) (*informal, especially NAmE*) to fail to make a successful start in a project, relationship, etc; to fail to get through the first stage

first·born /ˈfɜːstbɔːn; *NAmE* ˈfɜːrstbɔːrn/ *noun* (*old-fashioned*) a person's first child ▶ **first·born** *adj.* [only before noun]: *their firstborn son*

ˌ**first ˈclass** *noun, adv.*

■ ***noun*** [U] **1** the best and most expensive seats or accommodation on a train, plane or ship: *There is more room in first class.* **2** (in Britain) the class of mail that is delivered most quickly: *First class costs more.* **3** (in the US) the class of mail that is used for letters **4** the highest standard of degree given by a British university

■ ***adv.* 1** using the best and most expensive seats or accommodation in a train, plane or ship: *to travel first class* **2** (in Britain) by the quickest form of mail: *I sent the package first class on Monday.* **3** (in the US) by the class of mail that is used for letters

ˌ**first-ˈclass** *adj.* **1** [usually before noun] in the best group; of the highest standard SYN **excellent**: *a first-class novel* ◇ *a first-class writer* ◇ *The car was in first-class condition.* ◇ *I know a place where the food is first-class.* **2** [only before noun] connected with the best and most expensive way of travelling on a train, plane or ship: *first-class rail travel* ◇ *a first-class cabin/seat/ticket* **3** [only before noun] (in Britain) connected with letters, packages, etc. that are delivered most quickly, or that cost more to send: ***first-class mail/post/postage/stamps*** **4** [only before noun] used to describe a university degree of the highest class from a British university: *She was awarded a first-class degree in English.*

ˈ**first cost** *noun* [C, U] (*economics*) = PRIME COST

ˌ**first ˈcousin** *noun* = COUSIN (1)

ˈ**first degree** *noun* (*especially BrE*) an academic qualification given by a university or college, for example a BA or BSc, that is given to sb who does not already have a degree in that subject: *What was your first degree in?* ◇ *to study geography at first-degree level*

ˌ**first-deˈgree** *adj.* [only before noun] **1** (*especially NAmE*) **~ murder, assault, robbery, etc.** murder, etc. of the most serious kind **2 ~ burns** burns of the least serious of three kinds, affecting only the surface of the skin ➲ compare SECOND-DEGREE, THIRD-DEGREE

ˌ**first ˈdown** *noun* (in AMERICAN FOOTBALL) **1** the first of a series of four DOWNS (= chances to move the ball forward ten yards) **2** the chance to start a new series of four DOWNS because your team has succeeded in going forward ten yards

ˌ**first eˈdition** *noun* one of the copies of a book that was produced the first time the book was printed

ˌ**first-ˈever** *adj.* [only before noun] never having happened or been experienced before: *his first-ever visit to London* ◇ *the first-ever woman vice-president*

the ˌfirst ˈfamily *noun* [sing.] the family of the President of the United States

ˌ**first ˈfinger** *noun* = INDEX FINGER

ˌ**first ˈfloor** (usually **the first floor**) *noun* [sing.] **1** (*BrE*) the level of a building above the ground level: *Menswear is on the first floor.* **2** (*NAmE*) (*BrE* ˌ**ground ˈfloor**) the floor of a building that is at the same level as the ground outside ▶ ˌ**first-ˈfloor** *adj.* [only before noun]: *a first-floor flat/apartment* ➲ note at FLOOR

ˌ**first-ˈfoot** *verb* **~ sb** to be the first person to enter sb's house in the New Year. First-footing is a Scottish custom. ▶ ˌ**first-ˈfooter** *noun*

ˈ**first fruit** *noun* [usually pl.] the first result of sb's work or effort

ˌ**first geneˈration** *noun* [sing.] **1** people who have left their country to go and live in a new country; the children of these people **2** the first type of a machine to be developed: *the first generation of personal computers* ▶ ˌ**first-geneˈration** *adj.*: *first-generation Caribbeans in the UK*

ˌ**first-ˈhand** *adj.* [only before noun] obtained or experienced yourself: *to have first-hand experience of poverty* ➲ compare SECOND-HAND ▶ ˌ**first-ˈhand** *adv.*: *to experience poverty first-hand*

ˌ**First ˈLady** *noun* [usually sing.] **1 the First Lady** (in the US) the wife of the President **2** (*NAmE*) the wife of the leader of a state **3** (usually **first lady**) the woman who is thought to be the best in a particular profession, sport, etc: *the first lady of country music*

ˌfirst ˈlanguage *noun* the language that you learn to speak first as a child; the language that you speak best: *His first language is Welsh.* ➲ compare SECOND LANGUAGE

ˌfirst lieuˈtenant *noun* **1** an officer in the navy with responsibility for managing a ship, etc. **2** an officer in the US army and AIR FORCE just below the rank of a captain **3** (*informal*) a person who is the next most important to sb

ˌfirst ˈlight *noun* [U] the time when light first appears in the morning **SYN** **dawn, daybreak**: *We left at first light.*

first·ly /ˈfɜːstli; *NAmE* ˈfɜːrst-/ *adv.* used to introduce the first of a list of points you want to make in a speech or piece of writing: *There are two reasons for this decision: firstly...* ➲ LANGUAGE BANK at FIRST

Which Word?

firstly / first of all / at first

- **Firstly** and **first (of all)** are used to introduce a series of facts, reasons, opinions, etc: *The brochure is divided into two sections, dealing firstly with basic courses and secondly with advanced ones.* **Firstly** is more common in *BrE* than in *NAmE*.
- **At first** is used to talk about the situation at the beginning of a period of time, especially when you are comparing it with a different situation at a later period: *Maggie had seen him nearly every day at first. Now she saw him much less.*

ˌfirst ˈmate (also **ˌfirst ˈofficer**) *noun* the officer on a commercial ship just below the rank of captain or MASTER

ˌfirst ˈminister (also **First Minister**) *noun* the leader of the ruling political party in some regions or countries, for example in Scotland

ˈfirst name (also **ˈgiven name** especially in *NAmE*) *noun* a name that was given to you when you were born, that comes before your family name: *His first name is Tom and his surname is Green.* ◇ *Please give all your first names.* ◇ (*BrE*) *to be* ***on first-name terms*** *with sb* (= to call them by their first name as a sign of a friendly informal relationship) ◇ (*NAmE*) *to be on* ***a first-name basis***

ˌFirst ˈNations *noun* [pl.] (*CanE*) the Aboriginal peoples of Canada, not including the Inuit or Metis

ˌfirst ˈnight *noun* **1** the first public performance of a play, film/movie, etc. **2** (*NAmE*) a public celebration of NEW YEAR'S EVE

ˌfirst ofˈfender *noun* a person who has been found guilty of a crime for the first time

ˌfirst ˈofficer *noun* = FIRST MATE

ˌfirst-ˌpast-the-ˈpost *adj.* [only before noun] (of a system of elections) in which only the person who gets the most votes is elected ➲ compare PROPORTIONAL REPRESENTATION

the ˌfirst ˈperson *noun* [sing.] **1** (*grammar*) a set of pronouns and verb forms used by a speaker to refer to himself or herself, or to a group including himself or herself: *'I am' is the first person singular of the present tense of the verb 'to be'.* ◇ *'I', 'me', 'we' and 'us' are first-person pronouns.* **2** a way of writing a novel, etc. as if one of the characters is telling the story using the word *I*: *a novel written* ***in the first person*** ➲ compare THE SECOND PERSON, THE THIRD PERSON

ˌfirst ˈprinciples *noun* [pl.] the basic ideas on which a theory, system or method is based: *I think we should go back to first principles.*

ˌfirst-ˈrate *adj.* of the highest quality **SYN** **excellent**: *a first-rate swimmer* ◇ *The food here is absolutely first-rate.*

ˌfirst reˈfusal *noun* [U] (*BrE*) the right to decide whether to accept or refuse sth before it is offered to others: *Will you give me first refusal on the car, if you decide to sell it?*

first responder /ˌfɜːst rɪˈspɒndə(r); *NAmE* ˌfɜːrst rɪˈspɑːndər/ *noun* (*especially NAmE*) a person such as a member of the police or fire department in a position to arrive first at an emergency, who has been trained to give basic medical treatment ➲ compare EMERGENCY SERVICES

ˈfirst school *noun* (in Britain) a school for children between the ages of 5 and 8 or 9

ˌfirst ˈstrike *noun* an attack on an enemy made before they attack you

ˈfirst-time *adj.* [only before noun] doing or experiencing sth for the first time: *houses for first-time buyers* ◇ *a computer program designed for first-time users*

ˌfirst-ˈtimer *noun* a person who does sth for the first time: *conference first-timers*

ˌFirst ˈWorld *noun* [sing.] the rich industrial countries of the world ➲ compare THE THIRD WORLD

the ˌFirst World ˈWar (also **ˌWorld War ˈI**) *noun* [sing.] the war that was fought mainly in Europe between 1914 and 1918

firth /fɜːθ; *NAmE* fɜːrθ/ *noun* (especially in Scottish place names) a narrow strip of the sea that runs a long way into the land, or a part of a river where it flows into the sea: *the Moray Firth* ◇ *the Firth of Clyde*

fis·cal /ˈfɪskl/ *adj.* connected with government or public money, especially taxes: ***fiscal policies/reforms*** ▸ **fis·cal·ly** *adv.* ➲ see also PROCURATOR FISCAL

ˌfiscal ˈyear (*NAmE*) (*BrE* **fiˌnancial ˈyear**, **ˈtax year**) *noun* [usually sing.] a period of twelve months over which the accounts and taxes of a company or a person are calculated

fish ⁰ᵚ /fɪʃ/ *noun, verb*

■ ***noun*** (*pl.* **fish** or **fishes**) **HELP** **Fish** is the usual plural form. The older form, **fishes**, can be used to refer to different kinds of fish. **1** ⁰ᵚ [C] a creature that lives in water, breathes through GILLS, and uses FINS and a tail for swimming: *They caught several fish.* ◇ ***tropical/marine/freshwater fish*** ◇ ***shoals*** (= groups) ***of fish*** ◇ ***a fish tank/pond*** ◇ *There are about 30 000 species of fish in the world.* ◇ *The list of endangered species includes nearly 600 fishes.* ◇ *Fish stocks in the Baltic are in decline.* ➲ COLLOCATIONS at LIFE ➲ VISUAL VOCAB page V10 ➲ see also COARSE FISH, FLATFISH, SEA FISH, SHELLFISH, WET FISH **2** ⁰ᵚ [U] the flesh of fish eaten as food: ***frozen/smoked/fresh fish*** ◇ *fish pie*

IDM **a ˌfish out of ˈwater** a person who feels uncomfortable or awkward because he or she is in surroundings that are not familiar **have bigger/other fish to ˈfry** to have more important or more interesting things to do **neither ˌfish nor ˈfowl** neither one thing nor another **an odd/a queer ˈfish** (*old-fashioned, BrE*) a person who is slightly strange or crazy **there are plenty more fish in the ˈsea** there are many other people or things that are as good as the one sb has failed to get ➲ more at BIG *adj.*, COLD *adj.*, DIFFERENT, DRINK *v.*, SHOOT *v.*

■ ***verb*** **1** ⁰ᵚ [I] to try to catch fish with a hook, nets, etc: *The trawler was fishing off the coast of Iceland.* ◇ **~ for sth** *You can fish for trout in this stream.* **2** ⁰ᵚ [I] **go fishing** to spend time fishing for pleasure: *Let's go fishing this weekend.* **3** [T] **~ sth** (**for sth**) to try to catch fish in the area of water mentioned: *They fished the loch for salmon.* **4** [I] **+ adv./prep.** to search for sth, using your hands: *She fished around in her bag for her keys.*

PHR V **ˈfish for sth** to try to get sth, or to find out sth, although you are pretending not to: *to fish for compliments/information* **ˌfish sth/sb↔ˈout** (**of sth**) to take or pull sth/sb out of a place: *She fished a piece of paper out of the pile on her desk.* ◇ *They fished a dead body out of the river.*

ˌfish and ˈchips *noun* [U] a dish of fish that has been fried in BATTER served with CHIPS/FRIES, and usually bought in the place where it has been cooked and eaten at home, etc, especially in Britain: *Three portions of fish and chips, please.* ◇ *a fish and chip shop*

fish·bowl /ˈfɪʃbəʊl; *NAmE* -boʊl/ *noun* = GOLDFISH BOWL

fish·cake /ˈfɪʃkeɪk/ *noun* (*especially BrE*) pieces of fish mixed with MASHED potato made into a flat round shape, covered with BREADCRUMBS and fried

fish·er /ˈfɪʃə(r)/ *noun* (*especially NAmE*) = FISHERMAN

fish·er·man /ˈfɪʃəmən; *NAmE* ˈfɪʃərmən/ *noun* (*pl.* **-men** /-mən/) a person who catches fish, either as a job or as a sport ➲ compare ANGLER

fisher·woman /ˈfɪʃəwʊmən; *NAmE* ˈfɪʃər-/ *noun* (*pl.* **-women** /-wɪmɪn/) a woman who catches fish, either as a job or as a sport ➲ compare ANGLER ➲ note at GENDER

fish·ery /ˈfɪʃəri/ *noun* (*pl.* **-ies**) **1** a part of the sea or a river where fish are caught in large quantities: *a herring fishery* ◇ ***coastal/freshwater fisheries*** **2** = FISH FARM: *a trout fishery*

fish-eye lens /ˌfɪʃaɪ ˈlenz/ *noun* a camera LENS with a wide angle that gives the view a curved shape

ˈfish farm (also **fish·ery**) *noun* a place where fish are bred as a business

ˌfish ˈfinger (*BrE*, *NAmE* **ˌfish ˈstick**) *noun* a long narrow piece of fish covered with BREADCRUMBS or BATTER, usually frozen and sold in packs

ˈfish hook *noun* a sharp metal hook for catching fish, that has a point which curves backwards to make it difficult to pull out ➲ picture at HOOK

fish·ing 0‑ᴡ /ˈfɪʃɪŋ/ *noun* [U] the sport or business of catching fish: *They often* ***go fishing.*** ◇ *deep-sea fishing* ◇ *a fishing boat* ◇ *fishing grounds* ◇ *We enjoyed a day's fishing by the river.*

ˈfishing line *noun* [C, U] a long thread with a sharp hook attached, that is used for catching fish

ˈfishing rod (also **rod**) (*NAmE* also **ˈfishing pole**) *noun* a long wooden or plastic stick with a fishing line and hook attached, that is used for catching fish

ˈfishing tackle *noun* [U] equipment used for catching fish

ˈfish knife *noun* a knife with a broad blade and without a sharp edge, used for eating fish ➲ VISUAL VOCAB page V19

fish·mon·ger /ˈfɪʃmʌŋɡə(r)/ *noun* (*especially BrE*) **1** a person whose job is to sell fish in a shop **2** **fish·mon·ger's** (*pl.* **fish·mon·gers**) a shop that sells fish

fish·net /ˈfɪʃnet/ *noun* [U] a type of cloth made of threads that produce a pattern of small holes like a net: *fishnet stockings*

ˈfish slice (*BrE*) (also **spat·ula** *NAmE*, *BrE*) *noun* a kitchen UTENSIL that has a broad flat blade with narrow holes in it, attached to a long handle, used for turning and lifting food when cooking ➲ VISUAL VOCAB page V23

ˌfish ˈstick (*NAmE*) (*BrE* **ˌfish ˈfinger**) *noun* a long narrow piece of fish covered with BREADCRUMBS or BATTER, usually frozen and sold in packs

fish·tail /ˈfɪʃteɪl/ *verb* [I] if a vehicle **fishtails**, the back end slides from side to side

fish·wife /ˈfɪʃwaɪf/ *noun* (*pl.* **-wives** /-waɪvz/) (*disapproving*) a woman with a loud voice and bad manners

fishy /ˈfɪʃi/ *adj.* (**fish·ier**, **fishi·est**) **1** (*informal*) that makes you suspicious because it seems dishonest SYN **suspicious**: *There's something fishy going on here.* **2** smelling or tasting like a fish: *What's that fishy smell?*

fis·sile /ˈfɪsaɪl; *NAmE* ˈfɪsl/ *adj.* (*physics*) capable of nuclear FISSION: *fissile material*

fis·sion /ˈfɪʃn/ *noun* [U] **1** (also **ˌnuclear ˈfission**) (*physics*) the act or process of splitting the NUCLEUS (= central part) of an atom, when a large amount of energy is released ➲ compare FUSION **2** (*biology*) the division of cells into new cells as a method of reproducing cells **3** (*chemistry*) the breaking of a chemical BOND between two atoms

fis·sure /ˈfɪʃə(r)/ *noun* (*technical*) a long deep crack in sth, especially in rock or in the earth ▶ **fis·sured** *adj.*

fist /fɪst/ *noun* a hand when it is tightly closed with the fingers bent into the PALM: *He punched me with his fist.* ◇ *She* ***clenched her fists*** *to stop herself trembling.* ◇ *He got into a* ***fist fight*** *in the bar.* ➲ see also HAM-FISTED, TIGHT-FISTED

IDM **make a better, good, poor, etc. fist of sth** (*BrE*, *old-fashioned*, *informal*) to make a good, bad, etc. attempt to do sth ➲ more at IRON *adj.*, MONEY

fist·ful /ˈfɪstfʊl/ *noun* a number or an amount of sth that can be held in a fist: *a fistful of coins*

fisti·cuffs /ˈfɪstɪkʌfs/ *noun* [pl.] (*old-fashioned* or *humorous*) a fight in which people hit each other with their FISTS

fis·tula /ˈfɪstjʊlə; *NAmE* ˈfɪstʃələ/ *noun* (*medical*) an opening between two organs of the body, or between an organ and the skin, that would not normally exist, caused by injury, disease, etc.

fit 0‑ᴡ /fɪt/ *verb*, *adj.*, *noun*

■ ***verb*** (**fit·ting**, **fit·ted**, **fit·ted**) (*NAmE* usually **fit·ting**, **fit**, **fit** except in the passive)

▸ RIGHT SIZE/TYPE **1** 0‑ᴡ [I, T] (not used in the progressive tenses) to be the right shape and size for sb/sth: *I tried the dress on but it didn't fit.* ◇ *That jacket fits well.* ◇ *a close-fitting dress* ◇ **~ sb/sth** *I can't find clothes to fit me.* ◇ *The key doesn't fit the lock.* **2** 0‑ᴡ [I] to be of the right size, type or number to go somewhere: *I'd like to have a desk in the room but it won't fit.* ◇ **+ adv./prep.** *All the kids will fit in the back of the car.* **3** [T, often passive] **~ sb** (**for sth**) to put clothes on sb and make them the right size and shape: *I'm going to be fitted for my wedding dress today.*

▸ PUT STH SOMEWHERE **4** 0‑ᴡ [T] to put or fix sth somewhere: **~ sth + adv./prep.** *They fitted a smoke alarm to the ceiling.* ◇ **~ sth with sth** *The rooms were all fitted with smoke alarms.* **5** 0‑ᴡ [I, T] to put or join sth in the right place: **~ + adv./prep.** *The glass fits on top of the jug to form a lid.* ◇ *How do these two parts* ***fit together****?* ◇ **~ sth + adv./prep.** *We fitted together the pieces of the puzzle.*

▸ AGREE/MATCH **6** 0‑ᴡ [I, T] (not used in the progressive tenses) to agree with, match or be suitable for sth; to make sth do this: *Something doesn't quite fit here.* ◇ **~ into sth** *His pictures don't fit into any category.* ◇ **~ sth** *The facts certainly fit your theory.* ◇ *The punishment ought to fit the crime.* ◇ **~ sth to sth** *We should fit the punishment to the crime.*

▸ MAKE SUITABLE **7** [T] (*especially BrE*) to make sb/sth suitable for a particular job: **~ sb/sth for sth** *His experience fitted him perfectly for the job.* ◇ **~ sb/sth to do sth** *His experience fitted him to do the job.* ➲ see also FITTED

IDM **fit** (**sb**) **like a ˈglove** to be the perfect size or shape for sb ➲ more at BILL *n.*, CAP *n.*, DESCRIPTION, FACE *n.*

PHR V **ˌfit sb/sth↔ˈin** | **ˌfit sb/sth ˈin/ˈinto sth** **1** 0‑ᴡ to find time to see sb or to do sth: *I'll try and fit you in after lunch.* ◇ *I had to fit ten appointments into one morning.* **2** 0‑ᴡ to find or have enough space for sb/sth in a place: *We can't fit in any more chairs.* **ˌfit ˈin** (**with sb/sth**) 0‑ᴡ to live, work, etc. in an easy and natural way with sb/sth: *He's never done this type of work before; I'm not sure how he'll fit in with the other people.* ◇ *Where do I fit in?* ◇ *Do these plans fit in with your arrangements?* **ˌfit sb/sth↔ˈout/ˈup** (**with sth**) to supply sb/sth with all the equipment, clothes, food, etc. they need SYN **equip**: *to fit out a ship before a long voyage* ◇ *The room has been fitted out with a stove and a sink.* **ˌfit sb↔ˈup** (**for sth**) (*BrE*, *informal*) to make it look as if sb is guilty of a crime they have not committed SYN **frame**: *I didn't do it—I've been fitted up!*

■ ***adj.*** (**fit·ter**, **fit·test**)

▸ HEALTHY **1** 0‑ᴡ healthy and strong, especially because you do regular physical exercise: *Top athletes have to be very fit.* ◇ **~** (**to do sth**) (*BrE*) *He won't be fit to play in the match on Saturday.* ◇ *She tries to* ***keep fit*** *by jogging every day.* ◇ **~** (**for sth**) (*BrE*) *He's had a bad cold and isn't fit enough for work yet.* ◇ *I feel really* ***fighting fit*** (= very healthy and full of energy). ◇ *The government aims to make British industry leaner and fitter* (= employing fewer people and with lower costs). OPP **unfit** ➲ SYNONYMS at WELL ➲ see also KEEP-FIT

▸ SUITABLE **2** 0‑ᴡ suitable; of the right quality; with the right qualities or skills: **~ for sb/sth** *The food was not fit for human consumption.* ◇ *It was a meal* ***fit for a king*** (= of very good quality). ◇ *The children seem to think I'm only fit for cooking and washing!* ◇ **~ to do sth** *Your car isn't fit to be on the road!* ◇ *He's so angry he's* ***in no fit state*** *to see any-*

one. ◇ (*formal*) *This is not a fit place for you to live.* OPP **unfit**

▸ READY **3** **~ to do sth** (*BrE, informal*) ready or likely to do sth extreme: *They worked until they were **fit to drop*** (= so tired that they were likely to fall down). ◇ *I've eaten so much I'm **fit to burst**.* ◇ *She was laughing **fit to burst*** (= very much).

▸ ATTRACTIVE **4** (*BrE, informal*) sexually attractive

IDM **(as) ˌfit as a ˈfiddle** (*informal*) in very good physical condition **see/think ˈfit (to do sth)** (*formal*) to consider it right or acceptable to do sth; to decide or choose to do sth: *You must do as you think fit* (= but I don't agree with your decision). ◇ *The newspaper did not see fit to publish my letter* (= and I criticize it for that). ➲ more at SURVIVAL

■ ***noun***

▸ ILLNESS **1** [C] a sudden attack of an illness, such as EPILEPSY, in which sb becomes unconscious and their body may make violent movements SYN **convulsion**: *to have an epileptic fit* ◇ *Her fits are now controlled by drugs.*

▸ OF COUGHING/LAUGHTER **2** [C] a sudden short period of coughing or of laughing, that you cannot control SYN **bout**: *a fit of coughing* ◇ *He had us all **in fits** (**of laughter**) with his jokes.*

▸ OF STRONG FEELING **3** [C] a short period of very strong feeling: *to act in a **fit of anger/rage/temper/pique*** ➲ see also HISSY FIT

▸ OF CLOTHING **4** [C, U] (often with an adjective) the way that sth, especially a piece of clothing, fits: *a **good/bad/close/perfect fit***

▸ MATCH **5** [C] **~ (between A and B)** the way that two things match each other or are suitable for each other: *We need to work out the best fit between the staff required and the staff available.*

IDM **by/in ˌfits and ˈstarts** frequently starting and stopping again; not continuously: *Because of other commitments I can only write my book in fits and starts.* **have/throw a ˈfit** (*informal*) to be very shocked, upset or angry: *Your mother would have a fit if she knew you'd been drinking!*

fit·ful /ˈfɪtfl/ *adj.* happening only for short periods; not continuous or regular: *a fitful night's sleep* ▸ **fit·ful·ly** /ˈfɪtfəli/ *adv.*: *to sleep fitfully*

fit·ment /ˈfɪtmənt/ *noun* [usually pl.] (*BrE, technical*) a piece of furniture or equipment, especially one that is made for and fixed in a particular place

fit·ness /ˈfɪtnəs/ *noun* [U] **1** the state of being physically healthy and strong: *a magazine on health and fitness* ◇ *a **fitness instructor/class/test*** ◇ *a high level of physical fitness* ➲ COLLOCATIONS at DIET **2** the state of being suitable or good enough for sth: **~ for sth** *He convinced us of his fitness for the task.* ◇ **~ to do sth** *There were doubts about her fitness to hold office.*

ˈfitness centre (*BrE*) (*NAmE* **ˈfitness center**) *noun* a place where people go to do physical exercise in order to stay or become healthy and fit

fit·ted /ˈfɪtɪd/ *adj.* **1** [only before noun] (*especially BrE*) (of furniture) built to be fixed into a particular space SYN **built-in**: ***fitted wardrobes/cupboards*** ➲ VISUAL VOCAB page V20 **2** [only before noun] (*especially BrE*) (of a room) with matching cupboards and other furniture built for the space and fixed in place: ***a fitted kitchen/bedroom*** **3** [only before noun] (of clothes) made to follow the shape of the body: *a fitted jacket* OPP **loose** **4** **~ for/to sth** | **~ to do sth** (*especially BrE*) suitable; with the right qualities and skills: *She was well fitted to the role of tragic heroine.* **5** **~ with sth** having sth as equipment: *Insurance costs will be reduced for houses fitted with window locks.*

ˌfitted ˈcarpet *noun* (*BrE*) a carpet that is cut and fixed to cover the floor of a room completely ➲ VISUAL VOCAB page V20 ➲ see also WALL-TO-WALL CARPET

fit·ter /ˈfɪtə(r)/ *noun* **1** a person whose job is to put together or repair equipment: *a gas fitter* **2** a person whose job is to cut and fit clothes or carpets, etc.

fit·ting /ˈfɪtɪŋ/ *adj., noun*

■ ***adj.*** **1** (*formal*) suitable or right for the occasion SYN **appropriate**: *The award was a **fitting tribute** to her years of devoted work.* ◇ *A fitting end to the meal would be a glass of port.* ◇ ***It is fitting that** the new centre for European studies should be in a university that teaches every European language.* **2** **-fitting** (in adjectives) having a particular FIT: *a tight-fitting dress*

■ ***noun*** **1** [usually pl.] a small part on a piece of equipment or furniture: *light fittings* ◇ *a pine cupboard with brass fittings* **2** [usually pl.] (*BrE*) items in a house such as a cooker, lights or shelves that are usually fixed but that you can take with you when you move to a new house ➲ compare FIXTURE **3** an occasion when you try on a piece of clothing that is being made for you to see if it fits

ˈfitting room (*NAmE* also **ˈdressing room**) *noun* a room or CUBICLE in a shop/store where you can put on clothes to see how they look

five 0→ /faɪv/ *number*

5: *There are only five cookies left.* ◇ *five of Sweden's top financial experts* ◇ *Ten people were invited but only five turned up.* ◇ *Do you have change for five dollars?* ◇ *a five-month contract* ◇ *Look at page five.* ◇ *Five and four is nine.* ◇ *Three fives are fifteen.* ◇ *I can't read your writing—is this meant to be a five?* ◇ *The bulbs are planted in threes or fives* (= groups of three or five). ◇ *We moved to America when I was five* (= five years old). ◇ *Shall we meet at five* (= at five o'clock), *then?* ➲ see also HIGH FIVE

IDM **ˌgive sb ˈfive** (*informal*) to hit the inside of sb's hand with your hand as a way of saying hello or to celebrate a victory: *Give me five!* ➲ more at NINE

ˌfive-and-ˈdime (also **ˈdime store**) *noun* (*old-fashioned, NAmE*) a shop/store that sells a range of cheap goods

ˌfive-a-ˈside *noun* [U] (*BrE*) a game of football (SOCCER) played indoors with five players on each team

five·fold /ˈfaɪvfəʊld; *NAmE* -foʊld/ *adj., adv.* ➲ -FOLD

ˌfive o'clock ˈshadow *noun* [sing.] (*informal*) the dark colour that appears on a man's chin and face when th hair has grown a little during the day

ˌfive ˈpence (also **ˌfive pence ˈpiece, 5p**) *noun* a British coin worth five pence: *Have you got a five pence?*

fiver /ˈfaɪvə(r)/ *noun* (*informal*) **1** (*BrE*) £5 or a five-pound note: *Can you lend me a fiver?* **2** (*NAmE, old-fashioned*) $5 or a five-dollar bill

fives /faɪvz/ *noun* [U] a game played especially in British PUBLIC SCHOOLS in which players hit a ball with their hand or a BAT against the walls of a COURT

ˈfive-star *adj.* [usually before noun] **1** having five stars in a system that measures quality. Five stars usually represents the highest quality: *a five-star hotel* **2** (*NAmE*) having the highest military rank, and wearing a uniform which has five stars on it: *a five-star general*

fix 0→ /fɪks/ *verb, noun*

■ ***verb***

▸ ATTACH **1** 0→ **~ sth (+ adv./prep.)** (*especially BrE*) to put sth firmly in a place so that it will not move: *to fix a shelf to the wall* ◇ *to fix a post in the ground* ◇ (*figurative*) *He noted every detail so as to fix the scene in his mind.*

▸ ARRANGE **2** 0→ **~ sth** to decide on a date, a time, an amount, etc. for sth SYN **set**: *Has the date of the next meeting been fixed?* ◇ *They fixed the rent at £100 a week.* ◇ *Their prices are fixed until the end of the year* (= will not change before then). **3** to arrange or organize sth: **~ sth (for sb)** *I'll fix a meeting.* ◇ **~ sth up (for sb)** *You have to fix visits up in advance with the museum.* ◇ **~ sth with sth** (*informal*) *Don't worry, I'll **fix it with** Sarah.* ◇ **~ (up) (for sb) to do sth** *I've fixed up (for us) to go to the theatre next week.*

▸ POSITION/TIME **4** **~ sth** to discover or say the exact position, time, etc. of sth: *We can fix the ship's exact position at the time the fire broke out.*

▸ REPAIR **5** 0→ **~ sth** to repair or correct sth: *The car won't start—can you fix it?* ◇ *I've fixed the problem.*

▸ FOOD/DRINK **6** (*especially NAmE*) to provide or prepare sth, especially food: **~ sb sth** *Can I fix you a drink?* ◇ **~ sth for sb** *Can I fix a drink for you?* ◇ **~ sth** *I'll fix supper.*

▸ HAIR/FACE **7** **~ sth** (*especially NAmE*) to make sth such as your hair or face neat and attractive: *I'll fix my hair and then I'll be ready.*

▸ RESULT **8** [often passive] **~ sth** (*informal*) to arrange the result of sth in a way that is not honest or fair: *I'm sure the race was fixed.*

▸ PUNISH **9** **~ sb** (*informal*) to punish sb who has harmed you and stop them doing you any more harm: *Don't worry—I'll fix him.*

▸ IN PHOTOGRAPHY **10** **~ sth** (*technical*) to treat film for cameras, etc. with a chemical so that the colours do not change or become less bright

▸ ANIMAL **11** **~ sth** (*NAmE, informal*) to make an animal unable to have young by means of an operation ➲ see also NEUTER

IDM ▸ **fix sb with a 'look, 'stare, 'gaze, etc.** to look directly at sb for a long time: *He fixed her with an angry stare.* ➲ more at AIN'T

PHR V ▸ **'fix on sb/sth** to choose sb/sth: *They've fixed on Paris for their honeymoon.* **'fix sth on sb/sth** [often passive] if your eyes or your mind are **fixed on** sth, you are looking at or thinking about sth with great attention **,fix sth↔'up** to repair, decorate or make sth ready: *They fixed up the house before they moved in.* **,fix sb 'up (with sb)** (*informal*) to arrange for sb to have a meeting with sb who might become a boyfriend or girlfriend **,fix sb 'up (with sth)** (*informal*) to arrange for sb to have sth; to provide sb with sth: *I'll fix you up with a place to stay.*

■ ***noun***

▸ SOLUTION **1** [C] (*informal*) a solution to a problem, especially an easy or temporary one: *There is no **quick fix** for the steel industry.*

▸ DRUG **2** [sing.] (*informal*) an amount of sth that you need and want frequently, especially an illegal drug such as HEROIN: *to get yourself a fix* ◇ *I need a fix of coffee before I can face the day.*

▸ DIFFICULT SITUATION **3** [sing.] a difficult situation SYN **mess**: *We've got ourselves **in a fix** about this.*

▸ ON POSITION **4** [sing.] the act of finding the position of a ship or an aircraft: *They managed to **get a fix** on the yacht's position.*

▸ UNDERSTANDING **5** [sing.] (*informal*) an act of understanding sth: *He tried to **get a fix** on the young man's motives, but he just couldn't understand him.*

▸ DISHONEST RESULT **6** [sing.] (*informal*) a thing that is dishonestly arranged; a trick: *Her promotion was a fix, I'm sure!*

fix·ated /fɪk'seɪtɪd/ *adj.* [not before noun] **~ (on sb/sth)** always thinking and talking about sb/sth in a way that is not normal

fix·ation /fɪk'seɪʃn/ *noun* **1** [C] a very strong interest in sb/sth, that is not normal or natural: *a mother fixation* ◇ **~ with/on sb/sth** *He's got this fixation with cleanliness.* **2** [U] (*technical*) the process of a gas becoming solid: *nitrogen fixation*

fixa·tive /'fɪksətɪv/ *noun* [C, U] **1** a substance that is used to prevent colours or smells from changing or becoming weaker, for example in photography, art or the making of PERFUME **2** a substance that is used to stick things together or keep things in position

fixed 🔑 /fɪkst/ *adj.*

1 🔑 staying the same; not changing or able to be changed: *fixed prices* ◇ *a fixed rate of interest* ◇ *people living on **fixed incomes*** ◇ *The money has been invested for a **fixed period**.* ➲ see also ABODE **2** 🔑 (often *disapproving*) (of ideas and wishes) held very firmly; not easily changed: *My parents had **fixed ideas** about what I should become.* **3** [only before noun] (of expressions on sb's face) not changing and not sincere: *He greeted all his guests with a fixed smile on his face.*

IDM ▸ **how are you, etc. 'fixed (for sth)?** (*informal*) used to ask how much of sth a person has, or to ask about arrangements: *How are you fixed for cash?* ◇ *How are we fixed for Saturday* (= have we arranged to do anything)?

fixed 'assets *noun* [pl.] (*business*) land, buildings and equipment that are owned and used by a company

fixed 'costs *noun* [pl.] (*business*) the costs that a business must pay that do not change even if the amount of work produced changes

fix·ed·ly /'fɪksɪdli/ *adv.* continuously, without looking away, but often with no real interest: *to **stare/gaze fixedly** at sb/sth*

,fixed-'term *adj.* [only before noun] a **fixed-term** contract, etc. is one that only lasts for the agreed period of time

,fixed-'wing *adj.* [only before noun] used to describe aircraft with wings that remain in the same position, rather than HELICOPTERS, etc.

fixer /'fɪksə(r)/ *noun* **1** (*informal*) a person who arranges things for other people, sometimes dishonestly: *a great political fixer* **2** a chemical substance used in photography to prevent a photograph from changing and becoming too dark

,fixer-'upper *noun* (*NAmE, informal*) a house or flat/apartment that is cheap because it needs a lot of repair work when you buy it

fix·ings /'fɪksɪŋz/ *noun* [pl.] (*NAmE*) = TRIMMINGS: *a hamburger with all the fixings*

fix·ity /'fɪksəti/ *noun* [U] (*formal*) the quality of being firm and not changing

fix·ture /'fɪkstʃə(r)/ *noun* **1** (*BrE*) a sports event that has been arranged to take place on a particular date and at a particular place: *an annual fixture* ◇ *Saturday's fixture against Liverpool* ◇ *the season's fixture list* **2** a thing such as a bath/BATHTUB or a toilet that is fixed in a house and that you do not take with you when you move house: (*BrE*) *The price of the house includes **fixtures and fittings**.* ◇ (*figurative*) *He has stayed with us so long he seems to have become **a permanent fixture**.* ➲ COLLOCATIONS at DECORATE ➲ compare FITTING

fizz /fɪz/ *verb, noun*

■ ***verb*** [I] when a liquid **fizzes**, it produces a lot of bubbles and makes a long sound like an 's': *Champagne was fizzing in the glass.* ◇ (*figurative*) *Share prices are fizzing.* ◇ **~ with sth** (*figurative*) *He started to fizz with enthusiasm.*

■ ***noun*** **1** [U, sing.] the small bubbles of gas in a liquid: (*figurative*) *There is plenty of fizz and sparkle in the show.* ◇ (*figurative*) *The fizz has gone out of the market.* **2** [U, sing.] the sound that is made by bubbles of gas in a liquid, or a sound similar to this: *the fizz of a firework* **3** [U] (*BrE, informal*) a drink that has a lot of bubbles of gas, especially CHAMPAGNE

fizz·er /'fɪzə(r)/ *noun* (*AustralE, NZE, informal*) a failure: *The party was a fizzer.*

fiz·zle /'fɪzl/ *verb* [I] when sth, especially sth that is burning, **fizzles**, it makes a sound like a long 's' SYN **hiss**

PHR V ▸ **,fizzle 'out** (*informal*) to gradually become less successful and end in a disappointing way

fizzy /'fɪzi/ *adj.* (*BrE*) (**fizz·ier, fizzi·est**) (of a drink) having bubbles of gas in it SYN **sparkling**: *fizzy drinks* OPP **still**

fjord (also **fiord**) /'fjɔːd; *NAmE* 'fjɔːrd/ *noun* a long narrow strip of sea between high CLIFFS, especially in Norway

flab /flæb/ *noun* [U] (*informal, disapproving*) soft, loose flesh on a person's body

flab·ber·gast·ed /'flæbəgɑːstɪd; *NAmE* 'flæbərgæstɪd/ *adj.* [not usually before noun] (*informal*) extremely surprised and/or shocked SYN **astonished**

flabby /'flæbi/ *adj.* (*informal, disapproving*) (**flab·bier, flab·bi·est**) **1** having soft, loose flesh; fat: *flabby thighs* **2** weak; with no strength or force: *a flabby grip* ◇ *a flabby argument*

flac·cid /'flæsɪd; 'flæk-/ *adj.* (*formal*) soft and weak; not firm and hard: *flaccid breasts*

flack /flæk/ *noun* **1** [U] = FLAK **2** [C] (*NAmE, informal*) = PRESS AGENT

flag 🔑 /flæg/ *noun, verb*

■ ***noun*** **1** 🔑 a piece of cloth with a special coloured design on it that may be the symbol of a particular country or organization, or may have a particular meaning. A flag can be attached to a pole or held in the hand: *the Italian flag* ◇ *the flag of Italy* ◇ *The hotel **flies the** European Union **flag**.* ◇ *The American **flag was flying**.* ◇ *All the **flags were at half mast*** (= in honour of a famous person who has died). ◇ *The black and white flag went down, and the race began.*

➲ VISUAL VOCAB page V2 ➲ see also BLUE FLAG **2** used to refer to a particular country or organization and its beliefs and values: *to swear allegiance to the flag* ◇ *He was working under the flag of the United Nations.* **3** 🔑 a piece of cloth that is attached to a pole and used as a signal or MARKER in various sports **4** a flower that is a type of IRIS and that grows near water: *yellow flags* **5** = FLAGSTONE

IDM **fly/show/wave the 'flag** to show your support for your country, an organization or an idea to encourage or persuade others to do the same **keep the 'flag flying** to represent your country or organization: *Our exporters keep the flag flying at international trade exhibitions.* ➲ more at RED *adj.*

■ ***verb*** (-gg-) **1** [T] **~ sth** to put a special mark next to information that you think is important: *I've flagged the paragraphs that we need to look at in more detail.* **2** [I] to become tired, weaker or less enthusiastic: *It had been a long day and the children were beginning to flag.* ◇ *Her confidence had never flagged.* ◇ ***flagging support/enthusiasm***

PHR V ˌ**flag sb/sth↔'down** to signal to the driver of a vehicle to stop by waving at them ˌ**flag sth↔'up** (*BrE*) to draw attention to sth: *The report flagged up the dangers of under-age drinking.*

'flag day *noun* **1** (*BrE*) a day when money is collected in public places for a charity, and people who give money receive a small paper STICKER **2 Flag Day** 14 June, the anniversary of the day in 1777 when the Stars and Stripes became the national flag of the United States

fla·gel·late /ˈflædʒəleɪt/ *verb* **~ sb/yourself** (*formal*) to WHIP yourself or sb else, especially as a religious punishment or as a way of experiencing sexual pleasure ▶ **fla·gel·la·tion** /ˌflædʒəˈleɪʃn/ *noun* [U]

ˌflag 'football *noun* [U] (*NAmE*) a type of AMERICAN FOOTBALL played without the usual form of TACKLING. A TACKLE is made instead by pulling a piece of cloth from an opponent's WAISTBAND. ➲ compare TOUCH FOOTBALL

flagged /flægd/ *adj.* covered with large flat stones (called FLAGSTONES): *a flagged floor*

ˌflag of con'venience *noun* a flag of a foreign country that is used by a ship from another country for legal or financial reasons

flagon /ˈflægən/ *noun* a large bottle or similar container, often with a handle, in which wine, etc. is sold or served

flag·pole /ˈflægpəʊl; *NAmE* -poʊl/ (also **flag·staff**) *noun* a tall pole on which a flag is hung ➲ VISUAL VOCAB page V2

fla·grant /ˈfleɪgrənt/ *adj.* (of an action) shocking because it is done in a very obvious way and shows no respect for people, laws, etc. SYN **blatant**: *a flagrant abuse of human rights* ◇ *He showed a flagrant disregard for anyone else's feelings.* ▶ **fla·grant·ly** *adv.*

fla·grante ➲ IN FLAGRANTE

flag·ship /ˈflægʃɪp/ *noun* **1** the main ship in a FLEET of ships in the navy **2** [usually sing.] the most important product, service, building, etc. that an organization owns or produces: *The company is opening a new flagship store in London.*

flag·staff /ˈflægstɑːf; *NAmE* -stæf/ *noun* = FLAGPOLE

flag·stone /ˈflægstəʊn; *NAmE* -stoʊn/ (also **flag**) *noun* a large flat square piece of stone that is used for floors, paths, etc.

'flag-waving *noun* [U] the expression of strong national feelings, especially in a way that people disapprove of

flail /fleɪl/ *verb, noun*

■ ***verb*** **1** [I, T] **~ (sth)** (**about/around**) to move around without control; to move your arms and legs around without control: *The boys flailed around on the floor.* ◇ *He was running along, his arms flailing wildly.* **2** [T] **~ sb/sth** to hit sb/sth very hard, especially with a stick

■ ***noun*** a tool that has a long handle with a stick swinging from it, used especially in the past to separate grains of WHEAT from their dry outer covering, by beating the WHEAT

flair /fleə(r); *NAmE* fler/ *noun* **1** [sing., U] **~ for sth** a natural ability to do sth well SYN **talent**: *He **has a flair for** languages.* **2** [U] a quality showing the ability to do things in an interesting way that shows imagination: *artistic flair* ◇ *She dresses with real flair.*

flak (also **flack**) /flæk/ *noun* [U] **1** guns on the ground that are shooting at enemy aircraft; bullets from these guns **2** (*informal*) severe criticism: *He's **taken a lot of flak** for his left-wing views.* ◇ *She **came in for a lot of flak** from the press.*

flake /fleɪk/ *noun, verb*

■ ***noun*** **1** a small, very thin layer or piece of sth, especially one that has broken off from sth larger: ***flakes of snow/paint*** ◇ *dried onion flakes* ➲ see also CORNFLAKES, SNOWFLAKE, SOAP FLAKES **2** (*NAmE, informal*) a person who is strange or unusual or who forgets things easily

■ ***verb*** **1** [I] **~ (off)** to fall off in small thin pieces: *You could see bare wood where the paint had flaked off.* ◇ *His skin was dry and flaking.* **2** [T, I] **~ (sth)** to break sth, especially fish or other food into small thin pieces; to fall into small thin pieces: *Flake the tuna and add to the sauce.* ◇ *flaked almonds*

PHR V ˌ**flake 'out 1** (*informal*) to lie down or fall asleep because you are extremely tired: *When I got home he'd already flaked out on the bed.* **2** (*NAmE, informal*) to begin to behave in a strange way

'flak jacket *noun* a heavy jacket without sleeves that has metal inside it to make it stronger, and is worn by soldiers and police officers to protect them from bullets

flaky /ˈfleɪki/ *adj.* **1** tending to break into small, thin pieces: *flaky pastry* ◇ *dry flaky skin* **2** (*NAmE, informal*) (of a person) behaving in a strange or unusual way; tending to forget things **3** (*especially BrE, informal, computing*) that does not work well or often stops working: *I found the software a bit flaky.* ▶ **flaki·ness** *noun* [U]

flambé /ˈflɒmbeɪ; *NAmE* flɑːmˈbeɪ/ *adj.* [after noun] (from *French*) (of food) covered with alcohol, especially BRANDY and allowed to burn for a short time ▶ **flambé** *verb* **~ sth** ➲ VISUAL VOCAB page V24

flam·boy·ant /flæmˈbɔɪənt/ *adj.* **1** (of people or their behaviour) different, confident and exciting in a way that attracts attention: *a **flamboyant gesture/style/personality*** **2** brightly coloured and noticeable: ***flamboyant clothes/designs*** ▶ **flam·boy·ance** /-ˈbɔɪəns/ *noun* [U] **flam·boy·ant·ly** *adv.*

flame 🔑 /fleɪm/ *noun, verb*

■ ***noun*** **1** 🔑 [C, U] a hot bright stream of burning gas that comes from sth that is on fire: *the tiny yellow flame of a match* ◇ *The flames were growing higher and higher.* ◇ *The building was **in flames*** (= was burning). ◇ *The plane **burst into flame(s)*** (= suddenly began burning strongly). ◇ *Everything **went up in flames*** (= was destroyed by fire). ➲ VISUAL VOCAB page V57 **2** [U] a bright red or orange colour: *a flame-red car* **3** [C] (*literary*) a very strong feeling: *a flame of passion* ➲ see also OLD FLAME **4** [C] (*informal*) an angry or insulting message sent to sb by email or on the Internet IDM see FAN *v.*

■ ***verb*** **1** [I] (**+ adj.**) (*literary*) to burn with a bright flame: *The logs flamed on the hearth.* ◇ (*figurative*) *Hope flamed in her.* **2** [I, T] (**+ adj.**) | **~ (sth)** (*literary*) (of a person's face) to become red as a result of a strong emotion; to make sth become red: *Her cheeks flamed with rage.* **3** [T] **~ sb** (*informal*) to send sb an angry or insulting message by email or on the Internet

fla·menco /fləˈmeŋkəʊ; *NAmE* -koʊ/ *noun* (*pl.* -os) **1** [U, C] a fast exciting Spanish dance that is usually danced to music played on a GUITAR: *flamenco dancing* ◇ *to dance the flamenco* **2** [U] the GUITAR music that is played for this dance

flame·proof /ˈfleɪmpruːf/ *adj.* made of or covered with a special material that will not burn easily

flame-retard·ant /ˈfleɪm rɪˌtɑːdənt; *NAmE* -ˌtɑːrd-/ *adj.* = FIRE-RETARDANT

'flame-thrower *noun* a weapon like a gun that shoots out burning liquid or flames and is often used for clearing plants from land

F

flam·ing /ˈfleɪmɪŋ/ *adj.* [only before noun] **1** full of anger: *a* ***flaming argument/temper*** **2** burning and covered in flames: *Flaming fragments were still falling from the sky.* **3** (*BrE, informal*) used to emphasize that you are annoyed: *You flaming idiot!* **4** bright red or orange in colour: *flaming (red) hair* ◊ *a flaming sunset*

fla·mingo /fləˈmɪŋɡəʊ; *NAmE* -ɡoʊ/ *noun* (*pl.* -oes or -os) a large pink bird with long thin legs and a long neck, that lives near water in warm countries

flam·mable /ˈflæməbl/ (also **in·flam·mable** especially in *BrE*) *adj.* that can burn easily: ***highly flammable*** *liquids* OPP **non-flammable**

F

flan /flæn/ *noun* [C, U] **1** (*especially BrE*) an open PIE made of PASTRY or cake filled with eggs and cheese, fruit, etc: *a mushroom/strawberry flan* ◊ *Have some more flan.* ➲ compare QUICHE, TART **2** (*NAmE*) (*BrE* **crème caramel**) a cold DESSERT (= a sweet dish) made from milk, eggs and sugar

flange /flændʒ/ *noun* an edge that sticks out from an object and makes it stronger or (as in a wheel of a train) keeps it in the correct position

flank /flæŋk/ *noun, verb*

■ ***noun*** **1** the side of sth such as a building or mountain **2** the left or right side of an army during a battle, or a sports team during a game **3** the side of an animal between the RIBS and the hip

■ ***verb*** **1 be flanked by sb/sth** to have sb/sth on one or both sides: *She left the courtroom flanked by armed guards.* **2 ~ sth** to be placed on one or both sides of sth: *They drove through the cotton fields that flanked Highway 17.*

flank·er /ˈflæŋkə(r)/ *noun* an attacking player in RUGBY or AMERICAN FOOTBALL

flan·nel /ˈflænl/ *noun* **1** [U] a type of soft light cloth, containing cotton or wool, used for making clothes: *a flannel shirt* ◊ *a grey flannel suit* **2** (also **face·cloth**) (both *BrE*) (*NAmE* **wash·cloth**) [C] a small piece of cloth used for washing yourself: *a face flannel* ➲ VISUAL VOCAB page V21 **3 flannels** [pl.] trousers/pants made of flannel **4** [U] (*BrE, informal*) words that do not have much meaning and that avoid telling sb what they want to know

flan·nel·ette /ˌflænəˈlet/ *noun* [U] a type of soft cotton cloth, used especially for making sheets and NIGHTCLOTHES

flap /flæp/ *noun, verb*

■ ***noun***

▸ FLAT PIECE OF PAPER, ETC. **1** [C] a flat piece of paper, cloth, metal, etc. that is attached to sth along one side and that hangs down or covers an opening: *the flap of an envelope* ◊ *I zipped the tent flaps shut.* ➲ see also CAT FLAP ➲ VISUAL VOCAB page V56

▸ MOVEMENT **2** [C, usually sing.] a quick often noisy movement of sth up and down or from side to side: *With a flap of its wings, the bird was gone.* ◊ *the flap of the sails*

▸ WORRY/EXCITEMENT **3** [sing.] (*informal, especially BrE*) a state of worry, confusion and excitement: *She* ***gets in a flap*** *over the slightest thing.*

▸ PUBLIC DISAGREEMENT **4** [sing.] (*NAmE*) public disagreement, anger or criticism caused by sth a public figure has said or done: *the flap about the President's business affairs*

▸ PART OF AIRCRAFT **5** [C] (*technical*) a part of the wing of an aircraft, on the rear of the wing, that can be moved up or down to control upward or downward movement ➲ VISUAL VOCAB page V43

▸ PHONETICS **6** [C] = TAP (6)

■ ***verb*** (-pp-)

▸ MOVE QUICKLY **1** [T, I] **~ (sth)** if a bird **flaps** its wings, or if its wings **flap**, they move quickly up and down SYN **beat**: *The bird flapped its wings and flew away.* ◊ *The gulls flew off, wings flapping.* **2** [I, T] to move or to make sth move up and down or from side to side, often making a noise: (**+ adv./prep.**) *The sails flapped in the breeze.* ◊ *Two large birds flapped* (= flew) *slowly across the water.* ◊ **~ sth** *She walked up and down, flapping her arms to keep warm.* ◊ *A gust of wind flapped the tents.*

▸ BE WORRIED/EXCITED **3** [I] (*BrE, informal*) to behave in an anxious or excited way: *There's no need to flap—I've got everything under control.*

▸ PHONETICS **4** [T] **~ sth** = TAP (7) IDM see EAR

flap·jack /ˈflæpdʒæk/ *noun* **1** [U, C] (*BrE*) a thick soft biscuit made from OATS, butter, sugar and SYRUP **2** [C] (*NAmE*) a thick PANCAKE

flap·per /ˈflæpə(r)/ *noun* a fashionable young woman in the 1920s who was interested in modern ideas and was determined to enjoy herself

flare /fleə(r); *NAmE* fler/ *verb, noun*

■ ***verb*** **1** [I] to burn brightly, but usually for only a short time or not steadily: *The match flared and went out.* ◊ *The fire flared into life.* ◊ (*figurative*) *Colour flared in her cheeks.* **2** [I] **~ (up)** (especially of anger and violence) to suddenly start or become much stronger SYN **erupt**: *Violence flared when the police moved in.* ◊ ***Tempers flared*** *towards the end of the meeting.* ➲ related noun FLARE-UP (1) **3** [T, I] (**+ speech**) to say sth in an angry and aggressive way: *'You should have told me!' she flared at him.* **4** [I] (of clothes) to become wider towards the bottom: *The sleeves are tight to the elbow, then flare out.* **5** [T, I] **~ (sth)** if a person or an animal **flares** their NOSTRILS (= the openings at the end of the nose), or if their nostrils **flare**, they become wider, especially as a sign of anger: *The horse backed away, its nostrils flaring with fear.*

PHR V ˌ**flare** ˈ**up** **1** (of flames, a fire, etc.) to suddenly start burning more brightly ➲ related noun FLARE-UP (3) **2** (of a person) to suddenly become angry ➲ related noun FLARE-UP (1) **3** (of an illness, injury, etc.) to suddenly start again or become worse ➲ related noun FLARE-UP (2)

■ ***noun*** **1** [usually sing.] a bright but unsteady light or flame that does not last long: *The flare of the match lit up his face.* **2** a device that produces a bright flame, used especially as a signal; a flame produced in this way: *The ship sent up distress flares to attract the attention of the coastguard.* **3** a shape that becomes gradually wider: *a skirt with a slight flare* **4 flares** (*BrE* also ˌ**flared** ˈ**trousers**) [pl.] (*informal*) trousers/pants that become very wide at the bottom of the legs: *a pair of flares*

flared /fleəd; *NAmE* flerd/ *adj.* (of clothes) wider at the bottom edge than at the top

ˈ**flare-up** *noun* [usually sing.] **1** a sudden expression of angry or violent feeling SYN **outburst**: *a flare-up of tension between the two sides* **2** (of an illness) a sudden painful attack, especially after a period without any problems or pain **3** the fact of a fire suddenly starting to burn again more strongly than before: *a flare-up of the bushfires*

flash 0‑w /flæʃ/ *verb, noun, adj.*

■ ***verb***

▸ SHINE BRIGHTLY **1** 0‑w [I, T] to shine very brightly for a short time; to make sth shine in this way: *Lightning flashed in the distance.* ◊ *the flashing blue lights of a police car* ◊ **+ adv./prep.** *A neon sign flashed on and off above the door.* ◊ **~ sth** *The guide flashed a light into the cave.*

▸ GIVE SIGNAL **2** 0‑w [T, I] to use a light to give sb a signal: **~ sth (at sb)** *Red lights flashed a warning at them.* ◊ **~ sb (sth)** *Red lights flashed them a warning.* ◊ **~ at sb** *Why is that driver flashing at us?*

▸ SHOW QUICKLY **3** [T] **~ sth at sb** to show sth to sb quickly: *He flashed his pass at the security officer.*

▸ MOVE QUICKLY **4** [I] **+ adv./prep.** to move or pass very quickly: *The countryside flashed past the train windows.* ◊ *A look of terror flashed across his face.*

▸ OF THOUGHTS/MEMORIES **5** [I] **+ adv./prep.** to come into your mind suddenly: *A terrible thought flashed through my mind.*

▸ ON SCREEN **6** [I, T] to appear on a television screen, computer screen, etc. for a short time; to make sth do this: *A message was flashing on his pager.* ◊ **~ (sth) (up)** *His name was flashed up on the screen.*

▸ SEND NEWS **7** [T] **~ sth + adv./prep.** to send information quickly by radio, computer, etc: *News of their triumph was flashed around the world.*

▸ SHOW EMOTION **8** [I] (**+ adv./prep.**) (*literary*) to show a strong emotion suddenly and quickly: *Her eyes flashed with anger.*

▸ OF A MAN **9** [I] (*informal*) if a man **flashes**, he shows his sexual organs in public

IDM **flash sb a 'smile, 'look, etc.** to smile, look, etc. at sb suddenly and quickly

PHR V **,flash sth a'round** (*disapproving*) to show sth to other people in order to impress them: *He's always flashing his money around.* **,flash 'back (to sth)** **1** if your mind **flashes back** to sth, you remember sth that happened in the past: *Her thoughts flashed back to their wedding day.* ➲ related noun FLASHBACK (2) **2** if a film/movie **flashes back** to sth, it shows things that happened at an earlier time, for example at an earlier part of sb's life ➲ related noun FLASHBACK (1) **3** to reply very quickly and/or angrily **,flash 'by/'past** (of time) to go very quickly: *The morning has just flashed by.* **'flash on sth** (*US, informal*) to suddenly remember or think of sth: *I flashed on an argument I had with my sister when we were kids.* **'flash on sb** [no passive] if sth **flashes on you**, you suddenly realize it: **it flashes on sb that...** *It flashed on me that he was the man I'd seen in the hotel.*

▪ ***noun***

▸ LIGHT **1** 🔑 [C] a sudden bright light that shines for a moment and then disappears: *a **flash of lightning*** ◇ *Flashes of light were followed by an explosion.* ◇ *There was **a blinding flash** and the whole building shuddered.*

▸ SIGNAL **2** 🔑 [C] the act of shining a light on sth, especially as a signal

▸ IN PHOTOGRAPHY **3** 🔑 [C, U] a piece of equipment that produces a bright light for a very short time, used for taking photographs indoors, when it is dark, etc; the use of this when taking a photograph: *a camera with a built-in flash* ◇ *I'll need flash for this shot.* ◇ *flash photography* ➲ VISUAL VOCAB page V35

▸ OF BRIGHT COLOUR **4** 🔑 [C] **~ of sth** the sudden appearance for a short time of sth bright: *a flash of white teeth* ◇ *On the horizon, she saw a flash of silver—the sea!*

▸ SUDDEN IDEA/EMOTION **5** [C] **~ of sth** a particular feeling or idea that suddenly comes into your mind or shows in your face: *a **flash of anger/inspiration, etc.***

▸ NEWS **6** [C] = NEWSFLASH

▸ ON UNIFORM **7** [C] (*BrE*) a band or small piece of cloth worn on a military uniform to show a person's rank

▸ ON BOOK/PACK **8** [C] a band of colour or writing across a book, pack, etc.

▸ COMPUTING **9 Flash™** [U] a program which creates moving images for websites

IDM **a ,flash in the 'pan** a sudden success that lasts only a short time and is not likely to be repeated **in/like a 'flash** very quickly and suddenly ➲ more at QUICK *adv.*

▪ ***adj.*** (*BrE, informal, disapproving*) attracting attention by being large or expensive, or by having expensive clothes, etc: *a flash car* ◇ *He's very flash, isn't he?*

flash·back /ˈflæʃbæk/ *noun* **1** [C, U] a part of a film/movie, play, etc. that shows a scene that happened earlier in time than the main story: *The events that led up to the murder were shown in a series of flashbacks.* ◇ *The reader is told the story **in flashback**.* **2** [C] a sudden, very clear, strong memory of sth that happened in the past that is so real you feel that you are living through the experience again

flash·bulb /ˈflæʃbʌlb/ *noun* a small electric BULB that can be attached to a camera to take photographs indoors or when it is dark

'flash card *noun* a card with a word or picture on it, that teachers use during lessons

'flash drive (also **US'B drive, 'pen drive**) (*NAmE* also **'thumb drive**) *noun* (*computing*) a small memory device that can be used to store data from a computer and to move it from one computer to another SYN **memory stick** ➲ VISUAL VOCAB page V54

flash·er /ˈflæʃə(r)/ *noun* **1** (*informal*) a man who shows his sexual organs in public, especially in order to shock or frighten women **2** a device that turns a light on and off quickly **3** (*NAmE*) a light on a vehicle that you can turn on and off quickly as a signal: *four-way flashers* (= four lights that flash together to warn other drivers of possible danger)

'flash flood *noun* a sudden flood of water caused by heavy rain

flash·gun /ˈflæʃgʌn/ *noun* a piece of equipment that holds and operates a bright light that is used to take photographs indoors or when it is dark

flash·ing /ˈflæʃɪŋ/ *noun* [U] (also **flashings** [pl.]) a strip of metal put on a roof where it joins a wall to prevent water getting through

flash·light /ˈflæʃlaɪt/ (*especially NAmE*) (*BrE* also **torch**) *noun* a small electric lamp that uses batteries and that you can hold in your hand

'flash memory *noun* [U] (*computing*) computer memory that does not lose data when the power supply is lost

F

flash·mob /ˈflæʃmɒb; *NAmE* -mɑːb/ *noun* a large group of people who arrange (by mobile/cell phone or email) to gather together in a public place at exactly the same time, spend a short time doing sth there and then quickly all leave at the same time ▸ **flash·mob·ber** *noun* **flash·mob·bing** *noun* [U]

flash·point /ˈflæʃpɔɪnt/ *noun* [C, U] a situation or place in which violence or anger starts and cannot be controlled: *Tension in the city is rapidly reaching flashpoint.* ◇ *potential flashpoints in the south of the country*

flashy /ˈflæʃi/ *adj.* (**flash·ier, flashi·est**) (*informal*, usually *disapproving*) **1** (of things) attracting attention by being bright, expensive, large, etc: *a flashy hotel* ◇ *I just want a good reliable car, nothing flashy.* **2** (of people) attracting attention by wearing expensive clothes, etc. **3** intended to impress by looking very skilful: *He specializes in flashy technique, without much depth.* ▸ **flash·ily** *adv.*: *flashily dressed*

flask /flɑːsk; *NAmE* flæsk/ *noun* **1** a bottle with a narrow top, used in scientific work for mixing or storing chemicals ➲ VISUAL VOCAB page V57 **2** (*BrE*) = VACUUM FLASK: *a **flask of tea/coffee*** ➲ compare THERMOS **3** (*especially NAmE*) (*BrE* also **'hip flask**) a small flat bottle made of metal or glass and often covered with leather, used for carrying alcohol

flat 🔑 /flæt/ *adj., noun, adv., verb*

▪ ***adj.*** (**flat·ter, flat·test**)

▸ LEVEL **1** 🔑 having a level surface, not curved or sloping: *low buildings with flat roofs* ◇ *People used to think the earth was flat.* ◇ *Exercise is the only way to get a flat stomach after having a baby.* ◇ *The sails hung limply in the flat calm* (= conditions at sea when there is no wind and the water is completely level). **2** 🔑 (of land) without any slopes or hills: *The road stretched ahead across the flat landscape.* **3** 🔑 (of surfaces) smooth and even; without lumps or holes: *I need a flat surface to write on.* ◇ *We found a large flat rock to sit on.*

▸ NOT HIGH **4** 🔑 broad but not very high: *Chapattis are a kind of flat Indian bread.* ◇ *flat shoes* (= with no heels or very low ones)

▸ DULL **5** dull; lacking interest or enthusiasm: *He felt very flat after his friends had gone home.*

▸ VOICE **6** not showing much emotion; not changing much in tone: *Her voice was flat and expressionless.*

▸ COLOURS/PICTURES **7** very smooth, with no contrast between light and dark, and giving no impression of depth: *Acrylic paints can be used to create large, flat blocks of colour.*

▸ BUSINESS **8** not very successful because very little is being sold: *The housing market has been flat for months.*

▸ REFUSAL/DENIAL **9** [only before noun] not allowing discussion or argument; definite: *Her request was met with a flat refusal.* ◇ *He gave a flat 'No!' to one reporter's question.*

▸ IN MUSIC **10** used after the name of a note to mean a note a SEMITONE/HALF TONE lower: *That note should be B flat, not B.* ➲ picture at MUSIC OPP **sharp** ➲ compare NATURAL **11** below the correct PITCH (= how high or low a note sounds): *The high notes were slightly flat.* OPP **sharp**

▸ DRINK **12** no longer having bubbles in it; not fresh: *The soda was warm and had gone flat.*

▸ BATTERY **13** (*BrE*) unable to supply any more electricity

▸ TYRE **14** not containing enough air, usually because of a hole
▸ FEET **15** with no natural raised curves underneath ➲ see also FLAT-FOOTED
▸ **flat·ness** *noun* [U]
IDM **and ˌthat's 'flat!** (*BrE, informal*) that is my final decision and I will not change my mind: *You can't go and that's flat!* **as ˌflat as a 'pancake** completely flat ➲ more at BACK *n.*, SPIN *n.*
■ ***noun***
▸ ROOMS **1** (*key*) [C] (*BrE*) a set of rooms for living in, including a kitchen, usually on one floor of a building: *Do you live in a flat or a house?* ◇ *They're renting a* ***furnished flat*** *on the third floor.* ◇ *a ground-floor flat* ◇ *a new* ***block of flats*** ◇ *Many large old houses have been converted into flats.* ◇ *Children from the flats* (= the block of flats) *across the street were playing outside.* ➲ COLLOCATIONS at HOUSE ➲ VISUAL VOCAB page V14 ➲ compare APARTMENT
▸ LEVEL PART **2** [sing.] **the ~ of sth** the flat level part of sth: *He beat on the door with the flat of his hand.* ◇ *the flat of a sword*
▸ LAND **3** [C, usually pl.] an area of low flat land, especially near water: *salt flats* ➲ see also MUDFLAT
▸ HORSE RACING **4 the flat, the Flat** [sing.] (*BrE*) the season for racing horses on flat ground with no jumps
▸ IN MUSIC **5** [C] a note played a SEMITONE/HALF TONE lower than the note that is named. The written symbol is (♭): *There are no sharps or flats in the key of C major.* OPP **sharp** ➲ compare NATURAL
▸ TYRE **6** [C] (*especially NAmE*) a tyre that has lost air, usually because of a hole: *We got a flat on the way home.* ◇ *We had to stop to fix a flat.*
▸ IN THEATRE **7** [C] (*technical*) a vertical section of SCENERY used on a theatre stage
▸ SHOES **8 flats** (also **flat·ties**) [pl.] (*informal*) shoes with a very low heel: *a pair of flats* ➲ VISUAL VOCAB page V52
IDM **on the 'flat** (*BrE*) on level ground, without hills or jumps (= for example in horse racing)
■ ***adv.*** (*comparative* **flat·ter**, no *superlative*)
▸ LEVEL **1** spread out in a level, straight position, especially against another surface: *Lie flat and breathe deeply.* ◇ *They pressed themselves flat against the tunnel wall as the train approached.*
▸ REFUSING/DENYING **2** (*BrE*) (*NAmE* **ˌflat 'out**) (*informal*) in a definite and direct way: *She told me flat she would not speak to me again.* ◇ *I made them a reasonable offer but they turned it down flat.*
▸ IN MUSIC **3** lower than the correct PITCH (= how high or low a note sounds): *He sings flat all the time.* OPP **sharp**
IDM **fall 'flat** if a joke, a story, or an event **falls flat**, it completely fails to amuse people or to have the effect that was intended **fall flat on your 'face 1** to fall so that you are lying on your front **2** to fail completely, usually causing embarrassment: *His next television venture fell flat on its face.* **flat 'broke** (*BrE* also **stony 'broke**) (*informal*) completely BROKE (= without money) **flat 'out** (*informal*) **1** as fast or as hard as possible: *Workers are working flat out to meet the rise in demand for new cars.* **2** (*especially NAmE*) in a definite and direct way; completely: *I told him flat out 'No'.* ◇ *It's a 30-year mortgage we just flat out can't handle.* ➲ see also FLAT-OUT *adj.* **in... 'flat** (*informal*) used with an expression of time to say that sth happened or was done very quickly, in no more than the time stated: *They changed the wheel in three minutes flat* (= in only three minutes).
■ ***verb*** (-tt-) [I] (*AustralE, NZE*) to live in or share a flat/apartment: *My sister Zoe flats in Auckland.*

flat·bed /'flætbed/ *noun* **1** (*computing*) = FLATBED SCANNER **2** (also **ˌflatbed 'truck, ˌflatbed 'trailer**) (*especially NAmE*) an open truck or TRAILER without high sides, used for carrying large objects

ˌflatbed 'scanner (also **flat'bed**) *noun* (*computing*) a SCANNER (= device for copying pictures and documents so that they can be stored on a computer) on which the picture or document can be laid flat for copying ➲ VISUAL VOCAB pages V54, V56

ˌflat 'cap *noun* (*BrE*) = CLOTH CAP

flat·car /'flætkɑː(r)/ *noun* (*NAmE*) a coach/car on a train without a roof or sides, used for carrying goods

ˌflat-'chested *adj.* (of a woman) having small breasts

flat·fish /'flætfɪʃ/ *noun* (*pl.* **flat·fish**) any sea fish with a flat body, for example a PLAICE

ˌflat-'footed *adj.* **1** without naturally raised curves (=ARCHES) under the feet **2** (*especially NAmE*) not prepared for what is going to happen: *They were* ***caught flat-footed*** *by the attack.*

flat·head /'flæthed/ *adj.* (of a SCREWDRIVER) with a straight end rather than a cross-shaped end ➲ compare PHILLIPS

flat·let /'flætlət/ *noun* (*BrE*) a very small flat/apartment

flat·line /'flætlaɪn/ *verb* (*informal*) **1** [I] to die **2** [I] to be at a low level and fail to improve or increase

flat·ly /'flætli/ *adv.* **1** in a way that is very definite and will not be changed SYN **absolutely**: *to* ***flatly deny/reject/oppose*** *sth* ◇ *I* ***flatly refused*** *to spend any more time helping him.* **2** in a dull way with very little interest or emotion: *'Oh, it's you,' she said flatly.*

flat·mate /'flætmeɪt/ (*BrE*) (*NAmE* **'room-mate**) *noun* a person who shares a flat/apartment with one or more others

ˌflat-'out *adj.* [only before noun] (*especially NAmE*) definite and direct; complete: *His story was full of contradictions and flat-out lies.* ▸ **ˌflat-'out** *adv.*: *She just flat-out hated me.* ➲ see also FLAT *adv.*

'flat-pack *noun* (*BrE*) a piece of furniture that is sold in pieces in a flat box and that you have to build yourself

ˌflat-'panel *adj.* = FLAT-SCREEN

'flat racing *noun* [U] the sport of horse racing over flat ground with no jumps ➲ compare STEEPLECHASE

ˌflat 'rate *noun* a price that is the same for everyone and in all situations: *Interest is charged at a flat rate of 11%.*

ˌflat-'screen (also **ˌflat-'panel**) *adj.* [only before noun] **~ television/TV/computer/monitor, etc.** a type of television or computer monitor that is very thin when compared with the traditional type ➲ VISUAL VOCAB pages V18, V54

ˌflat 'spin *noun* (*technical*) a movement of an aircraft in which it goes gradually downwards while flying around in almost horizontal circles
IDM **in a flat 'spin** very confused, worried or excited

flat·ten /'flætn/ *verb* **1** [I, T] to become or make sth become flat or flatter: *The cookies will flatten slightly while cooking.* ◇ **~ sth** *These exercises will help to flatten your stomach.* ◇ *He flattened his hair down with gel.* **2** [T] **~ sth** to destroy or knock down a building, tree, etc: *Most of the factory was flattened by the explosion.* **3** [T] **~ sb** (*informal*) to defeat sb easily in a competition, an argument, etc. SYN **smash, thrash**: *Our team was flattened this evening!* **4** [T] **~ sb** (*informal*) to hit sb very hard so that they fall down: *He flattened the intruder with a single punch.* ◇ *I'll flatten you if you do that again!*
PHR V **ˌflatten sth/yourself a'gainst/'on sb/sth** to press sth/your body against sb/sth: *She flattened her nose against the window and looked in.* ◇ *Greg flattened himself against the wall to let me pass.* **ˌflatten 'out 1** to gradually become completely flat: *The hills first rose steeply then flattened out towards the sea.* **2** to stop growing or going up: *Export growth has started to flatten out.* **ˌflatten sth↔'out** to make sth completely flat

flat·ter /'flætə(r)/ *verb* **1** [T] **~ sb** to say nice things about sb, often in a way that is not sincere, because you want them to do sth for you or you want to please them: *Are you trying to flatter me?* **2** [T] **~ yourself (that...)** to choose to believe sth good about yourself and your abilities, especially when other people do not share this opinion: *'How will you manage without me?' 'Don't flatter yourself.'* **3** [T] **~ sb** to make sb seem more attractive or better than they really are: *That colour doesn't flatter many people.* ◇ *The scoreline flattered England* (= they did not deserve to get such a high score). ▸ **flat·ter·er** /'flætərə(r)/ *noun*
IDM **be/feel 'flattered** to be pleased because sb has made you feel important or special: *He was flattered by her atten-*

tion. ◇ *I felt flattered at being asked to give a lecture.* **ˌflatter to deˈceive** (*BrE*) if sth **flatters to deceive**, it appears to be better, more successful, etc. than it really is

flat·ter·ing /ˈflætərɪŋ/ *adj.* **1** making sb look more attractive: *a flattering dress* **2** saying nice things about sb/sth: *flattering remarks* **3** making sb feel pleased and special: *I found it flattering that he still recognized me after all these years.*

flat·tery /ˈflætəri/ *noun* [U] praise that is not sincere, especially in order to obtain sth from sb: *You're too intelligent to fall for his flattery.*
IDM **flattery will get you ˈeverywhere/ˈnowhere** (*informal, humorous*) praise that is not sincere will/will not get you what you want

flat·ties /ˈflætiz/ *noun* [pl.] = FLAT *n.* (8)

ˈflat-top *noun* a HAIRSTYLE in which the hair is cut short and flat across the top ➲ VISUAL VOCAB page V49

flatu·lence /ˈflætjʊləns; *NAmE* -tʃə-/ *noun* [U] an uncomfortable feeling caused by having too much gas in the stomach

flatu·lent /ˈflætjʊlənt; *NAmE* -tʃə-/ *adj.* **1** (*disapproving*) sounding important and impressive in a way that exaggerates the truth or facts **2** suffering from too much gas in the stomach

flat·ware /ˈflætweə(r); *NAmE* -wer/ *noun* [U] (*NAmE*) **1** = SILVERWARE **2** flat dishes such as plates and SAUCERS

flat·worm /ˈflætwɜːm; *NAmE* -wɜːrm/ *noun* a very simple WORM with a flat body

flaunt /flɔːnt/ *verb* (*disapproving*) **1** [T] **~ sth** to show sth you are proud of to other people, in order to impress them: *He did not believe in flaunting his wealth.* ◇ *She openly flaunted her affair with the senator.* **2** [T] **~ yourself** to behave in a confident and sexual way to attract attention
IDM **if you've ˌgot it, ˈflaunt it** (*humorous, saying*) used to tell sb that they should not be afraid of allowing other people to see their qualities and abilities

flaut·ist /ˈflɔːtɪst; *NAmE* ˈflaʊtɪst/ (*BrE*) (*NAmE* **flut·ist**) *noun* a person who plays the FLUTE

fla·von·oid /ˈfleɪvənɔɪd/ *noun* (*chemistry*) a type of substance that is found in some plants such as tomatoes, which is thought to protect against some types of cancer and heart disease

fla·vour 🔑 (*especially US* **fla·vor**) /ˈfleɪvə(r)/ *noun, verb*
■ ***noun*** **1** 🔑 [U] how food or drink tastes **SYN** **taste**: *The tomatoes **give** extra **flavour** to the sauce.* ◇ *It is stronger **in flavour** than other Dutch cheeses.* **2** 🔑 [C] a particular type of taste: *This yogurt comes in ten different flavours.* ◇ *a wine with a delicate fruit flavour* **3** (*NAmE*) = FLAVOURING **4** 🔑 [sing.] a particular quality or atmosphere **SYN** **ambience**: *the distinctive flavour of South Florida* ◇ *Foreign visitors help to **give a** truly international **flavour** to the occasion.* **5** [sing.] **a/the ~ of sth** an idea of what sth is like: *I have tried to convey something of the flavour of the argument.* **6** (*computing*) a particular type of sth, especially computer software
IDM **flavour of the ˈmonth** (*especially BrE*) a person or thing that is very popular at a particular time
■ ***verb*** 🔑 **~ sth (with sth)** to add sth to food or drink to give it more flavour or a particular flavour

fla·voured (*especially US* **fla·vored**) /ˈfleɪvəd; *NAmE* -vərd/ *adj.* **1 -flavoured** having the type of flavour mentioned: *lemon-flavoured sweets/candy* **2** having had flavour added to it: *flavoured yogurt*

fla·vour·ing (*especially US* **fla·vor·ing**) /ˈfleɪvərɪŋ/ (*NAmE* also **fla·vor**) *noun* [U, C] a substance added to food or drink to give it a particular flavour: *orange/vanilla flavouring* ◇ *This food contains no artificial flavourings.*

fla·vour·less (*especially US* **fla·vor·less**) /ˈfleɪvələs; *NAmE* -ərləs/ *adj.* having no flavour: *The meat was tough and flavourless.*

fla·vour·some /ˈfleɪvəsəm; *NAmE* -vərs-/ (*especially US* **fla·vor·ful** /ˈfleɪvəfʊl; *NAmE* -vərf-/) *adj.* having a lot of flavour

flaw /flɔː/ *noun* **1** a mistake in sth that means that it is not correct or does not work correctly **SYN** **defect, fault**: *The argument is full of fundamental flaws.* ◇ **~ in sth** *The report reveals **fatal flaws** in security at the airport.* **2 ~ (in sth)** a crack or fault in sth that makes it less attractive or valuable **3 ~ (in sb/sth)** a weakness in sb's character: *There is always a flaw in the character of a tragic hero.*

flawed /flɔːd/ *adj.* having a flaw; damaged or spoiled: ***seriously/fundamentally/fatally flawed*** ◇ *a flawed argument* ◇ *the book's flawed heroine*

flaw·less /ˈflɔːləs/ *adj.* without FLAWS and therefore perfect **SYN** **perfect**: *a flawless complexion/performance* ◇ *Her English is almost flawless.* ▶ **flaw·less·ly** *adv.*

flax /flæks/ *noun* [U] **1** a plant with blue flowers, grown for its STEM that is used to make thread and its seeds that are used to make LINSEED OIL **2** threads from the STEM of the flax plant, used to make LINEN

flax·en /ˈflæksn/ *adj.* (*literary*) (of hair) pale yellow **SYN** **blonde**

flax·seed /ˈflækssiːd/ *noun* [U, C] the seeds of the flax plant, eaten as a health food or used to make LINSEED OIL

ˈflaxseed oil *noun* [U] = LINSEED OIL

flay /fleɪ/ *verb* **1 ~ sth/sb** to remove the skin from an animal or person, usually when they are dead **2 ~ sb** to hit or WHIP sb very hard so that some of their skin comes off **3 ~ sb/yourself** (*formal*) to criticize sb/yourself severely

flea /fliː/ *noun* a very small jumping insect without wings, that bites animals and humans and sucks their blood: *The dog has fleas.*
IDM **with a ˈflea in your ear** if sb sends a person away **with a flea in their ear**, they tell them angrily to go away ➲ VISUAL VOCAB page V11

flea·bag /ˈfliːbæg/ *noun* (*informal*) **1** a person who looks poor and does not take care of their appearance **2** an animal that is in poor condition **3** (*especially NAmE*) a hotel that is cheap and dirty

ˈflea-bitten *adj.* (*informal*) in poor condition and with an unpleasant appearance

ˈflea market *noun* an outdoor market that sells SECOND-HAND (= old or used) goods at low prices

flea·pit /ˈfliːpɪt/ *noun* (*old-fashioned, BrE, informal*) an old and dirty cinema or theatre

fleck /flek/ *noun, verb*
■ ***noun*** [usually pl.] **~ (of sth)** **1** a very small area of a particular colour: *His hair was dark, with flecks of grey.* **2** a very small piece of sth: *flecks of dust/foam/dandruff*
■ ***verb*** [usually passive] **~ sth (with sth)** to cover or mark sth with small areas of a particular colour or with small pieces of sth: *The fabric was red, flecked with gold.* ◇ *His hair was flecked with paint.*

flec·tion = FLEXION

fled *past tense, past part.* of FLEE

fledged /fledʒd/ *adj.* (of birds) able to fly ➲ see also FULLY-FLEDGED

fledg·ling (*BrE* also **fledge·ling**) /ˈfledʒlɪŋ/ *noun* **1** a young bird that has just learnt to fly **2** (usually before another noun) a person, an organization or a system that is new and without experience: *fledgling democracies*

flee /fliː/ *verb* (**fled, fled** /fled/) [I, T, no passive] to leave a person or place very quickly, especially because you are afraid of possible danger: *She burst into tears and fled.* ◇ **~ from sb/sth** *a camp for refugees fleeing from the war* ◇ **~ to.../into...** *He fled to London after an argument with his family.* ◇ **~ sth** *He was caught trying to flee the country.* ➲ compare FLY *v.* (12)

fleece /fliːs/ *noun, verb*
■ ***noun*** **1** [C] the wool coat of a sheep; this coat when it has been removed from a sheep (by SHEARING) **2** [U, C] a type of soft warm cloth that feels like sheep's wool; a jacket or SWEATSHIRT that is made from this cloth: *a fleece lining* ◇ *a bright red fleece*

F

■ *verb* ~ sb (*informal*) to take a lot of money from sb by charging them too much: *Some local shops have been fleecing tourists.*

fleecy /ˈfliːsi/ *adj.* [usually before noun] made of soft material, like the wool coat of a sheep; looking like this: *a fleecy sweatshirt* ◇ *a blue sky with fleecy clouds*

fleet /fliːt/ *noun, adj.*

■ *noun* **1** [C] a group of military ships commanded by the same person **2** [C] a group of ships fishing together: ***a fishing/whaling fleet*** **3 the fleet** [sing.] all the military ships of a particular country: *a reduction in the size of the British fleet* **4** [C] ~ (**of sth**) a group of planes, buses, taxis, etc. travelling together or owned by the same organization: *the company's new fleet of vans*

■ *adj.* (*literary*) able to run fast: *fleet of foot* ◇ *fleet-footed*

ˌFleet ˈAdmiral (*US*) (*BrE* **ˌAdmiral of the ˈFleet**) *noun* an admiral of the highest rank in the navy: *Fleet Admiral William Hunter*

fleet·ing /ˈfliːtɪŋ/ *adj.* [usually before noun] lasting only a short time SYN **brief**: *a **fleeting glimpse/smile*** ◇ *a **fleeting moment** of happiness* ◇ *We paid a **fleeting visit** to Paris.* ▶ **fleet·ing·ly** *adv.*

ˈFleet Street *noun* [U] a street in central London where many national newspapers used to have their offices (now used to mean British newspapers and journalists in general)

Flem·ish /ˈflemɪʃ/ *noun* [U] the Dutch language as spoken in northern Belgium

flesh 0-w /fleʃ/ *noun, verb*

■ *noun* **1** 0-w [U] the soft substance between the skin and bones of animal or human bodies: *The trap had cut deeply into the rabbit's flesh.* ◇ *Tigers are **flesh-eating** animals.* ◇ *the smell of rotting flesh* **2** [U] the skin of the human body: *His fingers closed around the soft flesh of her arm.* ◇ ***flesh-coloured*** (= a light brownish pink colour) **3** 0-w [U] the soft part of fruit and vegetables, especially when it is eaten ➲ VISUAL VOCAB page V26 **4 the flesh** [sing.] (*literary*) the human body when considering its physical and sexual needs, rather than the mind or soul: *the pleasures/sins of the flesh*

IDM **ˌflesh and ˈblood** when you say that sb is **flesh and blood**, you mean that they are a normal human with needs, emotions and weaknesses: *Listening to the cries was more than flesh and blood could stand.* **your (ˌown) ˌflesh and ˈblood** a person that you are related to **in the ˈflesh** if you see sb **in the flesh**, you are in the same place as them and actually see them rather than just seeing a picture of them **make your ˈflesh creep** to make you feel afraid or full of disgust **put flesh on** (**the bones of**) **sth** to develop a basic idea, etc. by giving more details to make it more complete: *The strength of the book is that it puts flesh on the bare bones of this argument.* ➲ more at POUND *n.*, PRESS *v.*, SPIRIT *n.*, THORN, WAY *n.*

■ *verb*

PHR V **ˌflesh sth↔ˈout** to add more information or details to a plan, an argument, etc: *These points were fleshed out in the later parts of the speech.*

flesh·ly /ˈfleʃli/ *adj.* [only before noun] (*literary*) connected with physical and sexual desires: ***fleshly temptations/pleasures***

flesh·pots /ˈfleʃpɒts; *NAmE* -pɑːts/ *noun* [pl.] (*humorous*) places supplying food, drink and sexual entertainment

ˈflesh wound *noun* an injury in which the skin is cut but the bones and organs inside the body are not damaged

fleshy /ˈfleʃi/ *adj.* **1** (of parts of the body or people) having a lot of flesh: *fleshy arms/lips* ◇ *a large fleshy man* **2** (of plants or fruit) thick and soft: ***fleshy fruit/leaves***

fleur-de-lis (also **fleur-de-lys**) /ˌflɜː də ˈliː; -ˈliːs; *NAmE* ˌflɜːr/ *noun* (*pl.* **fleurs-de-lis** /ˌflɜː də ˈliː; -ˈliːs; *NAmE* ˌflɜːr/) (from *French*) a design representing a flower with three PETALS joined together at the bottom, often used in COATS OF ARMS

flew *past tense of* FLY

flex /fleks/ *verb, noun*

■ *verb* [T, I] ~ (**sth**) to bend, move or stretch an arm or a leg, or contract a muscle, especially in order to prepare for a physical activity: *to flex your fingers/feet/legs* ◇ *He stood on the side of the pool flexing his muscles.*

IDM **flex your ˈmuscles** to show sb how powerful you are, especially as a warning or threat

■ *noun* (*BrE*) (also **cord** *NAmE, BrE*) [C, U] a piece of wire that is covered with plastic, used for carrying electricity to a piece of equipment: *an electric flex* ◇ *a length of flex* ➲ picture at CORD

flex·ible AW /ˈfleksəbl/ *adj.* **1** (*approving*) able to change to suit new conditions or situations: *a more **flexible approach*** ◇ *flexible working hours* ◇ *Our plans need to be flexible enough to cater for the needs of everyone.* ◇ *You need to be more flexible and imaginative in your approach.* **2** able to bend easily without breaking: *flexible plastic tubing* OPP **inflexible** ▶ **flexi·bil·ity** AW /ˌfleksəˈbɪləti/ *noun* [U]: *Computers offer a much greater degree of flexibility in the way work is organized.* ◇ *exercises to develop the flexibility of dancers' bodies* **flex·ibly** *adv.*

flex·ion (also **flec·tion**) /ˈflekʃn/ *noun* [U] the action of bending sth

flexi·time /ˈfleksitaɪm/ (*especially BrE*) (*NAmE* usually **flex·time** /ˈflekstaɪm/) *noun* [U] a system in which employees work a particular number of hours each week or month but can choose when they start and finish work each day: *She works flexitime.*

flex·or /ˈfleksə(r); *NAmE* also ˈfleksɔːr/ (also **ˈflexor muscle**) *noun* (*anatomy*) a muscle that allows you to bend part of your body ➲ compare EXTENSOR

flib·ber·ti·gib·bet /ˈflɪbətidʒɪbɪt; ˌflɪbətiˈdʒɪbɪt; *NAmE* -bər-/ *noun* (*informal*) a person who is not serious enough or talks a lot about silly things

flick /flɪk/ *verb, noun*

■ *verb* **1** [T] ~ **sth + adv./prep.** to hit sth with a sudden quick movement, especially using your finger and thumb together, or using your hand: *She flicked the dust off her collar.* ◇ *The horse was flicking flies away with its tail.* ◇ *James flicked a peanut at her.* ◇ *Please don't flick ash on the carpet!* **2** [I, T] to move or make sth move with sudden quick movements: **+ adv./prep.** *The snake's tongue flicked out.* ◇ *Her eyes flicked from face to face.* ◇ ~ **sth** (**+ adv./prep.**) *He lifted his head, flicking his hair off his face.* ◇ *The horse moved off, flicking its tail.* **3** [T] to smile or look at sb suddenly and quickly ~ **a smile/look, etc. at sb**: *She flicked a nervous glance at him.* ◇ ~ **sb a smile/look, etc.** *She flicked him a nervous glance.* **4** [T] to press a button or switch quickly in order to turn a machine, etc. on or off SYN **flip**: ~ **sth** *He flicked a switch and all the lights went out.* ◇ ~ **sth on/off** *She flicked the TV on.* **5** [T] to move sth up and down with a sudden movement so that the end of it hits sth: ~ **A** (**with B**) *He flicked me with a wet towel.* ◇ ~ **B** (**at A**) *He flicked a wet towel at me.* ◇ *to flick a whip*

PHR V **ˌflick ˈthrough sth** (*especially BrE*) **1** to turn the pages of a book, etc. quickly and look at them without reading everything SYN **flip through**: *I've only had time to flick through your report but it seems to be fine.* **2** to keep changing television channels quickly to see what programmes are on SYN **flip through**: *Flicking through the channels, I came across an old war movie.*

■ *noun* **1** [C, usually sing.] a small sudden, quick movement or hit, for example with a WHIP or part of the body: *Bell's flick into the penalty area helped to create the goal.* ◇ *All this information is available **at the flick of a switch*** (= by simply turning on a machine). ◇ *He threw the ball back with a quick **flick of the wrist**.* **2** [sing.] **a ~ through sth** a quick look through the pages of a book, magazine, etc. SYN **flip**: *I had a flick through the catalogue while I was waiting.* **3** [C] (*old-fashioned, informal*) a film/movie **4 the flicks** [pl.] (*old-fashioned, BrE, informal*) a cinema

flicker /ˈflɪkə(r)/ *verb, noun*

■ *verb* **1** [I] (of a light or a flame) to keep going on and off as it shines or burns: *The lights flickered and went out.* ◇ *the flickering screen of the television* **2** [I] **+ adv./prep.** (of an emotion, a thought, etc.) to be expressed or appear somewhere for a short time: *Anger flickered in his eyes.* **3** [I] to

move with small quick movements: *Her eyelids flickered as she slept.*
■ **noun** [usually sing.] **~ (of sth) 1** a light that shines in an unsteady way: *the flicker of a television/candle* **2** a small, sudden movement with part of the body: *the flicker of an eyelid* **3** a feeling or an emotion that lasts for only a very short time: *a **flicker of hope/doubt/interest*** ◇ *A flicker of a smile crossed her face.*

'flick knife (*BrE*) (also **switch·blade** *NAmE, BrE*) *noun* a knife with a blade inside the handle that jumps out quickly when a button is pressed

flier *noun* = FLYER

flies /flaɪz/ *noun* [pl.] **1** *pl.* of FLY **2** (*BrE*) = FLY *n.* (3) **3 the flies** the space above the stage in a theatre, used for lights and for storing SCENERY

flight 0→ /flaɪt/ *noun, verb*
■ **noun**
▸ JOURNEY BY AIR **1** 0→ [C] a journey made by air, especially in a plane: *a **smooth/comfortable/bumpy flight*** ◇ ***a domestic/an international flight*** ◇ *a hot-air balloon flight* ◇ *We met on a flight from London to Paris.* ➲ see also IN-FLIGHT
▸ PLANE **2** 0→ [C] a plane making a particular journey: *We're booked on the same flight.* ◇ *Flight BA 4793 is now boarding at Gate 17.* ◇ *If we leave now, I can catch the earlier flight.* ◇ ***mercy/relief flights*** (= planes taking help to countries where there is a war) ➲ COLLOCATIONS at TRAVEL
▸ FLYING **3** 0→ [U] the act of flying: *the age of supersonic flight* ◇ *flight safety* ◇ *The bird is easily recognized **in flight*** (= when it is flying) *by the black band at the end of its tail.*
▸ MOVEMENT OF OBJECT **4** [U] the movement or direction of an object as it travels through the air: *the flight of a ball*
▸ OF STEPS **5** [C] a series of steps between two floors or levels: *She fell down **a flight of stairs/steps** and hurt her back.*
▸ RUNNING AWAY **6** [U, sing.] the act of running away from a dangerous or difficult situation: *the flight of refugees from the advancing forces* ◇ *The main character is a journalist in flight from a failed marriage.*
▸ OF FANCY/IMAGINATION **7** [C] **~ of fancy/imagination** an idea or a statement that shows a lot of imagination but is not practical or sensible
▸ GROUP OF BIRDS/AIRCRAFT **8** [C] a group of birds or aircraft flying together: *a flight of geese* ◇ *an aircraft of the Queen's flight*
IDM **in the first/top 'flight** among the best of a particular group ➲ see also TOP-FLIGHT **put sb to 'flight** (*old-fashioned*) to force sb to run away **take 'flight** to run away: *The gang took flight when they heard the police car.*
■ **verb** [usually passive] **~ sth** (*BrE, sport*) to kick, hit or throw a ball through the air in a skilful way: *He equalized with a beautifully flighted shot.*

'flight attendant *noun* a person whose job is to serve and take care of passengers on an aircraft

'flight crew *noun* [C+sing./pl. v.] the people who work on a plane during a flight

'flight deck *noun* **1** an area at the front of a large plane where the pilot sits to use the controls and fly the plane ➲ VISUAL VOCAB page V43 **2** a long flat surface on top of a ship that carries aircraft (= an AIRCRAFT CARRIER) where they take off and land

'flight jacket (*US*) (*BrE* **'flying jacket**) *noun* a short leather jacket with a warm LINING and COLLAR, originally worn by pilots

flight·less /'flaɪtləs/ *adj.* [usually before noun] (of birds or insects) unable to fly

,flight lieu'tenant *noun* (*abbr.* Flt. Lt.) an officer of fairly high rank in the British AIR FORCE: *Flight Lieutenant Richard Clarkson*

'flight path *noun* the route taken by an aircraft through the air

'flight recorder *noun* = BLACK BOX

'flight sergeant *noun* a member of the British AIR FORCE, just below the rank of an officer: *Flight Sergeant Bob Andrews*

'flight simulator *noun* a device that reproduces the conditions that exist when flying an aircraft, used for training pilots

flighty /'flaɪti/ *adj.* (*informal*) a **flighty** woman is one who cannot be relied on because she is always changing activities, ideas and partners without treating them seriously

flim·flam /'flɪmflæm/ *noun* [U] (*old-fashioned, informal*) nonsense

flimsy /'flɪmzi/ *adj.* (**flim·sier, flim·si·est**) **1** badly made and not strong enough for the purpose for which it is used SYN **rickety**: *a flimsy table* **2** (of material) thin and easily torn: *a flimsy piece of paper/fabric/plastic* **3** difficult to believe SYN **feeble**: *a **flimsy excuse/explanation*** ◇ *The evidence against him is pretty flimsy.* ▸ **flim·sily** *adv.* **flim·si·ness** *noun* [U]

flinch /flɪntʃ/ *verb* [I] to make a sudden movement with your face or body as a result of pain, fear, surprise, etc: *He met my gaze without flinching.* ◇ **~ at sth** *He flinched at the sight of the blood.* ◇ **~ away** *She flinched away from the dog.* ➲ see also UNFLINCHING
PHR V **'flinch from sth | 'flinch from doing sth** (often used in negative sentences) to avoid thinking about or doing sth unpleasant: *He never flinched from facing up to trouble.*

fling /flɪŋ/ *verb, noun*
■ **verb** (**flung, flung** /flʌŋ/) **1 ~ sb/sth + adv./prep.** to throw sb/sth somewhere with force, especially because you are angry SYN **hurl**: *Someone had flung a brick through the window.* ◇ *He flung her to the ground.* ◇ *The door was suddenly flung open.* ◇ *He had his enemies **flung into prison**.* ➲ SYNONYMS at THROW **2 ~ yourself/sth + adv./prep.** to move yourself or part of your body suddenly and with a lot of force: *She flung herself onto the bed.* ◇ *He flung out an arm to stop her from falling.* **3 ~ sth (at sb)** | **+ speech** to say sth to sb in an aggressive way SYN **hurl**: *They were flinging insults at each other.* ➲ see also FAR-FLUNG
PHR V **'fling yourself at sb** (*informal, disapproving*) to make it too obvious to sb that you want to have a sexual relationship with them **'fling yourself into sth** to start to do sth with a lot of energy and enthusiasm: *They flung themselves into the preparations for the party.* **,fling sth↔'off/'on** (*informal*) to take off or put on clothing in a quick and careless way: *He flung off his coat and collapsed on the sofa.* **,fling sb↔'out** (*BrE, informal*) to make sb leave a place suddenly SYN **throw out** **,fling sth↔'out** (*BrE, informal*) to get rid of sth that you do not want any longer SYN **throw out**
■ **noun** [usually sing.] (*informal*) **1** a short period of enjoyment when you do not allow yourself to worry or think seriously about anything: *He was determined to have one last fling before retiring.* **2 ~ (with sb)** a short sexual relationship with sb ➲ see also HIGHLAND FLING

flint /flɪnt/ *noun* **1** [U, C] a type of very hard grey stone that can produce a SPARK when it is hit against steel: *prehistoric flint implements* ◇ *His eyes were as hard as flint.* **2** [C] a piece of flint or hard metal that is used to produce a SPARK

flint·lock /'flɪntlɒk; *NAmE* -lɑːk/ *noun* a gun used in the past that produced a SPARK from a flint when the TRIGGER was pressed

flinty /'flɪnti/ *adj.* **1** showing no emotion: *a **flinty look/gaze/stare*** **2** containing flint: ***flinty pebbles/soils***

flip /flɪp/ *verb, noun, adj.*
■ **verb** (-pp-) **1** [I, T] to turn over into a different position with a sudden quick movement; to make sth do this: *The plane flipped and crashed.* ◇ (*figurative*) *She felt her heart flip* (= with excitement, etc.). ◇ **~ sth (+ adj.)** *He flipped the lid open and looked inside the case.* ➲ see also FLIP OVER **2** [T] to press a button or switch in order to turn a machine, etc. on or off SYN **flick**: **~ sth** *to flip a switch* ◇ **~ sth on/off** *She reached over and flipped off the light.* **3** [T] to throw sth somewhere using your thumb and/or fingers SYN **toss** **~ a coin**: *They flipped a coin to decide who would get the ticket.* ◇ **~ sth + adv./prep.** *He flipped the keys onto the desk.* **4** [I] **~ (out)** (*informal*) to become very angry, excited

F

or unable to think clearly: *She finally flipped under the pressure.*

IDM ˌ**flip your ˈlid** (*informal*) to become very angry and lose control of what you are saying or doing SYN **go mad**

PHR V ˌ**flip ˈover** to turn onto the other side or upside down: *The car hit a tree and flipped over.* ◇ *He flipped over and sat up.* ˌ**flip sth↔ˈover** to turn sth onto the other side or upside down: *The wind flipped over several cars.* ˈ**flip through sth** **1** to turn the pages of a book, etc. quickly and look at them without reading everything SYN **flick through**: *She flipped through the magazine looking for the letters page.* **2** (*especially NAmE*) to keep changing television channels quickly to see what shows are on SYN **flick through**: *Flipping through the channels, I came across an old war movie.*

■ ***noun*** **1** [C] a small quick hit with a part of the body that causes sth to turn over: *The whole thing was decided on the **flip of a coin**.* **2** [C] a movement in which the body turns over in the air SYN **somersault**: *The handstand was followed by a back flip.* ◇ (*figurative*) *Her heart did a flip.* **3** [sing.] **~ through sth** a quick look through the pages of a book, magazine, etc. SYN **flick**: *I had a quick flip through the report while I was waiting.*

■ ***adj.*** (*informal*) = FLIPPANT: *a **flip answer/comment*** ◇ *Don't be flip with me.*

ˈ**flip chart** *noun* large sheets of paper fixed at the top to a stand so that they can be turned over, used for presenting information at a talk or meeting ➲ VISUAL VOCAB page V56

ˈ**flip-flop** *noun, verb*

■ ***noun*** (*NAmE* also **thong**) a type of SANDAL (= open shoe) that has a piece of leather, etc. that goes between the big toe and the toe next to it: *a pair of flip-flops* ➲ VISUAL VOCAB page V52

■ ***verb*** (-pp-) [I] **~ (on sth)** (*informal, especially NAmE*) to change your opinion about sth, especially when you then hold the opposite opinion: *The vice-president was accused of flip-flopping on several major issues.*

ˈ**flip-flopper** /ˈflɪpflɒpə(r); *NAmE* -flɑːpər/ *noun* (*informal, especially NAmE*) a person, especially a politician, who suddenly changes his or her opinion or policy ➲ see also U-TURN

flip·pant /ˈflɪpənt/ (also *informal* **flip**) *adj.* showing that you do not take sth as seriously as other people think you should: *a **flippant answer/attitude*** ◇ *Sorry, I didn't mean to sound flippant.* ▶ **flip·pancy** /-ənsi/ *noun* [U] **flip·pant·ly** *adv.*

flip·per /ˈflɪpə(r)/ *noun* [usually pl.] **1** a flat part of the body of some sea animals such as SEALS and TURTLES, used for swimming ➲ VISUAL VOCAB page V11 **2** a long flat piece of rubber or plastic that you wear on your foot to help you swim more quickly, especially below the surface of the water ➲ VISUAL VOCAB page V34

ˈ**flip phone** *noun* a small mobile/cell phone with a cover that opens upwards

flip·ping /ˈflɪpɪŋ/ *adj., adv.* (*BrE, informal*) used as a mild swear word by some people to emphasize sth or to show that they are annoyed: *I hate this flipping hotel!* ◇ *Flipping kids!* ◇ *It's flipping cold today!*

ˈ**flip side** *noun* [usually sing.] **~ (of/to sth)** **1** different and less welcome aspects of an idea, argument or action **2** (*old-fashioned*) the side of a record that does not have the main song or piece of music on it

flirt /flɜːt; *NAmE* flɜːrt/ *verb, noun*

■ ***verb*** [I] **~ (with sb)** to behave towards sb as if you find them sexually attractive, without seriously wanting to have a relationship with them

PHR V ˈ**flirt with sth** **1** to think about or be interested in sth for a short time but not very seriously: *She flirted with the idea of becoming an actress when she was younger.* **2** to take risks or not worry about a dangerous situation that may happen: *to flirt with danger/death/disaster*

■ ***noun*** [usually sing.] a person who flirts with a lot of people: *She's a real flirt.*

flir·ta·tion /flɜːˈteɪʃn; *NAmE* flɜːrˈt-/ *noun* **1** [C, U] **~ with sth** a short period of time during which sb is involved or interested in sth, often not seriously: *a brief and unsuccessful flirtation with the property market* **2** [U] behaviour that shows you find sb sexually attractive but are not serious about them: *Frank's efforts at flirtation had become tiresome to her.* **3** [C] **~ (with sb)** a short sexual relationship with sb that is not taken seriously

flir·ta·tious /flɜːˈteɪʃəs; *NAmE* flɜːrˈt-/ (also *informal* **flirty**) *adj.* behaving in a way that shows a sexual attraction to sb that is not serious: *a flirtatious young woman* ◇ *a flirtatious smile* ▶ **flir·ta·tious·ly** *adv.* **flir·ta·tious·ness** *noun* [U]

flit /flɪt/ *verb, noun*

■ ***verb*** (-tt-) **1** [I] to move lightly and quickly from one place or thing to another: **~ from A to B** *Butterflies flitted from flower to flower.* ◇ *He flits from one job to another.* ◇ **+ adv./prep.** *A smile flitted across his face.* ◇ *A thought flitted through my mind.* **2** [I] (*ScotE*) to change the place where you live: *I had to change schools every time my parents flitted.*

■ ***noun***

IDM **do a moonlight/midnight ˈflit** (*BrE, informal*) to leave a place suddenly and secretly at night, usually in order to avoid paying money that you owe to sb

float 🔑 /fləʊt; *NAmE* floʊt/ *verb, noun*

■ ***verb***

▸ ON WATER/IN AIR **1** 🔑 [I] **+ adv./prep.** to move slowly on water or in the air SYN **drift**: *A group of swans floated by.* ◇ *The smell of new bread floated up from the kitchen.* ◇ *Beautiful music came floating out of the window.* ◇ (*figurative*) *An idea suddenly floated into my mind.* ◇ (*figurative*) *People seem to float in and out of my life.* **2** 🔑 [I] to stay on or near the surface of a liquid and not sink: *Wood floats.* ◇ **~ in/on sth** *A plastic bag was floating in the water.* ◇ *Can you float on your back?* **3** [T] to make sth move on or near the surface of a liquid: **~ sth** *There wasn't enough water to float the ship.* ◇ **~ sth + adv./prep.** *They float the logs down the river to the towns.*

▸ WALK LIGHTLY **4** [I] **+ adv./prep.** (*literary*) to walk or move in a smooth and easy way SYN **glide**: *She floated down the steps to greet us.*

▸ SUGGEST IDEA **5** [T] **~ sth** to suggest an idea or a plan for other people to consider: *They floated the idea of increased taxes on alcohol.*

▸ BUSINESS/ECONOMICS **6** [T] **~ sth** (*business*) to sell shares in a company or business to the public for the first time: *The company was floated on the stock market in 2007.* ◇ *Shares were floated at 585p.* **7** [T, I] **~ (sth)** (*economics*) if a government **floats** its country's money or allows it to **float**, it allows its value to change freely according to the value of the money of other countries

IDM **float sb's ˈboat** (*informal*) to be what sb likes: *You can listen to whatever kind of music floats your boat.* ➲ more at AIR *n.*

PHR V ˌ**float aˈbout/aˈround** (usually used in the progressive tenses) if an idea, etc. is **floating around**, it is talked about by a number of people or passed from one person to another

■ ***noun***

▸ VEHICLE **1** a large vehicle on which people dressed in special COSTUMES are carried in a festival: *a carnival float*

▸ IN FISHING **2** a small light object attached to a FISHING LINE that stays on the surface of the water and moves when a fish has been caught

▸ FOR SWIMMING **3** a light object that floats in the water and is held by a person who is learning to swim to stop them from sinking

▸ DRINK **4** (*NAmE*) a drink with ice cream floating in it: *a Coke float*

▸ MONEY **5** (*especially BrE*) a sum of money consisting of coins and notes of low value that is given to sb before they start selling things so that they can give customers change

▸ BUSINESS **6** = FLOTATION

float·er /ˈfləʊtə(r); *NAmE* ˈfloʊt-/ *noun* (*medical*) a very small object inside a person's eye which they see moving up and down

float·ing /ˈfləʊtɪŋ; *NAmE* ˈfloʊt-/ *adj.* [usually before noun] not fixed permanently in one particular position or place: ***floating exchange rates*** ◇ *a* ***floating population*** (= one in which people frequently move from one place to another) ◇ (*medical*) *a floating kidney*

ˌfloating ˈrib (also **ˌfalse ˈrib**) *noun* (*anatomy*) any of the lower RIBS which are not attached to the BREASTBONE

ˌfloating ˈvoter (*BrE*) (*NAmE* **ˈswing voter**) *noun* a person who does not always vote for the same political party and who has not decided which party to vote for in an election

floaty /ˈfləʊti; *NAmE* ˈfloʊti/ *adj.* (of cloth or clothing) very light and thin

flock /flɒk; *NAmE* flɑːk/ *noun, verb*
- ***noun*** **1** [C+sing./pl. v.] **~ (of sth)** a group of sheep, GOATS or birds of the same type ➲ compare HERD **2** [C+sing./pl. v.] **~ (of sb)** a large group of people, especially of the same type: *a flock of children/reporters* ◇ *They came in flocks to see the procession.* **3** [C+sing./pl. v.] (*literary*) the group of people who regularly attend the church of a particular priest, etc. **4** [U] small pieces of soft material used for filling CUSHIONS, chairs, etc. **5** [U] small pieces of soft material on the surface of paper or cloth that produce a raised pattern: *flock wallpaper*
- ***verb*** [I] to go or gather together somewhere in large numbers: **+ adv./prep.** *Thousands of people flocked to the beach this weekend.* ◇ *Huge numbers of birds had flocked together by the lake.* ◇ **~ to do sth** *People flocked to hear him speak.* IDM see BIRD

floe /fləʊ; *NAmE* floʊ/ *noun* = ICE FLOE

flog /flɒg; *NAmE* flɑːg/ *verb* (-gg-) **1** [often passive] **~ sb** to punish sb by hitting them many times with a WHIP or stick: *He was publicly flogged for breaking the country's alcohol laws.* **2** (*BrE, informal*) to sell sth to sb: **~ sth (to sb)** *She flogged her guitar to another student.* ◇ **~ sth (off)** *We buy them cheaply and then flog them off at a profit.* ◇ **~ sb sth** *I had a letter from a company trying to flog me insurance.* IDM **ˌflog a dead ˈhorse** (*BrE, informal*) to waste your effort by trying to do sth that is no longer possible **ˌflog sth to ˈdeath** (*BrE, informal*) to use an idea, a story, etc. so often that it is no longer interesting

flog·ging /ˈflɒgɪŋ; *NAmE* ˈflɑːg-/ *noun* [C, U] a punishment in which sb is hit many times with a WHIP or stick: *a public flogging*

flood 🔑 /flʌd/ *noun, verb*
- ***noun***
- ▸ WATER **1** 🔑 [C, U] a large amount of water covering an area that is usually dry: *The heavy rain has caused floods in many parts of the country.* ◇ *flood damage* ◇ *Police have issued* ***flood warnings*** *for Nevada.* ◇ *The river is* ***in flood*** (= has more water in it than normal and has caused a flood). ➲ see also FLASH FLOOD
- ▸ LARGE NUMBER **2** 🔑 [C] **~ (of sth)** a very large number of things or people that appear at the same time: *a flood of complaints* ◇ *a flood of refugees* ◇ *The child was* ***in floods of tears*** (= crying a lot).
- ***verb***
- ▸ FILL WITH WATER **1** 🔑 [I, T] if a place **floods** or sth **floods** it, it becomes filled or covered with water: *The cellar floods whenever it rains heavily.* ◇ **~ sth** *If the pipe bursts it could flood the whole house.*
- ▸ OF RIVER **2** 🔑 [I, T] to become so full that it spreads out onto the land around it: *When the Ganges floods, it causes considerable damage.* ◇ **~ sth** *The river flooded the valley.*
- ▸ LARGE NUMBERS **3** 🔑 [I] **~ in/into/out of sth** to arrive or go somewhere in large numbers SYN **pour**: *Refugees continue to flood into neighbouring countries.* ◇ *Telephone calls* ***came flooding in*** *from all over the country.* **4** [T, usually passive] **~ sb/sth with sth** to send sth somewhere in large numbers: *The office was flooded with applications for the job.* **5** [T] to become or make sth become available in a place in large numbers: **~ sth** *Cheap imported goods are* ***flooding the market.*** ◇ **~ sth with sth** *A man who planned to flood Britain with cocaine was jailed for 15 years.*
- ▸ OF FEELING/THOUGHT **6** 🔑 [I, T] to affect sb suddenly and strongly: **+ adv./prep.** *A great sense of relief flooded over him.* ◇ *Memories of her childhood* ***came flooding back.*** ◇ **~ sb with sth** *The words flooded him with self-pity.*
- ▸ OF LIGHT/COLOUR **7** 🔑 [I, T] to spread suddenly into sth; to cover sth: **+ adv./prep.** *She drew the curtains and the sunlight flooded in.* ◇ **~ sth** *She looked away as the colour flooded her cheeks.* ◇ **be flooded with sth** *The room was flooded with evening light.*
- ▸ ENGINE **8** [I, T] **~ (sth)** if an engine **floods** or if you **flood** it, it becomes so full of petrol/gas that it will not start ▸ **flood·ed** 🔑 *adj.*: *flooded fields* **flood·ing** 🔑 *noun* [U]: *There will be heavy rain with flooding in some areas.*

PHR V **ˌflood sb↔ˈout** [usually passive] to force sb to leave their home because of a flood

flood·gate /ˈflʌdgeɪt/ *noun* [usually pl.] a gate that can be opened or closed to control the flow of water on a river: (*figurative*) *If the case is successful, it may* ***open the floodgates*** *to more damages claims against the industry* (= start sth that will be difficult to stop).

flood·light /ˈflʌdlaɪt/ *noun, verb*
- ***noun*** [usually pl.] a large powerful lamp, used for lighting sports grounds, theatre stages and the outside of buildings: *a match played* ***under floodlights*** ▸ **flood·light·ing** *noun* [U]: *The floodlighting had been turned off.*
- ***verb*** (**flood·lit, flood·lit** /-lɪt/) [usually passive] **~ sth** to light a place or a building using floodlights: *The swimming pool is floodlit in the evenings.* ◇ *floodlit tennis courts*

ˈflood·plain /ˈflʌdpleɪn/ *noun* an area of flat land beside a river that regularly becomes flooded when there is too much water in the river

ˈflood tide *noun* a very high rise in the level of the sea as it moves in towards the coast ➲ compare HIGH TIDE

flood·water /ˈflʌdwɔːtə(r); *NAmE* also -wɑːtər/ *noun* [U] (also **floodwaters** [pl.]) water that covers land after there has been a flood: *The floodwaters have now receded.*

floor 🔑 /flɔː(r)/ *noun, verb*
- ***noun***
- ▸ OF ROOM **1** 🔑 [C, usually sing.] the surface of a room that you walk on: *a* ***wooden/concrete/marble, etc. floor*** ◇ *ceramic floor tiles* ◇ *The body was lying on the kitchen floor.* ◇ *The alterations should give us extra floor space.*
- ▸ OF VEHICLE **2** (*NAmE* also **floor·board**) [C, usually sing.] the bottom surface of a vehicle: *The floor of the car was covered in cigarette ends.*
- ▸ LEVEL OF BUILDING **3** 🔑 [C] all the rooms that are on the same level of a building: *Her office is* ***on the second floor.*** ◇ *the Irish guy who lives two floors above* ◇ *There is a lift to all floors.* ◇ *Their house is* ***on three floors*** (= it has three floors). ➲ note at STOREY ➲ see also GROUND FLOOR
- ▸ OF THE SEA/FORESTS **4** 🔑 [C, usually sing.] the ground at the bottom of the sea, a forest, etc: *the* ***ocean/valley/cave/forest floor***
- ▸ IN PARLIAMENT, ETC. **5 the floor** [sing.] the part of a building where discussions or debates are held, especially in a parliament; the people who attend a discussion or debate: *Opposition politicians registered their protest on the floor of the House.* ◇ *We will now take any questions from the floor.*
- ▸ AREA FOR WORK **6** [C, usually sing.] an area in a building that is used for a particular activity: *on the floor of the Stock Exchange* (= where trading takes place) ➲ see also DANCE FLOOR, FACTORY FLOOR, SHOP FLOOR
- ▸ FOR WAGES/PRICES **7** [C, usually sing.] the lowest level allowed for wages or prices: *Prices have* ***gone through the floor*** (= fallen to a very low level). ➲ compare CEILING (2)

IDM **get/be given/have the ˈfloor** to get/be given/have the right to speak during a discussion or debate **ˌhold the ˈfloor** to speak during a discussion or debate, especially for a long time so that nobody else is able to say anything **ˌtake (to) the ˈfloor** to start dancing on a DANCE FLOOR: *Couples took the floor for the last dance of the evening.* **wipe/mop the ˈfloor with sb** (*informal*) to defeat sb completely in an argument or a competition ➲ more at GROUND FLOOR
- ***verb***
- ▸ SURPRISE/CONFUSE **1 ~ sb** to surprise or confuse sb so that they are not sure what to say or do

▸ HIT **2** [usually passive] **~ sb** to make sb fall down by hitting them, especially in a sport
▸ BUILDING/ROOM **3** [usually passive] **~ sth** to provide a building or room with a floor
▸ DRIVING **4 ~ the accelerator** to press the ACCELERATOR pedal of a car hard

Synonyms

floor

ground • land • earth

These are all words for the surface that you walk on.

floor the surface of a room that you walk on: *She was sitting on the floor watching TV.*

ground (often **the ground**) the solid surface of the earth that you walk on: *I found her lying on the ground.* ◇ *The rocket crashed a few seconds after it* ***left the ground***.

land the surface of the earth that is not sea: *It was good to be back on* ***dry land*** *again.* ◇ *They fought both at sea and* ***on land***.

earth (often **the earth**) the solid surface of the world that is made of rock, soil, sand, etc: *You could feel the earth shake as the truck came closer.*

GROUND, LAND OR EARTH?

Ground is the normal word for the solid surface that you walk on when you are not in a building or vehicle. You can use **earth** if you want to draw attention to the rock, soil etc. that the ground is made of. **Land** is only used when you want to contrast it with the sea: ~~*the land beneath our feet*~~ ◇ ~~*feel the land shake*~~ ◇ ~~*sight ground/earth*~~ ◇ ~~*travel by ground/earth*~~

PATTERNS

- **on/under** the floor/ground/earth
- **bare** floor/ground/earth
- to **drop/fall to** the floor/the ground/(the) earth
- to **reach** the floor/the ground/land

British/American

floor

- In *BrE* the floor of a building at street level is the **ground floor**, the one above it is the **first floor** and the one below it is the **basement**, or **lower ground floor** in a public building.
- In *NAmE* the floor at street level is usually called the **first floor**, the one above it is the **second floor** and the one below it is the **basement**. In public buildings the floor at street level can also be called the **ground floor**.

➲ note at STOREY

floor·board /ˈflɔːbɔːd; *NAmE* ˈflɔːrbɔːrd/ *noun* **1** a long flat piece of wood in a wooden floor: *bare/polished floorboards* ➲ VISUAL VOCAB page V18 **2** [usually sing.] (*NAmE*) = FLOOR (2): *a car floorboard* ◇ *He had his foot to the floorboard* (= was going very fast).

floor·cloth /ˈflɔːklɒθ; *NAmE* ˈflɔːrklɔːθ/ *noun* (*BrE*) a cloth for cleaning floors

floor·ing /ˈflɔːrɪŋ/ *noun* [U] material used to make the floor of a room: *vinyl/wooden flooring* ◇ *kitchen/bathroom flooring*

ˈ**floor lamp** (*BrE* also ˈ**standard lamp**) *noun* a tall lamp that stands on the floor ➲ VISUAL VOCAB page V18

ˈ**floor manager** *noun* the person responsible for the lighting and other technical arrangements for a television production

ˈ**floor plan** *noun* (*technical*) a drawing of the shape of a room or building, as seen from above, showing the position of the furniture, etc.

ˈ**floor show** *noun* a series of performances by singers, dancers, etc. at a restaurant or club

floozy (also **flooz·ie**) /ˈfluːzi/ *noun* (*pl.* **-ies**) (*old-fashioned, informal, disapproving*) a woman who has sexual relationships with many different men

flop /flɒp; *NAmE* flɑːp/ *verb, noun*

■ ***verb*** (**-pp-**) **1** [I] **~ into/on sth** | **~ (down/back)** to sit or lie down in a heavy and sudden way because you are very tired: *Exhausted, he flopped down into a chair.* **2** [I] **+ adv./prep.** to fall, move or hang in a heavy or awkward way, without control: *Her hair flopped over her eyes.* ◇ *The young man flopped back, unconscious.* ◇ *The fish were flopping around in the bottom of the boat.* **3** [I] (*informal*) to be a complete failure: *The play flopped on Broadway.*

■ ***noun*** (*informal*) a film/movie, play, party, etc. that is not successful OPP **hit** ➲ see also BELLYFLOP

flop·house /ˈflɒphaʊs; *NAmE* ˈflɑːp-/ (*NAmE*) (*BrE* **doss-house**) *noun* (*informal*) a cheap place to stay for people who have no home

floppy /ˈflɒpi; *NAmE* ˈflɑːpi/ *adj.* (**flop·pier, flop·piest**) hanging or falling loosely; not hard and stiff: *a floppy hat*

ˌ**floppy ˈdisk** (also **floppy** *pl.* **-ies**) (also **disk·ette**) *noun* a flat disk inside a plastic cover, that is used to store data in the form that a computer can read, and that can be removed from the computer ➲ compare HARD DISK

flora /ˈflɔːrə/ *noun* [U] (*technical*) the plants of a particular area, type of environment or period of time: *alpine flora* ◇ *rare species of* ***flora and fauna*** (= plants and animals)

floral /ˈflɔːrəl/ *adj.* [usually before noun] **1** consisting of pictures of flowers; decorated with pictures of flowers: *wallpaper with a* ***floral design/pattern*** ◇ *a floral dress* **2** made of flowers: *a* ***floral arrangement/display*** ◇ ***Floral tributes*** *were sent to the church.*

flor·en·tine /ˈflɒrəntaɪn; -tiːn; *NAmE* ˈflɔːrəntiːn; -tɪn/ *adj., noun*

■ ***adj.*** (of food) served on SPINACH: *eggs florentine*

■ ***noun*** a biscuit/cookie containing nuts and fruit, half covered in chocolate

floret /ˈflɒrət; *NAmE* ˈflɔː-/ *noun* a flower part of some vegetables, for example BROCCOLI and CAULIFLOWER. Each vegetable has several florets coming from one main STEM. ➲ VISUAL VOCAB page V27

flori·bunda /ˌflɒrɪˈbʌndə; *NAmE* ˌflɔːr-/ *noun* (*technical*) a plant, especially a ROSE, with flowers that grow very close together in groups

florid /ˈflɒrɪd; *NAmE* ˈflɔː-; ˈflɑː-/ *adj.* **1** (of a person's face) red: *a florid complexion* **2** (usually *disapproving*) having too much decoration or detail: *florid language* ▸ **florid·ly** *adv.*

florin /ˈflɒrɪn; *NAmE* ˈflɔː-; ˈflɑː-/ *noun* an old British coin worth two SHILLINGS (= now 10p)

flor·ist /ˈflɒrɪst; *NAmE* ˈflɔː-/ *noun* **1** a person who owns or works in a shop/store that sells flowers and plants **2 flor·ist's** (*pl.* **flor·ists**) a shop/store that sells flowers and plants: *I've ordered some flowers from the florist's.*

floss /flɒs; *NAmE* flɔːs; flɑːs/ *noun, verb*

■ ***noun*** [U] **1** = DENTAL FLOSS **2** thin silk thread ➲ see also CANDYFLOSS

■ ***verb*** [I, T] **~ (sth)** to clean between your teeth with DENTAL FLOSS

flo·ta·tion /fləʊˈteɪʃn; *NAmE* floʊ-/ *noun* **1** (also **float**) [C, U] (*business*) the process of selling shares in a company to the public for the first time in order to raise money: *plans for (a) flotation on the stock exchange* ◇ *a stock-market flotation* **2** [U] the act of floating on or in water

floˈtation ˌtank *noun* a container filled with salt water in which people float in the dark as a way of relaxing

flo·tilla /fləˈtɪlə; *NAmE* floʊˈt-/ *noun* a group of boats or small ships sailing together

flot·sam /ˈflɒtsəm; *NAmE* ˈflɑːt-/ *noun* [U] **1** parts of boats, pieces of wood or rubbish/garbage, etc. that are found on land near the sea or floating on the sea; any kind of rubbish/garbage: *The beaches are wide and filled with interesting* ***flotsam and jetsam***. ➲ compare JETSAM **2** people who have no home or job and who move from place to place, often rejected by society: *the human flotsam of inner cities*

flounce /flaʊns/ *verb, noun*
- **verb** [I] (**+ adv./prep.**) to move somewhere in a way that draws attention to yourself, for example because you are angry or upset: *She flounced out of the room.*
- **noun 1** a strip of cloth that is sewn around the edge of a skirt, dress, curtain, etc. **2** a quick and exaggerated movement that you make when you are angry or want people to notice you: *She left the room with a flounce.* ▶ **flounced** *adj.*: *a flounced skirt*

floun·der /ˈflaʊndə(r)/ *verb, noun*
- **verb 1** [I, T] (**+ speech**) to struggle to know what to say or do or how to continue with sth: *His abrupt change of subject left her floundering helplessly.* **2** [I] to have a lot of problems and to be in danger of failing completely: *At that time the industry was floundering.* **3** [I] (**+ adv./prep.**) to struggle to move or get somewhere in water, mud, etc: *She was floundering around in the deep end of the swimming pool.*
- **noun** (*pl.* **floun·der** or **floun·ders**) a small flat sea fish that is used for food

flour 0→ /ˈflaʊə(r)/ *noun, verb*
- **noun** 0→ [U] a fine white or brown powder made from grain, especially WHEAT, and used in cooking for making bread, cakes, etc. ➲ see also PLAIN FLOUR, SELF-RAISING FLOUR
- **verb** [usually passive] **~ sth** to cover sth with a layer of flour: *Roll the dough on a lightly floured surface.*

flour·ish /ˈflʌrɪʃ; *NAmE* ˈflɜːrɪʃ/ *verb, noun*
- **verb 1** [I] to develop quickly and be successful or common SYN **thrive**: *Few businesses are flourishing in the present economic climate.* **2** [I] to grow well; to be healthy and happy SYN **thrive**: *These plants flourish in a damp climate.* ◇ *(especially BrE) I'm glad to hear you're all flourishing.* **3** [T] **~ sth** to wave sth around in a way that makes people look at it
- **noun 1** [usually sing.] an exaggerated movement that you make when you want sb to notice you: *He opened the door for her with a flourish.* **2** [usually sing.] an impressive act or way of doing sth: *The season ended with a flourish for Rooney, when he scored in the final minute of the match.* **3** details and decoration that are used in speech or writing: *a speech full of rhetorical flourishes* **4** a curved line, that is used as decoration, especially in writing **5** [usually sing.] a loud short piece of music, that is usually played to announce an important person or event: *a flourish of trumpets*

floury /ˈflaʊəri/ *adj.* **1** covered with flour: *floury hands* **2** like flour; tasting of flour: *a floury texture* **3** (of potatoes) soft and light when they are cooked

flout /flaʊt/ *verb* **~ sth** to show that you have no respect for a law, etc. by openly not obeying it SYN **defy**: *Motorists regularly **flout the law**.* ◇ *to **flout authority/convention***

flow 0→ /fləʊ; *NAmE* floʊ/ *noun, verb*
- **noun** [C, usually sing., U]
- ▸ CONTINUOUS MOVEMENT **1** 0→ **~ (of sth/sb)** the steady and continuous movement of sth/sb in one direction: *She tried to stop the flow of blood from the wound.* ◇ *an endless flow of refugees into the country* ◇ *to improve traffic flow* (= make it move faster) ◇ *to control the direction of flow*
- ▸ PRODUCTION/SUPPLY **2** 0→ **~ (of sth)** the continuous production or supply of sth: *the flow of goods and services to remote areas* ◇ *to encourage the free flow of information* ◇ *data flow* ➲ see also CASH FLOW
- ▸ OF SPEECH/WRITING **3** continuous talk by sb: *You've interrupted my flow—I can't remember what I was saying.* ◇ *As usual, Tom was **in full flow**.* **4 ~ of sth** the way that words and ideas are linked together in speech or writing: *Too many examples can interrupt the smooth flow of the text.*
- ▸ OF THE SEA **5** the movement of the sea towards the land: *the **ebb and flow** of the tide*

IDM **go with the ˈflow** (*informal*) to be relaxed and not worry about what you should do ➲ more at EBB *n.*

- **verb**
- ▸ MOVE CONTINUOUSLY **1** 0→ [I] (of liquid, gas or electricity) to move steadily and continuously in one direction: *She lost control and the tears began to flow.* ◇ **+ adv./prep.** *It's here that the river flows down into the ocean.* ◇ *Blood flowed from a cut on her head.* ◇ *This can prevent air from flowing freely to the lungs.* **2** 0→ [I] (**+ adv./prep.**) (of people or things) to move or pass continuously from one place or person to another, especially in large numbers or amounts: *Constant streams of traffic flowed past.* ◇ *Election results flowed in throughout the night.*
- ▸ OF IDEAS/CONVERSATION **3** [I] to develop or be produced in an easy and natural way: *Conversation flowed freely throughout the meal.*
- ▸ BE AVAILABLE EASILY **4** [I] to be available easily and in large amounts: *It was obvious that money flowed freely in their family.* ◇ *The party got livelier as the drink began to flow.*
- ▸ OF FEELING **5** [I] **+ adv./prep.** to be felt strongly by sb: *Fear and excitement suddenly flowed over me.*
- ▸ OF CLOTHES/HAIR **6** [I] **~ (down/over sth)** to hang loosely and freely: *Her hair flowed down over her shoulders.* ◇ *long flowing skirts*
- ▸ OF THE SEA **7** [I] (of the TIDE in the sea/ocean) to come in towards the land OPP **ebb** *v.*

PHR V **ˈflow from sth** (*formal*) to come or result from sth

ˈflow chart (also **ˈflow diagram**) *noun* a diagram that shows the connections between the different stages of a process or parts of a system

flower 0→ /ˈflaʊə(r)/ *noun, verb*
- **noun 1** 0→ the coloured part of a plant from which the seed or fruit develops. Flowers usually grow at the end of a STEM and last only a short time: *The plant has a beautiful bright red flower.* ◇ *The roses are **in flower** early this year.* ◇ *The crocuses are late **coming into flower**.* ➲ COLLOCATIONS at LIFE ➲ VISUAL VOCAB page V9 **2** 0→ a plant grown for the beauty of its flowers: *a garden full of flowers* ◇ *a **flower garden/show*** **3** 0→ a flower with its STEM that has been picked as a decoration: *I **picked some flowers**.* ◇ *a **bunch of flowers*** ◇ *a **flower arrangement*** ➲ see also BOUQUET

IDM **the flower of sth** (*literary*) the finest or best part of sth

- **verb 1** [I] (of a plant or tree) to produce flowers SYN **bloom**: *This particular variety flowers in July.* ◇ *early-flowering spring bulbs* **2** [I] (*literary*) to develop and become successful SYN **blossom**

ˈflower arranging *noun* [U] the art of arranging cut flowers in an attractive way

ˈflower bed *noun* a piece of ground in a garden/yard or park where flowers are grown ➲ VISUAL VOCAB page V16

flowered /ˈflaʊəd; *NAmE* ˈflaʊərd/ *adj.* [usually before noun] decorated with patterns of flowers

flower·ing /ˈflaʊərɪŋ/ *noun* **1** [U] the time when a plant has flowers **2** [C, usually sing.] **~ of sth** the time when sth, especially a period of new ideas in art, music, science, etc, reaches its most complete and successful stage of development

flower·pot /ˈflaʊəpɒt; *NAmE* ˈflaʊərpɑːt/ *noun* a container made of plastic or CLAY for growing plants in ➲ VISUAL VOCAB page V16

ˈflower power *noun* [U] the culture connected with young people of the 1960s and early 1970s who believed in love and peace and were against war

flowery /ˈflaʊəri/ *adj.* [usually before noun] **1** covered with flowers or decorated with pictures of flowers **2** smelling or tasting of flowers **3** (usually *disapproving*) (of speech or writing) too complicated; not expressed in a clear and simple way

flown *past part.* of FLY

ˈflow-on *noun, adj.* (*AustralE, NZE*)
- **noun** an increase in pay or an improvement in working conditions that is made because one has already been given in a similar job
- **adj. flow-on** effects, etc. are ones that happen as a result of sth else

fl oz *abbr.* (*pl.* **fl oz**) (in writing) FLUID OUNCE: *Add 8 fl oz water.*

F

flu 0- /fluː/ (often **the flu**) (also *formal* **in·flu·enza**) *noun* [U] an infectious disease like a very bad cold, that causes fever, pains and weakness: *The whole family has the flu.* ◇ (*BrE*) *She's got flu.* ➲ COLLOCATIONS at ILL

flub /flʌb/ *verb* (-bb-) [T, I] **~ (sth)** (*NAmE, informal*) to do sth badly or make a mistake SYN **fluff, bungle**: *She flubbed the first line of the song.* ▶ **flub** *noun*

fluc·tu·ate AW /ˈflʌktʃueɪt/ *verb* [I] to change frequently in size, amount, quality, etc, especially from one extreme to another SYN **vary**: *fluctuating prices* ◇ **~ between A and B** *During the crisis, oil prices fluctuated between $20 and $40 a barrel.* ◇ **+ adv./prep.** *Temperatures can fluctuate by as much as 10 degrees.* ◇ *My mood seems to fluctuate from day to day.* ▶ **fluc·tu·ation** AW /ˌflʌktʃuˈeɪʃn/ *noun* [C, U]: **~ (in/of sth)** *wild fluctuations in interest rates*

F

flue /fluː/ *noun* a pipe or tube that takes smoke, gas or hot air away from a fire, a HEATER or an oven

flu·ency /ˈfluːənsi/ *noun* [U, sing.] **1** the quality of being able to speak or write a language, especially a foreign language, easily and well: *Fluency in French is required for this job.* **2** the quality of doing sth in a smooth and skilful way: *The team lacked fluency during the first half.*

flu·ent /ˈfluːənt/ *adj.* **1 ~ (in sth)** able to speak, read or write a language, especially a foreign language, easily and well: *She's fluent in Polish.* ◇ *a* ***fluent speaker/reader*** **2** (of a language, especially a foreign language) expressed easily and well: *He speaks fluent Italian.* **3** (of an action) done in a smooth and skilful way: *fluent handwriting* ◇ *fluent movements* ▶ **flu·ent·ly** *adv.*

fluff /flʌf/ *noun, verb*

■ ***noun*** [U] **1** (*BrE*) (also **lint** *NAmE, BrE*) small pieces of wool, cotton, etc. that gather on clothes and other surfaces **2** soft animal fur or bird feathers, that is found especially on young animals or birds **3** (*informal, especially NAmE*) entertainment that is not serious and is not considered to have great value

■ ***verb*** **1 ~ sth** (*informal*) to do sth badly or to fail at sth SYN **bungle**: *He completely fluffed an easy shot* (= in sport). ◇ *Most actors fluff their lines occasionally.* **2 ~ sth (out/up)** to shake or brush sth so that it looks larger and/or softer: *The female sat on the eggs, fluffing out her feathers.* ◇ *Let me fluff up your pillows for you.*

fluffy /ˈflʌfi/ *adj.* (**fluf·fier, fluf·fiest**) **1** like fluff; covered in fluff: *a little fluffy kitten* **2** (of food) soft, light and containing air: *Beat the butter and sugar until soft and fluffy.* **3** looking as if it is soft and light: *fluffy white clouds* **4** (*informal, disapproving*) light and not serious; having no substance, depth or power: *a fluffy film/movie* ◇ *a fluffy argument*

flu·gel·horn /ˈfluːglhɔːn; *NAmE* -hɔːrn/ *noun* a BRASS musical instrument like a small TRUMPET

fluid /ˈfluːɪd/ *noun, adj.*

■ ***noun*** [C, U] (*formal* or *technical*) a liquid; a substance that can flow: *body fluids* (= for example, blood) ◇ *The doctor told him to drink plenty of fluids.* ◇ *cleaning fluid*

■ ***adj.*** **1** (*formal*) (of movements, designs, music, etc.) smooth and elegant SYN **flowing**: *a loose, fluid style of dancing* ◇ *fluid guitar playing* ◇ *the fluid lines of the drawing* **2** (*formal*) (of a situation) likely to change; not fixed: *a fluid political situation* **3** (*technical*) that can flow freely, as gases and liquids do: *a fluid consistency*

flu·id·ity /fluˈɪdəti/ *noun* [U] **1** (*formal*) the quality of being smooth and elegant: *She danced with great fluidity of movement.* **2** (*formal*) the quality of being likely to change: *the fluidity of human behaviour* ◇ *social fluidity* **3** (*technical*) the quality of being able to flow freely, as gases and liquids do

ˌfluid ˈounce *noun* (*abbr.* **fl oz**) a unit for measuring liquids. There are 20 fluid ounces in a British pint and 16 in an American pint.

fluke /fluːk/ *noun* [usually sing.] (*informal*) a lucky or unusual thing that happens by accident, not because of planning or skill: *They are determined to show that their last win was no fluke.* ◇ *a fluke goal* ▶ **fluky** (also **flukey**) /ˈfluːki/ *adj.*

flume /fluːm/ *noun* **1** a narrow channel made to carry water for use in industry **2** a water CHUTE (= a tube for sliding down) at an AMUSEMENT PARK or a swimming pool

flum·mery /ˈflʌməri/ *noun* [U] nonsense, especially praise that is silly or not sincere: *She hated the flummery of public relations.*

flum·mox /ˈflʌməks/ *verb* [usually passive] (not used in the progressive tenses) **~ sb** (*informal*) to confuse sb so that they do not know what to say or do: *I was flummoxed by her question.* ▶ **flum·moxed** *adj.*

flung *past tense, past part.* of FLING

flunk /flʌŋk/ *verb* (*informal, especially NAmE*) **1** [T, I] **~ (sth)** to fail an exam, a test or a course: *I flunked math in second grade.* **2** [T] **~ sb** to make sb fail an exam, a test, or a course by giving them a low mark/grade: *She's flunked 13 of the 18 students.*

PHR V **ˌflunk ˈout (of sth)** (*NAmE, informal*) to have to leave a school or college because your marks/grades are not good enough

flun·key (also **flunky**) /ˈflʌŋki/ *noun* (*pl.* -eys or -ies) **1** (*disapproving*) a person who tries to please sb who is important and powerful by doing small jobs for them **2** (*old-fashioned*) a servant in uniform

fluor·es·cent /ˌflɔːˈresnt; ˌflʊəˈr-; *NAmE* also ˌflʊˈr-/ *adj.* **1** (of substances) producing bright light by using some forms of RADIATION: *a fluorescent lamp* (= one that uses such a substance) ◇ *fluorescent lighting* **2** (of a colour, material, etc.) appearing very bright when light shines on it; that can be seen in the dark: *fluorescent armbands worn by cyclists* ➲ SYNONYMS at BRIGHT ➲ compare PHOSPHORESCENT ▶ **fluor·es·cence** *noun* [U]

fluorid·ation /ˌflɔːrɪˈdeɪʃn; *BrE* also ˌflʊər-; *NAmE* also ˌflʊr-/ *noun* [U] the practice of adding fluoride to drinking water to prevent tooth decay

fluor·ide /ˈflɔːraɪd; *BrE* also ˈflʊər-; *NAmE* also ˈflʊr-/ *noun* a chemical containing fluorine that protects teeth from decay and is often added to TOOTHPASTE and sometimes to drinking water

fluor·ine /ˈflɔːriːn; *BrE* also ˈflʊər-; *NAmE* also ˈflʊr-/ *noun* [U] (*symb.* F) a chemical element. Fluorine is a poisonous pale yellow gas and is very REACTIVE.

flur·ried /ˈflʌrid; *NAmE* ˈflɜːrid/ *adj.* nervous and confused, especially because there is too much to do SYN **flustered**

flurry /ˈflʌri; *NAmE* ˈflɜːri/ *noun* (*pl.* -ies) **1** [usually sing.] an occasion when there is a lot of activity, interest, excitement, etc. within a short period of time: *a sudden* ***flurry of activity*** ◇ *Her arrival caused a* ***flurry of excitement.*** ◇ *A* ***flurry of shots*** *rang out in the darkness.* **2** a small amount of snow, rain, etc. that falls for a short time and then stops: ***snow flurries*** ◇ *flurries of snow* **3** a sudden short movement of paper or cloth, especially clothes: *The ladies departed in a flurry of silks and satins.*

flush /flʌʃ/ *verb, noun, adj.*

■ ***verb*** **1** [I, T] (of a person or their face) to become red, especially because you are embarrassed, angry or hot: *She flushed with anger.* ◇ **+ adj.** *Sam felt her cheeks flush red.* ◇ **~ sth** *A rosy blush flushed her cheeks.* **2** [I, T] **~ (sth)** when a toilet **flushes** or you **flush** it, water passes through it to clean it, after a handle, etc. has been pressed **3** [T] to clean sth by causing water to pass through it: **~ sth out (with sth)** *Flush the pipe out with clean water.* ◇ **~ sth through sth** *Flush clean water through the pipe.* **4** [T] **+ adv./prep.** to get rid of sth with a sudden flow of water: *They flushed the drugs down the toilet.* ◇ *Drinking lots of water will help to flush toxins out of the body.*

PHR V **ˌflush sb/sth ˈout (of sth)** | **ˌflush sb/sth↔ˈout** to force a person or an animal to leave the place where they are hiding

■ ***noun*** **1** [C, usually sing.] a red colour that appears on your face or body because you are embarrassed, excited or hot: *A pink flush spread over his cheeks.* ➲ see also HOT FLUSH **2** [C, usually sing.] a sudden strong feeling; the hot feeling on your face or body caused by this: *a **flush of anger/embarrassment/enthusiasm/guilt*** **3** [sing.] the act of cleaning a toilet with a sudden flow of water: *Give the toilet a flush.* **4** [C] (in card games) a set of cards that a player has that are all of the same SUIT

IDM **(in) the first flush of sth** (*formal*) (at) a time when sth is new, exciting and strong: *in the first **flush of youth/enthusiasm/romance***

■ ***adj.*** [not before noun] **1** (*informal*) having a lot of money, usually for a short time **2 ~ with sth** (of two surfaces) completely level with each other: *Make sure the paving stones are flush with the lawn.*

flushed /flʌʃt/ *adj.* (of a person) red; with a red face: *flushed cheeks* ◇ *Her face was flushed with anger.* ◇ (*figurative*) *He was **flushed with success*** (= very excited and pleased) *after his first novel was published.*

flus·ter /ˈflʌstə(r)/ *verb, noun*

■ ***verb*** [often passive] **~ sb** to make sb nervous and/or confused, especially by giving them a lot to do or by making them hurry ▸ **flus·tered** *adj.* SYN **flurried**: *She arrived late, looking hot and flustered.*

■ ***noun*** [sing.] (*BrE*) a state of being nervous and confused

flute /fluːt/ *noun* **1** a musical instrument of the WOODWIND group, shaped like a thin pipe. The player holds it sideways and blows across a hole at one end. ➲ VISUAL VOCAB page V30 **2 champagne ~** a tall narrow glass used for drinking CHAMPAGNE ➲ VISUAL VOCAB page V19

fluted /ˈfluːtɪd/ *adj.* (especially of a round object) with a pattern of curves cut around the outside: *fluted columns* ▸ **flut·ing** *noun* [U]

flut·ist /ˈfluːtɪst/ (*NAmE*) (*BrE* **flaut·ist**) *noun* a person who plays the FLUTE

flut·ter /ˈflʌtə(r)/ *verb, noun*

■ ***verb*** **1** [I, T] to move lightly and quickly; to make sth move in this way: *Flags fluttered in the breeze.* ◇ *Her eyelids fluttered but did not open.* ◇ **~ sth** *He fluttered his hands around wildly.* ◇ *She **fluttered her eyelashes** at him* (= tried to attract him in order to persuade him to do sth). **2** [I, T] **~ (sth)** when a bird or an insect **flutters** its wings, or its wings **flutter**, the wings move lightly and quickly up and down **3** [I] **+ adv./prep.** (of a bird or an insect) to fly somewhere moving the wings quickly and lightly: *The butterfly fluttered from flower to flower.* **4** [I] (of your heart, etc.) to beat very quickly and not regularly: *I could feel a fluttering pulse.* ◇ (*figurative*) *The sound of his voice in the hall made her heart flutter.*

■ ***noun*** **1** [C, usually sing.] a quick, light movement: *the flutter of wings* ◇ *with a flutter of her long, dark eyelashes* ◇ (*figurative*) *to feel a flutter of panic in your stomach* **2** [C, usually sing.] **~ (on sth)** (*BrE, informal*) a small bet: *to have a flutter on the horses* **3** [sing.] a state of nervous or confused excitement: *Her sudden arrival caused quite a flutter.* **4** [C] a very fast HEARTBEAT, caused when sb is nervous or excited: *Her heart gave a flutter when she saw him.* **5** [U] (*medical*) a medical condition in which you have a fast, unsteady HEARTBEAT **6** [U] (*technical*) rapid changes in the PITCH or volume of recorded sound ➲ compare WOW

flu·vial /ˈfluːviəl/ *adj.* (*technical*) connected with rivers

flux /flʌks/ *noun* **1** [U] continuous movement and change: *Our society is **in a state of flux**.* **2** [C, usually sing., U] (*technical*) a flow; an act of flowing: *a flux of neutrons*

fly 🔑 /flaɪ/ *verb, noun, adj.*

■ ***verb*** (**flies**, **fly·ing**, **flew** /fluː/, **flown** /fləʊn; *NAmE* floʊn/)

HELP In sense 15 **flied** is used for the past tense and past participle.

▸ OF BIRD/INSECT **1** 🔑 [I] (**+ adv./prep.**) to move through the air, using wings: *A stork flew slowly past.* ◇ *A wasp had flown in through the window.*

▸ AIRCRAFT/SPACECRAFT **2** 🔑 [I] (**+ adv./prep.**) (of an aircraft or a SPACECRAFT) to move through air or space: *They were on a plane flying from London to New York.* ◇ *to fly at the speed of sound* ◇ *Lufthansa fly to La Paz from Frankfurt.* **3** 🔑 [I] to travel in an aircraft or a SPACECRAFT: *Is this the first time that you've flown?* ◇ **~ (from...) (to...)** *I'm flying to Hong Kong tomorrow.* ◇ **+ noun** *I always fly business class.* ◇ *We're flying KLM.* **4** 🔑 [T, I] **~ (sth)** to control an aircraft, etc. in the air: *a pilot trained to fly large passenger planes* ◇ *children flying kites* ◇ *He's learning to fly.* **5** [T] **+ adv./prep.** to transport goods or passengers in a plane: *The stranded tourists were finally flown home.* ◇ *He had flowers specially flown in for the ceremony.* **6** [T] **~ sth** to travel over an ocean or area of land in an aircraft: *to fly the Atlantic*

▸ MOVE QUICKLY/SUDDENLY **7** 🔑 [I] (**+ adv./prep.**) to go or move quickly: *The train was flying along.* ◇ *She gasped and her hand flew to her mouth.* ◇ *It's late—I must fly.* **8** 🔑 [I] (**+ adv./prep.**) to move suddenly and with force: (**+ adv./prep.**) *A large stone came flying in through the window.* ◇ *Several people were hit by flying glass.* ◇ **+ adj.** *David gave the door a kick and it flew open.*

▸ OF TIME **9** 🔑 [I] to seem to pass very quickly: *Doesn't time fly?* ◇ **~ by/past** *Summer has just flown by.*

▸ FLAG **10** [I, T] if a flag **flies**, or if you **fly** it, it is displayed, for example on a long pole: *Flags were flying at half mast on all public buildings.* ◇ **~ sth** *to fly the Stars and Stripes*

▸ MOVE FREELY **11** [I] to move around freely: *hair flying in the wind*

▸ OF STORIES/RUMOURS **12** [I] to be talked about by many people

▸ ESCAPE **13** [T, I] **~ (sth)** (*formal*) to escape from sb/sth: *Both suspects have flown the country.* ➲ compare FLEE

▸ OF PLAN **14** [I] (*NAmE*) to be successful: *It remains to be seen whether his project will fly.*

▸ IN BASEBALL **15** (**flies**, **flying**, **flied**, **flied**) [I, T] **~ (sth)** to hit a ball high into the air

IDM **fly the ˈcoop** (*informal, especially NAmE*) to escape from a place **fly ˈhigh** to be successful **fly in the face of ˈsth** to oppose or be the opposite of sth that is usual or expected: *Such a proposal is flying in the face of common sense.* **fly into a ˈrage, ˈtemper, etc.** to become suddenly very angry **(go) fly a/your ˈkite** (*NAmE, informal*) used to tell sb to go away and stop annoying you or INTERFERING **ˌfly the ˈnest 1** (of a young bird) to become able to fly and leave its nest **2** (*informal*) (of sb's child) to leave home and live somewhere else **fly off the ˈhandle** (*informal*) to suddenly become very angry **go ˈflying** (*BrE, informal*) to fall, especially as a result of not seeing sth under your feet: *Someone's going to go flying if you don't pick up these toys.* **let ˈfly (at sb/sth) (with sth)** to attack sb by hitting them or speaking angrily to them: *He let fly at me with his fist.* ◇ *She let fly with a stream of abuse.* ➲ more at BIRD, CROW *n.*, FLAG *n.*, PIG *n.*, SEAT *n.*, TANGENT, TIME *n.*, WINDOW

PHR V **ˈfly at sb** (of a person or an animal) to attack sb suddenly

■ ***noun*** (*pl.* **flies**)

▸ INSECT **1** 🔑 [C] a small flying insect with two wings. There are many different types of fly: *A fly was buzzing against the window.* ◇ *Flies rose in thick black swarms.*

▸ IN FISHING **2** [C] a fly or sth made to look like a fly, that is put on a hook and used as BAIT to catch fish: *fly fishing*

▸ ON TROUSERS/PANTS **3** [sing.] (*BrE* also **flies**) an opening down the front of a pair of trousers/pants that fastens with a ZIP or buttons and is usually covered over by a strip of material: *Your fly is undone!* ◇ *Your flies are undone!* ➲ VISUAL VOCAB page V51

▸ ON TENT **4** [C] a piece of material that covers the entrance to a tent ➲ see also FLIES

IDM **die/fall/drop like ˈflies** (*informal*) to die or fall down in very large numbers: *People were dropping like flies in the intense heat.* **a/the fly in the ˈointment** a person or thing that spoils a situation or an occasion that is fine in all other ways **a fly on the ˈwall** a person who watches others without being noticed: *I'd love to be a fly on the wall when he tells her the news.* ◇ *fly-on-the-wall documentaries* (= in which people are filmed going about their normal lives as if the camera were not there) **(there are) no flies on ˈsb** (*informal*) the person mentioned is clever and not easily tricked **not harm/hurt a ˈfly** to be kind and gentle and unwilling to cause unhappiness **on the ˈfly** (*informal*) if you do sth **on the fly**, you do it quickly while sth else is happening, and without thinking about it very much

■ ***adj.*** (*informal*) **1** (*BrE*) clever and showing good judgement about people, especially so that you can get an advantage for yourself **2** (*NAmE*) fashionable and attractive

ˌfly ˈagaric (also **ˌfly aˈgaric**) *noun* [U] a poisonous MUSHROOM with a red top with white spots

fly·away /ˈflaɪəweɪ/ *adj.* (especially of hair) soft and fine; difficult to keep tidy

ˈfly ball *noun* (in BASEBALL) a ball that is hit high into the air

fly·blown /ˈflaɪbləʊn; *NAmE* -bloʊn/ *adj.* (*BrE*) dirty and in bad condition; not fit to eat

ˈfly boy *noun* (*NAmE, informal*) a pilot, especially one in the AIR FORCE

F

ˈfly-by *noun* (*pl.* **fly-bys**) **1** the flight of a SPACECRAFT near a planet to record data **2** (*NAmE*) (also **ˈflyover**) (both *NAmE*) (*BrE* **ˈfly-past**) a special flight by a group of aircraft, for people to watch at an important ceremony

ˈfly-by-night *adj.* [only before noun] (of a person or business) dishonest and only interested in making money quickly ▸ **ˈfly-by-night** *noun*

fly·catch·er /ˈflaɪkætʃə(r)/ *noun* a small bird that catches insects while it is flying

ˈfly-drive *adj., noun* (*BrE*)
■ ***adj.*** [only before noun] (of a holiday/vacation) organized by a travel company at a fixed price that includes your flight to a place, a car to drive while you are there and somewhere to stay: *a fly-drive break*
■ ***noun*** a fly-drive holiday

flyer (also **flier**) /ˈflaɪə(r)/ *noun* **1** (*informal*) a person who flies an aircraft (usually a small one, not a passenger plane) **2** a person who travels in a plane as a passenger: *frequent flyers* **3** a person who operates sth such as a model aircraft or a KITE from the ground **4** a thing, especially a bird or an insect, that flies in a particular way: *Butterflies can be strong flyers.* **5** a small sheet of paper that advertises a product or an event and is given to a large number of people **6** (*informal*) a person, an animal or a vehicle that moves very quickly: *Ford's flashy new flyer* **7** = FLYING START ➲ see also HIGH-FLYER

ˈfly fishing *noun* [U] the sport of fishing in a river or lake using an artificial fly at the end of the line to attract and catch the fish

ˌfly ˈhalf *noun* = STAND-OFF HALF

fly·ing 0‒ /ˈflaɪɪŋ/ *adj., noun*
■ ***adj.*** 0‒ [only before noun] able to fly: *flying insects*
IDM **with ˌflying ˈcolours** very well; with a very high mark/grade: *She passed the exam with flying colours.* ORIGIN In the past, a ship returned to port after a victory in battle decorated with flags (= colours).
■ ***noun*** [U] **1** 0‒ travelling in an aircraft: *I'm terrified of flying.* **2** 0‒ operating the controls of an aircraft: *flying lessons*

ˈflying boat *noun* a large plane that can take off from and land on water

ˌflying ˈbuttress *noun* (*architecture*) a half ARCH of brick or stone that supports the outside wall of a large building such as a church

ˌflying ˈdoctor *noun* (especially in Australia) a doctor who travels in an aircraft to visit patients who live far from a town: *A **flying doctor service** operates in remote regions.*

ˌflying ˈfish *noun* a tropical sea fish that can rise and move forwards above the surface of the water, using its FINS (= flat parts that stick out from its body) as wings

ˌflying ˈfox *noun* a large BAT (= an animal like a mouse with wings) that lives in hot countries and eats fruit

ˈflying jacket (*BrE*) (*US* **ˈflight jacket**) *noun* a short leather jacket with a warm LINING and COLLAR, originally worn by pilots

ˌflying ˈleap *noun* a long high jump made while you are running quickly: *to take a flying leap into the air*

ˈflying machine *noun* an aircraft, especially one that is unusual or was built a long time ago

ˈflying officer *noun* an officer of lower rank in the British AIR FORCE: *Flying Officer Ian Wall*

ˌflying ˈpicket *noun* (*BrE*) a worker on strike who can go quickly to other factories, etc. to help persuade the workers there to join the strike

ˌflying ˈsaucer *noun* a round SPACECRAFT that some people claim to have seen and that some people believe comes from another planet ➲ compare UFO

ˈflying squad *noun* (usually **the Flying Squad**) a group of police officers in Britain who are ready to travel very quickly to the scene of a serious crime

ˌflying ˈsquirrel *noun* a small animal like a SQUIRREL which travels through the air between trees, spreading out the skin between its front and back legs to stop itself from falling too quickly

ˌflying ˈstart (also *less frequent* **flyer**) *noun* [sing.] a very fast start to a race, competition, etc.
IDM **get off to a ˌflying ˈstart | get off to a ˈflyer** to make a very good start; to begin sth well

ˈflying suit *noun* a piece of clothing that covers the whole body, worn by the pilot and CREW of a military or light aircraft

ˌflying ˈvisit *noun* (*BrE*) a very short visit

fly·leaf /ˈflaɪliːf/ *noun* (*pl.* **fly·leaves**) an empty page at the beginning or end of a book

fly·over /ˈflaɪəʊvə(r); *NAmE* -oʊvər/ *noun* **1** (*BrE*) (*NAmE* **over·pass**) a bridge that carries one road over another one **2** (*NAmE*) = FLY-BY

ˈflyover country *noun* [U] (also **the ˈflyover states** [pl.]) (*informal, disapproving*) (in the US) the area in the middle of the country between the states on the coasts: *It's an area most New Yorkers know as flyover country.*

fly·paper /ˈflaɪpeɪpə(r)/ *noun* [C, U] a strip of sticky paper that you hang in a room to catch flies

ˈfly-past (*BrE*) (*NAmE* **ˈfly-by, ˈflyover**) *noun* a special flight by a group of aircraft, for people to watch at an important ceremony

ˈfly-post *verb* [I, T] **~ (sth)** (*BrE*) to put up pieces of paper that advertise sth in public places, without official permission ▸ **ˈfly-posting** *noun* [U] **ˈfly-poster** *noun*

fly·sheet /ˈflaɪʃiːt/ *noun* (*BrE*) an extra sheet of material on the outside of a tent that keeps the rain out

ˈfly-tip *verb* (**-pp-**) [I] (*BrE*) to leave waste somewhere illegally ▸ **ˈfly-tipping** *noun* [U] **ˈfly-tipper** *noun*

fly·weight /ˈflaɪweɪt/ *noun* a BOXER, WRESTLER, etc. of the lightest class, usually weighing between 48 and 51 kilograms

fly·wheel /ˈflaɪwiːl/ *noun* a heavy wheel in a machine or an engine that helps to keep it working smoothly and at a steady speed

FM *abbr.* **1** /ˌef ˈem/ frequency modulation (a method of broadcasting high-quality sound by radio): *Radio 1 FM* **2** (in writing) FIELD MARSHALL

foal /fəʊl; *NAmE* foʊl/ *noun, verb*
■ ***noun*** a very young horse or DONKEY
IDM **in foal** (of a female horse) pregnant
■ ***verb*** [I] to give birth to a foal

foam /fəʊm; *NAmE* foʊm/ *noun, verb*
■ ***noun*** **1** (also **ˌfoam ˈrubber**) [U] a soft light rubber material, full of small holes, that is used for seats, MATTRESSES, etc: *a foam mattress* ◇ *foam packaging* **2** [U] a mass of very small air bubbles on the surface of a liquid SYN **froth**: *a glass of beer with a good head of foam* ◇ *The breaking waves left the beach covered with foam.* ➲ VISUAL VOCAB page V4 **3** [U, C] a chemical substance that forms or produces a soft mass of very small bubbles, used for washing, shaving, or putting out fires, for example: *shaving foam* ➲ picture at FROTH
■ ***verb*** [I] (of a liquid) to have or produce a mass of small bubbles SYN **froth**
IDM **foam at the ˈmouth 1** (especially of an animal) to have a mass of small bubbles in and around its mouth, es-

pecially because it is sick or angry **2** (*informal*) (of a person) to be very angry

foamy /ˈfəʊmi; *NAmE* ˈfoʊmi/ *adj.* consisting of or producing a mass of small bubbles; like foam

FOB /ˌef əʊ ˈbiː; *NAmE* oʊ/ *noun* (becoming *old-fashioned, informal, offensive, especially NAmE*) the abbreviation for 'fresh off the boat' (a person who has recently come to a country as an IMMIGRANT and does not speak or behave like people who have lived there a long time)

fob /fɒb; *NAmE* fɑːb/ *verb, noun*

▪ ***verb*** (-bb-)

PHR V **ˌfob sb↔ˈoff (with sth)** **1** to try to stop sb asking questions or complaining by telling them sth that is not true: *Don't let him fob you off with any more excuses.* ◇ *She wouldn't be fobbed off this time.* **2** to give sb sth that is not what they want or is of worse quality than they want: *He was unaware that he was being fobbed off with out-of-date stock.*

▪ ***noun*** **1** a short chain that is attached to a watch that is carried in a pocket **2** (also ˈ**fob watch**) a watch that is attached to a fob **3** a small decorative object that is attached to a KEY RING, etc.

f.o.b. *abbr.* (in writing) FREE ON BOARD

focal /ˈfəʊkl; *NAmE* ˈfoʊkl/ *adj.* [only before noun] central; very important; connected with or providing a focus

fo·cal·ize (*BrE* also **-ise**) /ˈfəʊkəlaɪz; *NAmE* ˈfoʊ-/ *verb* **~ sth** (*formal*) to make sth focus or concentrate on a particular thing ▸ **fo·cal·iza·tion, -isa·tion** /ˌfəʊkəlaɪˈzeɪʃn; *NAmE* ˌfoʊ-/ *noun* [U, C]

ˌfocal ˈlength *noun* (*physics*) the distance between the centre of a mirror or a LENS and its FOCUS

ˈfocal point *noun* **1** a thing or person that is the centre of interest or activity: *In rural areas, the school is often the focal point for the local community.* ◇ *He quickly became the focal point for those who disagreed with government policy.* **2** (*technical*) = FOCUS

fo'c'sle = FORECASTLE

focus 🔑 AW /ˈfəʊkəs; *NAmE* ˈfoʊ-/ *verb, noun*

▪ ***verb*** (-s- or -ss-) **1** 🔑 [I, T] to give attention, effort, etc. to one particular subject, situation or person rather than another: **~ (on/upon sb/sth)** *The discussion focused on three main problems.* ◇ *Each exercise focuses on a different grammar point.* ◇ **~ sth (on/upon sb/sth)** *The visit helped to focus world attention on the plight of the refugees.* **2** 🔑 [I, T] (of your eyes, a camera, etc.) to adapt or be adjusted so that things can be seen clearly; to adjust sth so that you can see things clearly: *It took a few moments for her eyes to focus in the dark.* ◇ **~ on sb/sth** *Let your eyes focus on objects that are further away from you.* ◇ *In this scene, the camera focuses on the actor's face.* ◇ **~ sth (on sb/sth)** *He focused his blue eyes on her.* ◇ *I quickly focused the camera on the children.* **3** [T] **~ sth (on sth)** (*technical*) to aim light onto a particular point using a LENS

▪ ***noun*** (*pl.* **fo·cuses** or **foci** /ˈfəʊsaɪ; *NAmE* ˈfoʊ-/) **1** 🔑 [U, C, usually sing.] the thing or person that people are most interested in; the act of paying special attention to sth and making people interested in it: *It was the main* ***focus of attention*** *at the meeting.* ◇ **~ for sth** *His comments provided a focus for debate.* ◇ **~ on sth** *We shall maintain our focus on the needs of the customer.* ◇ *In today's lecture the focus will be on tax structures within the European Union.* ◇ *The incident* ***brought*** *the problem of violence in schools* ***into sharp focus.*** ◇ *What we need now is a* ***change of focus*** (= to look at things in a different way). **2** 🔑 [U] a point or distance at which the outline of an object is clearly seen by the eye or through a LENS: *The children's faces are badly* ***out of focus*** (= not clearly shown) *in the photograph.* ◇ *The binoculars were not* ***in focus*** (= were not showing things clearly). **3** (also ˈ**focal point**) [C] (*physics*) a point at which waves of light, sound, etc. meet after REFLECTION or REFRACTION; the point from which waves of light, sound, etc. seem to come **4** [C] (*geology*) the point at which an EARTHQUAKE starts to happen

fo·cused (also **fo·cussed**) /ˈfəʊkəst; *NAmE* ˈfoʊ-/ *adj.* with your attention directed to what you want to do; with very clear aims: *She should do well in her studies this year—she's very focused.*

ˈfocus group *noun* a small group of people, specially chosen to represent different social classes, etc, who are asked to discuss and give their opinions about a particular subject. The information obtained is used by people doing MARKET RESEARCH, for example about new products or for a political party.

fod·der /ˈfɒdə(r); *NAmE* ˈfɑːd-/ *noun* [U] **1** food for horses and farm animals **2** (*disapproving*) (often after a noun) people or things that are considered to have only one use: *Without education, these children will end up as factory fodder* (= only able to work in a factory). ◇ *This story will be more fodder for the gossip columnists.* ➲ see also CANNON FODDER

foe /fəʊ; *NAmE* foʊ/ *noun* (*old-fashioned* or *formal*) an enemy

foehn = FÖHN

foe·tal (*BrE*) (also **fetal** *NAmE, BrE*) /ˈfiːtl/ *adj.* [only before noun] connected with a foetus; typical of a foetus: *foetal abnormalities* ◇ *She lay curled up in a* ***foetal position.***

foe·tid = FETID

foe·tus (*BrE*) (also **fetus** *NAmE, BrE*) /ˈfiːtəs/ *noun* a young human or animal before it is born, especially a human more than eight weeks after FERTILIZATION

fog /fɒg; *NAmE* fɔːg; fɑːg/ *noun, verb*

▪ ***noun*** [U, C] **1** a thick cloud of very small drops of water in the air close to the land or sea, that is very difficult to see through: ***Dense/thick fog*** *is affecting roads in the north and visibility is poor.* ◇ ***freezing fog*** ◇ ***Patches of fog*** *will clear by mid-morning.* ◇ *We get heavy fogs on this coast in winter.* ◇ *The town was covered in a thick* ***blanket of fog.*** ◇ *The* ***fog*** *finally* ***lifted*** (= disappeared). ➲ COLLOCATIONS at WEATHER ➲ compare MIST **2** a state of confusion, in which things are not clear: *He went through the day with his mind* ***in a fog.***

▪ ***verb*** (-gg-) **1** [I, T] **~ (sth) (up)** if a glass surface **fogs** or **is fogged** up, it becomes covered in steam or small drops of water so that you cannot see through **2** [T] **~ sth** to make sb/sth confused or less clear: *I tried to clear the confusion that was fogging my brain.* ◇ *The government was trying to* ***fog the real issues*** *before the election.*

fog·bound /ˈfɒgbaʊnd; *NAmE* ˈfɔːg-; ˈfɑːg-/ *adj.* unable to operate because of fog; unable to travel or to leave a place because of fog: *a fogbound airport* ◇ *fogbound passengers* ◇ *She spent hours fogbound in Brussels.*

fogey (also **fogy**) /ˈfəʊgi; *NAmE* ˈfoʊgi/ *noun* (*pl.* **fogeys, fo·gies**) a person with old-fashioned ideas that he or she is unwilling to change: *He sounds like such an* ***old fogey!***

foggy /ˈfɒgi; *NAmE* ˈfɔːgi; ˈfɑːgi/ *adj.* (**fog·gier, fog·gi·est**) not clear because of FOG: *foggy conditions* ◇ *a foggy road*

IDM **not have the ˈfoggiest (idea)** (*informal*) to not know anything at all about sth: *'Do you know where she is?' 'Sorry, I haven't the foggiest.'*

fog·horn /ˈfɒghɔːn; *NAmE* ˈfɔːghɔːrn; ˈfɑːg-/ *noun* an instrument that makes a loud noise to warn ships of danger in FOG: *He's got a voice like a foghorn* (= a loud unpleasant voice).

ˈfog lamp (*BrE*) (also ˈ**fog light** *NAmE, BrE*) *noun* a very bright light on the front or back of a car to help the driver to see or be seen in FOG

fogy = FOGEY

föhn (also **foehn**) /fɜːn/ *noun* (usually **the föhn**) [sing.] a hot wind that blows in the Alps

foi·ble /ˈfɔɪbl/ *noun* a silly habit or a strange or weak aspect of a person's character, that is considered harmless by other people SYN **idiosyncrasy**: *We have to tolerate each other's little foibles.*

ˌfoie ˈgras *noun* [U] ➲ PÂTÉ DE FOIE GRAS

foil /fɔɪl/ *noun, verb*

▪ ***noun*** **1** (*BrE* also **ˌsilver ˈfoil**) [U] metal made into very thin sheets that is used for covering or wrapping things, especially food: (*BrE*) *aluminium foil* ◇ (*NAmE*) *aluminum foil* ➲ see also TINFOIL **2** [U] paper that is covered in very thin sheets of metal: *The chocolates are individually wrapped in gold foil.* **3** [C] **~ (for sb/sth)** a person or thing that contrasts with, and therefore emphasizes, the qualities of another person or thing: *The pale walls provide a perfect foil for the furniture.* **4** [C] a long thin light SWORD used in the sport of FENCING ➲ VISUAL VOCAB page V39

■ ***verb*** [often passive] to stop sth from happening, especially sth illegal; to prevent sb from doing sth SYN **thwart**: **~ sth** *to foil a plan/crime/plot* ◇ *Customs officials foiled an attempt to smuggle the paintings out of the country.* ◇ **~ sb (in sth)** *They were foiled in their attempt to smuggle the paintings.*

foist /fɔɪst/ *verb*

PHR V **ˈfoist sb/sth on/upon sb** to force sb to accept sb/sth that they do not want: *The title for her novel was foisted on her by the publishers.*

fold 0-w /fəʊld; *NAmE* foʊld/ *verb, noun*

■ ***verb*** **1** 0-w [T] to bend sth, especially paper or cloth, so that one part lies on top of another part: **~ sth (up)** *He folded the map up and put it in his pocket.* ◇ *First,* ***fold*** *the paper* ***in half/in two.*** ◇ **~ sth (back, down, over, etc.)** *The blankets had been folded down.* ◇ *a pile of neatly folded clothes* ◇ *The bird folded its wings.* OPP **unfold** ➲ see also FOLD-UP **2** 0-w [T, I] to bend sth so that it becomes smaller or flatter and can be stored or carried more easily; to bend or be able to bend in this way: **~ sth (away/down/up)** *The bed can be folded away during the day.* ◇ **~ (away/up)** *The table folds up when not in use.* ◇ (*figurative*) *When she heard the news, her legs just folded under her* (= she fell). ◇ **+ adj.** *The ironing board folds flat for easy storage.* **3** [T] to wrap sth around sb/sth: **~ A in B** *She gently folded the baby in a blanket.* ◇ **~ B round/over A** *She folded a blanket around the baby.* **4** [I] (of a company, a play, etc.) to close because it is not successful

IDM **fold sb in your ˈarms** (*literary*) to put your arms around sb and hold them against your body **fold your ˈarms** to put one of your arms over the other one and hold them against your body **fold your ˈhands** to bring or hold your hands together: *She kept her hands folded in her lap.*

PHR V **ˌfold sth↔ˈin** | **ˌfold sth ˈinto sth** (in cooking) to add one substance to another and gently mix them together: *Fold in the beaten egg whites.*

■ ***noun*** **1** 0-w [C] a part of sth, especially cloth, that is folded or hangs as if it had been folded: *the folds of her dress* ◇ *loose folds of skin* **2** [C] a mark or line made by folding sth, or showing where sth should be folded **3** [C] an area in a field surrounded by a fence or wall where sheep are kept for safety **4 the fold** [sing.] a group of people with whom you feel you belong or who share the same ideas or beliefs: *He called on former Republican voters to return to the fold.* **5** [C] (*geology*) a curve or bend in the line of the layers of rock in the earth's CRUST **6** [C] (*BrE*) a hollow place among hills or mountains

IDM **aˌbove/beˌlow the ˈfold** in/not in a position where you see it first, for example in the top/bottom part of a newspaper page or web page: *Your ad will be placed above the fold for prominent exposure.* ➲ compare ABOVE-THE-FOLD, BELOW-THE-FOLD

-fold *suffix* (in adjectives and adverbs) multiplied by; having the number of parts mentioned: *to increase tenfold*

fold·away /ˈfəʊldəweɪ; *NAmE* ˈfoʊld-/ *adj.* = FOLDING

fold·er /ˈfəʊldə(r); *NAmE* ˈfoʊld-/ *noun* **1** a cardboard or plastic cover for holding loose papers, etc. ➲ VISUAL VOCAB page V56 **2** (in some computer systems) a way of organizing and storing computer files

fold·ing 0-w /ˈfəʊldɪŋ; *NAmE* ˈfoʊ-/ (also *less frequent* **fold·away**) *adj.* [only before noun] (of a piece of furniture, a bicycle, etc.) that can be folded, so that it can be carried or stored in a small space: *a folding chair* ◇ *a foldaway bed*

ˈfold-up *adj.* [only before noun] (of an object) that can be made smaller by closing or folding so that it takes up less space

fo·li·age /ˈfəʊliɪdʒ; *NAmE* ˈfoʊ-/ *noun* [U] the leaves of a tree or plant; leaves and branches together: *dense green foliage* ➲ VISUAL VOCAB page V8

fo·liar /ˈfəʊliə(r); *NAmE* ˈfoʊ-/ *adj.* (*technical*) relating to leaves: *foliar colour*

folic acid /ˌfɒlɪk ˈæsɪd; ˌfəʊ-; *NAmE* ˌfoʊ-/ *noun* [U] a VITAMIN found in green vegetables, LIVER and KIDNEY, needed by the body for the production of red blood cells

folio /ˈfəʊliəʊ; *NAmE* ˈfoʊlioʊ/ *noun* (*pl.* **-os**) **1** a book made with large sheets of paper, especially as used in early printing **2** (*technical*) a single sheet of paper from a book

folk /fəʊk; *NAmE* foʊk/ *noun, adj.*

■ ***noun*** **1** (also **folks** especially in *NAmE*) [pl.] (*informal*) people in general: *ordinary working-class folk* ◇ *I'd like a job working with* ***old folk*** *or kids.* ◇ *the folks back home* (= from the place where you come from) **2 folks** [pl.] (*informal*) a friendly way of addressing more than one person: *Well, folks, what are we going to do today?* **3 folks** [pl.] (*informal, especially NAmE*) the members of your family, especially your parents: *How are your folks?* **4** [pl.] people from a particular country or region, or who have a particular way of life: *country folk* ◇ *townsfolk* ◇ *farming folk* **5** (also **ˈfolk music**) [U] music in the traditional style of a country or community: ***a folk festival/concert***

■ ***adj.*** [only before noun] **1** (of art, culture, etc.) traditional and typical of the ordinary people of a country or community: *folk art* ◇ *a folk museum* **2** based on the beliefs of ordinary people: *folk wisdom* ◇ *Garlic is widely used in Chinese folk medicine.*

ˈfolk dance *noun* [C, U] a traditional dance of a particular area or country; a piece of music for such a dance

ˈfolk etymology (also **ˌpopular etyˈmology**) *noun* [U, C] a process by which a word is changed, for example because of a mistaken belief that it is related to another word, or to make a foreign word sound more familiar: *Folk etymology has created the cheeseburger and the beanburger, but the first hamburgers were in fact named after the city of Hamburg.*

ˈfolk hero *noun* a person that people in a particular place admire because of sth special he or she has done

folk·lore /ˈfəʊklɔː(r); *NAmE* ˈfoʊk-/ *noun* [U] the traditions and stories of a country or community: *Irish/Indian folklore* ◇ *The story rapidly became part of family folklore.*

folk·lor·ist /ˈfəʊklɔːrɪst; *NAmE* ˈfoʊk-/ *noun* a person who studies folklore, especially as an academic subject

ˌfolk ˈmemory *noun* [C, U] a memory of sth in the past that the people of a country or community never forget

ˈfolk music *noun* [U] = FOLK

ˌfolk ˈrock *noun* [U] a style of music that combines elements of folk music and rock

ˈfolk singer *noun* a person who sings folk songs

ˈfolk song *noun* **1** a song in the traditional style of a country or community **2** a type of song that became popular in the US in the 1960s, played on a GUITAR and often about political topics

folksy /ˈfəʊksi; *NAmE* ˈfoʊksi/ *adj.* **1** (*especially NAmE*) simple, friendly and informal: *They wanted the store to have a folksy small-town image.* **2** (sometimes *disapproving*) done or made in a traditional style that is typical of simple customs in the past: *a folksy ballad*

ˈfolk tale *noun* a very old traditional story from a particular place that was originally passed on to people in a spoken form

fol·licle /ˈfɒlɪkl; *NAmE* ˈfɑːl-/ *noun* one of the very small holes in the skin which hair grows from

fol·low 0-w /ˈfɒləʊ; *NAmE* ˈfɑːloʊ/ *verb*

▸ **GO AFTER** **1** 0-w [T, I] **~ (sb/sth)** to come or go after or behind sb/sth: *He followed her into the house.* ◇ *Follow me please. I'll show you the way.* ◇ *I think we're being followed.* ◇ (*figurative*) *She followed her mother into the medical profession.*

◇ *Wherever she led, they followed.* ◇ *Sam walked in, with the rest of the boys following closely behind.*

▸ HAPPEN/DO AFTER **2** 🔑 [T, I] **~ (sth/sb)** to come after sth/sb else in time or order; to happen as a result of sth else: *The first two classes are followed by a break of ten minutes.* ◇ *I remember little of the days that followed the accident.* ◇ *A period of unrest followed the president's resignation.* ◇ *A detailed news report will follow shortly.* ◇ ***There followed*** *a short silence.* ◇ *The opening hours are* ***as follows*** ... ◇ *A new proposal followed on from the discussions.* **3** 🔑 [T] to do sth after sth else: **~ sth with sth** *Follow your treatment with plenty of rest.* ◇ **~ sth up with sth** *They follow up their March show with four UK dates next month.*

▸ BE RESULT **4** 🔑 [I, T] (not usually used in the progressive tenses) to be the logical result of sth: **~ (from sth)** *I don't see how that follows from what you've just said.* ◇ **it follows that...** *If a = b and b = c it follows that a = c.*

▸ OF PART OF MEAL **5** 🔑 [T, I] **~ (sth)** to come or be eaten after another part: *The main course was followed by fresh fruit.* HELP This pattern is usually used in the passive.: *I'll have soup and fish* ***to follow***.

▸ ROAD/PATH **6** 🔑 [T] **~ sth** to go along a road, path, etc: *Follow this road until you get to the school, then turn left.* **7** 🔑 [T] **~ sth** (of a road, path, etc.) to go in the same direction as sth or parallel to sth: *The lane follows the edge of a wood for about a mile.*

▸ ADVICE/INSTRUCTIONS **8** 🔑 [T] **~ sth** to accept advice, instructions, etc. and do what you have been told or shown to do: *to* ***follow a diet/recipe*** ◇ *He has trouble* ***following*** *simple* ***instructions***. ◇ *Why didn't you* ***follow*** *my* ***advice***?

▸ ACCEPT/COPY **9** 🔑 [T] **~ sth** to accept sb/sth as a guide, a leader or an example; to copy sb/sth: *They followed the teachings of Buddha.* ◇ *He always followed the latest fashions* (= dressed in fashionable clothes). ◇ *I don't want you to follow my example and rush into marriage.* ◇ *The movie follows the book faithfully.*

▸ UNDERSTAND **10** 🔑 [I, T] to understand an explanation or the meaning of sth: **~ (sb)** *Sorry, I don't follow.* ◇ *Sorry, I don't follow you.* ◇ **~ sth** *The plot is almost impossible* ***to follow***. ➲ SYNONYMS at UNDERSTAND

▸ WATCH/LISTEN **11** 🔑 [T] **~ sb/sth** to watch or listen to sb/sth very carefully: *The children were following every word of the story intently.* ◇ *Her eyes followed him everywhere* (= she was looking at him all the time).

▸ BE INTERESTED IN **12** 🔑 [T] **~ sth** to take an active interest in sth and be aware of what is happening: *Have you been following the basketball championships?* ◇ *Millions of people followed the trial on TV.*

▸ OF BOOK/MOVIE **13** [T] **~ sth** to be concerned with the life or development of sb/sth: *The novel follows the fortunes of a village community in Scotland.*

▸ PATTERN/COURSE **14** [T] **~ sth** to develop or happen in a particular way: *The day followed the usual pattern.*

IDM **follow in sb's 'footsteps** to do the same job, have the same style of life, etc. as sb else, especially sb in your family: *She works in television, following in her father's footsteps.* **follow your 'nose 1** to be guided by your sense of smell **2** to go straight forward: *The garage is a mile ahead up the hill—just follow your nose.* **3** to act according to what seems right or reasonable, rather than following any particular rules **follow 'suit 1** (in card games) to play a card of the same SUIT that has just been played **2** to act or behave in the way that sb else has just done ➲ more at ACT *n.*

PHR V **ˌfollow sb aˈround/aˈbout** to keep going with sb wherever they go: *Will you stop following me around!* **ˌfollow 'on** to go somewhere after sb else has gone there: *You go to the beach with the kids and I'll follow on when I've finished work.* **ˌfollow 'through** (in TENNIS, GOLF, etc.) to complete a stroke by continuing to move the club, RACKET, etc. after hitting the ball ➲ related noun FOLLOW-THROUGH (1) **ˌfollow 'through (with sth)** | **ˌfollow sth↔'through** to finish sth that you have started ➲ related noun FOLLOW-THROUGH (2) **ˌfollow sth↔'up 1** 🔑 to add to sth that you have just done by doing sth else: *You should follow up your phone call with an email or a letter.* **2** to find out more about sth that sb has told you or suggested to you SYN **investigate**: *The police are following up several leads after their TV appeal for information.* ➲ related noun FOLLOW-UP

fol·low·er /ˈfɒləʊə(r); *NAmE* ˈfɑːloʊ-/ *noun* **1** a person who supports and admires a particular person or set of ideas: *the followers of Mahatma Gandhi* **2** a person who is very interested in a particular activity and follows all the recent news about it: *keen followers of football* ◇ *a follower of fashion* **3** a person who does things after sb else has done them first: *She is a leader, not a follower.*

fol·low·ing 🔑 /ˈfɒləʊɪŋ; *NAmE* ˈfɑːloʊɪŋ/ *adj., noun, prep.*

▪ ***adj.*** **the following... 1** 🔑 next in time: *the following afternoon/month/year/week* ◇ *They arrived on Monday evening and we got there the following day.* **2** 🔑 that is/are going to be mentioned next: *Answer the following questions.* ➲ LANGUAGE BANK at FIRST

IDM **a ˌfollowing 'wind** a wind blowing in the same direction as a ship or other vehicle that helps it move faster

▪ ***noun*** **1** 🔑 [usually sing.] a group of supporters: *The band has a huge following in Italy.* **2** 🔑 **the following** (used with either a singular or a plural verb, depending on whether you are talking about one thing or person or several things or people) the thing or things that you will mention next; the person or people that you will mention next: *The following is a summary of events.* ◇ *The following have been chosen to take part: Watts, Hodges and Lennox.*

▪ ***prep.*** 🔑 after or as a result of a particular event: *He took charge of the family business following his father's death.*

ˌfollow-'on *noun* [sing.] (in CRICKET) a second INNINGS (= a period during which a team is BATTING) that a team is made to play immediately after its first, if it fails to reach a particular score ▸ **ˌfollow-'on** *verb* [I]

ˌfollow-the-'leader (also **ˌfollow-my-'leader**) *noun* [U] a children's game in which people follow the person in front of them in a line, going wherever they go

ˌfollow-'through *noun* **1** [U, sing.] (in TENNIS, GOLF, etc.) the final part of a stroke after the ball has been hit **2** [U] the actions that sb takes in order to complete a plan: *The project could fail if there is inadequate follow-through.*

'follow-up *noun* [C, U] an action or a thing that continues sth that has already started or comes after sth similar that was done earlier: *The book is a follow-up to her excellent television series.* ▸ **'follow-up** *adj.* [only before noun]: *a follow-up study*

folly /ˈfɒli; *NAmE* ˈfɑːli/ *noun* (*pl.* **-ies**) **1** [U, C] a lack of good judgement; the fact of doing sth stupid; an activity or idea that shows a lack of judgement SYN **stupidity**: *an act of sheer folly* ◇ *Giving up a secure job seems to be the height of folly.* ◇ **~ (to do sth)** *It would be folly to turn the offer down.* ◇ *the follies of youth* **2** [C] a building that has no practical purpose but was built in the past for decoration, often in the garden of a large country house

fo·ment /fəʊˈment; *NAmE* foʊ-/ *verb* **~ sth** (*formal*) to create trouble or violence or make it worse SYN **incite**: *They accused him of fomenting political unrest.*

fond /fɒnd; *NAmE* fɑːnd/ *adj.* (**fond·er, fond·est**) **1 ~ of sb** feeling affection for sb, especially sb you have known for a long time: *Over the years, I have* ***grown quite fond of*** *her.* ➲ SYNONYMS at LOVE **2 ~ of (doing) sth** finding sth pleasant or enjoyable, especially sth you have liked or enjoyed for a long time: *fond of music/cooking* ◇ *We had* ***grown fond of*** *the house and didn't want to leave.* ➲ SYNONYMS at LIKE **3 ~ of (doing) sth** liking to do sth which other people find annoying or unpleasant, and doing it often: *Sheila's very fond of telling other people what to do.* ◇ *He's rather too fond of the sound of his own voice* (= he talks too much). **4** [only before noun] kind and loving SYN **affectionate**: *a* ***fond look/embrace/farewell*** ◇ *I have very* ***fond memories*** *of my time in Spain* (= I remember it with affection and pleasure). **5** [only before noun] **~ hope** a hope about sth that is not likely to happen: *I waited all day* ***in the fond hope that*** *she would change her mind.* ▸ **fond·ness** *noun* [U, sing.]: *He will be remembered by the staff with great fond-*

ness. ◇ **~ for sb/sth** *a fondness for animals* IDM see ABSENCE

fon·dant /ˈfɒndənt; *NAmE* ˈfɑːn-/ *noun* **1** [U] a thick sweet soft mixture made from sugar and water, used especially to cover cakes: *fondant icing* **2** [C] a soft sweet/candy that melts in the mouth, made of fondant

fon·dle /ˈfɒndl; *NAmE* ˈfɑːndl/ *verb* **~ sb/sth** to touch and move your hand gently over sb/sth, especially in a sexual way, or in order to show love SYN **caress**

fond·ly /ˈfɒndli; *NAmE* ˈfɑːndli/ *adv.* **1** in a way that shows great affection SYN **affectionately**: *He looked at her fondly.* ◇ *I fondly remember my first job as a reporter.* **2** in a way that shows hope that is not reasonable or realistic: *I fondly imagined that you cared for me.*

F

fon·due /ˈfɒndjuː; *NAmE* fɑːnˈduː/ *noun* [C, U] **1** a Swiss dish of melted cheese and wine into which pieces of bread are DIPPED **2** a dish of hot oil into which small pieces of meat, vegetables, etc. are DIPPED

font /fɒnt; *NAmE* fɑːnt/ *noun* **1** a large stone bowl in a church that holds water for the ceremony of BAPTISM **2** (*technical*) the particular size and style of a set of letters that are used in printing, etc.

fon·ta·nelle (*US* usually **fon·ta·nel**) /ˌfɒntəˈnel; *NAmE* ˌfɑːn-/ *noun* (*anatomy*) a space between the bones of a baby's SKULL, which makes a soft area on the top of the baby's head

food 0‑w /fuːd/ *noun*
1 0‑w [U] things that people or animals eat: ***a shortage of food/food shortages*** ◇ *food and drink* ◇ *the food industry* **2** 0‑w [C, U] a particular type of food: *Do you like Italian food?* ◇ ***frozen foods*** ◇ *a can of* ***dog food*** (= for a dog to eat) ◇ *He's* ***off his food*** (= he does not want to eat anything). ➲ see also CONVENIENCE FOOD, FAST FOOD, FUNCTIONAL FOOD, HEALTH FOOD, JUNK FOOD, SEAFOOD, SOUL FOOD, WHOLEFOOD

IDM **food for ˈthought** an idea that makes you think seriously and carefully

ˈfood bank *noun* (in the US) a place where poor people can go to get free food

ˈfood chain *noun* (usually **the food chain**) a series of living creatures in which each type of creature feeds on the one below it in the series: *Insects are fairly low down (on) the food chain.*

foodie /ˈfuːdi/ *noun* (*informal*) a person who is very interested in cooking and eating different kinds of food

ˈfood mile *noun* a measurement of the distance food has to be transported from the producer to the consumer and the fuel that this uses: *We keep food miles to a minimum by sourcing products locally.*

ˈfood poisoning *noun* [U] an illness of the stomach caused by eating food that contains harmful bacteria

ˈfood processor *noun* a piece of equipment that is used to mix or cut up food ➲ VISUAL VOCAB page V22

ˈfood science *noun* [U] the scientific study of food, for example what it is made of, the effects it has on our body, and how to prepare it and store it safely

ˈfood stamp *noun* (*US*) a piece of paper that is given by the government to poor people, for them to buy food with

food·stuff /ˈfuːdstʌf/ *noun* [usually pl.] (*technical*) any substance that is used as food: *basic foodstuffs*

ˈfood web *noun* (*technical*) a system of FOOD CHAINS that are related to and depend on each other

fool /fuːl/ *noun, verb, adj.*
■ ***noun*** **1** [C] a person who you think behaves or speaks in a way that lacks intelligence or good judgement SYN **idiot**: *Don't be such a fool!* ◇ *I* ***felt a fool*** *when I realized my mistake.* ◇ *He told me he was an actor and I* ***was fool enough to*** *believe him.* **2** [C] (in the past) a man employed by a king or queen to entertain people by telling jokes, singing songs, etc. SYN **jester** **3** [U, C] (*BrE*) (usually in compounds) a cold light DESSERT (= a sweet dish) made from fruit that is cooked and crushed and mixed with cream or CUSTARD: *rhubarb fool*

IDM **act/play the ˈfool** to behave in a stupid way in order to make people laugh, especially in a way that may also annoy them: *Quit playing the fool and get some work done!* **any fool can/could…** (*informal*) used to say that sth is very easy to do: *Any fool could tell she was lying.* **be ˌno/ˌnobody's ˈfool** to be too intelligent or know too much about sth to be tricked by other people: *She's nobody's fool when it comes to dealing with difficult patients.* **a ˌfool and his ˌmoney are soon ˈparted** (*saying*) a person who is not sensible usually spends money too quickly or carelessly, or is cheated by others **fools rush ˈin** (**where angels fear to ˈtread**) (*saying*) people with little experience try to do the difficult or dangerous things which more experienced people would not consider doing **make a ˈfool of sb** to say or do sth deliberately so that people will think that sb is stupid: *Can't you see she's making a fool of you?* ➲ SYNONYMS at CHEAT **make a ˈfool of yourself** to do sth stupid which makes other people think that you are a fool: *I made a complete fool of myself in front of everyone!* **ˌmore fool ˈsb** (**for doing sth**) (*informal*) used to say that you think that sb was stupid to do sth, especially when it causes them problems: *'He's not an easy person to live with.' 'More fool her for marrying him!'* (**there's**) **ˌno fool like an ˈold fool** (*saying*) an older person who behaves in a stupid way is worse than a younger person who does the same thing, because experience should have taught him or her not to do it ➲ more at SUFFER

■ ***verb*** **1** [T] to trick sb into believing sth that is not true: **~ sb** *You don't fool me!* ◇ *She certainly* ***had me fooled****—I really believed her!* ◇ **~ yourself** *You're fooling yourself if you think none of this will affect you.* ◇ **~ sb into doing sth** *Don't be fooled into thinking they're going to change anything.* **2** [I] to say or do stupid or silly things, often in order to make people laugh: **~ (about/around)** *Stop fooling around and sit down!* ◇ **~ (about/around) with sth** *If you fool about with matches, you'll end up getting burned.*

IDM **you could have fooled ˈme** (*informal*) used to say that you do not believe sth that sb has just told you: *'I'm trying as hard as I can!' 'You could have fooled me!'*

PHR V **ˌfool aˈround** **1** (*BrE* also **ˌfool aˈbout**) to waste time instead of doing sth that you should be doing SYN **mess around** **2 ~ (with sb)** to have a sexual relationship with another person's partner; to have a sexual relationship with sb who is not your partner SYN **mess around**: *She's been fooling around with a married man.*

■ ***adj.*** [only before noun] (*informal*) showing a lack of intelligence or good judgement SYN **silly, stupid, foolish**: *That was a damn fool thing to do!*

fool·hardy /ˈfuːlhɑːdi; *NAmE* -hɑːrdi/ *adj.* (*disapproving*) taking unnecessary risks SYN **reckless**: *It would be foolhardy to sail in weather like this.* ▶ **fool·hardi·ness** *noun* [U]

fool·ish /ˈfuːlɪʃ/ *adj.* **1** (of actions or behaviour) not showing good sense or judgement SYN **silly, stupid**: *She's just a vain, foolish woman.* ◇ *I was foolish enough to believe what Jeff told me.* ◇ *The accident was my fault—****it would be foolish*** *to pretend otherwise.* ◇ *How could she have been so foolish as to fall in love with him?* ◇ *a foolish idea/dream/mistake* ◇ *It was a very foolish thing to do.* **2** [not usually before noun] made to feel or look silly and embarrassed SYN **silly, stupid**: *I felt foolish and a failure.* ◇ *He's afraid of looking foolish in front of his friends.* ▶ **fool·ish·ly** *adv.*: *We foolishly thought that everyone would speak English.* ◇ *Foolishly, I allowed myself to be persuaded to enter the contest.* **fool·ish·ness** *noun* [U]: *Jenny had to laugh at her own foolishness.*

fool·proof /ˈfuːlpruːf/ *adj.* (of a plan, machine, method, etc.) very well designed and easy to use so that it cannot fail and you cannot use it wrongly SYN **infallible**: *This recipe is foolproof—it works every time.*

fools·cap /ˈfuːlskæp/ *noun* [U] (*BrE*) a large size of paper for writing on

ˌfool's ˈerrand *noun* [sing.] a task that has no hope of being done successfully: *He sent me* ***on a fool's errand.***

ˌfool's ˈgold *noun* [U] **1** a yellow mineral found in rock, which looks like gold but is not valuable, also called **iron pyrites** ➲ see also PYRITES **2** something that you think is valuable or will earn you a lot of money, but which has no chance of succeeding

ˌfool's ˈparadise *noun* [usually sing.] a state of happiness that is based on sth that is false or cannot last although the happy person does not realize it

foos·ball /ˈfuːzbɔːl/ (*NAmE*) (*BrE* **ˈtable football**) *noun* [U] an indoor game for two people or teams, played by moving rows of small models of football (SOCCER) players in order to move a ball on a board that has marks like a football (SOCCER) field

foot 0-w /fʊt/ *noun, verb*

■ ***noun*** (*pl.* **feet** /fiːt/)

▸ PART OF BODY **1** 0-w [C] the lowest part of the leg, below the ankle, on which a person or an animal stands: *My feet are aching.* ◇ *to get/rise* ***to your feet*** (= stand up) ◇ *I've been* ***on my feet*** (= standing or walking around) *all day.* ◇ *We came* ***on foot*** (= we walked). ◇ *walking around the house* ***in bare feet*** (= not wearing shoes or socks) ◇ *Please* ***wipe your feet*** (= your shoes) *on the mat.* ◇ *a* ***foot pump*** (= operated using your foot, not your hand) ◇ *a* ***foot passenger*** (= one who travels on a FERRY without a car) ➲ **SYNONYMS** at STAND ➲ **COLLOCATIONS** at PHYSICAL ➲ **VISUAL VOCAB** page V48 ➲ see also ATHLETE'S FOOT, BAREFOOT, CLUB FOOT, UNDERFOOT

▸ -FOOTED **2** (in adjectives and adverbs) having or using the type or number of foot/feet mentioned: *bare-footed* ◇ *four-footed* ◇ *a left-footed shot into the corner* ➲ see also FLAT-FOOTED, SURE-FOOTED

▸ PART OF SOCK **3** [C, usually sing.] the part of a sock, STOCKING, etc. that covers the foot

▸ BASE/BOTTOM **4** 0-w [sing.] **the ~ of sth** the lowest part of sth; the base or bottom of sth: *the* ***foot of the stairs/page/mountain*** ◇ *The nurse hung a chart at the* ***foot of the bed*** (= the part of the bed where your feet normally are when you are lying in it). ➲ **SYNONYMS** at BOTTOM

▸ MEASUREMENT **5** 0-w (*pl.* **feet** or **foot**) (*abbr.* **ft**) a unit for measuring length equal to 12 inches or 30.48 centimetres: *a 6-foot high wall* ◇ *We're flying at 35 000 feet.* ◇ *'How tall are you?' 'Five foot nine'* (= five feet and nine inches).

▸ -FOOTER **6** (in compound nouns) a person or thing that is a particular number of feet tall or long: *His boat is an eighteen-footer.*

▸ IN POETRY **7** [sing.] (*technical*) a unit of rhythm in a line of poetry containing one stressed syllable and one or more syllables without stress. Each of the four divisions in the following line is a foot: *For ˈmen / may ˈcome / and ˈmen / may ˈgo.*

IDM **be rushed/run off your ˈfeet** to be extremely busy; to have too many things to do **fall/land on your ˈfeet** to be lucky in finding yourself in a good situation, or in getting out of a difficult situation **feet ˈfirst 1** with your feet touching the ground before any other part of your body: *He landed feet first.* **2** (*humorous*) if you leave a place **feet first**, you are carried out after you are dead: *You'll have to carry me out feet first!* **get/have a/your ˌfoot in the ˈdoor** to manage to enter an organization, a field of business, etc. that could bring you success: *I always wanted to work in TV but it took me two years to get a foot in the door.* **get/start off on the right/wrong ˈfoot (with sb)** (*informal*) to start a relationship well/badly: *I seem to have got off on the wrong foot with the new boss.* **get your ˈfeet wet** (*especially NAmE, informal*) to start doing sth that is new for you: *At that time he was a young actor, just getting his feet wet.* **have feet of ˈclay** to have a fault or weakness in your character **have/keep your ˈfeet on the ground** to have a sensible and realistic attitude to life **have/keep a foot in both ˈcamps** to be involved in or connected with two different or opposing groups **have ˌone foot in the ˈgrave** (*informal*) to be so old or ill/sick that you are not likely to live much longer **...my ˈfoot!** (*informal, humorous*) a strong way of saying that you disagree completely with what has just been said: *'Ian can't come because he's tired.' 'Tired my foot! Lazy more like!'* **on your ˈfeet** completely well or in a normal state again after an illness or a time of trouble: *Sue's back on her feet again after her operation.* ◇ *The new chairman hopes to get the company back on its feet within six months.* ➲ note at STAND **put your best foot ˈforward** to make a great effort to do sth, especially if it is difficult or you are feeling tired **put your ˈfeet up** to sit down and relax, especially with your feet raised and supported: *After a hard day's work, it's nice to get home and put your feet up.* **put your ˈfoot down 1** to be very strict in opposing what sb wishes to do: *You've got to put your foot down and make him stop seeing her.* **2** (*BrE*) to drive faster: *She put her foot down and roared past them.* **put your ˈfoot in it** (*BrE*) (also **put your foot in your ˈmouth** *NAmE, BrE*) to say or do sth that upsets, offends or embarrasses sb: *I really put my foot in it with Ella—I didn't know she'd split up with Tom.* **put a foot ˈwrong** (usually used in negative sentences) to make a mistake: *In the last two games he has hardly put a foot wrong.* **set ˈfoot in/on sth** to enter or visit a place: *the first man to set foot on the moon* ◇ *I vowed never to set foot in the place again.* **set sb/sth on their/its ˈfeet** to make sb/sth independent or successful: *His business sense helped set the club on its feet again.* **stand on your own (two) ˈfeet** to be independent and able to take care of yourself: *When his parents died he had to learn to stand on his own two feet.* **under your ˈfeet** in the way; stopping you from working, etc: *I don't want you kids under my feet while I'm cooking.* ➲ more at BOOT *n.*, COLD *adj.*, DRAG *v.*, FIND *v.*, GRASS *n.*, GROUND *n.*, HAND *n.*, HEAD *n.*, ITCHY, LEFT *adj.*, PATTER *n.*, PULL *v.*, SHOE *n.*, SHOOT *v.*, SIT, STOCKING, SWEEP *v.*, THINK *v.*, VOTE *v.*, WAIT *v.*, WALK *v.*, WEIGHT *n.*, WORLD

■ ***verb***

IDM **foot the ˈbill** (*informal*) to be responsible for paying the cost of sth: *Once again it will be the taxpayer who has to foot the bill.*

foot·age /ˈfʊtɪdʒ/ *noun* [U] part of a film showing a particular event: *old film footage of the moon landing*

ˌfoot-and-ˈmouth disease (*NAmE* also **ˌhoof-and-ˈmouth disease**) *noun* [U] a disease of cows, sheep, etc, which causes sore places on the mouth and feet

foot·ball 0-w /ˈfʊtbɔːl/ *noun*

1 0-w [U] (also *formal* **Asˌsociation ˈfootball**) (both *BrE*) (also **soc·cer** *NAmE, BrE*) (also *BrE informal* **footy, footie**) a game played by two teams of 11 players, using a round ball which players kick up and down the playing field. Teams try to kick the ball into the other team's goal: *to* ***play football*** ◇ *a* ***football match/team/stadium*** ➲ **VISUAL VOCAB** page V36 ➲ see also GAELIC FOOTBALL **2** 0-w [U] (*NAmE*) = AMERICAN FOOTBALL, CANADIAN FOOTBALL ➲ **VISUAL VOCAB** page V36 **3** 0-w [C] a large round or OVAL ball made of leather or plastic and filled with air ➲ **VISUAL VOCAB** page V36 **4** [C] (always used with an adjective) an issue or a problem that frequently causes argument and disagreement: *Health care should not become a political football.*

ˈfootball boot *noun* (*BrE*) a leather shoe with pieces of rubber on the bottom to stop it slipping, worn for playing football (SOCCER) ➲ compare CLEATS

foot·baller /ˈfʊtbɔːlə(r)/ *noun* (*BrE*) a person who plays football (SOCCER), especially as a profession

foot·ball·ing /ˈfʊtbɔːlɪŋ/ *adj.* [only before noun] (*BrE*) connected with the game of football (SOCCER): *footballing skills*

ˈfootball pools (also **the pools**) *noun* [pl.] a form of gambling in Britain in which people try to win money by saying what the results of football (SOCCER) matches will be: *They've had a big win on the football pools.*

foot·brake /ˈfʊtbreɪk/ *noun* a BRAKE in a vehicle which is operated using your foot

foot·bridge /ˈfʊtbrɪdʒ/ *noun* a narrow bridge used only by people who are walking ➲ **VISUAL VOCAB** page V2

foot·er /ˈfʊtə(r)/ *noun* **1** a line or block of text that is automatically added to the bottom of every page that is printed from a computer ➲ compare HEADER **2** a line at the bottom of a page on the Internet: *a website footer*

foot·fall /ˈfʊtfɔːl/ *noun* **1** [C] (*literary*) the sound of the steps made by sb walking **2** [U] (*BrE, business*) the number of people that visit a particular shop/store, shopping

F

centre, etc. over a period of time: *a campaign to increase footfall*

ˈfoot fault *noun* (in TENNIS) a mistake that is made by not keeping behind the line when SERVING

foot·hill /ˈfʊthɪl/ *noun* [usually pl.] a hill or low mountain at the base of a higher mountain or range of mountains: *the foothills of the Himalayas* ➲ VISUAL VOCAB page V5

foot·hold /ˈfʊthəʊld; *NAmE* -hoʊld/ *noun* **1** a crack, hole or branch where your foot can be safely supported when climbing **2** [usually sing.] a strong position in a business, profession, etc. from which sb can make progress and achieve success: *The company is eager to **gain a foothold** in Europe.*

footie /ˈfʊti/ *noun* [U] (*BrE, informal*) = FOOTBALL (1)

foot·ing /ˈfʊtɪŋ/ *noun* [sing.] **1** the position of your feet when they are safely on the ground or some other surface: *She **lost her footing** (= she slipped or lost her balance) and fell backwards into the water.* ◇ *I slipped and struggled to regain my footing.* **2** the basis on which sth is established or organized: *The company is now **on a sound** financial **footing**.* ◇ *The country has been **on a war footing** (= prepared for war) since March.* **3** the position or status of sb/sth in relation to others; the relationship between two or more people or groups: *The two groups must meet **on an equal footing**.* ◇ *They were demanding to be treated **on the same footing** as the rest of the teachers.*

foot·lights /ˈfʊtlaɪts/ *noun* [pl.] a row of lights along the front of the stage in a theatre

foot·ling /ˈfuːtlɪŋ/ *adj.* (*old-fashioned, informal*) not important and likely to make you annoyed

foot·loose /ˈfʊtluːs/ *adj.* free to go where you like or do what you want because you have no responsibilities: *Bert was a footloose, unemployed actor.* ◇ *Ah, I was still **footloose and fancy-free** (= free to enjoy myself) in those days.*

foot·man /ˈfʊtmən/ *noun* (*pl.* **-men** /-mən/) a male servant in a house in the past, who opened the door to visitors, served food at table, etc.

foot·note /ˈfʊtnəʊt; *NAmE* -noʊt/ *noun* **1** an extra piece of information that is printed at the bottom of a page in a book ➲ WRITING TUTOR page WT11 **2** (of an event or a person) that may be remembered but only as sth/sb that is not important

foot·path /ˈfʊtpɑːθ; *NAmE* -pæθ/ *noun* **1** (*BrE*) a path that is made for people to walk along, especially in the country: *a public footpath* ➲ VISUAL VOCAB page V2 **2** (*AustralE, NZE*) = PAVEMENT

foot·plate /ˈfʊtpleɪt/ *noun* (*BrE*) the part of a steam train's engine where the driver stands

foot·print /ˈfʊtprɪnt/ *noun* **1** [usually pl.] a mark left on a surface by a person's foot or shoe or by an animal's foot: *footprints in the sand* ◇ *muddy footprints on the kitchen floor* **2** the amount of space that sth fills, for example the amount of space that a computer takes up on a desk **3** the area on the earth in which a signal from a communications SATELLITE can be received

foot·rest /ˈfʊtrest/ *noun* a support for your foot or feet, for example on a motorcycle or when you are sitting down

the Foot·sie™ /ˈfʊtsi/ *noun* = FTSE INDEX

foot·sie /ˈfʊtsi/ *noun* (*informal*)
IDM **play ˈfootsie with sb** to touch sb's feet lightly with your own feet, especially under a table, as an expression of affection or sexual interest

ˈfoot soldier *noun* **1** a soldier who fights on foot, not on a horse or in a vehicle **2** a person in an organization who does work that is important but boring, and who has no power or responsibility

foot·sore /ˈfʊtsɔː(r)/ *adj.* (*formal*) having sore or tired feet, especially after walking a long way

foot·step /ˈfʊtstep/ *noun* [usually pl.] the sound or mark made each time your foot touches the ground when you are walking or running: *the sound of footsteps on the stairs* ◇ *footsteps in the snow* IDM see FOLLOW

foot·stool /ˈfʊtstuːl/ *noun* a low piece of furniture used for resting your feet on when you are sitting ➲ VISUAL VOCAB page V18

foot·sure /ˈfʊtʃʊə(r); -ʃɔː(r); *NAmE* -ʃʊr/ *adj.* = SURE-FOOTED

foot·way /ˈfʊtweɪ/ *noun* (*BrE, formal*) a flat part at the side of a road for people to walk on SYN **pavement, sidewalk**

foot·wear /ˈfʊtweə(r); *NAmE* -wer/ *noun* [U] things that people wear on their feet, for example shoes and boots: *Be sure to wear the correct footwear to prevent injuries to your feet.*

foot·work /ˈfʊtwɜːk; *NAmE* -wɜːrk/ *noun* [U] **1** the way in which a person moves their feet when playing a sport or dancing **2** the ability to react quickly and skilfully to a difficult situation: *It was going to take some deft political footwork to save the situation.*

footy /ˈfʊti/ *noun* [U] (*BrE, informal*) = FOOTBALL (1)

fop /fɒp; *NAmE* fɑːp/ *noun* (*old-fashioned*) a man who is too interested in his clothes and the way he looks ▸ **fop·pish** *adj.*

for 🔑 /fə(r); *strong form* fɔː(r)/ *prep., conj.*

■ *prep.* HELP For the special uses of **for** in phrasal verbs, look at the entries for the verbs. For example **fall for sb** is in the phrasal verb section at **fall**. **1** 🔑 used to show who is intended to have or use sth or where sth is intended to be put: *There's a letter for you.* ◇ *It's a book for children.* ◇ *We got a new table for the dining room.* ◇ *This is the place for me* (= I like it very much). **2** 🔑 in order to help sb/sth: *What can I do for you* (= how can I help you)? ◇ *Can you translate this letter for me?* ◇ *I took her classes for her while she was sick.* ◇ *soldiers fighting for their country* **3** 🔑 concerning sb/sth: *They are anxious for her safety.* ◇ *Fortunately for us, the weather changed.* **4** 🔑 as a representative of: *I am speaking for everyone in this department.* **5** 🔑 employed by: *She's working for IBM.* **6** 🔑 meaning: *Shaking your head for 'No' is not universal.* **7** 🔑 in support of sb/sth: *Are you for or against the proposal?* ◇ *They voted for independence in a referendum.* ◇ *There's a strong case for postponing the exam.* ◇ *I'm **all for** people having fun.* ➲ compare AGAINST (2) **8** 🔑 used to show purpose or function: *a machine for slicing bread* ◇ *Let's go for a walk.* ◇ *Are you learning English for pleasure or for your work?* ◇ *What did you do that for* (= Why did you do that)? **9** 🔑 used to show a reason or cause: *The town is famous for its cathedral.* ◇ *She gave me a watch for my birthday.* ◇ *He got an award for bravery.* ◇ *I couldn't speak for laughing.* **10** 🔑 in order to obtain sth: *He came to me for advice.* ◇ *For more information, call this number.* ◇ *There were over fifty applicants for the job.* **11** 🔑 in exchange for sth: *Copies are available for two dollars each.* ◇ *I'll swap these two bottles for that one.* **12** 🔑 considering what can be expected from sb/sth: *The weather was warm for the time of year.* ◇ *She's tall for her age.* ◇ *That's too much responsibility for a child.* **13 better, happier, etc. ~ sth** better, happier, etc. following sth: *You'll feel better for a good night's sleep.* ◇ *This room would look more cheerful for a spot of paint.* **14** 🔑 used to show where sb/sth is going: *Is this the bus for Chicago?* ◇ *She knew she was destined for a great future.* **15** 🔑 used to show a length of time: *I'm going away for a few days.* ◇ *That's all the news there is **for now**.* **16** 🔑 used to show that sth is arranged or intended to happen at a particular time: *an appointment for May 12* ◇ *We're invited for 7.30.* **17** 🔑 used to show the occasion when sth happens: *I'm warning you for the last time—stop talking!* **18** 🔑 used to show a distance: *The road went on for miles and miles.* **19** 🔑 used to say how difficult, necessary, pleasant, etc. sth is that sb might do or has done: *It's useless **for** us **to** continue.* ◇ *There's no need **for** you **to** go.* ◇ *For her to have survived such an ordeal was remarkable.* ◇ *The box is **too** heavy **for** me to lift.* ◇ *Is it clear **enough for** you **to** read?* **20** used to show who can or should do sth: *It's not for me to say why he left.* ◇ *How to spend the money is for you to decide.*

IDM **be ˈin for it** (*BrE* also **be ˈfor it**) (*informal*) to be going to get into trouble or be punished: *We'd better hurry or we'll be in for it.* **for 'all 1** despite: *For all its clarity of style, the book is not easy reading.* **2** used to say that sth is not important or of no interest or value to you/sb: ***For all I know** she's still living in Boston.* ◇ *You can do what you like, for all I care.* ◇ *For all the good it's done we might as well not have bothered.* **there's/that's... for you** (often *ironic*) used to say that sth is a typical example of its kind: *She might at least have called to explain. There's gratitude for you.*

■ ***conj.*** (*old-fashioned* or *literary*) used to introduce the reason for sth mentioned in the previous statement: *We listened eagerly, for he brought news of our families.* ◇ *I believed her —for surely she would not lie to me.*

for·age /ˈfɒrɪdʒ; *NAmE* ˈfɔː-; ˈfɑː-/ *verb, noun*

■ ***verb* 1** [I] **~ (for sth)** (especially of an animal) to search for food **2** [I] **~ (for sth)** (of a person) to search for sth, especially using the hands SYN **rummage**

■ ***noun*** [U] food for horses and cows: ***forage crops/grass***

foray /ˈfɒreɪ; *NAmE* ˈfɔː-; ˈfɑː-/ *noun* **1 ~ (into sth)** an attempt to become involved in a different activity or profession: *the company's first foray into the computer market* **2 ~ (into sth)** a short sudden attack made by a group of soldiers **3 ~ (to/into...)** a short journey to find a particular thing or to visit a new place SYN **expedition**: *weekend shopping forays to France*

for·bade *past tense of* FORBID

for·bear *verb, noun*

■ ***verb*** /fɔːˈbeə(r); *NAmE* fɔːrˈber/ (**for·bore** /fɔːˈbɔː(r); *NAmE* fɔːrˈb-/, **for·borne** /fɔːˈbɔːn; *NAmE* fɔːrˈbɔːrn/) [I, T] (*formal*) to stop yourself from saying or doing sth that you could or would like to say or do: **~ (from sth/from doing sth)** *He wanted to answer back, but he forbore from doing so.* ◇ **~ to do sth** *She forbore to ask any further questions.*

■ ***noun*** = FOREBEAR

for·bear·ance /fɔːˈbeərəns; *NAmE* fɔːrˈber-/ *noun* [U] (*formal*) the quality of being patient and sympathetic towards other people, especially when they have done sth wrong

for·bear·ing /fɔːˈbeərɪŋ; *NAmE* fɔːrˈber-/ *adj.* (*formal*) showing forbearance SYN **patient**: *Thank you for being so forbearing.*

for·bid /fəˈbɪd; *NAmE* fərˈb-/ *verb* (**for·bade** /fəˈbæd; fəˈbeɪd; *NAmE* fərˈb-/, **for·bid·den** /fəˈbɪdn; *NAmE* fərˈb-/) **1** to order sb not to do sth; to order that sth must not be done: **~ sb (from doing sth)** *He forbade them from mentioning the subject again.* ◇ **~ sth** *Her father forbade the marriage.* ◇ **~ sb to do sth** *You are all forbidden to leave.* ◇ **~ sb sth** *My doctor has forbidden me sugar.* ◇ **~ (sb) doing sth** *She knew her mother would forbid her going.* OPP **allow, permit 2 ~ sth** | **~ sb to do sth** (*formal*) to make it difficult or impossible to do sth SYN **prohibit**: *Lack of space forbids further treatment of the topic here.*

IDM **God/Heaven for'bid (that...)** (*informal*) used to say that you hope that sth will not happen: *'Maybe you'll end up as a lawyer, like me.' 'God forbid!'* HELP Some people find this use offensive.

for·bid·den /fəˈbɪdn; *NAmE* fərˈb-/ *adj.* not allowed: *Photography is **strictly forbidden** in the museum.* ◇ *The conversation was in danger of wandering into forbidden territory* (= topics that they were not allowed to talk about).

IDM **for,bidden 'fruit** a thing that is not allowed and that therefore seems very attractive

for·bid·ding /fəˈbɪdɪŋ; *NAmE* fərˈb-/ *adj.* seeming unfriendly and frightening and likely to cause harm or danger: *a **forbidding appearance/look/manner*** ◇ *The house looked dark and forbidding.* ▶ **for·bid·ding·ly** *adv.*

for·bore *past tense of* FORBEAR

for·borne *past part. of* FORBEAR

force 🔑 /fɔːs; *NAmE* fɔːrs/ *noun, verb*

WORD FAMILY
force *noun, verb*
forceful *adj.*
forcefully *adv.*
forced *adj.* (≠ unforced)
forcible *adj.*
forcibly *adv.*
enforce *verb*

■ ***noun***

▸ VIOLENT ACTION **1** 🔑 [U] violent physical action used to obtain or achieve sth: *The release of the hostages could not be achieved without the use of force.* ◇ *The rioters were taken away **by force**.* ◇ *The ultimatum contained the threat of military force.* ◇ *We will achieve much more by persuasion than by **brute force**.*

▸ PHYSICAL STRENGTH **2** 🔑 [U] the physical strength of sth that is shown as it hits sth else: *the **force of the blow/explosion/collision*** ◇ *The shopping centre took the **full force** of the blast.*

▸ STRONG EFFECT **3** 🔑 [U] the strong effect or influence of sth: *They realized the force of her argument.* ◇ *He controlled himself by **sheer force of will**.* ◇ *She spoke with force and deliberation.*

▸ SB/STH WITH POWER **4** 🔑 [C] a person or thing that has a lot of power or influence: ***economic/market forces*** ◇ *the **forces of good/evil*** ◇ *Ron is **the driving force*** (= the person who has the most influence) *behind the project.* ◇ *She's **a force to be reckoned with*** (= a person who has a lot of power and influence and should therefore be treated seriously). ◇ *The expansion of higher education should be a powerful **force for change**.*

▸ AUTHORITY **5** [U] the authority of sth: *These guidelines do not have **the force of law**.* ◇ *The court ruled that these standards have force in British law.*

▸ GROUP OF PEOPLE **6** 🔑 [C+sing./pl. v.] a group of people who have been organized for a particular purpose: *a member of the **sales force*** ◇ *A large proportion of the **labour force*** (= all the people who work in a particular company, area, etc.) *is unskilled.* ➲ see also WORKFORCE

▸ MILITARY **7** 🔑 [C+sing./pl. v.] a group of people who have been trained to protect other people, usually by using weapons: *a member of the security forces* ◇ ***rebel/government forces*** ◇ *a peace-keeping force* ➲ see also AIR FORCE, POLICE FORCE, TASK FORCE **8 the forces** [pl.] (*BrE*) the army, navy and AIR FORCE: *allied forces* ➲ see also THE ARMED FORCES **9 forces** [pl.] the weapons and soldiers that an army, etc. has, considered as things that may be used: *strategic nuclear forces.*

▸ POLICE **10 the force** [sing.] (*BrE*) the police force: *He joined the force twenty years ago.*

▸ PHYSICS **11** 🔑 [C, U] an effect that causes things to move in a particular way: *The moon exerts a force on the earth.* ◇ *the force of gravity* ◇ *magnetic/centrifugal force*

▸ OF WIND **12** [C, usually sing.] a unit for measuring the strength of the wind: *a force 9 gale* ◇ *a gale force wind* ➲ see also TOUR DE FORCE

IDM **bring sth into 'force** to cause a law, rule, etc. to start being used: *They are hoping to bring the new legislation into force before the end of the year.* **come/enter into 'force** 🔑 (of a law, rule, etc.) to start being used: *When do the new regulations come into force?* **force of 'habit** if you do sth from or out of **force of habit**, you do it automatically and in a particular way because you have always done it that way in the past **the forces of 'nature** the power of the wind, rain, etc, especially when it causes damage or harm **in 'force 1** (of people) in large numbers: *Protesters turned out in force.* **2** 🔑 (of a law, rule, etc.) being used: *The new regulations are now in force.* **join/combine 'forces (with sb)** to work together in order to achieve a shared aim: *The two firms joined forces to win the contract.* ➲ more at SPENT

■ ***verb***

▸ MAKE SB DO STH **1** 🔑 [often passive] to make sb do sth that they do not want to do SYN **compel**: **~ sb into doing sth** *The President was forced into resigning.* ◇ **~ sb/yourself to do sth** *The President was forced to resign.* ◇ *I **was forced to** take a taxi because the last bus had left.* ◇ *She forced herself to be polite to them.* ◇ **~ sb into sth** *Ill health forced him into early retirement.* ◇ **~ sb** *He didn't force me—I wanted to go.* ◇ **~ yourself** (*informal, humorous*) *'I shouldn't really have any more.' 'Go on—force yourself!'* ◇ **~ sth** *Public pressure managed to force a change in the government's position.*

▸ USE PHYSICAL STRENGTH **2** 🔑 to use physical strength to move sb/sth into a particular position: **~ sth** *to **force a lock/window/door*** (= to break it open using force) ◇ *to **force an entry*** (= to enter a building using force) ◇ **~ sth + adv./prep.** *She **forced her way** through the crowd of reporters.* ◇ *He tried to force a copy of his book into my hand.* ◇ **~ sth + adj.** *The door had been **forced open**.*

F

▸ MAKE STH HAPPEN **3** to make sth happen, especially before other people are ready: **~ sth** *He was in a position where he had to force a decision.* ◇ **~ sth + adv./prep.** *Building a new road here will force house prices down.*
▸ A SMILE/LAUGH **4 ~ sth** to make yourself smile, laugh, etc. rather than doing it naturally: *She managed to force a smile.*
▸ FRUIT/PLANTS **5 ~ sth** to make fruit, plants, etc. grow or develop faster than normal by keeping them in special conditions: *forced rhubarb* ◇ (*figurative*) *It is unwise to force a child's talent.*

IDM **force sb's 'hand** to make sb do sth that they do not want to do or make them do it sooner than they had intended **'force the issue** to do sth to make people take a decision quickly **force the 'pace** (*especially BrE*) **1** to run very fast in a race in order to make the other people taking part run faster **2** to make sb do sth faster than they want to: *The demonstrations have succeeded in forcing the pace of change.* ➲ more at THROAT

PHR V **,force sth↔'back** to make yourself hide an emotion: *She swallowed hard and forced back her tears.* **,force sth↔'down 1** to make yourself eat or drink sth that you do not really want **2** to make a plane, etc. land, especially by threatening to attack it **'force sb/sth on/upon sb** to make sb accept sth that they do not want: *to force your attentions/opinions/company on sb* **,force sth 'out of sb** to make sb tell you sth, especially by threatening them: *I managed to force the truth out of him.*

forced /fɔːst; *NAmE* fɔːrst/ *adj.* **1** happening or done against sb's will: *forced relocation to a job in another city* ◇ *a forced sale of his property* **2** not sincere; not the result of genuine emotions: *She said she was enjoying herself but her smile was forced.* ➲ see also UNFORCED

,forced 'entry *noun* [U, C] an occasion when sb enters a building illegally, using force

,forced 'labour (*especially US* **,forced 'labor**) *noun* [U] **1** hard physical work that sb, often a prisoner or SLAVE, is forced to do **2** prisoners or SLAVES who are forced to work: *The mines were manned by forced labour from conquered countries.*

,forced 'landing *noun* an act of having to land an aircraft unexpectedly in order to avoid a crash: *to make a forced landing*

,forced 'march *noun* a long march, usually made by soldiers in difficult conditions

,force-'feed *verb* **~ sb** to use force to make sb, especially a prisoner, eat or drink, by pushing food or drink down their throat

'force field *noun* (often used in stories about space travel) a barrier that you cannot see

force·ful /'fɔːsfl; *NAmE* 'fɔːrsfl/ *adj.* **1** (of people) expressing opinions firmly and clearly in a way that persuades other people to believe them SYN **assertive**: *a forceful woman/speaker* ◇ *a forceful personality* **2** (of opinions, etc.) expressed firmly and clearly so that other people believe them: *a forceful argument/speech* **3** using force: *the forceful suppression of minorities* ▸ **force·ful·ly** /-fəli/ *adv.*: *He argued his case forcefully.* **force·ful·ness** *noun* [U]

force ma·jeure /,fɔːs mæ'ʒɜː(r); *NAmE* ,fɔːrs/ *noun* [U] (from *French, law*) unexpected circumstances, such as war, that can be used as an excuse when they prevent sb from doing sth that is written in a contract

force·meat /'fɔːsmiːt; *NAmE* 'fɔːrs-/ *noun* [U] a mixture of meat or vegetables cut into very small pieces, which is often placed inside a chicken, etc. before it is cooked to give it flavour

'force-out *noun* (in BASEBALL) a situation in which a player running to a BASE is out because a FIELDER is holding the ball at the base

for·ceps /'fɔːseps; *NAmE* 'fɔːrs-/ *noun* [pl.] an instrument used by doctors, with two long thin parts for picking up and holding things: *a pair of forceps* ◇ ***a forceps delivery*** (= a birth in which the baby is delivered with the help of forceps)

for·cible /'fɔːsəbl; *NAmE* 'fɔːrs-/ *adj.* [only before noun] involving the use of physical force: *forcible repatriation* ◇ *The police checked all windows and doors for signs of forcible entry.*

for·cibly /'fɔːsəbli; *NAmE* 'fɔːrs-/ *adv.* **1** in a way that involves the use of physical force: *Supporters were forcibly removed from the court.* **2** in a way that makes sth very clear: *It struck me forcibly how honest he'd been.*

ford /fɔːd; *NAmE* fɔːrd/ *noun, verb*
■ ***noun*** a shallow place in a river where it is possible to drive or walk across
■ ***verb*** **~ sth** to walk or drive across a river or stream

fore /fɔː(r)/ *noun, adj., adv.*
■ ***noun***
IDM **be/come to the 'fore** (*BrE*) (*NAmE* **be at the 'fore**) to be/become important and noticed by people; to play an important part: *She has always been to the fore at moments of crisis.* ◇ *The problem has come to the fore again in recent months.* **bring sth to the 'fore** to make sth become noticed by people
■ ***adj.*** [only before noun] (*technical*) located at the front of a ship, an aircraft or an animal ➲ compare AFT, HIND
■ ***adv.*** **1** at or towards the front of a ship or an aircraft ➲ compare AFT **2 Fore!** used in the game of GOLF to warn people that they are in the path of a ball that you are hitting

fore- /fɔː(r)/ *combining form* (in nouns and verbs) **1** before; in advance: *foreword* ◇ *foretell* **2** in the front of: *the foreground of the picture*

fore·arm[1] /'fɔːrɑːm; *NAmE* -ɑːrm/ *noun* the part of the arm between the elbow and the wrist ➲ VISUAL VOCAB page V48

fore·arm[2] /,fɔːr'ɑːm; *NAmE* -'ɑːrm/ *verb* IDM see FOREWARN

fore·bear (also **for·bear**) /'fɔːbeə(r); *NAmE* 'fɔːrber/ *noun* [usually pl.] (*formal* or *literary*) a person in your family who lived a long time ago SYN **ancestor**

fore·bod·ing /fɔː'bəʊdɪŋ; *NAmE* fɔːr'boʊ-/ *noun* [U, C] a strong feeling that sth unpleasant or dangerous is going to happen: *She had **a sense of foreboding** that the news would be bad.* ◇ *He knew from her face that his forebodings had been justified.* ▸ **fore·bod·ing** *adj.*: *a foreboding feeling that something was wrong*

fore·brain /'fɔːbreɪn; *NAmE* 'fɔːr-/ *noun* (*anatomy*) the front part of the brain

fore·cast 0‑ᵚ /'fɔːkɑːst; *NAmE* 'fɔːrkæst/ *noun, verb*
■ ***noun*** 0‑ᵚ a statement about what will happen in the future, based on information that is available now: *sales forecasts* ◇ *The forecast said there would be sunny intervals and showers.* ➲ see also WEATHER FORECAST
■ ***verb*** 0‑ᵚ (**fore·cast, fore·cast** or **fore·cast·ed, fore·cast·ed**) to say what you think will happen in the future based on information that you have now SYN **predict**: **~ sth** *Experts are forecasting a recovery in the economy.* ◇ *Snow is forecast for tomorrow.* ◇ **~ sth to do sth** *Temperatures were forecast to reach 40°C.* ◇ **~ that...** *The report forecasts that prices will rise by 3% next month.* ◇ **~ how, what, etc...** *It is difficult to forecast how the markets will react.* ➲ COLLOCATIONS at WEATHER ➲ LANGUAGE BANK at EXPECT

fore·cast·er /'fɔːkɑːstə(r); *NAmE* 'fɔːrkæstər/ *noun* a person who says what is expected to happen, especially sb whose job is to forecast the weather: *a weather forecaster* ◇ *an economic forecaster*

fore·castle (also **fo'c'sle**) /'fəʊksl; *NAmE* 'foʊksl/ *noun* the front part of a ship below the DECK, where the sailors live

fore·close /fɔː'kləʊz; *NAmE* fɔːr'kloʊz/ *verb* **1** [I, T] **~ (on sb/sth)** | **~ sth** (*finance*) (especially of a bank) to take control of sb's property because they have not paid back money that they borrowed to buy it ➲ COLLOCATIONS at HOUSE **2** [T] **~ sth** (*formal*) to reject sth as a possibility SYN **exclude**

fore·clos·ure /fɔːˈkləʊʒə(r); *NAmE* fɔːrˈkloʊ-/ *noun* [U, C] (*finance*) the act of foreclosing on money that has been borrowed; an example of this

fore·court /ˈfɔːkɔːt; *NAmE* ˈfɔːrkɔːrt/ *noun* (*BrE*) a large open space in front of a building, for example a PETROL/GAS STATION or hotel, often used for parking cars on

fore·doomed /fɔːˈduːmd; *NAmE* fɔːrˈd-/ *adj.* **~ (to sth)** (*formal*) that will not be successful, as if FATE has decided this from the beginning: *Any attempt to construct an ideal society is foredoomed to failure.*

fore·father /ˈfɔːfɑːðə(r); *NAmE* ˈfɔːrf-/ *noun* [usually pl.] (*formal* or *literary*) a person (especially a man) in your family who lived a long time ago SYN **ancestor**

fore·fend = FORFEND (1)

fore·fin·ger /ˈfɔːfɪŋgə(r); *NAmE* ˈfɔːrf-/ *noun* the finger next to the thumb SYN **index finger**

fore·foot /ˈfɔːfʊt; *NAmE* ˈfɔːrfʊt/ *noun* (*pl.* **forefeet** /-fiːt/) either of the two front feet of an animal that has four feet

fore·front /ˈfɔːfrʌnt; *NAmE* ˈfɔːrf-/ *noun* [sing.]
IDM **at/in/to the ˈforefront (of sth)** in or into an important or leading position in a particular group or activity: *Women have always been at the forefront of the Green movement.* ◇ *The new product took the company to the forefront of the computer software field.* ◇ *The court case was constantly in the forefront of my mind* (= I thought about it all the time).

fore·gather (also **for·gather**) /ˌfɔːˈgæðə(r); *NAmE* ˌfɔːrˈg-/ *verb* [I] (*formal*) to meet together in a group

fore·go = FORGO

fore·going /ˈfɔːgəʊɪŋ; *NAmE* ˈfɔːrgoʊɪŋ/ *adj.* [only before noun] (*formal*) **1** used to refer to sth that has just been mentioned: *the foregoing discussion* **2 the foregoing** *noun* [sing.+ sing./pl. v.] what has just been mentioned OPP **following**

fore·gone /ˈfɔːgɒn; *NAmE* ˈfɔːrgɔːn/ *adj.*
IDM **a ˌforegone conˈclusion** if you say that sth is **a foregone conclusion**, you mean that it is a result that is certain to happen

fore·ground /ˈfɔːgraʊnd; *NAmE* ˈfɔːrg-/ *noun*, *verb*
▪ ***noun* the foreground** **1** [C, usually sing.] the part of a view, picture, etc. that is nearest to you when you look at it: *The figure **in the foreground** is the artist's mother.* **2** [sing.] an important position that is noticed by people: *Inflation and interest rates will be very much **in the foreground of** their election campaign.* ➲ compare BACKGROUND
IDM **in the ˈforeground** (*computing*) (of a computer program) being used at the present time and appearing in front of any other programs on the screen ➲ compare IN THE BACKGROUND
▪ ***verb* ~ sth** to give particular importance to sth: *The play foregrounds the relationship between father and daughter.*

fore·hand /ˈfɔːhænd; *NAmE* ˈfɔːrh-/ *noun* [usually sing.] (in TENNIS, etc.) a way of hitting a ball in which the inner part of the hand (= the PALM) faces the ball as it is hit: *She has a strong forehand.* ◇ *a forehand volley* ◇ *He served to his opponent's forehand.* ➲ compare BACKHAND

fore·head /ˈfɔːhed; ˈfɒrɪd; *NAmE* ˈfɔːrhed; ˈfɔːred/ *noun* the part of the face above the eyes and below the hair SYN **brow** ➲ COLLOCATIONS at PHYSICAL ➲ VISUAL VOCAB page V48

for·eign 0‑ᵂ /ˈfɒrən; *NAmE* ˈfɔːrən; ˈfɑːrən/ *adj.*
1 0‑ᵂ in or from a country that is not your own: *a foreign accent/language/student* ◇ *a foreign-owned company* ◇ *foreign holidays* ◇ *You could tell she was foreign by the way she dressed.* **2** 0‑ᵂ [only before noun] dealing with or involving other countries: ***foreign affairs/news/policy/trade*** ◇ ***foreign aid*** ◇ *a **foreign correspondent*** (= one who reports on foreign countries in newspapers or on television) OPP **domestic, home** **3 ~ to sb/sth** (*formal*) not typical of sb/sth; not known to sb/sth and therefore seeming strange: *Dishonesty is foreign to his nature.* **4 ~ object/body** (*formal*) an object that has entered sth by accident and should not be there: *Tears help to protect the eye from potentially harmful foreign bodies.*

the ˌForeign and ˈCommonwealth Office *noun* [sing.+ sing./pl. v.] (*abbr.* FCO) the British government department that deals with relations with other countries. It used to be called **the Foreign Office** and it is still often referred to as this.

for·eign·er /ˈfɒrənə(r); *NAmE* ˈfɔːr-; ˈfɑːr-/ *noun* (sometimes *offensive*) **1** a person who comes from a different country: *The fact that I was a foreigner was a big disadvantage.* **2** a person who does not belong in a particular place: *I have always been regarded as a foreigner by the local folk.*

ˌforeign exˈchange *noun* **1** [U, C] the system of exchanging the money of one country for that of another country; the place where money is exchanged: *The euro fell on the foreign exchanges yesterday.* **2** [U] money that is obtained using this system: *our largest source of foreign exchange*

the ˈForeign Office *noun* [sing.+ sing./pl. v.] = THE FOREIGN AND COMMONWEALTH OFFICE

ˌforeign-reˈturned *adj.* (*IndE*, *informal*) (of a person) educated or trained in a foreign country, and having returned to India

the ˌForeign ˈSecretary *noun* the British government minister in charge of the FOREIGN AND COMMONWEALTH OFFICE

ˈForeign Service *noun* (*NAmE*) = DIPLOMATIC SERVICE

fore·know·ledge /fɔːˈnɒlɪdʒ; *NAmE* fɔːrˈnɑːl-/ *noun* [U] (*formal*) knowledge of sth before it happens

fore·land /ˈfɔːlənd; *NAmE* ˈfɔːr-/ *noun* [sing., U] **1** an area of land which lies in front of sth **2** an area of land which sticks out into the sea

fore·leg /ˈfɔːleg; *NAmE* ˈfɔːrleg/ (also **fore·limb** /ˈfɔːlɪm; *NAmE* ˈfɔːr-/) *noun* either of the two front legs of an animal that has four legs

fore·lock /ˈfɔːlɒk; *NAmE* ˈfɔːrlɑːk/ *noun* **1** a piece of hair that grows at the front of the head and hangs down over the FOREHEAD **2** a part of a horse's MANE that grows forwards between its ears
IDM **touch/tug your ˈforelock (to sb)** (*BrE*, *disapproving*) to show too much respect for sb, especially because you are anxious about what they think of you ORIGIN In the past people of the lower classes either took off their hats or pulled on their forelocks to show respect.

fore·man /ˈfɔːmən; *NAmE* ˈfɔːrmən/, **fore·woman** /ˈfɔːwʊmən; *NAmE* ˈfɔːrw-/ *noun* (*pl.* **-men** /-mən/, **-women** /-wɪmɪn/) **1** a worker who is in charge of a group of other factory or building workers **2** a person who acts as the leader of a JURY in court ➲ note at GENDER

fore·most /ˈfɔːməʊst; *NAmE* ˈfɔːrmoʊst/ *adj.*, *adv.*
▪ ***adj.*** the most important or famous; in a position at the front: *the world's foremost authority on the subject* ◇ *The Prime Minister was foremost among those who condemned the violence.* ◇ *This question has been foremost in our minds recently.*
▪ ***adv.*** IDM see FIRST *adv.*

fore·name /ˈfɔːneɪm; *NAmE* ˈfɔːrn-/ *noun* (*formal*) a person's first name rather than the name that they share with the other members of their family (= their SURNAME): *Please check that your surname and forenames have been correctly entered.*

fore·noon /ˈfɔːnuːn; *NAmE* ˈfɔːr-/ *noun* (*NAmE*, *ScotE*) the morning

fo·ren·sic /fəˈrensɪk; -ˈrenzɪk/ *adj.* [only before noun] **1** connected with the scientific tests used by the police when trying to solve a crime: ***forensic evidence/medicine/science/tests*** ◇ *the forensic laboratory* ◇ *a forensic pathologist* ➲ COLLOCATIONS at CRIME **2** connected with or used in court: *a forensic psychiatrist* (= one who examines people who have been accused of a crime)

fore·play /ˈfɔːpleɪ; *NAmE* ˈfɔːrp-/ *noun* [U] sexual activity, such as touching the sexual organs and kissing, that takes place before people have sex

fore·run·ner /ˈfɔːrʌnə(r)/ *noun* **~ (of sb/sth)** a person or thing that came before and influenced sb/sth else that is similar; a sign of what is going to happen: *Country music was undoubtedly one of the forerunners of rock and roll.*

fore·sail /ˈfɔːseɪl; ˈfɔːsl; *NAmE* ˈfɔːrseɪl; ˈfɔːrsl/ *noun* [usually sing.] the main sail on the MAST of a ship which is nearest the front (called the **foremast**)

fore·see /fɔːˈsiː; *NAmE* fɔːrˈsiː/ *verb* (**fore·saw** /fɔːˈsɔː; *NAmE* fɔːrˈsɔː/, **fore·seen** /fɔːˈsiːn; *NAmE* fɔːrˈsiːn/) to think sth is going to happen in the future; to know about sth before it happens SYN **predict**: **~ sth** *We do not foresee any problems.* ◇ *The extent of the damage could not have been foreseen.* ◇ **~ (that)...** *No one could have foreseen (that) things would turn out this way.* ◇ **~ how, what, etc...** *It is impossible to foresee how life will work out.* ◇ **~ sb/sth doing sth** *I just didn't foresee that happening.* ➲ compare UNFORESEEN

fore·see·able /fɔːˈsiːəbl; *NAmE* fɔːrˈs-/ *adj.* that you can predict will happen; that can be foreseen: ***foreseeable risks/consequences*** OPP **unforeseeable**

IDM **for/in the foreseeable 'future** for/in the period of time when you can predict what is going to happen, based on the present circumstances: *The statue will remain in the museum for the foreseeable future.* ◇ *It's unlikely that the hospital will be closed in the foreseeable future* (= soon).

fore·shadow /fɔːˈʃædəʊ; *NAmE* fɔːrˈʃædoʊ/ *verb* **~ sth** (*formal*) to be a sign of sth that will happen in the future

fore·shore /ˈfɔːʃɔː(r); *NAmE* ˈfɔːrʃ-/ *noun* [C, usually sing., U] **1** (on a beach or by a river) the part of the SHORE between the highest and lowest levels reached by the water **2** the part of the SHORE between the highest level reached by the water and the area of land that has buildings, plants, etc. on it

fore·short·en /fɔːˈʃɔːtn; *NAmE* fɔːrˈʃɔːrtn/ *verb* **1 ~ sth/sb** (*technical*) to draw, photograph, etc. objects or people so that they look smaller or closer together than they really are **2 ~ sth** (*formal*) to end sth before it would normally finish SYN **curtail**: *a foreshortened education*

fore·sight /ˈfɔːsaɪt; *NAmE* ˈfɔːrs-/ *noun* [U] (*approving*) the ability to predict what is likely to happen and to use this to prepare for the future: *She had had the foresight to prepare herself financially in case of an accident.* ➲ compare HINDSIGHT

fore·skin /ˈfɔːskɪn; *NAmE* ˈfɔːrs-/ *noun* the loose piece of skin that covers the end of a man's PENIS

for·est 🔑 /ˈfɒrɪst; *NAmE* ˈfɔːr-; ˈfɑːr-/ *noun* **1** 🔑 [C, U] a large area of land that is thickly covered with trees: *a tropical forest* ◇ *a forest fire* ◇ *Thousands of hectares of forest are destroyed each year.* ➲ see also RAINFOREST ➲ VISUAL VOCAB page V4 **2** [C] **~ (of sth)** a mass of tall narrow objects that are close together: *a forest of television aerials*

IDM **not see the ˌforest for the 'trees** (*NAmE*) (*BrE* **not see the ˌwood for the 'trees**) to not see or understand the main point about sth, because you are paying too much attention to small details

fore·stall /fɔːˈstɔːl; *NAmE* fɔːrˈs-/ *verb* **~ sth/sb** (*formal*) to prevent sth from happening or sb from doing sth by doing sth first: *Try to anticipate what your child will do and forestall problems.*

for·ested /ˈfɒrɪstɪd; *NAmE* ˈfɔːr-; ˈfɑːr-/ *adj.* covered in forest: ***thickly forested** hills* ◇ *The province is **heavily forested** and sparsely populated.*

for·est·er /ˈfɒrɪstə(r); *NAmE* ˈfɔːr-; ˈfɑːr-/ *noun* a person who works in a forest, taking care of the trees, planting new ones, etc.

for·est·ry /ˈfɒrɪstri; *NAmE* ˈfɔːr-; ˈfɑːr-/ *noun* [U] the science or practice of planting and taking care of trees and forests

fore·taste /ˈfɔːteɪst; *NAmE* ˈfɔːrt-/ *noun* [sing.] **a ~ (of sth)** a small amount of a particular experience or situation that shows you what it will be like when the same thing happens on a larger scale in the future: *They were unaware that the street violence was just a foretaste of what was to come.*

fore·tell /fɔːˈtel; *NAmE* fɔːrˈtel/ *verb* (**fore·told, fore·told** /fɔːˈtəʊld; *NAmE* fɔːrˈtoʊld/) (*literary*) to know or say what will happen in the future, especially by using magic powers: **~ sth** *to foretell the future* ◇ **~ that...** *The witch foretold that she would marry a prince.* ◇ **~ what, when, etc ...** *None of us can foretell what lies ahead.*

fore·thought /ˈfɔːθɔːt; *NAmE* ˈfɔːrθ-/ *noun* [U] careful thought to make sure that things are successful in the future: *Some forethought and preparation is necessary before you embark on the project.* IDM see MALICE

fore·told *past tense, past part.* of FORETELL

for·ever 🔑 /fərˈevə(r)/ *adv.* **1** 🔑 (*BrE* also **for ever**) used to say that a particular situation or state will always exist: *I'll love you forever!* ◇ *After her death, their lives changed forever.* ◇ *Just keep telling yourself that it won't last forever.* **2** 🔑 (*BrE* also **for ever**) (*informal*) a very long time: *It takes her forever to get dressed.* **3** (*informal*) used with verbs in the progressive tenses to say that sb does sth very often and in a way that is annoying to other people: *She's forever going on about how poor they are.*

fore·warn /fɔːˈwɔːn; *NAmE* fɔːrˈwɔːrn/ *verb* [often passive] **~ sb (of sth)** | **~ sb that...** (*formal*) to warn sb about sth bad or unpleasant before it happens: *The commander had been forewarned of the attack.* ▸ **fore·warn·ing** *noun* [U, C]

IDM **foreˌwarned is fore'armed** (*saying*) if you know about problems, dangers, etc. before they happen, you can be better prepared for them

fore·woman *noun* ➲ FOREMAN

fore·word /ˈfɔːwɜːd; *NAmE* ˈfɔːrwɜːrd/ *noun* a short introduction at the beginning of a book ➲ compare PREFACE

for·feit /ˈfɔːfɪt; *NAmE* ˈfɔːrfət/ *verb, noun, adj.*

- ***verb* ~ sth** to lose sth or have sth taken away from you because you have done sth wrong: *If you cancel your flight, you will forfeit your deposit.* ◇ *He has forfeited his right to be taken seriously.*
- ***noun*** something that a person has to pay, or sth that is taken from them, because they have done sth wrong
- ***adj.*** [not before noun] (*formal*) taken away from sb as a punishment

for·feit·ure /ˈfɔːfɪtʃə(r); *NAmE* ˈfɔːrfətʃər/ *noun* [U] (*law*) the act of forfeiting sth: *the forfeiture of property*

for·fend /fɔːˈfend; *NAmE* fɔːr-/ *verb* **1** (also **fore·fend**) **~ sth** (*NAmE*) to prevent sth **2 ~ sth** (*old use*) to prevent sth or keep sth away

IDM **Heaven/God for'fend (that)...** (*humorous* or *old use*) used to say that you are frightened of the idea of sth happening: *Heaven forfend that students are encouraged to think!*

for·gather *verb* [I] = FOREGATHER

for·gave *past tense* of FORGIVE

forge /fɔːdʒ; *NAmE* fɔːrdʒ/ *verb, noun*

- ***verb* 1** [T] **~ sth** to put a lot of effort into making sth successful or strong so that it will last: *a move to forge new links between management and workers* ◇ *Strategic alliances are being forged with major European companies.* ◇ *She forged a new career in the music business.* **2** [T] **~ sth** to make an illegal copy of sth in order to cheat people: *to forge a passport/banknote/cheque* ◇ *He's getting good at forging his mother's signature.* ➲ COLLOCATIONS at CRIME ➲ compare COUNTERFEIT **3** [T] **~ sth (from sth)** to shape metal by heating it in a fire and hitting it with a hammer; to make an object in this way: *swords forged from steel* **4** [I] **+ adv./prep.** (*formal*) to move forward in a steady but powerful way: *He forged through the crowds to the front of the stage.* ◇ *She forged into the lead* (= in a competition, race, etc.).

PHR V **ˌforge a'head (with sth)** to move forward quickly; to make a lot of progress quickly: *The company is forging ahead with its plans for expansion.*

- ***noun* 1** a place where objects are made by heating and shaping pieces of metal, especially one where a BLACKSMITH works **2** a large piece of equipment used for heating metals in; a building or part of a factory where this is found

for·ger /ˈfɔːdʒə(r); *NAmE* ˈfɔːrdʒ-/ *noun* a person who makes illegal copies of money, documents, etc. in order to cheat people ➲ compare COUNTERFEITER

for·gery /ˈfɔːdʒəri; *NAmE* ˈfɔːrdʒ-/ *noun* **1** [U] the crime of copying money, documents, etc. in order to cheat people SYN **fake 2** [C] something, for example a document, piece of paper money, etc, that has been copied in order to cheat people: *Experts are dismissing claims that the painting is a forgery.* ➲ compare COUNTERFEIT

for·get 0‑w /fəˈget; *NAmE* fərˈg-/ *verb* (**for·got** /fəˈgɒt; *NAmE* fərˈgɑːt/, **for·got·ten** /fəˈgɒtn; *NAmE* fərˈgɑːtn/)
▸ EVENTS/FACTS **1** 0‑w [I, T] (not usually used in the progressive tenses) to be unable to remember sth that has happened in the past or information that you knew in the past: **~ (about sth)** *I'd completely forgotten about the money he owed me.* ◇ *Before I forget, there was a call from Italy for you.* ◇ **~ sth** *I never forget a face.* ◇ *Who could forget his speech at last year's party?* ◇ **~ (that)...** *She keeps forgetting (that) I'm not a child any more.* ◇ ***I was forgetting*** (= I had forgotten) *(that) you've been here before.* ◇ **~ where, how, etc...** *I've forgotten where they live exactly.* ◇ *I forget how much they paid for it.* ◇ **~ (sb) doing sth** *I'll never forget hearing this piece of music for the first time.* ◇ **it is forgotten that...** *It should not be forgotten that people used to get much more exercise.*
▸ TO DO STH **2** 0‑w [I, T] to not remember to do sth that you ought to do, or to bring or buy sth that you ought to bring or buy: **~ (about sth)** *'Why weren't you at the meeting?' 'Sorry—I forgot.'* ◇ **~ to do sth** *Take care, and don't forget to write.* ◇ *I forgot to ask him for his address.* ◇ **~ sth/sb** *I forgot my purse* (= I did not remember to bring it). ◇ *'Hey, don't forget me!'* (= don't leave without me) ◇ ***Aren't you forgetting something?*** (= I think you have forgotten to do sth) HELP You cannot use **forget** if you want to mention the place where you have left something: *I've left my book at home.* ◇ *~~I've forgotten my book at home.~~*
▸ STOP THINKING ABOUT STH **3** 0‑w [I, T] to deliberately stop thinking about sb/sth: **~ (about sb/sth)** *Try to forget about what happened.* ◇ *Could you possibly forget about work for five minutes?* ◇ **~ sb/sth** *Forget him!* ◇ *Let's forget our differences and be friends.* ◇ **~ (that)...** *Forget (that) I said anything!* **4** [I, T] to stop thinking that sth is a possibility: **~ about sth** *If I lose this job, we can forget about buying a new car.* ◇ **~ sth** *'I was hoping you might be able to lend me the money.' 'You can forget that!'*
▸ YOURSELF **5** [T] **~ yourself** to behave in a way that is not socially acceptable: *I'm forgetting myself. I haven't offered you a drink yet!*
IDM **and don't (you) forˈget it** (*informal*) used to tell sb how they should behave, especially when they have been behaving in a way you do not like: *You're a suspect, not a detective, and don't you forget it.* **forˈget it** (*informal*) **1** used to tell sb that sth is not important and that they should not worry about it: *'I still owe you for lunch yesterday.' 'Forget it.'* **2** used to tell sb that you are not going to repeat what you said: *'Now, what were you saying about John?' 'Forget it, it doesn't matter.'* **3** used to emphasize that you are saying 'no' to sth: *'Any chance of you helping out here?' 'Forget it, I've got too much to do.'* **4** used to tell sb to stop talking about sth because they are annoying you: *Just forget it, will you!* **not forgetting...** (*BrE*) used to include sth in the list of things that you have just mentioned: *I share the house with Jim, Ian and Sam, not forgetting Spike, the dog.* ➲ more at FORGIVE

for·get·ful /fəˈgetfl; *NAmE* fərˈg-/ *adj.* **1** often forgetting things SYN **absent-minded**: *She has become very forgetful in recent years.* **2 ~ of sb/sth** (*formal*) not thinking about sb/sth that you should be thinking about ▸ **for·get·ful·ly** /-fəli/ *adv.* **for·get·ful·ness** *noun* [U]

forˈget-me-not *noun* a small wild plant with light blue flowers

for·get·table /fəˈgetəbl; *NAmE* fərˈg-/ *adj.* not interesting or special and therefore easily forgotten: *an instantly forgettable tune* OPP **unforgettable**

for·giv·able /fəˈgɪvəbl; *NAmE* fərˈg-/ *adj.* that you can understand and forgive SYN **excusable**: *His rudeness was forgivable in the circumstances.* OPP **unforgivable**

for·give 0‑w /fəˈgɪv; *NAmE* fərˈgɪv/ *verb* (**for·gave** /fəˈgeɪv; *NAmE* fərˈg-/, **for·given** /fəˈgɪvn; *NAmE* fərˈg-/)
1 0‑w [T, I] to stop feeling angry with sb who has done sth to harm, annoy or upset you; to stop feeling angry with yourself: **~ sb/yourself (for sth/for doing sth)** *I'll never forgive her for what she did.* ◇ *I'd never forgive myself if she heard the truth from someone else.* ◇ **~ (sth)** *I can't forgive that type of behaviour.* ◇ *We all have to learn to forgive.* ◇ **~ sb sth** *She'd forgive him anything.* **2** 0‑w [T] used to say in a polite way that you are sorry if what you are doing or saying seems rude or silly: **~ me** *Forgive me, but I don't see that any of this concerns me.* ◇ **~ me for doing sth** *Forgive me for interrupting, but I really don't agree with that.* ◇ **~ my ...** *Forgive my ignorance, but what exactly does the company do?* ◇ **~ my doing sth** *Forgive my interrupting but I really don't agree with that.* **3** [T] **~ (sb) sth** (*formal*) (of a bank, country, etc.) to say that sb does not need to pay back money that they have borrowed: *The government has agreed to forgive a large part of the debt.*
IDM **sb could/might be forgiven for doing sth** used to say that it is easy to understand why sb does or thinks sth, although they are wrong: *Looking at the crowds out shopping, you could be forgiven for thinking that everyone has plenty of money.* **forˌgive and forˈget** to stop feeling angry with sb for sth they have done to you and to behave as if it had not happened

for·give·ness /fəˈgɪvnəs; *NAmE* fərˈg-/ *noun* [U] the act of forgiving sb; willingness to forgive sb: *to pray for God's forgiveness* ◇ *the forgiveness of sins* ◇ *He begged forgiveness for what he had done.*

for·giv·ing /fəˈgɪvɪŋ; *NAmE* fərˈg-/ *adj.* willing to forgive: *She had not inherited her mother's forgiving nature.* ◇ **~ of sth** *The public was more forgiving of the president's difficulties than the press and fellow politicians.*

forgo (also **forego**) /fɔːˈgəʊ; *NAmE* fɔːrˈgoʊ/ *verb* (**for·went** /fɔːˈwent; *NAmE* fɔːrˈwent/, **for·gone** /fɔːˈgɒn; *NAmE* fɔːrˈgɔːn/) **~ sth** (*formal*) to decide not to have or do sth that you would like to have or do: *No one was prepared to forgo their lunch hour to attend the meeting.*

for·got *past tense* of FORGET

for·got·ten *past part.* of FORGET

fork 0‑w /fɔːk; *NAmE* fɔːrk/ *noun, verb*
■ ***noun*** **1** 0‑w a tool with a handle and three or four sharp points (called PRONGS), used for picking up and eating food: *to eat with a **knife and fork*** ➲ VISUAL VOCAB page V19 **2** a garden tool with a long or short handle and three or four sharp metal points, used for digging ➲ VISUAL VOCAB page V16 ➲ see also PITCHFORK **3** a place where a road, river, etc. divides into two parts; either of these two parts: *Shortly before dusk they reached a fork and took the left-hand track.* ◇ *Take the right fork.* **4** a thing shaped like a fork, with two or more long parts: *a jagged fork of lightning* ➲ see also TUNING FORK **5** either of two metal supporting pieces into which a wheel on a bicycle or motorcycle is fitted ➲ VISUAL VOCAB page V41
■ ***verb*** **1** [I] (not used in the progressive tenses) (+ **adv./prep.**) (of a road, river, etc.) to divide into two parts that lead in different directions: *The path forks at the bottom of the hill.* ◇ *The road forks right after the bridge.* **2** [I] + **adv./prep.** (not used in the progressive tenses) (of a person) to turn left or right where a road, etc. divides into two: *Fork right after the bridge.* **3** [T] (+ **adv./prep.**) to move, carry or dig sth using a fork: *Clear the soil of weeds and fork in plenty of compost.*
PHR V **ˌfork ˈout (for sth)** | **ˌfork ˈout sth (for/on sth)** (*informal*) to spend a lot of money on sth, especially unwillingly: *Why fork out for a taxi when there's a perfectly good bus service?* ◇ *We've forked out a small fortune on their education.*

forked /fɔːkt; *NAmE* fɔːrkt/ *adj.* with one end divided into two parts, like the shape of the letter 'Y': *a bird with a* *forked tail* ◇ *the forked tongue of a snake* ➲ VISUAL VOCAB page V11

ˌ**forked ˈlightning** *noun* [U] the type of LIGHTNING that is like a line that divides into smaller lines near the ground ➲ compare SHEET LIGHTNING

fork·ful /ˈfɔːkfʊl; *NAmE* ˈfɔːrk-/ *noun* the amount that a fork holds

fork·lift truck /ˌfɔːklɪft ˈtrʌk; *NAmE* ˌfɔːrk-/ (also **fork·lift**) *noun* a vehicle with special equipment on the front for moving and lifting heavy objects ➲ VISUAL VOCAB page V46

for·lorn /fəˈlɔːn; *NAmE* fərˈlɔːrn/ *adj.* **1** (of a person) appearing lonely and unhappy: *She looked so forlorn, standing there in the rain.* **2** (of a place) not cared for and with no people in it: *Empty houses quickly take on a forlorn look.* **3** unlikely to succeed, come true, etc: *She waited* ***in the forlorn hope*** *that he would one day come back to her.* ◇ *His father smiled weakly* ***in a forlorn attempt*** *to reassure him that everything was all right.* ▶ **for·lorn·ly** *adv.*

form 0-w /fɔːm; *NAmE* fɔːrm/ *noun, verb*

■ ***noun***

▸ TYPE **1** 0-w [C] a type or variety of sth: *forms of transport/government/energy* ◇ *one of the most common forms of cancer* ◇ *all the millions of different life forms on the planet today* ➲ see also ART FORM

▸ WAY STH IS/LOOKS **2** 0-w [C, U] the particular way sth is, seems, looks or is presented: *The disease can take several different forms.* ◇ *Help* ***in the form of*** *money will be very welcome.* ◇ *Help arrived* ***in the form of*** *two police officers.* ◇ *The training programme* ***takes the form of*** *a series of workshops.* ◇ *Most political questions involve morality* ***in some form or other.*** ◇ *We need to come to* ***some form of*** *agreement.* ◇ *I'm opposed to censorship* ***in any shape or form.*** ◇ *This dictionary is also available in electronic form.*

▸ DOCUMENT **3** 0-w [C] an official document containing questions and spaces for answers: *an* ***application/entry/order form*** ◇ *(especially BrE) to* ***fill in a form*** ◇ *(especially NAmE) to* ***fill out a form*** ◇ *I filled in/out a form on their website.* ◇ *to complete a form* ◇ (*BrE*) *a* ***booking form*** ◇ (*NAmE*) *a* ***reservation form***

▸ SHAPE **4** 0-w [C] the shape of sb/sth; a person or thing of which only the shape can be seen: *her slender form* ◇ *The human form has changed little over the last 30 000 years.* ◇ *They made out a shadowy form in front of them.*

▸ ARRANGEMENT OF PARTS **5** [U] the arrangement of parts in a whole, especially in a work of art or piece of writing: *In a novel, form and content are equally important.* ➲ SYNONYMS at STRUCTURE

▸ BEING FIT/HEALTHY **6** [U] (*BrE*) how fit and healthy sb is; the state of being fit and healthy: *After six months' training the whole team is in superb form.* ◇ *I really need to get back* ***in form.*** ◇ *The horse was clearly* ***out of form.***

▸ PERFORMANCE **7** [U] how well sb/sth is performing; the fact that sb/sth is performing well: *Midfielder Elliott has shown disappointing form recently.* ◇ ***On current/present form*** *the party is heading for another election victory.* ◇ *She signalled her return to form with a convincing victory.* ◇ *He's right* ***on form*** (= performing well) *as a crazy science teacher in his latest movie.* ◇ *The whole team was* ***on good form*** *and deserved the win.* ◇ *She was* ***in great form*** (= happy and cheerful and full of energy) *at the wedding party.*

▸ WAY OF DOING THINGS **8** [U, C] (*especially BrE*) the usual way of doing sth: *What's the form when you apply for a research grant?* ◇ *conventional social forms* ◇ ***True to form*** (= as he usually does) *he arrived an hour late.* ◇ *Partners of employees are invited* ***as a matter of form.*** **9** [U] **good/bad ~** (*old-fashioned, BrE*) the way of doing things that is socially acceptable/not socially acceptable

▸ OF WORD **10** [C] a way of writing or saying a word that shows, for example, if it is plural or in a particular tense: *the infinitive form of the verb*

▸ IN SCHOOL **11** (*BrE, old-fashioned*) a class in a school: *Who's your form teacher?* ➲ see also SIXTH FORM **12** **-former** (in compounds) (*BrE, old-fashioned*) a student in the form mentioned at school: *a third-former* ➲ see also SIXTH-FORMER

IDM **take ˈform** (*formal*) to gradually form into a particular shape; to gradually develop: *In her body a new life was taking form.* ➲ more at SHAPE *n.*

■ ***verb***

▸ START TO EXIST **1** 0-w [I, T] (especially of natural things) to begin to exist and gradually develop into a particular shape; to make sth begin to exist in a particular shape: *Flowers appeared, but fruits failed to form.* ◇ *Storm clouds are forming on the horizon.* ◇ **~ sth** *These hills were formed by glaciation.* **2** 0-w [I, T] to start to exist and develop; to make sth start to exist and develop: *A plan formed in my head.* ◇ **~ sth** *I formed many close friendships at college.* ◇ *I didn't see enough of the play to form an opinion about it.* ➲ SYNONYMS at MAKE

▸ MAKE SHAPE/FORM **3** 0-w [T, often passive] to produce sth in a particular way or make it have a particular shape: **~ sth** *Bend the wire so that it forms a 'V'.* ◇ *Rearrange the letters to form a new word.* ◇ *Games can help children learn to form letters.* ◇ *Do you know how to form the past tense?* ◇ **~ sth into sth** *Form the dough into balls with your hands.* ◇ **~ sth from/of sth** *The chain is formed from 136 links.* **4** 0-w [T, I] to move or arrange objects or people so that they are in a group with a particular shape; to become arranged in a group like this: **~ sb/sth (up) (into sth)** *to* ***form a line/queue/circle*** ◇ *First get students to form groups of four.* ◇ **~ (up) (into sth)** *Queues were already forming outside the theatre.* ◇ *The teams formed up into lines.*

▸ HAVE FUNCTION/ROLE **5** 0-w [T] **~ sth** to have a particular function or pattern: *The trees form a natural protection from the sun's rays.* **6** *linking verb* **+ noun** to be sth: *The castle forms the focal point of the city.* ◇ *The survey* ***formed part of*** *a larger programme of research.* ◇ *These drawings will* ***form the basis of*** *the exhibition.*

▸ ORGANIZATION **7** 0-w [T, I] **~ (sth)** to start a group of people, such as an organization, a committee, etc; to come together in a group of this kind: *They hope to form the new government.* ◇ *He formed a band with some friends from school.* ◇ *a newly-formed political party* ◇ *The band formed in 2007.*

▸ HAVE INFLUENCE ON **8** [T] **~ sth** to have an influence on the way that sth develops SYN **mould**: *Positive and negative experiences form a child's character.*

for·mal 0-w /ˈfɔːml; *NAmE* ˈfɔːrml/ *adj.* **1** 0-w (of a style of dress, speech, writing, behaviour, etc.) very correct and suitable for official or important occasions: *formal evening dress* ◇ *The dinner was a formal affair.* ◇ *He kept the tone of the letter formal and businesslike.* ◇ *She has a very formal manner, which can seem unfriendly.* OPP **informal** **2** 0-w official; following an agreed or official way of doing things: *formal legal processes* ◇ *to make a* ***formal apology/complaint/request*** ◇ *Formal diplomatic relations between the two countries were re-established in December.* ◇ *It is time to put these arrangements on a slightly more formal basis.* **3** 0-w (of education or training) received in a school, college or university, with lessons, exams, etc, rather than gained just through practical experience: *He has no formal teaching qualifications.* ◇ *Young children are beginning their formal education sometimes as early as four years old.* **4** concerned with the way sth is done rather than what is done: *Getting approval for the plan is a purely formal matter; nobody will seriously oppose it.* ◇ *Critics have concentrated too much on the formal elements of her poetry, without really looking at what it is saying.* **5** (of a garden, room or building) arranged in a regular manner, according to a clear, exact plan: *delightful formal gardens, with terraced lawns and an avenue of trees* OPP **informal** ▶ **for·mal·ly** 0-w /-məli/ *adv.*: *'How do you do?' she said formally.* ◇ *The accounts were formally approved by the board.* ◇ *Although not formally trained as an art historian, he is widely respected for his knowledge of the period.*

for·mal·de·hyde /fɔːˈmældɪhaɪd; *NAmE* fɔːrˈm-/ *noun* [U] **1** (*symb.* CH_2O) a gas with a strong smell **2** (also *technical* **for·mal·in** /ˈfɔːməlɪn; *NAmE* ˈfɔːrm-/) a liquid made by mixing formaldehyde and water, used for preserving BIOLOGICAL SPECIMENS, making plastics and as a DISINFECTANT

for·mal·ism /ˈfɔːməlɪzəm; *NAmE* ˈfɔːrm-/ *noun* [U] a style or method in art, music, literature, science, etc. that pays more attention to the rules and the correct arrangement and appearance of things than to inner meaning and feelings ▸ **for·mal·ist** /ˈfɔːməlɪst; *NAmE* ˈfɔːrm-/ *noun* **for·mal·ist** *adj.* [usually before noun]: *formalist theory*

for·mal·ity /fɔːˈmæləti; *NAmE* fɔːrˈm-/ *noun* (*pl.* -ies) **1** [C, usually pl.] a thing that you must do as a formal or official part of a legal process, a social situation, etc: *to go through all the formalities necessary in order to get a gun licence* ◇ *Let's skip the formalities and get down to business.* **2** [C, usually sing.] a thing that you must do as part of an official process, but which has little meaning and will not affect what happens: *He already knows he has the job so the interview is a mere formality.* **3** [U] correct and formal behaviour: *Different levels of formality are appropriate in different situations.* ◇ *She greeted him with stiff formality.*

for·mal·ize (*BrE* also **-ise**) /ˈfɔːməlaɪz; *NAmE* ˈfɔːrm-/ *verb* **1 ~ sth** to make an arrangement, a plan or a relationship official: *They decided to formalize their relationship by getting married.* **2 ~ sth** to give sth a fixed structure or form by introducing rules: *The college has a highly formalized system of assessment.* ▸ **for·mal·iza·tion, -isa·tion** /ˌfɔːməlaɪˈzeɪʃn; *NAmE* ˌfɔːrmələˈz-/ *noun* [U]

for·mat AW /ˈfɔːmæt; *NAmE* ˈfɔːrmæt/ *noun, verb*

■ ***noun*** **1** the general arrangement, plan, design, etc. of sth: *The format of the new quiz show has proved popular.* **2** the shape and size of a book, magazine, etc: *They've brought out the magazine in a new format.* **3** (*computing*) the way in which data is stored or held to be worked on by a computer

■ ***verb*** (-tt-) **1 ~ sth** to prepare a computer disk so that data can be recorded on it **2 ~ sth** (*technical*) to arrange text in a particular way on a page or a screen

for·ma·tion /fɔːˈmeɪʃn; *NAmE* fɔːrˈm-/ *noun* **1** [U] the action of forming sth; the process of being formed: *the formation of a new government* ◇ *evidence of recent star formation in the galaxy* **2** [C] a thing that has been formed, especially in a particular place or in a particular way: *rock formations* **3** [U, C] a particular arrangement or pattern: *aircraft flying **in formation*** ◇ *formation flying* ◇ *The team usually plays in a 4-4-2 formation.*

for·ma·tive /ˈfɔːmətɪv; *NAmE* ˈfɔːrm-/ *adj.* [only before noun] having an important and lasting influence on the development of sth or of sb's character: *the **formative years** of childhood*

for·mer 🔑 /ˈfɔːmə(r); *NAmE* ˈfɔːrm-/ *adj.* [only before noun]

1 🔑 that used to exist in earlier times: *in former times* ◇ *the countries of the former Soviet Union* ◇ *This beautiful old building has been restored to **its former glory**.* **2** 🔑 that used to have a particular position or status in the past: *the former world champion* ◇ *my former boss/colleague/wife* **3** 🔑 **the former...** used to refer to the first of two things or people mentioned: *The former option would be much more sensible.* ➲ compare LATTER **4** 🔑 **the former** *pron.* the first of two things or people mentioned: *He had to choose between giving up his job and giving up his principles. He chose the former.* ➲ compare LATTER

IDM **be a shadow/ghost of your former ˈself** to not have the strength, influence, etc. that you used to have

for·mer·ly 🔑 /ˈfɔːməli; *NAmE* ˈfɔːrmərli/ *adv.* in earlier times SYN **previously**: *Namibia, formerly known as South West Africa* ◇ *I learnt that the house had formerly been an inn.* ◇ *John Marsh, formerly of London Road, Leicester, now living in France*

For·mica™ /fɔːˈmaɪkə; *NAmE* fɔːrˈm-/ *noun* [U] a hard plastic that can resist heat, used for covering work surfaces, etc.

for·mic acid /ˌfɔːmɪk ˈæsɪd; *NAmE* ˌfɔːrmɪk/ *noun* [U] (*chemistry*) an acid made from CARBON MONOXIDE and steam. It is also present in a liquid produced by some ANTS.

for·mid·able /ˈfɔːmɪdəbl; fəˈmɪd-; *NAmE* ˈfɔːrm-; fərˈm-/ *adj.* if people, things or situations are **formidable**, you feel fear and/or respect for them, because they are impressive or powerful, or because they seem very difficult: *In debate he was a formidable opponent.* ◇ *She has a formidable list of qualifications.* ◇ *The two players together make a formidable combination.* ◇ *The task was a formidable one.* ◇ *They had to overcome formidable obstacles.* ▸ **for·mid·ably** /-əbli/ *adv.*: *He now has the chance to prove himself in a formidably difficult role.* ◇ *She's formidably intelligent.*

form·less /ˈfɔːmləs; *NAmE* ˈfɔːrm-/ *adj.* without a clear or definite shape or structure: *formless dreams* ▸ **form·less·ness** *noun* [U]

for·mula 🔑 AW /ˈfɔːmjələ; *NAmE* ˈfɔːrm-/ *noun* (*pl.* **for·mu·las** or, especially in scientific use, **for·mu·lae** /-liː/) **1** 🔑 [C] (*mathematics*) a series of letters, numbers or symbols that represent a rule or law: *This formula is used to calculate the area of a circle.* **2** 🔑 [C] (*chemistry*) letters and symbols that show the parts of a chemical COMPOUND, etc: *CO is the formula for carbon monoxide.* **3** 🔑 [C] a particular method of doing or achieving sth: *They're trying to work out a **peace formula** acceptable to both sides in the dispute.* ◇ **~ for sth/for doing sth** *There's no **magic formula** for a perfect marriage.* **4** 🔑 [C] a list of the things that sth is made from, giving the amount of each substance to use: *the secret formula for the blending of the whisky* **5** (also **ˈformula milk**) [U, C] (*especially NAmE*) a type of liquid food for babies, given instead of breast milk **6** [C] a class of racing car, based on engine size, etc: *Formula One racing™* **7** [C] a fixed form of words used in a particular situation: *legal formulae* ◇ *The minister keeps coming out with the same tired formulas.*

for·mu·la·ic /ˌfɔːmjuˈleɪɪk; *NAmE* ˌfɔːrm-/ *adj.* (*formal*) made up of fixed patterns of words or ideas: *Traditional stories make use of formulaic expressions like 'Once upon a time...'.*

for·mu·late AW /ˈfɔːmjuleɪt; *NAmE* ˈfɔːrm-/ *verb* **1** to create or prepare sth carefully, giving particular attention to the details: **~ sth** *to **formulate a policy/theory/plan/proposal*** ◇ *The compost is specially formulated for pot plants.* ◇ **~ sth to do sth** *This new kitchen cleaner is formulated to cut through grease and dirt.* **2 ~ sth** to express your ideas in carefully chosen words: *She has lots of good ideas, but she has difficulty formulating them.* ▸ **for·mu·la·tion** AW /ˌfɔːmjuˈleɪʃn; *NAmE* ˌfɔːrm-/ *noun* [U, C]: *the formulation of new policies*

for·ni·cate /ˈfɔːnɪkeɪt; *NAmE* ˈfɔːrn-/ *verb* [I] (*formal, disapproving*) to have sex with sb that you are not married to ▸ **for·ni·ca·tion** /ˌfɔːnɪˈkeɪʃn; *NAmE* ˌfɔːrn-/ *noun* [U] **for·ni·ca·tor** *noun*

for·sake /fəˈseɪk; *NAmE* fərˈs-/ *verb* (**for·sook** /fəˈsʊk; *NAmE* fərˈs-/, **for·saken** /fəˈseɪkən; *NAmE* fərˈs-/) (*literary*) **1 ~ sb/sth** (**for sb/sth**) to leave sb/sth, especially when you have a responsibility to stay SYN **abandon**: *He had made it clear to his wife that he would never forsake her.* **2 ~ sth** (**for sb/sth**) to stop doing sth, or leave sth, especially sth that you enjoy SYN **renounce**: *She forsook the glamour of the city and went to live in the wilds of Scotland.* ➲ see also GODFORSAKEN

for·sooth /fəˈsuːθ; *NAmE* fərˈ-/ *adv.* (*old use* or *humorous*) used to emphasize a statement, especially in order to show surprise

for·swear /fɔːˈsweə(r); *NAmE* fɔːrˈswer/ *verb* (**for·swore** /fɔːˈswɔː(r); *NAmE* fɔːrˈs-/, **for·sworn** /fɔːˈswɔːn; *NAmE* fɔːrˈswɔːrn/) **~ sth** (*formal* or *literary*) to stop doing or using sth; to make a promise that you will stop doing or using sth SYN **renounce**: *The group forswears all worldly possessions.* ◇ *The country has not forsworn the use of chemical weapons.*

for·sythia /fɔːˈsaɪθiə; *NAmE* fərˈsɪθiə/ *noun* [U, C] a bush that has small bright yellow flowers in the early spring

fort /fɔːt; *NAmE* fɔːrt/ *noun* **1** a building or buildings built in order to defend an area against attack ➲ VISUAL VOCAB page V13 **2** (*NAmE*) a place where soldiers live and have their training: *Fort Drum*

IDM **hold the ˈfort** (*BrE*) (*NAmE* **hold down the ˈfort**)

F

(*informal*) to have the responsibility for sth or care of sb while other people are away or out: *Why not have a day off? I'll hold the fort for you.*

forte /ˈfɔːteɪ; *NAmE* fɔːrt/ *noun, adv.*

■ ***noun*** [sing.] a thing that sb does particularly well: *Languages were never my forte.*

■ ***adv.*** (*music*) played or sung loudly **OPP piano** ▸ **forte** *adj.*

For·tean /ˈfɔːtiən; *NAmE* ˈfɔːrt-/ *adj.* involving or relating to things that cannot be explained by science **SYN paranormal**

forth /fɔːθ; *NAmE* fɔːrθ/ *adv.* (*literary* except in particular idioms and phrasal verbs) **1** away from a place; out: *They set forth at dawn.* ◇ *Huge chimneys belched forth smoke and grime.* **2** towards a place; forwards: *Water gushed forth from a hole in the rock.* ➲ see also BRING FORTH

IDM from that day/time 'forth (*literary*) beginning on that day; from that time ➲ more at BACK *adv.*, SO *adv.*

the ˌForth 'Bridge *noun*

IDM like painting the Forth 'Bridge (*BrE*) used to describe a job that never seems to end because by the time you get to the end you have to start at the beginning again **ORIGIN** From the name of a very large bridge over the river Forth in Scotland.

forth·com·ing AW /ˌfɔːθˈkʌmɪŋ; *NAmE* ˌfɔːrθ-/ *adj.* **1** [only before noun] going to happen, be published, etc. very soon: *the forthcoming elections* ◇ *a list of forthcoming books* ◇ *the band's forthcoming UK tour* **2** [not before noun] ready or made available when needed: *Financial support was not forthcoming.* **3** [not before noun] willing to give information about sth: *She's never very forthcoming about her plans.* **OPP unforthcoming**

forth·right /ˈfɔːθraɪt; *NAmE* ˈfɔːrθ-/ *adj.* direct and honest in manner and speech **SYN frank**: *a woman of forthright views* ▸ **forth·right·ly** *adv.* **forth·right·ness** *noun* [U]

forth·with /ˌfɔːθˈwɪθ; -ˈwɪð; *NAmE* ˌfɔːrθ-/ *adv.* (*formal*) immediately; at once: *The agreement between us is terminated forthwith.*

for·ti·eth ➲ FORTY

for·ti·fi·ca·tion /ˌfɔːtɪfɪˈkeɪʃn; *NAmE* ˌfɔːrt-/ *noun* **1** [C, usually pl.] a tower, wall, gun position, etc. built to defend a place against attack: *the ramparts and fortifications of the Old Town* **2** [U] the act of fortifying or making sth stronger: *plans for the fortification of the city*

for·tify /ˈfɔːtɪfaɪ; *NAmE* ˈfɔːrt-/ *verb* (**for·ti·fies, for·ti·fy·ing, for·ti·fied, for·ti·fied**) **1 ~ sth** (**against sb/sth**) to make a place more able to resist attack, especially by building high walls: *a fortified town* **2 ~ sb/yourself** (**against sb/sth**) to make sb/yourself feel stronger, braver, etc: *He fortified himself against the cold with a hot drink.* **3** to make a feeling or an attitude stronger: *The news merely fortified their determination.* **4 ~ sth** (**with sth**) to increase the strength or quality of food or drink by adding sth to it: *Sherry is **fortified wine*** (= wine with extra alcohol added). ◇ *cereal fortified with extra vitamins*

for·ti·ori ➲ A FORTIORI

for·tis·simo /fɔːˈtɪsɪməʊ; *NAmE* fɔːrˈtɪsɪmoʊ/ *adv.* (*abbr.* ff) (*music*) played or sung very loudly **OPP pianissimo**

for·ti·tude /ˈfɔːtɪtjuːd; *NAmE* ˈfɔːrtətuːd/ *noun* [U] (*formal*) courage shown by sb who is suffering great pain or facing great difficulties **SYN bravery, courage**

Fort Knox /ˌfɔːt ˈnɒks; *NAmE* ˌfɔːrt ˈnɑːks/ *noun*

IDM be like/as safe as Fort 'Knox (of a building) to be strongly built, often with many locks, strong doors, guards, etc, so that it is difficult for people to enter and the things kept there are safe: *This home of yours is like Fort Knox.* **ORIGIN** From the name of the military base in Kentucky where most of the US's store of gold is kept.

fort·night /ˈfɔːtnaɪt; *NAmE* ˈfɔːrt-/ *noun* [usually sing.] (*BrE*) two weeks: *a fortnight's holiday* ◇ *a fortnight ago* ◇ *in a fortnight's time* ◇ *He's had three accidents in the past fortnight.*

fort·night·ly /ˈfɔːtnaɪtli; *NAmE* ˈfɔːrt-/ *adj.* (*BrE*) happening once a fortnight: *Meetings take place at fortnightly intervals.* ▸ **fort·night·ly** *adv.*: *The committee meets fortnightly.*

fort·ress /ˈfɔːtrəs; *NAmE* ˈfɔːrt-/ *noun* a building or place that has been made stronger and protected against attack: *a fortress town enclosed by four miles of ramparts* ◇ *Fear of terrorist attack has turned the conference centre into a fortress.*

for·tuit·ous /fɔːˈtjuːɪtəs; *NAmE* fɔːrˈtuː-/ *adj.* (*formal*) happening by chance, especially a lucky chance that brings a good result ▸ **for·tuit·ous·ly** *adv.*

for·tu·nate /ˈfɔːtʃənət; *NAmE* ˈfɔːrtʃ-/ *adj.* having or bringing an advantage, an opportunity, a piece of good luck, etc. **SYN lucky**: **~** (**to do sth**) *I have been fortunate enough to visit many parts of the world as a lecturer.* ◇ **~** (**in having...**) *I was fortunate in having a good teacher.* ◇ *Remember those less fortunate than yourselves.* ◇ **~** (**for sb**) (**that...**) ***It was** very **fortunate** for him that I arrived on time.* **OPP unfortunate**

for·tu·nate·ly /ˈfɔːtʃənətli; *NAmE* ˈfɔːrtʃ-/ *adv.* by good luck **SYN luckily**: *I was late, but fortunately the meeting hadn't started.* ◇ *Fortunately for him, he was very soon offered another job.* **OPP unfortunately**

for·tune 0‑w /ˈfɔːtʃuːn; *NAmE* ˈfɔːrtʃən/ *noun*

1 0‑w [U] chance or luck, especially in the way it affects people's lives: *I have **had the good fortune to** work with some brilliant directors.* ◇ ***By a stroke of fortune** he found work almost immediately.* ◇ ***Fortune smiled on me*** (= I had good luck). **2** 0‑w [C] a large amount of money: *He **made a fortune** in real estate.* ◇ *She inherited a share of the family fortune.* ◇ *A car like that costs **a small fortune**.* ◇ *You don't have to **spend a fortune** to give your family tasty, healthy meals.* ◇ *She is hoping her US debut will be the first step on the road to **fame and fortune**.* ◇ *That ring must be **worth a fortune**.* **3** 0‑w [C, usually pl., U] the good and bad things that happen to a person, family, country, etc: *the changing fortunes of the film industry* ◇ *the fortunes of war* ◇ *a reversal of fortune(s)* **4** [C] a person's FATE or future: *She can **tell your fortune** by looking at the lines on your hand.* **IDM** see HOSTAGE, SEEK ➲ see also SOLDIER OF FORTUNE

'fortune cookie *noun* a thin hollow biscuit/cookie, served in Chinese restaurants, containing a short message that predicts what will happen to you in the future

'fortune hunter *noun* a person who tries to become rich by marrying sb with a lot of money

'fortune-teller *noun* a person who claims to have magic powers and who tells people what will happen to them in the future

forty 0‑w /ˈfɔːti; *NAmE* ˈfɔːrti/

1 0‑w *number* 40 **2** *noun* **the for·ties** [pl.] numbers, years or temperatures from 40 to 49 ▸ **fortieth** 0‑w /ˈfɔːtiəθ; *NAmE* ˈfɔːrt-/ *ordinal number, noun* **HELP** There are examples of how to use ordinal numbers at the entry for **fifth**.

IDM in your forties between the ages of 40 and 49

the ˌforty-ninth 'parallel *noun* the line on a map that is 49° north of the EQUATOR, thought of as forming the border between western Canada and the US

ˌforty 'winks *noun* [pl.] (*informal*) a short sleep, especially during the day: *I'll feel much better when I've had forty winks.*

forum /ˈfɔːrəm/ *noun* **1 ~** (**for sth**) a place where people can exchange opinions and ideas on a particular issue; a meeting organized for this purpose: *Television is now an important forum for political debate.* ◇ *an Internet forum* ◇ *to hold an international forum on drug abuse* ➲ COLLOCATIONS at EMAIL **2** (in ancient Rome) a public place where meetings were held

for·ward 0‑w /ˈfɔːwəd; *NAmE* ˈfɔːrwərd/ *adv., adj., verb, noun*

■ ***adv.*** **1** 0‑w (also **for·wards** especially in *BrE*) towards a place or position that is in front: *She **leaned forward** and kissed him on the cheek.* ◇ *He took two steps forward.* ◇ *They ran forward to welcome her.* **OPP back, backward(s)** **2** 0‑w towards a good result: *We consider this agreement to* be an important **step forward**. ◇ Cutting our costs is the only **way forward**. ◇ We are not getting any **further forward** with the discussion. ◇ The project will **go forward** (= continue) as planned. **OPP** **backward(s)** **3** towards the future; ahead in time: ***Looking forward,*** we hope to expand our operations in several of our overseas branches. ◇ The next scene takes the story forward five years. ◇ (*old use*) from this day forward **4** earlier; sooner: *It was decided to bring the meeting forward two weeks.* **5** (*technical*) in or towards the front part of a ship or plane: *The main cabin is situated forward of* (= in front of) *the mast.* ➲ see also LOOK FORWARD, PUT FORWARD

IDM **ˌgoing/ˌmoving ˈforward** (*formal* or *business*) in the future, starting from now: *We have a very solid financial position going forward.* ➲ more at BACKWARD(S), CLOCK *n.*, FOOT *n.*

■ ***adj.*** **1** [only before noun] directed or moving towards the front: *The door opened, blocking his* ***forward movement.*** ◇ *a* ***forward pass*** (= in a sports game) **2** [only before noun] (*technical*) located in front, especially on a ship, plane or other vehicle: *the forward cabins* ◇ *A bolt may have fallen off the plane's forward door.* **3** relating to the future: *the forward movement of history* ◇ *A little* ***forward planning*** *at the outset can save you a lot of expense.* ◇ *The plans are still* ***no further forward*** *than they were last month.* **4** behaving towards sb in a manner which is too confident or too informal: *I hope you don't think I'm being too forward.* ➲ compare BACKWARD

■ ***verb*** **1** (*formal*) to send or pass goods or information to sb: **~ sth to sb** *We will be forwarding our new catalogue to you next week.* ◇ **~ sb sth** *We will be forwarding you our new catalogue next week.* ◇ **~ sth** *to forward a request/complaint/proposal* **2** to send a letter, etc. received at the address a person used to live at to their new address **SYN** **send on**: **~ sth (to sb)** *Could you forward any mail to us in New York?* ◇ **~ (sth)** *I put 'please forward' on the envelope.* **3** **~ sth** (*formal*) to help to improve or develop sth **SYN** **further**: *He saw the assignment as a way to forward his career.* ➲ see also FAST-FORWARD

■ ***noun*** an attacking player whose position is near the front of a team in some sports ➲ compare BACK

ˈforwarding address *noun* a new address to which letters should be sent on from an old address that sb has moved away from

ˈforward-looking *adj.* (*approving*) planning for the future; willing to consider modern ideas and methods

for·ward·ness /ˈfɔːwədnəs; *NAmE* ˈfɔːrwərd-/ *noun* [U] behaviour that is too confident or too informal

ˈforward slash *noun* the symbol (/) used in computer commands and in Internet addresses to separate the different parts ➲ compare BACKSLASH

for·went *past tense* of FORGO

fos·sick /ˈfɒsɪk; *NAmE* ˈfɑːs-/ *verb* (*AustralE, NZE, informal*) **1** [I] **~ (through sth)** to search through sth: *He spent ages fossicking through the documents.* **2** [I] to search for gold in mines that are no longer used

fos·sil /ˈfɒsl; *NAmE* ˈfɑːsl/ *noun* **1** the remains of an animal or a plant which have become hard and turned into rock: *fossils over two million years old* **2** (*informal, disapproving*) an old person, especially one who is unable to accept new ideas or adapt to changes

ˈfossil fuel *noun* [C, U] fuel such as coal or oil, that was formed over millions of years from the remains of animals or plants ➲ compare BIOMASS ➲ VISUAL VOCAB page V6

fos·sil·ize (*BrE* also **-ise**) /ˈfɒsəlaɪz; *NAmE* ˈfɑːs-/ *verb* **1** [T, usually passive, I] **~ (sth)** to become or make sth become a fossil: *fossilized bones* **2** [I, T] **~ (sb/sth)** (*disapproving*) to become, or make sb/sth become, fixed and unable to change or develop ▶ **fos·sil·iza·tion, -isa·tion** /ˌfɒsəlaɪˈzeɪʃn; *NAmE* ˌfɑːsələˈz-/ *noun* [U]

fos·ter /ˈfɒstə(r); *NAmE* ˈfɔːs-; ˈfɑːs-/ *verb, adj.*

■ ***verb*** **1** [T] **~ sth** to encourage sth to develop **SYN** **encourage, promote**: *The club's aim is to foster better relations within the community.* **2** [T, I] **~ (sb)** (*especially BrE*) to take another person's child into your home for a period of time, without becoming his or her legal parents: *They have fostered over 60 children during the past ten years.* ◇ *We couldn't adopt a child, so we decided to foster.* ➲ COLLOCATIONS at CHILD ➲ compare ADOPT

■ ***adj.*** [only before noun] used with some nouns in connection with the fostering of a child: *a* ***foster mother/father/family*** ◇ ***foster parents*** ◇ *a* ***foster child*** ◇ *a* ***foster home*** ◇ ***foster care***

fought *past tense, past part.* of FIGHT

foul /faʊl/ *adj., verb, noun*

■ ***adj.*** (**foul·er, foul·est**) **1** dirty and smelling bad: ***foul air/breath*** ◇ *a* ***foul-smelling*** *prison* ➲ SYNONYMS at DISGUSTING **2** (*especially BrE*) very unpleasant; very bad: *She's in a* ***foul mood.*** ◇ *His boss has a* ***foul temper.*** ◇ *This tastes foul.* **3** (of language) including rude words and swearing **SYN** **offensive**: ***foul language*** ◇ *I'm sick of her* ***foul mouth*** (= habit of swearing). ◇ *He called her the foulest names imaginable.* **4** (of weather) very bad, with strong winds and rain: *a foul night* **5** (*literary*) very evil or cruel **SYN** **abominable**: *a* ***foul crime/murder*** ▶ **foul·ly** /ˈfaʊlli/ *adv.*: *He swore foully.* ◇ *She had been foully murdered during the night.* **foul·ness** *noun* [U]: *The air was heavy with the stink of damp and foulness.*

IDM **fall foul of ˈsb/ˈsth** to get into trouble with a person or an organization because of doing sth wrong or illegal: *to fall foul of the law* ➲ more at CRY *v.*, FAIR *adj.*

■ ***verb*** **1** [T] **~ sb** (in sport) to do sth to another player that is against the rules of the game: *He was fouled inside the penalty area.* **2** [I, T] **~ (sth)** (in BASEBALL) to hit the ball outside the playing area **3** [T] **~ sth** to make sth dirty, especially with waste matter from the body: *Do not permit your dog to foul the grass.* **4** [T, I] to become caught or twisted in sth and stop it working or moving: **~ sth (up)** *The rope fouled the propeller.* ◇ **~ (up)** *A rope fouled up* (= became twisted) *as we pulled the sail down.*

PHR V **ˌfoul ˈup** (*informal*) to make a lot of mistakes; to do sth badly: *I've fouled up badly again, haven't I?* ➲ related noun FOUL-UP **ˌfoul sth↔ˈup** (*informal*) to spoil sth, especially by doing sth wrong ➲ related noun FOUL-UP

■ ***noun*** (in sport) an action that is against the rules of the game: *It was a clear foul by Ford on the goalkeeper.* ◇ (*NAmE*) *to hit a foul* (= in BASEBALL, a ball that is too far left or right, outside the lines that mark the side of the field) ➲ see also PROFESSIONAL FOUL

ˈfoul ball *noun* (in BASEBALL) a hit that goes outside the allowed area

ˈfoul line *noun* **1** (in BASEBALL) either of two lines that show the area inside which the ball must be hit **2** (in BASKETBALL) a line from which a player is allowed to try to throw the ball into the BASKET after a foul

ˌfoul-ˈmouthed *adj.* using rude, offensive language: *a foul-mouthed racist*

ˌfoul ˈplay *noun* [U] **1** criminal or violent activity that causes sb's death: *Police immediately began an investigation, but did not suspect foul play* (= did not suspect that the person had been murdered). **2** (*BrE*) dishonest or unfair behaviour, especially during a sports game

ˈfoul-up *noun* (*informal*) a problem caused by bad organization or a stupid mistake

found **AW** /faʊnd/ *verb* **1** **~ sth** to start sth, such as an organization or an institution, especially by providing money **SYN** **establish**: *to found a club/company* ◇ *Her family founded the college in 1895.* **2** **~ sth** to be the first to start building and living in a town or country: *The town was founded by English settlers in 1790.* **3** [usually passive] **~ sth (on sth)** to base sth on sth: *Their marriage was founded on love and mutual respect.* ➲ see also ILL-FOUNDED, UNFOUNDED, WELL FOUNDED **4** **~ sth** (*technical*) to melt metal and pour it into a MOULD; to make objects using this process ➲ see also FIND *v.*

foun·da·tion **AW** /faʊnˈdeɪʃn/ *noun* **1** [C, usually pl.] a layer of bricks, concrete, etc. that forms the solid underground base of a building: *The builders are now beginning* ***to lay the foundations*** *of the new school.* ◇ *The explosion shook the foundations of the houses nearby.* ➲ SYNONYMS at BOTTOM **2** [C, U] a principle, an idea or a fact that sth is based on and that it grows from: *Respect and friendship provide a* ***solid foundation*** *for marriage.* ◇ *The rumour is totally* ***without foundation*** (= not based on any facts). ◇ *These stories* ***have no foundation*** (= are not based on any facts). ➲ SYNONYMS at BASIS **3** [C] an organization that is established to provide money for a particular purpose, for example for scientific research or charity: *The money will go to the San Francisco AIDS Foundation.* **4** [U] the act of starting a new institution or organization SYN **establishment**: *The organization has grown enormously since its foundation in 1955.* **5** [U] a skin-coloured cream that is put on the face underneath other make-up ➲ VISUAL VOCAB page V49

IDM **shake/rock the 'foundations of sth | shake/rock sth to its 'foundations** to cause people to question their basic beliefs about sth: *This issue has shaken the foundations of French politics.*

foun'dation course *noun* (*BrE*) a general course at a college that prepares students for longer or more difficult courses

foun'dation stone *noun* a large block of stone that is put at the base of an important new public building in a special ceremony: *to lay the foundation stone of the new museum*

foun·der /'faʊndə(r)/ *noun, verb*

▪ ***noun*** a person who starts an organization, institution, etc. or causes sth to be built: *the founder and president of the company*

▪ ***verb*** (*formal*) **1** [I] **~ (on sth)** (of a plan, etc.) to fail because of a particular problem or difficulty: *The peace talks foundered on a basic lack of trust.* **2** [I] **~ (on sth)** (of a ship) to fill with water and sink: *Our boat foundered on a reef.*

ˌfounder 'member (*BrE*) (*NAmE* **ˌcharter 'member**) *noun* one of the first members of a society, an organization, etc, especially one who helped start it

ˌfounding 'father *noun* **1** (*formal*) a person who starts or develops a new movement, institution or idea **2 Founding Father** a member of the group of people who wrote the Constitution of the US in 1787

found·ling /'faʊndlɪŋ/ *noun* (*old-fashioned*) a baby who has been left by its parents and who is found and taken care of by sb else

foun·dry /'faʊndri/ *noun* (*pl.* **-ies**) a factory where metal or glass is melted and made into different shapes or objects: *an iron foundry* ◇ *foundry workers* ➲ SYNONYMS at FACTORY

fount /faʊnt/ *noun* **~ (of sth)** (*literary* or *humorous*) the place where sth important comes from SYN **source**: *She treats him as if he were* ***the fount of all knowledge.***

foun·tain /'faʊntən; *NAmE* 'faʊntn/ *noun* **1** a structure from which water is sent up into the air by a PUMP, used to decorate parks and gardens/yards ➲ VISUAL VOCAB page V2 ➲ see also DRINKING FOUNTAIN **2** a strong flow of liquid or of another substance that is forced into the air: *The amplifier exploded in a fountain of sparks.* **3** a rich source or supply of sth: *Tourism is a fountain of wealth for the city.*

foun·tain·head /'faʊntənhed; *NAmE* -tnhed/ *noun* (*literary*) a source or origin

'fountain pen *noun* a pen with a container that you fill with ink that flows to a NIB ➲ VISUAL VOCAB page V56

four /fɔː(r)/

1 *number* 4 HELP There are examples of how to use numbers at the entry for **five**. **2** *noun* a group of four people or things: *to* ***make up a four*** *at tennis* ◇ *a coach and four* (= four horses) **3** *noun* (in CRICKET) a shot that scores four RUNS **4** *noun* a team of four people who ROW a long narrow boat in races; the boat that they row

IDM **on all 'fours** (of a person) bent over with hands and knees on the ground: *We were crawling around on all fours.* **these four 'walls** used when you are talking about keeping sth secret: *Don't let this go further than these four walls* (= Don't tell anyone else who is not in the room now).

ˌfour-by-'four (also **4x4**) *noun* a vehicle with FOUR-WHEEL DRIVE (= a system in which power is given to all four wheels)

ˌfour-colour 'process *noun* (*technical*) a way of reproducing natural colours in photographs and printing using COLOUR SEPARATION

ˌfour-di'mension·al *adj.* having four DIMENSIONS, usually length, width, depth, and time

four·fold /'fɔːfəʊld; *NAmE* 'fɔːrfoʊld/ *adj., adv.* ➲ -FOLD

ˌfour-letter 'word *noun* a short word that is considered rude or offensive, especially because it refers to sex or other functions of the body SYN **swear word**

ˌfour-poster 'bed (also **ˌfour-'poster**) *noun* a large bed with a tall post at each of the four corners, a cover over the top and curtains around the sides ➲ VISUAL VOCAB page V20

four·some /'fɔːsəm; *NAmE* 'fɔːrsəm/ *noun* [C+sing./pl. v.] a group of four people taking part in a social activity or sport together: *Can you* ***make up a foursome*** *for tennis tomorrow?*

ˌfour-'square *adj.* **1** (of a building) square in shape, solid and strong **2** (of a person) firm, steady and determined ▸ **ˌfour-'square** *adv.*: *I stand four-square with the President on this issue.*

'four-star *adj.* [usually before noun] **1** having four stars in a system that measures quality. The highest quality is shown by either four or five stars: *a four-star hotel* **2** (*NAmE*) having the second-highest military rank, and wearing a uniform that has four stars on it: *a four-star general*

'four-stroke *adj.* (*technical*) (of an engine or vehicle) with a PISTON that makes four up and down movements in each power CYCLE ➲ compare TWO-STROKE

four·teen /ˌfɔː'tiːn; *NAmE* ˌfɔːr't-/ *number* 14 ▸ **four·teenth** /ˌfɔː'tiːnθ; *NAmE* ˌfɔːr't-/ *ordinal number, noun* HELP There are examples of how to use ordinal numbers at the entry for **fifth**.

the ˌFourteenth A'mendment *noun* [sing.] a change made to the US Constitution in 1866 that gave all Americans equal rights and allowed former SLAVES to become citizens

fourth /fɔːθ; *NAmE* fɔːrθ/ *ordinal number, noun*

▪ ***ordinal number*** 4th HELP There are examples of how to use ordinal numbers at the entry for **fifth**.

▪ ***noun*** (*especially NAmE*) = QUARTER

the ˌfourth di'mension *noun* [sing.] **1** (used by scientists and writers of SCIENCE FICTION) time **2** an experience that is outside normal human experience

the ˌfourth e'state *noun* [sing.] newspapers and journalists in general and the political influence that they have SYN **the press**

fourth·ly /'fɔːθli; *NAmE* 'fɔːrθ-/ *adv.* used to introduce the fourth of a list of points you want to make in a speech or piece of writing

the ˌFourth of Ju'ly *noun* [sing.] a national holiday in the US when people celebrate the anniversary of the Declaration of Independence in 1776 ➲ see also INDEPENDENCE DAY

ˌfour-way 'stop *noun* (*SAfrE*) a place where two roads cross each other, at which there are signs indicating that vehicles must stop before continuing

ˌfour-wheel 'drive (*especially NAmE* **ˌall-wheel 'drive**) *noun* [U, C] a system in which power is applied to all four wheels of a vehicle, making it easier to control; a vehicle with this system: *a car with four-wheel drive* ◇ *We rented a four-wheel drive to get around the island.* ➲ VISUAL VOCAB page V42 ➲ see also FOUR-BY-FOUR

ˌfour-'wheeler (*NAmE*) (*BrE* **'quad bike**) *noun* a motorcycle with four large wheels, used for riding over rough ground, often for fun ➲ see also ATV

fowl /faʊl/ *noun* **1** [C, U] (*pl.* **fowl** or **fowls**) a bird that is kept for its meat and eggs, for example a chicken: *fowl such as turkeys and ducks* **2** [C] (*old use*) any bird ➲ see also GUINEAFOWL, WATERFOWL, WILDFOWL IDM see FISH *n.*

fox /fɒks; *NAmE* fɑːks/ *noun, verb*
■ ***noun* 1** [C] a wild animal of the dog family, with reddish-brown fur, a pointed face and a thick heavy tail ➲ see also FLYING FOX, VIXEN **2** [U] the skin and fur of the fox, used to make coats, etc. **3** [C] (often *disapproving*) a person who is clever and able to get what they want by influencing or tricking other people: *He's a wily old fox.* **4** [C] (*informal*) an attractive young woman
■ ***verb* ~ sb** (*informal, especially BrE*) to be too difficult for sb to understand or solve; to trick or confuse sb: *The last question foxed even our panel of experts.*

foxed /fɒkst; *NAmE* fɑːkst/ *adj.* **1** unable to understand or solve sth: *I must admit I'm completely foxed.* **2** (of the paper of old books or prints) covered with brown spots

fox·glove /ˈfɒksglʌv; *NAmE* ˈfɑːks-/ *noun* [C, U] a tall plant with purple or white flowers shaped like bells growing up its STEM

fox·hole /ˈfɒkshəʊl; *NAmE* ˈfɑːkshoʊl/ *noun* a hole in the ground that soldiers use as a shelter against the enemy or as a place to fire back from ➲ compare HOLE

fox·hound /ˈfɒkshaʊnd; *NAmE* ˈfɑːks-/ *noun* a dog with a very good sense of smell, that is trained to hunt FOXES

ˈfox-hunting (*BrE* also **hunt·ing**) *noun* [U] a sport in which FOXES are hunted by specially trained dogs and by people on horses. Fox-hunting with dogs is now illegal in the UK: *to go fox-hunting* ▶ **ˈfox hunt** *noun*: *a ban on fox hunts*

ˌfox ˈterrier *noun* a small dog with short hair

fox·trot /ˈfɒkstrɒt; *NAmE* ˈfɑːkstrɑːt/ *noun* a formal dance for two people together, with both small fast steps and longer slow ones; a piece of music for this dance

foxy /ˈfɒksi; *NAmE* ˈfɑːksi/ *adj.* **1** like a FOX in appearance **2** (*informal, especially NAmE*) (of a woman) sexually attractive SYN **sexy 3** clever at tricking others SYN **cunning**

foyer /ˈfɔɪeɪ; *NAmE* ˈfɔɪər/ *noun* **1** a large open space inside the entrance of a theatre or hotel where people can meet or wait SYN **lobby 2** (*NAmE*) an entrance hall in a private house or flat/apartment

Fr (also **Fr.** especially in *NAmE*) *abbr.* Father (used in front of the name of some Christian priests): *Fr (Paul) O'Connor*

fra·cas /ˈfrækɑː; *NAmE* ˈfreɪkəs/ *noun* (*pl.* **fra·cas** /-kɑːz/, *NAmE* **fra·cases**) [usually sing.] a noisy argument or fight, usually involving several people

frac·tal /ˈfræktl/ *noun* (*mathematics, physics*) a curve or pattern that includes a smaller curve or pattern which has exactly the same shape

frac·tion /ˈfrækʃn/ *noun* **1** a small part or amount of sth: *Only a small fraction of a bank's total deposits will be withdrawn at any one time.* ◇ *She hesitated for the merest fraction of a second.* HELP If **fraction** is used with a plural noun, the verb is usually plural: *Only a fraction of cars in the UK* ***use*** *leaded petrol.* If it is used with a singular noun that represents a group of people, the verb can be singular or plural in *BrE*, but is usually singular in *NAmE*: *A tiny fraction of the population never* ***vote/votes***. **2** a division of a number, for example ⅝ ➲ LANGUAGE BANK at PROPORTION ➲ compare INTEGER ➲ see also VULGAR FRACTION

frac·tion·al /ˈfrækʃənl/ *adj.* **1** (*formal*) very small; not important SYN **minimal**: *a fractional decline in earnings* **2** (*mathematics*) of or in fractions: *a fractional equation*

ˌfractional distilˈlation *noun* [U] (*chemistry*) the process of separating the parts of a liquid mixture by heating it. As the temperature goes up, each part in turn becomes a gas, which then cools as it moves up a tube and can be collected as a liquid.

frac·tion·al·ly /ˈfrækʃənəli/ *adv.* to a very small degree: *He was just fractionally ahead at the finishing line.*

frac·tious /ˈfrækʃəs/ *adj.* (*especially BrE*) **1** bad-tempered or easily upset, especially by small things SYN **irritable**: *Children often get fractious and tearful when tired.* **2** (*formal*) making trouble and complaining: *The six fractious republics are demanding autonomy.*

frac·ture /ˈfræktʃə(r)/ *noun, verb*
■ ***noun* 1** [C] a break in a bone or other hard material: *a fracture of the leg/skull* ◇ *a* ***compound/simple fracture*** (= one in which the broken bone comes/does not come through the skin) ➲ COLLOCATIONS at INJURY ➲ see also GREENSTICK FRACTURE **2** [U] the fact of sth breaking, especially a bone: *Old people's bones are more prone to fracture.*
■ ***verb* 1** [I, T] to break or crack; to make sth break or crack: *His leg fractured in two places.* ◇ **~ sth** *She fell and fractured her skull.* ◇ *a fractured pipeline* **2** [I, T] (*formal*) (of a society, an organization, etc.) to split into several parts so that it no longer functions or exists; to split a society or an organization, etc. in this way: *Many people predicted that the party would fracture and split.* ◇ **~ sth (into sth)** *The company was fractured into several smaller groups.* ▶ **frac·tured** *adj.* [usually before noun]: *He suffered a badly fractured arm.* ◇ (*figurative*) *They spoke a sort of fractured German.*

frae·nu·lum (*BrE*) = FRENULUM

fra·gile /ˈfrædʒaɪl; *NAmE* -dʒl/ *adj.* **1** easily broken or damaged: *fragile china/glass/bones* **2** weak and uncertain; easily destroyed or spoilt: *a* ***fragile alliance/ceasefire/relationship*** ◇ *The economy remains extremely fragile.* **3** delicate and often beautiful: *fragile beauty* ◇ *The woman's fragile face broke into a smile.* **4** not strong and likely to become ill/sick: *Her father is now 86 and in fragile health.* ◇ (*BrE, informal*) *I'm feeling a bit fragile after last night* (= not well, perhaps because of drinking too much alcohol). ▶ **fra·gil·ity** /frəˈdʒɪləti/ *noun* [U]: *the fragility of the human body*

frag·ment *noun, verb*
■ ***noun*** /ˈfrægmənt/ a small part of sth that has broken off or comes from sth larger: *Police found fragments of glass near the scene.* ◇ *The shattered vase lay in fragments on the floor.* ◇ *I overheard a fragment of their conversation.*
■ ***verb*** /frægˈment/ [I, T] **~ (sth)** to break or make sth break into small pieces or parts ▶ **frag·men·ta·tion** /ˌfrægmenˈteɪʃn/ *noun* [U]: *the fragmentation of the country into small independent states* **frag·ment·ed** *adj.*: *a fragmented society*

frag·men·tary /ˈfrægməntri; *NAmE* -teri/ *adj.* (*formal*) made of small parts that are not connected or complete: *There is only fragmentary evidence to support this theory.*

ˌfragmenˈtation grenade (also **ˌfragmenˈtation bomb**) *noun* a bomb that breaks into very small pieces when it explodes

fra·grance /ˈfreɪgrəns/ *noun* **1** [C, U] a pleasant smell: *The bath oil comes in various fragrances.* **2** [C] a liquid that you put on your skin in order to make yourself smell nice SYN **perfume**: *an exciting new fragrance from Dior*

fra·grant /ˈfreɪgrənt/ *adj.* having a pleasant smell: *fragrant herbs/flowers/oils* ◇ *The air was fragrant with scents from the sea and the hills.* ▶ **fra·grant·ly** *adv.*

fraidy cat /ˈfreɪdi kæt/ *noun* (*US, informal, disapproving*) = SCAREDY-CAT

frail /freɪl/ *adj.* (**frail·er**, **frail·est**) **1** (especially of an old person) physically weak and thin: *Mother was becoming too frail to live alone.* **2** weak; easily damaged or broken: *the frail stems of the flowers* ◇ *Human nature is frail.*

frailty /ˈfreɪlti/ *noun* (*pl.* **-ies**) **1** [U] weakness and poor health: *Increasing frailty meant that she was more and more confined to bed.* **2** [U, C] (*formal*) weakness in a person's character or moral standards: *human frailty* ◇ *the frailties of human nature*

frame O-w /freɪm/ *noun, verb*
■ ***noun***
▸ BORDER **1** O-w [C] a strong border or structure of wood, metal, etc. that holds a picture, door, piece of glass, etc. in position: *a picture frame* ◇ *aluminium window frames* ➲ picture at EDGE
▸ STRUCTURE **2** O-w [C] the supporting structure of a piece of furniture, a building, a vehicle, etc. that gives it its shape: *the frame of an aircraft/a car/a bicycle* ➲ VISUAL VOCAB page V41 ➲ see also CLIMBING FRAME
▸ OF GLASSES **3** [C, usually pl.] a structure of plastic or metal that holds the LENSES in a pair of glasses: *gold-rimmed frames*
▸ PERSON/ANIMAL'S BODY **4** [C, usually sing.] the form or struc-

F

ture of a person or animal's body: *to have a* ***small/slender/large frame***
▸ GENERAL IDEAS **5** [sing.] the general ideas or structure that form the background to sth: *In this course we hope to look at literature in the frame of its social and historical context.* ➲ see also TIME FRAME
▸ OF FILM/MOVIE **6** [C] one of the single photographs that a film or video is made of
▸ OF PICTURE STORY **7** [C] a single picture in a COMIC STRIP
▸ COMPUTING **8** [C] one of the separate areas on an Internet page that you can SCROLL through (= read by using the mouse to move the text up or down)
▸ IN GARDEN **9** [C] = COLD FRAME
▸ IN SNOOKER/BOWLING **10** [C] a single section of play in the game of SNOOKER, etc, or in BOWLING

IDM **be in/out of the 'frame** be taking part/not taking part in sth: *We won our match, so we're still in the frame for the championship.*

■ ***verb***
▸ MAKE BORDER **1** 🔑 [usually passive] **~ sth** to put or make a frame or border around sth: *The photograph had been framed.* ◇ *Her blonde hair framed her face.* ◇ *He stood there, head back, framed against the blue sky.*
▸ PRODUCE FALSE EVIDENCE **2** [usually passive] **~ sb** (**for sth**) to produce false evidence against an innocent person so that people think he or she is guilty SYN **fit up**: *He says he was framed.*
▸ DEVELOP PLAN/SYSTEM **3 ~ sth** (*formal*) to create and develop sth such as a plan, a system or a set of rules
▸ EXPRESS STH **4 ~ sth** to express sth in a particular way: *You'll have to be careful how you frame the question.*
▸ **framed** *adj.* (often in compounds): *a framed photograph* ◇ *a timber-framed house* (= with a supporting structure of wood)

frames

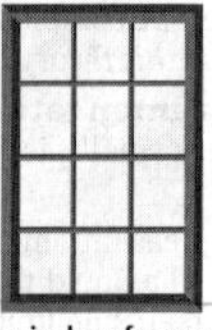
window frame

picture frame

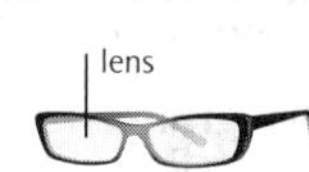

frames

bicycle frame

cold frame

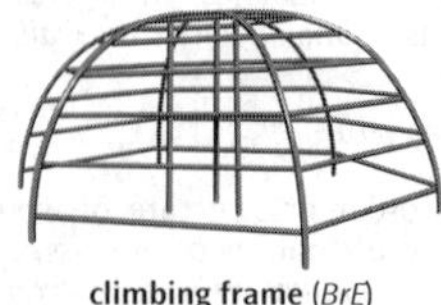
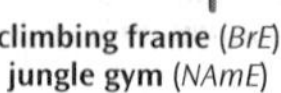
climbing frame (*BrE*)
jungle gym (*NAmE*)

Zimmer frame™ (*BrE*)
walker (*NAmE*)

ˌframe of 'mind *noun* [sing.] the way you feel or think about sth at a particular time: *We'll discuss this when you're in a better frame of mind.*

ˌframe of 'reference *noun* (*pl.* **frames of reference**) a particular set of beliefs, ideas or experiences that affects how a person understands or judges sth

'frame tent (*BrE*) (*NAmE* **'wall tent**) *noun* a large tent with a roof and walls that do not slope much ➲ compare DOME TENT, RIDGE TENT

'frame-up *noun* (*informal*) a situation in which false evidence is produced in order to make people think that an innocent person is guilty of a crime

frame·work AW /ˈfreɪmwɜːk; *NAmE* -wɜːrk/ *noun* **1** the parts of a building or an object that support its weight and give it shape ➲ SYNONYMS at STRUCTURE **2 ~** (**of/for sth**) a set of beliefs, ideas or rules that is used as the basis for making judgements, decisions, etc: *The report provides a framework for further research.* ➲ COLLOCATIONS at SCIENTIFIC **3** the structure of a particular system: *We need to establish a legal framework for the protection of the environment.* ◇ *the basic framework of society*

franc /fræŋk/ *noun* the unit of money in Switzerland and several other countries (replaced in 2002 in France, Belgium and Luxembourg by the euro)

fran·chise /ˈfræntʃaɪz/ *noun, verb*
■ ***noun*** **1** [C, U] formal permission given by a company to sb who wants to sell its goods or services in a particular area; formal permission given by a government to sb who wants to operate a public service as a business: *a* ***franchise agreement/company*** ◇ *a catering/rail franchise* ◇ *In the reorganization, Southern Television lost their franchise.* ◇ *to operate a business* ***under franchise*** ➲ COLLOCATIONS at BUSINESS **2** [C] a business or service run under franchise: *They operate franchises in London and Paris.* ◇ *a burger franchise* **3** [U] (*formal*) the right to vote in a country's elections: *universal adult franchise* ➲ see also ENFRANCHISE
■ ***verb*** [usually passive] **~ sth** (**out**) (**to sb/sth**) to give or sell a franchise (1) to sb: *Catering has been franchised (out) to a private company.* ◇ *franchised restaurants* ▸ **fran·chis·ing** *noun* [U]

fran·chisee /ˌfræntʃaɪˈziː/ *noun* a person or company that has been given a franchise

fran·chiser (also **fran·chisor**) /ˈfræntʃaɪzə(r)/ *noun* a company or an organization that gives sb a franchise

Fran·cis·can /frænˈsɪskən/ *noun, adj.*
■ ***noun*** a member of a religious organization started in 1209 by St Francis of Assisi in Italy
■ ***adj.*** relating to St Francis or to this organization: *a Franciscan monk*

fran·cium /ˈfrænsiəm/ *noun* [U] (*symb.* **Fr**) a chemical element. Francium is a RADIOACTIVE metal.

Franco- /ˈfræŋkəʊ; *NAmE* ˈfræŋkoʊ/ *combining form* (in nouns and adjectives) French; France: *the Franco-Prussian War* ◇ *Francophile*

franco·phone /ˈfræŋkəfəʊn; *NAmE* -foʊn/ *adj.* [only before noun] speaking French as the main language ▸ **franco·phone** *noun*: *Canadian francophones*

fran·gi·pani /ˌfrændʒiˈpæni; -ˈpɑːni/ *noun* **1** [U, C] a tropical American tree or bush with groups of white, pink, or yellow flowers **2** [U] a PERFUME that is made from the frangipani plant

frank /fræŋk/ *adj., verb*
■ ***adj.*** (**frank·er**, **frank·est** HELP **more frank** is also common) honest and direct in what you say, sometimes in a way that other people might not like: *a full and frank discussion* ◇ *a frank admission of guilt* ◇ *He was very frank about his relationship with the actress.* ◇ ***To be frank with you,*** *I think your son has little chance of passing the exam.* ➲ SYNONYMS at HONEST ▸ **frank·ness** *noun* [U]: *They outlined their aims with disarming frankness.*
■ ***verb*** [often passive] **~ sth** to stamp a mark on an envelope, etc. to show that the cost of posting it has been paid or does not need to be paid

Fran·ken·food /ˈfræŋkənfuːd/ (also **'Frankenstein food**) *noun* [C, U] (*informal, disapproving*) food that has been GENETICALLY MODIFIED

Fran·ken·stein /ˈfræŋkənstaɪn/ *noun* (also **ˌFrankenstein's 'monster**, **ˌFrankenstein 'monster**) used to talk about sth that sb creates or invents that goes out of control and becomes dangerous, often destroying the person who created it ORIGIN From the novel *Frankenstein* by Mary Shelley in which a scientist called Frankenstein makes a creature from pieces of dead bodies and brings it to life.

frank·furt·er /ˈfræŋkfɜːtə(r); *NAmE* -fɜːrt-/ (*NAmE* also **wie·ner**, *informal* **wee·nie**) *noun* a long thin smoked SAUSAGE with a reddish-brown skin, often eaten in a long bread roll as a HOT DOG

frank·in·cense /ˈfræŋkɪnsens/ *noun* [U] a substance that is burnt to give a pleasant smell, especially during religious ceremonies

ˈfranking machine (*especially BrE*) (*NAmE* usually **ˈpostage meter**) *noun* a machine that prints an official mark on a letter to show that the cost of posting it has been paid, or does not need to be paid

frank·ly /ˈfræŋkli/ *adv.* **1** in an honest and direct way that people might not like: *He spoke frankly about the ordeal.* ◇ *They frankly admitted their responsibility.* **2** used to show that you are being honest about sth, even though people might not like what you are saying: *Frankly, I couldn't care less what happens to him.* ◇ ***Quite frankly,*** *I'm not surprised you failed.*

fran·tic /ˈfræntɪk/ *adj.* **1** done quickly and with a lot of activity, but in a way that is not very well organized **SYN** **hectic**: *a* ***frantic dash/search/struggle*** ◇ *They made* ***frantic attempts*** *to revive him.* ◇ *Things are frantic in the office right now.* **2** unable to control your emotions because you are extremely frightened or worried about sth **SYN** **beside yourself**: *frantic with worry* ◇ *Let's go back. Your parents must be* ***getting frantic*** *by now.* ◇ *The children are driving me frantic* (= making me very annoyed). ▸ **fran·tic·al·ly** /-kli/ *adv.*: *They worked frantically to finish on time.*

frappé /ˈfræpeɪ; *NAmE* fræˈpeɪ/ *adj.*, *noun* (from *French*)

■ ***adj.*** [after noun] (of drinks) served cold with a lot of ice: *coffee frappé*

■ ***noun*** a drink or sweet food served cold with very small pieces of ice

frat /fræt/ *noun* (*NAmE, informal*) = FRATERNITY (2): *a frat boy* (= a member of a fraternity)

fra·ter·nal /frəˈtɜːnl; *NAmE* -ˈtɜːrnl/ *adj.* [usually before noun] **1** connected with the relationship that exists between people or groups that share the same ideas or interests: *a fraternal organization/society* **2** connected with the relationship that exists between brothers: *fraternal rivalry* ▸ **fra·ter·nal·ly** *adv.*

fraˌternal ˈtwin (also **ˌnon-iˌdentical ˈtwin** (*technical* **ˌdizyˌgotic ˈtwin**) *noun* either of two children or animals born from the same mother at the same time but not from the same egg ➲ compare IDENTICAL TWIN, MONOZYGOTIC TWIN

fra·ter·nity /frəˈtɜːnəti; *NAmE* -ˈtɜːrn-/ *noun* (*pl.* -ies) **1** [C+sing./pl. v.] a group of people sharing the same profession, interests or beliefs: *members of* ***the medical/banking/racing, etc. fraternity*** **2** (also *NAmE informal* **frat**) [C] a club for a group of male students at an American college or university ➲ compare SORORITY **3** [U] (*formal*) a feeling of friendship and support that exists between the members of a group: *the ideals of liberty, equality and fraternity*

frat·er·nize (*BrE* also **-ise**) /ˈfrætənaɪz; *NAmE* -tərn-/ *verb* [I] **~ (with sb)** to behave in a friendly manner, especially towards sb that you are not supposed to be friendly with: *She was accused of fraternizing with the enemy.* ▸ **frat·er·niza·tion**, **-isa·tion** /ˌfrætənaɪˈzeɪʃn; *NAmE* -tərnəˈz-/ *noun* [U]

frat·ri·cide /ˈfrætrɪsaɪd/ *noun* [U, C] **1** (*formal*) the crime of killing your brother or sister; a person who is guilty of this crime ➲ compare MATRICIDE, PARRICIDE, PATRICIDE **2** the crime of killing people of your own country or group; a person who is guilty of this crime ▸ **frat·ri·cidal** /ˌfrætrɪˈsaɪdl/ *adj.*: *to be engaged in a fratricidal struggle*

fraud /frɔːd/ *noun* **1** [U, C] the crime of cheating sb in order to get money or goods illegally: *She was charged with credit card fraud.* ◇ *property that has been obtained by fraud* ◇ *a $100 million fraud* ➲ COLLOCATIONS at CRIME **2** [C] a person who pretends to have qualities, abilities, etc. that they do not really have in order to cheat other people: *He's nothing but a liar and a fraud.* ◇ *She felt a fraud accepting their sympathy* (= because she was not really sad). **3** [C] something that is not as good, useful, etc. as people claim it is

ˈfraud squad *noun* [sing.+ sing./pl. v.] (*BrE*) part of a police force that investigates fraud

fraud·ster /ˈfrɔːdstə(r)/ *noun* (*BrE*) a person who commits fraud

fraudu·lent /ˈfrɔːdjələnt; *NAmE* -dʒə-/ *adj.* (*formal*) intended to cheat sb, usually in order to make money illegally: *fraudulent advertising* ◇ *fraudulent insurance claims* ▸ **fraudu·lence** /ˈfrɔːdjələns; *NAmE* -dʒə-/ *noun* [U] **fraudu·lent·ly** /ˈfrɔːdjələntli; *NAmE* -dʒə-/ *adv.*

fraught /frɔːt/ *adj.* **1 ~ with sth** filled with sth unpleasant: *a situation* ***fraught with danger/difficulty/problems*** **2** (*especially BrE*) causing or feeling worry and anxiety **SYN** **tense**: *She looked/sounded fraught.* ◇ *There was a fraught silence.* ◇ *Things are as fraught as ever in the office.*

fray /freɪ/ *verb, noun*

■ ***verb*** **1** [I, T] if cloth **frays** or sth **frays** it, the threads in it start to come apart: *The cuffs of his shirt were fraying.* ◇ *This material frays easily.* ◇ **~ sth** *It was fashionable to fray the bottoms of your jeans.* **2** [I, T] **~ (sth)** if sb's nerves or TEMPER **frays** or sth **frays** them, the person starts to get irritated or annoyed: *As the debate went on, tempers began to fray.* ▸ **frayed** *adj.*: *frayed denim shorts* ◇ *Tempers were getting very frayed.*

IDM **ˌfray at/around the ˈedges/ˈseams** to start to come apart or to fail: *Support for the leader was fraying at the edges.*

■ ***noun*** **the fray** [sing.] a fight, a competition or an argument, especially one that is exciting or seen as a test of your ability: *They were ready for the fray.* ◇ *to* ***enter/join the fray*** ◇ *At 71, he has now retired from the political fray.*

fraz·zle /ˈfræzl/ *noun*

IDM **be burnt, worn, etc. to a ˈfrazzle** (*informal*) to be completely burnt/extremely tired

fraz·zled /ˈfræzld/ *adj.* (*informal*) tired and easily annoyed: *They finally arrived home, hot and frazzled.*

freak /friːk/ *noun, adj., verb*

■ ***noun*** **1** (*informal*) a person with a very strong interest in a particular subject: *a* ***health/fitness/jazz, etc. freak*** ➲ see also CONTROL FREAK **2** (*disapproving*) a person who is considered to be unusual because of the way they behave, look or think: *She was treated like a freak because she didn't want children.* ◇ *He's going out with a real freak.* **3** (also **ˌfreak of ˈnature**) (sometimes *offensive*) a person, an animal, a plant or a thing that is not physically normal **4** a very unusual and unexpected event: *By some* ***freak of fate*** *they all escaped without injury.*

■ ***adj.*** [only before noun] (of an event or the weather) very unusual and unexpected: *a* ***freak accident/storm/occurrence*** ◇ *freak weather conditions*

■ ***verb*** [I, T] (*informal*) if sb **freaks** or if sth **freaks** them, they react very strongly to sth that makes them suddenly feel shocked, surprised, frightened, etc: **~ (out)** *My parents really freaked when they saw my hair.* ◇ **~ sb (out)** *Snakes really freak me out.*

freak·ing /ˈfriːkɪŋ/ *adv., adj.* [only before noun] (*NAmE, taboo, slang*) a swear word that many people find offensive, used to emphasize a comment or an angry statement to avoid saying 'fucking'

freak·ish /ˈfriːkɪʃ/ *adj.* very strange, unusual or unexpected: *freakish weather/behaviour* ▸ **freak·ish·ly** *adv.*

ˈfreak show *noun* **1** a small show at a FAIR, where people pay to see people or animals with strange physical characteristics **2** (*disapproving*) an event that people watch because it is very strange

freaky /ˈfriːki/ *adj.* (*informal*) very strange or unusual

freckle /ˈfrekl/ *noun* [usually pl.] a small, pale brown spot on a person's skin, especially on their face, caused by the sun ➲ compare MOLE ▸ **freckled** /ˈfrekld/ *adj.*: *a freckled face/schoolgirl*

F

free 🔑 /friː/ *adj., verb, adv.*
■ ***adj.*** (freer /ˈfriːə(r)/, freest /ˈfriːɪst/)
▸ NOT CONTROLLED **1** 🔑 not under the control or in the power of sb else; able to do what you want: *I have no ambitions other than to have a happy life and be free.* ◇ *Students have a* ***free choice*** *of courses in their final year.* ◇ **~ to do sth** *You are free to come and go as you please.* ◇ (*informal*) *'Can I use the phone?' 'Please,* ***feel free*** (= of course you can use it).' **2** 🔑 not restricted or controlled by anyone else; able to do or say what you want: *A true democracy complete with* ***free speech*** *and a free press was called for.* ◇ *the country's first free election* ◇ *They gave me free access to all the files.*
▸ NOT PRISONER **3** 🔑 (of a person) not a prisoner or SLAVE: *He walked out of jail* ***a free man.***
▸ ANIMAL/BIRD **4** 🔑 not tied up or in a CAGE: *The researchers* ***set*** *the birds* ***free.***
▸ NO PAYMENT **5** 🔑 costing nothing: *Admission is free.* ◇ ***free samples/tickets/advice*** ◇ *We're offering a fabulous* ***free gift*** *with each copy you buy.* ◇ *You can't expect people to work* ***for free*** (= without payment).
▸ NOT BLOCKED **6** 🔑 clear; not blocked: *Ensure there is a free flow of air around the machine.*
▸ WITHOUT STH **7** 🔑 **~ from/of sth** not containing or affected by sth harmful or unpleasant: *free from difficulty/doubt/fear* ◇ *free from artificial colours and flavourings* ◇ *It was several weeks before he was completely free of pain.* **8** 🔑 **-free** (in adjectives) without the thing mentioned: *virtually fat-free yogurt* ◇ *tax-free earnings* ◇ *a trouble-free life*
▸ NOT ATTACHED/TRAPPED **9** 🔑 **~ (of sth)** not attached to sth or trapped by sth: *Pull gently on the free end of the rope.* ◇ *They had to be* ***cut free*** *from their car after the accident.* ◇ *She finally managed to pull herself free.*
▸ NOT BEING USED **10** 🔑 not being used: *He held out his free hand and I took it.* ◇ *Is this seat free?*
▸ NOT BUSY **11** 🔑 **~ (for sth)** (of a person or time) without particular plans or arrangements; not busy: *If Sarah is free for lunch I'll take her out.* ◇ *Keep Friday night free for my party.* ◇ *What do you like to do in your* ***free time*** (= when you are not working)?
▸ READY TO GIVE **12 ~ with sth** (often *disapproving*) ready to give sth, especially when it is not wanted: *He's too free with his opinions.*
▸ TRANSLATION **13** a **free** translation is not exact but gives the general meaning ➲ compare LITERAL
IDM **free and ˈeasy** informal; relaxed: *Life was never going to be so free and easy again.* **get, have, etc. a free ˈhand** to get, have, etc. the opportunity to do what you want to do and to make your own decisions: *I was given a free hand in designing the syllabus.* **get, take, etc. a free ˈride** to get or take sth without paying because sb else is paying for it **it's a free ˈcountry** (*informal*) used as a reply when sb suggests that you should not do sth: *It's a free country; I'll say what I like!* **there's no such ˌthing as a free ˈlunch** (*informal*) used to say that it is not possible to get sth for nothing ➲ more at HOME *adv.*, REIN *n.*
■ ***verb***
▸ PRISONER **1** 🔑 **~ sb (from sth)** to allow sb to leave prison or somewhere they have been kept against their will **SYN** **release**: *By the end of May nearly 100 of an estimated 2 000 political prisoners had been freed.* ◇ *The hijackers agreed to free a further ten hostages.*
▸ SB/STH TRAPPED **2** 🔑 **~ sb/sth/yourself (from sth)** to move sb/sth that is caught or fixed on sth **SYN** **release**: *Three people were freed from the wreckage.* ◇ *She struggled to free herself.*
▸ REMOVE STH **3** 🔑 **~ sb/sth of/from sb/sth** to remove sth that is unpleasant or not wanted from sb/sth **SYN** **rid**: *These exercises help free the body of tension.* ◇ *The police are determined to free the town of violent crime.* ◇ *The centre aims to free young people from dependency on drugs.*
▸ MAKE AVAILABLE **4 ~ sb/sth (up)** to make sb/sth available for a particular purpose: *We freed time each week for a project meeting.* ◇ *The government has promised to free up more resources for education.* **5 ~ sb to do sth** to give sb the extra time to do sth that they want to do: *Winning the prize freed him to paint full-time.*
■ ***adv.***
▸ WITHOUT PAYMENT **1** 🔑 (also ˌ**free of ˈcharge**) without payment: *Children under five travel free.*
▸ NOT TRAPPED **2** 🔑 away from or out of a position in which sb/sth is stuck or trapped: *The wagon broke free from the train.* ➲ see also SCOT-FREE
IDM **make free with ˈsth** (*disapproving*) to use sth a lot, even though it does not belong to you **run ˈfree** (of an animal) to be allowed to go where it likes; not tied to anything or kept in a CAGE ➲ more at WALK *v.*

ˌ**free ˈagent** *noun* a person who can do whatever they want because they are not responsible to or for anyone else

free·base /ˈfriːbeɪs/ *noun* [U] (*slang*) a specially prepared form of the powerful illegal drug COCAINE

free·bas·ing /ˈfriːbeɪsɪŋ/ *noun* [U] (*slang*) the activity of smoking freebase

free·bie /ˈfriːbi/ *noun* (*informal*) something that is given to sb without payment, usually by a company: *He took all the freebies that were on offer.* ◇ *a freebie holiday*

free·boot·er /ˈfriːbuːtə(r)/ *noun* a person who takes part in a war in order to steal goods and money ▸ **free·boot·ing** *adj., noun* [U]

free·born /ˈfriːbɔːn; *NAmE* -bɔːrn/ *adj.* [only before noun] (*formal*) not born as a SLAVE

ˌ**Free ˈChurch** *noun* a Christian Church that does not belong to the established Church in a particular country

free·dom 🔑 /ˈfriːdəm/ *noun*
1 🔑 [U, C] **~ (of sth)** the right to do or say what you want without anyone stopping you: ***freedom of speech/thought/expression/worship*** ◇ *a threat to* ***press/academic, etc. freedom*** ◇ *rights and freedoms guaranteed by the constitution* **2** 🔑 [U, sing.] the state of being able to do what you want, without anything stopping you: **~ (of sth)** ***freedom of action/choice*** ◇ *Thanks to the automobile, Americans soon had a freedom of movement previously unknown.* ◇ **~ (to do sth)** *complete freedom to do as you wish* **3** 🔑 [U] the state of not being a prisoner or SLAVE: *He finally won his freedom after twenty years in jail.* **4** 🔑 [U] **~ from sth** the state of not being affected by the thing mentioned: ***freedom from fear/pain/hunger, etc.*** **5** [sing.] **the ~ of sth** permission to use sth without restriction: *I was given the freedom of the whole house.*
IDM **the freedom of the ˈcity** (in Britain) an honour that is given to sb by a city as a reward for work they have done ➲ see also FREEMAN **IDM** see MANOEUVRE *n.*

ˈ**freedom fighter** *noun* a name used to describe a person who uses violence to try to remove a government from power, by people who support this ➲ compare GUERRILLA

ˌ**freedom of asˈsembly** *noun* [U] the right to have public meetings which is guaranteed by law in the US

ˌ**freedom of associˈation** *noun* [U] the right to meet people and to form organizations without needing permission from the government

ˌ**freedom of inforˈmation** *noun* [U] the right to see any information that a government has about people and organizations

ˌ**free ˈenterprise** *noun* [U] an economic system in which private businesses compete with each other without much government control ➲ compare PRIVATE ENTERPRISE

ˌ**free ˈfall** *noun* [U] **1** the movement of an object or a person falling through the air without engine power or a PARACHUTE: *a free fall display* **2** a sudden drop in the value of sth that cannot be stopped: *Share prices have gone into free fall.*

ˌ**free-ˈfloating** *adj.* not attached to or controlled by anything: *a free-floating exchange rate*

Free·fone™ *noun* [U] = FREEPHONE

ˈ**free-for-all** *noun* [sing.] **1** a situation in which there are no rules or controls and everyone acts for their own advantage: *The lowering of trade barriers has led to a free-for-all among exporters.* **2** a noisy fight or argument in which a lot of people take part

ˈfree form (also ˌ**free ˈmorpheme**) *noun* (*linguistics*) a unit of language that can be used by itself: *The plural 's' is not a free form, as it must always be attached to a noun.*

ˈfree-form *adj.* [only before noun] (of art or music) not created according to standard forms or structures: *a free-form jazz improvisation*

free·gan /ˈfriːɡən/ *noun* a person who only eats food that they can get for free and that would otherwise be thrown out or wasted

free·hand /ˈfriːhænd/ *adj.* [only before noun] drawn without using a ruler or other instruments: *a freehand drawing* ▸ **free·hand** *adv.*: *to draw freehand*

free·hold /ˈfriːhəʊld; *NAmE* -hoʊld/ *noun* [C, U] (*law*) (*especially BrE*) the fact of owning a building or piece of land for a period of time that is not limited ▸ **free·hold** *adj.*: *a freehold property* **free·hold** *adv.*: *to buy a house freehold* ➲ compare LEASEHOLD

free·hold·er /ˈfriːhəʊldə(r); *NAmE* -hoʊld-/ *noun* (*law*) (*especially BrE*) a person who owns the freehold of a building or piece of land ➲ compare LEASEHOLDER

ˌ**free ˈhouse** *noun* (in Britain) a pub that can sell different types of beer because it is not owned and controlled by one particular BREWERY (= a company producing beer) ➲ compare TIED HOUSE

ˌ**free ˈkick** *noun* (in football (SOCCER) and RUGBY) an opportunity to kick the ball without any opposition, that is given to one team when the other team does sth wrong: *to take a free kick*

free·lance /ˈfriːlɑːns; *NAmE* -læns/ *adj., verb*

- ***adj.*** earning money by selling your work or services to several different organizations rather than being employed by one particular organization: *a freelance journalist* ◇ *freelance work* ➲ COLLOCATIONS at JOB ▸ **free·lance** *adv.*: (*especially BrE*) *I work freelance from home.*
- ***verb*** [I] to earn money by selling your work to several different organizations

free·lancer /ˈfriːlɑːnsə(r); *NAmE* -lænsər/ (also **free·lance**) *noun* a person who works freelance

free·load·er /ˈfriːləʊdə(r); *NAmE* -loʊd-/ *noun* (*informal, disapproving*) a person who is always accepting free food and accommodation from other people without giving them anything in exchange ▸ **free·load** *verb* [I] **free·load·ing** *adj., noun* [U]

ˌ**free ˈlove** *noun* [U] (*old-fashioned*) the practice of having sex without being married or having several sexual relationships at the same time

free·ly 🔑 /ˈfriːli/ *adv.*
1 🔑 without anyone trying to prevent or control sth: *the country's first freely elected president* ◇ *EU citizens can now travel freely between member states.* **2** 🔑 without anything stopping the movement or flow of sth: *When the gate is raised, the water can flow freely.* ◇ *Traffic is now moving more freely following an earlier accident.* ◇ *The book is now* ***freely available*** *in the shops* (= it is not difficult to get a copy). ◇ (*figurative*) *The wine flowed freely* (= there was a lot of it to drink). **3** 🔑 without trying to avoid the truth even though it might be unpleasant or embarrassing: *I freely admit that I made a mistake.* **4** 🔑 in an honest way without worrying about what people will say or do: *For the first time he was able to speak freely without the fear of reprisals against his family.* **5** 🔑 in a willing and generous way: *Millions of people gave freely in response to the appeal for the victims of the earthquake.* **6** a piece of writing that is translated **freely** is not translated exactly but the general meaning is given

free·man /ˈfriːmən/ *noun* (*pl.* **-men** /-mən/) **1** (*BrE*) a person who has been given the FREEDOM of a particular city as a reward for the work that they have done **2** a person who is not a SLAVE

ˌ**free ˈmarket** *noun* an economic system in which the price of goods and services is affected by supply and demand rather than controlled by a government: *She was a supporter of the* ***free market economy.***

ˌ**free marketˈeer** *noun* a person who believes that prices should be allowed to rise and fall according to supply and demand and not be controlled by the government

Free·mason /ˈfriːmeɪsn/ (also **Mason**) *noun* a man belonging to a secret society whose members help each other and communicate using secret signs

Free·mason·ry /ˈfriːmeɪsnri/ *noun* [U] **1** the system and practices of Freemasons **2 freemasonry** the friendship that exists between people who have the same profession or interests: *the freemasonry of actors*

ˌ**free ˈmorpheme** *noun* (*linguistics*) = FREE FORM

ˌ**free on ˈboard** *adj.* (*abbr.* **f.o.b.**) (*business*) including the cost of putting goods onto a ship in the price

ˌ**free ˈpardon** *noun* (*BrE, law*) = PARDON

ˌ**free ˈperiod** *noun* (*BrE*) a period of time in a school day when a student or teacher does not have a class

Free·phone (also **Free·fone™**) /ˈfriːfəʊn; *NAmE* -foʊn/ *noun* [U] (in Britain) a system in which the cost of a telephone call is paid for by the organization being called, rather than by the person making the call ➲ compare TOLL-FREE

ˌ**free ˈport** *noun* a port at which tax is not paid on goods that have been brought there temporarily before being sent to a different country

Free·post /ˈfriːpəʊst; *NAmE* -poʊst/ *noun* [U] (in Britain) a system in which the cost of sending a letter is paid for by the organization receiving it, rather than by the person sending it

ˌ**free ˈradical** *noun* (*chemistry*) an atom or group of atoms that has an ELECTRON that is not part of a pair, causing it to take part easily in chemical reactions. Free radicals in the body are thought to be one of the causes of diseases such as cancer. ➲ see also ANTIOXIDANT (1)

ˌ**free-ˈrange** *adj.* [usually before noun] connected with a system of farming in which animals are kept in natural conditions and can move around freely: *free-range chickens* ◇ *free-range eggs* ➲ compare BATTERY (4), BATTERY FARM

free·ride /ˈfriːraɪd/ (also ˈ**freeride board**) *noun* a type of SNOWBOARD used for riding on all types of snow

ˌ**freeˈrunning** *noun* [U] the activity or art of moving through a city by running, jumping and climbing under, around and through things in a way that is as elegant as possible ➲ compare PARKOUR

ˌ**free ˈsafety** *noun* (in AMERICAN FOOTBALL) a defending player who can try to stop any attacking player rather than one particular attacking player

free·sia /ˈfriːʒə; ˈfriːziə/ *noun* a plant with yellow, pink, white or purple flowers with a sweet smell, which are also called freesias

ˌ**free ˈspirit** *noun* a person who is independent and does what they want instead of doing what other people do

ˌ**free-ˈstanding** *adj.* **1** not supported by or attached to anything: *a free-standing sculpture* **2** not a part of sth else: *a free-standing adult education service*

free·style /ˈfriːstaɪl/ *noun, verb*

- ***noun*** [U] **1** a swimming race in which people taking part can use any stroke they want (usually CRAWL): *the men's 400 m freestyle* **2** (often used as an adjective) a sports competition in which people taking part can use any style that they want: *freestyle skiing*
- ***verb*** [I] to RAP, play music, dance, etc. by inventing it as you do it, rather than by planning it in advance or following fixed patterns SYN **improvise**

free·think·er /ˌfriːˈθɪŋkə(r)/ *noun* a person who forms their own ideas and opinions rather than accepting those of other people, especially in religious teaching ▸ ˌ**free·ˈthink·ing** *adj.* [only before noun]

ˌ**free ˈthrow** *noun* (in BASKETBALL) an attempt to throw a ball into the BASKET without any player trying to stop you, that you are allowed after a FOUL

F

ˌ**free-to-ˈair** (*BrE*) *adj.* [usually before noun] (of television programmes) that you do not have to pay to watch: *The company provides more than 20 free-to-air channels.*

ˌ**free ˈtrade** *noun* [U] a system of international trade in which there are no restrictions or taxes on imports and exports ➲ **COLLOCATIONS** at INTERNATIONAL

ˌ**free ˈverse** *noun* [U] (*technical*) poetry without a regular rhythm or RHYME ➲ compare BLANK VERSE

ˌ**free ˈvote** *noun* (in Britain) a vote by members of parliament in which they can vote according to their own beliefs rather than following the policy of their political party

free·ware /ˈfriːweə(r); *NAmE* -wer/ *noun* [U] (*computing*) computer software that is offered free for anyone to use ➲ compare SHAREWARE

free·way /ˈfriːweɪ/ (also **ex·press·way**) *noun* (in the US) a wide road, where traffic can travel fast for long distances. You can only enter and leave freeways at special RAMPS: *a freeway exit* ◇ *an accident on the freeway*

free·wheel /ˌfriːˈwiːl/ *verb* [I] (+ **adv./prep.**) to ride a bicycle without using the PEDALS: *I freewheeled down the hill to the village.*

free·wheel·ing /ˌfriːˈwiːlɪŋ/ *adj.* [only before noun] (*informal*) not concerned about rules or the possible results of what you do: *a freewheeling lifestyle*

ˌ**free ˈwill** *noun* [U] the power to make your own decisions without being controlled by God or FATE
IDM **of your own free ˈwill** because you want to do sth rather than because sb has told or forced you to do it: *She left of her own free will.*

freeze 0-w /friːz/ *verb, noun*

■ ***verb*** (froze /frəʊz; *NAmE* froʊz/, fro·zen /ˈfrəʊzn; *NAmE* ˈfroʊzn/)

▸ BECOME ICE **1** 0-w [I, T] to become hard, and often turn to ice, as a result of extreme cold; to make sth do this: *Water freezes at 0°C.* ◇ *It's so cold that even the river has frozen.* ◇ **~ sth** *The cold weather had frozen the ground.* ◇ **+ adj.** *The clothes **froze solid** on the washing-line.* **OPP** **thaw**

▸ OF PIPE/LOCK/MACHINE **2** 0-w [I, T] if a pipe, lock or machine **freezes**, or sth **freezes** it, it becomes blocked with frozen liquid and therefore cannot be used: **~ (up)** *The pipes have frozen, so we've got no water.* ◇ **~ sth (up)** *Ten degrees of frost had frozen the lock on the car.*

▸ OF WEATHER **3** 0-w [I] when **it freezes**, the weather is at or below 0° Celsius: *It may freeze tonight, so bring those plants inside.*

▸ BE VERY COLD **4** 0-w [I, T] to be very cold; to be so cold that you die: *Every time she opens the window we all freeze.* ◇ *Two men **froze to death** on the mountain.* ◇ **~ sb** *Two men were frozen to death on the mountain.*

▸ FOOD **5** 0-w [T] **~ sth** to keep food at a very low temperature in order to preserve it: *Can you freeze this cake?* ◇ *These meals are ideal for home freezing.* **6** 0-w [I] to be able to be kept at a very low temperature: *Some fruits freeze better than others.*

▸ STOP MOVING **7** 0-w [I] to stop moving suddenly because of fear, etc: *I froze with terror as the door slowly opened.* ◇ (*figurative*) *The smile froze on her lips.* ◇ *The police officer shouted 'Freeze!' and the man dropped the gun.*

▸ COMPUTER **8** [I] when a computer screen **freezes**, you cannot move any of the images, etc. on it, because there is a problem with the system

▸ FILM/MOVIE **9** [T] **~ sth** to stop a film/movie or video in order to look at a particular picture: *Freeze the action there!* ➲ see also FREEZE-FRAME

▸ WAGES/PRICES **10** [T] **~ sth** to hold wages, prices, etc. at a fixed level for a period of time **SYN** **peg**: *Salaries have been frozen for the current year.*

▸ MONEY/BANK ACCOUNT **11** [T] **~ sth** to prevent money, a bank account, etc. from being used by getting a court order which bans it: *The company's assets have been frozen.*

IDM **freeze your ˈblood | make your ˈblood freeze** to make you extremely frightened or shocked ➲ more at TRACK *n.*

PHR V ˌ**freeze sb↔ˈout (of sth)** (*informal*) to be deliberately unfriendly to sb, creating difficulties, etc. in order to stop or DISCOURAGE them from doing sth or taking part in sth ˌ**freeze ˈover** to become completely covered by ice: *The lake freezes over in winter.*

■ ***noun***

▸ OF WAGES/PRICES **1** the act of keeping wages, prices, etc. at a particular level for a period of time: ***a wage/price freeze***

▸ STOPPING STH **2** [usually sing.] **~ (on sth)** the act of stopping sth: *a freeze on imports*

▸ COLD WEATHER **3** [usually sing.] (*BrE*) an unusually cold period of weather during which temperatures stay below 0° Celsius: *Farmers still talk about the **big freeze** of '99.* **4** (*NAmE*) a short period of time, especially at night, when the temperature is below 0° Celsius: *A freeze warning was posted for Thursday night.*

ˈ**freeze-dry** *verb* [usually passive] **~ sth** to preserve food or drink by freezing and drying it very quickly

ˈ**freeze-frame** *noun* [U] the act of stopping a moving film at one particular FRAME (= picture)

freezer /ˈfriːzə(r)/ (*BrE* also ˌ**deep ˈfreeze**) (*US* also **Deepfreeze™**, ˌ**deep ˈfreezer**) *noun* a large piece of electrical equipment in which you can store food for a long time at a low temperature so that it stays frozen ➲ see also FRIDGE-FREEZER

freez·ing /ˈfriːzɪŋ/ *adj.* **1** extremely cold: *It's freezing in here!* ◇ *I'm freezing!* ➲ **SYNONYMS** at COLD **2** [only before noun] having temperatures that are below 0° Celsius: *freezing fog* ◇ *freezing temperatures* ➲ **SYNONYMS** at COLD
▸ **freez·ing** *adv.*: (*informal*) *It's freezing cold outside.*

ˈ**freezing point** *noun* **1** (also **freez·ing**) [U] 0° Celsius, the temperature at which water freezes: *Tonight temperatures will fall well below freezing (point).* **2** [C, usually sing.] the temperature at which a particular liquid freezes: *the freezing point of polar sea water*

freight /freɪt/ *noun, verb*

■ ***noun*** [U] goods that are transported by ships, planes, trains or lorries/trucks; the system of transporting goods in this way: *to send goods by air freight* ◇ *a freight business* ◇ *passenger and freight transportation services*

■ ***verb*** **1 ~ sth** to send or carry goods by air, sea or train **2** [usually passive] **~ sth with sth** (*literary*) to fill sth with a particular mood or tone: *Each word was freighted with anger.*

ˈ**freight car** (*NAmE*) (*BrE* **wagon**) *noun* a railway/railroad truck for carrying goods

freight·er /ˈfreɪtə(r)/ *noun* a large ship or plane that carries goods

ˈ**freight train** (*BrE* also ˈ**goods train**) *noun* a train that carries only goods ➲ **VISUAL VOCAB** page V47

French /frentʃ/ *adj., noun*

■ ***adj.*** of or connected with France, its people or its language
IDM **take French ˈleave** (*BrE*) to leave work without asking permission first

■ ***noun*** the language of France and some other countries
IDM **excuse/pardon my ˈFrench** (*informal*) used to say that you are sorry for swearing

ˌ**French ˈbean** *noun* (*BrE*) = GREEN BEAN

ˌ**French ˈbraid** (*NAmE*) (*BrE* ˌ**French ˈplait**) *noun* a HAIRSTYLE for women in which all the hair is gathered into one large PLAIT/BRAID down the back of the head ➲ **VISUAL VOCAB** page V49

ˌ**French ˈbread** *noun* [U] white bread in the shape of a long thick stick

ˌ**French ˈCanada** *noun* [U] the part of Canada where most French-speaking Canadians live, especially Quebec

ˌ**French Caˈnadian** *noun* a Canadian whose first language is French ▸ ˌ**French Caˈnadian** *adj.*

ˌ**French ˈdoor** *noun* (*especially NAmE*) a glass door, often one of a pair, that leads to a room, a garden/yard or a BALCONY ➲ **VISUAL VOCAB** page V15

ˌ**French ˈdressing** *noun* [U, C] a mixture of oil, VINEGAR, etc. used to add flavour to a salad **SYN** **vinaigrette**

ˌ**French ˈfry** (also **fry**) (both *especially NAmE*) (*BrE* also **chip**) *noun* [usually pl.] a long thin piece of potato fried in oil or fat

ˌFrench ˈhorn (also **horn** especially in *BrE*) *noun* a BRASS musical instrument that consists of a long tube curled around in a circle with a wide opening at the end ➲ VISUAL VOCAB page V30

ˌFrench ˈkiss *noun* a kiss during which people's mouths are open and their tongues touch

ˌFrench ˈletter *noun* (*old-fashioned, BrE, informal*) = CONDOM

ˌFrench ˈloaf *noun* = BAGUETTE

ˌFrench ˈplait (*BrE*) (*NAmE* **ˌFrench ˈbraid**) *noun* a HAIRSTYLE for women in which all the hair is gathered into one large PLAIT/BRAID down the back of the head ➲ VISUAL VOCAB page V49

ˌFrench ˈpleat (*BrE*) (*NAmE* **ˌFrench ˈtwist**) *noun* a HAIRSTYLE for women in which all the hair is lifted up at the back of the head, twisted and held in place

ˌFrench ˈpolish *noun* [U] (*BrE*) a type of VARNISH (= transparent liquid) that is painted onto wooden furniture to give it a hard shiny surface ▸ **ˌFrench ˈpolish** *verb* **~ sth**

ˌFrench ˈpress (*NAmE*) (*BrE* **cafe·tière**) *noun* a special glass container for making coffee with a metal FILTER that you push down ➲ VISUAL VOCAB page V22

ˌFrench ˈstick *noun* = BAGUETTE ➲ picture at STICK

ˌFrench ˈtoast *noun* [U] slices of bread that have been covered with a mixture of egg and milk and then fried

ˌFrench ˈtwist (*NAmE*) (*BrE* **ˌFrench ˈpleat**) *noun* a HAIRSTYLE for women in which all the hair is lifted up at the back of the head, twisted and held in place ➲ VISUAL VOCAB page V49

ˌFrench ˈwindow *noun* [usually pl.] a glass door, usually one of a pair, that leads to a garden/yard or BALCONY ➲ VISUAL VOCAB page V15

fre·net·ic /frəˈnetɪk/ *adj.* involving a lot of energy and activity in a way that is not organized: *a scene of frenetic activity* ▸ **fre·net·ic·al·ly** /-kli/ *adv.*

frenu·lum /ˈfrenjələm; *BrE* also ˈfriːn-/ (*BrE* also **frae·nu·lum**) /ˈfriːn-/ *noun* (*anatomy*) a small fold of skin that prevents an organ from moving too much, for example the fold of skin under the tongue

fren·zied /ˈfrenzid/ *adj.* [usually before noun] involving a lot of activity and strong emotions in a way that is often violent or frightening and not under control: *a frenzied attack* ◇ *frenzied activity* ▸ **fren·zied·ly** *adv.*

frenzy /ˈfrenzi/ *noun* [C, usually sing., U] (*pl.* -ies) **~ (of sth)** a state of great activity and strong emotion that is often violent or frightening and not under control: *in a* ***frenzy of activity/excitement/violence*** ◇ *The speaker worked the crowd up* ***into a frenzy.*** ◇ *an outbreak of patriotic frenzy* ◇ *a killing frenzy* ➲ see also FEEDING FRENZY

fre·quency /ˈfriːkwənsi/ *noun* (*pl.* -ies) **1** [U, C] the rate at which sth happens or is repeated: *Fatal road accidents have decreased in frequency over recent years.* ◇ *a society with a* ***high/low frequency*** (= happening often/not very often) *of stable marriages* ◇ *The program can show us* ***word frequency*** (= how often words occur in a language). **2** [U] the fact of sth happening often: *the alarming frequency of computer errors* ◇ *Objects like this turn up at sales with surprising frequency.* **3** [C, U] (*technical*) the rate at which a sound or ELECTROMAGNETIC wave VIBRATES (= moves up and down): *a* ***high/low frequency*** **4** [C, U] (*technical*) the number of radio waves for every second of a radio signal: *a frequency band* ◇ *There are only a limited number of broadcasting frequencies.*

fre·quent 🔑 *adj., verb*

■ ***adj.*** 🔑 /ˈfriːkwənt/ happening or doing sth often: *He is a frequent visitor to this country.* ◇ *Her calls became less frequent.* ◇ *There is a frequent bus service into the centre of town.* ◇ *How frequent is this word* (= how often does it occur in the language)? OPP **infrequent**

■ ***verb*** /friˈkwent/ **~ sth** (*formal*) to visit a particular place often: *We met in a local bar much frequented by students.*

fre·quent·ly 🔑 /ˈfriːkwəntli/ *adv.* often: *Buses run frequently between the city and the airport.* ◇ *some of the most frequently asked questions about the Internet* OPP **infrequently**

fresco /ˈfreskəʊ; *NAmE* -koʊ/ *noun* (*pl.* -oes or -os) [C, U] a picture that is painted on a wall while the PLASTER is still wet; the method of painting in this way ➲ COLLOCATIONS at ART ➲ see also AL FRESCO

fresh 🔑 /freʃ/ *adj., adv.*

■ ***adj.*** (fresh·er, fresh·est)

▸ FOOD **1** 🔑 (usually of food) recently produced or picked and not frozen, dried or preserved in tins or cans: *Is this milk fresh?* ◇ *fresh bread/flowers* ◇ *Eat plenty of fresh fruit and vegetables.* ◇ *vegetables fresh from the garden* ◇ *Our chefs use only the freshest produce available.*

▸ NEW **2** 🔑 made or experienced recently: *fresh tracks in the snow* ◇ *Let me write it down while it's still* ***fresh in my mind.*** **3** 🔑 [usually before noun] new or different in a way that adds to or replaces sth: *fresh evidence* ◇ *I think it's time we tried a fresh approach.* ◇ *a fresh coat of paint* ◇ *Could we order some fresh coffee?* ◇ *This is the opportunity he needs to* ***make a fresh start*** (= to try sth new after not being successful at sth else).

▸ CLEAN/COOL **4** 🔑 [usually before noun] pleasantly clean, pure or cool: *a toothpaste that leaves a nice fresh taste in your mouth* ◇ *Let's go and get some* ***fresh air*** (= go outside where the air is cooler).

▸ WATER **5** 🔑 [usually before noun] containing no salt: *There is a shortage of fresh water on the island.* ➲ see also FRESH-WATER

▸ WEATHER **6** 🔑 (of the wind) quite strong and cold SYN **brisk**: *a fresh breeze* **7** (*BrE*) quite cold with some wind: *It's fresh this morning, isn't it?*

▸ CLEAR/BRIGHT **8** 🔑 looking clear, bright and attractive: *He looked fresh and neat in a clean white shirt.* ◇ *a collection of summer dresses in fresh colours* ◇ *a fresh complexion*

▸ FULL OF ENERGY **9** [not usually before noun] full of energy: *Regular exercise will help you feel fresher and fitter.* ◇ *I managed to sleep on the plane and arrived feeling* ***as fresh as a daisy.***

▸ JUST FINISHED **10 ~ from sth** having just come from a particular place; having just had a particular experience: *students fresh from college* ◇ *fresh from her success at the Olympic Games*

▸ RUDE/CONFIDENT **11** [not before noun] **~ (with sb)** (*informal*) rude and too confident in a way that shows a lack of respect for sb or a sexual interest in sb: *Don't get fresh with me!*

▸ **fresh·ness** *noun* [U]: *We guarantee the freshness of all our produce.* ◇ *the cool freshness of the water* ◇ *I like the freshness of his approach to the problem.* IDM see BLOOD, BREATH, HEART

■ ***adv.***

IDM **fresh out of sth** (*informal, especially NAmE*) having recently finished a supply of sth: *Sorry, we're fresh out of milk.*

fresh·en /ˈfreʃn/ *verb* **1** [T] **~ sth (up)** to make sth cleaner, cooler, newer or more pleasant: *The walls need freshening up with white paint.* ◇ *The rain had freshened the air.* ◇ *Using a mouthwash freshens the breath.* **2** [T] **~ sth (up)** (*especially NAmE*) to add more liquid to a drink, especially an alcoholic one ➲ see also TOP UP **3** [I] (of the wind) to become stronger and colder: *The wind will freshen tonight.*

PHR V **ˌfreshen ˈup** | **ˌfreshen yourself ˈup** to wash and make yourself look clean and tidy: *I'll just go and freshen up before supper.*

fresh·ener /ˈfreʃnə(r)/ *noun* [U, C] (often in compounds) a thing that makes sth cleaner, purer or more pleasant: *air freshener*

fresh·er /ˈfreʃə(r)/ *noun* (*BrE, informal*) a student who has just started his or her first term at a university

ˈfresh-faced *adj.* having a young, healthy-looking face: *fresh-faced kids*

fresh·ly 🔑 /ˈfreʃli/ *adv.* usually followed by a past participle showing that sth has been made, prepared, etc. recently: *freshly brewed coffee*

fresh·man /ˈfreʃmən/ *noun* (*pl.* **-men** /-mən/) **1** (*especially NAmE*) a student who is in his or her first year at a university or college, or in the ninth grade at school: *high school/college freshmen* ◇ *during my freshman year* ➲ compare SOPHOMORE **2** (*CanE*) a first-year student at a university or college

fresh·water /ˈfreʃwɔːtə(r)/ *adj.* [only before noun] **1** living in water that is not the sea and is not salty: *freshwater fish* **2** having water that is not salty: *freshwater lakes* ➲ compare SALT WATER

fret /fret/ *verb, noun*

■ ***verb*** (-tt-) [I, T] **~ (about/over sth)** | **~ (that...)** (*especially BrE*) to be worried or unhappy and not able to relax: *Fretting about it won't help.* ◇ *Her baby starts to fret as soon as she goes out of the room.*

■ ***noun*** **1** one of the bars on the long thin part of a GUITAR, etc. Frets show you where to press the strings with your fingers to produce particular sounds. ➲ VISUAL VOCAB page V31 **2** (also ˈ**sea fret**) (*NEngE*) MIST or FOG that comes in from the sea

fret·ful /ˈfretfl/ *adj.* behaving in a way that shows you are unhappy or uncomfortable SYN **restless** ▸ **fret·ful·ly** *adv.*

fret·saw /ˈfretsɔː/ *noun* a SAW with a thin blade that is used for cutting patterns in wood, metal, etc.

fret·ted /ˈfretɪd/ *adj.* (*technical*) (especially of wood or stone) decorated with patterns

fret·work /ˈfretwɜːk; *NAmE* -wɜːrk/ *noun* [U] patterns cut into wood, metal, etc. to decorate it; the process of making these patterns

Freud·ian /ˈfrɔɪdiən/ *adj.* **1** connected with the ideas of Sigmund Freud about the way the human mind works, especially his theories of unconscious sexual feelings **2** (of sb's speech or behaviour) showing your secret thoughts or feelings, especially those connected with sex

ˌFreudian ˈslip *noun* something you say by mistake but which is believed to show your true thoughts ORIGIN This expression is named after Sigmund Freud and his theories of unconscious thought.

fri·able /ˈfraɪəbl/ *adj.* (*technical*) easily broken up into small pieces: *friable soil*

friar /ˈfraɪə(r)/ *noun* a member of one of several Roman Catholic religious communities of men who in the past travelled around teaching people about Christianity and lived by asking other people for food (= by BEGGING) ➲ compare MONK

fri·ary /ˈfraɪəri/ *noun* (*pl.* -ies) a building in which friars live

fric·as·see /ˈfrɪkəsiː/ *noun* [C, U] a hot dish consisting of small pieces of meat and vegetables that are cooked and served in a thick white sauce

frica·tive /ˈfrɪkətɪv/ (*BrE*) (*NAmE* **spir·ant**) *noun* (*phonetics*) a speech sound made by forcing breath out through a narrow space in the mouth with the lips, teeth or tongue in a particular position, for example /f/ and /ʃ/ in *fee* and *she* ▸ **frica·tive** *adj.* ➲ compare PLOSIVE

fric·tion /ˈfrɪkʃn/ *noun* **1** [U] the action of one object or surface moving against another: *Friction between moving parts had caused the engine to overheat.* **2** [U] (*physics*) the RESISTANCE (= the force that stops sth moving) of one surface to another surface or substance moving over or through it: *The force of friction slows the spacecraft down as it re-enters the earth's atmosphere.* **3** [U, C] **~ (between A and B)** disagreement or a lack of friendship among people who have different opinions about sth SYN **tension**: *conflicts and frictions that have still to be resolved*

ˈfriction tape *noun* [U] (*US*) = INSULATING TAPE

Fri·day 🔑 /ˈfraɪdeɪ; -di/ *noun* [C, U] (*abbr.* Fri.) the day of the week after Thursday and before Saturday HELP To see how **Friday** is used, look at the examples at **Monday**. ORIGIN Originally translated from the Latin for 'day of the planet Venus' *Veneris dies* and named after the Germanic goddess *Frigga*.

fridge 🔑 /frɪdʒ/ (*BrE*) (*NAmE* or *formal* **re·friger·ator**) (*US* also *old-fashioned* **ice·box**) *noun* a piece of electrical equipment in which food is kept cold so that it stays fresh: *This dessert can be served straight from the fridge.* ➲ VISUAL VOCAB page V22

ˌfridge-ˈfreezer *noun* (*BrE*) a piece of kitchen equipment that consists of a fridge/refrigerator and a FREEZER together

fried *past tense, past part.* of FRY

friend 🔑 /frend/ *noun*

▸ PERSON YOU LIKE **1** 🔑 a person you know well and like, and who is not usually a member of your family: *This is my friend Tom.* ◇ *Is he **a friend of yours**?* ◇ *She's an **old friend*** (= I have known her a long time). ◇ *He's one of my **best friends**.* ◇ *a **close/good friend*** ◇ *a **childhood/family/lifelong friend*** ◇ *I heard about it through **a friend of a friend**.* ◇ *She has a wide **circle of friends**.* ➲ see also BEFRIEND, BOYFRIEND, FAIR-WEATHER, FALSE FRIEND, GIRLFRIEND, PENFRIEND, SCHOOL FRIEND

▸ SUPPORTER **2** a person who supports an organization, a charity, etc, especially by giving or raising money; a person who supports a particular idea, etc: *the Friends of St Martin's Hospital* ◇ *a friend of democracy*

▸ NOT ENEMY **3** a person who has the same interests and opinions as yourself, and will help and support you: *You're among friends here—you can speak freely.*

▸ SILLY/ANNOYING PERSON **4** (*ironic*) used to talk about sb you do not know who has done sth silly or annoying: *I wish our friend at the next table would shut up.*

▸ IN PARLIAMENT/COURT **5** (in Britain) used by a member of parliament to refer to another member of parliament or by a lawyer to refer to another lawyer in a court of law: *my **honourable friend**, the member for Henley* (= in the House of Commons) ◇ *my **noble friend*** (= in the House of Lords) ◇ *my **learned friend*** (= in a court of law)

▸ IN RELIGION **6 Friend** a member of the Society of Friends SYN **Quaker**

IDM **be/make ˈfriends (with sb)** 🔑 to be/become a friend of sb: *We've been friends for years.* ◇ *They had a quarrel, but they're friends again now.* ◇ *Simon finds it hard to make friends with other children.* **be (just) good ˈfriends** used to say that two friends are not having a romantic relationship with each other **a ˌfriend in ˈneed (is a ˌfriend inˈdeed)** (*saying*) a friend who gives you help when you need it (is a true friend) **have ˌfriends in high ˈplaces** to know important people who can help you ➲ more at MAN *n.*

friend·less /ˈfrendləs/ *adj.* without any friends

friend·ly 🔑 /ˈfrendli/ *adj., noun*

■ ***adj.*** (**friend·lier**, **friend·li·est**) **1** 🔑 behaving in a kind and pleasant way because you like sb or want to help them: *a warm and friendly person* ◇ **~ to/toward(s) sb** *Everyone was very friendly towards me.* OPP **unfriendly** **2** 🔑 showing kindness; making you feel relaxed and as though you are among friends: *a **friendly smile/welcome*** ◇ *a small hotel with a friendly atmosphere* OPP **unfriendly** **3** 🔑 **~ (with sb)** treating sb as a friend: *We soon became friendly with the couple next door.* ◇ *She was **on friendly terms** with most of the hospital staff.* **4** 🔑 (especially of the relationship between countries) not treating sb/sth as an enemy: *to maintain **friendly relations** with all countries* OPP **hostile** **5** 🔑 (often in compound adjectives) that is helpful and easy to use; that helps sb/sth or does not harm it: *This software is much friendlier than the previous version.* ◇ *environmentally-friendly farming methods* ◇ *ozone-friendly cleaning materials* ➲ see also USER-FRIENDLY **6** 🔑 in which the people, teams, etc. taking part are not seriously competing against each other: *a friendly argument* ◇ *friendly rivalry* ◇ (*BrE*) *It was only a friendly match.* ▸ **friend·li·ness** *noun* [U]

■ ***noun*** (*pl.* -ies) (also ˈ**friendly match**) (both *BrE*) a game of football (SOCCER) etc. that is not part of an important competition

ˌfriendly ˈfire *noun* [U] in a war, if people are killed or injured by **friendly fire**, they are hit by a bomb or weapon that is fired by their own side

ˈfriendly society *noun* (in Britain) an organization that people pay regular amounts of money to, and which gives them money when they are ill/sick or old

friend·ship 🔑 /ˈfrendʃɪp/ *noun*
1 🔑 [C] a relationship between friends: *a **close/lasting/lifelong friendship** ◇ friendships formed while she was at college* ◇ **~ with sb** *He seemed to have already **struck up*** (= begun) ***a friendship** with Jo.* ◇ **~ between A and B** *It's the story of an extraordinary friendship between a boy and a seal.* **2** 🔑 [U] the feeling or relationship that friends have; the state of being friends: *Your friendship is very important to me.* ◇ *a conference to promote international friendship*

frier = FRYER

Frie·sian /ˈfriːʒn/ (*BrE*) (*NAmE* **Hol·stein**) *noun* a type of black and white cow that produces a lot of milk

frieze /friːz/ *noun* **1** a border that goes around the top of a room or building with pictures or CARVINGS on it **2** a long narrow picture, usually put up in a school, that children have made or that teaches them sth

frig·ate /ˈfrɪgət/ *noun* a small fast ship in the navy that travels with other ships in order to protect them

frig·ging /ˈfrɪgɪŋ/ *adv., adj.* [only before noun] (*taboo, slang*) a swear word that many people find offensive, used to emphasize a comment or an angry statement to avoid saying 'fucking': *It's frigging cold outside.* ◇ *Mind your own frigging business!*

fright /fraɪt/ *noun* **1** [U] a feeling of fear: *to cry out **in fright*** ◇ *He was shaking **with fright**.* ➲ SYNONYMS at FEAR ➲ see also STAGE FRIGHT **2** [C] an experience that makes you feel fear: *You **gave me a fright** jumping out at me like that.* ◇ *I got the **fright of my life**.*
IDM **look a ˈfright** (*old-fashioned, BrE*) to look ugly or ridiculous **take ˈfright (at sth)** (*formal*) to be frightened by sth: *The birds took fright and flew off.*

fright·en 🔑 /ˈfraɪtn/ *verb*
[T, I] **~ (sb)** | **~ sb to do sth** to make sb suddenly feel afraid: *Sorry, I didn't mean to frighten you.* ◇ *She's not easily frightened.* ◇ *She **doesn't frighten easily*** (= it is not easy to make her afraid). IDM see DAYLIGHTS, DEATH, LIFE
PHR V ˌ**frighten sb/sth↔aˈway/ˈoff** | ˌ**frighten sb/sth aˈway from sth** **1** 🔑 to make a person or an animal go away by making them feel afraid: *He threatened the intruders with a gun and frightened them off.* **2** 🔑 to make sb afraid or nervous so that they no longer want to do sth: *The high prices have frightened off many customers.* ˈ**frighten sb into sth/into doing sth** to make sb do sth by making them afraid

Synonyms

frighten

scare • alarm • terrify

These words all mean to make sb afraid.

frighten to make sb feel afraid, often suddenly: *He brought out a gun and frightened them off.*

scare to make sb feel afraid: *They managed to scare the bears away.*

alarm to make sb anxious or afraid: *It alarms me that nobody takes this problem seriously.* NOTE **Alarm** is used when sb has a feeling that sth unpleasant or dangerous might happen in the future; the feeling is often more one of worry than actual fear.

terrify to make sb feel extremely afraid: *Flying terrified her.*

FRIGHTEN OR SCARE?

Scare is slightly more informal than **frighten**.

PATTERNS

- to frighten/scare sb/sth **away/off**
- to frighten/scare/terrify sb **into** doing sth
- **It** frightens/scares/alarms/terrifies me **that...**
- **It** frightens/scares/alarms/terrifies me **to** think, see, etc.

fright·ened 🔑 /ˈfraɪtnd/ *adj.*
afraid; feeling fear: *a frightened child* ◇ *Don't be frightened.* ◇ *He sounded frightened.* ◇ **~ of sth** *What are you frightened of?* ◇ **~ of doing sth** *I'm frightened of walking home alone in the dark.* ◇ **~ to do sth** *I'm too frightened to ask him now.* ◇ **~ that...** *She was frightened that the plane would crash.* ◇ **~ for sb** *I'm frightened for him* (= that he will be hurt, etc.). ◇ (*informal*) *I'd never do that. I'd be **frightened to death**.* ➲ SYNONYMS at AFRAID IDM see SHADOW *n.*, WIT

fright·en·ers /ˈfraɪtnəz; *NAmE* -nərz/ *noun*
IDM **put the ˈfrighteners on sb** (*BrE, slang*) to threaten sb in order to make them do what you want

fright·en·ing 🔑 /ˈfraɪtnɪŋ/ *adj.*
making you feel afraid: *a frightening experience/prospect/thought* ◇ ***It's frightening** to think it could happen again.* ▶ **fright·en·ing·ly** *adv.*

fright·ful /ˈfraɪtfl/ *adj.* (*old-fashioned, especially BrE*) **1** (*informal*) used to emphasize how bad sth is SYN **awful, terrible**: *It was absolutely frightful!* ◇ *This room's in a frightful mess.* **2** very serious or unpleasant SYN **awful, terrible**: *a frightful accident*

fright·ful·ly /ˈfraɪtfəli/ *adv.* (*old-fashioned, especially BrE*) very; extremely SYN **awfully, frightfully**: *I'm frightfully sorry.*

ˈ**fright wig** *noun* a WIG with the hair standing up or sticking out, especially worn by a CLOWN

fri·gid /ˈfrɪdʒɪd/ *adj.* **1** (of a woman) not able to enjoy sex **2** very cold: *frigid air* **3** not showing any feelings of friendship or kindness SYN **frosty**: *a frigid voice* ◇ *There was a frigid atmosphere in the room.* ▶ **fri·gid·ly** *adv.*

fri·gid·ity /frɪˈdʒɪdəti/ *noun* [U] (in a woman) the lack of the ability to enjoy sex

ˈ**frigid zone** *noun* [C, usually sing.] (*technical*) the area inside the Arctic Circle or Antarctic Circle ➲ compare TEMPERATE ZONE, TORRID ZONE

frill /frɪl/ *noun* **1** (*BrE*) [C] a narrow strip of cloth with a lot of folds that is attached to the edge of a dress, curtain, etc. to decorate it: *a white blouse with frills at the cuffs* SYN **ruffle** **2 frills** [pl.] things that are not necessary but are added to make sth more attractive or interesting: *a simple meal with no frills* ➲ see also NO-FRILLS

frilled /frɪld/ *adj.* (*BrE*) decorated with frills SYN **ruffled**

frilly /ˈfrɪli/ *adj.* having a lot of frills: *a frilly blouse*

fringe /frɪndʒ/ *noun, verb*
■ ***noun*** **1** [C, usually sing.] (*BrE*) (*NAmE* **bangs** [pl.]) the front part of sb's hair that is cut so that it hangs over their FOREHEAD ➲ VISUAL VOCAB page V49 **2** [C] a strip of hanging threads attached to the edge of sth to decorate it **3** [C] a narrow strip of trees, buildings, etc. along the edge of sth: *a fringe of woodland* ◇ *Along the coast, an industrial fringe had already developed.* **4** [C] (*BrE*) the outer edge of an area or a group: *on the northern fringe of the city* ◇ *the urban/rural fringe* ◇ *the fringes of society* ◇ *Nina remained on the fringe of the crowd.* **5** [sing.] (usually **the fringe**) groups of people, events and activities that are not part of the main group or activity: *Street musicians have been gathering as part of the festival fringe.* ◇ *fringe meetings at the party conference* IDM see LUNATIC *adj.*
■ ***verb*** [usually passive] **~ sth** to form a border around sth: *The beach was fringed by coconut palms.* ▶ **fringed** *adj.*: *a carpet with a fringed edge*

ˈ**fringe benefit** *noun* [usually pl.] extra things that an employer gives you as well as your wages: *The fringe benefits include free health insurance.*

ˌ**fringe ˈmedicine** *noun* [U] any type of treatment which is not accepted by many people as being part of Western medicine, for example one using plants instead of artificial drugs

ˌ**fringe ˈtheatre** *noun* [U, C] (*BrE*) plays, often by new writers, that are unusual and question the way people think; a theatre where such plays are performed ➲ compare OFF-BROADWAY

frip·pery /ˈfrɪpəri/ *noun* [C, usually pl., U] (*pl.* -ies) (*disapproving, especially BrE*) objects, decorations and other items that are considered unnecessary and expensive

Fris·bee™ /ˈfrɪzbi/ *noun* a light plastic object, shaped like a plate, that is thrown from one player to another in a game ➲ VISUAL VOCAB page V32

fri·sée /ˈfriːzeɪ; *NAmE* friːˈzeɪ/ *noun* = CHICORY (2)

Fris·ian /ˈfriːʒn/ *noun* [U] the traditional language of the region of Frisia in NW Europe, closely related to German, Dutch and English

frisk /frɪsk/ *verb* **1** [T] **~ sb** to pass your hands over sb's body to search them for hidden weapons, drugs, etc. **2** [I] **~ (around)** (of animals) to run and jump in a lively and happy way SYN **gambol, skip**: *Lambs frisked in the fields.*

frisky /ˈfrɪski/ *adj.* (frisk·ier, friski·est) **1** (of people or animals) full of energy; wanting to play: *a frisky puppy* **2** (*informal*) wanting to enjoy yourself in a sexual way

fris·son /ˈfriːsɒ̃; *NAmE* friːˈsɔːn/ *noun* [usually sing.] (from *French*) a sudden strong feeling, especially of excitement or fear

fri·til·lary /frɪˈtɪləri; *NAmE* ˈfrɪtleri/ *noun* (*pl.* fri·til·lar·ies) **1** a plant with flowers shaped like bells **2** a BUTTERFLY with orange-brown and black wings

frit·ter /ˈfrɪtə(r)/ *verb, noun*

■ *verb*

PHR V ˌ**fritter sth↔aˈway (on sth)** to waste time or money on things that are not important: *He frittered away the millions his father had left him.*

■ *noun* (usually in compounds) a piece of fruit, meat or vegetable that is covered with BATTER and fried

fritz /frɪts/ *noun*

IDM **on the ˈfritz** (*NAmE, informal*) not working: *The TV is on the fritz again.*

fri·vol·ity /frɪˈvɒləti; *NAmE* -ˈvɑːl-/ *noun* (*pl.* -ies) (often *disapproving*) [U, C] behaviour that is silly or amusing, especially when this is not suitable: *It was just a piece of harmless frivolity.* ◇ *I can't waste time on such frivolities.*

frivo·lous /ˈfrɪvələs/ *adj.* (*disapproving*) **1** (of people or their behaviour) silly or amusing, especially when such behaviour is not suitable: ***frivolous comments/suggestions*** ◇ *Sorry, I was being frivolous.* **2** having no useful or serious purpose: ***frivolous pastimes/pleasures*** ▸ **frivo·lous·ly** *adv.*

frizz /frɪz/ *verb, noun*

■ *verb* [I, T] **~ (sth)** (*informal*) (of hair) to curl very tightly; to make hair do this ▸ **frizzy** *adj.* (friz·zi·er, friz·zi·est): *frizzy hair*

■ *noun* [U] (*disapproving*) hair that is very tightly curled

friz·zle /ˈfrɪzl/ *verb* **~ sth** to heat sth until it forms curls or until it burns: *frizzled hair* ◇ *frizzled bacon*

fro /frəʊ; *NAmE* froʊ/ *adv.* IDM see TO *adv.*

frock /frɒk; *NAmE* frɑːk/ *noun* (*old-fashioned, especially BrE*) a dress: *a party frock*

ˈ**frock coat** *noun* a long coat worn in the past by men, now worn only for special ceremonies

frog /frɒg; *NAmE* frɔːg; frɑːg/ *noun* **1** a small animal with smooth skin, that lives both on land and in water (= is an AMPHIBIAN). Frogs have very long back legs for jumping, and no tail: *the croaking of frogs* ➲ VISUAL VOCAB page V11 **2 Frog** (*informal*) an offensive word for a French person

IDM **have, etc. a ˈfrog in your throat** to lose your voice or be unable to speak clearly for a short time

frog·ging /ˈfrɒgɪŋ; *NAmE* ˈfrɔːg-; ˈfrɑːg-/ *noun* [U] a decorative fastening on a coat consisting of a long wooden button and a LOOP

frog·let /ˈfrɒglət; *NAmE* ˈfrɔːg-; ˈfrɑːg-/ *noun* **1** a type of small frog **2** a small frog that has recently changed from being a TADPOLE

frog·man /ˈfrɒgmən; *NAmE* ˈfrɔːg-; ˈfrɑːg-/ *noun* (*pl.* -men /-mən/) (*BrE*) a person who works underwater, wearing a rubber suit, FLIPPERS, and special equipment to help them breathe: *Police frogmen searched the lake for the murder weapon.* ➲ compare DIVER

frog·march /ˈfrɒgmɑːtʃ; *NAmE* ˈfrɔːgmɑːrtʃ; ˈfrɑːg-/ *verb* **~ sb + adv./prep.** (*BrE*) to force sb to go somewhere by holding their arms tightly so they have to walk along with you: *He was grabbed by two men and frogmarched out of the hall.*

frog·spawn /ˈfrɒgspɔːn; *NAmE* ˈfrɔːg-; ˈfrɑːg-/ *noun* [U] an almost transparent substance that looks like jelly and contains the eggs of a FROG ➲ VISUAL VOCAB page V11

fro·ing /ˈfrəʊɪŋ; *NAmE* ˈfroʊɪŋ/ *noun* IDM see TOING

frolic /ˈfrɒlɪk; *NAmE* ˈfrɑːl-/ *verb, noun*

■ *verb* (-ck-) [I] to play and move around in a lively, happy way: *children frolicking on the beach*

■ *noun* [C, U] (*old-fashioned*) a lively and enjoyable activity during which people forget their problems and responsibilities: *It was just a harmless frolic.*

frolic·some /ˈfrɒlɪksəm; *NAmE* ˈfrɑːl-/ *adj.* (especially *literary*) playing in a lively happy way: *frolicsome lambs*

from 0-w /frəm; *strong form* frɒm; *NAmE* frʌm; frɑːm/ *prep.*

HELP For the special uses of **from** in phrasal verbs, look at the entries for the verbs. For example **keep sth from sb** is in the phrasal verb section at **keep**. **1** 0-w used to show where sb/sth starts: *She began to walk away from him.* ◇ *Has the train from Bristol arrived?* **2** 0-w used to show when sth starts: *We're open from 8 to 7 every day.* ◇ *He was blind from birth.* **3** 0-w used to show who sent or gave sth/sb: *a letter from my brother* ◇ *information from witnesses* ◇ *the man from (= representing) the insurance company* **4** 0-w used to show what the origin of sb/sth is: *I'm from Italy.* ◇ *documents from the sixteenth century* ◇ *quotations from Shakespeare* ◇ *heat from the sun* **5** 0-w used to show the material that sth is made of: *Steel is made from iron.* **6** 0-w used to show how far apart two places are: *100 metres from the scene of the accident* **7** 0-w used to show sb's position or point of view: *You can see the island from here.* ◇ *From a financial point of view the project was a disaster.* **8** 0-w **~ sth (to sth)** used to show the range of sth: *The temperature varies from 30 degrees to minus 20.* ◇ *The store sells everything from shoelaces to computers.* ◇ *Conditions vary from school to school.* **9** 0-w **~ sth (to sth)** used to show the state or form of sth/sb before a change: *Things have gone* ***from bad to worse.*** ◇ *translating from English to Spanish* ◇ *You need a break from routine.* **10** 0-w used to show that sb/sth is separated or removed: *The party was ousted from power after eighteen years.* **11** 0-w used to show that sth is prevented: *She saved him from drowning.* **12** 0-w used to show the reason for sth: *She felt sick from tiredness.* **13** 0-w used to show the reason for making a judgement: *You can tell a lot about a person from their handwriting.* ◇ *From what I heard the company's in deep trouble.* **14** 0-w used when distinguishing between two people or things: *Is Portuguese very different from Spanish?* ◇ *I can't tell one twin from the other.*

IDM **from... on** 0-w starting at the time mentioned and continuously after that: ***From now on*** *you can work on your own.* ◇ *She never spoke to him again from that day on.*

from·age frais /ˌfrɒmɑːʒ ˈfreɪ; *NAmE* frəˈmɑːʒ/ *noun* [U] (from *French*) a type of very soft cheese, similar to YOGURT

frond /frɒnd; *NAmE* frɑːnd/ *noun* **1** a long leaf of some plants or trees, especially PALMS or FERNS. Fronds are often divided into parts along the edge. **2** a long piece of SEAWEED that looks like one of these leaves

front 0-w /frʌnt/ *noun, adj., verb*

■ *noun*

▸ FORWARD PART/POSITION **1** 0-w [C, usually sing.] (usually **the front**) the part or side of sth that faces forward; the side of sth that you look at first: *The front of the building was covered with ivy.* ◇ *The book has a picture of Rome* ***on the front.*** ◇ *The front of the car was badly damaged.* ➲ see also SHOPFRONT, Y-FRONTS **2** 0-w **the front** [sing.] the position that is in the direction that sb/sth is facing: *Keep your eyes to the front and walk straight ahead.* ◇ *There's a garden* ***at the front of*** *the house.* **3** 0-w **the front** [sing.] the part of sth that is furthest forward: *I prefer to travel* ***in the front of*** *the car (= next to the driver).* ◇ *The teacher made me move*

my seat to the front of the classroom. ◇ *Write your name in the front of the book* (= the first few pages).
▸ CHEST **4** 🗝 **sb's front** [sing.] the part of sb's body that faces forwards; sb's chest: *She was lying on her front.* ◇ *I spilled coffee down my front.*
▸ SIDE OF BUILDING **5** [C] **the west, north, south, east, etc. ~** the side of a large building, especially a church, that faces west, north, etc: *the west front of the cathedral*
▸ EDGE OF SEA/LAKE **6 the front** [sing.] (*BrE*) the road or area of land along the edge of the sea, a lake or a river: *Couples walked hand in hand along the front.* ➲ see also SEAFRONT
▸ IN WAR **7** [C, usually sing.] an area where fighting takes place during a war: *More British troops have been sent to the front.* ◇ *to serve at the front* ◇ *fighting a war on two fronts* ➲ see also FRONT LINE, HOME FRONT
▸ AREA OF ACTIVITY **8** [C] a particular area of activity: *Things are looking unsettled on the economic front.* ◇ *Progress has been made **on all fronts**.*
▸ HIDING TRUE FEELINGS **9** [sing.] behaviour that is not genuine, done in order to hide your true feelings or opinions: *Rudeness is just a front for her shyness.* ◇ *It's not always easy to **put on a** brave **front** for the family.* ◇ *The prime minister stressed the need to **present a united front*** (= show people that all members of the group have the same opinion about things).
▸ HIDING STH ILLEGAL **10** [C, usually sing.] **~ (for sth)** a person or an organization that is used to hide an illegal or secret activity: *The travel company is just a front for drug trafficking.*
▸ POLITICAL ORGANIZATION **11 Front** [sing.] used in the names of some political organizations: *the Animal Liberation Front* ➲ see also POPULAR FRONT
▸ WEATHER **12** [C] the line where a mass of cold air meets a mass of warm air: *a **cold/warm front***
IDM **ˌfront and ˈcenter** (*NAmE*) in or into the most important position **in ˈfront** *adv.* **1** 🗝 in a position that is further forward than sb/sth but not very far away: *Their house is the one with the big garden in front.* **2** 🗝 in first place in a race or competition: *The blue team is currently in front with a lead of six points.* **in ˈfront of** *prep.* **1** 🗝 in a position that is further forward than sb/sth but not very far away: *The car in front of me stopped suddenly and I had to brake.* ◇ *The bus stops right in front of our house.* ◇ *He was standing in front of me in the line.* ◇ *She spends all day **sitting in front of*** (= working at) *her computer.* **2** 🗝 if you do sth **in front of** sb, you do it when they are there: *Please don't talk about it in front of the children.* **3** 🗝 **~ sb** (of time) still to come; not yet passed: *Don't give up. You still have your whole life in front of you.* **out ˈfront 1** in the part of a theatre, restaurant, etc. where the public sits: *There's only a small audience out front tonight.* **2** (also *BrE informal* **out the ˈfront**) in the area near to the entrance to a building: *I'll wait for you out (the) front.* **up ˈfront** (*informal*) **1** as payment in advance: *We'll pay you half up front and the other half when you've finished the job.* **2** (in sports) in a forward position: *to play up front* ➲ see also UPFRONT ➲ more at BACK *n.*, CASH *n.*, EYE *n.*, LEAD[1] *v.*
■ ***adj.*** [only before noun] **1** 🗝 on or at the front of sth: *front teeth* ◇ *the front wheels of the car* ◇ *We had seats in the front row.* ◇ *an animal's front legs* ◇ *Let's go through to the **front room*** (= the main room in a house where people sit and entertain guests). ◇ *a front-seat passenger* ➲ compare BACK, HIND *adj.* **2** (*phonetics*) (of a vowel) produced with the front of the tongue in a higher position than the back, for example /iː/ in English ➲ compare BACK, CENTRAL
IDM **on the ˈfront burner** (*informal, especially NAmE*) (of an issue, a plan, etc.) being given a lot of attention because it is considered important: *Anything that keeps education on the front burner is good.* ➲ compare ON THE BACK BURNER at BACK *adj.*
■ ***verb***
▸ FACE STH **1** [T, I] to face sth or be in front of sth; to have the front pointing towards sth: **~ sth** *The cathedral fronts the city's main square.* ◇ **~ onto sth** *The line of houses fronted straight onto the road.*
▸ COVER FRONT **2** [T, usually passive] **~ sth** to have the front covered with sth: *a glass-fronted bookcase*
▸ LEAD GROUP **3** [T] **~ sth** to lead or represent an organization, a group, etc: *He fronts a multinational company.* ◇ *A former art student fronted the band* (= was the main singer).
▸ PRESENT TV PROGRAMME **4** [T] **~ sth** (*especially BrE*) to present a television programme, a show, etc.
▸ GRAMMAR **5** [T] **~ sth** (*linguistics*) to give more importance to a part of a sentence by placing it at or near the beginning of the sentence, as in 'That I would like to see.'
PHR V **ˈfront for sb/sth** to represent a group or an organization and try to hide its secret or illegal activities: *He fronted for them in several illegal property deals.*

Which Word?

in front of / in the front of

- **In front of** can mean the same as **outside**, but not **opposite**: *I'll meet you in front of/outside your hotel.* ◇ *There's a bus stop in front of the house* (= on the same side of the road). ◇ *There's a bus stop opposite the house* (= on the other side of the road).
- **In/at the front (of sth)** means 'in the most forward part of something': *The driver sits at the front of the bus.* ◇ *Put the shortest flowers in the front (of the bunch).*

front·age /ˈfrʌntɪdʒ/ *noun* **1** [C, U] the front of a building, especially when this faces a road or river: *the baroque frontage of Milan Cathedral* **2** [U] (*especially NAmE*) land that is next to a building, a street or an area of water: *They bought two miles of river frontage along the Colorado.*
ˈfrontage road *noun* (*NAmE*) = SERVICE ROAD
front·al /ˈfrʌntl/ *adj.* [only before noun] **1** connected with the front of sth: *Airbags protect the driver in the event of a severe frontal impact.* **2** (also **ˌfull-ˈfrontal**) a **frontal** attack or a criticism is very strong and direct: *They launched a frontal attack on company directors.* **3** connected with a weather FRONT: *a cold frontal system* **4** (*medical*) connected with the front part of the head: *the frontal lobes of the brain* ▸ **front·al·ly** /-təli/ *adv.*
ˌfrontal ˈlobe *noun* (*anatomy*) either of the two parts at the front of the brain that are concerned with behaviour, learning and personality
the ˌfront ˈbench *noun* [C+sing./pl. v.] the most important members of the government and the opposition in the British parliament, who sit in the front rows of seats: *an Opposition front-bench spokesman on defence* ➲ compare BACK BENCH
front·bench·er /ˌfrʌntˈbentʃə(r)/ *noun* an important member of the government or the opposition in the British parliament, who sits in the front rows of seats ➲ compare BACKBENCHER
ˌfront ˈdesk *noun* the desk inside the entrance of a hotel, an office building, etc. where guests or visitors go when they first arrive ➲ compare RECEPTION
ˌfront ˈdoor *noun* the main entrance to a house, usually at the front: *There's someone at the front door.* ➲ VISUAL VOCAB page V15
ˈfront-end *adj.* [only before noun] (*computing*) (of a device or program) directly used by a user, and allowing the user to use other devices or programs ➲ compare BACK-END
ˌfront-ˌend ˈloader *noun* (*especially NAmE*) a large vehicle with machinery for digging worked by a system of HYDRAULICS
fron·tier /ˈfrʌntɪə(r); *NAmE* frʌnˈtɪr/ *noun* **1** (*BrE*) [C] a line that separates two countries, etc; the land near this line: **~ (between A and B)** *the frontier between the land of the Saxons and that of the Danes* ◇ **~ (with sth)** *a customs post on the frontier with Italy* ◇ *a **frontier town/zone/post*** ➲ SYNONYMS at BORDER **2 the frontier** [sing.] the edge of land where people live and have built towns, beyond which the country is wild and unknown, especially in the western US in the 19th century: *a remote frontier settlement* **3** [C, usually pl.] **~ (of sth)** the limit of sth, especially

the limit of what is known about a particular subject or activity: *to* ***push back the frontiers*** *of science* (= to increase knowledge of science) ◇ *to* ***roll back the frontiers*** *of government* (= to limit the powers of the government)

fron·tiers·man /ˈfrʌntɪərzmən; *NAmE* frʌnˈtɪrz-/ *noun* (*pl.* **-men** /-mən/) a man living on the frontier especially one who lived in the western US during the 19th century

fron·tis·piece /ˈfrʌntɪspiːs/ *noun* [usually sing.] a picture at the beginning of a book, on the page opposite the page with the title on it

the ˌfront ˈline *noun* [sing.] an area where the enemies are facing each other during a war and where fighting takes place: *Tanks have been deployed all along the front line.* ◇ *front-line troops*

IDM **in the front line (of sth)** doing work that will have an important effect on sth: *a life spent in the front line of research*

ˌfront-ˈload *verb* **1 ~ sth** (*business*) to spread the costs of a project so that more of the money is spent in the earlier stages: *a need to front-load budget spending* ◇ *the positive effects of front-loading funds* **2 ~ sth** to organize work on a project or information in a document so that the more important work or information is done or placed first: *Teach your students to front-load their research.*

front·man /ˈfrʌntmæn/ *noun* (*pl.* **-men** /-men/) **1** a person who represents an organization and tries to make its activities seem acceptable to the public, although in fact they may be illegal: *He acted as a frontman for a drugs cartel.* **2** the leader of a group of musicians **3** (*BrE*) a person who presents a television programme

ˌfront ˈoffice *noun* [sing.] (*especially NAmE*) the part of a business concerned with managing things or dealing with the public

ˌfront-of-ˈhouse *noun* [U] (*BrE*) **1** the parts of a theatre that are used by the audience **2** (often used as an adjective) the business of dealing with an audience at a theatre, for example selling tickets and programmes

ˌfront ˈpage *noun* the first page of a newspaper, where the most important news is printed: *The story was on the front pages of all the tabloids.* ▶ **ˈfront-page** *adj.* [only before noun]: *The divorce made* ***front-page news.***

ˌfront ˈrunner *noun* a person, an animal or an organization that seems most likely to win a race or competition

ˌfront-wheel ˈdrive *noun* [U] a system in which power from the engine is sent to the front wheels of a vehicle ➲ compare REAR-WHEEL DRIVE

frost /frɒst; *NAmE* frɔːst/ *noun, verb*

■ ***noun*** **1** [U, C] a weather condition in which the temperature drops below 0°C (=FREEZING POINT) so that a thin white layer of ice forms on the ground and other surfaces, especially at night: *It will be a clear night with some* ***ground frost.*** ◇ *a* ***sharp/hard/severe frost*** ◇ *There were ten degrees of frost* (= the temperature dropped to -10°C) *last night.* ◇ *frost damage* **2** [U] the thin white layer of ice that forms when the temperature drops below 0°C: *The car windows were covered with frost.* ➲ see also HOAR FROST

■ ***verb*** **1** [T, I] to cover sth or to become covered with a thin white layer of ice: **~ sth (over/up)** *The mirror was frosted up.* ◇ **~ (over/up)** *The windows had frosted over.* **2** [T] **~ sth** (*especially NAmE*) to cover a cake with ICING/FROSTING

frost·bite /ˈfrɒstbaɪt; *NAmE* ˈfrɔːst-/ *noun* [U] a medical condition in which parts of the body, especially the fingers and toes, become damaged as a result of extremely cold temperatures ▶ **frost·bit·ten** /ˈfrɒstbɪtn; *NAmE* ˈfrɔːst-/ *adj.*

frost·ed /ˈfrɒstɪd; *NAmE* ˈfrɔːstɪd/ *adj.* **1** [only before noun] (of glass) that has been given a rough surface, so that it is difficult to see through **2** (*especially NAmE*) (of cakes, etc.) covered with ICING/FROSTING **3** covered with FROST: *the frosted garden* **4** containing very small shiny pieces: *frosted eyeshadow*

frost·ing /ˈfrɒstɪŋ; *NAmE* ˈfrɔːst-/ *noun* [U] **1** (*NAmE*) = ICING **2** [U] (*BrE*) the crime of stealing a vehicle that has been left with the engine running in cold weather so that the engine warms up

frosty /ˈfrɒsti; *NAmE* ˈfrɔːsti/ *adj.* (**frost·ier, frosti·est**) **1** (of the weather) extremely cold; cold with FROST: *a frosty morning* ◇ *He breathed in the frosty air.* **2** covered with FROST: *frosty fields* **3** unfriendly, in a way that suggests that sb does not approve of sth: *a* ***frosty look/reply*** ◇ *The latest proposals were given a frosty reception.* ▶ **frost·ily** /-ɪli/ *adv.*: *'No, thank you,' she said frostily.*

froth /frɒθ; *NAmE* frɔːθ/ *noun, verb*

■ ***noun*** **1** [U] a mass of small bubbles, especially on the surface of a liquid SYN **foam**: *a glass of beer with thick froth on top* **2** [U] ideas, activities, etc. that seem attractive and enjoyable but have no real value **3** [sing.] **~ of sth** something that looks like a mass of small bubbles on liquid: *a froth of black lace*

■ ***verb*** **1** [I, T] **~ (sth)** if a liquid **froths**, or if sb/sth **froths** it, a mass of small bubbles appears on the surface: *a cup of frothing coffee* **2** [I] to produce a lot of SALIVA (= liquid in your mouth): *The dog was* ***frothing at the mouth.*** ◇ (*figurative*) *He* ***frothed at the mouth*** (= was very angry) *when I asked for more money.*

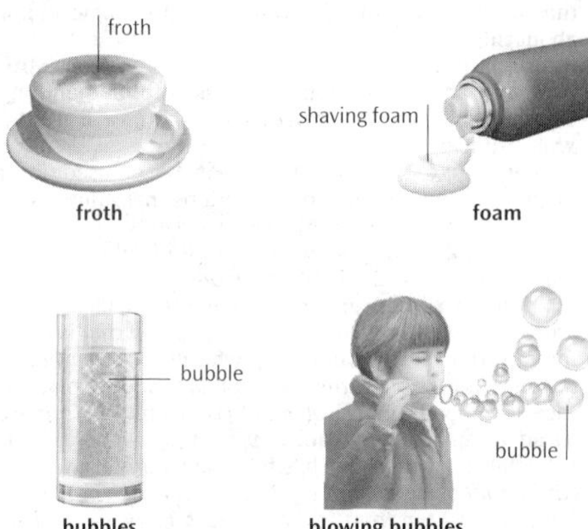

frothy /ˈfrɒθi; *NAmE* ˈfrɔːθi/ *adj.* **1** (of liquids) having a mass of small bubbles on the surface: *frothy coffee* **2** seeming attractive and enjoyable but having no real value: *frothy romantic novels* **3** (of clothes or cloth) light and delicate

frown /fraʊn/ *verb, noun*

■ ***verb*** [I, T] to make a serious, angry or worried expression by bringing your EYEBROWS closer together so that lines appear on your FOREHEAD: **~ (at sb/sth)** *What are you frowning at me for?* ◇ **+ speech** *'I don't understand,' she frowned.*

PHR V **ˈfrown on/upon sb/sth** to disapprove of sb/sth: *In her family, any expression of feeling was frowned upon.*

■ ***noun*** [usually sing.] a serious, angry or worried expression on a person's face that causes lines on their FOREHEAD: *She looked up* ***with a*** *puzzled* ***frown*** *on her face.* ◇ *a slight* ***frown of disapproval/concentration, etc.***

frow·sty /ˈfraʊsti/ *adj.* (*BrE*) smelling bad because there is no fresh air SYN **fusty, musty**: *a small frowsty office*

froze *past tense* of FREEZE

fro·zen 0━ /ˈfrəʊzn; *NAmE* ˈfroʊzn/ *adj.* **1** 0━ [usually before noun] (of food) kept at a very low temperature in order to preserve it: *frozen peas* **2** 0━ [not usually before noun] (of people or parts of the body) extremely cold: *I'm absolutely frozen!* ◇ *You look* ***frozen stiff.*** **3** 0━ (of rivers, lakes, etc.) with a layer of ice on the surface **4** 0━ (especially of ground) so cold that it has become very hard: *The ground was* ***frozen solid.*** **5** 0━ **~ with/in sth** unable to move because of a strong emotion such as fear or horror: *She stared at him, frozen with shock.* ➲ see also FREEZE *v.*

FRS /ˌef ɑːr ˈes/ *abbr.* **1** (*NAmE*) FEDERAL RESERVE SYSTEM **2** (*BrE*) Fellow of the Royal Society (a title given to important British scientists)

fruc·tose /ˈfrʌktəʊs; -təʊz; *NAmE* -toʊs; -toʊz/ *noun* [U] (*chemistry*) a type of sugar found in fruit juice and HONEY

fru·gal /ˈfruːɡl/ *adj.* **1** using only as much money or food as is necessary: *a **frugal existence/life*** OPP **extravagant** **2** (of meals) small, plain and not costing very much SYN **meagre**: *a frugal lunch of bread and cheese* ▸ **fru·gal·ity** /fruˈɡæləti/ *noun* [U] **fru·gal·ly** /-ɡəli/ *adv.*: *to **live/eat frugally***

fruit /fruːt/ *noun, verb*

▪ ***noun*** **1** [C, U] the part of a plant that consists of one or more seeds and flesh, can be eaten as food and usually tastes sweet: *tropical fruits, such as bananas and pineapples* ◇ *Eat plenty of fresh fruit and vegetables.* ◇ *a **piece of fruit*** (= an apple, an orange, etc.) ◇ *fruit juice* ◇ *fruit trees* ➲ **VISUAL VOCAB** page V26 ➲ compare VEGETABLE ➲ see also DRIED FRUIT, FIRST FRUIT, SOFT FRUIT **2** [C] (*technical*) a part of a plant or tree that is formed after the flowers have died and in which seeds develop **3** [C, usually pl.] (*literary*) all the natural things that the earth produces **4** [C] (*offensive*) an offensive word for a HOMOSEXUAL man

IDM **the fruit/fruits of sth** the good results of an activity or a situation: *to enjoy the fruits of your labours* (= the rewards for your hard work) ◇ *The book is the fruit of years of research.* ➲ more at BEAR *v.*, FORBIDDEN

▪ ***verb*** [I] (*technical*) (of a tree or plant) to produce fruit

fruit·ar·ian /fruːˈteəriən; *NAmE* -ˈter-/ *noun* a person who eats only fruit ➲ compare VEGETARIAN

ˈ**fruit bat** *noun* a BAT (= an animal like a mouse with wings) that lives in hot countries and eats fruit

ˈ**fruit cake** *noun* **1** [C, U] a cake containing dried fruit **2 fruitcake** [C] (*informal*) a person who behaves in a strange or crazy way: *She's **nutty as a fruitcake**.*

ˌ**fruit ˈcocktail** *noun* [U] a mixture of pieces of fruit in liquid, sold in tins

ˌ**fruit ˈcup** *noun* [U, C] **1** (*BrE*) a drink consisting of fruit juices and pieces of fruit **2** (*NAmE*) = FRUIT SALAD

fruit·er·er /ˈfruːtərə(r)/ *noun* (*old-fashioned, especially BrE*) a person who owns or manages a shop/store selling fruit ➲ compare GREENGROCER

ˈ**fruit fly** *noun* a small fly that eats plants that are decaying, especially fruit

fruit·ful /ˈfruːtfl/ *adj.* **1** producing many useful results SYN **productive**: *a fruitful collaboration/discussion* OPP **fruitless** **2** (*literary*) (of land or trees) producing a lot of crops ▸ **fruit·ful·ly** /ˈfruːtfəli/ *adv.* **fruit·ful·ness** /ˈfruːtfəlnəs/ *noun* [U]

fruiti·ness /ˈfruːtinəs/ *noun* [U] (especially of wine) the quality of tasting or smelling strongly of fruit

fru·ition /fruˈɪʃn/ *noun* [U] (*formal*) the successful result of a plan, a process or an activity: *After months of hard work, our plans finally **came to fruition**.* ◇ *His extravagant ideas were never **brought to fruition**.*

fruit·less /ˈfruːtləs/ *adj.* producing no useful results SYN **unproductive**: *a **fruitless attempt/search*** ◇ *Our efforts to persuade her proved fruitless.* OPP **fruitful** ▸ **fruit·less·ly** *adv.*

ˈ**fruit machine** (*BrE*) (also ˌ**one-armed ˈbandit**, ˈ**slot machine** *NAmE, BrE*) *noun* a gambling machine that you put coins into and that gives money back if particular pictures appear together on the screen

ˌ**fruit ˈsalad** (*NAmE* also ˌ**fruit ˈcup**) *noun* [U, C] a cold DESSERT (= a sweet dish) consisting of small pieces of different types of fruit

fruity /ˈfruːti/ *adj.* (**fruit·ier**, **fruiti·est**) **1** smelling or tasting strongly of fruit: *The wine from this region is rich and fruity.* **2** (of a voice or laugh) deep and pleasant in quality **3** (*NAmE, informal*) (of people) slightly crazy

frump /frʌmp/ *noun* (*disapproving*) a woman who wears clothes that are not fashionable ▸ **frumpy** (also *less frequent* **frump·ish**) *adj.*: *frumpy clothes* ◇ *a frumpy housewife*

frus·trate /frʌˈstreɪt; *NAmE* ˈfrʌstreɪt/ *verb* **1 ~ sb** to make sb feel annoyed or impatient because they cannot do or achieve what they want: *What frustrates him is that there's too little money to spend on the project.* **2 ~ sb/sth** to prevent sb from doing sth; to prevent sth from happening or succeeding SYN **thwart**: *The rescue attempt was frustrated by bad weather.*

frus·trated /frʌˈstreɪtɪd; *NAmE* ˈfrʌstreɪtɪd/ *adj.* **1** feeling annoyed and impatient because you cannot do or achieve what you want: *It's very easy to get frustrated in this job.* ◇ **~ at/with sth** *They felt frustrated at the lack of progress.* **2** (of an emotion) having no effect; not being satisfied: *He stamped his foot in frustrated rage.* ◇ *frustrated desires* **3** [only before noun] unable to be successful in a particular career: *a frustrated artist* **4** not satisfied sexually

frus·trat·ing /frʌˈstreɪtɪŋ; *NAmE* ˈfrʌstreɪtɪŋ/ *adj.* causing you to feel annoyed and impatient because you cannot do or achieve what you want: *It's frustrating to have to wait so long.* ▸ **frus·trat·ing·ly** *adv.*: *Progress was frustratingly slow.*

frus·tra·tion /frʌˈstreɪʃn/ *noun* **1** [U] the feeling of being frustrated: *Dave thumped the table **in frustration**.* ◇ *She couldn't stand the frustration of not being able to help.* ◇ *sexual frustration* **2** [C, usually pl.] something that causes you to feel frustrated: *Every job has its difficulties and frustrations.* ◇ *Inevitably she took out her frustrations on the children.* **3** [U] **~ of sth** (*formal*) the fact that sth is preventing sth/sb from succeeding: *the frustration of all his ambitions*

fry /fraɪ/ *verb, noun*

▪ ***verb*** (**fries**, **fry·ing**, **fried**, **fried**) **1** [T, I] **~ (sth)** to cook sth in hot fat or oil; to be cooked in hot fat or oil: *fried fish* ◇ *the smell of bacon frying* ➲ related noun FRY-UP ➲ **COLLOCATIONS** at COOKING ➲ **VISUAL VOCAB** page V24 ➲ see also STIR-FRY **2** [I] (*informal*) to be burnt by the sun: *You'll fry on the beach if you're not careful.* IDM see FISH *n.*

▪ ***noun*** **1** [pl.] very small young fish ➲ see also SMALL FRY **2** [C] (usually **fries** [pl.]) (*especially NAmE*) = FRENCH FRY: *Would you like ketchup with your fries?*

fryer (also **frier**) /ˈfraɪə(r)/ *noun* **1** a large deep pan used for frying food in: *a deep-fat fryer* **2** (*NAmE*) a young chicken that is suitable for frying

ˈ**frying pan** (*NAmE* also **fry·pan**, **skil·let**) *noun* a large shallow pan with a long handle, used for frying food in ➲ **VISUAL VOCAB** page V24

IDM **out of the ˈfrying pan into the ˈfire** (*saying*) from a bad situation to one that is worse

ˈ**fry-up** *noun* (*BrE, informal*) a meal of fried food, such as BACON and eggs

FT (also **F/T**) *abbr.* (in writing) FULL-TIME: *The course is 1 year FT, 2 years PT.* ➲ compare PT

Ft (also **Ft.** especially in *NAmE*) *abbr.* FORT: *Ft William*

ft (*BrE*) (also **ft.** *NAmE, BrE*) *abbr.* (in writing measurements) feet; foot: *The room is 12ft × 9ft.*

the FTC /ˌef tiː ˈsiː/ *abbr.* the Federal Trade Commission (the US government organization that is responsible for making sure that there is fair competition in business)

FTP /ˌef tiː ˈpiː/ *abbr.* file transfer protocol (a set of rules for sending files from one computer to another on the Internet)

the FTSE index™ /ˈfʊtsi ɪndeks/ (also **the FT index** /ˌef ˈtiː/, **the Fiˌnancial Times ˈindex**, **the Foot·sie™**) *noun* [sing.] a figure that shows the relative price of shares on the London Stock Exchange

fuch·sia /ˈfjuːʃə/ *noun* [C, U] a small bush with flowers in two colours of red, purple or white, that hang down

fuck /fʌk/ *verb, noun*

▪ ***verb*** (*taboo, slang*) **1** [I, T] **~ (sb)** to have sex with sb **2** [I, T] a swear word that many people find offensive that is used to express anger, disgust or surprise: *Oh, fuck! I've lost my keys.* ◇ **~ sb/sth** *Fuck it! We've missed the train.* ◇ *Fuck you—I'm leaving.*

IDM ˌ**fuck ˈme** used to express surprise

PHR V ˌ**fuck aˈround** (*BrE* also ˌ**fuck aˈbout**) to waste time by behaving in a silly way HELP A more polite, informal way of saying this is **mess about** (*BrE*) or **mess around** (*NAmE, BrE*). ˌ**fuck sb aˈround** (*BrE* also ˌ**fuck sb aˈbout**) to treat sb in a way that is deliberately not helpful to them or wastes their time HELP A more polite, informal way of saying this is **mess sb about/around** (*BrE*). **ˌfuck ˈoff** (usually used in orders) to go away: *Why don't you just fuck off?* **ˌfuck ˈup** to do sth badly or make a bad mistake: *You've really fucked up this time!* HELP A more polite way to express this is **mess up**. **ˌfuck sb↔ˈup** to upset or confuse sb so much that they are not able to deal with problems in their life: *My parents' divorce really fucked me up.* HELP A more polite way to express this is **mess sb up**. **ˌfuck sth↔ˈup** to do sth badly or spoil sth: *I completely fucked up my exams.* HELP A more polite, informal way of saying this is **mess sth up**. **ˈfuck with sb** to treat sb badly in a way that makes them annoyed: *Don't fuck with him.* HELP A more polite way to express this is **mess with sb**.

F

■ ***noun*** (*taboo, slang*) **1** [C, usually sing.] an act of sex **2 the fuck** [sing.] used for emphasis, or to show that you are angry, annoyed or surprised: *What the fuck are you doing?* ◊ *Let's get the fuck out of here!*

IDM **not give a ˈfuck (about sb/sth)** to not care at all about sb/sth ➲ see also F-WORD

ˌfuck ˈall *noun* [U] (*BrE, taboo, slang*) a phrase that many people find offensive, used to mean 'none at all' or 'nothing at all': *You've done fuck all today.* ◊ *These instructions make fuck all sense to me.*

fuck·er /ˈfʌkə(r)/ *noun* (*taboo, slang*) a very offensive word used to insult sb

fuck·ing /ˈfʌkɪŋ/ *adj., adv.* (*taboo, slang*) a swear word that many people find offensive that is used to emphasize a comment or an angry statement: *I'm fucking sick of this fucking rain!* ◊ *He's a fucking good player.*

IDM **ˈfucking well** (*especially BrE*) used to emphasize an angry statement or an order: *You're fucking well coming whether you want to or not.*

fud·dled /ˈfʌdld/ *adj.* unable to think clearly, usually as a result of being old or drinking alcohol

fuddy-duddy /ˈfʌdi dʌdi/ *noun* (*pl.* **fuddy-duddies**) (*informal*) a person who has old-fashioned ideas or habits ▸ **fuddy-duddy** *adj.*

fudge /fʌdʒ/ *noun, verb*

■ ***noun*** **1** [U] a type of soft brown sweet/candy made from sugar, butter and milk **2 a fudge** [sing.] (*especially BrE*, rather *informal*) a way of dealing with a situation that does not really solve the problems but is intended to appear to do so: *This solution is a fudge rushed in to win cheers at the party conference.*

■ ***verb*** [T, I] **~ (on) sth** (rather *informal*) to avoid giving clear and accurate information, or a clear answer: *I asked how long he was staying, but he fudged the answer.* ◊ *Politicians are often very clever at* ***fudging the issue***.

fuel 🔑 /ˈfjuːəl/ *noun, verb*

■ ***noun*** **1** 🔑 [U, C] any material that produces heat or power, usually when it is burnt: ***solid fuel*** (= wood, coal, etc.) ◊ *nuclear fuels* ◊ *a car with high* ***fuel consumption*** ➲ see also FOSSIL FUEL **2** [U] a thing that is said or done that makes sth, especially an argument, continue or get worse: *The new information adds fuel to the debate over safety procedures.* ◊ *The revelations gave new fuel to angry opponents of the proposed law.* ◊ *His remarks simply* ***added fuel to the fire/flames*** *of her rage.*

■ ***verb*** (**-ll-**, *US* **-l-**) **1** [T] **~ sth** to supply sth with material that can be burnt to produce heat or power: *Uranium is used to fuel nuclear plants.* ◊ *oil-fuelled power stations* **2** [T, I] **~ (sth) (up)** to put petrol/gas into a vehicle: *The helicopter was already fuelled (up) and ready to go.* **3** [T] **~ sth** to increase sth; to make sth stronger SYN **stoke**: *to* ***fuel speculation/rumours/fears*** ◊ *Higher salaries helped to fuel inflation.*

ˈfuel cell *noun* a device that produces electricity directly from a fuel, such as HYDROGEN, by its reaction with another chemical, such as OXYGEN, without any burning, in order to supply power to a vehicle or machine

ˈfuel injection *noun* [U] a system of putting fuel into the engine of a car under pressure as a way of improving its performance

ˈfuel rod *noun* (*technical*) a long thin piece of fuel used in a nuclear power station

fufu /ˈfuːfuː/ *noun* [U] (*WAfrE*) a smooth white food often eaten with soups or STEWS and made by boiling and crushing the roots of plants such as COCOYAMS and CASSAVA

fug /fʌg/ *noun* [sing.] (*BrE, informal*) air in a room that is hot and smells unpleasant because there are too many people in the room or because people are smoking

fugal /ˈfjuːgl/ *adj.* (*music*) similar to or related to a FUGUE

fu·gi·tive /ˈfjuːdʒətɪv/ *noun, adj.*

■ ***noun*** **~ (from sb/sth)** a person who has escaped or is running away from somewhere and is trying to avoid being caught: *a fugitive from justice*

■ ***adj.*** [only before noun] **1** trying to avoid being caught: *a fugitive criminal* **2** (*literary*) lasting only for a very short time SYN **fleeting**: *a* ***fugitive idea/thought***

fugue /fjuːg/ *noun* a piece of music in which one or more tunes are introduced and then repeated in a complicated pattern

-ful *suffix* **1** (in adjectives) full of; having the qualities of; tending to: *sorrowful* ◊ *masterful* ◊ *forgetful* **2** (in nouns) an amount that fills sth: *handful* ◊ *spoonful*

ful·crum /ˈfʊlkrəm; ˈfʌlk-/ *noun* (*pl.* **ful·crums** or **ful·cra** /ˈfʊlkrə; ˈfʌlk-/) **1** (*physics*) the point on which a LEVER turns or is supported **2** [usually sing.] the most important part of an activity or a situation

ful·fil (*BrE*) (*NAmE* **ful·fill**) /fʊlˈfɪl/ *verb* (**ful·fill·ing, ful·filled, ful·filled**) **1 ~ sth** to do or achieve what was hoped for or expected: *to* ***fulfil*** *your* ***dream/ambition/potential*** **2 ~ sth** (*formal*) to do or have what is required or necessary: *to* ***fulfil a duty/an obligation/a promise*** ◊ *to* ***fulfil the terms/conditions*** *of an agreement* ◊ *No candidate fulfils all the criteria for this position.* **3 ~ sth** to have a particular role or purpose: *Nursery schools should* ***fulfil the function*** *of preparing children for school.* **4 ~ sb/yourself** to make sb feel happy and satisfied with what they are doing or have done: *I need a job that really fulfils me.* ◊ *He was able to fulfil himself through his painting.* ▸ **ful·fil·ment** (*BrE*) (*NAmE* **ful·fill·ment**) *noun* [U]: *the fulfilment of a dream* ◊ *to find personal fulfilment* ➲ SYNONYMS at SATISFACTION

ful·filled /fʊlˈfɪld/ *adj.* feeling happy and satisfied that you are doing sth useful with your life: *He doesn't feel fulfilled in his present job.* OPP **unfulfilled**

ful·fil·ling /fʊlˈfɪlɪŋ/ *adj.* causing sb to feel satisfied and useful: *a fulfilling experience* OPP **unfulfilling** ➲ SYNONYMS at SATISFYING

full 🔑 /fʊl/ *adj., adv.*

■ ***adj.*** (**full·er, fullest**)

▸ WITH NO EMPTY SPACE **1** 🔑 **~ (of sth)** containing or holding as much or as many as possible; having no empty space: *a full bottle of wine* ◊ *She could only nod, because her mouth was full.* ◊ *My suitcase was full of books.* ◊ *There were cardboard boxes* ***stuffed full of*** *clothes.* ◊ (*BrE*) *Sorry, the hotel is* ***full up*** *tonight.*

▸ HAVING A LOT **2** 🔑 **~ of sth** having or containing a large number or amount of sth: *The sky was full of brightly coloured fireworks.* ◊ ***Life is full of*** *coincidences.* ◊ *Our new brochure is* ***crammed full of*** *inspirational ideas.* ◊ *animals* ***pumped full of*** *antibiotics* ◊ *She was full of admiration for the care she had received.* ◊ *He smiled, his eyes full of laughter.*

▸ TALKING A LOT **3 ~ of sth** (of a person) thinking or talking a lot about a particular thing: *He was full of his new job and everything he'd been doing.*

▸ WITH FOOD **4** 🔑 (*BrE* also **ˌfull ˈup**) having had enough to eat: *No more for me, thanks—I'm full up.* ◊ *The kids still weren't full, so I gave them an ice cream each.* ◊ *You can't run* ***on a full stomach***.

▸ COMPLETE **5** 🔑 [usually before noun] complete; with nothing missing: *Full details are available on request.* ◊ *I still don't think we've heard* ***the full story***. ◊ *a full English breakfast* ◊ *A full refund will be given if the item is faulty.* ◊ *Fill in your full name and address.* ◊ *The country applied for full membership of the European Union.*

▸ AS MUCH AS POSSIBLE **6** 🔑 [usually before noun] to the highest level or greatest amount possible SYN **maximum**:

*Many people don't use their computers to their **full potential**. ◇ measures to achieve **full employment** ◇ Students should **take full advantage of** the university's facilities. ◇ She came round the corner **at full speed**.*
▸ BUSY **7** busy; involving a lot of activities: *He'd had a very **full life**. ◇ Her life was too full to find time for hobbies.*
▸ FOR EMPHASIS **8** [only before noun] used to emphasize an amount or a quantity: *She is a full four inches shorter than her sister.*
▸ MOON **9** appearing as a complete circle: *The moon was full, the sky clear.* ➲ see also FULL MOON
▸ FAT **10** (of a person or part of the body) large and round. 'Full' is sometimes used to avoid saying 'fat': *He kissed her full sensual lips. ◇ They specialize in clothes for women with a fuller figure.*
▸ CLOTHES **11** made with plenty of cloth; fitting loosely: *a full skirt*
▸ TONE/VOICE/FLAVOUR **12** deep, strong and rich: *He draws a unique full sound from the instrument. ◇ the full fruity flavour of the wine*
IDM Most idioms containing **full** are at the entries for the nouns and verbs in the idioms, for example **full of the joys of spring** is at **joy**. **'full of it** (*informal, disapproving, especially NAmE*) (of a person) not telling the truth; tending to exaggerate things: *'You are so full of it!' she retorted furiously.* **'full of yourself** (*disapproving*) very proud; thinking only of yourself **in full** including the whole of sth: *The address must be printed in full.* **to the full** (*NAmE* usually **to the fullest**) to the greatest possible degree: *I've always believed in living life to the full.*
■ ***adv.*** **~ in/on sth** directly: *She looked him full in the face.*

full·back /ˈfʊlbæk/ *noun* **1** [C] one of the defending players in football (SOCCER), HOCKEY or RUGBY whose position is near the goal they are defending **2** [C] the attacking player in AMERICAN FOOTBALL whose position is behind the QUARTERBACK and beside the HALFBACKS **3** [U] the position a fullback plays at: *Hunter is at fullback.*

ˌfull ˈbeam *noun* [U] (*BrE*) the brightest light that a vehicle's HEADLIGHTS can give, usually used when there are no street lights and no other traffic: *Even with the lights on full beam I couldn't see very far.*

ˌfull-ˈblooded *adj.* [only before noun] **1** involving very strong feelings or actions; done in an enthusiastic way: *a full-blooded attack* **2** having parents, grandparents, etc. from only one race or country: *a full-blooded Scotsman*

ˌfull-ˈblown *adj.* [only before noun] having all the characteristics of sb/sth; fully developed: *full-blown AIDS ◇ The border dispute turned into a full-blown crisis.*

ˌfull ˈboard (*BrE*) (*NAmE* **Aˌmerican ˈplan**) *noun* [U] a type of accommodation in a hotel, etc. that includes all meals: *Do you require full or half board?* ➲ compare BED AND BREAKFAST, EUROPEAN PLAN, HALF BOARD

ˌfull-ˈbodied *adj.* having a pleasantly strong taste or sound: *a full-bodied red wine ◇ a full-bodied string section*

ˌfull-ˈcolour (*especially US* **ˌfull-ˈcolor**) *adj.* [only before noun] printed using colours rather than just black and white

ˌfull-court ˈpress *noun* [sing.] (*NAmE*) **1** (in BASKETBALL) a way of attacking in which the members of a team stay close to their opponents over the whole area of play **2** (*informal*) a strong effort to influence sb or a group of people by putting pressure on them

ˌfull-ˈcream *adj.* (*BrE*) (of milk) with none of the fat taken away

full·er's earth /ˌfʊləz ˈɜːθ; *NAmE* ˌfʊlərz ˈɜːrθ/ *noun* [U] a type of CLAY used for cleaning cloth and making it thicker

ˌfull ˈface *adj., adv.* showing the whole of sb's face; not in PROFILE: *a full-face* ***view/portrait***

ˌfull-ˈfat *adj.* [usually before noun] (*especially BrE*) (of milk, cheese, etc.) without any of the fat removed

ˌfull-ˈfledged (*especially NAmE*) (*BrE* also **ˌfully ˈfledged**) *adj.* completely developed; with all the qualifications necessary for sth

ˌfull ˈforward *noun* (in AUSTRALIAN RULES football) an attacking player who plays near the opposing team's goal

ˌfull-ˈfrontal *adj., noun*
■ ***adj.*** [only before noun] **1** showing the whole of the front of a person's body: *full-frontal nudity* **2** = FRONTAL (2)
■ ***noun*** a picture or a scene in a film/movie which shows the naked body of a person from the front

ˌfull-ˈgrown *adj.* (of people, animals or plants) having reached the greatest size to which they can grow and stopped growing

ˌfull ˈhouse *noun* **1** an occasion in a theatre, cinema/movie theater, etc. when there are no empty seats: *They played to a full house.* **2** (in the card game of POKER) three cards of one kind and two of another kind

ˌfull-ˈlength *adj., adv.*
■ ***adj.*** [only before noun] **1** (of a mirror or picture) showing the whole of a person's body: *a full-length portrait* **2** (of a book, play, etc.) not made shorter; of the usual length: *a full-length novel* **3** (of curtains or a window) reaching the ground **4** (of clothing) reaching a person's ankles: *a full-length skirt*
■ ***adv.*** a person who is lying **full-length** is lying flat with their legs straight: *He was sprawled full-length across the bed.*

ˌfull ˈmarks *noun* [pl.] (*BrE*) the highest mark/grade in a test, etc. (when you get nothing wrong): *She got full marks in the exam.* ◇ (*figurative*) ***Full marks to** Bill for an excellent idea!* (= he deserves praise)

ˌfull ˈmoon *noun* [C, usually sing., U] the moon when it appears as a full circle; a time when this happens ➲ compare HALF-MOON, HARVEST MOON, NEW MOON

full·ness /ˈfʊlnəs/ *noun* [U, sing.] **1** (of the body or part of the body) the quality of being large and round: *the fullness of her lips* **2** (of colours, sounds and flavours) the quality of being deep and rich **3** the quality of being complete and satisfying: *the fullness of life*
IDM **in the fullness of ˈtime** when the time is appropriate, usually after a long period

ˌfull-ˈon *adj.* (*informal*) used to say that sth is done to the greatest possible degree: *It was a full-on night out with the boys.*

ˌfull-ˈpage *adj.* [only before noun] filling a complete page of a newspaper or magazine: *a full-page ad*

ˌfull ˈpoint *noun* = FULL STOP

ˈfull professor *noun* (*NAmE*) = PROFESSOR (1)

ˌfull-ˈscale *adj.* [only before noun] **1** that is as complete and thorough as possible: *a full-scale attack* **2** that is the same size as sth that is being copied: *a full-scale model*

ˌfull-ˈsize (also **ˌfull-ˈsized**) *adj.* [usually before noun] not made smaller; of the usual size: *a full-size model ◇ a full-size snooker table*

ˌfull ˈstop *noun, adv.*
■ ***noun*** (also *less frequent* **stop**) (also **ˌfull ˈpoint**) (all *BrE*) (*NAmE* **period**) the mark (.) used at the end of a sentence and in some abbreviations, for example *e.g.*
IDM **come to a full ˈstop** to stop completely
■ ***adv.*** (*BrE*) (also **period** *NAmE, BrE*) (*informal*) used at the end of a sentence to emphasize that there is nothing more to say about a subject: *I've already told you—we can't afford it, full stop!*

ˌfull-ˈterm *adj.* (*technical*) **1** (of a PREGNANCY) lasting the normal length of time **2** (of a baby) born after a PREGNANCY lasting the normal length of time

ˌfull ˈtime *noun* [U] (*BrE*) the end of a sports game: *The referee blew his whistle for full time. ◇ The full-time score was 1-1.* ➲ compare HALF-TIME

ˌfull-ˈtime *adj., adv.* (*abbr.* FT) for all the hours of a week during which people normally work or study, rather than just for a part of it: *students in full-time education ◇ a full-time employee ◇ a full-time job ◇ Looking after a child is a full-time job* (= hard work that takes a lot of time). *◇ She works full-time and still manages to run a home.* ➲ compare PART-TIME

ˌfull-ˈtimer *noun* a person who works full-time

ˌ**full 'toss** *noun* (in CRICKET) a ball that reaches the BATSMAN without touching the ground and is easy to hit

fully 0-w /ˈfʊli/ *adv.*
1 0-w completely: *She had* ***fully recovered*** *from the accident.* ◇ *We are* ***fully aware*** *of the dangers.* ◇ ***I fully understand*** *your motives.* **2** (*formal*) (used to emphasize an amount) the whole of; as much as: *The disease affects fully 30 per cent of the population.*

ˌ**fully 'fledged** (*BrE*) (also ˌ**full-'fledged** *NAmE, BrE*) *adj.* [usually before noun] completely developed; with all the qualifications necessary for sth: *the emergence of a fully fledged market economy* ◇ *She was now a fully fledged member of the teaching profession.*

F

ful·mar /ˈfʊlmə(r)/ *noun* a grey and white bird that lives near the sea

ful·min·ate /ˈfʊlmɪneɪt; ˈfʌl-/ *verb* [I] **~ against (sb/sth)** (*formal*) to criticize sb/sth angrily ▸ **ful·min·ation** /ˌfʊlmɪˈneɪʃn; ˌfʌl-/ *noun* [C, U]

ful·some /ˈfʊlsəm/ *adj.* (*disapproving*) too generous in praising or thanking sb, or in saying sorry, so that you do not sound sincere: *a fulsome apology* ◇ *He was fulsome in his praise of the Prime Minister.* ▸ **ful·some·ly** *adv.*

fum·ble /ˈfʌmbl/ *verb, noun*
▪ ***verb*** **1** [I, T] to use your hands in an awkward way when you are doing sth or looking for sth: **~ (at/with/in sth)** (**for sth**) *She fumbled in her pocket for a handkerchief.* ◇ *He fumbled with the buttons on his shirt.* ◇ **~ around** *She was fumbling around in the dark looking for the light switch.* ◇ **~ sth** (**+ adv./prep.**) *He fumbled the key into the ignition.* ◇ **~ to do sth** *I fumbled to zip up my jacket.* **2** [I, T] to have difficulty speaking clearly or finding the right words to say: **~ (for sth)** *During the interview, she fumbled helplessly for words.* ◇ **~ sth** *to fumble an announcement* **3** [T] **~ sth** (especially in sport) to drop a ball or to fail to stop or kick it
▪ ***noun*** **1** [sing.] (also **fum·bling** [C, usually pl.]) an awkward action using the hands **2** [C] (*NAmE*) the action of dropping the ball while it is in play in AMERICAN FOOTBALL

fum·bling /ˈfʌmblɪŋ/ *adj.* awkward, uncertain or hesitating: *a fumbling schoolboy*

fume /fjuːm/ *verb* **1** [I, T] to be very angry about sth: **~ (at/over/about sb/sth)** *She sat in the car, silently fuming at the traffic jam.* ◇ **~ (with sth)** *He was fuming with indignation.* ◇ **+ speech** *'This is intolerable!' she fumed.* **2** [I] to produce smoke or fumes

fumes /fjuːmz/ *noun* [pl.] (also *less frequent* **fume** [U]) smoke, gas, or sth similar that smells strongly or is dangerous to breathe in: ***diesel/petrol/exhaust fumes*** ➲ VISUAL VOCAB page V7: *to be overcome by smoke and fumes* ◇ *Clouds of toxic fumes escaped in a huge chemical factory blaze.* ◇ *The body of a man was found in a* ***fume-filled*** *car yesterday.*

fu·mi·gate /ˈfjuːmɪɡeɪt/ *verb* **~ sth** to use special chemicals, smoke or gas to destroy the harmful insects or bacteria in a place: *to fumigate a room* ▸ **fu·mi·ga·tion** /ˌfjuːmɪˈɡeɪʃn/ *noun* [U, C]

fun 0-w /fʌn/ *noun, adj.*
▪ ***noun*** [U] **1** 0-w enjoyment; pleasure; a thing that gives enjoyment or pleasure and makes you feel happy: *We had a lot of fun at Sarah's party.* ◇ *Sailing is* ***good fun.*** ◇ ***Have fun!*** (= Enjoy yourself) ◇ *I decided to learn Spanish, just* ***for fun.*** ◇ *I didn't do all that work just* ***for the fun of it.*** ◇ *It's not much fun going to a party on your own.* ◇ *'What fun!' she said with a laugh.* ◇ *Walking three miles in the pouring rain is* ***not my idea of fun.*** ◇ *'What do you say to a weekend in New York?' 'Sounds like fun.'* **2** 0-w behaviour or activities that are not serious but come from a sense of enjoyment: *She's very lively and* ***full of fun.*** ◇ *We didn't mean to hurt him. It was just* ***a bit of fun.*** ◇ *It wasn't serious - it was all done* ***in fun.*** ➲ SYNONYMS at ENTERTAINMENT
IDM **fun and 'games** (*informal*) activities that are not serious and that other people may disapprove of **make 'fun of sb/sth** 0-w to laugh at sb/sth or make other people laugh at them, usually in an unkind way: *It's cruel to make fun of people who stammer.* ➲ more at FIGURE *n.*, POKE *v.*
▪ ***adj.*** 0-w amusing or enjoyable: *She's really fun to be with.* ◇ *This game looks fun!* ◇ *There are lots of fun things for young people to do here.*

Synonyms

fun

pleasure • (a) good time • enjoyment • (a) great time

These are all words for the feeling of enjoying yourself, or activities or time that you enjoy.

fun (*rather informal*) the feeling of enjoying yourself; activities that you enjoy: *We had a lot of fun at Sarah's party.* ◇ *Sailing is* ***good/great fun.***

pleasure (*rather formal*) the feeling of enjoying yourself or being satisfied: *Reading for pleasure and reading for study are not the same.*

(a) good time (*rather informal*) a time that you spend enjoying yourself: *We had a good time in Spain.*

enjoyment (*rather formal*) the feeling of enjoying yourself: *I get a lot of enjoyment from music.*

PLEASURE OR ENJOYMENT?

Enjoyment usually comes from an activity that you do; **pleasure** can come from sth that you do or sth that happens: *He beamed with pleasure at seeing her.* ◇ ~~*He beamed with enjoyment at seeing her.*~~

(a) great time (*rather informal*) a time that you spend enjoying yourself very much: *We had a really great time together.*

PATTERNS

- to do sth **for** fun/pleasure/enjoyment
- **great** fun/pleasure/enjoyment
- to **have** fun/a good time/a great time
- to **get** pleasure/enjoyment **from** sth
- to **spoil** the fun/sb's pleasure/sb's enjoyment

func·tion 0-w AW /ˈfʌŋkʃn/ *noun, verb*
▪ ***noun*** **1** 0-w [C, U] a special activity or purpose of a person or thing: *to* ***fulfil/perform a function*** ◇ ***bodily functions*** (= for example eating, sex, using the toilet) ◇ *The function of the heart is to pump blood through the body.* ◇ *This design aims for harmony of form and function.* **2** 0-w [C] a social event or official ceremony: *The hall provided a venue for weddings and other functions.* **3** [C] (*mathematics*) a quantity whose value depends on the varying values of others. In the statement 2x=y, y is a function of x: (*figurative*) *Salary is* ***a function of*** *age and experience.* **4** [C] (*computing*) a part of a program, etc. that performs a basic operation
▪ ***verb*** 0-w [I] (**+ adv./prep.**) (rather *formal*) to work in the correct way SYN **operate**: *Despite the power cuts, the hospital continued to function normally.* ◇ *We now have a functioning shower.* ◇ *Many children can't function effectively in large classes.*
PHR V **'function as sb/sth** 0-w to perform the action or the job of the thing or person mentioned: *The sofa also functions as a bed.*

func·tion·al AW /ˈfʌŋkʃənl/ *adj.* **1** practical and useful; with little or no decoration SYN **utilitarian**: *Bathrooms don't have to be purely functional.* ◇ *The office was large and functional rather than welcoming.* **2** having a special purpose; making it possible for sb to do sth or for sth to happen: *a functional disorder* (= an illness caused when an organ of the body fails to perform its function) ◇ *a functional approach to language learning* ◇ *These units played a key functional role in the military operation.* **3** (especially of a machine, an organization or a system) working; able to work: *The hospital will soon be fully functional.* ▸ **func·tion·al·ly** AW /-ʃənəli/ *adv.*

ˈ**functional food** *noun* [C, U] (also **nutra·ceut·ical**) food that has had substances that are good for your health specially added to it

ˌ**functional 'grammar** *noun* [U] (*linguistics*) grammar that analyses how language is used to communicate

func·tion·al·ism /ˈfʌŋkʃənəlɪzəm/ *noun* [U] the idea or belief that the most important thing about the style or design of a building or object is how it is going to be used, not how it will look ▸ **func·tion·al·ist** /-ʃənəlɪst/ *noun* **func·tion·al·ist** *adj.* [usually before noun]

func·tion·al·ity /ˌfʌŋkʃəˈnæləti/ *noun* (*pl.* -ies) **1** [U] the quality in sth of being very suitable for the purpose it was designed for SYN **practicality 2** [U] the purpose that sth is designed for or expected to perform: *Manufacturing processes may be affected by the functionality of the product.* **3** [U, C] (*computing*) the range of functions that a computer or other electronic system can perform: *new software with additional functionality*

func·tion·ary /ˈfʌŋkʃənəri; *NAmE* -neri/ *noun* (*pl.* -ies) (often *disapproving*) a person with official duties SYN **official**: ***party/state/government functionaries***

ˈ**function key** *noun* (*computing*) one of several keys on a computer keyboard, each marked with 'F' and a number, that can be used to do sth, such as save a file or get to the 'help' function in a program

ˈ**function word** (also **func·tor**) *noun* (*grammar*) a word that is important to the grammar of a sentence rather than its meaning, for example 'do' in 'we do not live here' ➲ compare CONTENT WORD

func·tor /ˈfʌŋktə(r)/ *noun* **1** (*mathematics*) a FUNCTION or a symbol such as + or × **2** (*grammar*) = FUNCTION WORD

fund 🔑 AW /fʌnd/ *noun, verb*

■ ***noun* 1** 🔑 [C] an amount of money that has been saved or has been made available for a particular purpose: *a disaster relief fund* ◇ *the company's pension fund* ◇ *the International Monetary Fund* **2** 🔑 **funds** [pl.] money that is available to be spent: *government funds* ◇ *The hospital is trying to raise funds for a new kidney machine.* ◇ *The project has been cancelled because of lack of funds* ◇ *I'm* ***short of funds*** *at the moment—can I pay you back next week?* ➲ COLLOCATIONS at FINANCE **3** [sing.] **~ of sth** an amount or a supply of sth: *a fund of knowledge*

■ ***verb*** 🔑 **~ sth** to provide money for sth, usually sth official: *a dance festival funded by the Arts Council* ◇ *The museum is privately funded.* ◇ *a government-funded programme*

fun·da·men·tal 🔑 AW /ˌfʌndəˈmentl/ *adj., noun*

■ ***adj.* 1** 🔑 serious and very important; affecting the most central and important parts of sth SYN **basic**: *There is a* ***fundamental difference*** *between the two points of view.* ◇ *A* ***fundamental change*** *in the organization of health services was required.* ◇ *a question of fundamental importance* **2** 🔑 **~ (to sth)** central; forming the necessary basis of sth SYN **essential**: *Hard work is fundamental to success.* **3** [only before noun] (*physics*) forming the source or base from which everything else is made; not able to be divided any further: *a fundamental particle*

■ ***noun*** [usually pl.] a basic rule or principle; an essential part: *the fundamentals of modern physics* ◇ *He taught me the fundamentals of the job.*

ˌ**fundamental** ˈ**force** *noun* (*technical*) a force that is a property (= characteristic) of everything in the universe. There are four fundamental forces including GRAVITY and ELECTROMAGNETISM.

fun·da·men·tal·ism /ˌfʌndəˈmentəlɪzəm/ *noun* [U] **1** the practice of following very strictly the basic rules and teachings of any religion **2** (in Christianity) the belief that everything that is written in the Bible is completely true ▸ **fun·da·men·tal·ist** /-ɪst/ *noun* **fun·da·men·tal·ist** /-ɪst/ *adj.*

fun·da·men·tal·ly AW /ˌfʌndəˈmentəli/ *adv.* **1** in every way that is important; completely: *The two approaches are fundamentally different.* ◇ *By the 1960s the situation had changed fundamentally.* ◇ *They remained fundamentally opposed to the plan.* **2** used when you are introducing a topic and stating sth important about it SYN **basically**: *Fundamentally, there are two different approaches to the problem.* **3** used when you are saying what is the most important thing about sb/sth SYN **basically**: *She is fundamentally a nice person, but she finds it difficult to communicate.*

fun·der AW /ˈfʌndə(r)/ *noun* a person or an organization that provides money for a particular purpose

fund·holding /ˈfʌndhəʊldɪŋ; *NAmE* -hoʊ-/ *noun* [U] a system in Britain in which the government gives GPs (= family doctors) an amount of money with which they can buy some hospital services ▸ ˈ**fund·holder** *noun*

fundi /ˈfʊndi:/ *noun* (*SAfrE*) a person who is very skilled at sth or who has gained a lot of knowledge about a particular subject: *a computer fundi* ◇ *He's become quite a fundi on wine.*

fund·ing AW /ˈfʌndɪŋ/ *noun* [U] money for a particular purpose; the act of providing money for such a purpose: *There have been large cuts in government funding for scientific research.*

ˈ**fund-raiser** *noun* **1** a person who collects money for a charity or an organization **2** a social event or an entertainment held in order to collect money for a charity or an organization ▸ ˈ**fund-raising** *noun* [U]

fu·neral 🔑 /ˈfju:nərəl/ *noun*

a ceremony, usually a religious one, for burying or CREMATING (= burning) a dead person: *Hundreds of people attended the funeral.* ◇ *a funeral procession* ◇ *a funeral march* (= a sad piece of music suitable for funerals)

IDM **it's** ˈ**your funeral** (*informal*) used to tell sb that they, and nobody else, will have to deal with the unpleasant results of their own actions

ˈ**funeral director** *noun* (*formal*) = UNDERTAKER

ˈ**funeral parlour** (*especially US* ˈ**funeral parlor**) (also ˈ**funeral home** *NAmE, BrE*) (*NAmE* also **mor·tu·ary**) *noun* a place where dead people are prepared for being buried or CREMATED (= burned) and where visitors can see the body

fu·ner·ary /ˈfju:nərəri; *NAmE* -reri/ *adj.* [only before noun] (*formal*) of or used at a funeral: ***funerary monuments/rites***

fu·ner·eal /fjuˈnɪəriəl; *NAmE* -ˈnɪr-/ *adj.* (*formal*) suitable for a funeral; sad: *a funereal atmosphere*

fun·fair /ˈfʌnfeə(r); *NAmE* -fer/ *noun* (*BrE*) = FAIR

fung·al /ˈfʌŋgl/ *adj.* of or caused by FUNGUS: *a fungal infection*

fun·gi·cide /ˈfʌŋgɪsaɪd; ˈfʌndʒɪ-/ *noun* [C, U] a substance that kills fungus

fun·goid /ˈfʌŋgɔɪd/ *adj.* (*technical*) like a FUNGUS: *a fungoid growth*

fun·gus /ˈfʌŋgəs/ *noun* (*pl.* **fungi** /ˈfʌŋgi:; -gaɪ; ˈfʌndʒaɪ/) **1** [C] any plant without leaves, flowers or green colouring, usually growing on other plants or on decaying matter. MUSHROOMS and MILDEW are both fungi. ➲ COLLOCATIONS at LIFE **2** [U, C] a covering of MOULD or a similar fungus, for example on a plant or wall: *fungus infections*

fun·house /ˈfʌnhaʊs/ *noun* (*especially NAmE*) a building at an AMUSEMENT PARK containing mirrors that produce strange images, moving floors, and other devices for scaring and amusing people

fu·nicu·lar /fju:ˈnɪkjələ(r)/ (also **fuˌnicular** ˈ**railway**) *noun* a railway on a steep slope, used to transport passengers up and down in special cars by means of a moving cable ➲ VISUAL VOCAB page V47

funk /fʌŋk/ *noun, verb*

■ ***noun* 1** [U] a type of dance music with a strong rhythm, developed by African American musicians in the 1960s **2** (also ˌ**blue** ˈ**funk**) [sing.] (*old-fashioned, informal*) a state of fear or anxiety **3** [C, usually sing.] (*NAmE*) a strong unpleasant smell

■ ***verb*** **~ sth** (*BrE, informal*) to avoid doing sth because you are afraid to or find it difficult

funky /fʌŋki/ *adj.* (**funk·ier, funki·est**) (*informal*) **1** (of pop music) with a strong rhythm that is easy to dance to: *a funky disco beat* **2** (*approving*) fashionable and unusual: *She wears really funky clothes.* **3** (*NAmE*) having a strong unpleasant smell

ˈ**fun-loving** *adj.* (of people) liking to enjoy themselves

fun·nel /ˈfʌnl/ *noun, verb*

■ ***noun* 1** a device that is wide at the top and narrow at the bottom, used for pouring liquids or powders into a small opening ➲ VISUAL VOCAB page V57 **2** (*BrE*) (also **smoke·stack** *NAmE, BrE*) a metal CHIMNEY, for example on a ship or an engine, through which smoke comes out

■ ***verb*** (-ll-, *especially US* -l-) [I, T] to move or make sth move

F

through a narrow space, or as if through a funnel: (**+ adv./prep.**) *Wind was funnelling through the gorge.* ◇ **~ sth** (**+ adv./prep.**) *Huge pipes funnel the water down the mountainside.* ◇ *Barricades funnelled the crowds towards the square.* ◇ (*figurative*) *Some $10 million in aid was funnelled into the country through government agencies.*

the fun·nies /ˈfʌniz/ *noun* [pl.] (*NAmE, informal*) the part of a newspaper where there are several COMIC STRIPS (= series of drawings that tell a funny story)

fun·nily /ˈfʌnəli/ *adv.* in a strange way
IDM **funnily eˈnough** used to show that you expect people to find a particular fact surprising: *Funnily enough, I met her only yesterday.*

F

Synonyms

funny

amusing • entertaining • witty • humorous • comic • hilarious

These words all describe sb/sth that makes you laugh or smile.

funny that makes you laugh: *a funny story* ◇ *He was a very funny guy.*

amusing funny and enjoyable: *It's a very amusing game to play.*

entertaining amusing and interesting: *It was a very entertaining evening.*

witty clever and amusing; able to say or write clever and amusing things: *a witty remark* ◇ *a witty public speaker*

humorous funny and entertaining; showing a sense of humour: *a humorous look at the world of fashion*

comic that makes you laugh: *Many of the scenes in the book are richly comic.*

hilarious extremely funny

FUNNY, AMUSING, HUMOROUS OR COMIC?

Amusing is the most general of these words because it includes the idea of being enjoyable as well as making people laugh and can be used to describe events, activities and occasions: *an amusing party/game/evening* ◇ ~~*a funny/humorous/comic party/game/evening*~~. **Humorous** is more about showing that you see the humour in a situation, than actually making people laugh out loud. **Comic** is used especially to talk about writing and drama or things that are funny in a deliberate and theatrical way. It is not used to describe people (except for *comic writers*). **Funny** can describe people, jokes and stories, things that happen, or anything that makes people laugh.

PATTERNS

- a(n) funny/amusing/entertaining/witty/humorous/comic **story**
- a(n) funny/amusing/entertaining/witty/humorous **speech**
- a(n) funny/entertaining/witty/humorous/comic **writer**
- a(n) funny/amusing/hilarious **joke**
- to **find sth** funny/amusing/entertaining/witty/humorous/hilarious

funny 0-ᴡ /ˈfʌni/ *adj.* (**fun·nier, fun·ni·est**)
▸ AMUSING **1** 0-ᴡ making you laugh; amusing: *a funny story* ◇ *That's the funniest thing I've ever heard.* ◇ *It's not funny! Someone could have been hurt.* ◇ *I was really embarrassed, but then I **saw the funny side of it**.* ◇ (*ironic*) *Oh **very funny**! You expect me to believe that?* ◇ ***'What's so funny?'** she demanded.* HELP Note that **funny** does not mean 'enjoyable': *The party was great fun.* ◇ ~~*The party was very funny.*~~
▸ STRANGE **2** 0-ᴡ difficult to explain or understand SYN **strange, peculiar**: *A funny thing happened to me today.* ◇ ***It's funny how** things never happen the way you expect them to.* ◇ ***That's funny**—he was here a moment ago and now he's gone.* ◇ ***The funny thing is** it never happened again after that.* ◇ *The engine's making a very funny noise.* ◇ *I'm pleased I didn't get that job, in a funny sort of way.*
▸ SUSPICIOUS/ILLEGAL **3** (*informal*) suspicious and probably illegal or dishonest: *I suspect there may be something funny going on.* ◇ *If there has been any **funny business**, we'll soon find out.*
▸ WITHOUT RESPECT **4** (*BrE*) humorous in a way that shows a lack of respect for sb SYN **cheeky**: *Don't you **get funny** with me!*
▸ ILL/SICK **5** (*informal*) slightly ill/sick: *I feel a bit funny today—I don't think I'll go to work.*
▸ CRAZY **6** (*BrE, informal*) slightly crazy; not like other people SYN **strange, peculiar**: *That Dave's a funny chap, isn't he?* ◇ *She went a bit funny after her husband died.*
▸ MACHINE **7** (*informal*) not working as it should: *My computer keeps **going funny**.*
IDM ˌ**funny ha-ˈha** (*informal*) used to show that 'funny' is being used with the meaning of 'amusing' ˌ**funny peˈculiar** (*BrE*) (*US* ˌ**funny ˈweird/ˈstrange**) (*informal*) used to show that 'funny' is being used with the meaning of 'strange'

ˈ**funny bone** *noun* [usually sing.] (*informal*) the part of the elbow containing a very sensitive nerve that is painful if you hit it against sth

ˈ**funny farm** *noun* (*informal, offensive*) a hospital for people who are mentally ill

ˌ**funny ˈmoney** *noun* [U] (*informal, disapproving*) **1** a CURRENCY (= the money used in one country) which is not worth much and whose value can change quickly **2** money that has been FORGED (= is not real) or stolen or that has come from illegal activities

ˈ**fun run** *noun* (*especially BrE*) an event in which people run a long distance, for fun, and to collect money for charity

fur 0-ᴡ /fɜː(r)/ *noun*
1 0-ᴡ [U] the soft thick mass of hair that grows on the body of some animals **2** 0-ᴡ [U] the skin of an animal with the fur still on it, used especially for making clothes: *a fur coat* ◇ *the fur trade* ◇ *a fur farm* (= where animals are bred and killed for their fur) ◇ *The animal is hunted for its fur.* ◇ *fur-lined gloves* **3** 0-ᴡ [U] an artificial material that looks and feels like fur **4** 0-ᴡ [C] a piece of clothing, especially a coat or jacket, made of real or artificial fur: *elegant ladies in furs* **5** (*BrE*) = SCALE *n.* (9) **6** [U] a greyish-white layer that forms on a person's tongue, especially when they are ill/sick ➲ see also FURRED

furi·ous /ˈfjʊəriəs; *NAmE* ˈfjʊr-/ *adj.* **1** very angry: **~ (at sth/sb)** *She was absolutely furious at having been deceived.* ◇ **~ (with sb/yourself)** *He was furious with himself for letting things get so out of control.* ◇ **~ (that...)** *I'm furious that I wasn't told about it.* **2** with great energy, speed or anger: *a furious debate* ◇ *She drove off at a furious pace.* ➲ see also FURY ▸ **furi·ous·ly** *adv.*: *furiously angry* ◇ *'Damn!' he said furiously.* ◇ *They worked furiously all weekend, trying to get it finished on time.* IDM see FAST *adj.*

furl /fɜːl; *NAmE* fɜːrl/ *verb* **~ sth** to roll and fasten sth such as a sail, a flag or an umbrella

fur·long /ˈfɜːlɒŋ; *NAmE* ˈfɜːrlɔːŋ; ˈfɜːrlɑːŋ/ *noun* (especially in horse racing) a unit for measuring distance, equal to 220 yards or 201 metres; one eighth of a mile

fur·lough /ˈfɜːləʊ; *NAmE* ˈfɜːrloʊ/ *noun* [U, C] **1** permission to leave your duties for a period of time, especially for soldiers working in a foreign country **2** (*NAmE*) permission for a prisoner to leave prison for a period of time **3** (*NAmE*) a period of time during which workers are told not to come to work, usually because there is not enough money to pay them ▸ **fur·lough** *verb* **~ sb**

fur·nace /ˈfɜːnɪs; *NAmE* ˈfɜːrnɪs/ *noun* **1** a space surrounded on all sides by walls and a roof for heating metal or glass to very high temperatures: *It's **like a furnace*** (= very hot) *in here!* ➲ see also BLAST FURNACE **2** (*especially NAmE*) = BOILER

fur·nish /ˈfɜːnɪʃ; *NAmE* ˈfɜːrnɪʃ/ *verb* **1 ~ sth** to put furniture in a house, room, etc: *The room was furnished with antiques.* ➲ COLLOCATIONS at DECORATE **2 ~ sb/sth with sth** | **~ sth** (*formal*) to supply or provide sb/sth with sth; to supply sth to sb: *She furnished him with the facts surrounding the case.*

fur·nished /ˈfɜːnɪʃt; *NAmE* ˈfɜːrnɪʃt/ *adj.* (of a house, room, etc.) containing furniture: *furnished accommodation* (= to rent complete with furniture) ◇ *The house was simply furnished.*

fur·nish·ings /ˈfɜːnɪʃɪŋz; *NAmE* ˈfɜːrn-/ *noun* [pl.] the furniture, carpets, curtains, etc. in a room or house: *soft furnishings* ◇ *The wallpaper should match the furnishings.*

fur·ni·ture 🔑 /ˈfɜːnɪtʃə(r); *NAmE* ˈfɜːrn-/ *noun* [U] objects that can be moved, such as tables, chairs and beds, that are put into a house or an office to make it suitable for living or working in: *a* ***piece of furniture*** ◇ ***garden/office, etc. furniture*** ◇ *We need to buy some new furniture.* ➲ see also DOOR FURNITURE, STREET FURNITURE IDM see PART *n.*

ˈ**furniture van** *noun* (*BrE*) = REMOVAL VAN

fur·ore /fjuˈrɔːri; ˈfjʊərɔː(r); *NAmE* ˈfjʊr-/ (also **furor** /ˈfjʊərɔː(r); *NAmE* ˈfjʊr-/ especially in *NAmE*) *noun* [sing.] great anger or excitement shown by a number of people, usually caused by a public event: **~ (among sb)** *His novel about Jesus caused a furore among Christians.* ◇ **~ (about/over sth)** *the recent furore over the tax increases* SYN **uproar**

furphy /ˈfɜːfi; *NAmE* ˈfɜːrfi/ *noun* (*pl.* -ies) (*AustralE*) a piece of information or a story, that people talk about but that may not be true SYN **rumour**

fur·red /fɜːd; *NAmE* fɜːrd/ *adj.* covered with fur or with sth that looks like fur: *a furred tongue*

fur·rier /ˈfʌriə(r)/ *noun* a person who prepares or sells clothes made from fur

fur·row /ˈfʌrəʊ; *NAmE* ˈfɜːroʊ/ *noun, verb*
- ***noun*** **1** a long narrow cut in the ground, especially one made by a PLOUGH for planting seeds in ➲ VISUAL VOCAB page V2 **2** a deep line in the skin of the face IDM see PLOUGH *v.*
- ***verb*** **1** [T] **~ sth** to make a furrow in the earth: *furrowed fields* **2** [I, T] **~ (sth)** (*formal*) if your BROWS OR EYEBROWS **furrow** or **are furrowed**, you pull them together, usually because you are worried, and so produce lines on your face

furry /ˈfɜːri/ *adj.* (fur·rier, fur·ri·est) **1** covered with fur: *small furry animals* **2** like fur: *The moss was soft and furry to the touch.*

fur·ther 🔑 /ˈfɜːðə(r); *NAmE* ˈfɜːrð-/ *adv., adj., verb*
- ***adv.*** **1** 🔑 (comparative of *far*) (*especially BrE*) at or to a greater distance SYN **farther**: *We had walked further than I had realized.* ◇ *Two miles further on we came to a small town.* ◇ *The hospital is further down the road.* ◇ *Can you stand a bit further away?* **2** 🔑 a longer way in the past or the future: *Think further back into your childhood.* ◇ *How will the company be doing ten years further on?* **3** 🔑 to a greater degree or extent: *The police decided to investigate further.* ◇ *My life is further complicated by having to work such long hours.* ◇ *Nothing could be* ***further from the truth.*** **4** (*formal*) in addition to what has just been said SYN **furthermore**: *Further, it is important to consider the cost of repairs.* ➲ note at FARTHER

IDM **go ˈfurther 1** to say more about sth, or make a more extreme point about it: *I would go even further and suggest that the entire government is corrupt.* **2** to last longer; to serve more people: *They watered down the soup to make it go further.* **go no ˈfurther | not go any ˈfurther** if you tell sb that a secret will **go no further**, you promise not to tell it to anyone else **take sth ˈfurther** to take more serious action about sth or speak to sb at a higher level about it: *I am not satisfied with your explanation and intend to take the matter further.* ➲ more at AFIELD
- ***adj.*** 🔑 (comparative of *far*) more; additional: *Cook for a further 2 minutes.* ◇ *Have you any further questions?* ◇ *For further details call this number.* ◇ *We have decided to take no further action.* ◇ *The museum is closed* ***until further notice*** (= until we say that it is open again). ➲ LANGUAGE BANK at ADDITION
- ***verb*** **~ sth** to help sth to develop or be successful: *They hoped the new venture would further the cause of cultural cooperation in Europe.* ◇ *She took the new job to further her career.*

fur·ther·ance /ˈfɜːðərəns; *NAmE* ˈfɜːrð-/ *noun* [U] (*formal*) the process of helping sth to develop or to be successful SYN **advancement**: *He took these actions purely* ***in (the) furtherance of*** *his own career.*

ˌ**further eduˈcation** *noun* [U] (*abbr.* FE) (*BrE*) education that is provided for people after leaving school, but not at a university ➲ compare HIGHER EDUCATION

fur·ther·more AW /ˌfɜːðəˈmɔː(r); *NAmE* ˌfɜːrðərˈmɔːr/ *adv.* (*formal*) in addition to what has just been stated. Furthermore is used especially to add a point to an argument. SYN **moreover**: *He said he had not discussed the matter with her. Furthermore, he had not even contacted her.* ➲ LANGUAGE BANK at ADDITION

fur·ther·most /ˈfɜːðəməʊst; *NAmE* ˈfɜːrðərmoʊst/ *adj.* (*formal*) located at the greatest distance from sth: *at the furthermost end of the street*

ˈ**further to** *prep.* (*formal*) used in letters, emails, etc. to refer to a previous letter, email, conversation, etc.: *Further to our conversation of last Friday, I would like to book the conference centre for 26 June.*

fur·thest /ˈfɜːðɪst; *NAmE* ˈfɜːrð-/ *adj., adv.* = FARTHEST

fur·tive /ˈfɜːtɪv; *NAmE* ˈfɜːrtɪv/ *adj.* (*disapproving*) behaving in a way that shows that you want to keep sth secret and do not want to be noticed SYN **stealthy**: *She cast a* ***furtive glance*** *over her shoulder.* ◇ *He looked sly and furtive.* ▶ **fur·tive·ly** *adv.* **fur·tive·ness** *noun* [U]

fury /ˈfjʊəri; *NAmE* ˈfjʊri/ *noun* **1** [U] extreme anger that often includes violent behaviour SYN **rage**: *Her eyes blazed with fury.* ◇ *Fury over tax increases* (= as a newspaper HEADLINE). ◇ (*figurative*) *There was no shelter from the fury of the storm.* **2** [sing.] a state of being extremely angry about sth SYN **rage**: *He flew into a fury when I refused.* **3 the Furies** [pl.] (in ancient Greek stories) three GODDESSES who punish people for their crimes ➲ see also FURIOUS

IDM **like fury** (*informal*) with great effort, power, speed, etc. ➲ more at HELL

furze /fɜːz; *NAmE* fɜːrz/ *noun* [U] (*BrE*) = GORSE

fuse /fjuːz/ *noun, verb*
- ***noun*** **1** a small wire or device inside a piece of electrical equipment that breaks and stops the current if the flow of electricity is too strong: *to change a fuse* ◇ *Check whether a fuse has blown.* **2** a long piece of string or paper which is lit to make a bomb or a FIREWORK explode **3** (*NAmE* also **fuze**) a device that makes a bomb explode when it hits sth or at a particular time: *He set the fuse to three minutes.* ◇ *The bombs inside were on a one-hour fuse.* IDM see BLOW *v.*, SHORT *n.*
- ***verb*** **1** [I, T] (*formal* or *technical*) when one thing **fuses** with another, or two things **fuse** or **are fused**, they are joined together to form a single thing: **~ (together)** *As they heal, the bones will fuse together.* ◇ **~ (into sth)** *Our different ideas fused into a plan.* ◇ **~ with sth** *The sperm fuses with the egg to begin the process of fertilization.* ◇ **~ sth (into sth)** *The two companies have been fused into a single organization.* ◇ *Atoms of hydrogen are fused to make helium.* **2** [I, T] **~ (sth)** (*technical*) when a substance, especially metal, **fuses**, or you **fuse** it, it is heated until it melts **3** [I, T] **~ (sth)** (*BrE*) to stop working or to make sth stop working because a fuse melts: *The lights have fused.* ◇ *I've fused the lights.* **4** [T, usually passive] **~ sth** to put a fuse in a CIRCUIT or in a piece of equipment: *Is this plug fused?*

ˈ**fuse box** *noun* a small box or cupboard that contains the fuses of the electrical system of a building

fu·sel·age /ˈfjuːzəlɑːʒ; *NAmE* ˈfjuːs-/ *noun* the main part of an aircraft in which passengers and goods are carried ➲ VISUAL VOCAB page V43

ˈ**fuse wire** *noun* [U] thin wire used in an electrical FUSE

fu·si·lier /ˌfjuːzəˈlɪə(r)/ *noun* (in the past) a soldier who carried a light gun

fu·sil·lade /ˌfjuːzəˈleɪd; *NAmE* -sə-/ *noun* a rapid series of shots fired from one or more guns; a rapid series of objects that are thrown SYN **barrage**: *a* ***fusillade of bullets/stones*** ◇ (*figurative*) *He faced a fusillade of questions from the waiting journalists.*

F

fu·sion /ˈfjuːʒn/ *noun* **1** [U, sing.] the process or result of joining two or more things together to form one: *the fusion of copper and zinc to produce brass* ◇ *The movie displayed a perfect fusion of image and sound.* **2** (also ˌ**nuclear** ˈ**fusion**) [U] (*physics*) the act or process of combining the NUCLEI (= central parts) of atoms to form a heavier NUCLEUS, with energy being released ➲ compare FISSION **3** [U] music that is a mixture of different styles, especially JAZZ and rock **4** [U] cooking that is a mixture of different styles: *French–Thai fusion*

ˈ**fusion bomb** *noun* a bomb that gets its energy from nuclear FUSION, especially a HYDROGEN BOMB

fu·sion·ist /ˈfjuːʒənɪst/ *noun* a musician who plays FUSION music

F

fuss /fʌs/ *noun, verb*

▪ ***noun*** **1** [U, sing.] unnecessary excitement, worry or activity: *He does what he's told without any fuss.* ◇ *All that fuss over a few pounds!* ◇ *It's a very ordinary movie—I don't know* ***what all the fuss is about*** (= why other people think it is so good). ◇ *It was all* ***a fuss about nothing****.* ◇ *We'd like a quiet wedding without any fuss.* **2** [sing.] anger or complaints about sth, especially sth that is not important: *I'm sorry for* ***making such a fuss*** *about the noise.* ◇ *Steve* ***kicks up a fuss*** *every time I even suggest seeing you.*

IDM **make a fuss of/over sb** to pay a lot of attention to sb, usually to show how much you like them: *They made a great fuss of the baby.* ◇ *The dog loves being made a fuss of.*

▪ ***verb*** **1** [I] to do things, or pay too much attention to things, that are not important or necessary: **~ (around)** *Stop fussing around and find something useful to do!* ◇ **~ (with/over sth)** *Don't fuss with your hair!* **2** [I] **~ (about sth)** to worry about things that are not very important: *Don't fuss, Mum, everything is all right.*

IDM **not be fussed (about sb/sth)** (*BrE, informal*) to not mind about sth; to not have feelings about sth SYN **not be bothered**: *It'd be good to be there, but I'm not that fussed.*

PHR V ˈ**fuss over sb** to pay a lot of attention to sb

fuss·pot /ˈfʌspɒt; *NAmE* -pɑːt/ (*BrE*) (*NAmE* **fuss·budget** /ˈfʌsbʌdʒɪt/) *noun* (*informal*) a person who is often worried about unimportant things and is difficult to please

fussy /ˈfʌsi/ *adj.* (**fuss·ier, fussi·est**) **1** too concerned or worried about details or standards, especially unimportant ones: *fussy parents* ◇ **~ (about sth)** *Our teacher is very fussy about punctuation.* ◇ *She's such a fussy eater.* ◇ *'Where do you want to go for lunch?' 'I'm not fussy* (= I don't mind).*'* **2** doing sth with small, quick, nervous movements: *a fussy manner* ◇ *the quick, fussy movements of her small hands* **3** having too much detail or decoration: *The costume designs are too fussy.* ▸ **fuss·ily** *adv.* **fussi·ness** *noun* [U]

fus·tian /ˈfʌstiən; *NAmE* -tʃən/ *noun* [U] **1** a thick strong cotton cloth with a slightly rough surface, used in the past for making clothes **2** (*literary*) language that sounds impressive but does not mean much

fusty /ˈfʌsti/ *adj.* (*disapproving*) **1** smelling old, damp or not fresh SYN **musty**: *a dark fusty room* **2** old-fashioned: *fusty ideas* ◇ *a fusty old professor*

fu·tile /ˈfjuːtaɪl; *NAmE* -tl/ *adj.* having no purpose because there is no chance of success SYN **pointless**: *a* ***futile attempt/exercise/gesture*** ◇ *Their efforts to revive him were futile.* ◇ ***It would be futile to*** *protest.* ◇ *My appeal proved futile.* ▸ **fu·tile·ly** *adv.* **fu·til·ity** /fjuːˈtɪləti/ *noun* [U]: *a sense of futility* ◇ *the futility of war*

fu·ton /ˈfuːtɒn; *NAmE* -tɑːn/ *noun* a Japanese MATTRESS, often on a wooden frame, that can be used for sitting on or rolled out to make a bed ➲ **VISUAL VOCAB** page V20

fu·ture 🔑 /ˈfjuːtʃə(r)/ *noun, adj.*

▪ ***noun*** **1** 🔑 **the future** [sing.] the time that will come after the present or the events that will happen then: *We need to plan for the future.* ◇ *What will the cities of the future look like?* ◇ *The movie is set in the future.* ◇ *The exchange rate is likely to fall* ***in the near future*** (= soon). ◇ *What does the future hold?* **2** 🔑 [C] what will happen to sb/sth at a later time: *Her future is uncertain.* ◇ *This deal could safeguard the futures of the 2 000 employees.* **3** 🔑 [sing., U] the possibility of being successful or surviving at a later time: *She has a* ***great future*** *ahead of her.* ◇ *I can't see any future in this relationship.* **4 futures** [pl.] (*finance*) goods or shares that are bought at agreed prices but that will be delivered and paid for at a later time: *oil futures* ◇ *the futures market* **5 the future** [sing.] (*grammar*) (also **the** ˌ**future** ˈ**tense**) the form of a verb that expresses what will happen after the present

IDM **in future** 🔑 (*BrE*) (*NAmE* **in the future**) from now on: *Please be more careful in future.* ◇ *In future, make sure the door is never left unlocked.* ➲ more at DISTANT, FORESEEABLE

▪ ***adj.*** 🔑 [only before noun] taking place or existing at a time after the present: *future generations* ◇ *at a future date* ◇ *future developments in computer software* ◇ *He met his future wife at law school.*

the ˌ**future** ˈ**perfect** (also **the** ˌ**future** ˌ**perfect** ˈ**tense**) *noun* [sing.] (*grammar*) the form of a verb that expresses an action completed before a particular point in the future, formed in English with *will have* or *shall have* and the past participle

ˈ**future-proof** *adj., verb*

▪ ***adj.*** (*business* or *technical*) designed to continue working or to be effective after changes that may happen in the future: *future-proof website design*

▪ ***verb*** **~ sth** to make sth future-proof: *The firm claims that it future-proofs its software.*

fu·tur·ism /ˈfjuːtʃərɪzəm/ *noun* [U] a movement in art and literature in the 1920s and 30s that did not try to show realistic figures and scenes but aimed to express confidence in the modern world, particularly in modern machines ▸ **fu·tur·ist** *noun* **fu·tur·ist** *adj.*: *futurist poets*

fu·tur·is·tic /ˌfjuːtʃəˈrɪstɪk/ *adj.* **1** extremely modern and unusual in appearance, as if belonging to a future time: *futuristic design* **2** imagining what the future will be like: *a futuristic novel*

fu·tur·ity /fjuˈtjʊərəti; *NAmE* -ˈtʊr-/ *noun* [U] (*formal*) the time that will come after the present and what will happen then: *a vision of futurity*

fu·tur·olo·gist /ˌfjuːtʃəˈrɒlədʒɪst; *NAmE* -ˈrɑːl-/ *noun* a person who is an expert in futurology

fu·tur·ology /ˌfjuːtʃəˈrɒlədʒi; *NAmE* -ˈrɑːl-/ *noun* [U] the study of how people will live in the future

fuze (*NAmE*) = FUSE *n.* (3)

fuzz /fʌz/ *noun* **1** [U] short soft fine hair or fur that covers sth, especially a person's face or arms SYN **down** **2** [sing.] a mass of hair in tight curls: *a fuzz of blonde hair* **3 the fuzz** [sing.+ sing./pl. v.] (*old-fashioned, slang*) the police **4** something that you cannot see clearly SYN **blur**: *I saw it as a dim fuzz through the binoculars.*

fuzz·box /ˈfʌzbɒks; *NAmE* -bɑːks/ *noun* a device that is used to change the sound of an electric GUITAR or other instrument by making the notes sound noisier and less clear

fuzzy /ˈfʌzi/ *adj.* (**fuzz·ier, fuzzi·est**) **1** covered with short soft fine hair or fur SYN **downy** **2** (of hair) in a mass of tight curls **3** not clear in shape or sound SYN **blurred**: *a fuzzy image* ◇ *The soundtrack is fuzzy in places.* **4** confused and not expressed clearly: ***fuzzy ideas/thinking*** ▸ **fuzz·ily** *adv.* **fuzzi·ness** *noun* [U]

ˌ**fuzzy** ˈ**logic** *noun* [U] (*computing*) a type of logic that is used to try to make computers behave like the human brain

FWIW *abbr.* (*informal*) used in writing to mean 'for what it's worth'

ˈ**F-word** *noun* [sing.] (*informal*) used to replace a word beginning with F that you do not want to say, especially the offensive swear word 'fuck': *He was shocked at how often she used the F-word.* ➲ compare C-WORD

FX /ˌef ˈeks/ *abbr.* **1** a short way of writing SPECIAL EFFECTS **2** a short way of writing FOREIGN EXCHANGE

-fy ➲ -IFY

FYI *abbr.* used in writing to mean 'for your information'

Gg

G /dʒiː/ *noun, abbr.*

■ ***noun*** (also **g**) [C, U] (*pl.* **Gs, G's, g's** /dʒiːz/) **1** the 7th letter of the English alphabet: *'Gold' begins with (a) G/'G'.* **2 G** (*music*) the fifth note in the SCALE of C MAJOR ➲ see also G AND T, G-STRING

■ ***abbr.*** **1** (*NAmE*) general audience (a label for a film/movie that is suitable for anyone, including children) **2** (*NAmE, informal*) $1 000

g *abbr.* **1** gram(s): *400g flour* **2** /dʒiː/ (*technical*) GRAVITY or a measurement of the force with which sth moves faster through space because of GRAVITY: *Spacecraft which are re-entering the earth's atmosphere are affected by g forces.*

gab /gæb/ *verb, noun*

■ ***verb*** (-bb-) (*informal*) [I] to talk for a long time about things that are not important

■ ***noun*** IDM see GIFT *n.*

gab·ar·dine (also **gab·er·dine**) /ˌgæbəˈdiːn; ˈgæbədiːn; *NAmE* -bərd-/ *noun* **1** [U] a strong material used especially for making RAINCOATS **2** [C] a coat, especially a RAINCOAT, made of gabardine

gab·ble /ˈgæbl/ *verb, noun*

■ ***verb*** [I, T] (*informal*) to talk quickly so that people cannot hear you clearly or understand you: *She was nervous and started to gabble.* ◇ **~ on/away** *They were gabbling on about the past.* ◇ **~ sth** *He was gabbling nonsense.* ◇ **+ speech** *'No, no, not all,' she gabbled.*

■ ***noun*** [sing.] fast speech that is difficult to understand, especially when a lot of people are talking at the same time

gabby /ˈgæbi/ *adj.* (*informal, disapproving*) talking a lot, especially about things that are not important

gab·fest /ˈgæbfest/ *noun* (*NAmE, informal*) an informal meeting to talk and exchange news; a long conversation

ga·bion /ˈgeɪbiən/ *noun* a large square container made of wire in which rocks are packed. Gabions are used for building structures outdoors, for example to support pieces of ground or control a flow of water.

gable /ˈgeɪbl/ *noun* the upper part of the end wall of a building, between the two sloping sides of the roof, that is shaped like a triangle ➲ VISUAL VOCAB page V15

gabled /ˈgeɪbld/ *adj.* having one or more gables: *a **gabled** house/roof*

ga·boon /gəˈbuːn/ (also **gaˌboon maˈhogany**) *noun* [U] the hard wood of a tropical African tree, used especially for making parts of musical instruments or small pieces of decoration

gad /gæd/ *verb* (-dd-)

PHRV **ˌgad aˈbout/aˈround** (*informal, especially BrE*) to visit different places and have fun, especially when you should be doing sth else

gad·about /ˈgædəbaʊt/ *noun* (*informal* often *humorous*) a person who is always going out socially or travelling for pleasure

gad·fly /ˈgædflaɪ/ *noun* (*pl.* -ies) (usually *disapproving*) a person who annoys or criticizes other people in order to make them do sth

gadget /ˈgædʒɪt/ *noun* a small tool or device that does sth useful

gadget·ry /ˈgædʒɪtri/ *noun* [U] (sometimes *disapproving*) a collection of modern tools and devices: *His desk is covered with electronic gadgetry.*

gado·lin·ium /ˌgædəˈlɪniəm/ *noun* [U] (*symb.* **Gd**) a chemical element. Gadolinium is a soft silver-white metal.

gad·zooks /gædˈzuːks/ *exclamation* (*old use*) used in the past to show that sb is surprised or annoyed

Gael·ic *noun* [U] **1** /ˈgælɪk; ˈgeɪlɪk/ the Celtic language of Scotland ➲ compare SCOTS **2** /ˈgeɪlɪk/ (also **ˌIrish ˈGaelic**) the Celtic language of Ireland ➲ compare ERSE, IRISH ▸ **Gael·ic** *adj.*

ˌGaelic ˈfootball *noun* [U] a game played mainly in Ireland between two teams of 15 players. The players of one team try to kick or hit a round ball into or over the other team's goal.

the Gael·tacht /ˈgeɪltəxt/ *noun* the parts of Ireland and Scotland where Gaelic is spoken by a large part of the population

gaff /gæf/ *noun* **1** a pole with a hook on the end used to pull large fish out of the water **2** (*BrE, slang*) the house, flat/apartment, etc. where sb lives IDM see BLOW *v.*

gaffe /gæf/ *noun* a mistake that a person makes in public or in a social situation, especially sth embarrassing SYN **faux pas**

gaf·fer /ˈgæfə(r)/ *noun* **1** (*BrE, informal*) a person who is in charge of a group of people, for example, workers in a factory, a sports team, etc. SYN **boss** **2** the person who is in charge of the electrical work and the lights when a film/movie or television programme is being made

ˈgaffer tape *noun* [U] (*BrE*) strong sticky tape with cloth on the back

gag /gæg/ *noun, verb*

■ ***noun*** **1** a piece of cloth that is put over or in sb's mouth to stop them speaking **2** an order that prevents sth from being publicly reported or discussed: *a press gag* ◇ *a **gag rule/order*** (= one given by a court of law) **3** (*informal*) a joke or a funny story, especially one told by a professional COMEDIAN SYN **joke**: *to **tell/crack a gag*** ◇ *a **running gag*** (= one that is regularly repeated during a performance) **4** (*especially NAmE*) a trick you play on sb: *It was just a gag —we didn't mean to upset anyone.*

■ ***verb*** (-gg-) **1** [T] **~ sb** to put a piece of cloth in or over sb's mouth to prevent them from speaking or shouting: *The hostages were **bound and gagged**.* **2** [T] **~ sb/sth** to prevent sb from speaking freely or expressing their opinion: *The new laws are seen as an attempt to gag the press.* ◇ *a **gagging order*** (= one given by a court of law) **3** [I] **~ (on sth)** to have the unpleasant feeling in your mouth and stomach as if you are going to VOMIT SYN **retch**: *She gagged on the blood that filled her mouth.*

IDM **be gagging for sth/to do sth** (*BrE, slang*) to want sth or want to do sth very much **be ˈgagging for it** (*BrE, slang*) to want very much to have sex

gaga /ˈgɑːgɑː/ *adj.* [not usually before noun] (*informal*) **1** (*offensive*) confused and not able to think clearly, especially because you are old: *He has gone completely gaga.* **2** slightly crazy because you are very excited about sb/sth, or very much in love: *The fans went totally gaga over the band.*

gage (*US*) = GAUGE

gag·gle /ˈgægl/ *noun* **1** a group of noisy people: *a **gaggle of tourists/schoolchildren*** **2** a group of GEESE

Gaia /ˈgaɪə/ *noun* [sing.] the Earth, considered as a single natural system which organizes and controls itself

gai·ety /ˈgeɪəti/ *noun* [U] (*old-fashioned*) the state of being cheerful and full of fun: *The colourful flags added to the gaiety of the occasion.* ➲ compare GAYNESS ➲ see also GAILY, GAY

gaily /ˈgeɪli/ *adv.* **1** in a bright and attractive way: *a gaily decorated room* **2** in a cheerful way: *gaily laughing children* ◇ *She waved gaily to the little crowd.* **3** without thinking or caring about the effect of your actions on other people: *She gaily announced that she was leaving the next day.* ➲ see also GAIETY, GAY

gain 🔑 /geɪn/ *verb, noun*

■ ***verb***

▸ OBTAIN/WIN **1** 🔑 [T] to obtain or win sth, especially sth that you need or want: **~ sth** *to **gain entrance/entry/access** to sth* ◇ *The country gained its independence ten years ago.* ◇ *The party gained over 50% of the vote.* ◇ **~ sb sth** *Her unusual talent gained her worldwide recognition.* **2** 🔑 [T, I] to obtain an advantage or benefit from sth or from doing sth: **~ sth (by/from sth)** *There is **nothing to be gained** from*

delaying the decision. ◇ **~ (by/from sth)** *Who **stands to gain** from this decision?*
▸ GET MORE **3** 🔑 [T] **~ sth** to gradually get more of sth: *to **gain** confidence/strength/experience* ◇ *I've **gained** weight recently.* OPP **lose**
▸ OF WATCH/CLOCK **4** [T, I] **~ (sth)** to go too fast: *My watch gains two minutes every 24 hours.* OPP **lose**
▸ OF CURRENCIES/SHARES **5** [T, I] to increase in value: **~ sth** *The shares gained 14p to 262p.* ◇ **~ against sth** *The euro gained against the dollar again today.*
▸ REACH PLACE **6** [T] **~ sth** (*formal*) to reach a place, usually after a lot of effort: *At last she gained the shelter of the forest.*
IDM **gain 'ground** to become more powerful or successful: *Sterling continues to gain ground against the dollar.* **gain 'time** to delay sth so that you can have more time to make a decision, deal with a problem, etc. ➲ more at VENTURE *v.*
PHR V **'gain in sth** to get more of a particular quality: *to gain in confidence* ◇ *His books have gained in popularity in recent years.* **'gain on sb/sth** to get closer to sb/sth that you are chasing
■ ***noun***
▸ INCREASE **1** 🔑 [C, U] an increase in the amount of sth, especially in wealth or weight: *a £3 000 gain from our investment* ◇ *Regular exercise helps prevent weight gain.*
▸ ADVANTAGE **2** 🔑 [C] an advantage or improvement: *efficiency gains* ◇ *These policies have resulted in great gains in public health.* ◇ *Our loss is their gain.* OPP **loss**
▸ PROFIT **3** [U] (often *disapproving*) financial profit: *He only seems to be interested in personal gain.* ◇ *It's amazing what some people will do **for gain**.* IDM see PAIN *n.*

gain·ful /ˈɡeɪnfl/ *adj.* (*formal*) used to describe useful work that you are paid for: *gainful employment* ▸ **gain·ful·ly** /-fəli/ *adv.*: *gainfully employed*

gain·say /ˌɡeɪnˈseɪ/ *verb* (**gain·says** /-ˈsez/, **gain·said**, **gain·said** /-ˈsed/) **~ sth** (*formal*) (often used in negative sentences) to say that sth is not true; to disagree with or deny sth SYN **deny**: *Nobody can gainsay his claims.*

gait /ɡeɪt/ *noun* [sing.] a way of walking: *He walked with a rolling gait.*

gai·ter /ˈɡeɪtə(r)/ *noun* [usually pl.] a cloth or leather covering for the leg between the knee and the ankle. Gaiters were worn by men in the past and are now mainly worn by people who go walking or climbing: *a pair of gaiters*

gal /ɡæl/ *noun* (*old-fashioned, informal, especially NAmE*) a girl or woman

gal. *abbr.* (in writing) gallon(s)

gala /ˈɡɑːlə; *NAmE* ˈɡeɪlə/ *noun* **1** a special public celebration or entertainment: *a charity gala* ◇ *a **gala dinner/night*** **2** (*BrE*) a sports competition, especially in swimming: *a swimming gala*

ga·lac·tic /ɡəˈlæktɪk/ *adj.* relating to a galaxy

galah /ɡəˈlɑː/ *noun* (*AustralE, informal*) a stupid person

gal·axy /ˈɡæləksi/ *noun* (*pl.* **-ies**) **1** [C] any of the large systems of stars, etc. in outer space **2 the Galaxy** (also **the ˌMilky ˈWay**) [sing.] the system of stars that contains our sun and its planets, seen as a bright band in the night sky **3** [C] (*informal*) a group of famous people, or people with a particular skill: *a galaxy of Hollywood stars*

gale /ɡeɪl/ *noun* an extremely strong wind: *The gale blew down hundreds of trees.* ◇ ***gale-force winds*** ◇ (*BrE*) *It's **blowing a gale** outside* (= a strong wind is blowing). ➲ COLLOCATIONS at WEATHER
IDM **gale(s) of laughter** the sound of people laughing very loudly: *His speech was greeted with gales of laughter.*

gall /ɡɔːl/ *noun, verb*
■ ***noun*** **1** rude behaviour showing a lack of respect that is surprising because the person behaving badly is not embarrassed SYN **impudence**: *Then they **had the gall to** complain!* **2** (*formal*) a bitter feeling full of hatred SYN **resentment** **3** a swelling on plants and trees caused by insects, disease, etc. **4** (*old-fashioned*) = BILE
■ ***verb* ~ sb | it galls sb to do sth | it galls sb that…** to make sb feel upset and angry, especially because sth is unfair: *It galls me to have to apologize to her.* ➲ see also GALLING

gal·lant *adj., noun*
■ ***adj.*** /ˈɡælənt/ **1** (*old-fashioned* or *literary*) brave, especially in a very difficult situation SYN **heroic**: *gallant soldiers* ◇ *She made a gallant attempt to hide her tears.* **2** (of a man) giving polite attention to women ▸ **gal·lant·ly** *adv.*: *She gallantly battled on alone.* ◇ *He bowed and gallantly kissed my hand.*
■ ***noun*** /ɡəˈlænt; ˈɡælənt/ (*old-fashioned*) a fashionable young man, especially one who gives polite attention to women

gal·lant·ry /ˈɡæləntri/ *noun* [U] (*formal*) **1** courage, especially in a battle: *a medal for gallantry* **2** polite attention given by men to women

ˈgall bladder *noun* an organ attached to the LIVER in which BILE is stored ➲ VISUAL VOCAB page V48

gal·leon /ˈɡæliən/ *noun* a large Spanish sailing ship, used between the 15th and the 17th centuries

gal·ler·ied /ˈɡælərid/ *adj.* (of a building) having a gallery (3)

gal·lery /ˈɡæləri/ *noun* (*pl.* **-ies**) **1** a room or building for showing works of art, especially to the public: ***an art/a picture gallery*** ◇ *the National Gallery* ➲ COLLOCATIONS at ART ➲ see also ART GALLERY **2** a small private shop/store where you can see and buy works of art **3** an upstairs area at the back or sides of a large hall where people can sit: *Relatives of the victim watched from the public gallery as the murder charge was read out in court.* ➲ see also PRESS GALLERY **4** the highest level in a theatre where the cheapest seats are **5** a long narrow room, especially one used for a particular purpose ➲ see also SHOOTING GALLERY **6** a level passage under the ground in a mine or CAVE
IDM **play to the ˈgallery** to behave in an exaggerated way to attract people's attention

gal·ley /ˈɡæli/ *noun* **1** a long flat ship with sails, usually ROWED by SLAVES or criminals, especially one used by the ancient Greeks or Romans in war **2** the kitchen on a ship or plane

Gal·lic /ˈɡælɪk/ *adj.* connected with or considered typical of France or its people: *Gallic charm*

gall·ing /ˈɡɔːlɪŋ/ *adj.* [not usually before noun] (of a situation or fact) making you angry because it is unfair: *It was galling to have to apologize to a man she hated.*

gal·lium /ˈɡæliəm/ *noun* [U] (*symb.* **Ga**) a chemical element. Gallium is a soft silver-white metal.

gal·li·vant /ˈɡælɪvænt/ *verb* [I] (usually used in the progressive tenses) **~ (about/around)** (*old-fashioned, informal*) to go from place to place enjoying yourself SYN **gad**: *You're too old to go gallivanting around Europe.*

gal·lon 🔑 /ˈɡælən/ *noun* (*abbr.* **gal.**) a unit for measuring liquid. In the UK, Canada and other countries it is equal to about 4.5 litres; in the US it is equal to about 3.8 litres. There are four QUARTS in a gallon.

gal·lop /ˈɡæləp/ *verb, noun*
■ ***verb*** **1** [I] (**+ adv./prep.**) when a horse or similar animal **gallops**, it moves very fast and each STRIDE includes a stage when all four feet are off the ground together ➲ compare CANTER **2** [I, T] to ride a horse very fast, usually at a gallop: (**+ adv./prep.**) *Jo galloped across the field towards him.* ◇ **~ sth** (**+ adv./prep.**) *He galloped his horse home.* ➲ compare CANTER **3** [I] (**+ adv./prep.**) (*informal*) (of a person) to run very quickly SYN **charge**: *She came galloping down the street.*
■ ***noun*** **1** [sing.] the fastest speed at which a horse can run, with a stage in which all four feet are off the ground together: *He rode off **at a gallop**.* ◇ *My horse suddenly **broke into a gallop**.* **2** [C] a ride on a horse at its fastest speed: *to go for a gallop* **3** [sing.] an unusually fast speed

gal·lop·ing /ˈɡæləpɪŋ/ *adj.* [only before noun] increasing or spreading rapidly: *galloping inflation*

gal·lows /ˈɡæləʊz; *NAmE* -loʊz/ *noun* (*pl.* **gal·lows**) a structure on which people, for example criminals, are killed by hanging: *to send a man to the gallows* (= to send him to his death by hanging)

ˌ**gallows 'humour** (*especially US* ˌ**gallows 'humor**) *noun* [U] jokes about unpleasant things like death

gall·stone /'gɔːlstəʊn; *NAmE* -stoʊn/ *noun* a hard painful mass that can form in the GALL BLADDER

Gal·lup poll™ /'gæləp pəʊl; *NAmE* poʊl/ *noun* a way of finding out public opinion by asking a typical group of people questions ORIGIN From G H Gallup, who invented it.

gal·ore /gə'lɔː(r)/ *adj.* [after noun] (*informal*) in large quantities: *There will be games and prizes galore.*

gal·oshes /gə'lɒʃɪz; *NAmE* -'lɑːʃ-/ *noun* [pl.] rubber shoes (no longer very common) that are worn over normal shoes in wet weather: *a pair of galoshes*

gal·umph /gə'lʌmf/ *verb* [I] + **adv./prep.** (*informal*) to move in an awkward, careless or noisy way

gal·van·ic /gæl'vænɪk/ *adj.* **1** (*technical*) producing an electric current by the action of a chemical on metal **2** (*formal*) making people react in a sudden and dramatic way

gal·van·ize (*BrE* also **-ise**) /'gælvənaɪz/ *verb* **1** ~ **sb (into sth/into doing sth)** to make sb take action by shocking them or by making them excited: *The urgency of his voice* ***galvanized them into action.*** **2** ~ **sth** (*technical*) to cover metal with ZINC in order to protect it from RUST: *a galvanized bucket* ◇ *galvanized steel*

gam·bit /'gæmbɪt/ *noun* **1** a thing that sb does, or sth that sb says at the beginning of a situation or conversation, that is intended to give them some advantage: *an* ***opening gambit*** (= the first thing you say) **2** a move or moves made at the beginning of a game of CHESS in order to gain an advantage later

gam·ble 0-w /'gæmbl/ *verb, noun*

■ ***verb*** **1** 0-w [I, T] to risk money on a card game, horse race, etc: ~ **(at/on sth)** *to* ***gamble at cards*** ◇ *to* ***gamble on the horses*** ◇ ~ **sth (at/on sth)** *I gambled all my winnings on the last race.* **2** 0-w [T, I] to risk losing sth in the hope of being successful: ~ **sth (on sth)** *He's gambling his reputation on this deal.* ◇ ~ **with/on sth** *It was wrong to gamble with our children's future.* ▸ **gam·bler** /'gæmblə(r)/ *noun*: *He was a* ***compulsive gambler*** (= found it difficult to stop).

PHR V ˌ**gamble sth↔a'way** to lose sth such as money, possessions, etc. by gambling '**gamble on sth/on doing sth** to take a risk with sth, hoping that you will be successful: *He gambled on being able to buy a ticket at the last minute.*

■ ***noun*** 0-w [sing.] an action that you take when you know there is a risk but when you hope that the result will be a success: *She knew she was* ***taking a gamble*** *but decided it was worth it.* ◇ *They invested money in the company right at the start and* ***the gamble paid off*** (= brought them success).

gam·bling 0-w /'gæmblɪŋ/ *noun* [U] the activity of playing games of chance for money and of betting on horses, etc: *heavy gambling debts*

gam·bol /'gæmbl/ *verb* (-ll-, *US* also -l-) [I] (**+ adv./prep.**) to jump or run about in a lively way: *lambs gambolling in the meadow*

game 0-w /geɪm/ *noun, adj.*

■ ***noun***

▸ ACTIVITY/SPORT **1** 0-w [C] an activity or a sport with rules in which people or teams compete against each other: *card games* ◇ *board games* ◇ *a* ***game of chance/skill*** ◇ ***ball games****, such as football or tennis* ◇ (*NAmE*) *We're going to the* ***ball game*** (=BASEBALL game). ➲ VISUAL VOCAB pages V32, V33 ➲ see also WAR GAME **2** 0-w [C] an occasion of playing a game: *to* ***play a game of*** *chess* ◇ *Saturday's League game against Swansea* ◇ *Let's* ***have a game of*** *table tennis.* ◇ *They're in training for the big game.* **3** [sing.] **sb's** ~ the way in which sb plays a game: *Maguire* ***raised his game*** *to collect the £40 000 first prize.* ◇ *Stretching exercises can help you avoid injury and improve your game.*

▸ SPORTS **4** 0-w **games** [pl.] a large organized sports event: *the Olympic Games* **5 games** [pl.] (*old-fashioned, BrE*) sport as a lesson or an activity at school: *I always hated games at school.*

▸ PART OF SPORTS MATCH **6** 0-w [C] a section of some games, such as TENNIS, which forms a unit in scoring: *two games all* (= both players have won two games)

▸ CHILDREN'S ACTIVITY **7** 0-w [C] a children's activity when they play with toys, pretend to be sb else, etc: *a game of cops and robbers* ➲ SYNONYMS at INTEREST

▸ FUN **8** [C] an activity that you do to have fun: *He was* ***playing games*** *with the dog.* ➲ SYNONYMS at INTEREST

▸ ACTIVITY, BUSINESS **9** [C] a type of activity or business: *How long have you been in this game?* ◇ *the game of politics* ◇ *I'm* ***new to this game*** *myself.* ◇ *Getting dirty was* ***all part of the game*** *to the kids.* ➲ see also WAITING GAME

▸ SECRET PLAN **10** [C] (*informal*) a secret and clever plan; a trick: *So* ***that's his game*** (= now I know what he has been planning).

▸ WILD ANIMALS/BIRDS **11** [U] wild animals or birds that people hunt for sport or food ➲ VISUAL VOCAB page V10 ➲ see also BIG GAME, FAIR GAME

IDM **be a 'game** to not be considered to be serious: *For her the whole project was* ***just a game.*** **be on the 'game** (*BrE, slang*) to be a PROSTITUTE **be**ˌ **out of the 'game** to no longer have a chance of winning a game or succeeding in an activity that you are taking part in **be** ˌ**still/**ˌ**back in the 'game** to still/once again have a good chance of winning a game or succeeding in an activity that you are taking part in: *The team was still in the game, just one goal down.* **the game is 'up** (*BrE, informal*) said to sb who has done sth wrong, when they are caught and the crime or trick has been discovered **game 'on** (*informal*) used after sth has happened that makes it clear that a contest is not yet decided and anyone could still win: *We were losing 2–0 with ten minutes to go, and then we scored. It was game on!* **give the 'game away** to tell a secret, especially by accident; to show sth that should be kept hidden **the only game in 'town** (*informal*) the most important thing of a particular type, or the only thing that is available **play the 'game** to behave in a fair and honest way **play sb's 'game** to do sth which helps sb else's plans, especially by accident, when you did not intend to help them **play (silly) 'games (with sb)** not to treat a situation seriously, especially in order to cheat sb: *Don't play silly games with me; I know you did it.* '**two can play at 'that game** (*saying*) used to tell sb who has played a trick on you that you can do the same thing to them **what's sb's/your 'game?** (*BrE, informal*) used to ask why sb is behaving as they are ➲ more at BEAT *v.*, CAT, FUN *n.*, MUG *n.*, NAME *n.*, NUMBER *n.*, RULE *n.*, SKIN *n.*, TALK *v.*, WORTH *adj.*

■ ***adj.*** ~ **(for sth/to do sth)** ready and willing to do sth new, difficult or dangerous: *She's game for anything.* ◇ *We need a volunteer for this exercise. Who's game to try?*

'**game bird** *noun* a bird that people hunt for sport or food

'**game-changer** *noun* (*NAmE*) a person, an idea or an event that completely changes the way a situation develops

game·keep·er /'geɪmkiːpə(r)/ *noun* a person whose job is to take care of and breed wild animals and birds that are kept on private land in order to be hunted IDM see POACHER

game·lan /'gæməlæn/ *noun* a traditional group of Indonesian musicians, playing instruments such as XYLOPHONES and GONGS

game·ly /'geɪmli/ *adv.* in a way that seems brave, although a lot of effort is involved: *She tried gamely to finish the race.*

'**game plan** *noun* a plan for success in the future, especially in sport, politics or business

game·play /'geɪmpleɪ/ *noun* [U] the features of a computer game, such as its story or the way it is played, rather than the images or sounds it uses

ˌ**game 'point** *noun* (especially in TENNIS) a point that, if won by a player, will win them the game

gamer /'geɪmə(r)/ *noun* (*informal*) **1** a person who likes playing computer games **2** (*NAmE*) (in sports) a player who is enthusiastic and works hard

'**game reserve** (also '**game park**) (both *BrE*) (*NAmE* '**game preserve**) *noun* a large area of land where wild animals can live in safety

'game show *noun* a television programme in which people play games or answer questions to win prizes

games·man·ship /'geɪmzmənʃɪp/ *noun* [U] the ability to win games by making your opponent less confident and using rules to your advantage

gam·ete /'gæmiːt/ *noun* (*biology*) a male or female cell that joins with a cell of the opposite sex to form a ZYGOTE (= a single cell that develops into a person, animal or plant)

'game theory *noun* [U] the part of mathematics that deals with situations in which people compete with each other, for example war or business

'game warden *noun* a person whose job is to manage and take care of the wild animals in a GAME RESERVE

G

gamey (also **gamy**) /'geɪmi/ *adj.* (of meat that has been hunted) having a strong flavour or smell as a result of being kept for some time before cooking

gam·ine /gæ'miːn/ *adj.* (*formal*) (of a young woman) thin and attractive; looking like a boy ▸ **gam·ine** *noun*

gam·ing /'geɪmɪŋ/ *noun* [U] **1** (*old-fashioned* or *law*) = GAMBLING: *He spent all night at the gaming tables.* **2** playing computer games ➲ see also WAR GAMING

gamma /'gæmə/ *noun* the third letter of the Greek alphabet (Γ, γ)

gamma globulin /ˌgæmə 'glɒbjʊlɪn; *NAmE* 'glɑːb-/ *noun* (*biology*) [U] a type of PROTEIN in the blood that gives protection against some types of diseases

ˌgamma radi'ation *noun* [U] (also **'gamma rays** [pl.]) (*physics*) high-energy RAYS of very short WAVELENGTH sent out by some RADIOACTIVE substances ➲ compare ALPHA RADIATION

gam·mon /'gæmən/ *noun* [U] (*BrE*) meat from the back leg or side of a pig that has been CURED (= preserved using salt or smoke), usually served in thick slices ➲ compare BACON, HAM, PORK

gammy /'gæmi/ *adj.* [usually before noun] (*old-fashioned, BrE, informal*) (of a leg or knee) injured

the gamut /'gæmət/ *noun* [sing.] the complete range of a particular kind of thing: *The network will provide the gamut of computer services to your home.* ◇ *She felt she had* ***run the (whole) gamut of*** *human emotions from joy to despair.*

gamy = GAMEY

Gan /gæn/ *noun* [U] a form of Chinese, spoken mainly in Jiangxi

gan·der /'gændə(r)/ *noun* a male GOOSE (= a bird like a large DUCK)
IDM **have/take a 'gander (at sth)** (*informal*) to look at sth ➲ more at SAUCE

G and T /ˌdʒiː ən 'tiː/ *noun* a drink consisting of GIN mixed with TONIC WATER

gang /gæŋ/ *noun, verb*
■ ***noun*** [C+sing./pl. v.] **1** an organized group of criminals: *criminal gang members and drug dealers* ◇ *a gang of pickpockets* ◇ *A four-man gang carried out the robbery.* **2** a group of young people who spend a lot of time together and often cause trouble or fight against other groups: *a gang of youths* ◇ *a street gang* **3** (*informal*) a group of friends who meet regularly: *The whole gang will be there.* **4** an organized group of workers or prisoners doing work together ➲ see also CHAIN GANG
■ ***verb***
PHR V **ˌgang to'gether** (*informal*) to join together in a group in order to have more power or strength **ˌgang 'up (on/against sb)** (*informal*) to join together in a group to hurt, frighten or oppose sb: *At school the older boys ganged up on him and called him names.*

'gang bang *noun* (*slang*) **1** an occasion when a number of people have sex with each other in a group **2** the RAPE of a person by a number of people one after the other ▸ **'gang-bang** *verb* **~ sb**

gang·bust·ers /'gæŋbʌstəz; *NAmE* -ərz/ *noun*
IDM **like 'gangbusters** (*NAmE, informal*) with a lot of energy and enthusiasm

gang·land /'gæŋlænd/ *noun* [sing.] the world of organized and violent crime: *gangland killings*

gan·gling /'gæŋglɪŋ/ (also **gan·gly** /'gæŋgli/) *adj.* (of a person) tall, thin and awkward in their movements SYN **lanky**: *a* ***gangling youth/adolescent***

gan·glion /'gæŋgliən/ *noun* (*pl.* **gan·glia** /-liə/) (*medical*) **1** a mass of nerve cells **2** a swelling in a TENDON, often at the back of the hand

gang·mas·ter /'gæŋmɑːstə(r); *NAmE* -mæs-/ *noun* (*BrE*) a person or company that organizes groups of workers on a temporary basis to do MANUAL work (= physical work using their hands), especially work on farms

gang·plank /'gæŋplæŋk/ *noun* a board placed between the side of a boat and land so people can get on and off

'gang rape *noun* [U, C] the RAPE of a person by a number of people one after the other ▸ **'gang-rape** *verb* **~ sb**

gan·grene /'gæŋgriːn/ *noun* [U] the decay that takes place in a part of the body when the blood supply to it has been stopped because of an illness or injury: *Gangrene set in and he had to have his leg amputated.* ▸ **gan·gren·ous** /'gæŋgrɪnəs/ *adj.*

gang·sta /'gæŋstə/ *noun* **1** [C] (*NAmE, slang*) a member of a street GANG **2** (also **ˌgangsta 'rap**) [U] a type of RAP music, typically with words about violence, guns, drugs and sex

gang·ster /'gæŋstə(r)/ *noun* a member of a group of violent criminals: *Chicago gangsters*

gang·way /'gæŋweɪ/ *noun* **1** (*BrE*) a passage between rows of seats in a theatre, an aircraft, etc. ➲ compare AISLE **2** a bridge placed between the side of a ship and land so people can get on and off

ganja /'gændʒə; 'gɑːn-/ *noun* [U] (*slang*) = MARIJUANA

gan·net /'gænɪt/ *noun* **1** a large bird that lives near the sea which catches fish by diving **2** (*BrE, informal*) a person who eats a lot

gan·try /'gæntri/ *noun* (*pl.* **-ies**) a tall metal frame that is used to support a CRANE, road signs, a SPACECRAFT while it is still on the ground, etc.

Gantt chart /'gænt tʃɑːt; *NAmE* tʃɑːrt/ *noun* (*business*) a chart used for managing the tasks involved in a project that shows when each stage should start and end and compares the amount of work done with the amount planned

gaol, gaoler (*BrE*) = JAIL, JAILER

gap 0➔ /gæp/ *noun*
~ (in/between sth) 1 0➔ a space between two things or in the middle of sth, especially because there is a part missing: *a gap in a hedge* ◇ *Leave a gap between your car and the next.* **2** 0➔ a period of time when sth stops, or between two events: *a gap in the conversation* ◇ *They met again after a gap of twenty years.* ◇ *There's a big* ***age gap*** *between them* (= a big difference in their ages). **3** 0➔ a difference that separates people, or their opinions, situation, etc: *the gap between rich and poor* ◇ *the gap between theory and practice* ➲ see also CREDIBILITY, GENERATION GAP **4** 0➔ a space where sth is missing: *His death left an enormous gap in my life.* ◇ *There were several gaps in my education.* ◇ *We think we've identified* ***a gap in the market*** (= a business opportunity to make or sell sth that is not yet available).
IDM see BRIDGE *v.*

gape /geɪp/ *verb* **1** [I] **~ (at sb/sth)** to stare at sb/sth with your mouth open because you are shocked or surprised **2** [I] to be or become wide open: *a* ***gaping hole/mouth/wound*** ◇ **~ open** *He stood yawning, his pyjama jacket gaping open.* ▸ **gape** *noun*

gap·per /'gæpə(r)/ *noun* (*BrE*) a young person who is spending a year working or travelling after leaving school and before going to university

ˌgap-'toothed *adj.* [usually before noun] having wide spaces between your teeth

ˈ**gap year** *noun* (*BrE*) a year that a young person spends working and/or travelling, often between leaving school and starting university: *I'm planning to take a gap year and go backpacking in India.*

gar·age 🔑 /ˈgærɑːʒ; -rɑːdʒ; -rɪdʒ; *NAmE* gəˈrɑːʒ; -ˈrɑːdʒ/ *noun, verb*

■ ***noun*** **1** 🔑 [C] a building for keeping one or more cars or other vehicles in: (*BrE*) *a house with a built-in garage* ◇ (*NAmE*) *a house with an attached garage* ◇ *a double garage* (= one for two cars) ◇ *a bus garage* ◇ *an underground garage* (= for example under an office building) ➲ VISUAL VOCAB page V15 **2** 🔑 [C] a place where vehicles are repaired and where you can buy a car or buy petrol/gas and oil: *a garage mechanic* ➲ see also PETROL STATION **3** [U] a type of HOUSE MUSIC

■ ***verb*** **~ sth** to put or keep a vehicle in a garage

ˌ**garage ˈrock** *noun* [U] a type of rock music played with a lot of energy, often by musicians who are not professionals

ˈ**garage sale** *noun* a sale of used clothes, furniture, etc, held in the garage of sb's house

garam masala /ˌgʌrəm məˈsɑːlə; *NAmE* ˌgɑːrɑːm/ *noun* [U] a mixture of spices with a strong flavour, used in S Asian cooking

garb /gɑːb; *NAmE* gɑːrb/ *noun* [U] (*formal* or *humorous*) clothes, especially unusual clothes or those worn by a particular type of person: *prison garb*

gar·bage 🔑 /ˈgɑːbɪdʒ; *NAmE* ˈgɑːrb-/ *noun* [U] **1** 🔑 (*especially NAmE*) waste food, paper, etc. that you throw away: *garbage collection* ◇ *Don't forget to take out the garbage.* ➲ COLLOCATIONS at ENVIRONMENT **2** 🔑 (*especially NAmE*) a place or container where waste food, paper, etc. can be placed: *Throw it in the garbage.* **3** 🔑 (*informal*) something stupid or not true SYN **rubbish** ➲ note at RUBBISH

IDM **garbage ˌin, garbage ˈout** (*abbr.* **GIGO**) used to express the idea that if wrong or poor quality data is put into a computer, wrong or poor quality data will come out of it

ˈ**garbage can** (also ˈ**trash can**) (both *NAmE*) (*BrE* **dust·bin**) *noun* a large container with a lid, used for putting rubbish/garbage in, usually kept outside the house ➲ note at RUBBISH

ˈ**garbage dis·posal** *noun* (*NAmE*) = WASTE-DISPOSAL UNIT

ˈ**garbage man** (also *formal* ˈ**garbage collector**) (both *NAmE*) (*BrE* **dust·man**, *informal* **bin·man**, *formal* ˈ**refuse collector**) *noun* a person whose job is to remove waste from outside houses, etc. ➲ note at RUBBISH

ˈ**garbage truck** (*NAmE*) (*BrE* **dust·cart**) *noun* a vehicle for collecting rubbish/garbage from outside houses, etc.

gar·banzo /gɑːˈbænzəʊ; *NAmE* gɑːrˈbɑːnzoʊ; -ˈbæn-/ (also **garˈbanzo ˌbean**) (both *NAmE*) *noun* (*pl.* **-os**) = CHICKPEA

garbed /gɑːbd; *NAmE* gɑːrbd/ *adj.* [not before noun] (*formal*) **~ (in sth)** dressed in a particular way: *brightly garbed*

gar·bled /ˈgɑːbld; *NAmE* ˈgɑːrbld/ *adj.* (of a message or story) told in a way that confuses the person listening, usually by sb who is shocked or in a hurry SYN **confused**: *He gave a garbled account of what had happened.* ◇ *There was a garbled message from her on my voicemail.*

garbo /ˈgɑːbəʊ; *NAmE* ˈgɑːrboʊ/ *noun* (*pl.* **-os**) (*AustralE, informal*) a person whose job is to remove waste from outside houses, etc. SYN **dustman, garbage collector**

Garda /ˈgɑːdə; *NAmE* ˈgɑːrdə/ *noun* **1 the Garda** [U] the police force of the Republic of Ireland **2** [C] (also **garda**) (*pl.* gardai /ˈgɑːdiː; *NAmE* ˈgɑːrdiː/) a police officer of the Republic of Ireland

gar·den 🔑 /ˈgɑːdn; *NAmE* ˈgɑːrdn/ *noun, verb*

■ ***noun*** **1** 🔑 [C] (*BrE*) (*NAmE* **yard**) a piece of land next to or around your house where you can grow flowers, fruit, vegetables, etc, usually with a LAWN (= an area of grass): *a* ***front/back garden*** ◇ *children playing in the garden* ◇ ***garden flowers/plants*** ◇ *out in the garden* ◇ *a rose garden* (= where only roses are grown) ➲ see also KITCHEN GARDEN, MARKET GARDEN, ROCK GARDEN, ROOF GARDEN **2** 🔑 [C] (*NAmE*) an area in a yard where you grow flowers or plants **3** 🔑 [C] (usually **gardens**) a public park: *the botanical gardens in Edinburgh* ➲ see also ZOOLOGICAL GARDEN **4 gardens** [sing.] (*abbr.* **Gdns**) (*BrE*) used in the name of streets: *39 Belvoir Gardens*

IDM **everything in the garden is ˈrosy** (*BrE, saying*) everything is fine ➲ more at COMMON *adj.*, LEAD[1] *v.*

■ ***verb*** [I] to work in a garden ▸ **gar·den·er** /ˈgɑːdnə(r); *NAmE* ˈgɑːrd-/ *noun*: *My wife's a keen gardener.* ◇ *We employ a gardener two days a week.* **gar·den·ing** /ˈgɑːdnɪŋ; *NAmE* ˈgɑːrd-/ *noun* [U]: *organic gardening* ◇ *gardening gloves* ◇ *a gardening programme on TV* ➲ VISUAL VOCAB page V35

ˈ**garden centre** *noun* (*BrE*) a place that sells plants, seeds, garden equipment, etc.

ˌ**garden ˈcity**, ˌ**garden ˈsuburb** *nouns* (*BrE*) a city or part of a city that has been specially designed to have a lot of open spaces, parks and trees

ˈ**garden egg** *noun* [C, U] (*WAfrE*) a type of AUBERGINE/EGGPLANT with purple, white or greenish-yellow skin

gar·denia /gɑːˈdiːniə; *NAmE* gɑːrˈd-/ *noun* a bush with shiny leaves and large white or yellow flowers with a sweet smell, also called gardenias

ˈ**gardening leave** *noun* [U] (*BrE*) a period during which sb does not work but remains employed by a company in order to prevent them working for another company: *She handed in her resignation and was put on three months' gardening leave.*

the ˌGarden of ˈEden *noun* [sing.] = EDEN

ˈ**garden party** *noun* a formal social event that takes place in the afternoon in a large garden

ˌ**garden ˈsalad** [U, C] (*NAmE*) a salad containing a variety of raw vegetables, especially LETTUCE

ˈ**garden-variety** (*NAmE*) (*BrE* ˌ**common or ˈgarden**) *adj.* [only before noun] ordinary; with no special features: *He is not one of your garden-variety criminals.*

gar·gan·tuan /gɑːˈgæntʃuən; *NAmE* gɑːrˈg-/ *adj.* [usually before noun] extremely large SYN **enormous**: *a* ***gargantuan appetite/meal***

gar·gle /ˈgɑːgl; *NAmE* ˈgɑːrgl/ *verb, noun*

■ ***verb*** [I] **~ (with sth)** to wash inside your mouth and throat by moving a liquid around at the back of your throat and then SPITTING it out

■ ***noun*** **1** [C, U] a liquid used for gargling: *an antiseptic gargle* **2** [sing.] an act of gargling or a sound like that made when gargling: *to have a gargle with salt water*

gar·goyle /ˈgɑːgɔɪl; *NAmE* ˈgɑːrg-/ *noun* an ugly figure of a person or an animal that is made of stone and through which water is carried away from the roof of a building, especially a church ➲ VISUAL VOCAB page V12

gar·ish /ˈgeərɪʃ; *NAmE* ˈgerɪʃ/ *adj.* very brightly coloured in an unpleasant way SYN **gaudy**: *garish clothes/colours* ▸ **gar·ish·ly** *adv.*: *garishly decorated/lit/painted*

gar·land /ˈgɑːlənd; *NAmE* ˈgɑːrl-/ *noun, verb*

■ ***noun*** a circle of flowers and leaves that is worn on the head or around the neck or is hung in a room as decoration

■ ***verb*** [usually passive] **~ sb/sth** (*literary*) to decorate sb/sth with a garland or garlands

gar·lic /ˈgɑːlɪk; *NAmE* ˈgɑːrlɪk/ *noun* [U] a vegetable of the onion family with a very strong taste and smell, used in cooking to give flavour to food: *a* ***clove of garlic*** (= one section of it) ▸ **gar·licky** *adj.*: *garlicky breath/food* ➲ VISUAL VOCAB page V27

ˌ**garlic ˈbread** *noun* [U] bread, usually in the shape of a stick, containing melted butter and garlic

gar·ment /ˈgɑːmənt; *NAmE* ˈgɑːrm-/ *noun* (*formal*) a piece of clothing: *a strange shapeless garment that had once been a jacket* ◇ ***woollen/winter/outer garments*** ➲ SYNONYMS at CLOTHES ➲ see also UNDERGARMENT

gar·ner /ˈgɑːnə(r); *NAmE* ˈgɑːrn-/ *verb* **~ sth** (*formal*) to obtain or collect sth such as information, support, etc. SYN **gather, acquire**

gar·net /ˈɡɑːnɪt; *NAmE* ˈɡɑːrn-/ *noun* a clear dark red SEMI-PRECIOUS STONE that is fairly valuable

gar·nish /ˈɡɑːnɪʃ; *NAmE* ˈɡɑːrnɪʃ/ *verb, noun*
■ ***verb*** **~ sth (with sth)** to decorate a dish of food with a small amount of another food ➲ COLLOCATIONS at COOKING
■ ***noun*** [C, U] a small amount of food that is used to decorate a larger dish of food

gar·otte (*BrE*) = GARROTTE

gar·ret /ˈɡærət/ *noun* a room, often a small dark unpleasant one, at the top of a house, especially in the roof ➲ compare ATTIC ➲ see also LOFT

gar·rison /ˈɡærɪsn/ *noun, verb*
■ ***noun*** [C+sing./pl. v.] a group of soldiers living in a town or FORT to defend it; the buildings these soldiers live in: *a garrison of 5 000 troops* ◇ *a garrison town* ◇ *Half the garrison is/are on duty.*
■ ***verb*** to put soldiers in a place in order to defend it from attack: **~ sth** *Two regiments were sent to garrison the town.* ◇ **~ sb + adv./prep.** *100 soldiers were garrisoned in the town.*

gar·rotte (*BrE* also **gar·otte**) (*US* also **gar·rote**) /ɡəˈrɒt; *NAmE* ɡəˈrɑːt/ *verb, noun*
■ ***verb*** **~ sb** to kill sb by putting a piece of wire, etc. around their neck and pulling it tight
■ ***noun*** a piece of wire, etc. used for garrotting sb

gar·rul·ous /ˈɡærələs; *BrE* also -rjʊl-/ *adj.* talking a lot, especially about unimportant things SYN **talkative** ▸ **gar·rul·ous·ly** *adv.*

gar·ter /ˈɡɑːtə(r); *NAmE* ˈɡɑːrt-/ *noun* **1** a band, usually made of ELASTIC, that is worn around the leg to keep up a sock or STOCKING **2** (*NAmE*) (*BrE* **sus·pend·er**) a short circle of ELASTIC for holding up a sock or STOCKING IDM see GUT *n.*

ˈgarter belt (*NAmE*) (*BrE* **suˈspender belt**) *noun* a piece of women's underwear like a belt, worn around the waist, used for holding STOCKINGS up

ˈgarter snake *noun* a harmless American snake with coloured lines along its back

gas 🔑 /ɡæs/ *noun, verb*
■ ***noun*** (*pl.* **gases** or *less frequent* **gas·ses**)
▸ NOT SOLID/LIQUID **1** 🔑 [C, U] any substance like air that is neither a solid nor a liquid, for example HYDROGEN and OXYGEN are both gases: *Air is a mixture of gases.* ◇ *CFC gases* ◇ *a* ***gas bottle/cylinder*** (= for storing gas) ➲ see also GREENHOUSE GAS **2** 🔑 [U] a particular type of gas or mixture of gases used as fuel for heating and cooking: *a* ***gas cooker/fire/furnace/oven/ring/stove*** ◇ *a* ***gas explosion/leak*** ◇ *gas central heating* ◇ (*BrE*) *Preheat the oven to gas mark 5* (= a particular temperature of a gas oven) ➲ see also CALOR GAS, COAL GAS, NATURAL GAS **3** [U] a particular type of gas used during a medical operation, to make the patient sleep or to make the pain less: *an anaesthetic gas* ◇ *During the birth she was given gas and air.* ➲ see also LAUGHING GAS **4** [U] a particular type of gas used in war to kill or injure people, or used by the police to control people: *a gas attack* ➲ see also CS GAS, NERVE GAS, TEAR GAS
▸ IN VEHICLE **5** 🔑 (also **gas·oline**) (both *NAmE*) (*BrE* **pet·rol**) [U] a liquid obtained from PETROLEUM, used as fuel in car engines, etc: *a gas station* ◇ *a gas pump* ◇ *to fill up the gas tank* **6 the gas** [sing.] (*especially NAmE*) = GAS PEDAL: ***Step on the gas****, we're late.*
▸ FUN **7** [sing.] (*especially NAmE*) a person or an event that is fun: *The party was a real gas.*
▸ IN STOMACH **8** (*NAmE*) (*BrE* **wind**) [U] air that you swallow with food or drink; gas that is produced in your stomach or INTESTINES that makes you feel uncomfortable IDM see COOK *v.*
■ ***verb*** (-ss-)
▸ KILL/HARM WITH GAS **1** [T] **~ sb/yourself** to kill or harm sb by making them breathe poisonous gas
▸ TALK **2** [I] (usually used in the progressive tenses) (*old-fashioned, informal*) to talk for a long time about things that are not important SYN **chat**

gas·bag /ˈɡæsbæɡ/ *noun* (*informal, humorous*) a person who talks a lot

ˈgas chamber *noun* a room that can be filled with poisonous gas for killing animals or people

ˈgas-cooled *adj.* [only before noun] using gas to keep the temperature cool: *gas-cooled nuclear reactors*

gas·eous /ˈɡæsiəs; ˈɡeɪsiəs/ *adj.* [usually before noun] like or containing gas: *a gaseous mixture* ◇ *in gaseous form*

ˌgas-ˈfired *adj.* [usually before noun] (*BrE*) using gas as a fuel: *gas-fired central heating*

ˌgas ˈgiant *noun* (*astronomy*) a large planet made mostly of the gases HYDROGEN and HELIUM, for example Jupiter or Saturn

ˈgas guzzler (also **guz·zler**) *noun* (*informal, especially NAmE*) a car that needs a lot of petrol/gas ▸ **ˈgas-guzzling** *adj.* [only before noun]

gash /ɡæʃ/ *noun, verb*
■ ***noun*** **~ (in/on sth)** a long deep cut in the surface of sth, especially a person's skin
■ ***verb*** **~ sth/sb** to make a long deep cut in sth, especially a person's skin: *He gashed his hand on a sharp piece of rock.*

gas·hold·er /ˈɡæshəʊldə(r); *NAmE* -hoʊl-/ *noun* = GASOMETER

gas·ket /ˈɡæskɪt/ *noun* a flat piece of rubber, etc. placed between two metal surfaces in a pipe or an engine to prevent steam, gas or oil from escaping: *The engine had* ***blown a gasket*** (= had allowed steam, etc. to escape). ◇ (*figurative, informal*) *He* ***blew a gasket*** *at the news* (= became very angry).

ˈgas lamp (also **gas·light**) *noun* a lamp in the street or in a house, that produces light from burning gas

gas·light /ˈɡæslaɪt/ *noun* **1** [U] light produced from burning gas: *In the gaslight she looked paler than ever.* **2** [C] = GAS LAMP

gas·man /ˈɡæsmæn/ *noun* (*pl.* **-men** /-men/) (*informal*) a man whose job is to visit people's houses to see how much gas they have used, or to fit and check gas equipment

ˈgas mantle *noun* = MANTLE

ˈgas mask *noun* a piece of equipment worn over the face as protection against poisonous gas

gaso·hol /ˈɡæsəhɒl; *NAmE* -hɔːl; -hɑːl/ *noun* [U] (*NAmE*) a mixture of petrol/gas and alcohol which can be used in cars

ˈgas oil *noun* [U] a type of oil obtained from PETROLEUM which is used as a fuel

gas·oline 🔑 (also **gas·olene**) /ˈɡæsəliːn/ *noun* [U] (*NAmE*) = GAS (5): ***I fill up*** *the tank* ***with gasoline*** *about once a week.* ◇ ***leaded/unleaded gasoline***

gas·om·eter /ɡæˈsɒmɪtə(r); *NAmE* -ˈsɑːm-/ (also **gas·hold·er**) *noun* a very large round container or building in which gas is stored and from which it is sent through pipes to other buildings

gasp /ɡɑːsp; *NAmE* ɡæsp/ *verb, noun*
■ ***verb*** **1** [I, T] to take a quick deep breath with your mouth open, especially because you are surprised or in pain: **~ (at sth)** *She gasped at the wonderful view.* ◇ *They gasped in astonishment at the news.* ◇ **+ speech** *'What was that noise?' he gasped.* **2** [I, T] to have difficulty breathing or speaking: **~ (for sth)** *He came to the surface of the water gasping for air.* ◇ **~ (sth) (out)** *She managed to gasp out her name.* ◇ **+ speech** *'Can't breathe,' he gasped.* **3 be gasping (for sth)** [I] (*BrE, informal*) to want or need sth very badly, especially a drink or a cigarette
■ ***noun*** a quick deep breath, usually caused by a strong emotion: *to give a* ***gasp of horror/surprise/relief*** ◇ *His breath came in short gasps.* IDM see LAST *det.*

ˈgas pedal (*especially NAmE*) (*BrE* also **ac·cel·er·ator**) *noun* the PEDAL in a car or other vehicle that you press with your foot to control the speed of the engine ➲ VISUAL VOCAB page V42

ˌ**gas-ˈpermeable** *adj.* allowing gases to pass through: *gas-permeable contact lenses*

ˈ**gas ring** *noun* (*especially BrE*) a round piece of metal with holes in it on the top of a gas cooker/stove, where the gas is lit to produce the flame for cooking ➲ picture at RING ➲ VISUAL VOCAB page V22

ˈ**gas station** (*NAmE*) (*BrE* ˈ**petrol station**) (also ˈ**filling station**, ˈ**service station** *NAmE, BrE*) *noun* a place at the side of a road where you take your car to buy petrol/gas, oil, etc.

gassy /ˈgæsi/ *adj.* **1** (*BrE*) (of drinks) containing too much gas in the form of bubbles **2** (*NAmE*) (of people) having a lot of gas in your stomach, etc.

gas·tric /ˈgæstrɪk/ *adj.* [only before noun] (*medical*) connected with the stomach: *a gastric ulcer* ◇ *gastric juices* (= the acids in your stomach that help you to DIGEST food)

ˌ**gastric ˈflu** *noun* [U] an illness affecting the stomach, which does not last long and is thought to be caused by a virus

gas·tri·tis /gæˈstraɪtɪs/ *noun* [U] (*medical*) an illness in which the inside of the stomach becomes swollen and painful

gastro·enter·itis /ˌgæstrəʊ ˌentəˈraɪtɪs; *NAmE* ˌgæstroʊ/ *noun* [U] (*medical*) an illness of the stomach and other food passages that causes DIARRHOEA and VOMITING

gas·tro·intest·inal /ˌgæstrəʊɪnˈtestɪnl; *NAmE* -roʊ-; *BrE* also ˌgæstrəʊɪnteˈstaɪnl/ *adj.* (*medical*) of or related to the stomach and INTESTINES

gas·tro·nom·ic /ˌgæstrəˈnɒmɪk; *NAmE* -ˈnɑːm-/ *adj.* [only before noun] connected with cooking and eating good food ▸ **gas·tro·nom·ic·al·ly** /-kli/ *adv.*

gas·tron·omy /gæˈstrɒnəmi; *NAmE* -ˈstrɑːn-/ *noun* [U] (*formal*) the art and practice of cooking and eating good food

gas·tro·pod /ˈgæstrəpɒd; *NAmE* -pɑːd/ *noun* (*biology*) a MOLLUSC such as a SNAIL or SLUG, that moves on one large foot ➲ VISUAL VOCAB page V11

gas·tro·pub /ˈgæstrəʊpʌb; *NAmE* -troʊ-/ *noun* (*BrE*) a pub which is well known for serving good food

gas·works /ˈgæswɜːks; *NAmE* -wɜːrks/ *noun* (*pl.* **gas·works**) [C+sing./pl. v.] a factory where gas for lighting and heating is made from coal

gate 0-π /geɪt/ *noun*
1 0-π [C] a barrier like a door that is used to close an opening in a fence or a wall outside a building: *an iron gate* ◇ *He pushed open the garden gate.* ◇ *A crowd gathered at the factory gates.* ◇ *the gates of the city* ➲ VISUAL VOCAB page V16 ➲ see also LYCHGATE, STARTING GATE **2** 0-π [C] an opening that can be closed by a gate or gates: *We drove through the palace gates.* **3** [C] a barrier that is used to control the flow of water on a river or CANAL: *a* ***lock/sluice gate*** **4** 0-π [C] a way out of an airport through which passengers go to get on their plane: *BA flight 726 to Paris is now boarding at gate 16.* **5** [C] the number of people who attend a sports event: *Tonight's game has attracted the largest gate of the season.* **6** (also ˈ**gate money**) [U] the amount of money made by selling tickets for a sports event: *Today's gate will be given to charity.* **7 -gate** (forming nouns from the names of people or places; used especially in newspapers) a political SCANDAL connected with the person or place mentioned ORIGIN From **Watergate**, the scandal in the United States that brought about the resignation of President Nixon in 1974. **8** (*computing*) = LOGIC GATE

gat·eau /ˈgætəʊ; *NAmE* gæˈtoʊ/ *noun* [C, U] (*pl.* **gat·eaux** /ˈgætəʊ; *NAmE* gæˈtoʊ/) a large cake filled with cream and usually decorated with fruit, nuts, etc: *a strawberry gateau* ◇ *Is there any gateau left?*

gate·crash /ˈgeɪtkræʃ/ (also *informal* **crash**) *verb* [T, I] ~ **(sth)** to go to a party or social event without being invited ▸ **gate·crash·er** *noun*

gated /ˈgeɪtɪd/ *adj.* [usually before noun] (of a road) having gates that need to be opened and closed by drivers

ˌ**gated comˈmunity** *noun* a group of houses surrounded by a wall or fence, with an entrance that is guarded

gate·fold /ˈgeɪtfəʊld; *NAmE* -foʊld/ *noun* a large page folded to fit a book or magazine that can be opened out for reading

gate·house /ˈgeɪthaʊs/ *noun* a house built at or over a gate, for example at the entrance to a park or castle

gate·keep·er /ˈgeɪtkiːpə(r)/ *noun* **1** a person whose job is to check and control who is allowed to go through a gate **2** a person, system, etc. that decides whether sb/sth will be allowed, or allowed to reach a particular place or person: *His secretary acts as a gatekeeper, reading all mail before it reaches her boss.*

gate·leg table /ˌgeɪtleg ˈteɪbl/ *noun* a table with extra sections that can be folded out to make it larger, supported on legs that swing out from the centre

G

ˈ**gate money** *noun* [U] = GATE (6)

gate·post /ˈgeɪtpəʊst; *NAmE* -poʊst/ *noun* a post to which a gate is attached or against which it is closed
IDM **between you, me and the ˈgatepost** (*BrE, informal*) used to show that what you are going to say next is a secret

gate·way /ˈgeɪtweɪ/ *noun* **1** an opening in a wall or fence that can be closed by a gate: *They turned through the gateway on the left.* **2** [usually sing.] **~ to/into...** a place through which you can go to reach another larger place: *Perth, the gateway to Western Australia* **3** [usually sing.] **~ to sth** a means of getting or achieving sth: *A good education is the gateway to success.* **4** (*computing*) a device that connects two computer networks that cannot be connected in any other way

gather 0-π /ˈgæðə(r)/ *verb*
▸ COME/BRING TOGETHER **1** 0-π [I, T] to come together, or bring people together, in one place to form a group: *A crowd soon gathered.* ◇ **+ adv./prep.** *His supporters gathered in the main square.* ◇ *Can you all* ***gather round****? I've got something to tell you.* ◇ *The whole family* ***gathered together*** *at Ray's home.* ◇ **be gathered + adv.prep.** *They were all* ***gathered round*** *the TV.* ◇ *A large crowd was gathered outside the studio.* ◇ *The kids were* ***gathered together*** *in one room.* **2** 0-π [T] to bring things together that have been spread around: **~ sth** *People slowly gathered their belongings and left the hall.* ◇ **~ sth together/up** *I waited while he gathered up his papers.* ➲ SYNONYMS at COLLECT
▸ COLLECT **3** 0-π [T] **~ sth** to collect information from different sources: *Detectives have spent months gathering evidence.* ➲ SYNONYMS at COLLECT **4** 0-π [T] **~ sth** to collect plants, fruit, etc. from a wide area: *to gather wild flowers*
▸ CROPS/HARVEST **5** [T] **~ sth (in)** (*formal* or *literary*) to pick or cut and collect crops to be stored: *It was late August and the harvest had been safely gathered in.*
▸ BELIEVE/UNDERSTAND **6** [T, I] (not used in the progressive tenses) to believe or understand that sth is true because of information or evidence you have: **~ (that)...** *I gather (that) you wanted to see me.* ◇ *I gather from your letter that you're not enjoying your job.* ◇ **~ (sth)** *'There's been a delay.' 'I gathered that.'* ◇ *'She won't be coming.'* ***'So I gather.'*** ◇ *You're self-employed, I gather.* ◇ ***As far as I can gather****, he got involved in a fight.* ◇ ***From what I can gather****, there's been some kind of problem.*
▸ INCREASE **7** [T] **~ sth** to increase in speed, force, etc: *The truck* ***gathered speed.*** ◇ *During the 1980s the green movement* ***gathered momentum.*** ◇ *Thousands of these machines are* ***gathering dust*** (= not being used) *in stockrooms.*
▸ OF CLOUDS/DARKNESS **8** [I] to gradually increase in number or amount: *The storm clouds were gathering.* ◇ *the gathering gloom of a winter's afternoon*
▸ CLOTHING **9** [T] to pull a piece of clothing tighter to your body: **~ sth around you/sth** *He gathered his cloak around him.* ◇ **~ sth up** *She gathered up her skirts and ran.* **10** [T] **~ sth (in)** to pull parts of a piece of clothing together in folds and sew them in place: *She wore a skirt gathered (in) at the waist.*
▸ HOLD SB **11** [T] **~ sb + adv./prep.** to pull sb towards you

and put your arms around them: *She gathered the child in her arms and held him close.* ◇ *He gathered her to him.*

▸ PREPARE YOURSELF **12** [T] **~ sth/yourself** to prepare yourself to do sth that requires effort: *I sat down for a moment to gather my strength.* ◇ *She was still trying to gather her thoughts together when the door opened.* ◇ *Fortunately the short delay gave him time to gather himself.*

IDM see ROLL *v.*

gath·er·er /ˈɡæðərə(r)/ *noun* a person who collects sth: *prehistoric hunters and gatherers*

gath·er·ing /ˈɡæðərɪŋ/ *noun* **1** [C] a meeting of people for a particular purpose: *a* ***social/family gathering*** ◇ *a gathering of religious leaders* **2** [U] the process of collecting sth: *methods of information gathering*

G

gathers /ˈɡæðəz; *NAmE* ˈɡæðərz/ *noun* [pl.] small folds that are sewn into a piece of clothing

ga·tor /ˈɡeɪtə(r)/ *noun* (*NAmE, informal*) = ALLIGATOR

GATT /ɡæt/ *noun* the General Agreement on Tariffs and Trade (in the past, an international organization that tried to encourage international trade and reduce taxes on imports; the agreement by which this organization was created. GATT was replaced by the WTO in 1994.)

gauche /ɡəʊʃ; *NAmE* ɡoʊʃ/ *adj.* awkward when dealing with people and often saying or doing the wrong thing: *a gauche schoolgirl/manner* ▸ **gauche·ness** (also **gauch·erie** /ˈɡəʊʃəri; *NAmE* ˌɡoʊʃəˈri/) *noun* [U]: *the gaucheness of youth*

gau·cho /ˈɡaʊtʃəʊ; *NAmE* -tʃoʊ/ *noun* (*pl.* -os) a S American COWBOY

gaudy /ˈɡɔːdi/ *adj.* (**gaud·ier, gaudi·est**) (*disapproving*) too brightly coloured in a way that lacks taste SYN **garish**: *gaudy clothes/colours* ▸ **gaud·ily** /ˈɡɔːdɪli/ *adv.*: *gaudily dressed/painted* **gaudi·ness** /ˈɡɔːdinəs/ *noun* [U]

gauge (*US* also **gage**) /ɡeɪdʒ/ *noun, verb*

■ ***noun*** **1** (often in compounds) an instrument for measuring the amount or level of sth: *a* ***fuel/petrol/temperature, etc.*** *gauge* ➲ VISUAL VOCAB page V42 **2** a measurement of the width or thickness of sth: *What gauge of wire do we need?* **3** (also **bore** especially in *BrE*) a measurement of the width of the BARREL of a gun: *a 12-gauge shotgun* **4** the distance between the rails of a railway/railroad track or the wheels of a train: ***standard gauge*** (= 56½ inches in Britain) ◇ *a* ***narrow gauge*** (= narrower than standard) *railway* **5** [usually sing.] **~ (of sth)** a fact or an event that can be used to estimate or judge sth: *Tomorrow's game against Arsenal will be a good gauge of their promotion chances.*

■ ***verb*** **1** to make a judgement about sth, especially people's feelings or attitudes: **~ sth** *They interviewed employees to gauge their reaction to the changes.* ◇ *He tried to gauge her mood.* ◇ **~ whether, how, etc...** *It was difficult to gauge whether she was angry or not.* **2 ~ sth** to measure sth accurately using a special instrument: *precision instruments that can gauge the diameter to a fraction of a millimetre* **3 ~ sth** | **~ how, what, etc...** to calculate sth approximately: *We were able to gauge the strength of the wind from the movement of the trees.*

gaunt /ɡɔːnt/ *adj.* **1** (of a person) very thin, usually because of illness, not having enough food, or worry: *a gaunt face* **2** (of a building) not attractive and without any decoration ▸ **gaunt·ness** *noun* [U]

gaunt·let /ˈɡɔːntlət/ *noun* **1** a metal glove worn as part of a suit of ARMOUR by soldiers in the Middle Ages **2** a strong glove with a wide covering for the wrist, used for example when driving: *motorcyclists with leather gauntlets*

IDM **run the ˈgauntlet** to be criticized or attacked by a lot of people, especially a group of people that you have to walk through: *Some of the witnesses had to run the gauntlet of television cameras and reporters.* ORIGIN This phrase refers to an old army punishment where a man was forced to run between two lines of soldiers hitting him. **take up the ˈgauntlet** to accept sb's invitation to fight or compete ORIGIN In the Middle Ages a knight threw his gauntlet at the feet of another knight as a challenge to fight. If he accepted the challenge, the other knight would pick up the glove. **throw down the ˈgauntlet** to invite sb to fight or compete with you

gauze /ɡɔːz/ *noun* **1** [U] a type of light transparent cloth, usually made of cotton or silk **2** [U] a type of thin cotton cloth used for covering and protecting wounds: *a gauze dressing* **3** [U, C] material made of a network of wire; a piece of this: *wire gauze* ➲ VISUAL VOCAB page V57 ▸ **gauzy** *adj.* [usually before noun]: *a gauzy material*

gave *past tense* of GIVE

gavel /ˈɡævl/ *noun* a small hammer used by a person in charge of a meeting or an AUCTION, or by a judge in court, in order to get people's attention

ga·vial /ˈɡeɪviəl/ *noun* = GHARIAL

ga·votte /ɡəˈvɒt; *NAmE* ɡəˈvɑːt/ *noun* a French dance that was popular in the past; a piece of music for this dance

Gawd /ɡɔːd/ *noun, exclamation* (*informal*) used in written English to show that the word 'God' is being pronounced in a particular way to express surprise, anger or fear: *For Gawd's sake hurry up!*

gawk /ɡɔːk/ *verb* [I] **~ (at sb/sth)** (*informal*) to stare at sb/sth in a rude or stupid way SYN **gape**

gawky /ˈɡɔːki/ *adj.* (especially of a tall young person) awkward in the way they move or behave ▸ **gawk·ily** /ˈɡɔːkɪli/ *adv.* **gawki·ness** /ˈɡɔːkinəs/ *noun* [U]

gawp /ɡɔːp/ *verb* [I] **~ (at sb/sth)** (*BrE, informal*) to stare at sb/sth in a rude or stupid way SYN **gape**

gay /ɡeɪ/ *adj., noun*

■ ***adj.*** **1** (of people, especially men) sexually attracted to people of the same sex SYN **homosexual**: *gay men* ◇ *I didn't know he was gay.* ◇ *Is she gay?* OPP **straight** **2** [only before noun] connected with people who are gay: *a* ***gay club/bar*** ◇ *the lesbian and gay community* **3** [not before noun] (*slang, disapproving,* sometimes *offensive*) (used especially by young people) boring and not fashionable or attractive: *She didn't like the ringtone—said it was gay.* ◇ *That is so gay!* **4** (**gayer, gayest**) (*old-fashioned*) happy and full of fun: *gay laughter* **5** (*old-fashioned*) brightly coloured: *The garden was gay with red geraniums.* ➲ see also GAIETY, GAILY

IDM **with ˈgay abandon** without thinking about the results or effects of a particular action

■ ***noun*** a person who is HOMOSEXUAL, especially a man

gay·dar /ˈɡeɪdɑː(r)/ *noun* [U] (*informal*) the ability that a HOMOSEXUAL person is supposed to have to recognize other people who are homosexual

gay·ness /ˈɡeɪnəs/ *noun* [U] the state of being HOMOSEXUAL ➲ compare GAIETY

ˌgay ˈpride *noun* [U] the feeling that HOMOSEXUAL people should not be ashamed of telling people that they are homosexual and should feel proud of themselves

gaze /ɡeɪz/ *verb, noun*

■ ***verb*** [I] **+ adv./prep.** to look steadily at sb/sth for a long time, either because you are very interested or surprised, or because you are thinking of sth else SYN **stare**: *She gazed at him in amazement.* ◇ *He sat for hours just* ***gazing into space.*** ➲ SYNONYMS at STARE

■ ***noun*** [usually sing.] a long steady look at sb/sth: *He* ***met her gaze*** (= looked at her while she looked at him). ◇ *She* ***dropped her gaze*** (= stopped looking). ➲ SYNONYMS at LOOK

gaz·ebo /ɡəˈziːbəʊ; *NAmE* -boʊ/ *noun* (*pl.* -os) a small building with open sides in a garden/yard, especially one with a view

gazebo

gaz·elle /ɡəˈzel/ *noun* (*pl.* **gaz·elle** or **gaz·elles**) a small ANTELOPE

gaz·ette /ɡəˈzet/ *noun* **1** an official newspaper published by a particular organization containing important information about decisions that have been made and people who have been employed **2 Gazette** used in the titles of some newspapers: *the Evening Gazette*

gaz·et·teer /ˌɡæzəˈtɪə(r); *NAmE* -ˈtɪr/ *noun* a list of place names published as a book or at the end of a book

ga·zil·lion /ɡəˈzɪljən/ *noun* (*NAmE, informal*) a very large number: *gazillion-dollar houses* ◇ *gazillions of copies*

gaz·pa·cho /ɡæzˈpætʃəʊ; *NAmE* ɡəzˈpɑːtʃoʊ/ *noun* [U] a cold Spanish soup made with tomatoes, peppers, CUCUMBERS, etc.

gaz·ump /ɡəˈzʌmp/ *verb* [usually passive] **~ sb** (*BrE*) when sb who has made an offer to pay a particular price for a house and who has had this offer accepted is **gazumped**, their offer is no longer accepted by the person selling the house, because sb else has made a higher offer ▸ **gaz·ump·ing** /ɡəˈzʌmpɪŋ/ *noun* [U] ➲ compare GAZUNDER

gaz·un·der /ɡəˈzʌndə(r)/ *verb* [often passive] **~ sb** (*BrE*) to offer a lower price for a house that you have already agreed to buy at a higher price, before the contract is signed: *The vendors were gazundered at the last minute.* ▸ **gaz·un·der·ing** *noun* [U] ➲ compare GAZUMP

GB *abbr.* **1** /ˌdʒiː ˈbiː/ Great Britain **2** (in writing) GIGABYTE: *a 750GB hard drive*

Gb (also **Gbit**) *abbr.* (in writing) GIGABIT

GBH /ˌdʒiː biː ˈeɪtʃ/ *abbr.* (*BrE, law*) GRIEVOUS BODILY HARM

GCE /ˌdʒiː siː ˈiː/ *noun* [C, U] the abbreviation for 'General Certificate of Education' (a British exam taken by students in England and Wales and some other countries in any of a range of subjects. GCE O levels were replaced in 1988 by GCSE exams.) ➲ compare O LEVEL, A LEVEL

GCSE /ˌdʒiː siː es ˈiː/ *noun* [C, U] the abbreviation for 'General Certificate of Secondary Education' (a British exam taken by students in England and Wales and some other countries, usually around the age of 16. GCSE can be taken in any of a range of subjects.): *She's got 10 GCSEs.* ◇ *He's doing German at GCSE.* ➲ compare A LEVEL

g'day /ɡəˈdeɪ/ *exclamation* (*AustralE, NZE*) hello

Gdns *abbr.* (*BrE*) (used in written addresses) Gardens: *7 Windsor Gdns*

GDP /ˌdʒiː diː ˈpiː/ *noun* the abbreviation for 'gross domestic product' (the total value of all the goods and services produced by a country in one year) ➲ compare GNP

GDR /ˌdʒiː diː ˈɑː(r)/ *abbr.* German Democratic Republic

gear 🔑 /ɡɪə(r); *NAmE* ɡɪr/ *noun, verb*

■ ***noun***

▸ IN VEHICLE **1** 🔑 [C, usually pl.] machinery in a vehicle that turns engine power (or power on a bicycle) into movement forwards or backwards: *Careless use of the clutch may damage the gears.* ➲ VISUAL VOCAB page V41 **2** 🔑 [U, C] a particular position of the gears in a vehicle that gives a particular range of speed and power: ***first/second, etc. gear*** ◇ ***reverse gear*** ◇ ***low/high gear*** ◇ (*BrE*) ***bottom/top gear*** ◇ (*BrE*) ***to change gear*** ◇ (*NAmE*) ***to shift gear*** ◇ *When parking on a hill, leave the car* ***in gear****.* ◇ *What gear are you in?* ◇ *He drove wildly, crashing through the gears like a maniac.* ➲ COLLOCATIONS at DRIVING

▸ EQUIPMENT/CLOTHES **3** 🔑 [U] the equipment or clothing needed for a particular activity: ***climbing/fishing/sports, etc. gear*** ➲ see also HEADGEAR, RIOT GEAR ➲ SYNONYMS at EQUIPMENT **4** [U] (*informal*) clothes: *wearing the latest gear* ➲ SYNONYMS at CLOTHES

▸ POSSESSIONS **5** [U] (*informal*) the things that a person owns: *I've left all my gear at Dave's house.*

▸ MACHINERY **6** [U] (often in compounds) a piece of machinery used for a particular purpose: ***lifting/towing/winding, etc. gear*** ➲ see also LANDING GEAR

▸ SPEED/EFFORT **7** [U, C] used to talk about the speed or effort involved in doing sth: (*BrE*) *The party organization is* ***moving into top gear*** *as the election approaches.* ◇ (*NAmE*) *to* ***move into high gear*** ◇ *Coming out of the final bend, the runner* ***stepped up a gear*** *to overtake the rest of the pack.*

▸ DRUGS **8** [U] (*slang*) illegal drugs

IDM **get into ˈgear | get sth into ˈgear** to start working, or to start sth working, in an efficient way **(slip/be thrown) out of ˈgear** (of emotions or situations) (to become) out of control: *She said nothing in case her temper slipped out of gear.* IDM see ASS

■ ***verb***

PHR V **ˈgear sth to/towards sth** [usually passive] to make, change or prepare sth so that it is suitable for a particular purpose: *The course had been geared towards the specific needs of its members.* **ˌgear ˈup (for/to sth) | ˌgear sb/sth↔ˈup (for/to sth)** to prepare yourself/sb/sth to do sth: *Cycle organizations are gearing up for National Bike Week.* ➲ see also GEARED

gear·box /ˈɡɪəbɒks; *NAmE* ˈɡɪrbɑːks/ *noun* the part containing the gears of a vehicle

geared /ɡɪəd; *NAmE* ɡɪrd/ *adj.* [not before noun] **1 ~ to/towards sth | ~ to do sth** designed or organized to achieve a particular purpose, or to be suitable for a particular group of people: *The programme is geared to preparing students for the world of work.* ◇ *The resort is geared towards children.* **2 ~ up (for sth) | ~ up (to do sth)** prepared and ready for sth: *We have people on board geared up to help with any problems.*

gear·head /ˈɡɪəhed; *NAmE* ˈɡɪrhed/ *noun* (*informal*) a person who is very enthusiastic about cars or new technical devices and equipment: *He's a total gearhead—can't keep away from the race track.*

gear·ing /ˈɡɪərɪŋ; *NAmE* ˈɡɪrɪŋ/ *noun* [U] **1** (*BrE*) (*NAmE* **le·ver·age**) (*finance*) the relationship between the amount of money that a company owes and the value of its shares **2** a particular set or arrangement of gears in a machine or vehicle

ˈgear lever (also **ˈgear·stick**) (both *BrE*) (*NAmE* **ˈgear shift**, **ˈstick shift**) *noun* a handle used to change the gears of a vehicle ➲ VISUAL VOCAB page V42

gecko /ˈɡekəʊ; *NAmE* ˈɡekoʊ/ *noun* (*pl.* **-os** or **-oes**) a small LIZARD (= a type of REPTILE) that lives in warm countries

GED /ˌdʒiː iː ˈdiː/ *noun* (in the US and Canada) the abbreviation for 'general equivalency diploma' or 'general educational development' (an official certificate that people who did not finish high school can get, after taking classes and passing an examination)

ged·dit? /ˈɡedɪt/ *abbr.* (*informal*) Do you get it? (= Do you understand the joke?)

gee /dʒiː/ *exclamation, verb*

■ ***exclamation*** (*especially NAmE*) a word that some people use to show that they are surprised, impressed or annoyed: *Gee, what a great idea!*

■ ***verb*** (*BrE*)

PHR V **ˌgee sb↔ˈup | ˌgee sb↔ˈon** to encourage sb to work harder, perform better, etc. **ˌgee ˈup** used to tell a horse to start moving or to go faster

ˈgee-gee *noun* (*BrE, informal*) (used especially by and to young children) a horse

geek /ɡiːk/ *noun* (*informal*) a person who is boring, wears clothes that are not fashionable, does not know how to behave in social situations, etc. SYN **nerd**: *a computer geek* ▸ **geeky** *adj.*

geese *pl.* of GOOSE

gee whiz /ˌdʒiː ˈwɪz/ *exclamation* (*old-fashioned, especially NAmE*) = GEE

gee·zer /ˈɡiːzə(r)/ *noun* (*informal*) **1** (*BrE*) a man: *Some geezer called Danny did it.* **2** (*NAmE*) an old man, especially one who is rather strange

Gei·ger count·er /ˈɡaɪɡə kaʊntə(r); *NAmE* ˈɡaɪɡər/ *noun* a device used for finding and measuring RADIOACTIVITY

gei·sha /ˈɡeɪʃə/ (also **ˈgeisha girl**) *noun* a Japanese woman who is trained to entertain men with conversation, dancing and singing

gel /dʒel/ *noun, verb*

■ ***noun*** [U, C] a thick substance like jelly, especially one used in products for the hair or skin: ***hair/shower gel***

■ *verb* (-ll-) **1** [I] (*BrE*) (also **jell** *NAmE, BrE*) (of two or more people) to work well together; to form a successful group: *We just didn't gel as a group.* **2** [I] (*BrE*) (also **jell** *NAmE, BrE*) (of an idea, a thought, a plan, etc.) to become clearer and more definite; to work well: *Ideas were beginning to gel in my mind.* ◇ *That day, everything gelled.* **3** [I] (also **jell** especially in *NAmE*) (*technical*) (of a liquid) to become thicker and more solid; to form a gel **4** [T, usually passive] **~ sth** to put gel on your hair

gel·atin /ˈdʒelətɪn/ (also **gel·atine** /ˈdʒelətiːn/) *noun* [U] a clear substance without any taste that is made from boiling animal bones and is used to make jelly, film for cameras, etc.

gel·at·in·ous /dʒəˈlætɪnəs/ *adj.* thick and sticky, like a jelly: *a gelatinous substance*

G

ˈgelatin paper *noun* [U] paper covered with gelatin, used in photography

geld /geld/ *verb* **~ sth** (*technical*) to remove the TESTICLES of a male animal, especially a horse SYN **castrate**

geld·ing /ˈgeldɪŋ/ *noun* a horse that has been CASTRATED ➲ compare STALLION

gel·ig·nite /ˈdʒelɪgnaɪt/ *noun* [U] a powerful EXPLOSIVE

gem /dʒem/ *noun* **1** (also *less frequent* **gem·stone** /ˈdʒemstəʊn; *NAmE* -stoʊn/) a PRECIOUS STONE that has been cut and polished and is used in jewellery SYN **jewel, precious stone**: *a crown studded with gems* **2** a person, place or thing that is especially good: *This picture is the gem* (= the best) *of the collection.* ◇ *a gem of a place* ◇ *She's a real gem!* ➲ compare JEWEL

gemin·ate /ˈdʒemɪneɪt; -nət/ *adj.* (*phonetics*) (of a speech sound) consisting of the same consonant pronounced twice, for example /kk/ in the middle of the word *backcomb*

Gem·ini /ˈdʒemɪnaɪ; -ni/ *noun* **1** [U] the third sign of the ZODIAC, the TWINS **2** [C] a person born when the sun is in this sign, that is between 22 May and 21 June

Gen. *abbr.* (in writing) GENERAL: *Gen.* (*Stanley*) *Armstrong*

gen /dʒen/ *noun, verb*

■ ***noun*** [U] **~ (on sth)** (*old-fashioned, BrE, informal*) information

■ ***verb*** (-nn-)

PHR V **ˌgen ˈup (on sth)** | **ˌgen sb/yourself ˈup (on sth)** (*old-fashioned, BrE, informal*) to find out or give sb information about sth

gen·darme /ˈʒɒndɑːm; *NAmE* ˈʒɑːndɑːrm/ *noun* (from *French*) a member of the French police force

gen·der AW /ˈdʒendə(r)/ *noun* **1** [C, U] the fact of being male or female, especially when considered with reference to social and cultural differences, not differences in biology: *issues of class, race and gender* ◇ *traditional concepts of gender* ◇ ***gender differences/relations/roles*** ➲ compare SEX *n.* (1) **2** [C, U] (*grammar*) (in some languages) each of the classes (MASCULINE, FEMININE and sometimes NEUTER) into which nouns, pronouns and adjectives are divided; the division of nouns, pronouns and adjectives into these different genders. Different genders may have different endings, etc: *In French the adjective must agree with the noun in number and gender.*

ˈgender bender *noun* (*informal*) a person who dresses and behaves like a member of the opposite sex

ˌgender reasˈsignment *noun* [U] the act of changing a person's sex by a medical operation in which parts of their body are changed so that they become like a person of the opposite sex

ˈgender-specific *adj.* connected with women only or with men only: *The report was redrafted to remove gender-specific language.*

gene /dʒiːn/ *noun* (*biology*) a unit inside a cell which controls a particular quality in a living thing that has been passed on from its parents: *a **dominant/recessive gene*** ◇ *genes that code for the colour of the eyes* ➲ see also GENETIC

IDM **be in the ˈgenes** to be a quality that your parents have passed on to you: *I've always enjoyed music—it's in the genes.*

More About

gender

Ways of talking about men and women

- When you are writing or speaking English it is important to use language that includes both men and women equally. Some people may be very offended if you do not.

The human race

- **Man** and **mankind** have traditionally been used to mean 'all men and women'. Many people now prefer to use **humanity**, **the human race**, **human beings** or **people**.

Jobs

- The suffix **-ess** in names of occupations such as **actress**, **hostess** and **waitress** shows that the person doing the job is a woman. Many people now avoid these. Instead you can use **actor** or **host**, (although **actress** and **hostess** are still very common) or a neutral word, such as **server** for *waiter* and *waitress*.
- Neutral words like **assistant**, **worker**, **person** or **officer** are now often used instead of *-man* or *-woman* in the names of jobs. For example, you can use **police officer** instead of *policeman* or *policewoman*, and **spokesperson** instead of *spokesman* or *spokeswoman*. Neutral words are very common in newspapers, on television and radio and in official writing, in both *BrE* and *NAmE*.
- When talking about jobs that are traditionally done by the other sex, some people say: **a male secretary/nurse/model** (NOT **man**) or **a woman/female doctor/barrister/driver**. However this is now not usually used unless you need to emphasize which sex the person is, or it is still unusual for the job to be done by a man/woman: *My daughter prefers to see a woman doctor.* ◇ *They have a male nanny for their kids.* ◇ *a female racing driver*

Pronouns

- **He** used to be considered to cover both men and women: *Everyone needs to feel he is loved*. This is not now acceptable. Instead, after **everybody**, **everyone**, **anybody**, **anyone**, **somebody**, **someone**, etc. one of the plural pronouns **they**, **them**, and **their** is often used: *Does everybody know what they want?* ◇ *Somebody's left their coat here.* ◇ *I hope nobody's forgotten to bring their passport with them.*
- Some people prefer to use **he or she**, **his or her**, or **him or her** in speech and writing: *Everyone knows what's best for him or herself.* **He/she** or **(s)he** can also be used in writing: *If in doubt, ask your doctor. He/she can give you more information.* (You may find that some writers just use 'she'.) These uses can seem awkward when they are used a lot. It is better to try to change the sentence, using a plural noun. Instead of saying: *A baby cries when he or she is tired* you can say *Babies cry when they are tired.*

ge·neal·ogist /ˌdʒiːniˈælədʒɪst/ *noun* a person who studies family history

ge·neal·ogy /ˌdʒiːniˈælədʒi/ *noun* (*pl.* -ies) **1** [U] the study of family history, including the study of who the ANCESTORS of a particular person were **2** [C] a particular person's line of ANCESTORS; a diagram that shows this ▸ **ge·nea·logic·al** /ˌdʒiːniəˈlɒdʒɪkl; *NAmE* -ˈlɑːdʒ-/ *adj.* [only before noun]: *a **genealogical chart/table/tree*** (= a chart with branches that shows a person's ANCESTORS)

ˈgene pool *noun* (*biology*) all of the GENES that are available within breeding populations of a particular SPECIES of animal or plant

gen·era *pl.* of GENUS

gen·eral 0‑w /ˈdʒenrəl/ *adj., noun*

■ ***adj.***

▸ AFFECTING ALL **1** 0‑w affecting all or most people, places or things: *The* ***general opinion*** *is that the conference was a success.* ◇ *the* ***general belief/consensus*** ◇ *books of* ***general interest*** (= of interest to most people) ◇ *The bad weather has been fairly general* (= has affected most areas).

▸ USUAL **2** 0‑w [usually before noun] normal; usual: *There is one exception to this general principle.* ◇ ***As a general rule*** (= usually) *he did what he could to be helpful.* ◇ *This opinion is common among the general population* (= ordinary people).

▸ NOT EXACT **3** 0‑w including the most important aspects of sth; not exact or detailed SYN **overall**: *I check the bookings to get a* ***general idea*** *of what activities to plan.* ◇ *I know how it works* ***in general terms.*** ◇ *They gave a general description of the man.* **4 the ~ direction/area** approximately, but not exactly, the direction/area mentioned: *They fired in the general direction of the enemy.*

▸ NOT LIMITED **5** 0‑w not limited to a particular subject, use or activity: *a general hospital* ◇ *general education* ◇ *We shall at this stage keep the discussion fairly general.* **6** not limited to one part or aspect of a person or thing: *a general anaesthetic* ◇ *The building was in a general state of disrepair.*

▸ HIGHEST IN RANK **7** [only before noun] (also **General**) [after noun] highest in rank; chief: *the general manager* ◇ *the Inspector General of Police* ➲ see also ATTORNEY GENERAL, DIRECTOR GENERAL, GOVERNOR GENERAL, SECRETARY GENERAL, SOLICITOR GENERAL, SURGEON GENERAL

IDM **in ˈgeneral 1** 0‑w usually; mainly: *In general, Japanese cars are very reliable and breakdowns are rare.* ➲ LANGUAGE BANK at CONCLUSION, GENERALLY **2** 0‑w as a whole: *This is a crucial year for your relationships in general and your love life in particular.*

■ ***noun*** (*abbr.* **Gen.**) an officer of very high rank in the army and the US AIR FORCE; the officer with the highest rank in the MARINES: *a four-star general* ◇ *General Tom Parker* ➲ see also BRIGADIER GENERAL, MAJOR GENERAL

ˌGeneral Aˈmerican *noun* [U] the way people speak English in most parts of the US, not including New England, New York, and the South

ˌGeneral Cerˌtificate of Eduˈcation *noun* = GCE

ˌGeneral Cerˌtificate of ˌSecondary Eduˈcation *noun* = GCSE

ˌgeneral ˈcounsel *noun* (in the US) the main lawyer who gives legal advice to a company

ˌgeneral deˈlivery (*NAmE*) (*BrE* **poste rest·ante**) *noun* [U] an arrangement in which a post office keeps a person's mail until they go to collect it, used especially when sb is travelling

ˌgeneral eˈlection *noun* an election in which all the people of a country vote to choose a government ➲ compare BY-ELECTION

ˌgeneral headˈquarters *noun* [U+sing./pl. v.] = GHQ

gen·er·al·ist /ˈdʒenrəlɪst/ *noun* a person who has knowledge of several different subjects or activities OPP **specialist**

gen·er·al·ity /ˌdʒenəˈræləti/ *noun* (*pl.* **-ies**) **1** [C, usually pl.] a statement that discusses general principles or issues rather than details or particular examples: *to speak in broad generalities* ◇ *As usual, he confined his comments to generalities.* **2 the generality** [sing.+ sing./pl. v.] (*formal*) most of a group of people or things: *This view is held by the generality of leading scholars.* **3** [U] (*formal*) the quality of being general rather than detailed or exact: *An account of such generality is of little value.*

gen·er·al·iza·tion (*BrE* also **-isa·tion**) /ˌdʒenrəlaɪˈzeɪʃn; *NAmE* -ləˈz-/ *noun* [C, U] a general statement that is based on only a few facts or examples; the act of making such statements: *a speech full of* ***broad/sweeping generalizations*** ◇ *to* ***make generalizations about*** *sth* ◇ *Try to avoid generalization.*

gen·er·al·ize (*BrE* also **-ise**) /ˈdʒenrəlaɪz/ *verb* **1** [I] **~ (from sth)** to use a particular set of facts or ideas in order to form an opinion that is considered valid for a different situation: *It would be foolish to generalize from a single example.* **2** [I] **~ (about sth)** to make a general statement about sth and not look at the details: *It is dangerous to generalize about the poor.* **3** [T, often passive] **~ sth (to sth)** (*formal*) to apply a theory, idea, etc. to a wider group or situation than the original one: *These conclusions cannot be generalized to the whole country.*

gen·er·al·ized (*BrE* also **-ised**) /ˈdʒenrəlaɪzd/ *adj.* [usually before noun] not detailed; not limited to one particular area: *a generalized discussion* ◇ *a* ***generalized disease/rash*** (= affecting the whole body)

ˌgeneral ˈknowledge *noun* [U] knowledge of facts about a lot of different subjects: *a general knowledge quiz*

gen·er·al·ly 0‑w /ˈdʒenrəli/ *adv.*

1 0‑w by or to most people: *The plan was generally welcomed.* ◇ *It is now generally accepted that...* ◇ *The new drug will be generally available from January.* ◇ *He was a generally unpopular choice for captain.* **2** 0‑w in most cases SYN **as a rule**: *I generally get up at six.* ◇ *The male is generally larger with a shorter beak.* **3** 0‑w without discussing the details of sth: *Let's talk just about investment generally.*

Language Bank

generally

Ways of saying 'in general'

- Women **generally** earn less than men.
- **Generally speaking**, jobs traditionally done by women are paid at a lower rate than those traditionally done by men.
- **In general/By and large**, women do not earn as much as men.
- Certain jobs, like nursing and cleaning, are still **mainly** carried out by women.
- Senior management posts are **predominantly** held by men.
- Most senior management posts **tend to** be held by men.
- Women are, **for the most part**, still paid less than men.
- Economic and social factors are, **to a large extent**, responsible for women being concentrated in low-paid jobs.

➲ Language Banks at CONCLUSION, EXCEPT, SIMILARLY

ˌgeneral ˈpractice *noun* [U, C] **1** (*especially BrE*) the work of a doctor who treats people in the community rather than at a hospital and who is not a specialist in one particular area of medicine; a place where a doctor like this works: *to be in general practice* ◇ *She runs a general practice in Hull.* **2** (*especially NAmE*) the work of a lawyer who deals with all kinds of legal cases and who is not a specialist in one particular area of law; the place where a lawyer like this works

ˌgeneral pracˈtitioner (also **ˌfamily pracˈtitioner**) (*abbr.* **GP**) (also *informal* **ˌfamily ˈdoctor**) (*especially BrE*) *noun* a doctor who is trained in general medicine and who treats patients in a local community rather than at a hospital

the ˌgeneral ˈpublic *noun* [sing.+ sing./pl. v.] ordinary people who are not members of a particular group or organization: *At that time, the general public was/were not aware of the health risks.* ◇ *The exhibition is not open to the general public.*

ˌgeneral-ˈpurpose *adj.* [only before noun] having a wide range of different uses: *a general-purpose farm vehicle*

gen·er·al·ship /ˈdʒenrəlʃɪp/ *noun* [U] the skill or practice of leading an army during a battle

ˌgeneral ˈstaff (often **the general staff**) *noun* [sing.+ sing./pl. v.] officers who advise a military leader and help to plan a military operation

G

,general 'store *noun* (*BrE* also **,general 'stores** [pl.]) a shop/store that sells a wide variety of goods, especially one in a small town or village

,general 'strike *noun* a period of time when most or all of the workers in a country go on strike

gen·er·ate 🔑 AW /'dʒenəreɪt/ *verb* **~ sth** to produce or create sth: *to* ***generate electricity/heat/ power*** ◇ *to* ***generate income/profit*** ◇ *We need someone to generate new ideas.* ◇ *The proposal has generated a lot of interest.* ➲ SYNONYMS at MAKE

gen·er·ation 🔑 AW /,dʒenə'reɪʃn/ *noun* **1** 🔑 [C+sing./pl. v.] all the people who were born at about the same time: *the* ***younger/older generation*** ◇ *My generation have grown up without the experience of a world war.* ◇ *I often wonder what* ***future generations*** *will make of our efforts.* **2** 🔑 [C] the average time in which children grow up, become adults and have children of their own, (usually considered to be about 30 years): *a generation ago* ◇ *My family have lived in this house* ***for generations.*** **3** 🔑 [C, U] a single stage in the history of a family: *stories passed down from generation to generation* ◇ *a* ***first-/second-generation*** *American* (= a person whose family has lived in America for one/two generations) **4** 🔑 [C, usually sing.] a group of people of similar age involved in a particular activity: *She has inspired a whole generation of fashion school graduates.* **5** [C, usually sing.] a stage in the development of a product, usually a technical one: *fifth-generation computing* ◇ ***a new generation of*** *vehicle* **6** [U] the production of sth, especially electricity, heat, etc: *the generation of electricity* ◇ *methods of income generation*

gen·er·ation·al /,dʒenə'reɪʃənl/ *adj.* [usually before noun] connected with a particular generation or with the relationship between different generations: *generational conflict*

the gene'ration gap *noun* [sing.] the difference in attitude or behaviour between young and older people that causes a lack of understanding: *a movie that is sure to bridge the generation gap*

Gene,ration 'X *noun* [U] the group of people who were born between the early 1960s and the middle of the 1970s, who seem to lack a sense of direction in life and to feel that they have no part to play in society

gen·era·tive /'dʒenərətɪv/ *adj.* (*formal*) that can produce sth: *generative processes*

,generative 'grammar *noun* [C, U] (*linguistics*) a type of grammar which describes a language by giving a set of rules which can be used to produce all the possible sentences in that language

gen·er·ator /'dʒenəreɪtə(r)/ *noun* **1** a machine for producing electricity: *The factory's emergency generators were used during the power cut.* ◇ *a wind generator* (= a machine that uses the power of the wind to produce electricity) **2** a machine for producing a particular substance: *The museum uses smells and smoke generators to create atmosphere.* ◇ (*figurative*) *The company is a major generator of jobs.* **3** (*BrE*) a company that produces electricity to sell to the public: *the UK's major electricity generator*

gen·er·ic /dʒə'nerɪk/ *adj.* **1** shared by, including or typical of a whole group of things; not specific: *'Vine fruit' is the* ***generic term*** *for currants and raisins.* **2** (of a product, especially a drug) not using the name of the company that made it: *The doctor offered me a choice of a branded or a generic drug.* ▸ **gen·er·ic·al·ly** /dʒə'nerɪkli/ *adv.*

gen·er·os·ity /,dʒenə'rɒsəti; *NAmE* -'rɑːs-/ *noun* [U, sing.] **~ (to/towards sb)** the fact of being generous (= willing to give sb money, gifts, time or kindness freely): *He treated them with generosity and thoughtfulness.*

gen·er·ous 🔑 /'dʒenərəs/ *adj.* (*approving*) **1** 🔑 giving or willing to give freely; given freely: *a generous benefactor* ◇ **~ (with sth)** *to be generous with your time* ◇ *to be generous in giving help* ◇ *a* ***generous gift/offer*** ◇ *It was* ***generous of him*** *to offer to pay for us both.* OPP **mean** **2** 🔑 more than is necessary; large SYN **lavish**: *a generous helping of meat* ◇ *The car has a generous amount of space.* **3** 🔑 kind in the way you treat people; willing to see what is good about sb/sth: *a generous mind* ◇ *He wrote a very generous assessment of my work.* ▸ **gen·er·ous·ly** 🔑 *adv.*: *Please give generously.* ◇ *a dress that is generously cut* (= uses plenty of material)

gen·esis /'dʒenəsɪs/ *noun* [sing.] (*formal*) the beginning or origin of sth

genet /'dʒenɪt/ *noun* a wild animal similar to a cat but with a longer tail and body and a pointed head. Genets are found in Africa, southern Europe and Asia and eat insects and small animals.

'gene therapy *noun* [U] (*medical*) a treatment in which normal GENES are put into cells to replace ones that are missing or not normal

gen·et·ic /dʒə'netɪk/ *adj.* connected with GENES (= the units in the cells of a living thing that control its physical characteristics) or GENETICS (= the study of genes): *genetic and environmental factors* ◇ *genetic abnormalities* ▸ **gen·et·ic·al·ly** /-kli/ *adv.*: *genetically engineered/determined/transmitted*

ge,netically 'modified *adj.* (*abbr.* GM) (of a plant, etc.) having had its genetic structure changed artificially, so that it will produce more fruit or not be affected by disease: *genetically modified foods* (= made from plants that have been changed in this way) ➲ COLLOCATIONS at FARMING

ge,netic 'code *noun* the arrangement of GENES that controls how each living thing will develop

ge,netic ,engi'neering *noun* [U] the science of changing how a living creature or plant develops by changing the information in its GENES

ge,netic 'fingerprinting (also **,DNA 'fingerprinting**) *noun* [U] the method of finding the particular pattern of GENES in an individual person, particularly to identify sb or find out if sb has committed a crime ▸ **ge,netic 'fingerprint** *noun*

gen·eti·cist /dʒə'netɪsɪst/ *noun* a scientist who studies genetics

gen·et·ics /dʒə'netɪks/ *noun* [U] the scientific study of the ways in which different characteristics are passed from each generation of living things to the next

Geneva Convention /dʒə,niːvə kən'venʃn/ *noun* [sing.] an international agreement which states how PRISONERS OF WAR should be treated

Gen·ghis Khan /,geŋgɪs 'kɑːn; ,dʒeŋ-/ *noun* [usually sing.] a person who is very cruel or has very RIGHT-WING political opinions: *Her politics are somewhere to the right of Genghis Khan.* ORIGIN From the name of the first ruler of the Mongol empire, who was born in the 12th century.

gen·ial /'dʒiːniəl/ *adj.* friendly and cheerful SYN **affable**: *a genial person* ◇ *a genial smile* ▸ **geni·al·ity** /,dʒiːni'æləti/ *noun* [U]: *an atmosphere of warmth and geniality* **geni·al·ly** /'dʒiːniəli/ *adv.*: *to smile genially*

genie /'dʒiːni/ *noun* (*pl.* **gen·ies** or **genii** /'dʒiːniaɪ/) (in Arabian stories) a spirit with magic powers, especially one that lives in a bottle or a lamp SYN **djinn**

geni·tal /'dʒenɪtl/ *adj.* [only before noun] connected with the outer sexual organs of a person or an animal: *the genital area* ◇ *genital infections*

geni·tals /'dʒenɪtlz/ (also **geni·talia** /,dʒenɪ'teɪliə/) *noun* [pl.] a person's sex organs that are outside their body

geni·tive /'dʒenətɪv/ *noun* (*grammar*) (in some languages) the special form of a noun, a pronoun or an adjective that is used to show possession or close connection between two things ➲ compare ABLATIVE, ACCUSATIVE, DATIVE, NOMINATIVE, POSSESSIVE, VOCATIVE ▸ **geni·tive** *adj.*

ge·nius /'dʒiːniəs/ *noun* (*pl.* **ge·niuses**) **1** [U] unusually great intelligence, skill or artistic ability: *the genius of Shakespeare* ◇ *a statesman of genius* ◇ *Her idea was* ***a stroke of genius.*** **2** [C] a person who is unusually intelligent or artistic, or who has a very high level of skill, especially in one area: *a* ***mathematical/comic, etc. genius*** ◇ *He's a genius at organizing people.* ◇ *You don't have to be a genius to see that they are in love!* **3** [sing.] **~ for sth/for doing sth** a special skill or ability: *He had a genius for making people feel at home.*

IDM **sb's good/evil 'genius** (*especially BrE*) a person or spirit who is thought to have a good/bad influence over you

geno·cide /ˈdʒenəsaɪd/ *noun* [U] the murder of a whole race or group of people ➲ COLLOCATIONS at WAR ▶ **geno·cidal** *adj.*

gen·ome /ˈdʒiːnəʊm; *NAmE* -oʊm/ *noun* (*biology*) the complete set of GENES in a cell or living thing: *the human genome*

geno·type /ˈdʒenətaɪp; ˈdʒiːn-/ *noun* (*biology*) the combination of GENES that a particular living thing carries, some of which may not be noticed from its appearance ➲ compare PHENOTYPE

genre /ˈʒɒ̃rə; ˈʒɒnrə; *NAmE* ˈʒɑːnrə/ *noun* (*formal*) a particular type or style of literature, art, film or music that you can recognize because of its special features

'genre painting *noun* [U, C] (*art*) a style of painting showing scenes from ordinary life that is associated with 17th century Dutch and Flemish artists; a painting done in this style

gent /dʒent/ *noun* (*BrE*) **1** (*old-fashioned* or *humorous*) a man; a gentleman: *a gent's hairdresser* ◇ *This way please, ladies and gents!* **2 a/the gents, a/the Gents** [sing.] (*informal*) a public toilet/bathroom for men: *Is there a gents near here?* ◇ *Where's the gents?*

gen·teel /dʒenˈtiːl/ *adj.* (sometimes *disapproving*) **1** (of people and their way of life) quiet and polite, often in an exaggerated way; from, or pretending to be from, a high social class: *a genteel manner* ◇ *Her genteel accent irritated me.* ◇ *He lived in genteel poverty* (= trying to keep the style of a high social class, but with little money). **2** (of places) quiet and old-fashioned and perhaps slightly boring ▶ **gen·teel·ly** /dʒenˈtiːlli/ *adv.*

gen·tian /ˈdʒenʃn/ *noun* [C, U] a small plant with bright blue flowers that grows in mountain areas

gen·tile /ˈdʒentaɪl/ (also **Gentile**) *noun* a person who is not Jewish ▶ **gen·tile** (also **Gentile**) *adj.* [only before noun]

gen·til·ity /dʒenˈtɪləti/ *noun* [U] (*formal*) **1** very good manners and behaviour; the fact of belonging to a high social class: *He took her hand with discreet gentility.* ◇ *She thinks expensive clothes are a mark of gentility.* **2** the fact of being quiet and old-fashioned: *the faded gentility of the town*

gen·tle 🔑 /ˈdʒentl/ *adj.* (**gent·ler** /ˈdʒentlə(r)/, **gent·lest** /ˈdʒentlɪst/)

1 🔑 calm and kind; doing things in a quiet and careful way: *a quiet and gentle man* ◇ *a gentle voice/laugh/touch* ◇ *She was the gentlest of nurses.* ◇ *He lived in a gentler age than ours.* ◇ *Be gentle with her!* ◇ *She agreed to come, after a little* ***gentle persuasion.*** ◇ *He looks scary but he's really a* ***gentle giant.*** **2** 🔑 (of weather, temperature, etc.) not strong or extreme: *a gentle breeze* ◇ *the gentle swell of the sea* ◇ *Cook over a gentle heat.* **3** 🔑 having only a small effect; not strong or violent: *We went for a gentle stroll.* ◇ *a little* ***gentle exercise*** ◇ *This soap is very gentle on the hands.* **4** 🔑 not steep or sharp: *a* ***gentle slope/curve/angle*** ➲ see also GENTLY ▶ **gentle·ness** /ˈdʒentlnəs/ *noun* [U]

gentle·folk /ˈdʒentlfəʊk; *NAmE* -foʊk/ *noun* [pl.] (*old-fashioned*) (in the past) people belonging to respected families of the higher social classes

gentle·man 🔑 /ˈdʒentlmən/ *noun* (*pl.* **-men** /-mən/)

1 🔑 [C] a man who is polite and well educated, who has excellent manners and always behaves well: *Thank you—you're a real gentleman.* ◇ *He's no gentleman!* ➲ compare LADY **2** 🔑 [C, usually pl.] (*formal*) used to address or refer to a man, especially sb you do not know: ***Ladies and gentlemen!*** *Can I have your attention, please?* ◇ *Gentlemen of the jury!* ◇ *Can I help you, gentlemen?* ◇ *There's a gentleman to see you.* HELP In more informal speech, you could say: *Can I help you?* ◇ *There's someone to see you.* **3** (*NAmE*) used to address or refer to a male member of a LEGISLATURE, for example the House of Representatives **4** (*old-fashioned*) a man from a high social class, especially one who does not need to work: *a country gentleman* ◇ *a gentleman farmer* (= one who owns a farm for pleasure, not as his main job) IDM see LEISURE

gentle·man·ly /ˈdʒentlmənli/ *adj.* (*approving*) behaving very well and showing very good manners; like a gentleman: *gentlemanly behaviour* ◇ *So far, the election campaign has been a very gentlemanly affair.*

ˌgentleman's aˈgreement (also **ˌgentlemen's aˈgreement**) *noun* an agreement made between people who trust each other, which is not written down and which has no legal force

gentle·woman /ˈdʒentlwʊmən/ *noun* (*pl.* **-women** /-wɪmɪn/) **1** (*old use*) a woman who belongs to a high social class; a woman who is well educated and has excellent manners **2** (*NAmE*) used to address or refer to a female member of a LEGISLATURE, for example the House of Representatives

gen·tly 🔑 /ˈdʒentli/ *adv.*

1 🔑 in a gentle way: *She held the baby gently.* ◇ *'You miss them, don't you?' he asked gently.* ◇ *Simmer the soup gently for 30 minutes.* ◇ *Massage the area* ***gently but firmly.*** ◇ *leaves moving gently in the breeze* ◇ *The path ran gently down to the sea.* **2 Gently!** (*BrE, informal*) used to tell sb to be careful: *Gently! You'll hurt the poor thing!* ◇ *Don't go too fast—****gently does it!***

gen·tri·fy /ˈdʒentrɪfaɪ/ *verb* (**gen·tri·fies, gen·tri·fy·ing, gen·tri·fied, gen·tri·fied**) [usually passive] **~ sth/sb** to change an area, a person, etc. so that they are suitable for, or can mix with, people of a higher social class than before: *Old working-class areas of the city are being gentrified.* ▶ **gen·tri·fi·ca·tion** *noun* [U]

gen·try /ˈdʒentri/ *noun* [pl.] (usually **the gentry**) (*old-fashioned*) people belonging to a high social class: *the local gentry* ◇ *the landed gentry* (= those who own a lot of land)

genu·flect /ˈdʒenjuflekt/ *verb* (*formal*) **1** [I] to move your body into a lower position by bending one or both knees, as a sign of respect during worship in a church **2** [I] **~ (to sth)** (*disapproving*) to show too much respect to sb/sth ▶ **genu·flec·tion** (*BrE* also **genu·flex·ion**) /ˌdʒenjuˈflekʃn/ *noun* [C, U]

genu·ine 🔑 /ˈdʒenjuɪn/ *adj.*

1 🔑 real; exactly what it appears to be; not artificial SYN **authentic**: *Is the painting a genuine Picasso?* ◇ *Fake designer watches are sold at a fraction of the price of* ***the genuine article.*** ◇ *Only genuine refugees can apply for asylum.* **2** 🔑 sincere and honest; that can be trusted: *He made a genuine attempt to improve conditions.* ◇ *genuine concern for others* ◇ *a very genuine person* ▶ **genu·ine·ly** 🔑 *adv.*: *genuinely sorry* **genu·ine·ness** *noun* [U]

genus /ˈdʒiːnəs/ *noun* (*pl.* **gen·era** /ˈdʒenərə/) (*biology*) a group into which animals, plants, etc. that have similar characteristics are divided, smaller than a family and larger than a SPECIES ➲ compare CLASS, KINGDOM, ORDER, PHYLUM ➲ see also GENERIC

geo- *combining form* (in nouns, adjectives and adverbs) of the earth: *geochemical* ◇ *geoscience*

geo·cen·tric /ˌdʒiːəʊˈsentrɪk; *NAmE* ˌdʒiːoʊ-/ *adj.* (*technical*) with the earth as the centre

geo·des·ic /ˌdʒiːəʊˈdesɪk; -ˈdiːsɪk; *NAmE* ˌdʒiːoʊ-/ *adj.* (*technical*) relating to the shortest possible line between two points on a curved surface

ˌgeoˌdesic ˈdome *noun* (*architecture*) a DOME which is built from panels whose edges form geodesic lines ➲ VISUAL VOCAB page V12

geog·raph·er /dʒiˈɒɡrəfə(r); *NAmE* -ˈɑːɡ-/ *noun* a person who studies geography; an expert in geography

geog·raphy 🔑 /dʒiˈɒɡrəfi; *NAmE* -ˈɑːɡ-/ *noun*

1 🔑 [U] the scientific study of the earth's surface, physical features, divisions, products, population, etc: ***human/physical/economic/social geography*** ◇ ***a geography lesson/department/teacher/textbook*** ◇ *a degree in geography* **2** 🔑 [sing.] the way in which the physical features of a place are arranged: *the geography of New York City* ◇ *Kim knew the geography of the building and strode along the corridor.* **3** [sing.] the way in which a particular aspect of life or society is influenced by geography or varies according to geography: *The geography of poverty and the geography of voting are connected.* ▶ **geo·graph·ic·al** /ˌdʒiːəˈgræfɪkl/ (also **geo·graph·ic** /ˌdʒiːəˈgræfɪk/) *adj.*: *The survey covers a wide* **geographical area**. ◇ *The importance of the town is due to its* **geographical location**. **geo·graph·ic·al·ly** /-kli/ *adv.*: *geographically remote areas*

geolo·gist /dʒiˈɒlədʒɪst; *NAmE* -ˈɑːl-/ *noun* a scientist who studies geology

geol·ogy /dʒiˈɒlədʒi; *NAmE* -ˈɑːl-/ *noun* **1** [U] the scientific study of the earth, including the origin and history of the rocks and soil of which the earth is made **2** [sing.] the origin and history of the rocks and soil of a particular area: *the geology of the British Isles* ▶ **geo·logic·al** /ˌdʒiːəˈlɒdʒɪkl; *NAmE* -ˈlɑːdʒ-/ (also **geo·logic** /ˌdʒiːəˈlɒdʒɪk; *NAmE* -ˈlɑːdʒ-/) *adj.*: *a geological survey* **geo·logic·al·ly** /ˌdʒiːəˈlɒdʒɪkli; *NAmE* -ˈlɑːdʒ-/ *adv.*

geo·mag·net·ism /ˌdʒiːəʊˈmægnətɪzəm; *NAmE* ˌdʒiːoʊ-/ *noun* [U] (*geology*) the study of the MAGNETIC characteristics of the earth ▶ **geo·mag·net·ic** /ˌdʒiːəʊmægˈnetɪk; *NAmE* ˌdʒiːoʊ-/ *adj.*

geo·mancy /ˈdʒiːəʊmænsi; *NAmE* ˈdʒiːoʊ-/ *noun* [U] **1** the art of arranging buildings and areas in a good or lucky position **2** a method of saying what will happen in the future using patterns on the ground

geo·met·ric /ˌdʒiːəˈmetrɪk/ (also *less frequent* **geo·met·ric·al** /-ɪkl/) *adj.* of GEOMETRY; of or like the lines, shapes, etc. used in GEOMETRY, especially because of having regular shapes or lines: *a geometric design* ▶ **geo·met·ric·al·ly** /ˌdʒiːəˈmetrɪkli/ *adv.*

geoˌmetric ˈmean *noun* the central number in a geometric progression

geoˌmetric proˈgression (also **geoˌmetric ˈseries**) *noun* a series of numbers in which each is multiplied or divided by a fixed number to produce the next, for example 1, 3, 9, 27, 81 ➲ compare ARITHMETIC PROGRESSION

geom·etry /dʒiˈɒmətri; *NAmE* -ˈɑːm-/ *noun* **1** [U] the branch of mathematics that deals with the measurements and relationships of lines, angles, surfaces and solids **2** [sing.] the measurements and relationships of lines, angles, etc. in a particular object or shape: *the geometry of a spider's web*

geo·phys·ics /ˌdʒiːəʊˈfɪzɪks; *NAmE* ˌdʒiːoʊ-/ *noun* [U] the scientific study of the earth's atmosphere, oceans and climate ▶ **geo·phys·ic·al** /-ˈfɪzɪkl/ *adj.*: *geophysical data* **geo·physi·cist** /-ˈfɪzɪsɪst/ *noun*

geo·pol·it·ics /ˌdʒiːəʊˈpɒlətɪks; *NAmE* ˌdʒiːoʊˈpɑːl-/ *noun* [U+sing./pl. v.] the political relations between countries and groups of countries in the world; the study of these relations ▶ **geo·pol·it·ical** /ˌdʒiːəʊpəˈlɪtɪkl; *NAmE* ˌdʒiːoʊ-/ *adj.*

Geor·die /ˈdʒɔːdi; *NAmE* ˈdʒɔːrdi/ *noun* (*BrE, informal*) **1** [C] a person from Tyneside in NE England **2** [U] a way of speaking, typical of people from Tyneside in NE England ▶ **Geor·die** *adj.*: *a Geordie accent*

geor·gette /ˌdʒɔːˈdʒet; *NAmE* ˌdʒɔːrˈdʒet/ *noun* [U] a type of thin silk or cotton cloth, used for making clothes

Geor·gian /ˈdʒɔːdʒən; *NAmE* ˈdʒɔːrdʒən/ *adj.* (especially of ARCHITECTURE and furniture) from the time of the British kings George I–IV (1714–1830): *a fine Georgian house*

geo·ther·mal /ˌdʒiːəʊˈθɜːml; *NAmE* ˌdʒiːoʊˈθɜːrml/ *adj.* (*geology*) connected with the natural heat of rock deep in the ground: *geothermal energy*

ge·ra·nium /dʒəˈreɪniəm/ *noun* a garden plant with a mass of red, pink or white flowers on the end of each STEM

ger·bil /ˈdʒɜːbɪl; *NAmE* ˈdʒɜːrbɪl/ *noun* a small desert animal like a mouse, that is often kept as a pet

geri·at·ric /ˌdʒeriˈætrɪk/ *noun* **1 geriatrics** [U] the branch of medicine concerned with the diseases and care of old people **2** [C] (*informal, offensive*) an old person, especially one with poor physical or mental health: *I'm not a geriatric yet, you know!* ▶ **geri·at·ric** *adj.*: *the geriatric ward* (= in a hospital) ◇ *a geriatric vehicle* (= old and in bad condition)

geria·tri·cian /ˌdʒeriəˈtrɪʃn/ *noun* a doctor who studies and treats the diseases of old people

germ /dʒɜːm; *NAmE* dʒɜːrm/ *noun* **1** [C, usually pl.] a very small living thing that can cause infection and disease: *Disinfectant kills germs.* ◇ *Dirty hands can be a breeding ground for germs.* **2** [sing.] **~ of sth** an early stage of the development of sth: *Here was the germ of a brilliant idea.* **3** [C] (*biology*) the part of a plant or an animal that can develop into a new one ➲ see also WHEATGERM

Ger·man /ˈdʒɜːmən; *NAmE* ˈdʒɜːrmən/ *adj., noun*
■ ***adj.*** from or connected with Germany
■ ***noun*** **1** [C] a person from Germany **2** [U] the language of Germany, Austria and parts of Switzerland

ger·mane /dʒɜːˈmeɪn; *NAmE* dʒɜːrˈm-/ *adj.* [not usually before noun] **~ (to sth)** (*formal*) (of ideas, remarks, etc.) connected with sth in an important or appropriate way **SYN relevant**: *remarks that are germane to the discussion*

Ger·man·ic /dʒɜːˈmænɪk; *NAmE* dʒɜːrˈm-/ *adj.* **1** connected with or considered typical of Germany or its people: *She had an almost Germanic regard for order.* **2** connected with the language family that includes German, English, Dutch and Swedish among others

ger·ma·nium /dʒɜːˈmeɪniəm; *NAmE* dʒɜːr-/ *noun* [U] (*symb.* Ge) a chemical element. Germanium is a shiny grey element that is similar to a metal (= is a METALLOID).

ˈGerman ˈmeasles (also **ru·bella**) *noun* [U] a mild infectious disease that causes a sore throat and red spots all over the body. It can seriously affect babies born to women who catch it soon after they become pregnant.

ˌGerman ˈshepherd (*especially NAmE*) (*BrE* also **Al·sa·tian**) *noun* a large dog, often trained to help the police, to guard buildings or (especially in the US) to help blind people find their way

ger·mi·cide /ˈdʒɜːmɪsaɪd; *NAmE* ˈdʒɜːrm-/ *noun* [C, U] a substance which destroys bacteria, etc. ▶ **ger·mi·cidal** /ˌdʒɜːmɪˈsaɪdl; *NAmE* ˌdʒɜːrm-/ *adj.*

ger·min·ate /ˈdʒɜːmɪneɪt; *NAmE* ˈdʒɜːrm-/ *verb* [I, T] **~ (sth)** when the seed of a plant **germinates** or **is germinated**, it starts to grow: (*figurative*) *An idea for a novel began to germinate in her mind.* ▶ **ger·min·ation** /ˌdʒɜːmɪˈneɪʃn; *NAmE* ˌdʒɜːrm-/ *noun* [U]

ˌgerm ˈwarfare *noun* [U] = BIOLOGICAL WARFARE

ger·on·toc·racy /ˌdʒerənˈtɒkrəsi; *NAmE* -ˈtɑːk-/ *noun* (*pl.* -ies) [C, U] a state, society, or group governed by old people; government by old people ▶ **ger·on·to·crat·ic** /dʒəˌrɒntəˈkrætɪk; *NAmE* -ˌrɑːntə-/ *adj.*

ger·ont·olo·gist /ˌdʒerɒnˈtɒlədʒɪst; *NAmE* -rənˈtɑːl-/ *noun* (*especially NAmE*) a person who studies the process of people growing old

ge·ron·tol·ogy /ˌdʒerɒnˈtɒlədʒi; *NAmE* -rənˈtɑːl-/ *noun* [U] the scientific study of OLD AGE and the process of growing old

ger·ry·man·der (also **jer·ry·man·der**) /ˈdʒerimændə(r)/ *verb* **~ sth** (*disapproving*) to change the size and borders of an area for voting in order to give an unfair advantage to one party in an election ▶ **ger·ry·man·der·ing** (also **jer·ry·man·der·ing**) *noun* [U]

ger·und /ˈdʒerənd/ *noun* (*grammar*) a noun in the form of the present participle of a verb (that is, ending in *-ing*) for example *travelling* in the sentence *I preferred travelling alone.*

ge·stalt /gəˈʃtælt; *NAmE* also -ˈʃtɑːlt/ *noun* (*psychology*) (from *German*) a set of things, such as a person's thoughts or experiences, that is considered as a single system which is different from the individual thoughts, experiences, etc. within it

ges·tate /dʒeˈsteɪt; *NAmE* ˈdʒesteɪt/ *verb* **~ sth** (*biology* or *medical*) to carry a young human or animal inside the WOMB until it is born

ges·ta·tion /dʒeˈsteɪʃn/ *noun* **1** [U, sing.] the time that the young of a person or an animal develops inside its mother's body until it is born; the process of developing inside the mother's body: *a baby born at 38 weeks' gestation* ◇ *The* **gestation period** *of a horse is about eleven months.* **2** [U] (*formal*) the process by which an idea or a plan develops SYN **development**

ges·ticu·late /dʒeˈstɪkjuleɪt/ *verb* [I] to move your hands and arms about in order to attract attention or make sb understand what you are saying: *He* **gesticulated wildly** *at the clock.* ▶ **ges·ticu·la·tion** /dʒeˌstɪkjuˈleɪʃn/ *noun* [C, U]: ***wild/frantic gesticulations***

ges·ture /ˈdʒestʃə(r)/ *noun, verb*

■ ***noun*** **1** [C, U] a movement that you make with your hands, your head or your face to show a particular meaning: *He* **made a** *rude* **gesture** *at the driver of the other car.* ◇ *She finished what she had to say with a gesture of despair.* ◇ *They communicated entirely by gesture.* **2** [C] something that you do or say to show a particular feeling or intention: *They sent some flowers as a gesture of sympathy to the parents of the child.* ◇ *It was a nice gesture* (= it was kind) *to invite his wife too.* ◇ *We do not accept responsibility but we will refund the money as a* **gesture of goodwill.** ◇ *The government has made a gesture towards public opinion* (= has tried to do sth that the public will like).

■ ***verb*** [I, T] to move your hands, head, face, etc. as a way of expressing what you mean or want: (**+ adv./prep.**) *'I see you read a lot,' he said, gesturing at the wall of books.* ◇ **~ to sb** (**to do sth**) | **~ for sb to do sth** *She gestured for them to come in.* ◇ **~** (**to sb**) (**that**)... *He gestured* (*to me*) *that it was time to go.* ◇ *They gestured that I should follow.*

ge·sund·heit /ɡəˈzʊndhaɪt/ *exclamation* (*NAmE*, from *German*) used when sb has SNEEZED to wish them good health

get 🔑 /ɡet/ *verb* (getting, got, got /ɡɒt; *NAmE* ɡɑːt/)

HELP In spoken *NAmE* the past participle **got·ten** /ˈɡɒtn/ /ˈɡɑːtn/ is almost always used.

▸ RECEIVE/OBTAIN **1** 🔑 [T, no passive] **~ sth** to receive sth: *I got a letter from Dave this morning.* ◇ *What* (= What presents) *did you get for your birthday?* ◇ *He gets* (= earns) *about $40 000 a year.* ◇ *This room gets very little sunshine.* ◇ *I* **got a shock** *when I saw the bill.* ◇ *I* **get the impression** *that he is bored with his job.* **2** 🔑 [T, no passive] to obtain sth: **~ sth** *Where did you get* (= buy) *that skirt?* ◇ *Did you manage to get tickets for the concert?* ◇ *She opened the door wider to get a better look.* ◇ *Try to get some sleep.* ◇ *He has just got a new job.* ◇ **~ sth for sb** *Did you get a present for your mother?* ◇ **~ sb/yourself sth** *Did you get your mother a present?* ◇ *Why don't you get yourself a car?* **3** 🔑 [T, no passive] **~ sth** (**for sth**) to obtain or receive an amount of money by selling sth: *How much did you get for your car?*

▸ BRING **4** 🔑 [T] to go to a place and bring sb/sth back SYN **fetch**: **~ sb/sth** *Quick—go and get a cloth!* ◇ *Somebody get a doctor!* ◇ *I have to go and get my mother from the airport* (= collect her). ◇ **~ sth for sb** *Get a drink for John.* ◇ **~ sb/yourself sth** *Get John a drink.*

▸ PUNISHMENT **5** [T, no passive] **~ sth** to receive sth as a punishment: *He got ten years* (= was sent to prison for ten years) *for armed robbery.*

▸ BROADCASTS **6** [T, no passive] **~ sth** to receive broadcasts from a particular television or radio station: *We can't get Channel 5 in our area.*

▸ BUY **7** [T, no passive] **~ sth** to buy sth, for example a newspaper or magazine, regularly SYN **take**: *Which newspaper do you get?*

▸ MARK/GRADE **8** 🔑 [T, no passive] **~ sth** to achieve or be given a particular mark/grade in an exam: *He got a 'C' in Chemistry and a 'B' in English.*

▸ ILLNESS **9** 🔑 [T, no passive] **~ sth** to become infected with an illness; to suffer from a pain, etc: *I got this cold off* (= from) *you!* ◇ *She gets* (= often suffers from) *really bad headaches.*

▸ CONTACT **10** [T, no passive] **~ sb** to be connected with sb by telephone: *I wanted to speak to the manager but I got his secretary instead.*

▸ STATE/CONDITION **11** 🔑 *linking verb* to reach a particular state or condition; to make sb/sth/yourself reach a particular state or condition: **+ adj.** *to get angry/bored/hungry/fat* ◇ *You'll soon* **get used to** *the climate here.* ◇ *We ought to go; it's getting late.* ◇ *to* **get dressed/undressed** (= to put your clothes on/take your clothes off) ◇ *They plan to* **get married** *in the summer.* ◇ *She's upstairs getting ready.* ◇ *I wouldn't go there alone; you might get* (= be) *mugged.* ◇ *My car got* (= was) *stolen at the weekend.* ◇ **~ sb/sth + adj.** *Don't get your dress dirty!* ◇ *He got his fingers caught in the door.* ◇ *She soon got the children ready for school.* ➲ SYNONYMS at BECOME **12** 🔑 [I] **~ to do sth** to reach the point at which you feel, know, are, etc. sth: *After a time you get to realize that these things don't matter.* ◇ *You'll like her once you* **get to know** *her.* ◇ *His drinking is getting to be a problem.* ◇ *She's getting to be an old lady now.*

▸ MAKE/PERSUADE **13** 🔑 [T] to make, persuade, etc. sb/sth to do sth: **~ sb/sth to do sth** *I couldn't get the car to start this morning.* ◇ *He got his sister to help him with his homework.* ◇ *You'll never get him to understand.* ◇ **~ sb/sth doing sth** *Can you really get that old car going again?* ◇ *It's not hard to get him talking—the problem is stopping him!*

▸ GET STH DONE **14** 🔑 [T] **~ sth done** to cause sth to happen or be done: *I must get my hair cut.* ◇ *I'll never get all this work finished.*

▸ START **15** [T] **~ doing sth** to start doing sth: *I got talking to her.* ◇ *We need to get going soon.*

▸ OPPORTUNITY **16** [I] **~ to do sth** (*informal*) to have the opportunity to do sth: *He got to try out all the new software.* ◇ *It's not fair—I never get to go first.*

▸ ARRIVE **17** 🔑 [I] **+ adv./prep.** to arrive at or reach a place or point: *We got to San Diego at 7 o'clock.* ◇ *You got in very late last night.* ◇ *What time did you get here?* ◇ *I haven't got very far with the book I'm reading.*

▸ MOVE/TRAVEL **18** 🔑 [I, T] to move to or from a particular place or in a particular direction, sometimes with difficulty; to make sb/sth do this: **+ adv./prep.** *The bridge was destroyed so we couldn't get across the river.* ◇ *She got into bed.* ◇ *He got down from the ladder.* ◇ *We didn't* **get** (= go) **to bed** *until 3 a.m.* ◇ *Where do we* **get on** *the bus?* ◇ *I'm* **getting off** (= leaving the train) *at the next station.* ◇ *Where have they* **got to** (= where are they)? ◇ *We must be* **getting home;** *it's past midnight.* ◇ **~ sb/sth + adv./prep.** *The general had to get his troops across the river.* ◇ *We couldn't get the piano through the door.* ◇ *We'd better call a taxi and get you home.* ◇ *I can't get the lid off.* **19** 🔑 [T, no passive] **~ sth** to use a bus, taxi, plane, etc: *We're going to be late—let's get a taxi.* ◇ *I usually get the bus to work.*

▸ MEAL **20** [T] (*especially BrE*) to prepare a meal: **~ sth** *Who's getting the lunch?* ◇ **~ sth for sb/yourself** *I must go home and get tea for the kids.* ◇ **~ sb/yourself sth** *I must go home and get the kids their tea.*

▸ TELEPHONE/DOOR **21** [T] **~ sth** (*informal*) to answer the telephone or a door when sb calls, knocks, etc: *Will you get the phone?*

▸ CATCH/HIT **22** [T] **~ sb** to catch or take hold of sb, especially in order to harm or punish them: *He was on the run for a week before the police got him.* ◇ *to get sb by the arm/wrist/throat* ◇ *She fell overboard and the sharks got her.* ◇ *He thinks everybody is* **out to get him** (= trying to harm him). ◇ (*informal*) ***I'll get you for that!*** **23** [T] **~ sb + adv./prep.** to hit or wound sb: *The bullet got him in the neck.*

▸ UNDERSTAND **24** [T, no passive] **~ sb/sth** (*informal*) to understand sb/sth: *I don't get you.* ◇ *She didn't get the joke.* ◇ *I* **don't get it**—*why would she do a thing like that?* ◇ *I* **get the message**—*you don't want me to come.* ➲ SYNONYMS at UNDERSTAND

▸ HAPPEN/EXIST **25** [T, no passive] **~ sth** (*informal*) used to say that sth happens or exists: ***You get*** (= There are) *all these kids hanging around in the street.* ◇ *They still get cases of typhoid there.*

▸ CONFUSE/ANNOY **26** [T, no passive] **~ sb** (*informal*) to make sb feel confused because they do not understand sth SYN **puzzle**: *'What's the capital of Bhutan?'* ***'You've got me there!'*** (= I don't know). **27** [T, no passive] **~ sb** (*informal*) to annoy sb: ***What gets me*** *is having to do the same* thing all day long. HELP **Get** is one of the most common words in English, but some people try to avoid it in formal writing.

IDM Most idioms containing **get** are at the entries for the nouns and adjectives in the idioms, for example **get sb's goat** is at **goat**. **be getting 'on** (*informal*) **1** (of a person) to be becoming old **2** (of time) to be becoming late: *The time's getting on—we ought to be going.* **be getting on for ...** (*especially BrE*) to be nearly a particular time, age or number: *It must be getting on for midnight.* ◇ *He's getting on for eighty.* **can't get 'over sth** (*informal*) used to say that you are shocked, surprised, amused, etc. by sth: *I can't get over how rude she was.* **get a'way from it all** (*informal*) to have a short holiday/vacation in a place where you can relax ,**get it 'on (with sb)** (*slang, especially NAmE*) to have sex with sb **'get it** (also **catch 'hell**) (both *NAmE*) (*BrE* **'catch it**) (*informal*) to be punished or spoken to angrily about sth ,**get it 'up** (*slang*) (of a man) to have an ERECTION **get sb 'going** (*BrE, informal*) to make sb angry, worried or excited **get sb nowhere/not get sb anywhere** to not help sb make progress or succeed: *This line of investigation is getting us nowhere.* ◇ *Being rude to me won't get you anywhere.* **get somewhere/anywhere/nowhere** to make some progress/no progress: *After six months' work on the project, at last I feel I'm getting somewhere.* ◇ *I don't seem to be getting anywhere with this letter.* **'get there** to achieve your aim or complete a task: *I'm sure you'll get there in the end.* ◇ *It's not perfect but **we're getting there*** (= making progress). ,**get 'this!** (*informal, especially NAmE*) used to say that you are going to tell sb sth that they will find surprising or interesting: *OK, get this guys—there are only two left!* **how selfish, stupid, ungrateful, etc. can you 'get?** (*informal*) used to express surprise or disapproval that sb has been so selfish, etc. **there's no getting a'way from sth | you can't get a'way from sth** you have to admit that sth unpleasant is true **what are you, was he, etc. 'getting at?** (*informal*) used to ask, especially in an angry way, what sb is/was suggesting: *I'm partly to blame? What exactly are you getting at?* **what has got into sb?** (*informal*) used to say that sb has suddenly started to behave in a strange or different way: *What's got into Alex? He never used to worry like that.*

PHR V ,**get a'bout** (*BrE*) = GET AROUND

,**get a'bove yourself** (*especially BrE*) to have too high an opinion of yourself

,**get a'cross (to sb)** | ,**get sth↔a'cross (to sb)** to be communicated or understood; to succeed in communicating sth: *Your meaning didn't really get across.* ◇ *He's not very good at getting his ideas across.*

,**get a'head (of sb)** to make progress (further than others have done): *She wants to get ahead in her career.* ◇ *He soon got ahead of the others in his class.*

,**get a'long 1** (usually used in the progressive tenses) to leave a place: *It's time we were getting along.* **2** = GET ON

,**get a'round 1** (*BrE* also ,**get a'bout**) to move from place to place or from person to person: *She gets around with the help of a stick.* ◇ *News soon got around that he had resigned.* **2** (*especially NAmE*) = GET ROUND

'get at sb (usually used in the progressive tenses) to keep criticizing sb: *He's always getting at me.* ◇ *She feels she's being got at.* **'get at sb/sth** to reach sb/sth; to gain access to sb/sth: *The files are locked up and I can't get at them.* **'get at sth** to learn or find out sth: *The truth is sometimes difficult to get at.*

,**get a'way 1** to have a holiday/vacation: *We're hoping to get away for a few days at Easter.* ➲ related noun GETAWAY **2** (*BrE, informal*) used to show that you do not believe or are surprised by what sb has said: *'These tickets didn't cost me a thing.' 'Get away!'* ,**get a'way (from...)** to succeed in leaving a place: *I won't be able to get away from the office before 7.* ,**get a'way (from sb/...)** 🔑 to escape from sb or a place ,**get a'way with sth 1** 🔑 to steal sth and escape with it: *Thieves got away with computer equipment worth $30 000.* ➲ related noun GETAWAY **2** 🔑 to receive a relatively light punishment: *He was lucky to get away with only a fine.* **3** 🔑 to do sth wrong and not be punished for it: *Don't be tempted to cheat—you'll never get away with it.* ◇ **~ doing sth** *Nobody gets away with insulting me like that.* **4** to manage with less of sth than you might expect to need: *After the first month, you should be able to get away with one lesson a week.*

,**get 'back** 🔑 to return, especially to your home: *What time did you get back last night?* ➲ SYNONYMS at RETURN ,**get sth↔'back** 🔑 to obtain sth again after having lost it: *She's got her old job back.* ◇ *I never lend books—you never get them back.* ,**get 'back (in)** (of a political party) to win an election after having lost the previous one ,**get 'back at sb** (*informal*) to do sth bad to sb who has done sth bad to you; to get REVENGE on sb: *I'll find a way of getting back at him!* ,**get 'back to sb** (*informal*) to speak or write to sb again later, especially in order to give a reply: *I'll find out and get back to you.* ,**get 'back to sth** to return to sth: *Could we get back to the question of funding?* ,**get back to'gether (with sb)** to start a relationship with sb again, especially a romantic relationship, after having finished a previous relationship with the same person: *I just got back together with my ex-girlfriend.*

,**get be'hind (with sth)** to fail to make enough progress or to produce sth at the right time: *I'm getting behind with my work.* ◇ *He got behind with the payments for his car.*

,**get 'by (on/in/with sth)** 🔑 to manage to live or do a particular thing using the money, knowledge, equipment, etc. that you have: *How does she get by on such a small salary?* ◇ *I can just about get by in German* (= I can speak basic German).

,**get 'down** (of children) (*BrE*) to leave the table after a meal ,**get sb 'down** (*informal*) to make sb feel sad or depressed ,**get sth↔'down 1** to swallow sth, usually with difficulty **2** to make a note of sth SYN **write down**: *Did you get his number down?* ,**get 'down to sth** to begin to do sth; to give serious attention to sth: *Let's **get down to business**.* ◇ *I like to **get down to work** by 9.* ◇ **~ doing sth** *It's time I got down to thinking about that essay.*

,**get 'in** | ,**get 'into sth 1** 🔑 to arrive at a place: *The train got in late.* ◇ *What time do you get into Heathrow?* **2** 🔑 to win an election: *The Republican candidate stands a good chance of getting in.* ◇ *She first got into Parliament* (= became an MP) *in 2005.* **3** 🔑 to be admitted to a school, university, etc: *She's got into Durham to study law.* ,**get sb↔'in** to call sb to your house to do a job ,**get sth↔'in 1** to collect or gather sth: *to **get the crops/harvest in*** **2** to buy a supply of sth: *Remember to get in some beers for this evening.* **3** to manage to do or say sth: *I got in an hour's work while the baby was asleep.* ◇ *She talks so much it's impossible to get a word in.* ,**get 'in on sth** to take part in an activity: *He's hoping to get in on any discussions about the new project.* ,**get 'in with sb** (*informal*) to become friendly with sb, especially in order to gain an advantage

,**get 'into sth 1** 🔑 to put on a piece of clothing, especially with difficulty: *I can't get into these shoes—they're too small.* **2** 🔑 to start a career in a particular profession: *What's the best way to get into journalism?* **3** 🔑 to become involved in sth; to start sth: *I got into conversation with an Italian student.* ◇ *to get into a fight* **4** 🔑 to develop a particular habit: *Don't let yourself get into bad habits.* ◇ *You should get into the routine of saving the document you are working on every ten minutes.* ◇ *How did she get into* (= start taking) *drugs?* **5** 🔑 (*informal*) to become interested in sth: *I'm really getting into jazz these days.* **6** to become familiar with sth; to learn sth: *I haven't really got into my new job yet.* ,**get 'into sth** | ,**get yourself/sb 'into sth** 🔑 to reach a particular state or condition; to make sb reach a particular state or condition: *He got into trouble with the police while he was still at school.* ◇ *Three people were rescued from a yacht which got into difficulties.* ◇ *She got herself into a real state* (= became very anxious) *before the interview.*

,**get 'off** | ,**get 'off sb** used especially to tell sb to stop touching you or another person: *Get off me, that hurts!* ,**get 'off** | ,**get sb 'off 1** to leave a place or start a journey; to help sb do this: *We got off straight after breakfast.* ◇ *He got the children off to school.* **2** (*BrE*) to fall asleep; to make sb do this: *I had great difficulty getting off to sleep.* ◇ *They couldn't get the baby off till midnight.* ,**get 'off** | ,**get 'off sth** to leave work with permission: *Could you get off (work) early tomorrow?* ,**get 'off sth** | ,**get sb 'off sth** to stop discussing a particular subject; to make sb do this: *Please can we get off the subject of dieting?* ◇ *I couldn't get him off politics once he had started.* **ˌget sth ˈoff** to send sth by post/mail: *I must get these letters off first thing tomorrow.* **ˌget ˈoff on sth** (*informal*) to be excited by sth, especially in a sexual way **ˌget ˈoff (with sth)** to have no or almost no injuries in an accident: *She was lucky to get off with just a few bruises.* **ˌget ˈoff (with sth) | ˌget sb ˈoff (with sth)** 🗝 to receive no or almost no punishment; to help sb do this: *He was lucky to get off with a small fine.* ◇ *A good lawyer might be able to get you off.* **ˌget ˈoff with sb** (*informal, especially BrE*) to have a sexual or romantic experience with sb; to start a sexual relationship with sb: *Steve got off with Tracey at the party.*

ˌget ˈon 1 🗝 (also **ˌget aˈlong**) used to talk or ask about how well sb is doing in a particular situation: *He's getting on very well at school.* ◇ ***How did you get on** at the interview?* **2** 🗝 to be successful in your career, etc: *Parents are always anxious for their children to get on.* ◇ *I don't know how he's going to **get on in life**.* **3** 🗝 (also **ˌget aˈlong**) to manage or survive: *We can get on perfectly well without her.* ◇ *I just can't get along without a secretary.* **ˌget ˈon to sb 1** to contact sb by telephone, letter or email: *The heating isn't working; I'll get on to the landlord about it.* **2** to become aware of sb's activities, especially when they have been doing sth bad or illegal: *He had been stealing money from the company for years before they got on to him.* **ˌget ˈon to sth** to begin to talk about a new subject: *It's time we got on to the question of costs.* **ˌget ˈon with sb | ˌget ˈon (together)** 🗝 (both *BrE*) (also **ˌget aˈlong with sb, ˌget aˈlong (together)** *NAmE, BrE*) to have a friendly relationship with sb: *She's never really got on with her sister.* ◇ *She and her sister have never really got on.* ◇ *We get along just fine together.* **ˌget ˈon with sth 1** 🗝 (also **ˌget aˈlong with sth**) used to talk or ask about how well sb is doing a task: *I'm not getting on very fast with this job.* **2** 🗝 to continue doing sth, especially after an interruption: *Be quiet and get on with your work.* ◇ (*informal*) *Get on with it! We haven't got all day.*

ˌget ˈout to become known: *If this gets out there'll be trouble.* **ˌget sth↔ˈout 1** to produce or publish sth: *Will we get the book out by the end of the year?* **2** to say sth with difficulty: *She managed to get out a few words of thanks.* **ˌget ˈout (of sth)** to leave or go out of a place: *You ought to get out of the house more.* ◇ *She screamed at me to get out.* **ˌget ˈout of sth 1** 🗝 to avoid a responsibility or duty: *We promised we'd go—we can't get out of it now.* ◇ **~ doing sth** *I wish I could get out of going to that meeting.* **2** 🗝 to stop having a particular habit: *I can't get out of the habit of waking at six in the morning.* **ˌget sth ˈout of sb** to persuade sb to tell or give you sth, especially by force: *The police finally got a confession out of her.* **ˌget sth ˈout of sb/sth** to gain or obtain sth good from sb/sth: *She seems to get a lot out of life.* ◇ *He always gets the best out of people.*

ˌget ˈover sth 🗝 to deal with or gain control of sth **SYN overcome**: *She can't get over her shyness.* ◇ *I think the problem can be got over without too much difficulty.* **ˌget ˈover sth/sb** 🗝 to return to your usual state of health, happiness, etc. after an illness, a shock, the end of a relationship, etc: *He was disappointed at not getting the job, but he'll get over it.* **ˌget ˈover yourself** (*informal*) to stop thinking that you are so important; to stop being so serious: *Just get over yourself and stop moaning!* ◇ *He needs to grow up a bit and get over himself.* **ˌget sth↔ˈover (to sb)** to make sth clear to sb: *He didn't really get his meaning over to the audience.* **ˌget sth ˈover (with)** (*informal*) to complete sth unpleasant but necessary: *I'll be glad to **get** the exam **over and done with**.*

ˌget ˈround/aˈround sb to persuade sb to agree or to do what you want, usually by doing nice things for them: *She knows how to get round her dad.* **ˌget ˈround/aˈround sth** 🗝 to deal with a problem successfully **SYN overcome**: *A clever lawyer might find a way of getting round that clause.* **ˌget ˈround/aˈround to sth** 🗝 to find the time to do sth: *I meant to do the ironing but I didn't get round to it.* ◇ **~ doing sth** *I hope to get around to answering your letter next week.*

ˈget through sth 1 🗝 to use up a large amount of sth: *We got through a fortune while we were in New York!* **2** to manage to do or complete sth: *Let's start—there's a lot to get through.* **ˌget ˈthrough (sth)** (*BrE*) to be successful in an exam, etc. **ˌget sb ˈthrough sth** to help sb to be successful in an exam: *She got all her students through the exam.* **ˌget ˈthrough (sth) | ˌget sth ˈthrough (sth)** to be officially accepted; to make sth be officially accepted: *They got the bill through Congress.* **ˌget ˈthrough (to sb) 1** 🗝 to reach sb: *Thousands of refugees will die if these supplies don't get through to them.* **2** 🗝 to make contact with sb by telephone: *I tried calling you several times but I couldn't get through.* **ˌget ˈthrough (to sth)** (of a player or team) to reach the next stage of a competition: *Moya has got through to the final.* **ˌget ˈthrough to sb** to make sb understand or accept what you say, especially when you are trying to help them: *I find it impossible to get through to her.* **ˌget ˈthrough with sth** to finish or complete a task

ˈget to sb (*informal*) to annoy or affect sb: *The pressure of work is beginning to get to him.*

ˌget sb/sth toˈgether to collect people or things in one place: *I'm trying to get a team together for Saturday.* **ˌget toˈgether (with sb)** (*informal*) to meet with sb socially or in order to discuss sth: *We must get together for a drink sometime.* ◇ *Management should get together with the union.* ➲ related noun GET-TOGETHER

ˌget ˈup 1 🗝 to stand up after sitting, lying, etc. **SYN rise**: *The class got up when the teacher came in.* ➲ SYNONYMS at STAND **2** if the sea or wind **gets up**, it increases in strength and becomes violent **ˌget ˈup | ˌget sb ˈup** 🗝 to get out of bed; to make sb get out of bed: *He always gets up early.* ◇ *Could you get me up at 6.30 tomorrow?* **ˌget yourself/sb ˈup as sth** [often passive] (*BrE*) to dress yourself/sb as sb/sth else: *She was got up as an Indian princess.* ➲ related noun GET-UP **ˌget sth↔ˈup** to arrange or organize sth: *We're getting up a party for her birthday.* **ˌget ˈup to sth 1** to reach a particular point: *We got up to page 72 last lesson.* **2** to be busy with sth, especially sth surprising or unpleasant: *What on earth will he get up to next?* ◇ *She's been getting up to her old tricks again!*

get·away /ˈgetəweɪ/ *noun* [usually sing.] **1** an escape from a difficult situation, especially after committing a crime: *to **make a quick getaway*** ◇ *a getaway car* **2** (*informal*) a short holiday/vacation; a place that is suitable for a holiday/vacation: *a romantic weekend getaway in New York* ◇ *the popular island getaway of Penang*

ˈget-out *noun* [usually sing.] (*BrE, informal*) a way of avoiding sth, especially a responsibility or duty: *He said he'd come but he's looking for a get-out.* ◇ *a **get-out clause** in the contract*

get·ting /ˈgetɪŋ/ *noun* [sing.]

IDM while the ˌgetting is ˈgood (*NAmE*) (*BrE* **while the ˌgoing is ˈgood**) before a situation changes and it is no longer possible to do sth

ˈget-together *noun* (*informal*) an informal meeting; a party

ˈget-up *noun* (*old-fashioned, informal*) a set of clothes, especially strange or unusual ones

ˌget-up-and-ˈgo *noun* [U] (*informal*) energy and determination to get things done

gew·gaw /ˈgjuːgɔː; *NAmE* also ˈguː-/ *noun* an object that attracts attention but has no value or use

gey·ser /ˈgiːzə(r); *NAmE* ˈgaɪzər/ *noun* **1** a natural SPRING that sometimes sends hot water or steam up into the air **2** (*BrE*) a piece of equipment in a kitchen or bathroom that heats water, usually by gas **3** (*SAfrE*) a large container in which water is stored and heated, usually by electricity, in order to provide hot water in a building

ghagra /ˈgʌgrɑː/ *noun* a long skirt, worn by women in S Asia

gha·rara /gʌˈrɑːrə/ *noun* loose wide trousers, worn with a KAMEEZ and DUPATTA by women in S Asia

ghar·ial /ˈgæriɑːl; ˌgʌriˈɑːl; *NAmE* ˈgeriəl/ (also **ga·vial**) *noun* a S Asian CROCODILE

G

ghastly /ˈɡɑːstli; *NAmE* ˈɡæstli/ *adj.* (**ghast·lier**, **ghast·li·est**) **1** (of an event) very frightening and unpleasant, because it involves pain, death, etc. SYN **horrible**: *a ghastly crime/murder* **2** (*informal*) (of an experience or a situation) very bad; unpleasant SYN **terrible**: *The weather was ghastly.* ◇ *It's all been a ghastly mistake.* **3** (*informal*) (of a person or thing) that you find unpleasant and dislike very much SYN **horrible**: *her ghastly husband* ◇ *This lipstick is a ghastly colour.* **4** [not usually before noun] ill/sick or upset SYN **terrible**: *I felt ghastly the next day.* **5** (*literary*) very pale in appearance, like a dead person: *His face was ghastly white.*

ghat /ɡɑːt/ *noun* (*IndE*) **1** [C] steps leading down to a river or lake **2** [C] a road or way over or through mountains **3 Ghats** [pl.] the mountains near the eastern and western coasts of India

G

ghee /ɡiː/ *noun* [U] a type of butter used in S Asian cooking

gher·kin /ˈɡɜːkɪn; *NAmE* ˈɡɜːrkɪn/ *noun* **1** (*BrE*) (*NAmE* **pickle**) a small CUCUMBER that has been preserved in VINEGAR before being eaten **2** (*NAmE*) a small CUCUMBER

ghetto /ˈɡetəʊ; *NAmE* ˈɡetoʊ/ *noun* (*pl.* **-os** or **-oes**) **1** an area of a city where many people of the same race or background live, separately from the rest of the population. Ghettos are often crowded, with bad living conditions: *a poor kid growing up in the ghetto* ◇ *The south coast of Spain has become something of a tourist ghetto.* **2** the area of a town where Jews were forced to live in the past: *the Warsaw ghetto*

ˈ**ghetto blaster** (also ˈ**boom box** especially in *NAmE*) *noun* (*informal*) a large radio and CD or CASSETTE player that can be carried around, especially to play loud music in public

ghil·lie *noun* = GILLIE

ghost /ɡəʊst; *NAmE* ɡoʊst/ *noun, verb*

▪ ***noun*** **1** [C] the spirit of a dead person that a living person believes they can see or hear: *Do you believe in ghosts* (= believe that they exist)? ◇ *the ghost of her father that had come back to haunt her* ◇ *He looked as if he had seen a ghost* (= looked very frightened). **2** [C] the memory of sth, especially sth bad: *The ghost of anti-Semitism still haunts Europe.* **3** [sing.] **~ of sth** a very slight amount of sth that is left behind or that you are not sure really exists: *There was a ghost of a smile on his face.* ◇ *You don't have a ghost of a chance* (= you have no chance). **4** [sing.] a second image on a television screen that is not as clear as the first, caused by a fault

IDM **give up the ˈghost 1** to die **2** (*humorous*) (of a machine) to stop working: *My car finally gave up the ghost.* ➲ more at FORMER

▪ ***verb*** **1** = GHOSTWRITE **2** [I] **+ adv./prep.** (*literary*) to move without making a sound: *They ghosted up the smooth waters of the river.*

ghost·ing /ˈɡəʊstɪŋ; *NAmE* ˈɡoʊ-/ *noun* [U] the appearance of a faint second image next to an image on a television screen, computer screen, etc.

ghost·ly /ˈɡəʊstli; *NAmE* ˈɡoʊstli/ *adj.* (**ghost·lier**, **ghost·li·est**) looking or sounding like a ghost; full of ghosts: *a ghostly figure* ◇ *ghostly footsteps* ◇ *the ghostly churchyard*

ˈ**ghost story** *noun* a story about ghosts that is intended to frighten you

ˈ**ghost town** *noun* a town that used to be busy and have a lot of people living in it, but is now empty

ˈ**ghost train** *noun* (*BrE*) a small train at a FUNFAIR that goes through a dark tunnel full of frightening things

ghost·write /ˈɡəʊstraɪt; *NAmE* ˈɡoʊst-/ (also **ghost**) *verb* [T, often passive, I] **~ (sth)** to write a book, an article, etc. for another person who publishes it as their own work: *Her memoirs were ghostwritten.*

ghost·writer /ˈɡəʊstraɪtə(r); *NAmE* ˈɡoʊst-/ *noun* a person who writes a book, etc. for another person, under whose name it is then published

ghoul /ɡuːl/ *noun* **1** (in stories) an evil spirit that opens graves and eats the dead bodies in them **2** (*disapproving*) a person who is too interested in unpleasant things such as death and disaster ▸ **ghoul·ish** /ˈɡuːlɪʃ/ *adj.*: *ghoulish laughter*

GHQ /ˌdʒiː eɪtʃ ˈkjuː/ *noun* [U] the abbreviation for 'general headquarters' (the main centre of a military organization): *He was posted to GHQ Cairo.*

GHz *abbr.* (in writing) GIGAHERTZ

GI /ˌdʒiː ˈaɪ/ *noun, abbr.*

▪ ***noun*** (*pl.* **GIs**) a soldier in the US armed forces

▪ ***abbr.*** GLYCAEMIC INDEX (= a system for measuring the effect of foods containing CARBOHYDRATES on the level of sugar in the blood): *The diet is based mainly on low GI foods.*

giant 🔑 /ˈdʒaɪənt/ *noun, adj.*

▪ ***noun*** **1** 🔑 (in stories) a very large strong person who is often cruel and stupid ➲ see also GIANTESS **2** 🔑 an unusually large person, animal or plant: *He's a giant of a man.* **3** a very large and powerful organization: *the multinational oil giants* **4** a person who is very good at sth: *literary giants*

▪ ***adj.*** 🔑 [only before noun] very large; much larger or more important than similar things usually are: *a giant crab* ◇ *a giant-size box of tissues* ◇ *a giant step towards achieving independence*

giant·ess /ˌdʒaɪənˈtes/ *noun* (in stories) a female giant

giant·ism /ˈdʒaɪəntɪzəm/ *noun* [U] = GIGANTISM

ˈ**giant-killer** *noun* (*BrE*) (especially in sports) a person or team that defeats another much stronger opponent

ˌ**giant ˈpanda** *noun* = PANDA (1)

ˌ**giant ˈslalom** *noun* a SLALOM SKIING competition over a long distance, with wide fast turns

GiB *abbr.* (in writing) GIBIBYTE

Gib (also **Gibit**) *abbr.* (in writing) GIBIBIT

gib·ber /ˈdʒɪbə(r)/ *verb* [I, T] (**+ speech**) to speak quickly in a way that is difficult to understand, often because of fear: *He cowered in the corner, gibbering with terror.* ◇ *By this time I was a **gibbering wreck**.*

gib·ber·ish /ˈdʒɪbərɪʃ/ *noun* [U] (*informal*) words that have no meaning or are impossible to understand SYN **nonsense**: *You were talking gibberish in your sleep.*

gib·bet /ˈdʒɪbɪt/ *noun* (*old-fashioned*) a vertical wooden structure on which criminals used to be hanged SYN **gallows**

gib·bon /ˈɡɪbən/ *noun* a small APE (= an animal like a large MONKEY without a tail) with long arms, that lives in SE Asia

gib·bous /ˈɡɪbəs/ *adj.* (*technical*) (of the moon) with the bright part bigger than a SEMICIRCLE and smaller than a circle

gibe = JIBE

gibi·bit /ˈɡɪbibɪt/ *noun* (*abbr.* **Gib**, **Gibit**) (*computing*) = GIGABIT (2)

gibi·byte /ˈɡɪbibaɪt/ *noun* (*abbr.* **GiB**) (*computing*) = GIGABYTE (2)

gib·lets /ˈdʒɪbləts/ *noun* [pl.] the inside parts of a chicken or other bird, including the heart and LIVER, that are usually removed before it is cooked

giddy /ˈɡɪdi/ *adj.* (**gid·dier**, **gid·di·est**) **1** [not usually before noun] feeling that everything is moving and that you are going to fall SYN **dizzy**: *When I looked down from the top floor, I felt giddy.* **2** [not usually before noun] **~ (with sth)** so happy and excited that you cannot behave normally: *She was giddy with happiness.* **3** [usually before noun] making you feel as if you were about to fall: *The kids were pushing the roundabout at a giddy speed.* ◇ (*figurative*) ***the giddy heights** of success* **4** (*old-fashioned*) (of people) not serious SYN **silly**: *Isabel's giddy young sister* ▸ **gid·di·ly** /ˈɡɪdɪli/ *adv.*: *She swayed giddily across the dance floor.* **gid·di·ness** /ˈɡɪdinəs/ *noun* [U]: *Symptoms include nausea and giddiness.*

ˌgiddy-ˈup *exclamation* used as a command to a horse to make it go faster

GIF™ /ɡɪf/ *noun* (*computing*) the abbreviation for 'Graphic Interchange Format' (a type of computer file that contains images and is used a lot on the Internet): *Send it as a GIF.*

gift /ɡɪft/ *noun, verb*
■ ***noun*** **1** a thing that you give to sb, especially on a special occasion or to say thank you SYN **present**: *The watch was a gift from my mother.* ◇ *Thank you for your generous gift.* ◇ *a **free gift** for every reader* ◇ *the gift of life* ◇ (*formal*) *The family **made a gift of** his paintings to the gallery.* ◇ *gifts of toys for the children* **2** a natural ability SYN **talent**: **~ (for sth)** *She has a great gift for music.* ◇ **~ (for doing sth)** *He has the gift of making friends easily.* ◇ *She can pick up a tune instantly on the piano. It's a gift.* **3** [usually sing.] (*informal*) a thing that is very easy to do or cheap to buy: *Their second goal was an absolute gift.* ◇ *At £500 it's a gift.*
IDM **be in the gift of sb** | **be in sb's ˈgift** (*especially BrE*) if sth such as an important job or a special right or advantage is **in sb's gift**, that person can decide who to give it to: *All such posts are in the gift of the managing director* (= only given by the managing director). **the gift of the ˈgab** (*BrE*) (*US* **a gift for/of ˈgab**) (*informal*, sometimes *disapproving*) the ability to speak easily and to persuade other people with your words **look a gift horse in the ˈmouth** (usually with negatives) (*informal*) to refuse or criticize sth that is given to you for nothing ➲ more at GOD
■ ***verb*** (*BrE*) (used especially in JOURNALISM) to give sth to sb without their having to make any effort to get it: **~ sb sth** *They gifted their opponents a goal.* ◇ **~ sth to sb** *They gifted a goal to their opponents.*

ˈgift certificate (*NAmE*) (*BrE* **ˈgift voucher**, **ˈgift token**) *noun* a piece of paper that is worth a particular amount of money and that can be exchanged for goods in a shop/store

gift·ed /ˈɡɪftɪd/ *adj.* **1** having a lot of natural ability or intelligence: *a **gifted musician/player, etc.*** ◇ *gifted children* **2 ~ with sth** having sth pleasant: *He was gifted with a charming smile.*

ˈgift shop *noun* a shop/store that sells goods that are suitable for giving as presents

ˈgift voucher (also **ˈgift token**) (both *BrE*) (*NAmE* **ˈgift certificate**) *noun* a piece of paper that is worth a particular amount of money and that can be exchanged for goods in a shop/store

ˈgift wrap *noun* [U] attractive coloured or patterned paper used for wrapping presents in

ˈgift-wrap *verb* (**-pp-**) [often passive] **~ sth** to wrap sth as a present for sb, especially in a shop/store: *Would you like the chocolates gift-wrapped?* ◇ *The store offers a gift-wrapping service.*

gig /ɡɪɡ/ *noun* **1** a performance by musicians playing popular music or JAZZ in front of an audience; a similar performance by a COMEDIAN: *to do a gig* ◇ *a White Stripes gig* ➲ **COLLOCATIONS** at MUSIC **2** (*NAmE, informal*) a job, especially a temporary one: *a gig as a basketball coach* **3** (*informal*) = GIGABYTE **4** a small light CARRIAGE with two wheels, pulled by one horse

giga- /ˈɡɪɡə-; ˈdʒɪɡə-/ *combining form* (in nouns; used in units of measurement) **1** 10^9, or 1 000 000 000: *gigahertz* **2** 2^{30}, or 1 073 741 824

giga·bit /ˈɡɪɡəbɪt/ *noun* (*abbr.* **Gb**, **Gbit**) (*computing*) **1** a unit of computer memory or data, equal to 10^9, or 1000^3, (= 1 000 000 000) BITS **2** (also **gibi·bit**) a unit of computer memory or data, equal to 2^{30}, or 1024^3, (= 1 073 741 824) BITS

giga·byte /ˈɡɪɡəbaɪt/ (also *informal* **gig**) *noun* (*abbr.* **GB**) (*computing*) **1** a unit of computer memory or data, equal to 10^9, or 1000^3, (= 1 000 000 000) BYTES **2** (also **gibi·byte**) a unit of computer memory or data, equal to 2^{30}, or 1024^3, (= 1 073 741 824) BYTES

giga·hertz /ˈɡɪɡəhɜːts; ˈdʒɪ-; *NAmE* -hɜːrts/ *noun* (*pl.* **giga·hertz**) (*abbr.* **GHz**) (*computing, physics*) a unit for measuring radio waves and the speed at which a computer operates; 1 000 000 000 HERTZ

gi·gan·tic /dʒaɪˈɡæntɪk/ *adj.* extremely large SYN **enormous, huge**

gi·gant·ism /dʒaɪˈɡæntɪzəm; ˈdʒaɪɡæntɪzəm/ (also **giant·ism**) *noun* [U] (*medical*) a condition in which sb grows to an unusually large size

gig·gle /ˈɡɪɡl/ *verb, noun*
■ ***verb*** [I, T] **~ (at/about sb/sth)** | **(+ speech)** to laugh in a silly way because you are amused, embarrassed or nervous: *The girls giggled at the joke.* ◇ *They giggled nervously as they waited for their turn.*
■ ***noun*** **1** [C] a slight silly repeated laugh: *She gave a nervous giggle.* ◇ *Matt collapsed into giggles and hung up the phone.* **2** [sing.] (*BrE, informal*) a thing that you think is amusing: *We only did it **for a giggle**.* **3 the giggles** [pl.] (*informal*) continuous giggling that you cannot control or stop: *I **get the giggles** when I'm nervous.* ◇ *She had a **fit of the giggles** and had to leave the room.*

G

gig·gly /ˈɡɪɡli/ *adj.* laughing a lot in a silly, nervous way

GIGO /ˈɡaɪɡəʊ; *NAmE* -ɡoʊ/ ➲ GARBAGE

gig·olo /ˈʒɪɡələʊ; ˈdʒɪ-; *NAmE* -loʊ/ *noun* (*pl.* **-os**) a man who is paid to be the lover of an older woman, usually one who is rich

gild /ɡɪld/ *verb* **1 ~ sth** (*literary*) to make sth look bright, as if covered with gold: *The golden light gilded the sea.* **2 ~ sth** to cover sth with a thin layer of gold or gold paint
IDM **gild the ˈlily** to spoil sth that is already good or beautiful by trying to improve it

gild·ed /ˈɡɪldɪd/ *adj.* [only before noun] **1** covered with a thin layer of gold or gold paint **2** (*literary*) rich and belonging to the upper classes: *the **gilded youth*** (= rich, upper-class young people) *of the Edwardian era*

gild·ing /ˈɡɪldɪŋ/ *noun* [U] a layer of gold or gold paint; the surface that this makes

gilet /ˈʒɪleɪ; ˈʒiː-/ *noun* a light thick jacket without sleeves

gill[1] /ɡɪl/ *noun* [usually pl.] one of the openings on the side of a fish's head that it breathes through ➲ **VISUAL VOCAB** page V10
IDM **to the ˈgills** (*informal*) completely full: *I was stuffed to the gills with chocolate cake.*

gill[2] /dʒɪl/ *noun* a unit for measuring liquids. There are four gills in a pint.

gil·lie (also **ghil·lie**) /ˈɡɪli/ *noun* (*ScotE*) a man or boy who helps sb who is shooting or fishing for sport in Scotland

gilt /ɡɪlt/ *noun* **1** [U] a thin layer of gold, or sth like gold that is used on a surface for decoration: *gilt lettering* **2 gilts** [pl.] (*BrE, finance*) gilt-edged investments **3** [C] (*especially NAmE*) a young female pig
IDM **take the gilt off the ˈgingerbread** (*BrE*) to do or be sth that makes a situation or achievement less attractive or impressive

ˌgilt-ˈedged *adj.* (*finance*) very safe: ***gilt-edged securities/shares/stocks*** (= investments that are considered safe because they have been sold by the government)

gim·crack /ˈdʒɪmkræk/ *adj.* [only before noun] badly made and of little value SYN **shoddy**

gim·let /ˈɡɪmlət/ *noun* a small tool for making holes in wood to put screws in: (*figurative*) *eyes like gimlets* (= looking very hard at things and noticing every detail)

gimme /ˈɡɪmi/ (*informal*)
■ a way of writing the way that the words 'give me' are sometimes spoken: *Gimme back my bike!*
■ ***noun*** [usually sing.] something that is very easy to do or achieve

gim·mick /ˈɡɪmɪk/ *noun* (often *disapproving*) an unusual trick or unnecessary device that is intended to attract attention or to persuade people to buy sth: *a **promotional/publicity/sales gimmick*** ▸ **gim·micky** /ˈɡɪmɪki/ *adj.*: *a gimmicky idea*

gim·mick·ry /ˈɡɪmɪkri/ *noun* [U] (*disapproving*) the use of gimmicks in selling, etc.

gin /dʒɪn/ *noun* **1** [U] an alcoholic drink made from grain and flavoured with JUNIPER BERRIES. Gin is usually drunk mixed with TONIC WATER or fruit juice. ➲ see also PINK GIN **2** [C] a glass of gin: *I'll have a gin and tonic, please.* **3** = COTTON GIN

gin·ger /ˈdʒɪndʒə(r)/ *noun, adj., verb*
- **noun** [U] **1** the root of the ginger plant used in cooking as a spice: *a teaspoon of ground ginger* ◇ (*BrE*) *ginger biscuits* ➲ VISUAL VOCAB page V28 **2** a light brownish-orange colour
- **adj.** (*BrE*) light brownish-orange in colour: *ginger hair* ◇ *a ginger cat*
- **verb**

PHR V ˌ**ginger sth/sb**↔ˈ**up** (*BrE*) to make sth/sb more active or exciting SYN **liven up**

G

ˌ**ginger ˈale** *noun* **1** [U] a clear FIZZY drink (= with bubbles) that does not contain alcohol, flavoured with ginger, and often mixed with alcoholic drinks **2** [C] a bottle or glass of ginger ale

ˌ**ginger ˈbeer** *noun* **1** [U] a FIZZY drink (= with bubbles) with a very small amount of alcohol in, flavoured with ginger **2** [C] a bottle or glass of ginger beer

gin·ger·bread /ˈdʒɪndʒəbred; *NAmE* -dʒərb-/ *noun* [U] a sweet cake or soft biscuit/cookie flavoured with GINGER: *a gingerbread man* (= a gingerbread biscuit/cookie in the shape of a person) IDM see GILT

ˈ**ginger group** *noun* (*BrE*) a group of people within a political party or an organization, who work to persuade other members to accept their policies or ideas

gin·ger·ly /ˈdʒɪndʒəli; *NAmE* -dʒərli/ *adv.* in a careful way, because you are afraid of being hurt, of making a noise, etc: *He opened the box gingerly and looked inside.*

ˈ**ginger nut** (*BrE*) (also ˈ**ginger snap** *NAmE, BrE*) *noun* a hard sweet biscuit/cookie flavoured with GINGER

gin·gery /ˈdʒɪndʒəri/ *adj.* like GINGER in colour or flavour

ging·ham /ˈɡɪŋəm/ *noun* [U] a type of cotton cloth with a pattern of white and coloured squares: *a blue and white gingham dress*

gin·gi·vitis /ˌdʒɪndʒɪˈvaɪtəs/ *noun* [U] (*medical*) a condition in which the GUMS around the teeth become painful, red and swollen

ginkgo /ˈɡɪŋkɡəʊ; *NAmE* -ɡoʊ/ (also **gingko** /ˈɡɪŋkəʊ; *NAmE* -koʊ/) *noun* (*pl.* **-os** or **-oes**) a Chinese tree with yellow flowers SYN **maidenhair tree**

gi·nor·mous /dʒaɪˈnɔːməs; *NAmE* -ˈnɔːrm-/ *adj.* (*BrE, informal*) extremely large

ˌ**gin ˈrummy** *noun* [U] a card game in which players try to get HANDS (= sets of cards) that add up to ten

gin·seng /ˈdʒɪnseŋ/ *noun* [U] a medicine obtained from a plant root that some people believe helps you stay young and healthy

ˈ**gin trap** *noun* a device for trapping small wild animals or birds

gippy tummy (also **gyppy tummy**) /ˌdʒɪpi ˈtʌmi/ *noun* (*old-fashioned, BrE, informal*) DIARRHOEA (= an illness in which waste matter is emptied from the body in liquid form) that affects visitors to hot countries

Gipsy = GYPSY

gir·affe /dʒəˈrɑːf; *NAmE* -ˈræf/ *noun* (*pl.* **gir·affe** or **gir·affes**) a tall African animal with a very long neck, long legs, and dark marks on its coat

gird /ɡɜːd; *NAmE* ɡɜːrd/ *verb* ~ **sth** (**with sth**) to surround sth with sth; to fasten sth around sb/sth

IDM **gird** (**up**) **your ˈloins** (*literary* or *humorous*) to get ready to do sth difficult: *The company is girding its loins for a plunge into the overseas market.*

PHR V **gird** (**yourself/sb/sth**) (**up**) **for sth** (*literary*) to prepare for sth difficult, especially a fight, contest, etc.

gird·er /ˈɡɜːdə(r); *NAmE* ˈɡɜːrd-/ *noun* a long strong iron or steel bar used for building bridges and the FRAMEWORK of large buildings

gir·dle /ˈɡɜːdl; *NAmE* ˈɡɜːrdl/ *noun, verb*
- **noun** **1** a piece of women's underwear that fits closely around the body from the waist to the top of the legs, designed to make a woman look thinner **2** (*literary*) a thing that surrounds sth else: *carefully tended lawns set in a girdle of trees* **3** (*old-fashioned*) a belt or thick string fastened around the waist to keep clothes in position
- **verb** ~ **sth** (*literary*) to surround sth: *A chain of volcanoes girdles the Pacific.*

girl 🔑 /ɡɜːl; *NAmE* ɡɜːrl/ *noun*
1 🔑 [C] a female child: *a* ***baby girl*** ◇ *a* ***little girl*** *of six* ◇ *Hello, girls and boys!* ➲ see also POSTER CHILD **2** 🔑 [C] a daughter: *Our youngest girl is at college.* **3** 🔑 [C] (sometimes *offensive*) a young woman: *Alex is not interested in girls yet.* ◇ *He married the girl next door.* **4** [C] (usually in compounds) (*old-fashioned, offensive*) a female worker: *an office girl* **5** [C] (*old-fashioned*) a man's girlfriend **6 girls** [pl.] (used especially as a form of address by women) a woman's female friends: *I'm having a night out with the girls.* ◇ *Good morning, girls!* **7** [sing.] **old ~** (often *offensive*) an old woman, especially sb's wife or mother: *How is the old girl these days?* IDM see BIG *adj.*

ˈ**girl band** (also ˈ**girl group**) *noun* a group of attractive young women who sing pop music and dance

ˌ**girl ˈFriday** *noun* a girl or a woman who is employed in an office to do several different jobs, helping other people

girl·friend 🔑 /ˈɡɜːlfrend; *NAmE* ˈɡɜːrl-/ *noun*
1 🔑 a girl or a woman that sb is having a romantic relationship with **2** 🔑 (*especially NAmE*) a woman's female friend: *I had lunch with a girlfriend.*

ˌ**Girl ˈGuide** *noun* (*old-fashioned, BrE*) = GUIDE

ˈ**Girl Guider** *noun* (*BrE*) = GUIDER

girl·hood /ˈɡɜːlhʊd; *NAmE* ˈɡɜːrl-/ *noun* [U] (*old-fashioned*) the time when sb is a girl; the fact of being a girl

girlie /ˈɡɜːli; *NAmE* ˈɡɜːrli/ *adj., noun* (*informal*)
- **adj.** [only before noun] **1** containing photographs of naked or nearly naked women, that are intended to make men sexually excited: *girlie magazines* **2** (*disapproving*) suitable for or like girls, not boys: *girlie games*
- **noun** a way of referring to a girl or young woman, that many women find offensive

girl·ish /ˈɡɜːlɪʃ; *NAmE* ˈɡɜːrlɪʃ/ *adj.* like a girl; of a girl: *a girlish giggle* ◇ *a girlish figure*

ˈ**girl power** *noun* [U] the idea that women should take control of their careers and lives

ˌ**Girl ˈScout** (*US*) (*BrE* **Guide**, *old-fashioned* ˌ**Girl ˈGuide**) *noun* a member of an organization (called **the Guides** or **the Girl Scouts**) which is similar to the SCOUTS and which trains girls in practical skills and does a lot of activities with them, for example camping

girn = GURN

giro /ˈdʒaɪrəʊ; *NAmE* -roʊ/ *noun* (*pl.* **-os**) (*BrE*) **1** [U] (*finance*) a system in which money can be moved from one bank or post office account to another by a central computer: *to pay by giro* ◇ *a* ***giro credit/payment/transfer*** **2** (also ˈ**giro cheque**) [C] a cheque that the government pays through the giro system to people who are unemployed or sick, or who have a very small income: *It is easy for families to run out of money before the weekly giro arrives.*

girth /ɡɜːθ; *NAmE* ɡɜːrθ/ *noun* **1** [U, C] the measurement around sth, especially a person's waist: *a man of enormous girth* ◇ *a tree one metre in girth/with a girth of one metre* **2** [C] a narrow piece of leather or cloth that is fastened around the middle of a horse to keep the seat (called a SADDLE) or a load in place

gismo = GIZMO

gist /dʒɪst/ *noun* (usually **the gist**) [sing.] ~ (**of sth**) the main or general meaning of a piece of writing, a speech or a conversation: *to get* (= understand) *the gist of an argument* ◇ *I missed the beginning of the lecture—can you give me the* gist of what he said? ◇ I'm afraid I don't quite follow your gist (= what you really mean).

git /gɪt/ *noun* (*BrE, slang*) a stupid or unpleasant man

give 0-w /gɪv/ *verb, noun*

■ ***verb*** (gave /geɪv/, given /ˈgɪvn/)

▸ HAND/PROVIDE **1** 0-w [T] to hand sth to sb so that they can look at it, use it or keep it for a time: **~ sth to sb** *Give the letter to your mother when you've read it.* ◇ *She gave her ticket to the woman at the check-in desk.* ◇ **~ sb sth** *Give your mother the letter.* ◇ *They were all given a box to carry.* **2** 0-w [T, I] to hand sth to sb as a present; to allow sb to have sth as a present: **~ sb sth** *What are you giving your father for his birthday?* ◇ *She was given a huge bunch of flowers.* ◇ *Did you give the waiter a tip?* ◇ **~ sth to sb** *We don't usually give presents to people at work.* ◇ **~ (sth)** *They say it's better to give than to receive.* **3** 0-w [T] to provide sb with sth: **~ sb sth** *They were all thirsty so I gave them a drink.* ◇ *Give me your name and address.* ◇ *We've been given a 2% pay increase.* ◇ *I was hoping you would give me a job.* ◇ *He was given a new heart in a five-hour operation.* ◇ *She wants a job that gives her more responsibility.* ◇ *Can I give you a ride to the station?* ◇ *They couldn't give me any more information.* ◇ *I'll give you* (= allow you to have) *ten minutes to prepare your answer.* ◇ *Don't give me any of that backchat* (= don't be rude). ◇ **~ sth to sb** *He gives Italian lessons to his colleagues.* ◇ *The reforms should give a better chance to the less able children.*

▸ MONEY **4** 0-w [I, T] to pay money to a charity, etc, to help people: *We need your help—please give generously.* ◇ **~ to sth** *They both gave regularly to charity.* ◇ **~ sth (to sth)** *I gave a small donation.* **5** 0-w [T] to pay in order to have or do sth: **~ sb sth (for sth)** *How much will you give me for the car?* ◇ **~ sth** *I'd give anything to see him again.* ◇ **~ sth for sth** *I gave £50 for the lot.*

▸ TREAT AS IMPORTANT **6** 0-w [T] to use time, energy, etc. for sb/sth: **~ sb/sth sth** *I gave the matter a lot of thought.* ◇ **~ sth to sb/sth** *I gave a lot of thought to the matter.* ◇ *The government has given top priority to reforming the tax system.*

▸ PUNISHMENT **7** 0-w [T] to make sb suffer a particular punishment: **~ sb sth** *The judge gave him a nine-month suspended sentence.* ◇ **~ sth to sb** *We discussed what punishment should be given to the boys.*

▸ ILLNESS **8** 0-w [T] to infect sb with an illness: **~ sb sth** *You've given me your cold.* ◇ **~ sth to sb** *She'd given the bug to all her colleagues.*

▸ PARTY/EVENT **9** 0-w [T] **~ sth** if you **give** a party, you organize it and invite people **10** 0-w [T] **~ sth** to perform sth in public: *She gave a reading from her latest volume of poetry.* ◇ *The President will be giving a press conference this afternoon.*

▸ DO/PRODUCE STH **11** 0-w [T] used with a noun to describe a particular action, giving the same meaning as the related verb: **~ sth** *She gave a shrug of her shoulders* (= she shrugged). ◇ *He turned to us and gave a big smile* (= smiled broadly). ◇ *She looked up from her work and gave a yawn* (= yawned). ◇ *He gave a loud cry* (= cried out loudly) *and fell to the floor.* ◇ *Her work has given pleasure to* (= pleased) *millions of readers.* ◇ **~ sb sth** *He gave her a kiss* (= kissed her). ◇ *I have to admit that the news gave us a shock* (= shocked us). ◇ *We'll give you all the help we can* (= help you in every way we can). HELP For other similar expressions, look up the nouns in each. For example, you will find **give your approval** at **approval**. **12** 0-w [T] **~ sb sth** to produce a particular feeling in sb: *All that driving has given me a headache.* ◇ *Go for a walk. It'll give you an appetite.*

▸ TELEPHONE CALL **13** 0-w [T] **~ sb sth** to make a telephone call to sb: *Give me a call tomorrow.* ◇ (*BrE*) *I'll give you a ring.*

▸ MARK/GRADE **14** 0-w [T] **~ sb/sth sth** | **~ sth (to sb/sth)** to judge sb/sth to be of a particular standard: *She had given the assignment an A.* ◇ *I give it ten out of ten for originality.*

▸ PREDICT HOW LONG **15** [T] **~ sb/sth sth** to predict that sth will last a particular length of time: *That marriage won't last. I'll give them two years, at the outside.*

▸ IN SPORT **16** [T] **~ sb/sth + adj.** to say that a player or the ball is in a particular position: *The umpire gave the ball out.*

▸ BEND **17** [I] to bend or stretch under pressure: *The branch began to give under his weight.* ◇ (*figurative*) *We can't go on like this—**something's got to give**.* **18** [I] to agree to change your mind or give up some of your demands: *You're going to have to give a little.*

IDM Most idioms containing **give** are at the entries for the nouns and adjectives in the idioms, for example, **give rise to sth** is at **rise** *n.* **don't give me ˈthat** (*informal*) used to tell sb that you do not accept what they say: *'I didn't have time to do it.' 'Oh, don't give me that!'* **ˌgive and ˈtake** to be willing, in a relationship, to accept what sb else wants and to give up some of what you want: *You're going to have to learn to give and take.* **give as good as you ˈget** to react with equal force when sb attacks or criticizes you: *She can give as good as she gets.* **give it up (for sb)** (*informal*) to show your approval of sb by clapping your hands: *Give it up for Eddie Murphy!* **ˈgive me sth/sb (any day/time)** (*informal*) used to say that you prefer a particular thing or person to the one that has just been mentioned: *We don't go out much. Give me a quiet night in front of the TV any day!* **give or ˈtake (sth)** if sth is correct **give or take** a particular amount, it is approximately correct: *It'll take about three weeks, give or take a day or so.* **give sb to believe/understand (that)...** [often passive] (*formal*) to make sb believe/understand sth: *I was given to understand that she had resigned.* **I give you...** used to ask people to drink a TOAST to sb: *Ladies and gentlemen, I give you Geoff Ogilby!* **I/I'll give you ˈthat** (*informal*) used when you are admitting that sth is true **what ˈgives?** (*informal*) what is happening?; what is the news?

PHR V **ˌgive sb aˈway** (in a marriage ceremony) to lead the BRIDE to the BRIDEGROOM and formally allow her to marry him: *The bride was given away by her father.* **ˌgive sth↔aˈway** **1** 0-w to give sth as a gift: *He gave away most of his money to charity.* ◇ (*informal*) *Check out the prices of our pizzas—we're virtually giving them away!* ➲ related noun GIVEAWAY **2** to present sth: *The mayor gave away the prizes at the school sports day.* **3** to carelessly allow sb to have an advantage: *They've given away two goals already.*

ˌgive sth/sb↔aˈway 0-w to make known sth that sb wants to keep secret SYN **betray**: *She gave away state secrets to the enemy.* ◇ *It was supposed to be a surprise but the children **gave the game away**.* ◇ *His voice gave him away* (= showed who he really was). ➲ related noun GIVEAWAY

ˌgive sb ˈback sth | **ˌgive sth↔ˈback (to sb)** **1** 0-w to return sth to its owner: *Could you give me back my pen?* ◇ *Could you give me my pen back?* ◇ *I picked it up and gave it back to him.* ◇ (*informal*) *Give it me back!* **2** 0-w to allow sb to have sth again: *The operation gave him back the use of his legs.*

ˌgive ˈin (to sb/sth) **1** 0-w to admit that you have been defeated by sb/sth: *The rebels were forced to give in.* **2** 0-w to agree to do sth that you do not want to do: *The authorities have shown no signs of giving in to the kidnappers' demands.*

ˌgive sth ˈin (to sb) (*BrE*) (also **ˌhand sth↔ˈin (to sb)** *BrE, NAmE*) to hand over sth to sb in authority: *Please give your work in before Monday.*

ˌgive ˈoff sth 0-w to produce sth such as a smell, heat, light, etc: *The flowers gave off a fragrant perfume.*

ˈgive on to/onto sth [no passive] (*BrE*) to have a view of sth; to lead directly to sth: *The bedroom windows give on to the street.* ◇ *This door gives onto the hall.*

ˌgive ˈout **1** to come to an end; to be completely used up: *After a month their food supplies gave out.* ◇ *Her patience finally gave out.* **2** to stop working: *One of the plane's engines gave out in mid-Atlantic.* ◇ *Her legs gave out and she collapsed.* **ˌgive sth↔ˈout** 0-w to give sth to a lot of people: *The teacher gave out the exam papers.* **ˌgive ˈout sth** **1** to produce sth such as heat, light, etc: *The radiator gives out a lot of heat.* **2** [often passive] (*especially BrE*) to tell people about sth or broadcast sth

ˌgive ˈover (*BrE, informal*) used to tell sb to stop doing sth: *Give over, Chris! You're hurting me.* ◇ **~ doing sth** *Give over complaining!* **ˌgive yourself ˈover to sth** (also **ˌgive yourself ˈup to sth**) to spend all your time doing sth or thinking about sth; to allow sth to completely control your life

ˌgive sth↔ˈover to sth [usually passive] to use sth for one particular purpose: *The gallery is given over to British art.*

ˌgive ˈup 0-w to stop trying to do sth: *They gave up without a fight.* ◇ *She doesn't give up easily.* ◇ *I give up—tell me the answer.* **ˌgive sb ˈup** **1** (also **ˌgive ˈup on sb** especially in

NAmE) to believe that sb is never going to arrive, get better, be found, etc: *There you are at last! We'd given you up.* ◇ *We hadn't heard from him for so long, we'd* **given him up for dead**. **2** to stop having a relationship with sb: *Why don't you give him up?* ˌ**give sth↔'up 1** 0‑ [no passive] to stop doing or having sth: *She didn't give up work when she had the baby.* ◇ *We'd* **given up hope** *of ever having children.* ◇ **~ doing sth** *You ought to give up smoking.* **2** to spend time on a task that you would normally spend on sth else: *I gave up my weekend to help him paint his apartment.* ˌ**give sth↔'up (to sb)** to hand sth over to sb else: *We had to give our passports up to the authorities.* ◇ *He gave up his seat to a pregnant woman* (= stood up to allow her to sit down). ˌ**give yourself/sb 'up (to sb)** to offer yourself/sb to be captured: *After a week on the run he gave himself up to the police.* ˌ**give yourself 'up to sth** = GIVE YOURSELF OVER TO STH ˌ**give 'up on sb 1** to stop hoping or believing that sb will change, get better, etc: *His teachers seem to have given up on him.* **2** (*especially NAmE*) = GIVE SB UP

G

■ ***noun*** [U] the ability of sth to bend or stretch under pressure: *The shoes may seem tight at first, but the leather has plenty of give in it.*

IDM ˌ**give and 'take 1** willingness in a relationship to accept what sb else wants and give up some of what you want **2** an exchange of words or ideas: *to encourage a lively give and take*

give·away /'ɡɪvəweɪ/ *noun, adj.*

■ ***noun*** (*informal*) **1** something that a company gives free, usually with sth else that is for sale **2** something that makes you guess the real truth about sth/sb: *She pretended she wasn't excited but the expression on her face was a* **dead** (= obvious) ***giveaway***.

■ ***adj.*** [only before noun] (*informal*) (of prices) very low

give·back /'ɡɪvbæk/ *noun* (*NAmE*) a situation in which workers agree to accept lower wages or fewer benefits at a particular time, in return for more money or benefits later

given /'ɡɪvn/ *adj., prep., noun*

■ ***adj.*** [usually before noun] **1** already arranged: *They were to meet at a given time and place.* **2** that you have stated and are discussing; particular: *We can find out how much money is spent on food in any given period.*

IDM **be given to sth/to doing sth** (*formal*) to do sth often or regularly: *He's given to going for long walks on his own.*

■ ***prep.*** when you consider sth: *Given his age* (= considering how old he is), *he's remarkably active.* ◇ *Given her interest in children, teaching seems the right job for her.* ▸ **given that** *conj.*: *It was surprising the government was re-elected, given that they had raised taxes so much.*

■ ***noun*** something that is accepted as true, for example when you are discussing sth, or planning sth

'**given name** *noun* (*especially NAmE*) = FIRST NAME

giver /'ɡɪvə(r)/ *noun* (often in compounds) a person or an organization that gives: *They are very generous givers to charity.*

gizmo (also **gismo**) /'ɡɪzməʊ; *NAmE* -moʊ/ *noun* (*informal*) (*pl.* -os) a general word for a small piece of equipment, often one that does sth in a new and clever way

giz·zard /'ɡɪzəd; *NAmE* -zərd/ *noun* the part of a bird's stomach in which food is broken up into smaller pieces before being DIGESTED

glacé /'ɡlæseɪ; *NAmE* ɡlæ'seɪ/ *adj.* [only before noun] (of fruit) preserved in sugar: *glacé fruits* ◇ *glacé cherries*

gla·cial /'ɡleɪʃl; 'ɡleɪsiəl/ *adj.* **1** [usually before noun] (*geology*) connected with the Ice Age: *the glacial period* (= the time when much of the northern half of the world was covered by ice) **2** (*technical*) caused or made by glaciers; connected with glaciers: *a glacial landscape* ◇ *glacial deposits/erosion* **3** (*formal*) very cold; like ice SYN **icy**: *glacial winds/temperatures* **4** (*formal*) (of people) cold and unfriendly; not showing feelings SYN **icy**: *Her expression was glacial.* ◇ *Relations between the two countries had always been glacial.*

gla·ci·ation /ˌɡleɪsi'eɪʃn/ *noun* [U] (*geology*) the process or result of land being covered by glaciers

gla·cier /'ɡlæsiə(r); *NAmE* 'ɡleɪʃər/ *noun* a large mass of ice, formed by snow on mountains, that moves very slowly down a valley ➲ VISUAL VOCAB page V4

Synonyms

glad

happy • pleased • delighted • proud • relieved • thrilled

These words all describe people feeling happy about sth that has happened or is going to happen.

glad [not usually before noun] happy about sth or grateful for it: *He was glad he'd come.* ◇ *She was glad when the meeting was over.*

happy pleased about sth nice that you have to do or sth that has happened to sb: *We are happy to announce the engagement of our daughter.*

pleased [not before noun] happy about sth that has happened or sth that you have to do: *She was very pleased with her exam results.* ◇ *You're coming? I'm so pleased.*

GLAD, HAPPY OR PLEASED?

Feeling **pleased** can suggest that you have judged sb/sth and approve of them. Feeling **glad** can be more about feeling grateful for sth. You cannot be 'glad with sb': ~~*The boss should be glad with you.*~~ **Happy** can mean glad, pleased or satisfied.

delighted very pleased about sth; very happy to do sth; showing your delight: *I'm delighted at your news.* NOTE **Delighted** is often used to accept an invitation: *'Can you stay for dinner?' 'I'd be delighted (to).'*

proud pleased and satisfied about sth that you own or have done, or are connected with: *proud parents* ◇ *He was* ***proud of*** *himself for not giving up.*

relieved feeling happy because sth unpleasant has stopped or has not happened; showing this: *You'll be relieved to know your jobs are safe.*

thrilled [not before noun] (*rather informal*) extremely pleased and excited about sth: *I was thrilled to be invited.*

DELIGHTED OR THRILLED?

Thrilled may express a stronger feeling than **delighted**, but **delighted** can be made stronger with *absolutely, more than* or *only too.* **Thrilled** can be made negative and ironic with *not exactly* or *less than*: *She was* ***not exactly thrilled*** *at the prospect of looking after her niece.*

PATTERNS

- glad/happy/pleased/delighted/relieved/thrilled **about** sth
- pleased/delighted/relieved/thrilled **at** sth
- glad/happy/pleased/delighted/thrilled **for** sb
- glad/happy/pleased/delighted/proud/relieved/thrilled **that.../to see/hear/find/know...**
- **very** glad/happy/pleased/proud/relieved
- **absolutely** delighted/thrilled

glad 0‑ /ɡlæd/ *adj.*

1 0‑ [not before noun] pleased; happy: *'I passed the test!' 'I'm so glad (for you).'* ◇ *She was glad when the meeting was over.* ◇ **~ about sth** *'He doesn't need the pills any more.' 'I'm glad about that.'* ◇ **~ to know, hear, see...** *I'm glad to hear you're feeling better.* ◇ **~ (that)...** *I'm glad (that) you're feeling better.* ◇ *He was glad he'd come.* ◇ *I'm so glad (that) you're safe!* ◇ **~ to do sth** *I'm glad to meet you. I've heard a lot about you.* ◇ *I've never been so glad to see anyone in my life!* **2** grateful for sth: **~ of sth** *She was very glad of her warm coat in the biting wind.* ◇ *I'd be glad of your help.* ◇ **~ if...** *I'd be glad if you could help me.* **3 ~ to do sth** very willing to do sth: *I'd be glad to lend you the money.* ◇ *If you'd like me to* help you, I'd **be only too glad to.** **4** [only before noun] (*old-fashioned*) bringing joy; full of joy: ***glad news/tidings***

IDM **I'm glad to say (that…)** (*informal*) used when you are commenting on a situation and saying that you are happy about it: *Most teachers, I'm glad to say, take their jobs very seriously.*

glad·den /ˈglædn/ *verb* (*old-fashioned*) to make sb feel pleased or happy: **~ sth** *The sight of the flowers* ***gladdened her heart.*** ◇ **it gladdens sb to do sth** *It gladdened him to see them all enjoying themselves.*

glade /gleɪd/ *noun* (*literary*) a small open area of grass in a wood or a forest ➲ VISUAL VOCAB page V4

ˈglad-hand *verb* [I, T] **~ (sb)** (especially of a politician) to say hello to sb in a friendly way, especially when this is not sincere ▶ **ˈglad-handing** *noun* [U]

gladi·ator /ˈglædieɪtə(r)/ *noun* (in ancient Rome) a man trained to fight other men or animals in order to entertain the public ▶ **gladia·tor·ial** /ˌglædiəˈtɔːriəl/ *adj.*: *gladiatorial combat*

gladi·olus /ˌglædiˈəʊləs; *NAmE* -ˈoʊləs/ *noun* (*pl.* **gladi·oli** /-laɪ/) a tall garden plant with long thin leaves and brightly coloured flowers growing up the STEM

glad·ly /ˈglædli/ *adv.* **1** willingly: *I would gladly pay extra for a good seat.* **2** happily; with thanks: *When I offered her my seat, she accepted it gladly.* IDM see SUFFER

glad·ness /ˈglædnəs/ *noun* [U] (*literary*) joy; happiness

ˈglad rags *noun* [pl.] (*old-fashioned, informal*) a person's best clothes, worn on a special occasion

glam·or·ize (*BrE* also **-ise**) /ˈglæməraɪz/ *verb* **~ sth** (usually *disapproving*) to make sth bad appear attractive or exciting: *Television tends to glamorize violence.*

glam·or·ous /ˈglæmərəs/ (also *informal* **glam**) *adj.* especially attractive and exciting, and different from ordinary things or people: *glamorous movie stars* ◇ *a glamorous job* OPP **unglamorous** ▶ **glam·or·ous·ly** *adv.*: *glamorously dressed*

glam·our (*NAmE* also **glamor**) /ˈglæmə(r)/ *noun* [U] **1** the attractive and exciting quality that makes a person, a job or a place seem special, often because of wealth or status: *hopeful young actors and actresses dazzled by the glamour of Hollywood* ◇ *Now that she's a flight attendant, foreign travel has lost its glamour for her.* **2** physical beauty that also suggests wealth or success: *Add a cashmere scarf under your jacket for a touch of glamour.*

ˈglamour model *noun* (*especially BrE*) a person, especially a woman, who is photographed wearing very few or no clothes in order to sexually excite the person looking at the photographs

glam rock /ˌglæm ˈrɒk; *NAmE* ˈrɑːk/ *noun* [U] a style of music popular in the 1970s, in which male singers wore unusual clothes and make-up

glance /glɑːns; *NAmE* glæns/ *verb, noun*

■ *verb* **1** [I] **+ adv./prep.** to look quickly at sth/sb: *She glanced at her watch.* ◇ *He glanced around the room.* ◇ *I glanced up quickly to see who had come in.* **2** [I] **~ at/down/over/through sth** to read sth quickly and not thoroughly SYN **scan**: *I only had time to glance at the newspapers.* ◇ *He glanced briefly down the list of names.* ◇ *She glanced through the report.*

PHR V **ˈglance on/off sth** (of light) to flash on a surface or be reflected off it **ˌglance ˈoff (sth)** to hit sth at an angle and move off it in a different direction: *The ball glanced off the post into the net.*

■ *noun* **~ (at sb/sth)** a quick look: *to* ***take/have a glance*** *at the newspaper headlines* ◇ *a* ***cursory/brief/casual/furtive glance*** ◇ *The sisters* ***exchanged glances*** (= looked at each other). ◇ *She shot him a* ***sideways glance.*** ◇ *He walked away* ***without a backward glance.*** ◇ *She* ***stole a glance*** (= looked secretly) *at her watch.* ➲ SYNONYMS at LOOK

IDM **at a (single) ˈglance** immediately; with only a quick look: *He could tell at a glance what was wrong.* **at first ˈglance** when you first look at or think about sth, often rather quickly: *At first glance the problem seemed easy.*

glan·cing /ˈglɑːnsɪŋ; *NAmE* ˈglænsɪŋ/ *adj.* [only before noun] hitting sth/sb at an angle, not with full force: *to strike somebody a* ***glancing blow***

gland /glænd/ *noun* an organ in a person's or an animal's body that produces a substance for the body to use. There are many different glands in the body: *a snake's poison glands* ◇ *Her glands are swollen.* ➲ see also PITUITARY ▶ **glan·du·lar** /ˈglændjələ(r); *NAmE* -dʒə-/ *adj.* [usually before noun]: *glandular tissue*

ˌglandular ˈfever *noun* [U] (*BrE*) = MONONUCLEOSIS

glans /glænz/ (*pl.* **glan·des** /ˈglændiːz/) *noun* (*anatomy*) the round part at the end of a man's PENIS or a woman's CLITORIS

glare /gleə(r); *NAmE* gler/ *verb, noun*

■ *verb* **1** [I] **~ (at sb/sth)** to look at sb/sth in an angry way SYN **glower**: *He didn't shout, he just glared at me silently.* **2** [I] to shine with a very bright unpleasant light

■ *noun* **1** [U, sing.] a very bright, unpleasant light: *the glare of the sun* ◇ *The rabbit was caught in the glare of the car's headlights.* ◇ *These sunglasses are designed to reduce glare.* ◇ (*figurative*) *The divorce was conducted* ***in the full glare of publicity*** (= with continuous attention from newspapers and television). **2** [C] a long, angry look: *to give sb a hostile glare* ➲ SYNONYMS at LOOK, STARE

glar·ing /ˈgleərɪŋ; *NAmE* ˈgler-/ *adj.* **1** [usually before noun] (of sth bad) very easily seen SYN **blatant**: *a* ***glaring error/omission/inconsistency/injustice*** ◇ *the most* ***glaring example*** *of this problem* **2** (of a light) very bright and unpleasant **3** angry; aggressive: *glaring eyes* ▶ **glar·ing·ly** *adv.*: *glaringly obvious*

glass 🔑 /glɑːs; *NAmE* glæs/ *noun, verb*

■ *noun*

▸ TRANSPARENT SUBSTANCE **1** 🔑 [U] a hard, usually transparent, substance used, for example, for making windows and bottles: *a* ***sheet/pane of glass*** ◇ ***frosted/toughened glass*** ◇ *a* ***glass bottle/dish/roof*** ◇ *I cut myself on a piece of* ***broken glass.*** ◇ *The vegetables are grown* ***under glass*** (= in a GREENHOUSE). ➲ see also CUT GLASS, PLATE GLASS, STAINED GLASS, GLAZIER

▸ FOR DRINKING **2** 🔑 [C] (often in compounds) a container made of glass, used for drinking out of: *a sherry glass* ◇ *a wine glass* ➲ VISUAL VOCAB page V19 **3** 🔑 [C] the contents of a glass: *a* ***glass of sherry/wine/water, etc.*** ◇ *He drank three whole glasses.*

▸ GLASS OBJECTS **4** 🔑 [U] objects made of glass: *We keep all our glass and china in this cupboard.* ◇ *She has a fine collection of Bohemian glass.* **5** [sing.] a protecting cover made of glass on a watch, picture or photograph frame, FIRE ALARM, etc: *In case of emergency, break the glass and press the button.*

▸ FOR EYES **6** 🔑 **glasses** (*NAmE* also **eye·glasses**) (also *old-fashioned* or *formal* **spec·tacles**, *informal* **specs** especially in *BrE*) [pl.] two LENSES in a frame that rests on the nose and ears. People wear glasses in order to be able to see better or to protect their eyes from bright light: *a* ***pair of glasses*** ◇ *dark glasses* ◇ ***I wear glasses*** *for driving.* ➲ see also FIELD GLASSES, MAGNIFYING GLASS, SUNGLASSES

▸ MIRROR **7** [C, usually sing.] (*old-fashioned*) a mirror ➲ see also LOOKING GLASS

▸ BAROMETER **8 the glass** [sing.] a BAROMETER IDM see PEOPLE *n.*, RAISE *v.*

■ *verb* **~ sb** (*BrE, informal*) to hit sb in the face with a glass

PHR V **ˌglass sth ˈin/ˈover** [usually passive] to cover sth with a roof or wall made of glass: *a glassed-in pool* ➲ compare GLAZE

ˈglass-blowing *noun* [U] the art or activity of blowing hot glass into shapes using a special tube ▶ **ˈglass-blower** *noun*

ˌglass ˈceiling *noun* [usually sing.] the way in which unfair attitudes can stop women, or other groups, from getting the best jobs in a company, etc. although there are no official rules to prevent them from getting these jobs

ˌglass ˈfibre (*BrE*) (*NAmE* **ˌglass ˈfiber**) *noun* [U] = FIBREGLASS

G

glass·ful /ˈglɑːsfʊl; *NAmE* ˈglæs-/ *noun* the amount that a drinking glass will hold

glass·house /ˈglɑːshaʊs; *NAmE* ˈglæs-/ *noun* (*BrE*) **1** a building with glass sides and a glass roof, for growing plants in; a type of large GREENHOUSE ➲ VISUAL VOCAB page V13 **2** (*slang*) a military prison

glass·ware /ˈglɑːsweə(r); *NAmE* ˈglæswer/ *noun* [U] objects made of glass

glassy /ˈglɑːsi; *NAmE* ˈglæsi/ *adj.* (**glass·ier, glassi·est**) **1** like glass; smooth and shiny: *a glassy lake* ◇ *a glassy material* **2** showing no feeling or emotion: *glassy eyes* ◇ *a* ***glassy look/stare*** ◇ *He looked flushed and* ***glassy-eyed***.

Glas·we·gian /glæzˈwiːdʒən/ *noun* a person from Glasgow in Scotland ▶ **Glas·we·gian** *adj.*

glau·coma /glɔːˈkəʊmə; *NAmE* glaʊˈkoʊmə; glɔː-/ *noun* [U] an eye disease that causes gradual loss of sight

glaze /gleɪz/ *verb, noun*
■ ***verb*** **1** [I] **~ (over)** if a person's eyes **glaze** or **glaze over**, the person begins to look bored or tired: *A lot of people's eyes glaze over if you say you are a feminist.* ◇ *'I'm feeling rather tired,' he said, his eyes glazing.* **2** [T] **~ sth** to fit sheets of glass into sth: *to glaze a window/house* ◇ *a glazed door* ➲ compare GLASS ➲ see also DOUBLE GLAZING **3** [T] **~ sth (with sth)** to cover sth with a glaze to give it a shiny surface: *Glaze the pie with beaten egg.* ◇ *glazed tiles* ◇ (*NAmE*) *a glazed doughnut*
■ ***noun*** [C, U] **1** a thin clear liquid put on CLAY objects such as cups and plates before they are finished, to give them a hard shiny surface **2** a thin liquid, made of egg, milk or sugar, for example, that is put on cake, bread, etc. to make it look shiny

glazed /gleɪzd/ *adj.* (especially of the eyes) showing no feeling or emotion; dull: *eyes glazed with boredom*

glaz·ier /ˈgleɪziə(r); *NAmE* -ʒər/ *noun* a person whose job is to fit glass into the frames of windows, etc.

gleam /gliːm/ *verb, noun*
■ ***verb*** **1** [I] to shine with a pale clear light: *The moonlight gleamed on the water.* ◇ *Her eyes gleamed in the dark.* ➲ SYNONYMS at SHINE **2** [I] to look very clean or bright: **~ (with sth)** *The house was gleaming with fresh white paint.* ◇ **+ adj.** *Her teeth gleamed white against the tanned skin of her face.* **3** [I] if a person's eyes **gleam** with a particular emotion, or an emotion **gleams** in a person's eyes, the person shows that emotion: **~ (with sth)** *His eyes gleamed with amusement.* ◇ **~ (in sth)** *Amusement gleamed in his eyes.*
■ ***noun*** [usually sing.] **1** a pale clear light, often reflected from sth: *the gleam of moonlight on the water* ◇ *A few gleams of sunshine lit up the gloomy afternoon.* ◇ *I saw the gleam of the knife as it flashed through the air.* **2** a small amount of sth: *a faint gleam of hope* ◇ *a serious book with an occasional gleam of humour* **3** an expression of a particular feeling or emotion that shows in sb's eyes SYN **glint**: *a gleam of triumph in her eyes* ◇ *a mischievous gleam in his eye* ◇ *The gleam in his eye made her uncomfortable* (= as if he was planning sth secret or unpleasant).

gleam·ing /ˈgliːmɪŋ/ *adj.* shining brightly: *gleaming white teeth*

glean /gliːn/ *verb* **~ sth (from sb/sth)** to obtain information, knowledge etc, sometimes with difficulty and often from various different places: *These figures have been gleaned from a number of studies.*

glean·ings /ˈgliːnɪŋz/ *noun* [pl.] information, knowledge etc, that you obtain from various different places, often with difficulty

glebe /gliːb/ *noun* (*old use*) **1** [C] a piece of land that provided an income for a priest **2** [U] land; fields

glee /gliː/ *noun* [U] a feeling of happiness, usually because sth good has happened to you, or sth bad has happened to sb else SYN **delight**: *He rubbed his hands* ***in glee*** *as he thought of all the money he would make.* ◇ *She couldn't disguise her glee at their embarrassment.*

glee·ful /ˈgliːfl/ *adj.* happy because of sth good you have done or sth bad that has happened to sb else: *a gleeful laugh* ▶ **glee·ful·ly** /-fəli/ *adv.*

glen /glen/ *noun* a deep narrow valley, especially in Scotland or Ireland

glib /glɪb/ *adj.* (*disapproving*) (of speakers and speech) using words that are clever, but are not sincere, and do not show much thought: *a glib salesman* ◇ *glib answers* ▶ **glib·ly** *adv.*

glide /glaɪd/ *verb, noun*
■ ***verb*** **1** [I] (**+ adv./prep.**) to move smoothly and quietly, especially as though it takes no effort: *Swans went gliding past.* ◇ *The skaters were gliding over the ice.* **2** [I] (**+ adv./prep.**) (of birds or aircraft) to fly using air currents, without the birds moving their wings or the aircraft using the engine: *An eagle was gliding high overhead.* ◇ *The plane managed to glide down to the runway.*
■ ***noun*** **1** [sing.] a continuous smooth movement: *the graceful glide of a skater* **2** [C] (*phonetics*) a speech sound made while moving the tongue from one position to another ➲ compare DIPHTHONG

glider /ˈglaɪdə(r)/ *noun* a light aircraft that flies without an engine ➲ VISUAL VOCAB page V43

glid·ing /ˈglaɪdɪŋ/ *noun* [U] the sport of flying in a glider

glim·mer /ˈglɪmə(r)/ *noun, verb*
■ ***noun*** **1** a faint unsteady light: *We could see a glimmer of light on the far shore.* **2** (also **glim·mer·ing**) a small sign of sth: *a* ***glimmer of hope*** ◇ *I caught the* ***glimmer of a smile*** *in his eyes.* ◇ *the* ***glimmering of an idea***
■ ***verb*** [I] to shine with a faint unsteady light: *The candles glimmered in the corner.* ◇ (*figurative*) *Amusement glimmered in his eyes.*

glimpse /glɪmps/ *noun, verb*
■ ***noun*** [usually sing.] **1 ~ (of sb/sth)** | **~ (at sb/sth)** a look at sb/sth for a very short time, when you do not see the person or thing completely: *He* ***caught a glimpse*** *of her in the crowd.* ◇ *I came up on deck to get my first glimpse of the island.* ➲ SYNONYMS at LOOK, SEE **2** a short experience of sth that helps you to understand it: **~ (into sth)** *a fascinating glimpse into life in the ocean* ◇ **~ (of sth)** *The programme gives us a rare glimpse of a great artist at work.*
■ ***verb*** **1 ~ sb/sth** to see sb/sth for a moment, but not very clearly SYN **catch sight of, spot**: *He'd glimpsed her through the window as he passed.* **2 ~ sth** to start to understand sth: *Suddenly she glimpsed the truth about her sister.*

glint /glɪnt/ *verb, noun*
■ ***verb*** **1** [I] (**+ adv./prep.**) to produce small bright flashes of light: *The sea glinted in the moonlight.* ◇ *The sun glinted on the windows.* ➲ SYNONYMS at SHINE **2** [I] **+ adv./prep.** if a person's eyes **glint** with a particular emotion, or an emotion **glints** in a person's eyes, the person shows that emotion, which is usually a strong one: *Her eyes glinted angrily.* ◇ *Hostility glinted in his eyes.*
■ ***noun*** **1** a sudden flash of light or colour shining from a bright surface: *the glint of the sun on the water* ◇ *golden glints in her red hair* ◇ *She saw a glint of silver in the grass.* **2** an expression in sb's eyes showing a particular emotion, often a negative one: *He had a wicked glint in his eye.* ◇ *a glint of anger*

glis·sando /glɪˈsændəʊ; *NAmE* -doʊ/ *noun* (*pl.* **glis·sandos** or **glis·sandi** /-diː/) (from *Italian*) a way of playing a series of notes so that each one slides into the next, making a smooth continuous sound

glis·ten /ˈglɪsn/ *verb* [I] (of sth wet) to shine: *Her eyes were glistening with tears.* ◇ *Sweat glistened on his forehead.* ◇ **+ adj.** *The road glistened wet after the rain.* ➲ SYNONYMS at SHINE IDM see GOLD *n.*

glis·ter /ˈglɪstə; *NAmE* ˈglɪstər/ *verb* [I] (*literary*) to shine brightly with little flashes of light, like a diamond SYN **glitter**

glitch /glɪtʃ/ *noun* (*informal*) a small problem or fault that stops sth working successfully

glit·ter /ˈglɪtə(r)/ *verb, noun*
■ ***verb*** **1** [I] to shine brightly with little flashes of light, like a diamond SYN **sparkle**: *The ceiling of the cathedral glittered with gold.* ◇ *The water glittered in the sunlight.* ➲ SYNONYMS at SHINE **2** [I] **~ (with sth)** (of the eyes) to shine brightly

with a particular emotion, usually a strong one: *His eyes glittered with greed.* IDM see GOLD *n.*

■ ***noun*** **1** [U] bright light consisting of many little flashes: *the glitter of diamonds* **2** [sing.] a bright expression in sb's eyes showing a particular emotion SYN **glint**: *There was a triumphant glitter in his eyes.* **3** [U] the attractive, exciting qualities that sb/sth, especially a rich and famous person or place, seems to have SYN **glamour**: *the superficial glitter of show business* **4** [U] very small shiny pieces of thin metal or paper that are stuck to things as a decoration: ***gold/silver glitter***

glit·ter·ati /ˌglɪtəˈrɑːti/ *noun* [pl.] (used in newspapers) fashionable, rich and famous people

glit·ter·ing /ˈglɪtərɪŋ/ *adj.* [usually before noun] **1** very impressive and successful: *He has a glittering career ahead of him.* **2** very impressive and involving rich and successful people: *a* ***glittering occasion/ceremony*** ◇ *a glittering array of stars* **3** shining brightly with many small flashes of light SYN **sparkling**: *glittering jewels*

glit·tery /ˈglɪtəri/ *adj.* shining brightly with many little flashes of light: *a glittery suit*

glitz /glɪts/ *noun* [U] (sometimes *disapproving*) the quality of appearing very attractive, exciting and impressive, in a way that is not always genuine: *the glitz and glamour of the music scene* ▶ **glitzy** *adj.*: *a glitzy, Hollywood-style occasion*

the gloam·ing /ˈgləʊmɪŋ; *NAmE* ˈgloʊ-/ *noun* [sing.] (*ScotE* or *literary*) the faint light after the sun sets SYN **twilight, dusk**

gloat /gləʊt; *NAmE* gloʊt/ *verb* [I] **~ (about/at/over sth)** to show that you are happy about your own success or sb else's failure, in an unpleasant way SYN **crow**: *She was still gloating over her rival's disappointment.* ▶ **gloat·ing** *adj.*: *a gloating look*

glob /glɒb; *NAmE* glɑːb/ *noun* (*informal*) a small amount of a liquid or substance in a round shape: *thick globs of paint on the floor*

global 0‑**π** AW /ˈgləʊbl; *NAmE* ˈgloʊbl/ *adj.* [usually before noun]

1 0‑**π** covering or affecting the whole world: *global issues* ◇ *The commission is calling for a global ban on whaling.* ◇ *the company's domestic and global markets* ➲ COLLOCATIONS at INTERNATIONAL **2** considering or including all parts of sth: *We need to take a more global approach to the problem.* ◇ *global searches on the database* ◇ *They sent a global email to all staff.* ▶ **glob·al·ly** AW /-bəli/ *adv.*: *We need to start thinking globally.*

glob·al·iza·tion (*BrE* also **-isa·tion**) AW /ˌgləʊbəlaɪˈzeɪʃn; *NAmE* ˌgloʊbələˈz-/ *noun* [U] the fact that different cultures and economic systems around the world are becoming connected and similar to each other because of the influence of large MULTINATIONAL companies and of improved communication ➲ COLLOCATIONS at INTERNATIONAL

glob·al·ize (*BrE* also **-ise**) /ˈgləʊbəlaɪz; *NAmE* ˈgloʊ-/ *verb* [I, T] **~ (sth)** (*economics*) if sth, for example a business company, **globalizes** or **is globalized**, it operates all around the world

ˌglobal ˈvillage *noun* [sing.] the whole world, looked at as a single community that is connected by electronic communication systems

ˌglobal ˈwarming *noun* [U] the increase in temperature of the earth's atmosphere, that is caused by the increase of particular gases, especially CARBON DIOXIDE ➲ COLLOCATIONS at ENVIRONMENT ➲ compare CLIMATE CHANGE ➲ see also GREENHOUSE EFFECT

globe AW /gləʊb; *NAmE* gloʊb/ *noun* **1** [C] an object shaped like a ball with a map of the world on its surface, usually on a stand so that it can be turned **2 the globe** [sing.] the world (used especially to emphasize its size): *tourists from every corner of the globe* **3** [C] a thing shaped like a ball

ˌglobe ˈartichoke *noun* = ARTICHOKE (1)

globe·trot·ting /ˈgləʊbtrɒtɪŋ; *NAmE* ˈgloʊbtrɑːtɪŋ/ *adj.* (*informal*) travelling in many countries all over the world: *a globetrotting journalist* ▶ **globe·trot·ter** *noun* **globe·trot·ting** *noun* [U]

globu·lar /ˈglɒbjələ(r); *NAmE* ˈglɑːb-/ *adj.* shaped like a ball, GLOBE or globule; consisting of globules

glob·ule /ˈglɒbjuːl; *NAmE* ˈglɑːb-/ *noun* a very small drop or ball of a liquid or of a solid that has been melted: *a globule of fat*

gloc·al·iza·tion (*BrE* also **-isa·tion**) /ˌgləʊkəlaɪˈzeɪʃn; *NAmE* ˌgloʊ-/ *noun* [U] the fact of adapting products or services that are available all over the world to make them suitable for local needs

glock·en·spiel /ˈglɒkənʃpiːl; *NAmE* ˈglɑːk-/ *noun* a musical instrument made of a row of metal bars of different lengths, that you hit with two small HAMMERS ➲ VISUAL VOCAB page V30 ➲ compare XYLOPHONE

glom /glɒm; *NAmE* glɑːm/ *verb* (**-mm-**) **~ sth** (*NAmE, informal*) to steal

PHR V **ˌglom ˈonto sth** **1** to develop a strong interest in sth: *Kids soon glom onto the latest trend.* **2** to become attached or stuck to sth

gloom /gluːm/ *noun* **1** [U, sing.] a feeling of being sad and without hope SYN **depression**: *The gloom deepened as the election results came in.* **2** [U] (*literary*) almost total DARKNESS: *We watched the boats come back in the gathering gloom.* IDM see DOOM *n.*, PILE *v.*

gloomy /ˈgluːmi/ *adj.* (**gloom·ier**, **gloomi·est**) **1** nearly dark, or badly lit in a way that makes you feel sad SYN **depressing**: *a gloomy room/atmosphere* ◇ *It was a wet and gloomy day.* **2** sad and without hope SYN **glum**: *a gloomy expression* ◇ *We sat in gloomy silence.* **3** without much hope of success or happiness in the future SYN **depressing**: *a* ***gloomy picture*** *of the country's economic future* ◇ *Suddenly, the future didn't look so gloomy after all.* ▶ **gloom·ily** /-ɪli/ *adv.*: *He stared gloomily at the phone.* **gloomi·ness** *noun* [U]

gloop /gluːp/ (*BrE*) (*NAmE* **glop** /glɒp; *NAmE* glɑːp/) *noun* [U] (*informal*) a thick wet substance that looks, tastes or feels unpleasant ▶ **gloopy** (*BrE*) (*NAmE* **gloppy**) *adj.*

glop /glɒp; *NAmE* glɑːp/ *noun* [U] (*informal, especially NAmE*) a thick wet substance that looks, tastes or feels unpleasant

glori·fied /ˈglɔːrɪfaɪd/ *adj.* [only before noun] making sb/sth seem more important or better than they are: *The restaurant was no more than a glorified fast-food cafe.*

glor·ify /ˈglɔːrɪfaɪ/ *verb* (**glori·fies**, **glori·fy·ing**, **glori·fied**, **glori·fied**) **1 ~ sth** (often *disapproving*) to make sth seem better or more important than it really is: *He denies that the movie glorifies violence.* **2 ~ sb** (*formal*) to praise and worship God ▶ **glori·fi·ca·tion** /ˌglɔːrɪfɪˈkeɪʃn/ *noun* [U]: *the glorification of war*

glori·ous /ˈglɔːriəs/ *adj.* **1** (*formal*) deserving or bringing great fame and success: *a glorious victory* ◇ *a glorious chapter in our country's history* ➲ compare INGLORIOUS **2** (*formal*) very beautiful and impressive SYN **splendid**: *a glorious sunset* **3** extremely enjoyable SYN **wonderful**: *a glorious trip to Rome* **4** (of weather) hot, with the sun shining: *They had three weeks of glorious sunshine.* ▶ **glori·ous·ly** *adv.*

glory /ˈglɔːri/ *noun, verb*

■ ***noun*** **1** [U] fame, praise or honour that is given to sb because they have achieved sth important: *Olympic glory in the 100 metres* ◇ *I do all the work and he gets all the glory.* ◇ *She wanted to enjoy her moment of glory.* ◇ *He came home a rich man,* ***covered in glory***. **2** [U] praise and worship of God: *'Glory to God in the highest'* **3** [U] great beauty: *The city was spread out beneath us* ***in all its glory***. ◇ *The house has now been restored to its* ***former glory***. **4** [C] a special cause for pride, respect or pleasure: *The temple is one of the glories of ancient Greece.* ◇ *Her long black hair is her* ***crowning glory*** (= most impressive feature). ➲ see also REFLECTED GLORY

G

■ *verb* (glor·ies, glory·ing, glor·ied, glor·ied)
PHR V **'glory in sth** to get great pleasure or enjoyment from sth SYN **revel**: *She gloried in her new-found independence.*

'glory days *noun* [pl.] a time in the past which people look back on as being better than the present

gloss /glɒs; *NAmE* glɑːs; glɔːs/ *noun, verb*
■ *noun* **1** [U, sing.] a shine on a smooth surface: *paper with a high gloss on one side* ◇ *The gel gives your hair a gloss.* ◇ *You can have the photos with either a gloss or a matt finish.* **2** [U] (often in compounds) a substance designed to make sth shiny: *lip gloss* **3** (also ˌ**gloss 'paint**) [U] paint which, when dry, has a hard shiny surface: *two coats of gloss* **4** [U, sing.] an attractive appearance that is only on the surface and hides what is not so attractive: *Beneath the gloss of success was a tragic private life.* ◇ *This scandal has taken the gloss off the occasion.* **5** [C] ~ (**on sth**) a way of explaining sth to make it seem more attractive or acceptable: *The director puts a Hollywood gloss on the civil war.* **6** [C] ~ (**on sth**) a note or comment added to a piece of writing to explain a difficult word or phrase
■ *verb* ~ **sth** (**as sth**) to add a note or comment to a piece of writing to explain a difficult word or idea
PHR V ˌ**gloss 'over sth** to avoid talking about sth unpleasant or embarrassing by not dealing with it in detail: *to gloss over a problem* ◇ *He glossed over any splits in the party.*

gloss·ary /ˈglɒsəri; *NAmE* ˈglɑːs-; ˈglɔːs-/ *noun* (*pl.* -ies) a list of technical or special words, especially those in a particular text, explaining their meanings

glossy /ˈglɒsi; *NAmE* ˈglɑːsi; ˈglɔːsi/ *adj., noun*
■ *adj.* (gloss·ier, glossi·est) **1** smooth and shiny: *glossy hair* ◇ *a* **glossy brochure/magazine** (= printed on shiny paper) **2** giving an appearance of being important and expensive: *the glossy world of fashion*
■ *noun* (*pl.* -ies) (*BrE, informal*) an expensive magazine printed on glossy paper, with a lot of colour photographs, etc.

glot·tal /ˈglɒtl; *NAmE* ˈglɑːtl/ *noun* (*phonetics*) a speech sound produced by the glottis ▸ **glot·tal** *adj.*

ˌ**glottal 'stop** *noun* (*phonetics*) a speech sound made by closing and opening the glottis, which in English sometimes takes the place of a /t/, for example in *butter*

glot·tis /ˈglɒtɪs; *NAmE* ˈglɑːt-/ *noun* (*anatomy*) the part of the throat that contains the VOCAL CORDS and the narrow opening between them

glove 🔑 /glʌv/ *noun*
a covering for the hand, made of wool, leather, etc. with separate parts for each finger and the thumb: *a pair of gloves* ◇ **rubber gloves** ◇ *gardening gloves* ➲ VISUAL VOCAB pages V17, V36, V39, V53 ➲ compare MITTEN ➲ see also BOXING, OVEN GLOVE
IDM **the gloves are off** used to say that sb is ready for a fight or an argument ➲ more at FIT *v.*, HAND *n.*, IRON *adj.*, KID *n.*

'glove compartment (also **'glove box**) *noun* a small space or shelf facing the front seats of a car, used for keeping small things in ➲ VISUAL VOCAB page V42

gloved /glʌvd/ *adj.* [usually before noun] (of a hand) wearing a glove

'glove puppet (*BrE*) (*NAmE* **'hand puppet**) *noun* a type of PUPPET that you put over your hand and move using your fingers ➲ VISUAL VOCAB page V32

glow /gləʊ; *NAmE* gloʊ/ *verb, noun*
■ *verb* **1** [I] (especially of sth hot or warm) to produce a dull, steady light: *The embers still glowed in the hearth.* ◇ *The strap has a fluorescent coating that* **glows in the dark**. ◇ **+ adj.** *A cigarette end glowed red in the darkness.* ➲ SYNONYMS at SHINE **2** [I] (of a person's body or face) to look or feel warm or pink, especially after exercise or because of excitement, embarrassment, etc: *Her cheeks were glowing.* ◇ ~ **with sth** *His face glowed with embarrassment.* **3** [I] ~ (**with sth**) to look very pleased or satisfied: *She was positively glowing with pride.* ◇ *He gave her a warm glowing smile.* **4** [I] to appear a strong, warm colour: ~ (**with sth**) *The countryside glowed with autumn colours.* ◇ **+ adj.** *The brick walls glowed red in the late afternoon sun.*
■ *noun* [sing.] **1** a dull steady light, especially from a fire that has stopped producing flames: *The city was just a red glow on the horizon.* ◇ *There was no light except for the occasional glow of a cigarette.* **2** the pink colour in your face when you have been doing exercise or feel happy and excited: *The fresh air had brought a healthy glow to her cheeks.* **3** a gold or red colour: *the glow of autumn leaves* **4** a feeling of pleasure and satisfaction: *When she looked at her children, she felt a glow of pride.*

glow·er /ˈglaʊə(r)/ *verb* [I] ~ (**at sb/sth**) to look in an angry, aggressive way SYN **glare** ▸ **glow·er** *noun*

glow·ing /ˈgləʊɪŋ; *NAmE* ˈgloʊɪŋ/ *adj.* giving enthusiastic praise: *a* **glowing account/report/review** ◇ *He spoke of her performance in the film* **in glowing terms** (= praising her highly). ▸ **glow·ing·ly** *adv.*

glow·stick /ˈgləʊstɪk; *NAmE* ˈgloʊ-/ (also **'light stick**) *noun* a plastic tube filled with chemicals that shines like a lamp when you bend it

'glow-worm *noun* a type of insect. The female has no wings and produces a green light at the end of the tail.

glu·cose /ˈgluːkəʊs; -kəʊz; *NAmE* -koʊs; -koʊz/ *noun* [U] a simple type of sugar that is an important energy source in living things and which is a part of many CARBOHYDRATES

glue 🔑 /gluː/ *noun, verb*
■ *noun* 🔑 [U, C] a sticky substance that is used for joining things together: *a tube of glue* ◇ *He sticks to her like glue* (= never leaves her). ➲ VISUAL VOCAB page V56
■ *verb* 🔑 to join two things together using glue SYN **stick**: ~ **A** (**to/onto B**) *She glued the label onto the box.* ◇ ~ **A and B** (**together**) *Glue the two pieces of cardboard together.* ◇ *Make sure the edges are glued down.*
IDM **be 'glued to sth** (*informal*) to give all your attention to sth; to stay very close to sth: *He spends every evening glued to the TV.* ◇ *Her eyes were glued to the screen* (= she did not stop watching it). ˌ**glued to the 'spot** not able to move, for example because you are frightened or surprised

ˌ**glue 'ear** *noun* [U] (*BrE*) a medical condition in which the tubes going from the nose to the ear are blocked with MUCUS

'glue-sniffing *noun* [U] the habit of breathing in the gases from some kinds of glue in order to produce a state of excitement; a type of SOLVENT ABUSE

gluey /ˈgluːi/ *adj.* sticky like glue; covered with glue

glug /glʌg/ *verb, noun* (*informal*)
■ *verb* (-gg-) **1** [I] **+ adv./prep.** (of liquid) to pour out quickly and noisily, especially from a bottle **2** [T] ~ **sth** (**down**) to drink sth quickly: *She glugged down a glass of water*
■ *noun* a small amount of a drink or liquid poured out

glum /glʌm/ *adj.* sad, quiet and unhappy SYN **gloomy**: *The players sat there with glum looks on their faces.* ▸ **glum·ly** *adv.*: *The three of us sat glumly looking out to sea.*

glut /glʌt/ *noun, verb*
■ *noun* [usually sing.] ~ (**of sth**) a situation in which there is more of sth than is needed or can be used SYN **surfeit**: *a glut of cheap DVDs on the market* OPP **shortage**
■ *verb* (-tt-) [usually passive] ~ **sth** (**with sth**) to supply or provide sth with too much of sth: *The market has been glutted with foreign cars.*

glu·ten /ˈgluːtn/ *noun* [U] a sticky substance that is a mixture of two PROTEINS and is left when STARCH is removed from flour, especially WHEAT flour: *We sell a range of* **gluten-free** *products* (= not containing gluten).

glutes /gluːts/ *noun* [pl.] (*informal*) the muscles in the BUTTOCKS that move the top of the leg

glu·teus /ˈgluːtiəs; *NAmE* also gluːˈtiəs/ (also **'gluteus muscle**) *noun* (*anatomy*) any of the three muscles in each BUTTOCK

glu·tin·ous /ˈgluːtənəs/ *adj.* sticky: *glutinous rice*

glut·ton /ˈglʌtn/ *noun* **1** (*disapproving*) a person who eats too much **2** ~ **for punishment/work** a person who enjoys doing difficult or unpleasant tasks ▸ **glut·ton·ous** /ˈglʌtənəs/ *adj.* SYN **greedy**

glut·tony /ˈɡlʌtəni/ *noun* [U] the habit of eating and drinking too much SYN **greed**

gly·caem·ic index (*BrE*) (*NAmE* **gly·cem·ic index**) /ɡlaɪˌsiːmɪk ˈɪndeks/ *noun* = GI *abbr.*

gly·cer·ine /ˈɡlɪsəriːn; -rɪn; *NAmE* -rən/ (*especially BrE*) (*US* usually **gly·cerin** /-rɪn; *NAmE* -rən/) *noun* [U] a thick sweet clear liquid made from fats and oils and used in medicines, beauty products and EXPLOSIVES

glyph /ɡlɪf/ *noun* a symbol CARVED out of stone, especially one from an ancient writing system

GM /ˌdʒiː ˈem/ *abbr.* **1** (*BrE*) GENETICALLY MODIFIED: *GM foods or 'Frankenstein foods' as they are popularly called* **2** grant-maintained (used in Britain to describe schools that receive money from central, not local, government)

gm (*BrE*) (also **gm.** *US, BrE*) *abbr.* (*pl.* **gm** or **gms**) gram(s)

GMAT /ˈdʒiːmæt/ *abbr.* Graduate Management Admissions Test (a test taken by GRADUATE students in the US who want to study for a degree in Business)

GMO /ˌdʒiː em ˈəʊ; *NAmE* ˈoʊ/ *noun* (*pl.* **GMOs**) the abbreviation for 'genetically modified organism' (a plant, etc. that has had its genetic structure changed artificially, so that it will produce more fruit or not be affected by disease)

GMT /ˌdʒiː em ˈtiː/ *noun* [U] the abbreviation for 'Greenwich Mean Time' (the time at Greenwich in England on the line of 0° LONGITUDE, used for calculating time everywhere in the world; also called Universal Time)

gnarled /nɑːld; *NAmE* nɑːrld/ *adj.* **1** (of trees) twisted and rough; covered with hard lumps: *a gnarled oak/branch/trunk* **2** (of a person or part of the body) bent and twisted because of age or illness: *gnarled hands*

gnarly /ˈnɑːli; *NAmE* ˈnɑːrli/ *adj.* (*NAmE, slang*) **1** very good; excellent: *Wow, man! That's totally gnarly!* **2** not very good

gnash /næʃ/ *verb*
IDM **gnash your ˈteeth** to feel very angry and upset about sth, especially because you cannot get what you want: *He'll be gnashing his teeth when he hears that we lost the contract.*

gnash·ers /ˈnæʃəz; *NAmE* -ʃərz/ *noun* [pl.] (*BrE, informal*) teeth

gnat /næt/ *noun* a small fly with two wings, that bites

gnaw /nɔː/ *verb* [T, I] to keep biting sth or chewing it hard, so that it gradually disappears: **~ sth** *The dog was gnawing a bone.* ◇ **~ through sth** *Rats had gnawed through the cable* ◇ **~ at/on sth** *She gnawed at her fingernails.* ◇ **~ away at/on sth** (*figurative*) *Self-doubt began to gnaw away at her confidence.*
PHR V **ˈgnaw at sb** to make sb feel anxious, frightened or uncomfortable over a long period of time: *The problem had been gnawing at him for months.*

gnaw·ing /ˈnɔːɪŋ/ *adj.* [only before noun] making you feel worried over a period of time: *gnawing doubts*

gneiss /naɪs/ *noun* [U] (*geology*) a type of METAMORPHIC rock formed at high pressure and temperature deep in the ground

gnoc·chi /ˈnjɒki; *NAmE* ˈnjɑːki/ *noun* [pl.] an Italian dish consisting of small balls of potato mixed with flour and boiled, usually eaten with a sauce

gnome /nəʊm; *NAmE* noʊm/ *noun* **1** (in stories) a creature like a small man with a pointed hat, who lives under the ground and guards gold and TREASURE **2** a plastic or stone figure of a gnome, used to decorate a garden

gno·mic /ˈnəʊmɪk; *NAmE* ˈnoʊ-/ *adj.* (*formal*) (of a person or a remark) clever and wise but sometimes difficult to understand

GNP /ˌdʒiː en ˈpiː/ *noun* the abbreviation for 'gross national product' (the total value of all the goods and services produced by a country in one year, including the total income from foreign countries) ➲ compare GDP

gnu /nuː; njuː/ *noun* (*pl.* **gnu** or **gnus**) = WILDEBEEST

GNVQ /ˌdʒiː en viː ˈkjuː/ *noun* the abbreviation for 'General National Vocational Qualification' (a qualification which until 2007 was taken in British schools by students aged 15–18 to prepare them for university or work) ➲ compare A LEVEL

go 🔑 /ɡəʊ; *NAmE* ɡoʊ/ *verb, noun*
■ *verb* (**goes** /ɡəʊz; *NAmE* ɡoʊz/, **went** /went/, **gone** /ɡɒn; *NAmE* ɡɔːn/) HELP **Been** is used as the past participle of **go** when sb has gone somewhere and come back.

▸ MOVE/TRAVEL **1** 🔑 [I] to move or travel from one place to another: **+ adv./prep.** *She went into her room and shut the door behind her.* ◇ *He goes to work by bus.* ◇ *I have to go to Rome on business.* ◇ *She has gone to China* (= is now in China or is on her way there). ◇ *She has been to China* (= she went to China and has now returned). ◇ *I think you should go to the doctor's.* ◇ *Are you going home for Christmas?* ◇ **~ to do sth** *She has gone to see her sister this weekend.* HELP In spoken English **go** can be used with **and** plus another verb to show purpose or to tell sb what to do: *I'll go and answer the door.* ◇ ***Go and get** me a drink!* The **and** is sometimes left out, especially in *NAmE*: ***Go ask** your mom!* **2** 🔑 [I] **~** (**to sth**) (**with sb**) to move or travel, especially with sb else, to a particular place or in order to be present at an event: *Are you going to Dave's party?* ◇ *Who else is going?* ◇ *His dog goes everywhere with him.* **3** 🔑 [I] to move or travel in a particular way or over a particular distance: **+ adv./prep.** *He's going too fast.* ◇ **+ noun** *We had gone about fifty miles when the car broke down.* **4** 🔑 [I] **~ flying, skidding, etc.** (**+ adv./prep.**) to move in a particular way or while doing sth else: *The car went skidding off the road into a ditch.* ◇ *She went sobbing up the stairs.* ◇ *She crashed into a waiter and his tray of drinks went flying.*

▸ LEAVE **5** 🔑 [I] to leave one place in order to reach another SYN **depart**: *I must be going now.* ◇ *They came at six and went at nine.* ◇ *Has she gone yet?* ◇ *He's been gone an hour* (= he left an hour a go). ◇ *When does the train go?* **6** 🔑 [I] **~ on sth** to leave a place and do sth different: *to **go on a journey/a tour/a trip/a cruise*** ◇ *Richard has gone on leave for two weeks.*

▸ VISIT/ATTEND **7** 🔑 [I] **~ to sth** to visit or attend a place for a particular purpose: (*BrE*) *I have to go to hospital for an operation.* ◇ (*NAmE*) *I have to go to the hospital.* ◇ *to go to prison* (= to be sent there as punishment for a crime) ◇ *Do you go to church* (= regularly attend church services)?

▸ SWIMMING/FISHING/JOGGING, ETC. **8** 🔑 [I] **~** (**for**) **sth** to leave a place or travel to a place in order to take part in an activity or a sport: *to **go for a walk/drive/swim/run*** ◇ *Shall we go for a drink* (= at a pub or bar) *after work?* ◇ *I have to go shopping this afternoon.* ◇ *We're going sailing on Saturday.*

▸ BE SENT **9** 🔑 [I] (**+ adv./prep.**) to be sent or passed somewhere: *I want this memo to go to all managers.*

▸ LEAD **10** 🔑 [I] **~** (**from...**) (**to...**) to lead or extend from one place to another: *I want a rope that will go from the top window to the ground.* ◇ *Where does this road go?*

▸ PLACE/SPACE **11** 🔑 [I] **+ adv./prep.** to have as a usual or correct position; to be placed: *This dictionary goes on the top shelf.* ◇ *Where do you want the piano to go* (= be put)? **12** 🔑 [I] **will/would not ~** (**in/into sth**) used to say that sth does/did not fit into a particular place or space: *My clothes won't all go in that one suitcase.* ◇ *He tried to push his hand through the gap but it wouldn't go.*

▸ NUMBERS **13** [I] if a number will **go into** another number, it is contained in that number an exact number of times: (**+ adj.**) *3 into 12 goes 4 times.* ◇ *7 into 15 won't go.* ◇ (*NAmE*) *7 into 15 doesn't go.* ◇ **~ into sth** *7 won't go into 15.*

▸ PROGRESS **14** 🔑 [I] **+ adv./prep.** used to talk about how well or badly sth makes progress or succeeds: *'How did your interview go?' 'It went very well, thank you.'* ◇ *Did everything go smoothly?* ◇ *How's it going* (= is your life enjoyable, successful, etc. at the moment)? ◇ *The way things are going the company will be bankrupt by the end of the year.*

▸ STATE/CONDITION **15** 🔑 [I] used in many expressions to show that sb/sth has reached a particular state/is no longer in a particular state: **~ to/into sth** *She went to sleep.* ◇ **~ out of sth** *That colour has gone out of fashion.* **16** 🔑 *linking verb* **+ adj.** to become different in a particular way, especially a bad way: *to go **bald/blind/mad/bankrupt, etc.***

G

◇ *Her hair is* **going grey**. ◇ *This milk has* **gone sour**. ◇ *The children* **went wild** *with excitement.* ➲ SYNONYMS at BECOME **17** [I] **+ adj.** to live or move around in a particular state: *to* **go naked/barefoot** ◇ *She cannot bear the thought of children going hungry.* **18** [I] **~ unnoticed, unreported, etc.** to not be noticed, reported, etc: *Police are worried that many crimes go unreported.*

▸ SONG/STORY **19** [I, T] used to talk about what tune or words a song or poem has or what happens in a story: **+ adv./prep.** *How does that song go?* ◇ *I forget how the next line goes.* ◇ **~ that...** *The story goes that she's been married five times.*

▸ SOUND/MOVEMENT **20** 🔑 [I] to make a particular sound or movement: **+ noun** *The gun went 'bang'.* ◇ **+ adv./prep.** *She went like this with her hand.* **21** 🔑 [I] to be sounded as a signal or warning: *The whistle went for the end of the game.*

▸ SAY **22** [T] **+ speech** (*informal*) (used when telling a story) to say: *I asked 'How much?' and he goes, 'Fifty' and I go, 'Fifty? You must be joking!'*

▸ START **23** [I] to start an activity: *I'll say 'One, two, three, go!' as a signal for you to start.* ◇ *As soon as he gets here we're ready to go.*

▸ MACHINE **24** 🔑 [I] if a machine **goes**, it works: *This clock doesn't go.*

▸ DISAPPEAR **25** 🔑 [I] to stop existing; to be lost or stolen SYN **disappear**: *Has your headache gone yet?* ◇ *I left my bike outside the library and when I came out again it had gone.*

▸ BE THROWN OUT **26** [I] **sb/sth must/has to/can ~** used to talk about wanting to get rid of sb/sth: *The old sofa will have to go.* ◇ *He's useless—he'll have to go.*

▸ NOT WORK **27** [I] to get worse; to become damaged or stop working correctly: *Her sight is beginning to go.* ◇ *His mind is going* (= he is losing his mental powers). ◇ *I was driving home when my brakes went.*

▸ DIE **28** [I] to die. People say 'go' to avoid saying 'die': *You can't take your money with you when you go.*

▸ MONEY **29** [I] when money **goes**, it is spent or used for sth: *I don't know where the money goes!* ◇ **~ on sth** *Most of my salary goes on the rent.* ◇ **~ to do sth** *The money will go to finance a new community centre.* **30** [I] **~ (to sb) (for sth)** to be sold: *We won't let the house go for less than $200 000.* ◇ *There was usually some bread* **going cheap** (= being sold cheaply) *at the end of the day.* **31** [I] **+ adv./prep.** to be willing to pay a particular amount of money for sth: *He's offered £3 000 for the car and I don't think he'll go any higher.* ◇ *I'll go to $1 000 but that's my limit.*

▸ HELP **32** [I] **~ to do sth** to help; to play a part in doing sth: *This all goes to prove my theory.* ◇ *It* (= what has just happened) ***just goes to show*** *you can't always tell how people are going to react.*

▸ BE AVAILABLE **33** **be going** [I] (*informal*) to be available: *There just aren't any jobs going in this area.*

▸ TIME **34** 🔑 [I] **+ adv./prep.** used to talk about how quickly or slowly time seems to pass: *Hasn't the time gone quickly?* ◇ *Half an hour went past while we were sitting there.*

▸ USE TOILET **35** [I] (*informal*) to use a toilet: *Do you need to go, Billy?*

IDM Most idioms containing **go** are at the entries for the nouns and adjectives in the idioms, for example **go it alone** is at **alone**. **anything goes** (*informal*) anything that sb says or does is accepted or allowed, however shocking or unusual it may be: *Almost anything goes these days.* **as people, things, etc. go** in comparison with the average person, thing, etc: *As teachers go, he's not bad.* **be going on (for) sth** (*BrE*) to be nearly a particular age, time or number: *It was going on (for) midnight.* **be going to do sth 1** 🔑 used to show what sb intends to do in the future: *We're going to buy a house when we've saved enough money.* **2** 🔑 used to show that sth is likely to happen very soon or in the future: *I think I'm going to faint.* ◇ *If the drought continues there's going to be a famine.* **don't go doing sth** (*informal*) used to tell or warn sb not to do sth: *Don't go getting yourself into trouble.* **enough/something to be going 'on with** (*BrE*) something that is enough for a short time: *£50 should be enough to be going on with.* **go all 'out for sth** | **go all out to 'do sth** to make a very great effort to get sth or do sth **go and do sth** used to show that you are angry or annoyed that sb has done sth stupid: *Trust him to go and mess things up!* ◇ *Why did you have to go and upset your mother like that?* ◇ ***You've really gone and done it*** (= done sth very stupid) *now!* **go 'off on one** (*BrE, informal*) to suddenly become very angry **go 'on (with you)** (*old-fashioned*) used to express the fact that you do not believe sth, or that you disapprove of sth **(have) a lot, nothing, etc. 'going for you** (to have) many/not many advantages: *You're young, intelligent, attractive—you have a lot going for you!* **ˌno 'go** (*informal*) not possible or allowed: *If the bank won't lend us the money it's no go, I'm afraid.* ➲ see also NO-GO AREA **not (even) 'go there** (*informal*) used to say that you do not want to talk about sth in any more detail because you do not even want to think about it: *Don't ask me to choose. I don't want to go there.* ◇ *'There was a problem with his parents, wasn't there?' 'Don't even go there!'* **to 'go 1** remaining; still left: *I only have one exam to go.* **2** (*NAmE, informal*) if you buy cooked food **to go** in a restaurant or shop/store, you buy it to take away and eat somewhere else: *Two pizzas to go.* **what ˌgoes around 'comes around** (*saying*) **1** the way sb behaves towards other people will affect the way those people behave towards them in the future **2** something that is not fashionable now will become fashionable again in the future **ˌwhere does sb ˌgo from 'here?** used to ask what action sb should take, especially in order to improve the difficult situation that they are in **ˌwho goes 'there?** used by a soldier who is guarding a place to order sb to say who they are: *Halt, who goes there?*

PHR V **ˌgo a'bout** (*BrE*) = GO AROUND **'go about sth** to continue to do sth; to keep busy with sth: *Despite the threat of war, people went about their business as usual.* **ˌgo a'bout sth** to start working on sth SYN **tackle**: *You're not going about the job in the right way.* ◇ **~ doing sth** *How should I go about finding a job?*

ˌgo 'after sb to chase or follow sb: *He went after the burglars.* ◇ *She left the room in tears so I went after her.* **ˌgo 'after sb/sth** to try to get sb/sth: *We're both going after the same job.*

ˌgo a'gainst sb to not be in sb's favour or not to their advantage: *The jury's verdict went against him.* **ˌgo a'gainst sb/sth** to resist or oppose sb/sth: *He would not go against his parents' wishes.* **ˌgo a'gainst sth** to be opposed to sth; to not fit or agree with sth: *Paying for hospital treatment goes against her principles.* ◇ *His thinking goes against all logic.*

ˌgo a'head 1 🔑 to travel in front of other people in your group and arrive before them: *I'll go ahead and tell them you're on the way.* **2** 🔑 to happen; to be done SYN **proceed**: *The building of the new bridge will go ahead as planned.* ➲ related noun GO-AHEAD **ˌgo a'head (with sth)** 🔑 to begin to do sth, especially when sb has given permission or has expressed doubts or opposition: *'May I start now?' 'Yes, go ahead.'* ◇ *The government intends to go ahead with its tax cutting plans*

ˌgo a'long 1 to continue with an activity: *He made up the story* **as he went along**. **2** to make progress; to develop: *Things are going along nicely.* **ˌgo a'long with sb/sth** to agree with sb/sth: *I don't go along with her views on private medicine.* ➲ SYNONYMS at AGREE

ˌgo a'round/'round 1 🔑 to spin or turn: *to go round in a circle* **2** 🔑 to be enough for everyone to have one or some: *There aren't enough chairs to go around.* **3** 🔑 (*BrE* also **ˌgo a'bout**) to often be in a particular state or behave in a particular way: *She often goes around barefoot.* ◇ **~ doing sth** *It's unprofessional to go round criticizing your colleagues.* **4** to spread from person to person: *There's a rumour going around that they're having an affair.* **ˌgo a'round/'round (to...)** 🔑 to visit sb or a place that is near: *I went round to the post office.* ◇ *I'm going around to my sister's* (= her house) *later.*

'go at sb to attack sb: *They went at each other furiously.* **'go at sth** to make great efforts to do sth; to work hard at sth: *They went at the job as if their lives depended on it.*

ˌgo a'way 1 🔑 to leave a person or place: *Just go away!* ◇ *Go away and think about it, then let me know.* **2** 🔑 to leave home for a period of time, especially for a holiday/vacation: *They've gone away for a few days.* ◇ *I'm going away on business.* **3** 🔑 to disappear: *The smell still hasn't gone away.*

ˌ**go ˈback** if two people **go back** a period of time (usually a long time), they have known each other for that time: *Dave and I go back twenty years.* ˌ**go ˈback (to…)** to return to a place: *She doesn't want to go back to her husband* (= to live with him again). ◇ *This toaster will have to go back* (= be taken back to the shop/store where it was bought) *—it's faulty.* ◇ *Of course we want to go back some day—it's our country, our real home.* ➲ SYNONYMS at RETURN ˌ**go ˈback (to sth) 1** 🔑 to consider sth that happened or was said at an earlier time: *Can I go back to what you said at the beginning of the meeting?* ◇ *Once you have made this decision, there will be* ***no going back*** (= you will not be able to change your mind). **2** 🔑 to have existed since a particular time or for a particular period: *Their family goes back to the time of the Pilgrim Fathers.* ˌ**go ˈback on sth** to fail to keep a promise; to change your mind about sth: *He never* ***goes back on his word*** (= never fails to do what he has said he will do). ˌ**go ˈback to sth** 🔑 to start doing sth again that you had stopped doing: *The kids go back to school next week.* ◇ **~ doing sth** *She's decided to go back to teaching.*

ˌ**go beˈfore** to exist or happen in an earlier time: *The present crisis is worse than any that have gone before.* ˈ**go before sb/sth** to be presented to sb/sth for discussion, decision or judgement: *My application goes before the planning committee next week.*

ˌ**go beˈyond sth** to be more than sth SYN **exceed**: *This year's sales figures go beyond all our expectations* (= are much better than we thought they would be).

ˌ**go ˈby** 🔑 (of time) to pass: *Things will get easier* ***as time goes by.*** ◇ *The weeks went slowly by.* ˈ**go by sth** to be guided by sth; to form an opinion from sth: *That's a good rule to go by.* ◇ ***If past experience is anything to go by,*** *they'll be late.*

ˌ**go ˈdown 1** to fall to the ground: *She tripped and went down with a bump.* **2** if a ship, etc. **goes down**, it disappears below the water SYN **sink 3** 🔑 when the sun or moon **goes down**, it disappears below the HORIZON SYN **set 4** if food or drink will/will not **go down**, it is easy/difficult to swallow: *A glass of wine would go down very nicely* (= I would very much like one). **5** 🔑 if the price of sth, the temperature, etc. **goes down**, it becomes lower SYN **fall**: *The price of oil is going down.* ◇ *Oil is going down in price.* OPP **go up 6** (*informal*) to get worse in quality: *The neighbourhood has gone down a lot recently.* **7** (*computing*) to stop working temporarily: *The system is going down in ten minutes.* **8** (*NAmE, informal*) to happen: *You really don't know what's going down?* ˌ**go ˈdown (from…)** (*BrE, formal*) to leave a university, especially Oxford or Cambridge, at the end of a term or after finishing your studies OPP **go up (to…)** ˌ**go ˈdown (in sth)** to be written in sth; to be recorded or remembered in sth: *It all goes down* (= she writes it all) *in her notebook.* ◇ *He will* ***go down in history*** *as a great statesman.* ˌ**go ˈdown (on sb)** (*slang*) to perform ORAL sex on sb (= to use the mouth to give sb sexual pleasure) ˌ**go ˈdown (to sb)** to be defeated by sb, especially in a game or competition: *Italy went down to Brazil by three goals to one.* ˌ**go ˈdown (to…) (from…)** to go from one place to another, especially further south or from a city or large town to a smaller place: *They've gone down to Brighton for a couple of days.* OPP **go up** ˌ**go ˈdown (with sb)** to be received in a particular way by sb: *The suggestion didn't go down very well with her boss.* ˌ**go ˈdown with sth** (*especially BrE*) to become ill/sick with sth SYN **catch**: *Our youngest boy has gone down with chickenpox.*

ˈ**go for sb** to attack sb: *She went for him with a knife.* ˈ**go for sb/sth 1** to apply to sb/sth: *What I said about Peter goes for you, too.* ◇ *They have a high level of unemployment —but* ***the same goes for*** *many other countries.* **2** to go to a place and bring sb/sth back: *She's gone for some milk.* **3** (*informal*) to be attracted by sb/sth; to like or prefer sb/sth: *She goes for tall slim men.* ◇ *I don't really go for modern art.* ˈ**go for sth 1** to choose sth: *I think I'll go for the fruit salad.* ➲ SYNONYMS at CHOOSE **2** to put a lot of effort into sth, so that you get or achieve sth: ***Go for it,*** *John! You know you can beat him.* ◇ *It sounds a great idea.* ***Go for it!***

ˌ**go ˈin 1** to enter a room, house, etc: *Let's go in, it's getting cold.* **2** if the sun or moon **goes in**, it disappears behind a cloud ˌ**go ˈin for sth 1** (*BrE*) to take an exam or enter a competition: *She's going in for the Cambridge First Certificate.* **2** to have sth as an interest or a hobby: *She doesn't go in for team sports.* ˌ**go ˈin with sb** to join sb in starting a business: *My brothers are opening a garage and they want me to go in with them.*

ˌ**go ˈinto sth 1** 🔑 (of a vehicle) to hit sth violently: *The car skidded and went into a tree.* **2** (of a vehicle or driver) to start moving in a particular way: *The plane went into a nosedive.* **3** 🔑 to join an organization, especially in order to have a career in it: *to go into the Army/the Church/Parliament* ◇ *to go into teaching* **4** to begin to do sth or behave in a particular way: *He went into a long explanation of the affair.* **5** to examine sth carefully: *We need to go into the question of costs.* **6** (of money, time, effort, etc.) to be spent on sth or used to do sth: *More government money needs to go into the project.* ◇ **~ doing sth** *Years of work went into researching the book.*

ˌ**go ˈoff 1** to leave a place, especially in order to do sth: *She went off to get a drink.* **2** 🔑 to be fired; to explode: *The gun went off by accident.* ◇ *The bomb went off in a crowded street.* ➲ SYNONYMS at EXPLODE **3** 🔑 if an alarm, etc. **goes off**, it makes a sudden loud noise **4** 🔑 if a light, the electricity, etc. **goes off**, it stops working: *Suddenly the lights went off.* ◇ *The heating goes off at night.* OPP **go on 5** (*BrE, informal*) to fall asleep: *Hasn't the baby gone off yet?* **6** 🔑 (*BrE*) if food or drink **goes off**, it becomes bad and not fit to eat or drink **7** (*BrE*) to get worse in quality: *Her books have gone off in recent years.* **8** to happen in a particular way: *The meeting* ***went off well.*** ˌ**go ˈoff (on sb)** (*NAmE, informal*) to suddenly become angry with sb ˌ**go ˈoff sb/sth** (*BrE, informal*) to stop liking sb/sth or lose interest in them: *Jane seems to be going off Paul.* ◇ *I've gone off beer.* ˌ**go ˈoff with sb** to leave your husband, wife, partner, etc. in order to have a relationship with sb else: *He went off with his best friend's wife.* ˌ**go ˈoff with sth** to take away from a place sth that does not belong to you: *He went off with $10 000 of the company's money.*

ˌ**go ˈon 1** when a performer **goes on**, they begin their performance: *She doesn't go on until Act 2.* **2** (in sport) to join a team as a SUBSTITUTE during a game: *Walcott went on in place of Rooney just before half-time.* **3** 🔑 when a light, the electricity, etc. **goes on**, it starts to work: *Suddenly all the lights went on.* OPP **go off 4** 🔑 (of time) to pass: *She became more and more talkative as the evening went on.* **5** 🔑 (usually **be going on**) to happen: ***What's going on*** *here?* **6** 🔑 if a situation **goes on**, it continues without changing: *This cannot be allowed to go on.* ◇ *How much longer will this hot weather go on for?* ◇ *We* ***can't go on like this****—we seem to be always arguing.* **7** 🔑 to continue speaking, often after a short pause: *She hesitated for a moment and then went on.* ◇ **+ speech** *'You know,' he went on, 'I think my brother could help you.'* **8** 🔑 used to encourage sb to do sth: *Go on! Have another drink!* ◇ *Go on—jump!* ˌ**go ˈon (ahead)** to travel in front of sb else: *You go on ahead—I'll catch you up in a few minutes.* ˈ**go on sth** (used in negative sentences and questions) to base an opinion or a judgement on sth: *The police don't have much to go on.* ˌ**go ˈon (about sb/sth)** (*informal*) to talk about sb/sth for a long time, especially in a boring or complaining way: *He* ***went on and on*** *about how poor he was.* ◇ *She does go on sometimes!* ˌ**go ˈon (at sb)** (*informal, especially BrE*) to complain to sb about their behaviour, work, etc. SYN **criticize**: *She goes on at him continually.* ˌ**go ˈon (with sth)** 🔑 to continue an activity, especially after a pause or break: *That's enough for now—let's go on with it tomorrow.* ˌ**go ˈon doing sth** 🔑 to continue an activity without stopping: *He said nothing but just went on working.* ˌ**go ˈon to sth** to pass from one item to the next: *Let's go on to the next item on the agenda.* ˌ**go ˈon to do sth** to do sth after completing sth else: *The book goes on to describe his experiences in the army.*

ˌ**go ˈout 1** 🔑 to leave your house to go to a social event: *She goes out a lot.* ◇ **~ doing sth** *He goes out drinking most evenings.* **2** when the TIDE **goes out**, it moves away from the land SYN **ebb** OPP **come in 3** to be sent: *Have the invitations gone out yet?* **4** (*BrE*) when a radio or television

G

programme **goes out**, it is broadcast **5** when news or information **goes out**, it is announced or published: **~ that** ... *Word went out that the director had resigned* **6** ⊶ if a fire or light **goes out**, it stops burning or shining ˌ**go 'out (of sth) 1** to fail to reach the next stage of a competition, etc: *She went out of the tournament in the first round.* **2** to be no longer fashionable or generally used: *Those skirts went out years ago.* ˌ**go 'out of sb/sth** (of a quality or a feeling) to be no longer present in sb/sth; to disappear from sb/sth: *All the fight seemed to go out of him.* ˌ**go 'out to sb** if your thoughts, etc. **go out to sb**, you think about them in a kind way and hope that the difficult situation that they are in will get better: **go 'out with sb** | ˌ**go 'out (together)** ⊶ (especially of young people) to spend time with sb and have a romantic or sexual relationship with them: *Tom has been going out with Lucy for six weeks.* ◇ *How long have Tom and Lucy been going out together?*

ˌ**go 'over sth 1** ⊶ to examine or check sth carefully: *Go over your work before you hand it in.* ➲ SYNONYMS at CHECK **2** to study sth carefully, especially by repeating it: *He went over the events of the day in his mind* (= thought about them carefully). ˌ**go 'over (to...)** to move from one place to another, especially when this means crossing sth such as a room, town or city: *He went over and shook hands with his guests.* ◇ *Many Irish people went over to America during the famine.* ˌ**go 'over to sb/sth** (in broadcasting) to change to a different person or place for the next part of a broadcast: *We are now going over to the news desk for an important announcement.* ˌ**go 'over to sth** to change from one side, opinion, habit, etc. to another: *Two Conservative MPs have gone over to the Liberal Democrats.* ˌ**go 'over (with sb)** (*NAmE*) to be received in a particular way by sb: *The news of her promotion went over well with her colleagues.*

ˌ**go 'round** = GO AROUND ˌ**go 'round (to...)** = GO AROUND (TO...)

ˌ**go 'through** if a law, contract, etc. **goes through**, it is officially accepted or completed: *The deal did not go through.* **go through sth 1** ⊶ to look at or examine sth carefully, especially in order to find sth: *I always start the day by going through my email.* ◇ *She went through the company's accounts, looking for evidence of fraud.* **2** ⊶ to study or consider sth in detail, especially by repeating it: *Let's go through the arguments again.* ◇ *Could we go through* (= practise) *Act 2 once more?* **3** ⊶ to perform a series of actions; to follow a method or procedure: *Certain formalities have to be gone through before you can emigrate.* **4** ⊶ to experience or suffer sth: *She's been going through a bad patch recently.* ◇ *He's amazingly cheerful considering all he's had to go through.* **5** to use up or finish sth completely: *The boys went through two whole loaves of bread.* ˌ**go 'through with sth** ⊶ to do what is necessary to complete a course of action, especially one that is difficult or unpleasant: *She decided not to go through with* (= not to have) *the operation.*

'**go to sb/sth** ⊶ to be given to sb/sth: *Proceeds from the concert will go to charity.* ◇ *All her property went to her eldest son* (= when she died).

ˌ**go to'gether** = GO WITH STH

'**go towards sth** to be used as part of the payment for sth: *The money will go towards a new car.* ◇ **~ doing sth** *Part of my pay cheque went towards buying an MP3 player.*

ˌ**go 'under 1** (of sth that floats) to sink below the surface **2** (*informal*) to become BANKRUPT (= be unable to pay what you owe): *The firm will go under unless business improves.*

ˌ**go 'up 1** to be built: *New offices buildings are going up everywhere.* **2** when the curtain across the stage in a theatre **goes up**, it is raised or opened **3** to be destroyed by fire or an explosion: *The whole building went up in flames.* **4** ⊶ if the price of sth, the temperature, etc. **goes up**, it becomes higher SYN **rise**: *The price of cigarettes is going up.* ◇ *Cigarettes are going up in price.* OPP **go down** ˌ**go 'up (to...)** (*BrE, formal*) to arrive at a university, especially Oxford or Cambridge, at the beginning of a term or in order to begin your studies OPP **go down (from...)** ˌ**go 'up (to...)** (**from...**) to go from one place to another, especially further north or to a city or large town from a smaller place: *When are you next going up to Scotland?* ◇ *We went up to London last weekend.* OPP **go down**

'**go with sb 1** (*old-fashioned, informal*) to have a sexual or romantic relationship with sb **2** (*informal*) to have sex with sb '**go with sth 1** to be included with or as part of sth: *A car goes with the job.* **2** to agree to accept sth, for example a plan or an offer: *You're offering £500? I think we can go with that.* **3** ⊶ (also **go (together)**) to combine well with sth SYN **match**: *Does this jacket go with this skirt?* ◇ *Those colours don't really go (together).* **4** ⊶ (also ˌ**go to'gether**) to exist at the same time or in the same place as sth; to be found together: *Disease often goes with poverty.* ◇ *Disease and poverty often go together.*

ˌ**go wi'thout (sth)** ⊶ to manage without sth that you usually have or need: *There wasn't time for breakfast, so I had to go without.* ◇ *How long can a human being go* (= survive) *without sleep?* ◇ **~ doing sth** *She went without eating for three days.*

■ ***noun*** (*pl.* **goes** /ɡəʊz; *NAmE* ɡoʊz/) **1** [C] (*BrE*) (also **turn** *NAmE, BrE*) a person's turn to move or play in a game or an activity: *Whose go is it?* ◇ *It's your go.* ◇ *'How much is it to play?' 'It's 50p a go.'* ◇ *Can I **have a go on** your new bike?* **2** [C] (*BrE*) (also **try** *NAmE, BrE*) an attempt at doing sth: *It took three goes to get it right.* ◇ *I doubt if he'll listen to advice from me, but **I'll give it a go*** (= I'll try but I don't think I will succeed). **3** [U] (*BrE*) energy and enthusiasm: *Mary's always got plenty of go.* ➲ see also GET-UP-AND-GO

IDM **at one 'go** (*BrE*) in one single attempt or try: *She blew out the candles at one go.* **be a 'go** (*NAmE, informal*) to be planned and possible or allowed: *I'm not sure if Friday's trip is a go.* **be all 'go** (*BrE, informal*) to be very busy or full of activity: *It was all go in the office today.* **be on the 'go** (also **be on the 'move**) (*informal*) to be very active and busy: *I've been on the go all day.* ◇ *Having four children keeps her on the go.* **first, second, etc. 'go** (*BrE*) at the first, second, etc. attempt: *I passed my driving test first go.* **have a 'go** (*informal, especially BrE*) to attack sb physically: *There were about seven of them standing round him, all waiting to have a go.* **have a 'go (at sth/at doing sth)** to make an attempt to do sth: *'I can't start the engine.' 'Let me have a go.'* ◇ *I'll have a go at fixing it tonight.* **have a 'go at sb** (*informal, BrE*) to criticize sb or complain about sb: *The boss had a go at me for being late for work.* **have sth on the 'go** (*BrE, informal*) to be in the middle of an activity or a project: *The award-winning novelist often has three or four books on the go at once.* **in one 'go** (*informal*) all together on one occasion: *I'd rather do the journey in one go, and not stop on the way.* ◇ *They ate the packet of biscuits all in one go.* **make a 'go of sth** (*informal*) to be successful in sth: *We've had a few problems in our marriage, but we're both determined to make a go of it.* ➲ more at LEAVE *v.*, LET *v.*

goad /ɡəʊd; *NAmE* ɡoʊd/ *verb, noun*

■ ***verb*** to keep irritating or annoying sb/sth until they react: **~ sb/sth** *Goaded beyond endurance, she turned on him and hit out.* ◇ **~ sb/sth into sth/into doing sth** *He finally goaded her into answering his question.*

PHR V ˌ**goad sb↔'on** to drive or encourage sb to do sth: *The boxers were goaded on by the shrieking crowd.*

■ ***noun* 1** a pointed stick used for making cows, etc. move forwards **2** something that makes sb do sth, usually by annoying them

'**go-ahead** *noun, adj.*

■ ***noun* the go-ahead** [sing.] (*informal*) permission for sb to start doing sth: *The council has **given the go-ahead** to start building.*

■ ***adj.*** [usually before noun] willing to try new ideas, methods, etc. and therefore likely to succeed: *a go-ahead company*

goal ⊶ AW /ɡəʊl; *NAmE* ɡoʊl/ *noun*

1 ⊶ (in sports) a frame with a net into which players must kick or hit the ball in order to score a point: *He headed the ball into an open goal* (= one that had nobody defending it). ◇ *Who is **in goal*** (= is the goalkeeper) *for Arsenal?* ➲ VISUAL VOCAB page V36 **2** ⊶ the act of kicking or hitting the ball into the goal; a point that is scored for this: *The **winning goal** was scored by Hill.* ◇ *Liverpool won by three goals to one.* ◇ *United conceded two goals in the first half.* ◇

a penalty goal ➲ see also DROP GOAL, GOLDEN GOAL, OWN GOAL **3** ⚷ something that you hope to achieve **SYN aim**: *to work towards a goal* ◇ *to **achieve/attain a goal*** ◇ *You need to **set yourself** some long-term **goals**.* ◇ *Our **ultimate goal** must be the preservation of the environment.* ➲ SYNONYMS at TARGET

goal·keep·er /ˈɡəʊlkiːpə(r); *NAmE* ˈɡoʊl-/ (also *informal* **goalie** /ˈɡəʊli; *NAmE* ˈɡoʊli/) (*NAmE* also **goal·tend·er**) (also *BrE informal* **keeper**) *noun* (in football (SOCCER), HOCKEY, etc.) a player whose job is to stop the ball from going into his or her own team's goal ➲ VISUAL VOCAB page V36 ▶ **goal·keep·ing** *noun* [U]: *goalkeeping techniques*

ˈ**goal kick** *noun* (in football (SOCCER)) a kick taken by one team after the ball has been kicked over their GOAL LINE by the other team without a goal being scored

goal·less /ˈɡəʊlləs; *NAmE* ˈɡoʊl-/ *adj.* [usually before noun] without either team scoring a goal: (*BrE*) *The match ended in a goalless draw.*

ˈ**goal line** *noun* (in football, HOCKEY, etc.) the line at either end of a sports field on which the goal stands or which the ball must cross to score a goal or TOUCHDOWN

goal·mouth /ˈɡəʊlmaʊθ; *NAmE* ˈɡoʊl-/ *noun* the area directly in front of a goal

ˈ**goal poacher** *noun* = POACHER (3)

goal·post /ˈɡəʊlpəʊst; *NAmE* ˈɡoʊlpoʊst/ (also **post**) *noun* one of the two vertical posts that form part of a goal
IDM **move, etc. the ˈgoalposts** (*BrE, informal, disapproving*) to change the rules for sth, or conditions under which it is done, so that the situation becomes more difficult for sb

goal·scorer /ˈɡəʊlskɔːrə(r); *NAmE* ˈɡoʊl-/ *noun* a player in a sports game who scores a goal

goal·tend·er /ˈɡəʊltendə(r); *NAmE* ˈɡoʊl-/ *noun* (*NAmE*) = GOALKEEPER

ˈ**go-around** (also ˈ**go-round**) *noun* **1** (*technical*) a path taken by a plane after an unsuccessful attempt at landing, in order to get into a suitable position to try to land again **2** (*NAmE, informal*) a disagreement or argument

goat /ɡəʊt; *NAmE* ɡoʊt/ *noun* **1** an animal with horns and a coat of hair, that lives wild in mountain areas or is kept on farms for its milk or meat: *a mountain goat* ◇ ***goat's milk/cheese*** ➲ see also BILLY GOAT, KID, NANNY GOAT **2 old ~** (*informal*) an unpleasant old man who is annoying in a sexual way
IDM **get sb's ˈgoat** (*informal*) to annoy sb very much ➲ more at SHEEP

goatee /ɡəʊˈtiː; *NAmE* ɡoʊ-/ *noun* a small pointed beard (= hair growing on a man's face) that is grown only on the chin ➲ VISUAL VOCAB page V49

goat·herd /ˈɡəʊthɜːd; *NAmE* ˈɡoʊthɜːrd/ *noun* a person whose job is to take care of a group of goats

goat·skin /ˈɡəʊtskɪn; *NAmE* ˈɡoʊt-/ *noun* [U] leather made from the skin of a goat

gob /ɡɒb; *NAmE* ɡɑːb/ *noun, verb*
▪ ***noun*** (*slang*) **1** (*BrE*) a rude way of referring to a person's mouth: *Shut your gob!* (= a rude way of telling sb to be quiet) **2** a small amount of a thick wet substance: *Gobs of spittle ran down his chin.* **3** [usually pl.] (*NAmE*) a large amount of sth: *great gobs of cash*
▪ ***verb*** (**-bb-**) [I] (*BrE, slang*) to blow SALIVA out of your mouth **SYN spit**

gob·bet /ˈɡɒbɪt; *NAmE* ˈɡɑːb-/ *noun* (*old-fashioned*) **~ (of sth)** a small amount of sth: *gobbets of food*

gob·ble /ˈɡɒbl; *NAmE* ˈɡɑːbl/ *verb* **1** [T, I] to eat sth very fast, in a way that people consider rude or GREEDY **SYN wolf**: **~ (sth)** *Don't gobble your food like that!* ◇ **~ sth up/down** *They gobbled down all the sandwiches.* **2** [I] when a TURKEY **gobbles**, it makes a noise in its throat
PHR V ˌ**gobble sth**↔ˈ**up** (*informal*) **1** to use sth very quickly: *Hotel costs gobbled up most of their holiday budget.* **2** if a business company, etc. **gobbles up** a smaller one, it takes control of it

gobble·de·gook (also **gobble·dy·gook**) /ˈɡɒbldiɡuːk; *NAmE* ˈɡɑːbl-/ *noun* [U] (*informal*) complicated language that is difficult to understand, especially when used in official documents: *It's all gobbledegook to me.*

ˈ**go-between** *noun* [C, U] a person who takes messages between one person or group and another: *to act as (a) go-between*

gob·let /ˈɡɒblət; *NAmE* ˈɡɑːb-/ *noun* a cup for wine, usually made of glass or metal, with a STEM and base but no handle

gob·lin /ˈɡɒblɪn; *NAmE* ˈɡɑːb-/ *noun* (in stories) a small ugly creature that likes to trick people or cause trouble

gob·shite /ˈɡɒbʃaɪt; *NAmE* ˈɡɑːb-/ *noun* (*BrE, taboo, slang*) a stupid person who talks nonsense

gob·smacked /ˈɡɒbsmækt; *NAmE* ˈɡɑːb-/ *adj.* (*BrE, informal*) so surprised that you do not know what to say

gob·stop·per /ˈɡɒbstɒpə(r); *NAmE* ˈɡɑːbstɑːpər/ (*BrE*) (*NAmE* **jaw·break·er**) *noun* a very large hard round sweet/candy

G

goby /ˈɡəʊbi; *NAmE* ˈɡoʊ-/ *noun* (*pl.* **goby** or **gob·ies**) a small sea fish with a SUCKER underneath

ˈ**go-cart** *noun* (*especially NAmE*) = GO-KART

god ⚷ /ɡɒd; *NAmE* ɡɑːd/ *noun*
1 ⚷ **God** [sing.] (not used with *the*) (in Christianity, Islam and Judaism) the BEING or spirit that is worshipped and is believed to have created the universe: *Do you **believe in God**?* ◇ *Good luck and **God bless you**.* ◇ *the Son of God* (= Christ) ➲ COLLOCATIONS at RELIGION **2** ⚷ [C] (in some religions) a BEING or spirit who is believed to have power over a particular part of nature or who is believed to represent a particular quality: *Mars was the Roman god of war.* ◇ *the rain god* ◇ *Greek gods* ➲ see also GODDESS **3** [C] a person who is loved or admired very much by other people: *To her fans she's a god.* ➲ see also GODDESS **4** [C] something to which too much importance or attention is given: *Money is his god.* **5 the gods** [pl.] (*BrE, informal*) the seats that are high up at the back of a theatre
IDM **by ˈGod!** (*old-fashioned, informal*) used to emphasize a feeling of determination or surprise **HELP** Some people find this use offensive. **God** | **God alˈmighty** | **God in ˈheaven** | **good ˈGod** | **my ˈGod** | **oh (dear) ˈGod** ⚷ (*informal*) used to emphasize what you are saying when you are surprised, shocked or annoyed: *God, what a stupid thing to do!* **HELP** Some people find this use offensive. **God ˈbless** used when you are leaving sb, to say that you hope they will be safe, etc.: *Goodnight, God bless.* **God ˌrest his/her ˈsoul** | **God ˈrest him/her** (*old-fashioned, informal*) used to show respect when you are talking about sb who is dead **God's gift (to sb/sth)** (*ironic*) a person who thinks that they are particularly good at sth or who thinks that sb will find them particularly attractive: *He seems to think he's God's gift to women.* **God ˈwilling** (*informal*) used to say that you hope that things will happen as you have planned and that there will be no problems: *I'll be back next week, God willing.* **play ˈGod** to behave as if you control events or other people's lives: *It is unfair to ask doctors to play God and end someone's life.* **to ˈGod/ˈgoodness/ˈHeaven** used after a verb to emphasize a particular hope, wish, etc.: *I wish to God you'd learn to pay attention!* **HELP** Some people find this use offensive. **ye ˈgods!** (*old-fashioned, informal*) used to show surprise, lack of belief, etc. ➲ more at ACT *n.*, FEAR *n.*, FORBID, GRACE *n.*, HELP *v.*, HONEST, KNOW *v.*, LAP *n.*, LOVE *n.*, MAN *n.*, NAME *n.*, PLEASE *v.*, THANK

ˈ**God-awful** *adj.* [usually before noun] (*informal*) extremely bad: *He made a God-awful mess of it!* **HELP** Some people find this use offensive.

god·child /ˈɡɒdtʃaɪld; *NAmE* ˈɡɑːd-/ *noun* (*pl.* **god·children** /ˈɡɒdtʃɪldrən; *NAmE* ˈɡɑːd-/) a child that a GODPARENT at a Christian BAPTISM ceremony promises to be responsible for and to teach about the Christian religion

god·dam (also **god·damn**) /ˈɡɒddæm; *NAmE* ˈɡɑːd-/ (also **god·damned** /ˈɡɒddæmd; *NAmE* ˈɡɑːd-/) *adj., adv.* (*taboo, slang*) a swear word that many people find offensive, used to show that you are angry or annoyed: *There's no need to be so goddam rude!* ◇ *Where's that goddamned pen?*

ˈgod-daughter *noun* a female GODCHILD

god·dess /ˈɡɒdes; -əs; *NAmE* ˈɡɑːdəs/ *noun* **1** a female god: *Diana, the goddess of hunting* **2** a woman who is loved or admired very much by other people: *a screen goddess* (= a female film/movie star)

god·father /ˈɡɒdfɑːðə(r); *NAmE* ˈɡɑːd-/ *noun* **1** a male GODPARENT **2** (often **Godfather**) a very powerful man in a criminal organization, especially the Mafia **3** **~ of sth** a person who began or developed sth: *He's the godfather of punk.*

ˈGod-fearing *adj.* [usually before noun] (*old-fashioned*) living a moral life based on religious principles

god·for·saken /ˈɡɒdfəseɪkən; *NAmE* ˈɡɑːdfər-/ *adj.* [only before noun] (of places) boring, depressing and ugly: *I can't stand living in this godforsaken hole.*

ˈGod-given *adj.* [usually before noun] given or created by God: *a God-given talent* ◇ *What gives you* ***a God-given right*** *to know all my business?*

god·head /ˈɡɒdhed; *NAmE* ˈɡɑːd-/ *noun* **the Godhead** [sing.] (*formal*) used in the Christian religion to mean God, including the Father, Son and HOLY SPIRIT

god·less /ˈɡɒdləs; *NAmE* ˈɡɑːd-/ *adj.* [usually before noun] not believing in or respecting God: *a godless generation/world* ▶ **god·less·ness** *noun* [U]

god·like /ˈɡɒdlaɪk; *NAmE* ˈɡɑːd-/ *adj.* like God or a god in some quality: *his godlike beauty*

godly /ˈɡɒdli; *NAmE* ˈɡɑːdli/ *adj.* [usually before noun] (*old-fashioned*) living a moral life based on religious principles: *a godly man* ▶ **god·li·ness** *noun* [U]

god·mother /ˈɡɒdmʌðə(r); *NAmE* ˈɡɑːd-/ *noun* a female GODPARENT ➲ see also FAIRY GODMOTHER

go·down /ˈɡəʊdaʊn; *NAmE* ˈɡoʊ-/ *noun* (*IndE*) a WAREHOUSE (= building where goods are stored)

god·par·ent /ˈɡɒdpeərənt; *NAmE* ˈɡɑːdperənt/ *noun* a person who promises at a Christian BAPTISM ceremony to be responsible for a child (= his or her GODCHILD) and to teach them about the Christian religion

ˌGod ˌSave the ˈKing/ˈQueen *noun* [U] the British national ANTHEM (= song)

ˈGod's country *noun* (*NAmE*) a beautiful and peaceful area that people love. Americans often use the expression to mean the US, especially the western states.

god·send /ˈɡɒdsend; *NAmE* ˈɡɑːd-/ *noun* [sing.] **~ (for sb/sth)** | **~ (to sb/sth)** something good that happens unexpectedly and helps sb/sth when they need help: *This new benefit has come as a godsend for low-income families.*

god·son /ˈɡɒdsʌn; *NAmE* ˈɡɑːd-/ *noun* a male GODCHILD

the ˈGod squad *noun* [sing.] (*informal, disapproving*) Christians, especially ones who try to make people share their beliefs

goer /ˈɡəʊə(r); *NAmE* ˈɡoʊər/ *noun* **1** **-goer** (in compounds) a person who regularly goes to the place or event mentioned: *a cinema-goer* ◇ *a moviegoer* **2** (*BrE, informal*) a woman who enjoys having sex frequently, especially with different men

ˌgo-faster ˈstripes *noun* [pl.] (*informal*) **1** coloured lines that can be stuck on the sides of cars **2** (*disapproving*) features that are added to a product to attract attention but which actually have no practical use

gofer (also **go·pher**) /ˈɡəʊfə(r); *NAmE* ˈɡoʊ-/ *noun* (*informal*) a person whose job is to do small boring tasks for other people in a company **SYN** **dogsbody**: *They call me the gofer—go for this, go for that…*

ˈgo-getter *noun* (*informal*) a person who is determined to succeed, especially in business

gogga /ˈxɒxə; ˈxɒxɒ; *NAmE* ˈxɑː-; ˈxɔːxɔː/ *noun* (*SAfrE, informal*) an insect

gog·gle /ˈɡɒɡl; *NAmE* ˈɡɑːɡl/ *verb* [I] **~ (at sb/sth)** (*old-fashioned, informal*) to look at sb/sth with your eyes wide open, especially because you are surprised or shocked

ˈgoggle-box *noun* (*BrE, old-fashioned, informal*) a television

ˌgoggle-ˈeyed *adj.* with your eyes wide open, staring at sth, especially because you are surprised

gog·gles /ˈɡɒɡlz; *NAmE* ˈɡɑːɡlz/ *noun* [pl.] a pair of glasses that fit closely to the face to protect the eyes from wind, dust, water, etc: *a pair of* ***swimming/ski/safety goggles*** ➲ VISUAL VOCAB page V39

ˈgo-go *adj.* **1** connected with a style of dancing to pop music in which women dance wearing very few clothes: *a go-go dancer* **2** (*NAmE, informal*) of a period of time when businesses are growing and people are making money fast: *the go-go years of the 1990s*

gogo /ˈɡɔːɡɔː/ *noun* (*SAfrE*) **1** a grandmother **2** the title for an older woman that is polite and shows affection

going /ˈɡəʊɪŋ; *NAmE* ˈɡoʊɪŋ/ *noun, adj.*

■ ***noun*** **1** [sing.] (*formal*) an act of leaving a place **SYN** **departure**: *We were all sad at her going.* **2** [U] (used with an adjective) the speed with which sb does sth; how difficult it is to do sth: *Walking four miles in an hour is pretty* ***good going*** *for me.* ◇ *She had her own company by 25—not* ***bad going!*** ◇ *It was* ***hard going*** *getting up at five every morning.* **3** [U] the condition of the ground, especially in horse racing: *The going is good to firm.* ➲ see also OUTGOINGS

IDM **when the ˌgoing gets ˈtough (the ˌtough get ˈgoing)** (*saying*) when conditions or progress become difficult (strong and determined people work even harder to succeed) **while the ˌgoing is ˈgood** (*BrE*) (*NAmE* **while the ˌgetting is ˈgood**) before a situation changes and it is no longer possible to do sth: *Don't you think we should quit while the going is good?* ➲ more at COMING, HEAVY

■ ***adj.*** **-going** (in compounds) going regularly to the place or event mentioned: *the theatre-going public* ➲ see also OCEAN-GOING, ONGOING, OUTGOING

IDM **a ˌgoing conˈcern** a business or an activity that is making a profit and is expected to continue to do well: *He sold the cafe* ***as a going concern.*** **the ˌgoing ˈrate (for sth)** the usual amount of money paid for goods or services at a particular time: *They pay slightly more than the going rate.*

ˌgoing-ˈover *noun* [sing.] (*informal*) **1** a thorough examination of sb/sth: *The garage gave the car a thorough going-over.* **2** a serious physical attack on sb: *The gang gave him a real going-over.*

ˌgoings-ˈon *noun* [pl.] (*informal*) activities or events that are strange, surprising or dishonest: *There were some strange goings-on next door last night.*

goitre (*especially US* **goi·ter**) /ˈɡɔɪtə(r)/ *noun* [U, C] a swelling of the throat caused by a disease of the THYROID GLAND

go-kart (*BrE*) (also **go-cart** *NAmE, BrE*) /ˈɡəʊ kɑːt; *NAmE* ˈɡoʊ kɑːrt/ *noun* a vehicle like a small low car with no roof or doors, used for racing

gold 🔑 /ɡəʊld; *NAmE* ɡoʊld/ *noun, adj.*

■ ***noun*** **1** 🔑 [U] (*symb.* **Au**) a chemical element. Gold is a yellow PRECIOUS METAL used for making coins, jewellery, decorative objects, etc: *a* ***gold bracelet/ring/watch, etc.*** ◇ *18-carat gold* ◇ *the country's gold reserves* ◇ *made of* ***solid/pure gold*** ➲ see also FOOL'S GOLD **2** [U] money, jewellery, etc. that is made of gold: *His wife was dripping with* (= wearing a lot of) *gold.* **3** 🔑 [U, C] the colour of gold: *I love the reds and golds of autumn.* **4** [U, C] = GOLD MEDAL: *The team look set to win Olympic gold.* ◇ *He won three golds and a bronze.*

IDM **ˌall that ˌglitters/ˌglistens is not ˈgold** (*saying*) not everything that seems good, attractive, etc. is actually good, etc. **a crock/pot of ˈgold** a large prize or reward that sb hopes for but is unlikely to get **(as) good as ˈgold** (*informal*) behaving in a way that other people approve of: *The kids have been as good as gold all day.* ➲ more at HEART, STREET, STRIKE *v.*, WORTH *adj.*

■ ***adj.*** 🔑 [only before noun] bright yellow in colour, like gold: *The company name was spelled out in gold letters.*

ˈgold brick *noun* (*US, informal*) a person who is lazy and tries to avoid work by pretending to be ill/sick

gold·brick /ˈɡəʊldbrɪk; *NAmE* ˈɡoʊld-/ *verb* [I] (*US, informal*) to be lazy and try to avoid work by pretending to be ill/sick

ˈgold card *noun* a type of credit card that enables a person to buy more goods and services than a normal card does

gold·crest /ˈɡəʊldkrest; *NAmE* ˈɡoʊld-/ *noun* a very small bird with yellow feathers sticking up from the top of its head

ˈgold-digger *noun* (*informal, disapproving*) a person who uses the fact that he or she is attractive to get money from a relationship with sb

ˌgold ˈdisc *noun* a gold record that is given to a singer or group that sells a particularly high number of records

ˈgold dust *noun* [U] gold in the form of powder
IDM **like ˈgold dust** (*BrE*) difficult to find or obtain: *Tickets for the final are like gold dust.*

gold·en /ˈɡəʊldən; *NAmE* ˈɡoʊldən/ *adj.* **1** (especially *literary*) made of gold: *a golden crown* **2** bright yellow in colour like gold: *golden hair* ◇ *miles of golden beaches* **3** special; wonderful: *golden memories* ◇ *Businesses have a* ***golden opportunity*** *to expand into new markets.* ◇ *Hollywood's* ***golden boy***
IDM **be ˈgolden** (*NAmE, informal*) in a situation where you are successful or do not have any problems: *He thinks once he gets the money he'll be golden.* ➲ more at KILL *v.*, MEAN *n.*, SILENCE *n.*

ˈgolden age *noun* [usually sing.] **~ (of sth)** a period during which sth is very successful, especially in the past: *the golden age of cinema*

ˌgolden ˈager *noun* (*informal*) an old person

ˌgolden anniˈversary *noun* (*US*) **1** (*BrE* **ˌgolden ˈjubilee**) the 50th anniversary of an important event **2** (*BrE* **ˌgolden ˈwedding**) (also **ˌgolden ˈwedding anniversary** *NAmE, BrE*) the 50th anniversary of a wedding

ˌgolden ˈeagle *noun* a large BIRD OF PREY (= a bird that kills other creatures for food) of the EAGLE family, with brownish feathers, that lives in northern parts of the world ➲ VISUAL VOCAB page V10

ˌgolden ˈgoal *noun* (in some football (SOCCER) competitions) the first goal scored during EXTRA TIME, which ends the game and gives victory to the team that scores the goal

ˌgolden ˈgoose *noun* something that provides sb with a lot of money, that they must be very careful with in order not to lose it: *An increase in crime could kill the golden goose of tourism.*

ˌgolden ˈhandcuffs *noun* [pl.] a large sum of money and other financial benefits that are given to sb to persuade them to continue working for a company rather than leaving to work for another company

ˌgolden ˈhandshake *noun* a large sum of money that is given to sb when they leave their job, or to persuade them to leave their job

ˌgolden helˈlo *noun* a large sum of money that is given to sb for accepting a job

ˌgolden ˈjubilee (*BrE*) (*US* **ˌgolden anniˈversary**) *noun* the 50th anniversary of an important event: *Queen Victoria's Golden Jubilee celebrations* ◇ *a party to mark the company's golden jubilee* ➲ compare DIAMOND JUBILEE, SILVER JUBILEE

ˌgolden ˈoldie *noun* (*informal*) **1** a song or film/movie that is quite old but still well known and popular **2** a person who is no longer young but still successful in their particular career, sport, etc.

ˌgolden ˈparachute *noun* (*informal*) part of a work contract in which a business person is promised a large amount of money if they have to leave their job

ˌgolden ˈraisin (*NAmE*) (*BrE* **sul·tana**) *noun* a small dried GRAPE without seeds, used in cakes, etc.

ˌgolden reˈtriever *noun* a large dog with thick yellow hair

ˌgolden ˈrule *noun* [usually sing.] an important principle that should be followed when doing sth in order to be successful: *The golden rule in tennis is to keep your eye on the ball.*

ˌgolden ˈsection *noun* (*technical*) the proportion that is considered to be the most attractive to look at when a line is divided into two

ˌgolden ˈsyrup (also **trea·cle**) (both *BrE*) *noun* [U] a very sweet thick yellow liquid made from sugar

ˌgolden ˈwedding (*BrE*) (*US* **ˌgolden anniˈversary**) (also **ˌgolden ˈwedding anniversary** *NAmE, BrE*) *noun* the 50th anniversary of a wedding: *The couple celebrated their golden wedding in January.* ➲ compare DIAMOND WEDDING, RUBY WEDDING, SILVER WEDDING

gold·field /ˈɡəʊldfiːld; *NAmE* ˈɡoʊld-/ *noun* an area where gold is found in the ground

gold·finch /ˈɡəʊldfɪntʃ; *NAmE* ˈɡoʊld-/ *noun* a small brightly coloured European bird of the FINCH family, with yellow feathers on its wings

gold·fish /ˈɡəʊldfɪʃ; *NAmE* ˈɡoʊld-/ *noun* (*pl.* **gold·fish**) a small orange or red fish. Goldfish are kept as pets in bowls or PONDS.

ˈgoldfish bowl (also **fish·bowl**) *noun* **1** a glass bowl for keeping fish in as pets **2** a situation in which people can see everything that happens and nothing is private: *Living in this goldfish bowl of publicity would crack the strongest marriage.*

ˌgold ˈleaf (also **ˌgold ˈfoil**) *noun* [U] gold that has been made into a very thin sheet and is used for decoration

ˌgold ˈmedal *noun* (also **gold**) a MEDAL made of gold that is given to the winner of a race or competition: *an Olympic gold medal winner* ➲ compare BRONZE MEDAL, SILVER MEDAL ▶ **ˌgold ˈmedallist** (*BrE*) (*NAmE* **ˌgold ˈmedalist**) *noun*: *an Olympic gold medallist*

ˈgold mine *noun* **1** a place where gold is dug out of the ground **2** a business or an activity that makes a large profit: *This restaurant is a potential gold mine.*

ˌgold ˈplate *noun* [U] **1** dishes, etc. made of gold **2** a thin layer of gold used to cover another metal; objects made in this way

ˌgold-ˈplated *adj.* covered with a thin layer of gold: *gold-plated earrings*

ˈgold reserve *noun* [usually pl.] an amount of gold kept by a country's bank in order to support the supply of money

ˈgold rush *noun* a situation in which a lot of people suddenly go to a place where gold has recently been discovered

gold·smith /ˈɡəʊldsmɪθ; *NAmE* ˈɡoʊld-/ *noun* a person who makes, repairs or sells articles made of gold

ˈgold standard *noun* **1** (usually **the gold standard**) [sing.] an economic system in which the value of money is based on the value of gold **2** [usually sing.] a high level of quality that others try to copy: *Articles like his are the gold standard of news reporting.*

golem /ˈɡəʊləm; ˈɡɔɪ-; *NAmE* ˈɡoʊ-/ *noun* **1** (in Jewish stories) a figure made of CLAY that comes to life **2** a machine that behaves like a human

golf /ɡɒlf; *NAmE* ɡɑːlf; ɡɔːlf/ *noun* [U] a game played over a large area of ground using specially shaped sticks to hit a small hard ball (a **golf ball**) into a series of 9 or 18 holes, using as few strokes as possible: *He enjoyed a* ***round of golf*** *on a Sunday morning.* ➲ see also CRAZY GOLF, MINI-GOLF ➲ VISUAL VOCAB page V34

ˈgolf club *noun* **1** (also **club**) a long metal stick with a piece of metal or wood at one end, used for hitting the ball in golf: *a set of golf clubs* ➲ VISUAL VOCAB page V34 **2** an organization whose members play golf; the place where these people meet and play golf: *Pine Ridge Golf Club* ◇ *We're going for lunch at the golf club.*

ˈgolf course (also **course**) *noun* a large area of land that is designed for playing golf on ➲ VISUAL VOCAB page V34

G

papers that tries to shock or excite readers rather than to give true information

golf·er /ˈɡɒlfə(r); *NAmE* ˈɡɑːl-; ˈɡɔːl-/ *noun* a person who plays golf ➲ VISUAL VOCAB page V34

golf·ing /ˈɡɒlfɪŋ; *NAmE* ˈɡɑːlf-; ˈɡɔːlf-/ *adj.* [only before noun] playing golf; connected with golf: *a golfing holiday* ▸ **golf·ing** *noun* [U]: *a week's golfing with friends*

ˈ**golf links** (also **links**) *noun* (*pl.* **golf links**) a golf course, especially one by the sea

Gol·iath /ɡəˈlaɪəθ/ *noun* a person or thing that is very large or powerful: *a Goliath of a man* ◇ *a Goliath of the computer industry* ORIGIN From **Goliath**, a giant in the Bible who is killed by the boy David with a stone.

gol·li·wog /ˈɡɒliwɒɡ; *NAmE* ˈɡɑːliwɑːɡ/ (also *informal* **golly** /ˈɡɒli; *NAmE* ˈɡɑːli/ *pl.* **-ies**) *noun* a DOLL (= a model of a person for a child to play with) made of cloth with a black face and short black hair, now often considered offensive to black people

G

golly /ˈɡɒli; *NAmE* ˈɡɑːli/ *exclamation* (*old-fashioned, informal*) used to express surprise: *Golly, you're early!*

gonad /ˈɡəʊnæd; *NAmE* ˈɡoʊ-/ *noun* (*anatomy*) a male sex organ that produces SPERM; a female sex organ that produces eggs

gon·dola /ˈɡɒndələ; *NAmE* ˈɡɑːn-; ɡɑːnˈdoʊlə/ *noun* **1** a long boat with a flat bottom and high parts at each end, used on CANALS in Venice ➲ VISUAL VOCAB page V45 **2** the part on a CABLE CAR or SKI LIFT where the passengers sit **3** (*especially NAmE*) the part of a hot air BALLOON or AIRSHIP where the passengers sit

gon·do·lier /ˌɡɒndəˈlɪə(r); *NAmE* ˌɡɑːndəˈlɪr/ *noun* a person whose job is to move and steer a gondola in Venice ➲ VISUAL VOCAB page V45

Gon·dwana /ɡɒnˈdwɑːnə; *NAmE* ɡɑːn-/ (also **Gon·dwana·land** /ɡɒnˈdwɑːnəlænd; *NAmE* ɡɑːn-/) *noun* [sing.] (*geology*) a very large area of land that existed in the southern HEMISPHERE millions of years ago. It was made up of the present Arabia, S America, Antarctica, Australia and India.

gone /ɡɒn; *NAmE* ɡɔːn/ *adj., prep.* ➲ see also GO *v.*

■ ***adj.*** [not before noun] **1** (of a thing) used up: *'Where's the coffee?' 'It's all gone.'* **2** (of a person) having left a place; away from a place: *'Is Tom here?' 'No, he was gone before I arrived'.* **3** (*formal*) used to say that a particular situation no longer exists: *The days are gone when you could leave your door unlocked at night.* **4** (*BrE, informal*) having been pregnant for the length of time mentioned: *She's seven months gone.* ◇ *How far gone are you?*

IDM ˌ**going**, ˌ**going**, ˈ**gone** (*BrE*) (also **going** ˈ**once, going** ˈ**twice**, ˈ**sold** *NAmE, BrE*) said by an AUCTIONEER to show that an item has been sold ➲ more at DEAD *adj.*

■ ***prep.*** (*BrE, informal*) later than the time mentioned SYN **past**: *It's gone six already.*

goner /ˈɡɒnə(r); *NAmE* ˈɡɔːn-/ *noun* (*informal*) a person who is going to die soon or who cannot be saved from a dangerous situation: *We were frantic. We thought you were a goner.*

gong /ɡɒŋ; *NAmE* ɡɑːŋ; ɡɔːŋ/ *noun* **1** a round piece of metal that hangs in a frame and makes a loud deep sound when it is hit with a stick. Gongs are used as musical instruments or to give signals, for example that a meal is ready. **2** (*BrE, informal*) an award or MEDAL given to sb for the work they have done

gonna /ˈɡənə; ˈɡɒnə; *NAmE* ˈɡɔːnə/ (*informal, non-standard*) a way of saying or writing 'going to' in informal speech, when it refers to the future: *What's she gonna do now?* HELP You should not write this form unless you are copying somebody's speech.

go·nor·rhoea (*BrE*) (*NAmE* **go·nor·rhea**) /ˌɡɒnəˈrɪə; *NAmE* ˌɡɑːnəˈriːə/ *noun* [U] a disease of the sexual organs, caught by having sex with an infected person ➲ see also VENEREAL DISEASE

gonzo journalism /ˈɡɒnzəʊ dʒɜːnəlɪzəm; *NAmE* ˈɡɑːnzoʊ dʒɜːrn-/ *noun* [U] (*NAmE, informal*) reporting in news-papers that tries to shock or excite readers rather than to give true information

goo /ɡuː/ *noun* [U] (*informal*) any unpleasant sticky wet substance ➲ see also GOOEY

good 🔑 /ɡʊd/ *adj., noun, adv.*

■ ***adj.*** (**bet·ter** /ˈbetə(r)/, **best** /best/)

▸ HIGH QUALITY **1** 🔑 of high quality or an acceptable standard: *a good book* ◇ *good food* ◇ *The piano was in good condition.* ◇ *Your work is just not good enough.* ◇ *The results were pretty good.* ◇ *Sorry, my English is not very good.* ◇ *This is* ***as good a*** *place* ***as any*** *to spend the night.* ◇ *You'll never marry her—she's much too good for you.*

▸ PLEASANT **2** 🔑 pleasant; that you enjoy or want: *Did you have a* ***good time*** *in London?* ◇ *It's good to see you again.* ◇ *This is very* ***good news.*** ◇ *Let's hope we have good weather tomorrow.* ◇ *We are still friends, though, which is good.* ◇ ***It's a good thing*** (= it's lucky) *you came early.*

▸ SENSIBLE/STRONG **3** 🔑 sensible, logical or strongly supporting what is being discussed: *Thank you,* ***good question.*** ◇ *Yes, that's a* ***good point.*** ◇ *I have* ***good reason*** *to be suspicious.* ◇ *What a* ***good idea!***

▸ FAVOURABLE **4** 🔑 showing or getting approval or respect: *The play had good reviews.* ◇ *The hotel has a good reputation.* ◇ *He comes from a good family.*

▸ SKILFUL **5** 🔑 able to do sth well: *to be a good actor/cook* ◇ **~ at sth** *to be good at languages/your job* ◇ **~ at doing sth** *Nick has always been good at finding cheap flights.* **6** 🔑 **~ with sth/sb** able to use sth or deal with people well: *She's good with her hands* (= able to make things, etc.). ◇ *He's very good with children.*

▸ MORALLY RIGHT **7** 🔑 morally right; behaving in a way that is morally right: *She has tried to lead a* ***good life.*** ◇ *a* ***good deed*** ◇ *Giving her that money was a good thing to do.* ◇ *He is a very good man.*

▸ FOLLOWING RULES **8** 🔑 following strictly a set of rules or principles: *It is* ***good practice*** *to supply a written report to the buyer.* ◇ *She was a good Catholic girl.*

▸ KIND **9** 🔑 willing to help; showing kindness to other people: **~** (**to sb**) *He was very good to me when I was ill.* ◇ **~** (**of sb**) (**to do sth**) *It was very good of you to come.* ◇ **~** (**about sth**) *I had to take a week off work but my colleagues were very good about it.*

▸ CHILD **10** 🔑 behaving well or politely: *You can stay up late if you're good.* ◇ *Get dressed now, there's a good girl.*

▸ HEALTHY **11** 🔑 healthy or strong: *Can you speak into my good ear?* ◇ *I don't feel too good today.* ◇ *'How are you?' 'I'm good.'* (= used as a general reply to a greeting)

▸ USEFUL/HELPFUL **12** 🔑 **~** (**for sb/sth**) having a useful or helpful effect on sb/sth: *Too much sun isn't good for you.* ◇ *It's probably good for you to get some criticism now and then.* ◇ (*informal*) *Shut your mouth,* ***if you know what's good for you*** (= used as a threat). **13** 🔑 **no ~ doing sth** | **no ~ to sb** not having a useful or helpful effect: *It's no good complaining—they never listen.* ◇ *This book is no good to me: I need the new edition.*

▸ SUITABLE **14** 🔑 suitable or appropriate: *Now is a good time to buy a house.* ◇ **~ for sth/to do sth** *She would be good for the job.* ◇ **~ for sb** *Can we change our meeting? Monday isn't good* (= convenient) *for me.*

▸ SHOWING APPROVAL **15** 🔑 (*informal*) used to show that you approve of or are pleased about sth that has been said or done, or to show that you want to move on to a new topic of conversation: *'Dinner's ready.' 'Good—I'm starving.'* ◇ *'I got the job.' 'Oh, good.'* ◇ *Good, I think we've come to a decision.* **16** 🔑 [only before noun] (*informal*) used as a form of praise: *Good old Jack!* ◇ *'I've ordered some drinks.' 'Good man!'*

▸ IN EXCLAMATIONS **17** (*informal*) used in exclamations: *Good heavens!* ◇ *Good God!*

▸ LARGE **18** [only before noun] great in number, amount or degree: *a good many people* ◇ *The kitchen is a good size.* ◇ *We spent a good while* (= quite a long time) *looking for the house.* ◇ *He devoted* ***a good deal of*** (= a lot of) *attention to the problem.* ◇ *There's* ***a good chance*** (= it is likely) *that I won't be here next year.*

▸ AT LEAST **19** not less than; rather more than: *We waited for a good hour.* ◇ *It's a good three miles to the station.*

▸ THOROUGH **20** [only before noun] thorough; complete: *We* had a good laugh about it afterwards. ◇ You'll feel better after a good sleep.

▸ AMUSING **21** [usually before noun] amusing: *a* ***good story/ joke*** ◇ *(informal) That's a good one!*

▸ FOR PARTICULAR TIME/DISTANCE **22 ~ for sth** having enough energy, health, strength, etc. to last for a particular length of time or distance: *You're good for* (= you will live) *a few years yet.* **23 ~ for sth** valid for sth: *The ticket is good for three months.*

▸ LIKELY TO PROVIDE **24 ~ for sth** likely to provide sth: *He's always good for a laugh.* ◇ *Bobby should be good for a few drinks.*

IDM Most idioms containing **good** are at the entries for the nouns and verbs in the idioms, for example **(as) good as gold** is at **gold**. **as 'good as** very nearly: *The matter is as good as settled.* ◇ *He as good as called me a coward* (= suggested that I was a coward without actually using the word 'coward'). **as ˌgood as it 'gets** used when you are saying that a situation is not going to get any better **good and...** *(informal)* completely: *I won't go until I'm good and ready.* **a good 'few** several: *There are still a good few empty seats.* **ˌgood for 'you, 'sb, 'them, etc.** *(especially AustralE* **good 'on you, etc.**) *(informal)* used to praise sb for doing sth well: *'I passed first time.' 'Good for you!'*

■ ***noun*** ➲ see also GOODS

▸ MORALLY RIGHT **1** 🔑 [U] behaviour that is morally right or acceptable: *the difference between good and evil* ◇ *Is religion always a force for good?* **2 the good** [pl.] people who live a moral life; people who are admired for the work they do to help other people: *a gathering of the great and the good*

▸ STH HELPFUL **3** 🔑 [U] something that helps sb/sth: *Cuts have been made* ***for the good of the company.*** ◇ *I'm only telling you this* ***for your own good.*** ◇ ***What's the good of*** (= how does it help you) *earning all that money if you don't have time to enjoy it?* ◇ ***What good is it*** *redecorating if you're thinking of moving?* ➲ see also DO-GOODER

IDM ˌ**all to the 'good** used to say that if sth happens, it will be good, even if it is not exactly what you were expecting: *If these measures also reduce unemployment, that is all to the good.* **be no 'good | not be any/much 'good 1** 🔑 to not be useful; to have no useful effect: *This gadget isn't much good.* ◇ *It's no good trying to talk me out of leaving.* ◇ *Was his advice ever any good?* **2** 🔑 to not be interesting or enjoyable: *His latest film isn't much good.* **do 'good | do sb 'good** 🔑 to have a useful effect; to help sb: *Do you think these latest changes will do any good?* ◇ *Don't you think talking to her would do some good?* ◇ *I'm sure a few days off would do you* ***a power of good*** (= improve your health). **for 'good** *(BrE* also **for ˌgood and 'all**) permanently: *This time she's leaving for good* (= she will never return). **to the 'good** used to say that sb now has a particular amount of money that they did not have before: *We are £500 to the good.* **up to no 'good** *(informal)* doing sth wrong or dishonest: *Those kids are always up to no good.* ➲ more at ILL *adj.*, POWER *n.*, WORLD

■ ***adv.*** *(especially NAmE, informal)* well: *'How's it going?' 'Pretty good.'* ◇ *(non-standard) Now, you listen to me good!*

Vocabulary Building

Good and very good

Instead of saying that something is **good** or **very good**, try to use more precise and interesting adjectives to describe things:

- **delicious/tasty** food
- an **exciting/entertaining/absorbing** movie
- an **absorbing**/a **fascinating**/an **informative** book
- a **pleasant**/an **enjoyable** trip
- a **skilful/talented/fine** player
- **impressive/high-quality** acting
- **useful/helpful** advice

In conversation you can use words like **great**, **super**, **wonderful**, **lovely** and **excellent**.

➲ note at NICE

Which Word?

good / goodness

- The noun **good** means actions and behaviour that are morally right. You can talk about a person doing **good**: *The charity does a lot of good.* ◇ *the difference between good and evil.*
- **Goodness** is the quality of being good. You can talk about a person's **goodness**: *Her goodness shone through.*

ˌ**good after'noon** *exclamation* used to say hello politely when people first see each other in the afternoon; in informal use people often just say *Afternoon*.

good·bye 🔑 /ˌɡʊdˈbaɪ/ *exclamation, noun* used when you are leaving sb or when sb else is leaving: *Goodbye! It was great to meet you.* ◇ *She didn't even* ***say goodbye*** *to her mother.* ◇ *We* ***waved*** *them* ***goodbye.*** ◇ *We've already said our goodbyes.* ◇ ***Kiss*** *me* ***goodbye!*** ◇ *(figurative) Take out our service contract and say goodbye to costly repair bills.* ➲ compare BYE IDM see KISS *v.*

ˌ**good 'day** *exclamation (old-fashioned, BrE)* used to say hello or goodbye politely when people first see each other or leave each other during the day: *Good day to you.*

ˌ**good 'evening** *exclamation* used to say hello politely when people first see each other in the evening; in informal use people often just say *Evening*.

good 'faith *noun* [U] the intention to be honest and helpful: *a gesture of good faith* ◇ *He acted* ***in good faith.***

'**good-for-nothing** *noun (informal)* a person who is lazy and has no skills: *an idle good-for-nothing* ▸ '**good-for-nothing** *adj.* [usually before noun]: *Where's that good-for-nothing son of yours?*

ˌ**Good 'Friday** *noun* [U, C] the Friday before Easter, the day when Christians remember the Crucifixion of Christ

ˌ**good-'hearted** *adj.* kind; willing to help other people

ˌ**good 'humour** *(especially US* ˌ**good 'humor**) *noun* [U, sing.] a cheerful mood: *Everyone admired her patience and unfailing good humour.* OPP **ill humour** ▸ ˌ**good-'humoured** *(especially US* ˌ**good-'humored**) *adj.*: *a good-humoured atmosphere* ˌ**good-'humoured·ly** *(especially US* ˌ**good-'humored·ly**) *adv.*

goodie = GOODY

good·ish /ˈɡʊdɪʃ/ *adj.* [only before noun] *(BrE, informal)* **1** quite good rather than very good: *'Is the salary good?' 'Goodish.'* **2** quite large in size or amount: *It'll be a goodish while yet before I've finished.*

ˌ**good-'looking** *adj.* (especially of people) physically attractive OPP **ugly**: *a good-looking man/couple* ◇ *She's strikingly good-looking.* ➲ SYNONYMS at BEAUTIFUL

ˌ**good 'looks** *noun* [pl.] the physical beauty of a person: *an actor famous for his rugged good looks*

good·ly /ˈɡʊdli/ *adj.* [only before noun] **1** *(old-fashioned, formal)* quite large in size or amount: *a goodly number* **2** *(old use)* physically attractive; of good quality

ˌ**good 'morning** *exclamation* used to say hello politely when people first see each other in the morning (in informal use people often just say *Morning* in this case); sometimes also used formally when people leave each other in the morning

ˌ**good 'name** *noun* [sing.] the good opinion that people have of sb/sth SYN **reputation**: *He told the police he didn't know her, to protect her good name.* ◇ *My election chances are not as important as the good name of the party.*

ˌ**good 'nature** *noun* [U] the quality of being kind, friendly and patient when dealing with people

ˌ**good-'natured** *adj.* kind, friendly and patient when dealing with people: *a good-natured person/discussion* ▸ ˌ**good-'natured·ly** *adv.*: *to smile good-naturedly*

G

ˌgood-ˈneighbour·li·ness *noun* [U] (*BrE*) good relations that exist between people who live in the same area or between countries that are near each other

good·ness /ˈɡʊdnəs/ *noun* [U] **1** the quality of being good: *the essential goodness of human nature* ◇ *evidence of God's goodness* ◇ (*formal*) *At least* **have the goodness** (= good manners) *to look at me when I'm talking to you.* ➲ note at GOOD **2** the part of sth that has a useful effect on sb/sth, especially sb's health: *These vegetables have had all the goodness boiled out of them.*

IDM **Goodness!** | **ˌGoodness ˈme!** | **ˌMy ˈgoodness!** | **ˌGoodness ˈgracious!** (*informal*) used to express surprise: *Goodness, what a big balloon!* ◇ *My goodness, you have been busy!* ◇ *Goodness me, no!* **out of the goodness of your ˈheart** from feelings of kindness, without thinking about what advantage there will be for you: *You're not telling me he offered to lend you the money out of the goodness of his heart?* ➲ more at GOD, HONEST, KNOW *v.*, THANK

good·night /ˌɡʊdˈnaɪt/ *exclamation* used when you are saying goodbye to sb late in the evening, or when they or you are going to bed; in informal use people often just say *Night.*

goodo /ˈɡʊdəʊ; *NAmE* -oʊ/ *adj.* (*AustralE, NZE, informal*) good

ˌgood old ˈboy *noun* (*NAmE, informal*) a man who is considered typical of white men in the southern states of the US

goods 🔑 /ɡʊdz/ *noun* [pl.]
1 🔑 things that are produced to be sold: *cheap/expensive goods* ◇ *leather/cotton/paper goods* ◇ *electrical/sports goods* ◇ *perishable/durable goods* ◇ *increased tax on* **goods and services** ➲ see also CONSUMER GOODS ➲ SYNONYMS at PRODUCT **2** 🔑 possessions that can be moved: **stolen goods** ◇ *The plastic bag contained all his* **worldly goods** (= everything he owned). ➲ SYNONYMS at THING **3** (*BrE*) things (not people) that are transported by rail or road: *a goods train* ◇ *a heavy goods vehicle* ➲ compare FREIGHT

IDM **be the ˈgoods** (*BrE, informal*) to be very good or impressive **deliver the ˈgoods** | **come up with the ˈgoods** (*informal*) to do what you have promised to do or what people expect or want you to do: *We expected great things of the England team, but on the day they simply failed to deliver the goods.*

ˌgoods and ˈchattels *noun* [pl.] (*BrE, law*) personal possessions that are not land or buildings

ˌgood ˈsense *noun* [U] ~ **(to do sth)** the ability to make the right decision about sth; good judgement: *a man of honour and good sense* ◇ *Keeping to a low-fat diet* **makes** *very* **good sense** (= is a sensible thing to do).

ˈgoods train *noun* (*BrE*) = FREIGHT TRAIN

ˌgood-ˈtempered *adj.* cheerful and not easily made angry

ˈgood-time *adj.* [only before noun] only interested in pleasure, and not in anything serious or important: *I was too much of a good-time girl to do any serious studying.*

good·will /ˌɡʊdˈwɪl/ *noun* [U] **1** friendly or helpful feelings towards other people or countries: *a spirit of goodwill in international relations* ◇ *a* **goodwill gesture/a gesture of goodwill** **2** the good relationship between a business and its customers that is calculated as part of its value when it is sold

goody /ˈɡʊdi/ *noun, exclamation*
▪ ***noun*** (also **goodie**) [usually pl.] (*pl.* -ies) (*informal*) **1** a thing that is very nice to eat: *a basket of goodies for the children* **2** anything that is attractive and that people want to have: *We're giving away lots of free goodies—T-shirts, hats and DVDs!* **3** a good person, especially in a book or a film/movie: *It's sometimes difficult to tell who are the goodies and who are the baddies.* OPP **baddy**
▪ ***exclamation*** (becoming *old-fashioned*) a word children use when they are excited or pleased about sth

ˈgoody bag (also **ˈgoodie bag**) *noun* **1** a bag containing sweets/candy and small presents, given to children to take home at the end of a party **2** a bag containing examples of a company's products, given away in order to advertise them

ˈgoody-goody *noun* (*pl.* goody-goodies) (*informal, disapproving*) (used especially by and about children) a person who behaves very well to please people in authority such as parents or teachers

ˌgoody-ˈtwo-shoes *noun* (*pl.* goody-two-shoes) (*informal, disapproving*) a person who always behaves well, and perhaps has a disapproving attitude to people who do not

gooey /ˈɡuːi/ *adj.* (*informal*) soft and sticky: *a gooey mess* ◇ *gooey cakes*

goof /ɡuːf/ *verb, noun*
▪ ***verb*** [I] (*informal, especially NAmE*) to make a stupid mistake: *Sorry, guys. I goofed.*

PHR V **ˌgoof aˈround** (*informal, especially NAmE*) to spend your time doing silly or stupid things SYN **mess around** **ˌgoof ˈoff** (*NAmE, informal*) to spend your time doing nothing, especially when you should be working
▪ ***noun*** (*informal, especially NAmE*) **1** a stupid mistake **2** a silly or stupid person

goof·ball /ˈɡuːfbɔːl/ *noun* (*NAmE, informal*) a stupid person ▶ **goof·ball** *adj.* [only before noun]: *This is just another of his goofball ideas.*

ˈgoof-off *noun* (*NAmE, slang*) a person who avoids work or responsibility

goofy /ˈɡuːfi/ *adj.* (*informal, especially NAmE*) silly; stupid: *a goofy grin*

goog /ɡuːɡ/ *noun* (*AustralE, NZE, informal*) an egg

google /ˈɡuːɡl/ *verb* [T, I] ~ **(sb/sth)** (*computing*) to type words into the SEARCH ENGINE Google® in order to find information about sb/sth: *You can google someone you've recently met to see what information is available about them on the Internet.* ◇ *I tried googling but couldn't find anything relevant.*

googly /ˈɡuːɡli/ *noun* (*pl.* -ies) (in CRICKET) a ball that is BOWLED so that it looks as if it will turn in one direction, but that actually turns the opposite way: (*figurative*) *He bowled the prime minister a googly* (= asked him a difficult question).

goo·gol /ˈɡuːɡɒl; *NAmE* -ɡɔːl/ *noun* (*mathematics*) the number 10^{100}, or 1 followed by 100 zeros

gook /ɡuːk/ *noun* **1** [U] (*informal*) any unpleasant sticky wet substance **2** [C] (*NAmE, taboo, slang*) an offensive word for a person from SE Asia

goolie (also **gooly**) /ˈɡuːli/ *noun* [usually pl.] (*pl.* -ies) (*BrE, slang*) a rude word for a man's TESTICLE

goon /ɡuːn/ *noun* (*informal*) **1** (*especially NAmE*) a criminal who is paid to frighten or injure people **2** (*old-fashioned, especially BrE*) a stupid or silly person

goose /ɡuːs/ *noun, verb*
▪ ***noun*** (*pl.* geese /ɡiːs/) **1** [C] a bird like a large DUCK with a long neck. Geese either live wild or are kept on farms. **2** [U] meat from a goose: *roast goose* **3** [C] a female goose ➲ compare GANDER **4** [C] (*old-fashioned, informal*) a silly person ➲ see also WILD GOOSE CHASE IDM see COOK *v.*, KILL *v.*, SAUCE, SAY *v.*
▪ ***verb*** (*informal*) **1** ~ **sb** to touch or squeeze sb's bottom **2** ~ **sth (along/up)** (*NAmE*) to make sth move or work faster

goose·berry /ˈɡʊzbəri; *NAmE* ˈɡuːsberi/ *noun* (*pl.* -ies) a small green fruit that grows on a bush with THORNS. Gooseberries taste sour and are usually cooked to make jam, PIES, etc. Children are sometimes told that babies come from 'under the gooseberry bush': *a gooseberry bush* ➲ VISUAL VOCAB page V26

IDM **play ˈgooseberry** (*BrE*) to be a third person with two people who have a romantic relationship and want to be alone together

goose·bumps /ˈɡuːsbʌmps/ *noun* [pl.] (*especially NAmE*) = GOOSE PIMPLES

ˈgoose egg *noun* (*NAmE, informal*) a score of zero in a game

ˈgoose pimples *noun* [pl.] (also *less frequent* **goose-flesh** [U]) (both *especially BrE*) (also **goose·bumps** especially in *NAmE*) a condition in which there are raised spots on your skin because you feel cold, frightened or excited: *It **gave me goose pimples** just to think about it.*

ˈgoose-step *noun* [sing.] (often *disapproving*) a way of marching, used by soldiers in some countries, in which the legs are raised high and straight ▸ **ˈgoose-step** *verb* (-pp-) [I]

GOP /ˌdʒiː əʊ ˈpiː; *NAmE* oʊ/ *abbr.* Grand Old Party (the Republican political party in the US)

go·pher /ˈɡəʊfə(r); *NAmE* ˈɡoʊ-/ *noun* **1** (also ˈ**ground squirrel**) a N American animal like a RAT, that lives in holes in the ground **2** = GOFER

gora /ˈɡɔːrə/ *noun* (*pl.* **goras** or **goray** /ˈɡɔːreɪ/) a word used by people from S Asia for a white person

Gor·dian knot /ˌɡɔːdiən ˈnɒt; *NAmE* ˌɡɔːrdiən ˈnɑːt/ *noun* a very difficult or impossible task or problem: *to **cut/untie the Gordian knot*** (= to solve a problem by taking action) ORIGIN From the legend in which King Gordius tied a very complicated knot and said that whoever undid it would become the ruler of Asia. Alexander the Great cut through the knot with his sword.

Gor·don Ben·nett /ˌɡɔːdn ˈbenət; *NAmE* ˌɡɔːrd-/ *exclamation* (*BrE*) people sometimes say **Gordon Bennett!** when they are annoyed or surprised about sth ORIGIN From James Gordon Bennett, an American newspaper owner and financial supporter of sports events.

gore /ɡɔː(r)/ *verb, noun*

■ ***verb* ~ sb/sth** (of an animal) to wound a person or another animal with a horn or TUSK: *He was gored by a bull.*

■ ***noun*** [U] thick blood that has flowed from a wound, especially in a violent situation: *The movie is not just **blood and gore*** (= scenes of violence)*; it has a thrilling story.* ➲ see also GORY

Gore·tex™ /ˈɡɔːteks; *NAmE* ˈɡɔːrt-/ *noun* [U] a light material that does not let water through but that allows air and water VAPOUR through, used for making outdoor and sports clothes

gorge /ɡɔːdʒ; *NAmE* ɡɔːrdʒ/ *noun, verb*

■ ***noun*** a deep narrow valley with steep sides SYN **canyon**: *the Rhine Gorge* ➲ VISUAL VOCAB page V4

IDM **sb's ˈgorge rises** (*formal*) somebody feels so angry about sth that they feel physically sick

■ ***verb*** [T, I] **~ (yourself) (on sth)** (sometimes *disapproving*) to eat a lot of sth, until you are too full to eat any more SYN **stuff yourself**

gor·geous /ˈɡɔːdʒəs; *NAmE* ˈɡɔːrdʒəs/ *adj.* **1** (*informal*) very beautiful and attractive; giving pleasure and enjoyment SYN **lovely**: *a gorgeous girl/man* ◇ *a gorgeous view* ◇ *gorgeous weather* (= warm and with a lot of sun) ◇ *You **look gorgeous!*** ◇ *It was **absolutely gorgeous**.* ➲ SYNONYMS at BEAUTIFUL **2** [usually before noun] (of colours, clothes, etc.) with very deep colours; impressive: *exotic birds with feathers of gorgeous colours* ▸ **gor·geous·ly** *adv.*

gor·gon /ˈɡɔːɡən; *NAmE* ˈɡɔːrɡən/ *noun* **1** (in ancient Greek stories) one of three sisters with snakes on their heads instead of hair, who can change anyone that looks at them into stone **2** an ugly woman who behaves in an aggressive and frightening way

Gor·gon·zola /ˌɡɔːɡənˈzəʊlə; *NAmE* ˌɡɔːrɡənˈzoʊlə/ *noun* [U] a type of Italian cheese with blue marks and a strong flavour

gor·illa /ɡəˈrɪlə/ *noun* **1** a very large powerful African APE (= an animal like a large MONKEY without a tail) covered with black or brown hair **2** (*informal*) a large aggressive man

gorm·less /ˈɡɔːmləs; *NAmE* ˈɡɔːrm-/ *adj.* (*BrE, informal*) stupid: *a gormless boy* ◇ *Don't just stand there looking gormless—do something!*

ˈgo-round *noun* = GO-AROUND

gorp /ɡɔːp; *NAmE* ɡɔːrp/ *noun* [U] (*NAmE*) a mixture of nuts, dried fruit, etc. eaten between meals to provide extra energy, especially by people on camping trips, etc.

gorse /ɡɔːs; *NAmE* ɡɔːrs/ (*BrE* also **furze**) *noun* [U] a bush with thin leaves with sharp points and small yellow flowers. Gorse often grows on land that is not used or cared for.

gory /ˈɡɔːri/ *adj.* (**gor·ier**, **gori·est**) **1** (*informal*) involving a lot of blood or violence; showing or describing blood and violence: *a gory accident* ◇ *the gory task of the pathologist* ◇ *a gory movie* ◇ (*humorous*) *He insisted on telling us all the **gory details** about their divorce* (= the unpleasant facts). **2** (*literary*) covered with blood SYN **bloodstained**: *a gory figure*

gosh /ɡɒʃ; *NAmE* ɡɑːʃ/ *exclamation* (*old-fashioned, informal*) people say **'Gosh!'** when they are surprised or shocked: *Gosh, is that the time?*

gos·hawk /ˈɡɒshɔːk; *NAmE* ˈɡɑːs-/ *noun* a large HAWK with short wings

gos·ling /ˈɡɒzlɪŋ; *NAmE* ˈɡɑːz-/ *noun* a young GOOSE (= a bird like a large DUCK)

ˌgo-ˈslow (*BrE*) (*NAmE* **slow·down**) *noun* a protest that workers make by doing their work more slowly than usual ➲ compare WORK-TO-RULE

gos·pel /ˈɡɒspl; *NAmE* ˈɡɑːspl/ *noun* **1** [C] (also **Gospel**) one of the four books in the Bible about the life and teaching of Jesus: *the Gospel according to St John* ◇ *St Mark's Gospel* **2** [sing.] (also **the Gospel**) the life and teaching of Jesus as explained in the Bible: ***preaching/spreading the gospel*** ➲ COLLOCATIONS at RELIGION **3** [C, usually sing.] a set of ideas that sb believes in and tries to persuade others to accept: *He preached a gospel of military strength.* **4** (also ˌ**gospel ˈtruth**) [U] (*informal*) the complete truth: *Is that gospel?* ◇ *Don't take his word as gospel.* **5** (also ˈ**gospel music**) [U] a style of religious singing developed by African Americans: *a gospel choir*

gos·samer /ˈɡɒsəmə(r); *NAmE* ˈɡɑːs-/ *noun* [U] **1** the very fine thread made by spiders **2** (*literary*) any very light delicate material: *a gown of gossamer silk* ◇ *the gossamer wings of a dragonfly*

gos·sip /ˈɡɒsɪp; *NAmE* ˈɡɑːsɪp/ *noun, verb*

■ ***noun*** **1** [U] (*disapproving*) informal talk or stories about other people's private lives, that may be unkind or not true: *Don't believe all the gossip you hear.* ◇ *Tell me all the **latest gossip!*** ◇ *The gossip was that he had lost a fortune on the stock exchange.* ◇ *It was **common gossip*** (= everyone said so) *that they were having an affair.* ◇ *She's a great one for **idle gossip*** (= she enjoys spreading stories about other people that are probably not true). **2** [C, usually sing.] a conversation about other people and their private lives: *I love a good gossip.* ➲ SYNONYMS at DISCUSSION **3** [C] (*disapproving*) a person who enjoys talking about other people's private lives ➲ SYNONYMS at SPEAKER ▸ **gos·sipy** /ˈɡɒsɪpi; *NAmE* ˈɡɑːs-/ *adj.*: *a gossipy letter/neighbour*

■ ***verb*** [I] to talk about other people's private lives, often in an unkind way: *I can't stand here gossiping all day.* ◇ **~ about sb/sth** *She's been gossiping about you.*

ˈgossip column *noun* a piece of writing in a newspaper about social events and the private and personal lives of famous people ▸ ˈ**gossip columnist** *noun*

got *past tense, past part.* of GET

gotcha /ˈɡɒtʃə; *NAmE* ˈɡɑːtʃə/ *exclamation* (*non-standard*) the written form of the way some people pronounce 'I've got you', which is not considered to be correct: *'Gotcha!' I yelled as I grabbed him by the arm.* (= used when you have caught sb, or have beaten them at sth). ◇ *'Don't let go.' 'Yeah, gotcha.'* (= Yes, I understand.) HELP You should not write this form unless you are copying somebody's speech.

goth /ɡɒθ; *NAmE* ɡɑːθ/ *noun* **1** [U] a style of rock music, popular in the 1980s, that developed from PUNK music. The words often expressed ideas about the end of the world, death or the DEVIL. **2** [C] a member of a group of people who listen to goth music and wear black clothes and black and white MAKE-UP ▸ **goth** (also **gothic**) *adj.*

Gotham /ˈɡɒθəm; *NAmE* ˈɡɑːθ-/ *noun* (*informal*) New York City

Goth·ic /ˈɡɒθɪk; *NAmE* ˈɡɑːθ-/ *adj., noun*

■ ***adj.*** **1** connected with the Goths (= a Germanic people

G

who fought against the Roman Empire) **2** (*architecture*) built in the style that was popular in western Europe from the 12th to the 16th centuries, and which has pointed ARCHES and windows and tall thin PILLARS: *a Gothic church* **3** (of a novel, etc.) written in the style popular in the 18th and 19th centuries, which described romantic adventures in mysterious or frightening surroundings **4** (of type and printing) having pointed letters with thick lines and sharp angles. German books used to be printed in this style. **5** connected with goths
▪ ***noun*** [U] **1** the Gothic style of ARCHITECTURE **2** Gothic printing type or printed letters

'go-to *adj.* [only before noun] (*especially NAmE*) used to refer to the person or place that sb goes to for help, advice or information: *He's the president's go-to guy on Asian politics.*

G

gotta /'gɒtə; *NAmE* 'gɑːtə/ (*informal, non-standard*) the written form of the word some people use to mean 'have got to' or 'have got a', which is not considered to be correct: *He's gotta go.* ◇ *Gotta cigarette?* HELP You should not write this form unless you are copying somebody's speech.

got·ten (*NAmE*) *past part.* of GET

gou·ache /gu'ɑːʃ; gwɑːʃ/ *noun* **1** [U] a method of painting using colours that are mixed with water and made thick with a type of glue; the paints used in this method **2** [C] a picture painted using this method

Gouda /'gaʊdə; *NAmE* 'guːdə/ *noun* [U] a type of Dutch cheese that is covered with yellow WAX

gouge /gaʊdʒ/ *verb, noun*
▪ ***verb*** **1** **~ sth (in sth)** to make a hole or cut in sth with a sharp object in a rough or violent way: *The lion's claws had gouged a wound in the horse's side.* ◇ *He had gouged her cheek with a screwdriver.* **2** **~ sb/sth** (*NAmE*) to force sb to pay an unfairly high price for sth; to raise prices unfairly: *Price gouging is widespread.*
PHR V **,gouge sth↔'out (of sth)** to remove or form sth by digging into a surface: *The man's eyes had been gouged out.* ◇ *Glaciers gouged out valleys from the hills.*
▪ ***noun*** **1** a sharp tool for making hollow areas in wood **2** a deep, narrow hole or cut in a surface

gou·jons /'guːdʒənz; 'guːʒ-/ *noun* [pl.] (*BrE*, from *French*) small pieces of fish or chicken fried in oil

gou·lash /'guːlæʃ/ *noun* [C, U] a hot spicy Hungarian dish of meat that is cooked slowly in liquid with PAPRIKA

gourd /gʊəd; gɔːd; *NAmE* gʊrd; gɔːrd/ *noun* a type of large fruit with hard skin and soft flesh. Gourds are often dried and used as containers. ➲ see also CALABASH

gour·mand /'gʊəmənd; *NAmE* 'gʊrmɑːnd/ *noun* (often *disapproving*) a person who enjoys eating and eats large amounts of food

gour·met /'gʊəmeɪ; *NAmE* 'gʊrm-/ *noun* a person who knows a lot about good food and wines and who enjoys choosing, eating and drinking them ▸ **gour·met** *adj.* [only before noun]: *gourmet food* (= of high quality and often expensive)

gout /gaʊt/ *noun* [U] a disease that causes painful swelling in the joints, especially of the toes, knees and fingers

gov·ern 🔑 /'gʌvn; *NAmE* 'gʌvərn/ *verb*
1 🔑 [T, I] **~ (sth)** to legally control a country or its people and be responsible for introducing new laws, organizing public services, etc: *The country is governed by elected representatives of the people.* ◇ *He accused the opposition party of being unfit to govern.* **2** [T, often passive] **~ sth** to control or influence sb/sth or how sth happens, functions, etc: *Prices are governed by market demand.* ◇ *All his decisions have been entirely governed by self-interest.* ◇ *We need changes in the law governing school attendance.* **3** [T] **~ sth** (*grammar*) if a word **governs** another word or phrase, it affects how that word or phrase is formed or used

gov·ern·ance /'gʌvənəns; *NAmE* -vərn-/ *noun* [U] (*technical*) the activity of governing a country or controlling a company or an organization; the way in which a country is governed or a company or institution is controlled

gov·ern·ess /'gʌvənəs; *NAmE* -vərn-/ *noun* (especially in the past), a woman employed to teach the children of a rich family in their home and to live with them ➲ compare TUTOR

gov·ern·ing /'gʌvənɪŋ; *NAmE* -vərn-/ *adj.* [only before noun] having the right and the authority to control sth such as a country or an institution: *The Conservatives were then the* ***governing party.*** ◇ *The school's* ***governing body*** (= the group of people who control the organization of the school) *took responsibility for the decision.*

gov·ern·ment 🔑 /'gʌvənmənt; *NAmE* -vərn-/ *noun*
1 🔑 [C+sing./pl. v.] (often **the Government**) (*abbr.* govt) the group of people who are responsible for controlling a country or a state: *to* ***lead/form a government*** ◇ *the last Conservative government* ◇ *the government of the day* ◇ *Foreign governments have been consulted about this decision.* ◇ *She has resigned from the Government.* ◇ *The Government has/have been considering further tax cuts.* ◇ ***government policies/officials/ministers*** ◇ ***a government department/agency/grant*** ◇ ***government expenditure/intervention*** ➲ COLLOCATIONS at POLITICS **2** 🔑 [U] a particular system or method of controlling a country: ***coalition/communist/democratic/totalitarian, etc.*** *government* ◇ *Democratic government has now replaced military rule.* ◇ ***central/federal government*** **3** 🔑 [U] the activity or the manner of controlling a country: *strong government* ◇ *The Democrats are now* ***in government*** *in the US.* ➲ see also BIG GOVERNMENT

gov·ern·men·tal /ˌgʌvn'mentl; *NAmE* ˌgʌvərn-/ *adj.* connected with government; of a government: *governmental agencies* ◇ *governmental actions*

ˌgovernment and 'binding theory (also **'binding theory**) *noun* [U] (*linguistics*) a theory of grammar based on the idea that a series of conditions relate the parts of a sentence together

ˌgovernment 'health warning *noun* **1** (in Britain) a notice that must by law appear on a product, especially a pack of cigarettes, that warns people that it is dangerous to their health **2** (also **'health warning**) (*BrE*) a warning that sth should be treated carefully because it may cause problems: *These figures should come with a government health warning.*

gov·ern·or 🔑 /'gʌvənə(r); *NAmE* -vərn-/ *noun*
1 🔑 (also **Governor**) a person who is the official head of a country or region that is governed by another country: *the former governor of the colony* ◇ *a provincial governor* **2** 🔑 (also **Governor**) a person who is chosen to be in charge of the government of a state in the US: *the governor of Arizona* ◇ *the Arizona governor* ◇ *Governor Bev Perdue* **3** 🔑 (*especially BrE*) a member of a group of people who are responsible for controlling an institution such as a school, a college or a hospital: *a school governor* ◇ *the board of governors of the college* **4** 🔑 (*BrE*) a person who is in charge of an institution: *a prison governor* ◇ *the governor of the Bank of England* ◇ (*informal*) *I can't decide. I'll have to ask the governor* (= the man in charge, who employs sb). ➲ see also GUV'NOR

ˌGovernor 'General *noun* (*pl.* **Governors General** or **Governor Generals**) the official representative in a country of the country that has or had political control over it, especially the representative of the British King or Queen in a Commonwealth country

govt (also **govt.** especially in *NAmE*) *abbr.* (in writing) government

ˌgo 'well *exclamation* (*SAfrE*) used to say goodbye to sb: *I hope you enjoy your holiday. Go well!*

gown /gaʊn/ *noun* **1** a woman's dress, especially a long one for special occasions: *an* ***evening/wedding gown*** **2** a long loose piece of clothing that is worn over other clothes by judges and (in Britain) by other lawyers, and by members of universities (at special ceremonies): *a graduation gown* **3** a piece of clothing that is worn over other clothes to protect them, especially in a hospital: *a surgeon's gown* ➲ see also DRESSING GOWN

gowned /gaʊnd/ *adj.* wearing a gown

goy /gɔɪ/ *noun* (*pl.* **goy·im** /ˈgɔɪɪm/ or **goys**) (*informal*, often *offensive*) a word used by Jewish people for a person who is not Jewish

GP /ˌdʒiː ˈpiː/ *noun* (*BrE*) the abbreviation for 'general practitioner' (a doctor who is trained in general medicine and who works in the local community, not in a hospital): *Go and see your GP as soon as possible.* ◇ *There are four GPs in our local practice.*

GPA /ˌdʒiː piː ˈeɪ/ *abbr.* (*NAmE*) GRADE POINT AVERAGE: *He graduated with a GPA of 3.8.*

Gp Capt *abbr.* GROUP CAPTAIN

GPRS /ˌdʒiː piː ɑːr ˈes/ *abbr.* general packet radio services (a way of sending electronic data as radio signals, used especially between mobile phones/cell phones and the Internet

GPS /ˌdʒiː piː ˈes/ *abbr.* global positioning system (a system by which signals are sent from SATELLITES to a special device, used to show the position of a person or thing on the surface of the earth very accurately): *The drivers all have GPS in the van.* ➲ compare SATNAV

grab 0-π /græb/ *verb, noun*

■ ***verb*** (**-bb-**) **1** 0-π [T, I] to take or hold sb/sth with your hand suddenly, firmly or roughly SYN **seize**: **~ (sth)** *She grabbed the child's hand and ran.* ◇ *He* ***grabbed hold of*** *me and wouldn't let go.* ◇ *Don't grab—there's plenty for everyone.* ◇ **~ sth from sb/sth** *Jim grabbed a cake from the plate.* **2** 0-π [I] to try to take hold of sth: **~ at sth** *She grabbed at the branch, missed and fell.* ◇ **~ for sth** *Kate grabbed for the robber's gun.* **3** [T, I] to take advantage of an opportunity to do or have sth SYN **seize**: **~ sth** *This was my big chance and I grabbed it with both hands.* ◇ **~ at sth** *He'll grab at any excuse to avoid doing the dishes.* **4** 0-π [T] **~ sth** to have or take sth quickly, especially because you are in a hurry: *Let's grab a sandwich before we go.* ◇ *I managed to grab a couple of hours' sleep on the plane.* ◇ ***Grab a seat****, I won't keep you a moment.* **5** 0-π [T] **~ sth** to take sth for yourself, especially in a selfish or GREEDY way: *By the time we arrived, someone had grabbed all the good seats.* **6** [T] **~ sb/sth** to get sb's attention: *I'll see if I can grab the waitress and get the bill.* ◇ *Glasgow's drugs problem has* ***grabbed the headlines tonight*** (= been published as an important story in the newspapers).

IDM **how does...grab you?** (*informal*) used to ask sb whether they are interested in sth or in doing sth: *How does the idea of a trip to Rome grab you?*

■ ***noun*** **1** [usually sing.] **~ (at/for sb/sth)** a sudden attempt to take or hold sb/sth: *He* ***made a grab for*** *her bag.* ➲ see also SMASH-AND-GRAB **2** (*computing*) a picture taken from a television or video film, stored as an image on a computer: *a screen grab from Wednesday's programme* **3** a piece of equipment which lifts and holds goods, for example the equipment that hangs from a CRANE

IDM **up for ˈgrabs** (*informal*) available for anyone who is interested: *There are £25 000 worth of prizes up for grabs in our competition!*

ˈgrab bag *noun* (*NAmE*) **1** (*BrE* **ˌlucky ˈdip**) a game in which people choose a present from a container of presents without being able to see what it is going to be **2** (*informal*) a mixed collection of things: *He offered a grab bag of reasons for his decision.*

grace /greɪs/ *noun, verb*

■ ***noun***

▸ OF MOVEMENT **1** [U] an attractive quality of movement that is smooth, elegant and controlled: *She moves with the natural grace of a ballerina.*

▸ BEHAVIOUR **2** [U] a quality of behaviour that is polite and pleasant and deserves respect: *He conducted himself with grace and dignity throughout the trial.* **3 graces** [pl.] (*especially BrE*) ways of behaving that people think are polite and acceptable: *He was not particularly well versed in the* ***social graces***.

▸ EXTRA TIME **4** [U] extra time that is given to sb to enable them to pay a bill, finish a piece of work, etc: *They've given me a month's grace to get the money.*

▸ OF GOD **5** [U] the kindness that God shows towards the human race: *It was only by the grace of God that they survived.* ➲ COLLOCATIONS at RELIGION

▸ PRAYER **6** [U, C] a short prayer that is usually said before a meal to thank God for the food: *Let's* ***say grace***.

▸ TITLE **7 His/Her/Your Grace** [C] used as a title of respect when talking to or about an ARCHBISHOP, a DUKE or a DUCHESS: *Good Morning, Your Grace.* ◇ *Their Graces the Duke and Duchess of Kent.* ➲ see also COUP DE GRÂCE, SAVING GRACE

IDM **be in sb's good ˈgraces** (*formal*) to have sb's approval and be liked by them **ˌfall from ˈgrace** to lose the trust or respect that people have for you, especially by doing sth wrong or immoral **sb's ˌfall from ˈgrace** a situation in which sb loses the trust or respect that people have for them, especially because of sth wrong or immoral that they have done **have the (good) grace to do sth** to be polite enough to do sth, especially when you have done sth wrong: *He didn't even have the grace to look embarrassed.* **there but for the grace of ˈGod (go ˈI)** (*saying*) used to say that you could easily have been in the same difficult or unpleasant situation that sb else is in **with (a) bad ˈgrace** in an unwilling and/or rude way: *He handed over the money with typical bad grace.* **with (a) good ˈgrace** in a willing and pleasant way: *You must learn to accept defeat with good grace.* ➲ more at AIR *n.*, STATE *n.*, YEAR

■ ***verb*** (*formal*) **1 ~ sth** to make sth more attractive; to decorate sth: *The table had once graced a duke's drawing room.* **2** (usually *ironic*) to bring honour to sb/sth; to be kind enough to attend or take part in sth: **~ sb/sth** *She is one of the finest players ever to have graced the game.* ◇ **~ sb/sth with sth** *Will you be* ***gracing us with your presence*** *tonight?*

ˌgrace and ˈfavour *adj.* [only before noun] (*BrE*) used to describe a house or flat/apartment that a king, queen or government has allowed sb to use

grace·ful /ˈgreɪsfl/ *adj.* **1** moving in a controlled, attractive way or having a smooth, attractive form: *The dancers were all tall and graceful.* ◇ *He gave a graceful bow to the audience.* ◇ *the graceful curves of the hills* **2** polite and kind in your behaviour, especially in a difficult situation: *His father had always taught him to be graceful in defeat.* ▸ **grace·ful·ly** /-fəli/ *adv.*: *The cathedral's white towers climb gracefully into the sky.* ◇ *I think we should just* ***give in gracefully***. **grace·ful·ness** *noun* [U]

grace·less /ˈgreɪsləs/ *adj.* **1** not knowing how to be polite and pleasant to other people: *a graceless, angry young man* **2** not pleasing or attractive to look at: *the graceless architecture of the 1960s* **3** moving in an awkward way: *She swam with a graceless stroke.* OPP **graceful** ▸ **grace·less·ly** *adv.*

ˈgrace note *noun* (*music*) an extra note which is not a necessary part of a tune, but which is played before one of the notes of the tune as decoration

gra·cious /ˈgreɪʃəs/ *adj.* **1** (of people or behaviour) kind, polite and generous, especially to sb of a lower social position: *a gracious lady* ◇ *a gracious smile* ◇ *He has not yet learned how to be gracious in defeat.* **2** [usually before noun] showing the comfort and easy way of life that wealth can bring: *gracious living* **3** [only before noun] (*BrE, formal*) used as a very polite word for royal people or their actions: *her gracious Majesty the Queen* **4 ~ (to sb)** (of God) showing kindness and MERCY: *a gracious act of God* **5** (becoming *old-fashioned*) used for expressing surprise: *Goodness gracious!* ◇ *'I hope you didn't mind my phoning you.' 'Good gracious, no, of course not.'* ▸ **gra·cious·ly** *adv.*: *She graciously accepted our invitation.* **gra·cious·ness** *noun* [U]

grad /græd/ *noun* (*informal, especially NAmE*) = GRADUATE

grad·able /ˈgreɪdəbl/ *adj.* (*grammar*) (of an adjective) that can be used in the comparative and superlative forms or be used with words like 'very' and 'less' OPP **non-gradable** ▸ **grad·abil·ity** /ˌgreɪdəˈbɪləti/ *noun* [U]

grad·ation /grəˈdeɪʃn/ *noun* **1** [C, U] (*formal*) any of the small changes or levels which sth is divided into; the process or result of sth changing gradually: *gradations of colour* ◇ *gradation in size* **2** (also **gradu·ation**) [C] a mark

G

showing a division on a scale: *the gradations on a thermometer*

grade 🔑 AW /ɡreɪd/ *noun, verb*

■ ***noun*** **1** 🔑 the quality of a particular product or material: *All the materials used were of the highest grade.* **2** 🔑 a level of ability or rank that sb has in an organization: *salary grades* (= levels of pay) ◇ *She's still only on a secretarial grade.* **3** 🔑 a mark given in an exam or for a piece of school work: (*BrE*) *She got good grades in her exams.* ◇ (*NAmE*) *She got good grades on her exams.* ◇ *70% of pupils got Grade C or above.* **4** 🔑 (in the US school system) one of the levels in a school with children of similar age: *Sam is in (the) second grade.* **5** (*technical*) how serious an illness is: ***low/high grade*** *fever* **6** (*especially NAmE*) = GRADIENT (1) **7** (*BrE*) a level of exam in musical skill

IDM **make the ˈgrade** (*informal*) to reach the necessary standard; to succeed: *About 10% of trainees fail to make the grade.*

■ ***verb*** **1** 🔑 [often passive] to arrange people or things in groups according to their ability, quality, size, etc: **~ sth/sb (by/according to sth)** *The containers are graded according to size.* ◇ **~ sth/sb from… to…** *Eggs are graded from small to extra large.* ◇ *Responses were graded from 1 (very satisfied) to 5 (not at all satisfied).* ◇ **~ sth (as) sth** *Ten beaches were graded as acceptable.* **2** 🔑 (*especially NAmE*) to give a mark/grade to a student or to a piece of their written work: **~ sb/sth** *I spent all weekend grading papers.* ◇ **~ sb/sth + noun** *The best students are graded A.* ➲ compare MARK

graded AW /ˈɡreɪdɪd/ *adj.* arranged in order or in groups according to difficulty, size, etc: *graded tests for language students* ◇ *graded doses of a drug*

ˈgrade point average *noun* [usually sing.] (*abbr.* **GPA**) the average of a student's marks/grades over a period of time in the US education system

grader /ˈɡreɪdə(r)/ *noun* (*NAmE*) **1 first, second, etc. ~** a student who is in the grade mentioned: *The play is open to all seventh and eighth graders.* **2** (*BrE* **mark·er**) a person who marks/grades students' work or exam papers

ˈgrade school *noun* (*informal*) = ELEMENTARY SCHOOL

gra·di·ent /ˈɡreɪdiənt/ *noun* **1** (also **grade** especially in *NAmE*) the degree to which the ground slopes, especially on a road or railway: *a steep gradient* ◇ *a hill with a gradient of 1 in 4 (or 25%)* **2** (*technical*) the rate at which temperature, pressure, etc. changes, or increases and decreases, between one region and another

grad·ing /ˈɡreɪdɪŋ/ *noun* [U] (*NAmE*) = MARKING (3)

gra·dio·meter /ˌɡreɪdiˈɒmɪtə(r); *NAmE* -ˈɑːm-/ *noun* **1** (*technical*) an instrument for measuring the angle of a slope **2** (*physics*) an instrument for measuring the changes in an energy field

ˈgrad school *noun* (*NAmE, informal*) = GRADUATE SCHOOL

grad·ual 🔑 /ˈɡrædʒuəl/ *adj.*
1 🔑 happening slowly over a long period; not sudden: *a gradual change in the climate* ◇ *Recovery from the disease is very gradual.* OPP **sudden** **2** (of a slope) not steep

grad·ual·ism /ˈɡrædʒuəlɪzəm/ *noun* [U] a policy of gradual change in society rather than sudden change or revolution ▸ **grad·ual·ist** *noun*

grad·ual·ly 🔑 /ˈɡrædʒuəli/ *adv.*
slowly, over a long period of time: *The weather gradually improved.* ◇ *Gradually, the children began to understand.*

gradu·ate *noun, verb*

■ ***noun*** /ˈɡrædʒuət/ (also *informal* **grad** especially in *NAmE*) **1 ~ (in sth)** a person who has a university degree: *a graduate in history* ◇ *a science graduate* ◇ *a graduate of Yale/a Yale graduate* ◇ *a graduate student/course* **2** (*NAmE*) a person who has completed their school studies: *a high school graduate* ➲ SYNONYMS at STUDENT

■ ***verb*** /ˈɡrædʒueɪt/ **1** [I, T] to get a degree, especially your first degree, from a university or college: **~ (in sth)** *Only three students graduated in Czech studies last year.* ◇ **~ (from…)** *She graduated from Harvard this year.* ◇ *He graduated from York with a degree in Psychology.* ◇ **~ sth** (*NAmE*) *She graduated college last year.* **2** [I, T] (*NAmE*) to complete a course in education, especially at HIGH SCHOOL: **~ (from…)** *Martha graduated from high school two years ago.* ◇ **~ sth** *Martha graduated high school two years ago.* **3** [T] **~ sb (from sth)** (*NAmE*) to give a degree, DIPLOMA, etc. to sb: *The college graduated 50 students last year.* **4** [I] **~ (from sth) to sth** to start doing sth more difficult or important than what you were doing before: *She recently graduated from being a dancer to having a small role in a movie.* ➲ COLLOCATIONS at EDUCATION

gradu·ated /ˈɡrædʒueɪtɪd/ *adj.* **1** divided into groups or levels on a scale: *graduated lessons/tests* **2** (of a container or measure) marked with lines to show measurements SYN **calibrated**: *a graduated jar*

ˌGraduate ˌManagement Adˈmissions Test ➲ GMAT

ˈgraduate school (also *informal* **ˈgrad school**) (both *NAmE*) *noun* a part of a college or university where you can study for a second or further degree

gradu·ation /ˌɡrædʒuˈeɪʃn/ *noun* **1** [U] the act of successfully completing a university degree, or studies at an American HIGH SCHOOL: *It was my first job after graduation.* **2** [U, C] a ceremony at which degrees, etc. are officially given out: *graduation day* ◇ *My whole family came to my graduation.* **3** [C] = GRADATION (2): *The graduations are marked on the side of the flask.*

Graeco- (*NAmE* usually **Greco-**) /ˈɡriːkəʊ-; *NAmE* -koʊ/ *combining form* (in adjectives) Greek

graf·fiti /ɡrəˈfiːti/ *noun* [U, pl.] drawings or writing on a wall, etc. in a public place: *The subway was covered in graffiti.*

graft /ɡrɑːft; *NAmE* ɡræft/ *noun, verb*

■ ***noun*** **1** [C] a piece cut from a living plant and fixed in a cut made in another plant, so that it grows there; the process or result of doing this **2** [C] a piece of skin, bone, etc. removed from a living body and placed in another part of the body which has been damaged; the process or result of doing this: *a skin graft* **3** [U] (*BrE, informal*) hard work: *Their success was the result of years of* ***hard graft***. **4** [U] (*especially NAmE*) the use of illegal or unfair methods, especially BRIBERY, to gain advantage in business, politics, etc; money obtained in this way

■ ***verb*** **1** [T] **~ sth (onto/to/into sth)** | **~ sth (on) (from sth)** to take a piece of skin, bone, etc. from one part of the body and attach it to a damaged part: *newly grafted tissue* ◇ *New skin had to be grafted on from his back.* **2** [T] **~ sth (onto sth)** to cut a piece from a living plant and attach it to another plant **3** [T] **~ sth (onto sth)** to make one idea, system, etc. become part of another one: *Old values are being grafted onto a new social class.* **4** [I] (*BrE, informal*) to work hard

graham cracker /ˈɡreɪəm krækə(r)/ *noun* (*NAmE*) a slightly sweet RECTANGULAR biscuit/cookie made with WHOLEMEAL flour

grail /ɡreɪl/ (also **the ˌHoly ˈGrail**) *noun* **1** [sing.] the cup or bowl believed to have been used by Jesus Christ before he died, that became a holy thing that people wanted to find **2** [C] a thing that you try very hard to find or achieve, but never will

grain 🔑 /ɡreɪn/ *noun*
1 🔑 [U, C] the small hard seeds of food plants such as WHEAT, rice, etc; a single seed of such a plant: *America's grain exports* ◇ *a few grains of rice* ➲ see also WHOLEGRAIN ➲ VISUAL VOCAB page V28 **2** 🔑 [C] a small hard piece of particular substances: *a* ***grain of salt/sand/sugar*** **3** [C] (used especially in negative sentences) a very small amount SYN **iota**: *There isn't* ***a grain of truth*** *in those rumours.* **4** [C] a small unit of weight, equal to 0.00143 of a pound or 0.0648 of a gram, used for example for weighing medicines **5** [U] the natural direction of lines in wood, cloth, etc. or of layers of rock; the pattern of lines that you can see: *to cut a piece of wood* ***along/across the grain*** **6** [U, C] how rough or smooth a surface feels: *wood of* ***coarse/fine grain***

IDM **be/go against the ˈgrain** to be or do sth different

from what is normal or natural: *It really goes against the grain to have to work on a Sunday.*

grained /greɪnd/ *adj.* (of wood, stone, etc.) **1** having noticeable lines or a pattern on the surface **2 -grained** having a TEXTURE of the type mentioned: *fine-grained stone*

grainy /ˈgreɪni/ *adj.* (**grain·ier, graini·est**) **1** (especially of photographs) not having completely clear images because they look as if they are made of a lot of small dots and marks: *The film is shot in grainy black and white.* **2** having a rough surface or containing small bits, seeds, etc: *grainy texture*

gram 0‑w /græm/ *noun*
1 0‑w (*BrE* also **gramme**) (*abbr.* **g, gm**) a unit for measuring weight. There are 1000 grams in one kilogram. **2 -gram** a thing that is written or drawn: *telegram* ◇ *hologram*

ˈ**gram flour** (also **besan**, ˈ**chickpea flour**) *noun* [U] flour made from CHICKPEAS

gram·mar 0‑w /ˈgræmə(r)/ *noun*
1 0‑w [U] the rules in a language for changing the form of words and joining them into sentences: *the basic rules of grammar* ◇ *English grammar* ➲ see also GENERATIVE GRAMMAR **2** 0‑w [U] a person's knowledge and use of a language: *His grammar is appalling.* ◇ *bad grammar* **3** 0‑w [C] a book containing a description of the rules of a language: *a French grammar*

gram·mar·ian /grəˈmeəriən; *NAmE* -ˈmer-/ *noun* a person who is an expert in the study of grammar

ˈ**grammar school** *noun* **1** (in Britain, especially in the past) a school for young people between the ages of 11 and 18 who are good at academic subjects **2** (*old-fashioned*) = ELEMENTARY SCHOOL

the ˌ**grammar trans**ˈ**lation method** *noun* [sing.] (*linguistics*) a traditional way of teaching a foreign language, in which the study of grammar is very important and very little teaching is in the foreign language

gram·mat·ical /grəˈmætɪkl/ *adj.* **1** connected with the rules of grammar: *a grammatical error* **2** correctly following the rules of grammar: *That sentence is not grammatical.* ▸ **gram·mat·ical·ly** /-kli/ *adv.*: *a grammatically correct sentence*

gramme (*BrE*) = GRAM

Grammy /ˈgræmi/ (*pl.* **Gram·mies** or **Grammys**) one of the awards for achievement in the music industry given every year by the US National Academy of Recording Arts and Sciences

gramo·phone /ˈgræməfəʊn; *NAmE* -foʊn/ *noun* (*old-fashioned*) = RECORD PLAYER

gran /græn/ *noun* (*BrE, informal*) grandmother: *Do you want to go to your gran's?* ◇ *Gran, can I have some more?*

Gran·ary™ /ˈgrænəri/ *adj.* [only before noun] (*BrE*) (of bread) containing whole grains of WHEAT

gran·ary /ˈgrænəri/ *noun* (*pl.* **-ies**) a building where grain is stored

grand 0‑w /grænd/ *adj., noun*
■ *adj.* (**grand·er, grand·est**) **1** 0‑w impressive and large or important: *It's not a very grand house.* ◇ *The wedding was a very grand occasion.* **2 Grand** [only before noun] used in the names of impressive or very large buildings, etc.: *the Grand Canyon* ◇ *We stayed at the Grand Hotel.* **3** 0‑w needing a lot of effort, money or time to succeed but intended to achieve impressive results: *a* ***grand design/plan/strategy*** ◇ *New Yorkers built their city* ***on a grand scale.*** **4** (of people) behaving in a proud way because they are rich or from a high social class **5** (*dialect* or *informal*) very good or enjoyable; excellent: *I had a grand day out at the seaside.* ◇ *Thanks. That'll be grand!* ◇ *Fred did a grand job of painting the house.* **6 Grand** used in the titles of people of very high social rank: *the Grand Duchess Elena* ➲ see also GRANDEUR ▸ **grand·ly** *adv.*: *He described himself grandly as a 'landscape architect'.* **grand·ness** *noun* [U]
IDM **a/the** ˌ**grand old** ˈ**age (of…)** a great age: *She finally learned to drive at the grand old age of 70.* **a/the** ˌ**grand old** ˈ**man (of sth)** a man who is respected in a particular profession that he has been involved in for a long time: *James Lovelock, the grand old man of environmental science*
■ *noun* **1** (*pl.* **grand**) (*informal*) $1000; £1000: *It'll cost you five grand!* **2** = GRAND PIANO ➲ see also CONCERT GRAND

gran·dad (also **grand·dad** especially in *NAmE*) /ˈgrændæd/ *noun* (*informal*) grandfather

ˌ**Grand** ˌ**Central** ˈ**Station** *noun* (*US*) used to describe a place that is very busy or crowded: *My hospital room was like Grand Central Station with everybody coming and going.* ORIGIN From the name of a very busy train station in New York City. ➲ compare PICCADILLY CIRCUS

grand·child 0‑w /ˈgræntʃaɪld/ *noun* (*pl.* **grand·chil·dren**)
a child of your son or daughter

grand·daddy (also **gran·daddy**) /ˈgrændædi/ *noun* (*pl.* **-ies**) (*NAmE, informal*) **1** = GRANDFATHER **2 the granddaddy** the first or greatest example of sth

grand·daugh·ter 0‑w /ˈgrændɔːtə(r)/ *noun*
a daughter of your son or daughter ➲ compare GRANDSON

ˌ**grand** ˈ**duchess** *noun* **1** the wife of a grand duke **2** (in some parts of Europe, especially in the past), a female ruler of a small independent state **3** (in Russia in the past) a daughter of the TSAR

ˌ**grand** ˈ**duke** *noun* **1** (in some parts of Europe, especially in the past), a male ruler of a small independent state: *The Grand Duke of Tuscany* **2** (in Russia in the past), a son of the TSAR ➲ compare ARCHDUKE

gran·dee /grænˈdiː/ *noun* **1** (in the past) a Spanish or Portuguese NOBLEMAN of high rank **2** a person of high social rank and importance

grand·eur /ˈgrændʒə(r); -djə(r)/ *noun* [U] **1** the quality of being great and impressive in appearance SYN **splendour**: *the grandeur and simplicity of Roman architecture* ◇ *The hotel had an air of faded grandeur.* **2** the importance or social status sb has or thinks they have: *He has a sense of grandeur about him.* ◇ *She is clearly suffering from* ***delusions of grandeur*** (= thinks she is more important than she really is). ➲ see also GRAND

grand·father 0‑w /ˈgrænfɑːðə(r)/ *noun*
the father of your father or mother ➲ see also GRANDAD, GRANDDADDY, GRANDPA ➲ compare GRANDMOTHER

ˌ**grandfather** ˈ**clock** *noun* an old-fashioned type of clock in a tall wooden case that stands on the floor ➲ picture at CLOCK

grand·ilo·quent /grænˈdɪləkwənt/ *adj.* (*formal, disapproving*) using long or complicated words in order to impress people SYN **pompous** ▸ **grand·ilo·quence** /-əns/ *noun* [U]

gran·di·ose /ˈgrændiəʊs; *NAmE* -oʊs/ *adj.* (*disapproving*) seeming very impressive but too large, complicated, expensive, etc. to be practical or possible: *The grandiose scheme for a journey across the desert came to nothing.* ◇ *a grandiose opera house*

ˌ**grand** ˈ**jury** *noun* (*law*) (in the US) a JURY which has to decide whether there is enough evidence against an accused person for a trial in court

grand·ma /ˈgrænmɑː/ *noun* (*informal*) grandmother

grand mal /ˌgrɒ̃ ˈmæl; *NAmE* ˌgræn ˈmɑːl; ˈmæl/ *noun* [U] (from *French, medical*) a serious form of EPILEPSY in which sb becomes unconscious for fairly long periods

ˌ**grand** ˈ**master** *noun* a CHESS player of the highest standard

grand·mother 0‑w /ˈgrænmʌðə(r)/ *noun*
the mother of your father or mother ➲ see also GRAN, GRANDMA, GRANNY ➲ compare GRANDFATHER IDM see TEACH

ˌ**grandmother** ˈ**clock** *noun* a clock similar to a GRANDFATHER CLOCK but smaller

ˌgrand ˈopera *noun* [U, C] OPERA in which everything is sung and there are no spoken parts

grand·pa /ˈgrænpɑː/ *noun* (*informal*) grandfather ➲ see also GRANDAD

grand·par·ent 🔑 /ˈgrænpeərənt; *NAmE* -perənt/ *noun* [usually pl.]
the father or mother of your father or mother: *The children are staying with their grandparents.*

ˌgrand ˈpiano (also **grand**) *noun* a large piano in which the strings are horizontal ➲ VISUAL VOCAB page V31 ➲ compare UPRIGHT PIANO

Grand Prix /ˌgrɒ̃ ˈpriː; *NAmE* ˌgrɑ̃ː/ *noun* (*pl.* **Grands Prix** /ˌgrɒ̃ ˈpriː; *NAmE* ˌgrɑ̃ː/) one of a series of important international races for racing cars or motorcycles

G

ˌgrand ˈslam *noun* **1** (also **Grand Slam**) a very important sports event, contest, etc: *a Grand Slam **tournament/cup/title*** **2** the winning of every part of a sports contest or all the main contests in a year for a particular sport: *Will France win the grand slam this year?* (= in RUGBY) **3** (also **grand ˌslam home ˈrun**) (in BASEBALL) a HOME RUN that is worth four points **4** (in card games, especially BRIDGE) the winning of all the TRICKS in a single game

grand·son 🔑 /ˈgrænsʌn/ *noun*
a son of your son or daughter ➲ compare GRANDDAUGHTER

grand·stand /ˈgrænstænd/ *noun* a large covered structure with rows of seats for people to watch sports events: *The game was played to a packed grandstand.* ◇ *From her house, we had a **grandstand view** (= very good view) of the celebrations.*

ˌgrandstand ˈfinish *noun* (*BrE*) (in sport) a close or exciting finish to a race or competition

grand·stand·ing /ˈgrænstændɪŋ/ *noun* [U] (*NAmE*) (especially in business, politics, etc.) the fact of behaving or speaking in a way that is intended to make people impressed in order to gain some advantage for yourself

ˌgrand ˈtotal *noun* the final total when a number of other totals have been added together

ˌgrand ˈtour *noun* **1** (often *humorous*) a visit around a building or house in order to show it to sb: *Steve took us on a grand tour of the house and garden.* **2** (also **Grand Tour**) a visit to the main cities of Europe made by rich young British or American people as part of their education in the past

ˌgrand ˈunified theory *noun* (*physics*) a single theory that tries to explain all the behaviour of SUBATOMIC PARTICLES

grange /greɪndʒ/ *noun* (*BrE*) (often as part of a name) a country house with farm buildings: *Thrushcross Grange*

gran·ita /grəˈniːtə/ *noun* [U, C] (from *Italian*) a drink or sweet dish made with crushed ice

gran·ite /ˈgrænɪt/ *noun* [U] a type of hard grey stone, often used in building

granny (also *less frequent* **gran·nie**) /ˈgræni/ *noun* (*pl.* -ies) (*informal*) grandmother ➲ see also GRANDMA ▸ **granny** (also *less frequent* **gran·nie**) *adj.*: *a pair of granny glasses*

ˈgranny flat *noun* (*BrE*) (also **ˈin-law apartment**, **ˈmother-in-law apartment**, **ˈin-law suite** all *NAmE*) (*informal*) a set of rooms for an old person, especially in a relative's house

ˈgranny knot *noun* an untidy double knot ➲ compare REEF KNOT

gran·ola /grəˈnəʊlə; *NAmE* -ˈnoʊ-/ *noun, adj.*
■ ***noun*** [U] (*especially NAmE*) a type of breakfast CEREAL made of grains, nuts, etc. that have been TOASTED
■ ***adj.*** [only before noun] (*NAmE, informal*) (of a person) eating healthy food, supporting the protection of the environment and having LIBERAL views

grant 🔑 AW /grɑːnt; *NAmE* grænt/ *verb, noun*
■ ***verb* 1** 🔑 [often passive] to agree to give sb what they ask for, especially formal or legal permission to do sth: **~ sth** *My request was granted.* ◇ **~ sb sth** *I was granted permission to visit the palace.* ◇ *She was granted a divorce.* ◇ *The bank finally granted me a £500 loan.* ◇ **~ sth to sb/sth** *The bank finally granted a £500 loan to me.* **2** to admit that sth is true, although you may not like or agree with it: **~ sb** *She's a smart woman, I grant you, but she's no genius.* ◇ **~ (sb) (that)...** *I grant you (that) it looks good, but it's not exactly practical.*
IDM **take it for ˈgranted (that...)** 🔑 to believe sth is true without first making sure that it is: *I just took it for granted that he'd always be around.* **take sb/sth for ˈgranted** 🔑 to be so used to sb/sth that you do not recognize their true value any more and do not show that you are grateful: *Her husband was always there and she just took him for granted.* ◇ *We take having an endless supply of clean water for granted.*
■ ***noun*** 🔑 **~ (to do sth)** a sum of money that is given by the government or by another organization to be used for a particular purpose: *student grants* (= to pay for their education) ◇ *He has been awarded a research grant.*

ˈgrant aid *noun* [U] (*BrE*) money given by the government to organizations or local areas ▸ **ˌgrant-ˈaided** *adj.*: *a grant-aided school*

grant·ed AW /ˈgrɑːntɪd; *NAmE* ˈgræn-/ *adv., conj.*
■ ***adv.*** used to show that you accept that sth is true, often before you make another statement about it: *'You could have done more to help.' 'Granted.'* ◇ *Granted, it's not the most pleasant of jobs but it has to be done.*
■ ***conj.* ~ (that...)** because of the fact that: *Granted that it is a simple test to perform, it should be easy to get results quickly.*

ˌgrant-in-ˈaid *noun* (*pl.* **ˌgrants-in-ˈaid**) a sum of money given to a local government or an institution, or to a particular person to allow them to study sth

ˌgrant-mainˈtained *adj.* (*abbr.* **GM**) (of a school in Britain) receiving financial support from central government rather than local government

granu·lar /ˈgrænjələ(r)/ *adj.* consisting of small GRANULES; looking or feeling like a collection of GRANULES

granu·lated sugar /ˌgrænjuleɪtɪd ˈʃʊgə(r)/ *noun* [U] white sugar in the form of small grains

gran·ule /ˈgrænjuːl/ *noun* [usually pl.] a small, hard piece of sth; a small grain: *instant coffee granules*

grape /greɪp/ *noun* a small green or purple fruit that grows in bunches on a climbing plant (called a VINE). Wine is made from grapes: *a bunch of grapes* ◇ ***black/white grapes*** (= grapes that are actually purple/green in colour) ➲ VISUAL VOCAB page V26 IDM see SOUR *adj.*

grape·fruit /ˈgreɪpfruːt/ *noun* (*pl.* **grapefruit** or **grapefruits**) [C, U] a large round yellow CITRUS fruit with a lot of slightly sour juice ➲ VISUAL VOCAB page V26

grape·shot /ˈgreɪpʃɒt; *NAmE* -ʃɑːt/ *noun* [U] a number of small iron balls that are fired together from a CANNON

grape·vine /ˈgreɪpvaɪn/ *noun* a climbing plant that produces GRAPES
IDM **on/through the ˈgrapevine** by talking in an informal way to other people: *I heard on the grapevine that you're leaving.*

graph /græf; *BrE* also grɑːf/ *noun* a planned drawing, consisting of a line or lines, showing how two or more sets of numbers are related to each other: *Plot a graph of height against age.* ◇ *The graph shows how house prices have risen since the 1980s.* ➲ LANGUAGE BANK at ILLUSTRATE ➲ WRITING TUTOR page WT16

graph·eme /ˈgræfiːm/ *noun* (*linguistics*) the smallest unit that has meaning in a writing system ➲ compare PHONEME

graph·ic /ˈgræfɪk/ *adj., noun*
■ ***adj.* 1** [only before noun] connected with drawings and design, especially in the production of books, magazines, etc: *graphic design* ◇ *a graphic designer* **2** (of descriptions, etc.) very clear and full of details, especially about sth unpleasant SYN **vivid**: *a **graphic account/description** of a battle* ◇ *He kept telling us about his operation, in the most **graphic detail**.*
■ ***noun*** a diagram or picture, especially one that appears on

a computer screen or in a newspaper or book ➲ compare GRAPHICS

graph·ic·al /ˈɡræfɪkl/ *adj.* **1** [only before noun] connected with art or computer graphics: *The system uses an impressive graphical interface.* **2** in the form of a diagram or graph: *a graphical presentation of results*

graph·ic·al·ly /ˈɡræfɪkli/ *adv.* **1** in the form of drawings or diagrams: *This data is shown graphically on the opposite page.* **2** very clearly and in great detail SYN **vividly**: *The murders are graphically described in the article.*

ˌgraphic ˈarts *noun* [U] art based on the use of lines and shades of colour ▶ **ˌgraphic ˈartist** *noun*

ˌgraphic ˈequalizer *noun* (*technical*) an electronic device or computer program that allows you to control the strength and quality of particular sound FREQUENCIES separately

ˌgraphic ˈnovel *noun* a novel in the form of a COMIC STRIP

graph·ics /ˈɡræfɪks/ *noun* [pl.] designs, drawings or pictures, that are used especially in the production of books, magazines, etc: *computer graphics* ◇ *Text and graphics are prepared separately and then combined.*

ˈgraphics adapter *noun* (*computing*) = VIDEO CARD

ˈgraphics card *noun* (*computing*) a CIRCUIT BOARD that allows a computer to show images on its screen

graph·ite /ˈɡræfaɪt/ *noun* [U] a soft black mineral that is a form of CARBON. Graphite is used to make pencils, to LUBRICATE machinery, and in nuclear REACTORS.

graph·ology /ɡræˈfɒlədʒi; *NAmE* -ˈfɑːl-/ *noun* [U] the study of HANDWRITING, for example as a way of learning more about sb's character

ˈgraph paper *noun* [U] paper with small squares of equal size printed on it, used for drawing GRAPHS and other diagrams

-graphy *combining form* (in nouns) **1** a type of art or science: *choreography* ◇ *geography* **2** a method of producing images: *radiography* **3** a form of writing or drawing: *calligraphy* ◇ *biography*

grappa /ˈɡræpə/ *noun* [U, C] a strong alcoholic drink from Italy, made from GRAPES

grap·ple /ˈɡræpl/ *verb* **1** [I, T] to take a firm hold of sb/sth and struggle with them: **~ (with sb/sth)** *Passers-by grappled with the man after the attack.* ◇ **~ sb/sth (+ adv./prep.)** *They managed to grapple him to the ground.* **2** [I] to try hard to find a solution to a problem: **~ with sth** *The new government has yet to grapple with the problem of air pollution.* ◇ **~ to do sth** *I was grappling to find an answer to his question.*

ˈgrappling iron (also **ˈgrappling hook**) *noun* a tool with several hooks attached to a long rope, used for dragging sth along or holding a boat still

grasp /ɡrɑːsp; *NAmE* ɡræsp/ *verb, noun*
- ***verb*** **1 ~ sb/sth** to take a firm hold of sb/sth SYN **grip**: *He grasped my hand and shook it warmly.* ◇ *Kay grasped him by the wrist.* ➲ note at HOLD **2** to understand sth completely: **~ sth** *They failed to grasp the importance of his words.* ◇ **~ how, why, etc...** *She was unable to grasp how to do it.* ◇ **~ that...** *It took him some time to grasp that he was now a public figure.* ➲ SYNONYMS at UNDERSTAND **3 ~ a chance/an opportunity** to take an opportunity without hesitating and use it: *I grasped the opportunity to work abroad.*

IDM **grasp the ˈnettle** (*BrE*) to deal with a difficult situation firmly and without hesitating ➲ more at STRAW

PHR V **ˈgrasp at sth 1** to try to take hold of sth in your hands: *She grasped at his coat as he rushed past her.* **2** to try to take an opportunity

- ***noun*** [usually sing.] **1** a firm hold of sb/sth or control over sb/sth SYN **grip**: *I grabbed him, but he slipped from my grasp.* ◇ *She felt a firm grasp on her arm.* ◇ *Don't let the situation escape from your grasp.* **2** a person's understanding of a subject or of difficult facts: *He has **a good grasp of** German grammar.* ◇ *These complex formulae are **beyond the grasp of** the average pupil.* **3** the ability to get or achieve sth: *Success was **within her grasp**.*

grasp·ing /ˈɡrɑːspɪŋ; *NAmE* ˈɡræs-/ *adj.* (*disapproving*) always trying to get money, possessions, power, etc. for yourself SYN **greedy**: *a grasping landlord*

grass 0➔ /ɡrɑːs; *NAmE* ɡræs/ *noun, verb*
- ***noun*** **1** 0➔ [U] a common wild plant with narrow green leaves and STEMS that are eaten by cows, horses, sheep, etc: ***a blade of grass*** ◇ *The dry grass caught fire.* **2** [C] any type of grass: *ornamental grasses* **3** 0➔ [sing., U] (usually **the grass**) an area of ground covered with grass: ***to cut/mow the grass*** ◇ *Don't walk **on the grass**.* ◇ ***Keep off the grass.*** (= on a sign) **4** [U] (*slang*) MARIJUANA **5** [C] (*BrE, informal*, usually *disapproving*) a person, usually a criminal, who tells the police about sb's criminal activities and plans ➲ compare SUPERGRASS

IDM **the grass is (always) greener on the other side (of the fence)** (*saying*) said about people who never seem happy with what they have and always think that other people have a better situation than they have **not let the grass grow under your feet** to not delay in getting things done **put sb out to ˈgrass** (*informal*) to force sb to stop doing their job, especially because they are old ➲ more at KICK *v.*, SNAKE *n.*

- ***verb*** [I] **~ (on sb)** (also **ˌgrass sb↔ˈup**) (both *BrE, informal*) to tell the police about sb's criminal activities

PHR V **ˌgrass sth↔ˈover** to cover an area with grass

ˌgrass ˈcourt *noun* a TENNIS COURT with a grass surface

ˈgrass·cutter /ˈɡrɑːskʌtə(r); *NAmE* ˈɡræs-/ (also **ˈcutting grass**) *noun* a name used in W Africa for a CANE RAT (= type of large RODENT that is used for food)

grassed /ɡrɑːst; *NAmE* ɡræst/ *adj.* covered with grass

grass·hop·per /ˈɡrɑːshɒpə(r); *NAmE* ˈɡræshɑːp-/ *noun* an insect with long back legs, that can jump very high and that makes a sound with its legs ➲ VISUAL VOCAB page V11 IDM see KNEE-HIGH

grass·land /ˈɡrɑːslænd; *NAmE* ˈɡræs-/ *noun* [U] (also **grasslands** [pl.]) a large area of open land covered with wild grass

ˌgrass ˈroots (*BrE*) *noun* [pl.] (often **the grass roots**) ordinary people in society or in an organization, rather than the leaders or people who make decisions: *the grass roots of the party* ◇ *We need support at grass-roots level.*

ˌgrass ˈskirt *noun* a skirt made of long grass, worn by dancers in the Pacific islands

ˈgrass snake *noun* a small harmless snake

ˌgrass ˈwidow *noun* a woman whose husband is away from home for long periods of time

grassy /ˈɡrɑːsi; *NAmE* ˈɡræsi/ *adj.* (**grass·ier, grassi·est**) covered with grass

grate /ɡreɪt/ *noun, verb*
- ***noun*** **1** a metal frame for holding the wood or coal in a FIREPLACE ➲ VISUAL VOCAB page V18 **2** (also **ˈsewer grate**) (both *US*) (*BrE* **drain**) a frame of metal bars over the opening to a DRAIN in the ground ➲ see also GRATING
- ***verb*** **1** [T] **~ sth** to rub food against a GRATER in order to cut it into small pieces: ***grated apple/carrot/cheese, etc.*** ➲ COLLOCATIONS at COOKING ➲ VISUAL VOCAB page V25 **2** [I] to irritate or annoy sb: **~ (on sb)** *Her voice really grates on me.* ◇ **~ (with sb)** *It grated with him when people implied he wasn't really British.* **3** [I, T] when two hard surfaces **grate** as they rub together, they make a sharp unpleasant sound; sb can also make one thing **grate** against another: *The rusty hinges grated as the gate swung back.* ◇ **~ sth (+ adv./prep.)** *He grated his knife across the plate.*

grate·ful 0➔ /ˈɡreɪtfl/ *adj.*
1 0➔ feeling or showing thanks because sb has done sth kind for you or has done as you asked: **~ (to sb) (for sth)** *I am extremely grateful to all the teachers for their help.* ◇ *We would be grateful for any information you can give us.* ◇ **~ (to do sth)** *She seems to think I should be grateful to have a*

WORD FAMILY
grateful *adj.* (≠ ungrateful)
gratefully *adv.*
gratitude *noun* (≠ ingratitude)

G

job at all. ◇ **~ (that...)** *He was grateful that she didn't tell his parents about the incident.* ◇ *Grateful thanks are due to the following people for their help...* ◇ *Kate gave him a grateful smile.* **2** used to make a request, especially in a letter or in a formal situation: ***I would be grateful if you could*** *send the completed form back as soon as possible.* ▸ **grate·ful·ly** /-fəli/ *adv.*: *He nodded gratefully.* ◇ *All donations will be gratefully received.* IDM see SMALL *adj.*

grater /ˈgreɪtə(r)/ *noun* a kitchen UTENSIL (= a tool) with a rough surface, used for GRATING food into very small pieces: *a **cheese/nutmeg grater*** ➲ VISUAL VOCAB pages V23, V25

grat·ifi·ca·tion /ˌgrætɪfɪˈkeɪʃn/ *noun* [U, C] (*formal*) the state of feeling pleasure when sth goes well for you or when your desires are satisfied; sth that gives you pleasure SYN **satisfaction**: *sexual gratification* ◇ *A feed will usually provide instant gratification to a crying baby.*

grat·ify /ˈgrætɪfaɪ/ *verb* (**grati·fies**, **grati·fy·ing**, **grati·fied**, **grati·fied**) **1** (*formal*) to please or satisfy sb: **it gratifies sb to do sth** *It gratified him to think that it was all his work.* ◇ **~ sb** *I was gratified by their invitation.* **2 ~ sth** (*formal*) to satisfy a wish, need, etc: *He only gave his consent in order to gratify her wishes.* ▸ **grati·fied** *adj.* [not usually before noun]: **~ (at sth)** | **~ (to find, hear, see, etc.)** *She was gratified to find that they had followed her advice.*

grati·fy·ing /ˈgrætɪfaɪɪŋ/ *adj.* (*formal*) pleasing and giving satisfaction: ***It is gratifying*** *to see such good results.* ➲ SYNONYMS at SATISFYING ▸ **grati·fy·ing·ly** *adv.*

gra·tin /ˈgrætæn; *NAmE* ˈgrætn/ *noun* [U] (from *French*) a cooked dish which is covered with a crisp layer of cheese or BREADCRUMBS ➲ see also AU GRATIN

grat·ing /ˈgreɪtɪŋ/ *noun, adj.*
- ***noun*** a flat frame with metal bars across it, used to cover a window, a hole in the ground, etc. ➲ see also GRATE (2)
- ***adj.*** (of a sound or sb's voice) unpleasant to listen to

gra·tis /ˈgrætɪs; ˈgreɪtɪs/ *adv.* done or given without having to be paid for SYN **free of charge**: *I knew his help wouldn't be given gratis.* ▸ **gra·tis** *adj.*: *a gratis copy of a book*

grati·tude /ˈgrætɪtjuːd; *NAmE* -tuːd/ *noun* [U] the feeling of being grateful and wanting to express your thanks: *He smiled at them* ***with gratitude***. ◇ **~ (to sb)** (**for sth**) *I would like to express my gratitude to everyone for their hard work.* ◇ *She was presented with the gift* ***in gratitude for*** *her long service.* ◇ *a deep sense of gratitude* ◇ ***I owe*** *you a great* ***debt of gratitude*** (= feel extremely grateful). OPP **ingratitude**

gra·tuit·ous /grəˈtjuːɪtəs; *NAmE* -ˈtuː-/ *adj.* (*disapproving*) done without any good reason or purpose and often having harmful effects SYN **unnecessary**: *gratuitous violence on television* ▸ **gra·tuit·ous·ly** *adv.*

gra·tu·ity /grəˈtjuːəti; *NAmE* -ˈtuː-/ *noun* (*pl.* **-ies**) **1** (*formal*) money that you give to sb who has provided a service for you SYN **tip** **2** (*BrE*) money that is given to employees when they leave their job

grave[1] /greɪv/ *noun, adj.* ➲ see also GRAVE[2]
- ***noun*** **1** a place in the ground where a dead person is buried: *We visited Grandma's grave.* ◇ *There were flowers on the grave.* **2** [sing.] (often **the grave**) (usually *literary*) death; a person's death: *Is there life beyond the grave* (= life after death)? ◇ *He followed her to the grave* (= died soon after her). ◇ *She smoked herself into an early grave* (= died young as a result of smoking).

IDM **turn in his/her ˈgrave** (*BrE*) (*NAmE* **roll in his/her ˈgrave**) (of a person who is dead) likely to be very shocked or angry: *My father would turn in his grave if he knew.* ➲ more at CRADLE *n.*, DIG *v.*, FOOT *n.*
- ***adj.*** (**graver**, **grav·est**) (*formal*) **1** (of situations, feelings, etc.) very serious and important; giving you a reason to feel worried: *The police have expressed grave concern about the missing child's safety.* ◇ *The consequences will be very grave if nothing is done.* ◇ *We were in grave danger.* **2** (of people) serious in manner, as if sth sad, important or worrying has just happened: *He looked very grave as he entered the room.* ➲ see also GRAVITY ➲ SYNONYMS at SERIOUS ▸ **grave·ly** *adv.*: *She is gravely ill.* ◇ *Local people are gravely concerned.* ◇ *He nodded gravely as I poured out my troubles.*

grave[2] /grɑːv/ (also ˌ**grave ˈaccent**) *noun* a mark placed over a vowel in some languages to show how it should be pronounced, as over the *e* in the French word *père* ➲ compare ACUTE ACCENT, CIRCUMFLEX, TILDE, UMLAUT ➲ see also GRAVE[1]

grave·dig·ger /ˈgreɪvdɪgə(r)/ *noun* a person whose job is to dig graves

gravel /ˈgrævl/ *noun* [U] small stones, often used to make the surface of paths and roads: *a gravel path* ◇ *a* ***gravel pit*** (= a place where gravel is taken from the ground)

grav·elled (*US* **grav·eled**) /ˈgrævld/ *adj.* (of a road, etc.) covered with gravel

grav·el·ly /ˈgrævəli/ *adj.* **1** full of or containing many small stones: *a dry gravelly soil* **2** (of a voice) deep and with a rough sound

gra·ven image /ˌgreɪvn ˈɪmɪdʒ/ *noun* (*disapproving*) a statue or image which people worship as a god or as if it were a god

grave·stone /ˈgreɪvstəʊn; *NAmE* -stoʊn/ *noun* a stone that is put on a grave in a vertical position, showing the name, etc. of the person buried there SYN **headstone** ➲ compare TOMBSTONE

grave·yard /ˈgreɪvjɑːd; *NAmE* -jɑːrd/ *noun* **1** an area of land, often near a church, where people are buried ➲ compare CEMETERY, CHURCHYARD **2** a place where things or people that are not wanted are sent or left

ˈgraveyard shift *noun* (*especially NAmE*) a period of time working at night or in the very early morning

gravid /ˈgrævɪd/ *adj.* (*technical*) pregnant

grav·itas /ˈgrævɪtɑːs; -tæs/ *noun* [U] (*formal*) the quality of being serious SYN **seriousness**: *a book of extraordinary gravitas*

gravi·tate /ˈgrævɪteɪt/ *verb* (*formal*)

PHR V **ˈgravitate to/toward(s) sb/sth** to move towards sb/sth that you are attracted to: *Many young people gravitate to the cities in search of work.*

gravi·ta·tion /ˌgrævɪˈteɪʃn/ *noun* [U] (*physics*) a force of attraction that causes objects to move towards each other

gravi·ta·tion·al /ˌgrævɪˈteɪʃənl/ *adj.* connected with or caused by the force of gravity: *a gravitational field* ◇ *the gravitational pull of the moon*

grav·ity /ˈgrævəti/ *noun* [U] **1** (*abbr.* g) the force that attracts objects in space towards each other, and that on the earth pulls them towards the centre of the planet, so that things fall to the ground when they are dropped: *Newton's law of gravity* ➲ see also CENTRE OF GRAVITY **2** (*formal*) extreme importance and a cause for worry SYN **seriousness**: *I don't think you realise the gravity of the situation.* ◇ *Punishment varies according to the gravity of the offence.* **3** (*formal*) serious behaviour, speech or appearance: *They were asked to behave with the gravity that was appropriate in a court of law.* ➲ see also GRAVE[1] *adj.*

gravy /ˈgreɪvi/ *noun* [U] **1** a brown sauce made by adding flour to the juices that come out of meat while it is cooking **2** (*NAmE, informal*) something, especially money, that is obtained when you do not expect it

ˈgravy boat *noun* a long low JUG used for serving and pouring gravy at a meal ➲ VISUAL VOCAB page V19

ˈgravy train *noun* (*informal*) a situation where people seem to be making a lot of money without much effort

gray /greɪ/ (*especially NAmE*) = GREY

gray·beard (*especially NAmE*) = GREYBEARD

gray·ish /ˈgreɪɪʃ/ *adj.* (*especially NAmE*) = GREYISH

gray·scale (*especially NAmE*) = GREYSCALE

graze /greɪz/ *verb, noun*
- ***verb*** **1** [I, T] (of cows, sheep, etc.) to eat grass that is growing in a field: *There were cows grazing beside the river.* ◇ **~ on sth** *The horses were grazing on the lush grass.* ◇ **~ sth** *The field had been grazed by sheep.* **2** [T] **~ sth** to put cows,

sheep, etc. in a field so that they can eat the grass there: *The land is used by local people to graze their animals.* ➲ COLLOCATIONS at FARMING **3** [I] **~ (on sth)** (*informal*) to eat small amounts of food many times during the day, often while doing other things, instead of eating three meals: *I have this really bad habit of grazing on junk food.* **4** [T] **~ sth (on sth)** to break the surface of your skin by rubbing it against sth rough: *I fell and grazed my knee.* ➲ COLLOCATIONS at INJURY **5** [T] **~ sth** to touch sth lightly while passing it: *The bullet grazed his cheek.*

■ ***noun*** a small injury where the surface of the skin has been slightly broken by rubbing against sth: *Adam walked away from the crash with just* ***cuts and grazes.***

gra·zier /ˈgreɪziə(r)/ *noun* a farmer who keeps animals that eat grass

graz·ing /ˈgreɪzɪŋ/ *noun* [U] land with grass that cows, sheep, etc. can eat

GRE /ˌdʒiː ɑːr ˈiː/ *abbr.* Graduate Record Examination (an examination taken by students who want to study for a further degree in the US)

grease /griːs/ *noun, verb*

■ ***noun*** [U] **1** any thick OILY substance, especially one that is used to make machines run smoothly: *Grease marks can be removed with liquid detergent.* ◇ *Her hands were covered with oil and grease.* ◇ *the grease in his hair* ➲ see also ELBOW GREASE **2** animal fat that has been made softer by cooking or heating: *plates covered with grease*

■ ***verb*** **~ sth** to rub grease or fat on sth: *to grease a cake tin/pan*

IDM **grease sb's ˈpalm** (*old-fashioned, informal*) to give sb money in order to persuade them to do sth dishonest SYN **bribe** **grease the ˈwheels** (*NAmE*) (*BrE* **oil the ˈwheels**) to help sth to happen easily and without problems, especially in business or politics

grease·ball /ˈgriːsbɔːl/ *noun* (*NAmE, taboo, slang*) a very offensive word for a person from southern Europe or Latin America

ˈgrease gun *noun* a tool for applying GREASE to moving parts of a machine, etc.

ˈgrease monkey *noun* (*informal*) an offensive or humorous word for a person whose job is repairing cars

grease·paint /ˈgriːspeɪnt/ *noun* [U] a thick substance used by actors as make-up

grease·proof paper /ˌgriːspruːf ˈpeɪpə(r)/ (*BrE*) (*NAmE* **ˈwax paper**) *noun* [U] paper that does not let GREASE, oil, etc. pass through it, used in cooking and for wrapping food in

greasy /ˈgriːsi; ˈgriːzi/ *adj.* (**greas·ier, greasi·est**) **1** covered in a lot of GREASE or oil: *greasy fingers/marks/overalls* **2** (*disapproving*) (of food) cooked with too much oil: *greasy chips* **3** (*disapproving*) (of hair or skin) producing too much natural oil: *long greasy hair* **4** (*informal, disapproving*) (of people or their behaviour) friendly in a way that does not seem sincere SYN **smarmy**

IDM **the greasy ˈpole** (*informal*) used to refer to the difficult way to the top of a profession

ˌgreasy ˈspoon *noun* (*informal*, often *disapproving*) a small cheap restaurant, usually one that is not very clean or attractive

great 🔑 /greɪt/ *adj., noun, adv.*

■ ***adj.*** (**great·er, great·est**)

▸ LARGE **1** 🔑 [usually before noun] very large; much bigger than average in size or quantity: *A great crowd had gathered.* ◇ *People were arriving in great numbers.* ◇ *The* ***great majority of*** (= most) *people seem to agree with this view.* ◇ *He must have fallen from a great height.* ◇ *She lived to a great age.* **2** 🔑 [only before noun] (*informal*) used to emphasize an adjective of size or quality: *There was a* ***great big*** *pile of books on the table.* ◇ *He cut himself a great thick slice of cake.* **3** 🔑 much more than average in degree or quantity: *a matter of great importance* ◇ *The concert had been a great success.* ◇ *Her death was a great shock to us all.* ◇ *It gives me great pleasure to welcome you here today.* ◇ *Take great care of it.* ◇ *You've been a great help.* ◇ *We are all* ***to a great extent*** *the products of our culture.* ➲ SYNONYMS at BIG

> **Synonyms**
>
> **great**
>
> **cool • fantastic • fabulous • terrific • brilliant • awesome**
>
> These are all informal words that describe sb/sth that is very good, pleasant, enjoyable, etc.
>
> **great** (*informal*) very good; giving a lot of pleasure: *We had a great time in Madrid.*
>
> **cool** (*informal*) used to show that you admire or approve of sth, often because it is fashionable, attractive or different: *I think their new song's really cool.*
>
> **fantastic** (*informal*) extremely good; giving a lot of pleasure: *'How was your holiday?' 'Fantastic!'*
>
> **fabulous** (*informal*) extremely good: *Jane's a fabulous cook.* (**Fabulous** is slightly more old-fashioned than the other words in this set.)
>
> **terrific** (*informal*) extremely good; wonderful: *She's doing a terrific job.*
>
> **brilliant** (*BrE, informal*) extremely good; wonderful: *'How was the show?' 'Brilliant!'*
>
> **awesome** (*informal, especially NAmE*) very good, impressive, or enjoyable: *The show was just awesome.*
>
> PATTERNS
>
> - to have a(n) great/cool/fantastic/fabulous/terrific/brilliant/awesome **time**
> - to **look/sound** great/cool/fantastic/fabulous/terrific/brilliant/awesome
> - **really** great/cool/fantastic/fabulous/terrific/brilliant/awesome
> - **absolutely** great/fantastic/fabulous/terrific/brilliant/awesome

▸ ADMIRED **4** 🔑 extremely good in ability or quality and therefore admired by many people: *He has been described as the world's greatest violinist.* ◇ *Sherlock Holmes, the great detective* ◇ *Great art has the power to change lives.*

▸ GOOD **5** 🔑 (*informal*) very good or pleasant: *He's a great bloke.* ◇ *It's great to see you again.* ◇ *What a great goal!* ◇ *We had a great time in Madrid.* ◇ *'I'll pick you up at seven.' 'That'll be great, thanks.'* ◇ (*ironic*) *Oh great, they left without us.* ◇ *You've been a great help, I must say* (= no help at all).

▸ IMPORTANT/IMPRESSIVE **6** 🔑 [only before noun] important and impressive: *The wedding was a great occasion.* ◇ *As the great day approached, she grew more and more nervous.* ◇ ***The great thing*** *is to get it done quickly.* ◇ *One great advantage of this metal is that it doesn't rust.*

▸ WITH INFLUENCE **7** 🔑 having high status or a lot of influence: *the great powers* (= important and powerful countries) ◇ *We can make this country great again.* ◇ *Alexander the Great*

▸ IN GOOD HEALTH **8** 🔑 in a very good state of physical or mental health: *She seemed in great spirits* (= very cheerful). ◇ ***I feel great*** *today.* ◇ *Everyone's in great form.*

▸ SKILLED **9** [not usually before noun] **~ at (doing) sth** (*informal*) able to do sth well: *She's great at chess.*

▸ USEFUL **10 ~ for (doing) sth** (*informal*) very suitable or useful for sth: *This gadget's great for opening jars.* ◇ *Try this cream—it's great for spots.*

▸ FOR EMPHASIS **11** [only before noun] used when you are emphasizing a particular description of sb/sth: *We are great friends.* ◇ *I've never been a great reader* (= I do not read much). ◇ *She's a great talker, isn't she?*

▸ FAMILY **12 great-** added to words for family members to show a further stage in relationship: *my great-aunt* (= my father's or mother's aunt) ◇ *her great-grandson* (= the grandson of her son or daughter) ◇ *my great-great-grandfather* (= the grandfather of my grandfather)

▸ LARGER ANIMALS/PLANTS **13** [only before noun] used in the

names of animals or plants which are larger than similar kinds: *the great tit*
▸ CITY NAME **14 Greater** used with the name of a city to describe an area that includes the centre of the city and a large area all round it: *Greater London*
▶ **great·ness** noun [U]
IDM **be going great 'guns** (*informal*) to be doing sth quickly and successfully: *Work is going great guns now.* **be a 'great one for (doing) sth** to do sth a lot; to enjoy sth: *I've never been a great one for writing letters.* ◇ *You're a great one for quizzes, aren't you?* **be no great 'shakes** (*informal*) to be not very good, efficient, suitable, etc. **,great and 'small** of all sizes or types: *all creatures great and small* **great ,minds think a'like** (*informal, humorous*) used to say that you and another person must both be very clever because you have had the same idea or agree about sth **the great ...in the 'sky** (*humorous*) used to refer to where a particular person is imagined to go when they die or a thing when it is no longer working, similar to the place they were connected with on earth: *Their pet rabbit had gone to the great rabbit hutch in the sky.* ➲ more at OAK, PAINS, SUM *n.*
■ ***noun*** [usually pl.] (*informal*) a very well-known and successful person or thing: *He was one of boxing's all-time greats.*
■ ***adv.*** (*informal, non-standard*) very well: *Well done. You did great.*

,great 'ape noun [usually pl.] one of the large animals which are most similar to humans (CHIMPANZEES, GORILLAS, and ORANG-UTANS)

,great 'auk noun a large bird similar to a PENGUIN, that no longer exists

the ,Great 'Bear noun [sing.] (*astronomy*) = URSA MAJOR

,Great 'Britain noun [U] England, Scotland and Wales, when considered as a unit HELP Sometimes 'Great Britain' (or 'Britain') is wrongly used to refer to the political state, officially called the 'United Kingdom of Great Britain and Northern Ireland' or the 'UK'.

great·coat /ˈgreɪtkəʊt; NAmE -koʊt/ noun a long heavy coat, especially one worn by soldiers

Great Dane /ˌgreɪt ˈdeɪn/ noun a very large dog with short hair

great·ly 0━ /ˈgreɪtli/ *adv.* (*formal*) (usually before a verb or participle) very much: *People's reaction to the film has varied greatly.* ◇ *a greatly increased risk* ◇ *Your help would be greatly appreciated.*

the ,Great 'War noun [sing.] (*old-fashioned*) = THE FIRST WORLD WAR

,great white 'shark noun a large aggressive SHARK with a brown or grey back, found in warm seas

the ,Great White 'Way noun (*informal*) a name for Broadway in New York City that refers to the many bright lights of its theatres

grebe /griːb/ noun a bird like a DUCK, that can also swim underwater: *a great crested grebe*

Gre·cian /ˈgriːʃn/ *adj.* from ancient Greece or like the styles of ancient Greece: *Grecian architecture*

,Grecian 'nose noun a straight nose that continues the line of the FOREHEAD

,Greco- *combining form* (*NAmE*) = GRAECO-

greed /griːd/ noun [U] (*disapproving*) **1** a strong desire for more wealth, possessions, power, etc. than a person needs: *His actions were motivated by greed.* ◇ **~ for sth** *Nothing would satisfy her greed for power.* **2** a strong desire for more food or drink when you are no longer hungry or thirsty: *I had another helping of ice cream out of pure greed.*

greedy /ˈgriːdi/ *adj.* (**greed·ier, greedi·est**) wanting more money, power, food, etc. than you really need: *You greedy pig! You've already had two helpings!* ◇ *He stared at the diamonds with greedy eyes.* ◇ **~ for sth** *The shareholders are greedy for profit.* ▶ **greed·ily** *adv.*: *She ate noisily and greedily.*
IDM **'greedy guts** (*BrE, informal*) used to refer to sb who eats too much

Greek /griːk/ noun **1** [C] a person from modern or ancient Greece **2** [U] the language of modern or ancient Greece **3** [C] (*NAmE*) a member of a FRATERNITY or a SORORITY at a college or university
IDM **it's all 'Greek to me** (*informal, saying*) I cannot understand it: *She tried to explain how the system works, but it's all Greek to me.*

,Greek 'cross noun a cross with all arms of the same length

,Greek 'salad noun [C, U] a salad that is made with tomatoes, OLIVES and FETA CHEESE

green 0━ /griːn/ *adj., noun, verb*
■ ***adj.*** (**green·er, green·est**)
▸ COLOUR **1** 0━ having the colour of grass or the leaves of most plants and trees: *green beans* ◇ *Wait for the light to turn green* (= on traffic lights).
▸ COVERED WITH GRASS **2** 0━ covered with grass or other plants: ***green fields/hills*** ◇ *After the rains, the land was green with new growth.*
▸ FRUIT **3** 0━ not yet ready to eat: *green tomatoes*
▸ POLITICS **4** 0━ concerned with the protection of the environment; supporting the protection of the environment as a political principle: *green politics* ◇ *Try to adopt a greener lifestyle.* ◇ *the Green Party*
▸ PERSON **5** (*informal*) (of a person) young and lacking experience: *The new trainees are still very green.* **6** (of a person or their skin) being a pale colour, as if the person is going to VOMIT: *It was a rough crossing and most of the passengers looked distinctly green.*
▶ **green·ness** noun [U]: *the greenness of the countryside* ◇ *Supermarkets have started proclaiming the greenness of their products.*
IDM **,green with 'envy** very jealous ➲ more at GRASS *n.*
■ ***noun***
▸ COLOUR **1** 0━ [U, C] the colour of grass and the leaves of most plants and trees: *the green of the countryside in spring* ◇ *The room was decorated in a combination of greens and blues.* ◇ *She was dressed all in green.*
▸ VEGETABLES **2 greens** [pl.] (*especially BrE*) green vegetables: *Eat up your greens.*
▸ AREA OF GRASS **3** [C] (*BrE*) an area of grass, especially in the middle of a town or village: *Children were playing on the village green.* ➲ VISUAL VOCAB page V3 **4** [C] (in GOLF) an area of grass cut short around a hole on a GOLF COURSE: *the 18th green* ◇ *Did the ball land on the green?* ➲ VISUAL VOCAB page V34 ➲ see also BOWLING GREEN, PUTTING GREEN
▸ POLITICS **5 the Greens** [pl.] the Green Party (= the party whose main aim is the protection of the environment)
■ ***verb***
▸ CREATE PARKS **1 ~ sth** to create parks and other areas with trees and plants in a city: *projects for greening the cities*
▸ POLITICS **2 ~ sb/sth** to make sb more aware of issues connected with the environment; to make sth appear friendly towards the environment: *an attempt to green industry bosses*
▶ **green·ing** noun [U]: *the greening of British politics*

,green 'audit noun an official examination of the effect of a company's business on the environment

green·back /ˈgriːnbæk/ noun (*NAmE, informal*) an American dollar note

,green 'bean (*BrE* also **,French 'bean**) (*NAmE* also **,string 'bean**) noun a type of BEAN which is a long thin green POD, cooked and eaten whole as a vegetable ➲ VISUAL VOCAB page V27

,green 'belt noun [U, C, usually sing.] (*especially BrE*) an area of open land around a city where building is strictly controlled: *New roads are cutting into the green belt.*

,Green Be'ret noun a member of the US army Special Forces

,green 'card noun **1** a document that legally allows sb from another country to live and work in the US **2** (*BrE*) an insurance document that you need when you drive your car in another country

green·ery /ˈɡriːnəri/ *noun* [U] attractive green leaves and plants: *The room was decorated with flowers and greenery.*

the ˌgreen-eyed ˈmonster *noun* (*informal*) used as a way of talking about JEALOUSY

green·field /ˈɡriːnfiːld/ *adj.* [only before noun] (*BrE*) used to describe an area of land that has not yet had buildings on it, but for which building development may be planned: *a greenfield site*

ˌgreen ˈfingers *noun* [pl.] (*BrE*) (*NAmE* **ˌgreen ˈthumb**) if you have **green fingers**, you are good at making plants grow ▸ **ˌgreen-ˈfingered** *adj.* (*BrE*)

green·fly /ˈɡriːnflaɪ/ *noun* [U, C] (*pl.* **green·flies** or **green·fly**) a small flying insect that is harmful to plants: *The roses have got greenfly.*

green·gage /ˈɡriːnɡeɪdʒ/ *noun* a small soft green fruit that is a type of PLUM: *a greengage tree*

green·gro·cer /ˈɡriːnɡrəʊsə(r); *NAmE* -ɡroʊ-/ *noun* (*especially BrE*) **1** a person who owns, manages or works in a shop/store selling fruit and vegetables ➲ compare FRUITERER **2 green·gro·cer's** (*pl.* **green·gro·cers**) a shop/store that sells fruit and vegetables

green·horn /ˈɡriːnhɔːn; *NAmE* -hɔːrn/ *noun* (*informal, especially NAmE*) a person who has little experience and can be easily tricked SYN **tenderfoot**

green·house /ˈɡriːnhaʊs/ *noun* a building with glass sides and a glass roof for growing plants in ➲ VISUAL VOCAB page V16

the ˈgreenhouse effect *noun* [sing.] the problem of the gradual rise in temperature of the earth's atmosphere, caused by an increase of gases such as CARBON DIOXIDE in the air surrounding the earth, which trap the heat of the sun ➲ COLLOCATIONS at ENVIRONMENT ➲ see also GLOBAL WARMING

ˌgreenhouse ˈgas *noun* any of the gases that are thought to cause the greenhouse effect, especially CARBON DIOXIDE ➲ COLLOCATIONS at ENVIRONMENT

green·ing /ˈɡriːnɪŋ/ *noun* [U] ➲ GREEN *v.*

green·ish /ˈɡriːnɪʃ/ *adj.* fairly green in colour

green·keep·er /ˈɡriːnkiːpə(r)/ (*NAmE* also **greens·keep·er**) *noun* a person whose job is to take care of a GOLF COURSE

ˌgreen ˈlight *noun* [sing.] permission for a project, etc. to start or continue SYN **go-ahead**: *The government has decided to* ***give the green light*** *to the plan.*

ˌgreen maˈnure *noun* [U, C] plants that are dug into the soil in order to improve its quality

ˌgreen ˈonion (also **scal·lion**) (both *NAmE*) (*BrE* **ˌspring ˈonion**) *noun* a type of small onion with a long green STEM and leaves. Green onions are often eaten raw in salads. ➲ VISUAL VOCAB page V27

ˌGreen ˈPaper *noun* (in Britain) a document containing government proposals on a particular subject, intended for general discussion ➲ compare WHITE PAPER

ˌgreen ˈpepper *noun* a hollow green fruit that is eaten, raw or cooked, as a vegetable

ˈgreen roof (also **ˈliving roof**) *noun* a type of roof that has plants growing on it that help to keep the building cool in summer and warm in winter

ˈgreen room *noun* a room in a theatre, television studio, etc. where the performers can relax when they are not performing

ˌgreen ˈsalad *noun* [C, U] (*BrE*) a salad that is made with raw green vegetables, especially LETTUCE: *Serve with a green salad.*

greens·keep·er /ˈɡriːnzkiːpə(r)/ *noun* (*NAmE*) = GREENKEEPER

greens·ward /ˈɡriːnswɔːd; *NAmE* -swɔːrd/ *noun* [U] (*literary*) a piece of ground covered with grass

ˌgreen ˈtea *noun* [U] a pale tea made from leaves that have been dried but not FERMENTED

ˌgreen ˈthumb (*NAmE*) (*BrE* **ˌgreen ˈfingers**) *noun* [sing.] if you have a **green thumb**, you are good at making plants grow

ˌgreen ˈvegetable *noun* [C, usually pl.] (*BrE* also **greens** [pl.]) a vegetable with dark green leaves, for example CABBAGE or SPINACH

green·wash /ˈɡriːnwɒʃ; *NAmE* -wɔːʃ/ *noun* [U] (*disapproving*) activities by a company or an organization that are intended to make people think that it is concerned about the environment, even if its real business actually harms the environment

the ˌgreen ˈwelly brigade *noun* [sing.+ sing./pl. v.] (*BrE, humorous, disapproving*) rich people who live in or like to visit the countryside ORIGIN From the green wellington boots that they often wear.

G

Green·wich Mean Time /ˌɡrenɪtʃ ˈmiːn taɪm; -nɪdʒ/ ➲ GMT

greet /ɡriːt/ *verb* **1** to say hello to sb or to welcome them: **~ sb** *He greeted all the guests warmly as they arrived.* ◇ **~ sb with sth** *She greeted us with a smile.* ➲ see also MEET-AND-GREET **2** [usually passive] to react to sb/sth in a particular way: **~ sb/sth** *Loud cheers greeted the news.* ◇ **~ sb/sth with sth** *The changes were greeted with suspicion.* ◇ **~ sb/sth as sth** *The team's win was greeted as a major triumph.* **3** [usually passive] **~ sb** (of sights, sounds or smells) to be the first thing that you see, hear or smell at a particular time: *When she opened the door she was greeted by a scene of utter confusion.*

greet·er /ˈɡriːtə(r)/ *noun* (*especially NAmE*) a person whose job is to meet and welcome people in a public place such as a restaurant or shop/store

greet·ing /ˈɡriːtɪŋ/ *noun* **1** [C, U] something that you say or do to greet sb: *She waved a friendly greeting.* ◇ *They* ***exchanged greetings*** *and sat down to lunch.* ◇ *He raised his hand* ***in greeting***. **2 greetings** [pl.] a message of good wishes for sb's health, happiness, etc: ***Christmas/birthday, etc.*** *greetings* ◇ *My mother sends her greetings to you all.* IDM see SEASON *n.*

ˈgreetings card (*BrE*) (*NAmE* **ˈgreeting card**) *noun* a card with a picture on the front and a message inside that you send to sb on a particular occasion such as their birthday

gre·gari·ous /ɡrɪˈɡeəriəs; *NAmE* -ˈɡer-/ *adj.* **1** liking to be with other people SYN **sociable 2** (*biology*) (of animals or birds) living in groups ▸ **gre·gari·ous·ly** *adv.* **gre·gari·ous·ness** *noun* [U]

Gre·gor·ian calendar /ɡrɪˌɡɔːriən ˈkælɪndə(r)/ *noun* [sing.] the system used since 1582 in Western countries of arranging the months in the year and the days in the months and of counting the years from the birth of Christ ➲ compare JULIAN CALENDAR

GreˌgorianˈChant *noun* [U, C] a type of church music for voices alone, used since the Middle Ages

grem·lin /ˈɡremlɪn/ *noun* an imaginary creature that people blame when a machine suddenly stops working

gren·ade /ɡrəˈneɪd/ *noun* a small bomb that can be thrown by hand or fired from a gun ➲ see also HAND GRENADE

grena·dier /ˌɡrenəˈdɪə(r); *NAmE* -ˈdɪr/ *noun* a soldier in the part of the British army known as the **Grenadiers** or **Grenadier Guards**

grena·dine /ˈɡrenədiːn/ *noun* [U] a sweet red liquid that is made from POMEGRANATES (= a tropical fruit with many seeds). It is drunk mixed with water or alcoholic drinks.

Gretna Green /ˌɡretnə ˈɡriːn/ *noun* a village in Scotland near the border with England, famous in the past as a place where English couples used to go to get married when they were not allowed to get married in England

grew *past tense* of GROW

grey 🗝 (*especially BrE*) (*NAmE* usually **gray**) /greɪ/ *adj., noun, verb*
■ **adj. 1** 🗝 having the colour of smoke or ASHES: *grey eyes/hair* ◇ *wisps of grey smoke* ◇ *a grey suit* **2** 🗝 [not usually before noun] having grey hair: *He's gone very grey.* **3** 🗝 (of the sky or weather) dull; full of clouds: *grey skies* ◇ *I hate these grey days.* **4** (of a person's skin colour) pale and dull, because they are ill/sick, tired or sad **5** without interest or variety; making you feel sad: *Life seems grey and pointless without him.* **6** (*disapproving*) not interesting or attractive: *The company was full of faceless grey men who all looked the same.* **7** [only before noun] connected with old people: *the grey vote* ◇ *grey power* ▶ **grey·ness** (*especially BrE*) (*NAmE* usually **gray·ness**) *noun* [U, sing.]
■ ***noun* 1** 🗝 [U, C] the colour of smoke or ASHES: *the dull grey of the sky* ◇ *dressed in grey* **2** [C] a grey or white horse: *She's riding the grey.*
■ **verb** [I] (of hair) to become grey: *His hair was greying at the sides.* ◇ *a tall woman with greying hair*

ˌgrey ˈarea (*especially BrE*) (*NAmE* usually **ˌgray ˈarea**) *noun* an area of a subject or situation that is not clear or does not fit into a particular group and is therefore difficult to define or deal with: *Exactly what can be called an offensive weapon is still a grey area.*

grey·beard (*especially BrE*) (*NAmE* usually **gray·beard**) /ˈgreɪbɪəd; *NAmE* -bɪrd/ *noun* (*informal*) an old man: *the greybeards of the art world*

ˌgrey-ˈhaired (*especially BrE*) (*NAmE* usually **ˌgray-ˈhaired**) *adj.* with grey hair

grey·hound /ˈgreɪhaʊnd/ *noun* a large thin dog with smooth hair and long thin legs, that can run very fast and is used in the sport of **greyhound racing**

grey·ish (*especially BrE*) (*NAmE* usually **gray·ish**) /ˈgreɪɪʃ/ *adj.* fairly grey in colour: *greyish hair*

ˌgrey ˈmarket (*NAmE* usually **ˌgray ˈmarket**) *noun* [usually sing.] **1** a system in which products are imported into a country and sold without the permission of the company that produced them **2** (*BrE*) old people, when they are thought of as customers for goods

ˈgrey matter (*especially BrE*) (*NAmE* usually **ˈgray matter**) *noun* [U] (*informal*) a person's intelligence

grey·scale (*especially BrE*) (*NAmE* usually **gray·scale**) /ˈgreɪskeɪl/ *adj.* (*technical*) **1** (of an image) produced using only shades of grey, not colour: *I've printed out the pictures **in greyscale**.* **2** (of a printer or SCANNER) producing images using only shades of grey, not colour

grid /grɪd/ *noun* **1** a pattern of straight lines, usually crossing each other to form squares: *New York's grid of streets* **2** a frame of metal or wooden bars that are parallel or cross each other ➲ see also CATTLE GRID **3** a pattern of squares on a map that are marked with letters or numbers to help you find the exact position of a place: *The **grid reference** is C8.* **4** (*especially BrE*) a system of electric wires or pipes carrying gas, for sending power over a large area: *the national grid* (= the electricity supply in a country) **5** (in motor racing) a pattern of lines marking the starting positions for the racing cars **6** (often **the Grid**) [sing.] (*computing*) a number of computers that are linked together using the Internet so that they can share power, data, etc. in order to work on difficult problems
IDM **ˌoff the ˈgrid** (*especially NAmE*) not using the public supplies of electricity, gas, water, etc: *The mountain cabin is entirely off the grid.* ➲ see also OFF-THE-GRID

grid·dle /ˈgrɪdl/ *noun* a flat round iron plate that is heated on a stove or over a fire and used for cooking

grid·iron /ˈgrɪdaɪən; *NAmE* -aɪərn/ *noun* **1** a frame made of metal bars that is used for cooking meat or fish on, over an open fire **2** (*NAmE*) a field used for AMERICAN FOOTBALL marked with a pattern of parallel lines

grid·lock /ˈgrɪdlɒk; *NAmE* -lɑːk/ *noun* [U] **1** a situation in which there are so many cars in the streets of a town that the traffic cannot move at all **2** (usually in politics) a situation in which people with different opinions are not able to agree with each other and so no action can be taken: *Congress is in gridlock.* ▶ **grid·locked** *adj.*

grief /griːf/ *noun* **1** [U, C] ~ (**over/at sth**) a feeling of great sadness, especially when sb dies: *She was overcome with grief when her husband died.* ◇ *They were able to share their common joys and griefs.* **2** [C, usually sing.] something that causes great sadness: *It was a grief to them that they had no children.* **3** [U] (*informal*) problems and worry: *He caused his parents a lot of grief.*
IDM **come to ˈgrief** (*informal*) **1** to end in total failure **2** to be harmed in an accident: *Several pedestrians came to grief on the icy pavement.* **give sb ˈgrief** (**about/over sth**) (*informal*) to be annoyed with sb and criticize their behaviour **good ˈgrief!** (*informal*) used to express surprise or shock: *Good grief! What a mess!*

ˈgrief-stricken *adj.* feeling extremely sad because of sth that has happened, especially the death of sb

griev·ance /ˈgriːvəns/ *noun* ~ (**against sb**) something that you think is unfair and that you complain or protest about: *Parents were invited to **air their grievances*** (= express them) *at the meeting.* ◇ *He had been **nursing a grievance** against his boss for months.* ◇ *Does the company have a formal **grievance procedure*** (= a way of telling sb your complaints at work)*?*

grieve /griːv/ *verb* **1** [I, T] to feel very sad, especially because sb has died: ~ (**for/over sb/sth**) *They are still grieving for their dead child.* ◇ *grieving relatives* ◇ ~ **sb/sth** *She grieved the death of her husband.* **2** [T] (*formal*) to make you feel very sad SYN **pain**: **it grieves sb that…** *It grieved him that he could do nothing to help her.* ◇ ~ **sb** *Their lack of interest grieved her.* ◇ **it grieves sb to do sth** *It grieved her to leave.* IDM see EYE *n.*

griev·ous /ˈgriːvəs/ *adj.* (*formal*) very serious and often causing great pain or suffering: *He had been the victim of a grievous injustice.* ▶ **griev·ous·ly** *adv.*: ***grievously hurt/wounded***

ˌgrievous ˌbodily ˈharm *noun* [U] (*abbr.* **GBH**) (*BrE, law*) the crime of causing sb serious physical injury ➲ compare ACTUAL BODILY HARM

grif·fin /ˈgrɪfɪn/ (also **grif·fon**, **gry·phon** /ˈgrɪfən/) *noun* (in stories) a creature with a LION's body and an EAGLE's wings and head

grift·er /ˈgrɪftə(r)/ *noun* (*especially US*) a person who tricks people into giving them money, etc.

grill /grɪl/ *noun, verb*
■ ***noun* 1** (*BrE*) the part of a cooker that directs heat downwards to cook food that is placed underneath it ➲ VISUAL VOCAB page V22 ➲ compare BROILER **2** a flat metal frame that you put food on to cook over a fire ➲ see also BARBECUE **3** a dish of grilled food, especially meat ➲ see also MIXED GRILL **4** (especially in names) a restaurant serving grilled food: *Harry's Bar and Grill* **5** = GRILLE
■ ***verb* 1** ~ **sth** (*BrE*) to cook food under or over a very strong heat: *Grill the sausages for ten minutes.* ◇ *grilled bacon* ➲ compare BROIL ➲ COLLOCATIONS at COOKING **2** ~ **sth** (*NAmE*) to cook food over a fire, especially outdoors: *grilled meat and shrimp* **3** ~ **sb** (**about sth**) to ask sb a lot of questions about their ideas, actions, etc, often in an unpleasant way: *They grilled her about where she had been all night.* ➲ see also GRILLING

grille (also **grill**) /grɪl/ *noun* a screen made of metal bars or wire that is placed in front of a window, door or piece of machinery in order to protect it: *a radiator grille* (= at the front of a car) ◇ *a security grille*

grill·ing /ˈgrɪlɪŋ/ *noun* [usually sing.] a period of being questioned closely about your ideas, actions, etc: *The minister faced a tough grilling at today's press conference.*

grilse /grɪls/ *noun* a SALMON (= a type of fish) that has returned to a river or lake after spending one winter in the sea

grim /grɪm/ *adj.* (**grim·mer**, **grim·mest**) **1** looking or sounding very serious: *a **grim face/look/smile*** ◇ *She looked grim.* ◇ *with a look of **grim determination** on his face* ◇ ***grim-faced** policemen* **2** unpleasant and depressing: *grim news* ◇ *We face the grim prospect of still higher unemployment.* ◇ *The outlook is pretty grim.* ◇ *Things are **look-***

ing grim for workers in the building industry. **3** (of a place or building) not attractive; depressing: *The house looked grim and dreary in the rain.* ◇ *the grim walls of the prison* **4** [not before noun] (*BrE, informal*) ill/sick: *I feel grim this morning.* **5** [not usually before noun] (*BrE, informal*) of very low quality: *Their performance was fairly grim, I'm afraid!* ▶ **grim·ly** *adv.*: *'It won't be easy,' he said grimly.* ◇ *grimly determined* **grim·ness** *noun* [U]

IDM **hang/hold on for/like grim 'death** (*BrE*) (also **hang/hold on for dear 'life** *NAmE, BrE*) (*informal*) to hold sb/sth very tightly because you are afraid

grim·ace /grɪˈmeɪs; ˈgrɪməs/ *verb, noun*

■ *verb* [I] **~ (at sb/sth)** to make an ugly expression with your face to show pain, disgust, etc: *He grimaced at the bitter taste.* ◇ *She grimaced as the needle went in.*

■ *noun* an ugly expression made by twisting your face, used to show pain, disgust, etc. or to make sb laugh: *to* ***make/give a grimace*** *of pain* ◇ *'What's that?' she asked with a grimace.*

grime /graɪm/ *noun* [U] dirt that forms a layer on the surface of sth SYN **dirt**: *a face covered with grime and sweat*

the ˌGrim 'Reaper *noun* an imaginary figure who represents death. It looks like a SKELETON, wears a long CLOAK and carries a SCYTHE.

grimy /ˈgraɪmi/ *adj.* (**grimi·er**, **grimi·est**) covered with dirt SYN **dirty**: *grimy hands/windows*

grin /grɪn/ *verb, noun*

■ *verb* (-nn-) [I, T] to smile widely: *They grinned with delight when they heard our news.* ◇ *He was* ***grinning from ear to ear.*** ◇ **~ at sb** *She grinned amiably at us.* ◇ **~ sth** *He grinned a wide grin.*

IDM **grin and 'bear it** (only used as an infinitive and in orders) to accept pain, disappointment or a difficult situation without complaining: *There's nothing we can do about it. We'll just have to grin and bear it.* ➲ more at EAR

■ *noun* a wide smile: *She gave a* ***broad grin.*** ◇ *a* ***wry/sheepish grin*** ◇ *'No,' he said* ***with a grin.*** ◇ ***Take that grin off your face!***

grind /graɪnd/ *verb, noun*

■ *verb* (**ground**, **ground** /graʊnd/)

▸ FOOD/FLOUR/COFFEE **1** [T] **~ sth (down/up)** | **~ sth (to/into sth)** to break or crush sth into very small pieces between two hard surfaces or using a special machine: *to grind coffee/corn* ➲ see also GROUND *adj.* **2** [T] **~ sth** to produce sth such as flour by crushing: *The flour is ground using traditional methods.* **3** [T] **~ sth** (*NAmE*) = MINCE

▸ MAKE SHARP/SMOOTH **4** [T] **~ sth** to make sth sharp or smooth by rubbing it against a hard surface: *a special stone for grinding knives*

▸ PRESS INTO SURFACE **5** [T] to press or rub sth into a surface: **~ sth into sth** *He ground his cigarette into the ashtray.* ◇ **~ sth in** *The dirt on her hands was ground in.*

▸ RUB TOGETHER **6** [I, T] to rub together, or to make hard objects rub together, often producing an unpleasant noise: **~ (together)** *Parts of the machine were grinding together noisily.* ◇ **~ sth (together)** *She* ***grinds her teeth*** *when she is asleep.* ◇ *He ground the gears on the car.*

▸ MACHINE **7** [T] **~ sth** to turn the handle of a machine that grinds sth: *to grind a pepper mill*

IDM **bring sth to a grinding 'halt** to make sth gradually go slower until it stops completely **grind to a 'halt** | **come to a grinding 'halt** to go slower gradually and then stop completely: *Production ground to a halt during the strike.* ➲ more at AXE *n.*

PHR V **ˌgrind sb↔'down** to treat sb in a cruel unpleasant way over a long period of time, so that they become very unhappy: *Don't let them grind you down.* ◇ *Years of oppression had ground the people down.* **ˌgrind 'on** to continue for a long time, when this is unpleasant: *The argument ground on for almost two years.* **ˌgrind sth↔'out** to produce sth in large quantities, often sth that is not good or interesting SYN **churn out**: *She grinds out romantic novels at the rate of five a year.*

■ *noun*

▸ BORING ACTIVITY **1** [sing.] (*informal*) an activity that is tiring or boring and takes a lot of time: *the* ***daily grind*** *of family life* ◇ *It's a long grind to the top of that particular profession.*

▸ OF MACHINES **2** [sing.] the unpleasant noise made by machines

▸ SWOT **3** (*US*) (*BrE* **swot**) [C] (*informal*) a person who spends too much time studying

grind·er /ˈgraɪndə(r)/ *noun* **1** a machine or tool for grinding a solid substance into a powder: *a coffee grinder* **2** a person whose job is to make knives sharper; a machine which does this ➲ see also ORGAN-GRINDER

grind·ing /ˈgraɪndɪŋ/ *adj.* [only before noun] (of a difficult situation) that never ends or improves: *grinding poverty*

grind·stone /ˈgraɪndstəʊn; *NAmE* -stoʊn/ *noun* a round stone that is turned like a wheel and is used to make knives and other tools sharp IDM see NOSE *n.*

gringo /ˈgrɪŋgəʊ; *NAmE* -goʊ/ *noun* (*pl.* -os) (*informal, disapproving*) used in Latin American countries to refer to a person from the US

griot /ˈgriːəʊ; *NAmE* ˈgriːoʊ/ *noun* (in W Africa, especially in the past) a person who sings or tells stories about the history and traditions of their people and community

grip /grɪp/ *noun, verb*

■ *noun*

▸ HOLDING TIGHTLY **1** [C, usually sing.] **~ (on sb/sth)** an act of holding sb/sth tightly; a particular way of doing this SYN **grasp**: *Keep a tight grip on the rope.* ◇ *to* ***loosen/release/relax your grip*** ◇ *She tried to* ***get a grip on*** *the icy rock.* ◇ *The climber slipped and* ***lost her grip.*** ◇ *She struggled from his grip.* ◇ *Try adjusting your grip on the racket.*

▸ CONTROL/POWER **2** [sing.] **~ (on sb/sth)** control or power over sb/sth: *The home team took a firm grip on the game.* ◇ *We need to tighten the grip we have on the market.*

▸ UNDERSTANDING **3** [sing.] **~ (on sth)** an understanding of sth SYN **grasp**: *I couldn't get a grip on what was going on.* ◇ *You need to keep a good grip on reality in this job.*

▸ MOVING WITHOUT SLIPPING **4** [U] the ability of sth to move over a surface without slipping: *These tyres give the bus better grip in slippery conditions.*

▸ PART OF OBJECT **5** [C] a part of sth that has a special surface so that it can be held without the hands slipping: *the grip on a golf club*

▸ FOR HAIR **6** [C] (*BrE*) = HAIRGRIP

▸ JOB IN THE MOVIES **7** [C] a person who prepares and moves the cameras, and sometimes the lighting equipment, when a film/movie is being made

▸ BAG **8** [C] (*old-fashioned*) a large soft bag, used when travelling

IDM **come/get to 'grips with sth** to begin to understand and deal with sth difficult: *I'm slowly getting to grips with the language.* **get/take a 'grip (on yourself)** to improve your behaviour or control your emotions after being afraid, upset or angry: *I have to take a grip on myself, he told himself firmly.* ◇ (*informal*) ***Get a grip!*** (= make an effort to control your emotions) **in the 'grip of sth** experiencing sth unpleasant that cannot be stopped: *a country in the grip of recession* **lose your 'grip (on sth)** to become unable to understand or control a situation: *Sometimes I feel I'm losing my grip.*

■ *verb* (-pp-)

▸ HOLD TIGHTLY **1** [T, I] to hold sth tightly SYN **grasp**: **~ sth** *'Please don't go,' he said, gripping her arm.* ◇ **~ on to sth** *She gripped on to the railing with both hands.* ➲ SYNONYMS at HOLD

▸ INTEREST/EXCITE **2** [T] **~ sb** to interest or excite sb; to hold sb's attention: *The book grips you from start to finish.* ◇ *I was totally gripped by the story.* ➲ see also GRIPPING

▸ HAVE POWERFUL EFFECT **3** [T] **~ sb/sth** (of an emotion or a situation) to have a powerful effect on sb/sth: *I was gripped by a feeling of panic.* ◇ *Terrorism has gripped the country for the past two years.*

▸ MOVE/HOLD WITHOUT SLIPPING **4** [T, I] **~ (sth)** to hold onto or to move over a surface without slipping: *tyres that grip the road*

gripe /graɪp/ *noun, verb*

■ *noun* (*informal*) a complaint about sth: *My only gripe about the hotel was the food.*

■ *verb* [I] ~ (**about sb/sth**) (*informal*) to complain about sb/sth in an annoying way: *He's always griping about the people at work.*

'Gripe Water™ *noun* [U] (*BrE*) medicine that is given to babies when they have stomach pains

grip·ing /'graɪpɪŋ/ *adj.* [only before noun] a **griping** pain is a sudden strong pain in your stomach

grip·ping /'grɪpɪŋ/ *adj.* exciting or interesting in a way that keeps your attention ➲ SYNONYMS at INTERESTING

grisly /'grɪzli/ *adj.* [usually before noun] (**gris·lier, gris·li·est**) extremely unpleasant and frightening and usually connected with death and violence: *a grisly crime*

grist /grɪst/ *noun*

IDM (**all**) **grist to the/sb's 'mill** (*BrE*) (*NAmE* (**all**) **grist for the/sb's 'mill**) something that is useful to sb for a particular purpose: *Political sex scandals are all grist to the mill of the tabloid newspapers.*

gris·tle /'grɪsl/ *noun* [U] a hard substance in meat that is unpleasant to eat: *a lump of gristle*

grit /grɪt/ *noun, verb*

■ *noun* [U] **1** very small pieces of stone or sand: *I had a piece of grit in my eye.* ◊ *They were spreading grit and salt on the icy roads.* **2** the courage and determination that makes it possible for sb to continue doing sth difficult or unpleasant

■ *verb* (-tt-) ~ **sth** to spread grit, salt or sand on a road that is covered with ice

IDM **grit your 'teeth 1** to bite your teeth tightly together: *She gritted her teeth against the pain.* ◊ *'Stop it!' he said through gritted teeth.* **2** to be determined to continue to do sth in a difficult or unpleasant situation: *It started to rain harder, but we gritted our teeth and carried on.*

grits /grɪts/ *noun* [pl.] CORN (MAIZE) that is partly crushed before cooking, often eaten for breakfast or as part of a meal in the southern US

grit·ter /'grɪtə(r)/ (*BrE*) (*US* **'salt truck**) *noun* a large vehicle used for putting salt, sand or GRIT on the roads in winter when there is ice on them

gritty /'grɪti/ *adj.* (**gritt·ier, grit·ti·est**) **1** containing or like GRIT: *a layer of gritty dust* **2** showing the courage and determination to continue doing sth difficult or unpleasant: *gritty determination* ◊ *a gritty performance from the British player* **3** showing sth unpleasant as it really is: *a gritty description of urban violence* ◊ *gritty realism* ➲ see also NITTY-GRITTY ▸ **grit·tily** *adv.* **grit·ti·ness** *noun* [U]

griz·zle /'grɪzl/ *verb* [I] (*BrE, informal*) (especially of a baby or child) to cry or complain continuously in a way that is annoying

griz·zled /'grɪzld/ *adj.* (*literary*) having hair that is grey or partly grey

griz·zly bear /ˌgrɪzli 'beə(r); *NAmE* 'ber/ (also **'griz·zly** *pl.* -ies) *noun* a large aggressive brown BEAR that lives in N America and parts of Russia

groan /grəʊn; *NAmE* groʊn/ *verb, noun*

■ *verb* **1** [I, T] to make a long deep sound because you are annoyed, upset or in pain, or with pleasure SYN **moan**: *He lay on the floor groaning.* ◊ ~ **with sth** *to groan with pain/pleasure* ◊ ~ **at sth** *We all groaned at his terrible jokes.* ◊ ~ **about sth** *They were all **moaning and groaning** (= complaining) about the amount of work they had.* ◊ + **speech** *'It's a complete mess!' she groaned.* **2** [I] to make a sound like a person groaning SYN **moan**: *The trees creaked and groaned in the wind.*

IDM **groan under the weight of sth** (*formal*) used to say that there is too much of sth

PHR V **'groan with sth** (*formal*) to be full of sth: *tables groaning with food*

■ *noun* a long deep sound made when sb/sth groans SYN **moan**: *She let out a groan of dismay.* ◊ *He fell to the floor with a groan.* ◊ *The house was filled with the cello's dismal squeaks and groans.*

groat /grəʊt; *NAmE* groʊt/ *noun* a silver coin used in Europe in the past

gro·cer /'grəʊsə(r); *NAmE* 'groʊ-/ *noun* **1** a person who owns, manages or works in a shop/store selling food and other things used in the home **2 gro·cer's** (*pl.* **gro·cers**) a shop/store that sells these things

gro·cery 🔑 /'grəʊsəri; *NAmE* 'groʊ-/ *noun* (*pl.* -ies) **1** 🔑 (*especially BrE*) (*NAmE* usually **'grocery store**) [C] a shop/store that sells food and other things used in the home. In American English ' grocery store ' is often used to mean 'supermarket'. **2** 🔑 **groceries** [pl.] food and other goods sold by a grocer or at a supermarket ➲ COLLOCATIONS at SHOPPING ▸ **gro·cery** *adj.* [only before noun]: *the grocery bill*

grog /grɒg; *NAmE* grɑːg/ *noun* [U] **1** a strong alcoholic drink, originally RUM, mixed with water **2** (*informal, AustralE, NZE*) any alcoholic drink, especially beer

groggy /'grɒgi; *NAmE* 'grɑːgi/ *adj.* [not usually before noun] (**grog·gier, grog·gi·est**) (*informal*) weak and unable to think or move well because you are ill/sick or very tired

groin /grɔɪn/ *noun* **1** the part of the body where the legs join at the top including the area around the GENITALS (= sex organs): *She kicked her attacker in the groin.* ◊ *He's been off all season with a groin injury.* ➲ VISUAL VOCAB page V48 **2** (*especially US*) = GROYNE

grok /grɒk; *NAmE* grɑːk/ (-kk-) *verb* ~ **sth** (*US, slang*) to understand sth completely using your feelings rather than considering the facts: *Children grok this show immediately but their parents take longer to get it.*

grom·met /'grɒmɪt; *NAmE* 'grɑːm-/ *noun* **1** a small metal ring placed around a hole in cloth or leather, to make it stronger **2** (*BrE*) (*NAmE* **tube**) a small tube placed in a child's ear in order to DRAIN liquid from it

groom /gruːm/ *verb, noun*

■ *verb* **1** ~ **sth** to clean or brush an animal: *to groom a horse/dog/cat* ◊ *The horses are all well fed and groomed.* **2** ~ **sth** (of an animal) to clean the fur or skin of another animal or itself: *a female ape grooming her mate* **3** to prepare or train sb for an important job or position: ~ **sb** (**for/as sth**) *Our junior employees are being groomed for more senior roles.* ◊ ~ **sb to do sth** *The eldest son is being groomed to take over when his father dies.* **4** ~ **sb** (of a person who is sexually attracted to children) to prepare a child for a meeting, especially using an Internet CHAT ROOM, with the intention of performing an illegal sexual act

■ *noun* **1** a person whose job is to feed and take care of horses, especially by brushing and cleaning them **2** = BRIDEGROOM

groomed /gruːmd/ *adj.* (usually following an adverb) used to describe the way in which a person cares for their clothes and hair: *She is always perfectly groomed.* ➲ see also WELL GROOMED

groom·ing /'gruːmɪŋ/ *noun* [U] **1** the things that you do to keep your clothes and hair clean and neat, or to keep an animal's fur or hair clean: *You should always pay attention to personal grooming.* **2** the process in which an adult develops a friendship with a child, particularly through the Internet, with the intention of having a sexual relationship

grooms·man /'gruːmzmən/ *noun* (*pl.* **-men** /-mən/) (*NAmE*) a friend of the BRIDEGROOM at a wedding, who has special duties

groove /gruːv/ *noun* **1** a long narrow cut in the surface of sth hard **2** (*informal*) a particular type of musical rhythm: *a jazz groove*

IDM **be** (**stuck**) **in a 'groove** (*BrE*) to be unable to change sth that you have been doing the same way for a long time and that has become boring

grooved /gruːvd/ *adj.* having a groove or grooves

groovy /'gruːvi/ *adj.* (*old-fashioned, informal*) fashionable, attractive and interesting

grope /grəʊp; *NAmE* groʊp/ *verb, noun*

■ *verb* **1** [I] ~ (**around**)(**for sth**) to try and find sth that you cannot see, by feeling with your hands: *He groped around in the dark for his other sock.* ◊ (*figurative*) *'It's so..., so...' I was groping for the right word to describe it.* **2** [T, I] to try and reach a place by feeling with your hands because you cannot see clearly ~ **your way + adv./prep.**: *He groped his way up the staircase in the dark.* ◊ + **adv./prep.** *She groped*

through the darkness towards the doors. **3** [T] **~ sb** (*informal*) to touch sb sexually, especially when they do not want you to
■ ***noun*** (*informal*) an act of groping sb (= touching them sexually)

gross /grəʊs; *NAmE* groʊs/ *adj., adv., verb, noun*
■ ***adj.*** (**gross·er, gross·est**) **1** [only before noun] being the total amount of sth before anything is taken away: ***gross weight*** (= including the container or wrapping) ◇ ***gross income/wage*** (= before taxes, etc. are taken away) ◇ *Investments showed a **gross profit** of 26%.* ➲ compare NET **2** [only before noun] (*formal* or *law*) (of a crime, etc.) very obvious and unacceptable: ***gross indecency/negligence/misconduct*** ◇ *a **gross violation** of human rights* **3** (*informal*) very unpleasant SYN **disgusting**: *'He ate it with mustard.' 'Oh, gross!'* ➲ SYNONYMS at DISGUSTING **4** very rude SYN **crude**: *gross behaviour* **5** very fat and ugly: *She's not just fat, she's positively gross!* ▸ **gross·ness** *noun* [U]
■ ***adv.*** in total, before anything is taken away: *She earns £25 000 a year gross.* ➲ compare NET
■ ***verb*** **~ sth** to earn a particular amount of money before tax has been taken off it: *It is one of the biggest grossing movies of all time.*
PHR V ˌ**gross sb 'out** (*NAmE, informal*) to be very unpleasant and make sb feel disgusted SYN **disgust**: *His bad breath really grossed me out.*
■ ***noun*** **1** (*pl.* **gross**) a group of 144 things: *two gross of apples* ◇ *to sell sth by the gross* **2** (*pl.* **grosses**) (*especially US*) a total amount of money earned by sth, especially a film/movie, before any costs are taken away

ˌ**gross doˌmestic 'product** *noun* [sing., U] = GDP

gross·ly /'grəʊsli; *NAmE* 'groʊsli/ *adv.* (*disapproving*) (used to describe unpleasant qualities) extremely: ***grossly overweight/unfair/inadequate*** ◇ *Press reports have been grossly exaggerated.*

ˌ**gross ˌnational 'product** *noun* [sing., U] = GNP

'**gross-out** *noun* (*especially NAmE, informal*) something disgusting: *They eat flies? What a gross-out!* ▸ '**gross-out** *adj.* [only before noun]: *gross-out movie scenes*

grot /grɒt; *NAmE* grɑːt/ *noun* [U] (*BrE, informal*) something unpleasant, dirty or of poor quality

gro·tesque /grəʊ'tesk; *NAmE* groʊ-/ *adj., noun*
■ ***adj.*** **1** strange in a way that is unpleasant or offensive: *a grotesque distortion of the truth* ◇ *It's grotesque to expect a person of her experience to work for so little money.* **2** extremely ugly in a strange way that is often frightening or amusing: *a grotesque figure* ◇ *tribal dancers wearing grotesque masks* ▸ **gro·tesque·ly** *adv.*
■ ***noun*** **1** [C] a person who is extremely ugly in a strange way, especially in a book or painting **2 the grotesque** [sing.] a style of art using grotesque figures and designs

grotto /'grɒtəʊ; *NAmE* 'grɑːtoʊ/ *noun* (*pl.* **-oes** or **-os**) a small CAVE, especially one that has been made artificially, for example in a garden

grotty /'grɒti; *NAmE* 'grɑːti/ *adj.* (*BrE, informal*) (**grot·tier, grot·ti·est**) unpleasant or of poor quality: *a grotty little hotel* ◇ *I'm feeling pretty grotty* (= ill).

grouch *noun* /graʊtʃ/ (*informal*) **1** a person who complains a lot **2** a complaint about sth unimportant ▸ **grouch** *verb* [I]

grouchy /'graʊtʃi/ *adj.* (*informal*) bad-tempered and often complaining

ground 0-w /graʊnd/ *noun, verb, adj.* ➲ see also GRIND *V.*
■ ***noun***
▸ SURFACE OF EARTH **1** 0-w (often **the ground**) [U] the solid surface of the earth: *I found her lying **on the ground**.* ◇ *He lost his balance and fell **to the ground**.* ◇ *2 metres **above/below ground*** ◇ *Most of the monkeys' food is found **at ground level**.* ◇ ***ground forces*** (= soldiers that fight on land, not in the air or at sea) ◇ *Houses and a luxury tourist hotel were **burned to the ground*** (= completely destroyed, so that there is nothing left). ➲ SYNONYMS at FLOOR
▸ SOIL **2** 0-w [U] soil on the surface of the earth: *fertile ground for planting crops* ➲ SYNONYMS at SOIL
▸ AREA OF LAND **3** 0-w [U] an area of open land: *The kids were playing on **waste ground** behind the school.* **4** 0-w [C] (often in compounds) (*BrE*) an area of land that is used for a particular purpose, activity or sport: *a **football/recreation/sports, etc. ground*** ◇ *ancient burial grounds* ➲ see also BREEDING GROUND, DUMPING GROUND, PARADE GROUND, STAMPING GROUND, TESTING GROUND ➲ SYNONYMS at LAND **5 grounds** [pl.] a large area of land or sea that is used for a particular purpose: *fishing grounds* ◇ *feeding grounds for birds*
▸ GARDENS **6** 0-w **grounds** [pl.] the land or gardens around a large building: *the hospital grounds*
▸ AREA OF KNOWLEDGE/IDEAS **7** 0-w [U] an area of interest, knowledge or ideas: *He managed to **cover a lot of ground** in a short talk.* ◇ *We had to **go over the same ground*** (= talk about the same things again) *in class the next day.* ◇ *You're **on dangerous ground*** (= talking about ideas that are likely to offend sb or make people angry) *if you criticize his family.* ◇ *I thought I was **on safe ground*** (= talking about a suitable subject) *discussing music with her.* ◇ *He was back **on familiar ground**, dealing with the customers.* ◇ *They are fighting the Conservatives **on their own ground**.* ➲ see also COMMON GROUND, MIDDLE GROUND
▸ GOOD REASON **8** 0-w [C, usually pl.] **~ for sth/for doing sth** a good or true reason for saying, doing or believing sth: *You have no grounds for complaint.* ◇ *What were his grounds for wanting a divorce?* ◇ *The case was dismissed **on the grounds that** there was not enough evidence.* ◇ *He retired from the job **on health grounds**.* ◇ *Employers cannot discriminate **on grounds of** age.* ➲ SYNONYMS at REASON
▸ IN LIQUID **9 grounds** [pl.] the small pieces of solid matter in a liquid that have fallen to the bottom: *coffee grounds*
▸ ELECTRICAL WIRE **10** (*NAmE*) (*BrE* **earth**) [C, usually sing.] a wire that connects an electric CIRCUIT with the ground and makes it safe
▸ BACKGROUND **11** [C] a background that a design is painted or printed on: *pink roses on a white ground*
IDM **cut the ground from under sb's 'feet** to suddenly spoil sb's idea or plan by doing sth to stop them from continuing with it **gain/make up 'ground (on sb/sth)** to gradually get closer to sb/sth that is moving or making progress in an activity: *The police car was gaining ground on the suspects.* ◇ *They needed to make up ground on their competitors.* **get (sth) off the 'ground** to start happening successfully; to make sth start happening successfully: *Without more money, the movie is unlikely to get off the ground.* ◇ *to get a new company off the ground* **give/lose 'ground (to sb/sth)** to allow sb to have an advantage; to lose an advantage for yourself: *They are not prepared to give ground on tax cuts.* ◇ *The Conservatives lost a lot of ground to the Liberal Democrats at the election.* **go to 'ground** (*BrE*) to hide, especially to escape sb who is chasing you **hold/stand your 'ground 1** to continue with your opinions or intentions when sb is opposing you and wants you to change: *Don't let him persuade you—stand your ground.* **2** to face a situation and refuse to run away: *It is not easy to hold your ground in front of someone with a gun.* **on the 'ground** in the place where sth is happening and among the people who are in the situation, especially a war: *On the ground, there are hopes that the fighting will soon stop.* ◇ *There's a lot of support for the policy on the ground.* **run/drive/work yourself into the 'ground** to work so hard that you become extremely tired **run sb/sth into the 'ground** to use sth so much that it is broken; to make sb work so hard that they are no longer able to work **thick/thin on the 'ground** (*BrE*) if people or things are **thick/thin on the ground**, there are a lot/not many of them in a place: *Customers are thin on the ground at this time of year.* ➲ more at EAR, FIRM *adj.*, FOOT *n.*, GAIN *v.*, HIT *v.*, MORAL *adj.*, NEUTRAL *adv.*, NEW, PREPARE, RIVET *v.*, SHIFT *v.*, STONY, SUIT *v.*
■ ***verb***
▸ BOAT **1** [T, I] **~ (sth)** when a boat **grounds** or sth **grounds** it, it touches the bottom of the sea and is unable to move: *The fishing boat had been grounded on rocks off the coast of Cornwall.*
▸ AIRCRAFT **2** [T, often passive] **~ sth** to prevent an aircraft

from taking off: *The balloon was grounded by strong winds.* ◇ *All planes out of Heathrow have been grounded by the strikes.*

▸ CHILD **3** [T, usually passive] **~ sb** to punish a child or young person by not allowing them to go out with their friends for a period of time: *You're grounded for a week!*

▸ ELECTRICITY **4** (*NAmE*) (*BrE* **earth**) [T, usually passive] **~ sth** to make electrical equipment safe by connecting it to the ground with a wire ➲ see also GROUNDED, GROUNDING

■ ***adj.*** [only before noun] (of food) cut, chopped or crushed into very small pieces or powder: *ground coffee* ◇ (*US*) *ground pork* ➲ see also HAMBURGER (2)

'ground ball *noun* = GROUNDER

ˌground 'beef *noun* [U] (*NAmE*) = HAMBURGER (2)

ground·break·ing /'graʊndbreɪkɪŋ/ *adj.* [only before noun] making new discoveries; using new methods: *a groundbreaking piece of research*

'ground cloth (*US*) (*BrE* **ground·sheet**) *noun* a large piece of material that does not let water through that is placed on the ground inside a tent

'ground control *noun* [U] the people and equipment on the ground that make sure that planes or SPACECRAFT take off and land safely

'ground cover *noun* [U] plants that cover the soil

'ground crew (also **'ground staff**) *noun* [C+sing./pl. v.] the people at an airport whose job is to take care of aircraft while they are on the ground

ground·ed /'graʊndɪd/ *adj.* having a sensible and realistic attitude to life: *Away from Hollywood, he relies on his family and friends to keep him grounded.*

IDM ▸ (**be**) **'grounded in/on sth** (to be) based on sth: *His views are grounded on the assumption that all people are equal.*

ground·er /'graʊndə(r)/ (also **'ground ball**) *noun* (in BASEBALL) a ball that runs along the ground after it has been hit

ˌground 'floor (*BrE*) (*NAmE* **ˌfirst 'floor**) *noun* the floor of a building that is at the same level as the ground outside: *a ground-floor window* ◇ *I live on the ground floor.* ➲ note at FLOOR

IDM ▸ **be/get in on the ground 'floor** to become involved in a plan, project, etc. at the beginning

ground·hog /'graʊndhɒg; *NAmE* -hɑːg; -hɔːg/ *noun* = WOODCHUCK

'Groundhog Day *noun* **1** (in N America) February 2, when it is said that the groundhog comes out of its hole at the end of winter. If the sun shines and the groundhog sees its shadow, it is said that there will be another six weeks of winter. **2** an event that is repeated without changing: *The Government lost the vote then and it can expect a Groundhog Day next time.* ORIGIN From the film/movie *Groundhog Day* about a man who lives the same day many times.

ground·ing /'graʊndɪŋ/ *noun* **1** [sing.] **~ (in sth)** the teaching of the basic parts of a subject: *a good grounding in grammar* **2** [U, C] the act of keeping a plane on the ground or a ship in a port, especially because it is not in a good enough condition to travel

ground·less /'graʊndləs/ *adj.* not based on reason or evidence SYN **unfounded**: *groundless allegations* ◇ *Our fears proved groundless.* ▸ **ground·less·ly** *adv.*

ground·nut /'graʊndnʌt/ *noun* (*BrE*) = PEANUT

ground·out /'graʊndaʊt/ *noun* (in BASEBALL) a situation in which a player hits the ball along the ground but a FIELDER touches first BASE with it before the player reaches the base

'ground plan *noun* **1** a plan of the ground floor of a building ➲ compare PLAN *n.* (4) **2** a plan for future action

'ground rent *noun* [U, C] (in Britain) rent paid by the owner of a building to the owner of the land on which it is built

'ground rule *noun* **1 ground rules** [pl.] the basic rules on which sth is based: *The new code of conduct lays down the ground rules for management-union relations.* **2** [C] (*NAmE, sport*) a rule for the playing of a game on a particular field, etc.

ground·sel /'graʊnsl/ *noun* [U] a wild plant with yellow flowers, sometimes used as food for animals and birds

ground·sheet /'graʊndʃiːt/ (*BrE*) (*US* **'ground cloth**) *noun* a large piece of material that does not let water through that is placed on the ground inside a tent

grounds·man /'graʊndzmən/ *noun* (*pl.* **-men** /-mən/) (*especially BrE*) a man whose job is to take care of a sports ground or large garden

'ground speed *noun* the speed of an aircraft relative to the ground ➲ compare AIRSPEED

'ground squirrel *noun* = GOPHER

'ground staff *noun* [C+sing./pl. v.] **1** (*BrE*) the people at a sports ground whose job it is to take care of the grass, equipment, etc. **2** = GROUND CREW

ground·stroke /'graʊndstrəʊk; *NAmE* -stroʊk/ *noun* (in TENNIS) a hit that is made after the ball has BOUNCED

ground·swell /'graʊndswel/ *noun* [sing.] **~ (of sth)** (*formal*) the sudden increase of a particular feeling among a group of people: *a groundswell of support* ◇ *There was a groundswell of opinion that he should resign.*

ground·water /'graʊndwɔːtə(r)/ *noun* [U] water that is found under the ground in soil, rocks, etc.

ground·work /'graʊndwɜːk; *NAmE* -wɜːrk/ *noun* [U] **~ (for sth)** work that is done as preparation for other work that will be done later: *Officials are* ***laying the groundwork*** *for a summit conference of world leaders.*

ˌground 'zero *noun* [U] **1** the point on the earth's surface where a nuclear bomb explodes **2 Ground Zero** the site of the World Trade Center in New York, destroyed on 11 September 2001 **3** the beginning; a starting point for an activity

group 🔑 /gruːp/ *noun, verb*

■ ***noun*** [C+sing./pl. v.] **1** 🔑 a number of people or things that are together in the same place or that are connected in some way: *a group of girls/trees/houses* ◇ *A group of us is/are going to the theatre this evening.* ◇ *Students stood around* ***in groups*** *waiting for their results.* ◇ *The residents formed a community action group.* ◇ *English is a member of the Germanic group of languages* ◇ *The proportion of single parent families varies between different income groups.* ◇ *a minority group* ◇ *ethnic groups* ◇ *a* ***group activity*** (= done by a number of people working together) ◇ *She asked her students to* ***get into groups*** *of four.* ◇ *to work* ***in groups*** ➲ see also SUBGROUP HELP There are many other compounds ending in **group**. You will find them at their place in the alphabet. **2** (*business*) a number of companies that are owned by the same person or organization: *a newspaper group* ◇ *the Burton group* ◇ *the group sales director* **3** (rather *old-fashioned*) a number of musicians who perform together, especially to play pop music: *She sings in a rock group.*

■ ***verb*** **1** [T, I] to gather into a group; to make sb/sth form a group: **~ sb/sth/yourself (round/around sb/sth)** *The children grouped themselves around their teacher.* ◇ **~ round/around sb/sth** *We all grouped around the tree for a photograph.* ◇ **~ (sb/sth) together** *The colleges grouped together to offer a wider range of courses.* **2** [T] **~ sb/sth (together)** to divide people or things into groups of people or things that are similar in some way: *The books are grouped together by subject.* ◇ *Contestants were grouped according to age and ability.*

ˌgroup 'captain *noun* (*abbr.* **Gp Capt**) an officer of high rank in the British AIR FORCE: *Group Captain (Jonathan) Sutton*

groupie /'gruːpi/ *noun* a person, especially a young woman, who follows pop or rock musicians or other famous people around and tries to meet them

group·ing /'gruːpɪŋ/ *noun* **1** [C] a number of people or organizations that have the same interests, aims or characteristics and are often part of a larger group: *These small* *nations constitute an important grouping within the EU.* **2** [U] the act of forming sth into a group

ˌgroup ˈpractice *noun* a group of several doctors or other medical workers who work together in the community and use the same building to see patients

ˌgroup ˈtherapy *noun* [U] a type of PSYCHIATRIC treatment in which people with similar personal problems meet together to discuss them

group·ware /ˈgruːpweə(r); *NAmE* -wer/ *noun* [U] (*computing*) software that is designed to help a group of people on different computers to work together

ˈgroup work *noun* [U] (*BrE*) work done by a group of people working together, for example students in a classroom

grouse /graʊs/ *noun, verb*

■ ***noun* 1** [C, U] (*pl.* **grouse**) a bird with a fat body and feathers on its legs, which people shoot for sport and food; the meat of this bird: *grouse shooting* ◇ *grouse moors* ◇ *roast grouse* **2** [C] (*informal*) a complaint

■ ***verb*** [I, T] **~ (about sb/sth)** | (**+ speech**) (*informal*) to complain about sb/sth in a way that other people find annoying **SYN** **grumble**

grout /graʊt/ (also **grout·ing**) *noun* [U] a substance that is used between the TILES on the walls of kitchens, bathrooms, etc. ▶ **grout** *verb* **~ sth**

grove /grəʊv; *NAmE* groʊv/ *noun* **1** (*literary*) a small group of trees: *a grove of birch trees* **2** a small area of land with fruit trees of particular types on it: *an olive grove* **3** used in the names of streets: *Elm Grove*

grovel /ˈgrɒvl; *NAmE* ˈgrɑːvl/ *verb* (**-ll-**, *especially US* **-l-**) **1** [I] **~ (to sb) (for sth)** (*disapproving*) to behave in a very HUMBLE way towards sb who is more important than you or who can give you sth you want **SYN** **crawl 2** [I] **+ adv./prep.** to move along the ground on your hands and knees, especially because you are looking for sth ▶ **grov·el·ling** (*especially US* **grov·el·ing**) *adj.* [only before noun]: *a grovelling letter of apology*

grow 🔑 /grəʊ; *NAmE* groʊ/ *verb* (**grew** /gruː/, **grown** /grəʊn; *NAmE* groʊn/)

▸ INCREASE **1** 🔑 [I] to increase in size, number, strength or quality: *The company profits grew by 5% last year.* ◇ *Fears are growing for the safety of a teenager who disappeared a week ago.* ◇ **~ in sth** *The family has* ***grown in size*** *recently.* ◇ *She is growing in confidence all the time.* ◇ **+ adj.** *The company is growing bigger all the time.*

▸ OF PERSON/ANIMAL **2** 🔑 [I] to become bigger or taller and develop into an adult: *You've grown since the last time I saw you!* ◇ *Nick's grown almost an inch in the last month.* ◇ **+ adj.** *to* ***grow bigger/taller***

▸ OF PLANT **3** 🔑 [I, T] to exist and develop in a particular place; to make plants grow: *The region is too dry for plants to grow.* ◇ *Tomatoes grow best in direct sunlight.* ◇ **~ sth** *I didn't know they grew rice in France.* ➲ see also HOME-GROWN

▸ OF HAIR/NAILS **4** 🔑 [I, T] to become longer; to allow sth to become longer by not cutting it: *I've decided to let my hair grow.* ◇ **~ sth** *I've decided to grow my hair.* ◇ *I didn't recognize him—he's grown a beard.*

▸ BECOME/BEGIN **5** 🔑 *linking verb* **+ adj.** to begin to have a particular quality or feeling over a period of time: *to grow old/bored/calm* ◇ *As time went on he grew more and more impatient.* ◇ *The skies grew dark and it began to rain.* **6** [I] **~ to do sth** to gradually begin to do sth: *I'm sure you'll grow to like her in time.*

▸ DEVELOP SKILLS **7** [I] **~ (as sth)** (of a person) to develop and improve particular qualities or skills: *She continues to grow as an artist.*

▸ BUSINESS **8** [T] **~ sth** to increase the size, quality or number of sth: *We are trying to grow the business.*

IDM **it/money doesn't grow on ˈtrees** (*saying*) used to tell sb not to use sth or spend money carelessly because you do not have a lot of it ➲ more at ABSENCE, GRASS *n.*

PHR V **ˌgrow aˈpart (from sb)** to stop having a close relationship with sb over a period of time **ˌgrow aˈway from sb** [no passive] to become less close to sb; to depend on sb or care for sb less: *When she left school she grew away from her mother.* **ˌgrow ˈback** to begin growing again after being cut off or damaged **ˌgrow ˈinto sth** [no passive] **1** to gradually develop into a particular type of person over a period of time **2** (of a child) to grow big enough to fit into a piece of clothing that used to be too big: *The dress is too long for her now but she'll grow into it.* **3** to become more confident in a new job, etc. and learn to do it better: *She's still growing into her new role as a mother.* **ˈgrow on sb** [no passive] if sb/sth **grows on** you, you start to like them or it more and more **ˌgrow ˈout** (of a HAIRSTYLE, etc.) to disappear as your hair grows: *I had a perm a year ago and it still hasn't grown out.* **ˌgrow sth↔ˈout** to allow your hair to grow in order to change the style: *I've decided to grow my layers out.* **ˌgrow ˈout of sth** [no passive] **1** (of a child) to become too big to fit into a piece of clothing **SYN** **outgrow**: *He's already grown out of his school uniform.* **2** to stop doing sth as you become older **SYN** **outgrow**: *Most children suck their thumbs but they grow out of it.* **3** to develop from sth: *The idea for the book grew out of a visit to India.* **ˌgrow ˈup 1** 🔑 (of a person) to develop into an adult: *She grew up in Boston* (= lived there as a child). ◇ *Their children have all grown up and left home now.* ◇ **~ to do sth** *He grew up to become a famous pianist.* ➲ related noun GROWN-UP[2] **2** 🔑 used to tell sb to stop behaving in a silly way: *Why don't you grow up?* ◇ *It's time you grew up.* **3** to develop gradually: *A closeness grew up between the two girls.* **IDM** see OAK

grow·bag (also **Gro-bag™**) /ˈgrəʊbæg; *NAmE* ˈgroʊ-/ *noun* a large plastic bag full of soil, used for growing plants

grow·er /ˈgrəʊə(r); *NAmE* ˈgroʊ-/ *noun* **1** a person or company that grows plants, fruit or vegetables to sell: *a tobacco grower* ◇ *All our vegetables are supplied by local growers.* **2** a plant that grows in the way mentioned: *a* ***fast/slow grower***

grow·ing /ˈgrəʊɪŋ; *NAmE* ˈgroʊɪŋ/ *adj.* [only before noun] increasing in size, amount or degree: *A* ***growing number*** *of people are returning to full-time education.* ◇ *one of the country's* ***fastest growing*** *industries* ◇ *There is growing concern over the safety of the missing teenager.*

ˈgrowing pains *noun* [pl.] **1** pains that some children feel in their arms and legs when they are growing **2** emotional anxieties felt by young people as they grow up **3** problems that are experienced by a company when it begins operating but that are not likely to last

ˈgrowing season *noun* [usually sing.] the period of the year during which the weather conditions are right for plants to grow

growl /graʊl/ *verb, noun*

■ ***verb* 1** [I] **~ (at sb/sth)** (of animals, especially dogs) to make a low sound in the throat, usually as a sign of anger **2** [T] to say sth in a low angry voice: **+ speech (at sb)** *'Who are you?' he growled at the stranger.* ◇ **~ sth (at sb)** *She growled a sarcastic reply.*

■ ***noun*** a deep angry sound made when sb/sth growls

grown /grəʊn; *NAmE* groʊn/ *adj.* [only before noun] (of a person) mentally and physically an adult: *It's pathetic that grown men have to resort to violence like this.* ➲ see also FULL-GROWN, HOME-GROWN, GROW *v.*

ˌgrown-ˈup[1] *adj.* **1** (of a person) mentally and physically an adult **SYN** **adult**: *What do you want to be when you're grown-up?* ◇ *She has a grown-up son.* **2** suitable for or typical of an adult: *The child was clearly puzzled at being addressed in such a grown-up way.*

ˈgrown-up[2] *noun* (used especially by and to children) an adult person **SYN** **adult**: *If you're good you can eat with the grown-ups.*

growth 🔑 /grəʊθ; *NAmE* groʊθ/ *noun*

1 🔑 [U] (of people, animals or plants) the process of growing physically, mentally or emotionally: *Lack of water will stunt the plant's growth.* ◇ *Remove dead leaves to encourage new growth.* ◇ *a concern with personal* (= mental and emotional) *growth and development* ◇ *growth hormones* (= designed to make sb/sth grow faster) **2** 🔑 [U] **~ (in/of sth)** an increase in the size, amount or degree of sth: *population* growth ◇ *the rapid growth in violent crime* **3** ⊶ [U] an increase in economic activity: *a disappointing year of little growth in Britain and America* ◇ *policies aimed at sustaining economic growth* ◇ *an annual growth rate of 10%* ◇ *a* ***growth area/industry*** ➲ COLLOCATIONS at ECONOMY **4** [C] a lump caused by a disease that forms on or inside a person, an animal or a plant: *a* ***malignant/cancerous growth*** **5** [U, C] something that has grown: *The forest's dense growth provides nesting places for a wide variety of birds.* ◇ *several days' growth of beard*

ˈgrowth ring *noun* a layer of wood, shell or bone developed in one year, or in another regular period of growth, that an expert can look at to find out how old sth is

groyne (*especially US* **groin**) /grɔɪn/ *noun* a low wall built out into the sea to prevent it from washing away sand and stones from the beach ➲ VISUAL VOCAB page V4

G

grub /grʌb/ *noun, verb*
■ ***noun*** **1** [C] the young form of an insect, that looks like a small fat WORM **2** [U] (*informal*) food: *Grub's up!* (= the meal is ready) ◇ *They serve good pub grub there.*
■ ***verb*** (-bb-) [I] **~ (around/about) (for sth)** to look for sth, especially by digging or by looking through or under other things: *birds grubbing for worms*
PHR V **ˌgrub sth↔ˈup/ˈout** to dig sth out of the ground

grub·ber /ˈgrʌbə(r)/ *noun* (in CRICKET) a ball that is BOWLED along the ground

grubby /ˈgrʌbi/ *adj.* (**grub·bier**, **grub·bi·est**) **1** rather dirty, usually because it has not been washed or cleaned: *grubby hands/clothes* ➲ SYNONYMS at DIRTY **2** unpleasant because it involves activities that are dishonest or immoral SYN **sordid**: *a grubby scandal* ▸ **grubbi·ness** *noun* [U]

ˈGrub Street *noun* used to refer to poor writers and journalists as a group, or the life they live ORIGIN From the name of a street in London where many poor writers lived in the 17th century.

grudge /grʌdʒ/ *noun, verb*
■ ***noun*** **~ (against sb)** a feeling of anger or dislike towards sb because of sth bad they have done to you in the past: *I* ***bear*** *him* ***no grudge***. ◇ *He* ***has a grudge against*** *the world.* ◇ *I don't* ***hold any grudges*** *now.* ◇ *He's a man with a grudge.* ◇ *England beat New Zealand in a* ***grudge match*** (= a match where there is strong dislike between the teams).
■ ***verb*** **1** to do or give sth unwillingly SYN **begrudge**: **~ doing sth** *I grudge having to pay so much tax.* ◇ **~ sth** *He grudges the time he spends travelling to work.* **2 ~ sb sth** to think that sb does not deserve to have sth SYN **begrudge**: *You surely don't grudge her her success?*

grudg·ing /ˈgrʌdʒɪŋ/ *adj.* [usually before noun] given or done unwillingly SYN **reluctant**: *He could not help feeling a grudging admiration for the old lady.* ▸ **grudg·ing·ly** (*also less frequent* **be·grudg·ing·ly**) *adv.*: *She grudgingly admitted that I was right.*

gruel /ˈgruːəl/ *noun* [U] a simple dish made by boiling OATS in milk or water, eaten especially in the past by poor people

gruel·ling (*especially BrE*) (*NAmE* usually **gruel·ing**) /ˈgruːəlɪŋ/ *adj.* very difficult and tiring, needing great effort for a long time SYN **punishing**: *a* ***gruelling journey/schedule*** ◇ *I've had a gruelling day.*

grue·some /ˈgruːsəm/ *adj.* very unpleasant and filling you with horror, usually because it is connected with death or injury: *a gruesome murder* ◇ *gruesome pictures of dead bodies* ◇ (*humorous*) *We spent a week in a gruesome apartment in Miami.* ▸ **grue·some·ly** *adv.*

gruff /grʌf/ *adj.* **1** (of a voice) deep and rough, and often sounding unfriendly **2** (of a person's behaviour) unfriendly and impatient: *Beneath his gruff exterior, he's really very kind-hearted.* ▸ **gruff·ly** *adv.*

grum·ble /ˈgrʌmbl/ *verb, noun*
■ ***verb*** **1** [I, T] to complain about sb/sth in a bad-tempered way: **~ (at/to sb) (about/at sb/sth)** *She's always grumbling to me about how badly she's treated at work.* ◇ **+ speech** *'I'll just have to do it myself,' he grumbled.* ◇ **~ that...** *They kept grumbling that they were cold.* ➲ SYNONYMS at COMPLAIN **2** [I] to make a deep continuous sound SYN **rumble**: *Thunder grumbled in the distance.* ▸ **grum·bler** /ˈgrʌmblə(r)/ *noun*
■ ***noun*** **1 ~ (about sth) | ~ (that...)** something that you complain about because you are not satisfied: *My main grumble is about the lack of privacy.* **2** a long low sound SYN **rumble**: *a distant grumble of thunder*

grum·bling /ˈgrʌmblɪŋ/ *noun* **1** [U] the act of complaining about sth: *We didn't hear any grumbling about the food.* **2 grumblings** [pl.] protests about sth that come from a number of people but that are not expressed very clearly

grump /grʌmp/ *noun* (*informal*) a bad-tempered person

grumpy /ˈgrʌmpi/ *adj.* (**grump·ier**, **grumpi·est**) (*informal*) bad-tempered ▸ **grump·ily** /ˈgrʌmpɪli/ *adv.*

grunge /grʌndʒ/ *noun* [U] **1** (*informal*) dirt of any kind SYN **grime** **2** (*also* **ˈgrunge rock**) a type of loud rock music, which was popular in the early 1990s **3** a style of fashion worn by people who like grunge music, usually involving clothes that look untidy

grungy /ˈgrʌndʒi/ *adj.* (*informal*) dirty in an unpleasant way

grunt /grʌnt/ *verb, noun*
■ ***verb*** **1** [I] (of animals, especially pigs) to make a short low sound in the throat **2** [I, T] (of people) to make a short low sound in your throat, especially to show that you are in pain, annoyed or not interested; to say sth using this sound: *He pulled harder on the rope, grunting with the effort.* ◇ *When I told her what had happened she just grunted and turned back to her book.* ◇ **~ sth** *He grunted something about being late and rushed out.* ◇ **+ speech** *'Thanks,' he grunted.*
■ ***noun*** **1** a short, low sound made by a person or an animal (especially a pig): *to give a* ***grunt of effort/pain*** **2** (*NAmE, informal*) a worker who does boring tasks for low pay **3** (*NAmE, informal*) a soldier of low rank

ˈgrunt work *noun* [U] (*informal*) hard boring work: *She has assistants to do the grunt work like research and proofreading.*

Gruy·ère /ˈgruːjɜː(r); *NAmE* -jər; ˈgriːjər/ *noun* [U] a type of Swiss cheese with a strong flavour

gryphon /ˈgrɪfən/ *noun* = GRIFFIN

GSM /ˌdʒiː es ˈem/ *abbr.* Global System/Standard for Mobile Communication(s) (an international system for DIGITAL communication by mobile/cell phone)

GSOH *abbr.* good sense of humour (used in personal advertisements)

ˈG spot *noun* a sensitive area inside a woman's VAGINA that is thought to give great sexual pleasure when touched

GST /ˌdʒiː es ˈtiː/ *noun* [U] (*CanE*) goods and services tax (a tax that is added to the price of goods and services)

ˈG-string *noun* a narrow piece of cloth that covers the sexual organs and is held up by a string around the waist

Gt (*also* **Gt.** especially in *NAmE*) *abbr.* (in names of places) Great: *Gt Britain* ◇ *Gt Yarmouth*

gua·ca·mole /ˌgwækəˈməʊleɪ; -li; *NAmE* -ˈmoʊ-/ *noun* [U] (from *Spanish*) a Mexican dish of crushed AVOCADO mixed with onion, tomatoes, CHILLIES, etc.

guano /ˈgwɑːnəʊ; *NAmE* -noʊ/ *noun* [U] the waste substance passed from the bodies of birds that live near the sea, used to make plants and crops grow well

guar·an·tee ⊶ AW /ˌgærənˈtiː/ *noun, verb*
■ ***noun*** **1** ⊶ a firm promise that you will do sth or that sth will happen SYN **assurance**: *to give a guarantee of good behaviour* ◇ *He gave me a guarantee that it would never happen again.* ◇ *They are demanding certain guarantees before they sign the treaty.* **2** ⊶ a written promise given by a company that sth you buy will be replaced or repaired without payment if it goes wrong within a particular period SYN **warranty**: *We provide a 5-year guarantee against rust.* ◇ *The watch is still* ***under guarantee***. ◇ *The television comes with a year's guarantee.* ◇ *a money-back guarantee* **3** ⊶ something that makes sth else certain to

happen: **~** (**of sth**) *Career success is no guarantee of happiness.* ◇ **~** (**that...**) *There's no guarantee that she'll come* (= she may not come). **4** money or sth valuable that you give or promise to a bank, for example, to make sure that you will do what you have promised: *We had to offer our house as a guarantee when getting the loan.* **5** a written promise to pay back money that sb else owes, or do sth that sb else promised to do, if they cannot do it themselves: *A close relative, usually a parent, can provide a guarantee for the loan.*

■ ***verb*** **1** to promise to do sth; to promise sth will happen: **~ sth** *Basic human rights, including freedom of speech, are now guaranteed.* ◇ **~** (**that**)... *We cannot guarantee (that) our flights will never be delayed.* ◇ **~ sb sth** *The ticket will guarantee you free entry.* ◇ **~ to do sth** *We guarantee to deliver your goods within a week.* **2** **~ sth** (**against sth**) to give a written promise to replace or repair a product free if it goes wrong: *This iron is guaranteed for a year against faulty workmanship.* **3** to make sth certain to happen: **~ sth** *Tonight's victory guarantees the team's place in the final.* ◇ **~ sb sth** *These days getting a degree doesn't guarantee you a job.* **4** **~** (**that**)... to be certain that sth will happen: *You can guarantee (that) the children will start being naughty as soon as they have to go to bed.* **5** to agree to be legally responsible for sth or for doing sth, especially for paying back money that sb else owes if they cannot pay it back themselves: **~ sth** *to guarantee a bank loan* ◇ **~ to do sth** *to guarantee to pay sb's debts* ◇ **~ that...** *I guarantee that he will appear in court.*

IDM **be guaran'teed to do sth** to be certain to have a particular result: *If we try to keep it a secret, she's guaranteed to find out.* ◇ *That kind of behaviour is guaranteed to make him angry.* ➲ SYNONYMS at CERTAIN

guar·an·tor /ˌgærən'tɔː(r)/ *noun* (*formal* or *law*) a person who agrees to be responsible for sb or for making sure that sth happens or is done: *The United Nations will act as guarantor of the peace settlement.*

guard /gɑːd; *NAmE* gɑːrd/ *noun, verb*

■ ***noun***

▸ PEOPLE WHO PROTECT **1** [C] a person, such as a soldier, a police officer or a prison officer, who protects a place or people, or prevents prisoners from escaping: *a* ***security guard*** ◇ ***border guard****s* ◇ *The prisoner slipped past the guards on the gate and escaped.* ◇ *A guard was posted outside the building.* ➲ compare WARDER ➲ see also BODYGUARD, COASTGUARD, LIFEGUARD **2** [C+sing./pl. v.] a group of people, such as soldiers or police officers, who protect sb/sth: *the captain of the guard* ◇ *the changing of the guard* (= when one group replaces another) ◇ *The guard is/are being inspected today.* ◇ *Fellow airmen provided a* ***guard of honour*** *at his wedding.* ◇ *The President always travels with an* ***armed guard****.* ➲ see also NATIONAL GUARD, OLD GUARD, REARGUARD **3** [U] the act or duty of protecting property, places or people from attack or danger; the act or duty of preventing prisoners from escaping: *a sentry* ***on guard*** (= at his or her post, on duty) ◇ *to do* ***guard duty*** ◇ *The escaped prisoner was brought back* ***under armed guard****.* ◇ *The terrorist was kept* ***under*** *police* ***guard****.* ◇ *One of the men* ***kept guard****, while the other broke into the house.* **4 the Guards** [pl.] (in Britain and some other countries) special REGIMENTS of soldiers whose original duty was to protect the king or queen

▸ AGAINST INJURY **5** [C] (often in compounds) something that covers a part of a person's body or a dangerous part of a machine to prevent injury: *Ensure the guard is in place before operating the machine.* ➲ see also FIREGUARD, MOUTHGUARD, MUDGUARD, SAFEGUARD, SHIN GUARD ➲ VISUAL VOCAB page V39

▸ ON TRAIN **6** [C] (*BrE*, becoming *old-fashioned*) = CONDUCTOR (2)

▸ IN BOXING/FENCING **7** [U] a position you take to defend yourself, especially in a sport such as BOXING or FENCING: *to drop/keep up your guard* ◇ (*figurative*) *In spite of the awkward questions the minister never let his guard fall for a moment.*

▸ IN BASKETBALL **8** [C] one of the two players on a BASKETBALL team who are mainly responsible for staying close to opposing players to stop them from scoring

▸ IN AMERICAN FOOTBALL **9** [C] one of the two players on an AMERICAN FOOTBALL team who play either side of the CENTRE FORWARD

IDM **be on your 'guard** to be very careful and prepared for sth difficult or dangerous **mount/stand/keep 'guard** (**over sb/sth**) to watch or protect sb/sth: *Four soldiers stood guard over the coffin.* **off** (**your**) **'guard** not careful or prepared for sth difficult or dangerous: *The lawyer's apparently innocent question was designed to* ***catch*** *the witness* ***off*** (***his***) ***guard****.*

■ ***verb*** **1** **~ sb/sth** to protect property, places or people from attack or danger: *The dog was guarding its owner's luggage.* ◇ *political leaders guarded by the police* ◇ *You can't get in; the whole place is guarded.* ◇ (*figurative*) *a closely guarded secret* **2** **~ sb** to prevent prisoners from escaping: *The prisoners were guarded by soldiers.*

PHR V **'guard against sth** to take care to prevent sth or to protect yourself from sth: *to guard against accidents/disease*

'guard dog *noun* a dog that is kept to guard a building

guard·ed /'gɑːdɪd; *NAmE* 'gɑːrdɪd/ *adj.* (of a person or a remark they make) careful; not showing feelings or giving much information SYN **cautious**: *a guarded reply* ◇ *You should be more guarded in what you say to reporters.* ◇ *They gave the news a guarded welcome* (= did not show great enthusiasm about it). OPP **unguarded** ▸ **guard·ed·ly** *adv.*

guard·house /'gɑːdhaʊs; *NAmE* 'gɑːrd-/ *noun* a building for soldiers who are guarding the entrance to a military camp or for keeping military prisoners in

guard·ian /'gɑːdiən; *NAmE* 'gɑːrd-/ *noun* **1** a person who protects sth SYN **custodian**: *Farmers should be guardians of the countryside.* ◇ *The police are guardians of law and order.* **2** a person who is legally responsible for the care of another person, especially a child whose parents have died

ˌguardian 'angel *noun* a spirit that some people believe protects and guides them, especially when they are in danger: (*figurative*) *A delightful guide was my guardian angel for the first week of the tour.*

guard·ian·ship /'gɑːdiənʃɪp; *NAmE* 'gɑːrd-/ *noun* [U] (*formal* or *law*) the state or position of being responsible for sb/sth

'guard rail *noun* **1** a rail placed on the edge of a path, a CLIFF or a boat to protect people and prevent them falling over the edge **2** (*NAmE*) (*BrE* **'crash barrier**) a strong low fence or wall at the side of a road or between the two halves of a major road such as a MOTORWAY or INTERSTATE

guard·room /'gɑːdruːm; -rʊm; *NAmE* 'gɑːrd-/ *noun* a room for soldiers who are guarding the entrance to a building or for keeping military prisoners in

guards·man /'gɑːdzmən; *NAmE* 'gɑːrd-/ *noun* (*pl.* **-men** /-mən/) a soldier in the Guards or in the National Guard in the US

'guard's van *noun* (*BrE*) the part of a train where the person who is in charge of the train rides

guava /'gwɑːvə/ *noun* the fruit of a tropical American tree, with yellow skin and pink flesh

gub·bins /'gʌbɪnz/ *noun* [U] (*old-fashioned, BrE, informal*) various things that are not important: *All the gubbins that came with the computer is still in the box.*

gu·ber·na·tor·ial /ˌguːbənə'tɔːriəl; *NAmE* -bərnə-/ *adj.* (*formal*) connected with the job of state governor in the US: *a gubernatorial candidate* ◇ *gubernatorial duties*

Guern·sey /'gɜːnzi; *NAmE* 'gɜːrnzi/ *noun* **1** a type of cow kept for its rich milk **2 guernsey** a thick sweater made with dark blue wool that has been specially treated so that it does not let water through, worn originally by FISHERMEN **3 guernsey** (*AustralE*) a football sweater, especially one of the type without sleeves worn by Australian Rules players

IDM **get a 'guernsey** (*AustralE, informal*) to be recognized as being good (originally meaning to be chosen for a football team)

G

guer·rilla (also **guer·illa**) /ɡəˈrɪlə/ *noun, adj.*

■ ***noun*** a member of a small group of soldiers who are not part of an official army and who fight against official soldiers, usually to try to change the government: *urban guerrillas* (= those who fight in towns) ◇ ***guerrilla war/warfare*** (= fought by guerrillas on one or both sides) ◇ *a guerrilla movement* ➲ compare FREEDOM FIGHTER

■ ***adj.*** [only before noun] organized in an informal way and without official permission or approval: *Guerrilla actors took to the streets in army fatigues to protest against the war.* ◇ *guerrilla marketing* (= marketing that uses unusual methods in order to achieve the greatest effect for the smallest amount of money)

guess 0ᴡ /ɡes/ *verb, noun*

■ ***verb* 1** 0ᴡ [I, T] to try and give an answer or make a judgement about sth without being sure of all the facts: *I don't really know. I'm just guessing.* ◇ **~ at sth** *We can only guess at her reasons for leaving.* ◇ **+ adj.** *He* ***guessed right/wrong.*** ◇ **~ (that)...** *I'd guess that she's about 30.* ◇ **~ where, who, etc...** *Can you guess where I've been?* ◇ **~ sth** *Can you guess his age?* **2** 0ᴡ [T] to find the right answer to a question or the truth without knowing all the facts: **~ sth** *She guessed the answer straight away.* ◇ **~ what, where, etc...** ***You'll never guess*** *what she told me.* ◇ **~ (that)...** *You would never guess (that) she had problems. She's always so cheerful.* ➲ see also SECOND-GUESS **3** 0ᴡ **I guess** [T, I] **~ (that)...** (*informal, especially NAmE*) to suppose that sth is true or likely: *I guess (that) you'll be looking for a new job now.* ◇ *'He didn't see me, I guess.'* ◇ *'Are you ready to go?' 'Yeah, I* ***guess so.****'* ◇ *'They aren't coming, then?'* ***'I guess not.'*** **4** 0ᴡ **guess...!** [T] used to show that you are going to say sth surprising or exciting: **~ sth** *Guess what! He's asked me out!* ◇ **~ who, where, etc...** *Guess who I've just seen!*

IDM **keep sb ˈguessing** (*informal*) to not tell sb about your plans or what is going to happen next: *It's the kind of book that keeps you guessing right to the end.*

■ ***noun*** 0ᴡ an attempt to give an answer or an opinion when you cannot be certain if you are right **~ (at sth)** (*BrE*): *to* ***have/make a guess*** *(at sth)* ◇ (*NAmE*) *to* ***take a guess*** ◇ *Go on! Have a guess!* ◇ **~ (about sth)** *The article is based on guesses about what might happen in the future.* ◇ *They might be here by 3—but that's just a* ***rough guess*** (= not exact). ◇ **~ (that...)** ***My guess is that*** *we won't hear from him again.* ◇ ***At a guess****, there were forty people at the party.* ◇ *If I might* ***hazard a guess****, I'd say she was about thirty.* ◇ *Who do you think I saw yesterday?* ***I'll give you three guesses.***

IDM **ˈanybody's/ˈanyone's guess** (*informal*) something that nobody can be certain about: *What will happen next is anybody's guess.* **your ˌguess is as good as ˈmine** (*informal*) used to tell sb that you do not know any more about a subject than the person that you are talking to does: *'Who's going to win?' 'Your guess is as good as mine.'* ➲ more at EDUCATED, MISS *v.*

ˈguessing game *noun* **1** a game in which you have to guess the answers to questions **2** a situation in which you do not know what is going to happen or what sb is going to do

guess·ti·mate (also **gues·ti·mate**) /ˈɡestɪmət/ *noun* (*informal*) an attempt to calculate sth that is based more on guessing than on information

guess·work /ˈɡeswɜːk; *NAmE* -wɜːrk/ *noun* [U] the process of trying to find an answer by guessing when you do not have enough information to be sure: *It was pure guesswork on our part.* ➲ see also CONJECTURE

guest 0ᴡ /ɡest/ *noun, verb*

■ ***noun* 1** 0ᴡ a person that you have invited to your house or to a particular event that you are paying for: *We have guests staying this weekend.* ◇ *more than 100 wedding guests* ◇ *I went to the theatre club as Helen's guest.* ◇ *He was the* ***guest of honour*** (= the most important person invited to an event). ◇ *Liz was not on the* ***guest list.*** **2** 0ᴡ a person who is staying at a hotel, etc: *We have accommodation for 500 guests.* ◇ *a* ***paying guest*** (= a person who is living in a private house, but paying as if they were in a hotel) ◇ *Guests should vacate their rooms by 10.30 a.m.* **3** a famous person or performer who takes part in a television show or concert: *a* ***guest artist/star/singer*** ◇ *Our special guest tonight is...* ◇ *He* ***made a guest appearance*** *on the show.* **4** a person who is invited to a particular place or organization, or to speak at a meeting: *The scientists are here as guests of our government.* ◇ *a* ***guest speaker***

IDM **be my ˈguest** (*informal*) used to give sb permission to do sth that they have asked to do: *'Do you mind if I use the phone?' 'Be my guest.'*

■ ***verb*** [I] **~ (on sth)** to take part in a television or radio show, a concert, a game, etc. as a visiting or temporary performer or player: *She guested on several chat shows while visiting Britain.*

ˈguest beer *noun* [U, C] (*BrE*) a beer that is not usually available in a particular pub, but which is served there for a limited period, often at a specially reduced price

ˈguest house *noun* **1** (*BrE*) a small hotel **2** (*NAmE*) a small house built near a large house, for guests to stay in

gues·ti·mate = GUESSTIMATE

ˈguest room *noun* a bedroom that is kept for guests to use

ˈguest worker *noun* a person, usually from a poor country, who comes to another richer country in order to work there

guff /ɡʌf/ *noun* [U] (*informal*) ideas or talk that you think are stupid SYN **nonsense**

guf·faw /ɡəˈfɔː/ *verb* [I, T] (**+ speech**) to laugh noisily: *They all guffawed at his jokes.* ▶ **guf·faw** *noun*: *She let out a loud guffaw.*

GUI /ˌdʒiː juː ˈaɪ; ˈɡuːi/ *abbr.* (*computing*) graphical user interface (a way of giving instructions to a computer using things that can be seen on the screen such as symbols and menus)

guid·ance /ˈɡaɪdns/ *noun* [U] **1 ~ (on sth)** help or advice that is given to sb, especially by sb older or with more experience: *guidance for teachers on how to use video in the classroom* ◇ *Activities all take place* ***under the guidance of*** *an experienced tutor.* ◇ (*NAmE*) *a guidance counselor* (= sb who advises students) ➲ see also MARRIAGE GUIDANCE **2** the process of controlling the direction of a ROCKET, etc, using electronic equipment: *a missile guidance system*

guide 0ᴡ /ɡaɪd/ *noun, verb*

■ ***noun***

▸ BOOK/MAGAZINE **1** 0ᴡ **~ (to sth)** a book, magazine, etc. that gives you information, help or instructions about sth: *a Guide to Family Health* ◇ *Let's have a look at the TV guide and see what's on.* **2** 0ᴡ (also **guide·book**) **~ (to sth)** a book that gives information about a place for travellers or tourists: *a guide to Italy* ◇ *travel guides*

▸ PERSON **3** 0ᴡ a person who shows other people the way to a place, especially sb employed to show tourists around interesting places: *a tour guide* ◇ *We hired a local guide to get us across the mountains.* **4** a person who advises you on how to live and behave: *a spiritual guide*

▸ STH THAT HELPS YOU DECIDE **5** something that gives you enough information to be able to make a decision about sth or form an opinion: ***As a rough guide****, allow half a cup of rice per person.* ◇ *I let my feelings be my guide.*

▸ GIRL **6 Guide** (also *old-fashioned* **ˌGirl ˈGuide**) (both *BrE*) (*US* **ˌGirl ˈScout**) a member of an organization (called **the Guides** or **the Girl Scouts**) which is similar to the SCOUTS and which trains girls in practical skills and does a lot of activities with them, for example camping ➲ compare BROWNIE

■ ***verb***

▸ SHOW THE WAY **1** 0ᴡ **~ sb (to/through/around sth)** to show sb the way to a place, often by going with them; to show sb a place that you know well: *She guided us through the busy streets to the cathedral.* ◇ *We were guided around the museums.* ➲ SYNONYMS at TAKE

▸ INFLUENCE BEHAVIOUR **2** 0ᴡ **~ sb** to direct or influence sb's behaviour: *He was always guided by his religious beliefs.*

▸ EXPLAIN **3** 0ᴡ **~ sb (through sth)** to explain to sb how to do sth, especially sth complicated or difficult: *The health and safety officer will guide you through the safety procedures.*

▸ HELP SB MOVE **4** 0ᴡ **~ sb/sth (+ adv./prep.)** to help sb to move in a particular direction; to move sth in a particular direction: *She took her arm and guided her across the busy road.* ◇ *He guided her hand to his face.* ➲ see also GUIDING

guide·book /ˈɡaɪdbʊk/ *noun* = GUIDE (2)

guided /ˈɡaɪdɪd/ *adj.* [usually before noun] that is led by sb who works as a guide: *a* ***guided tour/walk***

ˌguided ˈmissile *noun* a MISSILE that can be controlled while in the air by electronic equipment

ˈguide dog (*NAmE* also **ˌSeeing ˈEye dog™**) *noun* a dog trained to guide a blind person

guide·line AW /ˈɡaɪdlaɪn/ *noun* **1 guidelines** [pl.] rules or instructions that are given by an official organization telling you how to do sth, especially sth difficult: *The government has* ***drawn up guidelines*** *on the treatment of the mentally ill.* **2** [C] something that can be used to help you make a decision or form an opinion: *The figures are a useful guideline when buying a house.*

Gui·der /ˈɡaɪdə(r)/ (also *old-fashioned* **ˌGirl ˈGuider**) *noun* (*BrE*) an adult leader in the Guides

guid·ing /ˈɡaɪdɪŋ/ *adj.* [only before noun] giving advice and help; having a strong influence on people: *She was inexperienced and needed a* ***guiding hand.*** ◇ *a guiding force*

guild /ɡɪld/ *noun* [C+sing./pl. v.] **1** an organization of people who do the same job or who have the same interests or aims: *the Screen Actors' Guild* **2** an association of skilled workers in the Middle Ages

guil·der /ˈɡɪldə(r)/ *noun* the former unit of money in the Netherlands (replaced in 2002 by the euro)

guild·hall /ˈɡɪldhɔːl/ *noun* (*BrE*) a building in which the members of a GUILD used to meet, now often used for meetings and performances

guile /ɡaɪl/ *noun* [U] (*formal*) the use of clever but dishonest behaviour in order to trick people SYN **deceit**

guile·less /ˈɡaɪlləs/ *adj.* (*formal*) behaving in a very honest way; not knowing how to trick people ▶ **guile·less·ly** *adv.*

guil·le·mot /ˈɡɪlɪmɒt; *NAmE* -mɑːt/ *noun* a black and white bird with a long narrow beak that lives near the sea

guil·lo·tine /ˈɡɪlətiːn/ *noun, verb*

■ *noun* **1** [sing.] a machine, originally from France, for cutting people's heads off. It has a heavy blade that slides down a wooden frame. **2** (*BrE*) (*US* **ˈpaper cutter**) [C] a device with a long blade for cutting paper **3** [sing.] (*BrE, politics*) the setting of a time limit on a debate in Parliament

■ *verb* **1 ~ sb** to kill sb by cutting off their head with a guillotine **2 ~ sth** (*BrE*) to cut paper using a guillotine **3 ~ sth** (*BrE, politics*) to limit the amount of time spent discussing a new law in Parliament: *to guillotine a bill*

guilt /ɡɪlt/ *noun, verb*

■ *noun* [U] **1 ~ (about sth)** the unhappy feelings caused by knowing or thinking that you have done sth wrong: *She had feelings of guilt about leaving her children and going to work.* ◇ *Many survivors were left with* ***a sense of guilt.*** ◇ *a* ***guilt complex*** (= an exaggerated sense of guilt) **2** the fact that sb has done sth illegal: *His guilt was proved beyond all doubt by the prosecution.* ◇ *an admission of guilt* OPP **innocence** **3** blame or responsibility for doing sth wrong or for sth bad that has happened: *The investigation will try to find out where the guilt for the disaster really lies.* ▶ **guilt·less** *adj.*

IDM **a ˈguilt trip** (*informal*) things you say to sb in order to make them feel guilty about sth: *Don't* ***lay a guilt trip*** *on your child about schoolwork.*

■ *verb*

PHR V **ˈguilt sb into sth/into doing sth** (*informal*) to make sb do sth by persuading them that it is wrong not to do it: *I only went because she guilted me into it.*

guilty 🔑 /ˈɡɪlti/ *adj.* (**guilt·ier**, **guilti·est**) HELP **more guilty** and **most guilty** are more common

1 🔑 **~ (about sth)** feeling ashamed because you have done sth that you know is wrong or have not done sth that you should have done: *I felt guilty about not visiting my parents more often.* ◇ *John had a guilty look on his face.* ◇ *I had a* ***guilty conscience*** *and could not sleep.* **2** 🔑 **~ (of sth)** having done sth illegal; being responsible for sth bad that has happened: *The jury* ***found*** *the defendant* ***not guilty*** *of the offence.* ◇ *He* ***pleaded guilty*** *to murder.* ◇ ***the guilty party*** (= the person responsible for sth bad happening) ◇ *We've all been guilty of selfishness at some time in our lives.* OPP **innocent** ➲ COLLOCATIONS at JUSTICE ▶ **guilt·ily** /-ɪli/ *adv.*

IDM **a guilty ˈsecret** a secret that sb feels ashamed about

guinea /ˈɡɪni/ *noun* an old British gold coin or unit of money worth 21 SHILLINGS (= now £1.05). Prices are sometimes still given in guineas, for example when buying or selling horses.

guinea·fowl /ˈɡɪnifaʊl/ *noun* [C, U] (*pl.* **guinea·fowl**) a bird of the PHEASANT family, that has dark grey feathers with white spots, and is often used for food; the meat of this bird: *roast guineafowl*

ˈguinea pig *noun* **1** a small animal with short ears and no tail, often kept as a pet **2** a person used in medical or other experiments: *Students in fifty schools are to act as guinea pigs for these new teaching methods.*

Guin·ness™ /ˈɡɪnɪs/ *noun* [U, C] a type of very dark brown beer, with a white HEAD (= top) on it

guise /ɡaɪz/ *noun* a way in which sb/sth appears, often in a way that is different from usual or that hides the truth about them/it: *His speech presented racist ideas* ***under the guise of*** *nationalism.* ◇ *The story appears in different guises in different cultures.*

gui·tar /ɡɪˈtɑː(r)/ *noun* a musical instrument that usually has six strings, that you play with your fingers or with a PLECTRUM: ***an acoustic/an electric/a classical, etc. guitar*** ◇ *a guitar player* ◇ *Do you* ***play the guitar?*** ◇ *She plays guitar in a band.* ◇ *As he sang, he strummed his guitar.* ➲ VISUAL VOCAB page V31 ➲ see also AIR GUITAR, BASS

gui·tar·ist /ɡɪˈtɑːrɪst/ *noun* a person who plays the guitar

Gu·ja·rati (also **Gu·je·rati**) /ˌɡuːdʒəˈrɑːti/ *noun* **1** [C] a person from the state of Gujarat in western India **2** [U] the language of Gujarat ▶ **Gu·ja·rati** (also **Gu·je·rati**) *adj.*

gulch /ɡʌltʃ/ *noun* (*especially NAmE*) a narrow valley with steep sides, that was formed by a fast stream flowing through it

gulf /ɡʌlf/ *noun* **1** [C] a large area of sea that is partly surrounded by land: *the Gulf of Mexico* **2 the Gulf** [sing.] the Persian Gulf, the area of sea between the Arabian PENINSULA and Iran: *the Gulf States* (= the countries with coasts on the Gulf) **3** [C, usually sing.] **~ (between A and B)** a large difference between two people or groups in the way that they think, live or feel: *The gulf between rich and poor is enormous.* **4** [C] a wide deep crack in the ground IDM see BRIDGE *v.*

the ˈGulf Stream *noun* [sing.] a warm current of water flowing across the Atlantic Ocean from the Gulf of Mexico towards Europe

gull /ɡʌl/ (also **sea·gull**) *noun* a bird with long wings and usually white and grey or black feathers that lives near the sea. There are several types of gull. ➲ VISUAL VOCAB page V10 ➲ see also HERRING GULL

Gul·lah /ˈɡʌlə/ *noun* [U] a language spoken by black people living on the coast of South Carolina, that is a combination of English and various W African languages

gul·let /ˈɡʌlɪt/ *noun* the tube through which food passes from the mouth to the stomach SYN **oesophagus** ➲ VISUAL VOCAB page V48

gul·lible /ˈɡʌləbl/ *adj.* too willing to believe or accept what other people tell you and therefore easily tricked SYN **naive** ▶ **gul·li·bil·ity** /ˌɡʌləˈbɪləti/ *noun* [U]

gully (also **gul·ley**) /ˈɡʌli/ *noun* (*pl.* **gul·lies**, **gul·leys**) **1** a small, narrow channel, usually formed by a stream or by rain **2** a deep DITCH

gulp /ɡʌlp/ *verb, noun*

■ *verb* **1** [T, I] **~ (sth)** | **~ sth down** to swallow large amounts of food or drink quickly: *He gulped down the rest of his tea and went out.* **2** [I, T] **(+ speech)** to swallow, but without eating or drinking anything, especially because of a strong

G

emotion such as fear or surprise: *She gulped nervously before trying to answer.* **3** [I, T] to breathe quickly and deeply, because you need more air: **~ (for sth)** *She came up gulping for air.* ◇ **~ sth (in)** *He leant against the car, gulping in the cold air.*

PHR V **ˌgulp sth↔ˈback** to stop yourself showing your emotions by swallowing hard: *She gulped back her tears and forced a smile.*

■ ***noun*** **1 ~ (of sth)** an amount of sth that you swallow or drink quickly: *He **took a gulp** of coffee.* **2** an act of breathing in or of swallowing sth: *'Can you start on Monday?' Amy gave a gulp. 'Of course,' she said.* ◇ *He drank the glass of whisky **in one gulp**.*

gum /ɡʌm/ *noun, verb*

■ ***noun*** **1** [C, usually pl.] either of the firm areas of flesh in the mouth to which the teeth are attached: *gum disease* ➲ VISUAL VOCAB page V48 **2** [U] a sticky substance produced by some types of tree **3** [U] a type of glue used for sticking light things together, such as paper **4** [U] = CHEWING GUM **5** [C] a firm transparent fruit-flavoured sweet/candy that you chew: *fruit gums*

IDM **by gum!** (*old-fashioned, BrE, informal*) used to show surprise

■ ***verb*** (-mm-) **~ A to B | ~ sth (down)** (rather *old-fashioned*) to spread glue on the surface of sth; to stick two things together with glue: *A large address label was gummed to the package.*

PHR V **ˌgum sth↔ˈup** [usually passive] (*BrE, informal*) to cover or fill sth with a sticky substance so that it stops moving or working as it should

gum·ball /ˈɡʌmbɔːl/ *noun* (*NAmE*) a small ball of CHEWING GUM that looks like a sweet/candy

gumbo /ˈɡʌmbəʊ; *NAmE* -boʊ/ *noun* [U] a thick chicken or SEAFOOD soup, usually made with the vegetable OKRA

gum·boil /ˈɡʌmbɔɪl/ *noun* a small swelling on the GUM in a person's mouth, over an infected area on the root of a tooth

gum·boot /ˈɡʌmbuːt/ *noun* (*old-fashioned, BrE*) = WELLINGTON

gum·drop /ˈɡʌmdrɒp; *NAmE* -drɑːp/ *noun* a sweet/candy that is like a small firm lump of jelly

gummed /ɡʌmd/ *adj.* [usually before noun] (of stamps, paper, etc.) covered with a type of glue that will become sticky when water is put on it

gummy /ˈɡʌmi/ *adj.* (*informal*) **1** sticky or covered in gum (3) **2** a **gummy** smile shows your teeth and gums

gump·tion /ˈɡʌmpʃn/ *noun* [U] (*old-fashioned, informal*) **1** the intelligence needed to know what to do in a particular situation **2** courage and determination

gum·shield /ˈɡʌmʃiːld/ (*BrE*) (*NAmE* **mouth·guard**) *noun* a cover that a sports player wears in his or her mouth to protect the teeth and GUMS

gum·shoe /ˈɡʌmʃuː/ *noun* (*old-fashioned, NAmE, informal*) = DETECTIVE (1)

ˈgum tree *noun* a EUCALYPTUS tree

IDM **be up a ˈgum tree** (*BrE, informal*) to be in a very difficult situation

gun 🔑 /ɡʌn/ *noun, verb*

■ ***noun*** **1** 🔑 [C] a weapon that is used for firing bullets or SHELLS: *to **fire a gun** at sb* ◇ *a toy gun* ◇ *anti-aircraft guns* ◇ *Look out, he's got a gun!* ◇ *Should police officers **carry guns**?* ◇ *He **pointed/aimed the gun** at her head.* ◇ *The police officers **drew their guns*** (= took them out so they were ready to use). ◇ *She **pulled a gun on** me* (= took out a gun and aimed it at me). ◇ *The **gun went off** by accident.* ◇ *a **gun battle** between rival gangs* ➲ see also AIRGUN, HANDGUN, MACHINE GUN, SHOTGUN, STUN GUN, SUB-MACHINE GUN, TOMMY GUN **2** [C] a tool that uses pressure to send out a substance or an object: *a staple gun* ➲ see also SPRAY GUN **3 the gun** [sing.] the signal to begin a race, that is made by firing a special gun, called a STARTING PISTOL, into the air **4** [C] (*informal, especially NAmE*) a person who is paid to shoot sb: *a hired gun* ➲ see also FLASHGUN, SON OF A GUN

IDM **hold/put a gun to sb's ˈhead** to force sb to do sth that they do not want to do, by making threats **under the ˈgun** (*NAmE, informal*) experiencing a lot of pressure: *I'm really under the gun today.* **(with) all/both guns ˈblazing** (*informal*) with a lot of energy and determination: *The champions came out (with) all guns blazing.* ➲ more at GREAT *adj.*, JUMP *v.*, SPIKE *v.*, STICK *v.*

■ ***verb*** (-nn-) **1** [I] (*NAmE*) (of an engine) to run very quickly: *a line of motorcycles with their engines gunning* **2** [T] **~ sth + adv./prep.** (*NAmE*) to start driving a vehicle very fast: *He gunned the cab through the red light.*

PHR V **be ˈgunning for sb** (*informal*) to be looking for an opportunity to blame or attack sb **be ˈgunning for sth** to be competing for or trying hard to get sth: *She's gunning for the top job.* **ˌgun sb↔ˈdown** [usually passive] to shoot sb, especially killing or seriously injuring them

gun·boat /ˈɡʌnbəʊt; *NAmE* -boʊt/ *noun* a small ship that is fitted with large guns

ˌgunboat diˈplomacy *noun* [U] a way of making another country accept your demands by using the threat of force

ˈgun carriage *noun* a support on wheels for a large heavy gun

ˈgun control *noun* [U] (*especially NAmE*) laws that restrict the sale and use of guns

ˈgun dog *noun* a dog trained to help in the sport of shooting, for example by finding birds that have been shot

gun·fight /ˈɡʌnfaɪt/ *noun* a fight between people using guns ▶ **gun·fight·er** *noun*

gun·fire /ˈɡʌnfaɪə(r)/ *noun* [U] the repeated firing of guns; the sound of guns firing: *an exchange of gunfire with the police* ◇ *I could hear gunfire.*

gunge /ɡʌndʒ/ (*BrE*) (also **gunk** *NAmE, BrE*) *noun* [U] (*informal*) any unpleasant, sticky or dirty substance ▶ **gungy** *adj.*

gung-ho /ˌɡʌŋ ˈhəʊ; *NAmE* ˈhoʊ/ *adj.* (*informal, disapproving*) too enthusiastic about sth, without thinking seriously about it, especially about fighting and war

gunk /ɡʌŋk/ (*especially NAmE*) (*BrE* also **gunge**) *noun* [U] (*informal*) any unpleasant, sticky or dirty substance ▶ **gunky** *adj.*

gun·man /ˈɡʌnmən/ *noun* (*pl.* **-men** /-mən/) a man who uses a gun to steal from or kill people

gun·metal /ˈɡʌnmetl/ *noun* [U] **1** a metal that is a mixture of COPPER, tin and ZINC **2** a dull blue-grey colour

gun·nel = GUNWALE

gun·ner /ˈɡʌnə(r)/ *noun* **1** a member of the armed forces who is trained to use large guns **2** a soldier in the British ARTILLERY (= the part of the army that uses large guns)

gun·nery /ˈɡʌnəri/ *noun* [U] (*technical*) the operation of large military guns

gunny /ˈɡʌni/ *noun* [U] a type of rough cloth used for making SACKS

gun·ny·sack /ˈɡʌnisæk/ *noun* (*NAmE*) a large bag made from rough material and used to store flour, potatoes, etc.

gun·point /ˈɡʌnpɔɪnt/ *noun*

IDM **at ˈgunpoint** while threatening sb or being threatened with a gun: *The driver was robbed at gunpoint.*

gun·pow·der /ˈɡʌnpaʊdə(r)/ (also **pow·der**) *noun* [U] EXPLOSIVE powder used especially in bombs or FIREWORKS

gun·run·ner /ˈɡʌnrʌnə(r)/ *noun* a person who secretly and illegally brings guns into a country ▶ **gun·run·ning** *noun* [U]

gun·ship /ˈɡʌnʃɪp/ *noun* an armed military HELICOPTER or other aircraft

gun·shot /ˈɡʌnʃɒt; *NAmE* -ʃɑːt/ *noun* **1** [U] the bullets that are fired from a gun: *gunshot wounds* **2** [C] the firing of a gun; the sound of it being fired: *I heard the sound of gunshots out in the street.* **3** [U] the distance that a bullet from a gun can travel: *He was **out of/within gunshot**.*

gun·sight /ˈɡʌnsaɪt/ *noun* a part of a gun that you look through in order to aim it accurately ➲ see also SIGHT *n.* (7)

gun·sling·er /ˈɡʌnslɪŋə(r)/ *noun* (*NAmE*) a person who is paid to kill people, especially in films/movies about the American Wild West

gun·smith /ˈɡʌnsmɪθ/ *noun* a person who makes and repairs guns

gun·wale (also **gun·nel**) /ˈɡʌnl/ *noun* the upper edge of the side of a boat or small ship

guppy /ˈɡʌpi/ *noun* (*pl.* -ies) a small FRESHWATER fish, commonly kept in AQUARIUMS

gur·dwa·ra /ɡɜːˈdwɑːrə; *NAmE* ɡɜːr-/ *noun* a building in which Sikhs worship

gur·gle /ˈɡɜːɡl; *NAmE* ˈɡɜːrɡl/ *verb, noun*
- ***verb*** **1** [I] to make a sound like water flowing quickly through a narrow space: *Water gurgled through the pipes.* ◇ *a gurgling stream* **2** [I] if a baby **gurgles**, it makes a noise in its throat when it is happy
- ***noun*** **1** a sound like water flowing quickly through a narrow space **2** the sound that babies make in the throat, especially when they are happy

Gur·kha /ˈɡɜːkə; *NAmE* ˈɡɜːrkə/ *noun* one of a group of people from Nepal who are known as good soldiers. Some Gurkhas are members of a REGIMENT in the British army.

gurn (also **girn**) /ɡɜːn; *NAmE* ɡɜːrn/ *verb* [I] (*especially BrE*) to make a ridiculous or unpleasant face ▶ **gurn·er** /ˈɡɜːnə(r); *NAmE* ˈɡɜːrn-/ *noun*

gur·ney /ˈɡɜːni; *NAmE* ˈɡɜːrni/ *noun* (*NAmE*) a type of TROLLEY which is used for moving patients in a hospital

guru /ˈɡʊruː/ *noun* **1** a Hindu or Sikh religious teacher or leader **2** (*informal*) a person who is an expert on a particular subject or who is very good at doing sth: *a **management/health/fashion, etc. guru***

gush /ɡʌʃ/ *verb, noun*
- ***verb*** **1** [I] **~ out of/from/into sth** | **~ out/in** to flow or pour suddenly and quickly out of a hole in large amounts: *blood gushing from a wound* ◇ *Water gushed out of the pipe.* **2** [T] **~ sth** (of a container/vehicle etc.) to suddenly let out large amounts of a liquid: *The tanker was gushing oil.* ◇ (*figurative*) *She absolutely gushed enthusiasm.* **3** [T, I] (+ **speech**) (*disapproving*) to express so much praise or emotion about sb/sth that it does not seem sincere: *'You are clever,' she gushed.*
- ***noun*** [usually sing.] **1 ~** (**of sth**) a large amount of liquid suddenly and quickly flowing or pouring out of sth: *a gush of blood* **2 ~** (**of sth**) a sudden strong expression of feeling: *a gush of emotion*

gush·er /ˈɡʌʃə(r)/ *noun* **1** (*NAmE*) an OIL WELL where the oil comes out quickly and in large quantities **2** a person who gushes (3)

gush·ing /ˈɡʌʃɪŋ/ *adj.* (*disapproving*) expressing so much enthusiasm, praise or emotion that it does not seem sincere ▶ **gush·ing·ly** *adv.*

gus·set /ˈɡʌsɪt/ *noun* an extra piece of cloth sewn into a piece of clothing to make it wider, stronger or more comfortable

gussy /ˈɡʌsi/ *verb* (**gus·sies**, **gussy·ing**, **gus·sied**, **gus·sied**)
PHR V **ˌgussy ˈup** (*NAmE, informal*) to dress yourself in an attractive way SYN **dress up**: *Even the stars get tired of gussying up for the awards.*

gust /ɡʌst/ *noun, verb*
- ***noun*** **1** a sudden strong increase in the amount and speed of wind that is blowing: *A **gust of wind** blew his hat off.* ◇ *The wind was blowing in gusts.* **2** a sudden strong expression of emotion: *a **gust of laughter***
- ***verb*** [I] (of the wind) to suddenly blow very hard: *winds gusting up to 60 mph*

gusto /ˈɡʌstəʊ; *NAmE* -toʊ/ *noun* [U] enthusiasm and energy in doing sth: *They sang **with gusto**.*

gusty /ˈɡʌsti/ *adj.* [usually before noun] with the wind blowing in GUSTS: *a gusty morning* ◇ *gusty winds*

gut /ɡʌt/ *noun, verb, adj.*
- ***noun*** **1** [C] the tube in the body through which food passes when it leaves the stomach SYN **intestine** **2 guts** [pl.] the organs in and around the stomach, especially in an animal: *I'll only cook fish if the guts have been removed.* **3** [C] (*informal*) a person's stomach, especially when it is large SYN **belly**: *Have you seen the gut on him!* ◇ *a **beer gut*** (= caused by drinking beer) **4 guts** [pl.] (*informal*) the courage and determination that it takes to do sth difficult or unpleasant: *He **doesn't have the guts** to walk away from a well-paid job.* **5** [C, usually pl.] the place where your natural feelings that make you react in a particular way are thought to be: *I had a feeling **in my guts** that something was wrong.* **6 guts** [pl.] the most important part of sth: *the guts of the problem* **7** [U] = CATGUT

IDM **have sb's ˌguts for ˈgarters** (*BrE, informal*) to be very angry with sb and punish them severely for sth they have done **slog/sweat/work your ˈguts out** (*informal*) to work very hard to achieve sth: *I slogged my guts out for the exam.* ➲ more at BUST *v.*, GREEDY *adj.*, HATE *v.*, SPILL *v.*
- ***verb*** (-tt-) **1** [usually passive] **~ sth** to destroy the inside or contents of a building or room: *a factory gutted by fire* ◇ *The house was completely gutted.* **2 ~ sth** to remove the organs from inside a fish or an animal to prepare it for cooking
- ***adj.*** [only before noun] based on feelings and emotions rather than thought and reason: *a **gut feeling/reaction*** ◇ *You have to work on **gut instinct**.*

gut·less /ˈɡʌtləs/ *adj.* lacking courage or determination

gut·ser /ˈɡʌtsə(r)/ *noun* (*AustralE, NZE, informal*) an occasion when sb/sth falls or knocks into sth
IDM **come a ˈgutser** to fail or be defeated

gutsy /ˈɡʌtsi/ *adj.* (*informal*) **1** showing courage and determination: *a **gutsy fighter/win*** **2** having strong and unusual qualities: *a gutsy red wine* ◇ *a gutsy song*

gut·ted /ˈɡʌtɪd/ *adj.* [not before noun] (*BrE, informal*) extremely sad or disappointed: *Disappointed? I was gutted!*

gut·ter /ˈɡʌtə(r)/ *noun, verb*
- ***noun*** **1** [C] a long curved channel made of metal or plastic that is fixed under the edge of a roof to carry away the water when it rains: *a **blocked/leaking gutter*** ➲ VISUAL VOCAB page V15 **2** [C] a channel at the edge of a road where water collects and is carried away to DRAINS **3 the gutter** [sing.] the bad social conditions or low moral standards sometimes connected with the lowest level of society: *She rose from the gutter to become a great star.* ◇ *the language of the gutter* (= used when swearing)
- ***verb*** [I] (*literary*) (of a flame or CANDLE) to burn in an unsteady way

gut·ter·ing /ˈɡʌtərɪŋ/ *noun* [U] the system of gutters on a building; the material used to make gutters: *a length of guttering*

the ˌgutter ˈpress *noun* [sing.] (*BrE, disapproving*) newspapers that print a lot of shocking stories about people's private lives rather than serious news

gut·ter·snipe /ˈɡʌtəsnaɪp; *NAmE* -tərs-/ *noun* (*informal, disapproving*) a poor and dirty child

gut·tur·al /ˈɡʌtərəl/ *adj.* (of a sound) made or seeming to be made at the back of the throat: *guttural consonants* ◇ *a low guttural growl*

ˈgut-wrench·ing *adj.* (*informal*) very unpleasant; making you feel very upset

guv /ɡʌv/ *exclamation* (*BrE, informal*) used by a man to address another man who is a customer, etc, meaning 'sir'

guv'nor /ˈɡʌvnə(r)/ *noun* (*BrE, informal*) (often used as a way of addressing sb) a man who is in a position of authority, for example your employer: *Do you want me to ask the guv'nor about it?* ➲ see also GOVERNOR

guy 🔑 /ɡaɪ/ *noun*
1 🔑 [C] (*informal*) a man: *a big/nice/tough guy* ◇ *a Dutch guy* ◇ *At the end of the film the bad guy gets shot.* ➲ see also FALL GUY, WISE GUY **2 guys** [pl.] (*informal, especially NAmE*) a group of people of either sex: *Come on, you guys, let's get going!* **3** [C] (in Britain) a model of a man dressed in old clothes that is burned on a BONFIRE on 5 November

G

during the celebrations for Bonfire Night **4** (also **'guy rope**) [C] a rope used to keep a pole or tent in a vertical position IDM see MR *abbr.*

Guy Fawkes night /'gaɪ fɔːks naɪt/ *noun* [U, C] Bonfire Night

guz·zle /'gʌzl/ *verb* [T, I] **~ (sth)** (*informal*, usually *disapproving*) to drink sth quickly and in large amounts. In British English it also means to eat food quickly and in large amounts: *The kids seem to be guzzling soft drinks all day.* ◇ (*figurative*) *My car guzzles fuel.*

guz·zler /'gʌzlə(r)/ *noun* (*informal, especially NAmE*) = GAS GUZZLER

gweilo /'gweɪləʊ; *NAmE* -loʊ/ *noun* (*pl.* -os) (*SEAsianE*) used in SE Asia to refer to a person from a foreign country, especially sb from the West

G

gybe (*especially BrE*) (*NAmE* usually **jibe**) /dʒaɪb/ *verb, noun*

■ ***verb*** [I] to change direction when sailing with the wind behind you, by swinging the sail from one side of the boat to the other

■ ***noun*** an act of gybing

gym /dʒɪm/ *noun* (*informal*) **1** (also *formal* **gym·na·sium**) [C] a room or hall with equipment for doing physical exercise, for example in a school: *to play basketball in the gym* ◇ *The school has recently built a new gym.* **2** [U] physical exercises done in a gym, especially at school: *I don't enjoy gym.* ◇ *gym shoes* **3** [C] = HEALTH CLUB: *I just joined a gym.* ◇ *I work out at the gym most days.* ➲ COLLOCATIONS at DIET

gym·khana /dʒɪm'kɑːnə/ *noun* (*BrE*) an event in which people riding horses take part in various competitions

gym·na·sium /dʒɪm'neɪziəm/ *noun* (*pl.* gym·na·siums or gym·na·sia /-ziə/) (*formal*) = GYM (1)

gym·nast /'dʒɪmnæst/ *noun* a person who performs gymnastics, especially in a competition

gym·nas·tics /dʒɪm'næstɪks/ *noun* [U] physical exercises that develop and show the body's strength and ability to move and bend easily, often done as a sport in competitions: *a gymnastics competition* ◇ (*figurative*) ***mental/verbal gymnastics*** (= quick or clever thinking or use of words) ➲ VISUAL VOCAB page V39 ▸ **gym·nas·tic** *adj.* [only before noun]

'gym shoe *noun* (*BrE* also **plim·soll, pump**) a light simple sports shoe made of CANVAS (= strong cotton cloth) with a rubber SOLE

gym·slip /'dʒɪmslɪp/ *noun* (*BrE*) a dress without sleeves worn over a shirt as a school uniform for girls, especially in the past

gy·nae·colo·gist (*BrE*) (*NAmE* **gyne·colo·gist**) /ˌgaɪnə'kɒlədʒɪst; *NAmE* -'kɑːl-/ *noun* a doctor who studies and treats the medical conditions and diseases of women

gy·nae·col·ogy (*BrE*) (*NAmE* **gyne·cology**) /ˌgaɪnə'kɒlədʒi; *NAmE* -'kɑːl-/ *noun* [U] the scientific study and treatment of the medical conditions and diseases of women, especially those connected with sexual REPRODUCTION ▸ **gy·nae·co·logic·al** (*BrE*) (*NAmE* **gyne-**) /ˌgaɪnəkə'lɒdʒɪkl; *NAmE* -'lɑːdʒ-/ *adj.*: *a gynaecological examination*

gyp /dʒɪp/ *noun, verb*

■ ***noun*** [sing.] (*NAmE, informal*) an act of charging too much money for sth: *That meal was a real gyp.*

IDM **give sb 'gyp** (*BrE, informal*) to cause sb a lot of pain: *My back's been giving me gyp lately.*

■ ***verb*** (-pp-) **~ sb** (*especially NAmE*) to cheat or trick sb, especially by taking their money

gyp·sum /'dʒɪpsəm/ *noun* [U] a soft white mineral like CHALK that is found naturally and is used in making PLASTER OF PARIS

Gypsy (also **Gipsy**) /'dʒɪpsi/ *noun* (*pl.* -ies) (sometimes *offensive*) **1** a member of a race of people, originally from Asia, who traditionally travel around and live in CARAVANS. Many people prefer to use the name Roma or Romani. **2** = TRAVELLER (2)

gyr·ate /dʒaɪ'reɪt; *NAmE* 'dʒaɪreɪt/ *verb* [I, T] to move around in circles; to make sth, especially a part of your body, move around: *They began gyrating to the music.* ◇ *The leaves gyrated slowly to the ground.* ◇ **~ sth** *As the lead singer gyrated his hips, the crowd screamed wildly.* ▸ **gyr·ation** /dʒaɪ'reɪʃn/ *noun* [C, usually pl., U]

gyro·scope /'dʒaɪrəskəʊp; *NAmE* -skoʊp/ (also *informal* **gyro** /'dʒaɪrəʊ; *NAmE* -roʊ/) *noun* a device consisting of a wheel that spins rapidly inside a frame and does not change position when the frame is moved. Gyroscopes are often used to keep ships and aircraft steady. ▸ **gyro·scop·ic** /ˌdʒaɪrə'skɒpɪk; *NAmE* -'skɑːpɪk/ *adj.*

H (also **h**) /eɪtʃ/ *noun, abbr.*
■ ***noun*** [C, U] (*pl.* **Hs, H's, h's** /ˈeɪtʃɪz/) the 8th letter of the English alphabet: *'Hat' begins with (an) H/'H'.* ➲ compare AITCH ➲ see also H-BOMB
■ ***abbr.*** (in writing) HENRY

ha[1] /hɑː/ *exclamation* **1** (also **hah**) the sound that people make when they are surprised or pleased or when they have discovered sth: *Ha! It serves you right!* ◇ *Ha! I knew he was hiding something.* **2** (also **ha! ha!**) the word for the sound that people make when they laugh **3** (also **ha! ha!**) (*informal, ironic*) used to show that you do not think that sth is funny: *Ha! Ha! Very funny! Now give me back my shoes.*

ha[2] *abbr.* (in writing) HECTARE

haar /hɑː(r)/ *noun* [sing.] a cold sea FOG on the east coast of England or Scotland

hab·eas cor·pus /ˌheɪbiəs ˈkɔːpəs; *NAmE* ˈkɔːrpəs/ *noun* [U] (from *Latin, law*) a law that states that a person who has been arrested should not be kept in prison longer than a particular period of time unless a judge in court has decided that it is right

hab·er·dash·er /ˈhæbədæʃə(r); *NAmE* ˈhæbərd-/ *noun* **1** (*old-fashioned, BrE*) a person who owns or works in a shop/store selling small articles for sewing, for example, needles, pins, cotton and buttons **2 hab·er·dash·er's** (*pl.* **hab·er·dash·ers**) a shop/store that sells these things **3** (*NAmE*) a person who owns, manages or works in a shop/store that makes and sells men's clothes

hab·er·dash·ery /ˌhæbəˈdæʃəri; *NAmE* ˈhæbərd-/ *noun* (*pl.* **-ies**) **1** [U] (*old-fashioned, BrE*) small articles for sewing, for example needles, pins, cotton and buttons **2** [U] (*old-fashioned, NAmE*) men's clothes **3** [C] a shop/store or part of a shop/store where haberdashery is sold

habit 🔑 /ˈhæbɪt/ *noun*
1 🔑 [C] a thing that you do often and almost without thinking, especially sth that is hard to stop doing: *You need to change your eating habits.* ◇ ***good/bad habits*** ◇ *He has the irritating habit of biting his nails.* ◇ *It's all right to borrow money occasionally, but don't* ***let it become a habit.*** ◇ *I'd prefer you not to* ***make a habit*** *of it.* ◇ *I'm not* ***in the habit of*** *letting strangers into my apartment.* ◇ *I've* ***got into the habit of*** *turning on the TV as soon as I get home.* ◇ *I'm trying to* ***break the habit*** *of staying up too late.* **2** 🔑 [U] usual behaviour: *I only do it* ***out of habit.*** ◇ *I'm a* ***creature of habit*** (= I have a fixed and regular way of doing things). **3** [C] (*informal*) a strong need to keep using drugs, alcohol or cigarettes regularly: *He began to finance his habit through burglary.* ◇ *She's tried to give up smoking but just can't* ***kick the habit.*** ◇ *a 50-a-day habit* **4** [C] a long piece of clothing worn by a MONK OR NUN **IDM** see FORCE *n.*

hab·it·able /ˈhæbɪtəbl/ *adj.* suitable for people to live in: *The house should be habitable by the new year.* **OPP** **uninhabitable**

habi·tat /ˈhæbɪtæt/ *noun* [C, U] the place where a particular type of animal or plant is normally found: *The panda's* ***natural habitat*** *is the bamboo forest.* ◇ *the destruction of wildlife habitat* ➲ COLLOCATIONS at ENVIRONMENT

habi·ta·tion /ˌhæbɪˈteɪʃn/ *noun* **1** [U] the act of living in a place: *They looked around for any signs of habitation.* ◇ *The houses were* ***unfit for human habitation*** (= not clean or safe enough for people to live in). **2** [C] (*formal*) a place where people live: *The road serves the scattered habitations along the coast.*

ˈhabit-forming *adj.* a **habit-forming** activity or drug is one that makes you want to continue doing it or taking it

ha·bit·ual /həˈbɪtʃuəl/ *adj.* **1** [only before noun] usual or typical of sb/sth: *They waited for his habitual response.* ◇ (*formal*) *a person's place of habitual residence* **2** (of an action) done, often in a way that is annoying or difficult to stop: *habitual complaining* ◇ *the habitual use of heroin* **3** [only before noun] (of a person) doing sth that has become a habit and is therefore difficult to stop: *a* ***habitual criminal/drinker/liar, etc.*** **HELP** Some speakers do not pronounce the 'h' at the beginning of **habitual** and use 'an' instead of 'a' before it. This now sounds old-fashioned.
▸ **ha·bit·ual·ly** /-tʃuəli/ *adv.*: *the dark glasses he habitually wore*

ha·bitu·ated /həˈbɪtʃueɪtɪd/ *adj.* **~ (to sth)** (*formal*) familiar with sth because you have done it or experienced it often **SYN** **accustomed**

ha·bi·tué /(h)æˈbɪtʃueɪ/ *noun* (from *French, formal*) a person who goes regularly to a particular place or event: *a(n) habitué of upmarket clubs* **SYN** **regular**

ha·ci·enda /ˌhæsiˈendə/ *noun* a large farm in a Spanish-speaking country

hack /hæk/ *verb, noun*
■ ***verb*** **1** [T, I] to cut sb/sth with rough, heavy blows: **~ sb/sth + adv./prep.** *I hacked the dead branches off.* ◇ *They were hacked to death as they tried to escape.* ◇ *We had to* ***hack our way*** *through the jungle.* ◇ **+ adv./prep.** *We hacked away at the bushes.* **2** [T] **~ sb/sth + adv./prep.** to kick sth roughly or without control: *He hacked the ball away.* **3** (*computing*) [I, T] to secretly find a way of looking at and/or changing information on sb else's computer system without permission: **~ into sth** *He hacked into the bank's computer.* ◇ **~ sth** *They had hacked secret data.* **4** [T] **can/can't hack it** (*informal*) to be able/not able to manage in a particular situation: *Lots of people leave this job because they can't hack it.* **5** [I] (usually **go hacking**) (*especially BrE*) to ride a horse for pleasure **6** [I] (*NAmE, informal*) to drive a taxi
■ ***noun*** **1** (*disapproving*) a writer, especially of newspaper articles, who does a lot of low quality work and does not get paid much **2** (*disapproving*) a person who does the hard and often boring work for an organization, especially a politician: *a party hack* **3** a horse for ordinary riding or one that can be hired **4** (*NAmE, informal*) a taxi **5** an act of hitting sth, especially with a cutting tool

ˌhacked ˈoff *adj.* [not before noun] (*BrE, informal*) extremely annoyed: *I'm really hacked off.* **SYN** **fed up**

hack·er /ˈhækə(r)/ *noun* a person who secretly finds a way of looking at and/or changing information on sb else's computer system without permission

ˌhacking ˈcough *noun* [sing.] a dry painful cough that is repeated often

ˈhacking jacket *noun* a short jacket worn for horse riding

hackles /ˈhæklz/ *noun* [pl.] the hairs on the back of the neck of a dog, cat, etc. that rise when the animal is afraid or angry
IDM **make sb's ˈhackles rise | raise sb's ˈhackles** to make sb angry **sb's ˈhackles rise** to become angry: *Ben felt his hackles rise as the speaker continued.*

hack·ney car·riage /ˈhækni kærɪdʒ/ (also **ˈhack·ney cab**) *noun* (*BrE*) a word used in official language for a taxi. In the past hackney carriages were carriages pulled by horses that were used as taxis.

hack·neyed /ˈhæknid/ *adj.* used too often and therefore boring **SYN** **clichéd**: *a* ***hackneyed phrase/subject***

hack·saw /ˈhæksɔː/ *noun* a tool with a narrow blade in a frame, used for cutting metal ➲ VISUAL VOCAB page V17

had /həd; əd; *strong form* hæd/ ➲ HAVE

had·dock /ˈhædək/ *noun* (*pl.* **had·dock**) [C, U] a sea fish like a COD but smaller, with white flesh that is used for food: *smoked haddock*

Hades /ˈheɪdiːz/ *noun* [U] (in ancient Greek stories) the land of the dead **SYN** **hell**

Had·ith /hæˈdiːθ/ *noun* (*pl.* **Had·ith** or **Had·iths**) (in Islam) **1** [sing.] a text containing things said by Muhammad and descriptions of his daily life, used by Muslims as a spiritual guide **2** [C] one of the things said by Muhammad, recorded in this text

hadn't /ˈhædnt/ *short form* had not

haem·atite (*BrE*) (*NAmE* **hema·tite**) /ˈhiːmətaɪt/ *noun* [U] (*geology*) a dark red rock from which iron is obtained

haema·tol·ogy (*BrE*) (*NAmE* **hema·tol·ogy**) /ˌhiːməˈtɒlədʒi; *NAmE* -ˈtɑːl-/ *noun* [U] the scientific study of the blood and its diseases ▸ **haem·ato·logic·al** (*BrE*) (*NAmE* **hem-**) /ˌhiːmətəˈlɒdʒɪkl; *NAmE* -ˈlɑːdʒ-/ *adj.* **haema·tolo·gist** (*BrE*) (*NAmE* **hem-**) /ˌhiːməˈtɒlədʒɪst; *NAmE* -ˈtɑːl-/ *noun*

haem·atoma (*BrE*) (*NAmE* **hema·toma**) /ˌhiːməˈtəʊmə; *NAmE* -ˈtoʊmə/ *noun* (*medical*) a swollen area on the body consisting of blood that has become thick

haemo- (*BrE*) (*NAmE* **hemo-**) /ˈhiːməʊ; *NAmE* -moʊ/ *combining form* (in nouns and adjectives) connected with blood: *haemophilia*

haemo·globin (*BrE*) (*NAmE* **hemo·globin**) /ˌhiːməˈɡləʊbɪn; *NAmE* -ˈɡloʊ-/ *noun* [U] a red substance in the blood that carries OXYGEN and contains iron

H

haemo·philia (*BrE*) (*NAmE* **hemo·philia**) /ˌhiːməˈfɪliə/ *noun* [U] a medical condition that causes severe loss of blood from even a slight injury because the blood fails to CLOT normally. It usually affects only men although it can be passed on by women.

haemo·phil·iac (*BrE*) (*NAmE* **hemo·phil·iac**) /ˌhiːməˈfɪliæk/ *noun* a person who suffers from haemophilia

haem·or·rhage (*BrE*) (*NAmE* **hem·or·rhage**) /ˈhemərɪdʒ/ *noun, verb*

▪ ***noun* 1** [C, U] a medical condition in which there is severe loss of blood from inside a person's body: *a massive **brain/cerebral haemorrhage*** ◇ *He was checked for any signs of haemorrhage.* **2** [C, usually sing.] **~ (of sb/sth)** a serious loss of people, money, etc. from a country, a group or an organization: *Poor working conditions have led to a steady haemorrhage of qualified teachers from our schools.*

▪ ***verb* 1** [I] to lose blood heavily, especially from the inside of the body; to have a haemorrhage **2** [T] **~ sb/sth** to lose money or people in large amounts at a fast rate

haem·or·rhagic (*BrE*) (*NAmE* **hem·or·rhagic**) /ˌheməˈrædʒɪk/ *adj.* (*medical*) happening with or caused by haemorrhage: *a haemorrhagic fever*

haem·or·rhoids (*BrE*) (*NAmE* **hem·or·rhoids**) /ˈhemərɔɪdz/ *noun* [pl.] (*medical*) painful swollen VEINS at or near the ANUS **SYN piles**

haf·nium /ˈhæfniəm/ *noun* [U] (*symb.* **Hf**) a RADIOACTIVE chemical element. Hafnium is a hard silver-grey metal.

haft /hɑːft; *NAmE* hæft/ *noun* the handle of a knife or weapon

hag /hæɡ/ *noun* (*offensive*) an ugly and/or unpleasant old woman ➲ see also FAG HAG

hag·gard /ˈhæɡəd; *NAmE* -ɡərd/ *adj.* looking very tired because of illness, worry or lack of sleep **SYN drawn**

hag·gis /ˈhæɡɪs/ *noun* [C, U] a Scottish dish that looks like a large round SAUSAGE made from the heart, lungs and LIVER of a sheep that are finely chopped, mixed with OATS, HERBS, etc. and boiled in a bag that is traditionally made from part of a sheep's stomach

hag·gle /ˈhæɡl/ *verb* [I] **~ (with sb) (over sth)** to argue with sb in order to reach an agreement, especially about the price of sth: *I left him in the market haggling over the price of a shirt.*

hagi·og·raph·er /ˌhæɡiˈɒɡrəfə(r); *NAmE* -ˈɑːɡ-/ *noun* (*formal*) **1** a person who writes the life story of a SAINT **2** a person who writes about another person's life in a way that praises them too much, and does not criticize them

hagi·og·raphy /ˌhæɡiˈɒɡrəfi; *NAmE* -ˈɑːɡ-/ *noun* (*pl.* -ies) [C, U] (*formal*) a book about the life of a person that praises them too much; this style of writing

hah = HA

haiku /ˈhaɪkuː/ *noun* (*pl.* **haiku** or **haikus**) (from *Japanese*) a poem with three lines and usually 17 syllables, written in a style that is traditional in Japan

hail /heɪl/ *verb, noun*

▪ ***verb* 1** [T, usually passive] to describe sb/sth as being very good or special, especially in newspapers, etc: **~ sb/sth as sth** *The conference was hailed as a great success.* ◇ **~ sb/sth + noun** *Teenager Matt Brown is being hailed a hero for saving a young child from drowning.* **2** [T] **~ sth** to signal to a taxi or a bus, in order to get the driver to stop: *to **hail a taxi/cab*** **3** [T] **~ sb** (*literary*) to call to sb in order to say hello to them or attract their attention: *A voice hailed us from the other side of the street.* **4** [I] when **it hails**, small balls of ice fall like rain from the sky: *It's hailing!*

PHR V **ˈhail from...** (*formal*) to come from or have been born in a particular place: *His father hailed from Italy.*

▪ ***noun* 1** [U] small balls of ice that fall like rain: *We drove through hail and snow.* **2** [sing.] **a ~ of sth** a large number or amount of sth that is aimed at sb in order to harm them: *a **hail of arrows/bullets*** ◇ *a hail of abuse*

Hail Mary /ˌheɪl ˈmeəri; *NAmE* ˈmeri/ *noun* (*pl.* **Hail Marys**) a Roman Catholic prayer to Mary, the mother of Jesus

hail·stone /ˈheɪlstəʊn; *NAmE* -stoʊn/ *noun* [usually pl.] a small ball of ice that falls like rain

hail·storm /ˈheɪlstɔːm; *NAmE* -stɔːrm/ *noun* a storm during which hail falls from the sky

hair 0‑ᴡ /heə(r); *NAmE* her/ *noun*

1 0‑ᴡ [U, C] the substance that looks like a mass of fine threads growing especially on the head; one of these threads growing on the body of people and some animals: ***fair/dark hair*** ◇ ***straight/curly/wavy hair*** ◇ *to **comb/brush** your **hair*** ◇ (*informal*) *I'll be down in a minute. I'm **doing*** (= brushing, arranging, etc.) ***my hair.*** ◇ *I'm **having my hair cut** this afternoon.* ◇ ***body/facial/pubic hair*** ◇ *There's a hair in my soup.* ◇ *The rug was covered with cat hairs.* ➲ COLLOCATIONS at FASHION, PHYSICAL ➲ VISUAL VOCAB pages V48, V49 ➲ see also CAMEL HAIR, HORSEHAIR **2 -haired** (in adjectives) having the type of hair mentioned: *dark-haired* ◇ *long-haired* **3** [C] a thing that looks like a fine thread growing on the leaves and STEMS of some plants

IDM **get in sb's ˈhair** (*informal*) to annoy sb by always being near them, asking them questions, etc. **the hair of the ˈdog (that ˈbit you)** (*informal*) alcohol that you drink in order to make you feel better when you have drunk too much alcohol the night before **keep your ˈhair on** (*BrE, informal*) used to tell sb to stop shouting and become calm when they are angry **let your ˈhair down** (*informal*) to relax and enjoy yourself, especially in a lively way **make sb's ˈhair stand on end** to shock or frighten sb: *a chilling tale that will make your hair stand on end* **not harm/touch a hair of sb's ˈhead** to not hurt sb physically in any way **not have a ˈhair out of place** (of a person) to look extremely clean and neat **not turn a ˈhair** to show no emotion when sth surprising, shocking, etc. happens ➲ more at HANG *v.*, HIDE *n.*, SPLIT *v.*, TEAR[1] *v.*

hair·band /ˈheəbænd; *NAmE* ˈherb-/ *noun* a strip of cloth or curved plastic worn by women in their hair, that fits closely over the top of the head and behind the ears

hair·brush /ˈheəbrʌʃ; *NAmE* ˈherb-/ *noun* a brush for making the hair tidy or smooth ➲ VISUAL VOCAB page V21

hair·cut /ˈheəkʌt; *NAmE* ˈherkʌt/ *noun* **1** the act of sb cutting your hair: *You need a haircut.* ◇ *I see you've had a haircut.* **2** the style in which sb's hair is cut: *What do you think of my new haircut?* ◇ *a trendy haircut* ➲ COLLOCATIONS at FASHION

hair·do /ˈheəduː; *NAmE* ˈherduː/ *noun* (*pl.* -os) (*old-fashioned, informal*) the style in which a woman's hair is arranged **SYN hairstyle**

hair·dress·er 0‑ᴡ /ˈheədresə(r); *NAmE* ˈherd-/ *noun* **1** 0‑ᴡ a person whose job is to cut, wash and shape hair **2** 0‑ᴡ **hairdresser's** (*pl.* **hair·dress·ers**) a place where you can get your hair cut, washed and shaped ➲ compare BARBER ▸ **hair·dress·ing** *noun* [U]

hair·dryer (also **hair·drier**) /ˈheədraɪə(r); *NAmE* ˈherd-/ *noun* a small machine used for drying your hair by blowing hot air over it

hair·grip /ˈheəɡrɪp; *NAmE* ˈherɡ-/ (also **grip**, ˈ**kirby grip**) (all *BrE*) (*NAmE* ˈ**bobby pin**) *noun* a small thin piece of metal or plastic folded in the middle, used by women for holding their hair in place ➲ compare HAIRPIN

hair·less /ˈheələs; *NAmE* ˈherləs/ *adj.* without hair

hair·line /ˈheəlaɪn; *NAmE* ˈherl-/ *noun* **1** the edge of a person's hair, especially at the front: *a receding hairline* **2** (often used as an adjective) a very thin crack or line: *a **hairline crack/fracture***

hair·net /ˈheənet; *NAmE* ˈhernet/ *noun* a net worn over the hair to keep it in place

hair·piece /ˈheəpiːs; *NAmE* ˈherp-/ *noun* a piece of false hair worn to make your own hair look longer or thicker

hair·pin /ˈheəpɪn; *NAmE* ˈherpɪn/ *noun* **1** a small thin piece of wire that is folded in the middle, used by women for holding their hair in place ➲ compare HAIRGRIP **2** = HAIRPIN BEND

ˌ**hairpin** ˈ**bend** (*BrE*) (*NAmE* ˌ**hairpin** ˈ**curve**, ˌ**hairpin** ˈ**turn**) (also **hair·pin** *BrE, NAmE*) *noun* a very sharp bend in a road, especially a mountain road

ˈ**hair-raising** *adj.* extremely frightening but often exciting: *a **hair-raising adventure/story***

ˈ**hair's breadth** *noun* [sing.] a very small amount or distance: *We won by a hair's breadth.* ◇ *They were within a hair's breadth of being killed.*

ˌ**hair** ˈ**shirt** *noun* a shirt made of rough cloth containing hair, worn in the past by people who wished to punish themselves for religious reasons

hair·slide /ˈheəslaɪd; *NAmE* ˈhers-/ (also **slide**) (both *BrE*) (*NAmE* **bar·rette**) *noun* a small decorative piece of metal or plastic used by women for holding their hair in place

ˈ**hair-splitting** *noun* [U] (*disapproving*) the act of giving too much importance to small and unimportant differences in an argument SYN **quibbling** IDM see SPLIT *v.*

hair·spray /ˈheəspreɪ; *NAmE* ˈhers-/ *noun* [U, C] a substance sprayed onto the hair to hold it in a particular style

hair·style /ˈheəstaɪl; *NAmE* ˈhers-/ *noun* the style in which sb's hair is cut or arranged ➲ COLLOCATIONS at FASHION

hair·styl·ist /ˈheəstaɪlɪst; *NAmE* ˈhers-/ *noun* a person whose job is to cut, wash and shape hair

hairy /ˈheəri; *NAmE* ˈheri/ *adj.* (**hair·ier**, **hairi·est**) **1** covered with a lot of hair: *a **hairy chest/monster*** ◇ *plants with hairy stems* **2** (*informal*) dangerous or frightening but often exciting: *Driving on icy roads can be pretty hairy.* ◇ *a hairy experience* ▸ **hairi·ness** *noun* [U]

hajj (also **haj**) /hædʒ/ *noun* (usually **the Hajj**) [sing.] the religious journey to Mecca that all Muslims try to make at least once in their lives

haka /ˈhɑːkə/ *noun* a traditional Maori war dance with singing. New Zealand RUGBY teams perform a version of it before games.

hake /heɪk/ *noun* [C, U] (*pl.* **hake**) a large sea fish that is used for food

ha·kim /hæˈkiːm/ *noun* a doctor in India and Muslim countries who uses HERBS and other traditional ways of treating illnesses

Hakka /ˈhækə/ (also **Kejia**) *noun* [U] a form of Chinese spoken by a group of people in SE China

halal /ˈhælæl/ *adj.* [only before noun] (of meat) from an animal that has been killed according to Muslim law: *halal meat* ◇ *a halal butcher* (= one who sells halal meat)

hal·berd /ˈhælbɜːd; *NAmE* -bərd/ *noun* a weapon used in the past which is a combination of a SPEAR and an AXE

hal·cyon /ˈhælsiən/ *adj.* [usually before noun] (*literary*) peaceful and happy: *the halcyon days of her youth*

hale /heɪl/ *adj.*
IDM ˌ**hale and** ˈ**hearty** (especially of an old person) strong and healthy

half 0‑ /hɑːf; *NAmE* hæf/ *noun, det., pron., adv.*
■ ***noun*** (*pl.* **halves** /hɑːvz; *NAmE* hævz/) **1** 0‑ either of two equal parts into which sth is or can be divided: *two and a half kilos* (2½) ◇ *One and a half hours are allowed for the exam.* ◇ *An hour and a half is allowed for the exam.* ◇ *The second half of the book is more exciting.* ◇ *I've divided the money **in half**.* ◇ *We'll need to reduce the weight **by half**.* ➲ see also HALVE **2** 0‑ either of two periods of time into which a sports game, concert, etc. is divided: *No goals were scored in the first half.* **3** = HALFBACK ➲ see also CENTRE HALF, SCRUM HALF **4** (*BrE, informal*) half a pint of beer or a similar drink: *Two halves of bitter, please.*
IDM **and a** ˈ**half** (*informal*) bigger, better, more important, etc. than usual: *That was a game and a half!* **do nothing/not do anything by** ˈ**halves** to do whatever you do completely and thoroughly: *You're expecting twins? Well, you never did do anything by halves.* **go half and** ˈ**half** | **go** ˈ**halves** (**with sb**) to share the cost of sth equally with sb: *We go halves on all the bills.* **the** ˈ**half of it** used in negative sentences to say that a situation is worse or more complicated than sb thinks: *'It sounds very difficult.' '**You don't know the half of it**.'* **how the other half** ˈ**lives** the way of life of a different social group, especially one much richer than you **too clever, etc. by** ˈ**half** (*BrE, informal, disapproving*) clever, etc. in a way that annoys you or makes you suspicious ➲ more at MIND *n.*, SIX, TIME *n.*
■ ***det., pron.* 1** 0‑ an amount equal to half of sth/sb: *half an hour* ◇ *Half (of) the fruit was bad.* ◇ *Half of the money was mine.* ◇ *He has a half share in the company.* ◇ *Out of 36 candidates, half passed.* ➲ LANGUAGE BANK at PROPORTION **2 ~ the time, fun, trouble, etc.** the largest part of sth: *Half the fun of gardening is never knowing exactly what's going to come up.* ◇ *Half the time you don't even listen to what I say.*
IDM **half a** ˌ**loaf is better than no** ˈ**bread** (*saying*) you should be grateful for sth, even if it is not as good, much, etc. as you really wanted; something is better than nothing **half a** ˈ**minute,** ˈ**second, etc.** (*informal*) a short time: *Hang on. I'll be ready in half a minute.* **half past** ˈ**one,** ˈ**two, etc.** 0‑ (*US* also **half after** ˈ**one,** ˈ**two, etc.**) (also *BrE informal* **half** ˈ**one,** ˈ**two, etc.**) 30 minutes after any hour on the clock
■ ***adv.* 1** 0‑ to the extent of half: *The glass was half full.* **2** 0‑ partly: *The chicken was only half cooked.* ◇ *half-closed eyes* ◇ *I'm half inclined to agree.*
IDM ˌ**half as** ˌ**many,** ˌ**much, etc. a**ˈ**gain** (*BrE*) (*US* **half a**ˈ**gain as much**) an increase of 50% of the existing number or amount: *Spending on health is half as much again as it was in 2009.* ˌ**not** ˈ**half** (*BrE, informal*) used to emphasize a statement or an opinion: *It wasn't half good* (= it was very good). ◇ *'Was she annoyed?' 'Not half!'* (= she was extremely annoyed). **not** ˈ**half as** | **not** ˈ**half such a** not nearly: *He is not half such a fool as they think.* **not half** ˈ**bad** (*informal*) (used to show surprise) not bad at all; good: *It really isn't half bad, is it?*

Grammar Point

half / whole / quarter

- **Quarter**, **half** and **whole** can all be nouns: *Cut the apple into quarters.* ◇ *Two halves make a whole.*
- **Whole** is also an adjective: *I've been waiting here for a whole hour.*
- **Half** is also a determiner: *Half (of) the work is already finished.* ◇ *They spent half the time looking for a parking space.* ◇ *Her house is half a mile down the road.* Note that you do not put *a* or *the* in front of **half** when it is used in this way: *I waited for half an hour* ◇ ~~*I waited for a half an hour.*~~
- **Half** can also be used as an adverb: *This meal is only half cooked.*

ˌ**half-and-**ˈ**half** *adj., adv., noun*
■ ***adj.*** being half one thing and half another: *I was in that half-and-half land where you are not completely asleep nor completely awake.* ▸ ˌ**half-and-**ˈ**half** *adv.*
■ ***noun*** [U] (*NAmE*) a mixture of milk and cream that is used in tea and coffee

ˌhalf-ˈarsed (*BrE*) (*NAmE* **ˈhalf-assed**) *adj.* (*slang*) **1** done without care or effort; not well planned **2** stupid

half·back /ˈhɑːfbæk; *NAmE* ˈhæf-/ (also **half**) *noun* **1** [C] one of the defending players in HOCKEY or RUGBY whose position is between those who play at the front of a team and those who play at the back **2** (also **tail·back**) [C] one of the two attacking players in AMERICAN FOOTBALL whose position is behind the QUARTERBACK and beside the FULLBACKS **3** (also **tail·back**) [U] the position a halfback plays at

ˌhalf-ˈbaked *adj.* [usually before noun] (*informal*) not well planned or considered: *a half-baked idea*

ˈhalf-bath *noun* (*NAmE*) a small room in a house, containing a WASHBASIN and a toilet SYN **powder room**

ˌhalf ˈboard *noun* [U] (*BrE*) a type of accommodation at a hotel, etc. that includes breakfast and an evening meal ➲ compare AMERICAN PLAN, EUROPEAN PLAN, BED AND BREAKFAST, FULL BOARD

H

ˈhalf-breed *noun* (*taboo, offensive*) a person whose parents are from different races, especially when one is white and the other is a Native American ▸ **ˈhalf-breed** *adj.* (*taboo, offensive*) HELP It is more acceptable to talk about 'a person **of mixed race**'.

ˈhalf-brother *noun* a person's **half-brother** is a boy or man with either the same mother or the same father as they have ➲ compare STEPBROTHER

ˈhalf-caste *noun* (*taboo, offensive*) a person whose parents are from different races ▸ **ˈhalf-caste** *adj.* (*taboo, offensive*) HELP It is more acceptable to talk about 'a person **of mixed race**'.

ˌhalf-ˈcentury *noun* **1** a period of 50 years **2** (in CRICKET) a score of 50

ˌhalf-ˈcock *noun*
IDM **go off at ˌhalf-ˈcock** (*BrE, informal*) to start before preparations are complete, so that the effect or result is not as it should be

ˌhalf-ˈcrown (also **ˌhalf a ˈcrown**) *noun* an old British coin worth 2½ SHILLINGS (= now 12½ pence)

ˌhalf ˈday *noun* a day on which people work only in the morning or in the afternoon: *Tuesday is her half day.*

ˌhalf ˈdollar *noun* a US coin worth 50 cents

ˌhalf-ˈhearted *adj.* done without enthusiasm or effort: *He made a **half-hearted attempt** to justify himself.* ▸ **ˌhalf-ˈhearted·ly** *adv.*

ˌhalf-ˈhour (also **ˌhalf an ˈhour**) *noun* a period of 30 minutes: *He should arrive within the next half-hour.* ◇ *a half-hour drive*

ˌhalf-ˈhourly *adj.* happening every 30 minutes: *a half-hourly bus service* ▸ **ˌhalf-ˈhourly** *adv.*: *The buses run half-hourly.*

ˈhalf-life *noun* [C] **1** (*physics*) the time taken for the RADIOACTIVITY of a substance to fall to half its original value **2** (*chemistry*) the time taken for the concentration of a REACTANT to fall to half of its original value in a chemical reaction

ˈhalf-light *noun* [sing., U] a dull light in which it is difficult to see things: *in the grey half-light of dawn*

ˌhalf ˈmast *noun*
IDM **at ˌhalf ˈmast** (of a flag) flown at the middle of the MAST as a sign of respect for a person who has just died: *Flags were flown at half mast on the day of his funeral.*

ˌhalf ˈmeasures *noun* [pl.] a policy or plan of action that is weak and does not do enough: *There are **no half measures** with this company.*

ˌhalf-ˈmoon *noun* **1** the moon when only half of it can be seen from the earth; the time when this happens ➲ compare FULL MOON, HARVEST MOON, NEW MOON **2** a thing that is shaped like a half-moon

ˈhalf note (*NAmE*) (*BrE* **minim**) *noun* (*music*) a note that lasts twice as long as a CROTCHET/QUARTER NOTE ➲ picture at MUSIC

ˈhalf pants *noun* [pl.] (*IndE, informal*) short trousers/pants SYN **shorts**

half·penny *noun* (*pl.* -ies) **1** (also **ha'penny**) /ˈheɪpni/ a British coin in use until 1971, worth half a penny. There were 480 halfpennies in a pound. **2** /ˈhɑːfpeni/ (also **half·pence** /ˌhɑːfˈpens/) a British coin in use between 1971 and 1984, worth half a penny. There were 200 halfpennies in a pound. IDM see SPOIL *v.*

ˈhalf-pipe *noun* a U-shaped structure or a U-shaped channel cut into snow, used for performing complicated movements in SKATEBOARDING, ROLLERBLADING and SNOWBOARDING

ˌhalf-ˈprice *adj.* costing half the usual price: *a half-price ticket* ▸ **ˌhalf-ˈprice** *adv.*: *Children aged under four go half-price.* **ˌhalf ˈprice** *noun* [U]: *Many items are at half price.*

ˈhalf-sister *noun* a person's **half-sister** is a girl or woman who has either the same mother or the same father as them ➲ compare STEPSISTER

ˈhalf step (also **ˈhalf-tone**) (both *NAmE*) (*BrE* **semi·tone**) *noun* (*music*) half a TONE on a musical SCALE, for example the INTERVAL between C and C♯ or between E and F ➲ compare STEP *n.* (10)

ˌhalf-ˈterm *noun* (in British schools) a short holiday/vacation in the middle of each term: *the **half-term break/holiday*** ◇ *What are you doing **at half-term**?*

ˌhalf-ˈtimbered *adj.* [usually before noun] (of a building) having walls that are made from a wooden frame filled with brick, stone, etc. so that the FRAMEWORK can still be seen

ˌhalf-ˈtime *noun* [U] a short period between the two halves of a sports game during which the players rest: *The score at half-time was two all.* ◇ *the half-time score* ➲ compare FULL TIME

ˈhalf-tone *noun* **1** (*technical*) a print of a black and white photograph in which the different shades of grey are produced from small and large black dots **2** (*NAmE, music*) = HALF STEP

ˈhalf-truth *noun* a statement that gives only part of the truth, especially when it is intended to cheat sb: *The newspaper reports are a mixture of gossip, lies and half-truths.*

ˈhalf-volley *noun* (in TENNIS and football (SOCCER)) a stroke or kick immediately after the ball has BOUNCED

half·way /ˌhɑːfˈweɪ; *NAmE* ˌhæf-/ *adv.* **1** at an equal distance between two points; in the middle of a period of time: *It's about halfway between London and Bristol.* ◇ *He left halfway through the ceremony.* ◇ *I'm afraid we're not even **halfway there** yet.* **2 ~ to/towards sth** | **~ to/towards doing sth** part of the way towards doing or achieving sth: *This only goes halfway to explaining what really happened.* **3 ~ decent** (*informal*) fairly, but not very, good: *Any halfway decent map will give you that information.* ▸ **half·way** *adj.*: *the **halfway point/stage*** IDM see MEET *v.*

ˌhalfway ˈhouse *noun* **1** [sing.] (*BrE*) something that combines the features of two very different things **2** [C] a place where prisoners, mental patients, etc. can stay for a short time after leaving a prison or hospital, before they start to live on their own again

ˈhalfway line *noun* a line across a sports field at an equal distance between the ends

half·wit /ˈhɑːfwɪt; *NAmE* ˈhæf-/ *noun* (*informal*) a stupid person SYN **idiot** ▸ **ˌhalf-ˈwitted** *adj.*

ˌhalf-ˈyearly *adj.* [only before noun] happening every six months; happening after the first six months of the year: *a half-yearly meeting* ◇ *the half-yearly sales figures* ▸ **ˌhalf-ˈyearly** *adv.*: *Interest will be paid half-yearly in June and December.*

hali·but /ˈhælɪbət/ *noun* [C, U] (*pl.* **hali·but**) a large flat sea fish that is used for food

hali·tosis /ˌhælɪˈtəʊsɪs; *NAmE* -ˈtoʊ-/ *noun* [U] (*medical*) a condition in which the breath smells unpleasant SYN **bad breath**

hall O▬ /hɔːl/ *noun*
1 O▬ (also **hall·way**) (*NAmE* also **entry**) a space or pas-

sage inside the entrance or front door of a building: *She ran into the hall and up the stairs.* ➲ see also ENTRANCE HALL **2** ⊶ (*NAmE* also **hall·way**) a passage in a building with rooms down either side SYN **corridor**: *I headed for Scott's office down the hall.* **3** ⊶ a building or large room for public meetings, meals, concerts, etc: *a **concert/banqueting/sports/exhibition, etc. hall*** ◇ *There are three dining halls on campus.* ◇ *The Royal Albert Hall* ◇ (*BrE*) *A jumble sale will be held in the village hall on Saturday.* ➲ see also CITY HALL, DANCE HALL, GUILDHALL, MUSIC HALL, TOWN HALL **4** (*BrE*) = HALL OF RESIDENCE: *She's living **in hall(s)**.* **5** (*BrE*) (often as part of a name) a large country house: *Haddon Hall*

hal·le·lu·jah /ˌhælɪˈluːjə/ (also **al·le·luia**) *noun* a song or shout of praise to God ▸ **hal·le·lu·jah** *exclamation*

hall·mark /ˈhɔːlmɑːk; *NAmE* -mɑːrk/ *noun, verb*

■ ***noun*** **1** a feature or quality that is typical of sb/sth: *Police said the explosion **bore all the hallmarks of** a terrorist attack.* **2** a mark put on gold, silver and PLATINUM objects that shows the quality of the metal and gives information about when and where the object was made

■ ***verb*** **~ sth** to put a hallmark on metal goods

hallo (*BrE*) = HELLO

ˌHall of ˈFame *noun* (*pl.* ˌHalls of ˈFame) (*especially NAmE*) **1** a place for people to visit, like a museum, with things connected with famous people from a particular sport or activity: *the Country Music Hall of Fame* **2** [sing.] the group of people who have done a particular activity or sport particularly well

ˌhall of ˈresidence (also **hall**) *noun* (*pl.* **halls of residence, halls**) (both *BrE*) (*NAmE* **dor·mi·tory**) a building for university or college students to live in

hal·loo /həˈluː/ *exclamation* **1** used to attract sb's attention **2** used in hunting to tell the dogs to start chasing an animal ▸ **hal·loo** *verb* [T, I] **~ (sb)**

hal·lowed /ˈhæləʊd; *NAmE* -loʊd/ *adj.* [only before noun] **1** (especially of old things) respected and important SYN **sacred**: *one of the theatre's most hallowed traditions* **2** that has been made holy: *to be buried in hallowed ground* SYN **sacred**

Hal·low·een (also **Hal·low·e'en**) /ˌhæləʊˈiːn; *NAmE* -loʊ-/ *noun* [C, U] the night of 31st October when it was believed in the past that dead people appeared from their graves, and which is now celebrated in the US, Canada and Britain by children who dress as GHOSTS, WITCHES, etc. ➲ see also TRICK OR TREAT

hal·lu·cin·ate /həˈluːsɪneɪt/ *verb* [I] to see or hear things that are not really there because of illness or drugs

hal·lu·cin·ation /həˌluːsɪˈneɪʃn/ *noun* **1** [C, U] the fact of seeming to see or hear sb/sth that is not really there, especially because of illness or drugs: *to have hallucinations* ◇ *High temperatures can cause hallucination.* **2** [C] something that is seen or heard when it is not really there: *Was the figure real or just a hallucination?* HELP Some speakers do not pronounce the 'h' at the beginning of **hallucination** and use 'an' instead of 'a' before it. This now sounds old-fashioned.

hal·lu·cin·atory /həˈluːsɪnətri; həˌluːsɪˈneɪtəri; *NAmE* həˈluːsənətɔːri/ *adj.* [only before noun] connected with or causing hallucinations: *a hallucinatory experience* ◇ *hallucinatory drugs*

hal·lu·cino·gen /həˈluːsɪnədʒən/ *noun* a drug, such as LSD, that affects people's minds and makes them see and hear things that are not really there ▸ **hal·lu·cino·gen·ic** /həˌluːsɪnəˈdʒenɪk/ *adj.*: ***hallucinogenic drugs/effects***

hall·way /ˈhɔːlweɪ/ *noun* **1** (*especially BrE*) = HALL (1) **2** (*NAmE*) = HALL (2)

halo /ˈheɪləʊ; *NAmE* -loʊ/ *noun* (*pl.* -oes or -os) **1** (in paintings, etc.) a circle of light shown around or above the head of a holy person: *She played the part of an angel, complete with wings and a halo.* ◇ (*figurative*) *a halo of white frizzy hair* **2** (*informal*) = CORONA

halo·gen /ˈhælədʒən/ *noun* (*chemistry*) any of a set of five chemical elements, including FLUORINE, CHLORINE and IODINE, that react with HYDROGEN to form acids from which simple salts can be made. Halogens, in the form of gas, are used in lamps and cookers/stoves.

halon /ˈheɪlɒn; *NAmE* -lɑːn/ *noun* (*chemistry*) a gas that is made up of CARBON and one or more halogens, used especially to stop fires

halt /hɔːlt; *BrE* also hɒlt/ *verb, noun*

■ ***verb*** [I, T] to stop; to make sb/sth stop: *She walked towards him and then halted.* ◇ *'Halt!' the Major ordered* (= used as a command to soldiers). ◇ **~ sb/sth** *The police were halting traffic on the parade route.* ◇ *The trial was halted after the first week.* IDM see TRACK *n.*

■ ***noun*** **1** [sing.] an act of stopping the movement or progress of sb/sth: *Work **came to a halt** when the machine broke down.* ◇ *The thought **brought her to an** abrupt **halt**.* ◇ *The car skidded to a halt.* ◇ *Strikes have led to **a halt in** production.* ◇ *They decided it was time to **call a halt to** the project* (= stop it officially). **2** [C] (*BrE*) a small train station in the country that has a platform but no buildings IDM see GRIND *v.*

hal·ter /ˈhɔːltə(r); *BrE* also ˈhɒlt-/ *noun* **1** a rope or narrow piece of leather put around the head of a horse for leading it with **2** (usually used as an adjective) a narrow piece of cloth around the neck that holds a woman's dress or shirt in position, with the back and shoulders not covered: *She was dressed in a halter top and shorts.*

halt·ing /ˈhɔːltɪŋ; *BrE* also ˈhɒlt-/ *adj.* [usually before noun] (especially of speech or movement) stopping and starting often, especially because you are not certain or are not very confident SYN **hesitant**: *a halting conversation* ◇ *a toddler's first few halting steps* ▸ **halt·ing·ly** *adv.*: *'Well...' she began haltingly.*

halve /hɑːv; *NAmE* hæv/ *verb* **1** [I, T] to reduce by a half; to make sth reduce by a half: *The shares have **halved in value**.* ◇ **~ sth** *The company is halving its prices.* **2** [T] **~ sth** to divide sth into two equal parts IDM see TROUBLE *n.*

halves *pl.* of HALF

halwa /ˈhælwɑː/ *noun* [U] a sweet food from S Asia, made from SEMOLINA or carrots, with ALMONDS and CARDAMOM

hal·yard /ˈhæljəd; *NAmE* -jərd/ *noun* (*technical*) a rope used for raising or taking down a sail or flag

ham /hæm/ *noun, verb*

■ ***noun*** **1** [C, U] the top part of a pig's leg that has been CURED (= preserved using salt or smoke) and is eaten as food; the meat from this: *The hams were cooked whole.* ◇ *a slice of ham* ◇ *a ham sandwich* ➲ compare BACON, GAMMON, PORK **2** [C] a person who sends and receives radio messages as a hobby rather than as a job: *a radio ham* **3** [C] (*informal*) (often used as an adjective) an actor who performs badly, especially by exaggerating emotions: *a ham actor* **4** [C, usually pl.] (*informal*) the back part of a person's leg above the knee ➲ see also HAMSTRING

■ ***verb*** (-mm-)

IDM **ˌham it ˈup** (*informal*) (especially of actors) when people **ham it up**, they deliberately exaggerate their emotions or movements

ham·burg·er /ˈhæmbɜːgə(r); *NAmE* -bɜːrg-/ (also **burger**) *noun* **1** (*BrE* also **beef·burg·er**) [C] finely chopped beef made into a flat round shape that is then fried, often served in a bread roll **2** (also ˈ**hamburger meat**) (both *US*) (*NAmE* also ˌ**ground ˈbeef**) (*BrE* **mince**) [U] beef that has been finely chopped in a special machine

ˌham-ˈfisted (*NAmE* also ˈ**ham-handed**) *adj.* (*informal*) lacking skill when using your hands or when dealing with people SYN **clumsy**: *his ham-fisted efforts to assist her*

ham·let /ˈhæmlət/ *noun* a very small village

ham·mer ⊶ /ˈhæmə(r)/ *noun, verb*

■ ***noun***

▸ TOOL **1** ⊶ [C] a tool with a handle and a heavy metal head, used for breaking things or hitting nails: (*figurative*) *The decision is a hammer blow for the steel industry.* ➲ **VISUAL VOCAB** page V17 ➲ see also SLEDGEHAMMER **2** [C] a tool with a handle and a wooden head, used by a person in

H

charge of an AUCTION (= a sale at which things are sold to the person who offers the most money) in order to get people's attention when sth is just being sold: *to come/go under the hammer* (= to be sold at AUCTION)
▸ IN PIANO **3** [C] a small wooden part inside a piano, that hits the strings to produce a sound
▸ IN GUN **4** [C] a part inside a gun that makes the gun fire
▸ SPORT **5** [C] a metal ball attached to a wire, thrown as a sport **6 the hammer** [sing.] the event or sport of throwing the hammer ➲ VISUAL VOCAB page V38
IDM ˌ**hammer and ˈtongs** if two people are **at it hammer and tongs** or **go at it hammer and tongs**, they argue or fight with a lot of energy and noise
■ *verb*
▸ HIT WITH TOOL **1** [I, T] to hit sth with a hammer: *I could hear somebody hammering next door.* ◇ **~ sth (in/into/onto sth)** *She hammered the nail into the wall.* ◇ **~ sth + adj.** *He was hammering the sheet of copper flat.*
▸ HIT MANY TIMES **2** [I, T] to hit sth hard many times, especially so that it makes a loud noise SYN **pound**: *Someone was hammering at the door.* ◇ *Hail was hammering down onto the roof.* ◇ (*figurative*) *I was so scared my heart was hammering* (= beating very fast) *in my chest.* ◇ **~ sth** *He hammered the door with his fists.* ➲ SYNONYMS at BEAT
▸ KICK/HIT BALL **3** [T] **~ sth (+ adv./prep.)** (*informal*) to kick or hit a ball very hard: *He hammered the ball into the net.*
▸ DEFEAT EASILY **4** [T] **~ sb** (*informal*) to defeat sb very easily: *Our team was hammered 5-1.*
PHR V ˌ**hammer aˈway at sth** to work hard in order to finish or achieve sth; to keep repeating sth in order to get the result that you want ˌ**hammer sth↔ˈhome 1** to emphasize a point, an idea, etc. so that people fully understand it **2** to kick a ball hard and score a goal ˌ**hammer sth ˈinto sb** to make sb learn or remember sth by repeating it many times ˌ**hammer ˈout sth 1** to discuss a plan, an idea, etc. until everyone agrees or a decision is made: *to hammer out a compromise* **2** to play a tune, especially on a piano, loudly and not very well

ˌ**hammer and ˈsickle** *noun* [sing.] tools representing the people who work in industry and farming, used on the flag of the former Soviet Union and as a symbol of Communism

ham·mered /ˈhæməd; *NAmE* -ərd/ *adj.* [not before noun] (*slang*) very drunk

ham·mer·head /ˈhæməhed; *NAmE* -mər-/ (also ˌ**hammerhead ˈshark**) *noun* a SHARK with flat parts sticking out from either side of its head with eyes at the ends

ham·mer·ing /ˈhæmərɪŋ/ *noun* **1** [U, sing.] the sound of sb hitting sth with a hammer or with their FISTS: *the sound of hammering from the next room* **2** [C, usually sing.] (*BrE, informal*) an act of defeating or criticizing sb severely: *Our team took a real hammering in the first half.*

ˈ**hammer price** *noun* the last and highest amount offered for sth at an AUCTION which is the price for which it is sold

ham·mock /ˈhæmək/ *noun* a type of bed made from a net or from a piece of strong material, with ropes at each end that are used to hang it between two trees, posts, etc. ➲ VISUAL VOCAB page V20

Hammond organ™ /ˌhæmənd ˈɔːgən; *NAmE* ˈɔːrg-/ *noun* a type of electronic organ

hammy /ˈhæmi/ *adj.* (**ham·mier**, **ham·mi·est**) (*informal*) (of a style of acting) artificial or exaggerated

ham·per /ˈhæmpə(r)/ *verb, noun*
■ *verb* [often passive] **~ sb/sth** to prevent sb from easily doing or achieving sth SYN **hinder**
■ *noun* **1** a large BASKET with a lid, especially one used to carry food in: *a picnic hamper* ➲ picture at BASKET **2** (*especially BrE*) a box or package containing food, sent as a gift: *a Christmas hamper* **3** (*NAmE*) a large BASKET that you keep your dirty clothes in until they are washed

ham·ster /ˈhæmstə(r)/ *noun* an animal like a large mouse, with large cheeks for storing food. Hamsters are often kept as pets.

ham·string /ˈhæmstrɪŋ/ *noun, verb*
■ *noun* **1** one of the five TENDONS behind the knee that connect the muscles of the upper leg to the bones of the lower leg: *a hamstring injury* ◇ *She's pulled a hamstring.* **2** a TENDON behind the middle joint (=HOCK) of the back leg of a horse and some other animals
■ *verb* (**ham·strung**, **ham·strung** /ˈhæmstrʌŋ/) [often passive] **~ sb/sth** to prevent sb/sth from working or taking action in the way that is needed

hand 🔑 /hænd/ *noun, verb*
■ *noun*
▸ PART OF BODY **1** 🔑 [C] the part of the body at the end of the arm, including the fingers and thumb: *Ian placed a hand on her shoulder.* ◇ ***Put your hand up** if you know the answer.* ◇ *Keep both hands on the steering wheel at all times.* ◇ *She was* **on** (**her**) **hands and knees** (=CRAWLING on the floor) *looking for an earring.* ◇ *Couples strolled past* **holding hands.** ◇ ***Give me your hand*** (= hold my hand) *while we cross the road.* ◇ *The crowd* **threw up their hands** (= lifted them into the air) *in dismay.* ◇ *He killed the snake* **with his bare hands** (= using only his hands). ◇ *a* **hand towel** (= a small towel for drying your hands on) ◇ *a* **hand drill** (= one that is used by turning a handle rather than powered by electricity) ➲ COLLOCATIONS at PHYSICAL ➲ VISUAL VOCAB page V48 ➲ see also LEFT-HAND, RIGHT-HAND
▸ -HANDED **2** (in adjectives) using the hand or number of hands mentioned: *a one-handed catch* ◇ *left-handed scissors* (= intended to be held in your left hand)
▸ HELP **3** 🔑 **a hand** [sing.] (*informal*) help in doing sth: *Let me* **give you a hand** *with those bags* (= help you to carry them). ◇ *Do you* **need a hand** *with those invoices?* ◇ *The neighbours are always willing to* **lend a hand.**
▸ ROLE IN SITUATION **4** [sing.] **~ in sth** the part or role that sb/sth plays in a particular situation; sb's influence in a situation: *Early reports suggest the hand of rebel forces in the bombings.* ◇ *Several of his colleagues* **had a hand in** *his downfall.* ◇ *This appointment was an attempt to* **strengthen her hand** *in policy discussions.*
▸ ON CLOCK/WATCH **5** [C] (usually in compounds) a part of a clock or watch that points to the numbers ➲ picture at CLOCK ➲ see also HOUR HAND, MINUTE HAND, SECOND HAND
▸ WORKER **6** [C] a person who does physical work on a farm or in a factory ➲ see also CHARGEHAND, FARMHAND, HIRED HAND, STAGEHAND
▸ SAILOR **7** [C] a sailor on a ship: *All hands on deck!* ➲ see also DECKHAND
▸ HAND- **8** (in compounds) by a person rather than a machine: *hand-painted pottery* ◇ *hand-knitted* ◇ *This item should be hand washed.* ➲ see also HANDMADE
▸ IN CARD GAMES **9** [C] a set of PLAYING CARDS given to one player in a game: *to be dealt a* **good/bad hand** ➲ VISUAL VOCAB page V32 **10** [C] one stage of a game of cards: *I'll have to leave after this hand.*
▸ WRITING **11** [sing.] (*old use*) a particular style of writing ➲ see also FREEHAND
▸ MEASUREMENT FOR HORSE **12** [C] a unit for measuring the height of a horse, equal to 4 inches or 10.16 centimetres ➲ see also DAB HAND, OLD HAND, SECOND-HAND, UNDERHAND
IDM **all** ˌ**hands on ˈdeck** (also **all** ˌ**hands to the ˈpump**) (*saying, humorous*) everyone helps or must help, especially in a difficult situation: *There are 30 people coming to dinner tonight, so it's all hands on deck.* (**close/near**) **at ˈhand** close to you in time or distance: *Help was at hand.* ◇ *The property is ideally located with all local amenities close at hand.* **at the hands of sb** | **at sb's hands** (*formal*) if you experience sth **at the hands of sb**, they are the cause of it **be good with your ˈhands** to be skilful at making or doing things with your hands **bind/tie sb hand and ˈfoot 1** to tie sb's hands and feet together so that they cannot move or escape **2** to prevent sb from doing what they want by creating rules, restrictions, etc. **by ˈhand 1** 🔑 by a person rather than a machine: *The fabric was painted by hand.* **2** 🔑 if a letter is delivered **by hand**, it is delivered by the person who wrote it, or sb who is sent by them, rather than by post/mail **fall into sb's ˈhands/the ˈhands of sb** (*formal*) to become controlled by sb: *The town fell into enemy hands.* ◇ *We don't want this document* **falling into**

Vocabulary Building

Using your hands

Touch

These verbs describe different ways of touching things:

feel	*I felt the bag to see what was in it.*
finger	*She fingered the silk delicately.*
handle	*Handle the fruit with care.*
rub	*She rubbed her eyes wearily.*
stroke	*The cat loves being stroked.*
pat	*He patted my arm and told me not to worry.*
tap	*Someone was tapping lightly at the door.*
squeeze	*I took his hand and squeezed it.*

Hold

You can use these verbs to describe taking something quickly:

grab	*I grabbed his arm to stop myself from falling.*
snatch	*She snatched the letter out of my hand.*

These verbs describe holding things tightly:

clasp	*Her hands were clasped behind her head.*
clutch	*The child was clutching a doll in her hand.*
grasp	*Grasp the rope with both hands and pull.*
grip	*He gripped his bag tightly and wouldn't let go.*

the wrong hands. **(at) first 'hand** by experiencing, seeing, etc. sth yourself rather than being told about it by sb else: *The President visited the area to see the devastation at first hand.* **get your 'hands dirty** to do physical work: *He's not frightened of getting his hands dirty.* **sb's 'hand (in marriage)** (*old-fashioned*) permission to marry sb, especially a woman: *He asked the general for his daughter's hand in marriage.* **ˌhand in 'glove (with sb)** working closely with sb, especially in a secret and/or illegal way **ˌhand in 'hand 1** if two people are **hand in hand**, they are holding each other's hand **2** if two things **go hand in hand**, they are closely connected and one thing causes the other: *Poverty and poor health often go hand in hand.* **ˌhands 'down** (*informal*) easily and without any doubt: *They **won hands down**.* ◇ *It is hands down the best movie this year.* ➲ see also HANDS-DOWN *adj.* **(get/take your) ˌhands 'off (sth/sb)** (*informal*) used to tell sb not to touch sth/sb: *Get your hands off my wife!* ◇ *Hey, hands off! That's my drink!* **ˌhands 'up!** (*informal*) **1** used to tell a group of people to raise one hand in the air if they know the answer to a question, etc.: *Hands up all those who want to go swimming.* **2** used by sb who is threatening people with a gun to tell them to raise both hands in the air **have your 'hands full** to be very busy or too busy to do sth else: *She certainly has her hands full with four kids in the house.* **have your 'hands tied** to be unable to do what you want to do because of rules, promises, etc: *I really wish I could help but my hands are tied.* **hold sb's 'hand** to give sb support in a difficult situation: *Do you want me to come along and hold your hand?* **in sb's capable, safe, etc. 'hands** being taken care of or dealt with by sb that you think you can rely on: *Can I leave these queries in your capable hands?* **in 'hand 1** if you have time or money **in hand**, it is left and available to be used **2** if you have a particular situation **in hand**, you are in control of it **3** the job, question, etc. **in hand** is the one that you are dealing with **4** if sb works a week, month, etc. **in hand**, they are paid for the work a week, etc. after they have completed it **in the hands of sb | in sb's 'hands** 🔑 being taken care of or controlled by sb: *The matter is now in the hands of my lawyer.* ◇ *At that time, the castle was in enemy hands.* **keep your 'hand in** to occasionally do sth that you used to do a lot so that you do not lose your skill at it: *She retired last year but still teaches the odd class to keep her hand in.* **lay/get your 'hands on sb** to catch sb that you are annoyed with: *Wait till I get my hands on him!* **lay/get your 'hands on sth** to find or get sth: *I know their address is here somewhere, but I can't lay my hands on it right now.* **many hands make light 'work** (*saying*) used to say that a job is made easier if a lot of people help **not do a hand's 'turn** (*old-fashioned*) to do no work: *She hasn't done a hand's turn all week.* **off your 'hands** no longer your responsibility **on either/every 'hand** (*literary*) on both/all sides; in both/all directions **on 'hand** available, especially to help: *The emergency services were on hand with medical advice.* **on your 'hands** if you have sb/sth **on your hands**, you are responsible for them or it: *Let me take care of the invitations—you've enough on your hands with the caterers.* **(on the 'one hand ...) on the 'other (hand)...** used to introduce different points of view, ideas, etc, especially when they are opposites: *On the one hand they'd love to have kids, but on the other, they don't want to give up their freedom.* ➲ LANGUAGE BANK at CONTRAST **out of 'hand 1** difficult or impossible to control: *Unemployment is getting out of hand.* **2** if you reject, etc. sth **out of hand**, you do so immediately without thinking about it fully or listening to other people's arguments: *All our suggestions were dismissed out of hand.* **ˌout of your 'hands** no longer your responsibility: *I'm afraid the matter is now out of my hands.* **ˌplay into sb's 'hands** to do exactly what an enemy, opponent, etc. wants so that they gain the advantage in a particular situation: *If we get the police involved, we'll be playing right into the protesters' hands.* **put your ˌhand in your 'pocket** (*BrE*) to spend money or give it to sb: *I've heard he doesn't like putting his hand in his pocket.* **(at) second, third, etc. 'hand** by being told about sth by sb else who has seen it or heard about it, not by experiencing, seeing, etc. it yourself: *I'm fed up of hearing about these decisions third hand!* **ˌtake sb in 'hand** to deal with sb in a strict way in order to improve their behaviour **take sth into your own 'hands** to deal with a particular situation yourself because you are not happy with the way that others are dealing with it **throw your 'hand in** (*informal*) to stop doing sth or taking part in sth, especially because you are not successful **to 'hand** that you can reach or get easily: *I'm afraid I don't have the latest figures to hand.* **turn your 'hand to sth** to start doing sth or be able to do sth, especially when you do it well: *Jim can turn his hand to most jobs around the house.* ➲ more at BIG *adj.*, BIRD, BITE *v.*, BLOOD *n.*, CAP *n.*, CASH *n.*, CHANGE *v.*, CLOSE[2] *adv.*, COURAGE, DEAD *adj.*, DEVIL, EAT, FIRM *adj.*, FOLD *v.*, FORCE *v.*, FREE *adj.*, HAT, HEAVY, HELP *v.*, IRON *adj.*, JOIN *v.*, KNOW *v.*, LAW, LIFE, LIFT *v.*, LIVE[1], MONEY, OFFER *v.*, OVERPLAY, PAIR *n.*, PALM *n.*, PUTTY, RAISE *v.*, SAFE *adj.*, SHOW *n.*, SHOW *v.*, SLEIGHT, STAY *v.*, TIME *n.*, TRY *v.*, UPPER *adj.*, WAIT *v.*, WASH *v.*, WHIP *n.*, WIN *v.*, WRING

■ ***verb*** 🔑 to pass or give sth to sb: **~ sth to sb** *She handed the letter to me.* ◇ **~ sb sth** *She handed me the letter.*

IDM **hand sth to sb on a 'plate** (*informal*) to give sth to sb without the person concerned making any effort: *Nobody's going to hand you success on a plate.* **have (got) to 'hand it to sb** (*informal*) used to say that sb deserves praise for sth: *You've got to hand it to her—she's a great cook.*

PHR V **ˌhand sth↔a'round/'round** 🔑 to offer or pass sth, especially food or drinks, to all the people in a group **ˌhand sth 'back (to sb)** 🔑 to give or return sth to the person who owns it or to where it belongs **ˌhand sth↔'down (to sb) 1** 🔑 [usually passive] to give or leave sth to sb who is younger than you **SYN** **pass down**: *These skills used to be handed down from father to son.* ➲ related noun HAND-ME-DOWN **2** to officially give a decision/statement, etc. **SYN** **announce**: *The judge has handed down his verdict.* **ˌhand sth↔'in (to sb)** 🔑 (*BrE* also **ˌgive sth 'in (to sb)**) to give sth to a person in authority, especially a piece of work or sth that is lost: *You must all hand in your projects by the end of next week.* ◇ *I handed the watch in to the police.* ◇ *to **hand in your notice/resignation*** (= formally tell your employer that you want to stop working for them) **ˌhand sb↔'off** (*BrE*) (also **ˌstraight-'arm**, **ˌstiff-'arm** both *NAmE*) (in sport) to push away a player who is trying to stop you, with your arm straight **ˌhand sth↔'on (to sb)** to give or leave sth for another person to use or deal with **SYN** **pass on** **ˌhand sth↔'out (to sb) 1** 🔑 to give a number of things to the members of a group **SYN** **distribute**: *Could*

H

you hand these books out, please? ➲ related noun HANDOUT **2** (*informal*) to give advice, a punishment, etc: *He's always handing out advice to people.* ˌ**hand ˈover (to sb)** | ˌ**hand sth↔ˈover (to sb)** to give sb else your position of power or the responsibility for sth: *She resigned and handed over to one of her younger colleagues.* ◇ *He finally handed over his responsibility for the company last year.* ➲ related noun HANDOVER ˌ**hand sb ˈover to sb** to let sb listen or speak to another person, especially on the telephone or in a news broadcast: *I'll hand you over to my boss.* ˌ**hand sb/sth↔ˈover (to sb)** 🗝 to give sth/sb officially or formally to another person: *He handed over a cheque for $200 000.* ◇ *They handed the weapons over to the police.* ➲ related noun HANDOVER

hand·bag /ˈhændbæg/ (*NAmE* also **purse**) *noun* a small bag for money, keys, etc, carried especially by women ➲ VISUAL VOCAB page V52

ˈ**hand baggage** *noun* [U] (*especially NAmE*) = HAND LUGGAGE

hand·ball /ˈhændbɔːl/ *noun* **1** [U] (*US* also ˈ**team handball**) a team game for two teams of seven players, usually played indoors, in which players try to score goals by throwing a ball with their hand **2** [U] (*NAmE*) a game in which players hit a small ball against a wall with their hand **3** [C, U] (in football (SOCCER)) the offence of touching the ball with your hands: *a penalty for handball*

hand·basin /ˈhændbeɪsn/ *noun* (*BrE*) a small bowl that has taps/faucets and is fixed to the wall, used for washing your hands in

hand·bas·ket /ˈhændbɑːskɪt; *NAmE* -bæs-/ *noun*
IDM **go to hell in a ˈhandbasket** (*NAmE*) = GO TO THE DOGS at DOG *n.*

hand·bell /ˈhændbel/ *noun* a small bell with a handle, especially one of a set used by a group of people to play tunes

hand·bill /ˈhændbɪl/ *noun* a small printed advertisement that is given to people by hand

hand·book /ˈhændbʊk/ *noun* a book giving instructions on how to use sth or information about a particular subject ➲ compare MANUAL

hand·brake /ˈhændbreɪk/ (*especially BrE*) (*NAmE* usually ˈ**emergency brake**, ˈ**parking brake**) *noun* a BRAKE in a vehicle that is operated by hand, used especially when the vehicle is not moving: *to put the handbrake on* ◇ *to take the handbrake off* ◇ *Is the handbrake on?* ➲ COLLOCATIONS at DRIVING ➲ VISUAL VOCAB page V42

hand·cart /ˈhændkɑːt; *NAmE* -kɑːrt/ *noun* = CART

hand·craft /ˈhændkrɑːft; *NAmE* -kræft/ *noun* (*NAmE*) = HANDICRAFT

hand·craf·ted /ˈhændkrɑːftɪd; *NAmE* -kræft-/ *adj.* skilfully made by hand, not by machine: *a handcrafted chair*

ˈ**hand cream** *noun* [U] cream that you put on your hands to prevent dry skin

hand·cuff /ˈhændkʌf/ *verb* [usually passive] **~ sb** to put handcuffs on sb or to fasten sb to sth/sb with handcuffs

hand·cuffs /ˈhændkʌfs/ (also *informal* **cuffs**) *noun* [pl.] a pair of metal rings joined by a chain, used for holding the wrists of a prisoner together: *a pair of handcuffs* ◇ *She was led away* ***in handcuffs***. ➲ see also GOLDEN HANDCUFFS

hand·ful /ˈhændfʊl/ *noun* **1** [C] **~ (of sth)** the amount of sth that can be held in one hand: *a handful of rice* **2** [sing.] **~ (of sb/sth)** a small number of people or things: *Only a handful of people came.* **3 a ~** [sing.] (*informal*) a person or an animal that is difficult to control: *Her children can be a real handful.*

ˈ**hand grenade** *noun* a small bomb that is thrown by hand

hand·grip /ˈhændgrɪp/ *noun* **1** a handle for holding sth **2** a soft bag with handles for carrying things while you are travelling

hand·gun /ˈhændgʌn/ *noun* a small gun that you can hold and fire with one hand

ˌ**hand-ˈheld** *adj.* [usually before noun] small enough to be held in the hand while being used ▸ ˈ**hand-held** *noun*: *I prefer to consult a dictionary on a hand-held.*

hand·hold /ˈhændhəʊld; *NAmE* -hoʊld/ *noun* something on the surface of a steep slope, wall, etc. that a person can hold when climbing up it

ˈ**hand-hot** *adj.* water that is **hand-hot** is hot, but not too hot to put your hand into

handi·cap /ˈhændikæp/ *noun, verb*

■ ***noun*** **1** [C, U] (becoming *old-fashioned*, sometimes *offensive*) a permanent physical or mental condition that makes it difficult or impossible to use a particular part of your body or mind SYN **disability**: *Despite her handicap, Jane is able to hold down a full-time job.* ◇ ***mental/physical/visual handicap*** ➲ note at DISABLED **2** [C] something that makes it difficult for sb to do sth SYN **obstacle**: *Not speaking the language proved to be a bigger handicap than I'd imagined.* **3** [C] (*sport*) a race or competition in which the most skilful must run further, carry extra weight, etc. in order to give all those taking part an equal chance of winning; the disadvantage that is given to sb you are competing against in such a race or competition **4** [C] (in GOLF) an advantage given to a weaker player so that competition is more equal when they play against a stronger player. It is expressed as a number related to the number of times a player hits the ball and gets lower as he/she improves.

■ ***verb*** (-pp-) [usually passive] **~ sb/sth** to make sth more difficult for sb to do: *British exports have been handicapped by the strong pound.*

handi·capped /ˈhændikæpt/ *adj.* (becoming *old-fashioned*, sometimes *offensive*) **1** suffering from a mental or physical handicap SYN **disabled**: *a visually handicapped child* ◇ *The accident left him physically handicapped.* ➲ see also MENTALLY HANDICAPPED **2 the handicapped** *noun* [pl.] people who are handicapped: *a school for the physically handicapped* ➲ note at DISABLED

han·di·craft /ˈhændikrɑːft; *NAmE* -kræft/ (*NAmE* also **hand·craft**) *noun* [C, usually pl., U] **1** activities such as sewing and making cloth that use skill with your hands and artistic ability to make things: *to teach handicrafts* ◇ *Her hobbies are music, reading and handicraft.* **2** things made in this way: *traditional handicrafts bought by tourists*

hand·ily /ˈhændɪli/ *adv.* **1** in a way that is HANDY (= convenient): *We're handily placed for the train station.* **2** (*especially NAmE*) easily: *He handily defeated his challengers.*

han·di·work /ˈhændiwɜːk; *NAmE* -wɜːrk/ *noun* [U] **1** work that you do, or sth that you have made, especially using your artistic skill: *We admired her exquisite handiwork.* **2** a thing done by a particular person or group, especially sth bad: *This looks like the handiwork of an arsonist.*

hand·job /ˈhænddʒɒb; *NAmE* -dʒɑːb/ *noun* (*taboo, slang*) the act of a person rubbing a man's PENIS with their hand to give sexual pleasure

hand·ker·chief /ˈhæŋkətʃɪf; -tʃiːf; *NAmE* -kərtʃ-/ *noun* (*pl.* **hand·ker·chiefs** or **hand·ker·chieves** /-tʃiːvz/) (also *informal* **hanky, han·kie**) a small piece of material or paper that you use for blowing your nose, etc.

han·dle 🗝 /ˈhændl/ *verb, noun*

■ ***verb***

▸ DEAL WITH **1** 🗝 [T] to deal with a situation, a person, an area of work or a strong emotion: **~ sth/sb** *A new man was appointed to handle the crisis.* ◇ *She's very good at handling her patients.* ◇ *The sale was handled by Adams Commercial.* ◇ *We can handle up to 500 calls an hour at our new offices.* ◇ *We all have to learn to handle stress.* ◇ *This matter has been handled very badly.* ◇ (*informal*) *'Any problems?' 'Nothing* ***I can't handle***.*'* ◇ (*informal*) *I've got to go. I can't* ***handle it*** *any more* (= deal with a difficult situation). ◇ **~ yourself** (*informal*) *You have to know how to handle yourself in this business* (= know the right way to behave).

▸ TOUCH WITH HANDS **2** 🗝 [T] **~ sth** to touch, hold or move sth with your hands: *Our cat hates being handled.* ◇ *The label on the box said: 'Fragile.* ***Handle with care***.*'*

▸ CONTROL **3** 🗝 [T] **~ sth** to control a vehicle, an animal, a tool, etc: *I wasn't sure if I could handle such a powerful car.* ◇ *She's a difficult horse to handle.* **4** [I] **~ well/badly** to be easy/difficult to drive or control: *The car handles well in any weather.*

▸ BUY/SELL **5** [T] **~ sth** to buy or sell sth SYN **deal in**: *They were arrested for* **handling stolen goods.**

■ ***noun***

▸ OF DOOR/DRAWER/WINDOW **1** 🗝 the part of a door, drawer, window, etc. that you use to open it: *She turned the handle and opened the door.* ➲ VISUAL VOCAB page V42

▸ OF CUP/BAG/TOOL **2** 🗝 the part of an object, such as a cup, a bag, or a tool that you use to hold it, or carry it: *the handle of a knife* ◇ *a broom handle* ➲ VISUAL VOCAB pages V19, V23, V52 ➲ see also LOVE HANDLES

▸ -HANDLED **3** (in adjectives) having the number or type of handle mentioned: *a long-handled spoon*

IDM **get/have a 'handle on sb/sth** (*informal*) to understand or know about sb/sth, especially so that you can deal with it or them later: *I can't get a handle on these sales figures.* **give sb a 'handle (on sth)** (*informal*) to give sb enough facts or knowledge for them to be able to deal with sth ➲ more at FLY *v.*

handles

knobs

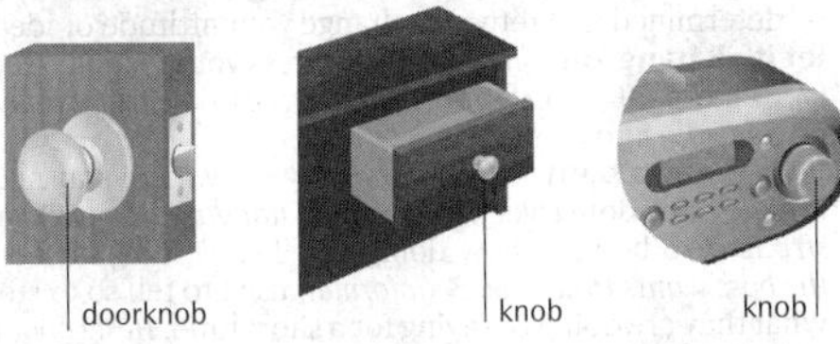

buttons

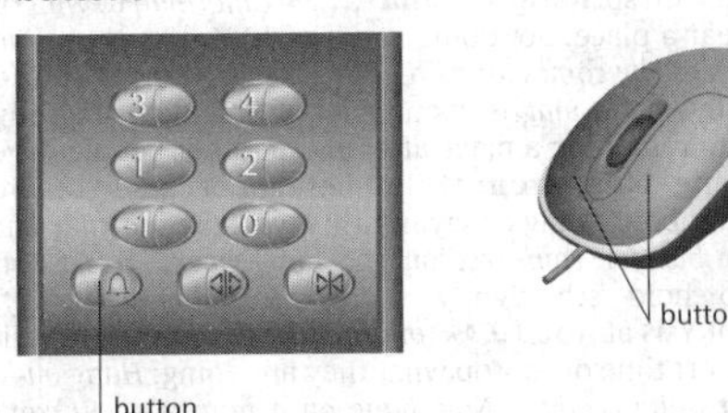

handle·bar /ˈhændlbɑː(r)/ *noun* [C] (also **handlebars** [pl.]) a metal bar, with a handle at each end, that you use for steering a bicycle or motorcycle: *to hold onto the handlebars* ➲ VISUAL VOCAB page V41 ➲ see also DROP HANDLEBARS

ˌhandlebar mousˈtache *noun* a MOUSTACHE that is curved upwards at each end

hand·ler /ˈhændlə(r)/ *noun* (especially in compounds) **1** a person who trains and controls animals, especially dogs **2** a person who carries or touches sth as part of their job: *airport baggage handlers* ◇ *food handlers* **3** (*especially NAmE*) a person who organizes sth or advises sb: *the President's campaign handlers*

hand·ling /ˈhændlɪŋ/ *noun* [U] **1** the way that sb deals with or treats a situation, a person, an animal, etc: *I was impressed by his handling of the affair.* ◇ *This horse needs firm handling.* **2** the action of organizing or controlling sth: *data handling on computer* **3** the action of touching, feeling or holding sth with your hands: *toys that can stand up to rough handling* **4** the cost of dealing with an order, delivering goods, booking tickets, etc: *a small handling charge* **5** the way in which a vehicle can be controlled by the driver: *a car designed for easy handling* **6** (also *BrE* **car·riage**) (*formal*) the act or cost of transporting goods from one place to another

ˈhand luggage (*especially BrE*) (also **ˈhand baggage, ˈcarry-on baggage** especially in *NAmE*) *noun* [U] small bags that you can keep with you on an aircraft

hand·made /ˌhændˈmeɪd/ *adj.* made by a person using their hands rather than by machines ➲ compare MACHINE-MADE

hand·maiden /ˈhændmeɪdn/ (also **hand·maid** /ˈhændmeɪd/) *noun* **1** (*old-fashioned*) a female servant **2** (*formal*) something that supports and helps sth else: *Mathematics was once dubbed the handmaiden of the sciences.*

ˈhand-me-down *noun* [usually pl.] (*especially NAmE*) = CAST-OFF: *She hated having to wear her sister's hand-me-downs.* ▸ **ˈhand-me-down** *adj.* (*especially NAmE*) = CAST-OFF

ˈhand-me-up *noun* an item that sb gives to an older member of their family because they no longer use it or because they have bought sth better to replace it

hand·off /ˈhændɒf; *NAmE* -ɔːf; -ɑːf/ *noun* **1** (especially in RUGBY) an act of preventing an opponent from TACKLING you by blocking them with your hand while keeping your arm straight **2** (in AMERICAN FOOTBALL) an act of giving the ball to another player on your team

hand·out /ˈhændaʊt/ *noun* **1** (sometimes *disapproving*) food, money or clothes that are given to a person who is poor **2** (often *disapproving*) money that is given to a person or an organization by the government, etc, for example to encourage commercial activity **3** a free document that gives information about an event or a matter of public interest, or that states the views of a political party, etc. ➲ see also PRESS RELEASE **4** a document that is given to students in class or people attending a talk, etc. and that contains a summary of the lesson/talk, a set of exercises, etc.

hand·over /ˈhændəʊvə(r); *NAmE* -oʊvər/ *noun* [C, U] **1** the act of moving power or responsibility from one person or group to another; the period during which this is done: *the smooth handover of power from a military to a civilian government* **2** the act of giving a person or thing to sb in authority: *the handover of the hostages*

hand·phone /ˈhændfəʊn; *NAmE* -foʊn/ *noun* used in SE Asia as the word for a mobile/cell phone

ˌhand-ˈpicked *adj.* carefully chosen for a special purpose

hand·print /ˈhændprɪnt/ *noun* a mark left by the flat part of someone's hand on a surface

ˈhand puppet (*NAmE*) (*BrE* **ˈglove puppet**) *noun* a type of PUPPET that you put over your hand and move using your fingers ➲ VISUAL VOCAB page V32

hand·rail /ˈhændreɪl/ *noun* a long narrow bar that you can hold onto for support, for example when you are going up or down stairs ➲ picture at STAIRCASE

hand·saw /ˈhændsɔː/ *noun* a SAW (= a tool with a long blade with sharp teeth along one edge) that is used with one hand only ➲ VISUAL VOCAB page V17

ˌhands-ˈdown *adj.* [only before noun] **~ winner/favourite/choice** (*informal*) easily the winner of a contest; definitely the one that people prefer: *These kits were hands-down favourites with our testers.* IDM see HAND *n.*

hand·set /ˈhændset/ *noun* **1** the part of a telephone that you hold close to your mouth and ear to speak into and listen ➲ compare RECEIVER **2** a mobile/cell phone or SMARTPHONE, especially the main part of the phone not including the battery or SIM CARD: *mobile handsets* ◇ *handset manufacturers* **3** a device that you hold in your hand to operate a television, etc. ➲ see also REMOTE CONTROL

ˈhands-free *adj.* (of a telephone, etc.) able to be used without needing to be held in the hand

hand·shake /ˈhændʃeɪk/ *noun* an act of shaking sb's hand with your own, used especially to say hello or goodbye or when you have made an agreement ➲ see also GOLDEN HANDSHAKE

ˌhands-ˈoff *adj.* [usually before noun] dealing with people or a situation by not becoming involved and by allowing people to do what they want to: *a hands-off approach to staff management* ➲ compare HANDS-ON

hand·some /ˈhænsəm/ *adj.* (**hand·somer, hand·som·est**) HELP **more handsome** and **most handsome** are more common **1** (of men) attractive SYN **good-looking**: *a handsome face* ◇ *He's the most handsome man I've ever met.* ◇ *He was aptly described as* ***'tall, dark, and handsome'****.* ➲ SYNONYMS at BEAUTIFUL **2** (of women) attractive, with large strong features rather than small delicate ones: *a tall, handsome woman* ➲ SYNONYMS at BEAUTIFUL **3** beautiful to look at: *a handsome horse/house/city* ◇ *The two of them made a* ***handsome couple****.* **4** large in amount or quantity: *a* ***handsome profit*** ◇ *He was elected by a handsome majority* (= a lot of people voted for him). **5** generous: *She paid him a handsome compliment.* ▶ **hand·some·ly** *adv.*: *a handsomely dressed man* ◇ *a handsomely produced book* ◇ *to be* ***paid/rewarded handsomely*** **hand·some·ness** *noun* [U]

ˌhands-ˈon *adj.* [usually before noun] doing sth rather than just talking about it: *hands-on computer training* ◇ *to gain* ***hands-on experience*** *of industry* ◇ *a hands-on style of management* ➲ compare HANDS-OFF

hand·spring /ˈhændsprɪŋ/ *noun* a movement in gymnastics in which you jump through the air landing on your hands, then again landing on your feet

hand·stand /ˈhændstænd/ *noun* a movement in which you balance on your hands and put your legs straight up in the air

ˌhand-to-ˈhand *adj.* **hand-to-hand** fighting involves physical contact with your opponent

ˌhand-to-ˈmouth *adj.* [usually before noun] if you have a **hand-to-mouth** life, you spend all the money you earn on basic needs such as food and do not have anything left IDM see LIVE[1]

hand·writ·ing /ˈhændraɪtɪŋ/ *noun* [U] **1** writing that is done with a pen or pencil, not printed or typed **2** a person's particular style of writing in this way: *I can't read his handwriting.*
IDM **the ˌhandwriting on the ˈwall** (*NAmE*) = THE WRITING ON THE WALL

hand·writ·ten /ˌhændˈrɪtn/ *adj.* written by hand, not printed or typed: *a handwritten note*

handy /ˈhændi/ *adj.* (**hand·ier, handi·est**) (*informal*) **1** easy to use or to do SYN **useful**: *a handy little tool* ◇ ***handy hints/tips*** *for removing stains* **2** [not before noun] located near to sb/sth; located or stored in a convenient place: *Always keep a first-aid kit handy.* ◇ *Have you got a pen handy?* ◇ **~ (for sth/for doing sth)** (*BrE*) *Our house is very handy for the station.* **3** [not before noun] skilful in using your hands or tools to make or repair things: *to be handy around the house* ➲ see also HANDILY ▶ **handi·ness** *noun* [U]
IDM **ˌcome in ˈhandy** (*informal*) to be useful: *The extra money came in very handy.* ◇ *Don't throw that away—it might come in handy.*

handy·man /ˈhændimæn/ *noun* (*pl.* **-men** /-men/) a man who is good at doing practical jobs inside and outside the house, either as a hobby or as a job

hang 🔑 /hæŋ/ *verb, noun*
■ *verb* (**hung, hung** /hʌŋ/ HELP In sense 4, **hanged** is used for the past tense and past participle.)
▸ ATTACH FROM TOP **1** 🔑 [T, I] to attach sth, or to be attached, at the top so that the lower part is free or loose: **~ sth + adv./prep.** *Hang your coat on the hook.* ◇ **~ sth up** *Shall I hang your coat up?* ◇ **~ sth (out)** (*BrE*) *Have you hung out the washing?* ◇ (*NAmE*) *Have you hung the wash?* ◇ **~ adv./prep.** *There were several expensive suits hanging in the wardrobe.*
▸ FALL LOOSELY **2** 🔑 [I] **~ adv./prep.** when sth **hangs** in a particular way, it falls in that way: *Her hair hung down to her waist.* ◇ *He had lost weight and the suit hung loosely on him.*
▸ BEND DOWNWARDS **3** 🔑 [I, T] to bend or let sth bend downwards: **~ adv./prep.** *The dog's tongue was hanging out.* ◇ *Children hung* (= were leaning) *over the gate.* ◇ *A cigarette hung from her lips.* ◇ **~ sth** *She* ***hung her head*** *in shame.*
▸ KILL SB **4** 🔑 (**hanged, hanged**) [T, I] **~ (sb/yourself)** to kill sb, usually as a punishment, by tying a rope around their neck and allowing them to drop; to be killed in this way: *He was the last man to be hanged for murder in this country.* ◇ *She had committed suicide by hanging herself from a beam.* ◇ *At that time you could hang for stealing.*
▸ PICTURES **5** 🔑 [T, I] **~ (sth)** to attach sth, especially a picture, to a hook on a wall; to be attached in this way: *We hung her portrait above the fireplace.* ◇ *Several of his paintings hang in the Tate Gallery.* **6** [T, usually passive] **~ sth with sth** to decorate a place by placing paintings, etc. on a wall: *The rooms were hung with tapestries.*
▸ WALLPAPER **7** [T] **~ sth** to stick WALLPAPER to a wall
▸ DOOR/GATE **8** [T] **~ sth** to attach a door or gate to a post so that it moves freely
▸ STAY IN THE AIR **9** [I] **+ adv./prep.** to stay in the air: *Smoke hung in the air above the city.*
IDM **ˈhang sth** (*BrE, informal*) used to say that you are not going to worry about sth: *Oh, let's get two and hang the expense!* **hang a ˈleft/ˈright** (*NAmE*) to take a left/right turn **hang by a ˈhair/ˈthread** (of a person's life) to be in great danger **hang (on) ˈin there** (*informal*) to remain determined to succeed even when a situation is difficult **hang on sb's ˈwords/on sb's every ˈword** to listen with great attention to sb you admire **hang ˈtough** (*NAmE*) to be determined and refuse to change your attitude or ideas **let it all hang ˈout** (*informal*) to express your feelings freely ➲ more at BALANCE *n.*, FIRE *n.*, GRIM, HEAVY *adv.*, LOOSE *adj.*, PEG *n.*, WELL *adv.*
PHR V **ˌhang aˈbout** (*BrE, informal*) **1** 🔑 to wait or stay near a place, not doing very much: *kids hanging about in the streets* **2** to be very slow doing sth: *I can't hang about—the boss wants to see me.* **3** (*informal*) used to tell sb to stop what they are doing or saying for a short time: *Hang about! There's something not quite right here.* **ˌhang aˈbout with sb** 🔑 (*BrE*) (*NAmE* **ˈhang with sb**) (*informal*) to spend a lot of time with sb **ˌhang aˈround (...)** 🔑 (*informal*) to wait or stay near a place, not doing very much: *You hang around here in case he comes, and I'll go on ahead.* **ˌhang aˈround with sb** 🔑 (*informal*) to spend a lot of time with sb **ˌhang ˈback** to remain in a place after all the other people have left **ˌhang ˈback (from sth)** to hesitate because you are nervous about doing or saying sth: *I was sure she knew the answer but for some reason she hung back.* **ˌhang ˈon 1** 🔑 to hold sth tightly: *Hang on tight—we're off!* ➲ SYNONYMS at HOLD **2** 🔑 (*informal*) used to ask sb to wait for a short time or to stop what they are doing: *Hang on—I'm not quite ready.* ◇ *Now hang on a minute—you can't really believe what you just said!* **3** to wait for sth to happen: *I haven't heard if I've got the job yet—they've kept me hanging on for days.* **4** (*informal*) used on the telephone to ask sb who is calling to wait until they can talk to the person they want: *Hang on—I'll just see if he's here.* **5** to continue doing sth in difficult circumstances: *The team hung on for victory.* **ˈhang on sth** to depend on sth: *A lot hangs on this decision.* **ˌhang ˈon to sth 1** 🔑 to hold sth tightly: *Hang on to that rope and don't let go.* **2** (*informal*) to keep sth, not sell it or give it away: *Let's hang on to those old photographs—they may be valuable.* **ˌhang ˈout** (*informal*) to spend a lot of time in a place: *The local kids hang out at the mall.* ➲ related noun HANG-OUT **ˌhang sth↔ˈout** (*especially BrE*) to attach things that you have washed to a piece of thin rope or wire, etc. outside so that they can dry; to attach sth such as a flag outside a window or in the street **ˌhang ˈover sb** if sth bad or unpleasant is **hanging over** you, you think about it and worry about it a lot

because it is happening or might happen: *The possibility of a court case is still hanging over her.* ˌ**hang toˈgether 1** to fit together well; to be the same as or CONSISTENT with each other: *Their accounts of what happened don't hang together.* **2** (of people) to support or help one another ˌ**hang ˈup** 0‑ to end a telephone conversation by putting the telephone RECEIVER down or switching the telephone off: *After I hung up I remembered what I'd wanted to say.* ˌ**hang sth↔ˈup** (*informal*) to finish using sth for the last time: *Ruth has hung up her dancing shoes.* ˌ**hang ˈup on sb** (*informal*) to end a telephone call by suddenly and unexpectedly putting the telephone down: *Don't hang up on me—we must talk!* ➲ see also HUNG UP

PHR V ˈ**hang with sb** (*NAmE*) (*BrE* ˌ**hang aˈbout with sb**) (*informal*) to spend a lot of time with sb

■ ***noun*** [sing.] the way in which a dress, piece of cloth, etc. falls or moves

IDM **get the ˈhang of sth** (*informal*) to learn how to do or to use sth; to understand sth: *It's not difficult once you get the hang of it.*

hangar /ˈhæŋə(r); ˈhæŋgə(r)/ *noun* a large building in which aircraft are kept

hang·dog /ˈhæŋdɒg; *NAmE* -dɔːg; -dɑːg/ *adj.* [only before noun] if a person has a **hangdog** look, they look sad or ashamed

hanger /ˈhæŋə(r)/ (also ˈ**coat hanger**, ˈ**clothes hanger**) *noun* a curved piece of wood, plastic or wire, with a hook at the top, that you use to hang clothes up on ➲ VISUAL VOCAB pages V20, V51

ˌ**hanger-ˈon** *noun* (*pl.* ˌhangers-ˈon) (often *disapproving*) a person who tries to be friendly with a famous person or who goes to important events, in order to get some advantage

ˈ**hang-glider** *noun* **1** the frame used in hang-gliding **2** a person who goes hang-gliding

ˈ**hang-gliding** *noun* [U] a sport in which you fly while hanging from a frame like a large KITE which you control with your body movements: *to go hang-gliding* ➲ VISUAL VOCAB page V40

hang·ing /ˈhæŋɪŋ/ *noun* **1** [U, C] the practice of killing sb as a punishment by putting a rope around their neck and hanging them from a high place; an occasion when this happens: *to sentence sb to death by hanging* ◇ *public hangings* **2** [C, usually pl.] a large piece of material that is hung on a wall for decoration: *wall hangings*

ˌ**hanging ˈbasket** *noun* a BASKET or similar container with flowers growing in it, that is hung from a building by a short chain or rope ➲ picture at BASKET ➲ VISUAL VOCAB page V15

ˌ**hanging ˈvalley** *noun* (*technical*) a valley which joins a deeper valley, often with a WATERFALL where the two valleys join

hang·man /ˈhæŋmən/ *noun* (*pl.* -men /-mən/) **1** [C] a man whose job is to hang criminals **2** [U] a game in which one player chooses a word and the other players try to guess it, letter by letter. Each time they guess wrongly, the first person draws one part of a man being hanged. The other players have to guess the word before the drawing is complete.

hang·nail /ˈhæŋneɪl/ *noun* a piece of skin near the bottom or at the side of your nail that is loose and sore

ˈ**hang-out** *noun* (*informal*) a place where sb lives or likes to go often **SYN** **haunt**

hang·over /ˈhæŋəʊvə(r); *NAmE* -oʊvər/ *noun* **1** the headache and sick feeling that you have the day after drinking too much alcohol: *She woke up with a terrible hangover.* **2** [usually sing.] **~ (from sth)** a feeling, custom, idea, etc. that remains from the past, although it is no longer practical or suitable: *the insecure feeling that was a hangover from her childhood* ◇ *hangover laws from the previous administration* ➲ see also HOLDOVER

the Hang Seng Index /ˌhæŋ ˈseŋ ɪndeks/ *noun* a figure that shows the relative price of shares on the Hong Kong Stock Exchange

ˈ**hang-up** *noun* (*informal*) **1 ~ (about sth)** an emotional problem about sth that makes you embarrassed or worried: *He's got a real hang-up about his height.* **2** (*NAmE*) a problem that delays sth being agreed or achieved

hank /hæŋk/ *noun* a long piece of wool, thread, rope, etc. that is wound into a large loose ball

han·ker /ˈhæŋkə(r)/ *verb* [I] to have a strong desire for sth: **~ after/for sth** *He had hankered after fame all his life.* ◇ **~ to do sth** *She hankered to go back to Australia.*

han·ker·ing /ˈhæŋkərɪŋ/ *noun* [usually sing.] **~ (for/after sth)** | **~ (to do sth)** a strong desire: *a hankering for a wealthy lifestyle*

hanky (also **han·kie**) /ˈhæŋki/ *noun* (*pl.* -ies) (*informal*) = HANDKERCHIEF

hanky-panky /ˌhæŋki ˈpæŋki/ *noun* [U] (*old-fashioned, informal*) **1** sexual activity that is not considered acceptable **2** dishonest behaviour

Han·sard /ˈhænsɑːd; *NAmE* -sɑːrd/ *noun* [U] (in the British, Canadian, Australian, New Zealand or South African parliaments) the official written record of everything that is said in the parliament

han·som /ˈhænsəm/ (also ˈ**hansom cab**) *noun* a CARRIAGE with two wheels, pulled by one horse, used in the past to carry two passengers

Ha·nuk·kah (also **Cha·nuk·kah**, **Cha·nuk·ah**) /ˈhænʊkə/ *noun* an eight-day Jewish festival and holiday in November or December when Jews remember the occasion when the TEMPLE in Jerusalem was DEDICATED again in 165 BC

ha'·penny = HALFPENNY

hap·haz·ard /hæpˈhæzəd; *NAmE* -zərd/ *adj.* (*disapproving*) with no particular order or plan; not organized well: *The books had been piled on the shelves in a haphazard fashion.* ◇ *The government's approach to the problem was haphazard.* ▶ **hap·haz·ard·ly** *adv.*

hap·less /ˈhæpləs/ *adj.* [only before noun] (*formal*) not lucky; unfortunate: *the hapless victims of exploitation*

hap·loid /ˈhæplɔɪd/ *adj.* (*biology*) (of a cell) containing the set of CHROMOSOMES from one parent only ➲ compare DIPLOID

ha'p'orth /ˈheɪpəθ; *NAmE* -pərθ/ *noun* [sing.] (*old-fashioned, BrE, informal*) a very small amount (in the past, an amount that could be bought for a HALFPENNY)

IDM see SPOIL *v.*

hap·pen 0‑ /ˈhæpən/ *verb*

1 0‑ [I] to take place, especially without being planned: *You'll never guess what's happened!* ◇ *Accidents like this happen all the time.* ◇ *Let's see what happens next week.* ◇ *I'll be there* **whatever happens**. ◇ *I don't know how this happened.* **2** 0‑ [I] to take place as the result of sth: *She pressed the button but nothing happened.* ◇ *What happens if nobody comes to the party?* ◇ *Just plug it in and* **see what happens**. **3** *linking verb* to do or be sth by chance: **~ to be/do sth** *She happened to be out when we called.* ◇ *You don't happen to know his name, do you?* ◇ **it happens that...** *It happened that she was out when we called.* **4** [T] **~ to be/do sth** used to tell sb sth, especially when you are disagreeing with them or annoyed by what they have said: *That happens to be my mother you're talking about!*

IDM **anything can/might ˈhappen** used to say that it is not possible to know what the result of sth will be **as it happens/happened** used when you say sth that is surprising, or sth connected with what sb else has just said: *I agree with you, as it happens.* ◇ *As it happens, I have a spare set of keys in my office.* **it (just) so happens that...** by chance: *It just so happened they'd been invited too.* ˌ**these things ˈhappen** used to tell sb not to worry about sth they have done: *'Sorry—I've spilt some wine.' 'Never mind. These things happen.'* ➲ more at ACCIDENT, EVENT, SHIT, WAIT *v.*

PHR V ˈ**happen on sth** (*old-fashioned*) to find sth by chance ˈ**happen to sb/sth** 0‑ to have an effect on sb/sth: *I hope nothing* (= nothing unpleasant) *has happened to them.* ◇ *It's* the best thing that has ever happened to me. ◇ What's happened to your car? ◇ Do you know what happened to Gill Lovecy (= have you any news about her)?

hap·pen·ing /ˈhæpənɪŋ/ *noun, adj.*
■ ***noun*** **1** [usually pl.] an event; something that happens, often sth unusual: *There have been strange happenings here lately.* **2** an artistic performance or event that is not planned
■ ***adj.*** [only before noun] (*informal*) where there is a lot of exciting activity; fashionable: *a happening place*

hap·pen·stance /ˈhæpənstæns; *BrE* also -stɑːns/ *noun* [U, C] (*literary*) chance, especially when it results in sth good

hap·pily 🔑 /ˈhæpɪli/ *adv.*
1 🔑 in a cheerful way; with feelings of pleasure or satisfaction: *children playing happily on the beach* ◇ *to be happily married* ◇ *I think we can manage quite happily on our own.* ◇ ***And they all lived happily ever after*** (= used as the end of a FAIRY TALE). **2** 🔑 by good luck SYN **fortunately**: *Happily, the damage was only slight.* **3** willingly: *I'll happily help, if I can.* **4** (*formal*) in a way that is suitable or appropriate: *This suggestion did not fit very happily with our existing plans.*

Synonyms

happy

satisfied • content • contented • joyful • blissful

These words all describe feeling, showing or giving pleasure or satisfaction.

happy feeling, showing or giving pleasure; satisfied with sth or not worried about it: *a happy marriage/ memory/ childhood* ◇ *I said I'd go, just to* ***keep him happy.***

satisfied pleased because you have achieved sth or because sth has happened as you wanted it to; showing this satisfaction: *She's never satisfied with what she's got.* ◇ *a satisfied smile*

content [not before noun] happy and satisfied with what you have: *I'm perfectly* ***content just to*** *lie in the sun.*

contented happy and comfortable with what you have; showing this: *a contented baby* ◇ *a long contented sigh*

CONTENT OR CONTENTED?

Being **contented** depends more on having a comfortable life; being **content** can depend more on your attitude to your life: you can *have to be content* or *learn to be content*. People or animals can be **contented** but only people can be **content**.

joyful (*rather formal*) very happy; making people very happy

blissful making people very happy; showing this happiness: *three blissful weeks away*

JOYFUL OR BLISSFUL?

Joy is a livelier feeling; **bliss** is more peaceful.

PATTERNS

- happy/satisfied/content/contented **with** sth
- a happy/satisfied/contented/blissful **smile**
- a happy/joyful **occasion/celebration**
- **to feel** happy/satisfied/content/contented/joyful
- **very/perfectly/quite** happy/satisfied/content/contented

happy 🔑 /ˈhæpi/ *adj.* (**hap·pier, hap·pi·est**)
▸ FEELING/GIVING PLEASURE **1** 🔑 feeling or showing pleasure; pleased: *a happy smile/face* ◇ *You don't look very happy today.* ◇ **~ to do sth** *We are happy to announce the engagement of our daughter.* ◇ **~ for sb** *I'm very happy for you.* ◇ **~ (that)...** *I'm happy (that) you could come.* ➲ SYNONYMS at GLAD **2** 🔑 giving or causing pleasure: *a happy marriage/ memory/childhood* ◇ *The story has a* ***happy ending.*** ◇ *Those were the happiest days of my life.*
▸ AT CELEBRATION **3** 🔑 if you wish sb a **Happy Birthday, Happy New Year**, etc. you mean that you hope they have a pleasant celebration
▸ SATISFIED **4** 🔑 satisfied that sth is good or right; not anxious: **~ (with sb/sth)** *Are you happy with that arrangement?* ◇ *I'm not happy with his work this term.* ◇ *She was happy enough with her performance.* ◇ **~ (about sb/sth)** *If there's anything you're not happy about, come and ask.* ◇ *I'm not too happy about her living alone.* ◇ *I said I'd go just to* ***keep him happy.***
▸ WILLING **5** 🔑 **~ to do sth** (*formal*) willing or pleased to do sth: *I'm happy to leave it till tomorrow.* ◇ *He will be* ***more than happy*** *to come with us.*
▸ LUCKY **6** lucky; successful SYN **fortunate**: *By* ***a happy coincidence,*** *we arrived at exactly the same time.* ◇ *He is* ***in the happy position of*** *never having to worry about money.*
▸ SUITABLE **7** (*formal*) (of words, ideas or behaviour) suitable and appropriate for a particular situation: *That wasn't the happiest choice of words.*
▸ **hap·pi·ness** 🔑 *noun* [U]: *to* ***find*** *true* ***happiness*** ◇ *Her eyes shone with happiness.* ➲ SYNONYMS at SATISFACTION
IDM **a ˌhappy eˈvent** the birth of a baby **a/the happy ˈmedium** something that is in the middle between two choices or two ways of doing sth **not a ˌhappy ˈbunny** (*BrE*) (*NAmE* **not a ˌhappy ˈcamper**) (*informal*) not pleased about a situation: *She wasn't a happy bunny at all.* **many happy reˈturns (of the ˈday)** used to wish sb a happy and pleasant birthday ➲ more at MEAN *n.*

WORD FAMILY
happy *adj.* (≠ unhappy)
happily *adv.* (≠ unhappily)
happiness *noun* (≠ unhappiness)

happy-clappy /ˌhæpi ˈklæpi/ *adj.* (*BrE*, often *disapproving*) connected with a Christian group which worships in a very loud and enthusiastic way, showing a lot of feeling

ˌhappy ˈfamilies *noun* [U] a children's card game played with special cards with pictures of family members on them. The aim is to get as many whole families as possible.
IDM **ˌplay happy ˈfamilies** to do things that normal happy families do, especially when you want it to appear that your family is happy: *I'm not going to play happy families just for the benefit of your parents.*

ˌhappy-go-ˈlucky *adj.* not caring or worrying about the future: *a happy-go-lucky attitude* ◇ *a happy-go-lucky sort of person*

ˈhappy hour *noun* [usually sing.] (*informal*) a time, usually in the early evening, when a pub or a bar sells alcoholic drinks at lower prices than usual

ˈhappy slapping *noun* (*BrE*) [U] the practice of several people attacking sb while another person in the group makes a film of the attack

hap·tic /ˈhæptɪk/ *adj.* (*technical*) relating to or involving the sense of touch: *Players use a haptic device such as a joystick to control the game.*

hara-kiri /ˌhærə ˈkɪri; *NAmE* ˌherə ˈkeri/ *noun* [U] (from *Japanese*) an act of killing yourself by cutting open your stomach with a SWORD, performed especially by the SAMURAI in Japan in the past, to avoid losing honour

har·am·bee /həˈræmbiː/ *noun* (*EAfrE*) **1** [C] a meeting that is held in order to collect money for sth, for example a community project: *They held a harambee meeting to raise funds for a new classroom.* **2** [U] the act of joining with other people to achieve a difficult task: *the spirit of harambee*

har·angue /həˈræŋ/ *verb, noun*
■ ***verb*** **~ sb** to speak loudly and angrily in a way that criticizes sb/sth or tries to persuade people to do sth
■ ***noun*** a long loud angry speech that criticizes sb/sth or tries to persuade people to do sth

har·ass /ˈhærəs; həˈræs/ *verb* **1** [often passive] **~ sb** to annoy or worry sb by putting pressure on them or saying or doing unpleasant things to them: *He has complained of being harassed by the police.* ◇ *She claims she has been* ***sexually harassed*** *at work.* **2** **~ sb/sth** to make repeated attacks on an enemy SYN **harry** ▸ **har·ass·ment** *noun* [U]: ***racial/sexual harassment***

har·assed /ˈhærəst; həˈræst/ *adj.* tired and anxious because you have too much to do: *a harassed-looking waiter* ◇ *harassed mothers with their children*

har·bin·ger /ˈhɑːbɪndʒə(r); *NAmE* ˈhɑːrb-/ *noun* **~ (of sth)** (*formal* or *literary*) a sign that shows that sth is going to happen soon, often sth bad

har·bour (*especially US* **har·bor**) /ˈhɑːbə(r); *NAmE* ˈhɑːrb-/ *noun, verb*

■ ***noun*** [C, U] an area of water on the coast, protected from the open sea by strong walls, where ships can shelter: *Several boats lay at anchor in the harbour.* ◇ *to* ***enter/leave harbour*** ➲ VISUAL VOCAB page V5

■ ***verb*** **1 ~ sb** to hide and protect sb who is hiding from the police: *Police believe someone must be harbouring the killer.* **2 ~ sth** to keep feelings or thoughts, especially negative ones, in your mind for a long time: *The arsonist may* ***harbour a grudge*** *against the company.* ◇ *She began to harbour doubts about the decision.* **3 ~ sth** to contain sth and allow it to develop: *Your dishcloth can harbour many germs.*

ˈharbour master (*especially US* **har·bor·mas·ter**) *noun* an official in charge of a harbour

hard 0‑ᵂ /hɑːd; *NAmE* hɑːrd/ *adj., adv.*

■ ***adj.*** (**hard·er, hard·est**)

▸ SOLID/STIFF **1** 0‑ᵂ solid, firm or stiff and difficult to bend or break: *Wait for the concrete to go hard.* ◇ *a hard mattress* ◇ *Diamonds are the hardest known mineral.* OPP **soft**

▸ DIFFICULT **2** 0‑ᵂ difficult to do, understand or answer: *a hard choice/question* ◇ **~ to do sth** *It is* ***hard to believe*** *that she's only nine.* ◇ *It's* ***hard to see*** *how they can lose.* ◇ *'When will the job be finished?' 'It's* ***hard to say.***' (= it is difficult to be certain) ◇ *I find his attitude very* ***hard to take*** (= difficult to accept). ◇ *We're finding reliable staff* ***hard to come by*** (= difficult to get). ◇ **~ for sb (to do sth)** *It's hard for old people to change their ways.* ◇ *It must be hard for her, bringing up four children on her own.* OPP **easy** **3** 0‑ᵂ full of difficulty and problems, especially because of a lack of money SYN **tough**: *Times were hard at the end of the war.* ◇ *She's had a hard life.* OPP **easy**

▸ NEEDING/USING EFFORT **4** 0‑ᵂ needing or using a lot of physical strength or mental effort: *It's* ***hard work*** *shovelling snow.* ◇ *I've had a long hard day.* ➲ SYNONYMS at DIFFICULT **5** 0‑ᵂ (of people) putting a lot of effort or energy into an activity: *She's a very hard worker.* ◇ *He's* ***hard at work*** *on a new novel.* ◇ *When I left they were all still* ***hard at it*** (= working hard). ➲ SYNONYMS at DIFFICULT **6** 0‑ᵂ done with a lot of strength or force: *He gave the door a good hard kick.* ◇ *a hard punch*

▸ WITHOUT SYMPATHY **7** 0‑ᵂ showing no sympathy or affection: *My father was a hard man.* ◇ *She gave me a hard stare.* ◇ *He said some very hard things to me.*

▸ NOT AFRAID **8** (*informal*) (of people) ready to fight and showing no signs of fear or weakness: *Come and get me if you think you're hard enough.* ◇ *You think you're really hard, don't you?*

▸ FACTS/EVIDENCE **9** [only before noun] definitely true and based on information that can be proved: *Is there any* ***hard evidence*** *either way?* ◇ *The newspaper story is based on* ***hard facts.***

▸ WEATHER **10** very cold and severe: *It had been a* ***hard winter.*** ◇ *There was a* ***hard frost*** *that night.* ➲ compare MILD

▸ DRINK **11** [only before noun] strongly alcoholic: ***hard liquor*** ◇ (*informal*) *a drop of* ***the hard stuff*** (= a strong alcoholic drink) ➲ compare SOFT DRINK

▸ WATER **12** containing CALCIUM and other mineral salts that make mixing with soap difficult: *a* ***hard water*** *area* ◇ *Our water is very hard.* OPP **soft**

▸ CONSONANTS **13** (*phonetics*) used to describe a letter *c* or *g* when pronounced as in 'cat' or 'go', rather than as in 'city' or 'giant' OPP **soft**

▸ **hard·ness** *noun* [U]: *water hardness* ◇ *hardness of heart*

IDM **be ˈhard on sb/sth** **1** 0‑ᵂ to treat or criticize sb in a very severe or strict way: *Don't be too hard on him—he's very young.* **2** 0‑ᵂ to be difficult for or unfair to sb/sth: *It's hard on people who don't have a car.* **3** to be likely to hurt or damage sth: *Looking at a computer screen all day can be very hard on the eyes.* **drive/strike a hard ˈbargain** to argue in an aggressive way and force sb to agree on the best possible price or arrangement **give sb a hard ˈtime** to deliberately make a situation difficult and unpleasant for sb: *They really gave me a hard time at the interview.* **ˌhard and ˈfast** (especially after a negative) that cannot be changed in any circumstances: *There are* ***no hard and fast rules*** *about this.* **(as) ˌhard as ˈnails** showing no sympathy, kindness or fear **ˌhard ˈcheese** (*BrE, informal*) used as a way of saying that you are sorry about sth, usually IRONICALLY (= you really mean the opposite) **ˌhard ˈgoing** difficult to understand or needing a lot of effort: *I'm finding his latest novel very hard going.* **ˌhard ˈluck/ˈlines** (*BrE*) used to tell sb that you feel sorry for them: *'Failed again, I'm afraid.' 'Oh, hard luck.'* **the ˈhard way** by having an unpleasant experience or by making mistakes: *She won't listen to my advice so she'll just have to* ***learn the hard way.*** **make hard ˈwork of sth** to use more time or energy on a task than is necessary **no hard ˈfeelings** used to tell sb you have been arguing with or have beaten in a contest that you would still like to be friendly with them: *It looks like I'm the winner again. No hard feelings, Dave, eh?* **play hard to ˈget** (*informal*) to make yourself seem more attractive or interesting by not immediately accepting an invitation to do sth **too much like hard ˈwork** needing too much effort: *I can't be bothered making a hot meal—it's too much like hard work.* ➲ more at ACT *n.*, JOB, LONG *adj.*, NUT *n.*, ROCK *n.*

■ ***adv.*** (**hard·er, hard·est**)

▸ WITH EFFORT **1** 0‑ᵂ with great effort; with difficulty: *to* ***work hard*** ◇ *You must* ***try harder.*** ◇ *She* ***tried her hardest*** *not to show how disappointed she was.* ◇ *Don't hit it so hard!* ◇ *He was still breathing hard after his run.* ◇ *Our victory was hard won* (= won with great difficulty).

▸ WITH FORCE **2** 0‑ᵂ with great force: (*figurative*) *Small businesses have been* ***hit hard/hard hit*** *by the recession.*

▸ CAREFULLY **3** 0‑ᵂ very carefully and thoroughly: *to think hard* ◇ *We thought* ***long and hard*** *before deciding to move house.*

▸ A LOT **4** heavily; a lot or for a long time: *It was* ***raining hard*** *when we set off.*

▸ LEFT/RIGHT **5** at a sharp angle to the left/right: *Turn hard right at the next junction.*

IDM **be/feel hard ˈdone by** (*informal*) to be or feel unfairly treated: *She has every right to feel hard done by—her parents have given her nothing.* **be ˌhard ˈpressed/ˈpushed to do sth | be hard ˈput (to it) to do sth** to find it very difficult to do sth: *He was hard put to it to explain her disappearance.* **be hard ˈup for sth** to have too few or too little of sth: *We're hard up for ideas.* ➲ see also HARD UP **ˈhard on sth** very soon after: *His death followed hard on hers.* **take sth ˈhard** to be very upset by sth: *He took his wife's death very hard.* ➲ more at DIE *v.*, HEEL *n.*

Which Word?

hard / hardly

- The adverb from the adjective **hard** is **hard**: *I have to work hard today.* ◇ *She has thought very hard about her future plans.* ◇ *It was raining hard outside.*
- **Hardly** is an adverb meaning 'almost not': *I hardly ever go to concerts.* ◇ *I can hardly wait for my birthday.* It cannot be used instead of **hard**: ~~*I've been working hardly today.*~~ ◇ ~~*She has thought very hardly about her future plans.*~~ ◇ ~~*It was raining hardly outside.*~~

➲ note at HARDLY

hard·back /ˈhɑːdbæk; *NAmE* ˈhɑːrd-/ (also **hard·cover** especially in *NAmE*) *noun* [C, U] a book that has a stiff cover: *What's the price of the hardback?* ◇ *It was published* ***in hardback*** *last year.* ◇ ***hardback books/editions*** ➲ compare PAPERBACK

hard·ball /ˈhɑːdbɔːl; *NAmE* ˈhɑːrd-/ *noun* (*NAmE*) **1** the game of BASEBALL (when contrasted with SOFTBALL) **2** used to refer to a way of behaving, especially in politics, that shows that a person is determined to get what they

H

want: *I want us to **play hardball** on this issue.* ◇ *hardball politics*

hard·bit·ten /ˌhɑːdˈbɪtn; *NAmE* ˌhɑːrd-/ *adj.* not easily shocked and not showing emotion, because you have experienced many unpleasant things

hard·board /ˈhɑːdbɔːd; *NAmE* ˈhɑːrdbɔːrd/ *noun* [U] a type of stiff board made by crushing very small pieces of wood together into thin sheets

ˌhard-ˈboiled *adj.* **1** (of an egg) boiled until the inside is hard ➲ compare SOFT-BOILED **2** (of people) not showing much emotion

ˌhard ˈby *prep.* (*old-fashioned*) very near sth ▶ **ˌhard ˈby** *adv.*

ˌhard ˈcandy (*NAmE*) (*BrE* **ˌboiled ˈsweet**) *noun* [U] a hard sweet/candy made from boiled sugar, often with fruit flavours

ˌhard ˈcash (*BrE*) (*NAmE* **ˌcold ˈcash**) *noun* [U] money, especially in the form of coins and notes, that you can spend

ˌhard-ˈcharging *adj.* [only before noun] working or performing with a lot of energy and skill: *He changed from a goofy kid to a hard-charging soldier.*

ˈhard cider (*NAmE*) (*BrE* **cider**) *noun* [U, C] an alcoholic drink made from the juice of apples

ˌhard-ˈcode *verb* **~ sth** (*computing*) to write data so that it cannot easily be changed

ˌhard ˈcopy *noun* [U, C] (*computing*) information from a computer that has been printed on paper ➲ VISUAL VOCAB page V56

ˌhard ˈcore *noun* (*BrE*) **1** [sing.+ sing./pl. v.] the small central group in an organization, or in a particular group of people, who are the most active or who will not change their beliefs or behaviour: *It's really only the hard core that bother(s) to go to meetings.* ◇ *A hard core of drivers ignores the law.* **2** [U] (usually **ˈhardcore**) small pieces of stone, brick, etc. used as a base for building roads on

ˌhard-ˈcore *adj.* [only before noun] **1** having a belief or a way of behaving that will not change: *hard-core party members* **2** showing or describing sexual activity in a detailed or violent way: *They sell **hard-core pornography**.* ➲ compare SOFT-CORE

ˌhard ˈcourt *noun* an area with a hard surface for playing TENNIS on, not grass

hard·cover /ˈhɑːdkʌvə(r); *NAmE* ˈhɑːrd-/ *noun* (*especially NAmE*) = HARDBACK

ˌhard ˈcurrency *noun* [U, C] money that is easy to exchange for money from another country, because it is not likely to lose its value

ˌhard ˈdisk *noun* a disk inside a computer that stores data and programs ➲ VISUAL VOCAB page V54 ➲ compare FLOPPY DISK

ˌhard ˈdisk recorder *noun* a DIGITAL recording system that records sound or video directly to a hard disk, without using tape

ˈhard-drinking *adj.* drinking a lot of alcohol

ˈhard drive *noun* (*computing*) a part of a computer that reads data on a HARD DISK

ˌhard ˈdrug *noun* [usually pl.] a powerful illegal drug, such as HEROIN, that some people take for pleasure and can become ADDICTED to ➲ compare SOFT DRUG

ˌhard-ˈearned *adj.* that you get only after a lot of work and effort: *hard-earned cash* ◇ *We finally managed a hard-earned draw.*

ˌhard-ˈedged *adj.* powerful, true to life and not affected by emotion: *the movie's hard-edged realism*

hard·en /ˈhɑːdn; *NAmE* ˈhɑːrdn/ *verb* **1** [I, T] to become or make sth become firm, stiff or solid: *The varnish takes a few hours to harden.* ◇ **~ sth** *a method for hardening and preserving wood* **2** [I, T] if your voice, face, etc. **hardens**, or you **harden** it, it becomes more serious or severe: *Her face hardened into an expression of hatred.* ◇ **~ sth** *He hardened his voice when he saw she wasn't listening.* **3** [I, T] if sb's feelings or attitudes **harden** or sb/sth **hardens** them, they become more fixed and determined: *Public attitudes to the strike have hardened.* ◇ *Their suspicions hardened into certainty.* ◇ **~ sth** *The incident hardened her resolve to leave the company.* **4** [T, usually passive] **~ sb/sth/yourself** to make sb less kind or less affected by extreme situations: *Joe sounded different, hardened by the war.* ◇ *They were **hardened criminals*** (= they showed no regret for their crimes). ◇ *In this job you have to **harden your heart** to pain and suffering.* ▶ **hard·en·ing** *noun* [U, sing.]: *hardening of the arteries* ◇ *a hardening of attitudes towards one-parent families*

ˌhard-ˈfaced *adj.* (*disapproving*) (of a person) showing no feeling or sympathy for other people

ˌhard-ˈfought *adj.* that involves fighting very hard: *a hard-fought battle/win/victory*

ˌhard ˈhat *noun* a hat worn by building workers, etc. to protect their heads ➲ VISUAL VOCAB page V53

ˌhard-ˈheaded *adj.* determined and not allowing your emotions to affect your decisions

ˌhard-ˈhearted *adj.* giving no importance to the feelings or problems of other people ➲ compare SOFT-HEARTED

ˌhard-ˈhitting *adj.* not afraid to talk about or criticize sb/sth in an honest and very direct way: *a hard-hitting speech*

ˌhard ˈlabour (*especially US* **ˌhard ˈlabor**) *noun* [U] punishment in prison that involves a lot of very hard physical work

ˌhard ˈleft *noun* [sing.+ sing./pl. v.] (*especially BrE*) the members of a LEFT-WING political party who have the most extreme opinions: *hard-left policies*

ˌhard ˈline *noun* [sing.] a strict policy or attitude: *the judge's hard line against drug dealers* ◇ *The government **took a hard line on** the strike.*

ˌhard-ˈline *adj.* [usually before noun] **1** (of a person) having very fixed beliefs and being unlikely or unwilling to change them: *a hard-line conservative* **2** (of ideas) very fixed and unlikely to change: *a hard-line attitude* ▶ **hard·liner** /ˌhɑːdˈlaɪnə(r); *NAmE* ˌhɑːrd-/ *noun*: *a Republican hardliner*

ˌhard-ˈluck story *noun* a story about yourself that you tell sb in order to get their sympathy or help

Grammar Point

hardly / scarcely / barely / no sooner

- **Hardly**, **scarcely** and **barely** can all be used to say that something is only just true or possible. They are used with words like *any* and *anyone*, with adjectives and verbs, and are often placed between *can, could, have, be*, etc. and the main part of the verb: *They have sold scarcely any copies of the book.* ◇ *I barely recognized her.* ◇ *His words were barely audible.* ◇ *I can hardly believe it.* ◇ ~~*I hardly can believe it.*~~
- **Hardly**, **scarcely** and **barely** are negative words and should not be used with *not* or other negatives: ~~*I can't hardly believe it.*~~
- You can also use **hardly**, **scarcely** and **barely** to say that one thing happens immediately after another: *We had hardly/scarcely/barely sat down at the table, when the phone rang.* In formal, written English, especially in a literary style, these words can be placed at the beginning of the sentence and then the subject and verb are turned around: *Hardly/Scarcely had we sat down at the table, when the phone rang.* Note that you usually use *when* in these sentences, not *than*. You can also use *before*: *I scarcely had time to ring the bell before the door opened.* **No sooner** can be used in the same way, but is always used with *than*: *No sooner had we sat down at the table than the phone rang.*
- **Hardly** and **scarcely** can be used to mean 'almost never', but **barely** is not used in this way: *She hardly (ever) sees her parents these days.* ◇ ~~*She barely sees her parents these days.*~~

hard·ly 0‑ /ˈhɑːdli; *NAmE* ˈhɑːrd-/ *adv.* **1** 0‑ almost no; almost not; almost none: *There's **hardly any** tea left.* ◇ *Hardly anyone has bothered to reply.* ◇ *She **hardly ever** calls me* (= almost never). ◇ *We hardly know each other.* ◇ ***Hardly a day goes by without** my thinking of her* (= I think of her almost every day). **2** 0‑ used especially after 'can' or 'could' and before the main verb, to emphasize that it is difficult to do sth: *I can hardly keep my eyes open* (= I'm almost falling asleep). ◇ *I **could hardly believe** it when I read the letter.* **3** 0‑ used to say that sth has just begun, happened, etc.: *We can't stop for coffee now, we've hardly started.* ◇ *We had hardly sat down to supper when the phone rang.* ◇ (*formal*) *Hardly had she spoken than she regretted it bitterly.* **4** 0‑ used to suggest that sth is unlikely or unreasonable or that sb is silly for saying or doing sth: *He is hardly likely to admit he was wrong.* ◇ *It's **hardly surprising** she was fired; she never did any work.* ◇ *It's **hardly the time** to discuss it now.* ◇ *You **can hardly** expect her to do it for free.* ◇ *'Couldn't you have just said no?' 'Well, hardly* (= of course not)*, she's my wife's sister.'* ➲ note at HARD

ˌhard-ˈnosed *adj.* not affected by feelings when trying to get what you want: *a hard-nosed journalist*

ˌhard of ˈhearing *adj.* [not before noun] **1** unable to hear very well **2 the hard of hearing** *noun* [pl.] people who are unable to hear very well: *subtitles for the deaf and the hard of hearing*

ˈhard-on *noun* (*taboo, slang*) an ERECTION (1)

ˌhard ˈporn *noun* [U] (*informal*) films/movies, pictures, books, etc. that show sexual activity in a very detailed and sometimes violent way ➲ compare SOFT PORN

ˌhard-ˈpressed *adj.* **1** having a lot of problems, especially too much work, and too little time or money **2 ~ to do sth** finding sth very difficult to do: *You would be hard-pressed to find a better secretary.*

ˌhard ˈright *noun* [sing.+ sing./pl. v.] (*especially BrE*) the members of a RIGHT-WING political party who have the most extreme opinions: *hard-right opinions*

ˌhard ˈrock *noun* [U] a type of loud rock music with a very strong beat, played on electric GUITARS

ˌhard ˈscience *noun* **1** [U] science that is based on the objective measurement and observation of physical facts or events **2** [C] a science that involves the objective measurement and observation of physical facts or events, such as physics and chemistry

hard·scrab·ble /ˌhɑːdˈskræbl; *NAmE* ˌhɑːrd-/ *adj.* (*NAmE*) not having enough of the basic things you need to live: *a **hardscrabble life/upbringing***

ˌhard ˈsell *noun* [sing.] a method of selling that puts a lot of pressure on the customer to buy ➲ compare SOFT SELL

hard·ship /ˈhɑːdʃɪp; *NAmE* ˈhɑːrd-/ *noun* [U, C] a situation that is difficult and unpleasant because you do not have enough money, food, clothes, etc: ***economic/financial, etc. hardship*** ◇ *People suffered many hardships during that long winter.* ◇ *It was **no hardship** to walk home on such a lovely evening.*

ˌhard ˈshoulder (*BrE*) (*US* **ˈbreakdown lane**) *noun* [sing.] a strip of ground with a hard surface beside a major road such as a MOTORWAY or INTERSTATE where vehicles can stop in an emergency: *to pull over onto the hard shoulder/into the breakdown lane*

hard·top /ˈhɑːdtɒp; *NAmE* ˈhɑːrdtɑːp/ *noun* a car with a metal roof

ˌhard ˈup *adj.* (*informal*) **1** having very little money, especially for a short period of time ➲ note at POOR **2 ~ (for sth)** lacking in sth interesting to do, talk about, etc: *'You could always go out with Steve.' 'I'm not that hard up!'*

hard·ware /ˈhɑːdweə(r); *NAmE* ˈhɑːrdwer/ *noun* [U] **1** (*computing*) the machinery and electronic parts of a computer system ➲ compare SOFTWARE **2** (*BrE* also **iron·mon·gery**) tools and equipment that are used in the house and garden/yard: *a hardware shop* **3** the equipment, machinery and vehicles used to do sth: *tanks and other military hardware*

ˈhardware dealer *noun* (*NAmE*) **1** (*BrE* becoming *old-fashioned* **iron·mon·ger**) a person who owns or works in a shop/store selling tools and equipment for the house and garden/yard **2** (*BrE* **ironmonger's**) a shop that sells tools and equipment for the house and garden/yard

ˌhard-ˈwearing *adj.* (*BrE*) that lasts a long time and remains in good condition: *a hard-wearing carpet*

ˌhard-ˈwired *adj.* **1** (*technical*) (of computer functions) built into the permanent system and not provided by software **2** (of a skill, quality or type of behaviour) present when you are born and not changing during your life: *Many aspects of morality appear to be hard-wired in the brain.*

ˌhard-ˈwon *adj.* [usually before noun] that you only get after fighting or working hard for it: *She was not going to give up her hard-won freedom so easily.*

hard·wood /ˈhɑːdwʊd; *NAmE* ˈhɑːrd-/ *noun* [U, C] hard heavy wood from a BROADLEAVED tree ➲ compare SOFTWOOD

ˌhard-ˈworking *adj.* putting a lot of effort into a job and doing it well: *hard-working nurses*

hardy /ˈhɑːdi; *NAmE* ˈhɑːrdi/ *adj.* (**har·dier**, **har·di·est**) **1** strong and able to survive difficult conditions and bad weather: *a hardy breed of sheep* **2** (of a plant) that can live outside through the winter ▶ **hardi·ness** *noun* [U]

hare /heə(r); *NAmE* her/ *noun, verb*
■ ***noun*** an animal like a large RABBIT with very strong back legs, that can run very fast ➲ picture at RABBIT IDM see MAD
■ ***verb*** [I] **+ adv./prep.** (*BrE*) to run or go somewhere very fast

hare·bell /ˈheəbel; *NAmE* ˈherbel/ (*ScotE* **blue·bell**) *noun* a wild plant with delicate blue flowers shaped like bells

ˈhare-brained *adj.* (*informal*) crazy and unlikely to succeed: *a **hare-brained scheme/idea/theory***

Hare Krishna /ˌhɑːreɪ ˈkrɪʃnə; ˌhæri/ *noun* **1** [U] a religious group whose members wear orange ROBES and use the name of the Hindu god Krishna in their worship **2** [C] a member of this religious group

hare·lip /ˈheəlɪp; *NAmE* ˈherlɪp/ *noun* an old-fashioned and now offensive word for CLEFT LIP

harem /ˈhɑːriːm; -rəm; *NAmE* ˈhærəm/ *noun* **1** the women or wives belonging to a rich man, especially in some Muslim societies in the past **2** the separate part of a traditional Muslim house where the women live **3** (*technical*) a group of female animals that share the same male for reproducing

hari·cot /ˈhærɪkəʊ; *NAmE* -koʊ/ (also **ˌharicot ˈbean**) (both *BrE*) (*NAmE* **ˈnavy bean**) *noun* a type of small white BEAN that is usually dried before it is sold and then left in water before cooking

hark /hɑːk; *NAmE* hɑːrk/ *verb* [I] (*old use*) used only as an order to tell sb to listen
PHR V **ˈhark at sb** (*BrE, informal*) used only as an order to draw attention to sb who has just said sth stupid or who is showing too much pride: *Just hark at him! Who does he think he is?* **ˌhark ˈback (to sth)** **1** to remember or talk about sth that happened in the past: *She's always harking back to how things used to be.* **2** to remind you of, or to be like, sth in the past: *The newest styles hark back to the clothes of the Seventies.*

har·ken = HEARKEN

Har·le·quin /ˈhɑːləkwɪn; *NAmE* ˈhɑːrl-/ *noun* an amusing character in some traditional plays, who wears special brightly coloured clothes with a diamond pattern

Har·ley Street /ˈhɑːli striːt; *NAmE* ˈhɑːrli/ *noun* a street in central London in which many private doctors have their offices where they talk to and examine patients: *a Harley Street doctor*

har·lot /ˈhɑːlət; *NAmE* ˈhɑːrlət/ *noun* (*old use, disapproving*) a PROSTITUTE, or a woman who looks and behaves like one

harm 🔑 /hɑːm; *NAmE* hɑːrm/ *noun, verb*
■ ***noun*** 🔑 [U] damage or injury that is caused by a person or an event: *He would never frighten anyone or* **cause** *them* **any harm**. ◇ *He may look fierce, but he* **means no harm**. ◇ *The court case will* **do serious harm to** *my business.* ◇ *The accident could have been much worse; luckily* **no harm was done**. ◇ *Don't worry, we'll see that the children* **come to no harm**. ◇ *I can't say I like Mark very much, but I don't* **wish him any harm**. ◇ *Hard work* **never did anyone any harm**. ◇ *Look, we're just going out for a few drinks,* **where's the harm in that?** ◇ *The treatment they gave him did him* **more harm than good**.
IDM **it wouldn't do sb any harm (to do sth)** used to suggest that it would be a good idea for sb to do sth: *It wouldn't do you any harm to smarten yourself up.* **ˌno ˈharm done** (*informal*) used to tell sb not to worry because they have caused no serious damage or injury **out of harm's ˈway** in a safe place where sb/sth cannot be hurt or injured or do any damage to sb/sth **there is no harm in (sb's) doing sth** | **it does no harm (for sb) to do sth** used to tell sb that sth is a good idea and will not cause any problems: *He may say no, but there's no harm in asking.* ◇ *It does no harm to ask.*
■ ***verb*** 🔑 **~ sb/sth** to hurt or injure sb or to damage sth: *He would never harm anyone.* ◇ *Pollution can harm marine life.* ◇ *These revelations will harm her chances of winning the election.* IDM see FLY *n.*, HAIR ➲ SYNONYMS at DAMAGE

harm·ful 🔑 /ˈhɑːmfl; *NAmE* ˈhɑːrmfl/ *adj.* (rather *formal*) causing damage or injury to sb/sth, especially to a person's health or to the environment: *the harmful effects of alcohol* ◇ *the sun's harmful ultra-violet rays* ◇ *Many household products are potentially harmful.* ◇ **~ to sb/sth** *Fruit juices can be harmful to children's teeth.* ▸ **harm·fully** /-fəli/ *adv.* **harm·ful·ness** *noun* [U]

harm·less 🔑 /ˈhɑːmləs; *NAmE* ˈhɑːrm-/ *adj.* **1** 🔑 **~ (to sb/sth)** unable or unlikely to cause damage or harm: *The bacteria is harmless to humans.* **2** 🔑 unlikely to upset or offend anyone SYN **innocuous**: *It's just a bit of harmless fun.* ▸ **harm·less·ly** *adv.*: *The missile fell harmlessly into the sea.* **harm·less·ness** *noun* [U]

har·mon·ic /hɑːˈmɒnɪk; *NAmE* hɑːrˈmɑːn-/ *adj., noun*
■ ***adj.*** [usually before noun] (*music*) relating to the way notes are played or sung together to make a pleasing sound
■ ***noun*** [usually pl.] (*music*) **1** a note that sounds together with the main note being played and is higher and quieter than that note **2** a high quiet note that can be played on some instruments like the VIOLIN by touching the string very lightly

har·mon·ica /hɑːˈmɒnɪkə; *NAmE* hɑːrˈmɑːn-/ (*BrE* also **ˈmouth organ**) *noun* a small musical instrument that you hold near your mouth and play by blowing or sucking air through it ➲ VISUAL VOCAB page V30

har·mo·ni·ous /hɑːˈməʊniəs; *NAmE* hɑːrˈmoʊ-/ *adj.* **1** (of relationships, etc.) friendly, peaceful and without any disagreement **2** arranged together in a pleasing way so that each part goes well with the others SYN **pleasing**: *a harmonious combination of colours* **3** (of sounds) very pleasant when played or sung together ▸ **har·mo·ni·ous·ly** *adv.*: *They worked very harmoniously together.*

har·mo·nium /hɑːˈməʊniəm; *NAmE* hɑːrˈmoʊ-/ *noun* a musical instrument like a small organ. Air is forced through metal pipes to produce the sound and the different notes are played on the keyboard.

har·mon·ize (*BrE* also **-ise**) /ˈhɑːmənaɪz; *NAmE* ˈhɑːrm-/ *verb* **1** [I] **~ (with sth)** if two or more things **harmonize** with each other or one thing **harmonizes** with the other, the things go well together and produce an attractive result: *The new building does not harmonize with its surroundings.* **2** [T] **~ sth** to make systems or rules similar in different countries or organizations: *the need to harmonize tax levels across the European Union* **3** [I] **~ (with sb/sth)** to play or sing music that combines with the main tune to make a pleasing sound ▸ **har·mon·iza·tion, -isa·tion** /ˌhɑːmənaɪˈzeɪʃn; *NAmE* ˌhɑːrmənəˈz-/ *noun* [U, C]

har·mony /ˈhɑːməni; *NAmE* ˈhɑːrm-/ *noun* (*pl.* **-ies**) **1** [U] a state of peaceful existence and agreement: *the need to* **be in harmony with** *our environment* ◇ *to live together in perfect harmony* ◇ **social/racial harmony** ➲ compare DISCORD **2** [U, C] (*music*) the way in which different notes that are played or sung together combine to make a pleasing sound: *to sing in harmony* ◇ *to study four-part harmony* ◇ *passionate lyrics and stunning vocal harmonies* ➲ compare DISCORD **3** [C, U] a pleasing combination of related things: *the harmony of colour in nature*

har·ness /ˈhɑːnɪs; *NAmE* ˈhɑːrnɪs/ *noun, verb*
■ ***noun*** **1** a set of strips of leather and metal pieces that is put around a horse's head and body so that the horse can be controlled and fastened to a CARRIAGE, etc. **2** a set of strips of leather, etc. for fastening sth to a person's body or to keep them from moving off or falling: *a safety harness*
IDM **in ˈharness** (*BrE*) doing your normal work, especially after a rest or a holiday **in harness (with sb)** (*BrE*) working closely with sb in order to achieve sth
■ ***verb*** **1** to put a harness on a horse or other animal; to attach a horse or other animal to sth with a harness: **~ sth** *to harness a horse* ◇ **~ sth to sth** *We harnessed two ponies to the cart.* ◇ (*figurative*) *In some areas, the poor feel harnessed to their jobs.* **2 ~ sth** to control and use the force or strength of sth to produce power or to achieve sth: *attempts to harness the sun's rays as a source of energy* ◇ *We must harness the skill and creativity of our workforce.*

harp /hɑːp; *NAmE* hɑːrp/ *noun, verb*
■ ***noun*** a large musical instrument with strings stretched on a vertical frame, played with the fingers ➲ VISUAL VOCAB page V30 ➲ see also JEW'S HARP
■ ***verb***
PHR V **ˌharp ˈon (about sth)** | **ˈharp on sth** to keep talking about sth in a boring or annoying way

harp·ist /ˈhɑːpɪst; *NAmE* ˈhɑːrp-/ *noun* a person who plays the harp

har·poon /hɑːˈpuːn; *NAmE* hɑːrˈp-/ *noun, verb*
■ ***noun*** a weapon like a SPEAR that you can throw or fire from a gun and is used for catching large fish, WHALES, etc.
■ ***verb*** **~ sth** to hit sth with a harpoon

harp·si·chord /ˈhɑːpsɪkɔːd; *NAmE* ˈhɑːrpsɪkɔːrd/ *noun* an early type of musical instrument similar to a piano, but with strings that are PLUCKED (= pulled), not hit

harp·si·chord·ist /ˈhɑːpsɪkɔːdɪst; *NAmE* ˈhɑːrpsɪkɔːrd-/ *noun* a person who plays the harpsichord

harpy /ˈhɑːpi; *NAmE* ˈhɑːrpi/ *noun* (*pl.* **-ies**) **1** (in ancient Greek and Roman stories) a cruel creature with a woman's head and body and a bird's wings and feet **2** a cruel woman

har·ri·dan /ˈhærɪdən/ *noun* (*old-fashioned* or *literary*) a bad-tempered unpleasant woman

har·rier /ˈhæriə(r)/ *noun* a BIRD OF PREY (= a bird that kills other creatures for food) of the HAWK family

har·row /ˈhærəʊ; *NAmE* -roʊ/ *noun* a piece of farming equipment that is pulled over land that has been PLOUGHED to break up the earth before planting ▸ **har·row** *verb* **~ sth**

har·row·ing /ˈhærəʊɪŋ; *NAmE* -roʊ-/ *adj.* very shocking or frightening and making you feel very upset

har·rumph /həˈrʌmf/ *verb* [I] (*informal*) to express disagreement or disapproval, especially by making a sound in your throat like a cough ▸ **har·rumph** *noun* [sing.]

harry /ˈhæri/ *verb* (**har·ries, harry·ing, har·ried, har·ried**) (*formal*) **1 ~ sb** to annoy or upset sb by continuously asking them questions or for sth SYN **harass**: *She has been harried by the press all week.* **2 ~ sb/sth** to make repeated attacks on an enemy SYN **harass**

harsh /hɑːʃ; *NAmE* hɑːrʃ/ *adj.* (**harsh·er, harsh·est**) **1** cruel, severe and unkind: *The punishment was harsh and unfair.* ◇ *The minister received some* **harsh criticism**. ◇ *the harsh treatment of slaves* ◇ *He regretted his harsh words.* ◇ *We had to face up to the* **harsh realities** *of life sooner or* later. **2** (of weather or living conditions) very difficult and unpleasant to live in: *a **harsh winter/wind/climate** ◇ the harsh conditions of poverty which existed for most people at that time* **3** too strong and bright; ugly or unpleasant to look at: *harsh colours ◇ She was caught in the harsh glare of the headlights. ◇ the harsh lines of concrete buildings* OPP **soft** **4** unpleasant to listen to: *a harsh voice* **5** too strong and rough and likely to damage sth: *harsh detergents* ▶ **harsh·ly** *adv.*: *She was treated very harshly. ◇ Alec laughed harshly.* **harsh·ness** *noun* [U]

hart /hɑːt; *NAmE* hɑːrt/ *noun* a male DEER, especially a RED DEER; a STAG ➲ compare BUCK, HIND

harum-scarum /ˌheərəm ˈskeərəm; *NAmE* ˌherəm ˈskerəm; ˌhærəm ˈskærəm/ *adj.* (*old-fashioned*) behaving in a wild and sometimes careless way

har·vest /ˈhɑːvɪst; *NAmE* ˈhɑːrv-/ *noun, verb*

■ ***noun*** **1** [C, U] the time of year when the crops are gathered in on a farm, etc; the act of cutting and gathering crops: *harvest time ◇ Farmers are extremely busy during the harvest.* **2** [C] the crops, or the amount of crops, cut and gathered: *the grain harvest ◇ a **good/bad harvest*** (= a lot of crops or few crops) ◇ (*figurative*) *The appeal produced a rich harvest of blankets, medicines and clothing.* IDM see REAP

■ ***verb*** **1** [I, T] **~ (sth)** to cut and gather a crop; to catch a number of animals or fish to eat ➲ COLLOCATIONS at FARMING **2** [T] **~ sth** (*medical*) to collect cells or TISSUE from sb's body for use in medical experiments or operations: *She had her eggs harvested and frozen for her own future use.*

har·vest·er /ˈhɑːvɪstə(r); *NAmE* ˈhɑːrv-/ *noun* **1** a machine that cuts and gathers grain ➲ see also COMBINE HARVESTER **2** (*old-fashioned*) a person who helps to gather in the crops

ˌharvest ˈfestival *noun* a service held in Christian churches when people thank God for the crops that have been gathered ➲ compare THANKSGIVING

ˌharvest ˈmoon *noun* [sing.] a full moon in the autumn/fall nearest the time when day and night are of equal length ➲ compare FULL MOON, HALF-MOON

has /həz; əz; *strong form* hæz/ ➲ HAVE

has-been /ˈhæz biːn/ *noun* (*informal, disapproving*) a person who is no longer as famous, successful or important as they used to be

hash /hæʃ/ *noun, verb*

■ ***noun*** **1** [U, C] a hot dish of cooked meat and potatoes that are cut into small pieces and mixed together **2** [U] (*informal*) = HASHISH **3** (also **ˈhash sign**) (both *BrE*) (*NAmE* **ˈpound sign**) [C] the symbol (#), especially one on a telephone

IDM **make a ˈhash of sth** (*informal*) to do sth badly: *I made a real hash of the interview.*

■ ***verb***

PHR V **ˌhash sth↔ˈout** (*informal, especially NAmE*) to discuss sth thoroughly in order to reach an agreement or decide sth

ˌhash ˈbrowns *noun* [pl.] (*NAmE*) a dish of chopped potatoes and onions, fried until they are brown

hash·ish /ˈhæʃiːʃ; hæˈʃiːʃ/ (also *informal* **hash**) *noun* [U] a drug made from the RESIN of the HEMP plant, which gives a feeling of being relaxed when it is smoked or chewed. Use of the drug is illegal in many countries. SYN **cannabis**

Has·id·ism (also **Has·sid·ism**) /ˈhæsɪdɪzəm/ *noun* [U] a form of the Jewish religion which has very strict beliefs ▶ **Hasid** (also **Has·sid**) /ˈhæsɪd/ *noun* **Has·id·ic** (also **Has·sid·ic**) /hæˈsɪdɪk/ *adj.*

hasn't /ˈhæznt/ *short form* has not

hasp /hɑːsp; *NAmE* hæsp/ *noun* a flat piece of metal with a long narrow hole in it, used with a PADLOCK to fasten doors, boxes, etc.

Has·sid·ism = HASIDISM

has·sium /ˈhæsiəm/ *noun* [U] (*symb.* **Hs**) a chemical element. Hassium is produced when atoms COLLIDE (= crash into each other).

has·sle /ˈhæsl/ *noun, verb*

■ ***noun*** [C, U] (*informal*) **1** a situation that is annoying because it involves doing sth difficult or complicated that needs a lot of effort: *Send them an email—it's a lot less hassle than phoning. ◇ legal hassles* **2** a situation in which people disagree, argue or annoy you: *Do as you're told and don't give me any hassle!*

■ ***verb* ~ sb (for sth/to do sth)** (*informal*) to annoy sb or cause them trouble, especially by asking them to do sth many times SYN **bother**: *Don't keep hassling me! I'll do it later.*

has·sock /ˈhæsək/ *noun* **1** a thick firm CUSHION on which you rest your knees when saying prayers in a church **2** (*NAmE*) (*BrE* **pouffe**) a large thick CUSHION used as a seat or for resting your feet on

hast /hæst/ **thou hast** (*old use*) a way of saying 'you have'

haste /heɪst/ *noun* [U] (*formal*) speed in doing sth, especially because you do not have enough time SYN **hurry**: *In her haste to complete the work on time, she made a number of mistakes. ◇ The letter had clearly been written **in haste**. ◇ After his first wife died, he married again with almost indecent haste. ◇* (*old-fashioned*) *She **made haste** to open the door.*

H

IDM **ˌmore ˈhaste, ˌless ˈspeed** (*BrE, saying*) you will finish doing sth sooner if you do not try to do it too quickly because you will make fewer mistakes ➲ more at MARRY

has·ten /ˈheɪsn/ *verb* **1** [I] **~ to do sth** to say or do sth without delay: *She saw his frown and hastened to explain. ◇ He has been described as a 'charmless bore'—not by me, I **hasten to add**.* **2** [T] **~ sth** (*formal*) to make sth happen sooner or more quickly: *The treatment she received may, in fact, have hastened her death. ◇ News of the scandal certainly hastened his departure from office.* **3** [I] **+ adv./prep.** (*literary*) to go or move somewhere quickly SYN **hurry**

hasty /ˈheɪsti/ *adj.* (**hasti·er, hasti·est**) **1** said, made or done very quickly, especially when this has bad results SYN **hurried**: *a hasty departure/meal/farewell ◇ Let's not make any hasty decisions.* **2 ~ in doing sth** (of a person) acting or deciding too quickly, without enough thought: *Perhaps I was too hasty in rejecting his offer.* IDM see BEAT *v.* ▶ **hasti·ly** /-ɪli/ *adv.*: *Perhaps I spoke too hastily. ◇ She hastily changed the subject.*

hat 0‑w /hæt/ *noun*

1 0‑w a covering made to fit the head, often with a BRIM, (= a flat edge that sticks out) and worn out of doors: *a **straw/woolly, etc. hat** ◇ to **put on/take off a hat*** ➲ VISUAL VOCAB page V53 **2** (*informal*) a position or role, especially an official or professional role, when you have more than one such role: *I'm wearing two hats tonight—parent and teacher. ◇ I'm telling you this with my lawyer's hat on, you understand.* ➲ see also OLD HAT

IDM **go hat in ˈhand (to sb)** (*NAmE*) (*BrE* **go cap in ˈhand (to sb)**) to ask sb for sth, especially money, in a very polite way that makes you seem less important **keep sth under your ˈhat** (*informal*) to keep sth secret and not tell anyone else **ˌmy ˈhat** (*old-fashioned, BrE*) used to express surprise **out of a/the ˈhat** if sth such as a name is picked **out of a/the hat**, it is picked at RANDOM from a container into which all the names are put, so that each name has an equal chance of being picked, in a competition, etc. **I take my ˈhat off to sb | hats off to sb** (both *especially BrE*) (*NAmE* usually **I tip my ˈhat to sb**) (*informal*) used to say that you admire sb very much for sth they have done **throw your ˈhat into the ring** to announce officially that you are going to compete in an election, a competition, etc. ➲ more at DROP *n.*, EAT, KNOCK *v.*, PASS *v.*, PULL *v.*, TALK *v.*

hat·band /ˈhætbænd/ *noun* a band of cloth placed around a hat as decoration

hat·box /ˈhætbɒks; *NAmE* -bɑːks/ *noun* a round box used for keeping a hat in, to stop it from being crushed or damaged

hatch /hætʃ/ *verb, noun*

■ ***verb*** **1** [I] **~ (out)** (of a young bird, fish, insect, etc.) to come out of an egg: *Ten chicks hatched (out) this morning.* **2** [I] **~ (out)** (of an egg) to break open so that a young bird, fish, insect, etc. can come out: *The eggs are about to hatch.*

➲ COLLOCATIONS at LIFE **3** [T] **~ sth** to make a young bird, fish, insect, etc. come out of an egg: *The female must find a warm place to hatch her eggs.* **4** [T] **~ sth (up)** to create a plan or an idea, especially in secret: *Have you been hatching up a deal with her?* IDM see COUNT *v.*

▪ ***noun*** **1** (also **hatch·way**) an opening or a door in the DECK of a ship or the bottom of an aircraft, through which goods to be carried are passed **2** an opening in a wall between two rooms, especially a kitchen and a DINING ROOM, through which food can be passed: *a serving hatch* **3** a door in an aircraft or a SPACECRAFT: *an escape hatch* **4** an opening or a door in a floor or ceiling: *a hatch to the attic*

IDM ˌ**down the ˈhatch** (*informal, saying*) used before drinking sth, especially to express good wishes before drinking alcohol ➲ more at BATTEN

hatch·back /ˈhætʃbæk/ *noun* a car with a sloping door at the back that opens upwards ➲ VISUAL VOCAB page V42

hatch·ery /ˈhætʃəri/ *noun* (*pl.* -ies) a place for HATCHING eggs as part of a business: *a trout hatchery*

hatchet /ˈhætʃɪt/ *noun* a small AXE (= a tool with a heavy blade for chopping things) with a short handle ➲ picture at AXE IDM see BURY

ˈ**hatchet-faced** *adj.* (*disapproving*) (of a person) having a long thin face and sharp features

ˈ**hatchet job** *noun* [usually sing.] **~ (on sb/sth)** (*informal*) strong criticism that is often unfair and is intended to harm sb/sth: *The press did a very effective hatchet job on her last movie.*

ˈ**hatchet man** *noun* (*informal*) a person employed by an organization to make changes that are not popular with the other people who work there

hatch·ling /ˈhætʃlɪŋ/ *noun* a baby bird or animal which has just come out of its shell

hatch·way /ˈhætʃweɪ/ *noun* = HATCH *n.* (1)

hate 🔑 /heɪt/ *verb, noun*

▪ ***verb*** (not used in the progressive tenses) **1** 🔑 to dislike sth very much: **~ sth** *I hate spinach.* ◇ *I hate Monday mornings.* ◇ *I **hate it** when people cry.* ◇ *He **hated it** in France* (= did not like the life there). ◇ *I **hate the way** she always criticizes me.* ◇ **~ doing sth** *She hates making mistakes.* ◇ **~ to do sth** *He hated to be away from his family.* ◇ *She's a person who hates to make mistakes.* ◇ *I **hate to think** what would have happened if you hadn't been there.* ◇ **~ sb/sth doing sth** *He hates anyone parking in his space.* ◇ **~ sb/sth to do sth** *She would have hated him to see how her hands shook.* ◇ *I'd hate anything to happen to him.* **2** 🔑 to dislike sb very much: **~ sb/yourself** *The two boys hated each other.* ◇ *He was her most hated enemy.* ◇ **~ sb/yourself for sth/for doing sth** *I hated myself for feeling jealous.* **3** [no passive] **~ to do sth** used when saying sth that you would prefer not to have to say, or when politely asking to do sth: ***I hate to say it**, but I don't think their marriage will last.* ◇ *I hate to trouble you, but could I use your phone?* ▸ **hater** *noun*: *I'm not a woman hater, I just don't like Joan.*

IDM **hate sb's ˈguts** (*informal*) to dislike sb very much

▪ ***noun*** **1** 🔑 [U] a very strong feeling of dislike for sb SYN **hatred**: *a look of hate* ◇ *a hate campaign* (= cruel comments made about sb over a period of time in order to damage their reputation) ◇ ***hate mail*** (= letters containing cruel comments) **2** [C] (*informal*) a person or thing that you hate: *Plastic flowers have always been a particular hate of mine.* IDM see PET *adj.*

Which Word?

hate / hatred

- These two words have a similar meaning. **Hatred** is more often used to describe a very strong feeling of dislike for a particular person or thing: *Her deep hatred of her sister was obvious.* ◇ *a cat's hatred of water.* **Hate** is more often used when you are talking about this feeling in a general way: *a look of pure hate* ◇ *people filled with hate.*

Synonyms

hate

dislike • can't stand • despise • can't bear • loathe • detest

These words all mean to have a strong feeling of dislike for sb/sth.

hate to have a strong feeling of dislike for sb/sth. NOTE Although **hate** is generally a very strong verb, it is also commonly used in spoken or informal English to talk about people or things that you dislike in a less important way, for example a particular type of food: *He hates violence in any form.* ◇ *I've always hated cabbage.*

dislike (*rather formal*) to not like sb/sth. NOTE **Dislike** is a rather formal word; it is less formal, and more usual, to say that you *don't like* sb/sth, especially in spoken English: *I don't like it when you phone me so late at night.*

can't stand (*rather informal*) used to emphasize that you really do not like sb/sth: *I can't stand his brother.* ◇ *She couldn't stand being kept waiting.*

despise to dislike and have no respect for sb/sth: *He despised himself for being so cowardly.*

can't bear used to say that you dislike sth so much that you cannot accept or deal with it: *I can't bear having cats in the house.*

CAN'T STAND OR CAN'T BEAR?

In many cases you can use either word, but **can't bear** is slightly stronger and slightly more formal than **can't stand**.

loathe to hate sb/sth very much: *They loathe each other.* NOTE **Loathe** is generally an even stronger verb than **hate**, but it can also be used more informally to talk about less important things, meaning 'really don't like': *Whether you **love or loathe** their music, you can't deny their talent.*

detest (*rather formal*) to hate sb/sth very much: *They absolutely detest each other.*

PATTERNS

- I hate/dislike/can't stand/can't bear/loathe/detest **doing sth**.
- I hate/can't bear **to do sth**.
- I hate/dislike/can't stand/can't bear **it when...**
- I **really** hate/dislike/can't stand/despise/can't bear/detest sb/sth
- I **absolutely** hate/can't stand/loathe/detest sb/sth

ˈ**hate crime** *noun* **1** [U] violent acts that are committed against people because they are of a different race, because they are HOMOSEXUAL, etc. **2** [C] a single act of this type: *the victim of a hate crime*

hate·ful /ˈheɪtfl/ *adj.* very unkind or unpleasant: *a hateful person/place/face* ◇ **~ to sb** *The idea of fighting against men of their own race was hateful to them.*

hath /hæθ/ (*old use*) = HAS

hat·pin /ˈhætpɪn/ *noun* a long pin used for fastening a hat to your hair, especially in the past

hat·red 🔑 /ˈheɪtrɪd/ *noun* [U, C] a very strong feeling of dislike for sb/sth: *He looked at me with intense hatred.* ◇ *There was fear and hatred in his voice.* ◇ **~ (for/of sb/sth)** *She felt nothing but hatred for her attacker.* ◇ *a profound hatred of war* ◇ **~ (towards sb)** *feelings of hatred towards the bombers* ◇ *racial hatred* (= between people from different races) ◇ *The debate simply revived old hatreds.* ➲ note at HATE

hat·stand /ˈhætstænd/ *noun* a vertical pole with large hooks around the top, for hanging hats and coats on

hat·ter /ˈhætə(r)/ *noun* (*old-fashioned*) a person who makes and sells hats IDM see MAD

ˈhat-trick *noun* three points, goals, etc. scored by the same player in a particular match or game; three successes achieved by one person: *to score a hat-trick*

haughty /ˈhɔːti/ *adj.* (**haught·ier**, **haught·iest**) behaving in an unfriendly way towards other people because you think that you are better than them **SYN arrogant**: *a **haughty face/look/manner*** ◇ *He replied with haughty disdain.* ▶ **haught·ily** /-ɪli/ *adv.* **haughti·ness** *noun* [U]

haul /hɔːl/ *verb, noun*

■ ***verb*** **1** to pull sth/sb with a lot of effort: **~ sth/sb** *The wagons were hauled by horses.* ◇ **~ sth/sb + adv./prep.** *He reached down and hauled Liz up onto the wall.* ➲ SYNONYMS at PULL **2 ~ yourself up/out of, etc.** to move yourself somewhere slowly and with a lot of effort: *She hauled herself out of bed.* **3 ~ sb + adv./prep.** to force sb to go somewhere they do not want to go: *A number of suspects have been hauled in for questioning.* **4** [usually passive] **~ sb (up) before sb/sth** to make sb appear in court in order to be judged: *He was hauled up before the local magistrates for dangerous driving.*

IDM haul sb over the ˈcoals (*BrE*) (*NAmE* **rake sb over the ˈcoals**) to criticize sb severely because they have done sth wrong

■ ***noun*** **1** a large amount of sth that has been stolen or that is illegal: *a haul of weapons* ◇ *a drugs haul* **2** (especially in sport) a large number of points, goals, etc: *His haul of 40 goals in a season is a record.* **3** [usually sing.] the distance covered in a particular journey: *They began the long slow haul to the summit.* ◇ *Our camp is only a short haul from here.* ◇ *Take the coast road—it'll be less of a haul* (= an easier journey). ➲ see also LONG HAUL, SHORT-HAUL **4** a quantity of fish caught at one time

haul·age /ˈhɔːlɪdʒ/ *noun* [U] (*BrE*) the business of transporting goods by road or railway; money charged for this: *the road haulage industry* ◇ *a **haulage firm/contractor*** ◇ *How much is haulage?*

haul·ier /ˈhɔːliə(r)/ (*BrE*) (*NAmE* **haul·er** /ˈhɔːlə(r)/) *noun* a person or company whose business is transporting goods by road or railway/railroad

haunch /hɔːntʃ/ *noun* **1 haunches** [pl.] the tops of the legs and BUTTOCKS; the similar parts at the back of the body of an animal that has four legs: *to crouch/squat **on your haunches*** **2** [C] a back leg and LOIN of an animal that has four legs, eaten as food: *a haunch of venison*

haunt /hɔːnt/ *verb, noun*

■ ***verb*** **1 ~ sth/sb** if the GHOST of a dead person **haunts** a place, people say that they have seen it there: *A headless rider haunts the country lanes.* **2 ~ sb** if sth unpleasant **haunts** you, it keeps coming to your mind so that you cannot forget it: *The memory of that day still haunts me.* ◇ *For years she was haunted by guilt.* **3 ~ sb** to continue to cause problems for sb for a long time: *That decision **came back to haunt him**.*

■ ***noun*** a place that sb visits often or where they spend a lot of time: *The pub is a favourite haunt of artists.*

haunt·ed /ˈhɔːntɪd/ *adj.* **1** (of a building) believed to be visited by GHOSTS: *a haunted house* **2** (of an expression on sb's face) showing that sb is very worried: *There was a haunted look in his eyes.*

haunt·ing /ˈhɔːntɪŋ/ *adj.* beautiful, sad or frightening in a way that cannot be forgotten: *a **haunting melody/experience/image*** ▶ **haunt·ing·ly** *adv.*

Hausa /ˈhaʊsə; -zə/ *noun* [U] a language spoken by the Hausa people of W Africa, especially in Nigeria and Niger, and also used in other parts of W Africa as a language of communication between different peoples

haute cou·ture /ˌəʊt kuˈtjʊə(r); *NAmE* ˌoʊt kuˈtʊr/ *noun* [U] (from *French*) the business of making fashionable and expensive clothes for women; the clothes made in this business

haute cuis·ine /ˌəʊt kwɪˈziːn; *NAmE* ˌoʊt/ *noun* [U] (from *French*) cooking of a very high standard

haut·eur /əʊˈtɜː(r); *NAmE* hɔːˈtɜːr; oʊˈt-/ *noun* [U] (*formal*) an unfriendly way of behaving towards other people suggesting that you think that you are better than they are

have 🔑 /həv; əv; *strong form* hæv/ *verb, auxiliary verb*
➲ IRREGULAR VERBS

■ ***verb*** (In some senses **have got** is also used, especially in British English.)

▸ OWN/HOLD **1** 🔑 (also **have got**) **~ sth** (not used in the progressive tenses) to own, hold or possess sth: *He had a new car and a boat.* ◇ *Have you got a job yet?* ◇ *I don't have that much money on me.* ◇ *She's got a BA in English.*

▸ CONSIST OF **2** 🔑 (also **have got**) **~ sth** (not used in the progressive tenses) be made up of: *In 2008 the party had 10 000 members.*

▸ QUALITY/FEATURE **3** 🔑 (also **have got**) (not used in the progressive tenses) to show a quality or feature: **~ sth** *The ham had a smoky flavour.* ◇ *The house has gas-fired central heating.* ◇ *They have a lot of courage.* ◇ **~ sth + adj.** *He's got a front tooth missing.* **4** 🔑 (also **have got**) **~ sth to do sth** (not used in the progressive tenses) to show a particular quality by your actions: *Surely she didn't have the nerve to say that to him?*

▸ RELATIONSHIP **5** 🔑 (also **have got**) **~ sb/sth** (not used in the progressive tenses) used to show a particular relationship: *He's got three children.* ◇ *Do you have a client named Peters?*

▸ STH AVAILABLE **6** 🔑 (also **have got**) **~ sth** (not used in the progressive tenses) to be able to make use of sth because it is available: *Have you got time to call him?* ◇ *We have no choice in the matter.*

▸ SHOULD/MUST **7** 🔑 (also **have got**) **~ sth** (not used in the progressive tenses) to be in a position where you ought to do sth: *We have a duty to care for the refugees.* **8** 🔑 (also **have got**) (not used in the progressive tenses) to be in a position of needing to do sth: **~ sth** *I've got a lot of homework tonight.* ◇ **~ sth to do** *I must go—I have a bus to catch.*

▸ HOLD **9** 🔑 (also **have got**) (not used in the progressive tenses) **~ sb/sth + adv./prep.** to hold sb/sth in the way mentioned: *She'd got him by the collar.* ◇ *He had his head in his hands.*

▸ PUT/KEEP IN A POSITION **10** 🔑 (also **have got**) **~ sth + adv./prep.** (not used in the progressive tenses) to place or keep sth in a particular position: *Mary had her back to me.* ◇ *I soon had the fish in a net.*

▸ FEELING/THOUGHT **11** 🔑 (also **have got**) (not used in the progressive tenses) **~ sth** to let a feeling or thought come into your mind: *He had the strong impression that someone was watching him.* ◇ *We've got a few ideas for the title.* ◇ (*informal*) ***I've got it!** We'll call it 'Word Magic'.*

▸ ILLNESS **12** 🔑 (also **have got**) **~ sth** (not used in the progressive tenses) to suffer from an illness or a disease: *I've got a headache.*

▸ EXPERIENCE **13** 🔑 **~ sth** to experience sth: *I went to a few parties and had a good time.* ◇ *I was having difficulty in staying awake.* ◇ *She'll have an accident one day.*

▸ EVENT **14** 🔑 **~ sth** to organize or hold an event: *Let's have a party.*

▸ EAT/DRINK/SMOKE **15** 🔑 **~ sth** to eat, drink or smoke sth: *to **have breakfast/lunch/dinner*** ◇ *I'll have the salmon* (= for example, in a restaurant). ◇ *I had a cigarette while I was waiting.*

▸ DO STH **16** 🔑 **~ sth** to perform a particular action: *I had a swim to cool down.* ◇ (*BrE*) *to **have a wash/shower/bath***

▸ GIVE BIRTH **17** 🔑 **~ sb/sth** to give birth to sb/sth: *She's going to have a baby.*

▸ EFFECT **18** 🔑 **~ sth** to produce a particular effect: *His paintings had a strong influence on me as a student.* ◇ *The colour green has a restful effect.*

▸ RECEIVE **19** 🔑 **~ sth** (not usually used in the progressive tenses) to receive sth from sb: *I had a letter from my brother this morning.* ◇ ***Can I have the bill**, please?* **20** 🔑 **~ sth** to be given sth; to have sth done to you: *I'm having treatment for my back problem.* ◇ *How many driving lessons have you had so far?* **21** 🔑 (also **have got**) (not used in the progressive tenses) **~ sth doing sth** to experience the effects of sb's actions: *We have orders coming in from all over the world.*

▸ HAVE STH DONE **22** 🔑 (used with a past participle) **~ sth done** to suffer the effects of what sb else does to you: *She*

H

had her bag stolen. **23** (used with a past participle) **~ sth done** to cause sth to be done for you by sb else: *You've had your hair cut!* ◇ *We're having our car repaired.* **24** to tell or arrange for sb to do sth for you: **~ sb do sth** *He had the bouncers throw them out of the club.* ◇ (*informal*) ***I'll have you know*** (= I'm telling you) *I'm a black belt in judo.* ◇ **~ sb + adv./prep.** *She's always having the builders in to do something or other.*

▸ ALLOW **25** (used in negative sentences, especially after *will not, cannot*, etc.) to allow sth; to accept sth without complaining: **~ sth** *I'm sick of your rudeness—I won't have it any longer!* ◇ **~ sb/sth doing sth** *We can't have people arriving late all the time.*

▸ PUT SB/STH IN A CONDITION **26** to cause sb/sth to be in a particular state; to make sb react in a particular way: **~ sb/sth + adj.** *I want to have everything ready in good time.* ◇ **~ sb/sth doing sth** *He had his audience listening attentively.*

▸ IN ARGUMENT **27** (also **have got**) **~ sb** (*informal*) (not used in the progressive tenses) to put sb at a disadvantage in an argument: ***You've got me there.*** *I hadn't thought of that.*

▸ SEX **28 ~ sb** (*slang*) to have sex with sb: *He had her in his office.*

▸ TRICK **29** [usually passive] **~ sb** (*informal*) to trick or cheat sb: *I'm afraid you've been had.*

▸ GUESTS **30** [no passive] **~ sb/sth** to take care of sb/sth in your home, especially for a limited period: *We're having the kids for the weekend.* **31** [no passive] **~ sb + adv./prep.** to entertain sb in your home: *We had some friends to dinner last night.*

▸ BE WITH **32** (also **have got**) **~ sb with you** (not used in the progressive tenses) to be with sb: *She had some friends with her.*

▸ FOR A JOB **33** [no passive] **~ sb as sth** to take or accept sb for a particular role: *Who can we have as treasurer?*

IDM Most idioms containing **have** are at the entries for the nouns and adjectives in the idioms, for example **have your eye on sb** is at **eye** *n.* **have 'done with sth** (*especially BrE*) to finish sth unpleasant so that it does not continue: *Let's have done with this silly argument.* **have 'had it** (*informal*) **1** to be in a very bad condition; to be unable to be repaired: *The car had had it.* **2** to be extremely tired: *I've had it! I'm going to bed.* **3** to have lost all chance of surviving sth: *When the truck smashed into me, I thought I'd had it.* **4** to be going to experience sth unpleasant: *Dad saw you scratch the car—you've had it now!* **5** to be unable to accept a situation any longer: ***I've had it (up to here) with him***—*he's done it once too often.* **have it 'off/a'way (with sb)** (*BrE, slang*) to have sex with sb **'have it (that...)** to claim that it is a fact that...: ***Rumour has it*** *that we'll have a new manager soon.* **have (got) it/that 'coming (to you)** to be likely to suffer the unpleasant effects of your actions and to deserve to do so: *It was no surprise when she left him—everyone knew he had it coming to him.* **have it 'in for sb** (*informal*) to not like sb and be unpleasant to them **have it 'in you (to do sth)** (*informal*) to be capable of doing sth: *Everyone thinks he has it in him to produce a literary classic.* ◇ *You were great. I didn't know you had it in you.* **have (got) 'nothing on sb/sth** (*informal*) to be not nearly as good as sb/sth ➲ see also HAVE STH ON SB **not 'having any** (*informal*) not willing to listen to or believe sth: *I tried to persuade her to wait but she wasn't having any.* **what 'have you** (*informal*) other things, people, etc. of the same kind: *There's room in the cellar to store old furniture and what have you.*

PHR V **,have (got) sth a'gainst sb/sth** (not used in the progressive tenses) to dislike sb/sth for a particular reason: *What have you got against Ruth? She's always been good to you.* **,have sb↔'back** to allow a husband, wife or partner that you are separated from to return **,have sth 'back** to receive sth that sb has borrowed or taken from you: *You can have your files back after we've checked them.* **,have (got) sth 'in** (not used in the progressive tenses) to have a supply of sth in your home, etc: *Have we got enough food in?* **,have sb 'on** (*informal*) to try to make sb believe sth that is not true, usually as a joke: *You didn't really, did you? You're not having me on, are you?* **,have (got) sth 'on** (not used in the progressive tenses) **1** to be wearing sth: *She had a red jacket on.* ◇ *He had nothing* (= no clothes) *on.* **2** to leave a piece of equipment working: *She has her TV on all day.* **3** to have arranged to do sth: *I can't see you this week—I've got a lot on.* **,have (got) sth 'on sb** [no passive] (*informal*) (not used in the progressive tenses) to know sth bad about sb, especially sth that connects them with a crime: *I'm not worried—they've got nothing on me.* **,have sth 'out** to cause sth, especially a part of your body, to be removed: *I had to have my appendix out.* **,have sth 'out (with sb)** to try to settle a disagreement by discussing or arguing about it openly: *I need to have it out with her once and for all.* **,have sb 'up (for sth)** (*BrE, informal*) [usually passive] to cause sb to be accused of sth in court: *He was had up for manslaughter.*

■ ***auxiliary verb*** used with the past participle to form perfect tenses: *I've finished my work.* ◇ *He's gone home, hasn't he?* ◇ *'Have you seen it?' 'Yes, I have/No, I haven't.'* ◇ *She'll have had the results by now.* ◇ *Had they left before you got there?* ◇ *If I hadn't seen it with my own eyes I wouldn't have believed it.* ◇ (*formal*) *Had I known that* (= if I had known that) *I would never have come.*

British/American

have you got? / do you have?

- **Have got** is the usual verb in *BrE* to show possession, etc. in positive statements in the present tense, in negative statements and in questions: *They've got a wonderful house.* ◇ *We haven't got a television.* ◇ *Have you got a meeting today?* Questions and negative statements formed with **do** are also common: *Do you have any brothers and sisters?* ◇ *We don't have a car.*
- **Have** is also used but is more formal: *I have no objection to your request.* ◇ *Have you an appointment?* Some expressions with **have** are common even in informal language: *I'm sorry, I haven't a clue.*
- In the past tense **had** is used in positive statements. In negatives and questions, forms with **did have** are usually used: *They had a wonderful house.* ◇ *We didn't have much time.* ◇ *Did she have her husband with her?*
- In *NAmE* **have** and forms with **do/does/did** are the usual way to show possession, etc. in positive statements, negatives and questions: *They have a wonderful house.* ◇ *We don't have a television.* ◇ *Do you have a meeting today?* **Have got** is not used in questions, but is used in positive statements, especially to emphasize that somebody has one thing rather than another: *'Does your brother have brown hair?' 'No, he's got blond hair.'*
- In both *BrE* and *NAmE* **have** and forms with **do/does** and **did** are used when you are referring to a habit or routine: *We don't often have time to talk.*

haven /ˈheɪvn/ *noun* a place that is safe and peaceful where people or animals are protected: *The hotel is a haven of peace and tranquility.* ◇ *The river banks are a haven for wildlife.* ➲ see also SAFE HAVEN, TAX HAVEN

the ,have-'nots *noun* [pl.] people who do not have money and possessions ➲ compare THE HAVES

haven't /ˈhævnt/ *short form* have not

hav·er·sack /ˈhævəsæk; *NAmE* -vərs-/ *noun* (*old-fashioned, BrE*) a bag that is carried on the back or over the shoulder, especially when walking in the country

the 'haves *noun* [pl.] people who have enough money and possessions: *the division between the haves and the have-nots* ➲ compare THE HAVE-NOTS

have to /ˈhæv tə; ˈhæf/ *modal verb* (**has to** /ˈhæz tə; ˈhæs/, **had to, had to** /ˈhæd tə; ˈhæt/)
1 (also **have got to**) used to show that you must do sth: *Sorry, I've got to go.* ◇ *Did she have to pay a fine?* ◇ *You don't have to knock—just walk in.* ◇ *I haven't got to leave till seven.* ◇ *First, you have to think logically about your fears.* ◇ ***I have to admit****, the idea of marriage scares me.* ◇ *Do you have to go?* ◇ (*especially BrE*) *Have you got to go?* **2** (also

have got to especially in *BrE*) used to give advice or recommend sth: *You simply have to get a new job.* ◇ *You've got to try this recipe—it's delicious.* **3** 0‑m (also **have got to** especially in *BrE*) used to say that sth must be true or must happen: *There has to be a reason for his strange behaviour.* ◇ *This war has got to end soon.* **4** used to suggest that an annoying event happens in order to annoy you, or that sb does sth in order to annoy you: *Of course, it had to start raining as soon as we got to the beach.* ◇ ***Do you have to*** *hum so loudly?* (= it is annoying) ➲ note at MODAL, MUST

havoc /ˈhævək/ *noun* [U] a situation in which there is a lot of damage, destruction or confusion: *The floods caused havoc throughout the area.* ◇ *Continuing strikes are beginning to* ***play havoc with*** *the national economy.* ◇ *These insects can* ***wreak havoc on*** *crops.*

haw /hɔː/ *verb* IDM see HUM *v.*

Ha·wai·ian shirt /həˌwaɪən ˈʃɜːt; *NAmE* ˈʃɜːrt/ (also **aˈloha shirt**) *noun* a loose cotton shirt with a brightly coloured pattern and short sleeves

hawk /hɔːk/ *noun, verb*

■ ***noun* 1** a strong fast BIRD OF PREY (= a bird that kills other creatures for food): *He waited,* ***watching her like a hawk*** (= watching her very closely). ➲ see also SPARROWHAWK **2** a person, especially a politician, who supports the use of military force to solve problems OPP **dove**

IDM see EYE *n.*

■ ***verb* 1** [T] **~ sth** to try to sell things by going from place to place asking people to buy them SYN **peddle** **2** [I, T] **~ (sth)** to get PHLEGM in your mouth when you cough

hawk·er /ˈhɔːkə(r)/ *noun* a person who makes money by hawking goods

ˌhawk-ˈeyed *adj.* (of a person) watching closely and carefully and noticing small details SYN **eagle-eyed**

hawk·ish /ˈhɔːkɪʃ/ *adj.* preferring to use military action rather than peaceful discussion in order to solve a political problem OPP **dovish**

haw·ser /ˈhɔːzə(r)/ *noun* (*technical*) a thick rope or steel cable used on a ship

haw·thorn /ˈhɔːθɔːn; *NAmE* -θɔːrn/ *noun* [U, C] a bush or small tree with THORNS, white or pink flowers and small dark red BERRIES

hay /heɪ/ *noun* [U] **1** grass that has been cut and dried and is used as food for animals: *a bale of hay* ➲ compare STRAW ➲ VISUAL VOCAB page V2 **2** (*NAmE, informal*) a small amount of money

IDM **make hay while the ˈsun shines** (*saying*) to make good use of opportunities, good conditions, etc. while they last ➲ more at HIT *v.*, ROLL *n.*

ˈhay fever *noun* [U] an illness that affects the nose, eyes and throat and is caused by POLLEN from plants that is breathed in from the air

hay·loft /ˈheɪlɒft; *NAmE* -lɔːft/ *noun* a place at the top of a farm building used for storing HAY

hay·mak·ing /ˈheɪmeɪkɪŋ/ *noun* [U] the process of cutting and drying grass to make HAY

hay·ride /ˈheɪraɪd/ *noun* (*NAmE*) a ride for pleasure on a CART filled with HAY, pulled by a horse or TRACTOR

hay·stack /ˈheɪstæk/ (also *less frequent* **hay·rick** /ˈheɪrɪk/) *noun* a large pile of HAY, used as a way of storing it until it is needed IDM see NEEDLE *n.* ➲ VISUAL VOCAB page V2

hay·wire /ˈheɪwaɪə(r)/ *adj.*

IDM **go ˈhaywire** (*informal*) to stop working correctly or become out of control: *After that, things started to go haywire.*

haz·ard /ˈhæzəd; *NAmE* -ərd/ *noun, verb*

■ ***noun*** a thing that can be dangerous or cause damage: *a* ***fire/safety hazard*** ◇ **~ (to sb/sth)** *Growing levels of pollution represent a serious* ***health hazard*** *to the local population.* ◇ **~ (of sth/of doing sth)** *Everybody is aware of the hazards of smoking.* ◇ ***hazard lights*** (= flashing lights on a car that warn other drivers of possible danger)

■ ***verb* 1** to make a suggestion or guess which you know may be wrong: **~ sth** *Would you like to* ***hazard a guess?*** ◇ **+ speech** *'Is it Tom you're going with?' she hazarded.* ◇ **~ that...** *I would hazard that she is the sole reason we are here.* **2 ~ sth** (*formal*) to risk sth or put it in danger SYN **endanger**: *Careless drivers hazard other people's lives as well as their own.*

haz·ard·ous /ˈhæzədəs; *NAmE* -ərdəs/ *adj.* involving risk or danger, especially to sb's health or safety: ***hazardous waste/chemicals*** ◇ *a hazardous journey* ◇ *It would be hazardous to invest so much.* ◇ *a list of products that are potentially hazardous to health*

ˈhazard pay (also **ˈdanger pay**) (both *US*) (*BrE* **ˈdanger money**) *noun* [U] extra pay for doing work that is dangerous

haze /heɪz/ *noun, verb*

■ ***noun* 1** [C, U] air that is difficult to see through because it contains very small drops of water, especially caused by hot weather: *a heat haze* **2** [sing.] air containing sth that makes it difficult to see through it: *a* ***haze of smoke/dust/steam*** **3** [sing.] a mental state in which your thoughts, feelings, etc. are not clear: *an alcoholic haze*

■ ***verb* 1** [I, T] **~ (sth)** to become covered or to cover sth in a HAZE **2 ~ sb** (*NAmE*) to play tricks on sb, especially a new student, or to give them very unpleasant things to do, sometimes as a condition for entering a FRATERNITY or SORORITY

hazel /ˈheɪzl/ *noun, adj.*

■ ***noun*** [C, U] a small tree that produces small nuts (called hazelnuts) that can be eaten

■ ***adj.*** (of eyes) greenish-brown or reddish-brown in colour

hazel·nut /ˈheɪzlnʌt/ (also **fil·bert** especially in *NAmE*) *noun* the small brown nut of the HAZEL tree ➲ VISUAL VOCAB page V28

hazy /ˈheɪzi/ *adj.* (**hazi·er, hazi·est**) **1** not clear because of HAZE: *a* ***hazy afternoon/sky*** ◇ ***hazy light/sunshine*** ◇ *The mountains were hazy in the distance.* **2** not clear because of a lack of memory, understanding or detail SYN **vague**: *a* ***hazy memory/idea*** ◇ *What happened next is all very hazy.* **3** (of a person) uncertain or confused about sth: *I'm a little hazy about what to do next.* ▸ **haz·ily** *adv.*: *'Why now?' she wondered hazily.*

ˈH-bomb *noun* = HYDROGEN BOMB

HCF /ˌeɪtʃ siː ˈef/ *abbr.* (*mathematics*) HIGHEST COMMON FACTOR

HCFC /ˌeɪtʃ siː ef ˈsiː/ *noun* (*chemistry*) the abbreviation for 'hydrochlorofluorocarbon' (a type of gas used especially in AEROSOLS (= types of container that release liquid in the form of a spray) instead of CFC, as it is less harmful to the layer of the gas OZONE in the earth's atmosphere)

HD /ˌeɪtʃ ˈdiː/ *abbr.* high-definition (used of television, film or video images that are extremely high quality, with very clear, sharp outlines and details): *The film was shot in HD.*

HDTV /ˌeɪtʃ diː tiː ˈviː/ *noun* [U] (*technical*) the abbreviation for 'high definition television' (technology that produces extremely clear images on a television screen)

HE (*BrE*) (also **H.E.** *US, BrE*) *abbr.* **1** Her/His EXCELLENCY: *HE the Australian Ambassador* **2** HIGHER EDUCATION

he 0‑m /hi; iː; i; *strong form* hiː/ *pron., noun*

■ ***pron.*** (used as the subject of a verb) **1** 0‑m a male person or animal that has already been mentioned or is easily identified: *Everyone liked my father—he was the perfect gentleman.* ◇ *He* (= the man we are watching) *went through that door.* **2** (becoming *old-fashioned*) a person, male or female, whose sex is not stated or known, especially when referring to sb mentioned earlier or to a group in general: *Every child needs to know that he is loved.* ◇ (*saying*) *He who* (= anyone who) *hesitates is lost.* ➲ note at GENDER **3 He** used when referring to God ➲ compare HIM

■ ***noun*** /hiː/ **1** [sing.] (*informal*) a male: *What a nice dog—is it a he or a she?* **2 he-** (in compound nouns) a male animal: *a he-goat*

head 0‑m /hed/ *noun, verb*

■ ***noun***

▸ PART OF BODY **1** 0‑m [C] the part of the body on top of the neck containing the eyes, nose, mouth and brain: *She* ***nodded her head*** *in agreement.* ◇ *He* ***shook his head*** *in disbelief.* ◇ *The boys* ***hung their heads*** *in shame.* ◇ *The driver suffered head injuries.* ◇ *She always* ***has her head in a book*** (= is always reading). ◇ *He still has* ***a good head of hair*** (= a lot of hair). ➲ COLLOCATIONS at PHYSICAL ➲ VISUAL VOCAB page V48 ➲ see also DEATH'S HEAD

▸ MIND **2** 🔑 [C] the mind or brain: *I sometimes wonder what goes on in that head of yours.* ◇ *I wish you'd* ***use your head*** (= think carefully before doing or saying sth). ◇ *The thought* ***never entered my head.*** ◇ *I can't work it out* ***in my head****—I need a calculator.* ◇ *I* ***can't get*** *that tune* ***out of my head.*** ◇ *When will you* ***get it into your head*** (= understand) *that I don't want to discuss this any more!* ◇ *For some reason, she's* ***got it into her head*** (= believes) *that the others don't like her.* ◇ *Who's been* ***putting*** *such weird ideas* ***into your head*** (= making you believe that)? ◇ *Try to* ***put*** *the exams* ***out of your head*** (= stop thinking about them) *for tonight.* ➲ see also HOTHEAD

H

▸ MEASUREMENT **3 a head** [sing.] the size of a person's or animal's head, used as a measurement of distance or height: *She's a good head taller than her sister.* ◇ *The favourite won* ***by a short head*** (= a distance slightly less than the length of a horse's head).

▸ PAIN **4** [C, usually sing.] (*informal*) a continuous pain in your head SYN **headache**: *I woke up with a really bad head this morning.*

▸ OF GROUP/ORGANIZATION **5** 🔑 [C, U] the person in charge of a group of people or an organization: *the* ***heads of government/state*** ◇ *She resigned as* ***head of department.*** ◇ *the* ***crowned heads*** (= the kings and queens) *of Europe* ◇ *the* ***head gardener/waiter, etc.*** ◇ (*BrE*) *the* ***head boy/girl*** (= a student who is chosen to represent the school)

▸ OF SCHOOL/COLLEGE **6** [C] (often **Head**) (*BrE*) the person in charge of a school or college SYN **headmaster, headmistress, head teacher**: *I've been called in to see the Head.* ◇ *the deputy head*

▸ SIDE OF COIN **7 heads** [U] the side of a coin that has a picture of the head of a person on it, used as one choice when a coin is TOSSED to decide sth ➲ compare TAILS *n.* (7)

▸ END OF OBJECT **8** [C, usually sing.] **~ (of sth)** the end of a long narrow object that is larger or wider than the rest of it: *the head of a nail* ➲ VISUAL VOCAB page V17 ➲ see also BEDHEAD

▸ TOP **9** [sing.] **~ of sth** the top or highest part of sth: *at the head of the page* ◇ *They finished the season at the head of their league.*

▸ OF RIVER **10** [sing.] **the ~ of the river** the place where a river begins SYN **source**

▸ OF TABLE **11** [sing.] **the ~ of the table** the most important seat at a table: *The President sat at the head of the table.*

▸ OF LINE OF PEOPLE **12** [sing.] **the ~ of sth** the position at the front of a line of people: *The prince rode at the head of his regiment.*

▸ OF PLANT **13** [C] **~ (of sth)** the mass of leaves or flowers at the end of a STEM: *Remove the dead heads to encourage new growth.*

▸ ON BEER **14** [sing.] the mass of small bubbles on the top of a glass of beer

▸ OF SPOT **15** [C] the part of a spot on your skin that contains a thick yellowish liquid (=PUS) ➲ see also BLACKHEAD

▸ IN TAPE/VIDEO RECORDER **16** [C] the part of a TAPE RECORDER or VIDEO RECORDER that touches the tape and changes the electrical signals into sounds and/or pictures

▸ NUMBER OF ANIMALS **17 ~ of sth** [pl.] used to say how many animals of a particular type are on a farm, in a HERD, etc.: *200 head of sheep*

▸ OF STEAM **18 a ~ of steam** [sing.] the pressure produced by steam in a confined space

▸ SEX **19** [U] (*taboo, slang*) ORAL sex (= using the mouth to give sb sexual pleasure): *to give head*

▸ LINGUISTICS **20** [C] the central part of a phrase, which has the same GRAMMATICAL function as the whole phrase. In the phrase 'the tall man in a suit', *man* is the head.

IDM **a/per 'head** 🔑 for each person: *The meal worked out at $20 a head.* **bang/knock your/their 'heads together** (*informal*) to force people to stop arguing and behave in a sensible way **be banging, etc. your head against a brick 'wall** (*informal*) to keep trying to do sth that will never be successful: *Trying to reason with them was like banging my head against a brick wall.* **be/stand head and 'shoulders above sb/sth** to be much better than other people or things **bite/snap sb's 'head off** (*informal*) to shout at sb in an angry way, especially without reason **bring sth to a 'head | come to a 'head** if you **bring** a situation **to a head** or if a situation **comes to a head**, you are forced to deal with it quickly because it suddenly becomes very bad **bury/hide your head in the 'sand** to refuse to admit that a problem exists or refuse to deal with it **can't make head nor 'tail of sth** to be unable to understand sth: *I couldn't make head nor tail of what he was saying.* **do sb's 'head in** (*BrE, informal*) to make you feel confused, upset and/or annoyed: *Shut up! You're doing my head in.* **do sth standing on your 'head** (*informal*) to be able to do sth very easily and without having to think too much **from ˌhead to 'foot/'toe** covering your whole body: *We were covered from head to foot in mud.* **get your 'head down** (*informal*) **1** (*BrE*) to sleep: *I managed to get my head down for an hour.* **2** = KEEP/GET YOUR HEAD DOWN **get your 'head round sth** (*BrE, informal*) to be able to understand or accept sth: *She's dead. I can't get my head round it yet.* **give sb their 'head** to allow sb to do what they want without trying to stop them **go head to 'head (with sb)** to deal with sb in a very direct and determined way **go to sb's 'head 1** (of alcohol) to make you feel drunk: *That glass of wine has gone straight to my head.* **2** (of success, praise, etc.) to make you feel too proud of yourself in a way that other people find annoying **have a good 'head on your shoulders** to be a sensible person **have a head for sth 1** to be good at sth: *to have* ***a head for figures/business*** **2** if sb does not **have a head for heights,** they feel nervous and think they are going to fall when they look down from a high place **have your head in the 'clouds 1** to be thinking about sth that is not connected with what you are doing **2** to have ideas, plans, etc. that are not realistic **have your 'head screwed on (the right way)** (*informal*) to be a sensible person **ˌhead 'first 1** moving forwards or downwards with your head in front of the rest of your body: *He fell head first down the stairs.* **2** without thinking carefully about sth before acting: *She got divorced and rushed head first into another marriage.* SYN **headlong** **head over heels in 'love** loving sb very much: *He's fallen head over heels in love with his boss.* **heads or 'tails?** used to ask sb which side of a coin they think will be facing upwards when it is TOSSED in order to decide sth by chance **'heads will roll (for sth)** (*informal, usually humorous*) used to say that some people will be punished because of sth that has happened **hold your 'head high | hold up your 'head** to be proud of or not feel ashamed about sth that you have done: *She managed to hold her head high and ignore what people were saying.* **in over your 'head** involved in sth that is too difficult for you to deal with: *After a week in the new job, I soon realized that I was in over my head.* **keep/get your 'head down** to avoid attracting attention to yourself **keep your 'head | keep a clear/cool 'head** to remain calm in a difficult situation **keep your 'head above water** to deal with a difficult situation, especially one in which you have financial problems, and just manage to survive **laugh, scream, etc. your 'head off** (*informal*) to laugh, etc. a lot and very loudly **lose your 'head** to become unable to act in a calm or sensible way **on your (own) head 'be it** used to tell sb that they will have to accept any unpleasant results of sth that they decide to do: *Tell him the truth if you want to, but on your own head be it!* **out of/off your 'head** (*BrE, informal*) **1** crazy **2** not knowing what you are saying or doing because of the effects of alcohol or drugs **over sb's 'head 1** too difficult or complicated for sb to understand: *A lot of the jokes went* (= were) *right over my head.* **2** to a higher position of authority than sb: *I couldn't help feeling jealous when she was promoted over my head.* **put our/your/their 'heads together** to think about or discuss sth as a group **stand/turn sth on its 'head** to make people think about sth in a completely different way **take it into your head to do sth** to suddenly decide to do sth, especially sth that other people think is stupid **take it into your head that ...** to suddenly start thinking sth, especially sth that other people think is stupid **turn sb's ˈhead** (of success, praise, etc.) to make a person feel too proud in a way that other people find annoying **two heads are better than ˈone** (*saying*) used to say that two people can achieve more than one person working alone ➲ more at BEAR *n.*, BLOCK *n.*, BOTHER *v.*, DRUM *v.*, EYE *n.*, GUN *n.*, HAIR, HEART, HIT *v.*, IDEA, KNOCK *v.*, LAUGH *v.*, NEED *v.*, OLD, PRICE *n.*, REAR *v.*, RING *v.*, ROOF *n.*, SCRATCH *v.*, THICK *adj.*, TOP *n.*

■ ***verb***

▸ MOVE TOWARDS **1** 🔑 [I] (also **be headed** especially in *NAmE*) + **adv./prep.** to move in a particular direction: *Where are we heading?* ◇ *Where are you two headed?* ◇ *Let's head back home.* ◇ *She headed for the door.* ◇ (*figurative*) *Can you forecast where the economy is heading?*

▸ GROUP/ORGANIZATION **2** 🔑 [T] **~ sth** (also **ˌhead sth↔ˈup**) to lead or be in charge of sth: *She has been appointed to head the research team.*

▸ LIST/LINE OF PEOPLE **3** [T] **~ sth** to be at the top of a list of names or at the front of a line of people: *Italy heads the table after two games.* ◇ *to **head a march/procession***

▸ BE AT TOP **4** [T, usually passive] **~ sth** to put a word or words at the top of a page or section of a book as a title: *The chapter was headed 'My Early Life'.*

▸ FOOTBALL **5** [T] **~ sth** to hit a football with your head: *Walsh headed the ball into an empty goal.*

PHR V **be ˈheading for sth** (also **be ˈheaded for sth** especially in *NAmE*) to be likely to experience sth bad: *They look as though they're heading for divorce.* **ˌhead sb↔ˈoff** to get in front of sb in order to make them turn back or change direction SYN **intercept**: *We'll head them off at the bridge!* **ˌhead sth↔ˈoff** to take action in order to prevent sth from happening: *He headed off efforts to replace him as leader.* **ˌhead sth↔ˈup** to lead or be in charge of a department, part of an organization, etc. ➲ see also HEAD *v.* (2)

-head /hed/ *suffix* (*informal*) (in nouns) a person who is very enthusiastic about a particular thing or is addicted to a particular drug: *The cybercafe was a nethead's dream.* ◇ *a gearhead* ◇ *a crackhead* ◇ *a smackhead* ◇ *a pothead*

head·ache 🔑 /ˈhedeɪk/ *noun*
1 🔑 a continuous pain in the head: *to suffer from headaches* ◇ *Red wine gives me a headache.* ◇ *I have **a splitting headache*** (= a very bad one). ➲ COLLOCATIONS at ILL **2** (*informal*) a person or thing that causes worry or trouble: *The real headache will be getting the bank to lend you the money.*

head·band /ˈhedbænd/ *noun* a strip of cloth worn around the head, especially to keep hair or sweat out of your eyes when playing sports

head·bang·er /ˈhedbæŋə(r)/ *noun* (*informal*) **1** a person who likes to shake their head violently up and down while listening to rock music **2** a stupid or crazy person ▸ **head·banging** *noun* [U]

head·board /ˈhedbɔːd; *NAmE* -bɔːrd/ *noun* the vertical board at the end of a bed where you put your head ➲ VISUAL VOCAB page V20

ˌhead ˈboy *noun* (in some British schools) the boy who is chosen each year to represent his school

head·butt /ˈhedbʌt/ *verb* **~ sb** (*especially BrE*) to deliberately hit sb hard with your head ▸ **head·butt** *noun*

head·case /ˈhedkeɪs/ *noun* (*BrE, informal*) a person who behaves in a strange way and who seems to be mentally ill

head·cheese /ˈhedtʃiːz/ (*NAmE*) (*BrE* **brawn**) *noun* [U] meat made from the head of a pig or CALF that has been boiled and pressed into a container, served cold in thin slices

head·count /ˈhedkaʊnt/ *noun* an act of counting the number of people who are at an event, employed by an organization, etc; the number of people that have been counted in this way: *to do a headcount* ◇ *What's the latest headcount?*

head·dress /ˈheddres/ *noun* a covering worn on the head on special occasions

head·ed /ˈhedɪd/ *adj.* **1** (of writing paper) having the name and address of a person, an organization, etc. printed at the top: *headed notepaper* **2 -headed** (in adjectives) having the type of head or number of heads mentioned: *a bald-headed man* ◇ *a three-headed monster* ➲ see also BIG-HEADED, CLEAR-HEADED, COOL-HEADED, EMPTY-HEADED, HARD-HEADED, LEVEL-HEADED, LIGHT-HEADED, PIG-HEADED, WRONG-HEADED

head·er /ˈhedə(r)/ *noun* **1** (in football (SOCCER)) an act of hitting the ball with your head **2** a line or block of text that is automatically added to the top of every page that is printed from a computer ➲ compare FOOTER

head·gear /ˈhedgɪə(r); *NAmE* -gɪr/ *noun* [U] anything worn on the head, for example a hat: *protective headgear*

ˌhead ˈgirl *noun* (in some British schools) the girl who is chosen each year to represent her school

head·hunt /ˈhedhʌnt/ *verb* **~ sb** to find sb who is suitable for a senior job and persuade them to leave their present job: *I was headhunted by a marketing agency.* ▸ **head·hunt·ing** *noun* [U]

head·hunt·er /ˈhedhʌntə(r)/ *noun* **1** a person whose job is to find people with the necessary skills to work for a particular company and to persuade them to join this company **2** a member of a people that collects the heads of the people they kill

head·ing /ˈhedɪŋ/ *noun* **1** a title printed at the top of a page or at the beginning of a section of a book: *chapter headings* **2** the subject of each section of a speech or piece of writing: *The company's aims can be grouped under three main headings.*

head·lamp /ˈhedlæmp/ *noun* (*especially BrE*) = HEADLIGHT

head·land /ˈhedlənd; -lænd/ *noun* a narrow piece of high land that sticks out from the coast into the sea SYN **promontory** ➲ VISUAL VOCAB page V4

head·less /ˈhedləs/ *adj.* [usually before noun] without a head: *a **headless body/corpse***

IDM **run around like a ˌheadless ˈchicken** to be very busy and active trying to do sth, but not very organized, with the result that you do not succeed

head·light /ˈhedlaɪt/ *noun* (also **head·lamp** especially in *BrE*) a large light, usually one of two, at the front of a vehicle; the BEAM from this light: *He dipped his headlights* (= directed the light downwards) *for the oncoming traffic.* ➲ VISUAL VOCAB page V42

head·line /ˈhedlaɪn/ *noun, verb*

■ ***noun*** **1** [C] the title of a newspaper article printed in large letters, especially at the top of the front page: *They ran the story under the headline 'Home at last!'.* ◇ *The scandal was in the headlines for several days.* ◇ *headline news* ➲ see also BANNER HEADLINE **2 the headlines** [pl.] a short summary of the most important items of news, read at the beginning of a news programme on the radio or television

IDM **grab/hit/make the ˈheadlines** to be an important item of news in newspapers or on the radio or television

■ ***verb*** **1** [T, usually passive] **~ sth + noun** to give a story or article a particular headline: *The story was headlined 'Back to the future.'* **2** [T, I] **~ (sth)** to be the main performer in a concert or show: *The concert is to be headlined by Steve Earle.*

head·lock /ˈhedlɒk; *NAmE* -lɑːk/ *noun* (in WRESTLING) a way of holding an opponent's head so that they cannot move: *He had him in a headlock.*

head·long /ˈhedlɒŋ; *NAmE* -lɔːŋ; -lɑːŋ/ *adv.* **1** with the head first and the rest of the body following SYN **head first**: *She **fell headlong** into the icy pool.* **2** without thinking carefully before doing sth: *The government is taking care not to **rush headlong into** another controversy.* **3** quickly and without looking where you are going: *He ran headlong into a police car.* ▸ **head·long** *adj.* [only before noun]: *a headlong dive/rush*

head·man /ˈhedmæn; -mən/ *noun* (*pl.* **-men** /-men; -mən/) the leader of a community SYN **chief**: *the village headman*

H

head·mas·ter /ˌhedˈmɑːstə(r); *NAmE* -ˈmæs-/, **head·mis·tress** /ˌhedˈmɪstrəs/ *noun* (*NAmE* usually **prin·ci·pal**) a teacher who is in charge of a school, especially a private school ➲ see also HEAD TEACHER

ˌhead ˈoffice *noun* [C, U+sing./pl. v.] the main office of a company; the managers who work there: *Their head office is in New York.* ◇ *I don't know what head office will think about this proposal.*

ˌhead of ˈstate *noun* (*pl.* **heads of state**) the official leader of a country who is sometimes also the leader of the government

ˌhead-ˈon *adj.* [only before noun] **1** in which the front part of one vehicle hits the front part of another vehicle: *a **head-on crash/collision*** **2** in which people express strong views and deal with sth in a direct way: *There was a **head-on confrontation** between management and unions.* ▸ **ˌhead-ˈon** *adv.*: *The cars **crashed head-on**.* ◇ *We hit the tree head-on.* ◇ *to **tackle a problem head-on*** (= without trying to avoid it)

head·phones /ˈhedfəʊnz; *NAmE* -foʊnz/ (also **ear·phones**) *noun* [pl.] a piece of equipment worn over or in the ears that makes it possible to listen to music, the radio, etc. without other people hearing it: *a **pair/set of headphones***

head·quar·tered /ˌhedˈkwɔːtəd; *NAmE* ˈhedkwɔːrtərd/ *adj.* [not before noun] having headquarters in a particular place: *News Corporation is headquartered in Sydney.*

head·quar·ters /ˌhedˈkwɔːtəz; *NAmE* ˈhedkwɔːrtərz/ *noun* [U+sing./pl. v., C] (*pl.* **head·quar·ters**) (*abbr.* **HQ**) a place from which an organization or a military operation is controlled; the people who work there: *The firm's headquarters is/are in London.* ◇ *Several companies have their headquarters in the area.* ◇ *I'm now based at headquarters.* ◇ *police headquarters* ◇ *Headquarters in Dublin has/have agreed.*

head·rest /ˈhedrest/ *noun* the part of a seat or chair that supports a person's head, especially on the front seat of a car ➲ VISUAL VOCAB page V42

head·room /ˈhedruːm; -rʊm/ *noun* [U] **1** the amount of space between the top of a vehicle and an object it drives under **2** the amount of space between the top of your head and the roof of a vehicle: *There's a lot of headroom for such a small car.*

ˈhead rush *noun* a thing or an experience that you find very exciting: *the physical head rush of being in love*

head·scarf /ˈhedskɑːf; *NAmE* -skɑːrf/ *noun* (*pl.* **head·scarves**) a square piece of cloth tied around the head by women or girls, usually with a knot under the chin

head·set /ˈhedset/ *noun* a pair of HEADPHONES, especially one with a MICROPHONE attached to it ➲ VISUAL VOCAB page V54

head·ship /ˈhedʃɪp/ *noun* **~** (**of sth**) **1** the position of being in charge of an organization: *the headship of the department* **2** (*BrE*) the position of being in charge of a school

head·stand /ˈhedstand/ *noun* a position in which a person has their head on the ground and their feet straight up in the air

ˌhead ˈstart *noun* [sing.] **~** (**on/over sb**) an advantage that sb already has before they start doing sth: *Being able to speak French gave her a head start over the other candidates.*

head·stone /ˈhedstəʊn; *NAmE* -stoʊn/ *noun* a piece of stone placed at one end of a grave, showing the name, etc. of the person buried there SYN **gravestone** ➲ compare TOMBSTONE

head·strong /ˈhedstrɒŋ; *NAmE* -strɔːŋ/ *adj.* (*disapproving*) a **headstrong** person is determined to do things their own way and refuses to listen to advice

ˈheads-up *noun* (*pl.* **heads-up** or **heads-ups**) **~** (**about sth**) (*especially NAmE*) a piece of information given in advance of sth or as advice: *Send everyone a heads-up about the changes well in advance.*

ˌhead ˈtable (*NAmE*) (*BrE* **ˌtop ˈtable**) *noun* the table at which the most important guests sit at a formal dinner

ˌhead ˈteacher *noun* (*BrE*) (*NAmE* **prin·ci·pal**) a teacher who is in charge of a school

ˌhead-to-ˈhead *adj.* [only before noun] in which two people or groups face each other directly in order to decide the result of a disagreement or competition: *a **head-to-head battle/clash/contest*** ▸ **ˌhead-to-ˈhead** *adv.*: *They are set to meet head-to-head in next week's final.*

head·waters /ˈhedwɔːtəz; *NAmE* -tərz/ *noun* [pl.] streams forming the source of a river

head·way /ˈhedweɪ/ *noun* [U]

IDM **make ˈheadway** to make progress, especially when this is slow or difficult: *We are making little headway with the negotiations.* ◇ *The boat was unable to make much headway against the tide.*

head·wind /ˈhedwɪnd/ *noun* a wind that is blowing towards a person or vehicle, so that it is blowing from the direction in which the person or vehicle is moving ➲ compare TAILWIND

head·word /ˈhedwɜːd; *NAmE* -wɜːrd/ *noun* (*technical*) a word that forms a HEADING in a dictionary, under which its meaning is explained

heady /ˈhedi/ *adj.* (**head·ier**, **headi·est**) **1** [usually before noun] having a strong effect on your senses; making you feel excited and confident SYN **intoxicating**: *the heady days of youth* ◇ *the heady scent of hot spices* ◇ *a heady mixture of desire and fear* ➲ SYNONYMS at EXCITING **2** [not before noun] (of a person) excited in a way that makes you do things without worrying about the possible results: *She felt heady with success.*

heal 0-w /hiːl/ *verb*

1 0-w [I, T] to become healthy again; to make sth healthy again: *It took a long time for the wounds to heal.* ◇ **~ up** *The cut healed up without leaving a scar.* ◇ **~ sth** *This will help to heal your cuts and scratches.* ◇ (*figurative*) *It was a chance to **heal the wounds** in the party* (= to repair the damage that had been done). **2** [T] **~ sb** (**of sth**) (*old use* or *formal*) to cure sb who is ill/sick; to make sb feel happy again: *the story of Jesus healing ten lepers of their disease* ◇ *I felt healed by his love.* **3** [T, I] **~** (**sth**) to put an end to sth or make sth easier to bear; to end or become easier to bear: *She was never able to heal the rift between herself and her father.* ◇ *The breach between them never really healed.*

heal·er /ˈhiːlə(r)/ *noun* **1** a person who cures people of illnesses and disease using natural powers rather than medicine: *a **faith/spiritual healer*** **2** something that makes a bad situation easier to deal with: *Time is a great healer.*

heal·ing /ˈhiːlɪŋ/ *noun* [U] the process of becoming or making sb/sth healthy again; the process of getting better after an emotional shock: *the healing process* ◇ *emotional healing* ➲ see also FAITH HEALING

health 0-w /helθ/ *noun* [U]

1 0-w the condition of a person's body or mind: *Exhaust fumes are bad for your health.* ◇ ***to be in poor/good/excellent/the best of health*** ◇ *Smoking can seriously **damage your health**.* ◇ ***mental health*** ➲ see also ILL HEALTH **2** 0-w the state of being physically and mentally healthy: *He was nursed back to health by his wife.* ◇ *She was glowing with health and clearly enjoying life.* ◇ *As long as you have your health, nothing else matters.* **3** 0-w the work of providing medical services: *All parties are promising to increase spending on health.* ◇ *the Health Minister* ◇ *the Department of Health* ◇ ***health insurance*** ◇ ***health and safety regulations*** (= laws that protect the health of people at work) **4** how successful sth is: *the health of your marriage/finances* IDM see CLEAN *adj.*, DRINK *v.*, PROPOSE, RUDE

ˈhealth care *noun* [U] the service of providing medical care: *the costs of health care for the elderly* ◇ ***health care workers/professionals***

ˈhealth centre (*BrE*) (*especially US* **ˈhealth ˌcenter**) *noun* a building where a group of doctors see their patients and where some local medical services have their offices

ˈhealth club *noun* (also **gym**) a private club where people go to do physical exercise in order to stay or become healthy and fit

ˈhealth farm *noun* (*especially BrE*) = HEALTH SPA

ˈhealth food *noun* [U, C, usually pl.] food that does not contain any artificial substances and is therefore thought to be good for your health

health·ful /ˈhelθfl/ *adj.* [usually before noun] (*formal* or *NAmE*) good for your health ▶ **health·ful·ly** *adv.*

ˈhealth service *noun* a public service providing medical care ➲ see also NATIONAL HEALTH SERVICE

ˈhealth spa (also **ˈhealth farm** especially in *BrE*) *noun* a place where people can stay for short periods of time in order to try to improve their health by eating special food, doing physical exercise, etc.

ˈhealth visitor *noun* (in Britain) a trained nurse whose job is to visit people in their homes, for example new parents, and give them advice on some areas of medical care

healthy 🔑 /ˈhelθi/ *adj.* (**health·ier**, **healthi·est**) **1** 🔑 having good health and not likely to become ill/sick: *a healthy child/animal/tree* ◇ ***Keep healthy** by eating well and exercising regularly.* OPP **unhealthy** ➲ SYNONYMS at WELL **2** 🔑 [usually before noun] good for your health: *a **healthy diet/climate/lifestyle*** OPP **unhealthy** **3** 🔑 [usually before noun] showing that you are in good health: *to have a healthy appetite* ◇ *a shampoo that keeps hair looking healthy* **4** normal and sensible: *The child showed a healthy curiosity.* ◇ *She has a healthy respect for her rival's talents.* ◇ *It's not healthy the way she clings to the past.* OPP **unhealthy** **5** successful and working well: *a healthy economy* ◇ *Your car doesn't sound very healthy.* **6** [usually before noun] large and showing success: *a healthy bank balance* ◇ *a healthy profit* ▶ **health·ily** *adv.*: *to eat healthily* **healthi·ness** *noun* [U]

heap /hiːp/ *noun, verb*

■ ***noun*** **1 ~ (of sth)** an untidy pile of sth: *The building was reduced to a heap of rubble.* ◇ *a compost heap* ◇ *His clothes lay **in a heap** on the floor.* ◇ *Worn-out car tyres were stacked **in heaps**.* ➲ see also SCRAPHEAP, SLAG HEAP **2** [usually pl.] (*informal*) a lot of sth: (*BrE*)*There's heaps of time before the plane leaves.* ◇ (*NAmE*)*I've got a heap of things to do.* **3** (*informal, humorous*) a car that is old and in bad condition

IDM **at the top/bottom of the ˈheap** high up/low down in the structure of an organization or a society: *These workers are at the bottom of the economic heap.* **collapse, fall, etc. in a ˈheap** to fall down heavily and not move **heaps ˈbetter, ˈmore, ˈolder, etc.** (*BrE, informal*) a lot better, etc: *Help yourself—there's heaps more.* ◇ *He looks heaps better than when I last saw him.*

■ ***verb*** **1 ~ sth (up)** to put things in an untidy pile: *Rocks were heaped up on the side of the road.* **2** to put a lot of sth in a pile on sth: **~ A on B** *She heaped food on my plate.* ◇ **~ B with A** *She heaped my plate with food.* **3** to give a lot of sth such as praise or criticism to sb: **~ A on B** *He **heaped praise** on his team.* ◇ **~ B with A** *He heaped his team with praise.*

IDM see SCORN *n.*

heap·ed /hiːpt/ (*especially BrE*) (*NAmE* usually **heap·ing**) *adj.* used to describe a spoon, etc. that has as much in it or on it as it can hold: *a heaped teaspoon of sugar* ◇ *heaping plates of scrambled eggs* ➲ compare LEVEL *adj.* (1)

hear 🔑 /hɪə(r); *NAmE* hɪr/ *verb* (**heard**, **heard** /hɜːd; *NAmE* hɜːrd/)

1 🔑 [I, T] (not used in the progressive tenses) to be aware of sounds with your ears: *I can't hear very well.* ◇ **~ sth/sb** *She heard footsteps behind her.* ◇ **~ sb/sth doing sth** *He could hear a dog barking.* ◇ **~ sb/sth do sth** *Did you hear him go out?* ◇ **~ what...** *Didn't you hear what I said?* ◇ **sb/sth is heard to do sth** *She has been heard to make threats to her former lover.* **2** 🔑 [T] (not used in the progressive tenses) to listen or pay attention to sb/sth: **~ sth** *Did you hear that play on the radio last night?* ◇ **~ sb/sth/yourself do sth** *Be quiet—**I can't hear myself think!*** (= it is so noisy that I can't think clearly) ◇ **~ what...** *We'd better hear what they have to say.* ◇ ***I hear what you're saying*** (= I have listened to your opinion), *but you're wrong.* **3** 🔑 [I, T] (not usually used in the progressive tenses) to be told about sth: *Haven't you heard? She resigned.* ◇ *'I'm getting married.' **'So I've heard.'*** ◇ *Things are going well **from what I hear**.* ◇ **~ about sb/sth** *I was sorry to hear about your accident.* ◇ *I've heard about people like you.* ◇ **~ sth** *We had heard nothing for weeks.* ◇ **~ (that)...** *I was surprised to hear (that) he was married.* ◇ *I hear you've been away this weekend.* ◇ **~ it said (that)...** *I've heard it said (that) they met in Italy.* ◇ **~ what, how, etc...** *Did you hear what happened?* **4** [T] **~ sth** to listen to and judge a case in court: *The appeal was heard in private.* ◇ *Today the jury began to hear the evidence.*

IDM **have you heard the one about...?** used to ask sb if they have heard a particular joke before **ˌhear! ˈhear!** used to show that you agree with or approve of what sb has just said, especially during a speech **hear ˈtell (of sth)** (*old-fashioned* or *formal*) to hear people talking about sth: *I've often heard tell of such things.* **I've heard it all beˈfore** (*informal*) used to say that you do not really believe sb's promises or excuses because they are the same ones you have heard before **let's hear it for...** (*informal*) used to say that sb/sth deserves praise: *Let's hear it for the teachers, for a change.* **not/never hear the ˈend of it** to keep being reminded of sth because sb is always talking to you about it: *If we don't get her a dog we'll never hear the end of it.* **you could hear a ˈpin drop** it was extremely quiet: *The audience was so quiet you could have heard a pin drop.* **(do) you ˈhear (me)?** (*informal*) used to tell sb in an angry way to pay attention and obey you: *You can't go—do you hear me?* ➲ more at LAST *n.*, THING, VOICE *n.*

PHR V **ˈhear from sb | ˈhear sth from sb** 🔑 to receive a letter, email, phone call, etc. from sb: *I look forward to hearing from you.* ◇ *I haven't heard anything from her for months.* **ˈhear of sb/sth | ˈhear sth of sb/sth** 🔑 to know about sb/sth because you have been told about them: *I've never heard of the place.* ◇ *She disappeared and was never heard of again.* ◇ ***The last I heard of** him he was living in Glasgow.* ◇ *This is **the first I've heard of** it!* **not ˈhear of sth** to refuse to let sb do sth, especially because you want to help them: *She wanted to walk home but I wouldn't hear of it.* ◇ **~ sb doing sth** *He wouldn't hear of my walking home alone* ➲ see also UNHEARD-OF **ˌhear sb ˈout** to listen until sb has finished saying what they want to say

hear·er /ˈhɪərə(r); *NAmE* ˈhɪr-/ *noun* a person who hears sth or who is listening to sb SYN **listener**

hear·ing 🔑 /ˈhɪərɪŋ; *NAmE* ˈhɪr-/ *noun*

1 🔑 [U] the ability to hear: *Her hearing is poor.* ◇ *He's **hearing-impaired*** (= not able to hear well). ➲ see also HARD OF HEARING **2** [C] an official meeting at which the facts about a crime, complaint, etc. are presented to the person or group of people who will have to decide what action to take: *a **court/disciplinary hearing*** ➲ COLLOCATIONS at JUSTICE **3** [sing.] an opportunity to explain your actions, ideas or opinions: *to get/give sb **a fair hearing*** ◇ *His views may be unfashionable but he deserves a hearing.*

IDM **in/within (sb's) ˈhearing** near enough to sb so that they can hear what is said SYN **within earshot**: *She shouldn't have said such things in your hearing.* ◇ *I had no reason to believe there was anyone within hearing.* **out of ˈhearing** too far away to hear sb/sth or to be heard: *She had moved out of hearing.*

ˈhearing aid *noun* a small device that fits inside the ear and makes sounds louder, used by people who cannot hear well: *to **have/wear a hearing aid***

ˈhearing dog *noun* a dog trained to make a deaf person (= person who cannot hear well) aware of sounds such as the ringing of a telephone or a DOORBELL

heark·en (also **hark·en**) /ˈhɑːkən; *NAmE* ˈhɑːrkən/ *verb* [I] **~ (to sb/sth)** (*old use*) to listen to sb/sth

hear·say /ˈhɪəseɪ; *NAmE* ˈhɪrseɪ/ *noun* [U] things that you have heard from another person but do not (definitely) know to be true: *We can't make a decision based on hearsay and guesswork.* ◇ *hearsay evidence*

hearse /hɜːs; *NAmE* hɜːrs/ *noun* a long vehicle used for carrying the coffin (= the box for the dead body) at a funeral

H

heart 🔑 /hɑːt; *NAmE* hɑːrt/ *noun*
▸ PART OF BODY **1** 🔑 [C] the organ in the chest that sends blood around the body, usually on the left in humans: *The patient's heart stopped beating for a few seconds.* ◇ ***heart trouble/failure*** ◇ *to have a weak heart* ◇ *I could feel my heart pounding in my chest* (= because of excitement, etc.). ➲ VISUAL VOCAB page V48 ➲ see also CORONARY HEART DISEASE, OPEN-HEART SURGERY **2** [C] (*literary*) the outside part of the chest where the heart is: *She clasped the photo to her heart.*
▸ FEELINGS/EMOTIONS **3** 🔑 [C] the place in a person where the feelings and emotions are thought to be, especially those connected with love: *She has a kind heart.* ◇ *Have you no heart?* ◇ *He returned with a* ***heavy heart*** (= sad). ◇ *Her novels tend to deal with* ***affairs of the heart***. ◇ *The story captured* ***the hearts and minds*** *of a generation.* ➲ see also BROKEN HEART
▸ -HEARTED **4** (in adjectives) having the type of character or personality mentioned: *cold-hearted* ◇ *kind-hearted*
▸ IMPORTANT PART **5** [sing.] **~ (of sth)** the most important part of sth: *the* ***heart of the matter/problem*** ◇ *The committee's report* ***went to the heart of*** *the government's dilemma.* ◇ *The distinction between right and wrong* ***lies at the heart of*** *all questions of morality.*
▸ CENTRE **6** [C, usually sing.] **~ (of sth)** the part that is in the centre of sth: *a quiet hotel* ***in the very heart of*** *the city*
▸ OF CABBAGE **7** [C] the smaller leaves in the middle of a CABBAGE, LETTUCE, etc.
▸ SHAPE **8** 🔑 [C] a thing shaped like a heart, often red and used as a symbol of love; a symbol shaped like a heart used to mean the verb 'love': *The words 'I love you' were written inside a big red heart.* ◇ (*informal*) *I ♥ New York.*
▸ IN CARD GAMES **9 hearts** [pl., U] one of the four sets of cards (called SUITS) in a PACK/DECK of cards, with red heart symbols on them: *the queen of hearts* ◇ *Hearts is/are trumps.* ➲ VISUAL VOCAB page V32 **10** [C] one card from the set of hearts: *Who played that heart?*

IDM **at 'heart** used to say what sb is really like even though they may seem to be sth different: *He's still a socialist at heart.* **break sb's 'heart** to make sb feel very unhappy: *She broke his heart when she called off the engagement.* ◇ *It breaks my heart to see you like this.* **by 'heart** 🔑 (*BrE* also **off by 'heart**) using only your memory: *I've dialled the number so many times I know it by heart.* ◇ *She's learnt the whole speech off by heart.* **close/dear/near to sb's 'heart** having a lot of importance and interest for sb **from the (bottom of your) 'heart** in a way that is sincere: *I beg you, from the bottom of my heart, to spare his life.* ◇ *It was clearly an offer that came from the heart.* **give sb (fresh) 'heart** to make sb feel positive, especially when they thought that they had no chance of achieving sth **give your 'heart to sb** to give your love to one person **have a 'heart!** (*informal*) used to ask sb to be kind and/or reasonable **have a heart of 'gold** to be a very kind person **have a heart of 'stone** to be a person who does not show others sympathy or pity **heart and 'soul** with a lot of energy and enthusiasm: *They threw themselves heart and soul into the project.* **your heart goes 'out to sb** used to say that you feel a lot of sympathy for sb: *Our hearts go out to the families of the victims.* **sb's heart is in their 'mouth** somebody feels nervous or frightened about sth **sb's heart is in the right 'place** used to say that sb's intentions are kind and sincere even though they sometimes do the wrong thing **your 'heart is not in sth** used to say that you are not very interested in or enthusiastic about sth **sb's heart 'leaps** used to say that sb has a sudden feeling of happiness or excitement **sb's heart misses a 'beat** used to say that sb has a sudden feeling of fear, excitement, etc. **sb's heart 'sinks** used to say that sb suddenly feels sad or depressed about sth: *My heart sank when I saw how much work there was left.* ◇ *She watched him go* ***with a sinking heart***. **in good 'heart** (*BrE*) happy and cheerful **in your 'heart (of 'hearts)** if you know sth **in your heart**, you have a strong feeling that it is true: *She knew in her heart of hearts that she was making the wrong decision.* **it does sb's 'heart good (to do sth)** it makes sb feel happy when they see or hear sth: *It does my heart good to see the old place being taken care of so well.* **let your ˌheart rule your 'head** to act according to what you feel rather than to what you think is sensible **lose 'heart** to stop hoping for sth or trying to do sth because you no longer feel confident **lose your 'heart (to sb/sth)** (*formal*) to fall in love with sb/sth **a man/woman after your own 'heart** a man/woman who likes the same things or has the same opinions as you **my heart 'bleeds (for sb)** (*ironic*) used to say that you do not feel sympathy or pity for sb: *'I have to go to Brazil on business.' 'My heart bleeds for you!'* **not have the 'heart (to do sth)** to be unable to do sth because you know that it will make sb sad or upset **off by 'heart** (*BrE*) = BY HEART **pour out/open your 'heart to sb** to tell sb all your problems, feelings, etc. **set your 'heart on sth | have your heart 'set on sth** to want sth very much **take 'heart (from sth)** to feel more positive about sth, especially when you thought that you had no chance of achieving sth: *The government can take heart from the latest opinion polls.* **take sth to 'heart** to be very upset by sth that sb says or does **ˌtear/ˌrip the 'heart out of sth** to destroy the most important part or aspect of sth **to your heart's con'tent** as much as you want: *a supervised play area where children can run around to their heart's content* **with all your 'heart/your whole 'heart** completely: *I hope with all my heart that things work out for you.* ➲ more at ABSENCE, CHANGE *n.*, CROSS *v.*, EAT, ETCH, EYE *n.*, FIND *v.*, GOODNESS, HOME *n.*, INTEREST *n.*, SICK *adj.*, SOB *v.*, STEAL *v.*, STRIKE *v.*, TEAR[1] *v.*, WARM *v.*, WAY *n.*, WEAR *v.*, WIN *v.*, YOUNG *adj.*

heart·ache /ˈhɑːteɪk; *NAmE* ˈhɑːrt-/ *noun* [U, C] a strong feeling of sadness or worry: *The relationship caused her a great deal of heartache.* ◇ *the heartaches of being a parent*

ˈheart attack *noun* a sudden serious medical condition in which the heart stops working normally, sometimes causing death ➲ COLLOCATIONS at ILL ➲ compare CORONARY THROMBOSIS

heart·beat /ˈhɑːtbiːt; *NAmE* ˈhɑːrt-/ *noun* **1** [C, U] the movement or sound of the heart as it sends blood around the body: *a* ***rapid/regular heartbeat*** **2** [sing.] **the ~ of sth** (*NAmE*) an important feature of sth, that is responsible for making it what it is: *The candidate said that he understood the heartbeat of the Hispanic community in California.*
IDM **a 'heartbeat away (from sth)** very close to sth **in a 'heartbeat** very quickly, without thinking about it: *If I was offered another job, I'd leave in a heartbeat.*

heart·break /ˈhɑːtbreɪk; *NAmE* ˈhɑːrt-/ *noun* [U, C] a strong feeling of sadness: *They suffered the heartbreak of losing a child through cancer.* ▸ **ˈheart·break·ing** *adj.*: *a heartbreaking story* ◇ *It's heartbreaking to see him wasting his life like this.*

heart·broken /ˈhɑːtbrəʊkən; *NAmE* ˈhɑːrtbroʊkən/ *adj.* extremely sad because of sth that has happened SYN **broken-hearted**

heart·burn /ˈhɑːtbɜːn; *NAmE* ˈhɑːrtbɜːrn/ *noun* [U] a pain that feels like sth burning in your chest caused by INDIGESTION

heart·en /ˈhɑːtn; *NAmE* ˈhɑːrtn/ *verb* [usually passive] **~ sb** to give sb encouragement or hope OPP **dishearten** ▸ **heart·en·ing** *adj.*: *It is heartening to see the determination of these young people.*

ˈheart failure *noun* [U] a serious medical condition in which the heart does not work correctly

heart·felt /ˈhɑːtfelt; *NAmE* ˈhɑːrt-/ *adj.* [usually before noun] showing strong feelings that are sincere SYN **sincere**: *a* ***heartfelt apology/plea/sigh*** ◇ ***heartfelt sympathy/thanks***

hearth /hɑːθ; *NAmE* hɑːrθ/ *noun* **1** the floor at the bottom of a FIREPLACE (= the space for a fire in the wall of a room); the area in front of this: *A log fire roared in the open hearth.* ◇ *The cat dozed in its favourite spot on the hearth.* ➲ VISUAL VOCAB page V18 **2** (*literary*) home and family life: *a longing for* ***hearth and home***

hearth·rug /ˈhɑːθrʌɡ; *NAmE* ˈhɑːrθ-/ *noun* a RUG (= a small carpet) placed on the floor in front of a FIREPLACE

heart·ily /ˈhɑːtɪli; *NAmE* ˈhɑːrt-/ *adv.* **1** with obvious enjoyment and enthusiasm: *to laugh/sing/eat heartily* **2** in a way that shows that you feel strongly about sth: *I heartily agree with her on this.* **3** extremely: *heartily glad/relieved*

heart·land /ˈhɑːtlænd; *NAmE* ˈhɑːrt-/ *noun* (also **heart·lands** [pl.]) **1** the central part of a country or an area: *the great Russian heartlands* **2** an area that is important for a particular activity or political party: *the industrial heartland of Germany* ◊ *the traditional Tory heartland of Britain's boardrooms*

heart·less /ˈhɑːtləs; *NAmE* ˈhɑːrt-/ *adj.* feeling no pity for other people SYN **cruel**: *What a heartless thing to say!* ▶ **heart·less·ly** *adv.* **heart·less·ness** *noun* [U]

ˌheart-ˈlung machine *noun* a machine that replaces the functions of the heart and lungs, for example during a medical operation on the heart

ˈheart-rending *adj.* [usually before noun] causing feelings of great sadness SYN **heartbreaking**: *a heart-rending story*

ˈheart-searching *noun* [U] the process of examining carefully your feelings or reasons for doing sth

heart·sick /ˈhɑːtsɪk; *NAmE* ˈhɑːrt-/ *adj.* [not usually before noun] (*literary*) extremely unhappy or disappointed

ˈheart-stopping *adj.* [usually before noun] causing feelings of great excitement or worry: *For one heart-stopping moment she thought they were too late.*

heart·strings /ˈhɑːtstrɪŋz; *NAmE* ˈhɑːrt-/ *noun* [pl.] strong feelings of love or pity: *to* ***tug/pull at sb's heartstrings*** (= to cause such feelings in sb)

ˈheart-throb *noun* (used especially in newspapers) a famous man, usually an actor or a singer, that a lot of women find attractive

ˌheart-to-ˈheart *noun* [usually sing.] a conversation in which two people talk honestly about their feelings and personal problems: *to have a heart-to-heart with sb* ▶ **ˌheart-to-ˈheart** *adj.*: *a heart-to-heart talk*

ˈheart-warming *adj.* causing feelings of happiness and pleasure

heart·wood /ˈhɑːtwʊd; *NAmE* ˈhɑːrt-/ *noun* [U] the hard older inner layers of the wood of a tree ➲ compare SAPWOOD

hearty /ˈhɑːti; *NAmE* ˈhɑːrti/ *adj., noun*

■ ***adj.*** (**heart·ier**, **hearti·est**) **1** [usually before noun] showing friendly feelings for sb: *a hearty welcome* **2** (sometimes *disapproving*) loud, cheerful and full of energy: *a hearty and boisterous fellow* ◊ *a hearty voice* **3** [only before noun] (of a meal or sb's APPETITE) large; making you feel full: *a hearty breakfast* ◊ *to have a hearty appetite* **4** [usually before noun] showing that you feel strongly about sth: *He nodded his head in hearty agreement.* ◊ *Hearty congratulations to everyone involved.* ◊ *a hearty dislike of sth* IDM see HALE ▶ **hearti·ness** *noun* [U]

■ ***noun*** (*pl.* -ies) (*BrE*, sometimes *disapproving*) a person who is loud, cheerful and full of energy, especially one who plays a lot of sport

heat 🔑 /hiːt/ *noun, verb*

■ ***noun***

▸ BEING HOT/TEMPERATURE **1** 🔑 [U, sing.] the quality of being hot: *He could feel the heat of the sun on his back.* ◊ *Heat rises.* ◊ *The fire gave out a fierce heat.* ➲ see also WHITE HEAT **2** 🔑 [U, C, usually sing.] the level of temperature: *to* ***increase/reduce the heat*** ◊ *Test the heat of the water before getting in.* ◊ *Set the oven to a* ***low/high/moderate*** *heat.* ➲ see also BLOOD HEAT **3** 🔑 [U] hot weather; the hot conditions in a building/vehicle, etc: *You should not go out in* ***the heat of the day*** (= at the hottest time). ◊ *to suffer from the heat* ◊ *the* ***afternoon/midday heat*** ◊ *The heat in the factory was unbearable.* ➲ see also PRICKLY HEAT

▸ FOR COOKING **4** 🔑 [U] a source of heat, especially one that you cook food on: *Return the pan to the heat and stir.*

▸ IN BUILDING/ROOM **5** 🔑 [U] (*especially NAmE*) = HEATING: *The heat wasn't on and the house was freezing.*

▸ STRONG FEELINGS **6** [U] strong feelings, especially of anger or excitement: *'No, I won't,' he said with heat in his voice.* ◊ *The chairman tried to take the heat out of the situation* (= to make people calmer). ◊ ***In the heat of the moment*** *she forgot what she wanted to say* (= because she was so angry or excited). ◊ *In the heat of the argument he said a lot of things he regretted later.*

▸ PRESSURE **7** [U] pressure on sb to do or achieve sth: ***The heat is on*** *now that the election is only a week away.* ◊ *United turned up the heat on their opponents with a second goal.* ◊ *Can she* ***take the heat*** *of this level of competition?*

▸ RACE **8** [C] one of a series of races or competitions, the winners of which then compete against each other in the next part of the competition: *a qualifying heat* ◊ *She won her heat.* ◊ *He did well in* ***the heats;*** *hopefully he'll do as well in the final.* ➲ see also DEAD HEAT

IDM **be on ˈheat** (*BrE*) (*NAmE* **be in ˈheat**) (of a female MAMMAL) to be in a sexual condition ready to reproduce **if you can't stand the ˈheat (get out of the ˈkitchen)** (*informal*) used to tell sb to stop trying to do sth if they find it too difficult, especially in order to suggest that they are less able than other people

■ ***verb*** 🔑 [T, I] **~ (sth)** to make sth hot or warm; to become hot or warm: *Heat the oil and add the onions.* ◊ *The system produced enough energy to heat several thousand homes.* ➲ COLLOCATIONS at COOKING

PHR V **ˌheat ˈup 1** 🔑 to become hot or warm SYN **warm up**: *The oven takes a while to heat up.* **2** (*especially NAmE*) (*BrE* also **ˌhot ˈup**) to become more exciting or to show an increase in activity: *The election contest is heating up.* **ˌheat sth↔ˈup** 🔑 to make sth hot or warm SYN **warm up**: *Just heat up the food in the microwave.*

heat·ed /ˈhiːtɪd/ *adj.* **1** (of a person or discussion) full of anger and excitement: *a* ***heated argument/debate*** ◊ *She became very heated.* **2** (of a room, building, etc.) made warmer using a heater: *a heated swimming pool* OPP **unheated** ▶ **heat·ed·ly** *adv.*: *'You had no right!' she said heatedly.*

heat·er /ˈhiːtə(r)/ *noun* a machine used for making air or water warmer: *a gas heater* ◊ *a water heater* ➲ see also IMMERSION HEATER, STORAGE HEATER

ˈheat exchanger *noun* (*technical*) a device for making heat pass from one liquid to another without allowing the liquids to mix

heath /hiːθ/ *noun* a large area of open land that is not used for farming and is covered with rough grass and other small wild plants

hea·then /ˈhiːðn/ *noun, adj.*

■ ***noun*** (*old-fashioned, offensive*) **1** used by people who have a strong religious belief as a way of referring to a person who has no religion or who believes in a religion that is not one of the world's main religions **2** used to refer to a person who shows lack of education

■ ***adj.*** (*old-fashioned, offensive*) connected with heathens: *heathen gods* ◊ *He set out to convert* ***the heathen*** (= people who are heathens).

hea·ther /ˈheðə(r)/ *noun* [U] a low wild plant with small purple, pink or white flowers, that grows on hills and areas of wild open land (=MOORLAND)

heath·land /ˈhiːθlənd; *NAmE* -lænd/ *noun* [U] **heath·lands** [pl.] a large area of heath

Heath Rob·in·son /ˌhiːθ ˈrɒbɪnsən; *NAmE* ˈrɑːb-/ (*BrE*) (*NAmE* **ˌRube ˈGold·berg**) *adj.* [only before noun] (*humorous*) (of machines and devices) having a very complicated design, especially when used to perform a very simple task; not practical: *a Heath Robinson contraption*

heat·ing 🔑 /ˈhiːtɪŋ/ *noun* [U] (*especially BrE*) (also **heat** especially in *NAmE*) the process of supplying heat to a room or building; a system used to do this: *Who turned the heating off?* ◊ *What type of heating do you have?* ◊ *a gas heating system* ◊ *heating bills* ➲ see also CENTRAL HEATING

heat·proof /ˈhiːtpruːf/ *adj.* that cannot be damaged by heat: *a heatproof dish*

ˈheat-resist·ant *adj.* not easily damaged by heat

ˈheat-seeking *adj.* [only before noun] (of a weapon) that moves towards the heat coming from the aircraft, etc. that it is intended to hit and destroy: *heat-seeking missiles*

H

heat·stroke /ˈhiːtstrəʊk; *NAmE* -stroʊk/ *noun* [U] an illness with fever and often loss of CONSCIOUSNESS, caused by being in too great a heat for too long

heat·wave /ˈhiːtweɪv/ *noun* a period of unusually hot weather

heave /hiːv/ *verb, noun*

■ ***verb*** **1** [T, I] to lift, pull or throw sb/sth very heavy with one great effort: **~ sth/sb/yourself + adv./prep.** *I managed to heave the trunk down the stairs.* ◇ *They heaved the body overboard.* ◇ **+ adv./prep.** *We all heaved on the rope.* **2** [I] to rise up and down with strong, regular movements: *The boat heaved beneath them.* ◇ **~ with sth** *Her shoulders heaved with laughter.* **3** [T] **~ a sigh, etc.** to make a sound slowly and often with effort: *We all **heaved a sigh of relief**.* **4** [I] to experience the tight feeling in your stomach that you get before you VOMIT: *The thought of it makes me heave.*

IDM **ˌheave into ˈsight/ˈview** (*formal*) (especially of ships) to appear, especially when moving gradually closer from a long way off: *A ship hove into sight.* HELP **Hove** is usually used for the past tense and past participle in this idiom.

PHR V **ˌheave ˈto** (*technical*) if a ship or its CREW (= the people sailing it) **heave to**, the ship stops moving HELP **Hove** is usually used for the past tense and past participle in this phrasal verb.

■ ***noun*** **1** [C] an act of lifting, pulling or throwing: *With a mighty heave he lifted the sack onto the truck.* **2** [U] (especially *literary*) a rising and falling movement: *the steady heave of the sea*

heave-ho /ˌhiːv ˈhəʊ; *NAmE* ˈhoʊ/ *noun* [sing.]

IDM **give sb the (old) heave-ˈho** (*informal*) to dismiss sb from their job; to end a relationship with sb

heaven 0-w /ˈhevn/ *noun*

1 0-w (also **Heaven**) [U] (used without *the*) (in some religions) the place believed to be the home of God where good people go when they die: *the kingdom of heaven* ◇ *I feel like I've died and gone to heaven.* **2** 0-w [U, C] (*informal*) a place or situation in which you are very happy: *This isn't exactly my idea of heaven!* ◇ *It was heaven being away from the office for a week.* ◇ *The island is truly **a heaven on earth**.* **3 the heavens** [pl.] (*literary*) the sky: *Four tall trees stretched up to the heavens.*

IDM **(Good) ˈHeavens!** | **ˌHeavens aˈbove!** (*informal*) used to show that you are surprised or annoyed: *Good heavens, what are you doing?* **the heavens ˈopened** it began to rain heavily **made in ˈheaven** (especially of a marriage or other relationship) seeming to be perfect ➲ more at FORBID, GOD, HELP *v.*, HIGH *adj.*, KNOW *v.*, MOVE *v.*, NAME *n.*, SEVENTH, THANK

heav·en·ly /ˈhevnli/ *adj.* **1** [only before noun] connected with heaven: *our heavenly Father* (= God) ◇ *the heavenly kingdom* **2** [only before noun] connected with the sky: ***heavenly bodies*** (= the sun, moon, stars and planets) **3** (*informal*) very pleasant SYN **wonderful**: *a heavenly morning/feeling* ◇ *This place is heavenly.*

ˌheaven-ˈsent *adj.* [usually before noun] happening unexpectedly and at exactly the right time

heav·en·ward /ˈhevnwəd; *NAmE* -wərd/ (also **heav·en·wards**) *adv.* (*literary*) towards heaven or the sky: *to **cast/raise your eyes heavenward*** (= to show you are annoyed or impatient)

heav·ily 0-w /ˈhevɪli/ *adv.*

1 0-w to a great degree; in large amounts: *It was raining heavily.* ◇ *to **drink/smoke** heavily* ◇ ***heavily armed** police* (= carrying a lot of weapons) ◇ *a **heavily pregnant** woman* (= one whose baby is nearly ready to be born) ◇ *They are both **heavily involved** in politics.* ◇ *He **relies heavily** on his parents.* ◇ *She has been **heavily criticized** in the press.* **2** with a lot of force or effort: *She fell heavily to the ground.* **3 ~ built** (of a person) with a large, solid and strong body **4** slowly and loudly: *She was now breathing heavily.* ◇ *He was snoring heavily.* **5** in a slow way that sounds as though you are worried or sad: *He sighed heavily.* **6** in a way that makes you feel uncomfortable or anxious: *Silence hung heavily in the room.* ◇ *The burden of guilt weighed heavily on his mind.* **7 ~ loaded/laden** full of or loaded with heavy things: *a heavily loaded van*

heav·ing /ˈhiːvɪŋ/ *adj.* [not before noun] **~ (with sb/sth)** full of sb/sth: *The place was heaving with journalists.*

heavy 0-w /ˈhevi/ *adj., noun, adv.*

■ ***adj.*** (heav·ier, heavi·est)

▸ WEIGHING A LOT **1** 0-w weighing a lot; difficult to lift or move: *She was struggling with a heavy suitcase.* ◇ *My brother is much heavier than me.* ◇ *He tried to push the heavy door open.* ◇ ***How heavy** is it* (= how much does it weigh)? ◇ (*especially NAmE*) *Many young people today are too heavy* (= fat). ◇ (*figurative*) *Her father carried a **heavy burden** of responsibility.* OPP **light**

▸ WORSE THAN USUAL **2** 0-w more or worse than usual in amount, degree, etc: *the noise of **heavy traffic*** ◇ ***heavy frost/rain/snow*** ◇ *the effects of **heavy drinking*** ◇ *There was heavy fighting in the capital last night.* ◇ *The penalty for speeding can be a **heavy fine**.* ◇ *She spoke with **heavy irony**.* OPP **light**

▸ NOT DELICATE **3** 0-w (of sb/sth's appearance or structure) large and solid; not delicate: *big, dark rooms full of heavy furniture* ◇ *He was tall and strong, with heavy features.*

▸ MATERIAL **4** 0-w (of the material or substance that sth is made of) thick: *heavy curtains* ◇ *a heavy coat* OPP **light**

▸ FULL OF STH **5 ~ with sth** (*literary*) full of or loaded with sth: *trees heavy with apples* ◇ *The air was heavy with the scent of flowers.* ◇ *His voice was heavy with sarcasm.*

▸ MACHINES **6** [usually before noun] (of machines, vehicles or weapons) large and powerful: *a wide range of engines and **heavy machinery*** ◇ ***heavy lorries/trucks***

▸ BUSY **7** 0-w [usually before noun] involving a lot of work or activity; very busy: *a **heavy schedule*** ◇ *She'd had a heavy day.*

▸ WORK **8** 0-w hard, especially because it requires a lot of physical strength: ***heavy digging/lifting***

▸ FALL/HIT **9** 0-w falling or hitting sth with a lot of force: *a **heavy fall/blow***

▸ MEAL/FOOD **10** 0-w large in amount or very solid: *a **heavy lunch/dinner*** ◇ *a heavy cake* OPP **light**

▸ DRINKER/SMOKER/SLEEPER **11** 0-w [only before noun] (of a person) doing the thing mentioned more, or more deeply, than usual: *a **heavy drinker/smoker*** ◇ *a heavy sleeper*

▸ SOUND **12** 0-w (of a sound that sb makes) loud and deep: ***heavy breathing/snoring*** ◇ *a **heavy groan/sigh***

▸ USING A LOT **13 ~ on sth** (*informal*) using a lot of sth: *Older cars are heavy on gas.* ◇ *Don't go so heavy on the garlic.*

▸ SERIOUS/DIFFICULT **14** (usually *disapproving*) (of a book, programme, style, etc.) serious; difficult to understand or enjoy: *We found the play very heavy.* ◇ *The discussion got a little heavy.*

▸ SEA/OCEAN **15** dangerous because of big waves, etc: *strong winds and heavy seas*

▸ AIR/WEATHER **16** hot and lacking fresh air, in a way that is unpleasant: *It's very heavy—I think there'll be a storm.*

▸ SOIL **17** wet, sticky and difficult to dig or to move over

▸ STRICT **18** (of a person) very strict and severe: *Don't be so heavy on her—it wasn't her fault.*

▸ **heavi·ness** *noun* [U]

IDM **get ˈheavy** (*informal*) to become very serious, because strong feelings are involved: *They started shouting at me. It got very heavy.* **ˌheavy ˈgoing** used to describe sb/sth that is difficult to deal with or understand: *She's a bit heavy going.* ◇ *I found the course rather heavy going.* **heavy ˈhand** a way of doing sth or of treating people that is much stronger and less sensitive than it needs to be: *the heavy hand of management* **a heavy ˈheart** a feeling of great sadness: *She left her children behind with a heavy heart.* **the ˈheavy mob/brigade** (*BrE, informal*) a group of strong, often violent people employed to do sth such as protect sb **a heavy ˈsilence/ˈatmosphere** a situation when people do not say anything, but feel embarrassed or uncomfortable **make heavy ˈweather of sth** to seem to find sth more difficult or complicated than it needs to be ➲ more at CROSS *n.*, TOLL *n.*

■ ***noun*** (*pl.* -ies) **1** [C] (*informal*) a large strong man whose job is to protect a person or place, often using violence **2** [U] (*ScotE*) strong beer, especially bitter: *a pint of heavy*

■ *adv.*

IDM **hang/lie 'heavy 1 ~ (on/in sth)** (of a feeling or sth in the air) to be very noticeable in a particular place in a way that is unpleasant: *Smoke lay heavy on the far side of the water.* ◇ *Despair hangs heavy in the stifling air.* **2 ~ on sb/sth** to cause sb/sth to feel uncomfortable or anxious: *The crime lay heavy on her conscience.*

ˌheavy 'breather *noun* a person who gets sexual pleasure from calling sb on the telephone and not speaking to them ▸ **ˌheavy 'breathing** *noun* [U]

ˌheavy-'duty *adj.* [only before noun] **1** not easily damaged and therefore suitable for hard physical work or to be used all the time: *a heavy-duty carpet* **2** (*informal, especially NAmE*) very serious or great in quantity: *I think you need some heavy-duty advice.*

ˌheavy 'goods vehicle *noun* (*BrE*) = HGV

ˌheavy-'handed *adj.* **1** not showing a sympathetic understanding of the feelings of other people: *a heavy-handed approach* **2** using unnecessary force: *heavy-handed police methods* **3** (of a person) using too much of sth in a way that can cause damage: *Don't be too heavy-handed with the salt.*

ˌheavy 'hitter *noun* (*informal, especially NAmE*) a person with a lot of power, especially in business or politics

ˌheavy 'industry *noun* [U, C] industry that uses large machinery to produce metal, coal, vehicles, etc. ➲ compare LIGHT INDUSTRY

ˌheavy 'metal *noun* **1** [U] a type of rock music with a very strong beat played very loud on electric GUITARS **2** [C] (*technical*) a metal that has a very high DENSITY (= the relation of its weight to its volume), such as gold or LEAD

ˌheavy 'petting *noun* [U] sexual activity that does not involve full SEXUAL INTERCOURSE

ˌheavy-'set *adj.* having a broad heavy body SYN **thickset**

'heavy water *noun* [U] (*chemistry*) water in which HYDROGEN is replaced by DEUTERIUM, used in nuclear reactions

heavy·weight /'heviweɪt/ *noun* **1** a BOXER of the heaviest class in normal use, weighing 79.5 kilograms or more: *a heavyweight champion* **2** a person or thing that weighs more than is usual **3** a very important person, organization or thing that influences others: *a political heavyweight* ◇ *a heavyweight journal*

Heb·raic /hi'breɪɪk/ *adj.* of or connected with the Hebrew language or people: *Hebraic poetry*

Heb·rew /'hi:bru:/ *noun* **1** a member of an ancient race of people living in what is now Israel and Palestine. Their writings and traditions form the basis of the Jewish religion. **2** the language traditionally used by the Hebrew people **3** a modern form of the Hebrew language which is the official language of modern Israel ➲ compare YIDDISH ▸ **Heb·rew** *adj.*

heck /hek/ *exclamation, noun* (*informal*) used to show that you are slightly annoyed or surprised: *Oh heck, I'm going to be late!* ◇ *We had to wait* **a heck of a** *long time!* ◇ ***Who the heck*** *are you?*

IDM **for the 'heck of it** (*informal*) just for pleasure rather than for a reason **what the 'heck!** (*informal*) used to say that you are going to do sth that you know you should not do: *It means I'll be late for work but what the heck!*

heckle /'hekl/ *verb* [T, I] **~ (sb)** to interrupt a speaker at a public meeting by shouting out questions or rude remarks SYN **barrack**: *He was booed and heckled throughout his speech.* ▸ **heck·ler** /'heklə(r)/ *noun* **heck·ling** *noun* [U]

hec·tare /'hekteə(r); *NAmE* -ter; *BrE* also 'hektɑ:(r)/ *noun* (*abbr.* **ha**) a unit for measuring an area of land; 10 000 square metres or about 2.5 ACRES

hec·tic /'hektɪk/ *adj.* very busy; full of activity: *to lead a hectic life* ◇ *a hectic schedule*

hecto·litre (*especially US* **hecto·liter**) /'hektəli:tə(r)/ *noun* (*abbr.* **hl**) a unit for measuring volume; 100 litres

hec·tor /'hektə(r)/ *verb* **~ sb | + speech** (*formal*) to try to make sb do sth by talking or behaving in an aggressive way SYN **bully** ▸ **hec·tor·ing** *adj.*: *a hectoring tone of voice*

he'd /hi:d/ *short form* **1** he had **2** he would

hedge /hedʒ/ *noun, verb*

■ ***noun* 1** a row of bushes or small trees planted close together, usually along the edge of a field, garden/yard or road: *a privet hedge* ➲ VISUAL VOCAB pages V2, V16 **2 ~ against sth** a way of protecting yourself against the loss of sth, especially money: *to buy gold as a hedge against inflation*

■ ***verb* 1** [I] to avoid giving a direct answer to a question or promising to support a particular idea, etc: *Just answer 'yes' or 'no'—and stop hedging.* **2** [T] **~ sth** to put a hedge around a field, etc. **3** [T, usually passive] **~ sb/sth (about/around) (with sth)** (*formal*) to surround or limit sb/sth: *His religious belief was always hedged with doubt.* ◇ *Their offer was hedged around with all sorts of conditions.*

IDM **ˌhedge your 'bets** to reduce the risk of losing or making a mistake by supporting more than one side in a competition, an argument, etc, or by having several choices available to you

PHR V **'hedge against sth** to do sth to protect yourself against problems, especially against losing money: *a way of hedging against currency risks* **ˌhedge sb/sth↔'in** to surround sb/sth with sth SYN **hem sb/sth in**: *The cathedral is now hedged in by other buildings.* ◇ (*figurative*) *Married life made him feel hedged in and restless.*

hedge·hog /'hedʒhɒg; *NAmE* -hɔ:g; -hɑ:g/ *noun* a small brown European animal with stiff parts like needles (called SPINES) covering its back. Hedgehogs are NOCTURNAL (= active mostly at night) and can roll into a ball to defend themselves when they are attacked.

hedge·row /'hedʒrəʊ; *NAmE* -roʊ/ *noun* (especially in Britain) a line of bushes planted along the edge of a field or road ➲ VISUAL VOCAB page V2

he·don·ism /'hi:dənɪzəm/ *noun* [U] the belief that pleasure is the most important thing in life ▸ **he·don·is·tic** /ˌhi:də'nɪstɪk/ *adj.*

he·don·ist /'hi:dənɪst/ *noun* a person who believes that pleasure is the most important thing in life

the heebie-jeebies /ˌhi:bi 'dʒi:biz/ *noun* [pl.] (*old-fashioned, informal*) a feeling of nervous fear or worry

heed /hi:d/ *verb, noun*

■ ***verb* ~ sb/sth** (*formal*) to pay careful attention to sb's advice or warning SYN **take notice of**

■ ***noun*** [U]

IDM **give/pay 'heed (to sb/sth) | take 'heed (of sb/sth)** (*formal*) to pay careful attention to sb/sth

heed·ful /'hi:dfl/ *adj.* **~ (of sb/sth)** (*formal*) paying careful attention to sb/sth

heed·less /'hi:dləs/ *adj.* [not usually before noun] **~ (of sb/sth)** (*formal*) not paying careful attention to sb/sth ▸ **heed·less·ly** *adv.*

hee-haw /'hi: hɔ:/ *noun* the way of writing the sound made by a DONKEY

heel 🔑 /hi:l/ *noun, verb*

■ ***noun***

▸ PART OF FOOT **1** 🔑 [C] the back part of the foot below the ankle ➲ VISUAL VOCAB page V48

▸ PART OF SOCK/SHOE **2** [C] the part of a sock, etc. that covers the heel **3** 🔑 [C] the raised part on the bottom of a shoe, boot, etc. that makes the shoe, etc. higher at the back: *shoes with a* **low/high heel** ◇ *a stiletto heel* ◇ *The sergeant clicked his heels and walked out.* ➲ VISUAL VOCAB page V52 ➲ compare SOLE *n.* (2)

▸ -HEELED **4** (in adjectives) having the type of heel mentioned: *high-heeled shoes* ➲ see also WELL HEELED

▸ SHOES **5 heels** [pl.] a pair of women's shoes that have high heels: *She doesn't often wear heels.* ➲ see also KITTEN HEELS

▸ PART OF HAND **6** [C] **~ of your hand/palm** the raised part of the inside of the hand where it joins the wrist ➲ VISUAL VOCAB page V48

▸ UNPLEASANT MAN **7** [C] (*old-fashioned, informal*) a man who is unpleasant to other people and cannot be trusted ➲ see also ACHILLES HEEL, DOWN AT HEEL

IDM **at/on sb's 'heels** following closely behind sb: *He fled from the stadium with the police at his heels.* **bring sb/sth to 'heel 1** to force sb to obey you and accept discipline **2** to make a dog come close to you **come to 'heel 1** (of a person) to agree to obey sb and accept their orders **2** (of a dog) to come close to the person who has called it **(hard/hot) on sb's/sth's 'heels** very close behind sb/sth; very soon after sth: *News of rising unemployment followed hard on the heels of falling export figures.* **,take to your 'heels** to run away from sb/sth **,turn/,spin on your 'heel** to turn around suddenly so that you are facing in the opposite direction **under the 'heel of sb** (*literary*) completely controlled by sb ➲ more at COOL *v.*, DIG *v.*, DRAG *v.*, HEAD *n.*, KICK *v.*, TREAD *v.*

■ *verb*

▸ REPAIR SHOE **1** [T] **~ sth** to repair the heel of a shoe, etc.

▸ OF BOAT **2** [I] **~ (over)** to lean over to one side: *The boat heeled over in the strong wind.*

Heely™ /ˈhiːli/ *noun* (*pl.* **Heelys**) (*especially BrE*) (also **'skate shoe** especially in *NAmE*) a sports shoe that has one or more wheels underneath it

heft /heft/ *verb, noun*

■ *verb* **1 ~ sth (+ adv./prep.)** to lift or carry sth heavy from one position to another: *The two men hefted the box into the car.* **2 ~ sth** to lift or hold sth in order to estimate its weight: *Anna took the old sword and hefted it in her hands.*

■ *noun* [U] (*NAmE*) the weight of sb/sth: *She was surprised by the sheer heft of the package.*

hefty /ˈhefti/ *adj.* (**heft·ier, hefti·est**) **1** (of a person or an object) big and heavy: *Her brothers were both hefty men in their forties.* **2** (of an amount of money) large; larger than usual or expected: *They sold it easily and made a hefty profit.* **3** using a lot of force: *He gave the door a hefty kick.* ▸ **heft·ily** *adv.*

he·gem·ony /hɪˈdʒeməni; -ˈge-; ˈhedʒɪməni; *NAmE* -moʊni/ *noun* [U, C] (*pl.* **-ies**) (*formal*) control by one country, organization, etc. over other countries, etc. within a particular group ▸ **hege·mon·ic** /ˌhedʒɪˈmɒnɪk; ˌhegɪ-; *NAmE* -ˈmɑːnɪk/ *adj.*: *hegemonic control*

He·gi·ra (also **He·ji·ra**) /ˈhedʒɪrə; hɪˈdʒaɪrə/ (also **Hijra**) *noun* [sing.] **1** (usually **the Hegira**) the occasion when Muhammad left Mecca to go to Medina in AD 622 **2** the period which began at this time; the Muslim ERA

heifer /ˈhefə(r)/ *noun* a young female cow, especially one that has not yet had a CALF

height 🔑 /haɪt/ *noun*

▸ MEASUREMENT **1** 🔑 [U, C] the measurement of how tall a person or thing is: *Height: 210 mm. Width: 57 mm. Length: 170 mm.* ◇ *Please state your height and weight.* ◇ *It is almost 2 metres* **in height**. ◇ *She is the same height as her sister.* ◇ *to be of* **medium/average height** ◇ *You can adjust the height of the chair.* ◇ *The table is available in several different heights.*

▸ BEING TALL **2** 🔑 [U] the quality of being tall or high: *She worries about her height* (= that she is too tall). ◇ *The height of the mountain did not discourage them.*

▸ DISTANCE ABOVE GROUND **3** 🔑 [C, U] a particular distance above the ground: *The plane flew* **at a height of** *3 000 metres.* ◇ *The stone was dropped* **from a great height**. ◇ *The aircraft was gaining height.* ◇ *to be at* **shoulder/chest/waist height**

▸ HIGH PLACE **4** 🔑 [C, usually pl.] (often used in names) a high place or position: *Brooklyn Heights* ◇ *He doesn't have* **a head for heights** (= is afraid of high places). ◇ *a fear of heights* ◇ *We looked out over the city from the heights of Edinburgh Castle.* ◇ *The pattern of the ancient fields is clearly visible* **from a height**.

▸ STRONGEST POINT/LEVEL **5** 🔑 [sing.] the point when sth is at its best or strongest: *He is at the height of his career.* ◇ *She is still at the* **height of her powers**. ◇ *I wouldn't go there* **in the height of summer**. ◇ *The fire* **reached its height** *around 2 a.m.* ◇ *The crisis was* **at its height** *in May.* **6 heights** [pl.] a better or greater level of sth; a situation where sth is very good: *Their success had reached* **new heights**. IDM see DIZZY

▸ EXTREME EXAMPLE **7** [sing.] **~ of sth** an extreme example of a particular quality: *It would be* **the height of folly** (= very stupid) *to change course now.* ◇ *She was dressed in* **the height of fashion**.

IDM **draw yourself up/rise to your full 'height** to stand straight and tall in order to show your determination or high status

height·en /ˈhaɪtn/ *verb* [I, T] if a feeling or an effect **heightens**, or sth **heightens** it, it becomes stronger or increases SYN **intensify**: *Tension has heightened after the recent bomb attack.* ◇ **~ sth** *The campaign is intended to heighten public awareness of the disease.*

hein·ous /ˈheɪnəs/ *adj.* [usually before noun] (*formal*) morally very bad: *a heinous crime* ▸ **hein·ous·ly** *adv.* **hein·ous·ness** *noun* [U]

heir /eə(r); *NAmE* er/ *noun* **~ (to sth)** | **~ (of sb) 1** a person who has the legal right to receive sb's property, money or title when that person dies: *to be heir to a large fortune* ◇ *the heir to the throne* (= the person who will be the next king or queen) **2** a person who is thought to continue the work or a tradition started by sb else: *the president's political heirs* HELP Use **an**, not **a**, before **heir**.

,heir ap'parent *noun* (*pl.* **heirs apparent**) **~ (to sth) 1** an HEIR whose legal right to receive sb's property, money or title cannot be taken away because it is impossible for sb with a stronger claim to be born **2** a person who is expected to take the job of sb when that person leaves

heir·ess /ˈeəres; -rəs; *NAmE* ˈer-/ *noun* **~ (to sth)** a female heir, especially one who has received or will receive a large amount of money HELP Use **an**, not **a**, before **heiress**.

heir·loom /ˈeəluːm; *NAmE* ˈerl-/ *noun, adj.*

■ *noun* a valuable object that has belonged to the same family for many years: *a family heirloom* HELP Use **an**, not **a**, before **heirloom**.

■ *adj.* [only before noun] (*NAmE*) **heirloom** plants are varieties which were commonly grown in the past but are no longer grown as commercial crops

,heir pre'sumptive *noun* (*pl.* **heirs presumptive**) an HEIR who may lose his or her legal right to receive sb's property, money or title if sb with a stronger claim is born

heist /haɪst/ *noun, verb*

■ *noun* (*informal, especially NAmE*) an act of stealing sth valuable from a shop/store or bank SYN **robbery**: *a bank heist*

■ *verb* **~ sth** (*informal, especially NAmE*) to steal sth valuable from a shop/store or bank

Hej·ira = HEGIRA

held *past tense, past part.* of HOLD

hel·ic·al /ˈhelɪkl; ˈhiːl-/ *adj.* (*technical*) like a HELIX

heli·cop·ter /ˈhelɪkɒptə(r); *NAmE* -kɑːp-/ (also *informal* **cop·ter, chop·per**) *noun* an aircraft without wings that has large blades on top that go round. It can fly straight up from the ground and can also stay in one position in the air: *He was rushed to the hospital* **by helicopter**. ◇ *a police helicopter* ◇ *a helicopter pilot* ➲ VISUAL VOCAB page V43

'helicopter view (*business*) a broad general view or description of a problem SYN 10 000-**foot view, overview**

he·lio·cen·tric /ˌhiːliəˈsentrɪk/ *adj.* (*astronomy*) with the sun as the centre: *the heliocentric model of the solar system*

he·lio·graph /ˈhiːliəgrɑːf; *NAmE* -græf/ *noun* **1** a device which gives signals by reflecting flashes of light from the sun **2** (also **he·lio·gram** /ˈhiːliəgræm/) a message which is sent using signals from a heliograph **3** a special camera which takes photographs of the sun

he·lio·trope /ˈhiːliətrəʊp; *NAmE* -troʊp/ *noun* **1** [C, U] a garden plant with pale purple flowers with a sweet smell **2** [U] a pale purple colour

heli·pad /ˈhelipæd/ (also **'helicopter pad**) *noun* a small area where HELICOPTERS can take off and land

heli·port /ˈhelipɔːt; *NAmE* -pɔːrt/ *noun* a place where HELICOPTERS take off and land

heli-skiing /ˈheliskiːɪŋ/ *noun* [U] the sport of flying in a HELICOPTER to a place where there is a lot of snow on a mountain in order to SKI there

he·lium /ˈhiːliəm/ *noun* [U] (*symb.* **He**) a chemical element. Helium is a very light gas that does not burn, often used to fill BALLOONS and to freeze food.

helix /ˈhiːlɪks/ *noun* (*pl.* **heli·ces** /ˈhiːlɪsiːz/) a shape like a SPIRAL or a line curved around a CYLINDER or CONE ➲ see also DOUBLE HELIX

helix

hell 0‑w /hel/ *noun* **1** 0‑w [sing.] (usually **Hell**) (used without *a* or *the*) in some religions, the place believed to be the home of DEVILS and where bad people go after death **2** 0‑w [U, sing.] a very unpleasant experience or situation in which people suffer very much: *The last three months have been hell.* ◇ *He went* **through hell** *during the trial.* ◇ *Her parents made her life hell.* ◇ *Being totally alone is my idea of* **hell on earth**. **3** 0‑w [U] a swear word that some people use when they are annoyed or surprised or to emphasize sth. Its use is offensive to some people.: *Oh hell, I've burned the pan.* ◇ *What the hell do you think you are doing?* ◇ *Go to hell!* ◇ *I can't really afford it, but, what the hell* (= it doesn't matter), *I'll get it anyway.* ◇ *He's as guilty as hell.* ◇ (*NAmE*) *'Do you understand?' 'Hell, no. I don't.'*
IDM **all ˈhell broke loose** (*informal*) suddenly there was a lot of noise, arguing, fighting or confusion: *There was a loud bang and then all hell broke loose.* **beat/kick (the) ˈhell out of sb/sth | knock ˈhell out of sb/sth** (*informal*) to hit sb/sth very hard: *He was a dirty player and loved to kick hell out of the opposition.* **(just) for the ˈhell of it** (*informal*) just for fun; for no real reason: *They stole the car just for the hell of it.* **from ˈhell** (*informal*) used to describe a very unpleasant person or thing; the worst that you can imagine: *They are the neighbours from hell.* **get the hell ˈout (of…)** (*informal*) to leave a place very quickly: *Let's get the hell out of here.* **give sb ˈhell** (*informal*) **1** to make life unpleasant for sb: *He used to give his mother hell when he was a teenager.* ◇ *My new shoes are giving me hell* (= are hurting me). **2** to shout at or speak angrily to sb: *Dad will give us hell when he sees that mess.* **go to hell in a ˈhandbasket** (*NAmE, informal*) = GO TO THE DOGS at DOG *n.* **hell for ˈleather** (*old-fashioned, BrE, informal*) as quickly as possible: *to ride hell for leather* **hell hath no ˈfury (like a woman ˈscorned)** (*BrE*) used to refer to sb, usually a woman, who has reacted very angrily to sth, especially the fact that her husband or lover has been UNFAITHFUL **(come) hell or high ˈwater** despite any difficulties: *I was determined to go, come hell or high water.* **Hell's ˈteeth** (*old-fashioned, BrE, informal*) used to express anger or surprise **like ˈhell 1** (*informal*) used for emphasis: *She worked like hell for her exams.* ◇ *My broken finger hurt like hell.* **2** (*informal*) used when you are refusing permission or saying that sth is not true: *'I'm coming with you.' 'Like hell you are'* (= you certainly are not). **a/one hell of a… | a/one helluva …** /ˈheləvə/ (*slang*) used to give emphasis to what a person is saying: *The firm was in a hell of a mess when he took over.* ◇ *It must have been one hell of a party.* ◇ *That's one helluva big house you've got.* **play (merry) ˈhell with sth/sb** (*BrE, informal*) to affect sth/sb badly **scare, annoy, etc. the ˈhell out of sb** (*informal*) to scare, annoy, etc. sb very much **to ˈhell and back** (*informal*) used to say that sb has been through a difficult situation: *We'd been to hell and back together and we were still good friends.* **to ˈhell with sb/sth** (*informal*) used to express anger or dislike and to say that you no longer care about sb/sth and will take no notice of them: *'To hell with him,' she thought, 'I'm leaving.'* ➲ more at BAT *n.*, BUG *v.*, CAT, CATCH *v.*, HOPE *n.*, PAY *v.*, RAISE *v.*, ROAD, SNOWBALL *n.*

he'll /hiːl/ *short form* he will

ˌhell-ˈbent *adj.* **~ on sth/on doing sth** determined to do sth even though the results may be bad: *He seems hell-bent on drinking himself to death.*

hel·le·bore /ˈhelɪbɔː(r)/ *noun* a poisonous plant with divided leaves and large green, white or purple flowers

Hel·lene /ˈheliːn/ *noun* a person from Greece, especially ancient Greece

Hel·len·ic /heˈlenɪk; -ˈliːn-/ *adj.* of or connected with ancient or modern Greece

Hel·len·is·tic /ˌhelɪˈnɪstɪk/ *adj.* of or connected with the Greek history, language and culture of the 4th–1st centuries BC

hell·fire /ˈhelfaɪə(r)/ *noun* [U] the fires which are believed by some religious people to burn in hell, where bad people go to be punished after they die

hell·hole /ˈhelhəʊl; *NAmE* -hoʊl/ *noun* (*informal*) a very unpleasant place

hel·lion /ˈheliən/ *noun* (*NAmE*) a badly behaved child who annoys other people

hell·ish /ˈhelɪʃ/ *adj.* (*informal, especially BrE*) extremely unpleasant

H

hello 0‑w (also **hullo** especially in *BrE*) (*BrE* also **hallo**) /həˈləʊ; *NAmE* həˈloʊ/ *exclamation, noun* (*pl.* -os)
1 0‑w used as a GREETING when you meet sb, when you answer the telephone or when you want to attract sb's attention: *Hello John, how are you?* ◇ *Hello, is there anybody there?* ◇ ***Say hello** to Liz for me.* ◇ *They exchanged hellos* (= said hello to each other) *and forced smiles.* **2** (*BrE*) used to show that you are surprised by sth: *Hello, hello, what's going on here?* **3** (*informal*) used to show that you think sb has said sth stupid or is not paying attention: *Hello? You didn't really mean that, did you?* ◇ *I'm like, 'Hello! Did you even listen?'* ➲ see also GOLDEN HELLO

More About

greetings

- **Hello** is the most usual word and is used in all situations, including answering the telephone.
- **Hi** is more informal and is now very common.
- **How are you?** or **How are you doing?** (*very informal*) often follow **Hello** and **Hi**: *'Hello, Mark.' 'Oh, hi, Kathy! How are you?'*
- **Good morning** is often used by members of a family or people who work together when they see each other for the first time in the day. It can also be used in formal situations and on the telephone. In informal speech, people may just say **Morning**.
- **Good afternoon** and **Good evening** are much less common. **Good night** is not used to greet somebody, but only to say goodbye late in the evening or when you are going to bed.
- If you are meeting someone for the first time, you can say **Pleased to meet you** or **Nice to meet you** (*less formal*). Some people use **How do you do?** in formal situations. The correct reply to this is **How do you do?**

hell·rais·er /ˈhelreɪzə(r)/ *noun* a person who causes trouble by behaving loudly and often violently, especially when they have drunk too much alcohol

ˌHell's ˈAngel *noun* a member of a group of people, usually men, who ride powerful motorcycles, wear leather clothes and used to be known for their wild and violent behaviour

hel·luva ➲ HELL

helm /helm/ *noun* a handle or wheel used for steering a boat or ship ➲ compare TILLER
IDM **at the ˈhelm 1** in charge of an organization, project, etc. **2** steering a boat or ship **take the ˈhelm 1** to take charge of an organization, project, etc. **2** to begin steering a boat or ship

hel·met /ˈhelmɪt/ *noun* a type of hard hat that protects the head, worn, for example, by a police officer, a soldier or a person playing some sports ➲ VISUAL VOCAB pages V36, V39, V41 ➲ see also CRASH HELMET

hel·met·ed /ˈhelmɪtɪd/ *adj.* [only before noun] wearing a helmet

helms·man /ˈhelmzmən/ *noun* (*pl.* -men /-mən/) a person who steers a boat or ship

help 🗝 /help/ *verb, noun*

■ ***verb***

▸ MAKE EASIER/BETTER **1** 🗝 [I, T] to make it easier or possible for sb to do sth by doing sth for them or by giving them sth that they need: *Help, I'm stuck!* ◇ **~ with sth** *He always helps with the housework.* ◇ **~ sb** *We must all try and help each other.* ◇ **~ sb with sth** *Jo will help us with some of the organization.* ◇ **~ (sb) in doing sth** *I need contacts that could help in finding a job.* ◇ **~ sb (to) do sth** *The college's aim is to help students (to) achieve their aspirations.* ◇ *This charity aims to help people (to) help themselves.* ◇ *Come and help me lift this box.* ◇ **~ (to) do sth** *She helped (to) organize the party.* HELP In verb patterns with a **to** infinitive, the 'to' is often left out, especially in informal or spoken English. **2** 🗝 [I, T] to improve a situation; to make it easier for sth to happen: ***It helped*** *being able to talk about it.* ◇ **~ sth** *It doesn't really **help matters** knowing that everyone is talking about us.* ◇ **~ (to) do sth** *This should help (to) reduce the pain.*

▸ SB TO MOVE **3** 🗝 [T] **~ sb + adv./prep.** to help sb move by letting them lean on you, guiding them, etc: *She helped him to his feet.* ◇ *We were helped ashore by local people.*

▸ GIVE FOOD/DRINK **4** 🗝 [T] to give yourself/sb food, drinks, etc: **~ yourself** *If you want another drink, just help yourself.* ◇ **~ yourself/sb to sth** *Can I help you to some more salad?*

▸ STEAL **5** [T] **~ yourself to sth** (*informal, disapproving*) to take sth without permission SYN **steal**: *He'd been helping himself to the money in the cash register.*

IDM **sb can (not) help (doing) sth | sb can not help but do sth** 🗝 used to say that it is impossible to prevent or avoid sth: *I can't help thinking he knows more than he has told us.* ◇ *She couldn't help but wonder what he was thinking.* ◇ ***It couldn't be helped*** (= there was no way of avoiding it and we must accept it). ◇ *I always end up having an argument with her, I don't know why, I just **can't help it**.* ◇ *I couldn't help it if the bus was late* (= it wasn't my fault). ◇ *She burst out laughing—she **couldn't help herself*** (= couldn't stop herself). **give/lend a ˌhelping ˈhand** to help sb **God/Heaven ˈhelp sb** (*informal*) used to say that you are afraid sb will be in danger or that sth bad will happen to them: *God help us if this doesn't work.* HELP Some people find this use offensive. **so ˈhelp me (God)** used to swear that what you are saying is true, especially in a court of law

PHR V **ˌhelp sb ˈoff/ˈon with sth** to help sb take off/put on a piece of clothing: *Let me help you off with your coat.* **ˌhelp ˈout | ˌhelp sb↔ˈout** 🗝 to help sb, especially in a difficult situation: *He's always willing to help out.* ◇ *When I bought the house, my sister helped me out with a loan.*

■ ***noun***

▸ MAKING EASIER/BETTER **1** 🗝 [U] the act of helping sb to do sth: *Thank you for all your help.* ◇ **~ (with sth)** *Do you need any help with that?* ◇ *Can I be **of any help** to you?* ◇ *None of this would have been possible without their help.* ◇ *She stopped smoking **with the help** of her family and friends.*

▸ ADVICE/MONEY **2** 🗝 [U] advice, money, etc. that is given to sb in order to solve their problems: *to **seek financial/legal/medical, etc. help*** ◇ **~ in doing sth** *The organization offers practical help in dealing with paperwork.* ◇ **~ with sth** *You should qualify for help with the costs of running a car.* ◇ *a **help key/screen*** (= a function on a computer that provides information on how to use the computer)

▸ BEING USEFUL **3** 🗝 [U] the fact of being useful: *The map wasn't **much help**.* ◇ ***With the help of*** *a ladder, neighbours were able to rescue the children from the blaze.* ◇ *Just shouting at him isn't going to be a lot of help.*

▸ FOR SB IN DANGER **4** 🗝 [U] the act of helping sb who is in danger: *Quick, get help!* ◇ *She screamed for help.*

▸ PERSON/THING **5** [sing.] **a ~ (to sb)** a person or thing that helps sb: *She was more of a hindrance than a help.* ◇ *Your advice was a big help.* ◇ (*ironic*) *You're a great help, I must say!*

▸ IN HOUSE **6 the help** [U+sing./pl. v.] (*especially NAmE*) the person or people who are employed by sb to clean their house, etc. ➲ see also HOME HELP

IDM **there is no ˈhelp for it** (*especially BrE*) it is not possible to avoid doing sth that may harm sb in some way: *There's no help for it. We shall have to call the police.*

ˈhelp desk *noun* a service, usually in a business company, that gives people information and help, especially if they are having problems with a computer

help·er /ˈhelpə(r)/ *noun* a person who helps sb to do sth: *a willing helper*

help·ful 🗝 /ˈhelpfl/ *adj.*

1 🗝 able to improve a particular situation SYN **useful**: ***helpful advice/information/suggestions*** ◇ *Sorry I can't be more helpful.* ◇ **~ (for sb) (to do sth)** *It would be helpful for me to see the damage for myself.* ◇ **~ in doing sth** *Role-play is helpful in developing communication skills.* ◇ **~ to sb** *The booklet should be very helpful to parents of disabled children.* **2** 🗝 (of a person) willing to help sb: *I called the police but they weren't very helpful.* ◇ *The staff couldn't have been more helpful.* OPP **unhelpful** ▸ **help·ful·ly** /-fəli/ *adv.*: *She helpfully suggested that I try the local library.* **help·ful·ness** *noun* [U]

help·ing /ˈhelpɪŋ/ *noun* **~ (of sth)** an amount of food given to sb at a meal SYN **serving**: *a **small/generous helping*** ◇ *We all had a **second helping** of pie.*

help·less /ˈhelpləs/ *adj.* **1** unable to take care of yourself or do things without the help of other people: *the helpless victims of war* ◇ *a helpless gesture/look* ◇ *He lay helpless on the floor.* ◇ *It's natural to feel helpless against such abuse.* ◇ *The worst part is being helpless to change anything.* **2** unable to control a strong feeling: ***helpless panic/rage*** ◇ **~ with sth** *The audience was **helpless with laughter**.* ▸ **help·less·ly** *adv.*: *They watched helplessly as their home went up in flames.* **help·less·ness** *noun* [U]: *a **feeling/sense of helplessness***

help·line /ˈhelplaɪn/ *noun* (*BrE*) a telephone service that provides advice and information about particular problems

help·mate /ˈhelpmeɪt/ (also **help·meet** /ˈhelpmiːt/) *noun* (*formal* or *literary*) a helpful partner, especially a wife

helter-skelter /ˌheltə ˈskeltə(r); *NAmE* ˌheltər/ *noun, adj.*

■ ***noun*** (*BrE*) a tall tower at a FAIRGROUND that has a path twisting around the outside of it from the top to the bottom for people to slide down

■ ***adj.*** [only before noun] done in a hurry and in a way that lacks organization: *a helter-skelter dash to meet the deadline* ▸ **helter-skelter** *adv.*

hem /hem/ *noun, verb*

■ ***noun*** the edge of a piece of cloth that has been folded over and sewn, especially on a piece of clothing: *to take up the hem of a dress* (= to make the dress shorter)

■ ***verb*** (-mm-) **~ sth** to make a hem on sth: *to hem a skirt*

IDM **ˌhem and ˈhaw** (*NAmE*) (*BrE* **ˌhum and ˈhaw**) (*informal*) to take a long time to make a decision or before you say sth

PHR V **ˌhem sb/sth↔ˈin** to surround sb/sth so that they cannot move or grow easily SYN **hedge sb/sth in**: *The village is hemmed in on all sides by mountains.* ◇ (*figurative*) *She felt hemmed in by all their petty rules and regulations.*

ˈhe-man *noun* (*pl.* **he-men**) (often *humorous*) a strong man with big muscles, especially one who likes to show other people how strong he is

hema·tite (*NAmE*) (*BrE* **haem·atite**) /ˈhiːmətaɪt/ *noun* [U] (*geology*) a dark red rock from which iron is obtained

hema·tol·ogy (*NAmE*) (*BrE* **haema·tol·ogy**) /ˌhiːməˈtɒlədʒi; *NAmE* -ˈtɑːl-/ *noun* [U] the scientific study of the blood and its diseases ▸ **hem·ato·logic·al** (*NAmE*) (*BrE* **haem-**) /ˌhiːmətəˈlɒdʒɪkl; *NAmE* -ˈlɑːdʒ-/ *adj.*

hema·tolo·gist (*NAmE*) (*BrE* **haem-**) /ˌhiːməˈtɒlədʒɪst; *NAmE* -ˈtɑːl-/ *noun*

hema·toma (*NAmE*) (*BrE* **haem·atoma**) /ˌhiːməˈtəʊmə; *NAmE* -ˈtoʊmə/ *noun* (*medical*) a swollen area on the body consisting of blood that has become thick

hemi·sphere /ˈhemɪsfɪə(r); *NAmE* -sfɪr/ *noun* **1** one half of the earth, especially the half above or below the EQUATOR: *the* ***northern/southern hemisphere*** **2** either half of the brain: *the* ***left/right cerebral hemisphere*** **3** one half of a SPHERE (= a round solid object)

hemi·spher·ic·al /ˌhemɪˈsferɪkl; *NAmE* also -ˈsfɪr-/ *adj.* shaped like a hemisphere

hem·line /ˈhemlaɪn/ *noun* the bottom edge of a dress or skirt; the length of a dress or skirt: *Shorter hemlines are back in this season.*

hem·lock /ˈhemlɒk; *NAmE* -lɑːk/ *noun* **1** [U, C] a poisonous plant with a mass of small white flowers growing at the end of a STEM that is covered in spots **2** [U] poison made from hemlock

hemo- (*NAmE*) (*BrE* **haemo-**) /ˈhiːməʊ; *NAmE* -moʊ/ *combining form* (in nouns and adjectives) connected with blood: *hemophilia*

hemp /hemp/ *noun* [U] a plant which is used for making rope and cloth, and also to make the drug CANNABIS

hen /hen/ *noun* **1** a female chicken, often kept for its eggs or meat: *a small flock of laying hens* ◇ *battery hens* **2** (especially in compounds) any female bird: *a hen pheasant* ➲ compare COCK ➲ see also MOORHEN

hence 🔑 AW /hens/ *adv.* (*formal*) for this reason: *We suspect they are trying to hide something, hence the need for an independent inquiry.* ➲ LANGUAGE BANK at THEREFORE
IDM **... days, weeks, etc. ˈhence** (*formal*) a number of days, etc. from now: *The true consequences will only be known several years hence.*

hence·forth /ˌhensˈfɔːθ; *NAmE* -ˈfɔːrθ/ (also **hence·for·ward** /ˌhensˈfɔːwəd; *NAmE* -ˈfɔːrwərd/) *adv.* (*formal*) starting from a particular time and at all times in the future: *Friday 31 July 1925 henceforth became known as 'Red Friday'.*

hench·man /ˈhentʃmən/ *noun* (*pl.* **-men** /-mən/) a faithful supporter of a powerful person, for example a political leader or criminal, who is prepared to use violence or become involved in illegal activities to help that person

hen·deca·syl·lable /ˌhendekəˈsɪləbl/ *noun* (*technical*) a line of poetry with eleven syllables ▶ **hen·deca·syl·lab·ic** /ˌhendekəsɪˈlæbɪk/ *adj.*

hen·dia·dys /henˈdaɪədɪs/ *noun* [U] (*grammar*) the use of two words joined with 'and' to express a single idea, for example 'nice and warm'

henge /hendʒ/ *noun* a circle of large vertical wooden or stone objects built in PREHISTORIC times

henna /ˈhenə/ *noun* [U] a reddish-brown DYE (= a substance used to change the colour of sth), used especially on the hair and skin

ˈhen party (also **ˈhen night**) *noun* (*BrE*, *informal*) a party for women only, especially one held for a woman who will soon get married ➲ compare STAG NIGHT

hen·pecked /ˈhenpekt/ *adj.* (*informal*) a man who people say is **henpecked** has a wife who is always telling him what to do, and is too weak to disagree with her

henry /ˈhenri/ *noun* (*pl.* **hen·ries** or **henrys**) (*abbr.* **H**) a unit for measuring the INDUCTANCE in an electric CIRCUIT

hep·at·ic /hɪˈpætɪk/ *adj.* (*biology*) connected with the LIVER

hepa·titis /ˌhepəˈtaɪtɪs/ *noun* [U] a serious disease of the LIVER. There are three main forms: **hepatitis A** (the least serious, caused by infected food), **hepatitis B** and **hepatitis C** (both very serious and caused by infected blood).

hepta·gon /ˈheptəgən; *NAmE* -gɑːn/ *noun* (*geometry*) a flat shape with seven straight sides and seven angles ▶ **hept·agon·al** /hepˈtægənl/ *adj.*

hept·ath·lon /hepˈtæθlən/ *noun* a sporting event, especially one for women, in which people compete in seven different sports ➲ compare BIATHLON, DECATHLON, PENTATHLON, TETRATHLON, TRIATHLON

her 🔑 /hə(r); ɜː(r); ə(r); *strong form* hɜː(r)/ *pron., det.*
■ ***pron.*** 🔑 used as the object of a verb, after the verb *be* or after a preposition to refer to a woman or girl who has already been mentioned or is easily identified: *We're going to call her Sophie.* ◇ *Please give her my regards.* ◇ *The manager will be free soon—you can wait for her here.* ◇ *That must be her now.* ➲ compare SHE ➲ note at GENDER
■ ***det.*** 🔑 (the possessive form of *she*) of or belonging to a woman or girl who has already been mentioned or is easily identified: *Meg loves her job.* ◇ *She broke her leg skiing.* ➲ see also HERS

her·ald /ˈherəld/ *verb, noun*
■ ***verb*** (*formal*) **1 ~ sth** to be a sign that sth is going to happen: *These talks could herald a new era of peace.* **2 ~ sb/sth (as sth)** [often passive] to say in public that sb/sth is good or important: *The report is being heralded as a blueprint for the future of transport.*
■ ***noun*** **1** something that shows that sth else is going to happen soon: *The government claims that the fall in unemployment is the herald of economic recovery.* **2** (in the past) a person who carried messages from a ruler

her·ald·ry /ˈherəldri/ *noun* [U] the study of the COATS OF ARMS and the history of old families ▶ **her·al·dic** /heˈrældɪk/ *adj.*

herb /hɜːb; *NAmE* ɜːrb; hɜːrb/ *noun* **1** a plant whose leaves, flowers or seeds are used to flavour food, in medicines or for their pleasant smell. PARSLEY, MINT and OREGANO are all herbs: *a herb garden* ◇ (*NAmE*) *an herb garden* ➲ VISUAL VOCAB page V28 **2** (*technical*) a plant with a soft STEM that dies down after flowering

herb·aceous /hɜːˈbeɪʃəs; *NAmE* ɜːrˈb-; hɜːrˈb-/ *adj.* (*technical*) connected with plants that have soft STEMS: *a herbaceous plant*

herˌbaceous ˈborder *noun* a piece of ground in a garden/yard containing plants that produce flowers every year without being replaced

herb·age /ˈhɜːbɪdʒ; *NAmE* ˈɜːrb-; ˈhɜːrb-/ *noun* [U] (*technical*) plants in general, especially grass that is grown for cows, etc. to eat

herb·al /ˈhɜːbl; *NAmE* ˈɜːrbl; ˈhɜːrbl/ *adj., noun*
■ ***adj.*** connected with or made from HERBS: ***herbal medicine/remedies***
■ ***noun*** a book about HERBS, especially those used in medicines

herb·al·ism /ˈhɜːblɪzəm; *NAmE* ˈɜːrbl-; ˈhɜːrbl-/ *noun* [U] the medical use of plants, especially as a form of ALTERNATIVE MEDICINE

herb·al·ist /ˈhɜːbəlɪst; *NAmE* ˈɜːrb-; ˈhɜːrb-/ *noun* a person who grows, sells or uses HERBS for medical purposes

ˌherbal ˈtea *noun* [U, C] a drink made from dried HERBS and hot water

herbi·cide /ˈhɜːbɪsaɪd; *NAmE* ˈɜːrb-; ˈhɜːrb-/ *noun* [C, U] a chemical that is poisonous to plants, used to kill plants that are growing where they are not wanted ➲ see also INSECTICIDE, PESTICIDE

herbi·vore /ˈhɜːbɪvɔː(r); *NAmE* ˈɜːrb-; ˈhɜːrb-/ *noun* any animal that eats only plants ➲ compare CARNIVORE, INSECTIVORE, OMNIVORE, VEGETARIAN ▶ **herb·iv·or·ous** /hɜːˈbɪvərəs; *NAmE* ɜːrˈb-; hɜːrˈb-/ *adj.*: *herbivorous dinosaurs*

Her·cu·lean /ˌhɜːkjuˈliːən; *NAmE* ˌhɜːrk-/ *adj.* [usually before noun] needing a lot of strength, determination or effort: *a Herculean task* ORIGIN From the Greek myth in which **Hercules** proved his courage and strength by completing twelve very difficult tasks (called the Labours of Hercules).

herd /hɜːd; *NAmE* hɜːrd/ *noun, verb*
■ ***noun*** **1** a group of animals of the same type that live and

feed together: *a **herd of cows/deer/elephants*** ◇ *a **beef/ dairy herd*** ➲ compare FLOCK **2** (usually *disapproving*) a large group of people of the same type: *She pushed her way through a herd of lunchtime drinkers.* ◇ *the **common herd*** (= ordinary people) ◇ *Why **follow the herd*** (= do and think the same as everyone else)? IDM see RIDE *v.*

■ ***verb*** **1** [I, T] to move or make sb/sth move in a particular direction: **+ adv./prep.** *We all herded on to the bus.* ◇ **~ sb/ sth + adv./prep.** *They were herded together into trucks and driven away.* **2** [T] **~ sth** to make animals move together as a group: *a shepherd herding his flock*

herd·er /ˈhɜːde(r); *NAmE* ˈhɜːrder/ *noun* a person whose job is to take care of a group of animals such as sheep and cows in the countryside

ˈherd instinct *noun* [sing.] the natural tendency in people or animals to behave or think like other people or animals

herds·man /ˈhɜːdzmən; *NAmE* ˈhɜːrd-/ *noun* (*pl.* -men /-mən/) a man whose job is to take care of a group of animals such as sheep and cows in the countryside

here 0→ /hɪə(r); *NAmE* hɪr/ *adv., exclamation*

■ ***adv.*** **1** 0→ used after a verb or preposition to mean 'in, at or to this position or place': *I live here.* ◇ *Put the box here.* ◇ *Let's get out of here.* ◇ *Come over here.* **2** 0→ now; at this point: *The countdown to Christmas **starts here**.* ◇ *Here the speaker paused to have a drink.* **3** 0→ used when you are giving or showing sth to sb: *Here's the money I promised you.* ◇ *Here's a dish that is simple and quick to make.* ◇ *Here is your opportunity.* ◇ ***Here comes** the bus.* ◇ *I can't find my keys. Oh, **here they are**.* ◇ ***Here we are*** (= we've arrived). **4** 0→ **~ to do sth** used to show your role in a situation: *I'm here to help you.* **5** (used after a noun, for emphasis): *My friend here saw it happen.*

IDM **by ˈhere** (*WelshE*) here; to here: *Come by here now!* **ˌhere and ˈthere** 0→ in various places: *Papers were scattered here and there on the floor.* **ˌhere ˈgoes** (*informal*) used when you are telling people that you are just going to do sth exciting, dangerous, etc. **here's to sb/sth** used to wish sb health or success, as you lift a glass and drink a TOAST: *Here's to your future happiness!* **ˌhere, ˌthere and ˈeverywhere** in many different places; all around **ˌhere we ˈgo** (*informal*) said when sth is starting to happen: *'Here we go,' thought Fred, 'she's sure to say something.'* **ˌhere we go aˈgain** (*informal*) said when sth is starting to happen again, especially sth bad **ˌhere you ˈare** 0→ (*informal*) used when you are giving sth to sb: *Here you are. This is what you were asking for.* **ˌhere you ˈgo** (*informal*) used when you are giving sth to sb: *Here you go. Four copies, is that right?* **neither ˈhere nor ˈthere** not important SYN **irrelevant**: *What might have happened is neither here nor there.* ➲ more at OUT *adv. prep.*

■ ***exclamation*** **1** (*BrE*) used to attract sb's attention: *Here, where are you going with that ladder?* **2** used when offering sth to sb: *Here, let me carry that for you.*

here·abouts /ˌhɪərəˈbaʊts; *NAmE* ˌhɪr-/ (*NAmE* also **here·about**) *adv.* near this place: *There aren't many houses hereabouts.*

here·after /ˌhɪərˈɑːftə(r); *NAmE* ˌhɪrˈæf-/ *adv., noun*

■ ***adv.*** **1** (also **here·in·after**) (*law*) (in legal documents, etc.) in the rest of this document **2** (*formal*) from this time; in future ➲ compare THEREAFTER **3** (*formal*) after death: *Do you believe in a life hereafter?*

■ ***noun* the hereafter** [sing.] a life believed to begin after death

here·by /ˌhɪəˈbaɪ; *NAmE* ˌhɪrˈbaɪ/ *adv.* (in legal documents, etc.) as a result of this statement, and in a way that makes sth legal

her·edi·tary /həˈredɪtri; *NAmE* -teri/ *adj.* **1** (especially of illnesses) given to a child by its parents before it is born: *a **hereditary illness/disease/condition/problem*** ◇ *Epilepsy is hereditary in her family.* **2** that is legally given to sb's child, when that person dies: *a **hereditary title/monarchy*** **3** holding a rank or title that is hereditary: ***hereditary peers/rulers***

her·ed·ity /həˈredəti/ *noun* [U] the process by which mental and physical characteristics are passed by parents to their children; these characteristics in a particular person: *the debate over the effects of heredity and environment*

here·in /ˌhɪərˈɪn; *NAmE* ˌhɪrˈɪn/ *adv.* (*formal* or *law*) in this place, document, statement or fact: *Neither party is willing to compromise and herein lies the problem.*

here·in·after /ˌhɪərɪnˈɑːftə(r); *NAmE* ˌhɪrɪnˈæf-/ *adv.* (*law*) = HEREAFTER (1)

here·of /ˌhɪərˈɒv; *NAmE* ˌhɪrˈʌv; -ˈɑːv/ *adv.* (*law*) of this: *a period of 12 months from the date hereof* (= the date of this document)

her·esy /ˈherəsi/ *noun* [U, C] (*pl.* -ies) **1** a belief or an opinion that is against the principles of a particular religion; the fact of holding such beliefs: *He was burned at the stake for heresy.* ◇ *the heresies of the early Protestants* ➲ COLLOCATIONS at RELIGION **2** a belief or an opinion that disagrees strongly with what most people believe: *The idea is heresy to most employees of the firm.*

her·et·ic /ˈherətɪk/ *noun* a person who is guilty of heresy ▸ **her·et·ical** /həˈretɪkl/ *adj.*: *heretical beliefs*

here·to /ˌhɪəˈtuː; *NAmE* ˌhɪrˈtuː/ *adv.* (*law*) to this

here·to·fore /ˌhɪətuˈfɔː(r); *NAmE* ˌhɪrt-/ *adv.* (*law* or *formal*) before this time

here·upon /ˌhɪərəˈpɒn; *NAmE* ˌhɪrəˈpɑːn/ *adv.* (*literary*) after this; as a direct result of this situation

here·with /ˌhɪəˈwɪð; -ˈwɪθ; *NAmE* ˌhɪrˈw-/ *adv.* (*formal*) with this letter, book or document: *I enclose herewith a copy of the policy.*

her·it·able /ˈherɪtəbl/ *adj.* (*law*) (of property) that can be passed from one member of a family to another

heri·tage /ˈherɪtɪdʒ/ *noun* [usually sing.] the history, traditions and qualities that a country or society has had for many years and that are considered an important part of its character: *Spain's rich cultural heritage* ◇ *The building is part of our national heritage.*

ˈheritage centre *noun* (*BrE*) a place where there are exhibitions that people visit to learn about life in the past

herm·aph·ro·dite /hɜːˈmæfrədaɪt; *NAmE* hɜːrˈm-/ *noun* a person, an animal or a flower that has both male and female sexual organs or characteristics ▸ **herm·aph·ro·dite** *adj.*

her·men·eut·ic /ˌhɜːməˈnjuːtɪk; *NAmE* ˌhɜːrməˈnjuːtɪk; -ˈnuː-/ *adj.* (*technical*) relating to the meaning of written texts

her·men·eut·ics /ˌhɜːməˈnjuːtɪks; *NAmE* ˌhɜːrməˈnjuːtɪks; -ˈnuː-/ *noun* [pl.] (*technical*) the area of study that analyses and explains written texts

her·met·ic /hɜːˈmetɪk; *NAmE* hɜːrˈm-/ *adj.* **1** (*technical*) tightly closed so that no air can escape or enter SYN **airtight** **2** (*formal, disapproving*) closed and difficult to become a part of: *the strange, hermetic world of the theatre* ▸ **her·met·ic·al·ly** /-kli/ *adv.*: *a hermetically sealed container*

her·mit /ˈhɜːmɪt; *NAmE* ˈhɜːrmɪt/ *noun* a person who, usually for religious reasons, lives a very simple life alone and does not meet or talk to other people.

her·mit·age /ˈhɜːmɪtɪdʒ; *NAmE* ˈhɜːrm-/ *noun* a place where a hermit lives or lived

ˈhermit crab *noun* a CRAB (= a sea creature with eight legs and, usually, a hard shell) that has no shell of its own and has to use the empty shells of other sea creatures

her·nia /ˈhɜːniə; *NAmE* ˈhɜːrniə/ *noun* [C, U] a medical condition in which part of an organ is pushed through a weak part of the body wall

hero 0→ /ˈhɪərəʊ; *NAmE* ˈhɪroʊ; ˈhiː-/ *noun* (*pl.* -oes) **1** 0→ a person, especially a man, who is admired by many people for doing sth brave or good: *a **war hero*** (= sb who was very brave during a war) ◇ *The Olympic team were given **a hero's welcome** on their return home.* ◇ *one of the country's **national heroes*** **2** 0→ the main male character in a story, novel, film/movie, etc: *The hero of the novel is a ten-year old boy.* **3** 0→ a person, especially a man, that you admire because of a particular quality or skill that they have: *my childhood hero* **4** (*NAmE*) = SUBMARINE (2) ➲ see also HEROINE

hero·ic /hə'rəʊɪk; *NAmE* -'roʊ-/ *adj.* **1** showing extreme courage and admired by many people SYN **courageous**: *a heroic figure* ◇ *Rescuers made* **heroic efforts** *to save the crew.* **2** showing great determination to succeed or to achieve sth, especially sth difficult: *We watched our team's heroic struggle to win back the cup.* **3** that is about or involves a hero: *a* **heroic story/poem** ◇ **heroic deeds/myths** **4** very large or great: *This was foolishness on a* **heroic scale**. ▶ **hero·ic·al·ly** /-kli/ *adv.*

he,roic 'couplet *noun* (*technical*) two lines of poetry one after the other that RHYME and usually contain ten syllables and five stresses

hero·ics /hə'rəʊɪks; *NAmE* -'roʊ-/ *noun* [pl.] **1** (*disapproving*) talk or behaviour that is too brave or dramatic for a particular situation: *Remember, no heroics, we just go in there and do our job.* **2** actions that are brave and determined: *Thanks to Bateman's heroics in the second half, the team won 2–0.*

her·oin /'herəʊɪn; *NAmE* -roʊ-/ *noun* [U] a powerful illegal drug made from MORPHINE, that some people take for pleasure and can become ADDICTED to: *a heroin addict*

hero·ine /'herəʊɪn; *NAmE* -roʊ-/ *noun* **1** a girl or woman who is admired by many for doing sth brave or good: *the heroines of the revolution* **2** the main female character in a story, novel, film/movie, etc: *The heroine is played by Demi Moore.* **3** a woman that you admire because of a particular quality or skill that she has: *Madonna was her teenage heroine.*

hero·ism /'herəʊɪzəm; *NAmE* -roʊ-/ *noun* [U] very great courage

heron /'herən/ *noun* a large bird with a long neck and long legs, that lives near water

'hero worship *noun* [U] great admiration for sb because you think they are extremely beautiful, intelligent, etc.

'hero-worship *verb* (-pp-) **~ sb** to admire sb very much because you think they are extremely beautiful, intelligent, etc.

her·pes /'hɜːpiːz; *NAmE* 'hɜːrp-/ *noun* [U] one of a group of infectious diseases, caused by a virus, that cause painful spots on the skin, especially on the face and sexual organs

herpes zoster /,hɜːpiːz 'zɒstə(r); *NAmE* ,hɜːrpiːz 'zɑːstər/ *noun* [U] (*medical*) **1** = SHINGLES **2** a virus which causes SHINGLES and CHICKENPOX

her·ring /'herɪŋ/ *noun* (*pl.* **her·ring** or **her·rings**) [U, C] a N Atlantic fish that swims in very large groups and is used for food: *shoals of herring* ◇ *fresh herring fillets* ◇ *pickled herrings* ➲ see also RED HERRING

her·ring·bone /'herɪŋbəʊn; *NAmE* -boʊn/ *noun* [U] a pattern used, for example, in cloth consisting of lines of V-shapes that are parallel to each other

'herring gull *noun* a large N Atlantic bird of the GULL family, with black tips to its wings

hers 0→ /hɜːz; ɜːz; *NAmE* hɜːrz; ɜːrz/ *pron.* of or belonging to her: *His eyes met hers.* ◇ *The choice was hers.* ◇ *a friend of hers* ➲ note at GENDER

her·self 0→ /hɜː'self; *NAmE* hɜːr's- *weak form* hə'self; *NAmE* hər's-/ *pron.*
1 0→ (the reflexive form of *she*) used when the woman or girl who performs an action is also affected by it: *She hurt herself.* ◇ *She must be very proud of herself.* **2** 0→ used to emphasize the female subject or object of a sentence: *She told me the news herself.* ◇ *Jane herself was at the meeting.*
IDM **be, seem, etc. her'self** (of a woman or girl) to be in a normal state of health or happiness; not influenced by other people: *She didn't seem quite herself this morning.* ◇ *She needed space to be herself.* (**all**) **by her'self** **1** alone; without anyone else: *She lives by herself.* **2** without help: *She runs the business by herself.* (**all**) **to her'self** for only her to have or use: *She wants a room all to herself.*

hertz /hɜːts; *NAmE* hɜːrts/ *noun* (*pl.* **hertz**) (*abbr.* **Hz**) a unit for measuring the FREQUENCY of sound waves

he's *short form* **1** /hiːz; hɪs; ɪz/ he is **2** /hiːz/ he has

hesi·tancy /'hezɪtənsi/ *noun* [U] the state or quality of being slow or uncertain in doing or saying sth: *I noticed a certain hesitancy in his voice.*

hesi·tant /'hezɪtənt/ *adj.* slow to speak or act because you feel uncertain, embarrassed or unwilling: *a hesitant smile* ◇ *the baby's first few hesitant steps* ◇ **~ about sth** *She's hesitant about signing the contract.* ◇ **~ to do sth** *Doctors are hesitant to comment on the new treatment.* ▶ **hesi·tant·ly** *adv.*

hesi·tate 0→ /'hezɪteɪt/ *verb*
1 0→ [I, T] to be slow to speak or act because you feel uncertain or nervous: *She hesitated before replying.* ◇ **~ about/over sth** *I didn't hesitate for a moment about taking the job.* ◇ **+ speech** *'I'm not sure,' she hesitated.* **2** 0→ [I] **~ to do sth** to be worried about doing sth, especially because you are not sure that it is right or appropriate: *Please do not hesitate to contact me if you have any queries.* ▶ **hesi·ta·tion** /,hezɪ'teɪʃn/ *noun* [U, C]: *She agreed* **without** *the slightest* **hesitation**. ◇ *I* **have no hesitation in** *recommending her for the job.* ◇ *He spoke fluently and without unnecessary hesitations.*
IDM **he who 'hesitates** (**is 'lost**) (*saying*) if you delay in doing sth you may lose a good opportunity

hes·sian /'hesiən; *NAmE* 'heʃn/ (*especially BrE*) (*NAmE* usually **bur·lap**) *noun* [U] a type of strong rough brown cloth, used especially for making SACKS

hetero- /'hetərəʊ-; *NAmE* -roʊ/ *combining form* (in nouns, adjectives and adverbs) other; different: *heterogeneous* ◇ *heterosexual* ➲ compare HOMO-

het·ero·dox /'hetərədɒks; *NAmE* -dɑːks/ *adj.* (*formal*) not following the usual or accepted beliefs and opinions ➲ compare ORTHODOX, UNORTHODOX ▶ **het·ero·doxy** *noun* [U, C] (*pl.* -ies)

het·ero·ge·neous /,hetərə'dʒiːniəs/ *adj.* (*formal*) consisting of many different kinds of people or things: *the heterogeneous population of the United States* OPP **homogeneous** ▶ **het·ero·gen·eity** /-dʒə'niːəti/ *noun* [U]

het·ero·nym /'hetərənɪm/ *noun* (*linguistics*) **1** one of two or more words that have the same spelling but different meanings and pronunciation, for example 'tear' meaning 'rip' and 'tear' meaning 'liquid from the eye' **2** one of two or more words that refer to the same thing, for example 'lift' and 'elevator'

het·ero·sex·ual /,hetərə'sekʃuəl/ *noun* a person who is sexually attracted to people of the opposite sex ➲ compare BISEXUAL, HOMOSEXUAL ▶ **het·ero·sex·ual** *adj.*: *a heterosexual relationship* **het·ero·sexu·al·ity** /,hetərə,sekʃu'æləti/ *noun* [U]

het·ero·zy·gote /,hetərə'zaɪgəʊt; *NAmE* -goʊt/ *noun* (*biology*) a living thing that has two varying forms of a particular GENE, and whose young may therefore vary in a particular characteristic ▶ **het·ero·zy·gous** /-gəs/ *adj.*

het up /,het 'ʌp/ *adj.* [not before noun] **~** (**about/over sth**) (*BrE, informal*) anxious, excited or slightly angry: *What are you getting so het up about?*

heur·is·tic /hju'rɪstɪk/ *adj.* (*formal*) **heuristic** teaching or education encourages you to learn by discovering things for yourself

heur·is·tics /hju'rɪstɪks/ *noun* [U] (*formal*) a method of solving problems by finding practical ways of dealing with them, learning from past experience

hew /hjuː/ *verb* (**hewed, hewed** or **hewn** /hjuːn/) **1 ~ sth** (*old-fashioned*) to cut sth large with a tool: *to hew wood* **2 ~ sth** (**out of sth**) (*formal*) to make or shape sth large by cutting: *roughly hewn timber frames* ◇ *The statues were hewn out of solid rock.*

hex /heks/ *verb* **~ sb** (*NAmE*) to use magic powers in order to harm sb ▶ **hex** *noun*: *to put a hex on sb* ➲ compare CURSE

H

hexa- /ˈheksə/ (also **hex-**) *combining form* (in nouns, adjectives and adverbs) six; having six

hexa·deci·mal /ˌheksəˈdesɪml/ (also **hex** /heks/) *adj.* (*computing*) a system for representing pieces of data using the numbers 0-9 and the letters A-F: *The number 107 is represented in hexadecimal as 6B.*

hexa·gon /ˈheksəgən; *NAmE* -gɑːn/ *noun* (*geometry*) a flat shape with six straight sides and six angles ➲ VISUAL VOCAB page V58 ▶ **hex·agon·al** /heksˈægənl/ *adj.*

hexa·gram /ˈheksəgræm/ *noun* (*geometry*) a shape made by six straight lines, especially a star made from two triangles with equal sides

hex·am·eter /hekˈsæmɪtə(r)/ *noun* (*technical*) a line of poetry with six stressed syllables

hey /heɪ/ *exclamation* (*informal*) **1** used to attract sb's attention or to express interest, surprise or anger: *Hey, can I just ask you something?* ◇ *Hey, leave my things alone!* **2** used to show that you do not really care about sth or that you think it is not important: *That's the third time I've been late this week—but hey!—who's counting?* **3** (*SAfrE*) used at the end of a statement, to show that you have finished speaking, or to form a question or invite sb to reply: *Thanks for your help, hey.* ◇ *My new bike's nice, hey?*
IDM **what the ˈhey!** (*NAmE, informal*) used to say that sth does not matter or that you do not care about it: *This is probably a bad idea, but what the hey!*

hey·day /ˈheɪdeɪ/ *noun* [usually sing.] the time when sb/sth had most power or success, or was most popular SYN **prime**: ***In its heyday****, the company ran trains every fifteen minutes.* ◇ *a fine example from the heyday of Italian cinema* ◇ *a picture of Brigitte Bardot in her heyday*

ˌhey ˈpresto *exclamation* (*BrE*) (*NAmE* **presto**) **1** something that people say when they have just done sth so quickly and easily that it seems to have been done by magic: *You just press the button and, hey presto, a perfect cup of coffee!* **2** something that people say just before they finish a magic trick

HFC /ˌeɪtʃ ef ˈsiː/ *noun* [C, U] the abbreviation for 'hydrofluorocarbon' (a type of gas used especially in AEROSOLS (= types of container that release liquid in the form of a spray). HFCs are not harmful to the layer of the gas OZONE in the earth's atmosphere.)

HGV /ˌeɪtʃ dʒiː ˈviː/ *abbr.* (*BrE*) heavy goods vehicle (a large vehicle such as a lorry/truck): *You need an HGV licence for this job.*

HHS /ˌeɪtʃ eɪtʃ ˈes/ *abbr.* Department of Health and Human Services (the US government department responsible for national health programmes and the SOCIAL SERVICES ADMINISTRATION)

hi 🔑 /haɪ/ *exclamation* (*informal*) used to say hello: *Hi guys!* ◇ ***Hi, there!*** *How're you doing?*

hia·tus /haɪˈeɪtəs/ *noun* [sing.] (*formal*) **1** a pause in activity when nothing happens **2** a space, especially in a piece of writing or in a speech, where sth is missing

hi·ber·nate /ˈhaɪbəneɪt; *NAmE* -bərn-/ *verb* [I] (of animals) to spend the winter in a state like deep sleep ➲ COLLOCATIONS at LIFE ▶ **hi·ber·na·tion** /ˌhaɪbəˈneɪʃn; *NAmE* -bərˈn-/ *noun* [U]

hi·bis·cus /hɪˈbɪskəs; haɪ-/ *noun* [U, C] (*pl.* **hi·bis·cus**) a tropical plant or bush with large brightly coloured flowers

hic·cup (also **hic·cough**) /ˈhɪkʌp/ *noun, verb*
■ ***noun*** **1** [C] a sharp, usually repeated, sound made in the throat, that is caused by a sudden movement of the DIAPHRAGM and that you cannot control: *She gave a loud hiccup.* **2** (**the**) **hiccups** [pl.] a series of hiccups: *I ate too quickly and got hiccups.* ◇ *He had the hiccups.* **3** [C] (*informal*) a small problem or temporary delay: *There was a slight hiccup in the timetable.*
■ ***verb*** [I] to have hiccups or a single hiccup

hick /hɪk/ *noun* (*informal, especially NAmE*) a person from the country who is considered to be stupid and to have little experience of life: *I was just a hick from Texas then.* ▶ **hick** *adj.*: *a hick town*

hickey /ˈhɪki/ (*NAmE*) (*BrE* ˈ**love bite**) *noun* a red mark on the skin that is caused by sb biting or sucking their partner's skin when they are kissing

hick·ory /ˈhɪkəri/ *noun* [U] the hard wood of the N American **hickory tree**

HICP /ˌeɪtʃ aɪ siː ˈpiː/ *abbr.* harmonized index of consumer prices (a list of the prices of some ordinary goods and services which shows how much these prices change each month. It is used by the European Central Bank and began to be used in the UK in 2003, where it is called the 'Consumer Price Index'.)

ˌhidden aˈgenda *noun* (*disapproving*) the secret intention behind what sb says or does: *There are fears of a hidden agenda behind this new proposal.*

Synonyms

hide

conceal • cover • disguise • mask • camouflage

These words all mean to put or keep sb/sth in a place where they/it cannot be seen or found, or to keep the truth or your feelings secret.

hide to put or keep sb/sth in a place where they/it cannot be seen or found; to keep sth secret, especially your feelings: *He hid the letter in a drawer.* ◇ *She managed to hide her disappointment.*

conceal (*formal*) to hide sb/sth; to keep sth secret: *The paintings were concealed beneath a thick layer of plaster.* ◇ *Tim could barely conceal his disappointment.* NOTE When it is being used to talk about emotions, **conceal** is often used in negative statements.

cover to place sth over or in front of sth in order to hide it: *She covered her face with her hands.*

disguise to hide or change the nature of sth, so that it cannot be recognized: *He tried to disguise his accent.*

mask to hide a feeling, smell, fact, etc. so that it cannot be easily seen or noticed: *She masked her anger with a smile.*

camouflage to hide sb/sth by making them/it look like the things around, or like sth else: *The soldiers camouflaged themselves with leaves and twigs.*

PATTERNS
- to hide/conceal/disguise/mask/camouflage sth **behind** sth
- to hide/conceal sth **under** sth
- to hide/conceal sth **from** sb
- to hide/conceal/disguise/mask **the truth/the fact that...**
- to hide/conceal/disguise/mask **your feelings**

hide 🔑 /haɪd/ *verb, noun*
■ ***verb*** (**hid** /hɪd/, **hid·den** /ˈhɪdn/) **1** 🔑 [T] to put or keep sb/sth in a place where they/it cannot be seen or found SYN **conceal**: **~ sb/sth** *He hid the letter in a drawer.* ◇ *I keep my private papers hidden.* ◇ **~ sb/sth from sth** *They hid me from the police in their attic.* **2** 🔑 [I, T] to go somewhere where you hope you will not be seen or found: *Quick, hide!* ◇ **+ adv./prep.** *I hid under the bed.* ◇ (*figurative*) *He hid behind a false identity.* ◇ **~ yourself** (**+ adv.prep.**) *She hides herself away in her office all day.* **3** 🔑 [T] to cover sth so that it cannot be seen SYN **conceal**: **~ sth + adv./prep.** *He hid his face in his hands.* ◇ **~ sth** *The house was hidden by trees.* ◇ *No amount of make-up could hide her age.* **4** 🔑 [T] **~ sth** to keep sth secret, especially your feelings SYN **conceal**: *She struggled to hide her disappointment.* ◇ *I have never tried to hide the truth about my past.* ◇ *They claim that they* ***have nothing to hide*** (= there was nothing wrong or illegal about what they did). ◇ *She felt sure the letter had some* ***hidden meaning.***

IDM **hide your light under a 'bushel** (*BrE*) to not let people know that you are good at sth ➲ more at HEAD *n.*, MULTITUDE

■ ***noun*** **1** [C] (*BrE*) a place from which people can watch wild animals or birds, without being seen by them **2** [C, U] an animal's skin, especially when it is bought or sold or used for leather: *boots made from buffalo hide* **3** [sing.] (*informal, especially NAmE*) used to refer to sb's life or safety when they are in a difficult situation: *All he's worried about is his own hide* (= himself).

IDM **have/tan sb's 'hide** (*old-fashioned, informal* or *humorous*) to punish sb severely **not see hide nor 'hair of sb/sth** (*informal*) not to see sb/sth for some time: *I haven't seen hide nor hair of her for a month.* IDM see SAVE *v.*

hide-and-seek /ˌhaɪd n ˈsiːk/ *noun* [U] a children's game in which one player covers his or her eyes while the other players hide, and then tries to find them

hide·away /ˈhaɪdəweɪ/ *noun* a place where you can go to hide or to be alone

hide·bound /ˈhaɪdbaʊnd/ *adj.* (*disapproving*) having old-fashioned ideas, rather than accepting new ways of thinking SYN **narrow-minded**

hid·eous /ˈhɪdiəs/ *adj.* very ugly or unpleasant SYN **revolting**: *a hideous face/building/dress* ◇ *Their new colour scheme is hideous!* ◇ *a hideous crime* ◇ *The whole experience had been like some hideous nightmare.* ▶ **hid·eous·ly** *adv.*: *His face was hideously deformed.*

hide·out /ˈhaɪdaʊt/ *noun* a place where sb goes when they do not want anyone to find them

hidey-hole (also **hidy-hole**) /ˈhaɪdi həʊl; *NAmE* -hoʊl/ *noun* (*informal*) a place where sb hides, especially in order to avoid being with other people

hid·ing /ˈhaɪdɪŋ/ *noun* **1** [U] the state of being hidden: *After the trial, she had to* **go into hiding** *for several weeks.* ◇ *He only* **came out of hiding** *ten years after the war was over.* ◇ *We spent months* **in hiding**. **2** [C, usually sing.] (*informal, especially BrE*) a physical punishment, usually involving being hit hard many times SYN **beating**: *to* ***give sb/get a*** (***good***) ***hiding*** ◇ (*figurative*) *The team got a hiding in their last game.*

IDM **on a ˌhiding to 'nothing** (*BrE, informal*) having no chance of success, or not getting much advantage even if you do succeed

'hiding place *noun* a place where sb/sth can be hidden

hie /haɪ/ *verb* (**hies**, **hying**, **hied**) [I] + **adv./prep.** (*old use*) to go quickly

hier·arch·ic·al AW /ˌhaɪəˈrɑːkɪkl; *NAmE* -ˈrɑːrk-/ *adj.* arranged in a hierarchy: *a* ***hierarchical society/structure/organization*** ▶ **hier·arch·ic·al·ly** /-kli/ *adv.*

hier·archy AW /ˈhaɪərɑːki; *NAmE* -rɑːrki/ *noun* (*pl.* **-ies**) **1** [C, U] a system, especially in a society or an organization, in which people are organized into different levels of importance from highest to lowest: *the* ***social/political hierarchy*** ◇ *She's quite high up in the management hierarchy.* **2** [C+sing./pl. v.] the group of people in control of a large organization or institution **3** [C] (*formal*) a system that ideas or beliefs can be arranged into: *a hierarchy of needs*

hiero·glyph /ˈhaɪərəglɪf/ *noun* a picture or symbol of an object, representing a word, syllable or sound, especially as used in ancient Egyptian and other writing systems ▶ **hiero·glyph·ic** /ˌhaɪərəˈglɪfɪk/ *adj.*

hiero·glyph·ics /ˌhaɪərəˈglɪfɪks/ *noun* [pl.] writing that uses hieroglyphs

hieroglyphics

hi-fi /ˈhaɪ faɪ/ *noun* [C, U] equipment for playing recorded music that produces high-quality STEREO sound ▶ **hi-fi** *adj.* [usually before noun]: *a hi-fi system* ➲ VISUAL VOCAB page V18

higgledy-piggledy /ˌhɪgldi ˈpɪgldi/ *adv.* (*informal*) in an untidy way that lacks any order: *Files were strewn higgledy-piggledy over the floor.* ▶ **higgledy-piggledy** *adj.*: *a higgledy-piggledy collection of houses*

high 🔑 /haɪ/ *adj.*, *noun*, *adv.*

■ ***adj.*** (**high·er**, **high·est**)

> **WORD FAMILY**
> **high** *adj., noun, adv.*
> **highly** *adv.*
> **height** *noun*
> **heighten** *verb*

▸ FROM BOTTOM TO TOP **1** 🔑 measuring a long distance from the bottom to the top: *What's the highest mountain in the US?* ◇ *The house has a high wall all the way round it.* ◇ *shoes with high heels* ◇ *He has a round face with a high forehead.* OPP **low** **2** 🔑 used to talk about the distance that sth measures from the bottom to the top: *How high is Everest?* ◇ *It's only a low wall—about a metre high.* ◇ *The grass was waist-high.*

▸ FAR ABOVE GROUND **3** 🔑 at a level which is a long way above the ground or above the level of the sea: *a high branch/shelf/window* ◇ *The rooms had high ceilings.* ◇ *They were flying at high altitude.* ◇ *the grasslands of the high prairies* OPP **low**

▸ GREATER THAN NORMAL **4** 🔑 greater or better than normal in quantity or quality, size or degree: *a high temperature/speed/price* ◇ *a high rate of inflation* ◇ *Demand is high at this time of year.* ◇ *a* **high level** *of pollution* ◇ *a* **high standard** *of craftsmanship* ◇ **high-quality** *goods* ◇ *A* **high degree** *of accuracy is needed.* ◇ *The tree blew over in the* **high winds**. ◇ *We had* **high hopes** *for the business* (= we believed it would be successful). ◇ *The cost in terms of human life was high.* ➲ compare LOW (4)

▸ CONTAINING A LOT **5** 🔑 **~ (in sth)** containing a lot of a particular substance OPP **low**: *foods which are high in fat* ◇ *a high potassium content* ◇ *a* **high-fat** *diet*

▸ RANK/STATUS **6** (usually before noun) near the top in rank or status: *She has held* **high office** *under three prime ministers.* ◇ *He has friends* **in high places** (= among people of power and influence). OPP **low**

▸ VALUABLE **7** of great value: *to play for high stakes* ◇ *My highest card is ten.*

▸ IDEALS/PRINCIPLES **8** (usually before noun) morally good: *a man of* ***high ideals/principles***

▸ APPROVING **9** (usually before noun) showing a lot of approval or respect for sb: *She is held in very high regard by her colleagues.* ◇ *You seem to have a* **high opinion** *of yourself!* OPP **low**

▸ SOUND **10** at the upper end of the range of sounds that humans can hear; not deep or low: *She has a high voice.* ◇ *That note is definitely too high for me.* OPP **low**

▸ OF PERIOD OF TIME **11** [only before noun] used to describe the middle or the most attractive part of a period of time: *high noon* ◇ *high summer*

▸ FOOD **12** (of meat, cheese, etc.) beginning to go bad and having a strong smell

▸ ON ALCOHOL/DRUGS **13** [not before noun] **~ (on sth)** (*informal*) behaving in an excited way because of the effects of alcohol or drugs

▸ PHONETICS **14** (*phonetics*) = CLOSE[2]

IDM **be/get on your high 'horse** (*informal*) to behave in a way that shows you think you are better than other people **have a 'high old time** (*old-fashioned, informal*) to enjoy yourself very much **high and 'dry** **1** (of a boat, etc.) in a position out of the water: *Their yacht was left high and dry on a sandbank.* **2** in a difficult situation, without help or money **high and 'mighty** (*informal*) behaving as though you think you are more important than other people **high as a 'kite** (*informal*) behaving in a very excited way, especially because of being strongly affected by alcohol or drugs **in high 'dudgeon** (*old-fashioned, formal*) in an angry or offended mood, and showing other people that you are angry: *He stomped out of the room in high dudgeon.* **smell, stink, etc. to high 'heaven** (*informal*) **1** to have a strong unpleasant smell **2** to seem to be very dishonest or morally unacceptable ➲ more at HELL, MORAL *adj.*, ORDER *n.*, PROFILE *n.*, TIME *n.*

■ *noun*
▸ LEVEL/NUMBER **1** the highest level or number: *Profits reached an* ***all-time high*** *last year.*
▸ WEATHER **2** an area of high air pressure; an ANTICYCLONE: *A high over southern Europe is bringing fine, sunny weather to all parts.* **3** the highest temperature reached during a particular day, week, etc: *Highs today will be in the region of 25°C.*
▸ FROM DRUGS **4** (*informal*) the feeling of extreme pleasure and excitement that sb gets after taking some types of drugs: *The high lasted all night.*
▸ FROM SUCCESS/ENJOYMENT **5** (*informal*) the feeling of extreme pleasure and excitement that sb gets from doing sth enjoyable or being successful at sth: *He was* ***on a real high*** *after winning the competition.* ◇ *the* ***highs and lows*** *of her acting career*
▸ SCHOOL **6** used in the name of a high school: *He graduated from Little Rock High in 1982.*

IDM **on 'high 1** (*formal*) in a high place: *We gazed down into the valley from on high.* **2** (*humorous*) the people in senior positions in an organization: *An order came down from on high that lunchbreaks were to be half an hour and no longer.* **3** in heaven: *The disaster was seen as a judgement from on high.*

■ *adv.* (high·er, high·est)
▸ FAR FROM GROUND/BOTTOM **1** at or to a position or level that is a long way up from the ground or from the bottom: *An eagle circled high overhead.* ◇ *I can't jump any higher.* ◇ *She never got very high in the company.* ◇ *His desk was* ***piled high*** *with papers.* ◇ *She's* ***aiming high*** (= hoping to be very successful) *in her exams.*
▸ VALUE/AMOUNT **2** at or to a large cost, value or amount: *Prices are expected to rise even higher this year.*
▸ SOUND **3** at a high PITCH: *I can't sing that high.* OPP **low**

IDM **,high and 'low** everywhere: *I've searched high and low for my purse.* **run 'high** (especially of feelings) to be strong and angry or excited: *Feelings ran high as the election approached.* ➲ more at FLY *v.*, HEAD *n.*, RIDE *v.*

Which Word?

high / tall

- **High** is used to talk about the measurement from the bottom to the top of something: *The fence is over five metres high.* ◇ *He has climbed some of the world's highest mountains.* You also use **high** to describe the distance of something from the ground: *How high was the plane when the engine failed?*
- **Tall** is used instead of **high** to talk about people: *My brother's much taller than me.* **Tall** is also used for things that are high and narrow such as trees: *She ordered cold beer in a tall glass.* ◇ *tall factory chimneys.* Buildings can be **high** or **tall**.

,high and 'tight *noun* (*US*) a military HAIRSTYLE in which the sides of the head are shaved and the top is cut very short

high·ball /'haɪbɔːl/ *noun, verb* (*NAmE*)
■ *noun* a strong alcoholic drink, such as WHISKY or GIN, mixed with FIZZY water (= with bubbles) or GINGER ALE, etc. and served with ice
■ *verb* (*informal*) **1** [I] + **adv./prep.** to go somewhere very quickly: *They highballed out of town.* **2** [T] **~ sth** to deliberately make an estimate of the cost, value, etc. of sth that is too high: *He thought she was highballing her salary requirements.* OPP **lowball**

'high beams *noun* [pl.] (*NAmE*) the lights on a car when they are pointing a long way ahead, not down at the road

,high-'born *adj.* (*old-fashioned* or *formal*) having parents who are members of the highest social class SYN **aristocratic** OPP **low-born**

high·boy /'haɪbɔɪ/ (*NAmE*) (*BrE* **tall·boy**) *noun* a tall piece of furniture with drawers, used for storing clothes in

high·brow /'haɪbraʊ/ *adj.* (sometimes *disapproving*) concerned with or interested in serious artistic or cultural ideas SYN **intellectual**: *highbrow newspapers* ◇ *highbrow readers* OPP **lowbrow** ➲ compare MIDDLEBROW

'high chair *noun* a special chair with long legs and a little seat and table, for a small child to sit in when eating ➲ VISUAL VOCAB page V19

,High 'Church *adj.* connected with the part of the Anglican Church that is most similar to the Roman Catholic Church in its beliefs and practices

,high-'class *adj.* **1** excellent; of good quality: *a high-class restaurant* ◇ *to stay in high-class accommodation* **2** connected with a high social class: *to come from a high-class background* OPP **low-class**

,high com'mand *noun* [usually sing.] the senior leaders of the armed forces of a country

,high com'mission *noun* **1** the office and the staff of an EMBASSY that represents the interests of one Commonwealth country in another **2** a group of people who are working for a government or an international organization on an important project: *the United Nations High Commission for Refugees*

,High Com'missioner *noun* **1** a person who is sent by one Commonwealth country to live in another, to protect the interests of their own country **2** a person who is head of an important international project: *the United Nations High Commissioner for Refugees*

,High 'Court (also **,High Court of 'Justice**) *noun* **1** a court in England and Wales that deals with the most serious CIVIL cases (= not criminal cases) **2** = THE SUPREME COURT

'high day *noun* (*old-fashioned*, *BrE*) the day of a religious festival
IDM **,high days and 'holidays** festivals and special occasions

,high-defi'nition *adj.* (*abbr.* **HD**) [only before noun] (*technical*) using or produced by a system that gives very clear detailed images: *high-definition television* ◇ *high-definition displays* ➲ see also HDTV

,high-'end *adj.* (*NAmE*) expensive and of high quality

High·er /'haɪə(r)/ *noun* (in Scotland) an exam in a particular subject at a higher level than STANDARD GRADE. Highers are usually taken around the age of 17 to 18.

high·er /'haɪə(r)/ *adj.* [only before noun] at a more advanced level; greater in rank or importance than others: *The case was referred to a higher court.* ◇ *higher mathematics* ◇ *My mind was on higher things.*

,higher 'animals, ,higher 'plants *noun* [pl.] (*technical*) animals and plants that have reached an advanced stage of development

,higher edu'cation *noun* [U] (*abbr.* **HE**) education and training at college and university, especially to degree level ➲ compare FURTHER EDUCATION

,higher-'up *noun* (*informal*) a person who has a higher rank or who is more senior than you

,highest common 'factor *noun* (*abbr.* **HCF**) (*mathematics*) the highest number that can be divided exactly into two or more numbers

,high ex'plosive *noun* [C, U] a very powerful substance that is used in bombs and can damage a very large area

high·fa·lu·tin /,haɪfə'luːtɪn/ *adj.* (*informal*) trying to be serious or important, but in a way that often appears silly and unnecessary SYN **pretentious**

,high fi'delity *noun* [U] (*old-fashioned*) = HI-FI

,high 'five *noun* (*especially NAmE*) an action to celebrate victory or to express happiness in which two people raise one arm each and hit their open hands together: *Way to go! High five!*

,high-'flown *adj.* (usually *disapproving*) (of language and ideas) very grand and complicated SYN **bombastic**: *His high-flown style just sounds absurd today.*

,high-'flyer (also **,high-'flier**) *noun* a person who has the desire and the ability to be very successful in their job or their studies: *academic high-flyers*

ˌ**high-ˈflying** *adj.* [only before noun] **1** very successful: *a high-flying career woman* **2** that flies very high in the air

ˌ**high-ˈgrade** *adj.* [usually before noun] of very good quality: *high-grade petrol*

ˈ**high ground** *noun* (usually **the high ground**) [sing.] the advantage in a discussion or an argument, etc: *The government is claiming the high ground in the education debate.* IDM see MORAL

ˌ**high-ˈhanded** *adj.* (of people or their behaviour) using authority in an unreasonable way, without considering the opinions of other people SYN **overbearing**

ˈ**high-hat** *noun* = HI-HAT ➲ VISUAL VOCAB page V30

ˌ**high ˈheels** *noun* [pl.] shoes that have very high heels, usually worn by women ▶ ˌ**high-ˈheeled** *adj.* [only before noun]: ***high-heeled shoes/boots***

ˌ**high ˈjinks** (*NAmE* also **hi·jinks**) *noun* [pl.] (*old-fashioned, informal*) lively and excited behaviour SYN **fun**

the ˈhigh jump *noun* [sing.] a sporting event in which people try to jump over a high bar that is gradually raised higher and higher: *She won a silver medal in the high jump.* ➲ VISUAL VOCAB page V38

IDM **be for the ˈhigh jump** (*BrE, informal*) to be going to be severely punished

high·land /ˈhaɪlənd/ *adj., noun*

■ ***adj.*** [only before noun] **1** connected with an area of land that has hills or mountains: *highland regions* **2 Highland** connected with the Highlands of Scotland ➲ compare LOWLAND

■ ***noun*** **1** [C, usually pl.] an area of land with hills or mountains **2 the Highlands** [pl.] the high mountain region of Scotland ➲ compare LOWLAND

ˌ**Highland ˈcattle** *noun* [pl.] cows of a breed with long rough hair and large horns. An individual animal is a **Highland cow**.

ˌ**Highland ˈdress** *noun* [U] traditional clothing worn by men in the Scottish Highlands, which includes a KILT and a SPORRAN (= a small decorated bag worn around the waist that hangs down at the front)

high·land·er /ˈhaɪləndə(r)/ *noun* **1** a person who comes from an area where there are a lot of mountains **2 High·land·er** a person who comes from the Scottish Highlands ➲ compare LOWLANDER

ˌ**Highland ˈfling** *noun* a fast Scottish dance that is danced by one person

ˌ**Highland ˈGames** *noun* [pl.] a Scottish event with traditional sports, dancing and music

ˌ**high-ˈlevel** *adj.* [usually before noun] **1** involving senior people: ***high-level talks/negotiations*** ◇ *high-level staff* **2** in a high position or place: *a high-level walk in the hills* **3** advanced: *a high-level course* **4** (*computing*) (of a computer language) similar to an existing language such as English, making it fairly simple to use OPP **low-level**

ˈ**high life** *noun* (also **the high life**) [sing., U] (also ˌ**high ˈliving** [U]) (sometimes *disapproving*) a way of life that involves going to parties and spending a lot of money on food, clothes, etc.

high·life /ˈhaɪlaɪf/ *noun* [U] a style of dance and music from W Africa influenced by rock and JAZZ and popular especially in the 1950s and 1960s

high·light 0‑w AW /ˈhaɪlaɪt/ *verb, noun*

■ ***verb*** **1** 0‑w **~ sth** to emphasize sth, especially so that people give it more attention: *The report highlights the major problems facing society today.* ➲ LANGUAGE BANK at EMPHASIS **2 ~ sth** to mark part of a text with a special coloured pen, or to mark an area on a computer screen, to emphasize it or make it easier to see: *I've highlighted the important passages in yellow.* **3 ~ sth** to make some parts of your hair a lighter colour than the rest by using a chemical substance on them

■ ***noun*** **1** 0‑w the best, most interesting or most exciting part of sth: *One of the highlights of the trip was seeing the Taj Mahal.* ◇ *The highlights of the match will be shown later this evening.* **2 highlights** [pl.] areas of hair that are lighter than the rest, usually because a chemical substance has been put on them ➲ compare LOWLIGHTS **3 highlights** [pl.] (*technical*) the light or bright part of a picture or photograph

high·light·er /ˈhaɪlaɪtə(r)/ *noun* **1** (also ˈ**highlighter pen**) a special pen used for marking words in a text in bright colours ➲ VISUAL VOCAB page V56 **2** a coloured substance that you put above your eyes or on your cheeks to make yourself more attractive

high·ly 0‑w /ˈhaɪli/ *adv.*

1 0‑w very: *highly successful/skilled/intelligent* ◇ *highly competitive/critical/sensitive* ◇ *It is **highly unlikely** that she'll be late.* **2** 0‑w at or to a high standard, level or amount: ***highly trained/educated*** ◇ *a **highly paid** job* **3** 0‑w with admiration or praise: *His teachers **think very highly of him*** (= have a very good opinion of him). ◇ *She **speaks highly of you.*** ◇ *Her novels are very highly regarded.*

ˌ**highly ˈstrung** (*BrE*) (*NAmE* ˌ**high-ˈstrung**) *adj.* (of a person or an animal) nervous and easily upset: *a sensitive and highly-strung child* ◇ *Their new horse is very highly strung.* ➲ compare NERVOUS

ˌ**high-ˈmainten·ance** *adj.* needing a lot of attention or effort: *a high-maintenance girlfriend* OPP **low-maintenance**

ˌ**high-ˈminded** *adj.* (of people or ideas) having strong moral principles ▶ ˌ**high-ˈminded·ness** *noun* [U]

High·ness /ˈhaɪnəs/ *noun* **His/Her/Your Highness** a title of respect used when talking to or about a member of the royal family ➲ see also ROYAL HIGHNESS

ˌ**high ˈnoon** *noun* **1** exactly twelve o'clock in the middle of the day **2** (*formal*) the most important stage of sth, when sth that will decide the future happens

ˌ**high-ˈoctane** *adj.* [only before noun] **1** (of fuel used in engines) of very good quality and very efficient **2** (*informal*) full of energy; powerful: *a high-octane athlete*

ˌ**high-perˈform·ance** *adj.* [only before noun] that can go very fast or do complicated things: *a **high-performance car/computer, etc.***

ˌ**high-ˈpitched** *adj.* (of sounds) very high: *a high-pitched voice/whistle* OPP **low-pitched**

ˈ**high point** (*BrE* also ˈ**high spot**) *noun* the most interesting, enjoyable or best part of sth: *It was the high point of the evening.* OPP **low point**

ˌ**high-ˈpowered** *adj.* **1** (of people) having a lot of power and influence; full of energy: *high-powered executives* **2** (of activities) important; with a lot of responsibility: *a high-powered job* **3** (also ˌ**high-ˈpower**) (of machines) very powerful: *a **high-powered car/computer, etc.***

ˌ**high ˈpressure** *noun* [U] **1** the condition of air, gas, or liquid that is kept in a small space by force: *Water is forced through the pipes at **high pressure**.* **2** a condition of the air which affects the weather, when the PRESSURE is higher than average ➲ compare LOW PRESSURE

ˌ**high-ˈpressure** *adj.* [only before noun] **1** that involves aggressive ways of persuading sb to do sth or to buy sth: *high-pressure sales techniques* **2** that involves a lot of worry and anxiety SYN **stressful**: *a high-pressure job* **3** using or containing a great force of a gas or a liquid: *a high-pressure water jet*

ˌ**high-ˈpriced** *adj.* [usually before noun] expensive: *high-priced housing/cars* OPP **low-priced**

ˌ**high ˈpriest** *noun* **1** the most important priest in the Jewish religion in the past **2** (*feminine* ˌ**high ˈpriestess**) an important priest in some other non-Christian religions: (*figurative*) *Janis Joplin was known as the High Priestess of Rock.*

ˌ**high-ˈprofile** *adj.* [usually before noun] receiving or involving a lot of attention and discussion on television, in newspapers, etc: *a high-profile campaign* ➲ see also PROFILE

ˌ**high-ˈranking** *adj.* senior; important: *a **high-ranking officer/official*** ◇ *a high-ranking post* OPP **low-ranking**

H

ˌhigh-resoˈlution (also **hi-res, high-res**) *adj.* (of a photograph or an image on a computer or television screen) showing a lot of clear sharp detail: *a high-resolution scan* OPP **low-resolution**

ˈhigh-rise *adj.* [only before noun] (of a building) very tall and having a lot of floors: *high-rise housing* ▸ **ˈhigh-rise** *noun*: *to live in a high-rise* ➲ compare LOW-RISE

ˌhigh-ˈrisk *adj.* [usually before noun] involving a lot of danger and the risk of injury, death, damage, etc: *a high-risk sport* ◇ *high-risk patients* (= who are very likely to get a particular illness) ➲ compare LOW-RISK

ˈhigh road *noun* [usually sing.] **1** (*old-fashioned, BrE*) a main or important road **2 ~ (to sth)** the most direct way: *This is the high road to democracy.*
IDM **take the ˈhigh road (in sth)** (*NAmE*) to take the most positive course of action: *He took the high road in his campaign.*

H

ˌhigh ˈroller *noun* (*NAmE, informal*) a person who spends a lot of money, especially on gambling

ˈhigh school *noun* [C, U] **1** (in the US and some other countries) a school for young people between the ages of 14 and 18 **2** often used in Britain in the names of schools for young people between the ages of 11 and 18: *Worthing High School* ➲ compare SECONDARY SCHOOL ➲ **COLLOCATIONS** at EDUCATION

the ˌhigh ˈseas *noun* [pl.] (*formal* or *literary*) the areas of sea that are not under the legal control of any one country

ˌhigh ˈseason *noun* [U, sing.] (*especially BrE*) the time of year when a hotel or tourist area receives most visitors ➲ compare LOW SEASON

ˌhigh-seˈcurity *adj.* [only before noun] **1** (of buildings and places) very carefully locked and guarded: *a high-security prison* **2** (of prisoners) kept in a prison that is very carefully locked and guarded

ˈhigh-sounding *adj.* (*especially BrE, often disapproving*) (of language or ideas) complicated and intended to sound important SYN **pretentious**

ˌhigh-ˈspeed *adj.* [only before noun] that travels, works or happens very fast: *a high-speed train* ◇ *a high-speed car chase*

ˌhigh-ˈspirit·ed *adj.* **1** (of people) very lively and active: *a high-spirited child* ◇ *high-spirited behaviour* **2** (of animals, especially horses) lively and difficult to control OPP **placid** ➲ see also SPIRIT

ˈhigh spot *noun* (*BrE*) = HIGH POINT

ˈhigh street (*BrE*) (*NAmE* **ˈmain street**) *noun* (especially in names) the main street of a town, where most shops/stores, banks, etc. are: *Peckham High Street* ◇ *106 High Street, Peckham* ◇ ***high-street banks/shops*** ➲ **VISUAL VOCAB** page V3

ˌhigh-ˈstrung (*NAmE*) (*BrE* **ˌhighly ˈstrung**) *adj.* (of a person or an animal) nervous and easily upset ➲ **SYNONYMS** at NERVOUS

ˌhigh ˈtable *noun* [C, U] (*BrE*) a table on a raised platform, where the most important people at a formal dinner sit to eat

high·tail /ˈhaɪteɪl/ *verb*
IDM **ˈhightail it** (*informal, especially NAmE*) to leave somewhere very quickly

ˌhigh ˈtea *noun* (*BrE*) a meal consisting of cooked food, bread and butter and cakes, usually with tea to drink, eaten in the late afternoon or early evening instead of dinner

ˌhigh-ˈtech (also **ˌhi-ˈtech**) *adj.* (*informal*) **1** using the most modern methods and machines, especially electronic ones: *high-tech industries* **2** (of designs, objects, etc.) very modern in appearance; using modern materials: *a high-tech table made of glass and steel* ➲ compare LOW-TECH

ˌhigh techˈnology *noun* [U] the most modern methods and machines, especially electronic ones; the use of these in industry, etc.

ˌhigh-ˈtension *adj.* [only before noun] carrying a very powerful electric current: ***high-tension wires/cables***

ˌhigh ˈtide *noun* [U, C] the time when the sea has risen to its highest level; the sea at this time: *You can't walk along this beach **at high tide**.* ➲ compare FLOOD TIDE, HIGH WATER OPP **low tide**

ˈhigh-tops *noun* [pl.] (*especially NAmE*) sports shoes that cover the ankle, worn especially for playing BASKETBALL ▸ **ˈhigh-top** *adj.* [usually before noun]: *high-top sneakers*

ˌhigh ˈtreason *noun* [U] = TREASON

ˈhigh-up *noun* (*BrE, informal*) an important person with a high rank

ˌhigh ˈwater *noun* [U] the time when the sea or the water in a river has risen to its highest level: *Fishing is good at high water.* ➲ compare HIGH TIDE IDM see HELL

ˌhigh-ˈwater mark *noun* a line or mark showing the highest point that the sea or FLOODWATER has reached: (*figurative*) *the high-water mark of Parisian fashion* (= the most successful time) ➲ compare LOW-WATER MARK

high·way 🔑 /ˈhaɪweɪ/ *noun*
1 🔑 (*especially NAmE*) a main road for travelling long distances, especially one connecting and going through cities and towns: *an interstate highway* ◇ *Highway patrol officers closed the road.* **2** (*BrE, formal*) a public road: *A parked car was obstructing the highway.*
IDM **ˌhighway ˈrobbery** (*informal, especially NAmE*) = DAYLIGHT ROBBERY at DAYLIGHT ➲ more at WAY *n.*

the ˌHighway ˈCode *noun* [sing.] (in Britain) the official rules for drivers and other users of public roads; the book that contains these rules

high·way·man /ˈhaɪweɪmən/ *noun* (*pl.* **-men** /-mən/) a man, usually on a horse and carrying a gun, who stole from travellers on public roads in the past

ˌhigh ˈwire *noun* [usually sing.] a rope or wire that is stretched high above the ground, and used by CIRCUS performers SYN **tightrope**

ˈhi-hat (also **ˈhigh-hat**) *noun* a pair of CYMBALS on a set of drums, operated by the foot ➲ **VISUAL VOCAB** page V30

hi·jab /hɪˈdʒɑːb/ *noun* **1** [C] a head covering worn in public by some Muslim women **2** [U] the religious system which controls the wearing of such clothing

hi·jack /ˈhaɪdʒæk/ *verb* **1 ~ sth** to use violence or threats to take control of a vehicle, especially a plane, in order to force it to travel to a different place or to demand sth from a government: *The plane was hijacked by two armed men on a flight from London to Rome.* ➲ **COLLOCATIONS** at CRIME **2 ~ sth** (*disapproving*) to use or take control of sth, especially a meeting, in order to advertise your own aims and interests ▸ **hi·jack·ing** (also **hi·jack**) *noun* [C, U]: *There have been a series of hijackings recently in the area.* ◇ *an unsuccessful hijack* ➲ compare CARJACKING

hi·jack·er /ˈhaɪdʒækə(r)/ *noun* a person who hijacks a plane or other vehicle

hi·jinks (*NAmE*) = HIGH JINKS

Hijra /ˈhɪdʒrə/ *noun* = HEGIRA

hike /haɪk/ *noun, verb*
■ ***noun* 1** a long walk in the country: *They went on a ten-mile hike through the forest.* ◇ *We could go into town but it's a real hike* (= a long way) *from here.* **2** (*informal*) a large or sudden increase in prices, costs, etc: *a **tax/price hike*** ◇ **~ in sth** *the latest hike in interest rates*
IDM **take a ˈhike** (*NAmE, informal*) a rude way of telling sb to go away
■ ***verb* 1** [I, T] to go for a long walk in the country, especially for pleasure: *strong boots for hiking over rough country* ◇ **~ sth** (*NAmE*) *to hike the Rockies* **2** [I] **go hiking** to spend time hiking for pleasure: *If the weather's fine, we'll go hiking this weekend.* **3** [T] **~ sth (up)** to increase prices, taxes, etc. suddenly by large amounts: *The government hiked up the price of milk by over 40%.*
PHR V **ˌhike sth↔ˈup** (*informal*) to pull or lift sth up, espe-

cially your clothing SYN **hitch up**: *She hiked up her skirt and waded into the river.*

hiker /ˈhaɪkə(r)/ *noun* a person who goes for long walks in the country for pleasure ➲ see also HITCHHIKER

hik·ing /ˈhaɪkɪŋ/ *noun* [U] the activity of going for long walks in the country for pleasure: *to go hiking* ◇ *hiking boots* ➲ VISUAL VOCAB page V52

hil·ari·ous /hɪˈleəriəs; *NAmE* -ˈler-/ *adj.* extremely funny: *a hilarious joke/story* ◇ *Lynn found the whole situation hilarious.* ◇ *Do you know Pete? He's hilarious.* ➲ SYNONYMS at FUNNY ▸ **hil·ari·ous·ly** *adv.*: *hilariously funny*

hil·ar·ity /hɪˈlærəti/ *noun* [U] a state of great AMUSEMENT which makes people laugh

hill 0- /hɪl/ *noun*
1 0- [C] an area of land that is higher than the land around it, but not as high as a mountain: *a region of gently rolling hills* ◇ *a* ***hill farm/town/fort*** ◇ *The house is built* ***on the side of a hill*** *overlooking the river.* ◇ *I love walking* ***in the hills*** (= in the area where there are hills). ➲ VISUAL VOCAB page V2 ➲ see also ANTHILL, FOOTHILL, MOLEHILL **2** 0- [C] a slope on a road: *Always take care when driving down* ***steep hills.*** ◇ *a hill start* (= the act of starting a vehicle on a slope) ➲ see also DOWNHILL, UPHILL **3 the Hill** [sing.] (*NAmE, informal*) = CAPITOL HILL
IDM **a ˌhill of ˈbeans** (*old-fashioned, NAmE, informal*) something that is not worth much **ˌover the ˈhill** (*informal*) (of a person) old and therefore no longer useful or attractive ➲ more at OLD

hill·billy /ˈhɪlbɪli/ *noun* (*pl.* **-ies**) (*NAmE, disapproving*) a person who lives in the mountains and is thought to be stupid by people who live in the towns

hil·lock /ˈhɪlək/ *noun* a small hill

hill·side /ˈhɪlsaɪd/ *noun* the side of a hill: *The crops will not grow on exposed hillsides.* ◇ *Our hotel was on the hillside overlooking the lake.*

ˈhill station *noun* a small town in the hills, especially in S Asia, where people go to find cooler weather in summer

hill·top /ˈhɪltɒp; *NAmE* -tɑːp/ *noun* the top of a hill: *the hilltop town of Urbino*

hill·walk·ing /ˈhɪlwɔːkɪŋ/ *noun* [U] the activity of walking on or up hills in the countryside for pleasure

hilly /ˈhɪli/ *adj.* (**hill·ier, hilli·est**) having a lot of hills: *a* ***hilly area/region***

hilt /hɪlt/ *noun* the handle of a SWORD, knife, etc. ➲ picture at SWORD
IDM **(up) to the ˈhilt** as much as possible: *We're mortgaged up to the hilt.* ◇ *They have promised to back us to the hilt.*

him 0- /hɪm; ɪm/ *pron.*
1 0- used as the object of a verb, after the verb *be* or after a preposition to refer to a male person or animal that has already been mentioned or is easily identified: *When did you see him?* ◇ *He took the children with him.* ◇ *I'm taller than him.* ◇ *It's him.* ➲ compare HE ➲ note at GENDER **2 Him** used when referring to God

him·self 0- /hɪmˈself/ *pron.*
1 0- (the reflexive form of *he*) used when the man or boy who performs an action is also affected by it: *He introduced himself.* ◇ *Peter ought to be ashamed of himself.* **2** 0- used to emphasize the male subject or object of a sentence: *The doctor said so himself.* ◇ *Did you see the manager himself?*
IDM **be, seem, etc. himˈself** (of a man or boy) to be in a normal state of health or happiness; not influenced by other people: *He didn't seem quite himself this morning.* ◇ *He needed space to be himself.* **(all) by himˈself 1** alone; without anyone else: *He lives all by himself.* **2** without help: *He managed to repair the car by himself.* **(all) to himˈself** for only him to have or use: *He has the house to himself during the week.*

hind /haɪnd/ *adj., noun*
▪ ***adj.*** [only before noun] the **hind** legs or feet of an animal with four legs are those at the back: *The horse reared up on its hind legs.* OPP **fore, front** IDM see TALK *v.*
▪ ***noun*** a female DEER, especially a RED DEER; a DOE ➲ compare HART

hind·brain /ˈhaɪndbreɪn/ *noun* (*anatomy*) the part of the brain near the base of the head

hin·der /ˈhɪndə(r)/ *verb* to make it difficult for sb to do sth or for sth to happen SYN **hamper**: **~ sb/sth** *a political situation that hinders economic growth* ◇ *Some teachers felt hindered by a lack of resources.* ◇ **~ sb/sth from sth/from doing sth** *An injury was hindering him from playing his best.* ➲ see also HINDRANCE

Hindi /ˈhɪndi/ *noun* [U] one of the official languages of India, spoken especially in northern India ▸ **Hindi** *adj.*

hind·limb /ˈhaɪndlɪm/ *noun* one of the legs at the back of an animal's body

hind·quar·ters /ˌhaɪndˈkwɔːtəz; *NAmE* -ˈkwɔːrtərz/ *noun* [pl.] the back part of an animal that has four legs, including its two back legs

hin·drance /ˈhɪndrəns/ *noun* **1** [C, usually sing.] a person or thing that makes it more difficult for sb to do sth or for sth to happen: *To be honest, she was more of a hindrance than a help.* ◇ **~ to sth/sb** *The high price is a major hindrance to potential buyers.* **2** [U] (*formal*) the act of making it more difficult for sb to do sth or for sth to happen: *They were able to complete their journey without further hindrance.* ➲ see also HINDER IDM see LET *n.*

hind·sight /ˈhaɪndsaɪt/ *noun* [U] the understanding that you have of a situation only after it has happened and that means you would have done things in a different way: ***With hindsight*** *it is easy to say they should not have released him.* ◇ *What looks obvious in hindsight was not at all obvious at the time.* ◇ *It's easy to criticize* ***with the benefit of hindsight.*** ➲ compare FORESIGHT

Hindu /ˈhɪnduː; ˌhɪnˈduː/ *noun* a person whose religion is Hinduism ▸ **Hindu** *adj.*: *a Hindu temple*

Hin·du·ism /ˈhɪnduːɪzəm/ *noun* [U] the main religion of India and Nepal which includes the worship of one or more gods and belief in REINCARNATION

hinge /hɪndʒ/ *noun, verb*
▪ ***noun*** a piece of metal, plastic, etc. on which a door, lid or gate moves freely as it opens or closes: *The door had been pulled off its hinges.*
▪ ***verb*** [usually passive] **~ sth** to attach sth with a hinge ▸ **hinged** *adj.*: *a hinged door/lid*
PHR V **ˈhinge on/upon sth** (of an action, a result, etc.) to depend on sth completely: *Everything hinges on the outcome of these talks.* ◇ **~ how, what, etc...** *His success hinges on how well he does at the interview.*

hinge

Hing·lish /ˈhɪŋglɪʃ/ *noun* [U] (*informal*) language which is a mixture of ENGLISH and HINDI, especially a type of English that includes many Hindi words

hint /hɪnt/ *noun, verb*
▪ ***noun*** **1** something that you say or do in an indirect way in order to show sb what you are thinking: *He gave a* ***broad hint*** (= one that was obvious) *that he was thinking of retiring.* ◇ *Should I* ***drop a hint*** (= give a hint) *to Matt?* **2** something that suggests what will happen in the future SYN **sign**: *At the first hint of trouble, they left.* **3** [usually sing.] **~ (of sth)** a small amount of sth SYN **suggestion, trace**: *a hint of a smile* ◇ *There was more than a hint of sadness in his voice.* ◇ *The walls were painted white with a hint of peach.* **4** [usually pl.] **~ (on sth)** a small piece of practical information or advice SYN **tip**: *handy hints on saving money*
IDM **take a/the ˈhint** to understand what sb wants you to do even though they tell you in an indirect way: *I thought they'd never go—some people just can't take a hint.* ◇ *Sarah hoped he'd take the hint and leave her alone.*
▪ ***verb*** [I, T] to suggest sth in an indirect way: **~ at sth** *What are you hinting at?* ◇ **~ (that)...** *They hinted (that) there might be more job losses.* ◇ **+ speech** *'I might know something about it,' he hinted.*

hin·ter·land /ˈhɪntəlænd; *NAmE* -tərl-/ *noun* [usually sing.] the areas of a country that are away from the coast, from the banks of a large river or from the main cities: *the rural/agricultural hinterland*

hip /hɪp/ *noun, adj., exclamation*
■ ***noun* 1** the area at either side of the body between the top of the leg and the waist; the joint at the top of the leg: *She stood with her hands on her hips.* ◇ *These jeans are too tight around the hips.* ◇ *a hip replacement operation* ◇ *the hip bone* ◇ *She broke her hip in the fall.* ➲ COLLOCATIONS at PHYSICAL ➲ VISUAL VOCAB page V48 **2 -hipped** (in adjectives) having hips of the size or shape mentioned: *large-hipped* ◇ *slim-hipped* **3** (also ˈ**rose hip**) the red fruit that grows on some types of wild ROSE bush IDM see SHOOT *v.*
■ ***adj.*** (**hip·per, hip·pest**) (*informal*) following or knowing what is fashionable in clothes, music, etc.
■ ***exclamation***
IDM **hip, hip, hooˈray!** (also *less frequent* **hip, hip, hurˈrah/hurˈray!**) used by a group of people to show their approval of sb. One person in the group says 'hip, hip' and the others then shout 'hooray'.: *'Three cheers for the bride and groom: Hip, hip…' 'Hooray!'*

ˈ**hip bath** *noun* a small bath/BATHTUB that you sit in rather than lie down in

ˈ**hip flask** (*BrE*) (also **flask** *NAmE, BrE*) *noun* a small flat bottle made of metal or glass and often covered with leather, used for carrying alcohol

ˈ**hip hop** *noun* [U] **1** a type of popular music with spoken words and a steady beat played on electronic instruments, originally played by young African Americans **2** the culture of the young African Americans and others who enjoy this type of music, including special styles of art, dancing, dress, etc.

ˈ**hip-huggers** (*NAmE*) (*BrE* **hip·sters**) *noun* [pl.] trousers/pants that cover the hips but not the waist ▸ ˈ**hip-hugger** *adj.* [only before noun]

ˈ**hip joint** *noun* the joint that connects the leg to the body, at the top of the THIGH bone

hip·pie (also **hippy**) /ˈhɪpi/ *noun* (*pl.* -ies) a person who rejects the way that most people live in Western society, often having long hair, wearing brightly coloured clothes and taking illegal drugs. The hippie movement was most popular in the 1960s.

hippo /ˈhɪpəʊ; *NAmE* ˈhɪpoʊ/ *noun* (*pl.* -os) (*informal*) = HIPPOPOTAMUS

hippo·cam·pus /ˌhɪpəˈkæmpəs/ *noun* (*pl.* **hippo·campi** /-paɪ; -pi/) (*anatomy*) either of the two areas of the brain thought to be the centre of emotion and memory

ˌ**hip ˈpocket** *noun* a pocket at the back or the side of a pair of trousers/pants or a skirt

the Hippo·crat·ic oath /ˌhɪpəkrætɪk ˈəʊθ; *NAmE* ˈoʊθ/ *noun* [sing.] the promise that doctors make to keep to the principles of the medical profession

hip·po·drome /ˈhɪpədrəʊm; *NAmE* -droʊm/ *noun* **1** (*BrE*) used in the names of some theatres and concert halls **2** (*NAmE*) an ARENA, especially one used for horse shows **3** a track in ancient Greece or Rome on which horse races or CHARIOT races took place

hippo·pot·amus /ˌhɪpəˈpɒtəməs; *NAmE* -ˈpɑːtə-/ (also *informal* **hippo**) *noun* (*pl.* **hippo·pot·amuses** /-məsɪz/ or **hip·po·pot·ami** /-maɪ/) a large heavy African animal with thick dark skin and short legs, that lives in rivers and lakes

hippy = HIPPIE

hip·sters /ˈhɪpstəz; *NAmE* -stərz/ (*BrE*) (*NAmE* ˈ**hip-huggers**) *noun* [pl.] trousers/pants that cover the hips but not the waist: *a pair of hipsters* ▸ **hip·ster** *adj.* [only before noun]: *hipster jeans*

hira·gana /ˌhɪrəˈɡɑːnə/ *noun* [U] (from *Japanese*) a set of symbols used in Japanese writing ➲ compare KATAKANA

hire /ˈhaɪə(r)/ *verb, noun*
■ ***verb* 1** [T] **~ sth** (*especially BrE*) to pay money to borrow sth for a short time: *to hire a car/room/video* ➲ note at RENT **2** [T, I] **~ (sb)** (*especially NAmE*) to give sb a job: *She was hired three years ago.* ◇ *He does the **hiring and firing** in our company.* ➲ COLLOCATIONS at JOB **3** [T] **~ sb/sth** to employ sb for a short time to do a particular job: *to hire a lawyer* ◇ *They hired a firm of consultants to design the new system.*
PHR V ˌ**hire sth↔ˈout** to let sb use sth for a short time, in return for payment ˌ**hire yourself ˈout (to sb)** to arrange to work for sb: *He hired himself out to whoever needed his services.*
■ ***noun* 1** [U] (*especially BrE*) the act of paying to use sth for a short time: *bicycles **for hire**, £2 an hour* ◇ *a **hire car*** ◇ *a **car hire** firm* ◇ *The price includes the hire of the hall.* ◇ *The costumes are **on hire from** the local theatre.* ➲ note at RENT **2** [C] (*especially NAmE*) a person who has recently been given a job by a company IDM see PLY *v.*

ˌ**hired ˈhand** *noun* (*NAmE*) a person who is paid to work on a farm

hire·ling /ˈhaɪəlɪŋ; *NAmE* ˈhaɪərlɪŋ/ *noun* (*disapproving*) a person who is willing to do anything or work for anyone as long as they are paid

ˌ**hire ˈpurchase** *noun* [U] (*BrE*) (*abbr.* **h.p., HP**) (*NAmE* **inˈstallment plan**) a method of buying an article by making regular payments for it over several months or years. The article only belongs to the person who is buying it when all the payments have been made: *a hire purchase agreement* ◇ *We're buying a new cooker **on hire purchase**.* ➲ compare CREDIT

hi-res (also **high-res**) /ˌhaɪ ˈrez/ *adj.* (*informal*) = HIGH-RESOLUTION

hir·sute /ˈhɜːsjuːt; *NAmE* ˈhɜːrsuːt/ *adj.* (*literary* or *humorous*) (especially of a man) having a lot of hair on the face or body SYN **hairy**

his /hɪz; ɪz/ *det., pron.*
■ ***det.*** (the possessive form of *he*) **1** of or belonging to a man or boy who has already been mentioned or is easily identified: *James has sold his car.* ◇ *He broke his leg skiing.* **2 His** of or belonging to God
■ ***pron.*** of or belonging to him: *He took my hand in his.* ◇ *The choice was his.* ◇ *a friend of his* ➲ note at GENDER

His·pan·ic /hɪˈspænɪk/ *adj., noun*
■ ***adj.*** of or connected with Spain or Spanish-speaking countries, especially those of Latin America
■ ***noun*** a person whose first language is Spanish, especially one from a Latin American country living in the US or Canada

His·pan·o- /hɪˈspænəʊ; *NAmE* -noʊ/ *combining form* (in nouns and adjectives) Spanish: *the Hispano-French border* ◇ *Hispanophile*

hiss /hɪs/ *verb, noun*
■ ***verb* 1** [I] **~ (at sb/sth)** to make a sound like a long 's': *The steam escaped with a loud hissing noise.* ◇ *The snake lifted its head and hissed.* **2** [T, I] **~ (sb/sth)** | **~ (sb/sth + adv./prep.)** to make a sound like a long 's' to show disapproval of sb/sth, especially an actor or a speaker: *He was booed and hissed off the stage.* **3** [I, T] to say sth in a quiet angry voice: **~ at sb** *He hissed at them to be quiet.* ◇ **+ speech** *'Leave me alone!' she hissed.*
■ ***noun*** a sound like a long 's'; this sound used to show disapproval of sb: *the hiss of the air brakes* ◇ *the snake's hiss* ◇ *The performance was met with boos and hisses.*

ˈ**hissy fit** *noun* [C, usually sing.] (*informal*) a state of being bad-tempered and unreasonable SYN **tantrum**: *She **threw a hissy fit** because her dressing room wasn't painted blue.*

his·ta·mine /ˈhɪstəmiːn/ *noun* [U] (*medical*) a chemical substance that is given out in the body in response to an injury or an ALLERGY ➲ see also ANTIHISTAMINE

histo·gram /ˈhɪstəɡræm/ *noun* (*technical*) a diagram which uses RECTANGLES (= bars) of different heights (and sometimes different widths) to show different amounts, so that they can be compared ➲ compare BAR CHART

his·tolo·gy /hɪˈstɒlədʒi; *NAmE* -ˈstɑːl-/ *noun* [U] the scientific study of the extremely small structures that form living TISSUE ▶ **his·tolo·gist** /hɪˈstɒlədʒɪst; *NAmE* -ˈstɑːl-/ *noun*

histo·path·ology /ˌhɪstəʊpəˈθɒlədʒi; *NAmE* ˌhɪstoʊpə-ˈθɑːl-/ *noun* [U] the study of changes in cells where disease is present

his·tor·ian /hɪˈstɔːriən/ *noun* a person who studies or writes about history; an expert in history HELP Some speakers do not pronounce the 'h' at the beginning of **historian** and use 'an' instead of 'a' before it. This now sounds old-fashioned.

his·tor·ic /hɪˈstɒrɪk; *NAmE* -ˈstɔːr-; -ˈstɑːr-/ *adj.* [usually before noun] **1** important in history; likely to be thought of as important at some time in the future: *a historic building/monument* ◇ *The area is of special historic interest.* ◇ *a historic occasion/decision/day/visit/victory* **2** of a period during which history was recorded: *in historic times* ➲ compare PREHISTORIC HELP Some speakers do not pronounce the 'h' at the beginning of **historic** and use 'an' instead of 'a' before it. This now sounds old-fashioned.

Which Word?

historic / historical

- **Historic** is usually used to describe something that is so important that it is likely to be remembered: *Today is a historic occasion for our country.* **Historical** usually describes something that is connected with the past or with the study of history, or something that really happened in the past: *I have been doing some historical research.* ◇ *Was Robin Hood a historical figure?*

his·tor·ic·al 0̶ /hɪˈstɒrɪkl; *NAmE* -ˈstɔːr-; -ˈstɑːr-/ *adj.* [usually before noun] **1** 0̶ connected with the past: *the historical background to the war* ◇ *You must place these events in their **historical context**.* **2** 0̶ connected with the study of history: ***historical documents/records/research*** ◇ *The building is of **historical importance**.* **3** 0̶ (of a book, film/movie, etc.) about people and events in the past: *a historical novel* HELP Some speakers do not pronounce the 'h' at the beginning of **historical** and use 'an' instead of 'a' before it. This now sounds old-fashioned. ▶ **his·tor·ic·al·ly** /-kli/ *adv.*: *The book is historically inaccurate.* ◇ *Historically, there has always been a great deal of rivalry between the two families.*

his·tori·cism /hɪˈstɒrɪsɪzəm; *NAmE* -ˈstɔːr-; -ˈstɑːr-/ *noun* [U] the theory that cultural and social events and situations can be explained by history

the hisˌtoric ˈpresent *noun* [sing.] (*grammar*) the simple present tense used to describe events in the past in order to make the description more powerful

his·tor·iog·raphy /hɪˌstɒriˈɒgrəfi; *NAmE* -ˌstɔːriˈɑːg-; -ˌstɑːr-/ *noun* [U] the study of writing about history ▶ **his·tori·og·raph·ical** /hɪˌstɒriəˈgræfɪkl; *NAmE* -ˌstɔːr-; -ˌstɑː-/ *adj.*

his·tory 0̶ /ˈhɪstri/ *noun* (*pl.* -ies) **1** 0̶ [U] all the events that happened in the past: *a turning point in human history* ◇ *one of the worst disasters in **recent history*** ◇ *a people with no **sense of history*** ◇ *Many people throughout history have dreamt of a world without war.* ◇ *The area was inhabited long before the dawn of **recorded history*** (= before people wrote about events). ◇ *These events changed the **course of history**.* **2** 0̶ [sing., U] the past events concerned in the development of a particular place, subject, etc: *the history of Ireland/democracy/popular music* ◇ *The **local history** of the area is fascinating.* ◇ *The school traces its history back to 1865.* **3** 0̶ [U] the study of past events as a subject at school or university: *a **history teacher*** ◇ *a degree in History* ◇ ***social/economic/political history*** ◇ ***ancient/medieval/modern history*** ◇ *She's studying **art history**.* ➲ see also NATURAL HISTORY **4** 0̶ [C] a written or spoken account of past events: *She's writing a new history of Europe.* ◇ *She went on to catalogue a long history of disasters.* **5** 0̶ [sing.] **~ (of sth)** a record of sth happening frequently in the past life of a person, family or place; the set of facts that are known about sb's past life: *He has a history of violent crime.* ◇ *There is a history of heart disease in my family.* ◇ *a patient's **medical history*** ➲ see also CASE HISTORY, LIFE HISTORY

IDM **be ˈhistory** (*informal*) to be dead or no longer important: *Another mistake like that and you're history.* ◇ *We won't talk about that—that's history.* ◇ *That's **past history** now.* **the ˈhistory books** the record of great achievements in history: *She has earned her place in the history books.* **history reˈpeats itself** used to say that things often happen later in the same way as before **make ˈhistory | go down in ˈhistory** to be or do sth so important that it will be recorded in history: *a discovery that made medical history* ➲ more at REST *n.*

his·tri·on·ic /ˌhɪstriˈɒnɪk; *NAmE* -ˈɑːnɪk/ *adj.* [usually before noun] (*formal, disapproving*) **histrionic** behaviour is very emotional and is intended to attract attention in a way that does not seem sincere ▶ **his·tri·on·ic·al·ly** /-kli/ *adv.* **his·tri·on·ics** *noun* [pl.]: *She was used to her mother's histrionics.*

H

hit 0̶ /hɪt/ *verb, noun*

■ *verb* (**hit·ting, hit, hit**)

▸ TOUCH SB/STH WITH FORCE **1** 0̶ [T] to bring your hand, or an object you are holding, against sb/sth quickly and with force: **~ sb/sth** *My parents never used to hit me.* ◇ **~ sb/sth with sth** *He hit the nail squarely on the head with the hammer.* ◇ *She hit him on the head with her umbrella.* **2** 0̶ [T] **~ sth/sb** to come against sth/sb with force, especially causing damage or injury: *The bus hit the bridge.* ◇ *I was hit by a falling stone.* **3** 0̶ [T] **~ sth (on/against sth)** to knock a part of your body against sth: *He hit his head on the low ceiling.* **4** 0̶ [T, often passive] **~ sb/sth** (of a bullet, bomb, etc. or a person using them) to reach and touch a person or thing suddenly and with force: *The town was hit by bombs again last night.* ◇ *He was hit by a sniper.*

▸ BALL **5** 0̶ [T] **~ sth (+ adv./prep.)** to bring a BAT, etc. against a ball and push it away with force: *She hit the ball too hard and it went out of the court.* ◇ *We've hit our ball over the fence!* **6** [T] **~ sth** (*sport*) to score points by hitting a ball: *to hit a home run*

▸ HAVE BAD EFFECT **7** 0̶ [T, I] **~ (sb/sth)** to have a bad effect on sb/sth: *The tax increases will certainly hit the poor.* ◇ *His death didn't really hit me at first.* ◇ *Rural areas have been worst hit by the strike.* ◇ *Spain was one of the **hardest hit** countries.* ◇ *A tornado hit on Tuesday night.*

▸ ATTACK **8** [T, I] **~ (sb/sth)** to attack sb/sth: *We hit the enemy when they least expected it.*

▸ REACH **9** [T] **~ sth** (*informal*) to reach a place: *Follow this footpath and you'll eventually hit the road.* ◇ *The President **hits town** tomorrow.* **10** [T] **~ sth** to reach a particular level: *Temperatures hit 40° yesterday.* ◇ *The euro hit a record low in trading today.*

▸ PROBLEM/DIFFICULTY **11** [T] **~ sth** (*informal*) to experience sth difficult or unpleasant: *We seem to have hit a problem.* ◇ *Everything was going well but then we hit trouble.*

▸ SUDDENLY REALIZE **12** [T] **~ sb** (*informal*) to come suddenly into your mind: *I couldn't remember where I'd seen him before, and then it suddenly hit me.*

▸ PRESS BUTTON **13** [T] **~ sth** (*informal*) to press sth such as a button to operate a machine, etc: *Hit the brakes!*

IDM **hit (it) ˈbig** (*informal*) to be very successful: *The band has hit big in the US.* **hit the ˈbuffers** (*informal*) if a plan, sb's career, etc. **hits the buffers**, it suddenly stops being successful **hit the ˈceiling/ˈroof** (*informal*) to suddenly become very angry **hit the ˈdeck** (*informal*) to fall to the ground **ˌhit the ground ˈrunning** (*informal*) to start doing sth and continue very quickly and successfully **hit the ˈhay/ˈsack** (*informal*) to go to bed **hit a/the ˈwall** to reach a point when you cannot continue or make any more progress: *We hit a wall and we weren't scoring.* **hit sb (straight/right) in the ˈeye** to be very obvious to sb **ˈhit it** (*informal*) used to tell sb to start doing sth, such as playing music: *Hit it, Louis!* **hit it ˈoff (with sb)** (*informal*) to have a good friendly relationship with sb: *We hit it off straight away.* **hit the ˈjackpot** to make or win a lot of money quickly and unexpectedly **hit the nail on the ˈhead** to say sth that is exactly right **hit the ˈroad/ˈtrail** (*informal*) to start a journey/trip **hit the 'roof** = GO THROUGH THE ROOF at ROOF **hit the 'spot** (*informal*) if sth **hits the spot** it does exactly what it should do **hit the 'streets | hit the 'shops/'stores** (*informal*) to become widely available for sale: *The new magazine hits the streets tomorrow.* **hit sb when they're 'down** to continue to hurt sb when they are already defeated **hit sb where it 'hurts** to affect sb where they will feel it most ➲ more at HEADLINE, HOME *adv.*, KNOW *v.*, MARK *n.*, NERVE *n.*, NOTE *n.*, PAY DIRT, SHIT *n.*, SIX, STRIDE *n.*

PHR V **,hit 'back (at sb/sth)** to reply to attacks or criticism SYN **retaliate**: *In a TV interview she hit back at her critics.* **'hit on sb** (*NAmE, slang*) to start talking to sb to show them that you are sexually attracted to them **'hit on/upon sth** [no passive] (rather *informal*) to think of a good idea suddenly or by chance: *She hit on the perfect title for her new novel.* **,hit 'out (at sb/sth)** to attack sb/sth violently by fighting them or criticizing them: *I just hit out blindly in all directions.* ◇ *In a rousing speech the minister hit out at racism in the armed forces.* **,hit sb 'up for sth | 'hit sb for sth** (*NAmE, informal*) to ask sb for money: *Does he always hit you up for cash when he wants new clothes?* **'hit sb with sth** (*informal*) to tell sb sth, especially sth that surprises or shocks them: *How much is it going to cost, then? Come on, hit me with it!*

■ ***noun***

▸ ACT OF HITTING **1** 🔑 an act of hitting sb/sth with your hand or with an object held in your hand: *Give it a good hit.* ◇ *He made the winning hit.* **2** 🔑 an occasion when sth that has been thrown, fired, etc. at an object reaches that object: *The bomber scored a* ***direct hit*** *on the bridge.* ◇ *We finished the first round with a score of two hits and six misses.*

▸ STH POPULAR **3** 🔑 a person or thing that is very popular: *The duo were a real hit in last year's show.* ◇ *a hit musical* ◇ *Her new series is a* ***smash hit***.

▸ POP MUSIC **4** 🔑 a successful pop song or record: *They are about to release an album of their greatest hits.* ◇ *She played all her old hits.* ◇ *a* ***hit record/single***

▸ OF DRUG **5** (*slang*) an amount of an illegal drug that is taken at one time

▸ MURDER **6** (*slang, especially NAmE*) a violent crime or murder ➲ see also HIT MAN

▸ COMPUTING **7** a result of a search on a computer, for example on the Internet: *How many hits did you get?*

IDM **be/make a 'hit (with sb)** to be liked very much by sb when they first meet you **take a 'hit** to be damaged or badly affected by sth: *The airline industry took a hit last year.*

Synonyms

hit

knock • bang • strike • bump • bash

These words all mean to come against sth with a lot of force.

hit to come against sth with force, especially causing damage or injury: *The boy was hit by a speeding car.*

knock to hit sth so that it moves or breaks; to put sb/sth into a particular state or position by hitting them/it: *Someone had knocked a hole in the wall.*

bang to hit sth in a way that makes a loud noise: *The baby was banging the table with his spoon.*

strike (*formal*) to hit sb/sth hard: *The ship struck a rock.*

bump to hit sb/sth accidentally: *In the darkness I bumped into a chair.*

bash (*informal*) to hit against sth very hard: *I braked too late, bashing into the car in front.*

PATTERNS

- to hit/knock/bang/bump/bash **against** sb/sth
- to knock/bang/bump/bash **into** sb/sth
- to hit/strike the **ground/floor/wall**

,hit-and-'miss (also **,hit-or-'miss**) *adj.* not done in a careful or planned way and therefore not likely to be successful

,hit-and-'run *adj.* [only before noun] **1** (of a road accident) caused by a driver who does not stop to help: *a* ***hit-and-run accident/death*** ◇ *a* ***hit-and-run driver*** (= one who causes an accident but drives away without helping) **2** (of a military attack) happening suddenly and unexpectedly so that the people attacking can leave quickly without being hurt: *hit-and-run raids* ▸ **,hit-and-'run** *noun*: *He was killed in a hit-and-run.*

hitch /hɪtʃ/ *verb, noun*

■ ***verb*** **1** [T, I] to get a free ride in a person's car; to travel around in this way, by standing at the side of the road and trying to get passing cars to stop: **~ sth** *They* ***hitched a ride*** *in a truck.* ◇ (*BrE* also) *They* ***hitched a lift.*** ◇ (**+ adv./prep.**) *We spent the summer hitching around Europe.* ➲ see also HITCHHIKE **2** [T] **~ sth (up)** to pull up a piece of your clothing SYN **hike up**: *She hitched up her skirt and waded into the river.* **3** [T] **~ yourself (up, etc.)** to lift yourself into a higher position, or the position mentioned: *She hitched herself up.* ◇ *He hitched himself onto the bar stool.* **4** [T] **~ sth (to sth)** to fix sth to sth else with a rope, a hook, etc: *She hitched the pony to the gate.*

IDM **get 'hitched** (*informal*) to get married

■ ***noun*** **1** a problem or difficulty that causes a short delay: *The ceremony went off* ***without a hitch.*** ◇ *a technical hitch* **2** a type of knot: *a clove hitch*

hitch·hike /ˈhɪtʃhaɪk/ *verb* [I] to travel by asking for free rides in other people's cars, by standing at the side of the road and trying to get passing cars to stop: *They hitchhiked around Europe.* ➲ see also HITCH ▸ **hitch·hiker** (also **hitch·er** /ˈhɪtʃə(r)/) *noun*: *He picked up two hitchhikers on the road to Bristol.*

,hi-'tech = HIGH-TECH

hither /ˈhɪðə(r)/ *adv.* (*old use*) to this place

IDM **,hither and 'thither | ,hither and 'yon** (especially *literary*) in many different directions

hith·er·to /ˌhɪðəˈtuː; *NAmE* ˌhɪðərˈtuː/ *adv.* (*formal*) until now; until the particular time you are talking about: *a hitherto unknown species of moth*

'hit list *noun* (*informal*) a list of people, organizations, etc. against whom some unpleasant action is being planned: *Which services are on the government's hit list?* ◇ *She was at the top of the terrorists' hit list for over two years.*

'hit man *noun* (*informal*) a criminal who is paid to kill sb

,hit-or-'miss *adj.* = HIT-AND-MISS

'hit-out *noun* (in AUSTRALIAN RULES football) a hit of the ball towards a player from your team after it has been BOUNCED by the UMPIRE

the 'hit parade *noun* (*old-fashioned*) a list published every week that shows which pop records have sold the most copies

'hit squad *noun* a group of criminals who are paid to kill a person

hit·ter /ˈhɪtə(r)/ *noun* (often in compounds) **1** (in sports) a person who hits the ball in the way mentioned: *a* ***big/long/hard hitter*** **2** (in politics or business) a person who is powerful: *the* ***heavy hitters*** *of Japanese industry*

HIV /ˌeɪtʃ aɪ ˈviː/ *noun* [U] the abbreviation for 'human immunodeficiency virus' (the virus that can cause AIDS): *to be infected with HIV* ◇ *to be* ***HIV-positive/HIV-negative*** (= to have had a medical test which shows that you are/are not infected with HIV)

hive /haɪv/ *noun, verb*

■ ***noun*** **1** (also **bee·hive**) [C] a structure made for BEES to live in **2** [C] the BEES living in a hive **3** [C, usually sing.] **a ~ of activity/industry** a place full of people who are busy **4 hives** [U] = URTICARIA

■ ***verb***

PHR V **,hive sth↔'off (to/into sth)** [often passive] (*especially BrE*) to separate one part of a group from the rest; to sell part of a business: *The IT department is being hived off into a new company.*

hiya /ˈhaɪjə/ *exclamation* used to say hello to sb in an informal way

hl *abbr.* HECTOLITRE(S)

HM (*BrE*) (also **H.M.** *US, BrE*) *abbr.* Her/His MAJESTY('S): *HM the Queen* ◇ *HM Customs*

hm *abbr.* HECTOMETRE(S)

HMG *abbr.* (*BrE*) Her Majesty's Government

hmm (also **hm, h'm**) /m; hm/ *exclamation* used in writing to show the sound that you make to express doubt or when you are hesitating

HMRC /ˌeɪtʃ em ɑː ˈsiː; *NAmE* -ɑːr-/ *abbr.* HM Revenue and Customs

ˌHM ˌRevenue and ˈCustoms *noun* [U] (*abbr.* **HMRC**) the government department in Britain that is responsible for collecting taxes. It replaced the INLAND REVENUE and HM CUSTOMS AND EXCISE in 2005. ➲ compare THE INTERNAL REVENUE SERVICE

HMS /ˌeɪtʃ em ˈes/ *abbr.* Her/His Majesty's Ship (used before the name of a ship in the British navy): *HMS Apollo*

HNC /ˌeɪtʃ en ˈsiː/ *noun* the abbreviation for 'Higher National Certificate' (a British university or college qualification, especially in a technical or scientific subject): *to do an HNC in electrical engineering*

HND /ˌeɪtʃ en ˈdiː/ *noun* the abbreviation for 'Higher National Diploma' (a British university or college qualification, especially in a technical or scientific subject): *to do an HND in fashion design*

ho /həʊ; *NAmE* hoʊ/ *noun* (*pl.* **hos** or **hoes**) (*NAmE, taboo, slang*) **1** a female PROSTITUTE **2** an offensive word used about a woman, especially one who you think has sex with a lot of men ORIGIN Short form of *whore*.

hoagie /ˈhəʊgi; *NAmE* ˈhoʊ-/ *noun* (*NAmE*) **1** a long piece of bread filled with meat, cheese and salad **2** a piece of bread used to make a hoagie

hoard /hɔːd; *NAmE* hɔːrd/ *noun, verb*
- ***noun*** ~ (**of sth**) a collection of money, food, valuable objects, etc, especially one that sb keeps in a secret place so that other people will not find or steal it
- ***verb*** [I, T] ~ (**sth**) to collect and keep large amounts of food, money, etc, especially secretly ▸ **hoard·er** *noun*

hoard·ing /ˈhɔːdɪŋ; *NAmE* ˈhɔːrd-/ *noun* **1** (*BrE*) (also **bill·board** *NAmE, BrE*) [C] a large board on the outside of a building or at the side of the road, used for putting advertisements on ➲ VISUAL VOCAB page V2 **2** [C] (*BrE*) a temporary fence made of boards that is placed around an area of land until a building has been built **3** [U] the act of hoarding things

hoar frost /ˈhɔː frɒst; *NAmE* ˈhɔːr frɔːst/ *noun* [U] a layer of small pieces of ice that look like white needles and that form on surfaces outside when temperatures are very low

hoarse /hɔːs; *NAmE* hɔːrs/ *adj.* (of a person or voice) sounding rough and unpleasant, especially because of a sore throat: *He shouted himself hoarse.* ◇ *a* ***hoarse cough/cry/scream*** ▸ **hoarse·ly** *adv.* **hoarse·ness** *noun* [U]

hoary /ˈhɔːri/ *adj.* [usually before noun] **1** (*old-fashioned*) very old and well known and therefore no longer interesting: *a hoary old joke* **2** (*literary*) (especially of hair) grey or white because a person is old

hoax /həʊks; *NAmE* hoʊks/ *noun, verb*
- ***noun*** an act intended to make sb believe sth that is not true, especially sth unpleasant: *a bomb hoax* ◇ *hoax calls*
- ***verb*** ~ **sb** to trick sb by making them believe sth that is not true, especially sth unpleasant ▸ **hoax·er** *noun*

hob /hɒb; *NAmE* hɑːb/ *noun* **1** (*BrE*) (*NAmE* **stove·top**) the top part of a cooker where food is cooked in pans; a similar surface that is built into a kitchen unit and is separate from the oven: *an electric/a gas hob* ➲ VISUAL VOCAB page V22 **2** a metal shelf at the side of a fire, used in the past for heating pans, etc. on

hob·ble /ˈhɒbl; *NAmE* ˈhɑːbl/ *verb* **1** [I] (+ **adv./prep.**) to walk with difficulty, especially because your feet or legs hurt SYN **limp**: *The old man hobbled across the road.* **2** [T] ~ **sth** to tie together two legs of a horse or other animal in order to stop it from running away **3** [T] ~ **sth** to make it more difficult for sb to do sth or for sth to happen

hobby 0‑ /ˈhɒbi; *NAmE* ˈhɑːbi/ *noun* (*pl.* **-ies**) an activity that you do for pleasure when you are not working: *Her hobbies include swimming and gardening.* ◇ *I only play jazz as a hobby.* ➲ SYNONYMS at INTEREST ➲ VISUAL VOCAB pages V34, V35

ˈhobby horse *noun* **1** (sometimes *disapproving*) a subject that sb feels strongly about and likes to talk about: *to* ***get on your hobby horse*** (= talk about your favourite subject) **2** a toy made from a long stick that has a horse's head at one end. Children pretend to ride on it.

hob·by·ist /ˈhɒbiɪst; *NAmE* ˈhɑːb-/ *noun* (*formal*) a person who is very interested in a particular hobby

hob·gob·lin /hɒbˈgɒblɪn; ˈhɒbgɒblɪn; *NAmE* ˈhɑːbgɑːb-/ *noun* (in stories) a small ugly creature that likes to trick people or cause trouble

hob·nail boot /ˌhɒbneɪl ˈbuːt; *NAmE* ˌhɑːb-/ (also **hob·nailed boot** /-neɪld/) *noun* [usually pl.] a heavy shoe whose SOLE is attached to the upper part with short heavy nails

hob·nob /ˈhɒbnɒb; *NAmE* ˈhɑːbnɑːb/ *verb* (**-bb-**) [I] ~ (**with sb**) (*informal*) to spend a lot of time with sb, especially sb who is rich and/or famous

hobo /ˈhəʊbəʊ; *NAmE* ˈhoʊboʊ/ *noun* (*pl.* **-os**) (*old-fashioned, especially NAmE*) **1** a person who travels from place to place looking for work, especially on farms **2** = TRAMP

Hob·son's choice /ˌhɒbsnz ˈtʃɔɪs; *NAmE* ˌhɑːb-/ *noun* [U] a situation in which sb has no choice because if they do not accept what is offered, they will get nothing ORIGIN From Tobias Hobson, a man who hired out horses in the 17th century. He gave his customers the choice of the horse nearest the stable door or none at all.

hock /hɒk; *NAmE* hɑːk/ *noun, verb*
- ***noun*** **1** [C] the middle joint of an animal's back leg **2** [U, C] (*BrE*) a German white wine **3** [U, C] (*especially NAmE*) = KNUCKLE (2) **4** [U] (*informal*) if sth that you own is in **hock**, you have exchanged it for money but hope to buy it back later

IDM **be in ˈhock** (**to sb**) to owe sb sth: *I'm in hock to the bank for £6 000.*
- ***verb*** ~ **sth** (*informal*) to leave a valuable object with sb in exchange for money that you borrow SYN **pawn**

hockey /ˈhɒki; *NAmE* ˈhɑːki/ *noun* [U] **1** (*BrE*) (*NAmE* **ˈfield hockey**) a game played on a field by two teams of 11 players, with curved sticks and a small hard ball. Teams try to hit the ball into the other team's goal: *to play hockey* ◇ *a* ***hockey stick/player/team*** **2** (*NAmE*) (*BrE* **ˈice hockey**) a game played on ice, in which players use long sticks to hit a hard rubber disc (called a PUCK) into the other team's goal ➲ VISUAL VOCAB page V36

hocus-pocus /ˌhəʊkəs ˈpəʊkəs; *NAmE* ˌhoʊkəs ˈpoʊkəs/ *noun* [U] language or behaviour that is nonsense and is intended to hide the truth from people

hod /hɒd; *NAmE* hɑːd/ *noun* an open box attached to a pole, used by building workers for carrying bricks on the shoulder

hodge·podge /ˈhɒdʒpɒdʒ; *NAmE* ˈhɑːdʒpɑːdʒ/ *noun* [sing.] (*NAmE*) = HOTCHPOTCH

Hodg·kin's dis·ease /ˈhɒdʒkɪnz dɪziːz; *NAmE* ˈhɑːdʒ-/ *noun* [U] a serious disease of the LYMPH NODES, LIVER and SPLEEN

hoe /həʊ; *NAmE* hoʊ/ *noun, verb*
- ***noun*** a garden tool with a long handle and a blade, used for breaking up soil and removing WEEDS (= plants growing where they are not wanted) ➲ VISUAL VOCAB page V16
- ***verb*** (**hoe·ing, hoed, hoed**) [T, I] ~ (**sth**) to break up soil, remove plants, etc. with a hoe: *to hoe the flower beds*

PHR V **hoe ˈin** (*AustralE, NZE, informal*) to eat with enthusiasm

H

hoe·down /ˈhəʊdaʊn; *NAmE* ˈhoʊ-/ *noun* (*NAmE*) **1** a social occasion when lively dances are performed **2** a lively dance

hog /hɒɡ; *NAmE* hɔːɡ; hɑːɡ/ *noun, verb*

■ ***noun*** **1** (*especially NAmE*) a pig, especially one that is kept and made fat for eating **2** (*BrE*) a male pig that has been CASTRATED (= had part of its sex organs removed) and is kept for its meat ➲ compare BOAR, SOW ➲ see also ROAD HOG, WARTHOG

IDM **go the whole ˈhog** (*informal*) to do sth thoroughly or completely

■ ***verb*** (-gg-) **~ sth** (*informal*) to use or keep most of sth yourself and stop others from using or having it: *to hog the road* (= to drive so that other vehicles cannot pass) ◊ *to hog the bathroom* (= to spend a long time in it so that others cannot use it)

Hog·ma·nay /ˈhɒɡmənеɪ; ˌhɒɡməˈneɪ; *NAmE* hɑːɡ-/ *noun* [U] (in Scotland) New Year's Eve (31 December) and the celebrations that happen on that day

H

hog·wash /ˈhɒɡwɒʃ; *NAmE* ˈhɔːɡwɑːʃ; ˈhɑːɡ-; -wɔːʃ/ *noun* [U] (*informal*) an idea, argument, etc. that you think is stupid

ho ho /ˌhəʊ ˈhəʊ; *NAmE* ˌhoʊ ˈhoʊ/ *exclamation* **1** used to show the sound of a deep laugh **2** used to show surprise: *Ho, ho! What have we here?*

ho-hum /ˌhəʊ ˈhʌm; *NAmE* ˌhoʊ/ *exclamation* used to show that you are bored

hoick /hɔɪk/ *verb* **~ sth** (**+ adv./prep.**) (*BrE, informal*) to lift or pull sth in a particular direction, especially with a quick sudden movement SYN **jerk**

the hoi pol·loi /ˌhɔɪ pəˈlɔɪ/ *noun* [pl.] (*disapproving* or *humorous*) an insulting word for ordinary people

hoist /hɔɪst/ *verb, noun*

■ ***verb*** **~ sth** (**+ adv./prep.**) to raise or pull sth up to a higher position, often using ropes or special equipment: *He hoisted himself onto a high stool.* ◊ *The cargo was hoisted aboard by crane.* ◊ *to* ***hoist a flag/sail***

IDM **be hoist/hoisted by/with your own peˈtard** to be hurt or to have problems as a result of your own plans to hurt or trick others

■ ***noun*** a piece of equipment used for lifting heavy things, or for lifting people who cannot stand or walk

hoity-toity /ˌhɔɪti ˈtɔɪti/ *adj.* (*old-fashioned, informal*) behaving in a way that suggests that you think you are more important than other people

hokey /ˈhəʊki; *NAmE* ˈhoʊki/ *adj.* (*NAmE, informal*) expressing emotions in a way that seems exaggerated or silly

hoki /ˈhəʊki; *NAmE* ˈhoʊki/ *noun* (*pl.* **hoki**) a fish found in the seas off New Zealand

hokum /ˈhəʊkəm; *NAmE* ˈhoʊ-/ *noun* [U] (*informal, especially NAmE*) **1** a film/movie, play, etc. that is not realistic and has no artistic qualities **2** an idea, argument, etc. that you think is stupid: *What a bunch of hokum!*

hold 🔑 /həʊld; *NAmE* hoʊld/ *verb, noun*

■ ***verb*** (**held, held** /held/)

▸ IN HAND/ARMS **1** 🔑 [T] **~ sb/sth** (**+ adv./prep.**) to carry sth; to have sb/sth in your hand, arms, etc: *She was holding a large box.* ◊ *I held the mouse by its tail.* ◊ *The girl held her father's hand tightly.* ◊ *He was holding the baby in his arms.* ◊ *The winning captain held the trophy in the air.* ◊ *We were* ***holding hands*** (= holding each other's hands). ◊ *The lovers held each other close.* **2** 🔑 [T] **~ sth** to put your hand on part of your body, usually because it hurts: *She groaned and held her head.*

▸ IN POSITION **3** 🔑 [T] to keep sb/sth in a particular position: **~ sth** (**+ adv./prep.**) *Hold your head up.* ◊ *Hold this position for a count of 10.* ◊ *The wood is held in position by a clamp.* ◊ *I had to hold my stomach in* (= pull the muscles flat) *to zip up my jeans.* ◊ **~ sth + adj.** *I'll hold the door open for you.*

▸ SUPPORT **4** 🔑 [T] **~ sb/sth** to support the weight of sb/sth: *I don't think that branch will hold your weight.*

▸ CONTAIN **5** 🔑 [T] **~ sb/sth** to have enough space for sth/sb; to contain sth/sb: *This barrel holds 25 litres.* ◊ *The plane holds about 300 passengers.*

▸ SB PRISONER **6** 🔑 [T] to keep sb and not allow them to leave: **~ sb** *Police are holding two men in connection with last Thursday's bank raid.* ◊ **~ sb + noun** *He was* ***held prisoner*** *for two years.*

▸ CONTROL **7** [T] **~ sth** to defend sth against attack; to have control of sth: *The rebels held the radio station.*

▸ REMAIN **8** [I] to remain strong and safe or in position: *They were afraid the dam wouldn't hold.* **9** [I] to remain the same: *How long will the fine weather hold?* ◊ *If their luck holds, they could still win the championship.*

▸ KEEP **10** 🔑 [T] **~ sth** to keep sb's attention or interest: *There wasn't much in the museum to hold my attention.* **11** [T] **~ sth** (**at sth**) to keep sth at the same level, rate, speed, etc: *Hold your speed at 70.* **12** 🔑 [T] **~ sth** to keep sth so that it can be used later: *records held on computer* ◊ *Our solicitor holds our wills.* ◊ *We can hold your reservation for three days.*

▸ OWN **13** 🔑 [T] **~ sth** (rather *formal*) to own or have sth: *Employees hold 30% of the shares.*

▸ JOB **14** 🔑 [T] **~ sth** to have a particular job or position: *How long has he held office?*

▸ RECORD/TITLE **15** 🔑 [T] **~ sth** to have sth you have gained or achieved: *Who holds the world record for the long jump?* ◊ *She held the title of world champion for three years.*

▸ OPINION **16** [T] to have a belief or an opinion about sb/sth: **~ sth** *He holds strange views on education.* ◊ **~ sb/sth + adv./prep./adj.** *She is* ***held in high regard*** *by her students* (= they have a high opinion of her). ◊ *firmly-held beliefs* **17** [T] (*formal*) to consider that sth is true: **~ that...** *I still hold that the government's economic policies are mistaken.* ◊ **~ sb/sth + adj.** *Parents will be* ***held responsible*** *for their children's behaviour.* ◊ **be held to be sth** *These vases are held to be the finest examples of Greek art.*

▸ MEETING **18** 🔑 [T, usually passive] **~ sth** to have a meeting, competition, conversation, etc: *The meeting will be held in the community centre.* ◊ *It's impossible to hold a conversation with all this noise.*

▸ ROAD/COURSE **19** [T] **~ the road** (of a vehicle) to be in close contact with the road and easy to control, especially when driven fast **20** [T] **~ a course** (of a ship or an aircraft) to continue to move in a particular direction

▸ IN MUSIC **21** [T] **~ sth** to make a note continue for a particular time

▸ ON TELEPHONE **22** [I, T] to wait until you can speak to the person you have telephoned: *That extension is busy right now. Can you hold?* ◊ **~ the line** *She asked me to hold the line.*

▸ STOP **23** [T] **~ sth** used to tell sb to stop doing sth or not to do sth: *Hold your fire!* (= don't shoot) ◊ *Hold the front page!* (= don't print it until a particular piece of news is available) ◊ (*NAmE, informal*) *Give me a hot dog, but hold the* (= don't give me any) *mustard.*

IDM Most idioms containing **hold** are at the entries for the nouns and adjectives in the idioms, for example **hold the fort** is at **fort**. **hold ˈgood** to be true: *The same argument does not hold good in every case.* **ˈhold it** (*informal*) used to ask sb to wait, or not to move: *Hold it a second—I don't think everyone's arrived yet.* **there is no ˈholding sb** a person cannot be prevented from doing sth: *Once she gets on to the subject of politics there's no holding her.*

PHR V **ˌhold sth aˈgainst sb** to allow sth that sb has done to make you have a lower opinion of them: *I admit I made a mistake—but don't hold it against me.*

ˌhold sb/sth↔ˈback 1 🔑 to prevent sb/sth from moving forward or crossing sth: *The police were unable to hold back the crowd.* **2** 🔑 to prevent the progress or development of sb/sth: *Do you think that mixed-ability classes hold back the better students?* **ˌhold sth↔ˈback 1** 🔑 to not tell sb sth they want or need to know: *to hold back information* **2** 🔑 to stop yourself from expressing how you really feel: *She just managed to hold back her anger.* ◊ *He bravely held back his tears.* **ˌhold ˈback** (**from doing sth**) | **ˌhold sb ˈback** (**from doing sth**) to hesitate or to make sb hesitate to act or speak: *She held back, not knowing how to break the terrible news.* ◊ *I wanted to tell him the truth, but something held me back.*

ˌhold sb↔ˈdown 1 to prevent sb from moving, using

force: *It took three men to hold him down.* **2** to prevent sb from having their freedom or rights: *The people are held down by a repressive regime.* ˌ**hold sth↔'down 1** to keep sth at a low level: *The rate of inflation must be held down.* **2** [no passive] to keep a job for some time: *He was unable to hold down a job after his breakdown.* **3** [no passive] (*NAmE, informal*) to limit sth, especially a noise: *Hold it down, will you? I'm trying to sleep!*

ˌ**hold 'forth** to speak for a long time about sth in a way that other people might find boring

ˌ**hold sth↔'in** to not express how you really feel: *to hold in your feelings/anger* OPP **let sth out**

ˌ**hold 'off 1** (of rain or a storm) to not start: *The rain held off just long enough for us to have our picnic.* **2** to not do sth immediately: *We could get a new computer now or hold off until prices are lower.* ◇ **~ doing sth** *Could you hold off making your decision for a few days?* ˌ**hold sb/sth↔'off** to stop sb/sth defeating you: *She held off all the last-minute challengers and won the race in a new record time.*

ˌ**hold 'on 1** (*informal*) used to tell sb to wait or stop SYN **wait**: *Hold on a minute while I get my breath back.* ◇ *Hold on! This isn't the right road.* **2** to survive in a difficult or dangerous situation: *They managed to hold on until help arrived.* **3** (*informal*) used on the telephone to ask sb to wait until they can talk to the person they want: *Can you hold on? I'll see if he's here.* ˌ**hold sth↔'on** to keep sth in position: *These nuts and bolts hold the wheels on.* ◇ *The knob is only held on by sticky tape.* ˌ**hold 'on (to sth/sb)** | ˌ**hold 'on to sth/sb** [no passive] to keep holding sth/sb: *Hold on and don't let go until I say so.* ◇ *He held on to the back of the chair to stop himself from falling.* ➲ SYNONYMS at HOLD ˌ**hold 'on to sth** | ˌ**hold 'onto sth 1** to keep sth that is an advantage for you; to not give or sell sth to sb else: *You should hold on to your oil shares.* ◇ *She took an early lead in the race and held on to it for nine laps.* **2** to keep sth for sb else or for longer than usual: *I'll hold on to your mail for you until you get back.*

ˌ**hold 'out 1** to last, especially in a difficult situation: *We can stay here for as long as our supplies hold out.* **2** to resist or survive in a dangerous or difficult situation: *The rebels held out in the mountains for several years.* ˌ**hold 'out sth** to offer a chance, hope or possibility of sth: *Doctors hold out little hope of her recovering.* ˌ**hold sth↔'out** to put your hand or arms, or sth in your hand, towards sb, especially to give or offer sth: *I held out my hand to steady her.* ◇ *He held out the keys and I took them.* ˌ**hold 'out for sth** [no passive] to cause a delay in reaching an agreement because you hope you will gain sth: *The union negotiators are holding out for a more generous pay settlement.* ˌ**hold 'out on sb** (*informal*) to refuse to tell or give sb sth

ˌ**hold sth↔'over** [usually passive] **1** to not deal with sth immediately; to leave sth to be dealt with later SYN **postpone**: *The matter was held over until the next meeting.* **2** to show a film/movie, play, etc. for longer than planned: *The movie proved so popular it was held over for another week.* ˌ**hold sth 'over sb** to use knowledge that you have about sb to threaten them or make them do what you want

'**hold sb to sth 1** to make sb keep a promise **2** to stop an opposing team scoring more points, etc. than you: *The league leaders were held to a 0–0 draw.*

ˌ**hold to'gether** | ˌ**hold sth↔to'gether 1** to remain, or to keep sth, united: *A political party should hold together.* ◇ *It's the mother who usually holds the family together.* **2** (of an argument, a theory or a story) to be logical or CONSISTENT: *Their case doesn't hold together when you look at the evidence.* ➲ compare HANG TOGETHER at HANG **3** if a machine or an object **holds together** or sth **holds it together**, the different parts stay together so that it does not break

ˌ**hold 'up** to remain strong and working effectively: *She's holding up well under the pressure.* ˌ**hold sb/sth↔'up** [often passive] **1** to support sb/sth and stop them from falling **2** to delay or block the movement or progress of sb/sth: *An accident is holding up traffic.* ◇ *My application was held up by the postal strike.* ➲ related noun HOLD-UP **3** to use or present sb/sth as an example: *She's always holding up her children as models of good behaviour.* ◇ *His ideas were held up to ridicule.* ˌ**hold up 'sth** to steal from a bank, shop/store, etc. using a gun ➲ related noun HOLD-UP

'**hold with sth** [no passive] (used in negative sentences or in questions) to agree with sth SYN **approve of**: *I don't hold with the use of force.* ◇ **~ doing sth** *They don't hold with letting children watch as much TV as they want.*

■ ***noun***

▸ WITH HAND **1** [sing., U] the action of holding sb/sth; the way you are holding sb/sth SYN **grip**: *His hold on her arm tightened.* ◇ *She tried to* ***keep hold of*** *the child's hand.* ◇ *Make sure you've got a steady hold on the camera.*

▸ IN SPORT **2** [C] a particular way of holding sb, especially in a sport such as WRESTLING or in a fight: *The wrestler put his opponent into a head hold.*

▸ POWER/CONTROL **3** [sing.] **~ (on/over sb/sth)** influence, power or control over sb/sth: *What she knew about his past gave her a hold over him.* ◇ *He struggled to get a hold of his anger.* ➲ see also STRANGLEHOLD

▸ IN CLIMBING **4** [C] a place where you can put your hands or feet when climbing ➲ see also FOOTHOLD, HANDHOLD, TOEHOLD

▸ ON SHIP/PLANE **5** [C] the part of a ship or plane where the goods being carried are stored ➲ VISUAL VOCAB page V43

Synonyms

hold

hold on • cling • clutch • grip • grasp • clasp • hang on

These words all mean to have sb/sth in your hands or arms.

hold to have sb/sth in your hand or arms: *She was holding a large box.* ◇ *I held the baby gently in my arms.*

hold on (to sb/sth) to continue to hold sb/sth; to put your hand on sb/sth and not take your hand away: *Hold on and don't let go until I say so.*

cling to hold on to sb/sth tightly, especially with your whole body: *Survivors* ***clung to*** *pieces of floating debris.*

clutch to hold sb/sth tightly, especially in your hand; to take hold of sth suddenly: *She stood there, the flowers still clutched in her hand.* ◇ *He felt himself slipping and* ***clutched at*** *a branch.*

grip to hold on to sth very tightly with your hand: *Grip the rope as tightly as you can.*

grasp to take hold of sth firmly: *He grasped my hand and shook it warmly.* NOTE The object of **grasp** is often sb's *hand* or *wrist*.

clasp (*formal*) to hold sb/sth tightly in your hand or in your arms: *They clasped hands* (= held each other's hands). ◇ *She clasped the children in her arms.* NOTE The object of **clasp** is often your *hands*, sb else's *hand* or another person.

hang on (to sth) to hold on to sth very tightly, especially in order to support yourself or stop yourself from falling: *Hang on tight. We're off!*

PATTERNS

- to hold/clutch/grip/clasp sth **in your hand/hands**
- to hold/catch/clasp sb/sth **in your arms**
- to hold/clutch/grip/grasp/clasp/hang **on to** sth
- to hold/cling/hang **on**
- to hold/clutch/clasp sb/sth **to** you
- to hold/hold on to/cling to/clutch/grip/grasp/clasp/hang on to sb/sth **tightly**
- to hold/hold on to/cling to/clutch/grip/grasp/clasp sb/sth **firmly**
- to hold/hold on to/clutch/grip/clasp/hang on to sb/sth **tight**

IDM **catch, get, grab, take, etc. (a) 'hold of sb/sth** to have or take sb/sth in your hands: *He caught hold of her wrists so she couldn't get away.* ◇ *Lee got hold of the dog by its collar.* ◇ *Quick, grab a hold of that rope.* ◇ *Gently, she took*

H

hold of the door handle and turned it. **get 'hold of sb** to contact or find sb: *Where have you been? I've been trying to get hold of you all day.* **get 'hold of sth 1** to find sth that you want or need: *I need to get hold of Tom's address.* ◇ *It's almost impossible to get hold of tickets for the final.* **2** to learn or understand sth **,no ,holds 'barred** with no rules or limits on what sb is allowed to do **on 'hold 1** delayed until a later time or date: *She **put** her career **on hold** to have a baby.* ◇ *The project is on hold until more money is available.* **2** if a person on the telephone is put **on hold**, they have to wait until the person that they want to talk to is free **take (a) 'hold** to begin to have complete control over sb/sth; to become very strong: *Panic took hold of him and he couldn't move.* ◇ *They got out of the house just before the flames took hold.* ◇ *It is best to treat the disease early before it takes a hold.* ➲ more at WRONG *adj.*

hold·all /ˈhəʊldɔːl; *NAmE* ˈhoʊ-/ (*BrE*) (*NAmE* **'duffel bag**) *noun* a large bag made of strong cloth or soft leather, used when you are travelling for carrying clothes, etc. ➲ VISUAL VOCAB page V52

hold·er /ˈhəʊldə(r); *NAmE* ˈhoʊ-/ *noun* (often in compounds) **1** a person who has or owns the thing mentioned: *a licence holder* ◇ *a season ticket holder* ◇ *the current holder of the world record* ◇ *holders of high office* ◇ *the holder of a French passport* ➲ see also RECORD HOLDER, TITLE-HOLDER **2** a thing that holds the object mentioned: *a pen holder* ➲ VISUAL VOCAB pages V19, V22, V56 ➲ see also CIGARETTE HOLDER

hold·ing /ˈhəʊldɪŋ; *NAmE* ˈhoʊ-/ *noun* **1** ~ **(in sth)** a number of shares that sb has in a company: *She has a 40% holding in the company.* ➲ see also FUNDHOLDING **2** an amount of property that is owned by a person, museum, library, etc: *one of the most important private holdings of Indian art* **3** a piece of land that is rented by sb and used for farming ➲ see also SMALLHOLDING

'holding company *noun* a company that is formed to buy shares in other companies which it then controls

'holding operation *noun* a course of action that is taken so that a particular situation stays the same or does not become any worse

'holding pattern *noun* the route that a plane travels while it is flying above an airport waiting for permission to land

hold·over /ˈhəʊldəʊvə(r); *NAmE* ˈhoʊldoʊvər/ *noun* (*NAmE*) a person who keeps a position of power, for example sb who had a particular position in one ADMINISTRATION and who still has it in the next

'hold-up *noun* **1** a situation in which sth is prevented from happening for a short time SYN **delay**: *What's the hold-up?* ◇ *We should finish by tonight, barring hold-ups.* ◇ (*BrE*) *Sorry I'm late. There was a hold-up on the motorway.* **2** (also **'stick-up** especially in *NAmE*) an act of stealing from a bank, etc. using a gun

hole 0‑w /həʊl; *NAmE* hoʊl/ *noun, verb*

■ ***noun***

▸ HOLLOW SPACE **1** 0‑w [C] a hollow space in sth solid or in the surface of sth: *He **dug a** deep **hole** in the garden.* ◇ *The bomb blew a huge hole in the ground.* ◇ *Water had collected in the holes in the road.*

▸ OPENING **2** 0‑w [C] a space or opening that goes all the way through sth: *to **drill/bore/punch/kick a hole** in sth* ◇ *There were holes in the knees of his trousers.* ◇ *The children climbed through a hole in the fence.* ◇ *a **bullet hole*** ◇ *the hole in the ozone layer* ➲ see also OZONE HOLE

▸ ANIMAL'S HOME **3** 0‑w [C] the home of a small animal: *a **rabbit/mouse, etc. hole*** ➲ compare FOXHOLE, PIGEONHOLE ➲ see also BOLT-HOLE

▸ UNPLEASANT PLACE **4** [C, usually sing.] (*informal, disapproving*) an unpleasant place to live or be in SYN **dump**: *I am not going to bring up my child in this hole.* ➲ see also HELL-HOLE

▸ IN GOLF **5** [C] a hollow in the ground that you must get the ball into; one of the sections of a GOLF COURSE with the TEE at the beginning and the hole at the end: *The ball rolled into the hole and she had won.* ◇ *an eighteen-hole golf course* ◇ *He liked to play a few holes after work.* ◇ *She won the first hole.* ➲ VISUAL VOCAB page V34

▸ FAULT/WEAKNESS **6** [C, usually pl.] a fault or weakness in sth such as a plan, law or story: *He was found not guilty because of holes in the prosecution case.* ◇ *I don't believe what she says—her story is full of holes.* ➲ see also LOOPHOLE

▸ EMPTY PLACE/POSITION **7** [sing.] a place or position that needs to be filled because sb/sth is no longer there: *After his wife left, there was a gaping hole in his life.* ◇ *Buying the new equipment left a big hole in the company's finances.*

HELP There are many other compounds ending in **hole**. You will find them at their place in the alphabet.

IDM **in a 'hole** (*informal*) in a difficult situation: *He had got himself into a hole and it was going to be difficult to get out of it.* **in the 'hole** (*NAmE, informal*) owing money SYN **in debt**: *We start the current fiscal year $30 million in the hole.* **make a 'hole in sth** to use up a large amount of sth that you have, especially money: *School fees can make a big hole in your savings.* ➲ more at ACE *n.*, BURN *v.*, DIG *v.*, PICK *v.*, SQUARE *adj.*

■ ***verb***

▸ MAKE A HOLE **1** [T, usually passive] ~ **sth** to make a hole or holes in sth, especially a boat or ship

▸ IN GOLF **2** [T, I] to hit a GOLF ball into the hole: ~ **sth** *She holed a 25 foot putt.* ◇ ~ **(out)** *She holed out from 25 feet.*

PHR V **,hole 'up** | **be ,holed 'up** (*informal*) to hide in a place: *He'll hole up now and move again tomorrow, after dark.* ◇ *We believe the gang are holed up in the mountains.*

,hole-and-'corner *adj.* done in secret because you want to avoid being noticed: *a hole-and-corner wedding*

hole-in-'one *noun* (*pl.* **holes-in-one**) an occasion in GOLF when a player hits the ball from the TEE into the hole using only one shot

,hole in the 'heart *noun* (*medical*) a condition in which a baby is born with a problem with the wall dividing the parts of its heart, so that it does not get enough OXYGEN in its blood

,hole in the 'wall *noun* [sing.] (*informal*) **1** (*BrE*) = CASH MACHINE **2** (*NAmE*) a small dark shop/store or restaurant ▸ **,hole-in-the-'wall** *adj.* [only before noun]: *hole-in-the-wall cash machines/restaurants*

holey /ˈhəʊli; *NAmE* ˈhoʊ-/ *adj.* a **holey** piece of clothing or material has a lot of holes in it

British/American

holiday / vacation

- You use **holiday** (or **holidays**) in *BrE* and **vacation** in *NAmE* to describe the regular periods of time when you are not at work or school, or time that you spend travelling or resting away from home: *I get four weeks' holiday/vacation a year.* ◇ *He's on holiday/vacation this week.* ◇ *I like to take my holiday/vacation in the winter.* ◇ *the summer holidays/vacation.*
- In *NAmE* a **holiday** (or a **public holiday**) is a single day when government offices, schools, banks and businesses are closed: *The school will be closed Monday because it's a holiday.* This is called a **bank holiday** in *BrE*.
- **The holidays** is used in *NAmE* to refer to the time in late December and early January that includes Christmas, Hanukkah and the New Year.
- **Vacation** in *BrE* is used mainly to mean one of the periods when universities are officially closed for the students.

holi·day 0‑w /ˈhɒlədeɪ; *NAmE* ˈhɑːl-; *BrE* also -di/ *noun, verb*

■ ***noun* 1** 0‑w [U] (also **holidays** [pl.]) (both *BrE*) (*NAmE* **vacation**) a period of time when you are not at work or school: *the **school/summer/Christmas, etc. holidays*** ◇ *I'm afraid Mr Walsh is away **on holiday** this week.* ◇ *The package includes 20 days' **paid holiday** a year.* ◇ ***holiday pay*** ◇ *a **holiday job*** (= done by students during the school holidays) **2** ⊶ [C] (*BrE*) (*NAmE* **vac·ation**) a period of time spent travelling or resting away from home: *a **camping/skiing/walking, etc. holiday** ◇ a **family holiday** ◇ a **foreign holiday** ◇ a **holiday cottage/home/resort** ◇ the holiday industry ◇ Where are you going **for your holidays** this year? ◇ They met while **on holiday** in Greece. ◇ We **went on holiday** together last summer.* ➲ COLLOCATIONS at TRAVEL ➲ see also BUSMAN'S HOLIDAY, PACKAGE TOUR **3** ⊶ [C] a day when most people do not go to work or school, especially because of a religious or national celebration: *a national holiday ◇ Today is a holiday in Wales.* ➲ see also BANK HOLIDAY, PUBLIC HOLIDAY **4** ⊶ **holidays** [pl.] (*NAmE*) the time in December and early January that includes Christmas, Hanukkah and New Year: *Happy Holidays!*

■ ***verb*** (*BrE*) (*NAmE* **vac·ation**) [I] (+ **adv./prep.**) to spend a holiday somewhere: *She was holidaying with her family in Ireland.*

'holiday camp *noun* (*BrE*) a place that provides accommodation and entertainment for large numbers of people who are on holiday/vacation

holi·day·maker /'hɒlədeɪmeɪkə(r); *NAmE* 'hɑːl-; *BrE* also -dimeɪ-/ *noun* (*BrE*) (*NAmE* **vac·ation·er**) a person who is visiting a place on holiday/vacation

holier-than-thou /ˌhəʊliə ðən 'ðaʊ; *NAmE* ˌhoʊliər/ *adj.* (*disapproving*) showing that you think that you are morally better than other people **SYN** **self-righteous**: *I can't stand his holier-than-thou attitude.*

holi·ness /'həʊlinəs; *NAmE* 'hoʊ-/ *noun* **1** [U] the quality of being holy **2** **His/Your Holiness** [C] a title of respect used when talking to or about the Pope and some other religious leaders: *His Holiness Pope Benedict XVI*

hol·ism /'həʊlɪzəm; 'hɒl-; *NAmE* 'hoʊl-; 'hɑːl-/ *noun* [U] **1** the idea that the whole of sth must be considered in order to understand its different parts ➲ compare ATOMISM **2** the idea that the whole of a sick person, including their body, mind and way of life, should be considered when treating them, and not just the SYMPTOMS (= effects) of the disease

hol·is·tic /həʊ'lɪstɪk; hɒ'l-; *NAmE* hoʊ'l-; hɑː'l-/ *adj.* **1** (*informal*) considering a whole thing or being to be more than a collection of parts: *a holistic approach to life* **2** (*medical*) treating the whole person rather than just the SYMPTOMS (= effects) of a disease: *holistic medicine* ▸ **hol·is·tic·al·ly** /-kli/ *adv.*

hol·land·aise sauce /ˌhɒləndeɪz 'sɔːs; *NAmE* ˌhɑːl-/ *noun* [U] a sauce made with butter, egg YOLKS (= yellow parts) and VINEGAR

hol·ler /'hɒlə(r); *NAmE* 'hɑːl-/ *verb* [I, T] (*informal, especially NAmE*) to shout loudly **SYN** **yell**: **~ (at sb)** *Don't holler at me!* ◇ **+ speech** *'Look out!' I hollered.* ◇ **~ sth** *He hollered something I couldn't understand.*

hol·low ⊶ /'hɒləʊ; *NAmE* 'hɑːloʊ/ *adj., noun, verb*

■ ***adj.*** **1** ⊶ having a hole or empty space inside: *a hollow ball/centre/tube ◇ The tree trunk was hollow inside. ◇ Her stomach felt hollow with fear.* **2** (of parts of the face) sinking deeply into the face: ***hollow eyes/cheeks*** *◇ hollow-eyed from lack of sleep* **3** [usually before noun] (of sounds) making a low sound like that made by an empty object when it is hit: *a hollow groan* **4** [usually before noun] not sincere: ***hollow promises/threats*** *◇ a hollow laugh ◇ Their appeals for an end to the violence had a **hollow ring**.* **5** [usually before noun] without real value: *to win a **hollow victory*** **IDM** see RING² *v.* ▸ **hol·low·ly** *adv.*: *to laugh hollowly* **hol·low·ness** *noun* [U]: *the hollowness of the victory*

■ ***noun*** **1** an area that is lower than the surface around it, especially on the ground: *muddy hollows ◇ The village lay secluded in a hollow of the hills* (= a small valley). *◇ She noticed the slight hollows under his cheekbones.* **2** a hole or a confined space in sth: *The squirrel disappeared into a hollow at the base of the tree.*

■ ***verb*** [usually passive] **~ sth** to make a flat surface curve in **PHR V** ˌ**hollow sth**↔'**out** **1** to make a hole in sth by removing part of it: *Hollow out the cake and fill it with cream.* **2** to form sth by making a hole in sth else: *The cave has been hollowed out of the mountainside.*

holly /'hɒli; *NAmE* 'hɑːli/ *noun* (*pl.* **-ies**) [U, C] a bush or small tree with hard shiny leaves with sharp points and bright red BERRIES in winter, often used as a decoration at Christmas: *a sprig of holly*

hol·ly·hock /'hɒlihɒk; *NAmE* 'hɑːlihɑːk/ *noun* a tall garden plant with white, yellow, red or purple flowers growing up its STEM

Hol·ly·wood /'hɒliwʊd; *NAmE* 'hɑːl-/ *noun* [U] the part of Los Angeles where the film/movie industry is based (used to refer to the US film/movie industry and the way of life that is associated with it) ➲ COLLOCATIONS at CINEMA

ˌ**Hollywood 'ending** *noun* (usually *disapproving*) an ending in a film/movie, novel, etc, which happens in the way you expect, is full of exaggerated happiness, pity or love, and may not be very realistic: *The film refuses to sell out and provide a Hollywood ending.*

hol·mium /'həʊlmiəm; *NAmE* 'hoʊl-/ *noun* [U] (*symb.* **Ho**) a chemical element. Holmium is a soft silver-white metal.

holo·caust /'hɒləkɔːst; *NAmE* 'hɑːlə-; 'hoʊlə-/ *noun* **1** [C] a situation in which many things are destroyed and many people killed, especially because of a war or a fire: *a nuclear holocaust* **2** **the Holocaust** [sing.] the killing of millions of Jews by the Nazis in the 1930s and 1940s

holo·gram /'hɒləgræm; *NAmE* 'hɑːl-; 'hoʊl-/ *noun* a special type of picture in which the objects seem to be THREE-DIMENSIONAL (= solid rather than flat)

holo·graph /'hɒləgrɑːf; *NAmE* 'hɑːləgræf; 'hoʊl-/ *noun* (*technical*) a piece of writing that has been written by hand by its author

holo·graph·ic /ˌhɒlə'græfɪk; *NAmE* ˌhɑːl-; ˌhoʊl-/ *adj.* [usually before noun] connected with holograms: *a holographic picture*

holo·phra·sis /ˌhɒlə'freɪsɪs; *NAmE* hə'lɑːfrəsɪs/ *noun* [U] (*linguistics*) the expression of a whole idea in a single word, for example a baby saying 'up' for 'I want you to pick me up' ▸ **holo·phras·tic** /ˌhɒlə'fræstɪk; *NAmE* ˌhɑːlə-; ˌhoʊlə-/ *adj.*

hols /hɒlz; *NAmE* hɑːlz/ *noun* [pl.] (*old-fashioned, BrE, informal*) holidays

Hol·stein /'hɒlstaɪn; -stiːn; *NAmE* 'hoʊl-/ (*NAmE*) (*BrE* **Frie·sian**) *noun* a type of black and white cow that produces a lot of milk

hol·ster /'həʊlstə(r); *NAmE* 'hoʊ-/ *noun, verb*

■ ***noun*** a leather case worn on a belt or on a narrow piece of leather under the arm, used for carrying a small gun

■ ***verb*** **~ sth** to put a gun in a holster

holy ⊶ /'həʊli; *NAmE* 'hoʊli/ *adj.* (**holi·er**, **holi·est**) **1** ⊶ [usually before noun] connected with God or a particular religion: *the **Holy Bible/Scriptures** ◇ holy ground ◇ a holy war* (= one fought to defend the beliefs of a particular religion) *◇ the holy city of Mecca ◇ Islam's holiest shrine* **OPP** **unholy** ➲ see also HOLY ORDERS **2** ⊶ good in a moral and religious way: *a holy life/man* **OPP** **unholy** **3** [only before noun] (*informal*) used to emphasize that you are surprised, afraid, etc.: *Holy cow! What was that?* ➲ see also HOLIER-THAN-THOU, HOLINESS

ˌ**Holy Com'munion** *noun* [U] = COMMUNION

the ˌ**Holy 'Father** *noun* [sing.] the POPE

the ˌ**Holy 'Ghost** *noun* [sing.] = THE HOLY SPIRIT

the ˌ**Holy 'Grail** *noun* [sing.] = GRAIL

the ˌ**holy of 'holies** *noun* [sing.] **1** the most holy part of a religious building **2** (*humorous*) a special room or building that can only be visited by important people

ˌ**holy 'orders** *noun* [pl.] the official position of being a priest: *to take holy orders* (= to become a priest)

Holy·rood /'hɒliruːd; *NAmE* 'hɑːl-/ *noun* [U] the Scottish parliament and government: *elections to Holyrood* **ORIGIN** From the name of the part of Edinburgh where the parliament building is.

the ˌ**Holy 'See** *noun* [sing.] **1** the job or authority of the Pope **2** the Roman Catholic court at the Vatican in Rome

H

the ˌHoly ˈSpirit (also **the ˌHoly ˈGhost**) *noun* [sing.] (in Christianity) God in the form of a spirit

ˌholy ˈwater *noun* [U] water that has been BLESSED by a priest

ˈHoly Week *noun* in the Christian Church, the week before Easter Sunday

ˌHoly ˈWrit *noun* [U] (*old-fashioned*) the Bible: (*figurative*) *You shouldn't take what he says as Holy Writ* (= accept that it is true without questioning it).

hom·age /ˈhɒmɪdʒ; *NAmE* ˈhɑːm-/ *noun* [U, C, usually sing.] **~ (to sb/sth)** (*formal*) something that is said or done to show respect for sb: *The kings of France* ***paid homage*** *to no one.* ◇ *He describes his book as 'a homage to my father'.* ◇ *They stood in silent homage around the grave.*

hom·bre /ˈɒmbreɪ; *NAmE* ˈɑːmb-/ *noun* (from Spanish, *NAmE, informal*) a man, especially one of a particular type: *Their quarterback is one tough hombre.*

H

hom·burg /ˈhɒmbɜːg; *NAmE* ˈhɑːmbɜːrg/ *noun* a man's soft hat with a narrow, curled BRIM

home 🔑 /həʊm; *NAmE* hoʊm/ *noun, adj., adv., verb*

■ ***noun***

▸ HOUSE, ETC. **1** 🔑 [C, U] the house or flat/apartment that you live in, especially with your family: *We are not far from my home now.* ◇ *Old people prefer to stay in their own homes.* ◇ *She leaves home at 7 every day.* ◇ *the family home* ◇ *While travelling she missed the comforts of home.* ◇ *He* ***left home*** (= left his parents and began an independent life) *at sixteen.* ◇ *Nowadays a lot of people* ***work from home.*** ◇ *I'll call you from home later.* ◇ (*figurative*) *We haven't found a home for all our books yet* (= a place where they can be kept). ◇ *stray dogs needing new homes* ➲ see also STAY-AT-HOME **2** 🔑 [C] a house or flat/apartment, etc, when you think of it as property that can be bought and sold: *a* ***holiday/summer home*** ◇ *A lot of new homes are being built on the edge of town.* ◇ *Private* ***home ownership*** *is increasing faster than ever.* ◇ *They applied for a home improvement loan.* ➲ COLLOCATIONS at DECORATE, HOUSE ➲ VISUAL VOCAB page V14 ➲ see also MOBILE HOME, SECOND HOME, STATELY HOME

▸ TOWN/COUNTRY **3** 🔑 [C, U] the town, district, country, etc. that you come from, or where you are living and that you feel you belong to: *I often think about my friends* ***back home.*** ◇ *Jane left England and made Greece her home.* ◇ *Jamaica is home to over two million people.*

▸ FAMILY **4** 🔑 [C] used to refer to a family living together, and the way it behaves: *She came from a violent home.* ◇ *He had always wanted a real home with a wife and children.* ➲ see also BROKEN HOME

▸ FOR OLD PEOPLE/CHILDREN **5** [C] a place where people who cannot care for themselves live and are cared for by others: *a* ***children's home*** ◇ *an* ***old people's home*** ◇ *a* ***retirement home*** ◇ *a home for the mentally ill* ◇ *She has lived* ***in a home*** *since she was six.* ➲ see also NURSING HOME, REST HOME

▸ FOR PETS **6** [C] a place where pets with no owner are taken care of: *a* ***dogs'/cats' home***

▸ OF PLANT/ANIMAL **7** [sing., U] the place where a plant or animal usually lives; the place where sb/sth can be found: *This region is the home of many species of wild flower.* ◇ *The tiger's home is in the jungle.* ◇ *The Rockies are home to bears and mountain lions.*

▸ WHERE STH FIRST DONE **8** [sing.] **the ~ of sth** the place where sth was first discovered, made or invented: *New Orleans, the home of jazz* ◇ *Greece, the home of democracy*

IDM **at ˈhome 1** 🔑 in a person's own house, flat/apartment, etc: *I phoned you last night, but you weren't at home.* ◇ *Oh no, I left my purse at home.* ◇ *He lived at home* (= with his parents) *until he was thirty.* **2** 🔑 comfortable and relaxed: *Sit down and* ***make yourself at home.*** ◇ *Simon feels very at home on a horse.* **3** (used especially in JOURNALISM) in sb's own country, not in a foreign country: *The president is not as popular at home as he is abroad.* **4** if a sports team plays **at home**, it plays in the town, etc. that it comes from: *Leeds are playing at home this weekend.* ◇ *Is the match on Saturday at home or away?* **away from ˈhome 1** away from a person's own house, flat/apartment, etc: *He works away from home during the week.* ◇ *I don't want to be away from home for too long.* **2** (*BrE*) if a sports team plays **away from home**, it plays in the town, etc. that its opponent comes from **a ˌhome from ˈhome** (*BrE*) (*NAmE* **a ˌhome away from ˈhome**) a place where you feel relaxed and comfortable as if you were in your own home **ˌhome is where the ˈheart is** (*saying*) a home is where the people you love are **home sweet ˈhome** (often *ironic*) used to say how pleasant your home is (especially when you really mean that it is not pleasant at all) **set up ˈhome** (*BrE*) (used especially about a couple) to start living in a new place: *They got married and set up home together in Hull.* **when he's, it's, etc. at ˈhome** (*BrE, humorous*) used to emphasize a question about sb/sth: *Who's she when she's at home?* (= I don't know her) ➲ more at CHARITY, CLOSE[2] *adj.*, EAT, ENGLISHMAN, SPIRITUAL

■ ***adj.*** [only before noun]

▸ WHERE YOU LIVE **1** connected with the place where you live: ***home life*** (= with your family) ◇ *a person's* ***home address/town*** ◇ *We offer customers a free* ***home delivery*** *service.*

▸ MADE/USED AT HOME **2** made or used at home: *home movies* ◇ *home cooking* ◇ *a home computer*

▸ OWN COUNTRY **3** (*especially BrE*) connected with your own country rather than foreign countries SYN **domestic**: *products for the home market* ◇ ***home news/affairs*** OPP **foreign**, **overseas**

▸ IN SPORT **4** connected with a team's own sports ground: *a* ***home match/win*** ◇ *the* ***home team*** ◇ *Rangers were playing in front of their* ***home crowd.*** ➲ compare AWAY

■ ***adv.***

▸ WHERE YOU LIVE **1** 🔑 to or at the place where you live: *Come on, it's time to* ***go home.*** ◇ *What time did you* ***get home*** *last night?* ◇ *The trip has been exhausting and I'll be glad to* ***be home.*** ◇ *After a month, they went* ***back home*** *to America.* ◇ *It was a lovely day so I walked home.* ◇ *Anna will drive me home after work.* ◇ *Hopefully the doctors will allow her home tomorrow.* ◇ (*NAmE*) *I like to* ***stay home*** *in the evenings.*

▸ INTO CORRECT POSITION **2** into the correct position: *She leaned on the door and pushed the bolt home.* ◇ *He drove the ball home* (= scored a goal) *from 15 metres.* ◇ *The torpedo struck home on the hull of the ship.*

IDM **be home and ˈdry** (*BrE*) (*NAmE* **be home ˈfree**) to have done sth successfully, especially when it was difficult: *I could see the finish line and thought I was home and dry.* **bring home the ˈbacon** (*informal*) to be successful at sth; to earn money for your family to live on **bring sth ˈhome to sb** to make sb realize how important, difficult or serious sth is: *The television pictures brought home to us the full horror of the attack.* **come ˈhome to sb** to become completely clear to sb, often in a way that is painful: *It suddenly came home to him that he was never going to see Julie again.* **sth comes home to ˈroost** (also **the chickens come home to ˈroost**) used to say that if sb says or does sth bad or wrong, it will affect them badly in the future **hit/strike ˈhome** if a remark, etc. **hits/strikes home**, it has a strong effect on sb, in a way that makes them realize what the true facts of a situation are: *Her face went pale as his words hit home.* ➲ more at COW *n.*, DRIVE *v.*, LIGHT *n.*, PRESS *v.*, RAM *v.*, ROMP *n.*, WRITE

■ ***verb***

PHR V **ˌhome ˈin on sth 1** to aim at sth and move straight towards it: *The missile homed in on the target.* **2** to direct your thoughts or attention towards sth: *I began to feel I was really homing in on the answer.*

ˌhome ˈbase *noun* [sing., U] **1** = HOME PLATE **2** the place where sb/sth usually lives, works or operates from

home·body /ˈhəʊmbɒdi; *NAmE* ˈhoʊmbɑːdi/ *noun* (*pl.* -ies) (*informal, especially NAmE*) a person who enjoys spending time at home

home·boy /ˈhəʊmbɔɪ; *NAmE* ˈhoʊm-/ (also **homie**) *noun* (*NAmE, informal*) a male friend from the same town as you; a member of your GANG (= a group of young people who go around together)

ˌhome ˈbrew *noun* [U] **1** beer that sb makes at home **2** something that sb makes at home rather than buying it: *The security software he uses is home brew.* ▸ **ˌhome-ˈbrew** (also **ˌhome-ˈbrewed**) *adj.*

home·buy·er /ˈhəʊmbaɪə(r); *NAmE* ˈhoʊm-/ *noun* a person who buys a house, flat/apartment, etc.

ˌhome ˈcinema (*BrE*) (*NAmE* **ˌhome ˈtheater**) *noun* [U] television and video equipment designed to give a similar experience to being in a cinema/movie theater, with high-quality pictures and sound and a large screen

home·com·ing /ˈhəʊmkʌmɪŋ; *NAmE* ˈhoʊm-/ *noun* **1** [C, U] the act of returning to your home after being away for a long time **2** [C] (*NAmE*) a social event that takes place every year at a HIGH SCHOOL, college or university for people who used to be students there

the ˌHome ˈCounties *noun* [pl.] the counties around London

ˌhome ecoˈnomics *noun* [U] cooking and other skills needed at home, taught as a subject in school

ˌhome ˈfront *noun* [sing.] the people who do not go to fight in a war but who stay in a country to work

IDM **on the ˈhome front** happening at home, or in your own country

home·girl /ˈhəʊmgɜːl; *NAmE* ˈhoʊmgɜːrl/ (also **homie**) *noun* (*NAmE, informal*) a female friend from the same town as you; a member of your GANG (= a group of young people who go around together)

ˌhome ˈground *noun* [sing., U] **1** (*BrE*) a sports ground that a team regularly plays on in their own area or town **2** a place where sb lives or works and where they feel confident, rather than a place that is not familiar to them: *I'd rather meet him here on my own home ground.*

ˌhome-ˈgrown *adj.* **1** (of plants, fruit and vegetables) grown in a person's garden: *home-grown tomatoes* **2** made, trained or educated in your own country, town, etc: *The team has a wealth of home-grown talent.*

ˌhome ˈhelp *noun* (*BrE*) a person whose job is to help old or sick people with cooking, cleaning, etc.

ˌhome imˈprovement *noun* [C, U] changes that are made to a house, that increase its value: *They've spent a lot of money on home improvements.* ◇ *home-improvement products* ➲ COLLOCATIONS at DECORATE

home·land /ˈhəʊmlænd; *NAmE* ˈhoʊm-/ *noun* **1** [usually sing.] the country where a person was born: *Many refugees have been forced to flee their homeland.* **2** (in the Republic of South Africa under the APARTHEID system in the past) one of the areas with some SELF-GOVERNMENT that were intended for a group of black African people to live in: *the Transkei homeland*

ˌHomeland Seˈcurity *noun* [U] the activities and organizations whose aim is to prevent TERRORIST attacks in the US: *the Department of Homeland Security*

home·less /ˈhəʊmləs; *NAmE* ˈhoʊm-/ *adj.* **1** having no home: *The scheme has been set up to help homeless people.* **2 the homeless** *noun* [pl.] people who have no home: *helping the homeless* ▸ **home·less·ness** *noun* [U]

ˌhome ˈloan *noun* (*informal*) = MORTGAGE

home·ly /ˈhəʊmli; *NAmE* ˈhoʊm-/ *adj.* (**home·lier, home·li·est**) **1** (*BrE, approving*) (of a place) making you feel comfortable, as if you were in your own home: *The hotel has a lovely homely feel to it.* **2** (*approving, especially BrE*) simple and good: *homely cooking* **3** (*BrE, approving*) (of a woman) warm and friendly and enjoying the pleasures of home and family: *His landlady was a kind, homely woman.* **4** (*NAmE, disapproving*) (of a person's appearance) not attractive SYN **plain**: *a homely child*

ˌhome-ˈmade *adj.* made at home, rather than produced in a factory and bought in a shop/store

home·maker /ˈhəʊmmeɪkə(r); *NAmE* ˈhoʊm-/ *noun* (*especially NAmE*) a person who works at home and takes care of the house and family ▸ **home·making** *noun* [U]

the ˈHome Office *noun* [sing.+ sing./pl. v.] the British government department that deals with the law, the police and prisons, and with decisions about who can enter the country

ˌhome ˈoffice *noun* a room in sb's home that is used for work

homeo·path (*BrE* also **hom·oeo-**) /ˈhəʊmiəpæθ; ˈhɒmi-; *NAmE* ˈhoʊ-; ˈhɑːm-/ *noun* a person who treats illness using homeopathic methods

hom·eop·athy (*BrE* also **hom·oeo-**) /ˌhəʊmiˈɒpəθi; ˌhɒm-; *NAmE* ˌhoʊmiˈɑːp-; ˌhɑːm-/ *noun* [U] a system of treating diseases or conditions using very small amounts of the substance that causes the disease or condition ▸ **homeo·path·ic** (*BrE* also **hom·oeo-**) /ˌhəʊmiəˈpæθɪk; ˌhɒm-; *NAmE* ˌhoʊm-; ˌhɑːm-/ *adj.*: *homeopathic medicines/remedies/treatments*

homeo·stasis (*BrE* also **hom·oeo-**) /ˌhəʊmiəˈsteɪsɪs; ˌhɒm-; *NAmE* ˌhoʊm-/ *noun* [U] (*biology*) the process by which the body reacts to changes in order to keep conditions inside the body, for example temperature, the same

home·own·er /ˈhəʊməʊnə(r); *NAmE* ˈhoʊmoʊ-/ *noun* a person who owns their house or flat/apartment

ˈhome page *noun* (*computing*) **1** the main page created by a company, an organization, etc. on the Internet from which connections to other pages can be made ➲ VISUAL VOCAB page V55 **2** a page on the Internet that you choose to appear first on your screen whenever you make a connection to the Internet

ˈhome plate (also **ˌhome ˈbase**) (*NAmE* also **plate**) *noun* (in BASEBALL) the place where the person hitting the ball stands and where they must return to after running around all the bases

homer /ˈhəʊmə(r); *NAmE* ˈhoʊm-/ *noun* (*NAmE, informal*) = HOME RUN: *He hit a homer.*

home·room /ˈhəʊmruːm; -rʊm; *NAmE* ˈhoʊm-/ *noun* [C, U] (*NAmE*) a room in a school where students go at the beginning of each school day, so that teachers can check who is in school; the time spent in this room

ˌhome ˈrule *noun* [U] the right of a country or region to govern itself, especially after another country or region has governed it

ˌhome ˈrun (also *NAmE informal* **homer**) *noun* (in BASEBALL) a hit that allows the person hitting the ball to run around all the bases without stopping

home·school·ing /ˌhəʊmˈskuːlɪŋ; *NAmE* ˌhoʊm-/ *noun* [U] the practice of educating children at home, not in schools ▸ **home·school** /ˌhəʊmˈskuːl; *NAmE* ˌhoʊm-/ *verb* **~ sb**

ˌHome ˈSecretary *noun* the British government minister in charge of the Home Office

ˌhome ˈshopping *noun* [U] the practice of ordering goods by phone or by email and having them delivered to your home

home·sick /ˈhəʊmsɪk; *NAmE* ˈhoʊm-/ *adj.* sad because you are away from home and you miss your family and friends: *I felt homesick for Scotland.* ▸ **home·sick·ness** *noun* [U]

home·spun /ˈhəʊmspʌn; *NAmE* ˈhoʊm-/ *adj.* **1** (especially of ideas) simple and ordinary; not coming from an expert **2** (of cloth) made at home

home·stay /ˈhəʊmsteɪ; *NAmE* ˈhoʊm-/ *noun* [C, U] an arrangement that provides accommodation for students or tourists in the home of a family in exchange for payment: *The trip includes a homestay in a traditional village.* ◇ *Live with an American family in homestay and learn the language and customs.*

home·stead /ˈhəʊmsted; *NAmE* ˈhoʊm-/ *noun, verb*

▪ ***noun* 1** a house with the land and buildings around it, especially a farm **2** (in the US in the past) a piece of land given to sb by the government on condition that they lived on it and grew crops on it

▪ ***verb*** [I] (*old-fashioned, NAmE*) to live and work on a homestead (2) ▸ **home·stead·er** *noun*

the ˌhome ˈstraight (*especially BrE*) (also **the ˌhome ˈstretch** especially in *NAmE*) *noun* [sing.] **1** the last part of

H

a race **2** the last part of an activity, etc. when it is nearly completed

ˌhome ˈtheater (*NAmE*) (*BrE* **ˌhome ˈcinema**) *noun* [U] television and video equipment designed to give a similar experience to being in a cinema/movie theater, with high-quality pictures and sound and a large screen

home·town /ˈhəʊmtaʊn; *NAmE* ˈhoʊm-/ *noun* the place where you were born or lived as a child

ˌhome ˈtruth *noun* [usually pl.] a true but unpleasant fact about a person, usually told to them by sb else: *It's time you told him a few home truths.*

ˈhome unit *noun* (*AustralE, NZE*) = UNIT (9)

home·ward /ˈhəʊmwəd; *NAmE* ˈhoʊmwərd/ *adj.* going towards home: *the homeward journey* ▸ **home·ward** (also **home·wards** especially in *BrE*) *adv.*: *Commuters were heading homeward at the end of the day.* ◇ *We drove homewards in silence.* ◇ *We were* ***homeward bound*** *at last.*

H

home·work 0-ᴡ /ˈhəʊmwɜːk; *NAmE* ˈhoʊmwɜːrk/ *noun* [U]
1 0-ᴡ work that is given by teachers for students to do at home: *I still haven't done my geography homework.* ◇ *How much homework do you get?* ◇ *I have to write up the notes* ***for homework.*** ➲ COLLOCATIONS at EDUCATION **2** (*informal*) work that sb does to prepare for sth: *You could tell that he had really* ***done his homework*** (= found out all he needed to know).

home·work·er /ˈhəʊmwɜːkə(r); *NAmE* ˈhoʊmwɜːrk-/ *noun* a person who works at home, often doing jobs that are not well paid such as making clothes for shops/stores ▸ **home·work·ing** *noun* [U]

homey (also **homy**) /ˈhəʊmi; *NAmE* ˈhoʊmi/ *adj., noun*
■ ***adj.*** (*informal, especially NAmE*) pleasant and comfortable, like home: *The hotel had a nice, homey atmosphere.*
■ ***noun*** = HOMIE

homi·cidal /ˌhɒmɪˈsaɪdl; *NAmE* ˌhɑːm-/ *adj.* likely to kill another person; making sb likely to kill another person: *a homicidal maniac* ◇ *He had clear homicidal tendencies.*

homi·cide /ˈhɒmɪsaɪd; *NAmE* ˈhɑːm-/ *noun* [C, U] (*especially NAmE, law*) the crime of killing sb deliberately SYN **murder** ➲ compare CULPABLE HOMICIDE, MANSLAUGHTER

homie (also **homey**) /ˈhəʊmi; *NAmE* ˈhoʊmi/ *noun* (*NAmE, informal*) a HOMEBOY or HOMEGIRL

hom·ily /ˈhɒməli; *NAmE* ˈhɑːm-/ (*pl.* -ies) *noun* (*formal, often disapproving*) a speech or piece of writing giving advice on the correct way to behave, etc: *She delivered a homily on the virtues of family life.*

hom·ing /ˈhəʊmɪŋ; *NAmE* ˈhoʊm-/ *adj.* [only before noun] **1** (of a bird or an animal) trained, or having a natural ability, to find the way home from a long distance away: *Many birds have a remarkable* ***homing instinct.*** **2** (of a MISSILE, etc.) fitted with an electronic device that enables it to find and hit the place or object it is aimed at: *a* ***homing device***

ˈhoming pigeon *noun* a PIGEON (= a type of bird) that has been trained to find its way home from a long distance away, and that people race against other pigeons for sport

hom·in·id /ˈhɒmɪnɪd; *NAmE* ˈhɑːm-/ *noun* (*technical*) a human, or a creature that lived in the past which humans developed from

hom·in·oid /ˈhɒmɪnɔɪd; *NAmE* ˈhɑːm-/ *noun* (*technical*) a human, or a creature related to humans

hom·iny /ˈhɒmɪni; *NAmE* ˈhɑːm-/ *noun* [U] dried CORN (MAIZE), boiled in water or milk, eaten especially in the southern states of the US

Homo /ˈhɒməʊ; ˈhəʊməʊ; *NAmE* ˈhoʊmoʊ/ *noun* (from *Latin, technical*) the GENUS (= group) of PRIMATES that includes early and modern humans

homo- /ˈhɒməʊ-; ˈhəʊm-; *NAmE* ˈhoʊmoʊ-/ *combining form* (in nouns, adjectives and adverbs) the same ➲ compare HETERO-

hom·oe·op·ath (*BrE*) = HOMEOPATH

hom·oe·op·athy (*BrE*) = HOMEOPATHY

hom·oeo·stasis (*BrE*) = HOMEOSTASIS

Homo erectus /ˌhɒməʊ ɪˈrektəs; ˌhəʊməʊ; *NAmE* ˌhoʊmoʊ/ *noun* [U] (from *Latin, technical*) an early form of human which was able to walk on two legs

homo·erot·ic /ˌhɒməʊɪˈrɒtɪk; ˌhəʊm-; *NAmE* ˌhoʊmoʊɪˈrɑːtɪk/ *adj.* relating to HOMOSEXUAL sex and sexual desire

homo·gen·eity /ˌhɒmədʒəˈniːəti; *NAmE* ˌhɑːm-/ *noun* [U] (*formal*) the quality of being homogeneous

homo·ge·neous /ˌhɒməˈdʒiːniəs; *NAmE* ˌhoʊm-/ *adj.* (*formal*) consisting of things or people that are all the same or all of the same type: *a homogeneous group/mixture/population* OPP **heterogeneous**

hom·ogen·ized (*BrE* also **-ised**) /həˈmɒdʒənaɪzd; *NAmE* həˈmɑːdʒ-/ *adj.* (of milk) treated so that the cream is mixed in with the rest

homo·graph /ˈhɒməgrɑːf; *NAmE* ˈhɑːməgræf/ *noun* (*grammar*) a word that is spelt like another word but has a different meaning from it, and may have a different pronunciation, for example *bow* /baʊ/, *bow* /bəʊ/, /boʊ/

Homo habilis /ˌhɒməʊ ˈhæbɪlɪs; ˌhəʊməʊ; *NAmE* ˌhoʊmoʊ/ *noun* [U] (from *Latin, technical*) an early form of human which was able to use tools

hom·olo·gous /həˈmɒləgəs; *NAmE* hoʊˈmɑːl-; he-/ *adj.* **~ (with sth)** (*technical*) similar in position, structure, etc. to sth else: *The seal's flipper is homologous with the human arm.*

homo·nym /ˈhɒmənɪm; *NAmE* ˈhɑːm-; ˈhoʊm-/ *noun* (*grammar*) a word that is spelt like another word (or pronounced like it) but which has a different meaning, for example *can* meaning 'be able' and *can* meaning 'put sth in a container'

homo·pho·bia /ˌhɒməˈfəʊbiə; ˌhəʊm-; *NAmE* ˌhoʊməˈfoʊ-/ *noun* [U] a strong dislike and fear of HOMOSEXUAL people ▸ **homo·pho·bic** *adj.*

homo·phone /ˈhɒməfəʊn; *NAmE* ˈhɑːməfoʊn/ *noun* (*grammar*) a word that is pronounced like another word but has a different spelling or meaning, for example *some, sum* /sʌm/

hom·oph·onous /həˈmɒfənəs; *NAmE* -ˈmɑːf-/ *adj.* (*linguistics*) (of a word) having the same pronunciation as another word but a different meaning or spelling: *'Bear' and 'bare' are homophonous.*

Homo sa·pi·ens /ˌhɒməʊ ˈsæpienz; ˌhəʊm-; *NAmE* ˌhoʊmoʊ ˈseɪp-; ˈsæp-/ *noun* [U] (from *Latin, technical*) the kind or SPECIES of human that exists now

homo·sex·ual /ˌhəʊməˈsekʃuəl; ˌhɒm-; *NAmE* ˌhoʊm-/ *noun* a person, usually a man, who is sexually attracted to people of the same sex: *a practising homosexual* ➲ compare BISEXUAL, GAY, HETEROSEXUAL, LESBIAN ▸ **homo·sex·ual** *adj.*: *a homosexual act/relationship*
homo·sexu·al·ity /ˌhəʊməˌsekʃuˈæləti; ˌhɒm-; *NAmE* ˌhoʊm-/ *noun* [U]

homo·zy·gote /ˌhɒməˈzaɪgəʊt; *NAmE* ˌhɑːməˈzaɪgoʊt/ *noun* (*biology*) a living thing that has only one form of a particular GENE, and whose young are more likely to share a particular characteristic ▸ **homo·zy·gous** /-gəs/ *adj.*

homy = HOMEY

Hon (also **Hon.** especially in *NAmE*) /ɒn; *NAmE* ɑːn/ *abbr.* **1** (*BrE*) HONORARY (used in official titles of jobs): *Hon Treasurer: D Shrimpton* **2** HONOURABLE: *the Hon Member for Bolsover*

hon·cho /ˈhɒntʃəʊ; *NAmE* ˈhɑːntʃoʊ/ *noun* (*pl.* -os) (*informal, especially NAmE*) the person who is in charge SYN **boss**: *Claude is the studio's* ***head honcho.***

hone /həʊn; *NAmE* hoʊn/ *verb* **1** to develop and improve sth, especially a skill, over a period of time: **~ sth** *She honed her debating skills at college.* ◇ *It was a finely honed piece of writing.* ◇ **~ sth to sth** *His body was honed to perfection.* **2 ~ sth (to sth)** to make a blade sharp or sharper SYN **sharpen**

hon·est ⊶ /ˈɒnɪst; *NAmE* ˈɑːn-/ *adj.* **1** ⊶ always telling the truth, and never stealing or cheating: *an honest man/woman* OPP **dishonest** **2** ⊶ not hiding the truth about sth: *an honest answer* ◇ **~ (about sth)** *Are you being completely honest about your feelings?* ◇ **~ (with sb)** *Thank you for being so honest with me.* ◇ *Give me your honest opinion.* ◇ ***To be honest*** (= what I really think is), *it was one of the worst books I've ever read.* ◇ ***Let's be honest**, she's only interested in Mike because of his money.* **3** ⊶ showing an honest mind or attitude: *She's got an honest face.* **4** (of work or wages) earned or resulting from hard work: *He hasn't done **an honest day's work** in his life.* ◇ *It's quite a struggle to make **an honest living**.* HELP Use **an**, not **a**, before **honest**.

IDM **honest!** (*informal*) used to emphasize that you are not lying: *I didn't mean it, honest!* **honest to ˈGod/ˈgoodness** used to emphasize that what you are saying is true: *Honest to God, Mary, I'm not joking.* HELP Some people find this use offensive. **make an honest ˈwoman of sb** (*old-fashioned, humorous*) to marry a woman after having had a sexual relationship with her

Synonyms

honest

frank • direct • open • outspoken • straight • blunt

These words all describe people saying exactly what they mean without trying to hide feelings, opinions or facts.

honest not hiding the truth about sth: *Thank you for being so honest with me.*

frank honest in what you say, sometimes in a way that other people might not like: *To be frank with you, I think your son has little chance of passing the exam.*

direct saying exactly what you mean in a way that nobody can pretend not to understand: *You'll have to get used to his direct manner.* NOTE Being **direct** is sometimes considered positive but sometimes it is used as a 'polite' way of saying that sb is rude.

open (*approving*) (of a person) not keeping thoughts and feelings hidden: *He was quite open about his reasons for leaving.*

outspoken saying exactly what you think, even if this shocks or offends people: *She was outspoken in her criticism of the plan.*

straight honest and direct: *I don't think you're being straight with me.*

blunt saying exactly what you think without trying to be polite: *She has a reputation for blunt speaking.*

WHICH WORD?

Honest and **frank** refer to *what* you say as much as *how* you say it: *a(n) honest/frank admission of guilt*. They are generally positive words, although it is possible to be *too* frank in a way that other people might not like. **Direct**, **outspoken** and **blunt** all describe sb's manner of saying what they think. **Outspoken** suggests that you are willing to shock people by saying what you believe to be right. **Blunt** and **direct** often suggest that you think honesty is more important than being polite. **Open** is positive and describes sb's character: *I'm a very open person.*

PATTERNS

- honest/frank/direct/open/outspoken/straight **about** sth
- honest/frank/direct/open/straight/blunt **with** sb
- a(n) honest/direct/straight/blunt **answer**
- a frank/direct/blunt **manner**

ˌhonest ˈbroker *noun* a person or country that tries to get other people or countries to reach an agreement or to solve a problem, without getting involved with either side

hon·est·ly ⊶ /ˈɒnɪstli; *NAmE* ˈɑːn-/ *adv.* **1** ⊶ in an honest way: *I can't believe he got that money honestly.* OPP **dishonestly** **2** ⊶ used to emphasize that what you are saying is true, however surprising it may seem: *I didn't tell anyone, honestly!* ◇ *I honestly can't remember a thing about last night.* ◇ *You can't honestly expect me to believe that!* **3** (*informal*) used to show that you disapprove of sth and are irritated by it: *Honestly! Whatever will they think of next?*

ˌhonest-to-ˈgoodness *adj.* [only before noun] (*approving*) simple and good: *honest-to-goodness country food*

hon·esty /ˈɒnəsti; *NAmE* ˈɑːn-/ *noun* [U] the quality of being honest: *She answered all my questions with her usual honesty.* ◇ *His honesty is not in question.*

IDM **in all ˈhonesty** used to state a fact or an opinion which, though true, may seem disappointing: *The book isn't, in all honesty, as good as I expected.*

honey /ˈhʌni/ *noun* **1** [U] a sweet sticky yellow substance made by BEES that is spread on bread, etc. like jam **2** [C] (*informal*) a way of addressing sb that you like or love: *Have you seen my keys, honey?* **3** [C] (*informal*) a person that you like or love and think is very kind: *He can be a real honey when he wants to be.* IDM see LAND *n.*

honey·bee /ˈhʌnibiː/ *noun* a BEE that makes honey

honey·comb /ˈhʌnikəʊm; *NAmE* -koʊm/ (also **comb**) *noun* [C, U] a structure of cells with six sides, made by BEES for holding their honey and their eggs

honey·combed /ˈhʌnikəʊmd; *NAmE* -koʊmd/ *adj.* **~ (with sth)** filled with holes, tunnels, etc.

honey·dew melon /ˌhʌnidjuː ˈmelən; *NAmE* -duː/ *noun* a type of MELON with a pale skin and green flesh

hon·eyed /ˈhʌnid/ *adj.* (*literary*) **1** (of words) soft and intended to please, but often not sincere **2** tasting or smelling like honey, or having the colour of honey

honey·moon /ˈhʌnimuːn/ *noun, verb*

■ ***noun*** [usually sing.] **1** a holiday/vacation taken by a couple who have just got married: *We went to Venice for our honeymoon.* ◇ *They're **on their honeymoon**.* **2** the period of time at the start of a new activity when nobody is criticized and people feel enthusiastic: *The **honeymoon period** for the government is now over.*

■ ***verb*** [I] + **adv./prep.** to spend your honeymoon somewhere ▸ **honey·moon·er** *noun*

honey·pot /ˈhʌnipɒt; *NAmE* -pɑːt/ *noun* [usually sing.] (*BrE*) a place, thing or person that a lot of people are attracted to

honey·suckle /ˈhʌnisʌkl/ *noun* [U, C] a climbing plant with white, yellow or pink flowers with a sweet smell

hongi /ˈhɒŋi; *NAmE* ˈhɑːŋi/ *noun* (*NZE*) a traditional Maori GREETING in which people press their noses together

honk /hɒŋk; *NAmE* hɑːŋk; hɔːŋk/ *noun, verb*

■ ***noun*** **1** the noise made by a GOOSE **2** the noise made by a car horn

■ ***verb*** **1** [I, T] if a car horn **honks** or you **honk** or **honk the horn**, the horn makes a loud noise SYN **hoot**: *honking taxis* ◇ **~ at sb/sth** *Why did he honk at me?* ◇ **~ sth** *People honked their horns as they drove past.* **2** [I] when a GOOSE **honks**, it makes a loud noise

honky /ˈhɒŋki; *NAmE* ˈhɑːŋ-; ˈhɔːŋ-/ *noun* (*pl.* **-ies**) (*NAmE, slang*) an offensive word for a white person, used by black people

honky-tonk /ˈhɒŋki tɒŋk; *NAmE* ˈhɑːŋki tɑːŋk; ˈhɔːŋki tɔːŋk/ *noun* **1** [C] (*NAmE*) a cheap, noisy bar or dance hall **2** [U] a type of lively JAZZ played on a piano

honor, hon·or·able (*especially US*) = HONOUR, HONOURABLE

hon·or·arium /ˌɒnəˈreəriəm; *NAmE* ˌɑːnəˈrer-/ *noun* (*pl.* **hon·or·aria** /-riə/) (*formal*) a payment made for sb's professional services HELP Use **an**, not **a**, before **honorarium**.

hon·or·ary /ˈɒnərəri; *NAmE* ˈɑːnəreri/ *adj.* (*abbr.* **Hon**) **1** (of a university degree, a rank, etc.) given as an honour, without the person having to have the usual qualifications: *an **honorary doctorate/degree*** **2** (of a position in an organization) not paid: *the honorary president* ◇ *The post of treasurer is a purely honorary position.* **3** treated

H

like a member of group without actually belonging to it: *She was treated as an honorary man.* HELP Use **an**, not **a**, before **honorary**.

hon·or·ee (*BrE* also **hon·our·ee**) /ˌɒnəˈriː; *NAmE* ˌɑːnəˈriː/ *noun* (*especially NAmE*) a person or thing that wins an award: *The author is a Pulitzer Prize honoree.* HELP Use **an**, not **a**, before **honoree**.

hon·or·if·ic /ˌɒnəˈrɪfɪk; *NAmE* ˌɑːnə-/ *adj.* (*formal*) showing respect for the person you are speaking to: *an honorific title* HELP Use **an**, not **a**, before **honorific**.

hon·oris causa /ɒˌnɔːrɪs ˈkaʊzɑː; *NAmE* əˌnɔːrəs ˈkɔːzə/ *adv.* (from *Latin*) (especially of a degree) given to a person as a sign of honour and respect, without their having to take an exam: *She was awarded a degree honoris causa.*

ˈhonor roll *noun* (*especially US*) **1** (*BrE* ˌ**roll of ˈhonour**) [usually sing.] a list of people who are being praised officially for sth they have done **2** a list of the best students in a college or HIGH SCHOOL

H

ˈhonor society *noun* (in the US) an organization for students with the best grades at school or college

ˈhonor system *noun* [sing.] (*NAmE*) an agreement in which people are trusted to obey rules

hon·our 🔑 (*especially US* **honor**) /ˈɒnə(r); *NAmE* ˈɑːnər/ *noun, verb*

■ ***noun*** HELP Use **an**, not **a**, before **honour**.

▸ RESPECT **1** 🔑 [U] great respect and admiration for sb: *the* ***guest of honour*** (= the most important one) ◇ *the* ***seat/place of honour*** (= given to the most important guest) ◇ *They stood in silence as a mark of honour to her.* ➲ see also MAID OF HONOUR, MATRON OF HONOUR

▸ PRIVILEGE **2** 🔑 [sing.] something that you are very pleased or proud to do because people are showing you great respect: *It was a great honour to be invited here today.* SYN **privilege** ➲ SYNONYMS at PLEASURE

▸ MORAL BEHAVIOUR **3** 🔑 [U] the quality of knowing and doing what is morally right: *a man of honour* ◇ *Proving his innocence has become a matter of honour.*

▸ REPUTATION **4** 🔑 [U] a good reputation; respect from other people: *upholding the honour of your country* ◇ *The family honour is at stake.* ➲ compare DISHONOUR **5** [sing.] **~ to sth/sb** a person or thing that causes others to respect and admire sth/sb: *She is an honour to the profession.*

▸ AWARD **6** 🔑 [C] an award, official title, etc. given to sb as a reward for sth that they have done: *the New Year's Honours list* (= in Britain, a list of awards and titles given on January 1 each year) ◇ *to win the highest honour* ◇ *He was buried* ***with full military honours*** (= with a special military service as a sign of respect). ➲ see also ROLL OF HONOUR

▸ AT UNIVERSITY/SCHOOL **7 honours, honors** [pl.] (*abbr.* **Hons**) (often used as an adjective) a university course that is of a higher level than a basic course (in the US also used to describe a class in school which is at a higher level than other classes): *an* ***honours degree/course*** ◇ *a First Class Honours degree* ◇ (*NAmE*) *I took an honors class in English.* **8 honours, honors** [pl.] if you pass an exam or GRADUATE from a university or school **with honours**, you receive a special mark/grade for having achieved a very high standard

▸ JUDGE/MAYOR **9 His/Her/Your Honour** [C] a title of respect used when talking to or about a judge or a US MAYOR: *No more questions, Your Honour.*

▸ IN CARD GAMES **10** [C, usually pl.] the cards that have the highest value

IDM **do sb an ˈhonour | do sb the ˈhonour (of doing sth)** (*formal*) to do sth to make sb feel very proud and pleased: *Would you do me the honour of dining with me?* **do the ˈhonours** to perform a social duty or ceremony, such as pouring drinks, making a speech, etc: *Would you do the honours and draw the winning ticket?* **have the ˈhonour of sth/of doing sth** (*formal*) to be given the opportunity to do sth that makes you feel proud and happy: *May I have the honour of the next dance?* **(there is) honour among ˈthieves** (*saying*) used to say that even criminals have standards of behaviour that they respect **(feel) honour-ˈbound to do sth** (*formal*) to feel that you must do sth because of your sense of moral duty: *She felt honour-bound to attend as she had promised to.* ➲ compare DUTY-BOUND **the honours are ˈeven** no particular person, team, etc. is doing better than the others in a competition, an argument, etc. **in ˈhonour of sb/sth | in sb's/sth's ˈhonour** in order to show respect and admiration for sb/sth: *a ceremony in honour of those killed in the explosion* ◇ *A banquet was held in her honour.* **on your ˈhonour** (*old-fashioned*) **1** used to promise very seriously that you will do sth or that sth is true: *I swear on my honour that I knew nothing about this.* **2** to be trusted to do sth: *You're on your honour not to go into my room.* ➲ more at POINT *n.*

■ ***verb***

▸ SHOW RESPECT **1 ~ sb (with sth)** to do sth that shows great respect for sb/sth: *The President honoured us with a personal visit.* ◇ *our honoured guests* ◇ (*ironic*) *I'm glad to see that you've decided to* ***honour us with your presence!***

▸ GIVE AWARD **2 ~ sb/sth (with sth) (for sth)** to give public praise, an award or a title to sb for sth they have done: *He has been honoured with a knighthood for his scientific work.*

▸ KEEP PROMISE **3 ~ sth** (*formal*) to do what you have agreed or promised to do: *I have every intention of honouring our contract.* ◇ *to honour a cheque* (= to keep an agreement to pay it)

IDM **be/feel honoured (to do sth)** to feel proud and happy: *I was honoured to have been mentioned in his speech.*

hon·our·able (*especially US* **hon·or·able**) /ˈɒnərəbl; *NAmE* ˈɑːnə-/ *adj.* **1** deserving respect and admiration: *a long and honourable career in government* ◇ *They managed an honourable 2–2 draw.* ◇ ***With a few honourable exceptions****, the staff were found to be incompetent.* **2** showing high moral standards: *an honourable man* **3** allowing sb to keep their good name and the respect of others: *an honourable compromise* ◇ *They urged her to* ***do the honourable thing*** *and resign.* ◇ *He received an honourable discharge from the army.* OPP **dishonourable 4 the Honourable** (*abbr.* **Hon**) [only before noun] (in Britain) a title used by a child of some ranks of the NOBILITY **5 the/my Honourable...** (*abbr.* **Hon**) [only before noun] (in Britain), a title used by Members of Parliament when talking about or to another Member during a debate: *If my Honourable Friend would give me a chance to answer,...* **6** (*abbr.* **Hon**) a title of respect used by an official of high rank: *the Honorable Alan Simpson, US senator* ➲ compare RIGHT HONOURABLE HELP Use **an**, not **a**, before **honourable.** ▸ **hon·our·ably** (*especially US* **hon·or·ably**) /-əbli/ *adv.*: *to behave honourably*

hon·our·ee (*especially US* **hon·or·ee**) /ˌɒnəˈriː; *NAmE* ˌɑːnəˈriː/ *noun* (*especially NAmE*) a person or thing that wins an award: *The author is a Pulitzer Prize honoree.*

Hons /ɒnz; *NAmE* ɑːnz/ *abbr.* (*BrE*) HONOURS (used after the name of a university degree): *Tim Smith BA (Hons)*

hooch /huːtʃ/ *noun* [U] (*informal, especially NAmE*) strong alcoholic drink, especially sth that has been made illegally

hood /hʊd/ *noun* **1** a part of a coat, etc. that you can pull up to cover the back and top of your head: *a jacket with a detachable hood* ➲ VISUAL VOCAB pages V50, V53 **2** a piece of cloth put over sb's face and head so that they cannot be recognized or so that they cannot see **3** a piece of coloured silk or fur worn over an academic GOWN to show the kind of degree held by the person wearing it **4** (*especially BrE*) a folding cover over a car, etc: *We drove all the way with the hood down.* ➲ picture at PUSHCHAIR **5** (*NAmE*) (*BrE* **bonnet**) the metal part over the front of a vehicle, usually covering the engine ➲ VISUAL VOCAB page V42 **6** a cover placed over a device or machine, for example, to protect it: *a lens hood* ◇ *an extractor hood* (= one that removes cooking smells from a kitchen) ➲ VISUAL VOCAB page V22 **7** (*slang, especially NAmE*) = HOODLUM (1) **8** (also **'hood**) (*slang, especially NAmE*) a neighbourhood, especially a person's own neighbourhood

-hood *suffix* (in nouns) **1** the state or quality of: *childhood* ◇ *falsehood* **2** a group of people of the type mentioned: *the priesthood*

hood·ed /ˈhʊdɪd/ *adj.* **1** having or wearing a hood: *a hooded jacket* ◇ *A hooded figure waited in the doorway.*

2 (of eyes) having large EYELIDS that always look as if they are partly closed

hood·lum /ˈhuːdləm/ *noun* (*informal*) **1** (also *slang* **hood** especially in *NAmE*) a violent criminal, especially one who is part of a GANG **2** a violent and noisy young man SYN **hooligan**

hoo·doo /ˈhuːduː/ *noun* (*pl.* **-oos**) (*especially US*) a person or thing that brings or causes bad luck

hood·wink /ˈhʊdwɪŋk/ *verb* **~ sb (into doing sth)** to trick sb: *She had been hoodwinked into buying a worthless necklace.*

hoody (also **hoodie**) /ˈhʊdi/ *noun* (*pl.* **-ies**) (*informal*) a jacket or a SWEATSHIRT with a HOOD ➲ VISUAL VOCAB page V51

hooey /ˈhuːi/ *noun* [U] (*informal, especially NAmE*) nonsense; stupid talk

hoof /huːf/ *noun, verb*

■ ***noun*** (*pl.* hoofs or hooves /huːvz/) the hard part of the foot of some animals, for example horses ➲ VISUAL VOCAB page V10

IDM **on the ˈhoof 1** meat that is sold, transported, etc. **on the hoof** is sold, etc. while the cow or sheep is still alive **2** (*BrE, informal*) if you do sth **on the hoof**, you do it quickly and without giving it your full attention because you are doing sth else at the same time

■ ***verb*** **~ sth** (*informal*) to kick a ball very hard or a long way

IDM **ˈhoof it** (*informal*) to go somewhere on foot; to walk somewhere: *We hoofed it all the way to 42nd Street.*

ˌhoof-and-ˈmouth disease *noun* [U] (*NAmE*) = FOOT-AND-MOUTH DISEASE

hoo-ha /ˈhuː hɑː/ *noun* [U, sing.] (*BrE, informal*) noisy excitement, especially about sth unimportant SYN **fuss**

hooks

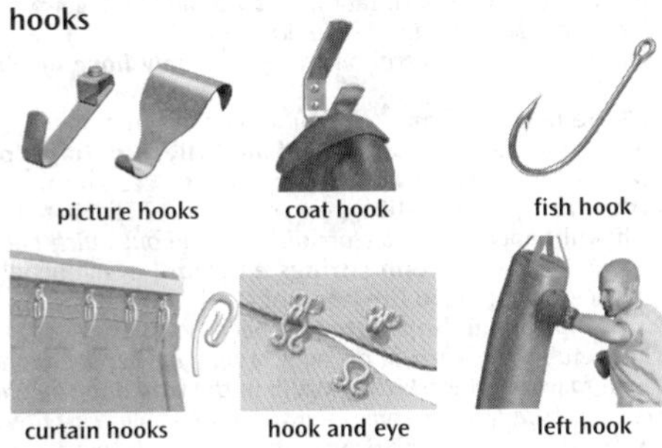

picture hooks | coat hook | fish hook | curtain hooks | hook and eye | left hook

hook 🔑 /hʊk/ *noun, verb*

■ ***noun*** **1** 🔑 a curved piece of metal, plastic or wire for hanging things on, catching fish with, etc: *a **picture/curtain/coat hook** ◇ a fish hook ◇ Hang your towel **on the hook**.* ➲ VISUAL VOCAB page V35 ➲ see also BOATHOOK **2** (in boxing) a short hard blow that is made with the elbow bent: *a left hook to the jaw* **3** (in CRICKET and GOLF) a way of hitting the ball so that it curves sideways instead of going straight ahead **4** a thing that is used to make people interested in sth: *The images are used as a hook to get children interested in science.*

IDM **by ˌhook or by ˈcrook** using any method you can, even a dishonest one **get (sb) off the ˈhook | let sb off the ˈhook** to free yourself or sb else from a difficult situation or a punishment **hook, line and ˈsinker** completely: *What I said was not true, but he fell for it* (= believed it) *hook, line and sinker.* **off the ˈhook** if you leave or take the telephone **off the hook**, you take the RECEIVER (= the part that you pick up) off the place where it usually rests, so that nobody can call you ➲ more at RING² *v.*, SLING *v.*

■ ***verb*** **1** [T, I] to fasten or hang sth on sth else using a hook; to be fastened or hanging in this way: **~ sth + adv./prep.** *We hooked the trailer to the back of the car.* ◇ **+ adv./prep.** *a dress that hooks at the back* **2** [T, I] to put sth, especially your leg, arm or finger, around sth else so that you can hold onto it or move it; to go around sth else in this way: **~ sth + adv./prep.** *He hooked his foot under the stool and dragged it over.* ◇ *Her thumbs were hooked into the pockets of her jeans.* ◇ **+ adv./prep.** *Suddenly an arm hooked around my neck.* **3** [T] **~ sth** to catch a fish with a hook: *It was the biggest pike I ever hooked.* ◇ (*figurative*) *She had managed to hook a wealthy husband.* **4** [T] **~ sth** (especially in GOLF, CRICKET or football (SOCCER)) to hit or kick a ball so that it goes to one side instead of straight ahead

PHR V **ˌhook ˈup (to sth) | ˌhook sb/sth↔ˈup (to sth)** to connect sb/sth to a piece of electronic equipment, to a power supply or to the Internet: *She was then hooked up to an IV drip.* ◇ *Check that the computer is hooked up to the printer.* ◇ *A large proportion of the nation's households are hooked up to the Internet.* **ˌhook ˈup with sb** (*informal*) **1** to meet sb and spend time with them **2** to start working with sb **ˌhook sb ˈup with sb/sth** (*informal*) to put sb in contact with sb who can help them; to get sth for sb that they want: *Can you hook me up with someone with a car?*

hoo·kah /ˈhʊkə/ *noun* a long pipe for smoking that passes smoke through a container of water to cool it

ˌhook and ˈeye *noun* (*pl.* **hooks and eyes**) a device for fastening clothes, consisting of a small thin piece of metal curved round, and a hook that fits into it ➲ picture at HOOK ➲ VISUAL VOCAB page V51

hooked /hʊkt/ *adj.* **1** curved; shaped like a hook: *a **hooked nose/beak/finger*** **2** [not before noun] **~ (on sth)** (*informal*) needing sth that is bad for you, especially a drug **3** [not before noun] **~ (on sth)** (*informal*) enjoying sth very much, so that you want to do it, see it, etc. as much as possible **4** having one or more hooks

hook·er /ˈhʊkə(r)/ *noun* **1** the player in a RUGBY team, whose job is to pull the ball out of the SCRUM with his foot **2** (*informal, especially NAmE*) a PROSTITUTE

hookey = HOOKY

ˈhook shot *noun* **1** (in BASKETBALL) a shot in which a player throws the ball towards the BASKET in a wide curve, by stretching their arm out to the side and throwing over their head **2** (in CRICKET) a shot in which a player hits the ball to the side by swinging the BAT across their chest

ˈhook-up *noun* a connection between two pieces of equipment, especially electronic equipment used in broadcasting, or computers: *a satellite hook-up between the major European networks*

hook·worm /ˈhʊkwɜːm; *NAmE* -wɜːrm/ *noun* **1** [C] a WORM that lives in the INTESTINES of humans and animals **2** [U] a disease caused by hookworms

hooky (also **hookey**) /ˈhʊki/ (*old-fashioned, NAmE*)

IDM **play ˈhooky** (*informal*) (*BrE* **play ˈtruant**) to stay away from school without permission

hooli·gan /ˈhuːlɪɡən/ *noun* a young person who behaves in an extremely noisy and violent way in public, usually in a group: *English football hooligans* ▸ **hooli·gan·ism** /-ɪzəm/ *noun* [U]

hoon /huːn/ *noun* (*AustralE, NZE, informal*) a man who behaves in a rude and aggressive way, especially one who drives in a dangerous way ▸ **hoon** *verb* [I]

hoop /huːp/ *noun* **1** a large ring of plastic, wood or iron: *a barrel bound with iron hoops* ◇ *hoop earrings* (= in the shape of a hoop) ➲ VISUAL VOCAB page V53 **2** the ring that the players throw the ball through in the game of BASKETBALL in order to score points: *Let's shoot some hoops.* ➲ VISUAL VOCAB page V36 **3** a large ring that was used as a children's toy in the past, or for animals or riders to jump through at a CIRCUS **4** = HULA HOOP **5** a small ARCH made of metal or plastic, put into the ground: *croquet hoops* ◇ *Grow lettuces under plastic stretched over wire hoops.* IDM see JUMP *v.*

hooped /huːpt/ *adj.* shaped like a hoop: *hooped earrings*

hoopla /ˈhuːplɑː/ *noun* **1** [U, sing.] (*informal, especially NAmE*) excitement about sth which gets a lot of public attention **2** [U] (*BrE*) (*NAmE* **ring·toss**) a game in which players try to throw rings over objects in order to win them as prizes

hoo·poe /ˈhuːpuː; -pəʊ; *NAmE* -poʊ/ *noun* an orange-pink bird with a long beak that curves downwards, black and white wings and a CREST on its head

hoo·ray /huˈreɪ/ *exclamation* **1** (also **hur·rah, hur·ray**) used to show that you are happy or that you approve of sth **2** (also **hoo·roo**) (*AustralE, NZE*) goodbye IDM see HIP *exclam.*

Hoo·ray Hen·ry /ˌhuːreɪ ˈhenri/ *noun* (*pl.* **Hoo·ray Hen·rys** or **Hoo·ray Hen·ries**) (*BrE, informal, disapproving*) a young upper-class man who enjoys himself in a loud and silly way

hoo·roo /həˈruː; hʌˈruː/ *exclamation* (*AustralE*) = HOORAY (2)

hoot /huːt/ *verb, noun*

■ ***verb*** **1** [I] to make a loud noise: *He had the audience **hooting with laughter**.* ◇ *Some people hooted in disgust.* **2** [I, T] (*BrE*) if a car horn **hoots** or you **hoot** or **hoot the horn**, the horn makes a loud noise SYN **honk**: *hooting cars* ◇ **~ at sb/sth** *Why did he hoot at me?* ◇ **~ sth** *Passing motorists hooted their horns.* ◇ *The train hooted a warning* (= the driver sounded the horn to warn people). **3** [I] when an OWL **hoots**, it makes a long calling sound

■ ***noun*** **1** [C] (*especially BrE*) a short loud laugh or shout: *The suggestion was greeted by **hoots of laughter**.* **2** [sing.] (*informal*) a situation or a person that you find very funny: *You ought to meet her—she's a hoot!* **3** the loud sound made by the horn of a vehicle **4** the cry of an OWL

IDM **not care/give a ˈhoot** | **not care/give two ˈhoots** (*informal*) not to care at all

hoote·nanny /ˈhuːtnæni/ *noun* (*pl.* **-ies**) (*especially US*) an informal social event at which people play FOLK MUSIC, sing and sometimes dance

hoot·er /ˈhuːtə(r)/ *noun* **1** (*BrE*, rather *old-fashioned*) the device in a vehicle, or a factory, that makes a loud noise as a signal **2** (*BrE, slang*) a person's nose, especially a large one **3** [usually pl.] (*NAmE, slang*) a woman's breast

Hoo·ver™ /ˈhuːvə(r)/ *noun* (*BrE*) = VACUUM CLEANER

hoo·ver /ˈhuːvə(r)/ *verb* [T, I] **~ (sth)** (*BrE*) to clean a carpet, floor, etc. with a vacuum cleaner SYN **vacuum**: *to hoover the carpet*

PHR V **ˌhoover sth↔ˈup** **1** to remove sth from a carpet, floor, etc. with a VACUUM CLEANER: *to hoover up all the dust* **2** (*informal*) to get or collect sth in large quantities: *The US and Canada usually hoover up most of the gold medals.* ▸ **hoo·ver·ing** *noun* [U]: *It's your turn to **do the hoovering**.*

hooves *pl.* of HOOF

hop /hɒp; *NAmE* hɑːp/ *verb, noun*

■ ***verb*** (**-pp-**) **1** [I] (**+ adv./prep.**) (of a person) to move by jumping on one foot: *I couldn't put my weight on my ankle and had to hop everywhere.* ◇ *kids hopping over puddles* **2** [I] **+ adv./prep.** (of an animal or a bird) to move by jumping with all or both feet together: *A robin was hopping around on the path.* **3** [I] **+ adv./prep.** (*informal*) to go or move somewhere quickly and suddenly: *Hop in, I'll drive you home.* ◇ *to **hop into/out** of bed* ◇ *I hopped on the next train.* ◇ *We hopped over to Paris for the weekend.* **4** [T] **~ a plane, bus, train, etc.** (*NAmE*) to get on a plane, bus, etc. **5** [I] **~ (from sth to sth)** to change from one activity or subject to another: *I like to hop from channel to channel when I watch TV.*

IDM **ˈhop it** (*old-fashioned, BrE, informal*) usually used in orders to tell sb to go away SYN **go away**: *Go on, hop it!* **hop ˈto it** (*NAmE, informal*) = JUMP TO IT

■ ***noun*** **1** [C] a short jump by a person on one foot: *He crossed the hall with a hop, skip and a jump.* **2** [C] a short jump by an animal or a bird with all or both feet together **3** [C] a short journey, especially by plane **4** [C] a tall climbing plant with green female flowers that are shaped like CONES **5** **hops** [pl.] the green female flowers of the hop plant that have been dried, used for making beer **6** [C] (*old-fashioned, informal*) a social event at which people dance in an informal way ➲ see also HIP HOP IDM see CATCH *v.*

hope 0-w /həʊp; *NAmE* hoʊp/ *verb, noun*

■ ***verb*** 0-w [I, T] to want sth to happen and think that it is possible: **~ (for sth)** *We are hoping for good weather on Sunday.* ◇ *All we can do now is wait and hope.* ◇ *'Do you think it will rain?' '**I hope not**.'* ◇ *'Will you be back before dark?' '**I hope so, yes**.'* ◇ **~ (that)...** *I hope (that) you're okay.* ◇ ***Let's hope** we can find a parking space.* ◇ **it is hoped (that)...** *It is hoped that over £10 000 will be raised.* ◇ **~ to do sth** *She is hoping to win the gold medal.* ◇ *We hope to arrive around two.* HELP **Hope** can be used in the passive in the form **it is hoped that....** **For** must always be used with **hope** in other passive sentences: *The improvement that had been hoped for never came.* ◇ *The hoped-for improvement never came.*

IDM **ˌhope against ˈhope (that...)** to continue to hope for sth although it is very unlikely to happen **ˌhope for the ˈbest** to hope that sth will happen successfully, especially where it seems likely that it will not **I should hope so/not** | **so I should hope** (*informal*) used to say that you feel very strongly that sth should/should not happen: *'Nobody blames you.' 'I should hope not!'* ➲ more at CROSS *v.*

■ ***noun*** **1** 0-w [U, C] a belief that sth you want will happen: **~ (of sth)** *There is now hope of a cure.* ◇ **~ (for sb/sth)** *Hopes for the missing men are fading.* ◇ **~ (that...)** *There is **little hope that** they will be found alive.* ◇ **~ (of doing sth)** *They have **given up hope** of finding any more survivors.* ◇ *She has **high hopes** of winning* (= is very confident about it). ◇ *The future is not without hope.* ◇ *Don't **raise your hopes** too high, or you may be disappointed.* ◇ *I'll do what I can, but don't **get your hopes up**.* ◇ *There is still a **glimmer of hope**.* ◇ *The situation is not good but we **live in hope** that it will improve.* **2** 0-w [C] **~ (of/for sth)** | **~ (for sb)** | **~ (that...)** | **~ (of doing sth)** something that you wish for: *She told me all her hopes, dreams and fears.* ◇ *They **have high hopes** for their children.* **3** [C, usually sing.] **~ (of sth)** | **~ (for sb)** a person, a thing or a situation that will help you get what you want: *He turned to her in despair and said, 'You're my **last hope**.'* ◇ *The operation was Kelly's **only hope of** survival.*

IDM **be beyond ˈhope (of sth)** to be in a situation where no improvement is possible **hold out little, etc. ˈhope (of sth/that...)** | **not hold out any, much, etc. ˈhope (of sth/that...)** to offer little, etc. reason for believing that sth will happen: *The doctors did not hold out much hope for her recovery.* **ˌhope springs eˈternal** (*saying*) people never stop hoping **in the hope of sth** | **in the hope that ...** (*NAmE* also **in hopes that...**) because you want sth to happen: *I called early in the hope of catching her before she went to work.* ◇ *He asked her again **in the vain hope** that he could persuade her to come* (= it was impossible). **not have a ˈhope (in ˈhell) (of doing sth)** (*informal*) to have no chance at all: *She doesn't have a hope of winning.* **ˌsome ˈhope!** (*BrE, informal*) used to say that there is no chance at all that sth will happen ➲ more at DASH *v.*, PIN *v.*

ˈhope chest *noun* (*NAmE*) items for the house collected by a woman, especially in the past, in preparation for her marriage (and often kept in a large CHEST) ➲ compare BOTTOM DRAWER

ˈhoped-for *adj.* [only before noun] wanted and thought possible: *The new policy did not bring the hoped-for economic recovery.*

hope·ful /ˈhəʊpfl; *NAmE* ˈhoʊp-/ *adj., noun*

■ ***adj.*** **1** [not usually before noun] (of a person) believing that sth you want will happen SYN **optimistic**: **~ (that...)** *I feel hopeful that we'll find a suitable house very soon.* ◇ **~ (about sth)** *He is not very hopeful about the outcome of the interview.* ◇ **~ (of doing sth)** (*BrE*) *She is hopeful of returning to work soon.* OPP **pessimistic** **2** [only before noun] (of a person's behaviour) showing hope: *a hopeful smile* **3** (of a thing) making you believe that sth you want will happen; bringing hope SYN **promising**: *The latest trade figures are a hopeful sign.* ◇ *The future did not seem very hopeful.* ▸ **hope·ful·ness** *noun* [U]

■ ***noun*** a person who wants to succeed at sth: *50 young hopefuls are trying for a place in the England team.*

hope·ful·ly /ˈhəʊpfəli; *NAmE* ˈhoʊp-/ *adv.* **1** used to express what you hope will happen: *Hopefully, we'll arrive before dark.* HELP Although this is the most common use of **hopefully**, it is a fairly new use and some people think it is not correct. **2** showing hope: *'Are you free tonight?' she asked hopefully.*

hope·less /ˈhəʊpləs; *NAmE* ˈhoʊp-/ *adj.* **1** if sth is **hopeless**, there is no hope that it will get better or succeed: *a hopeless situation* ◇ ***It's hopeless** trying to convince her.* ◇ *Most of the students are making good progress, but Michael is **a hopeless case**.* ◇ *He felt that his life was a hopeless mess.* **2** (*BrE, informal*) extremely bad SYN **terrible**: *The buses are absolutely hopeless these days!* **3** (*especially BrE*) (of people) very bad (at sth); with no ability or skill SYN **terrible**: *a hopeless driver* ◇ **~ at sth** *I'm hopeless at science.* **4** feeling or showing no hope: *She felt lonely and hopeless.* ▸ **hope·less·ly** *adv.*: *hopelessly outnumbered* ◇ *They were hopelessly lost.* ◇ *to be hopelessly in love* ◇ *'I'll never manage it,' he said hopelessly.* **hope·less·ness** *noun* [U]: *a **sense/feeling of hopelessness***

Hopi /ˈhəʊpi; *NAmE* ˈhoʊpi/ *noun* (*pl.* **Hopi** or **Hopis**) a member of a Native American people, many of whom live in the US state of Arizona

hop·per /ˈhɒpə(r); *NAmE* ˈhɑːp-/ *noun* a container shaped like a V, that holds grain, coal, or food for animals, and lets it out through the bottom

hop·ping /ˈhɒpɪŋ; *NAmE* ˈhɑːp-/ *adj., adv.*

■ ***adj.*** (*NAmE, informal*) very lively or busy: *The clubs in town are really hopping.*

■ ***adv.***

IDM ˌ**hopping** ˈ**mad** (*informal*) very angry

hop·scotch /ˈhɒpskɒtʃ; *NAmE* ˈhɑːpskɑːtʃ/ *noun* [U] a children's game played on a pattern of squares marked on the ground. Each child throws a stone into a square then HOPS (= jumps on one leg) and jumps along the empty squares to pick up the stone again.

horde /hɔːd; *NAmE* hɔːrd/ *noun* (sometimes *disapproving*) a large crowd of people: *There are always hordes of tourists here in the summer.* ◇ *Football fans turned up **in hordes**.*

hori·zon /həˈraɪzn/ *noun* **1 the horizon** [sing.] the furthest that you can see, where the sky seems to meet the land or the sea: *The sun sank below the horizon.* ◇ *A ship appeared on the horizon.* ➲ VISUAL VOCAB page V4 **2** [C, usually pl.] the limit of your desires, knowledge or interests: *She wanted to travel to **broaden her horizons**.* ◇ *The company needs new horizons now.*

IDM **on the hoˈrizon** likely to happen soon: *There's trouble looming on the horizon.*

hori·zon·tal 🔑 /ˌhɒrɪˈzɒntl; *NAmE* ˌhɔːrəˈzɑːntl; ˌhɑːr-/ *adj., noun*

■ ***adj.*** 🔑 flat and level; going across and parallel to the ground rather than going up and down: *horizontal lines* ➲ compare VERTICAL ▸ **hori·zon·tal·ly** /-təli/ *adv.*: *Cut the cake in half horizontally and spread jam on one half.*

■ ***noun*** **1 the hori·zon·tal** [U] a horizontal position: *He shifted his position from the horizontal.* **2** [C] a horizontal line or surface

Hor·licks™ /ˈhɔːlɪks; *NAmE* ˈhɔːrl-/ *noun* **1** [U] powder that contains MALT that you mix with hot milk to make a drink **2** [U, C] a drink made by mixing Horlicks powder with hot milk

IDM **make a ˈhorlicks of sth** (*old-fashioned, BrE, informal*) to do sth badly

hor·mone /ˈhɔːməʊn; *NAmE* ˈhɔːrmoʊn/ *noun* a chemical substance produced in the body or in a plant that encourages growth or influences how the cells and TISSUES function; an artificial substance that has similar effects: *growth hormones* ◇ *a hormone imbalance* ◇ *Oestrogen is a female sex hormone.* ▸ **hor·mo·nal** /hɔːˈməʊnl; *NAmE* hɔːrˈmoʊnl/ *adj.* [usually before noun]: *the hormonal changes occurring during pregnancy*

ˌ**hormone reˈplacement therapy** *noun* [U] = HRT

horn 🔑 /hɔːn; *NAmE* hɔːrn/ *noun, verb*

■ ***noun*** **1** 🔑 [C] a hard pointed part that grows, usually in pairs, on the heads of some animals, such as sheep and cows. Horns are often curved. ➲ VISUAL VOCAB page V10 **2** [U] the hard substance of which animal horns are made **3** 🔑 [C] a simple musical instrument that consists of a curved metal tube that you blow into: *a hunting horn* **4** [C] (*especially BrE*) = FRENCH HORN: *a horn concerto* **5** 🔑 [C] a device in a vehicle for making a loud sound as a warning or signal: *to **honk your car horn*** ◇ (*BrE*) *to **sound/toot** your **horn*** ➲ VISUAL VOCAB page V42 ➲ see also FOGHORN

IDM **blow/toot your own ˈhorn** (*NAmE, informal*) = BLOW YOUR OWN TRUMPET at BLOW *v.* **draw/pull your ˈhorns in** to start being more careful in your behaviour, especially by spending less money than before **on the horns of a diˈlemma** in a situation in which you have to make a choice between things that are equally unpleasant ➲ more at BULL, LOCK *v.*

■ ***verb***

PHR V ˌ**horn ˈin** (**on sb/sth**) (*NAmE, informal*) to involve yourself in a situation that does not concern you: *I'm sure she doesn't want us horning in on her business.*

horn·beam /ˈhɔːnbiːm; *NAmE* ˈhɔːrn-/ *noun* [C, U] a tree with smooth grey BARK and hard wood

horn·bill /ˈhɔːnbɪl; *NAmE* ˈhɔːrn-/ *noun* a tropical bird with a very large curved beak

horned /hɔːnd; *NAmE* hɔːrnd/ *adj.* having horns or having sth that looks like horns

hor·net /ˈhɔːnɪt; *NAmE* ˈhɔːrnɪt/ *noun* a large WASP (= a black and yellow flying insect) that has a very powerful sting

IDM **a ˈhornets' nest** a difficult situation in which a lot of people get very angry: *His letter to the papers **stirred up a** real **hornets' nest**.*

ˌ**horn of ˈplenty** *noun* = CORNUCOPIA

horn·pipe /ˈhɔːnpaɪp; *NAmE* ˈhɔːrn-/ *noun* a fast dance for one person, traditionally performed by sailors; the music for the dance

ˈ**horn-rimmed** *adj.* (of a pair of glasses) with frames made of material that looks like horn

horny /ˈhɔːni; *NAmE* ˈhɔːrni/ *adj.* **1** (*informal*) sexually excited: *to feel horny* **2** (*informal*) sexually attractive: *to look horny* **3** made of a hard substance like horn: *the bird's horny beak* **4** (of skin, etc.) hard and rough: *horny hands*

hor·ol·ogy /hɒˈrɒlədʒi; *NAmE* həˈrɑːl-/ *noun* [U] **1** the study and measurement of time **2** the art of making clocks and watches

horo·scope /ˈhɒrəskəʊp; *NAmE* ˈhɔːrəskoʊp; ˈhɑːr-/ *noun* a description of what is going to happen to sb in the future, based on the position of the stars and the planets when the person was born

hor·ren·dous /hɒˈrendəs; *NAmE* hɔːˈr-; hɑːˈr-/ *adj.* **1** extremely shocking SYN **horrific, horrifying**: *horrendous injuries* **2** (*informal*) extremely unpleasant and unacceptable SYN **terrible**: *horrendous traffic* HELP Some speakers do not pronounce the 'h' at the beginning of **horrendous** and use 'an' instead of 'a' before it. This now sounds old-fashioned. ➲ SYNONYMS at TERRIBLE ▸ **hor·ren·dous·ly** *adv.*: *horrendously expensive*

hor·rible /ˈhɒrəbl; *NAmE* ˈhɔːr-; ˈhɑːr-/ *adj.* **1** (*informal*) very bad or unpleasant; used to describe sth that you do not like: *horrible weather/children/shoes* ◇ *The coffee tasted horrible.* ◇ *I've got a horrible feeling she lied to us.* ➲ SYNONYMS at TERRIBLE **2** making you feel very shocked and frightened SYN **terrible**: *a horrible crime/nightmare* **3** (*informal*) (of people or their behaviour) unfriendly, unpleasant or unkind SYN **nasty, obnoxious**: *a horrible man* ◇ *My sister was being horrible to me all day.* ◇ *What a horrible thing to say!* ▸ **hor·ribly** /-əbli/ *adv.*: *It was horribly painful.* ◇ *The experiment went horribly wrong.*

hor·rid /ˈhɒrɪd; *NAmE* ˈhɔːr-; ˈhɑːr-/ *adj.* (*old-fashioned* or *informal, especially BrE*) very unpleasant or unkind SYN **horrible**: *a horrid child* ◇ *a horrid smell* ◇ *Don't be so horrid to your brother.*

hor·rif·ic /həˈrɪfɪk/ *adj.* **1** extremely bad and shocking or frightening SYN **horrifying**: *a **horrific murder/accident/attack, etc.*** ◇ *Her injuries were horrific.* **2** (*informal*) very bad or unpleasant SYN **horrendous**: *We had a horrific trip.* HELP Some speakers do not pronounce the 'h' at the beginning of **horrific** and use 'an' instead of 'a' before it. This now sounds old-fashioned. ▶ **hor·rif·ic·al·ly** /-kli/ *adv.*

hor·rify /ˈhɒrɪfaɪ; *NAmE* ˈhɔːr-; ˈhɑːr-/ *verb* (**hor·ri·fies, hor·ri·fy·ing, hor·ri·fied, hor·ri·fied**) to make sb feel extremely shocked, disgusted or frightened SYN **appal**: **~ sb** *The whole country was horrified by the killings.* ◇ **it horrifies sb to do sth** *It horrified her to think that he had killed someone.* ◇ **it horrifies sb that…** *It horrified her that he had actually killed someone.* ▶ **hor·ri·fied** *adj.*: *He was horrified when he discovered the conditions in which they lived.* ◇ *She gazed at him in horrified disbelief.*

hor·ri·fy·ing /ˈhɒrɪfaɪɪŋ; *NAmE* ˈhɔːr-; ˈhɑːr-/ *adj.* making you feel extremely shocked, disgusted or frightened SYN **horrific**: *a* ***horrifying sight/experience/story*** ◇ *It's horrifying to see such poverty.* ▶ **hor·ri·fy·ing·ly** *adv.*

hor·ror 0‑ /ˈhɒrə(r); *NAmE* ˈhɔːr-; ˈhɑːr-/ *noun* **1** 0‑ [U] a feeling of great shock, fear or disgust: *People watched* ***in horror*** *as the plane crashed to the ground.* ◇ *With a look of horror, he asked if the doctor thought he had cancer.* ◇ *The thought of being left alone filled her with horror.* ◇ *She recoiled in horror at the sight of an enormous spider.* ◇ ***To his horror,*** *he could feel himself starting to cry* (= it upset him very much). ◇ *Her eyes were wide with horror.* **2** 0‑ [sing.] a great fear or hatred of sth: **~ of sth** *a horror of deep water* ◇ **~ of doing sth** *Most people have a horror of speaking in public.* **3** 0‑ [U] **the ~ of sth** the very unpleasant nature of sth, especially when it is shocking or frightening: ***The full horror of*** *the accident was beginning to become clear.* ◇ *In his dreams he relives the horror of the attack.* **4** 0‑ [C, usually pl.] a very unpleasant or frightening experience: *the horrors of war* **5** 0‑ [U] a type of book, film/movie, etc. that is designed to frighten people: *In this section you'll find horror and science fiction.* ◇ *a* ***horror film/movie*** ➲ see also HORROR STORY **6** [C] (*BrE, informal*) a child who behaves badly: *Her son is a little horror.*
IDM **ˌhorror of ˈhorrors** (*BrE, humorous* or *ironic*) used to emphasize how bad a situation is: *I stood up to speak and—horror of horrors—realized I had left my notes behind.* ➲ more at SHOCK *n.*

ˈhorror story *noun* **1** a story about strange and frightening things that is designed to entertain people **2** (*informal*) a report that describes an experience of a situation as very unpleasant: *horror stories about visits to the dentist*

ˈhorror-struck (also **ˈhorror-stricken**) *adj.* suddenly feeling very shocked, frightened or disgusted

hors de com·bat /ˌɔː də ˈkɒ̃bɑː; *NAmE* ˌɔːr də koʊmˈbɑː/ *adj.* (from *French, formal*) unable to fight or to take part in an activity, especially because you are injured

hors d'oeuvre /ˌɔː ˈdɜːv; *NAmE* ˌɔːr ˈdɜːrv/ *noun* [C, U] (*pl.* **hors d'oeuvres** /ˌɔː ˈdɜːv; *NAmE* ˌɔːr ˈdɜːrv/) (from *French*) a small amount of food, usually cold, served before the main part of a meal ➲ compare STARTER

horse 0‑ /hɔːs; *NAmE* hɔːrs/ *noun, verb*
■ ***noun*** **1** 0‑ a large animal with four legs, a MANE (= long thick hair on its neck) and a tail. Horses are used for riding on, pulling CARRIAGES, etc: *He mounted his horse and rode off.* ◇ *a horse and cart* ➲ see also COLT, FILLY, FOAL, GELDING, MARE, STALLION **2 the horses** [pl.] (*informal*) horse racing: *He lost a lot of money on the horses* (= by gambling on races). **3** = VAULTING HORSE ➲ see also CLOTHES HORSE, HOBBY HORSE, QUARTER HORSE, ROCKING HORSE, SEA HORSE, STALKING HORSE, TROJAN HORSE, WHITE HORSES
IDM **(straight) from the horse's ˈmouth** (*informal*) (of information) given by sb who is directly involved and therefore likely to be accurate **hold your ˈhorses** (*informal*) used to tell sb that they should wait a moment and not be so excited that they take action without thinking about it first **ˌhorses for ˈcourses** (*BrE*) the act of matching people with suitable jobs or tasks ORIGIN This expression refers to the fact that horses race better on a track that suits them. **a one, two, three, etc. horse ˈrace** a competition or an election in which there are only one, two, etc. teams or candidates with a chance of winning **you can ˌlead/ˌtake a horse to ˌwater, but you ˌcan't make it ˈdrink** (*saying*) you can give sb the opportunity to do sth, but you cannot force them to do it if they do not want to ➲ more at BACK *v.*, BARN *n.*, CART *n.*, CHANGE *v.*, DARK *adj.*, DRIVE *v.*, EAT, FLOG, GIFT *n.*, HIGH *adj.*, STABLE DOOR *n.*, WILD *adj.*, WISH *n.*
■ ***verb***
PHR V **ˌhorse aˈbout/aˈround** (*informal*) to play in a way that is noisy and not very careful so that you could hurt sb or damage sth SYN **fool around**

horse·back /ˈhɔːsbæk; *NAmE* ˈhɔːrs-/ *noun, adj.*
■ ***noun***
IDM **on ˈhorseback** sitting on a horse; using horses: *a soldier on horseback*
■ ***adj.*** [only before noun] sitting on a horse: *a horseback tour* ▶ **horse·back** *adv.*: *to ride horseback*

ˈhorseback riding *noun* [U] (*NAmE*) = RIDING

horse·box /ˈhɔːsbɒks; *NAmE* ˈhɔːrsbɑːks/ *noun* (*BrE*) a vehicle for transporting horses in, sometimes pulled behind another vehicle ➲ see also HORSE TRAILER

ˌhorse ˈchestnut *noun* **1** a large tall tree with spreading branches, white or pink flowers and nuts that grow inside cases which are covered with SPIKES ➲ VISUAL VOCAB page V8 ➲ see also CHESTNUT **2** the smooth brown nut of the horse chestnut tree ➲ compare CONKER

ˈhorse-drawn *adj.* [only before noun] (of a vehicle) pulled by a horse or horses

horse·flesh /ˈhɔːsfleʃ; *NAmE* ˈhɔːrs-/ *noun* [U] horses, especially when being bought or sold

horse·fly /ˈhɔːsflaɪ; *NAmE* ˈhɔːrs-/ *noun* (*pl.* -ies) a large fly that bites horses and cows

horse·hair /ˈhɔːsheə(r); *NAmE* ˈhɔːrsher/ *noun* [U] hair from the MANE or tail of a horse, used, in the past, for filling MATTRESSES, chairs, etc.

horse·man /ˈhɔːsmən; *NAmE* ˈhɔːrs-/ *noun* (*pl.* -men /-mən/) a rider on a horse; a person who can ride horses: *a good horseman* ➲ see also HORSEWOMAN

horse·man·ship /ˈhɔːsmənʃɪp; *NAmE* ˈhɔːrs-/ *noun* [U] skill in riding horses

horse·play /ˈhɔːspleɪ; *NAmE* ˈhɔːrs-/ *noun* [U] rough noisy play in which people push or hit each other for fun

horse·power /ˈhɔːspaʊə(r); *NAmE* ˈhɔːrs-/ *noun* [C, U] (*pl.* horse·power) (*abbr.* h.p.) a unit for measuring the power of an engine: *a powerful car with a 170 horsepower engine*

ˈhorse race *noun* a race between horses with riders

ˈhorse racing *noun* [U] a sport in which horses with riders race against each other ➲ VISUAL VOCAB page V38

horse·rad·ish /ˈhɔːsrædɪʃ; *NAmE* ˈhɔːrs-/ *noun* [U] **1** a hard white root vegetable that has a taste like pepper **2** (*BrE* also **ˌhorseradish ˈsauce**) a sauce made from horseradish, that is eaten with meat: *roast beef and horseradish*

ˈhorse riding *noun* [U] (*BrE*) = RIDING

horse·shoe /ˈhɔːsʃuː; ˈhɔːʃʃuː; *NAmE* ˈhɔːrʃ-; ˈhɔːrs-/ *noun* (also **shoe**) **1** a piece of curved iron that is attached with nails to the bottom of a horse's foot. A horseshoe is often used as a symbol of good luck. **2** anything shaped like a horseshoe: *a horseshoe bend in the river*

ˈhorse-trading *noun* [U] the activity of discussing business with sb using clever or secret methods in order to reach an agreement that suits you

ˈhorse trailer *noun* (*NAmE*) a vehicle for transporting horses in, pulled by another vehicle ➲ see also HORSEBOX

horse·whip /ˈhɔːswɪp; *NAmE* ˈhɔːrs-/ *noun, verb*
■ ***noun*** a long stick with a long piece of leather attached to the end that is used to control or train horses
■ ***verb*** (-pp-) **~ sb** to beat sb with a horsewhip

horse·woman /ˈhɔːswʊmən; *NAmE* ˈhɔːrs-/ *noun* (*pl.* -women /-wɪmɪn/) a woman rider on a horse; a woman who can ride horses well: *a good horsewoman*

horsey (also **horsy**) /ˈhɔːsi; *NAmE* ˈhɔːrsi/ *adj.* **1** interested in and involved with horses or horse racing **2** connected with horses; like a horse: *She had a long, horsey face.*

horti·cul·ture /ˈhɔːtɪkʌltʃə(r); *NAmE* ˈhɔːrt-/ *noun* [U] the study or practice of growing flowers, fruit and vegetables: *a college of agriculture and horticulture* ➲ compare GARDENING ▸ **horti·cul·tural** /ˌhɔːtɪˈkʌltʃərəl; *NAmE* ˌhɔːrt-/ *adj.*: *a horticultural show* **horti·cul·tur·al·ist**, **horti·cul·tur·ist** *noun*

hos·anna (also **hos·annah**) /həʊˈzænə; *NAmE* hoʊ-/ *exclamation* used in worship to express praise, joy and love for God, especially in the Christian and Jewish religions ▸ **hos·anna** *noun*

hose /həʊz; *NAmE* hoʊz/ *noun, verb*

■ ***noun*** **1** (also **hose·pipe** /ˈhəʊzpaɪp; *NAmE* ˈhoʊz-/) [C, U] (*BrE*) a long tube made of rubber, plastic, etc, used for putting water onto fires, gardens, etc: *a garden hose* ◇ *a length of hose* ➲ VISUAL VOCAB page V16 ➲ see also FIRE HOSE **2** [pl.] = HOSIERY **3** [pl.] trousers/pants that fit tightly over the legs, worn by men in the past: *doublet and hose*

■ ***verb*** **~ sth** to wash or pour water on sth using a hose: *Firemen hosed the burning car.*

PHR V ˌ**hose sth↔ˈdown** to wash sth using a hose

ho·siery /ˈhəʊziəri; *NAmE* ˈhoʊʒəri/ (also **hose**) *noun* [U] used especially in shops/stores as a word for TIGHTS, STOCKINGS and socks: *the hosiery department*

hos·pice /ˈhɒspɪs; *NAmE* ˈhɑːs-/ *noun* a hospital for people who are dying: *an AIDS hospice*

hos·pit·able /hɒˈspɪtəbl; ˈhɒspɪtəbl; *NAmE* hɑːˈs-; ˈhɑːs-/ *adj.* **1 ~ (to/towards sb)** (of a person) pleased to welcome guests; generous and friendly to visitors SYN **welcoming**: *The local people are very hospitable to strangers.* **2** having good conditions that allow things to grow; having a pleasant environment: *a hospitable climate* OPP **inhospitable** ▸ **hos·pit·ably** /-əbli/ *adv.*

hos·pital 🔑 /ˈhɒspɪtl; *NAmE* ˈhɑːs-/ *noun* a large building where people who are ill/sick or injured are given medical treatment and care: (*BrE*) *He had to go* ***to hospital*** *for treatment.* ◇ (*NAmE*) *He had to go* ***to the hospital*** *for treatment.* ◇ *to* ***be admitted to (the) hospital*** ◇ *to* ***be discharged from (the) hospital*** ◇ *The injured were* ***rushed to (the) hospital*** *in an ambulance.* ◇ *He died in (the) hospital.* ◇ *I'm going to the hospital to visit my brother.* ◇ *a* ***psychiatric/mental hospital*** ◇ ***hospital doctors/nurses/staff*** ◇ *There is an urgent need for more hospital beds.* ➲ see also COTTAGE HOSPITAL

British/American

hospital

- In *BrE* you say **to hospital** or **in hospital** when you talk about somebody being there as a patient: *I had to go to hospital.* ◇ *She spent two weeks in hospital.*
- In *NAmE* you need to use **the**: *I had to go to the hospital.* ◇ *She spent two weeks in the hospital.*

ˌ**hospital ˈcorners** *noun* [pl.] a way of folding the sheets at the corners of a bed tightly and neatly, in a way that they are often folded in a hospital

hos·pi·tal·ity /ˌhɒspɪˈtæləti; *NAmE* ˌhɑːs-/ *noun* [U] **1** friendly and generous behaviour towards guests: *Thank you for your kind hospitality.* **2** food, drink or services that are provided by an organization for guests, customers, etc: *We were entertained in the company's* ***hospitality suite.*** ◇ *the hospitality industry* (= hotels, restaurants, etc.)

hos·pi·tal·ize (*BrE* also **-ise**) /ˈhɒspɪtəlaɪz; *NAmE* ˈhɑːs-/ *verb* [usually passive] **~ sb** to send sb to a hospital for treatment ▸ **hos·pi·tal·iza·tion**, **-isa·tion** /ˌhɒspɪtəlaɪˈzeɪʃn; *NAmE* ˌhɑːspɪtələˈz-/ *noun* [U]: *a long period of hospitalization*

host 🔑 /həʊst; *NAmE* hoʊst/ *noun, verb*

■ ***noun*** **1** 🔑 [C] a person who invites guests to a meal, a party, etc. or who has people staying at their house: *Ian, our host, introduced us to the other guests.* ➲ see also HOSTESS **2** 🔑 [C] a country, a city or an organization that holds and arranges a special event: *The college is* ***playing host to*** *a group of visiting Russian scientists.* **3** 🔑 [C] a person who introduces a television or radio show, and talks to guests SYN **compère**: *a TV game show host* ➲ see also ANNOUNCER, PRESENTER **4** [C] (*technical*) an animal or a plant on which another animal or plant lives and feeds **5** [C] **~ of sb/sth** a large number of people or things: *a host of possibilities* **6** [C] the main computer in a network that controls or supplies information to other computers that are connected to it: *transferring files from the host to your local computer* **7 the Host** [sing.] the bread that is used in the Christian service of COMMUNION, after it has been BLESSED

■ ***verb*** **1** 🔑 **~ sth** to organize an event to which others are invited and make all the arrangements for them: *South Africa hosted the World Cup finals.* **2** 🔑 **~ sth** to introduce a television or radio programme, a show, etc. SYN **compère** **3 ~ sth** to organize a party that you have invited guests to: *to host a dinner* **4 ~ sth** to store a website on a computer connected to the Internet, usually in return for payment: *a company that builds and hosts e-commerce sites*

hos·tage /ˈhɒstɪdʒ; *NAmE* ˈhɑːs-/ *noun* a person who is captured and held prisoner by a person or group, and who may be injured or killed if people do not do what the person or group is asking: *Three children were* ***taken hostage*** *during the bank robbery.* ◇ *He was* ***held hostage*** *for almost a year.* ◇ *The government is negotiating the release of the hostages.*

IDM **a** ˌ**hostage to** ˈ**fortune** something that you have, or have promised to do, that could cause trouble or worry in the future

ˈ**hostage-taker** *noun* a person, often one of a group, who captures sb and holds them prisoner, and who may injure or kill them if people do not do what the person is asking ▸ ˈ**hostage-taking** *noun* [U]

hos·tel /ˈhɒstl; *NAmE* ˈhɑːstl/ *noun* **1** a building that provides cheap accommodation and meals to students, workers or travellers ➲ see also YOUTH HOSTEL **2** (*BrE*) (also **shel·ter** *NAmE, BrE*) a building, usually run by a charity, where people who have no home can stay for a short time: *a hostel for the homeless*

hos·tel·ry /ˈhɒstəlri; *NAmE* ˈhɑːs-/ (*pl.* **-ies**) *noun* (*old use* or *humorous*) a pub or hotel

host·ess /ˈhəʊstəs; -es; *NAmE* ˈhoʊstəs/ *noun* **1** a woman who invites guests to a meal, a party, etc; a woman who has people staying at her home: *Mary was always the perfect hostess.* **2** a woman who is employed to welcome and entertain men at a NIGHTCLUB **3** a woman who introduces and talks to guests on a television or radio show SYN **compère** ➲ note at GENDER **4** (*NAmE*) a woman who welcomes the customers in a restaurant ➲ see also HOST

hos·tile /ˈhɒstaɪl; *NAmE* ˈhɑːstl; -taɪl/ *adj.* **1** very unfriendly or aggressive and ready to argue or fight: *The speaker got a hostile reception from the audience.* ◇ **~ to/towards sb/sth** *She was openly hostile towards her parents.* **2 ~ (to sth)** strongly rejecting sth SYN **opposed to**: *hostile to the idea of change* **3** making it difficult for sth to happen or to be achieved: *hostile conditions for plants to grow in* **4** belonging to a military enemy: *hostile territory* **5** (*business*) (of an offer to buy a company, etc.) not wanted by the company that is to be bought: *a hostile takeover bid*

hos·til·ity /hɒˈstɪləti; *NAmE* hɑːˈs-/ *noun* **1** [U] unfriendly or aggressive feelings or behaviour: **~ (to/towards sb/sth)** *feelings of hostility towards people from other backgrounds* ◇ **~ (between A and B)** *There was* ***open hostility*** *between the two schools.* **2** [U] **~ (to/towards sth)** strong and angry opposition towards an idea, a plan or a situation: *public hostility to nuclear power* **3 hostilities** [pl.] (*formal*) acts of fighting in a war: *the* ***start/outbreak of hostilities*** *between the two sides* ◇ *a* ***cessation of hostilities*** (= an end to fighting) ➲ COLLOCATIONS at WAR

host·ler /ˈhɒslə(r); *NAmE* ˈhɑːs-/ *noun* (*NAmE*) = OSTLER

hot 🔑 /hɒt; *NAmE* hɑːt/ *adj., verb*

■ ***adj.*** (**hot·ter**, **hot·test**)

▸ TEMPERATURE **1** 🔑 having a high temperature; producing heat: *Do you like this hot weather?* ◇ *It's hot today, isn't it?* ◇

H

It was hot and getting hotter. ◇ *It was the hottest July on record.* ◇ *a hot dry summer* ◇ *Be careful—the plates are hot.* ◇ *All rooms have hot and cold water.* ◇ *a hot bath* ◇ *a hot meal* (= one that has been cooked) ◇ *I couldn't live in a hot country* (= one which has high average temperatures). ◇ *Cook in a very hot oven.* ◇ *Eat it while it's hot.* ◇ *I touched his forehead. He felt hot and feverish.* ➲ see also BAKING HOT, BOILING HOT, PIPING HOT, RED-HOT, WHITE-HOT **2** 🔑 (of a person) feeling heat in an unpleasant or uncomfortable way: *Is anyone too hot?* ◇ *I feel hot.* ◇ *Her cheeks were hot with embarrassment.* **3** 🔑 making you feel hot: *London was hot and dusty.* ◇ *a long hot journey*

▸ FOOD WITH SPICES **4** 🔑 containing pepper and spices and producing a burning feeling in your mouth: *hot spicy food* ◇ *You can make a curry hotter simply by adding chillies.* ◇ *hot mustard* **OPP** **mild**

▸ CAUSING STRONG FEELINGS **5** involving a lot of activity, argument or strong feelings: *Today we enter the hottest phase of the election campaign.* ◇ *The environment has become a very hot issue.* ◇ *Competition is getting hotter day by day.*

▸ DIFFICULT/DANGEROUS **6** difficult or dangerous to deal with and making you feel worried or uncomfortable: *When things got too hot most journalists left the area.* ◇ *They're making life hot for her.*

▸ POPULAR **7** (*informal*) new, exciting and very popular: *This is one of the hottest clubs in town.* ◇ *They are one of this year's hot new bands.* ◇ *The couple are Hollywood's **hottest property**.*

▸ NEWS **8** fresh, very recent and usually exciting: *I've got some hot gossip for you!* ◇ *a story that is **hot off the press*** (= has just appeared in the newspapers)

▸ TIP/FAVOURITE **9** [only before noun] likely to be successful: *She seems to be the **hot favourite** for the job.* ◇ *Do you have any **hot tips** for today's race?*

▸ GOOD AT STH/KNOWING A LOT **10** [not before noun] **~ at/on sth** (*informal*) very good at doing sth; knowing a lot about sth: *Don't ask me—I'm **not too hot on** British history.*

▸ ANGER **11** if sb has a **hot temper** they become angry very easily

▸ SEXUAL EXCITEMENT **12** feeling or causing sexual excitement: *You were as hot for me as I was for you.* ◇ *I've got a **hot date** tonight.*

▸ SHOCKING/CRITICAL **13** containing scenes, statements, etc. that are too shocking or too critical and are likely to cause anger or disapproval: *Some of the nude scenes were regarded as too hot for Broadway.* ◇ *The report was highly critical of senior members of the Cabinet and was considered too hot to publish.* ➲ see also HOT STUFF

▸ STRICT **14** [not before noun] **~ on sth** thinking that sth is very important and making sure that it always happens or is done: *They're very hot on punctuality at work.*

▸ MUSIC **15** (of music, especially JAZZ) having a strong and exciting rhythm

▸ GOODS **16** stolen and difficult to get rid of because they can easily be recognized: *I'd never have touched those CDs if I'd known they were hot.*

▸ IN CHILDREN'S GAMES **17** [not before noun] used in children's games to say that the person playing is very close to finding a person or thing, or to guessing the correct answer: *You're getting hot!*

IDM **be ˌhot to ˈtrot** (*informal*) **1** to be very enthusiastic about starting an activity **2** to be excited in a sexual way **be in/get into hot ˈwater** (*informal*) to be in or get into trouble **go hot and ˈcold** to experience a sudden feeling of fear or anxiety: *When the phone rang I just went hot and cold.* **go/sell like hot ˈcakes** to sell quickly or in great numbers **(all) hot and ˈbothered** (*informal*) in a state of anxiety or confusion because you are under too much pressure, have a problem, are trying to hurry, etc. **hot on sb's/sth's ˈheels** following sb/sth very closely: *He turned and fled with Peter hot on his heels.* ◇ *Further successes came hot on the heels of her first best-selling novel.* **hot on sb's/sth's ˈtracks/ˈtrail** (*informal*) close to catching or finding the person or thing that you have been chasing or searching for **hot under the ˈcollar** (*informal*) angry or embarrassed: *He got very hot under the collar when I asked him where he'd been all day.* **in hot purˈsuit (of sb)** following sb closely and determined to catch them: *She sped away in her car with journalists in hot pursuit.* **not so/too ˈhot** **1** not very good in quality: *Her spelling isn't too hot.* **2** not feeling well: *'How are you today?' 'Not so hot, I'm afraid.'* ➲ more at BLOW *v.*, CAT, HEEL *n.*, STRIKE *v.*

▪ ***verb*** (-tt-)

PHR V **ˌhot ˈup** (*BrE*) (also **ˌheat ˈup** *NAmE, BrE*) (*informal*) to become more exciting or to show an increase in activity: *Things are really hotting up in the election campaign.*

ˌhot ˈair *noun* [U] (*informal*) claims, promises or statements that sound impressive but have no real meaning or truth

ˌhot-ˈair balloon *noun* = BALLOON (2) ➲ VISUAL VOCAB page V43

hot·bed /ˈhɒtbed; *NAmE* ˈhɑːt-/ *noun* [usually sing.] **~ of sth** a place where a lot of a particular activity, especially sth bad or violent, is happening: *The area was a hotbed of crime.*

ˌhot-ˈblooded *adj.* (of a person) having strong emotions and easily becoming very excited or angry **SYN** **passionate** ➲ compare WARM-BLOODED

ˈhot button *noun* (*NAmE, informal*) a subject or issue that people have strong feelings about and argue about a lot: *Race has always been a hot button in this country's history.* ◇ *the hot-button issue of nuclear waste disposal*

ˌhot ˈchocolate (*BrE* also **choc·olate**) *noun* [U, C] a drink made by mixing chocolate powder with hot water or milk; a cup of this drink: *Two coffees and a hot chocolate, please.*

hotch·potch /ˈhɒtʃpɒtʃ; *NAmE* ˈhɑːtʃpɑːtʃ/ (*especially BrE*) (*NAmE* usually **hodge·podge**) *noun* [sing.] (*informal*) a number of things mixed together without any particular order or reason

ˌhot cross ˈbun *noun* a small sweet bread roll that contains CURRANTS and has a pattern of a cross on top, traditionally eaten in Britain around Easter

ˌhot-ˈdesking *noun* [U] the practice in an office of giving desks to workers when they are required, rather than giving each worker their own desk

ˈhot dog (*BrE* also **ˌhot ˈdog**) *noun* **1** a hot SAUSAGE served in a long bread roll **2** (*NAmE*) a person who performs clever or dangerous tricks while SKIING, SNOWBOARDING or SURFING: *He's a real hot dog.*

ˈhot-dog *verb* (-gg-) [I] (*NAmE, informal*) to perform clever or dangerous tricks while SKIING, SNOWBOARDING or SURFING

hotel 🔑 /həʊˈtel; *NAmE* hoʊ-/ *noun*
1 🔑 a building where people stay, usually for a short time, paying for their rooms and meals: *We stayed at/in a hotel.* ◇ ***hotel rooms/guests*** ◇ *a **two-star/five-star, etc. hotel*** ◇ *a **luxury hotel*** ◇ *a friendly, family-run hotel* ➲ COLLOCATIONS at TRAVEL **2** (*AustralE, NZE*) a pub **3** (*IndE*) a restaurant **HELP** Some speakers do not pronounce the 'h' at the beginning of **hotel** and use 'an' instead of 'a' before it. This now sounds old-fashioned.

ho·tel·ier /həʊˈteliə(r); -lieɪ; *NAmE* hoʊˈteljər; ˌoʊtelˈjeɪ/ *noun* a person who owns or manages a hotel

hot·fix /ˈhɒtfɪks; *NAmE* ˈhɑːt-/ *noun* (*computing*) a file that is used to correct a fault in a computer program

ˌhot ˈflush (*BrE*) (*NAmE* **ˌhot ˈflash**) *noun* a sudden hot and uncomfortable feeling in the skin, especially experienced by women during the MENOPAUSE

hot·foot /ˈhɒtfʊt; *NAmE* ˈhɑːt-/ *adv., verb*
▪ ***adv.*** moving quickly and in a hurry: *He had just arrived hotfoot from London.*
▪ ***verb***
IDM **ˈhotfoot it** (*informal*) to walk or run somewhere quickly: *When the police arrived, they hotfooted it out of there.*

hot·head /ˈhɒthed; *NAmE* ˈhɑːt-/ *noun* a person who often acts too quickly, without thinking of what might happen ▸ **ˌhot-ˈheaded** *adj.*

hot·house /ˈhɒthaʊs; *NAmE* ˈhɑːt-/ *noun* **1** a heated building, usually made of glass, used for growing delicate plants in: *hothouse flowers* **2** a place or situation that encourages the rapid development of sb/sth, especially ideas and emotions

'hot key *noun* (*computing*) a key on a computer keyboard that you can press to perform a set of operations quickly, rather than having to press a number of different keys

hot·line /ˈhɒtlaɪn; *NAmE* ˈhɑːt-/ *noun* **1** a special telephone line that people can use in order to get information or to talk about sth **2** a direct telephone line between the heads of government in different countries

hot·link /ˈhɒtlɪŋk; *NAmE* ˈhɑːt-/ *noun* = HYPERLINK

hot·list /ˈhɒtlɪst; *NAmE* ˈhɑːt-/ *noun* **1** a list of popular, fashionable or important people or things **2** (*computing*) a personal list of your favourite or most frequently visited websites that you store on your computer

hotly /ˈhɒtli; *NAmE* ˈhɑːtli/ *adv.* **1** done in an angry or excited way or with a lot of strong feeling: *a hotly debated topic* ◇ *Recent reports in the press have been hotly denied.* ◇ *'Nonsense!' he said hotly.* ◇ *The results were hotly disputed.* **2** done with a lot of energy and determination SYN **closely**: *hotly contested elections* ◇ *She ran out of the shop, **hotly pursued** by the store detective.*

'hot pants *noun* [pl.] very short, tight women's SHORTS

hot·plate /ˈhɒtpleɪt; *NAmE* ˈhɑːt-/ *noun* a flat, heated metal surface, for example on a cooker/stove, that is used for cooking food or for keeping it hot

hot·pot /ˈhɒtpɒt; *NAmE* ˈhɑːtpɑːt/ *noun* **1** [C, U] (*BrE*) a hot dish of meat, potato, onion, etc. cooked slowly in liquid in the oven **2** [C] (*NAmE*) a small electric pot that you can use to heat water or food

,hot po'tato *noun* [usually sing.] (*informal*) a problem, situation, etc. that is difficult and unpleasant to deal with

'hot rod *noun* a car that has been changed and improved to give it extra power and speed

hots /hɒts; *NAmE* hɑːts/ *noun* [pl.]
IDM **get/have the 'hots for sb** (*informal*) to be sexually attracted to sb

the 'hot seat *noun* [sing.] (*informal*) if sb is **in the hot seat**, they have to take responsibility for important or difficult decisions and actions

hot·shot /ˈhɒtʃɒt; *NAmE* ˈhɑːtʃɑːt/ *noun* (*informal*) a person who is extremely successful in their career or at a particular sport ▸ **hot·shot** *adj.* [only before noun]: *a hotshot lawyer*

'hot spot *noun* (*informal*) **1** a place where fighting is common, especially for political reasons **2** a place where there is a lot of activity or entertainment **3** (*NAmE*) a place that is very hot and dry, where a fire has been burning or is likely to start **4** (*computing*) an area on a computer screen that you can click on to start an operation such as loading a file **5** a place in a hotel, restaurant, airport, etc. that is fitted with a special device that enables you to connect a computer to the Internet without using wires

,hot 'stuff *noun* [U] (*informal, especially BrE*) **1** a person who is sexually attractive: *She's pretty hot stuff.* **2** a film/movie, book, etc. which is exciting in a sexual way **3 ~ (at sth)** a person who is very skilful at sth: *She's really hot stuff at tennis.* **4** something that is likely to cause anger or disagreement: *These new proposals are proving to be hot stuff.*

,hot-'tempered *adj.* (*especially BrE*) tending to become very angry easily

hot·tie (also **hotty**) /ˈhɒti; *NAmE* ˈhɑːti/ *noun* (*informal*) a person who is very sexually attractive

'hot tub *noun* a heated bath/BATHTUB, often outside, that several people can sit in together to relax

,hot-'water bottle *noun* a rubber container that is filled with hot water and put in a bed to make it warm

'hot-wire *verb* **~ sth** (*informal*) to start the engine of a vehicle by using a piece of wire instead of a key

Hou·dini /huːˈdiːni/ *noun* a person or an animal that is very good at escaping ORIGIN From Harry Houdini, a famous performer in the US who escaped from ropes, chains, boxes, etc.

hou·mous = HUMMUS

hound /haʊnd/ *noun, verb*
■ ***noun*** a dog that can run fast and has a good sense of smell, used for hunting ➲ see also AFGHAN HOUND, BLOODHOUND, FOXHOUND, GREYHOUND, WOLFHOUND
■ ***verb* ~ sb** to keep following sb and not leave them alone, especially in order to get sth from them or ask them questions SYN **harass**: *They were hounded day and night by the press.*
PHR V **,hound sb 'out (of sth)** | **'hound sb from sth** [usually passive] to force sb to leave a job or a place, especially by making their life difficult and unpleasant

'hound dog *noun* (*NAmE*) (especially in the southern US) a dog used in hunting

hounds·tooth /ˈhaʊndztuːθ/ *noun* [U] a type of large pattern with pointed shapes, often in black and white, used especially in cloth for jackets and suits

hour 0➔ /ˈaʊə(r)/ *noun*
HELP Use **an**, not **a**, before **hour**. **1** 0➔ [C] (*abbr.* **hr**, **hr.**) 60 minutes; one of the 24 parts that a day is divided into: *It will take about an hour to get there.* ◇ *The interview lasted half an hour.* ◇ *It was a three-hour exam.* ◇ *I waited **for an hour** and then I left.* ◇ *He'll be back **in an hour**.* ◇ *We're paid **by the hour**.* ◇ *The minimum wage was set at £5.80 **an hour**.* ◇ *Top speed is 120 miles **per hour**.* ◇ *York was within an hour's drive.* ◇ *Chicago is two hours away* (= it takes two hours to get there). ◇ *We're four hours ahead of New York* (= referring to the time difference). ◇ *We hope to be there **within the hour*** (= in less than an hour). **2** 0➔ [C, usually sing.] a period of about an hour, used for a particular purpose: *I use the Internet at work, during my **lunch hour**.* ➲ see also HAPPY HOUR, RUSH HOUR **3** 0➔ **hours** [pl.] a fixed period of time during which people work, an office is open, etc: ***Opening hours** are from 10 to 6 each day.* ◇ *Most people in this kind of job tend to work **long hours**.* ◇ *What are your **office hours**?* ◇ *a hospital's **visiting hours*** ◇ *Britain's **licensing hours*** (= when pubs are allowed to open) *used to be very restricted.* ◇ *This is the only place to get a drink **after hours*** (= after the normal closing time for pubs). ◇ *Clients can now contact us by email **out of hours*** (= when the office is closed). **4** 0➔ **hours** [pl.] a long time: *It took hours getting there.* ◇ *I've been waiting **for hours**.* ◇ *'How long did it last?' 'Oh, **hours and hours**.'* **5** [sing.] a particular point in time: *You can't turn him away at this hour of the night.* **6** [C, usually sing.] the time when sth important happens: *This was often thought of as the country's **finest hour**.* ◇ *She thought her **last hour** had come.* ◇ *Don't desert me in my **hour of need**.* **7 the hour** [sing.] the time when it is exactly 1 o'clock, 2 o'clock, etc: *There's a bus every hour **on the hour**.* ◇ *The clock **struck the hour**.* **8 hours** [pl.] used when giving the time according to the 24-hour clock, usually in military or other official language: *The first missile was launched at 2300 hours* (= at 11 p.m.). HELP This is pronounced '23 hundred hours'.
IDM **'all hours** any time, especially a time which is not usual or suitable: *He's started staying out **till all hours*** (= until very late at night). ◇ *She thinks she can call me **at all hours of the day and night**.* **keep... 'hours** if you keep regular, strange, etc. **hours**, the times at which you do things (especially getting up or going to bed) are regular, strange, etc. **the 'small/'early hours** (also **the wee small 'hours** *ScotE, NAmE* also **the wee 'hours**) the period of time very early in the morning, soon after midnight: *We worked well into the small hours.* ◇ *The fighting began in the early hours of Saturday morning.* ➲ more at ELEVENTH, EVIL, KILL *v.*, UNEARTHLY, UNGODLY

hour·glass /ˈaʊəɡlɑːs; *NAmE* ˈaʊərɡlæs/ *noun, adj.*
■ ***noun*** a glass container holding sand that takes exactly an hour to pass through a small opening between the top and bottom sections ➲ compare EGG TIMER
■ ***adj.*** [only before noun] a woman who has an **hourglass** figure, shape, etc. has large breasts and hips and a small waist

'hour hand *noun* the small hand on a clock or watch that points to the hour ➲ picture at CLOCK

hour·ly /ˈaʊəli; *NAmE* ˈaʊərli/ *adj., adv.* HELP Use **an**, not **a**, before **hourly**.
■ ***adj.*** [only before noun] **1** done or happening every hour: *an hourly bus service* ◇ *Trains leave at hourly intervals.* **2** an **hourly wage, fee, rate, etc.** is the amount that you earn every hour or pay for a service every hour: *an hourly rate of $30 an hour*
■ ***adv.*** every hour: *Reapply sunscreen hourly and after swimming.* ◇ *Dressings are changed four hourly* (= every four hours) *to help prevent infection.*

house 🔑 *noun, verb*
■ ***noun*** /haʊs/ (*pl.* houses /ˈhaʊzɪz/)
▸ BUILDING **1** 🔑 [C] a building for people to live in, usually for one family: *He went into the house.* ◇ *a two-bedroom house* ◇ *Let's have the party* ***at my house.*** ◇ *house prices* ◇ *What time do you leave the house in the morning* (= to go to work)? ◇ (*BrE*) *We're* ***moving house*** (= leaving our house and going to live in a different one). ➲ COLLOCATIONS at DECORATE ➲ VISUAL VOCAB page V15 ➲ see also PENTHOUSE, SAFE HOUSE, SHOW HOUSE **2** 🔑 [sing.] all the people living in a house SYN **household**: *Be quiet or you'll wake the whole house!* **3** [C] (in compounds) a building used for a particular purpose, for example for holding meetings in or keeping animals or goods in: *an opera house* ◇ *a henhouse* ➲ see also DOGHOUSE, DOSSHOUSE, HALFWAY HOUSE, HOTHOUSE, LIGHTHOUSE, MADHOUSE, OUTHOUSE, STOREHOUSE, WAREHOUSE **4 House** [sing.] (*BrE*) used in the names of office buildings: *Their offices are on the second floor of Chester House.*
▸ COMPANY/INSTITUTION **5** [C] (in compounds) a company involved in a particular kind of business; an institution of a particular kind: *a* ***fashion/banking/publishing, etc. house*** ◇ *a religious house* (= a CONVENT or a MONASTERY) ◇ *I work* ***in house*** (= in the offices of the company that I work for, not at home) ➲ see also CLEARING HOUSE, IN-HOUSE
▸ RESTAURANT **6** [C] (in compounds) a restaurant: *a steakhouse* ◇ *a coffee house* ◇ *a bottle of* ***house wine*** (= the cheapest wine available in a particular restaurant, sometimes not listed by name) ➲ see also FREE HOUSE, PUBLIC HOUSE, ROADHOUSE, TIED HOUSE
▸ PARLIAMENT **7** [C] (often **House**) a group of people who meet to discuss and make the laws of a country: *Legislation requires approval by both houses of parliament.* ➲ see also LOWER HOUSE, UPPER HOUSE **8 the House** [sing.] the House of Commons or the House of Lords in Britain; the House of Representatives in the US
▸ IN DEBATE **9 the house** [sing.] a group of people discussing sth in a formal debate: *I urge the house to vote against the motion.*
▸ IN THEATRE **10** [C] the part of a theatre where the audience sits; the audience at a particular performance: *playing to a* ***full/packed/empty house*** (= to a large/small audience) ◇ *The spotlight faded and the house lights came up.* ➲ see also FRONT-OF-HOUSE, FULL HOUSE
▸ IN SCHOOL **11** [C] (in some British schools) an organized group of students of different ages who compete against other groups in sports competitions, etc. and who may, in BOARDING SCHOOLS, live together in one building
▸ FAMILY **12** [C] (usually **the House of...**) an old and famous family: *the House of Windsor* (= the British royal family)
▸ MUSIC **13** [U] = HOUSE MUSIC ➲ see also ACID HOUSE, ART-HOUSE, OPEN HOUSE, POWERHOUSE HELP There are many other compounds ending in **house**. You will find them at their place in the alphabet.
IDM **bring the ˈhouse down** to make everyone laugh or CHEER, especially at a performance in the theatre **get on like a ˈhouse on fire** (*BrE*) (*NAmE* **get along like a ˈhouse on fire**) (*informal*) (of people) to become friends quickly and have a very friendly relationship **go all round the ˈhouses** (*BrE, informal*) to do sth or ask a question in a very complicated way instead of in a simple, direct way **keep ˈhouse** to cook, clean and do all the other jobs around the house **on the ˈhouse** drinks or meals that are **on the house** are provided free by the pub/bar or restaurant and you do not have to pay **put/set your (own) ˈhouse in order** to organize your own business or improve your own behaviour before you try to criticize sb else **set up ˈhouse** to make a place your home: *They set up house together in a small flat in Brighton.* ➲ more at CLEAN *v.*, DRY *n.*, EAT, PEOPLE *n.*, SAFE *adj.*
■ ***verb*** /haʊz/
▸ PROVIDE HOME **1 ~ sb** to provide a place for sb to live: *The government is committed to housing the refugees.*
▸ KEEP STH **2 ~ sth** to be the place where sth is kept or where sth operates from: *The gallery houses 2 000 works of modern art.* ◇ *The museum is housed in the Old Court House.*

Collocations

Moving house

Renting
- **live in** a rented/(*especially NAmE*) rental property
- **rent/share/move into** a furnished house/(*BrE*) flat/(*especially NAmE*) apartment
- **rent** a studio/(*BrE*) a studio flat/(*especially NAmE*) a studio apartment/(*BrE*) a bedsit
- **find/get** a housemate/(*BrE*) a flatmate/(*NAmE*) a roommate
- **sign/break** the lease/rental agreement/contract
- **extend/renew/terminate** the lease/(*BrE*) tenancy
- **afford/pay** the rent/the bills/(*NAmE*) the utilities
- (*especially BrE*) **fall behind with**/(*especially NAmE*) **fall behind on** the rent
- **pay/lose/return** a damage deposit/(*NAmE*) security deposit
- **give/receive** a month's/two-weeks' notice to leave/vacate the property

Being a landlord
- **have a flat/apartment/room** (*BrE*) to let/(*especially NAmE*) for rent
- **rent (out)/lease (out)**/(*BrE*) **let (out)/sublet** a flat/apartment/house/property
- **collect/increase/raise** the rent
- **evict** the existing tenants
- **attract/find** new/prospective tenants
- **invest in** rental property/(*BrE*) property to let/(*BrE*) the buy-to-let market

Buying
- **buy/acquire/purchase** a house/(a) property/(*especially NAmE*) (a piece of) prime real estate
- **call/contact/use** (*BrE*) an estate agent/(*NAmE*) a Realtor™/(*NAmE*) a real estate agent/broker
- **make**/(*BrE*) **put in** an offer on a house
- **put down/save for** (*BrE*) a deposit on a house
- **make/put/save for** (*especially NAmE*) a down payment on a house/home
- **apply for/arrange/take out** a mortgage/home loan
- **(struggle to) pay** the mortgage
- **make/meet/keep up/cover** the monthly mortgage payments/(*BrE also*) repayments
- (*BrE*) **repossess**/(*especially NAmE*) **foreclose on** sb's home/house

Selling
- **put your house/property** on the market/up for sale/up for auction
- **increase/lower** your price/the asking price
- **have/hold/hand over** the deed/(*especially BrE*) deeds of/to the house, land, etc.

ˈhouse arrest *noun* [U] the state of being a prisoner in your own house rather than in a prison: *to* ***be under house arrest*** ◇ *She was* ***placed under house arrest.***

house·boat /ˈhaʊsbəʊt; *NAmE* -boʊt/ *noun* a boat that people can live in, usually kept at a particular place on a river or CANAL ➲ VISUAL VOCAB page V14

house·bound /ˈhaʊsbaʊnd/ *adj.* **1** unable to leave your house because you cannot walk very far as a result of being ill/sick or old **2 the housebound** *noun* [pl.] people who are housebound

house·boy /ˈhaʊsbɔɪ/ *noun* a young male servant in a house

house·break·ing /ˈhaʊsbreɪkɪŋ/ *noun* [U] (*especially BrE*) the crime of entering a house illegally by using force, in order to steal things from it SYN **burglary** ▸ **house·break·er** /ˈhaʊsbreɪkə(r)/ *noun*

ˈhouse-broken (*NAmE*) (*BrE* **ˈhouse-trained**) *adj.* (of pet cats or dogs) trained to DEFECATE and URINATE outside the house or in a special box

house·coat /ˈhaʊskəʊt; *NAmE* -koʊt/ *noun* a long loose piece of clothing, worn in the house by women

ˈhouse dust mite *noun* = DUST MITE

house·fly /ˈhaʊsflaɪ/ *noun* (*pl.* **-ies**) a common fly that lives in houses

house·ful /ˈhaʊsfʊl/ *noun* [sing.] a large number of people in a house: *He grew up in a houseful of women.* ◇ *They had a houseful so we didn't stay.*

ˈhouse guest *noun* a person who is staying in your house for a short time

house·hold 0→ /ˈhaʊshəʊld; *NAmE* -hoʊld/ *noun* all the people living together in a house or flat/apartment: *Most households now own at least one car.* ◇ ***low-income/one-parent, etc. households*** ◇ *the* ***head of the household*** ▸ **house·hold** 0→ *adj.* [only before noun]: ***household bills/chores/goods*** (= connected with looking after a house and the people living in it)

house·hold·er /ˈhaʊshəʊldə(r); *NAmE* -hoʊld-/ *noun* (*formal*) a person who owns or rents the house that they live in

ˌhousehold ˈname (also *less frequent* **ˌhousehold ˈword**) *noun* a name that has become very well known: *She became a household name in the 1960s.*

ˈhouse-hunting *noun* [U] the activity of looking for a house to buy ▸ **ˈhouse-hunter** *noun*

ˈhouse husband *noun* a man who stays at home to cook, clean, take care of the children, etc. while his wife or partner goes out to work ➲ compare HOUSEWIFE

house·keep·er /ˈhaʊskiːpə(r)/ *noun* **1** a person, usually a woman, whose job is to manage the shopping, cooking, cleaning, etc. in a house or an institution **2** a person whose job is to manage the cleaning of rooms in a hotel

house·keep·ing /ˈhaʊskiːpɪŋ/ *noun* [U] **1** the work involved in taking care of a house, especially shopping and managing money **2** the department in a hotel, a hospital, an office building, etc. that is responsible for cleaning the rooms, etc: *Call housekeeping and ask them to bring us some clean towels.* **3** (also **ˈhousekeeping money** especially in *BrE*) the money used to buy food, cleaning materials and other things needed for taking care of a house **4** jobs that are done to enable an organization or computer system to work well: *Most large companies now use computers for accounting and housekeeping operations.*

house·maid /ˈhaʊsmeɪd/ *noun* (*old-fashioned*) a female servant in a large house who cleans the rooms, etc. and often lives there

house·man /ˈhaʊsmən/ *noun* (*pl.* **-men** /-mən/) **1** (*old-fashioned, BrE*) = HOUSE OFFICER **2** (*NAmE*) a man employed to do general jobs in a house, hotel, etc.

ˈhouse martin *noun* a small black and white European bird like a SWALLOW

house·mas·ter /ˈhaʊsmɑːstə(r); *NAmE* -mæs-/, **house·mis·tress** /ˈhaʊsmɪstrəs/ *noun* (*especially BrE*) a teacher in charge of a group of children, (called a HOUSE), in a school, especially a private school

house·mate /ˈhaʊsmeɪt/ *noun* a person that you share a house with, but who is not one of your family

ˈhouse music (also **house**) *noun* [U] a type of electronic dance music with a fast beat

ˌhouse of ˈcards *noun* [sing.] **1** a plan, an organization, etc. that is so badly arranged that it could easily fail **2** a structure built out of PLAYING CARDS

the ˌHouse of ˈCommons (also **the Com·mons**) *noun* **1** [sing.+ sing./pl. v.] (in Britain and Canada) the part of Parliament whose members are elected by the people of the country **2** [sing.] the building where the members of the House of Commons meet ➲ compare THE HOUSE OF LORDS

ˈhouse officer *noun* (in Britain) a doctor who has finished medical school and who is working at a hospital to get further practical experience ➲ compare INTERN

ˌhouse of ˈGod *noun* [usually sing.] (*pl.* **houses of God**) (*literary*) a church or other religious building

the ˌHouse of ˈLords (also **the Lords**) *noun* **1** [sing.+ sing./pl. v.] (in Britain) the part of Parliament whose members are not elected by the people of the country **2** [sing.] the building where members of the House of Lords meet ➲ compare THE HOUSE OF COMMONS

the ˌHouse of Repreˈsentatives *noun* [sing.] the largest part of Congress in the US, or of the Parliament in Australia, whose members are elected by the people of the country ➲ compare SENATE (1)

ˈhouse party *noun* a party held at a large house in the country where guests stay for a few days; the guests at this party

ˈhouse plant (*BrE* also **ˈpot plant**) *noun* a plant that you grow in a pot and keep indoors ➲ VISUAL VOCAB page V18

ˈhouse-proud *adj.* spending a lot of time making your house look clean and attractive, and thinking that this is important

house·room /ˈhaʊsruːm; -rʊm/ *noun* [U] space in a house for sb/sth
IDM **not give sth ˈhouseroom** (*BrE*) to not like sth and not want it in your house

ˈhouse-sit *verb* (-tt-) [I] to live in sb's house while they are away in order to take care of it for them

the ˌHouses of ˈParliament *noun* [pl.] (in Britain) the Parliament that consists of both the HOUSE OF COMMONS and the HOUSE OF LORDS; the buildings in London where the British Parliament meets

ˌhouse ˈstyle *noun* [U, C] the way a company such as a PUBLISHER prefers its written materials to be expressed and arranged

ˌhouse-to-ˈhouse *adj.* [only before noun] visiting every house in a particular area: *a* ***house-to-house collection/search*** ◇ *The police are making house-to-house enquiries.*

ˈhouse-trained (*BrE*) (*NAmE* **ˈhouse-broken**) *adj.* (of pet cats or dogs) trained to DEFECATE and URINATE outside the house or in a special box

house·wares /ˈhaʊsweəz; *NAmE* -werz/ *noun* [pl.] (*NAmE*) (in shops/stores) small items used in the house, especially kitchen equipment

ˈhouse-warming *noun* a party given by sb who has just moved into a new house

house·wife /ˈhaʊswaɪf/ *noun* (*pl.* **-wives** /-waɪvz/) a woman who stays at home to cook, clean, take care of the children, etc. while her husband or partner goes out to work ➲ compare HOUSE HUSBAND ▸ **house·wife·ly** *adj.*

house·work /ˈhaʊswɜːk; *NAmE* -wɜːrk/ *noun* [U] the work involved in taking care of a home and family, for example cleaning and cooking: *to do the housework*

hous·ing 0→ /ˈhaʊzɪŋ/ *noun*
1 0→ [U] houses, flats/apartments, etc. that people live in, especially when referring to their type, price or condition: ***public/private housing*** ◇ *poor housing conditions* ◇ *the housing shortage* ◇ *the* ***housing market*** (= the activity of buying and selling houses, etc.) **2** 0→ [U] the job of providing houses, flats/apartments, etc. for people to live in: *the*

H

housing department ◇ *the council's housing policy* **3** [C] a hard cover that protects part of a machine: *a car's rear axle housing*

'housing association *noun* (in Britain) an organization that owns houses, flats/apartments, etc. and helps people to rent or buy them at a low price

'housing benefit *noun* [U, C] (in Britain) money given by the government to people who do not earn much, to help them pay for a place to live in

'housing estate (*BrE*) (also **'housing development** *NAmE, BrE*) *noun* an area in which a large number of houses or flats/apartments are planned and built together at the same time: *They live on a housing estate.*

'housing project (also **pro·ject**) (both *NAmE*) *noun* a group of houses or flats/apartments built for poor families, usually with government money

hove *past tense, past part.* of HEAVE

hovel /ˈhɒvl; *NAmE* ˈhʌvl/ *noun* (*disapproving*) a house or room that is not fit to live in because it is dirty or in very bad condition

hover /ˈhɒvə(r); *NAmE* ˈhʌvər/ *verb* **1** [I] (+ **adv./prep.**) (of birds, HELICOPTERS, etc.) to stay in the air in one place: *A hawk hovered over the hill.* **2** [I] (+ **adv./prep.**) (of a person) to wait somewhere, especially near sb, in a shy or uncertain manner: *He hovered nervously in the doorway.* **3** [I] + **adv./prep.** to stay close to sth, or to stay in an uncertain state: *Temperatures hovered around freezing.* ◇ *He hovered on the edge of consciousness.* ◇ *A smile hovered on her lips.*

hov·er·craft /ˈhɒvəkrɑːft; *NAmE* ˈhʌvərkræft/ *noun* a vehicle that travels just above the surface of water or land, held up by air being forced downwards ➲ VISUAL VOCAB page V44 ➲ compare HYDROFOIL

ˌHO'V lane /ˌeɪtʃ əʊ ˈviː leɪn; *NAmE* oʊ/ *noun* (*especially NAmE*) high-occupancy vehicle lane (a part of the road that may only be used by vehicles that are carrying two or more people)

how 🔑 /haʊ/ *adv.*
1 🔑 in what way or manner: *How does it work?* ◇ *He did not know how he ought to behave.* ◇ *I'll show you how to load the software.* ◇ *'Her behaviour was very odd.' '**How so?**'* ◇ *It's funny how* (= that) *people always remember him.* ◇ *Do you remember how* (= that) *the kids always loved going there?* ◇ ***How ever** did you get here so quickly?* ➲ compare HOWEVER **2** 🔑 used to ask about sb's health: *How are you?* ◇ *How are you feeling now?* **3** 🔑 used to ask whether sth is successful or enjoyable: *How was your trip?* ◇ *How did they play?* **4** 🔑 used before an adjective or adverb to ask about the amount, degree, etc. of sth, or about sb's age: ***How often** do you go swimming?* ◇ *I didn't know how much to bring.* ◇ ***How much** are those earrings* (= What do they cost)? ◇ ***How many** people were there?* ◇ *How old is she?* **5** 🔑 used to express surprise, pleasure, etc.: *How kind of you to help!* ◇ *How he wished he had been there!* **6** 🔑 in any way in which SYN **however**: *I'll dress how I like in my own house!*

IDM **how about...?** **1** 🔑 used when asking for information about sb/sth: *I'm not going. How about you?* **2** 🔑 used to make a suggestion: *How about a break?* ◇ *How about going for a meal?* ◇ (*especially NAmE*) *How about we go for a meal?* **how 'can/'could you!** (*informal*) used to show that you strongly disapprove of sb's behaviour or are very surprised by it: *Ben! How could you? After all they've done for us!* ◇ *Ugh! How can you eat that stuff?* **how 'come?** 🔑 (*informal*) used to ask the reason for sth: *'I think you owe me some money.' 'How come?'* **ˌhow do you 'do** 🔑 (becoming *old-fashioned*) used as a formal GREETING when you meet sb for the first time. The usual reply is also *How do you do?* **ˌhow's 'that?** (*informal*) **1** used to ask the reason for sth: *'I left work early today.' 'How's that* (= Why)*?'* **2** used when asking sb's opinion of sth: *I'll tuck your sheets in for you. How's that? Comfortable?* ◇ *Two o'clock on the dot! **How's that for** punctuality!*

how·dah /ˈhaʊdə/ *noun* a seat for riding on the back of an ELEPHANT or a CAMEL, often for more than one person

howdy /ˈhaʊdi/ *exclamation* (*NAmE, informal*, often *humorous*) used to say hello: *Howdy, partner.*

how·ever 🔑 /haʊˈevə(r)/ *adv.*
1 🔑 used with an adjective or adverb to mean 'to whatever degree': *He wanted to take no risks, however small.* ◇ *She has the window open, however cold it is outside.* ◇ *However carefully I explained, she still didn't understand.* HELP When **ever** is used to emphasize **how**, meaning 'In what way or manner?', it is usually written as a separate word: ***How ever** did you get here so quickly?* **2** 🔑 in whatever way: *However you look at it, it's going to cost a lot.* **3** 🔑 used to introduce a statement that contrasts with sth that has just been said: *He was feeling bad. He went to work, however, and tried to concentrate.* ◇ *We thought the figures were correct. However, we have now discovered some errors.*

Language Bank

however

Ways of saying 'but'

- Politicians have promised to improve road safety. So far, **however**, little has been achieved.
- **Despite** clear evidence from road safety studies, no new measures have been introduced.
- Politicians have promised to improve road safety. **In spite of this/Despite this**, little has been achieved so far.
- **Although** politicians have promised to improve road safety, little has been achieved so far.
- Some politicians claim that the new transport policy has been a success. **In fact**, it has been a total disaster.
- Government campaigns have had a measure of success, **but the fact remains that** large numbers of accidents are still caused by careless drivers.

➲ Language Bank at NEVERTHELESS

how·itz·er /ˈhaʊɪtsə(r)/ *noun* a heavy gun that fires SHELLS high into the air for a short distance

howl /haʊl/ *verb, noun*
▪ *verb* **1** [I] (of a dog, WOLF, etc.) to make a long, loud cry **2** [I] **~ (in/with sth)** to make a loud cry when you are in pain, angry, amused, etc: *to howl in pain* ◇ *We howled with laughter.* ◇ *The baby was howling* (= crying loudly) *all the time I was there.* **3** [I] (of the wind) to blow hard and make a long loud noise: *The wind was howling around the house.* **4** [T] **~ sth** | **+ speech** to say sth loudly and angrily: *The crowd howled its displeasure.*

PHR V **ˌhowl sb↔'down** to prevent a speaker from being heard by shouting angrily SYN **shout sb down**

▪ *noun* **1** a long loud cry made by a dog, WOLF, etc. **2** a loud cry showing that you are in pain, angry, amused, etc: *to let out a howl of anguish* ◇ *The suggestion was greeted with **howls of laughter**.* **3** a long loud sound made when the wind is blowing strongly: *They listened to the howl of the wind through the trees.*

howl·er /ˈhaʊlə(r)/ *noun* (*informal, especially BrE*) a stupid mistake, especially in what sb says or writes SYN **glaring error**: *The report is full of howlers.* ➲ SYNONYMS at MISTAKE

howl·ing /ˈhaʊlɪŋ/ *adj.* [only before noun] **1** (of a storm, etc.) very violent, with strong winds: *a **howling gale/storm/wind*** **2** (*informal*) very great or extreme: *a howling success* ◇ *She flew into a howling rage.*

'how-to *adj.* [only before noun] providing detailed instructions or advice on how to do sth: *how-to books on computing* ▸ **'how-to** *noun* (*pl.* -os): *Visit our downloads page for free how-tos and tutorials.*

how·zat /ˌhaʊˈzæt/ *exclamation* used in CRICKET to tell the UMPIRE that you think the other team's BATSMAN is out

how·zit /ˈhaʊzɪt/ *exclamation* (*SAfrE, informal*) used to say hello when you meet sb: *Howzit Mandla, how's it going?* ◇ *Please say howzit to Nicki for me.*

h.p. /ˌeɪtʃ ˈpiː/ *abbr.* **1** HORSEPOWER **2** (also **HP**) (*BrE*) HIRE PURCHASE

HQ /ˌeɪtʃ ˈkjuː/ *abbr.* HEADQUARTERS: *See you back at HQ.* ◇ *police HQ*

HR /ˌeɪtʃ ˈɑː(r)/ *abbr.* HUMAN RESOURCES

hr (also **hr.** especially in *NAmE*) *abbr.* (*pl.* **hrs** or **hr**) (in writing) hour: *Cover and chill for 1 hr.*

HRH /ˌeɪtʃ ɑːr ˈeɪtʃ/ *abbr.* His/Her ROYAL HIGHNESS: *HRH Prince Harry*

HRT /ˌeɪtʃ ɑː ˈtiː; *NAmE* ɑːr/ *noun* [U] the abbreviation for 'hormone replacement therapy' (medical treatment for women going through the MENOPAUSE in which HORMONES are added to the body)

Hsiang /ʃiːˈæŋ/ *noun* [U] = XIANG

HTML /ˌeɪtʃ tiː em ˈel/ *abbr.* (*computing*) Hypertext Mark-up Language (a system used to mark text for World Wide Web pages in order to obtain colours, style, pictures, etc.)

HTTP (also **http**) /ˌeɪtʃ tiː tiː ˈpiː/ *abbr.* (*computing*) Hypertext Transfer Protocol (the set of rules that control the way data is sent and received over the Internet)

hua·rache /wæˈrɑːtʃi; wəˈr-/ *noun* a type of SANDAL (= open shoe) made of many narrow strips of leather twisted together

hub /hʌb/ *noun* **1** [usually sing.] **~ (of sth)** the central and most important part of a particular place or activity: *the commercial hub of the city* ◇ *to be at the hub of things* (= where things happen and important decisions are made) ◇ *a hub airport* (= a large important one where people often change from one plane to another) **2** the central part of a wheel ➲ VISUAL VOCAB page V41

hub·bub /ˈhʌbʌb/ *noun* [sing., U] **1** the loud sound made by a lot of people talking at the same time: *It was difficult to hear what he was saying over the hubbub.* **2** a situation in which there is a lot of noise, excitement and activity: *the hubbub of city life*

hubby /ˈhʌbi/ *noun* (*pl.* -ies) (*informal*) = HUSBAND

hub·cap /ˈhʌbkæp/ *noun* a round metal cover that fits over the HUB of a vehicle's wheel ➲ VISUAL VOCAB page V42

hu·bris /ˈhjuːbrɪs/ *noun* [U] (*literary*) the fact of sb being too proud. In literature, a character with this pride ignores warnings and laws and this usually results in their DOWNFALL and death.

huckle·berry /ˈhʌklbəri; *NAmE* -beri/ *noun* (*pl.* -ies) a small soft round purple N American fruit. The bush it grows on is also called a huckleberry.

huck·ster /ˈhʌkstə(r)/ *noun* (*old-fashioned, NAmE*) **1** (*disapproving*) a person who uses aggressive or annoying methods to sell sth **2** a person who sells things in the street or by visiting people's houses

HUD /ˌeɪtʃ juː ˈdiː/ *abbr.* Department of Housing and Urban Development (the US government department in charge of financial programmes to build houses and to help people buy their own homes)

hud·dle /ˈhʌdl/ *verb, noun*

▪ ***verb*** **1** [I] **~ (up/together)** (**+ adv./prep.**) (of people or animals) to gather closely together, usually because of cold or fear: *We huddled together for warmth.* ◇ *They all huddled around the fire.* **2** [I] **~ (up)** (**+ adv./prep.**) to hold your arms and legs close to your body, usually because you are cold or frightened: *I huddled under a blanket on the floor.* ▸ **hud·dled** *adj.*: *People were huddled together around the fire.* ◇ *huddled figures in shop doorways* ◇ *We found him huddled on the floor.*

▪ ***noun*** **1** a small group of people, objects or buildings that are close together, especially when they are not in any particular order: *People stood around in huddles.* ◇ *The track led them to a huddle of outbuildings.* **2** (in AMERICAN FOOTBALL) a time when the players gather round to hear the plan for the next part of the game

IDM **get/go into a ˈhuddle (with sb)** to move close to sb so that you can talk about sth without other people hearing

hue /hjuː/ *noun* **1** (*literary* or *technical*) a colour; a particular shade of a colour: *His face took on an unhealthy whitish hue.* ◇ *Her paintings capture the subtle hues of the countryside in autumn.* ➲ SYNONYMS at COLOUR **2** (*formal*) a type of belief or opinion: *supporters of every political hue*

IDM **ˌhue and ˈcry** strong public protest about sth

huff /hʌf/ *verb, noun*

▪ ***verb*** [T, I] (**+ speech**) to say sth or make a noise in a way that shows you are offended or annoyed: *'Well, nobody asked you,' she huffed irritably.*

IDM **ˌhuff and ˈpuff** (*informal*) **1** to breathe in a noisy way because you are very tired: *Jack was huffing and puffing to keep up with her.* **2** to make it obvious that you are annoyed about sth without doing anything to change the situation: *After much huffing and puffing, she finally agreed to help.*

▪ ***noun***

IDM **in a ˈhuff** (*informal*) in a bad mood, especially because sb has annoyed or upset you: *She went off in a huff.*

huffy /ˈhʌfi/ *adj.* (*informal*) in a bad mood, especially because sb has annoyed or upset you ▸ **huff·ily** *adv.*

hug /hʌg/ *verb, noun*

▪ ***verb*** (**-gg-**) **1** [T, I] **~ (sb)** to put your arms around sb and hold them tightly, especially to show that you like or love them SYN **embrace**: *They hugged each other.* ◇ *She hugged him tightly.* ◇ *They put their arms around each other and hugged.* **2** [T] **~ sth** to put your arms around sth and hold it close to your body: *She sat in the chair, hugging her knees.* ◇ *He hugged the hot-water bottle to his chest.* **3** [T] **~ sth** (of a path, vehicle, etc.) to keep close to sth for a distance: *The track hugs the coast for a mile.* **4** [T] **~ sth** to fit tightly around sth, especially a person's body: *figure-hugging jeans*

▪ ***noun*** an act of putting your arms around sb and holding them tightly, especially to show that you like or love them: *She gave her mother a big hug.* ◇ *He stopped to receive **hugs and kisses** from the fans.* ➲ see also BEAR HUG

huge 🔑 /hjuːdʒ/ *adj.*

1 🔑 extremely large in size or amount; great in degree SYN **enormous, vast**: *a huge crowd* ◇ *He gazed up at her with huge brown eyes.* ◇ *huge debts* ◇ *huge amounts of data* ◇ *The sums of money involved are potentially huge.* ◇ *The party was a huge success.* ◇ *This is going to be a huge problem for us.* **2** (*informal*) very successful: *I think this band is going to be huge.*

huge·ly /ˈhjuːdʒli/ *adv.* **1** extremely: *hugely entertaining/important/popular/successful* **2** very much: *They intended to invest hugely in new technology.* ◇ *He turned around, grinning hugely.*

huh /hʌ/ *exclamation* **1** people use **Huh?** at the end of questions, suggestions, etc, especially when they want sb to agree with them: *So you won't be coming tonight, huh?* ◇ *Let's get out of here, huh?* **2** people say **Huh!** to show anger, surprise, disagreement, etc. or to show that they are not impressed by sth: *Huh! Is that all you've done?* **3** (*NAmE*) (*BrE* **eh**) people say **Huh?** to show that they have not heard what sb has just said: *'Are you feeling OK?' 'Huh?'*

hula hoop (*US* **Hula-Hoop™**) /ˈhuːlə huːp/ *noun* a large plastic ring that you spin around your waist by moving your hips

hulk /hʌlk/ *noun* **1** the main part of an old vehicle, especially a ship, that is no longer used: *the hulk of a wrecked ship* **2** a very large person, especially one who moves in an awkward way: *a great hulk of a man* **3** a very large object, especially one that causes you to feel nervous or afraid

hulk·ing /ˈhʌlkɪŋ/ *adj.* [only before noun] very large or heavy, often in a way that causes you to feel nervous or afraid: *a hulking figure crouching in the darkness* ◇ *I don't want that hulking great computer in my office.*

hull /hʌl/ *noun, verb*

▪ ***noun*** the main, bottom part of a ship, that goes in the

H

water: *a* ***wooden/steel hull*** ◇ *They climbed onto the upturned hull and waited to be rescued.* ➲ VISUAL VOCAB page V44
▪ ***verb*** **~ sth** to remove the outer covering of PEAS, BEANS, etc. or the ring of leaves attached to STRAWBERRIES

hul·la·ba·loo /ˌhʌləbəˈluː/ *noun* [sing.] a lot of loud noise, especially made by people who are annoyed or excited about sth SYN **commotion, uproar**

hullo (*especially BrE*) = HELLO

hum /hʌm/ *verb, noun*
▪ ***verb*** (-mm-) **1** [I, T] to sing a tune with your lips closed: *She was humming softly to herself.* ◇ **~ sth** *What's that tune you're humming?* ➲ COLLOCATIONS at MUSIC **2** [I] to make a low continuous sound: *The computers were humming away.* **3** [I] to be full of activity: *The streets were beginning to hum with life.*
IDM **ˌhum and ˈhaw** (*BrE*) (*NAmE* **ˌhem and ˈhaw**) (*informal*) to take a long time to make a decision or before you say sth
▪ ***noun*** [sing.] **~ (of sth)** a low continuous sound: *the* ***hum of bees/traffic/voices*** ◇ *The room filled with the hum of conversation.*

human 🔑 /ˈhjuːmən/ *adj., noun*
▪ ***adj.*** **1** 🔑 [only before noun] of or connected with people rather than animals, machines or gods: *the* ***human body/brain*** ◇ ***human anatomy/activity/behaviour/experience*** ◇ *a terrible loss of* ***human life*** ◇ *Contact with other people is a basic* ***human need.*** ◇ *This food is not fit for* ***human consumption.*** ◇ ***human geography*** (= the study of the way different people live around the world) ◇ *The hostages were used as a* ***human shield*** (= a person or group of people that is forced to stay in a particular place where they would be hurt or killed if their country attacked it). ◇ *Firefighters formed a* ***human chain*** (= a line of people) *to carry the children to safety.* ◇ ***Human remains*** (= the body of a dead person) *were found inside the house.* **2** 🔑 showing the weaknesses that are typical of people, which means that other people should not criticize the person too much: ***human weaknesses/failings*** ◇ *We must allow for* ***human error.*** ◇ ***It's only human*** *to want the best for your children.* **3** 🔑 having the same feelings and emotions as most ordinary people: *He's really very human when you get to know him.* ◇ *The public is always attracted to politicians who have* ***the human touch*** (= the ability to make ordinary people feel relaxed when they meet them). ➲ compare INHUMAN, NON-HUMAN
IDM **the ˈhuman face of...** a person who is involved in a subject, issue, etc. and makes it easier for ordinary people to understand and have sympathy with it: *He is the human face of party politics.* **with a human ˈface** that considers the needs of ordinary people: *This was science with a human face.* ➲ more at MILK *n.*
▪ ***noun*** 🔑 (also **ˌhuman ˈbeing**) a person rather than an animal or a machine: *Dogs can hear much better than humans.* ◇ *That is no way to treat another human being.*

hu·mane /hjuːˈmeɪn/ *adj.* showing kindness towards people and animals by making sure that they do not suffer more than is necessary: *a caring and humane society* ◇ *the humane treatment of refugees* ◇ *the humane killing of animals* OPP **inhumane** ▶ **hu·mane·ly** *adv.*: *to treat sb humanely* ◇ *meat that has been humanely produced* ◇ *The dog was humanely destroyed.*

ˌhuman ˈinterest *noun* [U] the part of a story in a newspaper, etc. that people find interesting because it describes the experiences, feelings, etc. of the people involved

hu·man·ism /ˈhjuːmənɪzəm/ *noun* [U] a system of thought that considers that solving human problems with the help of reason is more important than religious beliefs. It emphasizes the fact that the basic nature of humans is good. ▶ **hu·man·is·tic** /ˌhjuːməˈnɪstɪk/ *adj.*: *humanistic ideals*

hu·man·ist /ˈhjuːmənɪst/ *noun* a person who believes in humanism

hu·mani·tar·ian /hjuːˌmænɪˈteəriən; *NAmE* -ˈter-/ *adj.* [usually before noun] concerned with reducing suffering and improving the conditions that people live in: *to provide* ***humanitarian aid*** *to the war zone* ◇ *humanitarian issues* ◇ *a humanitarian organization* ◇ *They are calling for the release of the hostages on* ***humanitarian grounds.*** ◇ *The expulsion of thousands of people represents a humanitarian catastrophe of enormous proportions.* ▶ **hu·mani·tar·ian** *noun* **hu·mani·tar·ian·ism** /-ɪzəm/ *noun* [U]

hu·man·ity /hjuːˈmænəti/ *noun* **1** [U] people in general: *crimes against humanity* ➲ note at GENDER **2** [U] the state of being a person rather than a god, an animal or a machine: *The story was used to emphasize the humanity of Jesus.* ◇ *united by a sense of common humanity* **3** [U] the quality of being kind to people and animals by making sure that they do not suffer more than is necessary; the quality of being HUMANE: *The judge was praised for his courage and humanity.* OPP **inhumanity** **4** **(the) humanities** [pl.] the subjects of study that are concerned with the way people think and behave, for example literature, language, history and philosophy ➲ compare SCIENCE

hu·man·ize (*BrE* also **-ise**) /ˈhjuːmənaɪz/ *verb* **~ sth** to make sth more pleasant or suitable for people; to make sth more HUMANE: *These measures are intended to humanize the prison system.*

hu·man·kind /ˌhjuːmənˈkaɪnd/ *noun* [U] people in general ➲ see also MANKIND

hu·man·ly /ˈhjuːmənli/ *adv.* within human ability; in a way that is typical of human behaviour, thoughts and feelings: *The doctors did all that was* ***humanly possible.*** ◇ *He couldn't humanly refuse to help her.*

ˌhuman ˈnature *noun* [U] the ways of behaving, thinking and feeling that are shared by most people and are considered to be normal: *Her kindness has restored my faith in human nature* (= the belief that people are good). ◇ ***It's only human nature*** *to be worried about change.*

hu·man·oid /ˈhjuːmənɔɪd/ *noun* a machine or creature that looks and behaves like a human ▶ **hu·man·oid** *adj.*

the ˌhuman ˈrace *noun* [sing.] all people, considered together as a group

ˌhuman reˈsources *noun* **1** [pl.] people's skills and abilities, seen as sth a company, an organization, etc. can make use of **2** (*abbr.* **HR**) [U+sing./pl. v.] the department in a company that deals with employing and training people SYN **personnel**: *the human resources director*

ˌhuman ˈright *noun* [usually pl.] one of the basic rights that everyone has to be treated fairly and not in a cruel way, especially by their government: *The country has a poor record on human rights.* ◇ *to campaign for human rights* ◇ ***human rights abuses/violations***

hum·ble /ˈhʌmbl/ *adj., verb*
▪ ***adj.*** (**hum·bler** /ˈhʌmblə(r)/, **hum·blest** /ˈhʌmblɪst/) **1** showing you do not think that you are as important as other people SYN **modest**: *Be humble enough to learn from your mistakes.* ◇ *my humble tribute to this great man* ➲ see also HUMILITY **2** (*ironic* or *humorous*) used to suggest that you are not as important as other people, but in a way that is not sincere or not very serious: ***In my humble opinion,*** *you were in the wrong.* ◇ ***My humble apologies.*** *I did not understand.* **3** having a low rank or social position: *a man of* ***humble birth/origins*** ◇ *a humble occupation* ◇ *the daughter of a humble shopkeeper* **4** (of a thing) not large or special in any way SYN **modest**: *a humble farmhouse* ◇ *The company has worked its way up from humble beginnings to become the market leader.* ▶ **hum·bly** /ˈhʌmbli/ *adv.*: *I would humbly suggest that there is something wrong here.* ◇ *'Sorry,' she said humbly.* IDM see EAT
▪ ***verb*** **1** **~ sb** to make sb feel that they are not as good or important as they thought they were: *He was humbled by her generosity.* ◇ *a humbling experience* **2** [usually passive] **~ sb** to easily defeat an opponent, especially a strong or powerful one: *The world champion was humbled last night in three rounds.* **3** **~ yourself** to show that you are not too proud to ask for sth, admit that you have been wrong, etc. ➲ see also HUMILITY

hum·bug /ˈhʌmbʌɡ/ *noun* **1** [U] (*old-fashioned*) dishonest language or behaviour that is intended to trick people: *political humbug* **2** [C] (*old-fashioned*) a person who is not sincere or honest **3** [C] (*BrE*) a hard sweet/candy made from boiled sugar, especially one that tastes of PEPPERMINT

hum·ding·er /ˌhʌmˈdɪŋə(r)/ *noun* [sing.] (*informal*) something that is very exciting or impressive: *It turned into a real humdinger of a game.*

hum·drum /ˈhʌmdrʌm/ *adj.* boring and always the same SYN **dull, tedious**: *a* ***humdrum existence/job/life***

hu·mec·tant /hjuːˈmektənt; *NAmE* also juː-/ *noun* (*technical*) **1** a substance added to foods to stop them from becoming dry **2** a substance added to skin cream to stop your skin from being dry

hu·merus /ˈhjuːmərəs/ *noun* (*pl.* **hu·meri** /ˈhjuːməraɪ/) (*anatomy*) the large bone in the top part of the arm between the shoulder and the elbow ➲ VISUAL VOCAB page V48

humid /ˈhjuːmɪd/ *adj.* (of the air or climate) warm and damp: *These ferns will grow best in a humid atmosphere.* ◇ *The island is hot and humid in the summer.*

humi·dex /ˈhjuːmɪdeks/ *noun* [sing.] (*CanE*) a scale that measures how unpleasant hot and HUMID weather feels to people

hu·midi·fier /hjuːˈmɪdɪfaɪə(r)/ *noun* a machine used for making the air in a room less dry ➲ see also DEHUMIDIFIER

hu·mid·ity /hjuːˈmɪdəti/ *noun* [U] **1** the amount of water in the air: ***high/low humidity*** ◇ *70% humidity* **2** conditions in which the air is very warm and damp: *These plants need heat and humidity to grow well.* ◇ *The humidity was becoming unbearable.*

hu·mili·ate /hjuːˈmɪlieɪt/ *verb* **~ sb/yourself/sth** to make sb feel ashamed or stupid and lose the respect of other people: *I didn't want to humiliate her in front of her colleagues.* ◇ *I've never felt so humiliated.* ◇ *The party was humiliated in the recent elections.* ▸ **hu·mili·at·ing** *adj.*: *a humiliating defeat* **hu·mili·ation** /hjuːˌmɪliˈeɪʃn/ *noun* [U, C]: *She suffered the humiliation of being criticized in public.*

hu·mil·ity /hjuːˈmɪləti/ *noun* [U] the quality of not thinking that you are better than other people; the quality of being humble: *Her first defeat was an early lesson in humility.* ◇ *an act of genuine humility*

Hum·int /ˈhjuːmɪnt/ *noun* [U] the activity or job of collecting secret information about people or governments ORIGIN A combination of *human* and *intelligence*.

hum·ming·bird /ˈhʌmɪŋbɜːd; *NAmE* -bɜːrd/ *noun* a small brightly coloured bird that lives in warm countries and that can stay in one place in the air by beating its wings very fast, making a continuous low sound (= a HUMMING sound)

hum·mock /ˈhʌmək/ *noun* (*BrE*) a small hill or pile of earth

hum·mus (also **hou·mous**) /ˈhʊməs; ˈhuːməs/ *noun* [U] a type of food, originally from the Middle East, that is a soft mixture of CHICKPEAS, SESAME seeds, oil, lemon juice and GARLIC

hu·mon·gous (also **hu·mun·gous**) /hjuːˈmʌŋɡəs/ *adj.* (*informal*) very big SYN **enormous**

humor, humor·less (*especially US*) = HUMOUR, HUMOURLESS

hu·mor·ist /ˈhjuːmərɪst/ *noun* a person who is famous for writing or telling amusing stories

hu·mor·ous 0‑w /ˈhjuːmərəs/ *adj.* funny and entertaining; showing a sense of humour: *He gave a humorous account of their trip to Spain.* ◇ *He had a wide mouth and humorous grey eyes.* ➲ SYNONYMS at FUNNY ▸ **hu·mor·ous·ly** *adv.*: *The poem humorously describes local characters and traditions.*

hu·mour 0‑w (*especially US* **hu·mor**) /ˈhjuːmə(r)/ *noun, verb*

▪ *noun* **1** 0‑w [U] the quality in sth that makes it funny or amusing; the ability to laugh at things that are amusing: *a story full of gentle humour* ◇ *She ignored his feeble attempt at humour.* ◇ *They failed to see the humour of the situation.* ◇ *I can't stand people with no* ***sense of humour****.* ◇ *She smiled with a rare flash of humour.* ◇ *She has her very own brand of humour.* ◇ *The film is only funny if you appreciate French humour* (= things that cause French people to laugh). **2** [C, U] (*formal*) the state of your feelings or mind at a particular time: *to be in the best of humours* ◇ *The meeting dissolved in* ***ill humour****.* ◇ *to be* ***out of humour*** (= in a bad mood) ➲ see also GOOD HUMOUR, GOOD-HUMOURED, ILL-HUMOURED **3** [C] (*old use*) one of the four liquids that were thought in the past to be in a person's body and to influence health and character

▪ *verb* **~ sb** to agree with sb's wishes, even if they seem unreasonable, in order to keep the person happy: *She thought it best to humour him rather than get into an argument.*

hu·mour·less (*especially US* **hu·mor·less**) /ˈhjuːmələs; *NAmE* -ərləs/ *adj.* not having or showing the ability to laugh at things that other people think are amusing ▸ **hu·mour·less·ly** (*especially US* **hu·mor·less·ly**) *adv.*

hump /hʌmp/ *noun, verb*

▪ *noun* **1** a large lump that sticks out above the surface of sth, especially the ground: *the dark hump of the mountain in the distance* ◇ (*BrE*) *a* ***road/speed/traffic hump*** (= a hump on a road that forces traffic to drive more slowly) **2** a large lump on the back of some animals, especially CAMELS **3** a large lump on the back of a person, caused by an unusual curve in the SPINE (= the row of bones in the middle of the back)

IDM **be over the ˈhump** to have done the most difficult part of sth **get/take the ˈhump** (*BrE, informal*) to become annoyed or upset about sth: *Fans get the hump when the team loses.*

▪ *verb* **1 ~ sth (+ adv./prep.)** (*BrE*) to carry sth heavy: *I've been humping furniture around all day.* **2 ~ sb** (*taboo, slang*) to have sex with sb

hump·back /ˈhʌmpbæk/ *noun* **1** = HUMPBACK WHALE **2** = HUNCHBACK

ˌhumpback ˈbridge (also **ˌhumpbacked ˈbridge**) *noun* (*BrE*) a small bridge that slopes steeply on both sides ➲ VISUAL VOCAB page V12

ˌhumpback ˈwhale (also **hump·back**) *noun* a large WHALE (= a very large sea animal) with a back shaped like a HUMP

humped /hʌmpt/ *adj.* having a HUMP or HUMPS; shaped like a HUMP: *a humped back* ◇ *He was tall and broad with humped shoulders.*

humph *exclamation* the way of writing the sound /həmf/ that people use to show they do not believe sth or do not approve of it

hu·mun·gous = HUMONGOUS

humus /ˈhjuːməs/ *noun* [U] a substance made from dead leaves and plants, added to soil to help plants grow

Hun /hʌn/ *noun* (*pl.* **Huns** or **the Hun**) (*informal*) an offensive word for a German person, used especially during the First and Second World Wars

hunch /hʌntʃ/ *verb, noun*

▪ *verb* [I, T] to bend the top part of your body forward and raise your shoulders and back: (**+ adv./prep.**) *She leaned forward, hunching over the desk.* ◇ **~ sth** *He* ***hunched his shoulders*** *and thrust his hands deep into his pockets.* ▸ **hunched** *adj.*: *a hunched figure* ◇ *He sat hunched over his breakfast.*

▪ *noun* a feeling that sth is true even though you do not have any evidence to prove it: *It seemed that the doctor's hunch had been right.* ◇ *I had a hunch (that) you'd be back.* ◇ *to follow/back your hunches*

hunch·back /ˈhʌntʃbæk/ (also **hump·back**) *noun* (*offensive*) a person who has a HUMP on their back ▸ **hunch·backed** /ˈhʌntʃbækt/ *adj.*

hun·dred 0‑w /ˈhʌndrəd/ *number* (*plural verb*) **1** 0‑w 100: *One hundred (of the children) have already been* *placed with foster families.* ◇ *There were just a hundred of them there.* ◇ *This vase is worth several hundred dollars.* ◇ *She must be over a hundred* (= a hundred years old). ◇ *Hundreds of thousands of people are at risk.* ◇ *a hundred-year lease* HELP You say **a, one, two, several, etc. hundred** without a final 's' on 'hundred'. **Hundreds (of...)** can be used if there is no number or quantity before it. Always use a plural verb with **hundred** or **hundreds**, except when an amount of money is mentioned: *Four hundred (people) are expected to attend.* ◇ *Two hundred (pounds) was withdrawn from the account.* **2** **a hundred** or **hundreds (of...)** (usually *informal*) a large amount: *hundreds of miles away* ◇ *for hundreds of years* ◇ *If I've said it once, I've said it a hundred times.* ◇ *I have **a hundred and one** things to do.* ◇ (*formal*) *Men died in their hundreds.* **3 the hundreds** [pl.] the numbers from 100 to 999: *We're talking about a figure in the low hundreds.* **4 the... hundreds** [pl.] the years of a particular century: *the early nineteen hundreds* (= written 'early 1900s') **5 one, two, three, etc. ~ hours** used to express whole hours in the 24-hour system: *twelve hundred hours* (= 12.00, midday)

H

IDM **a/one 'hundred per cent** **1** in every way SYN **completely**: *I'm not a hundred per cent sure.* ◇ *My family supports me one hundred per cent.* **2** (*BrE*) completely fit and healthy: *I still don't feel a hundred per cent.* **give a 'hundred (and ten) per cent** to put as much effort into sth as you can: *Every player gave a hundred per cent tonight.* ➲ more at NINETY

,hundreds and 'thousands (*BrE*) (*NAmE* **sprinkles**) *noun* [pl.] extremely small pieces of coloured sugar, used to decorate cakes, etc.

hun·dredth /ˈhʌndrədθ; -ətθ/ *ordinal number, noun*

■ ***ordinal number*** 100th: *her hundredth birthday*

■ ***noun*** each of one hundred equal parts of sth: *a/one hundredth of a second*

hun·dred·weight /ˈhʌndrədweɪt/ *noun* (*pl.* **hun·dred·weight**) (*abbr.* **cwt**) a unit for measuring weight equal to 112 pounds in the UK and 100 pounds in the US. There are 20 hundredweight in a ton.

hung /hʌŋ/ *adj.* [only before noun] **1** (of a parliament or council) (*BrE*) in which no political party has more elected members than all the other parties added together **2** (of a JURY) unable to agree about whether sb is guilty of a crime ➲ see also HANG *v.*

hun·ger /ˈhʌŋɡə(r)/ *noun, verb*

■ ***noun*** **1** [U] the state of not having enough food to eat, especially when this causes illness or death SYN **starvation**: *Around fifty people die of hunger every day in the camp.* ◇ *The organization works to alleviate world hunger and disease.* **2** [U] the feeling caused by a need to eat: *hunger pangs* ◇ *I felt faint with hunger.* **3** [sing.] **~ (for sth)** (*formal*) a strong desire for sth: *a hunger for knowledge* ◇ *Nothing seemed to satisfy their hunger for truth.*

■ ***verb***

PHR V **'hunger for/after sth/sb** (*literary*) to have a strong desire or need for sth/sb

'hunger strike *noun* [C, U] the act of refusing to eat for a long period of time in order to protest about sth: *to **be on / go on hunger strike*** ▸ **'hunger striker** *noun*

hung·over /ˌhʌŋˈəʊvə(r)/ *adj.* [not usually before noun] a person who is **hungover** is feeling ill/sick because they drank too much alcohol the night before ➲ see also HANGOVER

hun·gry /ˈhʌŋɡri/ *adj.* (**hun·grier, hun·gri·est**) **1** feeling that you want to eat sth: *I'm really hungry.* ◇ *Is anyone getting hungry?* ◇ *All this talk of food is making me hungry.* ◇ *I have a hungry family to feed.* **2** not having enough food to eat: *Thousands are **going hungry** because of the failure of this year's harvest.* **3 the hungry** *noun* [pl.] people who do not have enough food to eat **4** [only before noun] causing you to feel that you want to eat sth: *All this gardening is hungry work.* **5** **~ (for sth)** having or showing a strong desire for sth: *Both parties are hungry for power.* ◇ *power-hungry* ◇ *The child is simply hungry for affection.* ◇ *His eyes had a wild hungry look in them.* ▸ **hun·grily** /ˈhʌŋɡrəli/ *adv.*: *They gazed hungrily at the display of food.* ◇ *He kissed her hungrily.*

,hung 'up *adj.* [not before noun] **~ (on/about sth/sb)** (*informal, disapproving*) very worried about sth/sb; thinking about sth/sb too much: *You're not still hung up on that girl?* ◇ *He's too hung up about fitness.*

hunk /hʌŋk/ *noun* **1** a large piece of sth, especially food, that has been cut or broken from a larger piece: *a hunk of bread/cheese/meat* **2** (*informal*) a man who is big, strong and sexually attractive: *He's a real hunk.*

hun·ker /ˈhʌŋkə(r)/ *verb*

PHR V **,hunker 'down** **1** (*especially NAmE*) to sit on your heels with your knees bent up in front of you SYN **squat**: *He hunkered down beside her.* **2** to prepare yourself to stay somewhere, keep an opinion, etc. for a long time **3** to refuse to change an opinion, way of behaving, etc.

hun·kers /ˈhʌŋkəz; *NAmE* -kərz/ *noun* [pl.]

IDM **on your 'hunkers** sitting on your heels with your knees bent up in front of you SYN **haunches**

hunky /ˈhʌŋki/ *adj.* (**hunk·ier, hunk·iest**) (of a man) big, strong and sexually attractive

hunky-dory /ˌhʌŋki ˈdɔːri/ *adj.* [not before noun] (*informal*) if you say that **everything is hunky-dory**, you mean that there are no problems and that everyone is happy

hunt /hʌnt/ *verb, noun*

■ ***verb*** **1** [I, T] to chase wild animals or birds in order to catch or kill them for food, sport or to make money: *Lions sometimes hunt alone.* ◇ **~ sth** *Whales are still being hunted and killed in the Arctic.* **2** [I] to look for sth that is difficult to find SYN **search**: *I've hunted everywhere but I can't find it.* ◇ **~ for sth** *She is still hunting for a new job.* **3** [T, I] to look for sb in order to catch them or harm them: **~ sb** *Police are hunting an escaped criminal.* ◇ **~ for sb** *Detectives are hunting for thieves who broke into a warehouse yesterday.* **4** [I, T] **~ (sth)** (in Britain) to chase and kill FOXES as a sport, riding horses and using dogs. FOX-HUNTING with dogs has been illegal in the UK since 2005.

PHR V **,hunt sb↔'down** to search for sb until you catch or find them, especially in order to punish or harm them **,hunt sth↔'down/'out** to search for sth until you find it

■ ***noun*** **1** [C, usually sing.] **~ (for sb/sth)** an act of looking for sb/sth that is difficult to find: ***The hunt is on** for a suitable candidate.* ◇ *Hundreds have joined a police hunt for the missing teenager.* ◇ (*BrE*) *a **murder hunt*** (= to find the person who has killed sb) ➲ see also TREASURE HUNT, WITCH-HUNT **2** [C] (often in compounds) an act of chasing wild animals to kill or capture them: *a tiger hunt* **3** [C] (in Britain) an event at which people ride horses and hunt FOXES with dogs as a sport, illegal in the UK since 2005: *There will be a hunt on Boxing Day.* ◇ *a hunt meeting* **4** [C+sing./pl. v.] (in Britain) a group of people who regularly hunt FOXES as a sport: *There are several different hunts in the area.*

IDM **be in the 'hunt** to have a chance of winning: *The team are back in the hunt for the league title.*

hunt·ed /ˈhʌntɪd/ *adj.* (of an expression on sb's face) showing that sb is very worried or frightened, as if they are being followed or chased: *His eyes had a hunted look.*

hunt·er /ˈhʌntə(r)/ *noun* **1** a person who hunts wild animals for food or sport; an animal that hunts its food **2** (usually in compounds) a person who looks for and collects a particular kind of thing: *a bargain hunter* ➲ see also HEADHUNTER **3** (*BrE*) a fast strong horse used in hunting FOXES **4** (*NAmE*) a dog used in hunting

,hunter-'gather·er *noun* a member of a group of people who do not live in one place but move around and live by hunting, fishing and gathering plants

hunt·ing /ˈhʌntɪŋ/ *noun* [U] **1** chasing and killing wild animals and birds as a sport or for food: *to go hunting* ◇ *Since 1977 otter hunting has been illegal.* **2** (*BrE*) = FOX-HUNTING **3** (in compounds) the process of looking for sth: *We're going house-hunting at the weekend.* ◇ *How's the job-hunting going?*

'hunting ground *noun* **1** a place where people with a particular interest can easily find what they want: *Crowd-*

*ed markets are a **happy hunting ground** for pickpockets.* **2** a place where wild animals are hunted

hunt·ress /ˈhʌntrəs/ *noun* (*literary*) a woman who hunts wild animals

hunts·man /ˈhʌntsmən/ *noun* (*pl.* **-men** /-mən/) a man who hunts wild animals

hur·dle /ˈhɜːdl; *NAmE* ˈhɜːrdl/ *noun, verb*

■ ***noun* 1** each of a series of vertical frames that a person or horse jumps over in a race: *His horse fell at the final hurdle.* ◇ *to **clear a hurdle*** (= jump over it successfully) **2 hur·dles** [pl.] a race in which runners or horses have to jump over hurdles: *the 300 m hurdles* ⊃ VISUAL VOCAB page V38 **3** a problem or difficulty that must be solved or dealt with before you can achieve sth SYN **obstacle**: *The next hurdle will be getting her parents' agreement.*

■ ***verb* 1** [T, I] to jump over sth while you are running: **~ sth** *He hurdled two barriers to avoid reporters.* ◇ **~ over sth** *to hurdle over a fence* **2** [I] to run in a hurdles race

hurd·ler /ˈhɜːdlə(r); *NAmE* ˈhɜːrd-/ *noun* a person or horse that runs in races over hurdles

hurd·ling /ˈhɜːdlɪŋ; *NAmE* ˈhɜːrd-/ *noun* [U] the sport of racing over HURDLES ⊃ VISUAL VOCAB page V38

hurdy-gurdy /ˈhɜːdi gɜːdi; *NAmE* ˈhɜːrdi gɜːrdi/ *noun* (*pl.* **-ies**) a small musical instrument that is played by turning a handle with one hand and pressing keys with the other

hurl /hɜːl; *NAmE* hɜːrl/ *verb* **1** [T] **~ sth/sb + adv./prep.** to throw sth/sb violently in a particular direction: *He hurled a brick through the window.* ⊃ SYNONYMS at THROW **2** [T] **~ abuse, accusations, insults, etc.** (**at sb**) to shout insults, etc. at sb: *Rival fans hurled abuse at each other.* **3** [I] (*NAmE, slang*) to VOMIT

hurl·ing /ˈhɜːlɪŋ; *NAmE* ˈhɜːrlɪŋ/ *noun* [U] an Irish ball game similar to HOCKEY played by two teams of 15 boys or men ⊃ compare CAMOGIE

hurly-burly /ˈhɜːli bɜːli; *NAmE* ˈhɜːrli bɜːrli/ *noun* [U] a very noisy and busy activity or situation: *He enjoys the hurly-burly of political debate.*

hur·rah /həˈrɑː/ (*BrE* **hur·ray** /həˈreɪ/) *exclamation* = HOORAY

hur·ri·cane /ˈhʌrɪkən; *NAmE* ˈhɜːrəkən; -keɪn/ *noun* a violent storm with very strong winds, especially in the western Atlantic Ocean: *hurricane-force winds* ◇ *Hurricane Betty is now approaching the coast of Florida.* ⊃ COLLOCATIONS at WEATHER ⊃ compare CYCLONE, TYPHOON

ˈhurricane lamp *noun* a type of lamp with glass sides to protect the flame inside from the wind

hur·ried /ˈhʌrid; *NAmE* ˈhɜːr-/ *adj.* [usually before noun] done too quickly because you do not have enough time: *I ate a hurried breakfast and left.* SYN **rushed** OPP **unhurried** ▶ **hur·ried·ly** *adv.*: *I hurriedly got up and dressed.*

hurry 🔑 /ˈhʌri; *NAmE* ˈhɜːri/ *verb, noun*

■ ***verb*** (**hur·ries, hurry·ing, hur·ried, hur·ried**) **1** 🔑 [I] to do sth more quickly than usual because there is not much time SYN **rush**: *You'll have to hurry if you want to catch that train.* ◇ *The kids hurried to open their presents.* HELP In spoken English **hurry** can be used with **and** plus another verb, instead of with **to** and the infinitive, especially to tell somebody to do something quickly: *Hurry and open your present—I want to see what it is!* **2** 🔑 [I] **+ adv./prep.** to move quickly in a particular direction SYN **rush**: *He picked up his bags and hurried across the courtyard.* ◇ *She hurried away without saying goodbye.* **3** 🔑 [T] to make sb do sth more quickly SYN **rush**: **~ sb** *I don't want to hurry you but we close in twenty minutes.* ◇ **~ sb into doing sth** *She was hurried into making an unwise choice.* **4** [T] **~ sth + adv./prep.** to deal with sth quickly SYN **rush**: *Her application was hurried through.* **5** [T, usually passive] **~ sth** to do sth too quickly SYN **rush**: *A good meal should never be hurried.*

PHR V **ˌhurry ˈon** to continue speaking without giving anyone else time to say anything **ˌhurry ˈup** (**with sth**) 🔑 to do sth more quickly because there is not much time: *I wish the bus would hurry up and come.* ◇ *Hurry up! We're going to be late.* ◇ *Hurry up with the scissors. I need them.* **ˌhurry sb/sth↔ˈup** to make sb do sth more quickly; to make sth happen more quickly: *Can you do anything to hurry my order up?*

■ ***noun*** 🔑 [U, sing.] the need or wish to get sth done quickly: *Take your time—there's no hurry.* ◇ ***In my hurry to** leave, I forgot my passport.* ◇ ***What's the hurry?** The train doesn't leave for an hour.*

IDM **in a ˈhurry 1** 🔑 very quickly or more quickly than usual: *He had to leave in a hurry.* **2** 🔑 not having enough time to do sth: *Sorry, I haven't got time to do it now—I'm in a hurry.* ◇ *Alice was **in a tearing hurry** as usual.* **in a ˈhurry to do sth** impatient to do sth: *My daughter is in such a hurry to grow up.* ◇ *Why are you in such a hurry to sell?* **in no ˈhurry** (**to do sth**) | **not in a/any ˈhurry** (**to do sth**) **1** having plenty of time: *I don't mind waiting—I'm not in any particular hurry.* **2** not wanting or not willing to do sth: *We were in no hurry to get back to work after the holiday.* **sb will not do sth again in a ˈhurry** (*informal*) used to say that sb does not want to do sth again because it was not enjoyable: *I won't be going there again in a hurry—the food was terrible.*

Synonyms

hurt

ache • burn • sting • tingle • itch • throb

These are all words that can be used when part of your body feels painful.

hurt (of part of your body) to feel painful; (of an action) to cause pain: *My feet hurt.* ◇ *Ouch! That hurt!*

ache to feel a continuous dull pain: *I'm aching all over.*

burn (of part of your body) to feel very hot and painful: *Our eyes were burning from the chemicals in the air.*

sting to make sb feel a sharp burning pain or uncomfortable feeling in part of their body; (of part of your body) to feel this pain: *My eyes were stinging from the smoke.*

tingle (of part of your body) to feel as if a lot of small sharp points are pushing into the skin there: *The cold air made her face tingle.*

itch to have an uncomfortable feeling on your skin that makes you want to scratch; to make your skin feel like this: *I itch all over.* ◇ *Does the rash itch?*

throb (of part of your body) to feel pain as a series of regular beats: *His head throbbed painfully.*

PATTERNS

- your **eyes** hurt/ache/burn/sting/itch
- your **skin** hurts/burns/stings/tingles/itches
- your **flesh** hurts/burns/stings/tingles
- your **head** hurts/aches/throbs
- your **stomach** hurts/aches
- to **really** hurt/ache/burn/sting/tingle/itch/throb
- to hurt/ache/sting/itch **badly/a lot**
- **It** hurts/stings/tingles/itches.

hurt 🔑 /hɜːt; *NAmE* hɜːrt/ *verb, adj., noun*

■ ***verb*** (**hurt, hurt**) **1** 🔑 [T, I] **~** (**sb/sth/yourself**) to cause physical pain to sb/yourself; to injure sb/yourself: *He hurt his back playing squash.* ◇ *Did you hurt yourself?* ◇ *Stop it. You're hurting me.* ◇ *My back is really hurting me today.* ◇ *My shoes hurt—they're too tight.* ⊃ SYNONYMS at INJURE ⊃ COLLOCATIONS at INJURY **2** 🔑 [I] to feel painful: *My feet hurt.* ◇ *Ouch! That hurt!* ◇ ***It hurts** when I bend my knee.* **3** 🔑 [I, T] to make sb unhappy or upset: *What really hurt was that he never answered my letter.* ◇ **~ sb/sth** *I'm sorry, I didn't mean to hurt you.* ◇ *I didn't want to **hurt his feelings**.* ◇ **it hurts** (**sb**) **to do sth** *It hurt me to think that he would lie to me.* **4** [I] **be hurting** (*informal*) to feel unhappy or upset: *I know you're hurting and I want to help you.* **5** [T] **~ sb/sth** to have a bad effect on sb/sth: *Many people on low incomes will be hurt by the government's plans.* ⊃ SYNONYMS at DAMAGE **6** [I] **be hurting** (**for sth**) (*NAmE*) to be in a

H

difficult situation because you need sth, especially money: *His campaign is already hurting for money.*

IDM **it won't/wouldn't 'hurt (sb/sth) (to do sth)** used to say that sb should do a particular thing: *It wouldn't hurt you to help with the housework occasionally.* ➲ more at FLY *n.*, HIT *v.*

■ ***adj.*** **1** injured physically: *None of the passengers were **badly hurt**.* OPP **unhurt** **2** upset and offended by sth that sb has said or done: *a **hurt look/expression*** ◇ *She was **deeply hurt** that she had not been invited.* ◇ *Martha's hurt pride showed in her eyes.*

■ ***noun*** [U, sing.] (rather *informal*) a feeling of unhappiness because sb has been unkind or unfair to you: *There was hurt and real anger in her voice.* ◇ *It was a hurt that would take a long time to heal.*

hurt·ful /ˈhɜːtfl; *NAmE* ˈhɜːrtfl/ *adj.* (of comments) making you feel upset and offended SYN **unkind**: *I cannot forget the hurtful things he said.* ◇ **~ to sb** *The bad reviews of her new book were very hurtful to her.* ▶ **hurt·ful·ly** /-fəli/ *adv.*: *He said, rather hurtfully, that he had better things to do than come and see me.*

H

hur·tle /ˈhɜːtl; *NAmE* ˈhɜːrtl/ *verb* [I] **+ adv./prep.** to move very fast in a particular direction: *A runaway car **came hurtling** towards us.*

hus·band /ˈhʌzbənd/ *noun, verb*

■ ***noun*** (also *informal* **hubby**) the man that a woman is married to; a married man: *This is my husband, Steve.* ➲ COLLOCATIONS at MARRIAGE

IDM **ˌhusband and ˈwife** a man and woman who are married to each other: *They lived together as husband and wife* (= as if they were married) *for years.* ◇ *a husband-and-wife team*

■ ***verb*** **~ sth** (*formal*) to use sth very carefully and make sure that you do not waste it

hus·band·ry /ˈhʌzbəndri/ *noun* **1** farming, especially when done carefully and well: ***animal/crop husbandry*** **2** (*old-fashioned*) the careful use of food, money and supplies

hush /hʌʃ/ *verb, noun*

■ ***verb*** **1** [I] (used especially in orders) to be quiet; to stop talking or crying: *Hush now and try to sleep.* **2** [T] **~ sb/sth** to make sb/sth become quieter; to make sb stop talking, crying, etc.

PHR V **ˌhush sth↔ˈup** to hide information about a situation because you do not want people to know about it: *He claimed that the whole affair had been hushed up by the council.*

■ ***noun*** [sing., U] a period of silence, especially following a lot of noise, or when people are expecting sth to happen: *There was **a deathly hush** in the theatre.* ◇ ***A hush descended** over the waiting crowd.* ◇ (*BrE, informal*) ***Can we have a bit of hush?*** (= please be quiet)

hushed /hʌʃt/ *adj.* **1** (of a place) quiet because nobody is talking; much quieter than usual: *A hushed courtroom listened as the boy gave evidence.* **2** [usually before noun] (of voices) speaking very quietly: *a hushed whisper*

ˌhush-ˈhush *adj.* (*informal*) secret and not known about by many people: *Their wedding was very hush-hush.*

ˈhush money *noun* [U] money that is paid to sb to prevent them from giving other people information that could be embarrassing or damaging

ˈhush puppy *noun* a small fried cake made of CORNMEAL, eaten especially in the southern US

husk /hʌsk/ *noun, verb*

■ ***noun*** the dry outer covering of nuts, fruits and seeds, especially of grain

■ ***verb*** **~ sth** to remove the husks from grain, seeds, nuts, etc.

husky /ˈhʌski/ *adj., noun*

■ ***adj.*** (**husk·ier**, **husk·iest**) **1** (of a person or their voice) sounding deep, quiet and rough, sometimes in an attractive way: *She spoke in a husky whisper.* **2** (*NAmE*) (of a man) big, strong and sexually attractive ▶ **husk·ily** *adv.* **huski·ness** *noun* [U]

■ ***noun*** (*NAmE* also **huskie**) (*pl.* **-ies**) a large strong dog with thick hair, used for pulling SLEDGES across snow

hus·sar /həˈzɑː(r)/ *noun* (in the past) a CAVALRY soldier who carried light weapons

hussy /ˈhʌsi/ *noun* (*pl.* **-ies**) (*old-fashioned, disapproving*) a girl or woman who behaves in a way that is considered shocking or morally wrong

hust·ings /ˈhʌstɪŋz/ *noun* **the hustings** [pl.] (*especially BrE*) the political meetings, speeches, etc. that take place in the period before an election: *Most candidates will be out **on the hustings** this week.*

hus·tle /ˈhʌsl/ *verb, noun*

■ ***verb*** **1** [T] **~ sb + adv./prep.** to make sb move quickly by pushing them in a rough aggressive way: *He grabbed her arm and hustled her out of the room.* **2** [T] **~ sb (into sth)** to force sb to make a decision before they are ready or sure **3** [T, I] **~ (sth)** (*informal, especially NAmE*) to sell or obtain sth, often illegally: *to hustle dope* ◇ *They survive by hustling on the streets.* **4** [I] (*NAmE, informal*) to act in an aggressive way or with a lot of energy **5** [I] (*NAmE*) to work as a PROSTITUTE

■ ***noun*** [U] busy noisy activity of a lot of people in one place: *We escaped from the **hustle and bustle** of the city for the weekend.*

hust·ler /ˈhʌslə(r)/ *noun* (*informal*) **1** (*especially NAmE*) a person who tries to trick sb into giving them money **2** (*NAmE*) a PROSTITUTE

hut /hʌt/ *noun* a small, simply built house or shelter: *a beach hut* ◇ *a wooden hut* ➲ VISUAL VOCAB page V13

hutch /hʌtʃ/ *noun* **1** a wooden box with a front made of wire, used for keeping RABBITS or other small animals in **2** (*NAmE*) a large piece of wooden furniture with shelves in the top part and cupboards below, used for displaying and storing cups, plates, etc.

hwyl /ˈhɔɪl/ *noun* [U] (*WelshE*) a strong feeling of emotion and enthusiasm

hya·cinth /ˈhaɪəsɪnθ/ *noun* a plant with a mass of small blue, white or pink flowers with a sweet smell that grow closely together around a thick STEM

hy·aena = HYENA

hy·brid /ˈhaɪbrɪd/ *noun* **1** an animal or plant that has parents of different SPECIES or varieties: *A mule is a hybrid of a male donkey and a female horse.* ➲ compare CROSS-BREED **2 ~ (between/of A and B)** something that is the product of mixing two or more different things SYN **mixture**: *The music was a hybrid of Western pop and traditional folk song.* **3** a vehicle that uses two different types of power, especially petrol/gas or DIESEL and electricity ➲ VISUAL VOCAB page V7 ▶ **hy·brid** *adj.*: *a hybrid car/vehicle*

hy·brid·ize (*BrE* also **-ise**) /ˈhaɪbrɪdaɪz/ *verb* [I, T] **~ (sth)** (*technical*) if an animal or a plant **hybridizes** or **is hybridized** with an animal or a plant of another SPECIES, they join together to produce a hybrid ▶ **hy·brid·iza·tion**, **-isa·tion** /ˌhaɪbrɪdaɪˈzeɪʃn; *NAmE* -dəˈzeɪ-/ *noun* [U]

hydel /ˈhaɪdel/ *abbr.* (*IndE*) HYDROELECTRIC

hydra /ˈhaɪdrə/ *noun* **1 Hydra** (in ancient Greek stories) a snake with several heads. As one head was cut off, another one grew. In the end it was killed by Hercules. **2** (*formal*) a thing that is very difficult to deal with, because it continues for a long time or because it has many different aspects **3** (*biology*) an extremely small water creature with a tube-shaped body and TENTACLES around its mouth

hy·dran·gea /haɪˈdreɪndʒə/ *noun* a bush with white, pink or blue flowers that grow closely together in the shape of a large ball

hy·drant /ˈhaɪdrənt/ *noun* = FIRE HYDRANT

hy·drate /ˈhaɪdreɪt; haɪˈdreɪt/ *verb* **~ sth** (*technical*) to make sth absorb water ▶ **hy·dra·tion** /haɪˈdreɪʃn/ *noun* [U] ➲ compare DEHYDRATE

hy·draul·ic /haɪˈdrɔːlɪk; *BrE* also -ˈdrɒl-/ *adj.* [usually before noun] **1** (of water, oil, etc.) moved through pipes, etc. under pressure: *hydraulic fluid* **2** (of a piece of machinery) operated by liquid moving under pressure: *hydraulic brakes* **3** connected with hydraulic systems: *hydraulic engineering* ▶ **hy·draul·ic·al·ly** /-kli/ *adv.*: *hydraulically operated doors*

hy·draul·ics /haɪˈdrɔːlɪks; *BrE* also -ˈdrɒl-/ *noun* **1** [pl.] machinery that works by the use of liquid moving under pressure **2** [U] the science of the use of liquids moving under pressure

hydr(o)- /ˈhaɪdr(əʊ); *NAmE* -dr(oʊ)/ *combining form* (in nouns, adjectives and adverbs) **1** connected with water **2** (*chemistry*) combined with HYDROGEN

hydro /ˈhaɪdrəʊ; *NAmE* -droʊ/ *noun* [U] (*CanE*) electricity: *to pay your hydro bill*

hydro·car·bon /ˌhaɪdrəˈkɑːbən; *NAmE* -ˈkɑːrb-/ *noun* (*chemistry*) a chemical made up of HYDROGEN and CARBON only. There are many different hydrocarbons found in petrol/gas, coal and natural gas.

hydro·chlor·ic acid /ˌhaɪdrəˌklɒrɪk ˈæsɪd; *NAmE* -ˌklɔːr-/ *noun* [U] (*chemistry*) (*symb.* **HCl**) an acid containing HYDROGEN and CHLORINE

hydro·chloro·fluoro·carbon /ˌhaɪdrəʊklɒrəʊˈflʊərəkɑːbən; *NAmE* ˌhaɪdroʊklɔːroʊˈflʊrəkɑːrbən/ *noun* (*chemistry*) = HCFC

hydro·cor·ti·sone /ˌhaɪdrəˈkɔːtɪzəʊn; *NAmE* -ˈkɔːrtɪzoʊn/ *noun* [U] a HORMONE produced in the body that is used in drugs to help with diseases of the skin and muscles

hydro·elec·tric /ˌhaɪdrəʊɪˈlektrɪk; *NAmE* ˌhaɪdroʊ-/ *adj.* using the power of water to produce electricity; produced by the power of water: *a hydroelectric plant* ◇ *hydroelectric power* ➲ VISUAL VOCAB page V7 ▶ **hydro·elec·tri·city** /-ɪˌlekˈtrɪsəti/ *noun* [U]

hydro·fluoro·car·bon /ˌhaɪdrəʊˈflʊərəʊkɑːbən; *NAmE* ˌhaɪdroʊˈflʊroʊkɑːrbən/ *noun* (*chemistry*) = HFC

hydro·foil /ˈhaɪdrəfɔɪl/ *noun* a boat which rises above the surface of the water when it is travelling fast ➲ VISUAL VOCAB page V44 ➲ compare HOVERCRAFT

hydro·gen /ˈhaɪdrədʒən/ *noun* [U] (*symb.* **H**) a chemical element. Hydrogen is a gas that is the lightest of all the elements. It combines with OXYGEN to form water.

hy·dro·gen·ated /haɪˈdrɒdʒəneɪtɪd; *NAmE* -ˈdrɑːdʒ-/ *adj.* (*chemistry*) **hydrogenated** oils have had hydrogen added to them

ˈhydrogen bomb (also **ˈH-bomb**) *noun* a very powerful nuclear bomb

ˌhydrogen peˈroxide *noun* [U] (*symb.* H_2O_2) (*chemistry*) = PEROXIDE

hy·drol·ogy /haɪˈdrɒlədʒi; *NAmE* -ˈdrɑːl-/ *noun* [U] (*technical*) the scientific study of the earth's water, especially its movement in relation to land

hy·droly·sis /haɪˈdrɒlɪsɪs; *NAmE* -ˈdrɑːl-/ *noun* [U] (*chemistry*) a reaction with water which causes a COMPOUND to separate into its parts

hydro·pho·bia /ˌhaɪdrəˈfəʊbiə; *NAmE* -ˈfoʊbiə/ *noun* [U] extreme fear of water, which happens with RABIES infection in humans ▶ **hydro·pho·bic** /ˌhaɪdrəˈfəʊbɪk; *NAmE* -ˈfoʊ-/ *adj.*

hydro·plane /ˈhaɪdrəpleɪn/ *noun, verb*

■ ***noun* 1** a light boat with an engine and a flat bottom, designed to travel fast over the surface of water **2** (*NAmE*) = SEAPLANE

■ ***verb* 1** (*NAmE*) (*BrE* **aqua·plane**) (of a motor vehicle) to slide out of control on a wet road **2** (of a boat) to travel fast over the surface of the water

hydro·plan·ing /ˈhaɪdrəpleɪnɪŋ/ (*NAmE*) (*BrE* **aqua·plan·ing**) *noun* [U] the fact of a vehicle sliding on a wet surface, so that it is out of control

hydro·pon·ics /ˌhaɪdrəˈpɒnɪks; *NAmE* -ˈpɑːn-/ *noun* [U] the process of growing plants in water or sand, rather than in soil

hydro·speed /ˈhaɪdrəʊspiːd; *NAmE* -droʊ-/ (*BrE* also **hydro·speed·ing**) *noun* [U] the sport of jumping into a river that is flowing fast, wearing equipment that allows you to float

hydro·ther·apy /ˌhaɪdrəʊˈθerəpi; *NAmE* ˌhaɪdroʊ-/ *noun* [U] the treatment of disease or injury by doing physical exercises in water

hy·drox·ide /haɪˈdrɒksaɪd; *NAmE* -ˈdrɑːks-/ *noun* (*chemistry*) a chemical consisting of a metal and a combination of OXYGEN and HYDROGEN

hyena (also **hy·aena**) /haɪˈiːnə/ *noun* a wild animal like a dog, that eats the meat of animals that are already dead and has a cry like a human laugh. Hyenas live in Africa and Asia.

hy·giene /ˈhaɪdʒiːn/ *noun* [U] the practice of keeping yourself and your living and working areas clean in order to prevent illness and disease: *food hygiene* ◇ *personal hygiene* ◇ *In the interests of hygiene, please wash your hands.*

hy·gien·ic /haɪˈdʒiːnɪk; *NAmE* usually -ˈdʒen-/ *adj.* clean and free of bacteria and therefore unlikely to spread disease: *Food must be prepared in hygienic conditions.* **OPP** **unhygienic** ▶ **hy·gien·ic·al·ly** /-kli/ *adv.*: *Medical supplies are disposed of hygienically.*

hy·gien·ist /haɪˈdʒiːnɪst/ (also **ˈdental hygienist** especially in *NAmE*) *noun* a person who works with a dentist and whose job is to clean people's teeth and give them advice about keeping them clean

hymen /ˈhaɪmən/ *noun* (*anatomy*) a piece of skin that partly covers the opening of the VAGINA in women who have never had sex

hymn /hɪm/ *noun* **1** a song of praise, especially one praising God and sung by Christians **2** [usually sing.] if a film/movie, book, etc. is a **hymn to sth**, it praises it very strongly **IDM** see SING *v.*

ˈhymn book (also *old-fashioned* **hym·nal** /ˈhɪmnəl/) *noun* a book of hymns

hype /haɪp/ *noun, verb*

■ ***noun*** [U] (*informal, disapproving*) advertisements and discussion on television, radio, etc. telling the public about a product and about how good or important it is: ***marketing/media hype*** ◇ *Don't believe all the hype—the book isn't that good.*

■ ***verb*** (*informal, disapproving*) to advertise sth a lot and exaggerate its good qualities, in order to get a lot of public attention for it: **~ sth** *This week his much hyped new movie opens in London.* ◇ **~ sth up** *The meeting was hyped up in the media as an important event.*

ˌhyped ˈup *adj.* (*informal*) (of a person) very worried or excited about sth that is going to happen

hyper /ˈhaɪpə(r)/ *adj.* (*informal*) excited and nervous; having too much nervous energy

hyper- /ˈhaɪpə(r)/ *prefix* (in adjectives and nouns) more than normal; too much: *hypercritical* ◇ *hypertension* ➲ compare HYPO-

hyper·active /ˌhaɪpərˈæktɪv/ *adj.* (especially of children and their behaviour) too active and only able to keep quiet and still for short periods ▶ **hyper·activ·ity** /ˌhaɪpərækˈtɪvəti/ *noun* [U]

hyper·bar·ic /ˌhaɪpəˈbærɪk; *NAmE* ˌhaɪpər-/ *adj.* (*physics*) (of gas) at a higher pressure than normal

hyper·bola /haɪˈpɜːbələ; *NAmE* -ˈpɜːr-/ *noun* (*pl.* **hyper·bolas** or **hyper·bolae** /-liː/) a SYMMETRICAL open curve ➲ VISUAL VOCAB page V58

hyper·bole /haɪˈpɜːbəli; *NAmE* -ˈpɜːrb-/ *noun* [U, C, usually sing.] a way of speaking or writing that makes sth sound better, more exciting, dangerous, etc. than it really is **SYN** **exaggeration**

hyper·bol·ic /ˌhaɪpəˈbɒlɪk; *NAmE* -pərˈbɑːl-/ *adj.* **1** (*mathematics*) of or related to a hyperbola **2** (of language) deliberately exaggerated; using hyperbole

hyper·cor·rec·tion /ˌhaɪpəkəˈrekʃn; *NAmE* -pərk-/ *noun* [U, C] (*linguistics*) the use of a wrong form or pronunciation of a word by sb who is trying to show that they can use language correctly. For example, the use of *I* instead of

H

me in the sentence 'They invited my husband and I to dinner'.

hyper·gly·caemia (*BrE*) (*NAmE* **hyper·gly·cemia**) /ˌhaɪpəglaɪˈsiːmiə; *NAmE* -pərg-/ *noun* [U] (*medical*) the condition of having too high a level of blood sugar

hyper·in·fla·tion /ˌhaɪpərɪnˈfleɪʃn/ *noun* [U] a situation in which prices rise very fast, causing damage to a country's economy

hyper·link /ˈhaɪpəlɪŋk; *NAmE* -pərl-/ (also **hot·link**) *noun* a place in an electronic document on a computer that is linked to another electronic document: *Click on the hyperlink.*

hyper·mar·ket /ˈhaɪpəmɑːkɪt; *NAmE* -pərmɑːrk-/ *noun* (*BrE*) a very large shop located outside a town, that sells a wide range of goods

hyper·media /ˌhaɪpəˈmiːdiə; *NAmE* -pərˈm-/ *noun* [U] (*computing*) a system that links text to files containing images, sound or video

H

hyper·nym /ˈhaɪpənɪm; *NAmE* -pərn-/ *noun* (*linguistics*) = SUPERORDINATE ➲ compare HYPONYM

hyper·sen·si·tive /ˌhaɪpəˈsensətɪv; *NAmE* -pərˈs-/ *adj.* ~ (**to sth**) **1** very easily offended: *He's hypersensitive to any kind of criticism.* **2** extremely physically sensitive to particular substances, medicines, light, etc: *Her skin is hypersensitive.* ▸ **hyper·sen·si·tiv·ity** /ˌhaɪpəˌsensəˈtɪvəti; *NAmE* -pərˌs-/ *noun* [U]

hyper·space /ˈhaɪpəspeɪs; *NAmE* -pərs-/ *noun* [U] **1** (*technical*) space which consists of more than three DIMENSIONS **2** (in stories) a situation in which it is possible to travel faster than light

hyper·ten·sion /ˌhaɪpəˈtenʃn; *NAmE* -pərˈt-/ *noun* [U] (*medical*) blood pressure that is higher than is normal

hyper·text /ˈhaɪpətekst; *NAmE* -pərt-/ *noun* [U] text stored in a computer system that contains links that allow the user to move from one piece of text or document to another ➲ see also HTML

hyper·thy·roid·ism /ˌhaɪpəˈθaɪrɔɪdɪzəm; *NAmE* -pərˈθ-/ *noun* [U] (*medical*) a condition in which the THYROID is too active, making the heart and other body systems function too quickly

hyper·trophy /haɪˈpɜːtrəfi; *NAmE* -ˈpɜːrt-/ *noun* [U] (*biology*) an increase in the size of an organ or TISSUE because its cells grow in size

hyper·ven·ti·late /ˌhaɪpəˈventɪleɪt; *NAmE* -pərˈv-/ *verb* [I] (*technical*) to breathe too quickly because you are very frightened or excited ▸ **hyper·ven·ti·la·tion** /ˌhaɪpəˌventɪˈleɪʃn; *NAmE* -pərˌven-/ *noun* [U]

hy·phen /ˈhaɪfn/ *noun* the mark (-) used to join two words together to make a new one, as in *back-up*, or to show that a word has been divided between the end of one line and the beginning of the next ➲ compare DASH

hy·phen·ate /ˈhaɪfəneɪt/ *verb* ~ **sth** to join two words together using a hyphen; to divide a word between two lines of text using a hyphen: *Is your name hyphenated?* ▸ **hy·phen·ation** /ˌhaɪfəˈneɪʃn/ *noun* [U]: *hyphenation rules*

hyp·no·sis /hɪpˈnəʊsɪs; *NAmE* -ˈnoʊ-/ *noun* [U] **1** an unconscious state in which sb can still see and hear and can be influenced to follow commands or answer questions: *She only remembered details of the accident* ***under hypnosis***. **2** = HYPNOTISM: *He uses hypnosis as part of the treatment.* ◇ *Hypnosis helped me give up smoking.*

hypno·ther·apy /ˌhɪpnəʊˈθerəpi; *NAmE* ˌhɪpnoʊ-/ *noun* [U] a kind of treatment that uses HYPNOSIS to help with physical or emotional problems

hyp·not·ic /hɪpˈnɒtɪk; *NAmE* -ˈnɑːt-/ *adj., noun*
■ ***adj.*** **1** making you feel as if you are going to fall asleep, especially because of a regular, repeated noise or movement SYN **mesmerizing, soporific**: *hypnotic music* ◇ *His voice had an almost hypnotic effect.* **2** [only before noun] connected with or produced by hypnosis: *a* ***hypnotic trance/state*** **3** (of a drug) making you sleep
■ ***noun*** (*technical*) a drug that makes you sleep; a SLEEPING PILL

hyp·no·tism /ˈhɪpnətɪzəm/ (also **hyp·no·sis**) *noun* [U] the practice of HYPNOTIZING a person (= putting them into an unconscious state)

hyp·no·tist /ˈhɪpnətɪst/ *noun* a person who hypnotizes people

hyp·no·tize (*BrE* also **-ise**) /ˈhɪpnətaɪz/ *verb* **1** ~ **sb** to produce a state of HYPNOSIS in sb **2** [usually passive] ~ **sb** (*formal*) to interest sb so much that they can think of nothing else SYN **mesmerize**

hypo- /ˈhaɪpəʊ; *NAmE* -poʊ/ (also **hyp-**) *prefix* (in adjectives and nouns) under; below normal: *hypodermic* ◇ *hypothermia* ➲ compare HYPER-

hypo·allergen·ic /ˌhaɪpəʊˌæləˈdʒenɪk; *NAmE* ˌhaɪpoʊˌælər-/ *adj.* (*technical*) **hypoallergenic** substances and materials are unlikely to cause an ALLERGIC reaction in the person who uses them

hypo·chon·dria /ˌhaɪpəˈkɒndriə; *NAmE* -ˈkɑːn-/ *noun* [U] a state in which sb worries all the time about their health and believes that they are ill/sick when there is nothing wrong with them

hypo·chon·driac /ˌhaɪpəˈkɒndriæk; *NAmE* -ˈkɑːn-/ *noun* a person who suffers from hypochondria: *Don't be such a hypochondriac!—there's nothing wrong with you.* ▸ **hypo·chon·driac** (also **hypo·chon·driacal** /ˌhaɪpəkɒnˈdraɪəkl; *NAmE* -ˌkɑːnˈd-/) *adj.*

hyp·oc·risy /hɪˈpɒkrəsi; *NAmE* hɪˈpɑːk-/ *noun* (*pl.* -**ies**) [U, C] (*disapproving*) behaviour in which sb pretends to have moral standards or opinions that they do not actually have: *He condemned the hypocrisy of those politicians who do one thing and say another.*

hypo·crite /ˈhɪpəkrɪt/ *noun* (*disapproving*) a person who pretends to have moral standards or opinions that they do not actually have ▸ **hypo·crit·ical** /ˌhɪpəˈkrɪtɪkl/ *adj.*: *It would be hypocritical of me to have a church wedding when I don't believe in God.* **hypo·crit·ic·al·ly** /-kli/ *adv.*

hypo·der·mic /ˌhaɪpəˈdɜːmɪk; *NAmE* -ˈdɜːrm-/ (also ˌ**hypodermic ˈneedle**, ˌ**hypodermic syˈringe**) *noun* a medical instrument with a long thin needle that is used to give sb an INJECTION under their skin ▸ **hypo·der·mic** *adj.*: *a hypodermic injection* (= one under the skin)

hypo·gly·caemia (*BrE*) (*NAmE* **hypo·gly·cemia**) /ˌhaɪpəʊglaɪˈsiːmiə; *NAmE* -poʊg-/ *noun* [U] (*medical*) the condition of having too low a level of blood sugar

hypo·nym /ˈhaɪpənɪm/ *noun* (*linguistics*) a word with a particular meaning that is included in the meaning of a more general word, for example 'dog' and 'cat' are **hyponyms** of 'animal' ➲ compare SUPERORDINATE

hypo·taxis /ˌhaɪpəʊˈtæksɪs; *NAmE* -poʊ-/ *noun* [U] (*grammar*) the use of SUBORDINATE CLAUSES ➲ compare PARATAXIS

hypot·en·use /haɪˈpɒtənjuːz; *NAmE* -ˈpɑːtənuːs; -njuːz/ *noun* (*geometry*) the side opposite the RIGHT ANGLE of a RIGHT-ANGLED triangle ➲ **VISUAL VOCAB** page V58

hypo·thal·amus /ˌhaɪpəˈθæləməs/ *noun* (*anatomy*) an area in the central lower part of the brain that controls body temperature, HUNGER, and the release of HORMONES

hypo·ther·mia /ˌhaɪpəˈθɜːmiə; *NAmE* -ˈθɜːrm-/ *noun* [U] a medical condition in which the body temperature is much lower than normal

hy·poth·esis AW /haɪˈpɒθəsɪs; *NAmE* -ˈpɑːθ-/ *noun* (*pl.* **hy·poth·eses** /-siːz/) **1** [C] an idea or explanation of sth that is based on a few known facts but that has not yet been proved to be true or correct SYN **theory**: ***to formulate/confirm a hypothesis*** ◇ *a hypothesis about the function of dreams* ➲ **COLLOCATIONS** at SCIENTIFIC **2** [U] guesses and ideas that are not based on certain knowledge SYN **speculation**: *It would be pointless to engage in hypothesis before we have the facts.*

hy·pothe·size (*BrE* also **-ise**) **AW** /haɪˈpɒθəsaɪz; *NAmE* -ˈpɑːθ-/ *verb* [T, I] **~ (sth)** | **~ that...** (*formal*) to suggest a way of explaining sth when you do not definitely know about it; to form a hypothesis: *The causes can be hypothesized but not proved.* ◇ *We can only hypothesize that the cases we know about are typical.*

hypo·thet·ic·al **AW** /ˌhaɪpəˈθetɪkl/ *adj.* based on situations or ideas which are possible and imagined rather than real and true: *a **hypothetical question/situation/example*** ◇ *Let us take the hypothetical case of Sheila, a mother of two...* ◇ *I wasn't asking about anybody in particular—it was a **purely hypothetical** question.* ▶ **hypo·thet·ic·al·ly** **AW** /-kli/ *adv.*

hypo·thy·roid·ism /ˌhaɪpəʊˈθaɪrɔɪdɪzəm; *NAmE* -poʊ-/ *noun* [U] (*medical*) a condition in which the THYROID is not active enough, making growth and mental development slower than normal

hyp·ox·aemia (*BrE*) (*NAmE* **hyp·ox·emia**) /ˌhaɪpɒkˈsiːmiə; *NAmE* -pɑːk-/ *noun* [U] (*medical*) a lower than normal amount of OXYGEN in the blood

hyp·oxia /haɪˈpɒksiə; *NAmE* -ˈpɑːk-/ *noun* [U] (*medical*) a condition in which not enough OXYGEN reaches the body's TISSUES

hys·ter·ec·tomy /ˌhɪstəˈrektəmi/ *noun* (*pl.* -ies) [C, U] a medical operation to remove a woman's WOMB

hys·teria /hɪˈstɪəriə; *NAmE* -ˈstɪr-/ *noun* [U] **1** a state of extreme excitement, fear or anger in which a person, or a group of people, loses control of their emotions and starts to cry, laugh, etc: *There was **mass hysteria** when the band came on stage.* ◇ *A note of hysteria crept into her voice.* **2** (*disapproving*) an extremely excited and exaggerated way of behaving or reacting to an event: *the usual media hysteria that surrounds royal visits* ◇ *public hysteria about AIDS* **3** (*medical*) a condition in which sb experiences violent or extreme emotions that they cannot control, especially as a result of shock

hys·ter·ic·al /hɪˈsterɪkl/ *adj.* **1** in a state of extreme excitement, and crying, laughing, etc. in an uncontrolled way: *hysterical screams* ◇ *a hysterical giggle* ◇ *He became almost hysterical when I told him.* ◇ *Let's not get hysterical.* ◇ (*disapproving*) *He thought I was being a hysterical female.* **2** (*informal*) extremely funny **SYN** **hilarious**: *She seemed to find my situation absolutely hysterical.* **HELP** Some speakers do not pronounce the 'h' at the beginning of **hysterical** and use 'an' instead of 'a' before it. This now sounds old-fashioned. ▶ **hys·ter·ic·al·ly** /-kli/ *adv.*: *to laugh/cry/scream/sob hysterically* ◇ *hysterically funny*

hys·ter·ics /hɪˈsterɪks/ *noun* [pl.] **1** an expression of extreme fear, excitement or anger that makes sb lose control of their emotions and cry, laugh, etc: *He went into hysterics when he heard the news.* **2** (*informal*) wild LAUGHTER: *She had the audience **in hysterics**.*

IDM **have hysterics** (*informal*) to be extremely upset and angry: *My mum'll have hysterics when she sees the colour of my hair.*

Hz *abbr.* (in writing) HERTZ

H

Ii

I 0-▬ /aɪ/ *noun, pron., symbol, abbr.*
■ ***noun*** (also **i**) [C, U] (*pl.* **Is, I's, i's** /aɪz/) the 9th letter of the English alphabet: *'Island' begins with (an) I/'I'.* IDM see DOT *v.*
■ ***pron.*** 0-▬ used as the subject of a verb when the speaker or writer is referring to himself/herself: *I think I'd better go now.* ◇ *He and I are old friends.* ◇ *When they asked me if I wanted the job, I said yes.* ◇ *I'm not going to fall, am I?* ◇ *I'm taller than her, aren't I?* ➲ see also ME
■ ***symbol*** (also **i**) the number 1 in ROMAN NUMERALS
■ ***abbr.*** (also **I.**) (especially on maps) Island(s); ISLE(S)

i- /aɪ/ *combining form* (in the names of products) (*computing*) INTERACTIVE (= allowing information to be passed continuously and in both directions between a computer and the person who uses it): *The i-writer teaches you how to plan and write essays.*

I-9 form /ˌaɪ ˈnaɪn fɔːm; *NAmE* fɔːrm/ *noun* (*US*) an official document that an employer must have which shows that an employee has the right to work in the US

-ial *suffix* (in adjectives) typical of: *dictatorial* ▶ **-ially** (in adverbs): *officially*

iam·bic /aɪˈæmbɪk/ *adj.* (*technical*) (of rhythm in poetry) in which one weak or short syllable is followed by one strong or long syllable: *a poem written in* ***iambic pentameters*** (= in lines of ten syllables, five short and five long)

iam·bus /aɪˈæmbəs/ *noun* (*pl.* **iambi** /-baɪ/, **iam·buses**) (also **iamb** /ˈaɪæm; ˈaɪæmb/) (*technical*) a unit of sound in poetry consisting of one weak or short syllable followed by one strong or long syllable

-ian, -an *suffix* **1** (in nouns and adjectives) from; typical of: *Bostonian* ◇ *Brazilian* ◇ *Shakespearian* ◇ *Libran* **2** (in nouns) a specialist in: *mathematician*

-iana, -ana *suffix* (in nouns) a collection of objects, facts, stories, etc. connected with the person, place, period, etc. mentioned: *Mozartiana* ◇ *Americana* ◇ *Victoriana*

IB /ˌaɪ ˈbiː/ *abbr.* INTERNATIONAL BACCALAUREATE: *to do the IB*

Iber·ian /aɪˈbɪəriən; *NAmE* -ˈbɪr-/ *adj.* relating to Spain and Portugal: *the Iberian peninsula*

ibex /ˈaɪbeks/ *noun* (*pl.* **ibex**) a mountain GOAT with long curved horns

ibid. (also **ib.**) *abbr.* in the same book or piece of writing as the one that has just been mentioned (from Latin 'ibidem')

-ibility ➲ -ABLE

ibis /ˈaɪbɪs/ *noun* (*pl.* **ibises**) a bird with a long neck, long legs and a long beak that curves downwards, that lives near water

-ible, -ibly ➲ -ABLE, -ABLY

Ibo /ˈiːbəʊ; *NAmE* ˈiːboʊ/ *noun* = IGBO

ibu·profen /ˌaɪbjuːˈprəʊfen; *NAmE* -ˈproʊ-/ *noun* [U] a drug used to reduce pain and INFLAMMATION

-ic *suffix* **1** (in adjectives and nouns) connected with: *scenic* ◇ *economic* ◇ *Arabic* **2** (in adjectives) that performs the action mentioned: *horrific* ◇ *specific* ▶ **-ical** (in adjectives): *comical* **-ically** (in adverbs): *physically*

ice 0-▬ /aɪs/ *noun, verb*
■ ***noun*** **1** 0-▬ [U] water that has frozen and become solid: *There was ice on the windows.* ◇ *The lake was covered with a* ***sheet of ice****.* ◇ *My hands are as cold as ice.* ➲ VISUAL VOCAB page V4 ➲ see also ICY, BLACK ICE, DRY ICE **2** [sing.] (usually **the ice**) a frozen surface that people SKATE on: *The dancers came out onto the ice.* ◇ *Both teams are on the ice, waiting for the whistle.* **3** 0-▬ [U] a piece of ice used to keep food and drinks cold: *I'll have lemonade please—no ice.* **4** [C] (*old-fashioned, especially BrE*) an ice cream **5** [U] (*NAmE*) a type of sweet food that consists of ice that has been crushed and flavoured
IDM **break the ˈice** to say or do sth that makes people feel more relaxed, especially at the beginning of a meeting, party, etc. ➲ see also ICEBREAKER (2) **cut no ˈice (with sb)** to have no influence or effect on sb: *His excuses cut no ice with me.* **on ˈice** **1** (of wine, etc.) kept cold by being surrounded by ice **2** (of a plan, etc.) not being dealt with now; waiting to be dealt with at a later time: *We've had to* ***put*** *our plans* ***on ice*** *for the time being.* **3** (of entertainment, etc.) performed by SKATERS on an ICE RINK: *Cinderella on ice* ➲ more at THIN *adj.*
■ ***verb*** **~ sth** to cover a cake with ICING
PHR V **ˌice ˈover/ˈup** | **ˌice sth↔ˈover/ˈup** to cover sth with ice; to become covered with ice

ˈice age (often **the Ice Age**) *noun* one of the long periods of time, thousands of years ago, when much of the earth's surface was covered in ice

ˈice axe (*BrE*) (*US* usually **ˈice ax**) *noun* a tool used by people climbing mountains for cutting steps into ice ➲ picture at AXE

ice·berg /ˈaɪsbɜːg; *NAmE* -bɜːrg/ *noun* an extremely large mass of ice floating in the sea IDM see TIP *n.*

ˌiceberg ˈlettuce *noun* a type of LETTUCE (= a salad vegetable) with crisp pale green leaves that form a tight ball

ice·block /ˈaɪsblɒk; *NAmE* -blɑːk/ *noun* (*AustralE, NZE*) a piece of flavoured ice on a stick

ˌice-ˈblue *adj.* (especially of eyes) very pale blue in colour

ˈice-bound *adj.* surrounded by or covered in ice

ice·box /ˈaɪsbɒks; *NAmE* -bɑːks/ *noun* (*old-fashioned, especially US*) = FRIDGE

ice·break·er /ˈaɪsbreɪkə(r)/ *noun* **1** a strong ship designed to break a way through ice, for example in the Arctic or Antarctic **2** a thing that you do or say, like a game or a joke, to make people feel less nervous when they first meet

ˈice bucket *noun* a container filled with ice and used for keeping bottles of wine, etc. cold

ˈice cap *noun* a layer of ice permanently covering parts of the earth, especially around the North and South Poles

ˌice-ˈcold *adj.* **1** as cold as ice; very cold: *ice-cold beer* ◇ *My hands were ice-cold.* **2** not having or showing any emotion: *His eyes had grown ice-cold.*

ˌice ˈcream 0-▬ (also **ˈice cream** especially in *NAmE*) *noun* [U, C]
a type of sweet frozen food made from milk fat, flavoured with fruit, chocolate, etc. and often eaten as a DESSERT; a small amount of this food intended for one person, often served in a container made of biscuit that is shaped like a CONE: *Desserts are served with cream or ice cream.* ◇ *Who wants an ice cream?*

ˈice cube *noun* a small, usually square, piece of ice used for making drinks cold

iced /aɪst/ *adj.* **1** (of drinks) made very cold; containing ice: *iced coffee/tea* **2** (of a cake, etc.) covered with ICING: *an iced cake*

ˈice dancing (also **ˈice dance**) *noun* [U] the sport of dancing on ice ▶ **ˈice dancer** *noun*

ˌiced ˈwater (*BrE*) (*NAmE* **ˈice water**) *noun* water with ice in it for drinking

ˈice field *noun* a large area of ice, especially one near the North or South Pole

ˈice floe (also **floe**) *noun* a large area of ice, floating in the sea

ˈice hockey (*BrE*) (*NAmE* **hockey**) *noun* [U] a game played on ice, in which players use long sticks to hit a hard rubber disc (called a PUCK) into the other team's goal ➲ VISUAL VOCAB page V36

ˈice house *noun* a building for storing ice in, especially in the past, usually underground or partly underground

ˌice ˈlolly (also *informal* **lolly**) (both *BrE*) (*NAmE* **Popsicle™**) *noun* a piece of ice flavoured with fruit, served on a stick

'ice pack *noun* a plastic container filled with ice that is used to cool parts of the body that are injured, etc.

'ice pick *noun* a tool with a very sharp point for breaking ice with

'ice rink (also **'skating rink, rink**) *noun* a specially prepared flat surface of ice, where you can ice-skate; a building where there is an ice rink ➲ VISUAL VOCAB pages V34, V36

'ice sheet *noun* (*technical*) a layer of ice that covers a large area of land for a long period of time

'ice shelf *noun* (*technical*) a layer of ice that is attached to land and covers a large area of sea

'ice skate (also **skate**) *noun* a boot with a thin metal blade on the bottom, that is used for SKATING on ice ➲ VISUAL VOCAB page V36

'ice-skate *verb* [I] to SKATE on ice ▸ **'ice skater** *noun*

'ice skating *noun* [U] = SKATING: *to go ice skating* ➲ VISUAL VOCAB page V34

'ice water (*NAmE*) (*BrE* **,iced 'water**) *noun* water with ice in it for drinking

icicle /'aɪsɪkl/ *noun* a pointed piece of ice that is formed when water freezes as it falls down from sth such as a roof

icily /'aɪsɪli/ *adv.* said or done in a very unfriendly way: *'I have nothing to say to you,' she said icily.*

icing /'aɪsɪŋ/ (*especially BrE*) (*NAmE* usually **frost·ing**) *noun* [U] a sweet mixture of sugar and water, milk, butter or egg white that is used to cover and decorate cakes ➲ see also ROYAL ICING

IDM **the icing on the 'cake**; (*US* also) **the frosting on the 'cake** something extra and not essential that is added to an already good situation or experience and that makes it even better

'icing sugar (*BrE*) (*US* **con'fectioner's sugar, 'powdered sugar**) *noun* [U] fine white powder made from sugar, that is mixed with water to make icing

icky /'ɪki/ *adj.* (**ick·ier, icki·est**) (*informal*) unpleasant (used especially about sth that is wet and sticky)

icon /'aɪkɒn; *NAmE* -kɑːn/ *noun* **1** (*computing*) a small symbol on a computer screen that represents a program or a file: *Click on the printer icon with the mouse.* ➲ VISUAL VOCAB page V55 **2** a famous person or thing that people admire and see as a symbol of a particular idea, way of life, etc: *Madonna and other pop icons of the 1980s* ◇ *a* ***feminist/gay icon*** (= sb that feminists/gay people admire) **3** (also **ikon**) (in the Orthodox Church) a painting or statue of a holy person that is also thought of as a holy object

icon·ic /aɪ'kɒnɪk; *NAmE* -'kɑːnɪk/ *adj.* acting as a sign or symbol of sth

icono·clast /aɪ'kɒnəklæst; *NAmE* -'kɑːnə-/ *noun* (*formal*) a person who criticizes popular beliefs or established customs and ideas

icono·clas·tic /aɪ,kɒnə'klæstɪk; *NAmE* ,kɑːnə-/ *adj.* (*formal*) criticizing popular beliefs or established customs and ideas ▸ **icono·clasm** /aɪ'kɒnəklæzəm; *NAmE* -'kɑːnə-/ *noun* [U]: *the iconoclasm of the early Christians*

icon·og·raphy /,aɪkə'nɒgrəfi; *NAmE* -'nɑːg-/ *noun* [U] the use or study of images or symbols in art

icon·ology /,aɪkə'nɒlədʒi; *NAmE* -'nɑːl-/ *noun* [U] the fact of a work of art being an image or symbol of sth

-ics *suffix* (in nouns) the science, art or activity of: *physics* ◇ *dramatics* ◇ *athletics*

ICT /,aɪ siː 'tiː/ *noun* [U] (*BrE*) the abbreviation for 'information and communications technology' (the study of the use of computers, the Internet, video, and other technology as a subject at school)

ICU /,aɪ siː 'juː/ *abbr.* intensive care unit (in a hospital)

icy /'aɪsi/ *adj.* (**icier, ici·est**) **1** very cold SYN **freezing**: *icy* ***winds/water*** ◇ *My feet were* ***icy cold.*** **2** covered with ice: *icy roads* **3** (of a person's voice, manner, etc.) not friendly or kind; showing feelings of dislike or anger: *My eyes met his icy gaze.* ➲ see also ICILY ▸ **ici·ness** *noun* [U]

ID /,aɪ 'diː/ *noun, verb*

■ ***noun* 1** [U, C] the abbreviation for 'identity' or 'identification' (an official way of showing who you are, for example a document with your name, date of birth and often a photograph on it): *You must carry ID at all times.* ◇ *The police checked IDs at the gate.* ◇ *an ID card* **2** [C] IDENTIFICATION: *The police need a witness to make a positive ID.* ➲ see also CALLER ID

■ ***verb*** (**ID's, ID'ing, ID'd, ID'd**) (*informal*) = IDENTIFY

Id = EID

id /ɪd/ *noun* (*psychology*) the part of the unconscious mind where many of a person's basic needs, feelings and desires are supposed to exist ➲ compare EGO, SUPEREGO

I'd /aɪd/ *short form* **1** I had **2** I would

I'D card *noun* = IDENTITY CARD

-ide *suffix* (*chemistry*) (in nouns) a COMPOUND of: *chloride*

idea 0‑w /aɪ'dɪə; *NAmE* -'diːə/ *noun*

▸ PLAN/THOUGHT **1** 0‑w [C] a plan, thought or suggestion, especially about what to do in a particular situation: *It would be* ***a good idea*** *to call before we leave.* ◇ **~ (of sth/of doing sth)** *I like the idea of living on a boat.* ◇ **~ (for sth)** *He already had an idea for his next novel.* ◇ *Her family expected her to go to college, but she had* ***other ideas.*** ◇ *The surprise party was Jane's idea.* ◇ ***It might be an idea*** (= it would be sensible) *to try again later.* ◇ *We've been toying with the idea of* (= thinking about) *getting a dog.* ◇ ***It seemed like a good idea at the time,*** *and then it all went horribly wrong.* ◇ *The latest* ***big idea*** *is to make women more interested in sport.*

▸ IMPRESSION **2** 0‑w [U, sing.] **~ (of sth)** a picture or an impression in your mind of what sb/sth is like: *The brochure should give you* ***a good idea of*** *the hotel.* ◇ *I had* ***some idea of*** *what the job would be like.* ◇ *She doesn't seem to have any idea of what I'm talking about.* ◇ *I don't want anyone* ***getting the wrong idea*** (= getting the wrong impression about sth). ◇ *An evening at home watching TV is not my idea of a good time.*

▸ OPINION **3** 0‑w [C] **~ (about sth)** an opinion or a belief about sth: *He has some very strange ideas about education.*

▸ FEELING **4** 0‑w [sing.] **~ (that...)** a feeling that sth is possible: *What gave you the idea that he'd be here?* ◇ *I have a pretty good idea where I left it—I hope I'm right.*

▸ AIM **5** 0‑w **the idea** [sing.] **~ of sth/of doing sth** the aim or purpose of sth: *You'll soon* ***get the idea*** (= understand). ◇ ***What's the idea*** *of the game?* ➲ SYNONYMS at PURPOSE

IDM **give sb i'deas | put i'deas into sb's head** to give sb hopes about sth that may not be possible or likely; to make sb act or think in an unreasonable way: *Who's been putting ideas into his head?* **have no i'dea | not have the faintest, first, etc. idea** 0‑w (*informal*) used to emphasize that you do not know sth: *'What's she talking about?' 'I've no idea.'* ◇ *He hasn't the faintest idea how to manage people.* **have the right i'dea** to have found a very good or successful way of living, doing sth, etc: *He's certainly got the right idea—retiring at 55.* **'that's an idea!** (*informal*) used to reply in a positive way to a suggestion that sb has made: *Hey, that's an idea! And we could get a band, as well.* **'that's the idea!** (*informal*) used to encourage people and to tell them that they are doing sth right: *That's the idea! You're doing fine.* **you have no i'dea...** (*informal*) used to show that sth is hard for sb else to imagine: *You've no idea how much traffic there was tonight.* ➲ more at BUCK *v.*

ideal 0‑w /aɪ'diːəl/ *adj., noun*

■ ***adj.* 1** 0‑w **~ (for sth)** perfect; most suitable: *This beach is ideal for children.* ◇ *She's the ideal candidate for the job.* ◇ *The trip to Paris will be an* ***ideal opportunity*** *to practise my French.* **2** 0‑w [only before noun] existing only in your imagination or as an idea; not likely to be real: *the search for ideal love* ◇ ***In an ideal world*** *there would be no poverty and disease.* IDM see WORLD ▸ **ideal·ly** /aɪ'diːəli/ *adv.*: *She's* ***ideally suited*** *for this job.* ◇ *Ideally, I'd like to live in New York, but that's not possible.*

■ ***noun* 1** 0‑w [C] an idea or standard that seems perfect, and worth trying to achieve or obtain: *political ideals* ◇ *She found it hard to live up to his high ideals.* **2** 0‑w [C, usually sing.] **~ (of sth)** a person or thing that you think is perfect: *It's my ideal of what a family home should be.*

ideal·ism /aɪˈdiːəlɪzəm/ *noun* [U] **1** the belief that a perfect life, situation, etc. can be achieved, even when this is not very likely: *He was full of youthful idealism.* **2** (*philosophy*) the belief that our ideas are the only things that are real and that we can know about ➲ compare MATERIALISM, REALISM ▶ **ideal·ist** *noun*: *He's too much of an idealist for this government.*

ideal·is·tic /ˌaɪdiəˈlɪstɪk/ *adj.* having a strong belief in perfect standards and trying to achieve them, even when this is not realistic: *She's still young and idealistic.* ▶ **ideal·is·tic·al·ly** /ˌaɪdiəˈlɪstɪkli/ *adv.*

ideal·ize (*BrE* also **-ise**) /aɪˈdiːəlaɪz/ *verb* **~ sb/sth** to consider or represent sb/sth as being perfect or better than they really are: *It is tempting to idealize the past.* ◇ *an idealized view of married life* ▶ **ideal·iza·tion**, **-isa·tion** /aɪˌdiːəlaɪˈzeɪʃn; *NAmE* -ləˈz-/ *noun* [U, C]

ide·ate /ˈaɪdieɪt/ *verb* (*formal*) **1** [T] **~ sth** to form an idea of sth; to imagine sth **2** [I] to form ideas; to think ▶ **idea·tion** /ˌaɪdiˈeɪʃn/ *noun* [U]

idée fixe /ˌiːdeɪ ˈfiːks/ *noun* (*pl.* **idées fixes** /ˌiːdeɪ ˈfiːks/) (from *French*) an idea or a desire which is so strong that you cannot think about anything else

idem /ˈɪdem/ *adv.* (from *Latin*) from the same book, article, author, etc. as the one that has just been mentioned

ident /ˈaɪdent/ *noun* (*BrE*) a piece of music or a short film that is broadcast between programmes so that people can recognize a radio station or television channel

iden·ti·cal AW /aɪˈdentɪkl/ *adj.* **1** similar in every detail: *a row of identical houses* ◇ *The two pictures are similar, although not identical.* ◇ **~ to sb/sth** *Her dress is almost identical to mine.* ◇ **~ with sb/sth** *The number on the card should be identical with the one on the chequebook.* ➲ LANGUAGE BANK at SIMILARLY **2 the identical** [only before noun] the same: *This is the identical room we stayed in last year.* ▶ **iden·ti·cal·ly** AW /-kli/ *adv.*: *The children were dressed identically.*

iˌdentical ˈtwin (also *technical* **monozyˌgotic ˈtwin**) *noun* either of two children or animals born from the same mother at the same time who have developed from a single egg. Identical twins are of the same sex and look very similar. ➲ compare DIZYGOTIC TWIN, FRATERNAL TWIN

iden·ti·fi·able AW /aɪˌdentɪˈfaɪəbl/ *adj.* that can be recognized: *identifiable characteristics* ◇ *The house is easily identifiable by the large tree outside.* OPP **unidentifiable**

iden·ti·fi·ca·tion AW /aɪˌdentɪfɪˈkeɪʃn/ *noun* **1** (*abbr.* **ID**) [U, C] the process of showing, proving or recognizing who or what sb/sth is: *The identification of the crash victims was a long and difficult task.* ◇ *Each product has a number for easy identification.* ◇ *an identification number* ◇ *Only one witness could make a positive identification.* **2** [U] the process of recognizing that sth exists, or is important: *The early identification of children with special educational needs is very important.* **3** (*abbr.* **ID**) [U] official papers or a document that can prove who you are: *Can I see some identification, please?* **4** [U, C] **~ (with sb/sth)** a strong feeling of sympathy, understanding or support for sb/sth: *her emotional identification with the play's heroine* ◇ *their increasing identification with the struggle for independence* **5** [U, C] **~ (of sb) (with sb/sth)** the process of making a close connection between one person or thing and another: *the voters' identification of the Democrats with high taxes*

iˌdentifiˈcation parade *noun* (also *informal* **iˈdentity parade**) (both *BrE*) (also **ˈline-up** *NAmE*, *BrE*) a row of people, including one person who is suspected of a crime, who are shown to a witness to see if he or she can recognize the criminal

iden·ti·fier /aɪˈdentɪfaɪə(r)/ *noun* (*computing*) a series of characters used to refer to a program or set of data within a program

iden·tify 🔑 AW /aɪˈdentɪfaɪ/ *verb* (**iden·ti·fies**, **iden·ti·fy·ing**, **iden·ti·fied**, **iden·ti·fied**)
1 🔑 (also *informal* **ID**) to recognize sb/sth and be able to say who or what they are: **~ sb/sth as sb/sth** *The bodies were identified as those of two suspected drug dealers.* ◇ **~ sb/sth** *She was able to identify her attacker.* ◇ *Passengers were asked to identify their own suitcases before they were put on the plane.* ◇ *Many of those arrested refused to* ***identify themselves*** (= would not say who they were). ◇ *First of all we must identify the problem areas.* **2** 🔑 to find or discover sb/sth: **~ sth** *Scientists have identified a link between diet and cancer.* ◇ *As yet they have not identified a buyer for the company.* ◇ **~ what, which, etc...** *They are trying to identify what is wrong with the present system.* **3 ~ sb/sth (as sb/sth)** to make it possible to recognize who or what sb/sth is: *In many cases, the clothes people wear identify them as belonging to a particular social class.*

PHR V **iˈdentify with sb** 🔑 to feel that you can understand and share the feelings of sb else SYN **sympathize with**: *I didn't enjoy the book because I couldn't identify with any of the main characters.* **iˈdentify sb with sth** to consider sb to be sth: *He was not the 'tough guy' the public identified him with.* **iˈdentify sth with sth** to consider sth to be the same as sth else SYN **equate**: *You should not identify wealth with happiness.* **be iˈdentified with sb/sth** | **iˈdentify yourself with sb/sth** to support sb/sth; to be closely connected with sb/sth: *The Church became increasingly identified with opposition to the regime.*

Synonyms

identify

know • recognize • name • make sb/sth out

These words all mean to be able to see or hear sb/sth and especially to be able to say who or what they are.

identify to be able to say who or what sb/sth is: *She was able to identify her attacker.*

know to be able to say who or what sth is when you see or hear it because you have seen or heard it before NOTE **Know** is used especially to talk about sounds that seem familiar and when sb recognizes the quality or opportunity that sb/sth represents: *I couldn't see who was speaking, but I knew the voice.* ◇ *She knows a bargain when she sees one.*

recognize to know who sb is or what sth is when you see or hear them/it, because you have seen or heard them/it before: *I recognized him as soon as he came in the room.*

name to say the name of sb/sth in order to show that you know who/what they are: *The victim has not yet been named.*

make sb/sth out to manage to see or hear sb/sth that is not very clear: *I could just make out a figure in the darkness.*

PATTERNS

- to identify/know/recognize sb/sth **by** sth
- to identify/recognize/name sb/sth **as** sb/sth
- to identify/know/recognize/make out **who/what/how...**
- to **easily/barely/just** identify/recognize/make out sb/sth

Iden·ti·kit™ /aɪˈdentɪkɪt/ (*BrE*) (*US* **com·pos·ite**, **comˈposite sketch**) *noun* a set of drawings of different features that can be put together to form the face of a person, especially sb wanted by the police, using descriptions given by people who saw the person; a picture made in this way ➲ compare E-FIT, PHOTOFIT

iden·tity 🔑 AW /aɪˈdentəti/ *noun* (*pl.* **-ies**)
1 🔑 [C, U] (*abbr.* **ID**) who or what sb/sth is: *The police are trying to discover the identity of the killer.* ◇ *Their identities were kept secret.* ◇ *She is innocent; it was* ***a case of mistaken identity.*** ◇ *Do you have any proof of identity?* ◇ *The thief used a false identity.* ◇ *She went through an* ***identity crisis*** *in her teens* (= was not sure of who she was or of her place in society). **2** 🔑 [C, U] the characteristics, feelings or beliefs that distinguish people from others: *a sense of* ***national/cultural/personal/group identity*** ◇ *a plan to strengthen*

the ***corporate identity*** *of the company* **3** [U] **~ (with sb/sth)** | **~ (between A and B)** the state or feeling of being very similar to and able to understand sb/sth: *an identity of interests* ◇ *There's a close identity between fans and their team.*

i'dentity card (also **I'D card**) *noun* a card with a person's name, date of birth, photograph, etc. on it that proves who they are

i'dentity parade *noun* (*BrE, informal*) = IDENTIFICATION PARADE

i'dentity theft *noun* [U] using sb else's name and personal information in order to obtain credit cards and other goods or to take money out of the person's bank accounts

ideograms

Chinese character for earth

Roman numeral three

wheelchair access sign

biohazard sign

ideo·gram /ˈɪdiəɡræm/ (also **ideo·graph** /ˈɪdiəɡrɑːf; *NAmE* -ɡræf/) *noun* **1** a symbol that is used in a writing system, for example Chinese, to represent the idea of a thing, rather than the sounds of a word **2** (*technical*) a sign or a symbol for sth

ideo·logue /ˈaɪdiəlɒɡ; ˈɪd-; *NAmE* -lɔːɡ; -lɑːɡ/ (also **ideolo·gist** /ˌaɪdiˈɒlədʒɪst; *NAmE* -ˈɑːl-/) *noun* (*formal*, sometimes *disapproving*) a person whose actions are influenced by belief in a set of principles (= by an ideology)

ideol·ogy **AW** /ˌaɪdiˈɒlədʒi; *NAmE* -ˈɑːl-/ *noun* [C, U] (*pl.* -ies) (sometimes *disapproving*) **1** a set of ideas that an economic or political system is based on: ***Marxist/capitalist ideology*** **2** a set of beliefs, especially one held by a particular group, that influences the way people behave: *the ideology of gender roles* ◇ *alternative ideologies* ▸ **ideo·logic·al** **AW** /ˌaɪdiəˈlɒdʒɪkl; *NAmE* -ˈlɑːdʒ-/ *adj.*: *ideological differences* **ideo·logic·al·ly** **AW** /-kli/ *adv.*: *ideologically correct*

ides /aɪdz/ *noun* [pl.] the middle day of the month in the ancient Roman system, from which other days were calculated: *the ides of March*

idi·ocy /ˈɪdiəsi/ *noun* (*pl.* -ies) (*formal*) **1** [U] very stupid behaviour; the state of being very stupid **SYN** **stupidity** **2** [C] a very stupid act, remark, etc: *the idiocies of bureaucracy*

idio·lect /ˈɪdiəlekt/ *noun* [C, U] (*linguistics*) the way that a particular person uses language ➲ compare DIALECT

idiom /ˈɪdiəm/ *noun* **1** [C] a group of words whose meaning is different from the meanings of the individual words: *'Let the cat out of the bag' is an idiom meaning to tell a secret by mistake.* ➲ SYNONYMS at WORD **2** [U, C] (*formal*) the kind of language and grammar used by particular people at a particular time or place **3** [U, C] (*formal*) the style of writing, music, art, etc. that is typical of a particular person, group, period or place: *the* ***classical/contemporary/popular idiom***

idiom·at·ic /ˌɪdiəˈmætɪk/ *adj.* **1** containing expressions that are natural to a NATIVE SPEAKER of a language: *She speaks fluent and idiomatic English.* **2** containing an idiom: *an idiomatic expression* ▸ **idiom·at·ic·al·ly** /-kli/ *adv.*

idio·syn·crasy /ˌɪdiəˈsɪŋkrəsi/ *noun* [C, U] (*pl.* -ies) a person's particular way of behaving, thinking, etc, especially when it is unusual; an unusual feature **SYN** **eccentricity**: *The car has its little idiosyncrasies.* ▸ **idio·syn·crat·ic** /ˌɪdiəsɪŋˈkrætɪk/ *adj.*: *His teaching methods are idiosyncratic but successful.*

idiot /ˈɪdiət/ *noun* **1** (*informal*) a very stupid person **SYN** **fool**: *When I lost my passport, I felt such an idiot.* ◇ *Not that switch, you idiot!* **2** (*old-fashioned, offensive*) a person with very low intelligence who cannot think or behave normally

idi·ot·ic /ˌɪdiˈɒtɪk; *NAmE* -ˈɑːtɪk/ *adj.* very stupid **SYN** **ridiculous**: *an idiotic question* ◇ *Don't be so idiotic!* ▸ **idi·ot·ic·al·ly** /-kli/ *adv.*

idiot sav·ant /ˌiːdjəʊ sæˈvɒ̃; *NAmE* ˌiːdjoʊ sæˈvɑ̃ː/ *noun* (*pl.* **idiot sav·ants** or **idiots sav·ants** /ˌiːdjəʊ sæˈvɒ̃; *NAmE* ˌiːdjoʊ sæˈvɑ̃ː/) (from *French*) a person who has severe LEARNING DIFFICULTIES, but who has an unusually high level of ability in a particular skill, for example in art or music, or in remembering things

idle /ˈaɪdl/ *adj., verb*

■ ***adj.*** **1** (of people) not working hard **SYN** **lazy**: *an idle student* **2** (of machines, factories, etc.) not in use: *to* ***lie/stand/remain idle*** **3** (of people) without work **SYN** **unemployed**: *Over ten per cent of the workforce is now idle.* **4** [usually before noun] with no particular purpose or effect; useless: ***idle chatter/curiosity*** ◇ *It was just an* ***idle threat*** (= not serious). ◇ ***It is idle to*** *pretend that their marriage is a success.* **5** [usually before noun] (of time) not spent doing work or sth particular: *In idle moments, he carved wooden figures.* **IDM** see DEVIL ▸ **idle·ness** *noun* [U]: *After a period of enforced idleness, she found a new job.*

■ ***verb*** **1** [T, I] to spend time doing nothing important: **~ sth** (**+ adv./prep.**) *They idled the days away, talking and watching television.* ◇ (**+ adv./prep.**) *They idled along by the river* (= walked slowly and with no particular purpose). **2** [I] (of an engine) to run slowly while the vehicle is not moving **SYN** **tick over**: *She left the car idling at the roadside.* **3** [T] **~ sb/sth** (*NAmE*) to close a factory, etc. or stop providing work for the workers, especially temporarily: *The strikes have idled nearly 4 000 workers.*

idler /ˈaɪdlə(r)/ *noun* a person who is lazy and does not work **SYN** **loafer**

idli /ˈɪdliː/ *noun* an Indian rice cake cooked using steam

idly /ˈaɪdli/ *adv.* without any particular reason, purpose or effort; doing nothing: *She sat in the sun, idly sipping a cool drink.* ◇ *He wondered idly what would happen.* ◇ *We can't* ***stand idly by*** (= do nothing) *and let people starve.*

idol /ˈaɪdl/ *noun* **1** a person or thing that is loved and admired very much: *a* ***pop/football/teen, etc. idol*** ◇ *the idol of countless teenagers* ◇ *a* ***fallen idol*** (= sb who is no longer popular) **2** a statue that is worshipped as a god

idol·atry /aɪˈdɒlətri; *NAmE* -ˈdɑːl-/ *noun* [U] **1** the practice of worshipping statues as gods **2** (*formal*) too much love or admiration for sb/sth: *football fans whose support for their team borders on idolatry* ▸ **idol·atrous** /aɪˈdɒlətrəs; *NAmE* -ˈdɑːl-/ *adj.*

idol·ize (*BrE* also **-ise**) /ˈaɪdəlaɪz/ *verb* **~ sb** to admire or love sb very much **SYN** **worship**: *a pop star idolized by millions of fans* ◇ *They idolize their kids.* ▸ **idol·iza·tion**, **-isa·tion** /ˌaɪdəlaɪˈzeɪʃn; *NAmE* -əˈzeɪʃn/ *noun* [U]

idyll /ˈɪdɪl; *NAmE* ˈaɪdl/ *noun* **1** (*literary*) a happy and peaceful place, event or experience, especially one connected with the countryside **2** a short poem or other piece of writing that describes a peaceful and happy scene

idyl·lic /ɪˈdɪlɪk; *NAmE* aɪˈd-/ *adj.* peaceful and beautiful; perfect, without problems: *a house set in idyllic surroundings* ◇ *to lead an idyllic existence* ◇ *The cottage sounds idyllic.* ▸ **idyl·lic·al·ly** /-kli/ *adv.*: *a house idyllically set in wooded grounds*

i.e. 0‑ˉ /ˌaɪ ˈiː/ *abbr.* used to explain exactly what the previous thing that you have mentioned means (from Latin 'id est'): *the basic essentials of life, i.e. housing, food and water*

Language Bank

i.e.

Explaining what you mean

- Some poems are mnemonics, **i.e.** they are designed to help you remember something.
- Some poems are mnemonics, **that is to say**, they are designed to help you remember something.
- Mnemonic poems, **that is** poems designed to help you remember something, are an excellent way to learn lists.
- A limerick's rhyme scheme is A–A–B–B–A. **In other words**, the first, second, and fifth lines all rhyme with one another, while the third and fourth lines have their own rhyme.
- In this exercise the reader is encouraged to work out the meaning, **or rather** the range of meanings, of the poem.
- This is a poem about death, **or, more precisely**, dying.
- He says his poems deal with 'the big issues', **by which he means** love, loss, grief and death.

➲ Language Bank at ABOUT

I

-ie ➲ -Y

IED /ˌaɪ iː ˈdiː/ *abbr.* improvised explosive device (a bomb made and used by people who are not members of the military forces of a country)

IELTS /ˈaɪelts/ *noun* [U] the abbreviation for 'International English Language Testing System' (a test that measures a person's ability to speak and write English at the level that is necessary to go to university in the UK, Ireland, Australia, Canada, South Africa and New Zealand)

if 🔑 /ɪf/ *conj., noun*

■ ***conj.*** **1** 🔑 used to say that one thing can, will or might happen or be true, depending on another thing happening or being true: *If you see him, give him this note.* ◇ *I'll only stay if you offer me more money.* ◇ *If necessary I can come at once.* ◇ *You can stay for the weekend if you like.* ◇ *If anyone calls, tell them I'm not at home.* ◇ *If he improved his IT skills, he'd* (= he would) *easily get a job.* ◇ *You would know what was going on if you'd* (= you had) *listened.* ◇ *They would have been here by now if they'd caught the early train.* ◇ *If I was in charge, I'd do things differently.* ◇ (rather *formal*) *If I were in charge...* ◇ ***Even if*** (= although) *you did see someone, you can't be sure it was him.* **2** 🔑 when; whenever; every time: *If metal gets hot it expands.* ◇ *She glares at me if I go near her desk.* **3** (*formal*) used with *will* or *would* to ask sb politely to do sth: *If you will sit down for a few moments, I'll tell the manager you're here.* ◇ *If you would care to leave your name, we'll contact you as soon as possible.* **4** 🔑 used after *ask, know, find out, wonder,* etc. to introduce one of two or more possibilities SYN **whether**: *Do you know if he's married?* ◇ *I wonder if I should wear a coat or not.* ◇ *He couldn't tell if she was laughing or crying.* ◇ *Listen to the tune and see if you can remember the words.* **5** 🔑 used after verbs or adjectives expressing feelings: *I am sorry if I disturbed you.* ◇ *I'd be grateful if you would keep it a secret.* ◇ *Do you mind if I turn the TV off?* **6** 🔑 used to admit that sth is possible, but to say that it is not very important: *If she has any weakness, it is her Italian.* ◇ ***So what if*** *he was late. Who cares?* **7** used before an adjective to introduce a contrast: *He's a good driver, if a little over-confident.* ◇ *We'll only do it once—**if at all**.* **8** 🔑 used to ask sb to listen to your opinion: *If you ask me, she's too scared to do it.* ◇ *If you think about it, those children must be at school by now.* ◇ *If you remember, Mary was always fond of animals.* **9** used before *could, may* or *might* to suggest sth or to interrupt sb politely: *If I may make a suggestion, perhaps we could begin a little earlier next week.*

IDM **ˌif and ˈwhen** used to say sth about an event that may or may not happen: *If and when we ever meet again I hope he remembers what I did for him.* **if ˈanything** used to express an opinion about sth, or after a negative statement to suggest that the opposite is true: *I'd say he was more like his father, if anything.* ◇ *She's not thin—if anything she's on the plump side.* **if ˌI were ˈyou** 🔑 used to give sb advice: *If I were you I'd start looking for another job.* **if ˈnot 1** 🔑 used to introduce a different suggestion, after a sentence with *if*: *I'll go if you're going. If not* (= if you are not) *I'd rather stay at home.* **2** 🔑 used after a *yes/no* question to say what will or should happen if the answer is 'no': *Are you ready? If not, I'm going without you.* ◇ *Do you want that cake? If not, I'll have it.* **3** used to suggest that sth may be even larger, more important, etc. than was first stated: *They cost thousands if not millions of pounds to build.* **if ˈonly** 🔑 used to say that you wish sth was true or that sth had happened: *If only I were rich.* ◇ *If only I knew her name.* ◇ *If only he'd remembered to send that letter.* ◇ *If only I had gone by taxi.* **it's not as if** used to say that sth that is happening is surprising: *I'm surprised they've invited me to their wedding—it's not as if I know them well.* **ˈonly if** (rather *formal*) used to state the only situation in which sth can happen: *Only if a teacher has given permission is a student allowed to leave the room.* ◇ *Only if the red light comes on is there any danger to employees.*

■ ***noun*** (*informal*) a situation that is not certain: *If he wins—and **it's a big if**—he'll be the first Englishman to win for fifty years.* ◇ *There are still a lot of **ifs and buts** before everything's settled.*

Grammar Point

if / whether

- Both **if** and **whether** are used in reporting questions which expect 'yes' or 'no' as the answer: *She asked if/whether I wanted a drink.*, although **whether** sounds more natural with particular verbs such as **discuss**, **consider** and **decide**. When a choice is offered between alternatives **if** or **whether** can be used: *We didn't know if/whether we should write or phone.* In this last type of sentence, **whether** is usually considered more formal and more suitable for written English.

iff /ɪf/ *conj.* (*mathematics*) an expression used in mathematics to mean 'if and only if'

iffy /ˈɪfi/ *adj.* (*informal*) **1** (*especially BrE*) not in perfect condition; bad in some way: *That meat smells a bit iffy to me.* **2** not certain: *The weather looks slightly iffy.*

-ify, -fy *suffix* (in verbs) to make or become: *purify* ◇ *solidify*

Igbo (also **Ibo**) /ˈiːbəʊ; *NAmE* ˈiːboʊ/ *noun* [U] a language spoken by the Igbo people of W Africa, especially in SE Nigeria

igloo /ˈɪgluː/ *noun* (*pl.* **-oos**) a small round house or shelter built from blocks of hard snow by the Inuit people of northern N America

ig·ne·ous /ˈɪgniəs/ *adj.* (*geology*) (of rocks) formed when MAGMA (= melted or liquid material lying below the earth's surface) becomes solid, especially after it has poured out of a VOLCANO

ig·nite /ɪgˈnaɪt/ *verb* [I, T] (*formal*) to start to burn; to make sth start to burn: *Gas ignites very easily.* ◇ (*figurative*) *Tempers ignited when the whole family spent Christmas together.* ◇ **~ sth** *Flames melted a lead pipe and ignited leaking gas.* ◇ (*figurative*) *His words ignited their anger.*

ig·ni·tion /ɪgˈnɪʃn/ *noun* **1** [C, usually sing.] the electrical system of a vehicle that makes the fuel begin to burn to start the engine; the place in a vehicle where you start this system: *to **turn the ignition on/off*** ◇ *to put the key **in the ignition*** ➲ COLLOCATIONS at DRIVING ➲ VISUAL VOCAB page V42 **2** [U] (*technical*) the action of starting to burn or of making sth burn: *The flames spread to all parts of the house within minutes of ignition.*

ig·noble /ɪgˈnəʊbl; *NAmE* -ˈnoʊ-/ *adj.* (*formal*) not good or honest; that should make you feel shame SYN **base**: *ignoble thoughts* ◇ *an ignoble person* OPP **noble**

ig·no·mini·ous /ˌɪgnəˈmɪniəs/ *adj.* (*formal*) that makes, or should make, you feel ashamed SYN **disgraceful**, **hu-**

miliating: *an ignominious defeat* ◇ *He made one mistake and his career came to an ignominious end.* ▶ **ig·no·mini·ous·ly** *adv.*

ig·no·miny /ˈɪɡnəmɪni/ *noun* [U] (*formal*) public shame and loss of honour SYN **disgrace**: *They suffered the ignominy of defeat.*

ig·nor·amus /ˌɪɡnəˈreɪməs/ *noun* (usually *humorous*) a person who does not have much knowledge: *When it comes to music, I'm a complete ignoramus.*

ig·nor·ance AW /ˈɪɡnərəns/ *noun* [U] **~ (of/about sth)** a lack of knowledge or information about sth: *widespread* ***ignorance of/about*** *the disease* ◇ *They fought a long battle against prejudice and ignorance.* ◇ *She was kept* ***in ignorance of*** *her husband's activities.* ◇ *Children often behave badly* ***out of/through ignorance.***
IDM **ˌignorance is ˈbliss** (*saying*) if you do not know about sth, you cannot worry about it: *Some doctors believe ignorance is bliss and don't give their patients all the facts.*

ig·nor·ant AW /ˈɪɡnərənt/ *adj.* **1** lacking knowledge or information about sth; not educated: *an ignorant person/question* ◇ *Never make your students feel ignorant.* ◇ **~ about sth** *He's ignorant about modern technology.* ◇ **~ of sth** *At that time I was ignorant of events going on elsewhere.* **2** (*informal*) with very bad manners SYN **uncouth**: *a rude, ignorant person* ▶ **ig·nor·ant·ly** *adv.*

ig·nore 🔑 AW /ɪɡˈnɔː(r)/ *verb*
1 🔑 **~ sth** to pay no attention to sth SYN **disregard**: *He ignored all the 'No Smoking' signs and lit up a cigarette.* ◇ *I made a suggestion but they chose to ignore it.* ◇ *We cannot afford to ignore their advice.* **2** 🔑 **~ sb** to pretend that you have not seen sb or that sb is not there SYN **take no notice of**: *She ignored him and carried on with her work.*

igu·ana /ɪˈɡwɑːnə/ *noun* a large tropical American LIZARD (= a type of REPTILE)

iguan·odon /ɪˈɡwɑːnədɒn; *NAmE* -dɑːn/ *noun* a large DINOSAUR

ike·bana /ˌɪkɪˈbɑːnə; ˌɪkeɪ-/ *noun* [U] (from *Japanese*) Japanese flower arranging, that has strict formal rules

ikon = ICON (3)

il- *prefix* ➲ IN-

ileum /ˈɪliəm/ *noun* (*pl.* **ilea** /ˈɪliə/) (*anatomy*) the third part of the small INTESTINE ➲ compare DUODENUM, JEJUNUM ▶ **ileal** /ˈɪliəl/ *adj.*

ilk /ɪlk/ *noun* [usually sing.] (sometimes *disapproving*) type; kind: *the world of media people* ***and their ilk*** ◇ *I can't stand him, or any others* ***of that ilk.***

ill 🔑 /ɪl/ *adj., adv., noun*
■ ***adj.*** **1** 🔑 (*especially BrE*) (*NAmE* usually **sick**) [not usually before noun] suffering from an illness or disease; not feeling well: *Her father is* ***seriously ill*** *in St Luke's hospital.* ◇ *She* ***was taken ill*** *suddenly.* ◇ *We both started to* ***feel ill*** *shortly after the meal.* ◇ *Uncle Harry is* ***terminally ill*** *with cancer* (= he will die from his illness). ◇ *the* ***mentally ill*** (= people with a mental illness) ◇ (*formal*) *He* ***fell ill*** *and died soon after.* ➲ see also ILLNESS **2** 🔑 [usually before noun] bad or harmful: *He resigned because of* ***ill health*** (= he was often ill). ◇ *She suffered no* ***ill effects*** *from the experience.* ◇ *a woman of* ***ill repute*** (= considered to be immoral) **3** (*formal*) that brings, or is thought to bring, bad luck: *a bird of ill omen*
IDM **ˌill at ˈease** feeling uncomfortable and embarrassed: *I* ***felt ill at ease*** *in such formal clothes.* **it's an ˌill ˈwind (that blows nobody any good)** (*saying*) no problem is so bad that it does not bring some advantage to sb ➲ more at FEELING
■ ***adv.*** **1** (especially in compounds) badly or in an unpleasant way: *The animals had been grossly ill-treated.* **2** (*formal*) badly; not in an acceptable way: *They live in an area ill served by public transport.* **3** (*formal*) only with difficulty: *We're wasting valuable time, time we can ill afford.*
IDM **speak/think ˈill of sb** (*formal*) to say or think bad things about sb: *Don't speak ill of the dead.*
■ ***noun*** **1** [usually pl.] (*formal*) a problem or harmful thing; an illness: *social/economic ills* ◇ *the ills of the modern world* **2** [U] (*literary*) harm; bad luck: *I may not like him, but I wish him no ill.*

Collocations

Illnesses

Becoming ill

- **catch** a cold/an infectious disease/the flu/(*BrE*) flu/pneumonia/a virus/(*informal*) a bug
- **get** (*BrE*) ill/(*NAmE*) sick/a disease/AIDS/breast cancer/a cold/the flu/(*BrE*) flu/a migraine
- **come down with** a cold/the flu/(*BrE*) flu
- **contract** a deadly disease/a serious illness/HIV/AIDS
- **be infected with** a virus/a parasite/HIV
- **develop** cancer/diabetes/a rash/an ulcer/symptoms of hepatitis
- **have** a heart attack/a stroke
- **provoke/trigger/produce** an allergic reaction
- **block/burst/rupture** a blood vessel
- **damage/sever** a nerve/an artery/a tendon

Being ill

- **feel** (*BrE*) ill/sick/nauseous/queasy
- **be running** (*BrE*) a temperature/(*NAmE*) a fever
- **have** a head cold/diabetes/heart disease/lung cancer/a headache/(*BrE*) a high temperature/(*NAmE*) a fever
- **suffer from** asthma/malnutrition/frequent headaches/bouts of depression/a mental disorder
- **be laid up with**/(*BrE*) **be in bed with** a cold/the flu/(*BrE*) flu/a migraine
- **nurse** a cold/a headache/a hangover
- **battle/fight** cancer/depression/addiction/alcoholism

Treatments

- **examine** a patient
- **diagnose** a condition/disease/disorder
- **be diagnosed with** cancer/diabetes/schizophrenia
- **prescribe/be given/be on/take** drugs/medicine/medication/pills/painkillers/antibiotics
- **treat sb for** cancer/depression/shock
- **have/undergo** an examination/an operation/surgery/a kidney transplant/therapy/chemotherapy/treatment for cancer
- **have/be given** an injection/(*BrE*) a flu jab/(*NAmE*) a flu shot/a blood transfusion/a scan/an X-ray
- **cure** a disease/an ailment/cancer/a headache/a patient
- **prevent** the spread of disease/further outbreaks/damage to the lungs
- **be vaccinated against** the flu/(*BrE*) flu/the measles/(*BrE*) measles/polio/smallpox
- **enhance/boost/confer/build** immunity to a disease

I'll /aɪl/ *short form* **1** I shall **2** I will

ˌill-adˈvised *adj.* not sensible; likely to cause difficulties in the future: *Her remarks were ill-advised, to say the least.* ◇ *You* ***would be ill-advised to*** *travel on your own.* ➲ compare WELL ADVISED ▶ **ˌill-adˈvised·ly** *adv.*

ˌill-asˈsort·ed *adj.* (of a group of people or things) not seeming suited to each other: *They seem an ill-assorted couple.*

ˌill-ˈbred *adj.* rude or badly behaved, especially because you have not been taught how to behave well OPP **well bred**

ˌill-conˈcealed *adj.* (*formal*) (of feelings or expressions of feeling) not hidden well from other people

ˌill-conˈceived *adj.* badly planned or designed

ˌill-conˈsid·ered *adj.* not carefully thought about or planned

ˌ**ill-deˈfined** *adj.* **1** not clearly described: *an ill-defined role* **2** not clearly marked or easy to see: *an ill-defined path* **OPP well defined**

ˌ**ill-disˈposed** *adj.* **~ (towards sb)** (*formal*) not feeling friendly towards sb **OPP well disposed**

il·legal 🔑 **AW** /ɪˈliːɡl/ *adj., noun*
■ ***adj.*** 🔑 not allowed by the law: *illegal immigrants/aliens* ◇ *It's illegal to drive through a red light.* **OPP legal** ▶ **il·legal·ly** 🔑 **AW** /-ɡəli/ *adv.*: *an illegally parked car* ◇ *He entered the country illegally.*
■ ***noun*** (*NAmE*) a person who lives or works in a country illegally

il·legal·ity **AW** /ˌɪliˈɡæləti/ *noun* (*pl.* **-ies**) **1** [U] the state of being illegal: *No illegality is suspected.* **2** [C] an illegal act ➲ compare LEGALITY

il·legible /ɪˈledʒəbl/ (also **un·read·able**) *adj.* difficult or impossible to read: *an illegible signature* **OPP legible** ▶ **il·legibly** *adv.* /-əbli/

il·legit·im·ate /ˌɪləˈdʒɪtəmət/ *adj.* **1** born to parents who are not married to each other **2** (*formal*) not allowed by a particular set of rules or by law **SYN unauthorized**: *illegitimate use of company property* **OPP legitimate** ▶ **il·legit·im·acy** /ˌɪləˈdʒɪtəməsi/ *noun* [U] **il·legit·im·ate·ly** *adv.*

ˌ**ill-eˈquipped** *adj.* **~ (for sth)** | **~ (to do sth)** not having the necessary equipment or skills

ˌ**ill-ˈfated** (also **fated**) *adj.* (*formal*) not lucky and ending sadly, especially in death or failure: *an ill-fated expedition*

ˌ**ill-ˈfitting** *adj.* not the right size or shape: *ill-fitting clothes*

ˌ**ill-ˈfounded** *adj.* (*formal*) not based on fact or truth: *All our fears proved ill-founded.* **OPP well founded**

ˌ**ill-ˈgotten** *adj.* (*old-fashioned* or *humorous*) obtained dishonestly or unfairly: ***ill-gotten gains*** (= money that was not obtained fairly)

ˌ**ill ˈhealth** *noun* [U] the poor condition of a person's body or mind: *He retired early* ***on grounds of ill health.*** ➲ SYNONYMS at ILLNESS

ˌ**ill ˈhumour** (*especially US* ˌ**ill ˈhumor**) *noun* [U, C] (*literary*) a bad mood **OPP good humour** ▶ ˌ**ill-ˈhumoured** (*especially US* ˌ**ill-ˈhumored**) *adj.*

il·lib·eral /ɪˈlɪbərəl/ *adj.* (*formal*) not allowing much freedom of opinion or action **SYN intolerant**: *illiberal policies*

il·licit /ɪˈlɪsɪt/ *adj.* **1** not allowed by the law **SYN illegal**: *illicit drugs* **2** not approved of by the normal rules of society: *an illicit love affair* ▶ **illicit·ly** *adv.*

ˌ**ill-inˈformed** *adj.* having or showing little knowledge of sth **OPP well informed**

il·lit·er·ate /ɪˈlɪtərət/ *adj., noun*
■ ***adj.*** **1** (of a person) not knowing how to read or write **OPP literate** **2** (of a document or letter) badly written, as if by sb without much education **3** (usually after a noun or adverb) not knowing very much about a particular subject area: *computer illiterate* ◇ *musically illiterate* ▶ **il·lit·er·acy** /ɪˈlɪtərəsi/ *noun* [U]
■ ***noun*** a person who is illiterate

ˌ**ill-ˈjudged** *adj.* (*formal*) that has not been carefully thought about; not appropriate in a particular situation

ˌ**ill-ˈmannered** *adj.* (*formal*) not behaving well or politely in social situations **SYN rude** **OPP well mannered**

ill·ness 🔑 /ˈɪlnəs/ *noun*
1 🔑 [U] the state of being physically or mentally ill: *mental illness* ◇ *I missed a lot of school through illness last year.* **2** 🔑 [C] a type or period of illness: ***minor/serious illnesses*** ◇ *childhood illnesses* ◇ *He died after a long illness.* ➲ SYNONYMS at DISEASE ➲ COLLOCATIONS at ILL

il·logic·al **AW** /ɪˈlɒdʒɪkl; *NAmE* -ˈlɑːdʒ-/ *adj.* not sensible or thought out in a logical way: *illogical behaviour/arguments* ◇ *She has an illogical fear of insects.* **OPP logical** ▶ **il·logic·al·ity** /ɪˌlɒdʒɪˈkæləti; *NAmE* -ˌlɑːdʒ-/ *noun* [U, C] **il·logic·al·ly** **AW** /-kli/ *adv.*

Synonyms

illness

sickness • **ill health** • **trouble**

These are all words for the state of being physically or mentally ill.

illness the state of being physically or mentally ill.

sickness illness; bad health: *I recommend you get insurance against sickness and unemployment.*

ILLNESS OR SICKNESS?

Sickness is used especially in contexts concerning work and insurance. It is commonly found with words such as *pay, leave, absence* and *insurance*. **Illness** has a wider range of uses and is found in more general contexts.

ill health (*rather formal*) the state of being physically ill or having lots of health problems: *She resigned because of ill health.* **NOTE** **Ill health** often lasts a long period of time.

trouble illness or pain: *heart trouble.* **NOTE** When **trouble** is used with this meaning, it is necessary to say which part of the body is affected.

PATTERNS

- **chronic** illness/sickness/ill health
- to **suffer from** illness/sickness/ill health/heart, etc. trouble

ˌ**ill-ˈomened** *adj.* (*formal*) (of an event or activity) seeming likely to be unlucky or unsuccessful because there are a lot of unlucky signs relating to it

ˌ**ill-preˈpared** *adj.* **1 ~ (for sth)** not ready, especially because you were not expecting sth to happen: *The team was ill-prepared for a disaster on that scale.* **2** badly planned or organized: *an ill-prepared speech*

ˌ**ill-ˈstarred** *adj.* (*formal*) not lucky and likely to bring unhappiness or to end in failure: *an ill-starred marriage*

ˌ**ill-ˈtempered** *adj.* (*formal*) angry and rude or irritated, especially when this seems unreasonable

ˌ**ill-ˈtimed** *adj.* done or happening at the wrong time: *an ill-timed visit* **OPP well timed**

ˌ**ill-ˈtreat** *verb* **~ sb** to treat sb in a cruel or unkind way ▶ ˌ**ill-ˈtreatment** *noun* [U]: *the ill-treatment of prisoners*

il·lu·min·ate /ɪˈluːmɪneɪt/ (also *less frequent* **il·lu·mine**) *verb* **1 ~ sth** (*formal*) to shine light on sth: *Floodlights illuminated the stadium.* ◇ *The earth is illuminated by the sun.* **2 ~ sth** (*formal*) to make sth clearer or easier to understand **SYN clarify**: *This text illuminates the philosopher's early thinking.* **3 ~ sth** to decorate a street, building, etc. with bright lights for a special occasion **4 ~ sth** (*literary*) to make a person's face, etc. seem bright and excited **SYN light up**: *Her smile illuminated her entire being.*

il·lu·min·ated /ɪˈluːmɪneɪtɪd/ *adj.* [usually before noun] **1** lit with bright lights: *the illuminated city at night* **2** (of books, etc.) decorated with gold, silver and bright colours in a way that was done in the past, by hand: *illuminated manuscripts*

il·lu·min·at·ing /ɪˈluːmɪneɪtɪŋ/ *adj.* helping to make sth clear or easier to understand: *We didn't find the examples he used particularly illuminating.*

il·lu·min·ation /ɪˌluːmɪˈneɪʃn/ *noun* **1** [U, C] light or a place that light comes from: *The only illumination in the room came from the fire.* **2 illuminations** [pl.] (*BrE*) bright coloured lights used to decorate a town or building for a special occasion: *Christmas illuminations* **3** [C, usually pl.] a coloured decoration, usually painted by hand, in an old book **4** [U] (*formal*) understanding or explanation of sth: *spiritual illumination*

il·lu·mine /ɪˈluːmɪn/ *verb* (*formal*) = ILLUMINATE

ˌ**ill-ˈused** *adj.* (*old-fashioned* or *formal*) badly treated

il·lu·sion /ɪˈluːʒn/ *noun* **1** [C, U] a false idea or belief, especially about sb or about a situation: *She's* ***under the illu-***

sion that (= believes wrongly that) *she'll get the job.* ◇ *The new president* ***has no illusions*** *about the difficulties facing her country* (= she knows that the country has serious problems). ◇ *He could no longer distinguish between illusion and reality.* **2** [C] something that seems to exist but in fact does not, or seems to be sth that it is not: *Mirrors in a room often give an illusion of space.* ◇ *The idea of absolute personal freedom is an illusion.* ➲ picture at OPTICAL ILLUSION

il·lu·sion·ist /ɪˈluːʒənɪst/ *noun* an entertainer who performs tricks that seem strange or impossible to believe

il·lu·sive /ɪˈluːsɪv/ *adj.* (*literary, rare*) not real although seeming to be SYN **illusory**: *There is an illusive sense of depth.* HELP *Illusive* is sometimes confused with *elusive* which has a different meaning.

il·lu·sory /ɪˈluːsəri/ *adj.* (*formal*) not real, although seeming to be: *an illusory sense of freedom*

il·lus·trate 🔑 AW /ˈɪləstreɪt/ *verb*
1 🔑 [usually passive] to use pictures, photographs, diagrams, etc. in a book, etc: **~ sth** *an illustrated textbook* ◇ **~ sth with sth** *His lecture was illustrated with photos taken during the expedition.* **2** 🔑 to make the meaning of sth clearer by using examples, pictures, etc: **~ sth** ***To illustrate my point****, let me tell you a little story.* ◇ *Last year's sales figures are illustrated in Figure 2.* ◇ **~ how, what, etc** *... Here's an example to illustrate what I mean.* ➲ LANGUAGE BANK at PROCESS **3** **~ sth** | **~ how, what, etc...** | **~ that...** to show that sth is true or that a situation exists SYN **demonstrate**: *The incident illustrates the need for better security measures.*

Language Bank

illustrate

Referring to a chart, graph or table

- This bar chart **illustrates** how many journeys people made on public transport over a three-month period.
- This table **compares** bus, train, and taxi use between April and June.
- The results **are shown** in the chart below.
- In this pie chart, the survey results **are broken down** by age.
- This pie chart **breaks down** the survey results by age.
- **As can be seen from** these results, younger people use buses more than older people.
- **According to** these figures, bus travel accounts for 60% of public transport use.
- **From** the data in the above graph, **it is apparent that** buses are the most widely used form of public transport.

➲ Language Banks at EVIDENCE, FALL, INCREASE, PROPORTION, SURPRISING

il·lus·tra·tion AW /ˌɪləˈstreɪʃn/ *noun* **1** [C] a drawing or picture in a book, magazine, etc. especially one that explains sth: *50 full-colour illustrations* **2** [U] the process of illustrating sth: *the art of book illustration* **3** [C, U] a story, an event or an example that clearly shows the truth about sth: *The statistics are a clear illustration of the point I am trying to make* ◇ *Let me,* ***by way of illustration****, quote from one of her poems.* ➲ SYNONYMS at EXAMPLE

il·lus·tra·tive AW /ˈɪləstrətɪv; *NAmE* ɪˈlʌs-/ *adj.* (*formal*) helping to explain sth or show it more clearly SYN **explanatory**: *an illustrative example*

il·lus·tra·tor /ˈɪləstreɪtə(r)/ *noun* a person who draws or paints pictures for books, etc.

il·lus·tri·ous /ɪˈlʌstriəs/ *adj.* (*formal*) very famous and much admired, especially because of what you have achieved SYN **distinguished**: *The composer was one of many illustrious visitors to the town.* ◇ *a long and illustrious career*

ˌill ˈwill *noun* [U] bad and unkind feelings towards sb: *I bear Sue no ill will.*

il·ly·whack·er /ˈɪliwækə(r)/ *noun* (*AustralE, informal*) a person who tricks others into giving him or her money, etc. SYN **confidence trickster**

ILO /ˌaɪ el ˈəʊ; *NAmE* ˈoʊ/ *abbr.* International Labour Organization (an organization within the United Nations concerned with work and working conditions)

I'm /aɪm/ *short form* I am

im- ➲ IN-

image 🔑 AW /ˈɪmɪdʒ/ *noun*
1 🔑 [C, U] the impression that a person, an organization or a product, etc. gives to the public: *His public image is very different from the real person.* ◇ *The advertisements are intended to improve the company's image.* ◇ *Image is very important in the music world.* ◇ *stereotyped images of women in children's books* **2** 🔑 [C] a mental picture that you have of what sb/sth is like or looks like: *images of the past* ◇ *I had a* ***mental image*** *of what she would look like.* **3** 🔑 [C] (*formal*) a copy of sb/sth in the form of a picture or statue: *Images of deer and hunters decorate the cave walls.* ◇ *a wooden image of the Hindu god Ganesh* **4** 🔑 [C] a picture of sb/sth seen in a mirror, through a camera, or on a television or computer: *He stared at his own image reflected in the water.* ◇ *Slowly, an image began to appear on the screen.* ➲ see also MIRROR IMAGE **5** 🔑 [C] a word or phrase used with a different meaning from its normal one, in order to describe sth in a way that produces a strong picture in the mind: *poetic images of the countryside*
IDM **be the image of sb/sth** to look very like sb/sth else: *He's the image of his father.* ➲ see also SPITTING IMAGE

im·agery AW /ˈɪmɪdʒəri/ *noun* [U] **1** language that produces pictures in the minds of people reading or listening: *poetic imagery* ➲ COLLOCATIONS at LITERATURE ➲ see also METAPHOR **2** (*formal*) pictures, photographs, etc: *satellite imagery* (= for example, photographs of the earth taken from space)

im·agin·able /ɪˈmædʒɪnəbl/ *adj.* **1** used with superlatives, and with *all* and *every*, to emphasize that sth is the best, worst, etc. that you can imagine, or includes every possible example: *The house has the most spectacular views imaginable.* ◇ *They stock every imaginable type of pasta.* **2** possible to imagine: *These technological developments were hardly imaginable 30 years ago.*

im·agin·ary 🔑 /ɪˈmædʒɪnəri; *NAmE* -neri/ *adj.* existing only in your mind or imagination: *imaginary fears* ◇ *The equator is an imaginary line around the middle of the earth.*

iˌmaginary ˈnumber *noun* (*mathematics*) a number expressed as the SQUARE ROOT of a negative number, especially the square root of -1 ➲ compare COMPLEX NUMBER, REAL NUMBER

im·agin·ation 🔑 /ɪˌmædʒɪˈneɪʃn/ *noun*
1 🔑 [U, C] the ability to create pictures in your mind; the part of your mind that does this: *a* ***vivid/fertile imagination*** ◇ *He's got no imagination.* ◇ *It doesn't* ***take much imagination*** *to guess what she meant.* ◇ *I won't tell you his reaction—****I'll leave that to your imagination****.* ◇ *Don't let your imagination run away with you* (= don't use too much imagination). ◇ *The new policies appear to have* ***caught the imagination*** *of the public* (= they find them interesting and exciting). ◇ *Nobody hates you—it's all* ***in your imagination****.* ◇ (*informal*) ***Use your imagination!*** (= used to tell sb that they will have to guess the answer to the question they have asked you, usually because it is obvious or embarrassing) **2** 🔑 [U] something that you have imagined rather than sth that exists: *She was no longer able to distinguish between imagination and reality.* ◇ *Is it my imagination or have you lost a lot of weight?* **3** 🔑 [U] the ability to have new and exciting ideas: *His writing lacks imagination.* ◇ ***With a little imagination****, you could turn this place into a palace.*
IDM **leave nothing/little to the imagiˈnation** (of clothes) to allow more of sb's body to be seen than usual:

I

Her tight-fitting dress left nothing to the imagination. ➲ more at FIGMENT, STRETCH *n.*

im·agina·tive /ɪˈmædʒɪnətɪv/ *adj.* having or showing new and exciting ideas SYN **inventive**: *an imaginative approach/idea/child* ◇ *recipes that make* ***imaginative use*** *of seasonal vegetables* OPP **unimaginative** ▸ **im·agina·tive·ly** *adv.*: *The stables have been imaginatively converted into offices.*

im·agine 🔑 /ɪˈmædʒɪn/ *verb* **1** 🔑 [T, I] to form a picture in your mind of what sth might be like: **~ sth** *The house was just as she had imagined it.* ◇ *I can't imagine life without the children now.* ◇ **~ (that)...** *Close your eyes and imagine (that) you are in a forest.* ◇ **~ what, how, etc...** *Can you imagine what it must be like to lose your job after 20 years?* ◇ **~ doing sth** *She imagined walking into the office and handing in her resignation.* ◇ *Imagine earning that much money!* ◇ **~ sb/sth doing sth** *I can just imagine him saying that!* ◇ **~ sb/sth to be/do sth** *I had imagined her to be older than that.* ◇ **~ (sb + adj./noun)** *I can imagine him really angry.* ◇ (*informal*) *'He was furious.' 'I* ***can imagine****.'* **2** 🔑 [T] to believe sth that is not true: **~ (that)...** *He's always imagining (that) we're talking about him behind his back.* ◇ **~ sth** *There's nobody there. You're* ***imagining things****.* **3** 🔑 [I, T] to think that sth is probably true SYN **suppose, assume**: *'Can we still buy tickets for the concert?' 'I* ***imagine so****.'* ◇ **~ (that)...** *I don't imagine (that) they'll refuse.*

Synonyms

imagine

think • see • envisage • envision

These words all mean to form an idea in your mind of what sb/sth might be like.

imagine to form an idea in your mind of what sb/sth might be like: *The house was just as she had imagined it.*

think to imagine sth that might happen or might have happened: *We couldn't think where you'd gone.* ◇ ***Just think*** *—this time tomorrow we'll be lying on a beach.*

see to consider sth as a future possibility; to imagine sb as sth: *I can't see her changing her mind.* ◇ *His colleagues see him as a future director.*

envisage (*especially BrE*) to imagine what will happen in the future: *I don't envisage working with him again.* NOTE The usual word for this in American English is **envision** (see below).

envision to imagine what a situation will be like in the future, especially a situation that you intend to work towards: *They envision an equal society, free from poverty and disease.* NOTE **Envision** is used especially in business and political contexts. In North American English it is also used as another form of the word **envisage**: *I don't envision working with him again.*

PATTERNS

- to imagine/see/envisage/envision sb/sth **as** sth
- to imagine/see/envisage/envision (sb) **doing sth**
- to imagine/think/see/envisage/envision **who/what/how...**
- to imagine/think/envisage/envision **that...**

im·agin·eer /ɪˌmædʒɪˈnɪə(r); *NAmE* -ˈnɪr/ *noun, verb*
▪ ***noun*** a person who invents sth exciting, especially a machine for people to ride on in a THEME PARK
▪ ***verb*** **~ sth** to invent sth exciting, especially a machine for people to ride on in a THEME PARK ▸ **im·agin·eer·ing** *noun* [U]

im·aging /ˈɪmɪdʒɪŋ/ *noun* [U] (*computing*) the process of capturing, storing and showing an image on a computer screen: *imaging software*

im·agin·ings /ɪˈmædʒɪnɪŋz/ *noun* [pl.] things that you imagine, that exist only in your mind

imago /ɪˈmeɪɡəʊ; ɪˈmɑːɡ-; *NAmE* -ɡoʊ/ *noun* **1** (*psychology*) a mental image of sb as being perfect that you do not realize you have and that influences your behaviour **2** (*pl.* **imagos** or **im·agi·nes** /ɪˈmeɪdʒɪniːz; ɪˈmɑːdʒ-/) the final and fully developed adult stage of an insect, especially one with wings

imam /ɪˈmɑːm/ *noun* (in Islam) **1** a religious man who leads the prayers in a MOSQUE **2 Imam** the title of a religious leader

IMAX™ /ˈaɪmæks/ *noun* **1** [U] technology which allows films/movies to be shown on extremely large screens **2** [C] a cinema/movie theater or screen that uses IMAX

im·bal·ance /ɪmˈbæləns/ *noun* [C, U] a situation in which two or more things are not the same size or are not treated the same, in a way that is unfair or causes problems: **~ (in/of sth)** *a global imbalance of/in power* ◇ **~ (between A and B)** *Attempts are being made to* ***redress*** (= put right) ***the imbalance*** *between our import and export figures.*

im·be·cile /ˈɪmbəsiːl; *NAmE* -sl/ *noun* **1** a rude way to describe a person that you think is very stupid SYN **idiot**: *They behaved like imbeciles.* **2** (*old-fashioned, offensive*) a person who has a very low level of intelligence ▸ **im·be·cile** (also **im·be·cil·ic**) *adj.* [usually before noun]: *imbecile remarks* **im·be·cil·ity** /ˌɪmbəˈsɪləti/ *noun* [U, C]

imbed = EMBED

im·bibe /ɪmˈbaɪb/ *verb* **1** [I, T] **~ (sth)** (*formal* or *humorous*) to drink sth, especially alcohol **2** [T] **~ sth** (*formal*) to absorb sth, especially information

im·bizo /ɪmˈbiːzəʊ; *NAmE* -zoʊ/ *noun* (*pl.* **-os**) (*SAfrE*) a meeting, especially one between politicians and members of the public, that is held in order to discuss general issues or a particular problem: *a government imbizo on poverty* ◇ *The minister of labour will be holding an imbizo with farmers in the area.*

im·bro·glio /ɪmˈbrəʊliəʊ; *NAmE* ɪmˈbroʊlioʊ/ *noun* (*pl.* **-os**) (*formal*) a complicated situation that causes confusion or embarrassment, especially one that is political

imbue /ɪmˈbjuː/ *verb* [often passive] **~ sb/sth (with sth)** (*formal*) to fill sb/sth with strong feelings, opinions or values SYN **infuse**: *Her voice was imbued with an unusual seriousness.* ◇ *He was imbued with a desire for social justice.*

IMF /ˌaɪ em ˈef/ *abbr.* International Monetary Fund (the organization within the United Nations which is concerned with trade and economic development)

imi·tate /ˈɪmɪteɪt/ *verb* **1 ~ sb/sth** to copy sb/sth: *Her style of painting has been imitated by other artists.* ◇ *Art imitates Nature.* ◇ *Teachers provide a model for children to imitate.* ◇ *No computer can imitate the complex functions of the human brain.* **2 ~ sb** to copy the way a person speaks or behaves, in order to amuse people SYN **mimic**: *She knew that the girls used to imitate her and laugh at her behind her back.*

imi·ta·tion /ˌɪmɪˈteɪʃn/ *noun* **1** [C] a copy of sth, especially sth expensive: *a* ***poor/cheap imitation*** *of the real thing* ◇ *This latest production is a* ***pale imitation*** *of the original* (= it is not nearly as good). ◇ *imitation leather/pearls* ➲ SYNONYMS at ARTIFICIAL **2** [U] the act of copying sb/sth: *A child learns to talk by imitation.* ◇ *Many corporate methods have been adopted by American managers* ***in imitation of*** *Japanese practice.* **3** [C] an act of copying the way sb talks and behaves, especially to make people laugh SYN **impersonation, impression**: *He* ***does an imitation*** *of Barack Obama.*

imi·ta·tive /ˈɪmɪtətɪv; *NAmE* -teɪtɪv/ *adj.* (*formal*, sometimes *disapproving*) that copies sb/sth: *movies that encourage imitative crime* ◇ *His work has been criticized for being imitative and shallow.*

imi·ta·tor /ˈɪmɪteɪtə(r)/ *noun* a person or thing that copies sb/sth else: *The band's success has inspired hundreds of would-be imitators.*

im·macu·late /ɪˈmækjələt/ *adj.* **1** extremely clean and tidy SYN **spotless**: *She always looks immaculate.* ◇ *an immaculate uniform/room* **2** containing no mistakes

SYN **perfect**: *an immaculate performance* ▸ **im·macu·late·ly** *adv.*: *immaculately dressed*

the Im,maculate Con'ception *noun* [sing.] (*religion*) the Christian belief that the Virgin Mary's soul was free from ORIGINAL SIN from the moment of her CONCEPTION

im·man·ent /ˈɪmənənt/ *adj.* (*formal*) present as a natural part of sth; present everywhere

im·ma·ter·ial /ˌɪməˈtɪəriəl; *NAmE* -ˈtɪr-/ *adj.* **1** [not usually before noun] not important in a particular situation **SYN** **irrelevant**: *The cost is immaterial.* ◇ **~ to sb/sth** *It is immaterial to me whether he stays or goes.* **2** (*formal*) not having a physical form: *an immaterial God* **OPP** **material**

im·ma·ture **AW** /ˌɪməˈtjʊə(r); *NAmE* -ˈtʃʊr; -ˈtʊr/ *adj.* **1** behaving in a way that is not sensible and is typical of people who are much younger: *immature behaviour* **2** not fully developed or grown: *immature plants* **OPP** **mature** ▸ **im·ma·tur·ity** **AW** /ˌɪməˈtjʊərəti; *NAmE* -ˈtʃʊr-; -ˈtʊr-/ *noun* [U]

im·meas·ur·able /ɪˈmeʒərəbl/ *adj.* (*formal*) too large, great etc. to be measured: *to cause immeasurable harm* ▸ **im·meas·ur·ably** /-bli/ *adv.*: *Housing standards improved immeasurably after the war.* ◇ *Stress has an immeasurably more serious effect on our lives than we realize.*

im·me·di·acy /ɪˈmiːdiəsi/ *noun* [U] (*formal*) **1** the quality in sth that makes it seem as if it is happening now, close to you and is therefore important, urgent, etc: *the* ***immediacy of*** *threat* ◇ *Email lacks the immediacy of online chat.* **2** lack of delay; speed: *Our aim is immediacy of response to emergency calls.*

im·me·di·ate 0-π /ɪˈmiːdiət/ *adj.*
1 0-π happening or done without delay **SYN** **instant**: *an* ***immediate reaction/response*** ◇ *to take* ***immediate action*** **2** 0-π [usually before noun] existing now and needing urgent attention: *Our immediate concern is to help the families of those who died.* ◇ *The effects of global warming, while not immediate, are potentially catastrophic.* ◇ *The hospital says she's out of* ***immediate danger.*** **3** 0-π [only before noun] next to or very close to a particular place or time: *in the* ***immediate vicinity*** ◇ *The prospects for the* ***immediate future*** *are good.* ◇ *The director is standing on her immediate right.* ◇ *my immediate predecessor in the job* (= the person who had the job just before me) **4** [only before noun] nearest in relationship or rank: *The funeral was attended by her* ***immediate family*** (= her parents, children, brothers and sisters) *only.* ◇ *He is my* ***immediate superior*** (= the person directly above me) *in the company.* **5** [only before noun] having a direct effect: *The immediate cause of death is unknown.* **IDM** see EFFECT *n.*

im·me·di·ate·ly 0-π /ɪˈmiːdiətli/ *adv., conj.*
▪ ***adv.*** **1** 0-π without delay **SYN** **at once**: *She answered almost immediately.* ◇ *The point of my question may not be immediately apparent.* **2** 0-π (usually with prepositions) next to or very close to a particular place or time: *Turn right immediately after the church.* ◇ *the years immediately before the war* **3** 0-π (usually with past participles) closely and directly: *Counselling is being given to those most immediately affected by the tragedy.*
▪ ***conj.*** (*especially BrE*) as soon as: *Immediately she'd gone, I remembered her name.*

im·me·mor·ial /ˌɪməˈmɔːriəl/ *adj.* (*formal* or *literary*) that has existed for longer than people can remember: *an immemorial tradition* ◇ *My family has lived in this area* ***from time immemorial*** (= for hundreds of years).

im·mense /ɪˈmens/ *adj.* extremely large or great **SYN** **enormous**: *There is still an immense amount of work to be done.* ◇ *The benefits are immense.* ◇ *a project of immense importance*

im·mense·ly /ɪˈmensli/ *adv.* extremely; very much **SYN** **enormously**: *immensely popular/difficult/grateful* ◇ *We enjoyed ourselves immensely.*

im·mens·ity /ɪˈmensəti/ *noun* [U] the large size of sth: *the immensity of the universe* ◇ *We were overwhelmed by the sheer immensity of the task.*

im·merse /ɪˈmɜːs; *NAmE* ɪˈmɜːrs/ *verb* **1** **~ sb/sth** (**in sth**) to put sb/sth into a liquid so that they or it are completely covered **2** **~ yourself/sb in sth** to become or make sb completely involved in sth: *She immersed herself in her work.* ◇ *Clare and Phil were immersed in conversation in the corner.*

im·mer·sion /ɪˈmɜːʃn; *NAmE* ɪˈmɜːrʃn; -ʒn/ *noun* [U] **1** **~** (**in sth**) the act of putting sb/sth into a liquid so that they or it are completely covered; the state of being completely covered by a liquid: *Immersion in cold water resulted in rapid loss of heat.* ◇ *baptism by total immersion* (= putting the whole body underwater) **2** **~** (**in sth**) the state of being completely involved in sth: *his long immersion in politics* ◇ *a two-week immersion course in French* (= in which the student will hear and use only French)

im'mersion heater *noun* (*BrE*) a device that provides hot water for a house by heating water in a tank

im·mer·sive /ɪˈmɜːsɪv; *NAmE* ɪˈmɜːrs-/ *adj.* (*technical*) used to describe a computer system or image that seems to surround the user

im·mi·grant **AW** /ˈɪmɪɡrənt/ *noun* a person who has come to live permanently in a country that is not their own: ***immigrant communities/families/workers*** ◇ *illegal immigrants* ➲ COLLOCATIONS at RACE ➲ compare EMIGRANT, MIGRANT

im·mi·grate **AW** /ˈɪmɪɡreɪt/ *verb* [I] **~** (**to...**) (**from...**) (*especially NAmE*) to come and live permanently in a country after leaving your own country ➲ compare EMIGRATE

im·mi·gra·tion **AW** /ˌɪmɪˈɡreɪʃn/ *noun* [U] **1** the process of coming to live permanently in a country that is not your own; the number of people who do this: *laws restricting immigration into the US* ◇ *a rise/fall in immigration* ◇ *immigration officers* ➲ COLLOCATIONS at RACE ➲ compare EMIGRATION **2** (also **immi'gration control**) the place at a port, an airport, etc. where the passports and other documents of people coming into a country are checked: *to go through immigration*

im·mi·nent /ˈɪmɪnənt/ *adj.* (especially of sth unpleasant) likely to happen very soon: *the imminent threat of invasion* ◇ *The system is* ***in imminent danger of*** *collapse.* ◇ *An announcement about his resignation is imminent.* ▸ **im·mi·nence** /-əns/ *noun* [U]: *the imminence of death* **im·mi·nent·ly** *adv.*

im·mis·cible /ɪˈmɪsəbl/ *adj.* (*technical*) (of liquids) that cannot be mixed together **OPP** **miscible**

im·mo·bile /ɪˈməʊbaɪl; *NAmE* ɪˈmoʊbl/ *adj.* **1** not moving **SYN** **motionless**: *She stood immobile by the window.* **2** unable to move: *His illness has left him completely immobile.* **OPP** **mobile** ▸ **im·mo·bil·ity** /ˌɪməˈbɪləti/ *noun* [U]

im·mo·bil·ize (*BrE* also **-ise**) /ɪˈməʊbəlaɪz; *NAmE* ɪˈmoʊ-/ *verb* **~ sth/sb** to prevent sth/sb from moving or from working normally: *a device to immobilize the car engine in case of theft* ◇ *Always immobilize a broken leg immediately.* ▸ **im·mo·bil·iza·tion, -isa·tion** /ɪˌməʊbəlaɪˈzeɪʃn; *NAmE* ɪˌmoʊbələˈz-/ *noun* [U]

im·mo·bil·izer (also **-iser**) /ɪˈməʊbəlaɪzə(r); *NAmE* ɪˈmoʊ-/ *noun* a device that is fitted to a car to stop it moving if sb tries to steal it

im·mod·er·ate /ɪˈmɒdərət; *NAmE* ɪˈmɑːd-/ *adj.* [usually before noun] (*formal, disapproving*) extreme; not reasonable **SYN** **excessive**: *immoderate drinking* **OPP** **moderate** ▸ **im·mod·er·ate·ly** *adv.*

im·mod·est /ɪˈmɒdɪst; *NAmE* ɪˈmɑːd-/ *adj.* **1** (*disapproving*) having or showing a very high opinion of yourself and your abilities **SYN** **conceited** **2** not considered to be socially acceptable by most people, especially concerning sexual behaviour: *an immodest dress* **OPP** **modest**

im·mol·ate /ˈɪməleɪt/ *verb* **~ sb** (*formal*) to kill sb by burning them ▸ **im·mol·ation** /ˌɪməˈleɪʃn/ *noun* [U]

im·moral 0-π /ɪˈmɒrəl; *NAmE* ɪˈmɔːr-; ɪˈmɑːr-/ *adj.*
1 0-π (of people and their behaviour) not considered to be good or honest by most people: *It's immoral to steal.* ◇ *There's nothing immoral about wanting to earn more money.* **2** 0-π not following accepted standards of sexual behaviour: *an immoral act/life/person* ◇ *They were charged*

I

with living off **immoral earnings** (= money earned by working as a PROSTITUTE). ➲ compare AMORAL, MORAL ▸ **im·mor·al·ity** /ˌɪməˈræləti/ *noun* [U, C] (*pl.* -ies): *the immorality of war* ◇ *a life of immorality* **im·mor·al·ly** /ɪˈmɒrəli; *NAmE* ɪˈmɔːr-; ɪˈmɑːr-/ *adv.*

im·mor·tal /ɪˈmɔːtl; *NAmE* ɪˈmɔːrtl/ *adj., noun*
▪ ***adj.*** **1** that lives or lasts for ever: *The soul is immortal.* OPP **mortal** **2** famous and likely to be remembered for ever: *the immortal Goethe* ◇ *In the immortal words of Henry Ford, 'If it ain't broke, don't fix it.'*
▪ ***noun*** **1** a person who is so famous that they will be remembered for ever: *She is one of the Hollywood immortals.* **2** a god or other BEING who is believed to live for ever

im·mor·tal·ity /ˌɪmɔːˈtæləti; *NAmE* ˌɪmɔːrˈt-/ *noun* [U] the state of being immortal: *belief in the immortality of the soul* ◇ *He is well on his way to showbusiness immortality.*

im·mor·tal·ize (*BrE* also **-ise**) /ɪˈmɔːtəlaɪz; *NAmE* ɪˈmɔːrt-/ *verb* **~ sb/sth (in sth)** to prevent sb/sth from being forgotten in the future, especially by mentioning them in literature, making films/movies about them, painting them, etc: *The poet fell in love with her and immortalized her in his verse.*

im·mov·able /ɪˈmuːvəbl/ *adj.* **1** [usually before noun] that cannot be moved: *an immovable object* **2** (of a person or an opinion, etc.) impossible to change or persuade: *On this issue he is completely immovable.*

im·mune /ɪˈmjuːn/ *adj.* [not usually before noun] **1 ~ (to sth)** that cannot catch or be affected by a particular disease or illness: *Adults are often immune to German measles.* **2 ~ (to sth)** not affected by sth: *You'll eventually become immune to criticism.* **3 ~ (from sth)** protected from sth and therefore able to avoid it SYN **exempt**: *No one should be immune from prosecution.*

imˌmune resˈponse *noun* (*biology*) the reaction of the body to the presence of an ANTIGEN (= a substance that can cause disease)

imˈmune system *noun* the system in your body that produces substances to help it fight against infection and disease

im·mun·ity /ɪˈmjuːnəti/ *noun* [U, C] (*pl.* -ies) **1** the body's ability to avoid or not be affected by infection and disease: **~ (to sth)** *immunity to infection* ◇ **~ (against sth)** *The vaccine provides longer immunity against flu.* ➲ COLLOCATIONS at ILL **2 ~ (from sth)** the state of being protected from sth: *The spies were all granted immunity from prosecution.* ◇ ***parliamentary/congressional immunity*** (= protection against particular laws that is given to politicians) ◇ *Officials of all member states receive certain privileges and immunities.* ➲ see also DIPLOMATIC IMMUNITY

im·mun·ize (*BrE* also **-ise**) /ˈɪmjunaɪz/ *verb* **~ sb/sth (against sth)** to protect a person or an animal from a disease, especially by giving them an INJECTION of a VACCINE ➲ compare INOCULATE, VACCINATE ▸ **im·mun·ization, -isa·tion** /ˌɪmjunaɪˈzeɪʃn; *NAmE* -nəˈz-/ *noun* [U, C]: *an immunization programme to prevent epidemics*

im·muno·defi·ciency /ˌɪmjuːnəʊdɪˈfɪʃnsi; *NAmE* -noʊd-/ (also **imˈmune deficiency**) *noun* [U] a medical condition in which your body does not have the normal ability to resist infection: *human immunodeficiency virus or HIV*

im·mun·ology /ˌɪmjuˈnɒlədʒi; *NAmE* -ˈnɑːl-/ *noun* [U] the scientific study of protection against disease ▸ **im·muno·logic·al** /ˌɪmjunəˈlɒdʒɪkl; *NAmE* -ˈlɑːdʒɪkl/ *adj.*

im·muno·sup·pres·sion /ˌɪmjunəʊsəˈpreʃn; *NAmE* -noʊ-/ *noun* [U] (*medical*) the act of stopping the body from reacting against ANTIGENS, for example in order to prevent the body from rejecting a new organ ▸ **im·muno·sup·pres·sant** /ˌɪmjunəʊsəˈpresənt; *NAmE* -noʊ-/ *noun*

im·mure /ɪˈmjʊə(r); *NAmE* ɪˈmjʊr/ *verb* **~ sb** (*literary*) to shut sb in a place so that they cannot get out SYN **imprison**

im·mut·able /ɪˈmjuːtəbl/ *adj.* (*formal*) that cannot be changed; that will never change SYN **unchangeable** ▸ **im·mut·abil·ity** /ɪˌmjuːtəˈbɪləti/ *noun* [U]

imp /ɪmp/ *noun* **1** (in stories) a small creature like a little man, that has magic powers and behaves badly **2** a child who behaves badly, but not in a serious way

im·pact 🔑 AW *noun, verb*
▪ ***noun*** /ˈɪmpækt/ [C, usually sing., U] **1** 🔑 **~ (of sth) (on sb/sth)** the powerful effect that sth has on sb/sth: *the environmental impact of tourism* ◇ *The report assesses the impact of AIDS on the gay community.* ◇ *Her speech made a profound impact on everyone.* ◇ *Businesses are beginning to feel the full impact of the recession.* **2** 🔑 the act of one object hitting another; the force with which this happens: *craters made by meteorite impacts* ◇ *The impact of the blow knocked Jack off balance.* ◇ *The bomb explodes* ***on impact*** (= when it hits something). ◇ *The car is fitted with* ***side impact*** *bars* (= to protect it from a blow from the side).
▪ ***verb*** /ɪmˈpækt/ **1** [I, T] to have an effect on sth SYN **affect**: **~ on/upon sth** *Her father's death impacted greatly on her childhood years.* ◇ **~ sth** (*business*) *The company's performance was impacted by the high value of the pound.* **2** [I, T] **~ (on/upon/with) sth** (*formal*) to hit sth with great force

im·pact·ed /ɪmˈpæktɪd/ *adj.* (of a tooth) that cannot grow correctly because it is under another tooth

im·pair /ɪmˈpeə(r); *NAmE* ɪmˈper/ *verb* **~ sth** (*formal*) to damage sth or make sth worse ➲ SYNONYMS at DAMAGE

im·paired /ɪmˈpeəd; *NAmE* ɪmˈperd/ *adj.* **1** damaged or not functioning normally: *impaired vision/memory* **2 -im·paired** having the type of physical or mental problem mentioned: *hearing-impaired children* ◇ *Nowadays we say someone is 'speech-impaired', not dumb.* ➲ note at DISABLED

im·pair·ment /ɪmˈpeəmənt; *NAmE* -ˈperm-/ *noun* [U, C] (*technical*) the state of having a physical or mental condition which means that part of your body or brain does not work correctly; a particular condition of this sort: *impairment of the functions of the kidney* ◇ *visual impairments*

im·pala /ɪmˈpɑːlə/ *noun* (*pl.* **im·pala** or **im·palas**) an African ANTELOPE with curled horns

im·pale /ɪmˈpeɪl/ *verb* **1 ~ sth (on sth)** to push a sharp pointed object through sth SYN **spear**: *She impaled a lump of meat on her fork.* **2 ~ sb/yourself on sth** if you **impale** yourself on sth, or **are impaled** on it, you have a sharp pointed object pushed into you and you may be caught somewhere by it: *He had fallen and been impaled on some iron railings.*

im·palp·able /ɪmˈpælpəbl/ *adj.* (*formal*) **1** that cannot be felt physically **2** very difficult to understand OPP **palpable**

im·panel (also **em·panel**) /ɪmˈpænl/ *verb* (-ll-, *US* -l-) **~ sb/sth** (*especially US*) to choose the members of a JURY in a court case; to choose sb as a member of a JURY

im·part /ɪmˈpɑːt; *NAmE* ɪmˈpɑːrt/ *verb* (*formal*) **1 ~ sth (to sb)** to pass information, knowledge, etc. to other people SYN **convey** **2 ~ sth (to sth)** to give a particular quality to sth SYN **lend**: *The spice imparts an Eastern flavour to the dish.*

im·par·tial /ɪmˈpɑːʃl; *NAmE* ɪmˈpɑːrʃl/ *adj.* not supporting one person or group more than another SYN **neutral, unbiased**: *an* ***impartial inquiry/observer*** ◇ *to give* ***impartial advice*** ◇ *As chairman, I must remain impartial.* OPP **partial** ▸ **im·par·ti·al·ity** /ˌɪmˌpɑːʃiˈæləti; *NAmE* -ˌpɑːrʃi-/ *noun* [U] **im·par·tial·ly** /-ʃəli/ *adv.*

im·pass·able /ɪmˈpɑːsəbl; *NAmE* -ˈpæs-/ *adj.* (of a road, an area etc.) impossible to travel on or through, especially because it is in bad condition or it has been blocked by sth OPP **passable**

im·passe /ˈæmpɑːs; *NAmE* ˈɪmpæs/ *noun* [usually sing.] a difficult situation in which no progress can be made because the people involved cannot agree what to do SYN **deadlock**: *to* ***break/end the impasse*** ◇ *Negotiations have* ***reached an impasse***.

im·pas·sioned /ɪm'pæʃnd/ *adj.* [usually before noun] (usually of speech) showing strong feelings about sth SYN **fervent**: *an **impassioned plea/speech/defence***

im·pas·sive /ɪm'pæsɪv/ *adj.* not showing any feeling or emotion SYN **emotionless**: *her **impassive expression/face*** ▶ **im·pas·sive·ly** *adv.*

im·pa·tient 0‑ /ɪm'peɪʃnt/ *adj.* **1** 0‑ annoyed or irritated by sb/sth, especially because you have to wait for a long time: *I'd been waiting for twenty minutes and I was getting impatient.* ◇ **~ (with sb/sth)** *Try not to be too impatient with her.* ◇ **~ (at sth)** *Sarah was becoming increasingly impatient at their lack of interest.* ◇ *He waved them away with an impatient gesture.* **2** 0‑ wanting to do sth soon; wanting sth to happen soon: **~ to do sth** *She was clearly impatient to leave.* ◇ **~ for sth** *impatient for change* **3 ~ of sb/sth** (*formal*) unable or unwilling to accept sth unpleasant: *impatient of criticism* ▶ **im·pa·tience** /ɪm'peɪʃns/ *noun* [U]: *She was bursting with impatience to tell me the news.* **im·pa·tient·ly** *adv.*: *We sat waiting impatiently for the movie to start.*

im·peach /ɪm'piːtʃ/ *verb* **1 ~ sb (for sth)** (of a court or other official body, especially in the US) to charge an important public figure with a serious crime **2 ~ sth** (*formal*) to raise doubts about sth SYN **question**: *to impeach sb's motives* ▶ **im·peach·ment** *noun* [U, C]

im·peach·able /ɪm'piːtʃəbl/ *adj.* (*especially US*) (of a crime) for which a politician or a person who works for the government can be impeached: *an impeachable offense*

im·pec·cable /ɪm'pekəbl/ *adj.* without mistakes or faults SYN **perfect**: ***impeccable manners/taste*** ◇ *Her written English is impeccable.* ◇ *He was dressed in a suit and an impeccable white shirt.* ▶ **im·pec·cably** /-bli/ *adv.*: *to behave impeccably* ◇ *impeccably dressed*

im·pe·cu·ni·ous /ˌɪmpɪ'kjuːniəs/ *adj.* (*formal* or *humorous*) having little or no money SYN **poor, penniless**

im·ped·ance /ɪm'piːdns/ *noun* [U] (*physics*) a measurement of the total RESISTANCE of a piece of electrical equipment, etc. to the flow of an ALTERNATING CURRENT

im·pede /ɪm'piːd/ *verb* [often passive] **~ sth** (*formal*) to delay or stop the progress of sth SYN **hinder, hamper**: *Work on the building was impeded by severe weather.*

im·pedi·ment /ɪm'pedɪmənt/ *noun* **1 ~ (to sth)** (*formal*) something that delays or stops the progress of sth SYN **obstacle**: *The level of inflation is a serious impediment to economic recovery.* **2** a physical problem that makes it difficult to speak normally: *a speech impediment*

im·pedi·menta /ɪmˌpedɪ'mentə/ *noun* [pl.] (*formal* or *humorous*) the bags and other equipment that you take with you, especially when travelling, and that are difficult to carry

impel /ɪm'pel/ *verb* (-ll-) (*formal*) if an idea or feeling **impels** you to do sth, you feel as if you are forced to do it: **~ sb to do sth** *He felt impelled to investigate further.* ◇ **~ sb (to sth)** *There are various reasons that impel me to that conclusion.*

im·pend·ing /ɪm'pendɪŋ/ *adj.* [only before noun] (usually of an unpleasant event) that is going to happen very soon SYN **imminent**: *his impending retirement* ◇ *warnings of **impending danger/disaster***

im·pene·trable /ɪm'penɪtrəbl/ *adj.* **1** that cannot be entered, passed through or seen through: *an impenetrable jungle* ◇ *impenetrable darkness* OPP **penetrable** **2** impossible to understand SYN **incomprehensible**: *an impenetrable mystery* ◇ **~ to sb** *Their jargon is impenetrable to an outsider.* ▶ **im·pene·tra·bil·ity** /ɪmˌpenɪtrə'bɪləti/ *noun* [U] **im·pene·trably** /-bli/ *adv.*

im·peni·tent /ɪm'penɪtənt/ *adj.* (*formal*) not feeling ashamed or sorry about sth bad you have done

im·pera·tive /ɪm'perətɪv/ *adj.*, *noun*
■ ***adj.*** **1** [not usually before noun] (*formal*) very important and needing immediate attention or action SYN **vital**: **~ (that ...)** *It is absolutely imperative that we finish by next week.* ◇ **~ (to do sth)** *It is imperative to continue the treatment for at least two months.* ⊃ LANGUAGE BANK at VITAL **2** (*formal*) expressing authority: *an imperative tone* **3** [only before noun] (*grammar*) expressing an order: *an imperative sentence*
■ ***noun*** **1** (*formal*) a thing that is very important and needs immediate attention or action: *the economic imperative of quality education for all* **2** (*grammar*) the form of a verb that expresses an order; a verb in this form: *In 'Go away!' the verb is **in the imperative**.* ◇ *'Go away!' is an imperative.*

im·per·cept·ible /ˌɪmpə'septəbl; *NAmE* -pər's-/ *adj.* (*formal*) very small and therefore unable to be seen or felt; OPP **perceptible**: *imperceptible changes in temperature* ▶ **im·per·cept·ibly** /-əbli/ *adv.*

im·per·fect /ɪm'pɜːfɪkt; *NAmE* -'pɜːrf-/ *adj.*, *noun*
■ ***adj.*** containing faults or mistakes; not complete or perfect SYN **flawed**: *an imperfect world* ◇ *an imperfect understanding of English* ◇ *All our sale items are slightly imperfect.* ▶ **im·per·fect·ly** *adv.*
■ ***noun*** **the imperfect** (also **the imˌperfect 'tense**) [sing.] (*grammar*) the verb tense that expresses action in the past that is not complete. It is often called the **past progressive** or **past continuous**: *In 'while I was washing my hair', the verb is **in the imperfect**.*

im·per·fec·tion /ˌɪmpə'fekʃn; *NAmE* -pər'f-/ *noun* [C, U] a fault or weakness in sb/sth: *They learned to live with each other's imperfections.*

im·per·ial /ɪm'pɪəriəl; *NAmE* -'pɪr-/ *adj.* [only before noun] **1** connected with an empire: *the imperial family/palace/army* ◇ *imperial power/expansion* **2** connected with the system for measuring length, weight and volume using pounds, inches, etc. ⊃ compare METRIC

im·peri·al·ism /ɪm'pɪəriəlɪzəm; *NAmE* -'pɪr-/ *noun* [U] (usually *disapproving*) **1** a system in which one country controls other countries, often after defeating them in a war: *Roman imperialism* **2** the fact of a powerful country increasing its influence over other countries through business, culture, etc: ***cultural/economic imperialism*** ▶ **im·peri·al·is·t** (also **im·peri·al·is·tic** /ɪmˌpɪəriə'lɪstɪk; *NAmE* -ˌpɪr-/) *adj.*: *an imperialist power* ◇ *imperialist ambitions*

im·peri·al·ist /ɪm'pɪəriəlɪst; *NAmE* -'pɪr-/ *noun* (usually *disapproving*) a person, such as a politician, who supports imperialism

im·peril /ɪm'perəl/ *verb* (-ll-, *US* -l-) **~ sth/sb** (*formal*) to put sth/sb in danger SYN **endanger**

im·peri·ous /ɪm'pɪəriəs; *NAmE* -'pɪr-/ *adj.* (*formal*) expecting people to obey you and treating them as if they are not as important as you: *an **imperious gesture/voice/command*** ▶ **im·peri·ous·ly** *adv.*: *'Get it now,' she demanded imperiously.*

im·per·ish·able /ɪm'perɪʃəbl/ *adj.* (*formal* or *literary*) that will last for a long time or forever SYN **enduring**

im·per·man·ent /ɪm'pɜːmənənt; *NAmE* -'pɜːrm-/ *adj.* (*formal*) that will not last or stay the same forever OPP **permanent** ▶ **im·per·man·ence** /-əns/ *noun* [U]

im·per·me·able /ɪm'pɜːmiəbl; *NAmE* -'pɜːrm-/ *adj.* **~ (to sth)** (*technical*) not allowing a liquid or gas to pass through OPP **permeable**

im·per·mis·sible /ˌɪmpɜː'mɪsəbl; *NAmE* -pɜːr'm-/ *adj.* that cannot be allowed: *an impermissible invasion of privacy* OPP **permissible**

im·per·son·al /ɪm'pɜːsənl; *NAmE* -'pɜːrs-/ *adj.* **1** (usually *disapproving*) lacking friendly human feelings or atmosphere; making you feel unimportant: *a vast impersonal organization* ◇ *an impersonal hotel room* ◇ *Business letters need not be formal and impersonal.* ◇ *a cold impersonal stare* **2** not referring to any particular person: *Let's keep the criticism general and impersonal.* **3** (*grammar*) an **impersonal** verb or sentence has 'it' or 'there' as the subject ▶ **im·per·son·al·ity** /ɪmˌpɜːsə'næləti; *NAmE* -ˌpɜːrs-/ *noun* [U]: *the cold impersonality of some modern cities* **im·per·son·ally** /ɪm'pɜːsənəli; *NAmE* -'pɜːrs-/ *adv.*

Language Bank

impersonal

Giving opinions using impersonal language

- **It is vital that** more is done to prevent the illegal trade in wild animals. ◇ (Compare: *We have to do more to stop people trading wild animals illegally.*)
- **It is clear that** more needs to be done to protect biodiversity. ◇ (Compare: *We clearly need to do more to protect biodiversity.*)
- **It is unfortunate that** the practice of keeping monkeys as pets still continues. ◇ (Compare: *It's absolutely terrible that people still keep monkeys as pets.*)
- **It is difficult** for many people **to** understand the reasons why certain individuals choose to hunt animals for sport. ◇ (Compare: *I can't understand why anyone would want to kill animals for fun.*)
- Unfortunately, **it would seem that** not enough is being done to support tiger conservation. ◇ (Compare: *Governments aren't doing enough to help tiger conservation.*)
- **There is no doubt that** the greatest threat to polar bears comes from global warming. ◇ (Compare: *I believe that the greatest threat...*)

➲ Language Banks at OPINION, PERHAPS, VITAL

I

im͵personal ˈpronoun *noun* (*grammar*) a pronoun (in English, the pronoun 'it') that does not refer to a person or thing or to any other part of the sentence, for example in 'it was raining'

im·per·son·ate /ɪmˈpɜːsəneɪt; *NAmE* -ˈpɜːrs-/ *verb* **~ sb** to pretend to be sb in order to trick people or to entertain them: *He was caught trying to impersonate a security guard.* ◇ *They do a pretty good job of impersonating Laurel and Hardy.* ▸ **im·per·son·ation** /ɪm͵pɜːsəˈneɪʃn; *NAmE* -͵pɜːrs-/ *noun* [C, U] **SYN** **impression**: *He did an extremely convincing impersonation of the singer.*

im·per·son·ator /ɪmˈpɜːsəneɪtə(r); *NAmE* -ˈpɜːrs-/ *noun* a person who copies the way another person talks or behaves in order to entertain people: *The show included a **female impersonator*** (= a man dressed as a woman).

im·per·tin·ent /ɪmˈpɜːtɪnənt; *NAmE* -ˈpɜːrtn-/ *adj.* rude and not showing respect for sb who is older or more important **SYN** **impolite**: *an impertinent question/child* ◇ *Would it be impertinent to ask why you're leaving?* ➲ SYNONYMS at RUDE ▸ **im·per·tin·ence** /-əns/ *noun* [U, C, usually sing.]: *She had the impertinence to ask my age!* **im·per·tin·ent·ly** *adv.*

im·per·turb·able /͵ɪmpəˈtɜːbəbl; *NAmE* -pərˈtɜːrb-/ *adj.* (*formal*) not easily upset or worried by a difficult situation; calm ▸ **im·per·turb·ability** /͵ɪmpə͵tɜːbəˈbɪləti; *NAmE* -pər͵tɜːrb-/ *noun* [U] **im·per·turb·ably** /-əbli/ *adv.*

im·per·vi·ous /ɪmˈpɜːviəs; *NAmE* -ˈpɜːrv-/ *adj.* **1 ~ to sth** not affected or influenced by sth: *impervious to criticism/pain* **2** (*technical*) not allowing a liquid or gas to pass through: *an **impervious rock/layer*** ◇ **~ to sth** *impervious to moisture*

im·pe·tigo /͵ɪmpɪˈtaɪɡəʊ; *NAmE* -ɡoʊ/ *noun* [U] an infectious disease that causes sore areas on the skin

im·petu·ous /ɪmˈpetʃuəs/ *adj.* acting or done quickly and without thinking carefully about the results **SYN** **rash, impulsive**: *an impetuous young woman* ◇ *an impetuous decision* ▸ **im·petu·os·ity** /ɪm͵petʃuˈɒsəti; *NAmE* -ˈɑːsəti/ *noun* [U] **im·petu·ous·ly** *adv.*

im·petus /ˈɪmpɪtəs/ *noun* **1** [U, sing.] something that encourages a process or activity to develop more quickly **SYN** **stimulus**: *The debate seems to have lost much of its initial impetus.* ◇ **~ to sth/to do sth** *to give (a) **new/fresh impetus** to sth* ◇ **~ for sth** *His articles provided the main impetus for change.* **2** [U] (*technical*) the force or energy with which sth moves

im·pinge /ɪmˈpɪndʒ/ *verb* [I] **~ (on/upon sth/sb)** (*formal*) to have a noticeable effect on sth/sb, especially a bad one **SYN** **encroach**: *He never allowed his work to impinge on his private life.*

im·pious /ˈɪmpiəs; ɪmˈpaɪəs/ *adj.* (*formal*) showing a lack of respect for God and religion **OPP** **pious** ▸ **im·pi·ety** /ɪmˈpaɪəti/ *noun* [U]

imp·ish /ˈɪmpɪʃ/ *adj.* showing a lack of respect for sb/sth in a way that is amusing rather than serious **SYN** **mischievous**: *an **impish grin/look*** ➲ see also IMP ▸ **imp·ish·ly** *adv.*

im·plac·able /ɪmˈplækəbl/ *adj.* **1** (of strong negative opinions or feelings) that cannot be changed: *implacable hatred* **2** (of a person) unwilling to stop opposing sb/sth: *an implacable enemy* ▸ **im·plac·ably** /ɪmˈplækəbli/ *adv.*: *to be implacably opposed to the plan*

im·plant *verb, noun*

- ***verb*** /ɪmˈplɑːnt; *NAmE* -ˈplænt/ **1** [T] **~ sth (in/into sth)** to fix an idea, attitude, etc. firmly in sb's mind: *Prejudices can easily become implanted in the mind.* **2** [T] **~ sth (in/into sth)** to put sth (usually sth artificial) into a part of the body for medical purposes, usually by means of an operation: *an electrode implanted into the brain* ➲ compare TRANSPLANT **3** [I] **~ (in/into sth)** (of an egg or an EMBRYO) to become fixed inside the body of a person or an animal so that it can start to develop ▸ **im·plant·ation** /͵ɪmplɑːnˈteɪʃn; *NAmE* -plæn-/ *noun* [U]
- ***noun*** /ˈɪmplɑːnt; *NAmE* -plænt/ something that is put into a person's body in a medical operation: *silicone breast implants* ➲ compare TRANSPLANT

im·plaus·ible /ɪmˈplɔːzəbl/ *adj.* not seeming reasonable or likely to be true: *an **implausible claim/idea/theory*** ◇ *It was all **highly implausible**.* **OPP** **plausible** ▸ **im·plaus·ibly** *adv.*

im·ple·ment **AW** *verb, noun*

- ***verb*** /ˈɪmplɪment/ **~ sth** (*formal*) to make sth that has been officially decided start to happen or be used **SYN** **carry out**: *to **implement changes/decisions/policies/reforms*** ▸ **im·ple·men·ta·tion** **AW** /͵ɪmplɪmenˈteɪʃn/ *noun* [U]: *the implementation of the new system*
- ***noun*** /ˈɪmplɪmənt/ (*formal*) a tool or an instrument, often one that is quite simple and that is used outdoors: *agricultural implements*

im·pli·cate **AW** /ˈɪmplɪkeɪt/ *verb* **1 ~ sb (in sth)** to show or suggest that sb is involved in sth bad or criminal **SYN** **incriminate**: *He tried to avoid saying anything that would implicate him further.* **2 ~ sth (in/as sth)** to show or suggest that sth is the cause of sth bad: *The results implicate poor hygiene as one cause of the outbreak.*

IDM **be implicated in sth** to be involved in a crime; to be responsible for sth bad: *Senior officials were implicated in the scandal.*

im·pli·ca·tion 0‑m **AW** /͵ɪmplɪˈkeɪʃn/ *noun* **1** 0‑m [C, usually pl.] **~ (of sth) (for sth)** a possible effect or result of an action or a decision: *They failed to consider the wider implications of their actions.* ◇ *The development of the site will **have implications for** the surrounding countryside.* **2** 0‑m [C, U] something that is suggested or indirectly stated (= sth that is implied): *The implication in his article is that being a housewife is greatly inferior to every other occupation.* ◇ *He criticized the Director and, **by implication**, the whole of the organization.* **3** [U] **~ (of sb) (in sth)** the fact of being involved, or of involving sb, in sth, especially a crime **SYN** **involvement**: *He resigned after his implication in a sex scandal.*

im·pli·ca·ture /ˈɪmplɪkətʃə(r)/ *noun* (*technical*) **1** [U] the act of suggesting that you feel or think sth is true, without saying so directly **2** [C] something that you can understand from what is said, but which is not stated directly: *An implicature of 'Some of my friends came' is 'Some of my friends did not come'.*

im·pli·cit **AW** /ɪmˈplɪsɪt/ *adj.* **1 ~ (in sth)** suggested without being directly expressed: *Implicit in his speech was the assumption that they were guilty.* ◇ *implicit criticism* **2 ~ (in sth)** forming part of sth (although perhaps not directly expressed): *The ability to listen is implicit in the teacher's role.* **3** complete and not doubted

SYN absolute: *She had the implicit trust of her staff.* ➲ compare EXPLICIT ▶ **im·pli·cit·ly** AW *adv.*: *It reinforces, implicitly or explicitly, the idea that money is all-important.* ◇ *I trust John implicitly.*

im·plode /ɪm'pləʊd; *NAmE* ɪm'ploʊd/ *verb* **1** [I] to burst or explode and collapse into the centre **2** [I] (of an organization, a system, etc.) to fail suddenly and completely ▶ **im·plo·sion** /ɪm'pləʊʒn; *NAmE* -'ploʊ-/ *noun* [C, U]

im·plore /ɪm'plɔː(r)/ *verb* (*formal* or *literary*) to ask sb to do sth in an anxious way because you want or need it very much **SYN beseech, beg**: **~ sb to do sth** *She implored him to stay.* ◇ **~ (sb) + speech** *'Help me,' he implored.* ◇ **~ sb** *Tell me it's true. I implore you.* ▶ **im·plor·ing** *adj.*: *She gave him an imploring look.*

imply 0‑ AW /ɪm'plaɪ/ *verb* (**im·plies, im·ply·ing, im·plied, im·plied**)
1 0‑ to suggest that sth is true or that you feel or think sth, without saying so directly: **~ (that)...** *Are you implying (that) I am wrong?* ◇ **~ sth** *I disliked the implied criticism in his voice.* ◇ **it is implied that...** *It was implied that we were at fault.* ➲ note at INFER **2** 0‑ to make it seem likely that sth is true or exists **SYN suggest**: **~ (that)...** *The survey implies (that) more people are moving house than was thought.* ◇ **it is implied that...** *It was implied in the survey that...* ◇ **~ sth** *The fact that she was here implies a degree of interest.* **3 ~ sth** (of an idea, action, etc.) to make sth necessary in order to be successful **SYN mean**: *The project implies an enormous investment in training.* ➲ see also IMPLICATION

im·pol·ite /ˌɪmpə'laɪt/ *adj.* not polite **SYN rude**: *Some people think it is impolite to ask someone's age.* ➲ SYNONYMS at RUDE ▶ **im·pol·ite·ly** *adv.* **im·pol·ite·ness** *noun* [U]

im·pol·it·ic /ɪm'pɒlətɪk; *NAmE* -'pɑːl-/ *adj.* (*formal*) not wise **SYN unwise**: *It would have been impolitic to refuse his offer.*

im·pon·der·able /ɪm'pɒndərəbl; *NAmE* -'pɑːn-/ *noun* [usually pl.] (*formal*) something that is difficult to measure or estimate: *We can't predict the outcome. There are too many imponderables.* ▶ **im·pon·der·able** *adj.*

im·port 0‑ *noun, verb*
■ ***noun*** /'ɪmpɔːt; *NAmE* 'ɪmpɔːrt/ **1** 0‑ [C, usually pl.] a product or service that is brought into one country from another: *food imports from abroad* **OPP export** ➲ COLLOCATIONS at ECONOMY **2** 0‑ [U, pl.] the act of bringing a product or service into one country from another: *The report calls for a ban on the import of hazardous waste.* ◇ *import controls* ◇ *an import licence* ◇ *imports of oil* **OPP export 3** [U] (*formal*) importance: *matters of great import* **4 the ~ (of sth)** [sing.] (*formal*) the meaning of sth, especially when it is not immediately clear: *It is difficult to understand the full import of this statement.*
■ ***verb*** /ɪm'pɔːt; *NAmE* ɪm'pɔːrt/ **1** 0‑ to bring a product, a service, an idea, etc. into one country from another: **~ sth** *The country has to import most of its raw materials.* ◇ **~ sth (from...) (into...)** *goods imported from Japan into the US* ◇ *customs imported from the West* **2 ~ sth (from...) (into...)** (*computing*) to get data from another program, changing its form so that the program you are using can read it **OPP export** ▶ **im·port·ation** /ˌɪmpɔː'teɪʃn; *NAmE* -pɔːr't-/ *noun* [U, C] **SYN import**: *a ban on the importation of ivory*

im·port·ance 0‑ /ɪm'pɔːtns; *NAmE* -'pɔːrt-/ *noun* [U] the quality of being important: *She* ***stressed the importance of*** *careful preparation.* ◇ *It's a matter* ***of the greatest importance*** *to me.* ◇ *They* ***attach*** *great* ***importance*** *to the project.* ◇ *the relative importance of the two ideas* ◇ *State your reasons in* ***order of importance.*** ◇ *He was very aware of his own importance* (= of his status).

im·port·ant 0‑ /ɪm'pɔːtnt; *NAmE* -'pɔːrt-/ *adj.*
1 0‑ having a great effect on people or things; of great value: *an important decision/factor* ◇ *I have an important announcement to make.* ◇ *Money played an important role in his life.* ◇ *Listening is an important part of the job.* ◇ *one of the most important collections of American art* ◇ ***It is important to*** *follow the manufacturer's instructions.* ◇ ***It is important that*** *he attend every day.* ◇ (*BrE*) ***It is important that*** *he should attend every day.* ◇ ***It is important for*** *him* ***to*** *attend every day.* ◇ **~ (to sb)** *It's very important to me that you should be there.* ◇ ***The important thing*** *is to keep trying.* ➲ LANGUAGE BANK at EMPHASIS **2** 0‑ (of a person) having great influence or authority: *an important member of the team* ◇ *He likes to feel important.* ▶ **im·port·ant·ly** 0‑ *adv.*: *More importantly, can he be trusted?* ◇ *She was sitting importantly behind a big desk.* ➲ LANGUAGE BANK at EMPHASIS

im·port·er /ɪm'pɔːtə(r); *NAmE* -'pɔːrt-/ *noun* a person, company, etc. that buys goods from another country in order to sell them in their own country: *a London-based importer of Italian food* ➲ compare EXPORTER

im·por·tun·ate /ɪm'pɔːtʃənət; *NAmE* -'pɔːrt-/ *adj.* (*formal*) asking for things many times in a way that is annoying

im·por·tune /ˌɪmpɔː'tjuːn; *NAmE* -pɔːr'tuːn/ *verb* **~ sb (for sth)** | **~ sb to do sth** (*formal*) to ask sb for sth many times and in a way that is annoying **SYN pester**

im·pose 0‑ AW /ɪm'pəʊz; *NAmE* ɪm'poʊz/ *verb*
1 0‑ [T] **~ sth (on/upon sth/sb)** to introduce a new law, rule, tax, etc; to order that a rule, punishment, etc. be used: *A new tax was imposed on fuel.* **2** 0‑ [T] **~ sth (on/upon sb/sth)** to force sb/sth to have to deal with sth that is difficult or unpleasant: *to* ***impose limitations/restrictions/constraints*** *on sth* ◇ *This system imposes additional financial burdens on many people.* **3** 0‑ [T] **~ sth (on/upon sb)** to make sb accept the same opinions, wishes, etc. as your own: *She didn't want to impose her values on her family.* ◇ *It was noticeable how a few people managed to* ***impose*** *their* ***will on*** *the others.* **4** [I] to expect sb to do sth for you or to spend time with you, when it may not be convenient for them: *'You must stay for lunch.' 'Well, thanks, but I don't want to impose...'* ◇ **~ on/upon sb/sth** *Everyone imposes on Dave's good nature.* **5** [T] **~ yourself (on/upon sb/sth)** to make sb/sth accept or be aware of your presence or ideas: *European civilization was the first to impose itself across the whole world.*

im·pos·ing /ɪm'pəʊzɪŋ; *NAmE* -'poʊz-/ *adj.* impressive to look at; making a strong impression: *a grand and imposing building* ◇ *a tall imposing woman*

im·pos·ition AW /ˌɪmpə'zɪʃn/ *noun* **1** [U] the act of introducing sth such as a new law or rule, or a new tax: *the imposition of martial law* ◇ *the imposition of tax on domestic fuel* **2** [C] an unfair or unreasonable thing that sb expects or asks you to do: *I'd like to stay if it's not too much of an imposition.*

im·pos·sible 0‑ /ɪm'pɒsəbl; *NAmE* -'pɑːs-/ *adj.*
1 0‑ that cannot exist or be done; not possible: ***almost/virtually impossible*** ◇ ***It's impossible for*** *me to be there before eight.* ◇ *It's impossible to prove.* ◇ ***I find it impossible*** *to lie to her.* ◇ *an* ***impossible dream/goal*** **OPP possible 2** 0‑ very difficult to deal with: *I've been placed in an* ***impossible position.*** ◇ *Honestly, you're impossible at times!* **3 the impossible** *noun* [sing.] a thing that is or seems impossible: *to attempt the impossible* ▶ **im·pos·si·bil·ity** /ɪmˌpɒsə'bɪləti; *NAmE* -ˌpɑːsə-/ *noun* [U, C, usually sing.] (*pl.* **-ies**): *the sheer impossibility of providing enough food for everyone* ◇ *a virtual impossibility* **im·pos·sibly** /ɪm'pɒsəbli; *NAmE* -'pɑːs-/ *adv.*: *an impossibly difficult problem* (= impossible to solve) ◇ *He was impossibly handsome* (= it was difficult to believe that he could be so handsome).

im·pos·tor (*BrE* also **im·pos·ter**) /ɪm'pɒstə(r); *NAmE* -'pɑːs-/ *noun* a person who pretends to be sb else in order to trick people

im·pos·ture /ɪm'pɒstʃə(r); *NAmE* -'pɑːs-/ *noun* [U, C] (*formal*) an act of tricking people deliberately by pretending to be sb else

im·po·tent /'ɪmpətənt/ *adj.* **1** having no power to change things or to influence a situation **SYN powerless**: *Without the chairman's support, the committee is impotent.* ◇ *She blazed with impotent rage.* **2** (of a man) unable to achieve an ERECTION and therefore unable to have full

I

sex ▸ **im·po·tence** /ˈɪmpətəns/ *noun* [U]: *a feeling of impotence in the face of an apparently insoluble problem* ◇ *male impotence* **im·po·tent·ly** *adv.*

im·pound /ɪmˈpaʊnd/ *verb* (*law*) **1** **~ sth** (of the police, courts of law, etc.) to take sth away from sb, so that they cannot use it SYN **confiscate**: *The car was impounded by the police after the accident.* **2** **~ sth** to shut up dogs, cats, etc. found on the streets in a POUND, until their owners collect them

im·pov·er·ish /ɪmˈpɒvərɪʃ; *NAmE* -ˈpɑːv-/ *verb* **1** **~ sb** to make sb poor: *These changes are likely to impoverish single-parent families even further.* **2** **~ sth** to make sth worse in quality: *Intensive cultivation has impoverished the soil.* ▸ **im·pov·er·ish·ment** *noun* [U]

im·pov·er·ished /ɪmˈpɒvərɪʃt; *NAmE* -ˈpɑːv-/ *adj.* **1** very poor; without money: *impoverished peasants* ◇ *the impoverished areas of the city* ➲ SYNONYMS at POOR **2** poor in quality, because sth is missing

im·prac·tic·able /ɪmˈpræktɪkəbl/ *adj.* impossible or very difficult to do; not practical in a particular situation: *It would be impracticable for each member to be consulted on every occasion.* ➲ compare IMPRACTICAL OPP **practicable** ▸ **im·prac·tic·abil·ity** /ɪmˌpræktɪkəˈbɪləti/ *noun* [U]

im·prac·ti·cal /ɪmˈpræktɪkl/ *adj.* **1** not sensible or realistic: *It was totally impractical to think that we could finish the job in two months.* **2** (of people) not good at doing things that involve using the hands; not good at planning or organizing things OPP **practical** ➲ compare IMPRACTICABLE ▸ **im·prac·ti·cal·ity** /ɪmˌpræktɪˈkæləti/ *noun* [U]

im·pre·ca·tion /ˌɪmprɪˈkeɪʃn/ *noun* (*formal*) a CURSE (= an offensive word that is used to express extreme anger)

im·pre·cise AW /ˌɪmprɪˈsaɪs/ *adj.* not giving exact details or making sth clear SYN **inaccurate**: *an imprecise definition* ◇ *imprecise information* ◇ *The witness's descriptions were too imprecise to be of any real value.* OPP **precise** ▸ **im·pre·cise·ly** *adv.*: *These terms are often used imprecisely and interchangeably.* **im·pre·ci·sion** /ˌɪmprɪˈsɪʒn/ *noun* [U]: *There is considerable imprecision in the terminology used.*

im·preg·nable /ɪmˈpregnəbl/ *adj.* **1** an **impregnable** building is so strongly built that it cannot be entered by force: *an impregnable fortress* **2** strong and impossible to defeat or change SYN **invincible**: *The team built up an impregnable 5–1 lead.*

im·preg·nate /ˈɪmpregneɪt; *NAmE* ɪmˈpreg-/ *verb* **1** [usually passive] **~ sth** (**with sth**) to make a substance spread through an area so that the area is full of the substance: *The pad is impregnated with insecticide.* **2** **~ sb/sth** (*formal*) to make a woman or female animal pregnant ▸ **im·preg·na·tion** /ˌɪmpregˈneɪʃn/ *noun* [U]

im·pres·ario /ˌɪmprəˈsɑːriəʊ; *NAmE* -rioʊ/ *noun* (*pl.* -os) a person who arranges plays in the theatre, etc, especially a person who manages a theatre, OPERA or BALLET company

im·press 0‑w /ɪmˈpres/ *verb*
1 0‑w [T, I] if a person or thing **impresses** you, you feel admiration for them or it: **~ (sb)** *We interviewed a number of candidates but none of them impressed us.* ◇ *The Grand Canyon never fails to impress.* ◇ *His sincerity impressed her.* ◇ **~ sb with sth/sb** *He impressed her with his sincerity.* ◇ **it impresses sb that...** *It impressed me that she remembered my name.* ◇ **sb is impressed that...** *I was impressed that she remembered my name.* ➲ see also IMPRESSED, IMPRESSIVE **2** [T] **~ sth on/upon sb** (*formal*) to make sb understand how important, serious, etc. sth is by emphasizing it: *He impressed on us the need for immediate action.* **3** [T] **~ sth/itself on/upon sth** (*formal*) to have a great effect on sth, especially sb's mind, imagination, etc: *Her words impressed themselves on my memory.*

im·pressed 0‑w /ɪmˈprest/ *adj.* feeling admiration for sb/sth because you think they are particularly good, interesting, etc: *I must admit I am impressed.* ◇ **~ by/with sb/sth** *We were all impressed by her enthusiasm.* ◇ *She was* ***suitably impressed*** (= as impressed as sb had hoped) *with the painting.* ➲ see also UNIMPRESSED

im·pres·sion 0‑w /ɪmˈpreʃn/ *noun*
▸ IDEA/OPINION **1** 0‑w an idea, a feeling or an opinion that you get about sb/sth, or that sb/sth gives you: ***a general/an overall impression*** ◇ ***an initial/a lasting impression*** ◇ **~ (of sb/sth)** *to get* ***a good/bad impression*** *of sb/sth* ◇ *My* ***first impression*** *of him was favourable.* ◇ *She* ***gives the impression*** *of being very busy.* ◇ **~ (that...)** *I did not* ***get the impression*** *that they were unhappy about the situation.* ◇ ***My impression is*** *that there are still a lot of problems.* ◇ *Try and smile. You don't want to* ***give people the wrong impression*** (= that you are not friendly).
▸ EFFECT **2** 0‑w the effect that an experience or a person has on sb/sth: *a* ***big impression*** ◇ **~ (on sb)** *His trip to India* ***made a*** *strong* ***impression*** *on him.* ◇ *My words* ***made no impression*** *on her.* ◇ *You'll have to play better than that if you really want to* ***make an impression*** (= to make people admire you).
▸ DRAWING **3** a drawing showing what a person looks like or what a place or a building will look like in the future: *This is an* ***artist's impression*** *of the new stadium.*
▸ AMUSING COPY OF SB **4** **~ (of sb)** an amusing copy of the way a person acts or speaks SYN **impersonation**: *He did an impression of Tom Hanks.*
▸ FALSE APPEARANCE **5** an appearance that may be false: *Clever lighting creates an impression of space in a room.*
▸ MARK **6** a mark that is left when an object is pressed hard into a surface
▸ BOOK **7** all the copies of a book that are printed at one time, with few or no changes to the contents since the last time the book was printed ➲ compare EDITION
IDM **(be) under the imˈpression that...** believing, usually wrongly, that sth is true or is happening: *I was under the impression that the work had already been completed.* ➲ SYNONYMS at THINK

im·pres·sion·able /ɪmˈpreʃənəbl/ *adj.* (of a person, especially a young one) easily influenced or affected by sb/sth: *children at an impressionable age*

Im·pres·sion·ism /ɪmˈpreʃənɪzəm/ *noun* [U] a style in painting developed in France in the late 19th century that uses colour to show the effects of light on things and to suggest atmosphere rather than showing exact details ▸ **Im·pres·sion·ist** *adj.* [usually before noun]: *Impressionist landscapes*

im·pres·sion·ist /ɪmˈpreʃənɪst/ *noun* **1** (usually **Impressionist**) an artist who paints in the style of Impressionism: *Impressionists such as Monet and Pissarro* **2** a person who entertains people by copying the way a famous person speaks or behaves

im·pres·sion·is·tic /ˌɪmpreʃəˈnɪstɪk/ *adj.* giving a general idea rather than particular facts or details

im·pres·sive 0‑w /ɪmˈpresɪv/ *adj.* (of things or people) making you feel admiration, because they are very large, good, skilful, etc: *an impressive building with a huge tower* ◇ *an impressive performance* ◇ *one of the most impressive novels of recent years* ◇ *She was very impressive in the interview.* OPP **unimpressive** ▸ **im·pres·sive·ly** *adv.*: *impressively high* ◇ *impressively organized*

im·pri·ma·tur /ˌɪmprɪˈmɑːtə(r)/ *noun* [sing.] (*formal*) official approval of sth, given by a person in a position of authority

im·print *verb, noun*
■ ***verb*** /ɪmˈprɪnt/ **1** **~ A in/on B** | **~ B with A** to have a great effect on sth so that it cannot be forgotten, changed, etc: *The terrible scenes were indelibly imprinted on his mind.* **2** **~ A in/on B** | **~ B with A** to print or press a mark or design onto a surface: *clothes imprinted with the logos of sports teams*
■ ***noun*** /ˈɪmprɪnt/ **1** **~ (of sth) (in/on sth)** a mark made by pressing or stamping sth onto a surface: *the imprint of a foot in the sand* **2** [usually sing.] **~ (of sth) (on sb/sth)** (*for-*

mal) the lasting effect that a person or an experience has on a place or a situation **3** (*technical*) the name of the PUBLISHER of a book, usually printed below the title on the first page

im·prison /ɪm'prɪzn/ *verb* [often passive] **~ sb** to put sb in a prison or another place from which they cannot escape **SYN jail**: *They were imprisoned for possession of drugs.* ◇ (*figurative*) *Some young mothers feel imprisoned in their own homes.* ➲ COLLOCATIONS at JUSTICE ▸ **im·pris·on·ment** /-mənt/ *noun* [U]: *to be sentenced to* ***life imprisonment*** *for murder*

im·prob·able /ɪm'prɒbəbl; *NAmE* -'prɑːb-/ *adj.* **1** not likely to be true or to happen **SYN unlikely**: *an improbable story* ◇ *It all sounded* ***highly improbable.*** ◇ **~ that...** *It seems improbable that the current situation will continue.* **OPP probable 2** seeming strange because it is not what you would expect **SYN unexpected**: *Her hair was an improbable shade of yellow.* ▸ **im·prob·abil·ity** /ɪm,prɒbə'bɪləti; *NAmE* -,prɑːbə-/ *noun* [U, C]: *the improbability of finding them alive* ◇ *statistical improbability* **im·prob·ably** /-əbli/ *adv.*: *He claimed, improbably, that he had never been there.* ◇ *an improbably happy end*

im·promptu /ɪm'prɒmptjuː; *NAmE* -'prɑːmptuː/ *adj.* done without preparation or planning **SYN improvised**: *an impromptu speech*

im·proper /ɪm'prɒpə(r); *NAmE* -'prɑːp-/ *adj.* (*formal*) **1** dishonest, or morally wrong: *improper business practices* ◇ *improper conduct* ◇ *There was nothing improper about our relationship* (= it did not involve sex). **OPP proper 2** not suited or appropriate to the situation **SYN inappropriate**: *It would be improper to comment at this stage.* **OPP proper 3** wrong; not correct: *improper use of the drug* ▸ **im·prop·er·ly** *adv.*: *to behave improperly* ◇ *He was improperly dressed for the occasion.* ◇ *improperly cooked meat*

im,proper 'fraction *noun* (*mathematics*) a FRACTION in which the top number is greater than the bottom number, for example 7/6

im·pro·pri·ety /,ɪmprə'praɪəti/ *noun* [U, C] (*pl.* **-ies**) (*formal*) behaviour or actions that are dishonest, morally wrong or not appropriate for a person in a position of responsibility **OPP propriety**

im·prove 🔑 /ɪm'pruːv/ *verb* [I, T] to become better than before; to make sth/sb better than before: *His quality of life has improved dramatically since the operation.* ◇ *The doctor says she should continue to improve* (= after an illness). ◇ **~ sth** *to improve standards* ◇ *The company needs to improve performance in all these areas.* ◇ *I need to improve my French.*

PHR V im'prove on/upon sth to achieve or produce sth that is of a better quality than sth else: *We've certainly improved on last year's figures.*

im·prove·ment 🔑 /ɪm'pruːvmənt/ *noun* **1** 🔑 [U] the act of making sth better; the process of sth becoming better: *Sales figures continue to show signs of improvement.* ◇ *We expect to see* ***further improvement*** *over the coming year.* ◇ **~ in/on/to sth** *There is still* ***room for improvement*** *in your work.* **2** 🔑 [C] a change in sth that makes it better; sth that is better than it was before: *a* ***significant/substantial/dramatic improvement*** ◇ *a* ***slight/steady improvement*** ◇ **~ in/on/to sth** *an improvement in Anglo-German relations* ◇ *This is a great improvement on your previous work.* ◇ *improvements to the bus service*

im·provi·dent /ɪm'prɒvɪdənt; *NAmE* -'prɑːv-/ *adj.* (*formal*) not thinking about or planning for the future; spending money in a careless way **OPP provident** ▸ **im·provi·dence** /-əns/ *noun* [U]

im·pro·vise /'ɪmprəvaɪz/ *verb* **1** [I, T] to make or do sth using whatever is available, usually because you do not have what you really need: *There isn't much equipment. We're going to have to improvise.* ◇ **~ sth** *We improvised some shelves out of planks of wood and bricks.* **2** [I, T] to invent music, the words in a play, a statement, etc. while you are playing or speaking, instead of planning it in advance: *'It'll be ready some time next week, I expect,' she said, improvising.* ◇ **~ on sth** *He improvised on the melody.* ◇ **~ sth** *an improvised speech* ▸ **im·pro·visa·tion** /,ɪmprəvaɪ'zeɪʃn; *NAmE* ɪm,prɑːvə'zeɪʃn/ *noun* [U, C]

im·pru·dent /ɪm'pruːdnt/ *adj.* (*formal*) not wise or sensible **SYN unwise**: *It would be imprudent to invest all your money in one company.* **OPP prudent** ▸ **im·pru·dence** /-ns/ *noun* [U] **im·pru·dent·ly** *adv.*

im·pu·dent /'ɪmpjədənt/ *adj.* (*formal*) rude; not showing respect for other people **SYN impertinent**: *an impudent young fellow* ◇ *an impudent remark* ▸ **im·pu·dence** /-əns/ *noun* [U]

im·pugn /ɪm'pjuːn/ *verb* **~ sth** (*formal*) to express doubts about whether sth is right, honest, etc. **SYN challenge**

im·pulse /'ɪmpʌls/ *noun* **1** [C, usually sing., U] **~ (to do sth)** a sudden strong wish or need to do sth, without stopping to think about the results: *He had a sudden impulse to stand up and sing.* ◇ *I resisted the impulse to laugh.* ◇ *Her first impulse was to run away.* ◇ *The door was open and* **on (an) impulse** *she went inside.* ◇ *He tends to act* **on impulse**. **2** [C] (*technical*) a force or movement of energy that causes sth else to react: ***nerve/electrical impulses*** **3** [C, usually sing., U] (*formal*) something that causes sb/sth to do sth or to develop and make progress: *to give an impulse to the struggling car industry*

'impulse buying *noun* [U] buying goods without planning to do so in advance, and without thinking about it carefully ▸ **'impulse buy** *noun*: *It was an impulse buy.*

im·pul·sion /ɪm'pʌlʃn/ *noun* (*formal*) **1** [C] a strong desire to do sth **2** [U] a reason for doing sth: *Lack of food and water provided much of the impulsion for their speed.*

im·pul·sive /ɪm'pʌlsɪv/ *adj.* (of people or their behaviour) acting suddenly without thinking carefully about what might happen because of what you are doing **SYN impetuous, rash**: *an* ***impulsive decision/gesture*** ◇ *You're so impulsive!* ◇ *He has an impulsive nature.* ▸ **im·pul·sive·ly** *adv.*: *Impulsively he reached out and took her hand.* **im·pul·sive·ness** *noun* [U]

im·pun·ity /ɪm'pjuːnəti/ *noun* [U] (*formal, disapproving*) if a person does sth bad **with impunity**, they do not get punished for what they have done

im·pure /ɪm'pjʊə(r); *NAmE* ɪm'pjʊr/ *adj.* **1** not pure or clean; not consisting of only one substance but mixed with one or more substances often of poorer quality: *impure gold* **2** (*old-fashioned* or *formal*) (of thoughts or feelings) morally bad, especially because they are connected with sex **OPP pure**

im·pur·ity /ɪm'pjʊərəti; *NAmE* -'pjʊr-/ *noun* (*pl.* **-ies**) **1** [C] a substance that is present in small amounts in another substance, making it dirty or of poor quality: *A filter will remove most impurities found in water.* **2** [U] the state of being dirty or not pure **OPP purity**

im·pute /ɪm'pjuːt/

PHR V im'pute sth to sb/sth (*formal*) to say, often unfairly, that sb is responsible for sth or has a particular quality **SYN attribute** ▸ **im·put·ation** /,ɪmpju'teɪʃn/ *noun* [U, C]

in 🔑 /ɪn/ *prep., adv., adj., noun*

■ ***prep.*** **HELP** For the special uses of **in** in phrasal verbs, look at the entries for the verbs. For example **deal in sth** is in the phrasal verb section at **deal**. **1** 🔑 at a point within an area or a space: *a country in Africa* ◇ *The kids were playing in the street.* ◇ *It's in that drawer.* ◇ *I read about it in the paper.* **2** 🔑 within the shape of sth; surrounded by sth: *She was lying in bed.* ◇ *sitting in an armchair* ◇ *Leave the key in the lock.* ◇ *Soak it in cold water.* **3** 🔑 into sth: *He dipped his brush in the paint.* ◇ *She got in her car and drove off.* **4** 🔑 forming the whole or part of sth/sb; contained within sth/sb: *There are 31 days in May.* ◇ *all the paintings in the collection* ◇ *I recognize his father in him* (= his character is similar to his father's). **5** 🔑 during a period of time: *in 2009* ◇ *in the 18th century* ◇ *in spring/summer/autumn/winter* ◇ *in the fall* ◇ *in March* ◇ *in the morning/afternoon/evening* ◇ *I'm getting forgetful in my old age.* **6** 🔑 after a particular length of time: *to return in a few minutes/hours/days/months.* ◇ *It will be ready in a week's* time (= one week from now). ◇ *She learnt to drive in three weeks* (= after three weeks she could drive). **7** (used in negative sentences or after *first, last*, etc.) for a particular period of time: *I haven't seen him in years.* ◇ *It's the first letter I've had in ten days.* **8** wearing sth: *dressed in their best clothes* ◇ *the man in the hat* ◇ *to be in uniform* ◇ *She was all in black.* **9** used to describe physical surroundings: *We went out in the rain.* ◇ *He was sitting alone in the darkness.* **10** used to show a state or condition: *I'm in love!* ◇ *The house is in good repair.* ◇ *I must put my affairs in order.* ◇ *a man in his thirties* ◇ *The daffodils were in full bloom.* **11** involved in sth; taking part in sth: *to act in a play* **12** used to show sb's job or profession: *He is in the army.* ◇ *She's in computers.* ◇ *in business* **13** used to show the form, shape, arrangement or quantity of sth: *a novel in three parts* ◇ *Roll it up in a ball.* ◇ *They sat in rows.* ◇ *People flocked in their thousands to see her.* **14** used to show the language, material, etc. used: *Say it in English.* ◇ *She wrote in pencil.* ◇ *Put it in writing.* ◇ *I paid in cash.* ◇ *He spoke in a loud voice.* **15** concerning sth: *She was not lacking in courage.* ◇ *a country rich in minerals* ◇ *three metres in length* **16** while doing sth; while sth is happening: *In attempting to save the child from drowning, she nearly lost her own life.* ◇ *In all the commotion I forgot to tell him the news.* **17** used to introduce the name of a person who has a particular quality: *We're losing a first-rate editor in Jen.* **18** used to show a rate or relative amount: *a gradient of one in five* ◇ *a tax rate of 22 pence in the pound*

IDM **in that** /ɪn ðət/ (*formal*) for the reason that; because: *She was fortunate in that she had friends to help her.*

■ ***adv.*** HELP For the special uses of **in** in phrasal verbs, look at the entries for the verbs. For example **fill in (for sb)** is in the phrasal verb section at **fill**. **1** contained within an object, an area or a substance: *We were locked in.* ◇ *I can't drink coffee with milk in.* **2** into an object, an area or a substance: *She opened the door and went in.* ◇ *The kids were playing by the river and one of them fell in.* **3** (of people) at home or at a place of work: *Nobody was in when we called.* OPP **out** **4** (of trains, buses, etc.) at the place where people can get on or off, for example the station: *The bus is due in* (= it should arrive) *at six.* **5** (of letters, etc.) received: *Applications must be in by April 30.* **6** (of the TIDE) at or towards its highest point on land: *Is the tide coming in or going out?* **7** elected: *Several new councillors got in at the last election.* **8** (in CRICKET, BASEBALL, etc.) if a team or team member is **in**, they are BATTING **9** (in TENNIS, etc.) if the ball is **in**, it has landed inside the line: *Her serve was just in.*

IDM **be in at sth** to be present when sth happens: *They were in at the start.* **be 'in for sth** (*informal*) to be going to experience sth soon, especially sth unpleasant: *He's in for a shock!* ◇ *I'm afraid we're in for a storm.* **be/get 'in on sth** (*informal*) to be/become involved in sth; to share or know about sth: *I'd like to be in on the plan.* ◇ *Is she in on the secret?* **be (well) 'in with sb** (*informal*) to be (very) friendly with sb, and likely to get an advantage from the friendship **ˌin and 'out (of sth)** going regularly to a place: *He was in and out of jail for most of his life.*

■ ***adj.*** [usually before noun] (*informal*) popular and fashionable: *Purple is the in colour this spring.* ◇ *Exotic pets are the in thing right now.* ◇ *Short skirts are in again.* ➲ see also IN-JOKE

■ ***noun***

IDM **an 'in to sth** = A WAY INTO STH at WAY *n.* **have an 'in with sb** (*especially NAmE*) to have influence with sb **the ˌins and 'outs (of sth)** all the details, especially the complicated or difficult ones: *the ins and outs of the problem* ◇ *He quickly learned the ins and outs of the job.*

in. *abbr.* (*pl.* in. or ins.) INCH: *Height: 6ft 2in.*

in- *prefix* /ɪn/ **1** (also **il-** /ɪl/, **im-** /ɪm/, **ir-** /ɪr/) (in adjectives, adverbs and nouns) not; the opposite of: *infinite* ◇ *illogical* ◇ *immorally* ◇ *irrelevance* **2** (also **im-** /ɪm/) (in verbs) to put into the condition mentioned: *inflame* ◇ *imperil*

-in *combining form* (in nouns) an activity in which many people take part: *a sit-in* ◇ *a teach-in*

in·abil·ity /ˌɪnəˈbɪləti/ *noun* [U, sing.] **~ (to do sth)** the fact of not being able to do sth: *the government's inability to provide basic services* ◇ *Some families go without medical treatment because of their inability to pay.* OPP **ability**

in ab·sen·tia /ˌɪn æbˈsenʃiə/ *adv.* (from *Latin*) while not present at the event being referred to: *Two foreign suspects will be tried in absentia.*

in·access·ible AW /ˌɪnækˈsesəbl/ *adj.* difficult or impossible to reach or to get: *They live in a remote area, inaccessible except by car.* ◇ **~ to sb/sth** *The temple is now inaccessible to the public.* ◇ (*figurative*) *The language of teenagers is often completely inaccessible to* (= not understood by) *adults.* OPP **accessible** ▶ **in·access·ibil·ity** /ˌɪnækˌsesəˈbɪləti/ *noun* [U]

in·accur·ate AW /ɪnˈækjərət/ *adj.* not exact or accurate; with mistakes: *an inaccurate statement* ◇ *inaccurate information* ◇ *All the maps we had were wildly inaccurate.* OPP **accurate** ▶ **in·accur·acy** AW /ɪnˈækjərəsi/ *noun* [C, U] (*pl.* -ies): *The article is full of inaccuracies.* ◇ *The writer is guilty of bias and inaccuracy.* ➲ SYNONYMS at MISTAKE **in·accur·ate·ly** *adv.*

in·action /ɪnˈækʃn/ *noun* [U] (usually *disapproving*) lack of action; the state of doing nothing about a situation or a problem

in·acti·vate /ɪnˈæktɪveɪt/ *verb* **~ sth** (*technical*) to make sth stop doing sth; to make sth no longer active

in·active /ɪnˈæktɪv/ *adj.* **1** not doing anything; not active: *Some animals are inactive during the daytime.* ◇ *politically inactive* ◇ *The volcano has been inactive for 50 years.* **2** not in use; not working: *an inactive oil well* **3** having no effect: *an **inactive drug/disease*** OPP **active** ▶ **in·activ·ity** /ˌɪnækˈtɪvəti/ *noun* [U]: *periods of enforced inactivity and boredom* ◇ *The inactivity of the government was deplorable.*

in·ad·equacy AW /ɪnˈædɪkwəsi/ *noun* (*pl.* -ies) **1** [U] **~ (of sth)** the state of not being enough or good enough: *the inadequacy of our resources* OPP **adequacy** **2** [U] a state of not being able or confident to deal with a situation: *a **feeling/sense of inadequacy*** **3** [C, usually pl.] **~ (of/in sth)** a weakness; a lack of sth: *gross inadequacies in the data* ◇ *He had to face up to his own inadequacies as a father.*

in·ad·equate AW /ɪnˈædɪkwət/ *adj.* **1** not enough; not good enough: *inadequate supplies* ◇ **~ for sth** *The system is inadequate for the tasks it has to perform.* ◇ **~ to do sth** *The food supplies are inadequate to meet the needs of the hungry.* OPP **adequate** **2** (of people) not able, or not confident enough, to deal with a situation SYN **incompetent**: *I felt **totally inadequate** as a parent.* ▶ **in·ad·equate·ly** AW *adv.*: *to be inadequately prepared/insured/funded*

in·ad·mis·sible /ˌɪnədˈmɪsəbl/ *adj.* (*formal*) that cannot be allowed or accepted, especially in court: *inadmissible evidence* OPP **admissible**

in·ad·vert·ent·ly /ˌɪnədˈvɜːtəntli; *NAmE* -ˈvɜːrt-/ *adv.* by accident; without intending to SYN **unintentionally**: *We had inadvertently left without paying the bill.* ▶ **in·ad·vert·ent** *adj.*: *an inadvertent omission* **in·ad·ver·tence** *noun* [U]

in·ad·vis·able /ˌɪnədˈvaɪzəbl/ *adj.* [not usually before noun] **~ (for sb) (to do sth)** (*formal*) not sensible or wise; that you would advise against: ***It is inadvisable to** bring children on this trip.* OPP **advisable**

in·ali·en·able /ɪnˈeɪliənəbl/ (also *less frequent* **un·ali·en·able**) *adj.* [usually before noun] (*formal*) that cannot be taken away from you: *the **inalienable right** to decide your own future*

in·am·or·ata /ɪnˌæməˈrɑːtə/ *noun* (from *Italian, formal* or *humorous*) a person's female lover

inane /ɪˈneɪn/ *adj.* stupid or silly; with no meaning: *an inane remark* ▶ **in·ane·ly** *adv.*: *to grin inanely* **in·an·ity** /ɪˈnænəti/ *noun* [U, C, usually pl.] (*pl.* -ies)

in·ani·mate /ɪnˈænɪmət/ *adj.* **1** not alive in the way that people, animals and plants are: *A rock is an inanimate ob-*

ject. **OPP** **animate 2** dead or appearing to be dead: *A man was lying inanimate on the floor.*

in·applic·able /ˌɪnəˈplɪkəbl; ɪnˈæplɪkəbl/ *adj.* [not before noun] **~ (to sb/sth)** that cannot be used, or that does not apply, in a particular situation: *These regulations are inapplicable to international students.* **OPP** **applicable**

in·appro·pri·ate **AW** /ˌɪnəˈprəʊpriət; *NAmE* -ˈproʊ-/ *adj.* not suitable or appropriate in a particular situation: ***inappropriate behaviour/language*** ◇ **~ (for sb/sth) (to do sth)** ***It would be inappropriate for me to*** *comment*. ◇ **~ to/for sth** *clothes inappropriate to the occasion* **OPP** **appropriate** ▸ **in·appro·pri·acy** **AW** *noun* [U] **in·appro·pri·ate·ly** **AW** *adv.*: *She was inappropriately dressed for a funeral.* **in·appro·pri·ate·ness** *noun* [U]

in·articu·late /ˌɪnɑːˈtɪkjələt; *NAmE* -ɑːrˈtɪk-/ *adj.* **1** (of people) not able to express ideas or feelings clearly or easily **2** (of speech) not using clear words; not expressed clearly: *an inarticulate reply* **OPP** **articulate** ▸ **in·articu·late·ly** *adv.*

in·as·much as /ˌɪnəzˈmʌtʃ əz/ *conj.* (*formal*) used to add a comment on sth that you have just said and to say in what way it is true: *He was a very unusual musician inasmuch as he was totally deaf.*

in·atten·tion /ˌɪnəˈtenʃn/ *noun* [U] (usually *disapproving*) lack of attention: *The accident was the result of a moment's inattention.*

in·atten·tive /ˌɪnəˈtentɪv/ *adj.* (*disapproving*) not paying attention to sth/sb: *an inattentive pupil* ◇ **~ to sth/sb** *inattentive to the needs of others* **OPP** **attentive** ▸ **in·atten·tive·ly** *adv.*

in·aud·ible /ɪnˈɔːdəbl/ *adj.* **~ (to sb)** that you cannot hear: *The whistle was inaudible to the human ear.* **OPP** **audible** ▸ **in·audi·bil·ity** /ɪnˌɔːdəˈbɪləti/ *noun* [U] **in·aud·ibly** /ɪnˈɔːdəbli/ *adv.*

in·aug·ural /ɪˈnɔːgjərəl/ *adj.* [only before noun] (of an official speech, meeting, etc.) first, and marking the beginning of sth important, for example the time when a new leader or parliament starts work, when a new organization is formed or when sth is used for the first time: *the President's inaugural address* ◇ *the inaugural meeting of the geographical society* ◇ *the inaugural flight of the space shuttle* ▸ **in·aug·ural** *noun* [C, usually sing.] (*especially NAmE*): *the presidential inaugural in January*

in·aug·ur·ate /ɪˈnɔːgjəreɪt/ *verb* **1 ~ sb (as sth)** | **~ sb + noun** to introduce a new public official or leader at a special ceremony: *He will be inaugurated (as) President in January.* **2 ~ sth** to officially open a building or start an organization with a special ceremony: *The new theatre was inaugurated by the mayor.* **3 ~ sth** (*formal*) to introduce a new development or an important change: *The moon landing inaugurated a new era in space exploration.* ▸ **in·aug·ur·ation** /ɪˌnɔːgjəˈreɪʃn/ *noun* [U, C]: *the President's inauguration* ◇ *an inauguration speech*

Iˌnauguˈration Day *noun* (in the US) 20 January, officially the first day of a new President's period of office

in·aus·pi·cious /ˌɪnɔːˈspɪʃəs/ *adj.* (*formal*) showing signs that the future will not be good or successful: *an inauspicious start* **OPP** **auspicious** ▸ **in·aus·pi·cious·ly** *adv.*

in·authen·tic /ˌɪnɔːˈθentɪk/ *adj.* not genuine; that you cannot believe or rely on **OPP** **authentic** ▸ **in·authen·ti·city** /ˌɪnɔːθenˈtɪsəti/ *noun* [U]

in·board /ˈɪnbɔːd; *NAmE* -bɔːrd/ *adj.* (*technical*) located on the inside of a boat, plane or car: *an inboard motor* **OPP** **outboard** ▸ **in·board** *adv.*

in·born /ˌɪnˈbɔːn; *NAmE* -ˈbɔːrn/ (also *less frequent* **in·bred**) *adj.* an **inborn** quality is one that you are born with **SYN** **innate**

in·bound /ˈɪnbaʊnd/ *adj.* (*formal*) travelling towards a place rather than leaving it: ***inbound flights/passengers*** **OPP** **outbound**

in·bounds /ˈɪnbaʊndz/ *adj.* (in BASKETBALL) relating to a throw that puts the ball into play again after it has gone out of play: *an inbounds pass*

ˈin box *noun* (*NAmE*) = IN TRAY

in·box /ˈɪnbɒks; *NAmE* -bɑːks/ *noun* (*computing*) the place on a computer where new email messages are shown: *I have a stack of emails in my inbox.* ➲ COLLOCATIONS at EMAIL

in·bred /ˌɪnˈbred/ *adj.* **1** produced by breeding among closely related members of a group of animals, people or plants: *an inbred racehorse* **2** = INBORN

in·breed·ing /ˈɪnbriːdɪŋ/ *noun* [U] breeding between closely related people or animals

in·built /ˈɪnbɪlt/ *adj.* [only before noun] an **inbuilt** quality exists as an essential part of sth/sb: *His height gives him an inbuilt advantage over his opponent.* ➲ compare BUILT-IN

ˌin-ˈbuilt *adj.* = BUILT-IN

Inc. /ɪŋk/ (also **inc**) *abbr.* Incorporated (used after the name of a company in the US): *Texaco Inc.*

inc. *abbr.* (*BrE*) = INCL.

in·cal·cul·able /ɪnˈkælkjələbl/ *adj.* (*formal*) very large or very great; too great to calculate: *The oil spill has caused incalculable damage to the environment.* ➲ compare CALCULABLE ▸ **in·cal·cul·ably** /-əbli/ *adv.*

in·can·des·cent /ˌɪnkænˈdesnt/ *adj.* **1** (*technical*) giving out light when heated: *incandescent lamps* **2** (*formal*) very bright: *incandescent white* **3** (*formal*) full of strong emotion: *an incandescent musical performance* ◇ *She was incandescent with rage.* ▸ **in·can·des·cence** /-sns/ *noun* [U]

in·can·ta·tion /ˌɪnkænˈteɪʃn/ *noun* [C, U] special words that are spoken or sung to have a magic effect; the act of speaking or singing these words

in·cap·able **AW** /ɪnˈkeɪpəbl/ *adj.* **1** not able to do sth: **~ of sth** *incapable of speech* ◇ **~ of doing sth** *The children seem to be* ***totally incapable*** *of working by themselves.* **2** not able to control yourself or your affairs; not able to do anything well: *He was found lying in the road, drunk and incapable.* ◇ *If people keep telling you you're incapable, you begin to lose confidence in yourself.* **OPP** **capable**

in·cap·aci·tate **AW** /ˌɪnkəˈpæsɪteɪt/ *verb* [usually passive] **~ sb/sth** (*formal*) to make sb/sth unable to live or work normally

in·cap·acity /ˌɪnkəˈpæsəti/ *noun* [U] (*formal*) **1 ~ (of sb/sth) (to do sth)** lack of ability or skill **SYN** **inability**: *their incapacity to govern effectively* **2** the state of being too ill/sick to do your work or take care of yourself: *She returned to work after a long period of incapacity.*

ˌin-ˈcar *adj.* [only before noun] relating to sth that you have or use inside a car, for example a radio or CD player: *in-car entertainment*

in·car·cer·ate /ɪnˈkɑːsəreɪt; *NAmE* -ˈkɑːrs-/ *verb* [usually passive] **~ sb (in sth)** (*formal*) to put sb in prison or in another place from which they cannot escape **SYN** **imprison** ▸ **in·car·cer·ation** /ɪnˌkɑːsəˈreɪʃn; *NAmE* -ˌkɑːrs-/ *noun* [U]

in·car·nate *adj., verb*

▪ ***adj.*** /ɪnˈkɑːnət; *NAmE* -ˈkɑːrn-/ (usually after nouns) (*formal*) in human form: *The leader seemed the devil incarnate.*

▪ ***verb*** /ˈɪnkɑːneɪt; *NAmE* -kɑːrn-/ **~ sth** (*formal*) to give a definite or human form to a particular idea or quality **SYN** **embody**

in·car·na·tion /ˌɪnkɑːˈneɪʃn; *NAmE* -kɑːrˈn-/ *noun* **1** [C] a period of life in a particular form: *one of the incarnations of Vishnu* ◇ *He believed he had been a prince in a previous incarnation.* ◇ (*figurative*) *I worked for her in her earlier incarnation* (= her previous job) *as a lawyer.* **2** [C] a person who represents a particular quality, for example, in human form **SYN** **embodiment**: *the incarnation of evil* **3** [sing., U] (also **the Incarnation**) (in Christianity) the act of God coming to earth in human form as Jesus

in·cau·tious /ɪnˈkɔːʃəs/ *adj.* (*formal*) done without thinking carefully about the results; not thinking about what might happen ▸ **in·cau·tious·ly** *adv.*

in·cen·di·ary /ɪnˈsendiəri; *NAmE* -dieri/ *adj., noun*

▪ ***adj.*** [only before noun] **1** designed to cause fires: *an incen-*

I

diary device/bomb/attack **2** (*formal*) causing strong feelings or violence SYN **inflammatory**: *incendiary remarks*
■ **noun** (*pl.* -ies) a bomb that is designed to make a fire start burning when it explodes SYN **firebomb**

in·cense *noun, verb*
■ **noun** /ˈɪnsens/ [U] a substance that produces a pleasant smell when you burn it, used particularly in religious ceremonies
■ **verb** /ɪnˈsens/ **~ sb** to make sb very angry: *The decision incensed the workforce.*

in·censed /ɪnˈsenst/ *adj.* very angry: *They were incensed at the decision.*

in·cen·tive AW /ɪnˈsentɪv/ *noun* [C, U] **~ (for/to sb/sth) (to do sth)** something that encourages you to do sth: *tax incentives to encourage savings* ◇ *There is no incentive for people to save fuel.* OPP **disincentive**

in·cen·tiv·ize (*BrE* also **-ise**) /ɪnˈsentɪvaɪz/ *verb* to encourage sb to behave in a particular way by offering them a reward: **~ sth** *ways to incentivize innovation* ◇ **~ sb to do sth** *You need to incentivize your existing customers to stay with you.*

in·cep·tion /ɪnˈsepʃn/ *noun* [sing.] (*formal*) the start of an institution, an organization, etc: *The club has grown rapidly since its inception in 2007.*

in·ces·sant /ɪnˈsesnt/ *adj.* (usually *disapproving*) never stopping SYN **constant**: *incessant noise/rain/chatter* ◇ *incessant meetings* ▸ **in·ces·sant·ly** *adv.*: *to talk incessantly*

in·cest /ˈɪnsest/ *noun* [U] sexual activity between two people who are very closely related in a family, for example, a brother and sister, or a father and daughter

in·ces·tu·ous /ɪnˈsestjuəs; *NAmE* -tʃuəs/ *adj.* **1** involving sex between two people in a family who are very closely related: *an incestuous relationship* **2** (*disapproving*) involving a group of people who have a close relationship and do not want to include anyone outside the group: *The music industry is an incestuous business.* ▸ **in·ces·tu·ous·ly** *adv.*

inch 0 /ɪntʃ/ *noun, verb*
■ **noun** **1** 0 (*abbr.* in.) a unit for measuring length, equal to 2.54 centimetres. There are 12 inches in a foot: *1.14 inches of rain fell last night.* ◇ *She's a few inches taller than me.* **2** 0 a small amount or distance: *He escaped death* **by an inch**. ◇ *The car missed us* **by inches**. ◇ *He was just inches away from scoring.*
IDM **every inch** **1** the whole of sth: *The doctor examined every inch of his body.* ◇ (*figurative*) *If they try to fire me I'll fight them* **every inch of the way**. **2** completely: *In his first game the young player already looked every inch a winner.* **give sb an ˈinch (and they'll take a ˈmile/ˈyard)** (*saying*) used to say that if you allow some people a small amount of freedom or power they will see you as weak and try to take a lot more **ˌinch by ˈinch** very slowly and with great care or difficulty: *She crawled forward inch by inch.* **not budge/give/move an ˈinch** to refuse to change your position, decision, etc. even a little: *We tried to negotiate a lower price but they wouldn't budge an inch.* **within an ˈinch of sth/of doing sth** very close to sth/doing sth: *She was within an inch of being killed.* ◇ *They beat him (to) within an inch of his life* (= very severely). ➲ more at TRUST *v.*
■ **verb** [I, T] to move or make sth move slowly and carefully in a particular direction: **+ adv./prep.** *She moved forward, inching towards the rope.* ◇ **~ sth + adv./prep.** *I inched the car forward.* ◇ *He* **inched his way** *through the narrow passage.*

in·charge /ˈɪntʃɑːdʒ; *NAmE* -tʃɑːrdʒ/ *noun* (*IndE*) the person who is officially responsible for a department, etc: *the incharge of the district hospital*

in·cho·ate /ɪnˈkəʊət; ˈɪnkəʊeɪt; *NAmE* -ˈkoʊ-/ *adj.* (*formal*) just beginning to form and therefore not clear or developed: *inchoate ideas*

in·cho·ative /ɪnˈkəʊətɪv; *NAmE* -ˈkoʊə-/ *adj.* (*grammar*) (of verbs) expressing a change of state that happens on its own. *Opened* in *the door opened* is an example of an inchoative verb. ➲ compare CAUSATIVE, ERGATIVE

in·ci·dence AW /ˈɪnsɪdəns/ *noun* **1** [C, usually sing.] **~ of sth** (*formal*) the extent to which sth happens or has an effect: *an area with a* **high incidence** *of crime* **2** [U] (*physics*) the way in which light meets a surface: *the angle of incidence*

in·ci·dent 0 AW /ˈɪnsɪdənt/ *noun*
1 0 [C] something that happens, especially sth unusual or unpleasant: *His bad behaviour was just an isolated incident.* ◇ *One particular incident sticks in my mind.* **2** 0 [C, U] a serious or violent event, such as a crime, an accident or an attack: *There was a shooting incident near here last night.* ◇ *The demonstration passed off* **without incident**. **3** 0 [C] a disagreement between two countries, often involving military forces: *a* **border/diplomatic incident**

in·ci·den·tal /ˌɪnsɪˈdentl/ *adj., noun*
■ **adj.** **1 ~ (to sth)** happening in connection with sth else, but not as important as it, or not intended: *The discovery was incidental to their main research.* ◇ **incidental music** (= music used with a play or a film/movie to give atmosphere) ◇ *You may be able to get help with* **incidental expenses** (= small costs that you get in connection with sth). **2 ~ to sth** (*technical*) happening as a natural result of sth: *These risks are incidental to the work of a firefighter.*
■ **noun** [usually pl.] something that happens in connection with sth else, but is less important: *You'll need money for incidentals such as tips and taxis.*

in·ci·den·tal·ly AW /ˌɪnsɪˈdentli/ *adv.* **1** used to introduce a new topic, or some extra information, or a question that you have just thought of SYN **by the way**: *Incidentally, have you heard the news about Sue?* **2** in a way that was not planned but that is connected with sth else: *The information was only discovered incidentally.*

ˈincident room *noun* (*BrE*) a room near where a serious crime has taken place where the police work to collect evidence and information

in·cin·er·ate /ɪnˈsɪnəreɪt/ *verb* [often passive] **~ sth** (*formal*) to burn sth until it is completely destroyed ▸ **in·cin·er·ation** /ɪnˌsɪnəˈreɪʃn/ *noun* [U]: *high-temperature incineration plants*

in·cin·er·ator /ɪnˈsɪnəreɪtə(r)/ *noun* a container which is closed on all sides for burning waste at high temperatures

in·cipi·ent /ɪnˈsɪpiənt/ *adj.* [usually before noun] (*formal*) just beginning: *signs of incipient unrest*

in·cise /ɪnˈsaɪz/ *verb* **~ sth (in/on/onto sth)** (*formal*) to cut words, designs, etc. into a surface ➲ compare ENGRAVE

in·ci·sion /ɪnˈsɪʒn/ *noun* [C, U] a sharp cut made in sth, particularly during a medical operation; the act of making a cut in sth: *Make a small incision below the ribs.*

in·ci·sive /ɪnˈsaɪsɪv/ *adj.* (*approving*) **1** showing clear thought and good understanding of what is important, and the ability to express this: ***incisive comments/criticism/analysis*** ◇ *an incisive mind* **2** showing sb's ability to take decisions and act with force: *an incisive performance* ▸ **in·ci·sive·ly** *adv.* **in·ci·sive·ness** *noun* [U]

in·ci·sor /ɪnˈsaɪzə(r)/ *noun* one of the eight sharp teeth at the front of the mouth that are used for biting ➲ compare CANINE, MOLAR

in·cite /ɪnˈsaɪt/ *verb* to encourage sb to do sth violent, illegal or unpleasant, especially by making them angry or excited: **~ sth** *to* ***incite crime/racial hatred/violence*** ◇ **~ sb (to sth)** *They were accused of inciting the crowd to violence.* ◇ **~ sb to do sth** *He incited the workforce to come out on strike.*

in·cite·ment /ɪnˈsaɪtmənt/ *noun* [U, C] **~ (to sth)** the act of encouraging sb to do sth violent, illegal or unpleasant: *incitement to racial hatred*

in·civil·ity /ˌɪnsəˈvɪləti/ *noun* [U, C] (*pl.* -ies) (*formal*) rude behaviour; rude remarks ➲ see also UNCIVIL

incl. (*BrE* also **inc.**) *abbr.* **1** (in advertisements) including; included: *transport not incl.* ◇ *£29.53 inc. tax* **2** INCLUSIVE: *Open 1 April to 31 October incl.*

in·clem·ent /ɪnˈklemənt/ *adj.* (*formal*) (of the weather) not pleasant; cold, wet, etc. OPP **clement** ▶ **in·clem·ency** /-ənsi/ *noun* [U]

in·clin·ation AW /ˌɪnklɪˈneɪʃn/ *noun* **1** [U, C] a feeling that makes you want to do sth: **~ (to do sth)** *He did not show the **slightest inclination** to leave.* ◇ *My **natural inclination** is to find a compromise.* ◇ *She had neither the time nor the inclination to help them.* ◇ **~ (towards/for sth)** *She lacked any inclination for housework.* ◇ *He was a loner by nature and **by inclination**.* ◇ *You must follow your own inclinations when choosing a career.* **2** [C] **~ to do sth** a tendency to do sth: *There is an inclination to treat geography as a less important subject.* **3** [C, usually sing., U] (*technical*) a degree of sloping: *an inclination of 45°* ◇ *the angle of inclination* **4** [C] a small downward movement, usually of the head

in·cline AW *verb, noun*

- ***verb*** /ɪnˈklaɪn/ (*formal*) **1** [I, T] to tend to think or behave in a particular way; to make sb do this: **~ to/towards sth** *I incline to the view that we should take no action at this stage.* ◇ **~ to do sth** *The government is more effective than we incline to think.* ◇ **~ sb to/towards sth** *Lack of money inclines many young people towards crime.* ◇ **~ sb to do sth** *His obvious sincerity inclined me to trust him.* **2** [T] **~ your head** to bend your head forward, especially as a sign of agreement, welcome, etc. **3** [I, T] **~ (sth) (to/towards sth)** to lean or slope in a particular direction; to make sth lean or slope: *The land inclined gently towards the shore.*
- ***noun*** /ˈɪnklaɪn/ (*formal*) a slope: *a **steep/slight incline***

in·clined AW /ɪnˈklaɪnd/ *adj.* **1** [not before noun] **~ (to do sth)** wanting to do sth: *She was inclined to trust him.* ◇ *He writes only when he feels inclined to.* ◇ *There'll be time for a swim if you **feel so inclined**.* **2** **~ to do sth** tending to do sth; likely to do sth: *He's inclined to be lazy.* ◇ *They'll be more inclined to listen if you don't shout.* **3** **~ to agree, believe, think, etc.** used when you are expressing an opinion but do not want to express it very strongly: *I'm inclined to agree with you.* **4** (used with particular adverbs) having a natural ability for sth; preferring to do sth: ***musically/academically inclined** children* **5** sloping; at an angle

in·clude 🔑 /ɪnˈkluːd/ *verb*

1 🔑 (not used in the progressive tenses) if one thing **includes** another, it has the second thing as one of its parts: **~ sth** *The tour included a visit to the Science Museum.* ◇ *Does the price include tax?* ◇ **~ doing sth** *Your duties include typing letters and answering the telephone.* **2** 🔑 to make sb/sth part of sth: **~ sb/sth (as/in/on sth)** *You should include some examples in your essay.* ◇ *We all went, **me included**.* ◇ **~ sb/sth as sth** *Representatives from the country were included as observers at the conference.* OPP **exclude**

in·clud·ing 🔑 /ɪnˈkluːdɪŋ/ *prep.* (*abbr.* incl.) having sth as part of a group or set: *I've got three days' holiday including New Year's Day.* ◇ *Six people were killed in the riot, including a policeman.* ◇ *It's £7.50, **not including** tax.* OPP **excluding** ➲ LANGUAGE BANK at E.G.

in·clu·sion /ɪnˈkluːʒn/ *noun* **1** [U] the fact of including sb/sth; the fact of being included: *His inclusion in the team is in doubt.* **2** [C] a person or thing that is included: *There were some surprising inclusions in the list.* OPP **exclusion**

in·clu·sive /ɪnˈkluːsɪv/ *adj.* **1** having the total cost, or the cost of sth that is mentioned, contained in the price: *The **fully inclusive** fare for the trip is £52.* ◇ **~ of sth** *The rent is inclusive of water and heating.* OPP **exclusive** **2** (**from**) **... to... inclusive** (*BrE*) including all the days, months, numbers, etc. mentioned: *We are offering free holidays for children aged two to eleven inclusive.* ◇ *The castle is open daily from May to October inclusive.* **3** including a wide range of people, things, ideas, etc: *The party must adopt more inclusive strategies and a broader vision.* OPP **exclusive** ▶ **in·clu·sive·ly** *adv.*: *The word 'men' can be understood inclusively* (= including men and women). **in·clu·sive·ness** *noun* [U]

in·cog·nito /ˌɪnkɒɡˈniːtəʊ; *NAmE* ˌɪnkɑːɡˈniːtoʊ/ *adv.* in a way that prevents other people from finding out who you are: *Movie stars often prefer to travel incognito.* ▶ **in·cog·nito** *adj.*: *an incognito visit*

British/American

inclusive / through

- In *BrE* **inclusive** is used to emphasize that you are including the days, months, numbers, etc. mentioned, especially in formal or official situations: *Answer questions 8 to 12 inclusive.* ◇ *The amusement park is open daily from May to October inclusive.*
- In *NAmE* **through** is used: *Answer questions 8 through 12.* ◇ *The amusement park is open (from) May through October.*
- **To** can also be used with this meaning in *BrE* and *NAmE*: *The park is open from 1 May to 31 October.*

in·co·her·ent AW /ˌɪnkəʊˈhɪərənt; *NAmE* ˌɪnkoʊˈhɪr-/ *adj.* **1** (of people) unable to express yourself clearly, often because of emotion: *She broke off, incoherent with anger.* OPP **coherent** **2** (of sounds) not clear and hard to understand SYN **unintelligible**: *Rachel whispered something incoherent.* **3** not logical or well organized: *an incoherent policy* OPP **coherent** ▶ **in·co·her·ence** /-əns/ *noun* [U] **in·co·her·ent·ly** AW *adv.*

in·come 🔑 AW /ˈɪnkʌm; -kəm/ *noun* [C, U] the money that a person, a region, a country, etc. earns from work, from investing money, from business, etc: *people **on high/low incomes*** ◇ *a weekly **disposable income*** (= the money that you have left to spend after tax, etc.) *of £200* ◇ *a rise in **national income*** ◇ *They receive a proportion of their income from the sale of goods and services.* ◇ *Tourism is a major **source of income** for the area.* ◇ ***higher/middle/lower income** groups* ➲ COLLOCATIONS at FINANCE ➲ compare EXPENDITURE

Synonyms

income

wage/wages • pay • salary • earnings

These are all words for money that a person earns or receives for their work.

income money that a person receives for their work, or from investments or business: *people on low incomes*

wage/wages money that employees get for doing their job, usually paid every week: *a weekly wage of £200*

pay money that employees earn for doing their job: *The job offers good rates of pay.*

salary money that employees earn for doing their job, usually paid every month.

WAGE, PAY OR SALARY?

Pay is the most general of these three words. Employees who work in factories, etc. get their **wages** each week. Employees who work in offices or professional people such as teachers or doctors receive a **salary** that is paid each month, but is usually expressed as an annual figure.

earnings money that a person earns from their work: *a rise in average earnings for factory workers*

PATTERNS

- (a) **high/low/basic** income/wage/pay/salary/earnings
- to **earn** an income/a wage/your pay/a salary
- to **be on** a(n) income/wage/salary of...

in·comer /ˈɪnkʌmə(r)/ *noun* (*BrE*) a person who comes to live in a particular place

ˌincome supˈport *noun* [U] (in Britain) the money that the government pays to people who have no income or a very low income

ˈincome tax *noun* [U, C] the amount of money that you pay to the government according to how much you earn: *The standard rate of income tax was cut to 23p in the pound.*

in·com·ing /ˈɪnkʌmɪŋ/ *adj.* [only before noun] **1** recently elected or chosen: *the* ***incoming government/president/administration*** OPP **outgoing** **2** arriving somewhere, or being received: ***incoming flights*** ◇ *the* ***incoming tide*** ◇ ***incoming calls/mail*** OPP **outgoing**

in·com·men·sur·able /ˌɪnkəˈmenʃərəbl/ *adj.* **~ (with sth)** (*formal*) if two things are **incommensurable**, they are so completely different from each other that they cannot be compared

in·com·men·sur·ate /ˌɪnkəˈmenʃərət/ *adj.* **~ (with sth)** (*formal*) not matching sth in size, importance, quality, etc. OPP **commensurate**

in·com·mode /ˌɪnkəˈməʊd; *NAmE* -ˈmoʊd/ *verb* **~ sb** (*formal*) to cause sb difficulties or problems: *We are very sorry to have incommoded you.*

in·com·mu·ni·cado /ˌɪnkəˌmjuːnɪˈkɑːdəʊ; *NAmE* -ˈkɑːdoʊ/ *adj.* without communicating with other people, because you are not allowed to or because you do not want to: *The prisoner has been* ***held incommunicado*** *for more than a week.*

I

in·com·par·able /ɪnˈkɒmprəbl; *NAmE* -ˈkɑːm-/ *adj.* so good or impressive that nothing can be compared to it SYN **matchless**: *the incomparable beauty of Lake Garda* ▸ **in·com·par·abil·ity** /ɪnˌkɒmpərəˈbɪləti; *NAmE* -ˌkɑːm-/ *noun* [U] **in·com·par·ably** /ɪnˈkɒmprəbli; *NAmE* -ˈkɑːm-/ *adv.*

in·com·pat·ible AW /ˌɪnkəmˈpætəbl/ *adj.* **1 ~ (with sth)** two actions, ideas, etc. that are **incompatible** are not acceptable or possible together because of basic differences: *The hours of the job are incompatible with family life.* ◇ *These two objectives are* ***mutually incompatible.*** **2** two people who are **incompatible** are very different from each other and so are not able to live or work happily together **3 ~ (with sth)** two things that are **incompatible** are of different types so that they cannot be used or mixed together: *New computer software is often incompatible with older computers.* ◇ *Those two blood groups are incompatible.* OPP **compatible** ▸ **in·com·pati·bil·ity** AW /ˌɪnkəmˌpætəˈbɪləti/ *noun* [U, C] (*pl.* **-ies**)

in·com·pe·tence /ɪnˈkɒmpɪtəns; *NAmE* -ˈkɑːm-/ *noun* [U] the lack of skill or ability to do your job or a task as it should be done: *professional incompetence* ◇ *police incompetence* ◇ *He was dismissed for incompetence.*

in·com·pe·tent /ɪnˈkɒmpɪtənt; *NAmE* -ˈkɑːm-/ *adj., noun*

- ***adj.*** not having the skill or ability to do your job or a task as it should be done: *an incompetent teacher* ◇ *his incompetent handling of the affair* ◇ *The Prime Minister was attacked as incompetent to lead.* OPP **competent** ▸ **in·com·pe·tent·ly** *adv.*
- ***noun*** a person who does not have the skill or ability to do their job or a task as it should be done

in·com·plete /ˌɪnkəmˈpliːt/ *adj., noun*

- ***adj.*** not having everything that it should have; not finished or complete: *an incomplete set of figures* ◇ *Spoken language contains many incomplete sentences.* OPP **complete** ▸ **in·com·plete·ly** *adv.*: *The causes of the phenomenon are still incompletely understood.* **in·com·plete·ness** *noun* [U]
- ***noun*** (*NAmE*) the grade that a student gets for a course of education when they have not completed all the work for that course

in·com·pre·hen·sible /ɪnˌkɒmprɪˈhensəbl; *NAmE* -ˌkɑːm-/ *adj.* **~ (to sb)** impossible to understand SYN **unintelligible**: *Some application forms can be incomprehensible to ordinary people.* ◇ *He found his son's actions totally incomprehensible.* OPP **comprehensible** ▸ **in·com·pre·hen·si·bil·ity** /ɪnˌkɒmprɪˌhensəˈbɪləti; *NAmE* -ˌkɑːm-/ *noun* [U] **in·com·pre·hen·sibly** /-səbli/ *adv.*

in·com·pre·hen·sion /ɪnˌkɒmprɪˈhenʃn; *NAmE* -ˌkɑːm-/ *noun* [U] the state of not being able to understand sb/sth: *Anna read the letter with incomprehension.*

in·con·ceiv·able AW /ˌɪnkənˈsiːvəbl/ *adj.* impossible to imagine or believe SYN **unthinkable**: ***It is inconceivable that*** *the minister was not aware of the problem.* OPP **conceivable** ▸ **in·con·ceiv·ably** AW *adv.*

in·con·clu·sive AW /ˌɪnkənˈkluːsɪv/ *adj.* not leading to a definite decision or result: *inconclusive evidence/results/tests* ◇ *inconclusive discussions* OPP **conclusive** ▸ **in·con·clu·sive·ly** AW *adv.*: *The last meeting had ended inconclusively.*

in·con·gru·ous /ɪnˈkɒŋgruəs; *NAmE* -ˈkɑːŋ-/ *adj.* strange, and not suitable in a particular situation SYN **inappropriate**: *Such traditional methods seem incongruous in our technical age.* ▸ **in·con·gru·ity** /ˌɪnkɒnˈgruːəti; *NAmE* ˌɪnkɑːn-/ *noun* [U, C] (*pl.* **-ies**): *She was struck by the incongruity of the situation.* **in·con·gru·ous·ly** *adv.*: *incongruously dressed*

in·con·se·quen·tial /ɪnˌkɒnsɪˈkwenʃl; *NAmE* -ˌkɑːn-/ *adj.* not important or worth considering SYN **trivial**: *inconsequential details* ◇ *inconsequential chatter* OPP **consequential** ▸ **in·con·se·quen·tial·ly** /-ʃəli/ *adv.*

in·con·sid·er·able /ˌɪnkənˈsɪdrəbl/ *adj.*
IDM **not inconˈsiderable** (*formal*) large; large enough to be considered important: *We have spent a not inconsiderable amount of money on the project already.*

in·con·sid·er·ate /ˌɪnkənˈsɪdərət/ *adj.* (*disapproving*) not giving enough thought to other people's feelings or needs SYN **thoughtless**: *inconsiderate behaviour* ◇ *It was inconsiderate of you not to call.* OPP **considerate** ▸ **in·con·sid·er·ate·ly** *adv.*

in·con·sist·ent AW /ˌɪnkənˈsɪstənt/ *adj.* **1** [not usually before noun] **~ (with sth)** if two statements, etc. are **inconsistent**, or one is **inconsistent with** the other, they cannot both be true because they give the facts in a different way: *The report is inconsistent with the financial statements.* ◇ *The witnesses' statements were inconsistent.* **2 ~ with sth** not matching a set of standards, ideas, etc: *Her behaviour was clearly inconsistent with her beliefs.* **3** (*disapproving*) tending to change too often; not staying the same: *inconsistent results* ◇ *Children find it difficult if a parent is inconsistent.* OPP **consistent** ▸ **in·con·sis·tency** AW /-ənsi/ *noun* [U, C] (*pl.* **-ies**): *There is some inconsistency between the witnesses' evidence and their earlier statements.* ◇ *I noticed a few minor inconsistencies in her argument.* **in·con·sist·ent·ly** *adv.*

in·con·sol·able /ˌɪnkənˈsəʊləbl; *NAmE* -ˈsoʊl-/ (also **un·con·sol·able**) *adj.* very sad and unable to accept help or comfort: *They were inconsolable when their only child died.* ▸ **in·con·sol·ably** /-əbli/ (also **un·con·sol·ably**) *adv.*: *to weep inconsolably*

in·con·spicu·ous /ˌɪnkənˈspɪkjuəs/ *adj.* not attracting attention; not easy to notice OPP **conspicuous** ▸ **in·con·spicu·ous·ly** *adv.*

in·con·stant /ɪnˈkɒnstənt; *NAmE* -ˈkɑːn-/ *adj.* (*formal*) **1** not faithful in love or friendship SYN **fickle** **2** that frequently changes OPP **constant** ▸ **in·con·stancy** AW /-ənsi/ *noun* [U]

in·con·test·able /ˌɪnkənˈtestəbl/ *adj.* (*formal*) that is true and cannot be disagreed with or denied SYN **indisputable**: *an incontestable right/fact* ▸ **in·con·test·ably** /-əbli/ *adv.*

in·con·tin·ence /ɪnˈkɒntɪnəns; *NAmE* -ˈkɑːn-/ *noun* [U] the lack of ability to control the BLADDER and BOWELS OPP **continence** ▸ **in·con·tin·ent** /-ənt; *NAmE* -ˈkɑːntɪnənt/ *adj.*: *Many of our patients are incontinent.*

in·con·tro·vert·ible /ˌɪnkɒntrəˈvɜːtəbl; *NAmE* ˌɪnkɑːntrəˈvɜːrt-/ *adj.* (*formal*) that is true and cannot be disagreed with or denied SYN **indisputable**: ***incontrovertible evidence/proof*** ▸ **in·con·tro·vert·ibly** /ˌɪnkɒntrəˈvɜːtəbli; *NAmE* ˌɪnkɑːntrəˈvɜːrt-/ *adv.*

in·con·veni·ence /ˌɪnkənˈviːniəns/ *noun, verb*

- ***noun*** **1** [U] trouble or problems, especially concerning what you need or would like yourself: *We apologize for the delay and regret any inconvenience it may have caused.* ◇ *I have already been put to considerable inconvenience.*

2 [C] a person or thing that causes problems or difficulties **SYN nuisance**: *I can put up with minor inconveniences.*
■ **verb ~ sb** (*formal*) to cause trouble or difficulty for sb: *I hope that we haven't inconvenienced you.*

in·con·veni·ent /ˌɪnkənˈviːniənt/ *adj.* causing trouble or problems, especially concerning what you need or would like yourself: *an* ***inconvenient time/place*** **OPP convenient** ▶ **in·con·veni·ent·ly** *adv.*

in·corp·or·ate **AW** /ɪnˈkɔːpəreɪt; *NAmE* -ˈkɔːrp-/ *verb* **1** to include sth so that it forms a part of sth: **~ sth** *The new car design incorporates all the latest safety features.* ◇ **~ sth in/into/within sth** *We have incorporated all the latest safety features into the design.* ◇ *Many of your suggestions have been incorporated in the plan.* **2** [often passive] **~ sth** (*business*) to create a legally recognized company: *The company was incorporated in 2008.* ▶ **in·corp·or·ation** **AW** /ɪnˌkɔːpəˈreɪʃn; *NAmE* -ˌkɔːrp-/ *noun* [U]: *the incorporation of foreign words into the language* ◇ *the articles of incorporation of the company*

in·corp·or·ated /ɪnˈkɔːpəreɪtɪd; *NAmE* -ˈkɔːrp-/ *adj.* (*abbr.* **Inc.**) (*business*) formed into a business company with legal status

in·cor·por·eal /ˌɪnkɔːˈpɔːriəl; *NAmE* -kɔːrˈp-/ *adj.* (*formal*) without a body or form

in·cor·rect /ˌɪnkəˈrekt/ *adj.* **1** not accurate or true: *incorrect information/spelling* ◇ *His version of what happened is incorrect.* **2** speaking or behaving in a way that does not follow the accepted standards or rules **OPP correct** ➲ see also POLITICALLY CORRECT ▶ **in·cor·rect·ly** *adv.*: *an incorrectly addressed letter* **in·cor·rect·ness** *noun* [U]

in·cor·ri·gible /ɪnˈkɒrɪdʒəbl; *NAmE* -ˈkɔːr-; -ˈkɑːr/ *adj.* (*disapproving* or *humorous*) having bad habits which cannot be changed or improved **SYN incurable**: *Her husband is an incorrigible flirt.* ◇ *You're incorrigible!* ▶ **in·cor·ri·gibly** /ɪnˈkɒrɪdʒəbli; *NAmE* -ˈkɔːr-; -ˈkɑːr/ *adv.*

in·cor·rupt·ible /ˌɪnkəˈrʌptəbl/ *adj.* **1** (of people) not able to be persuaded to do sth wrong or dishonest, even if sb offers them money **2** that cannot decay or be destroyed **OPP corruptible** ▶ **in·cor·rupt·ibil·ity** /ˌɪnkəˌrʌptəˈbɪləti/ *noun* [U]

Language Bank

increase

Describing an increase

- Student numbers in English language schools in this country **increased** from 66 000 in 2008 to just over 84 000 in 2009.
- The number of students **increased** by almost 30% compared with the previous year.
- Student numbers **shot up/increased dramatically** in 2009.
- The proportion of Spanish students **rose sharply** from 5% in 2008 to 14% in 2009.
- There was a significant **rise** in student numbers in 2009.
- The 2009 figure was 84 000, **an increase of** 28% on the previous year.
- The 2009 figure was 84 000, 28 per cent **up** on the previous year.
- As the chart shows, this can partly be explained by **a dramatic increase** in students from Spain.

➲ Language Banks at EXPECT, FALL, ILLUSTRATE, PROPORTION

in·crease 0‑w *verb, noun*
■ **verb** 0‑w /ɪnˈkriːs/ [I, T] to become or to make sth greater in amount, number, value, etc: **~ (from A) (to B)** *The population has increased from 1.2 million to 1.8 million.* ◇ *increasing levels of carbon dioxide in the earth's atmosphere* ◇ *The price of oil increased.* ◇ **~ in sth** *Oil increased in price.* ◇ **~ by sth** *The rate of inflation increased by 2%.* ◇ **~ with sth** *Disability increases with age* (= the older sb is, the more likely they are to be disabled). ◇ **~ sth (from A) (to B)** *We need to increase productivity.* ◇ **~ sth (by sth)** *They've increased the price by 50%.* **OPP decrease** ▶ **in·creased** *adj.* [only before noun]: *increased demand*
■ **noun** 0‑w /ˈɪŋkriːs/ [C, U] **~ (in sth)** a rise in the amount, number or value of sth: *an increase in spending* ◇ *an increase of 2p in the pound on income tax* ◇ *an increase of nearly 20%* ◇ *a* ***significant/substantial increase*** *in sales* ◇ ***price/tax/wage increases*** ◇ *Homelessness is* ***on the increase*** (= increasing). **OPP decrease**

in·creas·ing·ly 0‑w /ɪnˈkriːsɪŋli/ *adv.* more and more all the time: *increasingly difficult/important/popular* ◇ *It is becoming increasingly clear that this problem will not be easily solved.* ◇ *Increasingly, training is taking place in the office rather than outside it.*

in·cred·ible /ɪnˈkredəbl/ *adj.* **1** impossible or very difficult to believe **SYN unbelievable**: *an incredible story* ◇ *It seemed incredible that she had been there a week already.* **2** (*informal*) extremely good or extremely large: *The hotel was incredible.* ◇ *an incredible amount of work*

in·cred·ibly /ɪnˈkredəbli/ *adv.* **1** extremely **SYN unbelievably**: *incredibly lucky/stupid/difficult/beautiful* **2** in a way that is very difficult to believe: *Incredibly, she had no idea what was going on.*

in·credu·lous /ɪnˈkredjələs; *NAmE* -dʒəl-/ *adj.* not willing or not able to believe sth; showing an inability to believe sth: *'Here?' said Kate, incredulous.* ◇ *an incredulous look* ➲ compare CREDULOUS ▶ **in·credu·lity** /ˌɪnkrəˈdjuːləti; *NAmE* -ˈduː-/ *noun* [U] **SYN disbelief**: *a look of surprise and incredulity* **in·credu·lous·ly** *adv.*: *He laughed incredulously.*

in·cre·ment /ˈɪŋkrəmənt/ *noun* **1** a regular increase in the amount of money that sb is paid for their job: *a salary of £25 K with annual increments* **2** (*formal*) an increase in a number or an amount ▶ **in·cre·men·tal** /ˌɪŋkrəˈmentl/ *adj.*: *incremental costs* **in·cre·men·tal·ly** /-təli/ *adv.*

in·crim·in·ate /ɪnˈkrɪmɪneɪt/ *verb* **~ sb** to make it seem as if sb has done sth wrong or illegal: *They were afraid of answering the questions and incriminating themselves.* ▶ **in·crim·in·at·ing** *adj.* [usually before noun]: *incriminating evidence* **in·crim·in·ation** /ɪnˌkrɪmɪˈneɪʃn/ *noun* [U]

ˈin-crowd *noun* [sing.] a small group of people within a larger group who seem to be the most popular or fashionable

in·crust·ation (also **en·crust·ation**) /ˌɪnkrʌˈsteɪʃn/ *noun* [U, C] the process of forming a hard outer covering or layer; the covering or layer that is formed

in·cu·bate /ˈɪŋkjubeɪt/ *verb* **1** [T] **~ sth** (of a bird) to sit on its eggs in order to keep them warm until they HATCH **2** [T] **~ sth** (*biology*) to keep cells, bacteria, etc. at a suitable temperature so that they develop **3** [T] **be incubating sth** (*medical*) to have an infectious disease developing inside you before SYMPTOMS (= signs of illness) appear **4** [I] (*medical*) (of a disease) to develop slowly without showing any signs

in·cu·ba·tion /ˌɪŋkjuˈbeɪʃn/ *noun* **1** [U] the HATCHING of eggs **2** [C] (also **incuˈbation period**) (*medical* or *biology*) the time between sb being infected with a disease and the appearance of the first SYMPTOMS (= signs) **3** [U] (*biology*) the development and growth of bacteria, etc.

in·cu·ba·tor /ˈɪŋkjubeɪtə(r)/ *noun* **1** a piece of equipment in a hospital which new babies are placed in when they are weak or born too early, in order to help them survive **2** a machine like a box where eggs are kept warm until the young birds are born

in·cu·bus /ˈɪŋkjʊbəs/ *noun* (*pl.* **in·cu·buses** or **in·cubi** /-baɪ/) **1** (*literary*) a problem that makes you worry a lot **2** a male evil spirit, supposed in the past to have sex with a sleeping woman ➲ compare SUCCUBUS

in·cul·cate /ˈɪnkʌlkeɪt; *NAmE* ɪnˈkʌl-/ *verb* (*formal*) to cause sb to learn and remember ideas, moral principles, etc, especially by repeating them often: **~ sth (in/into sb)** *to inculcate a sense of responsibility in sb* ◇ **~ sb with sth** *to* inculcate sb with a sense of responsibility ▸ **in·cul·ca·tion** /ˌɪnkʌlˈkeɪʃn/ *noun* [U]

in·cum·bency /ɪnˈkʌmbənsi/ *noun* (*pl.* -ies) (*formal*) an official position or the time during which sb holds it

in·cum·bent /ɪnˈkʌmbənt/ *noun, adj.*
- ***noun*** a person who has an official position: *the* ***present incumbent*** *of the White House*
- ***adj.* 1** [only before noun] having an official position: *the incumbent president* **2** [not before noun] **~ upon/on sb** (*formal*) necessary as part of sb's duties: *It was incumbent on them to attend.*

incur /ɪnˈkɜː(r)/ *verb* (-rr-) (*formal*) **1 ~ sth** if you **incur** sth unpleasant, you are in a situation in which you have to deal with it: *She had incurred the wrath of her father by marrying without his consent* **2 ~ sth** if you **incur** costs, you have to pay them: *You risk incurring bank charges if you exceed your overdraft limit.*

in·cur·able /ɪnˈkjʊərəbl; *NAmE* -ˈkjʊr-/ *adj.* **1** that cannot be cured: *an* ***incurable disease/illness*** OPP **curable** **2** that cannot be changed SYN **incorrigible**: *She's an incurable optimist.* ▸ **in·cur·ably** /-əbli/ *adv.*: *incurably ill/romantic*

I

in·curi·ous /ɪnˈkjʊəriəs; *NAmE* -ˈkjʊr-/ *adj.* (*formal*) having no interest in knowing or discovering things ▸ **in·curi·ous·ly** *adv.*

in·cur·sion /ɪnˈkɜːʃn; *NAmE* ɪnˈkɜːrʒn/ *noun* **~ (into sth)** (*formal*) **1** a sudden attack on a place by foreign armies, etc. **2** the sudden appearance of sth in a particular area of activity that is either not expected or not wanted

Ind. *abbr.* (*BrE, politics*) INDEPENDENT: *G Green (Ind.)*

in·daba /ɪnˈdɑːbə/ *noun* (*SAfrE*) **1** a large meeting at which politicians, professional people, etc. have discussions about an important subject: *a national indaba on land reform* **2** (*informal*) a difficulty or matter that concerns you: *I don't care what he does. That's his indaba!*

in·debt·ed /ɪnˈdetɪd/ *adj.* **1 ~ (to sb) (for sth)** (*formal*) grateful to sb for helping you: *I am* ***deeply indebted*** *to my family for all their help.* **2** (of countries, governments, etc.) owing money to other countries or organizations: *a list of the fifteen most* ***heavily indebted*** *nations* ▸ **in·debt·ed·ness** *noun* [U]

in·decency /ɪnˈdiːsnsi/ *noun* (*pl.* -ies) **1** [U] behaviour that is thought to be morally or sexually offensive: *an act of* ***gross indecency*** (= a sexual act that is a criminal offence) **2** [C, usually sing.] an indecent act, expression, etc.

in·decent /ɪnˈdiːsnt/ *adj.* **1** (of behaviour, talk, etc.) thought to be morally offensive, especially because it involves sex or being naked: *indecent conduct/photos* ➲ compare DECENT **2** (of clothes) showing parts of the body that are usually covered: *That skirt of hers is positively indecent.* **3** not done in the appropriate or usual amount of time: *They left the funeral with almost* ***indecent haste*** (= too quickly). ▸ **in·decent·ly** *adv.*: *He was charged with indecently assaulting five women.*

inˌdecent asˈsault *noun* [C, U] (*law*) a sexual attack on sb but one that does not include RAPE

inˌdecent exˈposure *noun* [U] (*law*) the crime of showing your sexual organs to other people in a public place

in·de·cipher·able /ˌɪndɪˈsaɪfrəbl/ *adj.* (of writing or speech) impossible to read or understand

in·deci·sion /ˌɪndɪˈsɪʒn/ (also *less frequent* **in·deci·sive·ness**) *noun* [U] the state of being unable to decide: *After a moment's indecision, he said yes.* ➲ compare DECISION

in·deci·sive /ˌɪndɪˈsaɪsɪv/ *adj.* **1** (of a person) unable to make decisions: *a weak and indecisive man* **2** not providing a clear and definite answer or result: *an indecisive battle* OPP **decisive** ▸ **in·deci·sive·ly** *adv.* **in·deci·sive·ness** *noun* [U] = INDECISION

in·dec·or·ous /ɪnˈdekərəs/ *adj.* (*formal*) (of behaviour) embarrassing or not socially acceptable

in·deed 0━ /ɪnˈdiːd/ *adv.*
1 0━ used to emphasize a positive statement or answer: *'Was he very angry?' 'Indeed he was.'* ◇ *'Do you agree?' 'Indeed I do/Yes, indeed.'* ◇ *'You said you'd help?' 'I did indeed—yes.'* ◇ *It is indeed a remarkable achievement.* **2** 0━ (*especially BrE*) used after *very* and an adjective or adverb to emphasize a statement, description, etc.: *Thank you very much indeed!* ◇ *I was very sad indeed to hear of your father's death.* **3** (*formal, especially BrE*) used to add information to a statement: *I don't mind at all. Indeed, I would be delighted to help.* **4** (*informal, especially BrE*) used to show that you are surprised at sth or that you find sth ridiculous: *A ghost indeed! I've never heard anything so silly.* **5** (*informal*) used when you are repeating a question that sb has just asked and showing that you do not know the answer: *'Why did he do it?' 'Why indeed?'* IDM see FRIEND

in·defat·ig·able /ˌɪndɪˈfætɪɡəbl/ *adj.* (*formal, approving*) never giving up or getting tired of doing sth: *an indefatigable defender of human rights* ▸ **in·defat·ig·ably** /ˌɪndɪˈfætɪɡəbli/ *adv.*

in·defens·ible /ˌɪndɪˈfensəbl/ *adj.* **1** that cannot be defended or excused because it is morally unacceptable: *indefensible behaviour* ◇ *The Prime Minister was accused of defending the indefensible.* **2** (of a place or building) impossible to defend from military attack

in·defin·able /ˌɪndɪˈfaɪnəbl/ *adj.* difficult or impossible to define or explain: *She has that indefinable something that makes an actress a star.* ▸ **in·defin·ably** /-əbli/ *adv.*

in·def·in·ite AW /ɪnˈdefɪnət/ *adj.* **1** lasting for a period of time that has no fixed end: *She will be away for the indefinite future.* **2** not clearly defined SYN **imprecise**: *an indefinite science*

inˌdefinite ˈarticle *noun* (*grammar*) the word *a* or *an* in English, or a similar word in another language ➲ compare DEFINITE ARTICLE

in·def·in·ite·ly AW /ɪnˈdefɪnətli/ *adv.* for a period of time with no fixed limit: *The trial was postponed indefinitely.*

inˌdefinite ˈpronoun *noun* (*grammar*) a pronoun that does not refer to any person or thing in particular, for example 'anything' and 'everyone'

in·del·ible /ɪnˈdeləbl/ *adj.* **1** impossible to forget or remove SYN **permanent**: *The experience made an indelible impression on me.* ◇ *Her unhappy childhood left an indelible mark.* **2** (of ink, pens, etc.) leaving a mark that cannot be removed SYN **permanent**: *an indelible marker* ▸ **in·del·ibly** /-əbli/ *adv.*: *That day is stamped indelibly on my memory.*

in·deli·cate /ɪnˈdelɪkət/ *adj.* (*formal*) likely to be thought rude or embarrassing: *an indelicate question* ▸ **in·deli·cacy** /-kəsi/ *noun* [U]

in·dem·nify /ɪnˈdemnɪfaɪ/ *verb* (**in·dem·ni·fies**, **in·dem·ni·fy·ing**, **in·dem·ni·fied**, **in·dem·ni·fied**) (*law*) **1 ~ sb (against sth)** to promise to pay sb an amount of money if they suffer any damage or loss **2 ~ sb (for sth)** to pay sb an amount of money because of the damage or loss that they have suffered ▸ **in·dem·ni·fi·ca·tion** /ɪnˌdemnɪfɪˈkeɪʃn/ *noun* [U]

in·dem·nity /ɪnˈdemnəti/ *noun* (*pl.* -ies) (*formal* or *law*) **1** [U] **~ (against sth)** protection against damage or loss, especially in the form of a promise to pay for any damage or loss that happens: *an indemnity clause/fund/policy* ◇ *indemnity insurance* **2** [C] a sum of money that is given as payment for damage or loss

in·dent *verb, noun*
- ***verb*** /ɪnˈdent/ **~ sth** to start a line of print or writing further away from the edge of the page than the other lines: *The first line of each paragraph should be indented.*
- ***noun*** /ˈɪndent/ **1 ~ (for sth)** (*business*) (*especially BrE*) an official order for goods or equipment **2** = INDENTATION

in·den·ta·tion /ˌɪndenˈteɪʃn/ *noun* **1** [C] a cut or mark on the edge or surface of sth: *The horse's hooves left deep indentations in the mud.* **2** (also **in·dent**) [C] a space left at the beginning of a line of print or writing **3** [U] the action of indenting sth or the process of being indented

in·dent·ed /ɪnˈdentɪd/ *adj.* (of an edge or a surface) an **indented** edge is not even, because parts of it are missing or have been cut away: *an indented coastline*

in·den·ture /ɪnˈdentʃə(r)/ *noun* a type of contract in the past that forced a servant or APPRENTICE to work for their employer for a particular period of time ▸ **in·den·tured** *adj.*

in·de·pend·ence /ˌɪndɪˈpendəns/ *noun* [U] **1** **~ (from sb/sth)** (of a country) freedom from political control by other countries: *Cuba gained independence from Spain in 1898.* **2** the time when a country gains freedom from political control by another country: *independence celebrations* ◇ *the first elections since independence* **3** the freedom to organize your own life, make your own decisions, etc. without needing help from other people: *He values his independence.* ◇ *a woman's financial independence* OPP **dependence**

Indeˈpendence Day *noun* 4 July, celebrated in the US as the anniversary of the day in 1776 when the Americans declared themselves independent of Britain ➲ see also THE FOURTH OF JULY

in·de·pend·ent /ˌɪndɪˈpendənt/ *adj., noun*

■ *adj.*

▸ COUNTRY **1** **~ (from/of sth)** (of countries) having their own government SYN **self-governing**: *Mozambique became independent in 1975.*

▸ SEPARATE **2** done or given by sb who is not involved in a situation and so is able to judge it fairly: *an* ***independent inquiry/witness*** ◇ *She went to a lawyer for some* ***independent advice.*** **3** **~ (of sb/sth)** not connected with or influenced by sth; not connected with each other: *The police force should be independent of direct government control.* ◇ *Two independent research bodies reached the same conclusions.*

▸ ORGANIZATION **4** supported by private money rather than government money: ***independent television/schools*** ◇ *the independent sector*

▸ PERSON **5** **~ (of sb/sth)** confident and free to do things without needing help from other people: *Going away to college has made me much more independent.* ◇ *She's a very independent-minded young woman.* ◇ *Students should aim to become more independent of their teachers.* OPP **dependent** **6** **~ (of sb/sth)** having or earning enough money so that you do not have to rely on sb else for help: *It was important to me to be financially independent of my parents.* ◇ *a man* ***of independent means*** (= with an income that he does not earn by working) OPP **dependent**

▸ POLITICIAN **7** not representing or belonging to a particular political party: *an independent candidate*

▸ **in·de·pend·ent·ly** *adv.*: **~ (of sb/sth)** *The two departments work independently of each other.* ◇ *It was the first time that she had lived independently.*

■ *noun* (*abbr.* **Ind.**) a member of parliament, candidate, etc. who does not belong to a particular political party

indeˌpendent ˈschool *noun* = PRIVATE SCHOOL

indeˌpendent ˈvariable *noun* (*mathematics*) a VARIABLE whose value does not depend on another variable

ˌin-ˈdepth *adj.* [usually before noun] very thorough and detailed: *an* ***in-depth discussion/study*** ➲ see also DEPTH

in·des·crib·able /ˌɪndɪˈskraɪbəbl/ *adj.* so extreme or unusual it is almost impossible to describe: *The pain was indescribable.* ▸ **in·des·crib·ably** /-əbli/ *adv.*: *indescribably beautiful/boring*

in·des·truct·ible /ˌɪndɪˈstrʌktəbl/ *adj.* that is very strong and cannot easily be destroyed: *plastic containers that are virtually indestructible* ◇ *an indestructible bond of friendship*

in·de·ter·min·ate /ˌɪndɪˈtɜːmɪnət; *NAmE* -ˈtɜːrm-/ *adj.* that cannot be identified easily or exactly: *She was a tall woman of indeterminate age.* ▸ **in·de·ter·min·acy** /-nəsi/ *noun* [U]

index AW /ˈɪndeks/ *noun, verb*

■ *noun* **1** (*pl.* **in·dexes**) a list of names or topics that are referred to in a book, etc, usually arranged at the end of a book in alphabetical order or listed in a separate file or book: *Look it up in the index.* ◇ *Author and subject indexes are available on a library database.* **2** (*BrE*) = CARD INDEX ➲ VISUAL VOCAB page V56 **3** (*pl.* **in·dexes** or **in·dices** /ˈɪndɪsiːz/) a system that shows the level of prices and wages, etc. so that they can be compared with those of a previous date: *the cost-of-living index* ◇ *The Dow Jones index fell 15 points this morning.* ◇ *stock-market indices* ◇ *house price indexes* **4** (*pl.* **in·dices** /ˈɪndɪsiːz/) a sign or measure that sth else can be judged by: *The number of new houses being built is a good index of a country's prosperity.* **5** (usually **indices** [pl.]) (*mathematics*) the small number written above a larger number to show how many times that number must be multiplied by itself. In the EQUATION $4^2 = 16$, the number 2 is an index.

■ *verb* **1** **~ sth** to make an index of documents, the contents of a book, etc; to add sth to a list of this type: *All publications are indexed by subject and title.* **2** [usually passive] **~ sth (to sth)** to link wages, etc. to the level of prices of food, clothing, etc. so that they both increase at the same rate

in·dex·ation /ˌɪndekˈseɪʃn/ *noun* [U] the linking of increases in wages, etc. to increases in prices

ˈindex card *noun* a small card that you can write information on and keep with other cards in a box or file ➲ see also CARD INDEX ➲ VISUAL VOCAB page V56

ˈindex finger (also **ˌfirst ˈfinger**) *noun* the finger next to the thumb SYN **forefinger** ➲ VISUAL VOCAB page V48 ➲ compare POINTER FINGER

ˌindex-ˈlinked *adj.* (*BrE*) (of wages, etc.) rising in value according to increases in the cost of living ▸ **ˌindex-ˈlinking** *noun* [U]

In·dian /ˈɪndiən/ *noun* **1** a person from India **2** (*old-fashioned, offensive*) = NATIVE AMERICAN **3** (*CanE*) a Native Canadian who is not Inuit or Metis ▸ **In·dian** *adj.* IDM see CHIEF *n.*, FILE *n.*

ˌIndian ˈcorn *noun* [U] (*especially NAmE*) a type of CORN (MAIZE) with large brown and yellow grains, not usually eaten but sometimes used to make decorations, for example at Thanksgiving

ˌIndian ˈink (also **ˌIndia ˈink**) *noun* [U] a very black ink used in drawing and technical drawing

ˌIndian ˈsummer *noun* **1** a period of dry warm weather in the autumn/fall **2** a pleasant period of success or improvement, especially later in sb's life

India rubber /ˌɪndiə ˈrʌbə(r)/ *noun* [U] (*old-fashioned*) natural rubber

in·di·cate AW /ˈɪndɪkeɪt/ *verb*

▸ SHOW **1** [T, I] to show that sth is true or exists: **~ sth** *Record profits in the retail market indicate a boom in the economy.* ◇ **~ (that...)** *Research indicates that eating habits are changing fast.* ◇ *Kingston-upon-Thames, as the name indicates, is situated on the banks of the Thames.* ◇ **~ how, what etc...** *Our results indicate how misleading it could be to rely on this method.*

▸ SUGGEST **2** [T] to be a sign of sth; to show that sth is possible or likely: **~ sth** *A red sky at night often indicates fine weather the next day.* ◇ **~ that...** *Early results indicate that the government will be returned to power.*

▸ MENTION **3** [T] to mention sth, especially in an indirect way: **~ (to sb) (that)...** *In his letter he indicated to us (that) he was willing to cooperate.* ◇ **~ sth (to sb)** *He indicated his willingness to cooperate.* ◇ **~ whether, when, etc...** *Has she indicated yet whether she would like to be involved?* ➲ SYNONYMS at DECLARE

▸ POINT TO **4** [T] (*formal*) to make sb notice sb/sth, especially by pointing or moving your head: **~ sb/sth (to sb)** *She took out a map and indicated the quickest route to us.* ◇ **~ where, which, etc...** *He indicated where the furniture was to go.* ◇ **~ that...** *She indicated that I was to sit down.*

▸ GIVE INFORMATION **5** [T] **~ sth** (*formal*) to represent information without using words: *The results are indicated in Table 2.* **6** [T] (*formal*) to give information in writing: **~ sth** *You are allowed 20kgs of baggage unless indicated otherwise* *on your ticket.* ◇ **~ which, where, etc...** *Please indicate clearly which colour you require.*

▸ SHOW MEASUREMENT **7** [T] **~ sth** | **~ how much, how many, etc...** (of an instrument for measuring things) to show a particular measurement: *When the temperature gauge indicates 90°F or more, turn off the engine.*

▸ IN VEHICLE **8** [I, T] (*BrE*) to show that your vehicle is going to change direction, by using lights or your arm SYN **signal**: *Always indicate before moving into another lane.* ◇ **~ sth** *He indicated left and then turned right.* ◇ **~ (that)...** *She indicated that she was turning right.*

▸ BE RECOMMENDED **9** [T, usually passive] **~ sth** (*formal*) to be necessary or recommended: *A course of chemotherapy was indicated.*

in·di·ca·tion 🔑 AW /ˌɪndɪˈkeɪʃn/ *noun* [C, U] a remark or sign that shows that sth is happening or what sb is thinking or feeling: **~ (of sth)** *They* ***gave no indication*** *of how the work should be done.* ◇ **~ (of doing sth)** *He shows every indication* (= clear signs) *of wanting to accept the post.* ◇ **~ (that...)** *There are clear indications that the economy is improving.* ◇ *All the indications are that the deal will go ahead as planned.* ➲ SYNONYMS at SIGN

in·di·ca·tive AW /ɪnˈdɪkətɪv/ *adj., noun*

■ ***adj.*** **1** [not usually before noun] **~ (of sth)** (*formal*) showing or suggesting sth: *Their failure to act is indicative of their lack of interest.* **2** [only before noun] (*grammar*) stating a fact

■ ***noun*** **the indicative** [sing.] (*grammar*) the form of a verb that states a fact: *In 'Ben likes school', the verb 'like' is in the indicative.*

in·di·ca·tor AW /ˈɪndɪkeɪtə(r)/ *noun* **1** a sign that shows you what sth is like or how a situation is changing: *The economic indicators are better than expected.* ➲ SYNONYMS at SIGN **2** a device on a machine that shows speed, pressure, etc: *a depth indicator* **3** (*BrE*) (*NAmE* ˈ**turn signal**) (also *informal* **blink·er** *NAmE, BrE*) a light on a vehicle that flashes to show that the vehicle is going to turn left or right ➲ VISUAL VOCAB page V42

in·dices *pl.* of INDEX

in·dict /ɪnˈdaɪt/ *verb* [usually passive] **~ sb (for sth)** | **~ sb (on charges/on a charge of sth)** (*especially NAmE, law*) to officially charge sb with a crime: *The senator was indicted for murder.* ◇ *She was indicted on charges of corruption.* ➲ COLLOCATIONS at JUSTICE

in·dict·able /ɪnˈdaɪtəbl/ *adj.* (*law*) **1** (of a crime) for which you can be indicted: *an indictable offense* **2** (of a person) able to be indicted

in·dict·ment /ɪnˈdaɪtmənt/ *noun* **1** [C, usually sing.] **~ (of/on sb/sth)** a sign that a system, society, etc. is very bad or very wrong: *The poverty in our cities is a damning indictment of modern society.* **2** [C] (*especially NAmE*) a written statement accusing sb of a crime **3** [U] (*especially NAmE*) the act of officially accusing sb of a crime: *This led to his indictment on allegations of conspiracy.*

indie /ˈɪndi/ *adj., noun*

■ ***adj.*** (of a company, person or product) not belonging to, working for or produced by a large organization; independent: *an indie publisher/newspaper* ◇ *indie music* ◇ *an indie band/record label*

■ ***noun*** a small independent company, or sth produced by such a company

in·dif·fer·ence /ɪnˈdɪfrəns/ *noun* [U, sing.] **~ (to sb/sth)** a lack of interest, feeling or reaction towards sb/sth: *his total indifference to what people thought of him* ◇ *What she said is* ***a matter of complete indifference*** *to me.* ◇ *Their father treated them with indifference.* ◇ *an indifference to the needs of others*

in·dif·fer·ent /ɪnˈdɪfrənt/ *adj.* **1** [not usually before noun] **~ (to sb/sth)** having or showing no interest in sb/sth: *The government cannot afford to be indifferent to public opinion.* **2** not very good SYN **mediocre**: *an indifferent meal* ◇ *The festival has the usual mixture of movies—****good, bad and indifferent****.* ▸ **in·dif·fer·ent·ly** *adv.*: *He shrugged indifferently.*

in·di·gen·ous /ɪnˈdɪdʒənəs/ *adj.* (*formal*) belonging to a particular place rather than coming to it from somewhere else SYN **native**: *the* ***indigenous peoples/languages*** *of the area* ◇ **~ to...** *The kangaroo is indigenous to Australia.*

in·di·gent /ˈɪndɪdʒənt/ *adj.* [usually before noun] (*formal*) very poor

in·di·gest·ible /ˌɪndɪˈdʒestəbl/ *adj.* **1** (of food) that cannot easily be DIGESTED in the stomach: *an indigestible meal* **2** (of facts, information, etc.) difficult to understand, and presented in a complicated way OPP **digestible**

in·di·ges·tion /ˌɪndɪˈdʒestʃən/ *noun* [U] pain caused by difficulty in DIGESTING food SYN **dyspepsia**

in·dig·nant /ɪnˈdɪɡnənt/ *adj.* feeling or showing anger and surprise because you think that you have been treated unfairly: *an indignant letter/look* ◇ **~ at/about sth** *She was very indignant at the way she had been treated.* ◇ **~ that...** *They were indignant that they hadn't been invited.* ➲ note at ANGRY ▸ **in·dig·nant·ly** *adv.*: *'I'm certainly not asking him!' she retorted indignantly.*

in·dig·na·tion /ˌɪndɪɡˈneɪʃn/ *noun* [U] **~ (at/about sth)** | **~ (that...)** a feeling of anger and surprise caused by sth that you think is unfair or unreasonable: *The rise in train fares has aroused public indignation.* ◇ *Joe quivered* ***with indignation*** *that Paul should speak to him like that.* ◇ *Some benefits apply only to men, much* ***to the indignation of*** *working women.* ◇ *to be full of* ***righteous indignation*** (= the belief that you are right to be angry even though other people do not agree)

in·dig·nity /ɪnˈdɪɡnəti/ *noun* [U, C] (*pl.* **-ies**) **~ (of sth/of doing sth)** a situation that makes you feel embarrassed or ashamed because you are not treated with respect; an act that causes these feelings SYN **humiliation**: *The chairman* ***suffered the indignity of*** *being refused admission to the meeting.* ◇ *the daily indignities of imprisonment*

in·digo /ˈɪndɪɡəʊ; *NAmE* -ɡoʊ/ *adj.* very dark blue in colour: *an indigo sky* ▸ **in·digo** *noun* [U]

in·dir·ect 🔑 /ˌɪndəˈrekt; -daɪˈr-/ *adj.* [usually before noun]

1 🔑 happening not as the main aim, cause or result of a particular action, but in addition to it: *the* ***indirect effects*** *of the war* ◇ *to find something out by* ***indirect methods*** ◇ *The building collapsed as an* ***indirect result*** *of the heavy rain.* ◇ *There would be some benefit, however indirect, to the state.* ◇ ***indirect costs*** (= costs that are not directly connected with making a product, for example training, heating, rent, etc.) **2** 🔑 avoiding saying sth in a clear and obvious way: *an indirect attack* **3** 🔑 not going in a straight line: *an* ***indirect route*** OPP **direct** ▸ **in·dir·ect·ly** 🔑 *adv.*: *The new law will affect us all, directly or indirectly.* **in·dir·ect·ness** *noun* [U]

ˌindirect ˈobject *noun* (*grammar*) a noun, noun phrase or pronoun in a sentence, used after some verbs, that refers to the person or thing that an action is done to or for: *In 'Give him the money', 'him' is the indirect object and 'money' is the direct object.*

ˌindirect ˈquestion (also **reˌported ˈquestion**) *noun* (*grammar*) a question in REPORTED SPEECH, for example *She asked where I was going.* HELP Do not put a question mark after an indirect question.

ˌindirect ˈspeech *noun* [U] (*grammar*) = REPORTED SPEECH ➲ compare DIRECT SPEECH

ˌindirect ˈtax *noun* [C, U] a tax that is paid as an amount added to the price of goods and services and not paid directly to the government ➲ compare DIRECT TAX ▸ **ˌindirect taˈxation** *noun* [U]

in·dis·cern·ible /ˌɪndɪˈsɜːnəbl; *NAmE* -ˈsɜːrn-/ *adj.* that cannot be seen, heard or understood

in·dis·cip·line /ɪnˈdɪsɪplɪn/ *noun* [U] (*formal*) a lack of control in the behaviour of a group of people

in·dis·creet AW /ˌɪndɪˈskriːt/ *adj.* not careful about what you say or do, especially when this embarrasses or offends sb OPP **discreet** ▸ **in·dis·creet·ly** *adv.*

in·dis·cre·tion AW /ˌɪndɪˈskreʃn/ *noun* **1** [C] an act or remark that is indiscreet, especially one that is not morally acceptable: *youthful indiscretions* **2** [U] the act of saying or doing sth without thinking about the effect it may have, especially when this embarrasses or offends sb: *He talked to the press in a moment of indiscretion.* ➲ compare DISCRETION

in·dis·crim·in·ate /ˌɪndɪˈskrɪmɪnət/ *adj.* **1** an **indiscriminate** action is done without thought about what the result may be, especially when it causes people to be harmed: *indiscriminate attacks on motorists by youths throwing stones* ◇ *Doctors have been criticized for their indiscriminate use of antibiotics.* **2** acting without careful judgement: *She's always been indiscriminate in her choice of friends.* ▶ **in·dis·crim·in·ate·ly** *adv.*: *The soldiers fired indiscriminately into the crowd.*

in·dis·pens·able /ˌɪndɪˈspensəbl/ *adj.* too important to be without SYN **essential**: *Cars have become an indispensable part of our lives.* ◇ **~ to sb/sth** *She made herself indispensable to the department.* ◇ **~ for sth/for doing sth** *A good dictionary is indispensable for learning a foreign language.* OPP **dispensable** ➲ SYNONYMS at ESSENTIAL ➲ LANGUAGE BANK at VITAL

in·dis·posed /ˌɪndɪˈspəʊzd; *NAmE* -ˈspoʊzd/ *adj.* (*formal*) **1** [not usually before noun] unable to do sth because you are ill/sick, or for a reason you do not want to give SYN **unwell 2** [not before noun] **~ to do sth** not willing to do sth

in·dis·pos·ition /ˌɪndɪspəˈzɪʃn/ *noun* [C, U] (*formal*) a slight illness that makes you unable to do sth

in·dis·put·able /ˌɪndɪˈspjuːtəbl/ *adj.* that is true and cannot be disagreed with or denied SYN **undeniable**: *indisputable evidence* ◇ *an indisputable fact* ◇ *It is indisputable that the crime rate has been rising.* ➲ compare DISPUTABLE ▶ **in·dis·put·ably** *adv.*: *This painting is indisputably one of his finest works.*

in·dis·sol·uble /ˌɪndɪˈsɒljəbl; *NAmE* -ˈsɑːl-/ *adj.* (*formal*) (of a relationship) that cannot be ended: *an indissoluble friendship* ▶ **in·dis·sol·ubly** /ˌɪndɪˈsɒljəbli; *NAmE* -ˈsɑːl-/ *adv.*: *indissolubly linked*

in·dis·tinct AW /ˌɪndɪˈstɪŋkt/ *adj.* that cannot be seen, heard or remembered clearly SYN **vague**, **hazy** ▶ **in·dis·tinct·ly** AW *adv.*

in·dis·tin·guish·able /ˌɪndɪˈstɪŋɡwɪʃəbl/ *adj.* **1 ~ (from sth)** if two things are **indistinguishable**, or one is **indistinguishable from** the other, it is impossible to see any differences between them: *The male of the species is almost indistinguishable from the female.* **2** not clear; not able to be clearly identified: *His words were indistinguishable.*

in·dium /ˈɪndiəm/ *noun* [U] (*symb.* **In**) a chemical element. Indium is a soft silver-white metal.

in·di·vid·ual 🔑 AW /ˌɪndɪˈvɪdʒuəl/ *adj.*, *noun*

■ *adj.* **1** 🔑 [only before noun] (often used after *each*) considered separately rather than as part of a group: *We interviewed **each individual** member of the community.* ◇ *The minister refused to comment on individual cases.* **2** 🔑 [only before noun] connected with one person; designed for one person: *respect for individual freedom* ◇ *an individual pizza* **3** (usually *approving*) typical of one particular person or thing in a way that is different from others SYN **distinctive**: *a highly individual style of dress*

■ *noun* **1** 🔑 a person considered separately rather than as part of a group: *The competition is open to both teams and individuals.* ◇ *Treatment depends on the individual involved.* ◇ *donations from private individuals* (= ordinary people rather than companies, etc.) **2** a person who is original and very different from others: *She's grown into quite an individual.* **3** (*informal*, usually *disapproving*) a person of a particular type, especially a strange one: *an odd-looking individual* ◇ *So this individual came up and demanded money.*

in·di·vidu·al·ism AW /ˌɪndɪˈvɪdʒuəlɪzəm/ *noun* [U] **1** the quality of being different from other people and doing things in your own way **2** the belief that individual people in society should have the right to make their own decisions, etc, rather than be controlled by the government: *Capitalism stresses innovation, competition and individualism.* ▶ **in·di·vidu·al·ist** AW /-əlɪst/ *noun*: *She's a complete individualist in her art.* **in·di·vidu·al·is·tic** AW /ˌɪndɪˌvɪdʒuəˈlɪstɪk/ (also **in·di·vidu·al·ist**) *adj.*: *an individualistic culture* ◇ *His music is highly individualistic and may not appeal to everyone.*

in·di·vidu·al·ity AW /ˌɪndɪˌvɪdʒuˈæləti/ *noun* [U] the qualities that make sb/sth different from other people or things: *She expresses her individuality through her clothes.*

in·di·vidu·al·ize (*BrE* also **-ise**) /ˌɪndɪˈvɪdʒuəlaɪz/ *verb* **~ sth** to make sth different to suit the needs of a particular person, place, etc: *to individualize children's learning* ▶ **in·di·vidu·al·iza·tion, -isa·tion** /ˌɪndɪvɪdʒuəlaɪˈzeɪʃn; *NAmE* -əˈzeɪʃn/ *noun* [U]

in·di·vidu·al·ized (*BrE* also **-ised**) /ˌɪndɪˈvɪdʒuəlaɪzd/ *adj.* designed for a particular person or thing; connected with a particular person or thing: *individualized teaching* ◇ *a highly individualized approach to management*

in·di·vidu·al·ly AW /ˌɪndɪˈvɪdʒuəli/ *adv.* separately, rather than as a group: *individually wrapped chocolates* ◇ *The manager spoke to them all individually.* ◇ *The hotel has 100 individually designed bedrooms.*

in·di·vidu·ate /ˌɪndɪˈvɪdʒueɪt/ *verb* **~ sb/sth** (*formal*) to make sb/sth clearly different from other people or things of the same type

in·di·vis·ible /ˌɪndɪˈvɪzəbl/ *adj.* that cannot be divided into separate parts OPP **divisible** ▶ **in·di·vis·ibil·ity** /ˌɪndɪˌvɪzəˈbɪləti/ *noun* [U] **in·di·vis·ibly** /ˌɪndɪˈvɪzəbli/ *adv.*

Indo- /ˈɪndəʊ; *NAmE* ˈɪndoʊ/ *combining form* (in nouns and adjectives) Indian: *the Indo-Pakistan border*

ˌIndo-Caˈnadian *noun* [C] (*CanE*) a Canadian who was born in S Asia, especially India, or whose family originally came from S Asia

in·doc·trin·ate /ɪnˈdɒktrɪneɪt; *NAmE* ɪnˈdɑːk-/ *verb* **~ sb (with sth)** | **~ sb (to do sth)** (*disapproving*) to force sb to accept a particular belief or set of beliefs and not allow them to consider any others: *They had been indoctrinated from an early age with their parents' beliefs.* ▶ **in·doc·trin·ation** /ɪnˌdɒktrɪˈneɪʃn; *NAmE* -ˌdɑːk-/ *noun* [U]: ***political/religious indoctrination***

ˌIndo-ˌEuroˈpean *adj.* of or connected with the family of languages spoken in most of Europe and parts of western Asia (including English, French, Latin, Greek, Swedish, Russian and Hindi)

in·do·lent /ˈɪndələnt/ *adj.* (*formal*) not wanting to work SYN **lazy** ▶ **in·do·lence** /-əns/ *noun* [U]

in·dom·it·able /ɪnˈdɒmɪtəbl; *NAmE* ɪnˈdɑːm-/ *adj.* (*formal, approving*) not willing to accept defeat, even in a difficult situation; very brave and determined

in·door 🔑 /ˈɪndɔː(r)/ *adj.* [only before noun] located, done or used inside a building: *an indoor swimming pool* ◇ *indoor games* ◇ *the world indoor 200 metres champion* OPP **outdoor**

in·doors 🔑 /ˌɪnˈdɔːz; *NAmE* ˌɪnˈdɔːrz/ *adv.* inside or into a building: *to **go/stay indoors*** ◇ *Many herbs can be grown indoors.* OPP **outdoors**

in·drawn /ˌɪnˈdrɔːn/ *adj.* (*literary*) **indrawn breath** is air that sb breathes in suddenly and quickly, expressing surprise or shock

in·dub·it·ably /ɪnˈdjuːbɪtəbli; *NAmE* -ˈduː-/ *adv.* (*formal*) in a way that cannot be doubted; without question SYN **undoubtedly**: *He was, indubitably, the most suitable candidate.* ▶ **in·dub·it·able** *adj.*: *indubitable proof*

in·duce AW /ɪnˈdjuːs; *NAmE* -duːs/ *verb* **1 ~ sb to do sth** (*formal*) to persuade or influence sb to do sth: *Nothing would induce me to take the job.* **2 ~ sth** (*formal*) to cause sth: *drugs which induce sleep* ◇ *a drug-induced coma* **3 ~ sb/sth** (*medical*) to make a woman start giving birth to her baby by giving her special drugs: *an induced labour* ◇ *We'll have to induce her.*

in·duce·ment /ɪnˈdjuːsmənt; *NAmE* ɪnˈduːsmənt/ *noun* [C, U] **~ (to/for sb) (to do sth)** something that is given to sb to persuade them to do sth SYN **incentive**: *financial in-*

I

ducements to mothers to stay at home ◇ There is little inducement for them to work harder. ◇ Government officials have been accused of accepting inducements (=BRIBES) from local businessmen.

in·duct /ɪn'dʌkt/ *verb* [often passive] **~ sb (into sth) (as sth)** (*formal*) **1** to formally give sb a job or position of authority, especially as part of a ceremony **2** to officially introduce sb into a group or an organization, especially the army **3** to introduce sb to a particular area of knowledge: *They were inducted into the skills of magic.*

in·duct·ee /ˌɪndʌk'tiː/ *noun* (*especially NAmE*) a person who is being, or who has just been, introduced into a special group of people, especially sb who has just joined the army

in·duc·tion **AW** /ɪn'dʌkʃn/ *noun* **1** [U, C] **~ (into sth)** the process of introducing sb to a new job, skill, organization, etc; a ceremony at which this takes place **2** [U, C] the act of making a pregnant woman start to give birth, using artificial means such as a special drug **3** [U] (*technical*) a method of discovering general rules and principles from particular facts and examples ➲ compare DEDUCTION **4** [U] (*physics*) the process by which electricity or MAGNETISM passes from one object to another without them touching

in'duction course *noun* (*BrE*) a training course for new employees, students, etc. that is designed to give them a general introduction to the business, school, etc.

in'duction loop *noun* a system in theatres, etc, which helps people who cannot hear well. A ring of wire around the room produces a signal that can be received directly by HEARING AIDS.

in·duct·ive /ɪn'dʌktɪv/ *adj.* **1** (*technical*) using particular facts and examples to form general rules and principles: *an inductive argument* ◇ *inductive reasoning* ➲ compare DEDUCTIVE **2** (*physics*) connected with the INDUCTION of electricity ▶ **in·duct·ive·ly** *adv.*: *a theory derived inductively from the data*

in·dulge /ɪn'dʌldʒ/ *verb* **1** [I, T] to allow yourself to have or do sth that you like, especially sth that is considered bad for you: **~ in sth** *They went into town to indulge in some serious shopping.* ◇ **~ yourself (with sth)** *I indulged myself with a long hot bath.* **2** [T] **~ sth** to satisfy a particular desire, interest, etc: *The inheritance enabled him to indulge his passion for art.* **3** [T] to be too generous in allowing sb to have or do whatever they like: **~ sb (with sth)** *She did not believe in indulging the children with presents.* ◇ **~ sth** *Her father had always* ***indulged her every whim.*** **4** [I] **~ in sth** to take part in an activity, especially one that is illegal

in·dul·gence /ɪn'dʌldʒəns/ *noun* **1** [U] (usually *disapproving*) the state or act of having or doing whatever you want; the state of allowing sb to have or do whatever they want: *to lead a life of indulgence* ◇ *Avoid excessive indulgence in sweets and canned drinks.* ◇ *There is no limit to the indulgence he shows to his grandchildren.* **2** [C] something that you allow yourself to have even though it is not essential: *The holiday was an extravagant indulgence.* ➲ see also SELF-INDULGENCE **3** [U] (*formal*) willingness to ignore the weaknesses in sb/sth **SYN** **patience**: *They begged the audience's indulgence.*

in·dul·gent /ɪn'dʌldʒənt/ *adj.* **1** (usually *disapproving*) tending to allow sb to have or do whatever they want: *indulgent parents* ◇ *an indulgent smile* ➲ see also SELF-INDULGENT **2** willing or too willing to ignore the weaknesses in sb/sth **SYN** **patient**: *to take an indulgent view of sth* ▶ **in·dul·gent·ly** *adv.*: *to laugh indulgently*

in·duna /ɪn'duːnə/ *noun* (*SAfrE*) a senior leader of a TRIBE

in·dus·trial O‑ /ɪn'dʌstriəl/ *adj.* [usually before noun]
1 O‑ connected with industry: *industrial unrest* ◇ *industrial output* ◇ *an industrial accident* ◇ *They had made* ***industrial quantities*** *of food* (= a lot). **2** O‑ used by industries: *industrial chemicals* **3** O‑ having many industries: *an industrial town* ◇ *an industrial society* ◇ *the world's leading industrial nations* ▶ **in·dus·tri·al·ly** /-əli/ *adv.*: *industrially advanced countries*

inˌdustrial 'action *noun* [U] (*especially BrE*) action that workers take, especially stopping work, to protest to their employers about sth

inˌdustrial archae'ology *noun* [U] the study of machines, factories, bridges, etc. used in the past in industry

inˌdustrial 'arts (also **shop**, **'shop class**) *noun* [U] (*NAmE*) a school subject in which students learn to make things from wood and metal using tools and machines

inˌdustrial e'state (*BrE*) (*NAmE* **inˌdustrial 'park**) *noun* an area especially for factories, on the edge of a town ➲ compare TRADING ESTATE

in·dus·tri·al·ism /ɪn'dʌstriəlɪzəm/ *noun* [U] (*technical*) an economic and social system based on industry

in·dus·tri·al·ist /ɪn'dʌstriəlɪst/ *noun* a person who owns or runs a large factory or industrial company

in·dus·tri·al·ize (*BrE* also **-ise**) /ɪn'dʌstriəlaɪz/ *verb* [T, I] **~ (sth)** if a country or an area **is industrialized** or if it **industrializes**, industries are developed there: *The southern part of the country was slow to industrialize.* ▶ **in·dus·tri·al·iza·tion, -isa·tion** /ɪnˌdʌstriəlaɪ'zeɪʃn; *NAmE* -lə'z-/ *noun* [U]: *the rapid industrialization of Japan* **in·dus·tri·al·ized, -ised** *adj.*: *an industrialized country*

inˌdustrial 'park (*NAmE*) (*BrE* **inˌdustrial e'state**) *noun* an area especially for factories, on the edge of a town

inˌdustrial re'lations *noun* [pl.] relations between employers and employees

the Inˌdustrial Revo'lution *noun* [sing.] the period in the 18th and 19th centuries in Europe and the US when machines began to be used to do work, and industry grew rapidly

in'dustrial-strength *adj.* (often *humorous*) very strong or powerful: *industrial-strength coffee*

inˌdustrial tri'bunal *noun* (*BrE*) = EMPLOYMENT TRIBUNAL

in·dus·tri·ous /ɪn'dʌstriəs/ *adj.* (*approving*) working hard; busy **SYN** **hard-working**: *an industrious student* ▶ **in·dus·tri·ous·ly** *adv.*

in·dus·try O‑ /'ɪndəstri/ *noun* (*pl.* -ies)
1 O‑ [U] the production of goods from raw materials, especially in factories: ***heavy/light industry*** ◇ *the needs of British industry* ◇ *She got a job* ***in industry.*** ➲ COLLOCATIONS at ECONOMY **2** O‑ [C] the people and activities involved in producing a particular thing, or in providing a particular service: *the steel industry* ◇ *the* ***catering/tourist, etc. industry*** ◇ *We need to develop local industries.* ◇ (*figurative*) *the Madonna industry* (= the large number of people involved in making Madonna successful) ➲ see also CAPTAIN OF INDUSTRY, COTTAGE INDUSTRY, HEAVY INDUSTRY, SUNRISE INDUSTRY, SUNSET INDUSTRY **3** [U] (*formal*) the quality of working hard: *We were impressed by their industry.*

Indy /'ɪndi/ (also **'Indy racing**, **'Indycar**, **'Indy car racing**) *noun* [U] motor racing around a track which is raised at both sides

Indy·car /'ɪndikɑː(r)/ *noun* **1** [U] = INDY **2** [C] a car used in Indy racing

in·ebri·ated /ɪ'niːbrieɪtɪd/ *adj.* (*formal* or *humorous*) drunk ▶ **in·ebri·ation** /ɪˌniːbri'eɪʃn/ *noun* [U]

in·ed·ible /ɪn'edəbl/ *adj.* that you cannot eat because it is of poor quality, or poisonous **OPP** **edible**

in·effable /ɪn'efəbl/ *adj.* (*formal*) too great or beautiful to describe in words: *ineffable joy*

in·ef·fect·ive /ˌɪnɪ'fektɪv/ *adj.* not achieving what you want to achieve; not having any effect: *The new drug was ineffective.* ◇ *ineffective management* ◇ **~ in doing sth** *The law proved ineffective in dealing with the problem.* **OPP** **effective** ▶ **in·ef·fect·ive·ness** *noun* [U] **in·ef·fect·ive·ly** *adv.*

in·ef·fec·tual /ˌɪnɪ'fektʃuəl/ *adj.* (*formal*) without the ability to achieve much; weak; not achieving what you want to: *an ineffectual teacher* ◇ *an ineffectual attempt to reform the law* ▶ **in·ef·fec·tu·al·ly** /-tʃuəli/ *adv.*

in·ef·fi·cient /ˌɪnɪˈfɪʃnt/ *adj.* not doing a job well and not making the best use of time, money, energy, etc: *an inefficient heating system* ◇ *inefficient government* ◇ *an extremely inefficient secretary* ◇ *inefficient use of time and energy* OPP **efficient** ▸ **in·ef·fi·ciency** /-ənsi/ *noun* [U, C] (*pl.* -ies): *waste and inefficiency in government* ◇ *inefficiencies in the system* **in·ef·fi·cient·ly** *adv.*

in·ele·gant /ɪnˈelɪɡənt/ *adj.* not attractive or elegant OPP **elegant** ▸ **in·ele·gant·ly** *adv.*

in·eli·gible /ɪnˈelɪdʒəbl/ *adj.* not having the necessary qualifications to have or to do sth: ~ (**for sth**) *ineligible for financial assistance* ◇ ~ (**to do sth**) *ineligible to vote* OPP **eligible** ▸ **in·eli·gi·bil·ity** /ɪnˌelɪdʒəˈbɪləti/ *noun* [U]

in·eluct·able /ˌɪnɪˈlʌktəbl/ *adj.* (*formal*) that you cannot avoid SYN **unavoidable** ▸ **in·eluct·ably** /-əbli/ *adv.*

inept /ɪˈnept/ *adj.* acting or done with no skill: *She was left feeling inept and inadequate.* ◇ *an inept remark* ▸ **in·ept·ly** *adv.*

in·epti·tude /ɪˈneptɪtjuːd; *NAmE* -tuːd/ *noun* [U] lack of skill: *the ineptitude of the police in handling the situation*

in·equal·ity /ˌɪnɪˈkwɒləti; *NAmE* -ˈkwɑːl-/ *noun* [U, C] (*pl.* -ies) the unfair difference between groups of people in society, when some have more wealth, status or opportunities than others: *inequality of opportunity* ◇ *economic inequalities between different areas* ◇ *racial inequality* OPP **equality** ➲ COLLOCATIONS at RACE ➲ see also UNEQUAL

in·equit·able /ɪnˈekwɪtəbl/ *adj.* (*formal*) not fair; not the same for everyone OPP **unfair**: *inequitable distribution of wealth* OPP **equitable**

in·equity /ɪnˈekwəti/ *noun* [C, U] (*pl.* -ies) (*formal*) something that is unfair; the state of being unfair SYN **injustice**

in·erad·ic·able /ˌɪnɪˈrædɪkəbl/ *adj.* (*formal*) (of a quality or situation) that cannot be removed or changed

inert /ɪˈnɜːt; *NAmE* ɪˈnɜːrt/ *adj.* **1** (*formal*) without power to move or act: *He lay inert with half-closed eyes.* **2** (*chemistry*) without active chemical or other properties (= characteristics)

iˌnert ˈgas *noun* (*chemistry*) = NOBLE GAS

in·er·tia /ɪˈnɜːʃə; *NAmE* ɪˈnɜːrʃə/ *noun* [U] **1** (usually *disapproving*) lack of energy; lack of desire or ability to move or change: *I can't seem to throw off this feeling of inertia.* ◇ *the forces of institutional inertia in the school system* **2** (*physics*) a property (= characteristic) of MATTER (= a substance) by which it stays still or, if moving, continues moving in a straight line unless it is acted on by a force outside itself

in·er·tial /ɪˈnɜːʃl; *NAmE* ɪˈnɜːrʃl/ *adj.* (*technical*) connected with or caused by inertia

iˈnertia reel *noun* a round device that one end of a car SEAT BELT is wound around so that it will move freely unless it is pulled suddenly, for example in an accident

in·escap·able /ˌɪnɪˈskeɪpəbl/ *adj.* (of a fact or a situation) that you cannot avoid or ignore SYN **unavoidable**: *an inescapable fact* ◇ *This leads to the inescapable conclusion that the two things are connected.* ▸ **in·escap·ably** /-əbli/ *adv.*

in·es·sen·tial /ˌɪnɪˈsenʃl/ *adj.* not necessary: *inessential luxuries* ▸ **in·es·sen·tial** *noun*: *Few people had spare cash for inessentials.* ➲ compare ESSENTIAL, NON-ESSENTIAL

in·estim·able /ɪnˈestɪməbl/ *adj.* (*formal*) too great to calculate: *The information he provided was* ***of inestimable value.***

in·ev·it·able 🔑 AW /ɪnˈevɪtəbl/ *adj.* **1** 🔑 that you cannot avoid or prevent SYN **unavoidable**: *It was an inevitable consequence of the decision.* ◇ ***It was inevitable that*** *there would be job losses.* ◇ *A rise in the interest rates seems inevitable.* **2** [only before noun] (often *humorous*) so frequent that you always expect it: *the English and their inevitable cups of tea* **3 the inevitable** *noun* [sing.] something that is certain to happen: *You have to accept the inevitable.* ◇ *The inevitable happened—I forgot my passport.* ▸ **in·ev·it·abil·ity** AW /ɪnˌevɪtəˈbɪləti/ *noun* [U, sing.]: *the inevitability of death* ◇ *There was an inevitability about their defeat.*

in·ev·it·ably 🔑 AW /ɪnˈevɪtəbli/ *adv.* **1** 🔑 as is certain to happen: *Inevitably, the press exaggerated the story.* **2** (often *humorous*) as you would expect: *Inevitably, it rained on the day of the wedding.*

in·exact /ˌɪnɪɡˈzækt/ *adj.* not accurate or exact: *an inexact description* ◇ *Economics is an inexact science.*

in·exac·ti·tude /ˌɪnɪɡˈzæktɪtjuːd; *NAmE* -tuːd/ *noun* [U] (*formal*) the quality of being not accurate or exact

in·ex·cus·able /ˌɪnɪkˈskjuːzəbl/ *adj.* too bad to accept or forgive SYN **unjustifiable**: *inexcusable rudeness* OPP **excusable** ▸ **in·ex·cus·ably** /-əbli/ *adv.*

in·ex·haust·ible /ˌɪnɪɡˈzɔːstəbl/ *adj.* that cannot be EXHAUSTED (= finished); very great: *an inexhaustible supply of good jokes* ◇ *Her energy is inexhaustible.*

in·ex·or·able /ɪnˈeksərəbl/ *adj.* (*formal*) (of a process) that cannot be stopped or changed SYN **relentless**: *the inexorable rise of crime* ▸ **in·ex·or·abil·ity** /ɪnˌeksərəˈbɪləti/ *noun* [U]: *the inexorability of progress* **in·ex·or·ably** /ɪnˈeksərəbli/ *adv.*: *events leading inexorably towards a crisis*

in·ex·pe·di·ent /ˌɪnɪkˈspiːdiənt/ *adj.* [not usually before noun] (*formal*) (of an action) not fair or right: *It would be inexpedient to raise taxes further.* OPP **expedient**

in·ex·pen·sive /ˌɪnɪkˈspensɪv/ *adj.* not costing a lot of money: *a relatively inexpensive hotel* OPP **expensive** ➲ SYNONYMS at CHEAP ▸ **in·ex·pen·sive·ly** *adv.*

in·ex·peri·ence /ˌɪnɪkˈspɪəriəns; *NAmE* -ˈspɪr-/ *noun* [U] lack of knowledge and experience: *His mistake was due to youth and inexperience.*

in·ex·peri·enced /ˌɪnɪkˈspɪəriənst; *NAmE* -ˈspɪr-/ *adj.* having little knowledge or experience of sth: *inexperienced drivers/staff* ◇ *inexperienced in modern methods* ◇ *a child too young and inexperienced to recognize danger* OPP **experienced**

in·ex·pert /ɪnˈekspɜːt; *NAmE* -pɜːrt/ *adj.* without much skill ➲ compare EXPERT ▸ **in·ex·pert·ly** *adv.*

in·ex·plic·able /ˌɪnɪkˈsplɪkəbl/ *adj.* that cannot be understood or explained SYN **incomprehensible**: *inexplicable behaviour* ◇ ***For some inexplicable reason*** *he gave up a fantastic job.* OPP **explicable** ▸ **in·ex·plic·ably** *adv.*: *inexplicably delayed/absent* ◇ *She inexplicably withdrew the offer.*

in·ex·press·ible /ˌɪnɪkˈspresəbl/ *adj.* (of feelings) too strong to be put into words: *inexpressible joy*

in ex·tre·mis /ˌɪn ɪkˈstriːmɪs/ *adv.* (from *Latin*, *formal*) **1** in a very difficult situation when very strong action is needed **2** at the moment of death

in·ex·tric·able /ˌɪnɪkˈstrɪkəbl; ɪnˈekstrɪkəbl/ *adj.* (*formal*) too closely linked to be separated: *an inextricable connection between the past and the present*

in·ex·tric·ably /ˌɪnɪkˈstrɪkəbli; ɪnˈekstrɪkəbli/ *adv.* if two things are **inextricably linked**, etc, it is impossible to separate them: *Europe's foreign policy is inextricably linked with that of the US.* ◇ *She had become inextricably involved in the campaign.*

in·fal·lible /ɪnˈfæləbl/ *adj.* **1** never wrong; never making mistakes: *infallible advice* ◇ *Doctors are not infallible.* OPP **fallible** **2** that never fails; always doing what it is supposed to do: *an infallible method of memorizing things* ▸ **in·fal·li·bil·ity** /ɪnˌfæləˈbɪləti/ *noun* [U]: *papal infallibility* **in·fal·libly** /-əbli/ *adv.*

in·fam·ous /ˈɪnfəməs/ *adj.* (*formal*) well known for being bad or evil SYN **notorious**: *a general who was infamous for his brutality* ◇ *the most infamous concentration camp* ◇ (*humorous*) *the infamous British sandwich* ➲ compare FAMOUS

in·famy /ˈɪnfəmi/ *noun* (*pl.* -ies) (*formal*) **1** [U] the state of being well known for sth bad or evil: *a day that will live in infamy* **2** [U, C] evil behaviour; an evil act: *scenes of horror and infamy*

in·fancy /ˈɪnfənsi/ *noun* [U] **1** the time when a child is a baby or very young: *to die* ***in infancy*** **2** the early development of sth: *a time when the cinema was still* ***in its infancy***

I

in·fant /ˈɪnfənt/ *noun, adj.*
■ ***noun*** **1** (*formal* or *technical*) a baby or very young child: *a nursery for infants under two* ◇ *their infant son* ◇ *She was seriously ill as an infant.* ◇ *the infant mortality rate* ◇ *Mozart was an* ***infant prodigy*** (= a child with unusual ability). **HELP** In *NAmE* **infant** is only used for a baby, especially a very young one. **2** (in British and Australian education) a child at school between the ages of four and seven: *an infant school* ◇ *infant teachers* ◇ *I've known her since we were in the infants* (= at infant school).
■ ***adj.*** [only before noun] **1** designed to be used by infants: *infant formula* (= milk for babies) **2** new and not yet developed: *infant industries*

in·fanti·cide /ɪnˈfæntɪsaɪd/ *noun* (*formal*) **1** [U, C] the crime of killing a baby; a person who is guilty of this crime **2** [U] (in some cultures) the practice of killing babies that are not wanted, for example because they are girls and not boys

in·fant·ile /ˈɪnfəntaɪl/ *adj.* **1** (*disapproving*) typical of a small child (and therefore not suitable for adults or older children) **SYN** **childish** **2** [only before noun] (*formal* or *technical*) connected with babies or very young children

in·fant·il·ism /ɪnˈfæntɪlɪzəm/ *noun* [U] (*psychology*) the fact of adults continuing to behave like children, in a way that is not normal

in·fanti·lize (*BrE* also **-ise**) /ɪnˈfæntɪlaɪz/ *verb* **~ sb** (*formal*) to treat sb as though they are a child

in·fan·try /ˈɪnfəntri/ *noun* [C+sing./pl. v.] soldiers who fight on foot: *infantry units* ◇ *The infantry was/were guarding the bridge.*

in·fan·try·man /ˈɪnfəntrimən/ *noun* (*pl.* -men /-mən/) a soldier who fights on foot

in·farc·tion /ɪnˈfɑːkʃn; *NAmE* -ˈfɑːrk-/ *noun* (*medical*) a condition in which the blood supply to an area of TISSUE is blocked and the TISSUE dies

in·fatu·ated /ɪnˈfætʃueɪtɪd/ *adj.* **~ (with sb/sth)** having a very strong feeling of love or attraction for sb/sth so that you cannot think clearly and in a sensible way **SYN** **besotted**: *She was completely infatuated with him.*

in·fatu·ation /ɪnˌfætʃuˈeɪʃn/ *noun* [C, U] **~ (with/for sb/sth)** very strong feelings of love or attraction for sb/sth, especially when these are unreasonable and do not last long: *It isn't love, it's just a passing infatuation.*

in·fect **0-w** /ɪnˈfekt/ *verb*
1 **0-w** to make a disease or an illness spread to a person, an animal or a plant: **~ sb/sth** *It is not possible to infect another person through kissing.* ◇ **~ sb/sth with sth** *people infected with HIV* **2** **0-w** **~ sth (with sth)** [usually passive] to make a substance contain harmful bacteria that can spread disease **SYN** **contaminate**: *eggs infected with salmonella* **3** **~ sth (with sth)** to make a computer virus spread to another computer or program **4** **~ sb (with sth)** to make sb share a particular feeling: *She infected the children with her enthusiasm for music.*

in·fected **0-w** /ɪnˈfektɪd/ *adj.*
1 containing harmful bacteria: *The wound from the dog bite had become infected.* ◇ *an infected water supply* **2** (*computing*) affected by a computer virus: *an infected PC*

in·fec·tion **0-w** /ɪnˈfekʃn/ *noun*
1 **0-w** [U] the act or process of causing or getting a disease: *to be exposed to infection* ◇ *to increase the* ***risk of infection*** ➲ see also CROSS-INFECTION **2** **0-w** [C] an illness that is caused by bacteria or a virus and that affects one part of the body: *an* ***ear/throat, etc. infection*** ◇ *to spread an infection* ➲ SYNONYMS at DISEASE ➲ compare CONTAGION

in·fec·tious **0-w** /ɪnˈfekʃəs/ *adj.*
1 **0-w** an **infectious** disease can be passed easily from one person to another, especially through the air they breathe: *Flu is highly infectious.* ◇ (*figurative*) *infectious laughter* **2** **0-w** [not usually before noun] if a person or an animal is **infectious**, they have a disease that can be spread to others: *I'm still infectious.* ➲ compare CONTAGIOUS ▸ **in·fec·tious·ly** *adv.*: *to laugh infectiously* **in·fec·tious·ness** *noun* [U]

in·fect·ive /ɪnˈfektɪv/ *adj.* (*medical*) able to cause infection

infer **AW** /ɪnˈfɜː(r)/ *verb* (-rr-) **1** to reach an opinion or decide that sth is true on the basis of information that is available **SYN** **deduce**: **~ sth (from sth)** *Much of the meaning must be inferred from the context.* ◇ **~ that...** *It is reasonable to infer that the government knew about these deals.* **2** **~ (that)... | ~ sth** (*non-standard*) to suggest indirectly that sth is true: *Are you inferring (that) I'm not capable of doing the job?*

Which Word?

infer / imply

- **Infer** and **imply** have opposite meanings. The two words can describe the same event, but from different points of view. If a speaker or writer **implies** something, they suggest it without saying it directly: *The article implied that the pilot was responsible for the accident.* If you **infer** something from what a speaker or writer says, you come to the conclusion that this is what he or she means: *I inferred from the article that the pilot was responsible for the accident.*
- **Infer** is now often used with the same meaning as **imply**. However, many people consider that a sentence such as *Are you inferring that I'm a liar?* is incorrect, although it is fairly common in speech.

in·fer·ence **AW** /ˈɪnfərəns/ *noun* **1** [C] something that you can find out indirectly from what you already know **SYN** **deduction**: *to* ***draw/make inferences*** *from the data* ◇ *The clear inference is that the universe is expanding.* ➲ COLLOCATIONS at SCIENTIFIC **2** [U] the act or process of forming an opinion, based on what you already know: *If he is guilty then,* ***by inference****, so is his wife* (= it is logical to think so, from the same evidence).

in·fer·ior /ɪnˈfɪəriə(r); *NAmE* -ˈfɪr-/ *adj., noun*
■ ***adj.*** **1** not good or not as good as sb/sth else: *of inferior quality* ◇ *inferior goods* ◇ *to make sb* ***feel inferior*** ◇ **~ to sb/sth** *Modern music is often considered inferior to that of the past.* **2** [usually before noun] (*formal*) of lower rank; lower: *an inferior officer* **OPP** **superior**
■ ***noun*** a person who is not as good as sb else; a person who is lower in rank or status

in·fer·ior·ity /ɪnˌfɪəriˈɒrəti; *NAmE* -ˌfɪriˈɔːr-; -ˈɑːr-/ *noun* [U] the state of not being as good as sb/sth else: *a sense of inferiority* ◇ *social inferiority* **OPP** **superiority**

inˌferiˈority complex *noun* a feeling that you are not as good, as important or as intelligent as other people

in·fer·nal /ɪnˈfɜːnl; *NAmE* ɪnˈfɜːrnl/ *adj.* **1** [only before noun] (*old-fashioned*) extremely annoying: *Stop that infernal noise!* **2** (*literary*) connected with hell ▸ **in·fer·nal·ly** /-nəli/ *adv.*

in·ferno /ɪnˈfɜːnəʊ; *NAmE* ɪnˈfɜːrnoʊ/ *noun* [usually sing.] (*pl.* -os) a very large dangerous fire that is out of control: *a* ***blazing/raging inferno***

in·fer·tile /ɪnˈfɜːtaɪl; *NAmE* ɪnˈfɜːrtl/ *adj.* **1** (of people, animals and plants) not able to have babies or produce young: *an infertile couple* **2** (of land) not able to produce good crops **OPP** **fertile** ▸ **in·fer·til·ity** /ˌɪnfɜːˈtɪləti; *NAmE* -fɜːrˈt-/ *noun* [U]: *an infertility clinic* ◇ *infertility treatment for couples*

in·fest /ɪnˈfest/ *verb* [usually passive] **~ sth** (especially of insects or animals such as RATS) to exist in large numbers in a particular place, often causing damage or disease: *shark-infested waters* ◇ *The kitchen was infested with ants.* ▸ **in·festa·tion** /ˌɪnfeˈsteɪʃn/ *noun* [C, U]: *an infestation of lice*

in·fi·del /ˈɪnfɪdəl/ *noun* (*old use*) an offensive way of referring to sb who does not believe in what the speaker considers to be the true religion

in·fi·del·ity /ˌɪnfɪˈdeləti/ *noun* [U, C] (*pl.* -ies) the act of not being faithful to your wife, husband or partner, by having sex with sb else SYN **unfaithfulness**: *marital infidelity* ◇ *She could not forgive his infidelities.* OPP **fidelity**

in·field /ˈɪnfiːld/ *noun, adv.*
- ***noun*** [sing.] the inner part of the field in BASEBALL, CRICKET and some other sports ➲ compare OUTFIELD
- ***adv.*** in or to the infield: *Ronaldo came infield from the right to score.*

in·fight·ing /ˈɪnfaɪtɪŋ/ *noun* [U] arguments and disagreements between people in the same group who are competing for power: *political infighting within the party*

in·fill /ˈɪnfɪl/ *noun* [U] **1** the filling in of a space with sth, especially the building of new houses in spaces between existing ones: *infill development* **2** the material used to fill in a space or a hole: *gravel infill* ▶ **in·fill** *verb* [I, T] **~ (sth)**

in·fil·trate /ˈɪnfɪltreɪt/ *verb* **1** [T, I] to enter or make sb enter a place or an organization secretly, especially in order to get information that can be used against it: **~ sth** *The headquarters had been infiltrated by enemy spies.* ◇ **~ sb into sth** *Rebel forces were infiltrated into the country.* ◇ **~ into sth** *The CIA agents successfully infiltrated into the terrorist organizations.* **2** [I, T] **~ (into) sth** (*technical*) (especially of liquids or gases) to pass slowly into sth: *Only a small amount of the rainwater actually infiltrates into the soil.* ▶ **in·fil·tra·tion** /ˌɪnfɪlˈtreɪʃn/ *noun* [U]: *the infiltration of terrorists from across the border* ◇ *the infiltration of rain into the soil*

in·fil·tra·tor /ˈɪnfɪltreɪtə(r)/ *noun* a person who secretly becomes a member of a group or goes to a place, to get information or to influence the group

in·fin·ite AW /ˈɪnfɪnət/ *adj., noun*
- ***adj.*** **1** very great; impossible to measure SYN **boundless**: *an infinite variety of plants* ◇ *a teacher with infinite patience* ◇ (*ironic*) *The company* ***in its infinite wisdom*** *decided to close the staff restaurant* (= they thought it was a good thing to do, but nobody else agreed). **2** without limits; without end: *an infinite universe* OPP **finite**
- ***noun*** [sing.] **1 the infinite** something that has no end **2 the Infinite** God

in·fin·ite·ly AW /ˈɪnfɪnətli/ *adv.* **1** (used especially in comparisons) very much: *Your English is infinitely better than my German.* **2** extremely; with no limit: *Human beings are infinitely adaptable.*

in·fini·tesi·mal /ˌɪnfɪnɪˈtesɪml/ *adj.* (*formal*) extremely small SYN **tiny**: *infinitesimal traces of poison* ◇ *an infinitesimal risk* ▶ **in·fini·tesi·mal·ly** /-məli/ *adv.*

in·fini·tive /ɪnˈfɪnətɪv/ *noun* (*grammar*) the basic form of a verb such as *be* or *run*. In English, an infinitive is used by itself, for example *swim* in *She can swim* (this use is sometimes called the **bare infinitive**), or with *to* (the **to-infinitive**) as in *She likes to swim*. IDM see SPLIT *v.*

in·fin·ity /ɪnˈfɪnəti/ *noun* (*pl.* -ies) **1** [U] (also **in·fin·it·ies** [pl.]) the state of having no end or limit: *the infinity/infinities of space* **2** [U] a point far away that can never be reached: *The landscape seemed to stretch into infinity.* **3** (*symb.* ∞) [U, C] (*mathematics*) a number larger than any other **4** [sing.] a large amount that is impossible to count: *an infinity of stars*

inˈfinity pool *noun* a swimming pool that is specially designed so that, when you are in it, the pool seems to stretch to the HORIZON (= where the sky seems to meet the land or sea)

in·firm /ɪnˈfɜːm; *NAmE* ɪnˈfɜːrm/ *adj.* **1** ill/sick and weak, especially over a long period or as a result of being old **2 the infirm** *noun* [pl.] people who are weak and ill/sick for a long period: *care for the elderly and infirm*

in·firm·ary /ɪnˈfɜːməri; *NAmE* -ˈfɜːrm-/ *noun* (*pl.* -ies) **1** (often used in names) a hospital **2** a special room in a school, prison, etc. for people who are ill/sick

in·firm·ity /ɪnˈfɜːməti; *NAmE* -ˈfɜːrm-/ *noun* [U, C] (*pl.* -ies) weakness or illness over a long period: *We all fear disability or infirmity.* ◇ *the infirmities of old age*

infix /ˈɪnfɪks/ *noun* (*grammar*) a letter or group of letters added to the middle of a word to change its meaning

in fla·grante /ˌɪn fləˈɡrænti/ *adv.* (from *Latin*, *literary* or *humorous*) if sb is found or caught **in flagrante**, they are discovered doing sth that they should not be doing, especially having sex

in·flame /ɪnˈfleɪm/ *verb* (*formal*) **1 ~ sb/sth** to cause very strong feelings, especially anger or excitement, in a person or in a group of people: *His comments have inflamed teachers all over the country.* **2 ~ sth** to make a situation worse or more difficult to deal with: *The situation was further inflamed by the arrival of the security forces.*

in·flamed /ɪnˈfleɪmd/ *adj.* **1** (of a part of the body) red, sore and hot because of infection or injury ➲ SYNONYMS at PAINFUL **2** (of people, feelings, etc.) very angry or excited

in·flam·mable /ɪnˈflæməbl/ *adj.* **1** (*especially BrE*) = FLAMMABLE: *inflammable material* **2** full of strong emotions or violence

in·flam·ma·tion /ˌɪnfləˈmeɪʃn/ *noun* [U, C] a condition in which a part of the body becomes red, sore and swollen because of infection or injury

in·flam·ma·tory /ɪnˈflæmətri; *NAmE* -tɔːri/ *adj.* **1** (*disapproving*) intended to cause very strong feelings of anger: *inflammatory remarks* **2** (*medical*) causing or involving inflammation

in·flat·able /ɪnˈfleɪtəbl/ *adj., noun*
- ***adj.*** needing to be filled with air or gas before you use it: *an inflatable mattress*
- ***noun*** **1** an inflatable boat **2** a large object made of plastic or rubber and filled with air or gas, used for children to play on, or as an advertisement for sth

inˌflatable ˈbouncer *noun* (*NAmE*) = BOUNCER

in·flate /ɪnˈfleɪt/ *verb* **1** [T, I] **~ (sth)** to fill sth or become filled with gas or air: *Inflate your life jacket by pulling sharply on the cord.* ◇ *The life jacket failed to inflate.* **2** [T] **~ sth** to make sth appear to be more important or impressive than it really is **3** [T, I] **~ (sth)** to increase the price of sth; to increase in price: *The principal effect of the demand for new houses was to inflate prices.* ◇ *Food prices are no longer inflating at the same rate as last year.* ➲ compare DEFLATE, REFLATE

in·flated /ɪnˈfleɪtɪd/ *adj.* **1** (especially of prices) higher than is acceptable or reasonable: *inflated prices/salaries* **2** (of ideas, claims, etc.) believing or claiming that sb/sth is more important or impressive than they really are: *He has an inflated sense of his own importance.*

in·fla·tion /ɪnˈfleɪʃn/ *noun* [U] **1** a general rise in the prices of services and goods in a particular country, resulting in a fall in the value of money; the rate at which this happens: *the fight against* ***rising inflation*** ◇ *to* ***control/curb inflation*** ◇ *to* ***reduce/bring down*** *inflation* ◇ *a high/low* ***rate of inflation*** ◇ *an* ***inflation rate*** *of 3%* ◇ *Wage increases must be* ***in line with inflation.*** ◇ *Inflation is currently running at 3%.* ➲ COLLOCATIONS at ECONOMY **2** the act or process of filling sth with air or gas: *life jackets with an automatic inflation device* OPP **deflation**

in·fla·tion·ary /ɪnˈfleɪʃənri; *NAmE* -neri/ *adj.* [usually before noun] causing or connected with a general rise in the prices of services and goods: *the inflationary effects of price rises* ◇ *Our economy is in an* ***inflationary spiral*** *of wage and price increases* (= a continuing situation in which an increase in one causes an increase in the other).

in·flect /ɪnˈflekt/ *verb* [I] (*grammar*) if a word **inflects**, its ending or spelling changes according to its GRAMMATICAL function in a sentence; if a language **inflects**, it has words that do this ▶ **in·flect·ed** *adj.* [usually before noun]: ***an inflected language/form/verb***

in·flec·tion (also **in·flex·ion** especially in *BrE*) /ɪnˈflekʃn/ *noun* [C, U] **1** a change in the form of a word, especially the ending, according to its GRAMMATICAL function in a sentence **2** a change in how high or low your voice is as you are speaking

in·flex·ible AW /ɪnˈfleksəbl/ *adj.* **1** (*disapproving*) that cannot be changed or made more suitable for a particular situation SYN **rigid**: *an inflexible attitude/routine/system*

I

2 (*disapproving*) (of people or organizations) unwilling to change their opinions, decisions, etc, or the way they do things: *He's completely inflexible on the subject.* **3** (of a material) difficult or impossible to bend SYN **stiff** OPP **flexible** ▸ **in·flex·ibil·ity** AW /ɪnˌfleksəˈbɪləti/ *noun* [U] **in·flex·ibly** /-əbli/ *adv.*

in·flict /ɪnˈflɪkt/ *verb* to make sb/sth suffer sth unpleasant: **~ sth on/upon sb/sth** *They inflicted a humiliating defeat on the home team.* ◇ *Heavy casualties were inflicted on the enemy.* ◇ (*humorous*) *Do you have to inflict that music on us?* ◇ **~ sth** *They surveyed the damage inflicted by the storm.* ▸ **in·flic·tion** /ɪnˈflɪkʃn/ *noun* [U]: *the infliction of pain*
PHR V **inˈflict yourself/sb on sb** (often *humorous*) to force sb to spend time with you/sb, when they do not want to: *Sorry to inflict myself on you again like this!* ◇ *She inflicted her nephew on them for the weekend.*

ˌin-ˈflight *adj.* [only before noun] provided or happening during a journey on a plane: *an in-flight meal/movie* ◇ *in-flight refuelling*

in·flow /ˈɪnfləʊ; *NAmE* -floʊ/ *noun* **1** [C, U] the movement of a lot of money, people or things into a place from somewhere else SYN **influx** **2** [sing., U] the movement of a liquid or of air into a place from somewhere else: *an inflow pipe* OPP **outflow**

in·flu·ence /ˈɪnfluəns/ *noun, verb*
■ *noun* **1** [U, C] **~ (on/upon sb/sth)** the effect that sb/sth has on the way a person thinks or behaves or on the way that sth works or develops: *to* ***have/exert*** *a strong* ***influence*** *on sb* ◇ *the influence of the climate on agricultural production* ◇ *What exactly is the influence of television on children?* **2** [U] the power that sb/sth has to make sb/sth behave in a particular way: **~ (over sb/sth)** *Her parents no longer have any real influence over her.* ◇ **~ (with sb)** *She could probably* ***exert her influence*** *with the manager and get you a job.* ◇ *He committed the crime* ***under the influence of*** *drugs.* **3** [C] a person or thing that affects the way a person behaves and thinks: *cultural influences* ◇ **~ (on sb/sth)** *Those friends are* ***a bad influence*** *on her.* ◇ *His first music teacher was a major influence in his life.*
IDM **under the ˈinfluence** having had too much alcohol to drink: *She was charged with driving under the influence.*
■ *verb* **1** to have an effect on the way that sb behaves or thinks, especially by giving them an example to follow: **~ sb/sth** *His writings have influenced the lives of millions.* ◇ *to be* ***strongly influenced*** *by sth* ◇ *Don't let me influence you either way.* ◇ **~ how, whether, etc...** *The wording of questions can influence how people answer.* ◇ **~ sb to do sth** *She was influenced to take up voluntary work by her teacher.* **2** **~ sth** | **~ how, where, etc...** to have an effect on a particular situation and the way that it develops: *A number of social factors influence life expectancy.*

ˈinfluence peddling *noun* [U] the illegal activity of a politician doing sth for sb in return for payment SYN **corruption**

in·flu·en·tial /ˌɪnfluˈenʃl/ *adj.* having a lot of influence on sb/sth: *a highly influential book* ◇ **~ in sth** *She is one of the most influential figures in local politics.* ◇ **~ in doing sth** *The committee was influential in formulating government policy on employment.*

in·flu·enza /ˌɪnfluˈenzə/ *noun* [U] (*formal*) = FLU

in·flux /ˈɪnflʌks/ *noun* [usually sing.] **~ (of sb/sth) (into...)** the fact of a lot of people, money or things arriving somewhere: *a* ***massive/sudden influx*** *of visitors* ◇ *the influx of wealth into the region*

info /ˈɪnfəʊ; *NAmE* ˈɪnfoʊ/ *noun* **1** [U] (*informal*) information: *Have you had any more info about the job yet?* **2** **info-** (in nouns) connected with information: *an infosheet* ◇ *We send all potential clients an infopack.*

info·bahn /ˈɪnfəʊbɑːn; *NAmE* ˈɪnfoʊ-/ *noun* (*informal*) = INFORMATION SUPERHIGHWAY

info·mer·cial /ˌɪnfəʊˈmɜːʃl; *NAmE* ˌɪnfoʊˈmɜːrʃl/ *noun* (*especially NAmE*) a long advertisement on television that tries to give a lot of information about a subject, so that it does not appear to be an advertisement

in·form /ɪnˈfɔːm; *NAmE* ɪnˈfɔːrm/ *verb*
1 to tell sb about sth, especially in an official way: **~ sb (of/about sth)** *Please inform us of any changes of address.* ◇ **~ sb that...** *I have been* ***reliably informed*** (= somebody I trust has told me) *that the couple will marry next year.* ◇ **~ sb + speech** *'He's already left,' she informed us.* ◇ **~ sb when, where, etc...** *I have not been informed when the ceremony will take place.* **2** **~ yourself (of/about sth)** to find out information about sth: *We need time to inform ourselves thoroughly of the problem.* **3** **~ sth** (*formal*) to have an influence on sth: *Religion informs every aspect of their lives.*
PHR V **inˈform on sb** to give information to the police or sb in authority about the illegal activities of sb: *He informed on his own brother.*

in·for·mal /ɪnˈfɔːml; *NAmE* ɪnˈfɔːrml/ *adj.*
1 relaxed and friendly; not following strict rules of how to behave or do sth: *an informal atmosphere* ◇ *an informal arrangement/meeting/visit* ◇ *Discussions are held on an informal basis within the department.* **2** (of clothes) suitable for wearing at home or when relaxing rather than for a special or an official occasion SYN **casual** OPP **formal** **3** (of language) suitable for normal conversation and writing to friends rather than for serious speech and letters: *an informal expression* ➲ compare FORMAL, SLANG ▸ **in·for·mal·ity** /ˌɪnfɔːˈmæləti; *NAmE* -fɔːrˈm-/ *noun* [U] **in·for·mal·ly** /ɪnˈfɔːməli; *NAmE* -ˈfɔːrm-/ *adv.*: *They told me informally* (= not officially) *that I had got the job.* ◇ *to dress informally*

inˌformal ˈsettlement *noun* (*SAfrE*) a place where people decide to live and build temporary shelters, often followed by more permanent houses. Sometimes informal settlements are supplied with water, electricity, etc. and people can become owners of individual pieces of land.

in·form·ant /ɪnˈfɔːmənt; *NAmE* -ˈfɔːrm-/ *noun* **1** a person who gives secret information about sb/sth to the police or a newspaper SYN **informer** **2** (*technical*) a person who gives sb information about sth, for example to help them with their research: *His informants were middle-class professional women.*

in·form·at·ics /ˌɪnfəˈmætɪks; *NAmE* ˌɪnfər-/ *noun* [U] = INFORMATION SCIENCE

in·for·ma·tion /ˌɪnfəˈmeɪʃn; *NAmE* ˌɪnfərˈm-/ (also *informal* **info**) *noun* [U]
1 **~ (on/about sb/sth)** facts or details about sb/sth: *a* ***piece of information*** ◇ *a source of information* ◇ *to* ***collect/gather/obtain/receive information*** ◇ *to* ***provide/give/pass on information*** ◇ *For* ***further information*** *on the diet, write to us at this address.* ◇ ***Our information is*** *that the police will shortly make an arrest.* ◇ *This leaflet is produced* ***for the information of*** (= to inform) *our customers.* ◇ *an information desk* ◇ *He refused to comment before he had seen all the* ***relevant information***. **2** (*NAmE, informal*) = DIRECTORY ENQUIRIES ▸ **in·for·ma·tion·al** /-ʃənl/ *adj.* [only before noun]: *the informational content of a book* ◇ *the informational role of the media*
IDM **for information ˈonly** written on documents that are sent to sb who needs to know the information in them but does not need to deal with them **for your inforˈmation** **1** (*abbr.* FYI) = FOR INFORMATION ONLY **2** (*informal*) used to tell sb that they are wrong about sth: *For your information, I don't even have a car.* ➲ more at MINE *n.*

inforˌmation ˈscience (also **in·form·at·ics**) *noun* [U] (*computing*) the study of processes for storing and obtaining information

inforˌmation superˈhighway (also **super·highway**, *informal* **info·bahn**) *noun* (*computing*) a large electronic network such as the Internet, used for sending information such as sound, pictures and video quickly in DIGITAL form

inforˌmation techˈnology *noun* [U] (*abbr.* IT) the study or use of electronic equipment, especially computers, for storing and analysing information

infor'mation theory *noun* [U] (*mathematics*) a theory that is used to calculate the most efficient way to send information over distances in the form of signals or symbols

in·forma·tive /ɪnˈfɔːmətɪv; *NAmE* -ˈfɔːrm-/ *adj.* giving useful information: *The talk was both informative and entertaining.* **OPP uninformative**

in·formed /ɪnˈfɔːmd; *NAmE* ɪnˈfɔːrmd/ *adj.* having or showing a lot of knowledge about a particular subject or situation: *an informed critic ◇ an* ***informed choice/decision/guess/opinion*** *◇ They are not* ***fully informed*** *about the changes. ◇* ***Keep me informed*** *of any developments.* **OPP uninformed** ➲ see also ILL-INFORMED, WELL INFORMED

in·form·er /ɪnˈfɔːmə(r); *NAmE* -ˈfɔːrm-/ *noun* a person who gives information to the police or other authority

info·tain·ment /ˌɪnfəʊˈteɪnmənt; *NAmE* ˌɪnfoʊ-/ *noun* [U] television programmes, etc. that present news and serious subjects in an entertaining way

infra- *prefix* (in adjectives) below or beyond a particular limit: *infrared* ➲ compare ULTRA-

in·frac·tion /ɪnˈfrækʃn/ *noun* [C, U] (*formal*) an act of breaking a rule or law **SYN infringement**: *minor infractions of EU regulations*

infra dig /ˌɪnfrə ˈdɪɡ/ *adj.* [not before noun] (*old-fashioned, informal*) considered to be below the standard of behaviour appropriate in a particular situation or to sb's social position

in·fra·red /ˌɪnfrəˈred/ *adj.* (*physics*) having or using ELECTROMAGNETIC waves which are longer than those of red light in the SPECTRUM, and which cannot be seen: *infrared radiation ◇ an infrared lamp* ➲ compare ULTRAVIOLET

in·fra·struc·ture **AW** /ˈɪnfrəstrʌktʃə(r)/ *noun* [C, U] the basic systems and services that are necessary for a country or an organization to run smoothly, for example buildings, transport and water and power supplies ▸ **in·fra·struc·tural** /ˌɪnfrəˈstrʌktʃərəl/ *adj.* [usually before noun]: *infrastructural development*

in·fre·quent /ɪnˈfriːkwənt/ *adj.* not happening often **SYN rare**: *her infrequent visits home ◇ Muggings are relatively infrequent in this area.* **OPP frequent** ▸ **in·fre·quent·ly** *adv.*: *This happens not infrequently* (= often).

in·fringe /ɪnˈfrɪndʒ/ *verb* (*formal*) **1** [T] **~ sth** (of an action, a plan, etc.) to break a law or rule: *The material can be copied without infringing copyright.* **2** [T, I] to limit sb's legal rights: **~ sth** *They said that compulsory identity cards would infringe civil liberties. ◇* **~ on/upon sth** *She refused to answer questions that infringed on her private affairs.* ▸ **in·fringe·ment** /-mənt/ *noun* [U, C]: *copyright infringement ◇ an infringement of liberty*

in·furi·ate /ɪnˈfjʊərieɪt; *NAmE* -ˈfjʊr-/ *verb* to make sb extremely angry **SYN enrage**: **~ sb** *Her silence infuriated him even more. ◇* **it infuriates sb that.../to do sth** *It infuriates me that she was not found guilty.*

in·furi·at·ing /ɪnˈfjʊərieɪtɪŋ; *NAmE* -ˈfjʊr-/ *adj.* making you extremely angry: *an infuriating child/delay ◇ It is infuriating to talk to someone who just looks out of the window.* ▸ **in·furi·at·ing·ly** *adv.*: *to smile infuriatingly ◇ Infuriatingly, the shop had just closed.*

in·fuse /ɪnˈfjuːz/ *verb* **1** [T] **~ A into B | ~ B with A** (*formal*) to make sb/sth have a particular quality: *Her novels are infused with sadness.* **2** [T] **~ sth** (*formal*) to have an effect on all parts of sth: *Politics infuses all aspects of our lives.* **3** [T, I] **~ (sth)** if you **infuse** HERBS, etc. or they **infuse**, you put them in hot water until the flavour has passed into the water **4** [T] **~ sth (into sth)** (*medical*) to slowly put a drug or other substance into a person's VEIN

in·fu·sion /ɪnˈfjuːʒn/ *noun* **1** [C, U] **~ of sth (into sth)** (*formal*) the act of adding sth to sth else in order to make it stronger or more successful: *a cash infusion into the business ◇ an infusion of new talent into science education ◇ The company needs an infusion of new blood* (= new employees with new ideas). **2** [C] a drink or medicine made by leaving HERBS, etc. in hot water **3** [C, U] (*medical*) an act of slowly putting a drug or other substance into a person's VEIN; the drug that is used in this way

-ing *suffix* used to make the present participle of regular verbs: *hating ◇ walking ◇ loving*

in·geni·ous /ɪnˈdʒiːniəs/ *adj.* **1** (of an object, a plan, an idea, etc.) very suitable for a particular purpose and resulting from clever new ideas: *an ingenious device ◇ ingenious ways of saving energy* **2** (of a person) having a lot of clever new ideas and good at inventing things: *an ingenious cook ◇ She's very ingenious when it comes to finding excuses.* ▸ **in·geni·ous·ly** *adv.*: *ingeniously designed*

in·génue /ˈænʒeɪnjuː; *NAmE* ˈændʒənuː/ *noun* (from *French*) an innocent young woman, especially in a film/movie or play

in·genu·ity /ˌɪndʒəˈnjuːəti; *NAmE* -ˈnuː-/ *noun* [U] the ability to invent things or solve problems in clever new ways **SYN inventiveness**

in·genu·ous /ɪnˈdʒenjuəs/ *adj.* (*formal*, sometimes *disapproving*) honest, innocent and willing to trust people **SYN naive**: *You're too ingenuous. ◇ an ingenuous smile ◇ It is ingenuous to suppose that money did not play a part in his decision.* ➲ compare DISINGENUOUS ▸ **in·genu·ous·ly** *adv.*

Inger·land /ˈɪŋɡəːlænd/ *noun* (*BrE, informal, non-standard, humorous*) a way of writing and saying England used by football fans as a name for the English national football (SOCCER) team

in·gest /ɪnˈdʒest/ *verb* **~ sth** (*technical*) to take food, drugs, etc. into your body, usually by swallowing ▸ **in·gest·ion** *noun* [U]

ingle·nook /ˈɪŋɡlnʊk/ *noun* a space at either side of a large FIREPLACE where you can sit

in·glori·ous /ɪnˈɡlɔːriəs/ *adj.* [usually before noun] (*literary*) causing feelings of shame **SYN shameful**: *an inglorious chapter in the nation's history* ➲ compare GLORIOUS ▸ **in·glori·ous·ly** *adv.*

ˈin-goal area *noun* [sing.] (in RUGBY) the area between the GOAL LINE and the line at the end of the field, inside which a player must put the ball in order to score a TRY

ingot /ˈɪŋɡət/ *noun* a solid piece of metal, especially gold or silver, usually shaped like a brick

in·grained /ɪnˈɡreɪnd/ *adj.* **1 ~ (in sb/sth)** (of a habit, an attitude, etc.) that has existed for a long time and is therefore difficult to change **SYN deep-rooted**: *ingrained prejudices* **2** (of dirt) under the surface of sth and therefore difficult to get rid of

in·grati·ate /ɪnˈɡreɪʃieɪt/ *verb* [no passive] **~ yourself (with sb)** (*disapproving*) to do things in order to make sb like you, especially sb who will be useful to you: *The first part of his plan was to ingratiate himself with the members of the committee.*

in·grati·at·ing /ɪnˈɡreɪʃieɪtɪŋ/ *adj.* (*disapproving*) trying too hard to please sb: *an ingratiating smile* ▸ **in·grati·at·ing·ly** *adv.*

in·grati·tude /ɪnˈɡrætɪtjuːd; *NAmE* -tuːd/ *noun* [U] the state of not feeling or showing that you are grateful for sth **OPP gratitude**

in·gre·di·ent 🔑 /ɪnˈɡriːdiənt/ *noun* **~ (of/in/for sth) 1** 🔑 one of the things from which sth is made, especially one of the foods that are used together to make a particular dish: *Coconut is a basic ingredient for many curries. ◇ Our skin cream contains only natural ingredients.* **2** 🔑 one of the things or qualities that are necessary to make sth successful: *the essential ingredients for success ◇ It has* ***all the ingredients*** *of a good mystery story.*

in·gress /ˈɪnɡres/ *noun* [U] (*formal*) the act of entering a place; the right to enter a place ➲ compare EGRESS

ˈin-group *noun* (usually *disapproving*) a small group of people in an organization or a society whose members share the same interests, language, etc. and try to keep other people out **SYN clique**

I

in·grow·ing /ˈɪnɡrəʊɪŋ; *NAmE* -ɡroʊ-/ (*BrE*) (also **in·grown** *NAmE, BrE*) *adj.* [only before noun] (of the nail of a toe) growing into the skin

in·habit /ɪnˈhæbɪt/ *verb* **~ sth** (*formal*) to live in a particular place: *some of the rare species that inhabit the area*

WORD FAMILY
inhabit *verb*
habitable *adj.* (≠ uninhabitable)
inhabited *adj.* (≠ uninhabited)
inhabitant *noun*

in·hab·it·ant /ɪnˈhæbɪtənt/ *noun* a person or an animal that lives in a particular place: *the oldest inhabitant of the village* ◇ *a town of 11 000 inhabitants*

in·habited /ɪnˈhæbɪtɪd/ *adj.* with people or animals living there: *The island is no longer inhabited.* ◇ *The building is now inhabited by birds.* OPP **uninhabited**

in·hal·ant /ɪnˈheɪlənt/ *noun* a drug or medicine that you breathe in

in·hale /ɪnˈheɪl/ *verb* [I, T] (rather *formal*) to take air, smoke, gas, etc. into your lungs as you breathe SYN **breathe in**: *She closed her eyes and inhaled deeply.* ◇ *He inhaled deeply on another cigarette.* ◇ **~ sth** *Local residents needed hospital treatment after inhaling fumes from the fire.* OPP **exhale** ▸ **in·hal·ation** /ˌɪnhəˈleɪʃn/ *noun* [U, C]: *Hundreds of children were treated for smoke inhalation.*

in·haler /ɪnˈheɪlə(r)/ (also *informal* **puff·er**) *noun* a small device containing medicine that you breathe in through your mouth, used by people who have problems with breathing

in·har·mo·ni·ous /ˌɪnhɑːˈməʊniəs; *NAmE* -hɑːrˈmoʊ-/ *adj.* (*formal*) not combining well together or with sth else

in·here /ɪnˈhɪə(r); *NAmE* ɪnˈhɪr/ *verb*
PHR V **inˈhere in sth** (*formal*) to be a natural part of sth: *the meaning which inheres in words*

in·her·ent AW /ɪnˈhɪərənt; -ˈher-; *NAmE* -ˈhɪr-/ *adj.* **~ (in sb/sth)** that is a basic or permanent part of sb/sth and that cannot be removed SYN **intrinsic**: *the difficulties inherent in a study of this type* ◇ *Violence is inherent in our society.* ◇ *an inherent weakness in the design of the machine* ▸ **in·her·ent·ly** AW /ɪnˈhɪərəntli; -ˈher-; *NAmE* -ˈhɪr-/ *adv.*: *an inherently unworkable system*

in·herit /ɪnˈherɪt/ *verb* **1** [T, I] **~ (sth) (from sb)** to receive money, property, etc. from sb when they die: *She inherited a fortune from her father.* ➲ compare DISINHERIT **2** [T] **~ sth (from sb)** to have qualities, physical features, etc. that are similar to those of your parents, grandparents, etc: *He has inherited his mother's patience.* ◇ *an inherited disease* **3** [T] **~ sth (from sb)** if you **inherit** a particular situation from sb, you are now responsible for dealing with it, especially because you have replaced that person in their job: *policies inherited from the previous administration*

in·herit·able /ɪnˈherɪtəbl/ *adj.* (*biology*) (of a feature or disease) capable of being passed from a parent to a child in the GENES: *inheritable characteristics*

in·her·it·ance /ɪnˈherɪtəns/ *noun* **1** [C, U] the money, property, etc. that you receive from sb when they die; the fact of receiving sth when sb dies: *She spent all her inheritance in a year.* ◇ *The title passes by inheritance to the eldest son.* ➲ COLLOCATIONS at FINANCE **2** [U, C, usually sing.] something from the past or from your family that affects the way you behave, look, etc: *our cultural inheritance* ◇ *Physical characteristics are determined by genetic inheritance.*

inˈheritance tax (*NAmE* also **eˈstate tax**) *noun* [U] tax that you must pay on the money or property that you receive from sb when they die

in·heri·tor /ɪnˈherɪtə(r)/ *noun* **1** [usually pl.] **~ of sth** a person who is affected by the work, ideas, etc. of people who lived before them SYN **heir**: *We are the inheritors of a great cultural tradition.* **2** a person who receives money, property, etc. from sb when they die SYN **heir**

in·hibit AW /ɪnˈhɪbɪt/ *verb* **1 ~ sth** (*formal*) to prevent sth from happening or make it happen more slowly or less frequently than normal: *A lack of oxygen may inhibit brain development in the unborn child.* **2 ~ sb (from sth/from doing sth)** to make sb nervous or embarrassed so that they are unable to do sth: *The managing director's presence inhibited them from airing their problems.*

in·hibit·ed /ɪnˈhɪbɪtɪd/ *adj.* unable to relax or express your feelings in a natural way: *Boys are often more inhibited than girls about discussing their problems.*

in·hib·ition AW /ˌɪnhɪˈbɪʃn; ˌɪnɪˈb-/ *noun* **1** [C, U] a shy or nervous feeling that stops you from expressing your real thoughts or feelings: *The children were shy at first, but soon lost their inhibitions.* ◇ *She had no inhibitions about making her opinions known.* **2** [U] (*formal*) the act of restricting or preventing a process or an action: *the inhibition of growth*

in·hibi·tor /ɪnˈhɪbɪtə(r)/ *noun* **1** (*chemistry*) a substance which delays or prevents a chemical reaction **2** (*biology*) a GENE which prevents another gene from being effective

in·hos·pit·able /ˌɪnhɒˈspɪtəbl; *NAmE* ˌɪnhɑːˈs-/ *adj.* **1** (of a place) difficult to stay or live in, especially because there is no shelter from the weather SYN **unwelcoming**: *inhospitable terrain* ◇ *an inhospitable climate* **2** (of people) not giving a friendly or polite welcome to guests OPP **hospitable**

ˌin-ˈhouse *adj.* [only before noun] existing or happening within a company or an organization: *an in-house magazine* ◇ *in-house language training*

in·human /ɪnˈhjuːmən/ *adj.* **1** lacking the qualities of kindness and pity; very cruel: *inhuman and degrading treatment* **2** not human; not seeming to be produced by a human and therefore frightening: *There was a strange inhuman sound.* ➲ compare HUMAN, NON-HUMAN, SUBHUMAN

in·hu·mane /ˌɪnhjuːˈmeɪn/ *adj.* not caring about the suffering of other people; very cruel SYN **callous**: *inhumane treatment of animals/prisoners* OPP **humane** ▸ **in·hu·mane·ly** *adv.*

in·human·ity /ˌɪnhjuːˈmænəti/ *noun* [U] cruel behaviour or treatment; the fact of not having the usual human qualities of kindness and pity: *man's inhumanity to man* ◇ *the inhumanity of the system* OPP **humanity**

in·huma·tion /ˌɪnhjuːˈmeɪʃn/ *noun* [U] (*technical*) the act of burying dead people, used especially in relation to ancient times

in·imi·cal /ɪˈnɪmɪkl/ *adj.* (*formal*) **1 ~ to sth** harmful to sth; not helping sth: *These policies are inimical to the interests of society.* **2** unfriendly: *an inimical stare*

in·im·it·able /ɪˈnɪmɪtəbl/ *adj.* too good or individual for anyone else to copy with the same effect: *John related in his own* ***inimitable way*** *the story of his trip to Tibet.*

ini·qui·tous /ɪˈnɪkwɪtəs/ *adj.* (*formal*) very unfair or wrong SYN **wicked**: *an iniquitous system/practice*

ini·quity /ɪˈnɪkwəti/ *noun* [U, C] (*pl.* -ies) (*formal*) the fact of being very unfair or wrong; sth that is very unfair or wrong: *the iniquity of racial prejudice* ◇ *the iniquities of the criminal justice system*

ini·tial 0‑w AW /ɪˈnɪʃl/ *adj., noun, verb*

▪ ***adj.*** 0‑w [only before noun] happening at the beginning; first: *an initial payment of £60 and ten instalments of £25* ◇ *in the* ***initial stages*** (= at the beginning) *of the campaign* ◇ *My* ***initial reaction*** *was to decline the offer.*

▪ ***noun*** **1** 0‑w [C] the first letter of a person's first name: *'What initial is it, Mrs Owen?' 'It's J, J for Jane.'* **2** 0‑w **initials** [pl.] the first letters of all of a person's names: *John Fitzgerald Kennedy was often known by his initials JFK.* ◇ *Just write your initials.*

▪ ***verb*** (-ll-, *especially US* -l-) **~ sth** to mark or sign sth with your initials: *Please initial each page and sign in the space provided.*

ini·tial·ize (*BrE* also **-ise**) /ɪˈnɪʃəlaɪz/ *verb* **~ sth** (*computing*) to make a computer program or system ready for use or FORMAT a disk ▸ **ini·tial·iza·tion, -isa·tion** /ɪˌnɪʃəlaɪˈzeɪʃn; *NAmE* -ləˈz-/ *noun* [U]

ini·tial·ly 0‑w AW /ɪˈnɪʃəli/ *adv.*
at the beginning: *Initially, the system worked well.* ◇ *The*

death toll was initially reported at around 250, but was later revised to 300.

ini·ti·ate AW *verb, noun*

■ ***verb*** /ɪˈnɪʃieɪt/ **1 ~ sth** (*formal*) to make sth begin SYN **set in motion**: *to initiate legal proceedings against sb* ◇ *The government has initiated a programme of economic reform.* **2 ~ sb** (**into sth**) to explain sth to sb and/or make them experience it for the first time: *Many of them had been initiated into drug use at an early age.* **3 ~ sb** (**into sth**) to make sb a member of a particular group, especially as part of a secret ceremony: *Hundreds are initiated into the sect each year.*

■ ***noun*** /ɪˈnɪʃiət/ a person who has been allowed to join a particular group, organization, or religion and is learning its rules and secrets

ini·ti·ation AW /ɪˌnɪʃiˈeɪʃn/ *noun* [U] **1** the act of sb becoming a member of a group, often with a special ceremony; the act of introducing sb to an activity or skill: *an initiation ceremony* ◇ **~ into sth** *her initiation into the world of marketing* **2** (*formal*) the act of starting sth: *the initiation of criminal proceedings*

ini·tia·tive 0-w AW /ɪˈnɪʃətɪv/ *noun*
1 0-w [C] a new plan for dealing with a particular problem or for achieving a particular purpose: *a United Nations peace initiative* ◇ *a government initiative to combat unemployment* **2** 0-w [U] the ability to decide and act on your own without waiting for sb to tell you what to do: *You won't get much help. You'll have to* ***use your initiative.*** ◇ *She did it* ***on her own initiative*** (= without anyone telling her to do it). **3** 0-w **the initiative** [sing.] the power or opportunity to act and gain an advantage before other people do: *to* ***seize/lose the initiative*** ◇ *It was up to the US to* ***take the initiative*** *in repairing relations.* **4** [C] (*NAmE, law*) (in some states of the US) a process by which ordinary people can suggest a new law by signing a PETITION

ini·ti·ator AW /ɪˈnɪʃieɪtə(r)/ *noun* (*formal*) the person who starts sth

in·ject /ɪnˈdʒekt/ *verb* **1** to put a drug or other substance into a person's or an animal's body using a SYRINGE: **~ sth** (**into yourself/sb/sth**) *Adrenaline was injected into the muscle.* ◇ **~ yourself/sb/sth** (**with sth**) *She has been injecting herself with insulin since the age of 16.* **2** to put a liquid into sth using a SYRINGE or similar instrument: **~ A** (**with B**) *The fruit is injected with chemicals to reduce decay.* ◇ **~ B** (**into A**) *Chemicals are injected into the fruit to reduce decay.* **3 ~ sth** (**into sth**) to add a particular quality to sth: *His comments injected a note of humour into the proceedings.* **4 ~ sth** (**into sth**) to give money to an organization, a project, etc. so that it can function: *They are refusing to inject any more capital into the industry.*

in·jec·tion /ɪnˈdʒekʃn/ *noun* **1** [C, U] an act of injecting sb with a drug or other substance: *to* ***give sb an injection*** ◇ *He was treated with penicillin injections.* ◇ *An anaesthetic was administered* ***by injection.*** ◇ *daily injections of insulin* ⊃ COLLOCATIONS at ILL **2** [C] a large sum of money that is spent to help improve a situation, business, etc: *The theatre faces closure unless it gets an urgent cash injection.* **3** [U, C] an act of forcing liquid into sth: *a fuel injection system*

inˌjection ˈmoulding (*BrE*) (*NAmE* **inˌjection ˈmolding**) *noun* [U] (*technical*) a way of shaping plastic or rubber by heating it and pouring it into a MOULD ▶ **inˌjection-ˈmoulded** (*NAmE* **inˌjection-ˈmolded**) *adj.*

ˈin-joke *noun* a joke that is only understood by a particular group of people

in·ju·di·cious /ˌɪndʒuˈdɪʃəs/ *adj.* (*formal*) not sensible or wise; not appropriate in a particular situation SYN **unwise**: *an injudicious remark* OPP **judicious** ▶ **in·ju·di·cious·ly** *adv.*

Injun /ˈɪndʒən/ *noun* (*US, taboo, slang*) an offensive word for a Native American

in·junc·tion /ɪnˈdʒʌŋkʃn/ *noun* **1** an official order given by a court which demands that sth must or must not be done: *to* ***seek/obtain an injunction*** ◇ **~ against sb** *The court* ***granted an injunction against*** *the defendants.* ⊃ compare RESTRAINING ORDER **2** (*formal*) a warning or an order from sb in authority

in·jure 0-w AW /ˈɪndʒə(r)/ *verb*
1 0-w **~ sb/sth/yourself** to harm yourself or sb else physically, especially in an accident: *He injured his knee playing hockey.* ◇ *Three people were killed and five injured in the crash.* ⊃ COLLOCATIONS at INJURY **2** 0-w **~ sth** to damage sb's reputation, pride, etc: *This could seriously injure the company's reputation.*

Synonyms

injure

wound • hurt • bruise • sprain • pull • strain

These words all mean to harm yourself or sb else physically, especially in an accident.

injure to harm yourself or sb else physically, especially in an accident: *He injured his knee playing hockey.* ◇ *Three people were injured in the crash.*

wound [often passive] (*rather formal*) to injure part of the body, especially by making a hole in the skin using a weapon: *50 people were seriously wounded in the attack.* NOTE **Wound** is often used to talk about people being hurt in war or in other attacks which affect a lot of people.

hurt to cause physical pain to sb/yourself; to injure sb/yourself: *Did you hurt yourself?*

INJURE OR HURT?

You can **hurt** or **injure** a part of the body in an accident. **Hurt** emphasizes the physical pain caused; **injure** emphasizes that the part of the body has been damaged in some way.

bruise to make a blue, brown or purple mark (= a bruise) appear on the skin after sb has fallen or been hit; to develop a bruise

sprain to injure part of your body, especially your ankle, wrist or knee, by suddenly bending it in an awkward way, causing pain and swelling

pull to damage a muscle, etc, by using too much force

strain to injure yourself or part of your body by making it work too hard: *Don't strain your eyes by reading in poor light.*

PATTERNS

- to injure/hurt/strain **yourself**
- to injure/hurt/sprain/pull/strain a **muscle**
- to injure/hurt/sprain your **ankle/foot/knee/wrist/hand**
- to injure/hurt/strain your **back/shoulder/eyes**
- to injure/hurt your **spine/neck**
- to be **badly/severely/slightly** injured/wounded/hurt/bruised/sprained

in·jured 0-w AW /ˈɪndʒəd; *NAmE* -dʒərd/ *adj.*
1 0-w physically hurt; having an injury: *an injured leg* ◇ *Luckily, she isn't injured.* ◇ *Carter is playing in place of the injured O'Reilly.* OPP **uninjured** **2 the injured** *noun* [pl.] the people injured in an accident, a battle, etc: *Ambulances took the injured to a nearby hospital.* **3** 0-w (of a person or their feelings) upset or offended because sth unfair has been done: *an* ***injured look/tone*** ◇ ***injured pride***

the ˌinjured ˈparty *noun* [sing.] (*law*) the person who has been treated unfairly, or the person who claims in court to have been treated unfairly

in·juri·ous /ɪnˈdʒʊəriəs; *NAmE* -ˈdʒʊr-/ *adj.* **~** (**to sb/sth**) (*formal*) causing or likely to cause harm or damage SYN **damaging**

in·jury 0-w AW /ˈɪndʒəri/ *noun* (*pl.* -ies)
1 0-w [C, U] harm done to a person's or an animal's body, for example in an accident: ***serious injury/injuries*** ◇ ***minor injuries*** ◇ *to* ***sustain injuries/an injury*** ◇ *to* ***escape injury*** ◇ **~** (**to sb/sth**) *injury to the head* ◇ *a head injury* ◇ *Two*

I

players are out of the team **because of injury**. ◇ There were **no injuries** in the crash (= no people injured). ◇ (BrE, informal) Don't do that. You'll **do yourself an injury** (= hurt yourself). **2** [U] (law) damage to a person's feelings: *Damages may be awarded for emotional injury.* IDM see ADD

Collocations

Injuries

Being injured

- **have** a fall/an injury
- **receive/suffer/sustain** a serious injury/a hairline fracture/(*especially BrE*) whiplash/a gunshot wound
- **hurt/injure** your ankle/back/leg
- **damage** the brain/an ankle ligament/your liver/the optic nerve/the skin
- **pull/strain/tear** a hamstring/ligament/muscle/tendon
- **sprain/twist** your ankle/wrist
- **break** a bone/your collarbone/your leg/three ribs
- **fracture/crack** your skull
- **break/chip/knock out/lose** a tooth
- **burst/perforate** your eardrum
- **dislocate** your finger/hip/jaw/shoulder
- **bruise/cut/graze** your arm/knee/shoulder
- **burn/scald** yourself/your tongue
- **bang/bump/hit/**(*informal*) **bash** your elbow/head/knee (on/against sth)

Treating injuries

- **treat sb for** burns/a head injury/a stab wound
- **examine/clean/dress/bandage/treat** a bullet wound
- **repair** a damaged/torn ligament/tendon/cartilage
- **amputate/cut off** an arm/a finger/a foot/a leg/a limb
- **put on/**(*formal*) **apply/take off** (*especially NAmE*) a Band-Aid™/(*BrE*) a plaster/a bandage
- **need/require/put in/**(*especially BrE*) **have (out)**/(*NAmE*) **get (out)** stitches
- **put on/rub on/**(*formal*) **apply** cream/ointment/lotion
- **have/receive/undergo** (*BrE*) physiotherapy/(*NAmE*) physical therapy

'injury time *noun* [U] (*BrE*) time added at the end of a game of football (SOCCER), HOCKEY, etc. because the game has been interrupted by injured players needing treatment

in·just·ice /ɪn'dʒʌstɪs/ *noun* [U, C] the fact of a situation being unfair and of people not being treated equally; an unfair act or an example of unfair treatment: *fighting against poverty and injustice* ◇ *a burning* ***sense of injustice*** ◇ *social injustice* ◇ *She was enraged at the injustice of the remark.* ◇ *The report exposes the injustices of the system.* OPP **justice**

IDM **do yourself/sb an in'justice** to judge yourself/sb unfairly: *We may have been doing him an injustice. This work is good.*

ink 0‑ᴡ /ɪŋk/ *noun, verb*

■ ***noun*** 0‑ᴡ [U, C] coloured liquid for writing, drawing and printing: *written* ***in ink*** ◇ *a pen and ink drawing* ◇ *different coloured inks* ➲ see also INKY

■ ***verb*** **1 ~ sth** to cover sth with ink so that it can be used for printing **2 ~ sth** (*NAmE, informal*) to sign a document, especially a contract: *The group has just inked a $10 million deal.*

PHR V **,ink sth↔'in** to write or draw in ink over sth that has already been written or drawn in pencil: (*figurative*) *The date for the presentation should have been inked in* (= made definite) *by now.*

'ink-blot test *noun* (*psychology*) = RORSCHACH TEST

ink·jet printer /'ɪŋkdʒet prɪntə(r)/ *noun* a printer that uses very small JETS to blow ink onto paper in order to form letters, numbers, etc.

ink·ling /'ɪŋklɪŋ/ *noun* [usually sing.] a slight knowledge of sth that is happening or about to happen SYN **suspicion**: **~ (of sth)** *He* ***had no inkling*** *of what was going on.* ◇ **~ (that ...)** *The first inkling I had that something was wrong was when I found the front door wide open.*

'ink-pad *noun* a thick piece of soft material full of ink, used with a rubber stamp ➲ VISUAL VOCAB page V56

ink·well /'ɪŋkwel/ *noun* a pot for holding ink that fits into a hole in a desk (used in the past)

inky /'ɪŋki/ *adj.* **1** black like ink: *the inky blackness of the cellar* **2** made dirty with ink: *inky fingers*

in·laid /,ɪn'leɪd/ *adj.* (of furniture, floors, etc.) decorated with designs of wood, metal, etc. that are set into the surface: *an inlaid wooden box* ◇ **~ with sth** *a box inlaid with gold*

in·land *adv., adj.*

■ ***adv.*** /,ɪn'lænd/ in a direction towards the middle of a country; away from the coast: *The town lies a few kilometres inland.* ◇ *We travelled further inland the next day.*

■ ***adj.*** /'ɪnlænd/ [usually before noun] located in or near the middle of a country, not near the edge or on the coast: *inland areas* ◇ *inland lakes* ➲ compare COASTAL

the ,Inland 'Revenue *noun* [sing.] the government department in Britain that was responsible for collecting taxes until 2005 when it was replaced by HM REVENUE AND CUSTOMS ➲ compare THE INTERNAL REVENUE SERVICE

'in-law apartment (also **'mother-in-law apartment**, **'in-law suite**) (all *NAmE*) (*BrE* **'granny flat**) *noun* (*informal*) a set of rooms for an old person, especially in a relative's house

'in-laws *noun* [pl.] (*informal*) your relatives by marriage, especially the parents of your husband or wife: *We're visiting my in-laws on Sunday.*

inlay *verb, noun*

■ ***verb*** /,ɪn'leɪ/ (**in·lay·ing, in·laid, in·laid** /,ɪn'leɪd/) [often passive] **~ A (with B)** | **~ B (in/into A)** to decorate the surface of sth by putting pieces of wood or metal into it in such a way that the surface remains smooth: *The lid of the box had been inlaid with silver.*

■ ***noun*** /'ɪnleɪ/ [C, U] a design or pattern on a surface made by setting wood or metal into it; the material that this design is made of: *The table was decorated with gold inlay.*

inlet /'ɪnlet/ *noun* **1** a narrow strip of water that stretches into the land from the sea or a lake, or between islands ➲ VISUAL VOCAB page V4 **2** (*technical*) an opening through which liquid, air or gas can enter a machine: *a fuel inlet* OPP **outlet**

,in-line 'skate (*BrE* also **Roll·er·blade™**) (*NAmE* also **Roller Blade™**) *noun* a type of boot with a line of small wheels attached to the bottom ➲ VISUAL VOCAB page V34 ▸ **,in-line 'skating** *noun* [U]

in loco par·en·tis /ɪn ,ləʊkəʊ pə'rentɪs; *NAmE* ,loʊkoʊ/ *adv.* (from *Latin, formal*) having the same responsibility for a child as a parent has

in·mate /'ɪnmeɪt/ *noun* one of the people living in an institution such as a prison or a mental hospital

in med·ias res /ɪn ,miːdiæs 'reɪz/ *adv.* (*formal*, from *Latin*) straight into the main part of a story or account without giving any introduction: *He began his story in medias res.*

in me·mor·iam /,ɪn mə'mɔːriəm/ *prep.* (from *Latin*) used to mean 'in memory of', for example on the stone over a grave

in·most /'ɪnməʊst; *NAmE* 'ɪnmoʊst/ *adj.* [only before noun] = INNERMOST

inn /ɪn/ *noun* **1** (*old-fashioned, BrE*) a pub, usually in the country and often one where people can stay the night **2** (*NAmE*) a small hotel, usually in the country **3 Inn** used in the names of many pubs, hotels and restaurants: *Holiday Inn*

in·nards /ˈɪnədz; *NAmE* ˈɪnərdz/ *noun* [pl.] (*informal*) **1** the organs inside the body of a person or an animal, especially the stomach SYN **entrails**, **guts** **2** the parts inside a machine

in·nate /ɪˈneɪt/ *adj.* (of a quality, feeling, etc.) that you have when you are born SYN **inborn**: *the innate ability to learn* ▶ **in·nate·ly** *adv.*: *He believes that humans are innately violent.*

inner 0-w /ˈɪnə(r)/ *adj.* [only before noun] **1** 0-w inside; towards or close to the centre of a place: *an inner courtyard* ◇ *inner London* ◇ *the inner ear* OPP **outer** **2** (of feelings, etc.) private and secret; not expressed or shown to other people: *She doesn't reveal much of her inner self.*

ˌinner ˈcircle *noun* the small group of people who have a lot of power in an organization, or who control it

ˌinner ˈcity *noun* the part near the centre of a large city, which often has social problems: *There are huge problems in our inner cities.* ◇ *an inner-city* ***area/school***

ˌinner ˈear *noun* (*anatomy*) the parts of the ear which form the organs of balance and hearing, including the COCHLEA

in·ner·most /ˈɪnəməʊst; *NAmE* ˈɪnərmoʊst/ *adj.* [only before noun] **1** (also *less frequent* **in·most**) most private, personal and secret: *I could not express my innermost feelings to anyone.* **2** nearest to the centre or inside of sth: *the innermost shrine of the temple* OPP **outermost**

ˈinner tube *noun* a rubber tube filled with air inside a tyre

in·ning /ˈɪnɪŋ/ *noun* (in BASEBALL) one of the nine periods of a game in which each team has a turn at BATTING

in·nings /ˈɪnɪŋz/ *noun* (*pl.* **in·nings**) (in CRICKET) a period of time in a game during which a team or a single player is BATTING

IDM **sb had a good ˈinnings** (*BrE, informal*) used about sb who has died to say that they had a long life

innit /ˈɪnɪt/ *exclamation* (*BrE, non-standard*) **1** a way of saying 'isn't it': *Cold, innit?* **2** a way of saying any QUESTION TAG, such as 'don't you?' or 'haven't you?': *You got it, innit?*

inn·keep·er /ˈɪnkiːpə(r)/ *noun* (*old-fashioned*) a person who owns or manages an INN

in·no·cence /ˈɪnəsns/ *noun* [U] **1** the fact of not being guilty of a crime, etc: *She* ***protested her innocence*** (= said repeatedly that she was innocent). ◇ *This new evidence will prove their innocence.* ◇ *I asked if she was married* ***in all innocence*** (= without knowing it was likely to offend or upset her). OPP **guilt** **2** lack of knowledge and experience of the world, especially of evil or unpleasant things: *Children lose their innocence as they grow older.*

in·no·cent 0-w /ˈɪnəsnt/ *adj., noun*

▪ ***adj.*** **1** 0-w not guilty of a crime, etc; not having done sth wrong: *They have imprisoned an innocent man.* ◇ ~ (**of sth**) *She was found innocent of any crime.* ◇ *He was the* ***innocent party*** (= person) *in the breakdown of the marriage.* OPP **guilty** **2** 0-w [only before noun] suffering harm or being killed because of a crime, war, etc. although not directly involved in it: *an innocent bystander* ◇ *innocent victims of a bomb blast* **3** 0-w having little experience of the world, especially of sexual matters, or of evil or unpleasant things SYN **naive**: *an innocent young child* **4** not intended to cause harm or upset sb SYN **harmless**: *It was all innocent fun.* ◇ *It was a perfectly innocent remark.* ▶ **in·no·cent·ly** *adv.*: *'Oh, Sue went too, did she?' I asked innocently* (= pretending I did not know that this was important).

▪ ***noun*** an innocent person, especially a young child

in·nocu·ous /ɪˈnɒkjuəs; *NAmE* ɪˈnɑːk-/ *adj.* (*formal*) **1** not intended to offend or upset anyone SYN **harmless**: *It seemed a perfectly innocuous remark.* **2** not harmful or dangerous: *an innocuous substance* SYN **harmless**

in·nov·ate AW /ˈɪnəveɪt/ *verb* [I, T] to introduce new things, ideas, or ways of doing sth: *We must constantly adapt and innovate to ensure success in a growing market.* ◇ ~ **sth** *to innovate new products* ▶ **in·nov·ator** AW /ˈɪnəveɪtə(r)/ *noun*

in·nov·ation AW /ˌɪnəˈveɪʃn/ *noun* **1** [U] ~ (**in sth**) the introduction of new things, ideas or ways of doing sth: *an age of technological innovation* **2** [C] ~ (**in sth**) a new idea, way of doing sth, etc. that has been introduced or discovered: *recent innovations in steel-making technology*

in·nova·tive AW /ˈɪnəveɪtɪv; *BrE* also ˈɪnəvətɪv/ (also *less frequent* **in·nov·atory** /ˌɪnəˈveɪtəri; *NAmE* also ˈɪnəvətɔːri/) *adj.* (*approving*) introducing or using new ideas, ways of doing sth, etc: *There will be a prize for the most innovative design.*

in·nu·endo /ˌɪnjuˈendəʊ; *NAmE* -doʊ/ *noun* [C, U] (*pl.* **-oes** or **-os**) (*disapproving*) an indirect remark about sb/sth, usually suggesting sth bad or rude; the use of remarks like this: *innuendoes about her private life* ◇ *The song is full of sexual innuendo.*

in·nu·mer·able /ɪˈnjuːmərəbl; *NAmE* ɪˈnuː-/ *adj.* too many to be counted; very many SYN **countless**: *Innumerable books have been written on the subject.*

in·nu·mer·ate /ɪˈnjuːmərət; *NAmE* ɪˈnuː-/ *adj.* unable to count or do simple mathematics OPP **numerate**

in·ocu·late /ɪˈnɒkjuleɪt; *NAmE* ɪˈnɑːk-/ *verb* ~ **sb** (**against sth**) to protect a person or an animal from catching a particular disease by INJECTING them with a mild form of the disease ➲ compare IMMUNIZE, VACCINATE ▶ **in·ocu·la·tion** /ɪˌnɒkjuˈleɪʃn; *NAmE* ɪˌnɑːk-/ *noun* [C, U]

in·offen·sive /ˌɪnəˈfensɪv/ *adj.* not likely to offend or upset anyone: *a shy, inoffensive young man* OPP **offensive**

in·op·er·able /ɪnˈɒpərəbl; *NAmE* ɪnˈɑːp-/ *adj.* **1** (of an illness, especially cancer) not able to be cured by a medical operation: *an inoperable brain tumour* **2** (*formal*) that cannot be used or made to work; not practical: *The policy was thought to be inoperable.* OPP **operable**

in·op·era·tive /ɪnˈɒpərətɪv; *NAmE* ɪnˈɑːp-/ *adj.* (*formal*) **1** (of a rule, system, etc.) not valid or able to be used **2** (of a machine) not working; not functioning correctly OPP **operative**

in·op·por·tune /ɪnˈɒpətjuːn; *NAmE* ɪnˌɑːpərˈtuːn/ *adj.* (*formal*) happening at a bad time SYN **inappropriate**, **inconvenient**: *They arrived at an inopportune moment.* OPP **opportune**

in·or·din·ate /ɪnˈɔːdɪnət; *NAmE* -ˈɔːrd-/ *adj.* (*formal*) far more than is usual or expected SYN **excessive** ▶ **in·or·din·ate·ly** *adv.*: *inordinately high prices*

in·or·gan·ic /ˌɪnɔːˈgænɪk; *NAmE* ˌɪnɔːrˈg-/ *adj.* not consisting of or coming from any living substances: *inorganic fertilizers* OPP **organic**

ˌinorganic ˈchemistry *noun* [U] the branch of chemistry that deals with substances that do not contain CARBON ➲ compare ORGANIC CHEMISTRY

in·pa·tient /ˈɪnpeɪʃnt/ *noun* a person who stays in a hospital while receiving treatment ➲ compare OUTPATIENT

input AW /ˈɪnpʊt/ *noun, verb*

▪ ***noun*** **1** [C, U] time, knowledge, ideas, etc. that you put into work, a project, etc. in order to make it succeed; the act of putting sth in: ~ (**into/to sth**) *Her specialist input to the discussions has been very useful.* ◇ *I'd appreciate your input on this.* ◇ ~ (**of sth**) *There has been a big input of resources into the project from industry.* **2** [U] (*computing*) the act of putting information into a computer; the information that you put in: *data input* ◇ *This program accepts input from most word processors.* **3** [C] (*technical*) a place or means for electricity, data, etc. to enter a machine or system ➲ compare OUTPUT

▪ ***verb*** (**in·put·ting**, **input**, **input** or **in·put·ting**, **in·put·ted**, **in·put·ted**) ~ **sth** to put information into a computer: *to* ***input text/data/figures*** ➲ compare OUTPUT

in·quest /ˈɪŋkwest/ *noun* **1** an official investigation to find out the cause of sb's death, especially when it has not happened naturally: *An inquest was held to discover the cause of death.* ◇ ~ (**on/into sth**) *a coroner's inquest into his death* **2** ~ (**on/into sth**) a discussion about sth that has failed: *An inquest was held on the team's poor performance.*

I

in·quire, in·quirer, in·quir·ing, in·quiry = ENQUIRE, ENQUIRER, ENQUIRING, ENQUIRY

in·qui·si·tion /ˌɪnkwɪˈzɪʃn/ *noun* **1 the Inquisition** [sing.] the organization set up by the Roman Catholic Church to punish people who opposed its beliefs, especially from the 15th to the 17th century **2** [C] (*formal* or *humorous*) a series of questions that sb asks you, especially when they ask them in an unpleasant way ➲ see also SPANISH INQUISITION

in·quisi·tive /ɪnˈkwɪzətɪv/ *adj.* **1** (*disapproving*) asking too many questions and trying to find out about what other people are doing, etc. SYN **curious**: *Don't be so inquisitive. It's none of your business!* **2** very interested in learning about many different things SYN **enquiring**: *an inquisitive mind* ▶ **in·quisi·tive·ly** *adv.* **in·quisi·tive·ness** *noun* [U]

in·quisi·tor /ɪnˈkwɪzɪtə(r)/ *noun* **1** a person who asks a lot of difficult questions, especially in a way that makes you feel threatened **2** an officer of the Inquisition of the Roman Catholic Church ▶ **in·quisi·tor·ial** /ɪnˌkwɪzəˈtɔːriəl/ *adj.*: *He questioned her in a cold inquisitorial voice.* **in·quisi·tor·ial·ly** *adv.*

in·quor·ate /ɪnˈkwɔːreɪt; -ət/ *adj.* (*BrE, technical*) a meeting that is **inquorate** does not have enough people present for them to make official decisions by voting OPP **quorate**

in·road /ˈɪnrəʊd; *NAmE* -roʊd/ *noun* **~ (into sth)** something that is achieved, especially by reducing the power or success of sth else: *This deal is their first major inroad into the American market.*

IDM **make inroads into/on sth** if one thing **makes inroads into** another, it has a noticeable effect on the second thing, especially by reducing it, or influencing it: *Tax rises have made some inroads into the country's national debt.*

in·rush /ˈɪnrʌʃ/ *noun* [usually sing.] a sudden flow towards the inside: *an inrush of air/water*

in·salu·bri·ous /ˌɪnsəˈluːbriəs/ *adj.* (of a place) dirty and with many things that need to be repaired, cleaned or replaced OPP **salubrious**

in·sane /ɪnˈseɪn/ *adj.* **1** seriously mentally ill and unable to live in normal society: *Doctors certified him as insane.* ◇ *The prisoners were slowly* ***going insane.*** OPP **sane** ➲ note at MENTALLY ILL **2 the insane** *noun* [pl.] people who are insane: *a hospital for the insane* **3** (*informal*) very stupid, crazy or dangerous: *I must have been insane to agree to the idea.* ◇ *This job is* ***driving me insane*** (= making me feel very angry). ➲ see also INSANITY ▶ **in·sane·ly** *adv.*: *He is insanely jealous.*

in·sani·tary /ɪnˈsænətri; *NAmE* -teri/ (also **un·sani·tary** especially in *NAmE*) *adj.* dirty and likely to spread disease OPP **sanitary**

in·san·ity /ɪnˈsænəti/ *noun* [U] **1** the state of being INSANE SYN **madness**: *He was found not guilty, by reason of insanity.* OPP **sanity** **2** actions that are very stupid and possibly dangerous SYN **madness, lunacy**: *It would be sheer insanity to attempt the trip in such bad weather.*

in·sati·able /ɪnˈseɪʃəbl/ *adj.* always wanting more of sth; not able to be satisfied: *an* ***insatiable appetite/curiosity/thirst*** ◇ *There seems to be an* ***insatiable demand*** *for more powerful computers.* ▶ **in·sati·ably** /-ʃəbli/ *adv.*

in·scribe /ɪnˈskraɪb/ *verb* to write or cut words, your name, etc. onto sth: **~ A (on/in B)** *His name was inscribed on the trophy.* ◇ **~ B (with A)** *The trophy was inscribed with his name.* ◇ *She signed the book and inscribed the words 'with grateful thanks' on it.*

in·scrip·tion /ɪnˈskrɪpʃn/ *noun* words written in the front of a book or cut in stone or metal

in·scrut·able /ɪnˈskruːtəbl/ *adj.* if a person or their expression is **inscrutable**, it is hard to know what they are thinking or feeling, because they do not show any emotion ▶ **in·scrut·abil·ity** /ɪnˌskruːtəˈbɪləti/ *noun* [U] **in·scrut·ably** /ɪnˈskruːtəbli/ *adv.*

in·seam /ˈɪnsiːm/ (*NAmE*) (*BrE* **ˌinside ˈleg**) *noun* [sing.] a measurement of the length of the inside of sb's leg, used for making or choosing trousers of the correct size

in·sect 🔑 /ˈɪnsekt/ *noun* any small creature with six legs and a body divided into three parts. Insects usually also have wings. ANTS, BEES and flies are all insects: *insect species* ◇ ***insect repellent*** (= a chemical that keeps insects away) ◇ *an* ***insect bite*** ➲ COLLOCATIONS at LIFE ➲ VISUAL VOCAB page V11 ➲ see also STICK INSECT HELP **Insect** is often used to refer to other small creatures, for example spiders, although this is not correct scientific language.

in·secti·cide /ɪnˈsektɪsaɪd/ *noun* [C, U] a chemical used for killing insects ➲ see also HERBICIDE, PESTICIDE ▶ **in·secti·cidal** /ɪnˌsektɪˈsaɪdl/ *adj.*

in·sect·ivore /ɪnˈsektɪvɔː(r)/ *noun* any animal that eats insects ➲ compare CARNIVORE, HERBIVORE, OMNIVORE ▶ **in·sect·iv·or·ous** /ˌɪnsekˈtɪvərəs/ *adj.*

in·se·cure AW /ˌɪnsɪˈkjʊə(r); *NAmE* -ˈkjʊr/ *adj.* **1** not confident about yourself or your relationships with other people: *He's very insecure about his appearance.* ◇ *She felt nervous and insecure.* **2** not safe or protected: *Jobs nowadays are much more insecure than they were ten years ago.* ◇ *As an artist he was always financially insecure.* ◇ *Insecure doors and windows* (= for example, without good locks) *make life easy for burglars.* OPP **secure** ▶ **in·se·cure·ly** *adv.* **in·secur·ity** AW /ˌɪnsɪˈkjʊərəti; *NAmE* -ˈkjʊr-/ *noun* [U, C] (*pl.* **-ies**): *feelings of insecurity* ◇ *job insecurity* ◇ *We all have our fears and insecurities.*

in·sem·in·ate /ɪnˈsemɪneɪt/ *verb* **~ sb/sth** (*technical*) to put SPERM into a woman or female animal in order to make her pregnant: *The cows are* ***artificially inseminated.*** ▶ **in·sem·in·ation** /ɪnˌsemɪˈneɪʃn/ *noun* [U] ➲ see also ARTIFICIAL INSEMINATION

in·sens·ibil·ity /ɪnˌsensəˈbɪləti/ *noun* [U] **1** (*formal*) the state of being unconscious **2** the fact of not being able to react to a particular thing: *insensibility to pain*

in·sens·ible /ɪnˈsensəbl/ *adj.* (*formal*) **1** [not before noun] **~ (to sth)** unable to feel sth or react to it: *insensible to pain/cold* **2** [not before noun] **~ (of sth)** not aware of a situation or of sth that might happen SYN **unaware**: *They were not insensible of the risks.* OPP **sensible** **3** unconscious as the result of injury, illness, etc: *He drank himself insensible.* ▶ **in·sens·ibly** /-əbli/ *adv.*

in·sensi·tive /ɪnˈsensətɪv/ *adj.* **1** not realizing or caring how other people feel, and therefore likely to hurt or offend them SYN **unsympathetic**: *an insensitive remark* ◇ **~ to sth** *She's completely insensitive to my feelings.* **2 ~ (to sth)** not aware of changing situations, and therefore of the need to react to them: *The government seems totally insensitive to the mood of the country.* **3 ~ (to sth)** not able to feel or react to sth: *insensitive to pain/cold* ◇ *He seems completely insensitive to criticism.* OPP **sensitive** ▶ **in·sensi·tive·ly** *adv.* **in·sensi·tiv·ity** /ɪnˌsensəˈtɪvəti/ *noun* [U]

in·sep·ar·able /ɪnˈseprəbl/ *adj.* **1 ~ (from sth)** not able to be separated: *Our economic fortunes are inseparable from those of Europe.* **2** if people are **inseparable**, they spend most of their time together and are very good friends ▶ **in·sep·ar·ab·il·ity** /ɪnˌseprəˈbɪləti/ *noun* [U] **in·sep·ar·ably** /ɪnˈseprəbli/ *adv.*: *Our lives were inseparably linked.*

in·sert 🔑 AW *verb, noun*

■ ***verb*** /ɪnˈsɜːt; *NAmE* ɪnˈsɜːrt/ **1** 🔑 **~ sth (in/into/between sth)** to put sth into sth else or between two things: *Insert coins into the slot and press for a ticket.* ◇ *They inserted a tube in his mouth to help him breathe.* **2** 🔑 to add sth to a piece of writing: **~ sth** *Position the cursor where you want to insert a word.* ◇ **~ sth into sth** *Later, he inserted another paragraph into his will.*

■ ***noun*** /ˈɪnsɜːt; *NAmE* ˈɪnsɜːrt/ **~ (in sth) 1** an extra section added to a book, newspaper or magazine, especially to advertise sth: *an 8-page insert on the new car models* **2** something that is put inside sth else, or added to sth else: *These inserts fit inside any style of shoe.*

in·ser·tion AW /ɪnˈsɜːʃn; NAmE ɪnˈsɜːrʃn/ *noun* **1** [U, C] **~ (in/into sth)** the act of putting sth inside sth else; a thing that is put inside sth else: *An examination is carried out before the insertion of the tube.* **2** [C, U] a thing that is added to a book, piece of writing, etc; the act of adding sth: *the insertion of an extra paragraph*

ˌin-ˈservice *adj.* [only before noun] (of training, courses of study, etc.) done while sb is working in a job, in order to learn new skills: *in-service training*

inset /ˈɪnset/ *noun, verb*

■ ***noun*** **1** a small picture, map, etc. inside a larger one: *For the Shetland Islands, see inset.* **2** something that is added on to sth else, or put inside sth else: *The windows have beautiful stained glass insets.*

■ ***verb*** (**in·set·ting, inset, inset**) **1** [usually passive] to fix sth into the surface of sth else, especially as a decoration: **~ A (with B)** *The tables were inset with ceramic tiles.* ◇ **~ B (into A)** *Ceramic tiles were inset into the tables.* **2 ~ sth (into sth)** to put a small picture, map, etc. inside the borders of a bigger one

in·shore /ˈɪnʃɔː(r)/ *adj.* [usually before noun] in the sea but close to the SHORE: *an inshore breeze* ◇ *an inshore lifeboat* (= that stays close to the land) ▶ **ˌinˈshore** *adv.*: *The boat came inshore* (= towards the land). ➲ compare OFFSHORE

in·side 🔑 /ˌɪnˈsaɪd/ *prep., adv., noun, adj.*

■ ***prep.*** (also **in·side of** especially in *NAmE*) **1** 🔑 on or to the inner part of sth/sb; within sth/sb: *Go inside the house.* ◇ *Inside the box was a gold watch.* ◇ *For years we had little knowledge of what life was like inside China.* ◇ *You'll feel better with a good meal inside you.* ◇ (*figurative*) *Inside most of us is a small child screaming for attention.* OPP **outside** **2** in less than the amount of time mentioned: *The job is unlikely to be finished inside (of) a year*

■ ***adv.*** **1** 🔑 on or to the inside: *She shook it to make sure there was nothing inside.* ◇ *We had to move inside* (= indoors) *when it started to rain.* ◇ (*figurative*) *I pretended not to care but I was screaming inside.* OPP **outside** **2** (*informal*) in prison: *He was sentenced to three years inside.*

■ ***noun*** **1** 🔑 [C, usually sing.] (usually **the inside**) the inner part, side or surface of sth: *The inside of the box was blue.* ◇ *The door was locked from the inside.* ◇ *The shell is smooth on the inside.* ◇ *the insides of the windows* OPP **the outside** **2 the inside** [sing.] the part of a road nearest the edge, that is used by slower vehicles: *He tried to overtake **on the inside**.* OPP **the outside** **3 the inside** [sing.] the part of a curved road or track nearest to the middle or shortest side of the curve: *The French runner is coming up fast on the inside.* OPP **the outside** **4 insides** [pl.] (*informal*) a person's stomach and BOWELS: *She was so nervous, her insides were like jelly.*

IDM **ˌinside ˈout** 🔑 with the part that is usually inside facing out: *You've got your sweater on inside out.* ◇ *Turn the bag inside out and let it dry.* ➲ compare BACK TO FRONT at BACK *n.* **on the inˈside** belonging to a group or an organization and therefore able to get information that is not available to other people: *The thieves must have had someone on the inside helping them.* **turn sth ˌinside ˈout** **1** to make a place very untidy when you are searching for sth: *The burglars had turned the house inside out.* **2** to cause large changes: *The new manager turned the old systems inside out.* ➲ more at KNOW *v.*

■ ***adj.*** [only before noun] **1** 🔑 forming the inner part of sth; not on the outside: *the inside pages of a newspaper* ◇ *an inside pocket* ◇ (*BrE*) *I was driving in the **inside lane*** (= the part nearest the edge, not the middle of the road). **2** known or done by sb in a group or an organization: *inside information* ◇ *Any newspaper would pay big money to get **the inside story** on her marriage.* ◇ *The robbery appeared to have been an **inside job**.*

ˌinside ˈleg (*BrE*) (*NAmE* **inseam**) *noun* [sing.] a measurement of the length of the inside of sb's leg, used for making or choosing trousers of the correct size

in·sider /ɪnˈsaɪdə(r)/ *noun* a person who knows a lot about a group or an organization, because they are part of it: *The situation was described by one insider as 'absolute chaos'.* ➲ compare OUTSIDER

inˌsider ˈtrading (also **inˌsider ˈdealing**) *noun* [U] the crime of buying or selling shares in a company with the help of information known only by those connected with the business, before this information is available to everybody

ˌinside ˈtrack *noun* [sing.] (*especially NAmE*) a position in which you have an advantage over sb else

in·sidi·ous /ɪnˈsɪdiəs/ *adj.* (*formal, disapproving*) spreading gradually or without being noticed, but causing serious harm: *the insidious effects of polluted water supplies* ▶ **in·sidi·ous·ly** *adv.*

in·sight AW /ˈɪnsaɪt/ *noun* **1** [U] (*approving*) the ability to see and understand the truth about people or situations: *a writer of great insight* ◇ *With a flash of insight I realized what the dream meant.* **2** [C, U] **~ (into sth)** an understanding of what sth is like: *The book gives us fascinating insights into life in Mexico.*

in·sight·ful AW /ˈɪnsaɪtfʊl/ *adj.* (*approving*) showing a clear understanding of a person or situation SYN **perceptive**

in·sig·nia /ɪnˈsɪgniə/ *noun* [U+sing./pl. v.] the symbol, BADGE or sign that shows sb's rank or that they are a member of a group or an organization: *the royal insignia* ◇ *His uniform bore the insignia of a captain.*

in·sig·nifi·cant AW /ˌɪnsɪgˈnɪfɪkənt/ *adj.* not big or valuable enough to be considered important: *an insignificant difference* ◇ *The levels of chemicals in the river are not insignificant.* ◇ *He made her feel insignificant and stupid.* OPP **significant** ▶ **in·sig·nifi·cance** /-kəns/ *noun* [U]: *Her own problems **paled into insignificance** beside this terrible news.* **in·sig·nifi·cant·ly** AW *adv.*

in·sin·cere /ˌɪnsɪnˈsɪə(r); NAmE -ˈsɪr/ *adj.* (*disapproving*) saying or doing sth that you do not really mean or believe: *an insincere smile* OPP **sincere** ▶ **in·sin·cere·ly** *adv.* **in·sin·cer·ity** /ˌɪnsɪnˈserəti/ *noun* [U]: *She accused him of insincerity.*

in·sinu·ate /ɪnˈsɪnjueɪt/ *verb* **1** to suggest indirectly that sth unpleasant is true SYN **imply**: **~ that...** *The article insinuated that he was having an affair with his friend's wife.* ◇ **~ sth** *What are you trying to insinuate?* ◇ *an insinuating smile* **2 ~ yourself into sth** (*formal, disapproving*) to succeed in gaining sb's respect, affection, etc. so that you can use the situation to your own advantage: *In the first act, the villain insinuates himself into the household of the man he intends to kill.* **3 ~ yourself/sth + adv./prep.** (*formal*) to slowly move yourself or a part of your body into a particular position or place: *She insinuated her right hand under his arm.*

in·sinu·ation /ɪnˌsɪnjuˈeɪʃn/ *noun* **1** [C] something that sb insinuates: *She resented the insinuation that she was too old for the job.* **2** [U] the act of insinuating sth

in·sipid /ɪnˈsɪpɪd/ *adj.* (*disapproving*) **1** having almost no taste or flavour SYN **flavourless**: *a cup of insipid coffee* **2** not interesting or exciting SYN **dull**: *After an hour of insipid conversation, I left.*

in·sist 🔑 /ɪnˈsɪst/ *verb*

1 🔑 [I, T] to demand that sth happens or that sb agrees to do sth: *I didn't really want to go but he insisted.* ◇ *'Please come with us.' 'Very well then, **if you insist**.'* ◇ **~ on sth/sb doing sth** (*formal*) *She insisted on his/him wearing a suit.* ◇ **~ that...** *He insists that she come.* ◇ (*BrE* also) *He insists that she should come.* ➲ SYNONYMS at DEMAND **2** 🔑 [I, T] to say firmly that sth is true, especially when other people do not believe you: **~ on sth** *He insisted on his innocence.* ◇ **~ (that)...** *He insisted (that) he was innocent.* ◇ **+ speech** *'It's true,' she insisted.*

PHR V **inˈsist on/upon sth** 🔑 to demand sth and refuse to be persuaded to accept anything else: *We insisted on a refund of the full amount.* ◇ **~ doing sth** *They insisted upon being given every detail of the case.* **inˈsist on doing sth** 🔑 to continue doing sth even though other people think it is annoying: *They insist on playing their music late at night.*

I

in·sist·ence /ɪn'sɪstəns/ *noun* [U] **~ (on sth/on doing sth)** | **~ (that...)** an act of demanding or saying sth firmly and refusing to accept any opposition or excuses: *their insistence on strict standards of behaviour* ◇ ***At her insistence,*** *the matter was dropped.*

in·sist·ent /ɪn'sɪstənt/ *adj.* **1** demanding sth firmly and refusing to accept any opposition or excuses: **~ (on sth/on doing sth)** *They were insistent on having a contract for the work.* ◇ **~ (that...)** *Why are you so insistent that we leave tonight?* ◇ *She didn't want to go but her brother was insistent.* **2** continuing for a long period of time in a way that cannot be ignored: *insistent demands* ◇ *the insistent ringing of the telephone* ▸ **in·sist·ent·ly** *adv.*

in situ /ˌɪn 'sɪtjuː; 'saɪt-; *NAmE* 'saɪtuː/ *adv.* (from *Latin*) in the original or correct place

in·so·bri·ety /ˌɪnsə'braɪəti/ *noun* [U] (*formal*) the state of being drunk; wild and noisy behaviour which is typical of this state OPP **sobriety**

in·so·far as /ˌɪnsə'fɑːr əz/ = IN SO FAR AS at FAR

in·sole /'ɪnsəʊl; *NAmE* 'ɪnsoʊl/ *noun* a piece of material shaped like your foot that is placed inside a shoe to make it more comfortable

in·so·lent /'ɪnsələnt/ *adj.* extremely rude and showing a lack of respect: *an insolent child/smile* ➲ SYNONYMS at RUDE ▸ **in·so·lence** /-əns/ *noun* [U]: *Her insolence cost her her job.* **in·so·lent·ly** *adv.*

in·sol·uble /ɪn'sɒljəbl; *NAmE* -'sɑːl-/ *adj.* **1** (*especially BrE*) (*US* usually **in·sol·vable** /ɪn'sɒlvəbl; *NAmE* -'sɑːl-/) (of a problem, mystery, etc.) that cannot be solved or explained **2 ~ (in sth)** (of a substance) that does not dissolve in a liquid OPP **soluble**

in·solv·ent /ɪn'sɒlvənt; *NAmE* -'sɑːl-/ *adj.* not having enough money to pay what you owe SYN **bankrupt**: *The company has been declared insolvent.* OPP **solvent** ▸ **in·solv·ency** /-ənsi/ *noun* [U, C] (*pl.* **-ies**)

in·som·nia /ɪn'sɒmniə; *NAmE* -'sɑːm-/ *noun* [U] the condition of being unable to sleep: *to suffer from insomnia* ➲ see also SLEEPLESSNESS

in·som·niac /ɪn'sɒmniæk; *NAmE* -'sɑːm-/ *noun* a person who finds it difficult to sleep

in·sou·ci·ance /ɪn'suːsiəns/ *noun* [U] (*formal*) the state of not being worried about anything SYN **nonchalance**: *She hid her worries behind an air of insouciance.* ▸ **in·sou·ci·ant** /-siənt/ *adj.*

Insp *abbr.* INSPECTOR (especially in the British police force): *Chief Insp (Paul) King*

in·spect AW /ɪn'spekt/ *verb* **1** to look closely at sth/sb, especially to check that everything is as it should be SYN **examine**: **~ sth/sb** *The teacher walked around inspecting their work.* ◇ *Make sure you inspect the goods before signing for them.* ◇ **~ sth/sb for sth** *The plants are regularly inspected for disease.* ➲ SYNONYMS at CHECK **2 ~ sth** to officially visit a school, factory, etc. in order to check that rules are being obeyed and that standards are acceptable: *Public health officials were called in to inspect the premises.* ➲ SYNONYMS at CHECK

in·spec·tion AW /ɪn'spekʃn/ *noun* [U, C] **1** an official visit to a school, factory, etc. in order to check that rules are being obeyed and that standards are acceptable: *Regular* ***inspections*** *are* ***carried out*** *at the prison.* ◇ *The head went on a* ***tour of inspection*** *of all the classrooms.* **2** the act of looking closely at sth/sb, especially to check that everything is as it should be SYN **examination**: *The documents are available* ***for inspection.*** ◇ ***On closer inspection,*** *the notes proved to be forgeries.* ◇ *Engineers* ***carried out*** *a thorough* ***inspection*** *of the track.*

in·spect·or AW /ɪn'spektə(r)/ *noun* **1** a person whose job is to visit schools, factories, etc. to check that rules are being obeyed and that standards are acceptable: *a* ***school/health/safety, etc. inspector*** ➲ see also TAX INSPECTOR **2** (*abbr.* **Insp**) an officer of middle rank in the POLICE FORCE: *Inspector Maggie Forbes* ➲ see also CHIEF INSPECTOR **3** (in Britain) a person whose job is to check tickets on a bus or train to make sure that they are valid **4** (*NAmE*) (*BrE* **sur·vey·or**) a person whose job is to examine a building to make sure it is in good condition, usually done for sb who is thinking of buying it

in·spect·or·ate /ɪn'spektərət/ *noun* [C+sing./pl. v.] (*especially BrE*) an official group of inspectors who work together on the same subject or at the same kind of institution: *The schools inspectorate has/have published a report on science teaching.*

inˌspector of 'taxes (also **'tax inspector**) *noun* (in Britain) a person who is responsible for collecting the tax that people must pay on the money they earn ➲ see also TAX COLLECTOR, TAXMAN

in·spir·ation /ˌɪnspə'reɪʃn/ *noun* **1** [U] **~ (to do sth)** | **~ (for sth)** the process that takes place when sb sees or hears sth that causes them to have exciting new ideas or makes them want to create sth, especially in art, music or literature: *Dreams can be a rich source of inspiration for an artist.* ◇ *Both poets* ***drew their inspiration from*** *the countryside.* ◇ *Looking for inspiration for a new dessert? Try this recipe.* **2** [C, usually sing.] **~ (for sth)** a person or thing that is the reason why sb creates or does sth: *He says my sister was the inspiration for his heroine.* ◇ *Clark was the inspiration behind Saturday's victory.* **3** [C, usually sing.] **~ (to/for sb)** a person or thing that makes you want to be better, more successful, etc: *Her charity work is an inspiration to us all.* **4** [C, usually sing., U] a sudden good idea: *He had an inspiration: he'd give her a dog for her birthday.* ◇ *It came to me in a* ***flash of inspiration.***

in·spir·ation·al /ˌɪnspə'reɪʃənl/ *adj.* providing inspiration: *an inspirational leader*

in·spire /ɪn'spaɪə(r)/ *verb* **1** to give sb the desire, confidence or enthusiasm to do sth well: **~ sb (with sth)** *The actors inspired the kids with their enthusiasm.* ◇ *The actors' enthusiasm inspired the kids.* ◇ **~ sb to sth** *His superb play inspired the team to a thrilling 5–0 win.* ◇ **~ sb to do sth** *By visiting schools, the actors hope to inspire children to put on their own productions.* **2** [usually passive] **~ sth** to give sb the idea for sth, especially sth artistic or that shows imagination: *The choice of decor was inspired by a trip to India.* **3** to make sb have a particular feeling or emotion: **~ sb (with sth)** *Her work didn't exactly* ***inspire me with confidence.*** ◇ **~ sth (in sb)** *As a general, he inspired great loyalty in his troops.*

in·spired /ɪn'spaɪəd; *NAmE* ɪn'spaɪərd/ *adj.* **1** having excellent qualities or abilities; produced with the help of INSPIRATION: *an inspired performance* ◇ *an* ***inspired choice/guess*** (= one that is right but based on feelings rather than knowledge) OPP **uninspired** **2 -inspired** used with nouns, adjectives and adverbs to form adjectives that show how sth has been influenced: *politically-inspired killings*

in·spir·ing /ɪn'spaɪərɪŋ/ *adj.* exciting and encouraging you to do or feel sth: *an inspiring teacher* ◇ (*informal*) *The book is less than inspiring.* OPP **uninspiring** ➲ see also AWE-INSPIRING

in·stabil·ity AW /ˌɪnstə'bɪləti/ *noun* [U, C, usually pl.] (*pl.* **-ies**) **1** the quality of a situation in which things are likely to change or fail suddenly: *political and economic instability* **2** a mental condition in which sb's behaviour is likely to change suddenly: ***mental/emotional instability*** OPP **stability** ➲ see also UNSTABLE

in·stall 0→ /ɪn'stɔːl/ *verb*
1 0→ **~ sth** to fix equipment or furniture into position so that it can be used: *He's getting a phone installed tomorrow.* ◇ *The hotel chain has recently installed a new booking system.* **2** 0→ **~ sth** to put a new program into a computer: *I'll need some help installing the software.* **3 ~ sb (as sth)** to put sb in a new position of authority, often with an official ceremony: *He was installed as President last May.* **4 ~ sb/yourself (+ adv./prep.)** to make sb/yourself comfortable in a particular place or position: *We installed ourselves in the front row.*

in·stal·la·tion /ˌɪnstə'leɪʃn/ *noun* **1** [U, C] the act of fixing equipment or furniture in position so that it can be used: *installation costs* ◇ *Installation of the new system will* *take several days.* **2** [C] a piece of equipment or machinery that has been fixed in position so that it can be used: *a heating installation* **3** [C] a place where specialist equipment is kept and used: *a military installation* **4** [U] the act of placing sb in a new position of authority, often with a ceremony: *the installation of the new vice chancellor* **5** [C] (*art*) a piece of modern SCULPTURE that is made using sound, light, etc. as well as objects

in'stallment plan (*NAmE*) (*BrE* **ˌhire 'purchase**) *noun* [U, C] a method of buying an article by making regular payments for it over several months or years. The article only belongs to the person who is buying it when all the payments have been made. ➲ compare CREDIT

in·stal·ment (*especially BrE*) (*NAmE* usually **in·stall·ment**) /ɪn'stɔːlmənt/ *noun* **1** one of a number of payments that are made regularly over a period of time until sth has been paid for: *We paid for the car* ***by/in instalments.*** ◇ *The final instalment on the loan is due next week.* ◇ *They were unable to keep up* (= continue to pay regularly) *the instalments.* ➲ **SYNONYMS** at PAYMENT ➲ **COLLOCATIONS** at FINANCE **2** one of the parts of a story that appears regularly over a period of time in a newspaper, on television, etc. **SYN** **episode**

in·stance 0‑π AW /'ɪnstəns/ *noun, verb*

■ ***noun*** 0‑π a particular example or case of sth: *The report highlights a number of instances of injustice.* ◇ *In most instances, there will be no need for further treatment.* ◇ *I would normally suggest taking time off work, but* ***in this instance*** *I'm not sure that would do any good.* ➲ **SYNONYMS** at EXAMPLE

IDM **for 'instance** 0‑π for example: *What would you do, for instance, if you found a member of staff stealing?* ➲ **LANGUAGE BANK** at EXAMPLE, E.G. **in the 'first instance** (*formal*) as the first part of a series of actions: *In the first instance, notify the police and then contact your insurance company.*

■ ***verb*** **~ sth** (*formal*) to give sth as an example

in·stant /'ɪnstənt/ *adj., noun*

■ ***adj.*** **1** [usually before noun] happening immediately **SYN** **immediate**: *She took an instant dislike to me.* ◇ *This account gives you instant access to your money.* ◇ *The show was an instant success.* **2** [only before noun] (of food) that can be made quickly and easily, usually by adding hot water: *instant coffee*

■ ***noun*** [usually sing.] **1** a very short period of time **SYN** **moment**: *I'll be back in an instant.* ◇ *Just for an instant I thought he was going to refuse.* **2** a particular point in time: *At that (very) instant, the door opened.* ◇ *I recognized her* ***the instant*** *(****that****)* (= as soon as) *I saw her.* ◇ *Come here* ***this instant!*** (= immediately)

in·stant·an·eous /ˌɪnstən'teɪniəs/ *adj.* happening immediately: *an instantaneous response* ◇ *Death was almost instantaneous.* ▶ **in·stant·an·eous·ly** *adv.*

in·stant·ly /'ɪnstəntli/ *adv.* immediately: *Her voice is instantly recognizable.* ◇ *The driver was killed instantly.*

ˌinstant 'messaging *noun* [U] a system on the Internet that allows people to exchange written messages with each other very quickly

ˌinstant 'replay (*NAmE*) (*BrE* **ˌaction 'replay**) *noun* part of sth, for example a sports game on television, that is immediately repeated, often more slowly, so that you can see a goal or another exciting or important moment again

in·stead 0‑π /ɪn'sted/ *adv.* in the place of sb/sth: *Lee was ill so I went instead.* ◇ *He didn't reply. Instead, he turned on his heel and left the room.* ◇ *She said nothing, preferring instead to save her comments till later.*

in'stead of 0‑π *prep.* in the place of sb/sth: *We just had soup instead of a full meal.* ◇ *Now I can walk to work instead of going by car.*

in·step /'ɪnstep/ *noun* **1** the top part of the foot between the ankle and toes ➲ **VISUAL VOCAB** page V48 **2** the part of a shoe that covers the instep

in·sti·gate /'ɪnstɪɡeɪt/ *verb* (*formal*) **1 ~ sth** (*especially BrE*) to make sth start or happen, usually sth official **SYN** **bring sth about**: *The government has instigated a programme of economic reform.* **2 ~ sth** to cause sth bad to happen: *They were accused of instigating racial violence.*

in·sti·ga·tion /ˌɪnstɪ'ɡeɪʃn/ *noun* [U] the act of causing sth to begin or happen: *An appeal fund was launched* ***at the instigation of*** *the President.* ◇ *It was done* ***at his instigation.***

in·sti·ga·tor /'ɪnstɪɡeɪtə(r)/ *noun* **~ (of sth)** a person who causes sth to happen, especially sth bad: *the instigators of the riots*

in·stil (*BrE*) (*NAmE* **in·still**) /ɪn'stɪl/ *verb* (-ll-) **~ sth (in/into sb)** to gradually make sb feel, think or behave in a particular way over a period of time: *to* ***instil confidence/discipline/fear*** *into sb*

in·stinct /'ɪnstɪŋkt/ *noun* [U, C] **1 ~ (for sth/for doing sth)** | **~ (to do sth)** a natural tendency for people and animals to behave in a particular way using the knowledge and abilities that they were born with rather than thought or training: *maternal instincts* ◇ *Children do not know* ***by instinct*** *the difference between right and wrong.* ◇ *His first instinct was to run away.* ◇ *Horses have a well-developed instinct for fear.* ◇ *Even at school, he showed he* ***had an instinct for*** (= was naturally good at) *business.* **2 ~ (that...)** a feeling that makes you do sth or believe that sth is true, even though it is not based on facts or reason **SYN** **intuition**: *Her instincts had been right.*

in·stinct·ive /ɪn'stɪŋktɪv/ *adj.* based on instinct, not thought or training: *instinctive knowledge* ◇ *She's an instinctive player.* ◇ *My instinctive reaction was to deny everything.* ▶ **in·stinct·ive·ly** *adv.*: *He knew instinctively that something was wrong.*

in·stinct·ual /ɪn'stɪŋktʃuəl/ *adj.* (*psychology*) based on natural instinct; not learned

in·sti·tute 0‑π AW /'ɪnstɪtjuːt; *NAmE* -tuːt/ *noun, verb*

■ ***noun*** 0‑π an organization that has a particular purpose, especially one that is connected with education or a particular profession; the building used by this organization: *a research institute* ◇ *the Institute of Chartered Accountants* ◇ *institutes of higher education*

■ ***verb*** **~ sth** (*formal*) to introduce a system, policy, etc. or start a process: *to institute criminal proceedings against sb* ◇ *The new management intends to institute a number of changes.*

in·sti·tu·tion 0‑π AW /ˌɪnstɪ'tjuːʃn; *NAmE* -'tuːʃn/ *noun*

1 0‑π [C] a large important organization that has a particular purpose, for example, a university or bank: *an* ***educational/financial, etc. institution*** ◇ *the Smithsonian Institution* **2** [C] (usually *disapproving*) a building where people with special needs are taken care of, for example because they are old or mentally ill: *a mental institution* ◇ *We want this to be like a home, not an institution.* **3** [C] a custom or system that has existed for a long time among a particular group of people: *the institution of marriage* **4** [U] the act of starting or introducing sth such as a system or a law: *the institution of new safety procedures* **5** [C] (*informal, humorous*) a person who is well known because they have been in a particular place or job for a long time: *You must know him—he's an institution around here!*

in·sti·tu·tion·al AW /ˌɪnstɪ'tjuːʃənl; *NAmE* -'tuː-/ *adj.* [usually before noun] connected with an institution: *institutional investors* ◇ *institutional care* ▶ **in·sti·tu·tion·al·ly** AW /-ʃənəli/ *adv.*

in·sti·tu·tion·al·ize (*BrE* also **-ise**) AW /ˌɪnstɪ'tjuːʃənəlaɪz; *NAmE* -'tuː-/ *verb* **1 ~ sb** to send sb who is not capable of living independently to live in a special building (= an institution) especially when it is for a long period of time **2 ~ sth** to make sth become part of an organized system, society or culture, so that it is considered normal ▶ **in·sti·tu·tion·al·iza·tion, -isa·tion** /ˌɪnstɪˌtjuːʃənəlaɪ'zeɪʃn; *NAmE* -ˌtuːʃənələ'z-/ *noun* [U]

in·sti·tu·tion·al·ized (*BrE* also **-ised**) AW /ˌɪnstɪ'tjuːʃənəlaɪzd; *NAmE* -'tuː-/ *adj.* **1** (usually *disapproving*) that has happened or been done for so long that it is considered normal: *institutionalized racism* **2** (of people) lacking the ability to live and think independently because they have spent so long in an institution: *institutionalized patients*

ˌin-ˈstore *adj.* [only before noun] within a large shop/store: *an in-store bakery*

in·struct AW /ɪnˈstrʌkt/ *verb* **1** (*formal*) to tell sb to do sth, especially in a formal or official way SYN **direct, order**: **~ sb to do sth** *The letter instructed him to report to headquarters immediately.* ◇ **~ sb where, what, etc...** *You will be instructed where to go as soon as the plane is ready.* ◇ **~ sb** *She arrived at 10 o'clock* ***as instructed.*** ◇ **~ that...** *He instructed that a wall be built around the city.* ◇ (*BrE* also) *He instructed that a wall should be built around the city.* ◇ **~ (sb) + speech** *'Put it there,' she instructed (them).* ➲ note at ORDER **2 ~ sb (in sth)** (*formal*) to teach sb sth, especially a practical skill: *All our staff have been instructed in sign language.* **3** [usually passive] **~ sb that...** (*formal*) to give sb information about sth: *We* ***have been instructed that*** *a decision will not be made before the end of the week.* **4 ~ sb (to do sth)** (*law*) to employ sb to represent you in a legal situation, especially as a lawyer

in·struc·tion 0→ AW /ɪnˈstrʌkʃn/ *noun, adj.*

■ *noun* **1** 0→ **instructions** [pl.] detailed information on how to do or use sth SYN **directions**: ***Follow the instructions*** *on the packet carefully.* ◇ *Always* ***read the instructions*** *before you start.* ◇ **~ on how to do sth** *The plant comes with* ***full instructions*** *on how to care for it.* **2** 0→ [C, usually pl.] **~ (to do sth)** | **~ (that...)** something that sb tells you to do SYN **order**: *to* ***ignore/carry out sb's instructions*** ◇ *I'm* ***under instructions*** *to keep my speech short.* **3** [C] a piece of information that tells a computer to perform a particular operation. **4** [U] **~ (in sth)** (*formal*) the act of teaching sth to sb: *religious instruction*

■ *adj.* [only before noun] giving detailed information on how to do or use sth (= giving instructions): *an* ***instruction book/manual***

in·struc·tion·al /ɪnˈstrʌkʃənl/ *adj.* [usually before noun] (*formal*) that teaches people sth: *instructional materials*

in·struct·ive AW /ɪnˈstrʌktɪv/ *adj.* giving a lot of useful information: *a most instructive experience* ◇ *It is instructive to see how other countries are tackling the problem.* ▸ **in·struct·ive·ly** *adv.*

in·struct·or AW /ɪnˈstrʌktə(r)/ *noun* **1** a person whose job is to teach sb a practical skill or sport: *a driving instructor* **2** (*NAmE*) a teacher below the rank of ASSISTANT PROFESSOR at a college or university

in·stru·ment 0→ /ˈɪnstrəmənt/ *noun*
1 0→ a tool or device used for a particular task, especially for delicate or scientific work: ***surgical/optical/precision, etc. instruments*** ◇ *instruments of torture* **2** 0→ = MUSICAL INSTRUMENT: *Is he learning an instrument?* ◇ ***brass/stringed, etc. instruments*** **3** 0→ a device used for measuring speed, distance, temperature, etc. in a vehicle or on a piece of machinery: *the flight instruments* ◇ *the instrument panel* **4** (*formal*) something that is used by sb in order to achieve sth; a person or thing that makes sth happen: **~ for sth/for doing sth** *The law is not the best instrument for dealing with family matters.* ◇ **~ of sth** *an instrument of change* **5 ~ of sb/sth** (*formal*) a person who is used and controlled by sb/sth that is more powerful: *an instrument of fate* **6** (*law*) a formal legal document

in·stru·men·tal /ˌɪnstrəˈmentl/ *adj., noun*

■ *adj.* **1 ~ (in sth/in doing sth)** important in making sth happen: *He was instrumental in bringing about an end to the conflict.* **2** made by or for musical instruments: *instrumental music* ▸ **in·stru·men·tal·ly** /-təli/ *adv.*

■ *noun* **1** a piece of music (usually popular music) in which only musical instruments are used with no singing **2** (*grammar*) (in some languages) the form of a noun, pronoun or adjective when it refers to a thing that is used to do sth

in·stru·men·tal·ist /ˌɪnstrəˈmentəlɪst/ *noun* a person who plays a musical instrument ➲ compare VOCALIST

in·stru·men·ta·tion /ˌɪnstrəmenˈteɪʃn/ *noun* [U] **1** a set of instruments used in operating a vehicle or a piece of machinery **2** the way in which a piece of music is written for a particular group of instruments

in·sub·or·din·ation /ˌɪnsəˌbɔːdɪˈneɪʃn; *NAmE* -ˌbɔːrd-/ *noun* [U] (*formal*) the refusal to obey orders or show respect for sb who has a higher rank SYN **disobedience** ▸ **in·sub·or·din·ate** /ˌɪnsəˈbɔːdɪnət; *NAmE* -ˈbɔːrd-/ *adj.*

in·sub·stan·tial /ˌɪnsəbˈstænʃl/ *adj.* **1** not very large, strong or important: *an insubstantial construction of wood and glue* ◇ *an insubstantial argument* **2** (*literary*) not real or solid: *as insubstantial as a shadow*

in·suf·fer·able /ɪnˈsʌfrəbl/ *adj.* extremely annoying, unpleasant and difficult to bear SYN **unbearable** ▸ **in·suf·fer·ably** /-əbli/ *adv.*: *insufferably hot*

in·suf·fi·cient AW /ˌɪnsəˈfɪʃnt/ *adj.* **~ (to do sth)** | **~ (for sth)** (*formal*) not large, strong or important enough for a particular purpose SYN **inadequate**: *insufficient time* ◇ *His salary is insufficient to meet his needs.* OPP **sufficient** ▸ **in·suf·fi·cient·ly** AW *adv.* **in·suf·fi·ciency** /-ʃənsi/ *noun* [U, sing.] (*technical*): *cardiac insufficiency*

in·su·lar /ˈɪnsjələ(r); *NAmE* ˈɪnsələr/ *adj.* **1** (*disapproving*) only interested in your own country, ideas, etc. and not in those from outside: *The British are often accused of being insular.* **2** (*technical*) connected with an island or islands: *the coastal and insular areas* ▸ **in·su·lar·ity** /ˌɪnsjuˈlærəti; *NAmE* -səˈl-/ *noun* [U]

in·su·late /ˈɪnsjuleɪt; *NAmE* -səl-/ *verb* **1 ~ sth (from/against sth)** to protect sth with a material that prevents heat, sound, electricity, etc. from passing through: *Home owners are being encouraged to insulate their homes to save energy.* ➲ COLLOCATIONS at DECORATE **2 ~ sb/sth from/against sth** to protect sb/sth from unpleasant experiences or influences SYN **shield**

in·su·lated /ˈɪnsjuleɪtɪd; *NAmE* -səl-/ *adj.* protected with a material that prevents heat, sound, electricity, etc. from passing through: *insulated wires* ◇ *a well-insulated house*

in·su·lat·ing /ˈɪnsjuleɪtɪŋ; *NAmE* ˈɪnsəleɪtɪŋ/ *adj.* [only before noun] preventing heat, sound, electricity, etc. from passing through: *insulating materials*

ˈinsulating tape (*US* also **ˈfriction tape**) *noun* [U] a strip of sticky material used for covering the ends of electrical wires to prevent the possibility of an electric shock

in·su·la·tion /ˌɪnsjuˈleɪʃn; *NAmE* -səˈl-/ *noun* [U] the act of protecting sth with a material that prevents heat, sound, electricity, etc. from passing through; the materials used for this: *Better insulation of your home will help to reduce heating bills.* ◇ *foam insulation* ➲ COLLOCATIONS at DECORATE

in·su·la·tor /ˈɪnsjuleɪtə(r); *NAmE* -səl-/ *noun* a material or device used to prevent heat, electricity, or sound from escaping from sth

in·su·lin /ˈɪnsjəlɪn; *NAmE* -səl-/ *noun* [U] a chemical substance produced in the body that controls the amount of sugar in the blood (by influencing the rate at which it is removed); a similar artificial substance given to people whose bodies do not produce enough naturally: *insulin-dependent diabetes*

in·sult 0→ *verb, noun*

■ *verb* 0→ /ɪnˈsʌlt/ **~ sb/sth** to say or do sth that offends sb: *I have never been so insulted in my life!* ◇ *She felt insulted by the low offer.*

■ *noun* 0→ /ˈɪnsʌlt/ a remark or an action that is said or done in order to offend sb: *The crowd were shouting insults at the police.* ◇ **~ to sb/sth** *His comments were seen as an insult to the president.* ◇ *The questions were an* ***insult to our intelligence*** (= too easy). IDM see ADD

in·sult·ing 0→ /ɪnˈsʌltɪŋ/ *adj.* causing or intending to cause sb to feel offended: *insulting remarks* ◇ **~ to sb/sth** *She was really insulting to me.*

in·su·per·able /ɪnˈsuːpərəbl; *BrE* also -ˈsjuː-/ *adj.* (*formal*) (of difficulties, problems, etc.) that cannot be dealt with successfully SYN **insurmountable**

in·sup·port·able /ˌɪnsəˈpɔːtəbl; *NAmE* -ˈpɔːrt-/ *adj.* so bad or difficult that you cannot accept it or deal with it **SYN** **intolerable**

in·sur·ance 🔑 /ɪnˈʃʊərəns; -ˈʃɔːr-; *NAmE* -ˈʃʊr-/ *noun*
1 🔑 [U, C] an arrangement with a company in which you pay them regular amounts of money and they agree to pay the costs, for example, if you die or are ill/sick, or if you lose or damage sth: ***life/car/travel/household, etc. insurance*** ◇ *to have adequate* ***insurance cover*** ◇ **~** (**against sth**) *to* ***take out insurance*** *against fire and theft* ◇ ***insurance premiums*** (= the regular payments made for insurance) ◇ *Can you claim for the loss* ***on your insurance****?* ➲ see also NATIONAL INSURANCE **2** 🔑 [U] the business of providing people with insurance: *an* ***insurance broker/company*** ◇ *He works in insurance.* **3** [U] money paid by or to an insurance company: *to pay insurance on your house* ◇ *When her husband died, she received £50 000 in insurance.* **4** [U, C] **~** (**against sth**) something you do to protect yourself against sth bad happening in the future: *At that time people had large families as an insurance against some children dying.*

in'surance adjuster (*NAmE*) (*BrE* **'loss adjuster**) *noun* a person who works for an insurance company and whose job is to calculate how much money sb should receive after they have lost sth or had sth damaged

in'surance policy *noun* a written contract between a person and an insurance company: *a travel insurance policy* ◇ (*figurative*) *Always make a backup disk as an insurance policy.*

in·sure /ɪnˈʃʊə(r); -ˈʃɔː(r); *NAmE* -ˈʃʊr/ *verb* **1** [T, I] to buy insurance so that you will receive money if your property, car, etc. gets damaged or stolen, or if you get ill/sick or die: **~ sth/yourself** (**for sth**) *The painting is insured for $1 million.* ◇ **~ sth/yourself** (**against sth**) *Luckily he had insured himself against long-term illness.* ◇ (*figurative*) *Having a lot of children is a way of insuring themselves against loneliness in old age.* ◇ **~ against sth** *We strongly recommend insuring against sickness or injury.* **2** [T] **~ sb/sth** to sell insurance to sb for sth: *The company can refuse to insure a property that does not have window locks.* **3** (*especially NAmE*) = ENSURE

in·sured /ɪnˈʃʊəd; -ˈʃɔːd; *NAmE* -ˈʃʊrd/ *adj.* **1** having insurance: *Was the vehicle insured?* ◇ **~ to do sth** *You're not insured to drive our car.* ◇ **~ against sth** *It isn't insured against theft.* **2 the insured** *noun* (*pl.* **the insured**) (*law*) the person who has made an agreement with an insurance company and who receives money if, for example, they are ill/sick or if they lose or damage sth

in·surer /ɪnˈʃʊərə(r); -ˈʃɔːr-; *NAmE* -ˈʃʊr-/ *noun* a person or company that provides people with insurance

in·sur·gency /ɪnˈsɜːdʒənsi; *NAmE* -ˈsɜːrdʒ-/ *noun* [U, C] (*pl.* **-ies**) an attempt to take control of a country by force **SYN** **rebellion** ➲ COLLOCATIONS at WAR ➲ see also COUNTER-INSURGENCY

in·sur·gent /ɪnˈsɜːdʒənt; *NAmE* -ˈsɜːrdʒ-/ *noun* [usually pl.] (*formal*) a person fighting against the government or armed forces of their own country **SYN** **rebel** ▸ **in·sur·gent** *adj.* **SYN** **rebellious**

in·sur·mount·able /ˌɪnsəˈmaʊntəbl; *NAmE* -sərˈm-/ *adj.* (*formal*) (of difficulties, problems, etc.) that cannot be dealt with successfully **SYN** **insuperable**

in·sur·rec·tion /ˌɪnsəˈrekʃn/ *noun* [C, U] a situation in which a large group of people try to take political control of their own country with violence **SYN** **uprising** ▸ **in·sur·rec·tion·ary** /ˌɪnsəˈrekʃənri; *NAmE* -neri/ *adj.*

in·tact /ɪnˈtækt/ *adj.* [not usually before noun] complete and not damaged **SYN** **undamaged**: *Most of the house* ***remains intact*** *even after two hundred years.* ◇ *He emerged from the trial with his reputation intact.*

in·take /ˈɪnteɪk/ *noun* **1** [U, C] the amount of food, drink, etc. that you take into your body: *high fluid intake* ◇ *to reduce your daily intake of salt* **2** [C, U] the number of people who are allowed to enter a school, college, profession, etc. during a particular period: *the annual student intake* **3** [C] a place where liquid, air, etc. enters a machine: *the* ***air/fuel intake*** **4** [C, usually sing.] an act of taking sth in, especially breath: *a sharp intake of breath*

in·tan·gible /ɪnˈtændʒəbl/ *adj.* **1** that exists but that is difficult to describe, understand or measure: *The old building had an intangible air of sadness about it.* ◇ *The benefits are intangible.* **2** (*business*) that does not exist as a physical thing but is still valuable to a company: ***intangible assets/property*** **OPP** **tangible** ▸ **in·tan·gible** *noun* [usually pl.]: *intangibles such as staff morale and goodwill*

in·te·ger /ˈɪntɪdʒə(r)/ *noun* (*mathematics*) a whole number, such as 3 or 4 but not 3.5 ➲ compare FRACTION

in·te·gral **AW** /ˈɪntɪɡrəl; ɪnˈteɡ-/ *adj.* **1** being an essential part of sth: *Music is* ***an integral part of*** *the school's curriculum.* ◇ **~ to sth** *Practical experience is integral to the course.* **2** [usually before noun] included as part of sth, rather than supplied separately: *All models have an integral CD player.* **3** [usually before noun] having all the parts that are necessary for sth to be complete: *an integral system* ▸ **in·te·gral·ly** /ˈɪntɪɡrəli; ɪnˈteɡ-/ *adv.*

ˌintegral 'calculus *noun* [U] (*mathematics*) a type of mathematics that deals with quantities that change in time. It is used to calculate a quantity between two particular moments. ➲ compare DIFFERENTIAL CALCULUS

in·te·grate **AW** /ˈɪntɪɡreɪt/ *verb* **1** [I, T] to combine two or more things so that they work together; to combine with sth else in this way: **~ into/with sth** *These programs will integrate with your existing software.* ◇ **~ A** (**into/with B**) | **~ A and B** *These programs can be integrated with your existing software.* **2** [I, T] to become or make sb become accepted as a member of a social group, especially when they come from a different culture: **~** (**into/with sth**) *They have not made any effort to integrate with the local community.* ◇ **~ sb** (**into/with sth**) *The policy is to integrate children with special needs into ordinary schools.* ➲ compare SEGREGATE

in·te·grated **AW** /ˈɪntɪɡreɪtɪd/ *adj.* [usually before noun] in which many different parts are closely connected and work successfully together: *an integrated transport system* (= including buses, trains, taxis, etc.) ◇ *an integrated school* (= attended by students of all races and religions)

ˌintegrated 'circuit *noun* (*physics*) a small MICROCHIP that contains a large number of electrical connections and performs the same function as a larger CIRCUIT made from separate parts

in·te·gra·tion **AW** /ˌɪntɪˈɡreɪʃn/ *noun* **1** [U, C] the act or process of combining two or more things so that they work together (= of integrating them): *The aim is to promote closer economic integration.* ◇ *His music is an integration of tradition and new technology.* **2** [U] the act or process of mixing people who have previously been separated, usually because of colour, race, religion, etc: *racial integration in schools* ➲ COLLOCATIONS at RACE

in·teg·rity **AW** /ɪnˈteɡrəti/ *noun* [U] **1** the quality of being honest and having strong moral principles: ***personal/professional/artistic integrity*** ◇ *to behave with integrity* **2** (*formal*) the state of being whole and not divided **SYN** **unity**: *to respect the territorial integrity of the nation*

in·tel·lect /ˈɪntəlekt/ *noun* **1** [U, C] the ability to think in a logical way and understand things, especially at an advanced level; your mind: *a man of considerable intellect* **2** [C] a very intelligent person: *She was one of the most formidable intellects of her time.*

in·tel·lec·tual /ˌɪntəˈlektʃuəl/ *adj., noun*
■ ***adj.*** **1** [usually before noun] connected with or using a person's ability to think in a logical way and understand things **SYN** **mental**: *intellectual curiosity* ◇ *an intellectual novel* **2** (of a person) well educated and enjoying activities in which you have to think seriously about things: *She's very intellectual.* ▸ **in·tel·lec·tual·ism** /ˌɪntəˈlektʃuəlɪzəm/ *noun* [U] (usually *disapproving*) **in·tel·lec·tu·al·ly** *adv.*: *intellectually challenging*
■ ***noun*** a person who is well educated and enjoys activities in which they have to think seriously about things

I

ˌ**intelˌlectual ˈproperty** *noun* [U] (*law*) an idea, a design, etc. that sb has created and that the law prevents other people from copying: *intellectual property rights*

in·tel·li·gence 0-w AW /ɪnˈtelɪdʒəns/ *noun* [U] **1** 0-w the ability to learn, understand and think in a logical way about things; the ability to do this well: *a person of* ***high/average/low intelligence*** ◇ *He didn't even have the intelligence to call for an ambulance.* ⊃ see also ARTIFICIAL INTELLIGENCE, EMOTIONAL INTELLIGENCE **2** 0-w secret information that is collected, for example about a foreign country, especially one that is an enemy; the people that collect this information: *intelligence reports* ◇ *the US Central Intelligence Agency*

inˈtelligence quotient *noun* = IQ

inˈtelligence test *noun* a test to measure how well a person is able to understand and think in a logical way about things

in·tel·li·gent 0-w AW /ɪnˈtelɪdʒənt/ *adj.* **1** 0-w good at learning, understanding and thinking in a logical way about things; showing this ability: *a* ***highly intelligent*** *child* ◇ *to ask an intelligent question* OPP **unintelligent** **2** 0-w (of an animal, a being, etc.) able to understand and learn things: *a search for intelligent life on other planets* **3** (*computing*) (of a computer, program, etc.) able to store information and use it in new situations: ***intelligent software/systems*** ▶ **in·tel·li·gent·ly** AW *adv.*

Synonyms

intelligent

smart • clever • brilliant • bright

These words all describe people who are good at learning, understanding and thinking about things, and the actions that show this ability.

- **intelligent** good at learning, understanding and thinking in a logical way about things; showing this ability: *He's a* ***highly intelligent*** *man.* ◇ *She asked a lot of intelligent questions.*
- **smart** (*especially NAmE*) quick at learning and understanding things; showing the ability to make good business or personal decisions: *She's smarter than her brother.* ◇ *That was a smart career move.*
- **clever** (*sometimes disapproving, especially BrE*) quick at learning and understanding things; showing this ability: *How clever of you to work it out!* ◇ *He's* ***too clever by half,*** *if you ask me.* NOTE People use **clever** in the phrase : *Clever boy/girl!* to tell a young child that they have learnt or done sth well. When used to or about an adult **clever** can be disapproving.
- **brilliant** extremely intelligent or skilful: *He's a brilliant young scientist.*
- **bright** intelligent; quick to learn: *She's probably the brightest student in the class.* NOTE **Bright** is used especially to talk about young people. Common collocations of **bright** include *girl, boy, kid, student, pupil.*

PATTERNS

- clever/brilliant **at** sth
- a(n) intelligent/smart/clever/brilliant/bright **child/boy/girl/man/woman**
- a(n) intelligent/smart/clever/brilliant **thing to do**

inˌtelligent deˈsign *noun* [U] the belief that the universe and living things were created by an intelligent being: *the legal battle about the teaching of intelligent design as science* ⊃ compare CREATIONISM

in·tel·li·gent·sia /ɪnˌtelɪˈdʒentsiə/ (usually **the intelligentsia**) *noun* [sing.+ sing./pl. v.] the people in a country or society who are well educated and are interested in culture, politics, literature, etc.

in·tel·li·gible /ɪnˈtelɪdʒəbl/ *adj.* ~ **(to sb)** that can be easily understood SYN **understandable**: *His lecture was readily intelligible to all the students.* OPP **unintelligible** ▶ **in·tel·li·gi·bil·ity** /ɪnˌtelɪdʒəˈbɪləti/ *noun* [U] **in·tel·li·gibly** *adv.*

in·tem·per·ate /ɪnˈtempərət/ *adj.* (*formal*) **1** showing a lack of control over yourself: *intemperate language* OPP **temperate** **2** (*especially NAmE*) regularly drinking too much alcohol ▶ **in·tem·per·ance** /-pərəns/ *noun* [U]

in·tend 0-w /ɪnˈtend/ *verb* **1** 0-w [I, T] to have a plan, result or purpose in your mind when you do sth: *We finished later than we had intended.* ◇ ~ **to do sth** *I* ***fully intended*** (= definitely intended) *to pay for the damage.* ◇ ~ **sb/sth to do sth** *The writer clearly intends his readers to identify with the main character.* ◇ ~ **doing sth** (*BrE*) *I don't intend staying long.* ◇ ~ **sth** *The company intends a slow-down in expansion.* ◇ ~ **sb sth** *He intended her no harm* (= it was not his plan to harm her). ◇ **it is intended that...** *It is intended that production will start next month.* ◇ ~ **that...** *We intend that production will start next month.* **2** 0-w [T] (rather *formal*) to plan that sth should have a particular meaning SYN **mean:** ~ **sth (by sth)** *What exactly did you intend by that remark?* ◇ ~ **sth (as sth)** *He intended it as a joke.*

WORD FAMILY
intend *verb*
intended *adj.* (≠ unintended)
intention *noun*
intentional *adj.* (≠ unintentional)
intentionally *adv.* (≠ unintentionally)

in·tend·ed 0-w /ɪnˈtendɪd/ *adj.* **1** 0-w [only before noun] that you are trying to achieve or reach: *the intended purpose* ◇ *the intended audience* ◇ *The bullet missed its intended target.* **2** 0-w planned or designed for sb/sth: ~ **for sb/sth** *The book is intended for children.* ◇ ~ **as sth** *The notes are intended as an introduction to the course.* ◇ ~ **to be/do sth** *This list is not intended to be a complete catalogue.* ⊃ see also UNINTENDED

in·tense AW /ɪnˈtens/ *adj.* **1** very great; very strong SYN **extreme**: *intense heat/cold/pain* ◇ *The President is under intense pressure to resign.* ◇ *the intense blue of her eyes* ◇ *intense interest/pleasure/desire/anger* **2** serious and often involving a lot of action in a short period of time: *intense competition* ◇ *It was a period of intense activity.* **3** (of a person) having or showing very strong feelings, opinions or thoughts about sb/sth: *an intense look* ◇ *He's very intense about everything.* ⊃ compare INTENSIVE ▶ **in·tense·ly** AW *adv.*: *She disliked him intensely.*

in·ten·si·fier /ɪnˈtensɪfaɪə(r)/ *noun* (*grammar*) a word, especially an adjective or an adverb, for example *so* or *very*, that makes the meaning of another word stronger

in·ten·sify AW /ɪnˈtensɪfaɪ/ *verb* (**in·ten·si·fies, in·ten·si·fy·ing, in·ten·si·fied, in·ten·si·fied**) [I, T] to increase in degree or strength; to make sth increase in degree or strength SYN **heighten**: *Violence intensified during the night.* ◇ ~ **sth** *The opposition leader has intensified his attacks on the government.* ▶ **in·tensi·fi·ca·tion** AW /ɪnˌtensɪfɪˈkeɪʃn/ *noun* [U, sing.]

in·ten·sity AW /ɪnˈtensəti/ *noun* (*pl.* -ies) **1** [U, sing.] the state or quality of being intense: *intensity of light/sound/colour* ◇ *intensity of feeling/concentration/relief* ◇ *He was watching her with an intensity that was unnerving.* ◇ *The storm resumed with even greater intensity.* **2** [U, C] (*technical*) the strength of sth, for example light, that can be measured: *varying intensities of natural light*

in·ten·sive AW /ɪnˈtensɪv/ *adj.* **1** involving a lot of work or activity done in a short time: *an intensive language course* ◇ *two weeks of intensive training* ◇ *intensive diplomatic negotiations* **2** extremely thorough; done with a lot of care: *His disappearance has been the subject of intensive investigation.* **3** (of methods of farming) aimed at producing as much food as possible using as little land or as little money as possible: *Traditionally reared animals grow more slowly than those reared under intensive farming conditions.* ◇ *intensive agriculture* ⊃ see also CAPITAL-INTENSIVE, LABOUR-INTENSIVE ▶ **in·ten·sive·ly** AW *adv.*: *This case has been intensively studied.* ◇ *intensively farmed land*

inˌtensive ˈcare *noun* [U] **1** continuous care and attention, often using special equipment, for people in hospital who are very seriously ill or injured: *She needed intensive care for several days.* ◇ *intensive care patients/beds* **2** (also **in,tensive 'care unit** [C]) (*abbr.* **ICU**) the part of a hospital that provides intensive care: *The baby was* ***in intensive care*** *for 48 hours.*

in·tent /ɪnˈtent/ *adj., noun*

■ ***adj.*** **1** showing strong interest and attention: *an* ***intent gaze/look*** ◇ *His eyes were suddenly intent.* **2** (*formal*) determined to do sth, especially sth that will harm other people: **~ on/upon sth** *They were intent on murder.* ◇ **~ on/upon doing sth** *Are you intent upon destroying my reputation?* **3 ~ on/upon sth** giving all your attention to sth: *I was so intent on my work that I didn't notice the time.* ▸ **in·tent·ly** *adv.*: *She looked at him intently.*

■ ***noun*** [U] **~ (to do sth)** (*formal* or *law*) what you intend to do SYN **intention**: *She denies possessing the drug with intent to supply.* ◇ *a* ***letter/statement of intent*** ◇ *His intent is clearly not to placate his critics.*

IDM **to all intents and 'purposes** (*BrE*) (*NAmE* **for all intents and 'purposes**) in the effects that sth has, if not in reality; almost completely: *By 1981 the docks had, to all intents and purposes, closed.* ◇ *The two items are, to all intents and purposes, identical.*

in·ten·tion 0‑w /ɪnˈtenʃn/ *noun* [C, U] what you intend or plan to do; your aim: **~ (of doing sth)** *I* ***have no intention of*** *going to the wedding.* ◇ *He left England* ***with the intention of*** *travelling in Africa.* ◇ *I* ***have every intention*** *of paying her back what I owe her.* ◇ **~ (to do sth)** *He has announced his intention to retire.* ◇ **~ (that…)** *It was not my intention that she should suffer.* ◇ *The original intention was to devote three months to the project.* ◇ *She's full of* ***good intentions*** *but they rarely work out.* ◇ *I did it* ***with the best*** (*of*) ***intentions*** (= meaning to help), *but I only succeeded in annoying them.* ➲ SYNONYMS at PURPOSE ➲ see also WELL INTENTIONED IDM see ROAD

in·ten·tion·al /ɪnˈtenʃənl/ *adj.* done deliberately SYN **deliberate, intended**: *I'm sorry I left you off the list —it wasn't intentional.* OPP **unintentional** ▸ **in·ten·tion·al·ly** /-ʃənəli/ *adv.*: *She would never intentionally hurt anyone.* ◇ *I kept my statement intentionally vague.*

inter /ɪnˈtɜː(r)/ *verb* (**-rr-**) [usually passive] **~ sb** (*formal*) to bury a dead person OPP **disinter** ➲ see also INTERMENT

inter- /ˈɪntə(r)/ *prefix* (in verbs, nouns, adjectives and adverbs) between; from one to another: *interface* ◇ *interaction* ◇ *international* ➲ compare INTRA-

inter·act AW /ˌɪntərˈækt/ *verb* **1** [I] **~ (with sb)** to communicate with sb, especially while you work, play or spend time with them: *Teachers have a limited amount of time to interact with each child.* **2** [I] **~ (with sth)** if one thing **interacts** with another, or if two things **interact**, the two things have an effect on each other: *Perfume interacts with the skin's natural chemicals.* ▸ **inter·action** AW /-ˈækʃn/ *noun* [U, C]: **~ (between sb/sth)** *the interaction between performers and their audience* ◇ **~ (with sb/sth)** *the interaction of bacteria with the body's natural chemistry*

inter·active AW /ˌɪntərˈæktɪv/ *adj.* **1** that involves people working together and having an influence on each other: *The school believes in interactive teaching methods.* **2** (*computing*) that allows information to be passed continuously and in both directions between a computer and the person who uses it: ***interactive systems/video*** ◇ ***an interactive whiteboard*** ➲ VISUAL VOCAB page V57 ▸ **inter·active·ly** AW *adv.* **inter·activ·ity** /ˌɪntərækˈtɪvəti/ *noun* [U]

inter alia /ˌɪntər ˈeɪliə/ *adv.* (from *Latin*, *formal*) among other things

inter·breed /ˌɪntəˈbriːd; *NAmE* -tərˈb-/ *verb* [I, T] **~ (sth) (with sth)** if animals from different SPECIES **interbreed**, or sb **interbreeds** them, they produce young together

inter·cede /ˌɪntəˈsiːd; *NAmE* -tərˈs-/ *verb* [I] **~ (with sb) (for/on behalf of sb)** (*formal*) to speak to sb in order to persuade them to have pity on sb else or to help settle an argument SYN **intervene**: *They interceded with the authorities on behalf of the detainees.* ▸ **inter·ces·sion** /ˌɪntəˈseʃn; *NAmE* -tərˈs-/ *noun* [U]: *the intercession of a priest*

inter·cept /ˌɪntəˈsept; *NAmE* -tərˈs-/ *verb* **~ sb/sth** to stop sb/sth that is going from one place to another from arriving: *Reporters intercepted him as he tried to leave the hotel.* ◇ *The letter was intercepted.* ▸ **inter·cep·tion** /ˌɪntəˈsepʃn; *NAmE* -tərˈs-/ *noun* [U, C]: *the interception of enemy radio signals*

inter·cept·or /ˌɪntəˈseptə(r); *NAmE* -tərˈs-/ *noun* a fast military plane that attacks enemy planes that are carrying bombs

inter·change *noun, verb*

■ ***noun*** /ˈɪntətʃeɪndʒ; *NAmE* -tərtʃ-/ **1** [C, U] the act of sharing or exchanging sth, especially ideas or information: *a continuous interchange of ideas* ◇ *electronic data interchange* **2** [C] a place where a road joins a major road such as a MOTORWAY or INTERSTATE, designed so that vehicles leaving or joining the road do not have to cross other lines of traffic

■ ***verb*** /ˌɪntəˈtʃeɪndʒ; *NAmE* -tərˈtʃ-/ **1** [T] **~ sth** to share or exchange ideas, information, etc. **2** [T, I] to put each of two things or people in the other's place; to move or be moved from one place to another in this way: **~ A and B** *to interchange the front and rear tyres of a car* ◇ **~ (A) (with B)** *to interchange the front tyres with the rear ones* ◇ *The front and rear tyres interchange* (= can be exchanged).

inter·change·able /ˌɪntəˈtʃeɪndʒəbl; *NAmE* -tərˈtʃ-/ *adj.* that can be exchanged, especially without affecting the way in which sth works: *The two words are virtually interchangeable* (= have almost the same meaning). ◇ **~ with sth** *The V8 engines are all interchangeable with each other.* ▸ **inter·change·abil·ity** /ˌɪntəˌtʃeɪndʒəˈbɪləti; *NAmE* -tərˌtʃ-/ *noun* [U] **inter·change·ably** *adv.*: *These terms are used interchangeably.*

inter·city /ˌɪntəˈsɪti; *NAmE* -tərˈs-/ *adj.* [usually before noun] (of transport) travelling between cities, usually with not many stops on the way: *an intercity rail service* ◇ *intercity travel*

inter·col·le·gi·ate /ˌɪntəkəˈliːdʒiət; *NAmE* ˌɪntərkə-/ *adj.* (*especially NAmE*) involving competition between colleges: *intercollegiate football*

inter·com /ˈɪntəkɒm; *NAmE* ˈɪntərkɑːm/ *noun* a system of communication by telephone or radio inside an office, plane, etc; the device you press or switch on to start using this system: *to announce sth* ***over the intercom*** ◇ *They called him on the intercom.*

inter·com·mu·ni·ca·tion /ˌɪntəkəˌmjuːnɪˈkeɪʃn; *NAmE* -tərkə-/ *noun* [U] the process of communicating between people or groups

inter·con·nect /ˌɪntəkəˈnekt; *NAmE* -tərkə-/ *verb* [T, I] to connect similar things; to be connected to or with similar things: **~ A with B** *Bad housing is interconnected with debt and poverty.* ◇ **~ A and B** *Bad housing, debt and poverty are interconnected.* ◇ **~ (with sth)** *separate bedrooms that interconnect* ▸ **inter·con·nec·tion** /-ˈnekʃn/ *noun* [C, U]: *interconnections between different parts of the brain*

inter·con·tin·en·tal /ˌɪntəˌkɒntɪˈnentl; *NAmE* ˌɪntərˌkɑːn-/ *adj.* [usually before noun] between continents: ***intercontinental flights/missiles/travel/trade***

inter·cos·tal /ˌɪntəˈkɒstl; *NAmE* ˌɪntərˈkɑːstl/ *adj.* (*anatomy*) located between the RIBS (= the curved bones that go around the chest): *intercostal muscles*

inter·course /ˈɪntəkɔːs; *NAmE* ˈɪntərkɔːrs/ *noun* [U] **1** = SEXUAL INTERCOURSE: *The prosecution stated that intercourse had occurred on several occasions.* ◇ *anal intercourse* **2** (*old-fashioned*) communication between people, countries, etc: *the importance of social intercourse between different age groups*

inter·cul·tural /ˌɪntəˈkʌltʃərəl; *NAmE* ˌɪntər-/ *adj.* existing or happening between different cultures

inter·cut /ˌɪntəˈkʌt; *NAmE* ˌɪntər-/ *verb* (**inter·cut·ting, inter·cut, inter·cut**) **~ sth (with sth)** (*technical*) to put a film/movie scene between two parts of a different scene: *Scenes of city life were intercut with interviews with local people.*

I

inter·de·nom·in·ation·al /ˌɪntədɪˌnɒmɪˈneɪʃənl; *NAmE* ˌɪntərdɪˌnɑːm-/ *adj.* shared by different religious groups (= different DENOMINATIONS)

inter·de·part·men·tal /ˌɪntəˌdiːpɑːtˈmentl; *NAmE* ˌɪntərˌdiːpɑːrt-/ *adj.* between departments; involving more than one department

inter·de·pend·ent /ˌɪntədɪˈpendənt; *NAmE* -tərdɪ-/ *adj.* that depend on each other; consisting of parts that depend on each other: *interdependent economies/organizations/relationships* ◇ *The world is becoming increasingly interdependent.* ▸ **inter·de·pend·ence** /-əns/ (also *less frequent* **inter·de·pend·ency** *pl.* -ies) *noun* [U, C]

inter·dict /ˈɪntədɪkt; *NAmE* ˈɪntərd-/ *noun* **1** (*law*) an official order from a court that orders you not to do sth **2** (*technical*) (in the Roman Catholic Church) an order banning sb from taking part in church services, etc.

inter·dic·tion /ˌɪntəˈdɪkʃn; *NAmE* -tərˈd-/ *noun* [U] (*formal, especially NAmE*) the act of stopping sth that is being transported from one place from reaching another place, especially by using force: *the Customs Service's drug interdiction programs*

inter·dis·cip·lin·ary /ˌɪntəˈdɪsəplɪnəri; *NAmE* ˌɪntərˈdɪsəplɪneri/ *adj.* involving different areas of knowledge or study: *interdisciplinary research* ◇ *an interdisciplinary approach*

inter·est 0-w /ˈɪntrəst; -trest/ *noun, verb*

■ ***noun***

▸ WANTING TO KNOW MORE **1** 0-w [sing., U] **~ (in sb/sth)** the feeling that you have when you want to know or learn more about sb/sth: *to* ***feel/have/show/express*** *(an)* ***interest*** *in sth* ◇ *Do your parents* ***take an interest in*** *your friends?* ◇ *By that time I had* ***lost*** *(****all****)* ***interest*** *in the idea.* ◇ *I watched* ***with interest.*** ◇ ***As a matter of interest*** (= I'd like to know), *what time did the party finish?* ◇ ***Just out of interest,*** *how much did it cost?* ➲ compare DISINTEREST

▸ ATTRACTION **2** 0-w [U] the quality that sth has when it attracts sb's attention or makes them want to know more about it: *There are many* ***places of interest*** *near the city.* ◇ *The subject* ***is of no interest*** *to me at all.* ◇ *These plants will add interest to your garden in winter.* ◇ *These documents are of great historical interest.* ◇ *to be of cultural/scientific interest* ➲ see also HUMAN INTEREST, LOVE INTEREST

▸ HOBBY **3** 0-w [C] an activity or a subject that you enjoy and that you spend your free time doing or studying: *Her main interests are music and tennis.* ◇ *He was a man of wide interests outside his work.* ➲ compare HOBBY

▸ MONEY **4** 0-w [U] **~ (on sth)** (*finance*) the extra money that you pay back when you borrow money or that you receive when you invest money: *to* ***pay interest*** *on a loan* ◇ *The money was repaid* ***with interest.*** ◇ ***interest charges/payments*** ◇ ***Interest rates*** *have risen by 1%.* ◇ ***high rates of interest*** ➲ see also COMPOUND INTEREST, SIMPLE INTEREST

▸ ADVANTAGE **5** [C, usually pl., U] a good result or an advantage for sb/sth: *to* ***promote/protect/safeguard*** *sb's* ***interests*** ◇ *She was acting entirely* ***in her own interests.*** ◇ *These reforms were* ***in the best interests of*** *local government.* ◇ *It is* ***in the public interest*** *that these facts are made known.* ➲ see also SELF-INTEREST

▸ SHARE IN BUSINESS **6** [C, usually pl.] **~ (in sth)** a share in a business or company and its profits: *She has business interests in France.* ◇ *American interests in Europe* (= money invested in European countries) ➲ see also CONTROLLING INTEREST

▸ CONNECTION **7** [C, U] **~ (in sth)** a connection with sth which affects your attitude to it, especially because you may benefit from it in some way: *I should, at this point,* ***declare my interest.*** ◇ *Organizations* ***have an interest in*** *ensuring that employee motivation is high.* ➲ compare DISINTEREST ➲ see also VESTED INTEREST

▸ GROUP OF PEOPLE **8** [C, usually pl.] a group of people who are in the same business or who share the same aims which they want to protect: *powerful farming interests* ◇ *relationships between local government and business interests*

IDM **do sth (back) with interest** to do the same thing to sb as they have done to you, but with more force, enthusiasm, etc. **have sb's interests at ˈheart** to want sb to be happy and successful even though your actions may not show this **in the interest(s) of sth** in order to help or achieve sth: *In the interest(s) of safety, smoking is forbidden.* ➲ more at CONFLICT *n.*

■ ***verb*** 0-w to attract your attention and make you feel interested; to make yourself give your attention to sth: **~ sb** *Politics doesn't interest me.* ◇ **~ sb/yourself in sth** *She has always interested herself in charity work.* ◇ **it interests sb to do sth** ***It may interest you to*** *know that Andy didn't accept the job.*

PHR V **ˈinterest sb in sth** to persuade sb to buy, do or eat sth: *Could I interest you in this model, Sir?*

Synonyms

interest

hobby • game • pastime

These are all words for activities that you do for pleasure in your spare time.

interest an activity or a subject that you do or study for pleasure in your spare time: *Her main interests are music and gardening.*

hobby an activity that you do for pleasure in your spare time: *His hobbies include swimming and cooking.*

game a children's activity when they play with toys, pretend to be sb else, etc; an activity that you do to have fun: *a game of cops and robbers* ◇ *He was playing games with the dog.*

pastime an activity that people do for pleasure in their spare time: *Eating out is the national pastime in France.*

INTEREST, HOBBY OR PASTIME?

A **hobby** is often more active than an **interest**: *His main hobby is football* (= he plays football). ◇ *His main interest is football* (= he watches and reads about football, and may or may not play it). **Pastime** is used when talking about people in general; when you are talking about yourself or an individual person it is more usual to use **interest** or **hobby**: ~~*Eating out is the national interest/hobby in France.*~~ ◇ ~~*Do you have any pastimes?*~~

PATTERNS

- a **popular** interest/hobby/pastime
- to **have/share** interests/hobbies
- to **take up/pursue** a(n) interest/hobby

Which Word?

interested / interesting / uninterested / disinterested / uninteresting

- The opposite of **interested** is **uninterested** or **not interested**: *He is completely uninterested in politics.* ◇ *I am not really interested in politics.*
- **Disinterested** means that you can be fair in judging a situation because you do not feel personally involved in it: *A solicitor can give you disinterested advice.* However, in speech it is sometimes used instead of **uninterested**, although this is thought to be incorrect.
- The opposite of **interesting** can be **uninteresting**: *The food was dull and uninteresting.* It is more common to use a different word such as **dull** or **boring**.

inter·est·ed 0-w /ˈɪntrəstɪd; -trest-/ *adj.*
1 0-w giving your attention to sth because you enjoy finding out about it or doing it; showing interest in sth and finding it exciting: **~ (in sth/sb)** *I'm very interested in history.* ◇ **~ (in doing sth)** *Anyone interested in joining the club should contact us at the address below.* ◇ **~ (to do sth)** *We would be interested to hear your views on this subject.* ◇ *an interested audience* ◇ *There's a talk on Italian art—are you*

interested (= would you like to go)? ◇ *He sounded genuinely interested.* **2** in a position to gain from a situation or be affected by it: *As an* ***interested party****, I was not allowed to vote.* ◇ *Interested groups will be given three months to give their views on the new development.*

ˌinterest-ˈfree *adj.* with no interest charged on money borrowed: *an interest-free loan* ◇ *interest-free credit*

ˈinterest group *noun* a group of people who work together to achieve sth that they are particularly interested in, especially by putting pressure on the government, etc: *a special interest group of US lumber producers* ➲ compare ADVOCACY GROUP, PRESSURE GROUP

inter·est·ing 🔑 /ˈɪntrəstɪŋ; -trest-/ *adj.* attracting your attention because it is special, exciting or unusual: *an interesting question/point/example* ◇ *interesting people/places/work* ◇ **~ (to do sth)** *It would be interesting to know what he really believed.* ◇ *It is particularly interesting to compare the two versions.* ◇ **~ (that...)** *I find it interesting that she claims not to know him.* ◇ *Can't we do something more interesting?* ◇ *Her account makes interesting reading.* ▶ **inter·est·ing·ly** *adv.*: *Interestingly, there are very few recorded cases of such attacks.* ➲ LANGUAGE BANK at SURPRISING

Synonyms

interesting

fascinating • compelling • stimulating • gripping • absorbing

These words all describe sb/sth that attracts or holds your attention because they are exciting, unusual or full of good ideas.

interesting attracting your attention because it is exciting, unusual or full of good ideas: *That's an interesting question, Daniel.*

fascinating extremely interesting or attractive: *The exhibition tells the fascinating story of the steam age.*

compelling (*rather formal*) so interesting or exciting that it holds your attention: *Her latest book makes compelling reading.*

stimulating full of interesting or exciting ideas; making people feel enthusiastic: *Thank you for a most stimulating discussion.*

gripping so exciting or interesting that it holds your attention completely: *His books are always so gripping.*

absorbing so interesting or enjoyable that it holds your attention: *Chess can be an extremely absorbing game.*

PATTERNS

- interesting/fascinating/stimulating **for** sb
- interesting/fascinating **to** sb
- interesting/fascinating **that...**
- interesting/fascinating **to see/hear/find/learn/know...**
- a(n) interesting/fascinating/compelling/gripping **story/read/book**
- a(n) interesting/fascinating/stimulating **experience/discussion/idea**
- **to find sth** interesting/fascinating/compelling/stimulating/gripping/absorbing

inter·face /ˈɪntəfeɪs; *NAmE* -tərf-/ *noun, verb*
■ *noun* **1** (*computing*) the way a computer program presents information to a user or receives information from a user, in particular the LAYOUT of the screen and the menus: *the user interface* **2** (*computing*) an electrical CIRCUIT, connection or program that joins one device or system to another: *the interface between computer and printer* **3 ~ (between A and B)** the point where two subjects, systems, etc. meet and affect each other: *the interface between manufacturing and sales*
■ *verb* [I, T] **~ (sth) (with sth)** | **~ A and B** (*computing*) to be connected with sth using an interface; to connect sth in this way: *The new system interfaces with existing telephone equipment.*

inter·faith /ˈɪntəfeɪθ; *NAmE* -tərf-/ *adj.* [only before noun] between or connected with people of different religions: *an interfaith memorial service*

inter·fere /ˌɪntəˈfɪə(r); *NAmE* ˌɪntərˈfɪr/ *verb* [I] to get involved in and try to influence a situation that does not concern you, in a way that annoys other people: *I wish my mother would stop interfering and let me make my own decisions.* ◇ **~ in sth** *The police are very unwilling to interfere in family problems.*
PHR V **interˈfere with sb 1** to illegally try to influence sb who is going to give evidence in court, for example by threatening them or offering them money **2** (*BrE*) to touch a child in a sexual way **interˈfere with sth 1** to prevent sth from succeeding or from being done or happening as planned: *She never allows her personal feelings to interfere with her work.* **2** to touch, use or change sth, especially a piece of equipment, so that it is damaged or no longer works correctly: *I'd get fired if he found out I'd been interfering with his records.*

inter·fer·ence /ˌɪntəˈfɪərəns; *NAmE* -tərˈfɪr-/ *noun* [U] **1 ~ (in sth)** the act of interfering: *They resent foreign interference in the internal affairs of their country.* **2** interruption of a radio signal by another signal on a similar WAVELENGTH, causing extra noise that is not wanted
IDM **run interference** (*NAmE*) **1** (in AMERICAN FOOTBALL) to clear the way for the player with the ball by blocking players from the opposing team **2** (*informal*) to help sb by dealing with problems for them so that they do not need to deal with them

inter·fer·ing /ˌɪntəˈfɪərɪŋ; *NAmE* -tərˈfɪr-/ *adj.* [usually before noun] (*disapproving*) involving yourself in an annoying way in other people's private lives: *She's an interfering busybody!*

inter·feron /ˌɪntəˈfɪərɒn; *NAmE* ˌɪntərˈfɪrɑːn/ *noun* [U] (*biology*) a substance produced by the body to prevent harmful viruses from causing disease

inter·gal·act·ic /ˌɪntəgəˈlæktɪk; *NAmE* -tərgə-/ *adj.* [only before noun] existing or happening between GALAXIES of stars: *intergalactic space/travel*

inter·gov·ern·men·tal /ˌɪntəˌgʌvənˈmentl; *NAmE* ˌɪntərˌgʌvərn-/ *adj.* [only before noun] concerning the governments of two or more countries: *an intergovernmental conference*

in·terim /ˈɪntərɪm/ *adj., noun*
■ *adj.* [only before noun] **1** intended to last for only a short time until sb/sth more permanent is found: *an interim government/measure/report* ◇ *The vice-president took power in* ***the interim period*** *before the election.* **2** (*finance*) calculated before the final results of sth are known SYN **provisional**: *interim figures/profits/results*
■ *noun*
IDM **in the interim** during the period of time between two events; until a particular event happens: *Despite everything that had happened in the interim, they had remained good friends.* ◇ *Her new job does not start until May and she will continue in the old job in the interim.*

in·ter·ior 🔑 /ɪnˈtɪəriə(r); *NAmE* -ˈtɪr-/ *noun, adj.*
■ *noun* **1** 🔑 [C, usually sing.] the inside part of sth: *the interior of a building/a car* OPP **exterior 2 the interior** [sing.] the central part of a country or continent that is a long way from the coast: *an expedition into the interior of Australia* **3 the Interior** [sing.] a country's own affairs rather than those that involve other countries: *the* ***Department/Minister of the Interior***
■ *adj.* 🔑 [only before noun] connected with the inside part of sth: *interior walls* OPP **exterior**

inˌterior ˈdecorator *noun* a person whose job is to design and/or decorate a room or the inside of a house, etc. with paint, paper, carpets, etc. ▶ **inˌterior decoˈration** *noun* [U]: *an interior decoration scheme*

inˌterior deˈsign *noun* [U] the art or job of choosing the paint, carpets, furniture, etc. to decorate the inside of a house ▶ **inˌterior deˈsigner** *noun*

I

in,terior 'monologue *noun* (in literature) a piece of writing that expresses a character's inner thoughts and feelings

inter·ject /ˌɪntəˈdʒekt; *NAmE* -tərˈdʒ-/ *verb* [T, I] **+ speech | ~ (sth)** (*formal*) to interrupt what sb is saying with your opinion or a remark: *'You're wrong,' interjected Susan.*

inter·jec·tion /ˌɪntəˈdʒekʃn; *NAmE* -tərˈdʒ-/ *noun* (*grammar*) a short sound, word or phrase spoken suddenly to express an emotion. *Oh!*, *Look out!* and *Ow!* are interjections. SYN **exclamation**

inter·lace /ˌɪntəˈleɪs; *NAmE* -tərˈl-/ *verb* [T, I] **~ (sth) (with sth)** (*formal*) to twist things together over and under each other; to be twisted together in this way: *Her hair was interlaced with ribbons and flowers.* ◇ *interlacing branches*

inter·lan·guage /ˈɪntəlæŋgwɪdʒ; *NAmE* -tərl-/ *noun* [U, C] (*linguistics*) a language system produced by sb who is learning a language, which has features of the language which they are learning and also of their first language

inter·leave /ˌɪntəˈliːv; *NAmE* -tərˈl-/ *verb* **~ sth (with sth)** to put sth, especially thin layers of sth, between things

inter·lin·ear /ˌɪntəˈlɪniə(r); *NAmE* -tərˈl-/ *adj.* (*technical*) written or printed between the lines of a text

inter·lin·gual /ˌɪntəˈlɪŋgwəl; *NAmE* -tərˈl-/ *adj.* **1** (*linguistics*) using, between, or relating to two different languages: *interlingual communication* **2** relating to an INTERLANGUAGE

inter·link /ˌɪntəˈlɪŋk; *NAmE* -tərˈl-/ *verb* [T, usually passive, I] **~ (sth) (with sth)** to connect things; to be connected with other things: *The two processes are interlinked.* ◇ *a series of short interlinking stories*

inter·lock /ˌɪntəˈlɒk; *NAmE* ˌɪntərˈlɑːk/ *verb* [I, T] **~ (sth) (with sth)** to fit or be fastened firmly together: *interlocking shapes/systems/pieces*

inter·locu·tor /ˌɪntəˈlɒkjətə(r); *NAmE* ˌɪntərˈlɑːk-/ *noun* (*formal*) **1** a person taking part in a conversation with you **2** a person or an organization that talks to another person or organization on behalf of sb else

inter·loper /ˈɪntələʊpə(r); *NAmE* ˈɪntərloʊpər/ *noun* a person who is present in a place or a situation where they do not belong SYN **intruder**

inter·lude /ˈɪntəluːd; *NAmE* -tərl-/ *noun* **1** a period of time between two events during which sth different happens: *a romantic interlude* (= a short romantic relationship) ◇ *Apart from a brief interlude of peace, the war lasted nine years.* **2** a short period of time between the parts of a play, film/movie, etc: *There will now be a short interlude.* **3** a short piece of music or a talk, etc. that fills this period of time: *a musical interlude*

inter·marry /ˌɪntəˈmæri; *NAmE* -tərˈm-/ *verb* (**inter·mar·ries, inter·marry·ing, inter·mar·ried, inter·mar·ried**) **1** [I] to marry sb of a different race or from a different country or a different religious group: *Blacks and whites often intermarried* (= married each other). ◇ **~ with sb** *They were not forbidden to intermarry with the local people.* **2** [I] to marry sb within your own family or group: *cousins who intermarry* ▸ **inter·mar·riage** /ˌɪntəˈmærɪdʒ/ *noun* [U, C]: *intermarriage between blacks and whites*

inter·medi·ary /ˌɪntəˈmiːdiəri; *NAmE* ˌɪntərˈmiːdieri/ *noun* (*pl.* -ies) **~ (between A and B)** a person or an organization that helps other people or organizations to make an agreement by being a means of communication between them SYN **mediator, go-between**: *Financial institutions act as intermediaries between lenders and borrowers.* ◇ *All talks have so far been conducted through an intermediary.* ▸ **inter·medi·ary** *adj.* [only before noun]: *to play an intermediary role in the dispute*

inter·medi·ate AW /ˌɪntəˈmiːdiət; *NAmE* -tərˈm-/ *adj.*, *noun*

■ ***adj.*** **1** [usually before noun] located between two places, things, states, etc: *an* ***intermediate stage/step*** *in a process* ◇ **~ between A and B** *Liquid crystals are considered to be intermediate between liquid and solid.* **2** having more than a basic knowledge of sth but not yet advanced; suitable for sb who is at this level: *an* ***intermediate skier/student, etc.*** ◇ *an intermediate coursebook* ◇ ***pre-/upper-intermediate*** *classes*

■ ***noun*** a person who is learning sth and who has more than a basic knowledge of it but is not yet advanced

,intermediate tech'nology *noun* [U] technology that is suitable for use in developing countries as it is cheap and simple and can use local materials

in·ter·ment /ɪnˈtɜːmənt; *NAmE* -ˈtɜːrm-/ *noun* [C, U] (*formal*) the act of burying a dead person SYN **burial** ➲ see also INTER *v.*

inter·mesh /ˌɪntəˈmeʃ; *NAmE* -tərˈm-/ *verb* [I] (of two objects or parts) to fit closely together: *intermeshing cogs*

inter·mezzo /ˌɪntəˈmetsəʊ; *NAmE* ˌɪntərˈmetsoʊ/ *noun* (*pl.* **inter·mezzi** /-ˈmetsiː/ or **inter·mezzos** /-ˈmetsəʊz; *NAmE* -ˈmetsoʊz/) (*music*) (from *Italian*) a short piece of music for the ORCHESTRA that is played between two parts in an OPERA or other musical performance

in·ter·min·able /ɪnˈtɜːmɪnəbl; *NAmE* -ˈtɜːrm-/ *adj.* lasting a very long time and therefore boring or annoying SYN **endless**: *an interminable speech/wait/discussion* ◇ *The drive seemed interminable.* ▸ **in·ter·min·ably** /-əbli/ *adv.*: *The meeting dragged on interminably.*

inter·min·gle /ˌɪntəˈmɪŋgl; *NAmE* -tərˈm-/ *verb* [T, I] (*formal*) to mix people, ideas, colours, etc. together; to be mixed in this way: **~ A with B** *The book intermingles fact with fiction.* ◇ **~ A and B** *The book intermingles fact and fiction.* ◇ **~ (with sb/sth)** *tourists and local people intermingling in the market square*

inter·mis·sion /ˌɪntəˈmɪʃn; *NAmE* -tərˈm-/ *noun* [C, U] **1** (*especially NAmE*) a short period of time between the parts of a play, film/movie, etc: *Coffee was served during the intermission.* ◇ (*NAmE*) *After intermission, the second band played.* HELP This meaning is only [U] in *NAmE*. **2** a period of time during which sth stops before continuing again: *This state of affairs lasted without intermission for a hundred years.*

inter·mit·tent /ˌɪntəˈmɪtənt; *NAmE* -tərˈm-/ *adj.* stopping and starting often over a period of time, but not regularly SYN **sporadic**: *intermittent bursts of applause* ◇ *intermittent showers* ▸ **inter·mit·tent·ly** *adv.*: *Protests continued intermittently throughout November.*

inter·mix /ˌɪntəˈmɪks; *NAmE* -tərˈm-/ *verb* [T, I] **~ (sth) (with sth)** to mix things together; to be mixed together: *Grass fields were intermixed with areas of woodland.*

in·tern *verb, noun*

■ ***verb*** /ɪnˈtɜːn; *NAmE* ɪnˈtɜːrn/ [often passive] **~ sb (in sth)** to put sb in prison during a war or for political reasons, although they have not been charged with a crime ➲ see also INTERNEE ▸ **in·tern·ment** /ɪnˈtɜːnmənt; *NAmE* -ˈtɜːrn-/ *noun* [U]: *the internment of suspected terrorists* ◇ *internment camps*

■ ***noun*** (also **in·terne**) /ˈɪntɜːn; *NAmE* ˈɪntɜːrn/ (*NAmE*) **1** an advanced student of medicine, whose training is nearly finished and who is working in a hospital to get further practical experience ➲ compare HOUSE OFFICER **2** a student or new GRADUATE who is getting practical experience in a job, for example during the summer holiday/vacation: *a summer intern at a law firm* ➲ see also INTERNSHIP

in·tern·al 0‑ AW /ɪnˈtɜːnl; *NAmE* ɪnˈtɜːrnl/ *adj.*
1 0‑ [only before noun] connected with the inside of sth: *the internal structure of a building* ◇ *internal doors* OPP **external** **2** 0‑ [only before noun] connected with the inside of your body: ***internal organs/injuries*** ◇ *The medicine is not for* ***internal use.*** OPP **external** **3** 0‑ [usually before noun] involving or concerning only the people who are part of a particular organization rather than people from outside it: *an internal inquiry* ◇ *the internal workings of government* ◇ *internal divisions within the company* OPP **external** **4** 0‑ [only before noun] connected with a country's own affairs rather than those that involve other countries SYN **domestic**: ***internal affairs/trade/markets*** ◇ *an* ***internal flight*** (= within a country) OPP **external** **5** coming from within a thing itself rather than

from outside it: *a theory which lacks* ***internal consistency*** (= whose parts are not in agreement with each other) ◇ *Some photos contain* ***internal evidence*** (= fashions, transport, etc.) *that may help to date them.* **6** happening or existing in your mind **SYN** **inner**: *internal rage* ▸ **in·tern·al·ly** AW /-nəli/ *adv.*: *internally connected rooms* ◇ *The new posts were only advertised internally.*

in,ternal-com'bustion engine *noun* a type of engine used in most cars that produces power by burning petrol/gas inside

in·tern·al·ize (*BrE* also **-ise**) AW /ɪn'tɜːnəlaɪz; *NAmE* -'tɜːrn-/ *verb* **~ sth** (*technical*) to make a feeling, an attitude, or a belief part of the way you think and behave ➲ compare EXTERNALIZE ▸ **in·tern·al·iza·tion, -isa·tion** /ɪn,tɜːnəlaɪ'zeɪʃn; *NAmE* -,tɜːrnələ'z-/ *noun* [U]

in,ternal 'market *noun* (*business*) a situation in which different departments, countries, etc. in the same organization buy goods and services from each other

the In,ternal 'Revenue Service *noun* [sing.] (*abbr.* **IRS**) (in the US) the government department that is responsible for collecting most national taxes, for example income tax ➲ compare HM REVENUE AND CUSTOMS

inter·nation·al 0-π /,ɪntə'næʃnəl; *NAmE* -tər'n-/ *adj., noun*

■ ***adj.*** 0-π [usually before noun] connected with or involving two or more countries: *international trade/law/sport* ◇ *an international airport/school/company* ◇ *international relations* ◇ *a pianist with an international reputation* ▸ **inter·nation·al·ly** /-nəli/ *adv.*: *internationally famous*

■ ***noun*** **1** (*BrE*) a sports competition involving teams from two countries: *the France-Scotland rugby international* **2** (*BrE*) a player who takes part in a sports competition against another country: *a former swimming international* **3** (*NAmE*) a person from a foreign country: *an English course for internationals*

the ,Inter,national Bacca'laureate™ *noun* [sing.] (*abbr.* **IB**) an exam which is taken by students in many different countries in the world around the age of 18 or 19, and which includes up to six subjects

the Inter,national 'Date Line (also **'Date Line**) *noun* [sing.] the imaginary line that goes from north to south through the Pacific Ocean. The date on the west side is different by one day from that on the east side.

the Inter·nation·ale /,ɪntənæʃə'nɑːl; *NAmE* -tərn-/ *noun* [sing.] an international SOCIALIST song written in France that was the official ANTHEM of the USSR until 1944

inter·nation·al·ism /,ɪntə'næʃnəlɪzəm; *NAmE* -tər'n-/ *noun* [U] the belief that countries should work together in a friendly way

inter·nation·al·ist /,ɪntə'næʃnəlɪst; *NAmE* -tər'n-/ *noun* **1** a person who believes that countries should work together in a friendly way **2** (*ScotE*) a player who takes part in a sports competition against another country: *a Scottish rugby internationalist* ▸ **inter·nation·al·ist** *adj.*

inter·nation·al·ize (*BrE* also **-ise**) /,ɪntə'næʃnəlaɪz; *NAmE* -tər'n-/ *verb* **~ sth** to bring sth under the control or protection of many nations; to make sth international ▸ **inter·nation·al·iza·tion, -isa·tion** /,ɪntə,næʃnəlaɪ'zeɪʃn; *NAmE* -tər,næʃnələ'z-/ *noun* [U]

the Inter,national Pho,netic 'Alphabet *noun* [sing.] (*abbr.* **IPA**) an alphabet that is used to show the pronunciation of words in any language

in·terne *noun* = INTERN

inter·necine /,ɪntə'niːsaɪn; *NAmE* -tər'n-/ *adj.* [only before noun] (*formal*) happening between members of the same group, country or organization: ***internecine struggles/warfare/feuds***

in·tern·ee /,ɪntɜː'niː; *NAmE* ,ɪntɜːr'niː/ *noun* a person who is put in prison for political reasons, usually without a trial (= who is INTERNED)

Inter·net 0-π (also **inter·net**) /'ɪntənet; *NAmE* -tərn-/ *noun* (usually **the Internet**) (also *informal* **the Net**) [sing.] an international computer network connecting other networks and computers from companies, universities, etc: *I looked it up* ***on the Internet.*** ◇ *You can buy our goods* ***over the Internet.*** ◇ *All the rooms have* ***access to the Internet/ Internet access.*** ◇ *an* ***Internet service provider*** (= a company that provides you with an Internet connection and

Collocations

International relations

Trade

- **facilitate/regulate** trade (with other countries)
- **form/join** a trading bloc
- **live in/compete in** a global/the world economy
- **support/promote** free trade
- **adopt/call for/oppose** protectionist measures
- **erect/impose/reduce/remove** trade barriers
- **impose/lift/raise/eliminate** import tariffs (on sth)
- **have/run** a huge/large/growing trade surplus/deficit
- **embrace/resist/drive** globalization

Politics and law

- **conduct/handle/talk about/discuss** foreign policy
- **pursue** an aggressive/a hawkish foreign policy
- **require/use/conduct** diplomacy
- **establish/break off/sever/restore** diplomatic relations
- **foster/promote/strengthen** regional cooperation
- **facilitate/achieve** economic/political integration
- **exercise/defend/protect/transfer/restore/regain** national/state/full/limited sovereignty
- **consolidate/extend/lose/retain** your power (in the region)
- **hold/maintain/change/alter/shift/be a shift in** the balance of power (in the region)
- **cause/create/open/expose/heal/repair** a deep/ growing/major/serious rift between X and Y

Meetings and agreements

- **have/hold/host/attend** an international conference/ an economic forum/a G20 summit
- **launch** a new round of global/multilateral/world trade negotiations
- **send/head/lead/meet** a high-level/an official/a trade delegation
- **begin/start/continue/resume** peace talks
- **be committed to/be opposed to/disrupt/undermine/ derail/sabotage** the peace process
- **negotiate/achieve** a lasting political settlement
- **broker/sign** a peace deal/agreement/treaty

Conflict

- **be/constitute/pose** a threat to global security
- **compromise/endanger/protect** national security
- **justify/be in favour of**/(*especially US*) **be in favor of/be against** military intervention
- **threaten/authorize/launch/take/support/oppose** unilateral/pre-emptive military action
- **impose/enforce/lift/end** economic sanctions/an arms embargo/a naval blockade
- **close/protect/secure/patrol** the border
- **lead/be involved in** a peacekeeping operation

Aid

- **negotiate/announce** a $15 billion aid package/an economic stimulus package
- **send/provide/request/cut off** military aid
- **bring/provide** emergency/humanitarian relief
- **deliver/distribute** medical supplies/(*BrE*) food parcels
- **fund/run** a foreign/a local/an international NGO
- **reduce/eradicate** child/global/world poverty

I

services such as email, etc.) ➲ COLLOCATIONS at EMAIL ➲ see also INTRANET, WWW

in·tern·ist /ɪnˈtɜːnɪst; *NAmE* -ˈtɜːrn-/ *noun* (*NAmE*) a doctor who is a specialist in the treatment of diseases of the organs inside the body and who does not usually do medical operations

in·tern·ment ➲ INTERN

in·tern·ship /ˈɪntɜːnʃɪp; *NAmE* -tɜːrn-/ *noun* (*NAmE*) **1** a period of time during which a student or new GRADUATE gets practical experience in a job, for example during the summer holiday/vacation: *an internship at a television station* ➲ compare PLACEMENT (2), WORK EXPERIENCE **2** a job that an advanced student of medicine, whose training is nearly finished, does in a hospital to get further practical experience

inter·oper·able /ˌɪntərˈɒpərəbl; *NAmE* -ˈɑːp-/ *adj.* (*technical*) (of computer systems or programs) able to exchange information

inter·pene·trate /ˌɪntəˈpenɪtreɪt; *NAmE* -tərˈp-/ *verb* [I, T] **~ (sth)** (*formal*) to spread completely through sth or from one thing to another in each direction ▸ **inter·pene·tra·tion** /ˌɪntəˌpenɪˈtreɪʃn; *NAmE* -tərˌp-/ *noun* [U, C]

inter·per·son·al /ˌɪntəˈpɜːsənl; *NAmE* -tərˈpɜːrs-/ *adj.* [only before noun] connected with relationships between people: *interpersonal skills*

inter·plan·et·ary /ˌɪntəˈplænɪtri; *NAmE* ˌɪntərˈplænəteri/ *adj.* [only before noun] between planets: *interplanetary travel*

inter·play /ˈɪntəpleɪ; *NAmE* -tərp-/ *noun* [U, sing.] **~ (of/between A and B)** (*formal*) the way in which two or more things or people affect each other SYN **interaction**: *the interplay between politics and the environment* ◇ *the subtle interplay of colours*

Inter·pol /ˈɪntəpɒl; *NAmE* ˈɪntərpɔːl; ˈɪntərpɑːl/ *noun* [sing.+ sing./pl. v.] an international organization that enables the police forces of different countries to help each other to solve crimes

in·ter·pol·ate /ɪnˈtɜːpəleɪt; *NAmE* -ˈtɜːrp-/ *verb* (*formal*) **1** **+ speech** | **~ sth** to make a remark that interrupts a conversation SYN **interject**: *'But why?' he interpolated.* **2** **~ sth (into sth)** to add sth to a piece of writing SYN **insert**: *The lines were interpolated into the manuscript at a later date.* **3** **~ sth** (*mathematics*) to add a value into a series by calculating it from surrounding known values ▸ **in·ter·pol·ation** /ɪnˌtɜːpəˈleɪʃn; *NAmE* -ˌtɜːrp-/ *noun* [U, C]

inter·pose /ˌɪntəˈpəʊz; *NAmE* ˌɪntərˈpoʊz/ *verb* (*formal*) **1** **+ speech** | **~ sth** to add a question or remark into a conversation: *'Just a minute,' Charles interposed. 'How do you know?'* **2** **~ sb/sth (between A and B)** to place sth between two people or things: *He quickly interposed himself between Mel and the doorway.*

in·ter·pret 🔑 AW /ɪnˈtɜːprɪt; *NAmE* -ˈtɜːrp-/ *verb* **1** 🔑 [T] **~ sth** to explain the meaning of sth: *The students were asked to interpret the poem.* **2** 🔑 [T] to decide that sth has a particular meaning and to understand it in this way: **~ sth as sth** *I didn't know whether to interpret her silence as acceptance or refusal.* ◇ **~ sth** *The data can be interpreted in many different ways.* ➲ compare MISINTERPRET **3** 🔑 [I] **~ (for sb)** to translate one language into another as you hear it: *She couldn't speak much English so her children had to interpret for her.* **4** [T] **~ sth** to perform a piece of music, a role in a play, etc. in a way that shows your feelings about its meaning: *He interpreted the role with a lot of humour.* ▸ **in·ter·pret·able** /ɪnˈtɜːprɪtəbl; *NAmE* -ˈtɜːrp-/ *adj.*: *interpretable data*

in·ter·pret·ation 🔑 AW /ɪnˌtɜːprɪˈteɪʃn; *NAmE* -ˌtɜːrp-/ *noun* [C, U] **1** 🔑 the particular way in which sth is understood or explained: *Her evidence suggests a different interpretation of the events.* ◇ *It is not possible for everyone to put their own interpretation on the law.* ◇ *Dreams are* **open to interpretation** (= they can be explained in different ways). **2** the particular way in which sb chooses to perform a piece of music, a role in a play, etc: *a modern interpretation of 'King Lear'*

in·ter·pret·ative AW /ɪnˈtɜːprɪtətɪv; *NAmE* ɪnˈtɜːrprəteɪtɪv/ (also **in·ter·pret·ive** /ɪnˈtɜːprɪtɪv; *NAmE* -ˈtɜːrp-/ especially in *NAmE*) *adj.* [usually before noun] (*formal*) connected with the particular way in which sth is understood, explained or performed; providing an interpretation: *an interpretative problem* ◇ *an interpretative exhibition*

in·ter·pret·er /ɪnˈtɜːprɪtə(r); *NAmE* -ˈtɜːrp-/ *noun* **1** a person whose job is to translate what sb is saying into another language: *Speaking* **through an interpreter**, *the President said that the talks were going well.* ◇ *a sign language interpreter* (= a person who translates what sb is saying into sign language for deaf people) ➲ compare TRANSLATOR **2** a person who performs a piece of music or a role in a play in a way that clearly shows their ideas about its meaning: *She is one of the finest interpreters of Debussy's music.* **3** (*computing*) a computer program that changes the instructions of another program into a form that the computer can understand and use

inter·racial /ˌɪntəˈreɪʃl/ *adj.* [only before noun] involving people of different races: *interracial marriage*

inter·reg·num /ˌɪntəˈregnəm/ *noun* [usually sing.] (*pl.* **inter·reg·nums**) (*formal*) a period of time during which a country, an organization, etc. does not have a leader and is waiting for a new one

inter·relate /ˌɪntərɪˈleɪt/ *verb* [I, T, usually passive] if two or more things **interrelate**, or if they are **interrelated**, they are closely connected and they affect each other: *a discussion of how the mind and body interrelate* ◇ **~ with sth** *a discussion of how the mind interrelates with the body* ◇ **be interrelated** *a discussion of how the mind and body are interrelated* ▸ **inter·related** *adj.*: *a number of interrelated problems*

inter·rela·tion·ship /ˌɪntərɪˈleɪʃnʃɪp/ (also **inter·rela·tion** /ˌɪntərɪˈleɪʃn/) *noun* [C, U] **~ (of/between A and B)** the way in which two or more things or people are connected and affect each other

in·ter·ro·gate /ɪnˈterəgeɪt/ *verb* **1** **~ sb** to ask sb a lot of questions over a long period of time, especially in an aggressive way: *He was interrogated by the police for over 12 hours.* **2** **~ sth** (*technical*) to obtain information from a computer or other machine ▸ **in·ter·ro·ga·tion** /ɪnˌterəˈgeɪʃn/ *noun* [U, C]: *He confessed after four days* **under interrogation**. ◇ *She hated her parents' endless interrogations about where she'd been.* ➲ SYNONYMS at INTERVIEW **in·ter·ro·ga·tor** *noun*

inter·roga·tive /ˌɪntəˈrɒgətɪv; *NAmE* -ˈrɑːg-/ *adj.*, *noun*

■ ***adj.*** **1** (*formal*) asking a question; in the form of a question: *an interrogative gesture/remark/sentence* **2** (*grammar*) used in questions: *interrogative pronouns/determiners/adverbs* (= for example, *who, which* and *why*) ▸ **inter·roga·tive·ly** *adv.*

■ ***noun*** (*grammar*) a question word, especially a pronoun or a determiner such as *who* or *which*

inter·roga·tory /ˌɪntəˈrɒgətri; *NAmE* -ˈrɑːg-/ *adj.*, *noun*

■ ***adj.*** seeming to be asking a question or demanding an answer to sth: *an interrogatory stare*

■ ***noun*** (*pl.* -ies) (*law*) a written question, asked by one party in a legal case, which must be answered by the other party

inter·rupt 🔑 /ˌɪntəˈrʌpt/ *verb* **1** 🔑 [I, T] to say or do sth that makes sb stop what they are saying or doing: *Sorry to interrupt, but there's someone to see you.* ◇ **~ with sth** *Would you mind not interrupting with questions all the time?* ◇ **~ sb/sth (with sth)** *I hope I'm not interrupting you.* ◇ *They were interrupted by a knock at the door.* ◇ **~ (sb) + speech** *'I have a question,' she interrupted.* **2** 🔑 [T] **~ sth** to stop sth for a short time: *The game was interrupted several times by rain.* ◇ *We interrupt this programme to bring you an important news bulletin.* **3** [T] **~ sth** to stop a line, surface, view, etc. from being even or continuous

inter·rup·tion 🔑 /ˌɪntəˈrʌpʃn/ *noun* [C, U] **1** 🔑 something that temporarily stops an activity or a situation; a time when an activity is stopped: *The birth of her son was a minor interruption to her career.* ◇ *an interruption to the power supply* ◇ *I managed to work for two hours* ***without interruption.*** **2** the act of interrupting sb/sth and of stopping them from speaking: *He ignored her interruptions.* ◇ *She spoke for 20 minutes* ***without interruption.***

inter·sect /ˌɪntəˈsekt; *NAmE* -tərˈs-/ *verb* **1** [I, T] (of lines, roads, etc.) to meet or cross each other: **~ (sth)** *a pattern of intersecting streets* ◇ *The lines intersect at right angles.* ◇ **~ with sth** *The path intersected with a busy road.* **2** [T, usually passive] **~ sth (with sth)** to divide an area by crossing it: *The landscape is intersected with spectacular gorges.*

inter·sec·tion /ˌɪntəˈsekʃn; *NAmE* -tərˈs-/ *noun* **1** [C] (*NAmE* or *formal*, *BrE*) a place where two or more roads, lines, etc. meet or cross each other: *Traffic lights have been placed at all major intersections.* **2** [U] the act of intersecting sth

inter·sex /ˈɪntəseks; *NAmE* -tərs-/ *noun* [U] (*medical*) the physical condition of being partly male and partly female

inter·sperse /ˌɪntəˈspɜːs; *NAmE* -tərˈspɜːrs/ *verb* **be interspersed with/in sth** to put sth in sth else or among or between other things: *Lectures will be interspersed with practical demonstrations.*

inter·state /ˈɪntəsteɪt; *NAmE* -tərs-/ *adj.*, *noun*
■ ***adj.*** [only before noun] between states, especially in the US: *interstate commerce*
■ ***noun*** (also ˌ**interstate ˈhighway**) (in the US) a wide road, with at least two lanes in each direction, where traffic can travel fast for long distances across many states. You can only enter and leave interstates at special RAMPS. ⮕ compare MOTORWAY

inter·stel·lar /ˌɪntəˈstelə(r); *NAmE* -tərˈst-/ *adj.* [only before noun] between the stars in the sky ⮕ compare STELLAR

in·ter·stice /ɪnˈtɜːstɪs; *NAmE* -ˈtɜːrs-/ *noun* [usually pl.] (*formal*) a small crack or space in sth

inter·sti·tial /ˌɪntəˈstɪʃl; *NAmE* -tərˈs-/ *adj.* (*medical*) in or related to small spaces between the parts of an organ or between groups of cells or TISSUES: *interstitial cells*

inter·text·ual·ity /ˌɪntətekstʃuˈæləti; *NAmE* ˌɪntər-/ *noun* [U] (*technical*) the relationship between texts, especially literary texts

inter·twine /ˌɪntəˈtwaɪn; *NAmE* -tərˈtw-/ *verb* [usually passive] **1** [I, T] if two or more things **intertwine** or are **intertwined**, they are twisted together so that they are very difficult to separate: *intertwining branches* ◇ **~ sth (with sth)** *a necklace of rubies intertwined with pearls* **2** [T, usually passive, I] **~ (sth)** to be or become very closely connected with sth/sb else: *Their political careers had become* ***closely intertwined.***

inter·val AW /ˈɪntəvl; *NAmE* ˈɪntərvl/ *noun*
1 a period of time between two events: *The interval between major earthquakes might be 200 years.* **2** (*BrE*) (also **inter·mis·sion** *NAmE*, *BrE*) a short period of time separating parts of a play, film/movie or concert: *There will be an interval of 20 minutes after the second act.* **3** [usually pl.] a short period during which sth different happens from what is happening the rest of the time: *She's delirious, but has lucid intervals.* ◇ (*BrE*) *The day should be mainly dry with sunny intervals.* **4** (*music*) a difference in PITCH (= how high or low a note sounds) between two notes: *an interval of one octave*
IDM **at (...) intervals 1** with time between: *Buses to the city leave* ***at regular intervals.*** ◇ *The runners started at 5-minute intervals.* **2** with spaces between: *Flaming torches were positioned at intervals along the terrace.*

ˈ**interval training** *noun* [U] sports training consisting of different activities which require different speeds or amounts of effort

inter·vene AW /ˌɪntəˈviːn; *NAmE* -tərˈv-/ *verb* **1** [I] to become involved in a situation in order to improve or help it: *She might have been killed if the neighbours hadn't intervened.* ◇ **~ in sth** *The President intervened personally in the crisis.* **2** [T, I] (**+ speech**) to interrupt sb when they are speaking in order to say sth: *'But,' she intervened, 'what about the others?'* **3** [I] to happen in a way that delays sth or prevents it from happening: *They were planning to get married and then the war intervened.* **4** [I] (*formal*) to exist between two events or places: *I saw nothing of her during the years that intervened.* ▸ **inter·ven·tion** AW /ˌɪntəˈvenʃn; *NAmE* -tərˈv-/ *noun* [U, C]: **~ (in sth)** *calls for government intervention to save the steel industry* ◇ ***armed/military intervention*** ⮕ COLLOCATIONS at INTERNATIONAL

inter·ven·ing /ˌɪntəˈviːnɪŋ; *NAmE* -tərˈv-/ *adj.* [only before noun] coming or existing between two events, dates, objects, etc: *Little had changed in the intervening years.*

inter·ven·tion·ism /ˌɪntəˈvenʃənɪzəm; *NAmE* -tərˈv-/ *noun* [U] the policy or practice of a government influencing the economy of its own country, or of becoming involved in the affairs of other countries ▸ **inter·ven·tion·ist** /-ʃənɪst/ *adj.*, *noun*: *interventionist policies*

Synonyms

interview

interrogation • **audience** • **consultation**

These are all words for a meeting or occasion when sb is asked for information, opinions or advice.

interview a formal meeting at which sb is asked questions, for example, to see if they are suitable for a particular job or course of study, or in order to find out their opinions about sth: *a job interview*

interrogation the process of asking sb a lot of questions, especially in an aggressive way, in order to get information; an occasion on which this is done: *He confessed after four days* ***under interrogation.***

audience a formal meeting with an important person: *The Pope granted her a private audience.*

consultation a meeting with an expert, especially a doctor, to get advice or treatment.

PATTERNS
- an **in-depth** interview/consultation
- a **police** interview/interrogation
- to **have/request** a(n) interview/audience/consultation with sb
- to **give/grant** sb a(n) interview/audience/consultation
- to **carry out/conduct** an interview/interrogation

inter·view /ˈɪntəvjuː; *NAmE* -tərv-/ *noun*, *verb*
■ ***noun*** **1** a formal meeting at which sb is asked questions to see if they are suitable for a particular job, or for a course of study at a college, university, etc: *a* ***job interview*** ◇ *to be* ***called for*** *(****an****)* ***interview*** ◇ **~ for a job, etc.** *He* ***has an interview*** *next week for the manager's job.* ⮕ COLLOCATIONS at JOB **2** a meeting (often a public one) at which a journalist asks sb questions in order to find out their opinions: *a* ***television/radio/newspaper interview*** ◇ **~ (with sb)** *an interview with the new Governor* ◇ *to* ***give an interview*** (= to agree to answer questions) ◇ *Yesterday,* ***in an interview*** *on German television, the minister denied the reports.* ◇ *to* ***conduct an interview*** (= to ask sb questions in public) ◇ *The interview was published in all the papers.* **3** **~ (with sb)** a private meeting between people when questions are asked and answered: *an interview with the careers adviser*
■ ***verb*** **1** [T, I] **~ (sb)** (**for a job, etc.**) to talk to sb and ask them questions at a formal meeting to find out if they are suitable for a job, course of study, etc: *Which post are you being interviewed for?* ◇ *We interviewed ten people for the job.* **2** [I] (*especially NAmE*) **~ (for a job, etc.)** to talk to sb and answer questions at a formal meeting to get a job, a place on a course of study, etc: *The website gives you tips on interviewing for colleges.* ◇ (*BrE, NAmE*) *If you don't interview well you are unlikely to get the job.* **3** [T] to ask sb questions about their life, opinions, etc, especially on the radio or television or for a newspaper or magazine: **~ sb about sth** *Next week, I will be interviewing Spielberg about his lat-*

est movie. ◇ ~ **sb** *The Prime Minister declined to be interviewed.* **4** [T] ~ **sb** (**about sth**) to ask sb questions at a private meeting: *The police are waiting to interview the injured man.* ▶ **inter·view·ing** *noun* [U]: *The research involves in-depth interviewing.* ◇ *interviewing techniques*

inter·view·ee /ˌɪntəvjuːˈiː; *NAmE* -tərv-/ *noun* the person who answers the questions in an interview

inter·view·er /ˈɪntəvjuːə(r); *NAmE* -tərv-/ *noun* the person who asks the questions in an interview

inter·war /ˌɪntəˈwɔː(r); *NAmE* -tərˈw-/ *adj.* [only before noun] happening or existing between the First and the Second World Wars: *the* ***interwar years/period***

inter·weave /ˌɪntəˈwiːv; *NAmE* -tərˈw-/ *verb* (**inter·wove** /-ˈwəʊv; *NAmE* -ˈwoʊv/, **inter·woven** /-ˈwəʊvn; *NAmE* -ˈwoʊvn/) [T, usually passive, I] ~ (**sth**) (**with sth**) to twist together two or more pieces of thread, wool, etc: *The blue fabric was interwoven with red and gold thread.* ◇ (*figurative*) *The problems are inextricably interwoven* (= very closely connected).

in·tes·tate /ɪnˈtesteɪt/ *adj.* (*law*) not having made a WILL (= a legal document that says what is to happen to a person's property when they die) ▶ **in·tes·tacy** /ɪnˈtestəsi/ *noun* [U]

inˌtestinal ˈfortitude *noun* (*NAmE, formal* or *humorous*) the courage and determination necessary to do sth difficult or unpleasant (used when you want to avoid using the word *guts*): *He did not have the intestinal fortitude to implement the changes.*

in·tes·tine /ɪnˈtestɪn/ *noun* [usually pl.] a long tube in the body between the stomach and the ANUS. Food passes from the stomach to the **small intestine** and from there to the **large intestine**. ➲ VISUAL VOCAB page V48 ▶ **in·tes·tinal** /ɪnˈtestɪnl; ˌɪnteˈstaɪnl/ *adj.* [usually before noun]

in·tim·acy /ˈɪntɪməsi/ *noun* (*pl.* **-ies**) **1** [U] the state of having a close personal relationship with sb **2** [C, usually pl.] a thing that a person says or does to sb that they know very well **3** [U] (*formal* or *law*) sexual activity, especially an act of SEXUAL INTERCOURSE

in·tim·ate *adj., verb, noun*

■ ***adj.*** /ˈɪntɪmət/ **1** (of people) having a close and friendly relationship: *intimate friends* ◇ *We're not* ***on intimate terms with*** *our neighbours.* **2** private and personal, often in a sexual way: *The article revealed* ***intimate details*** *about his family life.* ◇ *the most intimate parts of her body* **3** (of a place or situation) encouraging close, friendly relationships, sometimes of a sexual nature: *an intimate restaurant* ◇ *He knew an intimate little bar where they would not be disturbed.* **4** (of knowledge) very detailed and thorough: *an intimate knowledge of the English countryside* **5** (of a link between things) very close: *an* ***intimate connection*** *between class and educational success* **6** ~ (**with sb**) (*formal* or *law*) having a sexual relationship with sb ▶ **in·tim·ate·ly** *adv.*: ***intimately connected/linked/related*** ◇ *an area of the country that he knew intimately* ◇ *She was* ***intimately involved*** *in the project.* ◇ *They touched each other intimately* (= in a sexual way).

■ ***verb*** /ˈɪntɪmeɪt/ (*formal*) to let sb know what you think or mean in an indirect way SYN **make known**: ~ **sth** (**to sb**) *He has already intimated to us his intention to retire.* ◇ ~ (**that**)... *He has already intimated (that) he intends to retire.*

■ ***noun*** /ˈɪntɪmət/ (*formal*) a close personal friend

in·tim·ation /ˌɪntɪˈmeɪʃn/ *noun* [C, U] (*formal*) the act of stating sth or of making it known, especially in an indirect way: *There was no intimation from his doctor that his condition was serious.*

in·timi·date /ɪnˈtɪmɪdeɪt/ *verb* ~ **sb** (**into sth/into doing sth**) to frighten or threaten sb so that they will do what you want: *They were accused of intimidating people into voting for them.* ◇ *She refused to be intimidated by their threats.* ▶ **in·timi·da·tion** /ɪnˌtɪmɪˈdeɪʃn/ *noun* [U]: *the intimidation of witnesses*

in·timi·dated /ɪnˈtɪmɪdeɪtɪd/ *adj.* [not usually before noun] feeling frightened and not confident in a particular situation: *We try to make sure children don't feel intimidated on their first day at school.*

in·timi·dat·ing /ɪnˈtɪmɪdeɪtɪŋ/ *adj.* frightening in a way which makes a person feel less confident: *an intimidating manner* ◇ ~ **for/to sb** *This kind of questioning can be very intimidating to children.*

in·timi·da·tory /ɪnˌtɪmɪˈdeɪtəri/ *adj.* (*formal*) intended to frighten or threaten sb

into /ˈɪntə; *before vowels* ˈɪntu; *strong form* ˈɪntuː/ *prep.*

HELP For the special uses of **into** in phrasal verbs, look at the entries for the verbs. For example **lay into sb/sth** is in the phrasal verb section at **lay**. **1** to a position in or inside sth: *Come into the house.* ◇ *She dived into the water.* ◇ *He threw the letter into the fire.* ◇ (*figurative*) *She turned and walked off into the night.* **2** in the direction of sth: *Speak clearly into the microphone.* ◇ *Driving into the sun, we had to shade our eyes.* **3** to a point at which you hit sb/sth: *The truck crashed into a parked car.* **4** to a point during a period of time: *She carried on working late into the night.* ◇ *He didn't get married until he was well into his forties.* **5** used to show a change in state: *The fruit can be made into jam.* ◇ *Can you translate this passage into German?* ◇ *They came into power in 2008.* ◇ *She was sliding into depression.* **6** used to show the result of an action: *He was shocked into a confession of guilt.* **7** about or concerning sth: *an inquiry into safety procedures* **8** used when you are dividing numbers: *3 into 24 is 8.*

IDM **be ˈinto sb for sth** (*US, informal*) to owe sb money or be owed money by sb: *By the time he'd fixed the leak, I was into him for $500.* ◇ *The bank was into her for $100 000.* **be ˈinto sth** (*informal*) to be interested in sth in an active way: *He's into surfing in a big way.*

in·toler·able /ɪnˈtɒlərəbl; *NAmE* -ˈtɑːl-/ *adj.* so bad or difficult that you cannot TOLERATE it; completely unacceptable SYN **unbearable**: *an intolerable burden/situation* ◇ *The heat was intolerable.* ▶ **in·toler·ably** /-əbli/ *adv.*: *intolerably hot*

in·toler·ant /ɪnˈtɒlərənt; *NAmE* -ˈtɑːl-/ *adj.* **1** ~ (**of sb/sth**) (*disapproving*) not willing to accept ideas or ways of behaving that are different from your own OPP **tolerant** **2** (*technical*) not able to eat particular foods, use particular medicines, etc: *recipes for people who are gluten intolerant* ▶ **in·toler·ance** /-əns/ *noun* [U, C]: *religious intolerance* ◇ *an intolerance to dairy products*

in·ton·ation /ˌɪntəˈneɪʃn/ *noun* **1** [U, C] (*phonetics*) the rise and fall of the voice in speaking, especially as this affects the meaning of what is being said: *intonation patterns* ◇ *In English, some questions have a rising intonation.* ➲ compare STRESS **2** [U] (*music*) the quality of playing or singing exactly in tune

in·tone /ɪnˈtəʊn; *NAmE* ɪnˈtoʊn/ *verb* ~ **sth** | + **speech** (*formal*) to say sth in a slow and serious voice without much expression: *The priest intoned the final prayer.*

in toto /ˌɪn ˈtəʊtəʊ; *NAmE* ˈtoʊtoʊ/ *adv.* (from *Latin, formal*) completely; including all parts

in·toxi·cant /ɪnˈtɒksɪkənt; *NAmE* -ˈtɑːk-/ *noun* (*technical*) a substance such as alcohol that produces false feelings of pleasure and a lack of control

in·toxi·cated /ɪnˈtɒksɪkeɪtɪd; *NAmE* -ˈtɑːk-/ *adj.* (*formal*) **1** under the influence of alcohol or drugs: (*NAmE*) *He was arrested for DWI* (= driving while intoxicated). **2** ~ (**by/with sth**) very excited by sth, so that you cannot think clearly: *intoxicated with success* ▶ **in·toxi·cate** *verb* ~ **sb**

in·toxi·cat·ing /ɪnˈtɒksɪkeɪtɪŋ; *NAmE* -ˈtɑːk-/ *adj.* (*formal*) **1** (of drink) containing alcohol **2** making you feel excited so that you cannot think clearly: *Power can be intoxicating.* ▶ **in·toxi·ca·tion** /ɪnˌtɒksɪˈkeɪʃn; *NAmE* -ˌtɑːk-/ *noun* [U]

intra- *prefix* (in adjectives and adverbs) inside; within: *intravenous* ◇ *intra-departmental* (= within a department) ➲ compare INTER-

in·tract·able /ɪnˈtræktəbl/ *adj.* (*formal*) (of a problem or a person) very difficult to deal with OPP **tractable** ▸ **in·tract·abil·ity** /ɪnˌtræktəˈbɪləti/ *noun* [U]

intra·mural /ˌɪntrəˈmjʊərəl; *NAmE* -ˈmjʊrəl/ *adj.* (*especially NAmE*) taking place within a single institution, especially a school or college: *Jeff played intramural basketball in high school.*

intra·mus·cu·lar /ˌɪntrəˈmʌskjələ(r)/ *adj.* (*medical*) happening inside a muscle or put into a muscle: *intramuscular pain* ◇ *an intramuscular injection*

intra·net /ˈɪntrənet/ *noun* (*computing*) a computer network that is private to a company, university, etc. but is connected to and uses the same software as the Internet

in·transi·gent /ɪnˈtrænsɪdʒənt; *NAmE* -ˈtrænz-/ *adj.* (*formal, disapproving*) (of people) unwilling to change their opinions or behaviour in a way that would be helpful to others SYN **stubborn** ▸ **in·transi·gence** /-əns/ *noun* [U]

in·transi·tive /ɪnˈtrænsətɪv/ *adj.* (*grammar*) (of verbs) used without a DIRECT OBJECT OPP **transitive**: *The verb 'die' as in 'He died suddenly', is intransitive.* ▸ **in·transi·tive·ly** *adv.*: *The verb is being used intransitively.*

intra·uter·ine /ˌɪntrəˈjuːtəraɪn/ *adj.* (*medical*) within the UTERUS

ˌintrauterine deˈvice *noun* = IUD

intra·ven·ous /ˌɪntrəˈviːnəs/ *adj.* (*abbr.* IV) (*medical*) (of drugs or food) going into a VEIN: *intravenous fluids* ◇ *an intravenous injection* ◇ *an intravenous drug user* ▸ **intra·ven·ous·ly** *adv.*

ˈin tray (*NAmE* also **ˈin box**) *noun* (in an office) a container on your desk for letters that are waiting to be read or answered ➲ compare OUT TRAY ➲ VISUAL VOCAB page V56

in·trench = ENTRENCH

in·trepid /ɪnˈtrepɪd/ *adj.* (*formal*, often *humorous*) very brave; not afraid of danger or difficulties SYN **fearless**: *an intrepid explorer*

in·tri·cacy /ˈɪntrɪkəsi/ *noun* **1** **in·tri·ca·cies** [pl.] **the ~ of sth** the complicated parts or details of sth: *the intricacies of economic policy* **2** [U] the fact of having complicated parts, details or patterns: *the intricacy of the design*

in·tri·cate /ˈɪntrɪkət/ *adj.* having a lot of different parts and small details that fit together: *intricate patterns* ◇ *an intricate network of loyalties and relationships* ▸ **in·tri·cate·ly** *adv.*: *intricately carved*

in·trigue *verb, noun*

■ *verb* /ɪnˈtriːɡ/ **1** [T, often passive] **~ sb** | **it intrigues sb that ...** to make sb very interested and want to know more about sth: *You've really intrigued me—tell me more!* **2** [I] **~ (with sb) (against sb)** (*formal*) to secretly plan with other people to harm sb

■ *noun* /ˈɪntriːɡ; ɪnˈtriːɡ/ **1** [U] the activity of making secret plans in order to achieve an aim, often by tricking people: *political intrigue* ◇ *The young heroine steps into a web of intrigue in the academic world.* **2** [C] a secret plan or relationship, especially one which involves sb else being tricked: *I soon learnt about all the intrigues and scandals that went on in the little town.* **3** [U] the atmosphere of interest and excitement that surrounds sth secret or important

in·trigued /ɪnˈtriːɡd/ *adj.* [not usually before noun] very interested in sth/sb and wanting to know more about it/them: *He was intrigued by her story.* ◇ **~ to do sth** *I'm intrigued to know what you thought of the movie.*

in·tri·guing /ɪnˈtriːɡɪŋ/ *adj.* very interesting because of being unusual or not having an obvious answer: *These discoveries raise intriguing questions.* ◇ *an intriguing possibility* ◇ *He found her intriguing.* ▸ **in·tri·guing·ly** *adv.*

in·trin·sic AW /ɪnˈtrɪnsɪk; -zɪk/ *adj.* belonging to or part of the real nature of sth/sb: *the intrinsic value of education* ◇ *These tasks were repetitive, lengthy and lacking any intrinsic interest.* ◇ **~ to sth** *Small local shops are intrinsic to the town's character.* ➲ compare EXTRINSIC ▸ **in·trin·sic·al·ly** AW /-kli/ *adv.*: *There is nothing intrinsically wrong with the idea* (= it is good in itself but there may be outside circumstances which mean it is not suitable).

intro /ˈɪntrəʊ; *NAmE* ˈɪntroʊ/ *noun* (*pl.* **-os**) (*informal*) an introduction to sth, especially to a piece of music or writing

intro·duce 🔑 /ˌɪntrəˈdjuːs; *NAmE* ˈduːs/ *verb*

▸ PEOPLE **1** 🔑 to tell two or more people who have not met before what each other's names are; to tell sb what your name is: **~ sb** *Can I introduce my wife?* ◇ **~ A to B (as sth)** *He introduced me to a Greek girl at the party.* ◇ **~ A and B** *We've already been introduced.* ◇ **~ yourself (to sb)** *Can I introduce myself? I'm Helen Robins.* ◇ *'Kay, this is Steve.' 'Yes, I know—we've already introduced ourselves.'*

▸ TV/RADIO SHOW **2** 🔑 **~ sb/sth** to be the main speaker in a television or radio show, who gives details about the show and who presents the people who are in it; to tell the audience the name of the person who is going to speak or perform: *The next programme will be introduced by Mary David.* ◇ *May I introduce my first guest on the show tonight ...*

▸ NEW EXPERIENCE **3** 🔑 to make sb learn about sth or do sth for the first time: **~ sb to sth** *The first lecture introduces students to the main topics of the course.* ◇ **~ sth (to sb)** *It was she who first introduced the pleasures of sailing to me.*

▸ NEW PRODUCT/LAW **4** 🔑 to make sth available for use, discussion, etc. for the first time SYN **bring in**: **~ sth** *The company is introducing a new range of products this year.* ◇ *The new law was introduced in 2007.* ◇ **~ sth into/to sth** *We want to introduce the latest technology into schools.*

▸ PLANT/ANIMAL/DISEASE **5** 🔑 **~ sth (to/into sth)** to bring a plant, an animal or a disease to a place for the first time: *Vegetation patterns changed when goats were introduced to the island.*

▸ START **6** 🔑 **~ sth** to be the start of sth new: *Bands from London introduced the craze for this kind of music.* ◇ *A slow theme introduces the first movement.*

▸ IN PARLIAMENT **7** **~ sth** to formally present a new law so that it can be discussed: *to introduce a bill (before Parliament)*

▸ ADD **8** **~ sth (into sth)** (*formal*) to put sth into sth: *Particles of glass had been introduced into the baby food.*

intro·duc·tion 🔑 /ˌɪntrəˈdʌkʃn/ *noun*

▸ BRINGING INTO USE/TO A PLACE **1** 🔑 [U] the act of bringing sth into use or existence for the first time, or of bringing sth to a place for the first time: *the introduction of new manufacturing methods* ◇ *the introduction of compulsory military service* ◇ *the 1 000th anniversary of the introduction of Christianity to Russia* **2** 🔑 [C] a thing that is brought into use or introduced to a place for the first time: *The book lists plants suitable for the British flower garden, among them many new introductions.*

▸ OF PEOPLE **3** 🔑 [C] **~ (to sb)** the act of making one person formally known to another, in which you tell each the other's name: *Introductions were made and the conversation started to flow.* ◇ *Our speaker today* ***needs no introduction*** (= is already well known). ◇ *a* ***letter of introduction*** (= a letter which tells sb who you are, written by sb who knows both you and the person reading the letter)

▸ FIRST EXPERIENCE **4** 🔑 [sing.] **~ (to sth)** a person's first experience of sth: *This album was my first introduction to modern jazz.*

▸ OF BOOK/SPEECH **5** 🔑 [C, U] **~ (to sth)** the first part of a book or speech that gives a general idea of what is to follow: *a brief introduction* ◇ *a book with an excellent introduction and notes* ◇ ***By way of introduction****, let me give you the background to the story.* ➲ compare PREFACE

▸ TO SUBJECT **6** 🔑 [C] **~ (to sth)** a book or course for people beginning to study a subject: *'An Introduction to Astronomy'* ◇ *It's a useful introduction to an extremely complex subject.*

▸ IN MUSIC **7** [C] (*music*) a short section at the beginning of a piece of music: *an eight-bar introduction*

intro·duc·tory /ˌɪntrəˈdʌktəri/ *adj.* **1** written or said at the beginning of sth as an introduction to what follows SYN **opening**: ***introductory chapters/paragraphs/remarks*** **2** intended as an introduction to a subject or an activity for people who have never done it before: ***intro-***

I

ductory courses/lectures **3** offered for a short time only, when a product is first on sale: *a special* ***introductory price*** *of just $10* ◇ *This* ***introductory offer*** *is for three days only.*

intro·spec·tion /ˌɪntrəˈspekʃn/ *noun* [U] the careful examination of your own thoughts, feelings and reasons for behaving in a particular way

intro·spect·ive /ˌɪntrəˈspektɪv/ *adj.* tending to think a lot about your own thoughts, feelings, etc.

intro·vert /ˈɪntrəvɜːt; *NAmE* -vɜːrt/ *noun* a quiet person who is more interested in their own thoughts and feelings than in spending time with other people **OPP** **extrovert** ▸ **intro·ver·sion** /ˌɪntrəˈvɜːʃn; *NAmE* -ˈvɜːrʒn/ *noun* [U]

intro·vert·ed /ˈɪntrəvɜːtɪd; *NAmE* -vɜːrt-/ (also **intro·vert**) *adj.* more interested in your own thoughts and feelings than in spending time with other people **OPP** **extrovert**

in·trude /ɪnˈtruːd/ *verb* (*formal*) **1** [I] to go or be somewhere where you are not wanted or are not supposed to be: *I'm sorry to intrude, but I need to talk to someone.* ◇ **~ into/on/upon sb/sth** *legislation to stop newspapers from intruding on people's private lives* **2** [I] **~ (on/into/upon sth)** to disturb sth or have an unpleasant effect on it: *The sound of the telephone intruded into his dreams.*

in·truder /ɪnˈtruːdə(r)/ *noun* **1** a person who enters a building or an area illegally **2** a person who is somewhere where they are not wanted: *The people in the room seemed to regard her as an unwelcome intruder.*

in·tru·sion /ɪnˈtruːʒn/ *noun* [U, C] **1** something that affects a situation or people's lives in a way that they do not want: **~ (on/upon sth)** *They claim the noise from the new airport is an intrusion on their lives.* ◇ **~ (into sth)** *This was another example of press intrusion into the affairs of the royals.* **2 ~ (into/on/upon sth)** (*formal*) the act of entering a place which is private or where you may not be wanted: *She apologized for the intrusion but said she had an urgent message.*

in·tru·sive /ɪnˈtruːsɪv/ *adj.* **1** too noticeable, direct, etc. in a way that is disturbing or annoying: *intrusive questions* ◇ *The constant presence of the media was very intrusive.* **2** (*phonetics*) (of a speech sound) produced in order to link two words together when speaking, for example the /r/ sound produced at the end of *law* by some English speakers in the phrase 'law and order'. Intrusive 'r' is not considered part of standard English.

in·tub·ate /ˈɪntjubeɪt; *NAmE* -tu-/ *verb* [T, I] **~ (sb/sth)** to put a tube into a hollow space in the body, for example to allow a person to breathe: *They managed to intubate the victim inside the wrecked car.* ◇ *to intubate the trachea* ◇ *We made the decision not to intubate.*

in·tuit /ɪnˈtjuːɪt; *NAmE* -ˈtuː-/ *verb* **~ that...** | **~ sth** | **~ what, why, etc...** (*formal*) to know that sth is true based on your feelings rather than on facts, what sb tells you, etc: *She intuited that something was badly wrong.*

in·tu·ition /ˌɪntjuˈɪʃn; *NAmE* -tu-/ *noun* **1** [U] the ability to know sth by using your feelings rather than considering the facts **2** [C] **~ (that...)** an idea or a strong feeling that sth is true although you cannot explain why: *I had an intuition that something awful was about to happen.*

in·tui·tive /ɪnˈtjuːɪtɪv; *NAmE* -ˈtuː-/ *adj.* **1** (of ideas) obtained by using your feelings rather than by considering the facts: *He had an intuitive sense of what the reader wanted.* **2** (of people) able to understand sth by using feelings rather than by considering the facts **3** (of computer software, etc.) easy to understand and to use ▸ **in·tui·tive·ly** *adv.*: *Intuitively, she knew that he was lying.*

Inuit /ˈɪnjuɪt; ˈɪnuɪt/ *noun* [pl.] (*sing.* **Inuk** /ˈɪnʊk/) a race of people from northern Canada and parts of Greenland and Alaska. The name is sometimes also wrongly used to refer to people from Siberia and S and W Alaska. ➲ compare ESKIMO

Inuk·ti·tut /ɪˈnʊktɪtʊt/ *noun* [U] the language of the Inuit people

in·un·date /ˈɪnʌndeɪt/ *verb* [usually passive] **1 ~ sb (with sth)** to give or send sb so many things that they cannot deal with them all **SYN** **overwhelm, swamp**: *We have been inundated with offers of help.* **2 ~ sth** (*formal*) to cover an area of land with a large amount of water **SYN** **flood** ▸ **in·un·da·tion** /ˌɪnʌnˈdeɪʃn/ *noun* [U, C]

inure /ɪˈnjʊə(r); *NAmE* ɪˈnjʊr/ *verb*
PHR V **iˈnure sb/yourself to sth** (*formal*) to make sb/yourself get used to sth unpleasant so that they/you are no longer strongly affected by it

in·vade /ɪnˈveɪd/ *verb* **1** [I, T] to enter a country, town, etc. using military force in order to take control of it: *Troops invaded on August 9th that year.* ◇ **~ sth** *When did the Romans invade Britain?* **2** [T] **~ sth** to enter a place in large numbers, especially in a way that causes damage or confusion: *Demonstrators invaded the government buildings.* ◇ *As the final whistle blew, fans began invading the field.* ◇ *The cancer cells may invade other parts of the body.* **3** [T] **~ sth** to affect sth in an unpleasant or annoying way: *Do the press have the right to* ***invade her privacy*** *in this way?* ➲ see also INVASION, INVASIVE

in·vader /ɪnˈveɪdə(r)/ *noun* an army or a country that enters another country by force in order to take control of it; a soldier fighting in such an army: *a foreign invader* ◇ *They prepared to repel the invaders.* ◇ (*figurative*) *The white blood cells attack cells infected with an invader.*

in·valid *adj., noun, verb*

▪ ***adj.*** /ɪnˈvælɪd/ **1** not legally or officially acceptable: *The treaty was declared invalid because it had not been ratified.* ◇ *People with invalid papers are deported to another country.* **2** not based on all the facts, and therefore not correct: *an invalid argument* **3** (*computing*) of a type that the computer cannot recognize: *An error code will be displayed if any invalid information has been entered.* ◇ *invalid characters* **OPP** **valid**

▪ ***noun*** /ˈɪnvəlɪd; *BrE* also ˈɪnvəliːd/ a person who needs other people to take care of them, because of illness that they have had for a long time: *She had been a delicate child and her parents had treated her as an invalid.* ◇ *his invalid wife*

▪ ***verb*** /ˈɪnvəlɪd; ˈɪnvəliːd/ **~ sb (out)** | **~ sb (out of sth)** (*BrE*) to force sb to leave the armed forces because of an illness or injury: *He was invalided out of the army in 1943.*

in·vali·date **AW** /ɪnˈvælɪdeɪt/ *verb* **1 ~ sth** to prove that an idea, a story, an argument, etc. is wrong: *This new piece of evidence invalidates his version of events.* **2 ~ sth** if you **invalidate** a document, contract, election, etc, you make it no longer legally or officially valid or acceptable **OPP** **validate** ▸ **in·vali·da·tion** /ɪnˌvælɪˈdeɪʃn/ *noun* [U]

in·val·id·ity **AW** /ˌɪnvəˈlɪdəti/ *noun* [U] **1** (*BrE, technical*) the state of being unable to take care of yourself because of illness or injury **2** (*formal*) the state of not being legally or officially acceptable ➲ compare VALIDITY

in·valu·able /ɪnˈvæljuəbl/ *adj.* extremely useful **SYN** **valuable**: *invaluable information* ◇ **~ to/for sb/sth** *The book will be invaluable for students in higher education.* ◇ **~ in sth** *The research should* ***prove invaluable*** *in the study of children's language.* ➲ compare VALUABLE
HELP **Invaluable** means 'very valuable or useful'. The opposite of **valuable** is **valueless** or **worthless**.

in·vari·able **AW** /ɪnˈveəriəbl; *NAmE* -ˈver-/ *adj.* always the same; never changing **SYN** **unchanging**: *Her routine was invariable.* ◇ *his invariable courtesy and charm* ◇ *an invariable principle* ➲ compare VARIABLE

in·vari·ably **AW** /ɪnˈveəriəbli; *NAmE* -ˈver-/ *adv.* always **SYN** **without fail**: *This acute infection of the brain is almost invariably fatal.* ◇ *This is not invariably the case.* ◇ *Invariably the reply came back, 'Not now!'*

in·vari·ant /ɪnˈveəriənt; *NAmE* -ˈver-/ *adj.* (*technical*) always the same; never changing **SYN** **invariable**

in·va·sion /ɪnˈveɪʒn/ *noun* [C, U] **1** the act of an army entering another country by force in order to take control of it: *the German invasion of Poland in 1939* ◇ *the threat of invasion* ◇ *an* ***invasion force/fleet*** ➲ COLLOCATIONS at WAR **2** the fact of a large number of people or things arriving somewhere, especially people or things that are disturbing or unpleasant: *the annual tourist invasion* ◇ *Farmers are struggling to cope with an invasion of slugs.* **3** an act or a process that affects sb/sth in a way that is not welcome: *The actress described the photographs of her as an* ***invasion of privacy.*** ➲ see also INVADE

in·va·sive /ɪnˈveɪsɪv/ *adj.* (*formal*) **1** (especially of diseases within the body) spreading very quickly and difficult to stop: *invasive cancer* **2** (of medical treatment) involving cutting into the body: *invasive surgery* ➲ see also INVADE **OPP** **non-invasive**

in·vec·tive /ɪnˈvektɪv/ *noun* [U] (*formal*) rude language and unpleasant remarks that sb shouts when they are very angry

in·veigh /ɪnˈveɪ/ *verb*
PHR V **inˈveigh against sb/sth** (*formal*) to criticize sb/sth strongly

in·vei·gle /ɪnˈveɪgl/ *verb* **~ sb/yourself (into sth/into doing sth)** (*formal*) to achieve control over sb in a clever and dishonest way, especially so that they will do what you want: *He* ***inveigled himself into her affections*** (= dishonestly made her love him).

in·vent 🔑 /ɪnˈvent/ *verb*
1 🔑 **~ sth** to produce or design sth that has not existed before: *Who invented the steam engine?* **2** 🔑 **~ sth** to say or describe sth that is not true, especially in order to trick people: *What excuse did he invent this time?* ◇ *Many children invent an imaginary friend.*

in·ven·tion 🔑 /ɪnˈvenʃn/ *noun*
1 🔑 [C] a thing or an idea that has been invented: *Fax machines were a wonderful invention at the time.* **2** 🔑 [U] the act of inventing sth: *Such changes have not been seen since the invention of the printing press.* **3** [C, U] the act of inventing a story or an idea and pretending that it is true; a story invented in this way: *This story is apparently a complete invention.* **4** [U] the ability to have new and interesting ideas: *John was full of invention—always making up new dance steps and sequences.* **IDM** see NECESSITY

in·vent·ive /ɪnˈventɪv/ *adj.* **1** (especially of people) able to think of new and interesting ideas **SYN** **imaginative**: *She has a highly inventive mind.* **2** (of ideas) new and interesting ▸ **in·vent·ive·ly** *adv.* **in·ven·tive·ness** *noun* [U]

in·vent·or /ɪnˈventə(r)/ *noun* a person who has invented sth or whose job is inventing things

in·ven·tory /ˈɪnvəntri; *NAmE* -tɔːri/ *noun, verb*
▪ ***noun*** (*pl.* -ies) **1** [C] a written list of all the objects, furniture, etc. in a particular building: *an inventory of the museum's contents* **2** [U] (*NAmE*) all the goods in a shop **SYN** **stock**: *The inventory will be disposed of over the next twelve weeks.* ◇ *inventory control* ➲ compare STOCKTAKING
▪ ***verb*** (**in·ven·tor·ies**, **in·ven·tory·ing**, **in·ven·tor·ied**, **in·ven·tor·ied**) **~ sth** (*formal*) to make a complete list of sth: *I've inventoried my father's collection of prints.*

in·verse /ˌɪnˈvɜːs; *NAmE* ˌɪnˈvɜːrs/ *adj.* **1** [only before noun] opposite in amount or position to sth else: *A person's wealth is often* ***in inverse proportion to*** *their happiness* (= the more money they have, the less happy they are). ◇ *There is often an* ***inverse relationship*** *between the power of the tool and how easy it is to use.* **2 the ˈinverse** *noun* [sing.] (*technical*) the exact opposite of sth ▸ **in·verse·ly** /ˌɪnˈvɜːsli; *NAmE* -ˈvɜːrs-/ *adv.*: *We regard health as inversely related to social class.*

in·ver·sion /ɪnˈvɜːʃn; *NAmE* ɪnˈvɜːrʃn; -ʒn/ *noun* [U, C] (*technical*) the act of changing the position or order of sth to its opposite, or of turning sth upside down: *the inversion of normal word order* ◇ *an inversion of the truth*

in·vert /ɪnˈvɜːt; *NAmE* ɪnˈvɜːrt/ *verb* **~ sth** (*formal*) to change the normal position of sth, especially by turning it upside down or by arranging it in the opposite order: *Place a plate over the cake tin and invert it.*

in·ver·te·brate /ɪnˈvɜːtɪbrət; *NAmE* -ˈvɜːrt-/ *noun* (*technical*) any animal with no BACKBONE, for example a WORM ➲ compare VERTEBRATE

inˌverted ˈcommas *noun* [pl.] (*BrE*) = QUOTATION MARKS
IDM **in inverted commas** (*informal*) used to show that you think a particular word, description, etc. is not true or appropriate: *The manager showed us to our 'luxury apartment', in inverted commas.*

inˌverted ˈsnobbery *noun* [U] (*BrE, disapproving*) the attitude that disapproves of everything connected with high social status and that is proud of low social status

in·vest 🔑 **AW** /ɪnˈvest/ *verb*
1 🔑 [I, T] to buy property, shares in a company, etc. in the hope of making a profit: **~ (in sth)** *Now is a good time to invest in the property market.* ◇ **~ sth (in sth)** *He invested his life savings in his daughter's business.* **2** 🔑 [I, T] (of an organization or government, etc.) to spend money on sth in order to make it better or more successful: **~ (in/on sth)** *The government has* ***invested heavily*** *in public transport.* ◇ **~ sth (in/on sth)** *The college is to invest $2 million in a new conference hall.* ◇ *In his time managing the club he has invested millions on new players.* **3** [T] **~ sth (in sth)** | **~ sth (in) doing sth** to spend time, energy, effort, etc. on sth that you think is good or useful: *She had invested all her adult life in the relationship.* **4** [T] (*formal*) to give sb power or authority, especially as part of their job: **~ sb (with sth)** *The new position invested her with a good deal of responsibility.* ◇ **~ sb (as sth)** *The interview was broadcast on the same day he was invested as President.* ➲ see also INVESTITURE
PHR V **inˈvest in sth** (*informal*, often *humorous*) to buy sth that is expensive but useful: *Don't you think it's about time you invested in a new coat?* **inˈvest sb/sth with sth** (*formal*) to make sb/sth seem to have a particular quality: *Being a model invests her with a certain glamour.*

in·ves·ti·gate 🔑 **AW** /ɪnˈvestɪgeɪt/ *verb*
1 🔑 [I, T] to carefully examine the facts of a situation, an event, a crime, etc. to find out the truth about it or how it happened: *The FBI has been called in to investigate.* ◇ (*informal*) *'What was that noise?' 'I'll go and investigate.'* ◇ **~ sth** *Police are investigating possible links between the murders.* ◇ **~ what, how, etc...** *Police are investigating what happened.* ➲ COLLOCATIONS at CRIME **2** 🔑 [T] **~ sb (for sth)** to try to find out information about sb's character, activities, etc: *This is not the first time he has been investigated by the police for fraud.* **3** 🔑 [T, I] to find out information and facts about a subject or problem by study or research: **~ (sth)** *Scientists are investigating the effects of diet on fighting cancer.* ◇ **~ how, what, etc...** *The research investigates how foreign speakers gain fluency.*

in·ves·ti·ga·tion 🔑 **AW** /ɪnˌvestɪˈgeɪʃn/ *noun* [C, U]
1 🔑 an official examination of the facts about a situation, crime, etc: *a* ***criminal/murder/police investigation*** ◇ *She is still* ***under investigation.*** ◇ **~ into sth** *The police have completed their investigations into the accident.* ➲ COLLOCATIONS at CRIME **2** 🔑 **~ (into sth)** a scientific or academic examination of the facts of a subject or problem **SYN** **enquiry**: *an investigation into the spending habits of teenagers*

in·ves·ti·ga·tive **AW** /ɪnˈvestɪgətɪv; *NAmE* -geɪtɪv/ (also *less frequent* **in·ves·ti·ga·tory** /ɪnˈvestɪgətəri; *NAmE* -gətɔːri/) *adj.* [usually before noun] involving examining an event or a situation to find out the truth: *The article was an excellent piece of* ***investigative journalism.*** ◇ *The police have full investigatory powers.*

in·ves·ti·ga·tor **AW** /ɪnˈvestɪgeɪtə(r)/ *noun* a person who examines a situation such as an accident or a crime to find out the truth: *air safety investigators* ◇ *a* ***private investigator*** (= a DETECTIVE)

in·ves·ti·ture /ɪnˈvestɪtʃə(r)/ *noun* [U, C] a ceremony at which sb formally receives an official title or special powers

in·vest·ment 🔑 **AW** /ɪnˈvestmənt/ *noun*
1 🔑 [U] the act of investing money in sth: *to* ***encourage*** *foreign* ***investment*** ◇ *investment income* ◇ **~ in sth** *This country needs investment in education.* ➲ COLLOCATIONS at ECONOMY **2** 🔑 [C] the money that you invest, or the thing that you invest in: *a minimum investment of $10 000* ◇ *a*

high ***return on my investments*** ◇ *Our investments are not doing well.* ◇ *We bought the house* ***as an investment*** (= to make money). ➲ COLLOCATIONS at BUSINESS **3** 🔑 [C] a thing that is worth buying because it will be useful or helpful: *A microwave is a* ***good investment.*** **4** [U, C] the act of giving time or effort to a particular task in order to make it successful: *The project has demanded considerable investment of time and effort.*

in'vestment bank (*NAmE*) (*BrE* ˌ**merchant 'bank**) *noun* a bank that deals with large businesses ▶ **inˌvestment 'banker** *noun* **inˌvestment 'banking** *noun* [U]

in·vest·or AW /ɪnˈvestə(r)/ *noun* a person or an organization that invests money in sth: *small investors* (= private people) ◇ *institutional investors*

in·vet·er·ate /ɪnˈvetərət/ *adj.* [usually before noun] (*formal*, often *disapproving*) **1** (of a person) always doing sth or enjoying sth, and unlikely to stop: *an inveterate liar* **2** (of a bad feeling or habit) done or felt for a long time and unlikely to change: *inveterate hostility*

in·vidi·ous /ɪnˈvɪdiəs/ *adj.* (*formal*) unpleasant and unfair; likely to offend sb or make them jealous: *We were* ***in the invidious position*** *of having to choose whether to break the law or risk lives.* ◇ *It would be invidious to single out any one person to thank.*

in·vigi·late /ɪnˈvɪdʒɪleɪt/ *verb* (*BrE*) (*NAmE* **proc·tor**) [T, I] **~ (sth)** to watch people while they are taking an exam to make sure that they have everything they need, that they keep to the rules, etc: *to invigilate an exam* ▶ **in·vigi·la·tion** /ɪnˌvɪdʒɪˈleɪʃn/ *noun* [U] **in·vigi·la·tor** /ɪnˈvɪdʒɪleɪtə(r)/ (*BrE*) (*NAmE* **proc·tor**) *noun*: *If you have a problem, ask the invigilator.*

in·vig·or·ate /ɪnˈvɪɡəreɪt/ *verb* **1** [often passive] **~ sb** to make sb feel healthy and full of energy: *The cold water invigorated him.* ◇ *They felt refreshed and invigorated after the walk.* **2 ~ sth** to make a situation, an organization, etc. efficient and successful: *They are looking into ways of invigorating the department.* ▶ **in·vig·or·at·ing** *adj.*: *an invigorating walk/shower*

in·vin·cible /ɪnˈvɪnsəbl/ *adj.* too strong to be defeated or changed SYN **unconquerable**: *The team seemed invincible.* ◇ *an invincible belief in his own ability* ▶ **in·vin·ci·bil·ity** /ɪnˌvɪnsəˈbɪləti/ *noun* [U]

in·viol·able /ɪnˈvaɪələbl/ *adj.* (*formal*) that must be respected and not attacked or destroyed: *the inviolable right to life* ◇ *inviolable territory* ◇ *an inviolable rule* ▶ **in·viol·abil·ity** /ɪnˌvaɪələˈbɪləti/ *noun* [U]

in·viol·ate /ɪnˈvaɪələt/ *adj.* (*formal*) that has been, or must be, respected and cannot be attacked or destroyed

in·vis·ible AW /ɪnˈvɪzəbl/ *adj.* **1** that cannot be seen: *a wizard who could make himself invisible* ◇ *She felt invisible in the crowd.* ◇ **~ to sb/sth** *stars invisible to the naked eye* OPP **visible** **2** (*economics*) connected with a service that a country provides, such as banks or TOURISM, rather than goods: *invisible earnings* ▶ **in·visi·bil·ity** AW /ɪnˌvɪzəˈbɪləti/ *noun* [U]: *The ink had faded to invisibility.* **in·vis·ibly** /ɪnˈvɪzəbli/ *adv.*: *He looked at me and nodded, almost invisibly.*

in·vi·ta·tion 🔑 /ˌɪnvɪˈteɪʃn/ *noun*
1 🔑 [C] a spoken or written request to sb to do sth or to go somewhere: *to* ***issue/extend an invitation*** ◇ *to* ***accept/turn down/decline an invitation*** ◇ **~ to sth** *an invitation to the party* ◇ **~ to do sth** *I have an* ***open invitation*** (= not restricted to a particular date) *to visit my friend in Japan.* **2** 🔑 [U] the act of inviting sb or of being invited: *A concert was held* ***at the invitation of*** *the mayor.* ◇ *Admission is* ***by invitation only.*** **3** 🔑 [C] a card or piece of paper that you use to invite sb to sth: *Have you ordered the wedding invitations yet?* **4** [sing.] **~ to sb (to do sth)** | **~ to sth** something that encourages sb to do sth, usually sth bad: *Leaving the doors unlocked is an* ***open invitation*** *to burglars.*

in·vi·ta·tion·al /ˌɪnvɪˈteɪʃənl/ *noun* (*especially NAmE*) (often used in names) a sports event that you can take part in only if you are invited ▶ **in·vi·ta·tion·al** *adj.*

in·vite 🔑 *verb, noun*
■ ***verb*** /ɪnˈvaɪt/ **1** 🔑 to ask sb to come to a social event: **~ sb to sth** *Have you been invited to their party?* ◇ **~ sb** *I'd have liked to have gone but I wasn't invited.* ◇ **~ sb to do sth** *They have invited me to go to Paris with them.* **2** 🔑 (*formal*) to ask sb formally to go somewhere or do sth: **~ sb (to/for sth)** *Successful candidates will be invited for interview next week.* ◇ **~ sth (from sb)** *He invited questions from the audience.* ◇ **~ sb to do sth** *Readers are invited to email their comments to us.* **3 ~ sth** | **~ sb/sth to do sth** to make sth, especially sth bad or unpleasant, likely to happen SYN **ask for**: *Such comments are just inviting trouble.* ➲ see also UNINVITED
PHR V **inˌvite sb aˈlong** to ask sb to go somewhere with you and other people: *I got myself invited along.* **inˌvite sb ˈback** **1** to ask sb to come to your home after you have been somewhere together: *After the movie, she invited me back for a drink.* **2** to ask sb to come to your home a second time, or to ask sb to come to your home after you have been to theirs **inˌvite sb ˈin/ˈup** to ask sb to come into your home, especially after you have been somewhere together **inˌvite sb ˈover/ˈround/aˈround** to ask sb to come to your home
■ ***noun*** /ˈɪnvaɪt/ (*informal*) an invitation: *Thanks for your invite.*

in·vit·ing /ɪnˈvaɪtɪŋ/ *adj.* making you want to do, try, taste, etc. sth SYN **attractive**: *an inviting smell* ◇ *The water looks really inviting.* ▶ **in·vit·ing·ly** *adv.*

in vitro /ɪn ˈviːtrəʊ; *NAmE* ˈviːtroʊ/ *adj.* (from *Latin*, *biology*) (of processes) taking place outside a living body, in scientific APPARATUS: *in vitro experiments* ◇ *the development of* ***in vitro fertilization*** ➲ see also IVF ▶ **in vitro** *adv.*: *an egg fertilized in vitro*

in vivo /ɪn ˈviːvəʊ; *NAmE* ˈviːvoʊ/ *adj.* (from *Latin*, *biology*) (of processes) taking place in a living body ▶ **in vivo** *adv.*

in·vo·ca·tion /ˌɪnvəˈkeɪʃn/ *noun* [U, C] **1** (*formal*) the act of asking for help, from a god or from a person in authority; the act of referring to sth or of calling for sth to appear **2** (*computing*) the act of making a particular function start

in·voice /ˈɪnvɔɪs/ *noun, verb*
■ ***noun*** a list of goods that have been sold, work that has been done etc, showing what you must pay SYN **bill**: *to* ***send/issue/settle an invoice*** *for the goods* ◇ *an invoice for £250* ➲ SYNONYMS at BILL
■ ***verb*** (*business*) to write or send sb a bill for work you have done or goods you have provided: **~ sb (for sth)** *You will be invoiced for these items at the end of the month.* ◇ **~ sth (to sb/sth)** *Invoice the goods to my account.*

in·voke AW /ɪnˈvəʊk; *NAmE* ɪnˈvoʊk/ *verb* **1 ~ sth (against sb)** to mention or use a law, rule, etc. as a reason for doing sth: *It is unlikely that libel laws will be invoked.* **2 ~ sb/sth** to mention a person, a theory, an example, etc. to support your opinions or ideas, or as a reason for sth: *She invoked several eminent scholars to back up her argument.* **3 ~ sth** to mention sb's name to make people feel a particular thing or act in a particular way: *His name was invoked as a symbol of the revolution.* **4 ~ sb** to make a request (for help) to sb, especially a god **5 ~ sth** to make sb have a particular feeling or imagine a particular scene SYN **evoke**: *The opening paragraph invokes a vision of England in the early Middle Ages.* HELP Some people think this use is not correct. **6 ~ sth** (*computing*) to begin to run a program, etc: *This command will invoke the HELP system.* **7 ~ sb/sth** to make evil appear by using magic

in·vol·un·tary /ɪnˈvɒləntri; *NAmE* ɪnˈvɑːlənteri/ *adj.* **1** an **involuntary** movement, etc. is made suddenly, without you intending it or being able to control it: *an involuntary cry of pain* OPP **voluntary** **2** happening without the person concerned wanting it to: *the involuntary repatriation of immigrants* ◇ *involuntary childlessness* ▶ **in·vol·un·tar·ily** /ɪnˈvɒləntrəli; *NAmE* ɪnˌvɑːlənˈterəli/ *adv.*

in·volve 🔑 AW /ɪnˈvɒlv; *NAmE* ɪnˈvɑːlv/ *verb*
1 🔑 if a situation, an event or an activity **involves** sth, that thing is an important or necessary part or result of it SYN **entail**: **~ sth** *Any investment involves an element of risk.* ◇ *Many of the crimes involved drugs.* ◇ **~ doing sth** *The test will involve answering questions about a photo-*

graph. ◇ **~ sb/sth doing sth** *The job involves me travelling all over the country.* ◇ (*formal*) *The job involves my travelling all over the country.* **2** 🔑 **~ sb/sth** if a situation, an event or an activity **involves** sb/sth, they take part in it or are affected by it: *There was a serious incident involving a group of youths.* ◇ *How many vehicles were involved in the crash?* **3** 🔑 to make sb take part in sth: **~ sb (in sth/in doing sth)** *We want to involve as many people as possible in the celebrations.* ◇ **~ yourself (in sth)** *Parents should involve themselves in their child's education.* **4 ~ sb (in sth)** to say or do sth to show that sb took part in sth, especially a crime **SYN implicate**: *His confession involved a number of other politicians in the affair.*

PHR V in'volve sb in sth to make sb experience sth, especially sth unpleasant: *You have involved me in a great deal of extra work.*

in·volved 🔑 **AW** /ɪn'vɒlvd; *NAmE* ɪn'vɑːlvd/ *adj.* **1** 🔑 [not before noun] **~ (in sth)** taking part in sth; being part of sth or connected with sth: *to* ***be/become/get involved*** *in politics* ◇ *We need to examine all the costs involved in the project first.* ◇ *We'll make our decision and contact the people involved.* ◇ *Some people tried to stop the fight but I didn't want to get involved.* **HELP** In this meaning, **involved** is often used after a noun. **OPP uninvolved** **2** 🔑 [not usually before noun] giving a lot of time or attention to sb/sth: **~ (with sth/sb)** *She was deeply involved with the local hospital.* ◇ **~ (in sth/sb)** *I was so involved in my book I didn't hear you knock.* ◇ *He's a very involved father* (= he spends a lot of time with his children). **OPP uninvolved** **3** 🔑 [not usually before noun] having a close personal relationship with sb: *They're not romantically involved.* ◇ **~ with sb/sth** *You're too emotionally involved with the situation.* **OPP uninvolved** **4** complicated and difficult to understand **SYN complex**: *an involved plot*

in·volve·ment 🔑 **AW** /ɪn'vɒlvmənt; *NAmE* -'vɑːlv-/ *noun* **1** 🔑 [U] **~ (in/with sth)** the act of taking part in sth **SYN participation**: *US involvement in European wars* **2** 🔑 [U, C] **~ (in/with sth)** the act of giving a lot of time and attention to sth you care about: *her growing involvement with contemporary music* **3** [C, U] **~ (with sb)** a romantic or sexual relationship with sb that you are not married to: *He spoke openly about his involvement with the singer.*

in·vul·ner·able /ɪn'vʌlnərəbl/ *adj.* that cannot be harmed or defeated; safe: *to be in an invulnerable position* ◇ **~ to sth** *The submarine is invulnerable to attack while at sea.* **OPP vulnerable** ▶ **in·vul·ner·abil·ity** /ɪnˌvʌlnərə'bɪləti/ *noun* [U]

in·ward /'ɪnwəd; *NAmE* -wərd/ *adj., adv.*
▪ ***adj.*** **1** [only before noun] inside your mind and not shown to other people: *an inward smile* ◇ *Her calm expression hid her inward panic.* **2** towards the inside or centre of sth: *an inward flow* ◇ *an inward curve* **OPP outward**
▪ ***adv.*** (also **in·wards** especially in *BrE*) **1** towards the inside or centre: *The door opens inwards.* **2** towards yourself and your interests: *Her thoughts turned inwards.* ◇ (*disapproving*) *an inward-looking person* (= one who is not interested in other people) **OPP outwards**

ˌinward in'vestment *noun* [U, C] (*business*) money that is invested in a particular country from outside it

in·ward·ly /'ɪnwədli; *NAmE* -wərd-/ *adv.* in your mind; secretly: *She groaned inwardly.* ◇ *I was inwardly furious.* **OPP outwardly**

in·ward·ness /'ɪnwədnəs; *NAmE* -wərd-/ *noun* [U] (*formal* or *literary*) interest in feelings and emotions rather than in the world around

in·yanga /ɪn'jɑːŋə/ *noun* (*pl.* **in·yangas** or **izin·yanga** /ˌɪzɪn'jɑːŋə/) (*SAfrE*) a person who treats people who are ill/sick using natural materials such as plants, etc. ➲ compare SANGOMA

in-your-'face *adj.* (*informal*) used to describe an attitude, a performance, etc. that is aggressive in style and deliberately designed to make people react strongly for or against it: *in-your-face action thrillers*

iod·ide /'aɪədaɪd/ *noun* [C] (*chemistry*) a chemical which contains iodine

iod·ine /'aɪədiːn; *NAmE* -daɪn/ *noun* [U] (*symb.* **I**) a chemical element. Iodine is a substance found in sea water. A liquid containing iodine is sometimes used as an ANTISEPTIC (= a substance used on wounds to prevent infection).

ion /'aɪən; *BrE* also 'aɪɒn; *NAmE* also 'aɪɑːn/ *noun* (*physics* or *chemistry*) an atom or a MOLECULE with a positive or negative electric charge caused by its losing or gaining one or more ELECTRONS

-ion (also **-ation, -ition, -sion, -tion, -xion**) *suffix* (in nouns) the action or state of: *hesitation* ◇ *competition* ◇ *confession*

ionic /aɪ'ɒnɪk; *NAmE* -'ɑːn-/ *adj.* **1** (*chemistry*) of or related to ions **2** (*chemistry*) (of a chemical BOND) using the electrical pull between positive and negative ions ➲ compare COVALENT **3 Ionic** (*architecture*) used to describe a style of ARCHITECTURE in ancient Greece that uses a curved decoration in the shape of a SCROLL

ion·ize (*BrE* also **-ise**) /'aɪənaɪz/ *verb* [T, I] **~ (sth)** (*technical*) to change sth or be changed into ions ▶ **ion·iza·tion, -isa·tion** /ˌaɪənaɪ'zeɪʃn; *NAmE* -nə'z-/ *noun* [U]

ion·izer (*BrE* also **-iser**) /'aɪənaɪzə(r)/ *noun* a device that is used to make air in a room fresh and healthy by producing negative IONS

iono·sphere /aɪ'ɒnəsfɪə(r); *NAmE* aɪ'ɑːnəsfɪr/ *noun* **the ionosphere** [sing.] a layer of the earth's atmosphere between about 80 and 1 000 kilometres above the surface of the earth, that reflects radio waves around the earth ➲ compare STRATOSPHERE

iota /aɪ'əʊtə; *NAmE* aɪ'oʊtə/ *noun* **1** [sing.] (usually used in negative sentences) an extremely small amount: *There is not one iota of truth* (= no truth at all) *in the story.* ◇ *I don't think that would help one iota.* **2** the 9th letter of the Greek alphabet (Ι, ι)

IOU /ˌaɪ əʊ 'juː; *NAmE* -oʊ-/ *noun* (*informal*) a written promise that you will pay sb the money you owe them (a way of writing 'I owe you'): *an IOU for £100*

IPA /ˌaɪ piː 'eɪ/ *abbr.* International Phonetic Alphabet (an alphabet that is used to show the pronunciation of words in any language)

IP address /ˌaɪ 'piː ədres/ *noun* (*computing*) a series of numbers separated by dots that identifies a particular computer connected to the Internet

IPO /ˌaɪ piː 'əʊ; *NAmE* 'oʊ/ *abbr.* (*business*) initial public offering (the act of selling shares in a company for the first time)

iPod™ /'aɪpɒd; *NAmE* -pɑːd/ *noun* a small piece of equipment that can store information taken from the Internet and that you carry with you, for example so that you can listen to music

ipso facto /ˌɪpsəʊ 'fæktəʊ; *NAmE* ˌɪpsoʊ 'fæktoʊ/ *adv.* (from *Latin, formal*) because of the fact that has been mentioned: *You cannot assume that a speaker of English is ipso facto qualified to teach English.*

IQ /ˌaɪ 'kjuː/ *noun* the abbreviation for 'intelligence quotient' (a measurement of a person's intelligence that is calculated from the results of special tests): *an IQ of 120* ◇ *to have a* ***high/low IQ*** ◇ *IQ tests*

ir- ➲ IN-

IRA /ˌaɪ ɑːr 'eɪ/ *abbr.* the abbreviation for 'Irish Republican Army' (an illegal organization which has fought for Northern Ireland to be united with the Republic of Ireland)

iras·cible /ɪ'ræsəbl/ *adj.* (*formal*) becoming angry very easily **SYN irritable** ▶ **iras·ci·bil·ity** /ɪˌræsə'bɪləti/ *noun* [U]

irate /aɪ'reɪt/ *adj.* very angry: *irate customers* ◇ *an irate phone call* ➲ SYNONYMS at ANGRY

IRC /ˌaɪ ɑː 'siː; *NAmE* ɑːr/ *abbr.* Internet Relay Chat (an area of the Internet where users can communicate directly with each other)

ire /ˈaɪə(r)/ *noun* [U] (*formal* or *literary*) anger SYN **wrath**: *to arouse/raise/provoke the ire of local residents* ◇ (*US*) *to draw the ire of local residents*

iri·des·cent /ˌɪrɪˈdesnt/ *adj.* (*formal*) showing many bright colours that seem to change in different lights: *a bird with iridescent blue feathers* ▸ **iri·des·cence** /-ˈdesns/ *noun* [U]

irid·ium /ɪˈrɪdiəm/ *noun* [U] (*symb.* **Ir**) a chemical element. Iridium is a very hard yellow-white metal, used especially in making ALLOYS.

irio /ˈɪrɪɒ; *NAmE* ˈɪrɪɑː/ *noun* [U] (*EAfrE*) a type of food made from a mixture of some or all of the following:MAIZE (CORN), BEANS, green vegetables and PEAS

iris /ˈaɪrɪs/ *noun* **1** the round coloured part that surrounds the PUPIL of your eye ➲ VISUAL VOCAB page V48 **2** a tall plant with long pointed leaves and large purple or yellow flowers ➲ VISUAL VOCAB page V9

Irish /ˈaɪrɪʃ/ *noun, adj.*

■ ***noun*** **1** (also ˌ**Irish ˈGaelic**, **Gaelic**) the Celtic language of Ireland ➲ compare ERSE **2 the Irish** [pl.] the people of Ireland

■ ***adj.*** of or connected with Ireland, its people or its language

ˌ**Irish ˈcoffee** *noun* **1** [U] hot coffee mixed with WHISKY and sugar, with thick cream on top **2** [C] a cup or glass of Irish coffee

ˌ**Irish ˈstew** *noun* [U, C] a hot dish of meat and vegetables boiled together

irk /ɜːk; *NAmE* ɜːrk/ *verb* **~ sb (to do sth)** | **it irks sb that...** (*formal* or *literary*) to annoy or irritate sb: *Her flippant tone irked him.*

irk·some /ˈɜːksəm; *NAmE* ˈɜːrk-/ *adj.* (*formal*) annoying or irritating SYN **tiresome**: *I found the restrictions irksome.*

IRL /ˌaɪ ɑːr ˈel/ *abbr.* in real life; not on the Internet (used in chat on the Internet): *If he did that IRL he'd have a bullet in his head.*

iroko /ɪˈrəʊkəʊ; *NAmE* ɪˈroʊkoʊ/ *noun* (*pl.* **-os**) **1** [C, U] a tall tree found in tropical W Africa that lives for many years. Some people believe that creatures with magic powers live in irokos. **2** [U] the wood from this tree, which is hard and used especially for outdoor building work

iron 0‑ /ˈaɪən; *NAmE* ˈaɪərn/ *noun, verb, adj.*

■ ***noun***

▸ METAL **1** 0‑ [U] (*symb.* **Fe**) a chemical element. Iron is a hard strong metal that is used to make steel and is also found in small quantities in blood and food: ***cast/wrought/corrugated iron*** ◇ ***iron gates/bars/railings*** ◇ *an* ***iron and steel*** *works* ◇ ***iron ore*** (= rock containing iron) ◇ *patients with* ***iron deficiency*** (= not enough iron in their blood) ◇ ***iron tablets*** (= containing iron prepared as a medicine) ◇ (*figurative*) *She had a* ***will of iron*** (= it was very strong).

▸ TOOL **2** 0‑ [C] a tool with a flat metal base that can be heated and used to make clothes smooth: *a steam iron* ➲ VISUAL VOCAB page V17 **3** [C] (usually in compounds) a tool made of iron or another metal ➲ see also BRANDING IRON, SOLDERING IRON, TIRE IRON

▸ FOR PRISONERS **4 irons** [pl.] chains or other heavy objects made of iron, attached to the arms and legs of prisoners, especially in the past

▸ IN GOLF **5** [C] one of the set of CLUBS (= sticks for hitting the ball with) that have a metal head ➲ compare WOOD

IDM **have several, etc. irons in the ˈfire** to be involved in several activities or areas of business at the same time, hoping that at least one will be successful ➲ more at PUMP *v.*, RULE *v.*, STRIKE *v.*

■ ***verb*** 0‑ [T, I] **~ (sth)** to make clothes, etc. smooth by using an iron: *I'll need to iron that dress before I can wear it.* ◇ *He was ironing when I arrived.* ➲ see also IRONING

PHR V ˌ**iron sth↔ˈout 1** to remove the CREASES (= folds that you do not want) from clothes, etc. by using an iron **2** to get rid of any problems or difficulties that are affecting sth: *There are still a few details that need ironing out.*

■ ***adj.*** [only before noun] very strong and determined: *She was known as the 'Iron Lady'.* ◇ *a man of* ***iron will***

IDM **an iron ˈfist/ˈhand (in a velvet ˈglove)** if you use the words **an iron fist/hand** when describing the way that sb behaves, you mean that they treat people severely. This treatment may be hidden behind a kind appearance (the **velvet glove**).

the ˈIron Age *noun* [sing.] the historical period about 3 000 years ago when people first used iron tools

iron·clad /ˈaɪənklæd; *NAmE* ˈaɪərn-/ *adj.* so strong that it cannot be challenged or changed: *an ironclad alibi/contract/excuse/guarantee* ◇ *His memo is ironclad proof he was involved.* ➲ compare CAST-IRON (2)

the ˌIron ˈCurtain *noun* [sing.] the name that people used for the border that used to exist between Western Europe and the COMMUNIST countries of Central and Eastern Europe

ˌ**iron-ˈgrey** (*especially BrE*) (also ˌ**iron-ˈgray** especially in *NAmE*) *adj.* dark grey in colour: *iron-grey hair*

iron·ic /aɪˈrɒnɪk; *NAmE* -ˈrɑːn-/ (also *less frequent* **iron·ic·al** /aɪˈrɒnɪkl; *NAmE* -ˈrɑːn-/) *adj.* **1** showing that you really mean the opposite of what you are saying; expressingIRONY: *an ironic comment* **2** (of a situation) strange or amusing because it is very different from what you expect: ***It's ironic that*** *she became a teacher—she used to hate school.* ➲ see also IRONY ▸ **iron·ic·al·ly** /aɪˈrɒnɪkli; *NAmE* -ˈrɑːn-/ *adv.*: *Ironically, the book she felt was her worst sold more copies than any of her others.* ◇ *He smiled ironically.*

iron·ing /ˈaɪənɪŋ; *NAmE* ˈaɪərnɪŋ/ *noun* [U] **1** the task of pressing clothes, etc. with an iron to make them smooth: *to* ***do the ironing*** **2** the clothes, etc. that you have just ironed or that need to be done: *a pile of ironing*

ˈ**ironing board** *noun* a long narrow board covered with cloth, and usually with folding legs, that you iron clothes on ➲ VISUAL VOCAB page V17

iron·mon·ger /ˈaɪənmʌŋɡə(r); *NAmE* ˈaɪərn-/ (*BrE*, becoming *old-fashioned*) (*NAmE* ˈ**hardware dealer**) *noun* **1** a person who owns or works in a shop/store selling tools and equipment for the house and garden/yard **2 ironmonger's** (*pl.* **iron·mon·gers**) a shop that sells tools and equipment for the house and garden/yard ▸ **iron·mon·gery** /-mʌŋɡəri/ *noun* [U] (*BrE*) = HARDWARE

ˌ**iron ˈrations** *noun* [pl.] (often *humorous*) a small amount of food that soldiers and people walking or climbing carry to use in an emergency

iron·stone /ˈaɪənstəʊn; *NAmE* ˈaɪərnstoʊn/ *noun* [U] a type of rock that contains iron

iron·work /ˈaɪənwɜːk; *NAmE* ˈaɪərnwɜːrk/ *noun* [U] things made of iron, such as gates, parts of buildings, etc.

iron·works /ˈaɪənwɜːks; *NAmE* ˈaɪərnwɜːrks/ *noun* (*pl.* **iron·works**) [C+sing./pl. v.] a factory where iron is obtained from ORE (= rock containing metal), or where heavy iron goods are made

irony /ˈaɪrəni/ *noun* (*pl.* **-ies**) **1** [U, C] the amusing or strange aspect of a situation that is very different from what you expect; a situation like this: ***The irony is that*** *when he finally got the job, he discovered he didn't like it.* ◇ *It was one of life's little ironies.* **2** [U] the use of words that say the opposite of what you really mean, often as a joke and with a tone of voice that shows this: *'England is famous for its food,' she said with* ***heavy irony.*** ◇ *There was a note of irony in his voice.* ◇ *She said it without a* ***hint/trace of irony.***

ir·radi·ance /ɪˈreɪdiəns/ *noun* [U] (*physics*) a measurement of the amount of light that comes from sth

ir·radi·ate /ɪˈreɪdieɪt/ *verb* **1 ~ sth** (*technical*) to treat food with GAMMA RADIATION in order to preserve it **2 ~ sth (with sth)** (*literary*) to make sth look brighter and happier: *faces irradiated with joy* ▸ **ir·radi·ation** /ɪˌreɪdiˈeɪʃn/ *noun* [U]

ir·ration·al AW /ɪˈræʃənl/ *adj.* not based on, or not using, clear logical thought SYN **unreasonable**: *an irrational fear* ◇ *You're being irrational.* OPP **rational** ▸ **ir·ration·al·ity** /ɪˌræʃəˈnæləti/ *noun* [U, C, usually sing.] **ir·ration·al·ly** /ɪˈræʃnəli/ *adv.*: *to behave irrationally*

ir,rational 'number (also **surd**) *noun* (*mathematics*) a number, for example π or the SQUARE ROOT of 2, that cannot be expressed as the RATIO of two whole numbers

ir·re·con·cil·able /ɪ'rekənsaɪləbl; ɪ,rekən'saɪləbl/ *adj.* (*formal*) **1** if differences or disagreements are **irreconcilable**, they are so great that it is not possible to settle them **2** if an idea or opinion is **irreconcilable** with another, it is impossible for sb to have both of them together: *This view is irreconcilable with common sense.* **3** people who are **irreconcilable** cannot be made to agree: *irreconcilable enemies*

ir·re·cov·er·able /,ɪrɪ'kʌvərəbl/ *adj.* (*formal*) that you cannot get back; lost: *irrecoverable costs* ◇ *irrecoverable loss of sight* **OPP** **recoverable** ▸ **ir·re·cov·er·ably** /-əbli/ *adv.*

ir·re·deem·able /,ɪrɪ'di:məbl/ *adj.* (*formal*) too bad to be corrected, improved or saved **SYN** **hopeless** ▸ **ir·re·deem·ably** /-əbli/ *adv.*: *irredeemably spoilt*

ir·re·du·cible /,ɪrɪ'dju:səbl; *NAmE* -'du:s-/ *adj.* (*formal*) that cannot be made smaller or simpler: *to cut staff to an irreducible minimum* ◇ *an irreducible fact* ▸ **ir·re·du·cibly** /-əbli/ *adv.*

ir·re·fut·able /,ɪrɪ'fju:təbl; ɪ'refjətəbl/ *adj.* (*formal*) that cannot be proved wrong and that must therefore be accepted: *irrefutable evidence* ▸ **ir·re·fut·ably** /-əbli/ *adv.*

ir·regu·lar /ɪ'regjələ(r)/ *adj.*, *noun*

■ ***adj.*** **1** not arranged in an even way; not having an even, smooth pattern or shape **SYN** **uneven**: *irregular teeth* ◇ *an irregular outline* **2** not happening at times that are at an equal distance from each other; not happening regularly: *irregular meals* ◇ *an irregular heartbeat* ◇ *irregular attendance at school* ◇ *He visited his parents* ***at irregular intervals***. **3** not normal; not according to the usual rules **SYN** **abnormal**: *an irregular practice* ◇ *His behaviour is highly irregular.* **4** (*grammar*) not formed in the normal way: *an irregular verb* **5** (of a soldier etc.) not part of a country's official army **OPP** **regular** ▸ **ir·regu·lar·ly** *adv.*

■ ***noun*** a soldier who is not a member of a country's official army

ir·regu·lar·ity /ɪ,regjə'lærəti/ *noun* (*pl.* -ies) **1** [C, U] an activity or a practice which is not according to the usual rules, or not normal: *alleged irregularities in the election campaign* ◇ *suspicion of financial irregularity* **2** [C, U] something that does not happen at regular intervals: *a slight irregularity in his heartbeat* **3** [U, C] something that is not smooth or regular in shape or arrangement: *The paint will cover any irregularity in the surface of the walls.* ➲ compare REGULARITY

ir·rele·vance **AW** /ɪ'reləvəns/ (also *less frequent* **ir·rele·vancy** /-ənsi/ *pl.* -ies) *noun* **1** [U] lack of importance to or connection with a situation: *the irrelevance of the curriculum to children's daily life* **OPP** **relevance** **2** [C, usually sing.] something that is not important to or connected with a situation: *His idea was rejected as an irrelevance.*

ir·rele·vant **AW** /ɪ'reləvənt/ *adj.* not important to or connected with a situation: ***totally/completely/largely irrelevant*** ◇ *irrelevant remarks* ◇ *Whether I believe you or not is irrelevant now.* ◇ **~ to sth/sb** *That evidence is irrelevant to the case.* ◇ *Many people consider politics irrelevant to their lives.* **OPP** **relevant** ▸ **ir·rele·vant·ly** *adv.*

ir·re·li·gious /,ɪrɪ'lɪdʒəs/ *adj.* (*formal*) without any religious belief; showing no respect for religion

ir·re·me·di·able /,ɪrɪ'mi:diəbl/ *adj.* (*formal*) too bad to be corrected or cured: *an irremediable situation* **OPP** **remediable** ▸ **ir·re·me·di·ably** /-əbli/ *adv.*

ir·rep·ar·able /ɪ'repərəbl/ *adj.* (of a loss, injury, etc.) too bad or too serious to repair or put right: *to cause* ***irreparable damage/harm*** *to your health* ◇ *Her death is an irreparable loss.* **OPP** **repairable** ▸ **ir·rep·ar·ably** /-əbli/ *adv.*: *irreparably damaged*

ir·re·place·able /,ɪrɪ'pleɪsəbl/ *adj.* too valuable or special to be replaced ➲ SYNONYMS at VALUABLE **OPP** **replaceable**

ir·re·press·ible /,ɪrɪ'presəbl/ *adj.* **1** (of a person) lively, happy and full of energy **SYN** **ebullient** **2** (of feelings, etc.) very strong; impossible to control or stop: *irrepressible confidence* ▸ **ir·re·press·ibly** /-əbli/ *adv.*

ir·re·proach·able /,ɪrɪ'prəʊtʃəbl; *NAmE* -'proʊ-/ *adj.* (of a person or their behaviour) free from fault and impossible to criticize **SYN** **blameless**

ir·re·sist·ible /,ɪrɪ'zɪstəbl/ *adj.* **1** so strong that it cannot be stopped or resisted: *I felt an irresistible urge to laugh.* ◇ *His arguments were irresistible.* **OPP** **resistible** **2** so attractive that you feel you must have it: *an irresistible bargain* ◇ *On such a hot day, the water was irresistible* (= it made you want to swim in it). ◇ **~ to sb** *The bright colours were irresistible to the baby.* ▸ **ir·re·sist·ibly** /-əbli/ *adv.*: *They were irresistibly drawn to each other.*

ir·reso·lute /ɪ'rezəlu:t/ *adj.* (*formal*) not able to decide what to do **OPP** **resolute** ▸ **ir·reso·lute·ly** *adv.* **ir·reso·lu·tion** /ɪ,rezə'lu:ʃn/ *noun* [U]

ir·re·spect·ive of /ɪrɪ'spektɪv əv/ *prep.* without considering sth or being influenced by it **SYN** **regardless of**: *Everyone is treated equally, irrespective of race.* ◇ *The weekly rent is the same irrespective of whether there are three or four occupants.*

ir·re·spon·sible /,ɪrɪ'spɒnsəbl; *NAmE* -'spɑ:n-/ *adj.* (*disapproving*) (of a person) not thinking enough about the effects of what they do; not showing a feeling of responsibility: *an irresponsible teenager* ◇ *an irresponsible attitude* ◇ ***It would be irresponsible to*** *ignore the situation.* **OPP** **responsible** ▸ **ir·re·spon·si·bil·ity** /,ɪrɪ,spɒnsə'bɪləti; *NAmE* -,spɑ:nsə-/ *noun* [U] **ir·re·spon·sibly** /-əbli/ *adv.*

ir·re·triev·able /,ɪrɪ'tri:vəbl/ *adj.* (*formal*) that you can never make right or get back: *an irretrievable situation* ◇ *the irretrievable breakdown of the marriage* ◇ *The money already paid is irretrievable.* **OPP** **retrievable** ▸ **ir·re·triev·ably** /-əbli/ *adv.*: *Some of our old traditions are irretrievably lost.*

ir·rev·er·ent /ɪ'revərənt/ *adj.* (usually *approving*) not showing respect to sb/sth that other people usually respect: *irreverent wit* ◇ *an irreverent attitude to tradition* ▸ **ir·rev·er·ence** /-əns/ *noun* [U] **ir·rev·er·ent·ly** *adv.*

ir·re·vers·ible **AW** /,ɪrɪ'vɜ:səbl; *NAmE* -'vɜ:rs-/ *adj.* that cannot be changed back to what it was before: *an irreversible change/decline/decision* ◇ *irreversible brain damage* (= that will not improve) **OPP** **reversible** ▸ **ir·re·vers·ibly** /-əbli/ *adv.*

ir·rev·oc·able /ɪ'revəkəbl/ *adj.* (*formal*) that cannot be changed **SYN** **final**: *an* ***irrevocable decision/step*** ▸ **ir·rev·oc·ably** /-əbli/ *adv.*: *irrevocably committed*

ir·ri·gate /'ɪrɪgeɪt/ *verb* **1 ~ sth** to supply water to an area of land through pipes or channels so that crops will grow: *irrigated land/crops* **2 ~ sth** (*medical*) to wash out a wound or part of the body with a flow of water or liquid ▸ **ir·ri·ga·tion** /,ɪrɪ'geɪʃn/ *noun* [U]: *irrigation channels*

ir·rit·able /'ɪrɪtəbl/ *adj.* getting annoyed easily; showing your anger **SYN** **bad-tempered**: *to be tired and irritable* ◇ *an irritable gesture* ▸ **ir·rit·abil·ity** /,ɪrɪtə'bɪləti/ *noun* [U] **ir·rit·ably** /-əbli/ *adv.*

,irritable 'bowel syndrome *noun* [U] a condition of the BOWELS that causes pain and DIARRHOEA or CONSTIPATION, often caused by stress or anxiety

ir·ri·tant /'ɪrɪtənt/ *noun* **1** (*technical*) a substance that makes part of your body sore **2** something that makes you annoyed or causes trouble ▸ **ir·ri·tant** *adj.* [usually before noun]: *irritant substances*

ir·ri·tate 0ᵂ /'ɪrɪteɪt/ *verb*

1 0ᵂ **~ sb** to annoy sb, especially by sth you continuously do or by sth that continuously happens: *The way she puts on that accent really irritates me.* **2** 0ᵂ **~ sth** to make your skin or a part of your body sore or painful: *Some drugs can irritate the lining of the stomach.* ▸ **ir·ri·tat·ing** 0ᵂ *adj.*: *I found her extremely irritating* ◇ *an irritating habit* ◇ *an irritating cough/rash* **ir·ri·tat·ing·ly** *adv.* **ir·ri·ta·tion** /,ɪrɪ'teɪʃn/ *noun* [U, C]: *He noted, with some irritation, that the letter had not been sent.* ◇ *a skin irritation*

ir·ri·tated 0→ /ˈɪrɪteɪtɪd/ *adj.*
~ (at/by/with sth) annoyed or angry: *She was getting more and more irritated at his comments.*

ir·rupt /ɪˈrʌpt/ *verb* [I] **+ adv./prep.** (*formal*) to enter or appear somewhere suddenly and with a lot of force: *Violence once again irrupted into their peaceful lives.* ▸ **ir·rup·tion** /ɪˈrʌpʃn/ *noun* [U, C]

IRS /ˌaɪ ɑːr ˈes/ *abbr.* Internal Revenue Service

Is. *abbr.* (especially on maps) Island(s); ISLE(S)

is /ɪz/ ➲ BE

ISA[1] /ˈaɪsə/ *noun* the abbreviation for 'Individual Savings Account' (a special account in Britain in which you can invest a limited amount each year without paying tax on the income)

ISA[2] /ˌaɪ es ˈeɪ/ *abbr.* Industry Standard Architecture (the usual international system used for connecting computers and other devices)

ISBN /ˌaɪ es biː ˈen/ *noun* the abbreviation for 'International Standard Book Number' (a number that identifies an individual book and its PUBLISHER)

I

is·chae·mia (*NAmE* **is·che·mia** /ɪˈskiːmiə/) *noun* [U] (*medical*) the situation when the supply of blood to an organ or part of the body, especially the heart muscles, is less than is needed

ISDN /ˌaɪ es diː ˈen/ *abbr.* integrated services digital network (a system for carrying sound signals, images, etc. along wires at high speed): *an ISDN Internet connection*

-ise ➲ -IZE

ish /ɪʃ/ *adv.* (*BrE, informal*) used after a statement to make it less definite: *I've finished. Ish. I still need to make the sauce.*

-ish 0→ *suffix* (in adjectives)
1 0→ from the country mentioned: *Turkish* ◇ *Irish* **2** 0→ (sometimes *disapproving*) having the nature of; like: *childish* **3** 0→ fairly; approximately: *reddish* ◇ *thirtyish* ▸ **-ishly** (in adverbs): *foolishly*

Islam /ˈɪzlɑːm; ɪzˈlɑːm/ *noun* [U] **1** the Muslim religion, based on belief in one God and REVEALED through Muhammad as the Prophet of Allah **2** all Muslims and Muslim countries in the world ▸ **Is·lam·ic** /ɪzˈlæmɪk; -ˈlɑːm-/ *adj.*: *Islamic law*

Is·lam·ist /ˈɪzləmɪst/ *noun* a person who believes strongly in the teachings of Islam ▸ **Is·lam·ism** /ˈɪzləmɪzəm/ *noun* [U] **Is·lam·ist** *adj.*

is·land 0→ /ˈaɪlənd/ *noun*
1 0→ (*abbr.* **I**, **I.**, **Is.**) a piece of land that is completely surrounded by water: *We spent a week on the Greek island of Kos.* ◇ *a remote island off the coast of Scotland* ➲ VISUAL VOCAB page V5 ➲ see also DESERT ISLAND **2** (*BrE*) = TRAFFIC ISLAND

is·land·er /ˈaɪləndə(r)/ *noun* a person who lives on an island, especially a small one

ˈ**island-hopping** *noun* [U] the activity of travelling from one island to another in an area that has lots of islands, especially as a tourist

isle /aɪl/ *noun* (*abbr.* **I**, **I.**, **Is.**) used especially in poetry and names to mean 'island': *the Isle of Skye* ◇ *the British Isles*

islet /ˈaɪlət/ *noun* a very small island

ism /ˈɪzəm/ *noun* (usually *disapproving*) used to refer to a set of ideas or system of beliefs or behaviour: *You're always talking in isms—sexism, ageism, racism.*

-ism *suffix* (in nouns) **1** the action or result of: *criticism* **2** the state or quality of: *heroism* **3** the teaching, system or movement of: *Buddhism* **4** unfair treatment or hatred for the reason mentioned: *racism* **5** a feature of language of the type mentioned: *an Americanism* ◇ *a colloquialism* **6** a medical condition or disease: *alcoholism*

isn't /ˈɪznt/ *short form* is not

ISO /ˌaɪ es ˈəʊ; *NAmE* ˈoʊ/ *abbr.* International Organization for Standardization (an organization established in 1946 to make the measurements used in science, industry and business standard throughout the world)

iso- /ˈaɪsəʊ; *NAmE* ˈaɪsoʊ/ *combining form* (in nouns, adjectives and adverbs) equal: *isotope* ◇ *isometric*

iso·bar /ˈaɪsəbɑː(r)/ *noun* (*technical*) a line on a weather map that joins places that have the same air pressure at a particular time

isol·ate AW /ˈaɪsəleɪt/ *verb* **1** to separate sb/sth physically or socially from other people or things: **~ sb/yourself/sth** *Patients with the disease should be isolated.* ◇ **~ sb/yourself/sth from sb/sth** *He was immediately isolated from the other prisoners.* ◇ *This decision will isolate the country from the rest of Europe.* **2 ~ sth (from sth)** (*formal*) to separate a part of a situation, problem, idea, etc. so that you can see what it is and deal with it separately: *It is possible to isolate a number of factors that contributed to her downfall.* **3 ~ sth (from sth)** (*technical*) to separate a single substance, cell, etc. from others so that you can study it: *Researchers are still trying to isolate the gene that causes this abnormality.*

isol·ated AW /ˈaɪsəleɪtɪd/ *adj.* **1** (of buildings and places) far away from any others SYN **remote**: *isolated rural areas* **2** without much contact with other people or other countries: *I felt very isolated in my new job.* ◇ *Elderly people easily become socially isolated.* ◇ *The decision left the country isolated from its allies.* **3** single; happening once: *The police said the attack was an isolated incident.*

isol·at·ing /ˈaɪsəleɪtɪŋ/ *adj.* (*linguistics*) = ANALYTIC

isol·ation AW /ˌaɪsəˈleɪʃn/ *noun* [U] **1** the act of separating sb/sth; the state of being separate: *geographical isolation* ◇ *an* ***isolation hospital/ward*** (= for people with infectious diseases) ◇ **~ (from sb/sth)** *The country has been threatened with complete isolation from the international community unless the atrocities stop.* ◇ *He lives in* ***splendid isolation*** (= far from, or in a superior position to, everyone else). **2 ~ (from sb/sth)** the state of being alone or lonely: *Many unemployed people experience feelings of isolation and depression.*
IDM **in isolation (from sb/sth)** separately; alone: *To make sense, these figures should not be looked at in isolation.*

isol·ation·ism AW /ˌaɪsəˈleɪʃənɪzəm/ *noun* [U] the policy of not becoming involved in the affairs of other countries or groups ▸ **isol·ation·ist** /-ʃənɪst/ *adj., noun*: *an isolationist foreign policy*

iso·mer /ˈaɪsəmə(r)/ *noun* **1** (*chemistry*) one of two or more COMPOUNDS which have the same atoms, but in different arrangements **2** (*physics*) one of two or more NUCLEI that have the same ATOMIC NUMBER, but different energy states ▸ **iso·mer·ic** /ˌaɪsəˈmerɪk/ *adj.* **iso·mer·ism** /ˈaɪsəmərɪzəm/ *noun* [U]

iso·met·ric /ˌaɪsəˈmetrɪk/ *adj.* **1** (*technical*) connected with a type of physical exercise in which muscles are made to work without the whole body moving **2** (*geometry*) connected with a style of drawing in three DIMENSIONS without PERSPECTIVE

iso·met·rics /ˌaɪsəˈmetrɪks/ *noun* [pl.] physical exercises in which the muscles work against each other or against a fixed object ▸ **iso·met·ric** *adj.*: *isometric exercises*

iso·prene /ˈaɪsəpriːn/ *noun* [U] a liquid HYDROCARBON obtained from PETROLEUM that is used to make artificial rubber. Isoprene is also found in natural rubber.

isos·celes tri·angle /aɪˌsɒsəliːz ˈtraɪæŋgl; *NAmE* -ˌsɑːs-/ *noun* (*geometry*) a triangle with two of its three sides the same length ➲ VISUAL VOCAB page V58

iso·therm /ˈaɪsəθɜːm; *NAmE* -θɜːrm/ *noun* (*technical*) a line on a weather map that joins places that have the same temperature at a particular time

iso·ton·ic /ˌaɪsəʊˈtɒnɪk; *NAmE* ˌaɪsoʊˈtɑːn-/ *adj.* (of a drink) with added minerals and salts, intended to replace those lost during exercise

iso·tope /ˈaɪsətəʊp; *NAmE* -toʊp/ *noun* (*physics, chemistry*) one of two or more forms of a chemical element which have the same number of PROTONS but a different number of NEUTRONS in their atoms. They have different physical

PROPERTIES (= characteristics) but the same chemical ones: *radioactive isotopes* ◇ *the many isotopes of carbon*

ISP /ˌaɪ es ˈpiː/ *abbr.* Internet Service Provider (a company that provides you with an Internet connection and services such as email, etc.)

I-spy /ˌaɪ ˈspaɪ/ *noun* [U] a children's game in which one player gives the first letter of a thing that they can see and the others have to guess what it is

Is·rael·ite /ˈɪzrəlaɪt; ˈɪzriə-/ *noun* a member of the ancient Hebrew nation described in the Bible

issue 0-w AW /ˈɪʃuː; *BrE* also ˈɪsjuː/ *noun, verb*

■ ***noun***

▸ TOPIC OF DISCUSSION **1** 0-w [C] an important topic that people are discussing or arguing about: *a* ***key/sensitive/ controversial issue*** ◇ *This is a* ***big issue****; we need more time to think about it.* ◇ *She usually writes about environmental issues.* ◇ *The union plans to* ***raise the issue*** *of overtime.* ◇ *The party was divided on this issue.* ◇ *You're just* ***avoiding the issue****.* ◇ *Don't* ***confuse the issue****.*

▸ PROBLEM/WORRY **2** 0-w [C] a problem or worry that sb has with sth: *Money is* ***not an issue****.* ◇ *I don't think my private life is the issue here.* ◇ *I'm not bothered about the cost—you're the one who's* ***making an issue*** *of it.* ◇ *Because I grew up in a dysfunctional family, anger is a big issue for me.* ◇ *She's always on a diet—she* ***has issues about*** *food.* ◇ *He still has* ***some issues with*** *women* (= has problems dealing with them). ◇ *If you have any issues, please call this number.*

▸ MAGAZINE/NEWSPAPER **3** 0-w [C] one of a regular series of magazines or newspapers: *the July issue of 'What Car?'* ◇ *The article appeared in issue 25.*

▸ OF STAMPS/COINS/SHARES **4** [C] a number or set of things that are supplied and made available at the same time: *The company is planning a new* ***share issue****.* ◇ *a special issue of stamps*

▸ MAKING AVAILABLE/KNOWN **5** [U] the act of supplying or making available things for people to buy or use: *I bought a set of the new stamps on the date of issue.* ◇ *the issue of blankets to the refugees* ◇ *the issue of a joint statement by the French and German foreign ministers*

▸ CHILDREN **6** [U] (*law*) children of your own: *He died without issue.*

IDM **be at ˈissue** to be the most important part of the subject that is being discussed: *What is at issue is whether she was responsible for her actions.* **take ˈissue with sb (about/on/over sth)** (*formal*) to start disagreeing or arguing with sb about sth: *I must take issue with you on that point.* ➲ more at FORCE *v.*

■ ***verb***

▸ MAKE KNOWN **1** 0-w **~ sth (to sb)** to make sth known formally: *They issued a joint statement denying the charges.* ◇ *The police have issued an appeal for witnesses.*

▸ GIVE **2** 0-w [often passive] to give sth to sb, especially officially: **~ sth** *to* ***issue passports/visas/tickets*** ◇ **~ sb with sth** *New members will be issued with a temporary identity card.* ◇ **~ sth to sb** *Work permits were issued to only 5% of those who applied for them.*

▸ LAW **3** **~ sth** to start a legal process against sb, especially by means of an official document: *to issue a writ against sb* ◇ *A warrant has been issued for his arrest.*

▸ MAGAZINE **4** **~ sth** to produce sth such as a magazine, article, etc: *We issue a monthly newsletter.*

▸ STAMPS/COINS/SHARES **5** **~ sth** to produce new stamps, coins, shares, etc. for sale to the public: *They issued a special set of stamps to mark the occasion.*

PHR V **ˈissue from sth** (*formal*) to come out of sth: *A weak trembling sound issued from his lips.* ▸ **is·suer** *noun*: *credit-card issuers*

-ist *suffix* (in nouns and some related adjectives) **1** a person who believes or practises sth: *atheist* **2** a member of a profession or business activity: *dentist* **3** a person who uses a thing: *violinist* **4** a person who does sth: *plagiarist*

-ista /ˈɪstə/ *suffix* (in nouns) a person who is very enthusiastic about sth: *fashionistas who are slaves to the latest trends*

isth·mus /ˈɪsməs/ *noun* a narrow strip of land, with water on each side, that joins two larger pieces of land

IT /ˌaɪ ˈtiː/ *noun* [U] the abbreviation for 'information technology' (the study and use of electronic processes and equipment to store and send information of all kinds, including words, pictures and numbers)

it 0-w /ɪt/ *pron.*

(used as the subject or object of a verb or after a preposition) **1** 0-w used to refer to an animal or a thing that has already been mentioned or that is being talked about now: *'Where's your car?' 'It's in the garage.'* ◇ *Did you see it?* ◇ *Start a new file and put this letter in it.* ◇ *Look! It's going up that tree.* ◇ *We have $500. Will it be enough for a deposit?* **2** 0-w used to refer to a baby, especially one whose sex is not known: *Her baby's due next month. She hopes it will be a boy.* **3** 0-w used to refer to a fact or situation that is already known or happening: *When the factory closes, it will mean 500 people losing their jobs.* ◇ *Yes, I was at home on Sunday. What about it?* (= Why do you ask?) ◇ *Stop it, you're hurting me!* **4** 0-w used to identify a person: *It's your mother on the phone.* ◇ *Hello, Peter, it's Mike here.* ◇ *Hi, it's me!* ◇ *Was it you who put these books on my desk?* **5** 0-w used in the position of the subject or object of a verb when the real subject or object is at the end of the sentence: *Does it matter what colour it is?* ◇ *It's impossible to get there in time.* ◇ *It's no use shouting.* ◇ *She finds it boring at home.* ◇ *It appears that the two leaders are holding secret talks.* ◇ *I find it strange that she doesn't want to go.* ➲ LANGUAGE BANK at IMPERSONAL **6** 0-w used in the position of the subject of a verb when you are talking about time, the date, distance, the weather, etc.: *It's ten past twelve.* ◇ *It's our anniversary.* ◇ *It's two miles to the beach.* ◇ *It's a long time since they left.* ◇ *It was raining this morning.* ◇ *It's quite warm at the moment.* **7** 0-w used when you are talking about a situation: *If it's convenient I can come tomorrow.* ◇ *It's good to talk.* ◇ *I like it here.* **8** 0-w used to emphasize any part of a sentence: *It's Jim who's the clever one.* ◇ *It's Spain that they're going to, not Portugal.* ◇ *It was three weeks later that he heard the news.* **9** exactly what is needed: *In this business, either you've got it or you haven't.* ➲ see also ITS

IDM **that is ˈit** **1** this/that is the important point, reason, etc: *That's just it—I can't work when you're making so much noise.* **2** 0-w this/that is the end: *I'm afraid that's it—we've lost.* **this is ˈit** **1** the expected event is just going to happen: *Well, this is it! Wish me luck.* **2** this is the main point: *'You're doing too much.' 'Well, this is it. I can't cope with any more work.'*

Ital·ian·ate /ɪˈtæljəneɪt/ *adj.* in an Italian style: *a Italianate villa*

Ital·ic /ɪˈtælɪk/ *adj.* [only before noun] of or connected with the branch of Indo-European languages that includes Latin and some other ancient languages of Italy, and the Romance languages

ital·ic /ɪˈtælɪk/ *adj.* (of printed or written letters) leaning to the right: *The example sentences in this dictionary are printed in italic type.* ◇ *Use an italic font.* ➲ compare ROMAN

itali·cize (*BrE* also **-ise**) /ɪˈtælɪsaɪz/ *verb* [often passive] **~ sth** to write or print sth in italics

ital·ics /ɪˈtælɪks/ *noun* [pl.] (also **italic** [sing.]) printed letters that lean to the right: *Examples in this dictionary are in italics.* ◇ *Use italics for the names of books or plays.* ➲ compare ROMAN

Italo- /ˈɪtələʊ; ɪˈtæləʊ; *NAmE* -loʊ/ *combining form* (with nouns and adjectives) Italian; Italian and something else: *Italo-Americans* ◇ *Italophiles*

itch /ɪtʃ/ *verb, noun*

■ ***verb*** **1** [I] to have an uncomfortable feeling on your skin that makes you want to scratch; to make your skin feel like this: *I itch all over.* ◇ *Does the rash itch?* ◇ *This sweater really itches.* ➲ SYNONYMS at HURT **2** [I] (*informal*) (often used in the progressive tenses) to want to do sth very much: **~ for sth** *The crowd was itching for a fight.* ◇ **~ to do sth** *He's itching to get back to work.*

■ ***noun*** **1** [C, usually sing.] an uncomfortable feeling on your skin that makes you want to scratch yourself: *to* ***get/have an itch*** **2** [sing.] **~ (to do sth)** (*informal*) a strong desire to do sth: *She has an itch to travel.* ◇ *the creative itch* IDM see SEVEN

itchy /ˈɪtʃi/ *adj.* having or producing an itch on the skin: *an itchy nose/rash* ◇ *I feel itchy all over.* ➲ SYNONYMS at PAINFUL ▶ **itchi·ness** *noun* [U]

IDM **(get/have) itchy ˈfeet** (*informal*) to want to travel or move to a different place; to want to do sth different

it'd /ˈɪtəd/ *short form* **1** it had **2** it would

-ite *suffix* (in nouns) (often *disapproving*) a person who follows or supports sb/sth: *Blairite* ◇ *Trotskyite*

item 🔑 AW /ˈaɪtəm/ *noun*
1 🔑 one thing on a list of things to buy, do, talk about, etc: *What's the next item on the agenda?* **2** 🔑 a single article or object: *Can I pay for each item separately?* ◇ *The computer was my largest single item of expenditure.* ◇ *This clock is a **collector's item*** (= because it is rare and valuable). **3** 🔑 a single piece of news in a newspaper, on television, etc: *an item of news/a news item*

IDM **be an item** (*informal*) to be involved in a romantic or sexual relationship: *Are they an item?*

I

item·ize (*BrE* also **-ise**) AW /ˈaɪtəmaɪz/ *verb* **~ sth** to produce a detailed list of things: *The report itemizes 23 different faults.* ◇ *an itemized phone bill* (= each call is shown separately)

it·er·ate /ˈɪtəreɪt/ *verb* [I] to repeat a MATHEMATICAL or COMPUTING process or set of instructions again and again, each time applying it to the result of the previous stage

it·er·ation /ˌɪtəˈreɪʃn/ *noun* **1** [U, C] the process of repeating a MATHEMATICAL or COMPUTING process or set of instructions again and again, each time applying it to the result of the previous stage **2** [C] a new version of a piece of computer software

it·in·er·ant /aɪˈtɪnərənt/ *adj.* [usually before noun] (*formal*) travelling from place to place, especially to find work: ***itinerant workers/musicians*** ◇ *to lead an itinerant life* ▶ **it·in·er·ant** *noun*: *homeless itinerants*

it·in·er·ary /aɪˈtɪnərəri; *NAmE* aɪˈtɪnəreri/ *noun* (*pl.* **-ies**) a plan of a journey, including the route and the places that you visit ➲ COLLOCATIONS at TRAVEL

-ition ➲ -ION

-itis *suffix* (in nouns) **1** (*medical*) a disease of: *tonsillitis* **2** (*informal*, especially *humorous*) too much of; too much interest in: *World Cup-itis*

it'll /ˈɪtl/ *short form* it will

its 🔑 /ɪts/ *det.*
belonging to or connected with a thing, an animal or a baby: *Turn the box on its side.* ◇ *Have you any idea of its value?* ◇ *The dog had hurt its paw.* ◇ *The baby threw its food on the floor.*

it's /ɪts/ *short form* **1** it is **2** it has

it·self 🔑 /ɪtˈself/ *pron.*
1 🔑 (the reflexive form of *it*) used when the animal or thing that does an action is also affected by it: *The cat was washing itself.* ◇ *Does the computer turn itself off?* ◇ *The company has got itself into difficulties.* ◇ *There's no need for the team to feel proud of itself.* **2** 🔑 used to emphasize an animal, a thing, etc.: *The village itself is pretty, but the surrounding countryside is rather dull.*

IDM **be ˌpatience, ˌhonesty, simˌplicity, etc. itˈself** to be an example of complete patience, etc: *The manager of the hotel was courtesy itself.* **(all) by itˈself 1** automatically; without anyone doing anything: *The machine will start by itself in a few seconds.* **2** alone: *The house stands by itself in an acre of land.* **in itˈself** considered separately from other things; in its true nature: *In itself, it's not a difficult problem to solve.* **to itˈself** not shared with others: *It doesn't have the market to itself.*

itty-bitty /ˌɪti ˈbɪti/ (also **itsy-bitsy** /ˌɪtsi ˈbɪtsi/) *adj.* [only before noun] (*informal, especially NAmE*) very small

ITV /ˌaɪ tiː ˈviː/ *abbr.* Independent Television (a group of British companies that produce programmes that are paid for by advertising)

-ity *suffix* (in nouns) the quality or state of: *purity* ◇ *oddity*

IUD /ˌaɪ juː ˈdiː/ (also **coil**) *noun* the abbreviation for 'intra-uterine device' (a small plastic or metal object placed inside a woman's UTERUS (= where a baby grows before it is born) to stop her becoming pregnant)

IV /ˌaɪ ˈviː/ *abbr., noun*
■ ***abbr.*** INTRAVENOUS, INTRAVENOUSLY
■ ***noun*** (*NAmE*) = DRIP (3)

I've /aɪv/ *short form* I have

-ive *suffix* (in nouns and adjectives) tending to; having the nature of: *explosive* ◇ *descriptive*

IVF /ˌaɪ viː ˈef/ *noun* [U] (*technical*) the abbreviation for 'in vitro fertilization' (a process which FERTILIZES an egg from a woman outside her body. The egg is then put inside her UTERUS to develop.) ➲ see also TEST-TUBE BABY

ivory /ˈaɪvəri/ (*pl.* **-ies**) *noun* **1** [U] a hard yellowish-white substance like bone that forms the TUSKS (= long teeth) of ELEPHANTS and some other animals: *a ban on the ivory trade* ◇ *an ivory chess set* **2** [C] an object made of ivory **3** [U] a yellowish-white colour

ˌivory ˈtower *noun* (*disapproving*) a place or situation where you are separated from the problems and practical aspects of normal life and therefore do not have to worry about or understand them: *academics living in ivory towers*

ivy /ˈaɪvi/ *noun* [U, C] (*pl.* **-ies**) a climbing plant, especially one with dark green shiny leaves with five points: *stone walls covered in ivy* ➲ VISUAL VOCAB page V9 ➲ see also POISON IVY

the ˌIvy ˈLeague *noun* [sing.] a group of eight traditional universities in the eastern US with high academic standards and a high social status ➲ compare OXBRIDGE ▶ **ˌIvy ˈLeague** *adj.*: *Ivy League colleges*

iwi /ˈiːwi/ *noun* (*pl.* **iwi**) (*NZE*) a Maori community or people

-ize, -ise *suffix* (in verbs) **1** to become, make or make like: *privatize* ◇ *fossilize* ◇ *Americanize* **2** to speak, think, act, treat, etc. in the way mentioned: *criticize* ◇ *theorize* ◇ *deputize* ◇ *pasteurize* **3** to place in: *hospitalize* ▶ **-ization, -isation** (in nouns): *immunization* **-izationally, -isationally** (in adverbs): *organizationally*

Jj

J (also **j**) /dʒeɪ/ *noun* [C, U] (*pl.* **Js, J's, j's** /dʒeɪz/) the 10th letter of the English alphabet: *'Jelly' begins with (a) J/'J'.*

ja /jɑː/ *exclamation* (*SAfrE, informal*) yes

jab /dʒæb/ *verb, noun*

■ ***verb*** (-bb-) [T, I] to push a pointed object into sb/sth, or in the direction of sb/sth, with a sudden strong movement **SYN prod**: **~ sb/sth (in sth) (with sth)** *She jabbed him in the ribs with her finger.* ◇ **~ sth in sth** *She jabbed her finger in his ribs.* ◇ **~ (at sb/sth) (with sth)** *He jabbed at the picture with his finger.* ◇ *The boxer jabbed at his opponent.*

■ ***noun* 1** a sudden strong hit with sth pointed or with a FIST (= a tightly closed hand): *She gave him a jab in the stomach with her elbow.* ◇ *a boxer's left jab* **2** (*BrE, informal*) an INJECTION to help prevent you from catching a disease: *a flu jab*

jab·ber /ˈdʒæbə(r)/ *verb* [I, T] **~ (about sth)** | **+ speech** (*disapproving*) to talk quickly and in an excited way so that it is difficult to understand what you are saying **SYN gabble**: *What is he jabbering about now?* ▶ **jab·ber** *noun* [U]

jaca·randa /ˌdʒækəˈrændə/ *noun* [C, U] a tropical tree with blue flowers and pleasant-smelling wood; the wood of this tree

jack /dʒæk/ *noun, verb, adj.*

■ ***noun* 1** [C] a device for raising heavy objects off the ground, especially vehicles so that a wheel can be changed **2** [C] an electronic connection between two pieces of electrical equipment **3** [C] (in a PACK/DECK of cards) a card with a picture of a young man on it, worth more than a ten and less than a queen: *the jack of clubs* ➲ VISUAL VOCAB page V32 **4** [C] (in the game of BOWLS) a small white ball towards which players roll larger balls **5 jacks** [pl.] a children's game in which players BOUNCE a small ball and pick up small metal objects, also called jacks, before catching the ball **6** (also **jack ˈshit**, *taboo*) [U] (*NAmE, slang*) (usually used in negative sentences) anything or nothing at all: *You don't know jack.* ➲ see also BLACKJACK, FLAPJACK, UNION JACK

IDM **a jack of ˈall trades** a person who can do many different types of work, but who perhaps does not do them very well ➲ more at ALL RIGHT *adj.*, WORK *n.*

■ ***verb* ~ sth** | **~ sb (for sth)** (*NAmE, informal*) to steal sth from sb, especially sth small or of low value: *Someone jacked my seat.*

PHR V **ˌjack sb aˈround** (*NAmE, informal*) to treat sb in a way that is deliberately not helpful to them or wastes their time: *Let's go. We're being jacked around here.* **ˌjack ˈin/ˈinto sth** (*informal*) to connect to a computer system: *I'm jacking into the Internet now.* **ˌjack sth↔ˈin** (*BrE, informal*) to decide to stop doing sth, especially your job: *After five years, he decided to* ***jack it all in***. **ˌjack ˈoff** (*taboo, slang*) (of a man) to MASTURBATE **ˌjack ˈup** (*informal*) to INJECT an illegal drug directly into your blood: *Drug users were jacking up in the stairwells.* **ˌjack sth↔ˈup 1** to lift sth, especially a vehicle, off the ground using a jack **2** (*informal*) to increase sth, especially prices, by a large amount

■ ***adj.*** [not before noun] **~ of sb/sth** (*AustralE*) tired of or bored with sb/sth

jackal /ˈdʒækl; -kɔːl/ *noun* a wild animal like a dog, that eats the meat of animals that are already dead and lives in Africa and Asia

jacka·napes /ˈdʒækəneɪps/ *noun* (*old use*) a person who is rude in an annoying way

jacka·roo /ˌdʒækəˈruː/ *noun* (*pl.* **-oos**) (*AustralE, NZE, informal*) a young man who is working on a farm in Australia/New Zealand to get experience ➲ compare JILLAROO

jack·ass /ˈdʒækæs/ *noun* (*informal, especially NAmE*) a stupid person: *Careful, you jackass!*

jack·boot /ˈdʒækbuːt/ *noun* **1** [C] a tall boot that reaches up to the knee, worn by soldiers, especially in the past **2 the jackboot** [sing.] used to refer to cruel military rule: *to be* ***under the jackboot of*** *a dictatorial regime*

ˈJack cheese *noun* [U] (*NAmE*) = MONTEREY JACK

jack·daw /ˈdʒækdɔː/ *noun* a black and grey bird of the CROW family

jacket 🔑 /ˈdʒækɪt/ *noun*

1 🔑 a piece of clothing worn on the top half of the body over a shirt, etc. that has sleeves and fastens down the front; a short, light coat: *a denim/tweed jacket* ◇ *I have to wear a jacket and tie to work.* ➲ VISUAL VOCAB page V50 ➲ see also BOMBER JACKET, DINNER JACKET, DONKEY JACKET, FLAK JACKET, LIFE JACKET, SMOKING JACKET, SPORTS JACKET, STRAITJACKET **2** (also **ˈdust jacket**) a loose paper cover for a book, usually with a design or picture on it **3** an outer cover around a hot water pipe, etc, for example to reduce loss of heat **4** (*BrE*) the skin of a baked potato: *potatoes baked in their jackets* **5** (*especially NAmE*) = SLEEVE (3)

ˌjacket poˈtato *noun* = BAKED POTATO

ˌJack ˈFrost *noun* [sing.] FROST, considered as a person: *Jack Frost was threatening to kill the new plants.*

jack·fruit /ˈdʒækfruːt/ *noun* **1** [C, U] a large tropical fruit **2** [C] the tree that jackfruits grow on

jack·ham·mer /ˈdʒækhæmə(r)/ (*NAmE*) (*BrE* **pneuˌmatic ˈdrill**) *noun* a large powerful tool, worked by air pressure, used especially for breaking up road surfaces

ˈjack-in-the-box *noun* a toy in the shape of a box with a figure inside on a spring that jumps up when you open the lid

jack·knife /ˈdʒæknaɪf/ *noun, verb*

■ ***noun*** (*pl.* **jack·knives** /-naɪvz/) a large knife with a folding blade

■ ***verb*** [I] to form a V-shape. For example if a lorry/truck that is in two parts **jackknifes**, the driver loses control and the back part moves towards the front part.

jack-o'-lantern /ˌdʒæk ə ˈlæntən; *NAmE* ˈdʒækə læntərn/ *noun* a PUMPKIN (= a large orange vegetable) with a face cut into it and a CANDLE put inside to shine through the holes

ˈjack plug *noun* a type of plug used to make a connection between the parts of a SOUND SYSTEM, etc.

jack·pot /ˈdʒækpɒt; *NAmE* -pɑːt/ *noun* a large amount of money that is the most valuable prize in a game of chance: *to win the jackpot* ◇ *jackpot winners* ◇ (*figurative*) *United* ***hit the jackpot*** (= were successful) *with a 5-0 win over Liverpool.*

jack·rab·bit /ˈdʒækræbɪt/ *noun* a large N American HARE (= an animal like a large RABBIT) with very long ears

Jack Robinson /ˌdʒæk ˈrɒbɪnsn; *NAmE* ˈrɑːb-/ *noun*

IDM **before you can say Jack ˈRobinson** (*old-fashioned*) very quickly; very soon

ˌjack ˈshit *noun* [U] (*NAmE, taboo, slang*) = JACK (6)

jack·sie (also **jack·sy**) /ˈdʒæksi/ *noun* (*BrE, informal*) your bottom (= the part of your body that you sit on)

jack·straw /ˈdʒækstrɔː/ (*NAmE*) (*BrE* **spilli·kins**) *noun* [U] a game in which you remove a small stick from a pile, without moving any of the other sticks

ˌJack ˈTar *noun* (*BrE, old-fashioned, informal*) a sailor

ˌJack the ˈLad *noun* [sing.] (*BrE, informal*) a young man who is very confident in a rude and noisy way, and enjoys going out with male friends, drinking alcohol and trying to attract women

Jaco·bean /ˌdʒækəˈbiːən/ *adj.* connected with the time when James I (1603–25) was King of England: *Jacobean drama*

Jaco·bite /ˈdʒækəbaɪt/ *noun* a supporter of King James II of England, Scotland and Ireland, or his son or grandson, after he was removed from power in 1688

Ja·cuzzi™ /dʒəˈkuːzi/ (also **spa** especially in *NAmE*) *noun* a large bath/BATHTUB with a PUMP that moves the water around, giving a pleasant feeling to your body

jade /dʒeɪd/ *noun* [U] **1** a hard stone that is usually green and is used in making jewellery and decorative objects: *a jade necklace* **2** objects made of jade: *a collection of Chinese jade* **3** (also ˌ**jade** ˈ**green**) a bright green colour

jaded /ˈdʒeɪdɪd/ *adj.* tired and bored, usually because you have had too much of sth: *I felt terribly jaded after working all weekend.* ◇ *It was a meal to tempt even the most jaded palate.*

jag /dʒæɡ/ *noun* (*informal, especially NAmE*) a short period of doing sth or of behaving in a particular way, especially in a way that you cannot control: *a crying jag*

jagged /ˈdʒæɡɪd/ *adj.* with rough, pointed, often sharp edges: *jagged rocks/peaks/edges*

jag·uar /ˈdʒæɡjuə(r)/ *noun* a large animal of the cat family, that has yellowish-brown fur with black rings and spots. Jaguars live in parts of Central and S America.

jail (*BrE* also **gaol**) /dʒeɪl/ *noun, verb*

▪ ***noun*** [U, C] a prison: *She spent a year in jail.* ◇ *He has been released from jail.* ◇ *a ten-year jail sentence* ◇ *Britain's overcrowded jails* ➲ COLLOCATIONS at JUSTICE ➲ note at SCHOOL

▪ ***verb*** [usually passive] **~ sb** (**for sth**) to put sb in prison SYN **imprison**: *He* ***was jailed for life*** *for murder.*

jail·bait /ˈdʒeɪlbeɪt/ *noun* [U] (*informal*) a girl or boy who is too young to have sex with legally

jail·bird /ˈdʒeɪlbɜːd; *NAmE* -bɜːrd/ *noun* (*old-fashioned, informal*) a person who has spent a lot of time in prison

jail·break /ˈdʒeɪlbreɪk/ *noun* (*especially NAmE*) an escape from prison, usually by several people

jail·er /ˈdʒeɪlə(r)/ (*BrE* also **gaol·er**) *noun* (*old-fashioned*) a person in charge of a prison and the prisoners in it

jail·house /ˈdʒeɪlhaʊs/ *noun* (*NAmE*) a prison

Jain /dʒeɪn/ *noun* a member of an Indian religion whose principles include not harming any living creature and a belief in REINCARNATION ▶ **Jain** *adj.* **Jain·ism** /ˈdʒeɪnɪzəm/ *noun* [U]

jala·peño /ˌhæləˈpeɪnjəʊ; *NAmE* ˌhɑːləˈpeɪnjoʊ/ (also ˌ**jala**ˌ**peño** ˈ**pepper**) *noun* (from *Spanish*) the small green fruit of a type of pepper plant, that has a very hot taste and is used in Mexican cooking

jal·opy /dʒəˈlɒpi; *NAmE* -ˈlɑːpi/ *noun* (*pl.* -ies) (*old-fashioned, informal*) an old car that is in bad condition

jam 🔑 /dʒæm/ *noun, verb*

▪ ***noun***

▸ SWEET FOOD **1** 🔑 [U, C] a thick sweet substance made by boiling fruit with sugar, often sold in JARS and spread on bread: *strawberry jam* ◇ *recipes for jams and preserves* ◇ (*BrE*) *a jam doughnut* ➲ compare JELLY, MARMALADE

▸ MANY PEOPLE/VEHICLES **2** [C] a situation in which it is difficult or impossible to move because there are so many people or vehicles in one particular place: *The bus was delayed in a five-mile jam.* ◇ *As fans rushed to leave, jams formed at all the exits.* ➲ see also TRAFFIC JAM

▸ MACHINE **3** [C] a situation in which a machine does not work because sth is stuck in one position: *There's a paper jam in the photocopier.*

IDM **be in a** ˈ**jam** (*informal*) to be in a difficult situation **jam to**ˈ**morrow** (*BrE, informal*) good things that are promised for the future but never happen: *They refused to settle for a promise of jam tomorrow.* ➲ more at MONEY

▪ ***verb*** (-mm-)

▸ PUSH WITH FORCE **1** [T] **~ sth + adv./prep.** to push sth somewhere with a lot of force: *He jammed his fingers in his ears.* ◇ *A stool had been jammed against the door.*

▸ STOP MOVING/WORKING **2** [I, T] to become unable to move or work; to make sth do this: **~** (**up**) *The photocopier keeps jamming up.* ◇ **~ sth** (**up**) *There's a loose part that keeps jamming the mechanism.* ◇ **+ adj.** *The valve has jammed shut.* ◇ **~ sth + adj.** *He jammed the door open with a piece of wood.*

▸ PUT INTO SMALL SPACE **3** [T, I] to put sb/sth into a small space where there is very little room to move SYN **squash, squeeze**: **~ sb/sth + adv./prep.** *Six of us were jammed into one small car.* ◇ *We were jammed together like sardines in a can.* ◇ *The cupboards were* ***jammed full*** *of old newspapers.* ◇ **+ adv./prep.** *Nearly 1 000 students jammed into the hall.* ➲ see also JAM-PACKED

▸ FILL WITH PEOPLE/THINGS **4** [T] **~ sth** (**up**) (**with sb/sth**) to fill sth with a large number of people or things so that it is unable to function as it should SYN **block**: *Viewers jammed the switchboard with complaints.*

▸ RADIO BROADCAST **5** [T] **~ sth** (*technical*) to send out radio signals to prevent another radio broadcast from being heard

▸ PLAY MUSIC **6** [I, T] **~** (**sth**) to play music with other musicians in an informal way without preparing or practising first

IDM **jam on the brake**(**s**) | **jam the brake**(**s**) **on** to operate the BRAKES on a vehicle suddenly and with force: *The car skidded as he jammed on the brakes.*

jamb /dʒæm/ *noun* a vertical post at the side of a door or window

jam·ba·laya /ˌdʒæmbəˈlaɪə/ *noun* [U] a spicy dish of rice, SEAFOOD, chicken, etc. from the southern US

jam·bo·ree /ˌdʒæmbəˈriː/ *noun* **1** a large party or celebration: *the movie industry's annual jamboree at Cannes* **2** a large meeting of SCOUTS or GUIDES

ˈ**jam jar** *noun* (*BrE*) a glass container for jam, etc.

jammed /dʒæmd/ *adj.* **1** [not before noun] not able to move SYN **stuck**: *I can't get the door open—it's completely jammed.* **2** (*especially NAmE*) very full; crowded SYN **jam-packed**: *Hundreds more people were waiting outside the jammed stadium.*

jammy /ˈdʒæmi/ *adj.* **1** covered with jam: *jammy fingers* **2** (*BrE, informal*) lucky, especially because sth good has happened to you without you making any effort

ˌ**jam-**ˈ**packed** *adj.* [not usually before noun] **~** (**with sb/sth**) (*informal*) very full or crowded: *The train was jam-packed with commuters.*

ˈ**jam session** *noun* an occasion when musicians perform in an informal way without practising first

Jane Doe /ˌdʒeɪn ˈdəʊ; *NAmE* ˈdoʊ/ *noun* [sing.] (*NAmE*) **1** used to refer to a woman whose name is not known or is kept secret, especially in a court of law **2** an average woman ➲ compare JOHN DOE

jan·gle /ˈdʒæŋɡl/ *verb, noun*

▪ ***verb*** **1** [I, T] to make an unpleasant sound, like two pieces of metal hitting each other; to make sth do this: *The shop bell jangled loudly.* ◇ **~ sth** *He jangled the keys in his pocket.* **2** [I, T] **~** (**sth**) if your nerves **jangle**, or if sb/sth **jangles** them, you feel anxious or upset: *She was suddenly wide awake, her nerves jangling.*

▪ ***noun*** [usually sing.] a hard noise like that of metal hitting metal

jani·tor /ˈdʒænɪtə(r)/ *noun* (*NAmE, ScotE*) = CUSTODIAN

Janu·ary 🔑 /ˈdʒænjuəri; *NAmE* -jueri/ *noun* [U, C] (*abbr.* **Jan.**)
the 1st month of the year, between December and February. HELP To see how **January** is used, look at the examples at **April**.

Jap /dʒæp/ *noun* (*taboo, slang*) an offensive word for a Japanese person

jape /dʒeɪp/ *noun* (*old-fashioned, BrE*) a trick or joke that is played on sb

ja·pon·ica /dʒəˈpɒnɪkə; *NAmE* -ˈpɑːn-/ *noun* a Japanese bush that is often grown in gardens/yards, and that has red flowers and pale yellow fruit

jar /dʒɑː(r)/ *noun, verb*

▪ ***noun*** **1** [C] a round glass container, with a lid, used for storing food, especially jam, HONEY, etc: *a storage jar* ➲ VISUAL VOCAB page V29 ➲ see also JAM JAR **2** [C] a jar and what it contains: *a jar of coffee* **3** [C] a tall container with a wide mouth, with or without handles, used in the past for carrying water, etc: *a water jar* ➲ see also BELL JAR **4** [C] (*BrE, informal*) a glass of beer: *Do you fancy a jar after work?* **5** [sing.] an unpleasant shock, especially from two things being suddenly shaken or hit: *The fall gave him a nasty jar.*

■ ***verb*** (-rr-) **1** [T, I] to give or receive a sudden sharp painful knock: **~ sth** *The jolt seemed to jar every bone in her body.* ◇ **~ (sth) (on sth)** *The spade jarred on something metal.* **2** [I, T] **~ (on sth) | ~ (sth)** to have an unpleasant or annoying effect SYN **grate**: *His constant moaning was beginning to jar on her nerves.* ◇ *There was a jarring note of triumph in his voice.* **3** [I] **~ (with sth)** to be different from sth in a strange or unpleasant way SYN **clash**: *Her brown shoes jarred with the rest of the outfit.*

jar·gon /ˈdʒɑːɡən; *NAmE* ˈdʒɑːrɡən/ *noun* [U] (often *disapproving*) words or expressions that are used by a particular profession or group of people, and are difficult for others to understand: ***medical/legal/computer, etc. jargon*** ◇ *Try to avoid using too much technical jargon.*

jar·head /ˈdʒɑːhed; *NAmE* ˈdʒɑːr-/ *noun* (*NAmE, informal*) a member of the US Marine Corps (= American soldiers trained to serve on land or at sea)

jas·mine /ˈdʒæzmɪn/ *noun* [U, C] a plant with white or yellow flowers with a sweet smell, sometimes used to make PERFUME and to flavour tea

jaun·dice /ˈdʒɔːndɪs/ *noun* [U] a medical condition in which the skin and the white parts of the eyes become yellow

jaun·diced /ˈdʒɔːndɪst/ *adj.* **1** not expecting sb/sth to be good or useful, especially because of experiences that you have had in the past: *He had a jaundiced view of life.* ◇ *She looked on politicians* ***with a jaundiced eye.*** **2** suffering from jaundice: *a* ***jaundiced patient/liver***

jaunt /dʒɔːnt/ *noun* (*old-fashioned* or *humorous*) a short journey that you make for pleasure SYN **excursion**

jaunty /ˈdʒɔːnti/ *adj.* **1** showing that you are feeling confident and pleased with yourself SYN **cheerful**: *a jaunty smile* **2** lively: *a jaunty tune* ▶ **jaunt·ily** *adv.*: *He set off jauntily, whistling to himself.* **jaunti·ness** *noun* [U]

jav·elin /ˈdʒævlɪn/ *noun* **1** [C] a light SPEAR (= a long stick with a pointed end) which is thrown in a sporting event **2 the javelin** [sing.] the event or sport of throwing a javelin as far as possible ➲ VISUAL VOCAB page V38

jaw /dʒɔː/ *noun, verb*

■ ***noun* 1** [C] either of the two bones at the bottom of the face that contain the teeth and move when you talk or eat: *the* ***top/upper jaw*** ◇ *the* ***bottom/lower jaw*** **2** [sing.] the lower part of the face; the lower jaw: *He has a strong square jaw.* ◇ *The punch broke my jaw.* ➲ VISUAL VOCAB page V48 **3 jaws** [pl.] the mouth and teeth of a person or an animal: *The alligator's jaws snapped shut.* **4 jaws** [pl.] the parts of a tool or machine that are used to hold things tightly: *the jaws of a vice*

IDM **sb's ˈjaw dropped/fell/sagged** used to say that sb suddenly looked surprised, shocked or disappointed **the jaws of ˈdeath, deˈfeat, etc.** (*literary*) used to describe an unpleasant situation that almost happens: *The team snatched victory from the jaws of defeat.* **the jaws of a tunnel, etc.** the narrow entrance to a tunnel, etc, especially one that looks dangerous

■ ***verb*** [I] (*informal*, often *disapproving*) to talk, especially to talk a lot or for a long time

jawan /dʒəˈwɑːn/ *noun* (*IndE*) a soldier of low rank

jaw·bone /ˈdʒɔːbəʊn; *NAmE* -boʊn/ *noun* the bone that forms the lower jaw SYN **mandible** ➲ VISUAL VOCAB page V48

jaw·break·er /ˈdʒɔːbreɪkə(r)/ (*NAmE*) (*BrE* **gob·stop·per**) *noun* a very large hard round sweet/candy

ˈjaw-dropping *adj.* (*informal*) so large or good that it is amazes you: *a jaw-dropping 5 million dollars* ◇ *The production is absolutely jaw dropping.* ▶ **ˈjaw-droppingly** *adv.*: *jaw-droppingly beautiful*

jaw·line /ˈdʒɔːlaɪn/ *noun* the outline of the lower jaw

jay /dʒeɪ/ *noun* a European bird of the CROW family, with bright feathers and a noisy call ➲ see also BLUEJAY

Jay·cee /ˈdʒeɪsiː/ *noun* (*NAmE, informal*) a member of the United States Junior Chamber, an organization for people between the ages of 21 and 39 that provides help in local communities in the US and other countries

jay·walk /ˈdʒeɪwɔːk/ *verb* [I] to walk along or across a street illegally or without paying attention to the traffic ▶ **jay·walk·er** *noun* **jay·walk·ing** *noun* [U]

jazz /dʒæz/ *noun, verb*

■ ***noun*** [U] a type of music with strong rhythms, in which the players often IMPROVISE (= make up the music as they are playing), originally created by African American musicians: *a* ***jazz band/club*** ◇ ***traditional/modern jazz*** ◇ *jazz musicians* ➲ COLLOCATIONS at MUSIC ➲ see also ACID JAZZ

IDM **and all that ˈjazz** (*informal*) and things like that: *How's it going? You know—love, life and all that jazz.*

■ ***verb***

PHR V **ˌjazz sth↔ˈup** (*informal*) **1** to make sth more interesting, exciting or attractive **2** to make a piece of music sound more modern, or more like popular music or jazz: *It's a jazzed up version of an old tune.*

jazzed /dʒæzd/ *adj.* [not before noun] (*informal*) excited: *I was jazzed to meet someone so famous.*

jazzy /ˈdʒæzi/ *adj.* (*informal*) **1** in the style of jazz: *a* ***jazzy melody/tune*** **2** (sometimes *disapproving*) brightly coloured and likely to attract attention SYN **snazzy**: *That's a jazzy tie you're wearing.*

JCB™ /ˌdʒeɪ siː ˈbiː/ *noun* (*BrE*) a powerful vehicle with a long arm for digging and moving earth

JCL /ˌdʒeɪ siː ˈel/ *abbr.* job control language (a computer language that lets the user state what tasks they want the OPERATING SYSTEM to do)

ˈJ-cloth™ *noun* a type of light cloth used for cleaning

JCR /ˌdʒeɪ siː ˈɑː(r)/ *abbr.* JUNIOR COMMON ROOM

jeal·ous 0‑ /ˈdʒeləs/ *adj.*

1 0‑ feeling angry or unhappy because sb you like or love is showing interest in sb else: *a* ***jealous wife/husband*** ◇ *He's only talking to her to make you jealous.* **2** 0‑ **~ (of sb/sth)** feeling angry or unhappy because you wish you had sth that sb else has SYN **envious**: *She's jealous of my success.* ◇ *Children often feel jealous when a new baby arrives.* **3 ~ (of sth)** wanting to keep or protect sth that you have because it makes you feel proud: *They are very jealous of their good reputation* (= they do not want to lose it). ▶ **jeal·ous·ly** *adv.*: *She eyed Natalia jealously.* ◇ *a* ***jealously guarded*** *secret*

jeal·ousy /ˈdʒeləsi/ *noun* (*pl.* -ies) **1** [U] a feeling of being jealous: *I felt sick with jealousy.* ◇ *sexual jealousy* **2** [C] an action or a remark that shows that a person is jealous: *I'm tired of her petty jealousies.*

jeans 0‑ /dʒiːnz/ *noun* [pl.]

trousers/pants made of strong cotton, especially DENIM: *a faded pair of blue jeans* ➲ VISUAL VOCAB page V51 ➲ see also DENIMS ORIGIN From **Janne**, the Old French name for Genoa, where the heavy cotton now used for jeans was first made.

Jeep™ /dʒiːp/ *noun* a small strong vehicle used, especially by the army, for driving over rough ground ➲ VISUAL VOCAB page V46

jee·pers /ˈdʒiːpəz; *NAmE* -pərz/ (also **ˌjeepers ˈcreepers**) *exclamation* (*especially NAmE, informal*) used to express surprise or shock: *Jeepers! That car nearly hit us!*

jeer /dʒɪə(r); *NAmE* dʒɪr/ *verb, noun*

■ ***verb*** [I, T] to laugh at sb or shout rude remarks at them to show that you do not respect them SYN **taunt**: *a jeering crowd* ◇ **~ at sb** *The police were jeered at by the waiting crowd.* ◇ **~ sb** *The players were jeered by disappointed fans.* ◇ **+ speech** *'Coward!' he jeered.*

■ ***noun*** [usually pl.] a rude remark that sb shouts at sb else to show that they do not respect or like them SYN **taunt**: *He walked on to the stage to be greeted with jeers and whistles.*

Jeez /dʒiːz/ *exclamation* (*informal, especially NAmE*) used to express anger, surprise, etc.

jehad = JIHAD

Je·ho·vah /dʒɪ'həʊvə; *NAmE* -'hoʊ-/ (also **Yah·weh**) *noun* the name of God that is used in the Old Testament of the Bible

Je,hovah's 'Witness *noun* a member of a religious organization based on Christianity, which believes that the end of the world is near and that only its members will be saved from being DAMNED

je·june /dʒɪ'dʒu:n/ *adj.* (*formal*) **1** too simple **SYN naive** **2** (of a speech, etc.) not interesting

je·junum /dʒɪ'dʒu:nəm/ *noun* (*anatomy*) the second part of the small INTESTINE ➲ compare DUODENUM, ILEUM ▸ **je·junal** /-'dʒu:nl/ *adj.*

Jek·yll and Hyde /,dʒekl ən 'haɪd/ *noun* [sing.] a person who is sometimes very pleasant (*Jekyll*) and sometimes very unpleasant (*Hyde*) or who leads two very separate lives **ORIGIN** From the story by Robert Louis Stevenson, *Dr Jekyll and Mr Hyde*, in which Dr Jekyll takes a drug which separates the good and bad sides of his personality into two characters. All the negative aspects go into the character of Mr Hyde.

jell (*especially NAmE*) (*BrE* usually **gel**) /dʒel/ *verb* **1** [I] (of two or more people) to work well together; to form a successful group: *We just didn't jell as a group.* **2** [I] (of an idea, a thought, a plan, etc.) to become clearer and more definite; to work well: *Ideas were beginning to jell in my mind.* ◇ *That day, everything jelled.* **3** [I] (*technical*) (of a liquid) to become thicker and more solid; to form a GEL

jel·lied /'dʒelid/ *adj.* [only before noun] (*especially BrE*) prepared or cooked in jelly: *jellied eels*

jelly 0‑ᴡ /'dʒeli/ (*pl.* -ies) *noun*
1 0‑ᴡ [U, C] (*BrE*) (*NAmE* **jello**, **Jell-O™** [U]) a cold sweet transparent food made from GELATIN, sugar and fruit juice, that shakes when it is moved: *jelly and ice cream* ◇ *a raspberry jelly* **2** [U] a substance like jelly made from GELATIN and meat juices, served around meat, fish, etc. **SYN aspic**: *chicken in jelly* **3** 0‑ᴡ [U, C] a type of jam that does not contain any pieces of fruit: *blackcurrant jelly* ➲ compare JAM **4** 0‑ᴡ [U] any thick sticky substance, especially a type of cream used on the skin ➲ see also PETROLEUM JELLY, ROYAL JELLY **5** (also **'jelly shoe**) [C] a light plastic shoe designed for wearing on the beach and in the sea ➲ VISUAL VOCAB page V52
IDM be/feel like 'jelly | **turn to 'jelly** (of legs or knees) to feel weak because you are nervous

'jelly baby *noun* (*BrE*) a small soft sweet/candy in the shape of a baby, made from GELATIN and flavoured with fruit

'jelly bean *noun* a small sweet/candy shaped like a BEAN, with a hard outside and a centre like jelly

jel·ly·fish /'dʒelifɪʃ/ *noun* (*pl.* **jel·ly·fish**) a sea creature with a body like jelly and long thin parts called TENTACLES that can give a sharp sting

'jelly roll (*NAmE*) (*BrE* **,Swiss 'roll**) *noun* a thin flat cake that is spread with jam, etc. and rolled up

jembe /'dʒembe/ *noun* **1** [C] (*EAfrE*) a farming tool with a long handle and a blade at one end, used for digging, breaking up soil or removing WEEDS (= plants growing where they are not wanted) **2** [C] a traditional W African drum **3** [U] a type of W African music

jemmy /'dʒemi/ (*BrE*) (*NAmE* **jimmy**) *noun* (*pl.* -ies) a short heavy metal bar used by thieves to force open doors and windows

je ne sais quoi /,ʒə nə seɪ 'kwɑ:/ *noun* [U] (from *French*, often *humorous*) a good quality that is difficult to describe: *He has that je ne sais quoi that distinguishes a professional from an amateur.*

jenny /'dʒeni/ *noun* (*pl.* -ies) a female DONKEY or ASS

jeop·ard·ize (*BrE* also **-ise**) /'dʒepədaɪz; *NAmE* -pərd-/ *verb* **~ sth/sb** (*formal*) to risk harming or destroying sth/sb **SYN endanger**: *He would never do anything to jeopardize his career.*

jeop·ardy /'dʒepədi; *NAmE* -pərdi/ *noun*
IDM in 'jeopardy in a dangerous position or situation and likely to be lost or harmed ➲ see also DOUBLE JEOPARDY

jere·miad /,dʒerɪ'maɪæd/ *noun* (*formal*) a very long sad complaint or list of complaints

jerk /dʒɜ:k; *NAmE* dʒɜ:rk/ *verb, noun*
▪ ***verb*** [T, I] to move or to make sth move with a sudden short sharp movement: **~ sth (+ adv./prep.)** *He jerked the phone away from her.* ◇ *She jerked her head up.* ◇ **+ adv./prep.** *The bus jerked to a halt.* ◇ *He grabbed a handful of hair and jerked at it.* ◇ **~ sth + adj.** *She got to the door and jerked it open.*
PHR V ,jerk sb a'round (*informal, especially NAmE*) to make things difficult for sb, especially by not being honest with them: *Consumers are often jerked around by big companies.* **,jerk 'off** (*taboo, slang*) (of a man) to MASTURBATE **,jerk 'out** | **,jerk sth↔'out** to say sth in a quick and awkward way because you are nervous
▪ ***noun*** **1** [C] a sudden quick sharp movement **SYN jolt**: *She sat up with a **jerk**.* **2** [C] (*informal*) a stupid person who often says or does the wrong thing **3** [U] meat that is MARINATED (= left in a mixture of oil and spices before being cooked) to give it a strong flavour and then cooked over a wood fire: *jerk chicken*

jer·kin /'dʒɜ:kɪn; *NAmE* 'dʒɜ:rkɪn/ *noun* (*BrE*) a short jacket without sleeves, especially one worn by men in the past

jerky /'dʒɜ:ki; *NAmE* 'dʒɜ:rki/ *adj., noun*
▪ ***adj.*** making sudden starts and stops and not moving smoothly ▸ **jerk·ily** /-ɪli/ *adv.*: *The car moved off jerkily.*
▪ ***noun*** [U] (*NAmE*) meat that has been cut into long strips and smoked or dried: *beef jerky*

jero·boam /,dʒerə'bəʊəm; *NAmE* -'boʊ-/ *noun* a wine bottle which holds four or six times as much wine as an ordinary bottle ➲ compare NEBUCHADNEZZAR, METHUSELAH

Jerry /'dʒeri/ *noun* (*pl.* -ies) (*taboo, BrE, slang*) an offensive word for a person from Germany, used especially during the First and Second World Wars

'jerry-built *noun* (*old-fashioned, disapproving*) built quickly and cheaply without caring about quality or safety

jer·ry·can /'dʒerikæn/ *noun* (*old-fashioned*) a large metal or plastic container with flat sides, used for carrying petrol/gas or water

jer·ry·man·der, **jer·ry·man·der·ing** = GERRYMANDER, GERRYMANDERING

jer·sey /'dʒɜ:zi; *NAmE* 'dʒɜ:rzi/ *noun* **1** [C] a shirt worn by sb playing a sports game ➲ VISUAL VOCAB page V36 **2** [C] a knitted piece of clothing made of wool or cotton for the upper part of the body, with long sleeves and no buttons; a type of sweater **3** [U] a type of soft fine knitted cloth used for making clothes: *made from 100% cotton jersey* **4 Jersey** [C] a type of light brown cow that produces high quality milk

Je·ru·sa·lem ar·ti·choke /dʒə,ru:sələm 'ɑ:tɪtʃəʊk; *NAmE* 'ɑ:rtətʃoʊk/ *noun* (*BrE* also **ar·ti·choke**) a light brown root vegetable that looks like a potato

jes·sie /'dʒesi/ (also **jessy**) *noun* (*pl.* -ies) (*BrE, old-fashioned, offensive*) a man or boy who is weak or who seems to behave too much like a woman

jest /dʒest/ *noun, verb*
▪ ***noun*** (*old-fashioned* or *formal*) something said or done to amuse people **SYN joke**
IDM in 'jest as a joke: *The remark was made half in jest.* ◇ *'Many a true word is spoken in jest,' thought Rosie* (= people often say things as a joke that are actually true).
▪ ***verb*** [I, T] **~ (about sth)** | **+ speech** (*formal* or *humorous*) to say things that are not serious or true, especially in order to make sb laugh **SYN joke**: *Would I jest about such a thing?*

jest·er /'dʒestə(r)/ *noun* a man employed in the past at the COURT of a king or queen to amuse people by telling jokes and funny stories: *the court jester*

Jes·uit /'dʒezjuɪt; *NAmE* 'dʒeʒəwət/ *noun* a member of the Society of Jesus, a Roman Catholic religious group: *a Jesuit priest*

Jesus /ˈdʒiːzəs/ (also **Jesus ˈChrist**) *noun* = CHRIST

jet /dʒet/ *noun, verb*

▪ ***noun* 1** [C] a plane driven by JET ENGINES: *a **jet aircraft/fighter/airliner** ◇ The accident happened as the jet was about to take off.* ➲ see also JUMBO (JET), JUMP JET **2** [C] a strong narrow stream of gas, liquid, steam or flame that comes very quickly out of a small opening. The opening is also called a jet: *The pipe burst and jets of water shot across the room. ◇ to clean the gas jets on the cooker* **3** [U] a hard black mineral that can be polished and is used in jewellery

▪ ***verb*** (-tt-) [I] **+ adv./prep.** (*informal*) to fly somewhere in a plane

ˌjet ˈblack *adj.* deep shiny black in colour

ˌjet ˈengine *noun* an engine that drives an aircraft forwards by pushing out a stream of gases behind it ➲ VISUAL VOCAB page V43

jet·foil /ˈdʒetfɔɪl/ *noun* a passenger boat which rises above the surface of the water when it is travelling fast and has JET ENGINES

ˈjet lag *noun* [U] the feeling of being tired and slightly confused after a long plane journey, especially when there is a big difference in the time at the place you leave and that at the place you arrive in ➲ COLLOCATIONS at TRAVEL ▸ **ˈjet-lagged** *adj.*

jet·liner /ˈdʒetlaɪnə(r)/ *noun* a large plane with a jet engine, that carries passengers

ˌjet-proˈpelled *adj.* driven by JET ENGINES

ˌjet proˈpulsion *noun* [U] the use of JET ENGINES for power

jet·sam /ˈdʒetsəm/ *noun* things that are thrown away, especially from a ship at sea and that float towards land ➲ compare FLOTSAM

the ˈjet set *noun* [sing.+ sing./pl. v.] rich and fashionable people who travel a lot

ˈjet-setter *noun* a rich, fashionable person who travels a lot ▸ **ˈjet-setting** *adj.* [usually before noun]: *her jet-setting millionaire boyfriend*

ˈJet Ski™ *noun* a vehicle with an engine, like a motorcycle, for riding across water ▸ **ˈjet-skiing** *noun* [U] ➲ VISUAL VOCAB page V40

ˈjet stream *noun* **1** (usually **the jet stream**) [sing.] a strong wind that blows high above the earth and that has an effect on the weather **2** [C] the flow of gases from a plane's engine

jet·ti·son /ˈdʒetɪsn/ *verb* **1 ~ sth** to throw sth out of a moving plane or ship to make it lighter: *to jettison fuel* **2 ~ sth/sb** to get rid of sth/sb that you no longer need or want SYN **discard**: *He was jettisoned as team coach after the defeat.* **3 ~ sth** to reject an idea, belief, plan, etc. that you no longer think is useful or likely to be successful SYN **abandon**

jetty /ˈdʒeti/ *noun* (*pl.* -ies) (*NAmE* also **dock**) a wall or platform built out into the sea, a river, etc, where boats can be tied and where people can get on and off boats ➲ VISUAL VOCAB page V5

Jet·way™ /ˈdʒetweɪ/ (*NAmE*) (*BrE* **ˈair bridge**) *noun* a bridge that can be moved and put against the door of an aircraft, so people can get on and off

Jew /dʒuː/ *noun* a member of the people and cultural community whose traditional religion is Judaism and who come from the ancient Hebrew people of Israel; a person who believes in and practises Judaism

jewel /ˈdʒuːəl/ *noun* **1** a PRECIOUS STONE such as a diamond, RUBY, etc. SYN **gem 2** [usually pl.] pieces of jewellery or decorative objects that contain PRECIOUS STONES: *The family jewels are locked away in a safe.* ➲ see also CROWN JEWELS **3** a small PRECIOUS STONE or piece of special glass that is used in the machinery of a watch **4** (*informal*) a person or thing that is very important or valuable ➲ compare GEM

IDM **the jewel in the ˈcrown** the most attractive or valuable part of sth

ˈjewel case *noun* a plastic box for holding a CD

jew·elled (*especially US* **jew·eled**) /ˈdʒuːəld/ *adj.* decorated with jewels

jew·el·ler (*especially US* **jew·el·er**) /ˈdʒuːələ(r)/ *noun* **1** a person who makes, repairs or sells jewellery and watches **2 jeweller's** (*pl.* jew·el·lers) a shop/store that sells jewellery and watches: *I bought it at the jeweller's near my office.*

jew·el·lery 0‑w (*especially US* **jew·el·ry**) /ˈdʒuːəlri/ *noun* [U]
objects such as rings and NECKLACES that people wear as decoration: ***silver/gold jewellery** ◇ She has some lovely **pieces of jewellery**.* ➲ COLLOCATIONS at FASHION ➲ VISUAL VOCAB page V53 ➲ see also COSTUME JEWELLERY

Jew·ess /ˈdʒuːəs/ *noun* (often *offensive*) an old-fashioned word for a Jewish woman

Jew·ish /ˈdʒuːɪʃ/ *adj.* connected with Jews or Judaism; believing in and practising Judaism: *We're Jewish. ◇ the local Jewish community* ▸ **Jew·ish·ness** *noun* [U]

Jewry /ˈdʒʊəri; *NAmE* ˈdʒʊri; ˈdʒuː-/ *noun* [U] (*formal*) Jewish people as a group: *British Jewry*

ˌJew's ˈharp *noun* a small musical instrument which is held between the teeth and played with a finger

Jez·ebel /ˈdʒezəbel/ *noun* (*old-fashioned*) a woman who is thought to be sexually immoral ORIGIN From the name of the wife of a king of Israel in the Bible, who wore make-up and was criticized by Elijah for worshipping the god Baal.

jib /dʒɪb/ *noun, verb*

▪ ***noun* 1** a small sail in front of the large sail on a boat ➲ VISUAL VOCAB page V45 **2** the arm of a CRANE that lifts things

▪ ***verb*** (-bb-) [I] **~ (at sth/at doing sth)** (*old-fashioned, informal*) to be unwilling to do or accept sth: *She agreed to attend but jibbed at making a speech.*

jibe (also **gibe**) /dʒaɪb/ *noun, verb*

▪ ***noun* 1 ~ (at sb/sth)** an unkind or insulting remark about sb: *He made several cheap jibes at his opponent during the interview.* **2** (*NAmE*) = GYBE

▪ ***verb* 1** [I, T] **~ (at sth)** | **~ that…** | **+ speech** to say sth that is intended to embarrass sb or make them look silly: *He jibed repeatedly at the errors they had made.* **2** [I] **~ (with sth)** (*NAmE, informal*) to be the same as sth or to match it: *Your statement doesn't jibe with the facts.* **3** (*NAmE*) = GYBE

jiffy /ˈdʒɪfi/ *noun* [usually sing.] (*informal*) (*pl.* -ies) a moment: *I'll be with you **in a jiffy*** (= very soon).

ˈJiffy bag™ *noun* **1** (*BrE*) a thick soft envelope for sending things that might break or tear easily **2** (*SAfrE*) a clear plastic bag used for storing things in, especially food

jig /dʒɪg/ *noun, verb*

▪ ***noun* 1** a quick lively dance; the music for this dance: *an Irish jig* **2** a device that holds sth in position and guides the tools that are working on it

▪ ***verb*** (-gg-) [I, T] **~ (sb/sth)** (**+ adv./prep.**) to move or to make sb/sth move up and down with short quick movements: *He jigged up and down with excitement.*

jig·ger /ˈdʒɪgə(r)/ *noun* = CHIGGER

jig·gered /ˈdʒɪgəd; *NAmE* -gərd/ *adj.* [not before noun]
IDM **I'll be jiggered!** (*old-fashioned, BrE, informal*) used to show surprise

jiggery-pokery /ˌdʒɪgəri ˈpəʊkəri; *NAmE* ˈpoʊk-/ *noun* [U] (*informal, especially BrE*) dishonest behaviour

jig·gle /ˈdʒɪgl/ *verb* [I, T] (*informal*) to move or make sth move up and down or from side to side with short quick movements: (**+ adv./prep.**) *Stop jiggling around! ◇ She jiggled with the lock.* ◇ **~ sth** (**+ adv./prep.**) *He stood jiggling his car keys in his hand.*

jig·saw /ˈdʒɪgsɔː/ *noun* **1** (also **ˈjigsaw puzzle**) (also **puz·zle** especially in *NAmE*) a picture printed on cardboard or wood, that has been cut up into a lot of small pieces of different shapes that you have to fit together again: *to do a jigsaw* ➲ VISUAL VOCAB page V33 **2** a mysterious situation in which it is not easy to understand all

J

the causes of what is happening; a complicated problem **3** a SAW (= a type of tool) with a fine blade for cutting designs in thin pieces of wood or metal

jihad (also **jehad**) /dʒɪ'hɑːd/ *noun* **1** (in Islam) a spiritual struggle within yourself to stop yourself breaking religious or moral laws **2** a holy war fought by Muslims to defend Islam

jiko /'dʒiːkɒ; *NAmE* -koː/ *noun* (*pl.* **-os**) (*EAfrE*) a container made of metal or CLAY and used for burning CHARCOAL or small pieces of wood. It is used for cooking or to give heat.

jil·bab /'dʒɪlbæb/ *noun* a full-length piece of clothing worn over other clothes by Muslim women

jill·aroo /ˌdʒɪlə'ruː/ *noun* (*pl.* **-oos**) (*AustralE, informal*) a young woman who is working on a farm in Australia/New Zealand to get experience ⇨ compare JACKAROO

jilt /dʒɪlt/ *verb* [often passive] **~ sb** to end a romantic relationship with sb in a sudden and unkind way: *He was jilted by his fiancée.* ◇ *a jilted bride/lover*

Jim Crow /ˌdʒɪm 'krəʊ; *NAmE* 'kroʊ/ *noun* [U] the former practice in the US of using laws that allowed black people to be treated unfairly and kept separate from white people, for example in schools **ORIGIN** From the title of a song that was sung by white entertainers who tried to look and sound like African Americans.

J

jim-jams /'dʒɪm dʒæmz/ *noun* [pl.] (*BrE, informal*) = PYJAMAS

jimmy /'dʒɪmi/ (*NAmE*) (*BrE* **jemmy**) *noun* (*pl.* **-ies**) a short heavy metal bar used by thieves to force open doors and windows

jin·gle /'dʒɪŋgl/ *noun, verb*

■ ***noun*** **1** [sing.] a sound like small bells ringing that is made when metal objects are shaken together: *the jingle of coins in his pocket* **2** [C] a short song or tune that is easy to remember and is used in advertising on radio or television

■ ***verb*** [I, T] **~ (sth)** to make a pleasant gentle sound like small bells ringing; to make sth do this: *The chimes jingled in the breeze.* ◇ *She jingled the coins in her pocket.*

jingo /'dʒɪŋgəʊ; *NAmE* -goʊ/ *noun*

IDM **by jingo** (*old-fashioned*) used to show surprise or determination

jin·go·ism /'dʒɪŋgəʊɪzəm; *NAmE* -goʊ-/ *noun* [U] (*disapproving*) a strong belief that your own country is best, especially when this is expressed in support of war with another country ▸ **jin·go·is·tic** /ˌdʒɪŋgəʊ'ɪstɪk; *NAmE* -goʊ-/ *adj.*

jink /dʒɪŋk/ *verb* [I] (**+ adv./prep.**) (*BrE, informal*) to move quickly while changing direction suddenly and often, especially in order to avoid sb/sth

jinks /dʒɪŋks/ *noun* ⇨ HIGH JINKS

jinx /dʒɪŋks/ *noun* [sing.] **~ (on sb/sth)** bad luck; sb/sth that is thought to bring bad luck in a mysterious way: *I'm convinced there's a jinx on this car.* ▸ **jinx** *verb* **~ sb/sth**

jinxed /dʒɪŋkst/ *adj.* (*informal*) having or bringing more bad luck than is normal: *The whole family seemed to be jinxed.*

jism /'dʒɪzəm/ (also **jis·som** /'dʒɪsəm/) *noun* [U] (*slang*) a man's SEMEN

JIT /ˌdʒeɪ aɪ 'tiː/ *abbr.* JUST-IN-TIME

jit·ter·bug /'dʒɪtəbʌg; *NAmE* -tər-/ *noun* a fast dance that was popular in the 1940s

jit·ters /'dʒɪtəz; *NAmE* -tərz/ (often **the jitters**) *noun* [pl.] (*informal*) feelings of being anxious and nervous, especially before an important event or before having to do sth difficult: *I always* ***get the jitters*** *before exams.*

jit·tery /'dʒɪtəri/ *adj.* (*informal*) anxious and nervous ⇨ SYNONYMS at NERVOUS

jiu-jitsu = JU-JITSU

jive /dʒaɪv/ *noun, verb*

■ ***noun*** **1** [U, sing.] a fast dance to music with a strong beat, especially popular in the 1950s **2** [U] (*NAmE, old-fashioned, informal*) nonsense: *to talk jive*

■ ***verb*** **1** [I] to dance to JAZZ or ROCK AND ROLL music **2** [I, T] **~ (sb)** (*NAmE, old-fashioned, informal*) to try to make sb believe sth that is not true **SYN** **kid**

Jnr *abbr.* = JR

Job /dʒəʊb; *NAmE* dʒoʊb/ *noun*

IDM **the patience of 'Job** the fact of being extremely patient and not complaining: *You need the patience of Job to deal with some of our customers.* **ORIGIN** From **Job**, a man in the Bible who experienced much suffering, including losing his family, his home and his possessions, but continued to believe in and trust God.

Synonyms

job

position • post • vacancy • appointment

These are all words for a position doing work for which you receive regular payment.

job a position doing work for which you receive regular payment: *He's trying to get a job in a bank.*

position (*rather formal*) a job: *a senior position in a large corporation*

JOB OR POSITION?

Position usually refers to a particular job within an organization, especially at a high level, and is not usually used about about jobs generally. It is also often used in job applications, descriptions and advertisements.

post a job, especially an important one in a large organization: *a key post in the new government*

vacancy a job that is available for sb to do: *We have several vacancies for casual workers.*

appointment (*rather formal, especially BrE*) a job or position of responsibility: *This is a permanent appointment, requiring commitment and hard work.*

PATTERNS

- a **permanent/temporary** job/position/post/vacancy/appointment
- a **full-time/part-time** job/position/post/vacancy/appointment
- to **have/have got** a(n) job/position/post/vacancy/appointment
- to **apply for/fill** a job/position/post/vacancy
- to **resign from/leave/quit** a job/position/post

job 0‒ **AW** /dʒɒb; *NAmE* dʒɑːb/ *noun*

▸ PAID WORK **1** 0‒ work for which you receive regular payment: *He's trying to* ***get a job.*** ◇ *She* ***took a job*** *as a waitress.* ◇ *His brother's just* ***lost his job.*** ◇ *a* ***summer/holiday/Saturday/vacation job*** ◇ *a* ***temporary/permanent job*** ◇ *I'm thinking of* ***applying for a*** *new* ***job.*** ◇ *The takeover of the company is bound to mean more* ***job losses.*** ◇ *Many women are in* ***part-time jobs.*** ◇ *Did they* ***offer you the job?*** ◇ *He certainly* ***knows his job*** (= is very good at his job). ◇ *I'm* ***only doing my job*** (= I'm doing what I am paid to do). ◇ *He's been* ***out of a job*** (= unemployed) *for six months now.* ◇ *She's never had a* ***steady job*** (= a job that is not going to end suddenly). ⇨ COLLOCATIONS at UNEMPLOYMENT

▸ TASK **2** 0‒ a particular task or piece of work that you have to do: *I've got various jobs around the house to do.* ◇ *Sorting these papers out is going to be a long job.* ◇ *The builder has a couple of jobs on at the moment.* ⇨ see also BLOW JOB, NOSE JOB ⇨ SYNONYMS at TASK

▸ DUTY **3** 0‒ [usually sing.] (rather *informal*) a responsibility or duty: *It's not my job to lock up!*

▸ CRIME **4** (*informal*) a crime, especially stealing: *a bank job* ◇ *an* ***inside job*** (= done by sb in the organization where the crime happens)

▸ OBJECT **5** (*informal*) a particular kind of thing: *It's real wood—not one of those plastic jobs.*

▸ COMPUTING **6** an item of work which is done by a computer as a single unit

Collocations

Jobs

Getting a job

- **look for** work
- **look for/apply for/go for** a job
- **get/pick up/complete/fill out/**(*BrE*) **fill in** an application (form)
- **send/email** your (*BrE*) CV/(*NAmE*) résumé/application/application form/covering letter
- **be called for/have/attend** an interview
- **offer sb** a job/work/employment/promotion
- **find/get/land** a job
- **employ/**(*especially NAmE*) **hire/recruit/**(*especially BrE*) **take on** staff/workers/trainees
- **recruit/appoint** a manager

Doing a job

- **arrive at/get to/leave** work/the office/the factory
- **start/finish** work/your shift
- **do/put in/work** overtime
- **have/gain/get/lack/need** experience/qualifications
- **do/get/have/receive** training
- **learn/pick up/improve/develop** (your) skills
- **cope with/manage/share/spread** the workload
- **improve your/achieve a better** work-life balance
- **have (no)** job satisfaction/job security

Building a career

- **have** a job/work/a career/a vocation
- **find/follow/pursue/**(*especially NAmE*) **live (out)** your vocation
- **enter/go into/join** a profession
- **choose/embark on/start/begin/pursue** a career
- **change** jobs/profession/career
- **be/**(*both especially BrE*) **work/go** freelance
- **do/take on** temp work/freelance work
- **do/be engaged in/be involved in** voluntary work

Leaving your job

- **leave/**(*especially NAmE*) **quit/resign from** your job
- **give up** work/your job/your career
- **hand in** your notice/resignation
- **plan to/be due to** retire in June/next year, etc.
- **take** early retirement

IDM **do the 'job** (*informal*) to be effective or successful in doing what you want: *This extra strong glue should do the job.* **do a good, bad, etc. 'job (on sth)** | **make a good, bad, etc. job of sth** to do sth well, badly, etc: *They did a very professional job.* ◇ *You've certainly made an excellent job of the kitchen* (= for example, painting it). **give sb/sth up as a bad 'job** (*informal*) to decide to stop trying to help sb or to do sth because there is no hope of success **good 'job!** (*especially NAmE, informal*) used to tell sb that they have done well at sth **a good 'job** (*informal*) used to say that you are pleased about a situation or that sb is lucky that sth happened: *It's a good job you were there to help.* **have a (hard/difficult) job doing/to do sth** to have difficulty doing sth: *You'll have a job convincing them that you're right.* ◇ *He had a hard job to make himself heard.* **a job of 'work** (*BrE, old-fashioned* or *formal*) work that you are paid to do or that must be done: *There was a job of work waiting for him that he was not looking forward to.* **jobs for the 'boys** (*BrE, informal, disapproving*) people use the expression **jobs for the boys** when they are criticizing the fact that sb in power has given work to friends or relatives **just the 'job** (*BrE*) (also **just the 'ticket** *NAmE, BrE*) (*informal, approving*) exactly what is needed in a particular situation **more than your 'job's worth (to do sth)** (*BrE, informal*) not worth doing because it is against the rules or because it might cause you to lose your job: *It's more than my job's worth to let you in without a ticket.* ➲ see also JOBSWORTH **on the 'job 1** while doing a particular job: *No sleeping on the job!* ◇ *on-the-job training* **2** (*BrE, slang*) having sex ➲ more at BEST *n.*, DEVIL, WALK *v.*

job·ber /ˈdʒɒbə(r); *NAmE* ˈdʒɑːb-/ (also **stock·job·ber**) *noun* (*finance*) (in Britain in the past) a person who worked on the STOCK EXCHANGE, buying shares, etc. from BROKERS and selling them to other brokers ➲ compare BROKER-DEALER

job·bie /ˈdʒɒbi; *NAmE* ˈdʒɑːbi/ *noun* (*informal*) used to refer to an object of a particular kind: *Her bikini was one of those expensive designer jobbies.*

job·bing /ˈdʒɒbɪŋ; *NAmE* ˈdʒɑːb-/ *adj.* [only before noun] (*BrE*) doing pieces of work for different people rather than a regular job: *a jobbing actor/builder*

job·centre /ˈdʒɒbsentə(r); *NAmE* ˈdʒɑːb-/ *noun* (*BrE*) a government office where people can get advice in finding work and where jobs are advertised

'job creation *noun* [U] the process of providing opportunities for paid work, especially for people who are unemployed

'job description *noun* a written description of the exact work and responsibilities of a job

'job-hunt *verb* [I] (usually used in the progressive tenses) to try to find a job: *At that time I had been job-hunting for six months.*

job·less /ˈdʒɒbləs; *NAmE* ˈdʒɑːb-/ *adj.* **1** without a job SYN **unemployed**: *The closure left 500 people jobless.* **2 the jobless** *noun* [pl.] people who are unemployed ▸ **job·less·ness** *noun* [U]

ˌjob 'lot *noun* (*informal*) a collection of different things, especially of poor quality, that are sold together

ˌjob satis'faction *noun* [U] the good feeling that you get when you have a job that you enjoy

'job seeker *noun* often used in official language in Britain to describe a person without a job who is trying to find one

ˌJobseeker's Al'lowance *noun* [U] (in Britain) money paid by the state to unemployed people who are looking for work ➲ see also UNEMPLOYMENT BENEFIT

'job-sharing *noun* [U] an arrangement for two people to share the hours of work and the pay of one job ▸ **'job-share** *noun*: *The company encourages job-shares and part-time working.* **'job-share** *verb* [I] **~ (with sb)**

jobs·worth /ˈdʒɒbzwɜːθ; *NAmE* ˈdʒɑːbzwɜːrθ/ *noun* (*BrE, informal, disapproving*) a person who follows the rules of a job exactly, even when this causes problems for other people, or when the rules are not sensible

Jock /dʒɒk; *NAmE* dʒɑːk/ *noun* (*informal*) a way of describing a person from Scotland, that can be offensive

jock /dʒɒk; *NAmE* dʒɑːk/ *noun* **1** (*NAmE*) a man or boy who plays a lot of sport **2** (*NAmE*) a person who likes a particular activity: *a computer jock* **3** = DISC JOCKEY ➲ compare SHOCK JOCK

jockey /ˈdʒɒki; *NAmE* ˈdʒɑːki/ *noun, verb*
- ***noun*** a person who rides horses in races, especially as a job ➲ VISUAL VOCAB page V38
- ***verb*** [I] **~ (with sb) (for sth)** | **~ (with sb) (to do sth)** to try all possible ways of gaining an advantage over other people: *The runners* ***jockeyed for position*** *at the start.* ◇ *The bands are constantly jockeying with each other for the number one spot.*

'jock itch *noun* (*NAmE, informal*) an infectious skin disease that affects the GROIN

jock·strap /ˈdʒɒkstræp; *NAmE* ˈdʒɑːk-/ (also **athˌletic sup'porter** especially in *NAmE*) *noun* a piece of men's underwear worn to support or protect the sexual organs while playing sports

joc·ose /dʒəˈkəʊs; *NAmE* -ˈkoʊs/ *adj.* (*formal*) humorous

jocu·lar /ˈdʒɒkjələ(r); *NAmE* ˈdʒɑːk-/ *adj.* (*formal*) **1** humorous: *a jocular comment* **2** (of a person) enjoying making people laugh SYN **jolly** ➲ see also JOKE ▶ **jocu·lar·ity** /ˌdʒɒkjəˈlærəti; NAmE ˌdʒɑːk-/ *noun* [U] **jocu·lar·ly** *adv.*

joc·und /ˈdʒɒkənd; ˈdʒəʊk-; NAmE ˈdʒɑːk-; ˈdʒoʊk-/ *adj.* (*formal*) cheerful

jodh·purs /ˈdʒɒdpəz; NAmE ˈdʒɑːdpərz/ *noun* [pl.] trousers/pants that are loose above the knee and tight from the knee to the ankle, worn when riding a horse: *a pair of jodhpurs*

Joe Bloggs /ˌdʒəʊ ˈblɒgz; NAmE ˌdʒoʊ ˈblɑːgz/ (*BrE*) (*NAmE* **Joe ˈBlow, John ˈDoe**) *noun* [sing.] (*informal*) a way of referring to a typical ordinary person

ˌJoe ˈPublic (*BrE*) (*NAmE* **John ˌQ. ˈPublic**) *noun* [U] (*informal*) people in general; the public

Joe Six·pack /ˌdʒəʊ ˈsɪkspæk; NAmE ˌdʒoʊ/ *noun* (*US, informal*) a man who is considered typical of a person who does MANUAL work: *Joe Sixpack doesn't care about that.*

joey /ˈdʒəʊi; NAmE ˈdʒoʊi/ *noun* a young KANGAROO, WALLABY or POSSUM ➲ VISUAL VOCAB page V10

jog /dʒɒg; NAmE dʒɑːg/ *verb, noun*

■ ***verb*** (-gg-) **1** (also **go jogging**) [I] to run slowly and steadily for a long time, especially for exercise: *I go jogging every evening.* **2** [T] ~ **sth/sb** to hit sth lightly and by accident SYN **nudge**: *Someone jogged her elbow, making her spill her coffee.*

IDM **jog sb's ˈmemory** to say or do sth that makes sb remember sth

PHR V **ˌjog aˈlong** (*BrE, informal*) to continue as usual with little or no excitement, change or progress

■ ***noun*** [sing.] **1** a slow run, especially one done for physical exercise: *I like to go for a jog after work.* **2** a light push or knock SYN **nudge**

jog·ger /ˈdʒɒgə(r); NAmE ˈdʒɑːg-/ *noun* **1** [C] a person who jogs regularly for exercise **2 joggers** [pl.] (*BrE*) soft loose trousers/pants, with ELASTIC at the waist, that you wear for doing exercise in

jog·ging /ˈdʒɒgɪŋ; NAmE ˈdʒɑːg-/ *noun* [U] the activity of running slowly and steadily as a form of exercise: *to go jogging* ➲ COLLOCATIONS at DIET ➲ VISUAL VOCAB page V35

ˈjogging suit *noun* = TRACKSUIT

jog·gle /ˈdʒɒgl; NAmE ˈdʒɑːgl/ *verb* [I, T] ~ **(sb/sth)** (*informal*) to move or to make sb/sth move quickly up and down or from one side to another

jog·trot /ˈdʒɒgtrɒt; NAmE ˈdʒɑːgtrɑːt/ *noun* [sing.] a slow steady run

john /dʒɒn; NAmE dʒɑːn/ *noun* (*informal, especially NAmE*) a toilet

ˌJohn ˈBull *noun* [U, C] (*old-fashioned*) a word that is used to refer to England or the English people, or to a typical Englishman

ˌJohn ˈDoe *noun* [usually sing.] (*NAmE*) **1** a name used for a person whose name is not known or is kept secret, especially in a court of law **2** an average man ➲ compare JANE DOE

John Han·cock /ˌdʒɒn ˈhæŋkɒk; NAmE ˌdʒɑːn ˈhæŋkɑːk/ *noun* (*NAmE, informal*) a person's signature

Johnny-come-lately /ˌdʒɒni kʌm ˈleɪtli; NAmE ˌdʒɑːni/ *noun* [sing.] (*disapproving* or *humorous*) a person who has only recently arrived in a place or started an activity, especially sb who is more confident than they should be

Johnny Reb /ˌdʒɒni ˈreb; NAmE ˌdʒɑːni/ *noun* (*NAmE, informal*) a name for a soldier who fought for the Confederate States in the American Civil War

John o'Groats /ˌdʒɒn əˈgrəʊts; NAmE ˌdʒɑːn əˈgroʊts/ *noun* a village in Scotland that is further north than any other place on the island of Great Britain ➲ compare LAND'S END

ˌJohn ˌQ. ˈPublic (*NAmE*) (*BrE* **Joe ˈPublic**) *noun* [U] (*informal*) people in general; the public

joie de vivre /ˌʒwʌ də ˈviːvrə/ *noun* [U] (from *French*) a feeling of great happiness and enjoyment of life

join 0→ /dʒɔɪn/ *verb, noun*

■ ***verb***

▸ CONNECT **1** 0→ [T, I] to fix or connect two or more things together: ~ **A to B** *Join one section of pipe to the next.* ◇ *The island is joined to the mainland by a bridge.* ◇ ~ **(A and B) (together/up)** *Join the two sections of pipe together.* ◇ *Draw a line joining (up) all the crosses.* ◇ *How do these two pieces join?*

▸ BECOME ONE **2** 0→ [I, T] if two things or groups **join**, or if one thing or group **joins** another, they come together to form one thing or group: *the place where the two paths join* ◇ ~ **sth** *The path joins the road near the trees.*

▸ CLUB/COMPANY **3** 0→ [T, I] ~ **(sth)** to become a member of an organization, a company, a club, etc: *I've joined an aerobics class.* ◇ *She joined the company three months ago.* ◇ (*figurative*) *to join the ranks of the unemployed* ◇ *It costs £20 to join.*

▸ DO STH WITH SB ELSE **4** 0→ [T] to take part in sth that sb else is doing or to go somewhere with them: ~ **sb (for sth)** *Will you join us for lunch?* ◇ *Do you mind if I join you?* ◇ ~ **sth** *Over 200 members of staff joined the strike.* ◇ *Members of the public joined the search for the missing boy.* ◇ ~ **sb in doing sth** *I'm sure you'll all join me in wishing Ted and Laura a very happy marriage.*

▸ TRAIN/PLANE **5** [T] ~ **sth** (*BrE*) if you **join** a train, plane, etc. you get on it

▸ ROAD/PATH/LINE **6** [T] ~ **sth** if you **join** a road or a line of people, you start to travel along it, or move into it

IDM **join ˈbattle (with sb)** (*formal*) to begin fighting sb: (*figurative*) *Local residents have joined battle with the council over the lack of parking facilities.* **join the ˈclub** (*informal*) used when sth bad that has happened to sb else has also happened to you: *So you didn't get a job either? Join the club!* **join ˈhands (with sb) 1** if two people **join hands**, they hold each other's hands **2** to work together in doing sth: *Education has been reluctant to join hands with business.* ➲ more at BEAT *v.*, FORCE *n.*

PHR V **ˌjoin ˈin (sth/doing sth)** | **ˌjoin ˈin (with sb/sth)** 0→ to take part in an activity with other people: *She listens but she never joins in.* ◇ *I wish he would join in with the other children.* **ˌjoin ˈup** (*BrE*) to become a member of the armed forces SYN **enlist** **ˌjoin ˈup (with sb)** to combine with sb else to do sth: *We'll join up with the other groups later.*

■ ***noun***

▸ CONNECTION a place where two things are fixed together: *The two pieces were stuck together so well that you could hardly see the join.*

ˌjoined-ˈup *adj.* [usually before noun] (*BrE*) **1 joined-up** writing is writing in which the letters in a word are joined to each other ➲ compare PRINTING **2** intelligent and involving good communication between different parts so that they can work together effectively: *We need more **joined-up thinking** in our approach to the environment.*

join·er /ˈdʒɔɪnə(r)/ *noun* **1** (*BrE*) a person whose job is to make the wooden parts of a building, especially window frames, doors, etc. ➲ compare CARPENTER **2** a person who joins an organization, club, etc: *All joiners will receive a welcome pack.*

join·ery /ˈdʒɔɪnəri/ *noun* [U] the work of a joiner or things made by a joiner

joint 0→ /dʒɔɪnt/ *adj., noun, verb*

■ ***adj.*** 0→ [only before noun] involving two or more people together: *a joint account* (= a bank account in the name of more than one person, for example a husband and wife) ◇ *The report was a **joint effort*** (= we worked on it together). ◇ *They finished in joint first place.* ◇ *They were joint owners of the house* (= they owned it together). ▶ **joint·ly** 0→ *adv.*: *The event was organized jointly by students and staff.*

■ ***noun*** **1** 0→ a place where two bones are joined together in the body in a way that enables them to bend and move: *inflammation of the knee joint* ➲ see also BALL-AND-SOCKET JOINT **2** 0→ a place where two or more parts of an object are joined together, especially to form a corner **3** (*BrE*) a piece of ROAST meat: *a joint of beef* ◇ *the Sunday joint* (= one traditionally eaten on a Sunday) **4** (*informal*) a place where people meet to eat, drink, dance, etc, especially one that is cheap: *a fast-food joint* **5** (*informal*) a cigarette containing MARIJUANA (= an illegal drug)

IDM **out of ˈjoint 1** (of a bone) pushed out of its correct position **2** not working or behaving in the normal way ➲ more at CASE *v.*, NOSE *n.*

■ ***verb*** **~ sth** to cut meat into large pieces, usually each containing a bone

ˌJoint ˌChiefs of ˈStaff *noun* [pl.] (in the US) the leaders of the ARMED FORCES who advise the President on military matters

ˌjoint deˈgree *noun* (in Britain and some other countries) a university course in which you study two subjects to the same standard

joint·ed /ˈdʒɔɪntɪd/ *adj.* [usually before noun] having parts that fit together and can move: *a doll with* ***jointed arms/legs***

ˈjoint family *noun* (*IndE*) a family structure in which grandparents, uncles, aunts and cousins are considered as a single unit living in one house

ˌjoint resoˈlution *noun* (in the US) a decision that has been approved by the Senate and the House of Representatives

ˌjoint-ˈstock company *noun* (*business*) a company that is owned by all the people who have shares in it

ˌjoint ˈventure *noun* (*business*) a business project or activity that is begun by two or more companies, etc, which remain separate organizations

joist /dʒɔɪst/ *noun* a long thick piece of wood or metal that is used to support a floor or ceiling in a building

jo·joba /həˈhəʊbə; həʊˈhəʊbə; *NAmE* hoʊˈhoʊbə/ *noun* **1** [U] oil from the seeds of an American plant, often used in COSMETICS **2** [U, C] the plant that produces these seeds

joke 🔑 /dʒəʊk; *NAmE* dʒoʊk/ *noun, verb*

■ ***noun*** **1** 🔑 something that you say or do to make people laugh, for example a funny story that you tell: *I can't* ***tell jokes.*** ◇ *She's always* ***cracking jokes.*** ◇ *They often* ***make jokes*** *at each other's expense.* ◇ *I didn't* ***get the joke*** (= understand it). ◇ *I wish he wouldn't tell* ***dirty jokes*** (= about sex). ◇ *I only did it* ***as a joke*** (= it was not meant seriously). ➲ see also IN-JOKE, PRACTICAL JOKE **2** [sing.] (*informal*) a person, thing or situation that is ridiculous or annoying and cannot be taken seriously: *This latest pay offer is a joke.* ➲ see also JOCULAR

IDM **be/get beyond a ˈjoke** to become annoying and no longer acceptable **be no ˈjoke** to be difficult or unpleasant: *It's no joke trying to find a job these days.* **the joke's on ˈsb** (*informal*) used to say that sb who tried to make another person look ridiculous now looks ridiculous instead **make a ˈjoke of sth** to laugh about sth that is serious or should be taken seriously **take a ˈjoke** to be able to laugh at a joke against yourself: *The trouble with her is she can't take a joke.*

■ ***verb*** **~ (with sb) (about sth) 1** 🔑 [I, T] to say sth to make people laugh; to tell a funny story: *She was laughing and joking with the children.* ◇ **~ about sth** *They often joked about all the things that could go wrong.* ◇ **+ speech** *'I cooked it myself, so be careful!' he joked.* **2** 🔑 [I, T] to say sth that is not true because you think it is funny: *I didn't mean that—I was* ***only joking.*** ◇ **~ that...** *She joked that she only loved him for his money.*

IDM **ˌjoking aˈpart/aˈside** (*BrE*) used to show that you are now being serious after you have said sth funny **you're ˈjoking | you must be ˈjoking** 🔑 (*informal*) used to show that you are very surprised at what sb has just said: *No way am I doing that. You must be joking!* ◇ *She's going out with Dan? You're joking!*

joker /ˈdʒəʊkə(r); *NAmE* ˈdʒoʊk-/ *noun* **1** a person who likes making jokes or doing silly things to make people laugh **2** (*informal*) a person that you think is stupid because they annoy you **3** an extra PLAYING CARD that is used in some card games, usually as a WILD CARD ➲ **VISUAL VOCAB** page V32

IDM **the ˌjoker in the ˈpack** a person or thing who could change the way that things will happen in a way that cannot be predicted

jokey (also **joky**) /ˈdʒəʊki; *NAmE* ˈdʒoʊki/ *adj.* (*informal*) amusing; making people laugh

jok·ing·ly /ˈdʒəʊkɪŋli; *NAmE* ˈdʒoʊk-/ *adv.* in a way that is intended to be amusing and not serious

jol /dʒɔːl/ *noun, verb* (*SAfrE, informal*)

■ ***noun*** a time of having fun; a party: *Have a jol!* ◇ *a New Year's Eve jol*

■ ***verb*** (-ll-) [I] to have fun: *We jolled all night.*

jol·lof rice /ˈdʒɒləf raɪs; *NAmE* ˈdʒɑːləf/ *noun* [U] a type of STEW eaten in W Africa made from rice, CHILLIES and meat or fish

jolly /ˈdʒɒli; *NAmE* ˈdʒɑːli/ *adj., adv., verb, noun*

■ ***adj.*** (**jol·lier, jol·li·est**) **1** happy and cheerful: *a jolly crowd/face/mood* **2** (*old-fashioned*) enjoyable: *a jolly evening/party/time* ▸ **jol·lity** /ˈdʒɒləti; *NAmE* ˈdʒɑːl-/ *noun* [U]: (*old-fashioned*) *scenes of high-spirits and jollity*

■ ***adv.*** (*old-fashioned, BrE, informal*) very: *That's a jolly good idea.*

IDM **jolly ˈgood!** (*old-fashioned, BrE, informal*) used to show that you approve of sth that sb has just said **ˈjolly well** (*old-fashioned, BrE*) used to emphasize a statement when you are annoyed about sth: *If you don't come now, you can jolly well walk home!*

■ ***verb*** (**jol·lies, jolly·ing, jol·lied, jol·lied**) (*BrE*)

PHR V **ˌjolly sb aˈlong** to encourage sb in a cheerful way **ˌjolly sb ˈinto sth/into ˈdoing sth** to persuade or encourage sb to do sth by making them feel happy about it **ˌjolly sb/sth ˈup** to make sb/sth more cheerful

■ ***noun*** (*BrE*) a trip that you make for enjoyment

IDM **get your ˈjollies** (*informal*) to get pleasure or have fun

the ˌJolly ˈRoger *noun* [sing.] a black flag with a white SKULL AND CROSSBONES on it, used in the past by PIRATES

jolt /dʒəʊlt; *NAmE* dʒoʊlt/ *verb, noun*

■ ***verb*** **1** [I, T] to move or to make sb/sth move suddenly and roughly SYN **jerk**: **(+ adv./prep.)** *The truck jolted and rattled over the rough ground.* ◇ *The bus jolted to a halt.* ◇ (*figurative*) *Her heart jolted when she saw him.* ◇ **~ sb/sth (+ adv./prep.)** *He was jolted forwards as the bus moved off.* **2** [T] to give sb a sudden shock, especially so that they start to take action or deal with a situation: **~ sb/sth (into sth)** *His remark jolted her into action.* ◇ **~ sb/sth (out of sth)** *a method of jolting the economy out of recession* ◇ **~ sb/sth + adj.** *I was suddenly jolted awake.*

■ ***noun*** [usually sing.] **1** a sudden rough movement SYN **jerk**: *The plane landed with a jolt.* **2** a sudden strong feeling, especially of shock or surprise: *a jolt of dismay*

Joneses /ˈdʒəʊnzɪz; *NAmE* ˈdʒoʊn-/ *noun* [pl.]

IDM **ˌkeep up with the ˈJoneses** (*informal*, often *disapproving*) to try to have all the possessions and social achievements that your friends and neighbours have

josh /dʒɒʃ; *NAmE* dʒɑːʃ/ *verb* [I, T] **~ (sb) | + speech** (*informal*) to gently make fun of sb or talk to them in a joking way SYN **tease**

joss stick /ˈdʒɒstɪk; *NAmE* ˈdʒɑːs-/ *noun* a thin wooden stick covered with a substance that burns slowly and produces a sweet smell

jos·tle /ˈdʒɒsl; *NAmE* ˈdʒɑːsl/ *verb* [T, I] **~ (sb)** to push roughly against sb in a crowd: *The visiting president was jostled by angry demonstrators.* ◇ *People were jostling, arguing and complaining.*

PHR V **ˈjostle for sth** to compete strongly and with force with other people for sth: *People in the crowd were jostling for the best positions.*

jot /dʒɒt; *NAmE* dʒɑːt/ *verb, noun*

■ ***verb*** (-tt-)

PHR V **ˌjot sth↔ˈdown** to write sth quickly: *I'll just jot down the address for you.*

■ ***noun***

IDM **not a/one ˈjot** used to mean 'not even a small amount' when you are emphasizing a negative statement: *There's not a jot of truth in what he says* (= none at all).

jot·ter /ˈdʒɒtə(r); *NAmE* ˈdʒɑːt-/ *noun* (*BrE*) **1** a small book used for writing notes in **2** (*ScotE*) an exercise book

jot·tings /ˈdʒɒtɪŋz; *NAmE* ˈdʒɑːt-/ *noun* [pl.] short notes that are written down quickly

J

joule /dʒuːl/ *noun* (*abbr.* **J**) (*physics*) a unit of energy or work

jour·nal AW /ˈdʒɜːnl; *NAmE* ˈdʒɜːrnl/ *noun* **1** a newspaper or magazine that deals with a particular subject or profession: *a **scientific/trade journal** ◇ the British Medical Journal* **2** used in the title of some newspapers: *the Wall Street Journal* **3** a written record of the things you do, see, etc. every day: *He **kept a journal** of his travels across Asia.* ➲ compare DIARY

jour·nal·ese /ˌdʒɜːnəˈliːz; *NAmE* ˌdʒɜːrn-/ *noun* [U] (usually *disapproving*) a style of language that is thought to be typical of that used in newspapers

jour·nal·ism /ˈdʒɜːnəlɪzəm; *NAmE* ˈdʒɜːrn-/ *noun* [U] the work of collecting and writing news stories for newspapers, magazines, radio or television

jour·nal·ist 🔑 /ˈdʒɜːnəlɪst; *NAmE* ˈdʒɜːrn-/ *noun* a person whose job is to collect and write news stories for newspapers, magazines, radio or television ➲ compare REPORTER

jour·nal·is·tic /ˌdʒɜːnəˈlɪstɪk; *NAmE* ˌdʒɜːrn-/ *adj.* [usually before noun] connected with the work of a journalist: *journalistic skills ◇ his journalistic background*

J

jour·ney 🔑 /ˈdʒɜːni; *NAmE* ˈdʒɜːrni/ *noun, verb*

■ ***noun*** 🔑 an act of travelling from one place to another, especially when they are far apart: *They went on a long train journey across India.* ◇ (*BrE*) *Did you have a good journey?* ◇ *on the **outward/return** journey* ◇ (*BrE*) *We **broke our journey*** (= stopped for a short time) *in Madrid.* ◇ (*BrE*) *Don't use the car for short journeys.* ◇ (*BrE*) *It's a day's journey by car.* ◇ (*BrE*) *I'm afraid you've had a wasted journey* (= you cannot do what you have come to do). ◇ (*BrE, informal*) *Bye! **Safe journey!*** (= used when sb is beginning a journey) ◇ (*figurative*) *The book describes a spiritual journey from despair to happiness.* ➲ SYNONYMS at TRIP

■ ***verb*** [I] (**+ adv./prep.**) (*formal* or *literary*) to travel, especially a long distance: *They journeyed for seven long months.*

jour·ney·man /ˈdʒɜːnimən; *NAmE* ˈdʒɜːrn-/ *noun* (*pl.* **-men** /-mən/) **1** (in the past) a person who was trained to do a particular job and who then worked for sb else **2** a person who has training and experience in a job but who is only average at it

journo /ˈdʒɜːnəʊ; *NAmE* ˈdʒɜːrnoʊ/ (*pl.* **-os**) *noun* (*BrE, slang*) a journalist

joust /dʒaʊst/ *verb* **1** [I] to fight on horses using a long stick (= a LANCE) to try to knock the other person off their horse, especially as part of a formal contest in the past **2** [I] (*formal*) to argue with sb, especially as part of a formal or public debate ▸ **joust** *noun*

Jove /dʒəʊv; *NAmE* dʒoʊv/ *noun*

IDM **by ˈJove** (*old-fashioned, informal, especially BrE*) used to express surprise or to emphasize a statement

jo·vial /ˈdʒəʊviəl; *NAmE* ˈdʒoʊ-/ *adj.* very cheerful and friendly ▸ **jovi·al·ity** /ˌdʒəʊviˈæləti; *NAmE* ˌdʒoʊ-/ *noun* [U] **jo·vial·ly** /-iəli/ *adv.*

jowl /dʒaʊl/ *noun* [usually pl.] the lower part of sb's cheek when it is fat and hangs down below their chin: *a man with heavy jowls* IDM see CHEEK *n.*

joy 🔑 /dʒɔɪ/ *noun*

1 🔑 [U] a feeling of great happiness SYN **delight**: *the sheer joy of being with her again ◇ to dance **for/with joy** ◇ I didn't expect them to **jump for joy** at the news* (= to be very pleased). ◇ *To his great joy, she accepted.* ➲ SYNONYMS at PLEASURE **2** [C] a person or thing that causes you to feel very happy: *the joys of fatherhood ◇ The game was a joy to watch.* **3** [U] (*BrE, informal*) (in questions and negative sentences) success or satisfaction: *We complained about our rooms but got no joy from the manager.* ◇ *'Any joy at the shops?' 'No, they didn't have what I wanted.'*

IDM **full of the joys of ˈspring** very cheerful ➲ more at PRIDE *n.*

joy·ful /ˈdʒɔɪfl/ *adj.* very happy; causing people to be happy ➲ SYNONYMS at HAPPY ▸ **joy·ful·ly** /-fəli/ *adv.* **joy·ful·ness** *noun* [U]

joy·less /ˈdʒɔɪləs/ *adj.* (*formal*) bringing no happiness; without joy: *a joyless childhood*

joy·ous /ˈdʒɔɪəs/ *adj.* (*literary*) very happy; causing people to be happy SYN **joyful**: *joyous laughter* ▸ **joy·ous·ly** *adv.*

joy·pad /ˈdʒɔɪpæd/ *noun* a device used with some computer games, with buttons that you use to move images on the screen

joy·rid·ing /ˈdʒɔɪraɪdɪŋ/ *noun* [U] the crime of stealing a car and driving it for pleasure, usually in a fast and dangerous way ▸ **joy·ride** *noun* **joy·rider** *noun*

joy·stick /ˈdʒɔɪstɪk/ *noun* **1** a stick with a handle used with some computer games to move images on the screen **2** (*informal*) a stick with a handle in an aircraft that is used to control direction or height

JP /ˌdʒeɪ ˈpiː/ *abbr.* JUSTICE OF THE PEACE: *Helen Alvey JP*

JPEG /ˈdʒeɪpeg/ *noun* (*computing*) **1** [U] the abbreviation for 'Joint Photographic Experts Group' (technology which reduces the size of files that contain images): *JPEG files* **2** [C] an image created using this technology: *You can download the pictures as JPEGs.*

Jr (also **Jnr**) (both *BrE*) (also **Jr.** *NAmE, BrE*) *abbr.* JUNIOR ➲ compare SR

jua kali /ˌdʒʊə ˈkæli/ *noun* [U] (in Kenya) the informal jobs that people do to earn money, for example making useful things from old metal and wood: *the **jua kali** sector*

ju·bi·lant /ˈdʒuːbɪlənt/ *adj.* feeling or showing great happiness because of a success ▸ **ju·bi·lant·ly** *adv.*

jubi·la·tion /ˌdʒuːbɪˈleɪʃn/ *noun* [U] a feeling of great happiness because of a success

ju·bi·lee /ˈdʒuːbɪliː/ *noun* a special anniversary of an event, especially one that took place 25 or 50 years ago; the celebrations connected with it ➲ see also DIAMOND JUBILEE, GOLDEN JUBILEE, SILVER JUBILEE

Ju·da·ism /ˈdʒuːdeɪɪzəm; *NAmE* -dəɪzəm/ *noun* [U] the religion of the Jewish people, based mainly on the Bible (= the Christian Old Testament) and the Talmud ▸ **Ju·da·ic** /dʒuːˈdeɪɪk/ *adj.* [only before noun]: *Judaic tradition*

Judas /ˈdʒuːdəs/ *noun* a person who treats a friend badly by not being loyal SYN **traitor**

jud·der /ˈdʒʌdə(r)/ *verb* [I] to shake violently: *He slammed on the brakes and the car juddered to a halt.*

judge 🔑 /dʒʌdʒ/ *noun, verb*

■ ***noun***

▸ IN COURT **1** 🔑 a person in a court who has the authority to decide how criminals should be punished or to make legal decisions: *a High Court judge ◇ a federal judge ◇ The case comes before Judge Cooper next week. ◇ The judge sentenced him to five years in prison.* ➲ compare JUSTICE OF THE PEACE, MAGISTRATE

▸ IN COMPETITION **2** 🔑 a person who decides who has won a competition: *the panel of judges at the flower show ◇ The judges' decision is final.*

▸ SB WHO GIVES OPINION **3** 🔑 [usually sing.] a person who has the necessary knowledge or skills to give their opinion about the value or quality of sb/sth: *She's a **good judge** of character.* ◇ *'I'm not sure that's a good way to do it.' '**Let me be the judge of that.**'*

■ ***verb***

▸ FORM OPINION **1** 🔑 [I, T] to form an opinion about sb/sth, based on the information you have: *As far as I can judge, all of them are to blame.* ◇ ***Judging by** her last letter, they are having a wonderful time.* ◇ ***To judge from** what he said, he was very disappointed.* ◇ **~ sb/sth (on sth)** *Schools should not be judged only on exam results.* ◇ *Each painting must be judged on its own merits.* ◇ **~ sb/sth + noun** *The tour was judged a great success.* ◇ **~ sb/sth to be/do sth** *The concert was judged to have been a great success.* ◇ **~ sb/sth + adj.** *They judged it wise to say nothing.* ◇ **~ that...** *He judged that the risk was too great.* ◇ **it is judged that...** *It was judged that the risk was too great.* ◇ **~ how, what, etc...** *It was hard to judge how great the risk was.*

▸ ESTIMATE **2** 🔑 [T] to guess the size, amount, etc. of sth:

~ how, what, etc... *It's difficult to judge how long the journey will take.* ◇ **~ sb/sth to be/do sth** *I judged him to be about 50.*
▸ IN COMPETITION **3** [T, I] **~ (sth)** to decide the result of a competition; to be the judge in a competition: *She was asked to judge the essay competition.*
▸ GIVE OPINION **4** [T, I] **~ (sb)** to give your opinion about sb, especially when you disapprove of them: *What gives you the right to judge other people?*
▸ IN COURT **5** [T] to decide whether sb is guilty or innocent in a court: **~ sth** *to judge a case* ◇ **~ sb + adj.** *to judge sb guilty/not guilty*
IDM **don't judge a ˌbook by its ˈcover** (*saying*) used to say that you should not form an opinion about sb/sth from their appearance only

judge·ment (also **judg·ment** especially in *NAmE*) /ˈdʒʌdʒmənt/ *noun*
1 [U] the ability to make sensible decisions after carefully considering the best thing to do: ***good/poor/sound judgement*** ◇ *She showed a lack of judgement when she gave Mark the job.* ◇ *It's not something I can give you rules for; you'll have to use your judgement.* ◇ *He achieved his aim* ***more by luck than judgement.*** ◇ *The accident was caused by an* ***error of judgement*** *on the part of the pilot.* **2** [C, U] **~ (of/about/on sth)** an opinion that you form about sth after thinking about it carefully; the act of making this opinion known to others: *He refused to* ***make a judgement*** *about the situation.* ◇ *Who am I to* ***pass judgement*** *on her behaviour?* (= to criticize it) ◇ *I'd like to* ***reserve judgement*** *until I see the report.* ◇ *It was,* ***in her judgement,*** *the wrong thing to do.* ◇ *I did it* ***against my better judgement*** (= although I thought it was perhaps the wrong thing to do). **3** (usually **judgment**) [C, U] the decision of a court or a judge: *a judgment from the European Court of Justice* ◇ *The judgment will be given tomorrow.* ◇ *The court has yet to* ***pass judgment*** (= say what its decision is) *in this case.* **4** [C, usually sing.] **~ (on sth)** (*formal*) something bad that happens to sb that is thought to be a punishment from God
IDM see SIT

judge·men·tal (*BrE*) (also **judg·men·tal** *NAmE, BrE*) /dʒʌdʒˈmentl/ *adj.* **1** (*disapproving*) judging people and criticizing them too quickly **2** (*formal*) connected with the process of judging things: *the judgemental process*

ˈjudgement call *noun* (*informal*) a decision you have to make where there is no clear rule about what the right thing to do is, so that you have to use your own judgement

ˈJudgement Day (also **the ˌDay of ˈJudgement, the ˌLast ˈJudgement**) *noun* the day at the end of the world when, according to some religions, God will judge everyone who has ever lived

ju·di·ca·ture /ˈdʒuːdɪkətʃə(r)/ *noun* (*law*) **1** [U] the system by which courts, trials, etc. are organized in a country **2 the judicature** [sing.+ sing./pl. v.] judges when they are considered as a group

ju·di·cial /dʒuˈdɪʃl/ *adj.* [usually before noun] connected with a court, a judge or legal judgement: *judicial powers* ◇ *the judicial process/system* ▸ **ju·di·cial·ly** /-ʃəli/ *adv.*

juˌdicial ˈactivism *noun* [U] (*law*) (in the US) the idea that it is not necessary to follow the exact words of the Constitution when new laws are made

juˌdicial reˈstraint *noun* [U] (*law*) (in the US) the idea that judges of the Supreme Court or other courts should not try to change a law that is allowed by the Constitution

juˌdicial reˈview *noun* (*law*) **1** [U] (in the US) the power of the Supreme Court to decide if sth is allowed by the Constitution **2** [C, U] (in Britain) a procedure in which a court examines an action or decision of a public body and decides whether it was right: *There is to be a judicial review of the visa changes.*

ju·di·ciary /dʒuˈdɪʃəri; *NAmE* -ʃieri/ *noun* (usually **the judiciary**) [C+sing./pl. v.] (*pl.* **-ies**) the judges of a country or a state, when they are considered as a group: *an independent judiciary* ➲ compare EXECUTIVE *n.* (3), LEGISLATURE

ju·di·cious /dʒuˈdɪʃəs/ *adj.* (*formal, approving*) careful and sensible; showing good judgement OPP **injudicious** ▸ **ju·di·cious·ly** *adv.*: *a judiciously worded letter*

judo /ˈdʒuːdəʊ; *NAmE* -doʊ/ *noun* [U] (from *Japanese*) a sport in which two people fight and try to throw each other to the ground: *He* ***does judo.*** ◇ *She's a* ***black belt in*** *judo.*

jug /dʒʌɡ/ *noun* **1** (*BrE*) (*NAmE* **pitch·er**) a container with a handle and a LIP, for holding and pouring liquids: *a milk/water jug* **2** (*NAmE*) a large round container with a small opening and a handle, for holding liquids: *a five-gallon jug of beer* **3** the amount of liquid contained in a jug: *She spilled a jug of water.* **4 jugs** [pl.] (*taboo, slang*) an offensive word for a woman's breasts

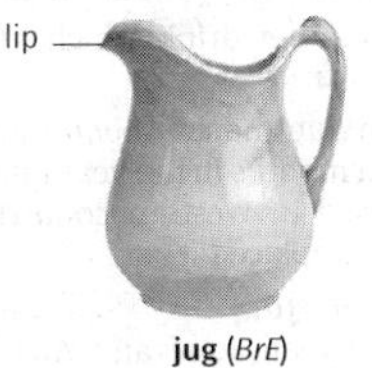

jug (*BrE*)
pitcher (*NAmE*)

pitcher (*BrE*)
jug (*NAmE*)

jug·ful /ˈdʒʌɡfʊl/ *noun* the amount of liquid contained in a jug

jugged hare /ˌdʒʌɡd ˈheə(r); *NAmE* ˈher/ *noun* [U] a hot dish made from HARE that has been cooked slowly in liquid in a container with a lid

jug·ger·naut /ˈdʒʌɡənɔːt; *NAmE* -ɡərn-/ *noun* **1** (*BrE, often disapproving*) a very large lorry/truck: *juggernauts roaring through country villages* **2** (*formal*) a large and powerful force or institution that cannot be controlled: *a bureaucratic juggernaut*

jug·gle /ˈdʒʌɡl/ *verb* **1** [I, T] to throw a set of three or more objects such as balls into the air and catch and throw them again quickly, one at a time: *My uncle taught me to juggle.* ◇ **~ with sth** *to juggle with balls* ◇ **~ sth** (*figurative*) *I was juggling books, shopping bags and the baby* (= I was trying to hold them all without dropping them). **2** [T, I] **~ (sth) (with sth)** to try to deal with two or more important jobs or activities at the same time so that you can fit all of them into your life: *Working mothers are used to juggling their jobs, their children's needs and their housework.* **3** [T] **~ sth** to organize information, figures, the money you spend, etc. in the most useful or effective way

jug·gler /ˈdʒʌɡlə(r)/ *noun* a person who juggles, especially an entertainer

jugu·lar /ˈdʒʌɡjələ(r)/ (also **jugular ˈvein**) *noun* any of the three large VEINS in the neck that carry blood from the head towards the heart
IDM **go for the ˈjugular** (*informal*) to attack sb's weakest point during a discussion, in an aggressive way

juice /dʒuːs/ *noun, verb*
■ ***noun*** **1** [U, C] the liquid that comes from fruit or vegetables; a drink made from this: *Add the juice of two lemons.* ◇ *a carton of apple juice* ◇ *Two orange juices, please.* **2** [C, usually pl., U] the liquid that comes out of a piece of meat when it is cooked **3** [C, usually pl.] the liquid in the stomach that helps you to DIGEST food: ***digestive/gastric juices*** **4** [U] (*informal, especially BrE*) petrol/gas **5** [U] (*NAmE, informal*) electricity IDM see STEW *v.*
■ ***verb*** **~ sth** to get the juice out of fruit or vegetables: *Juice two oranges.*
PHR V **juice sth↔ˈup** (*informal, especially NAmE*) to make sth more exciting or interesting

ˈjuice bar *noun* a cafe serving drinks made from freshly squeezed fruit

juicer /ˈdʒuːsə(r)/ *noun* **1** a piece of electrical equipment for getting the juice out of fruit or vegetables **2** (*NAmE*) (*BrE* **ˈlemon-squeezer**) a kitchen UTENSIL (= a tool) for squeezing juice out of a fruit ➲ VISUAL VOCAB page V23

juicy /ˈdʒuːsi/ *adj.* (juici·er, juici·est) **1** (*approving*) containing a lot of juice and good to eat: *soft juicy pears* ◇ *The meat was tender and juicy.* **2** (*informal*) interesting because you find it shocking or exciting: *juicy gossip* **3** (*informal*) attractive because it will bring you a lot of money or satisfaction: *a juicy prize*

ju-jitsu (also **jiu-jitsu**) /dʒuː ˈdʒɪtsuː/ *noun* [U] a Japanese system of fighting from which the sport of JUDO was developed

juju /ˈdʒuːdʒuː/ *noun* **1** [C] an object used in W African magic **2** [U] a type of magic in W Africa **3** [U] a type of Nigerian music that uses GUITARS and drums

juke·box /ˈdʒuːkbɒks; *NAmE* -bɑːks/ *noun* a machine in a pub, bar, etc. that plays music when you put coins into it

julep /ˈdʒuːlep/ *noun* [U, C] **1** a sweet drink which may contain alcohol or medicine **2** = MINT JULEP

Ju·lian cal·en·dar /ˌdʒuːliən ˈkælɪndə(r)/ *noun* [sing.] the system of arranging days and months in the year introduced by Julius Caesar, and used in Western countries until the GREGORIAN CALENDAR replaced it

July 0‑ /dʒuˈlaɪ/ *noun* [U, C] (*abbr.* **Jul.**) the 7th month of the year, between June and August HELP To see how **July** is used, look at the examples at **April**.

J

jum·ble /ˈdʒʌmbl/ *verb, noun*
■ *verb* [usually passive] **~ sth** (**together/up**) to mix things together in a confused or untidy way: *Books, shoes and clothes were **jumbled together** on the floor.* ▸ **jum·bled** *adj.*: *a jumbled collection of objects* ◇ *jumbled thoughts*
■ *noun* **1** [sing.] **~** (**of sth**) an untidy or confused mixture of things: *a jumble of books and paper* ◇ *The essay was a meaningless jumble of ideas.* **2** [U] (*BrE*) a collection of old or used clothes, etc. that are no longer wanted and are going to be taken to a jumble sale

ˈjumble sale (*BrE*) (also **ˈrummage sale** *NAmE, BrE*) *noun* a sale of old or used clothes, etc. to make money for a church, school or other organization

jumbo /ˈdʒʌmbəʊ; *NAmE* -boʊ/ *noun, adj.*
■ *noun* (*pl.* -os) (also **ˌjumbo ˈjet**) a large plane that can carry several hundred passengers, especially a Boeing 747
■ *adj.* [only before noun] (*informal*) very large; larger than usual: *a jumbo pack of cornflakes*

jump 0‑ /dʒʌmp/ *verb, noun*
■ *verb*
▸ MOVE OFF/TO GROUND **1** 0‑ [I] to move quickly off the ground or away from a surface by pushing yourself with your legs and feet: *'Quick, jump!' he shouted.* ◇ **+ adv./prep.** *to jump into the air/over a wall/into the water* ◇ *The children were jumping up and down with excitement.* ◇ *She jumped down from the chair.* ◇ *The pilot jumped from the burning plane* (= with a PARACHUTE). ◇ **+ noun** *She has jumped 2.2 metres.*
▸ PASS OVER STH **2** 0‑ [T] to pass over sth by jumping: **~ sth** *Can you jump that gate?* ◇ *His horse fell as it jumped the last hurdle.* ◇ **~ sth + adv./prep.** *I jumped my horse over all the fences.* SYN **leap**
▸ MOVE QUICKLY **3** 0‑ [I] **+ adv./prep.** to move quickly and suddenly: *He **jumped to his feet** when they called his name.* ◇ *She jumped up and ran out of the room.* ◇ *Do you want a ride? Jump in.* **4** 0‑ [I] to make a sudden movement because of surprise, fear or excitement: *A loud bang made me jump.* ◇ *Her heart jumped when she heard the news.*
▸ INCREASE **5** 0‑ [I] to rise suddenly by a large amount SYN **leap**: **~ by...** *Prices jumped by 60% last year.* ◇ **~** (**from...**) (**to...**) *Sales jumped from $2.7 billion to $3.5 billion.*
▸ CHANGE SUDDENLY **6** 0‑ [I] **~** (**about**) (**from sth to sth**) to change suddenly from one subject to another: *I couldn't follow the talk because he kept jumping about from one topic to another.* ◇ *The story then jumps from her childhood in New York to her first visit to London.*
▸ LEAVE OUT **7** [T] **~ sth** to leave out sth and pass to a further point or stage: *You seem to have jumped several steps in the argument.*
▸ OF MACHINE/DEVICE **8** [I] (**+ adv./prep.**) to move suddenly and unexpectedly, especially out of the correct position: *The needle jumped across the dial.* ◇ *The film jumped during projection.*
▸ ATTACK **9** [T, I] **~** (**on**) **sb** (*informal*) to attack sb suddenly: *The thieves jumped him in a dark alleyway.*
▸ VEHICLE **10** [T] **~ sth** (*NAmE*) to get on a vehicle very quickly: *to jump a bus* **11** (*NAmE*) = JUMP-START
▸ BE LIVELY **12 be jumping** [I] (*informal*) to be very lively: *The bar's jumping tonight.*

IDM **be ˈjumping up and down** (*informal*) to be very angry or excited about sth **jump down sb's ˈthroat** (*informal*) to react very angrily to sb **jump the ˈgun** to do sth too soon, before the right time **jump the ˈlights** (*BrE*) (also **run a** (**red**) **ˈlight**, **run the ˈlights** *NAmE, BrE*) (*informal*) to fail to stop at a red traffic light **jump out of your ˈskin** (*informal*) to move violently because of a sudden shock **jump the ˈqueue** (*BrE*) (*US* **jump the ˈline**) to go to the front of a line of people without waiting for your turn **jump the ˈrails** (of a train) to leave the rails suddenly **jump ˈship 1** to leave the ship on which you are serving, without permission **2** to leave an organization that you belong to, suddenly and unexpectedly **jump through ˈhoops** to do sth difficult or complicated in order to achieve sth **jump ˈto it** (*NAmE* also **hop ˈto it**) (*informal*) used to tell sb to hurry and do something quickly ➲ more at BANDWAGON, CONCLUSION, DEEP *adj.*

PHR V **ˈjump at sb** (*NAmE*) = JUMP ON SB **ˈjump at sth** to accept an opportunity, offer, etc. with enthusiasm SYN **leap at**

PHR V **ˌjump ˈin 1** to interrupt a conversation: *Before she could reply Peter jumped in with an objection.* **2** to start to do sth very quickly without spending a long time thinking first **ˈjump on sb** (*NAmE* also **ˈjump at sb**) (*informal*) to criticize sb **ˌjump ˈout at sb** to be very obvious and easily noticed SYN **leap out at**: *The mistake in the figures jumped out at me.*

■ *noun*
▸ MOVEMENT **1** 0‑ an act of jumping: *a jump of over six metres* ◇ *The story takes a jump back in time.* ◇ *Somehow he survived the jump from the third floor of the building.* ◇ *to do a parachute jump* ◇ *a ski jump champion* ◇ *I sat up **with a jump*** (= quickly and suddenly). ◇ *The negotiations took a jump forward yesterday* (= they made progress). ➲ see also HIGH JUMP, LONG JUMP, SKI JUMP, TRIPLE JUMP
▸ BARRIER **2** 0‑ a barrier like a narrow fence that a horse or a runner has to jump over in a race or competition: *The horse fell at the last jump.* ➲ VISUAL VOCAB page V38
▸ INCREASE **3** 0‑ **~** (**in sth**) a sudden increase in amount, price or value: *a 20 per cent jump in pre-tax profits* ◇ *unusually large price jumps*

IDM **to keep, etc. one jump ahead** (**of sb**) to keep your advantage over sb, especially your COMPETITORS, by taking action before they do or by making sure you know more than they do ➲ more at HIGH JUMP, RUNNING *adj.*

ˈjump ball *noun* (in BASKETBALL) a ball that the REFEREE throws up between two opposing players to begin play

jump·cut /ˈdʒʌmpkʌt/ *noun* (*technical*) (in films/movies) a sudden change from one scene to another

ˈjumped-up *adj.* [only before noun] (*BrE, informal, disapproving*) thinking you are more important than you really are, particularly because you have risen in social status

jump·er /ˈdʒʌmpə(r)/ *noun* **1** (*BrE*) a knitted piece of clothing made of wool or cotton for the upper part of the body, with long sleeves and no buttons: *a woolly jumper* ➲ VISUAL VOCAB page V51 **2** (*NAmE*) = PINAFORE **3** a person, an animal or an insect that jumps: *He's a good jumper.*

ˈjumper cable (*NAmE*) (*BrE* **jump lead**) *noun* [usually pl.] one of two cables that are used to start a car when it has no power in its battery. The jump cables connect the battery to the battery of another car.

ˌjumping-ˈoff point (also **jumping-ˈoff place**) *noun* a place from which to start a journey or new activity

ˈjump jet *noun* an aircraft that can take off and land by going straight up or down, without needing a RUNWAY

jump lead /ˈdʒʌmp liːd/ (*BrE*) (*NAmE* **ˈjumper cable**) *noun* [usually pl.] one of two cables that are used to start a car when it has no power in its battery. The jump leads connect the battery to the battery of another car.

ˈjump-off (*NAmE* also **ˈride-off**) *noun* (in the sport of SHOWJUMPING) an extra part of a competition in which horses that have the same score jump again to decide the winner

ˈjump rope *noun*, **ˌjump ˈrope** *verb* (*NAmE*) ➲ SKIPPING ROPE, SKIP ➲ **VISUAL VOCAB** page V32

ˈjump shot *noun* (in BASKETBALL) a shot made while jumping

ˈjump-start (*NAmE* also **jump**) *verb* **1** **~ sth** to start the engine of a car by connecting the battery to the battery of another car with JUMP LEADS **2** **~ sth** to put a lot of energy into starting a process or an activity or into making it start more quickly

jump·suit /ˈdʒʌmpsuːt; *BrE* also -sjuːt/ *noun* a piece of clothing that consists of trousers/pants and a jacket or shirt sewn together in one piece, worn especially by women

jumpy /ˈdʒʌmpi/ *adj.* (*informal*) nervous and anxious, especially because you think that sth bad is going to happen

junc·tion /ˈdʒʌŋkʃn/ *noun* **1** (*especially BrE*) (*NAmE* usually **inter·sec·tion**) the place where two or more roads or railway/railroad lines meet: *It was near the junction of City Road and Old Street.* ◇ *Come off the motorway at junction 6.* **2** a place where two or more cables, rivers or other things meet or are joined: *a telephone junction box*

junc·ture /ˈdʒʌŋktʃə(r)/ *noun* (*formal*) a particular point or stage in an activity or a series of events: *The battle had reached a crucial juncture.* ◇ ***At this juncture**, I would like to make an important announcement.*

June 🔑 /dʒuːn/ *noun* [U, C] (*abbr.* **Jun.**) the 6th month of the year, between May and July **HELP** To see how **June** is used, look at the examples at **April**.

jun·gle /ˈdʒʌŋgl/ *noun* **1** [U, C] an area of tropical forest where trees and plants grow very thickly: *The area was covered in dense jungle.* ◇ *the jungles of South-East Asia* ◇ *jungle warfare* ◇ *Our garden is a complete jungle.* **2** [sing.] an unfriendly or dangerous place or situation, especially one where it is very difficult to be successful or to trust anyone: *It's a jungle out there—you've got to be strong to succeed.* ➲ see also CONCRETE JUNGLE **3** (also **ˈjungle music**) [U] a type of electronic dance music developed in Britain in the early 1990s, which has a fast drum beat and a strong slower BASS beat **IDM** see LAW

ˈjungle gym (*NAmE*) (*BrE* **ˈclimbing frame**) *noun* a structure made of metal bars joined together for children to climb and play on ➲ picture at FRAME ➲ **VISUAL VOCAB** page V32

jun·gli /ˈdʒʌŋgli/ *adj.* (*IndE*) wild; not educated

jun·ior 🔑 /ˈdʒuːniə(r)/ *adj.*, *noun*

■ ***adj.***

▸ OF LOW RANK **1** 🔑 [usually before noun] having a low rank in an organization or a profession: *junior employees* ◇ **~ to sb** *She is junior to me.*

▸ IN SPORT **2** 🔑 [only before noun] connected with young people below a particular age, rather than with adults, especially in sports: *the world junior tennis championships*

▸ SON **3 Junior** (*abbr.* **Jnr**, **Jr.**) (especially in US) used after the name of a man who has the same name as his father, to avoid confusion ➲ compare THE YOUNGER at YOUNG *adj.* (6)

▸ SCHOOL/COLLEGE **4** [only before noun] (*BrE*) (of a school or part of a school) for children under the age of 11 or 13 **5** [only before noun] (*NAmE*) connected with the year before the last year in a HIGH SCHOOL or college: *I spent my junior year in France.* ➲ compare SENIOR

■ ***noun***

▸ LOW LEVEL JOB **1** 🔑 [C] (*especially BrE*) a person who has a job at a low level within an organization: *office juniors*

▸ IN SPORT **2** 🔑 [C] a young person below a particular age, rather than an adult: *She has coached many of our leading juniors.*

▸ IN SCHOOL/COLLEGE **3** [C] (*BrE*) a child who goes to JUNIOR SCHOOL **4** [C] (*NAmE*) a student in the year before the last year at HIGH SCHOOL or college ➲ compare SOPHOMORE

▸ SON **5** [sing.] (*NAmE*, *informal*) a person's young son: *I leave junior with Mom when I'm at work.*

IDM **be...years sb's ˈjunior** | **be sb's junior (by...)** to be younger than sb, by the number of years mentioned: *She's four years his junior.* ◇ *She's his junior by four years.*

ˌjunior ˈcollege *noun* (in the US) a college that offers programmes that are two years long. Some students go to a university or a college offering four-year programmes after they have finished studying at a junior college.

ˌjunior ˈcommon room *noun* (*abbr.* **JCR**) (*BrE*) a room in a college, used for social purposes by students who have not yet taken their first degree

ˈjunior doctor *noun* (in Britain) a doctor who has finished medical school and who is working at a hospital to get further practical experience ➲ compare HOUSE OFFICER, INTERN

ˌjunior ˈhigh school (also **ˌjunior ˈhigh**) *noun* [C, U] (in the US) a school for young people between the ages of 12 and 14 ➲ compare SENIOR HIGH SCHOOL

ˈjunior school *noun* [C, U] (in Britain) a school for children between the ages of 7 and 11

ju·ni·per /ˈdʒuːnɪpə(r)/ *noun* [U, C] a bush with purple BERRIES that are used in medicine and to flavour GIN

junk /dʒʌŋk/ *noun*, *verb*

■ ***noun*** **1** [U] things that are considered useless or of little value **SYN** **rubbish/garbage**: *I've cleared out all that old junk in the attic.* ◇ *There's nothing but junk on the TV.* ◇ (*informal, disapproving*) *Is this all your junk* (= are these all your things)? ➲ **SYNONYMS** at THING **2** [U] = JUNK FOOD **3** [C] a Chinese boat with a square sail and a flat bottom

■ ***verb*** **~ sth** (*informal*) to get rid of sth because it is no longer valuable or useful

ˈjunk bond *noun* (*business*) a type of BOND that pays a high rate of interest because there is a lot of risk involved, often used to raise money quickly in order to buy the shares of another company

jun·ket /ˈdʒʌŋkɪt/ *noun* (*informal, disapproving*) a trip that is made for pleasure by sb who works for the government, etc. and that is paid for using public money

ˈjunk food (also **junk**) *noun* [U] (also **junk foods** [pl.]) (*informal, disapproving*) food that is quick and easy to prepare and eat but that is thought to be bad for your health

junkie /ˈdʒʌŋki/ *noun* (*informal*) a drug ADDICT (= a person who is unable to stop taking dangerous drugs)

ˈjunk mail *noun* [U] (*disapproving*) advertising material that is sent to people who have not asked for it ➲ compare SPAM

ˌjunk ˈscience *noun* [U] (*disapproving*) used to refer to ideas and theories that seem to be well researched and scientific but in fact have little evidence to support them

ˈjunk shop *noun* (*especially BrE*) a shop that buys and sells old furniture and other objects, at cheap prices

junky /ˈdʒʌŋki/ *adj.* (*informal, especially NAmE*) of poor quality or of little value

junk·yard /ˈdʒʌŋkjɑːd; *NAmE* -jɑːrd/ (*especially NAmE*) (*BrE* also **scrap·yard**) *noun* a place where old cars, machines, etc. are collected, so that parts of them, or the metal they are made of, can be sold to be used again

junta /ˈdʒʌntə; *NAmE* ˈhʊntə/ *noun* a military government that has taken power by force

Ju·pi·ter /ˈdʒuːpɪtə(r)/ *noun* the largest planet of the SOLAR SYSTEM, fifth in order of distance from the sun ➲ **VISUAL VOCAB** page V59

J

Jur·as·sic /dʒʊˈræsɪk/ *adj.* (*geology*) of the PERIOD between around 208 to 146 million years ago, when the largest known dinosaurs lived; of the rocks formed during this time ▸ **the Jur·as·sic** *noun* [sing.]

jur·id·ic·al /dʒʊəˈrɪdɪkl; *NAmE* dʒʊˈr-/ *adj.* [usually before noun] (*formal*) connected with the law, judges or legal matters

jur·is·dic·tion /ˌdʒʊərɪsˈdɪkʃn; *NAmE* ˌdʒʊr-/ *noun* (*formal*) **1** [U, C] **~ (over sb/sth)** | **~ (of sb/sth) (to do sth)** the authority that an official organization has to make legal decisions about sb/sth **2** [C] an area or a country in which a particular system of laws has authority ▸ **jur·is·dic·tion·al** *adj.*

jur·is·pru·dence /ˌdʒʊərɪsˈpruːdns; *NAmE* ˌdʒʊr-/ *noun* [U] (*technical*) the scientific study of law: *a professor of jurisprudence*

jur·ist /ˈdʒʊərɪst; *NAmE* ˈdʒʊr-/ *noun* (*formal*) a person who is an expert in law

juror /ˈdʒʊərə(r); *NAmE* ˈdʒʊr-/ *noun* a member of a jury

jury /ˈdʒʊəri; *NAmE* ˈdʒʊri/ *noun* [C+sing./pl. v.] (*pl.* -ies) **1** (also **panel**, **ˈjury panel** especially in *NAmE*) a group of members of the public who listen to the facts of a case in a court and decide whether or not sb is guilty of a crime: ***members of the jury*** ◇ *to **be/sit/serve on a jury*** ◇ *The jury has/have returned a verdict of guilty.* ◇ *the right to trial **by jury*** ➲ COLLOCATIONS at JUSTICE ➲ see also GRAND JURY **2** a group of people who decide who is the winner of a competition

IDM **the jury is (still) ˈout on sth** used when you are saying that sth is still not certain

ˈjury duty (*BrE* usually **ˈjury service**) *noun* [U] a period of time spent as a member of a jury in court

jus /ʒuː; *NAmE* also dʒuːs/ *noun* [U] (from *French*) a thin sauce, especially one made from meat juices

just 🔑 /dʒʌst/ *adv., adj.*

■ ***adv.*** **1** 🔑 exactly: *This jacket is just my size.* ◇ *This gadget is **just the thing** for getting those nails out.* ◇ ***Just my luck*** (= the sort of bad luck I usually have). *The phone's not working.* ◇ *You're **just in time**.* ◇ **~ like...** *She looks just like her mother.* ◇ **~ what...** *It's just what I wanted!* ◇ **~ as...** *It's just as I thought.* ◇ (*BrE*) *It's **just on** six* (= exactly six o'clock). **2** 🔑 **~ as...** at the same moment as: *The clock struck six just as I arrived.* **3** 🔑 **~ as good, nice, easily, etc.** no less than; equally: *She's just as smart as her sister.* ◇ *You can get there just as cheaply by plane.* **4** 🔑 **(only) ~** | **~ after, before, under, etc. sth** by a small amount: *I got here just after nine.* ◇ *I only just caught the train.* ◇ *Inflation fell to just over 4 per cent.* **5** 🔑 used to say that you/sb did sth very recently: *I've just heard the news.* ◇ *When you arrived he had only just left.* ◇ *She has just been telling us about her trip to Rome.* ◇ (*especially NAmE*) *I just saw him a moment ago.* ➲ note at ALREADY **6** 🔑 at this/that moment; now: *I'm just finishing my book.* ◇ *I was just beginning to enjoy myself when we had to leave.* ◇ *I'm just off* (= I am leaving now). **7** 🔑 **~ about/going to do sth** going to do sth only a few moments from now or then: *The water's just about to boil.* ◇ *I was just going to tell you when you interrupted.* **8** 🔑 simply: *It was just an ordinary day.* ◇ *I **can't just** drop all my commitments.* ◇ *This essay is **just not good enough**.* ◇ *I didn't mean to upset you. **It's just that** I had to tell somebody.* ◇ *This is not **just another** disaster movie—it's a masterpiece.* ◇ ***Just because** you're older than me **doesn't mean** you know everything.* **9** 🔑 only: **~ (for sth)** *I decided to learn Japanese **just for fun**.* ◇ **~ (to do sth)** *I waited an hour just to see you.* ◇ *There is just one method that might work.* ◇ *'Can I help you?' 'No thanks, **I'm just looking**.'* (= in a shop/store) **10** (*informal*) really; completely: *The food was just wonderful!* ◇ *I can just imagine his reaction.* **11** used in orders to get sb's attention, give permission, etc.: *Just listen to what I'm saying, will you!* ◇ *Just help yourselves.* **12** used to make a polite request, excuse, etc.: *Could you just help me with this box, please?* ◇ *I've just got a few things to do first.* **13 could/might/may ~** used to show a slight possibility that sth is true or will happen: *Try his home number—he might just be there.* **14** used to agree with sb: *'He's very pompous.' 'Isn't he just?'*

IDM **could/might just as well...** used to say that you/sb would have been in the same position if you had done sth else, because you got little benefit or enjoyment from what you did do: *The weather was so bad we might just as well have stayed at home.* **it is just as ˈwell (that...)** it is a good thing: *It is just as well that we didn't leave any later or we'd have missed him.* **just about** (*informal*) **1** 🔑 almost; very nearly: *I've met just about everyone.* ◇ *'Did you reach your sales target?' 'Just about.'* **2** 🔑 approximately: *She should be arriving just about now.* **just a ˈminute/ˈmoment/ˈsecond** 🔑 (*informal*) used to ask sb to wait for a short time: *'Is Mr Burns available?' 'Just a second, please, I'll check.'* **just like ˈthat** suddenly, without warning or explanation **just ˈnow 1** 🔑 at this moment: *Come and see me later—I'm busy just now.* **2** 🔑 during this present period: *Business is good just now.* **3** 🔑 only a short time ago: *I saw her just now.* **4** (*SAfrE, informal*) later; in a short period of time **just ˈso** done or arranged very accurately or carefully: *He liked polishing the furniture and making everything just so.* **just ˈthen** 🔑 at that moment: *Just then, someone knocked at the front door.* **not just ˈyet** not now but probably quite soon: *I can't give you the money just yet.* **I, etc. would just as soon do sth** used to say that you would equally well like to do sth as do sth else that has been suggested: *I'd just as soon stay at home as go out tonight.* ➲ more at CASE *n.*, JOB

■ ***adj.*** [usually before noun] **1** that most people consider to be morally fair and reasonable SYN **fair**: *a **just decision/law/society*** **2 the just** *noun* [pl.] people who are just **3** appropriate in a particular situation: *a **just reward/punishment*** ◇ *I think she got her **just deserts*** (= what she deserved). OPP **unjust** ▸ **just·ly** *adv.*: *to be treated justly* ◇ *to be justly proud of sth*

just·ice 🔑 /ˈdʒʌstɪs/ *noun*

1 🔑 [U] the fair treatment of people: *laws based on the principles of justice* ◇ *They are demanding equal rights and justice.* OPP **injustice** ➲ see also POETIC JUSTICE, ROUGH JUSTICE **2** 🔑 [U] the quality of being fair or reasonable: *Who can deny the justice of their cause?* OPP **injustice** **3** 🔑 [U] the legal system used to punish people who have committed crimes: *the criminal justice system* ◇ *The European Court of Justice* ◇ (*BrE*) *They were accused of attempting to **pervert the course of justice**.* ◇ (*NAmE*) *They were accused of attempting to **obstruct justice**.* ➲ see also MISCARRIAGE OF JUSTICE **4** (also **Just·ice**) [C] (*NAmE*) a judge in a court (also used before the name of a judge) ➲ see also CHIEF JUSTICE **5 Just·ice** [C] (*BrE, CanE*) used before the name of a judge in a COURT OF APPEAL: *Mr Justice Davies*

IDM **bring sb to ˈjustice** to arrest sb for a crime and put them on trial in court **do justice to ˈsb/ˈsth; do sb/sth ˈjustice 1** to treat or represent sb/sth fairly, especially in a way that shows how good, attractive, etc. they are: *That photo doesn't do you justice.* **2** to deal with sb/sth correctly and completely: *You cannot do justice to such a complex situation in just a few pages.* **do yourself ˈjustice** to do sth as well as you can in order to show other people how good you are: *She didn't do herself justice in the exam.* ➲ more at PERVERT *v.*

ˌJustice of the ˈPeace *noun* (*pl.* **Justices of the Peace**) (*abbr.* **JP**) (*formal*) an official who acts as a judge in the lowest courts of law SYN **magistrate**

jus·ti·ciary /dʒʌˈstɪʃəri; *NAmE* dʒəˈstɪʃieri/ *noun* (*pl.* -ies) **1** (*ScotE*) [C] a judge or similar officer **2** [U] the process by which justice is done

jus·ti·fi·able AW /ˈdʒʌstɪfaɪəbl; ˌdʒʌstɪˈfaɪəbl/ *adj.* existing or done for a good reason, and therefore acceptable SYN **legitimate**: *justifiable pride* ▸ **jus·ti·fi·ably** AW /-əbli/ *adv.*: *The university can be justifiably proud of its record.*

ˌjustifiable ˈhomicide *noun* [U] (*law*) in some countries, a killing which is not a criminal act, for example because you were trying to defend yourself ➲ compare CULPABLE HOMICIDE

jus·ti·fi·ca·tion AW /ˌdʒʌstɪfɪˈkeɪʃn/ *noun* [U, C] **~ (for sth/doing sth)** a good reason why sth exists or is done: *I can see no possible justification for any further tax increases.*

Collocations

Criminal justice

Breaking the law

- **break/violate/obey/uphold** the law
- **be investigated/arrested/tried for** a crime/a robbery/fraud
- **be arrested/**(*especially NAmE*) **indicted/convicted** on charges of rape/fraud/(*especially US*) felony charges
- **be arrested** on suspicion of arson/robbery/shoplifting
- **be accused of/be charged with** murder/(*especially NAmE*) homicide/four counts of fraud
- **face** two charges of indecent assault
- **admit** your guilt/liability/responsibility (for sth)
- **deny** the allegations/claims/charges
- **confess to** a crime
- **grant/be refused/be released on/skip/jump** bail

The legal process

- **stand/await/bring sb to/come to/be on** trial
- **take sb to/come to/settle sth out of** court
- **face/avoid/escape** prosecution
- **seek/retain/have the right to/be denied access to** legal counsel
- **hold/conduct/attend/adjourn** a hearing/trial
- **sit on/influence/persuade/convince** the jury
- **sit/stand/appear/be put/place sb** in the dock
- **plead** guilty/not guilty to a crime
- **be called to/enter** (*BrE*) the witness box
- **take/put sb on** the stand/(*NAmE*) the witness stand
- **call/subpoena/question/cross-examine** a witness
- **give/hear** the evidence against/on behalf of sb
- **raise/withdraw/overrule** an objection
- **reach** a unanimous/majority verdict
- **return/deliver/record** a verdict of not guilty/unlawful killing/accidental death
- **convict/acquit** the defendant of the crime
- **secure** a conviction/your acquittal
- **lodge/file** an appeal
- **appeal (against)/challenge/uphold/overturn** a conviction/verdict

Sentencing and punishment

- **pass** sentence on sb
- **carry/face/serve** a seven-year/life sentence
- **receive/be given** the death penalty
- **be sentenced to** ten years (in prison/jail)
- **carry/impose/pay** a fine (of $3 000)/a penalty (of 14 years imprisonment)
- **be imprisoned/jailed for** drug possession/fraud/murder
- **do/serve** time/ten years
- **be sent to/put sb in/be released from** jail/prison
- **be/put sb/spend X years** on death row
- **be granted/be denied/break (your)** parole

➲ more collocations at CRIME

◇ *He was getting angry—and* ***with some justification.***
➲ SYNONYMS at REASON

IDM **in justifi'cation (of sb/sth)** as an explanation of why sth exists or why sb has done sth: *All I can say in justification of her actions is that she was under a lot of pressure at work.*

jus·ti·fied 0-w AW /ˈdʒʌstɪfaɪd/ *adj.* **1** 0-w **~ (in doing sth)** having a good reason for doing sth: *She felt fully justified in asking for her money back.* **2** 0-w existing or done for a good reason: *His fears proved justified.* OPP **unjustified**

jus·tify 0-w AW /ˈdʒʌstɪfaɪ/ *verb* (**jus·ti·fies, jus·ti·fy·ing, jus·ti·fied, jus·ti·fied**) **1** 0-w to show that sb/sth is right or reasonable: **~ (sb/sth) doing sth** *How can they justify paying such huge salaries?* ◇ **~ sth** *Her success had justified the faith her teachers had put in her.* **2** 0-w **~ sth/yourself (to sb)** | **~ (sb/sth) doing sth** to give an explanation or excuse for sth or for doing sth SYN **defend**: *The Prime Minister has been asked to justify the decision to Parliament.* ◇ *You don't need to justify yourself to me.* **3 ~ sth** (*technical*) to arrange lines of printed text so that one or both edges are straight IDM see END *n.*

ˌjust-ˌin-ˈtime *adj.* (*abbr.* JIT) (*business*) used to describe a system in which parts or materials are only delivered to a factory just before they are needed

jut /dʒʌt/ *verb* (-tt-) [I, T] to stick out further than the surrounding surface, objects, etc; to make sth stick out SYN **protrude, project: ~ (out) (from, into, over sth)** *A row of small windows jutted out from the roof.* ◇ *A rocky headland jutted into the sea.* ◇ *a jutting chin* ◇ **~ sth (out)** *She jutted her chin out stubbornly.*

jute /dʒuːt/ *noun* [U] FIBRES (= thin threads) from a plant, also called jute, used for making rope and rough cloth

ju·ven·ile /ˈdʒuːvənaɪl; *NAmE* -vənl/ *adj., noun*
■ ***adj.* 1** [only before noun] (*formal* or *law*) connected with young people who are not yet adults: *juvenile crime/employment* ◇ *juvenile offenders* **2** (*disapproving*) silly and more typical of a child than an adult SYN **childish**: *juvenile behaviour* ◇ *Don't be so juvenile!*
■ ***noun*** (*formal* or *law*) a young person who is not yet an adult

ˌjuvenile ˈcourt *noun* a court that deals with young people who are not yet adults

ˌjuvenile deˈlinquent *noun* a young person who is not yet an adult and who is guilty of committing a crime ▸ **juvenile deˈlinquency** *noun* [U]

ju·ven·ilia /ˌdʒuːvəˈnɪliə/ *noun* [pl.] (*formal*) writing, poetry, works of art, etc. produced by a writer or an artist when he/she was still young

juxta·pose /ˌdʒʌkstəˈpəʊz; *NAmE* -ˈpoʊz/ *verb* [usually passive] **~ A and/with B** (*formal*) to put people or things together, especially in order to show a contrast or a new relationship between them: *In the exhibition, abstract paintings are juxtaposed with shocking photographs.* ▸ **juxta·pos·ition** /ˌdʒʌkstəpəˈzɪʃn/ *noun* [U, C]: *the juxtaposition of realistic and surreal situations in the novel*

J

K k

K /keɪ/ *noun, abbr.*
■ ***noun*** (also **k**) [C, U] (*pl.* Ks, K's, k's /keɪz/) the 11th letter of the English alphabet: *'King' begins with (a) K/'K'.*
■ ***abbr.*** (*pl.* K) **1** (*informal*) one thousand: *She earns 40K* (= £40 000) *a year.* **2** kilometre(s): *a 10K race* **3** (*computing*) kilobyte(s) **4** KELVIN(S)
■ ***symbol*** the symbol for the chemical element potassium

K-12 /ˌkeɪ 'twelv/ *adj.* (in the US) relating to education from KINDERGARTEN (= the class that prepares children for school) to 12th GRADE

ka·baddi /'kʌbədi/ *noun* [U] a S Asian sport played by teams of seven players on a round sand court. A player from one team tries to capture a player from the other team and must hold his/her breath while running.

Kab·ba·lah (also **Ca·bala**, **Qa·ba·lah**) /kə'bɑːlə; 'kæbələ/ *noun* (in Judaism) the ancient tradition of explaining holy texts through MYSTICAL means

ka·buki /kə'buːki/ *noun* [U] (from *Japanese*) traditional Japanese theatre, in which songs, dance and MIME are performed by men

ka-ching /kə'tʃɪŋ/ (*BrE* also **ker-ching**) (*NAmE* also **cha-ching**) *exclamation* (*informal*) used to say that sb is getting a lot of money: *The money was rolling in, ka-ching, ka-ching!* ◇ *Ka-ching! I just got my first cheque.* ORIGIN A way of representing the noise made by a CASH REGISTER.

kaffee·klatsch /'kæfeɪklætʃ/ *noun* (*NAmE*, from *German*) a social event at which people drink coffee

Kaf·fir /'kæfə(r)/ *noun* (*taboo, slang*) a very offensive word for a black African

kaf·fi·yeh = KEFFIYEH

kafir /'kæfɪə(r); *NAmE* 'kæfər/ *noun* a word used by Muslims to refer to a person who is not a Muslim, that can be considered offensive

Kaf·ka·esque /ˌkæfkə'esk/ *adj.* used to describe a situation that is confusing and frightening, especially one involving complicated official rules and systems that do not seem to make any sense: *My attempt to get a new passport turned into a Kafkaesque nightmare.* ORIGIN From the name of the Czech writer Franz Kafka, whose novels often describe situations like this.

kaf·tan (also **caf·tan**) /'kæftæn/ *noun* **1** a long loose piece of clothing, usually with a belt at the waist, worn by men in Arab countries **2** a woman's long loose dress with long wide sleeves

ka·goul = CAGOULE

ka·huna /kə'huːnə/ *noun* (*NAmE, informal*) an important person; the person in charge

kai /kaɪ/ *noun* (*NZE, informal*) food

kai·ser /'kaɪzə(r)/ *noun* (from *German*) **1 Kaiser** (in the past) a ruler of Germany, of Austria, or of the Holy Roman Empire: *Kaiser Wilhelm* **2** (also **'kaiser roll**) (*NAmE*) a crisp bread roll

kai·zen /ˌkaɪ'zen/ *noun* [U] (*business*) (from *Japanese*) the practice of continuously improving the way in which a company operates

kajal /'kʌdʒəl/ *noun* [U] a type of black make-up used by S Asian women, that is put around the edge of the eyes to make them more noticeable and attractive

ka·kuro /ˌkɑː'kʊərəʊ; *NAmE* -'kʊroʊ/ *noun* (*pl.* -os) [C, U] (from *Japanese*) a number puzzle in which you have to put numbers into white spaces in a diagram so that their total is the number given in a black space: *She loves doing kakuros.* ➲ compare SUDOKU

Ka·lash·ni·kov /kə'læʃnɪkɒf; *NAmE* -kɔːf/ *noun* a type of RIFLE (= a long gun) that can fire bullets very quickly

kale /keɪl/ *noun* [U] (*NAmE* also **'collard greens**) a dark green vegetable like a CABBAGE

kal·eido·scope /kə'laɪdəskəʊp; *NAmE* -skoʊp/ *noun* **1** [C] a toy consisting of a tube that you look through with loose pieces of coloured glass and mirrors at the end. When the tube is turned, the pieces of glass move and form different patterns **2** [sing.] a situation, pattern, etc. containing a lot of different parts that are always changing ▸ **kal·eido·scop·ic** /kəˌlaɪdə'skɒpɪk; *NAmE* -'skɑːpɪk/ *adj.*

ka·meez /kə'miːz/ *noun* (*pl.* **ka·meez** or **ka·meezes**) a piece of clothing like a long shirt worn by many people from S Asia

kami·kaze /ˌkæmɪ'kɑːzi/ *adj.* [only before noun] (from *Japanese*) used to describe the way soldiers attack the enemy, knowing that they too will be killed SYN **suicidal**: *a kamikaze pilot/attack* ◇ (*figurative*) *He made a kamikaze run across three lanes of traffic.*

kanga = KHANGA

kan·ga·roo /ˌkæŋgə'ruː/ (also *informal* **roo**) *noun* (*pl.* -oos) a large Australian animal with a strong tail and back legs, that moves by jumping. The female carries its young in a pocket of skin (called a POUCH) on the front of its body. ➲ VISUAL VOCAB page V10

ˌkangaroo 'court *noun* (*disapproving*) an illegal court that punishes people unfairly

kanji /'kændʒi; 'kɑːn-/ *noun* [U, C] (*pl.* **kanji**) (from *Japanese*) a Japanese system of writing based on Chinese symbols, called CHARACTERS; a symbol in this system

Kan·nada /'kænədə/ (also **Kan·ar·ese** /ˌkænə'riːz/) *noun* [U] a language spoken in Karnataka in SW India

kanzu /'kænzuː/ *noun* (in E Africa) a long loose piece of outer clothing made from white cloth and worn by men

kao·lin /'keɪəlɪn/ (also **ˌchina 'clay**) *noun* [U] a type of fine white CLAY used in some medicines and in making PORCELAIN for cups, plates, etc.

kapok /'keɪpɒk; *NAmE* -pɑːk/ *noun* [U] a soft white material used for filling CUSHIONS, soft toys, etc.

kappa /'kæpə/ *noun* the 10th letter of the Greek alphabet (Κ, κ)

kaput /kə'pʊt/ *adj.* [not before noun] (*informal*) not working correctly; broken: *The truck's kaput.*

kara·bin·er /ˌkærə'biːnə(r)/ *noun* a metal ring that can open to allow a rope to pass through, used by rock CLIMBERS to attach themselves safely to things

kara·oke /ˌkæri'əʊki; *NAmE* -'oʊki/ *noun* [U] (from *Japanese*) a type of entertainment in which a machine plays only the music of popular songs so that people can sing the words themselves: *a karaoke machine/night/bar*

karat (*NAmE*) = CARAT

kar·ate /kə'rɑːti/ *noun* [U] a Japanese system of fighting in which you use your hands and feet as weapons: *a karate chop* (= a blow with the side of the hand)

karma /'kɑːmə; *NAmE* 'kɑːrmə/ *noun* [U] **1** (in Buddhism and Hinduism) the sum of sb's good and bad actions in one of their lives, believed to decide what will happen to them in the next life **2 good/bad ~** (*informal*) the good/bad effect of doing a particular thing, being in a particular place, etc: *Vegetarians believe that eating meat is bad karma.*

kart /kɑːt; *NAmE* kɑːrt/ *noun* a small motor vehicle used for racing

kart·ing /'kɑːtɪŋ; *NAmE* 'kɑːrt-/ *noun* [U] the sport of racing in karts

kas·bah (also **cas·bah**) /'kæzbɑː/ *noun* a castle on high ground in a N African city or the area around it

ka·tab·ol·ism = CATABOLISM

kata·kana /ˌkætə'kɑːnə/ *noun* [U] (from *Japanese*) a set of symbols used in Japanese writing, used especially to write foreign words or to represent noises ➲ compare HIRAGANA

kayak /'kaɪæk/ *noun* a light CANOE in which the part where you sit is covered over ➲ VISUAL VOCAB page V45 ▸ **kayak·ing** *noun* [U]: *to go kayaking*

kayo /keɪ'əʊ; *NAmE* -'oʊ/ *noun* (*pl.* -os) = KO

kazoo /kəˈzuː/ *noun* (*pl.* -oos) a small simple musical instrument consisting of a hollow pipe with a hole in it, that makes a BUZZING sound when you sing into it

KB (also **K**) *abbr.* (in writing) KILOBYTE

Kb (also **Kbit**) *abbr.* (in writing) KILOBIT

Kbps *abbr.* (in writing) kilobits per second (a unit for measuring the speed of a MODEM)

KC /ˌkeɪ ˈsiː/ *noun* the highest level of BARRISTER, who can speak for the government in court in Britain. KC is the abbreviation for 'King's Counsel' and is used when there is a king in Britain. ➲ compare QC

kebab /kɪˈbæb/ (also ˈ**shish kebab** especially in *NAmE*) *noun* small pieces of meat and vegetables cooked on a wooden or metal stick ➲ see also DONER KEBAB

kedg·eree /ˈkedʒəriː/ *noun* [U] a hot dish of rice, fish and eggs cooked together

keel /kiːl/ *noun, verb*

■ ***noun*** the long piece of wood or steel along the bottom of a ship, on which the frame is built, and which sometimes sticks out below the bottom and helps to keep it in a vertical position in the water **IDM** see EVEN *adj.*

■ ***verb*** [I, T] ~ (**sth**) (**over**) (of a ship or boat) to fall over sideways; to make sth fall over sideways **SYN** **capsize**

PHR V ˌ**keel** ˈ**over** to fall over unexpectedly, especially because you feel ill/sick: *Several of them keeled over in the heat.*

keel·haul /ˈkiːlhɔːl/ *verb* **1** ~ **sb** (*old use*) to punish a sailor by pulling him under a ship, from one side to the other or from one end to the other **2** ~ **sb** (*humorous*) to punish sb very severely or speak very angrily to sb

keen 0-π /kiːn/ *adj., verb*

■ ***adj.*** (**keen·er**, **keen·est**)

▸ EAGER/ENTHUSIASTIC **1** 0-π (*especially BrE*) wanting to do sth or wanting sth to happen very much **SYN** **eager**: ~ (**to do sth**) *John was very keen to help.* ◇ ~ (**that…**) *We are keen that our school should get involved too.* ◇ ~ (**on doing sth**) *I wasn't too keen on going to the party.* **2** 0-π [usually before noun] (*especially BrE*) enthusiastic about an activity or idea, etc: *a keen sportsman* ◇ *one of the keenest supporters of the team*

▸ LIKING SB/STH **3** 0-π (*BrE, informal*) liking sb/sth very much; very interested in sb/sth: ~ **on sb/sth** *Tom's very keen on Anna.* ◇ ~ **on doing sth** *She's not keen on being told what to do.* ➲ SYNONYMS at LIKE

▸ CLEVER **4** [only before noun] quick to understand: *a* ***keen mind/intellect*** **SYN** **sharp, acute**

▸ IDEAS/FEELINGS **5** [usually before noun] strong or deep: *a keen sense of tradition* ◇ *He took a* ***keen interest*** *in his grandson's education.*

▸ SENSES **6** [only before noun] highly developed **SYN** **sharp**: *Dogs have a keen sense of smell.* ◇ *My friend has* ***a keen eye for*** (= is good at noticing) *a bargain.*

▸ COMPETITION **7** involving people competing very hard with each other for sth: *There is keen competition for places at the college.*

▸ PRICES **8** (*especially BrE*) kept low in order to compete with other prices **SYN** **competitive**

▸ WIND **9** (*literary*) extremely cold

▸ KNIFE **10** [usually before noun] (*literary*) having a sharp edge or point **SYN** **sharp**

▸ **keen·ly** *adv.*: *a keenly fought contest* ◇ *We were keenly aware of the danger.* **keen·ness** *noun* [U]

IDM (**as**) ˌ**keen as** ˈ**mustard** (*BrE, informal*) wanting very much to do well at sth; enthusiastic ➲ more at MAD

■ ***verb*** [I] (usually used in the progressive tenses) (*old-fashioned*) to make a loud high sad sound, when sb has died

keep 0-π /kiːp/ *verb, noun*

■ ***verb*** (**kept**, **kept** /kept/)

▸ STAY **1** 0-π [I, T] to stay in a particular condition or position; to make sb/sth do this: + **adj.** *We huddled together to keep warm.* ◇ + **adv./prep.** *The notice said 'Keep off* (= Do not walk on) *the grass'.* ◇ *Keep left along the wall.* ◇ ~ **sb/sth** + **adj.** *She kept the children amused for hours.* ◇ ~ **sb/sth** (+ **adv./prep.**) *He kept his coat on.* ◇ *Don't* ***keep us in suspense***—*what happened next?* ◇ *She had trouble* ***keeping her balance.*** ◇ ~ **sb/sth doing sth** *I'm very sorry to* ***keep you waiting.***

▸ CONTINUE **2** 0-π [I] to continue doing sth; to do sth repeatedly: ~ **doing sth** *Keep smiling!* ◇ ~ **on doing sth** *Don't keep on interrupting me!*

▸ DELAY **3** [T] ~ **sb** to delay sb **SYN** **hold sb up**: *You're an hour late—what kept you?*

▸ NOT GIVE BACK **4** 0-π [T] ~ **sth** to continue to have sth and not give it back or throw it away: *Here's a five dollar bill—please* ***keep the change.*** ◇ *I keep all her letters.*

▸ SAVE FOR SB **5** 0-π [T] (*especially BrE*) to save sth for sb: ~ **sth for sb** *Please keep a seat for me.* ◇ ~ **sb sth** *Please keep me a seat.*

▸ PUT/STORE **6** 0-π [T] ~ **sth** + **adv./prep.** to put or store sth in a particular place: *Keep your passport in a safe place.*

▸ SHOP/RESTAURANT **7** [T] ~ **sth** (*especially BrE*) to own and manage a shop/store or restaurant: *Her father kept a grocer's shop.*

▸ ANIMALS **8** [T] ~ **sth** to own and care for animals: *to* ***keep bees/goats/hens***

▸ ABOUT HEALTH **9** [I] + **adv./prep.** (*informal*) used to ask or talk about sb's health: ***How is*** *your mother* ***keeping?*** ◇ *We're all keeping well.*

▸ OF FOOD **10** [I] to remain in good condition: *Finish off the pie—it won't keep.* ◇ (*informal, figurative*) *'I'd love to hear about it, but I'm late already.' 'That's OK—****it'll keep*** (= I can tell you about it later).*'*

▸ SECRET **11** 0-π [T] ~ **a secret** | ~ **sth secret** (**from sb**) to know sth and not tell it to anyone: *Can you keep a secret?* ◇ *She kept her past secret from us all.*

▸ PROMISE/APPOINTMENT **12** 0-π [T] ~ **your promise/word** | ~ **an appointment** to do what you have promised to do; to go where you have agreed to go: *She kept her promise to visit them.* ◇ *He failed to keep his appointment at the clinic.*

▸ DIARY/RECORD **13** 0-π [T] ~ **a diary, an account, a record, etc.** to write down sth as a record: *She kept a diary for over twenty years.* ◇ *Keep a note of where each item can be found.*

▸ SUPPORT SB **14** 0-π [T] ~ **sb/yourself** to provide what is necessary for sb to live; to support sb by paying for food, etc: *He scarcely earns enough to keep himself and his family.*

▸ PROTECT **15** [T] (*formal*) to protect sb from sth: ~ **sb** *May the Lord bless you and keep you* (= used in prayers in the Christian Church). ◇ ~ **sb from sth** *His only thought was to keep the boy from harm.*

▸ IN SPORT **16** [T] ~ **goal/wicket** (*BrE*) (in football (SOCCER), HOCKEY, CRICKET, etc.) to guard or protect the goal or WICKET ➲ see also GOALKEEPER, WICKETKEEPER

IDM Most idioms containing **keep** are at the entries for the nouns and adjectives in the idioms, for example **keep house** is at **house**. ˌ**keep** ˈ**going 1** 0-π to make an effort to live normally when you are in a difficult situation or when you have experienced great suffering: *You just have to keep yourself busy and keep going.* **2** 0-π (*informal*) used to encourage sb to continue doing sth: *Keep going, Sarah, you're nearly there.* ˌ**keep sb** ˈ**going** (*informal*) to be enough for sb until they get what they are waiting for: *Have an apple to keep you going till dinner time.*

PHR V ˌ**keep sb** ˈ**after** (*NAmE*) (*BrE* ˌ**keep sb**↔ˈ**back**) to make a student stay at school after normal hours as a punishment

ˌ**keep** ˈ**at sth** to continue working at sth: *Come on, keep at it, you've nearly finished!* ˌ**keep sb** ˈ**at sth** to make sb continue working at sth: *He kept us at it all day.*

ˌ**keep aˈway (from sb/sth)** to avoid going near sb/sth: *Keep away from the edge of the cliff.* ˌ**keep sb/sth aˈway (from sb/sth)** to prevent sb/sth from going somewhere: *Her illness kept her away from work for several weeks.*

ˌ**keep ˈback (from sb/sth)** to stay at a distance from sb/sth: *Keep well back from the road.* ˌ**keep sb**↔ˈ**back 1** (*BrE*) (*NAmE* ˌ**keep sb** ˈ**after**) to make a student stay at school after normal hours as a punishment **2** (*NAmE*) to make a student repeat a year at school because of poor marks/grades ˌ**keep sb**↔ˈ**back (from sb/sth)** to make sb stay at a distance from sb/sth: *Barricades were erected to keep back the crowds.* ˌ**keep sth**↔ˈ**back 1** to prevent a feeling, etc. from being expressed **SYN** **restrain**: *She was unable to*

K

keep back her tears. **2** to continue to have a part of sth: *He kept back half the money for himself.* **ˌkeep sth↔ˈback (from sb)** to refuse to tell sb sth: *I'm sure she's keeping something back from us.*

ˌkeep ˈdown to hide yourself by not standing up straight: *Keep down! You mustn't let anyone see you.* **ˌkeep sb↔ˈdown** to prevent a person, group, etc. from expressing themselves freely **SYN** **oppress**: *The people have been kept down for years by a brutal regime.* **ˌkeep sth↔ˈdown** **1** to make sth stay at a low level; to avoid increasing sth: *to keep down wages/prices/the cost of living* ◇ *Keep your voice down—I don't want anyone else to hear.* ◇ *Keep the noise down* (= be quiet). **2** to not bring sth back through the mouth from the stomach; to not VOMIT: *She's had some water but she can't keep any food down.*

ˈkeep from sth | ˈkeep yourself from sth to prevent yourself from doing sth: **~ doing sth** *She could hardly keep from laughing.* ◇ *I just managed to keep myself from falling.* **ˈkeep sb from sth** to prevent sb from doing sth: *I hope I'm not keeping you from your work.* ◇ **~ doing sth** *The church bells keep me from sleeping.* **ˈkeep sth from sb** to avoid telling sb sth: *I think we ought to keep the truth from him until he's better.* **ˈkeep sth from sth** to make sth stay out of sth: *She could not keep the dismay from her voice.*

ˌkeep ˈin with sb (*BrE, informal*) to make sure that you stay friendly with sb, because you will get an advantage from doing so **ˌkeep sth↔ˈin** to avoid expressing an emotion **SYN** **restrain**: *He could scarcely keep in his indignation.* **ˌkeep sb ˈin** to make sb stay indoors or in a particular place **ˈkeep sb/yourself in sth** to provide sb/yourself with a regular supply of sth

ˌkeep ˈoff if rain, snow, etc. **keeps off**, it does not fall **ˌkeep ˈoff sth** **1** to avoid eating, drinking or smoking sth: *I'm trying to keep off fatty foods.* **2** to avoid mentioning a particular subject: *It's best to keep off politics when my father's around.* **ˌkeep sb/sth↔ˈoff | ˌkeep sb/sth ˈoff sb/sth** to prevent sb/sth from coming near, touching, etc. sb/sth: *They lit a fire to keep off wild animals.* ◇ *Keep your hands off* (= do not touch) *me!*

ˌkeep ˈon to continue: *Keep on until you get to the church.* **ˌkeep sb↔ˈon** to continue to employ sb **ˌkeep sth ˈon** to continue to rent a house, flat/apartment, etc. **ˌkeep ˈon (at sb) (about sb/sth)** (*especially BrE*) to speak to sb often and in an annoying way about sb/sth **SYN** **go on, nag**: *He does keep on so!* ◇ *I'll do it—just don't keep on at me about it!*

ˌkeep ˈout (of sth) 🔑 to not enter a place; to stay outside: *The sign said 'Private Property—Keep Out!'* **ˌkeep sb/sth↔ˈout (of sth)** to prevent sb/sth from entering a place: *Keep that dog out of my study!* **ˌkeep ˈout of sth | ˌkeep sb ˈout of sth** 🔑 to avoid sth; to prevent sb from being involved in sth or affected by sth: *That child can't keep out of mischief.* ◇ *Keep the baby out of the sun.*

ˈkeep to sth **1** to avoid leaving a path, road, etc. **SYN** **stick to sth**: *Keep to the track—the land is very boggy around here.* **2** to talk or write only about the subject that you are supposed to talk or write about: *Nothing is more irritating than people who do not* ***keep to the point.*** **3** to do what you have promised or agreed to do: *to keep to an agreement/an undertaking/a plan* **4** to stay in and not leave a particular place or position: *She's nearly 90 and mostly keeps to her room.* **ˌkeep (yourself) to yourˈself** to avoid meeting people socially or becoming involved in their affairs: *Nobody knows much about him; he keeps himself very much to himself.* **ˌkeep sth to yourˈself** to not tell other people about sth: *I'd be grateful if you kept this information to yourself.*

ˌkeep sb ˈunder to control or OPPRESS sb: *The local people are kept under by the army.*

ˌkeep ˈup if particular weather **keeps up**, it continues without stopping: *The rain kept up all afternoon.* **ˌkeep ˈup (with sb/sth)** 🔑 to move, make progress or increase at the same rate as sb/sth: *Slow down—I can't keep up!* ◇ *I can't keep up with all the changes.* ◇ *Wages are not keeping up with inflation.* **ˌkeep ˈup with sb** to continue to be in contact with sb: *How many of your old school friends do you keep up with?* **ˌkeep ˈup with sth** **1** 🔑 to learn about or be aware of the news, current events, etc: *She likes to keep up with the latest fashions.* **2** 🔑 to continue to pay or do sth regularly: *If you do not keep up with the payments you could lose your home.* **ˌkeep sb ˈup** to prevent sb from going to bed: *I hope we're not keeping you up.* **ˌkeep sth↔ˈup** **1** 🔑 to make sth stay at a high level: *The high cost of raw materials is keeping prices up.* **2** 🔑 to continue sth at the same, usually high, level: *The enemy kept up the bombardment day and night.* ◇ *We're having difficulty keeping up our mortgage payments.* ◇ *Well done!* ***Keep up the good work/ Keep it up!*** **3** to make sth remain at a high level: *They sang songs to keep their spirits up.* **4** to continue to use or practise sth: *to keep up old traditions* ◇ *Do you still keep up your Spanish?* **5** to take care of a house, garden/yard, etc. so that it stays in good condition **SYN** **maintain** ➲ related noun UPKEEP

■ ***noun*** **1** [U] food, clothes and all the other things that a person needs to live; the cost of these things: *It's about time you got a job to* ***earn your keep.*** **2** [C] a large strong tower, built as part of an old castle

IDM **for ˈkeeps** (*informal*) for ever: *Is it yours for keeps or does he want it back?* ➲ more at EARN

keep·er /ˈkiːpə(r)/ *noun* **1** (especially in compounds) a person whose job is to take care of a building, its contents or sth valuable: *the keeper of geology at the museum* ➲ see also SHOPKEEPER **2** a person whose job is to take care of animals, especially in a ZOO ➲ see also GAMEKEEPER, ZOOKEEPER **3** (*BrE, informal*) = GOALKEEPER, WICKET-KEEPER **IDM** see FINDER

ˌkeep-ˈfit *noun* [U] (*BrE*) physical exercises that you do, usually in a class with other people, in order to improve your strength and to stay healthy: *a keep-fit class*

keep·ing /ˈkiːpɪŋ/ *noun*

IDM **in sb's ˈkeeping** being taken care of by sb ➲ see also SAFE KEEPING **in ˈkeeping (with sth)** appropriate or expected in a particular situation; in agreement with sth: *The latest results are in keeping with our earlier findings.* **out of ˈkeeping (with sth)** not appropriate or expected in a particular situation; not in agreement with sth: *The painting is out of keeping with the rest of the room.*

keep·sake /ˈkiːpseɪk/ *noun* a small object that sb gives you so that you will remember them **SYN** **memento**

kef·fi·yeh (also **kaf·fi·yeh**) /kəˈfiːjə/ *noun* a square of cloth worn on the head by Arab men and fastened by a band

keg /keg/ *noun* **1** [C] a round wooden or metal container with a flat top and bottom, used especially for storing beer, like a BARREL but smaller **2** [U] (*BrE*) = KEG BEER

ˈkeg beer (*BrE* also **keg**) *noun* [U, C] (in Britain) beer served from metal containers, using gas pressure

keis·ter /ˈkiːstə(r)/ *noun* (*NAmE, informal*) the part of the body that you sit on **SYN** **bottom**

Kejia /keɪˈdʒjɑː/ *noun* = HAKKA

kelim /kəˈliːm; ˈkelɪm; *NAmE* kiːˈliːm; ˈkeləm/ *noun* = KILIM

kelp /kelp/ *noun* [U] a type of brown SEAWEED, sometimes used as a FERTILIZER to help plants grow

kel·pie /ˈkelpi/ *noun* **1** (in Scottish stories) a water spirit **2** an Australian SHEEPDOG

kel·vin /ˈkelvɪn/ *noun* (*abbr.* K) (*pl.* **kelvin** or **kelvins**) a unit for measuring temperature. One kelvin is equal to one degree Celsius, but the **Kelvin scale** starts at ABSOLUTE ZERO and water freezes at 273.15 kelvin.

the ˌKelvin ˈscale *noun* [sing.] a scale of temperature in which water freezes at 273.15 degrees

ken /ken/ *noun, verb*

■ ***noun***

IDM **beyond your ken** (*old-fashioned*) if sth is **beyond your ken**, you do not know enough about it to be able to understand it

■ ***verb*** (-nn-) [I, T] **~ (sth) | ~ (that)... | ~ what, where, etc...** (*ScotE, NEngE*) to know **HELP** **Kent** is the usual form of the past tense used in Scotland.

kendo /ˈkendəʊ; *NAmE* -doʊ/ *noun* [U] (from *Japanese*) a Japanese form of the sport of FENCING, using light wooden weapons

ken·nel /ˈkenl/ *noun* **1** (*NAmE* **dog·house**) a small shelter for a dog to sleep in **2** (usually **kennels**) [C+sing./pl. v.] a place where people can leave their dogs to be taken care of when they go on holiday/vacation; a place where dogs are bred: *We put the dog* ***in kennels*** *when we go away.* ➲ see also BOARDING KENNEL

kept *past tense, past part.* of KEEP

ˌkept ˈwoman *noun* (*old-fashioned*, usually *humorous*) a woman who is given money and a home by a man who visits her regularly to have sex

kera·tin /ˈkerətɪn/ *noun* [U] (*biology*) a PROTEIN that forms hair, feathers, horns, HOOFS, etc.

kerb (*BrE*) (*NAmE* **curb**) /kɜːb; *NAmE* kɜːrb/ *noun* the edge of the raised path at the side of a road, usually made of long pieces of stone: *The bus mounted the kerb* (= went onto the PAVEMENT/SIDEWALK) *and hit a tree.* ➲ VISUAL VOCAB page V3

ˈkerb-crawling *noun* [U] (*BrE*) the crime of driving slowly along a road in order to find a PROSTITUTE ▸ **ˈkerb-crawler** *noun*

kerb·side (*BrE*) (*NAmE* **curb·side**) /ˈkɜːbsaɪd; *NAmE* ˈkɜːrb-/ *noun* [U] the side of the street or path near the kerb: *to stand at the kerbside*

kerb·stone (*BrE*) (*NAmE* **curb·stone**) /ˈkɜːbstəʊn; *NAmE* ˈkɜːrbstoʊn/ *noun* a block of stone or concrete in a kerb/curb

ker·chief /ˈkɜːtʃɪf; *NAmE* ˈkɜːrtʃɪf/ *noun* (*old-fashioned*) a square piece of cloth worn on the head or around the neck

ker-ching /kəˈtʃɪŋ/ *exclamation* (*BrE, informal*) = KA-CHING

ker·fuf·fle /kəˈfʌfl; *NAmE* kərˈf-/ *noun* [sing.] (*BrE, informal*) unnecessary excitement or activity SYN **commotion, fuss**

ker·nel /ˈkɜːnl; *NAmE* ˈkɜːrnl/ *noun* **1** the inner part of a nut or seed **2** the central, most important part of an idea or a subject

kero·sene (also **kero·sine**) /ˈkerəsiːn/ *noun* [U] a type of fuel oil that is made from PETROLEUM and that is used in the engines of planes and for heat and light. In British English it is usually called PARAFFIN when it is used for heat and light: *a kerosene lamp*

kes·trel /ˈkestrəl/ *noun* a small BIRD OF PREY (= a bird that kills other creatures for food) of the FALCON family

KET /ket/ *noun* [U] the abbreviation for 'Key English Test' (a British test, set by the University of Cambridge, that measures a person's ability to speak and write English as a foreign language at a basic level)

keta·mine /ˈkiːtəmiːn/ (also *informal* **ket** /kiːt/) *noun* [U] a substance that is used as an ANAESTHETIC, and also as a drug that is taken illegally for pleasure

ketch /ketʃ/ *noun* a sailing boat with two MASTS (= posts to support the sails)

ketchup /ˈketʃəp/ *noun* [U] a thick cold sauce made from tomatoes, usually sold in bottles

ket·tle /ˈketl/ *noun* a container with a lid, handle and a SPOUT, used for boiling water: *an electric kettle* ◇ (*BrE*) *I'll* ***put the kettle on*** (= start boiling some water) *and make some tea.* ➲ VISUAL VOCAB page V22 IDM see DIFFERENT, POT *n.*

kettle·drum /ˈketldrʌm/ *noun* a large metal drum with a round bottom and a thin plastic top that can be made looser or tighter to produce different musical notes. A set of kettledrums is usually called TIMPANI. ➲ VISUAL VOCAB page V30

Kev·lar™ /ˈkevlɑː(r)/ *noun* [U] an artificial substance used to give strength to tyres and other rubber products

key 🔑 /kiː/ *noun, verb, adj.*

■ ***noun***

▸ TOOL FOR LOCK **1** 🔑 a specially shaped piece of metal used for locking a door, starting a car, etc: *to* ***insert/turn the key*** *in the lock* ◇ *the car keys* ◇ *a bunch of keys* ◇ *the spare key to the front door* ◇ *We'll have a duplicate key cut* (= made).

▸ MOST IMPORTANT THING **2** 🔑 [usually sing.] a thing that makes you able to understand or achieve sth SYN **secret**: **~ (to sth)** *The key to success is preparation.* ◇ **~ (to doing sth)** *The driver of the car probably holds the key to solving the crime.* ◇ (*especially NAmE*) ***The key is,*** *how long can the federal government control the inflation rate?*

▸ ON COMPUTER **3** 🔑 any of the buttons that you press to operate a computer or TYPEWRITER: *Press the return key to enter the information.*

▸ ON MUSICAL INSTRUMENT **4** 🔑 any of the wooden or metal parts that you press to play a piano and some other musical instruments ➲ VISUAL VOCAB page V30

▸ MUSIC **5** a set of related notes, based on a particular note. Pieces of music are usually written mainly using a particular key: *a sonata in the key of E flat major* ➲ compare SCALE *n.* (7)

▸ ANSWERS **6** 🔑 a set of answers to exercises or problems: *Check your answers in the key at the back of the book.*

▸ ON MAP **7** an explanation of the symbols used on a map or plan ➲ see also LOW-KEY IDM see LOCK *n.*

■ ***verb*** **1** 🔑 **~ sth (in)** | **~ sth (into sth)** to put information into a computer using a keyboard SYN **enter**: *Key (in) your password.* **2** to deliberately damage a car by scratching it with a key

PHR V **ˈkey sb/sth to sth** [usually passive] (*especially NAmE*) to make sb/sth suitable or appropriate for a particular purpose SYN **gear**: *The classes are keyed to the needs of advanced students.*

■ ***adj.*** 🔑 [usually before noun] most important; essential SYN **critical, vital**: *the* ***key issue/factor/point*** ◇ *He was a* ***key figure*** *in the campaign.* ◇ *She played a* ***key role*** *in the dispute.* ◇ *'Caution' is the* ***key word*** *in this situation.* ◇ *Good communication is key to our success.* ◇ *His contribution could be key.* ➲ SYNONYMS at MAIN

keys

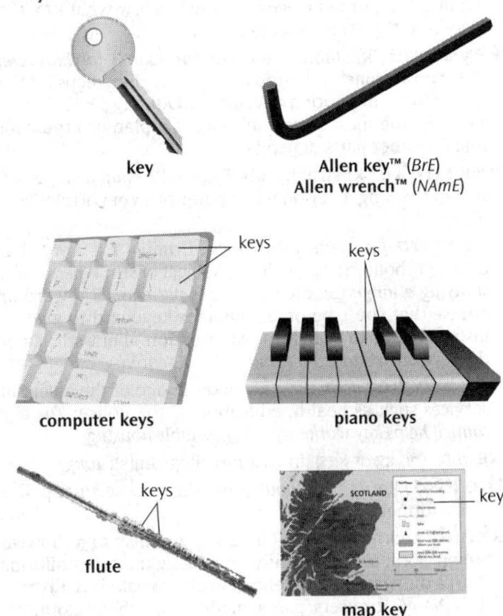

key·board 🔑 /ˈkiːbɔːd; *NAmE* -bɔːrd/ *noun, verb*

■ ***noun*** **1** 🔑 the set of keys for operating a computer or TYPEWRITER ➲ VISUAL VOCAB page V54 **2** 🔑 the set of black and white keys on a piano or other musical instrument ➲ VISUAL VOCAB page V31 **3** 🔑 an electronic musical instrument that has keys like a piano and can be made to play in different styles or to sound like different instruments ➲ compare SYNTHESIZER

■ *verb* [T, I] ~ (**sth**) to type information into a computer ▶ **key·board·ing** *noun* [U]

key·board·er /ˈkiːbɔːdə(r); *NAmE* -bɔːrd-/ *noun* a person whose job is to type data into a computer

key·board·ist /ˈkiːbɔːdɪst; *NAmE* -bɔːrd-/ *noun* a person who plays an electronic musical instrument with a keyboard

ˈkey card *noun* (*especially NAmE*) = SWIPE CARD

ˌkeyed ˈup *adj.* [not before noun] nervous and excited, especially before an important event

key·hole /ˈkiːhəʊl; *NAmE* -hoʊl/ *noun* the hole in a lock that you put a key in

ˌkeyhole ˈsurgery *noun* [U] (*especially BrE*) medical operations which involve only a very small cut being made in the patient's body

key·log·ger /ˈkiːlɒɡə(r); *NAmE* -lɔːɡ-; -lɑːɡ-/ *noun* (*computing*) a computer program that records all the keys that a user hits so that it is possible to discover secret information such as code words

key·note /ˈkiːnəʊt; *NAmE* -noʊt/ *noun* **1** [usually sing.] the central idea of a book, a speech, etc: *Choice is the keynote of the new education policy.* ◇ *a* ***keynote speech/speaker*** (= a very important one, introducing a meeting or its subject) **2** (*music*) the note on which the KEY is based ▶ **key·noter** *noun*: *For the first time, a woman will be the keynoter at the convention this year.*

K

key·pad /ˈkiːpæd/ *noun* a small set of buttons with numbers on used to operate a telephone, television, etc; the buttons on the right of a computer keyboard

key·pal /ˈkiːpæl/ *noun* (*informal*) a person that you regularly send emails to, often sb you have never met

ˈkey ring *noun* a small ring that you put keys on to keep them together ➲ picture at RING

ˈkey signature *noun* (*music*) the set of marks at the beginning of a printed piece of music to show what KEY the piece is in ➲ picture at MUSIC

key·stone /ˈkiːstəʊn; *NAmE* -stoʊn/ *noun* **1** (*architecture*) the central stone at the top of an ARCH that keeps all the other stones in position ➲ VISUAL VOCAB page V12 **2** [usually sing.] the most important part of a plan or argument that the other parts depend on

key·stroke /ˈkiːstrəʊk; *NAmE* -stroʊk/ *noun* a single action of pressing a key on a computer or TYPEWRITER keyboard

key·word /ˈkiːwɜːd; *NAmE* -wɜːrd/ *noun* **1** a word that tells you about the main idea or subject of sth: *When you're studying a language, the keyword is patience.* **2** a word or phrase that you type on a computer keyboard to give an instruction or to search for information about sth: *Enter the keyword 'restaurants' and click on Search.*

ˌkey ˈworker *noun* (*BrE*) a worker in one of the essential services such as health, education or the police: *The city council helps key workers find affordable housing.*

kg *abbr.* (*pl.* **kg** or **kgs**) (in writing) kilogram(s): *10kg*

the KGB /ˌkeɪ dʒiː ˈbiː/ *noun* [sing.] the state security police of the former USSR

khaki /ˈkɑːki/ *noun* **1** [U] a strong greenish or yellowish brown cloth, used especially for making military uniforms **2** [U] a dull greenish or yellowish brown colour **3 khakis** [pl.] (*NAmE*) trousers/pants made from khaki cloth: *He wore a pair of baggy khakis.* ▶ **khaki** *adj.*: *khaki uniforms*

khan /kɑːn/ *noun* a title given to rulers in some Muslim countries

khan·ate /ˈkɑːneɪt/ *noun* **1** the area which is ruled by a khan **2** the position of a khan

khanga (also **kanga**) /ˈkæŋɡə/ (also **lesso**) *noun* (*EAfrE*) a large piece of light cloth with designs printed on it and worn by women around the waist and legs or over the head and shoulders

khazi /ˈkɑːzi/ (also **kharzy** /ˈkɑːzi; *NAmE* ˈkɑːrzi/) *noun* (*pl.* **-ies**) (*old-fashioned, BrE, slang*) a toilet

kHz *abbr.* (in writing) KILOHERTZ

kia ora /ˌkiə ˈɔːrə/ *exclamation* (*NZE*) a GREETING wishing good health

KiB *abbr.* (in writing) KIBIBYTE

Kib (also **Kibit**) *abbr.* (in writing) KIBIBIT

kib·bled /ˈkɪbld/ *adj.* [usually before noun] (of grain) crushed into rough pieces

kib·butz /kɪˈbʊts/ *noun* (*pl.* **kib·butz·im** /ˌkɪbʊtˈsiːm/) (in Israel) a type of farm or factory where a group of people live together and share all the work, decisions and income

kibi·bit /ˈkɪbibɪt/ *noun* (*abbr.* **Kib, Kibit**) (*computing*) = KILOBIT (2)

kibi·byte /ˈkɪbibaɪt/ *noun* (*abbr.* **KiB**) (*computing*) = KILOBYTE (2)

kib·itz /ˈkɪbɪts/ *verb* (*NAmE, informal*) **1** [I, T] (usually *disapproving*) to watch other people doing sth and make comments or give advice about it, often in an annoying way: *It is rude to kibitz during a serious game.* ◇ ~ **sth** *I paused to kibitz a poker game.* **2** [I] to talk in a friendly informal way: *We sat around and kibitzed until about eleven.* ▶ **kib·itz·er** *noun*: *The kibitzers were second-guessing each move.*

kibla = QIBLAH

ki·bosh /ˈkaɪbɒʃ; *NAmE* -bɑːʃ/ *noun* [sing.]

IDM **put the ˈkibosh on sth** (*informal*) to stop sth from happening; to spoil sb's plans

kick 0‑ /kɪk/ *verb, noun*

■ *verb* **1** 0‑ [T, I] to hit sb/sth with your foot: ~ (**sb/sth**) *She was punched and kicked by her attackers.* ◇ *Stop kicking—it hurts!* ◇ ~ **sb/sth + adv./prep./adj.** *The boys were kicking a ball around in the yard.* ◇ *Vandals had kicked the door down.* **2** 0‑ [T, I] ~ (**sth**) to move your legs as if you were kicking sth: *The dancers kicked their legs in the air.* ◇ *The child was dragged away,* ***kicking and screaming***. **3** [T] ~ **yourself** (*informal*) to be annoyed with yourself because you have done sth stupid, missed an opportunity, etc: *He'll kick himself when he finds out he could have had the job.* **4** [T] ~ **sth** (in sports such as football (SOCCER) and RUGBY) to score points by kicking the ball: *to* ***kick a penalty/goal***

IDM **kick (some/sb's) ˈass** (*slang, especially NAmE*) to punish or defeat sb **kick the ˈbucket** (*informal* or *humorous*) to die **kick the ˈhabit, ˈdrug, ˈbooze, etc.** to stop doing sth harmful that you have done for a long time **kick your ˈheels** (*BrE*) to have nothing to do while you are waiting for sb/sth: *We were kicking our heels, waiting for some customers.* **kick sb in the ˈteeth** to treat sb badly or fail to give them help when they need it **kick sth into the long ˈgrass/into ˈtouch** (*BrE*) to reject, remove or stop dealing with a problem: *He tends to deal with disputes by kicking them into the long grass.* **kick over the ˈtraces** (*old-fashioned, BrE*) to start to behave badly and refuse to accept any discipline or control **kick up a ˈfuss, ˈstink, etc.** (*informal*) to complain loudly about sth **kick up your ˈheels** (*informal, especially NAmE*) to be relaxed and enjoy yourself **kick sb upˈstairs** (*informal*) to move sb to a job that seems to be more important but which actually has less power or influence **kick sb when they're ˈdown** to continue to hurt sb when they are already defeated, etc. ➲ more at ALIVE, HELL

PHR V **ˌkick aˈbout/aˈround** (*informal*) **1** (usually used in the progressive tenses) to be lying somewhere not being used: *There's a pen kicking around on my desk somewhere.* **2** to go from one place to another with no particular purpose: *They spent the summer kicking around Europe.* **ˌkick sb aˈround** (*informal*) to treat sb in a rough or unfair way **ˌkick sth aˈbout/aˈround** (*informal*) to discuss an idea, a plan, etc. in an informal way **ˈkick against sth** to protest about or resist sth: *Young people often kick against the rules.* **ˌkick ˈback** (*especially NAmE*) to relax: *Kick back and enjoy the summer.* **ˌkick ˈin** (*informal*) **1** to begin to take effect: *Reforms will kick in later this year.* **2** (also **ˌkick ˈin sth**) (both *NAmE*) to give your share of money or help **ˌkick ˈoff 1** when a football (SOCCER) game or a team, etc. **kicks off**, the game starts ➲ related noun KICK-OFF ➲ SYNONYMS at START **2** to suddenly become angry or violent

ˌkick ˈoff (with sth) (*informal*) to start: *What time shall we kick off?* ◇ *Tom will kick off with a few comments.* ➲ related noun KICK-OFF ˌkick sth↔ˈoff to remove sth by kicking: *to kick off your shoes* ˌkick ˈoff sth to start a discussion, a meeting, an event, etc. **SYN** open ˌkick ˈout (at sb/sth) **1** to try to hit sb/sth with your legs because you are angry or upset **2** to react violently to sb/sth that makes you angry or upset ˌkick sb ˈout (of sth) (*informal*) to make sb leave or go away (from somewhere) ˌkick ˈup (*especially NAmE*) (of wind or a storm) to become stronger ˌkick sth↔ˈup to make sth, especially dust, rise from the ground

■ ***noun*** **1** a movement with the foot or the leg, usually to hit sth with the foot: *the first kick of the game* ◇ *She gave him a kick on the shin.* ◇ *He aimed a kick at the dog.* ◇ *If the door won't open, give it a kick.* ◇ (*slang*) *She needs a **kick up the backside*** (= she needs to be strongly encouraged to do sth or to behave better). ➲ see also FREE KICK, PENALTY KICK, SPOT KICK **2** (*informal*) a strong feeling of excitement and pleasure **SYN** thrill: *I **get a kick out of** driving fast cars.* ◇ *He **gets his kicks from** hurting other people.* ◇ *What do you do **for kicks**?* **3** [usually sing.] (*informal*) the strong effect that a drug or an alcoholic drink has: *This drink has quite a kick.*

IDM **a kick in the ˈteeth** (*informal*) a great disappointment; sth that hurts sb/sth emotionally

ˈkick-ass (also **ˈass-kicking**) *adj.* (*slang, especially NAmE*) **1** powerful and aggressive: *the film's kick-ass heroine* ◇ *his reputation as a kick-ass coach* **2** extremely good and successful: *a kick-ass visual feast* ◇ *truly kick-ass quality*

kick·back /ˈkɪkbæk/ *noun* (*informal, especially NAmE*) money paid illegally to sb in return for work or help **SYN** bribe

kick·ball /ˈkɪkbɔːl/ *noun* [U] a game that is based on BASEBALL in which players kick the ball instead of hitting it with a BAT

ˈkick-boxing *noun* [U] a form of BOXING in which the people fighting each other can kick as well as punch (= hit with their hands)

ˈkick drum *noun* (*informal*) a large drum played using a PEDAL

kick·er /ˈkɪkə(r)/ *noun* **1** a person who kicks, especially the player in a sports team who kicks the ball to try to score points, for example in RUGBY **2** (*NAmE, informal*) a surprising end to a series of events

kick·ing /ˈkɪkɪŋ/ *adj., noun*

■ ***adj.*** (*informal*) full of life and excitement: *The club was really kicking last night.*

■ ***noun*** [sing.] an act of kicking sb hard and repeatedly, especially when they are lying on the ground: *They gave him a good kicking.*

ˈkick-off *noun* **1** [C, U] the start of a game of football (SOCCER): *The kick-off is at 3.* **2** [sing.] (*informal*) the start of an activity

kick·stand /ˈkɪkstænd/ *noun* a long straight piece of metal fixed to a bicycle or a motorcycle, which is kept horizontal while the bicycle is being ridden but which can be moved to a vertical position when you need to stand the bicycle somewhere ➲ VISUAL VOCAB page V41

ˈkick-start *verb, noun*

■ ***verb*** **1** ~ sth to start a motorcycle by pushing down a LEVER with your foot **2** ~ sth to do sth to help a process or project start more quickly: *The government's attempt to kick-start the economy has failed.*

■ ***noun*** **1** (also **ˈkick-starter**) the part of a motorcycle that you push down with your foot in order to start it **2** a quick start that you give to sth by taking some action

ˈkick-turn *noun* **1** (in SKIING) a turn made by lifting and turning each SKI separately so that you face the opposite direction **2** a turn made with the front wheels of a SKATEBOARD off the ground

kid /kɪd/ *noun, verb, adj.*

■ ***noun*** **1** [C] (*informal*) a child or young person: *A bunch of kids were hanging around outside.* ◇ *a kid of 15* ◇ *She's a bright kid.* ◇ *How are the kids* (= your children)? ◇ *Do you have any kids?* **HELP** **Kid** is much more common than **child** in informal and spoken *NAmE*. ➲ COLLOCATIONS at CHILD **2** [C] a young GOAT **3** [U] soft leather made from the skin of a young GOAT

IDM **handle/treat, etc. sb with kid ˈgloves** to deal with sb in a very careful way so that you do not offend or upset them **ˈkids' stuff** (*BrE*) (*NAmE* **ˈkid stuff**) something that is so easy to do or understand that it is thought to be not very serious or only suitable for children ➲ more at NEW

■ ***verb*** (-dd-) (*informal*) **1** [I, T] (usually used in the progressive tenses) to tell sb sth that is not true, especially as a joke **SYN** joke: *I thought he was kidding when he said he was going out with a rock star.* ◇ *I didn't mean it. I was **only kidding**.* ◇ ~ sb *I'm not kidding you. It does work.* **2** [T] to allow sb/yourself to believe sth that is not true **SYN** deceive: ~ sb/yourself *They're kidding themselves if they think it's going to be easy.* ◇ ~ sb/yourself (that)... *I tried to kid myself (that) everything was normal.*

IDM **ˌno ˈkidding** (*informal*) **1** used to emphasize that sth is true or that you agree with sth that sb has just said: *'It's cold!' 'No kidding!'* **2** used to show that you mean what you are saying: *I want the money back tomorrow. No kidding.* **you're ˈkidding | you must be ˈkidding** (*informal*) used to show that you are very surprised at sth that sb has just said

PHR V **ˌkid aˈround** (*especially NAmE*) to behave in a silly way

■ ***adj.*** ~ **sister/brother** (*informal, especially NAmE*) a person's younger sister/brother

kid·die (also **kiddy**) /ˈkɪdi/ (*pl.* -ies) *noun* (*informal*) a young child: *a kiddies' party*

kid·nap /ˈkɪdnæp/ *verb* (-pp-, *US* also -p-) ~ sb to take sb away illegally and keep them as a prisoner, especially in order to get money or sth else for returning them **SYN** abduct, seize: *Two businessmen have been kidnapped by terrorists.* ▸ **kid·napper** *noun*: *The kidnappers are demanding a ransom of $1 million.* **kid·nap·ping** (also **kidnap**) *noun* [U, C]: *He admitted the charge of kidnap.* ◇ *the kidnapping of 12 US citizens*

kid·ney /ˈkɪdni/ *noun* **1** [C] either of the two organs in the body that remove waste products from the blood and produce URINE: *a kidney infection* ➲ VISUAL VOCAB page V48 **2** [U, C] the kidneys of some animals that are cooked and eaten: *steak and kidney pie*

ˈkidney bean *noun* a type of reddish-brown BEAN shaped like a kidney that is usually dried before it is sold and then left in water before cooking ➲ VISUAL VOCAB page V27

ˈkidney machine *noun* a machine that does the work of a KIDNEY for sb whose kidneys are damaged or have been removed

kid·ol·ogy /kɪˈdɒlədʒi; *NAmE* -ˈdɑːl-/ *noun* [U] (*especially BrE, humorous*) the art or practice of making people believe sth which is not true

kid·ult /ˈkɪdʌlt/ *noun* (*informal*) an adult who likes doing or buying things that are usually thought more suitable for children

kike /kaɪk/ *noun* (*taboo, slang, especially NAmE*) a very offensive word for a Jew

kikoi /kɪˈkɔɪ/ *noun* (*EAfrE*) a large piece of strong coloured cloth used mainly as an item of clothing around the waist and legs or over the shoulders

kilim /kɪˈliːm; ˈkiːlɪm; *NAmE* kiːˈliːm; ˈkɪləm/ (also **kelim**) *noun* a type of Turkish carpet or RUG

kill /kɪl/ *verb, noun*

■ ***verb*** **1** [T, I] ~ (sb/sth/yourself) to make sb/sth die: *Cancer kills thousands of people every year.* ◇ *Three people were killed in the crash.* ◇ *He tried to kill himself with sleeping pills.* ◇ *I bought a spray to kill the weeds.* ◇ (*informal*) *My mother will kill me* (= be very angry with me) *when she finds out.* ◇ *Don't kill yourself trying to get the work done by tomorrow. It can wait.* ◇ *Tiredness while driving can kill.* **2** [T] ~ sth to destroy or spoil sth or make it stop: *to kill a rumour* ◇ *Do you agree that television kills conversation?* ◇

K

The defeat last night killed the team's chances of qualifying. **3** [T] **~ sb | it kills sb to do sth** (*informal*) (usually used in the progressive tenses and not used in the passive) to cause sb pain or suffering: *My feet are killing me.* **4** [T] **~ sb** (*NAmE*) to make sb laugh a lot: *Stop it! You're killing me!*

IDM **kill the goose that lays the golden 'egg/'eggs** (*saying*) to destroy sth that would make you rich, successful, etc. **,kill or 'cure** (*BrE*) used to say that what you are going to do will either be very successful or fail completely **kill 'time | kill an 'hour, a couple of 'hours, etc.** to spend time doing sth that is not important while you are waiting for sth else to happen: *We killed time playing cards.* **kill two birds with one 'stone** to achieve two things at the same time with one action **,kill sb/sth with 'kindness** to be so kind to sb/sth that you in fact harm them **,kill yourself 'laughing** (*BrE*) to laugh a lot: *He was killing himself laughing.* ➲ more at CURIOSITY, DRESSED, LOOK *n.*, TIME *n.*

PHR V **,kill sb/sth↔'off 1** to make a lot of plants, animals, etc. die: *Some drugs kill off useful bacteria in the user's body.* **2** to stop or get rid of sth: *He has effectively killed off any political opposition.*

■ ***noun*** [usually sing.] **1** an act of killing, especially when an animal is hunted or killed: *A cat often plays with a mouse before the kill.* ◇ *The plane prepared to* ***move in for the kill.*** ◇ *I was* ***in at the kill*** *when she finally lost her job* (= present at the end of an unpleasant process). **2** an animal that has been hunted and killed: *lions feeding on their kill*

kill·er /ˈkɪlə(r)/ *noun* **1** a person, an animal or a thing that kills: *Police are hunting his killer.* ◇ *Heart disease is the biggest killer in Scotland.* ◇ *an electric insect killer* ◇ *The players lacked* ***the killer instinct.*** ➲ see also LADYKILLER, SERIAL KILLER **2** (*informal*) something that is very difficult, very exciting or very skilful: *The exam was a real killer.* ◇ *The new movie is a killer.*

,killer appli'cation (also **,killer 'app**) *noun* (*computing*) a computer program that is so popular that it encourages people to buy or use the OPERATING SYSTEM, etc. that it runs on

,killer 'bee *noun* a type of BEE that is very aggressive

'killer cell *noun* (*biology*) a white blood cell which destroys infected cells or cancer cells

'killer whale (also **orca**) *noun* a black and white WHALE that eats meat

kill·ing /ˈkɪlɪŋ/ *noun, adj.*

■ ***noun*** an act of killing sb deliberately SYN **murder**: *brutal killings* ➲ COLLOCATIONS at CRIME ➲ see also MERCY KILLING

IDM **,make a 'killing** (*informal*) to make a lot of money quickly

■ ***adj.*** making you very tired SYN **exhausting**: *a killing schedule*

'killing fields *noun* [pl.] a place where very many people were killed, for example during a war

kill·joy /ˈkɪldʒɔɪ/ *noun* (*disapproving*) a person who likes to spoil other people's enjoyment

kiln /kɪln/ *noun* a large oven for baking CLAY and bricks, drying wood and grain, etc.

kilo /ˈkiːləʊ; *NAmE* ˈkiːloʊ/ *noun* (*pl.* **-os**) = KILOGRAM

kilo- /ˈkɪləʊ; *NAmE* ˈkɪloʊ/ *combining form* (in nouns; used in units of measurement) **1** one thousand: *kilojoule* **2** 2^{10}, or 1024

kilo·bit /ˈkɪləbɪt/ *noun* (*abbr.* **Kb, Kbit**) (*computing*) **1** a unit for measuring computer memory or data, equal to 10^3, or 1000 BITS ➲ see also KBPS **2** (also **kibi·bit**) a unit for measuring computer memory or data, equal to 2^{10}, or 1024 BITS

kilo·byte /ˈkɪləbaɪt/ *noun* (*abbr.* **K, KB**) (*computing*) **1** a unit for measuring computer memory or data, equal to 10^3, or 1000 BYTES **2** (also **kibi·byte**) a unit for measuring computer memory or data, equal to 2^{10}, or 1024 BYTES

kilo·gram (*BrE* also **kilo·gramme**) /ˈkɪləɡræm/ (also **kilo**) *noun* (*abbr.* **kg**) a unit for measuring weight; 1000 grams: *2 kilograms of rice* ◇ *Flour is sold by the kilogram.*

kilo·hertz /ˈkɪləhɜːts; *NAmE* -hɜːrts/ *noun* (*abbr.* **kHz**) (*pl.* **kilo·hertz**) a unit for measuring radio waves

kilo·joule /ˈkɪlədʒuːl/ *noun* (*abbr.* **kJ**) a measurement of the energy that you get from food; 1000 JOULES

kilo·metre (*especially US* **kilo·meter**) /ˈkɪləmiːtə(r); *BrE* also kɪˈlɒmɪtə(r); *NAmE* also kɪˈlɑːm-/ *noun* (*abbr.* **k, km**) a unit for measuring distance; 1000 metres

kilo·watt /ˈkɪləwɒt; *NAmE* -wɑːt/ *noun* (*abbr.* **kW**) a unit for measuring electrical power; 1000 WATTS

,kilowatt-'hour *noun* (*abbr.* **kWh**) a unit for measuring electrical energy equal to the power provided by one kilowatt in one hour

kilt /kɪlt/ *noun* a skirt made of TARTAN cloth that reaches to the knees and is traditionally worn by Scottish men; a similar skirt worn by women

kilt·ed /ˈkɪltɪd/ *adj.* wearing a kilt

kil·ter /ˈkɪltə(r)/ *noun* [U]

IDM **out of 'kilter 1** not agreeing with or the same as sth else: *His views are out of kilter with world opinion.* **2** no longer continuing or working in the normal way: *Long flights throw my sleeping pattern out of kilter for days.*

ki·mono /kɪˈməʊnəʊ; *NAmE* kɪˈmoʊnoʊ/ *noun* (*pl.* **-os**) (from *Japanese*) a traditional Japanese piece of clothing like a long loose dress with wide sleeves, worn on formal occasions; a DRESSING GOWN or ROBE in this style

kin /kɪn/ *noun* [pl.] (*old-fashioned* or *formal*) your family or your relatives ➲ compare KINDRED ➲ see also NEXT OF KIN IDM see KITH

Grammar Point

kind / sort

- Use the singular (**kind/sort**) or plural (**kinds/sorts**) depending on the word you use before them: *each/one/every kind of animal* ◇ *all/many/other sorts of animals.*
- **Kind/sort of** is followed by a singular or uncountable noun: ***This kind of question*** *often appears in the exam.* ◇ ***That sort of behaviour*** *is not acceptable.*
- **Kinds/sorts of** is followed by a plural or uncountable noun: ***These kinds of questions*** *often appear in the exam.* ◇ ***These sorts of behaviour*** *are not acceptable.*
- Other variations are possible but less common: ***These kinds of question*** *often appear in the exam.* ◇ ***These sort of things*** *don't happen in real life.* (This example is very informal and is considered incorrect by some people.)
- Note also that these examples are possible, especially in spoken English: *The shelf was full of* ***the sort of books*** *I like to read.* ◇ *He faced* ***the same kind of problems*** *as his predecessor.* ◇ *There are many* ***different sorts of animal*** *on the island.* ◇ ***What kind of camera*** *is this?* ◇ ***What kind/kinds of cameras*** *do you sell?* ◇ *There were* ***three kinds of cakes/cake*** *on the plate.*

kind /kaɪnd/ *noun, adj.*

■ ***noun*** [C, U] a group of people or things that are the same in some way; a particular variety or type: *three kinds of cakes/cake* ◇ *music of* ***all/various/different kinds*** ◇ *Exercises of this kind are very popular.* ◇ *What kind of house do you live in?* ◇ *They sell all* ***kinds of things.*** ◇ *The school is the first* ***of its kind*** *in Britain.* ◇ *She isn't* ***that kind of*** *girl.* ◇ *The regions differ in size, but not* ***in kind.*** ◇ *I need to buy paper and pencils, that* ***kind of thing.*** ◇ *I'll never have* ***that kind of*** *money* (= as much money as that). ◇ (*formal*) *Would you like a drink* ***of some kind?***

IDM **in 'kind 1** (of a payment) consisting of goods or services, not money **2** (*formal*) with the same thing: *She insulted him and he responded in kind.* **a 'kind of** (*informal*) used to show that sth you are saying is not exact: *I had a kind of feeling this might happen.* **'kind of** (*informal*) (also **'kinda** /'kaɪndə/) slightly; in some ways: *That made me feel kind of stupid.* ◇ *I like him, kind of.* **nothing of the 'kind/'sort** used to emphasize that the situation is very different from what has been said: *'I was terrible!' 'You were nothing of the kind.'* **of a 'kind 1** (*disapproving*) not as good as it could be: *You're making progress of a kind.* **2** very similar: *They're two of a kind—both workaholics!* **one of a 'kind** the only one like this SYN **unique**: *My father was one of a kind—I'll never be like him.* **something of the/that 'kind** something like what has been said: *'He's resigning.' 'I'd suspected something of the kind.'*

■ ***adj.*** (**kind·er**, **kind·est**) **1** caring about others; gentle, friendly and generous: *a very kind and helpful person* ◇ *a kind heart/face* ◇ *a kind action/gesture/comment* ◇ *You've been very kind.* ◇ ~ (**to sb/sth**) *kind to animals* ◇ (*figurative*) *Soft water is kinder to your hair.* ◇ (*figurative*) *The weather was very kind to us.* ◇ ~ (**of sb**) (**to do sth**) *It was really kind of you to help me.* ◇ (*formal*) *Thank you for your kind invitation.* ◇ (*formal*) *'Do have another.' 'That's very kind of you* (= thank you).*'* OPP **unkind 2** (*formal*) used to make a polite request or give an order: *Would you be kind enough to close the window?* ➲ see also KINDLY, KINDNESS

kin·der /'kɪndə(r)/ *noun* (*AustralE, informal*) = KINDERGARTEN

kin·der·gar·ten /'kɪndəgɑːtn; *NAmE* -dərgɑːrtn/ *noun* (from *German*) **1** (*especially NAmE*) a school or class to prepare children aged five for school **2** (*BrE, AustralE, NZE*) = NURSERY SCHOOL

ˌkind-'hearted *adj.* kind and generous

kin·dle /'kɪndl/ *verb* **1** [I, T] to start burning; to make a fire start burning: *We watched as the fire slowly kindled.* ◇ ~ **sth** *to kindle a fire/flame* **2** [T, I] ~ (**sth**) to make sth such as an interest, emotion, etc. start to grow in sb; to start to be felt by sb: *It was her teacher who kindled her interest in music.* ◇ *Suspicion kindled within her.*

kind·ling /'kɪndlɪŋ/ *noun* [U] small dry pieces of wood, etc. used to start a fire

kind·ly /'kaɪndli/ *adv., adj.*

■ ***adv.* 1** in a kind way: *She spoke kindly to them.* ◇ *He has kindly agreed to help.* **2** (*old-fashioned, formal*) used to ask or tell sb to do sth, especially when you are annoyed: *Kindly leave me alone!* ◇ *Visitors are kindly requested to sign the book.*

IDM **look 'kindly on/upon sth/sb** (*formal*) to approve of sth/sb: *He hoped they would look kindly on his request.* **not take 'kindly to sth/sb** to not like sth/sb: *She doesn't take kindly to sudden change.*

■ ***adj.*** [only before noun] (*old-fashioned* or *literary*) kind and caring ▸ **kind·li·ness** *noun* [U]

kind·ness /'kaɪndnəs/ *noun*

1 [U] the quality of being kind: *to treat sb with kindness and consideration* **2** [C] a kind act: *I can never repay your many kindnesses to me.* IDM see KILL *v.*, MILK *n.*

kin·dred /'kɪndrəd/ *noun, adj.*

■ ***noun*** (*old-fashioned* or *formal*) **1** [pl.] your family and relatives ➲ compare KIN **2** [U] the fact of being related to another person: *ties of kindred*

■ ***adj.*** [only before noun] (*formal*) very similar; related: *food and kindred products* ◇ *I knew I'd found **a kindred spirit*** (= a person with similar ideas, opinions, etc.).

kindy /'kɪndi/ *noun* (*pl.* **-ies**) (*AustralE, NZE, informal*) = KINDERGARTEN

kin·esis /kɪ'niːsɪs; kaɪ-/ *noun* [U] (*technical*) movement

kin·et·ic /kɪ'netɪk; *BrE* also kaɪ-/ *adj.* [usually before noun] (*technical*) of or produced by movement: *kinetic energy*

kiˌnetic 'art *noun* [U] (*art*) art, especially SCULPTURE, with parts that move

king /kɪŋ/ *noun*

1 the male ruler of an independent state that has a royal family: *the kings and queens of England* ◇ *to **be crowned king*** ◇ *King George V* **2** ~ (**of sth**) a person, an animal or a thing that is thought to be the best or most important of a particular type: *the king of comedy* ◇ *The lion is the king of the jungle.* **3** used in compounds with the names of animals or plants to describe a very large type of the thing mentioned: *a king penguin* **4** the most important piece used in the game of CHESS, that can move one square in any direction ➲ VISUAL VOCAB page V33 **5** a PLAYING CARD with the picture of a king on it ➲ VISUAL VOCAB page V32

IDM **a ˌking's 'ransom** (*literary*) a very large amount of money SYN **fortune** IDM see ENGLISH, EVIDENCE, UNCROWNED

king·dom /'kɪŋdəm/ *noun* **1** a country ruled by a king or queen: *the United Kingdom* ◇ *the kingdom of God* (= heaven) **2** an area controlled by a particular person or where a particular thing or idea is important **3** one of the three traditional divisions of the natural world: *the animal, vegetable and mineral kingdoms* **4** (*biology*) one of the five major groups into which all living things are organized

IDM **blow sb/sth to kingdom 'come** (*informal*) to completely destroy sb/sth with an explosion **till/until kingdom 'come** (*old-fashioned*) for ever

king·fish /'kɪŋfɪʃ/ *noun* a long FRESHWATER fish with two parts that function as lungs and make it able to breathe air

king·fish·er /'kɪŋfɪʃə(r)/ *noun* a bird with a long beak, that catches fish in rivers. The European kingfisher is small and brightly coloured and the American kingfisher is larger and blue-grey in colour.

K

'king-hit *noun* (*AustralE, NZE, informal*) a hard KNOCKOUT blow ▸ **'king-hit** *verb* (-tt-) ~ **sb**

king·ly /'kɪŋli/ *adj.* (*literary*) like a king; connected with or good enough for a king SYN **regal**

king·maker /'kɪŋmeɪkə(r)/ *noun* a person who has a very strong political influence and is able to bring sb else to power as a leader

king·pin /'kɪŋpɪn/ *noun* the most important person in an organization or activity

ˌKing's 'Bench *noun* the word for QUEEN'S BENCH when the UK has a king

ˌKing's 'Counsel *noun* = KC

ˌKing's 'English *noun* [U] the word for QUEEN'S ENGLISH when the UK has a king

ˌKing's 'evidence *noun* [U] the word for QUEEN'S EVIDENCE when the UK has a king

king·ship /'kɪŋʃɪp/ *noun* [U] the state of being a king; the official position of a king

'king-size (also **'king-sized**) *adj.* [usually before noun] very large; larger than normal when compared with a range of sizes: *a king-size bed* ◇ *a king-sized headache*

the ˌKing's 'speech *noun* the word for THE QUEEN'S SPEECH when the UK has a king

kink /kɪŋk/ *noun, verb*

■ ***noun* 1** a bend or twist in sth that is usually straight: *a dog with a kink in its tail* ◇ (*figurative*) *We need to iron out the kinks in the new system.* **2** (*informal, disapproving*) an unusual feature in a person's character or mind, especially one that does not seem normal **3** (*NAmE*) = CRICK

■ ***verb*** [I, T] ~ (**sth**) to develop or make sth develop a bend or twist

kinky /'kɪŋki/ *adj.* (*informal*, usually *disapproving*) used to describe sexual behaviour that most people would consider strange or unusual

kins·folk /'kɪnzfəʊk; *NAmE* -foʊk/ *noun* [pl.] (*formal* or *old-fashioned*) a person's relatives

kin·ship /'kɪnʃɪp/ *noun* (*formal*) **1** [U] the fact of being related in a family: *the ties of kinship* **2** [U, sing.] a feeling of being close to sb because you have similar origins or attitudes SYN **affinity**

kins·man /'kɪnzmən/, **kins·woman** /'kɪnzwʊmən/ *nouns* (*pl.* **-men** /-mən/, **-women** /-wɪmɪn/) (*old-fashioned* or *literary*) a relative

kiondo /ˈkjɒndɒ; *NAmE* ˈkjɑːndɑː/ *noun* (*pl.* -os) (*EAfrE*) a bag with one or two long handles and made from SISAL (= dried grass twisted together) or other materials

kiosk /ˈkiːɒsk; *NAmE* -ɑːsk/ *noun* **1** a small shop/store, open at the front, where newspapers, drinks, etc. are sold. In some countries kiosks also sell food and things used in the home. SYN **stand 2** (*old-fashioned, BrE*) a public telephone box SYN **booth**

kip /kɪp/ *noun, verb*
- ***noun*** [U, C, usually sing.] (*BrE, informal*) sleep: *I must get some kip.* ◇ *Why don't you have a quick kip?*
- ***verb*** (-pp-) [I] (*BrE, informal*) to sleep: *You can kip on the sofa, if you like.*

kip·pa (also **kipa, kipah, kip·pah**) /kɪˈpɑː/ *noun* = YARMULKE

kip·per /ˈkɪpə(r)/ *noun* a HERRING (= a type of fish) that has been preserved using salt, then smoked

ˌkipper ˈtie *noun* (*BrE*) a brightly coloured tie that is very wide

Kir™ /kɪə(r); kɪr/ *noun* [U, C] an alcoholic drink made by mixing white wine with CASSIS

kirby grip /ˈkɜːbi ɡrɪp; *NAmE* ˈkɜːrbi/ *noun* (*BrE*) = HAIRGRIP

kirk /kɜːk; *NAmE* kɜːrk/ *noun* **1** [C] (*ScotE*) church: *the parish kirk* **2 the Kirk** [sing.] a name often used for the official Church of Scotland

K

kir·pan /kɪəˈpɑːn; *NAmE* kɪr-/ *noun* a pointed knife that is worn by SIKH men as a sign of their religion

kirsch /kɪəʃ; *NAmE* kɪrʃ/ *noun* [U] a strong alcoholic drink made from CHERRIES

kis·met /ˈkɪzmet/ *noun* [U] (*literary*) the idea that everything that happens to you in your life is already decided and that you cannot do anything to change or control it SYN **destiny, fate**

kiss 0‑π /kɪs/ *verb, noun*
- ***verb* 1** 0‑π [I, T] to touch sb with your lips as a sign of love, affection, sexual desire, etc, or when saying hello or goodbye: *They stood in a doorway kissing* (= kissing each other). ◇ *Do people in Britain kiss when they meet?* ◇ **~ sb** *Go and kiss your mother goodnight.* ◇ *She kissed him on both cheeks.* ◇ *He lifted the trophy up and kissed it.* ➲ see also AIR KISS **2** [T] **~ sth** (*literary*) to gently move or touch sth: *The sunlight kissed the warm stones.*

IDM **ˌkiss and ˈtell** a way of referring to sb talking publicly, usually for money, about a past sexual relationship with sb famous **kiss sb's ˈarse** (*BrE*) (*NAmE* **kiss sb's ˈass, kiss ˈass**) (*taboo, slang*) to be very nice to sb in order to persuade them to help you or to give you sth HELP A more polite way to express this is **lick sb's boots**. **ˌkiss sth ˈbetter** (*informal*) to take away the pain of an injury by kissing it: *Come here and let me kiss it better.* **kiss sth goodˈbye | kiss goodˈbye to sth** (*informal*) to accept that you will lose sth or be unable to do sth: *Well, you can kiss goodbye to your chances of promotion.*

PHR V **ˌkiss sth↔aˈway** to stop sb feeling sad or angry by kissing them: *He kissed away her tears.*
- ***noun*** 0‑π the act of kissing sb/sth: *Come here and* **give me a kiss!** ◇ *a kiss on the cheek* ◇ *We were greeted with* **hugs and kisses.**

IDM **the kiss of ˈdeath** (*informal*, especially *humorous*) an event that seems good, but is certain to make sth else fail **the kiss of ˈlife** (*BrE*) a method of helping sb who has stopped breathing to breathe again by placing your mouth on theirs and forcing air into their lungs SYN **mouth-to-mouth resuscitation** IDM see STEAL *v.*

kis·ser /ˈkɪsə(r)/ *noun* **1 good, bad, etc. ~** a person who is very good, bad, etc. at kissing **2** (*informal*) a person's mouth

ˈkiss-off *noun* [usually sing.] (*NAmE, informal*) an occasion when sb is suddenly told they are no longer wanted, especially by a lover or by a company: *She gave her husband the kiss-off.* ◇ *He got the kiss-off from his job.*

kisso·gram /ˈkɪsəɡræm/ *noun* a humorous message on your birthday, etc, delivered by sb dressed in a special COSTUME who kisses you, arranged as a surprise by your friends

the ˈKISS principle *noun* [sing.] (*especially US*) the idea that products and advertising should be as simple as possible ORIGIN Formed from the first letters of the expression 'Keep it simple, stupid'.

Ki·swa·hili /ˌkiːswəˈhiːli; ˌkɪswɑːˈh-/ *noun* [U] = SWAHILI

kit /kɪt/ *noun, verb*
- ***noun* 1** [C] a set of parts ready to be made into sth: *a kit for a model plane* **2** [C, U] a set of tools or equipment that you use for a particular purpose: *a first-aid kit* ◇ *a drum kit* ➲ SYNONYMS at EQUIPMENT ➲ see also TOOLKIT **3** [U] (*BrE*) a set of clothes and equipment that you use for a particular activity: *sports kit*

IDM **get your ˈkit off** (*BrE, slang*) to take your clothes off ➲ more at CABOODLE
- ***verb*** (-tt-)

PHR V **ˌkit sb ˈout/ˈup (in/with sth)** [usually passive] (*BrE*) to give sb the correct clothes and/or equipment for a particular activity: *They were all kitted out in brand-new ski outfits.*

kit·bag /ˈkɪtbæɡ/ *noun* (*especially BrE*) a long narrow bag, usually made of CANVAS in which soldiers, etc. carry their clothes and other possessions

kit·chen 0‑π /ˈkɪtʃɪn/ *noun*
a room in which meals are cooked or prepared: *She's in the kitchen.* ◇ *We ate at the kitchen table.* ➲ VISUAL VOCAB page V22 ➲ see also SOUP KITCHEN

IDM **everything but the kitchen ˈsink** (*informal, humorous*) a very large number of things, probably more than is necessary ➲ more at HEAT *n.*

kit·chen·ette /ˌkɪtʃɪˈnet/ *noun* a small room or part of a room used as a kitchen, for example in a flat/apartment

ˌkitchen ˈgarden *noun* (*BrE*) a part of a garden/yard where you grow vegetables and fruit for your own use

ˈkitchen paper (also **ˈkitchen roll, ˈkitchen towel**) (all *BrE*) (*NAmE* **ˌpaper ˈtowel**) *noun* [U] thick paper on a roll, used for cleaning up liquid, food, etc. ➲ VISUAL VOCAB page V22

ˌkitchen ˈporter *noun* (*BrE*) a person who works in the kitchen of a restaurant, hotel, etc, washing plates and doing other simple jobs

ˌkitchen-ˈsink *adj.* [only before noun] (of plays, films, novels, etc.) dealing with ordinary life and ordinary people, especially when this involves describing the boring or difficult side of their lives: *a kitchen-sink drama*

kit·chen·ware /ˈkɪtʃɪnweə(r); *NAmE* -wer/ *noun* [U] used in shops/stores to describe objects that you use in a kitchen, such as pans, bowls, etc.

kite /kaɪt/ *noun, verb*
- ***noun* 1** a toy made of a light frame covered with paper, cloth, etc, that you fly in the air at the end of one or more long strings: *to fly a kite* ➲ VISUAL VOCAB page V32 **2** a BIRD OF PREY (= a bird that kills other creatures for food) of the HAWK family IDM see FLY *v.*, HIGH *adj.*
- ***verb*** **~ sth** (*NAmE, informal*) to use an illegal cheque to obtain money or to dishonestly change the amount written on a cheque: *to kite checks* ◇ *check kiting*

kite·surf·ing /ˈkaɪtsɜːfɪŋ; *NAmE* -sɜːrf-/ (also **kite·board·ing** /ˈkaɪtbɔːdɪŋ; *NAmE* -bɔːrd-/) *noun* [U] the sport of riding on water while standing on a short wide board and being pulled along by wind power, using a large kite ➲ VISUAL VOCAB page V40

kith /kɪθ/ *noun*

IDM **kith and kin** (*old-fashioned*) friends and relatives

kitsch /kɪtʃ/ *noun* [U] (*disapproving*) works of art or objects that are popular but that are considered to have no real artistic value and to be lacking in good taste, for example because they are SENTIMENTAL ▶ **kitsch** (also **kitschy**) *adj.*

kit·ten /ˈkɪtn/ *noun* a young cat

IDM **have ˈkittens** (*BrE, informal*) to be very anxious, angry or upset about sth

'kitten heels *noun* [pl.] small thin curved heels on women's shoes ➲ VISUAL VOCAB page V52

kit·ten·ish /'kɪtnɪʃ/ *adj.* (*old-fashioned*) (of a woman) lively, and trying to attract men's attention

kit·ti·wake /'kɪtiweɪk/ *noun* a bird that lives in groups on sea CLIFFS

kitty /'kɪti/ *noun* (*pl.* -ies) **1** (*informal*) if money is put in a **kitty**, a group of people all give an amount and the money is spent on sth they all agree on: *We each put £50 in the kitty to cover the bills.* **2** (in card games, etc.) the sum of money that all the players bet, which is given to the winner **3** (*informal*) a way of referring to a cat

,kitty-'corner(ed) *adj., adv.* (*NAmE, informal*) = CATTY-CORNER(ED)

kiwi /'ki:wi:/ *noun* **1 Kiwi** (*informal*) a person from New Zealand **2** a New Zealand bird with a long beak, short wings and no tail, that cannot fly **3** = KIWI FRUIT

'kiwi fruit *noun* (*pl.* kiwi fruit) (also **kiwi**) a small fruit with thin brown skin covered with small hairs, soft green flesh and black seeds ➲ VISUAL VOCAB page V26

kJ *abbr.* KILOJOULE(S)

KKK /,keɪ keɪ 'keɪ/ *abbr.* KU KLUX KLAN

klap /klʌp/ *verb* (-pp-) **~ sb/sth** (*SAfrE, informal*) to hit sb/sth: *I'll klap you!* ▸ **klap** *noun*: *to give sb a klap*

Klaxon™ /'klæksn/ *noun* (*BrE*) a horn, originally on a vehicle, that makes a loud sound as a warning

Klee·nex™ /'kli:neks/ *noun* [U, C] (*pl.* **Klee·nex**) a paper HANDKERCHIEF; a TISSUE: *a box of Kleenex* ◇ *Here, have a Kleenex to dry your eyes.*

klep·to·mania /,kleptə'meɪniə/ *noun* [U] a mental illness in which sb has a strong desire, which they cannot control, to steal things ▸ **klep·to·maniac** /,kleptə'meɪniæk/ *noun*: *She's a kleptomaniac.*

klick (also **click**) /klɪk/ *noun* (*NAmE, informal*) a kilometre: *We're twenty klicks south of your position.*

kludge /klu:dʒ/ *noun* (*computing*) a solution to a computer problem that has been quickly and badly put together ▸ **kludge** *verb* [I, T] **~ (sth)**

klutz /klʌts/ *noun* (*informal, especially NAmE*) a person who often drops things, is not good at sport(s), etc. ▸ **klutzy** /'klʌtsi/ *adj.*

km *abbr.* (*pl.* **km** or **kms**) (in writing) kilometre(s)

knack /næk/ *noun* [sing.] (*informal*) **1** a special skill or ability that you have naturally or can learn: *It's easy, once you've got the knack.* ◇ **~ of/for (doing) sth** *He's got a real knack for making money.* **2 ~ of doing sth** (*BrE*) a habit of doing sth: *She has the unfortunate knack of always saying the wrong thing.*

knacker /'nækə(r)/ *verb* (*BrE, slang*) **1 ~ sb** to make sb very tired SYN **exhaust 2 ~ sb/sth** to injure sb or damage sth ▸ **knacker·ing** *adj.* [not usually before noun]: (*BrE, informal*) *I don't do aerobics any more—it's too knackering.*

knack·ered /'nækəd; *NAmE* -kərd/ *adj.* (*BrE, slang*) **1** [not usually before noun] extremely tired SYN **exhausted, worn out 2** too old or broken to use

'knacker's yard (also **the knackers**) *noun* [usually sing.] (*old-fashioned, BrE*) a place where old and injured horses are taken to be killed

knap·sack /'næpsæk/ *noun* (*old-fashioned* or *NAmE*) a small RUCKSACK

knave /neɪv/ *noun* **1** (*old-fashioned*) = JACK (3): *the knave of clubs* **2** (*old use*) a dishonest man or boy

knead /ni:d/ *verb* **1 ~ sth** to press and stretch DOUGH, wet CLAY, etc. with your hands to make it ready to use ➲ VISUAL VOCAB page V25 **2 ~ sth** to rub and squeeze muscles, etc. especially to relax them or to make them less painful

knee 🔑 /ni:/ *noun, verb*
▪ *noun* **1** 🔑 the joint between the top and bottom parts of the leg where it bends in the middle: *a knee injury* ◇ *I grazed my knee when I fell.* ◇ *He* **went down on one knee** *and asked her to marry him.* ◇ *She was* **on her knees** *scrubbing the kitchen floor.* ➲ VISUAL VOCAB page V48 **2** 🔑 the part of a piece of clothing that covers the knee: *These jeans are torn at the knee.* ◇ *a knee patch* **3** 🔑 the top surface of the upper part of the legs when you are sitting down SYN **lap**: *Come and sit on Daddy's knee.*
IDM **bring sb to their 'knees** to defeat sb, especially in a war **bring sth to its 'knees** to badly affect an organization, etc. so that it can no longer function: *The strikes brought the industry to its knees.* **put sb over your 'knee** to punish sb by making them lie on top of your knee and hitting their bottom ➲ more at BEE, BEND *v.*, MOTHER *n.*, WEAK
▪ *verb* (**kneed, kneed**) **~ sb/sth** to hit or push sb/sth with your knee: *He kneed his attacker in the groin.*

knee·cap /'ni:kæp/ *noun, verb*
▪ *noun* the small bone that covers the front of the knee SYN **patella** ➲ VISUAL VOCAB page V48
▪ *verb* (-pp-) **~ sb** to shoot or break sb's kneecaps as a form of punishment that is not official and is illegal ▸ **knee·cap·ping** *noun* [C, U]

,knee-'deep *adj.* up to your knees: *The snow was knee-deep in places.* ◇ (*figurative*) *I was knee-deep in work.* ▸ **,knee-'deep** *adv.*: *I waded in knee-deep.*

,knee-'high *adj.* high enough to reach your knees
IDM **knee-high to a 'grasshopper** (*informal, humorous*) very small; very young

'knee-jerk *adj.* [only before noun] (*disapproving*) produced automatically, without any serious thought: *It was* **a knee-jerk reaction** *on her part.*

kneel /ni:l/ *verb* (**knelt, knelt** /nelt/) (*NAmE* also **kneeled, kneeled**) [I] to be in or move into a position where your body is supported on your knee or knees: *a kneeling figure* ◇ **~ (down)** *We knelt (down) on the ground to examine the tracks.*

'knee-length *adj.* long enough to reach your knees: *knee-length shorts/socks*

'knees-up *noun* [usually sing.] (*BrE, informal*) a noisy party, with dancing

'knee trembler *noun* (*informal*) an act of sex that is done standing up

knell /nel/ *noun* [sing.] = DEATH KNELL

knelt *past tense, past part.* of KNEEL

knew *past tense* of KNOW

knick·er·bockers /'nɪkəbɒkəz; *NAmE* 'nɪkərbɑ:kərz/ (*NAmE* also **knick·ers**) *noun* [pl.] short loose trousers/pants that fit tightly just below the knee, worn especially in the past

knick·ers /'nɪkəz; *NAmE* -kərz/ *noun* [pl.] **1** (*BrE*) (also **pan·ties** *NAmE, BrE*) a piece of women's underwear that covers the body from the waist to the tops of the legs: *a pair of knickers* **2** (*NAmE*) = KNICKERBOCKERS ▸ **knick·er** *adj.* [only before noun]: *knicker elastic*
IDM **get your 'knickers in a twist** (*BrE, slang*) to become angry, confused or upset ➲ more at WET *v.*

knick-knack /'nɪk næk/ *noun* [usually pl.] (sometimes *disapproving*) a small decorative object in a house SYN **ornament**

knife 🔑 /naɪf/ *noun, verb*
▪ *noun* 🔑 (*pl.* **knives** /naɪvz/) a sharp blade with a handle, used for cutting or as a weapon: *knives and forks* ◇ *a sharp knife* ◇ *a bread knife* (= one for cutting bread) ◇ *She was murdered in a frenzied knife attack.* ➲ VISUAL VOCAB pages V19, V23 ➲ see also FLICK KNIFE, JACKKNIFE, PALETTE KNIFE, PAPERKNIFE, PENKNIFE, STANLEY KNIFE
IDM **the 'knives are out (for sb)** the situation has become so bad that people are preparing to make one person take the blame, for example by taking away their job **like a knife through 'butter** (*informal*) easily; without meeting any difficulty **put/stick the 'knife in | put/stick the 'knife into sb** (*informal*) to be very unfriendly to sb and try to harm them **turn/twist the 'knife (in the wound)** to say or do sth unkind deliberately; to make sb who is

K

unhappy feel even more unhappy **under the 'knife** (*informal*) having a medical operation

■ ***verb*** **~ sb** to injure or kill sb with a knife SYN **stab**

'knife-edge *noun* [usually sing.] the sharp edge of a knife

IDM **on a 'knife-edge 1** (of a situation, etc.) finely balanced between success and failure: *The economy is balanced on a knife-edge.* **2** (of a person) very worried or anxious about the result of sth

knife·point /ˈnaɪfpɔɪnt/ *noun*

IDM **at 'knifepoint** while being threatened, or threatening sb, with a knife: *She was raped at knifepoint.*

knight /naɪt/ *noun, verb*

■ ***noun* 1** (in the Middle Ages) a man of high social rank who had a duty to fight for his king. Knights are often shown in pictures riding horses and wearing ARMOUR. ➲ see also BLACK KNIGHT, WHITE KNIGHT **2** (in Britain) a man who has been given a special honour by the king or queen and has the title *Sir* before his name ➲ compare BARONET **3** a piece used in the game of CHESS that is shaped like a horse's head ➲ VISUAL VOCAB page V33

IDM **a knight in shining 'armour** (usually *humorous*) a man who saves sb, especially a woman, from a dangerous situation

■ ***verb*** [usually passive] **~ sb** to give sb the rank and title of a knight: *He was knighted by the Queen for his services to industry.*

K

,knight 'errant *noun* (*pl.* **,knights 'errant**) (in the Middle Ages) a KNIGHT who travelled around, looking for adventure

knight·hood /ˈnaɪthʊd/ *noun* (in Britain) the rank or title of a KNIGHT: *He received a knighthood in the New Year's Honours list.*

knight·ly /ˈnaɪtli/ *adj.* [usually before noun] (*literary*) consisting of knights; typical of a knight SYN **chivalrous**

knit O-- /nɪt/ *verb, noun*

■ ***verb*** (**knit·ted, knit·ted**) HELP In senses 3 and 4 **knit** is usually used for the past tense and past participle. **1** O-- [T, I] to make clothes, etc. from wool or cotton thread using two long thin knitting needles or a machine: **~ (sth)** *I knitted this cardigan myself.* ◇ *Lucy was sitting on the sofa, knitting.* ◇ **~ sb sth** *She's knitting the baby a shawl.* **2** [T, I] **~ (sth)** to use a basic STITCH in knitting: *Knit one row, purl one row.* **3** [T, I] **~ (sb/sth) (together)** to join people or things closely together or to be joined closely together: *a **closely/tightly knit community*** (= one in which relationships are very close) ◇ *Society is knit together by certain commonly held beliefs.* **4** [I, T] **~ (sth)** (of broken bones) to grow together again to form one piece; to make broken bones grow together again SYN **mend**: *The bone failed to knit correctly.*

IDM **knit your 'brow(s)** to move your EYEBROWS together, to show that you are thinking hard, feeling angry, etc. SYN **frown**

■ ***noun*** [usually pl.] a piece of clothing that has been knitted: *winter knits*

knit·ted O-- /ˈnɪtɪd/ (also **knit**) *adj.* made by knitting wool or thread: *knitted gloves* ◇ *a white knit dress* ◇ *a hand-knitted sweater* ◇ *a cotton-knit shirt*

knit·ter /ˈnɪtə(r)/ *noun* a person who knits

knit·ting O-- /ˈnɪtɪŋ/ *noun* [U]

1 O-- an item that is being knitted: *Where's my knitting?*
2 O-- the activity of knitting

'knitting needle *noun* a long thin stick with a round end that you use for knitting by hand ➲ VISUAL VOCAB page V35

knit·wear /ˈnɪtweə(r); *NAmE* -wer/ *noun* [U] items of clothing that have been knitted

knives *pl.* of KNIFE

knob /nɒb; *NAmE* nɑːb/ *noun* **1** a round switch on a machine such as a television that you use to turn it on and off, etc: *the volume control knob* **2** a round handle on a door or a drawer **3** a round lump on the surface or end of sth ➲ picture at HANDLE **4** (*especially BrE*) a small lump of sth such as butter **5** (*BrE, taboo, slang*) a PENIS

IDM **with 'knobs on** (*BrE, slang*) used to say that sth is a more complicated version of what you mention: *It isn't art—it's just a horror movie with knobs on!*

knob·bly /ˈnɒbli; *NAmE* ˈnɑːbli/ (*especially NAmE* **knobby** /ˈnɒbi; *NAmE* ˈnɑːbi/) *adj.* having small hard lumps: *knobbly knees*

knock O-- /nɒk; *NAmE* nɑːk/ *verb, noun*

■ ***verb***

▸ AT DOOR/WINDOW **1** O-- [I] to hit a door, etc. firmly in order to attract attention SYN **rap**: *He knocked three times and waited.* ◇ **~ at/on sth** *Somebody was knocking on the window.*

▸ HIT **2** O-- [T, I] to hit sth, often by accident, with a short, hard blow: **~ sth (against/on sth)** *Be careful you don't knock your head on this low beam.* ◇ **~ against/on sth** *Her hand knocked against the glass.* **3** [T] to put sb/sth into a particular state by hitting them/it: **~ sb/sth + adj.** *The blow knocked me flat.* ◇ *He was knocked senseless by the blow.* ◇ **~ sb/sth doing sth** *She knocked my drink flying.* ◇ **~ sb/sth + adv./prep.** *The two rooms had been knocked into one* (= the wall between them had been knocked down). ➲ SYNONYMS at HIT **4** O-- [T] to hit sth so that it moves or breaks: **~ sth + adv./prep.** *He'd knocked over a glass of water.* ◇ *I knocked the nail into the wall.* ◇ *They had to knock the door down to get in.* ◇ *The boys were knocking* (= kicking) *a ball around in the back yard.* ◇ **~ sth** (*figurative*) *The criticism had knocked* (= damaged) *her self-esteem.* ➲ SYNONYMS at HIT **5** [T] **~ sth + adv./prep.** to make a hole in sth by hitting it hard: *They managed to knock a hole in the wall.*

▸ OF HEART/KNEES **6** [I] if your heart **knocks**, it beats hard; if your knees **knock**, they shake, for example from fear: *My heart was knocking wildly.*

▸ OF ENGINE/PIPES **7** [I] to make a regular sound of metal hitting metal, especially because there is sth wrong

▸ CRITICIZE **8** [T] **~ sb/sth** (*informal*) to criticize sb/sth, especially when it happens unfairly: *The newspapers are always knocking the England team.* ◇ *'E-books?' **'Don't knock it**—there's a great future in e-books.'*

IDM **I'll knock your 'block/'head off!** (*BrE, informal*) used to threaten sb that you will hit them **knock sb 'dead** (*informal*) to impress sb very much: *You look fabulous—you'll knock 'em dead tonight.* **knock sb/sth into a cocked 'hat** (*old-fashioned, BrE*) to be very much better than sb/sth **knock it 'off!** (*informal*) used to tell sb to stop making a noise, annoying you, etc. **knock sb off their 'pedestal/'perch** to make sb lose their position as sb/sth successful or admired **knock sth on the 'head** (*BrE, informal*) to stop sth from happening; to stop doing sth: *The recession knocked on the head any idea of expanding the company.* **,knock on 'wood** (*NAmE, saying*) (*BrE* **,touch 'wood**) used when you have just mentioned some way in which you have been lucky in the past, to avoid bringing bad luck **knock sb 'sideways** (*informal*) to surprise or shock sb so much that they are unable to react immediately **knock 'spots off sb/sth** (*BrE, informal*) to be very much better than sb/sth **knock the 'stuffing out of sb** (*informal*) to make sb lose their confidence and enthusiasm **you could have knocked me down with a 'feather** (*informal*) used to express surprise ➲ more at DAYLIGHTS, HEAD *n.*, HELL, SENSE *n.*, SHAPE *n.*, SIX, SOCK *n.*

PHR V **,knock a'round...** (*BrE* also **,knock a'bout...**) (*informal*) **1** to travel and live in various places: *He spent a few years knocking around Europe.* **2** used to say that sth is in a place but you do not know exactly where: *It must be knocking around here somewhere.* **,knock a'round with sb/together** (*BrE* also **,knock a'bout with sb/together**) (*informal*) to spend a lot of time with sb/together **,knock sb/sth a'round** (*BrE* also **,knock sb/sth a'bout**) (*informal*) to hit sb/sth repeatedly; to treat sb/sth roughly

,knock sb 'back 1 (*BrE*) to prevent sb from achieving sth or making progress, especially by rejecting them or sth that they suggest or ask ➲ related noun KNOCK-BACK **2** (*BrE*) to surprise or shock sb: *Hearing the news really knocked me back.* **,knock sb 'back sth** (*BrE, informal*) to cost sb a lot of money: *That house must have knocked them* *back a bit.* ˌ**knock sth↔ˈback** (*informal*) to drink sth quickly, especially an alcoholic drink

ˌ**knock sb ˈdown (from sth) (to sth)** (*informal*) to persuade sb to reduce the price of sth: *I managed to knock him down to $400.* ˌ**knock sb↔ˈdown/ˈover** 🔑 to hit sb and make them fall to the ground: *She was knocked down by a bus.* ◇ *He knocked his opponent down three times in the first round.* ˌ**knock sth↔ˈdown** 🔑 to destroy a building by breaking its walls SYN **demolish**: *These old houses are going to be knocked down.* ˌ**knock sth↔ˈdown (from sth) (to sth)** (*informal*) to reduce the price of sth: *He knocked down the price from $80 to $50.* ➲ see also KNOCK-DOWN

ˌ**knock ˈoff** | ˌ**knock ˈoff sth** (*informal*) to stop doing sth, especially work: *Do you want to knock off early today?* ◇ *What time do you knock off work?* ◇ *Let's knock off for lunch.* ˌ**knock sb↔ˈoff** (*slang*) to murder sb ˌ**knock sth↔ˈoff 1** (*informal*) to complete sth quickly and without much effort: *He knocks off three novels a year.* **2** (*BrE, slang*) to steal sth; to steal from a place: *to knock off a DVD player* ◇ *to knock off a bank* ˌ**knock sth↔ˈoff** | ˌ**knock sth↔ˈoff sth** (*informal*) to reduce the price or value of sth: *They knocked off $60 because of a scratch.* ◇ *The news knocked 13% off the company's shares.*

ˌ**knock sb↔ˈout 1** 🔑 to make sb fall asleep or become unconscious: *The blow knocked her out.* **2** (in boxing) to hit an opponent so that they cannot get up within a limited time and therefore lose the fight ➲ related noun KNOCKOUT **3** (*informal*) to surprise and impress sb very much: *The movie just knocked me out.* ➲ related noun KNOCKOUT ˌ**knock sb/yourself ˈout** to make sb/yourself very tired SYN **wear out** ˌ**knock sb↔ˈout (of sth)** to defeat sb so that they cannot continue competing SYN **eliminate**: *England had been knocked out of the World Cup.* ➲ see also KNOCKOUT ˌ**knock sth↔ˈout** (*informal*) to produce sth, especially quickly and easily: *He knocks out five books a year.*

ˌ**knock sb↔ˈover** = KNOCK SB DOWN

ˌ**knock sth↔toˈgether 1** (*informal*) to make or complete sth quickly and often not very well: *I knocked some bookshelves together from old planks.* **2** (*BrE*) to make two rooms or buildings into one by removing the wall between them: *The house consists of two cottages knocked together.*

ˌ**knock ˈup** (in TENNIS, etc.) to practise for a short time before the start of a game ˌ**knock sb↔ˈup 1** (*BrE, informal*) to wake sb by knocking on their door **2** (*informal, especially NAmE*) to make a woman pregnant ˌ**knock sth↔ˈup** to prepare or make sth quickly and without much effort: *She knocked up a meal in ten minutes.*

■ ***noun***

▸ **AT DOOR/WINDOW 1** 🔑 the sound of sb hitting a door, window, etc. with their hand or with sth hard to attract attention: *There was a* ***knock on/at*** *the door.*

▸ **HIT 2** 🔑 a sharp blow from sth hard SYN **bang**: *He got a nasty knock on the head.*

IDM **take a (hard, nasty, etc.) ˈknock** to have an experience that makes sb/sth less confident or successful; to be damaged

knock·about /ˈnɒkəbaʊt; *NAmE* ˈnɑːk-/ *adj.* [usually before noun] (*BrE*) **knockabout** entertainment involves people acting in a deliberately silly way, for example falling over or hitting other people, in order to make the audience laugh SYN **slapstick**

ˈ**knock-back** *noun* (*informal*) a difficulty or problem that makes you feel less confident that you will be successful in sth that you are doing, especially when sb rejects you or sth you suggest or ask

ˈ**knock-down** *adj., noun*

■ ***adj.*** [only before noun] (*informal*) **1** (of prices, etc.) much lower than usual SYN **rock-bottom 2** using a lot of force: *a knock-down punch*

■ ***noun* 1** (in boxing) an act of falling to the ground after being hit **2** (in football (SOCCER)) an act of hitting a high ball down to the ground or to another player

ˌ**knock-down-ˈdrag-out** *adj.* [only before noun] (*NAmE, informal*) (of a fight or an argument) very aggressive and unpleasant

knock·er /ˈnɒkə(r); *NAmE* ˈnɑːk-/ *noun* **1** (also ˈ**door knocker**) [C] a metal object attached to the outside of the door of a house, etc. which you hit against the door to attract attention ➲ VISUAL VOCAB page V15 **2** [C] (*informal*) a person who is always criticizing sb/sth **3 knockers** [pl.] (*taboo, slang*) an offensive word for a woman's breasts

ˈ**knocking copy** *noun* [U] (*BrE, informal*) advertising in which an opponent's product is criticized

ˈ**knocking shop** *noun* (*BrE, informal*) a BROTHEL (= place where people can pay for sex)

ˌ**knock-ˈkneed** *adj.* having legs that turn towards each other at the knees

ˌ**knock ˈknees** *noun* [pl.] legs that turn towards each other at the knees

ˌ**knock-ˈon** *adj.* (*especially BrE*) causing other events to happen one after another in a series: *The increase in the price of oil had* ***a knock-on effect*** *on the cost of many other goods.*

knock·out /ˈnɒkaʊt; *NAmE* ˈnɑːk-/ *noun, adj.*

■ ***noun* 1** (*abbr.* **KO**) (in boxing) a blow that makes an opponent fall to the ground and be unable to get up, so that he or she loses the fight **2** (*informal*) a person or thing that is very attractive or impressive

■ ***adj.*** [only before noun] **1** (*especially BrE*) a **knockout** competition is one in which the winning player/team at each stage competes in the next stage and the losing one no longer takes part in the competition: *the knockout stages of the tournament* **2** a **knockout** blow is one that hits sb so hard that they can no longer get up

ˈ**knock-up** *noun* (*BrE*) a short practice before a game, especially of TENNIS

knoll /nəʊl; *NAmE* noʊl/ *noun* a small round hill SYN **mound**

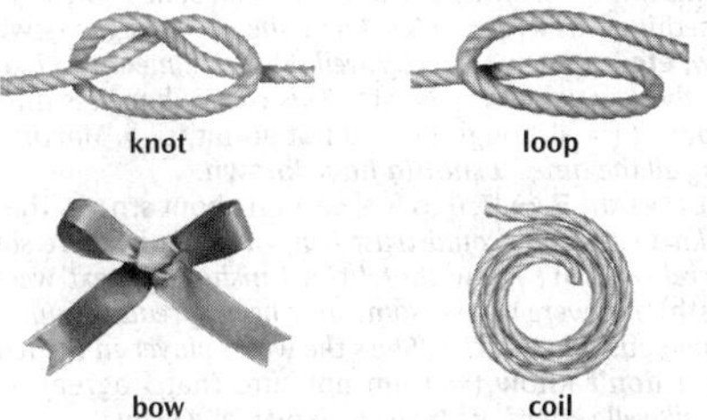

knot 🔑 /nɒt; *NAmE* nɑːt/ *noun, verb*

■ ***noun***

▸ **IN STRING/ROPE 1** 🔑 a join made by tying together two pieces or ends of string, rope, etc: *to* ***tie a knot*** ◇ *Tie the two ropes together with a knot.* ◇ (*figurative*) *hair full of knots and tangles* (= twisted in a way that is difficult to COMB)

▸ **OF HAIR 2** a way of twisting hair into a small round shape at the back of the head: *She had her hair in a knot.*

▸ **IN WOOD 3** a hard round spot in a piece of wood where there was once a branch

▸ **GROUP OF PEOPLE 4** a small group of people standing close together

▸ **OF MUSCLES 5** a tight, hard feeling in the stomach, throat, etc. caused by nerves, anger, etc: *My stomach was in knots.* ◇ *I could feel a knot of fear in my throat.*

▸ **SPEED OF BOAT/PLANE 6** a unit for measuring the speed of boats and aircraft; one NAUTICAL MILE per hour IDM see RATE *n.*, TIE *v.*

■ ***verb*** (-tt-)

▸ **TIE WITH KNOT 1** [T] **~ sth** to fasten sth with a knot or knots: *He carefully knotted his tie.*

▸ **TWIST 2** [I] to become twisted into a knot SYN **tangle 3** [T] **~ sth** to twist hair into a particular shape: *She wore her hair loosely knotted on top of her head.*

▸ **MUSCLES 4** [I, T] **~ (sth)** if muscles, etc. **knot** or sth **knots** them, they become hard and painful because of fear, excitement, etc: *She felt her stomach knot with fear.*

IDM **get ˈknotted** (*BrE, informal, slang*) a rude way of tell-

K

ing sb to go away or of telling them that you are annoyed with them

knotty /ˈnɒti; *NAmE* ˈnɑːti/ *adj.* (**knot·tier, knot·ti·est**) **1** complicated and difficult to solve SYN **thorny**: *a knotty problem* **2** having parts that are hard and twisted together: *the knotty roots of the old oak tree*

know /nəʊ; *NAmE* noʊ/ *verb, noun*

■ ***verb*** (**knew** /njuː; *NAmE* nuː/, **known** /nəʊn; *NAmE* noʊn/) (not used in the progressive tenses)

▸ HAVE INFORMATION **1** [T, I] to have information in your mind as a result of experience or because you have learned or been told it: **~ sth** *Do you know his address?* ◇ *The cause of the fire is not yet known.* ◇ ***All I know*** *is that she used to work in a bank* (= I have no other information about her). ◇ **~ (that)...** *I know (that) people's handwriting changes as they get older.* ◇ **it is known that...** *It is widely known that CFCs can damage the ozone layer.* ◇ **~ where, what, etc...** *I knew where he was hiding.* ◇ *I didn't know what he was talking about.* ◇ **~ (of/about sth)** *'You've got a flat tyre.' 'I know.'* ◇ *'What's the answer?' 'I don't know.'* ◇ *'There's no one in.'* ***'How do you know?'*** ◇ *You know about Amanda's baby, don't you?* ◇ ***I don't know about you, but*** *I'm ready for something to eat.* ◇ ***I know of*** *at least two people who did the same thing.* ◇ *'Is anyone else coming?'* ***'Not that I know of.'*** ◇ *'Isn't that his car?'* ***'I wouldn't know./How should I know?'*** (= I don't know and I am not the person you should ask.) ◇ (*informal*) *'What are you two whispering about?'* ***'You don't want to know'*** (= because you would be shocked or wouldn't approve). ◇ **~ to do sth** *Does he know to come here* (= that he should come here) *first?* ◇ **~ sb/sth to be/do sth** *We know her to be honest.* ◇ *Two women are known to have died.* ➲ see also NEED-TO-KNOW

▸ REALIZE **2** [T, I] to realize, understand or be aware of sth: **~ (that)...** *As soon as I walked in the room I knew (that) something was wrong.* ◇ *She knew she was dying.* ◇ **~ what, how, etc...** *I knew perfectly well what she meant.* ◇ *I know exactly how you feel.* ◇ **~ (sth)** *This case is hopeless* ***and he knows it*** (= although he will not admit it). ◇ *'Martin was lying all the time.'* ***'I should have known.'***

▸ FEEL CERTAIN **3** [T, I] to feel certain about sth: **~ (that)...** *He knew (that) he could trust her.* ◇ *I know it's here somewhere!* ◇ *I don't know that I can finish it by next week.* ◇ **~ (sth)** *'You were right—someone's been spreading rumours about you.' 'I knew it!'* ◇ *'She's the worst player in the team.' 'Oh,* ***I don't know*** (= I am not sure that I agree) *—she played well yesterday.'* ➲ see also DON'T-KNOW

▸ BE FAMILIAR **4** [T] **~ sb/sth** to be familiar with a person, place, thing, etc: *I've known David for 20 years.* ◇ *Do you two know each other* (= have you met before)? ◇ *She's very nice when you* ***get to know*** *her.* ◇ ***Knowing Ben,*** *we could be waiting a long time* (= it is typical of him to be late). ◇ *This man* ***is known to the police*** (= as a criminal). ◇ *I know Paris well.* ◇ *Do you know the play* (= have you seen or read it before)? ◇ *The new rules could mean the end of football* ***as we know it*** (= in the form that we are familiar with).

▸ REPUTATION **5** [T, usually passive] to think that sb/sth is a particular type of person or thing or has particular characteristics: **~ sb/sth as sth** *It's known as the most dangerous part of the city.* ◇ **~ sb/sth for sth** *She is best known for her work on the human brain.* ◇ **~ sb/sth to be/do sth** *He's known to be an outstanding physicist.*

▸ GIVE NAME **6** [T] **~ sb/sth as sth** [usually passive] to give sb/sth a particular name or title: *The drug is commonly known as Ecstasy.* ◇ *Peter Wilson, also known as 'the Tiger'*

▸ RECOGNIZE **7** [T] **~ sb/sth** to be able to recognize sb/sth: *I couldn't see who was speaking, but I knew the voice.* ◇ *She knows a bargain when she sees one.* ➲ SYNONYMS at IDENTIFY

▸ DISTINGUISH **8** [T] **~ sb/sth from sb/sth** to be able to distinguish one person or thing from another SYN **differentiate**: *I hope we have taught our children to know right from wrong.*

▸ SKILL/LANGUAGE **9** [T] to have learned a skill or language and be able to use it: **~ sth** *Do you know any Japanese?* ◇ **~ how, what, etc...** *Do you know how to use spreadsheets?*

▸ EXPERIENCE **10** [T] (only used in the perfect tenses) to have seen, heard or experienced sth: **~ sb/sth (to) do sth** *I've never known it (to) snow in July before.* ◇ **be known to do sth** *He has been known to spend all morning in the bathroom.* **11** [T] **~ sth** to have personal experience of sth: *He has known both poverty and wealth.* ◇ *She may be successful now, but she has* ***known what it is like to be*** *poor.*

IDM **before you know where you ˈare** very quickly or suddenly: *We were whisked off in a taxi before we knew where we were.* **be not to ˈknow** to have no way of realizing or being aware that you have done sth wrong: *'I'm sorry, I called when you were in bed.' 'Don't worry—you weren't to know.'* **for all you, I, they, etc. know** (*informal*) used to emphasize that you do not know sth and that it is not important to you: *She could be dead for all I know.* **God/goodness/Heaven knows** (*informal*) **1** used to emphasize that you do not know sth: *God knows what else they might find.* ◇ *'Where are they?' 'Goodness knows.'* HELP Some people may find the use of **God knows** offensive. **2** used to emphasize the truth of what you are saying: *She ought to pass the exam—goodness knows she's been working hard enough.* **I don't know how, why, etc...** (*informal*) used to criticize sb's behaviour: *I don't know how you can say things like that.* **I know** (*informal*) **1** /aɪ ˈnəʊ; *NAmE* aɪ ˈnoʊ/ used to agree with sb or to show sympathy: *'What a ridiculous situation!' 'I know.'* **2** /ˈaɪ nəʊ; *NAmE* ˈaɪ noʊ/ used to introduce a new idea or suggestion: *I know, let's see what's on at the theatre.* **know sth as well as ˈI do** used to criticize sb by saying that they should realize or understand sth: *You know as well as I do that you're being unreasonable.* **know sb/sth ˈbackwards** (*informal, especially BrE*) to know sb/sth extremely well: *She must know the play backwards by now.* **know ˈbest** to know what should be done, etc. better than other people: *The doctor told you to stay in bed, and she knows best.* **know better (than that/than to do sth)** to be sensible enough not to do sth: *He knows better than to judge by appearances.* **know sb by ˈsight** to recognize sb without knowing them well **know ˈdifferent/ˈotherwise** (*informal*) to have information or evidence that the opposite is true: *He says he doesn't care about what the critics write, but I know different.* **know full ˈwell** to be very aware of a fact and unable to deny or ignore it: *He knew full well what she thought of it.* **know sb/sth inside ˈout | know sb/sth like the back of your ˈhand** (*informal*) to be very familiar with sth: *This is where I grew up. I know this area like the back of my hand.* **know your own ˈmind** to have very firm ideas about what you want to do **know your ˈstuff** (*informal*) to know a lot about a particular subject or job **know your way aˈround** to be familiar with a place, subject, etc. **know what you're ˈtalking about** (*informal*) to have knowledge about sth from your own experience **know which side your ˈbread is buttered** (*informal*) to know where you can get an advantage for yourself **let it be known/make it known that...** (*formal*) to make sure that people are informed about sth, especially by getting sb else to tell them: *The President has let it be known that he does not intend to run for election again.* **let sb ˈknow** to tell sb about sth: *Let me know how I can help.* **make yourself ˈknown to sb** to introduce yourself to sb: *I made myself known to the hotel manager.* **not know any ˈbetter** to behave badly, usually because you have not been taught the correct way to behave **not know your ˌarse from your ˈelbow** (*BrE, taboo, slang*) to be very stupid or completely lacking in skill **not know ˈbeans about sth** (*NAmE, informal*) to know nothing about a subject **not know the first thing aˈbout sb/sth** to know nothing at all about sb/sth **not know sb from ˈAdam** (*informal*) to not know at all who sb is **not know what ˈhit you** (*informal*) to be so surprised by sth that you do not know how to react **not know where to ˈlook** (*informal*) to feel great embarrassment and not know how to react **not know whether you're ˈcoming or ˈgoing** (*informal*) to be so excited or confused that you cannot behave or think in a sensible way **not know you are ˈborn** (*BrE, informal*) to have an easy life without realizing how easy it is: *You people without kids don't know you're born.* **there's no ˈknowing** used to say that it is impossible to say what might happen: *There's no knowing how he'll react.* **what does... know?** used to say that sb knows nothing about the subject you are talking about: *What does he know about football, anyway?* **what do you 'know?** (*informal*) used to express surprise: *Well, what do you know? Look who's here!* **,you 'know** (*informal*) **1** used when you are thinking of what to say next: *Well, you know, it's difficult to explain.* **2** used to show that what you are referring to is known or understood by the person you are speaking to: *Guess who I've just seen? Maggie! You know—Jim's wife.* ◇ *You know that restaurant round the corner? It's closed down.* **3** used to emphasize sth that you are saying: *I'm not stupid, you know.* **you 'know something/'what?** (*informal*) used to introduce an interesting or surprising opinion, piece of news, etc.: *You know something? I've never really enjoyed Christmas.* **you know 'who/'what** (*informal*) used to refer to sb/sth without mentioning a name **you never know** (*informal*) used to say that you can never be certain about what will happen in the future, especially when you are suggesting that sth good might happen ➲ more at ANSWER *n.*, COST *n.*, DAY, DEVIL, FAR *adv.*, LORD *n.*, OLD, PAT *adv.*, ROPE *n.*, THING, TRUTH

■ ***noun***

IDM **in the 'know** (*informal*) having more information about sth than most people: *Somebody in the know told me he's going to resign.*

'know-all (*BrE*) (also **'know-it-all** *NAmE, BrE*) *noun* (*informal, disapproving*) a person who behaves as if they know everything

Know·bot™ /'nəʊbɒt; *NAmE* 'noʊbɑːt/ *noun* (*computing*) a program that is designed to search for data in a large number of DATABASES when a user of a network has asked for information

'know-how *noun* [U] (*informal*) knowledge of how to do sth and experience in doing it: *We need skilled workers and technical know-how.*

know·ing /'nəʊɪŋ; *NAmE* 'noʊ-/ *adj.* [usually before noun] showing that you know or understand about sth that is supposed to be secret: *a knowing smile* ➲ compare UNKNOWING

know·ing·ly /'nəʊɪŋli; *NAmE* 'noʊ-/ *adv.* **1** while knowing the truth or likely result of what you are doing SYN **deliberately**: *She was accused of knowingly making a false statement to the police.* **2** in a way that shows that you know or understand about sth that is supposed to be secret: *He glanced at her knowingly.*

'know-it-all (*especially NAmE*) (*BrE* also **'know-all**) *noun* (*informal, disapproving*) a person who behaves as if they know everything

know·ledge /'nɒlɪdʒ; *NAmE* 'nɑːl-/ *noun*
1 [U, sing.] the information, understanding and skills that you gain through education or experience: *practical/medical/scientific knowledge* ◇ **~ of/about sth** *He has a wide knowledge of painting and music.* ◇ *There is a lack of knowledge about the tax system.* **2** [U] the state of knowing about a particular fact or situation: *She sent the letter* ***without my knowledge.*** ◇ *The film was made with the Prince's* ***full knowledge*** *and approval.* ◇ *She was impatient* ***in the knowledge that*** *time was limited.* ◇ *I went to sleep* ***secure in the knowledge*** *that I was not alone in the house.* ◇ *They could relax* ***safe in the knowledge*** *that they had the funding for the project.* ◇ *He* ***denied all knowledge of*** *the affair.* **3 ~ economy/industry/worker** working with information rather than producing goods

IDM **be common/public 'knowledge** to be sth that everyone knows, especially in a particular community or group **come to sb's 'knowledge** (*formal*) to become known by sb: *It has come to our knowledge that you have been taking time off without permission.* **to your 'knowledge** from the information you have, although you may not know everything: *'Are they divorced?' 'Not to my knowledge.'* ➲ more at BEST *n.*

know·ledge·able /'nɒlɪdʒəbl; *NAmE* 'nɑːl-/ *adj.* **~ (about sth)** knowing a lot SYN **well informed**: *She is very knowledgeable about plants.* ▸ **know·ledge·ably** /-əbli/ *adv.*

known /nəʊn; *NAmE* noʊn/ *adj.* [only before noun] known about, especially by a lot of people: *He's a known thief.* ◇ *The disease has no known cure.* ➲ see also KNOW *v.*

knuckle /'nʌkl/ *noun, verb*

■ ***noun*** **1** [C] any of the joints in the fingers, especially those connecting the fingers to the rest of the hand ➲ VISUAL VOCAB page V48 **2** (also **hock** especially in *NAmE*) [U, C] a piece of meat from the lower part of an animal's leg, especially a pig

IDM **near the 'knuckle** (*BrE, informal*) (of a remark, joke, etc.) concerned with sex in a way that is likely to offend people or make them feel embarrassed ➲ more at RAP *n.*, RAP *v.*

■ ***verb***

PHR V **,knuckle 'down (to sth)** (*informal*) to begin to work hard at sth SYN **get down to**: *I'm going to have to knuckle down to some serious study.* **,knuckle 'under (to sb/sth)** (*informal*) to accept sb else's authority

'knuckle-dragger *noun* (*informal*) a stupid man who thinks and behaves in simple, basic ways

knuckle·dust·er /'nʌkldʌstə(r)/ *noun* (*NAmE* also **,brass 'knuckles**) a metal cover that is put on the fingers and used as a weapon

knuckle·head /'nʌklhed/ *noun* (*NAmE, informal*) a person who behaves in a stupid way

,knuckle 'sandwich *noun* (*slang*) a punch in the mouth

KO (also **kayo**) /,keɪ 'əʊ; *NAmE* 'oʊ/ *abbr.* KNOCKOUT

koala /kəʊ'ɑːlə; *NAmE* koʊ-/ (also **ko,ala 'bear**) *noun* an Australian animal with thick grey fur, large ears and no tail. Koalas live in trees and eat leaves. ➲ VISUAL VOCAB page V10

kofta /'kɒftə; *NAmE* 'kɔːf-/ *noun* [U, C] a S Asian dish of meat, fish or cheese mixed with spices, crushed and shaped into balls; one of these balls

kohl /kəʊl; *NAmE* koʊl/ *noun* [U] a black powder that is used especially in Eastern countries. It is put around the eyes to make them more attractive.

kohl·rabi /,kəʊl'rɑːbi; *NAmE* ,koʊl-/ *noun* [U] a vegetable of the CABBAGE family whose thick round white STEM is eaten

koi /kɔɪ/ *noun* (*pl.* **koi**) a large fish originally from Japan, often kept in fish PONDS

'kola nut *noun* = COLA NUT

kombi (also **combi**) /'kɒmbi; *NAmE* 'kɑːm-/ *noun* (*SAfrE*) a vehicle that looks like a van, has windows at the sides and carries about ten people

Ko·modo dragon /kə,məʊdəʊ 'drægən; *NAmE* kə,moʊdoʊ/ *noun* a very large LIZARD from Indonesia

kook /kuːk/ *noun* (*informal, especially NAmE*) a person who acts in a strange or crazy way ▸ **kooky** *adj.*

kooka·burra /'kʊkəbʌrə; *NAmE* -bɜːrə/ *noun* an Australian bird that makes a strange laughing cry

Koori /'kʊəri; *NAmE* 'kʊri/ *noun* (*AustralE*) an Aboriginal person from the south-east of Australia

kop /kɒp; *NAmE* kɑːp/ *noun* **1** (*SAfrE, informal*) a head **2** (*SAfrE*) (especially in place names) a hill **3** (usually **the Kop**) (*BrE*) (especially in the past) an area of steps at a football (SOCCER) team's ground where that team's supporters stand to watch the game

kop·pie /'kɒpi; *NAmE* 'kɑːpi/ *noun* (*SAfrE*) a small hill: *They went for a walk up the koppie.*

kora /'kɔːrə/ *noun* a W African musical instrument with 21 strings that pass over a bowl-shaped body and are attached to a long wooden part

Koran (also **Qur'an**) /kə'rɑːn/ *noun* **the Koran** [sing.] the holy book of the Islamic religion, written in Arabic, containing the word of Allah as REVEALED to the Prophet Muhammad ▸ **Kor·an·ic** /kə'rænɪk/ *adj.*

korf·ball /'kɔːfbɔːl; *NAmE* 'kɔːrf-/ *noun* [U] a game similar to BASKETBALL, played by two teams of eight players, four men and four women

K

korma /ˈkɔːmə; *NAmE* ˈkɔːrmə/ *noun* [U, C] a S Asian dish or sauce made with cream or YOGURT, and often ALMONDS: *chicken korma*

ko·sher /ˈkəʊʃə(r); *NAmE* ˈkoʊ-/ *adj.* **1** (of food) prepared according to the rules of Jewish law **2** (*informal*) honest or legal: *Their business deals are not always completely kosher.*

kow·tow /ˌkaʊˈtaʊ/ *verb* [I] **~ (to sb/sth)** (*informal, disapproving*) to show sb in authority too much respect and be too willing to obey them

KP /ˌkeɪ ˈpiː/ *noun* [U] (*NAmE*) work done by soldiers in the kitchen, usually as a punishment: *The sergeant assigned him to KP.* ORIGIN From 'kitchen police', a name for the soldiers.

kph /ˌkeɪ piː ˈeɪtʃ/ *abbr.* kilometres per hour

kraal /krɑːl/ *noun* (*SAfrE*) **1** a traditional African village of HUTS surrounded by a fence **2** an area surrounded by a fence in which animals are kept: *a cattle kraal*

kra·ken /ˈkrɑːkən/ *noun* an extremely large imaginary creature which is said to appear in the sea near Norway

Kraut /kraʊt/ *noun* (*taboo, slang*) an offensive word for a person from Germany

krill /krɪl/ *noun* [pl.] very small SHELLFISH that live in the sea around the Antarctic and are eaten by WHALES

kris /kriːs/ *noun* a Malay or Indonesian knife with a blade with little curves on its edge

K

Kriss Kringle /ˌkrɪs ˈkrɪŋgl/ *noun* (*NAmE*) = SANTA CLAUS ORIGIN From *Christkindl*, the German for 'Christ child'.

krona /ˈkrəʊnə; *NAmE* ˈkroʊnə/ *noun* (*pl.* **kro·nor** /-nɔː(r); -nə(r)/) the unit of money in Sweden and Iceland

krone /ˈkrəʊnə; *NAmE* ˈkroʊnə/ *noun* (*pl.* **kro·ner** /-nə(r)/) the unit of money in Denmark and Norway

kryp·ton /ˈkrɪptɒn; *NAmE* -tɑːn/ *noun* [U] (*symb.* **Kr**) a chemical element. Krypton is a gas that does not react with anything, used in FLUORESCENT lights and LASERS.

kryp·ton·ite /ˈkrɪptənaɪt/ *noun* [U] a chemical element that exists only in stories, especially in stories about Superman, a character with special powers which he loses when he is near to kryptonite

kudos /ˈkjuːdɒs; *NAmE* ˈkuːdɑːs/ *noun* [U] the admiration and respect that goes with a particular achievement or position SYN **prestige**: *the kudos of playing for such a famous team*

kudu /ˈkuːduː/ *noun* (*pl.* **kudu** or **kudus**) a large greyish or brownish African ANTELOPE with white stripes on its sides. The male kudu has long twisted horns.

kudzu /ˈkʊdzuː/ *noun* [U] a climbing plant with purple flowers that grows very fast and is used as a food and in medicines

Ku Klux Klan /ˌkuː klʌks ˈklæn/ *noun* [sing.+ sing./pl. v.] (*abbr.* **KKK**) a secret organization of white men in the southern states of the US who use violence to oppose social change and equal rights for black people

kulfi /ˈkʊlfi/ *noun* [C, U] a type of S Asian ice cream, usually served in the shape of a CONE

kum·quat /ˈkʌmkwɒt; *NAmE* -kwɑːt/ *noun* a fruit like a very small orange with sweet skin that is eaten, and sour flesh

kung fu /ˌkʌŋ ˈfuː/ *noun* [U] (from *Chinese*) a Chinese system of fighting without weapons, similar to KARATE

kurta /ˈkɜːtə; *NAmE* ˈkɜːrtə/ *noun* a loose shirt, worn by men or women in S Asia

kvetch /kvetʃ/ *verb* [I] (*NAmE, informal*) to complain about sth all the time SYN **moan, whine**

kW *abbr.* (*pl.* **kW**) (in writing) KILOWATT(S): *a 2kW electric fire*

kwaito /ˈkwaɪtəʊ; *NAmE* -toʊ/ *noun* [U] a type of South African dance music, often with words that are spoken or shouted rather than sung

Kwan·zaa /ˈkwænzɑː/ *noun* [U] a cultural festival that is celebrated in the US by some African Americans from December 26 to January 1 ORIGIN From a phrase in Swahili that means 'first fruits'.

kwashi·or·kor /ˌkwɒʃiˈɔːkɔː(r); ˌkwæʃ-; *NAmE* ˌkwɑːʃiˈɔːrkər/ *noun* [U] a dangerous form of MALNUTRITION that is caused by not eating enough PROTEIN

kwela /ˈkwelə/ *noun* [U] a type of South African JAZZ music in which the main part is usually played on a PENNY WHISTLE (= a type of long whistle with holes in it that you can cover with your fingers to produce different notes)

kWh *abbr.* (*pl.* **kWh**) (in writing) KILOWATT-HOUR(S)

kylie /ˈkaɪli/ *noun* (*AustralE*) a BOOMERANG

L /el/ *noun, abbr., symbol*

■ ***noun*** (also **l**) [C, U] (*pl.* Ls, L's, l's /elz/) the 12th letter of the English alphabet: *'Lion' begins with (an) L/'L'.* ➲ see also L-PLATE

■ ***abbr.*** **1** **L.** (especially on maps) Lake: *L. Windermere* **2** (especially for sizes of clothes) large: *S M and L* (= small, medium and large)

■ ***symbol*** (also **l**) the number 50 in ROMAN NUMERALS

l *abbr.* **1** (*pl.* l) (in writing) litre(s) **2** (also **l.**) (*pl.* ll) (in writing) line (on a page in a book)

LA (also **L.A.**) /ˌel ˈeɪ/ *abbr.* the city of Los Angeles

la = LAH ➲ see also À LA

laa·ger /ˈlɑːɡə(r)/ *noun* (*SAfrE*) (in the past) a group of WAGONS that were put into a circle in order to protect people in the middle: *They drew their wagons into a laager and set up camp.* ◇ *a* ***laager mentality*** (= one that is not willing to accept new ideas)

Lab. *abbr.* (in British politics) Labour

lab 0➛ /læb/ *noun* (*informal*) = LABORATORY: *science labs* ◇ *a lab technician* ◇ *a lab coat* (= a white coat worn by scientists, etc. working in a laboratory)

label

price tag

ticket

label 0➛ AW /ˈleɪbl/ *noun, verb*

■ ***noun*** **1** 0➛ a piece of paper, etc. that is attached to sth and that gives information about it SYN **tag, ticket**: *The washing instructions are on the label.* ◇ *price/address labels* ◇ *We tested various supermarkets'* ***own label*** *pasta sauces* (= those marked with the name of the shop/store where they are sold). ◇ *He'll only wear clothes with a* ***designer label.*** ➲ VISUAL VOCAB page V29 **2** (*disapproving*) a word or phrase that is used to describe sb/sth in a way that seems too general, unfair or not correct: *I hated the label 'housewife'.* **3** a company that produces and sells music, CDs, etc: *the Virgin record label* ◇ *It's his first release for a major label.*

■ ***verb*** (-ll-, *especially US* -l-) [often passive] **1** 0➛ **~ sth** to fix a label on sth or write information on sth: *We carefully labelled each item with the contents and the date.* ◇ *The file was labelled 'Private'.* **2** to describe sb/sth in a particular way, especially unfairly: **~ sb/sth (as) sth** | **~ sb/sth + noun** *He was labelled (as) a traitor by his former colleagues.* ◇ **~ sb/sth + adj.** *It is unfair to label a small baby as naughty.*

labia /ˈleɪbiə/ *noun* [pl.] the four folds of skin at the entrance to a woman's VAGINA

la·bial /ˈleɪbiəl/ *noun* (*phonetics*) a speech sound made with the lips, for example /m/, /p/ and /v/ in *me, pea* and *very* ▶ **la·bial** *adj.*

la·bio·den·tal /ˌleɪbiəʊˈdentl; *NAmE* -bioʊ-/ *noun* (*phonetics*) a speech sound made by placing the top teeth against the bottom lip, for example /f/ and /v/ in *fan* and *van* ▶ **la·bio·den·tal** *adj.*

la·bio·velar /ˌleɪbiəʊˈviːlə(r); *NAmE* -bioʊ-/ *noun* (*phonetics*) a speech sound made using the lips and soft PALATE, for example /w/ in *we* ▶ **la·bio·velar** *adj.*

labor AW (*especially US*) = LABOUR

la·bora·tory 0➛ /ləˈbɒrətri; *NAmE* ˈlæbrətɔːri/ *noun* (*pl.* -ies) (also *informal* **lab**) a room or building used for scientific research, experiments, testing, etc: *a research laboratory* ◇ ***laboratory experiments/tests*** ➲ see also LANGUAGE LABORATORY

ˈ**Labor Day** *noun* a public holiday in the US and Canada on the first Monday of September, in honour of working people ➲ compare MAY DAY

Synonyms

label

tag • sticker

These are all words for a piece of paper, fabric or plastic that is attached to sth and gives information about it.

label a small piece of paper, fabric or plastic that is attached to sth in order to show what it is or give information about it: *The washing instructions are on the label.* ◇ *address labels* ◇ *He'll only wear clothes with a* ***designer label.***

tag (often used in compounds) a small piece of paper, fabric or plastic that is attached to sth, or that sb wears, in order to give information about it/them: *Everyone at the conference had to wear a name tag.*

LABEL OR TAG?

Labels in clothes are usually made of fabric and sewn in. **Tags** on clothes are usually made of cardboard and cut off before you wear the clothes. A *name tag* can be stuck or tied onto sb to show who they are: *All babies in the hospital have name tags tied round their ankles.*

Price tag is much more frequent than *price label* and is used for both literal and figurative meanings: *What does the price tag say?* ◇ *There is a £20 million price tag on the team's star player.* A **label** can also be a **sticker** that you put on an envelope.

sticker a sticky label with a picture or message on it, that you stick on to sth.

PATTERNS

- a **price** label/tag/sticker
- to **have** a label/tag/sticker
- to **attach/put on/stick on** a label/tag/sticker
- The label/tag/sticker **says...**

la·bored, la·bor·er, la·bor·ing (*especially US*) = LABOURED, LABOURER, LABOURING

la·bori·ous /ləˈbɔːriəs/ *adj.* taking a lot of time and effort SYN **onerous, taxing**: *a* ***laborious task/process*** ◇ *Checking all the information will be slow and laborious.* ▶ **la·bori·ous·ly** *adv.*

ˈ**labor union** *noun* (*NAmE*) = UNION

la·bour 0➛ AW (*especially US* **labor**) /ˈleɪbə(r)/ *noun, verb*

■ ***noun***

▸ WORK **1** 0➛ [U] work, especially physical work: ***manual labour*** (= work using your hands) ◇ *The price will include the labour and materials.* ◇ *The company wants to keep down* ***labour costs.*** ◇ *The workers voted to* ***withdraw their labour*** (= to stop work as a means of protest). ◇ *He was sentenced to two years in a* ***labour camp*** (= a type of prison where people have to do hard physical work). **2** [C, usually pl.] (*formal*) a task or period of work: *He was so exhausted from the day's labours that he went straight to bed.*

▸ PEOPLE WHO WORK **3** 0➛ [U] the people who work or are available for work in a country or company: *a shortage of labour* ◇ *Employers are using immigrants as* ***cheap labour.*** ◇ *Repairs involve* ***skilled labour,*** *which can be expensive.* ◇ *good* ***labour relations*** (= the relationship between workers and employers)

▸ HAVING BABY **4** [U, C, usually sing.] the period of time or the process of giving birth to a baby: *Jane was* ***in labour*** *for ten hours.* ◇ *She* ***went into labour*** *early.* ◇ *labour pains*

▸ POLITICS **5** **Labour** [sing.+ sing./pl. v.] (*abbr.* **Lab.**) the British Labour Party: *He always votes Labour.* ◇ *Labour was/were in power for many years.*

IDM **a ˌlabour of ˈlove** a hard task that you do because you want to, not because it is necessary

■ *verb*

▸ STRUGGLE **1** [I] to try very hard to do sth difficult: **~ (away)** *He was in his study labouring away over some old papers.* ◇ **~ to do sth** *They laboured for years to clear their son's name.*

▸ WORK HARD **2** [I] to do hard physical work: *We laboured all day in the fields.* ◇ (*old-fashioned*) *the labouring classes* (= the working class)

▸ MOVE WITH DIFFICULTY **3** [I] (**+ adv./prep.**) to move with difficulty and effort SYN **struggle**: *The horses laboured up the steep slope.*

IDM **labour the ˈpoint** to continue to repeat or explain sth that has already been said and understood

PHR V **ˈlabour under sth** (*formal*) to believe sth that is not true: *to* ***labour under a misapprehension/delusion, etc.*** ◇ *He's still labouring under the impression that he's written a great book.*

la·boured (*especially US* **la·bored**) /ˈleɪbəd; *NAmE* -bərd/ *adj.* **1** (of breathing) slow and taking a lot of effort **2** (of writing, speaking, etc.) not natural and seeming to take a lot of effort

la·bour·er (*especially US* **la·bor·er**) /ˈleɪbərə(r)/ *noun* a person whose job involves hard physical work that is not skilled, especially work that is done outdoors

ˈlabour force (*especially US* **ˈlabor force**) *noun* [C+sing./pl. v.] all the people who work for a company or in a country SYN **workforce**: *a skilled/an unskilled labour force*

la·bour·ing (*especially US* **la·bor·ing**) /ˈleɪbərɪŋ/ *noun* [U] hard physical work that is not skilled: *a labouring job*

ˌlabour-inˈtensive (*especially US* **ˌlabor-inˈtensive**) *adj.* (of work) needing a lot of people to do it: *labour-intensive methods* ➲ compare CAPITAL-INTENSIVE

ˈlabour market (*especially US* **ˈlabor market**) *noun* the number of people who are available for work in relation to the number of jobs available: *young people about to enter the labour market*

the ˈLabour Party (also **Labour**) *noun* [sing.+ sing./pl. v.] one of the main British political parties, on the political left, that has traditionally represented the interests of working people: *the Labour Party leader*

ˈlabour-saving (*especially US* **ˈlabor-saving**) *adj.* [usually before noun] designed to reduce the amount of work or effort needed to do sth: *modern labour-saving devices such as washing machines and dishwashers*

Lab·ra·dor /ˈlæbrədɔː(r)/ *noun* a large dog that can be yellow, black or brown in colour, often used by blind people as a guide: *a* ***golden/black/chocolate Labrador***

la·bur·num /ləˈbɜːnəm; *NAmE* -ˈbɜːrn-/ *noun* [C, U] a small tree with hanging bunches of yellow flowers

laby·rinth /ˈlæbərɪnθ/ *noun* (*formal*) a complicated series of paths, which it is difficult to find your way through: *We lost our way in the labyrinth of streets.* ◇ (*figurative*) *a labyrinth of rules and regulations* ➲ compare MAZE ▸ **laby·rin·thine** /ˌlæbəˈrɪnθaɪn; *NAmE* also -θɪn/ *adj.*: (*formal*) *labyrinthine corridors* ◇ *labyrinthine legislation*

lace /leɪs/ *noun, verb*

■ *noun* **1** [U] a delicate material made from threads of cotton, silk, etc. that are twisted into a pattern of holes: *a lace handkerchief* ◇ *a tablecloth edged with lace* ◇ *lace curtains* ➲ see also LACY **2** [C] = SHOELACE: *Your laces are undone.* ➲ VISUAL VOCAB page V51

■ *verb* **1** [I, T] to be fastened with laces; to fasten sth with laces: **~ (up)** *She was wearing a dress that laced up at the side.* ◇ **~ sth (up)** *He was sitting on the bed lacing up his shoes.* ➲ see also LACE-UP **2** [T] **~ sth** to put a lace through the holes in a shoe, a boot, etc. ➲ related noun LACE-UP **3** [T] **~ sth (with sth)** to add a small amount of alcohol, a drug, poison, etc. to a drink SYN **spike**: *He had laced her milk with rum.* **4** [T] **~ sth (with sth)** to add a particular quality to a book, speech, etc: *Her conversation was laced with witty asides.* **5** [T] **~ sth** to twist sth together with another thing: *They sat with their fingers laced.*

la·cer·ate /ˈlæsəreɪt/ *verb* (*formal*) **1 ~ sth** to cut skin or flesh with sth sharp: *His hand had been badly lacerated.* **2 ~ sb** to criticize sb very severely ▸ **la·cer·ation** /ˌlæsəˈreɪʃn/ *noun* [C, U]: *She suffered multiple lacerations to the face.*

ˈlace-up *noun* [usually pl.] (*especially BrE*) a shoe that is fastened with laces: *a pair of lace-ups* ◇ *lace-up boots* ➲ compare OXFORD ➲ VISUAL VOCAB page V52

lace·wing /ˈleɪswɪŋ/ *noun* an insect that has large transparent wings with lines on

lach·ry·mose /ˈlækrɪməʊs; *NAmE* -moʊs/ *adj.* (*formal*) having a tendency to cry easily SYN **tearful**

lack 🔑 /læk/ *noun, verb*

■ *noun* 🔑 [U, sing.] **~ (of sth)** the state of not having sth or not having enough of sth SYN **dearth, shortage**: *a lack of food/money/skills* ◇ *The trip was cancelled* ***through lack of*** (= because there was not enough) *interest.* ◇ *There was* ***no lack of*** *volunteers.* IDM see TRY *v.*

■ *verb* 🔑 [no passive] **~ sth** to have none or not enough of sth: *Some houses still lack basic amenities such as bathrooms.* ◇ *He lacks confidence.* ◇ *She has the determination that her brother lacks.* ➲ see also LACKING

IDM **ˌlack (for) ˈnothing** (*formal*) to have everything that you need ➲ more at COURAGE

lacka·dai·si·cal /ˌlækəˈdeɪzɪkl/ *adj.* not showing enough care or enthusiasm

lackey /ˈlæki/ *noun* **1** (*old-fashioned*) a servant **2** (*disapproving*) a person who is treated like a servant or who behaves like one

lack·ing 🔑 /ˈlækɪŋ/ *adj.* [not before noun]
1 🔑 **~ (in sth)** having none or not enough of sth: *She's not usually lacking in confidence.* ◇ *The book is completely lacking in originality.* ◇ *He was taken on as a teacher but was* ***found lacking*** (= was thought not to be good enough). **2** 🔑 not present or not available SYN **missing**: *I feel there is something lacking in my life.*

lack·lustre (*especially US* **lack·lus·ter**) /ˈlæklʌstə(r)/ *adj.* not interesting or exciting; dull: *a lacklustre performance* ◇ *lacklustre hair*

la·con·ic /ləˈkɒnɪk; *NAmE* -ˈkɑːn-/ *adj.* using only a few words to say sth ▸ **la·con·ic·al·ly** /-kli/ *adv.*

lac·quer /ˈlækə(r)/ *noun, verb*

■ *noun* [U] **1** a liquid that is used on wood or metal to give it a hard shiny surface **2** (*old-fashioned*) a liquid that is sprayed on the hair so that it stays in place SYN **hairspray**

■ *verb* **1 ~ sth** to cover sth such as wood or metal with lacquer **2 ~ sth** (*old-fashioned, BrE*) to put lacquer on your hair

la·crosse /ləˈkrɒs; *NAmE* -ˈkrɔːs; -ˈkrɑːs/ *noun* [U] a game played on a field by two teams of ten players who use sticks with curved nets on them to catch, carry, and throw the ball

lac·tate /lækˈteɪt/ *verb* [I] (*technical*) (of a woman or female animal) to produce milk from the breasts to feed a baby or young animal ▸ **lac·ta·tion** /lækˈteɪʃn/ *noun* [U]: *the period of lactation*

lac·tic acid /ˌlæktɪk ˈæsɪd/ *noun* [U] an acid that forms in sour milk and is also produced in the muscles during hard exercise

lacto·ba·cil·lus /ˌlæktəʊbəˈsɪləs; *NAmE* -toʊ-/ *noun* (*biology*) a type of bacteria that produces lactic acid

lac·tose /ˈlæktəʊs; -təʊz; *NAmE* -toʊs; -toʊz/ *noun* [U] (*chemistry*) a type of sugar found in milk and used in some baby foods

la·cuna /ləˈkjuːnə; *NAmE* also -ˈkuː-/ *noun* (*pl.* **-nae** /-niː/ or **la·cu·nas**) (*formal*) a place where sth is missing in a piece of writing or in an idea, a theory, etc. SYN **gap**

lacy /ˈleɪsi/ *adj.* made of or looking like LACE: *lacy underwear*

lad /læd/ *noun* **1** [C] (*old-fashioned* or *informal, BrE*) a boy or young man: *Things have changed since I was a lad.* ◇ *He's a nice lad.* ➲ compare LASS **2 the lads** [pl.] (*BrE, informal*) a group of friends that a man works with or spends free time with: *to go to the pub with the lads* **3** [C, usually sing.] (*BrE, informal*) a lively young man, especially one who is very interested in women and having sex, drinks a lot of alcohol and enjoys sport: *Tony was **a bit of a lad**—always had an eye for the women.* ➲ see also LADDISH **4** [C] (*BrE*) a person who works in a stable ➲ see also STABLE BOY

lad·der /ˈlædə(r)/ *noun, verb*

■ ***noun*** **1** a piece of equipment for climbing up and down a wall, the side of a building, etc, consisting of two lengths of wood or metal that are joined together by steps or RUNGS: *to **climb up/fall off a ladder*** ➲ VISUAL VOCAB page V17 ➲ see also STEPLADDER **2** [usually sing.] a series of stages by which you can make progress in your life or career: *to move up or down the **social ladder** ◇ the **career ladder** ◇ (BrE) to get onto the **property ladder*** (= buy your first home) **3** (*BrE*) (*NAmE* **run**) a long thin hole in TIGHTS or STOCKINGS where some threads have broken **4** (also ˈ**ladder tournament**) a competition in a particular sport or game in which teams or players are arranged in a list and they can move up the list by defeating one of the teams or players above

■ ***verb*** [I, T] **~ (sth)** (*BrE*) if TIGHTS or STOCKINGS **ladder** or you **ladder** them, a long thin hole appears in them

lad·die /ˈlædi/ *noun* (*informal, especially ScotE*) a boy ➲ compare LASS

lad·dish /ˈlædɪʃ/ *adj.* (*informal*) behaving in a way that is supposed to be typical of a young man

laden /ˈleɪdn/ *adj.* **~ (with sth) 1** heavily loaded with sth: *passengers laden with luggage ◇ The trees were laden with apples. ◇ a **heavily/fully laden** truck* ➲ compare UNLADEN **2** (*literary*) full of sth, especially sth unpleasant: *His voice was soft, yet laden with threat.* **3 -laden** used to form adjectives showing that sth is full of, or loaded with, the thing mentioned: *calorie-laden cream cakes*

lad·ette /lædˈet/ *noun* (*BrE, informal*) a young woman who enjoys drinking alcohol, sport or other activities usually considered to be typical of young men

la-di-da (also **lah-di-da**) /ˌlɑː di ˈdɑː/ *adj., exclamation*

■ ***adj.*** (*informal, especially BrE*) used to describe a way of speaking or behaving that is typical of upper-class people but that is not natural or sincere SYN **affected**

■ ***exclamation*** used when sb is irritating you, because they seem to think they are more important then they really are

ˈ**ladies' man** (also ˈ**lady's man**) *noun* a man who enjoys spending time with women and thinks he is attractive to them

ladle /ˈleɪdl/ *noun, verb*

■ ***noun*** a large deep spoon with a long handle, used especially for serving soup ➲ VISUAL VOCAB page V23

■ ***verb* ~ sth** to place food on a plate with a large spoon or in large quantities

PHR V ˌ**ladle sth**↔ˈ**out** (sometimes *disapproving*) to give sb a lot of sth, especially money or advice SYN **dole sth out**

la dolce vita /lɑː ˌdɒltʃeɪ ˈviːtə; *NAmE* ˌdoul-/ *noun* [sing.] (from *Italian*) a life of pleasure and expensive things, without any worries

lady 🔑 /ˈleɪdi/ (*pl.* -ies) *noun*

1 🔑 [C] a word used to mean 'woman' that some people, especially older people, consider is more polite: *There's a lady waiting to see you. ◇ He was with an attractive young lady. ◇ the ladies' golf championship ◇ (BrE) a tea lady* (= a woman who serves tea in an office) ◇ (*NAmE, approving*) *She's a tough lady. ◇ a lady doctor/golfer* HELP Some women object to the way **lady** is used in some of these examples and prefer it to be avoided if possible: *a doctor/ a woman doctor ◇ There's someone waiting to see you.* ➲ see also BAG LADY, CLEANING LADY, DINNER LADY, FIRST LADY, LEADING LADY, LUNCH LADY, OLD LADY **2** 🔑 [C] a woman who is polite and well educated, has excellent manners and always behaves well: *His wife was a real lady.* ➲ compare GENTLEMAN **3** 🔑 [C, usually pl.] (*formal*) used when speaking to or about a girl or woman, especially sb you do not know: *Can I take your coats, ladies? ◇ Could I have your attention, **ladies and gentlemen**?* HELP Some women do not like **ladies** used on its own, as in the first example, and prefer it to be left out. **4** [sing.] (*especially NAmE*) an informal way to talk to a woman, showing a lack of respect: *Listen, lady, don't shout at me.* **5** [C] (*old-fashioned*) (in Britain) a woman belonging to a high social class: *the lords and ladies of the court ◇ a lady's maid* **6 Lady** [C] (in Britain) a title used by a woman who is a member of the NOBILITY, or by sb who has been given the title 'lady' as an honour. The wives and daughters of some members of the NOBILITY and the wives of KNIGHTS are also called 'Lady': *Lady Howe ◇ Lady Jane Grey* ➲ compare LORD, SIR **7 a/the ladies** [U] (*BrE*) (*NAmE* ˈ**ladies' room** [C]) a toilet/bathroom for women in a public building or place: *Could you tell me where the ladies is?* **8 Our Lady** a title used to refer to Mary, the mother of Christ, especially in the Roman Catholic Church: *Our Lady of Lourdes* IDM see FAT *adj.*, LEISURE

lady·bird /ˈleɪdibɜːd; *NAmE* -bɜːrd/ (*BrE*) (*NAmE* **lady·bug** /ˈleɪdibʌg/) *noun* a small flying insect, usually red with black spots ➲ VISUAL VOCAB page V11

lady·boy /ˈleɪdibɔɪ/ *noun* (*informal*) a TRANSVESTITE or TRANSSEXUAL

lady·finger /ˈleɪdifɪŋgə(r)/ *noun* (*NAmE*) a small long thin cake made with eggs, sugar and flour

ˌ**lady-in-ˈwaiting** *noun* (*pl.* **ladies-in-waiting**) a woman who goes to places with, and helps, a queen or princess

lady·kill·er /ˈleɪdikɪlə(r)/ *noun* (*old-fashioned* or *informal*) a man who is sexually attractive and successful with women, but who does not stay in a relationship with anyone for long

lady·like /ˈleɪdilaɪk/ *adj.* (*old-fashioned*) polite and quiet; typical of what is supposed to be socially acceptable for a woman SYN **refined**: *ladylike behaviour ◇ Her language was not very ladylike.*

ˌ**lady ˈmayor** *noun* = MAYORESS

lady·ship /ˈleɪdiʃɪp/ *noun* **1 Her/Your Ladyship** a title used when talking to or about a woman who is a member of the NOBILITY: *Does Your Ladyship require anything?* **2** (*BrE, informal*) a way of talking to or about a girl or woman that you think is trying to be too important: *Perhaps her ladyship would like to hang up her own clothes today!* ➲ compare LORDSHIP

ˈ**lady's man** *noun* = LADIES' MAN

lag /læg/ *verb, noun*

■ ***verb*** (-gg-) **1** [I] **~ (behind sb/sth)** | **~ (behind)** to move or develop slowly or more slowly than other people, organizations, etc. SYN **trail**: *The little boy lagged behind his parents. ◇ We still lag far behind many of our competitors in using modern technology.* **2** [T] **~ sth (with sth)** (*BrE*) to cover pipes, etc. with a special material to stop the water in them from freezing, or to save heat SYN **insulate**

■ ***noun*** = TIME LAG ➲ see also JET LAG, OLD LAG

lager /ˈlɑːgə(r)/ *noun* (*BrE*) **1** [U, C] a type of light pale beer that usually has a lot of bubbles: *a pint of lager ◇ German lagers* **2** [C] a glass, can or bottle of this

ˈ**lager lout** *noun* (*BrE*) a young man who drinks too much alcohol and then behaves in a noisy and unpleasant way

lag·gard /ˈlægəd; *NAmE* -gərd/ *noun* (*old-fashioned*) a slow and lazy person, organization, etc.

la·goon /ləˈguːn/ *noun* **1** a lake of salt water that is separated from the sea by a REEF or an area of rock or sand ➲ VISUAL VOCAB page V4 **2** (*NAmE*) a small area of fresh water near a lake or river **3** (*technical*) an artificial area built to hold waste water before it is treated at a SEWAGE WORKS

lah (also **la**) /lɑː/ *noun* (*music*) the 6th note of a MAJOR SCALE

lah-di-dah = LA-DI-DA

laid *past tense, past part.* of LAY

ˌ**laid-ˈback** *adj.* (*informal*) calm and relaxed; seeming not to worry about anything SYN **easy-going**: *a laid-back attitude to life*

lain *past part.* of LIE[1]

lair /leə(r); *NAmE* ler/ *noun* [usually sing.] **1** a place where a wild animal sleeps or hides **2** a place where sb goes to hide or to be alone SYN **den, hideout**

laird /leəd; *NAmE* lerd/ *noun* (in Scotland) a person who owns a large area of land

lairy /'leəri; *NAmE* 'leri/ *adj.* (*BrE, informal*) behaving in a way that seems too loud and confident

laissez-faire /ˌleseɪ 'feə(r); *NAmE* 'fer/ *noun* [U] (from *French*) the policy of allowing private businesses to develop without government control ▸ **laissez-faire** *adj.*: *a laissez-faire economy* ◇ *They have a laissez-faire approach to bringing up their children* (= they give them a lot of freedom).

laity /'leɪəti/ *noun* **the laity** [sing.+ sing./pl. v.] all the members of a Church who are not CLERGY ➲ see also LAYMAN

lake 🔑 /leɪk/ *noun* (*abbr.* L.) a large area of water that is surrounded by land: *We swam in the lake.* ◇ *Lake Ontario* ◇ (*figurative*) *a wine lake* (= a large supply of wine that is not being used) ➲ VISUAL VOCAB page V4

lake·side /'leɪksaɪd/ *noun* [sing.] the area around the edge of a lake: *We went for a walk by the lakeside.* ◇ *a lakeside hotel*

lakh /læk/ *noun* (*IndE*) a hundred thousand

la-la land /'lɑː lɑː lænd/ (also **cloud·land**) (both *NAmE*) (*BrE* ˌ**cloud** '**cuckoo land**) *noun* [U] (*informal, disapproving*) if you say that sb is living **in la-la land**, you mean that they do not understand what a situation is really like, but think it is much better than it is

lam /læm/ *noun, verb*

■ ***noun***

IDM **on the 'lam** (*NAmE, informal*) escaping from sb, especially from the police

■ ***verb*** (-mm-)

PHR V ˌ**lam 'into sb** (*BrE, informal*) to attack sb violently with blows or words: *She really lammed into her opponent during the debate.*

lama /'lɑːmə/ *noun* **1** a title given to a spiritual leader in Tibetan Buddhism **2** a Buddhist MONK from Tibet or Mongolia

Lama·ism /'lɑːməɪzəm/ *noun* [U] Tibetan Buddhism

lamb /læm/ *noun, verb*

■ ***noun*** **1** [C] a young sheep **2** [U] meat from a young sheep: *a leg of lamb* ◇ *lamb chops* ➲ compare MUTTON **3** [C] (*informal*) used to describe or address sb with affection or pity: *You poor lamb!*

IDM **(like) a lamb/lambs to the 'slaughter** used to describe people who are going to do sth dangerous without realizing it ➲ more at MUTTON, WELL *adv.*

■ ***verb*** [I] (of a sheep) to give birth to a lamb

lam·bada /læm'bɑːdə/ *noun* a fast Brazilian dance performed by couples who hold each other closely

lam·baste (also **lam·bast**) /læm'beɪst/ *verb* **~ sb/sth** (*formal*) to attack or criticize sb/sth very severely, especially in public SYN **lay into**

lambda /'læmdə/ *noun* the 11th letter of the Greek alphabet (Λ, λ)

lambs·wool /'læmzwʊl/ *noun* [U] soft fine wool from lambs, used for knitting clothes: *a lambswool sweater*

lame /leɪm/ *adj.* **1** (of people or animals) unable to walk well because of an injury to the leg or foot **2** (of an excuse, explanation, etc.) weak and difficult to believe SYN **feeble, unconvincing** ▸ **lame·ness** *noun* [U]: *The disease has left her with permanent lameness.*

lamé /'lɑːmeɪ; *NAmE* lɑː'meɪ/ *noun* [U] a type of cloth into which gold or silver thread has been twisted

lame·brain /'leɪmbreɪn/ *noun* (*informal, especially NAmE*) a stupid person ▸ **lame·brain** (also **lame·brained**) *adj.*: *They invented some lamebrain scheme to get rich quick.*

ˌ**lame 'duck** *noun* **1** a person or an organization that is not very successful and that needs help **2** (*US, informal*) a politician or government whose period of office will soon end and who will not be elected again: *a **lame-duck president/administration***

lame·ly /'leɪmli/ *adv.* in a way that does not sound very confident, or that does not persuade other people SYN **feebly**: *'I must have made a mistake,' she said lamely.*

lam·ent /lə'ment/ *verb, noun*

■ ***verb* ~ sth | ~ that... | + speech** (*formal*) to feel or express great sadness or disappointment about sb/sth SYN **bemoan, bewail**: *In the poem he laments the destruction of the countryside.*

■ ***noun*** (*formal*) a song, poem or other expression of great sadness for sb who has died or for sth that has ended

lam·ent·able /'læməntəbl; lə'ment-/ *adj.* (*formal*) very disappointing SYN **deplorable, regrettable**: *She shows a lamentable lack of understanding.* ▸ **lam·ent·ably** /-əbli/ *adv.*

lam·en·ta·tion /ˌlæmən'teɪʃn/ *noun* [C, U] (*formal*) an expression of great sadness or disappointment

lam·ented /lə'mentɪd/ *adj.* (*formal* or *humorous*) (of sb/sth that has died or disappeared) missed very much: *her late lamented husband* ◇ *the last edition of the much lamented newspaper*

lamin·ate /'læmɪnət/ *noun* [U, C] a material that is laminated

lamin·ated /'læmɪneɪtɪd/ *adj.* **1** (of wood, plastic, etc.) made by sticking several thin layers together **2** covered with thin transparent plastic for protection: *laminated membership cards*

lam·ing·ton /'læmɪŋtən/ *noun* (*AustralE, NZE*) a square piece of SPONGE cake that has been put in liquid chocolate and covered with small pieces of COCONUT

lamp 🔑 /læmp/ *noun, verb*

■ ***noun*** **1** 🔑 a device that uses electricity, oil or gas to produce light: *a **table/desk/bicycle, etc. lamp*** ◇ *to **switch on/turn off a lamp*** ◇ *a **street lamp*** ➲ VISUAL VOCAB pages V18, V56 ➲ see also FOG LAMP, HURRICANE LAMP, LAVA LAMP, STANDARD LAMP **2** an electrical device that produces RAYS of heat and that is used for medical or scientific purposes: *an **infra-red/ultraviolet lamp*** ➲ see also BLOWLAMP, SUNLAMP

■ ***verb*** (*BrE, informal*) to hit sb very hard: **~ sb** *The guy lamped me.* ◇ **~ sb sth** *I'd have lamped her one!*

lamp·light /'læmplaɪt/ *noun* [U] light from a lamp

lamp·lit /'læmplɪt/ *adj.* [usually before noun] given light by lamps; seen by the light from lamps: *a lamplit room* ◇ *a lamplit figure in the chair*

lam·poon /læm'puːn/ *verb, noun*

■ ***verb* ~ sb/sth** to criticize sb/sth publicly in an amusing way that makes them or it look ridiculous SYN **satirize**: *His cartoons mercilessly lampooned the politicians of his time.*

■ ***noun*** a piece of writing that criticizes sb/sth and makes them or it look ridiculous

'**lamp post** *noun* (*especially BrE*) a tall post in the street with a lamp at the top: *The car skidded and hit a lamp post.* ➲ compare STREET LIGHT ➲ VISUAL VOCAB page V2

lam·prey /'læmpri/ *noun* a FRESHWATER fish with a round mouth that attaches itself to other fish and sucks their blood

lamp·shade /'læmpʃeɪd/ *noun* a decorative cover for a lamp that is used to make the light softer or to direct it ➲ VISUAL VOCAB page V18

LAN /læn/ *noun* (*computing*) the abbreviation for 'local area network' (a system for communicating by computer within a large building or group of buildings) ➲ compare WAN

lance /lɑːns; *NAmE* læns/ *noun, verb*

■ ***noun*** a weapon with a long wooden handle and a pointed metal end that was used by people fighting on horses in the past

■ ***verb*** **1** [T] **~ sth** to cut open an infected place on sb's body with a sharp knife in order to let out the PUS (= a yellow substance produced by infection): *to lance an abscess* **2** [I] **+ adv./prep.** (of a pain) to move suddenly and quickly and be very sharp: *Pain lanced through his body.*

ˌlance ˈcorporal *noun* a member of one of the lower ranks in the British army: *Lance Corporal Alan Smith*

lan·cer /ˈlɑːnsə(r); *NAmE* ˈlæn-/ *noun* in the past, a member of a REGIMENT that used LANCES

lan·cet /ˈlɑːnsɪt; *NAmE* ˈlæn-/ *noun* a knife with a sharp point and two sharp edges, used by doctors for cutting skin and flesh

land 🔑 /lænd/ *noun, verb*

■ ***noun***

▸ SURFACE OF EARTH **1** 🔑 [U] the surface of the earth that is not sea: *It was good to be back* ***on land.*** ◇ *We made the journey* ***by land,*** *though flying would have been cheaper.* ◇ *In the distance the crew sighted land.* ◇ *The elephant is the largest living land animal.* ➲ SYNONYMS at FLOOR, SOIL ➲ see also DRY LAND

▸ AREA OF GROUND **2** 🔑 [U] (also **lands** [pl.]) an area of ground, especially of a particular type or used for a particular purpose SYN **terrain:** ***fertile/arid/stony, etc. land*** ◇ ***flat/undulating/hilly, etc. land*** ◇ ***agricultural/arable/industrial, etc. land*** ◇ *The land was very dry and hard after the long, hot summer.* ◇ *The land rose to the east.* ◇ *a piece of* ***waste/derelict land*** ◇ *Some of the country's richest grazing lands are in these valleys.* **3** 🔑 [U] (also *formal* **lands** [pl.]) the area of ground that sb owns, especially when you think of it as property that can be bought or sold: *The price of land is rising rapidly.* ◇ *During the war their lands were occupied by the enemy.* ➲ see also NO-MAN'S-LAND

▸ COUNTRYSIDE **4 the land** [U] used to refer to the countryside and the way people live in the country as opposed to in cities: *At the beginning of the 20th century almost a third of the population* ***lived off the land*** (= grew or produced their own food). ◇ *Many people leave the land to find work in towns and cities.* ➲ SYNONYMS at COUNTRY

▸ COUNTRY/REGION **5** [C] (*literary*) used to refer to a country or region in a way which appeals to the emotions or the imagination: *She longed to return to her* ***native land.*** ◇ *They dreamed of travelling to* ***foreign lands.*** ◇ *America is the land of freedom and opportunity.* ➲ see also CLOUD CUCKOO LAND, CLUBLAND, DOCKLAND, DREAMLAND, FAIRYLAND, NEVER-NEVER LAND, THE PROMISED LAND, WONDERLAND HELP There are many other compounds ending in **land.** You will find them at their place in the alphabet.

IDM **in the land of the ˈliving** (often *humorous*) awake or alive or no longer ill/sick **the land of ˌmilk and ˈhoney** a place where life is pleasant and easy and people are very happy **in the ˌland of ˈNod** (*old-fashioned, humorous*) asleep: *Pete and Jo were still in the land of Nod, so I went out for a walk in the morning sunshine.* **see, etc. how the ˈland lies** (*BrE*) to find out about a situation: *Let's wait and see how the land lies before we do anything.* ➲ more at LIE *n.*, LIVE[1], SPY *v.*

■ ***verb***

▸ OF BIRD/PLANE/INSECT **1** 🔑 [I] to come down through the air onto the ground or another surface: *The plane landed safely.* ◇ *A fly landed on his nose.* OPP **take off**

▸ OF PILOT **2** 🔑 [T] **~ sth** to bring a plane down to the ground in a controlled way: *The pilot landed the plane safely.*

▸ ARRIVE IN PLANE/BOAT **3** 🔑 [I] to arrive somewhere in a plane or a boat: *We shall be landing shortly. Please fasten your seatbelts.* ◇ *The troops landed at dawn.* ◇ *They were the first men to land on the moon.* ◇ *The ferry is due to land at 3 o'clock.* **4** [T] **~ sb/sth** to put sb/sth on land from an aircraft, a boat, etc: *The troops were landed by helicopter.*

▸ FALL TO GROUND **5** 🔑 [I] to come down to the ground after jumping, falling or being thrown: *I fell and landed heavily at the bottom of the stairs.* ◇ *A large stone landed right beside him.*

▸ DIFFICULTIES **6** [I] **+ adv./prep.** to arrive somewhere and cause difficulties that have to be dealt with: *Why do complaints always* ***land on my desk*** (= why do I always have to deal with them)*?*

▸ JOB **7** [T] (*informal*) to succeed in getting a job, etc, especially one that a lot of other people want: **~ sth** *He's just landed a starring role in Spielberg's next movie.* ◇ **~ sb/yourself sth** *She's just landed herself a company directorship.*

▸ FISH **8** [T] **~ sth** to catch a fish and bring it out of the water on to the land

IDM **land a ˈblow, ˈpunch, etc.** to succeed in hitting sb/sth: *She landed a punch on his chin.* ➲ more at FOOT *n.*

PHR V **ˈland in sth | ˈland sb/yourself in sth** (*informal*) to get sb/yourself into a difficult situation: *She was arrested and landed in court.* ◇ *His hot temper has landed him in trouble before.* ◇ *Now you've really* ***landed me in it!*** (= got me into trouble) **ˌland ˈup in, at...** (*informal*) to reach a final position or situation, sometimes after other things have happened SYN **end up**: *We travelled around for a while and landed up in Seattle.* ◇ *He landed up in a ditch after he lost control of his car.* **ˈland sb/yourself with sth/sb** (*informal*) to give sb/yourself sth unpleasant to do, especially because nobody else wants to do it: *As usual, I got landed with all the boring jobs.*

Synonyms

land

lot • ground • space • plot

These words all mean an area of land that is used for a particular purpose.

- **land** an area of ground, especially one that is used for a particular purpose: *agricultural land*
- **lot** (*NAmE*) a piece of land that is used or intended for a particular purpose: *building lots* ◇ *a parking lot*
- **ground** an area of land that is used for a particular purpose : *The kids were playing on waste ground near the school.* ◇ *the site of an ancient burial ground*

LAND, LOT OR GROUND?

Land is used for large areas of open land in the country, especially when it is used for farming. A **lot** is often a smaller piece of land in a town or city, especially one intended for building or parking on. **Ground** is any area of open land; a **ground** is an area of land designed or used for a particular purpose or activity.

- **space** a large area of land that has no buildings on it: *The city has plenty of open space.* ◇ *the* ***wide open spaces*** *of the Canadian prairies*
- **plot** a small piece of land used or intended for a particular purpose: *She bought a small* ***plot of land*** *to build a house.* ◇ *a vegetable plot*

LOT OR PLOT?

Either a **lot** or a **plot** can be used for building on. Only a **plot** can also be used for growing vegetables or burying people.

PATTERNS

- an **open** space
- **open/empty/vacant/waste/derelict** land/ground
- a/an **empty/vacant** lot/plot

ˈland agent *noun* (*especially BrE*) a person whose job is to manage land, farms, etc. for sb else

lan·dau /ˈlændɔː; -aʊ/ *noun* a CARRIAGE with four wheels and a roof that folds down in two sections, that is pulled by horses

ˈland-based *adj.* [usually before noun] located on or living on the land: *land-based missiles* ◇ *land-based animals*

land·ed /ˈlændɪd/ *adj.* [only before noun] **1** owning a lot of land: *the landed gentry* **2** including a large amount of land: *landed estates*

ˌlanded ˈimmigrant *noun* (*CanE*) a person from another country who has permission to live permanently in Canada

land·fall /ˈlændfɔːl/ *noun* **1** [U, C] (*literary*) the land that you see or arrive at first after a journey by sea or by air: *After three weeks they* ***made landfall*** *on the coast of Ireland.* **2** [C] = LANDSLIDE

land·fill /ˈlændfɪl/ *noun* **1** [C, U] an area of land where large amounts of waste material are buried under the earth: *The map shows the position of the new landfills.* ◇ *a landfill site* ➲ VISUAL VOCAB page V6 **2** [U] the process of burying large amounts of waste material: *the choice of landfill or incineration* **3** [U] waste material that will be buried

land·form /ˈlændfɔːm; *NAmE* -fɔːrm/ *noun* (*geology*) a natural feature of the earth's surface

land·hold·ing /ˈlændhəʊldɪŋ; *NAmE* -hoʊld-/ *noun* [C, U] (*technical*) a piece of land that sb owns or rents; the fact of owning or renting land ▸ **land·hold·er** *noun*: *farmers and landholders*

land·ing /ˈlændɪŋ/ *noun* **1** [C] the area at the top of a set of stairs where you arrive before you go into an upstairs room or move onto another set of stairs ➲ picture at STAIRCASE **2** [C, U] an act of bringing an aircraft or a SPACECRAFT down to the ground after a journey: *a perfect/smooth/safe landing* ◇ *the first Apollo* ***moon landing*** ◇ *The pilot was forced to make* ***an emergency landing.*** ◇ *a landing site* OPP **take-off** ➲ see also CRASH LANDING **3** [C] an act of bringing soldiers to land in an area that is controlled by the enemy **4** (*BrE* also ˈ**landing stage**) [C] a flat wooden platform on the water where boats let people get on and off, and load and unload goods SYN **jetty**

ˈ**landing craft** *noun* (*pl.* **landing craft**) a boat with a flat bottom, carried on a ship. Landing craft open at one end so soldiers and equipment can be brought to land.

L

ˈ**landing gear** *noun* [U] = UNDERCARRIAGE

ˈ**landing lights** *noun* [pl.] **1** bright lamps on a plane that are switched on before it lands **2** lights that are arranged along the sides of a RUNWAY to guide a pilot when he or she is landing a plane

ˈ**landing page** *noun* (*computing*) the part of a website that you reach first when you click on a link on the Internet: *Have a different landing page for each advertising campaign.*

ˈ**landing stage** (*BrE*) (also **landing** *NAmE, BrE*) *noun* a flat wooden platform on the water where boats let people get on and off, and load and unload goods SYN **jetty**

ˈ**landing strip** *noun* = AIRSTRIP

land·lady /ˈlændleɪdi/ *noun* (*pl.* -ies) **1** a woman from whom you rent a room, a house, etc. **2** (*BrE*) a woman who owns or manages a pub or a GUEST HOUSE SYN **proprietor** ➲ compare LANDLORD

land·less /ˈlændləs/ *adj.* [usually before noun] not owning land for farming; not allowed to own land

land·line /ˈlændlaɪn/ *noun* a telephone connection that uses wires carried on poles or under the ground, in contrast to a mobile/cell phone: *I'll call you later on the landline.* ➲ COLLOCATIONS at PHONE

land·locked /ˈlændlɒkt; *NAmE* -lɑːkt/ *adj.* almost or completely surrounded by land: *Switzerland is completely landlocked.*

land·lord /ˈlændlɔːd; *NAmE* -lɔːrd/ *noun* **1** a person or company from whom you rent a room, a house, an office, etc. **2** (*BrE*) a man who owns or manages a pub or a GUEST HOUSE SYN **proprietor** ➲ compare LANDLADY

land·lub·ber /ˈlændlʌbə(r)/ *noun* (*informal*) a person with not much knowledge or experience of the sea or sailing

land·mark /ˈlændmɑːk; *NAmE* -mɑːrk/ *noun* **1** something, such as a large building, that you can see clearly from a distance and that will help you to know where you are: *The Empire State Building is a familiar landmark on the New York skyline.* **2** ~ (**in sth**) an event, a discovery, an invention, etc. that marks an important stage in sth SYN **milestone**: *The ceasefire was seen as a major landmark in the fight against terrorism.* ◇ *a* ***landmark decision/ruling*** *in the courts* **3** (*especially NAmE*) a building or a place that is very important because of its history, and that should be preserved SYN **monument**

ˈ**land mass** *noun* (*technical*) a large area of land, for example a continent

land·mine /ˈlændmaɪn/ *noun* a bomb placed on or under the ground, which explodes when vehicles or people move over it

ˈ**land office** (*NAmE*) (*BrE* ˈ**land registry**) *noun* a government office that keeps a record of areas of land and who owns them

land·owner /ˈlændəʊnə(r); *NAmE* -oʊn-/ *noun* a person who owns land, especially a large area of land ▸ **land·owner·ship** (also **land·owning**) *noun* [U]: *private landownership* **land·owning** *adj.* [only before noun]: *the great landowning families*

ˈ**land reform** *noun* [U, C] the principle of dividing land for farming into smaller pieces so that more people can own some

ˈ**land registry** (*BrE*) (*NAmE* ˈ**land office**) *noun* a government office that keeps a record of areas of land and who owns them

ˈ**Land Rover™** (also ˈ**Land-Rover™**) *noun* a strong vehicle used for travelling over rough ground

land·scape 0‑w /ˈlændskeɪp/ *noun, verb*

■ ***noun*** **1** 0‑w [C, usually sing.] everything you can see when you look across a large area of land, especially in the country: *the* ***bleak/rugged/dramatic, etc. landscape*** *of the area* ◇ *the woods and fields that are typical features of the English landscape* ◇ *an* ***urban/industrial landscape*** ◇ (*figurative*) *We can expect changes in the* ***political landscape.*** ➲ SYNONYMS at COUNTRY **2** 0‑w [C, U] a painting of a view of the countryside; this style of painting: *an artist famous for his landscapes* ➲ COLLOCATIONS at ART ➲ compare TOWNSCAPE **3** [U] (*technical*) the way of printing a document in which the top of the page is one of the longer sides: *Select the landscape option when printing the file.* ➲ compare PORTRAIT IDM see BLOT *n.*

■ ***verb*** ~ **sth** to improve the appearance of an area of land by changing the design and planting trees, flowers, etc.

ˌ**landscape ˈarchitect** *noun* a person whose job is planning and designing the environment, especially so that roads, buildings, etc. combine with the landscape in an attractive way ▸ ˌ**landscape ˈarchitecture** *noun* [U]

ˌ**landscape ˈgardener** *noun* a person whose job is designing and creating attractive parks and gardens ▸ ˌ**landscape ˈgardening** *noun* [U]

ˌ**Land's ˈEnd** *noun* a place in Cornwall that is further west than any other place in England ➲ compare JOHN O'GROATS

land·slide /ˈlændslaɪd/ *noun* **1** (also **land·fall**) a mass of earth, rock, etc. that falls down the slope of a mountain or a CLIFF ➲ see also LANDSLIP **2** an election in which one person or party gets very many more votes than the other people or parties: *She was expected to win* ***by a landslide.*** ◇ *a landslide victory* ➲ COLLOCATIONS at VOTE

land·slip /ˈlændslɪp/ *noun* a mass of rock and earth that falls down a slope, usually smaller than a landslide

land·ward /ˈlændwəd; *NAmE* -wərd/ *adj.* [only before noun] facing the land; away from the sea ▸ **land·ward** (also **land·wards**) *adv.*: *After an hour, the ship turned landward.*

ˈ**land yacht** *noun* **1** a small vehicle with a sail and no engine, that is used on land **2** (*NAmE, informal*) a large car

lane 0‑w /leɪn/ *noun*

1 0‑w a narrow road in the country: *winding country lanes* ◇ *We drove along a muddy lane to reach the farmhouse.* ➲ VISUAL VOCAB page V3 ➲ see also MEMORY LANE **2** 0‑w (especially in place names) a street, often a narrow one with buildings on both sides: *The quickest way is through the back lanes behind the bus station.* ◇ *Park Lane* **3** 0‑w a section of a wide road, that is marked by painted white lines, to keep lines of traffic separate: *the* ***inside/middle lane*** ◇ *the* ***northbound/southbound lane*** ◇ *to change lanes* ◇ *She signalled and pulled over into the slow lane.* ◇ *a four-lane highway* ➲ see also BUS LANE, CYCLE LANE, FAST LANE, OUTSIDE LANE, PASSING LANE **4** a narrow marked section of a track or a swimming pool that is used by one person taking part in a race: *The Australian in lane four is* *coming up fast from behind.* ➲ VISUAL VOCAB pages V34, V38 **5** a route used by ships or aircraft on regular journeys: *one of the world's busiest* ***shipping/sea lanes*** IDM see FAST LANE

lan·gous·tine /ˈlɒŋgʊstiːn; *NAmE* ˈlɑːŋ-/ (also ˌ**Norway** ˈ**lobster**, ˌ**Dublin Bay** ˈ**prawn**) *noun* a type of SHELLFISH like a small LOBSTER

lan·guage 🔑 /ˈlæŋgwɪdʒ/ *noun*
▸ OF A COUNTRY **1** 🔑 [C] the system of communication in speech and writing that is used by people of a particular country or area: *the Japanese language* ◇ *It takes a long time to learn to* ***speak a language*** *well.* ◇ *Italian is my* ***first language.*** ◇ *All the children must learn a* ***foreign language.*** ◇ *She* ***has a good command of the*** *Spanish* ***language.*** ◇ *a qualification in* ***language teaching*** ◇ *They fell in love in spite of* ***the language barrier*** (= the difficulty of communicating when people speak different languages). ◇ *Why study Latin? It's a* ***dead language*** (= no longer spoken by anyone). ◇ *Is English an* ***official language*** *in your country?* ➲ see also MODERN LANGUAGE
▸ COMMUNICATION **2** 🔑 [U] the use by humans of a system of sounds and words to communicate: *theories about the origins of language* ◇ *a study of* ***language acquisition*** *in two-year-olds*
▸ STYLE OF SPEAKING/WRITING **3** 🔑 [U] a particular style of speaking or writing: ***bad/foul/strong language*** (= words that people may consider offensive) ◇ ***literary/poetic language*** ◇ *the language of the legal profession* ◇ *Give your instructions in everyday language.* ➲ see also BAD LANGUAGE
▸ MOVEMENTS/SYMBOLS/SOUND **4** 🔑 [C, U] a way of expressing ideas and feelings using movements, symbols and sound: *the language of mime* ◇ *the* ***language of dolphins/bees*** ➲ see also BODY LANGUAGE, SIGN LANGUAGE
▸ COMPUTING **5** 🔑 [C, U] a system of symbols and rules that is used to operate a computer: *a programming language*
IDM **mind/watch your** ˈ**language** to be careful about what you say in order not to upset or offend sb: *Watch your language, young man!* **speak/talk the same** ˈ**language** to be able to communicate easily with another person because you share similar opinions and experience

Synonyms

language

vocabulary • terms • wording • terminology

These are all terms for the words and expressions people use when they speak or write, or for a particular style of speaking or writing.

language a particular style of speaking or writing: *Give your instructions in everyday language.* ◇ *the language of the legal profession*

vocabulary all the words that a person knows or uses, or all the words in a particular language; the words that people use when they are talking about a particular subject: *to have a wide/limited vocabulary* ◇ *The word has become part of advertising vocabulary.*

terms a way of expressing yourself or of saying sth: *I'll try to explain in simple terms.*

wording [usually sing.] the words that are used in a piece of writing or speech, especially when they have been carefully chosen: *It was the standard form of wording for a consent letter.*

terminology (*rather formal*) the set of technical words or expressions used in a particular subject; words used with particular meanings: *medical terminology* ◇ *Scientists are constantly developing new terminologies.* NOTE *Literary/poetic terminology* is used for talking about literature or poetry. *Literary/poetic language* is used for writing in a literary or poetic style.

PATTERNS
- **formal/informal/everyday** language/vocabulary/terms
- **business/scientific/technical/specialized** language/vocabulary/terminology
- A word **enters** the language/the vocabulary.

ˌ**language engiˈneering** *noun* [U] (*computing*) the use of computers to process languages for industrial purposes

ˈ**language laboratory** *noun* a room in a school or college that contains special equipment to help students learn foreign languages by listening to tapes or CDs, watching videos or DVDs, recording themselves, etc.

ˈ**language transfer** *noun* [U] (*linguistics*) the process of using your knowledge of your first language or another language that you know when speaking or writing a language that you are learning

langue /lɒ̃g; *NAmE* lɑːŋg/ *noun* (*linguistics*) (from *French*) a language considered as a communication system of a particular community, rather than the way individual people speak ➲ compare PAROLE

lan·guid /ˈlæŋgwɪd/ *adj.* moving slowly in an elegant manner, not needing energy or effort: *a languid wave of the hand* ◇ *a languid afternoon in the sun* ▸ **lan·guid·ly** *adv.*: *He moved languidly across the room.*

lan·guish /ˈlæŋgwɪʃ/ *verb* (*formal*) **1** [I] ~ (**in sth**) to be forced to stay somewhere or suffer sth unpleasant for a long time: *She continues to languish in a foreign prison.* **2** [I] to become weaker or fail to make progress: *The share price languished at 102p.*

lan·guor /ˈlæŋgə(r)/ *noun* [U, sing.] (*literary*) the pleasant state of feeling lazy and without energy: *A delicious languor was stealing over him.* ▸ **lan·guor·ous** /ˈlæŋgərəs/ *adj.*: *a languorous pace of life* **lan·guor·ous·ly** *adv.*

La Niña /lɑː ˈniːnjə/ *noun* [U] the cooling of the water in the central and eastern Pacific Ocean that happens every few years and that affects the weather in many parts of the world ➲ compare EL NIÑO

lank /læŋk/ *adj.* **1** (of hair) straight, dull and not attractive **2** (*SAfrE, informal*) large in number or amount: *I've got lank work to do.*

lanky /ˈlæŋki/ *adj.* (**lank·ier**, **lank·iest**) (of a person) having long thin arms and legs and moving in an awkward way: *a tall, lanky teenager* SYN **gangling**

lano·lin /ˈlænəlɪn/ *noun* [U] an oil that comes from sheep's wool and is used to make skin creams

lan·tern /ˈlæntən; *NAmE* -tərn/ *noun* a lamp in a transparent case, often a metal case with glass sides, that has a handle, so that you can carry it outside ➲ see also CHINESE LANTERN

ˌ**lantern** ˈ**jaw** *noun* a long thin JAW with a large chin ▸ ˌ**lantern-**ˈ**jawed** *adj.*

lanth·anum /ˈlænθənəm/ *noun* [U] (*symb.* La) a chemical element. Lanthanum is a silver-white metal.

lan·yard /ˈlænjɑːd; ˈlænjəd; *NAmE* -jərd/ *noun* **1** a string that you wear around your neck or wrist for holding sth: *A lanyard is useful for carrying your ID card.* ◇ *a whistle lanyard* **2** a piece of equipment that you wear around your neck to hold the wire of an IPOD: *lanyard headphones for use with your iPod* **3** a rope used to fasten sth, for example the sail of a ship

lap /læp/ *noun, verb*
■ ***noun*** [C] **1** [usually sing.] the top part of your legs that forms a flat surface when you are sitting down: *There's only one seat so you'll have to sit* ***on my lap.*** ◇ *She sat with her hands* ***in her lap.*** **2** one journey from the beginning to the end of a track used for running, etc: *the fastest lap on record* ◇ *She has completed six laps.* ◇ *He was overtaken on the final lap.* ◇ *to do a* ***lap of honour*** (= go around the track again to celebrate winning) ◇ (*NAmE*) *to do a* ***victory lap*** **3** a section of a journey, or of a piece of work, etc: *They're off on the first lap of their round-the-world tour.* ◇ *We've nearly finished. We're* ***on the last lap.***
IDM **drop/dump sth in sb's** ˈ**lap** (*informal*) to make sth the responsibility of another person: *They dropped the problem firmly back in my lap.* **sth drops/falls into sb's lap** somebody has the opportunity to do sth pleasant without having made any effort: *My dream job just fell into my lap.* **in**

L

the lap of the 'gods if the result of sth is **in the lap of the gods**, you do not know what will happen because it depends on luck or things you cannot control **in the lap of 'luxury** in easy, comfortable conditions, and enjoying the advantages of being rich

■ ***verb*** (-pp-) **1** [I] (of water) to touch sth gently and regularly, often making a soft sound: *The waves lapped around our feet.* ◇ *the sound of water lapping against the boat* **2** [T] **~ sth** (of animals) to drink sth with quick movements of the tongue **3** [T] **~ sb** (in a race) to pass another runner on a track who is one or more laps behind you

PHR V **,lap sth↔'up 1** (*informal*) to accept or receive sth with great enjoyment, without thinking about whether it is good, true or sincere: *It's a terrible movie but audiences everywhere are lapping it up.* ◇ *She simply lapped up all the compliments.* **2** to drink all of sth with great enjoyment: *The calf lapped up the bucket of milk.*

lapa /'lɑːpə/ *noun* (*SAfrE*) a shelter without walls on all sides, usually made of wooden poles and covered with THATCH (= dry grass), especially used as a place for relaxing and eating meals

lapar·os·copy /,læpə'rɒskəpi; *NAmE* -'rɑːs-/ *noun* (*pl.* -ies) (*medical*) an examination of the inside of the body using a tube-shaped instrument that can be put through the wall of the ABDOMEN

lapar·ot·omy /,læpə'rɒtəmi; *NAmE* -'rɑːt-/ *noun* (*pl.* -ies) (*medical*) a cut in the ABDOMEN in order to perform an operation or an examination

L

'lap belt *noun* a type of SEAT BELT that goes across your waist

'lap dancing *noun* [U] sexually exciting dancing or STRIPTEASE which is performed close to, or sitting on, a customer in a bar or club

lap·dog /'læpdɒg; *NAmE* -dɔːg; -dɑːg/ *noun* **1** a pet dog that is small enough to be carried **2** (*disapproving*) a person who is under the control of another person or group SYN **poodle**

lapel /lə'pel/ *noun* one of the two front parts of the top of a coat or jacket that are joined to the COLLAR and are folded back ➲ VISUAL VOCAB page V50

lapi·dary /'læpɪdəri; *NAmE* -deri/ *adj.* **1** (*formal*) (especially of written language) elegant and exact SYN **concise**: *in lapidary style* **2** (*technical*) connected with stones and the work of cutting and polishing them

lapis laz·uli /,læpɪs 'læzjʊli; *NAmE* 'læzəli/ *noun* [U] a bright blue stone, used in making jewellery

lap·sang sou·chong /,læpsæŋ 'suːʃɒŋ; *NAmE* -ʃɑːŋ/ *noun* [U] a type of tea that has a taste like smoke

lapse /læps/ *noun, verb*

■ ***noun* 1** a small mistake, especially one that is caused by forgetting sth or by being careless: *a* ***lapse of concentration/memory*** ◇ *A momentary lapse in the final set cost her the match.* **2** a period of time between two things that happen SYN **interval**: *After a lapse of six months we met up again.* **3** an example or period of bad behaviour from sb who normally behaves well

■ ***verb* 1** [I] (of a contract, an agreement, etc.) to be no longer valid because the period of time that it lasts has come to an end: *She had allowed her membership to lapse.* **2** [I] to gradually become weaker or come to an end SYN **expire**: *His concentration lapsed after a few minutes.* **3** [I] **~ (from sth)** to stop believing in or practising your religion: *He lapsed from Judaism when he was a student.* ▶ **lapsed** *adj.* [only before noun]: *a lapsed subscription* ◇ *lapsed faith* ◇ *a lapsed Catholic*

PHR V **'lapse into sth 1** to gradually pass into a worse or less active state or condition: *to* ***lapse into unconsciousness/a coma*** ◇ *She* ***lapsed into silence*** *again.* **2** to start speaking or behaving in a different way, often one that is less acceptable: *He soon lapsed back into his old ways.*

lap·top /'læptɒp; *NAmE* -tɑːp/ *noun* a small computer that can work with a battery and be easily carried SYN **notebook** ➲ VISUAL VOCAB pages V54, V56 ➲ compare DESKTOP COMPUTER, NETBOOK, SUBNOTEBOOK

lap·wing /'læpwɪŋ/ (also **pee·wit**) *noun* a black and white bird with a row of feathers (called a CREST) standing up on its head

lar·ceny /'lɑːsəni; *NAmE* 'lɑːrs-/ *noun* [U, C] (*pl.* -ies) (*law*) (*NAmE* or *old-fashioned, BrE*) the crime of stealing sth from sb; an occasion when this takes place SYN **theft**: *The couple were charged with* ***grand/petty larceny*** (= stealing things that are valuable/not very valuable).

larch /lɑːtʃ; *NAmE* lɑːrtʃ/ *noun* [C, U] a tree with sharp pointed leaves that fall in winter and hard dry fruit called CONES

lard /lɑːd; *NAmE* lɑːrd/ *noun, verb*

■ ***noun*** [U] a firm white substance made from the melted fat of pigs that is used in cooking

■ ***verb* ~ sth** to put small pieces of fat on or into sth before cooking it

PHR V **'lard sth with sth** [usually passive] (often *disapproving*) to include a lot of a particular kind of word or expressions in a speech or in a piece of writing: *His conversation was larded with Russian proverbs.*

lard·ass /'lɑːdɑːs; *NAmE* 'lɑːrdæs/ *noun* (*informal, especially NAmE, offensive*) a fat person, especially sb who is thought of as lazy

lar·der /'lɑːdə(r); *NAmE* 'lɑːrd-/ *noun* (*especially BrE*) a cupboard/closet or small room in a house, used for storing food, especially in the past SYN **pantry**

large 0→ /lɑːdʒ; *NAmE* lɑːrdʒ/ *adj., verb*

■ ***adj.*** **(larger, larg·est) 1** 0→ big in size or quantity: *a large area/family/house/car/appetite* ◇ *a large number of people* ◇ *very large sums of money* ◇ *He's a very large child for his age.* ◇ *A large proportion of old people live alone.* ◇ *Women usually do the larger share of the housework.* ◇ *Brazil is the world's largest producer of coffee.* ◇ *Who's the rather large* (= fat) *lady in the hat?* **2** 0→ (*abbr.* L) used to describe one size in a range of sizes of clothes, food, products used in the house, etc.: *small, medium, large* **3** 0→ wide in range and involving many things: *a large and complex issue* ◇ *Some drugs are being used on a much larger scale than previously.* ◇ *If we look at the larger picture of the situation, the differences seem slight.* ➲ SYNONYMS at BIG ▶ **large·ness** *noun* [U]

IDM **at 'large 1** (used after a noun) as a whole; in general: *the opinion of the public at large* **2** (of a dangerous person or animal) not captured; free: *Her killer is still at large.* **by and 'large** used when you are saying something that is generally, but not completely, true: *By and large, I enjoyed my time at school.* ➲ LANGUAGE BANK at GENERALLY **give/have it 'large** (*BrE, slang*) to enjoy yourself, especially by dancing and drinking alcohol **in 'large part | in large 'measure** (*formal*) to a great extent: *Their success is due in large part to their determination.* **(as) large as 'life** (*humorous*) used to show surprise at seeing sb/sth: *I hadn't seen her for fifteen years and then there she was, (as) large as life.* **,larger than 'life** looking or behaving in a way that is more interesting or exciting than other people, and so is likely to attract attention SYN **flamboyant**: *He's a larger than life character.* ➲ more at LOOM *v.*, WRIT *v.*

■ ***verb***

IDM **'large it | large it 'up** (*BrE, slang*) to enjoy yourself, especially by dancing and drinking alcohol

large·ly 0→ /'lɑːdʒli; *NAmE* 'lɑːrdʒli/ *adv.* to a great extent; mostly or mainly: *the manager who is largely responsible for the team's victory* ◇ *It was* ***largely a matter of*** *trial and error.* ◇ *He resigned largely because of the stories in the press.*

,large-'scale *adj.* [usually before noun] **1** involving many people or things, especially over a wide area: *large-scale development* ◇ *the large-scale employment of women* **2** (of a map, model, etc.) drawn or made to a scale that shows a small area of land or a building in great detail OPP **small-scale**

lar·gesse (also **lar·gess**) /lɑː'dʒes; *NAmE* lɑːr'dʒes/ *noun* [U] (*formal* or *humorous*) the act or quality of being generous with money; money that you give to people who have less than you: *She is not noted for her largesse* (= she is not generous). ◇ *to dispense largesse to the poor*

lar·gish /ˈlɑːdʒɪʃ; *NAmE* ˈlɑːrdʒɪʃ/ *adj.* fairly large

largo /ˈlɑːɡəʊ; *NAmE* ˈlɑːrɡoʊ/ *adv., adj., noun* (*music*) (from *Italian*)
- **adv., adj.** (used as an instruction) in a slow, serious way
- **noun** (*pl.* **-os**) a piece of music to be performed in a slow, serious way

lark /lɑːk; *NAmE* lɑːrk/ *noun, verb*
- **noun 1** a small brown bird with a pleasant song ➲ see also SKYLARK **2** [usually sing.] (*informal*) a thing that you do for fun or as a joke: *The boys didn't mean any harm—they just did it for a lark.* **3** (*BrE, informal*) (used after another noun) an activity that you think is a waste of time or that you do not take seriously: *Perhaps this riding lark would be more fun than she'd thought.*

IDM **be/get up with the ˈlark** (*old-fashioned, BrE*) to get out of bed very early in the morning **blow/sod that for a lark** (*BrE, slang*) used by sb who does not want to do sth because it involves too much effort: *Sod that for a lark! I'm not doing any more tonight.*
- **verb**

PHR V **ˌlark aˈbout/aˈround** (*old-fashioned, informal, especially BrE*) to enjoy yourself by behaving in a silly way SYN **mess about/around**

lark·spur /ˈlɑːkspɜː(r); *NAmE* ˈlɑːrk-/ *noun* [C, U] a tall garden plant with blue, pink or white flowers growing up its STEM

lar·ney (also **lar·nie**) /ˈlɑːni; *NAmE* ˈlɑːr-/ *adj.* (*SAfrE*) very smart; expensive: *We were invited to a larney function.* ◇ *a larney hotel*

lar·ri·kin /ˈlærɪkɪn/ *noun* (*AustralE, NZE*) a person who ignores the normal rules of society or of an organization

larva /ˈlɑːvə; *NAmE* ˈlɑːrvə/ *noun* (*pl.* **lar·vae** /ˈlɑːviː; *NAmE* ˈlɑːrviː/) an insect at the stage when it has just come out of an egg and looks like a short fat WORM ▸ **lar·val** /ˈlɑːvl; *NAmE* ˈlɑːrvl/ *adj.* [only before noun]: *an insect in its larval stage* ➲ VISUAL VOCAB page V11

la·ryn·geal /ləˈrɪndʒiəl/ *adj.* (*biology, phonetics*) related to or produced by the larynx

laryn·gi·tis /ˌlærɪnˈdʒaɪtɪs/ *noun* [U] an infection of the larynx that makes speaking painful

lar·ynx /ˈlærɪŋks/ *noun* (*pl.* **la·ryn·ges** /ləˈrɪndʒiːz/) (*anatomy*) the area at the top of the throat that contains the VOCAL CORDS SYN **voice box** ➲ VISUAL VOCAB page V48

la·sagne (also **la·sagna**) /ləˈzænjə/ *noun* **1** [U] large flat pieces of PASTA **2** [U, C] an Italian dish made from layers of lasagne, finely chopped meat and/or vegetables and white sauce

la·scivi·ous /ləˈsɪviəs/ *adj.* (*formal, disapproving*) feeling or showing strong sexual desire: *a lascivious person* ◇ *lascivious thoughts* ▸ **la·scivi·ous·ly** *adv.* **la·scivi·ous·ness** *noun* [U]

laser /ˈleɪzə(r)/ *noun* a device that gives out light in which all the waves OSCILLATE (= change direction and strength) together, typically producing a powerful beam of light that can be used for cutting metal, in medical operations, etc: *a laser beam* ◇ *a laser navigation device* ◇ *The barcodes on the products are read by lasers.* ◇ *a* ***laser show*** (=lasers used as entertainment) ◇ *She's had* ***laser surgery*** *on her eye.*

laser·disc (also **laser·disk**) /ˈleɪzədɪsk; *NAmE* ˈleɪzər-/ *noun* a plastic disc like a large CD on which large amounts of information, such as video or music, can be stored, and which can be read by a laser

ˈlaser gun *noun* a piece of equipment which uses a laser to read a BAR CODE or to find out how fast a vehicle or other object is moving

ˈlaser printer *noun* a printer that produces good quality printed material by means of a laser

lash /læʃ/ *verb, noun*
- **verb 1** [I, T] to hit sb/sth with great force SYN **pound**: **+ adv./prep.** *The rain lashed at the windows.* ◇ **~ sth** *Huge waves lashed the shore.* ➲ SYNONYMS at BEAT **2** [T] **~ sb/sth** to hit a person or an animal with a WHIP, rope, stick, etc. SYN **beat 3** [T] **~ sb/sth** to criticize sb/sth in a very angry way SYN **attack 4** [T] **~ sth + adv./prep.** to fasten sth tightly to sth else with ropes: *Several logs had been lashed together to make a raft.* ◇ *During the storm everything on deck had to be lashed down.* **5** [I, T] **~ (sth)** to move or to move sth quickly and violently from side to side: *The crocodile's tail was lashing furiously from side to side.*

PHR V **ˌlash ˈout (at sb/sth) 1** to suddenly try to hit sb: *She suddenly lashed out at the boy.* **2** to criticize sb in an angry way: *In a bitter article he lashed out at his critics.* **ˌlash ˈout on sth** (*BrE, informal*) to spend a lot of money on sth
- **noun 1** = EYELASH: *her long dark lashes* **2** a hit with a WHIP, given as a form of punishment: *They each received 20 lashes for stealing.* ◇ (*figurative*) *to feel the lash of sb's tongue* (= to be spoken to in an angry and critical way) **3** the thin leather part at the end of a WHIP

lash·ing /ˈlæʃɪŋ/ *noun* **1 lashings** [pl.] (*BrE, informal*) a large amount of sth, especially of food and drink: *a bowl of strawberries with lashings of cream* **2** [C] an act of hitting sb with a WHIP as a punishment: (*figurative*) *He was given a severe tongue-lashing* (= angry criticism). **3** [C, usually pl.] a rope used to fasten sth tightly to sth else

lass /læs/ (also **las·sie** /ˈlæsi/) *noun* (*ScotE, NEngE*) a girl; a young woman ➲ compare LAD, LADDIE

lassa fever /ˈlæsə fiːvə(r)/ *noun* [U] a serious disease, usually caught from RATS and found especially in W Africa

lassi /ˈlæsi/ *noun* [U] a S Asian drink made from YOGURT

las·si·tude /ˈlæsɪtjuːd; *NAmE* -tuːd/ *noun* [U] (*formal*) a state of feeling very tired in mind or body; lack of energy

lasso /læˈsuː; ˈlæsəʊ; *NAmE* ˈlæsoʊ/ *noun, verb*
- **noun** (*pl.* **-os** or **-oes**) a long rope with one end tied into a LOOP that is used for catching horses, cows, etc.
- **verb ~ sth** to catch an animal using a lasso

last[1] 🔑 /lɑːst; *NAmE* læst/ *det., adv., noun, verb* ➲ see also LAST[2]
- **det. 1** 🔑 happening or coming after all other similar things or people: *We caught the last bus home.* ◇ *It's the last house on the left.* ◇ *She was last to arrive.* **2** 🔑 [only before noun] most recent: *last night/Tuesday/month/summer/year* ◇ *her last book* ◇ *This last point is crucial.* ◇ *The* ***last time*** *I saw him was in May.* **3** 🔑 [only before noun] only remaining SYN **final**: *This is our last bottle of water.* ◇ *He knew this was his last hope of winning.* **4** used to emphasize that sb/sth is the least likely or suitable: ***The last thing she needed*** *was more work.* ◇ *He's the* ***last person*** *I'd trust with a secret.*

IDM **be on your/its last ˈlegs** to be going to die or stop functioning very soon; to be very weak or in bad condition **the day, week, month, etc. before ˈlast** the day, week, etc. just before the most recent one; two days, weeks, etc. ago: *I haven't seen him since the summer before last.* **every last...** every person or thing in a group: *We spent every last penny we had on the house.* **have the last ˈlaugh** to be successful when you were not expected to be, making your opponents look stupid **in the last reˈsort** when there are no other possible courses of action SYN **at a pinch**: *In the last resort we can always walk home.* **your/the last ˈgasp** the point at which you/sth can no longer continue living, fighting, existing, etc. ➲ see also LAST-GASP **the ˌlast ˈminute/ˈmoment** the latest possible time before an important event: *They changed the plans at the last minute.* ◇ *Don't leave your decision to the last moment.* **a/your last reˈsort** the person or thing you rely on when everything else has failed: *I've tried everyone else and now you're my last resort.* **the ˌlast ˈword (in sth)** the most recent, fashionable, advanced, etc. thing: *These apartments are the last word in luxury.* ➲ more at ANALYSIS, BREATH, FAMOUS, LONG *adj.*, MAN *n.*, STRAW, THING, WEEK, WORD *n.*
- **adv. 1** 🔑 after anyone or anything else; at the end: *He came last in the race.* ◇ *They arrived last of all.* **2** 🔑 most recently: *When did you see him last?* ◇ *I saw him last/I last saw him in New York two years ago.* ◇ *They last won the cup in 2006.*

IDM **ˌlast but not ˈleast** used when mentioning the last

L

person or thing of a group, in order to say that they are not less important than the others: *Last but not least, I'd like to thank all the catering staff.* **,last 'in, ,first 'out** used, for example in a situation when people are losing their jobs, to say that the last people to be employed will be the first to go ➲ more at FIRST *adv.*, LAUGH *v.*

■ ***noun* the last** (*pl.* **the last**) **1** 0‑ᵂ the person or thing that comes or happens after all other similar people or things: *Sorry I'm late—am I the last?* ◇ *They were the last to arrive.* **2** 0‑ᵂ **~ of sth** the only remaining part or items of sth: *These are the last of our apples.*

IDM **at (long) 'last** after much delay, effort, etc; in the end **SYN** **finally**: *At last we're home!* ◇ *At long last the cheque arrived.* ➲ note at LASTLY **hear/see the 'last of sb/sth** to hear/see sb/sth for the last time: *That was the last I ever saw of her.* ◇ *Unfortunately, I don't think we've heard the last of this affair.* **the last I 'heard** used to give the most recent news you have about sb/sth: *The last I heard he was still working at the garage.* **next/second to 'last** (*BrE* also **,last but 'one**) the one before the last one: *She finished second to last.* **to/till the 'last** until the last possible moment, especially until death: *He died protesting his innocence to the last.* ➲ more at BREATHE, FIRST *n.*

■ ***verb* 1** 0‑ᵂ [I] (not used in the progressive tenses) to continue for a particular period of time: *The meeting only lasted (for) a few minutes.* ◇ *Each game lasts about an hour.* ◇ *How long does the play last?* **2** 0‑ᵂ [I, T] to continue to exist or to function well: *This weather won't last.* ◇ *He's making a big effort now, and I hope it lasts.* ◇ **~ sb** *These shoes should last you till next year.* **3** 0‑ᵂ [I, T] to survive sth or manage to stay in the same situation, despite difficulties: *She won't last long in that job.* ◇ **~ (out)** *Can you last (out) until I can get help?* ◇ **~ (out) sth** *Doctors say that she probably won't last out the night* (= she will probably die before the morning). ◇ *He was injured early on and didn't last the match.* **4** 0‑ᵂ [I, T] to be enough for sb to use, especially for a particular period of time: **~ (out)** *Will the coffee last out till next week?* ◇ **~ sb (out)** *We've got enough food to last us (for) three days.*

L

Which Word?

last / take

Last and **take** are both used to talk about the length of time that something continues.

- **Last** is used to talk about the length of time that an event continues: *How long do you think this storm will last?* ◇ *The movie lasted over two hours.* **Last** does not always need an expression of time: *His annoyance won't last.* **Last** is also used to say that you have enough of something: *We don't have enough money to last until next month.*
- **Take** is used to talk about the amount of time you need in order to go somewhere or do something. It must be used with an expression of time: *It takes (me) at least an hour to get home from work.* ◇ *How long will the flight take?* ◇ *The water took ages to boil.*

last[2] /lɑːst; *NAmE* læst/ *noun* a block of wood or metal shaped like a foot, used in making and repairing shoes ➲ see also LAST[1]

,last 'call *noun* **1** (*especially NAmE*) (*BrE* also **,last 'orders**) the last opportunity for people to buy drinks in a pub or a bar before it closes **2** the final request at an airport for passengers to get on their plane

,last-'ditch *adj.* [only before noun] used to describe a final attempt to achieve sth, when there is not much hope of succeeding: *She underwent a heart transplant in a* ***last-ditch attempt*** *to save her.*

,last-'gasp *adj.* [only before noun] done or achieved at the last possible moment: *a last-gasp 2-1 victory*

last·ing /ˈlɑːstɪŋ; *NAmE* ˈlæstɪŋ/ *adj.* [usually before noun] continuing to exist or to have an effect for a long time **SYN** **durable**: *Her words left a* ***lasting impression*** *on me.* ◇ *I formed several lasting friendships at college.* ◇ *The training was of no lasting value.* ➲ see also LONG-LASTING ▸ **last·ing·ly** *adv.*

the ,Last 'Judgement *noun* [sing.] = JUDGEMENT DAY

last·ly /ˈlɑːstli; *NAmE* ˈlæstli/ *adv.* **1** used to introduce the final point that you want to make **SYN** **finally**: *Lastly, I'd like to ask you about your plans.* ➲ LANGUAGE BANK at FIRST **2** at the end; after all the other things that you have mentioned: *Lastly, add the lemon juice.*

Which Word?

lastly / at last

- **Lastly** is used to introduce the last in a list of things or the final point you are making: *Lastly, I would like to thank my parents for all their support.*
- **At last** is used when something happens after a long time, especially when there has been some difficulty or delay: *At last, after twenty hours on the boat, they arrived at their destination.* You can also use **finally**, **eventually** or **in the end** with this meaning, but not *lastly*.

,last-'minute *adj.* [usually before noun] done, decided or organized just before sth happens or before it is too late: *a last-minute holiday*

'last name *noun* your family name ➲ compare SURNAME

,last 'orders *noun* [pl.] (*BrE*) (also **,last 'call** *NAmE, BrE*) the last opportunity for people to buy drinks in a pub or a bar before it closes: *'Last orders, please!'*

the ,last 'post *noun* [sing.] (*BrE*) a tune played on a BUGLE at military funerals and at the end of the day in military camps

the ,last 'rites *noun* [pl.] a Christian religious ceremony that a priest performs for, and in the presence of, a dying person: *to administer the last rites to sb* ◇ *to receive the last rites*

lat. *abbr.* (in writing) LATITUDE

latch /lætʃ/ *noun, verb*

■ ***noun* 1** a small metal bar that is used to fasten a door or a gate. You raise it to open the door, and drop it into a metal hook to fasten it: *He lifted the latch and opened the door.* **2** (*especially BrE*) a type of lock on a door that needs a key to open it from the outside: *She listened for his key in the latch.*

IDM **on the 'latch** (*BrE*) closed but not locked: *Can you leave the door on the latch so I can get in?*

■ ***verb* ~ sth** to fasten sth with a latch

PHR V **,latch 'on (to sth)** | **,latch 'onto sth** (*informal*) to understand an idea or what sb is saying: *It was a difficult concept to grasp, but I soon latched on.* **,latch 'on (to sb/sth)** | **,latch 'onto sb/sth** (*informal*) **1** to become attached to sb/sth: *antibodies that latch onto germs* **2** to join sb and stay in their company, especially when they would prefer you not to be with them **3** to develop a strong interest in sth: *She always latches on to the latest craze.*

latch·key /ˈlætʃkiː/ *noun* a key for the front or the outer door of a house, etc.

'latchkey child (also **'latchkey kid**) *noun* (*usually disapproving*) a child who is at home alone after school because both parents are at work

late 0‑ᵂ /leɪt/ *adj., adv.*

■ ***adj.*** (**later**, **lat·est**) **1** 0‑ᵂ [only before noun] near the end of a period of time, a person's life, etc: *in the late afternoon* ◇ *in late summer* ◇ *She married in her late twenties* (= when she was 28 or 29). ◇ *In later life he started playing golf.* ◇ *The school was built in the late 1970s.* **OPP** **early** **2** 0‑ᵂ [not usually before noun] arriving, happening or done after the expected, arranged or usual time: *I'm sorry I'm late.* ◇ *She's late for work every day.* ◇ *My flight was an hour late.* ◇ *We apologize for the late arrival of this train.* ◇ *Because of the cold weather the crops are later this year.* ◇ *Interest will be charged for late payment.* ◇ *Here is a late news flash.*

OPP **early 3** 🔑 near the end of the day: *Let's go home—it's getting late.* ◇ *Look at the time—it's much later than I thought.* ◇ *What are you doing up at this* **late hour**? ◇ *What is the latest time I can have an appointment?* ◇ *I've had too many* **late nights** *recently* (= when I've gone to bed very late). **OPP** **early 4** [only before noun] (*formal*) (of a person) no longer alive: *her late husband* ◇ *the late Paul Newman* ▸ **late·ness** /ˈleɪtnəs/ *noun* [U]: *They apologized for the lateness of the train.* ◇ *Despite the lateness of the hour, the children were not in bed.* ➲ see also LATER, LATEST

IDM **be too ˈlate** 🔑 happening after the time when it is possible to do sth: *It's too late to save her now.* ◇ *Buy now before it's too late.*

■ ***adv.*** (*comparative* **later**, no *superlative*) **1** 🔑 after the expected, arranged or usual time: *I got up late.* ◇ *Can I stay up late tonight?* ◇ *She has to work late tomorrow.* ◇ *The big stores are open later on Thursdays.* ◇ *She married late.* ◇ *The birthday card arrived three days late.* **2** 🔑 near the end of a period of time, a person's life, etc: *late in March/the afternoon* ◇ *It happened late last year.* ◇ **As late as** (= as recently as) *the 1950s, tuberculosis was still a fatal illness.* ◇ *He became an author* **late in life**. **3** 🔑 near the end of the day: *There's a good film on late.* ◇ *Late that evening, there was a knock at the door.* ◇ *Share prices fell early on but rose again late in the day.* **OPP** **early** ➲ see also LATER

IDM **ˌbetter ˌlate than ˈnever** (*saying*) used especially when you, or sb else, arrive/arrives late, or when sth such as success happens late, to say that this is better than not coming or happening at all **ˌlate in the ˈday** (*disapproving*) after the time when an action could be successful: *He started working hard much too late in the day—he couldn't possibly catch up.* **late of...** (*formal*) until recently working or living in the place mentioned: *Professor Jones, late of Oxford University* **of ˈlate** (*formal*) recently: *I haven't seen him of late.* **too ˈlate** 🔑 after the time when it is possible to do sth successfully: *She's left it too late to apply for the job.* ◇ *I realized the truth too late.* ➲ more at NIGHT, SOON

Grammar Point

late / lately

- **Late** and **lately** are both adverbs, but **late** is used with similar meanings to the adjective **late**, whereas **lately** can only mean 'recently': *We arrived two hours late.* ◇ *I haven't heard from him lately.* **Lately** is usually used with a perfect tense of the verb.
- Look also at the idioms **be too late** (at the adjective) and **too late** (at the adverb).

late·comer /ˈleɪtkʌmə(r)/ *noun* a person who arrives late

late·ly /ˈleɪtli/ *adv.* recently; in the recent past: *Have you seen her lately?* ◇ *It's only lately that she's been well enough to go out.* ◇ (*BrE*) *I haven't been sleeping well just lately.* ◇ *She had lately returned from India.*

ˌlate-ˈnight *adj.* [only before noun] happening late at night; available after other things finish: *a late-night movie* ◇ *late-night shopping*

la·tent /ˈleɪtnt/ *adj.* [usually before noun] existing, but not yet very noticeable, active or well developed: *latent disease* ◇ *These children have a huge reserve of latent talent.* ▸ **la·tency** /ˈleɪtənsi/ *noun* [U]

later 🔑 /ˈleɪtə(r)/ *adv., adj.*

■ ***adv.*** **1** 🔑 at a time in the future; after the time you are talking about: *See you later.* ◇ *I met her again three years later.* ◇ *His father died later that year.* ◇ *We're going to Rome later in the year.* ◇ *She later became a doctor.* **OPP** **earlier** **2 Later!** (*informal*) a way of saying goodbye, used by young people: *Later, guys!*

IDM **later ˈon** 🔑 (*informal*) at a time in the future; after the time you are talking about: *I'm going out later on.* ◇ *Much later on, she realized what he had meant.* **not/no later than...** by a particular time and not after it: *Please arrive no later than 8 o'clock.*

■ ***adj.*** [only before noun] **1** 🔑 coming after sth else or at a time in the future: *This is discussed in more detail in a later chapter.* ◇ *The match has been postponed to a later date.* **2** 🔑 near the end of a period of time, life, etc: *the later part of the seventeenth century* ◇ *She found happiness in her later years.* **OPP** **earlier** **IDM** see SOON

lat·eral /ˈlætərəl/ *adj., noun*

■ ***adj.*** [usually before noun] (*technical*) connected with the side of sth or with movement to the side: *the lateral branches of a tree* ◇ *lateral eye movements* ▸ **lat·eral·ly** /ˈlætərəli/ *adv.*

■ ***noun*** (also **ˌlateral ˈconsonant**) (*phonetics*) a consonant sound which is produced by placing a part of the tongue against the PALATE so that air flows around it on both sides, for example /l/ in *lie*

ˌlateral ˈthinking *noun* [U] (*especially BrE*) a way of solving problems by using your imagination to find new ways of looking at the problem

lat·est 🔑 /ˈleɪtɪst/ *adj., noun*

■ ***adj.*** 🔑 [only before noun] the most recent or newest: *the latest unemployment figures* ◇ *the latest craze/fashion/trend* ◇ *her latest novel* ◇ *Have you heard the latest news?*

■ ***noun*** 🔑 [U] **the latest** (*informal*) the most recent or the newest thing or piece of news: *This is the latest in robot technology.* ◇ *Have you heard the latest?*

IDM **at the ˈlatest** no later than the time or the date mentioned: *Applications should be in by next Monday at the latest.*

latex /ˈleɪteks/ *noun* [U] **1** a thick white liquid that is produced by some plants and trees, especially rubber trees. Latex becomes solid when exposed to air, and is used to make medical products: *latex gloves* **2** an artificial substance similar to this that is used to make paints, glues, etc.

lath /lɑːθ; *NAmE* læθ/ *noun* (*pl.* **laths** /lɑːθs; *NAmE* læðz/) a thin narrow strip of wood that is used to support PLASTER (= material used for covering walls) on the inside walls and the ceilings of buildings

lathe /leɪð/ *noun* a machine that shapes pieces of wood or metal by holding and turning them against a fixed cutting tool

la·ther /ˈlɑːðə(r); *NAmE* ˈlæð-/ *noun, verb*

■ ***noun*** [U, sing.] a white mass of small bubbles that is produced by mixing soap with water

IDM **get into a ˈlather | work yourself into a ˈlather** (*BrE, informal*) to get anxious or angry about sth, especially when it is not necessary **in a ˈlather** (*BrE, informal*) in a nervous, angry or excited state **SYN** **worked up**

■ ***verb*** **1** [T] **~ sth** to cover sth with lather: *I lathered my face and started to shave.* **2** [I] to produce lather: *Soap does not lather well in hard water.*

lathi /ˈlɑːtiː/ *noun* (*IndE*) a long thick stick, especially one used as a weapon or by the police

Latin /ˈlætɪn; *NAmE* ˈlætn/ *noun, adj.*

■ ***noun*** **1** [U] the language of ancient Rome and the official language of its empire **2** [C] a person from countries where languages that have developed from Latin, such as Spanish, Portuguese, Italian or French, are spoken **3** [U] music of a kind that came originally from Latin America, typically with strong dance rhythms

■ ***adj.*** **1** of or in the Latin language: *Latin poetry* **2** connected with or typical of the countries or peoples using languages developed from Latin, such as Spanish, Portuguese, Italian or French: *a Latin temperament*

La·tina /læˈtiːnə/ *noun* a woman or girl, especially one who is living in the US, who comes from Latin America, or whose family came from there ➲ compare LATINO ▸ **Latina** *adj.* [usually before noun]

ˌLatin Aˈmerica *noun* [U] the parts of the Americas in which Spanish or Portuguese is the main language ➲ note at AMERICAN ➲ compare SOUTH AMERICA

Lat·in·ate /ˈlætɪneɪt/ *adj.* (of words or language) from Latin, or relating to Latin: *formal Latinate terms*

ˌLatin ˈlover *noun* (*informal*) a man from the Mediterranean region or from Latin America who is considered a good lover

La·tino /læˈtiːnəʊ; *NAmE* -noʊ/ *noun* (*pl.* -os) a person, especially one who is living in the US, who comes from Latin America, or whose family came from there ➲ compare CHICANO ▸ **La·tino** *adj.* [usually before noun]

lati·tude /ˈlætɪtjuːd; *NAmE* -tuːd/ *noun* **1** (*abbr.* **lat.**) [U] the distance of a place north or south of the EQUATOR (= the line around the world dividing north and south), measured in degrees ➲ compare LONGITUDE **2 lati·tudes** [pl.] a region of the world that is a particular distance from the EQUATOR: *the northern latitudes* **3** [U] (*formal*) freedom to choose what you do or the way that you do it SYN **liberty** ➲ see also LEEWAY

la·trine /ləˈtriːn/ *noun* a toilet in a camp, etc, especially one made by digging a hole in the ground

latte /ˈlɑːteɪ/ *noun* = CAFFÈ LATTE

lat·ter 0‑w /ˈlætə(r)/ *adj., noun*

■ **adj. 1** 0‑w being the second of two things, people or groups that have just been mentioned, or the last in a list: *The latter point is the most important.* **2** nearer to the end of a period of time than the beginning: *the latter half of the year* ➲ compare FORMER

■ ***noun*** 0‑w **the latter** (*pl.* the latter) the second of two things, people or groups that have just been mentioned, or the last in a list: *He presented two solutions. The latter seems much better.* ◇ *The town has a concert hall and two theatres. The latter were both built in the 1950s.*

ˈlatter-day *adj.* [only before noun] being a modern version of a person or thing in the past: *a latter-day Robin Hood*

L

lat·ter·ly /ˈlætəli; *NAmE* -tərli/ *adv.* (*formal*) **1** most recently: *Latterly his painting has shown a new freedom of expression.* **2** towards the end of a period of time: *Her health declined rapidly and latterly she never left the house.*

lat·tice /ˈlætɪs/ *noun* [U, C] (also **ˈlat·tice·work** [U]) a structure that is made of strips of wood or metal that cross over each other with spaces shaped like a diamond between them, used, for example, as a fence; any structure or pattern like this: *a low wall of stone latticework* ◇ *a lattice of branches* ▸ **lat·ticed** /ˈlætɪst/ *adj.*

ˌlattice ˈwindow (also **ˌlat·ticed ˈwindow**) *noun* a window with small pieces of glass shaped like diamonds in a FRAMEWORK of metal strips

laud /lɔːd/ *verb* **~ sb/sth** (*formal*) to praise sb/sth

laud·able /ˈlɔːdəbl/ *adj.* (*formal*) deserving to be praised or admired, even if not really successful SYN **commendable**: *a laudable aim/attempt* ▸ **laud·ably** /-əbli/ *adv.*

laud·anum /ˈlɔːdənəm/ *noun* [U] a drug made from OPIUM. In the past, people used to take laudanum to reduce pain and anxiety, and to help them sleep.

laud·atory /ˈlɔːdətəri; *NAmE* -tɔːri/ *adj.* (*formal*) expressing praise or admiration

laugh 0‑w /lɑːf; *NAmE* læf/ *verb, noun*

■ ***verb* 1** 0‑w [I, T] to make the sounds and movements of your face that show you are happy or think sth is funny: *to* ***laugh loudly/aloud/out loud*** ◇ **~ (at/about sth)** *You never laugh at my jokes!* ◇ *The show was hilarious—I couldn't stop laughing.* ◇ *She always* ***makes me laugh.*** ◇ *He* ***burst out laughing*** (= suddenly started laughing). ◇ *She laughed to cover her nervousness.* ◇ *I told him I was worried but he laughed scornfully.* ◇ **+ speech** *'You're crazy!' she laughed.* **2** [I] **be laughing** (*informal*) used to say that you are in a very good position, especially because you have done sth successfully: *If we win the next game we'll be laughing.*

IDM **don't make me ˈlaugh** (*informal*) used to show that you think what sb has just said is impossible or stupid: *'Will your dad lend you the money?' 'Don't make me laugh!'* **he who laughs ˌlast laughs ˈlongest** (*saying*) used to tell sb not to be too proud of their present success; in the end another person may be more successful **laugh all the way to the ˈbank** (*informal*) to make a lot of money easily and feel very pleased about it **laugh in sb's ˈface** to show in a very obvious way that you have no respect for sb **laugh like a ˈdrain** (*BrE*) to laugh very loudly **laugh on the other side of your ˈface** (*BrE, informal*) to be forced to change from feeling pleased or satisfied to feeling disappointed or annoyed **laugh sb/sth out of ˈcourt** (*BrE, informal*) to completely reject an idea, a story, etc. that you think is not worth taking seriously at all **laugh till/until you ˈcry** to laugh so long and hard that there are tears in your eyes **laugh up your ˈsleeve** (**at sb/sth**) (*informal*) to be secretly amused about sth **laugh your ˈhead off** to laugh very loudly and for a long time **not know whether to ˌlaugh or ˈcry** (*informal*) to be unable to decide how to react to a bad or unfortunate situation **you ˌhave/you've ˌgot to ˈlaugh** (*informal*) used to say that you think there is a funny side to a situation: *Well, I'm sorry you've lost your shoes, but you've got to laugh, haven't you?* ➲ more at KILL *v.*, PISS *v.*

PHR V **ˈlaugh at sb/sth** 0‑w to make sb/sth seem stupid or not serious by making jokes about them/it SYN **ridicule**: *Everybody laughs at my accent.* ◇ *She is not afraid to laugh at herself* (= is not too serious about herself). **ˌlaugh sth↔ˈoff** (*informal*) to try to make people think that sth is not serious or important, especially by making a joke about it: *He laughed off suggestions that he was going to resign.*

■ ***noun* 1** 0‑w [C] the sound you make when you are amused or happy: *to* ***give a laugh*** ◇ *a short/nervous/hearty laugh* ◇ *His first joke* ***got the biggest laugh*** *of the night.* ➲ see also BELLY LAUGH **2 a laugh** [sing.] (*informal*) an enjoyable and amusing occasion or thing that happens: *Come to the karaoke night—it should be a good laugh.* ◇ *And he didn't realize it was you? What a laugh!* **3 a laugh** [sing.] a person who is amusing and fun to be with: *Paula's a good laugh, isn't she?*

IDM **do sth for a ˈlaugh/for ˈlaughs** to do sth for fun or as a joke: *I just did it for a laugh, but it got out of hand.* **have a (good) ˈlaugh (about sth)** to find sth amusing: *I was angry at the time but we had a good laugh about it afterwards.* ➲ more at BARREL *n.*, LAST *det.*

Vocabulary Building

Different ways of laughing

- **cackle** to laugh in a loud, unpleasant way, especially in a high voice
- **chuckle** to laugh quietly, especially because you are thinking about something funny
- **giggle** to laugh in a silly way because you are amused, embarrassed or nervous
- **guffaw** to laugh noisily
- **roar** to laugh very loudly
- **snigger/snicker** to laugh in a quiet unpleasant way, especially at something rude or at someone's problems or mistakes
- **titter** to laugh quietly, especially in a nervous or embarrassed way

You can also **be convulsed with laughter** or **dissolve into laughter** when you find something very funny. In *BrE* people also **shriek with laughter** or **howl with laughter**.

laugh·able /ˈlɑːfəbl; *NAmE* ˈlæf-/ *adj.* silly or ridiculous, and not worth taking seriously SYN **absurd** ▸ **laugh·ably** /-əbli/ *adv.*

laugh·ing /ˈlɑːfɪŋ; *NAmE* ˈlæfɪŋ/ *adj.* showing AMUSEMENT or happiness: *his laughing blue eyes* ◇ *laughing faces*

IDM **be no laughing ˈmatter** to be sth serious that you should not joke about ➲ more at DIE *v.*, SPLIT *v.*

ˈlaughing gas *noun* [U] (*informal*) = NITROUS OXIDE

laugh·ing·ly /ˈlɑːfɪŋli; *NAmE* ˈlæf-/ *adv.* **1** in an amused way: *He laughingly agreed.* **2** used to show that you think a particular word is not at all a suitable way of describing something and therefore seems ridiculous: *I finally reached what we laughingly call civilization.*

ˈlaughing stock *noun* [usually sing.] a person that everyone laughs at because they have done sth stupid: *I can't wear that! I'd be a laughing stock.*

ˌ**laugh-out-ˈloud** *adj.* (*abbr.* LOL) [only before noun] (*informal*) extremely funny: *a laugh-out-loud moment* ◇ *The best scenes in the movie are laugh-out-loud funny.* HELP The abbreviation **LOL** is also used in text messages, emails or Internet chat, to show that you think sth is funny or do not mean it seriously.

laugh·ter /ˈlɑːftə(r); *NAmE* ˈlæf-/ *noun* [U] the act or sound of laughing: *to* ***roar with laughter*** ◇ ***tears/gales/peals/shrieks of laughter*** ◇ *to* ***burst/dissolve into laughter*** ◇ *a house full of laughter* (= with a happy atmosphere) IDM see SPLIT *v.*

launch 🔑 /lɔːntʃ/ *verb, noun*

■ ***verb*** **1** 🔑 **~ sth** to start an activity, especially an organized one: *to* ***launch an appeal/an inquiry/an investigation/a campaign*** ◇ *to* ***launch an attack/invasion*** **2** 🔑 **~ sth** to make a product available to the public for the first time: *a party to launch his latest novel* ◇ *The new model will be launched in July.* **3** 🔑 **~ sth** to put a ship or boat into the water, especially one that has just been built: *The Navy is to launch a new warship today.* ◇ *The lifeboat was launched immediately.* **4** 🔑 **~ sth** to send sth such as a SPACECRAFT, weapon, etc. into space, into the sky or through water: *to launch a communications satellite* ◇ *to* ***launch a missile/rocket/torpedo*** **5 ~ yourself at, from, etc. sth | ~ yourself forwards, etc.** to jump forwards with a lot of force: *Without warning he launched himself at me.* **6 ~ sth** (*computing*) to start a computer program: *You can launch programs and documents from your keyboard.*

PHR V ˈ**launch into sth** | ˈ**launch yourself into sth** to begin sth in an enthusiastic way, especially sth that will take a long time: *He launched into a lengthy account of his career.* ˌ**launch** ˈ**out** to do sth new in your career, especially sth more exciting: *It's time I launched out on my own.*

■ ***noun*** **1** 🔑 [usually sing.] the action of launching sth; an event at which sth is launched: *the successful launch of the Ariane rocket* ◇ *a product launch* ◇ *The official launch date is in May.* **2** a large boat with a motor

launch·er /ˈlɔːntʃə(r)/ *noun* (often in compounds) a device that is used to send a ROCKET, a MISSILE, etc. into the sky: *a rocket launcher*

ˈ**launch pad** (also ˈ**launching pad**) *noun* a platform from which a SPACECRAFT, etc. is sent into the sky: (*figurative*) *She regards the job as a launch pad for her career in the media.*

laun·der /ˈlɔːndə(r)/ *verb* **1 ~ sth** (*formal*) to wash, dry and iron clothes, etc: *freshly laundered sheets* **2 ~ sth** to move money that has been obtained illegally into foreign bank accounts or legal businesses so that it is difficult for people to know where the money came from

laun·der·ette (also **laun·drette**) /lɔːnˈdret/ (both *BrE*) (*NAmE* **Laun·dro·mat™** /ˈlɔːndrəmæt/) *noun* a place where you can wash and dry your clothes in machines that you operate by putting in coins

laun·dry /ˈlɔːndri/ *noun* (*pl.* **-ies**) **1** [U] clothes, sheets, etc. that need washing, that are being washed, or that have been washed recently SYN **washing**: *a pile of* ***clean/dirty laundry*** ◇ *a* ***laundry basket/room*** **2** [U, sing.] the process or the job of washing clothes, sheets, etc: *to do the laundry* ◇ *The hotel has a laundry service.* **3** [C] a business or place where you send sheets, clothes, etc. to be washed

ˈ**laundry list** *noun* a long list of people or things: *a laundry list of problems*

Laur·asia /lɔːˈreɪʃə; -ʒə/ *noun* [sing.] (*geology*) a very large area of land that existed in the northern HEMISPHERE millions of years ago. It was made up of the present N America, Greenland, Europe and most of Asia.

laure·ate /ˈlɒriət; *NAmE* ˈlɔːr-; ˈlɑːr-/ *noun* **1** a person who has been given an official honour or prize for sth important they have achieved: *a Nobel laureate* **2** = POET LAUREATE

laurel /ˈlɒrəl; *NAmE* ˈlɔːr-; ˈlɑːr-/ *noun* **1** [U, C] a bush with dark smooth shiny leaves that remain on the bush and stay green through the year **2 laurels** [pl.] honour and praise given to sb because of sth that they have achieved

IDM **look to your** ˈ**laurels** to be careful that you do not lose the success or advantage that you have over other people **rest/sit on your** ˈ**laurels** (usually *disapproving*) to feel so satisfied with what you have already achieved that you do not try to do any more

ˈ**laurel wreath** *noun* a ring of laurel leaves that was worn on the head in the past as a sign of victory

lav /læv/ *noun* (*BrE, informal*) a toilet

lava /ˈlɑːvə/ *noun* [U] **1** hot liquid rock that comes out of a VOLCANO: *molten lava* **2** this type of rock when it has cooled and become hard

lav·age /ˈlævɪdʒ; læˈvɑːʒ/ *noun* (*medical*) the process of washing a space inside the body such as the stomach or COLON

ˈ**lava lamp** *noun* an electric lamp that contains a liquid in which a coloured substance like oil moves up and down in shapes that keep changing ➲ VISUAL VOCAB page V18

lava·tor·ial /ˌlævəˈtɔːriəl/ *adj.* (*especially BrE*) **lavatorial** humour refers in a rude way to parts of the body, going to the toilet, etc.

lav·atory /ˈlævətri; *NAmE* -tɔːri/ *noun* (*pl.* **-ies**) (*old-fashioned* or *formal*) **1** (*especially BrE*) a toilet, or a room with a toilet in it: *There's a bathroom and a lavatory upstairs.* **2** (*BrE*) a public building or part of a building, with toilets in it: *The nearest public lavatory is at the station.*

lav·en·der /ˈlævəndə(r)/ *noun* [U] **1** a garden plant or bush with bunches of purple flowers with a sweet smell **2** the flowers of the lavender plant that have been dried, used for making sheets, clothes, etc. smell nice: *lavender oil* **3** a pale purple colour

lav·ish /ˈlævɪʃ/ *adj., verb*

■ ***adj.*** **1** large in amount, or impressive, and usually costing a lot of money SYN **extravagant, luxurious**: *lavish gifts/costumes/celebrations* ◇ *They lived a very* ***lavish lifestyle.*** ◇ *They rebuilt the house on an even more* ***lavish scale*** *than before.* **2 ~ (with/in sth)** giving or doing sth generously: *He was lavish in his praise for her paintings.* ▶ **lav·ish·ly** *adv.*: *lavishly illustrated*

■ ***verb***

PHR V ˈ**lavish sth on/upon sb/sth** to give a lot of sth, often too much, to sb/sth: *She lavishes most of her attention on her youngest son.*

law 🔑 /lɔː/ *noun*

▸ SYSTEM OF RULES **1** 🔑 (also **the law**) [U] the whole system of rules that everyone in a country or society must obey: *If they entered the building they would be* ***breaking the law.*** ◇ *In Sweden it is* ***against the law*** *to hit a child.* ◇ *Defence attorneys can use any means* ***within the law*** *to get their client off.* ◇ *British schools are now required* ***by law*** *to publish their exam results.* ◇ *The reforms have recently* ***become law.*** ◇ *Do not think you are* ***above the law*** (= think that you cannot be punished by the law). ◇ *the need for better* ***law enforcement*** ◇ (*humorous*) *Kate's* ***word was law*** *in the Brown household.* ➲ COLLOCATIONS at JUSTICE **2** 🔑 [U] a particular branch of the law: ***company/international/tax, etc. law*** ➲ see also CANON LAW, CASE LAW, CIVIL LAW, COMMON LAW, PRIVATE LAW, STATUTE LAW

▸ ONE RULE **3** 🔑 [C] a rule that deals with a particular crime, agreement, etc: **~ (against sth)** *the 1996 law against the hiring of illegal immigrants* ◇ **~ (on sth)** *The government has introduced some tough new laws on food hygiene.* ◇ ***strict*** *gun* ***laws*** ◇ *a* ***federal/state law*** ◇ *to* ***pass a law*** (= officially make it part of the system of laws) ◇ (*informal*) *There ought to be a law against it!* ➲ see also BY-LAW, LICENSING LAWS

▸ SUBJECT/PROFESSION **4** 🔑 [U] the study of the law as a subject at university, etc; the profession of being a lawyer: *Jane is studying law.* ◇ (*NAmE*) *He's in* ***law school.*** ◇ (*BrE*) *He's at law school.* ◇ *What made you go into law?* ◇ *a law firm*

▸ POLICE **5** 🔑 **the law** [sing.] used to refer to the police and the legal system: *Jim is always getting into trouble with the law.*

▸ OF ORGANIZATION/ACTIVITY **6** [C] one of the rules which

L

controls an organization or activity: *the laws of the Church* ◇ *The first law of kung fu is to defend yourself.* ◇ *the laws of cricket*

▸ OF GOOD BEHAVIOUR **7** [C] a rule for good behaviour or how you should behave in a particular place or situation: *moral laws* ◇ *the unspoken laws of the street*

▸ IN BUSINESS/NATURE/SCIENCE **8** 0‑ᴡ [C] the fact that sth always happens in the same way in an activity or in nature SYN **principle**: *the laws of supply and demand* ◇ *the law of gravity* **9** [C] a scientific rule that sb has stated to explain a natural process: *the first law of thermodynamics* ⇨ see also MURPHY'S LAW, PARKINSON'S LAW, SOD'S LAW, LEGAL, LEGALIZE, LEGISLATE

IDM **be a law unto your'self** to behave in an independent way and ignore rules or what other people want you to do **go to 'law** (*BrE*) to ask a court to settle a problem or disagreement **,law and 'order** 0‑ᴡ a situation in which people obey the law and behave in a peaceful way: *The government struggled to maintain law and order.* ◇ *After the riots, the military was brought in to restore law and order.* ◇ *They claim to be the party of law and order.* **the ,law of 'averages** the principle that one thing will happen as often as another if you try enough times: *Keep applying and by the law of averages you'll get a job sooner or later.* **the ,law of the 'jungle** a situation in which people are prepared to harm other people in order to succeed **lay down the 'law** to tell sb with force what they should or should not do **take the law into your own 'hands** to do sth illegal in order to punish sb for doing sth wrong, instead of letting the police deal with them **there's no 'law against sth** (*informal*) used to tell sb who is criticizing you that you are not doing anything wrong: *I'll sing if I want to—there's no law against it.* ⇨ more at LETTER *n.*, POSSESSION, RULE *n.*, WRONG *adj.*

L

'law-abiding *adj.* obeying and respecting the law: *law-abiding citizens*

law·break·er /'lɔːbreɪkə(r)/ *noun* a person who does not obey the law ▸ **law·break·ing** *noun* [U]

'law court *noun* (*BrE*) = COURT OF LAW ⇨ note at COURT

law·ful /'lɔːfl/ *adj.* (*formal*) allowed or recognized by law; legal: *his lawful heir* OPP **unlawful** ▸ **law·ful·ly** /-fəli/ *adv.*: *a lawfully elected government* **law·ful·ness** *noun* [U]

lawks /lɔːks/ *exclamation* (*old-fashioned, BrE*) used to show that you are surprised, angry or impatient

law·less /'lɔːləs/ *adj.* **1** (of a country or an area) where laws do not exist or are not obeyed: *lawless streets* ◇ *the lawless days of the revolution* **2** (of people or their actions) without respect for the law SYN **anarchic**, **wild**: *lawless gangs* ▸ **law·less·ness** *noun* [U]

'law lord *noun* (*BrE*) a member of the British House of Lords who was qualified to perform its legal work. In 2009 the law lords' role was taken over by the judges of the new Supreme Court.

law·maker /'lɔːmeɪkə(r)/ *noun* a person in government who makes the laws of a country SYN **legislator**

law·man /'lɔːmæn/ *noun* (*pl.* -men /-men/) (*especially US*) an officer responsible for keeping law and order, especially a SHERIFF

lawn /lɔːn/ *noun* **1** [C] an area of ground covered in short grass in a garden/yard or park, or used for playing a game on: *In summer we have to mow the lawn twice a week.* ◇ *a croquet lawn* ⇨ VISUAL VOCAB page V16 **2** [U] a type of fine cotton or LINEN cloth used for making clothes

'lawn bowling *noun* [U] (*NAmE*) = BOWLS

'lawn chair *noun* (*especially NAmE*) a chair that can be folded and that people use when sitting outside

lawn·mow·er /'lɔːnməʊə(r); *NAmE* -moʊ-/ (also **mower**) *noun* a machine for cutting the grass on LAWNS ⇨ VISUAL VOCAB page V16

'lawn sign *noun* (*NAmE*) a board that people put outside their house in order to advertise sth or to show that they support a particular politician or political party

,lawn 'tennis *noun* [U] (*formal*) = TENNIS

law·ren·cium /lɒ'rensiəm; *NAmE* lɔː'r-/ *noun* [U] (*symb.* Lr) a chemical element. Lawrencium is a RADIOACTIVE metal.

law·suit /'lɔːsuːt; *BrE* also -sjuːt/ (also **suit**) *noun* a claim or complaint against sb that a person or an organization can make in court: *He **filed a lawsuit** against his record company.*

law·yer 0‑ᴡ /'lɔːjə(r)/ *noun* a person who is trained and qualified to advise people about the law and to represent them in court, and to write legal documents

More About

lawyers

- **Lawyer** is a general term for a person who is qualified to advise people about the law, to prepare legal documents for them and/or to represent them in a court of law.
- In England and Wales, a **lawyer** who is qualified to speak in the higher courts of law is called a **barrister**. In Scotland a **barrister** is called an **advocate**.
- In *NAmE* **attorney** is a more formal word used for a **lawyer** and is used especially in job titles: *district attorney.*
- **Counsel** is the formal legal word used for a lawyer who is representing someone in court: *counsel for the prosecution.*
- **Solicitor** is the *BrE* term for a lawyer who gives legal advice and prepares documents, for example when you are buying a house, and sometimes has the right to speak in a court of law.
- In *NAmE* **solicitor** is only used in the titles of some lawyers who work for the government: *Solicitor General.*

lax /læks/ *adj.* **1** (*disapproving*) not strict, severe or careful enough about work, rules or standards of behaviour SYN **slack**, **careless**: *lax security/discipline* ◇ *a lax attitude to health and safety regulations* **2** (*phonetics*) (of a speech sound) produced with the muscles of the speech organs relaxed OPP **tense** ▸ **lax·ity** /'læksəti/ *noun* [U]

laxa·tive /'læksətɪv/ *noun* a medicine, food or drink that makes sb empty their BOWELS easily ▸ **laxa·tive** *adj.*

lay 0‑ᴡ /leɪ/ *verb, adj., noun* ⇨ see also LIE *v.*

■ ***verb*** (**laid**, **laid** /leɪd/)

▸ PUT DOWN/SPREAD **1** 0‑ᴡ [T] to put sb/sth in a particular position, especially when it is done gently or carefully: **~ sb/sth (+ adv./prep.)** *She laid the baby down gently on the bed.* ◇ *He laid a hand on my arm.* ◇ *The horse laid back its ears.* ◇ *Relatives laid wreaths on the grave.* ◇ **~ sb/sth + adj.** *The cloth should be laid flat.* HELP Some speakers confuse this sense of **lay** with **lie**, especially in the present and progressive tenses. However, **lay** has an object and **lie** does not: *She was lying on the beach.* ◇ ~~*She was laying on the beach.*~~ ◇ *Why don't you lie on the bed?* ◇ ~~*Why don't you lay on the bed?*~~ In the past tenses **laid** (from: *lay*) is often wrongly used for **lay** or **lain** (from: *lie*): *She had lain there all night.* ◇ ~~*She had laid there all night.*~~ **2** 0‑ᴡ [T] **~ sth (down)** to put sth down, especially on the floor, ready to be used: *to **lay a carpet/cable/pipe*** ◇ *The foundations of the house are being laid today.* ◇ (*figurative*) *They had laid the groundwork for future development.* **3** 0‑ᴡ [T] to spread sth on sth; to cover sth with a layer of sth: **~ A (on/over B)** *Before they started they laid newspaper on the floor.* ◇ *The grapes were laid to dry on racks.* ◇ **~ B with A** *The floor was laid with newspaper.*

▸ EGGS **4** 0‑ᴡ [T, I] **~ (sth)** if a bird, an insect, a fish, etc. **lays** eggs, it produces them from its body: *The cuckoo lays its eggs in other birds' nests.* ◇ *new-laid eggs* ◇ *The hens are not laying well* (= not producing many eggs).

▸ TABLE **5** 0‑ᴡ [T] **~ sth** (*BrE*) to arrange knives, forks, plates, etc. on a table ready for a meal SYN **set**: *to lay the table*

▸ PRESENT PROPOSAL **6** [T] **~ sth + adv./prep.** to present a

proposal, some information, etc. to sb for them to think about and decide on: *The bill was laid before Parliament.*
▸ DIFFICULT SITUATION **7** [T] **~ sth + adv./prep.** (*formal*) to put sb/sth in a particular position or state, especially a difficult or unpleasant one **SYN** **place**: *to **lay a responsibility/burden** on sb* ◇ *to lay sb under an obligation to do sth*
▸ WITH NOUNS **8** [T] **~ sth + adv./prep.** used with a noun to form a phrase that has the same meaning as the verb related to the noun: *to lay the blame on sb* (= to blame sb) ◇ *Our teacher lays great stress on good spelling* (= stresses it strongly).
▸ PLAN/TRAP **9** [T] **~ sth** to prepare sth in detail: *to lay a trap for sb* ◇ *She began to **lay her plans** for her escape.* ◇ *Bad weather can upset even the **best-laid** plans.*
▸ HAVE SEX **10** [T, often passive] **~ sb** (*slang*) to have sex with sb: *He went out hoping to **get laid** that night.*
▸ FIRE **11** [T] **~ sth** to prepare a fire by arranging wood, sticks or coal
▸ BET **12** [T] to bet money on sth; to place a bet: **~ sth** *to lay a bet* ◇ **~ sth on sth** *She had laid $100 on the favourite.* ◇ **~ (sb) sth (that)...** *I'll lay you any money you like (that) he won't come.* **HELP** This pattern is not used in the passive.
IDM Idioms containing **lay** are at the entries for the nouns and adjectives in the idioms, for example **lay sth bare** is at **bare**.
PHR V **ˌlay aˈbout sb (with sth)** (*BrE*) to attack sb violently: *The gang laid about him with sticks.* **ˌlay aˈbout you/yourself (with sth)** (*BrE*) to hit sb/sth without control or move your arms or legs violently in all directions: *She laid about herself with her stick to keep the dogs off.* **ˌlay sth↔aˈside** (*formal*) **1** to put sth on one side and not use it or think about it **SYN** **set aside**: *He laid aside his book and stood up.* ◇ (*figurative*) *Doctors have to lay their personal feelings aside.* **2** (also **ˌlay sth ˈby**) to keep sth to use, or deal with later **SYN** **put aside**: *They had laid money aside for their old age.* **ˌlay sth↔ˈdown 1** to put sth down or stop using it **SYN** **put down**: *She laid the book down on the table.* ◇ *Both sides were urged to lay down their arms* (= stop fighting). **2** (*formal*) to stop doing a job, etc: *to lay down your duties* **3** if you **lay down** a rule or a principle, you state officially that people must obey it or use it: *You can't lay down hard and fast rules.* ◇ **it is laid down that...** *It is laid down that all candidates must submit three copies of their dissertation.* **4** [usually passive] to produce sth that is stored and gradually increases: *If you eat too much, the surplus is laid down as fat.* **ˌlay sth↔ˈin/ˈup** to collect and store sth to use in the future: *to lay in food supplies* **ˌlay ˈinto sb/sth** (*informal*) to attack sb violently with blows or words: *His parents really laid into him for wasting so much money.* **ˌlay ˈoff | ˌlay ˈoff sb/sth** (*informal*) used to tell sb to stop doing sth: *Lay off me will you—it's nothing to do with me.* ◇ **~ doing sth** *Lay off bullying Jack.* **ˌlay ˈoff sth** (*informal*) to stop using sth: *I think you'd better lay off fatty foods for a while.* **ˌlay sb↔ˈoff** to stop employing sb because there is not enough work for them to do **SYN** **make sb redundant** ➲ related noun LAY-OFF **ˌlay sth↔ˈon** (*BrE, informal*) to provide sth for sb, especially food or entertainment: *to lay on food and drink* ◇ *A bus has been laid on to take guests to the airport.* **ˌlay sth ˈon sb** (*informal*) to make sb have to deal with sth unpleasant or difficult: *Stop laying a guilt trip on me* (= making me feel guilty). **ˌlay sb↔ˈout 1** to knock sb unconscious **2** to prepare a dead body to be buried **ˌlay sth↔ˈout 1** to spread sth out so that it can be seen easily or is ready to use: *He laid the map out on the table.* ◇ **+ adj.** *Lay the material out flat.* **2** [often passive] to plan how sth should look and arrange it in this way: *The gardens were laid out with lawns and flower beds.* ◇ *a well-laid-out magazine* ➲ related noun LAYOUT **3** to present a plan, an argument, etc. clearly and carefully **SYN** **set out**: *All the terms and conditions are laid out in the contract.* **4** (*informal*) to spend money **SYN** **fork out**: *I had to lay out a fortune on a new car.* ➲ related noun OUTLAY **ˌlay ˈover (at/in...)** (*NAmE*) to stay somewhere for a short time during a long journey ➲ related noun LAYOVER ➲ see also STOP OVER **ˌlay sb ˈup** [usually passive] if sb is **laid up**, they are unable to work, etc. because of an illness or injury: *She's laid up with a broken leg.* **ˌlay sth ↔ ˈup 1** = LAY STH IN **2** if you **lay up** problems or trouble for yourself, you do sth that will cause you problems later **3** to stop using a ship or other vehicle while it is being repaired
■ **adj.** [only before noun] **1** not having expert knowledge or professional qualifications in a particular subject: *His book explains the theory for the lay public.* **2** not in an official position in the Church: *a lay preacher* ➲ see also LAYMAN, LAYPERSON, LAYWOMAN
■ **noun** **1** (*taboo, informal*) a partner in sex, especially a woman: ***an easy lay*** (= a person who is ready and willing to have sex) ◇ *to be a great lay* **2** (*old use*) a poem that was written to be sung, usually telling a story
IDM **the ˌlay of the ˈland** (*NAmE*) (*BrE* **the ˌlie of the ˈland**) **1** the way the land in an area is formed and what physical characteristics it has **2** the way a situation is now and how it is likely to develop

lay·about /ˈleɪəbaʊt/ *noun* (*old-fashioned, BrE, informal*) a lazy person who does not do much work

lay·away /ˈleɪəweɪ/ *noun* [U] (*NAmE*) a system of buying goods in a store, where the customer pays a small amount of the price for an article and the store keeps the goods until the full price has been paid

ˈlay-by *noun* **1** [C] (*BrE*) an area at the side of a road where vehicles may stop for a short time ➲ compare REST AREA **2** [U] (*AustralE, NZE, SAfrE*) a system of paying some money for an article so that it is kept for you and you can pay the rest of the money later: *You could secure it on lay-by.*

layer 🔑 **AW** /ˈleɪə(r); ˈleə(r); *NAmE* ˈler/ *noun, verb*
■ **noun** **1** 🔑 a quantity or thickness of sth that lies over a surface or between surfaces: *A thin layer of dust covered everything.* ◇ *How many layers of clothing are you wearing?* **2** 🔑 a level or part within a system or set of ideas: *There were too many layers of management in the company.* ◇ *the layers of meaning in the poem*
■ **verb** [often passive] **~ sth** to arrange sth in layers: *Layer the potatoes and onions in a dish.* ◇ *Her hair had been layered* (= cut to several different lengths). ➲ VISUAL VOCAB page V49

lay·ette /leɪˈet/ *noun* a set of clothes and other things for a new baby

lay·man /ˈleɪmən/ *noun* (*pl.* **-men** /-mən/) (also **lay·per·son**) **1** a person who does not have expert knowledge of a particular subject: *a book written for professionals and laymen alike* ◇ *to explain sth **in layman's terms*** (= in simple language) **2** a person who is a member of a Church but is not a priest or member of the CLERGY ➲ see also LAYWOMAN ➲ note at GENDER

ˈlay-off *noun* **1** an act of making people unemployed because there is no more work left for them to do **2** a period of time when sb is not working or not doing sth that they normally do regularly: *an eight-week lay-off with a broken leg*

lay·out /ˈleɪaʊt/ *noun* [usually sing.] the way in which the parts of sth such as the page of a book, a garden or a building are arranged: *the layout of streets* ◇ *the magazine's attractive new page layout*

lay·over /ˈleɪəʊvə(r); *NAmE* -oʊ-/ (*NAmE*) (*BrE* **stop·over**) *noun* a short stay somewhere between two parts of a journey

lay·per·son /ˈleɪpɜːsn; *NAmE* -pɜːrsn/ *noun* (also **ˈlay person**) (*pl.* **lay people** or **lay·persons**) = LAYMAN: *The layperson cannot really understand mental illness.*

ˈlay-up *noun* **1** (in BASKETBALL) a shot made with one hand from under or beside the BASKET **2** (in GOLF) a shot made from a difficult position to a position that will allow an easier next shot

lay·woman /ˈleɪwʊmən/ *noun* (*pl.* **-women** /-wɪmɪn/) a woman who is a member of a Church but is not a priest or a member of the CLERGY ➲ see also LAYMAN, LAYPERSON ➲ note at GENDER

Laz·a·rus /ˈlæzərəs/ *noun* used to refer to sb who improves or starts to be successful again after a period of failure **ORIGIN** From the story of **Lazarus** in the Bible. He was a man who died but was then brought back to life by Jesus Christ.

L

laze /leɪz/ *verb* [I] to relax and do very little: *We lazed by the pool all day.* ◇ **~ about/around** *I've spent the afternoon just lazing around.*

PHR V **'laze sth↔away** to spend time relaxing and doing very little SYN **lounge**: *They lazed away the long summer days.*

lazy 🔑 /'leɪzi/ *adj.* (lazi·er, lazi·est) **1** 🔑 (*disapproving*) unwilling to work or be active; doing as little as possible SYN **idle**: *He was not stupid, just lazy.* ◇ *I was feeling too lazy to go out.* **2** 🔑 not involving much energy or activity; slow and relaxed: *We spent a lazy day on the beach.* **3** (*disapproving*) showing a lack of effort or care: *a lazy piece of work* **4** (*literary*) moving slowly SYN **torpid**: *the lazy river* ▸ **lazi·ly** *adv.*: *She woke up and stretched lazily.* **lazi·ness** *noun* [U]

lazy·bones /'leɪzibəʊnz; *NAmE* -boʊnz/ *noun* [sing.] (*old-fashioned, informal*) used to refer to a lazy person: *Come on, lazybones, get up!*

ˌlazy 'eye *noun* an eye that does not see well because it is not used enough

ˌlazy 'Susan *noun* a round plate or TRAY on a base, which can be spun around so that the objects on it can be easily reached

lb (*BrE*) (*NAmE* **lb.**) *abbr.* (*pl.* **lb** or **lbs**) a pound in weight, equal to about 454 grams (from Latin 'libra').

lbw /ˌel biː 'dʌbljuː/ *abbr.* (in CRICKET) leg before wicket (When the ball hits a player's leg instead of hitting his or her BAT, and would have hit the WICKET if the leg had not stopped it, then that player is **out lbw** and has to stop BATTING.)

l.c. /ˌel 'siː/ *abbr.* **1** in the piece of text that has been quoted (from Latin 'loco citato') **2** (in writing) LETTER OF CREDIT **3** (in writing) LOWER CASE

LCD /ˌel siː 'diː/ *abbr.* **1** liquid crystal display (a way of showing information in electronic equipment. An electric current is passed through a special liquid and numbers and letters can be seen on a small screen.): *a pocket calculator with LCD* ◇ *an LCD screen* **2** LEAST/LOWEST COMMON DENOMINATOR

lea /liː/ *noun* (*literary*) an open area of land covered in grass

leach /liːtʃ/ *verb* (*technical*) **1** [I] **~ (from sth) (into sth)** | **~ out/away** (of chemicals, minerals, etc.) to be removed from soil, etc. by water passing through it: *Nitrates leach from the soil into rivers.* **2** [T] **~ sth (from sth) (into sth)** | **~ sth out/away** (of a liquid) to remove chemicals, minerals, etc. from soil: *The nutrient is quickly leached away.*

lead[1] 🔑 /liːd/ *verb, noun* ➲ see also LEAD[2]

■ *verb* (led, led /led/)

▸ SHOW THE WAY **1** 🔑 [I, T] to go with or in front of a person or an animal to show the way or to make them go in the right direction SYN **guide**: *If you lead, I'll follow.* ◇ **~ sb/sth + adv./prep.** *He led us out into the grounds.* ◇ *The receptionist **led the way** to the boardroom.* ◇ *She led the horse back into the stable.* ◇ (*figurative*) *I tried to lead the discussion back to the main issue.* ➲ SYNONYMS at TAKE

▸ CONNECT TWO THINGS **2** 🔑 [I] **~ from/to sth (to/from sth)** to connect one object or place to another: *the pipe leading from the top of the water tank* ◇ *The wire led to a speaker.*

▸ OF ROAD/PATH/DOOR **3** 🔑 [I, T] to go in a particular direction or to a particular place: **+ adv./prep.** *A path led up the hill.* ◇ *Which door leads to the yard?* ◇ **~ sb + adv./prep.** *The track led us through a wood.*

▸ CAUSE **4** 🔑 [I] **~ to sth** to have sth as a result SYN **result in**: *Eating too much sugar can lead to health problems.* ➲ LANGUAGE BANK at CAUSE **5** 🔑 [T] to be the reason why sb does or thinks sth: **~ sb (to sth)** *What led you to this conclusion?* ◇ *He's too **easily led*** (= easily persuaded to do or think sth). ◇ **~ sb to do sth** *This has led scientists to speculate on the existence of other galaxies.* ◇ *The situation is far worse than we had been **led to believe**.*

▸ LIFE **6** 🔑 [T] **~ sth** to have a particular type of life: *to lead a quiet life/a life of luxury/a miserable existence*

▸ BE BEST/FIRST **7** 🔑 [T, I] to be the best at sth; to be in first place: **~ (sb/sth) (in sth)** *The department led the world in cancer research.* ◇ *We **lead the way** in space technology.* ◇ **~ (sb/sth) by sth** *The champion is leading (her nearest rival) by 18 seconds.*

▸ BE IN CONTROL **8** 🔑 [T, I] **~ (sth)** to be in control of sth; to be the leader of sth: *to lead an expedition* ◇ *to lead a discussion* ◇ *Who will lead the party in the next election?*

▸ IN CARD GAMES **9** [I, T] to play first; to play sth as your first card: *It's your turn to lead.* ◇ **~ sth** *to lead the ten of clubs*

IDM **lead sb by the 'nose** to make sb do everything you want; to control sb completely **lead sb a (merry) 'dance** (*BrE*) to cause sb a lot of trouble or worry **lead from the 'front** to take an active part in what you are telling or persuading others to do **lead (sb) nowhere** to have no successful result for sb: *This discussion is leading us nowhere.* **lead sb up/down the garden 'path** to make sb believe sth which is not true SYN **mislead** IDM see BLIND *adj.*, HORSE *n.*, LIFE, THING

PHR V **ˌlead 'off (from) sth** to start at a place and go away from it: *narrow streets leading off from the main square* **ˌlead 'off** | **ˌlead sth↔'off** to start sth: *Who would like to lead off the debate?* **ˌlead sb 'on** (*informal*) to make sb believe sth which is not true, especially that you love them or find them attractive **ˌlead 'up to sth** to be an introduction to or the cause of sth: *the weeks leading up to the exam* ◇ *the events leading up to the strike* **'lead with sth 1** (of a newspaper) to have sth as the main item of news **2** (in boxing) to use a particular hand to begin an attack: *to **lead with your right/left***

■ *noun*

▸ FIRST PLACE **1** 🔑 **the lead** [sing.] the position ahead of everyone else in a race or competition: *She **took the lead** in the second lap.* ◇ *He has gone **into the lead**.* ◇ *The Democrats now appear to be **in the lead**.* ◇ *to **hold/lose the lead*** ◇ *The lead car is now three minutes ahead of the rest of the field.* **2** 🔑 [sing.] **~ (over sb/sth)** the amount or distance that sb/sth is in front of sb/sth else SYN **advantage**: *He managed to **hold a lead** of two seconds over his closest rival.* ◇ *The polls have given Labour a five-point lead.* ◇ *a **commanding/comfortable lead*** ◇ *to **increase/widen your lead*** ◇ *Manchester lost their early two-goal lead.*

▸ EXAMPLE **3** [sing.] an example or action for people to copy: *If one bank raises interest rates, all the others will **follow their lead**.* ◇ *If we **take the lead** in this* (= start to act), *others may follow.* ◇ *You go first, I'll take my lead from you.*

▸ INFORMATION **4** [C] a piece of information that may help to find out the truth or facts about a situation, especially a crime SYN **clue**: *The police will **follow up** all possible **leads**.*

▸ ACTOR/MUSICIAN **5** [C] the main part in a play, film/movie, etc; the person who plays this part: *Who is **playing the lead**?* ◇ *the **male/female lead*** ◇ *a lead role* ◇ *the lead singer in a band*

▸ FOR DOG **6** (*BrE*) (also **leash** *NAmE, BrE*) [C] a long piece of leather, chain or rope used for holding and controlling a dog: *Dogs must be kept on a lead in the park.*

▸ FOR ELECTRICITY **7** [C] (*BrE*) a long piece of wire, usually covered in plastic, that is used to connect a piece of electrical equipment to a source of electricity ➲ see also EXTENSION LEAD, JUMP LEAD

lead[2] /led/ *noun* ➲ see also LEAD[1] **1** [U] (*symb.* **Pb**) a chemical element. Lead is a heavy soft grey metal, used especially in the past for water pipes or to cover roofs. **2** [C, U] the thin black part of a pencil that marks paper ➲ VISUAL VOCAB page V56

IDM **go ˌdown like a lead bal'loon** (*informal*) to be very unsuccessful; to not be accepted by people ➲ more at SWING *v.*

lead·ed /'ledɪd/ *adj.* [usually before noun] **1** (of petrol, metal, etc.) with lead added to it OPP **unleaded 2** with a cover or a frame of lead: *a leaded roof*

ˌleaded 'light (also **ˌleaded 'window**) *noun* [usually pl.] (*BrE*) a window made from small pieces of glass that are arranged in diamond shapes and are separated by strips of LEAD

lead·en /'ledn/ *adj.* (*literary*) **1** dull grey in colour, like LEAD: *leaden skies* **2** dull, heavy or slow: *a leaden heart* (= because you are sad)

lead·er 0-w /'li:də(r)/ *noun*
1 0-w a person who leads a group of people, especially the head of a country, an organization, etc: *a* ***political/spiritual, etc. leader*** ◇ *the leader of the party* ◇ *union leaders* ◇ *He was not a* ***natural leader.*** ◇ *She's a* ***born leader.*** **2** 0-w a person or thing that is the best, or in first place in a race, business, etc: *She was among the leaders of the race from the start.* ◇ *The company is a* ***world leader*** *in electrical goods.* ➲ see also MARKET LEADER **3** (*BrE*) (also **con·cert·master** *NAmE, BrE*) the most important VIOLIN player in an ORCHESTRA **4** (*BrE*) = EDITORIAL

'leader board *noun* a sign showing the names and scores of the top players, especially in a GOLF competition

lead·er·less /'li:dələs; *NAmE* -dərl-/ *adj.* without a leader: *Her sudden death left the party leaderless.*

the ˌLeader of the 'House *noun* [sing.] (in Britain) a member of the government who is responsible for deciding what is discussed in Parliament

lead·er·ship /'li:dəʃɪp; *NAmE* -dərʃ-/ *noun* **1** [U] the state or position of being a leader: *a leadership contest* ◇ *The party thrived* ***under his leadership.*** **2** [U] the ability to be a leader or the qualities a good leader should have: ***leadership qualities/skills*** ◇ *Strong leadership is needed to captain the team.* **3** [C+sing./pl. v.] a group of leaders of a particular organization, etc: *The party leadership is/are divided.*

lead-free /ˌled 'fri:/ *adj.* (of petrol, paint, etc.) without any of the metal LEAD added to it

lead guitar /ˌli:d gɪ'tɑ:(r)/ *noun* [U] a GUITAR style that consists mainly of SOLOS and tunes rather than only CHORDS ➲ compare RHYTHM GUITAR

lead-in /'li:d ɪn/ *noun* an introduction to a subject, story, show, etc.

lead·ing[1] 0-w /'li:dɪŋ/ *adj.* [only before noun]
1 0-w most important or most successful: *leading experts* ◇ *She was offered the* ***leading role*** *in the new TV series.* ◇ *He* ***played a leading part*** *in the negotiations.* **2** 0-w ahead of others in a race or contest: *She started the last lap just behind the leading group.* ◇ *These are the leading first-round scores.*

lead·ing[2] /'ledɪŋ/ *noun* [U] (*technical*) the amount of white space between lines of printed text

ˌleading 'article (also **lead·er**) *noun* (both *BrE*) = EDITORIAL

ˌleading 'edge *noun* **1** [sing.] the most important and advanced position in an area of activity, especially technology: *at the leading edge of scientific research* **2** [C] (*technical*) the front or forward edge of sth moving, especially an aircraft wing ➲ VISUAL VOCAB page V43 ▶ **ˌleading-'edge** *adj.* [only before noun] SYN **cutting edge**: *leading-edge technology*

ˌleading 'lady, ˌleading 'man *noun* the actor with the main female or male part in a play or film/movie

ˌleading 'light *noun* an important, active or respected person in a particular area of activity: *She's one of the leading lights in the opera world.*

ˌleading 'question *noun* a question that you ask in a particular way in order to get the answer you want

'lead-off *adj.* (*NAmE*) being the first of a series: *the lead-off track on the album*

lead shot /ˌled 'ʃɒt; *NAmE* -'ʃɑ:t/ *noun* = SHOT (3)

lead story /'li:d stɔ:ri/ *noun* the main or first item of news in a newspaper, magazine or news broadcast

lead time /'li:d taɪm/ *noun* the time between starting and completing a production process

leaf 0-w /li:f/ *noun, verb*
■ ***noun*** (*pl.* **leaves** /li:vz/) **1** 0-w [C] a flat green part of a plant, growing from a STEM or branch or from the root: *lettuce/cabbage/oak leaves* ◇ *The trees are just* ***coming into leaf.*** ◇ *the dead leaves of autumn/the fall* ➲ COLLOCATIONS at LIFE ➲ VISUAL VOCAB page V8 ➲ see also BAY LEAF, FIG LEAF **2 -leaf, -leafed, -leaved** (in adjectives) having leaves of the type or number mentioned: *a four-leaf clover* ◇ *a broad-leaved plant* **3** [C] a sheet of paper, especially a page in a book ➲ see also FLYLEAF, LOOSE-LEAF, OVERLEAF **4** [U] metal, especially gold or silver, in the form of very thin sheets: *gold leaf* **5** [C] a part of a table that can be lifted up or pulled into position in order to make the table bigger
IDM **take a leaf from/out of sb's 'book** to copy sb's behaviour and do things in the same way that they do, because they are successful SYN **emulate** IDM see NEW
■ ***verb***
PHR V **'leaf through sth** to quickly turn over the pages of a book, etc. without reading them or looking at them carefully

leaf·less /'li:fləs/ *adj.* having no leaves SYN **bare**

leaf·let /'li:flət/ *noun, verb*
■ ***noun*** a printed sheet of paper or a few printed pages that are given free to advertise or give information about sth SYN **booklet, pamphlet**: *a leaflet on local places of interest*
■ ***verb*** [I, T] ~ **(sb/sth)** to give out leaflets to people: *We did a lot of leafleting in the area.*

'leaf mould (*BrE*) (*NAmE* **'leaf mold**) *noun* [U] soil consisting mostly of dead, decayed leaves

leafy /'li:fi/ *adj.* (**leaf·ier, leafi·est**) **1** having a lot of leaves: *Eat plenty of leafy green vegetables.* **2** (*approving*) (of a place) having a lot of trees and plants: *leafy suburbs* **3** made by a lot of leaves or trees: *We sat in the leafy shade of an oak tree.*

league 0-w /li:g/ *noun*
1 0-w a group of sports teams who all play each other to earn points and find which team is best: *major league baseball* ◇ *United were league champions last season.* ➲ see also MINOR-LEAGUE **2** (*informal*) a level of quality, ability, etc: *As a painter, he is* ***in a league of his own*** (= much better than others). ◇ *They're* ***in a different league*** *from us.* ◇ *When it comes to cooking, I'm* ***not in*** *her* ***league*** (= she is much better than me). ◇ *A house like that is* ***out of our league*** (= too expensive for us). **3** a group of people or nations who have combined for a particular purpose SYN **alliance**: *the League of Nations* ◇ *a meeting of the Women's League for Peace* ➲ see also IVY LEAGUE **4** (*old use*) a unit for measuring distance, equal to about 3 miles or 4 000 metres
IDM **in 'league (with sb)** making secret plans with sb

'league table *noun* (*BrE*) **1** a table that shows the position of sports teams and how successfully they are performing in a competition **2** a table that shows how well institutions such as schools or hospitals are performing in comparison with each other

leak /li:k/ *verb, noun*
■ ***verb*** **1** [I, T] to allow liquid or gas to get in or out through a small hole or crack: *a leaking pipe* ◇ *The roof was leaking.* ◇ **~ sth** *The tank had leaked a small amount of water.* **2** [I] (of a liquid or gas) to get in or out through a small hole or crack in sth: *Water had started to leak into the cellar.* **3** [T] **~ sth (to sb)** to give secret information to the public, for example by telling a newspaper SYN **disclose**: *The contents of the report were leaked to the press.* ◇ *a leaked document*
PHR V **ˌleak 'out** (of secret information) to become known to the public: *Details of the plan soon leaked out.*
■ ***noun*** **1** a small hole or crack that lets liquid or gas flow in or out of sth by accident: *a leak in the roof* ◇ *a leak in the gas pipe* ➲ COLLOCATIONS at DECORATE **2** liquid or gas that escapes through a hole in sth: *a gas leak* ◇ *oil leaks/leaks of oil* **3** a deliberate act of giving secret information to the newspapers, etc: *a leak to the press about the government plans on tax* **4** (*slang*) an act of passing URINE from the body: *to* ***have/take a leak*** IDM see SPRING *v.*

leak·age /'li:kɪdʒ/ *noun* [C, U] an amount of liquid or gas escaping through a hole in sth; an occasion when there is a leak: *a leakage of toxic waste into the sea* ◇ *Check bottles for leakage before use.*

leaky /'li:ki/ *adj.* having holes or cracks that allow liquid or gas to escape: *a leaky roof*

lean 0-w /li:n/ *verb, adj., noun*
■ ***verb*** (**leaned, leaned**) (*BrE* also **leant, leant** /lent/) **1** 0-w [I]

L

(**+ adv./prep.**) to bend or move from a vertical position: *I leaned back in my chair.* ◇ *The tower is leaning dangerously.* ◇ *A man was leaning out of the window.* **2** [I] to rest on or against sth for support: **~ against sth** *A shovel was leaning against the wall.* ◇ **~ on sth** *She walked slowly, leaning on her son's arm.* **3** [T] **~ sth against/on sth** to make sth rest against sth in a sloping position: *Can I lean my bike against the wall?* IDM see BACKWARDS

PHR V **'lean on sb/sth 1** to depend on sb/sth for help and support SYN **rely on**: *He leans heavily on his family.* **2** to try to influence sb by threatening them: *The government has been leaning on the TV company not to broadcast the show.* **'lean to/towards/toward sth** to have a tendency to prefer sth, especially a particular opinion or interest: *The UK leant towards the US proposal.*

■ ***adj.*** (**lean·er, lean·est**) **1** (usually *approving*) (of people, especially men, or animals) without much flesh; thin and fit: *a lean, muscular body* ◇ *He was tall, lean and handsome.* **2** (of meat) containing little or no fat **3** [usually before noun] (of a period of time) difficult and not producing much money, food, etc: *a* ***lean period/spell*** ◇ *The company recovered well after going through several* ***lean years***. **4** (of organizations, etc.) strong and efficient because the number of employees has been reduced: *The changes made the company leaner and more competitive.* ▶ **lean·ness** /'liːnnəs/ *noun* [U]

■ ***noun*** [U] the part of meat that has little or no fat

lean·ing /'liːnɪŋ/ *noun* [usually pl.] **~ (toward(s) sth)** a tendency to prefer sth or to believe in particular ideas, opinions, etc. SYN **inclination, tendency**: *a leaning towards comedy rather than tragedy* ◇ *a person with socialist leanings*

'lean-to *noun* (*pl.* -tos /-tuːz/) a small building with its roof leaning against the side of a large building, wall or fence: *a lean-to garage*

leap /liːp/ *verb, noun*

■ ***verb*** (**leapt, leapt** /lept/) or (**leaped, leaped**) **1** [I, T] to jump high or a long way: **+ adv./prep.** *A dolphin leapt out of the water.* ◇ *We leapt over the stream.* ◇ **~ sth** *The horse leapt a five-foot wall.* **2** [I] **+ adv./prep.** to move or do sth suddenly and quickly: *She leapt out of bed.* ◇ *He leapt across the room to answer the door.* ◇ *I* ***leapt to my feet*** (= stood up quickly). ◇ *They* ***leapt into action*** *immediately.* ◇ (*figurative*) *She was quick to* ***leap to my defence*** (= speak in support of me). ◇ *The photo seemed to* ***leap off the page*** (= it got your attention immediately). ◇ *His name* ***leapt out at me*** (= I saw it immediately). **3** [I] **~ (in sth) (from...) (to...)** to increase suddenly and by a large amount SYN **shoot up**: *The shares leapt in value from 476p to close at 536p.*

IDM **,look before you 'leap** (*saying*) used to advise sb to think about the possible results or dangers of sth before doing it ➲ more at CONCLUSION, HEART

PHR V **'leap at sth** to accept a chance or an opportunity quickly and with enthusiasm SYN **jump at**: *I leapt at the chance to go to France.*

■ ***noun* 1** a long or high jump: *a leap of six metres* ◇ *She took a* ***flying leap*** *and landed on the other side of the stream.* ◇ (*figurative*) *His heart gave a sudden leap when he saw her.* ◇ (*figurative*) *Few people successfully make the leap from television to the movies.* **2 ~ (in sth)** a sudden large change or increase in sth: *a leap in profits* ➲ see also QUANTUM LEAP

IDM **by/in ,leaps and 'bounds** very quickly; in large amounts: *Her health has improved in leaps and bounds.* **a leap in the 'dark** an action or a risk that you take without knowing anything about the activity or what the result will be

leap·frog /'liːpfrɒg; *NAmE* -frɔːg; -frɑːg/ *noun, verb*

■ ***noun*** [U] a children's game in which players take turns to jump over the backs of other players who are bending down

■ ***verb*** (-gg-) [T, I] **~ (sb/sth)** to get to a higher position or rank by going past sb else or by missing out some stages: *The win allowed them to leapfrog three teams to gain second place.*

'leap year *noun* one year in every four years when February has 29 days instead of 28

learn /lɜːn; *NAmE* lɜːrn/ *verb* (**learnt, learnt** /lɜːnt; *NAmE* lɜːrnt/) or (**learned, learned**)

1 [T, I] to gain knowledge or skill by studying, from experience, from being taught, etc: **~ sth** *to learn a language/a musical instrument/a skill* ◇ **~ sth from sb/sth** *I learned a lot from my father.* ◇ **~ sth from doing sth** *You can learn a great deal just from watching other players.* ◇ **~ (about sth)** *She's very keen to learn about Japanese culture.* ◇ *The book is about how children learn.* ◇ **~ to do sth** *He's learning to dance.* ◇ **~ how, what, etc...** *Today we learnt how to use the new software.* **2** [I, T] to become aware of sth by hearing about it from sb else SYN **discover**: **~ of/about sth** *I learnt of her arrival from a close friend.* ◇ **~ (that)...** *We were very surprised to learn (that) she had got married again.* ◇ **~ who, what, etc...** *We only learned who the new teacher was a few days ago.* ◇ **~ sth** *How did they react when they learned the news?* ◇ **it is learned that...** *It has been learned that 500 jobs are to be lost at the factory.* **3** [T] **~ sth** to study and repeat sth in order to be able to remember it SYN **memorize**: *We have to learn one of Hamlet's speeches for school tomorrow.* **4** [I, T] to gradually change your attitudes about sth so that you behave in a different way: **~ (from sth)** *I'm sure she'll learn from her mistakes.* ◇ **~ (that)...** *He'll just have to learn (that) he can't always have his own way.* ◇ **~ to do sth** *I soon learned not to ask too many questions.*

IDM **,learn (sth) the 'hard way** to find out how to behave by learning from your mistakes or from unpleasant experiences, rather than from being told **learn your 'lesson** to learn what to do or not to do in the future because you have had a bad experience in the past ➲ more at COST *n.*, LIVE[1], ROPE *n.*

Vocabulary Building

Learning

- **learn** *He's learning Spanish/to swim.*
- **study** *She studied chemistry for three years.*
- **revise** (*BrE*) (*NAmE* **review**) *In this class we'll revise/review what we did last week.*
- **practise** (*BrE*) (*NAmE* **practice**) *If you practise speaking English, you'll soon improve.*
- **rehearse** *We only had two weeks to rehearse the play.*

learn·ed /'lɜːnɪd; *NAmE* 'lɜːrnɪd/ *adj.* [usually before noun] **1** (*formal*) having a lot of knowledge because you have studied and read a lot: *a learned professor* ➲ see also FRIEND (5) **2** (*formal*) connected with or for learned people; showing and expressing deep knowledge SYN **scholarly**: *a learned journal* **3** /lɜːnd; *NAmE* lɜːrnd/ developed by training or experience; not existing at birth: *a learned skill*

learn·er /'lɜːnə(r); *NAmE* 'lɜːrn-/ *noun* **1** a person who is finding out about a subject or how to do sth: *a* ***slow/quick learner*** ◇ *a dictionary for learners of English* ◇ *learner-centred teaching methods* **2** (also **,learner 'driver**) a person who is learning to drive a car

'learner's permit (*NAmE*) (*BrE* **pro,visional 'licence**) *noun* an official document that you must have when you start to learn to drive

learn·ing /'lɜːnɪŋ; *NAmE* 'lɜːrnɪŋ/ *noun* [U] **1** the process of learning sth: *computer-assisted learning* ◇ *Last season was a learning experience for me.* ➲ see also DISTANCE LEARNING **2** knowledge that you get from reading and studying: *a woman of great learning*

'learning curve *noun* the rate at which you learn a new subject or a new skill; the process of learning from the mistakes you make

'learning difficulties *noun* [pl.] mental problems that people may have from birth, or that may be caused by illness or injury, that affect their ability to learn things

'learning disability *noun* [usually pl.] a mental problem that people may have from birth, or that may be caused by illness or injury, that affects their ability to learn things

lease /liːs/ *noun, verb*
■ ***noun*** a legal agreement that allows you to use a building, a piece of equipment or some land for a period of time, usually in return for rent: *to* ***take out a lease*** *on a house* ◇ *The* ***lease expires/runs out*** *next year.* ◇ *Under* ***the terms of the lease****, you have to pay maintenance charges.* ➲ COLLOCATIONS at HOUSE
IDM **a (ˌnew) lease of 'life** (*BrE*) (*NAmE* **a (ˌnew) lease on 'life**) the chance to live or last longer, or with a better quality of life: *Since her hip operation she's had a new lease of life.*
■ ***verb*** to use or let sb use sth, especially property or equipment, in exchange for rent or a regular payment SYN **rent**: **~ sth** *We lease all our computer equipment.* ◇ **~ sth from sb** *They lease the land from a local farmer.* ◇ **~ sb sth** *A local farmer leased them the land.* ◇ **~ sth (out) (to sb)** *Parts of the building are leased out to tenants.* ▶ **leas·ing** *noun* [U]: *car leasing* ◇ *a leasing company*

lease·back /ˈliːsbæk/ (*US* also **re·ver·sion**) *noun* [U] (*law*) the process of allowing the former owner of a property to continue to use it if they pay rent to the new owner; a legal agreement where this happens

lease·hold /ˈliːshəʊld; *NAmE* -hoʊld/ *adj., noun*
■ ***adj.*** (*especially BrE*) (of property or land) that can be used for a limited period of time, according to the arrangements in a LEASE: *a leasehold property* ▶ **lease·hold** *adv.*: *to purchase land leasehold* ➲ compare FREEHOLD
■ ***noun*** [U] (*especially BrE*) the right to use a building or a piece of land according to the arrangements in a LEASE: *to obtain/own the leasehold of a house* ➲ compare FREEHOLD

lease·hold·er /ˈliːshəʊldə(r); *NAmE* -hoʊld-/ *noun* (*especially BrE*) a person who is allowed to use a building or a piece of land according to the arrangements in a LEASE ➲ compare FREEHOLDER

leash /liːʃ/ *noun, verb*
■ ***noun*** (*especially NAmE*) (*BrE* also **lead**) a long piece of leather, chain or rope used for holding and controlling a dog: *All dogs must be kept* ***on a leash*** *in public places.* IDM see STRAIN *v.*
■ ***verb*** **~ sth** to control an animal, especially a dog, with a LEAD/LEASH

least 0-■ /liːst/ *det., pron., adv.*
■ ***det., pron.*** 0-■ (usually **the least**) smallest in size, amount, degree, etc: *He's the best teacher, even though he has the least experience.* ◇ *She never had the least idea what to do about it.* ◇ *He gave (the) least of all towards the wedding present.* ◇ *How others see me is* ***the least of*** *my worries* (= I have more important things to worry about). ◇ *It's* ***the least I can do*** *to help* (= I feel I should do more).
IDM **at the (very) 'least** used after amounts to show that the amount is the lowest possible: *It'll take a year, at the very least.* **ˌnot in the 'least** not at all: *Really, I'm not in the least tired.* ◇ *'Do you mind if I put the television on?' 'No, not in the least.'* ➲ more at SAY *v.*
■ ***adv.*** 0-■ to the smallest degree: *He always turns up just when you least expect him.* ◇ *She chose the least expensive of the hotels.* ◇ *I never hid the truth,* ***least of all*** *from you.*
IDM **at 'least 1** 0-■ not less than: *It'll cost at least 500 dollars.* ◇ *She must be at least 40.* ◇ *Cut the grass at least once a week in summer.* ◇ *I've known her at least as long as you have.* **2** 0-■ used to add a positive comment about a negative situation: *She may be slow but at least she's reliable.* **3** 0-■ even if nothing else is true or you do nothing else: *You could at least listen to what he says.* ◇ *Well, at least they weren't bored.* **4** 0-■ used to limit or make what you have just said less definite SYN **anyway**: *They seldom complained—officially at least.* ◇ *It works, at least I think it does.* **not 'least** especially: *The documentary caused a lot of bad feeling, not least among the workers whose lives it described.* ➲ more at LAST *adv.*, LINE *n.*, SAY *v.*

ˌleast ˌcommon de'nominator *noun* (*NAmE*) = LOWEST COMMON DENOMINATOR

ˌleast ˌcommon 'multiple *noun* (*NAmE*) = LOWEST COMMON MULTIPLE

least·ways /ˈliːstweɪz/ *adv.* (*NAmE, informal*) at least: *It isn't cheap to get there, leastways not at this time of year.*

lea·ther 0-■ /ˈleðə(r)/ *noun*
1 0-■ [U, C] material made by removing the hair or fur from animal skins and preserving the skins using special processes: *a leather jacket* ◇ *The soles are made of leather.* ◇ *a leather-bound book* ➲ VISUAL VOCAB page V50 **2 leathers** [pl.] clothes made from leather, especially those worn by people riding motorcycles ➲ see also CHAMOIS LEATHER, PATENT LEATHER IDM see HELL

lea·ther·back /ˈleðəbæk; *NAmE* -ðərb-/ (also **ˌleather-back 'turtle, ˌleathery 'turtle**) *noun* a very large sea TURTLE with a shell that looks like leather

lea·ther·ette /ˌleðəˈret/ *noun* [U] an artificial material that looks and feels like leather

lea·thery /ˈleðəri/ *adj.* that looks or feels hard and tough like leather: *leathery skin*

leave 0-■ /liːv/ *verb, noun*
■ ***verb*** (**left, left** /left/)
▸ PLACE/PERSON **1** 0-■ [I, T] to go away from a person or a place: *Come on, it's time we left.* ◇ **~ for...** *The plane leaves for Dallas at 12.35.* ◇ **~ sth** *I hate leaving home.* ◇ *The plane leaves Heathrow at 12.35.*
▸ HOME/JOB/SCHOOL **2** 0-■ [I, T] to stop living at a place, belonging to a group, working for an employer, etc: *My secretary has threatened to leave.* ◇ **~ sth** (*BrE*) *Some children leave school at 16.*
▸ WIFE/HUSBAND **3** 0-■ [T] **~ sb (for sb)** to leave your wife, husband or partner permanently: *She's leaving him for another man.*
▸ STH TO DO LATER **4** 0-■ [T] to not do sth or deal with sth immediately: **~ sth** *Leave the dishes—I'll do them later.* ◇ **~ sth until...** *Why do you always leave everything until the last moment?*
▸ SB/STH IN CONDITION/PLACE **5** 0-■ [T] to make or allow sb/sth to remain in a particular condition, place, etc: **~ sb/sth (+ adj.)** *Leave the door open, please.* ◇ *The bomb blast left 25 people dead.* ◇ **~ sb/sth doing sth** *Don't leave her waiting outside in the rain.* ◇ **~ sb/sth to do sth** *Leave the rice to cook for 20 minutes.* **6** 0-■ [T] to make sth happen or remain as a result: **~ sth** *Red wine leaves a stain.* ◇ **~ sb with sth** *She left me with the impression that she was unhappy with her job.* ◇ **~ sb sth** *I'm afraid you leave me no choice.* **7** 0-■ **be left** [T] to remain to be used, sold, etc: *Is there any coffee left?* ◇ *How many tickets do you have left?* ◇ **~ of sth** (*figurative*) *They are fighting to save what is left of their business.* ◇ **~ to sb** *The only course of action left to me was to notify her employer.* **8** 0-■ [T] to go away from a place without taking sth/sb with you: **~ sth/sb (+ adv./prep.)** *I've left my bag on the bus.* ◇ **~ sth/sb behind** *Don't leave any of your belongings behind.* ◇ *He wasn't well, so we had to leave him behind.*
▸ MATHEMATICS **9** [T] **~ sth** to have a particular amount remaining: *Seven from ten leaves three.*
▸ AFTER DEATH **10** [T] **~ sb** to have family remaining after your death: *He leaves a wife and two children.* **11** 0-■ [T] to give sth to sb when you die SYN **bequeath**: **~ sth (to sb)** *She left £1 million to her daughter.* ◇ **~ sb sth** *She left her daughter £1 million.*
▸ RESPONSIBILITY TO SB **12** 0-■ [T] to allow sb to take care of sth: **~ sb/sth + adv./prep.** *You can leave the cooking to me.* ◇ *She left her assistant in charge.* ◇ ***Leave it with me****—I'm sure I can sort it out.* ◇ *'Where shall we eat?' 'I'll leave it entirely (up) to you* (= you can decide).*'* ◇ *They left me with all the clearing up.* ◇ **~ sb/sth to do sth** *I was left to cope on my own.*
▸ DELIVER **13** 0-■ [T] to deliver sth and then go away: **~ sth (for sb)** *Someone left this note for you.* ◇ **~ sb sth** *Someone left you this note.*
IDM Most idioms containing **leave** are at the entries for the nouns and adjectives in the idioms, for example **leave sb in the lurch** is at **lurch**. **ˌleave 'go (of sth)** (*BrE, informal*) to stop holding on to sth SYN **let go**: *Leave go of my arm—*

L

you're hurting me! **leave it at 'that** (*informal*) to say or do nothing more about sth: *We'll never agree, so let's just leave it at that.* **,leave it 'out** (*BrE, informal*) used to tell sb to stop doing sth ➲ more at TAKE

PHR V **,leave sth↔a'side** to not consider sth: *Leaving the expense aside, do we actually need a second car?* **,leave sb/sth be'hind 1** [usually passive] to make much better progress than sb: *Britain is being left behind in the race for new markets.* **2** to leave a person, place or state permanently: *She knew that she had left childhood behind.* ➲ see also LEAVE (8) **,leave 'off** (*informal*) to stop doing sth: *Start reading from where you left off last time.* ◇ **~ doing sth** *He left off playing the piano to answer the door.* **,leave sb/sth↔'off (sth)** to not include sb/sth on a list, etc: *You've left off a zero.* ◇ *We left him off the list.* **,leave sb/sth 'out (of sth)** 🔑 to not include or mention sb/sth in sth: *Leave me out of this quarrel, please.* ◇ *He hadn't been asked to the party and was feeling very left out.* ◇ *She left out an 'm' in 'accommodation'.* **be ,left 'over (from sth)** 🔑 to remain when all that is needed has been used: *There was lots of food left over.* ➲ related noun LEFTOVER

■ ***noun*** [U] **1** a period of time when you are allowed to be away from work for a holiday/vacation or for a special reason: *to take a month's* ***paid/unpaid leave*** ◇ *soldiers home* ***on leave*** ◇ *to be on* ***maternity/study leave*** ◇ *How much* ***annual leave*** *do you get?* ➲ see also COMPASSIONATE LEAVE, SICK LEAVE **2** (*formal*) official permission to do sth: *to be absent* ***without leave*** ◇ **~ to do sth** *The court granted him leave to appeal against the sentence.* ◇ *She asked for* ***leave of absence*** (= permission to be away from work) *to attend a funeral.*

IDM **,by/,with your 'leave** (*formal*) with your permission **take ,leave of your 'senses** (*old-fashioned*) to start behaving as if you are crazy **take (your) 'leave (of sb)** (*formal*) to say goodbye: *With a nod and a smile, she took leave of her friends.* **without a ,by your 'leave; without so much as a ,by your 'leave** (*old-fashioned*) without asking permission; rudely ➲ more at BEG, FRENCH

-leaved /-li:vd/ ➲ LEAF

leaven /'levn/ *noun, verb*

■ ***noun*** [U] a substance, especially YEAST, that is added to bread before it is cooked to make it rise: (*figurative*) *A few jokes add leaven to a boring speech.*

■ ***verb*** [often passive] **~ sth (with sth)** (*formal*) to make sth more interesting or cheerful by adding sth to it: *Her speech was leavened with a touch of humour.*

leav·er /'li:və(r)/ *noun* (often in compounds) a person who is leaving a place: *school-leavers*

leaves *pl.* of LEAF

'leave-taking *noun* [U, C, usually sing.] (*formal*) the act of saying goodbye **SYN** **farewell**

leav·ings /'li:vɪŋz/ *noun* [pl.] something that you leave because you do not want it, especially food

lech /letʃ/ *noun, verb* (*BrE, informal, disapproving*)

■ ***noun*** a man who shows an unpleasant sexual interest in sb

■ ***verb***

PHR V **'lech after sb** (*BrE*) to show an unpleasant sexual interest in sb

lech·er /'letʃə(r)/ *noun* (*disapproving*) a man who is always thinking about sex and looking for sexual pleasure ▸ **lech·ery** *noun* [U]

lech·er·ous /'letʃərəs/ *adj.* (*disapproving*) having too much interest in sexual pleasure **SYN** **lustful, lascivious**

leci·thin /'lesɪθɪn/ *noun* [U] a natural substance found in animals, plants and in egg YOLKS. Lecithin is used as an ingredient in some foods.

lec·tern /'lektən; *NAmE* -tərn/ (*NAmE* also **po·dium**) *noun* a stand for holding a book, notes, etc. when you are reading in church, giving a talk, etc.

lec·tor /'lektɔ:(r)/ *noun* a person who teaches in a university, especially sb who teaches their own language in a foreign country ➲ compare LECTRICE

lec·trice /lek'tri:s; *NAmE* 'lektrɪs/ *noun* a female LECTOR in a university

lec·ture 🔑 **AW** /'lektʃə(r)/ *noun, verb*

■ ***noun*** **~ (to sb) (on/about sth) 1** 🔑 a talk that is given to a group of people to teach them about a particular subject, often as part of a university or college course: *to* ***deliver/give a lecture*** *to first-year students* ◇ *to attend a* ***series of lectures*** *on Jane Austen* ◇ *a* ***lecture room/hall*** ➲ SYNONYMS at SPEECH ➲ COLLOCATIONS at EDUCATION **2** a long angry talk that sb gives to one person or a group of people because they have done sth wrong: *I know I should stop smoking—don't give me a lecture about it.*

■ ***verb*** **1** [I] **~ (in/on sth)** to give a talk or a series of talks to a group of people on a subject, especially as a way of teaching in a university or college: *She lectures in Russian literature.* **2** [T] **~ sb (about/on sth)** | **~ sb (about doing sth)** to criticize sb or tell them how you think they should behave, especially when it is done in an annoying way: *He's always lecturing me about the way I dress.*

lec·tur·er **AW** /'lektʃərə(r)/ *noun* **1** a person who gives a lecture: *She's a superb lecturer.* **2** (especially in Britain) a person who teaches at a university or college: *He's a lecturer in French at Oxford.*

lec·ture·ship /'lektʃəʃɪp; *NAmE* -tʃərʃ-/ *noun* the position of lecturer at a British university or college: *a lectureship in media studies*

'lecture theatre (*BrE*) (*NAmE* **'lecture theater**) *noun* a large room with rows of seats on a slope, where lectures are given

LED /,el i: 'di:/ *abbr.* light emitting diode (a device that produces a light on electrical and electronic equipment): *A single red LED shows that the power is switched on.*

led /led/ **1** *past tense, past part.* of LEAD **2 -led** (in adjectives) influenced or organized by: *a consumer-led society* ◇ *student-led activities*

ledge /ledʒ/ *noun* **1** a narrow flat piece of rock that sticks out from a CLIFF: *seabirds nesting on rocky ledges* **2** a narrow flat shelf fixed to a wall, especially one below a window: *She put the vase of flowers on the window ledge.* ➲ see also SILL

ledger /'ledʒə(r)/ *noun* a book in which a bank, a business, etc. records the money it has paid and received: *to enter figures in the* ***purchase/sales ledger***

lee /li:/ *noun* **1** [sing.] the side or part of sth that provides shelter from the wind ➲ compare LEEWARD, WINDWARD **2 lees** [pl.] the substance that is left at the bottom of a bottle of wine, a container of beer, etc. **SYN** **dregs**

leech /li:tʃ/ *noun* **1** a small WORM that usually lives in water and that attaches itself to other creatures and sucks their blood. Leeches were used in the past by doctors to remove blood from sick people. **2** (*disapproving*) a person who depends on sb else for money, or takes the profit from sb else's work

leek /li:k/ *noun* a vegetable like a long onion with many layers of wide flat leaves that are white at the bottom and green at the top. Leeks are eaten cooked. The leek is a national symbol of Wales. ➲ VISUAL VOCAB page V27

leer /lɪə(r); *NAmE* lɪr/ *verb, noun*

■ ***verb*** [I] **~ (at sb)** to look or smile at sb in an unpleasant way that shows an evil or sexual interest in them

■ ***noun*** an unpleasant look or smile that shows sb is interested in a person in an evil or sexual way: *He looked at her with an evil leer.*

leery /'lɪəri; *NAmE* 'lɪri/ *adj.* (*informal*) **~ (of sth/sb)** | **~ (of doing sth)** suspicious or careful about sth/sb, and trying to avoid doing it or dealing with them **SYN** **wary**: *The government is leery of changing the current law.*

lee·ward /'li:wəd; *NAmE* -wərd; *or, in nautical use,* 'lu:əd; *NAmE* -ərd/ *adj., noun*

■ ***adj.*** on the side of sth that is sheltered from the wind: *a harbour on the leeward side of the island* ▸ **lee·ward** *adv.* ➲ compare WINDWARD

■ ***noun*** [U] the side or direction that is sheltered from the wind ➲ compare WINDWARD

Lego™ /ˈlegəʊ; *NAmE* -goʊ/ *noun* [U] a children's toy that consists of small coloured bricks that fit together

ˈleg-pull *noun* a joke played on sb, usually by making them believe sth that is not true

leg·room /ˈlegruːm; ˈlegrʊm/ *noun* [U] the amount of space available for your legs when you are sitting in a car, plane, theatre, etc.

leg·ume /ˈlegjuːm; lɪˈgjuːm/ *noun* (*technical*) any plant that has seeds in long PODS. PEAS and BEANS are legumes.

leg·um·in·ous /lɪˈgjuːmɪnəs/ *adj.* [usually before noun] (*technical*) relating to plants of the legume family

ˈleg-up *noun*
IDM **give sb a ˈleg-up** (*BrE, informal*) **1** to help sb to get on a horse, over a wall, etc. by allowing them to put their foot in your hands and lifting them up **2** to help sb to improve their situation

ˈleg warmer *noun* [usually pl.] a kind of sock without a foot that covers the leg from the ankle to the knee, often worn when doing exercise

leg·work /ˈlegwɜːk; *NAmE* -wɜːrk/ *noun* [U] (*informal*) difficult or boring work that takes a lot of time and effort, but that is thought to be less important

leis·ure /ˈleʒə(r); *NAmE* ˈliːʒər/ *noun* [U] time that is spent doing what you enjoy when you are not working or studying: *These days we have more money and more leisure to enjoy it.* ◇ ***leisure activities/interests/pursuits***
IDM **at ˈleisure 1** with no particular activities; free: *Spend the afternoon at leisure in the town centre.* **2** without hurrying: *Let's have lunch so we can talk at leisure.* **at your ˈleisure** (*formal*) when you have the time to do sth without hurrying: *I suggest you take the forms away and read them at your leisure.* **a ˌgentleman/ˌlady of ˈleisure** (*humorous*) a man/woman who does not have to work

ˈleisure centre *noun* (*BrE*) a public building where people can go to do sports and other activities in their free time

leis·ured /ˈleʒəd; *NAmE* ˈliːʒərd/ *adj.* **1** [only before noun] not having to work and therefore having a lot of time to do what you enjoy: *the leisured classes* **2** = LEISURELY

leis·ure·ly /ˈleʒəli; *NAmE* ˈliːʒərli/ (also **leis·ured**) *adj.* [usually before noun] done without hurrying: *a leisurely meal* ◇ *They set off at a leisurely pace.* ▸ **leis·ure·ly** *adv.*: *Couples strolled leisurely along the beach.*

ˈleisure suit *noun* (*NAmE*) an informal suit consisting of a shirt and trousers/pants made of the same cloth, popular in the 1970s

leis·ure·wear /ˈleʒəweə(r); *NAmE* ˈliːʒərwer/ *noun* [U] (used especially by shops/stores and clothes companies) informal clothes worn for relaxing or playing sports in

leit·motif (also **leit·motiv**) /ˈlaɪtməʊtiːf; *NAmE* -moʊ-/ *noun* (from *German*) **1** (*music*) a short tune in a piece of music that is often repeated and is connected with a particular person, thing or idea **2** an idea or a phrase that is repeated often in a book or work of art, or is typical of a particular person or group

lek·got·la /leˈxɒtlə; *NAmE* -ˈxɑːt-/ *noun* (*SAfrE*) an important meeting of politicians or government officials

lek·ker /ˈlekə(r)/ *adj., adv.* (*SAfrE, informal*)
■ ***adj.*** good or nice; tasting good: *It was lekker to see you again.* ◇ *a lekker meal*
■ ***adv.*** very: *I'm lekker full.*

lemma /ˈlemə/ *noun* (*pl.* **lem·mas** or **lem·mata** /-mətə/) **1** (*technical*) a statement that is assumed to be true in order to test the truth of another statement **2** (*linguistics*) the basic form of a word, for example the singular form of a noun or the infinitive form of a verb, as it is shown at the beginning of a dictionary entry

lem·ming /ˈlemɪŋ/ *noun* a small animal like a mouse, that lives in cold northern countries. Sometimes large groups of lemmingsMIGRATE (= move from one place to another) in search of food. Many of them die on these journeys and there is a popular belief that lemmings kill themselves by jumping off CLIFFS: *Lemming-like we rushed into certain disaster.*

lemon 🔑 /ˈlemən/ *noun, adj.*
■ ***noun*** **1** 🔑 [C, U] a yellow CITRUS fruit with a lot of sour juice. Slices of lemon and lemon juice are used in cooking and drinks: *lemon tea* ◇ *a gin and tonic with ice and lemon* ◇ *Squeeze the juice of half a lemon over the fish.* ◇ *a lemon tree* ➲ VISUAL VOCAB page V26 **2** 🔑 [U] lemon juice or a drink made from lemon ➲ see also BITTER LEMON **3** 🔑 (also **ˌlemon ˈyellow**) [U] a pale yellow colour **4** [C] (*informal, especially NAmE*) a thing that is useless because it does not work as it should SYN **dud** **5** [C] (*BrE*) a stupid person SYN **idiot**
■ ***adj.*** (also **ˌlemon ˈyellow**) pale yellow in colour

lem·on·ade /ˌleməˈneɪd/ *noun* **1** [U] (*BrE*) a sweet FIZZY drink (= with bubbles) with a lemon flavour **2** [U] a drink made from lemon juice, sugar and water **3** [C] a glass or bottle of lemonade ➲ compare ORANGEADE

ˈlemon balm *noun* [U] a HERB with leaves that taste of lemon

ˌlemon ˈcurd *noun* [U] (*BrE*) a thick sweet yellow substance made from lemon, sugar, eggs and butter, spread on bread, etc. or used to fill cakes

ˈlemon grass *noun* [U] a type of grass with a lemon flavour that grows in hot countries and is used especially in SE Asian cooking

ˌlemon ˈsole *noun* a common European FLATFISH, often eaten as food

ˈlemon-squeezer (*BrE*) (*NAmE* **juicer**) *noun* a kitchen UTENSIL (= a tool) for squeezing juice out of a fruit ➲ VISUAL VOCAB page V23

lem·ony /ˈleməni/ *adj.* tasting or smelling of lemon: *a lemony flavour*

lemur /ˈliːmə(r)/ *noun* an animal like a MONKEY, with thick fur and a long tail, that lives in trees in Madagascar

lend 🔑 /lend/ *verb* (**lent, lent** /lent/)
1 🔑 [T] to give sth to sb or allow them to use sth that belongs to you, which they have to return to you later SYN **loan**: **~ (out) sth (to sb)** *I've lent the car to a friend.* ◇ **~ sb sth** *Can you lend me your car this evening?* ◇ *Has he returned that book you lent him?* ➲ note at BORROW **2** 🔑 [T, I] (of a bank or financial institution) to give money to sb on condition that they pay it back over a period of time and pay interest on it SYN **loan**: **~ (sth) (to sb)** *The bank refused to lend the money to us.* ◇ **~ sb sth** *They refused to lend us the money.* ➲ compare BORROW **3** [T] (*formal*) to give a particular quality to a person or a situation: **~ sth (to sb/sth)** *The setting sun lent an air of melancholy to the scene.* ◇ **~ sb/sth sth** *Her presence lent the occasion a certain dignity.* **4** [T] to give or provide help, support, etc: **~ sth (to sb/sth)** *I was more than happy to lend my support to such a good cause.* ◇ **~ sb/sth sth** *He came along to lend me moral support.*
IDM **lend an ˈear (to sb/sth)** to listen in a patient and sympathetic way to sb **lend (sb) a (helping) ˈhand (with sth)** (*informal*) to help sb with sth: *I went over to see if I could lend a hand.* **lend ˈcolour to sth** (*BrE*) to make sth seem true or probable: *Most of the available evidence lends colour to this view.* **lend your name to sth** (*formal*) **1** to let it be known in public that you support or agree with sth: *I am more than happy to lend my name to this campaign.* **2** to have a place named after you **lend supˈport, ˈweight, ˈcredence, etc. to sth** to make sth seem more likely to be true or genuine: *This latest evidence lends support to her theory.* ➲ more at HELP *v.*
PHR V **ˈlend itself to sth** to be suitable for sth: *Her voice doesn't really lend itself well to blues singing.*

lend·er /ˈlendə(r)/ *noun* (*finance*) a person or an organization that lends money ➲ compare BORROWER ➲ see also MONEYLENDER

lend·ing /ˈlendɪŋ/ *noun* [U] (*finance*) the act of lending money: *Lending by banks rose to $10 billion last year.*

ˈlending library *noun* a public library from which you can borrow books and take them away to read at home ➲ compare REFERENCE LIBRARY

L

ˈlending rate *noun* (*finance*) the rate of interest that you must pay when you borrow money from a bank or another financial organization

length 0-ᵣ /leŋθ/ *noun*
▸ SIZE/MEASUREMENT **1** 0-ᵣ [U, C] the size or measurement of sth from one end to the other: *This room is twice the length of the kitchen.* ◇ *The river is 300 miles* ***in length.*** ◇ *The snake usually reaches a length of 100 cm.* ◇ *He ran the entire length of the beach* (= from one end to the other). ◇ *Did you see the length of his hair?* ➲ compare BREADTH, WIDTH
▸ TIME **2** 0-ᵣ [U, C] the amount of time that sth lasts: *We discussed shortening the length of the course.* ◇ *He was disgusted at* ***the length of time*** *he had to wait.* ◇ *She got a headache if she had to read* ***for any length of time*** (= for a long time). ◇ *Size of pension depends partly on length of service with the company.* ◇ *Each class is 45 minutes* ***in length.***
▸ OF BOOK/MOVIE **3** 0-ᵣ [U, C] the amount of writing in a book, or a document, etc; the amount of time that a film/movie lasts: *Her novels vary in length.*
▸ -LENGTH **4** (in adjectives) having the length mentioned: *shoulder-length hair* ➲ see also FULL-LENGTH, KNEE-LENGTH
▸ OF SWIMMING POOL **5** [C] the distance from one end of a swimming pool to the other: *He swims 50 lengths a day.* ➲ compare WIDTH
▸ IN RACE **6** [C] the size of a horse or boat from one end to the other, when it is used to measure the distance between two horses or boats taking part in a race: *The horse won by two clear lengths.*
▸ LONG THIN PIECE **7** [C] a long thin piece of sth: *a* ***length of rope/string/wire*** ➲ see also LONG *adj.*
IDM **at ˈlength | at... length 1** for a long time and in detail: *He quoted at length from the report.* ◇ *We have already discussed this matter at great length.* **2** (*literary*) after a long time: *'I'm still not sure,' he said at length.* **go to any, some, great, etc. ˈlengths (to do sth)** to put a lot of effort into doing sth, especially when this seems extreme: *She goes to extraordinary lengths to keep her private life private.* **the length and ˈbreadth of...** in or to all parts of a place: *They have travelled the length and breadth of Europe giving concerts.* ➲ more at ARM *n.*

length·en /ˈleŋθən/ *verb* [I, T] to become longer; to make sth longer: *The afternoon shadows lengthened.* ◇ **~ sth** *I need to lengthen this skirt.* OPP **shorten**

length·ways /ˈleŋθweɪz/ (also **length·wise** /ˈleŋθwaɪz/) *adv.* in the same direction as the longest side of sth: *Cut the banana in half lengthways.* ➲ compare WIDTHWAYS

lengthy /ˈleŋθi/ *adj.* (**length·ier**, **lengthi·est**) very long, and often too long, in time or size: *lengthy delays* ◇ *the lengthy process of obtaining a visa* ◇ *a lengthy explanation*

le·ni·ent /ˈliːniənt/ *adj.* not as strict as expected when punishing sb or when making sure that rules are obeyed: *a* ***lenient sentence/fine*** ◇ *The judge was far too lenient with him.* ▸ **le·ni·ency** /-ənsi/ (also *less frequent* **le·ni·ence**) *noun* [U]: *She appealed to the judge for leniency.* **le·ni·ent·ly** *adv.*: *to treat sb leniently*

Lenin·ism /ˈlenɪnɪzəm/ *noun* [U] the political and economic policies of Lenin, the first leader of the Soviet Union, which were based on Marxism ▸ **Lenin·ist** /ˈlenɪnɪst/ *noun, adj.*

lens /lenz/ *noun* **1** a curved piece of glass or plastic that makes things look larger, smaller or clearer when you look through it: *a pair of glasses with tinted lenses* ◇ *a camera with an adjustable lens* ◇ *a* ***lens cap/cover*** ➲ picture at BINOCULARS, FRAME ➲ VISUAL VOCAB page V54 ➲ see also FISHEYE LENS, TELEPHOTO LENS, WIDE-ANGLE LENS, ZOOM LENS **2** (*informal*) = CONTACT LENS: *Have you got your lenses in?* **3** (*anatomy*) the transparent part of the eye, behind the PUPIL, that focuses light so that you can see clearly ➲ VISUAL VOCAB page V48

lens·man /ˈlenzmən/ *noun* (*pl.* **-men** /-mən/) a professional photographer or CAMERAMAN

Lent /lent/ *noun* [U] in the Christian Church, the period of 40 days from Ash Wednesday to the day before Easter, during which some Christians give up some type of food or activity that they enjoy in memory of Christ's suffering

lent *past tense, past part.* of LEND

len·tigo /lenˈtaɪɡəʊ; *NAmE* -ɡoʊ/ *noun* [U] (*medical*) a condition in which small brown areas appear on the skin, usually in old people ➲ see also LIVER SPOT

len·til /ˈlentl/ *noun* a small green, orange or brown seed that is usually dried and used in cooking, for example in soup or STEW

Leo /ˈliːəʊ; *NAmE* ˈliːoʊ/ *noun* **1** [U] the fifth sign of the ZODIAC, the Lion **2** [C] (*pl.* **-os**) a person born when the sun is in this sign, that is between 23 July and 22 August, approximately

leo·nine /ˈliːənaɪn/ *adj.* (*literary*) like a LION

leop·ard /ˈlepəd; *NAmE* -ərd/ *noun* a large animal of the cat family, that has yellowish-brown fur with black spots. Leopards live in Africa and southern Asia. ➲ compare LEOPARDESS
IDM **a leopard cannot change its ˈspots** (*saying*) people cannot change their character, especially if they have a bad character

ˈleopard-crawl *verb* [I] **+ adv./prep.** (*SAfrE*) (often used about soldiers) to move with your body as close to the ground as possible, using your elbows and knees to push you forward

leop·ard·ess /ˈlepədes; *NAmE* -ərd-/ *noun* a female leopard

leo·tard /ˈliːətɑːd; *NAmE* -tɑːrd/ *noun* a piece of clothing that fits tightly over the body from the neck down to the tops of the legs, usually covering the arms, worn by dancers, women doing physical exercises, etc.

LEP /ˌel iː ˈpiː/ *abbr.* [only before noun] (*NAmE, technical*) Limited English Proficient (used to describe students who cannot speak English very well): *schools with large numbers of LEP children*

leper /ˈlepə(r)/ *noun* **1** a person suffering from LEPROSY **2** a person that other people avoid because they have done sth that these people do not approve of

lep·re·chaun /ˈleprəkɔːn/ *noun* (in Irish stories) a creature like a little man, with magic powers

lep·rosy /ˈleprəsi/ *noun* [U] an infectious disease that causes painful white areas on the skin and can destroy nerves and flesh ➲ see also LEPER

lep·rous /ˈleprəs/ *adj.* affected by LEPROSY

les·bian /ˈlezbiən/ (also *informal* **lezzy, lezzie**) *noun* a woman who is sexually attracted to other women: *lesbians and gays* ➲ compare GAY, HOMOSEXUAL ▸ **les·bian** *adj.*: *the lesbian and gay community* ◇ *a lesbian relationship* **les·bian·ism** *noun* [U]

lese-majesty /ˌliːz ˈmædʒəsti; *NAmE* ˌleɪz/ *noun* [U] (from *French, formal*) the act or crime of insulting the king, queen or other ruler

le·sion /ˈliːʒn/ *noun* (*medical*) damage to the skin or part of the body caused by injury or by illness: *skin/brain lesions*

less 0-ᵣ /les/ *det., pron., adv., prep.*
▪ ***det., pron.*** 0-ᵣ used with uncountable nouns to mean 'a smaller amount of': *less butter/time/importance* ◇ *He was advised to smoke fewer cigarettes and drink less beer.* ◇ *We have less to worry about now.* ◇ *It is* ***less of*** *a problem* ***than*** *I'd expected.* ◇ *We'll be there in* ***less than no time*** (= very soon). ◇ *The victory was* ***nothing less than*** *a miracle.*
HELP People often use **less** with countable nouns: *There were less cars on the road then.* This is not considered correct by some people, and **fewer** should be used instead.
IDM **ˌless and ˈless** 0-ᵣ smaller and smaller amounts: *As time passed, she saw less and less of all her old friends at home.* **ˌless is ˈmore** (*saying*) include only what is essential in order to create an effective product or result: *His simple, elegant paintings reflect his principle that less is more.* **no ˈless** (often *ironic*) used to suggest that sth is surprising or impressive: *She's having lunch with the Director, no less.* **no less than...** used to emphasize a large amount: *The guide contains details of no less than 115 hiking routes.*
▪ ***adv.*** 0-ᵣ to a smaller degree; not so much: *less expensive/*

likely/intelligent ◇ less often/enthusiastically ◇ I read much less now than I used to. ◇ The receptionist was **less than** (= not at all) helpful. ◇ She wasn't **any the less** happy for (= she was perfectly happy) being on her own. ◇ That this is a positive stereotype makes it **no less a** stereotype, and therefore unacceptable.

IDM **even/much/still 'less** and certainly not: *No explanation was offered, still less an apology.* **ˌless and 'less** continuing to become smaller in amount: *She found the job less and less attractive.* ➲ more at MORE *adv.*

■ ***prep.*** used before a particular amount that must be taken away from the amount just mentioned SYN **minus**: *a monthly salary of $2 000 less tax and insurance*

-less /-ləs/ *suffix* (in adjectives) **1** without: *treeless* ◇ *meaningless* **2** not doing; not affected by: *tireless* ◇ *selfless* ▶ **-less·ly** (in adverbs): *hopelessly* **-less·ness** (in nouns): *helplessness*

les·see /leˈsiː/ *noun* (*law*) a person who has use of a building, an area of land, etc. on a LEASE ➲ compare LESSOR

less·en /ˈlesn/ *verb* [I, T] to become or make sth become smaller, weaker, less important, etc. SYN **diminish**: *The noise began to lessen.* ◇ **~ sth** *to lessen the risk/impact/effect of sth* ▶ **less·en·ing** *noun* [sing., U]: *a lessening of tension*

less·er /ˈlesə(r)/ *adj.* [only before noun] **1** not as great in size, amount or importance as sth/sb else: *people of lesser importance* ◇ *They were all involved* ***to a greater or lesser degree*** (= some were more involved than others). ◇ *The law was designed to protect wives, and, to a lesser extent, children.* ◇ *He was encouraged to plead guilty to the lesser offence.* **2** used in the names of some types of animals, birds and plants which are smaller than similar kinds OPP **greater** ▶ **less·er** *adv.*: *one of the lesser-known Caribbean islands*

IDM **the ˌlesser of two ˈevils | the ˌlesser ˈevil** the less unpleasant of two unpleasant choices

lesso /ˈlesəʊ; *NAmE* ˈlesoʊ/ *noun* (*pl.* -os) = KHANGA

les·son /ˈlesn/ *noun*
1 a period of time in which sb is taught sth: *She gives piano lessons.* ◇ *All new students are given* ***lessons in/on*** *how to use the library.* ◇ *I'm* ***having/taking*** *driving lessons.* ◇ (*especially BrE*) *Our first lesson on Tuesdays is French.* ◇ (*especially BrE*) *What did we do last lesson?* ➲ COLLOCATIONS at EDUCATION ➲ compare CLASS **2** something that is intended to be learned: *The course book is divided into 30 lessons.* ◇ *Other countries can* ***teach us a lesson*** *or two on industrial policy.* **3** an experience, especially an unpleasant one, that sb can learn from so that it does not happen again in the future: *a salutary lesson* ◇ *The accident* ***taught me a lesson*** *I'll never forget.* ◇ **~ to sb** *Let that be a* ***lesson to you*** (= so that you do not make the same mistake again). ➲ see also OBJECT LESSON **4** a passage from the Bible that is read to people during a church service
IDM see LEARN

les·sor /leˈsɔː(r)/ *noun* (*law*) a person who gives sb the use of a building, an area of land, etc. on a LEASE ➲ compare LESSEE

lest /lest/ *conj.* (*formal* or *literary*) **1** in order to prevent sth from happening: *He gripped his brother's arm lest he be trampled by the mob.* **2** used to introduce the reason for the particular emotion mentioned SYN **in case**: *She was afraid lest she had revealed too much.*

let /let/ *verb, noun*
■ ***verb*** (**let·ting, let, let**)
▸ ALLOW **1** [no passive] to allow sb to do sth or sth to happen without trying to stop it: **~ sb/sth do sth** *Let them splash around in the pool for a while.* ◇ *Don't let her upset you.* ◇ *Let your body relax.* ◇ **~ sb/sth** *He'd eat chocolate all day long if I let him.* **2** to give sb permission to do sth: **~ sb/sth do sth** *They won't let him leave the country.* ◇ **~ sb/sth** *She wanted to lend me some money but I wouldn't let her.* **3** **~ sb/sth + adv./prep.** to allow sb/sth to go somewhere: *to let sb into the house* ◇ *I'll give you a key so that you can let yourself in.* ◇ *Please let me past.* ◇ *The cat wants to be let out.*
▸ MAKING SUGGESTIONS **4** **let's** [no passive] **~ (do sth)** used for making suggestions: *Let's go to the beach.* ◇ *Let's not tell her what we did.* ◇ (*BrE*) *Don't let's tell her what we did.* ◇ *I don't think we'll make it, but let's try anyway.* ◇ *'Shall we check it again?' 'Yes, let's.'*
▸ OFFERING HELP **5** [no passive] **~ sb/sth do sth** used for offering help to sb: *Here, let me do it.* ◇ *Let us get those boxes down for you.*
▸ MAKING REQUESTS **6** [no passive] **~ sb/sth do sth** used for making requests or giving instructions: *Let me have your report by Friday.*
▸ CHALLENGING **7** [no passive] **~ sb/sth do sth** used to show that you are not afraid or worried about sb doing sth: *If he thinks he can cheat me, just let him try!*
▸ WISHING **8** [no passive] **~ sb/sth do sth** (*literary*) used to express a strong wish for sth to happen: *Let her come home safely!*
▸ INTRODUCING STH **9** [no passive] **~ sb/sth do sth** used to introduce what you are going to say or do: *Let me give you an example.* ◇ *Let me just finish this and then I'll come.*
▸ IN CALCULATING **10** [no passive] **~ sb/sth do sth** (*technical*) used to say that you are supposing sth to be true when you calculate sth: *Let line AB be equal to line CD.*
▸ HOUSE/ROOM **11** **~ sth (out) (to sb)** (*especially BrE*) to allow sb to use a house, room, etc. in return for regular payments: *I let the spare room.* ◇ *They decided to let out the smaller offices at low rents.* ➲ COLLOCATIONS at HOUSE ➲ note at RENT

IDM Most idioms containing **let** are at the entries for the nouns and adjectives in the idioms, for example **let alone** is at **alone**. **ˌlet ˈfall sth** to mention sth in a conversation, by accident or as if by accident SYN **drop**: *She let fall a further heavy hint.* **ˌlet sb ˈgo 1** to allow sb to be free SYN **free**: *Will they let the hostages go?* **2** to make sb have to leave their job: *They're having to let 100 employees go because of falling profits.* **ˌlet sb/sth ˈgo | ˌlet ˈgo (of sb/sth) 1** to stop holding sb/sth: *Don't let the rope go.* ◇ *Don't let go of the rope.* ◇ *Let go! You're hurting me!* **2** to give up an idea or an attitude, or control of sth: *It's time to let the past go.* ◇ *It's time to let go of the past.* **ˌlet sth ˈgo** to stop taking care of a house, garden, etc: *I'm afraid I've let the garden go this year.* **ˌlet yourself ˈgo 1** to behave in a relaxed way without worrying about what people think of your behaviour: *Come on, enjoy yourself, let yourself go!* **2** to stop being careful about how you look and dress, etc: *He has let himself go since he lost his job.* **let sb ˈhave it** (*informal*) to attack sb physically or with words **let it ˈgo (at ˈthat)** to say or do no more about sth: *I don't entirely agree, but I'll let it go at that.* ◇ *I thought she was hinting at something, but I let it go.* **ˌlet me ˈsee/ˈthink** used when you are thinking or trying to remember sth: *Now let me see —where did he say he lived?* **let us ˈsay** used when making a suggestion or giving an example: *I can let you have it for, well let's say £100.*

PHR V **ˌlet sb↔ˈdown** to fail to help or support sb as they had hoped or expected: *I'm afraid she let us down badly.* ◇ *This machine won't let you down.* ◇ *He trudged home feeling lonely and let down.* ➲ related noun LET-DOWN **ˌlet sb/sth↔ˈdown** to make sb/sth less successful than they/it should be: *She speaks French very fluently, but her pronunciation lets her down.* **ˌlet sth↔ˈdown 1** to let or make sth go down: *We let the bucket down by a rope.* **2** to make a dress, skirt, coat, etc. longer, by reducing the amount of material that is folded over at the bottom OPP **take up** **3** (*BrE*) to allow the air to escape from sth deliberately: *Some kids had let my tyres down.* **ˌlet sb/yourself ˈin for sth** (*informal*) to involve sb/yourself in sth that is likely to be unpleasant or difficult: *I volunteered to help, and then I thought 'Oh no, what have I let myself in for!'* **ˌlet sb ˈin on sth | ˌlet sb ˈinto sth** (*informal*) to allow sb to share a secret: *Are you going to let them in on your plans?* **ˌlet sth ˈinto sth** to put sth into the surface of sth so that it does not stick out from it: *a window let into a wall* **ˌlet sb ˈoff (with sth)** to not punish sb for sth they have done wrong, or to give them only a light punishment: *They let us off lightly.* ◇ *She was let off with a warning.* **ˌlet sb ˈoff sth** (*BrE*) to allow sb not to do sth or not to go somewhere: *He let us off homework today.* **ˌlet sth ˈoff** to fire a gun or make a bomb, etc. explode: *The boys were letting off fire-*

works. ˌ**let ˈon (to sb)** (*informal*) to tell a secret: *I'm getting married next week, but please don't let on to anyone.* ◊ **~ that…** *She let on that she was leaving.* ˌ**let ˈout** (*NAmE*) (of school classes, films/movies, meetings, etc.) to come to an end, so that it is time for people to leave: *The movie has just let out.* ˌ**let sb ˈout** to make sb stop feeling that they are involved in sth or have to do sth: *They think the attacker was very tall—so that lets you out.* ➲ related noun LET-OUT ˌ**let sth ˈout 1** to give a cry, etc: *to* ***let out a scream*** *of terror* ◊ *to* ***let out a gasp*** *of delight* **OPP hold in 2** to make a shirt, coat, etc. looser or larger **OPP take in** ˌ**let ˈup** (*informal*) **1** to become less strong: *The pain finally let up.* **2** to make less effort: *We mustn't let up now.* ➲ related noun LET-UP

■ ***noun***

▸ IN TENNIS **1** a SERVE that lands in the correct part of the COURT but must be taken again because it has touched the top of the net

▸ HOUSE/ROOM **2** (*BrE*) an act of renting a house, etc: *a* ***long-term/short-term let***

IDM **without ˌlet or ˈhindrance** (*formal* or *law*) without being prevented from doing sth; freely

-let *suffix* (in nouns) small; not very important: *booklet* ◊ *piglet* ◊ *starlet*

ˈ**let-down** *noun* [C, usually sing., U] (*informal*) something that is disappointing because it is not as good as you expected it to be **SYN disappointment, anticlimax**

le·thal /ˈliːθl/ *adj.* **1** causing or able to cause death **SYN deadly, fatal**: *a lethal dose of poison* ◊ *a lethal weapon* ◊ (*figurative*) *The closure of the factory dealt a lethal blow to the town.* **2** (*informal*) causing or able to cause a lot of harm or damage: *You and that car—it's a lethal combination!* ▸ **le·thal·ly** /ˈliːθəli/ *adv.*

leth·argy /ˈleθədʒi; *NAmE* ˈleθərdʒi/ *noun* [U] the state of not having any energy or enthusiasm for doing things **SYN listlessness, inertia** ▸ **leth·ar·gic** /ləˈθɑːdʒɪk; *NAmE* -ˈθɑːrdʒ-/ *adj.*: *The weather made her lethargic.*

Lethe /ˈliːθi/ *noun* [U] (in ancient Greek stories) an imaginary river whose water, when drunk, was thought to make the dead forget their life on Earth

ˈ**let-out** *noun* [sing.] (*BrE*) an event or a statement that allows sb to avoid having to do sth: *Good—we have a let-out now.* ◊ *a let-out clause* (= in a contract)

let's /lets/ *short form* let us: *Let's break for lunch.*

let·ter 🔑 /ˈletə(r)/ *noun, verb*

■ ***noun*** **1** 🔑 a message that is written down or printed on paper and usually put in an envelope and sent to sb: *a* ***business/thank-you, etc. letter*** ◊ ***a letter of*** *complaint* ◊ (*BrE*) *to* ***post a letter*** ◊ (*NAmE*) *to* ***mail a letter*** ◊ *There's a letter for you from your mother.* ◊ *You will be notified* ***by letter.*** **HELP** You will find compounds ending in **letter** at their place in the alphabet. ➲ WRITING TUTOR page WT24 **2** 🔑 a written or printed sign representing a sound used in speech: *'B' is the second letter of the alphabet.* ◊ *Write your name* ***in capital/block letters.*** **3** (*NAmE*) a sign in the shape of a letter that is sewn onto clothes to show that a person plays in a school or college sports team

IDM **the ˌletter of the ˈlaw** (often *disapproving*) the exact words of a law or rule rather than its general meaning: *They insist on sticking to the letter of the law.* **to the ˈletter** doing/following exactly what sb/sth says, paying attention to every detail: *I followed your instructions to the letter.*

■ ***verb*** **1** [T, usually passive] **~ sth (+ noun)** to give a letter to sth as part of a series or list: *the stars lettered Alpha and Beta* **2** [T, usually passive] **~ sth (in sth)** to print, paint, sew, etc. letters onto sth: *a black banner lettered in white* **3** [I] (*NAmE*) to receive a letter made of cloth that you sew onto your clothes for playing in a school or college sports team

ˈ**letter bomb** *noun* a small bomb that is sent to sb hidden in a letter that explodes when the envelope is opened ➲ see also PARCEL BOMB

ˈ**letter box** *noun* (*BrE*) **1** (*NAmE* ˈ**mail slot**) a narrow opening in a door or wall through which mail is delivered ➲ VISUAL VOCAB page V15 **2** (*NAmE* ˈ**mail·box**) a small box near the main door of a building or by the road, which mail is delivered to **3** = POSTBOX ➲ compare PILLAR BOX

letter boxes

postbox (*BrE*) letter box (*BrE*) mail slot (*NAmE*)

mailboxes (*NAmE*)

let·ter·box /ˈletəbɒks; *NAmE* ˈletərbɑːks/ *noun, verb*

■ ***noun*** [U] = WIDESCREEN

■ ***verb*** **~ sth** to present a film/movie on television with the width a lot greater than the height, and with a black band at the top and bottom: *a letterboxed edition*

ˈ**letter carrier** *noun* (*NAmE*) = MAIL CARRIER

let·ter·head /ˈletəhed; *NAmE* -tərh-/ *noun* the name and address of a person, a company or an organization printed at the top of their writing paper

let·ter·ing /ˈletərɪŋ/ *noun* [U] **1** letters or words that are written or printed in a particular style: *Gothic lettering* **2** the process of writing, drawing or printing letters or words

ˌ**letter of ˈcredit** *noun* (*pl.* **letters of credit**) (*finance*) a letter from a bank that allows you to get a particular amount of money from another bank

ˈ**letter opener** *noun* (*especially NAmE*) = PAPERKNIFE

ˌ**letter-ˈperfect** *adj.* (*NAmE*) **1** correct in all details **2** (*BrE* ˌ**word-ˈperfect**) able to remember and repeat sth exactly without making any mistakes

ˈ**letter-size** (also **letter**) *adj.* (*NAmE*) (of paper) 8½ inches (215.9 mm) wide and 11 inches (279.4 mm) long

let·ting /ˈletɪŋ/ *noun* (*BrE*) a period of time when you let a house or other property to sb else: *holiday lettings*

let·tuce /ˈletɪs/ *noun* [U, C] a plant with large green leaves that are eaten raw, especially in salad. There are many types of lettuce: *a bacon, lettuce and tomato sandwich* ◊ *Buy a lettuce and some tomatoes.* ➲ VISUAL VOCAB page V27

ˈ**let-up** *noun* [U, sing.] **~ (in sth)** a period of time during which sth stops or becomes less strong, difficult, etc; a reduction in the strength of sth **SYN lull**: *There is no sign of a let-up in the recession.*

leuco·cyte (also **leuko·cyte**) /ˈluːkəsaɪt; *BrE* also -kəʊs-/ *noun* (*biology*) = WHITE BLOOD CELL

leu·kae·mia (*BrE*) (*NAmE* **leu·ke·mia**) /luːˈkiːmiə/ *noun* [U] a serious disease in which too many white blood cells are produced, causing weakness and sometimes death

levee /ˈlevi/ *noun* (*NAmE*) **1** a low wall built at the side of a river to prevent it from flooding **2** a place on a river where boats can let passengers on or off

level 🔑 /ˈlevl/ *noun, adj., verb*

■ ***noun***

▸ AMOUNT **1** 🔑 [C] the amount of sth that exists in a particular situation at a particular time: *a test that checks the level of alcohol in the blood* ◊ *a relatively* ***low/high level*** *of crime* ◊ ***low/high*** *pollution* ***levels*** ◊ *Profits were* ***at the same level*** *as the year before.*

▸ STANDARD **2** 🔑 [C, U] a particular standard or quality: *a* ***high level of*** *achievement* ◊ *a computer game with 15 levels* ◊ *What is the level of this course?* ◊ *He studied French to* ***degree level.*** ◊ *Both players are* ***on a level*** (= of the same standard). ◊ *I refuse to* ***sink to their level*** (= behave as badly as them). ➲ see also A LEVEL, ENTRY-LEVEL

▸ RANK IN SCALE **3** 🔑 [U, C] a position or rank in a scale of size or importance: *a decision taken at board level* ◊ *Discussions are currently being held at national level.*

▸ POINT OF VIEW **4** 🔑 [C] a particular way of looking at, reacting to or understanding sth: *On a more personal level, I*

would like to thank Jean for all the help she has given me. ◇ *Fables can be understood on various levels.*
▸ HEIGHT **5** [C, U] the height of sth in relation to the ground or to what it used to be: *the level of water in the bottle* ◇ *The cables are buried one metre below* ***ground level.*** ◇ *The floodwater nearly reached roof level.* ◇ *The tables are not* ***on a level*** (= the same height). ➲ see also EYE LEVEL, SEA LEVEL
▸ FLOOR/LAYER **6** [C] a floor of a building; a layer of ground: *The library is all on one level.* ◇ *Archaeologists found pottery in the lowest level of the site.* ◇ *a multi-level parking lot* ➲ see also SPLIT-LEVEL
▸ TOOL **7** [C] = SPIRIT LEVEL
IDM **on the 'level** (*NAmE* also **on the ˌup and 'up**) (*informal*) honest; legal SYN **above board**: *I'm not convinced he's on the level.* ◇ *Are you sure this deal is on the level?*
■ ***adj.***
▸ FLAT **1** having a flat surface that does not slope: *Pitch the tent on level ground.* ◇ *Add a* ***level tablespoon*** *of flour* (= enough to fill the spoon but not so much that it goes above the level of the edge of the spoon). ➲ compare HEAPED
▸ EQUAL **2** having the same height, position, value, etc. as sth: *Are these pictures level?* ◇ **~ with sth** *This latest rise is intended to keep wages level with inflation.* ◇ *She* ***drew level with*** (= came beside) *the police car.* **3 ~** (**with sb**) (*especially BrE, sport*) having the same score as sb: *A good second round brought him level with the tournament leader.* ◇ *France took an early lead but Wales soon* ***drew level*** (= scored the same number of points).
▸ VOICE/LOOK **4** not showing any emotion; steady SYN **even**: *a level gaze* ➲ see also LEVELLY
IDM **be ˌlevel 'pegging** (*BrE*) having the same score: *The contestants were level pegging after round 3.* **do/try your level 'best** (**to do sth**) to do as much as you can to try to achieve sth **a ˌlevel 'playing field** a situation in which everyone has the same opportunities
■ ***verb*** (-ll-, *especially US* -l-)
▸ MAKE FLAT **1** [T] **~ sth** (**off/out**) to make sth flat or smooth: *If you're laying tiles, the floor will need to be levelled first.*
▸ DESTROY **2** [T] **~ sth** to destroy a building or a group of trees completely by knocking it down SYN **raze**: *The blast levelled several buildings in the area.*
▸ MAKE EQUAL **3** [T, I] **~** (**sth**) to make sth equal or similar: (*BrE*) *Davies levelled the score at 2 all.*
▸ POINT **4** [T] **~ sth** (**at sb**) to point sth, especially a gun, at sb: *I had a gun levelled at my head.*
IDM **ˌlevel the 'playing field** to create a situation where everyone has the same opportunities
PHR V **'level sth against/at sb** to say publicly that sb is to blame for sth, especially a crime or a mistake: *The speech was intended to answer the charges levelled against him by his opponents.* **ˌlevel sth↔'down** to make standards, amounts, etc. be of the same low or lower level: *Teachers are accused of levelling standards down to suit the needs of less able students.* **ˌlevel 'off/'out 1** to stop rising or falling and remain horizontal: *The plane levelled off at 1 500 feet.* ◇ *After the long hill, the road levelled out.* **2** to stay at a steady level of development or progress after a period of sharp rises or falls: *Sales have levelled off after a period of rapid growth.* **ˌlevel sth↔'up** to make standards, amounts, etc. be of the same high or higher level **'level with sb** (*informal*) to tell sb the truth and not hide any unpleasant facts from them

ˌlevel 'crossing (*BrE*) (*NAmE* **'railroad crossing**) *noun* a place where a road crosses a railway/railroad line

ˌlevel-'headed *adj.* calm and sensible; able to make good decisions even in difficult situations

lev·el·ler (*especially US* **lev·el·er**) /'levələ(r)/ *noun* [usually sing.] an event or a situation that makes everyone equal whatever their age, importance, etc: *death, the great leveller*

lev·el·ly /'levəli/ *adv.* in a calm and steady way: *She looked at him levelly.*

lever /'li:və(r); *NAmE* 'levər/ *noun, verb*
■ ***noun*** **1** a handle used to operate a vehicle or piece of machinery: *Pull the lever towards you to adjust the speed.* ➲ see also GEAR LEVER **2** a long piece of wood, metal, etc. used for lifting or opening sth by sb placing one end of it under an object and pushing down on the other end **3 ~** (**for/against sth**) an action that is used to put pressure on sb to do sth they do not want to do: *The threat of sanctions is our most powerful lever for peace.*
■ ***verb*** to move sth with a lever SYN **prise**: **~ sth + adv./prep.** *I levered the lid off the pot with a knife.* ◇ **~ sth + adj.** *They managed to lever the door open.*

le·ver·age /'li:vərɪdʒ; *NAmE* 'lev-/ *noun, verb*
■ ***noun*** [U] **1** (*formal*) the ability to influence what people do: *diplomatic leverage* **2** (*technical*) the act of using a lever to open or lift sth; the force used to do this **3** (*NAmE*) (*BrE* **gear·ing**) (*finance*) the relationship between the amount of money that a company owes and the value of its shares
■ ***verb*** **~ sth** (*business*) to get as much advantage or profit as possible from sth that you have: *The company needs to leverage its resources.*

ˌleveraged 'buyout *noun* (*business*) (*especially NAmE*) the act of a small company buying a larger company using money that is borrowed based on the value of this larger company

lev·eret /'levərət/ *noun* a young HARE

le·via·than /lə'vaɪəθən/ *noun* **1** (in the Bible) a very large sea MONSTER **2** (*literary*) a very large and powerful thing: *the leviathan of government bureaucracy*

Levi's™ /'li:vaɪz/ *noun* [pl.] a US make of jeans (= trousers/pants made of DENIM)

levi·tate /'levɪteɪt/ *verb* [I, T] **~** (**sth**) to rise and float in the air with no physical support, especially by means of magic or by using special mental powers; to make sth rise in this way ▸ **levi·ta·tion** /ˌlevɪ'teɪʃn/ *noun* [U]

lev·ity /'levəti/ *noun* [U] (*formal*) behaviour that shows a lack of respect for sth serious and that treats it in an amusing way SYN **frivolity**

levy AW /'levi/ *noun, verb*
■ ***noun*** (*pl.* -ies) **~** (**on sth**) an extra amount of money that has to be paid, especially as a tax to the government: *to* ***put/impose a levy*** *on oil imports*
■ ***verb*** (**lev·ies, levy·ing, lev·ied, lev·ied**) **~ sth** (**on sb/sth**) to use official authority to demand and collect a payment, tax, etc: *a tax levied by the government on excess company profits*

lewd /lu:d; *BrE* also lju:d/ *adj.* referring to sex in a rude and offensive way SYN **obscene**: *lewd behaviour/jokes/suggestions* ▸ **lewd·ly** *adv.* **lewd·ness** *noun* [U]

lex·eme /'leksi:m/ (also **ˌlexical 'unit**) *noun* (*linguistics*) a word or several words that have a meaning that is not expressed by any of its separate parts

lex·ic·al /'leksɪkl/ *adj.* [usually before noun] (*linguistics*) connected with the words of a language: ***lexical items*** (= words and phrases) ▸ **lex·ic·al·ly** /-kli/ *adv.*

'lexical meaning *noun* [U, C] the meaning of a word, without paying attention to the way that it is used or to the words that occur with it

ˌlexical 'unit *noun* = LEXEME

lexi·cog·raph·er /ˌleksɪ'kɒɡrəfə(r); *NAmE* -'kɑ:ɡ-/ *noun* a person who writes and EDITS dictionaries

lexi·cog·raphy /ˌleksɪ'kɒɡrəfi; *NAmE* -'kɑ:ɡ-/ *noun* [U] the theory and practice of writing dictionaries

lexi·col·ogy /ˌleksɪ'kɒlədʒi; *NAmE* -'kɑ:l-/ *noun* [U] the study of the form, meaning and behaviour of words

lexi·con /'leksɪkən; *NAmE* also -kɑ:n/ *noun* **1** (also **the lexicon**) [sing.] (*linguistics*) all the words and phrases used in a particular language or subject; all the words and phrases used and known by a particular person or group of people: *the lexicon of finance and economics* **2** [C] a list of words on a particular subject or in a language in alphabetical order: *a lexicon of technical scientific terms* **3** [C] a dictionary, especially one of an ancient language, such as Greek or Hebrew

L

lexis /ˈleksɪs/ *noun* [U] (*linguistics*) all the words and phrases of a particular language SYN **vocabulary**

ley /leɪ/ *noun* **1** (also ˈ**ley line**) an imaginary line that is believed to follow the route of an ancient track and to have special powers **2** (*technical*) an area of land where grass is grown temporarily instead of crops

Ley·land cy·press /ˌleɪlənd ˈsaɪprəs/ (also **ley·landii** /leɪˈlændiaɪ/) *noun* a tree (a type of CONIFER) that grows very quickly, often used to divide gardens

lezzy (also **lezzie**) /ˈlezi/ *noun* (*pl.* **lez·zies**) *adj.* (*informal, especially BrE*) = LESBIAN

l.h. *abbr.* (in writing) LEFT HAND

li·abil·ity /ˌlaɪəˈbɪləti/ *noun* (*pl.* -ies) **1** [U] **~ (for sth)** | **~ (to do sth)** the state of being legally responsible for sth: *The company cannot accept liability for any damage caused by natural disasters.* **2** [C, usually sing.] (*informal*) a person or thing that causes you a lot of problems: *Since his injury, Jones has become more of a liability than an asset to the team.* **3** [C, usually pl.] the amount of money that a person or company owes: *The company is reported to have liabilities of nearly $90 000.* ➲ compare ASSET

li·able /ˈlaɪəbl/ *adj.* [not before noun] **1 ~ (for sth)** legally responsible for paying the cost of sth: *You will be liable for any damage caused.* ◇ *The court ruled he could not be held personally liable for his wife's debts.* **2 ~ to do sth** likely to do sth: *We're all liable to make mistakes when we're tired.* ◇ *The bridge is liable to collapse at any moment.* **3 ~ to sth** likely to be affected by sth SYN **prone**: *You are more liable to injury if you exercise infrequently.* **4 ~ to sth** likely to be punished by law for sth: *Offenders are liable to fines of up to $500.* **5 ~ for/to sth** | **~ to do sth** having to do sth by law: *People who earn under a certain amount are not liable to pay tax.*

li·aise /liˈeɪz/ *verb* **1** [I] **~ (with sb)** (*especially BrE*) to work closely with sb and exchange information with them: *He had to liaise directly with the police while writing the report.* **2** [I] **~ (between A and B)** to act as a link between two or more people or groups: *Her job is to liaise between students and teachers.*

li·aison /liˈeɪzn; *NAmE* liˈeɪzɑːn; ˈliəzɑːn/ *noun* **1** [U, sing.] **~ (between A and B)** a relationship between two organizations or different departments in an organization, involving the exchange of information or ideas: *Our role is to ensure liaison between schools and parents.* ◇ *We work **in close liaison with** the police.* **2** [C] **~ (to/with sb/sth)** a person whose job is to make sure there is a good relationship between two groups or organizations: *the White House liaison to organized labor* **3** [C] **~ (with sb)** a secret sexual relationship, especially if one or both partners are married SYN **affair**

liˈaison officer *noun* a person whose job is to make sure that there is a good relationship between two groups of people, organizations, etc. ➲ see also LIAISON (2)

liar /ˈlaɪə(r)/ *noun* a person who tells lies

lib /lɪb/ *noun* (*informal*) the abbreviation for 'liberation' (used in the names of organizations demanding greater freedom, equal rights, etc.): *women's lib*

li·ba·tion /laɪˈbeɪʃn/ *noun* (*formal*) (in the past) a gift of wine to a god

Lib Dem /ˌlɪb ˈdem/ *abbr.* (in British Politics) LIBERAL DEMOCRAT: *I voted Lib Dem.*

libel /ˈlaɪbl/ *noun, verb*

■ ***noun*** [U, C] the act of printing a statement about sb that is not true and that gives people a bad opinion of them: *He sued the newspaper for libel.* ◇ *a libel action* (= a case in a court of law) ➲ compare SLANDER

■ ***verb*** (-ll-, *especially US* -l-) **~ sb** to publish a written statement about sb that is not true: *He claimed he had been libelled in an article the magazine had published.* ➲ compare SLANDER

li·bel·lous (*especially US* **li·bel·ous**) /ˈlaɪbələs/ *adj.* containing a LIBEL about sb: *a libellous statement*

lib·eral AW /ˈlɪbərəl/ *adj., noun*

■ ***adj.***

▸ RESPECTING OTHER OPINIONS **1** willing to understand and respect other people's behaviour, opinions, etc, especially when they are different from your own; believing people should be able to choose how they behave: *liberal attitudes/views/opinions*

▸ POLITICS **2** wanting or allowing a lot of political and economic freedom and supporting gradual social, political or religious change: *Some politicians want more liberal trade relations with Europe.* ◇ *liberal democracy* ◇ *liberal theories* ◇ *a liberal politician* **3 Liberal** connected with the British Liberal Party in the past, or of a Liberal Party in another country

▸ GENEROUS **4 ~ (with sth)** generous; given in large amounts SYN **lavish**: *She is very liberal with her money.* ◇ *I think Sam is too liberal with his criticism* (= he criticizes people too much).

▸ EDUCATION **5** concerned with increasing sb's general knowledge and experience rather than particular skills: *a liberal education*

▸ NOT EXACT **6** not completely accurate or exact SYN **free**: *a liberal translation of the text* ◇ *a **liberal interpretation** of the law*

▸ **lib·er·al·ly** AW /-rəli/ *adv.*: *Apply the cream liberally.* ◇ *The word 'original' is liberally interpreted in copyright law.*

■ ***noun***

▸ SB WHO RESPECTS OTHERS **1** a person who understands and respects other people's opinions and behaviour, especially when they are different from their own

▸ POLITICS **2** a person who supports political, social and religious change: *Reform is popular with middle-class liberals.* **3 Liberal** (*politics*) a member of the British Liberal Party in the past, or of a Liberal Party in another country

ˌliberal ˈarts *noun* [pl.] (*especially NAmE*) subjects of study that develop students' general knowledge and ability to think, rather than their technical skills

ˌLiberal ˈDemocrat *noun* (*abbr.* **Lib Dem**) a member or supporter of the Liberal Democrats

the ˌLiberal ˈDemocrats *noun* [pl.] (*abbr.* **Lib Dems**) one of the main British political parties, in favour of some political and social change, but not extreme ➲ compare THE CONSERVATIVE PARTY, THE LABOUR PARTY

lib·er·al·ism AW /ˈlɪbərəlɪzəm/ *noun* [U] liberal opinions and beliefs, especially in politics

lib·er·al·ity /ˌlɪbəˈræləti/ *noun* [U] (*formal*) **1** respect for political, religious or moral views, even if you do not agree with them **2** the quality of being generous

lib·er·al·ize (*BrE* also **-ise**) AW /ˈlɪbrəlaɪz/ *verb* **~ sth** to make sth such as a law or a political or religious system less strict ▸ **lib·er·al·ization, -isa·tion** AW /ˌlɪbrəlaɪˈzeɪʃn; *NAmE* -ləˈz-/ *noun* [U]

lib·er·ate AW /ˈlɪbəreɪt/ *verb* **1 ~ sb/sth (from sb/sth)** to free a country or a person from the control of sb else: *The city was liberated by the advancing army.* **2 ~ sb (from sth)** to free sb from sth that restricts their enjoyment of life: *Writing poetry liberated her from the routine of everyday life.* ▸ **lib·er·ation** AW /ˌlɪbəˈreɪʃn/ *noun* [U, sing.]: *a war of liberation* ◇ *liberation from poverty* ◇ *women's liberation* **lib·er·ator** AW *noun*

lib·er·ated AW /ˈlɪbəreɪtɪd/ *adj.* free from the restrictions of traditional ideas about social and sexual behaviour

libeˌration theˈology *noun* [U] a Christian movement, developed mainly by Latin American Catholics, which deals with social justice and the problems of people who are poor, as well as with spiritual matters

lib·er·tar·ian /ˌlɪbəˈteəriən; *NAmE* -bərˈter-/ *noun* a person who strongly believes that people should have the freedom to do and think as they like

lib·er·tine /ˈlɪbətiːn; *NAmE* -bərt-/ *noun* (*formal, disapproving*) a person, usually a man, who leads an immoral life and is interested in pleasure, especially sexual pleasure

lib·erty /ˈlɪbəti; *NAmE* -bərti/ *noun* (*pl.* -ies) **1** [U] freedom to live as you choose without too many restrictions from government or authority: *the fight for justice and liberty* **2** [U] the state of not being a prisoner or a SLAVE: *He had to endure six months' loss of liberty.* **3** [C] the legal right and freedom to do sth: *The right to vote should be a liberty enjoyed by all.* ◇ *People fear that security cameras could infringe personal liberties.* ➲ see also CIVIL LIBERTY **4** [sing.] an act or a statement that may offend or annoy sb, especially because it is done without permission or does not show respect: *He* ***took the liberty of*** *reading my files while I was away.* ◇ *They've got a liberty, not even sending me a reply.*

IDM **at liberty** (*formal*) (of a prisoner or an animal) no longer in prison or in a CAGE SYN **free** **at liberty to do sth** (*formal*) having the right or freedom to do sth SYN **free**: *You are at liberty to say what you like.* **take 'liberties with sb/sth** **1** to make important and unreasonable changes to sth, especially a book: *The movie takes considerable liberties with the novel that it is based on.* **2** (*old-fashioned*) to be too friendly with sb, especially in a sexual way

li·bid·in·ous /lɪˈbɪdɪnəs/ *adj.* (*formal*) having or expressing strong sexual feelings

li·bido /lɪˈbiːdəʊ; ˈlɪbɪdəʊ; *NAmE* -doʊ/ *noun* (*pl.* -os) [U, C, usually sing.] (*technical*) sexual desire: *loss of libido*

Libra /ˈliːbrə/ *noun* **1** [U] the 7th sign of the ZODIAC, the SCALES **2** [C] a person born when the sun is in this sign, that is between 23 September and 22 October, approximately ▸ **Li·bran** *noun, adj.*

li·brar·ian /laɪˈbreəriən; *NAmE* -ˈbrer-/ *noun* a person who is in charge of or works in a library ▸ **li·brar·ian·ship** *noun* [U]: *a degree in librarianship*

li·brary 0‑w /ˈlaɪbrəri; ˈlaɪbri; *NAmE* -breri/ *noun* (*pl.* -ies)
1 0‑w a building in which collections of books, CDs, newspapers, etc. are kept for people to read, study or borrow: *a* ***public/reference/university, etc. library*** ◇ *a* ***library book*** ◇ *a* ***toy library*** (= for borrowing toys from) **2** a room in a large house where most of the books are kept **3** (*formal*) a personal collection of books, CDs, etc: *a new edition to add to your library* **4** a series of books, recordings, etc. produced by the same company and similar in appearance: *a library of children's classics*

the ˌLibrary of 'Congress *noun* [sing.] the US national library

li·bret·tist /lɪˈbretɪst/ *noun* a person who writes the words for an OPERA or a musical play

li·bretto /lɪˈbretəʊ; *NAmE* -toʊ/ *noun* (*pl.* -os or **li·bretti** /-tiː/) (*music*) the words that are sung or spoken in an OPERA or a musical play

lice *pl.* of LOUSE

li·cence 0‑w AW (*especially US* **li·cense**) /ˈlaɪsns/ *noun*
1 0‑w [C] an official document that shows that permission has been given to do, own or use sth: *a driving licence* ◇ ~ (**for sth**) *a licence for the software* ◇ *Is there a licence fee?* ◇ *James lost his licence for six months* (= had his licence taken away by the police as a punishment). ◇ ~ (**to do sth**) *You need a licence to fish in this river.* ◇ *a licence holder* (= a person who has been given a licence) **2** [U, sing.] ~ (**to do sth**) (*formal*) freedom to do or say whatever you want, often sth bad or unacceptable: *Lack of punishment seems to give youngsters licence to break the law.* **3** [U] (*formal*) freedom to behave in a way that is considered sexually immoral

IDM **artistic/poetic 'licence** the freedom of artists or writers to change facts in order to make a story, painting, etc. more interesting or beautiful **a licence to print 'money** (*disapproving*) used to describe a business which makes a lot of money with little effort **under 'licence** (of a product) made with the permission of a company or an organization

li·cense 0‑w AW /ˈlaɪsns/ *verb, noun*
■ ***verb*** 0‑w (*BrE* also *less frequent* **li·cence**) to give sb official permission to do, own, or use sth: ~ **sth** *The new drug has not yet been licensed in the US.* ◇ (*BrE*) *licensing hours* (= the times when alcohol can be sold at a pub, etc.) ◇ ~ **sb/sth to do sth** *They had licensed the firm to produce the drug.*
■ ***noun*** 0‑w (*NAmE*) = LICENCE: *a driver's license* ◇ *a license for the software* ◇ *a license holder* (= a person who has been given a license)

li·censed AW /ˈlaɪsnst/ *adj.* **1** (*BrE*) having official permission to sell alcoholic drinks: *a licensed restaurant* **2** that you have official permission to own: *Is that gun licensed?* **3** having official permission to do sth: *She is licensed to fly solo.*

ˌlicensed 'victualler *noun* = VICTUALLER

li·cen·see /ˌlaɪsənˈsiː/ *noun* **1** (*BrE*) a person who has a licence to sell alcoholic drinks **2** a person or company that has a licence to make sth or to use sth

'license number (*NAmE*) (*BrE* **regi'stration number**, **regis·tra·tion**) *noun* the series of letters and numbers that are shown on a LICENSE PLATE at the front and back of a vehicle to identify it

'license plate (*NAmE*) (*BrE* **'number plate**) *noun* a metal or plastic plate on the front and back of a vehicle that shows its LICENSE NUMBER ➲ VISUAL VOCAB page V42

'licensing laws *noun* [pl.] British laws that state where and when alcoholic drinks can be sold

li·cen·ti·ate /laɪˈsenʃiət/ *noun* (*technical*) a person with official permission to work in a particular profession

li·cen·tious /laɪˈsenʃəs/ *adj.* (*formal, disapproving*) behaving in a way that is considered sexually immoral ▸ **li·cen·tious·ness** *noun* [U]

li·chee = LYCHEE

li·chen /ˈlaɪkən; ˈlɪtʃən/ *noun* [U, C] a very small grey or yellow plant that spreads over the surface of rocks, walls and trees and does not have any flowers ➲ VISUAL VOCAB page V9 ➲ compare MOSS

lich·gate ➲ LYCHGATE

licit /ˈlɪsɪt/ *adj.* (*formal*) allowed or legal OPP **illicit** ▸ **licit·ly** *adv.*

lick /lɪk/ *verb, noun*
■ ***verb*** **1** [T] to move your tongue over the surface of sth in order to eat it, make it wet or clean it: ~ **sth** *He licked his fingers.* ◇ *I'm tired of licking envelopes.* ◇ *The cat sat licking its paws.* ◇ ~ **sth + adj.** *She licked the spoon clean.* **2** [T] ~ **sth + adv./prep.** to eat or drink sth by licking it: *The cat licked up the milk.* ◇ *She licked the honey off the spoon.* **3** [T, I] (of flames) to touch sth lightly: ~ **sth** *Flames were soon licking the curtains.* ◇ ~ **at sth** *The flames were now licking at their feet.* **4** [T] ~ **sb/sth** (*informal*) to easily defeat sb or deal with sth: *We thought we* ***had them licked.*** ◇ *It was a tricky problem but I think we've licked it.*

IDM **lick sb's 'boots** (also *taboo, slang* **lick sb's 'arse**) (*disapproving*) to show too much respect for sb in authority because you want to please them SYN **crawl** **lick your 'wounds** to spend time trying to get your strength or confidence back after a defeat or disappointment ➲ more at LIP, SHAPE *n.*
■ ***noun*** **1** [C] an act of licking sth with the tongue: *Can I have a lick of your ice cream?* **2** [sing.] **a ~ of paint** (*informal*) a small amount of paint, used to make a place look better: *What this room needs is a lick of paint.* **3** [C] (*informal*) a short piece of music which is part of a song and is played on a GUITAR: *a* ***guitar/blues lick***

IDM **a lick and a 'promise** (*informal*) the act of performing a task quickly and carelessly, especially of washing or cleaning sth quickly **at a (fair) 'lick** (*informal*) fast; at a high speed

lickety-split /ˌlɪkəti ˈsplɪt/ *adv.* (*NAmE, old-fashioned, informal*) very quickly; immediately

lick·ing /ˈlɪkɪŋ/ *noun* [sing.] (*informal*) a severe defeat in a battle, game, etc. SYN **thrashing**

lick·spit·tle /ˈlɪkspɪtl/ *noun* (*old-fashioned, disapproving*) a person who tries to gain the approval of an important person

lic·orice *noun* [U] (*especially NAmE*) = LIQUORICE

lid 0‑π /lɪd/ *noun*
1 0‑π a cover over a container that can be removed or opened by turning it or lifting it: *a dustbin lid* ◇ *I can't get the lid off this jar.* ➲ VISUAL VOCAB pages V19, V24, V29, V31 **2** = EYELID
IDM **keep a/the 'lid on sth 1** to keep sth secret or hidden **2** to keep sth under control: *The government is keeping the lid on inflation.* **lift the 'lid on sth | take/blow the 'lid off sth** to tell people unpleasant or shocking facts about sth: *Her article lifts the lid on child prostitution.* **put the (tin) 'lid on sth/things** (*BrE, informal*) to be the final act or event that spoils your plans or hopes ➲ more at FLIP *v.*

Synonyms

lid

top • cork • cap • plug

These are all words for a cover for a container.

lid a cover over a container that can be removed or opened by turning or lifting it: *a jar with a tight-fitting lid*

top a thing that you put over the end of sth such as a pen or bottle in order to close it

cork a small round object made of cork or plastic that is used for closing bottles, especially wine bottles

cap (often in compounds) a top for a pen or a protective cover for sth such as the lens of a camera

plug a round piece of material that you put into a hole in order to block it; a flat round rubber or plastic thing that you put into the hole of a sink in order to stop the water from flowing out: *a bath plug*

PATTERNS
- a **tight-fitting** lid/top/cap
- a **screw** top/cap
- a **pen** lid/top
- to **put on/screw on/take off/unscrew** the lid/top/cap
- to **pull out** the cork/plug

lid·ded /'lɪdɪd/ *adj.* [usually before noun] **1** (of containers) having a lid **2** (*literary*) used to describe a person's expression when their EYELIDS appear large or their eyes are almost closed: *heavily-lidded eyes* ◇ *his lidded gaze*

lido /'li:dəʊ; *NAmE* -doʊ/ *noun* (*pl.* -os) (*BrE*) a public outdoor swimming pool or part of a beach used by the public for swimming, water sports, etc.

lido·caine /'lɪdəkeɪn; *BrE* also -dəʊk-/ (also **lig·no·caine**) *noun* [U] a substance used as a LOCAL ANAESTHETIC, for example to stop people feeling pain when teeth are removed

lie[1] 0‑π /laɪ/ *verb, noun* ➲ see also LIE[2]
■ *verb* (lies, lying, lay /leɪ/, lain /leɪn/) **1** 0‑π [I] (of a person or an animal) to be or put yourself in a flat or horizontal position so that you are not standing or sitting: **+ adv./prep.** *to lie on your back/side/front* ◇ **+ adj.** *The cat was lying fast asleep by the fire.* **2** 0‑π [I] (of a thing) to be or remain in a flat position on a surface: **+ adv./prep.** *Clothes were lying all over the floor.* ◇ **+ adj.** *The book lay open on his desk.* **3** 0‑π [I] to be, remain or be kept in a particular state: **+ adj.** *Snow was lying thick on the ground.* ◇ *These machines have lain idle since the factory closed.* ◇ **+ adv./prep.** *a ship lying at anchor* ◇ *I'd rather use my money than leave it lying in the bank.* **4** 0‑π [I] **+ adv./prep.** (of a town, natural feature, etc.) to be located in a particular place: *The town lies on the coast.* **5** [I] **+ adv./prep.** to be spread out in a particular place: *The valley lay below us.* **6** [I] **~ (in sth)** (of ideas, qualities, problems, etc.) to exist or be found: *The problem lies in deciding when to intervene.* **7** [I] (*BrE*) to be in a particular position during a competition: **+ adv./prep.** *Thompson is lying in fourth place.* ◇ **+ adj.** *After five games the German team are lying second.* ➲ compare LAY
IDM **lie a'head/in 'store** to be going to happen to sb in the future: *You are young and your whole life lies ahead of you.* **lie in 'state** (of the dead body of an important person) to be placed on view in a public place before being buried **lie in 'wait (for sb)** to hide, waiting to surprise, attack or catch sb: *He was surrounded by reporters who had been lying in wait for him.* **lie 'low** (*informal*) to try not to attract attention to yourself **take sth lying 'down** to accept an insult or offensive act without protesting or reacting ➲ more at BED *n.*, BOTTOM *n.*, HEAVY *adv.*, LAND *n.*, SLEEP *v.*
PHR V **lie a'round** (*BrE* also **lie a'bout**) **1** 0‑π to be left somewhere in an untidy or careless way, not put away in the correct place: *Don't leave toys lying around—someone might trip over them.* **2** 0‑π (of a person) to spend time doing nothing and being lazy ➲ related noun LAYABOUT **,lie 'back** to do nothing except relax: *You don't have to do anything—just lie back and enjoy the ride.* **,lie be'hind sth** to be the real reason for sth, often hidden: *What lay behind this strange outburst?* **,lie 'down** 0‑π to be or get into a flat position, especially in bed, in order to sleep or rest: *Go and lie down for a while.* ◇ *He lay down on the sofa and soon fell asleep.* ➲ related noun LIE-DOWN **,lie 'in** (*BrE*) (also **,sleep 'in** *NAmE, BrE*) to stay in bed after the time you usually get up: *It's a holiday tomorrow, so you can lie in.* ➲ related noun LIE-IN **'lie with sb (to do sth)** (*formal*) to be sb's duty or responsibility: *It lies with you to accept or reject the proposals.*
■ *noun*
IDM **the ,lie of the 'land** (*BrE*) (*NAmE* **the ,lay of the 'land**) **1** the way the land in an area is formed and what physical characteristics it has **2** the way a situation is now and how it is likely to develop: *Check out the lie of the land before you make a decision.*

lie[2] 0‑π /laɪ/ *verb, noun* ➲ see also LIE[1]
■ *verb* 0‑π (lies, lying, lied, lied) [I] to say or write sth that you know is not true: *You could see from his face that he was lying.* ◇ **~ (to sb) (about sth)** *Don't lie to me!* ◇ *She lies about her age.* ◇ *The camera cannot lie* (= give a false impression). ➲ see also LIAR
IDM **lie through your 'teeth** (*informal*) to say sth that is not true at all: *The witness was clearly lying through his teeth.* **lie your way into/out of sth** to get yourself into or out of a situation by lying
■ *noun* 0‑π a statement made by sb knowing that it is not true: *to* **tell a lie** ◇ *The whole story is nothing but* **a pack of lies**. ◇ *a* **barefaced lie** (= a lie that is deliberate and shocking) ➲ see also WHITE LIE
IDM **give the lie to sth** (*formal*) to show that sth is not true **I tell a 'lie** (*BrE, informal*) used to say that sth you have just said is not true or correct: *We first met in 2006, no, I tell a lie, it was 2007.* ➲ more at LIVE[1], TISSUE

Lieb·frau·milch /'li:bfraʊmɪlʃ; -mɪlk; -mɪltʃ/ *noun* [U, C] (from *German*) a type of German white wine

lied /li:d/ *noun* (*pl.* **lieder** /'li:də(r)/) (from *German*) a German song for one singer and piano

'lie detector (also *technical*) (*formal* **poly·graph**) *noun* a piece of equipment that is used, for example by the police, to find out if sb is telling the truth

,lie-'down *noun* [sing.] (*BrE, informal*) a short rest, especially on a bed

lief /li:f/ *adv.* (*old use*) willingly; happily: *I would as lief kill myself as betray my master.*

liege /li:dʒ/ (also **,liege 'lord**) *noun* (*old use*) a king or lord

,lie-'in *noun* (*BrE*) a time when you stay in bed longer than normal in the morning

lien /'li:ən/ *noun* [U] **~ (in/over sth)** (*law*) the right to keep sb's property until a debt is paid

lieu /lu:; *BrE* also lju:/ *noun* (*formal*)
IDM **in lieu (of sth)** instead of: *They took cash in lieu of the prize they had won.* ◇ *We work on Saturdays and have a day off in lieu during the week.*

Lieut. (also **Lt**) (both *BrE*) (*NAmE* **Lt.**) *abbr.* (in writing) LIEUTENANT

lieu·ten·ant /lef'tenənt; *NAmE* lu:'t-/ *noun* (*abbr.* **Lieut.**, **Lt**) **1** an officer of middle rank in the army, navy, or AIR FORCE: *Lieutenant Paul Fisher* ➲ see also FLIGHT LIEU-

TENANT, SECOND LIEUTENANT, SUB LIEUTENANT **2** (in compounds) an officer just below the rank mentioned: *a lieutenant colonel* **3** (in the US) a police officer of fairly high rank **4** a person who helps sb who is above them in rank or who performs their duties when that person is unable to

lieu,tenant 'colonel *noun* an officer of middle rank in the US army, US AIR FORCE or British army

lieu,tenant com'mander *noun* an officer of middle rank in the navy

lieu,tenant 'general *noun* an officer of very high rank in the army

Lieu,tenant-'Govern·or *noun* (in Canada) the representative of the CROWN (2) in a PROVINCE

life 0-w /laɪf/ *noun* (*pl.* lives /laɪvz/)

▸ STATE OF LIVING **1** 0-w [U] the ability to breathe, grow, reproduce, etc. which people, animals and plants have before they die and which objects do not have: *life and death* ◇ *The body was cold and showed* ***no signs of life.*** ◇ *My father died last year—I wish I could bring him* ***back to life.*** ◇ *In spring the countryside bursts into life.* **2** 0-w [U, C] the state of being alive as a human; an individual person's existence: *The floods caused a massive* ***loss of life*** (= many people were killed). ◇ *He* ***risked his life*** *to save his daughter from the fire.* ◇ *Hundreds of lives were threatened when the building collapsed.* ◇ *The operation* ***saved her life.*** ◇ *My grandfather* ***lost his life*** (= was killed) *in the war.* ◇ *Several attempts have been made on the President's life* (= several people have tried to kill him).

▸ LIVING THINGS **3** 0-w [U] living things: ***plant/animal life*** ◇ ***marine/pond life*** ◇ *Is there intelligent life on other planets?*

▸ PERIOD OF TIME **4** 0-w [C, U] the period between sb's birth and their death; a part of this period: *He's lived here* ***all his life.*** ◇ *I've lived in England for most of my life.* ◇ *to have a* ***long/short life*** ◇ *He became very weak towards the end of his life.* ◇ *Brenda took up tennis* ***late in life.*** ◇ *He will spend* ***the rest of his life*** (= until he dies) *in a wheelchair.* ◇ *There's no such thing as a job* ***for life*** *any longer.* ◇ *She is a* ***life member*** *of the club.* ◇ *in* ***early/adult life*** ➲ see also CHANGE OF LIFE **5** 0-w [C] (used with an adjective) a period of sb's life when they are in a particular situation or job: *She has been an accountant all her* ***working life.*** ◇ *He met a lot of interesting people during his life as a student.* ◇ *They were very happy throughout their* ***married life.*** **6** 0-w [C] the period of time when sth exists or functions: *The International Stock Exchange* ***started life as*** *a London coffee shop.* ◇ *They could see that the company had a limited life* (= it was going to close). ◇ *In Italy the average life of a government is eleven months.* ➲ see also SHELF LIFE

▸ PUNISHMENT **7** [U] the punishment of being sent to prison for life; life IMPRISONMENT: *The judge* ***gave him life.***

▸ EXPERIENCE/ACTIVITIES **8** 0-w [U] the experience and activities that are typical of all people's existences: *the worries of everyday life* ◇ *He is young and has little* ***experience of life.*** ◇ *Commuting is a part of* ***daily life*** *for many people.* ◇ *Jill wants to travel and see life for herself.* ◇ *We bought a dishwasher* ***to make life easier.*** ◇ *In London life can be hard.* ◇ *In* ***real life*** (= when she met him) *he wasn't how she had imagined him at all.* ◇ *Life isn't like in the movies, you know.* **9** 0-w [U, C] the activities and experiences that are typical of a particular way of living: ***country/city life*** ◇ *She enjoyed political life.* ◇ ***family/married life*** ◇ *How do you find life in Japan?* **10** 0-w [C] a person's experiences during their life; the activities that form a particular part of a person's life: *He has had* ***a good life.*** ◇ ***a hard/an easy life*** ◇ *My* ***day-to-day life*** *is not very exciting.* ◇ ***a life of*** *luxury* ◇ *Her* ***daily life*** *involved meeting lots of people.* ◇ *Many of these children have led very* ***sheltered lives*** (= they have not had many different experiences). ◇ *They emigrated to* ***start a new life*** *in Canada.* ◇ *He doesn't like to talk about his* ***private life.*** ◇ *She has a full* ***social life.*** ◇ *articles about the* ***love lives*** *of the stars* ➲ see also SEX LIFE

▸ ENERGY/EXCITEMENT **11** 0-w [U] the quality of being active and exciting SYN **vitality**: *This is a great holiday resort that is* ***full of life.***

▸ IN ART **12** [U] a living model or a real object or scene that people draw or paint: *She had lessons in drawing from life.* ◇ *a* ***life class*** (= one in which art students draw a naked man or woman) ➲ see also STILL LIFE

▸ STORY OF LIFE **13** [C] a story of sb's life SYN **biography**: *She wrote a life of Mozart.*

▸ IN CHILDREN'S GAMES **14** [C] one of a set number of chances before a player is out of a game: *He's lost two lives, so he's only got one left.*

IDM **be sb's 'life** be the most important person or thing to sb: *My children are my life.* ◇ *Writing is his life.* **bring sb/sth to 'life** to make sb/sth more interesting or exciting: *The new teacher really brought French to life for us.* ◇ *Flowers can bring a dull room back to life.* **come to 'life 1** to become more interesting, exciting or full of activity: *The match finally came to life in the second half.* **2** to start to act or move as if alive: *In my dream all my toys came to life.* **for dear 'life | for your 'life** as hard or as fast as possible: *She was holding on to the rope for dear life.* ◇ *Run for your life!* **for the 'life of you** (*informal*) however hard you try: *I cannot for the life of me imagine why they want to leave.*

Collocations

The living world

Animals

- animals **mate/breed/reproduce/feed (on sth)**
- fish/amphibians **swim/spawn** (= lay eggs)
- birds **fly/migrate/nest/sing**
- insects **crawl/fly/bite/sting**
- insects/bees/locusts **swarm**
- bees **collect/gather** nectar/pollen
- spiders **spin/weave** a web
- snakes/lizards **shed their skins**
- bears/hedgehogs/frogs **hibernate**
- insect larvae **grow/develop/pupate**
- an egg/a chick/a larva **hatches**
- **attract/find/choose** a mate
- **produce/release** eggs/sperm
- **lay/fertilize/incubate/hatch** eggs
- **inhabit** a forest/a reef/the coast
- **mark/enter/defend** (a) territory
- **stalk/hunt/capture/catch/kill** prey

Plants and fungi

- trees/plants **grow/bloom/blossom/flower**
- a seed **germinates/sprouts**
- leaves/buds/roots/shoots **appear/develop/form**
- flower buds **swell/open**
- a fungus **grows/spreads/colonizes sth**
- **pollinate/fertilize** a flower/plant
- **produce/release/spread/disperse** pollen/seeds/spores
- **produce/bear** fruit
- **develop/grow/form** roots/shoots/leaves
- **provide/supply/absorb/extract/release** nutrients
- **perform/increase/reduce** photosynthesis

Bacteria and viruses

- bacteria/microbes/viruses **grow/spread/multiply**
- bacteria/microbes **live/thrive** in/on sth
- bacteria/microbes/viruses **evolve/colonize sth/cause disease**
- bacteria **break sth down/convert sth (into sth)**
- a virus **enters/invades** sth/the body
- a virus **mutates/evolves/replicates (itself)**
- be **infected with/contaminated with/exposed to** a new strain of a virus/drug-resistant bacteria
- **contain/carry/harbour** (*especially US*) **harbor** bacteria/a virus
- **kill/destroy/eliminate** harmful/deadly bacteria

L

frighten/scare the 'life out of sb to frighten sb very much **full of 'beans/'life** having a lot of energy **get a 'life** (*informal*) used to tell sb to stop being boring and to do sth more interesting **lay down your 'life (for sb/sth)** (*literary*) to die in order to save sb/sth SYN **sacrifice yourself** **lead/live the life of 'Riley** (*old-fashioned*, often *disapproving*) to live an enjoyable and comfortable life with no problems or responsibilities **life after 'death** the possibility or belief that people continue to exist in some form after they die **the life and 'soul of the party, etc.** (*BrE*) the most amusing and interesting person at a party, etc. **life is 'cheap** (*disapproving*) used to say that there is a situation in which it is not thought to be important if people somewhere die or are treated badly **(have) a life of its 'own** (of an object) seeming to move or function by itself without a person touching or working it **life's too 'short** (*informal*) used to say that it is not worth wasting time doing sth that you dislike or that is not important **make life 'difficult (for sb)** to cause problems for sb **the 'man/'woman in your life** (*informal*) the man or woman that you are having a sexual or romantic relationship with **not on your 'life** (*informal*) used to refuse very firmly to do sth **take sb's 'life** to kill sb **take your (own) 'life** to kill yourself **take your life in your 'hands** to risk being killed: *You take your life in your hands just crossing the road here.* **that's 'life** (*informal*) used when you are disappointed about sth but know that you must accept it **where there's 'life (, there's 'hope)** (*saying*) in a bad situation you must not give up hope because there is always a chance that it will improve ➲ more at BET *v.*, BREATH, BREATHE, CHANGE *n.*, DEPART, DOG *n.*, END *v.*, FACT, FEAR *n.*, FIGHT *v.*, INCH *n.*, KISS *n.*, LARGE, LEASE, LIGHT *n.*, MATTER *n.*, MISERY, NINE, RISK *v.*, SAVE *v.*, SLICE *n.*, SPRING *v.*, STAFF *n.*, STORY, TIME *n.*, TRUE *adj.*, VARIETY, WALK *n.*, WAY *n.*

ˌlife-and-'death (also **ˌlife-or-'death**) *adj.* [only before noun] extremely serious, especially when there is a situation in which people might die: *a life-and-death decision/struggle*

'life assurance *noun* [U] (*BrE*) = LIFE INSURANCE

life·belt /'laɪfbelt/ *noun* **1** (*BrE*) a large ring made of material that floats well, that is used to rescue sb who has fallen into water, to prevent them from DROWNING **2** (*NAmE*) a special belt worn to help sb float in water ➲ see also LIFE JACKET, LIFE PRESERVER

life·blood /'laɪfblʌd/ *noun* [U] **1 ~ (of sth)** the thing that keeps sth strong and healthy and is necessary for successful development: *Tourism is the lifeblood of the city.* **2** (*literary*) a person's blood, when it is thought of as the thing that is necessary for life

life·boat /'laɪfbəʊt; *NAmE* -boʊt/ *noun* **1** a special boat that is sent out to rescue people who are in danger at sea: *a **lifeboat crew/station*** ➲ VISUAL VOCAB page V44 **2** a small boat carried on a ship in order to save the people on board if the ship sinks

life·buoy /'laɪfbɔɪ; *NAmE* also -buːi/ *noun* a piece of material that floats well, used to rescue sb who has fallen into water, by keeping them above water

'life coach (also **coach**) *noun* a person who is employed by sb to give them advice about how to achieve the things they want in their life and work ▸ **'life coaching** (also **coaching**) *noun* [U]

'life cycle *noun* **1** (*biology*) the series of forms into which a living thing changes as it develops: *the life cycle of the butterfly* **2** the period of time during which sth, for example a product, is developed and used

'life-enhancing *adj.* making you feel happier and making life more enjoyable

'life expectancy (also **ˌexpectation of 'life**) *noun* [U, C] the number of years that a person is likely to live; the length of time that sth is likely to exist or continue for

'life force *noun* [U] **1** the force that gives sb/sth their strength or energy: *He looked very ill—his life force seemed to have drained away.* **2** the force that keeps all life in existence: *In Hindi philosophy the life force is known as prana.*

'life form *noun* (*technical*) a living thing such as a plant or an animal

'life-giving *adj.* [usually before noun] (*literary*) that gives life or keeps sth alive

life·guard /'laɪfgɑːd; *NAmE* -gɑːrd/ (*AustralE, NZE* **lifesaver, 'surf lifesaver**) *noun* a person who is employed at a beach or a swimming pool to rescue people who are in danger in the water

ˌlife 'history *noun* all the events that happen in the life of a person, animal or plant

'life insurance (*BrE* also **'life assurance**) *noun* [U] a type of insurance in which you make regular payments so that you receive a sum of money when you are a particular age, or so that your family will receive a sum of money when you die: *a life insurance policy*

'life jacket (*NAmE* also **'life vest**) *noun* a jacket without sleeves, that can be filled with air, designed to help you float if you fall in water ➲ VISUAL VOCAB page V45

life·less /'laɪfləs/ *adj.* **1** (*formal*) dead or appearing to be dead SYN **inanimate** **2** not living; not having living things growing on or in it: *lifeless machines* ◇ *a lifeless planet* **3** dull; lacking the qualities that make sth/sb interesting and full of life SYN **lacklustre**: *his lifeless performance on stage*

life·like /'laɪflaɪk/ *adj.* exactly like a real person or thing SYN **realistic**: *a lifelike statue/drawing/toy*

life·line /'laɪflaɪn/ *noun* **1** a line or rope thrown to rescue sb who is in difficulty in the water **2** a line attached to sb who goes deep under the sea **3** something that is very important for sb and that they depend on: *The extra payments are a lifeline for most single mothers.*

life·long /'laɪflɒŋ; *NAmE* -lɔːŋ; -lɑːŋ/ *adj.* [only before noun] lasting or existing all through your life

ˌlife-or-'death *adj.* = LIFE-AND-DEATH

ˌlife 'peer *noun* (in Britain) a person who is given the title of PEER (= 'Lord' or 'Lady') but who cannot pass it on to their son or daughter

'life preserver *noun* (*NAmE*) a piece of material that floats well, or a jacket made of such material, used to rescue a person who has fallen into water, by keeping them above water

lifer /'laɪfə(r)/ *noun* (*informal*) a person who has been sent to prison for their whole life

'life raft *noun* an open rubber boat filled with air, used for rescuing people from sinking ships or planes

life·saver /'laɪfseɪvə(r)/ *noun* **1** a thing that helps sb in a difficult situation; sth that saves sb's life: *The new drug is a potential lifesaver.* **2** (also **'surf lifesaver**) (*AustralE, NZE*) = LIFEGUARD

'life-saving *adj.*, *noun*

- ***adj.*** [usually before noun] that is going to save sb's life: *a life-saving heart operation*
- ***noun*** [U] the skills needed to save sb who is in water and is DROWNING: *a life-saving qualification*

'life sciences *noun* [pl.] the sciences concerned with studying humans, animals or plants ➲ compare EARTH SCIENCE, NATURAL SCIENCE, PHYSICAL SCIENCE

'life sentence *noun* the punishment by which sb spends the rest of their life in prison

'life-size (also **'life-sized**) *adj.* the same size as a person or thing really is: *a life-size statue*

life·span /'laɪfspæn/ *noun* the length of time that sth is likely to live, continue or function: *Worms have a lifespan of a few months.*

'life story *noun* the story that sb tells you about their whole life

life·style /'laɪfstaɪl/ *noun* [C, U] the way in which a person or a group of people lives and works: *a **comfortable/healthy/lavish, etc. lifestyle*** ◇ *It was a big change in lifestyle when we moved to the country.* ◇ *the lifestyle section of* *the newspaper* (= the part which deals with clothes, furniture, hobbies, etc.)

ˌlife supˈport *noun* [U] the fact of sb being on a life-support machine: *Families want the right to refuse life support.* ◇ *She's critically ill,* ***on life support***.

ˌlife-supˈport machine (also **ˌlife-supˈport system**) *noun* a piece of equipment that keeps sb alive when they are extremely ill/sick and cannot breathe without help: *He was put on a life-support machine in intensive care.*

ˌlife's ˈwork (*BrE*) (*NAmE* **life·work** /ˌlaɪfˈwɜːk; *NAmE* ˈwɜːrk/) *noun* [sing.] the main purpose or activity in a person's life, or their greatest achievement

ˈlife-threaten·ing *adj.* that is likely to kill sb: *His heart condition is not life-threatening.*

life·time /ˈlaɪftaɪm/ *noun* the length of time that sb lives or that sth lasts: *His diary was not published during his lifetime.* ◇ *a lifetime of experience* ◇ *in the lifetime of the present government*

IDM **the chance, etc. of a ˈlifetime** a wonderful opportunity, etc. that you are not likely to get again **once in a ˈlifetime** used to describe sth special that is not likely to happen to you again: *An opportunity like this comes once in a lifetime.* ◇ *a once-in-a-lifetime experience*

ˈlife vest *noun* (*NAmE*) = LIFE JACKET

lift 0‑ᵣ /lɪft/ *verb, noun*

▪ ***verb***

▸ RAISE **1** 0‑ᵣ [T, I] to raise sb/sth or be raised to a higher position or level: **~ sb/sth (up)** (**+ adv./prep.**) *He stood there with his arms lifted above his head.* ◇ *I lifted the lid of the box and peered in.* ◇ (*figurative*) *John lifted his eyes* (= looked up) *from his book.* ◇ **~ (up)** *Her eyebrows lifted. 'Apologize? Why?'*

▸ MOVE SB/STH **2** 0‑ᵣ [T] **~ sb/sth (+ adv./prep.)** to take hold of sb/sth and move them/it to a different position: *I lifted the baby out of the chair.* ◇ *He lifted the suitcase down from the rack.* **3** [T] **~ sb/sth (+ adv./prep.)** to transport people or things by air: *The survivors were lifted to safety by helicopter.* ➲ see also AIRLIFT

▸ REMOVE LAW/RULE **4** 0‑ᵣ [T] **~ sth** to remove or end restrictions: *to* ***lift a ban/curfew/blockade*** ◇ *Martial law has now been lifted.*

▸ HEART/SPIRITS **5** [I, T] to become or make sb more cheerful: *His heart lifted at the sight of her.* ◇ **~ sth** *The news lifted our spirits.*

▸ OF MIST/CLOUDS **6** [I] to rise and disappear **SYN** **disperse**: *The fog began to lift.* ◇ (*figurative*) *Gradually my depression started to lift.*

▸ STEAL **7** [T] **~ sth** (**from sb/sth**) (*informal*) to steal sth: *He had been lifting electrical goods from the store where he worked.* ➲ see also SHOPLIFT

▸ COPY IDEAS/WORDS **8** [T] **~ sth** (**from sth**) to use sb's ideas or words without asking permission or without saying where they come from **SYN** **plagiarize**: *She lifted most of the ideas from a book she had been reading.*

▸ VEGETABLES **9** [T] **~ sth** to dig up vegetables or plants from the ground: *to lift potatoes*

▸ INCREASE **10** [T, I] **~ (sth)** to make the amount or level of sth greater; to become greater in amount or level: *Interest rates were lifted yesterday.*

IDM **not lift/raise a finger/hand** (**to do sth**) (*informal*) to do nothing to help sb: *The children never lift a finger to help around the house.*

PHR V **ˌlift ˈoff** (of a ROCKET or, less frequently, an aircraft) to leave the ground and rise into the air ➲ related noun LIFT-OFF

▪ ***noun***

▸ MACHINE **1** 0‑ᵣ (*BrE*) (*NAmE* **ele·va·tor**) [C] a machine that carries people or goods up and down to different levels in a building or a mine: *It's on the sixth floor—let's* ***take the lift***. ➲ see also CHAIRLIFT, DRAG LIFT, SKI LIFT

▸ FREE RIDE **2** 0‑ᵣ (*BrE*) (*NAmE* **ride**) [C] a free ride in a car, etc. to a place you want to get to: *I'll* ***give you a lift*** *to the station.* ◇ *She* ***hitched a lift*** *on a truck.*

▸ HAPPIER FEELING **3** [sing.] a feeling of being happier or more confident than before **SYN** **boost**: *Passing the exam gave him a real lift.*

▸ RISING MOVEMENT **4** [sing.] a movement in which sth rises or is lifted up: *the puzzled lift of his eyebrows*

▸ ON AIRCRAFT **5** [U] the upward pressure of air on an aircraft when flying ➲ compare DRAG

ˈlift-off *noun* [C, U] the act of a SPACECRAFT leaving the ground and rising into the air **SYN** **blast-off**: *Ten minutes to lift-off.*

liga·ment /ˈlɪɡəmənt/ *noun* a strong band of TISSUE in the body that connects bones and supports organs and keeps them in position: *I've torn a ligament.* ➲ COLLOCATIONS at INJURY

li·gate /lɪˈɡeɪt; *NAmE* laɪˈɡ-/ *verb* **~ sth** (*medical*) to tie up an ARTERY or other BLOOD VESSEL or tube in the body, with a LIGATURE ▸ **li·ga·tion** *noun* [U]

liga·ture /ˈlɪɡətʃə(r)/ *noun* (*technical*) something that is used for tying sth very tightly, for example to stop the loss of blood from a wound

lig·ger /ˈlɪɡə(r)/ *noun* (*BrE, informal*) a person who always takes the opportunity to go to a free party or event that is arranged by a company to advertise its products

light 0‑ᵣ /laɪt/ *noun, adj., verb, adv.*

▪ ***noun***

▸ FROM SUN/LAMPS **1** 0‑ᵣ [U] the energy from the sun, a lamp, etc. that makes it possible to see things: ***bright/dim light*** ◇ *a room with good* ***natural light*** ◇ *in the fading light of a summer's evening* ◇ *The light was beginning to fail* (= it was beginning to get dark). ◇ *She could just see* ***by the light of*** *the candle.* ◇ *Bring it* ***into the light*** *so I can see it.* ◇ ***a beam/ray of light*** ◇ *The knife gleamed as it* ***caught the light*** (= as the light shone on it). ➲ see also FIRST LIGHT **2** 0‑ᵣ [C] a particular type of light with its own colour and qualities: *A cold grey light crept under the curtains.* ➲ see also THE NORTHERN LIGHTS

▸ LAMP **3** 0‑ᵣ [C] a thing that produces light, especially an electric light: *to* ***turn/switch the lights on/off*** ◇ *to* ***turn out the light***(*s*) ◇ *Suddenly all the* ***lights went out***. ◇ *It was an hour before the* ***lights came on*** *again.* ◇ *to* ***turn down/dim the lights*** ◇ *A light was still burning in the bedroom.* ◇ ***ceiling/wall lights*** ◇ *Keep going—the lights* (= traffic lights) *are green.* ◇ *Check your car before you drive to make sure that your lights are working.* ➲ VISUAL VOCAB page V41 ➲ see also BRAKE LIGHT, GREEN LIGHT, HEADLIGHT, LEADING LIGHT, RED LIGHT

▸ FOR CIGARETTE **4** 0‑ᵣ [sing.] a match or device with which you can light a cigarette: (*BrE*) *Have you got a light?* ◇ (*NAmE, BrE*) *Do you have a light?*

▸ EXPRESSION IN EYES **5** [sing.] an expression in sb's eyes which shows what they are thinking or feeling: *There was a soft light in her eyes as she looked at him.*

▸ IN PICTURE **6** [U] light colours in a picture, which contrast with darker ones: *the artist's use of light and shade*

▸ WINDOW **7** [C] (*architecture*) a window or an opening to allow light in: *leaded lights* ➲ see also SKYLIGHT

IDM **according to sb's/sth's ˈlights** (*formal*) according to the standards which sb sets for himself or herself **be/go out like a ˈlight** (*informal*) to go to sleep very quickly **be in sb's ˈlight** to be between sb and a source of light: *Could you move—you're in my light.* **bring sth to ˈlight** to make new information known to people: *These facts have only just been brought to light.* **cast/shed/throw ˈlight on sth** to make a problem, etc. easier to understand: *Recent research has thrown new light on the causes of the disease.* **come to ˈlight** to become known to people: *New evidence has recently come to light.* **in ˌa good, bad, favourable, etc. ˈlight** if you see sth or put sth **in a good, bad, etc. light**, it seems good, bad, etc: *You must not view what happened in a negative light.* ◇ *They want to present their policies in the best possible light.* **in the light of sth** (*BrE*) (*NAmE* **in light of sth**) after considering sth: *He rewrote the book in the light of further research.* **the lights are ˈon but nobody's ˈhome** (*saying, humorous*) used to describe sb who is stupid, not thinking clearly or not paying attention **light at the end of the ˈtunnel** something that shows you are nearly at the end of a long and difficult time or situation (**the**) **light ˈdawned** (**on sb**) somebody suddenly understood or began to understand sth: *I puzzled over the problem for ages before the light suddenly dawned.* **the light of sb's 'life** the person sb loves more than any other **run a (red) 'light | run the 'lights** (both *especially NAmE*) (*BrE* also **jump the 'lights**) (*informal*) to fail to stop at a red traffic light **see the 'light 1** to finally understand or accept sth, especially sth obvious **2** to begin to believe in a religion **see the 'light (of 'day)** to begin to exist or to become publicly known about: *He's written a lot of good material that has never seen the light of day.* **set 'light to sth** (*especially BrE*) to make sth start burning SYN **ignite**: *A spark from the fire had set light to a rug.* ➲ more at BRIGHT *adj.*, COLD *adj.*, HIDE *v.*, JUMP *v.*, SWEETNESS

■ ***adj.*** (light·er, light·est)

▸ WITH NATURAL LIGHT **1** full of light; having the natural light of day: *We'll leave in the morning as soon as **it's light**.* ◇ *It **gets light** at about 5 o'clock.* ◇ *It was a light spacious apartment at the top of the building.* OPP **dark**

▸ COLOURS **2** pale in colour: *light blue eyes* ◇ *Lighter shades suit you best.* ◇ *People with pale complexions should avoid wearing light colours.* OPP **dark**

▸ WEIGHT **3** easy to lift or move; not weighing very much: *Modern video cameras are light and easy to carry.* ◇ *Carry this bag—it's the lightest.* ◇ *He's lost a lot of weight—he's three kilos lighter than he was.* ◇ *The little girl was **as light as a feather**.* ◇ *The aluminium body is 12% lighter than if built with steel.* OPP **heavy 4** [usually before noun] of less than average or usual weight: *light summer clothes* ◇ *Only light vehicles are allowed over the old bridge.* OPP **heavy 5** used with a unit of weight to say that sth weighs less than it should do: *The delivery of potatoes was several kilos light.*

▸ GENTLE **6** [usually before noun] gentle or delicate; not using much force: *She felt a light tap on her shoulder.* ◇ *the sound of quick light footsteps* ◇ *You only need to apply light pressure.* ◇ *As a boxer, he was always **light on his feet*** (= quick and elegant in the way he moved). OPP **heavy**

▸ WORK/EXERCISE **7** [usually before noun] easy to do; not making you tired: *After his accident he was moved to lighter work.* ◇ *some light housework* ◇ *You are probably well enough to take a little light exercise.*

▸ NOT GREAT **8** not great in amount, degree, etc: *light traffic* ◇ *The forecast is for light showers.* ◇ *light winds* ◇ *Trading on the stock exchange was light today.* OPP **heavy**

▸ NOT SEVERE/SERIOUS **9** not severe: *He was convicted of assaulting a police officer but he got off with a **light sentence**.* **10** entertaining rather than serious and not needing much mental effort: ***light reading** for the beach* ◇ *a concert of light classical music* **11** not serious: *She kept her tone light.* ◇ *This programme looks at the **lighter side** of politics.* ◇ *We all needed a little **light relief** at the end of a long day* (= something amusing or entertaining that comes after sth serious or boring). ◇ ***On a lighter note**, we end the news today with a story about a duck called Quackers.*

▸ CHEERFUL **12** [usually before noun] free from worry; cheerful: *I left the island with a light heart.*

▸ FOOD **13** (of a meal) small in quantity: *a **light supper/snack**.* ◇ *I just want something light for lunch.* OPP **heavy 14** not containing much fat or not having a strong flavour and therefore easy for the stomach to DIGEST: *Stick to a light diet.* ➲ see also LITE **15** containing a lot of air: *This pastry is so light.*

▸ DRINK **16** low in alcohol: *a light beer* **17** (*IndE*) (of tea or coffee) containing a lot of water SYN **weak**: *I don't like my coffee too light.* OPP **strong**

▸ SLEEP **18** [only before noun] a person in a **light** sleep is easy to wake: *She drifted into a light sleep.* ◇ *I've always been a light sleeper.* OPP **deep**

▶ **light·ness** *noun* [U] ➲ see also LIGHTLY

IDM **be light on sth** (*BrE*) to not have enough of sth: *We seem to be light on fuel.* **a light touch** the ability to deal with sth in a delicate and relaxed way: *She handles this difficult subject with a light touch.* **make 'light of sth** to treat sth as not being important and not serious **make light 'work of sth** to do sth quickly and with little effort ➲ more at HAND *n.*

■ ***verb*** (lit, lit /lɪt/ HELP **Lighted** is also used for the past tense and past participle, especially in front of nouns.)

▸ START TO BURN **1** [T] **~ sth** to make sth start to burn: *She lit a candle.* ◇ *The candles were lit.* ◇ *I put a lighted match to the letter and watched it burn.* **2** [I] to start to burn: *The fire wouldn't light.*

▸ GIVE LIGHT **3** [T, usually passive] **~ sth** to give light to sth or to a place: *The stage was lit by bright spotlights.* ◇ ***well/badly lit** streets* **4** [T] **~ sth** (*literary*) to guide sb with a light: *Our way was lit by a full moon.*

PHR V **'light on/upon sth** (*literary*) to see or find sth by accident: *His eye lit upon a small boat on the horizon.* **ˌlight 'up | ˌlight sth↔'up 1** (*informal*) to begin to smoke a cigarette: *They all lit up as soon as he left the room.* ◇ *He sat back and lit up a cigarette.* **2** to become or to make sth become bright with light or colour: *There was an explosion and the whole sky lit up.* **3** if sb's eyes or face **light up**, or sth **lights them up**, they show happiness or excitement: *His eyes lit up when she walked into the room.* ◇ *A smile lit up her face.*

■ ***adv.*** IDM see TRAVEL *v.*

Which Word?

light / lighting

- The noun **light** has several different meanings and is used in many phrases. **Lighting** can only be used to talk about the type of light in a place or how lights are used to achieve a particular effect: *the lighting system* ◇ *the movie's interesting lighting effects* ◇ *The lighting at the disco was fantastic.*

ˌlight 'aircraft *noun* (*pl.* **light aircraft**) a small plane with seats for no more than about six passengers ➲ VISUAL VOCAB page V43

'light bulb *noun* = BULB ➲ VISUAL VOCAB page V7

ˌlight-'coloured (*especially US* **ˌlight-'colored**) *adj.* pale in colour; not dark

light·ed /'laɪtɪd/ *adj.* **1** a **lighted** CANDLE, cigarette, match, etc. is burning **2** a **lighted** window is bright because there are lights on inside the room OPP **unlit**

light·en /'laɪtn/ *verb* **1** [T] **~ sth** to reduce the amount of work, debt, worry, etc. that sb has SYN **lessen**: *equipment to **lighten the load** of domestic work* ◇ *The measures will lighten the tax burden on small businesses.* **2** [I, T] to become or make sth become brighter or lighter in colour: *The sky began to lighten in the east.* ◇ **~ sth** *Use bleach to lighten the wood.* **3** [I, T] to feel or make sb feel less sad, worried or serious SYN **cheer**: **~ (up)** *My mood gradually lightened.* ◇ **~ sth (up)** *She told a joke to lighten the atmosphere.* **4** [T] **~ sth** to make sth lighter in weight

PHR V **ˌlighten 'up** (*informal*) used to tell sb to become less serious or worried about sth: *Come on, John. Lighten up!*

light·er /'laɪtə(r)/ *noun* **1** (also **ciga'rette lighter**) a small device that produces a flame for lighting cigarettes, etc. **2** a boat with a flat bottom used for carrying goods to and from ships in HARBOUR

ˌlight-'fingered *adj.* (*informal*) likely to steal things

ˌlight-'footed *adj.* moving quickly and easily, in an elegant way

ˌlight-'headed *adj.* not completely in control of your thoughts or movements; slightly faint: *After four glasses of wine he began to feel light-headed.*

ˌlight-'hearted *adj.* **1** intended to be amusing or easily enjoyable rather than too serious: *a light-hearted speech* **2** cheerful and without problems: *She felt light-hearted and optimistic.* ▶ **ˌlight-'hearted·ly** *adv.*

light·house /'laɪthaʊs/ *noun* a tower or other building that contains a strong light to warn and guide ships near the coast ➲ VISUAL VOCAB pages V5, V13

ˌlight 'industry *noun* [U, C] industry that produces small or light objects such as things used in the house ➲ compare HEAVY INDUSTRY

light·ing /ˈlaɪtɪŋ/ *noun* [U] **1** the arrangement or type of light in a place: ***electric/natural lighting*** ◇ ***good/poor lighting*** ◇ *The play had excellent sound and lighting effects.* **2** the use of electric lights in a place: *the cost of heating and lighting* ◇ *street lighting* ➲ note at LIGHT

ˈlighting engineer *noun* a person who works in television, the theatre, etc. and whose job is to control and take care of the lights

light·ly 🔑 /ˈlaɪtli/ *adv.*
1 🔑 gently; with very little force or effort: *He kissed her lightly on the cheek.* **2** 🔑 to a small degree; not much: *It began to snow lightly.* ◇ *She tended to sleep lightly nowadays* (= it was easy to disturb her). ◇ *I try to eat lightly* (= not to eat heavy or GREASY food). **3** in a way that sounds as though you are not particularly worried or interested SYN **nonchalantly**: *'I'll be all right,' he said lightly.* **4** without being seriously considered: *This is not a problem we should **take lightly**.*
IDM **get off/be let off ˈlightly** (*informal*) to be punished or treated in a way that is less severe than you deserve or may have expected

ˈlight meter *noun* a device used to measure how bright the light is before taking a photograph

light·ning /ˈlaɪtnɪŋ/ *noun, adj.*
■ ***noun*** [U] a flash, or several flashes, of very bright light in the sky caused by electricity: *a **flash of lightning*** ◇ *a violent storm with **thunder and lightning*** ◇ *He was **struck by lightning** and killed.* ◇ ***Lightning strikes** caused scores of fires across the state.* ➲ COLLOCATIONS at WEATHER
IDM **lightning never strikes (in the same place) twice** (*saying*) an unusual or unpleasant event is not likely to happen in the same place or to the same people twice **like (greased) ˈlightning** very fast
■ ***adj.*** [only before noun] very fast or sudden

ˈlightning bug *noun* (*NAmE*) = FIREFLY

ˈlightning conductor (*BrE*) (*NAmE* **ˈlightning rod**) *noun* a long straight piece of metal or wire leading from the highest part of a building to the ground, put there to prevent lightning damaging the building

ˈlightning rod *noun* **1** (*NAmE*) = LIGHTNING CONDUCTOR **2** (*especially NAmE*) a person or thing that attracts criticism, especially if the criticism is then not directed at sb/sth else

ˌlightning ˈstrike *noun* **1** an incident in which LIGHTNING hits sb/sth **2** (*BrE*) a strike by a group of workers that is sudden and without warning

ˈlight pen *noun* **1** a piece of equipment, shaped like a pen, that is sensitive to light and that can be used to pass information to a computer when it touches the screen **2** a similar piece of equipment that is used for reading BAR CODES

ˈlight pollution *noun* [U] the existence of too much artificial light in the environment, for example from street lights, which makes it difficult to see the stars

light·ship /ˈlaɪtʃɪp/ *noun* a small ship that stays at a particular place at sea and that has a powerful light on it to warn and guide other ships

ˈlight show *noun* a display of changing coloured lights, for example at a pop concert

ˈlight stick *noun* = GLOWSTICK

ˈlight water *noun* [U] **1** (*chemistry*) water that contains the normal amount of DEUTERIUM ➲ compare HEAVY WATER **2** (*technical*) a type of FOAM (= mass of bubbles) used to put out fires

light·weight /ˈlaɪtweɪt/ *adj., noun*
■ ***adj.*** **1** made of thinner material and less heavy than usual: *a lightweight jacket* **2** (*disapproving*) not very serious or impressive: *a lightweight book* ◇ *He was considered too lightweight for the job.*
■ ***noun*** **1** a BOXER weighing between 57 and 61 kilograms, heavier than a FEATHERWEIGHT: *a lightweight champion* **2** a person or thing that weighs less than is usual **3** (*informal, disapproving*) a person or thing of little importance or influence: *a political lightweight* ◇ *He's an intellectual lightweight* (= he does not think very deeply or seriously).

ˈlight year *noun* **1** (*astronomy*) the distance that light travels in one year, 9.4607×10^{12} kilometres: *The nearest star to earth is about 4 light years away.* **2 light years** [pl.] a very long time: *Full employment still seems light years away.*

lig·nite /ˈlɪɡnaɪt/ *noun* [U] a soft brown type of coal

lig·no·caine /ˈlɪɡnəkeɪn; *BrE* also -nəʊk-/ *noun* [U] = LIDOCAINE

lik·able (*especially NAmE*) = LIKEABLE

like 🔑 /laɪk/ *prep., verb, conj., noun, adj., adv.*
■ ***prep.*** **1** 🔑 similar to sb/sth: *She's wearing a dress like mine.* ◇ *He's very like his father.* ◇ *She looks **nothing like*** (= not at all like) *her mother.* ◇ *That sounds like* (= I think I can hear) *him coming now.* **2** 🔑 used to ask sb's opinion of sb/sth: *What's it like studying in Spain?* ◇ *This new girlfriend of his—what's she like?* **3** 🔑 used to show what is usual or typical for sb: *It's just like her to tell everyone about it.* **4** 🔑 in the same way as sb/sth: *Students were angry at being treated like children.* ◇ *He ran like the wind* (= very fast). ◇ *You do it like this.* ◇ *I, like everyone else, had read these stories in the press.* ◇ *Don't look at me like that.* ◇ (*informal*) *The candles are arranged **like so*** (= in this way). ➲ LANGUAGE BANK at SIMILARLY **5** 🔑 for example: *anti-utopian novels like 'Animal Farm' and '1984'* ➲ note at AS
IDM **more like...** used to give a number or an amount that is more accurate than one previously mentioned: *He believes the figure should be more like $10 million.* **more ˈlike (it)** (*informal*) **1** better; more acceptable: *This is more like it! Real food—not that canned muck.* **2** used to give what you think is a better description of sth: *Just talking? Arguing more like it.* **what is sb ˈlike?** (*BrE, informal*) used to say that sb has done sth annoying, silly, etc: *Oh, what am I like? I just completely forgot it.*
■ ***verb*** (not usually used in the progressive tenses) **1** 🔑 [T] to find sb/sth pleasant, attractive or of a good enough standard; to enjoy sth: **~ sb/sth** *She's nice. I like her.* ◇ *Do you like their new house?* ◇ *Which tie do you like best?* ◇ *How did you like Japan* (= did you find it pleasant)? ◇ *I don't like the way he's looking at me.* ◇ *You've got to go to school, whether you like it or not.* ◇ **~ doing sth** *She's never liked swimming.* ◇ **~ sb/sth doing sth** *I didn't like him taking all the credit.* ◇ (*formal*) *I didn't like his taking all the credit.* ◇ **~ to do sth** *I like to see them enjoying themselves.* ◇ **~ it when...** *I like it when you do that.* ➲ SYNONYMS at LOVE **2** 🔑 [T, no passive] to prefer to do sth; to prefer sth to be made or to happen in a particular way: **~ to do sth** *At weekends I like to sleep late.* ◇ **~ sth + adj.** *I like my coffee strong.* **3** 🔑 [T, no passive] **what/whatever sb ~** to want: *Do what you like—I don't care.* ◇ *You can dye your hair whatever colour you like.* **4** 🔑 [T] used in negative sentences to mean 'to be unwilling to do sth': **~ to do sth** *I didn't like to disturb you.* ◇ **~ doing sth** *He doesn't like asking his parents for help.* **5** 🔑 [T, I] used with *would* or *should* as a polite way to say what you want or to ask what sb wants: **~ sth** *Would you like a drink?* ◇ **~ to do sth** *I'd like to think it over.* ◇ *Would you like to come with us?* ◇ (*formal*) *We would like to apologize for the delay.* ◇ *How can they afford it? That's what I'd like to know.* ◇ **~ sb/sth to do sth** *We'd like you to come and visit us.* ◇ **~ for sb to do sth** (*NAmE*) *I'd like for us to work together.* ➲ note at WANT
IDM **how would ˈyou like it?** used to emphasize that sth bad has happened to you and you want some sympathy: *How would you like it if someone called you a liar?* **if you ˈlike** (*informal*) **1** 🔑 used to politely agree to sth or to suggest sth: *'Shall we stop now?' 'If you like.'* ◇ *If you like, we could go out this evening.* **2** used when you express sth in a new way or when you are not confident about sth: *It was, if you like, the dawn of a new era.* **I like ˈthat!** (*old-fashioned, informal*) used to protest that sth that has been said is not true or fair: *'She called you a cheat.' 'Well, I like that!'* **I/I'd like to think** used to say that you hope or believe that sth is true: *I like to think I'm broad-minded.* **ˌwhat's ˌnot to ˈlike?** (*informal, humorous*) used to say that sth is very good or enjoyable: *You get paid to eat chocolate. So what's not to like!*

L

■ *conj.* (*informal*) **1** ⊶ in the same way as: *No one sings the blues like she did.* ◇ *It didn't turn out like I intended.* ◇ ***Like I said*** (= as I said before), *you're always welcome to stay.* **2** ⊶ as if: *She acts like she owns the place.* HELP You will find more information about this use of **like** at the entries for the verbs **act, behave, feel, look** and **sound** and in the note at **as**.

■ ***noun*** **1 likes** [pl.] the things that you like: *We all have different* ***likes and dislikes***. **2** [sing.] a person or thing that is similar to another: *jazz, rock* ***and the like*** (= similar types of music) ◇ *a man whose like we shall not see again* ◇ *You're not comparing* ***like with like***. **3 the likes of sb/sth** (*informal*) used to refer to sb/sth that is considered as a type, especially one that is considered as good as sb/sth else: *She didn't want to associate with the likes of me.*

■ ***adj.*** [only before noun] (*formal*) having similar qualities to another person or thing: *a chance to meet people of like mind* (= with similar interests and opinions) ◇ *She responded in like manner.*

■ ***adv.*** **1** used in very informal speech, for example when you are thinking what to say next, explaining sth, or giving an example of sth: *It was, like, weird.* ◇ *It was kind of scary, like.* ◇ *It's really hard. Like I have no time for my own work.* **2** used in very informal speech to show that what you are saying may not be exactly right but is nearly so: *I'm leaving in like twenty minutes.* ◇ *It's going to cost like a hundred dollars.* **3 I'm, he's, she's, etc. ~** used in very informal speech, to mean 'I say', 'he/she says', etc.: *And then I'm like 'No Way!'* **4** used in informal speech instead of *as* to say that sth happens in the same way: *There was silence, but not like before.* ➲ note at AS

IDM **(as) like as 'not | like e'nough | most/very 'like** (*old-fashioned*) quite probably: *She would be in bed by now, as like as not.*

Synonyms

like

love • be fond of • be keen on sth • adore

These words all mean to find sth pleasant, attractive or satisfactory, or to enjoy sth.

like to find sth pleasant, attractive or satisfactory; to enjoy sth: *Do you like their new house?* ◇ *I like to see them enjoying themselves.*

love to like or enjoy sth very much: *He loved the way she smiled.*

be fond of sth to like or enjoy sth, especially sth you have liked or enjoyed for a long time: *We were fond of the house and didn't want to leave.*

be keen on sth (*BrEinformal*) (often used in negative statements) to like or enjoy sth: *I'm not keen on spicy food.* ◇ *She's not keen on being told what to do.*

adore (*informal*) to like or enjoy sth very much: *She adores working with children.*

LOVE OR ADORE?

Adore is more informal than **love**, and is used to express a stronger feeling.

PATTERNS

- to like/love/be fond of/be keen on/adore **doing sth**
- to like/love **to do sth**
- to like/love sth **very much**
- **I** like/love/adore **it** here/there/when...
- to like/love/adore **the way** sb does sth
- to **really** like/love/adore sb/sth
- to be **really** fond of/keen on sth

-like *combining form* (in adjectives) similar to; typical of: *childlike* ◇ *shell-like*

like·able (*especially BrE*) (also **lik·able** *NAmE, BrE*) /ˈlaɪkəbl/ *adj.* pleasant and easy to like: *a very likeable man*

like·li·hood /ˈlaɪklihʊd/ *noun* [U, sing.] the chance of sth happening; how likely sth is to happen SYN **probability**: *There is very little likelihood of that happening.* ◇ ***In all likelihood*** (= very probably) *the meeting will be cancelled.* ◇ ***The likelihood is*** *that* (= it is likely that) *unemployment figures will continue to fall.*

like·ly ⊶ /ˈlaɪkli/ *adj., adv.*

■ ***adj.*** (**like·lier, like·li·est**) HELP **more likely** and **most likely** are the usual forms **1** ⊶ probable or expected: *the most likely outcome* ◇ **~ (to do sth)** *Tickets are likely to be expensive.* ◇ **~ (that...)** *It's* ***more than likely that*** *the thieves don't know how much it is worth.* ◇ *They might refuse to let us do it, but it's* ***hardly likely***. ➲ LANGUAGE BANK at EXPECT **2** seeming suitable for a purpose SYN **promising**: *She seems the most likely candidate for the job.*

IDM **a 'likely story** (*informal, ironic*) used to show that you do not believe what sb has said

■ ***adv.***

IDM **as ˌlikely as 'not | most/very 'likely** very probably: *As likely as not she's forgotten all about it.* **not 'likely!** (*informal, especially BrE*) used to disagree strongly with a statement or suggestion: *Me? Join the army? Not likely!*

Grammar Point

likely

- In standard *BrE* the adverb **likely** must be used with a word such as *most, more* or *very*: *We will most likely see him later.* In informal *NAmE* **likely** is often used on its own: *We will likely see him later.* ◇ *He said that he would likely run for President.*

ˌlike-'minded *adj.* having similar ideas and interests

liken /ˈlaɪkən/ *verb*

PHR V **'liken sth/sb to sth/sb** (*formal*) to compare one thing or person to another and say they are similar: *Life is often likened to a journey.*

like·ness /ˈlaɪknəs/ *noun* **1** [C, U] the fact of being similar to another person or thing, especially in appearance; an example of this SYN **resemblance**: *Joanna bears a strong likeness to her father.* ◇ *Do you notice any family likeness between them?* **2** [C, usually sing.] a painting, drawing, etc. of a person, especially one that looks very like them: *The drawing is said to be* ***a good likeness*** *of the girl's attacker.*

likes *noun* ➲ LIKE *n.* (1)

like·wise AW /ˈlaɪkwaɪz/ *adv.* **1** (*formal*) the same; in a similar way: *He voted for the change and he expected his colleagues to* ***do likewise***. **2** (*formal*) also: *Her second marriage was likewise unhappy.* **3** (*informal*) used to show that you feel the same towards sb or about sth: *'Let me know if you ever need any help.' 'Likewise.'*

lik·ing /ˈlaɪkɪŋ/ *noun* [sing.] **~ (for sb/sth)** the feeling that you like sb/sth; the enjoyment of sth SYN **fondness**: *He* ***had a liking for*** *fast cars.* ◇ *She had* ***taken a liking to him*** *on their first meeting.*

IDM **for your 'liking** if you say, for example, that sth is too hot **for your liking**, you mean that you would prefer it to be less hot: *The town was too crowded for my liking.* **to sb's 'liking** (*formal*) suitable, and how sb likes sth: *The coffee was just to his liking.*

lilac /ˈlaɪlək/ *noun* **1** [U, C] a bush or small tree with purple or white flowers with a sweet smell that grow closely together in the shape of a CONE **2** [U] a pale purple colour ▸ **lilac** *adj.*: *a lilac dress*

Lil·li·pu·tian /ˌlɪlɪˈpjuːʃn/ *adj.* (*formal*) extremely small SYN **diminutive, tiny** ORIGIN From the land of **Lilliput**, in Jonathan Swift's *Gulliver's Travels*, where the people are only 15 cm high.

lilo /ˈlaɪləʊ; *NAmE* -loʊ/ (also **Li-Lo™**) *noun* (*pl.* -os) (*BrE*) a plastic or rubber bed that is filled with air and used when camping or for floating on water

lilt /lɪlt/ *noun* [sing.] **1** the pleasant way in which a person's voice rises and falls: *Her voice had a soft Welsh lilt to it.* **2** a regular rising and falling pattern in music, with a strong rhythm ▸ **lilt·ing** *adj.*

lily /ˈlɪli/ *noun* (*pl.* -ies) a large white or brightly coloured flower with PETALS that curl back from the centre. There are many types of lily. ➲ VISUAL VOCAB page V9 ➲ see also WATER LILY IDM see GILD

lily-livered /ˈlɪli lɪvəd; *NAmE* -vərd/ *adj.* (*old-fashioned*) lacking courage SYN **cowardly**

ˌlily of the ˈvalley *noun* [C, U] (*pl.* **lilies of the valley**) a plant with small white flowers shaped like bells

ˈlily pad *noun* a round floating leaf of a WATER LILY

ˌlily-ˈwhite *adj.* **1** almost pure white in colour: *lily-white skin* **2** morally perfect: *They want me to conform, to be lily-white.*

lima bean /ˈliːmə biːn/ *noun* (*NAmE*) a type of round, pale green BEAN. Several lima beans grow together inside a flat POD.

limb /lɪm/ *noun* **1** an arm or a leg; a similar part of an animal, such as a wing: *an artificial limb* ◇ *For a while, she lost the use of her limbs.* **2 -limbed** (in adjectives) having the type of limbs mentioned: *long-limbed* ◇ *loose-limbed* **3** a large branch of a tree ➲ VISUAL VOCAB page V8

IDM **out on a ˈlimb** (*informal*) not supported by other people: *Are you prepared to **go out on a limb*** (= risk doing sth that other people are not prepared to do) *and make your suspicions public?* **tear/rip sb ˌlimb from ˈlimb** (often *humorous*) to attack sb very violently ➲ more at RISK *v.*

limba /ˈlɪmbə/ *noun* = AFARA

lim·ber /ˈlɪmbə(r)/ *verb*

PHR V **ˌlimber ˈup** to do physical exercises in order to stretch and prepare your muscles before taking part in a race, sporting activity, etc. SYN **warm up**

lim·bic sys·tem /ˈlɪmbɪk sɪstəm/ *noun* (*biology*) a system of nerves in the brain involving several different areas, concerned with basic emotions such as fear and anger and basic needs such as the need to eat and to have sex

limbo /ˈlɪmbəʊ; *NAmE* -boʊ/ *noun* **1** [C] a West Indian dance in which you lean backwards and go under a bar which is made lower each time you go under it **2** [U, sing.] a situation in which you are not certain what to do next, cannot take action, etc, especially because you are waiting for sb else to make a decision: *the limbo of the stateless person* ◇ *His life seemed stuck **in limbo**; he could not go forward and he could not go back.*

lime /laɪm/ *noun, verb*

■ ***noun*** **1** (also **quick·lime**) [U] a white substance obtained by heating LIMESTONE, used in building materials and to help plants grow **2** [C, U] a small green fruit, like a lemon, with a lot of sour juice, used in cooking and in drinks; the juice of this fruit: *lime juice* ◇ *slices of lime* ➲ VISUAL VOCAB page V26 **3** (also **ˈlime tree**) [C] a tree on which limes grow **4** (also **ˈlime tree**, **ˈlinden tree**, **linden**) [C] a large tree with light green heart-shaped leaves and yellow flowers: *an avenue of limes* **5** [U] = LIME GREEN

■ ***verb*** **~ sth** to add the substance lime to soil, especially in order to control the acid in it

lime·ade /laɪmˈeɪd/ *noun* [U, C] **1** a sweet FIZZY drink (= with bubbles) with a LIME flavour **2** a drink made from LIME juice, sugar and water

ˌlime ˈgreen *adj.* (also **lime**) bright yellowish green in colour ▸ **ˌlime ˈgreen** (also **lime**) *noun* [U]

lime·light /ˈlaɪmlaɪt/ (usually **the limelight**) *noun* [U] the centre of public attention: *to be **in the limelight*** ◇ *to stay **out of the limelight*** ◇ *to **steal/hog the limelight*** (= take attention away from other people)

lim·er·ick /ˈlɪmərɪk/ *noun* a humorous short poem, with two long lines that RHYME with each other, followed by two short lines that rhyme with each other and ending with a long line that rhymes with the first two

lime·scale /ˈlaɪmskeɪl/ *noun* [U] (*BrE*) the hard white substance that is left by water on the inside of pipes, etc.

lime·stone /ˈlaɪmstəʊn; *NAmE* -stoʊn/ *noun* [U] a type of white stone that contains CALCIUM, used in building and in making CEMENT

ˈlime water *noun* [U] (*chemistry*) a liquid containing CALCIUM HYDROXIDE which shows the presence of CARBON DIOXIDE by turning white

Limey /ˈlaɪmi/ *noun* (*old-fashioned, NAmE*) a slightly insulting word for a British person

Synonyms

limit

restriction • control • constraint • restraint • limitation

These are all words for sth that limits what you can do or what can happen.

limit the greatest or smallest amount of sth that is allowed: *The EU has set strict limits on pollution levels.* ◇ *the speed limit*

restriction (*rather formal*) a rule or law that limits what you can do: *There are no restrictions on the amount of money you can withdraw.*

control (often in compounds) the act of limiting or managing sth; a method of doing this: *arms control*

constraint (*rather formal*) a fact or decision that limits what you can do: *We have to work within severe constraints of time and money.*

restraint (*rather formal*) a decision, a rule, an idea, etc. that limits what you can do; the act of limiting sth because it is necessary or sensible to do so: *The government has imposed export restraints on some products.* ◇ *The unions are unlikely to accept any sort of wage restraint.*

limitation the act or process of limiting sth; a rule, fact or condition that limits sth: *They would resist any limitation of their powers.*

RESTRICTION, CONSTRAINT, RESTRAINT OR LIMITATION?

These are all things that limit what you can do. A **restriction** is rule or law that is made by sb in authority. A **constraint** is sth that exists rather than sth that is made, although it may exist as a result of sb's decision. A **restraint** is also sth that exists: it can exist outside yourself, as the result of sb else's decision; but it can also exist inside you, as a fear of what other people may think or as your own feeling about what is acceptable: *moral/social/cultural restraints.* A **limitation** is more general and can be a rule that sb makes or a fact or condition that exists.

PATTERNS

- limits/restrictions/controls/constraints/restraints/limitations **on** sth
- limits/limitations **to** sth
- **severe** limits/restrictions/controls/constraints/restraints/limitations
- **tight** limits/restrictions/controls/constraints
- **to impose/remove** limits/restrictions/controls/constraints/restraints/limitations
- **to lift** restrictions/controls/constraints/restraints

limit 🔑 /ˈlɪmɪt/ *noun, verb*

■ ***noun*** **1** 🔑 **~ (to sth)** a point at which sth stops being possible or existing: *There is a limit to the amount of pain we can bear.* ◇ *The team performed **to the limit** of its capabilities.* ◇ *She knew the limits of her power.* ◇ *to push/stretch/test sb/sth **to the limit*** ◇ *His arrogance **knew*** (= had) ***no limits.*** **2** 🔑 **~ (on sth)** the greatest or smallest amount of sth that is allowed SYN **restriction**: *a **time/speed/age limit*** ◇ *The EU has **set** strict **limits** on levels of pollution.* ◇ *They were travelling at a speed that was double the **legal limit**.* ◇ *You can't drive—you're **over the limit*** (= you have drunk more alcohol than is legal when driving). **3** the furthest edge of an area or a place: *We were reaching the limits of civilization.* ◇ *the **city limits*** (= the imaginary line which

L

officially divides the city from the area outside) ➲ see also OFF-LIMITS

IDM **be the 'limit** (*old-fashioned, informal*) to be extremely annoying **within 'limits** to some extent; with some restrictions: *I'm willing to help, within limits.* ➲ more at SKY

■ *verb* **1** ~ **sth** (**to sth**) to stop sth from increasing beyond a particular amount or level SYN **restrict**: *measures to limit carbon dioxide emissions from cars* ◇ *The amount of money you have to spend will limit your choice.* **2** ~ **yourself/sb** (**to sth**) to restrict or reduce the amount of sth that you or sb can have or use: *Families are limited to four free tickets each.* ◇ *I've limited myself to 1 000 calories a day to try and lose weight.*

PHR V **'limit sth to sb/sth** [usually passive] to make sth exist or happen only in a particular place or within a particular group: *Violent crime is not limited to big cities.* ◇ *The teaching of history should not be limited to dates and figures.*

limi·ta·tion /ˌlɪmɪˈteɪʃn/ *noun* **1** [U] the act or process of limiting or controlling sb/sth SYN **restriction**: *They would resist any limitation of their powers.* ➲ SYNONYMS at LIMIT ➲ see also DAMAGE LIMITATION **2** [C] ~ (**on sth**) a rule, fact or condition that limits sth SYN **curb, restraint**: *to impose limitations on imports* ◇ *Disability is a physical limitation on your life.* ➲ see also STATUTE OF LIMITATIONS **3** [C, usually pl.] a limit on what sb/sth can do or how good they or it can be: *This technique is useful but it* ***has its limitations.***

limit·ed /ˈlɪmɪtɪd/ *adj.* **1** not very great in amount or extent: *We are doing our best with the limited resources available.* **2** ~ (**to sth**) restricted to a particular limit of time, numbers, etc: *This offer is for a limited period only.* ➲ see also LTD

ˌlimited 'company (also **ˌlimited lia'bility company**) *noun* (in Britain) a company whose owners only have to pay a limited amount of its debts ➲ see also LTD

ˌlimited e'dition *noun* a fixed, usually small, number of copies of a book, picture, etc. produced at one time

ˌlimited lia'bility *noun* [U] (*law*) the legal position of having to pay only a limited amount of your or your company's debts

limit·ing /ˈlɪmɪtɪŋ/ *adj.* putting limits on what is possible: *Lack of cash is a limiting factor.*

limit·less /ˈlɪmɪtləs/ *adj.* without a limit; very great SYN **infinite**: *the limitless variety of consumer products* ◇ *The possibilities were almost limitless.*

limo /ˈlɪməʊ; *NAmE* ˈlɪmoʊ/ *noun* (*pl.* -**os**) (*informal*) = LIMOUSINE

lim·ou·sine /ˈlɪməziːn; ˌlɪməˈziːn/ (also *informal* **limo**) *noun* **1** a large expensive comfortable car: *a long black chauffeur-driven limousine* ➲ see also STRETCH LIMO **2** (*especially NAmE*) a van or small bus that takes people to and from an airport

limp /lɪmp/ *adj., verb, noun*

■ *adj.* **1** lacking strength or energy: *His hand went limp and the knife clattered to the ground.* ◇ *She felt limp and exhausted.* **2** not stiff or firm: *The hat had become limp and shapeless.* ▶ **limp·ly** *adv.*: *Her hair* ***hung limply*** *over her forehead.*

■ *verb* **1** [I] to walk slowly or with difficulty because one leg is injured: *She had twisted her ankle and was limping.* ◇ + **adv./prep.** *Matt limped painfully off the field.* **2** [I] + **adv./prep.** to move slowly or with difficulty after being damaged: *The plane limped back to the airport.* ◇ (*figurative*) *The government was limping along in its usual way.*

■ *noun* [usually sing.] a way of walking in which one leg is used less than normal because it is injured or stiff: *to walk with a* ***slight/pronounced limp***

lim·pet /ˈlɪmpɪt/ *noun* a small SHELLFISH that sticks very tightly to rocks: *The Prime Minister clung to his job like a limpet, despite calls for him to resign.*

lim·pid /ˈlɪmpɪd/ *adj.* (*literary*) (of liquids, etc.) clear SYN **transparent**: *limpid eyes/water*

ˌlimp-'wristed *adj.* (*informal*) an offensive word for HOMOSEXUAL

LINC /lɪŋk/ *abbr.* Language Instruction for Newcomers to Canada (free language classes provided by the government to people from other countries who come to live in Canada)

linch·pin (also **lynch·pin**) /ˈlɪntʃpɪn/ *noun* a person or thing that is the most important part of an organization, a plan, etc, because everything else depends on them or it

Lin·coln's Birth·day /ˌlɪŋkənz ˈbɜːθdeɪ; *NAmE* ˈbɜːrθ-/ *noun* [U] (in some US states) a legal holiday on 12 February in memory of the birthday of Abraham Lincoln

linc·tus /ˈlɪŋktəs/ *noun* [U] (*BrE*) thick liquid medicine that you take for a sore throat or a cough: *cough linctus*

lin·den /ˈlɪndən/ (also **'linden tree**) *noun* = LIME

line /laɪn/ *noun, verb*

■ *noun*

▸ LONG THIN MARK **1** [C] a long thin mark on a surface: *a* ***straight/wavy/dotted/diagonal line*** ◇ *a* ***vertical/horizontal line*** ◇ ***parallel lines*** ◇ *Draw a thick black line across the page.* **2** [C] a long thin mark on the ground to show the limit or border of sth, especially of a playing area in some sports: *The ball* ***went over the line.*** ◇ *Be careful not to* ***cross the line*** (= the broken line painted down the middle of the road). ◇ *Your feet must be behind the line when you serve* (= in TENNIS). ◇ *They were all waiting on the* ***starting line.*** ➲ see also FINISHING LINE, GOAL LINE, SIDELINE, TOUCHLINE **3** [C] a mark like a line on sb's skin that people usually get as they get older SYN **wrinkle**: *He has* ***fine lines*** *around his eyes.*

▸ DIVISION **4** [C] an imaginary limit or border between one place or thing and another: *He was convicted of illegally importing weapons across* ***state lines.*** ◇ *a* ***district/county line*** ◇ ***lines of longitude and latitude*** ➲ see also COASTLINE, DATE LINE, DIVIDING LINE, PICKET LINE, TREELINE, WATERLINE **5** [C] the division between one area of thought or behaviour and another: *We want to cut across lines of race, sex and religion.* ◇ *There is* ***a fine line between*** *showing interest in what someone is doing and interfering in it.* ➲ see also RED LINE

▸ SHAPE **6** [C] the edge, outline or shape of sb/sth: *He traced the line of her jaw with his finger.* ◇ *a beautiful sports car with sleek lines* ➲ see also BIKINI LINE

▸ ROW OF PEOPLE/THINGS **7** [C] a row of people or things next to each other or behind each other: *a long line of trees* ◇ *The children all stood* ***in a line.*** ◇ *They were stuck in a line of traffic.* **8** [C] (*NAmE*) a QUEUE of people: *to* ***stand/wait in line*** *for sth* ◇ *A line formed at each teller window.*

▸ IN FACTORY **9** [C] a system of making sth, in which the product moves from one worker to the next until it is finished ➲ see also ASSEMBLY LINE, PRODUCTION LINE

▸ SERIES **10** [C, usually sing.] a series of people, things or events that follow one another in time: *She came from* ***a long line of*** *doctors.* ◇ *to pass sth down through the* ***male/female line*** ◇ *This novel is the latest in a long line of thrillers that he has written.* **11** [C, usually sing.] a series of people in order of importance: *Orders came down the line from the very top.* ◇ *a line of command* ◇ *He is second* ***in line*** *to the chairman.* ◇ *to be* ***next in line*** *to the throne* ➲ see also LINE MANAGER

▸ WORDS **12** [C] (*abbr.* l) a row of words on a page or the empty space where they can be written; the words of a song or poem: *Look at line 5 of the text.* ◇ *Write the title of your essay on the top line.* ◇ *I can only remember the first two lines of that song.* ➲ see also BOTTOM LINE **13** [C] the words spoken by an actor in a play or film/movie: *to learn your lines* ◇ *a line from the film 'Casablanca'* **14 lines** [pl.] (*BrE*) (in some schools) a punishment in which a child has to write out a particular sentence a number of times **15** [C] (*informal*) a remark, especially when sb says it to achieve a particular purpose: *Don't give me that line about having to work late again.* ◇ (*BrE*) *That's the worst* ***chat-up line*** *I've ever heard.*

▸ ROPE/WIRE/PIPE **16** [C] a long piece of rope, thread, etc, especially when it is used for a particular purpose: *a* ***fishing line*** ◇ *He hung the towels out* ***on the line*** (= clothes line). ◇ *They dropped the sails and threw a line to a man on the dock.* ➲ see also LIFELINE **17** [C] a pipe or thick wire that carries water, gas or electricity from one place to another ➲ see also POWER LINE

▸ TELEPHONE **18** 🔑 [C] a telephone connection; a particular telephone number: *Your bill includes line rental.* ◇ *The company's lines have been jammed* (= busy) *all day with people making complaints.* ◇ *I was talking to John when the* **line** *suddenly* **went dead.** ◇ *If you* **hold the line** (= stay on the telephone and wait), *I'll see if she is available.* ➲ see also HELPLINE, HOTLINE, LANDLINE, OFFLINE, ONLINE

▸ RAILWAY/RAILROAD **19** 🔑 [C] a railway/railroad track; a section of a railway/railroad system: *The train was delayed because a tree had fallen across the line.* ◇ *a branch line* ◇ *the East Coast line* ➲ see also MAIN LINE

▸ ROUTE/DIRECTION **20** 🔑 [C, usually sing.] the direction that sb/sth is moving or located in: *Just keep going* ***in a straight line****; you can't miss it.* ◇ *The town is in a direct line between London and the coast.* ◇ *Please move; you're right in my* ***line of vision*** (= the direction I am looking in). ◇ *They followed the line of the river for three miles.* ◇ *Be careful to stay out of the* ***line of fire*** (= the direction sb is shooting in). **21** [C] a route from one place to another especially when it is used for a particular purpose: *Their aim was to block guerrilla* ***supply lines.***

▸ ATTITUDE/ARGUMENT **22** [C, usually sing.] an attitude or a belief, especially one that sb states publicly: *The government is* ***taking a firm line on*** *terrorism.* ◇ *He supported the* ***official line*** *on education.* ➲ see also HARD LINE, PARTY LINE **23** [C] a method or way of doing or thinking about sth: *I don't follow your* ***line of reasoning.*** ◇ *She decided to try a different* ***line of argument*** (= way of persuading sb of sth). ◇ *sb's first* ***line of attack/defence*** ◇ *The police are pursuing a new* ***line of enquiry/inquiry*** (= way of finding out information).

▸ ACTIVITY **24** [sing.] a type or area of business, activity or interest: *My* ***line of work*** *pays pretty well.* ◇ *You can't do much in the art line without training.* ➲ see also SIDELINE

▸ PRODUCT **25** [C] a type of product: *We are starting a new line in casual clothes.* ◇ *Some lines sell better than others.*

▸ TRANSPORT **26** [C] (often used in names) a company that provides transport for people or goods: *a* ***shipping/bus line*** ➲ see also AIRLINE

▸ SOLDIERS **27** [C] a row or series of military defences where the soldiers are fighting during a war: *The regiment was sent to fight in* ***the front line*** (= the position nearest the enemy). ◇ *They were trapped* ***behind enemy lines*** (= in the area controlled by the enemy).

▸ DRUGS **28** [C] (*slang*) an amount of COCAINE that is spread out in a thin line, ready to take

IDM **along/down the 'line** (*informal*) at some point during an activity or a process: *Somewhere along the line a large amount of money went missing.* ◇ *We'll make a decision on that further down the line.* **along/on (the)... 'lines 1** (*informal*) in the way that is mentioned: *The new system will operate* ***along the same lines*** *as the old one.* ◇ *They voted along class lines.* **2** (*informal*) similar to the way or thing that is mentioned: *Those aren't his exact words, but he said something along those lines.* **be, come, etc. on 'line 1** to be working or functioning: *The new working methods will come on line in June.* **2** using or connected to a computer or the Internet; communicating with other people by computer: *All the new homes are on line.* ➲ see also ONLINE **bring sb/sth, come, get, fall, etc. into 'line (with sb/sth)** to behave or make sb/sth behave in the same way as other people or how they should behave: *Britain must be brought into line with the rest of Europe on taxes.* **in (a) 'line (with sth)** in a position that forms a straight line with sth: *An eclipse happens when the earth and moon are in line with the sun.* **in 'line for sth** likely to get sth: *She is in line for promotion.* **in the ˌline of 'duty** while doing a job: *A policeman was injured in the line of duty yesterday.* **in 'line with sth** similar to sth or so that one thing is closely connected with another: *Annual pay increases will be in line with inflation.* **ˌlay it on the 'line** (*informal*) to tell sb clearly what you think, especially when they will not like what you say: *The manager laid it on the line—some people would have to lose their jobs.* **(choose, follow, take, etc.) the line of least re'sistance** (to choose, etc.) the easiest way of doing sth **(put sth) on the 'line** (*informal*) at risk: *If we don't make a profit, my job is on the line.* **out of 'line (with sb/sth) 1** not forming a straight line **2** different from sth: *London prices are way out of line with the rest of the country.* **3** (*NAmE*) (*BrE* **ˌout of 'order**) (*informal*) behaving in a way that is not acceptable or right **walk/tread a fine/thin line** to be in a difficult or dangerous situation where you could easily make a mistake: *He was walking a fine line between being funny and being rude.* ➲ more at BATTLE *n.*, DRAW *v.*, END *n.*, FIRING LINE, FIRM *adj.*, FRONT LINE, HARD *adj.*, HOOK *n.*, JUMP *v.*, OVERSTEP, PITCH *v.*, READ *v.*, SIGN *v.*, STEP *v.*, TOE *v.*

■ ***verb***

▸ COVER INSIDE **1** [often passive] **~ sth (with sth)** to cover the inside of sth with a layer of another material to keep it clean, make it stronger, etc: *Line the pan with greaseproof paper.* **2 ~ sth** to form a layer on the inside of sth: *the membranes that line the nose*

▸ FORM ROWS **3** [often passive] to form lines or rows along sth: **~ sth** *Crowds of people lined the streets to watch the race.* ◇ **~ sth with sth** *The walls were lined with books.* ➲ see also LINED

IDM **line your (own)/sb's 'pockets** to get richer or make sb richer, especially by taking unfair advantage of a situation or by being dishonest

PHR V **ˌline 'up** to stand in a line or row; to form a QUEUE/LINE: *Line up, children!* ◇ *Cars lined up waiting to board the ship.* **ˌline sb/sth↔'up 1** to arrange people or things in a straight line or row: *The suspects were lined up against the wall.* ◇ *He lined the bottles up along the shelf.* **2** to arrange for an event or activity to happen, or arrange for sb to be available to do sth: *Mark had a job lined up when he left college.* ◇ *I've got a lot lined up this week* (= I'm very busy). ◇ *She's lined up a live band for the party.* **ˌline sth↔'up (with sth)** to move one thing into a correct position in relation to another thing

lin·eage /ˈlɪniɪdʒ/ *noun* [U, C] (*formal*) the series of families that sb comes from originally SYN **ancestry**

lin·eal /ˈlɪniəl/ *adj.* [only before noun] (*formal*) coming in a direct line from an earlier or later generation of the same family as sb: *a lineal descendant of the company's founder*

lin·ea·ments /ˈlɪniəmənts/ *noun* [pl.] (*formal*) the typical features of sth

lin·ear /ˈlɪniə(r)/ *adj.* **1** of or in lines: *In his art he broke the laws of scientific linear perspective.* **2** going from one thing to another in a single series of stages: *Students do not always progress in a linear fashion.* OPP **non-linear** **3** of length: *linear measurement* (= for example metres, feet, etc.) **4** (*mathematics*) able to be represented by a straight line on a GRAPH: *linear equations* ▸ **lin·ear·ity** /ˌlɪniˈærəti/ *noun* [U]: *She abandoned the linearity of the conventional novel.* **lin·ear·ly** *adv.*

ˌLinear ˈB *noun* [U] the later of two early forms of writing found on stones in Crete

line·back·er /ˈlaɪnbækə(r)/ *noun* (in AMERICAN FOOTBALL) a DEFENSIVE player who tries to TACKLE members of the other team

ˈline-caught *adj.* (of fish) caught with a hook, not in a net: *We sell only line-caught wild fish.*

lined /laɪnd/ *adj.* **1** (of skin, especially on the face) having folds or lines because of age, worry, etc. SYN **wrinkled**: *a deeply lined face* **2** (of paper) having lines printed or drawn across it: *Lined paper helps keep handwriting neat.* **3** (of clothes) having a LINING inside them: *a lined skirt* **4 -lined** having the object mentioned along an edge or edges, or as a LINING: *a tree-lined road*

ˈline dancing *noun* [U] a type of dancing originally from the US, in which people dance in lines, all doing a complicated series of steps at the same time

ˈline drawing *noun* a drawing that consists only of lines

ˈline drive *noun* (in BASEBALL) a powerful hit in a straight line near to the ground

line·man /ˈlaɪnmən/ *noun* (*pl.* **-men** /-mən/) (*NAmE*) **1** a player in the front line of an AMERICAN FOOTBALL team **2** = LINESMAN (2)

L

ˈline management *noun* [U] (*BrE*) the system of organizing a company, etc. in which information and instructions are passed from each employee and manager to the person one rank above or below them ▶ **ˈline manager** *noun*: *Review your training needs with your line manager.*

linen /ˈlɪnɪn/ *noun* [U] **1** a type of cloth made from FLAX, used to make high-quality clothes, sheets, etc: *a linen tablecloth* **2** sheets, TABLECLOTHS, PILLOWCASES, etc: (*BrE*) *a linen cupboard* ◇ (*NAmE*) *a linen closet* ➲ see also BEDLINEN IDM see WASH *v.*

ˌline of ˈsight (also **ˌline of ˈvision**, **ˈsight-line**) *noun* an imaginary line that goes from sb's eye to sth that they are looking at: *There was a column directly in my line of sight, so I could only see half the stage.*

ˈline-out *noun* (in RUGBY) a situation that happens when the ball goes out of play, when players from opposing teams stand in lines and jump to try to catch the ball when it is thrown back in

ˈline printer *noun* a machine that prints very quickly, producing a complete line of print at a time

liner /ˈlaɪnə(r)/ *noun* **1** a large ship that carries passengers: *an ocean liner* ◇ *a luxury cruise liner* ➲ VISUAL VOCAB page V44 **2** (especially in compounds) a piece of material used to cover the inside surface of sth: *bin/nappy liners* **3** = EYELINER

ˈliner note (*BrE* also **ˈsleeve note**) *noun* [usually pl.] information about the music or the performers that comes with a CD or is printed on the cover of a record

L

lines·man /ˈlaɪnzmən/ *noun* (*pl.* **-men** /-mən/) **1** an official who helps the REFEREE in some games that are played on a field or court, especially in deciding whether or where a ball crosses one of the lines. Linesmen are now officially called **referee's assistants** in football (SOCCER). **2** (*BrE*) (*NAmE* **line·man**) a person whose job is to repair telephone or electricity power lines

ˈline-up *noun* [usually sing.] **1** the people who are going to take part in a particular event: *an impressive line-up of speakers* ◇ *the starting line-up* (= the players who will begin the game) **2** a set of items, events etc. arranged to follow one another SYN **programme**: *A horror movie completes this evening's TV line-up.* **3** (*especially NAmE*) (*BrE* also **iˌdentifiˈcation parade**, *informal* **iˈdentity parade**) a row of people, including one person who is suspected of a crime, who are shown to a witness to see if he or she can recognize the criminal

ling /lɪŋ/ *noun* [U] a low plant that is a type of HEATHER and that grows on areas of wild open land (=MOORLAND)

-ling /lɪŋ/ *suffix* (in nouns) (sometimes *disapproving*) small; not important: *duckling* ◇ *princeling*

lin·ger /ˈlɪŋgə(r)/ *verb* **1** [I] to continue to exist for longer than expected: *The faint smell of her perfume lingered in the room.* ◇ **~ on** *The civil war lingered on well into the 1930s.* **2** [I] (**+ adv./prep.**) to stay somewhere for longer because you do not want to leave; to spend a long time doing sth: *She lingered for a few minutes to talk to Nick.* ◇ *We lingered over breakfast on the terrace.* **3** [I] **~ (on sb/sth)** to continue to look at sb/sth or think about sth for longer than usual: *His eyes lingered on the diamond ring on her finger.* **4** [I] **~ (on)** to stay alive but become weaker: *He lingered on for several months after the heart attack.*

lin·ge·rie /ˈlænʒəri; *NAmE* ˌlɑːndʒəˈreɪ/ *noun* [U] (used especially by shops/stores) women's underwear

lin·ger·ing /ˈlɪŋgərɪŋ/ *adj.* slow to end or disappear: *a painful and lingering death* ◇ *a last lingering look* ◇ *lingering doubts* ◇ *a lingering smell of machine oil* ▶ **lin·ger·ing·ly** *adv.*

lingo /ˈlɪŋgəʊ; *NAmE* -goʊ/ *noun* [sing.] (*informal*) **1** a language, especially a foreign language: *He doesn't speak the lingo.* **2** (*especially NAmE*) expressions used by a particular group of people SYN **jargon**: *baseball lingo*

lin·gua franca /ˌlɪŋgwə ˈfræŋkə/ *noun* [usually sing.] (*linguistics*) a shared language of communication used between people whose main languages are different: *English has become a lingua franca in many parts of the world.*

lin·gual /ˈlɪŋgwəl/ *adj.* **1** (*anatomy*) related to the tongue **2** related to speech or language **3** (*phonetics*) (of a speech sound) produced using the tongue ▶ **lin·gual·ly** /ˈlɪŋgwəli/ *adv.*

lin·guist /ˈlɪŋgwɪst/ *noun* **1** a person who knows several foreign languages well: *She's an excellent linguist.* ◇ *I'm afraid I'm no linguist* (= I find foreign languages difficult). **2** a person who studies languages or LINGUISTICS

lin·guis·tic /lɪŋˈgwɪstɪk/ *adj.* connected with language or the scientific study of language: *linguistic and cultural barriers* ◇ *a child's innate linguistic ability* ◇ *new developments in linguistic theory* ▶ **lin·guis·tic·al·ly** *adv.*

lin·guis·tics /lɪŋˈgwɪstɪks/ *noun* [U] the scientific study of language or of particular languages: *a course in applied linguistics*

lini·ment /ˈlɪnəmənt/ *noun* [C, U] a liquid, especially one made with oil, that you rub on a painful part of your body to reduce the pain

lin·ing /ˈlaɪnɪŋ/ *noun* **1** [C] a layer of material used to cover the inside surface of sth: *a pair of leather gloves with fur linings* ➲ VISUAL VOCAB page V50 **2** [U] the covering of the inner surface of a part of the body: *the stomach lining* IDM see CLOUD *n.*

link 🔑 AW /lɪŋk/ *noun, verb*

■ ***noun*** **1** 🔑 **~ (between A and B)** a connection between two or more people or things: *Police suspect there may be a link between the two murders.* ◇ *evidence for a strong causal link between exposure to sun and skin cancer* ➲ see also MISSING LINK **2** 🔑 a relationship between two or more people, countries or organizations: **~ (with sth)** *to establish **trade links** with Asia* ◇ **~ (between A and B)** *Social customs provide a vital link between generations.* **3** 🔑 a means of travelling or communicating between two places: *a high-speed **rail link*** ◇ *a link road* ◇ *a video link* ◇ *The speech was broadcast via a **satellite link**.* **4** 🔑 (*computing*) a place in an electronic document that is connected to another electronic document or to another part of the same document: *To visit similar websites to this one, click on the links at the bottom of the page.* ➲ VISUAL VOCAB page V55 ➲ see also HYPERLINK **5** each ring of a chain ➲ picture at ROPE ➲ see also CUFFLINK

IDM **a link in the ˈchain** one of the stages in a process or a line of argument ➲ more at WEAK

■ ***verb*** [often passive] **1** 🔑 to make a physical or electronic connection between one object, machine, place, etc. and another SYN **connect**: **~ A to B** *The video cameras are linked to a powerful computer.* ◇ **~ A with B** *The Channel Tunnel links Britain with the rest of Europe.* ◇ **~ A and B (together)** *When computers are networked, they are linked together so that information can be transferred between them.* **2** 🔑 if sth **links** two things, facts or situations, or they **are linked**, they are connected in some way: **~ A to/with B** *Exposure to ultraviolet light is **closely linked** to skin cancer.* ◇ **~ A and B** *The two factors are **directly linked**.* ◇ *The personal and social development of the child are **inextricably linked*** (= they depend on each other). **3 ~ A to/with B | ~ A and B** to state that there is a connection or relationship between two things or people SYN **associate**: *Detectives have linked the break-in to a similar crime in the area last year.* ◇ *Newspapers have linked his name with the singer.* **4 ~ A and B** to join two things by putting one through the other: *The two girls **linked arms** as they strolled down the street.*

PHR V **ˌlink ˈup (with sb/sth)** to join or become joined with sb/sth: *The two spacecraft will link up in orbit.* ◇ *The bands have linked up for a charity concert.* ➲ related noun LINK-UP

link·age AW /ˈlɪŋkɪdʒ/ *noun* **1** [U, C] **~ (between A and B)** the act of linking things; a link or system of links SYN **connection**: *This chapter explores the linkage between economic development and the environment.* **2** [C] a device that links two or more things

ˈlinking verb (also **cop·ula**) *noun* (*grammar*) a verb such as *be* or *become* that connects a subject with the adjective or noun (called the COMPLEMENT) that describes it: *In 'She became angry', the verb 'became' is a linking verb.*

link·man /ˈlɪŋkmæn/ *noun* (*pl.* **-men** /-men/) (*BrE*) **1** a person who helps two people or groups of people to communicate with each other **2** a person who works on the radio or television introducing the programmes or telling people about future programmes

links /lɪŋks/ *noun* = GOLF LINKS

ˈ**link-up** *noun* a connection formed between two things, for example two companies or two broadcasting systems: *a live satellite link-up with the conference*

Lin·naean (also **Lin·nean**) /lɪˈneɪən; -ˈniːən/ *adj.* (*biology*) relating to the system of naming and arranging living things into scientific groups which was invented by Carolus Linnaeus (Carl von Linné)

lin·net /ˈlɪnɪt/ *noun* a small brown and grey bird of the FINCH family

lino /ˈlaɪnəʊ; *NAmE* -noʊ/ *noun* [U] (*BrE, informal*) = LINOLEUM

lino·cut /ˈlaɪnəʊkʌt; *NAmE* -noʊ-/ *noun* a design or shape cut in a piece of LINO, used to make a print; a print made in this way

li·no·leum /lɪˈnəʊliəm; *NAmE* -ˈnoʊ-/ (also *BrE informal* **lino**) *noun* [U] a type of strong material with a hard shiny surface, used for covering floors

Lino·type™ /ˈlaɪnəʊtaɪp; *NAmE* -noʊ-/ *noun* a machine used in the past for printing newspapers, that produces a line of words as one strip of metal

lin·seed oil /ˌlɪnsiːd ˈɔɪl/ (also **flax·seed oil**) *noun* [U] an oil made from FLAX seeds, used in paint or to protect wood, etc.

lint /lɪnt/ *noun* [U] **1** (*especially BrE*) a type of soft cotton cloth used for covering and protecting wounds **2** (*technical*) short fine FIBRES that come off the surface of cloth when it is being made **3** (*especially NAmE*) (*BrE* usually **fluff**) small soft pieces of wool, cotton, etc. that stick on the surface of cloth

lin·tel /ˈlɪntl/ *noun* (*architecture*) a piece of wood or stone over a door or window, that forms part of the frame

Linux™ /ˈlɪnəks/ *noun* [U] (*computing*) an OPERATING SYSTEM based on UNIX that is available free in the basic version

lion /ˈlaɪən/ *noun* a large powerful animal of the cat family, that hunts in groups and lives in parts of Africa and southern Asia. Lions have yellowish-brown fur and the male has a MANE (= long thick hair round its neck). ➲ VISUAL VOCAB page V10 ➲ compare LIONESS ➲ see also MOUNTAIN LION
IDM **the ˈlion's den** a difficult situation in which you have to face a person or people who are unfriendly or aggressive towards you **the ˈlion's share (of sth)** (*BrE*) the largest or best part of sth when it is divided ➲ more at BEARD *v.* ➲ see also THE BRITISH LIONS

lion·ess /ˈlaɪənes/ *noun* a female lion

lion·ize (*BrE* also **-ise**) /ˈlaɪənaɪz/ *verb* **~ sb** (*formal*) to treat sb as a famous or important person

lip 0-ᴡ /lɪp/ *noun*
1 0-ᴡ [C] either of the two soft edges at the opening to the mouth: *The assistant pursed her lips.* ◇ *your* ***upper/lower/top/bottom lip*** ◇ *She kissed him* ***on the lips.*** ◇ *Not a drop of alcohol* ***passed my lips*** (= I didn't drink any). ➲ COLLOCATIONS at PHYSICAL ➲ VISUAL VOCAB page V48 **2 -lipped** (in adjectives) having the type of lips mentioned: *thin-lipped* ◇ *thick-lipped* ➲ see also TIGHT-LIPPED **3** [C] **~ (of sth)** the edge of a container or a hollow place in the ground SYN **rim**: *He ran his finger around the lip of the cup.* ◇ *Lava bubbled a few feet below the lip of the crater.* ➲ picture at JUG **4** [U] (*informal*) words spoken to sb that are rude and show a lack of respect for that person SYN **cheek**: *Don't let him* ***give you any lip!***
IDM **lick/smack your ˈlips** **1** to move your tongue over your lips, especially before eating sth good **2** (*informal*) to show that you are excited about sth and want it to happen soon: *They were licking their lips at the thought of clinching the deal.* **my lips are ˈsealed** used to say that you will not repeat sb's secret to other people **on everyone's ˈlips** if sth is **on everyone's lips**, they are all talking about it ➲ more at BITE *v.*, PASS *v.*, READ *v.*, SLIP *n.*, STIFF *adj.*

lip·ase /ˈlaɪpeɪz/ *noun* [U] (*chemistry*) an ENZYME (= a chemical substance in the body) that makes fats change into acids and alcohol

ˈ**lip gloss** *noun* [U, C] a substance that is put on the lips to make them look shiny ➲ VISUAL VOCAB page V49

lipid /ˈlɪpɪd/ *noun* (*chemistry*) any of a group of natural substances which do not dissolve in water, including plant oils and STEROIDS

ˈ**lip liner** *noun* [U] a substance that is put on the outline of the lips, to prevent LIPSTICK from spreading ➲ VISUAL VOCAB page V49

lipo·pro·tein /ˈlɪpəprəʊtiːn; ˈlaɪ-; *NAmE* -proʊ-/ *noun* (*biology*) a PROTEIN that combines with a lipid and carries it to another part of the body in the blood

lipo·some /ˈlɪpəsəʊm; ˈlaɪ-; *NAmE* -soʊm/ *noun* a very small bag formed of lipid MOLECULES, used to carry a drug to a particular part of the body

lipo·suc·tion /ˈlɪpəʊsʌkʃn; ˈlaɪ-; *NAmE* ˈlaɪpoʊ-; ˈlɪ-/ *noun* [U] a way of removing fat from sb's body by using SUCTION

lippy /ˈlɪpi/ *adj.*, *noun*
▪ ***adj.*** (*BrE, informal*) showing a lack of respect in the way that you speak to sb SYN **cheeky**
▪ ***noun*** [U] (*BrE, informal*) = LIPSTICK

ˈ**lip-read** *verb* [I, T] **~ (sb)** to understand what sb is saying by watching the way their lips move ▶ ˈ**lip-reading** *noun* [U]

lip·salve /ˈlɪpsælv/ *noun* [U] (*BrE*) a substance in the form of a stick, like a LIPSTICK, that you put on your lips to stop them becoming sore

ˈ**lip service** *noun* [U] if sb pays **lip service** to sth, they say that they approve of it or support it, without proving their support by what they actually do: *All the parties pay lip service to environmental issues.*

lip·stick /ˈlɪpstɪk/ *noun* [U, C] a substance made into a small stick, used for colouring the lips; a small stick of this substance: *She was wearing bright red lipstick.* ➲ picture at STICK ➲ VISUAL VOCAB page V49

ˌ**lipstick ˈlesbian** *noun* (*informal*) a LESBIAN who is a fashionable and attractive woman: *the lipstick lesbian stereotype*

lip-sync (also **lip-synch**) /ˈlɪp sɪŋk/ *verb* [I, T] to move your mouth, without speaking or singing, so that its movements match the sound on a recorded song, etc: **~ (to sth)** *She lip-synced to a Beatles song.* ◇ **~ sth** *He lip-synced 'Return to Sender'.*

li·quefy /ˈlɪkwɪfaɪ/ *verb* (**li·que·fies, li·que·fy·ing, li·que·fied, li·que·fied**) [I, T] **~ (sth)** (*formal*) to become liquid; to make sth liquid

li·queur /lɪˈkjʊə(r); *NAmE* -ˈkɜːr/ (*NAmE* also **cor·dial**) *noun* **1** [U, C] a strong sweet alcoholic drink, sometimes flavoured with fruit. It is usually drunk in very small glasses after a meal. **2** [C] a glass of liqueur

li·quid 0-ᴡ /ˈlɪkwɪd/ *noun, adj.*
▪ ***noun*** 0-ᴡ [U, C] a substance that flows freely and is not a solid or a gas, for example water or oil: *She poured the dark brown liquid down the sink.* ◇ *the transition from liquid to vapour* ➲ see also WASHING-UP LIQUID
▪ ***adj.*** **1** 0-ᴡ in the form of a liquid; not a solid or a gas: *liquid soap* ◇ *liquid nitrogen* ◇ *The detergent comes in powder or* ***liquid form.*** ◇ *a bar selling snacks and* ***liquid refreshment*** (= drinks) **2** (*finance*) in cash, or that can easily be changed into cash: *liquid assets* **3** (*literary*) clear, like water SYN **limpid**: *liquid blue eyes* **4** (*literary*) (of sounds) clear, pure and flowing: *the liquid song of a blackbird*

li·quid·ate /ˈlɪkwɪdeɪt/ *verb* **1** [I, T] **~ (sth)** to close a business and sell everything it owns in order to pay debts **2** [T] **~ sth** (*finance*) to sell sth in order to get money: *to liquidate*

L

assets **3** [T] **~ sth** (*finance*) to pay a debt **4** [T] **~ sb/sth** to destroy or remove sb/sth that causes problems SYN **annihilate**: *The government tried to liquidate the rebel movement and failed.*

li·quid·ation /ˌlɪkwɪˈdeɪʃn/ *noun* [U] **1** (*BrE, AustralE, law*) the process of closing a company, selling what it owns and paying its debts: *The company has* ***gone into liquidation.*** ➲ COLLOCATIONS at BUSINESS ➲ compare CHAPTER 11 **2** (*finance*) the action of selling sth to get money or to avoid losing money: *Falling prices may lead to further liquidation of stocks.*

li·quid·ator /ˈlɪkwɪdeɪtə(r)/ *noun* a person responsible for closing down a business and using any profits from the sale to pay its debts

ˌliquid ˌcrystal disˈplay *noun* = LCD

li·quid·ity /lɪˈkwɪdəti/ *noun* [U] (*finance*) the state of owning things of value that can easily be exchanged for cash

li·quid·ize (*BrE* also **-ise**) /ˈlɪkwɪdaɪz/ *verb* **~ sth** (*especially BrE*) to crush fruit, vegetables, etc. into a thick liquid SYN **purée**

li·quid·izer (*BrE* also **-iser**) /ˈlɪkwɪdaɪzə(r)/ *noun* (*BrE*) = BLENDER

ˌliquid ˈparaffin (*BrE*) (*NAmE* **ˈmineral oil**) *noun* [U] a liquid with no colour and no smell that comes from PETROLEUM and is used in medicines and COSMETICS

li·quor /ˈlɪkə(r)/ *noun* [U] **1** (*especially NAmE*) strong alcoholic drink SYN **spirits**: *hard liquor* ◇ *She drinks wine and beer but no liquor.* **2** (*BrE, technical*) any alcoholic drink: *intoxicating liquor*

li·quor·ice (*especially BrE*) (*NAmE* usually **lic·orice**) /ˈlɪkərɪʃ; -rɪs/ *noun* [U, C] a firm black substance with a strong flavour, obtained from the root of a plant, used in medicine and to make sweets/candy; a sweet/candy made from this substance

li·quor·ice all·sorts /ˌlɪkərɪʃ ˈɔːlsɔːts; -rɪs; *NAmE* -sɔːrts/ *noun* [pl.] (*BrE*) brightly coloured sweets/candy made with liquorice

ˈliquor store (also **ˈpackage store**) (both *US*) (*BrE* **ˈoff-licence**) *noun* a shop that sells alcoholic drinks in bottles and cans to take away

lira /ˈlɪərə; *NAmE* ˈlɪrə/ *noun* (*pl.* **lire** /ˈlɪərə; *NAmE* ˈlɪreɪ/) (*abbr.* **l.**) the unit of money in Malta, Syria and Turkey, and formerly in Italy (replaced there in 2002 by the euro)

lisle /laɪl/ *noun* [U] a fine smooth cotton thread used especially for making TIGHTS and STOCKINGS

lisp /lɪsp/ *noun, verb*

▪ ***noun*** [usually sing.] a speech fault in which the sound 's' is pronounced 'th': *She spoke with a slight lisp.*

▪ ***verb*** [I, T] (**+ speech**) to speak with a lisp

lis·som (also **lis·some**) /ˈlɪsəm/ *adj.* (*literary*) (of sb's body) thin and attractive SYN **lithe**

list 🔑 /lɪst/ *noun, verb*

▪ ***noun*** **1** 🔑 [C] a series of names, items, figures, etc, especially when they are written or printed: *a* ***shopping/wine/price list*** ◇ *to* ***make a list*** *of things to do* ◇ (*formal*) *to* ***draw up a list*** ◇ *Is your name* ***on the list?*** ◇ *Having to wait hours came* ***high on the list*** *of complaints.* ➲ see also A-LIST, HIT LIST, LAUNDRY LIST, MAILING LIST, SHORTLIST, WAITING LIST, WAIT LIST **2** [sing.] the fact of a ship leaning to one side IDM see DANGER

▪ ***verb*** **1** 🔑 [T] **~ sth** to write a list of things in a particular order: *We were asked to list our ten favourite songs.* ◇ *Towns in the guide are listed alphabetically.* **2** [T] **~ sb/sth** to mention or include sb/sth in a list: *The koala is listed among Australia's endangered animals.* ◇ *soldiers listed as missing* **3** [I, T] **~ (at sth)** | **~ sth** (*NAmE*) to be put or put sth in a list of things for sale: *This CD player lists at $200.* **4** [I] (of a ship) to lean to one side

ˌlisted ˈbuilding *noun* (*BrE*) a building that is officially protected because it has artistic or historical value ➲ see also LANDMARK

lis·ten 🔑 /ˈlɪsn/ *verb, noun*

▪ ***verb*** **1** 🔑 [I] to pay attention to sb/sth that you can hear: *Listen! What's that noise? Can you hear it?* ◇ *Sorry, I wasn't really listening.* ◇ **~ to sb/sth** *to listen to music* ◇ *I listened carefully to her story.* HELP You cannot 'listen sth' (without 'to'): *I'm fond of listening to classical music.* ◇ ~~*I'm fond of listening classical music.*~~ **2** 🔑 [I] **~ (to sb/sth)** to take notice of what sb says to you so that you follow their advice or believe them: *None of this would have happened if you'd listened to me.* ◇ *Why won't you* ***listen to reason?*** **3** 🔑 [I] (*informal*) used to tell sb to take notice of what you are going to say: *Listen, there's something I have to tell you.*

PHR V **ˈlisten (ˈout) for sth** to be prepared to hear a particular sound: *Can you listen out for the doorbell?* **ˌlisten ˈin (on/to sth)** **1** to listen to a conversation that you are not supposed to hear: *You shouldn't listen in on other people's conversations.* **2** to listen to a radio broadcast **ˌlisten ˈup** (*informal, especially NAmE*) used to tell people to listen carefully because you are going to say sth important

▪ ***noun*** [usually sing.] an act of listening: *Have a listen to this.*

lis·ten·able /ˈlɪsnəbl/ *adj.* (*informal*) pleasant to listen to

lis·ten·er /ˈlɪsənə(r)/ *noun* **1** a person who listens: *a good listener* (= sb who you can rely on to listen with attention or sympathy) **2** a person listening to a radio programme

ˈlistening post *noun* a place where people who are part of an army listen to enemy communications to try to get information that will give them an advantage

lis·teria /lɪˈstɪəriə; *NAmE* -ˈstɪr-/ *noun* [U] a type of bacteria that makes people sick if they eat infected food

list·ing /ˈlɪstɪŋ/ *noun* **1** [C] a list, especially an official or published list of people or things, often arranged in alphabetical order: *a comprehensive listing of all airlines* **2 list·ings** [pl.] information in a newspaper or magazine about what films/movies, plays, etc. are being shown in a particular town or city: *a listings magazine* **3** [C] a position or an item on a list: (*business*) *The company is seeking a stock exchange listing* (= for trading shares).

list·less /ˈlɪstləs/ *adj.* having no energy or enthusiasm SYN **lethargic**: *The illness left her feeling listless and depressed.* ▸ **list·less·ly** *adv.* **list·less·ness** *noun* [U]

ˈlist price *noun* [usually sing.] (*business*) the price at which goods are advertised for sale, for example in a CATALOGUE

lit *past tense, past part.* of LIGHT

lit·any /ˈlɪtəni/ *noun* (*pl.* **-ies**) **1** a series of prayers to God for use in church services, spoken by a priest, etc, with set responses by the people **2 ~ (of sth)** (*formal*) a long boring account of a series of events, reasons, etc: *a litany of complaints*

lit·chi (*especially US*) = LYCHEE

lite /laɪt/ *adj.* (*informal*) **1** (*especially NAmE*) (of food or drink) containing fewer CALORIES than other types of food, and therefore less likely to make you fat (a way of spelling 'light'): *lite ice cream* **2** (used after a noun) (*disapproving*) used to say that a thing is similar to sth else but lacks many of its serious or important qualities: *I would describe this movie as 'Hitchcock lite'.*

liter (*NAmE*) = LITRE

lit·er·acy /ˈlɪtərəsi/ *noun* [U] the ability to read and write: *a campaign to promote adult literacy* ◇ *basic literacy skills* OPP **illiteracy** ➲ see also COMPUTER LITERACY

lit·eral /ˈlɪtərəl/ *adj.* **1** [usually before noun] being the basic or usual meaning of a word or phrase: *I am not referring to 'small' people in the literal sense of the word.* ◇ *The literal meaning of 'petrify' is 'turn to stone'.* ➲ compare FIGURATIVE, METAPHORICAL **2** [usually before noun] that follows the original words exactly: *a literal translation* ➲ compare FREE **3** (*disapproving*) lacking imagination: *Her interpretation of the music was too literal.* ▸ **lit·er·al·ness** *noun* [U]

lit·er·al·ly /ˈlɪtərəli/ *adv.* **1** in a literal way SYN **exactly**: *The word 'planet' literally means 'wandering body'.* ◇ *When I told you to 'get lost' I didn't expect to* ***be taken literally.*** **2** used to emphasize the truth of sth that may seem surprising: *There are literally hundreds of prizes to win.* **3** (*informal*) used to emphasize a word or phrase, even if it is not actually true in a literal sense: *I literally jumped out of my skin.*

lit·er·ary /ˈlɪtərəri; *NAmE* -reri/ *adj.* **1** connected with literature: ***literary criticism/theory*** **2** (of a language or style of writing) suitable for or typical of a work of literature: *It was Chaucer who really turned English into a literary language.* **3** liking literature very much; studying or writing literature: *a literary man*

ˈ**literary agent** *noun* a person whose job is to represent authors and persuade companies to publish their work

lit·er·ate /ˈlɪtərət/ *adj.* able to read and write **OPP illiterate** ➲ see also NUMERATE, COMPUTER-LITERATE

lit·er·ati /ˌlɪtəˈrɑːti/ **the literati** *noun* [pl.] (*formal*) educated and intelligent people who enjoy literature

Collocations

Literature

Being a writer

- **write/publish** literature/poetry/fiction/a book/a story/a poem/a novel/a review/an autobiography
- **become** a writer/novelist/playwright
- **find/have** a publisher/an agent
- **have** a new book out
- **edit/revise/proofread** a book/text/manuscript
- **dedicate** a book/poem to...

Plot, character and atmosphere

- **construct/create/weave/weave sth into** a complex narrative
- **advance/drive** the plot
- **introduce/present** the protagonist/a character
- **describe/depict/portray** a character (as...)/(sb as) a hero/villain
- **create** an exciting/a tense atmosphere
- **build/heighten** the suspense/tension
- **evoke/capture** the pathos of the situation
- **convey** emotion/an idea/an impression/a sense of...
- **engage** the reader
- **seize/capture/grip** the (reader's) imagination
- **arouse/elicit** emotion/sympathy (in the reader)
- **lack** imagination/emotion/structure/rhythm

Language, style and imagery

- **use/employ** language/imagery/humour/(*especially US*) humor/an image/a symbol/a metaphor/a device
- **use/adopt/develop** a style/technique
- **be rich in/be full of** symbolism
- **evoke** images of.../a sense of.../a feeling of...
- **create/achieve** an effect
- **maintain/lighten** the tone
- **introduce/develop** an idea/a theme
- **inspire** a novel/a poet/sb's work/sb's imagination

Reading and criticism

- **read** an author/sb's work/fiction/poetry/a text/a poem/a novel/a chapter/a passage
- **review** a book/a novel/sb's work
- **give sth/get/have/receive** a good/bad review
- **be hailed (as)/be recognized as** a masterpiece
- **quote** a phrase/line/stanza/passage/author
- **provoke/spark** discussion/criticism
- **study/interpret/understand** a text/passage
- **translate** sb's work/a text/a passage/a novel/a poem

lit·era·ture 🔑 /ˈlɪtrətʃə(r); *NAmE* also -tʃʊr/ *noun* [U]
1 🔑 pieces of writing that are valued as works of art, especially novels, plays and poems (in contrast to technical books and newspapers, magazines, etc.): *French literature* ◇ *great* ***works of literature*** **2** ~ (**on sth**) pieces of writing or printed information on a particular subject: *I've read all the available literature on keeping rabbits.* ◇ *sales literature*

lithe /laɪð/ *adj.* (of a person or their body) moving or bending easily, in a way that is elegant ▸ **lithe·ly** *adv.*

lith·ium /ˈlɪθiəm/ *noun* [U] (*symb.* Li) a chemical element. Lithium is a soft, very light, silver-white metal used in batteries and ALLOYS.

litho·graph /ˈlɪθəɡrɑːf; *NAmE* -ɡræf/ *noun* a picture printed by lithography

lith·og·raphy /lɪˈθɒɡrəfi; *NAmE* -ˈθɑːɡ-/ *noun* (also *informal* **litho** /ˈlaɪθəʊ; *NAmE* -θoʊ/) [U] the process of printing from a smooth surface, for example a metal plate, that has been specially prepared so that ink only sticks to the design to be printed ▸ **litho·graph·ic** /ˌlɪθəˈɡræfɪk/ *adj.*

lith·ology /lɪˈθɒlədʒi; *NAmE* lɪˈθɑːl-/ *noun* [U] the study of the general physical characteristics of rocks

litho·sphere /ˈlɪθəsfɪə(r); *NAmE* -sfɪr/ *noun* [sing.] (*geology*) the layer of rock that forms the outer part of the earth

liti·gant /ˈlɪtɪɡənt/ *noun* (*law*) a person who is making or defending a claim in court

liti·gate /ˈlɪtɪɡeɪt/ *verb* [I, T] ~ (**sth**) (*law*) to take a claim or disagreement to court ▸ **liti·ga·tor** *noun*

liti·ga·tion /ˌlɪtɪˈɡeɪʃn/ *noun* [U] (*law*) the process of making or defending a claim in court: *The company has been in litigation with its previous auditors for a full year.*

li·ti·gious /lɪˈtɪdʒəs/ *adj.* (*formal, disapproving*) too ready to take disagreements to court ▸ **li·ti·gious·ness** *noun* [U]

lit·mus /ˈlɪtməs/ *noun* [U] a substance that turns red when it touches an acid and blue when it touches an ALKALI: *litmus paper*

ˈ**litmus test** *noun* **1** (*especially NAmE*) = ACID TEST: *The outcome will be seen as a litmus test of government concern for conservation issues.* **2** a test using litmus

li·to·tes /laɪˈtəʊtiːz; *NAmE* -ˈtoʊ-/ *noun* [U] (*technical*) the use of a negative or weak statement to emphasize a positive meaning, for example *he wasn't slow to accept the offer* (= he was quick to accept the offer) ➲ compare UNDERSTATEMENT

litre 🔑 (*especially US* **liter**) /ˈliːtə(r)/ *noun* (*abbr.* **l**) a unit for measuring volume, equal to 1.76 British pints or 2.11 American pints: *3 litres of water* ◇ *a litre bottle of wine* ◇ *a car with a 3.5 litre engine*

lit·ter /ˈlɪtə(r)/ *noun, verb*

▪ ***noun*** **1** [U] small pieces of rubbish/garbage such as paper, cans and bottles, that people have left lying in a public place: *There will be fines for people who* ***drop litter.*** **2** [sing.] ~ **of sth** a number of things that are lying in an untidy way: *The floor was covered with a litter of newspapers, clothes and empty cups.* **3** [U] a dry substance that is put in a shallow open box for pets, especially cats, to use as a toilet when they are indoors: *cat litter* ◇ (*BrE*) *a litter tray* ◇ (*NAmE*) *a litter box* **4** [C] a number of baby animals that one mother gives birth to at the same time: *a litter of puppies* ◇ *the runt* (= the smallest and weakest baby) *of the litter* **5** [U] the substance, especially STRAW, that is used for farm animals to sleep on **6** [C] a kind of chair or bed that was used in the past for carrying important people

▪ ***verb*** **1** [T] ~ **sth** to be spread around a place, making it look untidy: *Piles of books and newspapers littered the floor.* ◇ *Broken glass littered the streets.* **2** [T, usually passive, I] ~ (**sth**) (**with sth**) to leave things in a place, making it look untidy: *The floor was littered with papers.* ◇ (*NAmE*) *He was arrested for littering.* **3** [T] **be littered with sth** to contain or involve a lot of a particular type of thing, usually sth bad: *Your essay is littered with spelling mistakes.*

ˈ**litter bin** (*BrE*) (*NAmE* ˈ**trash can**) *noun* a container for people to put rubbish/garbage in, in the street or in a public building ➲ VISUAL VOCAB page V2

L

'litter lout (*BrE*) (also **'lit·ter·bug** *NAmE, BrE*) *noun* (*informal, disapproving*) a person who leaves LITTER in public places

lit·tle 0→ /'lɪtl/ *adj., det., pron., adv.*

■ ***adj.*** [usually before noun] HELP The forms **littler** /'lɪtlə(r)/ and **littlest** /'lɪtlɪst/ are rare. It is more common to use **smaller** and **smallest**. **1** 0→ not big; small; smaller than others: *a little house* ◇ *a little group of tourists* ◇ *a little old lady* ◇ *the classic little black dress* ◇ *'Which do you want?' 'I'll take the little one.'* ◇ *She gave a little laugh.* ◇ (*BrE*) *We should manage, with **a little bit** of luck.* ◇ *Here's **a little something*** (= a small present) *for your birthday.* **2** 0→ used after an adjective to show affection or dislike, especially in a PATRONIZING way (= one that suggests that you think you are better than sb): *The **poor little thing**! It's lost its mother.* ◇ *What a nasty little man!* ◇ *She's a good little worker.* ◇ *He'd become **quite the little** gentleman.* **3** 0→ young: ***a little boy/girl*** ◇ *my **little brother/sister*** (= younger brother/sister) ◇ *I lived in America when I was little.* **4** 0→ (of distance or time) short: *A **little while** later the phone rang.* ◇ *Shall we walk a little way?* **5** 0→ not important; not serious: *I can't remember every little detail.* ◇ *You soon get used to the little difficulties.* ▶ **little·ness** *noun* [U]

IDM **a little 'bird told me** (*informal*) used to say that sb told you sth but you do not want to say who it was ➲ more at OAK, WONDER *n.*

■ ***det., pron.*** **1** 0→ used with uncountable nouns to mean 'not much': *There was little doubt in my mind.* ◇ *Students have **little or no** choice in the matter.* ◇ *I understood little of what he said.* ◇ *She said **little or nothing*** (= hardly anything) *about her experience.* ◇ *Tell him **as little as possible**.* **2** 0→ **a little** used with uncountable nouns to mean 'a small amount', 'some': *a little milk/sugar/tea* ◇ *If you have any spare milk, could you give me a little?* ◇ *I've only read a little of the book so far.* ◇ (*formal*) *It caused **not a little/no little*** (= a lot of) *confusion.* ◇ *After a little* (= a short time) *he got up and left.*

IDM **,little by 'little** 0→ slowly; gradually: *Little by little the snow disappeared.* ◇ *His English is improving little by little.*

■ ***adv.*** (less, least) **1** 0→ not much; only slightly: *He is little known as an artist.* ◇ *I slept very little last night.* ◇ ***Little did I know*** *that this spelled the end of my career.* **2** 0→ **a little (bit)** to a small degree: *She seemed a little afraid of going inside.* ◇ *These shoes are a little (bit) too big for me.* ◇ (*informal*) *Everything has become **just that little bit** harder.* ◇ (*formal*) *She felt tired and **more than a little** worried.* ➲ note at BIT

the ,Little 'Bear *noun* = URSA MINOR

,Little 'Englander *noun* (usually *disapproving*) an English person who believes England (or, in practice, Britain) should not get involved in international affairs

,little 'finger *noun* the smallest finger of the hand SYN **pinky** ➲ VISUAL VOCAB page V48

IDM **twist/wrap/wind sb around your little 'finger** (*informal*) to persuade sb to do anything that you want

'Little League *noun* [sing., U] (in the US) a BASEBALL league for children

'little people *noun* [pl.] **1** all the people in a country who have no power **2** extremely small people, who will never grow to a normal size because of a physical problem **3 the little people** small imaginary people with magic powers SYN **fairies**

lit·toral /'lɪtərəl/ *noun* (*technical*) the part of a country that is near the coast ▶ **lit·toral** *adj.* [only before noun]: *littoral states*

lit·urgy /'lɪtədʒi; *NAmE* 'lɪtərdʒi/ *noun* (*pl.* -ies) a fixed form of public worship used in churches ▶ **li·tur·gic·al** /lɪ'tɜːdʒɪkl; *NAmE* -'tɜːrdʒ-/ *adj.* **li·tur·gic·al·ly** /-kli/ *adv.*

liv·able *adj.* = LIVEABLE

live[1] 0→ /lɪv/ *verb* ➲ see also LIVE[2]

▸ IN A PLACE **1** 0→ [I] **+ adv./prep.** to have your home in a particular place: *to live in a house* ◇ *Where do you live?* ◇ *She needs to find **somewhere to live**.* ◇ *We used to live in London.* ◇ *Both her children still live at home.* ◇ (*BrE, informal*) *Where do these plates live* (= where are they usually kept)?

▸ BE ALIVE **2** 0→ [I] to remain alive: *The doctors said he only had six months to live.* ◇ *Spiders can live for several days without food.* ◇ **~ to do sth** *She lived to see her first grandchild.* **3** 0→ [I] to be alive, especially at a particular time: *When did Handel live?* ◇ *He's the greatest player who ever lived.*

▸ TYPE OF LIFE **4** 0→ [I, T] to spend your life in a particular way: *He lived in poverty most of his life.* ◇ **~ sth** *She lived a very peaceful life.* ◇ **+ noun** *She lived and died a single woman.*

▸ BE REMEMBERED **5** 0→ [I] to continue to exist or be remembered SYN **remain**: *This moment will live in our memory for many years to come.* ◇ *Her words have lived with me all my life.*

▸ HAVE EXCITEMENT **6** [I] to have a full and exciting life: *I don't want to be stuck in an office all my life—I want to live!*

IDM **,live and 'breathe sth** to be very enthusiastic about sth: *He just lives and breathes football.* **live and 'let live** (*saying*) used to say that you should accept other people's opinions and behaviour even though they are different from your own **live by your 'wits** to earn money by clever or sometimes dishonest means **live (from) ,hand to 'mouth** to spend all the money you earn on basic needs such as food without being able to save any money **live in the 'past** to behave as though society, etc. has not changed, when in fact it has **live in 'sin** (*old-fashioned* or *humorous*) to live together and have a sexual relationship without being married **live it 'up** (*informal*) to enjoy yourself in an exciting way, usually spending a lot of money **live a 'lie** to keep sth important about yourself a secret from other people, so that they do not know what you really think, what you are really like, etc. **live off the fat of the 'land** to have enough money to be able to afford expensive things, food, drink, etc. **live off the 'land** to eat whatever food you can grow, kill or find yourself **,live to fight another 'day** (*saying*) used to say that although you have failed or had a bad experience, you will continue **you haven't 'lived** used to tell sb that if they have not had a particular experience their life is not complete: *You've never been to New York? You haven't lived!* **you live and 'learn** used to express surprise at sth new or unexpected you have been told ➲ more at BORROW, CLOVER, HALF *n.*, LIFE, LONG *adv.*, PEOPLE *n.*, POCKET *n.*, ROUGH *adv.*

PHR V **'live by sth** to follow a particular belief or set of principles: *That's a philosophy I could live by.* **'live by doing sth** to earn money or to get the things you need by doing a particular thing: *a community that lives by fishing* **,live sth↔'down** to be able to make people forget about sth embarrassing you have done: *She felt so stupid. She'd never be able to live it down.* **'live for sb/sth** to think that sb/sth is the main purpose of or the most important thing in your life: *She lives for her work.* ◇ *After his wife died, he had nothing to live for.* **,live 'in** to live at the place where you work or study: *They have an au pair living in.* ➲ see also LIVE-IN **'live off sb/sth** (often *disapproving*) to receive the money you need to live from sb/sth because you do not have any yourself: *She's still living off her parents.* ◇ *to live off welfare* **'live off sth** to have one particular type of food as the main thing you eat in order to live: *He seems to live off junk food.* **,live 'on** to continue to live or exist: *She died ten years ago but her memory lives on.* **'live on sth 1** 0→ to eat a particular type of food to live: *Small birds live mainly on insects.* **2** (often *disapproving*) to eat only or a lot of a particular type of food: *She lives on burgers.* **3** 0→ to have enough money for the basic things you need to live: *You can't live on forty pounds a week.* **,live 'out** to live away from the place where you work or study: *Some college students will have to live out.* **,live 'out sth 1** to actually do what you have only thought about doing before: *to live out your fantasies* **2** to spend the rest of your life in a particular way: *He lived out his days alone.* **,live 'through sth** 0→ to experience a disaster or other unpleasant situation and survive it: *He has lived through two world wars.* **'live together** (also **'live with sb**) **1** 0→ to live in the same house **2** 0→ to share a home and have a sexual relationship without being married SYN **cohabit** **,live 'up to sth** to do as well as or be as good as other people expect you to: *He failed to live up to his parents' expectations.* ◇ *The team called 'The No-Hopers' certainly lived up to its name.* 'live with sb = LIVE TOGETHER 'live with sth to accept sth unpleasant: *I just had to learn to live with the pain.*

live² /laɪv/ *adj., adv.* ➲ see also LIVE¹

■ ***adj.*** [usually before noun]

▸ NOT DEAD **1** living; not dead: *live animals* ◇ *the number of live births* (= babies born alive) ◇ *We saw a **real live** rattlesnake!*

▸ NOT RECORDED **2** (of a broadcast) sent out while the event is actually happening, not recorded first and broadcast later: *live coverage of the World Cup* **3** (of a performance) given or made when people are watching, not recorded: *The club has live music most nights.* ◇ *a live recording made at Wembley Arena* ◇ *the band's new live album* ◇ *It was the first interview I'd done in front of a **live audience*** (= with people watching).

▸ ELECTRICITY **4** (of a wire or device) connected to a source of electrical power: *That terminal is live.*

▸ BULLETS/MATCHES **5** still able to explode or light; ready for use: *live ammunition*

▸ COALS **6 live** coals are burning or are still hot and red

▸ YOGURT **7 live** YOGURT still contains the bacteria needed to turn milk into YOGURT

▸ QUESTION/SUBJECT **8** of interest or importance at the present time: *Pollution is still very much a live issue.*

▸ INTERNET **9** (of an electronic link) functioning correctly, so that it is connected to another document or page on the Internet: *Here are some live links to other aviation-related web pages.*

IDM **a live 'wire** a person who is lively and full of energy

■ ***adv.*** broadcast at the time of an actual event; played or recorded at an actual performance: *The show is going out live.*

IDM **go 'live** (*computing*) (of a computer system) to become OPERATIONAL (= ready to be used)

live·able (also **liv·able**) /'lɪvəbl/ *adj.* **1** (*BrE* also **live·able in** [not before noun]) (of a house, etc.) fit to live in SYN **habitable**: *safer and more liveable residential areas* ◇ *The place looks liveable in.* **2** (of life) worth living SYN **endurable** **3** [not before noun] **~ with** that can be dealt with: *The problem is paying the mortgage—everything else is liveable with.* **4** [only before noun] (of a wage, etc.) enough to live on: *a liveable salary*

live action /ˌlaɪv 'ækʃn/ *noun* [U] part of a film/movie that is made using real people or animals, rather than using drawings, models or computers ▸ **ˌlive-'action** *adj.* [only before noun]: *a live-action movie*

'lived-in *adj.* (of a place) that has been used so continuously for so long that it does not look new: (*approving*) *The room had a comfortable, lived-in feel about it.*

live-in /'lɪv ɪn/ *adj.* **1** (of an employee) living in the house where they work: *a live-in nanny* **2 ~ lover, boyfriend, girlfriend, etc.** a person who lives with their sexual partner but is not married to them

live·li·hood /'laɪvlihʊd/ *noun* [C, usually sing., U] a means of earning money in order to live SYN **living**: *Communities on the island depended on whaling for their livelihood.* ◇ *a **means/source of livelihood***

live·long /'lɪvlɒŋ; *NAmE* -lɔːŋ; -lɑːŋ/ *adj.*

IDM **the livelong 'day** (*literary*) the whole length of the day

live·ly /'laɪvli/ *adj.* (**live·lier, live·li·est**)

1 full of life and energy; active and enthusiastic SYN **animated, vivacious**: *an intelligent and lively young woman* ◇ *a lively and enquiring mind* ◇ *He showed a lively interest in politics.* **2** (of a place, an event, etc.) full of interest or excitement SYN **bustling**: *a lively bar* ◇ *a lively debate* **3** (of colours) strong and definite: *a lively shade of pink* **4** (*especially BrE*) busy and active: *They do a lively trade in souvenirs and gifts.* ▸ **live·li·ness** *noun* [U]

liven /'laɪvn/ *verb*

PHR V **ˌliven 'up** | **ˌliven sb/sth 'up** to become or to make sb/sth more interesting or exciting: *The game didn't liven up till the second half.* ◇ *Let's put some music on to liven things up.*

liver /'lɪvə(r)/ *noun* **1** [C] a large organ in the body that cleans the blood and produces BILE ➲ VISUAL VOCAB page V48 **2** [U, C] the liver of some animals that is cooked and eaten: *liver and onions* ◇ *chicken livers*

'liver fluke *noun* a small WORM which, in an adult form, lives in the LIVER of people or animals, often causing disease

liv·er·ied /'lɪvərid/ *adj.* **1** (*BrE*) painted in a LIVERY: *liveried aircraft* **2** wearing LIVERY: *liveried servants*

Liv·er·pud·lian /ˌlɪvə'pʌdliən; *NAmE* ˌlɪvər'p-/ *noun* a person from Liverpool in NW England ▸ **Liv·er·pud·lian** *adj.*

'liver sausage (*BrE*) (*NAmE* **liv·er·wurst** /'lɪvəwɜːst; *NAmE* 'lɪvərwɜːrst/) *noun* [U] a type of soft SAUSAGE made from finely chopped LIVER, usually spread cold on bread

'liver spot *noun* a small brown spot on the skin, especially found in older people

liv·ery /'lɪvəri/ *noun* [U, C] (*pl.* **-ies**) **1** (*BrE*) the colours in which the vehicles, aircraft, etc. of a particular company are painted **2** a special uniform worn by servants or officials, especially in the past

'livery stable *noun* a place where people can pay to keep their horses or can hire a horse

lives *pl.* of LIFE

live·stock /'laɪvstɒk; *NAmE* -stɑːk/ *noun* [U, pl.] the animals kept on a farm, for example cows or sheep ➲ VISUAL VOCAB page V2

live·ware /'laɪvweə(r); *NAmE* -wer/ *noun* [U] (*informal*) people who work with computers, rather than the programs or computers with which they work

livid /'lɪvɪd/ *adj.* **1** extremely angry SYN **furious** **2** dark bluish-grey in colour: *a livid bruise*

liv·ing /'lɪvɪŋ/ *adj., noun*

■ ***adj.*** **1** alive now: *all **living things*** ◇ *living organisms* ◇ *the finest living pianist* **2** [only before noun] used or practised now: *living languages* (= those still spoken) ◇ *a living faith*

IDM **be living 'proof of sth/that...** to show by your actions or qualities that a particular fact is true: *He is living proof that not all engineers are boring.* **within/in ˌliving 'memory** at a time, or during the time, that is remembered by people still alive: *the coldest winter in living memory* ➲ more at DAYLIGHTS

■ ***noun*** **1** [C, usually sing.] money to buy the things that you need in life: *She **earns her living** as a freelance journalist.* ◇ *to **make a good/decent/meagre living*** ◇ *What do you **do for a living?*** ◇ *to **scrape/scratch a living** from part-time tutoring* **2** [U] a way or style of life: *everyday living* ◇ *communal living* ◇ *plain living* ◇ *Their **standard of living** is very low.* ◇ *The **cost of living** has risen sharply.* ◇ *poor **living conditions/standards*** **3 the living** [pl.] people who are alive now: *the living and the dead* IDM see LAND *n.* **4** [C] (*BrE*) (especially in the past) a position in the Church as a priest and the income and house that go with this SYN **benefice**

ˌliving 'death *noun* [sing.] a life that is worse than being dead

ˌliving 'hell *noun* [sing.] a very unpleasant situation that causes a lot of suffering and lasts a long time

'living roof *noun* = GREEN ROOF

'living room (*BrE* also **'sitting room**) *noun* a room in a house where people sit together, watch television, etc. SYN **lounge**

ˌliving 'wage *noun* [sing.] a wage that is high enough for sb to buy the things they need in order to live

ˌliving 'will *noun* a document stating your wishes concerning medical treatment in the case that you become so ill/sick that you can no longer make decisions about it, in particular asking doctors to stop treating you and let you die

L

liz·ard /ˈlɪzəd; *NAmE* -ərd/ *noun* a small REPTILE with a rough skin, four short legs and a long tail

ll *abbr.* (in writing) lines (the plural form of 'l')

llama /ˈlɑːmə/ *noun* a S American animal kept for its soft wool or for carrying loads

LLB (*BrE*) (*NAmE* **LL.B**) /ˌel el ˈbiː/ *noun* the abbreviation for 'Bachelor of Laws' (a first university degree in law)

LLD (*BrE*) (*NAmE* **LL.D**) /ˌel el ˈdiː/ *noun* the abbreviation for 'Doctor of Laws' (the highest university degree in law)

LLM (*BrE*) (*NAmE* **LL.M**) /ˌel el ˈem/ *noun* the abbreviation for 'Master of Laws' (a second university degree in law)

lm *abbr.* LUMEN

LMS /ˌel em ˈes/ *noun* the abbreviation for 'learning management system' (a software system for managing training and education using the Internet)

lo /ləʊ; *NAmE* loʊ/ *exclamation* (*old use* or *humorous*) used for calling attention to a surprising thing
IDM **ˌlo and beˈhold** (*humorous*) used for calling attention to a surprising or annoying thing

load 🔑 /ləʊd; *NAmE* loʊd/ *noun, verb*
■ ***noun***
▸ STH CARRIED **1** 🔑 [C] something that is being carried (usually in large amounts) by a person, vehicle, etc. SYN **cargo**: *The trucks waited at the warehouse to pick up their loads.* ◇ *The women came down the hill with their loads of firewood.* ◇ *These backpacks are designed to* ***carry a heavy load.*** ◇ *A lorry* ***shed its load*** (= accidentally dropped its load) *on the motorway.* **2** 🔑 [C] (often in compounds) the total amount of sth that sth can carry or contain: *a busload of tourists* ◇ *They ordered three truckloads of sand.* ◇ *He put half a load of washing in the machine.* ◇ *The plane took off with a* ***full load.***
▸ WEIGHT **3** [C, usually sing.] the amount of weight that is pressing down on sth: *a load-bearing wall* ◇ *Modern backpacks spread the load over a wider area.*
▸ LARGE AMOUNT **4** 🔑 [sing.] (*BrE* also **loads** [pl.]) **~ (of sth)** (*informal*) a large number or amount of sb/sth; plenty: *She's got loads of friends.* ◇ *There's loads to do today.* ◇ *He wrote loads and loads of letters to people.* ◇ *Uncle Jim brought a whole load of presents for the kids.*
▸ RUBBISH/NONSENSE **5** 🔑 [sing.] **~ of rubbish, garbage, nonsense, etc.** (*informal, especially BrE*) used to emphasize that sth is wrong, stupid, bad, etc.: *You're talking a load of rubbish.*
▸ WORK **6** [C] an amount of work that a person or machine has to do: *Teaching loads have increased in all types of school.* ➲ see also CASELOAD, WORKLOAD
▸ RESPONSIBILITY/WORRY **7** [C, usually sing.] a feeling of responsibility or worry that is difficult to deal with SYN **burden**: *She thought she would not be able to* ***bear the load*** *of bringing up her family alone.* ◇ *Knowing that they had arrived safely* ***took a load off my mind.***
▸ ELECTRICAL POWER **8** [C] the amount of electrical power that is being supplied at a particular time
IDM **get a load of sb/sth** (*informal*) used to tell sb to look at or listen to sb/sth: *Get a load of that dress!*
■ ***verb***
▸ GIVE/RECEIVE LOAD **1** 🔑 [T, I] to put a large quantity of things or people onto or into sth: **~ sth** *We loaded the car in ten minutes.* ◇ *Can you help me load the dishwasher?* ◇ **~ sth (up) (with sth)** *Men were loading up a truck with timber.* ◇ **~ sth/sb (into/onto sth)** *Sacks were being loaded onto the truck.* ◇ **~ (up)** | **~ (up with sth)** *We finished loading and set off.* OPP **unload 2** [I] to receive a load: *The ship was still loading.* OPP **unload 3** 🔑 [T] **~ sb with sth** to give sb a lot of things, especially things they have to carry: *They loaded her with gifts.*
▸ GUN/CAMERA **4** 🔑 [T, I] to put sth into a weapon, camera or other piece of equipment so that it can be used: **~ sth (into sth)** *She loaded film into the camera.* ◇ **~ sth (with sth)** *She loaded the camera with film.* ◇ **~ (sth)** *Is the gun loaded?* OPP **unload**
▸ COMPUTING **5** [T, I] **~ (sth)** to put data or a program into the memory of a computer: *Have you loaded the software?* ◇ *Wait for the game to load.* ➲ compare DOWNLOAD
IDM **load the ˈdice (against sb)** [usually passive] to put sb at a disadvantage: *He has always felt that the dice were loaded against him in life.*
PHR V **ˌload sb/sth ˈdown (with sth)** [usually passive] to give sb/sth a lot of heavy things to carry SYN **weigh down**: *She was loaded down with bags of groceries.*

load·ed /ˈləʊdɪd; *NAmE* ˈloʊd-/ *adj.*
▸ FULL **1** carrying a load; full and heavy SYN **laden**: *a fully loaded truck* ◇ **~ (with sth)** *a truck loaded with supplies* ◇ *She came into the room carrying a loaded tray.* **2 ~ with sth** (*informal*) full of a particular thing, quality or meaning: *cakes loaded with calories*
▸ RICH **3** [not before noun] (*informal*) very rich: *Let her pay—she's loaded.*
▸ ADVANTAGE/DISADVANTAGE **4 ~ in favour of sb/sth** | **~ against sb/sth** acting either as an advantage or a disadvantage to sb/sth in a way that is unfair: *a system that is loaded in favour of the young* (= gives them an advantage)
▸ WORD/STATEMENT **5** having more meaning than you realize at first and intended to make you think in a particular way: *It was a* ***loaded question*** *and I preferred not to comment.*
▸ GUN/CAMERA **6** containing bullets, film, etc: *a loaded shotgun*
▸ DRUNK **7** (*informal, especially NAmE*) very drunk

load·ing /ˈləʊdɪŋ; *NAmE* ˈloʊd-/ *noun* [U, C] **1** (*AustralE, NZE*) extra money that sb is paid for their job because they have special skills or qualifications **2** an extra amount of money that you must pay in addition to the usual price: *The 2% loading for using the card abroad has been removed.*

ˈload line *noun* = PLIMSOLL LINE

ˈload-shedding *noun* [U] the practice of stopping the supply of electricity for a period of time because the demand is greater than the supply

load·star *noun* = LODESTAR

load·stone *noun* = LODESTONE

loaf /ləʊf; *NAmE* loʊf/ *noun, verb*
■ ***noun*** (*pl.* **loaves** /ləʊvz; *NAmE* loʊvz/) an amount of bread that has been shaped and baked in one piece: *a loaf of bread* ◇ *Two white loaves, please.* ◇ *a sliced loaf* ➲ see also COTTAGE LOAF, FRENCH LOAF, MEAT LOAF IDM see HALF *det.*, USE *v.*
■ ***verb*** [I] **~ (about/around)** (*informal*) to spend your time not doing anything, especially when you should be working SYN **hang about/around**: *A group of kids were loafing around outside.*

loaf·er /ˈləʊfə(r); *NAmE* ˈloʊf-/ *noun* **1** a person who wastes their time rather than working **2** a flat leather shoe that you can put on your foot without fastening it ➲ VISUAL VOCAB page V52

loam /ləʊm; *NAmE* loʊm/ *noun* [U] (*technical*) good quality soil containing sand, CLAY and decayed vegetable matter ▸ **loamy** *adj.*

loan 🔑 /ləʊn; *NAmE* loʊn/ *noun, verb*
■ ***noun*** **1** 🔑 [C] money that an organization such as a bank lends and sb borrows: *to* ***take out/repay a loan*** (= to borrow money/pay it back) ◇ ***bank loans*** *with low interest rates* ◇ *It took three years to repay my* ***student loan*** (= money lent to a student). ◇ *a car loan* (= a loan to buy a car) ➲ COLLOCATIONS at FINANCE **2** 🔑 [sing.] **~ (of sth)** the act of lending sth; the state of being lent: *I even* ***gave her the loan of*** *my car.* ◇ *an exhibition of paintings* ***on loan*** (= borrowed) *from private collections*
■ ***verb*** **1** (*especially NAmE*) to lend sth to sb, especially money: **~ sth (to sb)** *The bank is happy to loan money to small businesses.* ◇ **~ sb sth** *A friend loaned me $1000.* **2** (*especially BrE*) to lend a valuable object to a museum, etc: **~ sth (out) (to sb/sth)** *This exhibit was kindly loaned by the artist's family.* ◇ **~ sb sth** *He loaned the museum his entire collection.*

ˈloan shark *noun* (*disapproving*) a person who lends money at very high rates of interest

ˈloan translation *noun* (*linguistics*) = CALQUE

loan·word /ˈləʊnwɜːd; *NAmE* ˈloʊnwɜːrd/ *noun* (*linguistics*) a word from another language used in its original form: *'Latte' is a loanword from Italian.*

loath (also *less frequent* **loth**) /ləʊθ; *NAmE* loʊθ/ *adj.* **~ to do sth** (*formal*) not willing to do sth: *He was loath to admit his mistake.*

loathe /ləʊð; *NAmE* loʊð/ *verb* (not used in the progressive tenses) **~ sb/sth | ~ doing sth** to dislike sb/sth very much **SYN detest**: *I loathe modern art.* ◇ *They loathe each other.* ➲ SYNONYMS at HATE

loath·ing /ˈləʊðɪŋ; *NAmE* ˈloʊð-/ *noun* [sing., U] **~ (for/of sb/sth)** (*formal*) a strong feeling of hatred: *She looked at her attacker with* ***fear and loathing***. ◇ *Many soldiers returned with a* ***deep loathing*** *of war.*

loath·some /ˈləʊðsəm; *NAmE* ˈloʊð-/ *adj.* (*formal*) extremely unpleasant; disgusting **SYN repulsive**

loaves *pl.* of LOAF

lob /lɒb; *NAmE* lɑːb/ *verb* (-bb-) **1 ~ sth + adv./prep.** (*informal*) to throw sth so that it goes quite high through the air: *Stones were lobbed over the wall.* ➲ SYNONYMS at THROW **2 ~ sth (+ adv./prep.)** (*sport*) to hit or kick a ball in a high curve through the air, especially so that it lands behind the person you are playing against: *He lobbed the ball over the defender's head.* ▶ **lob** *noun*: *to play a lob*

lobby /ˈlɒbi; *NAmE* ˈlɑːbi/ *noun, verb*

■ ***noun*** (*pl.* -ies) **1** [C] a large area inside the entrance of a public building where people can meet and wait **SYN foyer**: *a hotel lobby* **2** [C] (in the British Parliament) a large hall that is open to the public and used for people to meet and talk to Members of Parliament **3** [C+sing./pl. v.] a group of people who try to influence politicians on a particular issue: *The gun lobby is/are against any change in the law.* **4** [C, sing.] (*BrE*) an organized attempt by a group of people to influence politicians on a particular issue **SYN pressure group**: *a recent lobby of Parliament by pensioners*

■ ***verb*** (**lob·bies, lobby·ing, lob·bied, lob·bied**) [T, I] **~ (sb) (for/against sth)** to try to influence a politician or the government and, for example, persuade them to support or oppose a change in the law: *Farmers will lobby Congress for higher subsidies.* ◇ *Women's groups are lobbying to get more public money for children.* ▶ **lobby·ist** /-ɪst/ *noun*: *political lobbyists*

lobe /ləʊb; *NAmE* loʊb/ *noun* **1** = EAR LOBE **2** a part of an organ in the body, especially the lungs or brain

lo·belia /ləʊˈbiːliə; *NAmE* loʊ-/ *noun* [C, U] a small garden plant with small blue, red or white flowers

lob·ola /ləˈbəʊlə; lɒˈbɔːlə; *NAmE* loʊˈb-/ *noun* [U] (*SAfrE*) in traditional African culture, a sum of money or number of CATTLE that a man's family pays to a woman's family in order that he can marry her: *to pay lobola*

lob·ot·om·ize (*BrE* also **-ise**) /ləˈbɒtəmaɪz; *NAmE* -ˈbɑːt-/ *verb* **1 ~ sb** to perform a LOBOTOMY on sb **2 ~ sb** to make sb less intelligent or less mentally active

lob·ot·omy /ləʊˈbɒtəmi; lə-; *NAmE* loʊˈbɑːt-/ *noun* (*pl.* -ies) a rare medical operation that cuts into part of a person's brain in order to treat mental illness

lob·ster /ˈlɒbstə(r); *NAmE* ˈlɑːb-/ *noun* **1** [C] a sea creature with a hard shell, a long body divided into sections, eight legs and two large CLAWS (= curved and pointed arms for catching and holding things). Its shell is black but turns bright red when it is boiled. ➲ picture at SHELLFISH **2** [U] meat from a lobster, used for food

ˈlobster pot *noun* a trap for lobsters that is shaped like a BASKET

local 🔑 /ˈləʊkl; *NAmE* ˈloʊkl/ *adj., noun*

■ ***adj.*** [usually before noun] **1** 🔑 belonging to or connected with the particular place or area that you are talking about or with the place where you live: *a local farmer* ◇ *A local man was accused of the murder.* ◇ *Our children go to the local school.* ◇ *a* ***local newspaper*** (= one that gives local news) ◇ ***local radio*** (= a radio station that broadcasts to one area only) ◇ *decisions made at local rather than national level* ◇ *It was difficult to understand the local dialect.* **2** affecting only one part of the body: *Her tooth was extracted under* ***local anaesthetic***. ▶ **lo·cal·ly** 🔑 /-kəli/ *adv.*: *to work locally* ◇ *Do you* ***live locally*** (= in this area)? ◇ *locally grown fruit*

■ ***noun*** **1** [usually pl.] a person who lives in a particular place or district: *The locals are very friendly.* **2** (*BrE, informal*) a pub near where you live: *I called in at my local on the way home.* **3** (*NAmE*) a branch of a TRADE/LABOR UNION **4** (*NAmE*) a bus or train that stops at all places on the route

lo·cal /ˌləʊ ˈkæl; *NAmE* ˌloʊ/ *adj.* (*informal*) = LOW-CAL

ˌlocal ˌarea ˈnetwork *noun* = LAN

ˌlocal auˈthority *noun* (*BrE*) the organization which is responsible for the government of an area in Britain

ˈlocal call *noun* a telephone call to a place that is near

ˌlocal ˈcolour (*especially US* **ˌlocal ˈcolor**) *noun* [U] the typical things, customs, etc. in a place that make it interesting, and that are used in a picture, story or film/movie to make it seem real

lo·cale /ləʊˈkɑːl; *NAmE* loʊˈkæl/ *noun* (*technical* or *formal*) a place where sth happens

ˌlocal ˈgovernment *noun* **1** [U] (*especially BrE*) the system of government of a town or an area by elected representatives of the people who live there **2** [C] (*NAmE*) the organization that is responsible for the government of a local area and for providing services, etc: *state and local governments*

lo·cal·ity /ləʊˈkæləti; *NAmE* loʊ-/ *noun* (*pl.* -ies) (*formal*) **1** the area that surrounds the place you are in or are talking about **SYN vicinity**: *people living in the locality of the power station* ◇ *There is no airport* ***in the locality***. **2** the place where sb/sth exists: *We talk of the brain as the locality of thought.* ◇ *The birds are found in over 70 different localities.*

lo·cal·ize (*BrE* also **-ise**) /ˈləʊkəlaɪz; *NAmE* ˈloʊ-/ *verb* **1 ~ sth** to limit sth or its effects to a particular area **SYN confine** **2 ~ sth** (*formal*) to find out where sth is: *animals' ability to localize sounds* ▶ **lo·cal·iza·tion, -isa·tion** /ˌləʊkəlaɪˈzeɪʃn; *NAmE* ˌloʊkələˈz-/ *noun* [U]

lo·cal·ized (*BrE* also **-ised**) /ˈləʊkəlaɪzd; *NAmE* ˈloʊ-/ *adj.* (*formal*) happening within one small area: *a localized infection* (= in one part of the body) ◇ *localized fighting*

ˈlocal time *noun* [U] the time of day in the particular part of the world that you are talking about: *We reach Delhi at 2 o'clock local time.*

lo·cate 🔑 **AW** /ləʊˈkeɪt; *NAmE* ˈloʊkeɪt/ *verb* **1** 🔑 [T] **~ sb/sth** to find the exact position of sb/sth: *The mechanic located the fault immediately.* ◇ *Rescue planes are trying to locate the missing sailors.* **2** 🔑 [T] **~ sth + adv./prep.** to put or build sth in a particular place **SYN site**: *They located their headquarters in Swindon.* ➲ compare RELOCATE **3** [I] **+ adv./prep.** (*especially NAmE*) to start a business in a particular place: *There are tax breaks for businesses that locate in rural areas.*

lo·cated 🔑 **AW** /ləʊˈkeɪtɪd; *NAmE* ˈloʊkeɪ-/ *adj.* [not before noun] if sth is **located** in a particular place, it exists there or has been put there **SYN situated**: *a small town located 30 miles south of Chicago* ◇ *The offices are conveniently located just a few minutes from the main station.*

lo·ca·tion 🔑 **AW** /ləʊˈkeɪʃn; *NAmE* loʊ-/ *noun* **1** 🔑 [C] a place where sth happens or exists; the position of sth: *a honeymoon in a secret location* ◇ *What is the exact location of the ship?* ➲ SYNONYMS at PLACE **2** [C, U] a place outside a film studio where scenes of a film/movie are made: *A mountain in the Rockies became the location for a film about Everest.* ◇ *The movie was shot entirely* ***on location*** *in Italy.* **3** [U] the act of finding the position of sb/sth

loca·tive /ˈlɒkətɪv; *NAmE* ˈlɑːk-/ *adj.* (*grammar*) (in some languages) the form of a noun, pronoun or adjective when it expresses the idea of place ➲ see also ACCUSATIVE, DATIVE, GENITIVE, NOMINATIVE, VOCATIVE

L

lo·ca·tor /ləʊˈkeɪtə(r); *NAmE* loʊˈkeɪtər; ˈloʊkeɪtər/ *noun* a device or system for finding sth: *The company lists 5 000 stores on the store locator part of its website.*

loc. cit. /ˌlɒk ˈsɪt; *NAmE* ˌlɑːk/ *abbr.* in the piece of text quoted (from Latin 'loco citato')

loch /lɒk; lɒx; *NAmE* lɑːk; lɑːx/ *noun* (in Scotland) a lake or a narrow strip of sea almost surrounded by land ➲ see also LOUGH

loci *pl.* of LOCUS

lock 0→ /lɒk; *NAmE* lɑːk/ *verb, noun*

■ ***verb*** **1** 0→ [T, I] **~ (sth)** to fasten sth with a lock; to be fastened with a lock: *Did you lock the door?* ◇ *This suitcase doesn't lock.* **2** 0→ [T] **~ sth + adv./prep.** to put sth in a safe place and lock it: *She locked her passport and money in the safe.* **3** [I, T] **~ (sth) (in/into/around, etc. sth)** | **~ (sth) (together)** to become or make sth become fixed in one position and unable to move: *The brakes locked and the car skidded.* ◇ *He locked his helmet into position with a click.* **4** [T] **be locked in/into sth** to be involved in a difficult situation, an argument, a disagreement, etc: *The two sides are locked into a bitter dispute.* ◇ *She felt locked in a loveless marriage.* **5** [T] **be locked together/in sth** to be held very tightly by sb: *They were locked in a passionate embrace.* **6** [T] **~ sth** (*computing*) to prevent computer data from being changed or looked at by sb without permission: *These files are locked to protect confidentiality.*

IDM **ˌlock ˈhorns (with sb) (over sth)** to get involved in an argument or a disagreement with sb: *The company has locked horns with the unions over proposed pay cuts.*

PHR V **ˌlock sb/sth aˈway** = LOCK SB/STH UP **ˌlock sb/yourself ˈin (...)** to prevent sb from leaving a place by locking the door: *At 9 p.m. the prisoners are locked in for the night.* **ˌlock ˈonto sth** (of a MISSILE, etc.) to find the thing that is being attacked and follow it **ˌlock sb/yourself ˈout (of sth)** to prevent sb from entering a place by locking the door: *I'd locked myself out of the house and had to break a window to get in.* **ˌlock sb ˈout** (of an employer) to refuse to allow workers into their place of work until they agree to particular conditions ➲ related noun LOCKOUT **ˌlock ˈup** | **ˌlock sth↔ˈup** 0→ to make a building safe by locking the doors and windows: *Don't forget to lock up at night.* ◇ *He locked up the shop and went home.* **ˌlock sb↔ˈup/aˈway** 0→ (*informal*) to put sb in prison ➲ related noun LOCK-UP **ˌlock sth↔ˈup/aˈway** **1** 0→ to put sth in a safe place that can be locked **2** to put money into an investment that you cannot easily turn into cash: *Their capital is all locked up in property.*

■ ***noun*** **1** 0→ [C] a device that keeps a door, window, lid, etc. shut, usually needing a key to open it: *She turned the key in the lock.* ➲ see also COMBINATION LOCK **2** 0→ [C] a device with a key that prevents a vehicle or machine from being used: *a bicycle lock* ◇ *a steering lock* **3** [U] a state in which the parts of a machine, etc. do not move **4** [U, sing.] (*BrE*) (on a car, etc.) the amount that the front wheels can be turned in one direction or the other in order to turn the vehicle: *I had the steering wheel* ***on full lock*** (= I had turned it as far as it would turn). **5** [C] a section of CANAL or river with a gate at either end, in which the water level can be changed so that boats can move from one level of the canal or river to another **6** [C] a few hairs that hang or lie together on your head: *John brushed a* ***lock of hair*** *from his eyes.* **7 locks** [pl.] (*literary*) a person's hair: *She shook her long, flowing locks.* **8** [C] (in RUGBY) a player in the second row of the SCRUM **9** [sing.] **a ~ (on sth)** (*NAmE*) total control of sth: *One company* ***had a virtual lock on*** *all orange juice sales in the state.* ➲ see also ARMLOCK, HEADLOCK

IDM **ˌlock, stock and ˈbarrel** including everything: *He sold the business lock, stock and barrel.* **(keep sth/put sth/be) under ˌlock and ˈkey** locked up safely somewhere; in prison: *We keep our valuables under lock and key.* ◇ *I will not rest until the murderer is under lock and key.* ➲ more at PICK *v.*

lock·able /ˈlɒkəbl; *NAmE* ˈlɑːk-/ *adj.* that you can lock with a key

lock·down /ˈlɒkdaʊn; *NAmE* ˈlɑːk-/ *noun* [C, U] (*especially NAmE*) an official order to control the movement of people or vehicles because of a dangerous situation: *a three-day lockdown of American airspace* ◇ *Prisoners have been placed on lockdown to prevent further violence at the jail.*

lock·er /ˈlɒkə(r); *NAmE* ˈlɑːk-/ *noun* a small cupboard that can be locked, where you can leave your clothes, bags, etc. while you play a sport or go somewhere ➲ VISUAL VOCAB page V57

ˈlocker room *noun* (*especially NAmE*) a room with lockers in it, at a school, GYM, etc, where people can change their clothes ➲ compare CHANGING ROOM

locket /ˈlɒkɪt; *NAmE* ˈlɑːk-/ *noun* a piece of jewellery in the form of a small case that you wear on a chain around your neck and in which you can put a picture, piece of hair, etc. ➲ VISUAL VOCAB page V53

ˈlock-in *noun* (*BrE*) an occasion when customers are locked in a bar or club after it has closed so that they can continue drinking privately

lock·jaw /ˈlɒkdʒɔː; *NAmE* ˈlɑːk-/ *noun* [U] (*old-fashioned, informal*) a form of the disease TETANUS in which the JAWS become stiff and closed

ˈlock-keeper *noun* a person who is in charge of a LOCK on a CANAL or river, and opens and closes the gates

lock·out /ˈlɒkaʊt; *NAmE* ˈlɑːk-/ *noun* a situation when an employer refuses to allow workers into their place of work until they agree to various conditions

lock·smith /ˈlɒksmɪθ; *NAmE* ˈlɑːk-/ *noun* a person whose job is making, fitting and repairing locks

lock·step /ˈlɒkstep; *NAmE* ˈlɑːk-/ *noun* [U] (*especially NAmE*) **1** a way of walking together where people move their feet at the same time: *The coffin was carried by six soldiers walking* ***in lockstep***. ◇ (*figurative*) *Politicians and the media are* ***marching in lockstep*** *on this issue* (= they agree). **2** a situation where things happen at the same time or change at the same rate: *a lockstep approach to teaching* ◇ *Cases of breathing difficulties increase* ***in lockstep with*** *air pollution.*

ˈlock-up *noun* **1** a small prison where prisoners are kept for a short time **2** (*BrE*) a small shop that the owner does not live in; a garage that is usually separate from other buildings and that is rented to sb ► **ˈlock-up** *adj.* [only before noun]: *a lock-up garage*

loco /ˈləʊkəʊ; *NAmE* ˈloʊkoʊ/ *noun, adj.*

■ ***noun*** (*pl.* -os) (*informal*) = LOCOMOTIVE ➲ see also IN LOCO PARENTIS

■ ***adj.*** [not before noun] (*slang, especially NAmE*) crazy

loco·mo·tion /ˌləʊkəˈməʊʃn; *NAmE* ˌloʊkəˈmoʊʃn/ *noun* [U] (*formal*) movement or the ability to move

loco·mo·tive /ˌləʊkəˈməʊtɪv; *NAmE* ˌloʊkəˈmoʊ-/ (also *informal* **loco**) *noun, adj.*

■ ***noun*** a railway engine that pulls a train: ***steam/diesel/electric locomotives*** ➲ VISUAL VOCAB page V47

■ ***adj.*** (*formal*) connected with movement

locum /ˈləʊkəm; *NAmE* ˈloʊ-/ *noun* (*BrE*) a doctor or priest who does the work of another doctor or priest while they are sick, on holiday, etc.

locus /ˈləʊkəs; *NAmE* ˈloʊ-/ *noun* (*pl.* **loci** /ˈləʊsaɪ; *NAmE* ˈloʊ-/) (*technical* or *formal*) the exact place where sth happens or which is thought to be the centre of sth

lo·cust /ˈləʊkəst; *NAmE* ˈloʊ-/ *noun* a large insect that lives in hot countries and flies in large groups, destroying all the plants and crops of an area: *a swarm of locusts*

lo·cu·tion /ləˈkjuːʃn/ *noun* (*technical*) **1** [U] a style of speaking **2** [C] a particular phrase, especially one used by a particular group of people

lode /ləʊd; *NAmE* loʊd/ *noun* a line of ORE (= metal in the ground or in rocks)

lode·star (also **load·star**) /ˈləʊdstɑː(r); *NAmE* ˈloʊd-/ *noun* **1** the POLE STAR (= a star that is used by sailors to guide a ship) **2** (*formal*) a principle that guides sb's behaviour or actions

lode·stone (also **load·stone**) /ˈləʊdstəʊn; *NAmE* ˈloʊdstoʊn/ *noun* a piece of iron that acts as a MAGNET

lodge /lɒdʒ; *NAmE* lɑːdʒ/ *noun, verb*
■ ***noun*** **1** [C] a small house in the country where people stay when they want to take part in some types of outdoor sport: *a hunting lodge* **2** [C] a small house at the gates of a park or in the land belonging to a large house **3** [C] a room at the main entrance to a building for the person whose job is to see who enters and leaves the building: *All visitors should report to the porter's lodge.* **4** [C+sing./pl. v.] the members of a branch of a society such as the Freemasons; the building where they meet: *a masonic lodge* **5** [C] the home of a BEAVER or an OTTER **6** [C] a Native American's tent or home built of LOGS
■ ***verb*** **1** [T] **~ sth (with sb) (against sb/sth)** (*formal*) to make a formal statement about sth to a public organization or authority SYN **register, submit**: *They lodged a compensation claim against the factory.* ◇ *Portugal has lodged a complaint with the International Court of Justice.* **2** [I] **+ adv./prep.** (*old-fashioned*) to pay to live in a room in sb's house SYN **board**: *He lodged with Mrs Brown when he arrived in the city.* **3** [T] **~ sb (+ adv./prep.)** to provide sb with a place to sleep or live SYN **accommodate**: *The refugees are being lodged at an old army base.* **4** [I, T] to become fixed or stuck somewhere; to make sth become fixed or stuck somewhere: **~ in sth** *One of the bullets lodged in his chest.* ◇ **~ sth in sth** *She lodged the number firmly in her mind.* **5** [T] **~ sth with sb/in sth** to leave money or sth valuable in a safe place SYN **deposit**: *Your will should be lodged with your lawyer.*

lodg·er /ˈlɒdʒə(r); *NAmE* ˈlɑːdʒ-/ *noun* (*especially BrE*) a person who pays rent to live in sb's house

lodg·ing /ˈlɒdʒɪŋ; *NAmE* ˈlɑːdʒ-/ *noun* (*especially BrE*) **1** [U] temporary accommodation: *full board and lodging* (= a room to stay in and all meals provided) **2** [C, usually pl.] (*old-fashioned*) a room or rooms in sb else's house that you rent to live in: *It was cheaper to live in lodgings than in a hotel.*

ˈlodging house *noun* (*old-fashioned, BrE*) a house in which lodgings can be rented

loft /lɒft; *NAmE* lɔːft; lɑːft/ *noun, verb*
■ ***noun*** **1** (*especially BrE*) a space just below the roof of a house, often used for storing things and sometimes made into a room: *a* ***loft conversion*** (= one that has been made into a room or rooms for living in) ➲ compare ATTIC, GARRET **2** an upper level in a church, or a farm or factory building: *the organ loft* **3** a flat/apartment in a former factory, etc, that has been made suitable for living in: *They lived in a SoHo loft.* **4** (*NAmE*) a part of a room that is on a higher level than the rest: *The children slept in a loft in the upstairs bedroom.*
■ ***verb*** **~ sth** (*sport*) to hit, kick or throw a ball very high into the air

lofty /ˈlɒfti; *NAmE* ˈlɔːfti; ˈlɑːfti/ *adj.* (**loft·ier, lofti·est**) (*formal*) **1** (of buildings, mountains, etc.) very high and impressive: *lofty ceilings/rooms/towers* **2** [usually before noun] (*approving*) (of a thought, an aim, etc.) deserving praise because of its high moral quality: ***lofty ambitions/ideals/principles*** **3** (*disapproving*) showing a belief that you are worth more than other people SYN **haughty**: *her lofty disdain for other people* ▶ **loft·ily** /-ɪli/ *adv.* **lofti·ness** *noun* [U]

log /lɒg; *NAmE* lɔːg; lɑːg/ *noun, verb*
■ ***noun*** **1** a thick piece of wood that is cut from or has fallen from a tree: *logs for the fire* ➲ VISUAL VOCAB page V8 **2** (also **log·book**) an official record of events during a particular period of time, especially a journey on a ship or plane: *The captain keeps a log.* **3** (*informal*) = LOGARITHM
IDM see EASY *adj.*, SLEEP *v.*
■ ***verb*** (-gg-) **1 ~ sth** to put information in an official record or write a record of events SYN **record**: *The police log all phone calls.* **2 ~ sth** to travel a particular distance or for a particular length of time SYN **clock up**: *The pilot has logged 1000 hours in the air.* **3 ~ sth** to cut down trees in a forest for their wood
PHR V **ˌlog ˈin/ˈon** (*computing*) to perform the actions that allow you to begin using a computer system: *You need a password to log on.* **ˌlog sb ↔ˈin/ˈon** (*computing*) to allow sb to begin using a computer system: *The system is unable to log you on.* **ˌlog ˈoff/ˈout** (*computing*) to perform the actions that allow you to finish using a computer system **ˌlog sb ↔ˈoff/ˈout** (*computing*) to cause sb to finish using a computer system

-log (*NAmE*) = -LOGUE

lo·gan·berry /ˈləʊgənbəri; *NAmE* ˈloʊgənberi/ *noun* (*pl.* -ies) a soft dark red fruit, like a large RASPBERRY, that grows on a bush

loga·rithm /ˈlɒgərɪðəm; *NAmE* ˈlɔːg-; ˈlɑːg-/ (also *informal* **log**) *noun* (*mathematics*) any of a series of numbers set out in lists which make it possible to work out problems by adding and SUBTRACTING instead of multiplying and dividing ▶ **loga·rith·mic** /ˌlɒgəˈrɪðmɪk; *NAmE* ˌlɔːg-; ˌlɑːg-/ *adj.*

log·book /ˈlɒgbʊk; *NAmE* ˈlɔːg-; ˈlɑːg-/ *noun* **1** (*BrE*, becoming *old-fashioned*) a document that records official details about a vehicle, especially a car, and its owner ➲ compare REGISTRATION **2** = LOG (2)

ˌlog ˈcabin *noun* a small house built of logs ➲ VISUAL VOCAB page V13

log·ger /ˈlɒgə(r); *NAmE* ˈlɔːg-; ˈlɑːg-/ *noun* = LUMBERJACK

log·ger·heads /ˈlɒgəhedz; *NAmE* ˈlɔːgər-; ˈlɑːg-/ *noun*
IDM **at loggerheads (with sb) (over sth)** in strong disagreement: *The two governments are still at loggerheads over the island.*

log·gia /ˈləʊdʒə; ˈlɒdʒiə; *NAmE* ˈloʊdʒə; ˈlɑːdʒiə/ *noun* (*BrE*) a room or GALLERY with one or more open sides, especially one that forms part of a house and has one side open to the garden

log·ging /ˈlɒgɪŋ; *NAmE* ˈlɔːg-; ˈlɑːg-/ *noun* [U] the work of cutting down trees for their wood

logic 0‑w AW /ˈlɒdʒɪk; *NAmE* ˈlɑːdʒɪk/ *noun*
1 0‑w [U] a way of thinking or explaining sth: *I fail to see the logic behind his argument.* ◇ *The two parts of the plan were governed by the same logic.* **2** 0‑w [U, sing.] sensible reasons for doing sth: *Linking the proposals in a single package did have a certain logic.* ◇ *a strategy based on sound commercial logic* ◇ *There is* ***no logic to/in*** *any of their claims.* **3** 0‑w [U] (*philosophy*) the science of thinking about or explaining the reason for sth using formal methods: *the rules of logic* **4** [U] (*computing*) a system or set of principles used in preparing a computer to perform a particular task

lo·gic·al 0‑w AW /ˈlɒdʒɪkl; *NAmE* ˈlɑːdʒ-/ *adj.*
1 0‑w (of an action, event, etc.) seeming natural, reasonable or sensible: *a logical thing to do in the circumstances* ◇ *It was a logical conclusion from the child's point of view.* **2** 0‑w following or able to follow the rules of logic in which ideas or facts are based on other true ideas or facts: *a logical argument* ◇ *Computer programming needs someone with a logical mind.* OPP **illogical** ▶ **logic·al·ly** AW /-kli/ *adv.*: *to argue logically*

-logical, -logic ➲ -OLOGY

ˌlogical ˈpositivism *noun* [U] (*philosophy*) the belief that the only problems which have meaning are those that can be solved using logical thinking

ˈlogic circuit *noun* (*computing*) a series of logic gates that performs operations on data that is put into a computer

ˈlogic gate (also **gate**) *noun* (*computing*) an electronic switch that reacts in one of two ways to data that is put into it. A computer performs operations by passing data through a very large number of logic gates.

lo·gi·cian AW /ləˈdʒɪʃn/ *noun* a person who studies or is skilled in logic

login /ˈlɒgɪn; *NAmE* ˈlɔːg-; ˈlɑːg-/ (also **logon**) *noun* **1** [U] the act of starting to use a computer system, usually by typing a name or word that you choose to use: *If you've forgotten your login ID, click this link.* **2** [C] the name that you use to enter a computer system: *Enter your login and password and press 'go'.*

-logist ➲ -OLOGY

lo·gis·tics /lə'dʒɪstɪks/ *noun* **1** [U+sing./pl. v.] ~ (**of sth**) the practical organization that is needed to make a complicated plan successful when a lot of people and equipment is involved: *the logistics of moving the company to a new building* **2** [U] (*business*) the business of transporting and delivering goods **3** [U] the activity of moving equipment, supplies and people for military operations: *a revolution in military logistics* ▸ **lo·gis·tic** (also **lo·gis·tic·al** /lə'dʒɪstɪkl/) *adj.*: *logistic support* ◇ *Organizing famine relief presents huge logistical problems.* **lo·gis·tic·al·ly** /-kli/ *adv.*

log·jam /'lɒgdʒæm; *NAmE* 'lɔ:g-; 'lɑ:g-/ *noun* **1** a difficult situation in which you cannot make progress easily because there are too many things to do SYN **bottleneck** **2** a mass of LOGS floating on a river and blocking it

logo /'ləʊgəʊ; *NAmE* 'loʊgoʊ/ *noun* (*pl.* -os) a printed design or symbol that a company or an organization uses as its special sign

log·off /'lɒgɒf; *NAmE* 'lɔ:gɔ:f; 'lɑ:g-; -ɑ:f/ (also **log·out**) *noun* [U] the act of finishing using a computer system

logo·gram /'lɒgəgræm; *NAmE* 'lɔ:g-; 'lɑ:g-/ (also **logo·graph** /'lɒgəgrɑ:f; *NAmE* 'lɔ:gəgræf; 'lɑ:gəgræf/) *noun* (*technical*) a symbol that represents a word or phrase, for example those used in ancient writing systems

logon /'lɒgɒn; *NAmE* 'lɔ:gɑ:n; 'lɑ:g-; -ɔ:n/ *noun* = LOGIN

log·out /'lɒgaʊt; *NAmE* 'lɔ:g-; 'lɑ:g-/ *noun* = LOGOFF

log·roll·ing /'lɒgrəʊlɪŋ; *NAmE* 'lɔ:groʊ-; 'lɑ:g-/ *noun* [U] (*NAmE*) **1** (in US politics) the practice of agreeing with sb that you will vote to pass a law that they support so that they will later vote to pass a law that you support **2** a sport in which two people stand on a LOG floating on water and try to knock each other off by moving the log with their feet

L

-logue (*NAmE* also **-log**) *combining form* (in nouns) talk or speech: *a monologue*

-logy ➲ -OLOGY

loin /lɔɪn/ *noun* **1** [U, C] a piece of meat from the back or sides of an animal, near the tail: *loin of pork* **2** **loins** [pl.] (*old-fashioned*) the part of the body around the hips between the waist and the tops of the legs **3** **loins** [pl.] (*literary*) a person's sex organs IDM see GIRD

loin·cloth /'lɔɪnklɒθ; *NAmE* -klɔ:θ; -klɑ:θ/ *noun* a piece of cloth worn around the body at the hips by men in some hot countries, sometimes as the only piece of clothing worn

loi·ter /'lɔɪtə(r)/ *verb* [I] to stand or wait somewhere especially with no obvious reason SYN **hang around**: *Teenagers were loitering in the street outside.*

LOL /ˌel əʊ 'el; *NAmE* oʊ/ *abbr.* LAUGH-OUT-LOUD

Lo·li·ta /ləʊ'li:tə; *NAmE* loʊ'-/ *noun* a young girl who behaves in a more sexually developed way than is usual for her age, which makes her sexually attractive to older men ORIGIN From the name of the main character in Vladimir Nabokov's novel *Lolita*.

loll /lɒl; *NAmE* lɑ:l/ *verb* **1** [I] **+ adv./prep.** to lie, sit or stand in a lazy, relaxed way: *He lolled back in his chair by the fire.* **2** [I] **+ adv./prep.** (of your head, tongue, etc.) to move or hang in a relaxed way: *My head lolled against his shoulder.*

lol·li·pop /'lɒlipɒp; *NAmE* 'lɑ:lipɑ:p/ (also *BrE informal* **lolly**) (also *NAmE informal* **suck·er**) *noun* a hard round or flat sweet/candy made of boiled sugar on a small stick

'lollipop man, **'lollipop lady** *noun* (*BrE, informal*) a person whose job is to help children cross a busy road on their way to and from school by holding up a sign on a stick telling traffic to stop

lol·lop /'lɒləp; *NAmE* 'lɑ:ləp/ *verb* [I] (+ **adv./prep.**) (*informal, especially BrE*) to walk or run with long awkward steps: *The dog came lolloping towards them.*

lolly /'lɒli; *NAmE* 'lɑ:li/ *noun* (*pl.* -ies) (*informal*) **1** [C] (*BrE*) = LOLLIPOP **2** [C] (*BrE*) = ICE LOLLY **3** [U] (*old-fashioned, BrE*) money **4** [C] (*AustralE, NZE*) a sweet or a piece of candy

Lon·don·er /'lʌndənə(r)/ *noun* a person from London in England

lone /ləʊn; *NAmE* loʊn/ *adj.* [only before noun] **1** without any other people or things SYN **solitary**: *a lone sailor crossing the Atlantic* **2** (*especially BrE*) without a husband, wife or partner to share the care of children SYN **single**: *a* ***lone mother/parent/father*** ➲ note at ALONE
IDM **a ˌlone 'wolf** a person who prefers to be alone

lone·ly 0-w /'ləʊnli; *NAmE* 'loʊn-/ *adj.* (**lone·lier**, **lone·li·est**)
1 0-w unhappy because you have no friends or people to talk to: *She lives alone and often feels lonely.* **2** 0-w (of a situation or period of time) sad and spent alone: *all those lonely nights at home watching TV* **3** 0-w [only before noun] (of places) where only a few people ever come or visit SYN **isolated**: *a lonely beach* ➲ note at ALONE
▸ **lone·li·ness** *noun* [U]: *a period of loneliness in his life*

ˌlonely 'hearts *adj.* [only before noun] a **lonely hearts column** in a newspaper, etc. is where people can advertise for a new lover or friend: *He placed a lonely hearts ad in a magazine.*

ˌlone-parent 'family *noun* = ONE-PARENT FAMILY

loner /'ləʊnə(r); *NAmE* 'loʊn-/ *noun* a person who is often alone or who prefers to be alone, rather than with other people

lone·some /'ləʊnsəm; *NAmE* 'loʊn-/ *adj.*, *noun*
■ ***adj.*** (*especially NAmE*) **1** unhappy because you are alone and do not want to be or because you have no friends: *I felt so lonesome after he left.* **2** (of a place) where not many people go; a long way from where people live: *a lonesome road* ➲ note at ALONE
■ ***noun***
IDM (**all**) **by/on your lonesome** (*informal*) alone: *Are you here all by your lonesome?*

long 0-w /lɒŋ; *NAmE* lɔ:ŋ; lɑ:ŋ/ *adj.*, *adv.*, *verb*

WORD FAMILY
long *adj., adv.*
length *noun*
lengthy *adj.*
lengthen *verb*

■ ***adj.*** (**long·er** /'lɒŋgə(r); *NAmE* 'lɔ:ŋ-; 'lɑ:ŋ-/, **long·est** /'lɒŋgɪst; *NAmE* 'lɔ:ŋ-; 'lɑ:ŋ-/)
▸ DISTANCE **1** 0-w measuring or covering a great length or distance, or a greater length or distance than usual: *She had long dark hair.* ◇ *He walked down the long corridor.* ◇ *It was the world's longest bridge.* ◇ *a* ***long journey/walk/drive/flight*** ◇ *We're* ***a long way*** *from anywhere here.* ◇ *It's a* ***long way away.*** ➲ VISUAL VOCAB page V49 OPP **short** **2** 0-w used for asking or talking about particular lengths or distances: ***How long*** *is the River Nile?* ◇ *The table is six feet long.* ◇ *The report is only three pages long.*
▸ TIME **3** 0-w lasting or taking a great amount of time or more time than usual: *He's been ill* (**for**) ***a long time.*** ◇ *There was a long silence before she spoke.* ◇ *I like it now the days are getting longer* (= it stays light for more time each day). ◇ *a* ***long book/film/list*** (= taking a lot of time to read/watch/deal with) ◇ *Nurses have to work* ***long hours*** (= for more hours in the day than is usual). ◇ (*NAmE*) *He stared at them* ***for the longest time*** (= for a very long time) *before answering.* OPP **short** **4** 0-w used for asking or talking about particular periods of time: ***How long*** *is the course?* ◇ *I think it's only three weeks long.* ◇ *How long a stay did you have in mind?* **5** 0-w seeming to last or take more time than it really does because, for example, you are very busy or not happy: *I'm tired. It's been a long day.* ◇ *We were married for ten long years.* OPP **short**
▸ CLOTHES **6** 0-w covering all or most of your legs or arms: *She usually wears long skirts.* ◇ *a long-sleeved shirt* OPP **short**
▸ VOWEL SOUNDS **7** (*phonetics*) taking more time to make than a short vowel sound in the same position OPP **short**
IDM **as long as your 'arm** (*informal*) very long: *There's a list of repairs as long as your arm.* **at long last** after a long time SYN **finally**: *At long last his prayers had been answered.* **at the 'longest** not longer than the particular time given: *It will take an hour at the longest.* **by a 'long way** by a great amount **go back a long 'way** (of two or more people) to have known each other for a long time: *We go back a long way, he and I.* **go a long 'way** (of money, food, etc.) to last a long time: *She seems to make her money go a long way.* ◇ *A small amount of this paint goes a long way* (= covers a large area). ◇ (*ironic*) *I find that* ***a little of*** *Jerry's company can* ***go a long way*** (= I quickly get tired of being with him). **have come a long 'way** to have made a lot of

progress: *We've come a long way since the early days of the project.* **have a long way to 'go** to need to make a lot of progress before you can achieve sth: *She still has a long way to go before she's fully fit.* **how long is a piece of 'string?** (*BrE, informal*) used to say that there is no definite answer to a question: *'How long will it take?' 'How long's a piece of string?'* **in the 'long run** concerning a longer period in the future: *This measure inevitably means higher taxes in the long run.* **it's a ˌlong 'story.** (*informal*) used to say that the reasons for sth are complicated and you would prefer not to give all the details **the long arm of sth** the power and/or authority of sth: *There is no escape from the long arm of the law.* **the long and (the) 'short of it** used when you are telling sb the essential facts about sth or what effect it will have, without explaining all the details **(pull, wear, etc.) a long 'face** (to have) an unhappy or disappointed expression **ˌlong in the 'tooth** (*humorous, especially BrE*) old or too old **ORIGIN** This originally referred to the fact that a horse's teeth appear to be longer as it grows older, because its gums shrink. **'long on sth** (*informal*) having a lot of a particular quality: *The government is long on ideas but short on performance.* **a 'long shot** an attempt or a guess that is not likely to be successful but is worth trying: *It's a long shot, but it just might work.* **long time no 'see** (*informal*) used to say hello to sb you have not seen for a long time **not by a 'long chalk** (*BrE*) (also **not by a 'long shot** *NAmE, BrE*) not nearly; not at all: *It's not over yet—not by a long chalk.* **take a long (cool/hard) 'look at sth** to consider a problem or possibility very carefully and without hurrying: *We need to take a long hard look at all the options.* **take the 'long view (of sth)** to consider what is likely to happen or be important over a long period of time rather than only considering the present situation **to cut a long story 'short** (*BrE*) (*NAmE* **to make a long story 'short**) (*informal*) used when you are saying that you will get to the point of what you are saying quickly, without including all the details ➲ more at BROAD *adj.*, KICK *v.*, TERM *n.*, WAY *n.*

■ ***adv.*** (**long·er** /'lɒŋgə(r); *NAmE* 'lɔːŋ-; 'lɑːŋ-/, **long·est** /'lɒŋgɪst; *NAmE* 'lɔːŋ-; 'lɑːŋ-/) **1** 🗝 for a long time: *Have you been here long?* ◇ *Stay as long as you like.* ◇ *The party went on long into the night.* ◇ *This may **take longer** than we thought.* ◇ *I won't **be long*** (= I'll return, be ready, etc. soon). ◇ ***How long** have you been waiting?* ◇ *These reforms are long overdue.* **2** 🗝 a long time before or after a particular time or event: *He retired long before the war.* ◇ *It wasn't long before she had persuaded him* (= it only took a short time). ◇ *We'll be home **before long*** (= soon). ◇ *The house was pulled down **long ago**.* ◇ *They had **long since*** (= a long time before the present time) *moved away.* **3** used after a noun to emphasize that sth happens for the whole of a particular period of time: *We had to wait **all day long**.* ◇ *The baby was crying **all night long**.* ◇ *They stayed up **the whole night long**.*

IDM **as/so 'long as** **1** 🗝 only if: *We'll go as long as the weather is good.* **2** 🗝 since; to the extent that: *So long as there is a demand for these drugs, the financial incentive for drug dealers will be there.* **for (so) 'long** 🗝 for (such) a long time: *Will you be away for long?* ◇ *I'm sorry I haven't written to you for so long.* **how long have you 'got?** (*BrE*) (*NAmE* **how long do you 'have?**) (*informal*) used to say that sth is going to take a long time to explain: *What do I think about it? How long have you got?* **long live sb/sth** used to say that you hope sb/sth will live or last for a long time **no/any 'longer** 🗝 used to say that sth which was possible or true before, is not now: *I can't wait any longer.* ◇ *He no longer lives here.* **so 'long** (*informal*) goodbye ➲ more at LAUGH *v.*

■ ***verb*** [I] to want sth very much especially if it does not seem likely to happen soon **SYN** **yearn**: **~ for sb/sth** *Lucy had always longed for a brother.* ◇ **~ for sb to do sth** *He longed for Pat to phone.* ◇ **~ to do sth** *I'm longing to see you again.* ➲ see also LONGED-FOR

long. *abbr.* (in writing) LONGITUDE

ˌlong-a'waited *adj.* that people have been waiting for for a long time: *her long-awaited new novel*

long·board /'lɒŋbɔːd; *NAmE* 'lɔːŋbɔːrd/ *noun* a long board used in SURFING

Which Word?

(for) long / (for) a long time

- Both **(for) long** and **(for) a long time** are used as expressions of time. In positive sentences **(for) a long time** is used: *We've been friends a long time.* **(For) long** is not used in positive sentences unless it is used with *too, enough, as, so, seldom*, etc: *I stayed out in the sun for too long.* ◇ *You've been waiting long enough.* Both **(for) long** and **(for) a long time** can be used in questions, but **(for) long** is usually preferred: *Have you been waiting long?*
- In negative sentences **(for) a long time** sometimes has a different meaning from **(for) long**. Compare: *I haven't been here for a long time* (= It is a long time since the last time I was here) and *I haven't been here long* (= I arrived here only a short time ago).

long·boat /'lɒŋbəʊt; *NAmE* 'lɔːŋboʊt; 'lɑːŋboʊt/ *noun* a large ROWING BOAT, used especially for travelling on the sea

long·bow /'lɒŋbəʊ; *NAmE* 'lɔːŋboʊ; 'lɑːŋboʊ/ *noun* a large BOW made of a long thin curved piece of wood that was used in the past for shooting arrows

ˌlong-'distance *adj.* [only before noun] **1** travelling or involving travel between places that are far apart: *a long-distance commuter* ◇ *long-distance flights* **2** operating between people and places that are far apart: *a long-distance phone call* ▶ **ˌlong 'distance** *adv.*: *It's a relaxing car to drive long distance.* ◇ *to call long distance*

ˌlong-ˌdistance 'footpath *noun* a route that people can walk along to see the countryside or the coast

ˌlong di'vision *noun* [U] (*mathematics*) a method of dividing one number by another in which all the stages involved are written down

ˌlong-drawn-'out (also *less frequent* **'long-drawn, ˌdrawn-'out**) *adj.* lasting a very long time, often too long **SYN** **protracted**: *long-drawn-out negotiations*

ˌlong 'drink *noun* a cold drink that fills a tall glass, such as LEMONADE or beer

'longed-for *adj.* [only before noun] that sb has been wanting or hoping for very much: *the birth of a longed-for baby*

lon·gev·ity /lɒn'dʒevəti; *NAmE* lɔːn-; lɑːn-/ *noun* [U] (*formal*) long life; the fact of lasting a long time: *We wish you both health and longevity.* ◇ *He prides himself on the longevity of the company.*

long·hair /'lɒŋheə(r); *NAmE* 'lɔːŋher; 'lɑːŋher/ *noun* a breed of cat with long hair ➲ compare SHORTHAIR

long·hand /'lɒŋhænd; *NAmE* 'lɔːŋ-; 'lɑːŋ-/ *noun* [U] ordinary writing, not typed or written in SHORTHAND

ˌlong 'haul *noun* [usually sing.] a difficult task that takes a long time and a lot of effort to complete: *She knows that becoming world champion is going to be a long haul.*

IDM **be in sth for the long 'haul** (*especially NAmE*) to be willing to continue doing a task until it is finished: *I promise I am in this for the long haul.* **over the long 'haul** (*especially NAmE*) over a long period of time

'long-haul *adj.* [only before noun] involving the transport of goods or passengers over long distances: ***long-haul flights/routes*** **OPP** **short-haul**

long·horn /'lɒŋhɔːn; *NAmE* -hɔːrn/ *noun* a type of cow with long horns

long·house /'lɒŋhaʊs; *NAmE* 'lɔːŋ-; 'lɑːŋ-/ *noun* **1** (in Britain) an old type of house in which people and animals lived together **2** (in the US) a traditional house used by some Native Americans

long·ing /'lɒŋɪŋ; *NAmE* 'lɔːŋ-/ *noun, adj.*

■ ***noun*** [C, U] a strong feeling of wanting sth/sb: **~ (for sb/sth)** *a longing for home* ◇ **~ (to do sth)** *She was filled with*

L

longing to hear his voice again. ◇ *romantic longings* ◇ *His voice was husky with longing* (= sexual desire).

■ ***adj.*** [only before noun] feeling or showing that you want sth very much: *He gave a longing look at the ice cream.* ▶ **long·ing·ly** *adv.*: *We looked longingly towards the hills.*

long·ish /ˈlɒŋɪʃ; *NAmE* ˈlɔːŋ-/ *adj.* [only before noun] fairly long: *longish hair* ◇ *There was a longish pause.*

lon·gi·tude /ˈlɒŋɡɪtjuːd; ˈlɒndʒɪ-; *NAmE* ˈlɑːndʒətuːd; ˈlɔːndʒətuːd/ *noun* [U] (*abbr.* **long.**) the distance of a place east or west of the Greenwich MERIDIAN, measured in degrees: *the longitude of the island* ➲ compare LATITUDE

lon·gi·tu·din·al /ˌlɒŋɡɪˈtjuːdɪnl; ˌlɒndʒɪ-; *NAmE* ˌlɑːndʒəˈtuːdnl; ˌlɔːndʒəˈtuːdnl/ *adj.* (*technical*) **1** going downwards rather than across: *The plant's stem is marked with thin green longitudinal stripes.* **2** concerning the development of sth over a period of time: *a longitudinal study of ageing* **3** connected with longitude: *the town's longitudinal position* ▶ **lon·gi·tu·din·al·ly** /-nəli/ *adv.*

longiˌtudinal ˈwave *noun* (*physics*) a wave that VIBRATES in the direction that it is moving ➲ compare TRANSVERSE WAVE

ˈlong johns *noun* [pl.] (*informal*) warm UNDERPANTS with long legs down to the ankles: *a pair of long johns*

the ˈlong jump (*NAmE* also **the ˈbroad jump**) *noun* [sing.] a sporting event in which people try to jump as far forward as possible after running up to a line

ˌlong-ˈlasting *adj.* that can or does last for a long time **SYN** **durable**: *long-lasting effects* ◇ *a long-lasting agreement*

ˌlong-ˈlife *adj.* **1** made to last longer than the ordinary type: *long-life batteries* **2** (*BrE*) made to remain fresh longer than the ordinary type: *long-life milk*

ˌlong-ˈlived *adj.* having a long life; lasting for a long time ➲ SYNONYMS at OLD

ˈlong-lost *adj.* [only before noun] that you have not seen or received any news of for a long time: *a long-lost friend*

ˈlong-range *adj.* [only before noun] **1** travelling a long distance: *long-range missiles* **2** made for a period of time that will last a long way into the future: *a long-range weather forecast* ◇ *long-range plans* ➲ compare SHORT-RANGE

ˈlong-running *adj.* [only before noun] that has been continuing for a long time: *a long-running dispute* ◇ *a long-running TV series*

ˈlong-serving *adj.* [only before noun] having had the job or position mentioned for a long time: *long-serving employees*

long·ship /ˈlɒŋʃɪp; *NAmE* ˈlɔːŋ-; ˈlɑːŋ-/ *noun* a long narrow ship used by the Vikings

long·shore drift /ˌlɒŋʃɔː ˈdrɪft; *NAmE* ˌlɔːŋʃɔːr; ˌlɑːŋ-/ *noun* [U] (*technical*) the movement of sand, etc. along a beach caused by waves hitting the beach at an angle

long·shore·man /ˈlɒŋʃɔːmən; *NAmE* ˈlɔːŋʃɔːrmən; ˈlɑːŋʃɔːrmən/ *noun* (*pl.* **-men** /-mən/) (*NAmE*) a man whose job is moving goods on and off ships

ˌlong-ˈsighted (*especially BrE*) (also **ˌfar-ˈsighted** especially in *NAmE*) *adj.* [not usually before noun] not able to see things that are close to you clearly **OPP** **short-sighted** ▶ **ˌlong-ˈsighted·ness** (also **ˌlong ˈsight**) *noun* [U]

ˌlong-ˈstanding *adj.* [usually before noun] that has existed or lasted for a long time: *a long-standing relationship*

ˈlong-stay *adj.* [usually before noun] **1** likely to need treatment or care for a long time: *long-stay patients* ◇ ***long-stay hospitals/institutions/wards*** (= for long-stay patients) **2** for people who wish to park their cars for a long period: *long-stay parking*

ˌlong-ˈsuffer·ing *adj.* bearing problems or another person's unpleasant behaviour with patience: *his long-suffering wife*

ˌlong-ˈterm *adj.* [usually before noun] **1** that will last or have an effect over a long period of time: *a long-term strategy* ◇ *the long-term effects of fertilizers* ◇ *a long-term investment* **2** that is not likely to change or be solved quickly: *long-term unemployment* ➲ compare SHORT-TERM

ˈlong-time *adj.* [only before noun] having been the particular thing mentioned for a long time: *his long-time colleague*

lon·gueurs /lɒŋˈɡɜːz; *NAmE* loʊŋˈɡɜːrz/ *noun* [pl.] (from *French, literary*) very boring parts or aspects of sth

ˈlong wave *noun* [U, C] (*abbr.* **LW**) a radio wave with a length of more than 1000 metres: *to broadcast* ***on long wave*** ➲ compare SHORT WAVE

long·ways /ˈlɒŋweɪz; *NAmE* ˈlɔːŋ-; ˈlɑːŋ-/ (also **long·wise** /ˈlɒŋwaɪz; *NAmE* ˈlɔːŋ-/) *adv.* in the same direction as the longest side of sth **SYN** **lengthways**

ˌlong weekˈend *noun* a holiday/vacation of three or four days from Friday or Saturday to Sunday or Monday

ˌlong-ˈwinded *adj.* (*disapproving*) (especially of talking or writing) continuing for too long and therefore boring **SYN** **tedious**

loo /luː/ *noun* (*pl.* **loos**) (*BrE, informal*) a toilet/bathroom: *She's gone to the loo.* ◇ *Can I use your loo, please?*

loo·fah /ˈluːfə/ *noun* a long rough bath SPONGE made from the dried fruit of a tropical plant ➲ VISUAL VOCAB page V21

look 🔑 /lʊk/ *verb, noun, exclamation*

■ ***verb***

▸ USE EYES **1** 🔑 [I] to turn your eyes in a particular direction: *If you look carefully you can just see our house from here.* ◇ **~ (at sb/sth)** *She looked at me and smiled.* ◇ *'Has the mail come yet?' 'I'll* ***look and see****.'* ◇ *Look! I'm sure that's Brad Pitt!* ◇ *Don't look now, but there's someone staring at you!* ➲ see also FORWARD-LOOKING

▸ SEARCH **2** 🔑 [I] to try to find sb/sth: *I can't find my book—I've looked everywhere.* ◇ **~ for sb/sth** *Where have you been? We've been looking for you.* ◇ *Are you still looking for a job?*

▸ PAY ATTENTION **3** 🔑 [I, T] to pay attention to sth: **~ (at sth)** *Look at the time! We're going to be late.* ◇ **~ where, what, etc...** *Can't you look where you're going?*

▸ APPEAR/SEEM **4** 🔑 *linking verb* to seem; to appear: **+ adj.** *to look pale/happy/tired* ◇ *That book looks interesting.* ◇ **~ (to sb) like sb/sth** *That looks like an interesting book.* ◇ **+ noun** *That looks an interesting book.* ◇ *You made me look a complete fool!* ➲ see also GOOD-LOOKING **5** 🔑 [I] (not usually used in the progressive tenses) to have a similar appearance to sb/sth; to have an appearance that suggests that sth is true or will happen: **~ (to sb) like sb/sth** *That photograph doesn't look like her at all.* ◇ *It looks like rain* (= it looks as if it's going to rain). ◇ **~ (to sb) as if.../as though** ... *You look as though you slept badly.* **HELP** In spoken English people often use **like** instead of **as if** or **as though** in this meaning, especially in *NAmE*: *You look like you slept badly.* This is not considered correct in written *BrE*. **6** 🔑 [I] to seem likely: **~ (to sb) as if.../as though...** *It doesn't look as if we'll be moving after all.* ◇ **~ (to sb) like...** (*informal*) *It doesn't look like we'll be moving after all.* **HELP** This use of **like** instead of **as if** or **as though** is not considered correct in written *BrE*.

▸ FACE **7** [I] **+ adv./prep.** to face a particular direction: *The house looks east.* ◇ *The hotel looks out over the harbour.*

IDM Most idioms containing **look** are at the entries for the nouns and adjectives in the idioms, for example **look daggers at sb** is at **dagger**. **be just ˈlooking** used in a shop/store to say that you are not ready to buy sth: *'Can I help you?' 'I'm just looking, thank you.'* **be looking to do sth** to try to find ways of doing sth: *The government is looking to reduce inflation.* **look ˈbad | not look ˈgood** to be considered bad behaviour or bad manners: *It looks bad not going to your own brother's wedding.* **look ˈbad (for sb)** to show that sth bad might happen: *He's had another heart attack; things are looking bad for him, I'm afraid.* **look ˈgood** to show success or that sth good might happen: *This year's sales figures are looking good.* **look ˈhere** (*old-fashioned*) used to protest about sth: *Now look here, it wasn't my fault.* **look how/what/who...** used to give an example that proves what you are saying or makes it clearer: *Look how lazy we've become.* ◇ *Be careful climbing that ladder. Look what happened last time.* **look sb ˌup and ˈdown** to look at sb in a careful or critical way **(not) look**

your'self to not have your normal healthy appearance: *You're not looking yourself today* (= you look tired or ill/sick). **never/not look 'back** (*informal*) to become more and more successful: *Her first novel was published in 2007 and since then she hasn't looked back.* **not much to 'look at** (*informal*) not attractive **to 'look at sb/sth** judging by the appearance of sb/sth: *To look at him you'd never think he was nearly fifty.*

PHR V **,look 'after yourself/sb/sth** (*especially BrE*) **1** to be responsible for or to take care of sb/sth: *Who's going to look after the children while you're away?* ◇ *I'm looking after his affairs while he's in hospital.* ◇ *Don't worry about me—I can look after myself* (= I don't need any help). ⊃ note at CARE **2** to make sure that things happen to sb's advantage: *He's good at looking after his own interests.*

,look a'head (to sth) to think about what is going to happen in the future

,look a'round/'round to turn your head so that you can see sth: *People came out of their houses and looked around.* **,look a'round/'round (sth)** to visit a place or building, walking around it to see what is there: *Let's look round the town this afternoon.* **,look a'round/'round for sth** to search for sth in a number of different places: *We're looking around for a house in this area.*

'look at sth 1 to examine sth closely: *Your ankle's swollen—I think the doctor ought to look at it.* ◇ *I haven't had time to look at* (= read) *the papers yet.* **2** to think about, consider or study sth: *The implications of the new law will need to be looked at.* **3** to view or consider sth in a particular way: *Looked at from that point of view, his decision is easier to understand.*

,look 'back (on sth) to think about sth in your past **SYN** **reflect on**: *to look back on your childhood*

,look 'down on sb/sth to think that you are better than sb/sth: *She looks down on people who haven't been to college.*

'look for sth to hope for sth; to expect sth: *We shall be looking for an improvement in your work this term.*

,look 'forward to sth to be thinking with pleasure about sth that is going to happen (because you expect to enjoy it): *I'm looking forward to the weekend.* ◇ **~ doing sth** *We're really looking forward to seeing you again.*

,look 'in (on sb) to make a short visit to a place, especially sb's house when they are ill/sick or need help: *She looks in on her elderly neighbour every evening.* ◇ *Why don't you look in on me next time you're in town?*

,look 'into sth to examine sth: *A working party has been set up to look into the problem.*

,look 'on to watch sth without becoming involved in it yourself: *Passers-by simply looked on as he was attacked.* ⊃ related noun ONLOOKER **'look on sb/sth as sb/sth** to consider sb/sth to be sb/sth: *She's looked on as the leading authority on the subject.* **'look on sb/sth with sth** to consider sb/sth in a particular way **SYN** **regard**: *They looked on his behaviour with contempt.*

,look 'out used to warn sb to be careful, especially when there is danger **SYN** **watch out**: *Look out! There's a car coming.* **,look 'out for sb** to take care of sb and make sure nothing bad happens to them **,look 'out for sb/sth 1** to try to avoid sth bad happening or doing sth bad **SYN** **watch out**: *You should look out for pickpockets.* ◇ *Do look out for spelling mistakes in your work.* **2** to keep trying to find sth or meet sb: *I'll look out for you at the conference.* ⊃ related noun LOOKOUT **,look 'out for sb/yourself** to think only of sb's/your own advantage, without worrying about other people: *You should look out for yourself from now on.* **,look sth↔'out (for sb/sth)** (*BrE*) to search for sth from among your possessions: *I'll look out those old photographs you wanted to see.*

,look sth↔'over to examine sth to see how good, big, etc. it is: *We looked over the house again before we decided we would rent it.*

,look 'round (*BrE*) to turn your head to see sb/sth behind you: *She looked round when she heard the noise.*

,look 'through sb [no passive] to ignore sb by pretending not to see them: *She just looked straight through me.* **'look through sth** [no passive] to examine or read sth quickly: *She looked through her notes before the exam.*

'look to sb for sth | 'look to sb to do sth (*formal*) to rely on or expect sb to provide sth or do sth: *We are looking to you for help.* **'look to sth** (*formal*) to consider sth and think about how to make it better: *We need to look to ways of improving our marketing.*

,look 'up (*informal*) (of business, sb's situation, etc.) to become better **SYN** **improve**: *At last things were beginning to look up.* **,look 'up (from sth)** to raise your eyes when you are looking down at sth: *She looked up from her book as I entered the room.* **,look sb↔'up** [no passive] (*informal*) to visit or make contact with sb, especially when you have not seen them for a long time: *Do look me up the next time you're in London.* **,look sth↔'up** to look for information in a dictionary or REFERENCE BOOK, or by using a computer: *Can you look up the opening times on the website?* ◇ *I looked it up in the dictionary.* **,look 'up to sb** to admire or respect sb

Synonyms

look

watch • see • view • observe

These words all mean to turn your eyes in a particular direction.

look to turn your eyes in a particular direction: *If you look carefully you can just see our house from here.* ◇ *She **looked at** me and smiled.*

watch to look at sb/sth for a time, paying attention to what happens: *to watch television* ◇ *Watch what I do, then you try.*

see to watch a game, television programme, performance, etc: *In the evening we went to see a movie.*

view (*formal*) to look at sth, especially when you look carefully; to watch television, a film/movie, etc: *People came from all over the world to view her work.*

WATCH, SEE OR VIEW?

You can *see/view a film/movie/programme* but you cannot: ~~*see/view television*~~. **View** is more formal than **see** and is used especially in business contexts.

observe (*formal*) to watch sb/sth carefully, especially to learn more about them or it: *The patients were observed over a period of several months.*

PATTERNS

- to look/watch **for** sb/sth
- to watch/observe **what/who/how...**
- to look/watch/view/observe (sb/sth) **with** amazement/surprise/disapproval, etc.
- to watch/see/view a **film/movie/show/programme**
- to watch/see a **match/game/fight**
- to look (at sb/sth)/watch (sb/sth)/observe sb/sth **carefully/closely**

■ ***noun***

▸ USING EYES **1** [C, usually sing.] **~ (at sb/sth)** an act of looking at sb/sth: *Here, **have a look** at this.* ◇ ***Take a look** at these figures!* ◇ *Make sure you get a **good look** at their faces.* ◇ ***One look** at his face and Jenny stopped laughing.* ◇ *A look passed between them* (= they looked at each other). ◇ *It's an interesting place. Do you want to take **a look around**?* ◇ *We'll be taking a **close look** at these proposals* (= examining them carefully).

▸ SEARCH **2** [C, usually sing.] **~ (for sth/sb)** an act of trying to find sth/sb: *I've **had a** good **look** for it, but I can't find it.*

▸ EXPRESSION **3** [C] an expression in your eyes or face: *a **look of** surprise* ◇ *He didn't like the look in her eyes.* ◇ *She had a worried look on her face.*

▸ APPEARANCE **4** [C, usually sing.] the way sb/sth looks; the appearance of sb/sth: *It's going to rain today **by the look of it*** (= judging by appearances). ◇ *Looks can be deceptive.* ◇ ***I don't like the look of** that guy* (= I don't trust him, judging by his appearance). **5** **looks** [pl.] a person's appear-

ance, especially when the person is attractive: *She has her father's* ***good looks***. ◇ *He* ***lost his looks*** (= became less attractive) *in later life.* ➲ see also GOOD-LOOKING
▸ FASHION **6** 0→ [sing.] a fashion; a style: *The punk look is back in fashion.* ◇ *They've given the place a completely new look.* ➲ see also WET LOOK
IDM **if looks could 'kill...** used to describe the very angry or unpleasant way sb is/was looking at you: *I don't know what I've done to upset him, but if looks could kill...* ➲ more at DIRTY *adj.*, LONG *adj.*
■ ***exclamation*** used to make sb pay attention to what you are going to say, often when you are annoyed: *Look, I think we should go now.* ◇ *Look, that's not fair.*

Synonyms

look

glance • gaze • stare • glimpse • glare

These are all words for an act of looking, when you turn your eyes in a particular direction.

look an act of looking at sb/sth: *Here, have a look at this.*

glance a quick look: *She stole a glance at her watch.*

gaze a long steady look at sb/sth: *She felt embarrassed under his steady gaze.*

stare a long look at sb/sth, especially in a way that is unfriendly or that shows surprise: *She gave the officer a blank stare and shrugged her shoulders.*

glimpse a look at sb/sth for a very short time, when you do not see the person or thing completely: *He caught a glimpse of her in the crowd.*

glare a long angry look at sb/sth: *She fixed her questioner with a hostile glare.*

PATTERNS
- a look/glance **at** sb/sth
- a **penetrating/piercing** look/glance/gaze/stare
- a **long** look/glance/stare
- a **brief** look/glance/glimpse
- to **have/get/take** a look/glance/glimpse
- to **avoid** sb's glance/gaze/stare

L

loom /lu:m/ *verb, noun*
■ ***verb*** **1** [I] (+ **adv./prep.**) to appear as a large shape that is not clear, especially in a frightening or threatening way: *A dark shape loomed up ahead of us.* **2** [I] to appear important or threatening and likely to happen soon: *There was a crisis looming.*
IDM **,loom 'large** to be worrying or frightening and seem hard to avoid: *The prospect of war loomed large.*
■ ***noun*** a machine for making cloth by twisting threads between other threads which go in a different direction

loon /lu:n/ *noun* **1** a large N American bird that eats fish and has a cry like a laugh **2** = LOONY

loonie /'lu:ni/ *noun* (*CanE*) the Canadian dollar or a Canadian one-dollar coin

loony /'lu:ni/ *adj., noun*
■ ***adj.*** (*informal*) crazy or strange
■ ***noun*** (*pl.* -ies) (also **loon**) (*informal*) a person who has strange ideas or who behaves in a strange way

'loony bin *noun* (*old-fashioned, slang*) a humorous and sometimes offensive way of referring to a hospital for people who are mentally ill

loop /lu:p/ *noun, verb*
■ ***noun*** **1** a shape like a curve or circle made by a line curving right round and crossing itself: *The road went in a huge loop around the lake.* **2** a piece of rope, wire, etc. in the shape of a curve or circle: *He tied a loop of rope around his arm.* ◇ *Make a loop in the string.* ◇ *a belt loop* (= on trousers/pants, etc. for holding a belt in place) ➲ picture at KNOT **3** a strip of film or tape on which the pictures and sound are repeated continuously: *The film is on a loop.* ◇ (*figurative*) *His mind kept turning in an endless loop.* **4** (*computing*) a set of instructions that is repeated again and again until a particular condition is satisfied **5** a complete CIRCUIT for electrical current **6** (*BrE*) a railway line or road that leaves the main track or road and then joins it again **7 the Loop** (*US, informal*) the business centre of the US city of Chicago
IDM **in the 'loop | out of the 'loop** (*informal*) part of a group of people that is dealing with sth important; not part of this group **knock/throw sb for a 'loop** (*NAmE, informal*) to shock or surprise sb
■ ***verb*** **1** [T] **~ sth + adv./prep.** to form or bend sth into a loop: *He looped the strap over his shoulder.* **2** [I] **+ adv./prep.** to move in a way that makes the shape of a loop: *The river loops around the valley.* ◇ *The ball looped high up in the air.*
IDM **,loop the 'loop** to fly or make a plane fly in a circle going up and down

look·alike /'lʊkəlaɪk/ *noun* (often used after a person's name) a person who looks very similar to the person mentioned: *an Elvis lookalike*

,look-and-'say *noun* [U] a method of teaching people to read based on the recognition of whole words, rather than on the association of letters with sounds ➲ compare PHONICS

look·er /'lʊkə(r)/ *noun* (*informal*) a way of describing an attractive person, usually a woman: *She's a real looker!*

'look-in *noun*
IDM **(not) get/have a 'look-in** (*BrE, informal*) (not) to get a chance to take part or succeed in sth: *She talks so much that nobody else can get a look-in.*

'looking glass *noun* (*old-fashioned*) a mirror

look·out /'lʊkaʊt/ *noun* **1** a place for watching from, especially for danger or an enemy coming towards you: *a* ***lookout point/tower*** **2** a person who has the responsibility of watching for sth, especially danger, etc: *One of the men stood at the door to act as a lookout.*
IDM **be 'sb's lookout** (*BrE, informal*) used to say that you do not think sb's actions are sensible, but that it is their own problem or responsibility.: *If he wants to waste his money, that's his lookout.* **be on the 'lookout (for sb/sth) | keep a 'lookout (for sb/sth)** (*informal*) to watch carefully for sb/sth in order to avoid danger, etc. or in order to find sth you want: *The public should be on the lookout for symptoms of the disease.*

,look-'see *noun* [sing.] (*informal, especially NAmE*) a quick look at sth: *Come and have a look-see.*

loop·hole /'lu:phəʊl; *NAmE* -hoʊl/ *noun* **~ (in sth)** a mistake in the way a law, contract, etc. has been written which enables people to legally avoid doing sth that the law, contract, etc. had intended them to do: *a legal loophole* ◇ *to close existing loopholes*

loopy /'lu:pi/ *adj.* (*informal*) **1** not sensible; strange SYN **crazy 2** (*BrE*) very angry SYN **furious**: *He'll* ***go loopy*** *when he hears!*

loose 0→ /lu:s/ *adj., verb, noun*
■ ***adj.*** (loos·er, loos·est)
▸ NOT FIXED/TIED **1** 0→ not firmly fixed where it should be; able to become separated from sth: *a loose button/tooth* ◇ *Check that the plug has not* ***come loose***. **2** 0→ not tied together; not held in position by anything or contained in anything: *She usually wears her hair loose.* ◇ *The potatoes were sold loose, not in bags.* **3** 0→ [not usually before noun] free to move around without control; not tied up or shut in somewhere: *The sheep had got out and were loose on the road.* ◇ *The horse had* ***broken loose*** (= escaped) *from its tether.* ◇ *During the night, somebody had cut the boat loose from its moorings.*
▸ CLOTHES **4** 0→ not fitting closely: *a loose shirt* OPP **tight**
▸ NOT SOLID/HARD **5** 0→ not tightly packed together; not solid or hard: *loose soil* ◇ *a fabric with a loose weave*
▸ NOT STRICT/EXACT **6** not strictly organized or controlled: *a* ***loose alliance/coalition/federation*** **7** not exact; not very careful: *a loose translation* ◇ *loose thinking*
▸ IMMORAL **8** [usually before noun] (*old-fashioned*) having or

involving an attitude to sexual relationships that people consider to be immoral: *a young man of loose morals*

▸ BALL **9** (*sport*) not in any player's control: *He pounced on a* **loose ball**.

▸ BODY WASTE **10** having too much liquid in it: *a baby with loose bowel movements*

▸ **loose·ness** *noun* [U]

IDM **break/cut/tear (sb/sth) 'loose from sb/sth** to separate yourself or sb/sth from a group of people or their influence, etc: *The organization broke loose from its sponsors.* ◇ *He cut himself loose from his family.* **hang/stay 'loose** (*informal, especially NAmE*) to remain calm; to not worry: *It's OK—hang loose and stay cool.* **have a loose 'tongue** to talk too much, especially about things that are private **let 'loose** (*BrE*) (*NAmE* **cut 'loose**) (*informal*) to do sth or to happen in a way that is not controlled: *Teenagers need a place to let loose.* **let 'loose sth** to make a noise or remark, especially in a loud or sudden way: *She let loose a stream of abuse.* **let sb/sth 'loose 1** to free sb/sth from whatever holds them/it in place: *She let her hair loose and it fell around her shoulders.* ◇ *Who's let the dog loose?* **2** to give sb complete freedom to do what they want in a place or situation: *He was at last let loose in the kitchen.* ◇ *A team of professionals were* **let loose on** *the project.* ➲ more at FAST *adv.*, HELL, SCREW *n.*

■ ***verb*** (*formal*)

▸ RELEASE **1 ~ sth (on/upon sb/sth)** to release sth or let it happen or be expressed in an uncontrolled way: *His speech loosed a tide of nationalist sentiment.*

▸ MAKE STH LOOSE **2 ~ sth** to make sth loose, especially sth that is tied or held tightly SYN **loosen**: *He loosed the straps that bound her arms.*

▸ FIRE BULLETS **3 ~ sth (off) (at sb/sth)** to fire bullets, arrows, etc. HELP Do not confuse this verb with **to lose** = 'to be unable to find sth'.

■ ***noun***

IDM **on the 'loose** (of a person or an animal) having escaped from somewhere; free SYN **at large**: *Three prisoners are still on the loose.*

'loose box *noun* (*BrE*) a small area in a building or a vehicle where a horse can move freely

ˌloose 'cannon *noun* a person, usually a public figure, who often behaves in a way that nobody can predict

ˌloose 'change *noun* [U] coins that you have in a pocket or a bag

ˌloose 'cover (*BrE*) (*NAmE* **'slip cover**) *noun* [usually pl.] a cover for a chair, etc. that you can take off, for example to wash it

ˌloose 'end *noun* [usually pl.] a part of sth such as a story that has not been completely finished or explained: *The play has too many loose ends.* ◇ *There are still a few loose ends to tie up* (= a few things to finish).

IDM **at a loose 'end** (*BrE*) (*NAmE* **at loose 'ends**) having nothing to do and not knowing what you want to do: *Come and see us, if you're at a loose end.*

ˌloose-'fitting *adj.* (of clothes) not fitting the body tightly

ˌloose 'forward *noun* (in RUGBY) a player who plays at the back of the SCRUM

ˌloose 'head *noun* (in RUGBY) the player in the front row of a team in the SCRUM who is nearest to where the ball is put in

ˌloose-'leaf *adj.* [usually before noun] (of a book, file, etc.) having pages that can be taken out and put in separately: *a loose-leaf binder*

ˌloose-'limbed *adj.* (*literary*) (of a person) moving in an easy, not stiff, way

loose·ly 🔑 /ˈluːsli/ *adv.*
1 🔑 in a way that is not firm or tight: *She fastened the belt loosely around her waist.* **2** 🔑 in a way that is not exact: *to use a term loosely* ◇ *The play is loosely based on his childhood in Russia.*

loos·en /ˈluːsn/ *verb* **1** [T, I] **~ (sth)** to make sth less tight or firmly fixed; to become less tight or firmly fixed SYN **slacken**: *First loosen the nuts, then take off the wheel.* ◇ *The rope holding the boat loosened.* **2** [T] **~ sth** to make a piece of clothing, hair, etc. loose, when it has been tied or fastened **3** [T] **~ your hands, hold, etc.** to hold sb/sth less tightly: *He loosened his grip and let her go.* ◇ (*figurative*) *The military regime has not loosened its hold on power.* **4** [T] **~ sth** to make sth weaker or less controlled than before SYN **relax**: *The party has loosened its links with big business.* OPP **tighten**

IDM **loosen sb's 'tongue** to make sb talk more freely than usual: *A bottle of wine had loosened Harry's tongue.*

PHR V **ˌloosen 'up** to relax and stop worrying: *Come on, Jo. Loosen up.* **ˌloosen 'up | ˌloosen sb/sth↔'up** to relax your muscles or parts of the body or to make them relax, before taking exercise, etc.

loot /luːt/ *verb, noun*

■ ***verb*** [T, I] **~ (sth)** to steal things from shops/stores or buildings after a RIOT, fire, etc: *More than 20 shops were looted.* ▸ **loot·er** /ˈluːtə(r)/ *noun* **loot·ing** *noun* [U]

■ ***noun*** [U] **1** money and valuable objects taken by soldiers from the enemy after winning a battle SYN **booty 2** (*informal*) money and valuable objects that have been stolen by thieves **3** (*informal*) money

lop /lɒp; *NAmE* lɑːp/ *verb* (**-pp-**) **~ sth** to cut down a tree, or cut some large branches off it

PHR V **ˌlop sth↔'off (sth) 1** to remove part of sth by cutting it, especially to remove branches from a tree SYN **chop 2** to make sth smaller or less by a particular amount: *They lopped 20p off the price.*

lope /ləʊp; *NAmE* loʊp/ *verb* [I] **+ adv./prep.** to run taking long relaxed steps: *The dog loped along beside her.* ◇ *He set off with a loping stride.* ▸ **lope** *noun* [usually sing.]

'lop-ears *noun* [pl.] ears that hang down at the side of an animal's head ▸ **'lop-eared** *adj.*: *a lop-eared rabbit*

lop·sided /ˌlɒpˈsaɪdɪd; *NAmE* ˌlɑːp-/ *adj.* having one side lower, smaller, etc. than the other: *a lopsided grin/mouth* ◇ (*figurative*) *The article presents a somewhat lopsided view of events.* ▸ **lop·sided·ly** *adv.*

lo·qua·cious /ləˈkweɪʃəs/ *adj.* (*formal*) talking a lot SYN **talkative** ▸ **lo·qua·city** /ləˈkwæsəti/ *noun* [U]

lo·quat /ˈləʊkwɒt; *NAmE* ˈloʊkwɑːt/ *noun* a round pale orange fruit that grows on bushes in China, Japan and the Middle East

lord 🔑 /lɔːd; *NAmE* lɔːrd/ *noun, verb*

■ ***noun* 1** 🔑 [C] (in Britain) a man of high rank in the NOBILITY (= people of high social class), or sb who has been given the title 'lord' as an honour ➲ compare LADY **2** 🔑 **Lord** (in Britain) the title used by a lord: *Lord Beaverbrook* **3 Lord** a title used for some high official positions in Britain: *the Lord Chancellor* ◇ *the Lord Mayor* **4 My Lord** (in Britain) a title of respect used when speaking to a judge, BISHOP or some male members of the NOBILITY (= people of high social class) ➲ compare LADY **5** a powerful man in MEDIEVAL Europe, who owned a lot of land and property: *a feudal lord* ◇ *the lord of the manor* ➲ see also OVERLORD, WARLORD **6** (usually **the Lord**) [sing.] a title used to refer to God or Christ: *Love the Lord with all your heart.* **7 Our Lord** [sing.] a title used to refer to Christ **8 the Lords** [sing.+ sing./pl. v.] = HOUSE OF LORDS: *The Lords has/have not yet reached a decision.* ➲ compare COMMONS ➲ see also LAW LORD

IDM **(good) 'Lord! | oh 'Lord!** *exclamation* used to show that you are surprised, annoyed or worried about sth: *Good Lord, what have you done to your hair!* **'Lord knows** ... used to emphasize what you are saying: *Lord knows, I tried to teach her.* **'Lord ('only) knows (what, where, why, etc.)...** (*informal*) used to say that you do not know the answer to sth: *'Why did she say that?' 'Lord knows!'* HELP Some people may find the use of **Lord** in these expressions offensive. IDM see DRUNK *adj.*, YEAR

■ ***verb***

IDM **'lord it over sb** (*disapproving*) to act as if you are better or more important than sb

ˌLord Lieu'tenant *noun* in the UK, an officer in charge of local government and local judges

lord·ly /ˈlɔːdli; *NAmE* ˈlɔːrd-/ *adj.* **1** behaving in a way that suggests that you think you are better than other people

L

SYN **haughty** **2** large and impressive; suitable for a lord SYN **imposing**: *a lordly mansion*

ˌLord ˈMayor *noun* the title of the mayor of the City of London and some other large British cities

lord·ship /ˈlɔːdʃɪp; *NAmE* ˈlɔːrd-/ *noun* **1 His/Your Lordship** a title of respect used when speaking to or about a judge, a BISHOP or a NOBLEMAN: *His Lordship is away on business.* ➲ compare LADYSHIP **2** (*BrE, informal*) a humorous way of talking to or about a boy or man that you think is trying to be too important: *Can his lordship manage to switch off the TV?* **3** [U] the power or position of a LORD

the ˌLord's ˈPrayer *noun* [sing.] the prayer that Jesus Christ taught the people who followed him, that begins 'Our Father...'

lore /lɔː(r)/ *noun* [U] knowledge and information related to a particular subject, especially when this is not written down; the stories and traditions of a particular group of people: *weather lore* ◇ *Celtic lore* ➲ see also FOLKLORE

lo-res /ˌləʊ ˈrez; *NAmE* ˌloʊ/ *adj.* = LOW-RESOLUTION

lor·gnette /lɔːˈnjet; *NAmE* lɔːrˈnjet/ *noun* an old-fashioned pair of glasses that you hold to your eyes on a long handle

lori·keet /ˈlɒrɪkiːt; *NAmE* ˈlɔːrəkiːt; ˈlɑːr-/ *noun* a small bird found mainly in New Guinea

lorry 0-w /ˈlɒri; *NAmE* ˈlɔːri; ˈlɑːri/ (*BrE*) *noun* (*pl.* -ies) (also **truck** *NAmE, BrE*)
a large vehicle for carrying heavy loads by road: *a lorry driver* ◇ *Emergency food supplies were brought in* **by lorry**. ◇ *a lorry load of frozen fish* ➲ VISUAL VOCAB page V46
IDM see BACK *n.*

L

lose 0-w /luːz/ *verb* (**lost, lost** /lɒst; *NAmE* lɔːst; lɑːst/)
▸ NOT FIND **1** 0-w [T] **~ sth/sb** to be unable to find sth/sb SYN **mislay**: *I've lost my keys.* ◇ *The tickets seem to have* **got lost**. ◇ *She lost her husband in the crowd.*
▸ HAVE STH/SB TAKEN AWAY **2** 0-w [T] **~ sth/sb** to have sth/sb taken away from you as a result of an accident, getting old, dying, etc: *She lost a leg in a car crash.* ◇ *to* **lose your hair/teeth** (= as a result of getting old) ◇ *He's* **lost his job**. ◇ *Some families* **lost everything** (= all they owned) *in the flood.* ◇ *They lost both their sons* (= they were killed) *in the war.* ◇ *The ship was* **lost at sea** (= it sank). ◇ *Many people* **lost their lives** (= were killed). **3** 0-w [T] **~ sth (to sb/sth)** to have sth taken away by sb/sth: *The company has lost a lot of business to its competitors.* **4** 0-w [T] **~ sth** to have to give up sth; to fail to keep sth: *You will lose your deposit if you cancel the order.* ◇ *Sit down or you'll lose your seat.*
▸ HAVE LESS **5** 0-w [T] **~ sth** to have less and less of sth, especially until you no longer have any of it: *He* **lost his nerve** *at the last minute.* ◇ *She seemed to have* **lost interest** *in food.* ◇ *At that moment he* **lost his balance** *and fell.* ◇ *I've lost ten pounds since I started this diet.* ◇ *The train was* **losing speed**.
▸ NOT WIN **6** 0-w [T, I] to be defeated; to fail to win a competition, a court case, an argument, etc: **~ sth** (**to sb**) *to lose a game/a race/an election/a battle/a war* ◇ **~ to sb** *We lost to a stronger team.* ◇ **~ (sth) (by sth)** *He lost by less than 100 votes.*
▸ NOT KEEP **7** 0-w [T, I] to fail to keep sth you want or need, especially money; to cause sb to fail to keep sth: **~ sth** *The business is losing money.* ◇ *Poetry always loses something in translation.* ◇ **~ sth (on sth/by doing sth)** *You have* **nothing to lose** *by telling the truth.* ◇ **~ on sth/by doing sth** *We lost on that deal.* ◇ **~ sb sth** *His carelessness lost him the job.*
▸ NOT UNDERSTAND/HEAR **8** [T] **~ sth** to fail to get, hear or understand sth: *His words were lost* (= could not be heard) *in the applause.* **9** [T] **~ sb** (*informal*) to be no longer understood by sb: *I'm afraid* **you've lost me** *there.*
▸ ESCAPE **10** [T] **~ sb/sth** to escape from sb/sth SYN **evade**, **shake off**: *We managed to lose our pursuers in the darkness.*
▸ TIME **11** [T] **~ sth** to waste time or an opportunity: *We lost twenty minutes changing a tyre.* ◇ *Hurry—***there's no time to lose***!* ◇ *He* **lost no time in** *setting out for London.* **12** [T, I] **~ (sth)** if a watch or clock **loses** or **loses time**, it goes too slowly or becomes a particular amount of time behind the correct time: *This clock loses two minutes a day.* OPP **gain**
IDM Most idioms containing **lose** are at the entries for the nouns and adjectives in the idioms, for example **lose your bearings** is at **bearing**. **ˈlose it** (*informal*) to be unable to stop yourself from crying, laughing, etc; to become crazy: *Then she just lost it and started screaming.*
PHR V **ˈlose yourself in sth** to become so interested in sth that it takes all your attention **ˌlose ˈout (on sth)** (*informal*) to not get sth you wanted or feel you should have: *While the stores make big profits, it's the customer who loses out.* **ˌlose ˈout to sb/sth** (*informal*) to not get business, etc. that you expected or used to get because sb/sth else has taken it: *Small businesses are losing out to the large chains.*

loser /ˈluːzə(r)/ *noun* **1** a person who is defeated in a competition: *winners and losers* ◇ *He's* **a good/bad loser** (= he accepts defeat well/badly). **2** (rather *informal*) a person who is regularly unsuccessful, especially when you have a low opinion of them: *She's one of life's losers.* ◇ *He's* **a born loser**. **3** a person who suffers because of a particular action, decision, etc: *The real losers in all of this are the students.*

loss 0-w /lɒs; *NAmE* lɔːs; lɑːs/ *noun*
1 0-w [U, C, usually sing.] the state of no longer having sth or as much of sth; the process that leads to this: *I want to report the loss of a package.* ◇ **loss of blood** ◇ **weight loss** ◇ *The closure of the factory will lead to a number of* **job losses**. ◇ *When she died I was filled with a* **sense of loss**. ◇ **loss of earnings** (= the money you do not earn because you are prevented from working) **2** 0-w [C] money that has been lost by a business or an organization: *The company has announced* **net losses** *of $1.5 million.* ◇ *We* **made a loss on** (= lost money on) *the deal.* ◇ *We are now operating* **at a loss**. OPP **profit** **3** 0-w [C, U] the death of a person: *The loss of his wife was a great blow to him.* ◇ *Enemy troops suffered* **heavy losses**. ◇ *The drought has led to widespread* **loss of life**. **4** 0-w [sing.] the disadvantage that is caused when sb leaves or when a useful or valuable object is taken away; a person who causes a disadvantage by leaving: *Her departure is a* **big loss** *to the school.* ◇ *She will be a* **great loss** *to the school.* ◇ *If he isn't prepared to accept this money, then* **that's his loss**. ➲ see also DEAD LOSS **5** [C] a failure to win a contest: *Brazil's 2–1 loss to Argentina*
IDM **at a ˈloss** not knowing what to say or do: *His comments left me* **at a loss for words**. ◇ *I'm at a loss what to do next.* **cut your ˈlosses** to stop doing sth that is not successful before the situation becomes even worse

ˈloss adjuster (*BrE*) (*NAmE* **inˈsurance adjuster**) *noun* a person who works for an insurance company and whose job is to calculate how much money sb should receive after they have lost sth or had sth damaged

ˈloss-leader *noun* an item that a shop/store sells at a very low price to attract customers

loss·less /ˈlɒsləs; *NAmE* ˈlɔːs-; ˈlɑːs-/ *adj.* (*technical*) involving no loss of data or electrical energy OPP **lossy**

ˈloss-making *adj.* (of a company or business) not making a profit; losing money

lossy /ˈlɒsi; *NAmE* ˈlɔːsi; ˈlɑːsi/ *adj.* (*technical*) involving the loss of data or electrical energy OPP **lossless**

lost 0-w /lɒst; *NAmE* lɔːst; lɑːst/ *adj.*
1 0-w unable to find your way; not knowing where you are: *We always* **get lost** *in London.* ◇ *We're completely lost.* **2** 0-w that cannot be found or brought back: *I'm still looking for that lost file.* ◇ *Your cheque must have* **got lost** *in the post.* **3** 0-w [usually before noun] that cannot be obtained; that cannot be found or created again: *The strike cost them thousands of pounds in* **lost business**. ◇ *She's trying to recapture her* **lost youth**. ◇ *He regretted the* **lost** (= wasted) **opportunity** *to apologize to her.* **4** 0-w [not before noun] unable to deal successfully with a particular situation: *We would* **be lost without** *your help.* ◇ *I felt so lost after my mother died.* ◇ *He's a* **lost soul** (= a person who does not seem to know what to do, and seems unhappy). **5** 0-w [not before noun] unable to understand sth because it is too complicated: *They spoke so quickly I just got lost.* ◇ *Hang on a minute—I'm lost.* ➲ see also LOSE *v.*
IDM **ˌall is not ˈlost** there is still some hope of making a bad

situation better **be lost for 'words** to be so surprised, confused, etc. that you do not know what to say **be 'lost in sth** to be giving all your attention to sth so that you do not notice what is happening around you: *to be lost in thought* **be 'lost on sb** to be not understood or noticed by sb: *His jokes were completely lost on most of the students.* **be lost to the 'world** to be giving all your attention to sth so that you do not notice what is happening around you **get 'lost** (*informal*) a rude way of telling sb to go away, or of refusing sth **give sb up for 'lost** (*formal*) to stop expecting to find sb alive **make up for lost 'time** to do sth quickly or very often because you wish you had started doing it sooner ➲ more at LOVE *n.*

ˌlost and 'found (*NAmE*) (*BrE* **ˌlost 'property**) *noun* [U] the place where items that have been found are kept until they are collected

ˌlost 'cause *noun* something that has failed or that cannot succeed

ˌlost 'property *noun* [U] (*BrE*) **1** items that have been found in public places and are waiting to be collected by the people who lost them: *a lost-property office* **2** (*NAmE* **ˌlost and 'found**) the place where items that have been found are kept until they are collected

lot 🔑 /lɒt; *NAmE* lɑːt/ *pron., det., adv., noun*

■ ***pron.*** 🔑 **a lot** (also *informal* **lots**) **~ (to do)** a large number or amount: *'How many do you need?' 'A lot.'* ◇ *Have some more cake. There's lots left.* ◇ *She still has* ***an awful lot*** (= a very large amount) *to learn.* ◇ *He has invited nearly a hundred people but a lot aren't able to come.* ➲ note at MANY, MUCH

■ ***det.*** 🔑 **a lot of** (also *informal* **lots of**) a large number or amount of sb/sth: *What a lot of presents!* ◇ *A lot of people are coming to the meeting.* ◇ *black coffee with lots of sugar* ◇ *I saw a lot of her* (= I saw her often) *last summer.* ➲ note at MANY, MUCH

■ ***adv.*** (*informal*) **1** 🔑 **a lot** (also *informal* **lots**) used with adjectives and adverbs to mean 'much': *I'm feeling a lot better today.* ◇ *I eat lots less than I used to.* **2** 🔑 **a lot** used with verbs to mean 'a great amount': *I care a lot about you.* ◇ *Thanks a lot for your help.* ◇ *I play tennis quite a lot* (= often) *in the summer.* ➲ note at MUCH

■ ***noun***

▸ WHOLE AMOUNT/NUMBER **1 the lot, the whole lot** [sing. + sing./pl. v.] (*informal*) the whole number or amount of people or things: *He's bought a new PC, colour printer, scanner—the lot.* ◇ *Get out of my house,* ***the lot of you!*** ◇ ***That's the lot!*** (= that includes everything) ◇ ***That's your lot!*** (= that's all you're getting)

▸ GROUP/SET **2** [C+sing./pl. v.] (*especially BrE*) a group or set of people or things: *The first lot of visitors has/have arrived.* ◇ *I have several lots of essays to mark this weekend.* ◇ (*informal*) *What do* ***you lot*** *want?*

▸ ITEMS TO BE SOLD **3** [C] an item or a number of items to be sold, especially at an AUCTION: *Lot 46: six chairs*

▸ AREA OF LAND **4** [C] an area of land used for a particular purpose: *a parking lot* ◇ *a vacant lot* (= one available to be built on or used for sth) ◇ (*especially NAmE*) *We're going to build a house on this lot.* ➲ SYNONYMS at LAND

▸ LUCK/SITUATION **5** [sing.] a person's luck or situation in life SYN **destiny**: *She was feeling dissatisfied with her lot.*

IDM **all 'over the lot** (*NAmE*) = ALL OVER THE PLACE at PLACE *n.* **a bad 'lot** (*old-fashioned, BrE*) a person who is dishonest **by 'lot** using a method of choosing sb to do sth in which each person takes a piece of paper, etc. from a container and the one whose paper has a special mark is chosen **draw/cast 'lots (for sth/to do sth)** to choose sb/sth by lot: *They drew lots for the right to go first.* **fall to sb's 'lot (to do sth)** (*formal*) to become sb's task or responsibility **throw in your 'lot with sb** to decide to join sb and share their successes and problems ➲ more at BEST *n.*

ˌlo-'tech *adj.* = LOW-TECH

loth = LOATH

Loth·ario /ləˈθeəriəʊ; ləˈθɑːriəʊ; *NAmE* ləˈθerioʊ; ləˈθɑːrioʊ/ *noun* (*pl.* **-os**) a man who has sex with a lot of women: *He has a reputation as the office Lothario.* ORIGIN From the name of a character in an 18th century play by Nicholas Rowe.

lo·tion /ˈləʊʃn; *NAmE* ˈloʊʃn/ *noun* [C, U] a liquid used for cleaning, protecting or treating the skin: (*a*) ***body/hand lotion*** ◇ *suntan lotion*

lotta /ˈlɒtə; *NAmE* ˈlɑːtə/ (also **lotsa** /ˈlɒtsə; *NAmE* ˈlɑːtsə/) (*informal, non-standard*) a written form of 'lot of' or 'lots of' that shows how it sounds in informal speech: *We're gonna have a lotta fun.* HELP You should not write this form unless you are copying somebody's speech.

lot·tery /ˈlɒtəri; *NAmE* ˈlɑːt-/ *noun* (*pl.* **-ies**) **1** [C] a way of raising money for a government, charity, etc. by selling tickets that have different numbers on them that people have chosen. Numbers are then chosen by chance and the people who have those numbers on their tickets win prizes: *the* ***national/state lottery*** ◇ *a lottery ticket* ➲ compare DRAW, RAFFLE **2** [sing.] (often *disapproving*) a situation whose success or result is based on luck rather than on effort or careful organization SYN **gamble**: *Some people think that marriage is a lottery.* ➲ see also POSTCODE LOTTERY

lotto /ˈlɒtəʊ; *NAmE* ˈlɑːtoʊ/ *noun* (*pl.* **lottos**) **1** [U] a game of chance similar to BINGO but with the numbers drawn from a container by the players instead of being called out **2** [C] a lottery

lotus /ˈləʊtəs; *NAmE* ˈloʊ-/ *noun* **1** a tropical plant with white or pink flowers that grows on the surface of lakes in Africa and Asia: *a lotus flower* ➲ VISUAL VOCAB page V9 **2** a picture in the shape of the lotus plant, used in art and ARCHITECTURE, especially in ancient Egypt **3** (in ancient Greek stories) a fruit that is supposed to make you feel happy and relaxed when you have eaten it, as if in a dream

'lotus position *noun* [sing.] a way of sitting with your legs crossed, used especially when people MEDITATE or do YOGA

louche /luːʃ/ *adj.* (*especially BrE, formal*) not socially acceptable, but often still attractive despite this

loud 🔑 /laʊd/ *adj., adv.*

■ ***adj.*** (**loud·er, loud·est**) **1** 🔑 making a lot of noise: *loud laughter* ◇ *a* ***deafeningly loud*** *bang* ◇ *She spoke in a very loud voice.* ◇ *That music's too loud—please turn it down.* **2** 🔑 (of a person or their behaviour) talking very loudly, too much and in a way that is annoying **3** (of colours, patterns, etc.) too bright and lacking good taste SYN **gaudy, garish** ▸ **loud·ly** 🔑 *adv.*: *She screamed as loudly as she could.* **loud·ness** *noun* [U]

■ ***adv.*** 🔑 (**loud·er, loud·est**) (*informal*) in a way that makes a lot of noise or can be easily heard SYN **loudly**: *Do you have to play that music so loud?* ◇ *You'll have to speak louder—I can't hear you.*

IDM **ˌloud and 'clear** in a way that is very easy to understand: *The message is coming through loud and clear.* **ˌout 'loud** 🔑 in a voice that can be heard by other people: *I laughed out loud.* ◇ *Please read the letter out loud.* ➲ compare ALOUD ➲ more at ACTION, CRY *v.*, THINK *v.*

Which Word?

loud / loudly / aloud

- **Loudly** is the usual adverb from the adjective **loud**: *The audience laughed loudly at the joke.*
- **Loud** is very common as an adverb in informal language. It is nearly always used in phrases such as **loud enough**, **as loud as** or with *too, very, so*, etc: *Don't play your music too loud.* ◇ *I shouted as loud as I could.*
- **Louder** is also used in informal styles to mean 'more loudly': *Can you speak louder?*
- **Out loud** is a common adverb meaning 'so that people can hear': *Can you read the letter out loud?* ◇ *He laughed out loud at his own joke.* **Aloud** has the same meaning but is fairly formal. It can also mean 'in a loud voice'.

L

loud·hail·er /ˌlaʊd'heɪlə(r)/ (*BrE*) (*NAmE* **bull·horn**) *noun* an electronic device, shaped like a horn, with a MICROPHONE at one end, that you speak into in order to make your voice louder so that it can be heard at a distance ➲ compare MEGAPHONE

loud·mouth /'laʊdmaʊθ/ *noun* (*informal*) a person who is annoying because they talk too loudly or too much in an offensive or stupid way ▸ **'loud-mouthed** *adj.*

loud·speak·er /ˌlaʊd'spiːkə(r)/ *noun* **1** a piece of equipment that changes electrical signals into sound, used in public places for announcing things, playing music, etc: *Their names were called* ***over the loudspeaker.*** ➲ see also PUBLIC ADDRESS SYSTEM, TANNOY **2** (*old-fashioned*) the part of a radio or piece of musical equipment that the sound comes out of SYN **speaker**

lough /lɒk; lɒx; *NAmE* lɑːk; lɑːx/ *noun* (in Ireland) a lake or a long strip of sea that is almost surrounded by land: *Lough Corrib* ➲ see also LOCH

lounge /laʊndʒ/ *noun, verb*

■ ***noun*** **1** a room for waiting in at an airport, etc: *the departure lounge* **2** a public room in a hotel, club, etc. for waiting or relaxing in: *the television lounge* **3** (*BrE*) a room in a private house for sitting and relaxing in SYN **living room, sitting room** ➲ see also SUN LOUNGE **4** (*BrE*) = LOUNGE BAR

■ ***verb*** [I] (+ **adv./prep.**) to stand, sit or lie in a lazy way SYN **laze around**: *Several students were lounging around, reading newspapers.*

L

'lounge bar (also **sal·oon**) (both *BrE*) *noun* a bar in a pub, hotel, etc. which is more comfortable than the other bars and where the drinks are usually more expensive ➲ compare PUBLIC BAR

'lounge lizard *noun* (*old-fashioned, informal*) a person who does no work and who likes to be with rich, fashionable people

loun·ger /'laʊndʒə(r)/ *noun* (*especially BrE*) a long comfortable chair that supports your legs, used for sitting or lying on, especially outdoors ➲ compare SUNLOUNGER

'lounge suit *noun* (*BrE*) a man's suit of matching jacket and trousers/pants, worn especially in offices and on fairly formal occasions

lour *verb* = LOWER²

louse /laʊs/ *noun, verb*

■ ***noun*** **1** (*pl.* **lice** /laɪs/) a small insect that lives on the bodies of humans and animals: *head lice* ➲ see also WOODLOUSE **2** (*pl.* louses) (*informal, disapproving*) a very unpleasant person

■ ***verb***

PHR V **ˌlouse sth↔'up** (*informal*) to spoil sth or do it very badly

lousy /'laʊzi/ *adj.* (**lous·ier, lousi·est**) (*informal*) **1** very bad SYN **awful, terrible**: *What lousy weather!* ◇ *She felt lousy* (= ill). **2** [only before noun] used to show that you feel annoyed or insulted because you do not think that sth is worth very much: *All she bought me was this lousy T-shirt.* **3 ~ with sth/sb** (*NAmE*) having too much of sth or too many people: *This place is lousy with tourists in August.*

lout /laʊt/ *noun* (*BrE*) a man or boy who behaves in a rude and aggressive way SYN **yob** ➲ see also LAGER LOUT, LITTER LOUT ▸ **lout·ish** *adj.*: *loutish behaviour*

louvre (*especially US* **lou·ver**) /'luːvə(r)/ *noun* one of a set of narrow strips of wood, plastic, etc. in a door or a window that are designed to let air and some light in, but to keep out strong light or rain; a door or a window that has these strips across it ▸ **louvred** (*especially US* **lou·vered**) *adj.*

lov·able (also **love·able**) /'lʌvəbl/ *adj.* having qualities that people find attractive and easy to love, often despite any faults SYN **endearing**: *a lovable child* ◇ *a lovable rogue*

love 🔑 /lʌv/ *noun, verb*

■ ***noun***

▸ AFFECTION **1** 🔑 [U] a strong feeling of deep affection for sb/sth, especially a member of your family or a friend: *a mother's love for her children* ◇ *love of your country* ◇ *He seems incapable of love.*

▸ ROMANTIC **2** 🔑 [U] a strong feeling of affection for sb that you are sexually attracted to: *a* ***love song/story*** ◇ *We're* ***in love!*** ◇ *She was* ***in love with him.*** ◇ *They* ***fell in love*** *with each other.* ◇ *It was* ***love at first sight*** (= they were attracted to each other the first time they met). ◇ *They're* ***madly in love.*** ◇ *Their love grew with the years.* ➲ COLLOCATIONS at MARRIAGE

▸ ENJOYMENT **3** 🔑 [U, sing.] the strong feeling of enjoyment that sth gives you: *a* ***love of*** *learning* ◇ *He's* ***in love with*** *his work.* ◇ *I* ***fell in love with*** *the house.*

▸ SB/STH YOU LIKE **4** 🔑 [C] a person, a thing or an activity that you like very much: *Take care, my love.* ◇ *He was* ***the love of my life*** (= the person I loved most). ◇ *I like most sports but tennis is my* ***first love.***

▸ FRIENDLY NAME **5** [C] (*BrE, informal*) a word used as a friendly way of addressing sb: *Can I help you, love?* ➲ compare DUCK

▸ IN TENNIS **6** [U] a score of zero (points or games): *40–love!* ◇ *She won the first set* ***six–love/six games to love.***

Synonyms

love

like • be fond of sb • adore • be devoted to sb • care for sb • dote on sb

These words all mean to have feelings of love or affection for sb.

love to have strong feelings of affection for sb: *I love you.*

like to find sb pleasant and enjoy being with them: *She's nice. I like her.*

be fond of sb to feel affection for sb, especially sb you have known for a long time: *I've always been very fond of your mother.*

adore to love sb very much: *It's obvious that she adores him.*

be devoted to sb to love sb very much and be loyal to them: *They are devoted to their children.*

care for sb to love sb, especially in a way that is based on strong affection or a feeling of wanting to protect them, rather than sex: *He cared for her more than she realized.* NOTE **Care for sb** is often used when sb has not told anyone about their feelings or is just starting to be aware of them. It is also used when sb wishes that sb loved them, or doubts that sb does: *If he really cared for you, he wouldn't behave like that.*

dote on sb to feel and show great love for sb, ignoring their faults: *He dotes on his children.*

PATTERNS

- to **really** love/like/adore/care for/dote on sb
- to be **really/genuinely** fond of/devoted to sb
- to love/like/care for sb **very much**

IDM **(just) for 'love | (just) for the 'love of sth** without receiving payment or any other reward: *They're all volunteers, working for the love of it.* **for the love of 'God** (*old-fashioned, informal*) used when you are expressing anger and the fact that you are impatient: *For the love of God, tell me what he said!* **give/send my love to sb** (*informal*) used to send good wishes to sb: *Give my love to Mary when you see her.* ◇ *Bob sends his love.* **'love from | lots of 'love (from)** (*informal*) used at the end of a letter to a friend or to sb you love, followed by your name: *Lots of love, Jenny* **love is 'blind** (*saying*) when you love sb, you cannot see their faults **make 'love (to sb)** to have sex: *It was the first time they had made love.* **not for love or/nor 'money** if you say you cannot do sth **for love nor money**, you mean it is completely impossible to do it: *We couldn't find a taxi for love nor money.* **there's little/no 'love lost between A and B** they do not like each other: *There's no love lost between her and her in-laws.* ➲ more at CUPBOARD, FAIR *adj.*, HEAD *n.*, LABOUR *n.*

■ *verb*

▸ FEEL AFFECTION **1** ~ **sb/sth** (not used in the progressive tenses) to have very strong feelings of affection for sb: *I love you.* ◇ *If you love each other, why not get married?* ◇ *Her much-loved brother lay dying of AIDS.* ◇ *He had become a well-loved member of staff.* ◇ *Relatives need time to grieve over* **loved ones** *they have lost.* ◇ *to love your country*

▸ LIKE/ENJOY **2** to like or enjoy sth very much SYN **adore**: ~ **sth** *I really love summer evenings.* ◇ ***I just love it when*** *you bring me presents!* ◇ *He* **loved the way** *she smiled.* ◇ *I* **love it** *in Spain* (= I like the life there). ◇ *It was one of his best-loved songs.* ◇ (*ironic*) ***You're going to love this.*** *They've changed their minds again.* ◇ ~ **doing sth** (especially in *BrE*) *My dad loves going to football games.* ◇ ~ **to do sth** (*especially NAmE*) *I love to go out dancing.* ◇ ~ **sb/sth to do sth** *He loved her to sing to him.* ➲ SYNONYMS at LIKE **3** **would love** used to say that you would very much like sth: ~ **to do sth** *Come on Rory, the kids would love to hear you sing.* ◇ *I haven't been to Brazil, but I'd love to go.* ◇ ~ **sb/sth to do sth** *I'd love her to come and live with us.* ◇ ~ **sth** *'Cigarette?' 'I'd love one, but I've just given up.'*

IDM ˌ**love you and ˈleave you** (*informal, humorous*) used to say that you must go, although you would like to stay longer: *Well, time to love you and leave you.*

ˈ**love affair** *noun* **1** a romantic and/or sexual relationship between two people who are in love and not married to each other **2** great enthusiasm for sth SYN **passion**: *the English love affair with gardening*

love·bird /ˈlʌvbɜːd; *NAmE* -bɜːrd/ *noun* **1** [C] a small African PARROT (= a bird with brightly coloured feathers) **2 lovebirds** [pl.] (*humorous*) two people who love each other very much and show this in their behaviour

ˈ**love bite** (*BrE*) (*NAmE* **hickey**) *noun* a red mark on the skin that is caused by sb biting or sucking their partner's skin when they are kissing

ˈ**love child** *noun* (used especially in newspapers, etc.) a child born to parents who are not married to each other

ˌ**loved-ˈup** *adj.* (*informal*) **1** happy and excited because of the effects of the illegal drug ECSTASY **2** full of romantic love for sb

ˈ**love handles** *noun* [pl.] (*informal, humorous*) extra fat on a person's waist

ˌ**love-ˈhate relationship** *noun* [usually sing.] a relationship in which your feelings for sb/sth are a mixture of love and hatred

ˈ**love-in** *noun* (*informal*) **1** (*old-fashioned*) a party at which people freely show their affection and sexual attraction for each other, associated with HIPPIES in the 1960s **2** (*disapproving*) an occasion when people are being especially pleasant to each other, in a way that you believe is not sincere

ˈ**love interest** *noun* [C, usually sing.] a character in a film/movie or story who has a romantic role, often as the main character's lover

love·less /ˈlʌvləs/ *adj.* without love: *a loveless marriage*

ˈ**love letter** *noun* a letter that you write to sb telling them that you love them

ˈ**love life** *noun* the part of your life that involves your romantic and sexual relationships

love·li·ness /ˈlʌvlinəs/ *noun* [U] (*formal*) the state of being very attractive SYN **beauty**

love·lorn /ˈlʌvlɔːn; *NAmE* -lɔːrn/ *adj.* (*literary*) unhappy because the person you love does not love you

love·ly /ˈlʌvli/ *adj., noun*

■ *adj.* (**love·lier, love·li·est**) HELP You can also use **more lovely** and **most lovely**. (*especially BrE*) **1** beautiful; attractive: *lovely countryside/eyes/flowers* ◇ *She* **looked** *particularly* **lovely** *that night.* ◇ *He has a lovely voice.* ➲ SYNONYMS at BEAUTIFUL **2** (*informal*) very enjoyable and pleasant; wonderful: *'Can I get you anything?' 'A cup of tea would be lovely.'* ◇ *What a lovely surprise!* ◇ *How lovely to see you!* ◇ *Isn't it a lovely day?* ◇ *We've had a lovely time.* ◇ *It's a lovely old farm.* ◇ *It's been lovely having you here.* ◇ (*ironic*) *You've got yourself into a lovely mess, haven't you?* ➲ SYNONYMS at WONDERFUL **3** (*informal*) (of a person) very kind, generous and friendly: *Her mother was a lovely woman.* HELP **Very lovely** is not very common and is only used about the physical appearance of a person or thing.

IDM **lovely and ˈwarm, ˈcold, ˈquiet, etc.** (*BrE, informal*) used when you are emphasizing that sth is good because of the quality mentioned: *It's lovely and warm in here.*

■ *noun* (*pl.* -ies) (*old-fashioned*) a beautiful woman

love·mak·ing /ˈlʌvmeɪkɪŋ/ *noun* [U] sexual activity between two lovers, especially the act of having sex

ˈ**love match** *noun* a marriage of two people who are in love with each other

ˈ**love nest** *noun* [usually sing.] (*informal*) a house or an apartment where two people who are not married but are having a sexual relationship can meet

lover /ˈlʌvə(r)/ *noun*

1 a partner in a sexual relationship outside marriage: *He denied that he was her lover.* ◇ *We were lovers for several years.* ◇ *The park was full of young lovers holding hands.* **2** (often in compounds) a person who likes or enjoys a particular thing: *a lover of music* ◇ *an art-lover* ◇ *a nature-lover*

ˈ**love seat** *noun* (*NAmE*) a comfortable seat with a back and arms, for two people to sit on ➲ VISUAL VOCAB page V18

love·sick /ˈlʌvsɪk/ *adj.* unable to think clearly or behave in a sensible way because you are in love with sb, especially sb who is not in love with you

ˈ**love triangle** *noun* [usually sing.] a situation that involves three people, each of whom loves at least one of the others, for example a married woman, her husband, and another man that she loves

lovey (also **luvvy**) /ˈlʌvi/ *noun* (*BrE, informal*) used as a friendly way of addressing sb: *Ruth, lovey, are you there?*

lovey-dovey /ˌlʌvi ˈdʌvi/ *adj.* (*informal*) expressing romantic love in a way that is slightly silly

lov·ing /ˈlʌvɪŋ/ *adj.* **1** feeling or showing love and affection for sb/sth SYN **affectionate, tender**: *a warm and loving family* ◇ *She chose the present with loving care.* **2 -loving** (in adjectives) enjoying the object or activity mentioned: *fun-loving young people* ▸ **lov·ing·ly** *adv.*: *He gazed lovingly at his children.* ◇ *The house has been lovingly restored.*

ˈ**loving cup** *noun* (*old use*) a large cup with two handles, which guests pass around and drink from

low /ləʊ; *NAmE* loʊ/ *adj., adv., noun, verb*

■ *adj.* (**lower, low·est**)

▸ NOT HIGH/TALL **1** not high or tall; not far above the ground: *a low wall/building/table* ◇ *a low range of hills* ◇ *low clouds* ◇ *flying at low altitude* ◇ *The sun was low in the sky.* OPP **high**

▸ NEAR BOTTOM **2** at or near the bottom of sth: *low back pain* ◇ *the lower slopes of the mountain* ◇ *temperatures in the low 20s* (= no higher than 21–23°) OPP **high**

▸ CLOTHING **3** not high at the neck: *a dress with a low neckline* ➲ see also LOW-CUT

▸ LEVEL/VALUE **4** (also **low-**) (often in compounds) below the usual or average amount, level or value: *low prices* ◇ *low-income families* ◇ *a low-cost airline* ◇ *the lowest temperature ever recorded* ◇ *a low level of unemployment* ◇ *Yogurt is usually very low in fat.* ◇ *low-fat yogurt* ◇ *low-tar cigarettes* OPP **high** **5** having a reduced amount or not enough of sth: *The reservoir was low after the long drought.* ◇ *Our supplies are* ***running low*** (= we only have a little left). ◇ *They were* ***low on*** *fuel.*

▸ SOUND **6** not high; not loud: *The cello is lower than the violin.* ◇ *They were speaking in low voices.* OPP **high**

▸ STANDARD **7** below the usual or expected standard: *students with low marks/grades in their exams* ◇ *a low standard of living* OPP **high**

▸ STATUS **8** below other people or things in importance or status: *low forms of life* (= creatures with a very simple structure) ◇ *jobs with low status* ◇ *Training was given a very low priority.* ◇ *the* ***lower classes*** *of society* OPP **high**

L

▸ OPINION **9** [usually before noun] not very good SYN **poor**: *She has a very low opinion of her own abilities.* OPP **high**
▸ DEPRESSED **10** weak or depressed; with very little energy SYN **down**: *I'm feeling really low.* ◇ *They were in low spirits.*
▸ NOT HONEST **11** (of a person) not honest SYN **disreputable**: *He mixes with some pretty low types.*
▸ LIGHT **12** not bright SYN **dim**: *The lights were low and romance was in the air.*
▸ IN VEHICLE **13** if a vehicle is in **low gear**, it travels at a slower speed in relation to the speed of the engine
▸ PHONETICS **14** (*phonetics*) = OPEN

IDM **at a low 'ebb** in a poor state; worse than usual: *Morale among teachers is at a low ebb.* **be brought 'low** (*old-fashioned*) to lose your wealth or your high position in society **lay sb 'low** if sb is **laid low** by/with an injury or illness, they feel very weak and are unable to do much **the ˌlowest of the 'low** people who are not respected at all because they are dishonest, immoral or not at all important ➲ more at PROFILE *n.*

■ *adv.* (lower, low·est)
▸ NOT HIGH **1** in or into a low position, not far above the ground: *to crouch/bend low* ◇ *a plane flying low over the town* ◇ *low-flying aircraft* ◇ *The sun sank lower towards the horizon.*
▸ NEAR BOTTOM **2** in or into a position near the bottom of sth: *a window set low in the wall* ◇ *The candles were burning low.*
▸ LEVEL **3** (especially in compounds) at a level below what is usual or expected: *low-priced goods* ◇ *a low-powered PC* ◇ *a very low-scoring game*
▸ SOUND **4** not high; not loudly: *He's singing an octave lower than the rest of us.* ◇ *Can you turn the music lower—you'll wake the baby.* IDM see HIGH *adv.*, LIE *v.*, SINK *v.*, STOOP *v.*

■ *noun*
▸ LEVEL/VALUE **1** a low level or point; a low figure: *The yen has fallen to* ***an all-time low*** *against the dollar.* ◇ *The temperature reached a record low in London last night.* ◇ *The government's popularity has hit a new low.*
▸ DIFFICULT TIME **2** a very difficult time in sb's life or career: *The break-up of her marriage marked* ***an all-time low*** *in her life.*
▸ WEATHER **3** an area of low pressure in the atmosphere: *Another low is moving in from the Atlantic.* OPP **high**

■ *verb* [I] (*literary*) when a cow **lows**, it makes a deep sound SYN **moo**

low·ball /ˈləʊbɔːl; *NAmE* ˈloʊ-/ *verb* **~ sth** (*NAmE, informal*) to deliberately make an estimate of the cost, value, etc. of sth that is too low: *He lowballed the cost of the project in order to obtain federal funding.* OPP **highball**

ˌlow-'born *adj.* (*old-fashioned* or *formal*) having parents who are members of a low social class OPP **high-born**

low·brow /ˈləʊbraʊ; *NAmE* ˈloʊ-/ *adj.* (usually *disapproving*) having no connection with or interest in serious artistic or cultural ideas OPP **highbrow** ➲ compare MIDDLEBROW

low-cal (also **lo-cal**) /ˌləʊ ˈkæl; *NAmE* ˌloʊ/ *adj.* (*informal*) (of food and drink) containing very few CALORIES

ˌLow 'Church *adj.* connected with the part of the Anglican Church that considers priests and the traditional forms and ceremonies of the Anglican Church to be less important than personal faith and worship

ˌlow-'class *adj.* **1** of poor quality **2** connected with a low social class OPP **high-class**

the 'Low Countries *noun* [pl.] the region of Europe which consists of the Netherlands, Belgium and Luxembourg (used especially in the past)

ˌlow-'cut *adj.* (of dresses etc.) with the top very low so that you can see the neck and the top of the chest

'low-down *adj.*, *noun*
■ *adj.* [only before noun] (*informal*) not fair or honest SYN **mean**: *What a dirty, low-down trick!*
■ *noun* **the low-down** [sing.] **~ on (sb/sth)** (*informal*) the true facts about sb/sth, especially those considered most important to know: *Jane gave me the low-down on the other guests at the party.*

'low-end *adj.* [usually before noun] at the cheaper end of a range of similar products

lower[1] /ˈləʊə(r); *NAmE* ˈloʊ-/ *adj.*, *verb* ➲ see also LOWER[2]
■ *adj.* [only before noun] **1** located below sth else, especially sth of the same type, or the other of a pair: *the lower deck of a ship* ◇ *His lower lip trembled.* **2** at or near the bottom of sth: *the mountain's lower slopes* **3** (of a place) located towards the coast, on low ground or towards the south of an area: *the lower reaches of the Nile* OPP **upper**
■ *verb* **1** [T] to let or make sth/sb go down: **~ sth** *He had to lower his head to get through the door.* ◇ *She lowered her newspaper and looked around.* ◇ **~ sth/sb + adv./prep.** *They lowered him down the cliff on a rope.* OPP **raise** **2** [T, I] **~ (sth)** to reduce sth or to become less in value, quality, etc: *He lowered his voice to a whisper.* ◇ *This drug is used to lower blood pressure.* ◇ *Her voice lowered as she spoke.* OPP **raise**

IDM **lower the 'bar** to set a new, lower standard of quality or performance: *In the current economic climate we may need to lower the bar on quotas.* OPP **raise the bar** ➲ compare SET THE BAR at BAR *n.* **'lower yourself (by doing sth)** (usually used in negative sentences) to behave in a way that makes other people respect you less SYN **demean**: *I wouldn't lower myself by working for him.* ➲ more at SIGHT *n.*, TEMPERATURE

lower[2] (also **lour**) /ˈlaʊə(r)/ *verb* [I] (*literary*) (of the sky or clouds) to be dark and threatening ➲ see also LOWER[1]

ˌlower 'case *noun* [U] (*technical*) (in printing and writing) small letters: *The text is all in lower case.* ◇ *lower-case letters* ➲ compare CAPITAL *adj.*, UPPER CASE

ˌlower'chamber *noun* = LOWER HOUSE

the ˌlower 'classes *noun* [pl.] (also **the ˌlower 'class** [sing.]) the groups of people who are considered to have the lowest social status and who have less money and/or power than other people in society ▶ **ˌlower 'class** *adj.*: *The new bosses were condemned as 'too lower class'.* ◇ *a lower-class accent* ➲ compare UPPER CLASS

ˌlower 'house (also **ˌlower 'chamber**) *noun* [sing.] the larger group of people who make laws in a country, usually consisting of elected representatives, such as the House of Commons in Britain or the House of Representatives in the US ➲ compare UPPER HOUSE

the ˌlower 'orders *noun* [pl.] (*old-fashioned*) people who are considered to be less important because they belong to groups with a lower social status

'lower school *noun* a school, or the classes in a school, for younger students, usually between the ages of 11 and 14 ➲ compare UPPER SCHOOL

ˌlowest ˌcommon de'nominator *noun* **1** (*NAmE* usually **ˌleast ˌcommon de'nominator**) (*mathematics*) the smallest number that the bottom numbers of a group of FRACTIONS can be divided into exactly **2** (*NAmE* also **ˌleast ˌcommon de'nominator**) (*disapproving*) something that is simple enough to seem interesting to, or to be understood by, the highest number of people in a particular group; the sort of people who are least intelligent or accept sth that is of low quality: *The school syllabus seems aimed at the lowest common denominator.*

ˌlowest ˌcommon 'multiple (*NAmE* usually **ˌleast ˌcommon 'multiple**) *noun* (*mathematics*) the smallest number that a group of numbers can be divided into exactly

ˌlow-'fat *adj.* [usually before noun] containing only a very small amount of fat

ˌlow-'grade *adj.* [usually before noun] **1** of low quality **2** (*medical*) of a less serious type: *a low-grade infection*

ˌlow-'impact *adj.* [usually before noun] **1** involving movements that do not put a lot of stress on the body: *low-impact aerobics* **2** not causing very many problems or changes, especially in the environment: *low-impact tourism*

ˌlow-ˈkey *adj.* not intended to attract a lot of attention: *Their wedding was a very low-key affair.*

low·land /ˈləʊlənd; *NAmE* ˈloʊ-/ *adj., noun*
■ ***adj.*** [only before noun] connected with an area of land that is fairly flat and not very high above sea level ➲ compare HIGHLAND
■ ***noun*** [pl., U] an area of land that is fairly flat and not very high above sea level: *the lowlands of Scotland* ◇ *Much of the region is lowland.* ➲ compare HIGHLAND

low·land·er /ˈləʊləndə(r); *NAmE* ˈloʊ-/ *noun* a person who comes from an area which is flat and low ➲ compare HIGHLANDER

ˌlow-ˈlevel *adj.* [usually before noun] **1** close to the ground: *low-level bombing attacks* **2** of low rank; involving people of junior rank: *a low-level job* ◇ *low-level negotiations* **3** not containing much of a particular substance especially RADIOACTIVITY: *low-level radioactive waste* **4** (*computing*) (of a computer language) similar to MACHINE CODE in form OPP **high-level**

ˈlow life *noun* [U] the life and behaviour of people who are outside normal society, especially criminals ▸ **ˈlow-life** *adj.*: *a low-life bar*

low·lights /ˈləʊlaɪts; *NAmE* ˈloʊl-/ *noun* [pl.] areas of hair that have been made darker than the rest, with the use of a chemical substance ➲ compare HIGHLIGHTS

lowly /ˈləʊli; *NAmE* ˈloʊli/ *adj.* (**low·lier**, **low·li·est**) (often *humorous*) low in status or importance SYN **humble, obscure**

ˌlow-ˈlying *adj.* (of land) not high, and usually fairly flat

ˌlow-ˈmaintenance *adj.* not needing much attention or effort: *a low-maintenance garden* OPP **high-maintenance**

ˌlow-ˈpaid *adj.* earning or providing very little money: *low-paid workers* ◇ *It is one of the lowest-paid jobs.*

ˌlow-ˈpitched *adj.* (of sounds) deep; low: *a low-pitched voice* OPP **high-pitched**

ˈlow point *noun* the least interesting, enjoyable or worst part of sth OPP **high point**

ˌlow ˈpressure *noun* [U] **1** the condition of air, gas or liquid that is kept in a container with little force: *Water supplies to the house are* ***at low pressure.*** **2** a condition of the air which affects the weather when the pressure is lower than average ➲ compare HIGH PRESSURE

ˌlow-ˈprofile *adj.* [only before noun] receiving or involving very little attention: *a low-profile campaign* ➲ see also PROFILE

ˌlow-ˈranking *adj.* junior; not very important: *a* ***low-ranking officer/official*** OPP **high-ranking**

ˌlow-ˈrent *adj.* (*especially NAmE*) of poor quality or low social status: *her low-rent boyfriend*

ˌlow-resoˈlution (also **lo-res, low-res** /ˌləʊ ˈrez; *NAmE* ˌloʊ/) *adj.* (of a photograph or an image on a computer or television screen) not showing a lot of clear detail: *a low-resolution scan* OPP **high-resolution**

ˈlow-rise *adj., noun*
■ ***adj.*** [only before noun] **1** (of a building) low, with only a few floors: *low-rise housing* ➲ compare HIGH-RISE **2** (of a pair of jeans, etc.) cut so that the top is much lower than waist-level
■ ***noun*** a low buuilding with only a few floors

ˌlow-ˈrisk *adj.* [usually before noun] involving only a small amount of danger and little risk of injury, death, damage, etc. SYN **safe**: *a low-risk investment* ◇ *low-risk patients* (= who are very unlikely to get a particular illness) OPP **high-risk**

ˈlow season (also **ˈoff season**) *noun* [U, sing.] (*especially BrE*) the time of year when a hotel or tourist area receives fewest visitors OPP **high season**

ˌlow ˈslung *adj.* very low and close to the ground

ˌlow-ˈtech (also **ˌlo-ˈtech**) *adj.* (*informal*) not involving the most modern technology or methods OPP **high-tech**

ˌlow ˈtide (also **ˌlow ˈwater**) *noun* [U, C] the time when the sea is at its lowest level; the sea at this time: *The island can only be reached* ***at low tide.*** OPP **high tide**

ˌlow-ˈwater mark *noun* a line or mark showing the lowest point that the sea reaches at low tide OPP **high-water mark**

lox /lɒks; *NAmE* lɑːks/ *noun* [U] (*NAmE*) smoked SALMON (= a type of fish)

loyal 🔑 /ˈlɔɪəl/ *adj.*
~ **(to sb/sth)** remaining faithful to sb/sth and supporting them or it SYN **true**: *a* ***loyal friend/supporter*** ◇ *She has always* ***remained loyal to*** *her political principles.* OPP **disloyal** ▸ **loy·al·ly** /ˈlɔɪəli/ *adv.*

loyal·ist /ˈlɔɪəlɪst/ *noun* **1** a person who is loyal to the ruler or government, or to a political party, especially during a time of change **2 Loyalist** a person who supports the union between Great Britain and Northern Ireland ➲ compare REPUBLICAN

loy·alty /ˈlɔɪəlti/ *noun* (*pl.* **-ies**) **1** [U] ~ **(to/towards sb/sth)** the quality of being faithful in your support of sb/sth: *They swore their loyalty to the king.* ◇ *Can I count on your loyalty?* **2** [C, usually pl.] a strong feeling that you want to be loyal to sb/sth: *a case of* ***divided loyalties*** (= with strong feelings of support for two different causes, people, etc.)

ˈloyalty card *noun* (*BrE*) a card given to customers by a shop/store to encourage them to shop there regularly. Each time they buy sth they collect points which will allow them to have an amount of money taken off goods they buy in the future.

loz·enge /ˈlɒzɪndʒ; *NAmE* ˈlɑːz-/ *noun* **1** (*geometry*) a figure with four sides in the shape of a diamond that has two opposite angles more than 90° and the other two less than 90° **2** a small sweet/candy, often in a lozenge shape, especially one that contains medicine and that you dissolve in your mouth: ***throat/cough lozenges***

LP /ˌel ˈpiː/ *noun* the abbreviation for 'long-playing record' (a record that plays for about 25 minutes each side and turns 33 times per minute)

LPG /ˌel piː ˈdʒiː/ *noun* [U] the abbreviation for 'liquefied petroleum gas' (a fuel which is a mixture of gases kept in a liquid form by the pressure in a container)

ˈL-plate *noun* (in Britain and some other countries) a white sign with a large red letter L on it, that you put on a car when you are learning to drive

LPN /ˌel piː ˈen/ *abbr.* (in the US) licensed practical nurse

LSAT /ˌel es eɪ ˈtiː/ *abbr.* Law School Admission Test (a test taken by students who want to study law in the US)

LSD /ˌel es ˈdiː/ (also *slang* **acid**) *noun* [U] a powerful illegal drug that affects people's minds and makes them see and hear things that are not really there

Lt (*BrE*) (*NAmE* **Lt.**) *abbr.* (in writing) LIEUTENANT: *Lt (Helen) Brown*

Ltd *abbr.* Limited (used after the name of a British company or business): *Pearce and Co. Ltd*

lu·bri·cant /ˈluːbrɪkənt/ (also *informal* **lube** /luːb/) *noun* [U, C] a substance, for example oil, that you put on surfaces or parts of a machine so that they move easily and smoothly

lu·bri·cate /ˈluːbrɪkeɪt/ *verb* ~ **sth** to put a lubricant on sth such as the parts of a machine, to help them move smoothly SYN **grease, oil** ▸ **lu·bri·ca·tion** /ˌluːbrɪˈkeɪʃn/ *noun* [U]

lu·bri·cious /luːˈbrɪʃəs/ *adj.* (*formal*) showing a great interest in sex in a way that is considered unpleasant or unacceptable SYN **lewd**

lucid /ˈluːsɪd/ *adj.* **1** clearly expressed; easy to understand SYN **clear**: *a lucid style/explanation* **2** able to think clearly, especially during or after a period of illness or confusion: *In a rare lucid moment, she looked at me and smiled.* ▸ **lu·cid·ity** /luːˈsɪdəti/ *noun* [U] **lu·cid·ly** *adv.*

Lu·ci·fer /ˈluːsɪfə(r)/ *noun* [sing.] the DEVIL SYN **Satan**

luck 🔑 /lʌk/ *noun, verb*
■ ***noun*** [U] **1** 🔑 good things that happen to you by chance, not because of your own efforts or abilities: ***With (any)***

luck, we'll be home before dark. ◊ (*BrE*) ***With a bit of luck****, we'll finish on time.* ◊ *So far I have had no luck with finding a job.* ◊ *I* ***could hardly believe my luck*** *when he said yes.* ◊ *It was* ***a stroke of luck*** *that we found you.* ◊ ***By sheer luck*** *nobody was hurt in the explosion.* ◊ *We* ***wish her luck*** *in her new career.* ◊ *You're* ***in luck*** (= lucky) *—there's one ticket left.* ◊ *You're* ***out of luck****. She's not here.* ◊ *What a piece of luck!* ➲ see also BEGINNER'S LUCK **2** chance; the force that causes good or bad things to happen to people **SYN fortune**: *to have* ***good/bad luck*** ➲ see also HARD-LUCK STORY

IDM any 'luck? (*informal*) used to ask sb if they have been successful with sth: *'Any luck?' 'No, they're all too busy to help.'* **as luck would 'have it** in the way that chance decides what will happen: *As luck would have it, the train was late.* **bad, hard, etc. luck (on sb)** used to express sympathy for sb: *Bad luck, Helen, you played very well.* ◊ *It's hard luck on him that he wasn't chosen.* **be down on your 'luck** (*informal*) to have no money because of a period of bad luck **the best of 'luck (with sth) | good 'luck (with sth)** (*informal*) used to wish sb success with sth: *The best of luck with your exams.* ◊ *Good luck! I hope it goes well.* **ˌbetter luck 'next time** (*informal*) used to encourage sb who has not been successful at sth **for 'luck 1** because you believe it will bring you good luck, or because this is a traditional belief: *Take something blue. It's for luck.* **2** (*informal*) for no particular reason: *I hit him once more for luck.* **good 'luck to sb** (*informal*) used to say that you do not mind what sb does as it does not affect you, but you hope they will be successful: *It's not something I would care to try myself but if she wants to, good luck to her.* **just my/sb's 'luck** (*informal*) used to show you are not surprised sth bad has happened to you, because you are not often lucky: *Just my luck to arrive after they had left.* **your/sb's 'luck is in** used to say that sb has been lucky or successful **the luck of the 'draw** the fact that chance decides sth, in a way that you cannot control **no such 'luck** used to show disappointment that sth you were hoping for did not happen ➲ more at HARD *adj.*, POT *n.*, PUSH *v.*, TOUGH *adj.*, TRY *v.*, WORSE *adj.*

■ ***verb***

PHR V ˌluck 'out (*NAmE, informal*) to be lucky: *I guess I really lucked out when I met her.*

luck·less /ˈlʌkləs/ *adj.* having bad luck **SYN unlucky**: *the luckless victim of the attack*

lucky /ˈlʌki/ *adj.* (**luck·ier, lucki·est**)
1 having good luck **SYN fortunate**: **~ (to do sth)** *His friend was killed and he knows he is lucky to be alive.* ◊ *She was lucky enough to be chosen for the team.* ◊ **~ (that...)** *You were lucky (that) you spotted the danger in time.* ◊ *You can* ***think yourself lucky*** *you didn't get mugged.* ◊ *She* ***counted herself lucky*** *that she still had a job.* ◊ *Mark is* ***one of the lucky ones****—he at least has somewhere to sleep.* ◊ *the lucky winners* **2** **~ (for sb) (that...)** being the result of good luck: ***It was lucky for us that*** *we were able to go.* ◊ *That was the luckiest escape of my life.* ◊ *a lucky guess* **3** bringing good luck: *a lucky charm* ▶ **luck·ily** /ˈlʌkɪli/ *adv.*: **~ (for sb)** *Luckily for us, the train was late.* ◊ *Luckily, I am a good swimmer.*

IDM lucky 'you, 'me, etc. (*informal*) used to show that you think sb is lucky to have sth, be able to do sth, etc.: *'I'm off to Paris.' 'Lucky you!'* **ˌyou'll be 'lucky** (*informal*) used to tell sb that sth that they are expecting probably will not happen: *'I was hoping to get a ticket for Saturday.' 'You'll be lucky.'* **ˌyou, etc. should be so 'lucky** (*informal*) used to tell sb that they will probably not get what they are hoping for, and may not deserve it ➲ more at STRIKE *v.*, THANK, THIRD

ˌlucky 'dip (*BrE*) (*NAmE* **'grab bag**) *noun* [usually sing.] a game in which people choose a present from a container of presents without being able to see what it is going to be

lu·cra·tive /ˈluːkrətɪv/ *adj.* producing a large amount of money; making a large profit: ***a lucrative business/contract/market*** ➲ SYNONYMS at SUCCESSFUL ▶ **lu·cra·tive·ly** *adv.*

Synonyms

luck

chance • coincidence • accident • fate • destiny

These are all words for things that happen or the force that causes them to happen.

luck the force that causes good or bad things to happen to people: *This ring has always brought me good luck.*

chance the way that some things happen without any cause that you can see or understand: *The results could simply be due to chance.*

coincidence the fact of two things happening at the same time by chance, in a surprising way: *They met through a series of strange coincidences.*

accident something that happens unexpectedly and is not planned in advance: *Their early arrival was just an accident.*

fate the power that is believed to control everything that happens and that cannot be stopped or changed: *Fate decreed that she would never reach America.*

destiny the power that is believed to control events: *I believe there's some force guiding us—call it God, destiny or fate.*

FATE OR DESTINY?

Fate can be kind, but this is an unexpected gift; just as often, **fate** is cruel and makes people feel helpless. **Destiny** is more likely to give people a sense of power: people who have *a strong sense of destiny* usually believe that they are meant to be great or do great things.

PATTERNS

- **by** ...luck/chance/coincidence/accident
- **It's no** coincidence/accident **that...**
- **pure/sheer** luck/chance/coincidence/accident
- **to believe in** luck/coincidences/fate/destiny

lucre /ˈluːkə(r)/ *noun* [U] (*disapproving*) money, especially when it has been obtained in a way that is dishonest or immoral: *the lure of* ***filthy lucre***

Lud·dite /ˈlʌdaɪt/ *noun* (*BrE, disapproving*) a person who is opposed to new technology or working methods **ORIGIN** Named after Ned **Lud**, one of the workers who destroyed machinery in factories in the early 19th century, because they believed it would take away their jobs.

ludic /ˈluːdɪk/ *adj.* (*formal*) showing a tendency to play and have fun, make jokes, etc, especially when there is no particular reason for doing this

ludi·crous /ˈluːdɪkrəs/ *adj.* unreasonable; that you cannot take seriously **SYN absurd, ridiculous**: *a ludicrous suggestion* ◊ *It was ludicrous to think that the plan could succeed.* ▶ **ludi·crous·ly** *adv.*: *ludicrously expensive* **ludi·crous·ness** *noun* [U]

ludo /ˈluːdəʊ; *NAmE* -doʊ/ *noun* [U] (*BrE*) a simple game played with DICE and COUNTERS on a special board, similar to the American game, PARCHEESI

lug /lʌg/ *verb, noun*

■ ***verb*** (-gg-) **~ sth + adv./prep.** (*informal*) to carry or drag sth heavy with a lot of effort: *I had to lug my bags up to the fourth floor.*

■ ***noun*** **1** (*technical*) a part of sth that sticks out, used as a handle or support **2** (also **lug·hole**) (both *BrE, humorous*) an ear

luge /luːʒ; luːdʒ/ *noun* **1** [C] a type of SLEDGE (= a vehicle for sliding over ice) for racing, used by one person lying on their back with their feet pointing forwards **2 the luge** [sing.] the event or sport of racing down a track of ice on a luge ➲ VISUAL VOCAB page V39

Luger™ /ˈluːgə(r)/ *noun* a type of small gun which was made in Germany

lug·gage /ˈlʌgɪdʒ/ (*especially BrE*) (also **bag·gage** especially in *NAmE*) *noun* [U]
bags, cases, etc. that contain sb's clothes and things when they are travelling: *There's room for one more piece of*

luggage. ◇ *You stay there with the luggage while I find a cab.* ➲ COLLOCATIONS at TRAVEL ➲ note at BAGGAGE ➲ see also HAND LUGGAGE, LEFT-LUGGAGE OFFICE

ˈluggage rack *noun* **1** a shelf for luggage above the seats in a train, bus, etc. ➲ picture at RACK **2** (*especially NAmE*) = ROOF RACK

ˈluggage van (*BrE*) (*NAmE* **ˈbaggage car**) *noun* a coach/car on a train for carrying passengers' luggage

lug·hole /ˈlʌɡhəʊl; *NAmE* -hoʊl/ *noun* (*BrE, humorous*) = LUG (2)

lu·gu·bri·ous /ləˈɡuːbriəs/ *adj.* sad and serious SYN **doleful**: *a lugubrious expression* ▸ **lu·gu·bri·ous·ly** *adv.*

lug·worm /ˈlʌɡwɜːm; *NAmE* -wɜːrm/ *noun* a large WORM that lives in the sand by the sea. Lugworms are often used as BAIT on a hook to catch fish.

luke·warm /ˌluːkˈwɔːm; *NAmE* -ˈwɔːrm/ *adj.* (often *disapproving*) **1** slightly warm SYN **tepid**: *Our food was only lukewarm.* ➲ SYNONYMS at COLD **2** not interested or enthusiastic: *a lukewarm response* ◇ **~ about sb/sth** *She was lukewarm about the plan.*

lull /lʌl/ *noun, verb*

▪ ***noun*** [usually sing.] **~ (in sth)** a quiet period between times of activity: *a* ***lull in the conversation/fighting*** ◇ *Just before an attack everything would go quiet but we knew it was just* ***the lull before the storm*** (= before a time of noise or trouble).

▪ ***verb*** **1** [T] **~ sb** to make sb relaxed and calm SYN **soothe**: *The vibration of the engine* ***lulled*** *the children* ***to sleep.*** **2** [T, I] **~ (sth)** to make sth, or to become, less strong: *His father's arrival lulled the boy's anxiety.*

PHR V **ˌlull sb ˈinto sth** to make sb feel confident and relaxed, especially so that they do not expect it when sb does sth bad or dishonest: *His friendly manner* ***lulled her into a false sense of security*** (= made her feel safe with him when she should not have).

lul·laby /ˈlʌləbaɪ/ *noun* (*pl.* **-ies**) a soft gentle song sung to make a child go to sleep

lum·bago /lʌmˈbeɪɡəʊ; *NAmE* -ɡoʊ/ *noun* [U] pain in the muscles and joints of the lower back

lum·bar /ˈlʌmbə(r)/ *adj.* [only before noun] (*medical*) relating to the lower part of the back

ˌlumbar ˈpuncture (*BrE*) (*NAmE* **ˈspinal tap**) *noun* the removal of liquid from the lower part of the SPINE with a hollow needle

lum·ber /ˈlʌmbə(r)/ *noun, verb*

▪ ***noun*** [U] **1** (*especially NAmE*) = TIMBER **2** (*BrE*) pieces of furniture, and other large objects that you do not use any more: *a* ***lumber room*** (= for storing lumber in)

▪ ***verb*** **1** [I] **+ adv./prep.** to move in a slow, heavy and awkward way: *A family of elephants lumbered by.* **2** [T, usually passive] **~ sb (with sb/sth)** (*informal*) to give sb a responsibility, etc, that they do not want and that they cannot get rid of: *When our parents went out, my sister got lumbered with me for the evening.*

lum·ber·ing /ˈlʌmbərɪŋ/ *adj.* moving in a slow, heavy and awkward way: *a lumbering dinosaur*

lum·ber·jack /ˈlʌmbədʒæk; *NAmE* -bərdʒ-/ (also **log·ger**) *noun* (especially in the US and Canada) a person whose job is cutting down trees or cutting or transporting wood

lum·ber·yard /ˈlʌmbəjɑːd; *NAmE* ˈlʌmbərjɑːrd/ (*NAmE*) (*BrE* **ˈtim·ber yard**) *noun* a place where wood for building, etc. is stored and sold

lu·men /ˈluːmen/ *noun* (*abbr.* **lm**) (*physics*) a unit for measuring the rate of flow of light

lu·mi·nance /ˈluːmɪnəns/ *noun* [U] (*physics*) the amount of light given out in a particular direction from a particular area

lu·mi·nary /ˈluːmɪnəri; *NAmE* -neri/ *noun* (*pl.* **-ies**) a person who is an expert or a great influence in a special area or activity

lu·mi·nes·cence /ˌluːmɪˈnesns/ *noun* [U] (*technical* or *literary*) a quality in sth that produces light ▸ **lu·mi·nes·cent** *adj.*

lu·mi·nous /ˈluːmɪnəs/ *adj.* **1** shining in the dark; giving out light: *luminous paint* ◇ *luminous hands on a clock* ◇ *staring with huge luminous eyes* ◇ (*figurative*) *the luminous quality of the music* **2** very bright in colour: *They painted the door a luminous green.* ➲ SYNONYMS at BRIGHT ▸ **lu·mi·nous·ly** *adv.* **lu·mi·nos·ity** /ˌluːmɪˈnɒsəti; *NAmE* -ˈnɑːs-/ *noun* [sing., U]

lumme /ˈlʌmi/ *exclamation* (*old-fashioned, BrE, informal*) used to show surprise or interest

lump 🔑 /lʌmp/ *noun, verb*

▪ ***noun*** **1** 🔑 a piece of sth hard or solid, usually without a particular shape: *a lump of coal/cheese/wood* ◇ *This sauce has lumps in it.* **2** (*BrE*) = SUGAR LUMP: *One lump or two?* **3** 🔑 a swelling under the skin, sometimes a sign of serious illness: *He was unhurt apart from a lump on his head.* ◇ *Check your breasts for lumps every month.* **4** (*informal, especially BrE*) a heavy, lazy or stupid person

IDM **have, etc. a lump in your throat** to feel pressure in the throat because you are very angry or emotional **take your ˈlumps** (*NAmE, informal*) to accept bad things that happen to you without complaining

▪ ***verb*** **~ A and B together | ~ A (in) with B** to put or consider different things together in the same group: *You can't lump all Asian languages together.*

IDM **ˈlump it** (*informal*) to accept sth unpleasant because there's no other choice: *I'm sorry you're not happy about it but you'll just have to lump it.* ◇ *That's the situation—**like it or lump it!***

lump·ec·tomy /ˌlʌmˈpektəmi/ *noun* (*pl.* **-ies**) an operation to remove a TUMOUR from sb's body, especially from a woman's breast

lump·en /ˈlʌmpən/ *adj.* (*BrE, literary*) looking heavy and awkward or stupid

lump·ish /ˈlʌmpɪʃ/ *adj.* heavy and awkward; stupid SYN **clumsy**

ˌlump ˈsum (also **ˌlump ˌsum ˈpayment**) *noun* an amount of money that is paid at one time and not on separate occasions

lumpy /ˈlʌmpi/ *adj.* full of lumps; covered in lumps: *lumpy sauce* ◇ *a lumpy mattress*

lu·nacy /ˈluːnəsi/ *noun* [U] **1** behaviour that is stupid or crazy SYN **madness**: *It's sheer lunacy driving in such weather.* **2** (*old-fashioned*) mental illness SYN **madness**

lunar /ˈluːnə(r)/ *adj.* [usually before noun] connected with the moon: *a lunar eclipse/landscape*

ˌlunar ˈcycle *noun* (*astronomy*) a period of 19 years, after which the new moon and full moon return to the same day of the year

ˌlunar ˈmonth *noun* the average time between one new moon and the next (about 29½days) ➲ compare CALENDAR MONTH

ˌlunar ˈyear *noun* a period of twelve lunar months (about 354 days)

lu·na·tic /ˈluːnətɪk/ *noun, adj.*

▪ ***noun*** **1** a person who does crazy things that are often dangerous SYN **maniac**: *This lunatic in a white van pulled out right in front of me!* **2** (*old-fashioned*) a person who is severely mentally ill (the use of this word is now offensive) ORIGIN Originally from the Latin *lunaticus* (*luna*= moon), because people believed that the changes in the moon made people go mad temporarily.

▪ ***adj.*** crazy, ridiculous or extremely stupid: *lunatic ideas* ◇ *a lunatic smile*

IDM **the ˌlunatic ˈfringe** *noun* [sing.+ sing./pl. v.] (*disapproving*) those members of a political or other group whose views are considered to be very extreme and crazy

ˈlunatic asylum *noun* (*old-fashioned, especially BrE*) an institution where mentally ill people live

L

lunch 0-π /lʌntʃ/ *noun, verb*
■ ***noun*** 0-π [U, C] a meal eaten in the middle of the day: *She's gone to lunch.* ◇ *I'm ready for some lunch.* ◇ *What shall we have* ***for lunch****?* ◇ *We serve hot and cold lunches.* ◇ *a one-hour* ***lunch break*** ◇ ***Let's do lunch*** (= have lunch together). ➲ COLLOCATIONS at RESTAURANT ➲ note at MEAL ➲ see also BAG LUNCH, BOX LUNCH, PACKED LUNCH, PLOUGHMAN'S LUNCH
IDM **,out to 'lunch** (*informal, especially NAmE*) behaving in a strange or confused way ➲ more at FREE *adj.*
■ ***verb*** [I] (*formal*) to have lunch, especially at a restaurant: *He lunched with a client at the Ritz.*

'lunch box *noun* **1** a container to hold a meal that you take away from home to eat **2** a small computer that you can carry around

lunch·eon /'lʌntʃən/ *noun* [C, U] a formal lunch or a formal word for lunch: *a charity luncheon* ◇ *Luncheon will be served at one, Madam.*

lunch·eon·ette /,lʌntʃə'net/ *noun* (*old-fashioned, NAmE*) a small restaurant serving simple meals

'luncheon meat *noun* [U] finely chopped cooked meat that has been pressed together in a container, usually sold in cans and served cold in slices

'luncheon voucher *noun* a ticket given by some employers in Britain that sb can exchange for food at some restaurants and shops/stores

'lunch home *noun* (*IndE*) a restaurant

'lunch hour *noun* the time around the middle of the day when you stop work or school to eat lunch: *I usually go to the gym during my lunch hour.*

'lunch lady (*US*) (*BrE* **'dinner lady**) *noun* a woman whose job is to serve meals to children in schools

lunch·room /'lʌntʃru:m; -rʊm/ *noun* (*NAmE*) a large room in a school or office where people eat lunch

lunch·time /'lʌntʃtaɪm/ *noun* [U, C] the time around the middle of the day when people usually eat lunch: *The package still hadn't arrived by lunchtime.* ◇ *a lunchtime concert* ◇ *The sandwich bar is generally packed at lunchtimes.*

lung 0-π /lʌŋ/ *noun*
either of the two organs in the chest that you use for breathing: *lung cancer* ➲ VISUAL VOCAB page V48

lunge /lʌndʒ/ *verb, noun*
■ ***verb*** [I] **~ (at/towards/for sb/sth)** | **~ (forward)** to make a sudden powerful forward movement, especially in order to attack sb or take hold of sth
■ ***noun*** [usually sing.] **1 ~ (at sb)** | **~ (for sb/sth)** a sudden powerful forward movement of the body and arm that a person makes towards another person or thing, especially when attacking or trying to take hold of them: *He made a lunge for the phone.* **2** (in the sport of FENCING) a THRUST made by putting one foot forward and making the back leg straight

lung·fish /'lʌŋfɪʃ/ *noun* (*pl.* **lung·fish**) a long fish that can breathe air and survive for a period of time out of water

lung·ful /'lʌŋfʊl/ *noun* the amount of sth such as air or smoke that is breathed in at one time

lungi /'lʊŋgi:/ *noun* a piece of clothing worn in S and SE Asia consisting of a piece of cloth, usually worn wrapped around the hips and reaching the ankles

lunk·head /'lʌŋkhed/ *noun* (*NAmE, informal*) a stupid person

lupin (*BrE*) (*NAmE* **lu·pine**) /'lu:pɪn/ *noun* a tall garden plant with many small flowers growing up its thick STEM

lu·pine /'lu:paɪn/ *adj.* (*formal*) like a WOLF; connected with a wolf or wolves

lupus /'lu:pəs/ *noun* [U] a disease that affects the skin or sometimes the joints

lurch /lɜ:tʃ; *NAmE* lɜ:rtʃ/ *verb, noun*
■ ***verb*** **1** [I] (**+ adv./prep.**) to make a sudden, unsteady movement forward or sideways SYN **stagger, sway**: *Suddenly the horse lurched to one side and the child fell off.* ◇ *The man lurched drunkenly out of the pub.* ◇ (*figurative*) *Their relationship seems to lurch from one crisis to the next.* **2** [I] if your heart or stomach **lurches**, you have a sudden feeling of fear or excitement
■ ***noun*** [usually sing.] a sudden strong movement that moves you forward or sideways and nearly makes you lose your balance: *The train gave a violent lurch.* ◇ *His heart gave a lurch when he saw her.*
IDM **leave sb in the 'lurch** (*informal*) to fail to help sb when they are relying on you to do so

lurch·er /'lɜ:tʃə(r); *NAmE* 'lɜ:rtʃ-/ *noun* (*BrE*) a dog that is a mixture of two different breeds of dog, one of which is usually a GREYHOUND

lure /lʊə(r); ljʊə(r); *NAmE* lʊr/ *verb, noun*
■ ***verb* ~ sb** (**+ adv./prep.**) (*disapproving*) to persuade or trick sb to go somewhere or to do sth by promising them a reward SYN **entice**: *The child was lured into a car but managed to escape.* ◇ *Young people are lured to the city by the prospect of a job and money.*
■ ***noun*** **1** [usually sing.] the attractive qualities of sth: *Few can resist* ***the lure of*** *adventure.* **2** a thing that is used to attract fish or animals, so that they can be caught

Lurex™ /'lʊəreks; 'ljʊə-; *NAmE* 'lʊr-/ *noun* [U] a type of thin metal thread; a cloth containing this thread, used for making clothes

lurgy /'lɜ:gi; *NAmE* 'lɜ:rgi/ *noun* (*pl.* **-ies**) [C, usually sing.] (*BrE, humorous*) a mild illness or disease: *I've caught some kind of lurgy.* ◇ *It's the* ***dreaded lurgy****!*

lurid /'lʊərɪd; 'ljʊər-; *NAmE* 'lʊr-/ *adj.* (*disapproving*) **1** too bright in colour, in a way that is not attractive **2** (especially of a story or piece of writing) shocking and violent in a way that is deliberate: *lurid headlines* ◇ *The paper gave all the lurid details of the murder.* ► **lur·id·ly** *adv.*

lurk /lɜ:k; *NAmE* lɜ:rk/ *verb, noun*
■ ***verb*** **1** [I] (**+ adv./prep.**) to wait somewhere secretly, especially because you are going to do sth bad or illegal SYN **skulk**: *Why are you lurking around outside my house?* ◇ *A crocodile was lurking just below the surface.* **2** [I] (**+ adv./prep.**) when sth unpleasant or dangerous **lurks**, it is present but not in an obvious way: *At night, danger lurks in these streets.* **3** [I] (*computing*) to read a discussion in a CHAT ROOM, etc. on the Internet, without taking part in it yourself
■ ***noun*** (*AustralE, NZE, informal*) a clever trick that is used in order to get sth

lurve /lɜ:v; *NAmE* lɜ:rv/ *noun* [U] (*BrE, informal, humorous*) a non-standard spelling of 'love', used especially to refer to romantic love: *It's Valentine's Day and lurve is in the air.*

lus·cious /'lʌʃəs/ *adj.* **1** having a strong pleasant taste SYN **delicious**: *luscious fruit* **2** (of cloth, colours or music) soft and deep or heavy in a way that is pleasing to feel, look at or hear SYN **rich**: *luscious silks and velvets* **3** (especially of a woman) sexually attractive: *a luscious young girl*

lush /lʌʃ/ *adj., noun*
■ ***adj.*** **1** (of plants, gardens, etc.) growing thickly and strongly in a way that is attractive; covered in healthy grass and plants SYN **luxuriant**: *lush vegetation* ◇ *the lush green countryside* **2** beautiful and making you feel pleasure; seeming expensive: *a lush apartment*
■ ***noun*** (*NAmE, informal*) = ALCOHOLIC

luso·phone /'lu:səfəʊn; *NAmE* -foʊn/ *adj.* (*linguistics*) speaking Portuguese as the main language

lust /lʌst/ *noun, verb*
■ ***noun*** (often *disapproving*) [U, C] **1 ~ (for sb)** very strong sexual desire, especially when love is not involved: *Their affair was driven by pure lust.* **2 ~ (for sth)** very strong desire for sth or enjoyment of sth: *to satisfy his* ***lust for power*** ◇ *She has a real* ***lust for life*** (= she really enjoys life). ➲ see also BLOODLUST
■ ***verb***
PHR V **'lust after/for sb/sth** (often *disapproving*) to feel an extremely strong, especially sexual, desire for sb/sth

lust·ful /'lʌstfl/ *adj.* (often *disapproving*) feeling or showing strong sexual desire SYN **lascivious**

lustre (*especially US* **lust·er**) /'lʌstə(r)/ *noun* [U] **1** the shining quality of a surface SYN **sheen**: *Her hair had lost* *its lustre.* **2** the quality of being special in a way that is exciting: *The presence of the prince added lustre to the occasion.* ➲ compare LACKLUSTRE

lus·trous /ˈlʌstrəs/ *adj.* (*formal*) soft and shining SYN **glossy**: *thick lustrous hair*

lusty /ˈlʌsti/ *adj.* healthy and strong SYN **vigorous**: *a lusty young man* ◇ *lusty singing* ▶ **lust·ily** /-ɪli/ *adv.*: *singing lustily*

lute /luːt/ *noun* an early type of musical instrument with strings, played like a GUITAR

lu·ten·ist (also **lu·tan·ist**) /ˈluːtənɪst/ *noun* a person who plays the lute

lu·te·tium /luːˈtiːʃiəm; *BrE* also -siəm/ *noun* [U] (*symb.* Lu) a chemical element. Lutetium is a rare silver-white metal used in the nuclear industry.

Lu·ther·an /ˈluːθərən/ *noun* a member of a Christian Protestant Church that follows the teaching of the 16th century German religious leader Martin Luther ▶ **Lu·ther·an** *adj.*

luv /lʌv/ *noun* **1** (*BrE*) a way of spelling 'love', when used as an informal way of addressing sb: *Never mind, luv.* **2** an informal way of spelling 'love', for example when ending a letter: *See you soon, lots of luv, Sue.*

luvvy (also **luv·vie**) /ˈlʌvi/ *noun* (*pl.* -ies) (*BrE, informal*) **1** (*disapproving*) an actor, especially when he or she behaves in a way that seems exaggerated and not sincere **2** = LOVEY

lux·uri·ant /lʌɡˈʒʊəriənt; *NAmE* -ˈʒʊr-/ *adj.* **1** (of plants or hair) growing thickly and strongly in a way that is attractive: *luxuriant vegetation* ◇ *thick, luxuriant hair* **2** (especially of art or the atmosphere of a place) rich in sth that is pleasant or beautiful: *the poet's luxuriant imagery* ▶ **lux·uri·ance** /-əns/ *noun* [U]: *the luxuriance of the tropical forest*

lux·uri·ant·ly /lʌɡˈʒʊəriəntli; *NAmE* -ˈʒʊr-/ *adv.* **1** in a way that is thick and attractive: *a tall, luxuriantly bearded man* **2** (especially of a way of moving your body) in a way that is comfortable and enjoyable: *She turned luxuriantly on her side, yawning.*

lux·uri·ate /lʌɡˈʒʊərieɪt; *NAmE* -ˈʒʊr-/ *verb*
PHR V **luˈxuriate in sth** to relax while enjoying sth very pleasant: *She luxuriated in all the attention she received.*

lux·uri·ous /lʌɡˈʒʊəriəs; *NAmE* -ˈʒʊr-/ *adj.* very comfortable; containing expensive and enjoyable things SYN **sumptuous**: *a luxurious hotel* ◇ *luxurious surroundings* OPP **spartan** ▶ **lux·uri·ous·ly** *adv.*: *luxuriously comfortable* ◇ *a luxuriously furnished apartment* ◇ *She stretched luxuriously on the bed.*

lux·ury /ˈlʌkʃəri/ *noun* (*pl.* -ies) **1** [U] the enjoyment of special and expensive things, particularly food and drink, clothes and surroundings: *Now we'll be able to live* ***in luxury*** *for the rest of our lives.* ◇ *to lead a* ***life of luxury*** ◇ *a luxury hotel* ◇ *luxury goods* **2** [C] a thing that is expensive and enjoyable but not essential SYN **extravagance**: *small luxuries like chocolate and flowers* ◇ *I love having a long, hot bath—it's one of* ***life's little luxuries.*** ◇ *It was a luxury if you had a washing machine in those days.* **3** [U, sing.] a pleasure or an advantage that you do not often have SYN **indulgence**: *We had the luxury of being able to choose from four good candidates for the job.* IDM see LAP *n.*

LW *abbr.* (*especially BrE*) LONG WAVE: *1 500m LW*

-ly *suffix* **1** (in adverbs) in the way mentioned: *happily* ◇ *stupidly* **2** (in adjectives) having the qualities of: *cowardly* ◇ *scholarly* **3** (in adjectives and adverbs) at intervals of: *hourly* ◇ *daily*

ly·chee (also **li·chee**) (also **lit·chi** especially in *US*) /ˌlaɪˈtʃiː; ˈlaɪtʃiː/ *noun* a small Chinese fruit with thick rough reddish skin, white flesh and a large seed inside ➲ VISUAL VOCAB page V26

lych·gate (also **lich·gate**) /ˈlɪtʃɡeɪt/ *noun* a gate with a roof at the entrance to a CHURCHYARD

Lycra™ /ˈlaɪkrə/ (also **span·dex**) *noun* [U] an artificial material that stretches, used for making clothes that fit close to the body

lye /laɪ/ *noun* [U] a chemical used in various industrial processes, including washing

lying *pres. part.* of LIE

ˌlying-ˈin *noun* [sing.] (*old-fashioned*) the period of time during which a woman in the past stayed in bed before and after giving birth to a child

ˌlying-in-ˈstate *noun* [U] the period when the dead body of a ruler is displayed to the public before being buried; the display of the body in this way

Lyme disease /ˈlaɪm dɪziːz/ *noun* [U] a serious disease that causes fever and pain in the joints of the body, caused by bacteria carried by TICKS (= small insects)

lymph /lɪmf/ *noun* [U] a clear liquid containing white blood cells that helps to clean the TISSUES of the body and helps to prevent infections from spreading ▶ **lymph·at·ic** /lɪmˈfætɪk/ *adj.* [only before noun]: *the lymphatic system*

ˈlymph node (also **ˈlymph gland**) *noun* one of the small round parts of the LYMPHATIC system that stores LYMPHOCYTES and helps fight infection

lympho·cyte /ˈlɪmfəsaɪt/ *noun* (*biology*) a type of small white blood cell with one round NUCLEUS, found especially in the LYMPHATIC system

lymph·oma /lɪmˈfəʊmə; *NAmE* -ˈfoʊ-/ *noun* [U] cancer of the LYMPH NODES

lynch /lɪntʃ/ *verb* **~ sb** if a crowd of people **lynch** sb whom they consider guilty of a crime, they capture them, do not allow them to have a trial in court, and kill them illegally, usually by hanging ▶ **lynch·ing** *noun* [C, U]

ˈlynch mob *noun* a crowd of people who gather to lynch sb

lynch·pin = LINCHPIN

lynx /lɪŋks/ *noun* (*pl.* lynx or lynxes) a wild animal of the cat family, with spots on its fur and a very short tail

lyre /ˈlaɪə(r)/ *noun* an ancient musical instrument with strings fastened in a frame shaped like a U. It was played with the fingers.

lyre·bird /ˈlaɪəbɜːd; *NAmE* ˈlaɪrbɜːrd/ *noun* a large Australian bird

lyric /ˈlɪrɪk/ *adj.*, *noun*

■ ***adj.*** **1** (of poetry) expressing a person's personal feelings and thoughts ➲ compare EPIC **2** connected with, or written for, singing

■ ***noun*** **1** [C] a lyric poem ➲ compare EPIC **2** **lyrics** [pl.] the words of a song: *music and lyrics by Rodgers and Hart*

lyr·ic·al /ˈlɪrɪkl/ *adj.* expressing strong emotion in a way that is beautiful and shows imagination SYN **expressive**: *a lyrical melody* ◇ *He began to* ***wax lyrical*** (= talk in an enthusiastic way) *about his new car.*

lyr·ic·al·ly /ˈlɪrɪkli/ *adv.* **1** in a way that expresses strong emotion **2** connected with the words of a song: *Both musically and lyrically it is very effective.*

lyri·cism /ˈlɪrɪsɪzəm/ *noun* [U] the expression of strong emotion in poetry, art, music, etc.

lyri·cist /ˈlɪrɪsɪst/ *noun* a person who writes the words of songs

L

Mm

M /em/ *noun, abbr., symbol*
■ ***noun*** (also **m**) [C, U] (*pl.* Ms, M's, m's /emz/) the 13th letter of the English alphabet: *'Milk' begins with (an) M/'M'.*
■ ***abbr.*** **1** (also **med.**) (especially for sizes of clothes) medium: *S M and L* (= small, medium and large) **2** (used with a number to show the name of a British MOTORWAY): *heavy traffic on the M25*
■ ***symbol*** (also **m**) the number 1000 in ROMAN NUMERALS

m (*BrE*) (also **m.** *NAmE, BrE*) *abbr.* **1** male **2** married **3** metre(s): *800m medium wave* **4** million(s): *population: 10m*

MA (*BrE*) (*NAmE* **M.A.**) /ˌem ˈeɪ/ *noun* the abbreviation for 'Master of Arts' (a second university degree in an ARTS subject, or, in Scotland, a first university degree in an arts subject): *to be/have/do an MA* ◇ (*BrE*) *Julie Bell MA*

ma /mɑː/ *noun* (*informal*) mother: *I'm going now, ma.* ◇ *'I want my ma,' sobbed the little girl.*

ma'am *noun* [sing.] **1** /mæm/ (*NAmE*) used as a polite way of addressing a woman: *'Can I help you, ma'am?'* ➲ compare SIR **2** /mɑːm/ (*BrE*) used when addressing the Queen or senior women officers in the police or army = MADAM

maas /mɑːs/ *noun* (*SAfrE*) = AMASI

Mac /mæk/ *noun* [sing.] (*NAmE, informal*) used to address a man whose name you do not know

mac (also **mack**) /mæk/ (also *old-fashioned* **mack·in·tosh**) *noun* (all *BrE*) a coat made of material that keeps you dry in the rain

ma·cabre /məˈkɑːbrə/ *adj.* unpleasant and strange because connected with death and frightening things **SYN** **ghoulish, grisly**: *a **macabre tale/joke/ritual***

mac·adam /məˈkædəm/ *noun* [U] a road surface made of layers of broken stones, mixed with TAR

maca·da·mia /ˌmækəˈdeɪmiə/ (also **maca'damia nut**) *noun* the round nut of an Australian tree ➲ VISUAL VOCAB page V28

ma·caque /məˈkæk; -ˈkɑːk/ *noun* a type of MONKEY that lives in Africa and Asia

maca·roni /ˌmækəˈrəʊni; *NAmE* -ˈroʊni/ *noun* [U] PASTA in the shape of hollow tubes

ˌmacaroni ˈcheese (*BrE*) (*NAmE* **ˌmacaroni and ˈcheese**) *noun* [U] a hot dish of macaroni in a cheese sauce

maca·roon /ˌmækəˈruːn/ *noun* a soft round sweet biscuit/cookie made with ALMONDS or COCONUT

macaw /məˈkɔː/ *noun* a large Central and S American tropical bird of the PARROT family, with bright feathers and a long tail

Mace™ /meɪs/ *noun* [U] a chemical that makes your eyes and skin sting, that some people, including police officers, carry in spray cans so that they can defend themselves against people attacking them

mace /meɪs/ *noun* **1** [C] a decorative stick, carried as a sign of authority by an official such as a mayor ➲ compare SCEPTRE **2** [C] a large heavy stick that has a head with metal points on it, used in the past as a weapon **3** [U] the dried outer covering of NUTMEGS (= the hard nuts of a tropical tree), used in cooking as a spice

ma·cer·ate /ˈmæsəreɪt/ *verb* [T, I] **~ (sth)** (*technical*) to make sth (especially food) soft by leaving it in a liquid; to become soft in this way

Mach /mɑːk; mæk/ *noun* [U] (often followed by a number) a measurement of speed, used especially for aircraft. Mach 1 is the speed of sound: *a fighter plane with a top speed of Mach 3* (= 3 times the speed of sound)

ma·chete /məˈʃeti/ *noun* a broad heavy knife used as a cutting tool and as a weapon

Ma·chia·vel·lian /ˌmækiəˈveliən/ *adj.* (*formal, disapproving*) using clever plans to achieve what you want, without people realizing what you are doing **SYN** **cunning, unscrupulous** **ORIGIN** From the name of **Niccolò Machiavelli**, an Italian politician (1469-1527), who explained in his book *The Prince*, that it was often necessary for rulers to use immoral methods in order to achieve power and success.

ma·chin·ation /ˌmæʃɪˈneɪʃn/ *noun* [usually pl.] (*disapproving*) a secret and complicated plan **SYN** **plot, intrigue**

ma·chine 🔑 /məˈʃiːn/ *noun, verb*
■ ***noun*** **1** 🔑 (often in compounds) a piece of equipment with moving parts that is designed to do a particular job. The power used to work a machine may be electricity, steam, gas, etc. or human power: *Machines have replaced human labour in many industries.* ◇ *to **operate/run a machine*** ◇ *How does this machine work?* ◇ *a **washing/sewing machine*** ◇ *a machine for making plastic toys* ◇ *I left a message on her answering machine.* ◇ *The potatoes are planted **by machine**.* ➲ see also VOTING MACHINE **2** 🔑 (*informal*) a particular machine, for example in the home, when you do not refer to it by its full name: *Just put those clothes in the machine* (= the washing machine). ◇ *The new machines* (= computers) *will be shipped next month.* **3** a group of people that control an organization or part of an organization: *the president's propaganda machine* **4** (often *disapproving*) a person who acts automatically, without allowing their feelings to show or to affect their work ➲ see also MECHANICAL, FRUIT MACHINE, SLOT MACHINE, TIME MACHINE **HELP** You will find other compounds ending in **machine** at their place in the alphabet. **IDM** see COG
■ ***verb*** [T, I] **~ (sth)** (*technical*) to make or shape sth with a machine: *This material can be cut and machined easily.*

maˈchine code (also **maˈchine language**) *noun* [C, U] (*computing*) a code in which instructions are written in the form of numbers so that a computer can understand and act on them

maˈchine gun *noun* a gun that automatically fires many bullets one after the other very quickly: *a **burst/hail of machine-gun fire***

maˈchine-gun *verb* (-nn-) **~ sb/sth** to shoot at sb/sth with a machine gun

maˌchine-ˈmade *adj.* made by a machine ➲ compare HANDMADE

maˌchine-ˈreadable *adj.* (of data) in a form that a computer can understand

ma·chin·ery 🔑 /məˈʃiːnəri/ *noun*
1 🔑 [U] machines as a group, especially large ones: ***agricultural/industrial machinery*** ◇ *a piece of machinery* **2** 🔑 [U] the parts of a machine that make it work **3** [U, sing.] the organization or structure of sth; the system for doing sth: **~ (of sth)** *the machinery of government* ◇ **~ (for doing sth)** *There is no machinery for resolving disputes.*

maˈchine tool *noun* a tool for cutting or shaping metal, wood, etc, driven by a machine

maˌchine transˈlation *noun* [U] the process of translating language by computer

ma·chin·ist /məˈʃiːnɪst/ *noun* **1** a person whose job is operating a machine, especially machines used in industry for cutting and shaping things, or a sewing machine **2** a person whose job is to make or repair machines

mach·ismo /məˈtʃɪzməʊ; *NAmE* mɑːˈtʃiːzmoʊ/ *noun* [U] (from *Spanish*, usually *disapproving*) aggressive male behaviour that emphasizes the importance of being strong rather than being intelligent and sensitive

macho /ˈmætʃəʊ; *NAmE* ˈmɑːtʃoʊ/ *adj.* (usually *disapproving*) male in an aggressive way: *He's too macho to ever admit he was wrong.* ◇ ***macho pride/posturing***

mack = MAC

mack·erel /ˈmækrəl/ *noun* [C, U] (*pl.* **mack·erel**) a sea fish with greenish-blue bands on its body, that is used for food: *smoked mackerel*

mack·in·tosh /ˈmækɪntɒʃ; *NAmE* -tɑːʃ/ *noun* (*old-fashioned*) = MAC

mac·ramé /məˈkrɑːmi/ *noun* [U] the art of tying knots in string in a decorative way, to make things

macro /ˈmækrəʊ; *NAmE* ˈmækroʊ/ *noun* (*pl.* -os) (*computing*) a single instruction in a computer program that automatically causes a complete series of instructions to be put into effect, in order to perform a particular task

macro- /ˈmækrəʊ; *NAmE* ˈmækroʊ/ *combining form* (in nouns, adjectives and adverbs) large; on a large scale: *macroeconomics* OPP **micro-**

macro·bi·ot·ic /ˌmækrəʊbaɪˈɒtɪk; *NAmE* -kroʊbaɪˈɑːt-/ *adj.* consisting of whole grains and vegetables grown without chemical treatment: *a macrobiotic diet*

macro·cosm /ˈmækrəʊkɒzəm; *NAmE* -kroʊkɑːz-/ *noun* any large complete structure that contains smaller structures, for example the universe ➲ compare MICROCOSM

macro·eco·nom·ics /ˌmækrəʊˌiːkəˈnɒmɪks; *NAmE* -kroʊˌekəˈnɑːm-/ *noun* [U] the study of large economic systems, such as those of whole countries or areas of the world ▸ **macro·eco·nom·ic** *adj.*: *macroeconomic policy*

mac·ron /ˈmækrɒn; *NAmE* ˈmeɪkrɑːn/ *noun* (*linguistics*) the mark (¯) which is placed over a vowel in some languages and in the International Phonetic Alphabet to show that the vowel is stressed or long

macro·phage /ˈmækrəfeɪdʒ/ *noun* (*biology*) a large cell that is able to remove harmful substances from the body, and is found in blood and TISSUE

Synonyms

mad

crazy • nuts • batty • out of your mind • (not) in your right mind

These are all informal words that describe sb who has a mind that does not work normally.

mad (*informal, especially BrE*) having a mind that does not work normally: *I thought I'd go mad if I stayed any longer.* NOTE **Mad** is an informal word used to suggest that sb's behaviour is very strange, often because of extreme emotional pressure. It is offensive if used to describe sb suffering from a real mental illness; use **mentally ill** instead. **Mad** is not usually used in this meaning in North American English; use **crazy** instead.

crazy (*informal, especially NAmE*) having a mind that does not work normally: *A crazy old woman rented the upstairs room.* NOTE Like **mad**, **crazy** is offensive if used to describe sb suffering from a real mental illness.

nuts [not before noun] (*informal*) mad: *That noise is driving me nuts!* ◇ *You guys are nuts!*

batty (*informal, especially BrE*) slightly mad, in a harmless way: *Her mum's completely batty.*

out of your mind (*informal*) unable to think or behave normally, especially because of extreme shock or anxiety: *She was out of her mind with grief.*

(not) in your right mind (*informal*) (not) mentally normal: ***No one in their right mind*** *would choose to work there.*

PATTERNS

- to be mad/crazy/nuts/out of your mind/not in your right mind **to do sth**
- to **go** mad/crazy/nuts/batty
- to **drive sb** mad/crazy/nuts/batty/out of their mind
- **completely** mad/crazy/nuts/batty/out of your mind

mad 🗝 /mæd/ *adj.* (mad·der, mad·dest)
1 🗝 (*especially BrE*) having a mind that does not work normally; mentally ill: *They realized that he had* ***gone mad.*** ◇ *Inventors are not mad scientists.* ◇ *I'll* ***go mad*** *if I have to wait much longer.* ◇ *She seemed to have gone* ***stark raving mad.*** ➲ see also BARKING MAD **2** 🗝 (*informal, especially BrE*) very stupid; not at all sensible: *You* ***must be mad*** *to risk it.* ◇ *It was a mad idea.* ◇ *'I'm going to buy some new clothes.' 'Well, don't* ***go mad*** (= spend more than is sensible).' **3** 🗝 [not before noun] **~ (at/with sb)** | **~ (about sth)** (*informal, especially NAmE*) very angry: *He* ***got mad*** *and walked out.* ◇ *She's* ***mad at me*** *for being late.* ◇ (*BrE*) *That noise is* ***driving me mad.*** ◇ (*BrE*) *He'll* ***go mad*** *when he sees the damage.* ➲ SYNONYMS at ANGRY **4** 🗝 [not usually before noun] **~ (about/on sth/sb)** (*BrE, informal*) liking sth/sb very much; very interested in sth: *to be mad on tennis* ◇ *He's always been mad about kids.* ◇ *football-mad boys* ◇ *She's completely power-mad.* **5** 🗝 done without thought or control; wild and excited: *The crowd made a* ***mad rush*** *for the exit.* ◇ *Only a* ***mad dash*** *got them to the meeting on time.* ◇ (*BrE*) *The team won and the fans* ***went mad.*** ◇ **~ with sth** (*BrE*) *to be* ***mad with anger/excitement/grief/love*** ➲ compare CRAZY
IDM **be mad for sb/sth** (*BrE, informal*) to like or want sb/sth very much: *Scott's mad for peanuts.* **like ˈcrazy/ˈmad** (*informal*) very fast, hard, much, etc: *I had to run like mad to catch the bus.* **(as) mad as a ˈhatter/a March ˈhare** (*informal*) (of a person) mentally ill; very silly ORIGIN From the Mad Hatter, a character in Lewis Carroll's *Alice's Adventures in Wonderland*. Because of the chemicals used in hat-making, workers often suffered from mercury poisoning, which can cause loss of memory and damage to the nervous system. A **March hare** was called mad because of the strange behaviour of hares during the mating season. **mad ˈkeen (on sth/sb)** (*BrE, informal*) liking sth/sb very much; very interested in sth: *He's mad keen on planes.* ➲ more at HOPPING *adv.*, RAVING

madam /ˈmædəm/ *noun* **1** [sing.] (*formal*) used when speaking or writing to a woman in a formal or business situation: *Can I help you, madam?* ◇ *Dear Madam* (= used like *Dear Sir* in a letter) ➲ see also MA'AM **2** [C] (*informal, disapproving, especially BrE*) a girl or young woman who expects other people to do what she wants: *She's a proper little madam.* **3** [C] a woman who is in charge of the PROSTITUTES in a BROTHEL

mad·cap /ˈmædkæp/ *adj.* [usually before noun] (*informal*) (of people, plans etc.) crazy and not caring about danger; not sensible SYN **reckless**: ***madcap schemes/escapades***

mad ˈcow disease *noun* [U] (*informal*) = BSE

mad·den /ˈmædn/ *verb* [usually passive] **~ sb/sth** to make a person or an animal very angry or crazy SYN **infuriate** ▸ **mad·den·ing** /ˈmædnɪŋ/ *adj.*: *maddening delays* **mad·den·ing·ly** *adv.*: *Progress is maddeningly slow.*

mad·ding /ˈmædɪŋ/ *adj.* (*literary*) behaving in a crazy way; making you feel angry or crazy
IDM **ˌfar from the madding ˈcrowd** in a quiet and private place

made /meɪd/ **1** *past tense, past part.* of MAKE **2** **-made** (in adjectives) made in the way, place, etc. mentioned: *well-made* ◇ *home-made* ➲ see also SELF-MADE
IDM **have (got) it ˈmade** (*informal*) to be sure of success; to have everything that you want **(be) ˈmade for sb/each other** to be completely suited to sb/each other: *Peter and Judy seem made for each other, don't they?* **what sb is ˈmade of** (*informal*) how sb reacts in a difficult situation

Ma·deira /məˈdɪərə; *NAmE* məˈdɪrə/ (also **Maˌdeira ˈwine**) *noun* **1** [U, C] a strong wine, often sweet, from the island of Madeira **2** [C] a glass of Madeira

Maˈdeira cake (*BrE*) (*NAmE* **ˈpound cake**) *noun* [U, C] a plain yellow cake made with eggs, fat, flour and sugar

mad·eleine /ˈmædleɪn; ˈmædlen/ *noun* a type of small cake

ˌmade to ˈmeasure *adj.* (of clothes, curtains, etc.) made specially to fit a particular person, window, etc.

ˌmade to ˈorder *adj.* (*especially NAmE*) (of clothes, furniture, etc.) made specially for a particular customer

ˈmade-up *adj.* **1** wearing make-up: *a heavily* ***made-up face/woman*** **2** not true or real; invented: *a* ***made-up story/word/name***

M

mad·house /'mædhaʊs/ *noun* **1** [usually sing.] (*informal*) a place where there is confusion and noise: *Don't work in that department; it's a madhouse.* **2** (*old use*) a hospital for people who are mentally ill

Madi·son Av·enue /ˌmædɪsn 'ævənjuː/ *noun* [U] the US advertising industry ORIGIN From the name of the street in New York where many advertising companies have their offices.

madly /'mædli/ *adv.* **1** (only used *after* a verb) in a way that shows a lack of control: *She was rushing around madly trying to put out the fire.* ◇ *His heart thudded madly against his ribs.* **2** (*informal*) very, extremely: ***madly excited/jealous*** ◇ *She's* ***madly in love*** *with him.*

mad·man /'mædmən/ *noun* (*pl.* **-men** /-mən/) a man who has a serious mental illness: *The killing was the act of a madman.* ◇ *He drove* ***like a madman.*** ◇ *Some madman* (= stupid person) *deleted all the files.* ➲ see also MADWOMAN

mad·ness /'mædnəs/ *noun* [U] **1** (*old-fashioned*) the state of having a serious mental illness SYN **insanity**: *There may be a link between madness and creativity.* **2** crazy or stupid behaviour that could be dangerous: *It would be sheer madness to trust a man like that.* ◇ *In a* ***moment of madness*** *she had agreed to go out with him.* IDM see METHOD

ma·donna /mə'dɒnə; *NAmE* mə'dɑːnə/ *noun* **1 the Madonna** [sing.] the Virgin Mary, mother of Jesus Christ **2** [C] a statue or picture of the Virgin Mary

ma·dras /mə'dræs; -'drɑːs; *NAmE* also 'mædrəs/ *noun* [U, C] a spicy Indian dish, usually containing meat: *chicken madras*

ma·dra·sa (also **ma·dra·sah** /mə'dræsə/) *noun* a college where the Islamic faith is taught

M

mad·ri·gal /'mædrɪgl/ *noun* a song for several singers, usually without musical instruments, popular in the 16th century

mad·woman /'mædwʊmən/ *noun* (*pl.* **-women** /-wɪmɪn/) a woman who has a serious mental illness ➲ see also MADMAN

mael·strom /'meɪlstrɒm; *NAmE* -strɑːm/ *noun* [usually sing.] **1** (*literary*) a situation full of strong emotions or confusing events, that is hard to control and makes you feel frightened **2** a very strong current of water that moves in circles SYN **whirlpool**

maes·tro /'maɪstrəʊ; *NAmE* -stroʊ/ *noun* (*pl.* **-os**) (often used as a way of addressing sb, showing respect) a great performer, especially a musician: *Maestro Giulini* ◇ *The winning goal was scored by the maestro himself.*

Mafia /'mæfiə; *NAmE* 'mɑːf-/ *noun* **1 the Mafia** [sing.+ sing./pl. v.] a secret organization of criminals, that is active especially in Sicily, Italy and the US **2 mafia** [C+sing./pl. v.] a group of people within an organization or a community who use their power to get advantages for themselves: *a member of the local mafia* ◇ *Politics is still dominated by the middle-class mafia.*

Mafi·oso /ˌmæfi'əʊsəʊ; *NAmE* ˌmɑːfi'oʊsoʊ/ *noun* (*pl.* **Mafi·osi** /-siː/) a member of the Mafia

maga·zine 🔑 /ˌmægə'ziːn; *NAmE* 'mægəziːn/ *noun* **1** 🔑 (also *informal* **mag** /mæg/) a type of large thin book with a paper cover that you can buy every week or month, containing articles, photographs, etc, often on a particular topic: *a* ***weekly/monthly magazine*** ◇ *a* ***magazine article/interview*** ◇ *an* ***online magazine*** ◇ *Her designer clothes were from the pages of a glossy fashion magazine.* **2** a radio or television programme that is about a particular topic: *a regional news magazine on TV* ◇ *a* ***magazine programme/program*** **3** the part of a gun that holds the bullets before they are fired **4** a room or building where weapons, EXPLOSIVES and bullets are stored

ma·genta /mə'dʒentə/ *adj.* reddish-purple in colour ▶ **ma·genta** *noun* [U]

mag·got /'mægət/ *noun* a creature like a small short WORM, that is the young form of a fly and is found in decaying meat and other food. Maggots are often used as BAIT on a hook to catch fish.

Magi /'meɪdʒaɪ/ **the Magi** *noun* [pl.] (in the Bible) the three wise men from the East who are said to have brought presents to the baby Jesus

magic 🔑 /'mædʒɪk/ *noun, adj., verb*

■ ***noun*** [U] **1** 🔑 the secret power of appearing to make impossible things happen by saying special words or doing special things: *Do you believe in magic?* ◇ *He suddenly appeared* ***as if by magic.*** ◇ *A passage was cleared through the crowd* ***like magic.*** ➲ see also BLACK MAGIC **2** 🔑 the art of doing tricks that seem impossible in order to entertain people SYN **conjuring** **3** 🔑 a special quality or ability that sb/sth has, that seems too wonderful to be real SYN **enchantment**: *dance and music which capture the magic of India* ◇ *Like all truly charismatic people, he can* ***work his magic on*** *both men and women.* ◇ *Our year in Italy was* ***pure/sheer*** *magic.* IDM see WEAVE *v.*

■ ***adj.*** **1** 🔑 having or using special powers to make impossible things happen or seem to happen: *a* ***magic spell/charm/potion/trick*** ◇ *There is no magic formula for passing exams—only hard work.* **2** 🔑 (*informal*) having a special quality that makes sth seem wonderful: *It was a magic moment when the two sisters were reunited after 30 years.* ◇ *She has a* ***magic touch*** *with the children and they do everything she asks.* ◇ *Trust is the magic ingredient in our relationship.* **3** [not before noun] (*BrE, informal*) very good or enjoyable: *'What was the trip like?' 'Magic!'*

■ ***verb*** (-ck-) **~ sb/sth + adv./prep.** to make sb/sth appear somewhere, disappear or turn into sth, by magic, or as if by magic

magic·al /'mædʒɪkl/ *adj.* **1** containing magic; used in magic: *magical powers* ◇ *Her words had a magical effect on us.* **2** (*informal*) wonderful; very enjoyable SYN **enchanting**: *a truly magical feeling* ◇ *We spent a magical week in Paris.* ▶ **ma·gic·al·ly** /-kli/ *adv.*

ˌmagical 'realism *noun* [U] = MAGIC REALISM

ˌmagic 'bullet *noun* **1** (*medical*) a medical treatment which works very quickly and effectively against a particular illness **2** a fast and effective solution to a serious problem

ˌmagic 'carpet *noun* (in stories) a carpet that can fly and carry people

ma·gi·cian /mə'dʒɪʃn/ *noun* **1** a person who can do magic tricks SYN **conjuror** **2** (in stories) a person who has magic powers SYN **sorcerer**

ˌmagic 'lantern *noun* a piece of equipment used in the past to make pictures appear on a white wall or screen

ˌmagic 'mushroom (*BrE* or becoming *old-fashioned*, *NAmE*) (*NAmE* usually *informal* **shroom**) *noun* a type of MUSHROOM that has an effect like some drugs and that may make people who eat it HALLUCINATE (= see things that are not there)

ˌmagic 'realism (also **ˌmagical 'realism**) *noun* [U] a style of writing that mixes realistic events with FANTASY

ˌmagic 'wand *noun* = WAND: *I wish I could* ***wave a magic wand*** *and make everything all right again.*

magis·ter·ial /ˌmædʒɪ'stɪəriəl; *NAmE* -'stɪr-/ *adj.* (*formal*) **1** (especially of a person or their behaviour) having or showing power or authority: *He talked with the magisterial authority of the head of the family.* **2** (of a book or piece of writing) showing great knowledge or understanding SYN **authoritative**: *his magisterial work 'The Roman Wall in Scotland'* **3** [only before noun] connected with a magistrate ▶ **magis·teri·al·ly** /-iəli/ *adv.*

the magis·tracy /'mædʒɪstrəsi/ *noun* [sing.+ sing./pl. v.] magistrates as a group

magis·trate /'mædʒɪstreɪt/ *noun* an official who acts as a judge in the lowest courts of law SYN **Justice of the Peace**: *a magistrates' court* ◇ *to come up before the magistrates*

magma /'mægmə/ *noun* [U] (*technical*) very hot liquid rock found below the earth's surface

Magna Carta /ˌmægnə 'kɑːtə; *NAmE* 'kɑːrtə/ *noun* a document officially stating the political and legal rights of the English people, that King John was forced to sign in 1215 (often referred to as the basis for modern English law)

magna cum laude /ˌmæɡnə kʊm ˈlɔːdiː; ˈlaʊdeɪ/ *adv., adj.* (from *Latin*) (in the US) at the second of the three highest levels of achievement that students can reach when they finish their studies at college: *She graduated magna cum laude from UCLA.* ➲ compare CUM LAUDE, SUMMA CUM LAUDE

mag·nani·mous /mæɡˈnænɪməs/ *adj.* (*formal*) kind, generous and forgiving, especially towards an enemy or a rival: *a magnanimous gesture* ◇ *He was magnanimous in defeat and praised his opponent's skill.* ▸ **mag·na·nim·ity** /ˌmæɡnəˈnɪməti/ *noun* [U]: *She accepted the criticism with magnanimity.* **mag·nani·mous·ly** *adv.*

mag·nate /ˈmæɡneɪt/ *noun* a person who is rich, powerful and successful, especially in business: *a* ***media/property/shipping magnate***

mag·ne·sia /mæɡˈniːʒə; *NAmE* -ʃə; *BrE* also -ziə/ *noun* [U] a white substance containing MAGNESIUM, used to help with INDIGESTION

mag·ne·sium /mæɡˈniːziəm/ *noun* [U] (*symb.* Mg) a chemical element. Magnesium is a light, silver-white metal that burns with a bright white flame.

mag·net /ˈmæɡnət/ *noun* **1** a piece of iron that attracts objects made of iron towards it, either naturally or because of an electric current that is passed through it ➲ VISUAL VOCAB page V57 **2** [usually sing.] **~ (for sb/sth)** a person, place or thing that sb/sth is attracted to: *In the 1990s the area became a magnet for new investment.* **3** an object with a magnetic surface that you can stick onto a metal surface: *fridge magnets of your favourite cartoon characters*

mag·net·ic /mæɡˈnetɪk/ *adj.* [usually before noun] **1** behaving like a magnet (1): *magnetic materials* ◇ *The block becomes magnetic when the current is switched on.* **2** connected with or produced by magnetism: ***magnetic properties/forces*** ◇ *a* ***magnetic disk*** (= one containing magnetic tape that stores information to be used by a computer) **3** that people find very powerful and attractive: *a magnetic personality* ▸ **mag·net·ic·al·ly** /-kli/ *adv.*

magˌnetic ˈcompass *noun* = COMPASS (1)

magˌnetic ˈfield *noun* an area around a MAGNET or MAGNETIC object, where there is a force that will attract some metals towards it

magˌnetic ˈmedia *noun* [pl., U] the different methods, for example MAGNETIC TAPE, that are used to store information for computers

magˌnetic ˈnorth *noun* [U] the direction that is approximately north as it is shown on a magnetic compass ➲ compare TRUE NORTH

magˌnetic ˈstorm *noun* a situation in which the magnetic field of the earth or of another planet, star, etc. is disturbed

magˌnetic ˈstrip *noun* a line of magnetic material on a plastic card, containing information

magˌnetic ˈtape *noun* [U] a type of plastic tape that is used for recording sound, pictures or computer information

mag·net·ism /ˈmæɡnətɪzəm/ *noun* [U] **1** a physical property (= characteristic) of some metals such as iron, produced by electric currents, that causes forces between objects, either pulling them towards each other or pushing them apart **2** the qualities of sth, especially a person's character, that people find powerful and attractive: *She exudes sexual magnetism.*

mag·net·ize (*BrE* also **-ise**) /ˈmæɡnətaɪz/ *verb* **1** [usually passive] **~ sth** (*technical*) to make sth metal behave like a MAGNET **2 ~ sb** to strongly attract sb: *Cities have a powerful magnetizing effect on young people.*

mag·neto /mæɡˈniːtəʊ; *NAmE* -ˈniːtoʊ/ *noun* (*pl.* **-os**) a small piece of equipment that uses MAGNETS (1) to produce the electricity that lights the fuel in the engine of a car, etc.

ˈmagnet school *noun* (*NAmE*) a school in a large city that offers extra courses in some subjects in order to attract students from other areas of the city

mag·ni·fi·ca·tion /ˌmæɡnɪfɪˈkeɪʃn/ *noun* **1** [U] the act of making sth look larger: *The insects were examined under magnification.* **2** [C, U] the degree to which sth is made to look larger; the degree to which sth is able to make things look larger: *a magnification of 10 times the actual size* ◇ ***high/low magnification*** ◇ *The telescope has a magnification of 50.*

mag·nifi·cent /mæɡˈnɪfɪsnt/ *adj.* extremely attractive and impressive; deserving praise SYN **splendid**: *The Taj Mahal is a magnificent building.* ◇ *She looked magnificent in her wedding dress.* ◇ *You've all done a magnificent job.* ▸ **mag·nifi·cence** /-sns/ *noun* [U]: *the magnificence of the scenery* **mag·nifi·cent·ly** *adv.*: *The public have responded magnificently to our appeal.*

mag·ni·fier /ˈmæɡnɪfaɪə(r)/ *noun* a piece of equipment that is used to make things look larger

mag·nify /ˈmæɡnɪfaɪ/ *verb* (**mag·ni·fies, mag·ni·fy·ing, mag·ni·fied, mag·ni·fied**) **1 ~ sth (to/by sth)** to make sth look bigger than it really is, for example by using a LENS or MICROSCOPE SYN **enlarge**: *bacteria magnified to 1 000 times their actual size* ◇ *an image magnified by a factor of 4* **2 ~ sth** to make sth bigger, louder or stronger: *The sound was magnified by the high roof.* ◇ *The dry summer has magnified the problem of water shortages.* **3 ~ sth** to make sth seem more important or serious than it really is SYN **exaggerate**

ˈmagnifying glass *noun* a round piece of glass, usually with a handle, that you look through and that makes things look bigger than they really are ➲ VISUAL VOCAB page V35

mag·ni·tude /ˈmæɡnɪtjuːd; *NAmE* -tuːd/ *noun* **~ (of sth)** **1** [U] (*formal*) the great size or importance of sth; the degree to which sth is large or important: *We did not realize the magnitude of the problem.* ◇ *a discovery* ***of the first magnitude*** **2** [C, U] (*astronomy*) the degree to which a star is bright: *The star varies in brightness by about three magnitudes.* **3** [C, U] (*geology*) the size of an EARTHQUAKE

mag·no·lia /mæɡˈnəʊliə; *NAmE* -ˈnoʊ-/ *noun* **1** [C] a tree with large white, pink or purple flowers that smell sweet **2** [U] (*BrE*) a very pale cream colour

mag·num /ˈmæɡnəm/ *noun* a bottle containing 1.5 litres of wine, etc.

ˌmagnum ˈopus *noun* [sing.] (from *Latin*) a large and important work of art, literature or music, especially one that people think is the best work ever produced by that artist, writer, etc.

mag·pie /ˈmæɡpaɪ/ *noun* a black and white bird with a long tail and a noisy cry. There is a popular belief that magpies like to steal small bright objects.

magus /ˈmeɪɡəs/ *noun* (*pl.* **magi** /ˈmeɪdʒaɪ/) **1** a member of the group to which priests in ancient Persia belonged **2** a man with magic powers

maha·raja (also **maha·ra·jah**) /ˌmɑːhəˈrɑːdʒə/ *noun* an Indian prince, especially one who ruled over one of the states of India in the past

maha·rani (also **maha·ra·nee**) /ˌmɑːhəˈrɑːniː/ *noun* the wife of a maharaja

Maha·rishi /ˌmɑːhəˈrɪʃi; -ˈriː-/ *noun* a Hindu spiritual leader or wise man

ma·hatma /məˈhætmə; -ˈhɑːt-/ *noun* **1** a holy person in S Asia who is respected by many people **2 the Ma·hatma** Mahatma Gandhi, the Indian spiritual leader who opposed British rule in India

Maha·yana /ˌmɑːhəˈjɑːnə/ (also **ˌMahaˌyana ˈBuddhism**) *noun* [U] one of the two major forms of Buddhism ➲ compare THERAVADA

mah·jong (also **mah·jongg** especially in *NAmE*) /mɑːˈdʒɒŋ; *NAmE* -ˈʒɑːŋ; -ˈʒɔːŋ/ *noun* [U] (from *Chinese*) a Chi-

M

nese game played with small pieces of wood with symbols on them

ma·hog·any /mə'hɒɡəni; *NAmE* -'hɑːɡ-/ *noun* [U] **1** the hard reddish-brown wood of a tropical tree, used for making furniture: *a mahogany table* **2** a reddish-brown colour: *skin tanned to a deep mahogany*

ma·hout /mə'haʊt/ *noun* a person who works with, rides and cares for an ELEPHANT

maid /meɪd/ *noun* **1** (often in compounds) a female servant in a house or hotel: *There is a maid to do the housework.* ➲ see also BARMAID, CHAMBERMAID, DAIRYMAID, HOUSEMAID, MILKMAID, NURSEMAID **2** (*old use*) a young woman who is not married ➲ see also OLD MAID

mai·dan /maɪ'dɑːn/ *noun* an open space in or near a town in S Asia, usually covered with grass

maid·en /'meɪdn/ *noun, adj.*
- ***noun*** **1** (*literary*) a young girl or woman who is not married: *stories of knights and fair maidens* **2** (also ˌ**maiden 'over**) (in CRICKET) an OVER in which no points are scored
- ***adj.*** [only before noun] being the first of its kind: *a **maiden flight/voyage*** (= the first journey made by a plane/ship) ◇ *a **maiden speech*** (= the first speech made by an MP in the parliaments of some countries)

ˌ**maiden 'aunt** *noun* (*old-fashioned*) an aunt who has not married

maid·en·hair /'meɪdnheə(r); *NAmE* -her/ (also ˌ**maidenhair 'fern**) *noun* [U, C] a type of FERN with long thin STEMS and delicate pale green leaves that are shaped like fans

'**maidenhair tree** *noun* = GINKGO

M

maid·en·head /'meɪdnhed/ *noun* (*old use*) **1** the state of being a VIRGIN **2** = HYMEN

'**maiden name** *noun* a woman's family name before marriage: *Kate kept her maiden name when she got married* (= did not change her surname to that of her husband).

ˌ**maid of 'honour** (*especially US* ˌ**maid of 'honor**) *noun* (*pl.* **maids of honour/honor**) (especially in the US) a young woman or girl who is not married and who is the main BRIDESMAID at a wedding ➲ compare MATRON OF HONOUR

maid·ser·vant /'meɪdsɜːvənt; *NAmE* -sɜːrv-/ *noun* (*old-fashioned*) a female servant in a house

mail 0⊸ /meɪl/ *noun, verb*
- ***noun*** [U] **1** 0⊸ (*BrE* also **post**) the official system used for sending and delivering letters, packages, etc: *a **mail service/train/van*** ◇ *the Royal Mail* ◇ *Your cheque is in the mail.* ◇ *We do our business **by mail**.* ➲ see also AIRMAIL, SNAIL MAIL, VOICEMAIL **2** 0⊸ (*BrE* also **post**) letters, packages, etc. that are sent and delivered: *There isn't much mail today.* ◇ *I sat down to open **the mail**.* ◇ *Is there a letter from them **in the mail**?* ◇ ***hate mail*** (= letters containing insults and threats) ➲ see also JUNK MAIL, SURFACE MAIL ➲ note at POST **3** 0⊸ messages that are sent or received on a computer: *Check regularly for new mail.* ➲ see also ELECTRONIC MAIL, EMAIL **4** used in the title of some newspapers: *the Mail on Sunday* **5** = CHAIN MAIL: *a coat of mail*
- ***verb*** **1** 0⊸ (*especially NAmE*) to send sth to sb using the POSTAL system: **~ sth (to sb/sth)** *Don't forget to mail that letter to your mother.* ◇ **~ sb sth** *Don't forget to mail your mother that letter.* ◇ **~ sb/sth** *The company intends to mail 50 000 households in the area.* ➲ note at POST **2** 0⊸ (*BrE*) to send a message to sb by email: **~ sb** *Please mail us at the following email address.* ◇ **~ sth (to sb/sth)** *The virus mails itself forward to everyone in your address book.* ◇ **~ sb sth** *Can you mail me that document you mentioned?*

PHR V ˌ**mail sth↔'out** to send out a large number of letters, etc. at the same time: *The brochures were mailed out last week.*

mail·bag /'meɪlbæɡ/ (*BrE* also **post·bag**) *noun* **1** a large strong bag that is used for carrying letters and packages **2** [usually sing.] all the letters, emails, etc. received by a newspaper, a TV station, a website, or an important person at a particular time or about a particular subject

'**mail bomb** *noun, verb*
- ***noun*** **1** (*NAmE*) = LETTER BOMB **2** an extremely large number of email messages that are sent to sb
- ***verb*** '**mail-bomb ~ sb/sth** to send sb an extremely large number of email messages: *The newspaper was mail-bombed by angry readers after the article was published.*

mail·box /'meɪlbɒks; *NAmE* -bɑːks/ *noun* **1** (*NAmE*) (*BrE* '**letter box**) a small box near the main door of a building or by the road, which mail is delivered to **2** (*NAmE*) (*BrE* **post·box**, '**letter box**) a public box, for example in the street, that you put letters into when you send them ➲ picture at LETTER BOX **3** the area of a computer's memory where email messages are stored

'**mail carrier** (also '**letter carrier**) (both *NAmE*) *noun* ➲ MAILMAN

'**mail drop** *noun* **1** (*especially NAmE*) an address where sb's mail is delivered, which is not where they live or work **2** (*NAmE*) a box in a building where sb's mail is kept for them to collect **3** (*BrE*) an occasion when mail is delivered

mail·er /'meɪlə(r)/ *noun* (*NAmE*) **1** = MAILING (2) **2** an envelope, box, etc. for sending small things by mail

mail·ing /'meɪlɪŋ/ *noun* **1** [U] the act of sending items by mail: *The strike has delayed the mailing of tax reminders.* ◇ *a mailing address* **2** (*NAmE* also **mailer**) [C] a letter or package that is sent by mail, especially one that is sent to a large number of people: *An order form is included in the mailing.*

'**mailing list** *noun* **1** a list of the names and addresses of people who are regularly sent information, advertising material, etc. by an organization: *I am already on your mailing list.* **2** a list of names and email addresses kept on a computer so that you can send a message to a number of people at the same time

mail·man /'meɪlmæn/ *noun* (*pl.* **-men** /-men/) (also '**mail carrier**, '**letter carrier**) (all *NAmE*) a person whose job is to collect and deliver letters, etc. ➲ see also POSTMAN ➲ note at GENDER

Mail·merge™ /'meɪlmɜːdʒ; *NAmE* -mɜːrdʒ/ *noun* [U] a computer program that allows names and addresses to be automatically added to letters and envelopes, so that letters with the same contents can be sent to many different people

ˌ**mail 'order** *noun* [U] a system of buying and selling goods through the mail: *All our products are available by mail order.* ◇ *a mail-order company* ◇ *a mail-order catalogue*

mail·shot /'meɪlʃɒt; *NAmE* -ʃɑːt/ *noun* advertising or information that is sent to a large number of people at the same time by mail

'**mail slot** (*NAmE*) (*BrE* '**letter box**) *noun* a narrow opening in a door or wall through which mail is delivered ➲ picture at LETTER BOX

maim /meɪm/ *verb* **~ sb** to injure sb seriously, causing permanent damage to their body SYN **incapacitate**: *Hundreds of people are killed or maimed in car accidents every week.*

main 0⊸ /meɪn/ *adj., noun*
- ***adj.*** 0⊸ [only before noun] being the largest or most important of its kind: *Be careful crossing the **main road**.* ◇ *the **main course*** (= of a meal) ◇ *We have our main meal at lunchtime.* ◇ *Reception is in the main building.* ◇ *Poor housing and unemployment are the main problems.* ◇ ***The main thing*** *is to stay calm.* IDM see EYE *n.*
- ***noun*** **1** [C] a large pipe that carries water or gas to a building; a large cable that carries electricity to a building: *a leaking gas main* ➲ see also WATER MAIN **2** a large pipe that carries waste/water and SEWAGE (= human waste, etc.) away from a building **3 the mains** [pl.] (*BrE*) the place where the supply of water, gas or electricity to a building or an area starts; the system of providing gas, water and electricity to a building or of carrying it away from a building: *The house is not yet connected to the mains.* ◇ *The electricity supply has been cut off **at the mains**.* ◇ *Plug the transformer into the mains* (= the place on a wall where electricity is brought into a room). ◇ ***mains gas/***

water/electricity ◇ *The shaver will run off batteries or mains.* ◇ *mains drainage*

IDM **in the 'main** used to say that a statement is true in most cases: *The service here is, in the main, reliable.*

Synonyms

main

major • key • central • principal • chief • prime

These words all describe sb/sth that is the largest or most important of its kind.

main [only before noun] largest or most important: *Be careful crossing the main road.* ◇ *The main thing is to remain calm.*

major [usually before noun] very large or important: *He played a major role in setting up the system.* NOTE **Major** is most often used after *a* with a singular noun, or no article with a plural noun. When it is used with *the* or *my/your/his/her/our/their* it means 'the largest or most important': *Our major concern here is combatting poverty.* In this meaning it is only used to talk about ideas or worries that people have, not physical things, and it is also more formal than **main**: ~~*Be careful crossing the major road.*~~ ◇ ~~*The major thing is to remain calm.*~~

key [usually before noun] most important; essential: *He was a key figure in the campaign.* NOTE **Key** is used most frequently in business and political contexts. It can be used to talk about ideas, or the part that sb plays in a situation, but not physical things. It is slightly more informal than **major**, especially when used after a noun and linking verb: *Speed is key at this point.*

central (*rather formal*) most important: *The central issue is that of widespread racism.* NOTE **Central** is used in a similar way to **key**, but is more formal. It is most frequently used in the phrase *sth is central to sth else.*

principal [only before noun] (*rather formal*) most important: *The principal reason for this omission is lack of time.* NOTE **Principal** is mostly used for statements of fact about which there can be no argument. To state an opinion, or to try to persuade sb of the facts as you see them, it is more usual to use **key** or **central**: *The key/central issue here is...*

chief [only before noun] (*rather formal*) most important: *Unemployment was the chief cause of poverty.*

prime [only before noun] (*rather formal*) most important; to be considered first: *My prime concern is to protect my property.*

PATTERNS

- a/the main/major/key/central/principal/chief/prime **aim/concern**
- a/the main/major/principal **road/town/city**
- the main/key **thing** is to...
- to be **of** major/key/central/prime **importance**

,main 'clause *noun* (*grammar*) a group of words that includes a subject and a verb and can form a sentence ➲ compare SUBORDINATE CLAUSE

the ,main 'drag *noun* [sing.] (*NAmE, informal*) the most important or the busiest street in a town

main·frame /'meɪnfreɪm/ (also **,mainframe com'puter**) *noun* a large powerful computer, usually the centre of a network and shared by many users ➲ compare MICROCOMPUTER, MINICOMPUTER, PERSONAL COMPUTER

the main·land /'meɪnlænd/ *noun* [sing.] the main area of land of a country, not including any islands near to it: *a boat* ***to/from the mainland*** ◇ *The Hebrides are to the west of the Scottish mainland.* ▶ **main·land** *adj.* [only before noun]: *mainland Greece*

,main 'line *noun* an important railway/railroad line between two cities ▶ **,main-'line** *adj.*: *a main-line station*

main·line /'meɪnlaɪn/ *adj., verb*

■ ***adj.*** (*especially NAmE*) belonging to the system, or connected with the ideas that most people accept or believe in SYN **mainstream**: ***mainline churches/faiths***

■ ***verb*** [T, I] **~** (**sth**) (*slang*) to take an illegal drug by INJECTING it into a VEIN: *At 18 he was mainlining heroin.*

main·ly 0-w /'meɪnli/ *adv.*

1 0-w more than anything else; also used to talk about the most important reason for sth SYN **chiefly**, **primarily**: *They eat mainly fruit and nuts.* ◇ *'Where do you export to?' 'France, mainly.'* ◇ *The population almost doubles in summer,* ***mainly because of*** *the jazz festival.* **2** 0-w in most cases; used to talk about the largest part of a group of people or things: *Anorexia is an illness that occurs mainly in adolescents.* ◇ *The people in the hotel were mainly foreign tourists.* ➲ LANGUAGE BANK at GENERALLY

,main 'man *noun* [sing.] (*informal*) a man who is important to you because he is a trusted friend or employee: *Of course I trust you—you're my main man!*

main·sail /'meɪnseɪl; 'meɪnsl/ *noun* the largest and most important sail on a boat or ship ➲ VISUAL VOCAB page V45

main·spring /'meɪnsprɪŋ/ *noun* **1** [usually sing.] **~** (**of sth**) (*formal*) the most important part of sth; the most important influence on sth **2** the most important spring in a watch, clock, etc.

main·stay /'meɪnsteɪ/ *noun* [usually sing.] **~** (**of sth**) a person or thing that is the most important part of sth and enables it to exist or be successful: *Cocoa is the country's economic mainstay.*

main·stream /'meɪnstriːm/ *noun, adj., verb*

■ ***noun*** **the mainstream** [sing.] the ideas and opinions that are thought to be normal because they are shared by most people; the people whose ideas and opinions are most accepted: *His radical views place him outside the mainstream of American politics.* ▶ **main·stream** *adj.* [usually before noun]: *mainstream education*

■ ***verb*** **1 ~ sth** to make a particular idea or opinion accepted by most people: *Vegetarianism has been mainstreamed.* **2 ~ sb** (*especially NAmE*) to include children with mental or physical problems in ordinary school classes

'main street *noun* (*NAmE*) **1** (*BrE* **'high street**) [C] (especially in names) the main street of a town, where most shops/stores, banks, etc. are ➲ VISUAL VOCAB page V3 **2 Main Street** [U] typical middle-class Americans: *Main Street won't be happy with this new program.*

main·tain 0-w AW /meɪn'teɪn/ *verb*

1 0-w **~ sth** to make sth continue at the same level, standard, etc. SYN **preserve**: *to* ***maintain law and order/standards/a balance*** ◇ *The two countries have always maintained close relations.* ◇ (*formal*) *She maintained a dignified silence.* ◇ *to maintain prices* (= prevent them falling or rising) **2** 0-w **~ sth** to keep a building, a machine, etc. in good condition by checking or repairing it regularly: *The house is large and difficult to maintain.* **3** 0-w to keep stating that sth is true, even though other people do not agree or do not believe it SYN **insist**: **~** (**that**)... *The men maintained (that) they were out of the country when the crime was committed.* ◇ **~ sth** *She has always* ***maintained her innocence.*** ◇ **+ speech** *'But I'm innocent!' she maintained.* ➲ LANGUAGE BANK at ARGUE **4** 0-w **~ sb/sth** to support sb/sth over a long period of time by giving money, paying for food, etc. SYN **keep**: *Her income was barely enough to maintain one child, let alone three.*

main·ten·ance AW /'meɪntənəns/ *noun* [U] **1 ~** (**of sth**) the act of keeping sth in good condition by checking or repairing it regularly: *The school pays for heating and the maintenance of the buildings.* ◇ *car maintenance* **2 ~** (**of sth**) the act of making a state or situation continue: *the maintenance of international peace* **3** (*law*) (*BrE*) money that sb must pay regularly to their former wife, husband or partner, especially when they have had children together: *He has to pay maintenance to his ex-wife.* ◇ *child maintenance* ◇ *a maintenance order* (= given by a court of law) ➲ see also ALIMONY

M

ˌ**main ˈverb** *noun* [usually sing.] (*grammar*) the verb in a MAIN CLAUSE

mai·son·ette /ˌmeɪzəˈnet/ *noun* (*BrE*) a flat/apartment with rooms on two floors within a building, usually with a separate entrance

maître d' /ˌmeɪtrə ˈdiː; *NAmE* also ˌmeɪtər/ *noun* (*pl.* **maître d's** /ˌmeɪtrə ˈdiːz; *NAmE* also ˌmeɪtər/) (also *formal* **maître d'hôtel** /ˌmeɪtrə dəʊˈtel; *NAmE* doʊˈtel; *NAmE* also ˌmeɪtər/ *pl.* **maîtres d'hôtel** /ˌmeɪtrə dəʊˈtel; *NAmE* doʊˈtel; *NAmE* also ˌmeɪtər/) (from *French, informal*) **1** a head waiter **2** a man who manages a hotel

maize /meɪz/ *noun* [U] **1** (*BrE*) (*NAmE* **corn**) a tall plant grown for its large yellow grains that are used for making flour or eaten as a vegetable; the grains of this plant ➲ VISUAL VOCAB page V28 ➲ see also CORN ON THE COB, SWEETCORN **2** (*especially NAmE*) = INDIAN CORN

Maj. *abbr.* (in writing) MAJOR: *Maj. (Tony) Davies* ◇ *Maj. Gen.* (= Major General)

ma·jes·tic /məˈdʒestɪk/ *adj.* impressive because of size or beauty SYN **awe-inspiring, splendid**: *a majestic castle/river/view* ▸ **ma·jes·tic·al·ly** /-kli/ *adv.*

maj·esty /ˈmædʒəsti/ *noun* (*pl.* -ies) **1** [U] the impressive and attractive quality that sth has: *the sheer majesty of St Peter's in Rome* ◇ *the majesty of the music* **2** [C] **His/Her/Your Majesty** a title of respect used when speaking about or to a king or queen **3** [U] royal power

major 🔑 AW /ˈmeɪdʒə(r)/ *adj., noun, verb*

■ ***adj.*** **1** 🔑 [usually before noun] very large or important: *a major road* ◇ *major international companies* ◇ *to play a major role in sth* ◇ *We have encountered major problems.* ◇ *There were calls for major changes to the welfare system.* OPP **minor** ➲ SYNONYMS at MAIN ➲ see also MINOR-LEAGUE **2** [not before noun] (*NAmE*) serious: *Never mind—it's not major.* **3** (*music*) based on a SCALE (= a series of eight notes) in which the third note is two whole TONES/STEPS higher than the first note: *the key of D major* ➲ compare MINOR **4** (*NAmE*) related to sb's main subject of study in college

■ ***noun*** **1** [C] (*abbr.* **Maj.**) an officer of fairly high rank in the army or the US AIR FORCE: *Major Smith* ◇ *He's a major in the US army.* ➲ see also DRUM MAJOR, SERGEANT MAJOR **2** [C] (*NAmE*) the main subject or course of a student at college or university: *Her major is French.* ➲ compare MINOR **3** [C] (*NAmE*) a student studying a particular subject as the main part of their course: *She's a French major.* **4 the majors** [pl.] (*sport*) (*NAmE*) the MAJOR LEAGUES

■ ***verb***

PHR V ˈ**major in sth** (*NAmE*) to study sth as your main subject at a university or college: *She majored in History at Stanford.* ˈ**major on sth** (*BrE*) to pay particular attention to one subject, issue, etc.

major-domo /ˌmeɪdʒə ˈdəʊməʊ; *NAmE* ˌmeɪdʒər ˈdoʊmoʊ/ *noun* (*pl.* -os) a senior servant who manages a large house

ma·jor·ette /ˌmeɪdʒəˈret/ *noun* (*especially NAmE*) = DRUM MAJORETTE

ˌ**major ˈgeneral** *noun* an officer of very high rank in the army or the US AIR FORCE: *Major General William Hunt*

ma·jor·ity 🔑 AW /məˈdʒɒrəti; *NAmE* -ˈdʒɔːr-; -ˈdʒɑːr-/ *noun* (*pl.* -ies)

1 🔑 [sing.+ sing./pl. v.] **~ (of sb/sth)** the largest part of a group of people or things: *The majority of people interviewed prefer TV to radio.* ◇ *The majority was/were in favour of banning smoking*. ◇ *This treatment is not available in the* ***vast majority*** *of hospitals.* ◇ *a majority decision* (= one that is decided by what most people want) ◇ *In the nursing profession, women are* ***in a/the majority.*** OPP **minority** ➲ see also MORAL MAJORITY, THE SILENT MAJORITY **2** 🔑 [C] (*BrE*) the number of votes by which one political party wins an election; the number of votes by which one side in a discussion, etc. wins: *She was elected* ***by/with a majority*** *of 749.* ◇ *a clear* (= large) *majority* ◇ **~ (over sb)** *They had a large majority over their nearest rivals.* ◇ *The government does not have an* ***overall majority*** (= more members than all the other parties added together). ◇ *The resolution was carried by a huge majority.* ➲ COLLOCATIONS at VOTE ➲ see also ABSOLUTE MAJORITY **3** 🔑 [C] (*NAmE*) the difference between the number of votes given to the candidate who wins the election and the total number of votes of all the other candidates ➲ see also PLURALITY **4** [U] (*law*) the age at which you are legally considered to be an adult

maˈ**jority leader** *noun* the leader of the political party that has the majority in either the House of Representatives or the Senate in the US

maˌ**jority ˈrule** *noun* [U] a system in which power is held by the group that has the largest number of members

maˌ**jority ˈverdict** *noun* (*law*) a decision made by a JURY in a court case that most members, but not all, agree with

ˈ**major league** (also ˈ**Major league**) *noun* (*NAmE*) a league of professional sports teams, especially in BASEBALL, that play at the highest level

ˈ**major-league** *adj.* [only before noun] (*NAmE*) **1** (*sport*) connected with teams that play in the major leagues, especially in BASEBALL: *a major-league team* **2** very important and having a lot of influence: *a major-league business*

major·ly /ˈmeɪdʒəli; *NAmE* -dʒərli/ *adv.* (used before an adjective) (*informal, especially NAmE*) very; extremely: *majorly disappointed*

Synonyms

make

do • create • develop • produce • generate • form

These words all mean to make sth from parts or materials, or to cause sth to exist or happen.

make to create or prepare sth by combining materials or putting parts together; to cause sth to exist or happen: *She makes her own clothes.* ◇ *She* ***made a good impression*** *on the interviewer.*

do (*rather informal*) to make or prepare sth, especially sth artistic or sth to eat: *He did a beautiful drawing of a house.* ◇ *Who's doing the food for the party?*

create to make sth exist or happen, especially sth new that did not exist before: *Scientists disagree about how the universe was created.*

MAKE OR CREATE?

Make is a more general word and is more often used for physical things: you would usually *make a table/dress/cake* but *create jobs/wealth*. You can use **create** for sth physical in order to emphasize how original or unusual the object is: *Try this new dish, created by our head chef.*

develop (used especially in business contexts) to think of and produce a new product: *to develop new software*

produce to make things to be sold; to create sth using skill: *a factory that produces microchips*

generate to produce or create sth, especially power, money or ideas: *to generate electricity* ◇ *Brainstorming is a good way of generating ideas.*

form [often passive] to make sth from sth else; to make sth into sth else: *Rearrange the letters to form a new word.* ◇ *The chain is formed from 136 links.*

PATTERNS

- to make/create/develop/produce/generate/form sth **from/out of** sth
- to make/form sth **into** sth
- to make/produce **wine**
- to create/develop a **new product**
- to create/produce/generate **income/profits/wealth**
- to produce/generate **electricity/heat/power**

make 🔑 /meɪk/ *verb, noun* ➲ see also MADE

■ ***verb*** (**made, made** /meɪd/)

▸ CREATE **1** 🔑 to create or prepare sth by combining materials or putting parts together: **~ sth** *to make a table/dress/*

cake ◇ *to make bread/cement/paper* ◇ *She makes her own clothes.* ◇ *made in France* (= on a label) ◇ **~ sth** (**out**) **of sth** *What's your shirt made of?* ◇ **~ sth from sth** *Wine is made from grapes.* ◇ **~ sth into sth** *The grapes are made into wine.* ◇ **~ sth for sb** *She made coffee for us all.* ◇ **~ sb sth** *She made us all coffee.* ➲ note at DO **2** ⊶ **~ sth** to write, create or prepare sth: *These regulations were made to protect children.* ◇ *My lawyer has been urging me to make a will.* ◇ *She has made* (= directed or acted in) *several movies.*

▸ A BED **3** ⊶ **~ a bed** to arrange a bed so that it is neat and ready for use

▸ CAUSE TO APPEAR/HAPPEN/BECOME/DO **4** ⊶ **~ sth** (**+ adv./prep.**) to cause sth to appear as a result of breaking, tearing, hitting or removing material: *The stone made a dent in the roof of the car.* ◇ *The holes in the cloth were made by moths.* **5** ⊶ **~ sth** to cause sth to exist, happen or be done: *to* ***make a noise/mess/fuss*** ◇ *She tried to* ***make a good impression*** *on the interviewer.* ◇ *I keep* ***making*** *the same* ***mistakes.*** **6** ⊶ **~ sb/sth/yourself + adj.** to cause sb/sth to be or become sth: *The news made him very happy.* ◇ *She made her objections clear.* ◇ *He* ***made it clear that*** *he objected.* ◇ *The full story was never* ***made public.*** ◇ *Can you* ***make yourself understood*** *in Russian?* ◇ *She couldn't* ***make herself heard*** *above the noise of the traffic.* ◇ *The terrorists* ***made it known that*** *tourists would be targeted.* **7** ⊶ **~ sb/sth do sth** to cause sb/sth to do sth: *She always makes me laugh.* ◇ *This dress makes me look fat.* ◇ *What makes you say that* (= why do you think so)? ◇ *Nothing will make me change my mind.* **8** ⊶ to cause sb/sth to be or become sth: **~ sth of sb/sth** *This isn't very important—I don't want to* ***make an issue of it.*** ◇ *Don't* ***make a habit of it.*** ◇ *You've* ***made a*** *terrible* ***mess of*** *this job.* ◇ *It's important to try and* ***make something of*** (= achieve sth in) *your life.* ◇ *We'll make a tennis player of you yet.* ◇ **~ sth + noun** *I made painting the house my project for the summer.* ◇ *She* ***made it her business*** *to find out who was responsible.*

▸ A DECISION/GUESS/COMMENT, ETC. **9** ⊶ **~ a decision, guess, comment, etc.** to decide, guess, etc. sth: *Come on! It's time we made a start.* HELP **Make** can be used in this way with a number of different nouns. These expressions are included at the entry for each noun.

▸ FORCE **10** ⊶ to force sb to do sth: **~ sb do sth** *They made me repeat the whole story.* ◇ **be made to do sth** *She must be made to comply with the rules.* ◇ **~ sb** *He never cleans his room and his mother never tries to make him.*

▸ REPRESENT **11** ⊶ to represent sb/sth as being or doing sth: **~ sb/sth + adj.** *You've made my nose too big* (= for example in a drawing). ◇ **~ sb/sth + noun** *He makes King Lear a truly tragic figure.*

▸ APPOINT **12** ⊶ **~ sb + noun** to elect or choose sb as sth: *She made him her assistant.*

▸ BE SUITABLE **13** ⊶ *linking verb* **~ sb/sth + noun** to become or develop into sth; to be suitable for sth: *She would have made an excellent teacher.* ◇ *This room would make a nice office.*

▸ EQUAL **14** ⊶ *linking verb* **+ noun** to add up to or equal sth: *5 and 7 make 12.* ◇ *A hundred cents make one euro.* **15** *linking verb* **+ noun** to be a total of sth: *That makes the third time he's failed his driving test!*

▸ MONEY **16** ⊶ **~ sth** to earn or gain money: *She makes $100 000 a year.* ◇ *to* ***make a profit/loss*** ◇ *We need to think of ways to* ***make money.*** ◇ *He* ***made a fortune*** *on the stock market.* ◇ *He* ***makes a living*** *as a stand-up comic.*

▸ CALCULATE **17** [no passive] **~ sth + noun** to think or calculate sth to be sth: *What time do you* ***make it?*** ◇ *I make that exactly $50.*

▸ REACH **18** [no passive] **~ sth** to manage to reach or go to a place or position: *Do you think we'll make Dover by 12?* ◇ *I'm sorry I couldn't make your party last night.* ◇ *He'll never make* (= get a place in) *the team.* ◇ *The story made* (= appeared on) *the front pages of the national newspapers.* ◇ *We just managed to* ***make the deadline*** (= to finish sth in time).

▸ STH SUCCESSFUL **19** **~ sth** to cause sth to be a success: *Good wine can make a meal.* ◇ *The news really* ***made my day.***

IDM Most idioms containing **make** are at the entries for the nouns and adjectives in the idioms, for example **make merry** is at **merry**. **make as if to do sth** to make a movement that makes it seem as if you are just going to do sth: *He made as if to speak.* **make 'do (with sth)** to manage with sth that is not really good enough: *We were in a hurry so we had to make do with a quick snack.* **make 'good** to become rich and successful **make sth 'good 1** to pay for, replace or repair sth that has been lost or damaged: *She promised to make good the damage.* **2** to do sth that you have promised, threatened, etc. to do SYN **fulfil** **'make it 1** ⊶ to be successful in your career: *He never really made it as an actor.* **2** ⊶ to succeed in reaching a place in time, especially when this is difficult: *The flight leaves in twenty minutes—we'll never make it.* **3** ⊶ to be able to be present at a place: *I'm sorry I won't be able to make it* (= for example, to a party) *on Saturday.* **4** ⊶ to survive after a serious illness or accident; to deal successfully with a difficult experience: *The doctors think he's going to make it.* ◇ *I don't know how I* ***made it through*** *the week.* **'make it with sb** (*NAmE, slang*) to have sex with sb **make like...** (*NAmE, informal*) to pretend to be, know or have sth in order to impress people: *He makes like he's the greatest actor of all time.* **make the 'most of sth/sb/yourself** to gain as much advantage, enjoyment, etc. as you can from sb/sth: *It's my first trip abroad so I'm going to make the most of it.* ◇ *She doesn't know how to make the most of herself* (= make herself appear in the best possible way). **make 'much of sth/sb** to treat sth/sb as very important: *He always makes much of his humble origins.* **ˌmake or 'break sb/sth** to be the thing that makes sb/sth either a success or a failure: *This movie will make or break him as a director.* ◇ *It's make-or-break time for the company.* **'make something of yourself** to be successful in your life

PHR V **'make for sth 1** to move towards sth SYN **head for** **2** to help to make sth possible: *Constant arguing doesn't make for a happy marriage.* ➲ see also BE MADE FOR SB/EACH OTHER at MADE

'make sb/sth into sb/sth ⊶ to change sb/sth into sb/sth SYN **turn into**: *We're making our attic into an extra bedroom.*

'make sth of sb/sth to understand the meaning or character of sb/sth: ***What do you make of*** *it all?* ◇ *I can't make anything of this note.* ◇ *I don't know* ***what to make of*** (= think of) *the new manager.*

ˌmake 'off to hurry away, especially in order to escape

ˌmake 'off with sth to steal sth and hurry away with it

ˌmake 'out 1 (*informal*) used to ask if sb managed well or was successful in a particular situation: *How did he make out while his wife was away?* **2 ~ (with sb)** (*NAmE, informal*) to kiss and touch sb in a sexual way; to have sex with sb

ˌmake sb 'out to understand sb's character **ˌmake sb/sth↔'out 1** to manage to see sb/sth or read or hear sth SYN **distinguish**: *I could just make out a figure in the darkness.* ◇ **~ what, who, etc...** *I could hear voices but I couldn't make out what they were saying.* ➲ SYNONYMS at IDENTIFY **2** to say that sth is true when it may not be SYN **claim**: *She's not as rich as people make out.* ◇ **~ that...** *He made out that he had been robbed.* ◇ **~ to be/do sth** *She makes herself out to be smarter than she really is.* **ˌmake sth↔'out 1** to write out or complete a form or document: *He made out a cheque for €100.* ◇ *The doctor made out a prescription for me.* **2** (used in negative sentences and questions) to understand sth; to see the reasons for sth: *How do you make that out* (= what are your reasons for thinking that)? ◇ **~ what, why, etc...** *I can't make out what she wants.*

ˌmake sth↔'over (to sb/sth) 1 to legally give sth to sb: *He made over the property to his eldest son.* **2** to change sth in order to make it look different or use it for a different purpose; to give sb a different appearance by changing their clothes, hair, etc. SYN **transform** ➲ related noun MAKEOVER

'make towards sth to start moving towards sth: *He made towards the door.*

ˌmake 'up | ˌmake yourself/sb↔'up to put powder, LIPSTICK, etc. on your/sb's face to make it more attractive or to prepare for an appearance in the theatre, on television, etc. ➲ related noun MAKE-UP (1) **ˌmake sth↔'up 1** ⊶ to form sth SYN **constitute**: *Women make up 56% of the student numbers.* ➲ related noun MAKE-UP ➲ SYNONYMS at

CONSIST OF ➲ LANGUAGE BANK at PROPORTION **2** to put sth together from several different things ➲ related noun MAKE-UP **3** 🗝 to invent a story, etc, especially in order to trick or entertain sb: *He made up some excuse about his daughter being sick.* ◇ *I told the kids a story, making it up as I went along.* ◇ *You made that up!* **4** to complete a number or an amount required: *We need one more person to make up a team.* **5** to replace sth that has been lost; to COMPENSATE for sth: *Can I leave early this afternoon and make up the time tomorrow?* **6** to prepare a medicine by mixing different things together **7** to prepare a bed for use; to create a temporary bed: *We made up the bed in the spare room.* ◇ *They made up a bed for me on the sofa.* **8** (*especially NAmE*) to clean a hotel room and make the bed: *The maid asked if she could make up the room.* **ˌmake ˈup for sth** 🗝 to do sth that corrects a bad situation SYN **compensate**: *Nothing can make up for the loss of a child.* ◇ *After all the delays, we were anxious to **make up for lost time**.* ◇ *Her enthusiasm makes up for her lack of experience.* **ˌmake ˈup (to sb) for sth** 🗝 to do sth for sb or give them sth because you have caused them trouble, suffering or disappointment and wish to show that you are sorry SYN **compensate**: *How can I make up for the way I've treated you?* ◇ (*informal*) *I'll **make it up to you**, I promise.* **ˌmake ˈup to sb** (*BrE, informal, disapproving*) to be pleasant to sb, praise them, etc. especially in order to get an advantage for yourself **ˌmake ˈup (with sb)** (*BrE* also **ˌmake it ˈup**) to end a disagreement with sb and become friends again: *Why don't you two **kiss and make up**?* ◇ *Has he made it up with her yet?* ◇ *Have they made it up yet?*

■ ***noun*** 🗝 **~ (of sth)** the name or type of a machine, piece of equipment, etc. that is made by a particular company: *What make of car does he drive?* ◇ *There are so many different makes to choose from.* ◇ *a Swiss make of watch*

IDM **on the ˈmake** (*informal, disapproving*) trying to get money or an advantage for yourself

ˈmake-believe *noun* [U] **1** (*disapproving*) imagining or pretending things to be different or more exciting than they really are SYN **fantasy**: *They live in a world of make-believe.* **2** imagining that sth is real, or that you are sb else, for example in a child's game: *'Let's play make-believe,' said Sam.*

make·over /ˈmeɪkəʊvə(r); *NAmE* -oʊ-/ *noun* [C, U] the process of improving the appearance of a person or a place, or of changing the impression that sth gives

maker /ˈmeɪkə(r)/ *noun* **1** [C] **~ (of sth)** (often in compounds) a person, company, or piece of equipment that makes or produces sth: *a **decision/law/policy maker*** ◇ *programme makers* ◇ *a new film/movie from the makers of 'Terminator'* ◇ *If it doesn't work, send it back to the maker.* ◇ *an electric coffee-maker* ◇ *one of the best winemakers in France* ➲ VISUAL VOCAB page V22 ➲ see also HOLIDAYMAKER, PEACEMAKER, TROUBLEMAKER **2 the, his, your, etc. Maker** [sing.] God IDM see MEET *v.*

make·shift /ˈmeɪkʃɪft/ *adj.* [usually before noun] used temporarily for a particular purpose because the real thing is not available SYN **provisional, improvised**: *A few cushions formed a makeshift bed.*

ˈmake-up 🗝 *noun*

1 🗝 [U] substances used especially by women to make their faces look more attractive, or used by actors to change their appearance: *eye make-up* ◇ *to **put on your make-up*** ◇ *She never **wears make-up**.* ◇ *a make-up artist* (= a person whose job is to put make-up on the faces of actors and models) ➲ COLLOCATIONS at FASHION ➲ VISUAL VOCAB page V49 **2** [sing.] the different qualities that combine to form sb's character or being: *Jealousy is not part of his make-up.* ◇ *a person's genetic make-up* **3** [sing.] **~ (of sth)** the different things, people, etc. that combine to form sth; the way in which they combine: *the make-up of a TV audience* ◇ (*technical*) *the page make-up of a text* (= the way in which the words and pictures are arranged on a page) **4** [C] (*NAmE*) a special exam taken by students who missed or failed an earlier one

make·weight /ˈmeɪkweɪt/ *noun* an unimportant person or thing that is only added or included in sth in order to make it the correct number, quantity, size, etc.

ˈmake-work *noun* [U] (*NAmE*) work that has little value but is given to people to keep them busy: *In some departments there is too much make-work.* ◇ *These are simply make-work schemes for accountants.*

mak·ing /ˈmeɪkɪŋ/ *noun* [U] **~ (of sth)** (often in compounds) the act or process of making or producing sth: *strategic decision making* ◇ *film-making* ◇ *dressmaking* ◇ *tea and coffee making facilities* ◇ *the making of social policy* ➲ see also HAYMAKING, NON-PROFIT

IDM **be the ˈmaking of sb** to make sb become a better or more successful person: *University was the making of Joe.* **have the ˈmakings of sth** to have the qualities that are necessary to become sth: *Her first novel has all the makings of a classic.* **in the ˈmaking** in the process of becoming sth or of being made: *This model was two years in the making.* ◇ *These events are **history in the making**.* **of your own ˈmaking** (of a problem, difficulty, etc.) created by you rather than by sb/sth else

ma·kuti /mæˈkuːti/ *noun* [pl.] the leaves of a PALM tree, used as a material to make fences, BASKETS, etc. and roofs, especially on the coast of E Africa: *a makuti roof*

mal- /mæl/ *combining form* (in nouns, verbs and adjectives) bad or badly; not correct or correctly: *malpractice* ◇ *malodorous* ◇ *malfunction*

mal·ach·ite /ˈmæləkaɪt/ *noun* [U] a green mineral that can be polished, used to make decorative objects

mal·adjust·ed /ˌmæləˈdʒʌstɪd/ *adj.* (especially of children) having mental and emotional problems that lead to unacceptable behaviour ➲ compare WELL ADJUSTED ▶ **mal·adjust·ment** /ˌmæləˈdʒʌstmənt/ *noun* [U]

mal·admin·is·tra·tion /ˌmælədˌmɪnɪˈstreɪʃn/ *noun* [U] (*formal*) the fact of managing a business or an organization in a bad or dishonest way

mal·adroit /ˌmæləˈdrɔɪt/ *adj.* (*formal*) done without skill, especially in a way that annoys or offends people SYN **clumsy**

mal·ady /ˈmælədi/ *noun* (*pl.* -ies) **1** (*formal*) a serious problem SYN **ill**: *Violent crime is only one of the maladies afflicting modern society.* **2** (*old use*) an illness

mal·aise /məˈleɪz/ *noun* [U, sing.] (*formal*) **1** the problems affecting a particular situation or group of people that are difficult to explain or identify: ***economic/financial/social malaise*** **2** a general feeling of being ill/sick, unhappy or not satisfied, without signs of any particular problem SYN **unease**: *a serious malaise among the staff*

mala·prop·ism /ˈmæləprɒpɪzəm; *NAmE* -prɑːp-/ *noun* an amusing mistake sb makes when they use a word which sounds similar to the word they wanted to use, but means sth different ORIGIN From Mrs Malaprop, a character in Richard Brinsley Sheridan's play *The Rivals*, who confuses words like this all the time.

mal·aria /məˈleəriə; *NAmE* -ˈler-/ *noun* [U] a disease that causes fever and SHIVERING (= shaking of the body) caused by the bite of some types of MOSQUITO ▶ **mal·ar·ial** /-iəl/ *adj.*: ***malarial insects/patients/regions***

ma·lar·key /məˈlɑːki; *NAmE* məˈlɑːrki/ *noun* [U] (*informal, disapproving*) behaviour or an idea that you think is nonsense or has no meaning

Ma·lay·alam /ˌmʌləˈjɑːləm; ˌmɑːlə-/ *noun* [U] a language spoken in Kerala in SW India

mal·con·tent /ˈmælkəntent; *NAmE* ˌmælkənˈtent/ *noun* [usually pl.] (*formal, disapproving*) a person who is not satisfied with a situation and who complains about it, or causes trouble in order to change it

male 🗝 /meɪl/ *adj., noun*

■ ***adj.* 1** 🗝 (*abbr.* m) belonging to the sex that does not give birth to babies; connected with this sex: *a male bird* ◇ *All the attackers were male, aged between 25 and 30.* ◇ *a **male nurse/model/colleague*** ◇ *male attitudes to women* ◇ ***male bonding*** (= the act of forming close friendships between men) ◇ *the **male menopause*** (= emotional and physical problems that affect some men at about the age of 50)

➲ compare MASCULINE ➲ see also ALPHA MALE **2** (*biology*) (of most plants) producing POLLEN: *a male flower* **3** (*technical*) (of electrical PLUGS, parts of tools, etc.) having a part that sticks out which is designed to fit into a hole, SOCKET, etc. ➲ compare FEMALE ▶ **male·ness** *noun* [U]: *the chromosome that determines maleness*

■ ***noun*** 🔑 a male person, animal or plant: *The male of the species has a white tail.* ◇ *a male-dominated profession* ◇ (*formal*) *The body is that of a white male aged about 40.* ➲ compare FEMALE

ˌmale ˈchauvinism (also **chauvinism**) *noun* [U] (*disapproving*) the belief held by some men that men are more important, intelligent, etc. than women

ˌmale ˈchauvinist (also **chauvinist**) *noun* (*disapproving*) a man who believes men are more important, intelligent, etc. than women: *I hate working for that* ***male chauvinist pig*** *Steve.*

mal·efac·tor /ˈmælɪfæktə(r)/ *noun* (*rare, formal*) a person who does wrong, illegal or immoral things

ma·levo·lent /məˈlevələnt/ *adj.* [usually before noun] having or showing a desire to harm other people SYN **malicious, wicked** OPP **benevolent** ▶ **ma·levo·lence** /-əns/ *noun* [U]: *an act of pure malevolence* **ma·levo·lent·ly** *adv.*

mal·for·ma·tion /ˌmælfɔːˈmeɪʃn; *NAmE* -fɔːrˈm-/ *noun* **1** [C] a part of the body that is not formed correctly: *Some foetal malformations cannot be diagnosed until late in pregnancy.* **2** [U] the state of not being correctly formed

mal·formed /ˌmælˈfɔːmd; *NAmE* -ˈfɔːrmd/ *adj.* (*technical*) badly formed or shaped

mal·func·tion /ˌmælˈfʌŋkʃn/ *verb* [I] (of a machine, etc.) to fail to work correctly ▶ **mal·func·tion** *noun* [C, U]

mal·ice /ˈmælɪs/ *noun* [U] a feeling of hatred for sb that causes a desire to harm them: *He sent the letter* ***out of malice.*** ◇ *She is entirely without malice.* ◇ *He certainly* ***bears you no malice*** (= does not want to harm you).

IDM **with ˌmalice aˈforethought** (*law*) with the deliberate intention of committing a crime or harming sb

ma·li·cious /məˈlɪʃəs/ *adj.* having or showing hatred and a desire to harm sb or hurt their feelings SYN **malevolent, spiteful**: ***malicious gossip/lies/rumours*** ◇ *He took malicious pleasure in telling me what she had said.* ▶ **ma·li·cious·ly** *adv.*

ma·lign /məˈlaɪn/ *verb, adj.*

■ ***verb*** **~ sb/sth** (*formal*) to say bad things about sb/sth publicly SYN **slander**: *She feels she has been* ***much maligned*** *by the press.*

■ ***adj.*** [usually before noun] (*formal*) causing harm: ***a malign force/influence/effect*** ➲ compare BENIGN

ma·lig·nancy /məˈlɪɡnənsi/ *noun* (*pl.* **-ies**) (*formal*) **1** [C] a malignant mass of TISSUE in the body SYN **tumour** **2** [U] the state of being malignant

ma·lig·nant /məˈlɪɡnənt/ *adj.* **1** (of a TUMOUR or disease) that cannot be controlled and is likely to cause death: *malignant cells* OPP **non-malignant** ➲ compare BENIGN **2** (*formal*) having or showing a strong desire to harm sb SYN **malevolent**

ma·lin·ger /məˈlɪŋɡə(r)/ *verb* (usually **be malingering**) [I] (*disapproving*) to pretend to be ill/sick, especially in order to avoid work ▶ **ma·lin·ger·er** *noun*

mall 🔑 /mɔːl; *BrE* also mæl/ *noun* (also **shopping mall**) (both *especially NAmE*) a large building or covered area that has many shops/stores, restaurants, etc. inside it: *Let's go to the mall.* ◇ *Some teenagers were hanging out at the mall.* ➲ COLLOCATIONS at SHOPPING ➲ compare ARCADE

mal·lam /ˈmæləm/ (also **Mallam**) *noun* (*WAfrE*) a Muslim religious teacher; sometimes used as a title of respect for anybody who is seen as wise or highly educated, for example a university teacher

mal·lard /ˈmælɑːd; *NAmE* ˈmælərd/ *noun* (*pl.* **mal·lards** or **mal·lard**) a common wild DUCK

mal·le·able /ˈmæliəbl/ *adj.* **1** (*technical*) (of metal, etc.) that can be hit or pressed into different shapes easily without breaking or cracking **2** (of people, ideas, etc.) easily influenced or changed ▶ **mal·le·abil·ity** /ˌmæliəˈbɪləti/ *noun* [U]

mal·let /ˈmælɪt/ *noun* **1** a hammer with a large wooden head ➲ VISUAL VOCAB page V17 **2** a hammer with a long handle and a wooden head, used for hitting the ball in the games of CROQUET and POLO ➲ VISUAL VOCAB page V38

mal·low /ˈmæləʊ; *NAmE* -loʊ/ *noun* [C, U] a plant with STEMS covered with small hairs and pink, purple or white flowers

mall·rat /ˈmɔːlræt/ *noun* (*NAmE, informal*) a young person who spends a lot of time in SHOPPING MALLS, often in a large group of friends

malm·sey /ˈmɑːmzi/ *noun* [U, C] a type of strong sweet wine

mal·nour·ished /ˌmælˈnʌrɪʃt; *NAmE* -ˈnɜːr-/ *adj.* in bad health because of a lack of food or a lack of the right type of food

mal·nu·tri·tion /ˌmælnjuːˈtrɪʃn; *NAmE* -nuː-/ *noun* [U] a poor condition of health caused by a lack of food or a lack of the right type of food ➲ compare NUTRITION

mal·odor·ous /ˌmælˈəʊdərəs; *NAmE* -ˈoʊdərəs/ *adj.* (*formal* or *literary*) having an unpleasant smell

mal·prac·tice /ˌmælˈpræktɪs/ *noun* [U, C] (*law*) careless, wrong or illegal behaviour while in a professional job: *medical malpractice* ◇ *a malpractice suit* ◇ *He is currently standing trial for alleged malpractices.*

malt /mɔːlt; *BrE* also mɒlt; *NAmE* mɔːlt/ *noun* **1** [U] grain, usually BARLEY, that has been left in water for a period of time and then dried, used for making beer, WHISKY, etc. **2** [U, C] = MALT WHISKY **3** [U, C] (*NAmE*) = MALTED MILK

malt·ed /ˈmɔːltɪd/ *adj.* [only before noun] **1** having been made into malt: *malted barley* **2** having had malt added to it

ˌmalted ˈmilk (*NAmE* also **malt**) *noun* [U, C] a hot or cold drink made from MALT and dried milk mixed with water or milk and usually sugar, sometimes ice cream and/or chocolate added

Mal·tese /ˈmɔːltiːz/ *adj., noun* (*pl.* **Mal·tese**)

■ ***adj.*** from or connected with Malta

■ ***noun*** **1** [C] a person from Malta **2** [U] the language of Malta

ˌMaltese ˈcross *noun* a cross whose arms are equal in length and have wide ends with V-shapes cut out of them

malt·house /ˈmɔːlthaʊs/ (also **malt·ings** /ˈmɔːltɪŋz/ *BrE*) *noun* a building in which MALT is prepared and stored

Mal·thusian /mælˈθjuːziən/ *adj.* related to the theory of Thomas Malthus that, since populations naturally grow faster than the supply of food, failure to control their growth leads to disaster

mal·tose /ˈmɔːltəʊz; -təʊs; *NAmE* -toʊz; -toʊs/ *noun* [U] (*biology*) a sugar that substances in the body make from STARCH (= a food substance found in flour, rice, potatoes, etc.)

mal·treat /ˌmælˈtriːt/ *verb* **~ sb/sth** to be very cruel to a person or an animal SYN **ill-treat** ▶ **mal·treat·ment** *noun* [U]

ˌmalt ˈvinegar *noun* [U] VINEGAR which is made from grain rather than from wine

ˌmalt ˈwhisky (also **malt**) *noun* [U, C] high quality WHISKY from Scotland; a glass of this

mal·ware /ˈmælweə(r); *NAmE* -wer/ *noun* [U] software such as a virus on a computer or computer network that the user does not know about or want ORIGIN A combination of *malicious* and *software*.

mam /mæm/ *noun* (*BrE, dialect, informal*) mother

mama (also **mamma**) /ˈmæmə/ *noun* **1** /*BrE* also məˈmɑː/ (*NAmE* or *BrE, old-fashioned*) mother ➲ see also MUMMY **2** in some places in Africa, a mother or older woman (often used as a title that shows respect): *Leave this work to us, mama.* ◇ *Miriam Makeba became known as Mama Africa.* ◇ *Mama Ngina Kenyatta*

M

ˈmama's boy (*NAmE*) (*BrE* **ˈmummy's boy**) *noun* (*disapproving*) a boy or man who depends too much on his mother

mamba /ˈmæmbə/ *noun* a black or green poisonous African snake

mambo /ˈmæmbəʊ; *NAmE* -boʊ/ *noun* (*pl.* **-os**) **1** a lively Latin American dance **2** a female VOODOO priest

mam·mal /ˈmæml/ *noun* any animal that gives birth to live babies, not eggs, and feeds its young on milk. Cows, humans and WHALES are all mammals. ➲ VISUAL VOCAB page V10 ▸ **mam·ma·lian** /mæˈmeɪliən/ *adj.*

mam·mary /ˈmæməri/ *adj.* [only before noun] (*biology*) connected with the breasts: *mammary glands* (= parts of the breast that produce milk)

mam·mo·gram /ˈmæməgræm/ *noun* an examination of a breast using X-RAYS to check for cancer

mam·mog·raphy /mæˈmɒgrəfi; *NAmE* -ˈmɑːg-/ *noun* [U] the use of X-RAYS to check for cancer in a breast

Mam·mon /ˈmæmən/ *noun* [U] (*formal, disapproving*) a way of talking about money and wealth when it has become the most important thing in sb's life and as important as a god

mam·moth /ˈmæməθ/ *noun, adj.*
- **noun** an animal like a large ELEPHANT covered with hair, that lived thousands of years ago and is now EXTINCT
- **adj.** [usually before noun] extremely large SYN **huge**: *a mammoth task* ◇ *a financial crisis of mammoth proportions*

mammy /ˈmæmi/ *noun* (*pl.* **-ies**) **1** (*dialect, informal*) mother **2** an offensive word used in the past in the southern states of the US for a black woman who cared for a white family's children

M

ˈmammy-wagon *noun* (*old-fashioned, WAfrE*) a lorry/truck with a roof and seats for people to travel in

mam·para /mʌmˈpʌrə/ *noun* (*SAfrE*) = MOMPARA

man 0-w /mæn/ *noun, verb, exclamation*
- **noun** (*pl.* **men** /men/)
- ▸ MALE PERSON **1** 0-w [C] an adult male human: *a good-looking young man* ◇ *the relationships between men and women* ➲ see also DIRTY OLD MAN, LADIES' MAN, MEN'S ROOM
- ▸ HUMANS **2** 0-w [U] humans as a group or from a particular period of history: *the damage caused by man to the environment* ◇ ***early/modern/Prehistoric man*** ➲ note at GENDER **3** [C] (*literary* or *old-fashioned*) a person, either male or female: *All men must die.*
- ▸ PARTICULAR TYPE OF MAN **4** [C] (in compounds) a man who comes from the place mentioned or whose job or interest is connected with the thing mentioned: *a Frenchman* ◇ *a businessman* ◇ *a medical man* ◇ *a sportsman* ➲ note at GENDER **5** [C] a man who likes or who does the thing mentioned: *a* ***betting/drinking/fighting man*** ➲ see also FAMILY MAN **6** [C] a man who works for or supports a particular organization, comes from a particular town, etc: *the BBC's man in Moscow* (= the man who reports on news from Moscow) ◇ *a loyal Republican Party man* ➲ see also RIGHT-HAND MAN, YES-MAN
- ▸ SOLDIER/WORKER **7** [C, usually pl.] a soldier or a male worker who obeys the instructions of a person of higher rank: *The officer refused to let his men take part in the operation.* **8** [C] a man who comes to your house to do a job: *the gas man* ◇ *The man's coming to repair the TV today.*
- ▸ FORM OF ADDRESS **9** [sing.] (*informal, especially NAmE*) used for addressing a male person: *Nice shirt, man!* ◇ *Hey man. Back off!* **10** [sing.] (*old-fashioned*) used for addressing a male person in an angry or impatient way: *Don't just stand there, man—get a doctor!*
- ▸ HUSBAND/BOYFRIEND **11** [C] (sometimes *disapproving*) a husband or sexual partner: *What's her new man like?* ◇ *I now pronounce you man and wife* (= you are now officially married). ➲ see also OLD MAN
- ▸ STRONG/BRAVE PERSON **12** [C] a person who is strong and brave or has other qualities that some people think are particularly male: *Come on, now—be a man.* ◇ *She's more of a man than he is.* ➲ see also HE-MAN, MUSCLEMAN, SUPERMAN
- ▸ SERVANT **13** [sing.] (*old-fashioned, formal*) a male servant: *My man will drive you home.*
- ▸ IN CHESS **14** [C] one of the figures or objects that you play with in a game such as CHESS ➲ see also CHESSMAN

IDM **as one ˈman** with everyone doing or thinking the same thing at the same time; in agreement **be sb's ˈman** to be the best or most suitable person to do a particular job, etc: *For a superb haircut, David's your man.* **be ˈman enough (to do sth/for sth)** to be strong or brave enough: *He was not man enough to face up to his responsibility.* **every man for himˈself** (*saying*) people must take care of themselves and not give or expect any help: *In business, it's every man for himself.* **make a ˈman (out) of sb** to make a young man develop and become more adult **a/the ˌman about ˈtown** a man who frequently goes to fashionable parties, clubs, theatres, etc. **ˌman and ˈboy** from when sb was young to when they were old or older: *He's been doing the same job for 50 years—man and boy.* **the ˌman (and/or ˌwoman) in the ˈstreet** an average or ordinary person, either male or female: *Politicians often don't understand the views of the man in the street.* **a ˌman of ˈGod/the ˈcloth** (*old-fashioned, formal*) a religious man, especially a priest or a CLERGYMAN **the ˌman of the ˈmatch** (*BrE, sport*) the member of a team who plays the best in a particular game **a ˌman of the ˈpeople** (especially of a politician) a man who understands and is sympathetic to ordinary people **man's best ˈfriend** a way of describing a dog **a ˌman's ˌhome is his ˈcastle** (*US*) (*BrE* **an ˌEnglishman's ˌhome is his ˈcastle**) (*saying*) a person's home is a place where they can be private and safe and do as they like **a ˈman's man** a man who is more popular with men than with women **be your own ˈman/ˈwoman** to act or think independently, not following others or being ordered **ˌman to ˈman** between two men who are treating each other honestly and equally: *I'm telling you all this man to man.* ◇ *a man-to-man talk* **one man's ˌmeat is another man's ˈpoison** (*saying*) used to say that different people like different things; what one person likes very much, another person does not like at all **separate/sort out the ˌmen from the ˈboys** to show or prove who is brave, skilful, etc. and who is not **to a ˈman | to the last ˈman** used to emphasize that sth is true of all the people being described: *They answered 'Yes,' to a man.* ◇ *They were all destroyed, to the last man.* **you can't keep a good man ˈdown** (*saying*) a person who is determined or wants sth very much will succeed ➲ more at GRAND *adj.*, HEART, MARKED, NEXT *adj.*, ODD *adj.*, PART *n.*, POOR, POSSESSED, SUBSTANCE, THING, WORD *n.*, WORLD
- **verb** (-nn-) **~ sth** to work at a place or be in charge of a place or a machine; to supply people to work somewhere SYN **crew, staff**: *Soldiers manned barricades around the city.* ◇ *The telephones are manned 24 hours a day by volunteers.*
- **exclamation** (*informal, especially NAmE*) used to express surprise, anger, etc: *Man, that was great!*

man·acle /ˈmænəkl/ *noun, verb*
- **noun** [usually pl.] one of two metal bands joined by a chain, used for fastening a prisoner's ankles or wrists together
- **verb** [usually passive] **~ sb/sth** to put manacles on sb's wrists or ankles, to stop them from escaping

man·age 0-w /ˈmænɪdʒ/ *verb*
- ▸ DO STH DIFFICULT **1** 0-w [T, I] to succeed in doing sth, especially sth difficult: **~ sth** *In spite of his disappointment, he managed a weak smile.* ◇ *I don't know exactly how we'll* ***manage it****, but we will, somehow.* ◇ *Can you manage another piece of cake?* (= eat one) ◇ **~ (to do sth)** *We managed to get to the airport in time.* ◇ *How did you manage to persuade him?* ◇ (*humorous*) *He always manages to say the wrong thing.* ◇ *We couldn't have managed without you.* ◇ *'Need any help?' 'No, thanks. I can manage.'* ➲ note at CAN[1]
- ▸ DEAL WITH PROBLEMS **2** 0-w [I] to be able to solve your problems, deal with a difficult situation, etc. SYN **cope**: *She's 82 and can't manage on her own any more.* ◇ **~ with/without sb/sth** *How do you manage without a car?*
- ▸ MONEY/TIME/INFORMATION **3** 0-w [I] **~ (on sth)** to be able to live without having much money: *He has to manage on less than £100 a week.* **4** 0-w [T] **~ sth** to use money, time, infor-

mation, etc. in a sensible way: *Don't tell me how to manage my affairs.* ◇ *a computer program that helps you manage data efficiently* **5** [T] **~ sth** to be able to do sth at a particular time: *Let's meet up again—can you manage next week sometime?*
▸ BUSINESS/TEAM **6** [T, I] **~ (sth)** to control or be in charge of a business, a team, an organization, etc: *to **manage a factory/bank/hotel/soccer team*** ◇ *to **manage a department/project*** ◇ *We need people who are good at managing.*
▸ CONTROL **7** [T] **~ sb/sth** to keep sb/sth under control; to be able to deal with sb/sth: *It's like trying to manage an unruly child.* ◇ *Can you manage that suitcase?*

man·age·able /ˈmænɪdʒəbl/ *adj.* possible to deal with or control: *Use conditioner regularly to make your hair soft and manageable.* ◇ *The debt has been reduced to a more manageable level.* OPP **unmanageable**

man·aged /ˈmænɪdʒd/ *adj.* [only before noun] carefully taken care of and controlled: *The money will be invested in managed funds.* ◇ *Only wood from managed forests is used in our furniture.*

man·age·ment /ˈmænɪdʒmənt/ *noun*
1 [U] the act of running and controlling a business or similar organization: *a career in management* ◇ ***hotel/project management*** ◇ *a management training course* ◇ *The report blames bad management.* **2** [C+sing./pl. v., U] the people who run and control a business or similar organization: *The management is/are considering closing the factory.* ◇ *The shop is now **under new management**.* ◇ ***junior/middle/senior management*** ◇ *a **management decision/job*** ◇ *My role is to act as a mediator between employees and management.* ◇ *Most managements are keen to avoid strikes.* **3** [U] the act or skill of dealing with people or situations in a successful way: ***classroom management*** ◇ ***time management*** (= the way in which you organize how you spend your time) ◇ *management of staff* ◇ *Diet plays an important role in the management of heart disease.*

man·ager /ˈmænɪdʒə(r)/ *noun*
1 a person who is in charge of running a business, a shop/store or a similar organization or part of one: *a **bank/hotel manager*** ◇ *the **sales/marketing/personnel manager*** ◇ *a meeting of area managers* ➲ see also MIDDLE MANAGER **2** a person who deals with the business affairs of an actor, a musician, etc. **3** a person who trains and organizes a sports team: *the new manager of Italy*

man·ager·ess /ˌmænɪdʒəˈres/ *noun* (*BrE*, becoming *old-fashioned*) a woman who is in charge of a small business, for example, a shop/store, restaurant or hotel ➲ note at GENDER

man·ager·ial /ˌmænəˈdʒɪəriəl; *NAmE* -ˈdʒɪr-/ *adj.* [usually before noun] connected with the work of a manager: *Does she have any managerial experience?*

ˌmanaging diˈrector *noun* (*abbr.* **MD**) (*especially BrE*) the person who is in charge of a business

ma·ñana /mænˈjɑːnə/ *adv.* (from *Spanish*) at some time in the future (used when a person cannot or will not say exactly when)

mana·tee /ˈmænətiː/ *noun* a large water animal with front legs and a strong tail but no back legs, that lives in America and Africa

ˈman bag *noun* a bag designed for men to carry money, keys, small pieces of equipment, etc.

ˈman boob *noun* [usually pl.] (*informal*) a man's breast that is large and fat

Man·cu·nian /mænˈkjuːniən/ *noun* a person from Manchester in NW England ▸ **Man·cu·nian** *adj.*

man·dala /ˈmændələ/ *noun* a round picture that represents the universe in some Eastern religions

man·da·rin /ˈmændərɪn/ *noun* **1** [C] a powerful official of high rank, especially in the CIVIL SERVICE SYN **bureaucrat** **2** [C] a government official of high rank in China in the past **3 Mandarin** [U] the standard form of Chinese, which is the official language of China **4** (also **ˌmandarin ˈorange**) [C] a type of small orange with loose skin that comes off easily

ˌmandarin ˈcollar *noun* a small COLLAR that stands up and fits closely around the neck

man·date *noun, verb*
▪ ***noun*** /ˈmændeɪt/ **1** the authority to do sth, given to a government or other organization by the people who vote for it in an election: **~ (to do sth)** *The election victory gave the party a clear mandate to continue its programme of reform.* ◇ **~ (for sth)** *a mandate for an end to the civil war* **2** the period of time for which a government is given power: *The presidential mandate is limited to two terms of four years each.* **3 ~ (to do sth)** (*formal*) an official order given to sb to perform a particular task: *The bank had no mandate to honour the cheque.* **4** the power given to a country to govern another country or region, especially in the past
▪ ***verb*** /ˈmændeɪt; ˌmænˈdeɪt/ [often passive] (*formal*) **1 ~ that…** | **~ sb (to do sth)** (*especially NAmE*) to order sb to behave, do sth or vote in a particular way: *The law mandates that imported goods be identified as such.* **2 ~ sb/sth to do sth** to give sb, especially a government or a committee, the authority to do sth: *The assembly was mandated to draft a constitution.*

man·dated /ˈmændeɪtɪd/ *adj.* [only before noun] (*formal*) **1** (of a country or state) placed under the rule of another country: *mandated territories* **2** required by law: *a mandated curriculum* **3** having a mandate to do sth: *a mandated government*

man·da·tory /ˈmændətəri; *NAmE* -tɔːri; *BrE* also mænˈdeɪtəri/ *adj.* (*formal*) required by law SYN **compulsory**: *The offence carries a mandatory life sentence.* ◇ **~ (for sb) (to do sth)** *It is mandatory for blood banks to test all donated blood for the virus.*

man·dazi /mænˈdɑːzi/ *noun* (*pl.* **man·dazi**) (*EAfrE*) a small cake made of fried DOUGH

man·dible /ˈmændɪbl/ *noun* (*anatomy*) **1** the JAWBONE ➲ VISUAL VOCAB page V48 **2** the upper or lower part of a bird's beak **3** either of the two parts that are at the front and on either side of an insect's mouth, used especially for biting and crushing food ➲ VISUAL VOCAB page V11

man·dir /ˈmændɪə(r); *NAmE* -dɪr/ *noun* (*IndE*) a TEMPLE

man·do·lin /ˈmændəlɪn; ˌmændəˈlɪn/ *noun* a musical instrument with metal strings (usually eight) arranged in pairs, and a curved back, played with a PLECTRUM ➲ VISUAL VOCAB page V31

man·drake /ˈmændreɪk/ *noun* [C, U] a poisonous plant used to make drugs, especially ones to make people sleep, thought in the past to have magic powers

man·drill /ˈmændrɪl/ *noun* a large W African MONKEY with a red and blue face

mane /meɪn/ *noun* **1** the long hair on the neck of a horse or a LION ➲ VISUAL VOCAB page V10 **2** (*informal* or *literary*) a person's long or thick hair

man·eater /ˈmæniːtə(r)/ *noun* **1** a wild animal that attacks and eats humans **2** (*humorous*) a woman who has many sexual partners ▸ **ˈman-eating** *adj.* [only before noun]: *a man-eating tiger*

man·eu·ver, **man·eu·ver·able**, **man·eu·ver·ing** (*especially US*) = MANOEUVRE, MANOEUVRABLE, MANOEUVRING

ˌman ˈFriday *noun* a male assistant who does many different kinds of work ➲ compare GIRL FRIDAY ORIGIN From a character in Daniel Defoe's novel *Robinson Crusoe* who is rescued by Crusoe and works for him.

man·ful·ly /ˈmænfəli/ *adv.* using a lot of effort in a brave and determined way ▸ **man·ful** *adj.* [only before noun]

manga /ˈmæŋgə/ *noun* [C, U] (from *Japanese*) a Japanese form of COMIC STRIP, often one with violent or sexual contents

man·ga·nese /ˈmæŋgəniːz/ *noun* [U] (*symb.* **Mn**) a chemical element. Manganese is a grey-white metal that breaks easily, used in making glass and steel.

mange /meɪndʒ/ *noun* [U] a skin disease which affects MAMMALS, caused by a PARASITE ➲ see also MANGY

M

man·ger /ˈmeɪndʒə(r)/ *noun* a long open box that horses and cows can eat from IDM see DOG *n.*

mange·tout /ˌmɑːnʒˈtuː/ (*BrE*) (*NAmE* **ˈsnow pea**) *noun* [usually pl.] a type of very small PEA that grows in long, flat green PODS that are cooked and eaten whole

man·gle /ˈmæŋgl/ *verb, noun*

■ ***verb*** [usually passive] **1 ~ sth** to crush or twist sth so that it is badly damaged: *His hand was mangled in the machine.* **2 ~ sth** to spoil sth, for example a poem or a piece of music, by saying it wrongly or playing it badly SYN **ruin** ▸ **man·gled** *adj.*: ***mangled bodies/remains***

■ ***noun*** (also **wring·er**) a machine with two ROLLERS (1) used especially in the past for squeezing the water out of clothes that had been washed

mango /ˈmæŋgəʊ; *NAmE* -goʊ/ *noun* [C, U] (*pl.* -oes or -os) a tropical fruit with smooth yellow or red skin, soft orange flesh and a large seed inside ➲ VISUAL VOCAB page V26

man·go·steen /ˈmæŋgəstiːn/ *noun* a tropical fruit with a thick reddish-brown skin and sweet white flesh with a lot of juice ➲ VISUAL VOCAB page V26

man·grove /ˈmæŋgrəʊv; *NAmE* -groʊv/ *noun* a tropical tree that grows in mud or at the edge of rivers and has roots that are above ground: *mangrove swamps*

mangy /ˈmeɪndʒi/ *adj.* [usually before noun] **1** (of an animal) suffering from MANGE: *a mangy dog* **2** (*informal*) dirty and in bad condition SYN **moth-eaten**: *a mangy old coat*

man·handle /ˈmænhændl/ *verb* **1 ~ sb** to push, pull or handle sb roughly: *Bystanders claim they were manhandled by security guards.* **2 ~ sth + adv./prep.** to move or lift a heavy object using a lot of effort SYN **haul**: *They were trying to manhandle an old sofa across the road.*

M

man·hat·tan /ˌmænˈhætn/ *noun* an alcoholic drink made by mixing WHISKY or another strong alcoholic drink with VERMOUTH

man·hole /ˈmænhəʊl; *NAmE* -hoʊl/ *noun* a hole in the street that is covered with a lid, used when sb needs to go down to examine the pipes or SEWERS below the street

man·hood /ˈmænhʊd/ *noun* **1** [U] the state or time of being an adult man rather than a boy **2** [U] the qualities that a man is supposed to have, for example courage, strength and sexual power: *Her new-found power was a threat to his manhood.* **3** [sing.] (*literary* or *humorous*) a man's PENIS. People use 'manhood' to avoid saying 'penis'. **4** [U] (*literary*) all the men of a country: *The nation's manhood died on the battlefields of World War I.* ➲ compare WOMANHOOD

ˈman-hour *noun* [usually pl.] the amount of work done by one person in one hour

man·hunt /ˈmænhʌnt/ *noun* an organized search by a lot of people for a criminal or a prisoner who has escaped

mania /ˈmeɪniə/ *noun* **1** [C, usually sing., U] **~ (for sth/for doing sth)** an extremely strong desire or enthusiasm for sth, often shared by a lot of people at the same time SYN **craze**: *He had a mania for fast cars.* ◇ *Football mania is sweeping the country.* **2** [U] (*psychology*) a mental illness in which sb has an OBSESSION about sth that makes them extremely anxious, violent or confused

-mania *combining form* (in nouns) mental illness of a particular type: *kleptomania* ▸ **-maniac** (in nouns): *a pyromaniac*

ma·niac /ˈmeɪniæk/ *noun* **1** (*informal*) a person who behaves in an extremely dangerous, wild or stupid way SYN **madman**: *He was driving* ***like a maniac.*** **2** a person who has an extremely strong desire or enthusiasm for sth, to an extent that other people think is not normal SYN **fanatic** **3** (*psychology*) a person suffering from mania: *a homicidal maniac* ▸ **ma·niac** *adj.* [only before noun]: *a maniac driver/fan/killer*

ma·ni·acal /məˈnaɪəkl/ *adj.* wild or violent: *maniacal laughter* ▸ **ma·ni·acal·ly** /-kli/ *adv.*

manic /ˈmænɪk/ *adj.* **1** (*informal*) full of activity, excitement and anxiety; behaving in a busy, excited, anxious way SYN **hectic**: *Things are manic in the office at the moment.* ◇ *The performers had a manic energy and enthusiasm.* **2** (*psychology*) connected with MANIA (2): *manic mood swings* ▸ **man·ic·al·ly** /-kli/ *adv.*: *I rushed around manically, trying to finish the housework.*

ˌmanic deˈpression *noun* [U] = BIPOLAR DISORDER

ˌmanic-deˈpres·sive *adj., noun* = BIPOLAR

Mani·chae·an (also **Mani·che·an**) /ˌmænɪˈkiːən/ *adj.* (*religion, philosophy*) based on the belief that there are two opposites in everything, for example good and evil or light and dark

mani·cure /ˈmænɪkjʊə(r); *NAmE* -kjʊr/ *noun, verb*

■ ***noun*** [C, U] the care and treatment of a person's hands and nails: *to have a manicure* ➲ compare PEDICURE

■ ***verb*** **~ sth** to care for and treat your hands and nails

mani·cured /ˈmænɪkjʊəd; *NAmE* -kjʊrd/ *adj.* **1** (of hands or fingers) with nails that are neatly cut and polished **2** (of gardens, a LAWN, etc.) very neat and well cared for

mani·cur·ist /ˈmænɪkjʊərɪst; *NAmE* -kjʊr-/ *noun* a person whose job is the care and treatment of the hands and nails

mani·fest /ˈmænɪfest/ *verb, adj., noun*

■ ***verb*** (*formal*) **1 ~ sth (in sth)** to show sth clearly, especially a feeling, an attitude or a quality SYN **demonstrate**: *Social tensions were manifested in the recent political crisis.* **2 ~ itself (in sth)** to appear or become noticeable SYN **appear**: *The symptoms of the disease manifested themselves ten days later.*

■ ***adj.*** **~ (to sb) (in sth)** (*formal*) easy to see or understand SYN **clear**: *His nervousness was manifest to all those present.* ◇ *The anger he felt is manifest in his paintings.* ▸ **mani·fest·ly** *adv.*: *manifestly unfair* ◇ *The party has manifestly failed to achieve its goal.*

■ ***noun*** (*technical*) a list of goods or passengers on a ship or an aircraft

mani·fest·ation /ˌmænɪfeˈsteɪʃn/ *noun* (*formal*) **1** [C, U] **~ (of sth)** an event, action or thing that is a sign that sth exists or is happening; the act of appearing as a sign that sth exists or is happening: *The riots are a clear manifestation of the people's discontent.* ◇ *Some manifestation of your concern would have been appreciated.* **2** [C] an appearance of a GHOST or spirit: *The church is the site of a number of supernatural manifestations.*

mani·festo /ˌmænɪˈfestəʊ; *NAmE* -ˈfestoʊ/ *noun* (*pl.* -os) a written statement in which a group of people, especially a political party, explain their beliefs and say what they will do if they win an election: *an election manifesto* ◇ *the party manifesto*

mani·fold /ˈmænɪfəʊld; *NAmE* -foʊld/ *adj., noun*

■ ***adj.*** (*formal*) many; of many different types: *The possibilities were manifold.*

■ ***noun*** (*technical*) a pipe or chamber with several openings for taking gases in and out of a car engine: *the exhaust manifold*

mani·kin (also **man·ni·kin**) /ˈmænɪkɪn/ *noun* **1** a model of the human body that is used for teaching art or medicine ➲ compare MANNEQUIN **2** (*old-fashioned*) a very small man SYN **dwarf**

Ma·nila (also **Ma·nilla**) /məˈnɪlə/ *noun* [U] strong brown paper, used especially for making envelopes

man·ioc /ˈmæniɒk; *NAmE* -ɑːk/ *noun* [U] = CASSAVA

ma·nipu·late AW /məˈnɪpjuleɪt/ *verb* **1** (*disapproving*) to control or influence sb/sth, often in a dishonest way so that they do not realize it: **~ sb/sth** *She uses her charm to manipulate people.* ◇ *As a politician, he knows how to manipulate public opinion.* ◇ **~ sb into sth/into doing sth** *They managed to manipulate us into agreeing to help.* **2 ~ sth** (*formal*) to control or use sth in a skilful way: *to manipulate the gears and levers of a machine* ◇ *Computers are very efficient at manipulating information.* **3 ~ sth** (*technical*) to move a person's bones or joints into the correct position ▸ **ma·nipu·la·tion** AW /məˌnɪpjuˈleɪʃn/ *noun* [U, C]: *Advertising like this is a cynical manipulation of the elderly.* ◇ *data manipulation* ◇ *manipulation of the bones of the back*

ma·nipu·la·tive AW /məˈnɪpjələtɪv; *NAmE* -leɪtɪv/ *adj.* **1** (*disapproving*) skilful at influencing sb or forcing sb to do what you want, often in an unfair way **2** (*formal*) connected with the ability to handle objects skilfully: *manipulative skills such as typing and knitting*

ma·nipu·la·tor /məˈnɪpjuleɪtə(r)/ *noun* (often *disapproving*) a person who is skilful at influencing people or situations in order to get what they want

man·kind /mænˈkaɪnd/ *noun* [U] all humans, thought about as one large group; the human race: *the history of mankind* ◇ *an invention for the good of all mankind* ➲ note at GENDER ➲ compare WOMANKIND ➲ see also HUMANKIND

manky /ˈmæŋki/ *adj.* (*BrE, informal*) dirty and unpleasant

manly /ˈmænli/ *adj.* (often *approving*) (**man·lier, man·li·est**) having the qualities or physical features that are admired or expected in a man ▶ **man·li·ness** *noun* [U]

ˌman-ˈmade *adj.* made by people; not natural SYN **artificial**: *a man-made lake* ◇ *man-made fibres such as nylon and polyester* ➲ SYNONYMS at ARTIFICIAL

manna /ˈmænə/ *noun* [U] (in the Bible) the food that God provided for the people of Israel during their 40 years in the desert: (*figurative*) *To the refugees, the food shipments were* ***manna from heaven*** (= an unexpected and very welcome gift).

manned /mænd/ *adj.* if a machine, a vehicle, a place or an activity is **manned**, it has or needs a person to control or operate it: *manned space flight* OPP **unmanned**

man·ne·quin /ˈmænɪkɪn/ *noun* **1** a model of a human body, used for displaying clothes in shops/stores ➲ compare MANIKIN **2** (*old-fashioned*) a person whose job is to wear and display new styles of clothes SYN **model**

man·ner 0▬ /ˈmænə(r)/ *noun*
1 0▬ [sing.] (*formal*) the way that sth is done or happens: *She answered* ***in a*** *businesslike* ***manner***. ◇ *The manner in which the decision was announced was extremely regrettable.* **2** 0▬ [sing.] the way that sb behaves towards other people: *to have an aggressive/a friendly/a relaxed manner* ◇ *His manner was polite but cool.* ➲ see also BEDSIDE MANNER **3** 0▬ **manners** [pl.] behaviour that is considered to be polite in a particular society or culture: *to have* ***good/bad manners*** ◇ *It is bad manners to talk with your mouth full.* ◇ *He* ***has no manners*** (= behaves very badly). ➲ see also TABLE MANNERS **4 manners** [pl.] (*formal*) the habits and customs of a particular group of people: *the social morals and manners of the seventeenth century*
IDM **all ˈmanner of sb/sth** many different types of people or things: *The problem can be solved in all manner of ways.* **in a manner of ˈspeaking** if you think about it in a particular way; true in some but not all ways: *All these points of view are related, in a manner of speaking.* **in the manner of sb/sth** (*formal*) in a style that is typical of sb/sth: *a painting in the manner of Raphael* (**as/as if**) **to the manner ˈborn** (*formal*) as if sth is natural for you and you have done it many times in the past **what manner of...** (*formal* or *literary*) what kind of...: *What manner of man could do such a terrible thing?*

man·nered /ˈmænəd; *NAmE* -nərd/ *adj.* **1** (*disapproving*) (of behaviour, art, writing, etc.) trying to impress people by being formal and not natural SYN **affected** **2 -mannered** (in compounds) having the type of manners mentioned: *a bad-mannered child* ➲ see also ILL-MANNERED, MILD-MANNERED, WELL MANNERED

man·ner·ism /ˈmænərɪzəm/ *noun* **1** [C] a particular habit or way of speaking or behaving that sb has but is not aware of: ***nervous/odd/irritating mannerisms*** **2** [U] too much use of a particular style in painting or writing **3 Mannerism** [U] a style in 16th century Italian art that did not show things in a natural way but made them look strange or out of their usual shape

man·ner·ist /ˈmænərɪst/ (usually **Man·ner·ist**) *adj.* (of painting or writing) in the style of Mannerism

man·ni·kin = MANIKIN

man·nish /ˈmænɪʃ/ *adj.* (usually *disapproving*) (of a woman or of sth belonging to a woman) having qualities that are thought of as typical of or suitable for a man

mano-a-mano /ˌmɑːnəʊ æ ˈmɑːnəʊ; *NAmE* ˌmɑːnoʊ ɑː ˈmɑːnoʊ/ *adv., noun* (*informal, especially NAmE*, from *Spanish*)
■ ***adv.*** with two people facing each other directly in order to decide an argument or a competition: *It's time to settle this mano-a-mano.*
■ ***noun*** (*pl.* mano-a-manos) a fight or contest, especially one between two people

man·oeuv·rable (*BrE*) (*NAmE* **man·euv·er·able**) /məˈnuːvərəbl/ *adj.* that can easily be moved into different positions: *a highly manoeuvrable vehicle* ▶ **man·oeuv·ra·bil·ity** (*BrE*) (*NAmE* **man·eu·ver·abil·ity**) *noun* [U]

man·oeuvre (*especially US* **man·eu·ver**) /məˈnuːvə(r)/ *noun, verb*
■ ***noun*** **1** [C] a movement performed with care and skill: *a* ***complicated/skilful manoeuvre*** ◇ *You will be asked to perform some standard manoeuvres during your driving test.* **2** [C, U] a clever plan, action or movement that is used to give sb an advantage SYN **move**: *diplomatic manoeuvres* ◇ *a complex manoeuvre in a game of chess* **3 manoeuvres** [pl.] military exercises involving a large number of soldiers, ships, etc: *The army is* ***on manoeuvres*** *in the desert.*
IDM **freedom of/room for maˈnoeuvre** the chance to change the way that sth happens and influence decisions that are made
■ ***verb*** **1** [I, T] to move or turn skilfully or carefully; to move or turn sth skilfully or carefully: **~** (**for sth**) *The yachts manoeuvred for position.* ◇ *There was very little room to manoeuvre.* ◇ **~ sth** (**+ adv./prep.**) *She manoeuvred the car carefully into the garage.* **2** [I, T] to control or influence a situation in a skilful but sometimes dishonest way: *The new laws have left us little* ***room to manoeuvre*** (= not much opportunity to change or influence a situation). ◇ **~ sth + adv./prep.** *She manoeuvred her way to the top of the company.*

man·oeuv·ring (*especially US* **man·eu·ver·ing**) /məˈnuːvərɪŋ/ *noun* [U, C] clever, skilful, and often dishonest ways of achieving your aims

ˌman of ˈletters *noun* a man who is a writer, or who writes about literature

ˌman-of-ˈwar *noun* (*pl.* ˌmen-of-ˈwar) a sailing ship used in the past for fighting

manor /ˈmænə(r)/ *noun* (*BrE*) **1** (also **ˈmanor house**) a large country house surrounded by land that belongs to it **2** an area of land with a manor house on it **3** (*slang*) an area in which sb works or for which they are responsible, especially officers at a police station

man·orial /məˈnɔːriəl/ *adj.* typical of or connected with a manor, especially in the past

man·power /ˈmænpaʊə(r)/ *noun* [U] the number of workers needed or available to do a particular job: *a need for* ***trained/skilled manpower*** ◇ *a manpower shortage*

man·qué /ˈmɒŋkeɪ; *NAmE* mɑːŋˈkeɪ/ *adj.* (following nouns) (from *French, formal* or *humorous*) used to describe a person who hoped to follow a particular career but who failed in it or never tried it: *He's really an artist manqué.*

man·sard /ˈmænsɑːd; *NAmE* -sɑːrd/ (also ˌ**mansard ˈroof**) *noun* (*technical*) a roof with a double slope in which the upper part is less steep than the lower part

manse /mæns/ *noun* the house of a Christian minister, especially in Scotland

man·ser·vant /ˈmænsɜːvənt; *NAmE* -sɜːrv-/ *noun* (*pl.* **men·ser·vants**) (*old-fashioned*) a male servant, especially a man's personal servant

man·sion /ˈmænʃn/ *noun* **1** [C] a large impressive house: *an 18th century country mansion* **2 Mansions** [pl.] (*BrE*) used in the names of blocks of flats: *2 Moscow Mansions, Cromwell Road*

ˈman-sized *adj.* [only before noun] suitable or large enough for a man: *a man-sized breakfast*

M

man·slaugh·ter /ˈmænslɔːtə(r)/ *noun* [U] (*law*) the crime of killing sb illegally but not deliberately ➲ compare CULPABLE HOMICIDE, HOMICIDE, MURDER

manta /ˈmæntə/ (also ˌ**manta ˈray**) *noun* a large fish that lives in tropical seas and swims by moving two parts like large flat wings

man·tel·piece /ˈmæntlpiːs/ (also **man·tel** especially in *NAmE* /ˈmæntl/) *noun* a shelf above a FIREPLACE ➲ VISUAL VOCAB page V18

man·tis /ˈmæntɪs/ *noun* (*pl.* **man·tises** or **man·tids** /ˈmæntɪdz/) = PRAYING MANTIS

man·tle /ˈmæntl/ *noun, verb*

■ ***noun*** **1** [sing.] **the ~ of sb/sth** (*literary*) the role and responsibilities of an important person or job, especially when they are passed on from one person to another: *The vice-president must now* ***take on the mantle*** *of supreme power.* **2** [C] (*literary*) a layer of sth that covers a surface: *hills with a mantle of snow* **3** [C] a loose piece of clothing without sleeves, worn over other clothes, especially in the past SYN **cloak, covering** **4** (also ˈ**gas mantle**) [C] a cover around the flame of a gas lamp that becomes very bright when it is heated **5** [sing.] (*geology*) the part of the earth below the CRUST and surrounding the core

■ ***verb* ~ sth** (*literary*) to cover the surface of sth

man·tra /ˈmæntrə/ *noun* a word, phrase or sound that is repeated again and again, especially during prayer or MEDITATION: *a Buddhist mantra*

man·trap /ˈmæntræp/ *noun* **1** a trap used in the past for catching people, especially people who tried to steal things from sb's land **2** any electronic device that is used to catch people who are doing sth dishonest

M

man·ual AW /ˈmænjuəl/ *adj., noun*

■ ***adj.*** **1** (of work, etc.) involving using the hands or physical strength: ***manual labour/jobs/skills*** ◊ *manual and non-manual workers* **2** operated or controlled by hand rather than automatically or using electricity, etc: *a manual gearbox* ◊ *My camera has manual and automatic functions.* **3** connected with using the hands: *manual dexterity* ▸ **manu·al·ly** AW /-juəli/ *adv.*: *manually operated*

■ ***noun*** a book that tells you how to do or operate sth, especially one that comes with a machine, etc. when you buy it: *a* ***computer/car/instruction manual*** ➲ compare HANDBOOK

IDM **on ˈmanual** not being operated automatically: *Leave the controls on manual.*

manu·fac·ture 🔑 /ˌmænjuˈfæktʃə(r)/ *verb, noun*

■ ***verb*** **1** 🔑 **~ sth** to make goods in large quantities, using machinery SYN **mass-produce**: *manufactured goods* **2 ~ sth** to invent a story, an excuse, etc: *a news story manufactured by an unscrupulous journalist* **3 ~ sth** (*technical*) to produce a substance: *Vitamins cannot be manufactured by our bodies.*

■ ***noun*** **1** [U] the process of producing goods in large quantities SYN **mass production**: *the manufacture of cars* **2 manufactures** [pl.] (*technical*) manufactured goods: *a major importer of cotton manufactures*

manu·fac·tur·er 🔑 /ˌmænjuˈfæktʃərə(r)/ *noun* a person or company that produces goods in large quantities SYN **maker**: *a car/computer manufacturer* ◊ *Always follow the manufacturer's instructions.* ◊ *Faulty goods should be returned to the manufacturers.*

manu·fac·tur·ing 🔑 /ˌmænjuˈfæktʃərɪŋ/ *noun* [U] the business or industry of producing goods in large quantities in factories, etc: *Many jobs in manufacturing were lost during the recession.*

ma·nure /məˈnjʊə(r); *NAmE* məˈnʊr/ *noun, verb*

■ ***noun*** [U] the waste matter from animals that is spread over or mixed with the soil to help plants and crops grow SYN **dung**

■ ***verb* ~ sth** to put manure on or in soil to help plants grow

manu·script /ˈmænjuskrɪpt/ *noun* (*abbr.* MS) **1** a copy of a book, piece of music, etc. before it has been printed: *an* ***unpublished/original manuscript*** ◊ *I read her poems* ***in manuscript.*** **2** a very old book or document that was written by hand before printing was invented: *medieval illuminated manuscripts*

ˈ**manuscript paper** *noun* [U] paper printed with STAVES for writing music on

Manx /mæŋks/ *adj.* of or connected with the Isle of Man, its people or the language once spoken there

ˌ**Manx ˈcat** *noun* a breed of cat with no tail

many 🔑 /ˈmeni/ *det., pron.*

1 🔑 used with plural nouns and verbs, especially in negative sentences or in more formal English, to mean 'a large number of'. Also used in questions to ask about the size of a number, and with 'as', 'so' and 'too'.: *We don't have very many copies left.* ◊ *You can't have one each. We haven't got many.* ◊ *Many people feel that the law should be changed.* ◊ *Many of those present disagreed.* ◊ ***How many*** *children do you have?* ◊ *There are* ***too many*** *mistakes in this essay.* ◊ *He made ten mistakes* ***in as many*** (= in ten) *lines.* ◊ *New drivers have* ***twice as many*** *accidents as experienced drivers.* ◊ *Don't take* ***so many.*** ◊ *I've known her for* ***a great many*** (= very many) *years.* ◊ *Even if one person is hurt that is* ***one too many.*** ◊ *It was one of my many mistakes.* ◊ *a many-headed monster* **2 the many** used with a plural verb to mean 'most people': *a government which improves conditions for the many* **3 many a** (*formal*) used with a singular noun and verb to mean 'a large number of': *Many a good man has been destroyed by drink.*

IDM **as many as...** 🔑 used to show surprise that the number of people or things involved is so large: *There were as many as 200 people at the lecture.* **have had ˌone too ˈmany** (*informal*) to be slightly drunk **many's the...** (*formal*) used to show that sth happens often: *Many's the time I heard her use those words.*

Grammar Point

many / a lot of / lots of

- **Many** is used only with countable nouns. It is used mainly in questions and negative sentences: *Do you go to many concerts?* ◊ ***How many*** *people came to the meeting?* ◊ *I don't go to many concerts.* Although it is not common in statements, it is used after *so*, *as* and *too*: *You made too many mistakes.*
- In statements **a lot of** or **lots of** (*informal*) are much more common: *I go to a lot of concerts.* ◊ *'How many CDs have you got?' 'Lots!'* However, they are not used with measurements of time or distance: *I stayed in England for many/quite a few/ten weeks.* ◊ ~~*I stayed in England a lot of weeks.*~~ When **a lot of/lots of** means 'many', it takes a plural verb: *Lots of people like Italian food.* You can also use **plenty of** (*informal*): *Plenty of stores stay open late.* These phrases can also be used in questions and negative sentences.
- **A lot of/lots of** is still felt to be informal, especially in *BrE*, so in formal writing it is better to use **many** or a **large number of** in statements.

➲ note at MUCH

Mao·ism /ˈmaʊɪzəm/ *noun* [U] the ideas of the 20th century Chinese COMMUNIST leader Mao Zedong ▸ **Mao·ist** /ˈmaʊɪst/ *noun, adj.*

Maori /ˈmaʊri/ *noun* **1** [C] a member of a race of people who were the original people living in New Zealand **2** [U] the language of the Maori people ▸ **Maori** *adj.*

map 🔑 /mæp/ *noun, verb*

■ ***noun*** 🔑 a drawing or plan of the earth's surface or part of it, showing countries, towns, rivers, etc: *a map of France* ◊ *a street map of Miami* ◊ *to* ***read a/the map*** (= understand the information on a map) ◊ *large-scale maps* ◊ *Can you find Black Hill* ***on the map?*** ◊ *I'll draw you a map of how to get to my house.* ➲ VISUAL VOCAB page V34 ➲ see also ROAD MAP

IDM **put sb/sth on the ˈmap** to make sb/sth famous or important: *The exhibition has helped put the city on the map.* ➲ more at WIPE *v.*

■ ***verb*** (-pp-) **1 ~ sth** to make a map of an area **SYN chart**: *an unexplored region that has not yet been mapped* **2 ~ sth** to discover or give information about sth, especially the way it is arranged or organized: *It is now possible to map the different functions of the brain.* ▶ **map·ping** *noun* [U]: *the mapping of the Indian subcontinent* ◇ *gene mapping*

PHR V **'map sth on/onto sth** to link a group of qualities, items, etc. with their source, cause, position on a scale, etc: *Grammar information enables students to map the structure of a foreign language onto their own.* **ˌmap sth↔'out** to plan or arrange sth in a careful or detailed way: *He has his career path clearly mapped out.*

maple /'meɪpl/ *noun* **1** [C, U] (also **'maple tree**) a tall tree with leaves that have five points and turn bright red or yellow in the autumn/fall. Maples grow in northern countries. **2** [U] the wood of the maple tree

'maple leaf *noun* **1** [C] the leaf of the maple tree, used as a symbol of Canada **2 the Maple Leaf** [sing.] the flag of Canada

ˌmaple 'syrup *noun* [U] a sweet sticky sauce made with liquid obtained from some types of maple tree, often eaten with PANCAKES

mar /mɑː(r)/ *verb* (-rr-) **~ sth** to damage or spoil sth good **SYN blight, ruin**: *The game was marred by the behaviour of drunken fans.*

ma·racas /mə'rækəz; *NAmE* -'rɑː-/ *noun* [pl.] a pair of simple musical instruments consisting of hollow balls containing BEADS or BEANS that are shaken to produce a sound ➲ VISUAL VOCAB page V30

mar·as·chino /ˌmærə'ʃiːnəʊ; -'skiːnəʊ; *NAmE* -noʊ/ *noun* (*pl.* -os) **1** [U, C] a strong sweet alcoholic drink made from black CHERRIES **2** (also **ˌmaraschino 'cherry**) [C] a preserved CHERRY used to decorate alcoholic drinks

Ma·ra·thi (also **Mah·ratti**) /mə'rɑːti; -'ræti/ *noun* [U] a language spoken in Maharashtra in western India

mara·thon /'mærəθən; *NAmE* -θɑːn/ *noun* **1** a long running race of about 42 kilometres or 26 miles: *the London marathon* ◇ *to run a marathon* **2** an activity or a piece of work that lasts a long time and requires a lot of effort and patience: *The interview was a real marathon.* **ORIGIN** From the story that in ancient Greece a messenger ran from Marathon to Athens (22 miles) with the news of a victory over the Persians. ▶ **mara·thon** *adj.* [only before noun]: *a marathon journey lasting 56 hours* ◇ *a marathon legal battle*

ma·raud·ing /mə'rɔːdɪŋ/ *adj.* [only before noun] (of people or animals) going around a place in search of things to steal or people to attack: *marauding wolves* ▶ **ma·raud·er** /mə'rɔːdə(r)/ *noun*

mar·ble /'mɑːbl; *NAmE* 'mɑːrbl/ *noun* **1** [U] a type of hard stone that is usually white and often has coloured lines in it. It can be polished and is used in building and for making statues, etc: *a **slab/block of marble*** ◇ *a **marble floor/sculpture*** **2** [C] a small ball of coloured glass that children roll along the ground in a game **3 marbles** [U] a game played with marbles: *Three boys were playing marbles.* **4 marbles** [pl.] (*informal*) a way of referring to sb's intelligence or mental ability: *He's **losing his marbles*** (= he's not behaving in a sensible way).

mar·bled /'mɑːbld; *NAmE* 'mɑːrbld/ *adj.* having the colours and/or patterns of marble: *marbled wallpaper*

marb·ling /'mɑːblɪŋ; *NAmE* 'mɑːrb-/ *noun* [U] the method of decorating sth with a pattern that looks like MARBLE

marc /mɑːk; *NAmE* mɑːrk/ *noun* **1** [U, sing.] the substance left after GRAPES have been pressed to make wine **2** [U, C] a strong alcoholic drink made from this substance

March 0ⁿ /mɑːtʃ; *NAmE* mɑːrtʃ/ *noun* [U, C] (*abbr.* Mar.) the 3rd month of the year, between February and April **HELP** To see how **March** is used, look at the examples at **April**. **IDM** see MAD

march 0ⁿ /mɑːtʃ; *NAmE* mɑːrtʃ/ *verb, noun*

■ ***verb*** **1** 0ⁿ [I] to walk with stiff regular steps like a soldier: (**+ adv./prep.**) *Soldiers were marching up and down outside the government buildings.* ◇ *Quick march!* (= the order to start marching) ◇ **+ noun** *They marched 20 miles to reach the capital.* **2** 0ⁿ [I] **+ adv./prep.** to walk somewhere quickly in a determined way: *She marched over to me and demanded an apology.* **3** 0ⁿ [I] to walk through the streets in a large group in order to protest about sth **SYN demonstrate** **4** [T] **~ sb + adv./prep.** to force sb to walk somewhere with you: *The guards marched the prisoner away.*

IDM **get your 'marching orders** (*BrE, informal*) to be ordered to leave a place, a job, etc. **give sb their 'marching orders** (*informal*) to order sb to leave a place, their job, etc. **march to (the beat of) a different 'drummer/'drum** to behave in a different way from other people; to have different attitudes or ideas: *She was a gifted and original artist who marched to a different drummer.*

PHR V **ˌmarch 'on** to move on or pass quickly: ***Time marches on*** *and we still have not made a decision.* **'march on...** to march to a place to protest about sth or to attack it: *Several thousand people marched on City Hall.*

■ ***noun*** **1** 0ⁿ [C] an organized walk by many people from one place to another, in order to protest about sth, or to express their opinions: *protest marches* ◇ *to go on a march* ➲ compare DEMONSTRATION **2** 0ⁿ [C] an act of marching; a journey made by marching: *The army began their long march to the coast.* **3** [sing.] **the ~ of sth** the steady development or forward movement of sth: *the **march of progress/technology/time*** **4** [C] a piece of music written for marching to: *a funeral march*

IDM **on the 'march** marching somewhere: *The enemy are on the march.* ➲ more at STEAL *v.*

march·er /'mɑːtʃə(r); *NAmE* 'mɑːrtʃ-/ *noun* a person who is taking part in a march as a protest **SYN demonstrator**

'marching band *noun* [C+sing./pl. v.] a group of musicians who play while they are marching

'marching season *noun* (in Northern Ireland) the time in July and August when PROTESTANT groups march through the streets in memory of victories over CATHOLICS in the 17th century

mar·chion·ess /ˌmɑːʃə'nes; *NAmE* ˌmɑːrʃ-/ *noun* **1** a woman who has the rank of a MARQUESS **2** the wife of a MARQUESS ➲ compare MARQUISE

'march past *noun* [sing.] a ceremony in which soldiers march past an important person, etc. **SYN parade**

Mardi Gras /ˌmɑːdi 'grɑː; *NAmE* 'mɑːrdi grɑː/ *noun* [U] (from *French*) the day before the beginning of Lent, celebrated as a holiday in some countries, with music and dancing in the streets ➲ compare SHROVE TUESDAY

mare /meə(r); *NAmE* mer/ *noun* a female horse or DONKEY ➲ compare BROOD MARE, FILLY, STALLION

IDM **a 'mare's nest** **1** a discovery that seems interesting but is found to have no value **2** a very complicated situation

mar·gar·ine /ˌmɑːdʒə'riːn; *NAmE* 'mɑːrdʒərən/ (also *BrE informal* **marge** /mɑːdʒ; *NAmE* mɑːrdʒ/) *noun* [U] a yellow substance like butter made from animal or vegetable fats, used in cooking or spread on bread, etc.

mar·ga·rita /ˌmɑːgə'riːtə; *NAmE* ˌmɑːrg-/ *noun* an alcoholic drink made by mixing fruit juice with TEQUILA

mar·gin **AW** /'mɑːdʒɪn; *NAmE* 'mɑːrdʒən/ *noun* [C] **1** the empty space at the side of a written or printed page: *the **left-hand/right-hand margin*** ◇ *a **narrow/wide margin*** ◇ *notes scribbled **in the margin*** **2** [usually sing.] the amount of time, or number of votes, etc. by which sb wins sth: *He won by a **narrow margin**.* ◇ *She beat the other runners **by a margin of** ten seconds.* **3** (*business*) = PROFIT MARGIN: *What are your average operating margins?* ◇ *a gross margin of 45%* **4** [usually sing.] an extra amount of sth such as time, space, money, etc. that you include in order to make sure that sth is successful: *a safety margin* ◇ *The narrow gateway left me little **margin for error** as I reversed the car.* ➲ see also MARGIN OF ERROR **5** (*formal*) the extreme edge or limit of a place: *the eastern margin of the Indian Ocean* **6** [usually pl.] the part that is not included in the main part of a group or situation **SYN fringe**: *people living **on the margins** of society* **7** (*AustralE, NZE*) an amount that is

M

added to a basic wage, paid for special skill or responsibility

mar·gin·al AW /ˈmɑːdʒɪnl; *NAmE* ˈmɑːrdʒ-/ *adj., noun*
- ***adj.*** **1** small and not important SYN **slight**: *a marginal improvement in weather conditions* ◇ *The story will only be of marginal interest to our readers.* **2** not part of a main or important group or situation: *marginal groups in society* **3** (*politics*) (*especially BrE*) won or lost by a very small number of votes and therefore very important or interesting as an indication of public opinion: *a* ***marginal seat/constituency*** **4** [only before noun] written in the margin of a page: ***marginal notes/comments*** **5** (of land) that cannot produce enough good crops to make a profit
- ***noun*** (*BrE*) a seat in a parliament, on a local council, etc. that was won by a very small number of votes: *a Labour marginal*

mar·gi·na·lia /ˌmɑːdʒɪˈneɪliə; *NAmE* ˌmɑːrdʒ-/ *noun* [pl.] **1** notes written in the MARGINS of a book, etc. **2** facts or details that are not very important

mar·gin·al·ize (*BrE* also **-ise**) /ˈmɑːdʒɪnəlaɪz; *NAmE* ˈmɑːrdʒ-/ *verb* **~ sb** to make sb feel as if they are not important and cannot influence decisions or events; to put sb in a position in which they have no power ▸ **mar·gin·al·iza·tion, -isa·tion** *noun* [U]: *the marginalization of the elderly*

mar·gin·al·ly AW /ˈmɑːdʒɪnəli; *NAmE* ˈmɑːrdʒ-/ *adv.* very slightly; not very much: *They now cost marginally more than they did last year.*

ˌmargin of ˈerror *noun* [usually sing.] an amount that you allow when you calculate sth, for the possibility that a number is not completely accurate: *The survey has a margin of error of 2.5%.*

mar·guer·ite /ˌmɑːɡəˈriːt; *NAmE* ˌmɑːrɡ-/ *noun* a small white garden flower with a yellow centre

mari·achi /ˌmæriˈɑːtʃi/ *noun* [C, U] a musician who plays traditional Mexican music, usually as part of a small group that travels from place to place; the type of music played by these musicians: *a mariachi band*

Mar·ian /ˈmeəriən; *NAmE* ˈmer-/ *adj.* (*religion*) relating to the Virgin Mary in the Christian church

mari·cul·ture /ˈmærɪkʌltʃə(r)/ *noun* [U] (*technical*) a type of farming in which fish or other sea animals and plants are bred or grown for food

Marie Celeste /ˌmæri sɪˈlest; ˌmɑːri/ *noun* [sing.] = MARY CELESTE

mari·gold /ˈmærigəʊld; *NAmE* -goʊld/ *noun* an orange or yellow garden flower. There are several types of marigold.

ma·ri·juana (also **ma·ri·huana**) /ˌmærəˈwɑːnə/ (also *informal* **pot**) *noun* [U] a drug (illegal in many countries) made from the dried leaves and flowers of the HEMP plant, which gives the person smoking it a feeling of being relaxed SYN **cannabis**

ma·rimba /məˈrɪmbə/ *noun* a musical instrument like a XYLOPHONE

mar·ina /məˈriːnə/ *noun* a specially designed HARBOUR for small boats and YACHTS ➲ **VISUAL VOCAB** page V4

mar·in·ade /ˌmærɪˈneɪd/ *noun* [C, U] a mixture of oil, wine, spices, etc, in which meat or fish is left before it is cooked in order to make it softer or to give it a particular flavour

marin·ate /ˈmærɪneɪt/ (also **mar·in·ade**) *verb* [T, I] **~ (sth)** if you **marinate** food or it **marinates**, you leave it in a marinade before cooking it

mar·ine /məˈriːn/ *adj., noun*
- ***adj.*** [only before noun] **1** connected with the sea and the creatures and plants that live there: *marine life* ◇ *a marine biologist* (= a scientist who studies life in the sea) **2** connected with ships or trade at sea
- ***noun*** a soldier who is trained to serve on land or at sea, especially one in the US Marine Corps or the British Royal Marines

mari·ner /ˈmærɪnə(r)/ *noun* (*old-fashioned* or *literary*) a sailor

mar·io·nette /ˌmæriəˈnet/ *noun* a PUPPET whose arms, legs and head are moved by strings

mari·tal /ˈmærɪtl/ *adj.* [only before noun] connected with marriage or with the relationship between a husband and wife: ***marital difficulties/breakdown***

ˌmarital ˈstatus *noun* [U] (*formal*) (used especially on official forms) the fact of whether you are single, married, etc: *questions about age, sex and marital status*

mari·time /ˈmærɪtaɪm/ *adj.* **1** connected with the sea or ships: *a maritime museum* **2** (*formal*) near the sea: *maritime Antarctica*

mar·joram /ˈmɑːdʒərəm; *NAmE* ˈmɑːrdʒ-/ *noun* [U] a plant with leaves that smell sweet and are used in cooking as a HERB, often when dried

mark 🔑 /mɑːk; *NAmE* mɑːrk/ *verb, noun*
- ***verb***
- ▸ WRITE/DRAW **1** 🔑 [T] to write or draw a symbol, line, etc. on sth in order to give information about it: **~ A (with B)** *Items marked with an asterisk can be omitted.* ◇ **~ B on A** *Prices are marked on the goods.* ◇ **~ sb/sth + adj.** *The teacher marked her absent* (= made a mark by her name to show that she was absent). ◇ *Why have you marked this wrong?* ◇ *Do not open any mail marked 'Confidential'.*
- ▸ SPOIL/DAMAGE **2** 🔑 [T, I] **~ (sth)** to make a mark on sth in a way that spoils or damages it; to become spoilt or damaged in this way: *A large purple scar marked his cheek.* ◇ *The surfaces are made from a material that doesn't mark.*
- ▸ SHOW POSITION **3** 🔑 [T] **~ sth** to show the position of sth SYN **indicate**: *The cross marks the spot where the body was found.* ◇ *The route has been marked in red.*
- ▸ CELEBRATE **4** 🔑 [T] **~ sth** to celebrate or officially remember an event that you consider to be important: *a ceremony to mark the 50th anniversary of the end of the war*
- ▸ SHOW CHANGE **5** [T] **~ sth** to be a sign that sth new is going to happen: *This speech may* ***mark a change in*** *government policy.* ◇ *The agreement marks a new phase in international relations.*
- ▸ GIVE MARK/GRADE **6** 🔑 [T, I] **~ (sth)** (*especially BrE*) to give marks to students' work: *I hate marking exam papers.* ◇ *I spend at least six hours a week marking.* ➲ compare GRADE
- ▸ GIVE PARTICULAR QUALITY **7** [T, usually passive] (*formal*) to give sb/sth a particular quality or character SYN **characterize**: **~ sb/sth** *a life marked by suffering* ◇ **~ sb/sth as sth** *He was marked as an enemy of the poor.*
- ▸ PAY ATTENTION **8** [T] (*old-fashioned*) used to tell sb to pay careful attention to sth: **~ sth** *There'll be trouble over this,* ***mark my words.*** ◇ **~ what, how, etc...** *You mark what I say, John.*
- ▸ IN SPORT **9** [T] **~ sb** (in a team game) to stay close to an opponent in order to prevent them from getting the ball: *Hughes was marking Taylor.* ◇ *Our defence had him closely marked.* ➲ see also MARKING

IDM **ˌmark ˈtime 1** to pass the time while you wait for sth more interesting: *I'm just marking time in this job—I'm hoping to get into journalism.* **2** (of soldiers) to make marching movements without moving forwards **ˌmark ˈyou** (*old-fashioned, informal, especially BrE*) used to remind sb of sth they should consider in a particular case: *She hasn't had much success yet. Mark you, she tries hard.*

PHR V **ˌmark sb ˈdown** (*BrE*) to reduce the mark/grade given to sb in an exam, etc: *She was marked down because of poor grammar.* **ˌmark sb ˈdown as sth** (*especially BrE*) to recognize sb as a particular type: *I hadn't got him marked down as a liberal.* **ˌmark sth↔ˈdown 1** to reduce the price of sth: *All goods have been marked down by 15%.* OPP **mark up** ➲ related noun MARKDOWN **2** to make a note of sth for future use or action: *The factory is already marked down for demolition.* **ˌmark sb/sth ˈoff (from sb/sth)** to make sb/sth seem different from other people or things: *Each of London's districts had a distinct character that marked it off from its neighbours.* **ˌmark sth↔ˈoff** to separate sth by marking a line between it and sth else: *The playing area was marked off with a white line.* **ˌmark sb ˈout as/for sth** to make people recognize sb as special in some way: *She was marked out for early promotion.* **ˌmark sth↔ˈout** to draw lines to show the edges of sth: *They* marked out a tennis court on the lawn. ˌ**mark sth↔'up** **1** to increase the price of sth: *Share prices were marked up as soon as trading started.* OPP **mark down** ➲ related noun MARK-UP **2** (*technical*) to mark or correct a text, etc, for example for printing: *to mark up a manuscript*

■ ***noun***

▸ SPOT/DIRT **1** a small area of dirt, a spot or a cut on a surface that spoils its appearance: *The children left dirty marks all over the kitchen floor.* ◇ *a burn/scratch mark* ◇ *Detectives found no marks on the body.* **2** a noticeable spot or area of colour on the body of a person or an animal which helps you to recognize them: *a horse with a white mark on its head* ◇ *He was about six feet tall, with no* ***distinguishing marks.*** ➲ SYNONYMS at PATCH ➲ see also BIRTHMARK, MARKING

▸ SYMBOL **3** a written or printed symbol that is used as a sign of sth, for example the quality of sth or who made or owns it: *punctuation marks* ◇ *Any piece of silver bearing his mark is extremely valuable.* ◇ *I put a mark in the margin to remind me to check the figure.* ➲ see also QUESTION MARK, EXCLAMATION MARK, TRADEMARK

▸ SIGN **4** a sign that a quality or feeling exists: *On the day of the funeral businesses remained closed as* ***a mark of respect.*** ◇ *Such coolness under pressure is the mark of a champion.*

▸ STANDARD/GRADE **5** (*especially BrE*) a number or letter that is given to show the standard of sb's work or performance or is given to sb for answering sth correctly: *to get a* ***good/poor mark*** *in English* ◇ *to give sb a* ***high/low mark*** ◇ *What's the* ***pass mark*** (= the mark you need in order to pass)? ◇ *I got* ***full marks*** (= the highest mark possible) *in the spelling test.* ◇ (*ironic*) *'You're wearing a tie!' '****Full marks for*** *observation.'* ➲ see also BLACK MARK, GRADE

▸ LEVEL **6** a level or point that sth reaches that is thought to be important: *Unemployment has passed the four million mark.* ◇ *She was leading at the half-way mark.*

▸ MACHINE/VEHICLE **7 Mark** (followed by a number) a particular type or model of a machine or vehicle: *the Mark II engine*

Synonyms

mark

stain • fingerprint • streak • speck • blot • smear • spot

These are all words for a small area of dirt or another substance on a surface.

mark a small area of dirt or other substance on the surface of sth, especially one that spoils its appearance: *The kids left dirty marks all over the kitchen floor.*

stain a dirty mark on sth that is difficult to remove, especially one made by a liquid: *blood stains*

fingerprint a mark on a surface made by the pattern of lines on the end of a person's finger, often used by the police to identify criminals: *Her fingerprints were all over the gun.*

streak a long thin mark or line that is a different colour from the surface it is on: *She had streaks of grey in her hair.*

speck a very small mark, spot or piece of a substance on sth: *There isn't a* ***speck of dust*** *anywhere in the house.*

blot a spot or dirty mark left on sth by a substance such as ink or paint being dropped on a surface

smear a mark made by sth such as oil or paint being spread or rubbed on a surface

spot a small dirty mark on sth: *There were grease spots all over the walls.*

PATTERNS

- a streak/speck/blot/smear/spot **of** sth
- a **greasy** mark/stain/smear
- a/an **ink** mark/stain/blot/spot
- a/an **grease** mark/stain/spot
- to **leave** a mark/stain/fingerprint/streak/speck/blot/smear

▸ IN GAS OVEN **8 Mark** (*BrE*) (followed by a number) a particular level of temperature in a gas oven: *Preheat the oven to gas Mark 6.*

▸ SIGNATURE **9** a cross made on a document instead of a signature by sb who is not able to write their name

▸ TARGET **10** (*formal*) a target: *Of the blows delivered, barely half found their mark.* ◇ *to* ***hit/miss the mark***

▸ GERMAN MONEY **11** = DEUTSCHMARK

IDM **be close to/near the 'mark** to be fairly accurate in a guess, statement, etc. **be off the 'mark** not to be accurate in a guess, statement, etc: *No, you're way off the mark.* **be on the 'mark** to be accurate or correct: *That estimate was right on the mark.* **get off the 'mark** to start scoring, especially in CRICKET: *Stewart got off the mark with a four.* ˌ**hit/ˌmiss the 'mark** to succeed/fail in achieving or guessing sth: *He blushed furiously and Robyn knew she had hit the mark.* ˌ**leave your/its/a 'mark (on sth/sb)** to have an effect on sth/sb, especially a bad one, that lasts for a long time: *Such a traumatic experience was bound to leave its mark on the children.* ˌ**make your/a 'mark (on sth)** to become famous and successful in a particular area **not be/feel ˌup to the 'mark** (*old-fashioned, BrE*) not to feel as well or lively as usual **on your ˌmarks, get ˌset, 'go!** used to tell runners in a race to get ready and then to start **quick/slow off the 'mark** fast/slow in reacting to a situation ˌ**up to the 'mark** (*BrE*) (*NAmE* ˌ**up to 'snuff**) as good as it/they should be SYN **up to scratch**: *Your work isn't really up to the mark.* ➲ more at OVERSTEP, TOE *v.*, WIDE *adj.*

mark·down /ˈmɑːkdaʊn; *NAmE* ˈmɑːrk-/ *noun* [usually sing.] a reduction in price

marked /mɑːkt; *NAmE* mɑːrkt/ *adj.* **1** easy to see SYN **noticeable, distinct**: *a* ***marked difference/improvement*** ◇ *a marked increase in profits* ◇ *She is quiet and studious,* ***in marked contrast to*** *her sister.* **2** (*linguistics*) (of a word or form of a word) showing a particular feature or style, such as being formal or informal OPP **unmarked** ▸ **mark·ed·ly** /ˈmɑːkɪdli; *NAmE* ˈmɑːrk-/ *adv.*: *Her background is markedly different from her husband's.* ◇ *This year's sales have risen markedly.*

IDM **a marked 'man/'woman** a person who is in danger because their enemies want to harm them

mark·er /ˈmɑːkə(r); *NAmE* ˈmɑːrk-/ *noun* **1** [C] an object or a sign that shows the position of sth: *a boundary marker* ◇ *He placed a marker where the ball had landed.* **2** [sing.] **a ~ (of/for sth)** a sign that sth exists or that shows what it is like: *Price is not always an accurate marker of quality.* **3** (*BrE* also **'marker pen**) a pen with a thick FELT tip ➲ VISUAL VOCAB page V56 **4** (*BrE*) (*NAmE* **grader**) a person who marks/grades students' work or exam papers **5** (*BrE*) (in team games, especially football (SOCCER)) a player who stays close to a player on the other team in order to stop them getting the ball

mar·ket /ˈmɑːkɪt; *NAmE* ˈmɑːrk-/ *noun, verb*

■ ***noun* 1** [C] an occasion when people buy and sell goods; the open area or building where they meet to do this: *a* ***fruit/flower/antiques market*** ◇ ***an indoor/a street market*** ◇ ***market stalls/traders*** ◇ *We buy our fruit and vegetables* ***at the market.*** ◇ *Thursday is* ***market day.*** ◇ *a* ***market town*** (= a town in Britain where a regular market is or was held) ➲ VISUAL VOCAB page V2 ➲ see also FARMERS' MARKET **2** [sing.] business or trade, or the amount of trade in a particular type of goods: *the world market in coffee* ◇ *They have increased their* ***share of the market*** *by 10%.* ◇ *the* ***property/job market*** (= the number and type of houses, jobs, etc. that are available) ◇ *They have* ***cornered the market in*** *sportswear* (= sell the most). ➲ COLLOCATIONS at BUSINESS **3** [C] a particular area, country or section of the population that might buy goods: *the Japanese market* ◇ *the* ***global/domestic market*** **4** [sing.] **~ (for sth)** the number of people who want to buy sth SYN **demand**: *a* ***growing/declining market*** *for second-hand cars* **5** (often **the market**) [sing.] people who buy and sell goods in competition with each other: *The market will decide if the TV station has any future.*

M

◇ *a **market-based/market-driven/market-led** economy* ➲ see also BLACK MARKET, MARKET FORCES **6** [C] = STOCK MARKET: *the futures market* ◇ *a market crash* HELP There are many other compounds ending in **market**. You will find them at their place in the alphabet.

IDM **in the 'market for sth** interested in buying sth: *I'm not in the market for a new car at the moment.* **on the 'market** available for people to buy: *to put your house on the market* ◇ *The house came on the market last year.* ◇ *There are hundreds of different brands on the market.* **on the open 'market** available to buy without any restrictions **play the 'market** to buy and sell STOCKS and shares in order to make a profit ➲ more at BUYER, PRICE *v.*, SELLER

■ ***verb*** **~ sth (to sb) (as sth)** to advertise and offer a product for sale; to present sth in a particular way and make people want to buy it SYN **promote**: *It is marketed as a low-alcohol wine.* ◇ *School meals need to be marketed to children in the same way as other food.* ➲ see also MARKETING

mar·ket·able /'mɑːkɪtəbl; *NAmE* 'mɑːrk-/ *adj.* easy to sell; attractive to customers or employers: ***marketable products/skills/qualifications*** ▸ **mar·ket·abil·ity** /ˌmɑːkɪtə'bɪləti; *NAmE* ˌmɑːrk-/ *noun* [U]

mar·ket·eer /ˌmɑːkɪ'tɪə(r); *NAmE* ˌmɑːrkə'tɪr/ *noun* (usually in compounds) a person who is in favour of a particular system of buying and selling: *a free marketeer* (= a person who believes in a FREE MARKET system of trade) ➲ see also BLACK MARKETEER

ˌmarket 'forces *noun* [pl.] a free system of trade in which prices and wages rise and fall without being controlled by the government

ˌmarket 'garden (*BrE*) (*US* **'truck farm**) *noun* a type of farm where vegetables are grown for sale ▸ **ˌmarket 'gardener** *noun* **ˌmarket 'gardening** *noun* [U]

mar·ket·ing 0-w /'mɑːkɪtɪŋ; *NAmE* 'mɑːrk-/ *noun* [U] the activity of presenting, advertising and selling a company's products in the best possible way: *a marketing campaign* ◇ *She works in **sales and marketing**.* ➲ COLLOCATIONS at BUSINESS ➲ see also DIRECT MARKETING ▸ **mar·ket·er** *noun*: *a company that is a developer and marketer of software*

'marketing mix *noun* (*business*) the combination of the features of a product, its price, the way it is advertised and where it is sold, each of which a company can adjust to persuade people to buy the product

ˌmarket 'leader *noun* **1** the company that sells the largest quantity of a particular kind of product **2** a product that is the most successful of its kind

mar·ket·place /'mɑːkɪtpleɪs; *NAmE* 'mɑːrk-/ *noun* **1 the marketplace** [sing.] the activity of competing with other companies to buy and sell goods, services, etc: *Companies must be able to survive in the marketplace.* ◇ *the education marketplace* **2** (also **ˌmarket 'square**) [C] an open area in a town where a market is held

ˌmarket 'price *noun* the price that people are willing to pay for sth at a particular time

ˌmarket re'search (also **ˌmarket 'research**) *noun* [U] the work of collecting information about what people buy and why

ˌmarket 'share *noun* [U, sing.] (*business*) the amount that a company sells of its products or services compared with other companies selling the same things: *They claim to have a 40% worldwide market share.* ➲ COLLOCATIONS at BUSINESS

ˌmarket 'value *noun* [U, sing.] what sth would be worth if it were sold

mark·ing /'mɑːkɪŋ; *NAmE* 'mɑːrk-/ *noun* **1** [C, usually pl.] a pattern of colours or marks on animals, birds or wood **2** [C, usually pl.] lines, colours or shapes painted on roads, vehicles, etc: *Road markings indicate where you can stop.* **3** [U] (*especially BrE*) (*NAmE* usually **grad·ing**) the activity of checking and correcting the written work or exam papers of students: *She does her marking in the evenings.* **4** [U] (in team games, especially football (SOCCER)) the practice of staying close to a player on the other team in order to stop them getting the ball

marks·man /'mɑːksmən; *NAmE* 'mɑːrk-/, **marks·woman** /'mɑːkswʊmən; *NAmE* 'mɑːrk-/ *noun* (*pl.* **-men** /-mən/, **-women** /-wɪmɪn/) a person who is skilled in accurate shooting

marks·man·ship /'mɑːksmənʃɪp; *NAmE* 'mɑːrk-/ *noun* [U] skill in shooting

mark·up /'mɑːkʌp; *NAmE* 'mɑːrk-/ *noun* **1** [usually sing.] an increase in the price of sth based on the difference between the cost of producing it and the price it is sold at: *an average markup of 10%* **2** [U] (*computing*) the symbols used in computer documents which give information about the structure of the document and tell the computer how it is to appear on the computer screen, or how it is to appear when printed: *a markup language*

marl /mɑːl; *NAmE* mɑːrl/ *noun* **1** [U, C] soil consisting of CLAY and LIME (1) **2** [U] a type of cloth with threads in it that are not of an even colour: *blue marl leggings*

mar·lin /'mɑːlɪn; *NAmE* 'mɑːrlɪn/ *noun* (*pl.* **mar·lin**) a large sea fish with a long sharp nose, that people catch for sport

mar·ma·lade /'mɑːməleɪd; *NAmE* 'mɑːrm-/ *noun* [U] jam/jelly made from oranges, lemons, etc, eaten especially for breakfast ➲ compare JAM (1)

Mar·mite™ /'mɑːmaɪt; *NAmE* 'mɑːrm-/ *noun* [U] (*BrE*) a dark substance made from YEAST and spread on bread, etc. SYN **yeast extract**: *Marmite sandwiches*

mar·mor·eal /mɑː'mɔːriəl; *NAmE* mɑːr'm-/ *adj.* (*literary*) made of or similar to MARBLE

mar·mo·set /'mɑːməzet; *NAmE* 'mɑːrm-/ *noun* a small MONKEY with a long thick tail, that lives in Central and S America

mar·mot /'mɑːmət; *NAmE* 'mɑːrmət/ *noun* a small European or American animal that lives in holes in the ground

ma·roon /mə'ruːn/ *adj., noun, verb*

■ ***adj.*** dark brownish-red in colour

■ ***noun*** **1** [U] a dark brownish-red colour **2** [C] a large FIREWORK that shoots into the air and makes a loud noise, used to attract attention, especially at sea

■ ***verb*** [usually passive] **~ sb** to leave sb in a place that they cannot escape from, for example an island SYN **strand**: *'Lord of the Flies' is a novel about English schoolboys marooned on a desert island.*

marque /mɑːk; *NAmE* mɑːrk/ *noun* (*formal*) a well-known make of a product, especially a car, that is expensive and fashionable: *the Porsche marque*

mar·quee /mɑː'kiː; *NAmE* mɑːr'kiː/ *noun, adj.*

■ ***noun*** **1** a large tent used at social events **2** (*NAmE*) a covered entrance to a theatre, hotel, etc. often with a sign on or above it

■ ***adj.*** [only before noun] (*especially NAmE*) (especially in sport) most important or most popular: *He is one of the marquee names in men's tennis.*

mar·quess (also **mar·quis**) /'mɑːkwɪs; *NAmE* 'mɑːrk-/ *noun* (in Britain) a NOBLEMAN of high rank between an EARL and a DUKE: *the Marquess of Bath* ➲ compare MARCHIONESS

mar·quet·ry /'mɑːkɪtri; *NAmE* 'mɑːrk-/ *noun* [U] patterns or pictures made of pieces of wood on the surface of furniture, etc; the art of making these patterns

mar·quis /'mɑːkwɪs; *NAmE* 'mɑːrk-/ *noun* **1** (in some European countries but not Britain) a NOBLEMAN of high rank between a COUNT and a DUKE **2** = MARQUESS

mar·quise /mɑː'kiːz; *NAmE* mɑːr'kiːz/ *noun* **1** the wife of a marquis **2** a woman who has the rank of a marquis ➲ compare MARCHIONESS

mar·ram grass /'mærəm grɑːs; *NAmE* græs/ (also **mar·ram**) *noun* [U] a type of grass that grows in sand, often planted to prevent sand DUNES from being destroyed by the wind, rain, etc.

mar·riage 0-w /'mærɪdʒ/ *noun*

1 0-w [C] the legal relationship between a husband and wife: *a **happy/unhappy marriage*** ◇ *All of her children's* *marriages ended in divorce.* ◇ *an* **arranged marriage** (= one in which the parents choose a husband or wife for their child) ◇ *She has two children by a previous marriage.* ➲ see also MIXED **2** [U] the state of being married: *They don't believe in marriage.* ◇ *My parents are celebrating 30 years of marriage.* **3** [C] the ceremony in which two people become husband and wife: *Their marriage took place in a local church.* HELP **Wedding** is more common in this meaning.

IDM **by 'marriage** when sb is related to you **by marriage**, they are married to sb in your family, or you are married to sb in their family ➲ more at HAND *n.*

Collocations

Marriage and divorce

Romance

- **fall/be** (madly/deeply/hopelessly) **in love** (with sb)
- **be/believe in/fall in** love at first sight
- **be/find** true love/the love of your life
- **suffer (from)** (the pains/pangs of) unrequited love
- **have/feel/show/express** great/deep/genuine affection for sb/sth
- **meet/marry** your husband/wife/partner/fiancé/fiancée/boyfriend/girlfriend
- **have/go on** a (blind) **date**
- **be going out with**/(*especially NAmE*) **dating** a guy/girl/boy/man/woman
- **move in with/live with** your boyfriend/girlfriend/partner

Weddings

- **get/be** engaged/married/divorced
- **arrange/plan** a wedding
- **have** a big wedding/a honeymoon/a happy marriage
- **have/enter into** an arranged marriage
- **call off/cancel/postpone** your wedding
- **invite sb to/go to/attend** a wedding/a wedding ceremony/a wedding reception
- **conduct/perform** a wedding ceremony
- **exchange** rings/wedding vows/marriage vows
- **congratulate/toast/raise a glass to** the happy couple
- **be/go on** honeymoon (with your wife/husband)
- **celebrate** your first (wedding) anniversary

Separation and divorce

- **be unfaithful to**/(*informal*) **cheat on** your husband/wife/partner/fiancé/fiancée/boyfriend/girlfriend
- **have** an affair (with sb)
- **break off/end** an engagement/a relationship
- **break up with/split up with**/(*informal*) **dump** your boyfriend/girlfriend
- **separate from/be separated from/leave/divorce** your husband/wife
- **annul/dissolve** a marriage
- **apply for/ask for/go through/get** a divorce
- **get/gain/be awarded/have/lose** custody of the children
- **pay** alimony/child support (to your ex-wife/husband)

mar·riage·able /ˈmærɪdʒəbl/ *adj.* (*old-fashioned*) suitable for marriage: *She had reached marriageable age.*

'marriage broker *noun* a person who is paid to arrange for two people to meet and marry

'marriage bureau *noun* (*old-fashioned, BrE*) an organization that introduces people who are looking for sb to marry

'marriage certificate (*BrE*) (*US* **'marriage license**) *noun* a legal document that proves two people are married

,marriage 'guidance *noun* [U] (*BrE*) advice that is given by specially trained people to couples with problems in their marriage

'marriage licence (*BrE*) (*NAmE* **'marriage license**) *noun* **1** a document that allows two people to get married **2** (*US*) (*BrE* **'marriage certificate**) a legal document that proves two people are married

,marriage of con'venience *noun* a marriage that is made for practical, financial or political reasons and not because the two people love each other

mar·ried /ˈmærid/ *adj.*
1 having a husband or wife: *a* **married man/woman** ◇ *Is he married?* ◇ *a happily married couple* ◇ *She's* **married** *to John.* ◇ *Rachel and David are* **getting married** *on Saturday.* ◇ *How long have you been married?* OPP **unmarried** ➲ COLLOCATIONS at MARRIAGE **2** [only before noun] connected with marriage: *Are you enjoying married life?* ◇ *Her married name* (= the family name of her husband) *is Jones.* **3 ~ to sth** very involved in sth so that you have no time for other activities or interests: *My brother is married to his job.*

mar·row /ˈmærəʊ; *NAmE* -roʊ/ *noun* **1** [U] = BONE MARROW **2** (*BrE*) [U, C] a large vegetable that grows on the ground. Marrows are long and thick with dark green skin and white flesh. ➲ VISUAL VOCAB page V27

mar·row·bone /ˈmærəʊbəʊn; *NAmE* ˈmæroʊboʊn/ *noun* a bone which still contains the MARROW (= the substance inside) and is used in making food

marry /ˈmæri/ *verb* (**mar·ries, marry·ing, mar·ried, mar·ried**)
1 [T, I] to become the husband or wife of sb; to get married to sb: **~ (sb)** *She married a German.* ◇ *He never married.* ◇ *I guess I'm* **not the marrying kind** (= the kind of person who wants to get married). ◇ **+ adj.** *They* **married young**. HELP It is more common to say: *They're* **getting married** *next month.* than: *They're* **marrying** *next month.* ➲ COLLOCATIONS at MARRIAGE **2** [T] **~ sb** to perform a ceremony in which a man and woman become husband and wife: *They were married by the local priest.* **3** [T] **~ sb (to sb)** to find a husband or wife for sb, especially your daughter or son **4** [T] **~ sth and/to/with sth** (*formal*) to combine two different things, ideas, etc. successfully SYN **unite**: *The music business marries art and commerce.*

> **WORD FAMILY**
> **marry** *verb*
> **marriage** *noun*
> **married** *adj.* (≠ unmarried)

IDM **marry in 'haste** (, **repent at 'leisure**) (*saying*) people who marry quickly, without really getting to know each other, may discover later that they have made a mistake **marry 'money** to marry a rich person

PHR V **,marry 'into sth** to become part of a family or group because you have married sb who belongs to it: *She married into the aristocracy.* **,marry sb↔'off (to sb)** (*disapproving*) to find a husband or wife for sb, especially your daughter or son **,marry sth↔'up (with sth)** to combine two things, people or parts of sth successfully

Mars /mɑːz; *NAmE* mɑːrz/ *noun* the planet in the SOLAR SYSTEM that is fourth in order of distance from the sun, between the Earth and Jupiter

Mar·sala /mɑːˈsɑːlə; *NAmE* mɑːrˈs-/ *noun* [U] a dark strong sweet wine from Sicily. It is usually drunk with the sweet course of a meal.

marsh /mɑːʃ; *NAmE* mɑːrʃ/ *noun* [C, U] an area of low land that is always soft and wet because there is nowhere for the water to flow away to: *Cows were grazing on the marshes.* ➲ VISUAL VOCAB page V3 ► **marshy** *adj.*: *marshy ground/land*

mar·shal /ˈmɑːʃl; *NAmE* ˈmɑːrʃl/ *noun, verb*
■ *noun* **1** (usually in compounds) an officer of the highest rank in the British army or AIR FORCE: *Field Marshal Lord Haig* ◇ *Marshal of the Royal Air Force* ➲ see also AIR CHIEF MARSHAL, AIR MARSHAL, AIR VICE-MARSHAL, FIELD MARSHAL **2** a person responsible for making sure that public events, especially sports events, take place without any problems, and for controlling crowds SYN **steward**

M

3 (in the US) an officer whose job is to put court orders into effect: *a federal marshal* **4** (in some US cities) an officer of high rank in a police or fire department
- *verb* (-ll-, *US* -l-) (*formal*) **1 ~ sth** to gather together and organize the people, things, ideas, etc. that you need for a particular purpose SYN **muster**: *They have begun* ***marshalling forces*** *to send relief to the hurricane victims.* ◇ *to* ***marshal your arguments/thoughts/facts*** **2 ~ sb** to control or organize a large group of people: *Police were brought in to marshal the crowd.*

ˈmarshalling yard *noun* (*BrE*) a place where railway WAGONS are connected, prepared, etc. to form trains

ˌMarshal of the ˌRoyal ˈAir Force *noun* the highest rank of officer in the British AIR FORCE

ˈmarsh gas *noun* [U] a gas that is produced in a marsh when plants decay

marsh·land /ˈmɑːʃlænd; *NAmE* ˈmɑːrʃ-/ *noun* [U, C] an area of soft wet land

marsh·mal·low /ˌmɑːʃˈmæləʊ; *NAmE* ˈmɑːrʃmeloʊ/ *noun* [C, U] a pink or white sweet/candy that feels soft and ELASTIC when you chew it

mar·su·pial /mɑːˈsuːpiəl; *NAmE* mɑːrˈs-/ *noun* any animal that carries its young in a pocket of skin (called a POUCH) on the mother's stomach. KANGAROOS and KOALAS are marsupials. ➲ VISUAL VOCAB page V10 ▶ **mar·su·pial** *adj.*

mart /mɑːt; *NAmE* mɑːrt/ *noun* (*especially NAmE*) a place where things are bought and sold: *a used car mart*

mar·ten /ˈmɑːtɪn; *NAmE* ˈmɑːrtn/ *noun* a small wild animal with a long body, short legs and sharp teeth. Martens live in forests and eat smaller animals: *a pine marten*

M

mar·tial /ˈmɑːʃl; *NAmE* ˈmɑːrʃl/ *adj.* (*formal*) [only before noun] connected with fighting or war

ˌmartial ˈart *noun* [usually pl.] any of the fighting sports that include JUDO and KARATE

ˌmartial ˈlaw *noun* [U] a situation where the army of a country controls an area instead of the police during a time of trouble: *to* ***declare/impose/lift martial law*** ◇ *The city remains firmly* ***under martial law.***

Mar·tian /ˈmɑːʃn; *NAmE* ˈmɑːrʃn/ *adj., noun*
- *adj.* (*astronomy*) related to or coming from the planet Mars
- *noun* an imaginary creature from the planet Mars

mar·tinet /ˌmɑːtɪˈnet; *NAmE* ˌmɑːrtnˈet/ *noun* (*formal*) a very strict person who demands that other people obey orders or rules completely

mar·tini /mɑːˈtiːni; *NAmE* mɑːrˈt-/ *noun* **1 Martini™** [U] a type of VERMOUTH **2** [U] an alcoholic drink made with GIN and VERMOUTH **3** [C] a glass of martini: *a dry martini*

ˌMartin ˌLuther ˌKing ˈJr. Day *noun* a national holiday in the US on the third Monday in January to celebrate the birthday of Martin Luther King, Jr., who was active in the struggle to win more rights for Black Americans

mar·tyr /ˈmɑːtə(r); *NAmE* ˈmɑːrt-/ *noun, verb*
- *noun* **1** a person who suffers very much or is killed because of their religious or political beliefs: *the early Christian martyrs* ◇ ***a martyr to*** *the cause of freedom* **2** (usually *disapproving*) a person who tries to get sympathy from other people by telling them how much he or she is suffering **3 ~ to sth** (*informal*) a person who suffers very much because of an illness, problem or situation: *She's a martyr to her nerves.*
- *verb* [usually passive] **~ sb** to kill sb because of their religious or political beliefs

mar·tyr·dom /ˈmɑːtədəm; *NAmE* ˈmɑːrtərdəm/ *noun* [U] the suffering or death of a martyr

mar·tyred /ˈmɑːtəd; *NAmE* ˈmɑːrtərd/ *adj.* [usually before noun] (*disapproving*) showing pain or suffering so that people will be kind and sympathetic towards you: *She wore a perpetually martyred expression.*

mar·vel /ˈmɑːvl; *NAmE* ˈmɑːrvl/ *noun, verb*
- *noun* **1** a wonderful and surprising person or thing SYN **wonder**: *the* ***marvels of nature/technology*** **2 marvels** [pl.] wonderful results or things that have been achieved SYN **wonders**: *The doctors have done marvels for her.*
- *verb* (-ll-, *US* -l-) [I, T] **~ (at sth)** | **~ that...** | **+ speech** to be very surprised or impressed by sth: *Everyone marvelled at his courage.*

mar·vel·lous (*US* **mar·vel·ous**) /ˈmɑːvələs; *NAmE* ˈmɑːrv-/ *adj.* extremely good; wonderful SYN **fantastic, splendid**: *This will be a marvellous opportunity for her.* ◇ *The weather was marvellous.* ◇ ***It's marvellous*** *what modern technology can do.* ▶ **mar·vel·lous·ly** (*US* **mar·vel·ous·ly**) *adv.*

Marx·ism /ˈmɑːksɪzəm; *NAmE* ˈmɑːrks-/ *noun* [U] the political and economic theories of Karl Marx (1818-83) which explain the changes and developments in society as the result of opposition between the social classes ▶ **Marx·ist** /ˈmɑːksɪst; *NAmE* ˈmɑːrks-/ *noun* **Marx·ist** *adj.*: ***Marxist theory/doctrine/ideology***

Mary Celeste /ˌmeəri sɪˈlest; *NAmE* ˌmeri/ (also **Marie Celeste**) *noun* [sing.] used to talk about a place where all the people who should be there have disappeared in a mysterious way: *Where is everyone? It's like the Mary Celeste here today.* ORIGIN From the name of the US ship *Mary Celeste*, which in 1872 was found at sea with nobody on board.

mar·zi·pan /ˈmɑːzɪpæn; ˌmɑːzɪˈpæn; *NAmE* ˈmɑːrtsəpæn; ˈmɑːrz-/ *noun* [U] a sweet firm substance, sometimes with yellow colour added, made from ALMONDS, sugar and eggs and used to make sweets/candy and to cover cakes

ma·sala /məˈsɑːlə/ *noun* [U] **1** a mixture of spices used in S Asian cooking **2** a dish made with masala: *chicken masala*

mas·cara /mæˈskɑːrə; *NAmE* -ˈskærə/ *noun* [U] a substance that is put on EYELASHES to make them look dark and thick ➲ VISUAL VOCAB page V49

mas·cot /ˈmæskət; *NAmE* -skɑːt/ *noun* an animal, a toy, etc. that people believe will bring them good luck, or that represents an organization, etc: *The team's mascot is a giant swan.* ◇ *Zakumi—the official mascot of the 2010 FIFA World Cup*

mas·cu·line /ˈmæskjəlɪn/ *adj., noun*
- *adj.* **1** having the qualities or appearance considered to be typical of men; connected with or like men: *He was handsome and strong, and very masculine.* ◇ *That suit makes her look very masculine.* ➲ compare FEMININE, MALE **2** (*grammar*) belonging to a class of words that refer to male people or animals and often have a special form: *'He' and 'him' are masculine pronouns.* **3** (*grammar*) (in some languages) belonging to a class of nouns, pronouns or adjectives that have masculine GENDER, not FEMININE or NEUTER: *The French word for 'sun' is masculine.*
- *noun* **1 the masculine** [sing.] the masculine GENDER (= form of nouns, adjectives and pronouns) **2** [C] a masculine word or word form ➲ compare FEMININE, NEUTER

mas·cu·lin·ity /ˌmæskjuˈlɪnəti/ *noun* [U] the quality of being masculine: *He felt it was a threat to his masculinity.*

mas·cu·lin·ize (*BrE* also **-ise**) /ˈmæskjələnaɪz/ *verb* **~ sth/sb** (*formal*) to make sth or sb more like a man

mash /mæʃ/ *noun, verb*
- *noun* **1** (*especially BrE*) = MASHED POTATO **2** [U] grain cooked in water until soft, used to feed farm animals **3** [U] a mixture of MALT grains and hot water, used for making beer, etc. **4** [sing.] **a ~ (of sth)** any food that has been crushed into a soft mass: *The soup was a mash of grain and vegetables.* ➲ see also MISHMASH
- *verb* **~ sth (up)** to crush food into a soft mass: *Mash the fruit up with a fork.* ➲ COLLOCATIONS at COOKING ➲ VISUAL VOCAB page V25 ▶ **mashed** *adj.*: *mashed banana*

ˌmashed poˈtato (also **ˌmashed poˈtatoes, mash** especially in *BrE*) *noun* [U] potatoes that have been boiled and crushed into a soft mass, often with butter and milk

mashup /ˈmæʃʌp/ *noun* a combination of elements from different sources used to create a new song, video, computer file, program, etc: *a video mashup*

mask /mɑːsk; *NAmE* mæsk/ *noun, verb*

■ ***noun* 1** a covering for part or all of the face, worn to hide or protect it: ***a gas/surgical mask*** ◇ *The robbers wore stocking masks.* ➲ VISUAL VOCAB pages V34, V36, V39 ➲ see also OXYGEN MASK **2** something that covers your face and has another face painted on it: *The kids were all wearing animal masks.* ➲ see also DEATH MASK **3** a thick cream made of various substances that you put on your face and neck in order to improve the quality of your skin: *a face mask* **4** [usually sing.] a manner or an expression that hides your true character or feelings: *He longed to throw off the mask of respectability.* ◇ *Her face was a cold blank mask.*

masks

surgical mask Halloween mask

■ ***verb* ~ sth** to hide a feeling, smell, fact, etc. so that it cannot be easily seen or noticed SYN **disguise, veil**: *She masked her anger with a smile.* ➲ SYNONYMS at HIDE

masked /mɑːskt; *NAmE* mæskt/ *adj.* wearing a MASK: *a masked gunman*

ˌmasked ˈball *noun* a formal party at which guests wear masks

ˈmasking tape *noun* [U] sticky tape that you use to keep an area clean or protected when you are painting around or near it

maso·chism /ˈmæsəkɪzəm/ *noun* [U] **1** the practice of getting sexual pleasure from being physically hurt ➲ compare SADISM **2** (*informal*) the enjoyment of sth that most people would find unpleasant or painful: *You spent the whole weekend in a tent in the rain? That's masochism!* ▸ **maso·chist** /-kɪst/ *noun* **maso·chis·tic** /ˌmæsəˈkɪstɪk/ *adj.*: ***masochistic behaviour/tendencies***

mason /ˈmeɪsn/ *noun* **1** a person who builds using stone, or works with stone **2 Mason** = FREEMASON

the Mason-Dixon Line /ˌmeɪsn ˈdɪksn laɪn/ *noun* [sing.] the border between the US states of Maryland and Pennsylvania that is thought of as the dividing line between the south of the US and the north. In the past it formed the northern border of the states where SLAVES were owned.

Ma·son·ic /məˈsɒnɪk; *NAmE* -ˈsɑːn-/ *adj.* connected with FREEMASONS

Mason·ite™ /ˈmeɪsənaɪt/ *noun* [U] a US make of board that is used in building, made of small pieces of wood that are pressed together and stuck with glue

ma·son·ry /ˈmeɪsənri/ *noun* [U] the parts of a building that are made of stone: *She was injured by falling masonry.* ◇ *He acquired a knowledge of carpentry and masonry* (= building with stone).

masque /mɑːsk; *NAmE* mæsk/ *noun* a play written in VERSE, often with music and dancing, popular in England in the 16th and 17th centuries

mas·quer·ade /ˌmæskəˈreɪd; *BrE* also ˌmɑːsk-/ *noun, verb*

■ ***noun* 1** (*formal*) a way of behaving that hides the truth or a person's true feelings **2** (*especially NAmE*) a type of party where people wear special COSTUMES and MASKS over their faces, to hide their identities

■ ***verb*** [I] **~ as sth** to pretend to be sth that you are not: *commercial advertisers masquerading as private individuals*

Mass /mæs/ *noun* **1** (sometimes **mass**) [U, C] (especially in the Roman Catholic Church) a ceremony held in memory of the last meal that Christ had with his DISCIPLES: *to go to Mass* ◇ *a priest **celebrating/saying Mass*** ➲ see also EUCHARIST, COMMUNION **2** [C] a piece of music that is written for the prayers, etc. of this ceremony: *Bach's Mass in B minor*

mass 🔑 /mæs/ *noun, adj., verb*

■ ***noun* 1** 🔑 [C] **~ (of sth)** a large amount of a substance that does not have a definite shape or form: *a mass of snow and rocks falling down the mountain* ◇ *The hill appeared as a black mass in the distance.* ◇ *The sky was full of dark masses of clouds.* **2** 🔑 [C, usually sing.] **~ of sth** a large amount or quantity of sth: *a mass of blonde hair* ◇ *I began sifting through the mass of evidence.* **3** 🔑 [sing.] **~ of sth** a large number of people or things grouped together, often in a confused way: *I struggled through the mass of people to the exit.* ◇ *The page was covered with a mass of figures.* **4** 🔑 **masses** [pl.] **~ (of sth)** (*informal*) a large number or amount of sth SYN **lots**: *There were masses of people in the shops yesterday.* ◇ *I've got masses of work to do.* ◇ *Don't give me any more. I've eaten masses!* **5 the masses** [pl.] the ordinary people in society who are not leaders or who are considered to be not very well educated: *government attempts to suppress dissatisfaction among the masses* ◇ *a TV programme that brings science to the masses* **6 the mass of sth** [sing.] the most; the majority: *The reforms are unpopular with the mass of teachers and parents.* **7** [U] (*technical*) the quantity of material that sth contains: *calculating the mass of a planet* HELP **Weight** is used in non-technical language for this meaning. ➲ see also BIOMASS, CRITICAL MASS, LAND MASS

IDM **be a ˈmass of** to be full of or covered with sth: *The rose bushes are a mass of flowers in June.* ◇ *Her arm was a mass of bruises.*

■ ***adj.*** 🔑 [only before noun] affecting or involving a large number of people or things: ***mass unemployment/production*** ◇ *weapons of mass destruction* ◇ *Their latest product is aimed at the **mass market**.* ➲ see also MASS-MARKET

■ ***verb*** [I, T] to come together in large numbers; to gather people or things together in large numbers: **(+ adv./prep.)** *Demonstrators had massed outside the embassy.* ◇ *Dark clouds massed on the horizon.* ◇ **~ sb/sth** *The general massed his troops for a final attack.* ▸ **massed** *adj.*: *the **massed ranks** of his political opponents*

mas·sacre /ˈmæsəkə(r)/ *noun, verb*

■ ***noun*** [C, U] **1** the killing of a large number of people especially in a cruel way: *the bloody massacre of innocent civilians* ◇ *Nobody survived the massacre.* **2** (*informal*) a very big defeat in a game or competition: *The game was a 10–0 massacre for our team.*

■ ***verb* 1 ~ sb** to kill a large number of people, especially in a cruel way **2 ~ sb** (*informal*) to defeat sb in a game or competition by a high score

mas·sage /ˈmæsɑːʒ; *NAmE* məˈsɑːʒ/ *noun, verb*

■ ***noun*** [U, C] the action of rubbing and pressing a person's body with the hands to reduce pain in the muscles and joints: *Massage will help the pain.* ◇ *a back massage* ◇ *to give sb a massage* ◇ *massage oils*

■ ***verb* 1 ~ sth** to rub and press a person's body with the hands to reduce pain in the muscles and joints: *He massaged the aching muscles in her feet.* ◇ (*figurative*) *to massage sb's ego* (= to make sb feel better, more confident, attractive, etc.) **2 ~ sth into sth** to rub a substance into the skin, hair, etc: *Massage the cream into your skin.* **3 ~ sth** (*disapproving*) to change facts, figures, etc. in order to make them seem better than they really are: *The government was accused of massaging the unemployment figures.*

ˈmassage parlour (*especially US* **masˈsage parlor**) *noun* **1** a place where you can pay to have a massage **2** a place that is supposed to offer the service of massage, but is also where men go to pay for sex with PROSTITUTES

masse ➲ EN MASSE

mas·seur /mæˈsɜː(r)/ *noun* a person whose job is giving people massage

mas·seuse /mæˈsɜːz; *NAmE* məˈsuːs/ *noun* a woman whose job is giving people massage

mas·sif /mæˈsiːf/ *noun* (*technical*) a group of mountains that form a large mass

mas·sive 🔑 /ˈmæsɪv/ *adj.*

1 🔑 very large, heavy and solid: *a massive rock* ◇ *the mas-*

M

sive walls of the castle **2** extremely large or serious: *The explosion made a massive hole in the ground.* ◇ *a massive increase in spending* ◇ *He suffered a massive heart attack.* ◇ (*BrE, informal*) *Their house is massive.* ◇ *They have a massive great house.* ▶ **mas·sive·ly** *adv.*

ˌmass-ˈmarket *adj.* [only before noun] (of goods etc.) produced for very large numbers of people

the ˌmass ˈmedia *noun* [pl.] sources of information and news such as newspapers, magazines, radio and television, that reach and influence large numbers of people

ˈmass noun *noun* (*grammar*) **1** an uncountable noun **2** a noun that is usually uncountable but can be made plural or used with *a* or *an* when you are talking about different types of sth. For example, *bread* is used as a mass noun in *the shop sells several different breads.*

ˈmass number *noun* (*chemistry*) the total number of PROTONS and NEUTRONS in an atom

ˌmass-proˈduce *verb* **~ sth** to produce goods in large quantities, using machinery ▶ **ˌmass-proˈduced** *adj.*: *mass-produced goods* **ˌmass proˈduction** *noun* [U]: *the mass production of consumer goods*

mast /mɑːst; *NAmE* mæst/ *noun* **1** a tall pole on a boat or ship that supports the sails ➲ VISUAL VOCAB page V45 **2** a tall metal tower with an AERIAL that sends and receives radio or television signals **3** a tall pole that is used for holding a flag IDM see NAIL *v.* ➲ see also HALF MAST

mast·ec·tomy /mæˈstektəmi/ *noun* (*pl.* -ies) a medical operation to remove a person's breast

mas·ter /ˈmɑːstə(r); *NAmE* ˈmæs-/ *noun, verb, adj.*

M

■ ***noun***

▸ OF SERVANTS **1** (*old-fashioned*) a man who has people working for him, often as servants in his home: *They lived in fear of their master.*

▸ PERSON IN CONTROL **2 ~ of sth** a person who is able to control sth: *She was no longer master of her own future.*

▸ SKILLED PERSON **3** **~ (of sth)** a person who is skilled at sth: *a master of disguise* ◇ *a master of the serve-and-volley game* ➲ see also PAST MASTER

▸ DOG OWNER **4** the male owner of a dog: *The dog saved its master's life.* ➲ compare MISTRESS

▸ TEACHER **5** (*BrE, old-fashioned*) a male teacher at a school, especially a private school: *the physics master* ➲ compare SCHOOLMASTER, MISTRESS

▸ UNIVERSITY DEGREE **6** **master's** (also **ˈmaster's degree**) a second university degree, or, in Scotland, a first university degree, such as an MA: *He has a Master's in Business Administration.* ➲ see also MA, MB, MBA, MSc **7** (usually **Master**) a person who has a master's degree: *a* ***Master of Arts/Science***

▸ CAPTAIN OF SHIP **8** the captain of a ship that transports goods

▸ FAMOUS PAINTER **9** a famous painter who lived in the past: *an exhibition of work by the French master, Monet* ➲ see also OLD MASTER

▸ ORIGINAL RECORD/TAPE/MOVIE **10** (often used as an adjective) a version of a record, tape, film/movie, etc. from which copies are made: *the master copy*

▸ TITLE **11 Master** (*old-fashioned*) a title used when speaking to or about a boy who is too young to be called *Mr* (also used in front of the name on an envelope, etc.) **12 Master** (in Britain) the title of the head of some schools and university colleges: *the Master of Wolfson College* **13 Master** a title used for speaking to or about some religious teachers or leaders HELP There are many other compounds ending in **master**. You will find them at their place in the alphabet.

IDM **be your own ˈmaster/ˈmistress** to be free to make your own decisions rather than being told what to do by sb else ➲ more at LORD, SERVE *v.*

■ ***verb***

▸ LEARN/UNDERSTAND **1 ~ sth** to learn or understand sth completely: *to* ***master*** *new* ***skills/techniques*** ◇ *French was a language he had never mastered.*

▸ CONTROL **2 ~ sth** to manage to control an emotion: *She struggled hard to master her temper.* **3 ~ sth/sb** to gain control of an animal or a person

■ ***adj.*** [only before noun]

▸ SKILLED **1 ~ baker/chef/mason, etc.** used to describe a person who is very skilled at the job mentioned

▸ MOST IMPORTANT **2** the largest and/or most important: *the* ***master bedroom*** ◇ *a* ***master file/switch***

mas·ter·class /ˈmɑːstəklɑːs; *NAmE* ˈmæstərklæs/ *noun* a lesson, especially in music, given by a famous expert to very skilled students

mas·ter·ful /ˈmɑːstəfl; *NAmE* ˈmæstərfl/ *adj.* **1** (of a person, especially a man) able to control people or situations in a way that shows confidence as a leader **2** = MASTERLY: *a masterful performance* ▶ **mas·ter·ful·ly** /-fəli/ *adv.*: *He took her arm masterfully and led her away.*

ˈmaster key (also **ˈpass key**) *noun* a key that can be used to open many different locks in a building

mas·ter·ly /ˈmɑːstəli; *NAmE* ˈmæstərli/ (also **mas·ter·ful**) *adj.* showing great skill or understanding: *a masterly performance* ◇ *Her handling of the situation was masterly.*

mas·ter·mind /ˈmɑːstəmaɪnd; *NAmE* ˈmæstərm-/ *noun, verb*

■ ***noun*** [usually sing.] an intelligent person who plans and directs a complicated project or activity (often one that involves a crime)

■ ***verb*** **~ sth** to plan and direct a complicated project or activity

ˌmaster of ˈceremonies *noun* (*abbr.* MC) a person who introduces guests or entertainers at a formal occasion

mas·ter·piece /ˈmɑːstəpiːs; *NAmE* ˈmæstərp-/ (also **mas·ter·work**) *noun* a work of art such as a painting, film/movie, book, etc. that is an excellent, or the best, example of the artist's work: *The museum houses several of his Cubist masterpieces.* ◇ *Her work is a masterpiece of* (= an excellent example of) *simplicity.*

ˈmaster plan *noun* [sing.] a detailed plan that will make a complicated project successful

ˈmaster's degree (also **master's**) *noun* a further university degree that you study for after a first degree

the Master's Tournament (also **the Master's**) *noun* a GOLF competition held in the US, in which skilled players are invited to compete

mas·ter·stroke /ˈmɑːstəstrəʊk; *NAmE* ˈmæstərstroʊk/ *noun* [usually sing.] something clever that you do that gives a successful result

mas·ter·work /ˈmɑːstəwɜːk; *NAmE* ˈmæstərwɜːrk/ *noun* = MASTERPIECE

mas·tery /ˈmɑːstəri; *NAmE* ˈmæst-/ *noun* **1** [U, sing.] **~ (of sth)** great knowledge about or understanding of a particular thing SYN **command**: *She has mastery of several languages.* **2** [U] **~ (of/over sb/sth)** control or power: *human mastery of the natural world*

mast·head /ˈmɑːsthed; *NAmE* ˈmæst-/ *noun* **1** the top of a MAST on a ship **2** the name of a newspaper at the top of the front page **3** (*NAmE*) the part of a newspaper or a news website which gives details of the people who work on it and other information about it

mas·tic /ˈmæstɪk/ *noun* [U] **1** a substance that comes from the BARK of a tree and is used in making VARNISH **2** a substance that is used in building to fill holes and keep out water

mas·ti·cate /ˈmæstɪkeɪt/ *verb* [I] (*technical*) to chew food ▶ **mas·ti·ca·tion** /ˌmæstɪˈkeɪʃn/ *noun* [U]

mas·tiff /ˈmæstɪf/ *noun* a large strong dog with short hair, often used to guard buildings

mas·titis /mæˈstaɪtɪs/ *noun* [U] (*medical*) painful swelling of the breast or UDDER usually because of infection

mas·tur·bate /ˈmæstəbeɪt; *NAmE* -stərb-/ *verb* **1** [I, T] **~ (yourself)** to give yourself sexual pleasure by rubbing your sexual organs **2** [T] **~ sb** to give sb sexual pleasure by rubbing their sexual organs ▶ **mas·tur·ba·tion** /ˌmæstə-

'beɪʃn; *NAmE* -stər'b-/ *noun* [U] **mas·tur·ba·tory** /ˌmæstə'beɪtəri; *NAmE* 'mæstərbətɔːri/ *adj.*

mat /mæt/ *noun, adj.*

■ ***noun*** **1** a small piece of thick carpet or strong material that is used to cover part of a floor: *Wipe your feet on the mat before you come in, please.* ➲ see also BATH MAT, DOORMAT, MOUSE MAT **2** a piece of thick material such as rubber or plastic used especially in some sports for people to lie on or fall onto: ***a judo/an exercise mat*** **3** a small piece of plastic, wood or cloth used on a table for decoration or to protect the surface from heat or damage: *a beer mat* ➲ see also TABLE MAT **4** a thick mass of sth that is stuck together: *a mat of hair* ➲ see also MATTED

IDM **go to the 'mat (with sb) (for sb/sth)** (*NAmE, informal*) to support or defend sb/sth in an argument with sb **take sb/sth to the 'mat** (*US, informal*) to get involved in an argument with sb/sth

■ ***adj.*** (*US*) = MATT

mata·dor /'mætədɔː(r)/ *noun* (from *Spanish*) a person who fights and kills the BULL in a BULLFIGHT

Mata Hari /ˌmɑːtə 'hɑːri/ *noun* an attractive female SPY ORIGIN From the name of a Dutch dancer who worked as a spy for the German government during the First World War.

ma·tatu /mæ'tætuː/ *noun* (in Kenya) a small bus used as a taxi

match 0-ᵚ /mætʃ/ *noun, verb*

■ ***noun***

▸ FOR LIGHTING FIRES **1** 0-ᵚ [C] a small stick made of wood or cardboard that is used for lighting a fire, cigarette, etc: *a box of matches* ◇ *to **strike a match*** (= to make it burn) ◇ *to **put a match to sth*** (= set fire to sth)

▸ IN SPORT **2** 0-ᵚ [C] (*especially BrE*) a sports event where people or teams compete against each other: (*BrE*) *a football match* ◇ (*NAmE, BrE*) *a tennis match* ◇ *They are playing an important match against Liverpool on Saturday.* ◇ *to **win/lose a match*** ➲ see also SHOOTING MATCH, SLANGING MATCH, TEST MATCH

▸ AN EQUAL **3** [sing.] **a ~ for sb | sb's match** a person who is equal to sb else in strength, skill, intelligence, etc: *I was **no match for** him at tennis.* ◇ *I was his match at tennis.*

▸ SB/STH THAT COMBINES WELL **4** 0-ᵚ [sing.] a person or thing that combines well with sb/sth else: *The curtains and carpet are a **good match**.* ◇ *Jo and Ian are **a perfect match** for each other.*

▸ STH THE SAME **5** [C] a thing that looks exactly the same as or very similar to sth else: *I've found a vase that is an exact match of the one I broke.*

▸ MARRIAGE **6** [C] (*old-fashioned*) a marriage or a marriage partner ➲ see also LOVE MATCH

IDM **find/meet your 'match (in sb)** to meet sb who is equal to, or even better than you in strength, skill or intelligence ➲ more at MAN *n.*

■ ***verb***

▸ COMBINE WELL **1** 0-ᵚ [T, I] **~ (sth)** if two things **match**, or if one thing **matches** another, they have the same colour, pattern, or style and therefore look attractive together: *The doors were painted blue to match the walls.* ◇ *a scarf with gloves **to match*** ◇ *None of these glasses match* (= they are all different). ➲ see also MATCHING

▸ BE THE SAME **2** 0-ᵚ [T, I] **~ (sth)** if two things **match** or if one thing **matches** another, they are the same or very similar: *Her fingerprints match those found at the scene of the crime.* ◇ *As a couple they are not very well matched* (= they are not very suitable for each other). ◇ *The two sets of figures don't match.*

▸ FIND STH SIMILAR/CONNECTED **3** 0-ᵚ [T] **~ sb/sth (to/with sb/sth)** to find sb/sth that goes together with or is connected with another person or thing: *The aim of the competition is to match the quote to the person who said it.*

▸ BE EQUAL/BETTER **4** [T] **~ sb/sth** to be as good, interesting, successful, etc. as sb/sth else SYN **equal**: *The profits made in the first year have never been matched.* ◇ *The teams were **evenly matched**.* **5** [T] **~ sth** to make sth the same or better than sth else: *The company was unable to match his current salary.*

▸ PROVIDE STH SUITABLE **6** [T] **~ sth** to provide sth that is suitable for or enough for a particular situation: *Investment in hospitals is needed now to match the future needs of the country.* IDM see MIX *v.*

PHR V **'match sth against sth** to compare sth with sth else in order to find things that are the same or similar: *New information is matched against existing data in the computer.* **'match sb/sth against/with sb/sth** to arrange for sb to compete in a game or competition against sb else: *We are matched against last year's champions in the first round.* **ˌmatch 'up (to sb/sth)** (usually used in negative sentences) to be as good, interesting, successful as sb/sth SYN **measure up**: *The trip failed to match up to her expectations.* **ˌmatch 'up (with sth)** 0-ᵚ to be the same or similar SYN **tally, agree**: *The suspects' stories just don't match up.* **ˌmatch sth↔'up (with sth)** 0-ᵚ to find things that belong together or that look attractive together: *She spent the morning matching up orders with invoices.*

match·book /'mætʃbʊk/ *noun* (*NAmE*) a piece of folded card containing matches and a surface to light them on

match·box /'mætʃbɒks; *NAmE* -bɑːks/ *noun* a small box for holding matches ➲ VISUAL VOCAB page V29

match·ing 0-ᵚ /'mætʃɪŋ/ *adj.* [only before noun] (of clothing, material, objects, etc.) having the same colour, pattern, style, etc. and therefore looking attractive together: *a pine table with four matching chairs*

match·less /'mætʃləs/ *adj.* (*formal*) so good that nothing can be compared with it SYN **incomparable**: ***matchless beauty/skill***

match·maker /'mætʃmeɪkə(r)/ *noun* a person who tries to arrange marriages or relationships between others ▸ **match·mak·ing** *noun* [U]

'match play *noun* [U] a way of playing GOLF in which your score depends on the number of holes that you win rather than the number of times you hit the ball in the whole game ➲ compare STROKE PLAY

ˌmatch 'point *noun* [U, C] (*especially in* TENNIS) a point that, if won by a player, will also win them the match

match·stick /'mætʃstɪk/ *noun* a single wooden match: *starving children with legs like matchsticks*

'matchstick figure (*BrE*) (*NAmE* **'stick figure**) *noun* a picture of a person drawn only with thin lines for the arms and legs, a circle for the head, etc.

match·wood /'mætʃwʊd/ *noun* [U] very small pieces of wood

mate 0-ᵚ /meɪt/ *noun, verb*

■ ***noun***

▸ FRIEND **1** 0-ᵚ [C] (*BrE, AustralE, informal*) a friend: *They've been best mates since school.* ◇ *I was with a mate.*

▸ FRIENDLY NAME **2** 0-ᵚ [C] (*BrE, AustralE, informal*) used as a friendly way of addressing sb, especially between men: *Sorry mate, you'll have to wait.* ◇ *All right, mate?*

▸ SB YOU SHARE WITH **3** 0-ᵚ [C] (in compounds) a person you share an activity or accommodation with: ***workmates/teammates/playmates/classmates*** ◇ *my **room-mate/flatmate*** ➲ see also RUNNING MATE, SOULMATE

▸ BIRD/ANIMAL **4** 0-ᵚ [C] either of a pair of birds or animals: *A male bird sings to attract a mate.*

▸ SEXUAL PARTNER **5** [C] (*informal*) a husband, wife or other sexual partner

▸ JOB **6** [C] (*BrE*) a person whose job is to help a skilled worker: *a **builder's/plumber's mate***

▸ ON SHIP **7** [C] an officer in a commercial ship below the rank of captain or MASTER ➲ see also FIRST MATE

▸ IN CHESS **8** [U] = CHECKMATE

■ ***verb***

▸ ANIMALS/BIRDS **1** 0-ᵚ [I] **~ (with sth)** (of two animals or birds) to have sex in order to produce young: *Do foxes ever mate with dogs?* ➲ see also MATING **2** [T] **~ sth (to/with sth)** to put animals or birds together so that they will have sex and produce young

▸ IN CHESS **3** [T] = CHECKMATE

M

ma·ter·ial 0‑w /mə'tɪəriəl; *NAmE* -'tɪr-/ *noun, adj.*
■ ***noun*** **1** 0‑w [U, C] cloth used for making clothes, curtains, etc. SYN **fabric**: *a piece of material* ◇ *'What material is this dress made of?' 'Cotton.'* ➲ note at FABRIC **2** 0‑w [C, U] a substance that things can be made from: ***building materials*** (= bricks, sand, glass, etc.) ➲ see also RAW MATERIAL **3** 0‑w [C, usually pl., U] things that are needed in order to do a particular activity: *teaching materials* ◇ *The company produces its own training material.* ◇ (*figurative*) *The teacher saw her as good university material* (= good enough to go to university). ➲ SYNONYMS at EQUIPMENT **4** 0‑w [U] information or ideas used in books, etc: *She's collecting material for her latest novel.* **5** [U] items used in a performance: *The band played all new material at the gig.*
■ ***adj.*** **1** 0‑w [only before noun] connected with money, possessions, etc. rather than with the needs of the mind or spirit: *material comforts* ◇ *changes in your material circumstances* OPP **spiritual** **2** 0‑w [only before noun] connected with the physical world rather than with the mind or spirit: *the material world* OPP **immaterial** **3** (*formal* or *law*) important and needing to be considered: *material evidence* ◇ **~ to sth** *She omitted information that was material to the case.* ➲ see also IMMATERIAL ▶ **ma·teri·ally** /-iəli/ *adv.*: *Materially they are no better off.* ◇ *Their comments have not materially affected our plans* (= in a noticeable or important way).

ma·teri·al·ism /mə'tɪəriəlɪzəm; *NAmE* -'tɪr-/ *noun* [U] **1** (usually *disapproving*) the belief that money, possessions and physical comforts are more important than spiritual values **2** (*philosophy*) the belief that only material things exist ➲ compare IDEALISM

ma·teri·al·ist /mə'tɪəriəlɪst; *NAmE* -'tɪr-/ *noun* **1** a person who believes that money, possessions and physical comforts are more important than spiritual values in life **2** a person who believes in the philosophy of materialism

ma·teri·al·is·tic /mə,tɪəriə'lɪstɪk; *NAmE* -,tɪr-/ *adj.* (*disapproving*) caring more about money and possessions than anything else

ma·teri·al·ize (*BrE* also **-ise**) /mə'tɪəriəlaɪz; *NAmE* -'tɪr-/ *verb* **1** [I] (usually used in negative sentences) to take place or start to exist as expected or planned: *The promotion he had been promised failed to materialize.* **2** [I] to appear suddenly and/or in a way that cannot be explained: *A tall figure suddenly materialized at her side.* ◇ (*informal*) *The train failed to materialize* (= it did not come). ▶ **ma·teri·al·iza·tion, -isa·tion** /mə,tɪəriəlaɪ'zeɪʃn; *NAmE* -,trɪələ'z-/ *noun* [U]

ma·ter·iel /mə,tɪəri'el; *NAmE* -,tɪr-/ *noun* [U] (*technical*) military weapons and equipment

ma·ter·nal /mə'tɜːnl; *NAmE* mə'tɜːrnl/ *adj.* **1** having feelings that are typical of a caring mother towards a child: *maternal love* ◇ *I'm not very maternal.* ◇ *She didn't have any maternal instincts.* **2** connected with being a mother: *Maternal age affects the baby's survival rate.* **3** [only before noun] related through the mother's side of the family: *my maternal grandfather* (= my mother's father) ▶ **ma·ter·nal·ly** /-nəli/ *adv.*: *She behaved maternally towards her students.* ➲ compare PATERNAL

ma·ter·nity /mə'tɜːnəti; *NAmE* -'tɜːrn-/ *noun* [U] the state of being or becoming a mother: *maternity clothes* (= clothes for women who are pregnant) ◇ *a **maternity ward/hospital*** (= one where women go to give birth to their babies)

ma'ternity leave *noun* [U] a period of time when a woman temporarily leaves her job to have a baby ➲ COLLOCATIONS at CHILD ➲ see also PARENTAL LEAVE, PATERNITY LEAVE

mate·ship /'meɪtʃɪp/ *noun* [U] (*AustralE, NZE, informal*) friendship, especially between men

matey /'meɪti/ *adj., noun*
■ ***adj.*** **~ (with sb)** (*BrE, informal*) friendly, sometimes in a way that is not completely sincere: *She started off being quite matey with everyone.*
■ ***noun*** (*BrE*) used by men as an informal way of addressing another man

math /mæθ/ (*NAmE*) (*BrE* **maths**) *noun* [U] **1** mathematics, especially as a subject in school: *a math teacher* **2** the process of calculating using numbers: *Is your math correct?*
IDM **do the 'math** to think carefully about sth before doing it so that you know all the relevant facts or figures: *If only someone had done the math!*

math·em·at·ician /,mæθəmə'tɪʃn/ *noun* a person who is an expert in mathematics

math·emat·ics 0‑w /,mæθə'mætɪks/ (*formal*) (also *BrE* **maths** /mæθs/) (also *NAmE* **math** /mæθ/) *noun* **1** 0‑w [U] the science of numbers and shapes. Branches of mathematics include ARITHMETIC, ALGEBRA, GEOMETRY and TRIGONOMETRY: *the school mathematics curriculum* **2** 0‑w [U+sing./pl. v.] the process of calculating using numbers: *He worked out the very difficult mathematics in great detail.* ▶ **math·emat·ic·al** /,mæθə'mætɪkl/ *adj.*: ***mathematical calculations/problems/models*** ◇ *to assess children's mathematical ability* **math·emat·ic·al·ly** /-kli/ *adv.*: *It's mathematically impossible.* ◇ *Some people are very mathematically inclined* (= interested in and good at mathematics).

maths /mæθs/ (*BrE*) (*NAmE* **math** /mæθ/) *noun* **1** [U] mathematics, especially as a subject in school: *The core subjects are English, Maths and Science.* ◇ *a maths teacher* **2** [U+sing./pl. v.] the process of calculating using numbers: *If my maths is/are right, the answer is 142.*
IDM **do the 'maths** to think carefully about sth before doing it so that you know all the relevant facts or figures: *Do the maths before you take on more debt.*

Ma·tilda /mə'tɪldə/ *noun* (*old use, AustralE, NZE*) a pack of things tied or wrapped together and carried by a BUSHMAN

mat·inee (also **mat·inée**) /'mætɪneɪ; *NAmE* ,mætn'eɪ/ *noun* an afternoon performance of a play, etc; an afternoon showing of a film/movie

'matinee idol (also **'matinée idol**) *noun* (*old-fashioned*) an actor who is popular with women

mat·ing /'meɪtɪŋ/ *noun* [U, C] sex between animals: *the mating season*

mat·ins (also **mat·tins**) /'mætɪnz; *NAmE* 'mætnz/ *noun* [U] the service of morning prayer, especially in the Anglican Church ➲ compare EVENSONG, VESPERS

ma·toke /mæ'tɒkə; *NAmE* mæ'tɑːkə/ *noun* [U] a type of green BANANA grown in Uganda and other places in E Africa and used for cooking; the cooked food made from this type of banana and eaten with STEW

ma·tri·arch /'meɪtriɑːk; *NAmE* -ɑːrk/ *noun* a woman who is the head of a family or social group ➲ compare PATRIARCH

ma·tri·arch·al /,meɪtri'ɑːkl; *NAmE* -'ɑːrkl/ *adj.* (of a society or system) controlled by women rather than men; passing power, property, etc. from mother to daughter rather than from father to son: *The animals live in matriarchal groups.* ➲ compare PATRIARCHAL

ma·tri·archy /'meɪtriɑːki; *NAmE* -ɑːrki/ *noun* (*pl.* **-ies**) a social system that gives power and authority to women rather than men ➲ compare PATRIARCHY

ma·tric /mə'trɪk/ *noun* [U] (*SAfrE*) **1** the final year of school: *We studied that book in matric.* **2** the work and examinations in the final year of school: *He passed matric with four distinctions.* ◇ *She's preparing to write matric.*

matri·ces *pl.* of MATRIX

ma,tric e'xemption *noun* [U] (*SAfrE*) the fact of successfully completing the final year of school and being able to study at university or college: *A senior certificate with matric exemption is required for entry to university.*

matri·cide /'mætrɪsaɪd/ *noun* [U, C] (*formal*) the crime of killing your mother; a person who is guilty of this crime ➲ compare FRATRICIDE, PARRICIDE, PATRICIDE

ma·tric·ulate /mə'trɪkjuleɪt/ *verb* **1** [I] (*formal*) to officially become a student at a university: *She matriculated in*

1995. **2** [I] (*SAfrE*) to successfully complete the final year of school ▸ **ma·tricu·la·tion** /məˌtrɪkjuˈleɪʃn/ *noun* [U]

matri·lin·eal /ˌmætrɪˈlɪniəl/ *adj.* (*technical*) used to describe the relationship between mother and children that continues in a family with each generation, or sth that is based on this relationship: *She traced her family history by matrilineal descent* (= starting with her mother, her mother's mother, etc.). ➲ compare PATRILINEAL

matri·mo·nial /ˌmætrɪˈməʊniəl; *NAmE* -ˈmoʊ-/ *adj.* [usually before noun] (*formal* or *technical*) connected with marriage or with being married: *matrimonial problems* ◇ *the matrimonial home*

matri·mony /ˈmætrɪməni; *NAmE* -moʊni/ *noun* [U] (*formal* or *technical*) marriage; the state of being married: *holy matrimony*

mat·rix /ˈmeɪtrɪks/ *noun* (*pl.* **matri·ces** /ˈmeɪtrɪsiːz/) **1** (*mathematics*) an arrangement of numbers, symbols, etc. in rows and columns, treated as a single quantity **2** (*formal*) the formal social, political, etc. situation from which a society or person grows and develops: *the European cultural matrix* **3** (*formal* or *literary*) a system of lines, roads, etc. that cross each other, forming a series of squares or shapes in between SYN **network**: *a matrix of paths* **4** (*technical*) a MOULD in which sth is shaped **5** (*computing*) a group of electronic CIRCUIT elements arranged in rows and columns like a GRID ➲ see also DOT MATRIX PRINTER **6** (*geology*) a mass of rock in which minerals, PRECIOUS STONES, etc. are found in the ground

ma·tron /ˈmeɪtrən/ *noun* **1** (*BrE*) a woman who works as a nurse in a school **2** (*old-fashioned, BrE*) a senior female nurse in charge of the other nurses in a hospital (now usually called a **senior nursing officer**) **3** (becoming *old-fashioned*) an older married woman

ma·tron·ly /ˈmeɪtrənli/ *adj.* (*disapproving*) (of a woman) no longer young, and rather fat

ˈmatron of honour (*especially US* **ˈmatron of honor**) *noun* [sing.] a married woman who is the most important BRIDESMAID at a wedding ➲ compare MAID OF HONOUR

matro·nym·ic /ˌmætrəˈnɪmɪk/ *noun* (*technical*) a name formed from the name of your mother or a female ANCESTOR especially by adding sth to the beginning or end of their name ➲ compare PATRONYMIC

matt (*BrE*) (*US* **mat**) (also **matte** *NAmE, BrE*) /mæt/ *adj.* (of a colour, surface, or photograph) not shiny: *a matt finish* ◇ *matt white paint* ◇ *Prints are available on matt or glossy paper.*

mat·ted /ˈmætɪd/ *adj.* (of hair, etc.) forming a thick mass, especially because it is wet and dirty

mat·ter 0‑ /ˈmætə(r)/ *noun, verb*

■ ***noun***

▸ SUBJECT/SITUATION **1** 0‑ [C] a subject or situation that you must consider or deal with SYN **affair**: *It's a private matter.* ◇ *They had important matters to discuss.* ◇ *She may need your help with some business matters.* ◇ *I always consulted him on matters of policy.* ◇ *It's* ***a matter for*** *the police* (= for them to deal with). ◇ *That's a matter for you to take up with your boss.* ◇ *Let's get on with the* ***matter in hand*** (= what we need to deal with now). ◇ *I wasn't prepared to* ***let the matter drop*** (= stop discussing it). ◇ *It was* ***no easy matter*** *getting him to change his mind.* ◇ *It should have been a simple matter to check.* ◇ (*ironic*) *And then there's* ***the little matter*** *of the fifty pounds you owe me.* ◇ (*formal*) *It was* ***a matter of*** *some concern to most of those present* (= something they were worried about). ◇ *I did not feel that we had got to* ***the heart of the matter*** (= the most important part). ◇ *And that is* ***the crux of the matter*** (= the most important thing about the situation). **2** 0‑ **matters** [pl.] the present situation, or the situation that you are talking about SYN **things**: *Unfortunately, there is nothing we can do to improve matters.* ◇ *I'd forgotten the keys, which didn't* ***help matters.*** ◇ *Matters were made worse by a fire in the warehouse.* ◇ *And then,* ***to make matters worse,*** *his parents turned up.* ◇ *I decided to* ***take matters into my own hands*** (= deal with the situation myself). ◇ ***Matters came to a head*** (= the situation became very difficult) *with his resignation.*

▸ PROBLEM **3** 0‑ **the matter** [sing.] used (to ask) if sb is upset, unhappy, etc. or if there is a problem: ***What's the matter?*** *Is there something wrong?* ◇ *Is* ***anything the matter?*** ◇ **~ with sb/sth** *Is* ***something the matter*** *with Bob? He seems very down.* ◇ *There's something the matter with my eyes.* ◇ *'We've bought a new TV.' 'What was the matter with the old one?'* ◇ ***What's the matter with you*** *today* (= why are you behaving like this)?

▸ A MATTER OF STH/OF DOING STH **4** 0‑ [sing.] a situation that involves sth or depends on sth SYN **question**: *Learning to drive is all a matter of coordination.* ◇ *Planning a project is just a matter of working out the right order to do things in.* ◇ *That's not a problem. It's* ***simply a matter of*** *letting people know in time.* ◇ *Some people prefer the older version to the new one. It's* ***a matter of taste.*** ◇ *She resigned over* ***a matter of principle.*** ◇ *The government must deal with this* ***as a matter of urgency.*** ◇ *Just* ***as a matter of interest*** (= because it is interesting, not because it is important), *how much did you pay for it?* ◇ *'I think this is the best so far.' 'Well, that's* ***a matter of opinion*** (= other people may think differently).

▸ SUBSTANCE **5** 0‑ [U] (*physics*) physical substance in general that everything in the world consists of; not mind or spirit: *to study the properties of matter* **6** [U] (*formal*) a substance or things of a particular sort: *Add plenty of organic matter to improve the soil.* ◇ *elimination of* ***waste matter*** *from the body* ◇ *She didn't approve of their choice of* ***reading matter.*** ➲ see also SUBJECT MATTER

IDM **as a matter of ˈfact** **1** 0‑ used to add a comment on sth that you have just said, usually adding sth that you think the other person will be interested in: *It's a nice place. We've stayed there ourselves, as a matter of fact.* **2** 0‑ used to disagree with sth that sb has just said SYN **actually**: *'I suppose you'll be leaving soon, then?' 'No, as a matter of fact I'll be staying for another two years.'* **be another/a different ˈmatter** 0‑ to be very different: *I know which area they live in, but whether I can find their house is a different matter.* **for ˈthat matter** used to add a comment on sth that you have just said: *I didn't like it much. Nor did the kids, for that matter.* **it's just/only a matter of ˈtime (before...)** used to say that sth will definitely happen, although you are not sure when: *It's only a matter of time before they bring out their own version of the software.* **(as) a matter of ˈcourse** (as) the usual and correct thing to do: *We always check people's addresses as a matter of course.* **a matter of ˈhours, ˈminutes, etc.** | **a matter of ˈinches, ˈmetres, etc.** only a few hours, minutes, etc: *It was all over in a matter of minutes.* ◇ *The bullet missed her by a matter of inches.* **a ˌmatter of ˌlife and ˈdeath** used to describe a situation that is very important or serious **a ˌmatter of ˈrecord** (*formal*) something that has been recorded as being true **no matter** used to say that sth is not important **no matter who, what, where, etc.** 0‑ used to say that sth is always true, whatever the situation is, or that sb should certainly do sth: *They don't last long no matter how careful you are.* ◇ *Call me when you get there, no matter what the time is.* ➲ more at FACT, LAUGHING

■ ***verb*** 0‑ [I, T] (not used in the progressive tenses) to be important or have an important effect on sb/sth: **~ (to sb)** *The children matter more to her than anything else in the world.* ◇ *'What did you say?' 'Oh, it doesn't matter'* (= it is not important enough to repeat).*'* ◇ *'I'm afraid I forgot that book again.' 'It doesn't matter* (= it is not important enough to worry about).*'* ◇ ***What does it matter*** *if I spent $100 on it —it's my money!* ◇ *As long as you're happy, that's* ***all that matters.*** ◇ *After his death, nothing seemed to matter any more.* ◇ *He's been in prison, you know—****not that it matters*** (= that information does not affect my opinion of him). ◇ **~ (to sb) who, what, etc...** *Does it really matter who did it?* ◇ ***It doesn't matter*** *to me what you do.* ◇ **~ (to sb) that ...** *It didn't matter that the weather was bad.*

ˌmatter-of-ˈfact *adj.* said or done without showing any emotion, especially in a situation in which you would expect sb to express their feelings SYN **unemotional**: *She*

M

told us the news of his death in a very matter-of-fact way. ▸ ˌmatter-of-ˈfactly adv.

mat·ting /ˈmætɪŋ/ noun rough WOVEN material for making MATS: coconut matting

mat·tins noun [U] = MATINS

mat·tock /ˈmætək/ noun a heavy garden tool with a long handle and a metal head, used for breaking up soil, cutting roots, etc.

mat·tress /ˈmætrəs/ noun the soft part of a bed, that you lie on: a **soft/hard mattress** ➲ VISUAL VOCAB page V20

mat·ur·ation AW /ˌmætʃuˈreɪʃn/ noun [U] (formal) **1** the process of becoming or being made mature (= ready to eat or drink after being left for a period of time) **2** the process of becoming adult ▸ **mat·ur·ation·al** AW adj.

ma·ture AW /məˈtʃʊə(r); -ˈtjʊə(r); NAmE -ˈtʃʊr; -ˈtʊr/ adj., verb

■ **adj.** HELP **maturer** is occasionally used instead of **more mature**

▸ SENSIBLE **1** (of a child or young person) behaving in a sensible way, like an adult: *Jane is very mature for her age.* ◇ *a mature and sensible attitude* OPP **immature**

▸ FULLY GROWN **2** (of a person, a tree, a bird or an animal) fully grown and developed: *sexually mature* ◇ *a mature oak/eagle/elephant* OPP **immature** ➲ SYNONYMS at OLD

▸ WINE/CHEESE **3** developed over a period of time to produce a strong, rich flavour

▸ NO LONGER YOUNG **4** used as a polite or humorous way of saying that sb is no longer young: *clothes for the mature woman* ◇ *a man of mature years*

▸ WORK OF ART **5** created late in an artist's life and showing great understanding and skill

▸ INSURANCE POLICY **6** (business) ready to be paid

▸ **ma·ture·ly** adv.

IDM **on mature reˈflection/consideˈration** (formal) after thinking about sth carefully and for a long time

■ **verb**

▸ BECOME FULLY GROWN **1** [I] to become fully grown or developed: *This particular breed of cattle matures early.* ◇ *Technology in this field has matured considerably over the last decade.*

▸ BECOME SENSIBLE **2** [I] to develop emotionally and start to behave like a sensible adult: *He has matured a great deal over the past year.*

▸ DEVELOP SKILL **3** [I] ~ **(into sth)** to fully develop a particular skill or quality: *She has matured into one of the country's finest actresses.*

▸ WINE/CHEESE **4** [I, T] ~ **(sth)** if wine, cheese, etc. **matures** or **is matured**, it develops over a period of time to produce a strong, rich flavour

▸ INSURANCE POLICY **5** [I] (business) to reach the date when it must be paid

maˌture ˈstudent noun (BrE) an adult student who goes to college or university some years after leaving school

ma·tur·ity AW /məˈtʃʊərəti; -ˈtjʊə-; NAmE -ˈtʃʊr-; -ˈtʊr-/ noun [U] **1** the quality of thinking and behaving in a sensible, adult manner: *He has maturity beyond his years.* ◇ *Her poems show great maturity.* ➲ compare IMMATURITY **2** (of a person, an animal, or a plant) the state of being fully grown or developed: *The forest will take 100 years to* **reach maturity**. ➲ compare IMMATURITY **3** (business) (of an insurance policy, etc.) the time when money you have invested is ready to be paid

matzo /ˈmætsəʊ; NAmE ˈmɑːtsoʊ/ noun [U, C] (pl. **-os**) a type of bread in the form of a large flat biscuit, traditionally eaten by Jews during Passover; one of these biscuits

maud·lin /ˈmɔːdlɪn/ adj. **1** talking in a silly, emotional way, often full of pity for yourself, especially when drunk SYN **sentimental** **2** (of a book, film/movie, or song) expressing or causing exaggerated emotions, especially in way that is not sincere SYN **sentimental**

maul /mɔːl/ verb **1** ~ **sb** (of an animal) to attack and injure sb by tearing their flesh SYN **savage** **2** ~ **sb/sth** to touch sb/sth in an unpleasant and/or violent way **3** ~ **sth/sb** to criticize sth/sb severely and publicly SYN **savage** **4** ~ **sb** (informal) to defeat sb easily SYN **trash** ▸ **maul·ing** noun [sing.]: *The play received a mauling from the critics.* ◇ *They face a mauling by last year's winners.*

maun·der /ˈmɔːndə(r)/ verb [I] ~ **(on)** **(about sth)** (BrE) to talk or complain about sth in a boring and/or annoying way

Maundy Thurs·day /ˌmɔːndi ˈθɜːzdeɪ; -di; NAmE ˈθɜːrz-/ noun [U, C] (in the Christian Church) the Thursday before Easter

mau·so·leum /ˌmɔːsəˈliːəm/ noun a special building made to hold the dead body of an important person or the dead bodies of a family: *the royal mausoleum*

mauve /məʊv; NAmE moʊv/ adj. pale purple in colour ▸ **mauve** noun [U]

maven /ˈmeɪvn/ noun (NAmE) an expert on sth

mav·er·ick /ˈmævərɪk/ noun a person who does not behave or think like everyone else, but who has independent, unusual opinions ▸ **mav·er·ick** adj. [only before noun]: *a maverick film director*

maw /mɔː/ noun **1** (literary) something that seems like a big mouth that swallows things up completely **2** (old-fashioned) an animal's stomach or throat

mawk·ish /ˈmɔːkɪʃ/ adj. (disapproving) expressing or sharing emotion in a way that is exaggerated or embarrassing SYN **sentimental**: *a mawkish poem* ▸ **mawk·ish·ness** noun [U]

max AW /mæks/ abbr., verb

■ **abbr.** **1** (also **max.** especially in NAmE) maximum: *max temperature 18°C* **2** at the most: (informal) *It'll cost $50 max.* OPP **min.**

IDM **to the ˈmax** to the highest level or greatest amount possible: *She believes in living life to the max.*

■ **verb**

PHR V ˌ**max (sth) ˈout** (NAmE, informal) to reach, or make sth reach, the limit at which nothing more is possible: *The car maxed out at 150 mph.*

maxi /ˈmæksi/ noun a long coat, dress or skirt that reaches to the ankles

max·illa /mækˈsɪlə/ noun (pl. **max·il·lae** /-liː/) (anatomy) the JAW ▸ **max·il·lary** /mækˈsɪləri/ adj.: *a maxillary fracture*

maxim /ˈmæksɪm/ noun a well-known phrase that expresses sth that is usually true or that people think is a rule for sensible behaviour

max·imal /ˈmæksɪml/ adj. [usually before noun] (technical) as great or as large as possible ➲ compare MINIMAL

maxi·mize (BrE also **-ise**) AW /ˈmæksɪmaɪz/ verb **1** ~ **sth** to increase sth as much as possible: *to* **maximize efficiency/fitness/profits** ◇ (computing) *Maximize the window to full screen.* **2** ~ **sth** to make the best use of sth: *to* **maximize opportunities/resources** OPP **minimize** ▸ **maxi·miza·tion**, **-isa·tion** AW /ˌmæksɪmaɪˈzeɪʃn; NAmE -məˈz-/ noun [U]

max·imum 🔑 AW /ˈmæksɪməm/ adj., noun

■ **adj.** 🔑 [only before noun] (abbr. **max**) as large, fast, etc. as is possible, or the most that is possible or allowed: *the* **maximum speed/temperature/volume** ◇ **For maximum effect** *do the exercises every day.* ◇ *a maximum security prison* ➲ compare MINIMUM

■ **noun** 🔑 [usually sing.] (pl. **max·ima** /ˈmæksɪmə/) (abbr. **max**) the greatest amount, size, speed, etc. that is possible, recorded or allowed: *a maximum of 30 children in a class* ◇ *The job will require you to use all your skills* **to the maximum**. ◇ *The July maximum* (= the highest temperature recorded in July) *was 30°C.* ◇ *What is the absolute maximum you can afford to pay?* ➲ compare MINIMUM

May 🔑 /meɪ/ noun [U, C] the fifth month of the year, between April and June HELP To see how **May** is used, look at the examples at **April**.

may 🔑 /meɪ/ *modal verb, noun*
■ ***modal verb*** (*negative* **may not**, *rare short form* **mayn't** /ˈmeɪənt/, *pt* **might** /maɪt/, *negative* **might not**, *rare short form* **mightn't** /ˈmaɪtnt/) **1** 🔑 used to say that sth is possible: *That may or may not be true.* ◇ *He may have* (= perhaps he has) *missed his train.* ◇ *They* ***may well*** *win.* ◇ *There is a range of programs on the market which may be described as design aids.* **2** 🔑 used when admitting that sth is true before introducing another point, argument, etc.: *He may be a good father but he's a terrible husband.* **3** 🔑 (*formal*) used to ask for or give permission: *May I come in?* ◇ *You may come in if you wish.* ➲ note at CAN[1] **4** (*formal*) used as a polite way of making a comment, asking a question, etc.: *You look lovely, if I may say so.* ◇ *May I ask why you took that decision?* ◇ *If I may just add one thing...* **5** (*formal*) used to express wishes and hopes: *May she rest in peace.* ◇ *Business has been thriving in the past year.* ***Long may it continue*** *to do so.* **6** (*formal*) used to say what the purpose of sth is: *There is a need for more resources so that all children may have a decent education.* ➲ note at MODAL
IDM **be that as it ˈmay** (*formal*) despite that SYN **nevertheless**: *I know that he has tried hard; be that as it may, his work is just not good enough.*
■ ***noun*** [U] the white or pink flowers of the HAWTHORN

maybe 🔑 /ˈmeɪbi/ *adv.*
1 🔑 used when you are not certain that sth will happen or that sth is true or is a correct number SYN **perhaps**: *Maybe he'll come, maybe he won't.* ◇ *'Are you going to sell your house?' 'Maybe.'* ◇ *It will cost two, maybe three hundred pounds.* ◇ *We go there maybe once or twice a month.* **2** 🔑 used when making a suggestion SYN **perhaps**: *I thought maybe we could go together.* ◇ *Maybe you should tell her.* **3** 🔑 used to agree with sb, and to add more information that should be thought about SYN **perhaps**: *'You should stop work when you have the baby.' 'Maybe, but I can't afford to.'* **4** 🔑 used when replying to a question or an idea, when you are not sure whether to agree or disagree SYN **perhaps**: *'I think he should resign.' 'Maybe.'*

ˈMay bug *noun* = COCKCHAFER

ˈMay Day *noun* the first day of May, celebrated as a spring festival and, in some countries, as a holiday in honour of working people ➲ compare LABOR DAY

May·day /ˈmeɪdeɪ/ *noun* [U] an international radio signal used by ships and aircraft needing help when they are in danger ORIGIN From the French *venez m'aider* 'come and help me'.

may·fly /ˈmeɪflaɪ/ *noun* (*pl.* **-ies**) a small insect that lives near water and only lives for a very short time

may·hem /ˈmeɪhem/ *noun* [U] confusion and fear, usually caused by violent behaviour or by some sudden shocking event: *There was absolute mayhem when everyone tried to get out at once.*

may·on·naise /ˌmeɪəˈneɪz; *NAmE* ˈmeɪəneɪz/ (*also informal* **mayo** /ˈmeɪəʊ; *NAmE* ˈmeɪoʊ/) *noun* [U] a thick cold white sauce made from eggs, oil and VINEGAR, used to add flavour to SANDWICHES, salads, etc: *egg mayonnaise* (= a dish made with hard-boiled eggs and mayonnaise)

mayor 🔑 /meə(r); *NAmE* ˈmeɪər/ *noun*
1 🔑 (in England, Wales and Northern Ireland) the head of a town, BOROUGH or county council, chosen by other members of the council to represent them at official ceremonies, etc: *the Lord Mayor of London* ➲ compare PROVOST **2** 🔑 the head of the government of a town or city, etc, elected by the public: *the Mayor of New York* ◇ *Mayor Bob Anderson* ▶ **may·oral** /ˈmeərəl; *NAmE* ˈmeɪə-/ *adj.* [only before noun]: ***mayoral robes/duties***

may·or·alty /ˈmeərəlti; *NAmE* ˈmeɪər-/ *noun* (*pl.* **-ies**) (*formal*) **1** the title or position of a mayor **2** the period of time during which a person is a mayor

may·or·ess /meəˈres; *NAmE* ˈmeɪərəs/ *noun* **1** (also ˌ**lady ˈmayor**) a woman who has been elected mayor ➲ note at GENDER **2** (in England, Wales and Northern Ireland) the wife of a mayor or a woman who helps a mayor at official ceremonies

may·pole /ˈmeɪpəʊl; *NAmE* -poʊl/ *noun* a decorated pole that people dance round in celebrations on MAY DAY

maze /meɪz/ *noun* **1** a system of paths separated by walls or HEDGES built in a park or garden, that is designed so that it is difficult to find your way through: *We got lost in the maze.* ◇ (*figurative*) *The building is a maze of corridors.* ➲ compare LABYRINTH **2** [usually sing.] a large number of complicated rules or details that are difficult to understand: *a maze of regulations* **3** (*NAmE*) a printed PUZZLE in which you have to draw a line that shows a way through a complicated pattern of lines

ma·zurka /məˈzɜːkə; *NAmE* məˈzɜːrkə/ *noun* a fast Polish dance for four or eight couples, or a piece of music for this dance

MB *abbr.* **1** /ˌem ˈbiː/ (in Britain) Bachelor of Medicine (a university degree in medicine): *Philip Watt MB* **2** (in writing) MEGABYTE: *512MB of memory*

Mb (also **Mbit**) *abbr.* (in writing) MEGABIT

MBA /ˌem biː ˈeɪ/ *noun* the abbreviation for 'Master of Business Administration' (a second university degree in business): *to do an MBA*

MBE /ˌem biː ˈiː/ *noun* the abbreviation for 'Member (of the Order) of the British Empire' (an award given to some people in Britain for a special achievement): *She was made an MBE in 2007.* ◇ *Jim Cronin MBE*

MC /ˌem ˈsiː/ *noun* **1** the abbreviation for MASTER OF CEREMONIES **2** **M.C.** the abbreviation for 'Member of Congress' **3** a person who speaks the words of a RAP song

MCAT /ˈemkæt/ *abbr.* Medical College Admission Test (a test that students must pass in order to study medicine in the US)

Mc·Carthy·ism /məˈkɑːθiɪzəm; *NAmE* -ˈkɑːrθ-/ *noun* [U] an aggressive investigation during the 1950s against people in the US government and other institutions who were thought to be COMMUNISTS, in which many people lost their jobs

McCoy /məˈkɔɪ/ *noun*
IDM **the real McˈCoy** (*informal*) something that is genuine and that has value, not a copy: *It's an American flying jacket, the real McCoy.*

ˈm-commerce *noun* [U] (*BrE, business*) the business of buying and selling products on the Internet by using mobile/cell phones and other similar technology: *m-tickets and other m-commerce products*

MD /ˌem ˈdiː/ *noun* **1** the abbreviation for 'Doctor of Medicine': *Paul Clark MD* **2** (*BrE*) the abbreviation for MANAGING DIRECTOR: *Where's the MD's office?*

MDF /ˌem diː ˈef/ *noun* [U] the abbreviation for 'medium density fibreboard' (a building material made of wood or other plant FIBRES pressed together to form boards)

MDT /ˌem diː ˈtiː/ *abbr.* MOUNTAIN DAYLIGHT TIME.

ME /ˌem ˈiː/ *noun, abbr.*
■ ***noun*** (*BrE*) (also ˌ**chronic faˈtigue syndrome** *NAmE, BrE*) [U] the abbreviation for 'myalgic encephalomyelitis' (an illness that makes people feel extremely weak and tired and that can last a long time)
■ ***abbr.*** (*NAmE*) MEDICAL EXAMINER

me 🔑 *pron., noun*
■ ***pron.*** 🔑 /mi; *strong form* miː/ the form of *I* that is used when the speaker or writer is the object of a verb or preposition, or after the verb *be*: *Don't hit me.* ◇ *Excuse me!* ◇ *Give it to me.* ◇ *You're taller than me.* ◇ *Hello, it's me.* ◇ *'Who's there?' 'Only me.'* HELP The use of **me** in the last three examples is correct in modern standard English. **I** in these sentences would be considered much too formal for almost all contexts, especially in *BrE*.
■ ***noun*** (also **mi**) /miː/ (*music*) the third note of a MAJOR SCALE

mea culpa /ˌmeɪə ˈkʊlpə/ *exclamation* (from *Latin*, often *humorous*) used when you are admitting that sth is your fault

mead /miːd/ *noun* [U] a sweet alcoholic drink made from HONEY and water, drunk especially in the past

M

meadow /ˈmedəʊ; NAmE -doʊ/ *noun* a field covered in grass, used especially for HAY: *water meadows* (= near a river) ➲ VISUAL VOCAB page V2

meadow·lark /ˈmedəʊlɑːk; NAmE -doʊlɑːrk/ *noun* a singing bird that lives on the ground

meagre (*especially US* **mea·ger**) /ˈmiːgə(r)/ *adj.* small in quantity and poor in quality SYN **paltry**: *a meagre diet of bread and water* ◇ *She supplements her meagre income by cleaning at night.*

meal 🔑 /miːl/ *noun*
1 🔑 [C] an occasion when people sit down to eat food, especially breakfast, lunch or dinner: *Try not to eat between meals.* ◇ *Lunch is his main meal of the day.* ◇ (*especially BrE*) *to* ***go out for a meal*** (= to go to a restaurant to have a meal) ◇ *What time would you like your evening meal?* ➲ COLLOCATIONS at RESTAURANT **2** 🔑 [C] the food that is eaten at a meal: *Enjoy your meal.* ◇ *a three-course meal* **3** [U] (often in compounds) grain that has been crushed to produce a powder, used as food for animals and for making flour ➲ see also BONEMEAL, OATMEAL, WHOLEMEAL
IDM **make a ˈmeal of sth** (*informal*) to spend a lot of time, energy, etc. doing sth in a way that other people think is unnecessary and/or annoying ➲ more at SQUARE *adj.*

More About

meals

- People use the words **dinner**, **lunch**, **supper** and **tea** in different ways depending on which English-speaking country they come from. In Britain it may also depend on which part of the country or which social class a person comes from.
- A meal eaten in the middle of the day is usually called **lunch**. If it is the main meal of the day it may also be called **dinner** in *BrE*, especially in the north of the country.
- A main meal eaten in the evening is usually called **dinner**, especially if it is a formal meal. **Supper** is also an evening meal, but more informal than **dinner** and usually eaten at home. It can also be a late meal or something to eat and drink before going to bed.
- In *BrE*, **tea** is a light meal in the afternoon with sandwiches, cakes, etc. and a cup of tea: *a cream tea.* It can also be a main meal eaten early in the evening, especially by children: *What time do the kids have their tea?*
- As a general rule, if **dinner** is the word someone uses for the meal in the middle of the day, they probably call the meal in the evening **tea** or **supper**. If they call the meal in the middle of the day **lunch**, they probably call the meal in the evening **dinner**.
- **Brunch**, a combination of breakfast and lunch, is becoming more common, especially as a meal where your guests serve themselves.

meal·ie /ˈmiːli/ *noun* [C, usually pl., U] (*SAfrE*) **1** = MAIZE **2** = CORN ON THE COB

ˌmeals on ˈwheels *noun* [pl.] a service that takes meals to old or sick people in their homes

ˈmeal ticket *noun* **1** (*informal*) a person or thing that you see only as a source of money and food: *He suspected that he was just a meal ticket for her.* **2** (*NAmE*) a card or ticket that gives you the right to have a cheap or free meal, for example at school

meal·time /ˈmiːltaɪm/ *noun* a time in the day when you eat a meal

meal·worm /ˈmiːlwɜːm; NAmE -wɜːrm/ *noun* a LARVA which is used to feed pet birds

mealy /ˈmiːli/ *adj.* (especially of vegetables or fruit) soft and dry when you eat them

ˌmealy-ˈmouthed *adj.* (*disapproving*) not willing or honest enough to speak in a direct or open way about what you really think: *mealy-mouthed politicians*

mean 🔑 /miːn/ *verb, adj., noun*
■ *verb* (**meant, meant** /ment/)
▸ HAVE AS MEANING **1** 🔑 (not used in the progressive tenses) to have sth as a meaning: **~ sth** *What does this sentence mean?* ◇ ***What is meant by*** *'batch processing'?* ◇ **~ sth to sb** *Does the name 'Jos Vos'* ***mean anything to you*** (= do you know who he is)? ◇ **~ (that)...** *The flashing light means (that) you must stop.*
▸ INTEND AS MEANING **2** 🔑 (not used in the progressive tenses) to intend to say sth on a particular occasion: **~ sth** *What did he mean by that remark?* ◇ *'Perhaps we should try another approach.'* ***'What do you mean?*** (= I don't understand what you are suggesting.)' ◇ ***What do you mean****, you thought I wouldn't mind?* (= of course I mind and I am very angry) ◇ ***What she means is*** *that there's no point in waiting here.* ◇ *I always found him a little strange,* ***if you know what I mean*** (= if you understand what I mean by 'strange'). ◇ ***I know what you mean*** (= I understand and feel sympathy). *I hated learning to drive too.* ◇ (*informal*) *It was like —weird.* ***Know what I mean?*** ◇ ***I see what you mean*** (= I understand although I may not agree), *but I still think it's worth trying.* ◇ ***See what I mean*** (= I was right and this proves it, doesn't it)? *She never agrees to anything I suggest.* ◇ *'But Pete doesn't know we're here!'* ***'That's what I mean!*** (= that's what I have been trying to tell you.)' ◇ *Do you mean Ann Smith or Mary Smith?* ◇ **~ (that)...** *Did he mean (that) he was dissatisfied with our service?* ◇ ***You mean*** (= are you telling me) *we have to start all over again?* ➲ LANGUAGE BANK at I.E.
▸ HAVE AS PURPOSE **3** 🔑 to have sth as a purpose or intention SYN **intend**: **~ sth** ***What did she mean by*** *leaving so early* (= why did she do it)? ◇ *Don't laugh!* ***I mean it*** (= I am serious). ◇ *He* ***means trouble*** (= to cause trouble). ◇ **~ sth as sth** *Don't be upset—I'm sure she meant it as a compliment.* ◇ **~ what...** *He* ***means what he says*** (= is not joking, exaggerating, etc.). ◇ **~ sth for sb/sth** *The chair was clearly meant for a child.* ◇ *Don't be angry. I'm sure she* ***meant it for the best*** (= intended to be helpful). ◇ **~ to do sth** *She means to succeed.* ◇ *I'm sorry I hurt you.* ***I didn't mean to.*** ◇ *I'm feeling very guilty—****I've been meaning*** *to call my parents for days, but still haven't got around to it.* ◇ **~ sb/sth to do sth** *I didn't mean you to read the letter.* ◇ ***You're meant to*** (= you are supposed to) *pay before you go in.* ◇ **~ (that)...** (*formal*) *I never meant (that) you should come alone.*
▸ INTEND SB TO BE/DO STH **4** 🔑 [often passive] to intend sb to be or do sth: **~ sb for sth/sb** *I was never* ***meant for*** *the army* (= did not have the qualities needed to become a soldier). ◇ *Duncan and Makiko* ***were meant for each other*** (= are very suitable as partners). ◇ **~ sb/sth to be sth** *His father meant him to be an engineer.* ◇ *She did everything to get the two of them together, but I guess it just wasn't* ***meant to be.***
▸ HAVE AS RESULT **5** 🔑 to have sth as a result or a likely result SYN **entail**: **~ sth** *Spending too much now will mean a shortage of cash next year.* ◇ **~ to be/do sth** *Do you have any idea* ***what it means to*** *be poor?* ◇ **~ (that)...** *We'll have to be careful with money but* ***that doesn't mean*** *(that) we can't enjoy ourselves.* ◇ **~ doing sth** *This new order will mean working overtime.* ◇ **~ sb/sth doing sth** *The injury could mean him missing next week's game.*
▸ BE IMPORTANT **6** 🔑 [no passive] **~ sth to sb** to be of value or importance to sb: *Your friendship means a great deal to me.* ◇ *$20* ***means a lot*** (= represents a lot of money) *when you live on $100 a week.* ◇ *Money* ***means nothing to him.*** ◇ *Her children* ***mean the world to her.***
IDM **be meant to be sth** 🔑 to be generally considered to be sth: *This restaurant is meant to be excellent.* **I mean** 🔑 (*informal*) used to explain or correct what you have just said: *It was so boring—I mean, nothing happened for the first hour!* ◇ *She's English—Scottish, I mean.* **mean ˈbusiness** (*informal*) to be serious in your intentions: *He has the look of a man who means business.* **mean (sb) no ˈharm | not mean (sb) any ˈharm** to not have any intention of hurting sb **mean to ˈsay** used to emphasize what you are saying or to ask sb if they really mean what they say: *I mean to say, you should have known how he would react!* ◇

Do you mean to say you've lost it? ˈ**mean well** (*usually disapproving*) to have good intentions, although their effect may not be good

■ ***adj.*** (**mean·er, mean·est**)

‣ NOT GENEROUS **1** (*BrE*) (*NAmE* **cheap**) not willing to give or share things, especially money: *She's always been mean with money.* OPP **generous** ➲ see also STINGY

‣ UNKIND **2** ~ (**to sb**) (of people or their behaviour) unkind, for example by not letting sb have or do sth: *Don't be so mean to your little brother!*

‣ ANGRY/VIOLENT **3** (*especially NAmE*) likely to become angry or violent: *That's a mean-looking dog.*

‣ SKILFUL **4** (*informal, especially NAmE*) very good and skilful: *He's a mean tennis player.* ◇ *She plays a mean game of chess.*

‣ AVERAGE **5** [only before noun] (*technical*) average; between the highest and the lowest, etc: *the mean temperature*

‣ INTELLIGENCE **6** (*formal*) (of a person's understanding or ability) not very great: *This should be clear even to the meanest intelligence.*

‣ POOR **7** (*literary*) poor and dirty in appearance: ***mean houses/streets*** **8** (*old-fashioned*) born into or coming from a low social class

▸ **mean·ly** *adj.* **mean·ness** *noun* [U]

IDM **be no mean...** (*approving*) used to say that sb is very good at doing sth: *His mother was a painter, and he's no mean artist himself.*

■ ***noun*** ➲ see also MEANS

‣ MIDDLE WAY **1** ~ (**between A and B**) a quality, condition, or way of doing sth that is in the middle of two extremes and better than either of them: *He needed to find a mean between frankness and rudeness.*

‣ AVERAGE **2** (also **arithˌmetic ˈmean**) (*mathematics*) the value found by adding together all the numbers in a group, and dividing the total by the number of numbers ➲ see also GEOMETRIC MEAN

IDM **the happy/golden ˈmean** (*approving*) a course of action that is not extreme

me·ander /miˈændə(r)/ *verb* **1** [I] (+ **adv./prep.**) (of a river, road, etc.) to curve a lot rather than being in a straight line: *The stream meanders slowly down to the sea.* **2** [I] (+ **adv./prep.**) to walk slowly and change direction often, especially without a particular aim SYN **wander** **3** [I] (+ **adv./prep.**) (of a conversation, discussion, etc.) to develop slowly and change subject often, in a way that makes it boring or difficult to understand ▸ **me·ander** *noun*: *the meanders of a river* ➲ VISUAL VOCAB page V4

me·ander·ings /miˈændrɪŋz/ *noun* [pl.] **1** a course that does not follow a straight line: *the **meanderings of a river/path*** **2** walking or talking without any particular aim: *his philosophical meanderings*

meanie (also **meany**) /ˈmiːni/ *noun* (*pl.* **-ies**) (*informal*) used especially by children to describe an unkind person who will not give them what they want

mean·ing 🔑 /ˈmiːnɪŋ/ *noun, adj.*

■ ***noun***

‣ OF SOUND/WORD/SIGN **1** 🔑 [U, C] ~ (**of sth**) the thing or idea that a sound, word, sign, etc. represents: *What's the meaning of this word?* ◇ *Words often have several meanings.* ◇ *'Honesty'? He doesn't **know the meaning of the word!***

‣ OF WHAT SB SAYS/DOES **2** 🔑 [U, C] the things or ideas that sb wishes to communicate to you by what they say or do: *I don't quite **get your meaning*** (= understand what you mean to say). ◇ *What's the meaning of this? I explicitly told you not to leave the room.*

‣ OF FEELING/EXPERIENCE **3** 🔑 [U] the real importance of a feeling or experience: *With Anna he learned the meaning of love.*

‣ OF BOOK/PAINTING **4** 🔑 [U, C] the ideas that a writer, artist, etc. wishes to communicate through a book, painting, etc: *several **layers of meaning*** ◇ *There are, of course, deeper meanings in the poem.*

‣ SENSE OF PURPOSE **5** 🔑 [U] the quality or sense of purpose that makes you feel that your life is valuable: *Her life seemed to have lost all meaning.* ◇ *Having a child gave new meaning to their lives.*

■ ***adj.*** [usually before noun] = MEANINGFUL (2)

mean·ing·ful /ˈmiːnɪŋfl/ *adj.* **1** serious and important: *a **meaningful relationship / discussion / experience*** **2** (also *less frequent* **mean·ing**) intended to communicate or express sth to sb, without any words being spoken: *She gave me a **meaningful look**.* **3** having a meaning that is easy to understand: *These statistics are not very meaningful.* ▸ **mean·ing·ful·ly** /-fəli/ *adv.* **mean·ing·ful·ness** *noun* [U]

mean·ing·less /ˈmiːnɪŋləs/ *adj.* **1** without any purpose or reason and therefore not worth doing or having SYN **pointless**: *a meaningless existence* ◇ *We fill up our lives with meaningless tasks.* **2** not considered important SYN **irrelevant**: *Fines are meaningless to a huge company like that.* **3** not having a meaning that is easy to understand: *To me that painting is completely meaningless.* ▸ **mean·ing·less·ly** *adv.* **mean·ing·less·ness** *noun* [U]

means 🔑 /miːnz/ *noun* (*pl.* **means**)

1 🔑 [C] ~ (**of sth/of doing sth**) an action, an object or a system by which a result is achieved; a way of achieving or doing sth: *Television is an effective means of communication.* ◇ *Is there any means of contacting him?* ◇ *Have you any **means of identification**?* ◇ *We needed to get to London but we had no **means of transport**.* **2** [pl.] the money that a person has: *People should pay **according to their means**.* ◇ *He doesn't have the means to support a wife and child.* ◇ *Private school fees are **beyond the means of most people*** (= more than they can afford). ◇ *Are the monthly repayments **within your means*** (= can you afford them)? ◇ *Try to **live within your means*** (= not spend more money than you have). ◇ *a **man of means*** (= a rich man)

IDM **by ˈall means** used to say that you are very willing for sb to have sth or do sth: *'Do you mind if I have a look?' 'By all means.'* **by means of sth** 🔑 (*formal*) with the help of sth: *The load was lifted by means of a crane.* **by ˈno means | not by ˈany (manner of) means** not at all: *She is by no means an inexperienced teacher.* ◇ *We haven't won yet, not by any means.* **a ˌmeans to an ˈend** a thing or action that is not interesting or important in itself but is a way of achieving sth else: *He doesn't particularly like the work but he sees it as a means to an end.* ➲ more at END *n.*, FAIR *adj.*, WAY *n.*

M

ˈ**means test** *noun* an official check of sb's wealth or income in order to decide if they are poor enough to receive money from the government, etc. for a particular purpose ▸ ˈ**means-test** *verb* **~ sb**

ˈ**means-tested** *adj.* paid to sb according to the results of a means test: *means-tested benefits*

meant *past tense, past part.* of MEAN

mean·time /ˈmiːntaɪm/ *noun, adv.*

■ ***noun***

IDM **for the ˈmeantime** (*BrE*) for a short period of time but not permanently: *I'm changing my email address but for the meantime you can use the old one.* **in the ˈmeantime** in the period of time between two times or two events SYN **meanwhile**: *My first novel was rejected by six publishers. In the meantime I had written a play.*

■ ***adv.*** (*informal*) = MEANWHILE: *I'll contact them soon. Meantime don't tell them I'm back.*

mean·while 🔑 /ˈmiːnwaɪl/ *adv., noun*

■ ***adv.*** **1** 🔑 (also *informal* **mean·time**) while sth else is happening: *Bob spent fifteen months alone on his yacht. Ann, meanwhile, took care of the children on her own.* **2** 🔑 (also *informal* **mean·time**) in the period of time between two times or two events: *The doctor will see you again next week. Meanwhile, you must rest as much as possible.* **3** 🔑 used to compare two aspects of a situation: *Stress can be extremely damaging to your health. Exercise, meanwhile, can reduce its effects.*

■ ***noun***

IDM **for the ˈmeanwhile** (*BrE*) for a short period of time but not permanently: *We need some new curtains, but these will do for the meanwhile.* **in the ˈmeanwhile** in the period of time between two times or two events: *I hope to go to medical school eventually. In the meanwhile, I am going to study chemistry.*

meany = MEANIE

mea·sles /ˈmiːzlz/ *noun* [U] an infectious disease, especially of children, that causes fever and small red spots that cover the whole body ➲ see also GERMAN MEASLES

measly /ˈmiːzli/ *adj.* (*informal, disapproving*) very small in size or quantity; not enough: *I get a measly £4 an hour.*

meas·ur·able /ˈmeʒərəbl/ *adj.* **1** that can be measured **2** [usually before noun] large enough to be noticed or to have a clear and noticeable effect: *measurable improvements* ▸ **meas·ur·ably** /-əbli/ *adv.*: *Working conditions have changed measurably in the last ten years.*

meas·ure ⚷ /ˈmeʒə(r)/ *verb, noun*

■ ***verb***

▸ SIZE/QUANTITY **1** ⚷ to find the size, quantity, etc. of sth in standard units: **~ sth** (**in sth**) *A ship's speed is measured in knots.* ◇ *a device that measures the level of radiation in the atmosphere* ◇ ***measuring equipment/instruments*** ◇ **~ sb/sth for sth** *He's gone to be measured for a new suit.* ◇ **~ how much, how long, etc...** *A dipstick is used to measure how much oil is left in an engine.* **2** ⚷ *linking verb* (not used in the progressive tenses) **+ noun** to be a particular size, length, amount, etc: *The main bedroom measures 12ft by 15ft.* ◇ *The pond measures about 2 metres across.*

▸ JUDGE **3** ⚷ **~ sth** | **~ how, what, etc...** to judge the importance, value or effect of sth SYN **assess**: *It is difficult to measure the success of the campaign at this stage.*

PHR V **ˈmeasure sb/sth against sb/sth** to compare sb/sth with sb/sth: *The figures are not very good when measured against those of our competitors.* **ˌmeasure sth↔ˈout** to take the amount of sth that you need from a larger amount: *He measured out a cup of milk and added it to the mixture.* **ˌmeasure ˈup** | **ˌmeasure sb/sth↔ˈup** to measure sb/sth: *We spent the morning measuring up and deciding where the furniture would go.* **ˌmeasure ˈup** (**to sth/sb**) (usually used in negative sentences and questions) to be as good, successful, etc. as expected or needed SYN **match up**: *Last year's intake just didn't measure up.* ◇ *The job failed to measure up to her expectations.*

■ ***noun***

▸ OFFICIAL ACTION **1** ⚷ [C] an official action that is done in order to achieve a particular aim: ***safety/security/austerity measures*** ◇ ***a temporary/an emergency measure*** ◇ **~** (**to do sth**) *We must take* ***preventive measures*** *to reduce crime in the area.* ◇ *The government is introducing tougher measures to combat crime.* ◇ *measures against racism* ◇ *Police in riot gear were in attendance as a* ***precautionary measure***. ➲ SYNONYMS at ACTION ➲ see also HALF MEASURES

▸ UNIT OF SIZE/QUANTITY **2** ⚷ [C, U] a unit used for stating the size, quantity or degree of sth; a system or a scale of these units: *weights and measures* ◇ *The Richter Scale is a measure of ground motion.* ◇ ***liquid/dry measure*** ◇ *Which measure of weight do pharmacists use?* **3** [C] (especially of alcohol) a standard quantity: *a generous measure of whisky*

▸ AMOUNT **4** [sing.] a particular amount of sth, especially a fairly large amount SYN **degree**: *A measure of technical knowledge is desirable in this job.* ◇ *She achieved some measure of success with her first book.*

▸ INSTRUMENT FOR MEASURING **5** [C] an instrument such as a stick, a long tape or a container that is marked with standard units and is used for measuring ➲ see also TAPE MEASURE

▸ WAY OF SHOWING/JUDGING **6** [sing.] a sign of the size or the strength of sth: *Sending flowers is a measure of how much you care.* **7** [C] a way of judging or measuring sth: *an accurate measure of ability* ◇ *Is this test a good measure of reading comprehension?*

▸ SUGGESTED NEW LAW **8** [C] (*NAmE*) a written suggestion, especially one for a new law made by the lawmakers of a state: *a motion to refer the measure to another committee* ◇ *a ballot measure* (= a change in the law that voters decide on)

▸ IN MUSIC **9** (*NAmE*) (*BrE* **bar**) [C] one of the short sections of equal length that a piece of music is divided into, and the notes that are in it ➲ picture at MUSIC

IDM **beyond ˈmeasure** (*formal*) very much: *He irritated me beyond measure.* **for good ˈmeasure** as an extra amount of sth in addition to what has already been done or given: *Use 50g of rice per person and an extra spoonful for good measure.* **full/short ˈmeasure** the whole of sth or less of sth than you expect or should have: *We experienced the full measure of their hospitality.* ◇ *The concert only lasted an hour, so we felt we were getting short measure.* **in full ˈmeasure** (*formal*) to the greatest possible degree **get/take/have the ˈmeasure of sb** | **get/have/take sb's ˈmeasure** (*formal*) to form an opinion about sb's character or abilities so that you can deal with them: *After only one game, the chess champion had the measure of his young opponent.* **in no small ˈmeasure** | **in some, equal, etc. ˈmeasure** (*formal*) to a large extent or degree; to some, etc. extent or degree: *The introduction of a new tax accounted in no small measure for the downfall of the government.* ◇ *Our thanks are due in equal measure to every member of the team.* **ˌmade to ˈmeasure** (*BrE*) made especially for one person according to particular measurements SYN **bespoke**: *You'll need to get a suit made to measure.* ◇ *a made-to-measure suit* ➲ more at LARGE

meas·ured /ˈmeʒəd; *NAmE* -ərd/ *adj.* [only before noun] slow and careful; controlled: *She replied in a measured tone to his threat.* ◇ *He walked down the corridor with measured steps.*

meas·ure·less /ˈmeʒələs; *NAmE* -ʒərl-/ *adj.* (*literary*) very great or without limits: *the measureless oceans*

meas·ure·ment ⚷ /ˈmeʒəmənt; *NAmE* ˈmeʒərm-/ *noun*

1 ⚷ [U] the act or the process of finding the size, quantity or degree of sth: *the metric system of measurement* ◇ *Accurate measurement is very important in science.* ➲ COLLOCATIONS at SCIENTIFIC **2** ⚷ [C, usually pl.] the size, length or amount of sth: *to take sb's* ***chest/waist measurement*** ◇ *Do you know your measurements* (= the size of parts of your body)? ◇ *The exact measurements of the room are 3 metres 20 by 2 metres 84.*

ˈmeasuring cup *noun* a metal or plastic container used in the US for measuring quantities when cooking ➲ VISUAL VOCAB page V23

ˈmeasuring jug *noun* (*BrE*) a glass or plastic container for measuring liquids when cooking ➲ VISUAL VOCAB page V23

ˈmeasuring spoon *noun* a metal or plastic spoon used in the US for measuring quantities when cooking ➲ VISUAL VOCAB page V23

ˈmeasuring tape *noun* = TAPE MEASURE

meat ⚷ /miːt/ *noun*

1 ⚷ [U, C] the flesh of an animal or a bird eaten as food; a particular type of this: *a* ***piece/slice of meat*** ◇ *horse meat* (= from a horse) ◇ *dog meat* (= for a dog) ◇ *meat-eating animals* ◇ *There's not much meat on this chop.* ◇ (*figurative, humorous*) *There's not much meat on her* (= she is very thin). ➲ see also LUNCHEON MEAT, MINCEMEAT, RED MEAT, SAUSAGE MEAT, WHITE MEAT **2** [U] **~** (**of sth**) the important or interesting part of sth SYN **substance**: *This chapter contains the real meat of the writer's argument.*

IDM **ˌmeat and ˈdrink to sb** something that sb enjoys very much ➲ more at DEAD, MAN *n.*

ˌmeat and poˈtatoes *noun* [U] (*NAmE*) the most basic and important aspects or parts of sth: *Issues like this are the newspaper's meat and potatoes.*

ˌmeat-and-poˈtatoes *adj.* [only before noun] (*NAmE*) **1** dealing with the most basic and important aspects of sth: *a meat-and-potatoes argument* **2** liking plain, simple things: *He's a real meat-and-potatoes guy.*

ˌmeat and twoˈ veg *noun* [U] (*BrE, informal*) a dish of meat with potatoes and another vegetable, considered as typical traditional British food

meat·ball /ˈmiːtbɔːl/ *noun* a small ball of finely chopped meat, usually eaten hot with a sauce

ˈmeat grinder *noun* (*NAmE*) = MINCER

ˌmeat ˈloaf *noun* [C, U] finely chopped meat, onions, etc. that are mixed together and shaped like a LOAF of bread and then baked

M

'meat packing *noun* [U] (*NAmE*) the process of killing animals and preparing the meat for sale

meaty /'mi:ti/ *adj.* (**meat·ier**, **meati·est**) **1** containing a lot of meat **2** smelling, or tasting like meat: *a meaty taste* **3** (*approving*) containing a lot of important or interesting ideas SYN **substantial**: *a meaty discussion* **4** (*informal*) large and fat; with a lot of flesh SYN **fleshy**: *a meaty hand* ◇ *big, meaty tomatoes*

mebi·bit /'mebibɪt/ *noun* (*abbr.* **Mib**, **Mibit**) (*computing*) = MEGABIT (2)

mebi·byte /'mebibaɪt/ *noun* (*abbr.* **MiB**) (*computing*) = MEGABYTE (2)

Mecca /'mekə/ *noun* **1** a city in Saudi Arabia that is the holiest city of Islam, being the place where the Prophet Muhammad was born **2** (usually **mecca**) a place that many people like to visit, especially for a particular reason: *The coast is a mecca for tourists.*

mech·an·ic /mə'kænɪk/ *noun* **1** [C] a person whose job is repairing machines, especially the engines of vehicles: *a car mechanic* **2 mechanics** [U] the science of movement and force ➲ see also QUANTUM MECHANICS **3 mechanics** [U] the practical study of machinery: *the school's car maintenance department where students learn basic mechanics* **4 the mechanics** [pl.] the way sth works or is done: *The exact mechanics of how payment will be made will be decided later.*

mech·an·ic·al /mə'kænɪkl/ *adj.* **1** operated by power from an engine: *a **mechanical device/toy/clock*** ◇ *mechanical parts* **2** connected with machines and engines: ***mechanical problems/defects*** ◇ *The breakdown was due to a mechanical failure.* **3** (*disapproving*) (of people's behaviour and actions) done without thinking, like a machine SYN **routine**: *a **mechanical gesture/response*** **4** connected with the physical laws of movement and cause and effect (= with MECHANICS): *mechanical processes* **5** (of a person) good at understanding how machines work ▸ **mech·an·ic·al·ly** /-kli/ *adv.*: *a mechanically powered vehicle* ◇ *She spoke mechanically, as if thinking of something else.* ◇ *He's always been mechanically minded.*

me,chanical engi'neering *noun* [U] the study of how machines are designed, built and repaired ▸ **me,chanical engi'neer** *noun*

mech·an·ism AW /'mekənɪzəm/ *noun* **1** a set of moving parts in a machine that performs a task: *a delicate watch mechanism* **2** a method or a system for achieving sth: *mechanisms for dealing with complaints from the general public* **3** a system of parts in a living thing that together perform a particular function: *the balance mechanism in the ears* ◇ *Pain acts as a natural **defence mechanism**.*

mech·an·is·tic /,mekə'nɪstɪk/ *adj.* (often *disapproving*) connected with the belief that all things in the universe can be explained as if they were machines: *the mechanistic philosophy that compares the brain to a computer* ▸ **mech·an·is·ti·cal·ly** /-kli/ *adv.*

mech·an·ize (*BrE* also **-ise**) /'mekənaɪz/ *verb* [usually passive] **~ sth** to change a process, so that the work is done by machines rather than people SYN **automate**: *The production process is now highly mechanized.* ▸ **mech·an·iza·tion, -isa·tion** /,mekənaɪ'zeɪʃn; *NAmE* -nə'z-/ *noun* [U]: *the increasing mechanization of farm work*

Med /med/ **the Med** *noun* [sing.] (*informal*) the Mediterranean Sea

med /med/ *adj.* (*informal, especially NAmE*) = MEDICAL: *a med student* ◇ *She's in med school.*

medal /'medl/ *noun, verb*

- ***noun*** a flat piece of metal, usually shaped like a coin, that is given to the winner of a competition or to sb who has been brave, for example in war: *to win a gold medal in the Olympics* ◇ *to award a medal for bravery* IDM see DESERVE
- ***verb*** (-ll-, *especially US* -l-) [I] to win a medal in a competition: *Evans has medalled at several international events.*

med·al·lion /mə'dæliən/ *noun* a piece of jewellery in the shape of a large flat coin worn on a chain around the neck ➲ VISUAL VOCAB page V53

med·al·list (*BrE*) (*US* **med·al·ist**) /'medəlɪst/ *noun* a person who has received a medal, usually for winning a competition in a sport: *an Olympic medallist* ◇ *a **gold/silver/bronze medallist***

,Medal of 'Freedom *noun* the highest award that the US gives to a CIVILIAN who has achieved sth very important

,Medal of 'Honor *noun* the highest award that the US gives to a member of the armed forces who has shown very great courage in a war

'medal play *noun* [U] = STROKE PLAY

med·dle /'medl/ *verb* (*disapproving*) **1** [I] **~ (in/with sth)** to become involved in sth that does not concern you SYN **interfere**: *He had no right to meddle in her affairs.* **2** [I] **~ (with sth)** to touch sth in a careless way, especially when it is not yours or when you do not know how to use it correctly: *Somebody had been meddling with her computer.* ▸ **med·dling** *noun* [U]

med·dler /'medlə(r)/ *noun* (*disapproving*) a person who tries to get involved in sth that does not concern them SYN **busybody**

meddle·some /'medlsəm/ *adj.* (*disapproving*) (of people) enjoying getting involved in situations that do not concern them SYN **interfering**

mede·vac /'medɪvæk/ *noun* [U] (*especially NAmE*) the movement of injured soldiers or other people to hospital in a HELICOPTER or other aircraft ➲ compare AIR AMBULANCE

media 🔑 AW /'mi:diə/ *noun*
1 🔑 **the media** [U+sing./pl. v.] the main ways that large numbers of people receive information and entertainment, that is television, radio, newspapers and the Internet: *the **news/broadcasting/national media*** ◇ *The trial was fully reported in the media.* ◇ *The media was/were accused of influencing the final decision.* ◇ *Any event attended by the actor received widespread **media coverage**.* ➲ see also MASS MEDIA, NEW MEDIA **2** *pl.* of MEDIUM

medi·aeval = MEDIEVAL

med·ial /'mi:diəl/ *adj.* (*technical*) located in the middle, especially of the body or of an organ

me·dian /'mi:diən/ *adj., noun*

- ***adj.*** [only before noun] (*technical*) **1** having a value in the middle of a series of values: *the **median age/price*** **2** located in or passing through the middle: *a **median point/line***
- ***noun*** **1** (*mathematics*) the middle value of a series of numbers arranged in order of size **2** (*geometry*) a straight line passing from a point of a triangle to the centre of the opposite side. **3** (also **'median strip**) (both *NAmE*) (*BrE* **,central reser'vation**) a narrow strip of land that separ-

M

ates the two sides of a major road such as a MOTORWAY or INTERSTATE

ˈmedia studies *noun* [U+sing./pl. v.] the study of newspapers, television, radio, etc. as a subject at school, etc.

me·di·ate AW /ˈmiːdieɪt/ *verb* **1** [I, T] to try to end a disagreement between two or more people or groups by talking to them and trying to find things that everyone can agree on: **~ (in sth)** *The Secretary-General was asked to mediate in the dispute.* ◇ **~ between A and B** *An independent body was brought in to mediate between staff and management.* ◇ **~ sth** *to* ***mediate differences/disputes/problems*** **2** [T] **~ sth** to succeed in finding a solution to a disagreement between people or groups SYN **negotiate**: *They mediated a settlement.* **3** [T, usually passive] **~ sth** (*formal* or *technical*) to influence sth and/or make it possible for it to happen: *Educational success is mediated by economic factors.* ▶ **me·di·ation** AW /ˌmiːdiˈeɪʃn/ *noun* [U]

me·di·ator /ˈmiːdieɪtə(r)/ *noun* a person or an organization that tries to get agreement between people or groups who disagree with each other

medic /ˈmedɪk/ *noun* **1** (*informal, especially BrE*) a medical student or doctor **2** (*NAmE*) a person who is trained to give medical treatment, especially sb in the armed forces

Me·dic·aid /ˈmedɪkeɪd/ *noun* [U] (in the US) the insurance system that provides medical care for poor people

med·ic·al 🔑 AW /ˈmedɪkl/ *adj., noun*

▪ ***adj.*** [usually before noun] **1** 🔑 connected with illness and injury and their treatment: ***medical advances/care/research*** ◇ *her* ***medical condition/history/records*** ◇ *the* ***medical profession*** ◇ *a* ***medical student/school*** ◇ *a medical certificate* (= a statement by a doctor that gives details of your state of health) ➲ see also MED **2** connected with ways of treating illness that do not involve cutting the body: *medical or surgical treatment* ▶ **med·ic·al·ly** AW /-kli/ *adv.*: ***medically fit/unfit***

▪ ***noun*** (also **ˌmedical examiˈnation**) a thorough examination of your body that a doctor does, for example, before you start a particular job ➲ see also EXAM

ˌmedical eˈxaminer *noun* (*abbr.* ME) (*NAmE*) a doctor whose job is to examine a dead body in order to find out the cause of death ➲ compare PATHOLOGIST

ˈmedical hall *noun* (*IndE, informal*) a chemist's shop/drugstore

ˈmedical officer *noun* (*abbr.* MO) a person, usually a doctor, employed in an organization to deal with medical and health matters

ˈmedical school (*NAmE* also **ˈmed school**, *informal*) *noun* a college where students study to obtain a degree in medicine

Medi·care /ˈmedɪkeə(r); *NAmE* -ker/ *noun* [U] **1** (in the US) the federal insurance system that provides medical care for people over 65 **2** (in Australia and Canada) the national medical care system for all people that is paid for by taxes (spelt 'medicare' in Canada)

medi·cate /ˈmedɪkeɪt/ *verb* **~ sb** to give sb medicine, especially a drug that affects their behaviour

medi·cated /ˈmedɪkeɪtɪd/ *adj.* containing a substance for preventing or curing infections of your skin or hair: ***medicated shampoo/soap***

medi·ca·tion /ˌmedɪˈkeɪʃn/ *noun* [U, C] a drug or another form of medicine that you take to prevent or to treat an illness: *to be* ***on medication*** ◇ *Are you currently taking any medication?* ◇ *Many flu medications are available without a prescription.* ➲ COLLOCATIONS at ILL

me·di·cin·al /məˈdɪsɪnl/ *adj.* helpful in the process of healing illness or infection: ***medicinal herbs/plants*** ◇ ***medicinal properties/use*** ◇ (*humorous*) *He claims he keeps a bottle of brandy only* ***for medicinal purposes.***

medi·cine 🔑 /ˈmedsn; -dɪsn/ *noun*

1 🔑 [U] the study and treatment of diseases and injuries: *advances in modern medicine* ◇ *to* ***study/practise medicine*** ◇ ***traditional/conventional/orthodox medicine*** ◇ ***alternative medicine*** ➲ see also AYURVEDIC MEDICINE, DEFENSIVE MEDICINE **2** 🔑 [U, C] a substance, especially a liquid that you drink or swallow in order to cure an illness: *Did you take your medicine?* ◇ *cough medicine* ◇ *Chinese herbal medicines* ➲ COLLOCATIONS at ILL

IDM **the best ˈmedicine** the best way of improving a situation, especially of making you feel happier: *Laughter is the best medicine.* **a taste/dose of your own ˈmedicine** the same bad treatment that you have given to others: *Let the bully have a taste of his own medicine.*

ˈmedicine ball *noun* a large heavy ball which is thrown and caught as a form of exercise

ˈmedicine man *noun* a person who is believed to have special magic powers of healing, especially among Native Americans ➲ compare WITCH DOCTOR

med·ico /ˈmedɪkəʊ; *NAmE* -koʊ/ *noun* (*pl.* -os) (*informal*) a doctor

medi·eval (also **medi·aeval**) /ˌmediˈiːvl; *NAmE* also ˌmiːd-/ *adj.* [usually before noun] connected with the Middle Ages (about AD 1000 to AD 1450): *medieval architecture/castles/manuscripts* ◇ *the literature of the late medieval period*

me·di·ocre /ˌmiːdiˈəʊkə(r); *NAmE* -ˈoʊkər/ *adj.* (*disapproving*) not very good; of only average standard: *a mediocre musician/talent/performance* ◇ *I thought the play was only mediocre.*

me·di·oc·rity /ˌmiːdiˈɒkrəti; *NAmE* -ˈɑːk-/ *noun* (*pl.* -ies) (*disapproving*) **1** [U] the quality of being average or not very good: *His acting career started brilliantly, then sank into mediocrity.* **2** [C] a person who is not very good at sth: *a brilliant leader, surrounded by mediocrities*

medi·tate /ˈmedɪteɪt/ *verb* **1** [I] **~ (on/upon sth)** to think deeply, usually in silence, especially for religious reasons or in order to make your mind calm **2** [T] **~ sth** (*formal*) to plan sth in your mind; to consider doing sth SYN **contemplate**: *They were meditating revenge.*

medi·ta·tion /ˌmedɪˈteɪʃn/ *noun* **1** [U] the practice of thinking deeply in silence, especially for religious reasons or in order to make your mind calm: *She found peace through yoga and meditation.* ◇ *He was deep* ***in meditation*** *and didn't see me come in.* **2** [C, usually pl.] **~ (on sth)** (*formal*) serious thoughts on a particular subject that sb writes down or speaks: *his meditations on life and art*

medi·ta·tive /ˈmedɪtətɪv; *NAmE* -teɪt-/ *adj.* (*formal*) thinking very deeply; involving deep thought SYN **thoughtful**: *She found him in a meditative mood.* ◇ *a meditative poem*

Medi·ter·ra·nean /ˌmedɪtəˈreɪniən/ *adj.* [only before noun] connected with the Mediterranean Sea or the countries and regions that surround it; typical of this area: *a Mediterranean country* ◇ *a Mediterranean climate*

me·dium 🔑 AW /ˈmiːdiəm/ *adj., noun*

▪ ***adj.*** 🔑 [usually before noun] (*abbr.* M) in the middle between two sizes, amounts, lengths, temperatures, etc. SYN **average**: *a* ***medium-size car/business/town*** ◇ *a man of* ***medium height/build*** ◇ *There are three sizes—small, medium and large.* ◇ *Cook over a medium heat for 15 minutes.* ◇ *a* ***medium dry*** *white wine* ◇ *Choose* ***medium to large*** *tomatoes.* IDM see TERM

▪ ***noun*** (*pl.* **media** /ˈmiːdiə/ or **me·diums**) **1** 🔑 a way of communicating information, etc. to people: *the* ***medium of radio/television*** ◇ ***electronic/audio-visual media*** ◇ *Television is the modern* ***medium of communication.*** ◇ *A T-shirt can be an excellent medium for getting your message across.* HELP The plural in this meaning is usually **media**. ➲ see also MEDIA, MASS MEDIA **2** 🔑 something that is used for a particular purpose: *English is the* ***medium of instruction*** (= the language used to teach other subjects). ◇ *Video is a good medium for learning a foreign language.* **3** the material or the form that an artist, a writer or a musician uses: *the* ***medium of paint/poetry/drama*** ◇ *Watercolour is his favourite medium.* **4** (*biology*) a substance that sth exists or grows in or that it travels through: *The bacteria were growing in a sugar medium.* **5** (*pl.* **me·diums**) a person who claims to be able to communicate with the spirits of dead people IDM see HAPPY

M

ˈmedium-sized *adj.* of average size: *a medium-sized saucepan*

ˈmedium-term *adj.* used to describe a period of time that is a few weeks or months into the future: *the government's medium-term financial strategy*

ˈmedium wave (*abbr.* MW) *noun* [U] (also **the medium wave** [sing.]) a band of radio waves with a length of between 100 and 1 000 metres: *648 m on (the) medium wave* ➲ compare SHORT WAVE

med·lar /ˈmedlə(r)/ *noun* a brownish fruit which is eaten when it has started to decay and become soft

med·ley /ˈmedli/ *noun* **1** a piece of music consisting of several songs or tunes played or sung one after the other: *a medley of Beatles hits* **2** a mixture of people or things of different kinds: *a* ***medley of flavours/smells*** **3** a swimming race in which each member of a team uses a different stroke: *the 4 × 100 metres medley*

ˈmed school *noun* (*NAmE, informal*) = MEDICAL SCHOOL

meek /miːk/ *adj.* (**meek·er**, **meek·est**) **1** quiet, gentle, and always ready to do what other people want without expressing your own opinion SYN **compliant, self-effacing**: *They called her Miss Mouse because she was so* ***meek and mild***. **2 the meek** *noun* [pl.] people who are meek ▶ **meek·ly** *adv.*: *He meekly did as he was told.* **meek·ness** *noun* [U]

meer·kat /ˈmɪəkæt; *NAmE* ˈmɪr-/ *noun* a small southern African animal with a long tail, which often stands up on its back legs. Meerkats are a type of MONGOOSE.

meet 0‑ᵲ /miːt/ *verb, noun*

■ ***verb*** (**met**, **met** /met/)

▸ BY CHANCE **1** 0‑ᵲ [I, T, no passive] to be in the same place as sb by chance and talk to them: *Maybe we'll meet again some time.* ◇ **~ sb** *Did you meet anyone in town?*

▸ BY ARRANGEMENT **2** 0‑ᵲ [I, T, no passive] to come together formally in order to discuss sth: *The committee meets on Fridays.* ◇ **~ sb** *The Prime Minister met other European leaders for talks.* ◇ **~ with sb** *The President met with senior White House aides.* **3** 0‑ᵲ [I, T, no passive] to come together socially after you have arranged it: **~ (for sth)** *Let's meet for a drink after work.* ◇ **~ sb (for sth)** *We're meeting them outside the theatre at 7.* **4** 0‑ᵲ [T] **~ sb/sth** to go to a place and wait there for a particular person to arrive: *Will you meet me at the airport?* ◇ *The hotel bus meets all incoming flights.* ◇ *I met him off the plane.*

▸ FOR THE FIRST TIME **5** 0‑ᵲ [T, no passive, I] **~ (sb)** to see and know sb for the first time; to be introduced to sb: *Where did you first meet your husband?* ◇ (*especially BrE*) ***Pleased to meet you.*** ◇ (*NAmE*) ***Nice meeting you.*** ◇ *There's someone I want you to meet.* ◇ *I don't think we've met.*

▸ IN CONTEST **6** [I, T, no passive] to play, fight, etc. together as opponents in a competition: *Smith and Jones met in last year's final.* ◇ **~ sb** *Smith met Jones in last year's final.*

▸ EXPERIENCE STH **7** [T] **~ sth** to experience sth, often sth unpleasant: *Others have met similar problems.* ◇ *How she* ***met her death*** *will probably never be known.* SYN **come across, encounter**

▸ TOUCH/JOIN **8** [I, T] to touch sth; to join: *The curtains don't meet in the middle.* ◇ **~ sth** *That's where the river meets the sea.* ◇ *His hand met hers.*

▸ SATISFY **9** [T] **~ sth** to do or satisfy what is needed or what sb asks for SYN **fulfil**: *How can we best* ***meet the needs*** *of all the different groups?* ◇ *Until these* ***conditions are met*** *we cannot proceed with the sale.* ◇ *I can't possibly meet that deadline.*

▸ PAY **10** [T] **~ sth** to pay sth: *The* ***cost will be met*** *by the company.*

IDM **meet sb's ˈeye(s)** | **meet sb's ˈgaze, ˈlook, etc.** | **people's ˈeyes meet** **1** [T, I] if you **meet sb's eye(s)**, you look directly at them as they look at you; if two people's **eyes meet**, they look directly at each other: *She was afraid to meet my eye.* ◇ *Their eyes met across the crowded room.* ◇ *She met his gaze without flinching.* **2** [T] **~ your eyes** if a sight **meets your eyes**, you see it: *A terrible sight met their eyes.* **meet sb halfˈway** to reach an agreement with sb by giving them part of what they want **meet your ˈMaker** (*especially humorous*) to die **there is more to sb/sth than meets the ˈeye** a person or thing is more complicated or interesting than you might think at first ➲ more at END *n.*, MATCH *n.*, RUBBER, TWAIN

PHR V ˌ**meet ˈup (with sb)** 0‑ᵲ (*rather informal*) to meet sb, especially by arrangement: *They met up again later for a drink.* ˈ**meet with sb** 0‑ᵲ to meet sb, especially for discussions: *The President met with senior White House aides.* ˈ**meet with sth** **1** to be received or treated by sb in a particular way: *Her proposal met with resistance from the Left.* ◇ *to meet with success/failure* **2** to experience sth unpleasant: *She was worried that he might have met with an accident.* ˈ**meet sth with sth** to react to sth in a particular way SYN **receive**: *His suggestion was met with howls of protest.*

■ ***noun*** **1** (*especially NAmE*) a sports competition: *a track meet* **2** (*BrE*) an event at which horse riders and dogs hunt FOXES. FOX-HUNTING with dogs is now illegal in the UK.

ˌ**meet-and-ˈgreet** *adj.* [only before noun] (of an event) arranged so that sb, especially a famous person, can meet and talk to people ▶ ˌ**meet and ˈgreet** *noun*

meet·ing 0‑ᵲ /ˈmiːtɪŋ/ *noun*

1 0‑ᵲ [C] an occasion when people come together to discuss or decide sth: *to* ***have/hold/call/attend a meeting*** ◇ *a* ***committee/staff meeting*** ◇ *What time is the meeting?* ◇ *Helen will* ***chair the meeting*** (= be in charge of it). ◇ *I'll be* ***in a meeting*** *all morning—can you take my calls?* ◇ *a meeting of the United Nations Security Council* **2 the meeting** [sing.] the people at a meeting: *The meeting voted to accept the pay offer.* **3** 0‑ᵲ [C] a situation in which two or more people meet together, because they have arranged it or by chance SYN **encounter**: *At our first meeting I was nervous.* ◇ *It was a* ***chance meeting*** *that would change my life.* ◇ *He remembered their childhood meetings with nostalgia.* **4** [C] (*BrE*) a sports event or set of races, especially for horses: *an athletics meeting* ◇ *a race meeting*

IDM **a meeting of ˈminds** a close understanding between people with similar ideas, especially when they meet to do sth or meet for the first time

ˈ**meeting house** *noun* a place where Quakers meet for worship

ˈ**meeting place** *noun* a place where people often meet: *The cafe is a popular meeting place for students.*

meg /meg/ *noun* (*informal*) = MEGABYTE: *more than 512 megs of memory* ◇ *24-meg broadband*

mega /ˈmegə/ *adj.* [usually before noun] (*informal*) very large or impressive SYN **huge, great**: *The song was a mega hit last year.* ▶ **mega** *adv.*: *They're mega rich.*

mega- /ˈmegə-/ *combining form* (in nouns) **1** very large or great: *a megastore* **2** (in units of measurement) one million: *a megawatt* **3** (in units of measurement) 2^{20}, or 1 048 576

mega·bit /ˈmegəbɪt/ *noun* (*abbr.* **Mb**, **Mbit**) (*computing*) **1** a unit of computer memory or data, equal to 10^6, or 1000^2, (= 1 000 000) BITS **2** (also **mebi·bit**) a unit of computer memory or data, equal to 2^{20}, or 1024^2, (= 1 048 576) BITS

mega·bucks /ˈmegəbʌks/ *noun* [pl.] (*informal*) a very large amount of money: *He earns megabucks.*

mega·byte /ˈmegəbaɪt/ (also *informal* **meg**) *noun* (*abbr.* MB) (*computing*) **1** a unit of computer memory or data, equal to 10^6, or 1000^2, (= 1 000 000) BYTES: *a 512-megabyte flash drive* **2** (also **mebi·byte**) a unit of computer memory or data, equal to 2^{20}, or 1024^2, (= 1 048 576) BYTES

mega·hertz /ˈmegəhɜːts; *NAmE* -hɜːrts/ *noun* (*pl.* **mega·hertz**) (*abbr.* **MHz**) a unit for measuring radio waves and the speed at which a computer operates; 1 000 000 HERTZ

mega·lith /ˈmegəlɪθ/ *noun* a very large stone, especially one put in a place that was used for ceremonies in ancient times ▶ **mega·lith·ic** /ˌmegəˈlɪθɪk/ *adj.*

meg·alo·mania /ˌmegələˈmeɪniə/ *noun* [U] **1** (*technical*) a mental illness or condition in which sb has an exaggerated belief in their own importance or power **2** a strong feeling that you want to have more and more power

M

meg·alo·maniac /ˌmeɡələˈmeɪniæk/ *noun* a person suffering from or showing megalomania ▸ **meg·alo·maniac** *adj.*

meg·alop·olis /ˌmeɡəˈlɒpəlɪs; *NAmE* -ˈlɑːp-/ *noun* (*formal*) a very large city or group of cities where a great number of people live

mega·phone /ˈmeɡəfəʊn; *NAmE* -foʊn/ *noun* a device for making your voice sound louder, that is wider at one end, like a CONE, and is often used at outside events ➲ compare LOUDHAILER

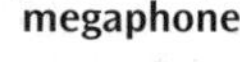

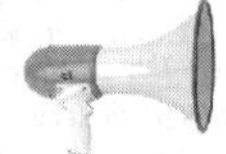

mega·pixel /ˈmeɡəpɪksl/ *noun* a million PIXELS (= very small individual areas on a computer screen), used to measure the quality of a DIGITAL screen or image: *a 12 megapixel digital camera*

mega·star /ˈmeɡəstɑː(r)/ *noun* (*informal*) a very famous singer, actor or entertainer

mega·store /ˈmeɡəstɔː(r)/ *noun* a very large shop, especially one that sells one type of product, for example computers or furniture

mega·ton (also **mega·tonne**) /ˈmeɡətʌn/ *noun* a unit for measuring the power of an EXPLOSIVE, equal to one million tons of TNT: *a one megaton nuclear bomb*

mega·watt /ˈmeɡəwɒt; *NAmE* -wɑːt/ *noun* (*abbr.* MW) a unit for measuring electrical power; one million WATTS

meh /me/ *exclamation, adj.* (*NAmE, informal*) used to show that you are not at all interested in or impressed by sth: *'So how was the movie?' 'Meh. The action scenes aren't awful, but there's nothing great about it.'* ◇ *She does an OK job on a meh song.*

M

mei·osis /maɪˈəʊsɪs; *NAmE* -ˈoʊs-/ *noun* [U] (*biology*) the division of a cell in two stages that results in four cells, each with half the number of CHROMOSOMES of the original cell

-meister /ˈmaɪstə(r)/ *combining form* (in nouns) (*informal*) a person thought of as skilled at a particular activity or important in a particular field: *a horror-meister*

meit·ner·ium /maɪtˈnɪəriəm; *NAmE* -ˈnɪr-/ *noun* [U] (*symb.* Mt) a RADIOACTIVE chemical element. Meitnerium is produced when atoms COLLIDE (= crash into each other).

mela·mine /ˈmeləmiːn/ *noun* [U] a strong hard plastic material, used especially for covering surfaces such as the tops of tables, and for making cups, etc.

mel·an·cho·lia /ˌmelənˈkəʊliə; *NAmE* -ˈkoʊ-/ *noun* (*old-fashioned*) a mental illness in which the patient is depressed and worried by unnecessary fears

mel·an·chol·ic /ˌmelənˈkɒlɪk; *NAmE* -ˈkɑːl-/ *adj.* (*old-fashioned* or *literary*) feeling or expressing sadness, especially when the sadness is like an illness

mel·an·choly /ˈmelənkəli; -kɒli; *NAmE* -kɑːli/ *noun, adj.*
- ***noun*** [U] (*formal*) a deep feeling of sadness that lasts for a long time and often cannot be explained: *A mood of melancholy descended on us.*
- ***adj.*** very sad or making you feel sadness SYN **mournful, sombre**: ***melancholy thoughts/memories*** ◇ *The melancholy song died away.*

me·lange /meɪˈlɑːnʒ/ *noun* (from *French, formal*) a mixture or variety of different things: *a melange of different cultures*

mel·anin /ˈmelənɪn/ *noun* [U] (*technical*) a dark substance in the skin and hair that causes the skin to change colour in the sun's light

mela·noma /ˌmeləˈnəʊmə; *NAmE* -ˈnoʊmə/ *noun* [C, U] (*medical*) a type of cancer that appears as a dark spot or TUMOUR on the skin

mela·to·nin /ˌmeləˈtəʊnɪn; *NAmE* -ˈtoʊ-/ *noun* [U] (*biology*) a HORMONE that causes changes in skin colour

meld /meld/ *verb* [I, T] **~ (A) with B | ~ (A and B) (together)** (*formal*) to combine with sth else; to make sth combine with sth else SYN **blend**

melee /ˈmeleɪ; *NAmE* ˈmeɪleɪ/ *noun* [sing.] (from *French*) a situation in which a crowd of people are rushing or pushing each other in a confused way

mel·lif·lu·ous /meˈlɪfluəs/ *adj.* (*formal*) (of music or of sb's voice) sounding sweet and smooth; very pleasant to listen to

mel·low /ˈmeləʊ; *NAmE* -loʊ/ *adj., verb*
- ***adj.*** (**mel·low·er, mel·low·est**) **1** (of colour or sound) soft, rich and pleasant: *mellow autumn colours* ◇ *Mellow music and lighting helped to create the right atmosphere.* **2** (of a taste or flavour) smooth and pleasant: *a mellow, fruity wine* **3** (of people) calm, gentle and reasonable because of age or experience: *Dad's certainly grown mellower with age.* **4** (*informal*) (of people) relaxed, calm and happy, especially after drinking alcohol: *After two glasses of wine, I was feeling mellow.*
- ***verb*** **1** [I, T] to become or make sb become less extreme in behaviour, etc, especially as a result of growing older: *She had mellowed a great deal since their days at college.* ◇ **~ sb** *A period spent working abroad had done nothing to mellow him.* **2** [I, T] **~ (sth)** to become, or make a colour become less bright, especially over a period of time **3** [I, T] **~ (sth)** to develop or make wine develop a pleasant and less bitter taste over a period of time

PHR V **ˌmellow ˈout** (*informal, especially NAmE*) to enjoy yourself by relaxing and not doing much

me·lod·ic /məˈlɒdɪk; *NAmE* -ˈlɑːd-/ *adj.* **1** [only before noun] connected with the main tune in a piece of music: *The melodic line is carried by the two clarinets.* **2** = MELODIOUS

me·lod·ica /məˈlɒdɪkə; *NAmE* -ˈlɑːd-/ *noun* a musical instrument that has a keyboard and a part that you blow into

me·lo·di·ous /məˈləʊdiəs; *NAmE* -ˈloʊ-/ (also **me·lod·ic**) *adj.* pleasant to listen to, like music: *a rich melodious voice* ▸ **me·lo·di·ous·ly** *adv.*

melo·dist /ˈmelədɪst/ *noun* a person who writes tunes; a person who is very good at writing tunes

melo·drama /ˈmelədrɑːmə/ *noun* [U, C] **1** a story, play or novel that is full of exciting events and in which the characters and emotions seem too exaggerated to be real: *a gripping Victorian melodrama* ◇ *Instead of tragedy, we got melodrama.* **2** events, behaviour, etc. which are exaggerated or extreme: *Her love of melodrama meant that any small problem became a crisis.*

melo·dra·mat·ic /ˌmelədrəˈmætɪk/ *adj.* (often *disapproving*) full of exciting and extreme emotions or events; behaving or reacting to sth in an exaggerated way: *a melodramatic plot full of deceit and murder* ▸ **melo·dra·mat·ic·al·ly** /-kli/ *adv.*

melo·dra·mat·ics /ˌmelədrəˈmætɪks/ *noun* [pl.] behaviour or events that are melodramatic: *Let's have no more melodramatics, if you don't mind.*

mel·ody /ˈmelədi/ *noun* (*pl.* -ies) **1** [C] a tune, especially the main tune in a piece of music written for several instruments or voices: *a haunting melody* ◇ *The melody is then taken up by the flutes.* ➲ COLLOCATIONS at MUSIC **2** [C] a piece of music or a song with a clear or simple tune: *old Irish melodies* **3** [U] the arrangement of musical notes in a tune: *a few bars of melody drifted towards us*

melon /ˈmelən/ *noun* [C, U] a large fruit with hard green, yellow or orange skin, sweet flesh and juice and a lot of seeds: *a slice of melon* ➲ see also HONEYDEW MELON, WATERMELON

melt 🔑 /melt/ *verb*
1 🔑 [I, T] to become or make sth become liquid as a result of heating: *The snow showed no sign of melting.* ◇ *melting ice* ◇ **~ sth** *The sun had melted the snow.* ◇ *First, melt two ounces of butter.* ➲ COLLOCATIONS at COOKING ➲ compare DEFROST, DE-ICE **2** [I, T] to become or to make a feeling, an emotion, etc. become gentler and less strong: *The tension in the room began to melt.* ◇ **~ sth** *Her trusting smile melted his heart.*

IDM ˌ**melt in your ˈmouth** (of food) to be soft and very good to eat ➲ more at BUTTER *n.*

PHR V ˌ**melt aˈway** | ˌ**melt sth↔aˈway** to disappear or make sth disappear gradually: *At the first sign of trouble, the crowd melted away.* ˌ**melt sth↔ˈdown** to heat a metal or WAX object until it is liquid, especially so that the metal or wax can be used to make sth else ➲ related noun MELTDOWN ˈ**melt into sth** to gradually become part of sth and therefore become difficult to see

melt·down /ˈmeltdaʊn/ *noun* [U, C] **1** a serious accident in which the central part of a nuclear REACTOR melts, causing harmful RADIATION to escape **2** (*economics*) a situation where sth fails or becomes weaker in a sudden or dramatic way: *The country is* ***in*** *economic* ***meltdown***. ◇ *a meltdown on the New York Stock Exchange*

melt·ing /ˈmeltɪŋ/ *adj.* [usually before noun] persuading you to feel love, pity or sympathy: *his melting eyes* ▶ **melt·ing·ly** *adv.*

ˈ**melting point** *noun* [U, C] the temperature at which a substance will melt

ˈ**melting pot** *noun* [usually sing.] a place or situation in which large numbers of people, ideas, etc. are mixed together: *the vast melting pot of American society*

IDM **in the ˈmelting pot** (*especially BrE*) likely to change; in the process of changing

mem·ber 🔑 /ˈmembə(r)/ *noun*
1 🔑 **~ (of sth)** a person, an animal or a plant that belongs to a particular group: *a* ***member of staff/society/the family*** ◇ *characteristics common to all members of the species* **2** 🔑 a person, a country or an organization that has joined a particular group, club or team: ***party/union members*** ◇ *a meeting of* ***member countries/states*** ◇ *How much does it cost to become a member?* ◇ **~ of sth** *an active member of the local church* **3** (*old use* or *literary*) a part of the body, especially an arm or a leg **4** a PENIS. People say 'member' to avoid saying 'penis'. **5 Member** (in Britain) a Member of Parliament: *the Hon. Member for Brent North* ➲ see also PRIVATE MEMBER

ˌ**Member of ˈParliament** *noun* = MP

mem·ber·ship 🔑 /ˈmembəʃɪp; *NAmE* -bərʃ-/ *noun*
1 🔑 [U] (*BrE*) **~ (of sth)** | (*NAmE*) **~ (in sth)** the state of being a member of a group, a club, an organization, etc: *Who is eligible to apply for membership of the association?* ◇ *a* ***membership card/fee*** **2** 🔑 [C+sing./pl. v.] the members, or the number of members, of a group, a club, an organization, etc: *The membership has/have not yet voted.* ◇ *The club has a membership of more than 500.*

mem·brane /ˈmembreɪn/ *noun* [C, U] **1** a thin layer of skin or TISSUE that connects or covers parts inside the body ➲ see also MUCOUS MEMBRANE **2** a very thin layer found in the structure of cells in plants **3** a thin layer of material used to prevent air, liquid, etc. from entering a particular part of sth: *a waterproof membrane* ▶ **mem·bran·ous** /ˈmembrənəs/ *adj.*

meme /miːm/ *noun* (*biology*) a type of behaviour that is passed from one member of a group to another, not in the GENES but by another means such as people copying it

me·mento /məˈmentəʊ; *NAmE* -toʊ/ *noun* (*pl.* -oes or -os) a thing that you keep or give to sb to remind you or them of a person or place **SYN** **souvenir**: *a memento of our trip to Italy*

me·mento mori /məˌmentəʊ ˈmɔːri; ˈmɔːraɪ; *NAmE* -toʊ/ *noun* (*pl.* **me·mento mori**) an object or symbol that reminds or warns you of death

memo /ˈmeməʊ; *NAmE* -moʊ/ *noun* (*pl.* -os) (also *formal* **memo·ran·dum**) **~ (to sb)** an official note from one person to another in the same organization: *to* ***write/send/circulate a memo***

mem·oir /ˈmemwɑː(r)/ *noun* **1 memoirs** [pl.] an account written by sb, especially sb famous, about their life and experiences **2** [C] (*formal*) a written account of sb's life, a place, or an event, written by sb who knows it well

mem·ora·bilia /ˌmemərəˈbɪliə/ *noun* [pl.] things that people collect because they once belonged to a famous person, or because they are connected with a particular interesting place, event or activity: *football/Beatles memorabilia*

mem·or·able /ˈmemərəbl/ *adj.* **~ (for sth)** special, good or unusual and therefore worth remembering or easy to remember **SYN** **unforgettable**: *a truly memorable occasion* ▶ **mem·or·ably** /-əbli/ *adv.*

memo·ran·dum /ˌmeməˈrændəm/ *noun* (*pl.* **memo·randa** /ˌmeməˈrændə/) **1** (*formal*) = MEMO: *an internal memorandum* **2** (*law*) a record of a legal agreement which has not yet been formally prepared and signed **3** a proposal or report on a particular subject for a person, an organization, a committee, etc: *a detailed memorandum to the commission on employment policy*

me·mor·ial /məˈmɔːriəl/ *noun, adj.*
■ ***noun*** **1** [C] a statue, stone, etc. that is built in order to remind people of an important past event or of a famous person who has died: *a* ***war memorial*** (= in memory of soldiers who died in a war) ◇ **~ to sb/sth** *a memorial to victims of the Holocaust* **2** [sing.] **~ to sb/sth** a thing that will continue to remind people of sb/sth: *The painting will be a lasting memorial to a remarkable woman.*
■ ***adj.*** [only before noun] created or done in order to remember sb who has died: *a* ***memorial statue/plaque/prize*** ◇ *The* ***memorial service*** *will be held at a local church.* ◇ *the John F Kennedy Memorial Hospital*

Meˈmorial Day *noun* a holiday in the US, usually the last Monday in May, in honour of members of the armed forces who have died in war ➲ see also REMEMBRANCE SUNDAY, VETERANS DAY

me·mor·ial·ize (*BrE* also **-ise**) /məˈmɔːriəlaɪz/ *verb* **~ sb/sth** (*formal*) to produce sth that will continue to exist and remind people of sb who has died or sth that has gone **SYN** **commemorate**

me·mor·iam /məˈmɔːriəm/ ➲ IN MEMORIAM

mem·or·ize (*BrE* also **-ise**) /ˈmeməraɪz/ *verb* **~ sth** to learn sth carefully so that you can remember it exactly: *to memorize a poem*

mem·ory 🔑 /ˈmeməri/ (*pl.* -ies) *noun*
▸ ABILITY TO REMEMBER **1** 🔑 [C, U] **~ (for sth)** your ability to remember things: *I have a bad memory for names.* ◇ *People have* ***short memories*** (= they soon forget). ◇ *He had a* ***long memory*** *for people who had disappointed him.* ◇ *She can recite the whole poem* ***from memory***. ◇ *He suffered loss of memory for weeks after the accident.* ◇ *Are you sure? Memory can play tricks on you.* **2** 🔑 [U] the period of time that sb is able to remember events: *There hasn't been peace in the country* ***in/within my memory***. ◇ *It was the worst storm in recent memory.* ◇ *This hasn't happened* ***in living memory*** (= nobody alive now can remember it happening).
▸ STH YOU REMEMBER **3** 🔑 [C] a thought of sth that you remember from the past **SYN** **recollection**: *childhood memories* ◇ *I have vivid memories of my grandparents.* ◇ *What is your earliest memory?* ◇ *The photos* ***bring back*** *lots of good* ***memories***. **4** [U] (*formal*) what is remembered about sb after they have died: *Her memory lives on* (= we still remember her).
▸ COMPUTING **5** 🔑 [C, U] the part of a computer where information is stored; the amount of space in a computer for storing information ➲ see also RAM

IDM **if (my) memory serves me well, correctly, etc.** if I remember correctly **in memory of sb** | **to the memory of sb** 🔑 intended to show respect and remind people of sb who has died: *He founded the charity in memory of his late wife.* ➲ more at ETCH, JOG *v.*, REFRESH, SIEVE *n.*

ˈ**memory bank** *noun* the memory of a device such as a computer

ˈ**memory card** *noun* an electronic device that can be used to store data, used especially with DIGITAL cameras, mobile/cell phones, music players, etc. ➲ compare SD CARD, SDHC CARD

M

ˌmemory ˈlane *noun*
IDM **a trip/walk down ˌmemory ˈlane** time that you spend thinking about and remembering the past or going to a place again in order to remind yourself of past experiences

ˈMemory Stick™ *noun* (*computing*) a CIRCUIT BOARD that can be put into a computer to give it more memory of the kind that does not lose data when the power supply is lost

ˈmemory stick *noun* (*especially BrE*) a small memory device that can be used to store data from a computer and to move it from one computer to another **SYN** **flash drive** ➲ VISUAL VOCAB page V54

mem·sahib /ˈmemsɑːb/ *noun* used in India, especially in the past, to address a married woman with high social status, often a European woman

men *pl.* of MAN

men·ace /ˈmenəs/ *noun, verb*
■ ***noun*** **1** [C, usually sing.] **~ (to sb/sth)** a person or thing that causes, or may cause, serious damage, harm or danger **SYN** **threat**: *a new initiative aimed at beating the menace of illegal drugs* **2** [U] an atmosphere that makes you feel threatened or frightened: ***a sense/an air/a hint of menace*** *in his voice* **3** [C, usually sing.] (*informal*) a person or thing that is annoying or causes trouble **SYN** **nuisance** **4 menaces** [pl.] (*law*) (*BrE*) threats that sb will cause harm if they do not get what they are asking for: *to demand money* ***with menaces***
■ ***verb*** **~ sth/sb** (*formal*) to be a possible danger to sth/sb **SYN** **threaten**: *The forests are being menaced by major development projects.*

men·acing /ˈmenəsɪŋ/ *adj.* seeming likely to cause you harm or danger **SYN** **threatening**: *a* ***menacing face/tone*** ◇ *At night, the dark streets become menacing.* ▶ **men·acing·ly** *adv.*: *The thunder growled menacingly.*

mé·nage /meɪˈnɑːʒ/ *noun* [usually sing.] (from *French*, *formal* or *humorous*) all the people who live together in one house **SYN** **household**

ménage à trois /ˌmeɪnɑːʒ ɑː ˈtrwʌ/ *noun* (*pl.* **ménages à trois** /ˌmeɪnɑːʒ ɑː ˈtrwʌ/) [usually sing.] (from *French*) a situation where three people, especially a husband, wife and lover, live together and have sexual relationships with each other

men·agerie /məˈnædʒəri/ *noun* a collection of wild animals

mend /mend/ *verb, noun*
■ ***verb*** **1** [T] **~ sth** (*BrE*) to repair sth that has been damaged or broken so that it can be used again: *Could you mend my bike for me?* ➲ see also FENCE-MENDING **2** [T] **~ sth** to repair a hole in a piece of clothing, etc: *He mended shoes for a living.* **3** [T] **~ sth** to find a solution to a problem or disagreement: *They tried to mend their differences.* **4** [I] (*old-fashioned, BrE*) (of a person) to improve in health after being ill/sick **SYN** **recover**: *He's mending slowly after the operation.* **5** [I] (of a broken bone) to heal
IDM **mend (your) fences (with sb)** to find a solution to a disagreement with sb **mend your ˈways** to stop behaving badly ➲ more at SAY *v.*
■ ***noun***
IDM **on the ˈmend** (*informal*) getting better after an illness or injury; improving after a difficult situation: *My leg is definitely on the mend now.* ◇ *Does he believe the economy's really on the mend?*

men·da·cious /menˈdeɪʃəs/ *adj.* (*formal*) not telling the truth **SYN** **lying**

men·da·city /menˈdæsəti/ *noun* [U] (*formal*) the act of not telling the truth **SYN** **lying**

men·del·evium /ˌmendəˈliːviəm; -ˈleɪv-/ *noun* [U] (*symb.* **Md**) a chemical element. Mendelevium is a RADIOACTIVE element that does not exist naturally.

mend·er /ˈmendə(r)/ *noun* (*BrE*) (usually in compounds) a person who mends sth: *road menders*

men·di·cant /ˈmendɪkənt/ *adj.* (*formal*) (especially of members of religious groups) living by asking people for money and food ▶ **men·di·cant** *noun*

men·folk /ˈmenfəʊk; *NAmE* -foʊk/ *noun* [pl.] (*old-fashioned*) men of a particular family or community: *a society sending its menfolk off to war* ➲ compare WOMENFOLK

me·nial /ˈmiːniəl/ *adj., noun*
■ ***adj.*** (usually *disapproving*) (of work) not skilled or important, and often boring or badly paid: ***menial jobs/work*** ◇ *menial tasks like cleaning the floor*
■ ***noun*** (*old-fashioned*) a person with a menial job

men·in·ges /məˈnɪndʒiːz/ *noun* [pl.] (*anatomy*) the three MEMBRANES (= thin layers of material) that surround the brain and SPINAL CORD

men·in·gi·tis /ˌmenɪnˈdʒaɪtɪs/ *noun* [U] a serious disease in which the TISSUES surrounding the brain and SPINAL CORD become infected and swollen, causing severe headache, fever and sometimes death

me·nis·cus /məˈnɪskəs/ *noun* (*pl.* **me·nisci** /-saɪ/) **1** (*physics*) the curved surface of a liquid in a tube **2** (*anatomy*) a thin layer of CARTILAGE between the surfaces of some joints, for example the knee

Men·non·ite /ˈmenənaɪt/ *noun* a member of a PROTESTANT religious group that lives in the US and Canada. Mennonites live a simple life and do not work as public officials or soldiers.

meno·pause /ˈmenəpɔːz/ (also *informal* **the ˈchange (of life)**) *noun* [U] (often **the menopause**) [sing.] the time during which a woman gradually stops MENSTRUATING, usually at around the age of 50: *to reach (the) menopause* ▶ **meno·pausal** /ˌmenəˈpɔːzl/ *adj.*: ***menopausal women/symptoms***

me·norah /mɪˈnɔːrə/ *noun* a traditional Jewish object to hold seven or nine CANDLES

mensch /menʃ/ *noun* (*NAmE, informal*) a good person, especially sb who does sth kind or helpful

men·ses /ˈmensiːz/ *noun* (often **the menses**) [pl.] (*technical*) the flow of blood each month from a woman's body

ˈmen's room *noun* (*NAmE*) a public toilet/bathroom for men

men·strual /ˈmenstruəl/ *adj.* connected with the time when a woman menstruates each month: *The average length of a woman's* ***menstrual cycle*** *is 28 days.* ◇ *menstrual blood* ◇ (*formal*) *a menstrual period* ➲ compare PREMENSTRUAL

men·stru·ate /ˈmenstrueɪt/ *verb* [I] (*formal*) when a woman **menstruates**, there is a flow of blood from her womb, usually once a month

men·stru·ation /ˌmenstruˈeɪʃn/ *noun* [U] (*formal*) the process or time of menstruating ➲ compare PERIOD

mens·wear /ˈmenzweə(r); *NAmE* -wer/ *noun* [U] used especially in shops/stores to describe clothes for men: *the menswear department*

-ment *suffix* (in nouns) the action or result of: *bombardment* ◇ *development* ▶ **-mental** (in adjectives): *governmental* ◇ *judgemental*

men·tal 🔑 **AW** /ˈmentl/ *adj.*
1 🔑 [usually before noun] connected with or happening in the mind; involving the process of thinking: *the mental process of remembering* ◇ *Do you have a* ***mental picture*** *of what it will look like?* ◇ ***I made a mental note*** *to talk to her about it.* ◇ *He has a complete* ***mental block*** (= difficulty in understanding or remembering) *when it comes to physics.* **2** 🔑 [usually before noun] connected with the state of health of the mind or with the treatment of illnesses of the mind **SYN** **psychological**: ***mental health*** ◇ *a* ***mental disorder/illness/hospital*** ◇ *She was suffering from physical and mental exhaustion.* ➲ compare PSYCHIATRIC **3** [not usually before noun] (*BrE, slang*) crazy: *Watch him. He's mental.* ◇ *My dad will* ***go mental*** (= be very angry) *when he finds out.*

ˌmental ˈage *noun* [C, usually sing.] the level of sb's ability to think, understand, etc. that is judged by comparison with the average ability for children of a particular age: *She is sixteen but* ***has a mental age of*** *five.* ➲ compare CHRONOLOGICAL

ˌmental aˈrithmetic *noun* [U] adding, multiplying, etc. numbers in your mind without writing anything down or using a CALCULATOR

men·tal·ity AW /menˈtæləti/ *noun* [usually sing.] (*pl.* -ies) the particular attitude or way of thinking of a person or group SYN **mindset**: *I cannot understand the mentality of football hooligans.* ◇ *a* ***criminal/ghetto mentality*** ➲ see also SIEGE MENTALITY

men·tal·ly 🗝 AW /ˈmentəli/ *adv.* connected with or happening in the mind: *mentally ill* ◇ *The baby is very mentally alert.* ◇ *Mentally, I began making a list of things I had to do.*

Synonyms

mentally ill

insane • neurotic • psychotic • disturbed • unstable

These words all describe sb who is suffering from a mental illness.

mentally ill suffering from an illness of the mind, especially in a way that affects the way you think and behave

insane [not usually before noun] (*rather formal*) suffering from a serious mental illness and unable to live in normal society: *The question is, was the man insane when he committed the crime?* NOTE In informal English **insane** can describe sb who is not suffering from a mental illness, but whose mind does not work normally, especially because they are under pressure. This meaning is used especially in the phrases *go insane* and *drive sb insane*.

neurotic (*medical*) suffering from or connected with neurosis (= a mental illness in which a person suffers strong feelings of fear and worry): *the treatment of anxiety in neurotic patients* NOTE In informal English **neurotic** is also used to describe sb who is not suffering from a mental illness, but is not behaving in a calm way because they are worried about sth: *She became neurotic about keeping the house clean.*

psychotic (*medical*) suffering from or connected with psychosis (= a serious mental illness in which thought and emotions lose connection with external reality). NOTE In informal English **psychotic** is sometimes used to describe anyone suffering from a mental illness, but in correct medical usage it only describes people who have difficulty relating to external reality. It contrasts with **neurotic** which describes people who are less seriously mentally ill and are still able to distinguish what is real from what is not.

disturbed mentally ill, especially because of very unhappy or shocking experiences: *He works with emotionally disturbed children.*

unstable having emotions and behaviour that are likely to change suddenly and unexpectedly

PATTERNS

- neurotic/psychotic/disturbed/unstable **behaviour**
- neurotic/psychotic **illnesses/disorders/symptoms/patients**
- **seriously** mentally ill/neurotic/psychotic/disturbed
- **emotionally/mentally** disturbed/unstable

ˌmentally ˈhandicapped *adj.* (*old-fashioned*) (of a person) slow to learn or to understand things because of a problem with the brain HELP It is now more usual to say that people with this kind of problem **have learning difficulties.**

men·tee /ˌmenˈtiː/ *noun* a person who is advised and helped by a more experienced person over a period of time: *the mentor/mentee relationship* ➲ compare MENTOR

men·thol /ˈmenθɒl; *NAmE* -θɔːl; -θɑːl/ *noun* [U] a substance that tastes and smells of MINT, that is used in some medicines for colds and to give a strong cool flavour to cigarettes, TOOTHPASTE, etc.

men·thol·ated /ˈmenθəleɪtɪd/ *adj.* containing menthol: *mentholated sweets*

men·tion 🗝 /ˈmenʃn/ *verb, noun*

■ ***verb*** 🗝 to write or speak about sth/sb, especially without giving much information: **~ sth/sb** (**to sb**) *Nobody mentioned anything to me about it.* ◇ *Sorry, I won't mention it again.* ◇ ***Now that you mention it****, she did seem to be in a strange mood.* ◇ **~ sth/sb as sth/sb** *His name has been mentioned as a future MP.* ◇ **~ where, why, etc...** *Did she mention where she was going?* ◇ **~ that...** *You mentioned in your letter that you might be moving abroad.* ◇ **~ doing sth** *Did I mention going to see Vicky on Sunday?* ➲ see also ABOVE-MENTIONED, AFOREMENTIONED

IDM **don't ˈmention it** 🗝 (*informal*) used as a polite answer when sb has thanked you for sth SYN **you're welcome**: *'Thanks for all your help.' 'Don't mention it.'* **not to mention** used to introduce extra information and emphasize what you are saying: *He has two big houses in this country, not to mention his villa in France.*

■ ***noun*** [U, C, usually sing.] an act of referring to sb/sth in speech or writing: *He* ***made no mention of*** *her work.* ◇ *The concert didn't even* ***get a mention*** *in the newspapers.* ◇ *Phil deserves (a)* ***special mention*** *for all the help he gave us.*

Synonyms

mention

refer to sb/sth • speak • cite • quote

These words all mean to write or speak about sb/sth, often in order to give an example or prove sth.

mention to write or speak about sth/sb, especially without giving much information: *Nobody mentioned anything to me about it.*

refer to sb/sth (*rather formal*) to mention or speak about sb/sth: *I promised not to refer to the matter again.*

speak to mention or describe sb/sth: *Witnesses* ***spoke of*** *a great ball of flame.*

cite (*formal*) to mention sth as a reason or an example, or in order to support what you are saying: *He cited his heavy workload as the reason for his breakdown.*

quote to mention an example of sth to support what you are saying: *Can you quote me an instance of when this happened?*

CITE OR QUOTE?

You can **cite** reasons or examples, but you can only **quote** examples: ~~*He quoted his heavy workload as the reason for his breakdown.*~~ **Cite** is a more formal word than **quote** and is often used in more formal situations, for example in descriptions of legal cases.

PATTERNS

- to mention/refer to/speak of/cite/quote sb/sth **as** sb/sth
- to mention/refer to/cite/quote a(n) **example/instance/case** of sth
- **frequently/often** mentioned/referred to/spoken of/cited/quoted
- the example mentioned/referred to/cited/quoted **above/earlier/previously**

men·tor /ˈmentɔː(r)/ *noun* an experienced person who advises and helps sb with less experience over a period of time ➲ compare MENTEE ▶ **men·tor·ing** *noun* [U]: *a mentoring programme*

menu 🗝 /ˈmenjuː/ *noun*

1 🗝 a list of the food that is available at a restaurant or to be served at a meal: *to ask* ***for/look*** *at the* ***menu*** ◇ *What's*

M

on the menu (= for dinner) *tonight?* ➲ COLLOCATIONS at RESTAURANT **2** 0‑w (*computing*) a list of possible choices that are shown on a computer screen: *a pull-down menu* ➲ see also DROP-DOWN MENU

'menu bar *noun* (*computing*) a horizontal bar at the top of a computer screen that contains PULL-DOWN menus such as 'File', 'Edit' and 'Help'

meow (*especially NAmE*) (*BrE* usually **miaow**) /mi'aʊ/ *noun* the crying sound made by a cat ➲ see also MEW ▸ **meow** (*especially NAmE*) (*BrE* usually **miaow**) *verb* [I]

MEP /ˌem iː 'piː/ *noun* the abbreviation for 'Member of the European Parliament': *the Labour MEP for South East Wales*

Meph·is·toph·elian /ˌmefɪstə'fiːliən; *NAmE* also ˌmefɪˌstɑːfə'liən/ *adj.* (*formal*) very evil; like the DEVIL ORIGIN From **Mephistopheles**, an evil spirit to whom, according to the German legend, Faust sold his soul.

mer·can·tile /'mɜːkəntaɪl; *NAmE* 'mɜːrk-; -tiːl/ *adj.* (*formal*) connected with trade and commercial affairs

mer·can·ti·lism /mɜː'kæntɪlɪzəm; *NAmE* mɜːr'k-/ *noun* [U] the economic theory that trade increases wealth ▸ **mer·can·ti·list** /-lɪst/ *adj.* **mer·can·ti·list** *noun*

Mer·ca·tor projection /mɜː'keɪtə prədʒekʃn; *NAmE* mɜːr'keɪtər/ *noun* [sing.] a traditional map of the world, on which the relative size of some countries is not accurate ➲ compare PETERS PROJECTION

mer·cen·ary /'mɜːsənəri; *NAmE* 'mɜːrsəneri/ *noun, adj.*
- ***noun*** (*pl.* -ies) a soldier who will fight for any country or group that offers payment: *foreign mercenaries* ◇ *mercenary soldiers*
- ***adj.*** (*disapproving*) only interested in making or getting money: *a **mercenary society/attitude*** ◇ *She's interested in him for purely mercenary reasons.*

M

mer·chan·dise *noun, verb*
- ***noun*** /'mɜːtʃəndaɪs; -daɪz; *NAmE* 'mɜːrtʃ-/ [U] **1** (*formal*) goods that are bought or sold; goods that are for sale in a shop/store: *a wide selection of merchandise* ➲ SYNONYMS at PRODUCT **2** things you can buy that are connected with or that advertise a particular event or organization: *official Olympic merchandise*
- ***verb*** /'mɜːtʃəndaɪz; *NAmE* 'mɜːrtʃ-/ **~ sth** to sell sth using advertising, etc.

mer·chan·dis·ing /'mɜːtʃəndaɪzɪŋ; *NAmE* 'mɜːrtʃ-/ *noun* [U] **1** (*especially NAmE*) the activity of selling goods, or of trying to sell them, by advertising or displaying them **2** products connected with a popular film/movie, person or event; the process of selling these goods: *millions of pounds' worth of Batman merchandising*

mer·chant /'mɜːtʃənt; *NAmE* 'mɜːrtʃ-/ *noun, adj.*
- ***noun*** **1** a person who buys and sells goods in large quantities, especially one who imports and exports goods: ***builders' merchants*** (= who sell supplies to the building trade) ◇ *a **coal/wine merchant*** ◇ *Venice was once a city of rich merchants.* ➲ see also SQUEEGEE MERCHANT **2** (*BrE, informal, disapproving*) a person who likes a particular activity: *a speed merchant* (= sb who likes to drive fast) ◇ *noise merchants* (= for example, a band who make a lot of noise) IDM see DOOM *n.*
- ***adj.*** [only before noun] connected with the transport of goods by sea: *merchant seamen*

mer·chant·able /'mɜːtʃəntəbl; *NAmE* 'mɜːrtʃ-/ *adj.* (*law*) in a good enough condition to be sold: *of merchantable quality*

ˌmerchant 'bank (*BrE*) (*NAmE* **in'vestment bank**) *noun* a bank that deals with large businesses ▸ **ˌmerchant 'banker** *noun* **ˌmerchant 'banking** *noun* [U]

mer·chant·man /'mɜːtʃəntmən; *NAmE* 'mɜːrtʃ-/ (*pl.* -men /-mən/) (also **'merchant ship**) *noun* a ship used for carrying goods for trade rather than a military ship

ˌmerchant 'navy (*BrE*) (*NAmE* **ˌmerchant ma'rine**) *noun* [C+sing./pl. v.] a country's commercial ships and the people who work on them

mer·ci·ful /'mɜːsɪfl; *NAmE* 'mɜːrs-/ *adj.* **1** ready to forgive people and show them kindness SYN **humane**: *a merciful God* ◇ *They asked her to be merciful to the prisoners.* **2** (of an event) seeming to be lucky, especially because it brings an end to sb's problems or suffering: *Death came as a merciful release.* ➲ see also MERCY

mer·ci·ful·ly /'mɜːsɪfəli; *NAmE* 'mɜːrs-/ *adv.* **1** used to show that you feel sb/sth is lucky because a situation could have been much worse SYN **thankfully**: *Deaths from the disease are mercifully rare.* ◇ *Mercifully, everyone arrived on time.* **2** in a kind way: *He was treated mercifully.*

mer·ci·less /'mɜːsɪləs; *NAmE* 'mɜːrs-/ *adj.* showing no kindness or pity SYN **cruel**: *a **merciless killer/attack*** ◇ *the merciless heat of the sun* ▸ **mer·ci·less·ly** *adv.* ➲ see also MERCY

mer·cur·ial /mɜː'kjʊəriəl; *NAmE* mɜːr'kjʊr-/ *adj.* **1** (*literary*) often changing or reacting in a way that is unexpected SYN **volatile**: *Emily's mercurial temperament made her difficult to live with.* **2** (*literary*) lively and quick: *a brilliant, mercurial mind* **3** (*technical*) containing MERCURY

Mer·cury /'mɜːkjəri; *NAmE* 'mɜːrk-/ *noun* the smallest planet in the SOLAR SYSTEM, nearest to the sun

mer·cury /'mɜːkjəri; *NAmE* 'mɜːrk-/ *noun* [U] (*symb.* **Hg**) a chemical element. Mercury is a poisonous silver liquid metal, used in THERMOMETERS.

mercy /'mɜːsi; *NAmE* 'mɜːrsi/ *noun* (*pl.* -ies) **1** [U] a kind or forgiving attitude towards sb that you have the power to harm or right to punish SYN **humanity**: *to **ask/beg/plead for mercy*** ◇ *They **showed no mercy** to their hostages.* ◇ *God **have mercy on** us.* ◇ *The troops are on **a mercy mission*** (= a journey to help people) *in the war zone.* **2** [C, usually sing.] (*informal*) an event or a situation to be grateful for, usually because it stops sth unpleasant: ***It's a mercy** she wasn't seriously hurt.* ➲ see also MERCIFUL, MERCILESS

IDM **at the mercy of sb/sth** not able to stop sb/sth harming you because they have power or control over you: *I'm not going to put myself at the mercy of the bank.* ◇ *We were at the mercy of the weather.* **leave sb/sth to the mercy/mercies of sb/sth** to leave sb/sth in a situation that may cause them to suffer or to be treated badly **throw yourself on sb's mercy** (*formal*) to put yourself in a situation where you must rely on sb to be kind to you and not harm or punish you ➲ more at SMALL *adj.*

'mercy killing *noun* [C, U] the act of killing sb out of pity, for example because they are in severe pain SYN **euthanasia**

mere 0‑w /mɪə(r); *NAmE* mɪr/ *adj., noun*
- ***adj.*** [only before noun] (*superlative* **mer·est**, no *comparative*) **1** 0‑w used when you want to emphasize how small, unimportant, etc. sb/sth is: *It took her a mere 20 minutes to win.* ◇ *A mere 2% of their budget has been spent on publicity.* ◇ *He seemed so young, a mere boy.* ◇ *You've got the job. The interview will be a mere formality.* **2** used when you are saying that the fact that a particular thing is present in a situation is enough to have an influence on that situation: *His mere presence* (= just the fact that he was there) *made her feel afraid.* ◇ *The **mere fact that** they were prepared to talk was encouraging.* ◇ *The **mere thought of** eating made him feel sick.* ◇ *The merest* (= the slightest) *hint of smoke is enough to make her feel ill.*
- ***noun*** (*BrE, literary*) (also used in names) a small lake

mere·ly 0‑w /'mɪəli; *NAmE* 'mɪrli/ *adv.* used meaning 'only' or 'simply' to emphasize a fact or sth that you are saying: *It is **not merely** a job, but a way of life.* ◇ *He said nothing, merely smiled and watched her.* ◇ *They agreed to go merely because they were getting paid for it.* ◇ *I'm merely stating what everybody knows anyway.*

mere·tri·cious /ˌmerə'trɪʃəs/ *adj.* (*formal*) seeming attractive, but in fact having no real value

merge /mɜːdʒ; *NAmE* mɜːrdʒ/ *verb* **1** [I, T] to combine or make two or more things combine to form a single thing: *The banks are set to merge next year.* ◇ *The two groups have merged to form a new party.* ◇ **~ with sth** *His department will merge with mine.* ◇ **~ into sth** *The villages expanded and merged into one large town.* ◇ **~ (A and B) (together)** *Fact* *and fiction merge together in his latest thriller.* ◇ **~ A with B** *His department will be merged with mine.* ◇ **~ sth** *The company was formed by merging three smaller firms.* **2** [I] **~ (into sth)** if two things **merge**, or if one thing **merges into** another, the differences between them gradually disappear so that it is impossible to separate them: *The hills merged into the dark sky behind them.*

IDM **merge into the 'background** (of a person) to behave quietly when you are with a group of people so that they do not notice you

mer·ger /'mɜːdʒə(r); *NAmE* 'mɜːrdʒ-/ *noun* [C] the act of joining two or more organizations or businesses into one: **~ (between/of A and B)** *a merger between the two banks* ◇ **~ (with sth)** *our proposed merger with the university* ➲ COLLOCATIONS at BUSINESS

me·rid·ian /mə'rɪdiən/ *noun* one of the lines that is drawn from the North Pole to the South Pole on a map of the world

mer·ingue /mə'ræŋ/ *noun* [U, C] a sweet white mixture made from egg whites and sugar, usually baked until crisp and used to make cakes; a small cake made from this mixture: *a lemon meringue pie*

me·rino /mə'riːnəʊ; *NAmE* -noʊ/ *noun* (*pl.* -os) **1** [C] a breed of sheep with long fine wool **2** [U] the wool of the merino sheep or a type of cloth made from this wool, used for making clothes

merit /'merɪt/ *noun, verb*

■ ***noun*** **1** [U] (*formal*) the quality of being good and of deserving praise, reward or admiration SYN **worth**: *a work of outstanding artistic merit* ◇ *The plan is entirely without merit.* ◇ *I want to get the job* ***on merit***. **2** [C, usually pl.] a good feature that deserves praise, reward or admiration SYN **strength**: *We will* ***consider each case on its*** **(*own*)** ***merits*** (= without considering any other issues, feelings, etc.). ◇ *They weighed up the* ***relative merits*** *of the four candidates.* **3** [C] (*BrE*) a mark/grade in an exam or for a piece of work at school or university which is excellent **4** [C] (*BrE*) a mark/grade given as a reward for good behaviour at school

■ ***verb*** (not used in the progressive tenses) **~ (doing) sth** (*formal*) to do sth to deserve praise, attention, etc. SYN **deserve**: *He claims that their success was not merited.* ◇ *The case does not merit further investigation.*

mer·it·oc·racy /ˌmerɪ'tɒkrəsi; *NAmE* -'tɑːk-/ *noun* (*pl.* -ies) **1** [C, U] a country or social system where people get power or money on the basis of their ability **2 the meritocracy** [sing.] the group of people with power in this kind of social system ▸ **mer·ito·crat·ic** /ˌmerɪtə'krætɪk/ *adj.*

meri·tori·ous /ˌmerɪ'tɔːriəs/ *adj.* (*formal*) deserving praise SYN **praiseworthy**

mer·lin /'mɜːlɪn; *NAmE* 'mɜːrlɪn/ *noun* a small BIRD OF PREY (= a bird that kills other creatures for food) of the FALCON family

mer·maid /'mɜːmeɪd; *NAmE* 'mɜːrm-/ *noun* (in stories) a creature with a woman's head and body, and a fish's tail instead of legs

mer·man /'mɜːmæn; *NAmE* 'mɜːr-/ *noun* (*pl.* -men /-men/) (in stories) a creature with a man's head and body and a fish's tail instead of legs, like a male MERMAID

mer·rily /'merəli/ *adv.* **1** in a happy, cheerful way: *They chatted merrily.* **2** without thinking about the problems that your actions might cause SYN **gaily**: *She carried on merrily, not realizing the offence she was causing.*

mer·ri·ment /'merimənt/ *noun* [U] (*formal*) happy talk, enjoyment and the sound of people laughing SYN **jollity, mirth**

merry /'meri/ *adj.* (**mer·rier, mer·ri·est**) **1** happy and cheerful SYN **cheery**: *a merry grin* **2 Merry Christmas** used at Christmas to say that you hope that sb has an enjoyable holiday **3** (*informal, especially BrE*) slightly drunk SYN **tipsy**

IDM **make 'merry** (*old-fashioned*) to enjoy yourself by singing, laughing, drinking, etc. **the ˌmore the 'merrier** (*saying*) the more people or things there are, the better the situation will be or the more fun people will have: *'Can I bring a friend to your party?' 'Sure—the more the merrier!'* ➲ more at EAT, HELL, LEAD[1] *v.*

'merry-go-round *noun* **1** (also **car·ou·sel** especially in *NAmE*) (*BrE* also **round·about**) a round platform with model horses, cars, etc. that turns around and around and that children ride on at a FAIRGROUND ➲ picture at ROUNDABOUT **2** (*NAmE*) (*BrE* **round·about**) a round platform for children to play on in a park, etc. that is pushed round while the children are sitting on it **3** continuous busy activity or a continuous series of changing events: *He was tired of the merry-go-round of romance and longed to settle down.*

merry·mak·ing /'merimeɪkɪŋ/ *noun* [U] (*literary*) fun and enjoyment with singing, laughing, drinking, etc. SYN **revelry**

mesa /'meɪsə/ *noun* (*pl.* **mesas**) a hill with a flat top and steep sides that is common in the south-west of the US

mes·cal /'meskæl; me'skæl/ *noun* = PEYOTE

mes·ca·line (also **mes·ca·lin**) /'meskəlɪn/ *noun* [U] a drug obtained from a type of CACTUS, that affects people's minds and makes them see and hear things that are not really there

mesh /meʃ/ *noun, verb*

■ ***noun*** **1** [U, C] material made of threads of plastic rope or wire that are twisted together like a net: *wire mesh over the door of the cage* **2** [C, usually sing.] a complicated situation or system that it is difficult to escape from SYN **web**

■ ***verb*** (*formal*) **1** [I, T] to fit together or match closely, especially in a way that works well; to make things fit together successfully: **~ (sth) (with sth)** *This evidence meshes with earlier reports of an organized riot.* ◇ **~ (sth) (together)** *His theories mesh together various political and religious beliefs.* **2** [I] (*technical*) (of parts of a machine) to fit together as they move: *If the cogs don't mesh correctly, the gears will keep slipping.*

mes·mer·ic /mez'merɪk/ *adj.* [usually before noun] (*formal*) having such a strong effect on people that they cannot give their attention to anything else SYN **hypnotic**

mes·mer·ize (*BrE* also **-ise**) /'mezməraɪz/ *verb* [usually passive] **~ sb** to have such a strong effect on you that you cannot give your attention to anything else SYN **fascinate** ▸ **mes·mer·iz·ing, -is·ing** *adj.*: *Her performance was mesmerizing.*

meso·phyll /'mezəfɪl; 'miːz-; *BrE* also 'mes-; miːs-/ *noun* [U] (*biology*) the material that the inside of a leaf is made of

meso·sphere /'mezəsfɪə(r); 'miːz-; *NAmE* -sfɪr/ *noun* [usually sing.] the part of the earth's atmosphere which is between 50 and 80 kilometres from the ground, between the STRATOSPHERE and the THERMOSPHERE

mes·quite /me'skiːt; 'meskiːt/ (also **me'squite tree**) *noun* a N American tree, often used for making CHARCOAL for GRILLING food: *mesquite-grilled chicken*

mess O- /mes/ *noun, verb*

■ ***noun***

▸ UNTIDY STATE **1** O- [C, usually sing.] a dirty or untidy state: *The room was* ***in a mess***. ◇ *The kids* ***made a mess*** *in the bathroom.* ◇ ***'What a mess!'*** *she said, surveying the scene after the party.* ◇ *My hair's a real mess!*

▸ DIFFICULT SITUATION **2** O- [C, usually sing.] a situation that is full of problems, usually because of a lack of organization or because of mistakes that sb has made: *The economy is* ***in a mess***. ◇ *I feel I've* ***made a mess of*** *things.* ◇ *The whole situation is a mess.* ◇ *Let's try to sort out the mess.* ◇ *The biggest question is how they got into this mess in the first place.*

▸ PERSON **3** [sing.] a person who is dirty or whose clothes and hair are not tidy: *You're a mess!* **4** [sing.] (*informal*) a person who has serious problems and is in a bad mental condition

▸ ANIMAL WASTE **5** [U, C] (*informal*) the EXCREMENT (= solid waste matter) of an animal, usually a dog or cat

▸ A LOT **6** [sing.] **a ~ of sth** (*NAmE, informal*) a lot of sth: *There's a mess of fish down there, so get your lines in the water.*

M

▸ ARMED FORCES **7** [C] (also **'mess hall** especially in *NAmE*) a building or room in which members of the armed forces have their meals: *the officers' mess*

■ *verb*

▸ MAKE UNTIDY **1** [T] **~ sth** (*informal, especially NAmE*) to make sth dirty or untidy: *Careful—you're messing my hair.*

▸ OF AN ANIMAL **2** [I] to empty its BOWELS somewhere that it should not

IDM **,no 'messing** (*informal*) used to say that sth has been done easily: *We finished in time, no messing.* **not mess a'round** (*BrE* also **not mess a'bout**) (*informal*) to do sth quickly, efficiently or in the right way: *When they decide to have a party they don't mess around.*

PHR V **,mess a'round** (*BrE* also **,mess a'bout**) **1** to behave in a silly and annoying way, especially instead of doing sth useful SYN **fool around**: *Will you stop messing around and get on with some work?* **2** to spend time doing sth for pleasure in a relaxed way: *We spent the day messing around on the river.* **,mess a'round with sb** (*BrE* also **,mess a'bout with sb**) to have a sexual relationship with sb, especially when you should not **,mess a'round with sth** (*BrE* also **,mess a'bout with sth**) **1** to touch or use sth in a careless and/or annoying way: *Who's been messing around with my computer?* **2** to spend time playing with sth, repairing sth, etc. **,mess sb a'bout/a'round** (*BrE*) to treat sb in an unfair and annoying way, especially by changing your mind a lot or not doing what you said you would **,mess 'up** | **,mess sth↔'up** to spoil sth or do it badly: *I've really messed up this time.* ◇ *If you cancel now you'll mess up all my arrangements.* **,mess sb↔'up 1** (*informal*) to cause sb to have serious emotional or mental problems **2** (*NAmE, informal*) to physically hurt sb, especially by hitting them: *He was messed up pretty bad by the other guy.* **,mess sth↔'up** to make sth dirty or untidy: *I don't want you messing up my nice clean kitchen.* **'mess with sb/sth** (usually used in negative sentences) to get involved with sb/sth that may be harmful: *I wouldn't mess with him if I were you.*

mes·sage 0-w /'mesɪdʒ/ *noun, verb*

■ *noun* **1** 0-w a written or spoken piece of information, etc. that you send to sb or leave for sb when you cannot speak to them yourself: *There were no messages for me at the hotel.* ◇ *We've had an urgent message saying that your father's ill.* ◇ *Jenny's not here at the moment.* ***Can I take a message?*** ◇ *I* ***left a message*** *on her voicemail.* ◇ *I've been trying to get you all day—don't you ever listen to your messages?* **~** (**from sb**) (**to sb**) ◇ *Messages of support have been arriving from all over the country* ◇ *a televised message from the President to the American people* ➲ see also ERROR MESSAGE **2** 0-w a piece of information sent in electronic form, for example by email or mobile/cell phone: *an email message* ◇ *There were four messages in my inbox.* ◇ *He sent me a message.* **3** 0-w [usually sing.] an important moral, social or political idea that a book, speech, etc. is trying to communicate: *a film with a strong religious message* ◇ *The campaign is trying to* ***get the message across*** *to young people that drugs are dangerous.* **4** a piece of information that is sent from the brain to a part of the body, or from a part of the body to the brain: *The message arrives in your brain in a fraction of a second.* **5 messages** [pl.] (*ScotE*) shopping: *to do the messages* ◇ *to go for the messages* ◇ *You can leave your messages* (= the things that you have bought) *here.*

IDM **get the 'message** (*informal*) to understand what sb is trying to tell you indirectly: *When he started looking at his watch, I got the message and left.* **on/off 'message** (of a politician) stating/not stating the official view of their political party

■ *verb* to send a TEXT MESSAGE to sb: **~ sb** *Fiona just messaged me.* ◇ **~ sb sth** *Brian messaged me the news.* ▸ **mes·saging** *noun* [U]: *a multimedia messaging service* ◇ *picture messaging*

'message board *noun* a place on a website where a user can write or read messages: *I posted a question on the message board.*

mes·sen·ger /'mesɪndʒə(r)/ *noun* a person who gives a message to sb or who delivers messages to people as a job: *He sent the order by messenger.* ◇ *a motorcycle messenger*
IDM see SHOOT *v.*

Mes·siah /mə'saɪə/ *noun* **1 the Messiah** [sing.] (in Christianity) Jesus Christ who was sent by God into the world to save people from evil and SIN **2 the Messiah** [sing.] (in Judaism) a king who will be sent by God to save the Jewish people **3 messiah** a leader who people believe will solve the problems of a country or the world SYN **saviour**: *He's seen by many as a political messiah.*

mes·si·an·ic /,mesi'ænɪk/ *adj.* (*formal*) **1** relating to a messiah **2** attempting to make big changes in society or to a political system in an extremely determined and enthusiastic way: *The reforms were carried out with an almost messianic zeal.*

Messrs (*BrE*) (*NAmE* **Messrs.**) /'mesəz; *NAmE* -sərz/ *abbr.* (used as the plural of 'Mr' before a list of names and before names of business companies): *Messrs Smith, Brown and Jones* ◇ *Messrs T Brown and Co*

messy /'mesi/ *adj.* (**mess·ier**, **messi·est**) **1** dirty and/or untidy SYN **chaotic**: *The house was always messy.* ◇ (*NAmE*) *Her long black hair was messy and dirty.* **2** making sb/sth dirty and/or untidy: *It was a messy job.* **3** (of a situation) unpleasant, confused or difficult to deal with: *The divorce was painful and messy.*

mes·tiza /me'sti:zə/ *noun* a female MESTIZO

mes·tizo /me'sti:zəʊ; *NAmE* -zoʊ/ *noun* (*pl.* **-os**) a Latin American who has both Spanish and Native American ANCESTORS

Met /met/ *abbr.* (*informal*) **1** METEOROLOGICAL: *the Met Office weather forecast service* **2 the Met** the Metropolitan Opera House (in New York) **3 the Met** the Metropolitan Police (the police force in London)

met *past tense, past part.* of MEET

meta- /'metə/ *combining form* (in nouns, adjectives and verbs) **1** connected with a change of position or state: *metamorphosis* ◇ *metabolism* **2** higher; beyond: *metaphysics* ◇ *metalanguage*

me·tab·ol·ism /mə'tæbəlɪzəm/ *noun* [U, sing.] (*biology*) the chemical processes in living things that change food, etc. into energy and materials for growth: *The body's metabolism is slowed down by extreme cold.* ▸ **meta·bol·ic** /,metə'bɒlɪk; *NAmE* -'bɑ:l-/ *adj.* [usually before noun]: *a* ***metabolic process/disorder*** ◇ *a* ***high/low metabolic rate***

me·tab·ol·ize (*BrE* also **-ise**) /mə'tæbəlaɪz/ *verb* **~ sth** (*biology*) to turn food, minerals, etc. in the body into new cells, energy and waste products by means of chemical processes

meta·car·pal /,metə'kɑ:pl; *NAmE* -'kɑ:rpl/ *noun* (*anatomy*) any of the five bones in the hand between the wrist and the fingers

meta·data /'metədeɪtə; -dɑ:tə; *NAmE* also -dætə/ *noun* [U] information that describes other information in order to help you understand or use it: *In the metadata she found the author and location of the file.*

meta·fic·tion /'metəfɪkʃn/ *noun* [U] a type of play, novel, etc. in which the author deliberately reminds the audience, reader, etc. that it is FICTION and not real life

metal 0-w /'metl/ *noun* [C, U]
a type of solid mineral substance that is usually hard and shiny and that heat and electricity can travel through, for example tin, iron and gold: *a piece of metal* ◇ *a* ***metal pipe/bar/box*** ◇ *The frame is made of metal.* ➲ see also HEAVY METAL, PRECIOUS METAL

meta·lan·guage /'metəlæŋgwɪdʒ/ *noun* [C, U] (*linguistics*) the words and phrases that people use to talk about or describe language or a particular language

'metal detector *noun* **1** an electronic device that you use to look for metal objects that are buried under the ground **2** an electronic machine that is used, for example at an airport, to see if people are hiding metal objects such as weapons

ˈ**metal fatigue** *noun* [U] weakness in metal that is frequently put under pressure that makes it likely to break

meta·lin·guis·tic /ˈmetəlɪŋɡwɪstɪk/ *adj.* (*linguistics*) related to metalanguage ▶ **meta·lin·guis·tics** /ˈmetəlɪŋɡwɪstɪks/ *noun* [U]

met·alled /ˈmetld/ *adj.* (of a road or track) made or repaired with small pieces of broken stone

me·tal·lic /məˈtælɪk/ *adj.* [usually before noun] **1** that looks, tastes or sounds like metal: ***metallic paint/colours/blue*** ◇ *a metallic taste* ◇ *a **metallic sound/click*** ◇ *a metallic voice* (= that sounds unpleasant) **2** made of or containing metal: *a metallic object* ◇ *metallic compounds*

met·al·loid /ˈmetlɔɪd/ (*BrE* also **semi·metal**) *noun* (*chemistry*) a chemical element which has properties both of metals and of other solid substances

me·tal·lur·gist /məˈtælədʒɪst; *NAmE* ˈmetlɜːrdʒɪst/ *noun* a scientist who studies metallurgy

me·tal·lurgy /məˈtælədʒi; *NAmE* ˈmetlɜːrdʒi/ *noun* [U] the scientific study of metals and their uses ▶ **me·tal·lur·gical** /ˌmetəˈlɜːdʒɪkl; *NAmE* ˌmetlˈɜːrdʒ-/ *adj.*

met·al·work /ˈmetlwɜːk; *NAmE* -wɜːrk/ *noun* [U] **1** the activity of making objects out of metal; objects that are made out of metal **2** the metal parts of sth: *cracks in the metalwork* ▶ **met·al·work·er** *noun*

meta·morph·ic /ˌmetəˈmɔːfɪk; *NAmE* -ˈmɔːrf-/ *adj.* (*geology*) (of rocks) formed by the action of heat or pressure

meta·morph·ose /ˌmetəˈmɔːfəʊz; *NAmE* -ˈmɔːrfoʊz/ *verb* [I, T] **~ (sth/sb) (from sth) (into sth)** (*formal*) to change or make sth/sb change into sth completely different, especially over a period of time **SYN** **transform**: *The caterpillar will eventually metamorphose into a butterfly.*

meta·mor·phosis /ˌmetəˈmɔːfəsɪs; *NAmE* -ˈmɔːrf-/ *noun* (*pl.* **meta·mor·phoses** /-əsiːz/) [C, U] (*formal*) a process in which sb/sth changes completely into sth different **SYN** **transformation**: *the metamorphosis of a caterpillar into a butterfly* ◇ *She had undergone an amazing metamorphosis from awkward schoolgirl to beautiful woman.*

meta·phor /ˈmetəfə(r); -fɔː(r)/ *noun* [C, U] a word or phrase used to describe sb/sth else, in a way that is different from its normal use, in order to show that the two things have the same qualities and to make the description more powerful, for example *She has a heart of stone*; the use of such words and phrases: *a game of football used as a metaphor for the competitive struggle of life* ◇ *the writer's striking use of metaphor* ➲ COLLOCATIONS at LITERATURE ➲ compare SIMILE

meta·phor·ical /ˌmetəˈfɒrɪkl; *NAmE* -ˈfɔːr-/ *adj.* connected with or containing metaphors: *metaphorical language* ➲ compare FIGURATIVE, LITERAL ▶ **meta·phor·ic·al·ly** /-kli/ *adv.*: *I'll leave you in Robin's capable hands—**metaphorically speaking**, of course!*

metaˌphysical ˈpoets *noun* [pl.] a group of 17th century English POETS who explored the nature of the world and human life, and who used images that were surprising at that time

meta·phys·ics /ˌmetəˈfɪzɪks/ *noun* [U] the branch of philosophy that deals with the nature of existence, truth and knowledge ▶ **meta·phys·ic·al** /ˌmetəˈfɪzɪkl/ *adj.*: ***metaphysical problems/speculation***

me·tas·ta·sis /məˈtæstəsɪs/ *noun* [U] (*medical*) the development of TUMOURS in different parts of the body resulting from cancer that has started in another part of the body ▶ **me·tas·ta·tic** /ˌmetəˈstætɪk/ *adj.*

meta·tar·sal /ˌmetəˈtɑːsl; *NAmE* -ˈtɑːrsl/ *noun* (*anatomy*) any of the bones in the part of the foot between the ankle and the toes

mete /miːt/ *verb*

PHR V ˌ**mete sth↔ˈout (to sb)** (*formal*) to give sb a punishment; to make sb suffer bad treatment: *Severe penalties were meted out by the court.* ◇ *the violence meted out to the prisoners*

me·teor /ˈmiːtiə(r); -iɔː(r)/ *noun* a piece of rock from outer space that makes a bright line across the night sky as it burns up while falling through the earth's atmosphere: *a meteor shower* ➲ see also SHOOTING STAR

me·teor·ic /ˌmiːtiˈɒrɪk; *NAmE* -ˈɔːr-/ *adj.* **1** achieving success very quickly: *a meteoric rise to fame* ◇ *a meteoric career* **2** connected with meteors: *meteoric craters*

me·teor·ite /ˈmiːtiəraɪt/ *noun* a piece of rock from outer space that hits the earth's surface

me·teor·olo·gist /ˌmiːtiəˈrɒlədʒɪst; *NAmE* -ˈrɑːl-/ *noun* a scientist who studies meteorology

me·teor·ology /ˌmiːtiəˈrɒlədʒi; *NAmE* -ˈrɑːl-/ *noun* [U] the scientific study of the earth's atmosphere and its changes, used especially in forecasting the weather (= saying what it will be like) ▶ **me·teoro·logic·al** /ˌmiːtiərəˈlɒdʒɪkl; *NAmE* -ˈlɑːdʒ-/ *adj.*

meter /ˈmiːtə(r)/ *noun, verb*

■ ***noun*** **1** (especially in compounds) a device that measures and records the amount of electricity, gas, water, etc. that you have used or the time and distance you have travelled, etc: *A man came to read the gas meter.* ◇ *The cab driver left the meter running while he waited for us.* ➲ see also LIGHT METER **2** = PARKING METER **3 -meter** (in compounds) a device for measuring the thing mentioned: *speedometer* ◇ *altimeter* ◇ *calorimeter* **4** (*NAmE*) = METRE: *Who holds the record in the 100 meters?*

■ ***verb*** **~ sth** to measure sth (for example how much gas, electricity, etc. has been used) using a meter

meth /meθ/ (also **crystal meth, crystal**) *noun* [U] (*informal*) a powerful illegal drug, METHAMPHETAMINE, that looks like small pieces of glass: *the growing meth problem in our rural communities*

metha·done /ˈmeθədəʊn; *NAmE* -doʊn/ *noun* [U] a drug that is used to treat people who are trying to stop taking the illegal drug HEROIN

meth·am·pheta·mine /ˌmeθæmˈfetəmiːn/ (also *informal* **meth**, ˈ**crystal meth**) *noun* [U] a powerful illegal drug

me·thane /ˈmiːθeɪn; *NAmE* ˈmeθ-/ *noun* [U] (*symb.* CH_4) a gas without colour or smell, that burns easily and is used as fuel. Natural gas consists mainly of methane.

metha·nol /ˈmeθənɒl; *NAmE* -nɔːl; -noʊl/ *noun* [U] (*symb.* CH_3OH) a poisonous form of alcohol formed when METHANE reacts with OXYGEN

methi·cil·lin /ˌmeθɪˈsɪlɪn/ *noun* [U] a drug that can be used against infections where PENICILLIN is not effective

me·thinks /mɪˈθɪŋks/ *verb* (*pt* **me·thought**) (not used in the perfect tenses) [I, T] **~ (that)...** (*old use* or *humorous*) I think

method 🔑 **AW** /ˈmeθəd/ *noun*

1 🔑 [C] a particular way of doing sth: **~ (of sth)** *a **reliable/effective/scientific method** of data analysis* ◇ **~ (of doing sth)** *a new method of solving the problem* ◇ ***traditional/alternative methods*** ◇ **~ (for sth/for doing sth)** *the best method for arriving at an accurate prediction of the costs* ➲ see also DIRECT METHOD **2** [U] the quality of being well planned and organized

IDM **there's (a) method in sb's madness** there is a reason for sb's behaviour and it is not as strange or as stupid as it seems

ˈ**method acting** *noun* [U] a method of preparing for a role in which an actor tries to experience the life and feelings of the character he or she will play ▶ ˈ**method actor** *noun*

meth·od·ic·al **AW** /məˈθɒdɪkl; *NAmE* -ˈθɑːd-/ *adj.* **1** done in a careful and logical way: *a **methodical approach/study*** **2** (of a person) doing things in a careful and logical way **SYN** **disciplined, precise**: *to have a methodical mind* ▶ **meth·od·ic·al·ly** /-kli/ *adv.*: *They sorted slowly and methodically through the papers.*

Meth·od·ist /ˈmeθədɪst/ *noun* a member of a Christian Protestant Church that broke away from the Church of England in the 18th century ▶ **Meth·od·ism** /ˈmeθədɪzəm/ *noun* [U] **Meth·od·ist** *adj.*: *a **Methodist church/preacher***

M

meth·od·ology AW /ˌmeθəˈdɒlədʒi; *NAmE* -ˈdɑːl-/ *noun* (*pl.* -ies) [C, U] (*formal*) a set of methods and principles used to perform a particular activity: *recent changes in the methodology of language teaching* ▸ **meth·odo·logic·al** AW /ˌmeθədəˈlɒdʒɪkl; *NAmE* -ˈlɑːdʒ-/ *adj.* [usually before noun]: *methodological problems* **meth·odo·logic·al·ly** /-kli/ *adv.*

meths /meθs/ *noun* [U] (*informal, especially BrE*) = METHYLATED SPIRIT

Me·thu·selah /məˈθjuːzələ/ *noun* used to describe a very old person: *I'm feeling older than Methuselah.* ORIGIN From Methuselah, a man in the Bible who is supposed to have lived for 969 years.

meth·yl·ated spirit /ˌmeθəleɪtɪd ˈspɪrɪt/ (also **meth·yl·ated spirits**) (also *informal* **meths**) *noun* [U] a type of alcohol that is not fit for drinking, used as a fuel for lighting and heating and for cleaning off dirty marks

me·ticu·lous /məˈtɪkjələs/ *adj.* paying careful attention to every detail SYN **fastidious, thorough**: ***meticulous planning/records/research*** ◇ **~ in sth/doing sth** *He's always meticulous in keeping the records up to date.* ◇ **~ about sth** *My father was meticulous about his appearance.* ▸ **me·ticu·lous·ly** *adv.*: *a meticulously planned schedule* ◇ *meticulously clean* **me·ticu·lous·ness** *noun* [U]

mé·tier /ˈmetieɪ; *NAmE* ˈmeɪt-/ *noun* [usually sing.] (from *French, formal*) a person's work, especially when they have a natural skill or ability for it

ˈ**me-time** *noun* [U] (*informal*) time when a person who is normally very busy relaxes or does sth they enjoy: *The spa is popular with women who want a bit of me-time.*

Metis /meɪˈtiː/ *noun* (*pl.* **Metis** /meɪˈtiː; meɪˈtiːz/) (*CanE*) (especially in Canada) a person with one Aboriginal parent and one European parent, or a person whose family comes from both Aboriginal and European backgrounds

me·ton·ymy /məˈtɒnəmi; *NAmE* -ˈtɑːn-/ *noun* [U] (*technical*) the act of referring to sth by the name of sth else that is closely connected with it, for example using *the White House* for *the US president*

ˌ**me-ˈtoo** *adj.* [only before noun] (*BrE, informal*) done or produced because of sth successful that sb else has done: *The magazine 'Hello!' gave rise to a number of me-too publications.*

metre 0-w (*especially US* **meter**) /ˈmiːtə(r)/ *noun* **1** 0-w [C] (*abbr.* m) a unit for measuring length; a hundred centimetres **2** [C, U] (*abbr.* m) used in the name of races: *She came second in the 200 metres.* ◇ *the 4 × 100 metre(s) relay* **3** [U, C] the arrangement of strong and weak stresses in lines of poetry that produces the rhythm; a particular example of this

met·ric /ˈmetrɪk/ *adj.* **1** based on the metric system: ***metric units/measurements/sizes*** ◇ *British currency went metric in 1971.* **2** made or measured using the metric system: *These screws are metric.* ⊃ compare IMPERIAL **3** = METRICAL

met·ric·al /ˈmetrɪkl/ (also **met·ric**) *adj.* connected with the rhythm of a poem, produced by the arrangement of stress on the syllables in each line

met·ri·ca·tion /ˌmetrɪˈkeɪʃn/ *noun* [U] the process of changing to using the metric system

the ˈmetric system *noun* [sing.] the system of measurement that uses the metre, the kilogram and the litre as basic units

ˌ**metric ˈton** *noun* = TONNE

metro /ˈmetrəʊ; *NAmE* ˈmetroʊ/ *noun, adj.*

■ ***noun*** (*pl.* -os) **1** (also **the Metro**) [sing.] an underground train system, especially the one in Paris: *to travel* ***on the metro/by metro*** ◇ *the Paris Metro* ◇ *a metro station* ⊃ note at UNDERGROUND **2** (*IndE*) a large or capital city, especially Delhi, Kolkata, Mumbai or Chennai: *Here are the temperatures recorded at the four metros at 5 o'clock this morning.*

■ ***adj.*** (*NAmE, informal*) = METROPOLITAN: *the New York metro areas*

me·trol·ogy /məˈtrɒlədʒi; *NAmE* -ˈtrɑːl-/ *noun* [U] the scientific study of measurement ▸ **me·tro·logic·al** /ˌmetrəˈlɒdʒɪkl; *NAmE* -ˈlɑːdʒ-/ *adj.*

met·ro·nome /ˈmetrənəʊm; *NAmE* -noʊm/ *noun* a device that makes a regular sound like a clock and is used by musicians to help them keep the correct rhythm when playing a piece of music ▸ **met·ro·nom·ic** /ˌmetrəˈnɒmɪk; *NAmE* -ˈnɑːm-/ *adj.*: *His financial problems hit the headlines with almost metronomic regularity.*

metronome

me·trop·olis /məˈtrɒpəlɪs; *NAmE* məˈtrɑːp-/ *noun* a large important city (often the capital city of a country or region)

met·ro·pol·itan /ˌmetrəˈpɒlɪtən; *NAmE* -ˈpɑːl-/ *adj.* [only before noun] **1** (also *NAmE informal* **metro**) connected with a large or capital city: *the New York metropolitan area* ◇ ***metropolitan districts/regions*** **2** connected with a particular country rather than with the other regions of the world that the country controls: ***metropolitan France/Spain***

met·ro·sex·ual /ˌmetrəˈsekʃuəl/ *noun* (*informal*) a HETEROSEXUAL man who lives in a city and is interested in things like fashion and shopping ▸ **met·ro·sex·ual** *adj.*

met·tle /ˈmetl/ *noun* [U] the ability and determination to do sth successfully despite difficult conditions: *The next game will be a real test of their mettle.*

IDM **on your ˈmettle** prepared to use all your skills, knowledge, etc. because you are being tested

mew /mjuː/ *noun* the soft high noise that a cat makes ▸ **mew** *verb* [I]: *The kitten mewed pitifully.*

mewl /mjuːl/ *verb* [I] to make a weak crying sound ▸ **mewl·ing** *noun* [U] **mewl·ing** *adj.*: *mewling babies*

mews /mjuːz/ *noun* (*pl.* **mews**) (*BrE*) a short, narrow street with a row of stables (= buildings used to keep horses in) that have been made into small houses

ˈ**mews house** (*BrE*) (*US* ˈ**carriage house**) *noun* a house in a mews

Mex·ican /ˈmeksɪkən/ *adj., noun*

■ ***adj.*** from or connected with Mexico

■ ***noun*** a person from Mexico

ˌ**Mexican ˈwave** (*BrE*) (*NAmE* **the ˈwave**) *noun* a continuous movement that looks like a wave on the sea, made by a large group of people, especially people watching a sports game, when one person after another stands up, raises their arms, and then sits down again

mez·za·nine /ˈmezəniːn; ˈmetsə-/ *noun* **1** a floor that is built between two floors of a building and is smaller than the other floors: *a bedroom on the mezzanine* ◇ *a mezzanine floor* **2** (*NAmE*) the first area of seats above the ground floor in a theatre; the first few rows of these seats ⊃ see also DRESS CIRCLE

mezzo-soprano /ˌmetsəʊ səˈprɑːnəʊ; *NAmE* ˌmetsoʊ səˈprɑːnoʊ; -ˈpræn-/ (also **mezzo**) *noun* (*pl.* **mezzo-sopranos, mezzos**) (from *Italian*) a singing voice with a range between SOPRANO and ALTO; a woman with a mezzo-soprano voice

mg *abbr.* (in writing) milligram(s)

Mgr (also **Mgr.** especially in *NAmE*) *abbr.* (in writing) MONSIGNOR

MHA /ˌem eɪtʃ ˈeɪ/ *abbr.* (*CanE*) Member of the House of Assembly (the parliament in Newfoundland and Labrador)

mhm /əmˈhm/ *exclamation* used to say 'yes', or to show sb that you are listening to them: *'Can I borrow your pen?' 'Mhm.'* ◇ *'I phoned Alan…' 'Mhm.' '…and he said he's going to come.'*

MHz *abbr.* (in writing) MEGAHERTZ

mi = ME *n*

MI5 /ˌem aɪ ˈfaɪv/ *noun* [U] the British government organization that deals with national security within Britain. Its official name is 'the Security Service'.

MI6 /ˌem aɪ ˈsɪks/ *noun* [U] the British government organization that deals with national security from outside Britain. Its official name is 'the Secret Intelligence Service'.

MIA /ˌem aɪ ˈeɪ/ *abbr.* (*especially NAmE*) (of a soldier) missing in action (missing after a battle)

miaow (*BrE*) (also **meow** *NAmE, BrE*) /miˈaʊ/ *noun* the crying sound made by a cat ➲ see also MEW ▶ **miaow** (*BrE*) (also **meow** *NAmE, BrE*) *verb* [I]

mi·asma /miˈæzmə; maɪˈæ-/ *noun* [C, usually sing., U] (*literary*) a mass of air that is dirty and smells unpleasant: *A miasma of stale alcohol hung around him.* ◇ (*figurative*) *the miasma of depression*

MiB *abbr.* (in writing) MEBIBYTE

Mib (also **Mibit**) *abbr.* (in writing) MEBIBIT

mic /maɪk/ *noun* (*informal*) = MICROPHONE

mica /ˈmaɪkə/ *noun* [U] a clear mineral that splits easily into thin flat layers and is used to make electrical equipment

mice *pl.* of MOUSE

Mich·ael·mas /ˈmɪklməs/ *noun* [U] (in the Christian Church) the holy day in honour of St Michael, 29 September

ˌMichaelmas ˈdaisy *noun* a plant that has blue, white, pink or purple flowers with dark centres, that appear in the autumn/fall

Michelin man /ˈmɪtʃəlɪn mæn; ˈmɪʃ-/ *noun*

IDM **like the/a ˈMichelin man** having a wide round body because of being very fat or wearing a lot of thick heavy clothes ORIGIN From the fat cartoon character made of tyres used as a symbol of the Michelin™ tyre company.

Mick /mɪk/ *noun* (*taboo, slang*) an offensive word for a person from Ireland

mickey /ˈmɪki/ *noun*

IDM **take the ˈmickey/ˈmick** (**out of sb**) (*BrE, informal*) to make sb look or feel silly by copying the way they talk, behave, etc. or by making them believe sth that is not true, often in a way that is not intended to be unkind SYN **tease, mock**

Mickey Finn /ˌmɪki ˈfɪn/ *noun* a drink containing a drug or a lot of alcohol, given to sb who does not realize what is in it

ˌMickey ˈMouse *adj.* (*disapproving*) not of high quality; too easy: *It's only a Mickey Mouse job.*

micro /ˈmaɪkrəʊ; *NAmE* -kroʊ/ *noun* (*pl.* -os) = MICROCOMPUTER

micro- /ˈmaɪkrəʊ; *NAmE* -kroʊ/ *combining form* **1** (in nouns, adjectives and adverbs) small; on a small scale: *microchip* ◇ *microorganism* OPP **macro- 2** (in nouns; used in units of measurement) one millionth: *a microlitre*

mi·crobe /ˈmaɪkrəʊb; *NAmE* -kroʊb/ *noun* an extremely small living thing that you can only see under a MICROSCOPE and that may cause disease ➲ COLLOCATIONS at LIFE

micro·biolo·gist /ˌmaɪkrəʊbaɪˈɒlədʒɪst; *NAmE* -kroʊbaɪˈɑːl-/ *noun* a scientist who studies microbiology

micro·biol·ogy /ˌmaɪkrəʊbaɪˈɒlədʒi; *NAmE* -kroʊbaɪˈɑːl-/ *noun* [U] the scientific study of very small living things, such as bacteria ▶ **micro·bio·logic·al** /ˌmaɪkrəʊˌbaɪəˈlɒdʒɪkl; *NAmE* -kroʊˌbaɪəˈlɑːdʒ-/ *adj.*

micro·blog·ging /ˈmaɪkrəʊblɒɡɪŋ; *NAmE* -kroʊblɑːɡ-/ *noun* [U] the activity of sending regular short messages, photos or videos over the Internet, either to a selected group of people, or so that they can be viewed by anyone, as a means of keeping people informed about your activities and thoughts ▶ **micro·blog** /ˈmaɪkrəʊblɒɡ; *NAmE* -kroʊblɑːɡ/ *noun* **micro·blog** *verb* [I] ➲ compare TWITTER

micro·chip /ˈmaɪkrəʊtʃɪp; *NAmE* -kroʊ-/ *noun, verb*

▪ ***noun*** (also **chip**) a very small piece of a material that is a SEMICONDUCTOR, used to carry a complicated electronic CIRCUIT

▪ ***verb*** (-pp-) **~ sth** to put a microchip under the skin of an animal as a way of identifying it

micro·cli·mate /ˈmaɪkrəʊklaɪmət; *NAmE* -kroʊ-/ *noun* (*technical*) the weather in a particular small area, especially when this is different from the weather in the surrounding area

micro·com·puter /ˈmaɪkrəʊkəmpjuːtə(r); *NAmE* -kroʊ-/ (also **micro**) *noun* a small computer that contains a MICROPROCESSOR ➲ compare MAINFRAME, MINICOMPUTER, PERSONAL COMPUTER

micro·cosm /ˈmaɪkrəʊkɒzəm; *NAmE* -kroʊkɑːz-/ *noun* a thing, a place or a group that has all the features and qualities of sth much larger: *The family is a microcosm of society.* ➲ compare MACROCOSM

IDM **in microcosm** on a small scale: *The developments in this town represent in microcosm what is happening in the country as a whole.*

micro·dot /ˈmaɪkrəʊdɒt; *NAmE* -kroʊdɑːt/ *noun* **1** a very small photograph about one millimetre in size, usually of a printed document **2** a very small round piece of a drug, especially the illegal drug LSD

micro·elec·tron·ics /ˌmaɪkrəʊɪˌlekˈtrɒnɪks; *NAmE* -kroʊɪˌlekˈtrɑːn-/ *noun* [U] the design, production and use of very small electronic CIRCUITS ▶ **micro·elec·tron·ic** *adj.* [only before noun]

micro·fibre (*especially US* **micro·fiber**) /ˈmaɪkrəʊfaɪbə(r); *NAmE* -roʊf-/ *noun* [U] a very light and warm artificial material that is used especially for making coats and jackets

micro·fiche /ˈmaɪkrəʊfiːʃ; *NAmE* -kroʊ-/ *noun* [U, C] a piece of film with written information on it in print of very small size. Microfiches can only be read with a special machine: *The directory is available **on microfiche**.*

micro·film /ˈmaɪkrəʊfɪlm; *NAmE* -kroʊ-/ *noun* [U, C] film used for storing written information on in print of very small size

micro·fi·nance /ˈmaɪkrəʊfaɪnæns; *NAmE* -kroʊ-/ *noun* [U] a system of providing services such as lending money and saving for people who are too poor to use banks

micro·gram /ˈmaɪkrəʊɡræm; *NAmE* -kroʊ-/ *noun* (*symb.* µg) a unit for measuring weight; a millionth of a gram

micro·light /ˈmaɪkrəʊlaɪt; *NAmE* -kroʊ-/ (*BrE*) (*NAmE* **ultra·light**) *noun* a very small light aircraft for one or two people ➲ VISUAL VOCAB page V43

micro·manage /ˈmaɪkrəʊmænɪdʒ; *NAmE* -kroʊ-/ *verb* [T, I] **~ (sth)** (*especially NAmE, disapproving*) to control every detail of a business, especially your employees' work: *The problem may be that you are micromanaging your team.* ◇ *bosses who micromanage* ▶ **micro·man·age·ment** *noun* [U] **micro·man·ager** *noun*

micro·meter /maɪˈkrɒmɪtə(r); *NAmE* -krɑːm-/ *noun* **1** (*especially US*) = MICROMETRE **2** a device used for measuring very small distances or spaces, using a screw with a very fine THREAD

micro·metre (*especially US* **micro·meter**) /ˈmaɪkrəʊmiːtə(r); *NAmE* -kroʊ-/ *noun* (*symb.* µm) a unit for measuring length, equal to one millionth of a metre

mi·cron /ˈmaɪkrɒn; *NAmE* -krɑːn/ *noun* (*old-fashioned*) = MICROMETRE

ˌmicro-ˈorganism *noun* (*technical*) a very small living thing that you can only see under a MICROSCOPE

micro·phone /ˈmaɪkrəfəʊn; *NAmE* -foʊn/ (also *informal* **mic, mike**) *noun* a device that is used for recording sounds or for making your voice louder when you are speaking or singing to an audience: *to speak into the microphone* ◇ *Their remarks were picked up by the hidden microphones.*

micro·por·tal /ˈmaɪkrəʊpɔːtl; *NAmE* ˈmaɪkroʊpɔːrtl/ *noun* (*computing*) a website that is used as a point of entry to the Internet where information has been collected that will be useful to a particular person or group

micro·pro·ces·sor /ˌmaɪkrəʊˈprəʊsesə(r); *NAmE* -kroʊˈproʊ-/ *noun* (*computing*) a small unit of a computer that contains all the functions of the CENTRAL PROCESSING UNIT

M

micro·scope /ˈmaɪkrəskəʊp; *NAmE* -skoʊp/ *noun* an instrument used in scientific study for making very small things look larger so that you can examine them carefully: *a microscope slide* ◇ *The bacteria were then examined* ***under a/the microscope.*** ◇ (*figurative*) *In the play, love and marriage are* ***put under the microscope.*** ➲ VISUAL VOCAB page V57 ➲ see also ELECTRON MICROSCOPE

micro·scop·ic /ˌmaɪkrəˈskɒpɪk; *NAmE* -ˈskɑːpɪk/ *adj.* **1** [usually before noun] extremely small and difficult or impossible to see without a microscope: *a* ***microscopic creature/particle*** ◇ (*humorous*) *The sandwiches were microscopic!* **2** [only before noun] using a microscope: *a* ***microscopic analysis/examination*** ▸ **micro·scop·ic·al·ly** /-kli/ *adv.*: *microscopically small creatures* ◇ *All samples are examined microscopically.*

micro·scopy /maɪˈkrɒskəpi; *NAmE* -ˈkrɑːs-/ *noun* [U] (*technical*) the use of MICROSCOPES to look at very small creatures, objects, etc.

micro·sec·ond /ˈmaɪkrəʊsekənd; *NAmE* -kroʊ-/ *noun* (*technical*) (*symb.* µs) one millionth of a second

micro·sur·gery /ˈmaɪkrəʊsɜːdʒəri; *NAmE* -kroʊsɜːr-/ *noun* [U] the use of extremely small instruments and MICROSCOPES in order to perform very detailed and complicated medical operations

micro·wave /ˈmaɪkrəweɪv/ *noun, verb*

■ ***noun*** **1** (also *formal* **ˌmicrowave ˈoven**) a type of oven that cooks or heats food very quickly using ELECTROMAGNETIC waves rather than heat: *Reheat the soup in the microwave.* ◇ ***microwave cookery/meals*** ➲ VISUAL VOCAB page V22 ➲ compare OVEN **2** (*technical*) an ELECTROMAGNETIC wave that is shorter than a radio wave but longer than a light wave

■ ***verb*** **~ sth** to cook or heat sth in a microwave ➲ COLLOCATIONS at COOKING ▸ **micro·wave·able** (also **micro·wav·able**) *adj.*: *microwaveable meals*

M

mic·tur·ate /ˈmɪktjʊreɪt; *NAmE* ˈmɪktʃə-/ *verb* [I] (*formal*) to URINATE ▸ **mic·tur·ition** /ˌmɪktjuˈrɪʃn; *NAmE* -tʃəˈrɪʃn/ *noun* [U]

MID /ˌem aɪ ˈdiː/ *noun* the abbreviation for 'mobile Internet device' (a small computer that you can hold in your hand, larger than a SMARTPHONE but smaller than a TABLET PC. MIDs offer Internet-based services mainly for personal rather than business use.) ➲ compare MOBILE DEVICE

mid /mɪd/ *prep.* (*literary*) = AMID

mid- 0⊸ /mɪd/ *combining form* (in nouns and adjectives) in the middle of: *mid-morning coffee* ◇ *She's in her mid-thirties.*

ˌmid-ˈair *noun* [U] a place in the air or the sky, not on the ground: *The bird caught the insects* ***in mid-air*** ▸ **ˌmid-ˈair** *adj.*: *a mid-air collision*

Midas touch /ˈmaɪdəs tʌtʃ/ *noun* (usually **the Midas touch**) [sing.] the ability to make a financial success of everything you do ORIGIN From the Greek myth in which King Midas was given the power to turn everything he touched into gold.

ˌmid-Atˈlantic *adj.* [only before noun] **1** connected with the area on the east coast of the US, that is near New York and immediately to the south of it: *the* ***mid-Atlantic states/coast*** **2** in the middle of the Atlantic ocean: (*figurative*) *a mid-Atlantic accent* (= a form of English that uses a mixture of British and American sounds)

mid·brain /ˈmɪdbreɪn/ *noun* (*anatomy*) a small central part of the brain

mid·day 0⊸ /ˌmɪdˈdeɪ/ *noun* [U] 12 o'clock in the middle of the day; the period around this time SYN **noon**: *The train arrives at midday.* ◇ *a midday meal* ◇ *the heat of the midday sun*

mid·den /ˈmɪdn/ *noun* a pile of waste near a house, in the past

mid·dle 0⊸ /ˈmɪdl/ *noun, adj.*

■ ***noun*** **1** 0⊸ **the middle** [sing.] the part of sth that is at an equal distance from all its edges or sides; a point or a period of time between the beginning and the end of sth: *a lake with an island* ***in the middle*** ◇ *He was standing in the middle of the room.* ◇ *The phone rang in the middle of the night.* ◇ *This chicken isn't cooked in the middle.* ◇ *His picture was* ***right/bang*** (= exactly) ***in the middle*** *of the front page.* ◇ *Take a sheet of paper and draw a line* ***down the middle.*** ◇ *I should have finished* ***by the middle of*** *the week.* ➲ see also MONKEY IN THE MIDDLE, PIGGY IN THE MIDDLE **2** [C, usually sing.] (*informal*) a person's waist: *He grabbed her around the middle.*

IDM **be in the middle of sth/of doing sth** to be busy doing sth: *They were in the middle of dinner when I called.* ◇ *I'm in the middle of writing a difficult letter.* **the middle of ˈnowhere** (*informal*) a place that is a long way from other buildings, towns, etc: *She lives on a small farm in the middle of nowhere.* **ˌsplit/diˌvide sth down the ˈmiddle** to divide sth into two equal parts: *The country was split down the middle over the strike* (= half supported it, half did not).

■ ***adj.*** 0⊸ [only before noun] in a position in the middle of an object, group of objects, people, etc; between the beginning and the end of sth: *Pens are kept in the middle drawer.* ◇ *She's the middle child of three.* ◇ *He was very successful in his middle forties.* ◇ *a middle-sized room* ◇ *the middle-income groups in society*

IDM **(steer, take, etc.) a middle ˈcourse | (find, etc.) a/the middle ˈway** (to take/find) an acceptable course of action that avoids two extreme positions

ˌmiddle ˈage *noun* [U] the period of your life when you are neither young nor old, between the ages of about 45 and 60: *a pleasant woman in* ***early/late middle age*** ➲ COLLOCATIONS at AGE

ˌmiddle-ˈaged *adj.* **1** (of a person) neither young nor old **2 the middle aged** *noun* [pl.] people who are middle-aged **3** (*disapproving*) (of a person's attitudes or behaviour) rather boring and old-fashioned

the ˌMiddle ˈAges *noun* [pl.] in European history, the period from about AD 1000 to AD 1450

ˌmiddle-age ˈspread (also **ˌmiddle-aged ˈspread**) *noun* [U] (*humorous*) the fat around the stomach that some people develop in middle age

ˌMiddle Aˈmerica *noun* [U] the middle class in the US, especially those people who represent traditional social and political values, and who come from small towns and SUBURBS rather than cities

middle·brow /ˈmɪdlbraʊ/ *adj.* [usually before noun] (usually *disapproving*) (of books, music, art, etc.) of good quality but not needing a lot of thought to understand ➲ compare HIGHBROW, LOWBROW

ˌmiddle ˈC *noun* [U] the musical note C near the middle of the piano keyboard

ˌmiddle ˈclass *noun* [C+sing./pl. v.] the social class whose members are neither very rich nor very poor and that includes professional and business people: *the* ***upper/lower middle class*** ◇ *the growth of the middle classes* ➲ compare UPPER CLASS, WORKING CLASS

ˌmiddle-ˈclass *adj.* **1** connected with the middle social class: *a* ***middle-class background/family/suburb*** **2** (*disapproving*) typical of people from the middle social class, for example having traditional views: *a middle-class attitude* ◇ *The magazine is very middle-class.*

the ˌmiddle ˈdistance *noun* [sing.] the part of a painting or a view that is neither very close nor very far away: *His eyes were fixed on a small house in the middle distance.*

ˌmiddle-ˈdistance *adj.* [only before noun] (*sport*) connected with running a race over a distance that is neither very short nor very long: *a middle-distance runner* (= for example, somebody who runs 800 or 1500 metre races)

ˌmiddle ˈear *noun* [sing.] the part of the ear behind the EARDRUM, containing the little bones that transfer sound VIBRATIONS

the ˌMiddle ˈEast (also *less frequent* **the ˌNear ˈEast**) *noun* [sing.] an area that covers SW Asia and NE Africa ➲ compare THE FAR EAST ▸ **ˌMiddle ˈEastern** (also *less frequent* **ˌNear ˈEastern**) *adj.*

ˌ**Middle ˈEngland** *noun* [U] the middle classes in England, especially people who have traditional social and political ideas and do not live in London

ˌ**Middle ˈEnglish** *noun* [U] an old form of English that was used between about AD 1150 and AD 1500 ➲ compare OLD ENGLISH

ˌ**Middle-Euroˈpean** *adj.* of or related to central Europe or its people

ˌ**middle ˈfinger** *noun* the longest finger in the middle of each hand ➲ VISUAL VOCAB page V48

ˈ**middle ground** *noun* [U] a set of opinions, decisions, etc. that two or more groups who oppose each other can agree on; a position that is not extreme: *Negotiations have failed to establish any middle ground.* ◇ *The ballet company now* ***occupies the middle ground between*** *classical ballet and modern dance.*

middle·man /ˈmɪdlmæn/ *noun* (*pl.* **-men** /-men/) **1** a person or a company that buys goods from the company that makes them and sells them to sb else: *Buy direct from the manufacturer and* ***cut out the middleman.*** **2** a person who helps to arrange things between people who do not want to talk directly to each other SYN **intermediary, go-between**

ˌ**middle ˈmanagement** *noun* [U+sing./pl. v.] the people who are in charge of small groups of people and departments within a business organization but who are not involved in making important decisions that will affect the whole organization ▶ ˌ**middle ˈmanager** *noun*

ˌ**middle ˈname** *noun* a name that comes between your first name and your family name

IDM **be sb's middle ˈname** (*informal*) used to say that sb has a lot of a particular quality: *'Patience' is my middle name!*

ˌ**middle-of-the-ˈroad** *adj.* (of people, policies, etc.) not extreme; acceptable to most people SYN **moderate**: *a middle-of-the-road newspaper* ◇ *Their music is very middle-of-the-road.*

ˌ**middle-ˈranking** *adj.* [only before noun] having a responsible job or position, but not one of the most important

ˈ**middle school** *noun* **1** (in Britain) a school for children between the ages of about 9 and 13 **2** (in the US) a school for children between the ages of about 11 and 14 ➲ compare UPPER SCHOOL

middle·ware /ˈmɪdlweə(r); *NAmE* -wer/ *noun* [U] (*computing*) software that allows different programs to work with each other

middle·weight /ˈmɪdlweɪt/ *noun* a BOXER weighing between 67 and 72.5 kilograms, heavier than a WELTERWEIGHT: *a middleweight champion*

the ˌ**Middle ˈWest** *noun* [sing.] = MIDWEST

mid·dling /ˈmɪdlɪŋ/ *adj.* [usually before noun] of average size, quality, status, etc. SYN **moderate, unremarkable**: *a golfer of middling talent* IDM see FAIR *adv.*

mid·field /ˈmɪdfiːld; ˌmɪdˈfiːld/ *noun* [U, C, sing.] the central part of a sports field; the group of players in this position: *He plays* (***in***) ***midfield.*** ◇ *The team's midfield looks strong.* ◇ *a midfield player* ▶ **mid·field·er** /ˌmɪdˈfiːldə(r)/ *noun*

midge /mɪdʒ/ *noun* a small flying insect that lives especially in damp places and that bites humans and animals

midget /ˈmɪdʒɪt/ *noun, adj.*

■ ***noun*** **1** (*taboo, offensive*) an extremely small person, who will never grow to a normal size because of a physical problem; a person suffering from DWARFISM **2** (*informal*) a very small person or animal

■ ***adj.*** [only before noun] very small

MIDI /ˈmɪdi/ *noun* [U] a connection or program that connects electronic musical instruments and computers

ˈ**midi system** *noun* (*BrE*) a SOUND SYSTEM with several parts that fit together into a small space

Mid·lands /ˈmɪdləndz/ *noun* **the Midlands** [sing.+ sing./pl. v.] the central part of a country, especially the central counties of England ▶ **Mid·land** *adj.* [only before noun]

mid·life /mɪdˈlaɪf/ *noun* [U] the middle part of your life when you are neither young nor old: *It is not difficult to take up a new career in midlife* ◇ *midlife stresses*

ˌ**midlife ˈcrisis** *noun* [usually sing.] the feelings of worry, disappointment or lack of confidence that a person may feel in the middle part of their life ➲ COLLOCATIONS at AGE

mid·night 🔑 /ˈmɪdnaɪt/ *noun* [U]

1 🔑 12 o'clock at night: *They had to leave* ***at midnight.*** ◇ *on the stroke of* ***midnight/shortly*** *after* ***midnight*** ◇ *She heard the clock strike midnight.* ◇ *We have to catch the midnight train.* **2** (*especially NAmE*) = MIDNIGHT BLUE

IDM see BURN *v.*, FLIT *n.*

ˌ**midnight ˈblue** (also **mid·night** especially in *NAmE*) *noun* [U] a very dark blue colour ▶ ˌ**midnight ˈblue** *adj.*

the ˌ**midnight ˈsun** *noun* [sing.] the sun that you can see in the middle of the summer near the North and South Poles

ˈ**mid-point** *noun* [usually sing.] the point that is at an equal distance between the beginning and the end of sth; the point that is at an equal distance between two things: *the mid-point of the decade* ◇ *At its mid-point, the race had no clear winner.* ◇ *the mid-point between the first number and the last*

ˌ**mid-ˈrange** *adj.* [only before noun] (especially of a product for sale) neither the best nor the worst that is available: *a mid-range computer*

mid·riff /ˈmɪdrɪf/ *noun* the middle part of the body between the chest and the waist: *a bare midriff*

mid·ship·man /ˈmɪdʃɪpmən/ *noun* (*pl.* **-men** /-mən/) a person training to be an officer in the navy: *Midshipman Paul Brooks*

ˌ**mid-ˈsized** (also ˌ**mid-ˈsize**) (both *especially NAmE*) *adj.* of average size, neither large nor small

midst /mɪdst/ *noun* (*formal*) (used after a preposition) the middle part of sth SYN **middle**: *Such beauty was unexpected* ***in the midst of*** *the city.*

IDM **in the midst of sth/of doing sth** while sth is happening or being done; while you are doing sth: *a country in the midst of a recession* ◇ *She discovered it in the midst of sorting out her father's things.* **in their/our/its/your midst** (*formal*) among or with them/us/it/you: *There is a traitor in our midst.*

mid·stream /ˌmɪdˈstriːm/ *noun* [U] the middle part of a river, stream, etc: *We anchored in midstream*

IDM (**in**) **midstream** in the middle of doing sth; while sth is still happening: *Their conversation was interrupted in midstream by the baby crying.* ➲ more at CHANGE *v.*

mid·sum·mer /ˌmɪdˈsʌmə(r)/ *noun* [U] the middle of summer, especially the period in June in northern parts of the world, in December in southern parts: *a midsummer evening*

ˌ**Midsummer's ˈDay** (*BrE*) (also ˌ**Midsummer ˈDay** *NAmE, BrE*) *noun* 24 June, in northern parts of the world

mid·term /ˌmɪdˈtɜːm; *NAmE* -ˈtɜːrm/ *adj.* [only before noun] **1** in the middle of the period that a government, a council, etc. is elected for: *midterm elections* **2** for or connected with a period of time that is neither long nor short; in the middle of a particular period: *a midterm solution* ◇ *midterm losses* ➲ see also LONG-TERM, SHORT-TERM **3** in the middle of one of the main periods of the academic year: *a* ***midterm examination/break*** ➲ see also HALF-TERM

mid·town /ˈmɪdtaʊn/ *noun* [U] (*NAmE*) the part of a city that is between the central business area and the outer parts: *a house in midtown* ◇ *midtown Manhattan* ➲ compare DOWNTOWN, UPTOWN

mid·way /ˌmɪdˈweɪ/ *adv.* in the middle of a period of time; between two places SYN **halfway**: *The goal was scored midway through the first half.* ▶ **mid·way** *adj.*: *to reach the midway point*

mid·week /ˌmɪdˈwiːk/ *noun* [U] the middle of the week: *to play a match* ***in midweek*** ◇ *By midweek he was too tired*

M

to go out. ◇ *a midweek defeat for the team* ▶ **mid·week** *adv.*: *It's cheaper to travel midweek.*

the Mid·west /ˌmɪd'west/ (also **the ˌMiddle 'West**) *noun* [sing.] the northern central part of the US ▶ **Mid·west·ern** /ˌmɪd'westən; *NAmE* -ərn/ *adj.*

mid·wife /'mɪdwaɪf/ *noun* (*pl.* **mid·wives** /-waɪvz/) a person, especially a woman, who is trained to help women give birth to babies ➲ compare DOULA

mid·wif·ery /ˌmɪd'wɪfəri; *NAmE* also -'waɪf-/ *noun* [U] the profession and work of a midwife

mid·win·ter /ˌmɪd'wɪntə(r)/ *noun* [U] the middle of winter, around December in northern parts of the world, June in southern parts: *midwinter weather*

mien /miːn/ *noun* [sing.] (*formal* or *literary*) a person's appearance or manner that shows how they are feeling

miffed /mɪft/ *adj.* [not before noun] (*informal*) slightly angry or upset SYN **annoyed**

might O-w /maɪt/ *modal verb, noun*

■ ***modal verb*** (*negative* **might not**, *short form* **mightn't** /'maɪtnt/) **1** O-w used as the past tense of *may* when reporting what sb has said: *He said he might come tomorrow.* **2** O-w used when showing that sth is or was possible: *He might get there in time, but I can't be sure.* ◇ *I know Vicky doesn't like the job, but I mightn't find it too bad.* ◇ *The pills might have helped him, if only he'd taken them regularly.* ◇ *He might say that now* (= it is true that he does), *but he can soon change his mind.* **3** O-w used to make a polite suggestion: *You might try calling the help desk.* ◇ *I thought we might go to the zoo on Saturday.* **4** O-w (*BrE*) used to ask permission politely: *Might I use your phone?* ◇ *If I might just say something...* **5** (*formal*) used to ask for information: *How might the plans be improved upon?* ◇ *And who might she be?* **6** used to show that you are annoyed about sth that sb could do or could have done: *I think you might at least offer to help!* ◇ *Honestly, you might have told me!* **7** used to say that you are not surprised by sth: *I might have guessed it was you!* **8** used to emphasize that an important point has been made: *'And where is the money coming from?' 'You* ***might well*** *ask!'* ➲ note at MODAL IDM see WELL

■ ***noun*** [U] (*formal* or *literary*) great strength, energy or power: *America's military might* ◇ *I pushed the rock* ***with all my might.***

IDM **ˌmight is 'right** (*saying*) having the power to do sth gives you the right to do it: *Their foreign policy is based on the principle that 'might is right'.*

'might-have-been *noun* [usually pl.] (*informal*) an event or situation that could have happened or that you wish had happened, but which did not

might·ily /'maɪtɪli/ *adv.* (*old-fashioned*) **1** very; very much: ***mightily impressed/relieved*** **2** (*formal*) with great strength or effort: *We have struggled mightily to win back lost trade.*

mighty /'maɪti/ *adj., adv.*

■ ***adj.*** (**might·ier**, **mighti·est**) **1** (especially *literary*) very strong and powerful: *a mighty warrior* ◇ *He struck him with a mighty blow across his shoulder.* **2** large and impressive SYN **great**: *the mighty Mississippi river* IDM see HIGH *adj.*, PEN *n.*

■ ***adv.*** (*informal, especially NAmE*) (with adjectives and adverbs) very SYN **really**: *mighty difficult* ◇ *driving mighty fast*

mi·graine /'miːgreɪn; 'maɪg-; *NAmE* 'maɪg-/ *noun* [U, C] a very severe type of headache which often makes a person feel sick and have difficulty in seeing: *severe migraine* ◇ *I'm getting a migraine.* ➲ COLLOCATIONS at ILL

mi·grant AW /'maɪgrənt/ *noun* **1** a person who moves from one place to another, especially in order to find work: *migrant workers* ➲ COLLOCATIONS at RACE ➲ compare EMIGRANT, IMMIGRANT ➲ see also ECONOMIC MIGRANT **2** a bird or an animal that moves from one place to another according to the season

mi·grate AW /maɪ'greɪt; *NAmE* 'maɪgreɪt/ *verb* **1** [I] (of birds, animals, etc.) to move from one part of the world to another according to the season: *Swallows migrate south in winter.* **2** [I] (of a lot of people) to move from one town, country, etc. to go and live and/or work in another SYN **emigrate**: *Thousands were forced to migrate from rural to urban areas in search of work.* **3** [I] (*technical*) to move from one place to another: *The infected cells then migrate to other areas of the body.* **4** [I, T] **~ (sb)** (*computing*) to change, or cause sb to change, from one computer system to another **5** [T] **~ sth** (*computing*) to move programs or HARDWARE from one computer system to another

mi·gra·tion AW /maɪ'greɪʃn/ *noun* [U, C] **1** the movement of large numbers of people, birds or animals from one place to another: *seasonal migration* ◇ *mass migrations* **2** the fact of changing from one computer system to another; the act of moving programs, etc. from one computer system to another

mi·gra·tory AW /'maɪgrətri; maɪ'greɪtəri; *NAmE* 'maɪgrətɔːri/ *adj.* (*technical*) connected with, or having the habit of, regular migration: ***migratory flights/birds***

mi·kado /mɪ'kɑːdəʊ; *NAmE* -doʊ/ *noun* (*pl.* **-os**) (from *Japanese*) a title given in the past to the EMPEROR of Japan

mike /maɪk/ *noun* (*informal*) = MICROPHONE ➲ see also OPEN MIKE

mi·lady /mɪ'leɪdi/ *noun* (*pl.* **-ies**) (*old use* or *humorous*) used when talking to or about a woman who is a member of the British NOBILITY or of high class ➲ compare MILORD

mil·age = MILEAGE

milch cow /'mɪltʃ kaʊ/ *noun* (*BrE*) a person, an organization or a product from which it is easy to make money

mild O-w /maɪld/ *adj., noun*

■ ***adj.*** (**mild·er**, **mild·est**) **1** O-w not severe or strong: *a* ***mild form*** *of the disease* ◇ *a* ***mild punishment/criticism*** ◇ *It's safe to take a mild sedative.* ◇ *Use a soap that is mild on the skin.* **2** O-w (of weather) not very cold, and therefore pleasant: *the mildest winter since records began* ◇ *a mild climate* ➲ compare HARD **3** O-w (of feelings) not great or extreme SYN **slight**: ***mild irritation/amusement/disapproval*** ◇ *She looked at him in mild surprise.* **4** (of people or their behaviour) gentle and kind; not usually getting angry or violent SYN **equable**: *a mild woman, who never shouted* **5** (of a flavour) not strong, spicy or bitter: *a mild curry* ◇ *mild cheese* OPP **hot** ▶ **mild·ness** *noun* [U]: *the mildness of a sunny spring day* ◇ *her mildness of manner*

■ ***noun*** [U] (*BrE*) a type of dark beer with a mild flavour: *Two pints of mild, please.* ➲ compare BITTER

mil·dew /'mɪldjuː; *NAmE* -duː/ *noun* [U] a very small white FUNGUS that grows on walls, plants, food, etc. in warm wet conditions

mil·dewed /'mɪldjuːd; *NAmE* -duːd/ *adj.* with MILDEW growing on it

mild·ly /'maɪldli/ *adv.* **1** slightly; not very much: ***mildly surprised/irritated/interested*** **2** in a gentle manner: *'I didn't mean to upset you' he said mildly.*

IDM **to put it 'mildly** used to show that what you are talking about is much more extreme, etc. than your words suggest: *The result was unfortunate, to put it mildly* (= it was extremely unfortunate).

ˌmild-'mannered *adj.* (of a person) gentle and not usually getting angry or violent

ˌmild 'steel *noun* [U] a type of steel containing very little CARBON which is very strong but not easy to shape

mile O-w /maɪl/ *noun*

1 O-w [C] a unit for measuring distance equal to 1 609 metres or 1760 yards: *a 20-mile drive to work* ◇ *an area of four square miles* ◇ *a mile-long procession* ◇ *The nearest bank is about half a mile down the road.* ◇ *We did about 30 miles a day on our cycling trip.* ◇ *The car must have been doing at least 100 miles an hour.* ◇ (*BrE*) *My car does 35 miles to the gallon.* ◇ (*NAmE*) *My car gets 35 miles to the gallon.* ➲ see also AIR MILES, MPH, NAUTICAL MILE **2** O-w **miles** [pl.] a large area or a long distance: *miles and miles of desert* ◇ *There isn't a house for miles around here.* ◇ *I'm not walking*

—*it's* **miles away**. **3** [C, usually pl.] (*informal*) very much; far: *I'm feeling miles better today, thanks.* ◇ *I'm miles behind with my work.* ◇ *She's taller than you by a mile.* **4 the mile** [sing.] a race over one mile: *He ran the mile in less than four minutes.* ◇ *a four-minute mile*

IDM **be ˈmiles away** (*informal*) to be thinking deeply about sth and not aware of what is happening around you **go the ˌextra ˈmile (for sb/sth)** to make a special effort to achieve sth, help sb, etc. **ˌmiles from ˈanywhere** (*informal*) in a place that is a long way from a town and surrounded only by a lot of open country, sea, etc: *We broke down miles from anywhere.* **run a ˈmile (from sb/sth)** (*informal*) to show that you are very frightened of doing sth **see, spot, tell, smell, etc. sth a ˈmile off** (*informal*) to see or realize sth very easily and quickly: *He's wearing a wig—you can see it a mile off.* **stand/stick out a ˈmile** to be very obvious or noticeable ➲ more at INCH *n.*, MISS *n.*

mile·age (also **mil·age**) /ˈmaɪlɪdʒ/ *noun* **1** [U, C, usually sing.] the distance that a vehicle has travelled, measured in miles: *My annual mileage is about 10 000.* ◇ *a used car with one owner and a low mileage* ◇ *The car rental included unlimited mileage, but not fuel.* ◇ *I get a* ***mileage allowance*** *if I use my car for work* (= an amount of money paid for each mile I travel). **2** [U, C] the number of miles that a vehicle can travel using a particular amount of fuel: *If you drive carefully you can get better mileage from your car.* **3** [U] (*informal*) the amount of advantage or use that you can get from a particular event or situation: *I don't think the press can get any more mileage out of that story.*

mile·om·eter *noun* = MILOMETER

mile·post /ˈmaɪlpəʊst; *NAmE* -poʊst/ *noun* (*especially NAmE*) **1** a post by the side of the road that shows how far it is to the next town, and to other places **2** = MILESTONE (1)

mile·stone /ˈmaɪlstəʊn; *NAmE* -stoʊn/ *noun* **1** (also **milepost** especially in *NAmE*) a very important stage or event in the development of sth SYN **landmark 2** a stone by the side of a road that shows how far it is to the next town and to other places

mi·lieu /miːˈljɜː/ *noun* [C, usually sing.] (*pl.* **mi·lieux** or **mi·lieus** /-ˈljɜːz/) (from *French, formal*) the social environment that you live or work in SYN **background**

mili·tant /ˈmɪlɪtənt/ *adj.* using, or willing to use, force or strong pressure to achieve your aims, especially to achieve social or political change: ***militant groups/leaders*** ▶ **mili·tancy** /-ənsi/ *noun* [U]: *a growing militancy amongst the unemployed* **mili·tant** *noun*: *Student militants were fighting with the police.* **mili·tant·ly** *adv.*

mili·tar·ism /ˈmɪlɪtərɪzəm/ *noun* [U] (usually *disapproving*) the belief that a country should have great military strength in order to be powerful ▶ **mili·tar·ist** *noun*: *Militarists ran the country.* **mili·tar·is·tic** /ˌmɪlɪtəˈrɪstɪk/ *adj.*: *militaristic government*

mili·tar·ize (*BrE* also **-ise**) /ˈmɪlɪtəraɪz/ *verb* [usually passive] **1 ~ sth** to send armed forces to an area: *a militarized zone* OPP **demilitarize 2 ~ sth** to make sth similar to an army: *a militarized police force* ▶ **mili·tar·iza·tion, -isa·tion** /ˌmɪlɪtəraɪˈzeɪʃn; *NAmE* -rəˈz-/ *noun* [U]

mili·tary 🔑 AW /ˈmɪlətri; *NAmE* -teri/ *adj., noun*

▪ ***adj.*** 🔑 [usually before noun] connected with soldiers or the armed forces: ***military training/intelligence*** ◇ *a military coup* ◇ *military uniform* ◇ *We may have to take military action.* ➲ COLLOCATIONS at WAR ➲ compare CIVILIAN ▶ **mili·tar·ily** *adv.*: *a militarily superior country* ◇ *We may have to intervene militarily in the area.*

▪ ***noun*** **the military** [sing.+ sing./pl. v.] soldiers; the armed forces: *The military was/were called in to deal with the riot.*

ˌmilitary ˈband *noun* a large group of soldiers who play wind instruments and drums, sometimes while marching ➲ compare CONCERT BAND

ˌmilitary poˈlice *noun* (*abbr.* MP) (often **the military police**) [pl.] the police force which is responsible for the army, navy, etc.

ˌmilitary ˈservice *noun* [U] **1** a period during which young people train in the armed forces: *to be* ***called up*** *for military service* ◇ *She has to* **do her military service**. **2** the time sb spends in the armed forces: *He's completed 30 years of active military service.*

mili·tate /ˈmɪlɪteɪt/ *verb*

PHR V **ˈmilitate against sth** (*formal*) to prevent sth; to make it difficult for sth to happen or exist SYN **hinder**: *The supervisor's presence militated against a relaxed atmosphere.*

mili·tia /məˈlɪʃə/ *noun* [sing.+ sing./pl. v.] a group of people who are not professional soldiers but who have had military training and can act as an army

mili·tia·man /məˈlɪʃəmən/ *noun* (*pl.* **-men** /-mən/) a member of a militia

milk 🔑 /mɪlk/ *noun, verb*

▪ ***noun*** [U] **1** 🔑 the white liquid produced by cows, GOATS and some other animals as food for their young and used as a drink by humans: *a* ***pint/litre of milk*** ◇ *a* ***bottle/carton of milk*** ◇ ***fresh/dried/powdered milk*** ◇ *Do you take milk in your tea?* ◇ *milk products* (= butter, cheese, etc.) ➲ see also BUTTERMILK, CONDENSED MILK, EVAPORATED MILK, MALTED MILK, SKIMMED MILK **2** 🔑 the white liquid that is produced by women and female MAMMALS for feeding their babies: *breast milk* **3** the white juice of some plants and trees, especially the COCONUT ➲ VISUAL VOCAB page V26 ➲ see also SOYA MILK

IDM **the milk of human ˈkindness** (*literary*) kind behaviour, considered to be natural to humans ➲ more at CRY *v.*, LAND *n.*

▪ ***verb*** **1 ~ sth** to take milk from a cow, GOAT, etc. **2** (*disapproving*) to obtain as much money, advantage, etc. for yourself as you can from a particular situation, especially in a dishonest way: **~ A (from B)** *She's milked a small fortune from the company over the years.* ◇ **~ B (of A)** *She's milked the company of a small fortune.* ◇ *I know he's had a hard time lately, but he's certainly* ***milking it for all it's worth*** (= using it as an excuse to do things that people would normally object to). IDM see DRY *n.*

ˈmilk chocolate *noun* [U] light brown chocolate made with milk ➲ compare DARK CHOCOLATE

ˈmilk float *noun* (*BrE*) a small electric vehicle used for delivering milk to people's houses

milk·ing /ˈmɪlkɪŋ/ *noun* [U] the process of taking milk from a cow, etc: ***milking machines/sheds***

milk·maid /ˈmɪlkmeɪd/ *noun* (in the past) a woman whose job was to take milk from cows and make butter and cheese

milk·man /ˈmɪlkmən/ *noun* (*pl.* **-men** /-mən/) (especially in Britain) a person whose job is to deliver milk to customers each morning

ˈmilk powder (also **ˌpowdered ˈmilk**) (both *BrE*) (*US* **ˌdry ˈmilk**) *noun* [U] dried milk in the form of a powder

ˌmilk ˈpudding *noun* [U, C] a PUDDING (= sweet dish) made with milk and rice, or with milk and another grain

ˈmilk round *noun* **1** (in Britain) the job of going from house to house regularly, delivering milk; the route taken by sb doing this job **2** (also **the milk round**) (in Britain) a series of visits that large companies make each year to colleges and universities, to talk to students who are interested in working for them

ˈmilk run *noun* (*informal*) **1** [C] (*especially BrE*) a regular journey that is easy and in which nothing unusual happens, especially one by plane **2 the milk run** [sing.] (*NAmE*) a plane or train journey with stops in many places: *We took the milk run back home.*

milk·shake /ˈmɪlkʃeɪk/ (also **shake**) *noun* a drink made of milk, and sometimes ice cream, with an added flavour of fruit or chocolate, which is mixed or shaken until it is full of bubbles: *a banana milkshake*

milk·sop /ˈmɪlksɒp; *NAmE* -sɑːp/ *noun* (*old-fashioned, disapproving*) a man or boy who is not brave or strong

ˈmilk tooth (*BrE*) (also **ˈbaby tooth** *NAmE, BrE*) *noun* any of the first set of teeth in young children that drop out and are replaced by others

M

milky /ˈmɪlki/ *adj.* **1** made of milk; containing a lot of milk: *a hot milky drink* ◇ *milky tea/coffee* **2** like milk: *milky* (= not clear) *blue eyes* ◇ *milky* (= white) *skin*

the ˌMilky ˈWay *noun* [sing.] = THE GALAXY

mill /mɪl/ *noun, verb*
■ *noun* **1** a building fitted with machinery for GRINDING grain into flour ➲ see also WATERMILL, WINDMILL **2** (often in compounds) a factory that produces a particular type of material: *a cotton/cloth/steel/paper mill* ◇ *mill owners/workers* ➲ SYNONYMS at FACTORY ➲ see also ROLLING MILL, SAWMILL **3** (often in compounds) a small machine for crushing or GRINDING a solid substance into powder: *a pepper mill* ➲ VISUAL VOCAB page V23 ➲ see also RUN-OF-THE-MILL, TREADMILL
IDM **go through the ˈmill | put sb through the ˈmill** to have or make sb have a difficult time ➲ more at GRIST
■ *verb* [often passive] **~ sth** to crush or GRIND sth in a mill
PHR V **ˌmill aˈround** (*BrE* also **ˌmill aˈbout**) (especially of a large group of people) to move around an area without seeming to be going anywhere in particular: *Fans were milling around outside the hotel.* ➲ see also MILLING

mil·len·ar·ian /ˌmɪlɪˈneəriən; *NAmE* -ˈner-/ *noun* a member of a religious group which believes in a future age of happiness and peace when Christ will return to Earth ▶ **mil·len·ar·ian** *adj.* **mil·len·ar·ian·ism** /-ˈneəriənɪzəm; *NAmE* -ˈner-/ *noun* [U]

mil·len·nium /mɪˈleniəm/ *noun* (*pl.* **mil·len·nia** /-niə/ or **mil·len·niums**) **1** a period of 1000 years, especially as calculated before or after the birth of Christ: *the second millennium AD* **2 the millennium** the time when one period of 1000 years ends and another begins: *How did you celebrate the millennium?*

mille·pede ➲ MILLIPEDE

mill·er /ˈmɪlə(r)/ *noun* a person who owns or works in a MILL for making flour

mil·let /ˈmɪlɪt/ *noun* [U] a type of plant that grows in hot countries and produces very small seeds. The seeds are used as food, mainly to make flour, and also to feed to birds and animals. ➲ VISUAL VOCAB page V28

milli- /ˈmɪli/ *combining form* (in nouns; used in units of measurement) one thousandth: *milligram*

milli·bar /ˈmɪlibɑː(r)/ *noun* a unit for measuring the pressure of the atmosphere. One thousand millibars are equal to one BAR.

milli·gram 🔑 (*BrE* also **milli·gramme**) /ˈmɪligræm/ *noun* (*abbr.* **mg**)
a unit for measuring weight; a 1000th of a gram

milli·litre (*especially US* **milli·liter**) /ˈmɪliliːtə(r)/ *noun* (*abbr.* **ml**) /mɪl/ a unit for measuring the volume of liquids and gases; a 1000th of a litre

milli·metre 🔑 (*especially US* **milli·meter**) /ˈmɪlimiːtə(r)/ *noun* (*abbr.* **mm**)
a unit for measuring length; a 1000th of a metre

mill·iner /ˈmɪlɪnə(r)/ *noun* a person whose job is making and/or selling women's hats

mill·in·ery /ˈmɪlɪnəri; *NAmE* ˈmɪlɪneri/ *noun* [U] **1** the work of a milliner **2** hats sold in shops/stores

mill·ing /ˈmɪlɪŋ/ *adj.* [only before noun] (of people) moving around in a large mass: *I had to fight my way through the milling crowd.*

mil·lion 🔑 /ˈmɪljən/ *number* (*plural verb*)
1 🔑 (*abbr.* **m**) 1 000 000: *a population of half a million* ◇ *tens of millions of dollars* ◇ *It must be worth a million* (= pounds, dollars, etc.) HELP You say **a, one, two, several, etc. million** without a final 's' on 'million'. **Millions (of...)** can be used if there is no number or quantity before it. Always use a plural verb with **million** or **millions**, except when an amount of money is mentioned: *Four million (people) were affected.* ◇ *Two million (pounds) was withdrawn from the account.* **2** 🔑 **a million** or **millions (of ...)** (*informal*) a very large amount: *I still have a million things to do.* ◇ *There were millions of people there.* ◇ *He made his **millions*** (= all his money) *on currency deals.* HELP There are more examples of how to use numbers at the entry for **hundred**.
IDM **look/feel like a million ˈdollars/ˈbucks** (*informal*) to look/feel extremely good **one, etc. in a ˈmillion** a person or thing that is very unusual or special: *He's a man in a million.*

mil·lion·aire /ˌmɪljəˈneə(r); *NAmE* -ˈner/ *noun* a person who has a million pounds, dollars, etc; a very rich person: *an oil millionaire* ◇ *She's a millionaire several times over.* ◇ *a millionaire businessman*

mil·lion·air·ess /ˌmɪljəˈneərəs; *NAmE* -ˈner-/ *noun* (*old-fashioned*) a woman who is a millionaire

mil·lionth 🔑 /ˈmɪljənθ/ *ordinal number, noun*
■ *ordinal number* 🔑 1 000 000th
■ *noun* 🔑 each of one million equal parts of sth: *a/one millionth of a second*

milli·pede (also **millepede**) /ˈmɪlɪpiːd/ *noun* a small creature like an insect, with a long thin body divided into many sections, each with two pairs of legs

milli·sec·ond /ˈmɪlisekənd/ *noun* (*technical*) a 1000th of a second: (*figurative*) *I hesitated a millisecond too long.*

mil·li·volt /ˈmɪlivəʊlt; -vɒlt; *NAmE* -voːlt/ *noun* (*physics*) a unit for measuring the force of an electric current; a 1000th of a VOLT

mill·pond /ˈmɪlpɒnd; *NAmE* -pɑːnd/ *noun* a small area of water used especially in the past to make the wheel of a MILL turn: *The sea was as calm as a millpond.*

ˌMills and ˈBoon™ *noun* a company that publishes popular romantic novels: *He was tall, dark and handsome, like a Mills and Boon hero.*

mill·stone /ˈmɪlstəʊn; *NAmE* -stoʊn/ *noun* one of two flat round stones used, especially in the past, to crush grain to make flour
IDM **a millstone around/round your ˈneck** a difficult problem or responsibility that it seems impossible to solve or get rid of: *My debts are a millstone around my neck.*

mill·stream /ˈmɪlstriːm/ *noun* a stream whose water turns a wheel that provides power for machinery in a WATERMILL

ˈmill wheel *noun* a large wheel that is turned by water and that makes the machinery of a MILL work

mil·om·eter (also **mile·ometer**) /maɪˈlɒmɪtə(r); *NAmE* -ˈlɑːm-/ (both *BrE*) (*NAmE* **odom·eter**) (also *informal* **the clock** *US, BrE*) *noun* an instrument in a vehicle that measures the number of miles it has travelled ➲ VISUAL VOCAB page V42

mi·lord /mɪˈlɔːd; *NAmE* -ˈlɔːrd/ *noun* (*old use* or *humorous*) used when talking to or about a man who is a member of the British NOBILITY ➲ compare MILADY

mime /maɪm/ *noun, verb*
■ *noun* (also *less frequent* **dumb·show**) [U, C] (especially in the theatre) the use of movements of your hands or body and the expressions on your face to tell a story or to act sth without speaking; a performance using this method of acting: *The performance consisted of dance, music and mime.* ◇ *a mime artist* ◇ *She performed a brief mime.*
■ *verb* **1** [T, I] to act, tell a story, etc. by moving your body and face but without speaking: **~ (sth)** *Each player has to mime the title of a movie, play or book.* ◇ **~ doing sth** *He mimed climbing a mountain.* **2** [I, T] **~ (to sth) | ~ (sth)** to pretend to sing a song that is actually being sung by sb else on a tape, etc: *The band was miming to a backing tape.*

mi·mesis /mɪˈmiːsɪs; maɪˈm-/ *noun* [U] **1** (*technical*) the way in which the real world and human behaviour is represented in art or literature **2** (*technical*) the fact of a particular social group changing their behaviour by copying the behaviour of another social group **3** (*biology*) the fact of a plant or animal developing a similar appearance to another plant or animal. **4** (*medical*) the fact of a set of SYMPTOMS suggesting that sb has a particular disease, when in fact that person has a different disease or none

mi·met·ic /mɪˈmetɪk/ *adj.* (*technical* or *formal*) copying the behaviour or appearance of sb/sth else

mimic /ˈmɪmɪk/ *verb, noun*

■ ***verb*** (-ck-) **1 ~ sb/sth | + speech** to copy the way sb speaks, moves, behaves, etc, especially in order to make other people laugh: *She's always mimicking the teachers.* ◇ *He mimicked her southern accent.* **2 ~ sth** (*technical* or *formal*) to look or behave like sth else **SYN imitate**: *The robot was programmed to mimic a series of human movements.*

■ ***noun*** a person or an animal that can copy the voice, movements, etc. of others

mim·ic·ry /ˈmɪmɪkri/ *noun* [U] the action or skill of being able to copy the voice, movements, etc. of others: *a talent for mimicry*

mi·mosa /mɪˈməʊzə; -ˈməʊsə; *NAmE* -ˈmoʊ-/ *noun* [C, U] **1** a tropical bush or tree with balls of yellow flowers and leaves that are sensitive to touch and light **2** (*NAmE*) (*BrE* ˌ**Buck's ˈFizz**) an alcoholic drink made by mixing SPARKLING white wine (= with bubbles) with orange juice

Min /mɪn/ *noun* [U] a form of Chinese spoken mainly in SE China

min. *abbr.* **1** (in writing) minute(s): *Cook for 8–10 min. until tender.* **2** (in writing) minimum: *min. charge £4.50* **OPP max**

min·aret /ˌmɪnəˈret/ *noun* a tall thin tower, usually forming part of a MOSQUE, from which Muslims are called to prayer

min·atory /ˈmɪnətəri; *NAmE* -tɔːri/ *adj.* (*formal*) threatening: *minatory words*

mince /mɪns/ *verb, noun*

■ ***verb*** **1** (*NAmE* also **grind**) [T] **~ sth** to cut food, especially meat, into very small pieces using a special machine (called a MINCER): *minced beef* **2** [I] **+ adv./prep.** (*disapproving*) to walk with quick short steps, in a way that is not natural: *He minced over to serve us.*

IDM not mince (your) ˈwords to say sth in a direct way even though it might offend other people

■ ***noun*** (*BrE*) [U] meat, especially beef, that has been finely chopped in a special machine: *a pound of mince* ➲ see also HAMBURGER (2)

mince·meat /ˈmɪnsmiːt/ *noun* [U] (*especially BrE*) a mixture of dried fruit, spices, etc. used especially for making PIES

IDM make ˈmincemeat of sb (*informal*) to defeat sb completely in a fight, an argument or a competition

ˌ**mince ˈpie** *noun* a small round PIE filled with mincemeat, traditionally eaten at Christmas, especially in Britain

min·cer /ˈmɪnsə(r)/ (*especially BrE*) (*NAmE* usually ˈ**meat grinder**) *noun* a machine for cutting food, especially meat, into very small pieces

min·cing /ˈmɪnsɪŋ/ *adj.* (*disapproving*) (of a way of walking or speaking) very delicate, and not natural: *short mincing steps*

mind 🔑 /maɪnd/ *noun, verb*

■ ***noun***

▸ ABILITY TO THINK **1** 🔑 [C, U] the part of a person that makes them able to be aware of things, to think and to feel: *the* ***conscious/subconscious mind*** ◇ *There were all kinds of thoughts running through my mind.* ◇ *There was no doubt in his mind that he'd get the job.* ◇ *'Drugs' are associated in most people's minds with drug abuse.* ◇ *She was in a disturbed* ***state of mind.*** ◇ *I could not have complete* ***peace of mind*** *before they returned.* ➲ see also FRAME OF MIND, PRESENCE OF MIND **2** 🔑 [C] your ability to think and reason; your intelligence; the particular way that sb thinks **SYN intellect**: *to have a* ***brilliant/good/keen mind*** ◇ *a* ***creative/evil/suspicious mind*** ◇ *She had a lively and enquiring mind.* ◇ *His mind is as sharp as ever.* ◇ *I've no idea how her mind works!* ◇ *He had the body of a man and the mind of a child.* ◇ *insights into the criminal mind* ➲ see also ONE-TRACK MIND

▸ INTELLIGENT PERSON **3** [C] a person who is very intelligent **SYN brain** ➲ see also MASTERMIND: *She was one of the greatest minds of her generation.*

▸ THOUGHTS **4** 🔑 [C] your thoughts, interest, etc: ***Keep your mind on*** *your work!* ◇ *Her mind is completely occupied by the new baby.* ◇ *The lecture dragged on and my mind wandered.* ◇ *He* ***gave his mind to*** *the arrangements for the next day.* ◇ *As for avoiding you,* ***nothing could be further from my mind*** (= I was not thinking of it at all).

▸ MEMORY **5** 🔑 [C, usually sing.] your ability to remember things: *When I saw the exam questions my* ***mind*** *just* ***went blank*** (= I couldn't remember anything). ◇ *Sorry—your name has gone right out of my mind.*

IDM be all in sb's/the ˈmind to be sth that only exists in sb's imagination: *These problems are all in your mind, you know.* **bear/keep sb/sth in ˈmind | bear/keep in ˈmind that...** 🔑 to remember sb/sth; to remember or consider that... **be bored, frightened, pissed, stoned, etc. out of your ˈmind** (*informal*) to be extremely bored, etc. **be/go ˌout of your ˈmind** 🔑 to be unable to think or behave in a normal way; to become crazy: (*informal*) *You're lending them money? You must be out of your tiny mind!* ➲ SYNONYMS at MAD **be in two ˈminds about sth/about doing sth** (*BrE*) (*NAmE* **be of two ˈminds about sth/about doing sth**) to be unable to decide what you think about sb/sth, or whether to do sth or not: *I was in two minds about the book* (= I didn't know if I liked it or not). ◇ *She's in two minds about accepting his invitation.* **be of one/the same ˈmind (about sb/sth)** to have the same opinion about sb/sth **be ˌout of your ˈmind with worry, etc.** to be extremely worried, etc. **bring/call sb/sth to ˈmind** (*formal*) **1** to remember sb/sth **SYN recall**: *She couldn't call to mind where she had seen him before.* **2** to remind you of sb/sth **SYN recall**: *The painting brings to mind some of Picasso's early works.* **come/spring to ˈmind** 🔑 if sth **comes/springs to mind**, you suddenly remember or think of it: *When discussing influential modern artists, three names immediately come to mind.* **have a good mind to do sth | have half a mind to do sth** **1** used to say that you think you will do sth, although you are not sure: *I've half a mind to come with you tomorrow.* **2** used to say that you disapprove of what sb has done and should do sth about it, although you probably will not: *I've a good mind to write and tell your parents about it.* **have sb/sth in ˈmind (for sth)** 🔑 to be thinking of sb/sth, especially for a particular job, etc: *Do you have anyone in mind for this job?* ◇ *Watching TV all evening wasn't exactly what I had in mind!* **have it in mind to do sth** (*formal*) to intend to do sth **have a mind of your ˈown** to have your own opinion and make your own decisions without being influenced by other people: *She has a mind of her own and isn't afraid to say what she thinks.* ◇ (*humorous*) *My computer seems to have a mind of its own!* **lose your ˈmind** 🔑 to become mentally ill **make up your ˈmind | make your ˈmind up** 🔑 to decide sth: *They're both beautiful—I can't make up my mind.* ◇ *Have you made up your minds where to go for your honeymoon?* ◇ *You'll never persuade him to stay—his* ***mind's made up*** (= he has definitely decided to go). ◇ *Come on—it's* ***make your mind up time!*** ˌ**mind over ˈmatter** the use of the power of your mind to deal with physical problems **your mind's ˈeye** your imagination: *He pictured the scene in his mind's eye.* **on your ˈmind** if sb/sth is **on your mind**, you are thinking and worrying about them/it a lot: *You've been on my mind all day.* ◇ *Don't bother your father tonight—he's* ***got a lot on his mind.*** **put/get sth out of your ˈmind** to stop thinking about sb/sth; to deliberately forget sb/sth: *I just can't get her out of my mind.* **put sb in mind of sb/sth** (*old-fashioned*) to make sb think of sb/sth; to remind sb of sb/sth **put/set sb's ˈmind at ease/rest** to do or say sth to make sb stop worrying about sth **SYN reassure** **put/set/turn your ˈmind to sth | set your ˈmind on sth** to decide you want to achieve sth and give this all your attention: *She could have been a brilliant pianist if she'd put her mind to it.* **take your mind off sth** to make you forget about sth unpleasant for a short time **SYN distract** **to ˈmy mind** in my opinion: *It was a ridiculous thing to do, to my mind.* ➲ more at BACK *n.*, BEND *v.*, BLOW *v.*, BOGGLE, CAST *v.*, CHANGE *v.*, CHANGE *n.*, CLOSE[1] *v.*, CROSS *v.*, ETCH, GREAT *adj.*, KNOW *v.*, MEETING, OPEN *adj.*, OPEN *v.*, PIECE *n.*, PREY *v.*, PUSH *v.*, RIGHT *adj.*, SIEVE *n.*, SIGHT *n.*, SLIP *v.*, SPEAK, STICK *v.*, TURN *n.*, UNSOUND

M

■ *verb*

▸ BE UPSET/ANNOYED **1** [T, I] (used especially in questions or with negatives; not used in the passive) to be upset, annoyed or worried by sth: **~ (sth)** *I don't mind the cold—it's the rain I don't like.* ◇ *I hope you don't mind the noise.* ◇ *He wouldn't have minded so much if she'd told him the truth.* ◇ **~ about sth** *Did she mind about not getting the job?* ◇ **~ doing sth** *Did she mind not getting the job?* ◇ **~ sb/sth doing sth** *Do your parents mind you leaving home?* ◇ (*formal*) *Do your parents mind your leaving home?* ◇ **~ how, what, etc...** *She never minded how hot it was.* ◇ **~ that...** *He minded that he hadn't been asked.*

▸ ASKING PERMISSION **2** [I, T] used to ask for permission to do sth, or to ask sb in a polite way to do sth: *Do you mind if I open the window?* ◇ **~ sb doing sth** *Are you married, if you don't mind me asking?* ◇ (*formal*) *Are you married, if you don't mind my asking?* ◇ **~ doing sth** *Would you mind explaining that again, please?* ◇ *Do you mind driving? I'm feeling pretty tired.*

▸ NOT CARE/WORRY **3** **not mind** [I, T, no passive] to not care or not be concerned about sth: *'Would you like tea or coffee?' 'I don't mind—either's fine.'* ◇ **~ sb** *Don't mind her—she didn't mean what she said.* ◇ *Don't mind me* (= don't let me disturb you) *—I'll just sit here quietly.*

▸ BE WILLING **4** **not mind doing sth** [T] to be willing to do sth: *I don't mind helping if you can't find anyone else.*

▸ WARNING **5** (*BrE*) (also **watch** *NAmE, BrE*) [T] used to tell sb to be careful about sth or warn them about a danger: **~ sth** *Mind* (= Don't fall on) *that step!* ◇ *Mind your head!* (= for example, be careful you don't hit it on a low ceiling) ◇ *Mind your language!* (= don't speak in a rude or offensive way) ◇ **~ how, where, etc...** *Mind how you go!* (= often used when you say goodbye to sb) ◇ *Mind where you're treading!* ◇ **~ (that)...** *Mind you don't cut yourself—that knife's very sharp.* ◇ *You must be home for dinner, mind.* HELP 'That' is nearly always left out in this pattern.

▸ OBEY **6** [T] **~ sb** (*NAmE, IrishE*) to pay attention to what sb says, and obey them: *And the moral of the story is: always mind your mother!*

▸ TAKE CARE OF **7** (*especially BrE*) (*NAmE* usually **watch**) [T] **~ sb/sth** to take care of sb/sth SYN **look after**: *Who's minding the children this evening?* ◇ *Could you mind my bags for a moment?*

IDM **,do you 'mind?** (*ironic*) used to show that you are annoyed about sth that sb has just said or done: *Do you mind? I was here before you.* **I don't mind ad'mitting, 'telling you..., etc.** used to emphasize what you are saying, especially when you are talking about sth that may be embarrassing for you: *I was scared, I don't mind telling you!* **I don't mind if I 'do** (*informal*) used to say politely that you would like sth you have been offered: *'Cup of tea, Brian?' 'I don't mind if I do.'* **if you ,don't 'mind | if you ,wouldn't 'mind 1** used to check that sb does not object to sth you want to do, or to ask sb politely to do sth: *I'd like to ask you a few questions, if you don't mind.* ◇ *Can you read that form carefully, if you wouldn't mind, and then sign it.* **2** (often *ironic*) used to show that you object to sth that sb has said or done: *I give the orders around here, if you don't mind.* **3** used to refuse an offer politely: *'Will you come with us tonight?' 'I won't, if you don't mind—I've got a lot of work to do.'* **if you ,don't mind me/my 'saying so ...** used when you are going to criticize sb or say sth that might upset them: *That colour doesn't really suit you, if you don't mind my saying so.* **I wouldn't mind sth/doing sth** used to say politely that you would very much like sth/to do sth: *I wouldn't mind a cup of coffee, if it's no trouble.* ◇ *I wouldn't mind having his money!* **,mind your ,own 'business** (*informal*) to think about your own affairs and not ask questions about or try to get involved in other people's lives: *'What are you reading?' 'Mind your own business!'* ◇ *I was just sitting there, minding my own business, when a man started shouting at me.* **mind the 'shop** (*BrE*) (*NAmE* **mind the 'store**) to be in charge of sth for a short time while sb is away: *Who's minding the shop while the boss is abroad?* **,mind 'you** (*informal*) used to add sth to what you have just said, especially sth that makes it less strong: *I've heard they're getting divorced. Mind you, I'm not surprised—they were always arguing.* **,mind your Ps and 'Qs** (*informal*) to behave in the most polite way you can **,never 'mind 1** (*especially BrE*) used to tell sb not to worry or be upset: *Have you broken it? Never mind, we can buy another one.* **2** used to suggest that sth is not important: *This isn't where I intended to take you—but never mind, it's just as good.* **3** used to emphasize that what is true about the first thing you have said is even more true about the second SYN **let alone**: *I never thought she'd win once, never mind twice!* **never mind (about) (doing) sth** used to tell sb they shouldn't think about sth or do sth because it is not as important as sth else, or because you will do it: *Never mind your car—what about the damage to my fence?* ◇ *Never mind washing the dishes—I'll do them later.* **,never you 'mind** (*informal*) used to tell sb not to ask about sth because you are not going to tell them: *'Who told you about it?' 'Never you mind!'* ◇ *Never you mind how I found out—it's true, isn't it?* ➲ more at LANGUAGE, STEP *n.*

PHR V **,mind 'out** (*BrE, informal*) used to tell sb to move so that you can pass SYN **watch out**: *Mind out—you're in the way there!* **,mind 'out (for sb/sth)** (*BrE*) used to warn sb of danger: *Have some of my plum jam—but mind out for the stones.*

'mind-bending *adj.* (*informal*) (especially of drugs) having a strong effect on your mind

'mind-blowing *adj.* (*informal*) very exciting, impressive or surprising: *Watching your baby being born is a mind-blowing experience.*

'mind-boggling *adj.* (*informal*) very difficult to imagine or to understand; extremely surprising: *a problem of mind-boggling complexity* ➲ compare BOGGLE

mind·ed /ˈmaɪndɪd/ *adj.* **1** (used with adjectives to form compound adjectives) having the way of thinking, the attitude or the type of character mentioned: *a fair-minded employer* ◇ *high-minded principles* ◇ *I appeal to all like-minded people to support me.* ➲ see also ABSENT-MINDED, BLOODY-MINDED, SINGLE-MINDED **2** (used with adverbs to form compound adjectives) having the type of mind that is interested in or able to understand the areas mentioned: *I'm not very politically minded.* **3** (used with nouns to form compound adjectives) interested in or enthusiastic about the thing mentioned: *a reform-minded government* **4** [not before noun] **~ (to do sth)** (*formal*) wishing or intending to do sth SYN **inclined**: *She was minded to accept their offer.*

mind·er /ˈmaɪndə(r)/ *noun* (*especially BrE*) a person whose job is to take care of and protect another person: *a star surrounded by her minders* ➲ see also CHILDMINDER

mind·ful /ˈmaɪndfl/ *adj.* **~ of sb/sth | ~ that...** (*formal*) remembering sb/sth and considering them or it when you do sth SYN **conscious**: *mindful of our responsibilities* ◇ *Mindful of the danger of tropical storms, I decided not to go out.*

'mind game *noun* something that you do or say in order to make sb feel less confident, especially to gain an advantage for yourself

mind·less /ˈmaɪndləs/ *adj.* **1** done or acting without thought and for no particular reason or purpose; SYN **senseless**: *mindless violence* ◇ *mindless vandals* **2** not needing thought or intelligence SYN **dull**: *a mindless and repetitive task* **3** **~ of sb/sth** (*formal*) not remembering sb/sth and not considering them or it when you do sth: *We explored the whole town, mindless of the cold and rain.* ▸ **mind·less·ly** *adv.*

'mind-numbing *adj.* very boring: *mind-numbing conversation* ▸ **mind-numbing·ly** *adv.*: *The lecture was mind-numbingly tedious.*

'mind-reader *noun* (often *humorous*) a person who knows what sb else is thinking without being told

mind·set /ˈmaɪndset/ *noun* a set of attitudes or fixed ideas that sb has and that are often difficult to change SYN **mentality**: *a conservative mindset* ◇ *the mindset of the computer generation*

mind·share /ˈmaɪndʃeə(r); *NAmE* -ʃer/ *noun* [U] (*business*) the extent of knowledge of a company or product among consumers, compared with their knowledge of others of the same type

M

mine 0-ᵀ /maɪn/ *pron., noun, verb*

■ ***pron.*** 0-ᵀ (the possessive form of *I*) **1** of or belonging to the person writing or speaking: *That's mine.* ◇ *He's a friend **of mine*** (= one of my friends). ◇ *She wanted one like mine* (= like I have). **2** (*BrE, informal*) my home: *Let's go back to mine after the show.*

■ ***noun*** **1** 0-ᵀ a deep hole or holes under the ground where minerals such as coal, gold, etc. are dug: *a **copper/diamond mine*** ➲ compare PIT, QUARRY ➲ see also MINING, COAL MINE, GOLD MINE **2** 0-ᵀ a type of bomb that is hidden under the ground or in the sea and that explodes when sb/sth touches it ➲ see also LANDMINE

IDM **a mine of inforˈmation (about/on sb/sth)** a person, book, etc. that can give you a lot of information on a particular subject

■ ***verb*** **1** [T, I] to dig holes in the ground in order to find and obtain coal, diamonds, etc: **~ sth (for sth)** *The area has been mined for slate for centuries.* ◇ **~ (for sth)** *They were mining for gold.* **2** [T] **~ sth** to place MINES *n.* (2) below the surface of an area of land or water; to destroy a vehicle with mines: *The coastal route had been mined.* ◇ *The UN convoy was mined on its way to the border.*

ˈmine dump *noun* (*SAfrE*) = DUMP (2)

mine·field /ˈmaɪnfiːld/ *noun* **1** an area of land or water where MINES (= bombs that explode when they are touched) have been hidden **2** a situation that contains hidden dangers or difficulties: *a legal minefield* ◇ *Tax can be a minefield for the unwary.*

mine·hunt·er /ˈmaɪnhʌntə(r)/ *noun* (*BrE*) a military ship for finding and destroying MINES (= bombs that explode when they are touched)

miner /ˈmaɪnə(r)/ *noun* a person who works in a mine taking out coal, gold, diamonds, etc. ➲ see also COAL MINER

min·eral 0-ᵀ /ˈmɪnərəl/ *noun*

1 0-ᵀ [C, U] a substance that is naturally present in the earth and is not formed from animal or vegetable matter, for example gold and salt. Some minerals are also present in food and drink and in the human body and are essential for good health: ***mineral deposits/extraction*** ◇ *the recommended intake of vitamins and minerals* ➲ COLLOCATIONS at DIET ➲ compare VEGETABLE **2** [C, usually pl.] (*BrE, formal*) (*NAmE* **soda**) a sweet drink in various flavours that has bubbles of gas in it and does not contain alcohol: *Soft drinks and minerals sold here.*

min·er·al·ogist /ˌmɪnəˈrælədʒɪst/ *noun* a scientist who studies mineralogy

min·er·al·ogy /ˌmɪnəˈrælədʒi/ *noun* [U] the scientific study of minerals ▸ **min·er·al·ogic·al** /ˌmɪnərəˈlɒdʒɪkl; *NAmE* -ˈlɑːdʒ-/ *adj.*

ˈmineral oil *noun* [U] **1** (*BrE*) = PETROLEUM **2** (*NAmE*) (*BrE* **ˌliquid ˈparaffin**) a liquid with no colour and no smell that comes from PETROLEUM and is used in medicines and COSMETICS

ˈmineral water *noun* **1** [U, C] water from a SPRING in the ground that contains mineral salts or gases: *A glass of mineral water, please.* **2** [C] a glass or bottle of mineral water

mine·shaft /ˈmaɪnʃɑːft; *NAmE* -ʃæft/ *noun* a deep narrow hole that goes down to a mine

min·es·trone /ˌmɪnəˈstrəʊni; *NAmE* -ˈstroʊ-/ *noun* [U] an Italian soup containing small pieces of vegetables and PASTA

mine·sweeper /ˈmaɪnswiːpə(r)/ *noun* a ship used for finding and clearing away MINES (= bombs that explode when they are touched)

mine·work·er /ˈmaɪnwɜːkə(r); *NAmE* -wɜːrk-/ *noun* a person who works in a mine

minge /mɪndʒ/ *noun* (*BrE, taboo, slang*) the female sex organs or PUBIC hair

ming·er /ˈmɪŋə(r)/ *noun* (*BrE, informal*) a person who is not attractive

min·ging /ˈmɪŋɪŋ/ *adj.* (*BrE, informal*) very bad, unpleasant or ugly

min·gle /ˈmɪŋgl/ *verb* **1** [I, T] to combine or make one thing combine with another: *The sounds of laughter and singing mingled in the evening air.* ◇ **~ (A) (with B)** *Her tears mingled with the blood on her face.* ◇ *He felt a kind of happiness mingled with regret.* ◇ **~ (A and B) (together)** *The flowers mingle together to form a blaze of colour.* ➲ SYNONYMS at MIX **2** [I] to move among people and talk to them, especially at a social event SYN **circulate**: *The princess was not recognized and mingled freely with the crowds.* ◇ *If you'll excuse me, I must go and mingle* (= talk to other guests).

mingy /ˈmɪndʒi/ *adj.* (*BrE, informal*) small, not generous SYN **stingy**

mini /ˈmɪni/ *noun* = MINISKIRT

mini- /ˈmɪni/ *combining form* (in nouns) small: *mini-break* (= a short holiday/vacation) ◇ *minigolf*

mini·ature /ˈmɪnətʃə(r); *NAmE* also -tʃʊr/ *adj., noun*

■ ***adj.*** [only before noun] very small; much smaller than usual: *miniature roses* ◇ *a rare breed of miniature horses* ◇ *It looks like a miniature version of James Bond's car.*

■ ***noun*** **1** a very small detailed painting, often of a person **2** a very small copy or model of sth; a very small version of sth: *brandy miniatures* (= very small bottles)

IDM **in miniature** on a very small scale: *a doll's house with everything in miniature* ◇ *Through play, children act out in miniature the dramas of adult life.*

ˈminiature golf *noun* [U] (*NAmE*) = MINIGOLF

mini·atur·ist /ˈmɪnɪtʃərɪst/ *noun* a painter who paints small works of art

mini·atur·ize (*BrE* also **-ise**) /ˈmɪnətʃəraɪz/ *verb* **~ sth** to make a much smaller version of sth ▸ **mini·atur·iza·tion, -isa·tion** /ˌmɪnətʃəraɪˈzeɪʃn; *NAmE* -rəˈzeɪ-/ *noun* [U] **mini·atur·ized, -ised** *adj.* [only before noun]: *a miniaturized listening device*

mini·bar /ˈmɪnibɑː(r)/ *noun* a small fridge/refrigerator in a hotel room, with drinks in it for guests to use

mini·beast /ˈmɪnibiːst/ *noun* (*BrE*) (used especially in schools) any small animal that does not have a BACKBONE: *minibeasts such as worms, snails, centipedes and spiders*

mini·bus /ˈmɪnibʌs/ *noun* a small vehicle with seats for about twelve people ➲ VISUAL VOCAB page V46

mini·cab /ˈmɪnikæb/ *noun* (*BrE*) a taxi that you have to order by telephone and cannot stop in the street

mini·cam /ˈmɪnikæm/ *noun* a video camera that is small enough to hold in one hand

mini·com·puter /ˈmɪnikəmpjuːtə(r)/ *noun* a computer that is smaller and slower than a MAINFRAME but larger and faster than a MICROCOMPUTER

mini·disc /ˈmɪnidɪsk/ *noun* a disc like a small CD that can record and play sound or data

mini·dress /ˈmɪnidres/ *noun* a very short dress

mini·golf /ˈmɪnigɒlf; *NAmE* -gɑːlf; -gɔːlf/ (*NAmE* also **ˈminiature golf**) (*BrE* also **ˈcrazy golf**) *noun* [U] a type of GOLF in which people go around a small course hitting a ball through or over little tunnels, hills, bridges and other objects

minim /ˈmɪnɪm/ (*BrE*) (*NAmE* **ˈhalf note**) *noun* (*music*) a note that lasts twice as long as a CROTCHET/QUARTER NOTE ➲ picture at MUSIC

min·imal AW /ˈmɪnɪməl/ *adj.* very small in size or amount; as small as possible: *The work was carried out at minimal cost.* ◇ *There's only a minimal amount of risk involved.* ◇ *The damage to the car was minimal.* ➲ compare MAXIMAL ▸ **min·im·al·ly** AW *adv.*: *minimally invasive surgery* ◇ *The episode was reported minimally in the press.*

min·im·al·ist AW /ˈmɪnɪməlɪst/ *noun* an artist, a musician, etc. who uses very simple ideas or a very small number of simple things in their work ▸ **min·im·al·ism** *noun* [U] **min·im·al·ist** *adj.*

ˌminimal ˈpair *noun* (*phonetics*) a pair of words, sounds, etc. which are distinguished from each other by only one feature, for example *pin* and *bin*

mini·mart /ˈmɪnimɑːt; *NAmE* -mɑːrt/ *noun* (*NAmE*) a small shop/store that sells food, newspapers, etc. and stays open very late

min·im·ize (*BrE* also **-ise**) AW /ˈmɪnɪmaɪz/ *verb* **1 ~ sth** to reduce sth, especially sth bad, to the lowest possible level: *Good hygiene helps to minimize the risk of infection.* OPP **maximize 2 ~ sth** to try to make sth seem less important than it really is SYN **play down**: *He always tried to minimize his own faults, while exaggerating those of others.* **3 ~ sth** to make sth small, especially on a computer screen: *Minimize any windows you have open.* OPP **maximize** ▸ **mini·miza·tion, -isa·ation** /ˌmɪnɪmaɪˈzeɪʃn; *NAmE* -məˈz-/ *noun* [U]

mini·moto (also **mini-moto**) /ˈmɪniməʊtəʊ; *NAmE* -moʊtoʊ/ *noun* (*pl.* -os) a small motorcycle about 60cm high that people ride for fun and in races, but not on public roads

min·imum 0-w AW /ˈmɪnɪməm/ *adj., noun*

■ ***adj.*** 0-w [usually before noun] (*abbr.* **min.**) the smallest that is possible or allowed; extremely small: *a **minimum charge/price** ◇ the minimum age for retirement ◇ The work was done with the minimum amount of effort.* OPP **maximum** ▸ **min·imum** *adv.*: *You'll need £200 minimum for your holiday expenses.*

■ ***noun*** (*pl.* **min·ima** /-mə/) [C, usually sing.] **1** 0-w (*abbr.* **min.**) the smallest or lowest amount that is possible, required or recorded: *Costs should **be kept to a minimum**. ◇ The class needs a minimum of six students to continue. ◇ As an **absolute minimum**, you should spend two hours in the evening studying. ◇ Temperatures will fall to a minimum of 10 degrees.* **2** 0-w [sing.] an extremely small amount: *He passed the exams with the minimum of effort.* OPP **maximum**

ˌminimum seˈcurity prison (*NAmE*) (*BrE* **ˌopen ˈprison**) *noun* a prison in which prisoners have more freedom than in ordinary prisons

ˌminimum ˈwage *noun* [sing.] the lowest wage that an employer is allowed to pay by law

min·ing /ˈmaɪnɪŋ/ *noun* [U] the process of getting coal and other minerals from under the ground; the industry involved in this: ***coal/diamond/gold/tin mining** ◇ a **mining company/community/engineer*** ➲ see also MINE

ˈmini-note *noun* = SUBNOTEBOOK

min·ion /ˈmɪniən/ *noun* (*disapproving* or *humorous*) an unimportant person in an organization who has to obey orders; a servant

ˌmini-ˈroundabout *noun* (*BrE*) a white circle painted on a road at a place where two or more roads meet, that all traffic must go around in the same direction

mini·ser·ies /ˈmɪnisɪəriːz; *NAmE* -sɪriːz/ *noun* (*pl.* **mini·ser·ies**) a television play that is divided into a number of parts and shown on different days

mini·skirt /ˈmɪniskɜːt; *NAmE* -skɜːrt/ (also **mini**) *noun* a very short skirt

min·is·ter 0-w /ˈmɪnɪstə(r)/ *noun, verb*

■ ***noun*** **1** 0-w (often **Minister**) (*BrE*) (in Britain and many other countries) a senior member of the government who is in charge of a government department or a branch of one: *the Minister of Education ◇ a meeting of EU Foreign Ministers ◇ senior ministers in the Cabinet ◇ cabinet ministers* ➲ see also FIRST MINISTER, PRIME MINISTER **2** 0-w (in some Protestant Christian Churches) a trained religious leader: *a Methodist minister* ➲ compare PASTOR, PRIEST, VICAR **3** a person, lower in rank than an AMBASSADOR, whose job is to represent their government in a foreign country

■ ***verb***

PHR V **ˈminister to sb/sth** (*formal*) to care for sb, especially sb who is sick or old, and make sure that they have everything they need SYN **tend**

min·is·ter·ial AW /ˌmɪnɪˈstɪəriəl; *NAmE* -ˈstɪr-/ *adj.* connected with a government minister or ministers: *decisions taken at ministerial level ◇ to **hold ministerial office*** (= to have the job of a government minister)

min·is·ter·ing /ˈmɪnɪstərɪŋ/ *adj.* [only before noun] (*formal*) caring for people: *She could not see herself in the role of **ministering angel**.*

ˌMinister of ˈState *noun* a British government minister but not one who is in charge of a department

min·is·tra·tions /ˌmɪnɪˈstreɪʃnz/ *noun* [pl.] (*formal* or *humorous*) the act of helping or caring for sb especially when they are ill/sick or in trouble

min·is·try 0-w AW /ˈmɪnɪstri/ *noun* (*pl.* -ies)

1 0-w [C] (*BrE*) a government department that has a particular area of responsibility: *the Ministry of Defence ◇ a ministry spokesperson* **2 the Ministry** [sing.+ sing./pl. v.] ministers of religion, especially Protestant ministers, when they are mentioned as a group **3** [C, usually sing.] the work and duties of a minister in the Church; the period of time spent working as a minister in the Church

mini·van (also **Mini Van™**) /ˈmɪnivæn/ (*especially NAmE*) (*BrE* **ˈpeople carrier**, **ˈpeople mover**) *noun* a large car, like a van, designed to carry up to eight people ➲ VISUAL VOCAB page V42

mink /mɪŋk/ *noun* (*pl.* **mink** or **minks**) **1** [C] a small wild animal with thick shiny fur, a long body and short legs. Mink are often kept on farms for their fur: *a mink farm* **2** [U] the skin and shiny brown fur of the mink, used for making expensive coats, etc: *a mink jacket* **3** [C] a coat or jacket made of mink

minke /ˈmɪŋki; -kə/ (also **ˈminke whale**) *noun* a small WHALE that is dark grey on top and white underneath

min·now /ˈmɪnəʊ; *NAmE* -noʊ/ *noun* **1** a very small FRESHWATER fish **2** a company or sports team that is small or unimportant

minor 0-w AW /ˈmaɪnə(r)/ *adj., noun, verb*

■ ***adj.*** **1** 0-w [usually before noun] not very large, important or serious: *a minor road ◇ minor injuries ◇ to undergo minor surgery ◇ youths imprisoned for minor offences ◇ There may be some minor changes to the schedule. ◇ Women played a relatively minor role in the organization.* OPP **major** **2** (*music*) based on a SCALE in which the third note is a SEMITONE/HALF TONE higher than the second note: *the key of C minor* ➲ compare MAJOR

■ ***noun*** **1** (*law*) a person who is under the age at which you legally become an adult and are responsible for your actions: *It is an offence to serve alcohol to minors.* **2** (*especially NAmE*) a subject that you study at university in addition to your MAJOR

■ ***verb***

PHR V **ˈminor in sth** (*NAmE*) to study sth at college, but not as your main subject ➲ compare MAJOR

mi·nor·ity 0-w AW /maɪˈnɒrəti; *NAmE* -ˈnɔːr-/ *noun* (*pl.* -ies)

1 0-w [sing.+ sing./pl. v.] the smaller part of a group; less than half of the people or things in a large group: *Only a small minority of students is/are interested in politics these days. ◇ minority shareholders in the bank* OPP **majority** **2** 0-w [C] a small group within a community or country that is different because of race, religion, language, etc: *the rights of **ethnic/racial minorities** ◇ minority languages ◇ a large German-speaking minority in the east of the country ◇ (NAmE) The school is 95 per cent minority* (= 95 per cent of children are not white Americans but from different groups). *◇ (NAmE) minority neighborhoods* (= where no or few white people live) ➲ COLLOCATIONS at RACE **3** [U] (*law*) the state of being under the age at which you are legally an adult

IDM **be in a/the miˈnority** 0-w to form much less than half of a large group **be in a minority of ˈone** (often *humorous*) to be the only person to have a particular opinion or to vote a particular way

miˌnority ˈgovernment *noun* [C, U] a government that has fewer seats in parliament than the total number held by all the other parties

miˌnority ˈleader *noun* (in the US Senate or House of Representatives) a leader of a political party that does not have a majority

'minor league (also **'Minor league**) *noun* (*NAmE*) a league of professional sports teams, especially in BASEBALL, that play at a lower level than the major leagues

'minor-league *adj.* [only before noun] (*NAmE*) **1** (*sport*) connected with teams in the minor leagues in BASEBALL: *a minor-league team* **2** not very important and having little influence: *a minor-league business*

Mi·no·taur /'maɪnətɔ:(r); 'mɪn-/ *noun* (in ancient Greek stories) an imaginary creature who was half man and half BULL

min·ster /'mɪnstə(r)/ *noun* (*BrE*) a large or important church: *York Minster*

min·strel /'mɪnstrəl/ *noun* a musician or singer in the Middle Ages

mint /mɪnt/ *noun, verb*

■ ***noun*** **1** [U] a plant with dark green leaves that have a fresh smell and taste and are added to food and drinks to give flavour, and used in cooking as a HERB and to decorate food: *mint-flavoured toothpaste* ◇ *I decorated the fruit salad with a sprig of mint.* ◇ *roast lamb with mint sauce* ➲ VISUAL VOCAB page V28 **2** [C] a sweet/candy flavoured with a type of mint called PEPPERMINT: *after-dinner mints* **3** [C] a place where money is made: *the Royal Mint* (= the one where British coins and notes are made) **4 a mint** [sing.] (*informal*) a large amount of money: *to* ***make/cost a mint***

IDM **in mint con'dition** new or as good as new; in perfect condition

■ ***verb*** **~ sth** to make a coin from metal

mint·ed /'mɪntɪd/ *adj.* **1 freshly/newly ~** recently produced, invented, etc: *a newly minted expression* **2** (of food) flavoured with mint **3** (*BrE, informal*) very rich

,mint 'julep (also **julep**) *noun* [U, C] an alcoholic drink made by mixing BOURBON with crushed ice, sugar and MINT

minty /'mɪnti/ *adj.* tasting or smelling of MINT: *a* ***minty flavour/smell***

min·uet /,mɪnju'et/ *noun* a slow elegant dance that was popular in the 17th and 18th centuries; a piece of music for this dance

minus /'maɪnəs/ *prep., noun, adj.*

■ ***prep.*** **1** used when you SUBTRACT (= take away) one number or thing from another one: *Seven minus three is four* (*7 – 3 = 4*). ◇ *the former Soviet Union, minus the Baltic republics and Georgia* **2** used to express temperature below zero degrees: *It was minus ten.* ◇ *The temperature dropped to minus 28 degrees centigrade* (*–28°C*). **3** (*informal*) without sth that was there before: *We're going to be minus a car for a while.* OPP **plus** IDM see PLUS *prep.*

■ ***noun*** **1** (also **'minus sign**) The symbol (–), used in mathematics **2** (*informal*) a negative quality; a disadvantage: *Let's consider the pluses and minuses of changing the system.* OPP **plus**

■ ***adj.*** **1** (*mathematics*) lower than zero: *a* ***minus figure/number*** **2** making sth seem negative and less attractive or good: *What are the car's* ***minus points*** (= the disadvantages)? ◇ ***On the minus side****, rented property is expensive and difficult to find.* **3** [not before noun] (used in a system of marks/grades) slightly lower than the mark/grade A, B, etc: *I got (a) B minus (B–) in the test.* OPP **plus**

min·us·cule /'mɪnəskju:l/ *adj.* extremely small

min·ute¹ O-w /'mɪnɪt/ *noun, verb* ➲ see also MINUTE²

■ ***noun***

▸ PART OF HOUR **1** O-w [C] (*abbr.* **min.**) each of the 60 parts of an hour, that are equal to 60 seconds: *It's four minutes to six.* ◇ *I'll be back in a few minutes.* ◇ *Boil the rice for 20 minutes.* ◇ *a ten-minute bus ride* ◇ *I enjoyed every minute of the party.*

▸ VERY SHORT TIME **2** O-w [sing.] (*informal*) a very short time: *It only takes a minute to make a salad.* ◇ ***Hang on a minute****—I'll just get my coat.* ◇ *I just have to finish this—I won't be a minute.* ◇ *Could I see you for a minute?* ◇ *I'll be with you* ***in a minute****, Jo.* ◇ *Typical English weather—one minute it's raining and the next minute the sun is shining.*

▸ EXACT MOMENT **3** O-w [sing.] an exact moment in time: *At that very minute, Tom walked in.*

▸ ANGLES **4** [C] each of the 60 equal parts of a degree, used in measuring angles: *37 degrees 30 minutes* (*37° 30'*)

▸ RECORD OF MEETING **5 the minutes** [pl.] a summary or record of what is said or decided at a formal meeting: *We read through the minutes of the last meeting.* ◇ *Who is going to* ***take the minutes*** (= write them)?

▸ SHORT NOTE **6** [C] a short note on a subject, especially one that recommends a course of action

IDM **(at) any 'minute ('now)** O-w very soon: *Hurry up! He'll be back any minute now.* **the minute (that)...** O-w as soon as...: *I want to see him the minute he arrives.* **,not for a/one 'minute** certainly not; not at all: *I don't think for a minute that she'll accept but you can ask her.* **this minute** O-w immediately; now: *Come down this minute!* ◇ *I don't know what I'm going to do yet—I've* ***just this minute*** *found out.* **to the 'minute** exactly: *The train arrived at 9.05 to the minute.* **,up to the 'minute** (*informal*) **1** fashionable and modern: *Her styles are always up to the minute.* **2** having the latest information: *The traffic reports are up to the minute.* ➲ see also UP-TO-THE-MINUTE ➲ more at BORN, JUST *adv.*, LAST *det.*, WAIT *v.*

■ ***verb*** **~ sth** | **~ that...** to write down sth that is said at a meeting in the official record (=the minutes): *I'd like that last remark to be minuted.*

mi·nute² /maɪ'nju:t; *NAmE* also -'nu:t/ *adj.* ➲ see also MINUTE¹ (*superlative* **minut·est**, no *comparative*) **1** extremely small SYN **tiny**: *minute amounts of chemicals in the water* ◇ *The kitchen on the boat is minute.* **2** very detailed, careful and thorough: *a* ***minute examination/inspection*** ◇ *She remembered everything* ***in minute detail/in the minutest detail****(s).* ▸ **mi·nute·ly** *adv.*: *The agreement has been examined minutely.*

'minute hand *noun* [usually sing.] the hand on a watch or clock that points to the minutes ➲ picture at CLOCK

Min·ute·man /'mɪnɪtmæn/ *noun* (*pl.* **-men** /-men/) (*US*) (during the American Revolution) a member of a group of men who were not soldiers but who were ready to fight immediately when they were needed

mi·nu·tiae /maɪ'nju:ʃii:; *NAmE* mɪ'nu:ʃii:/ *noun* [pl.] very small details: *the minutiae of the contract*

minx /mɪŋks/ *noun* [sing.] (*old-fashioned* or *humorous*) a girl or young woman who is clever at getting what she wants, and does not show respect

MIPS /mɪps/ *abbr.* (*computing*) million instructions per second (a unit for measuring computer speed)

miraa /'mɪrɑ:/ *noun* [U] (*EAfrE*) a form of KHAT

mir·acle /'mɪrəkl/ *noun* **1** [C] an act or event that does not follow the laws of nature and is believed to be caused by God SYN **wonder** **2** [sing.] (*informal*) a lucky thing that happens that you did not expect or think was possible SYN **wonder**: *an economic miracle* ◇ ***It's a miracle (that)*** *nobody was killed in the crash.* ◇ *It would take a miracle to make this business profitable.* ◇ *a* ***miracle cure/drug*** **3** [C] **~ of sth** a very good example or product of sth SYN **wonder**: *The car is a miracle of engineering.*

IDM **work/perform 'miracles** to achieve very good results: *Her exercise programme has worked miracles for her.*

mi·racu·lous /mɪ'rækjələs/ *adj.* like a miracle; completely unexpected and very lucky SYN **extraordinary, phenomenal**: *miraculous powers of healing* ◇ *She's made a miraculous recovery.* ▸ **mi·racu·lous·ly** *adv.*: *They miraculously survived the plane crash.*

mir·age /'mɪrɑ:ʒ; mɪ'rɑ:ʒ; *NAmE* mə'rɑ:ʒ/ *noun* **1** an effect caused by hot air in deserts or on roads, that makes you think you can see sth, such as water, which is not there **2** a hope or wish that you cannot make happen because it is not realistic SYN **illusion**: *His idea of love was a mirage.*

Mi·randa /mɪ'rændə/ *adj.* (in the US) relating to the fact that the police must tell sb who has been arrested about their rights, including the right not to answer questions, and warn them that anything they say may be used as evidence against them: *The police read him his Miranda rights.*

M

ORIGIN From the decision of the Supreme Court on the case of Miranda v the State of Arizona in 1966.

mire /ˈmaɪə(r)/ *noun* [U] an area of deep mud SYN **bog**: *The wheels sank deeper into the mire.* ◇ (*figurative*) *My name had been dragged through the mire* (= my reputation was ruined). ◇ (*figurative*) *The government was sinking deeper and deeper* ***into the mire*** (= getting further into a difficult situation).

mired /ˈmaɪəd; *NAmE* ˈmaɪərd/ *adj.* [not before noun] **~ in sth** (*literary*) **1** in a difficult or unpleasant situation that you cannot escape from: *The country was mired in recession.* **2** stuck in deep mud

mir·ror 🔑 /ˈmɪrə(r)/ *noun, verb*
- ***noun* 1** 🔑 [C] a piece of special flat glass that reflects images, so that you can see yourself when you look in it: *He looked at himself* ***in the mirror.*** ◇ *a rear-view mirror* (= in a car, so that the driver can see what is behind) ◇ (*BrE*) *a wing mirror* (= on the side of a car) ◇ (*NAmE*) *a side-view mirror* ➲ VISUAL VOCAB pages V20, V41, V49 **2** 🔑 **a ~ of sth** [sing.] something that shows what sth else is like: *The face is the mirror of the soul.*
- ***verb* 1 ~ sth** to have features that are similar to sth else and which show what it is like SYN **reflect**: *The music of the time mirrored the feeling of optimism in the country.* **2 ~ sb/sth** to show the image of sb/sth on the surface of water, glass, etc. SYN **reflect**: *She saw herself mirrored in the window.*

mir·ror·ball /ˈmɪrəbɔːl; *NAmE* ˈmɪrər-/ *noun* a decoration consisting of a large ball covered in small mirrors that hangs from the ceiling and turns to produce lighting effects

mir·rored /ˈmɪrəd; *NAmE* -rərd/ *adj.* [only before noun] having a mirror or mirrors or behaving like a mirror: ***mirrored doors/sunglasses***

ˌmirror ˈimage *noun* an image of sth that is like a REFLECTION of it, either because it is exactly the same or because the right side of the original object appears on the left and the left side appears on the right

ˈmirror site (also **mir·ror**) *noun* (*computing*) a website which is a copy of another website but has a different address on the Internet

mirth /mɜːθ; *NAmE* mɜːrθ/ *noun* [U] happiness, fun and the sound of people laughing SYN **merriment**: *The performance produced much mirth among the audience.*

mirth·less /ˈmɜːθləs; *NAmE* ˈmɜːrθ-/ *adj.* (*formal*) showing no real enjoyment or AMUSEMENT: *a* ***mirthless laugh/smile*** ▸ **mirth·less·ly** *adv.*

MIS /ˌem aɪ ˈes/ *abbr.* (*computing*) management information system (a system that stores information for use by business managers)

mis- /mɪs/ *prefix* (in verbs and nouns) bad or wrong; badly or wrongly: *misbehaviour* ◇ *misinterpret*

mis·ad·ven·ture /ˌmɪsədˈventʃə(r)/ *noun* **1** [U] (*BrE, law*) death caused by accident, rather than as a result of a crime: *a verdict of* ***death by misadventure*** **2** [C, U] (*formal*) bad luck or a small accident SYN **mishap**

mis·aligned /ˌmɪsəˈlaɪnd/ *adj.* not in the correct position in relation to sth else: *a misaligned vertebra* ▸ **mis·align·ment** /ˌmɪsəˈlaɪnmənt/ *noun* [U]: *The tests revealed a slight misalignment of the eyes.*

mis·an·thrope /ˈmɪsənθrəʊp; *NAmE* -θroʊp/ *noun* (*formal*) a person who hates and avoids other people

mis·an·throp·ic /ˌmɪsənˈθrɒpɪk; *NAmE* -ˈθrɑːp-/ *adj.* (*formal*) hating and avoiding other people ▸ **mis·an·thropy** /mɪˈsænθrəpi/ *noun* [U]

mis·ap·pli·ca·tion /ˌmɪsæplɪˈkeɪʃn/ *noun* [U, C] (*formal*) the use of sth for the wrong purpose or in the wrong way

mis·ap·ply /ˌmɪsəˈplaɪ/ *verb* (**mis·ap·plies, mis·ap·ply·ing, mis·ap·plied, mis·ap·plied**) [usually passive] **~ sth** (*formal*) to use sth for the wrong purpose or in the wrong way

mis·ap·pre·hen·sion /ˌmɪsæprɪˈhenʃn/ *noun* [U, C] (*formal*) a wrong idea about sth, or sth you believe to be true that is not true: *I was* ***under the misapprehension that*** *the course was for complete beginners.*

mis·ap·pro·pri·ate /ˌmɪsəˈprəʊprieɪt; *NAmE* -ˈproʊ-/ *verb* **~ sth** (*formal*) to take sb else's money or property for yourself, especially when they have trusted you to take care of it SYN **embezzle** ➲ compare APPROPRIATE *v.* ▸ **mis·ap·pro·pri·ation** /ˌmɪsəˌprəʊpriˈeɪʃn; *NAmE* -ˌproʊ-/ *noun* [U]

mis·be·got·ten /ˌmɪsbɪˈɡɒtn; *NAmE* -ˈɡɑːtn/ *adj.* [usually before noun] (*formal*) badly designed or planned

mis·be·have /ˌmɪsbɪˈheɪv/ *verb* [I, T] to behave badly: *Any child caught misbehaving was made to stand at the front of the class.* ◇ **~ yourself** *I see the dog has been misbehaving itself again.* OPP **behave** ▸ **mis·be·hav·iour** (*BrE*) (*NAmE* **mis·be·hav·ior**) /ˌmɪsbɪˈheɪvjə(r)/ *noun* [U]

mis·cal·cu·late /ˌmɪsˈkælkjuleɪt/ *verb* **1** [T, I] to estimate an amount, a figure, a measurement, etc. wrongly: **~ (sth)** *They had seriously miscalculated the effect of inflation.* ◇ **~ how long, how much, etc...** *He had miscalculated how long the trip would take.* **2** [T, I] **~ (sth)** | **~ how, what, etc...** to judge a situation wrongly SYN **misjudge**: *She miscalculated the level of opposition to her proposals.* ▸ **mis·cal·cu·la·tion** /ˌmɪskælkjuˈleɪʃn/ *noun* [C, U]: *to make a miscalculation*

mis·car·riage /ˈmɪskærɪdʒ; *BrE* also ˌmɪsˈk-/ *noun* [C, U] the process of giving birth to a baby before it is fully developed and able to survive; an occasion when this happens: *to have a miscarriage* ◇ *The pregnancy ended in miscarriage at 11 weeks.* ➲ COLLOCATIONS at CHILD ➲ compare ABORTION

misˌcarriage of ˈjustice *noun* [U, C] (*law*) a situation in which a court makes a wrong decision, especially when sb is punished when they are innocent

mis·carry /ˌmɪsˈkæri/ *verb* (**mis·car·ries, mis·carry·ing, mis·car·ried, mis·car·ried**) **1** [I, T] **~ (sth)** to give birth to a baby before it is fully developed and able to live: *The shock caused her to miscarry.* **2** [I] (*formal*) (of a plan) to fail SYN **come to nothing**

mis·cast /ˌmɪsˈkɑːst; *NAmE* -ˈkæst/ *verb* (**mis·cast, mis·cast**) [usually passive] **~ sb (as sb/sth)** to choose an actor to play a role for which they are not suitable

mis·ce·gen·ation /ˌmɪsɪdʒəˈneɪʃn/ *noun* [U] (*formal*) the fact of children being produced by parents who are of different races, especially when one parent is white

mis·cel·lan·eous /ˌmɪsəˈleɪniəs/ *adj.* [usually before noun] consisting of many different kinds of things that are not connected and do not easily form a group SYN **diverse, various**: *a sale of miscellaneous household items* ◇ *She gave me some money to cover any miscellaneous expenses.*

mis·cel·lany /mɪˈseləni; *NAmE* ˈmɪsəleɪni/ *noun* [sing.] (*formal*) a group or collection of different kinds of things SYN **assortment**

mis·chance /ˌmɪsˈtʃɑːns; *NAmE* -ˈtʃæns/ *noun* [U, C] (*formal*) bad luck

mis·chief /ˈmɪstʃɪf/ *noun* [U] **1** bad behaviour (especially of children) that is annoying but does not cause any serious damage or harm: *Those children are always* ***getting into mischief.*** ◇ *I try to* ***keep out of mischief.*** ◇ *It's very quiet upstairs; they must be* ***up to some mischief!*** **2** the wish or tendency to behave or play in a way that causes trouble: *Her eyes were full of mischief.* **3** (*formal*) harm or injury that is done to sb or to their reputation: *The incident caused a great deal of political mischief.*

IDM **ˌdo yourself a ˈmischief** (*BrE, informal*) to hurt yourself physically: *Watch how you use those scissors—you could do yourself a mischief!* **make ˈmischief** to do or say sth deliberately to upset other people, or cause trouble between them

ˈmischief-making *noun* [U] the act of deliberately causing trouble for people, such as harming their reputation

mis·chiev·ous /ˈmɪstʃɪvəs/ *adj.* **1** enjoying playing tricks and annoying people SYN **naughty**: *a mischievous* boy ◇ *a **mischievous grin/smile/look*** **2** (*formal*) (of an action or a statement) causing trouble, such as damaging sb's reputation: ***mischievous lies/gossip*** ▶ **mis·chiev·ous·ly** *adv.*

mis·cible /ˈmɪsəbl/ *adj.* (*technical*) (of liquids) that can be mixed together **OPP immiscible**

mis·con·ceive /ˌmɪskənˈsiːv/ *verb* **~ sth** (*formal*) to understand sth in the wrong way **SYN misunderstand**

mis·con·ceived /ˌmɪskənˈsiːvd/ *adj.* badly planned or judged; not carefully thought about: *a misconceived education policy* ◇ *their misconceived expectations of country life*

mis·con·cep·tion /ˌmɪskənˈsepʃn/ *noun* [C, U] **~ (about sth)** a belief or an idea that is not based on correct information, or that is not understood by people: *frequently held misconceptions about the disease* ◇ *a **popular misconception*** (= one that a lot of people have) ◇ *Let me deal with some **common misconceptions**.* ◇ *views based on misconception and prejudice* ➲ compare PRECONCEPTION

mis·con·duct /ˌmɪsˈkɒndʌkt; *NAmE* -ˈkɑːn-/ *noun* [U] (*formal*) **1** unacceptable behaviour, especially by a professional person: *a doctor accused of **gross misconduct*** (= very serious misconduct) ◇ *professional misconduct* **2** bad management of a company, etc: *misconduct of the company's financial affairs*

mis·con·struc·tion /ˌmɪskənˈstrʌkʃn/ *noun* [U, C] (*formal*) a completely wrong understanding of sth

mis·con·strue /ˌmɪskənˈstruː/ *verb* **~ sth (as sth)** (*formal*) to understand sb's words or actions wrongly **SYN misinterpret**: *It is easy to misconstrue confidence as arrogance.*

mis·count /ˌmɪsˈkaʊnt/ *verb* [T, I] **~ (sth)** to count sth wrongly: *The votes had been miscounted.*

mis·cre·ant /ˈmɪskriənt/ *noun* (*literary*) a person who has done sth wrong or illegal

mis·deed /ˌmɪsˈdiːd/ *noun* [usually pl.] (*formal*) a bad or evil act **SYN wrongdoing**

mis·de·mean·our (*especially US* **mis·de·meanor**) /ˌmɪsdɪˈmiːnə(r)/ *noun* **1** (*formal*) an action that is bad or unacceptable, but not very serious: *youthful misdemeanours* **2** (*law*) (*especially US*) a crime that is not considered to be very serious ➲ compare FELONY

mis·diag·nose /mɪsˈdaɪəgnəʊz; *NAmE* -noʊz/ *verb* **~ sth (as sth)** to give an explanation of the nature of an illness or a problem that is not correct: *Her depression was misdiagnosed as stress.* ▶ **mis·diag·nosis** /ˌmɪsdaɪəgˈnəʊsɪs; *NAmE* -ˈnoʊ-/ *noun* (*pl.* **mis·diag·noses** /-siːz/)

mis·dial /ˌmɪsˈdaɪəl/ *verb* (**-ll-**, *NAmE* **-l-**) [I, T] **~ (sth)** to call the wrong telephone number by mistake

mis·dir·ect /ˌmɪsdəˈrekt; -daɪˈrekt/ *verb* **1** [usually passive] **~ sth** to use sth in a way that is not appropriate to a particular situation: *Their efforts over the past years have been largely misdirected.* **2 ~ sb/sth** to send sb/sth in the wrong direction or to the wrong place **3 ~ sb/sth** (*law*) (of a judge) to give a JURY (= the group of people who decide if sb is guilty of a crime) wrong information about the law ▶ **mis·dir·ec·tion** /ˌmɪsdəˈrekʃn; -daɪˈrek-/ *noun* [U]

mise en scène /ˌmiːz ɒn ˈsen; *NAmE* ɑːn/ *noun* [sing.] (from *French*) **1** the arrangement of furniture, SCENERY, LIGHTING, etc. used on the stage for a play in the theatre, or in front of the camera in a film/movie **2** (*formal*) the place or scene where an event takes place: *Venice provided the mise-en-scène for the conference.*

miser /ˈmaɪzə(r)/ *noun* (*disapproving*) a person who loves money and hates spending it

mis·er·able /ˈmɪzrəbl/ *adj.* **1** very unhappy or uncomfortable: *We were cold, wet and thoroughly miserable.* ◇ *Don't look so miserable!* ◇ *She knows how to **make life miserable** for her employees.* **2** making you feel very unhappy or uncomfortable **SYN depressing**: *miserable housing conditions* ◇ *I spent a miserable weekend alone at home.* ◇ *What a miserable day!* (= cold and wet) ◇ *The play was **a miserable failure**.* **3** [only before noun] (*disapproving*) (of a person) always unhappy, bad-tempered and unfriendly **SYN grumpy**: *He was a miserable old devil.* **4** too small in quantity **SYN paltry**: *How can anyone live on such a miserable wage?* ▶ **mis·er·ably** /-əbli/ *adv.*: *They wandered around miserably.* ◇ *a miserably cold day* ◇ *He **failed miserably** as an actor.* **IDM** see SIN *n.*

miser·ly /ˈmaɪzəli; *NAmE* -ərli/ *adj.* (*disapproving*) **1** (of a person) hating to spend money **SYN mean 2** (of a quantity or amount) too small **SYN paltry**

mis·ery /ˈmɪzəri/ *noun* (*pl.* **-ies**) **1** [U] great suffering of the mind or body **SYN distress**: *Fame brought her nothing but misery.* **2** [U] very poor living conditions **SYN poverty**: *The vast majority of the population lives in utter misery.* **3** [C] something that causes great suffering of mind or body: *the miseries of unemployment* **4** [C] (*BrE, informal*) a person who is always unhappy and complaining: *Don't be such an old misery!*

IDM make sb's life a ˈmisery to behave in a way that makes sb else feel very unhappy **put an animal, a bird, etc. out of its ˈmisery** to kill a creature because it has an illness or injury that cannot be treated **put sb out of their ˈmisery** (*informal*) to stop sb worrying by telling them sth that they are anxious to know: *Put me out of my misery—did I pass or didn't I?*

mis·file /ˌmɪsˈfaɪl/ *verb* **~ sth** to put away a document in the wrong place: *The missing letter had been misfiled.*

mis·fire /ˌmɪsˈfaɪə(r)/ *verb* **1** [I] (of a plan or joke) to fail to have the effect that you had intended **SYN go wrong** **2** (also **miss**) [I] (of an engine) to not work correctly because the petrol/gas does not burn at the right time **3** [I] (of a gun, etc.) to fail to send out a bullet, etc. when fired ➲ compare BACKFIRE

mis·fit /ˈmɪsfɪt/ *noun* a person who is not accepted by a particular group of people, especially because their behaviour or their ideas are very different: *a social misfit*

mis·for·tune /ˌmɪsˈfɔːtʃuːn; *NAmE* -ˈfɔːrtʃ-/ *noun* **1** [U] bad luck: *He has known great misfortune in his life.* ◇ *We **had the misfortune to** run into a violent storm.* **2** [C] an unfortunate accident, condition or event **SYN blow, disaster**: *She bore her misfortunes bravely.*

mis·giv·ing /ˌmɪsˈgɪvɪŋ/ *noun* [C, usually pl., U] **~ about sth/about doing sth** feelings of doubt or anxiety about what might happen, or about whether or not sth is the right thing to do: *I had grave misgivings about making the trip.* ◇ *I read the letter with a sense of misgiving.*

mis·govern /ˌmɪsˈgʌvn; *NAmE* -ˈgʌvərn/ *verb* **~ sth** to govern a country or state badly or unfairly ▶ **mis·gov·ern·ment** /ˌmɪsˈgʌvənmənt; *NAmE* -ˈgʌvərn-/ *noun* [U]

mis·guided /ˌmɪsˈgaɪdɪd/ *adj.* wrong because you have understood or judged a situation badly **SYN inappropriate**: *She only did it in a misguided attempt to help.* ▶ **mis·guided·ly** *adv.*

mis·handle /ˌmɪsˈhændl/ *verb* **1 ~ sth** to deal badly with a problem or situation **SYN mismanage**: *The entire campaign had been badly mishandled.* **2 ~ sb/sth** to touch or treat sb/sth in a rough and careless way: *The equipment could be dangerous if mishandled.* ▶ **mis·hand·ling** *noun* [U]: *the government's mishandling of the economy*

mis·hap /ˈmɪshæp/ *noun* [C, U] a small accident or piece of bad luck that does not have serious results: *a slight mishap* ◇ *a series of mishaps* ◇ *I managed to get home **without (further) mishap**.*

mis·hear /ˌmɪsˈhɪə(r); *NAmE* -ˈhɪr/ *verb* (**mis·heard**, **mis·heard** /-ˈhɜːd; *NAmE* -ˈhɜːrd/) [T, I] **~ (sb)** | **~ what...** to fail to hear correctly what sb says, so that you think they said sth else: *You may have misheard her—I'm sure she didn't mean that.* ◇ *I thought he said he was coming today, but I must have misheard.*

mis·hit /ˌmɪsˈhɪt/ *verb* (**mis·hit·ting**, **mis·hit**, **mis·hit**) **~ sth** (in a game) to hit the ball badly so that it does not go where you had intended ▶ **mis·hit** /ˈmɪshɪt/ *noun*

mish·mash /ˈmɪʃmæʃ/ *noun* [sing.] (*informal*, usually *disapproving*) a confused mixture of different kinds of things, styles, etc.

M

mis·in·form /ˌmɪsɪnˈfɔːm; *NAmE* -ˈfɔːrm/ *verb* [often passive] **~ sb (about sth)** to give sb wrong information about sth: *They were deliberately misinformed about their rights.* ◇ *a misinformed belief* (= based on wrong information) ▸ **mis·in·for·ma·tion** /ˌmɪsɪnfəˈmeɪʃn/ *noun* [U]: *a campaign of misinformation*

mis·in·ter·pret AW /ˌmɪsɪnˈtɜːprɪt; *NAmE* -ˈtɜːrp-/ *verb* **~ sth (as sth/doing sth)** to understand sth/sb wrongly SYN **misconstrue, misread**: *His comments were misinterpreted as a criticism of the project.* ➲ compare INTERPRET ▸ **mis·in·ter·pret·ation** AW /ˌmɪsɪntɜːprɪˈteɪʃn; *NAmE* -tɜːrp-/ *noun* [U, C]: *A number of these statements could be **open to misinterpretation*** (= could be understood wrongly).

mis·judge /ˌmɪsˈdʒʌdʒ/ *verb* [T, I] **1 ~ sb/sth | ~ how, what, etc...** to form a wrong opinion about a person or situation, especially in a way that makes you deal with them or it unfairly: *She now realizes that she misjudged him.* **2 ~ sth | ~ how long, how far, etc...** to estimate sth such as time or distance wrongly: *He misjudged the distance and his ball landed in the lake.* ▸ **mis·judge·ment** (also **mis·judg·ment**) *noun* [C, U]

mis·lay /ˌmɪsˈleɪ/ *verb* (**mis·laid, mis·laid** /-ˈleɪd/) **~ sth** (*formal, especially BrE*) to put sth somewhere and then be unable to find it again, especially for only a short time SYN **lose**: *I seem to have mislaid my keys.*

mis·lead /ˌmɪsˈliːd/ *verb* (**mis·led, mis·led** /-ˈled/) **~ sb (about sth) | ~ sb (into doing sth)** to give sb the wrong idea or impression and make them believe sth that is not true SYN **deceive**: *He deliberately misled us about the nature of their relationship.*

mis·lead·ing /ˌmɪsˈliːdɪŋ/ *adj.* giving the wrong idea or impression and making you believe sth that is not true SYN **deceptive**: ***misleading information/advertisements*** ▸ **mis·lead·ing·ly** *adv.*: *These bats are sometimes misleadingly referred to as 'flying foxes'.*

mis·man·age /ˌmɪsˈmænɪdʒ/ *verb* **~ sth** to deal with or manage sth badly SYN **mishandle** ▸ **mis·man·age·ment** *noun* [U]: *accusations of corruption and financial mismanagement*

mis·match /ˈmɪsmætʃ/ *noun* **~ (between A and B)** a combination of things or people that do not go together well or are not suitable for each other: *a mismatch between people's real needs and the available facilities* ▸ **mis·match** /ˌmɪsˈmætʃ/ *verb* [often passive]: **~ sb/sth** *They made a mismatched couple.*

mis·name /ˌmɪsˈneɪm/ *verb* [usually passive] **~ sb/sth** to give sb/sth a name that is wrong or not appropriate

mis·nomer /ˌmɪsˈnəʊmə(r); *NAmE* -ˈnoʊ-/ *noun* a name or a word that is not appropriate or accurate: *'Villa' was **something of a misnomer**—the place was no more than an old farmhouse.*

miso /ˈmiːsəʊ; *NAmE* -soʊ/ *noun* [U] a substance made from BEANS, used in Japanese cooking

mis·ogyn·ist /mɪˈsɒdʒɪnɪst; *NAmE* -ˈsɑːdʒ-/ *noun* (*formal*) a man who hates women ▸ **mis·ogyn·is·tic** /mɪˌsɒdʒɪˈnɪstɪk/ (also **mis·ogyn·ist**) *adj.*: *misogynistic attitudes* **mis·ogyny** *noun* [U]

mis·place /ˌmɪsˈpleɪs/ *verb* **~ sth** to put sth somewhere and then be unable to find it again, especially for a short time SYN **mislay**

mis·placed /ˌmɪsˈpleɪst/ *adj.* **1** not appropriate or correct in the situation: ***misplaced confidence/optimism/fear*** **2** (of love, trust, etc.) given to a person who does not deserve or return those feelings: *misplaced loyalty*

mis·print /ˈmɪsprɪnt/ *noun* a mistake such as a spelling mistake that is made when a book, etc. is printed ➲ SYNONYMS at MISTAKE

mis·pro·nounce /ˌmɪsprəˈnaʊns/ *verb* **~ sth** to pronounce a word wrongly ▸ **mis·pro·nun·ci·ation** /ˌmɪsprənʌnsiˈeɪʃn/ *noun* [C, U]

mis·quote /ˌmɪsˈkwəʊt; *NAmE* -ˈkwoʊt/ *verb* **~ sb/sth** to repeat what sb has said or written in a way that is not correct: *The senator claims to have been misquoted in the article.* ▸ **mis·quo·ta·tion** /ˌmɪskwəʊˈteɪʃn; *NAmE* -kwoʊ-/ *noun* [C, U]

mis·read /ˌmɪsˈriːd/ *verb* (**mis·read, mis·read** /-ˈred/) **1** to understand sb/sth wrongly SYN **misinterpret**: **~ sth** *I'm afraid I completely misread the situation.* ◇ **~ sth as sth** *His confidence was misread as arrogance.* **2 ~ sth (as sth)** to read sth wrongly: *I misread the 1 as a 7.*

mis·re·port /ˌmɪsrɪˈpɔːt; *NAmE* -ˈpɔːrt/ *verb* **~ sth | ~ what, how, etc... | it is misreported that...** to give a report of an event, etc. that is not correct: *The newspapers misreported the facts of the case.*

mis·rep·re·sent /ˌmɪsˌreprɪˈzent/ *verb* [often passive] (*formal*) to give information about sb/sth that is not true or complete so that other people have the wrong impression about them/it: **~ sb/sth** *He felt that the book misrepresented his opinions.* ◇ **~ sb/sth as sth** *In the article she was misrepresented as an uncaring mother.* ◇ **~ what, how, etc ...** *The report misrepresented what the group believes.* ▸ **mis·rep·re·sen·ta·tion** /ˌmɪsˌreprɪzenˈteɪʃn/ *noun* [C, U]: *a deliberate misrepresentation of the facts*

mis·rule /ˌmɪsˈruːl/ *noun* [U] (*formal*) bad government: *The regime finally collapsed after 25 years of misrule.*

miss 🔑 /mɪs/ *verb, noun*

■ ***verb***

▸ NOT HIT, CATCH, ETC. **1** 🔑 [T, I] to fail to hit, catch, reach, etc. sth: **~ (sb/sth)** *How many goals has he missed this season?* ◇ *The bullet missed her by about six inches.* ◇ *She threw a plate at him and only **narrowly missed**.* ◇ **~ doing sth** *She narrowly missed hitting him.*

▸ NOT HEAR/SEE **2** 🔑 [T] **~ sth** to fail to hear, see or notice sth: *The hotel is the only white building on the road—**you can't miss it**.* ◇ *Don't miss next week's issue!* ◇ *I missed her name.* ◇ *Your mother will know who's moved in—she **doesn't miss much**.*

▸ NOT UNDERSTAND **3** 🔑 [T] **~ sth** to fail to understand sth: *He completely missed the joke.* ◇ *You're **missing the point*** (= failing to understand the main part) *of what I'm saying.*

▸ NOT BE/GO SOMEWHERE **4** 🔑 [T] **~ sth** to fail to be or go somewhere: *She hasn't missed a game all year.* ◇ *You missed a good party last night* (= because you did not go). ◇ *'Are you coming to the school play?' **'I wouldn't miss it for the world.'***

▸ NOT DO STH **5** 🔑 [T] **~ sth** to fail to do sth: *You can't afford to miss meals* (= not eat meals) *when you're in training.* ◇ *to miss a turn* (= to not play when it is your turn in a game) **6** 🔑 [T] **~ (doing) sth** to not take the opportunity to do sth: *The sale prices were **too good to miss**.* ◇ *It was an opportunity **not to be missed**.*

▸ BE LATE **7** 🔑 [T] **~ sth/sb | ~ doing sth** to be or arrive too late for sth: *If I don't leave now I'll miss my plane.* ◇ *Sorry I'm late—have I missed anything?* ◇ *'Is Ann there?' 'You've just missed her* (= she has just left).*'*

▸ FEEL SAD **8** 🔑 [T] to feel sad because you can no longer see sb or do sth that you like: **~ sb/sth** *She will be greatly missed when she leaves.* ◇ *What did you miss most when you were in France?* ◇ **~ (sb/sth) doing sth** *I don't miss getting up at six every morning!*

▸ NOTICE STH NOT THERE **9** [T] **~ sb/sth** to notice that sb/sth is not where they/it should be: *When did you first miss the necklace?* ◇ *We seem to be missing some students this morning.*

▸ AVOID STH BAD **10** [T] to avoid sth unpleasant SYN **escape**: **~ sth** *If you go now you should miss the crowds.* ◇ **~ doing sth** *He fell and just missed knocking the whole display over.*

▸ OF ENGINE **11** = MISFIRE

IDM **he, she, etc. doesn't miss a 'trick** (*informal*) used to say that sb notices every opportunity to gain an advantage **ˌmiss the 'boat** (*informal*) to be unable to take advantage of sth because you are too late: *If you don't buy now, you may find that you've missed the boat.* **ˌmiss your 'guess** (*NAmE, informal*) to make a mistake: ***Unless I miss my guess**, your computer needs a new hard drive.* ➲ more at HEART, MARK *n.*

PHR V **ˌmiss sb/sth↔'out** 🔑 (*BrE*) to fail to include sb/sth in sth SYN **omit**: *I'll just read through the form again to* *make sure I haven't missed anything out.* ˌ**miss** ˈ**out (on sth)** to fail to benefit from sth useful or enjoyable by not taking part in it: *Of course I'm coming—I don't want to miss out on all the fun!*

■ ***noun***

▸ TITLE/FORM OF ADDRESS **1** ⊶ **Miss** used before the family name, or the first and family name, of a woman who is not married, in order to speak or write to her politely: *That's all, thank you, Miss Lipman.* ➲ compare MRS, MS **2 Miss** a title given to the winner of a beauty contest in a particular country, town, etc.: *Miss Brighton* ◇ *the Miss World contest* **3 Miss** (*informal*) used especially by men to address a young woman when they do not know her name: *Will that be all, Miss?* **4 Miss** (*BrE, informal*) used as a form of address by children in some schools to a woman teacher, whether she is married or not: *Good morning, Miss!* ➲ compare SIR **5** (*old-fashioned*) a girl or young woman

▸ NOT HIT, CATCH, ETC. **6** a failure to hit, catch or reach sth: *He scored two goals and had another two* ***near misses***.

IDM **give sth a** ˈ**miss** (*informal, especially BrE*) to decide not to do sth, eat sth, etc: *I think I'll give badminton a miss tonight.* **a** ˌ**miss is as** ˌ**good as a** ˈ**mile** (*saying*) there is no real difference between only just failing in sth and failing in it badly because the result is still the same

mis·sal /ˈmɪsl/ *noun* a book that contains the prayers etc. that are used at MASS in the Roman Catholic Church

mis·sel thrush = MISTLE THRUSH

mis·sha·pen /ˌmɪsˈʃeɪpən/ *adj.* with a shape that is not normal or natural: *misshapen feet*

mis·sile /ˈmɪsaɪl; *NAmE* ˈmɪsl/ *noun* **1** a weapon that is sent through the air and that explodes when it hits the thing that it is aimed at: *nuclear missiles* ◇ *a* ***missile base/site*** ➲ COLLOCATIONS at WAR ➲ see also BALLISTIC MISSILE, CRUISE MISSILE, GUIDED MISSILE **2** an object that is thrown at sb to hurt them SYN **projectile**

miss·ing ⊶ /ˈmɪsɪŋ/ *adj.*

1 ⊶ that cannot be found or that is not in its usual place, or at home SYN **lost**: *I never found the missing piece.* ◇ *My gloves have been missing for ages.* ◇ *Two files have* ***gone missing***. ◇ *They still hoped to find their missing son.* ◇ (*especially BrE*) *Our cat's* ***gone missing*** *again.* **2** ⊶ that has been removed, lost or destroyed and has not been replaced: *The book has two pages* ***missing/missing*** *pages.* ◇ *He didn't notice there was anything missing from his room until later on.* **3** ⊶ (of a person) not present after an accident, battle, etc. but not known to have been killed: *He was reported* ***missing, presumed dead***. ◇ *Many soldiers were listed as* ***missing in action***. **4** ⊶ not included, often when it should have been: *Fill in the missing words in this text.* ◇ *There were several candidates missing from the list.*

ˌ**missing** ˈ**link** *noun* **1** [C] something, such as a piece of information, that is necessary for sb to be able to understand a problem or in order to make sth complete **2 the missing link** [sing.] an animal similar to humans that was once thought to exist at the time that APES were developing into humans

ˌ**missing** ˈ**person** *noun* (*pl.* **missing persons**) a person who has disappeared from their home and whose family are trying to find them with the help of the police

mis·sion /ˈmɪʃn/ *noun, verb*

■ ***noun***

▸ OFFICIAL JOB/GROUP **1** [C] an important official job that a person or group of people is given to do, especially when they are sent to another country: *a trade mission to China* ◇ *a fact-finding mission* ◇ *a mercy mission to aid homeless refugees* **2** [C] a group of people doing such a job; the place where they work: *the head of the British mission in Berlin*

▸ TEACHING CHRISTIANITY **3** [C, U] the work of teaching people about Christianity, especially in a foreign country; a group of people doing such work: *a Catholic mission in Africa* ◇ *Gandhi's attitude to mission and conversion* **4** [C] a building or group of buildings used by a Christian mission

▸ YOUR DUTY **5** [C] particular work that you feel it is your duty to do SYN **vocation**: *Her* ***mission in life*** *was to work with the homeless.* ➲ SYNONYMS at TASK

▸ OF ARMED FORCES **6** [C] an important job that is done by a soldier, group of soldiers, etc: *The squadron flew on a reconnaissance mission.* ➲ COLLOCATIONS at WAR

▸ SPACE FLIGHT **7** [C] a flight into space: *a US space mission* ◇ *mission control* (= the people on earth who control and communicate with the people on the mission)

▸ TASK **8** [C] (*BrE, informal*) a task or journey that is very difficult and takes a long time to complete: *It's a mission to get there.*

IDM ˌ**mission ac**ˈ**complished** used when you have successfully completed what you have had to do

■ ***verb*** [I] **+ adv./prep.** (*informal*) to go on a long and difficult journey, especially one that involves going to many different places: *We had to mission round all the bars until we found him.*

mis·sion·ary /ˈmɪʃənri; *NAmE* -neri/ *noun* (*pl.* -ies) a person who is sent to a foreign country to teach people about Christianity: *Baptist missionaries* ◇ *missionary work* ◇ (*figurative*) *She spoke about her new project with* ***missionary zeal*** (= with great enthusiasm).

the ˈ**missionary position** *noun* [sing.] a position for having sex in which a man and a woman face each other, with the man lying on top of the woman

ˌ**mission-**ˈ**critical** *adj.* essential for an organization to function successfully: *mission-critical employees*

ˈ**mission statement** *noun* an official statement of the aims of a company or an organization

mis·sis *noun* = MISSUS

mis·sive /ˈmɪsɪv/ *noun* (*formal* or *humorous*) a letter, especially a long or an official one

mis·spell /ˌmɪsˈspel/ *verb* (**mis·spelled, mis·spelled** or **mis·spelt, mis·spelt** /ˌmɪsˈspelt/) **~ sth** to spell a word wrongly ▸ **mis·spell·ing** *noun* [C, U]

mis·spend /ˌmɪsˈspend/ *verb* (**mis·spent, mis·spent** /-ˈspent/) [usually passive] **~ sth** to spend time or money in a careless rather than a useful way SYN **waste**: *He joked that being good at cards was the sign of* ***a misspent youth*** (= having wasted his time when he was young).

mis·step /ˌmɪsˈstep/ *noun* (*NAmE*) a mistake; a wrong action

mis·sus /ˈmɪsɪz/ *noun* (*BrE*) **1** (also **mis·sis**) (*informal*, becoming *old-fashioned*) (used after 'the', 'my', 'your', 'his') a man's wife: *How's the missus* (= your wife)? **2** (*informal*) (used especially by young people) girlfriend: *My missus doesn't like computer games.* ◇ *my current missus* **3** (also **mis·sis**) (*slang*, becoming *old-fashioned*) used by some people as a form of address to a woman whose name they do not know: *Is this your bag, missus?*

missy /ˈmɪsi/ *noun* used when talking to a young girl, especially to express anger or affection: *Don't you speak to me like that, missy!*

mist /mɪst/ *noun, verb*

■ ***noun*** **1** [U, C] a cloud of very small drops of water in the air just above the ground, that make it difficult to see: *The hills were* ***shrouded in mist***. ◇ *Early morning mist patches will soon clear.* ◇ *The origins of the story are* ***lost in the mists of time*** (= forgotten because it happened such a long time ago). ◇ (*figurative*) *She gazed at the scene through a mist of tears.* ➲ COLLOCATIONS at WEATHER ➲ compare FOG ➲ see also MISTY **2** [sing.] a fine spray of liquid, for example, from an AEROSOL can

■ ***verb*** **1** [T, I] **~ (sth) (up)** | **~ (over)** when sth such as glass **mists** or **is misted**, it becomes covered with very small drops of water, so that it is impossible to see through it: *The windows were misted up with condensation.* ◇ *As he came in from the cold, his glasses misted up.* **2** [I, T] if your eyes **mist** or sth **mists** them, they fill with tears: **~ (over/up)** *Her eyes misted over as she listened to the speech.* ◇ **~ sth (up)** *Tears misted his eyes.* **3** [T] **~ sth** to spray the leaves of a plant with very small drops of water

mis·take ⊶ /mɪˈsteɪk/ *noun, verb*

■ ***noun*** **1** ⊶ an action or an opinion that is not correct, or that produces a result that you did not want: *It's easy to* ***make a mistake***. ◇ *This letter is addressed to someone else—*

M

there must be some mistake. ◇ *It would be a mistake to ignore his opinion.* ◇ *Don't worry, we all* ***make mistakes.*** ◇ *You must try to* ***learn from your mistakes.*** ◇ *Leaving school so young was the biggest mistake of my life.* ◇ *I* ***made the mistake of*** *giving him my address.* ◇ *It was a big mistake on my part to have trusted her.* ◇ *a* ***great/serious/terrible mistake*** ◇ *It's a* ***common mistake*** (= one that a lot of people make). **2** 🔑 a word, figure, etc. that is not said or written down correctly SYN **error**: *It's a common mistake among learners of English.* ◇ *The waiter* ***made a mistake*** (**in**) *adding up the bill.* ◇ *Her essay is full of* ***spelling mistakes.***

IDM **and 'no mistake** (*old-fashioned, especially BrE*) used to show that you are sure about the truth of what you have just said: *This is a strange business and no mistake.* **by mi'stake** 🔑 by accident; without intending to: *I took your bag instead of mine by mistake.* **ˌmake no mi'stake** (**about sth**) used to emphasize what you are saying, especially when you want to warn sb about sth: *Make no mistake (about it), this is one crisis that won't just go away.* **in mi'stake for sth** thinking that sth is sth else: *Children may eat pills in mistake for sweets.*

■ ***verb*** 🔑 (**mis·took** /mɪ'stʊk/, **mis·taken** /mɪ'steɪkən/) to not understand or judge sb/sth correctly SYN **misconstrue**: **~ sb/sth** *I admit that I mistook his intentions.* ◇ ***There was no mistaking*** (= it was impossible to mistake) *the bitterness in her voice.* ◇ **~ sb/sth as sb/sth** *I mistook her offer as a threat.* ◇ **~ what...** *Sorry—I mistook what you said.*

PHR V **mi'stake sb/sth for sb/sth** 🔑 to think wrongly that sb/sth is sb/sth else SYN **confuse**: *I think you must be mistaking me for someone else.*

M

Synonyms

mistake

error • inaccuracy • slip • howler • misprint

These are all words for a word, figure or fact that is not said, written down or typed correctly.

mistake a word or figure that is not said or written down correctly: *It's a common mistake among learners of English.* ◇ *spelling mistakes*

error (*rather formal*) a word, figure, etc. that is not said or written down correctly: *There are too many errors in your work.* NOTE **Error** is a more formal way of saying **mistake**.

inaccuracy (*rather formal*) a piece of information that is not exactly correct: *The article is full of inaccuracies.*

slip a small mistake, usually made by being careless or not paying attention

howler (*informal, especially BrE*) a stupid mistake, especially in what sb says or writes: *The report is full of howlers.* NOTE A **howler** is usually an embarrassing mistake which shows that the person who made it does not know sth that they really should know.

misprint a small mistake in a printed text

PATTERNS

- a(n) mistake/error/inaccuracy/slip/howler/misprint **in** sth
- to **make** a(n) mistake/error/slip/howler
- to **contain/be full of** mistakes/errors/inaccuracies/howlers/misprints

mis·taken 🔑 /mɪ'steɪkən/ *adj.*
1 🔑 [not usually before noun] **~** (**about sb/sth**) wrong in your opinion or judgement: *You are completely mistaken about Jane.* ◇ *Unless I'm very much mistaken, that's Paul's wife over there.* **2** 🔑 based on a wrong opinion or bad judgement SYN **misguided**: ***mistaken views/ideas*** ◇ *I told her my secret* ***in the mistaken belief*** *that I could trust her.* ▶ **mis·taken·ly** *adv.*: *He mistakenly believed that his family would stand by him.*

miˌstaken i'dentity *noun* [U] a situation in which you think wrongly that you recognize sb or have found the person you are looking for: *He was shot in what seems to have been* ***a case of mistaken identity.***

mis·ter /'mɪstə(r)/ *noun* **1 Mister** the full form, not often used in writing, of the abbreviation *Mr* **2** (*informal*) used, especially by children, to address a man whose name they do not know: *Please, mister, can we have our ball back?*

mis·time /ˌmɪs'taɪm/ *verb* **~ sth** to do sth at the wrong time, especially when this makes sth bad or unpleasant happen: *The horse completely mistimed the jump and threw its rider.* ▶ **mis·tim·ing** *noun* [U]: *The failure of the talks was mainly due to insensitivity and mistiming.*

mis·tle thrush (also **mis·sel thrush**) /'mɪsl θrʌʃ/ *noun* a large THRUSH (= a type of bird) with spots on its front

mistle·toe /'mɪsltəʊ; 'mɪzl-; *NAmE* -toʊ/ *noun* [U] a plant with small shiny white BERRIES that grows on other trees and is often used as a decoration at Christmas: *the tradition of kissing under the mistletoe*

mis·took *past tense* of MISTAKE

mis·tral /'mɪstrəl; mɪ'strɑːl/ *noun* [sing.] a strong cold wind that blows through southern France, mainly in winter

mis·treat /ˌmɪs'triːt/ *verb* **~ sb/sth** to treat a person or an animal in a cruel, unkind or unfair way SYN **ill-treat, maltreat** ▶ **mis·treat·ment** *noun* [U]

mis·tress /'mɪstrəs/ *noun* **1** a man's (usually a married man's) **mistress** is a woman that he is having a regular sexual relationship with and who is not his wife **2** (*BrE, old-fashioned*) a female teacher in a school, especially a private school: *the Biology mistress* **3** (in the past) the female head of a house, especially one who employed servants: *the mistress of the house* **4** the female owner of a dog or other animal **5** (*formal*) a woman who is in a position of authority or control, or who is highly skilled in sth: *She wants to be mistress of her own affairs* (= to organize her own life). ➲ compare MASTER

mis·trial /ˌmɪs'traɪəl/ *noun* (*law*) **1** a trial that is not considered valid because of a mistake in the way it has been conducted **2** (*NAmE*) a trial in which the JURY cannot reach a decision

mis·trust /ˌmɪs'trʌst/ *verb, noun*

■ ***verb*** **~ sb/sth** to have no confidence in sb/sth because you think they may be harmful; to not trust sb/sth SYN **distrust** ➲ note at DISTRUST

■ ***noun*** [U, sing.] a feeling that you cannot trust sb/sth SYN **suspicion**: *a climate of mistrust and fear* ◇ *She has a deep mistrust of strangers.* ▶ **mis·trust·ful** /-fl/ *adj.*: **~** (**of sb/sth**) *Some people are very mistrustful of computers.* **mis·trust·ful·ly** /-fəli/ *adv.*

misty /'mɪsti/ *adj.* **1** with a lot of MIST: *a misty morning* **2** not clear or bright SYN **blurred**: *misty memories* ◇ (*literary*) *His eyes grew misty* (= full of tears) *as he talked.*

ˌmisty-'eyed *adj.* feeling full of emotion, as if you are going to cry

mis·un·der·stand /ˌmɪsʌndə'stænd; *NAmE* -dər's-/ *verb* (**mis·un·der·stood, mis·un·der·stood** /-'stʊd/) [T, I] **~** (**sb/sth**) | **~ what, how, etc...** to fail to understand sb/sth correctly: *I completely misunderstood her intentions.* ◇ *Don't misunderstand me—I am grateful for all you've done.* ◇ *I thought he was her husband—I must have misunderstood.*

mis·un·der·stand·ing /ˌmɪsʌndə'stændɪŋ; *NAmE* -dər's-/ *noun* **1** [U, C] a situation in which a comment, an instruction, etc. is not understood correctly: *There must be some misunderstanding—I thought I ordered the smaller model.* ◇ **~ of/about sth** *There is still a fundamental misunderstanding about the real purpose of this work.* ◇ **~ between A and B** *All contracts are translated to avoid any misunderstanding between the companies.* **2** [C] a slight disagreement or argument: *We had a little misunderstanding over the bill.*

mis·un·der·stood /ˌmɪsʌndə'stʊd/ *adj.* having qualities that people do not see or fully understand: *a much misunderstood illness* ◇ *She felt very alone and misunderstood.*

mis·use *noun, verb*
■ ***noun*** /ˌmɪsˈjuːs/ [U, C, usually sing.] (*formal*) the act of using sth in a dishonest way or for the wrong purpose SYN **abuse**: ***alcohol/drug misuse*** ◇ *the* ***misuse of power/authority***
■ ***verb*** /ˌmɪsˈjuːz/ (*formal*) **1 ~ sth** to use sth in the wrong way or for the wrong purpose SYN **abuse, ill-treat**: *individuals who misuse power for their own ends* **2 ~ sb** to treat sb badly and/or unfairly

mite /maɪt/ *noun* **1** a very small creature like a spider that lives on plants, animals, carpets, etc: *house dust mites* ➲ see also DUST MITE **2** a small child or animal, especially one that you feel sorry for: *Poor little mite!* **3** (*old-fashioned*) a small amount of sth: *The place looked* ***a mite*** (= a little) *expensive.*

miter (*NAmE*) = MITRE

miti·gate /ˈmɪtɪɡeɪt/ *verb* **~ sth** (*formal*) to make sth less harmful, serious, etc. SYN **alleviate**: *action to mitigate poverty* ◇ *Soil erosion was mitigated by the planting of trees.*

miti·gat·ing /ˈmɪtɪɡeɪtɪŋ/ *adj.* [only before noun] **~ circumstances/factors** (*law* or *formal*) circumstances or factors that provide a reason that explains sb's actions or a crime, and make them easier to understand so that the punishment may be less severe

miti·ga·tion /ˌmɪtɪˈɡeɪʃn/ *noun* [U] (*formal*) a reduction in how unpleasant, serious, etc. sth is
IDM **in mitiˈgation** (*law*) with the aim of making a crime seem less serious or easier to forgive: *In mitigation, the defence lawyer said his client was seriously depressed at the time of the assault.*

mi·to·chon·drion /ˌmaɪtəʊˈkɒndriən; *NAmE* ˌmaɪtoʊˈkɑːn-/ *noun* (*pl.* **mitochondria** /ˌmaɪtəʊˈkɒndriə; *NAmE* ˌmaɪtoʊˈkɑːn-/) (*biology*) a small part found in most cells, in which the energy in food is released ▶ **mito·chon·drial** /-driəl/ *adj.*: *mitochondrial DNA*

mi·tosis /maɪˈtəʊsɪs; *NAmE* -ˈtoʊs-/ *noun* [U] (*biology*) the process of cell division

mitre (*especially US* **miter**) /ˈmaɪtə(r)/ *noun, verb*
■ ***noun*** **1** a tall pointed hat worn by BISHOPS at special ceremonies as a symbol of their position and authority **2** (also ˈ**mitre joint**) a corner joint, formed by two pieces of wood each cut at an angle, as in a picture frame ➲ picture at DOVETAIL
■ ***verb*** **~ sth** (*technical*) to join two pieces of wood together with a mitre joint

mitt /mɪt/ *noun* **1** = MITTEN **2** (in BASEBALL) a large thick leather glove worn for catching the ball **3** [usually pl.] (*slang*) a hand: *I'd love to get my mitts on one of those.*

mit·ten /ˈmɪtn/ (also **mitt**) *noun* a type of glove that covers the four fingers together and the thumb separately ➲ VISUAL VOCAB page V53

Mitty ➲ WALTER MITTY

mix 🔑 /mɪks/ *verb, noun*
■ ***verb***
▸ COMBINE **1** 🔑 [I, T] if two or more substances **mix** or you **mix** them, they combine, usually in a way that means they cannot easily be separated: *Oil and water do not mix.* ◇ **~ with sth** *Oil does not mix with water.* ◇ **~ A and B (together)** *Mix all the ingredients together in a bowl.* ◇ *If you mix blue and yellow, you get green.* ◇ **~ A with B** *I don't like to* ***mix business with pleasure*** (= combine social events with doing business). **2** 🔑 [T] to prepare sth by combining two or more different substances: **~ sth** *With this range of paints, you can mix your own colours.* ◇ **~ sth for sb** *Why don't you mix a cocktail for our guests?* ◇ **~ sb sth** *Why don't you mix our guests a cocktail?* **3** 🔑 [I] if two or more things, people or activities **do not mix**, they are likely to cause problems or danger if they are combined: *Children and fireworks don't mix.*
▸ MEET PEOPLE **4** 🔑 [I] **~ (with sb)** to meet and talk to different people, especially at social events SYN **socialize**: *They don't mix much with the neighbours.*
▸ MUSIC/SOUNDS **5** [T] **~ sth** (*technical*) to combine different recordings of voices and/or instruments to produce a single piece of music
IDM **be/get mixed ˈup in sth** 🔑 to be/become involved in sth, especially sth illegal or dishonest **be/get mixed ˈup with sb** to be/become friendly with or involved with sb that other people do not approve of ˌ**mix and ˈmatch** to combine things in different ways for different purposes: *You can mix and match courses to suit your requirements.* ˈ**mix it (with sb)** (*BrE*) (*NAmE* ˌ**mix it ˈup (with sb)**) (*informal*) to argue with sb or cause trouble
PHR V ˌ**mix sth↔ˈin (with sth)** to add one substance to others, especially in cooking: *Mix the remaining cream in with the sauce.* ˈ**mix sth into sth** to combine one substance with others, especially in cooking: *Mix the fruit into the rest of the mixture.* ˈ**mix sth into/to sth** to produce sth by combining two or more substances, especially in cooking SYN **blend**: *Add the milk and mix to a smooth dough.* ˌ**mix sth↔ˈup** 🔑 to change the order or arrangement of a group of things, especially by mistake or in a way that you do not want SYN **muddle**: *Someone has mixed up all the application forms.* ➲ related noun MIX-UP ˌ**mix sb/sth ˈup (with sb/sth)** 🔑 to think wrongly that sb/sth is sb/sth else SYN **confuse**: *I think you must be mixing me up with someone else.* ➲ see also MIXED UP

Synonyms

mix

stir • **mingle** • **blend**

These words all refer to substances, qualities, ideas or feelings combining or being combined.

mix to combine two or more substances, qualities, ideas or feelings, usually in a way that means they cannot easily be separated; to be combined in this way: *Mix all the ingredients together in a bowl.* ◇ *Oil and water do not mix.*

stir to move a liquid or substance around, using a spoon or sth similar, in order to mix it thoroughly: *She stirred her tea.*

mingle to combine or be combined. NOTE **Mingle** can be used to talk about sounds, colours, feelings, ideas, qualities or substances. It is used in written English to talk about how a scene or event appears to sb or how they experience it: *The sounds of laughter and singing mingled in the evening air.* ◇ *He felt a kind of happiness mingled with regret.*

blend to mix two or more substances or flavours together; to be mixed together: *Blend the flour with the milk to make a smooth paste.*

MIX OR BLEND?

If you **blend** things when you are cooking you usually combine them more completely than if you just **mix** them. **Mix** can be used to talk about colours, feelings or qualities as well as food and substances. In this meaning **blend** is mostly used in the context of cooking. It is also used to talk about art, music, fashion, etc. with the meaning of 'combine in an attractive way'.

PATTERNS

- to mix/mingle/blend (sth) **with** sth
- to mix/stir/mingle/blend sth **into** sth
- to mix/stir/mingle/blend sth **together**
- to mix/stir/blend **ingredients**
- to mix/mingle/blend **flavours**
- to mix/blend **colours**
- mixed/mingled **feelings**
- to mix/stir/blend sth **thoroughly/well/gently**

■ ***noun***
▸ COMBINATION **1** 🔑 [C, usually sing.] a combination of different people or things SYN **blend**: *a school with a good social mix of children* ◇ *The town offers a fascinating mix of old and new.* ◇ *a pair of wool mix socks* (= made of wool and other materials) **2** 🔑 [C, U] a combination of things that you

M

need to make sth, often sold as a powder to which you add water, etc: *a cake mix* ◇ *cement mix*

▸ IN POPULAR MUSIC **3** [C] = REMIX **4** [sing.] the particular way that instruments and voices are arranged in a piece of music **5** [C] an arrangement of several songs or pieces of music into one continuous piece, especially for dancing

mixed /mɪkst/ *adj.*
1 having both good and bad qualities or feelings: *The weather has been very mixed recently.* ◇ *I still* ***have mixed feelings*** *about going to Brazil* (= I am not sure what to think). ◇ *The play was given a* ***mixed reception*** *by the critics* (= some liked it, some did not). ◇ *British athletes had mixed fortunes in yesterday's competition.* **2** [only before noun] consisting of different kinds of people, for example, people from different races and cultures: *a mixed community* ◇ *people of mixed race* ◇ *a mixed marriage* (= between two people of different races or religions) **3** [only before noun] consisting of different types of the same thing: *a mixed salad* **4** [usually before noun] of or for both males and females: *a mixed school* ◇ *I'd rather not talk about it in mixed company.*

ˌmixed-aˈbility *adj.* [usually before noun] with or for students who have different levels of ability: *a mixed-ability class* ◇ *mixed-ability teaching*

ˌmixed ˈbag *noun* [sing.] (*informal*) a collection of things or people of very different types

ˌmixed ˈblessing *noun* [usually sing.] something that has advantages and disadvantages

ˌmixed ˈdoubles *noun* [U+sing./pl. v.] (in TENNIS, etc.) a game in which a man and a woman play together against another man and woman

M

ˌmixed eˈconomy *noun* an economic system in a country in which some companies are owned by the state and some are private

ˌmixed ˈfarming *noun* [U] a system of farming in which farmers both grow crops and keep animals

ˌmixed ˈgrill *noun* (*BrE*) a hot dish of different types of meat and vegetables that have been GRILLED: *a mixed grill of bacon, sausages, tomatoes and mushrooms*

ˌmixed ˈmetaphor *noun* a combination of two or more METAPHORS or idioms that produces a ridiculous effect, for example, 'He put his foot down with a firm hand.'

ˌmixed ˈnumber *noun* (*mathematics*) a number consisting of a whole number and a PROPER FRACTION, for example 3¼

ˌmixed ˈrace *adj.* (*especially BrE*) (*NAmE* usually **biracial**) concerning or containing members of two different races: *a mixed-race child* (= with parents of different races)

ˌmixed ˈup *adj.* (*informal*) confused because of mental, emotional or social problems: *a* ***mixed-up kid/teenager***

mixer /ˈmɪksə(r)/ *noun* **1** a machine or device used for mixing things: *a food mixer* ◇ (*BrE*) *a mixer tap* (= one in which hot and cold water can be mixed together before it comes out of the pipe) ➲ see also CEMENT MIXER **2** a drink such as fruit juice that is not alcoholic and that can be mixed with alcohol: *low-calorie mixers* **3** (*technical*) a device used for mixing together different sound or picture signals in order to produce a single sound or picture; a person whose job is to operate this device

IDM **a good/bad ˈmixer** a person who finds it easy/difficult to talk to people they do not know, for example at a party

ˈmixing bowl *noun* a large bowl for mixing food in

ˈmixing desk *noun* a piece of electronic equipment for mixing sounds, used especially when recording music or to improve its sound after recording it

mix·ture /ˈmɪkstʃə(r)/ *noun*
1 [C, usually sing.] a combination of different things: *The city is a mixture of old and new buildings.* ◇ *We listened to the news with a mixture of surprise and horror.* **2** [C, U] a substance made by mixing other substances together: *cake mixture* ◇ *Add the eggs to the mixture and beat well.* ➲ see also COUGH MIXTURE **3** [C] (*technical*) a combination of two or more substances that mix together without any chemical reaction taking place ➲ compare COMPOUND *n.* **4** [U] the act of mixing different substances together

ˈmix-up *noun* (*informal*) a situation that is full of confusion, especially because sb has made a mistake SYN **muddle**: *There has been a mix-up over the dates.*

miz·zen (also **mizen**) /ˈmɪzn/ *noun* (*technical*) **1** (also **miz·zen·mast** /ˈmɪznmɑːst; *NAmE* -mæst/) the MAST of a ship that is behind the main mast **2** (also **miz·zen·sail** /ˈmɪznseɪl/) a sail on the mizzen of a ship

ml *abbr.* (*pl.* **ml** or **mls**) MILLILITRE(S): *25ml water*

MLA /ˌem el ˈeɪ/ *abbr.* (in Canada and Northern Ireland) Member of the Legislative Assembly

M'lud /məˈlʌd/ *noun* (*BrE*) used when speaking to the judge in court: *My client pleads guilty, M'lud.*

mm *abbr., exclamation*
▪ ***abbr.*** MILLIMETRE(S): *rainfall 6mm* ◇ *a 35mm camera*
▪ ***exclamation*** (also **mmm**) the way of writing the sound /m/ that people make to show that they are listening to sb or that they agree, they are thinking, they like sth, they are not sure, etc: *Mm, I know what you mean.* ◇ *Mm, what lovely cake!* ◇ *Mmm, I'm not so sure that's a good idea.*

MMR /ˌem em ˈɑː(r)/ *abbr.* MEASLES, MUMPS, RUBELLA: *an MMR jab* (= a VACCINE given to small children to prevent these three diseases)

MMS /ˌem em ˈes/ *noun* [U, C] the abbreviation for 'Multimedia Messaging Service' (a system for sending colour pictures and sounds as well as short written messages from one mobile/cell phone to another): *an MMS message* ◇ *He sent me an MMS.*

MNA /ˌem en ˈeɪ/ *abbr.* (*CanE*) Member of the National Assembly

mne·mon·ic /nɪˈmɒnɪk; *NAmE* -ˈmɑːn-/ *noun* a word, sentence, poem, etc. that helps you to remember sth ▸ **mne·mon·ic** *adj.* [only before noun]: *a mnemonic device*

MO (*BrE*) (also **M.O.** *US, BrE*) /ˌem ˈəʊ; *NAmE* ˈoʊ/ *abbr.* **1** MEDICAL OFFICER **2** MODUS OPERANDI

mo /məʊ; *NAmE* moʊ/ *noun* [sing.] (*BrE, informal*) a very short period of time SYN **moment**: *See you in a mo!*

moa /ˈməʊə; *NAmE* ˈmoʊə/ *noun* a large bird that could not fly, that was found in New Zealand but is now EXTINCT (= no longer exists)

moan /məʊn; *NAmE* moʊn/ *verb, noun*
▪ ***verb*** **1** [I, T] (of a person) to make a long deep sound, usually expressing unhappiness, suffering or sexual pleasure SYN **groan**: *The injured man was lying on the ground, moaning.* ◇ **~ in/with sth** *to* ***moan in/with pain*** ◇ **+ speech** *'I might never see you again,' she moaned.* **2** [I, T] **~ (at sb)** (*informal*) to complain about sth in a way that other people find annoying SYN **grumble, whine**: **~ (on) (about sth) (to sb)** *What are you moaning on about now?* ◇ **~ (at sb) (about sth)** *They're always* ***moaning and groaning*** *about how much they have to do.* ◇ **~ that...** *Bella moaned that her feet were cold.* ➲ SYNONYMS at COMPLAIN **3** [I] (*literary*) (especially of the wind) to make a long deep sound ▸ **moan·er** *noun*
▪ ***noun*** **1** [C] a long deep sound, usually expressing unhappiness, suffering or sexual pleasure SYN **groan**: *a low* ***moan of despair/anguish*** **2** [C] (*informal*) a complaint about sth: *We had a good moan about work.* ◇ *His letters are full of the usual moans and groans.* **3** [sing.] (*literary*) a long deep sound, especially the sound that is made by the wind

moat /məʊt; *NAmE* moʊt/ *noun* a deep wide channel that was dug around a castle, etc. and filled with water to make it more difficult for enemies to attack ➲ VISUAL VOCAB page V13 ▸ **moat·ed** *adj.* [usually before noun]: *a moated manor house*

mob /mɒb; *NAmE* mɑːb/ *noun, verb*
▪ ***noun*** **1** [C, sing.+ sing./pl. v.] a large crowd of people, especially one that may become violent or cause trouble: *an* ***angry/unruly mob*** ◇ *The mob was/were preparing to storm the building.* ◇ *an excited mob of fans* ◇ **mob rule** (= a situation in which a mob has control, rather than people

in authority) ➲ see also LYNCH MOB **2** [C, usually sing.] (*informal*) a group of people who are similar in some way SYN **gang**: *All the usual mob were there.* **3 the Mob** [sing.] (*informal*) the people involved in organized crime; the MAFIA **4** [C] (*AustralE, NZE*) a group of animals SYN **flock, herd**: *a mob of cattle* IDM see HEAVY *adj.*

■ ***verb*** (-bb-) [usually passive] **1 ~ sth** if a crowd of birds or animals **mob** another bird or animal, they gather round it and attack it **2 ~ sb** if a person is **mobbed** by a crowd of people, the crowd gathers round them in order to see them and try and get their attention SYN **besiege**

ˈmob cap *noun* a light cotton cap covering all the hair, worn by women in the 18th and 19th centuries

mo·bile 🔑 /ˈməʊbaɪl; *NAmE* ˈmoʊbl/ *adj., noun*

■ ***adj.*** **1** 🔑 [usually before noun] that is not fixed in one place and can be moved easily and quickly: *mobile equipment* ◊ *a* ***mobile shop/library*** (= one inside a vehicle) ➲ compare STATIONARY **2** [not usually before noun] (of a person) able to move or travel around easily: *a kitchen especially designed for the elderly or people who are less mobile* ◊ *You really need to be mobile* (= have a car) *if you live in the country.* OPP **immobile 3** (of people) able to change your social class, your job or the place where you live easily: *a highly mobile workforce* (= people who can move easily from place to place) ➲ see also UPWARDLY MOBILE **4** (of a face or its features) changing shape or expression easily and often

■ ***noun*** **1** (*BrE*) = MOBILE PHONE: *Call me on my mobile.* ◊ *What's your mobile number?* ◊ *the mobile networks* (= companies that provide mobile phone services) **2** a decoration made from wire, etc. that is hung from the ceiling and that has small objects hanging from it which move when the air around them moves ➲ VISUAL VOCAB page V20

ˌmobile deˈvice *noun* any small computing device that will fit into your pocket, such as a PDA or SMARTPHONE ➲ compare MID

ˌmobile ˈhome *noun* **1** (*especially NAmE*) (also **trailer** *NAmE*) a small building for people to live in that is made in a factory and moved to a permanent place ➲ VISUAL VOCAB page V14 **2** (*BrE*) (*NAmE* **trailer**) a large CARAVAN that can be moved, sometimes with wheels, that is usually parked in one place and used for living in ➲ VISUAL VOCAB page V14

ˌmobile ˈlibrary (*BrE*) (*NAmE* **book·mobile**) *noun* a van/truck that contains a library and travels from place to place so that people in different places can borrow books

ˌmobile ˈphone 🔑 (also **mo·bile**) (both *BrE*) (also **cell phone**, **ˈcellular phone**, *informal* **cell** *NAmE, BrE*) *noun*
a telephone that does not have wires and works by radio, that you can carry with you and use anywhere: *Please make sure all mobile phones are switched off during the performance.* ➲ COLLOCATIONS at PHONE

mo·bil·ity /məʊˈbɪləti; *NAmE* moʊ-/ *noun* [U] **1** the ability to move easily from one place, social class, or job to another: ***social/geographical/career mobility*** ➲ see also UPWARD MOBILITY **2** the ability to move or travel around easily: *An electric wheelchair has given her greater mobility.*

mo·bil·ize (*BrE* also **-ise**) /ˈməʊbəlaɪz; *NAmE* ˈmoʊ-/ *verb* **1** [T, I] **~ (sb)** to work together in order to achieve a particular aim; to organize a group of people to do this SYN **rally**: *The unions mobilized thousands of workers in a protest against the cuts.* **2** [T] **~ sth** to find and start to use sth that is needed for a particular purpose SYN **marshal**: *They were unable to mobilize the resources they needed.* **3** [T, I] **~ (sb/sth)** if a country **mobilizes** its army, or if a country or army **mobilizes**, it makes itself ready to fight in a war: *The troops were ordered to mobilize.* ➲ compare DEMOBILIZE
▸ **mo·bil·iza·tion, -isa·tion** /ˌməʊbəlaɪˈzeɪʃn; *NAmE* ˌmoʊbələˈz-/ *noun* [U]

Mö·bius strip (also **Moe·bius strip**) /ˈmɜːbiəs strɪp/ *noun* a surface with one continuous side, formed by joining the ends of a strip of material after twisting one end through 180 degrees

Möbius strip

mob·log /ˈmɒblɒɡ; ˈməʊ-; *NAmE* -blɑːɡ/ *noun* (*computing*) (*BrE*) a website that belongs to a particular person who puts pictures and other material from a mobile/cell phone

mob·ster /ˈmɒbstə(r); *NAmE* ˈmɑːb-/ *noun* a member of a group of people who are involved in organized crime

moc·ca·sin /ˈmɒkəsɪn; *NAmE* ˈmɑːk-/ *noun* a flat shoe that is made from soft leather and has large STITCHES around the front, of a type originally worn by Native Americans ➲ VISUAL VOCAB page V52

mocha /ˈmɒkə; *NAmE* ˈmoʊkə/ *noun* **1** [U] a type of coffee of very good quality **2** [C, U] a drink made or flavoured with this, often with chocolate added

mock /mɒk; *NAmE* mɑːk/ *verb, adj., noun*

■ ***verb*** **1** [T, I] **~ (sb/sth)** | **~ (sb) + speech** to laugh at sb/sth in an unkind way, especially by copying what they say or do SYN **make fun of**: *He's always mocking my French accent.* ◊ *The other children mocked her, laughing behind their hands.* ◊ *You can mock, but at least I'm willing to have a try!* **2** [T] **~ sth** (*formal*) to show no respect for sth: *The new exam mocked the needs of the majority of children.*
▸ **mock·er** *noun*

■ ***adj.*** [only before noun] **1** not sincere SYN **sham**: ***mock horror/surprise*** **2** that is a copy of sth; not real: *a mock election* ◊ *a* ***mock interview/examination*** (= used to practise for the real one)

■ ***noun*** (*informal*) (in Britain) a practice exam that you do before the official one: *The mocks are in November.* ◊ *What did you get in the mock?*

mock·ers /ˈmɒkəz; *NAmE* ˈmɑːkərz/ *noun* [pl.]
IDM **put the ˈmockers on sth/sb** (*BrE, informal*) to stop sth from happening; to bring bad luck to sth/sb: *We were going to have a barbecue but the rain put the mockers on that idea.*

mock·ery /ˈmɒkəri; *NAmE* ˈmɑːk-/ *noun* **1** [U] comments or actions that are intended to make sb/sth seem ridiculous SYN **ridicule, scorn**: *She couldn't stand any more of their mockery.* **2** [sing.] (*disapproving*) an action, a decision, etc. that is a failure and that is not as it is supposed to be SYN **travesty**: *It was a mockery of a trial.*
IDM **make a ˈmockery of sth** to make sth seem ridiculous or useless: *The trial made a mockery of justice.*

mock·ing /ˈmɒkɪŋ; *NAmE* ˈmɑːk-/ *adj.* (of behaviour, an expression, etc.) showing that you think sb/sth is ridiculous SYN **contemptuous**: *a mocking smile* ◊ *Her voice was faintly mocking.* ▸ **mock·ing·ly** *adv.*

mock·ing·bird /ˈmɒkɪŋbɜːd; *NAmE* ˈmɑːkɪŋbɜːrd/ *noun* a grey and white American bird that can copy the songs of other birds

mock·ney /ˈmɒkni; *NAmE* ˈmɑːkni/ *noun* [U] (*BrE, informal*, often *disapproving*) a way of speaking English by educated people from London which copies the words and sounds of COCKNEY speech (= a way of speaking typical of the East End of London): *She speaks in this ridiculous mockney accent.*

ˈmock-up *noun* a model or a copy of sth, often the same size as it, that is used for testing, or for showing people what the real thing will look like

MOD /ˌem əʊ ˈdiː; *NAmE* oʊ/ *abbr.* Ministry of Defence (the government department in Britain that is responsible for defence)

mod /mɒd; *NAmE* mɑːd/ *noun* a member of a group of young people, especially in Britain in the 1960s, who wore neat, fashionable clothes and rode MOTOR SCOOTERS ➲ compare ROCKER

modal /ˈməʊdl; *NAmE* ˈmoʊdl/ (also **modal ˈverb, modal auˈxiliary, modal auˈxiliary verb**) *noun* (*grammar*) a verb such as *can*, *may* or *will* that is used with another verb (not a modal) to express possibility, permission, intention, etc. ▸ **modal** *adj.* ➲ compare AUXILIARY

mo·dal·ity /məʊˈdæləti; *NAmE* moʊˈd-/ *noun* (*pl.* -ies) **1** [C] (*formal*) the particular way in which sth exists, is ex-

M

perienced or is done: *They are researching a different modality of treatment for the disease.* **2** [U] (*linguistics*) the idea expressed by modals **3** [C] (*biology*) the kind of senses that the body uses to experience things: *the visual and auditory modalities*

Grammar Point

modal verbs

- The **modal verbs** are **can, could, may, might, must, ought to, shall, should, will** and **would. Dare, need, have to** and **used to** also share some of the features of modal verbs.
- Modal verbs have only one form. They have no *-ing* or *-ed* forms and do not add *-s* to the 3rd person singular form: *He can speak three languages.* ◇ *She will try and visit tomorrow.*
- Modal verbs are followed by the infinitive of another verb without **to**. The exceptions are **ought to** and **used to**: *You must find a job.* ◇ *You ought to stop smoking.* ◇ *I used to smoke but I gave up two years ago.*
- Questions are formed without **do/does** in the present, or **did** in the past: *Can I invite Mary?* ◇ *Should I have invited Mary?*
- Negative sentences are formed with **not** or the short form **-n't** and do not use **do/does** or **did**.

You will find more help with how to use modal verbs at the dictionary entries for each verb.

mod cons /ˌmɒd ˈkɒnz; *NAmE* ˌmɑːd ˈkɑːnz/ *noun* [pl.] (*BrE, informal*) (especially in advertisements) the things in a house or flat/apartment that make living there easier and more comfortable

mod·ding /ˈmɒdɪŋ; *NAmE* ˈmɑːdɪŋ/ *noun* [U] (*computing*) (*informal*) the activity of changing a piece of computer equipment or a computer program so that it works in a way that was not intended by the producer: *There are stiff penalties for illegal modding.* ▸ **mod** /mɒd; *NAmE* mɑːd/ *verb* (-dd-): **~ sth** *a specially modded system*

mode AW /məʊd; *NAmE* moʊd/ *noun* **1** [C] a particular way of doing sth; a particular type of sth: *a mode of communication* ◇ *a mode of behaviour* ◇ *environment-friendly modes of transport* **2** [C, U] the way in which a piece of equipment is set to perform a particular task: *Switch the camera into the automatic mode.* **3** [U] a particular way of feeling or behaving: *to be in holiday mode* **4** [C, usually sing.] a particular style or fashion in clothes, art, etc: *a pop video made by a director who really understands the mode* ➲ see also À LA MODE, MODISH **5** [sing.] (*technical*) a set of notes in music which form a SCALE: ***major/minor mode*** **6** [sing.] (*mathematics*) the value that appears most frequently in a series of numbers

model O‑w /ˈmɒdl; *NAmE* ˈmɑːdl/ *noun, verb*

■ ***noun***

▸ SMALL COPY **1** O‑w a copy of sth, usually smaller than the original object: *a **working model*** (= one in which the parts move) *of a fire engine* ◇ *a model aeroplane* ◇ *The architect had produced a **scale model** of the proposed shopping complex.* ➲ VISUAL VOCAB page V35

▸ DESIGN **2** O‑w a particular design or type of product: *The latest models will be on display at the motor show.*

▸ DESCRIPTION OF SYSTEM **3** a simple description of a system, used for explaining how sth works or calculating what might happen, etc: *a mathematical model for determining the safe level of pesticides in food* ➲ COLLOCATIONS at SCIENTIFIC

▸ EXAMPLE TO COPY **4** O‑w something such as a system that can be copied by other people: *The nation's constitution provided a model that other countries followed.* **5** (*approving*) a person or thing that is considered an excellent example of sth: *It was a model of clarity.* ◇ *a model student* ◇ *a model farm* (= one that has been specially designed to work well) ➲ see also ROLE MODEL

▸ FASHION **6** O‑w a person whose job is to wear and show new styles of clothes and be photographed wearing them: *a fashion model* ◇ *a male model*

▸ FOR ARTIST **7** O‑w a person who is employed to be painted, drawn, photographed, etc. by an artist or photographer

■ ***verb*** (-ll-, *especially US* -l-)

▸ WORK AS MODEL **1** [I] to work as a model for an artist or in the fashion industry

▸ CLOTHES **2** [T] **~ sth** to wear clothes in order to show them to people who might want to buy them: *The wedding gown is being modelled for us by the designer's daughter.*

▸ CREATE COPY **3** [T] **~ sth** to create a copy of an activity, a situation, etc. so that you can study it before dealing with the real thing SYN **simulate**: *The program can model a typical home page for you.*

▸ CLAY, ETC. **4** [T] **~ sth** to shape CLAY, etc. in order to make sth: *a statue modelled in bronze*

PHR V ˈ**model yourself on sb** to copy the behaviour, style, etc. of sb you like and respect in order to be like them: *As a politician, he modelled himself on Churchill.* ˈ**model sth on/after sth** to make sth so that it looks, works, etc. like sth else: *The country's parliament is modelled on the British system.*

ˈ**model home** (*NAmE*) (*BrE* ˈ**show house**, ˈ**show home**) *noun* a house in a group of new houses that has been painted and filled with furniture, so that people who might want to buy one of the houses can see what they will be like

mod·el·ler (*especially US* **mod·el·er**) /ˈmɒdələ(r); *NAmE* ˈmɑːd-/ *noun* **1** a person who makes models of objects **2** a person who makes a simple description of a system or a process that can be used to explain it, etc.

mod·el·ling (*especially US* **mod·el·ing**) /ˈmɒdəlɪŋ; *NAmE* ˈmɑːd-/ *noun* [U] **1** the work of a fashion model: *a career in modelling* ◇ *a modelling agency* **2** the activity of making models of objects: *clay modelling* **3** the work of making a simple description of a system or a process that can be used to explain it, etc: ***mathematical/statistical/computer modelling***

ˌ**model** ˈ**village** *noun* **1** a small model of a village, or a collection of small models of famous buildings arranged like a village **2** (*old use*) a village with good-quality houses, especially one built in the past by an employer for workers to live in

modem /ˈməʊdem; *NAmE* ˈmoʊ-/ *noun* a device that connects one computer system to another using a telephone line so that data can be sent

mod·er·ate *adj., verb, noun*

■ ***adj.*** /ˈmɒdərət; *NAmE* ˈmɑːd-/ **1** that is neither very good, large, hot, etc. nor very bad, small, cold, etc: *students of moderate ability* ◇ *Even moderate amounts of the drug can be fatal.* ◇ *The team enjoyed only moderate success last season.* ◇ *Cook over a moderate heat.* **2** having or showing opinions, especially about politics, that are not extreme: ***moderate views/policies*** ◇ *a moderate socialist* **3** staying within limits that are considered to be reasonable by most people: *a moderate drinker* ◇ *moderate wage demands* OPP **immoderate**

■ ***verb*** /ˈmɒdəreɪt; *NAmE* ˈmɑːd-/ **1** [I, T] (*formal*) to become or make sth become less extreme, severe, etc: *By evening the wind had moderated slightly.* ◇ **~ sth** *We agreed to moderate our original demands.* **2** [T, I] **~** (**sth**) (*BrE*) to check that an exam has been marked fairly and in the same way by different people **3** [T, I] **~** (**sth**) to be in charge of a discussion or debate and make sure it is fair: *The television debate was moderated by a law professor.* ◇ *a moderated newsgroup*

■ ***noun*** /ˈmɒdərət; *NAmE* ˈmɑːd-/ a person who has opinions, especially about politics, that are not extreme

mod·er·ate·ly /ˈmɒdərətli; *NAmE* ˈmɑːd-/ *adv.* **1** to an average extent; fairly but not very SYN **reasonably**: *a moderately successful career* ◇ *She only did moderately well in the exam.* ◇ *Cook in a moderately hot oven.* **2** within reasonable limits: *He only drinks (alcohol) moderately.*

mod·er·ation /ˌmɒdəˈreɪʃn; *NAmE* ˌmɑːd-/ *noun* [U] **1** the quality of being reasonable and not being extreme: *There was a call for moderation on the part of the trade* *unions.* ◇ *Alcohol should only ever be taken* ***in moderation*** (= in small quantities). **2** (*BrE*) (in education) the process of making sure that the same standards are used by different people in marking exams, etc.

mod·er·ator /ˈmɒdəreɪtə(r); *NAmE* ˈmɑːd-/ *noun* **1** a person whose job is to help the two sides in a disagreement to reach an agreement ➲ see also MEDIATOR **2** (*especially NAmE*) a person whose job is to make sure that a discussion or a debate is fair **3** (*BrE*) a person whose job is to make sure that an exam is marked fairly **4** (*computing*) a person who is responsible for preventing offensive material from being published on a website: *moderators of online discussion groups* **5 Moderator** a religious leader in the Presbyterian Church who is in charge of the Church council

mod·ern 🔑 /ˈmɒdn; *NAmE* ˈmɑːdərn/ *adj.* **1** 🔑 [only before noun] of the present time or recent times SYN **contemporary**: *the modern industrial world* ◇ *Modern European history* ◇ *modern Greek* ◇ *Stress is a major problem of modern life.* **2** 🔑 [only before noun] (of styles in art, music, fashion, etc.) new and intended to be different from traditional styles SYN **contemporary**: ***modern art/architecture/drama/jazz*** **3** 🔑 (usually *approving*) using the latest technology, designs, materials, etc. SYN **up-to-date**: *a modern computer system* ◇ *modern methods of farming* ◇ *the most modern, well-equipped hospital in London* **4** (of ways of behaving, thinking, etc.) new and not always accepted by most members of society: *She has very modern ideas about educating her children.*

ˌmodern ˈdance *noun* [U] a form of dance that was developed in the early 20th century by people who did not like the restrictions of traditional BALLET

ˌmodern-ˈday *adj.* [only before noun] **1** of the present time SYN **contemporary**: *modern-day America* **2** used to describe a modern form of sb/sth, usually sb/sth bad or unpleasant, that existed in the past: *It has been called modern-day slavery.*

ˌmodern ˈEnglish *noun* [U] the English language in the form it has been in since about 1500

mod·ern·ism /ˈmɒdənɪzəm; *NAmE* ˈmɑːdərn-/ *noun* [U] **1** modern ideas or methods **2** a style and movement in art, ARCHITECTURE and literature popular in the middle of the 20th century in which modern ideas, methods and materials were used rather than traditional ones ➲ compare POSTMODERNISM ▸ **mod·ern·ist** /ˈmɒdənɪst; *NAmE* ˈmɑːdərn-/ *adj.* [only before noun]: *modernist art* **mod·ern·ist** *noun*

mod·ern·is·tic /ˌmɒdəˈnɪstɪk; *NAmE* ˌmɑːdərˈn-/ *adj.* (of a painting, building, piece of furniture, etc.) painted, designed, etc. in a very modern style

mod·ern·ity /məˈdɜːnəti; *NAmE* -ˈdɜːrn-/ *noun* [U] the condition of being new and modern

mod·ern·ize (*BrE* also **-ise**) /ˈmɒdənaɪz; *NAmE* ˈmɑːdərn-/ *verb* **1** [T] **~ sth** to make a system, methods, etc. more modern and more suitable for use at the present time SYN **update**: *The company is investing $9 million to modernize its factories.* **2** [I] to start using modern equipment, ideas, etc: *Unfortunately we lack the resources to modernize.* ▸ **mod·ern·iza·tion, -isa·tion** /ˌmɒdənaɪˈzeɪʃn; *NAmE* ˌmɑːdərnəˈz-/ *noun* [U]

ˌmodern ˈlanguage *noun* (*especially BrE*) a language that is spoken or written now, especially a European language, such as French or Spanish, that you study at school, university or college: *the department of modern languages* ◇ *a degree in modern languages*

mod·est /ˈmɒdɪst; *NAmE* ˈmɑːd-/ *adj.* **1** not very large, expensive, important, etc: *modest improvements/reforms* ◇ *He charged a relatively modest fee.* ◇ *a modest little house* ◇ *The research was carried out on a modest scale.* **2** (*approving*) not talking much about your own abilities or possessions: *She's very modest about her success.* ◇ *You're too modest!* OPP **immodest** **3** (of people, especially women, or their clothes) shy about showing much of the body; not intended to attract attention, especially in a sexual way SYN **demure**: *a modest dress* OPP **immodest** ▸ **mod·est·ly** *adv.*

mod·esty /ˈmɒdəsti; *NAmE* ˈmɑːd-/ *noun* [U] **1** the fact of not talking much about your abilities or possessions: *He accepted the award with characteristic modesty.* ◇ *I hate false* (= pretended) *modesty.* **2** the action of behaving or dressing so that you do not show your body or attract sexual attention **3** the state of being not very large, expensive, important, etc: *They tried to disguise the modesty of their achievements.*

modi·cum /ˈmɒdɪkəm; *NAmE* ˈmɑːd-; ˈmɔːd-/ *noun* [sing.] (*formal*) a fairly small amount, especially of sth good or pleasant: *They should win, given a modicum of luck.*

modi·fi·ca·tion AW /ˌmɒdɪfɪˈkeɪʃn; *NAmE* ˌmɑːd-/ *noun* [U, C] **~ (of/to/in sth)** the act or process of changing sth in order to improve it or make it more acceptable; a change that is made SYN **adaptation**: *Considerable modification of the existing system is needed.* ◇ *It might be necessary to make a few slight modifications to the design.*

modi·fier /ˈmɒdɪfaɪə(r); *NAmE* ˈmɑːd-/ *noun* (*grammar*) a word or group of words that describes a noun phrase or restricts its meaning in some way: ➲ compare POSTMODIFIER, PREMODIFIER

mod·ify AW /ˈmɒdɪfaɪ; *NAmE* ˈmɑːd-/ *verb* (**modi·fies, modi·fy·ing, modi·fied, modi·fied**) **1 ~ sth** to change sth slightly, especially in order to make it more suitable for a particular purpose SYN **adapt**: *The software we use has been modified for us.* ◇ *Patients are taught how to modify their diet.* **2 ~ sth** to make sth less extreme SYN **adjust**: *to* ***modify*** *your* ***behaviour/language/views*** **3 ~ sth** (*grammar*) a word, such as an adjective or adverb, that **modifies** another word or group of words describes it or restricts its meaning in some way: *In 'walk slowly', the adverb 'slowly' modifies the verb 'walk'.*

mod·ish /ˈməʊdɪʃ; *NAmE* ˈmoʊ-/ *adj.* (sometimes *disapproving*) fashionable

modu·lar /ˈmɒdjələ(r); *NAmE* ˈmɑːdʒə-/ *adj.* **1** (of a course of study, especially at a British university or college) consisting of separate units from which students may choose several: *a modular course* **2** (of machines, buildings, etc.) consisting of separate parts or units that can be joined together

modu·late /ˈmɒdjuleɪt; *NAmE* ˈmɑːdʒə-/ *verb* **1** [T] **~ sth** (*formal*) to change the quality of your voice in order to create a particular effect by making it louder, softer, lower, etc. **2** [I] **~ (from sth) (to/into sth)** (*music*) to change from one musical KEY (= set of notes) to another **3** [T] **~ sth** (*technical*) to affect sth so that it becomes more regular, slower, etc: *drugs that effectively modulate the disease process* **4** [T] **~ sth** (*technical*) to change the rate at which a sound wave or radio signal VIBRATES (= the FREQUENCY) so that it is clearer ▸ **modu·la·tion** /ˌmɒdjuˈleɪʃn; *NAmE* ˌmɑːdʒəˈl-/ *noun* [U, C]

mod·ule /ˈmɒdjuːl; *NAmE* ˈmɑːdʒul/ *noun* **1** a unit that can form part of a course of study, especially at a college or university in Britain: *The course consists of ten core modules and five optional modules.* **2** (*computing*) a unit of a computer system or program that has a particular function **3** one of a set of separate parts or units that can be joined together to make a machine, a piece of furniture, a building, etc. **4** a unit of a SPACECRAFT that can function independently of the main part: *the lunar module*

modus op·er·andi /ˌməʊdəs ˌɒpəˈrændiː; *NAmE* ˌmoʊdəs ˌɑːpə-/ *noun* [sing.] (from *Latin*, *formal*) (*abbr.* **MO**) a particular method of working

modus vi·vendi /ˌməʊdəs vɪˈvendiː; *NAmE* ˌmoʊdəs/ *noun* [sing.] (from *Latin*, *formal*) an arrangement that is made between people, institutions or countries who have very different opinions or ideas, so that they can live or work together without arguing

Moe·bius strip *noun* = MÖBIUS STRIP

mog·gie (also **moggy**) /ˈmɒgi; *NAmE* ˈmɑːgi/ *noun* (*pl.* **-ies**) (*BrE*, *informal*) a cat

M

mogul /ˈməʊgl; *NAmE* ˈmoʊgl/ *noun* **1** a very rich, important and powerful person SYN **magnate**: *a movie mogul* **2 Mogul** (also **Mo·ghul, Mug·hal** /ˈmuːgɑːl/) a member of the Muslim race that ruled much of India from the 16th to the 19th century **3** a raised area of hard snow that you jump over when you are SKIING

mo·hair /ˈməʊheə(r); *NAmE* ˈmoʊher/ *noun* [U] soft wool or cloth made from the fine hair of the ANGORA GOAT, used for making clothes: *a mohair sweater*

Mo·ham·med *noun* = MUHAMMAD

Mo·hawk /ˈməʊhɔːk; *NAmE* ˈmoʊ-/ *noun* (*pl.* **Mohawk** or **Mohawks**) a member of a Native American people, many of whom live in New York State and Canada

Mo·hi·can /məʊˈhiːkən; *NAmE* moʊ-/ (*especially BrE*) (also **Mo·hawk** especially in *NAmE* /ˈməʊhɔːk; *NAmE* ˈmoʊ-/) *noun* a way of cutting the hair in which the head is shaved except for a strip of hair in the middle that is sometimes made to stick up

moi /mwɑː/ *exclamation* (*humorous*, from *French*) me: *'Did you eat all the biscuits?' 'Who? Moi?'*

moire /mwɑː(r); *NAmE* also ˈmɔɪər/ (also **moiré** /ˈmwɑːreɪ/) *noun* [U] a type of silk cloth with a pattern on its surface like small waves

moist /mɔɪst/ *adj.* slightly wet: *warm moist air* ◇ *a rich moist cake* ◇ *Water the plants regularly to keep the soil moist.* ◇ *Her eyes were moist* (= with tears). ➲ SYNONYMS at WET ▸ **moist·ness** *noun* [U]

mois·ten /ˈmɔɪsn/ *verb* [T, I] ~ (**sth**) to become or make sth slightly wet: *He moistened his lips before he spoke.*

mois·ture /ˈmɔɪstʃə(r)/ *noun* [U] very small drops of water that are present in the air, on a surface or in a substance: *the skin's natural moisture* ◇ *a material that is designed to* ***absorb/retain moisture***

mois·tur·ize (*BrE* also **-ise**) /ˈmɔɪstʃəraɪz/ *verb* [T, I] ~ (**sth**) to put a special cream on your skin to make it less dry: *a* ***moisturizing cream/lotion*** ◇ *a product that soothes and moisturizes*

mois·tur·izer (*BrE* also **-iser**) /ˈmɔɪstʃəraɪzə(r)/ *noun* [C, U] a cream that is used to make the skin less dry

mojo /ˈməʊdʒəʊ; *NAmE* ˈmoʊdʒoʊ/ *noun* (*pl.* **mojos**) (*especially NAmE*) **1** [U] magic power **2** [C] a small object, or a collection of small objects in a bag, that is believed to have magic powers **3** [U] the power of sb's attractive personality

molar /ˈməʊlə(r); *NAmE* ˈmoʊ-/ *noun* any of the twelve large teeth at the back of the mouth used for crushing and chewing food ➲ compare CANINE, INCISOR

mo·las·ses /məˈlæsɪz/ (*NAmE*) (*BrE* **trea·cle**) *noun* [U] a thick black sweet sticky liquid produced when sugar is REFINED (= made pure), used in cooking

mold (*especially US*) (*BrE, CanE* **mould**) /məʊld; *NAmE* moʊld/ *noun, verb*

■ ***noun*** **1** [C] a container that you pour a liquid or soft substance into, which then becomes solid in the same shape as the container, for example when it is cooled or cooked: *A clay mold is used for casting bronze statues.* ◇ *Pour the chocolate into a heart-shaped mold.* ◇ *They* ***broke the mold*** *when they made you* (= there is nobody like you). **2** [C, usually sing.] a particular style showing the characteristics, attitudes or behaviour that are typical of sb/sth: *a hero in the 'Superman' mold* ◇ *He is cast in a different mold from his predecessor.* ◇ *She doesn't fit (into) the traditional mold of an academic.* **3** [U, C] a fine soft green, grey or black substance like fur that grows on old food or on objects that are left in warm wet air: *There's mold on the cheese.* ◇ *molds and fungi* ◇ *mold growth* ➲ see also LEAF MOULD

IDM **break the ˈmold (of sth)** to change what people expect from a situation, especially by acting in a dramatic and original way

■ ***verb*** **1** [T] to shape a soft substance into a particular form or object by pressing it or by putting it into a mold: ~ **A (into B)** *First, mold the clay into the desired shape.* ◇ ~ **B (from/out of/in A)** *The figure had been molded in clay.* **2** [T] to strongly influence the way sb's character, opinions, etc. develop: ~ **sb/sth** *The experience had molded and coloured her whole life.* ◇ ~ **sb/sth into sb/sth** *He molded them into a superb team.* **3** [I, T] ~ (**sth**) **to sth** to fit or make sth fit tightly around the shape of sth: *The fabric molds to the body.*

mol·der (*especially US*) (*BrE, CanE* **moulder**) /ˈməʊldə(r); *NAmE* ˈmoʊ-/ *verb* [I] to decay slowly and steadily: *The room smelt of disuse and moldering books.*

mold·ing (*especially US*) (*BrE, CanE* **mould·ing**) /ˈməʊldɪŋ; *NAmE* ˈmoʊ-/ *noun* a decorative strip of plastic, stone, wood, etc. around the top edge of a wall, on a door, etc.

moldy (*especially US*) (*BrE, CanE* **mouldy**) /ˈməʊldi; *NAmE* ˈmoʊ-/ *adj.* **1** covered with or containing MOLD: ***moldy bread/cheese*** ◇ *Strawberries* ***go moldy*** *very quickly.* **2** old and not in good condition

mole /məʊl; *NAmE* moʊl/ *noun* **1** a small animal with dark grey fur, that is almost blind and digs tunnels under the ground to live in ➲ see also MOLEHILL **2** a small dark brown mark on the skin, sometimes slightly higher than the skin around it ➲ compare FRECKLE **3** a person who works within an organization and secretly passes important information to another organization or country **4** (*chemistry*) a unit for measuring the amount of substance

mol·ecule /ˈmɒlɪkjuːl; *NAmE* ˈmɑːl-/ *noun* (*chemistry*) the smallest unit, consisting of a group of atoms, into which a substance can be divided without a change in its chemical nature: *A molecule of water consists of two atoms of hydrogen and one atom of oxygen.* ▸ **mo·lecu·lar** /məˈlekjələ(r)/ *adj.* [only before noun]: ***molecular structure/biology***

mole·hill /ˈməʊlhɪl; *NAmE* ˈmoʊl-/ *noun* a small pile of earth that a MOLE leaves on the surface of the ground when it digs underground IDM see MOUNTAIN

mole·skin /ˈməʊlskɪn; *NAmE* ˈmoʊl-/ *noun* [U] a type of strong cotton cloth with a soft surface, used for making clothes

mo·lest /məˈlest/ *verb* **1** ~ **sb** to attack sb, especially a child, sexually SYN **abuse 2** ~ **sb** (*old-fashioned*) to attack sb physically ▸ **mo·lest·ation** /ˌmɒleˈsteɪʃn; *NAmE* ˌmoʊ-/ *noun* [U] **mo·lest·er** /məˈlestə(r)/ *noun*: *a child molester*

moll /mɒl; *NAmE* mɑːl/ *noun* (*old-fashioned, slang*) the female friend of a criminal

mol·lify /ˈmɒlɪfaɪ; *NAmE* ˈmɑːl-/ *verb* (**mol·li·fies, mol·li·fy·ing, mol·li·fied, mol·li·fied**) ~ **sb** (*formal*) to make sb feel less angry or upset SYN **placate**

mol·lusc (*BrE*) (*US* **mol·lusk**) /ˈmɒləsk; *NAmE* ˈmɑːl-/ *noun* (*technical*) any creature with a soft body that is not divided into different sections, and usually a hard outer shell. SNAILS and SLUGS are molluscs. ➲ compare BIVALVE, SHELLFISH

molly·cod·dle /ˈmɒlikɒdl; *NAmE* ˈmɑːlikɑːdl/ *verb* (*disapproving*, becoming *old-fashioned*) ~ **sb** to protect sb too much and make their life too comfortable and safe ➲ compare CODDLE

Molo·tov cock·tail /ˌmɒlətɒf ˈkɒkteɪl; *NAmE* ˌmɑːlətɔːf ˈkɑːk-; ˌmɔːl-/ (*BrE* also **ˈpetrol bomb**) *noun* a simple bomb that consists of a bottle filled with petrol/gas and a piece of cloth in the end that is made to burn just before the bomb is thrown

molt (*especially US*) (*BrE, CanE* **moult**) /məʊlt; *NAmE* moʊlt/ *verb* [I] (of a bird or an animal) to lose feathers or hair before new feathers or hair grow

mol·ten /ˈməʊltən; *NAmE* ˈmoʊl-/ *adj.* (of metal, rock, or glass) heated to a very high temperature so that it becomes liquid

mo·lyb·denum /məˈlɪbdənəm/ *noun* [U] (*symb.* Mo) a chemical element. Molybdenum is a silver-grey metal that breaks easily and is used in some ALLOY steels.

mom 0‑ /mɒm; *NAmE* mɑːm/ *noun* (*NAmE*) (*BrE* **mum**) (*informal*)
a mother: *Where's my mom?* ◇ *Mom and Dad* ◇ *Are you listening, Mom?* ➲ see also SOCCER MOM

ˌmom-and-ˈpop *adj.* [only before noun] (*NAmE*) (of a shop/store or business) owned and run by a husband and wife, or by a family

mo·ment ⚿ /ˈməʊmənt; *NAmE* ˈmoʊ-/ *noun* **1** ⚿ a very short period of time: *Could you* ***wait a moment****, please?* ◇ ***One moment, please*** (= Please wait a short time). ◇ *He thought* ***for a moment*** *before replying.* ◇ *I'll be back* ***in a moment****.* ◇ *We arrived* ***not a moment too soon*** (= almost too late). ◇ ***Moments later*** (= a very short time later), *I heard a terrible crash.* ➲ see also SENIOR MOMENT **2** ⚿ [sing.] an exact point in time: *We're busy* ***at the moment*** (= now). ◇ *I agreed* ***in a moment of*** *weakness.* ◇ ***At that very moment****, the phone rang.* ◇ ***From that moment on****, she never felt really well again.* **3** ⚿ [C] a particular occasion; a time for doing sth: *I'm waiting for* ***the right moment*** *to tell him the bad news.* ◇ *That was one of the happiest moments of my life.* ◇ *Have I caught you at a bad moment?*
IDM **(at) any ˈmoment (ˈnow)** ⚿ very soon: *Hurry up! He'll be back any moment now.* **at this moment in ˈtime** (*informal*) now, at the present time: *At this moment in time, I don't know what my decision will be.* **for the ˈmoment/ˈpresent** for now; for a short time: *This house is big enough for the moment, but we'll have to move if we have children.* **have its/your ˈmoments** to have short times that are better, more interesting, etc. than others: *The job isn't exciting all the time, but it has its moments.* **the ˌmoment of ˈtruth** a time when sb/sth is tested, or when important decisions are made **the moment (that)...** as soon as...: *I want to see him the moment he arrives.* **ˌnot for a/one ˈmoment** certainly not; not at all: *I don't think for a moment that she'll accept but you can ask her.* **of ˈmoment** very important: *matters of great moment* **of the ˈmoment** (of a person, a job, an issue, etc.) famous, important and talked about a lot now: *She's the fashion designer of the moment.* ➲ more at EVIL, JUST *adv.*, LAST *det.*, NOTICE *n.*, PSYCHOLOGICAL, SPUR *n.*, WAIT *v.*

mo·ment·ar·ily /ˈməʊməntrəli; *NAmE* ˌmoʊmənˈterəli/ *adv.* **1** for a very short time SYN **briefly**: *He paused momentarily.* **2** (*NAmE*) very soon; in a moment: *I'll be with you momentarily.*

mo·ment·ary /ˈməʊməntri; *NAmE* ˈmoʊmənteri/ *adj.* lasting for a very short time SYN **brief**: *a momentary lapse of concentration* ◇ *momentary confusion*

mo·men·tous /məˈmentəs; *NAmE* moʊˈm-/ *adj.* very important or serious, especially because there may be important results SYN **historic**: *a* ***momentous decision/event/occasion***

mo·men·tum /məˈmentəm; *NAmE* moʊˈm-/ *noun* [U] **1** the ability to keep increasing or developing: *The fight for his release* ***gathers momentum*** *each day.* ◇ *They began to* ***lose momentum*** *in the second half of the game.* **2** a force that is gained by movement: *The vehicle* ***gained momentum*** *as the road dipped.* **3** (*technical*) the quantity of movement of a moving object, measured as its mass multiplied by its speed

momma /ˈmɒmə; *NAmE* ˈmɑːmə/ *noun* (*NAmE, informal*) = MOMMY

mommy /ˈmɒmi; *NAmE* ˈmɑːmi/ *noun* (*pl.* **-ies**) (also **momma**) (both *NAmE*) (*BrE* **mummy**) (*informal*) a child's word for a mother

mom·para /mɒmˈpʌrə; *NAmE* mɑːm-/ (also **mam·para**) *noun* (*SAfrE*) an insulting name for a person that you think is stupid

mon- ➲ MONO-

monad /ˈmɒnæd; ˈməʊn-; *NAmE* ˈmɑːn-; ˈmoʊn-/ *noun* (*philosophy*) a single simple thing that cannot be divided, for example an atom or a person

mon·arch /ˈmɒnək; *NAmE* ˈmɑːnərk; -ɑːrk/ *noun* a person who rules a country, for example a king or a queen

mo·nar·chic·al /məˈnɑːkɪkl; *NAmE* -ˈnɑːrk-/ *adj.* [usually before noun] (*formal*) connected with a ruler such as a king or a queen or with the system of government by a king or queen

mon·arch·ist /ˈmɒnəkɪst; *NAmE* ˈmɑːnərk-/ *noun* a person who believes that a country should be ruled by a king or queen ▶ **mon·arch·ist** *adj.*

mon·archy /ˈmɒnəki; *NAmE* ˈmɑːnərki/ *noun* (*pl.* **-ies**) **1 the monarchy** [sing.] a system of government by a king or a queen: *plans to abolish the monarchy* ➲ COLLOCATIONS at POLITICS **2** [C] a country that is ruled by a king or a queen: *There are several constitutional monarchies in Europe.* ➲ compare REPUBLIC **3 the monarchy** [sing.] the king or queen of a country and their family

mon·as·tery /ˈmɒnəstri; *NAmE* ˈmɑːnəsteri/ *noun* (*pl.* **-ies**) a building in which MONKS (= members of a male religious community) live together ➲ COLLOCATIONS at RELIGION

mo·nas·tic /məˈnæstɪk/ *adj.* **1** connected with MONKS or monasteries **2** (of a way of life) simple and quiet and possibly CELIBATE SYN **ascetic**

mo·nas·ti·cism /məˈnæstɪsɪzəm/ *noun* [U] the way of life of MONKS in MONASTERIES

Mon·day ⚿ /ˈmʌndeɪ; -di/ *noun* [C, U] (*abbr.* **Mon.**) the day of the week after Sunday and before Tuesday, the first day of the working week: *It's Monday today, isn't it?* ◇ *She started work* ***last Monday****.* ◇ *Are you busy* ***next Monday****?* ◇ ***Monday morning/afternoon/evening*** ◇ *We'll discuss this at Monday's meeting.* ◇ *Do we still have Monday's paper?* ◇ *I work Monday to Friday.* ◇ *I work Mondays to Fridays.* ◇ ***On Monday(s)*** (= Every Monday) *I do yoga.* ◇ *I always do yoga* ***on a Monday****.* ◇ *He was born on a Monday.* ◇ *I went to Paris on Thursday, and came back the following Monday.* ◇ *We'll meet* ***on Monday****.* ◇ (*BrE*) *'When did the accident happen?' 'It was the Monday* (= the Monday of the week we are talking about).*'* ◇ (*BrE*) *Come back Monday week* (= a week after next Monday). ◇ (*informal* or *NAmE*) *We'll meet Monday.* ORIGIN From the Old English for 'day of the moon', translated from Latin *lunae dies.*

M

ˌMonday morning ˈquarterback *noun* (*NAmE, informal, disapproving*) a person who criticizes or comments on an event after it has happened ORIGIN The quarterback directs the play in an American football match and matches are usually played at the weekend.

mon·et·ar·ism /ˈmʌnɪtərɪzəm/ *noun* [U] the policy of controlling the amount of money available in a country as a way of keeping the economy strong

mon·et·ar·ist /ˈmʌnɪtərɪst/ *noun* a person who supports monetarism ▶ **mon·et·ar·ist** *adj.*: *a monetarist economic policy*

mon·et·ary /ˈmʌnɪtri; *NAmE* -teri/ *adj.* [only before noun] connected with money, especially all the money in a country: ***monetary policy/growth*** ◇ *an item of little monetary value* ◇ *closer European political, monetary and economic union* ➲ SYNONYMS at ECONOMIC

money ⚿ /ˈmʌni/ *noun* **1** ⚿ [U] what you earn by working or selling things, and use to buy things: *to* ***borrow/save/spend/earn money*** ◇ *How much money is there in my account?* ◇ *The money is much better in my new job.* ◇ *If the item is not satisfactory, you will get your money back.* ◇ *We'll need to raise more money* (= collect or borrow it) *next year.* ◇ *Can you lend me some money until tomorrow?* ◇ *Be careful with that —it* ***cost a lot of money****.* ➲ COLLOCATIONS at FINANCE **2** ⚿ [U] coins or paper notes: *I counted the money carefully.* ◇ *Where can I change my money into dollars?* ➲ see also FUNNY MONEY, PAPER MONEY, READY MONEY **3** ⚿ [U] a person's wealth including their property: *He lost all his money.* ◇ *The family made their money in the 18th century.* **4 moneys** or **monies** [pl.] (*law* or *old use*) sums of money: *a statement of all monies paid into your account* HELP You will find other compounds ending in **money** at their place in the alphabet.
IDM **be in the ˈmoney** (*informal*) to have a lot of money to spend **for ˈmy money** (*informal*) in my opinion: *For my money, he's one of the greatest comedians of all time.* **get your ˈmoney's worth** to get enough value or enjoyment out of sth, considering the amount of money, time, etc. that you are spending on it **good ˈmoney** a lot of money; money that you earn with hard work: *Thousands of people*

paid good money to watch the band perform. ◇ *Don't waste good money on that!* **have money to 'burn** to have so much money that you do not have to be careful with it **'made of money** (*informal*) very rich **make 'money** 0‑w to earn a lot of money; to make a profit: *The movie should make money.* ◇ *There's money to be made from tourism.* **make/lose money ˌhand over 'fist** to make/lose money very fast and in large quantities **money for 'jam/old 'rope** (*BrE, informal*) money that is earned very easily, for sth that needs little effort **money is no 'object** money is not sth that needs to be considered, because there is plenty of it available: *She travels around the world as if money is no object.* **money 'talks** (*saying*) people who have a lot of money have more power and influence than others **on the 'money** correct; accurate: *His prediction was* ***right on the money.*** **put 'money into sth** to invest money in a business or a particular project: *We would welcome interest from anyone prepared to put money into the club.* **put your 'money on sb/sth 1** to bet that a particular horse, dog, etc. will win a race **2** to feel very sure that sth is true or that sb will succeed: *He'll be there tonight. I'd put money on it.* **put your money where your 'mouth is** (*informal*) to support what you say by doing sth practical; to show by your actions that you really mean sth **throw your 'money about/around** (*informal*) to spend money in a careless and obvious way **throw good money after 'bad** (*disapproving*) to spend more money on sth, when you have wasted a lot on it already **throw 'money at sth** (*disapproving*) to try to deal with a problem or improve a situation by spending money on it, when it would be better to deal with it in other ways: *It is inappropriate simply to throw money at these problems.* ➲ more at BEST *n.*, CAREFUL, COIN *v.*, COLOUR *n.*, EASY *adj.*, FOOL *n.*, GROW, LICENCE *n.*, LOVE *n.*, MARRY, OBJECT, PAY *v.*, POT *n.*, ROLL *v.*, RUN *n.*, TIME *n.*

Synonyms

money

cash • change

These are all words for money in the form of coins or paper notes.

money money in the form of coins or paper notes: *I counted the money carefully.* ◇ *Where can I change my money into dollars?* ◇ ***paper money*** (= money that is made of paper, not coins)

cash money in the form of coins or paper notes: *How much cash do you have on you?* ◇ *Payments can be made by cheque or* ***in cash.***

MONEY OR CASH?

If it is important to contrast money in the form of coins and notes and money in other forms, use **cash**: *How much money/cash do you have on you?* ◇ ~~*Payments can be made by cheque or in money.*~~ ◇ ~~*Customers are offered a discount if they pay money.*~~

change the money that you get back when you have paid for sth giving more money than the amount it costs; coins rather than paper money: *The ticket machine doesn't give change.* ◇ *I don't have any* ***small change*** (= coins of low value).

PATTERNS

- to **draw out/get out/take out/withdraw** money/cash
- **ready** money/cash (= money that you have available to spend immediately)

ˌmoney-back guaran'tee *noun* an official promise by a shop/store, etc. to return the money you have paid for sth if it is not of an acceptable standard

money·bags /'mʌnibægz/ *noun* (*pl.* **money·bags**) (*informal, humorous*) a very rich person

money

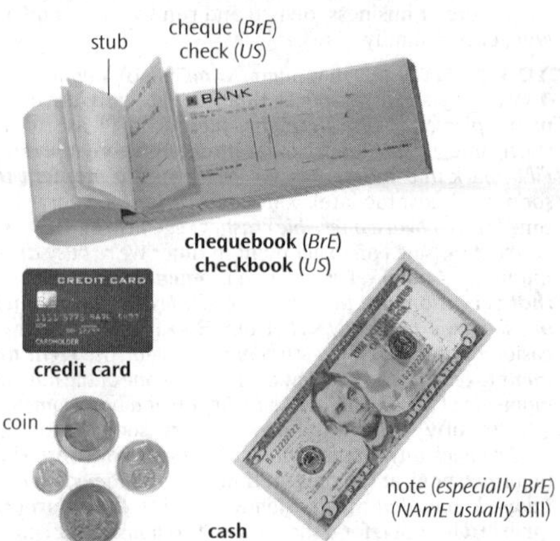

'money box *noun* (*especially BrE*) a small closed box with a narrow opening and sometimes with a lock and key, into which children put coins as a way of saving money ➲ compare PIGGY BANK

mon·eyed (also **mon·ied**) /'mʌnid/ *adj.* [only before noun] (*formal*) having a lot of money **SYN** **rich**: *the moneyed classes*

'money-grubbing (also **'money-grabbing**) *adj.* [only before noun] (*informal, disapproving*) trying to get a lot of money ▸ **'money-grubber** (also **'money-grabber**) *noun*

money·lend·er /'mʌnilendə(r)/ *noun* (*old-fashioned*) a person whose business is lending money, usually at a very high rate of interest

money·maker /'mʌnimeɪkə(r)/ *noun* a product, business, etc. that produces a large profit ▸ **money·mak·ing** *adj.*: *a moneymaking movie* **money·mak·ing** *noun* [U]

'money market *noun* the banks and other institutions that lend or borrow money, and buy and sell foreign money

'money order (*especially NAmE*) (*BrE* also **'postal order**) *noun* an official document that you can buy at a bank or a post office and send to sb so that they can exchange it for money

'money-saving *adj.* [only before noun] that helps you spend less money: ***money-saving offers/tips***

'money-spinner *noun* (*BrE, informal*) something that earns a lot of money

'money supply *noun* [sing., U] (*economics*) the total amount of money that exists in the economy of a country at a particular time

mon·gol /'mɒŋgəl; *NAmE* 'mɑːŋ-/ (*NAmE* usually **mon·goloid** /'mɒŋgəlɔɪd; *NAmE* 'mɑːŋ-/) *noun* (*old-fashioned*) an offensive word for a person with DOWN'S SYNDROME ▸ **mon·gol·ism** *noun* [U]

mon·goose /'mɒŋguːs; *NAmE* 'mɑːŋ-/ *noun* (*pl.* **mon·gooses** /-sɪz/) a small tropical animal with fur, that kills snakes, RATS, etc.

mon·grel /'mʌŋgrəl/ (*especially BrE*) (also **mutt** especially in *NAmE*) *noun* a dog that is a mixture of different breeds

mon·ied = MONEYED

moni·ker /'mɒnɪkə(r); *NAmE* 'mɑːn-/ *noun* (*humorous*) a name

mon·ism /'mɒnɪzəm; 'məʊn-; *NAmE* 'mɑːn-; 'moʊn-/ *noun* (*religion*) the belief that there is only one god

moni·tor 0‑w **AW** /'mɒnɪtə(r); *NAmE* 'mɑːn-/ *noun, verb*

■ ***noun* 1** 0‑w a television screen used to show particular kinds of information; a screen that shows information from a computer: *The details of today's flights are displayed on the monitor.* ◇ *a PC with a 17-inch colour monitor* ➲ **VISUAL VOCAB** page V54 ➲ see also VDU **2** a piece of equipment used to check or record sth: *a heart monitor* **3** a student in a school who performs special duties, such as helping the teacher **4** a person whose job is to check that sth is done fairly and honestly, especially in a foreign country: *UN monitors declared the referendum fair.* **5** a large tropical LIZARD (= a type of REPTILE)

▪ ***verb*** **1** ~ **sth** | ~ **what, how, etc...** to watch and check sth over a period of time in order to see how it develops, so that you can make any necessary changes SYN **track**: *Each student's progress is closely monitored.* **2** ~ **sth** to listen to telephone calls, foreign radio broadcasts, etc. in order to find out information that might be useful

monk /mʌŋk/ *noun* a member of a religious group of men who often live apart from other people in a MONASTERY and who do not marry or have personal possessions: ***Benedictine/Buddhist monks*** ➲ compare FRIAR, NUN ➲ see also MONKISH

mon·key /ˈmʌŋki/ *noun* **1** an animal with a long tail, that climbs trees and lives in hot countries. There are several types of monkey and they are related to APES and humans. **2** *(informal)* a child who is active and likes playing tricks on people: *Come here, you cheeky little monkey!* **3** *(BrE, slang)* £500

IDM **I don't/couldn't give a ˈmonkey's** *(BrE, slang)* used to say, in a way that is not very polite, that you do not care about sth, or are not at all interested in it **make a ˈmonkey (out) of sb** to make sb seem stupid ➲ more at BRASS

ˈmonkey business *noun* [U] *(informal)* dishonest or silly behaviour

ˈmonkey chanting *noun* [U] *(BrE)* abuse of a black player by white people who are watching a contest, especially a football (SOCCER) game

ˌmonkey in the ˈmiddle *(NAmE)* *(BrE* **ˌpiggy in the ˈmiddle, ˌpig in the ˈmiddle**) *noun* **1** a children's game where two people throw a ball to each other over the head of another person who tries to catch it **2** a person who is caught between two people or groups who are fighting or arguing

ˈmonkey nut *noun (BrE)* a PEANUT with its shell still on

ˈmonkey puzzle (also **ˈmonkey puzzle tree**) *noun* a CONIFER tree with leaves like scales, that are thin, tough and very sharp

ˌmonkey's ˈwedding *noun (SAfrE)* used to describe a period of time when it is raining while the sun is shining: *Look! It's a monkey's wedding!*

ˈmonkey wrench *(BrE* also **ˌadjustable ˈspanner**) *noun* a tool that can be adjusted to hold and turn things of different widths ➲ VISUAL VOCAB page V17 ➲ compare SPANNER, WRENCH

IDM **throw a ˈmonkey wrench in/into sth** (also **throw a ˈwrench in/into sth**) *(NAmE, informal)* to do sth to spoil sb's plans

monk·ish /ˈmʌŋkɪʃ/ *adj.* like a MONK; connected with MONKS

mono /ˈmɒnəʊ; *NAmE* ˈmɑːnoʊ/ *adj., noun*

▪ ***adj.*** (also **mono·phon·ic**) *(music)* recording or producing sound which comes from only one direction: *a mono recording* ➲ compare STEREO

▪ ***noun*** [U] **1** a system of recording or producing sound which comes from only one direction: *recorded in mono* ➲ compare STEREO **2** *(NAmE, informal)* = MONONUCLEOSIS

mono- /ˈmɒnəʊ; *NAmE* ˈmɑːnoʊ/ (also **mon-**) *combining form* (in nouns and adjectives) one; single: *monorail* ◇ *monogamy*

mono·chrome /ˈmɒnəkrəʊm; *NAmE* ˈmɑːnəkroʊm/ *adj.* **1** (of photographs, etc.) using only black, white and shades of grey: ***monochrome illustrations/images*** ◇ *(figurative) a dull monochrome life* **2** using different shades of one colour ▸ **mono·chro·mat·ic** /ˌmɒnəkrəˈmætɪk; *NAmE* ˌmɑːnəkroʊˈm-/ *adj.*: *a monochromatic colour scheme* **mono·chrome** *noun* [U]: *an artist who works in monochrome*

mon·ocle /ˈmɒnəkl; *NAmE* ˈmɑːn-/ *noun* a single glass LENS for one eye, held in place by the muscles around the eye and used by people in the past to help them see clearly

mono·coty·ledon /ˌmɒnəʊˌkɒtɪˈliːdn; *NAmE* ˌmɑːnoʊˌkɑːt-/ (also **mono·cot** /ˈmɒnəkɒt; *NAmE* ˈmɑːnəkɑːt/) *noun (biology)* a plant whose seeds form EMBRYOS that produce a single leaf ➲ compare DICOTYLEDON

mono·cul·ture /ˈmɒnəkʌltʃə(r); *NAmE* ˈmɑːn-/ *noun* **1** [U] the practice of growing only one type of crop on a certain area of land **2** [C, U] a society consisting of people who are all the same race, all share the same beliefs, etc: *a global economic monoculture*

mono·cycle /ˈmɒnəsaɪkl; *NAmE* ˈmɑːn-/ *noun* = UNICYCLE

mono·cyte /ˈmɒnəsaɪt; *NAmE* ˈmɑːn-/ *noun (biology)* a type of large white blood cell with a simple round NUCLEUS that can remove harmful substances from the body

mon·og·amy /məˈnɒɡəmi; *NAmE* məˈnɑːɡ-/ *noun* [U] **1** the fact or custom of being married to only one person at a particular time ➲ compare BIGAMY, POLYGAMY **2** the practice or custom of having a sexual relationship with only one partner at a particular time ▸ **mon·og·am·ous** /məˈnɒɡəməs; *NAmE* məˈnɑːɡ-/ *adj.*: *a monogamous marriage* ◇ *Most birds are monogamous.*

mono·glot /ˈmɒnəɡlɒt; *NAmE* ˈmɑːnəɡlɑːt/ *noun (technical)* a person who speaks only one language ➲ compare POLYGLOT

mono·gram /ˈmɒnəɡræm; *NAmE* ˈmɑːn-/ *noun* two or more letters, usually the first letters of sb's names, that are combined in a design and marked on items of clothing, etc. that they own ▸ **mono·grammed** *adj.*: *a monogrammed handkerchief*

mono·graph /ˈmɒnəɡrɑːf; *NAmE* ˈmɑːnəɡræf/ *noun (technical)* a detailed written study of a single subject, usually in the form of a short book

mono·lin·gual /ˌmɒnəˈlɪŋɡwəl; *NAmE* ˌmɑːnə-/ *adj.* speaking or using only one language: *a monolingual dictionary* ➲ compare BILINGUAL, MULTILINGUAL

mono·lith /ˈmɒnəlɪθ; *NAmE* ˈmɑːn-/ *noun* **1** a large single vertical block of stone, especially one that was shaped into a column by people living in ancient times, and that may have had some religious meaning **2** (often *disapproving*) a single, very large organization, etc. that is very slow to change and not interested in individual people ▸ **mono·lith·ic** /ˌmɒnəˈlɪθɪk; *NAmE* ˌmɑːnə-/ *adj.*: *a monolithic block* ◇ *the monolithic structure of the state*

mono·logue *(NAmE* also **mono·log**) /ˈmɒnəlɒɡ; *NAmE* ˈmɑːnəlɔːɡ; -lɑːɡ/ *noun* **1** [C] a long speech by one person during a conversation that stops other people from speaking or expressing an opinion: *He went into a long monologue about life in America.* **2** [U, C] a long speech in a play, film/movie, etc. spoken by one actor, especially when alone **3** [C, U] a dramatic story, especially in VERSE, told or performed by one person: *a dramatic monologue* ➲ compare DIALOGUE, SOLILOQUY

mono·mania /ˌmɒnəˈmeɪniə; *NAmE* ˈmɑːn-/ *noun* [U] *(psychology)* too much interest in or enthusiasm for just one thing so that it is not healthy

mono·nucle·osis /ˌmɒnəʊˌnjuːkliˈəʊsɪs; *NAmE* ˌmɑːnoʊˌnuːkliˈoʊsɪs/ *(NAmE or BrE, medical)* *(NAmE informal* **mono**) *(BrE* **ˌglandular ˈfever**) *noun* [U] an infectious disease that causes swelling of the LYMPH GLANDS and makes the person feel very weak for a long time

mono·phon·ic /ˌmɒnəˈfɒnɪk; *NAmE* ˌmɑːnəˈfɑːnɪk/ *adj.* *(music)* = MONO

mono·plane /ˈmɒnəpleɪn; *NAmE* ˈmɑː-/ *noun* an early type of plane with one set of wings ➲ compare BIPLANE

mon·op·ol·ist /məˈnɒpəlɪst; *NAmE* məˈnɑːp-/ *noun (technical)* a person or company that has a MONOPOLY

mon·op·ol·is·tic /məˌnɒpəˈlɪstɪk; *NAmE* məˌnɑːpə-/ *adj. (formal)* controlling or trying to get complete control over sth, especially an industry or a company

mon·op·ol·ize *(BrE* also **-ise**) /məˈnɒpəlaɪz; *NAmE* məˈnɑːp-/ *verb* **1** ~ **sth** to have or take control of the largest part of sth so that other people are prevented from sharing

M

it: *Men traditionally monopolized jobs in the printing industry.* ◊ *As usual, she completely monopolized the conversation.* **2 ~ sb** to have or take a large part of sb's attention or time so that they are unable to speak to or deal with other people ▶ **mon·op·ol·iza·tion, -isa·tion** /mə,nɒpəlaɪ'zeɪʃn; *NAmE* mə,nɑːpələ'z-/ *noun* [U]

mon·op·oly /mə'nɒpəli; *NAmE* mə'nɑːp-/ *noun* (*pl.* -ies) **1 ~ (in/of/on sth)** (*business*) the complete control of trade in particular goods or the supply of a particular service; a type of goods or a service that is controlled in this way: *In the past central government had a monopoly on television broadcasting.* ◊ *Electricity, gas and water were considered to be natural monopolies.* ➲ compare DUOPOLY **2** [usually sing.] **~ in/of/on sth** the complete control, possession or use of sth; a thing that belongs only to one person or group and that other people cannot share: *Managers do not have a monopoly on stress.* ◊ *A good education should not be the monopoly of the rich.* **3 Monopoly™** a BOARD GAME in which players have to pretend to buy and sell land and houses, using pieces of paper that look like money

Mo'nopoly money *noun* [U] money that does not really exist or has no real value: *Inflation was so high that the notes were like Monopoly money.* ORIGIN From the toy money used in the board game *Monopoly™*.

mono·rail /'mɒnəʊreɪl; *NAmE* 'mɑːnoʊ-/ *noun* **1** [U] a railway/railroad system in which trains travel along a track consisting of a single rail, usually one placed high above the ground **2** [C] a train used in a monorail system

mono·so·dium glu·ta·mate /,mɒnə,səʊdiəm 'gluːtəmeɪt; *NAmE* ,mɑːnə,soʊ-/ *noun* [U] (*abbr.* MSG) a chemical that is sometimes added to food to improve its flavour

mono·syl·lab·ic /,mɒnəsɪ'læbɪk; *NAmE* ,mɑːn-/ *adj.* **1** having only one syllable: *a monosyllabic word* **2** (of a person or their way of speaking) saying very little, in a way that appears rude to other people

mono·syl·lable /'mɒnəsɪləbl; *NAmE* 'mɑːn-/ *noun* a word with only one syllable, for example, 'it' or 'no'

mono·the·ism /'mɒnəʊθiɪzəm; *NAmE* 'mɑːnoʊ-/ *noun* [U] the belief that there is only one God ➲ compare POLYTHEISM ▶ **mono·the·ist** /'mɒnəʊθiɪst; *NAmE* 'mɑːnoʊ-/ *noun* **mono·the·is·tic** /,mɒnəʊθi'ɪstɪk; *NAmE* ,mɑːnoʊ-/ *adj.*

mono·tone /'mɒnətəʊn; *NAmE* 'mɑːnətoʊn/ *noun, adj.*
■ ***noun*** [sing.] a dull sound or way of speaking in which the tone and volume remain the same and therefore seem boring: *He spoke in a flat monotone.*
■ ***adj.*** [only before noun] without any changes or differences in sound or colour: *He spoke in a monotone drawl.* ◊ *monotone engravings*

mon·ot·on·ous /mə'nɒtənəs; *NAmE* mə'nɑːt-/ *adj.* never changing and therefore boring SYN **dull, repetitious**: *a **monotonous voice/diet/routine*** ◊ *monotonous work* ◊ *New secretaries came and went with **monotonous regularity**.* ▶ **mon·ot·on·ous·ly** *adv.*

mon·ot·ony /mə'nɒtəni; *NAmE* mə'nɑːt-/ *noun* [U] boring lack of variety: *She watches television to relieve the monotony of everyday life.*

mono·treme /'mɒnətriːm; *NAmE* 'mɑːn-/ *noun* (*technical*) a class of animal including the ECHIDNA and the PLATYPUS, which lays eggs, but also gives milk to its babies

mono·un·sat·ur·ated fat /,mɒnəʊʌn,sætʃəreɪtɪd 'fæt; *NAmE* ,mɑːnoʊ-/ *noun* [C, U] a type of fat found, for example, in OLIVES and nuts, which does not encourage the harmful development of CHOLESTEROL ➲ see also POLYUNSATURATED FAT, SATURATED FAT, TRANS-FATTY ACID, UNSATURATED FAT

mono·zyg·ot·ic twin /,mɒnəʊzaɪ'gɒtɪk twɪn; *NAmE* ,mɑːnoʊzaɪ'gɑːtɪk/ (also **mono·zyg·ous twin** /,mɒnəʊ'zaɪgəs twɪn; *NAmE* ,mɑːnoʊ-/) *adj.* (*technical*) = IDENTICAL TWIN ➲ compare DIZYGOTIC TWIN

the Mon·roe Doc·trine /mən,rəʊ 'dɒktrɪn; *NAmE* mən,roʊ 'dɑːk-/ *noun* a part of US foreign policy that states that the US will act to protect its own interests in N and S America ORIGIN From the name of US President James Monroe, who first stated the policy in 1823.

Mon·si·gnor /mɒn'siːnjə(r); *NAmE* mɑːn-/ *noun* (*abbr.* Mgr) used as a title when speaking to or about a priest of high rank in the Roman Catholic Church

mon·soon /,mɒn'suːn; *NAmE* ,mɑːn-/ *noun* **1** a period of heavy rain in summer in S Asia; the rain that falls during this period **2** a wind in S Asia that blows from the southwest in summer, bringing rain, and the north-east in winter

mons pubis /,mɒnz 'pjuːbɪs; *NAmE* ,mɑːnz/ (also **mons Ven·eris** /,mɒnz 'venərɪs; *NAmE* ,mɑːnz/) *noun* (*formal*) the curved area of fat over the joint of the PUBIC bones, especially in women

mon·ster /'mɒnstə(r); *NAmE* 'mɑːn-/ *noun, adj.*
■ ***noun*** **1** (in stories) an imaginary creature that is very large, ugly and frightening: *a monster with three heads* ◊ *prehistoric monsters* **2** an animal or a thing that is very large or ugly: *Their dog's an absolute monster!* **3** a person who is very cruel and evil **4** (*humorous*) a child who behaves badly
■ ***adj.*** [only before noun] (*informal*) unusually large SYN **giant**: *monster mushrooms*

,monster 'truck *noun* an extremely large PICKUP TRUCK with very large wheels, often used for racing

mon·stros·ity /mɒn'strɒsəti; *NAmE* mɑːn'strɑːs-/ *noun* (*pl.* -ies) something that is very large and very ugly, especially a building SYN **eyesore**: *a concrete monstrosity*

mon·strous /'mɒnstrəs; *NAmE* 'mɑːn-/ *adj.* **1** considered to be shocking and unacceptable because it is morally wrong or unfair SYN **outrageous**: *a **monstrous lie/injustice*** **2** very large SYN **gigantic**: *a monstrous wave* **3** very large, ugly and frightening SYN **horrifying**: *a **monstrous figure/creature*** ▶ **mon·strous·ly** *adv.*: *monstrously unfair* ◊ *a monstrously fat man*

mont·age /,mɒn'tɑːʒ; 'mɒn-; *NAmE* ,mɑːn'tɑːʒ/ *noun* **1** [C] a picture, film/movie or piece of music or writing that consists of many separate items put together, especially in an interesting or unusual combination: *a photographic montage* **2** [U] the process of making a montage

mon·tane /'mɒnteɪn; *NAmE* 'mɑːn-/ *adj.* [only before noun] (*technical*) connected with mountains

Mon·terey Jack /,mɒntəreɪ 'dʒæk; *NAmE* ,mɑːn-/ (*NAmE* also **'Jack cheese**) *noun* [U] a type of white American cheese with a mild flavour

month 0- /mʌnθ/ *noun*
1 0- [C] any of the twelve periods of time into which the year is divided, for example May or June: *the month of August* ◊ *We're moving house **next month**.* ◊ *She earns $1 000 **a month**.* ◊ *The rent is £300 **per month**.* ◊ *Have you read this month's 'Physics World'?* ◊ *Prices continue to rise **month after month*** (= over a period of several months). ◊ *Her anxiety mounted **month by month*** (= as each month passed). ➲ see also CALENDAR MONTH **2** 0- [C] a period of about 30 days, for example, 3 June to 3 July: *The baby is three months old.* ◊ *a three-month-old baby* ◊ *They lived in Toronto during their first few months of marriage.* ◊ *several months later* ◊ *a six-month contract* ◊ *a month-long strike* ◊ *He visits Paris once or twice a month.* ➲ see also LUNAR MONTH **3** 0- **months** [pl.] a long time, especially a period of several months: *He had to wait for months for the visas to come through.* ◊ *It will be months before we get the results.*
IDM **in a ,month of 'Sundays** (*informal*) used to emphasize that sth will never happen: *You won't find it, not in a month of Sundays.* ➲ more at FLAVOUR *n.*

month·ly /'mʌnθli/ *adj., adv., noun*
■ ***adj.*** **1** happening once a month or every month: *a **monthly meeting/visit/magazine*** **2** paid, valid or calculated for one month: *a monthly salary of £1 000* ◊ *a monthly season ticket* ◊ *Summers are hot, with monthly averages above 22°C.*
■ ***adv.*** every month or once a month: *She gets paid monthly.*

■ **noun** (*pl.* -ies) a magazine published once a month: *the fashion monthlies*

monty /ˈmɒnti; *NAmE* ˈmɑːnti/ *noun*
IDM **the ˌfull ˈmonty** the full amount that people expect or want: *They'll do the full monty* (= take off all their clothes) *if you pay them enough.*

monu·ment /ˈmɒnjumənt; *NAmE* ˈmɑːn-/ *noun* **1 ~ (to sb/sth)** a building, column, statue, etc. built to remind people of a famous person or event: *A monument to him was erected in St Paul's Cathedral.* **2** a building that has special historical importance: *an ancient monument* **3 ~ to sth** a thing that remains as a good example of sb's qualities or of what they did: *These recordings are a monument to his talent as a pianist.*

monu·men·tal /ˌmɒnjuˈmentl; *NAmE* ˌmɑːn-/ *adj.* **1** [usually before noun] very important and having a great influence, especially as the result of years of work SYN **historic**: *Gibbon's monumental work 'The Rise and Fall of the Roman Empire'* **2** [only before noun] very large, good, bad, stupid, etc. SYN **major**: *a book of monumental significance* ◇ *We have a monumental task ahead of us.* ◇ *It seems like an act of monumental folly.* **3** [only before noun] appearing in or serving as a monument: *a **monumental inscription/tomb*** ◇ *a **monumental mason*** (= a person who makes monuments)

monu·men·tal·ly /ˌmɒnjuˈmentəli; *NAmE* ˌmɑːn-/ *adv.* (used to describe negative qualities) extremely: ***monumentally difficult/stupid***

moo /muː/ *noun* (*pl.* **moos**) the long deep sound made by a cow ▶ **moo** *verb* [I]

mooch /muːtʃ/ *verb* (*informal*) **1** [I] **+ adv./prep.** (*BrE*) to walk slowly with no particular purpose; to be somewhere not doing very much SYN **potter**: *He's happy to mooch around the house all day.* **2** [I, T] **~ (sth) (off sb)** (*NAmE*) to get money, food, etc. from sb else instead of paying for it yourself SYN **cadge**: *He's always mooching off his friends.*

mood 0→ /muːd/ *noun*
1 0→ [C] the way you are feeling at a particular time: *She's **in a good mood** today* (= happy and friendly). ◇ *He's always **in a bad mood*** (= unhappy, or angry and impatient). ◇ *to be in a **foul/filthy mood*** ◇ *Some addicts suffer violent **mood swings*** (= changes of mood) *if deprived of the drug.* ◇ *I'm just not **in the mood for** a party tonight.* ◇ *I'm not really **in the mood to** go out tonight.* ◇ *He was **in no mood for** being polite to visitors.* **2** [C] a period of being angry or impatient: *I wonder why he's **in such a mood** today.* ◇ *She was **in one of her moods*** (= one of her regular periods of being angry or impatient). **3** 0→ [sing.] the way a group of people feel about sth; the atmosphere in a place or among a group of people: *The mood of the meeting was distinctly pessimistic.* ◇ *The movie captures the mood of the interwar years perfectly.* **4** [C] (*grammar*) any of the sets of verb forms that show whether what is said or written is certain, possible, necessary, etc. **5** [C] (*grammar*) one of the categories of verb use that expresses facts, orders, questions, wishes or conditions: *the **indicative/imperative/subjunctive mood***

ˈmood-altering *adj.* (of drugs) having an effect on your mood: *mood-altering substances*

ˈmood music *noun* [U] music intended to create a particular atmosphere, especially a relaxed or romantic one

moody /ˈmuːdi/ *adj.* (**mood·ier**, **moodi·est**) **1** having moods that change quickly and often: *Moody people are very difficult to deal with.* **2** bad-tempered or upset, often for no particular reason SYN **grumpy**: *Why are you so moody today?* **3** (of a film/movie, piece of music or place) suggesting particular emotions, especially sad ones ▶ **mood·ily** /-ɪli/ *adv.*: *He stared moodily into the fire.* **moodi·ness** *noun* [U]

mooli /ˈmuːli/ (also **dai·kon**) *noun* [U, C] a long white root vegetable that you can eat ➲ VISUAL VOCAB page V27

moon 0→ /muːn/ *noun, verb*
■ **noun 1** 0→ (usually **the moon**), (also **the Moon**) [sing.] the round object that moves around the earth once every 27½ days and shines at night by light reflected from the sun: *the surface of the moon* ◇ *a moon landing* **2** 0→ [sing.] the moon as it appears in the sky at a particular time: *a crescent moon* ◇ *There's no moon tonight* (= no moon can be seen). ◇ *By the light of the moon I could just make out shapes and outlines.* ➲ see also FULL MOON, HALF-MOON, NEW MOON **3** [C] a natural SATELLITE that moves around a planet other than the earth: *How many moons does Jupiter have?*
IDM **ask, cry, etc. for the ˈmoon** (*BrE, informal*) to ask for sth that is difficult or impossible to get or achieve **many ˈmoons ago** (*literary*) a very long time ago **over the ˈmoon** (*informal, especially BrE*) extremely happy and excited ➲ more at ONCE *adv.*, PROMISE *v.*
■ **verb** [I] (*informal*) to show your bottom to people in a public place as a joke or an insult
PHR V **ˌmoon aˈbout/aˈround** (*BrE, informal*) to spend time doing nothing or walking around with no particular purpose, especially because you are unhappy **ˈmoon over sb** (*informal*) to spend time thinking about sb that you love, especially when other people think this is silly or annoying SYN **pine for**

moon·beam /ˈmuːnbiːm/ *noun* a stream of light from the moon

ˈMoon Boot™ *noun* a thick warm boot made of cloth or plastic, worn in snow or cold weather

moong /muːŋ/ *noun* = MUNG

Moonie /ˈmuːni/ *noun* an offensive word for a member of the Unification Church

moonie /ˈmuːni/ *noun*
IDM **do a ˈmoonie** (*BrE, informal*) to show your naked bottom in public

moon·less /ˈmuːnləs/ *adj.* without a moon that can be seen: *a **moonless night/sky***

moon·light /ˈmuːnlaɪt/ *noun, verb*
■ **noun** [U] the light of the moon: *to go for a walk by **moonlight/in the moonlight*** IDM see FLIT *n.*
■ **verb** (**moon·lighted**, **moon·lighted**) [I] (*informal*) to have a second job that you do secretly, usually without paying tax on the extra money that you earn

moon·lit /ˈmuːnlɪt/ *adj.* lit by the moon: *a **moonlit night/beach***

moon·scape /ˈmuːnskeɪp/ *noun* **1** a view of the surface of the moon **2** an area of land that is empty, with no trees, water, etc, and looks like the surface of the moon

moon·shine /ˈmuːnʃaɪn/ *noun* [U] **1** (*old-fashioned, NAmE*) WHISKY or other strong alcoholic drinks made and sold illegally **2** (*informal*) silly talk SYN **nonsense**

moon·stone /ˈmuːnstəʊn; *NAmE* -stoʊn/ *noun* [C, U] a smooth white shiny SEMI-PRECIOUS stone

moon·struck /ˈmuːnstrʌk/ *adj.* slightly crazy, especially because you are in love

moon·walk /ˈmuːnwɔːk/ *verb* **1** [I] to walk on the moon **2** [I] to do a dance movement which consists of walking backwards, sliding the feet smoothly over the floor ▶ **moon·walk** *noun*

Moor /mɔː(r); mʊə(r); *NAmE* mʊr/ *noun* a member of a race of Muslim people living in NW Africa who entered and took control of part of Spain in the 8th century ▶ **Moor·ish** *adj.*: *the Moorish architecture of Cordoba*

moor /mɔː(r); mʊə(r); *NAmE* mʊr/ *noun, verb*
■ **noun** (*especially BrE*) **1** [C, usually pl.] a high open area of land that is not used for farming, especially an area covered with rough grass and HEATHER: *the North York moors* ◇ *to go for a walk on the moors* **2** [U] = MOORLAND: *moor and rough grassland*
■ **verb** [I, T] to attach a boat, ship, etc. to a fixed object or to the land with a rope, or ANCHOR it SYN **tie up**: *We moored off the north coast of the island.* ◇ **~ sth (to sth)** *A number of fishing boats were moored to the quay.*

moor·hen /ˈmɔːhen; ˈmʊə-; *NAmE* ˈmʊrhen/ *noun* a small black bird with a short reddish-yellow beak that lives on or near water

moor·ing /ˈmɔːrɪŋ; ˈmʊər-; *NAmE* ˈmʊr-/ *noun* **1 moor·ings** [pl.] the ropes, chains, etc. by which a ship or boat is

M

MOORED: *The boat slipped its moorings and drifted out to sea.* **2** [C] the place where a ship or boat is MOORED: *private moorings* ◇ *to find a mooring* ◇ *mooring ropes*

moor·land /ˈmɔːlənd; ˈmʊə-; *NAmE* ˈmʊrlənd/ (also **moor**) *noun* [U, C, usually pl.] (*especially BrE*) land that consists of MOORS: *walking across open moorland*

moose /muːs/ *noun* (*pl.* **moose**) a large DEER that lives in N America. In Europe and Asia it is called an ELK. ➲ picture at ELK

ˈ**moose milk** *noun* (*CanE*) **1** [U, C] an alcoholic drink made by mixing RUM with milk **2** [U] any strong alcoholic drink which is made at home

moot /muːt/ *adj., verb*

▪ **adj.** (*NAmE*) unlikely to happen and therefore not worth considering: *He argued that the issue had become moot since the board had changed its policy.*

IDM **a moot ˈpoint/ˈquestion** (*BrE, NAmE*) a matter about which there may be disagreement or confusion

▪ **verb** [usually passive] **~ sth** (*formal*) to suggest an idea for people to discuss SYN **propose, put forward**

ˈ**moot court** *noun* (*especially NAmE*) a MOCK court in which law students practise trials

mop /mɒp; *NAmE* mɑːp/ *noun, verb*

▪ **noun 1** a tool for washing floors that has a long handle with a bunch of thick strings or soft material at the end: *a mop and bucket* ➲ VISUAL VOCAB page V17 **2** a kitchen UTENSIL (= a tool) for washing dishes, that has a short handle with soft material at one end **3** a mass of thick, often untidy, hair: *a mop of curly red hair*

▪ **verb** (-pp-) **1 ~ sth** to clean sth with a mop: *She wiped all the surfaces and mopped the floor.* **2 ~ sth (from sth)** to remove liquid from the surface of sth using a cloth: *He took out a handkerchief to* **mop his brow** (= to remove the sweat). IDM see FLOOR *n.*

PHR V ˌ**mop sth/sb**↔ˈ**up** to remove the liquid from sth using sth that absorbs it: *Do you want some bread to mop up that sauce?* ◇ (*figurative*) *A number of smaller companies were mopped up* (= taken over) *by the American multinational.* ◇ (*figurative*) *New equipment mopped up* (= used up) *what was left of this year's budget.* ˌ**mop sb/sth**↔ˈ**up 1** to complete or end sth by dealing with the final parts: *There are a few things that need mopping up before I can leave.* **2** to get rid of the last few people who continue to oppose you, especially by capturing or killing them: *Troops combed the area to mop up any remaining resistance.*

mope /məʊp; *NAmE* moʊp/ *verb* [I] to spend your time doing nothing and feeling sorry for yourself SYN **brood**: *Moping won't do any good!*

PHR V ˌ**mope aˈbout/aˈround** (...) (*disapproving*) to spend time walking around a place with no particular purpose, especially because you feel sorry for yourself: *Instead of moping around the house all day, you should be out there looking for a job.*

moped /ˈməʊped; *NAmE* ˈmoʊ-/ *noun* a motorcycle with a small engine and also PEDALS

mop·pet /ˈmɒpɪt; *NAmE* ˈmɑːp-/ *noun* (*informal*) an attractive small child, especially a girl

mo·quette /mɒˈket; *NAmE* moʊ-/ *noun* [U] a type of thick cloth with a soft surface made of a mass of small threads, used for making carpets and covering furniture

MOR /ˌem əʊ ˈɑː(r); *NAmE* oʊ/ *noun* [U] music that is pleasant to listen to, but is not exciting or original (the abbreviation for 'middle-of-the-road')

mo·raine /məˈreɪn; *BrE* also mɒˈreɪn/ *noun* [U, C] (*technical*) a mass of earth, stones, etc, carried along by a GLACIER and left when it melts

moral 0‑w /ˈmɒrəl; *NAmE* ˈmɔːr-; ˈmɑːr-/ *adj., noun*

▪ **adj. 1** 0‑w [only before noun] concerned with principles of right and wrong behaviour: *a* **moral issue/dilemma/question** ◇ *traditional moral values* ◇ *a decline in* **moral standards** ◇ *moral philosophy* ◇ *a deeply religious man with a highly developed* **moral sense** ◇ *The newspapers were full of* **moral outrage** *at the weakness of other countries.* **2** 0‑w [only before noun] based on your own sense of what is right and fair, not on legal rights or duties SYN **ethical**: **moral responsibility/duty** ◇ *Governments have at least a* **moral obligation** *to answer these questions.* ◇ (*BrE*) *The job was to call on all her diplomatic skills and* **moral courage** (= the courage to do what you think is right). **3** 0‑w following the standards of behaviour considered acceptable and right by most people SYN **good, honourable**: *He led a very moral life.* ◇ *a very moral person* ➲ compare AMORAL, IMMORAL **4** [only before noun] able to understand the difference between right and wrong: *Children are not naturally moral beings.*

IDM **take, claim, seize, etc. the moral ˈhigh ground** to claim that your side of an argument is morally better than your opponents' side; to argue in a way that makes your side seem morally better

▪ **noun 1 morals** [pl.] standards or principles of good behaviour, especially in matters of sexual relationships: *Young people these days have no morals.* ◇ *The play was considered an affront to* **public morals**. ◇ (*old-fashioned*) *a woman of* **loose morals** (= with a low standard of sexual behaviour) **2** [C] a practical lesson that a story, an event or an experience teaches you: *And the moral is that crime doesn't pay.*

mor·ale /məˈrɑːl; *NAmE* -ˈræl/ *noun* [U] the amount of confidence and enthusiasm, etc. that a person or a group has at a particular time: *to* **boost/raise/improve morale** ◇ *Morale amongst the players is very high at the moment.* ◇ *Staff are suffering from low morale.*

ˌ**moral ˈfibre** (*BrE*) (*NAmE* ˌ**moral ˈfiber**) *noun* [U] the inner strength to do what you believe to be right in difficult situations

mor·al·ist /ˈmɒrəlɪst; *NAmE* ˈmɔːr-/ *noun* **1** (often *disapproving*) a person who has strong ideas about moral principles, especially one who tries to tell other people how they should behave **2** a person who teaches or writes about moral principles

mor·al·is·tic /ˌmɒrəˈlɪstɪk; *NAmE* ˌmɔːr-/ *adj.* (usually *disapproving*) having or showing very fixed ideas about what is right and wrong, especially when this causes you to judge other people's behaviour

mor·al·ity /məˈræləti/ *noun* (*pl.* **-ies**) **1** [U] principles concerning right and wrong or good and bad behaviour: *matters of* **public/private morality** ◇ *Standards of morality seem to be dropping.* **2** [U] the degree to which sth is right or wrong, good or bad, etc. according to moral principles: *a debate on the morality of abortion* **3** [U, C] a system of moral principles followed by a particular group of people SYN **ethics** ➲ compare IMMORALITY

moˈrality play *noun* a type of play that was popular in the 15th and 16th centuries and was intended to teach a moral lesson, using characters to represent good and bad qualities

mor·al·ize (*BrE* also **-ise**) /ˈmɒrəlaɪz; *NAmE* ˈmɔːr-; ˈmɑːr-/ *verb* [I] (usually *disapproving*) to tell other people what is right and wrong especially in order to emphasize that your opinions are correct SYN **preach**

mor·al·ly 0‑w /ˈmɒrəli; *NAmE* ˈmɔːr-/ *adv.* according to principles of good behaviour and what is considered to be right or wrong: *to act morally* ◇ **morally right/wrong/justified/unacceptable** ◇ *He felt morally responsible for the accident.*

the ˌ**moral maˈjority** *noun* [sing.+ sing./pl. v.] the largest group of people in a society, considered as having very traditional ideas about moral matters, religion, sexual behaviour, etc.

ˌ**moral supˈport** *noun* [U] the act of giving encouragement by showing your approval and interest, rather than by giving financial or practical support: *My sister came along just to give me some moral support.*

ˌ**moral ˈvictory** *noun* a situation in which your ideas or principles are proved to be right and fair, even though you may not have succeeded where practical results are concerned

mor·ass /məˈræs/ *noun* [usually sing.] (*formal*) **1** an unpleasant and complicated situation that is difficult to escape from SYN web **2** a dangerous area of low soft wet land SYN **bog, quagmire**

mora·tor·ium /ˌmɒrəˈtɔːriəm; *NAmE* ˌmɔːr-/ *noun* (*pl.* -riums or -toria /-riə/) **~ (on sth)** a temporary stopping of an activity, especially by official agreement: *The convention called for a two-year moratorium on commercial whaling.*

moray /mɒˈreɪ; ˈmɒreɪ; *NAmE* ˈmɔːreɪ/ (also ˌ**moray ˈeel**) *noun* a type of EEL that hides among rocks in tropical waters

mor·bid /ˈmɔːbɪd; *NAmE* ˈmɔːrbɪd/ *adj.* **1** having or expressing a strong interest in sad or unpleasant things, especially disease or death: *He had a morbid fascination with blood.* ◇ *'He might even die.' 'Don't be so morbid.'* **2** (*medical*) connected with disease ▶ **mor·bid·ity** /mɔːˈbɪdəti; *NAmE* mɔːrˈb-/ *noun* [U] **mor·bid·ly** *adv.*

mor·dant /ˈmɔːdnt; *NAmE* ˈmɔːrdnt/ *adj.* (*formal*) critical and unkind, but funny SYN **caustic**: *His mordant wit appealed to students.* ▶ **mor·dant·ly** *adv.*

more 🔑 /mɔː(r)/ *det., pron., adv.*

■ ***det., pron.*** 🔑 (used as the comparative of 'much', 'a lot of', 'many') **~ (sth/of sth) (than...)** a larger number or amount of: *more bread/cars* ◇ *Only two more days to go!* ◇ *people with more money than sense* ◇ *I can't stand much more of this.* ◇ *She earns a lot more than I do.* ◇ *There is room for* ***no more than*** *three cars.* ◇ *I hope we'll see more of you* (= see you again or more often).

IDM ˌ**more and ˈmore** 🔑 continuing to become larger in number or amount: *More and more people are using the Internet.* ◇ *She spends more and more time alone in her room.*

■ ***adv.*** **~ (than...)** **1** 🔑 used to form the comparative of adjectives and adverbs with two or more syllables: *She was far more intelligent than her sister.* ◇ *He read the letter more carefully the second time.* **2** 🔑 to a greater degree than sth else; to a greater degree than usual: *I like her more than her husband.* ◇ *a course for more advanced students* ◇ *It had more the appearance of a deliberate crime than of an accident.* ◇ *Could you repeat that* ***once more*** (= one more time)? ◇ *I had no complaints and* ***no more*** (= neither) *did Tom.* ◇ *Signing the forms is* ***little more than*** (= only) *a formality.* ◇ *I'm* ***more than*** *happy* (= extremely happy) *to take you there in my car.* ◇ *She was* ***more than a little*** *shaken* (= extremely shaken) *by the experience.* ◇ (*formal*) *I will torment you* ***no more*** (= no longer). ➲ see also ANY MORE

IDM ˌ**more and ˈmore** 🔑 continuing to become larger in number or amount SYN **increasingly**: *I was becoming more and more irritated by his behaviour.* ˌ**more or ˈless** **1** 🔑 almost: *I've more or less finished the book.* **2** 🔑 approximately: *She could earn $200 a night, more or less.* **the more, less, etc..., the more, less, etc...** 🔑 used to show that two things change to the same degree: *The more she thought about it, the more depressed she became.* ◇ *The less said about the whole thing, the happier I'll be.* **what is ˈmore** used to add a point that is even more important: *You're wrong, and what's more you know it!* ➲ LANGUAGE BANK at ADDITION

more·ish /ˈmɔːrɪʃ/ *adj.* (*BrE, informal*) if food or drink is **moreish**, it tastes so good that you want to have more of it

morel /məˈrel/ (also **moˌrel ˈmushroom**) *noun* a type of MUSHROOM that you can eat, with a top that is full of holes

more·over 🔑 /mɔːrˈəʊvə(r); *NAmE* -ˈoʊvər/ *adv.* (*formal*)
used to introduce some new information that adds to or supports what you have said previously SYN **in addition**: *A talented artist, he was, moreover, a writer of some note.* ➲ LANGUAGE BANK at ADDITION

mores /ˈmɔːreɪz/ *noun* [pl.] (*formal*) the customs and behaviour that are considered typical of a particular social group or community SYN **conventions**

morgue /mɔːg; *NAmE* mɔːrg/ *noun* **1** (*BrE*) a building in which dead bodies are kept before they are buried or CREMATED (= burned) ➲ compare MORTUARY **2** a place where dead bodies that have been found are kept until they can be identified

MORI™ /ˈmɒri; *NAmE* ˈmɔːri/ *noun* Market and Opinion Research International (an organization that finds out public opinion by asking a typical group of people questions): *A MORI poll showed that 68% of people opposed the ban.*

mori·bund /ˈmɒrɪbʌnd; *NAmE* ˈmɔːr-; ˈmɑːr-/ *adj.* (*formal*) **1** (of an industry, an institution, a custom, etc.) no longer effective and about to come to an end completely **2** in a very bad condition; dying: *a* ***moribund patient/tree***

Mor·mon /ˈmɔːmən; *NAmE* ˈmɔːrmən/ *noun* a member of a religion formed by Joseph Smith in the US in 1830, officially called 'the Church of Jesus Christ of Latter-day Saints': *a* ***Mormon church/chapel***

morn /mɔːn; *NAmE* mɔːrn/ *noun* [usually sing.] (*literary*) morning

morn·ing 🔑 /ˈmɔːnɪŋ; *NAmE* ˈmɔːrnɪŋ/ *noun*
1 🔑 the early part of the day from the time when people wake up until midday or before lunch: *They left for Spain early this morning.* ◇ *See you* ***tomorrow morning.*** ◇ *I prefer coffee* ***in the morning.*** ◇ *She woke every morning at the same time.* ◇ *Our group meets on Friday mornings.* ◇ *I walk to work most mornings.* ◇ *We got the news* ***on the morning of*** *the wedding.* ◇ *He's been in a meeting all morning.* ◇ *the morning papers* ➲ see also GOOD MORNING **2** 🔑 the part of the day from midnight to midday: *I didn't get home until two in the morning!* ◇ *He died in the early hours of Sunday morning.* **3 mornings** *adv.* in the morning of each day: *I only work mornings.*

IDM **in the ˈmorning** **1** 🔑 during the morning of the next day; tomorrow morning: *I'll give you a call in the morning.* **2** 🔑 between midnight and midday: *It must have happened at about five o'clock in the morning.* **morning, noon and ˈnight** at all times of the day and night (used to emphasize that sth happens very often or that it happens continuously): *She talks about him morning, noon and night.* ◇ *The work continues morning, noon and night.* ➲ more at OTHER *adj.*

ˌ**morning-ˈafter** *adj.* [only before noun] **1** happening the next day, after an exciting or important event: *After his election victory, the president held a morning-after news conference.* **2** used to describe how sb feels the next morning, after an occasion when they have drunk too much alcohol: *a morning-after headache*

ˌ**morning-ˈafter pill** *noun* a drug that a woman can take some hours after having sex in order to avoid becoming pregnant

ˈ**morning coat** (*BrE*) (*NAmE* **cut·away**) *noun* a black or grey jacket for men, short at the front and very long at the back, worn as part of morning dress ➲ compare TAILS (6)

ˈ**morning dress** *noun* [U] clothes worn by a man on very formal occasions, for example a wedding, including a morning coat and dark trousers/pants

ˌ**morning ˈglory** *noun* [C, U] a climbing plant with flowers shaped like TRUMPETS that open in the morning and close in late afternoon

ˈ**morning room** *noun* (*old-fashioned, especially BrE*) (in some large houses, especially in the past) a room that you sit in in the morning

ˈ**morning sickness** *noun* [U] the need to VOMIT that some women feel, often only in the morning, when they are pregnant, especially in the first months

the ˌmorning ˈstar *noun* [sing.] the planet Venus, when it shines in the east before the sun rises

ˈ**morning suit** *noun* (*BrE*) a suit worn by a man on very formal occasions, for example a wedding, including a morning coat and dark trousers/pants

mo·rocco /məˈrɒkəʊ; *NAmE* məˈrɑːkoʊ/ *noun* [U] fine soft leather made from the skin of a GOAT, used especially for making shoes and covering books

moron /ˈmɔːrɒn; *NAmE* -rɑːn/ *noun* (*informal*) an offensive way of referring to sb that you think is very stupid: *They're*

M

a bunch of morons. ◇ *You moron—now look what you've done!* ▶ **mor·on·ic** /məˈrɒnɪk; *NAmE* -ˈrɑːn-/ *adj.*: *a moronic stare* ◇ *a moronic TV programme*

mor·ose /məˈrəʊs; *NAmE* məˈroʊs/ *adj.* unhappy, bad-tempered and not talking very much SYN **gloomy**: *She just sat there looking morose.* ▶ **mor·ose·ly** *adv.*

morph /mɔːf; *NAmE* mɔːrf/ *verb* **1** [I, T] **~ (sth) (into sth)** to change smoothly from one image to another using computer ANIMATION; to make an image change in this way **2** [I, T] **~ (sb/sth) (into sb/sth)** to change, or make sb/sth change into sth different

mor·pheme /ˈmɔːfiːm; *NAmE* ˈmɔːrf-/ *noun* (*grammar*) the smallest unit of meaning that a word can be divided into: *The word 'like' contains one morpheme but 'un-like-ly' contains three.*

mor·phine /ˈmɔːfiːn; *NAmE* ˈmɔːrf-/ (also *old-fashioned* **mor·phia** /ˈmɔːfiə; *NAmE* ˈmɔːrf-/) *noun* [U] a powerful drug that is made from OPIUM and used to reduce pain

morph·ology /mɔːˈfɒlədʒi; *NAmE* mɔːrˈfɑːl-/ *noun* [U] **1** (*biology*) the form and structure of animals and plants, studied as a science **2** (*linguistics*) the forms of words, studied as a branch of linguistics ➲ compare GRAMMAR, SYNTAX ▶ **mor·pho·logic·al** /ˌmɔːfəˈlɒdʒɪkl; *NAmE* ˌmɔːrfəˈlɑːdʒ-/ *adj.*

mor·ris dance /ˈmɒrɪs dɑːns; *NAmE* ˈmɔːrɪs dæns; ˈmɑːrɪs dæns/ *noun* a traditional English dance that is performed by people wearing special clothes decorated with bells and carrying sticks that they hit together ▶ **ˈmorris dancer** *noun* **ˈmorris dancing** *noun* [U]

mor·row /ˈmɒrəʊ; *NAmE* ˈmɔːr-; ˈmɑːroʊ/ *noun* **the morrow** [sing.] (*old-fashioned, literary*) the next day; tomorrow: *We had to leave* ***on the morrow.*** ◇ *Who knows what the morrow* (= the future) *will bring?*

M

Morse code /ˌmɔːs ˈkəʊd; *NAmE* ˌmɔːrs ˈkoʊd/ *noun* [U] a system for sending messages, using combinations of long and short sounds or flashes of light to represent letters of the alphabet and numbers

mor·sel /ˈmɔːsl; *NAmE* ˈmɔːrsl/ *noun* a small amount or a piece of sth, especially food: *a tasty morsel of food* ◇ *He ate it all, down to the last morsel.*

mor·tal /ˈmɔːtl; *NAmE* ˈmɔːrtl/ *adj., noun*

■ ***adj.*** **1** that cannot live for ever and must die: *We are all mortal.* OPP **immortal** **2** (*literary*) causing death or likely to cause death; very serious: *a* ***mortal blow/wound*** ◇ *to be in mortal danger* ◇ (*figurative*) *Her reputation suffered a mortal blow as a result of the scandal.* ➲ compare FATAL **3** [only before noun] (*formal*) lasting until death SYN **deadly**: *mortal enemies* ◇ *They were locked* ***in mortal combat*** (= a fight that will only end with the death of one of them). **4** [only before noun] (*formal*) (of fear, etc.) extreme: *We lived* ***in mortal dread*** *of him discovering our secret.*

■ ***noun*** (often *humorous*) a human, especially an ordinary person with little power or influence SYN **human being**: *old stories about gods and mortals* ◇ (*humorous*) *Such things are not for* ***mere mortals*** *like ourselves.* ◇ (*humorous*) *She can deal with complicated numbers in her head, but we* ***lesser mortals*** *need calculators!*

mor·tal·ity /mɔːˈtæləti; *NAmE* mɔːrˈt-/ *noun* (*pl.* -ies) **1** [U] the state of being human and not living for ever: *After her mother's death, she became acutely aware of her own mortality.* **2** [U] the number of deaths in a particular situation or period of time: *the infant mortality rate* (= the number of babies that die at or just after birth) ◇ *Mortality from lung cancer is still increasing.* **3** [C] (*technical*) a death: *hospital mortalities* (= deaths in hospital)

mor·tal·ly /ˈmɔːtəli; *NAmE* ˈmɔːrt-/ *adv.* (*literary*) **1** causing or resulting in death SYN **fatally**: ***mortally wounded/ill*** **2** extremely: ***mortally afraid/offended***

ˌmortal ˈsin *noun* [C, U] (in the Roman Catholic Church) a very serious SIN for which you can be sent to HELL unless you CONFESS and are forgiven

mor·tar /ˈmɔːtə(r); *NAmE* ˈmɔːrt-/ *noun, verb*

■ ***noun*** **1** [U] a mixture of sand, water, LIME and CEMENT used in building for holding bricks and stones together **2** [C] a heavy gun that fires bombs and SHELLS high into the air; the bombs that are fired by this gun: *to come under* ***mortar fire/attack*** **3** [C] a small hard bowl in which you can crush substances such as seeds and grains into powder with a special object (called a PESTLE) ➲ **VISUAL VOCAB** pages V23, V57 IDM see BRICK *n.*

■ ***verb*** [I, T] **~ (sb/sth)** to attack sb/sth using a mortar

ˈmortar board *noun* a black hat with a stiff square top, worn by some university teachers and students at special ceremonies ➲ **VISUAL VOCAB** page V53 ➲ compare CAP (4)

mort·gage /ˈmɔːɡɪdʒ; *NAmE* ˈmɔːrɡ-/ *noun, verb*

■ ***noun*** (also *informal* **ˌhome ˈloan**) a legal agreement by which a bank or similar organization lends you money to buy a house, etc, and you pay the money back over a particular number of years; the sum of money that you borrow: *to* ***apply for/take out/pay off a mortgage*** ◇ *mortgage rates* (= of interest) ◇ *a mortgage on the house* ◇ *a mortgage of £60 000* ◇ *monthly mortgage payments* ➲ **COLLOCATIONS** at HOUSE

■ ***verb*** **~ sth** to give a bank, etc. the legal right to own your house, land, etc. if you do not pay the money back that you have borrowed from the bank to buy the house or land: *He had to mortgage his house to pay his legal costs.*

ˈmortgage bond *noun* (*SAfrE*) = BOND (4)

mort·ga·gee /ˌmɔːɡɪˈdʒiː; *NAmE* ˌmɔːrɡ-/ *noun* (*technical*) a person or an organization that lends money to people to buy houses, etc.

mort·ga·gor /ˈmɔːɡɪdʒɔː(r); *NAmE* ˈmɔːrɡ-/ *noun* (*technical*) a person who borrows money from a bank or a similar organization to buy a house, etc.

mor·ti·cian /mɔːˈtɪʃn; *NAmE* mɔːrˈt-/ *noun* (*NAmE*) = UNDERTAKER

mor·tify /ˈmɔːtɪfaɪ; *NAmE* ˈmɔːrt-/ *verb* (**mor·ti·fies, mor·ti·fy·ing, mor·ti·fied, mor·ti·fied**) [usually passive] **~ sb (to do sth)** | **it mortifies sb that...** to make sb feel very ashamed or embarrassed SYN **humiliate**: *She* ***was mortified to*** *realize he had heard every word she said.* ▶ **mor·ti·fi·ca·tion** /ˌmɔːtɪfɪˈkeɪʃn; *NAmE* ˌmɔːrt-/ *noun* [U] **mor·ti·fy·ing** *adj.*: *How mortifying to have to apologize to him!*

mor·tise (also **mor·tice**) /ˈmɔːtɪs; *NAmE* ˈmɔːrtɪs/ *noun* (*technical*) a hole cut in a piece of wood, etc. to receive the end of another piece of wood, so that the two are held together ➲ see also TENON

ˈmortise lock *noun* a lock that is fitted inside a hole cut into the edge of a door, not one that is screwed into the surface of one side

mor·tu·ary /ˈmɔːtʃəri; *NAmE* ˈmɔːrtʃueri/ *noun* (*pl.* -ies) **1** a room or building, for example part of a hospital, in which dead bodies are kept before they are buried or CREMATED (= burned) **2** (*NAmE*) = FUNERAL PARLOUR ➲ compare MORGUE

mo·saic /məʊˈzeɪɪk; *NAmE* moʊ-/ *noun* [C, U] a picture or pattern made by placing together small pieces of glass, stone, etc. of different colours: *a Roman mosaic* ◇ *a design in mosaic* ◇ *mosaic tiles* ◇ (*figurative*) *A mosaic of fields, rivers and woods lay below us.*

Mo·selle (*NAmE* usually **Mosel**) /məʊˈzel; *NAmE* moʊ-/ *noun* [U, C] a type of German white wine

Moses basket /ˈməʊzɪz bɑːskɪt; *NAmE* ˈmoʊzɪz bæskɪt/ (*BrE*) (*NAmE* **bas·sinet**) *noun* a BASKET for a small baby to sleep in

mosey /ˈməʊzi; *NAmE* ˈmoʊzi/ *verb* [I] **+ adv./prep.** (*informal*) to go in a particular direction slowly and with no definite purpose: *He moseyed on over to the bar.*

mosh /mɒʃ; *NAmE* mɑːʃ/ *verb* [I] to dance and jump up and down violently or without control at a concert where rock music is played

ˈmosh pit *noun* the place, just in front of the stage, where the audience at a concert of rock music moshes

Mos·lem /ˈmɒzləm; *NAmE* ˈmɑːz-/ *noun* = MUSLIM ▸ **Mos·lem** *adj.* = MUSLIM HELP The form **Moslem** is sometimes considered old-fashioned. Use **Muslim.**

mosque /mɒsk; *NAmE* mɑːsk/ *noun* a building in which Muslims worship

mos·quito /məˈskiːtəʊ; *NAmE* -toʊ; *BrE* also mɒs-/ *noun* (*pl.* **-oes** or **-os**) a flying insect that bites humans and animals and sucks their blood. One type of mosquito can spread the disease MALARIA: *a mosquito bite* ➲ VISUAL VOCAB page V11

mosˈquito net *noun* a net that you hang over a bed, etc. to keep mosquitoes away from you

moss /mɒs; *NAmE* mɔːs/ *noun* [U, C] a very small green or yellow plant without flowers that spreads over damp surfaces, rocks, trees, etc: *moss-covered walls* ➲ VISUAL VOCAB page V9 ➲ compare LICHEN ➲ see also SPANISH MOSS IDM see ROLL *v.*

mossy /ˈmɒsi; *NAmE* ˈmɔːsi/ *adj.* covered with moss

most 0▬ /məʊst; *NAmE* moʊst/ *det., pron., adv.*

▪ ***det., pron.*** (used as the superlative of 'much', 'a lot of', 'many') **1** 0▬ the largest in number or amount: *Who do you think will get (the) most votes?* ◇ *She had the most money of all of them.* ◇ *I spent most time on the first question.* ◇ *Who ate the most?* ◇ *The director has* **the most to lose**. HELP **The** can be left out in informal *BrE.* **2** 0▬ more than half of sb/sth; almost all of sb/sth: *I like most vegetables.* ◇ *Most classical music sends me to sleep.* ◇ *As most of you know, I've decided to resign.* ◇ *Most of the people I had invited turned up.* ◇ *There are thousands of verbs in English and most (of them) are regular.* HELP **The** is not used with **most** in this meaning.

IDM **at (the) ˈmost** not more than: *As a news item it merits a short paragraph at most.* ◇ *There were 50 people there, at the very most.*

▪ ***adv.*** **1** 0▬ used to form the superlative of adjectives and adverbs of two or more syllables: *the most boring/beautiful part* ◇ *It was the people with the least money who gave most generously.* HELP When **most** is followed only by an adverb, **the** is not used: *This reason is mentioned most frequently,* but: *This is* **the most** *frequently mentioned reason.* **2** 0▬ to the greatest degree: *What did you enjoy (the) most?* ◇ *It was what she wanted* **most of all**. HELP **The** is often left out in informal English. **3** (*formal*) very; extremely; completely: *It was most kind of you to meet me.* ◇ *We shall most probably never meet again.* ◇ *This technique looks easy, but it most certainly is not.* **4** (*NAmE, informal*) almost: *I go to the store most every day.*

-most *suffix* (in adjectives) the furthest: *inmost* (= the furthest in) ◇ *southernmost* ◇ *topmost* (= the furthest up/nearest to the top)

ˌmost favoured ˈnation *noun* a country to which another country allows the most advantages in trade, because they have a good relationship

most·ly 0▬ /ˈməʊstli; *NAmE* ˈmoʊ-/ *adv.* mainly; generally: *The sauce is mostly cream.* ◇ *We're mostly out on Sundays.*

MOT /ˌem əʊ ˈtiː; *NAmE* oʊ/ (also **MOT test**) *noun* the abbreviation for 'Ministry of Transport' a (test that any vehicle in Britain over three years old must take in order to make sure that it is safe and in good condition): *I've got to take the car in for its MOT.* ◇ *to* **pass/fail the MOT**

mote /məʊt; *NAmE* moʊt/ *noun* (*old-fashioned*) a very small piece of dust SYN **speck**

motel /məʊˈtel; *NAmE* moʊ-/ (also **ˈmotor lodge**) (*NAmE* also **ˈmotor inn**) *noun* a hotel for people who are travelling by car, with space for parking cars near the rooms

motet /məʊˈtet; *NAmE* moʊ-/ *noun* a short piece of church music, usually for voices only ➲ compare CANTATA

moth /mɒθ; *NAmE* mɔːθ/ *noun* a flying insect with a long thin body and four large wings, like a BUTTERFLY, but less brightly coloured. Moths fly mainly at night and are attracted to bright lights. ➲ VISUAL VOCAB page V11

moth·ball /ˈmɒθbɔːl; *NAmE* ˈmɔːθ-/ *noun, verb*

▪ ***noun*** a small white ball made of a chemical with a strong smell, used for keeping moths away from clothes

IDM **in ˈmothballs** stored and not in use, often for a long time

▪ ***verb*** [usually passive] **~ sth** to decide not to use or develop sth, for a period of time, especially a piece of equipment or a plan: *The original proposal had been mothballed years ago.* SYN **shelve**

ˈmoth-eaten *adj.* **1** (of clothes, etc.) damaged or destroyed by moths **2** (*informal, disapproving*) very old and in bad condition SYN **shabby**

mother 0▬ /ˈmʌðə(r)/ *noun, verb*

▪ ***noun*** **1** 0▬ a female parent of a child or animal; a person who is acting as a mother to a child: *I want to buy a present for my mother and father.* ◇ *the relationship between mother and baby* ◇ *She's the mother of twins.* ◇ *a mother of three* (= with three children) ◇ *an expectant* (= pregnant) *mother* ◇ *She was a wonderful mother to both her natural and adopted children.* ◇ *the mother chimpanzee caring for her young* **2** the title of a woman who is head of a CONVENT (= a community of NUNS) ➲ see also MOTHER SUPERIOR

IDM **at your ˌmother's ˈknee** when you were very young: *I learnt these songs at my mother's knee.* **the ˈmother of (all) sth** (*informal*) used to emphasize that sth is very large, unpleasant, important, etc.: *I got stuck in the mother of all traffic jams.* ➲ more at NECESSITY, OLD

▪ ***verb*** **~ sb/sth** to care for sb/sth because you are their mother, or as if you were their mother: *He was a disturbed child who needed mothering.* ◇ *Stop mothering me!*

mother·board /ˈmʌðəbɔːd; *NAmE* ˈmʌðərbɔːrd/ *noun* (*computing*) the main board of a computer, containing all the CIRCUITS

ˈmother country *noun* [sing.] **1** the country where you or your family were born and which you feel a strong emotional connection with **2** the country that controls or used to control the government of another country

ˈmother figure *noun* an older woman that you go to for advice, support, help, etc, as you would to a mother ➲ see also FATHER FIGURE

mother·fuck·er /ˈmʌðəfʌkə(r); *NAmE* -ðərf-/ *noun* (*taboo, slang, especially NAmE*) an offensive word used to insult sb, especially a man, and to show anger or dislike

ˌmother ˈhen *noun* (usually *disapproving*) a woman who likes to care for and protect people and who worries about them a lot

mother·hood /ˈmʌðəhʊd; *NAmE* -ðərh-/ *noun* [U] the state of being a mother: *Motherhood suits her.*

mother·ing /ˈmʌðərɪŋ/ *noun* [U] the act of caring for and protecting children or other people: *an example of* **good/poor mothering**

ˈMother·ing Sun·day *noun* [U, C] (*BrE,* becoming *old-fashioned*) = MOTHER'S DAY

ˈmother-in-law *noun* (*pl.* **mothers-in-law**) the mother of your husband or wife ➲ compare FATHER-IN-LAW

ˈmother-in-law apartment *noun* (*NAmE*) = IN-LAW APARTMENT

mother·land /ˈmʌðəlænd; *NAmE* -ðərl-/ *noun* (*formal*) the country that you were born in and that you feel a strong emotional connection with ➲ see also FATHERLAND

mother·less /ˈmʌðələs; *NAmE* -ðərl-/ *adj.* having no mother because she has died or does not live with you

ˈmother lode *noun* [usually sing.] (*especially NAmE*) a very rich source of gold, silver, etc. in a mine: (*figurative*) *Her own experiences have provided her with a mother lode of material for her songs.*

mother·ly /ˈmʌðəli; *NAmE* -ərli/ *adj.* having the qualities of a good mother; typical of a mother SYN **maternal**: *motherly love* ◇ *She was a kind, motherly woman.*

ˌMother ˈNature *noun* [U] the natural world, when you consider it as a force that affects the world and humans

ˌmother-of-ˈpearl (also **pearl**) *noun* [U] the hard smooth shiny substance in various colours that forms a

M

layer inside the shells of some types of SHELLFISH and is used in making buttons, decorative objects, etc.

ˈMother's Day *noun* a day on which mothers traditionally receive cards and gifts from their children, celebrated in Britain on the fourth Sunday in Lent and in the US on the 2nd Sunday in May

ˈmother ship *noun* a large ship or SPACECRAFT that smaller ones go out from

ˌmother's ˈmilk *noun* [U] a thing that a person really needs or enjoys: *Jazz is mother's milk to me.*

ˌmother's ˈruin *noun* [U] (*old-fashioned, BrE, informal*) the alcoholic drink GIN

ˌMother Suˈperior *noun* a woman who is the head of a female religious community, especially a CONVENT (= a community of NUNS)

ˌmother-to-ˈbe *noun* (*pl.* **mothers-to-be**) a woman who is pregnant

ˌmother ˈtongue *noun* the language that you first learn to speak when you are a child SYN **first language**

motif /məʊˈtiːf; *NAmE* moʊ-/ *noun* **1** a design or a pattern used as a decoration: *wallpaper with a flower motif* **2** a subject, an idea or a phrase that is repeated and developed in a work of literature or a piece of music ➲ see also LEITMOTIF SYN **theme**

mo·tion 0‑ᴡ /ˈməʊʃn; *NAmE* ˈmoʊʃn/ *noun, verb*

■ ***noun*** **1** 0‑ᴡ [U, sing.] the act or process of moving or the way sth moves: *Newton's laws of motion* ◇ *The swaying motion of the ship was making me feel seasick.* ◇ (*formal*) *Do not alight while the train is still* ***in motion*** (= moving). ◇ *Rub the cream in with a circular motion.* ➲ see also SLOW MOTION **2** [C] a particular movement made usually with your hand or your head, especially to communicate sth SYN **gesture**: *At a single motion of his hand, the room fell silent.* **3** [C] a formal proposal that is discussed and voted on at a meeting: ***to table/put forward a motion*** ◇ *to propose a motion* (= to be the main speaker in favour of a motion) ◇ *The* ***motion was adopted/carried*** *by six votes to one.* **4** [C] (*BrE, formal*) an act of emptying the BOWELS; the waste matter that is emptied from the bowels

IDM **go through the ˈmotions (of doing sth)** to do or say sth because you have to, not because you really want to **set/put sth in ˈmotion** to start sth moving: *They set the machinery in motion.* ◇ (*figurative*) *The wheels of change have been set in motion.*

■ ***verb*** [I, T] to make a movement, usually with your hand or head to show sb what you want them to do: **~ to sb (to do sth)** *I motioned to the waiter.* ◇ **~ (for) sb to do sth** *He motioned for us to follow him.* ◇ **~ sb + adv./prep.** *She motioned him into her office.*

mo·tion·less /ˈməʊʃnləs; *NAmE* ˈmoʊʃn-/ *adj.* not moving; still: *She stood absolutely motionless.*

ˌmotion ˈpicture *noun* (*especially NAmE*) a film/movie that is made for the cinema

ˈmotion sickness *noun* [U] the unpleasant feeling that you are going to VOMIT, that some people have when they are moving, especially in a vehicle

mo·tiv·ate AW /ˈməʊtɪveɪt; *NAmE* ˈmoʊ-/ *verb* **1** [often passive] **~ sb** to be the reason why sb does sth or behaves in a particular way: *He is motivated entirely by self-interest.* **2** to make sb want to do sth, especially sth that involves hard work and effort: **~ sb** *She's very good at motivating her students.* ◇ **~ sb to do sth** *The plan is designed to motivate employees to work more efficiently.* **3** **~ sth** (*SAfrE, formal*) to give reasons for sth that you have stated: *Please motivate your answer to question 5.* ▶ **mo·tiv·ated** AW *adj.*: *a racially motivated attack* ◇ *a highly motivated student* (= one who is very interested and works hard) OPP **unmotivated** **mo·tiv·ation** AW /ˌməʊtɪˈveɪʃn; *NAmE* ˌmoʊ-/ *noun* [C, U]: *What is the* ***motivation behind*** *this sudden change?* ◇ *Most people said that pay was their main motivation for working.* ◇ *He's intelligent enough but he lacks motivation.* ◇ (*SAfrE*) *All research proposals must be accompanied by a full motivation.* **mo·tiv·ation·al** /-ʃənl/ *adj.*: (*formal*) *an important motivational factor* **mo·tiv·ator** /ˈməʊtɪveɪtə(r); *NAmE* ˈmoʊ-/ *noun*: *Desire for status can be a powerful motivator.*

mo·tive AW /ˈməʊtɪv; *NAmE* ˈmoʊ-/ *noun, adj.*

■ ***noun* ~ (for sth)** a reason for doing sth: *There seemed to be no motive for the murder.* ◇ *I'm suspicious of his motives.* ◇ *the profit motive* (= the desire to make a profit) ◇ *I have an* ***ulterior motive*** *in offering to help you.* ➲ SYNONYMS at REASON ▶ **mo·tive·less** *adj.*: *an apparently* ***motiveless murder/attack***

■ ***adj.*** [only before noun] (*technical*) causing movement or action: ***motive power/force*** (= for example, electricity, to operate machinery)

mot juste /ˌməʊ ˈʒuːst; *NAmE* ˌmoʊ/ *noun* (*pl.* **mots justes** /ˌməʊ ˈʒuːst; *NAmE* ˌmoʊ/) (from *French*) the exact word that is appropriate for the situation

mot·ley /ˈmɒtli; *NAmE* ˈmɑːtli/ *adj.* (*disapproving*) consisting of many different types of people or things that do not seem to belong together: *The room was filled with a motley collection of furniture and paintings.* ◇ *The audience was a* ***motley crew*** *of students and tourists.*

moto·cross /ˈməʊtəʊkrɒs; *NAmE* ˈmoʊtoʊkrɔːs; ˈmoʊtoʊkrɑːs/ (*BrE* also **scram·bling**) *noun* [U] the sport of racing motorcycles over rough ground

moto·neur·on /ˌməʊtəˈnjʊərɒn; *NAmE* ˌmoʊtəˈnjuːrɑːn; -ˈnuː-/ *noun* = MOTOR NEURON

motor 0‑ᴡ /ˈməʊtə(r); *NAmE* ˈmoʊ-/ *noun, adj., verb*

■ ***noun*** **1** 0‑ᴡ a device that uses electricity, petrol/gas, etc. to produce movement and makes a machine, a vehicle, a boat, etc. work: *an electric motor* ◇ *He started the motor.* ➲ see also OUTBOARD MOTOR **2** (*BrE, old-fashioned* or *humorous*) a car

■ ***adj.*** [only before noun] **1** having an engine; using the power of an engine: *motor vehicles* **2** (*especially BrE*) connected with vehicles that have engines: *the* ***motor industry/trade*** ◇ *a motor accident* ◇ *motor insurance* ◇ *motor fuel* **3** (*technical*) connected with movement of the body that is produced by muscles; connected with the nerves that control movement: *uncoordinated motor activity* ◇ *Both motor and sensory functions are affected.*

■ ***verb*** [I] **+ adv./prep.** (*old-fashioned, BrE*) to travel by car, especially for pleasure ▶ **motor·ing** *noun* [U]: *They're planning a motoring holiday to France this year.*

motor·bike 0‑ᴡ /ˈməʊtəbaɪk; *NAmE* ˈmoʊtərb-/ *noun*

1 0‑ᴡ (*especially BrE*) = MOTORCYCLE: *Ben drove off on his motorbike.* **2** (*NAmE*) a bicycle which has a small engine

motor·boat /ˈməʊtəbəʊt; *NAmE* ˈmoʊtərboʊt/ *noun* a small fast boat driven by an engine

motor·cade /ˈməʊtəkeɪd; *NAmE* ˈmoʊtərk-/ *noun* a line of vehicles including one or more that famous or important people are travelling in: *The President's motorcade glided by.*

ˈmotor car *noun* (*BrE, formal*) a car

motor·cycle 0‑ᴡ /ˈməʊtəsaɪkl; *NAmE* ˈmoʊtərs-/ (also **motor·bike** especially in *BrE*) *noun*

a road vehicle with two wheels, driven by an engine, with one seat for the driver and a seat for a passenger behind the driver: *motorcycle racing* ◇ *a motorcycle accident* ➲ COLLOCATIONS at DRIVING ➲ VISUAL VOCAB page V41

motor·cyc·ling /ˈməʊtəsaɪklɪŋ; *NAmE* ˈmoʊtərs-/ *noun* [U] the sport of riding motorcycles

motor·cyc·list /ˈməʊtəsaɪklɪst; *NAmE* ˈmoʊtərs-/ *noun* a person riding a motorcycle: *a police motorcyclist* ◇ *leather-clad motorcyclists*

motor·home /ˈməʊtəhəʊm; *NAmE* ˈmoʊtərhoʊm/ (*NAmE* also **RV**, **recreˌational ˈvehicle**) (*BrE* also **camper**, **ˈcamper van**) *noun* a large vehicle designed for people to live and sleep in when they are travelling ➲ VISUAL VOCAB page V46

motor·ing /ˈməʊtərɪŋ; *NAmE* ˈmoʊ-/ *adj.* [only before noun] connected with driving a car: *a motoring offence*

motor·ist /ˈməʊtərɪst; *NAmE* ˈmoʊ-/ *noun* a person driving a car ➲ compare PEDESTRIAN

motor·ized (*BrE* also **-ised**) /ˈməʊtəraɪzd; *NAmE* ˈmoʊ-/ *adj.* [only before noun] **1** having an engine: *motorized vehicles* ◊ *a motorized wheelchair* **2** (of groups of soldiers, etc.) using vehicles with engines: ***motorized forces/divisions***

ˈ**motor lodge** (*NAmE* also ˈ**motor inn**) *nouns* = MOTEL

motor·mouth /ˈməʊtəmaʊθ; *NAmE* ˈmoʊtərm-/ *noun* (*pl.* **motor·mouths** /-maʊðz/) (*informal*) a person who talks loudly and too much

ˌ**motor ˈneuron** (also **moto·neur·on**) *noun* (*biology*) a nerve cell which sends signals to a muscle or GLAND

ˌ**motor ˈneuron disease** (also ˌ**motoˈneuron disease**) *noun* [U] a disease in which the nerves and muscles become gradually weaker until the person dies

ˈ**motor park** *noun* (*WAfrE*) a station for passengers to get or off buses or taxis: *Passengers are set down at Molete Motor Park.*

ˈ**motor pool** (*especially US*) (*BrE* also ˈ**car pool**) *noun* a group of cars owned by a company or an organization, that its staff can use

ˈ**motor racing** (*especially BrE*) (*NAmE* usually ˈ**auto racing**) *noun* [U] the sport of racing fast cars on a special track

ˈ**motor scooter** (*especially NAmE*) (*BrE* also **scoot·er**) *noun* a light motorcycle, usually with small wheels and a curved metal cover at the front to protect the rider's legs ➲ VISUAL VOCAB page V41

motor·sport /ˈməʊtəspɔːt; *NAmE* ˈmoʊtərspɔːrt/ *noun* [U] (*especially BrE*) (*NAmE* usually **motorsports** [pl.]) the sport of racing fast cars or motorcycles on a special track

ˈ**motor vehicle** *noun* any road vehicle driven by an engine

motor·way /ˈməʊtəweɪ; *NAmE* ˈmoʊtərweɪ/ *noun* [C, U] (in Britain) a wide road, with at least two lanes in each direction, where traffic can travel fast for long distances between large towns. You can only enter and leave motorways at special JUNCTIONS: ***busy/congested motorways*** ◊ *Join the motorway at Junction 19.* ◊ *Leave the motorway at the next exit.* ◊ *A nine-mile stretch of motorway has been closed.* ◊ *a* ***motorway service area / service station*** ➲ compare INTERSTATE

Mo·town™ /ˈməʊtaʊn; *NAmE* ˈmoʊ-/ *noun* [U] a style of music popular in the 1960s and 1970s, produced by a black music company based in Detroit ORIGIN From the informal name for the city of Detroit.

motte /mɒt; *NAmE* mɑːt/ *noun* the small hill on which the FORT is built in a motte-and-bailey castle

ˌ**motte-and-ˌbailey ˈcastle** *noun* an old type of castle that consists of a FORT on a small hill surrounded by an outer wall

mot·tled /ˈmɒtld; *NAmE* ˈmɑːtld/ *adj.* marked with shapes of different colours without a regular pattern

motto /ˈmɒtəʊ; *NAmE* ˈmɑːtoʊ/ *noun* (*pl.* **-oes** or **-os**) a short sentence or phrase that expresses the aims and beliefs of a person, a group, an institution, etc. and is used as a rule of behaviour: *The school's motto is: 'Duty, Honour, Country'.* ◊ *'Live and let live.' That's my motto.*

mould (*especially US* **mold**) /məʊld; *NAmE* moʊld/ *noun, verb*

■ ***noun*** **1** [C] a container that you pour a liquid or soft substance into, which then becomes solid in the same shape as the container, for example when it is cooled or cooked: *A clay mould is used for casting bronze statues.* ◊ *Pour the chocolate into a heart-shaped mould.* ◊ *They* ***broke the mould*** *when they made you* (= there is nobody like you). **2** [C, usually sing.] a particular style showing the characteristics, attitudes or behaviour that are typical of sb/sth: *a hero in the 'Superman' mould* ◊ *He is cast in a different mould from his predecessor.* ◊ *She doesn't fit* (*into*) *the traditional mould of an academic.* **3** [U, C] a fine soft green, grey or black substance like fur that grows on old food or on objects that are left in warm wet air: *There's mould on the cheese.* ◊ *moulds and fungi* ◊ *mould growth* ➲ see also LEAF MOULD

IDM **break the ˈmould (of sth)** to change what people expect from a situation, especially by acting in a dramatic and original way

■ ***verb*** **1** [T] to shape a soft substance into a particular form or object by pressing it or by putting it into a mould: **~ A (into B)** *First, mould the clay into the desired shape.* ◊ **~ B (from/out of/in A)** *The figure had been moulded in clay.* **2** [T] to strongly influence the way sb's character, opinions, etc. develop: **~ sb/sth** *The experience had moulded and coloured her whole life.* ◊ **~ sb/sth into sb/sth** *He moulded them into a superb team.* **3** [I, T] **~ (sth) to sth** to fit or make sth fit tightly around the shape of sth: *The fabric moulds to the body.*

mould·er (*US* **mol·der**) /ˈməʊldə(r); *NAmE* ˈmoʊ-/ *verb* [I] to decay slowly and steadily: *The room smelt of disuse and mouldering books.*

mould·ing (*especially US* **mold·ing**) /ˈməʊldɪŋ; *NAmE* ˈmoʊ-/ *noun* a decorative strip of plastic, stone, wood, etc. around the top edge of a wall, on a door, etc.

mouldy (*especially US* **moldy**) /ˈməʊldi; *NAmE* ˈmoʊ-/ *adj.* **1** covered with or containing MOULD: ***mouldy bread/cheese*** ◊ *Strawberries* ***go mouldy*** *very quickly.* **2** old and not in good condition

moult (*especially US* **molt**) /məʊlt; *NAmE* moʊlt/ *verb* [I] (of a bird or an animal) to lose feathers or hair before new feathers or hair grow

mound /maʊnd/ *noun* **1** a large pile of earth or stones; a small hill: *a Bronze Age burial mound* ◊ *The castle was built on top of a natural grassy mound.* **2** a pile SYN **heap**: *a small* ***mound of rice/sand*** **3 ~ of sth** (*informal*) a large amount of sth SYN **heap**: *I've got a mound of paperwork to do.* **4** (in BASEBALL) the small hill where the player who throws the ball (called the PITCHER) stands

mount 🔑 /maʊnt/ *verb, noun*

■ ***verb***

▸ ORGANIZE **1** 🔑 [T] **~ sth** to organize and begin sth SYN **arrange**: *to* ***mount a protest/campaign/an exhibition***

▸ INCREASE **2** 🔑 [I] to increase gradually: *Pressure is mounting on the government to change the law.* ◊ *The death toll continues to mount.* ➲ see also MOUNTING

▸ GO UP STH **3** 🔑 [T] **~ sth** (*formal*) to go up sth, or up on to sth that is raised SYN **ascend**: *She slowly mounted the steps.* ◊ *He mounted the platform and addressed the crowd.*

▸ BICYCLE/HORSE **4** 🔑 [T, I] **~ (sth)** (rather *formal*) to get on a bicycle, horse, etc. in order to ride it: *He mounted his horse and rode away.* OPP **dismount** ➲ see also MOUNTED

▸ PICTURE/JEWEL, ETC. **5** [T] **~ sth (on/onto/in sth)** to fix sth into position on sth, so that you can use it, look at it or study it: *The specimens were mounted on slides.* ◊ *The diamond is mounted in gold.*

▸ OF MALE ANIMAL **6** [T] **~ sth** to get onto the back of a female animal in order to have sex IDM see GUARD *n.*

PHR V ˌ**mount ˈup** to increase gradually in size and quantity SYN **build up**: *Meanwhile, my debts were mounting up.*

■ ***noun***

▸ MOUNTAIN **1** 🔑 **Mount** (*abbr.* **Mt**) (used in modern English only in place names) a mountain or a hill: *Mt Everest* ◊ *St Michael's Mount*

▸ HORSE **2** (*formal* or *literary*) a horse that you ride on

▸ FOR DISPLAYING/SUPPORTING STH **3** something such as a piece of card or glass that you put sth on or attach sth to, to display it **4** (also **mount·ing**) something that an object stands on or is attached to for support: *an* ***engine/gun mount***

moun·tain 🔑 /ˈmaʊntən; *NAmE* ˈmaʊntn/ *noun* **1** 🔑 a very high hill, often with rocks near the top: *a* ***chain/range of mountains*** ◊ *to climb a mountain* ◊ *We spent a week walking* ***in the mountains.*** ◊ *to enjoy the* ***mountain air/scenery*** ◊ ***mountain roads/streams/villages*** ◊ *a* ***mountain rescue team*** ➲ VISUAL VOCAB pages V4, V5 **2 ~ of sth** (*informal*) a very large amount or number of sth: *a mountain of work* ◊ *We made mountains of sandwiches.* ◊ *the problem of Europe's butter mountain* (=

M

the large amount of butter that has to be stored because it is not needed)

IDM **make a ˌmountain out of a ˈmolehill** (*disapproving*) to make an unimportant matter seem important

ˌmountain ˈash *noun* = ROWAN

ˈmountain bike *noun* a bicycle with a strong frame, wide tyres and many gears, designed for riding on rough ground ▸ **ˈmountain biking** *noun* [U] ➲ VISUAL VOCAB page V41

moun·tain·board /ˈmaʊntənbɔːd; *NAmE* ˈmaʊntn-bɔːrd/ (also **ˌall-terrain ˈboard**) *noun* a short narrow board with wheels like a SKATEBOARD that can be used for going down mountains ▸ **moun·tain·board·ing** *noun* [U]

ˌMountain ˈDaylight Time *noun* [U] (*abbr.* **MDT**) the time used in summer in parts of the US and Canada near the Rocky Mountains that is eight hours earlier than GMT

moun·tain·eer /ˌmaʊntəˈnɪə(r); *NAmE* -tnˈɪr/ *noun* a person who climbs mountains as a sport

moun·tain·eer·ing /ˌmaʊntəˈnɪərɪŋ; *NAmE* -tnˈɪrɪŋ/ *noun* [U] the sport or activity of climbing mountains: *to go mountaineering* ◇ *a mountaineering expedition*

ˈmountain lion *noun* (*NAmE*) = PUMA

ˈmountain man *noun* (*NAmE*) a man who lives alone in the mountains, especially one who catches and kills animals for their fur

moun·tain·ous /ˈmaʊntənəs/ *adj.* **1** having many mountains: ***a mountainous region/terrain*** **2** very large in size or amount; like a mountain SYN **huge**: *mountainous waves*

M

moun·tain·side /ˈmaʊntənsaɪd/ *noun* the side or slope of a mountain: *Tracks led up the mountainside.*

ˌMountain ˈStandard Time *noun* [U] (*abbr.* **MST**) the time used in winter in parts of the US and Canada near the Rocky Mountains that is seven hours earlier than GMT

ˈMountain time *noun* [U] the standard time in the parts of the US and Canada that are near the Rocky Mountains

moun·tain·top /ˈmaʊntəntɒp; *NAmE* ˈmaʊntntɑːp/ *noun* the top of a mountain ▸ **moun·tain·top** *adj.* [only before noun]: *a mountaintop ranch*

moun·te·bank /ˈmaʊntɪbæŋk/ *noun* (*old-fashioned*) a person who tries to trick people, especially in order to get their money

mount·ed /ˈmaʊntɪd/ *adj.* [only before noun] **1** (of a person, especially a soldier or a police officer) riding a horse: *mounted policemen* **2** placed on sth or attached to sth for display or support: *a mounted photograph* **3 -mounted** (in compounds) attached to the thing mentioned for support: *a ceiling-mounted fan* ➲ see also WALL-MOUNTED

Moun·tie /ˈmaʊnti/ *noun* (*informal*) a member of the Royal Canadian Mounted Police

mount·ing /ˈmaʊntɪŋ/ *adj., noun*

■ ***adj.*** [only before noun] increasing, often in a manner that causes or expresses anxiety SYN **growing**: ***mounting excitement/concern/tension*** ◇ *There is mounting evidence of serious effects on people's health.*

■ ***noun*** = MOUNT: *The engine came loose from its mountings.*

mourn /mɔːn; *NAmE* mɔːrn/ *verb* [T, I] to feel and show sadness because sb has died; to feel sad because sth no longer exists or is no longer the same SYN **grieve for**: **~ sth** *He was still mourning his brother's death.* ◇ *They mourn the passing of a simpler way of life.* ◇ **~ (for sb/sth)** *Today we mourn for all those who died in two world wars.* ◇ *She mourned for her lost childhood.*

mourn·er /ˈmɔːnə(r); *NAmE* ˈmɔːrn-/ *noun* a person who attends a funeral, especially a friend or a relative of the dead person

mourn·ful /ˈmɔːnfl; *NAmE* ˈmɔːrnfl/ *adj.* very sad SYN **melancholy**: *mournful eyes* ◇ *mournful music* ◇ *I couldn't bear the mournful look on her face.* ▸ **mourn·ful·ly** /-fəli/ *adv.*: *The dog looked mournfully after its owner.*

mourn·ing /ˈmɔːnɪŋ; *NAmE* ˈmɔːrn-/ *noun* [U] **1** sadness that you show and feel because sb has died SYN **grief**: *The government announced a day of national mourning for the victims.* ◇ *She was still* ***in mourning*** *for her husband.* **2** clothes that people wear to show their sadness at sb's death

mouse 0‑ /maʊs/ *noun, verb*

■ ***noun*** (*pl.* **mice** /maɪs/) **1** 0‑ a small animal that is covered in fur and has a long thin tail. Mice live in fields, in people's houses or where food is stored: *a field mouse* ◇ *a house mouse* ◇ *The stores were overrun with rats and mice.* ◇ *She crept upstairs,* ***quiet as a mouse***. ◇ *He was a weak little mouse of a man.* ➲ see also DORMOUSE **2** 0‑ (*pl. also* **mouses**) (*computing*) a small device that is moved by hand across a surface to control the movement of the CURSOR on a computer screen: *Click the left mouse button twice to highlight the program.* ◇ *Use the mouse to drag the icon to a new position.* ➲ VISUAL VOCAB pages V54, V56 IDM see CAT

■ ***verb***

PHR V **ˌmouse over sth** (*computing*) to use the mouse to move over sth on a computer screen: *Mouse over the link in the original message.* ▸ **mouse·over** /ˈmaʊsəʊvə(r); *NAmE* -oʊ-/ *noun*: *the use of mouseovers in web design*

ˈmouse mat (*BrE*) (*especially NAmE* **ˈmouse pad**) *noun* a small square of plastic that is the best kind of surface on which to use a computer mouse ➲ VISUAL VOCAB page V56

ˈmouse potato *noun* (*informal, disapproving*) a person who spends too much time using a computer

mouser /ˈmaʊsə(r)/ *noun* a cat that catches mice

mouse·trap /ˈmaʊstræp/ *noun* a trap with a powerful spring that is used, for example in a house, for catching mice

mousey = MOUSY

mous·saka /muːˈsɑːkə/ *noun* [U, C] a Greek dish made from layers of AUBERGINE and finely chopped meat with cheese on top

mousse /muːs/ *noun* [C, U] **1** a cold DESSERT (= a sweet dish) made with cream and egg whites and flavoured with fruit, chocolate, etc; a similar dish flavoured with fish, vegetables, etc: *a* ***chocolate/strawberry mousse*** ◇ ***salmon/mushroom mousse*** **2** a substance that is sold in AEROSOLS, for example the light white substance that is used on hair to give it a particular style or to improve its condition

mous·tache /məˈstɑːʃ/ (*especially US* **mus·tache**) *noun* **1** a line of hair that a man allows to grow on his upper lip ➲ COLLOCATIONS at PHYSICAL ➲ VISUAL VOCAB page V49 **2 moustaches** [pl.] a very long moustache ➲ compare BEARD

mous·tached /məˈstɑːʃt/ (*especially US* **mus·tached**) *adj.* [usually before noun] having a moustache ➲ compare MUSTACHIOED

mous·tachi·oed = MUSTACHIOED

mousy (also **mousey**) /ˈmaʊsi/ *adj.* (*disapproving*) **1** (of hair) of a dull brown colour **2** (usually *disapproving*) (of people) shy and quiet; without a strong personality

mouth 0‑ *noun, verb*

■ ***noun*** /maʊθ/ (*pl.* **mouths** /maʊðz/)

▸ PART OF FACE **1** 0‑ the opening in the face used for speaking, eating, etc; the area inside the head behind this opening: *She* ***opened her mouth*** *to say something.* ◇ *His mouth twisted into a wry smile.* ◇ *Their* ***mouths fell open*** (= they were surprised). ◇ *Don't* ***talk with your mouth full*** (= when eating). ◇ *The creature was foaming* ***at the mouth***. ➲ VISUAL VOCAB page V48 ➲ see also FOOT-AND-MOUTH DISEASE

▸ PERSON NEEDING FOOD **2** a person considered only as sb who needs to be provided with food: *Now there would be another* ***mouth to feed***. ◇ *The world will not be able to support all these extra* ***hungry mouths***.

▸ ENTRANCE/OPENING **3** 0‑ **~ (of sth)** the entrance or opening of sth: *the mouth of a cave/pit* ➲ see also GOALMOUTH

▸ OF RIVER **4** 0‑ the place where a river joins the sea

▸ WAY OF SPEAKING **5** a particular way of speaking: *He has a foul mouth on him!* ◇ *Watch your mouth!* (= stop saying

things that are rude and/or offensive) ➲ see also LOUDMOUTH
▸ -MOUTHED **6** (in adjectives) having the type or shape of mouth mentioned: *a wide-mouthed old woman* ◇ *a narrow-mouthed cave* ➲ see also OPEN-MOUTHED **7** (in adjectives) having a particular way of speaking: *a rather crude-mouthed individual* ➲ see also FOUL-MOUTHED, MEALY-MOUTHED

IDM **be all 'mouth** (*informal*) if you say sb is **all mouth**, you mean that they talk a lot about doing sth, but are, in fact, not brave enough to do it **down in the 'mouth** unhappy and depressed **keep your 'mouth shut** (*informal*) to not talk about sth to sb because it is a secret or because it will upset or annoy them: *I've warned them to keep their mouths shut about this.* ◇ *Now she's upset—why couldn't you keep your mouth shut?* **out of the ˌmouths of 'babes (and 'sucklings)** (*saying*) used when a small child has just said sth that seems very wise or clever **run off at the 'mouth** (*NAmE, informal*) to talk too much, in a way that is not sensible ➲ more at BIG *adj.*, BORN, BREAD, BUTTER *n.*, FOAM *v.*, FOOT *n.*, GIFT, HEART, HORSE *n.*, LIVE[1], MELT, MONEY, SHOOT *v.*, SHUT *v.*, TASTE *n.*, WATCH *v.*, WORD *n.*

■ **verb** /maʊð/ **1** **~ sth** | **+ speech** to move your lips as if you were saying sth, but without making a sound: *He mouthed a few obscenities at us and then moved off.* **2** **~ sth** | **+ speech** (*disapproving*) to say sth that you do not really feel, believe or understand: *They're just mouthing empty slogans.*

PHR V **ˌmouth 'off (at/about sth)** (*informal*) to talk or complain loudly about sth

mouth·ful /'maʊθfʊl/ *noun* **1** [C] an amount of food or drink that you put in your mouth at one time: *She took a mouthful of water.* **2** [sing.] (*informal*) a word or a phrase that is long and complicated or difficult to pronounce

IDM **give sb a 'mouthful** (*informal, especially BrE*) to speak angrily to sb, perhaps swearing at them **say a 'mouthful** (*NAmE, informal*) to say sth important using only a few words

mouth·guard /'maʊθɡɑːd; *NAmE* -ɡɑːrd/ (*NAmE*) (*BrE* **gum·shield**) *noun* a cover that a sports player wears in his/her mouth to protect the teeth and GUMS

'mouth organ *noun* (*BrE*) = HARMONICA

mouth·piece /'maʊθpiːs/ *noun* **1** the part of the telephone that is next to your mouth when you speak **2** the part of a musical instrument that you place between your lips ➲ VISUAL VOCAB page V30 **3** **~ (of/for sb)** a person, newspaper, etc. that speaks on behalf of another person or group of people: *The newspaper has become the official mouthpiece of the opposition party.* ◇ *The Press Secretary serves as the President's mouthpiece.*

ˌmouth-to-ˌmouth reˌsusci'tation (also **ˌmouth-to-'mouth**) *noun* [U] the act of breathing into the mouth of an unconscious person in order to fill their lungs with air SYN **the kiss of life** ➲ compare ARTIFICIAL RESPIRATION

'mouth ulcer (*BrE*) (*NAmE* **'canker sore**) *noun* a small sore area in the mouth

mouth·wash /'maʊθwɒʃ; *NAmE* -wɔːʃ; -wɑːʃ/ *noun* [C, U] a liquid used to make the mouth fresh and healthy

'mouth-watering *adj.* (*approving*) **mouth-watering** food looks or smells so good that you want to eat it immediately SYN **tempting**: *a mouth-watering display of cakes* ◇ (*figurative*) *mouth-watering travel brochures*

mouthy /'maʊθi; -ði/ *adj.* (*informal, disapproving*) used to describe a person who talks a lot, sometimes expressing their opinions strongly and in a rude way

mov·able (also **move·able**) /'muːvəbl/ *adj., noun*

■ **adj.** **1** that can be moved from one place or position to another: *movable partitions* ◇ *a doll with a movable head* **2** (*law*) (of property) able to be taken from one house, etc. to another

■ **noun** [C, usually pl.] (*law*) a thing that can be moved from one house, etc. to another; a personal possession

ˌmovable 'feast *noun* a religious festival, such as Easter, whose date changes from year to year

move ⚷ /muːv/ *verb, noun*

■ **verb**

▸ CHANGE POSITION **1** ⚷ [I, T] to change position or make sb/sth change position in a way that can be seen, heard or felt: *Don't move—stay perfectly still.* ◇ *The bus was already moving when I jumped onto it.* ◇ **+ adv./prep.** *He could hear someone moving around in the room above.* ◇ *Phil moved towards the window.* ◇ ***You can hardly move** in this pub on Saturdays* (= because it is so crowded). ◇ ***You can't move for** books in her room.* ◇ **~ sth** *I can't move my fingers.* ◇ **~ sth + adv./prep.** *We moved our chairs a little nearer.*

▸ CHANGE IDEAS/TIME **2** ⚷ [I, T] to change; to change sth SYN **shift**: (**+ adv./prep.**) *The government has not moved on this issue.* ◇ **~ sth (+ adv./prep.)** *Let's move the meeting to Wednesday.*

▸ MAKE PROGRESS **3** ⚷ [I] **~ (on/ahead)** to make progress in the way or direction mentioned SYN **progress**: *Time is moving on.* ◇ *Share prices moved ahead today.* ◇ *Things are not moving as fast as we hoped.*

▸ TAKE ACTION **4** [I] to take action; to do sth SYN **act**: *The police moved quickly to dispel the rumours.* ➲ SYNONYMS at ACTION

▸ CHANGE HOUSE/JOB **5** ⚷ [I, T] to change the place where you live, have your work, etc: *We don't like it here so we've decided to move.* ◇ **~ (from...) (to...)** *The company's moving to Scotland.* ◇ **~ away** *She's been all on her own since her daughter moved away.* ◇ **~ house** (*BrE*) *We moved house last week.* **6** ⚷ [T] **~ sb (from...) (to...)** to make sb change from one job, class, etc. to another SYN **transfer**: *I'm being moved to the New York office.*

▸ IN BOARD GAMES **7** ⚷ [I, T] (in CHESS and other board games) to change the position of a piece: *It's your turn to move.* ◇ **~ sth** *She moved her queen.*

▸ CAUSE STRONG FEELINGS **8** ⚷ [T] to cause sb to have strong feelings, especially of sympathy or sadness: **~ sb** *We were **deeply moved** by her plight.* ◇ **~ sb to sth** *Grown men were **moved to tears** at the horrific scenes.* ➲ see also MOVING

▸ MAKE SB DO STH **9** [T] (*formal*) to cause sb to do sth SYN **prompt**: **~ sb to do sth** *She felt moved to address the crowd.* ◇ **~ sb** *He works **when the spirit moves him*** (= when he wants to).

▸ SUGGEST FORMALLY **10** [T] (*formal*) to suggest sth formally so that it can be discussed and decided SYN **put forward**: **~ sth** *The Opposition moved an amendment to the Bill.* ◇ **~ that...** *I move that a vote be taken on this.*

IDM **get 'moving** (*informal*) to begin, leave, etc. quickly: *It's late—we'd better get moving.* **get sth 'moving** (*informal*) to cause sth to make progress: *The new director has really got things moving.* **move heaven and 'earth** to do everything you possibly can in order to achieve sth **move with the 'times** to change the way you think and behave according to changes in society ➲ more at ASS, FORWARD *adv.*

PHR V **ˌmove a'long** to go to a new position, especially in order to make room for other people: *The bus driver asked them to move along.* **ˌmove 'in** | **ˌmove 'into sth** ⚷ to start to live in your new home: *Our new neighbours moved in yesterday.* OPP **move out** **'move in sth** to live, spend your time, etc. in a particular social group: *She only moves in the best circles.* **ˌmove 'in (on sb/sth)** to move towards sb/sth from all directions, especially in a threatening way: *The police moved in on the terrorists.* **ˌmove 'in with sb** to start living with sb in the house or flat/apartment where they already live **ˌmove 'off** (especially of a vehicle) to start moving; to leave **ˌmove 'on (to sth)** to start doing or discussing sth new: *I've been in this job long enough—it's time I moved on.* ◇ *Can we move on to the next item on the agenda?* **ˌmove sb 'on** (of police, etc.) to order sb to move away from the scene of an accident, etc. **ˌmove 'out** ⚷ to leave your old home OPP **move in** **ˌmove 'over** ⚷ (also **ˌmove 'up**) to change your position in order to make room for sb: *There's room for another one if you move up a bit.*

■ **noun**

▸ ACTION **1** ⚷ **~ (towards/to sth)** | **~ (to do sth)** an action that you do or need to do to achieve sth: *This latest move by the government has aroused fierce opposition.* ◇ *The management have made no move to settle the strike.* ◇ *Getting a*

M

job in marketing was a good ***career move.*** ➲ see also FALSE MOVE
▸ CHANGE OF POSITION **2** 🗝 [usually sing.] a change of place or position: *Don't* ***make a move!*** ◇ *Every move was painful.* ◇ *She felt he was watching her* ***every move.*** ➲ see also MOVEMENT
▸ CHANGE OF IDEAS/BEHAVIOUR **3** **~ to/away from sth** a change in ideas, attitudes or behaviour SYN **shift, trend**: *There has been a move away from nuclear energy.*
▸ CHANGE OF HOUSE/JOB **4** 🗝 an act of changing the place where you live or work: *What's the date of your move?* ◇ *Their move from Italy to the US has not been a success.* ◇ *Her new job is just a sideways move.*
▸ IN BOARD GAMES **5** an act of changing the position of a piece in CHESS or other games that are played on a board: *The game was over in only six moves.* ◇ *It's your move.*
IDM **be on the 'move** **1** to be travelling from place to place **2** to be moving; to be going somewhere: *The car was already on the move.* ◇ *The firm is on the move to larger offices.* **3** = BE ON THE GO **get a 'move on** (*informal*) you tell sb to **get a move on** when you want them to hurry **make the first 'move** to do sth before sb else, for example in order to end an argument or to begin sth: *If he wants to see me, he should make the first move.* **make a 'move** (*BrE, informal*) to begin a journey or a task: *It's getting late—we'd better make a move.* **make a 'move on sb** (*informal*) **1** to try to start a sexual relationship with sb **2** (*sport*) to try to pass sb who is front of you in a race **make a, your, etc. 'move** to do the action that you intend to do or need to do in order to achieve sth: *The rebels waited until nightfall before they made their move.*

move·able *adj.* = MOVABLE

move·ment 🗝 /'mu:vmənt/ *noun*
▸ CHANGING POSITION **1** 🗝 [C, U] an act of moving the body or part of the body: ***hand/eye movements*** ◇ *She observed the gentle movement of his chest as he breathed.* ◇ *Loose clothing gives you greater freedom of movement.* ◇ *There was a sudden movement in the undergrowth.* **2** 🗝 [C, U] an act of moving from one place to another or of moving sth from one place to another: *enemy troop movements* ◇ *laws to allow free movement of goods and services*
▸ GROUP OF PEOPLE **3** 🗝 [C+sing./pl. v.] a group of people who share the same ideas or aims: *the* ***women's/peace movement*** ◇ *the Romantic movement* (= for example in literature) ◇ *a mass movement for change* ➲ COLLOCATIONS at POLITICS
▸ PERSON'S ACTIVITIES **4** **movements** [pl.] a person's activities over a period of time, especially as watched by sb else: *The police are keeping a close watch on the suspect's movements.*
▸ CHANGE OF IDEAS/BEHAVIOUR **5** [sing.] **~ (away from/towards sth)** a gradual change in what people in society do or think SYN **trend**: *a movement towards greater sexual equality*
▸ PROGRESS **6** [U] **~ (in sth)** progress, especially in a particular task: *It needs cooperation from all the countries to get any movement in arms control.*
▸ CHANGE IN AMOUNT **7** [U, C] **~ (in sth)** a change in amount: *There has been no movement in oil prices.*
▸ MUSIC **8** [C] any of the main parts that a long piece of music is divided into: *the slow movement of the First Concerto*
▸ OF BOWELS **9** [C] (*technical*) = BOWEL MOVEMENT

mover /'mu:və(r)/ *noun* **1** a person or thing that moves in a particular way: *a great mover on the dance floor* ➲ see also PRIME MOVER **2** a machine or a person that moves things from one place to another, especially sb who moves furniture from one house to another: *an earth mover* ◇ *professional furniture movers* ➲ see also REMOVER
IDM **,movers and 'shakers** people with power in important organizations

movie 🗝 /'mu:vi/ *noun* (*especially NAmE*)
1 🗝 [C] a series of moving pictures recorded with sound that tells a story, shown at the cinema/movie theater SYN **film**: *to make a horror movie* ◇ *Have you seen the latest Miyazaki movie?* ◇ *a famous* ***movie director/star*** ➲ COLLOCATIONS at CINEMA ➲ see also ROAD MOVIE **2** 🗝 **the movies** [pl.] = THE CINEMA (2): *Let's go to the movies.* **3** 🗝 **the movies** [pl.] = CINEMA (3): *I've always wanted to work in the movies.*

movie·goer /'mu:vigəʊə(r); *NAmE* -goʊ-/ *noun* (*especially NAmE*) = FILM-GOER

'movie star *noun* (*especially NAmE*) = FILM STAR

'movie theater 🗝 (also **theater**) *noun* (*NAmE*) = THEATER (2): *The documentary opens tomorrow in movie theaters nationwide.*

mov·ing 🗝 /'mu:vɪŋ/ *adj.*
1 🗝 causing you to have deep feelings of sadness or sympathy: *a deeply moving experience* **2** 🗝 [only before noun] (of things) changing from one place or position to another: *the moving parts of a machine* ◇ *fast-moving water* ◇ *a moving target* ▸ **mov·ing·ly** *adv.*: *She described her experiences in Africa very movingly.*

'moving van (*NAmE*) (*BrE* **re'moval van**, **'furniture van**) *noun* a large van used for moving furniture from one house to another

mow /məʊ; *NAmE* moʊ/ *verb* (**mowed**, **mown** /məʊn; *NAmE* moʊn/ or **mowed**) [T, I] **~ (sth)** to cut grass, etc. using a machine or tool with a special blade or blades: *I mow the lawn every week in summer.* ◇ *the smell of new-mown hay*
PHR V **,mow sb↔'down** to kill sb using a vehicle or a gun, especially when several people are all killed at the same time

mower /'məʊə(r); *NAmE* 'moʊ-/ *noun* (especially in compounds) a machine that cuts grass: *a lawnmower* ◇ *a* ***motor/rotary mower***

moxie /'mɒksi; *NAmE* 'mɑ:ksi/ *noun* [U] (*NAmE, informal*) courage, energy and determination

moz·za·rella /,mɒtsə'relə; *NAmE* ,mɑ:ts-/ *noun* [U] a type of soft white Italian cheese with a mild flavour

moz·zie /'mɒzi; *NAmE* 'mɑ:zi; 'mɔ:zi/ *noun* (*pl.* **-ies**) (*informal*) a MOSQUITO

MP /,em 'pi:/ *noun* **1** the abbreviation for 'Member of Parliament' (a person who has been elected to represent the people of a particular area in a parliament): *Michael Phillips MP* ◇ *Write to your local MP to protest.* ◇ *Conservative/Labour MPs* ◇ *the MP for Oxford East* ◇ *a Euro-MP* **2** a member of the MILITARY POLICE

MP3 /,em pi: 'θri:/ *noun* [C, U] a method of reducing the size of a computer file containing sound, or a file that is reduced in size in this way

MP'3 player *noun* a piece of computer equipment that can open and play MP3 files ➲ VISUAL VOCAB page V54

MP4 /,em pi: 'fɔ:(r)/ *noun* [C, U] a method of reducing the size of a computer file containing sound and images; a file that is reduced in size in this way

MPEG /'empeg/ *noun* (*computing*) **1** [U] technology which reduces the size of files that contain video images or sounds: *an MPEG file* **2** [C] a file produced using this technology

mpg /,em pi: 'dʒi:/ *abbr.* miles per gallon (used for saying how much petrol/gas a vehicle uses): *It does 40 mpg.* ◇ (*NAmE*) *It gets 40 mpg.*

mph /,em pi: 'eɪtʃ/ *abbr.* miles per hour: *a 60 mph speed limit*

MPV /,em pi: 'vi:/ *noun* the abbreviation for 'multi-purpose vehicle' (a large car like a van) SYN **people carrier**

Mr 🗝 (*BrE*) (also **Mr.** *NAmE, BrE*) /'mɪstə(r)/ *abbr.*
1 🗝 a title that comes before a man's family name, or before his first and family names together: *Mr Brown* ◇ *Mr John Brown* ◇ *Mr and Mrs Brown* **2** a title used to address a man in some official positions: *Thank you, Mr Chairman.* ◇ *Mr. President* ➲ see also MISTER
IDM **,Mr 'Nice Guy** (*informal*) a way of describing a man who is very honest and thinks about the wishes and feelings of other people: *I was tired of helping other people. From now on it was* ***no more Mr Nice Guy*** (= I would stop being pleasant and kind). **Mr 'Right** (*informal*) the man who would be the right husband for a particular woman:

M

I'm not getting married in a hurry—I'm waiting for Mr Right to come along.

ˌMr. ˈCharlie *noun* (*US, slang, offensive*) a name used by African Americans for a white man

ˌMr. ˈClean *noun* (*US, informal*) a man, especially a politician, who is considered to be very honest and good: *The scandal destroyed his image as Mr. Clean.*

Mr Fixit /ˌmɪstə ˈfɪksɪt/ *noun* (*BrE, informal*) a person who organizes things and solves problems

MRI /ˌem ɑːr ˈaɪ/ *abbr.* (*medical*) magnetic resonance imaging (a method of using a strong MAGNETIC FIELD to produce an image of the inside of a person's body): *an MRI scan*

Mrs 0‑ (*BrE*) (also **Mrs.** *NAmE, BrE*) /ˈmɪsɪz/ *abbr.* a title that comes before a married woman's family name or before her first and family names together: *Mrs Hill* ◇ *Mrs Susan Hill* ◇ *Mr and Mrs Hill* ➲ compare MISS, MS

MRSA /ˌem ɑːr es ˈeɪ/ *noun* [U] the abbreviation for 'methicillin-resistant Staphylococcus aureus' (a type of bacteria that cannot be killed by standard ANTIBIOTICS): *rising rates of MRSA infections in hospitals* ➲ see also SUPERBUG

MS (*NAmE* also **M.S.**) /ˌem ˈes/ *abbr.* **1** MULTIPLE SCLEROSIS **2** MANUSCRIPT **3** = MSc

Ms 0‑ (*BrE*) (also **Ms.** *NAmE, BrE*) /mɪz; məz/ *abbr.* a title that comes before a woman's family name or before her first and family names together, and that can be used when you do not want to state whether she is married or not: *Ms Murphy* ◇ *Ms Jean Murphy* ➲ compare MISS, MRS

MSc /ˌem es ˈsiː/ (*BrE*) (*NAmE* **M.S., MS**) *noun* the abbreviation for 'Master of Science' (a second university degree in science): (*BrE*) *to* ***be/have/do an MSc*** ◇ (*BrE*) *J Stevens MSc*

MSG /ˌem es ˈdʒiː/ *abbr.* MONOSODIUM GLUTAMATE

MSM /ˌem es ˈem/ *noun* [U+sing./pl. v.] (*computing*) the abbreviation for 'mainstream media' (traditional media such as newspapers and broadcasting): *The line is beginning to blur between influential blogs and MSM.*

MSP /ˌem es ˈpiː/ *noun* the abbreviation for 'Member of the Scottish Parliament': *Alex Neil MSP* ◇ *Write to your local MSP to protest.* ◇ *Labour MSPs*

MST /ˌem es ˈtiː/ *abbr.* MOUNTAIN STANDARD TIME

Mt (also **Mt.** especially in *NAmE*) *abbr.* (especially on maps) MOUNT: *Mt Kenya*

MTV™ /ˌem tiː ˈviː/ *abbr.* music television (a television channel that shows music videos and other light entertainment programmes)

mu /mjuː/ *noun* the 12th letter of the Greek alphabet (M, μ)

much 0‑ /mʌtʃ/ *det., pron., adv.*

■ ***det., pron.*** 0‑ used with uncountable nouns, especially in negative sentences to mean 'a large amount of sth', or after 'how' to ask about the amount of sth. It is also used with 'as', 'so' and 'too'.: *I don't have much money with me.* ◇ *'Got any money?'* ***'Not much.'*** ◇ ***How much*** *water do you need?* ◇ ***How much is it*** (= What does it cost)? ◇ *Take* ***as much*** *time* ***as*** *you like.* ◇ *There was* ***so much*** *traffic* ***that*** *we were an hour late.* ◇ *I've got far* ***too much to*** *do.* ◇ (*formal*) *I lay awake for much of the night.* ◇ (*formal*) *There was much discussion about the reasons for the failure.*

IDM **as ˈmuch** the same: *Please help me get this job—you know I would do as much for you.* ◇ *'Roger stole the money.' 'I* ***thought as much.'*** **as much as sb can do** used to say that sth is difficult to do: *No dessert for me, thanks. It was as much as I could do to finish the main course.* **not much ˈin it** used to say that there is little difference between two things: *I won, but there wasn't much in it* (= our scores were nearly the same). **ˈnot much of a…** not a good…: *He's not much of a tennis player.* **ˈthis much** used to introduce sth positive or definite: *I'll say this much for him—he never leaves a piece of work unfinished.*

■ ***adv.*** 0‑ (**more, most**) to a great degree: *Thank you* ***very much*** *for the flowers.* ◇ *I would very much like to see you again.* ◇ *He isn't in the office much* (= often). ◇ *You worry* ***too much.*** ◇ *My new job is* ***much the same as*** *the old one.* ◇ ***Much to*** *her surprise he came back the next day.* ◇ *She's much better today.* ◇ *The other one was* ***much too*** *expensive.* ◇ *Nikolai's English was* ***much the worst.*** ◇ *We are* ***very much aware*** *of the lack of food supplies.* ◇ *I'm* ***not much good at*** *tennis.* ◇ *He was much loved by all who knew him.* ◇ *an appeal to raise much-needed cash*

IDM **ˈmuch as** although: *Much as I would like to stay, I really must go home.* ➲ more at LESS *adv.*

Grammar Point

much / a lot of / lots of

- **Much** is used only with uncountable nouns. It is used mainly in questions and negative sentences: *Do you have much free time?* ◇ ***How much*** *experience have you had?* ◇ *I don't have much free time.*
- In statements **a lot of** or **lots of** (*informal*) is much more common: *'How much (money) does she earn?* ◇ *She earns a lot of money.* You can also use **plenty (of)**. These phrases can also be used in questions and negative sentences.
- **A lot of/lots of** is still felt to be informal, especially in *BrE*, so in formal writing it is better to use **much, a great deal of** or **a large amount of**.
- **Very much** and **a lot** can be used as adverbs: *I miss my family very much.* ◇ ~~*I miss very much my family.*~~ ◇ *I miss my family a lot.* ◇ *Thanks a lot.* In negative sentences you can use **much**: *I didn't enjoy the film (very) much.*

➲ note at MANY

much·ness /ˈmʌtʃnəs/ *noun*

IDM **ˌmuch of a ˈmuchness** very similar; almost the same: *The two candidates are much of a muchness—it's hard to choose between them.*

muck /mʌk/ *noun, verb*

■ ***noun*** **1** waste matter from farm animals SYN **manure**: *to spread muck on the fields* **2** (*informal, especially BrE*) dirt or mud: *Can you wipe the muck off the windows?* **3** (*informal, especially BrE*) something very unpleasant: *I can't eat this muck!*

IDM **where there's ˌmuck there's ˈbrass** (*BrE, saying*) used to say that a business activity that is unpleasant or dirty can bring in a lot of money

■ ***verb***

PHR V **ˌmuck aˈbout/aˈround** (*BrE, informal*) to behave in a silly way, especially when you should be working or doing sth else SYN **mess about/around** **ˌmuck aˈbout/aˈround with sth** (*BrE, informal, disapproving*) to do sth, especially to a machine, so that it does not work correctly SYN **mess about/around**: *Who's mucking around with my radio?* **ˌmuck sb aˈbout/aˈround** (*BrE, informal*) to treat sb badly, especially by changing your mind a lot, or by not being honest SYN **mess sb about/around**: *They've really mucked us about over our car insurance.* **ˌmuck ˈin** (*BrE, informal*) **1** to work with other people in order to complete a task: *If we all muck in, we could have the job finished by the end of the week.* **2** to share food, accommodation, etc. with other people: *We didn't have much money, but everyone just mucked in together.* **ˌmuck ˈout** | **ˌmuck sth↔ˈout** to clean out the place where an animal lives **ˌmuck sth↔ˈup** (*informal, especially BrE*) **1** to do sth badly so that you fail to achieve what you wanted or hoped to achieve SYN **mess sth up**: *He completely mucked up his English exam.* **2** to spoil a plan or an arrangement SYN **mess sth up** **3** to make sth dirty: *I don't want you mucking up my nice clean floor.*

muck·er /ˈmʌkə(r)/ *noun* **1** (*BrE, informal*) used when talking to or about a friend to refer to them: *It's my old mucker John!* **2** (*old-fashioned, NAmE, informal*) a person who is rough and does not have good manners

muck·rak·ing /ˈmʌkreɪkɪŋ/ *noun* [U] (*informal, disapproving*) the activity of looking for information about people's private lives that they do not wish to make public

M

mucky /ˈmʌki/ *adj.* (*informal, especially BrE*) **1** dirty: *mucky hands* **2** sexually offensive SYN **obscene**: *mucky books/jokes*

ˌmucous ˈmembrane *noun* (*anatomy*) a thin layer of skin that covers the inside of the nose and mouth and the outside of other organs in the body, producing mucus to prevent these parts from becoming dry

mucus /ˈmjuːkəs/ *noun* [U] a thick liquid that is produced in parts of the body, such as the nose, by a mucous membrane ▶ **mu·cous** /ˈmjuːkəs/ *adj.*: *mucous glands*

MUD /mʌd/ *noun* (*computing*) the abbreviation for 'multi-user dungeon/dimension' (a computer game played over the Internet by several players at the same time)

mud 0-w /mʌd/ *noun* [U]
wet earth that is soft and sticky: *The car wheels got stuck in the mud.* ◇ *Your boots are covered in mud.* ◇ ***mud bricks/huts*** (= made of dried mud) ➲ SYNONYMS at SOIL
IDM **fling, sling, etc. ˈmud (at sb)** to criticize sb or accuse sb of bad or shocking things in order to damage their reputation, especially in politics ➲ see also MUD-SLINGING **ˌmud ˈsticks** (*saying*) people remember and believe the bad things they hear about other people, even if they are later shown to be false ➲ more at CLEAR *adj.*, NAME *n.*

mud·bath /ˈmʌdbɑːθ; *NAmE* -bæθ/ *noun* **1** a bath in hot mud that contains a lot of minerals, which is taken, for example, to help with RHEUMATISM **2** a place where there is a lot of mud: *Heavy rain turned the campsite into a mudbath.*

mud·dle /ˈmʌdl/ *verb, noun*
■ ***verb*** (*especially BrE*) **1** to put things in the wrong order or mix them up: **~ sth** *Don't do that—you're muddling my papers.* ◇ **~ sth up** *Their letters were all muddled up together in a drawer.* **2 ~ sb (up)** to confuse sb: *Slow down a little—you're muddling me.* **3 ~ sb/sth (up) | ~ A (up) with B** to confuse one person or thing with another SYN **mix up**: *I muddled the dates and arrived a week early.* ◇ *He* ***got all muddled up*** *about what went where.* ◇ *They look so alike, I always* ***get them muddled up***.
PHR V **ˌmuddle aˈlong** (*especially BrE*) to continue doing sth without any clear plan or purpose: *We can't just keep muddling along like this.* **ˌmuddle ˈthrough** to achieve your aims even though you do not know exactly what you are doing and do not have the correct equipment, knowledge, etc: *We'll muddle through somehow.*
■ ***noun*** (*especially BrE*) **1** [C, usually sing.] a state of mental confusion: *Can you start from the beginning again—I'm* ***in a muddle***. **2** [C, usually sing., U] **~ (about/over sth)** a situation in which there is confusion about arrangements, etc. and things are done wrong: *There was a muddle over the theatre tickets.* ◇ *There followed a long period of confusion and muddle.* **3** [C, usually sing., U] a state of confusion in which things are untidy SYN **mess**: *My papers are all* ***in a muddle***.

mud·dled /ˈmʌdld/ *adj.* (*especially BrE*) confused: *He gets muddled when the teacher starts shouting.* ◇ *muddled thinking*

ˌmuddle-ˈheaded *adj.* confused or with confused ideas: *muddle-headed thinkers*

mud·dling /ˈmʌdlɪŋ/ *adj.* (*especially BrE*) causing confusion; difficult to understand

muddy /ˈmʌdi/ *adj., verb*
■ ***adj.*** (**mud·dier, mud·di·est**) **1** full of or covered in mud: *a* ***muddy field/track*** ◇ ***muddy boots/knees*** ➲ SYNONYMS at DIRTY **2** (of a liquid) containing mud; not clear: *muddy water* ◇ *a muddy pond* **3** (of colours) not clear or bright: ***muddy green/brown***
■ ***verb*** (**mud·dies, muddy·ing, mud·died, mud·died**) **~ sth** to make sth muddy
IDM **muddy the ˈwaters, ˈissue, etc.** (*disapproving*) to make a simple situation confused and more complicated than it really is

mud·flap /ˈmʌdflæp/ *noun* one of a set of pieces of FLEXIBLE material that are fixed behind the wheels of a car, motorcycle, etc. to prevent them from throwing up mud, stones or water

mud·flat /ˈmʌdflæt/ *noun* [usually pl.] an area of flat muddy land that is covered by the sea when it comes in at HIGH TIDE

mud·guard /ˈmʌdgɑːd; *NAmE* -gɑːrd/ (*BrE*) (*NAmE* **fender**) *noun* a curved cover over a wheel of a bicycle

ˈmud pack *noun* a substance containing CLAY that you put on your face and take off after a short period of time, used to improve the condition of your skin

ˌmud ˈpie *noun* wet earth that is made into the shape of a PIE as part of a game played by children

mud·slide /ˈmʌdslaɪd/ *noun* a large amount of mud sliding down a mountain, often destroying buildings and injuring or killing people below

ˈmud-slinging *noun* [U] (*disapproving*) the act of criticizing sb and accusing them of sth in order to damage their reputation

muesli /ˈmjuːzli/ *noun* [U] a mixture of grains, nuts, dried fruit, etc. served with milk and eaten for breakfast

muez·zin /muːˈezɪn; mjuː-/ *noun* a man who calls Muslims to prayer, usually from the tower of a MOSQUE

muff /mʌf/ *noun, verb*
■ ***noun*** a short tube of fur or other warm material that you put your hands into to keep them warm in cold weather ➲ see also EARMUFFS
■ ***verb*** **~ sth** (*informal, disapproving*) to miss an opportunity to do sth well: *He muffed his lines* (= he forgot them or said them wrongly). ◇ *It was a really simple shot, and I muffed it.*

muf·fin /ˈmʌfɪn/ *noun* **1** (*BrE*) (*NAmE* **ˌEnglish ˈmuffin**) a type of round flat bread roll, usually TOASTED and eaten hot with butter **2** a small cake in the shape of a cup, often containing small pieces of fruit, etc: *a blueberry muffin*

muf·fle /ˈmʌfl/ *verb* **1 ~ sth** to make a sound quieter or less clear: *He tried to muffle the alarm clock by putting it under his pillow.* **2 ~ sb/sth (up) in sth** to wrap or cover sb/sth in order to keep them/it warm: *She muffled the child up in a blanket.*

muf·fled /ˈmʌfld/ *adj.* (of sounds) not heard clearly because sth is in the way that stops the sound from travelling easily: *muffled voices from the next room*

muf·fler /ˈmʌflə(r)/ *noun* **1** (*old-fashioned*) a thick piece of cloth worn around the neck for warmth SYN **scarf** **2** (*NAmE*) (*BrE* **si·len·cer**) a device that is fixed to the EXHAUST of a vehicle in order to reduce the amount of noise that the engine makes ➲ VISUAL VOCAB page V41

mufti /ˈmʌfti/ *noun* **1** [C] (also **Mufti**) a Muslim who is an expert in legal matters connected with Islam **2** [U] (*old-fashioned*) ordinary clothes worn by people such as soldiers who wear uniform in their job: *officers in mufti*

mug /mʌg/ *noun, verb*
■ ***noun*** **1** a tall cup for drinking from, usually with straight sides and a handle, used without a SAUCER: *a coffee mug* ◇ *a beer mug* (= a large glass with a handle) ➲ VISUAL VOCAB page V19 **2** a mug and what it contains: *a mug of coffee* **3** (*slang*) a person's face: *I never want to see his ugly mug again.* **4** (*informal*) a person who is stupid and easy to trick: *They made me look a complete mug.* ◇ *He's no mug.*
IDM **a ˈmug's game** (*disapproving, especially BrE*) an activity that is unlikely to be successful or make a profit
■ ***verb*** (**-gg-**) **1** [T] **~ sb** to attack sb violently in order to steal their money, especially in a public place: *She had been mugged in the street in broad daylight.* **2** [I] **~ (for sb/sth)** (*informal, especially NAmE*) to make silly expressions with your face or behave in a silly, exaggerated way, especially on the stage or before a camera: *to mug for the cameras*
PHR V **ˌmug sth↔ˈup | ˌmug ˈup on sth** (*BrE, informal*) to learn sth, especially in a short time for a particular purpose, for example an exam

mug·ger /ˈmʌgə(r)/ *noun* a person who threatens or attacks sb in order to steal their money, especially in a public place

mug·ging /ˈmʌgɪŋ/ *noun* [U, C] the crime of attacking sb violently, or threatening to do so, in order to steal their money, especially in a public place: *Mugging is on the increase.* ◇ *There have been several muggings here recently.*

mug·gins /ˈmʌɡɪnz/ *noun* [sing.] (*BrE, informal, humorous*) used without 'a' or 'the' to refer to yourself when you feel stupid because you have let yourself be treated unfairly: *And muggins here had to clean up all the mess.*

muggy /ˈmʌɡi/ *adj.* (of weather) warm and damp in an unpleasant way SYN **close**: *a muggy August day*

Mug·hal /ˈmuːɡɑːl/ *noun* = MOGUL

mug·shot /ˈmʌɡʃɒt; *NAmE* -ʃɑːt/ *noun* (*informal*) a photograph of sb's face kept by the police in their records to identify criminals

mug·wump /ˈmʌɡwʌmp/ *noun* (*NAmE*, often *disapproving*) a person who cannot decide how to vote or who refuses to support a political party

Mu·ham·mad (also **Mo·ham·med**) /məˈhæmɪd/ *noun* the Arab PROPHET through whom the Koran was REVEALED and the religion of Islam established and completed

mu·ja·hi·deen (also **mu·ja·hi·din**) /ˌmuːdʒəhəˈdiːn/ *noun* [pl.] (in some Muslim countries) soldiers fighting in support of their strong Muslim beliefs

muk·luk /ˈmʌklʌk/ *noun* (*CanE*) a high soft winter boot that is traditionally made with the skin of SEALS

mu·latto /mjuˈlætəʊ; məˈl-; *NAmE* -toʊ/ *noun* (*pl.* **-os** or **-oes**) (*offensive*) a person with one black parent and one white parent

mul·berry /ˈmʌlbəri; *NAmE* -beri/ *noun* (*pl.* **-ies**) **1** (also ˈ**mulberry tree**) [C] a tree with broad dark green leaves and BERRIES that can be eaten. SILKWORMS (that make silk) eat the leaves of the white mulberry. **2** [C] the small purple or white BERRY of the mulberry tree **3** [U] a deep reddish-purple colour

mulch /mʌltʃ/ *noun, verb*

■ ***noun*** [C, U] material, for example, decaying leaves, that you put around a plant to protect its base and its roots, to improve the quality of the soil or to stop WEEDS growing

■ ***verb*** **~ sth** to cover the soil or the roots of a plant with a mulch

mule /mjuːl/ *noun* **1** an animal that has a horse and a DONKEY as parents, used especially for carrying loads: *He's as* ***stubborn as a mule.*** **2** (*slang*) a person who is paid to take drugs illegally from one country to another **3** a SLIPPER (= a soft shoe for wearing indoors) that is open around the heel ⊃ VISUAL VOCAB page V52

mule·teer /ˌmjuːləˈtɪə(r); *NAmE* -ˈtɪr/ *noun* a person who controls MULES (= the animals) and makes them go in the right direction

mul·ish /ˈmjuːlɪʃ/ *adj.* unwilling to change your mind or attitude or to do what other people want you to do SYN **stubborn**

mull /mʌl/ *verb*

PHR V ˌ**mull sth↔ˈover** to spend time thinking carefully about a plan or proposal SYN **consider**: *I need some time to mull it over before making a decision.*

mul·lah /ˈmʌlə; ˈmʊlə/ *noun* a Muslim teacher of religion and holy law

mulled /mʌld/ *adj.* [only before noun] **mulled** wine has been mixed with sugar and spices and heated

mul·let /ˈmʌlɪt/ *noun* **1** (*pl.* **mul·let**) [C, U] a sea fish that is used for food. The two main types are **red mullet** and **grey mullet**. **2** [C] (*informal*) a HAIRSTYLE for men in which the hair is short at the front and sides and long at the back

mul·li·ga·tawny /ˌmʌlɪɡəˈtɔːni/ *noun* [U] a hot spicy soup, originally from India ORIGIN From a Tamil word meaning 'pepper water'.

mul·lion /ˈmʌliən/ *noun* (*architecture*) a solid vertical piece of stone, wood or metal between two parts of a window ▸ **mul·lioned** /ˈmʌliənd/ *adj.* [only before noun]: *mullioned windows*

multi- /ˈmʌlti/ *combining form* (in nouns and adjectives) more than one; many: *multicoloured* ◇ *a multimillionaire* ◇ *a multimillion-dollar business* ◇ *a multi-ethnic society*

ˌ**multi-ˈaccess** *adj.* (*computing*) allowing several people to use the same system at the same time

multi·buy /ˈmʌltibaɪ/ *adj.* (*BrE*) used for describing items in a shop/store that are cheaper if you buy several of them: *Click here to see some of our multibuy offers.* ▸ **multi·buy** *noun*

multi·cast /ˈmʌltikɑːst; *NAmE* -kæst/ *verb* **~ sth** (*technical*) to send data across a computer network to several users at the same time ▸ **multi·cast** *noun* [U, C]

multi·chan·nel /ˈmʌltitʃænl/ *adj.* having or using many different television or communication channels

multi·col·oured (*especially US* **multi·col·ored**) /ˌmʌltiˈkʌləd; *NAmE* -ˈkʌlərd/ (*BrE* also **multi·col·our**) (*US* also **multi·col·or**) *adj.* consisting of or decorated with many colours, especially bright ones: *a multicoloured dress*

multi·cul·tural /ˌmʌltiˈkʌltʃərəl/ *adj.* for or including people of several different races, religions, languages and traditions: *We live in a multicultural society.* ◇ *a multicultural approach to education* ⊃ COLLOCATIONS at RACE

multi·cul·tural·ism /ˌmʌltiˌkʌltʃərəlɪzəm/ *noun* [U] the practice of giving importance to all cultures in a society ⊃ COLLOCATIONS at RACE

multi·di·men·sion·al AW /ˌmʌltidaɪˈmenʃənl; -dɪ-/ *adj.* having several DIMENSIONS (= measurements in space): *multidimensional space*

multi·dis·cip·lin·ary /ˌmʌltidɪsəˈplɪnəri; *NAmE* -ˈdɪsəpləneri/ *adj.* involving several different subjects of study: *a multidisciplinary course*

multi·fa·cet·ed /ˌmʌltiˈfæsɪtɪd/ *adj.* (*formal*) having many different aspects to be considered: *a complex and multifaceted problem*

multi·fari·ous /ˌmʌltɪˈfeəriəs; *NAmE* -ˈfer-/ *adj.* (*formal*) of many different kinds; having great variety: *the multifarious life forms in the coral reef* ◇ *a vast and multifarious organization*

multi·func·tion·al /ˌmʌltiˈfʌŋkʃənl/ *adj.* having several different functions: *a multifunctional device*

multi·grain /ˈmʌltiɡreɪn/ *adj.* containing several different types of grain: *multigrain bread*

multi·gym /ˈmʌltidʒɪm/ (*BrE*) *noun* a piece of equipment which can be used to exercise different parts of the body

multi·lat·eral /ˌmʌltiˈlætərəl/ *adj.* **1** in which three or more groups, nations, etc. take part: *multilateral negotiations* **2** having many sides or parts ⊃ compare BILATERAL, TRILATERAL, UNILATERAL

multi·lat·eral·ism /ˌmʌltiˈlætərəlɪzəm/ *noun* [U] (*politics*) the policy of trying to make multilateral agreements in order to achieve nuclear DISARMAMENT

multi·lin·gual /ˌmʌltiˈlɪŋɡwəl/ *adj.* **1** speaking or using several different languages: ***multilingual translators/communities/societies*** ◇ *a multilingual classroom* **2** written or printed in several different languages: *a multilingual phrase book* ⊃ compare BILINGUAL, MONOLINGUAL

multi·media /ˌmʌltiˈmiːdiə/ *adj.* [only before noun] **1** (in computing) using sound, pictures and film in addition to text on a screen: ***multimedia systems/products*** ◇ *the multimedia industry* (= producing CD-ROMs etc.) **2** (in teaching and art) using several different ways of giving information or several different materials: *a multimedia approach to learning* ▸ **multi·media** *noun* [U]: *the use of multimedia in museums*

multi·mill·ion·aire /ˌmʌltimɪljəˈneə(r); *NAmE* -ˈner/ *noun* a person who has money and possessions worth several million pounds, dollars, etc.

multi·nation·al /ˌmʌltiˈnæʃnəl/ *adj., noun*

■ ***adj.*** existing in or involving many countries: ***multinational companies/corporations*** ◇ *A multinational force is being sent to the trouble spot.*

■ ***noun*** a company that operates in several different countries, especially a large and powerful company

M

multi·party /ˌmʌltiˈpɑːti; *NAmE* -ˈpɑːrti/ *adj.* [only before noun] involving several different political parties

mul·tiple /ˈmʌltɪpl/ *adj., noun*

■ ***adj.*** [only before noun] many in number; involving many different people or things: *multiple copies of documents* ◇ *a multiple entry visa* ◇ *to suffer multiple injuries* (= in many different places in the body) ◇ *a multiple birth* (= several babies born to a mother at one time) ◇ *a multiple pile-up* (= a crash involving many vehicles) ◇ *a house in **multiple ownership/occupancy*** (= owned/occupied by several different people or families)

■ ***noun* 1** (*mathematics*) a quantity that contains another quantity an exact number of times: *14, 21 and 28 are all multiples of 7.* ◇ *18 is the lowest **common multiple** of 6 and 9.* ◇ *Traveller's cheques are available in multiples of €10* (= to the value of €10, €20, €30, etc.). **2** (also ˌ**multiple ˈstore**) (both *BrE*) = CHAIN STORE

ˌ**multiple-ˈchoice** *adj.* (of questions) showing several possible answers from which you must choose the correct one

ˌ**multiple-persoˈnality disorder** (also *less frequent* ˌ**split-persoˈnality disorder**) *noun* (*psychology*) a rare condition in which a person seems to have one or more different personalities

ˌ**multiple scleˈrosis** *noun* [U] (*abbr.* MS) a disease of the nervous system that gets worse over a period of time with loss of feeling and loss of control of movement and speech

multi·plex /ˈmʌltɪpleks/ (*BrE* also ˌ**multiplex ˈcinema**) *noun* a large cinema/movie theater with several separate rooms with screens

multi·pli·ca·tion /ˌmʌltɪplɪˈkeɪʃn/ *noun* [U] the act or process of multiplying: *the multiplication sign* (×) ◇ *Multiplication of cells leads to rapid growth of the organism.* ➲ compare DIVISION

ˌ**multipliˈcation table** (also **table**) *noun* a list showing the results when a number is multiplied by a set of other numbers, especially 1 to 12, in turn

multi·pli·city /ˌmʌltɪˈplɪsəti/ *noun* [sing., U] (*formal*) a great number and variety of sth: *This situation can be influenced by a multiplicity of different factors.*

multi·plier /ˈmʌltɪplaɪə(r)/ *noun* (*mathematics*) a number by which another number is multiplied

multi·ply 0‑ᴡ /ˈmʌltɪplaɪ/ *verb* (**multi·plies, multi·ply·ing, multi·plied, multi·plied**)
1 0‑ᴡ [I, T] to add a number to itself a particular number of times: *The children are already learning to multiply and divide.* ◇ **~ A by B** *2 multiplied by 4 is/equals/makes 8* (2 × 4 = 8) ◇ **~ A and B** (**together**) *Multiply 2 and 6 together and you get 12.* **2** 0‑ᴡ [I, T] to increase or make sth increase very much in number or amount: *Our problems have multiplied since last year.* ◇ **~ sth** *Cigarette smoking multiplies the risk of cancer.* **3** [I, T] (*biology*) to reproduce in large numbers; to make sth do this: *Rabbits multiply rapidly.* ◇ **~ sth** *It is possible to multiply these bacteria in the laboratory.*

multi·pro·ces·sor /ˌmʌltiˈprəʊsesə(r); *NAmE* -ˈprɑːs-; -ˈproʊ-/ *noun* a computer with more than one CENTRAL PROCESSING UNIT

ˌ**multi-ˈpurpose** *adj.* able to be used for several different purposes: *a **multi-purpose tool/machine*** ➲ see also MPV

multi·racial /ˌmʌltiˈreɪʃl/ *adj.* including or involving several different races of people: *a multiracial society*

ˌ**multi-ˈskilling** *noun* [U] (*business*) the fact of a person being trained in several different jobs which require different skills

ˌ**multi-storey ˈcar park** (also ˌ**multi-ˈstorey**) (both *BrE*) (*NAmE* ˈ**parking garage**) *noun* a large building with several floors for parking cars in

multi·task /ˌmʌltiˈtɑːsk; *NAmE* -ˈtæsk/ *verb* **1** [I] (of a computer) to operate several programs at the same time **2** [I] to do several things at the same time: *Women seem to be able to multitask better than men.*

multi·tasking /ˌmʌltiˈtɑːskɪŋ; *NAmE* -ˈtæsk-/ *noun* [U] **1** (*computing*) the ability of a computer to operate several programs at the same time **2** the ability to do several things at the same time

multi·track /ˈmʌltitræk/ *adj.* (*technical*) relating to the mixing of several different pieces of music

multi·tude /ˈmʌltɪtjuːd; *NAmE* -tuːd/ *noun* (*formal*) **1** [C] **~** (**of sth/sb**) an extremely large number of things or people: *a multitude of possibilities* ◇ *a multitude of birds* ◇ *These elements can be combined in a multitude of different ways.* ◇ *The region attracts tourists in their multitudes.* **2 the multitude** [sing.+ sing./pl. v.] (also **the multitudes** [pl.]) (sometimes *disapproving*) the mass of ordinary people: *It was an elite that believed its task was to enlighten the multitude.* ◇ *to feed the starving multitudes* **3** [C] (*literary*) a large crowd of people SYN **throng**: *He preached to the assembled multitude.*

IDM **cover/hide a multitude of sins** (often *humorous*) to hide the real situation or facts when these are not good or pleasant

multi·tu·di·nous /ˌmʌltɪˈtjuːdɪnəs; *NAmE* -ˈtuːdɪnəs/ *adj.* (*formal*) extremely large in number

ˌ**multi-ˈuser** *adj.* (*computing*) able to be used by more than one person at the same time: *a multi-user software licence*

multi·vita·min /ˌmʌltiˈvɪtəmɪn; *NAmE* -ˈvaɪt-/ *noun* a pill or medicine containing several VITAMINS

ˌ**multi-ˈword** *adj.* [only before noun] (*linguistics*) consisting of more than one word: *multi-word units such as 'fall in love'*

mum 0‑ᴡ /mʌm/ *noun, adj.*

■ ***noun*** 0‑ᴡ (*BrE*) (*NAmE* **mom**) (*informal*) a mother: *My mum says I can't go.* ◇ *Happy Birthday, Mum.* ◇ *A lot of **mums and dads** have the same worries.*

■ ***adj.***

IDM **keep mum** (*informal*) to say nothing about sth; to stay quiet: *He kept mum about what he'd seen.* ˌ**mum's the ˈword!** (*informal*) used to tell sb to say nothing about sth and keep it secret

mum·ble /ˈmʌmbl/ *verb, noun*

■ ***verb*** [I, T] to speak or say sth in a quiet voice in a way that is not clear SYN **mutter**: **~** (**to sb/yourself**) *I could hear him mumbling to himself.* ◇ **~ sth** (**to sb/yourself**) *She mumbled an apology and left.* ◇ **+ speech** *'Sorry,' she mumbled.* ◇ **~ that...** *She mumbled that she was sorry.*

■ ***noun*** [usually sing.] (also **mum·bling** [C, usually pl., U]) speech or words that are spoken in a quiet voice in a way that is not clear: *He spoke in a low mumble, as if to himself.* ◇ *They tried to make sense of her mumblings.*

mumbo jumbo /ˌmʌmbəʊ ˈdʒʌmbəʊ; *NAmE* ˌmʌmboʊ ˈdʒʌmboʊ/ *noun* [U] (*informal, disapproving*) language or a ceremony that seems complicated and important but is actually without real sense or meaning; nonsense

mum·mer /ˈmʌmə(r)/ *noun* an actor in an old form of drama without words

mum·mify /ˈmʌmɪfaɪ/ *verb* (**mum·mi·fies, mum·mi·fy·ing, mum·mi·fied, mum·mi·fied**) [usually passive] **~ sth** to preserve a dead body by treating it with special oils and wrapping it in cloth SYN **embalm**

mummy /ˈmʌmi/ *noun* (*pl.* **-ies**) **1** (*BrE*) (*NAmE* **mommy, momma**) (*informal*) a child's word for a mother: *'I want my mummy!' he wailed.* ◇ *It hurts, Mummy!* ◇ *Mummy and Daddy will be back soon.* **2** a body of a human or an animal that has been mummified: *an Egyptian mummy*

ˈ**mummy's boy** (*BrE*) (*NAmE* ˈ**mama's boy**) *noun* (*disapproving*) a boy or man who depends too much on his mother

mumps /mʌmps/ *noun* [U] a disease, especially of children, that causes painful swellings in the neck

mumsy /ˈmʌmzi/ *adj.* (*BrE, informal*) having a comfortable, but dull and old-fashioned appearance: *a mumsy dress*

munch /mʌntʃ/ *verb* [I, T] to eat sth steadily and often noisily, especially sth crisp SYN **chomp**: **~ on/at sth** *She* *munched on an apple.* ◇ **~ sth** *He sat in a chair munching his toast.* ◇ *I* ***munched my way through*** *a huge bowl of cereal.*

Munch·ausen's syn·drome /ˈmʊntʃaʊzənz sɪndrəʊm; *NAmE* -droʊm/ *noun* [U] a mental condition in which sb keeps pretending that they are ill/sick in order to receive hospital treatment

munch·ies /ˈmʌntʃɪz/ *noun* [pl.] (*informal*) small pieces of food for eating with drinks at a party
IDM **have the ˈmunchies** (*informal*) to feel hungry

mun·dane /mʌnˈdeɪn/ *adj.* (often *disapproving*) not interesting or exciting SYN **dull, ordinary**: *a* ***mundane task/job*** ◇ *I lead a pretty mundane existence.* ◇ *On a more mundane level, can we talk about the timetable for next week?*

mung /mʌŋ; muːŋ/ (also **moong**) *noun* **1** (also **ˈmung bean**) a small round green BEAN **2** the tropical plant that produces these beans

mu·ni·ci·pal /mjuːˈnɪsɪpl/ *adj.* [usually before noun] connected with or belonging to a town, city or district that has its own local government: ***municipal elections/councils*** ◇ *municipal workers* ◇ *the Los Angeles Municipal Art Gallery*

mu·ni·ci·pal·ity /mjuːˌnɪsɪˈpæləti/ *noun* (*pl.* -ies) (*formal*) a town, city or district with its own local government; the group of officials who govern it

mu·nifi·cent /mjuːˈnɪfɪsnt/ *adj.* (*formal*) extremely generous: *a* ***munificent patron/gift/gesture*** ▶ **mu·nifi·cence** /-sns/ *noun* [U]

mu·ni·tions /mjuːˈnɪʃnz/ *noun* [pl.] military weapons, AMMUNITION and equipment: *a shortage of munitions* ◇ *a munitions factory* ▶ **mu·ni·tion** *adj.* [only before noun]: *a munition store*

munt·jac (also **munt·jak**) /ˈmʌntdʒæk/ *noun* a type of small DEER, originally from SE Asia

mup·pet /ˈmʌpɪt/ *noun* (*BrE, informal*) a stupid person

mural /ˈmjʊərəl; *NAmE* ˈmjʊrəl/ *noun* a painting, usually a large one, done on a wall, sometimes on an outside wall of a building ▶ **mural** *adj.*: *mural paintings*

mur·der 🔑 /ˈmɜːdə(r); *NAmE* ˈmɜːrd-/ *noun, verb*
■ ***noun*** **1** 🔑 [U, C] the crime of killing sb deliberately SYN **homicide**: *He was found guilty of murder.* ◇ *She has been charged with the* ***attempted murder*** *of her husband.* ◇ *to* ***commit*** *(****a****)* ***murder*** ◇ *a* ***murder case/investigation/trial*** ◇ *The rebels were responsible for the* ***mass murder*** *of 400 civilians.* ◇ *What was the* ***murder weapon?*** ◇ *The play is a* ***murder mystery.*** ➲ COLLOCATIONS at CRIME ➲ compare MANSLAUGHTER **2** [U] (*informal*) used to describe sth that is difficult or unpleasant: *It's murder trying to get to the airport at this time of day.* ◇ *It was murder* (= very busy and unpleasant) *in the office today.*
IDM **get away with ˈmurder** (*informal*, often *humorous*) to do whatever you want without being stopped or punished ➲ more at SCREAM *v.*
■ ***verb*** **1** 🔑 **~ sb** to kill sb deliberately and illegally: *He denies murdering his wife's lover.* ◇ *The murdered woman was well known in the area.* **2 ~ sth** to spoil sth because you do not do it very well SYN **butcher**: *Critics accused him of murdering the English language* (= writing or speaking it very badly). **3 ~ sb** (*BrE, informal*) to defeat sb completely, especially in a team sport SYN **thrash**
IDM **I could murder a...** (*informal, especially BrE*) used to say that you very much want to eat or drink sth: *I could murder a beer.* **sb will ˈmurder you** (*informal*) used to warn sb that another person will be very angry with them

mur·der·er /ˈmɜːdərə(r); *NAmE* ˈmɜːrd-/ *noun* a person who has killed sb deliberately and illegally SYN **killer**: *a convicted murderer* ◇ *a mass murderer* (= who has killed a lot of people)

mur·der·ess /ˈmɜːdəres; *NAmE* ˈmɜːrd-/ *noun* (*old-fashioned*) a woman who has killed sb deliberately and illegally; a female murderer

mur·der·ous /ˈmɜːdərəs; *NAmE* ˈmɜːrd-/ *adj.* intending or likely to murder SYN **savage**: *a* ***murderous villain/tyrant*** ◇ *a murderous attack* ◇ *She gave him* ***a murderous look*** (= a very angry one). ▶ **mur·der·ous·ly** *adv.*

murk /mɜːk; *NAmE* mɜːrk/ *noun* (usually **the murk**) [U] DARKNESS caused by smoke, FOG, etc. SYN **gloom**

murky /ˈmɜːki; *NAmE* ˈmɜːrki/ *adj.* (**murk·ier, murki·est**) **1** (of a liquid) not clear; dark or dirty with mud or another substance SYN **cloudy**: *She gazed into the murky depths of the water.* **2** (of air, light, etc.) dark and unpleasant because of smoke, FOG, etc: *a murky night* **3** (*disapproving* or *humorous*) (of people's actions or character) not clearly known and suspected of not being honest: *He had a somewhat murky past.* ◇ *the murky world of arms dealing*

mur·mur /ˈmɜːmə(r); *NAmE* ˈmɜːrm-/ *verb, noun*
■ ***verb*** **1** [T, I] **~ (sth)** | **+ speech** | **~ that...** to say sth in a soft quiet voice that is difficult to hear or understand: *She murmured her agreement.* ◇ *He murmured something in his sleep.* ◇ *She was murmuring in his ear.* **2** [I] to make a quiet continuous sound: *The wind murmured in the trees.* **3** [I] **~ (against sb/sth)** (*literary*) to complain about sb/sth, but not openly
■ ***noun*** **1** [C] a quietly spoken word or words: *She answered in a faint murmur.* ◇ *Murmurs of 'Praise God' went around the circle.* **2** [C] (also **mur·mur·ings** [pl.]) a quiet expression of feeling: *a* ***murmur of agreement/approval/complaint*** ◇ *He paid the extra cost* ***without a murmur*** (= without complaining at all). ◇ *polite murmurings of gratitude* **3** (also **mur·mur·ing**) [sing.] a low continuous sound in the background: *the distant murmur of traffic* **4** [C] (*medical*) a faint sound in the chest, usually a sign of damage or disease in the heart: *a heart murmur*

Murphy's Law /ˌmɜːfiz ˈlɔː; *NAmE* ˌmɜːrfiz/ *noun* (*humorous*) a statement of the fact that, if anything can possibly go wrong, it will go wrong

mur·ram /ˈmʌrəm/ *noun* [U] a type of reddish soil that is often used to make roads in Africa

Mus·ca·det /ˈmʌskədeɪ; ˈmʊsk-/ *noun* [U, C] a type of dry white French wine

mus·cat /ˈmʌskæt/ *noun* [U, C] **1** a type of wine, especially a strong sweet white wine **2** a type of GRAPE which can be eaten or used to make wine or RAISINS

mus·ca·tel /ˌmʌskəˈtel/ (also **mus·ca·delle, mus·ca·del** /-ˈdel/) *noun* [U, C] a type of GRAPE used in sweet white wines and for drying to make RAISINS

muscle 🔑 /ˈmʌsl/ *noun, verb*
■ ***noun*** **1** 🔑 [C, U] a piece of body TISSUE that you contract and relax in order to move a particular part of the body; the TISSUE that forms the muscles of the body: *a* ***calf/neck/thigh muscle*** ◇ *to* ***pull/tear/strain a muscle*** ◇ *This exercise will work the muscles of the lower back.* ◇ *He* ***didn't move a muscle*** (= stood completely still). ➲ COLLOCATIONS at INJURY **2** [U] physical strength: *He's an intelligent player but lacks the muscle of older competitors.* **3** [U] the power and influence to make others do what you want: *to exercise* ***political/industrial/financial muscle*** ▶ **muscled** *adj.*: *heavily muscled shoulders* IDM see FLEX *v.*
■ ***verb***
PHR V **ˌmuscle ˈin (on sb/sth)** (*informal, disapproving*) to involve yourself in a situation when you have no right to do so, in order to get sth for yourself

ˈmuscle-bound *adj.* having large stiff muscles as a result of too much exercise

muscle·man /ˈmʌslmæn/ *noun* (*pl.* -men /-men/) a big strong man, especially one employed to protect sb/sth

mus·cu·lar /ˈmʌskjələ(r)/ *adj.* **1** connected with the muscles: ***muscular tension/power/tissue*** **2** (also *informal* **muscly** /ˈmʌsli/) having large strong muscles: ***a muscular body/build/chest*** ◇ *He was tall, lean and muscular.*

muscular dystrophy /ˌmʌskjələ ˈdɪstrəfi; *NAmE* -lər/ *noun* [U] a medical condition that some people are born with in which the muscles gradually become weaker

mus·cu·lat·ure /ˈmʌskjələtʃə(r)/ *noun* [U, sing.] (*biology*) the system of muscles in the body or part of the body

muse /mjuːz/ *noun, verb*
■ ***noun*** **1** a person or spirit that gives a writer, painter, etc. ideas and the desire to create things SYN **inspiration**: *He felt that his muse had deserted him* (= that he could no longer write, paint, etc.). **2 Muse** (in ancient Greek and

Roman stories) one of the nine GODDESSES who encouraged poetry, music and other branches of art and literature
- *verb* (*formal*) **1** [I] ~ (**about/on/over/upon sth**) to think carefully about sth for a time, ignoring what is happening around you SYN **ponder**: *I sat quietly, musing on the events of the day.* ➲ see also MUSING **2** [T] + **speech** | ~ **that...** to say sth to yourself in a way that shows you are thinking carefully about it: *'I wonder why?' she mused.*

mu·seum 0‑m /mjuˈziːəm/ *noun* a building in which objects of artistic, cultural, historical or scientific interest are kept and shown to the public: *a museum of modern art* ◇ *a science museum* ➲ VISUAL VOCAB page V2

muˈseum piece *noun* **1** an object that is of enough historical or artistic value to have in a museum **2** (*humorous*) a thing or person that is old-fashioned, or old and no longer useful

mush /mʌʃ/ *noun* **1** [U, sing.] (usually *disapproving*) a soft thick mass or mixture: *The vegetables had turned to mush.* ◇ *His insides suddenly felt like mush.* **2** [U] (*NAmE*) a type of thick PORRIDGE made from CORN (MAIZE)

musher /ˈmʌʃə(r)/ *noun* (*NAmE*) a person who drives a dog SLED

mush·room /ˈmʌʃrʊm; -ruːm/ *noun, verb*
- *noun* a FUNGUS with a round flat head and short STEM. Many mushrooms can be eaten: *a field mushroom* (= the most common type that is eaten, often just called a 'mushroom', and often grown to be sold) ◇ *fried mushrooms* ◇ *cream of mushroom soup* ➲ VISUAL VOCAB page V27 ➲ see also BUTTON MUSHROOM, TOADSTOOL
- *verb* **1** [I] to rapidly grow or increase in number: *We expect the market to mushroom in the next two years.* **2** (usually **go mushrooming**) [I] to gather mushrooms in a field or wood

ˈmushroom cloud *noun* a large cloud, shaped like a mushroom, that forms in the air after a nuclear explosion

mushy /ˈmʌʃi/ *adj.* (**mush·ier**, **mushi·est**) **1** soft and thick, like mush: *Cook until the fruit is soft but not mushy.* **2** (*informal, disapproving*) too emotional in a way that is embarrassing SYN **sentimental**: *mushy romantic novels*

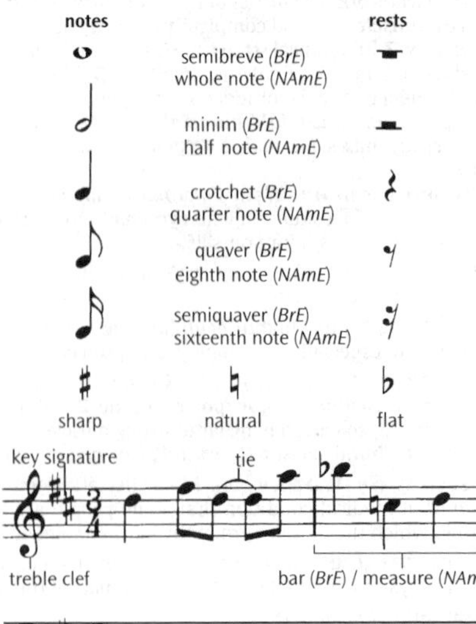

ˌmushy ˈpeas *noun* [pl.] (*BrE*) cooked PEAS that are made into a soft mixture

music 0‑m /ˈmjuːzɪk/ *noun* [U]
1 0‑m sounds that are arranged in a way that is pleasant or exciting to listen to. People sing music or play it on instruments: ***pop/dance/classical/church music*** ◇ *to listen to music* ◇ *She could hear music playing somewhere.* ◇ *It was a charming* ***piece of music.*** ◇ *the popularity of Mozart's music* ◇ *He wrote the music but I don't know who wrote the words.* ◇ *The poem has been* ***set to music.*** ◇ *Every week they get together to* ***make music*** (= to play music or sing). ➲ see also CHAMBER MUSIC, COUNTRY MUSIC, ROCK MUSIC, SOUL MUSIC **2** 0‑m the art of writing or playing music: *to study music* ◇ *a career in music* ◇ *music lessons* ◇ *the* ***music business/industry*** **3** 0‑m the written or printed signs that represent the sounds to be played or sung in a piece of music: *Can you* ***read music*** (= understand the signs in order to play or sing a piece of music)? ◇ *I had to play it without the music.* ◇ *The music was still open on the piano* (= the paper or book with the musical notes on it). ➲ see also SHEET MUSIC

IDM **music to your ˈears** news or information that you are very pleased to hear ➲ more at FACE *v.*

Collocations

Music

Listening
- **listen to/enjoy/love/be into** music/classical music/jazz/pop/hip-hop, etc.
- **listen to** the radio/an MP3 player/a CD
- **put on/play** a CD/a song/some music
- **turn down/up** the music/radio/volume/bass
- **go to** a concert/festival/gig/performance/recital
- **copy/burn/rip** music/a CD/a DVD
- **download** music/an album/a song/a demo/a video

Playing
- **play** a musical instrument/the piano/percussion/a note/a riff/the melody/a concerto/a duet/by ear
- **sing** an anthem/a ballad/a solo/an aria/the blues/in a choir/soprano/alto/tenor/bass/out of tune
- **hum** a tune/a theme tune/a lullaby
- **accompany** a singer/choir
- **strum** a chord/guitar

Performing
- **form/start/get together/join/quit/leave** a band
- **give** a performance/concert/recital
- **do** a concert/recital/gig
- **play** a concert/gig/festival/venue
- **perform** (*BrE*) at/in a concert/(*especially NAmE*) a concert
- **appear** at a festival/live
- **go on/embark on** a (world) tour

Recording
- **write/compose** music/a ballad/a melody/a tune/a song/a theme song/an opera/a symphony
- **land/get/sign** a record deal
- **be signed to/be dropped by** a record company
- **record/release/put out** an album/a single/a CD
- **be top of/top** the charts
- **get to/go straight to/go straight in at/enter the charts** at number one

mu·sic·al 0‑m /ˈmjuːzɪkl/ *adj., noun*
- *adj.* **1** 0‑m [only before noun] connected with music; containing music: *the musical director of the show* ◇ ***musical talent/ability/skill*** ◇ ***musical styles/tastes*** ◇ *a* ***musical production/entertainment*** **2** 0‑m (of a person) with a natural skill or interest in music: *She's very musical.* OPP **unmusical** **3** (of a sound) pleasant to listen to, like music: *a musical voice* OPP **unmusical**

■ ***noun*** (also *old-fashioned* ˌ**musical ˈcomedy**) a play or a film/movie in which part or all of the story is told using songs and often dancing

ˈ**musical box** *noun* (*especially BrE*) = MUSIC BOX

ˌ**musical ˈchairs** *noun* [U] **1** a children's game in which players run round a row of chairs while music is playing. Each time the music stops, players try to sit down on one of the chairs, but there are always more players than chairs. **2** (*often disapproving*) a situation in which people frequently exchange jobs or positions

ˌ**musical diˈrector** *noun* the person who is in charge of the music in a show in the theatre

ˌ**musical ˈinstrument** (also **in·stru·ment**) *noun* an object used for producing musical sounds, for example a piano or a drum: *Most pupils learn (to play) a musical instrument.* ◇ *the instruments of the orchestra* ➲ VISUAL VOCAB pages V30, V31

mu·sic·al·ity /ˌmjuːzɪˈkæləti/ *noun* [U] (*formal*) skill and understanding in performing music

music·al·ly /ˈmjuːzɪkli/ *adv.* **1** in a way that is connected with music: *musically gifted* ◇ *Musically speaking, their latest album is nothing special.* **2** with musical skill: *He plays really musically.* **3** in a way that is pleasant to listen to, like music: *to **laugh/speak musically***

ˈ**music box** (also ˈ**musical box** especially in *BrE*) *noun* a box containing a device that plays a tune when the box is opened

ˈ**music hall** *noun* (*BrE*) **1** (also **vaude·ville** *NAmE, BrE*) [U] a type of entertainment popular in the late 19th and early 20th centuries, including singing, dancing and comedy **2** (*NAmE* ˈ**vaudeville theater**) [C] a theatre used for popular entertainment in the late 19th and early 20th centuries

mu·si·cian 🔑 /mjuˈzɪʃn/ *noun* a person who plays a musical instrument or writes music, especially as a job: *a **jazz/rock musician***

mu·si·cian·ship /mjuˈzɪʃnʃɪp/ *noun* [U] skill in performing or writing music

mu·sic·ology /ˌmjuːzɪˈkɒlədʒi; *NAmE* -ˈkɑːl-/ *noun* [U] the study of the history and theory of music ▸ **mu·sic·olo·gist** /ˌmjuːzɪˈkɒlədʒɪst; *NAmE* -ˈkɑːl-/ *noun*

ˈ**music stand** *noun* a frame, especially one that you can fold, that is used for holding sheets of music while you play a musical instrument

ˈ**music video** *noun* = VIDEO (4)

mus·ing /ˈmjuːzɪŋ/ *noun* [U, C, usually pl.] a period of thinking carefully about sth or telling people your thoughts about it: *We had to sit and listen to his musings on life.*

musk /mʌsk/ *noun* [U] a substance with a strong smell that is used in making some PERFUMES. It is produced naturally by a type of male DEER. ▸ **musky** *adj.*: *a musky perfume* (= smelling of or like musk)

mus·ket /ˈmʌskɪt/ *noun* an early type of long gun that was used by soldiers in the past

mus·ket·eer /ˌmʌskəˈtɪə(r); *NAmE* -ˈtɪr/ *noun* a soldier who uses a musket

ˈ**musk ox** *noun* a large animal of the cow family that is covered with hair and has curved horns.

musk·rat /ˈmʌskræt/ *noun* a N American water animal that has a strong smell and is hunted for its fur

Mus·lim /ˈmʊzlɪm; ˈmʌz-; -ləm/ *noun* a person whose religion is Islam ▸ **Mus·lim** *adj.* ➲ see also MOSLEM

mus·lin /ˈmʌzlɪn/ *noun* [U] a type of fine cotton cloth that is almost transparent, used, especially in the past, for making clothes and curtains

muso /ˈmjuːzəʊ; *NAmE* -zoʊ/ *noun* (*pl.* **-os**) (*BrE, informal*) a person who plays, or is very interested in, music and knows a lot about it

mus·quash /ˈmʌskwɒʃ; *NAmE* -skwɑːʃ; -skwɔːʃ/ *noun* [U] the fur of the MUSKRAT

muss /mʌs/ *verb* **~ sth (up)** (*NAmE*) to make sb's clothes or hair untidy: *Hey, don't muss up my hair!*

mus·sel /ˈmʌsl/ *noun* a small SHELLFISH that can be eaten, with a black shell in two parts ➲ picture at SHELLFISH

Grammar Point

must / have (got) to / must not / don't have to

Necessity and Obligation

- **Must** and **have (got) to** are used in the present to say that something is necessary or should be done. **Have to** is more common in *NAmE*, especially in speech: *You must be home by 11 o'clock.* ◇ *I must wash the car tomorrow.* ◇ *I have to collect the children from school at 3 o'clock.* ◇ *Nurses have to wear a uniform.*
- In *BrE* there is a difference between them. **Must** is used to talk about what the speaker or listener wants, and **have (got) to** about rules, laws and other people's wishes: *I must finish this essay today. I'm going out tomorrow.* ◇ *I have to finish this essay today. We have to hand them in tomorrow.*
- There are no past or future forms of **must**. To talk about the past you use **had to** and **has had to**: *I had to wait half an hour for a bus.* **Will have to** is used to talk about the future, or **have to** if an arrangement has already been made: *We'll have to borrow the money we need.* ◇ *I have to go to the dentist tomorrow.*
- Questions with **have to** are formed using **do**: *Do the children have to wear a uniform?* In negative sentences both **must not** and **don't have to** are used, but with different meanings. **Must not** is used to tell somebody not to do something: *Passengers must not smoke until the signs have been switched off.* The short form **mustn't** is used especially in *BrE*: *You mustn't leave the gate open.* **Don't have to** is used when it is not necessary to do something: *You don't have to pay for the tickets in advance.* ◇ *She doesn't have to work at weekends.*

➲ note at NEED

Certainty

- Both **must** and **have to** are used to say that you are certain about something. **Have to** is the usual verb used in *NAmE* and this is becoming more frequent in *BrE* in this meaning: *He has (got) to be the worst actor on TV!* ◇ (*BrE*) *This must be the most boring party I've ever been to.* If you are talking about the past, use **must have**: *Your trip must have been fun!*

must 🔑 *modal verb, noun*

■ ***modal verb***

■ /məst; *strong form* mʌst/ (*negative* **must not**, *short form* **mustn't** /ˈmʌsnt/) **1** 🔑 used to say that sth is necessary or very important (sometimes involving a rule or a law): *All visitors must report to reception.* ◇ *Cars must not park in front of the entrance* (= it is not allowed). ◇ (*formal*) *I must ask you not to do that again.* ◇ *You mustn't say things like that.* ◇ *I must go to the bank and get some money.* ◇ ***I must admit*** (= I feel that I should admit) *I was surprised it cost so little.* ◇ (*especially BrE*) *Must you always question everything I say?* (= it is annoying) ◇ *'Do we have to finish this today?' 'Yes, you must.'* HELP Note that the negative for the last example is: *'No, you don't have to.'* **2** 🔑 used to say that sth is likely or logical: *You must be hungry after all that walking.* ◇ *He must have known* (= surely he knew) *what she wanted.* ◇ *I'm sorry, she's not here. She must have left already* (= that must be the explanation). **3** 🔑 (*especially BrE*) used to recommend that sb does sth because you think it is a good idea: *You simply must read this book.* ◇ *We must get together soon for lunch.* ➲ note at MODAL

IDM **if you ˈmust (do sth)** used to say that sb may do sth but you do not really want them to: *'Can I smoke?' 'If you*

M

must.' ◇ *It's from my boyfriend,* ***if you must know.*** **must-see/must-read/must-have, etc.** used to tell people that sth is so good or interesting that they should see, read, get it, etc.: *Sydney is one of the world's must-see cities.* ◇ *The magazine is a must-read in the show business world.* ➲ more at NEED *n.*

■ ***noun*** /mʌst/ [usually sing.] (*informal*) something that you must do, see, buy, etc: *His new novel is a must for all lovers of crime fiction.*

mus·tache (*NAmE*) (*BrE* **mous·tache**) /məˈstɑːʃ/ *noun* **1** a line of hair that a man allows to grow on his upper lip ➲ VISUAL VOCAB page V49 **2 mustaches** [pl.] a very long mustache ➲ compare BEARD

mus·tached (*NAmE*) (*BrE* **mous·tached**) /məˈstɑːʃt/ *adj.* [usually before noun] having a mustache ➲ compare MUSTACHIOED

mus·tachi·oed (also **mous·tachi·oed**) /məˈstæʃiəʊd; *NAmE* -ʃioʊd/ *adj.* (*literary*) having a large moustache with curls at the ends

mus·tang /ˈmʌstæŋ/ *noun* a small American wild horse

mus·tard /ˈmʌstəd; *NAmE* -tərd/ *noun* [U] **1** a thick cold yellow or brown sauce that tastes hot and spicy and is usually eaten with meat: *a jar of mustard* ◇ *mustard powder* ◇ ***French/English mustard*** **2** a small plant with yellow flowers, grown for its seeds that are crushed to make mustard **3** (*BrE*) the leaves of the mustard plant that are eaten raw in salads: *mustard and cress* (= leaves of white mustard grown with CRESS) **4** a brownish-yellow colour ▸ **mus·tard** *adj.*: *a mustard sweater*

IDM **(not) cut the ˈmustard** to (not) be as good as expected or required: *I didn't cut the mustard as a hockey player.* ➲ more at KEEN *adj.*

M

ˈmustard gas *noun* [U] a poisonous gas that burns the skin, used in chemical weapons, for example during the First World War

ˈmustard greens *noun* [pl.] the dark green leaves of a type of MUSTARD plant, that are cooked or eaten raw in salads, especially in the Southern US

mus·ter /ˈmʌstə(r)/ *verb, noun*

■ ***verb*** **1** [T] **~ sth (up)** to find as much support, courage, etc. as you can SYN **summon**: *We mustered what support we could for the plan.* ◇ *She left the room* ***with all the*** *dignity* ***she could muster.*** **2** [I, T] to come together, or bring people, especially soldiers, together for example for military action SYN **gather**: *The troops mustered.* ◇ **~ sb/sth** *to muster an army* **3** [T] **~ sth** (*AustralE, NZE*) to gather together sheep or cows

■ ***noun*** a group of people, especially soldiers, that have been brought together: ***muster stations*** (= parts of a building, a ship, etc. that people must go to if there is an emergency)

IDM see PASS *v.*

musty /ˈmʌsti/ *adj.* (**must·ier, musti·est**) smelling damp and unpleasant because of a lack of fresh air SYN **dank**: *a musty room*

mut·able /ˈmjuːtəbl/ *adj.* (*formal*) that can change; likely to change ▸ **mut·abil·ity** /ˌmjuːtəˈbɪləti/ *noun* [U]

mu·tant /ˈmjuːtənt/ *adj., noun*

■ ***adj.*** (*biology*) (of a living thing) different in some way from others of the same kind because of a change in its GENETIC structure: *a mutant gene*

■ ***noun*** **1** (*biology*) a living thing with qualities that are different from its parents' qualities because of a change in its GENETIC structure **2** (*informal*) (in stories about space, the future, etc.) a living thing with an unusual and frightening appearance because of a change in its GENETIC structure

mu·tate /mjuːˈteɪt; *NAmE* ˈmjuːteɪt/ *verb* **1** [I, T] to develop or make sth develop a new form or structure, because of a GENETIC change: **~ (into sth)** *the ability of the virus to mutate into new forms* ◇ **~ sth** *mutated genes* **2** [I] **~ (into sth)** to change into a new form: *Rhythm and blues mutated into rock and roll.* ➲ see also MUTATION

mu·ta·tion /mjuːˈteɪʃn/ *noun* **1** [U, C] (*biology*) a process in which the GENETIC material of a person, a plant or an animal changes in structure when it is passed on to children, etc, causing different physical characteristics to develop; a change of this kind: *cells affected by mutation* ◇ *genetic mutations* **2** [U, C] a change in the form or structure of sth: (*linguistics*) *vowel mutation*

mu·ta·tis mu·tan·dis /mjuːˌtɑːtɪs mjuːˈtændɪs; muː-/ *adv.* (from *Latin, formal*) (used when you are comparing two or more things or situations) making the small changes that are necessary for each individual case, without changing the main points: *The same contract, mutatis mutandis, will be given to each employee* (= the contract is basically the same for everybody, but the names, etc. are changed).

mute /mjuːt/ *adj., noun, verb*

■ ***adj.*** **1** not speaking SYN **silent**: *a look of mute appeal* ◇ *The child sat mute in the corner of the room.* **2** (*old-fashioned*) (of a person) unable to speak SYN **dumb**

■ ***noun*** **1** (*music*) a device made of metal, rubber or plastic that you use to make the sound of a musical instrument softer **2** (*old-fashioned*) a person who is not able to speak

■ ***verb*** **1 ~ sth** to make the sound of sth, especially a musical instrument, quieter or softer, sometimes using a mute: *He muted the strings with his palm.* **2 ~ sth** to make sth weaker or less severe SYN **tone down**: *She thought it better to mute her criticism.*

ˈmute button *noun* **1** a button on a telephone that you press in order to stop yourself from being heard by the person at the other end of the line (while you speak to sb else) **2** a button that you press in order to switch off a television's sound

muted /ˈmjuːtɪd/ *adj.* **1** (of sounds) quiet; not as loud as usual: *They spoke in muted voices.* **2** (of emotions, opinions, etc.) not strongly expressed: *The proposals received only a muted response.* **3** (of colours, light, etc.) not bright: *a dress in muted shades of blue* **4** (of musical instruments) used with a mute: *muted trumpets*

mute·ly /ˈmjuːtli/ *adv.* without speaking SYN **silently**

muti /ˈmuːti/ *noun* [U] (*SAfrE*) **1** African medicines or magic CHARMS that are prepared from plants, animals, etc. **2** any kind of medicine

mu·ti·late /ˈmjuːtɪleɪt/ *verb* **1 ~ sb/sth** to damage sb's body very severely, especially by cutting or tearing off part of it: *The body had been badly mutilated.* **2 ~ sth** to damage sth very badly SYN **vandalize**: *Intruders slashed and mutilated several paintings.* ▸ **mu·ti·la·tion** /ˌmjuːtɪˈleɪʃn/ *noun* [U, C]: *Thousands suffered death or mutilation in the bomb blast.*

mu·tin·eer /ˌmjuːtəˈnɪə(r); *NAmE* -ˈnɪr/ *noun* a person who takes part in a MUTINY

mu·tin·ous /ˈmjuːtənəs/ *adj.* **1** refusing to obey the orders of sb in authority; wanting to do this SYN **rebellious**: *mutinous workers* ◇ *a mutinous expression* **2** taking part in a mutiny ▸ **mu·tin·ous·ly** *adv.*

mu·tiny /ˈmjuːtəni/ *noun, verb*

■ ***noun*** (*pl.* **-ies**) [U, C] the act of refusing to obey the orders of sb in authority, especially by soldiers or sailors: *Discontent among the ship's crew finally led to the outbreak of mutiny.* ◇ *the famous movie 'Mutiny on the Bounty'* ◇ *We have a family mutiny on our hands!*

■ ***verb*** (**mu·tin·ies, mu·tiny·ing, mu·tin·ied, mu·tin·ied**) [I] (especially of soldiers or sailors) to refuse to obey the orders of sb in authority

mut·ism /ˈmjuːtɪzəm/ *noun* [U] (*medical*) a medical condition in which a person is unable to speak

mutt /mʌt/ *noun* (*informal, especially NAmE*) a dog, especially one that is not of a particular breed SYN **mongrel**

mut·ter /ˈmʌtə(r)/ *verb, noun*

■ ***verb*** **1** [T, I] to speak or say sth in a quiet voice that is difficult to hear, especially because you are annoyed about sth: **+ speech** *'How dare she,' he muttered under his breath.* ◇ **~ (sth) (to sb/yourself) (about sth)** *She just sat there muttering to herself.* ◇ *I muttered something about needing to get back to work.* ◇ **~ that...** *He muttered that he was sorry.* **2** [I, T] **~ (about sth)** | **~ that...** to complain about sth, without saying publicly what you think SYN **grumble**: *Workers continued to mutter about the management.*

▪ ***noun*** [usually sing.] a quiet sound or words that are difficult to hear: *the soft mutter of voices*

mut·ter·ing /ˈmʌtərɪŋ/ *noun* [U] **1** (also **mutterings** [pl.]) complaints that you express privately rather than openly: *There have been mutterings about his leadership.* **2** words that you speak very quietly to yourself

mut·ton /ˈmʌtn/ *noun* [U] meat from a fully grown sheep ➲ compare LAMB

IDM **mutton dressed as ˈlamb** (*BrE, informal, disapproving*) used to describe a woman who is trying to look younger than she really is, especially by wearing clothes that are designed for young people

ˌmutton ˈchops (also **ˌmutton chop ˈwhiskers**) *noun* [pl.] hair at the sides of a man's face which is grown so that it is very wide and round in shape at the bottom

mu·tual AW /ˈmjuːtʃuəl/ *adj.* **1** used to describe feelings that two or more people have for each other equally, or actions that affect two or more people equally: ***mutual respect/understanding*** ◇ ***mutual support/aid*** ◇ *I don't like her, and I think **the feeling is mutual*** (= she doesn't like me either). **2** [only before noun] shared by two or more people: *We met at the home of a mutual friend.* ◇ *They soon discovered a mutual interest in music.* ▸ **mu·tu·al·ity** /ˌmjuːtʃuˈæləti/ *noun* [U, C] (*formal*)

ˈmutual fund (*NAmE*) (*BrE* **ˌunit ˈtrust**) *noun* a company that offers a service to people by investing their money in various different businesses

mu·tu·al·ly AW /ˈmjuːtʃuəli/ *adv.* felt or done equally by two or more people: *a **mutually beneficial/supportive** relationship* ◇ *Can we find a mutually convenient time to meet?* ◇ *The two views are not **mutually exclusive*** (= both can be true at the same time).

Muzak™ /ˈmjuːzæk/ *noun* [U] (often *disapproving*) continuous recorded music that is played in shops, restaurants, airports, etc. ➲ compare PIPE *v.*

muz·zle /ˈmʌzl/ *noun, verb*

▪ ***noun* 1** the nose and mouth of an animal, especially a dog or a horse ➲ VISUAL VOCAB page V10 ➲ compare SNOUT **2** a device made of leather or plastic that you put over the nose and mouth of an animal, especially a dog, to prevent it from biting people **3** the open end of a gun, where the bullets come out

▪ ***verb* 1** [usually passive] **~ sth** to put a muzzle over a dog's head to prevent it from biting people **2 ~ sb/sth** to prevent sb from expressing their opinions in public as they want to SYN **gag**: *They accused the government of muzzling the press.*

muzzy /ˈmʌzi/ *adj.* (*BrE, informal*) **1** unable to think in a clear way: *a muzzy head* ◇ *Those drugs made me feel muzzy.* **2** not clear: *a muzzy voice* ◇ *muzzy plans*

MV /ˌem ˈviː/ *abbr.* (*BrE*) (used before the name of a ship) motor vessel: *the MV Puma*

MVP /ˌem viː ˈpi/ *abbr.* (*especially NAmE*) most valuable player (the best player in a team): *He has just earned his fourth MVP award this season.*

MW *abbr.* **1** MEDIUM WAVE **2** (*pl.* MW) MEGAWATT(S)

MWA /ˌem dʌbljuː ˈeɪ/ *abbr.* Member of the Welsh Assembly

mwah (also **mwa**) /mwɑː/ *exclamation* used to represent the sound that some people make when they kiss sb on the cheek

mwa·limu /mwɑːˈliːmuː/ *noun* (*EAfrE*) **1** a teacher **2 Mwalimu** a title or form of address for sb who is respected as a teacher: *Mwalimu Julius Nyerere*

mwethya /mˈweθjə/ *noun* (*pl.* **mwethya**) (*EAfrE*) a group of people who are involved with projects in a community, for example building a school or repairing roads

my 0‑ᴡ /maɪ/ *det.* (the possessive form of *I*)
1 0‑ᴡ of or belonging to the speaker or writer: *Where's my passport?* ◇ *My feet are cold.* **2** used in exclamations to express surprise, etc.: *My goodness! Look at the time!* **3** used when addressing sb, to show affection: ***my dear/darling/love*** **4** used when addressing sb that you consider to have a lower status than you: *My dear girl, you're wrong.*

my·al·gia /maɪˈældʒə/ *noun* [U] (*medical*) pain in a muscle ▸ **my·al·gic** /-dʒɪk/ *adj.* ➲ see also ME

my·al·gic en·ceph·alo·my·eli·tis /maɪˌældʒɪk enˌsefələʊmaɪəˈlaɪtɪs; *NAmE* -ˌsefəlem-/ *noun* [U] = ME

my·col·ogy /maɪˈkɒlədʒi; *NAmE* -ˈkɑːl-/ *noun* [U] the scientific study of FUNGI ➲ see also FUNGUS

mye·lin /ˈmaɪəlɪn/ *noun* [U] (*biology*) a mixture of PROTEINS and fats that surrounds many nerve cells, increasing the speed at which they send signals

mye·loma /ˌmaɪəˈləʊmə; *NAmE* -ˈloʊmə/ (*pl.* **mye·lo·mas** or **mye·lo·mata** /-mətə/) *noun* (*medical*) a type of cancer found as a TUMOUR inside the bone

mynah /ˈmaɪnə/ (also **ˈmynah bird**) *noun* a SE Asian bird with dark feathers, that can copy human speech

my·opia /maɪˈəʊpiə; *NAmE* -ˈoʊpiə/ *noun* [U] **1** (*technical*) the inability to see things clearly when they are far away SYN **short sight, short-sightedness 2** (*formal, disapproving*) the inability to see what the results of a particular action or decision will be; the inability to think about anything outside your own situation SYN **short-sightedness** ▸ **my·opic** /maɪˈɒpɪk; *NAmE* -ˈɑːpɪk/ *adj.*: (*technical*) *a **myopic child/eye*** ◇ (*disapproving*) *a myopic strategy* ◇ *myopic voters* ➲ see also SHORT-SIGHTED **my·opic·al·ly** /maɪˈɒpɪkli; *NAmE* -ˈɑːpɪk-/ *adv.*

myr·iad /ˈmɪriəd/ *noun* (*literary*) an extremely large number of sth: *Designs are available in a myriad of colours.* ▸ **myr·iad** *adj.*: *the myriad problems of modern life*

myrrh /mɜː(r)/ *noun* [U] a sticky substance with a sweet smell that comes from trees and is used to make PERFUME and INCENSE

myr·tle /ˈmɜːtl; *NAmE* ˈmɜːrtl/ *noun* [U, C] a bush with shiny leaves, pink or white flowers and bluish-black BERRIES

my·self 0‑ᴡ /maɪˈself/ *pron.*
1 0‑ᴡ (the reflexive form of *I*) used when the speaker or writer is also the person affected by an action: *I cut myself on a knife.* ◇ *I wrote a message to myself.* ◇ *I found myself unable to speak.* ◇ *I haven't been feeling myself recently* (= I have not felt well). ◇ *I needed space to be myself* (= not influenced by other people). **2** 0‑ᴡ used to emphasize the fact that the speaker is doing sth: *I'll speak to her myself.* ◇ *I myself do not agree.*

IDM **(all) by myˈself 1** alone; without anyone else: *I live by myself* **2** without help: *I painted the room all by myself.* **(all) to myˈself** for the speaker or writer alone; not shared: *I had a whole pizza to myself.*

My·Space™ /ˈmaɪspeɪs/ *noun* a SOCIAL NETWORKING website

mys·teri·ous 0‑ᴡ /mɪˈstɪəriəs; *NAmE* -ˈstɪr-/ *adj.*
1 0‑ᴡ difficult to understand or explain; strange: *He died in mysterious circumstances.* ◇ *A mysterious illness is affecting all the animals.* **2** 0‑ᴡ (especially of people) strange and interesting because you do not know much about them SYN **enigmatic**: *A mysterious young woman is living next door.* **3** (of people) not saying much about sth, especially when other people want to know more: *He was being very mysterious about where he was going.* ▸ **mys·teri·ous·ly** *adv.*: *My watch had mysteriously disappeared.* ◇ *Mysteriously, the streets were deserted.* ◇ *She was silent, smiling mysteriously.* **mys·teri·ous·ness** *noun* [U]

mys·tery 0‑ᴡ /ˈmɪstri/ *noun* (*pl.* -ies)
1 0‑ᴡ [C] something that is difficult to understand or to explain: *It is one of the great **unsolved mysteries** of this century.* ◇ *Their motives remain a mystery.* ◇ ***It's a** complete **mystery** to me why they chose him.* **2** 0‑ᴡ [C] (often used as an adjective) a person or thing that is strange and interesting because you do not know much about them or it: *He's a bit of a mystery.* ◇ *There was a **mystery guest** on the programme.* ◇ *The band was financed by a mystery backer.* ◇ (*BrE*) *a **mystery tour*** (= when you do not know where you are going) **3** 0‑ᴡ [U] the quality of being difficult to understand or to explain, especially when this makes sb/

M

sth seem interesting and exciting: *Mystery surrounds her disappearance.* ◇ *His past is* ***shrouded in mystery*** (= not much is known about it). ◇ *The dark glasses give her an* ***air of mystery.*** **4** [C] a story, a film/movie or a play in which crimes and strange events are only explained at the end: *I enjoy murder mysteries.* **5 mysteries** [pl.] secret religious ceremonies; secret knowledge: (*figurative*) *the teacher who initiated me into the mysteries of mathematics* **6** [C] a religious belief that cannot be explained or proved in a scientific way: *the mystery of creation*

'mystery play (also **'miracle play**) *noun* a type of play that was popular between the 11th and 14th centuries and was based on events in the Bible or the lives of the Christian SAINTS

ˌmystery 'shopper *noun* a person whose job is to visit or telephone a shop/store or other business pretending to be a customer, in order to get information on the quality of the service, the facilities, etc. ▶ **ˌmystery 'shopping** *noun* [U]

mys·tic /'mɪstɪk/ *noun* a person who tries to become united with God through prayer and MEDITATION and so understand important things that are beyond normal human understanding

mys·tic·al /'mɪstɪkl/ (also *less frequent* **mys·tic** /'mɪstɪk/) *adj.* **1** having spiritual powers or qualities that are difficult to understand or to explain: ***mystical forces/powers*** ◇ *mystic beauty* ◇ *Watching the sun rise over the mountain was an almost mystical experience.* **2** connected with mysticism: *the mystical life* ▶ **mys·tic·al·ly** /-kli/ *adv.*

mys·ti·cism /'mɪstɪsɪzəm/ *noun* [U] the belief that knowledge of God and of real truth can be found through prayer and MEDITATION rather than through reason and the senses: *Eastern mysticism*

mys·tify /'mɪstɪfaɪ/ *verb* (**mys·ti·fies, mys·ti·fy·ing, mys·ti·fied, mys·ti·fied**) **~ sb** to make sb confused because they do not understand sth **SYN baffle**: *They were totally mystified by the girl's disappearance.* ▶ **mys·ti·fi·ca·tion** /ˌmɪstɪfɪ'keɪʃn/ *noun* [U]: *He looked at her in mystification.* **mys·ti·fy·ing** *adj.*

mys·tique /mɪ'stiːk/ *noun* [U, sing.] the quality of being mysterious or secret that makes sb/sth seem interesting or attractive: *The mystique surrounding the monarchy has gone for ever.*

myth /mɪθ/ *noun* [C, U] **1** a story from ancient times, especially one that was told to explain natural events or to describe the early history of a people; this type of story **SYN legend**: *ancient Greek myths* ◇ *a creation myth* (= that explains how the world began) ◇ *the heroes of myth and legend* **2** something that many people believe but that does not exist or is false **SYN fallacy**: *It is time to dispel the myth of a classless society* (= to show that it does not exist). ◇ *Contrary to* ***popular myth****, women are not worse drivers than men.* ➲ see also URBAN MYTH

myth·ic /'mɪθɪk/ *adj.* **1** = MYTHICAL (1,2) **2** (also **myth·ic·al**) that has become very famous, like sb/sth in a myth **SYN legendary**: *Scott of the Antarctic was a national hero of mythic proportions.*

myth·ic·al /'mɪθɪkl/ *adj.* [usually before noun] **1** (also *less frequent* **myth·ic**) existing only in ancient myths **SYN legendary**: ***mythical beasts/heroes*** **2** (also *less frequent* **myth·ic**) that does not exist or is not true **SYN fictitious**: *the mythical 'rich uncle' that he boasts about* **3** = MYTHIC (2)

mytho·logic·al /ˌmɪθə'lɒdʒɪkl; *NAmE* -'lɑːdʒ-/ *adj.* [usually before noun] connected with ancient MYTHS: ***mythological subjects/figures/stories***

myth·ology /mɪ'θɒlədʒi; *NAmE* -'θɑːl-/ *noun* (*pl.* **-ies**) [U, C] **1** ancient MYTHS in general; the ancient MYTHS of a particular culture, society, etc: *Greek mythology* ◇ *a study of the religions and mythologies of ancient Rome* **2** ideas that many people think are true but that do not exist or are false: *the popular mythology that life begins at forty*

myxo·ma·tosis /ˌmɪksəmə'təʊsɪs; *NAmE* -'toʊ-/ *noun* [U] an infectious disease of RABBITS that usually causes death

mzee /m'ziː/ *noun* (*EAfrE*) **1** a person who is respected because of their age, experience or authority; an ELDER **2 Mzee** a title for a man that shows respect: *Mzee Kenyatta*

M

Nn

N /en/ *noun, abbr., symbol*
■ ***noun*** (also **n**) (*pl.* **Ns, N's, n's** /enz/) **1** [C, U] the 14th letter of the English alphabet: *'Night' begins with (an) N/'N'.* **2** [U] (*mathematics*) used to represent a number whose value is not mentioned: *The equation is impossible for any value of n greater than 2.* ➲ see also NTH
■ ***abbr.*** **1** (*NAmE* also **No.**) north; northern: *N Ireland* **2** NEWTON(S)
■ ***symbol*** the symbol for the chemical element nitrogen

n. *abbr.* noun

n/a *abbr.* **1** not applicable (used on a form as an answer to a question that does not apply to you) **2** not available

NAACP /ˌen dʌbəl ˌeɪ siː ˈpiː/ *abbr.* National Association for the Advancement of Colored People (an organization in the US that works for the rights of African Americans)

NAAFI /ˈnæfi/ *noun* [sing.] the abbreviation for 'Navy, Army and Air Force Institutes' (an organization which provides shops and places to eat for British soldiers)

naan *noun* [U] = NAN²

naar·tjie /ˈnɑːtʃi; *NAmE* ˈnɑːrtʃi/ *noun* (*SAfrE*) a type of small orange with a loose skin that you can remove easily

nab /næb/ *verb* (**-bb-**) (*informal*) **1** **~ sb** to catch or arrest sb who is doing sth wrong SYN **collar**: *He was nabbed by the police for speeding.* **2** **~ sth** to take or get sth: *Who's nabbed my drink?*

nabob /ˈneɪbɒb; *NAmE* -bɑːb/ *noun* **1** a Muslim ruler or officer in the Mogul empire **2** a rich or important person

nachos /ˈnætʃəʊz; *NAmE* -tʃoʊz/ *noun* [pl.] (from *Spanish*) a Mexican dish of crisp pieces of TORTILLA served with BEANS, cheese, spices, etc.

nada /ˈnɑːdə/ *noun* [U] (from *Spanish, informal, especially NAmE*) nothing: *What is it worth? Zero, zilch, nada!*

nadir /ˈneɪdɪə(r); *NAmE* -dɪr/ *noun* [sing.] (*formal*) the worst moment of a particular situation: *the nadir of his career* ◇ *Company losses reached their nadir in 2009.* OPP **zenith**

nae /neɪ/ *det.* (*ScotE*) no: *We have nae money.* ▶ **nae** *adv.*: *It's nae (= not) bad.*

naff /næf/ *adj.* (*BrE, informal*) lacking style, taste, quality, etc: *There was a naff band playing.*

nag /næg/ *verb, noun*
■ ***verb*** (**-gg-**) **1** [I, T] to keep complaining to sb about their behaviour or keep asking them to do sth SYN **pester**: **~ (at sb)** *Stop nagging—I'll do it as soon as I can.* ◇ **~ sb (to do sth)** *She had been nagging him to paint the fence.* **2** [I, T] to worry or irritate you continuously: **~ at sb** *A feeling of unease nagged at her.* ◇ **~ sb** *Doubts nagged me all evening.*
■ ***noun*** (*old-fashioned, informal*) a horse

na·gana /nəˈgɑːnə/ *noun* [U] (*EAfrE*) a serious illness that cows can get from a type of fly (= a TSETSE FLY)

nag·ging /ˈnægɪŋ/ *adj.* [only before noun] **1** continuing for a long time and difficult to cure or remove: *a* ***nagging pain/doubt*** **2** complaining: *a nagging voice*

nah /nɑː/ *exclamation* (*slang*) = NO

naiad /ˈnaɪæd/ *noun* (*pl.* **naiads** or **nai·ades** /-diːz/) (in ancient stories) a water spirit

nail 0-π /neɪl/ *noun, verb*
■ ***noun*** **1** 0-π thin hard layer covering the outer tip of the fingers or toes: *Stop biting your nails!* ◇ *nail clippers* ➲ VISUAL VOCAB page V48 ➲ see also FINGERNAIL, TOENAIL **2** 0-π a small thin pointed piece of metal with a flat head, used for hanging things on a wall or for joining pieces of wood together: *She hammered the nail in.* ➲ COLLOCATIONS at DECORATE ➲ VISUAL VOCAB page V17 ➲ compare SCREW (1), TACK (3)
IDM **a nail in sb's/sth's ˈcoffin** something that makes the end or failure of an organization, sb's plans, etc. more likely to happen **on the ˈnail** (*BrE, informal*) (of payment) without delay: *They're good customers who always pay on the nail.* ➲ more at FIGHT *v.*, HARD *adj.*, HIT *v.*, TOUGH *adj.*
■ ***verb*** **1** **~ sth (+ adv./prep./adj.)** to fasten sth to sth with a nail or nails: *I nailed the sign to a tree.* **2** **~ sb** (*informal*) to catch sb and prove they are guilty of a crime or of doing sth bad: *The police haven't been able to nail the killer.* **3** **~ sth** (*informal*) to prove that sth is not true: *We must nail this lie.* **4** **~ sth** (*NAmE, informal*) to achieve sth or do sth right, especially in sport: *He nailed a victory in the semi-finals.*
IDM **nail your colours to the ˈmast** (*especially BrE*) to say publicly and firmly what you believe or who you support
PHR V **ˌnail sth↔ˈdown** **1** to fasten sth down with a nail or nails **2** to reach an agreement or a decision, usually after a lot of discussion: *All the parties seem anxious to nail down a ceasefire.* **ˌnail sb↔ˈdown (to sth)** to force sb to give you a definite promise or tell you exactly what they intend to do SYN **pin down**: *She says she'll come, but I can't nail her down to a specific time.* **ˌnail sth↔ˈup** **1** to fasten sth to a wall, post, etc. with a nail or nails **2** to put nails into a door or window so that it cannot be opened

ˈnail bar *noun* a place where you can pay to have your nails shaped, coloured and made more attractive

ˈnail-biting *adj.* [usually before noun] making you feel very excited or anxious because you do not know what is going to happen: *a nail-biting finish* ◇ *It's been a nail-biting couple of weeks waiting for my results.*

ˈnail brush *noun* a small stiff brush for cleaning your nails ➲ VISUAL VOCAB page V21

ˈnail clippers *noun* [pl.] a small tool for cutting the nails on your fingers and toes ➲ VISUAL VOCAB page V21

ˈnail file *noun* a small metal tool with a rough surface for shaping your nails ➲ VISUAL VOCAB page V21 ➲ see also EMERY BOARD

ˈnail polish (*BrE* also **ˈnail varnish**) *noun* [U] clear or coloured liquid that you paint on your nails to make them look attractive: *nail polish/varnish remover*

ˈnail scissors *noun* [pl.] small scissors that are usually curved, used for cutting the nails on your fingers and toes: *a pair of nail scissors* ➲ VISUAL VOCAB page V21

naive (also **naïve**) /naɪˈiːv/ *adj.* **1** (*disapproving*) lacking experience of life, knowledge or good judgement and willing to believe that people always tell you the truth: *to be politically naive* ◇ *I can't believe you were so naive as to trust him!* ◇ *a naive question* **2** (*approving*) (of people and their behaviour) innocent and simple SYN **artless**: *Their approach to life is refreshingly naive.* ➲ compare SOPHISTICATED **3** (*technical*) (of art) in a style which is deliberately very simple, often uses bright colours and is similar to that produced by a child ▶ **naive·ly** (also **naïve·ly**) *adv.*: *I naively assumed that I would be paid for the work.* **naiv·ety** (also **naïv·ety**) /naɪˈiːvəti/ *noun* [U]: *They laughed at the naivety of his suggestion.* ◇ *She has lost none of her naivety.*

naked 0-π /ˈneɪkɪd/ *adj.*
1 0-π not wearing any clothes SYN **bare**: *a naked body* ◇ *naked shoulders* ◇ *They often wandered around the house* ***stark naked*** (= completely naked). ◇ *They found him* ***half naked*** *and bleeding to death.* ◇ *The prisoners were* ***stripped naked***. ➲ see also BUCK NAKED **2** [usually before noun] without the usual covering SYN **bare**: *a naked light* ◇ *a naked sword* ◇ *Mice are born naked* (= without fur). ◇ (*BrE*) *a naked flame* HELP In American English this is called an *open flame.* **3** [only before noun] (of emotions, attitudes, etc.) expressed strongly and not hidden: *naked aggression* ◇ *the naked truth* **4** [not usually before noun] unable to protect yourself from being harmed, criticized, etc. SYN **helpless**: *He still felt naked and drained after his ordeal.* ▶ **naked·ly** *adv.*: *nakedly aggressive* **naked·ness** *noun* [U]
IDM **the naked ˈeye** the normal power of your eyes without the help of an instrument: *The planet should be visible* ***with/to the naked eye***.

na·mas·kar /ˌnʌmʌsˈkɑː(r)/ *noun* [U] (*IndE*) a way of GREETING sb in which the hands are placed together as in prayer and the head is bent forwards

namby-pamby /ˌnæmbi ˈpæmbi/ *adj.* (*informal, disapproving*) weak and too emotional

Synonyms

naked / bare

Both these words can be used to mean 'not covered with clothes' and are frequently used with the following nouns:

naked ~	bare ~
body	feet
man	arms
fear	walls
aggression	branches
flame	essentials

- **Naked** is more often used to describe a person or their body and **bare** usually describes a part of the body.
- **Bare** can also describe other things with nothing on them: *bare walls* ◇ *a bare hillside.* **Naked** can mean 'without a protective covering': *a naked sword.*
- **Bare** can also mean 'just enough': *the bare minimum.* **Naked** can be used to talk about strong feelings that are not hidden: *naked fear.* Note also the idiom: *(visible) to/with **the naked eye.***

name 0‑ /neɪm/ *noun, verb*

▪ ***noun*** **1** 0‑ a word or words that a particular person, animal, place or thing is known by: *What's your name?* ◇ *What is/was the name, please?* (= a polite way of asking sb's name) ◇ *Please write your full **name and address** below.* ◇ *Do you know the name of this flower?* ◇ *Rubella is just another name for German measles.* ◇ *Are you changing your name when you get married?* ➲ see also ASSUMED NAME, BRAND NAME, CODE NAME, FAMILY NAME, FILENAME, FIRST NAME, FORENAME, HOUSEHOLD NAME, MAIDEN NAME, MIDDLE NAME, NICKNAME, PEN-NAME, PET NAME, PLACE NAME, SURNAME, TRADE NAME, USERNAME **2** [usually sing.] a reputation that sb/sth has; the opinion that people have about sb/sth: *She first **made her name** as a writer of children's books.* ◇ *He's **made** quite **a name for himself*** (= become famous). ◇ *The college has a **good name for** languages.* ◇ *This kind of behaviour **gives** students **a bad name.*** **3** (in compound adjectives) having a name or a reputation of the kind mentioned, especially one that is known by a lot of people: *a big-name company* ◇ *brand-name goods* ➲ see also HOUSEHOLD NAME **4** a famous person: *Some of the biggest names in the art world were at the party.*

IDM **by 'name** using the name of sb/sth: *She asked for you by name.* ◇ *The principal knows all the students by name.* ◇ *I only know her by name* (= I have heard about her but I have not met her). **by the name of...** (*formal*) who is called: *a young actor by the name of Tom Rees* **enter sb's/your 'name (for sth)** | **put sb's/your 'name down (for sth)** to apply for a place at a school, in a competition, etc. for sb or yourself: *Have you entered your name for the quiz yet?* **give your 'name to sth** to invent sth which then becomes known by your name **go by the name of...** to use a name that may not be your real one **have your/sb's 'name on it** | **with your/sb's 'name on it** (*informal*) if sth **has your name on it**, or there is sth **with your name on it**, it is intended for you: *He took my place and got killed. It should have been me—that bullet had my name on it.* ◇ *Are you coming for dinner this evening? I've got a steak here with your name on it!* **in ˌall but 'name** used to describe a situation which exists in reality but that is not officially recognized: *He runs the company in all but name.* **in 'God's/'Heaven's name** | **in the name of 'God/'Heaven** used especially in questions to show that you are angry, surprised or shocked: *What in God's name was that noise?* ◇ *Where in the name of Heaven have you been?* **in the name of 'sb/'sth** | **in sb's/sth's 'name 1** 0‑ for sb; showing that sth officially belongs to sb: *We reserved two tickets in the name of Brown.* ◇ *The car is registered in my name.* **2** using the authority of sb/sth; as a representative of sb/sth: *I arrest you in the name of the law.* **3** used to give a reason or an excuse for doing sth, often when what you are doing is wrong: *crimes committed in the name of religion* **in 'name only** officially recognized but not existing in reality: *He's party leader in name only.* **sb's name is 'mud** (*informal*, usually *humorous*) used to say that sb is not liked or popular because of sth they have done **the name of the 'game** (*informal*) the most important aspect of an activity; the most important quality needed for an activity: *Hard work is the name of the game if you want to succeed in business.* **a name to 'conjure with** (*BrE*) **1** (*NAmE* **a name to 'reckon with**) a person or thing that is well known and respected in a particular field: *Miyazaki is still a name to conjure with among anime fans.* **2** (*humorous*) used when you mention a name that you think is difficult to remember or pronounce: *He comes from Tighnabruaich—now there's a name to conjure with!* **put a 'name to sb/sth** to know or remember what sb/sth is called: *I recognize the tune but I can't put a name to it.* **take sb's name in 'vain** to show a lack of respect when using sb's name: (*humorous*) *Have you been taking my name in vain again?* **(have sth) to your 'name** to have or own sth: *an Olympic athlete with five gold medals to his name* ◇ *She doesn't have a penny/cent to her name* (= she is very poor). **under the name (of)...** using a name that may not be your real name ➲ more at ANSWER *v.*, BIG *adj.*, CALL *v.*, DOG *n.*, DROP *v.*, LEND, MIDDLE NAME, NAME *v.*, REJOICE, ROSE *n.*

More About

names and titles

Names

- Your **name** is either your whole name or one part of your name: *My name is Maria.* ◇ *His name is Tom Smith.*
- Your **last name** or **family name** (also called **surname** in *BrE*) is the name that all members of your family share.
- Your **first name/names** (*formal* **forename**) is/are the name(s) your parents gave you when you were born. In *BrE* some people use the expression **Christian name(s)** to refer to a person's first name(s).
- Your **middle name(s)** is/are any name your parents gave you other than the one that is placed first. The initial of this name is often used as part of your name, especially in America: *John T. Harvey*
- Your **full name** is all your names, usually in the order: first + middle + last name
- A woman's **maiden name** is the family name she had before she got married. Some women keep this name after they are married and do not use their husband's name. In North America, married women often use their maiden name followed by their husband's family name: *Hillary Rodham Clinton.*

Titles

- **Mr** (for both married and unmarried men)
- **Mrs** (for married women)
- **Miss** (for unmarried women)
- **Ms** (a title that some women prefer to use as it does not distinguish between married and unmarried women)
- **Doctor**, **Professor**, **President**, **Vice-President**, **Reverend** (or **Rev**), etc.

The correct way to talk to someone is:

- first name, if you know them well: *Hello, Maria.*
- or title + surname: *Hello, Mr Brown.*
- or *Doctor* (medical), *Professor*, etc. on its own: *Thank you, Doctor.* This is only used for a very limited number of titles.

▪ ***verb*** **1** 0‑ to give a name to sb/sth SYN **call**: **~ sb/sth (after sb)** | (*NAmE* also) **~ sb/sth (for sb)** *He was named after his father* (= given his father's first name). ◇ **~ sb/sth + noun** *They named their son John.* **2** 0‑ to say the name of sb/sth SYN **identify**: **~ sb/sth** *The victim has not yet been named.* ◇ *Can you name all the American states?* ◇ **~ sb/sth as sb/sth** *The missing man has been named as James Kelly.* ➲ SYNONYMS at IDENTIFY **3 ~ sth** to state sth exactly SYN **specify**: *Name your price.* ◇ *They're engaged, but they haven't yet* ***named the day*** (= chosen the date for their wedding). ◇ *Activities available include squash, archery and swimming,* ***to name but a few.*** ◇ *Chairs, tables, cabinets—* ***you name it****, she makes it* (= she makes anything you can imagine). **4** to choose sb for a job or position SYN **nominate**: **~ sb (as) sth | ~ sb + noun** *I had no hesitation in naming him (as) captain.* ◇ **~ sb (to sth)** *When she resigned, he was named to the committee in her place.*

IDM ˌ**name and** ˈ**shame** (*BrE*) to publish the names of people or organizations who have done sth wrong or illegal **name** ˈ**names** to give the names of the people involved in sth, especially sth wrong or illegal

ˈ**name-calling** *noun* [U] the act of using rude or insulting words about sb

name·check /ˈneɪmtʃek/ *noun, verb*

■ ***noun*** an occasion when the name of a person or thing is mentioned or included in a list: *She started her speech by giving a namecheck to all the people who had helped her.*

■ ***verb*** **~ sb/sth** to mention or include sb/sth in a list: *The songs namecheck other artists and bands.* ◇ *The book was namechecked in today's paper.*

ˈ**name day** *noun* a day which is special for a Christian with a particular name because it is the day which celebrates a SAINT with the same name

ˈ**name-dropping** *noun* [U] (*disapproving*) the act of mentioning the names of famous people you know or have met in order to impress other people ▸ ˈ**name-drop** *verb* [I] ➲ see also DROP NAMES

name·less /ˈneɪmləs/ *adj.* **1** [usually before noun] having no name; whose name you do not know: *a nameless grave* ◇ *thousands of nameless and faceless workers* **2** whose name is kept secret SYN **anonymous**: *a nameless source in the government* ◇ *a well-known public figure* ***who shall remain nameless*** **3** [usually before noun] (*literary*) difficult or too unpleasant to describe: *nameless horrors* ◇ *a nameless longing*

name·ly /ˈneɪmli/ *adv.* used to introduce more exact and detailed information about sth that you have just mentioned: *We need to concentrate on our target audience, namely women aged between 20 and 30.*

name·plate /ˈneɪmpleɪt/ *noun* **1** a sign on the door or the wall of a building showing the name of a company or the name of a person who is living or working there **2** a piece of metal or plastic on an object showing the name of the person who owns it, made it or presented it

name·sake /ˈneɪmseɪk/ *noun* a person or thing that has the same name as sb/sth else: *Unlike his more famous namesake, this Gordon Brown has little interest in politics.*

ˈ**name tag** *noun* a small piece of plastic, paper or metal that you wear, with your name on it

ˈ**name tape** *noun* a small piece of cloth that is sewn or stuck onto a piece of clothing and that has the name of the owner on it

nan[1] /næn/ *noun* (*BrE*) = NANNY (2)

nan[2] (also **naan**) /nɑːn/ (also ˈ**nan bread**, ˈ**naan bread**) *noun* [U] a type of soft flat S Asian bread

nana[1] (*BrE* also **nanna**) /ˈnænə/ *noun* (*informal*) = NANNY (2)

nana[2] /ˈnɑːnə/ *noun* (*old-fashioned, BrE, informal*) a stupid person SYN **idiot**: *I felt a right nana.*

nancy /ˈnænsi/ *noun* (*pl.* **-ies**) (also ˈ**nancy boy**, **nance** /næns/) (*taboo, slang, especially BrE*) an offensive word for a HOMOSEXUAL man, or a man who behaves in a way that is thought to be typical of women

nanny /ˈnæni/ *noun* (*pl.* **-ies**) **1** a woman whose job is to take care of young children in the children's own home **2** (also **nan**) (both *BrE*) (used by children, especially as a form of address) a grandmother: *When is Nanny coming to stay?* ◇ *my nan and grandad* ➲ see also GRANNY

IDM **the** ˈ**nanny state** (*BrE*) a disapproving way of talking about the fact that government seems to get too much involved in people's lives and to protect them too much, in a way that limits their freedom

ˈ**nanny goat** *noun* a female GOAT ➲ compare BILLY GOAT

nanny·ing /ˈnæniɪŋ/ *noun* [U] **1** the job of being a child's NANNY **2** (*BrE, disapproving*) the fact of helping and protecting sb too much

nano- /ˈnænəʊ; *NAmE* ˈnænoʊ/ *combining form* (*technical*) (in nouns and adjectives; used especially in units of measurement) one billionth: *nanosecond*

nano·metre (*especially US* **nano·meter**) /ˈnænəʊmiːtə(r); *NAmE* ˈnænoʊ-/ *noun* (*abbr.* **nm**) one thousand millionth of a metre

nano·par·ticle /ˈnænəʊpɑːtɪkl; *NAmE* ˈnænoʊpɑːrt-/ *noun* a piece of matter less than 100 NANOMETRES long

nano·scale /ˈnænəʊskeɪl; *NAmE* ˈnænoʊ-/ *adj.* [usually before noun] of a size that can be measured in nanometres: *nanoscale particles/devices/electronics*

nano·sec·ond /ˈnænəʊsekənd; *NAmE* ˈnænoʊ-/ *noun* (*abbr.* **ns**) one thousand millionth of a second

nano·tech·nol·ogy /ˌnænəʊtekˈnɒlədʒi; *NAmE* ˌnænoʊtekˈnɑːlədʒi/ *noun* [U] the branch of technology that deals with structures that are less than 100 NANOMETRES long. Scientists often build these structures using individual MOLECULES of substances. ▸ **nano·tech·nolo·gist** *noun* **nano·tech·no·logic·al** /ˌnænəʊˌteknəˈlɒdʒɪkl; *NAmE* ˌnænoʊˌteknəˈlɑːdʒɪkl/ *adj.*: *nanotechnological research*

nap /næp/ *noun, verb*

■ ***noun*** **1** [C] a short sleep, especially during the day SYN **snooze**: *to* ***take/have a nap*** ➲ SYNONYMS at SLEEP ➲ compare SIESTA ➲ see also CATNAP, POWER NAP **2** [sing.] the short fine threads on the surface of some types of cloth, usually lying in the same direction **3** [C] (*BrE*) advice given by an expert on which horse is most likely to win a race

■ ***verb*** (**-pp-**) [I] to sleep for a short time, especially during the day IDM see CATCH *v.*

napa *noun* [U] = NAPPA

na·palm /ˈneɪpɑːm/ *noun* [U] a substance like jelly, made from petrol/gas, that burns and is used in making bombs

nape /neɪp/ *noun* [sing.] **~ (of sb's neck)** the back of the neck: *Her hair was cut short at the nape of her neck.* ➲ VISUAL VOCAB page V48

naph·tha /ˈnæfθə/ *noun* [U] a type of oil that starts burning very easily, used as fuel or in making chemicals

naph·tha·lene /ˈnæfθəliːn; *NAmE* also ˈnæpθə-/ *noun* [U] (*chemistry*) a substance used in products that keep MOTHS away from clothes, and in industrial processes

nap·kin /ˈnæpkɪn/ *noun* **1** (also ˈ**table napkin**) a piece of cloth or paper used at meals for protecting your clothes and cleaning your lips and fingers SYN **serviette** ➲ VISUAL VOCAB page V19 **2** (*NAmE*) = SANITARY NAPKIN **3** (*BrE, old-fashioned* or *formal*) = NAPPY

nappa (also **napa**) /ˈnæpə/ *noun* [U] a type of soft leather made from the skin of sheep or GOATS

nappe /næp/ *noun* [U] (*geology*) a thin layer of rock that lies on top of a different type of rock

nappy /ˈnæpi/ *noun* (*pl.* **-ies**) (*BrE*) (*NAmE* **di·aper**) a piece of soft cloth or other thick material that is folded around a baby's bottom and between its legs to absorb and hold its body waste: *I'll change her nappy.* ◇ *a disposable nappy* (= one that is made to be used once only) ◇ *nappy rash* ➲ COLLOCATIONS at CHILD

narc /nɑːk; *NAmE* nɑːrk/ (also **narco** /ˈnɑːkəʊ; *NAmE* ˈnɑːrkoʊ/) *noun* (*NAmE, informal*) a police officer whose job is to stop people selling or using drugs illegally

nar·cis·sism /ˈnɑːsɪsɪzəm; *NAmE* ˈnɑːrs-/ *noun* [U] (*formal, disapproving*) the habit of admiring yourself too much, especially your appearance ▸ **nar·cis·sis·tic** /ˌnɑːsɪˈsɪstɪk;

N

NAmE ˌnɑːrs-/ *adj.* **ORIGIN** From the Greek myth in which **Narcissus**, a beautiful young man, fell in love with his own reflection in a pool. He died and was changed into the flower which bears his name.

nar·cis·sus /nɑːˈsɪsəs; *NAmE* nɑːrˈs-/ *noun* (*pl.* **nar·cissi** /nɑːˈsɪsaɪ; *NAmE* nɑːrˈs-/) a plant with white or yellow flowers that appear in spring. There are many types of narcissus, including the DAFFODIL.

nar·co·lepsy /ˈnɑːkəʊlepsi; *NAmE* ˈnɑːrkoʊ-/ *noun* [U] (*medical*) a condition in which sb falls into a deep sleep when they are in relaxing surroundings

nar·co·sis /nɑːˈkəʊsɪs; *NAmE* nɑːrˈkoʊsɪs/ *noun* [U] (*medical*) a state caused by drugs in which sb is unconscious or keeps falling asleep

nar·cot·ic /nɑːˈkɒtɪk; *NAmE* nɑːrˈkɑː-/ *noun, adj.*

■ ***noun*** **1** (*formal*) a powerful illegal drug that affects the mind in a harmful way. HEROIN and COCAINE are narcotics: *a narcotics agent* (= a police officer investigating the illegal trade in drugs) **2** (*medical*) a substance that relaxes you, reduces pain or makes you sleep: *a mild narcotic*

■ ***adj.*** **1** (of a drug) that affects your mind in a harmful way **2** (of a substance) making you sleep: *a mild narcotic effect*

nark /nɑːk; *NAmE* nɑːrk/ *noun* (*BrE, slang*) a person who is friendly with criminals and who gives the police information about them

narked /nɑːkt; *NAmE* nɑːrkt/ *adj.* [not usually before noun] (*old-fashioned, BrE, informal*) annoyed

narky /ˈnɑːki; *NAmE* ˈnɑːrki/ *adj.* (**nark·ier**, **narki·est**) (*BrE, informal*) easily becoming angry or annoyed

nar·rate /nəˈreɪt; *NAmE* also ˈnæreɪt/ *verb* **1 ~ sth** (*formal*) to tell a story **SYN** **relate**: *She entertained them by narrating her adventures in Africa.* **2 ~ sth** to speak the words that form the text of a DOCUMENTARY film or programme: *The film was narrated by Andrew Sachs.*

N

nar·ra·tion /nəˈreɪʃn; næˈr-/ *noun* (*formal*) **1** [U, C] the act or process of telling a story, especially in a novel, a film/movie or a play **2** [C] a description of events that is spoken during a film/movie, a play, etc. or with music: *He has recorded the narration for the production.*

nar·ra·tive /ˈnærətɪv/ *noun* (*formal*) **1** [C] a description of events, especially in a novel **SYN** **story**: *a gripping narrative of their journey up the Amazon* ➲ **COLLOCATIONS** at LITERATURE **2** [U] the act, process or skill of telling a story: *The novel contains too much dialogue and not enough narrative.* ▶ **nar·ra·tive** *adj.* [only before noun]: *narrative fiction*

nar·ra·tor /nəˈreɪtə(r)/ *noun* a person who tells a story, especially in a book, play or film/movie; the person who speaks the words in a television programme but who does not appear in it: *a first-person narrator*

nar·row 🗝 /ˈnærəʊ; *NAmE* -roʊ/ *adj., verb*

■ ***adj.*** (**nar·row·er**, **nar·row·est**) **1** 🗝 measuring a short distance from one side to the other, especially in relation to length: *narrow streets* ◇ *a narrow bed/doorway/shelf* ◇ *narrow shoulders/hips* ◇ *There was only a narrow gap between the bed and the wall.* ◇ (*figurative*) *the narrow confines of prison life* **OPP** **broad**, **wide** **2** 🗝 [usually before noun] only just achieved or avoided: *a* ***narrow victory*** ◇ *He lost the race by the* ***narrowest of margins.*** ◇ *She was elected by a* ***narrow majority.*** ◇ *He had a* ***narrow escape*** *when his car skidded on the ice.* **3** 🗝 limited in a way that ignores important issues or the opinions of other people: *narrow interests* ◇ *She has a very narrow view of the world.* **OPP** **broad** **4** 🗝 limited in variety or numbers **SYN** **restricted**: *The shop sells only a narrow range of goods.* ◇ *a narrow circle of friends* **OPP** **wide** **5** limited in meaning; exact: *I am using the word 'education' in the narrower sense.* **OPP** **broad** ▶ **nar·row·ness** *noun* [U]: *The narrowness of the streets caused many traffic problems.* ◇ *We were surprised by the narrowness of our victory.* ◇ *His attitudes show a certain narrowness of mind.* **IDM** see STRAIGHT *n.*

■ ***verb*** [I, T] to become or make sth narrower: *This is where the river narrows.* ◇ *The gap between the two teams has narrowed to three points.* ◇ *Her* ***eyes narrowed*** (= almost closed) *menacingly.* ◇ **~ sth** *He narrowed his eyes at her.* ◇ *We need to try and narrow the health divide between rich and poor.*

PHR V ˌ**narrow sth**↔ˈ**down** (**to sth**) to reduce the number of possibilities or choices: *We have narrowed down the list to four candidates.*

Synonyms

narrow / thin

These adjectives are frequently used with the following nouns:

narrow ~	**thin ~**
road	man
entrance	legs
bed	ice
stairs	line
majority	layer
victory	material
range	cream

- **Narrow** describes something that is a short distance from side to side. **Thin** describes people, or something that has a short distance through it from one side to the other.
- **Thin** is also used of things that are not as thick as you expect. **Narrow** can be used with the meanings 'only just achieved' and 'limited'.

nar·row·band /ˈnærəʊbænd; *NAmE* -roʊ-/ *noun* [U] (*technical*) signals that use a narrow range of FREQUENCIES ➲ compare BROADBAND

nar·row·boat /ˈnærəʊbəʊt; *NAmE* ˈnæroʊboʊt/ *noun* (*BrE*) a long narrow boat, used on CANALS ➲ **VISUAL VOCAB** page V44

nar·row·cast /ˈnærəʊkɑːst; *NAmE* ˈnæroʊkæst/ *verb* [I] (*technical*) to send information by television or the Internet to a particular group of people ➲ compare BROADCAST

ˈ**narrow gauge** *noun* [U] a size of railway/railroad track that is not as wide as the standard track that is used in Britain and the US: *a narrow-gauge railway*

nar·row·ly /ˈnærəʊli; *NAmE* -roʊ-/ *adv.* **1** only by a small amount: *The car narrowly missed a cyclist.* ◇ *She narrowly escaped injury.* ◇ *The team lost narrowly.* **2** (sometimes *disapproving*) in a way that is limited: *a narrowly defined task* ◇ *a narrowly specialized education* **3** closely; carefully: *She looked at him narrowly.*

ˌ**narrow-ˈminded** *adj.* (*disapproving*) not willing to listen to new ideas or to the opinions of others **SYN** **bigoted**, **intolerant**: *a narrow-minded attitude* ◇ *a narrow-minded nationalist* **OPP** **broad-minded**, **open-minded** ▶ ˌ**narrow-ˈminded·ness** *noun* [U]

nar·rows /ˈnærəʊz; *NAmE* -roʊz/ *noun* [pl.] a narrow channel that connects two larger areas of water

nar·whal /ˈnɑːwəl; *NAmE* ˈnɑːrwɑːl/ *noun* a small white WHALE from the Arctic region. The male narwhal has a long TUSK (= outer tooth).

nary /ˈneəri; *NAmE* ˈneri/ *adj.* (*old use* or *dialect*) not a; no

NASA /ˈnæsə/ *abbr.* National Aeronautics and Space Administration (a US government organization that does research into space and organizes space travel)

nasal /ˈneɪzl/ *adj.* **1** connected with the nose: *the nasal passages* ◇ *a nasal spray* **2** (of sb's voice) sounding as if it is produced partly through the nose: *a nasal accent* **3** (*phonetics*) (of a speech sound) produced by sending a stream of air through the nose. The nasal consonants in English are /m/, /n/ and /ŋ/, as in *sum*, *sun* and *sung*.

na·sal·ize (*BrE* also **-ise**) /ˈneɪzəlaɪz/ *verb* **~ sth** (*phonetics*) to produce a speech sound, especially a vowel, with the air in the nose VIBRATING ▶ **na·sal·iz·ation**, **-is·ation** /ˌneɪzəlaɪˈzeɪʃn/ *noun* [U]

nas·cent /ˈnæsnt/ *adj.* (*formal*) beginning to exist; not yet fully developed

the NASDAQ /ˈnæzdæk/ *noun* [sing.] National Association of Securities Dealers Automated Quotations (a computer system in the US that supplies the current price of shares to the people who sell them)

na·stur·tium /nəˈstɜːʃəm; *NAmE* -ˈstɜːrʃ-/ *noun* a garden plant with round flat leaves and red, orange or yellow flowers that are sometimes eaten in salads

nasty /ˈnɑːsti; *NAmE* ˈnæsti/ *adj.* (**nas·tier**, **nas·ti·est**) **1** very bad or unpleasant: *a nasty accident* ◇ *The news gave me a nasty shock.* ◇ *I had a nasty feeling that he would follow me.* ◇ *He had a nasty moment when he thought he'd lost his passport.* ◇ *This coffee has a nasty taste.* ◇ *Don't buy that coat —it looks **cheap and nasty**.* **2** unkind; unpleasant SYN **mean**: *to make nasty remarks about sb* ◇ *the nastier side of her character* ◇ *to have a nasty temper* ◇ *Don't be so nasty to your brother.* ◇ *That was a nasty little trick.* ◇ *Life has a **nasty habit** of repeating itself.* **3** dangerous or serious: *a nasty bend* (= dangerous for cars going fast) ◇ *a nasty injury* **4** offensive; in bad taste: *to have a nasty mind* ◇ *nasty jokes* ➲ see also VIDEO NASTY ▶ **nas·tily** /-ɪli/ *adv.*: *'I hate you,' she said nastily.* **nas·ti·ness** *noun* [U]
IDM **get/turn ˈnasty** **1** to become threatening and violent: *You'd better do what he says or he'll turn nasty.* **2** to become bad or unpleasant: *It looks as though the weather is going to turn nasty again.* **a nasty piece of ˈwork** (*BrE, informal*) a person who is unpleasant, unkind or dishonest ➲ more at TASTE *n.*

natal /ˈneɪtl/ *adj.* [only before noun] (*formal*) relating to the place where or the time when sb was born: *her natal home*

na·tal·ity /nəˈtæləti/ *noun* [U] (*technical*) the number of births every year for every 1 000 people in the population SYN **birth rate**

natch /nætʃ/ *adv.* (*slang*) used to say that sth is obvious or exactly as you would expect SYN **naturally**: *He was wearing the latest T-shirt, natch.*

na·tion O-w /ˈneɪʃn/ *noun*
1 O-w [C] a country considered as a group of people with the same language, culture and history, who live in a particular area under one government: *an independent nation* ◇ *the African nations* **2** O-w [sing.] all the people in a country SYN **population**: *The entire nation, it seemed, was watching TV.* ▶ **na·tion·hood** /ˈneɪʃnhʊd/ *noun* [U]: *Citizenship is about the sense of nationhood.*

na·tion·al O-w /ˈnæʃnəl/ *adj., noun*
■ **adj.** [usually before noun] **1** O-w connected with a particular nation; shared by a whole nation: *national and local newspapers* ◇ *national and international news* ◇ *national and regional politics* ◇ *a national election* ◇ *These buildings are part of our national heritage.* ◇ *They are afraid of losing their national identity.* **2** O-w owned, controlled or paid for by the government: *a national airline/museum/theatre*
■ ***noun*** (*technical*) a citizen of a particular country: *Polish nationals living in Germany*

ˌnational ˈanthem *noun* the official song of a nation that is sung on special occasions

the ˌNational Asˌsembly for ˈWales *noun* = THE WELSH ASSEMBLY

ˌnational conˈvention *noun* a meeting held by a political party, especially in the US, to choose a candidate to take part in the election for President

ˌnational ˈcostume *noun* [C, U] (also **ˌnational ˈdress** [U]) the clothes traditionally worn by people from a particular country, especially on special occasions or for formal ceremonies

the ˌnational curˈriculum *noun* [sing.] (in Britain) a programme of study in all the main subjects that children aged 5 to 16 in state schools must follow

ˌnational ˈdebt *noun* [usually sing.] the total amount of money that the government of a country owes

the ˌNational ˈFront *noun* [sing.+ sing./pl. v.] (in Britain) a small political party with extreme views, especially on issues connected with race

ˌnational ˈgrid *noun* [sing.] (*BrE*) the system of power lines that joins the places where electricity is produced, and takes electricity to all parts of the country

the ˌNational ˈGuard *noun* [sing.] **1** a small army, often used to protect a political leader **2** the army in each state of the US that can be used by the federal government if needed

the ˌNational ˈHealth Service *noun* [sing.] (*abbr.* NHS) the public health service in Britain that provides medical care and is paid for by taxes: *I got my glasses on the National Health (Service).*

ˌNational Inˈsurance *noun* [U] (*abbr.* NI) (in Britain) a system of payments that have to be made by employers and employees to provide help for people who are sick, old or unemployed

na·tion·al·ism /ˈnæʃnəlɪzəm/ *noun* [U] **1** the desire by a group of people who share the same race, culture, language, etc. to form an independent country: *Scottish nationalism* **2** (sometimes *disapproving*) a feeling of love for and pride in your country; a feeling that your country is better than any other

na·tion·al·ist /ˈnæʃnəlɪst/ *noun* **1** a person who wants their country to become independent: *Scottish nationalists* **2** (sometimes *disapproving*) a person who has a great love for and pride in their country; a person who has a feeling that their country is better than any other ▶ **na·tion·al·ist** *adj.*: *nationalist sentiments*

na·tion·al·is·tic /ˌnæʃnəˈlɪstɪk/ *adj.* (usually *disapproving*) having very strong feelings of love for and pride in your country, so that you think that it is better than any other

na·tion·al·ity /ˌnæʃəˈnæləti/ *noun* (*pl.* **-ies**) **1** [U, C] the legal right of belonging to a particular nation: *to **take/have/hold** French **nationality*** ◇ *All applicants will be considered regardless of age, sex, religion or nationality.* ◇ *The college attracts students of all nationalities.* ◇ *She has **dual nationality*** (= is a citizen of two countries). **2** [C] a group of people with the same language, culture and history who form part of a political nation: *Kazakhstan alone contains more than a hundred nationalities.*

na·tion·al·ize (*BrE* also **-ise**) /ˈnæʃnəlaɪz/ *verb* **~ sth** to put an industry or a company under the control of the government, which becomes its owner: *nationalized industries* OPP **denationalize, privatize** ▶ **na·tion·al·iza·tion, -isa·tion** /ˌnæʃnəlaɪˈzeɪʃn; *NAmE* -ləˈz-/ *noun* [U, C]

the ˌNational ˈLeague *noun* (in the US) one of the two organizations for professional BASEBALL ➲ see also AMERICAN LEAGUE

na·tion·al·ly /ˈnæʃnəli/ *adv.* relating to a country as a whole; relating to a particular country: *The programme was broadcast nationally.* ◇ *Meetings were held locally and nationally.* ◇ *He's a talented athlete who competes nationally and internationally.*

the ˌNational ˈMotto *noun* [sing.] the official US motto 'In God we trust'

ˌnational ˈpark *noun* an area of land that is protected by the government for people to visit because of its natural beauty and historical or scientific interest

ˌnational ˈservice *noun* [U] the system in some countries in which young people have to do military training for a period of time SYN **military service**: *to do your national service*

ˌNational ˈSocialism *noun* [U] (*politics*) the policies of the German Nazi party ▶ **ˌNational ˈSocialist** *noun, adj.*

ˌnational ˈtrail *noun* a long route through beautiful country where people can walk or ride

the ˌNational ˈTrust *noun* an organization that owns and takes care of places of historical interest or natural beauty in England, Wales and Northern Ireland, so that people can go and visit them

N

ˌ**nation ˈstate** *noun* a group of people with the same culture, language, etc. who have formed an independent country

na·tion·wide /ˌneɪʃnˈwaɪd/ *adj.* happening or existing in all parts of a particular country: *a nationwide campaign* ▶ **na·tion·wide** *adv.*: *The company has over 500 stores nationwide.*

na·tive /ˈneɪtɪv/ *adj., noun*

■ ***adj.*** **1** [only before noun] connected with the place where you were born and lived for the first years of your life: *your* ***native land/country/city*** ◇ *It is a long time since he has visited his native Chile.* ◇ *Her native language is Korean.* ➲ see also NATIVE SPEAKER **2** [only before noun] connected with the place where you have always lived or have lived for a long time: *native Berliners* **3** [only before noun] (sometimes *offensive*) connected with the people who originally lived in a country before other people, especially white people, came there: *native peoples* ◇ *native art* **4** **~ (to...)** (of animals and plants) existing naturally in a place SYN **indigenous**: *the native plants of America* ◇ *The tiger is native to India.* ◇ *native species* **5** [only before noun] that you have naturally without having to learn it SYN **innate**: *native cunning*

IDM **go ˈnative** (often *humorous*) (of a person staying in another country) to try to live and behave like the local people

■ ***noun*** **1** a person who was born in a particular country or area: *a native of New York* **2** a person who lives in a particular place, especially sb who has lived there a long time SYN **local**: *You can always tell the difference between the tourists and the natives.* ◇ *She speaks Italian like a native.* **3** (*old-fashioned, offensive*) a word used in the past by Europeans to describe a person who lived in a place originally, before white people arrived there: *disputes between early settlers and natives* **4** an animal or a plant that lives or grows naturally in a particular area: *The kangaroo is a native of Australia.*

ˌ**Native Aˈmerican** (also **Aˌmerican ˈIndian**) *noun* a member of any of the races of people who were the original people living in America ▶ ˌ**Native Aˈmerican** *adj.*: *Native American languages*

ˌ**Na·tive Caˈn·adian** *noun* (*CanE*) an Aboriginal Canadian; a Canadian Indian, Inuit or Metis

ˌ**native ˈspeaker** *noun* a person who speaks a language as their first language and has not learned it as a foreign language

na·tiv·ity /nəˈtɪvəti/ *noun* **1 the Nativity** [sing.] the birth of Jesus Christ, celebrated by Christians at Christmas **2** a picture or a model of the baby Jesus Christ and the place where he was born

naˈtivity play *noun* a play about the birth of Jesus Christ, usually performed by children at Christmas

NATO /ˈneɪtəʊ; *NAmE* -toʊ/ (also **Nato**) *abbr.* North Atlantic Treaty Organization. NATO is an organization to which many European countries and the US and Canada belong. They agree to give each other military help if necessary.

nat·ter /ˈnætə(r)/ *verb* [I] **~ (away/on)** **(about sth)** (*BrE, informal*) to talk for a long time, especially about unimportant things SYN **chat** ▶ **nat·ter** *noun* [sing.]: (*BrE, informal*) *to have a good natter*

natty /ˈnæti/ *adj.* (*old-fashioned, informal*) **1** neat and fashionable: *a natty suit* **2** well designed; clever: *a natty little briefcase* ▶ **nat·tily** *adv.*

nat·ural ⚿ /ˈnætʃrəl/ *adj., noun*

■ ***adj.***

▸ IN NATURE **1** ⚿ [only before noun] existing in nature; not made or caused by humans: *natural disasters* ◇ ***the natural world*** (= of trees, rivers, animals and birds) ◇ *a country's* ***natural resources*** (= its coal, oil, forests, etc.) ◇ *wildlife in its natural habitat* ◇ *natural yogurt* (= with no flavour added) ◇ *My hair soon grew back to its natural colour* (= after being DYED). ◇ *The clothes are available in warm natural colours.* ➲ compare SUPERNATURAL

▸ EXPECTED **2** ⚿ normal; as you would expect: *to die of* ***natural causes*** (= not by violence, but normally, of old age) ◇ *He thought social inequality was all part of the natural order of things.* ◇ *She was the natural choice for the job.* ➲ compare UNNATURAL

▸ BEHAVIOUR **3** ⚿ used to describe behaviour that is part of the character that a person or an animal was born with: *the natural agility of a cat* ◇ *the natural processes of language learning* ◇ *It's* ***only natural*** *to worry about your children.*

▸ ABILITY **4** ⚿ [only before noun] having an ability that you were born with: *He's a natural leader.*

▸ RELAXED **5** relaxed and not pretending to be sb/sth different: *It's difficult to look natural when you're feeling nervous.*

▸ PARENTS/CHILDREN **6** [only before noun] (of parents or their children) related by blood: *His natural mother was unable to care for him so he was raised by an aunt.* **7** [only before noun] (*old use* or *formal*) (of a son or daughter) born to parents who are not married SYN **illegitimate**: *She was a natural daughter of King James II.*

▸ BASED ON HUMAN REASON **8** [only before noun] based on human reason alone: ***natural justice/law***

▸ IN MUSIC **9** used after the name of a note to show that the note is neither SHARP nor FLAT. The written symbol is (♮).: *B natural* ➲ picture at MUSIC

■ ***noun***

▸ PERSON **1** **~ (for sth)** a person who is very good at sth without having to learn how to do it, or who is perfectly suited for a particular job: *She took to flying like a natural.* ◇ *He's a natural for the role.*

▸ IN MUSIC **2** a normal musical note, not its SHARP or FLAT form. The written symbol is (♮).

ˈ**natural-born** *adj.* [only before noun] having a natural ability or skill that you have not had to learn

ˌ**natural ˈchildbirth** *noun* [U] a method of giving birth to a baby in which a woman chooses not to take drugs and does special exercises to make her relaxed

ˌ**natural ˈgas** *noun* [U] gas that is found under the ground or the sea and that is used as a fuel

ˌ**natural ˈhistory** *noun* [U, C] the study of plants and animals; an account of the plant and animal life of a particular place: *the Natural History Museum* ◇ *He has written a natural history of Scotland.*

nat·ur·al·ism /ˈnætʃrəlɪzəm/ *noun* [U] **1** a style of art or writing that shows people, things and experiences as they really are **2** (*philosophy*) the theory that everything in the world and life is based on natural causes and laws, and not on spiritual or SUPERNATURAL ones

nat·ur·al·ist /ˈnætʃrəlɪst/ *noun* a person who studies animals, plants, birds and other living things

nat·ur·al·is·tic /ˌnætʃrəˈlɪstɪk/ *adj.* **1** (of artists, writers, etc. or their work) showing things as they appear in the natural world **2** copying the way things are in the natural world: *to study behaviour in laboratory and naturalistic settings*

nat·ur·al·ize (*BrE* also **-ise**) /ˈnætʃrəlaɪz/ *verb* [usually passive] **1** [T] **~ sb** to make sb who was not born in a particular country a citizen of that country **2** [T] **~ sth** to introduce a plant or an animal to a country where it is not NATIVE **3** [I] (of a plant or an animal) to start growing or living naturally in a country where it is not NATIVE ▶ **nat·ur·al·iza·tion, -isa·tion** /ˌnætʃrəlaɪˈzeɪʃn; *NAmE* -ləˈz-/ *noun* [U]

ˌ**natural ˈlanguage** *noun* [C, U] a language that has developed in a natural way and is not designed by humans

ˌ**natural ˈlanguage processing** *noun* [U] (*abbr.* NLP) the use of computers to process natural languages, for example for translating

ˌ**natural ˈlaw** *noun* [U] a set of moral principles on which human behaviour is based

nat·ur·al·ly ⚿ /ˈnætʃrəli/ *adv.*

1 ⚿ in a way that you would expect SYN **of course**: *Naturally, I get upset when things go wrong.* ◇ *After a while, we naturally started talking about the children.* ◇ *'Did you complain about the noise?' 'Naturally.'* **2** ⚿ without special help, treatment or action by sb: *naturally occurring chem-*

icals ◇ *plants that grow naturally in poor soils* **3** 🔑 as a normal, logical result of sth: *This leads naturally to my next point.* **4** 🔑 in a way that shows or uses abilities or qualities that a person or an animal is born with: *to be naturally artistic* ◇ *a naturally gifted athlete* **5** in a relaxed and normal way: *Just act naturally.*

IDM **come 'naturally (to sb/sth)** if sth **comes naturally** to you, you are able to do it very easily and very well: *Making money came naturally to him.*

nat·ur·al·ness /ˈnætʃrəlnəs/ *noun* [U] **1** the state or quality of being like real life: *The naturalness of the dialogue made the book so true to life.* **2** the quality of behaving in a normal, relaxed or innocent way: *Teenagers lose their childhood simplicity and naturalness.* **3** the style or quality of happening in a normal way that you would expect: *the naturalness of her reaction*

ˌnatural ˈnumber *noun* (*mathematics*) a positive whole number such as 1, 2, or 3, and sometimes also zero

ˌnatural phiˈlosophy *noun* [U] (*old use*) the study of the physical world, which developed into the natural sciences

ˌnatural ˈscience *noun* [C, U] a science concerned with studying the physical world. Chemistry, biology and physics are all natural sciences. ➲ compare EARTH SCIENCE, LIFE SCIENCES

ˌnatural seˈlection *noun* [U] the process by which plants, animals, etc. that can adapt to their environment survive and reproduce, while the others disappear

ˌnatural ˈwastage (*BrE*) (also **at·tri·tion** *NAmE, BrE*) *noun* [U] the process of reducing the number of people who are employed by an organization by, for example, not replacing people who leave their jobs

na·ture 🔑 /ˈneɪtʃə(r)/ *noun*

> **WORD FAMILY**
> **nature** *noun*
> **natural** *adj.* (≠ unnatural)
> **naturally** *adv.* (≠ unnaturally)

▸ PLANTS, ANIMALS **1** 🔑 (often **Nature**) [U] all the plants, animals and things that exist in the universe that are not made by people: *the beauties of nature* ◇ *man-made substances not found in nature* ◇ *nature conservation* **HELP** You cannot use 'the nature' in this meaning: ~~*the beauties of the nature*~~. It is often better to use another appropriate word, for example **the countryside**, **the scenery** or **wildlife**: *We stopped to admire the scenery.* ◇ ~~*We stopped to admire the nature.*~~ **2** 🔑 (often **Nature**) [U] the way that things happen in the physical world when it is not controlled by people: *the **forces/laws of nature*** ◇ *Just let nature take its course.* ◇ *Her illness was Nature's way of telling her to do less.* ➲ see also MOTHER NATURE

▸ CHARACTER **3** 🔑 [C, U] the usual way that a person or an animal behaves that is part of their character: *It's **not in his nature** to be unkind.* ◇ *She is very sensitive **by nature**.* ◇ *We appealed to his **better nature*** (= his kindness). ➲ see also GOOD NATURE, HUMAN NATURE, SECOND NATURE

▸ BASIC QUALITIES **4** 🔑 [sing.] the basic qualities of a thing: *the changing nature of society* ◇ *It's difficult to define the exact nature of the problem.* ◇ *My work is very specialized **in nature**.*

▸ TYPE/KIND **5** [sing.] a type or kind of sth: *books of a scientific nature* ◇ *Don't worry about things of that nature.*

▸ -NATURED **6** (in adjectives) having the type of character or quality mentioned: *a good-natured man*

IDM **against ˈnature** not natural; not moral: *Murder is a crime against nature.* **(get, go, etc.) back to ˈnature** to return to a simple kind of life in the country, away from cities **in the nature of ˈsth** similar to sth; a type of sth; in the style of sth: *His speech was in the nature of an apology.* **in the ˈnature of things** in the way that things usually happen: *In the nature of things, young people often rebel against their parents.* ➲ more at CALL *n.*, FORCE *n.*

ˈnature reserve *noun* an area of land where the animals and plants are protected

ˈnature strip *noun* (*AustralE*) a piece of public land between the edge of a house, or other building, and the street, usually planted with grass

ˈnature trail *noun* a path through countryside which you can follow in order to see the interesting plants and animals that are found there

na·tur·ism /ˈneɪtʃərɪzəm/ *noun* [U] (*especially BrE*) = NUDISM

na·tur·ist /ˈneɪtʃərɪst/ *noun* (*especially BrE*) = NUDIST

na·tur·op·athy /ˌneɪtʃəˈrɒpəθi; *NAmE* -ˈrɑːp-/ *noun* [U] a system for treating diseases or conditions using natural foods and herbs and various other techniques, rather than artificial drugs ▸ **na·turo·path** /ˈneɪtʃərəpæθ/ *noun*: *A medical herbalist or naturopath will be able to advise on individual treatment plans.* **na·turo·path·ic** /ˌneɪtʃərəˈpæθɪk/ *adj.* [only before noun]: *naturopathic medicine* ◇ *a naturopathic physician*

naught *noun* = NOUGHT

naughty /ˈnɔːti/ *adj.* (**naugh·tier**, **naugh·ti·est**) **1** (especially of children) behaving badly; not willing to obey: *a naughty boy/girl* ◇ (*humorous*) *I'm being very naughty—I've ordered champagne!* **2** (*informal*, often *humorous*) slightly rude; connected with sex **SYN** **risqué**: *a naughty joke/word* ▸ **naugh·tily** *adv.* **naugh·ti·ness** *noun* [U]

nau·sea /ˈnɔːziə; ˈnɔːsiə/ *noun* [U] the feeling that you have when you want to VOMIT, for example because you are ill/sick or are disgusted by sth: *A wave of nausea swept over her.* ◇ *Nausea and vomiting are common symptoms.* ➲ see also AD NAUSEAM

nau·se·ate /ˈnɔːzieɪt; ˈnɔːsieɪt/ *verb* **1** **~ sb** to make sb feel that they want to VOMIT **2** **~ sb** to make sb feel disgusted **SYN** **revolt**, **sicken**: *I was nauseated by the violence in the movie.* ▸ **nau·se·at·ing** *adj.*: *a nauseating smell* ◇ *his nauseating behaviour* **nau·se·at·ing·ly** *adv.*

nau·se·ous /ˈnɔːziəs; ˈnɔːsiəs; *NAmE* ˈnɔːʃəs/ *adj.* **1** feeling as if you want to VOMIT: *She felt dizzy and nauseous.* **2** making you feel as if you want to VOMIT: *a nauseous smell*

naut·ical /ˈnɔːtɪkl/ *adj.* connected with ships, sailors and sailing: *nautical terms*

ˌnautical ˈmile (also **ˈsea mile**) *noun* a unit for measuring distance at sea; 1 852 metres

naut·ilus /ˈnɔːtɪləs/ *noun* a creature with a shell that lives in the sea. It has TENTACLES around its mouth and its shell fills with gas to help it float.

Nav·ajo (also **Nava·ho**) /ˈnævəhəʊ; *NAmE* -hoʊ/ *noun* (*pl.* **Nav·ajo** or **Nav·ajos**) a member of the largest group of Native American people, most of whom live in the US states of Arizona, New Mexico and Utah

naval /ˈneɪvl/ *adj.* connected with the navy of a country: *a naval base/officer/battle*

Nava·rat·ri /ˌnævəˈrætri/ (also **Nava·rat·ra** /-trə/) *noun* a Hindu festival lasting for nine nights, which takes place in the autumn/fall

nave /neɪv/ *noun* the long central part of a church where most of the seats are ➲ compare TRANSEPT

navel /ˈneɪvl/ (also *informal* **ˈbelly button**) (*BrE* also **ˈtummy button**) *noun* the small hollow part or lump in the middle of the stomach where the UMBILICAL CORD was cut at birth ➲ **VISUAL VOCAB** page V48

ˈnavel-gazing *noun* [U] (*disapproving*) the fact of thinking too much about a single issue and how it could affect you, without thinking about other things that could also affect the situation

ˌnavel ˈorange *noun* a large orange without seeds that has a part at the top that looks like a navel

nav·ig·able /ˈnævɪɡəbl/ *adj.* (of rivers, etc.) wide and deep enough for ships and boats to sail on ▸ **nav·ig·abil·ity** /ˌnævɪɡəˈbɪləti/ *noun* [U]

navi·gate /ˈnævɪɡeɪt/ *verb* **1** [I, T] to find your position or the position of your ship, plane, car etc. and the direction you need to go in, for example by using a map: *to navigate by the stars* ◇ *I'll drive, and you can navigate.* ◇ **~ your way ...** *How do you navigate your way through a forest?* **2** [T] **~**

N

sth to sail along, over or through a sea, river etc: *The river became too narrow and shallow to navigate.* **3** [T] **~ sth** to find the right way to deal with a difficult or complicated situation: *We next had to navigate a complex network of committees.* **4** [I, T] **~** (**sth**) (*computing*) to find your way around on the Internet or on a particular website

navi·ga·tion /ˌnævɪˈɡeɪʃn/ *noun* [U] **1** the skill or the process of planning a route for a ship or other vehicle and taking it there: *navigation systems* ◇ *an expert in navigation* **2** the movement of ships or aircraft: *the right of navigation through international waters* ▶ **nav·iga·tion·al** /-ʃənl/ *adj.*: *navigational aids*

navi·ga·tor /ˈnævɪɡeɪtə(r)/ *noun* a person who navigates, for example on a ship or an aircraft

navvy /ˈnævi/ *noun* (*pl.* -ies) (*BrE*) a person employed to do hard physical work, especially building roads, etc.

navy 0‑ᴡ /ˈneɪvi/ *noun* (*pl.* -ies)
1 0‑ᴡ [C+sing./pl. v.] the part of a country's armed forces that fights at sea, and the ships that it uses: *the British and German navies* ◇ *He's joined* ***the navy/the Navy.*** ◇ *an officer in* ***the navy/the Navy*** ◇ *The navy is/are considering buying six new warships.* ➲ COLLOCATIONS at WAR ➲ see also NAVAL (2) **2** [U] = NAVY BLUE

ˈnavy bean (*NAmE*) (*BrE* **hari·cot**, **ˌharicot ˈbean**) *noun* a type of small white BEAN that is usually dried before it is sold and then left in water before cooking

ˌnavy ˈblue (also **navy**) *adj.* very dark blue in colour: *a navy blue suit* ▶ **ˌnavy ˈblue** (also **navy**) *noun* [U]: *She was dressed in navy blue.*

naw /nɔː/ *exclamation* (*informal*) no, used when answering a question: *'Want some toast?' 'Naw.'*

nawab /nəˈwɑːb/ *noun* **1** an Indian ruler during the Mogul empire **2** (*IndE*) a Muslim with high social status or rank

N

Naxa·lite /ˈnæksəlaɪt/ *noun* (in India) a member of a group which believes in political revolution in order to change the system of how land is owned. It took its name from Naxalbari in West Bengal, where it started.

nay /neɪ/ *adv.* **1** (*old-fashioned*) used to emphasize sth you have just said by introducing a stronger word or phrase: *Such a policy is difficult, nay impossible.* **2** (*old use* or *dialect*) no ➲ compare YEA

Nazi /ˈnɑːtsi/ *noun* **1** a member of the National Socialist party which controlled Germany from 1933 to 1945 **2** (*disapproving*) a person who uses their power in a cruel way; a person with extreme and unreasonable views about race ▶ **Nazi** *adj.* **Naz·ism** /ˈnɑːtsɪzəm/ *noun* [U]

NB (*BrE*) (also **N.B.** *US*, *BrE*) /ˌen ˈbiː/ *abbr.* used in writing to make sb take notice of a particular piece of information that is important (from Latin 'nota bene'): *NB The office will be closed from 1 July.*

NBA /ˌen biː ˈeɪ/ *abbr.* National Basketball Association (the US organization responsible for professional BASKETBALL)

NBC /ˌen biː ˈsiː/ *abbr.* National Broadcasting Company (a US company that produces television and radio programmes): *NBC News*

NCO /ˌen siː ˈəʊ; *NAmE* ˈoʊ/ *abbr.* non-commissioned officer (a soldier who has a rank such as CORPORAL or SERGEANT)

NCT /ˌen siː ˈtiː/ *noun* (in Britain) the abbreviation for 'National Curriculum Test' (a test taken by children at the ages of 7 and 11, also called SAT)

ndugu /nˈdʊɡʊ/ *noun* (*EAfrE*) (usually **Ndugu**) (in Tanzania) a title for a man or woman that shows respect

NE *abbr.* north-east; north-eastern: *NE England*

Ne·an·der·thal /niˈændətɑːl; *NAmE* -dɑːrt-/ (also **neanderthal**) *adj.* **1** used to describe a type of human being who used stone tools and lived in Europe during the early period of human history **2** (*disapproving*) very old-fashioned and not wanting any change: *neanderthal attitudes* **3** (*disapproving*) (of a man) unpleasant, rude and not behaving in a socially acceptable way ▶ **Ne·an·der·thal** *noun*

neap tide /ˈniːp taɪd/ (also **neap**) *noun* a TIDE in the sea in which there is only a very small difference between the level of the water at HIGH TIDE and that at LOW TIDE

Which Word?

near / close

- The adjectives **near** and **close** are often the same in meaning, but in some phrases only one of them may be used: *the near future* ◇ *a near neighbour* ◇ *a near miss* ◇ *a close contest* ◇ *a close encounter* ◇ *a close call.* **Close** is more often used to describe a relationship between people: *a close friend* ◇ *close family* ◇ *close links.* You do not usually use **near** in this way.

near 0‑ᴡ /nɪə(r); *NAmE* nɪr/ *adj.*, *adv.*, *prep.*, *verb*
■ ***adj.*** (**near·er**, **near·est**) HELP In senses 1 to 4 **near** and **nearer** do not usually go before a noun; **nearest** can go either before or after a noun. **1** 0‑ᴡ a short distance away SYN **close**: *His house is very near.* ◇ *Where's the nearest bank?* ➲ note at NEXT **2** 0‑ᴡ a short time away in the future: *The conflict is unlikely to be resolved* ***in the near future*** (= very soon). **3** 0‑ᴡ coming next after sb/sth: *She has a 12-point lead over her nearest rival.* **4** 0‑ᴡ (usually **nearest**) similar; most similar: *He was* ***the nearest thing to*** (= the person most like) *a father she had ever had.* ➲ see also O.N.O. **5** 0‑ᴡ [only before noun] (no comparative or superlative) close to being sb/sth: *The election proved to be a near disaster for the party.* ◇ *a near impossibility* **6** 0‑ᴡ **~ relative/relation** used to describe a close family connection: *Only the nearest relatives were present at the funeral.* ▶ **nearness** *noun* [U]: *the nearness of death*
IDM **your ˌnearest and ˈdearest** (*informal*) your close family and friends **a ˌnear ˈthing** a situation in which you are successful, but which could also have ended badly: *Phew! That was a near thing! It could have been a disaster.* ◇ *We won in the end but it was a near thing.* **to the nearest ...** followed by a number when counting or measuring approximately: *We calculated the cost to the nearest 50 dollars.*
■ ***adv.*** (**near·er**, **near·est**) **1** 0‑ᴡ at a short distance away: *A bomb exploded somewhere near.* ◇ *She took a step nearer.* ◇ *Visitors came from* ***near and far.*** **2** 0‑ᴡ a short time away in the future: *The exams are* ***drawing near.*** **3** (especially in compounds) almost: *a near-perfect performance* ◇ *I'm as near certain as can be.*
IDM **as near as** as accurately as: *There were about 3 000 people there, as near as I could judge.* **as ˌnear as ˈdamn it/ˈdammit** (*BrE*, *informal*) used to say that an amount is so nearly correct that the difference does not matter: *It will cost £350, or as near as dammit.* **near eˈnough** (*BrE*, *informal*) used to say that sth is so nearly true that the difference does not matter: *We've been here twenty years, near enough.* **not anywhere near/nowhere near** far from; not at all: *The job doesn't pay anywhere near enough for me.* **so ˌnear and ˌyet so ˈfar** used to comment on sth that was almost successful but in fact failed ➲ more at PRETTY *adv.*
■ ***prep.*** (also **near to**, **near·er** (**to**), **near·est** (**to**)) HELP **Near to** is not usually used before the name of a place, person, festival, etc. **1** 0‑ᴡ at a short distance away from sb/sth: *Do you live near here?* ◇ *Go and sit nearer (to) the fire.* ➲ note at NEXT **2** 0‑ᴡ a short period of time from sth: *My birthday is very near Christmas.* ◇ *I'll think about it* ***nearer*** *(to)* ***the time*** (= when it is just going to happen). **3** 0‑ᴡ used before a number to mean 'approximately', 'just below or above': *Share prices are near their record high of last year.* ◇ *Profits fell from $11 million to nearer $8 million.* **4** 0‑ᴡ similar to sb/sth in quality, size, etc: *Nobody else comes near her in intellect.* ◇ *He's nearer 70 than 60.* ◇ *This colour is nearest (to) the original.* **5** 0‑ᴡ **~** (**doing**) **sth** close to a particular state: *a state near (to) death* ◇ *She was* ***near to tears*** (= almost crying). ◇ *We* ***came near to*** *being killed.*
IDM see HAND *n.*, HEART, MARK *n.*
■ ***verb*** [T, I] **~** (**sth**) (rather *formal*) to come close to sth in time or space SYN **approach**: *The project is* ***nearing comple-***

tion. ◇ *She was* **nearing the end** *of her life.* ◇ *We neared the top of the hill.* ◇ *As Christmas neared, the children became more and more excited.*

near·by 🔑 /ˌnɪəˈbaɪ; *NAmE* ˌnɪrˈbaɪ/ *adj., adv.*
■ ***adj.*** 🔑 [usually before noun] near in position; not far away: *Her mother lived in a nearby town.* ◇ *There were complaints from nearby residents.*
■ ***adv.*** 🔑 a short distance from sb/sth; not far away: *They live nearby.* ◇ *The car is parked nearby.*

ˌnear-ˌdeath exˈperience *noun* an occasion when you almost die, which is often remembered as leaving your body or going down a tunnel

the ˌNear ˈEast *noun* [sing.] = THE MIDDLE EAST

near·ly 🔑 /ˈnɪəli; *NAmE* ˈnɪrli/ *adv.*
almost; not quite; not completely: *The bottle's nearly empty.* ◇ *I've worked here for nearly two years.* ◇ *It's nearly time to leave.* ◇ *The audience was nearly all men.* ◇ *He's nearly as tall as you are.* ◇ *They're nearly always late.* ◇ *She very nearly died.* ➲ SYNONYMS at ALMOST
IDM **not ˈnearly** 🔑 much less than; not at all: *It's not nearly as hot as last year.* ◇ *There isn't nearly enough time to get there now.* ➲ more at PRETTY *adv.*

ˌnear ˈmiss *noun* **1** a situation when a serious accident or a disaster very nearly happens **2** a bomb or a shot that nearly hits what it is aimed at but misses it: (*figurative*) *He should have won the match—it was a near miss.* ➲ see also CLOSE/NEAR THING at THING

near·side /ˈnɪəsaɪd; *NAmE* ˈnɪrs-/ *adj.* [only before noun] (*BrE*) (for a driver) on the side that is nearest the edge of the road: *the car's nearside doors* ◇ *Keep to the nearside lane.* ▸ **the near·side** *noun* [sing.]: *The driver lost control and veered to the nearside.* OPP **offside**

near·sight·ed /ˌnɪəˈsaɪtɪd; *NAmE* ˌnɪr-/ *adj.* (*especially NAmE*) = SHORT-SIGHTED OPP **far-sighted** ▸ **near·sight·ed·ness** *noun* [U]

neat 🔑 /niːt/ *adj.* (**neat·er**, **neat·est**)
1 🔑 tidy and in order; carefully done or arranged: *a neat desk* ◇ *neat handwriting* ◇ *neat rows of books* ◇ *She was wearing a neat black suit.* ◇ *They sat in her* **neat and tidy** *kitchen.* **2** 🔑 (of people) liking to keep things tidy and in order; looking tidy or doing things in a tidy way: *Try and be neater!* **3** small, with a pleasing shape or appearance SYN **trim**: *her neat figure* **4** simple but clever: *a neat explanation* ◇ *a neat solution to the problem* **5** (*NAmE, informal*) good; excellent: *It's a really neat movie.* ◇ *We had a great time—it was pretty neat.* **6** (*BrE*) (*NAmE* **straight**) (especially of alcoholic drinks) not mixed with water or anything else: *neat whisky* ▸ **neat·ly** 🔑 *adv.*: *neatly folded clothes* ◇ *The box fitted neatly into the drawer.* ◇ *She summarized her plan very neatly.* **neat·ness** *noun* [U]

neat·en /ˈniːtn/ *verb* **~ sth** to make sth tidy

neb·bish /ˈnebɪʃ/ *noun* (*NAmE, informal*) a man who behaves in an anxious and nervous way and without confidence

neb·ula /ˈnebjələ/ *noun* (*pl.* **nebu·lae** /-liː/) (*astronomy*) a mass of dust or gas that can be seen in the night sky, often appearing very bright; a bright area in the night sky caused by a large cloud of stars that are far away

nebu·lous /ˈnebjələs/ *adj.* (*formal*) not clear SYN **vague**: *a nebulous concept*

ne·ces·sar·ies /ˈnesəsəriz; *NAmE* ˈnesəseriz/ *noun* [pl.] (*old-fashioned*) the things that you need, especially in order to live

ne·ces·sar·ily 🔑 /ˌnesəˈserəli; *BrE* also ˈnesəsərəli/ *adv.*
used to say that sth cannot be avoided: *The number of places available is necessarily limited.*
IDM **ˌnot necesˈsarily** 🔑 used to say that sth is possibly true but not definitely or always true: *The more expensive articles are not necessarily better.* ◇ *Biggest doesn't necessarily mean best.* ◇ *'We're going to lose.' 'Not necessarily.'*

ne·ces·sary 🔑 /ˈnesəsəri; *NAmE* -seri/ *adj.*
1 🔑 **~ (for sb/sth) (to do sth)** that is needed for a purpose or a reason SYN **essential**: *It may be necessary to buy a new one.* ◇ *It doesn't seem necessary for us to meet.* ◇ *Only use your car when absolutely necessary.* ◇ ***If necessary**, you can contact me at home.* ◇ *I'll make the necessary arrangements.* **2** 🔑 [only before noun] that must exist or happen and cannot be avoided SYN **inevitable**: *This is a necessary consequence of progress.*
IDM **a ˌnecessary ˈevil** a thing that is bad or that you do not like but which you must accept for a particular reason

ne·ces·si·tate /nəˈsesɪteɪt/ *verb* (*formal*) to make sth necessary: **~ sth** *Recent financial scandals have necessitated changes in parliamentary procedures.* ◇ **~ doing sth** *Increased traffic necessitated widening the road.* ◇ **~ sb/sth doing sth** *His new job necessitated him/his getting up at six.*

ne·ces·sity /nəˈsesəti/ *noun* **1** [U] the fact that sth must happen or be done; the need for sth: **~ (for sth)** *We recognize the necessity for a written agreement.* ◇ **~ (of sth/of doing sth)** *We were discussing the necessity of employing more staff.* ◇ **~ (for sb) to do sth** *There had never been any necessity for her to go out to work.* ◇ *This is,* **of necessity**, *a brief and incomplete account.* **2** [C] a thing that you must have and cannot manage without: *Many people cannot even afford* **basic necessities** *such as food and clothing.* ◇ *Air-conditioning is an absolute necessity in this climate.* **3** [C, usually sing.] a situation that must happen and that cannot be avoided: *Living in London, he felt, was an unfortunate necessity.*
IDM **neˌcessity is the ˌmother of inˈvention** (*saying*) a difficult new problem forces people to think of a solution to it ➲ more at VIRTUE

neck 🔑 /nek/ *noun, verb*

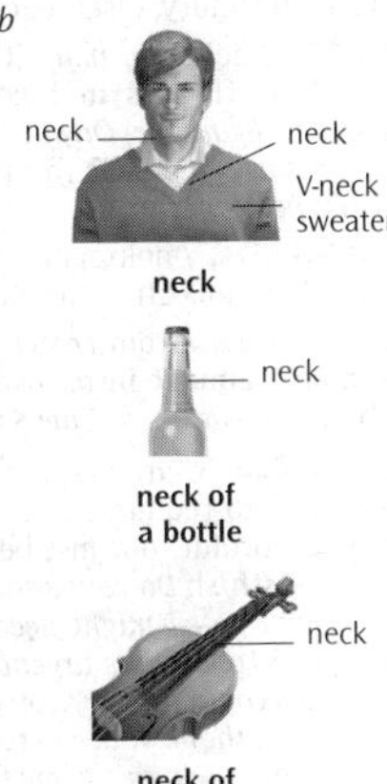

neck
neck of a bottle
neck of a violin

■ ***noun*** **1** 🔑 [C] the part of the body between the head and the shoulders: *He tied a scarf around his neck.* ◇ *Giraffes have very long necks.* ◇ *She* **craned** (= stretched) **her neck** *to get a better view.* ◇ *He broke his neck in the fall.* ◇ *Somebody's going to* **break their neck** (= injure themselves) *on these steps.* ➲ COLLOCATIONS at PHYSICAL ➲ VISUAL VOCAB page V48 **2** [C] the part of a piece of clothing that fits around the neck: *What neck size do you take?* ➲ see also CREW NECK, POLO NECK, TURTLENECK, V-NECK ➲ VISUAL VOCAB page V51 **3 -necked** (in adjectives) having the type of neck mentioned: *a round-necked sweater* ➲ see also OPEN-NECKED, STIFF-NECKED **4** [C] **~ (of sth)** a long narrow part of sth: *the neck of a bottle* ◇ *a neck of land* **5** [U] **~ (of sth)** the neck of an animal, cooked and eaten: *neck of lamb* ➲ see also BOTTLENECK, REDNECK, ROUGHNECK
IDM **be up to your neck in sth** to have a lot of sth to deal with: *We're up to our neck in debt.* ◇ *He's in it* (= trouble) *up to his neck.* **by a ˈneck** if a person or an animal wins a race **by a neck**, they win it by a short distance **ˌget it in the ˈneck** (*BrE, informal*) to be shouted at or punished because of sth that you have done **ˌneck and ˈneck (with sb/sth)** (also **ˌnip and ˈtuck (with sb)** especially in *US*) level with sb in a race or competition **ˌneck of the ˈwoods** (*informal*) a particular place or area: *He's from your neck of the woods* (= the area where you live). ➲ more at BLOCK *n.*, BRASS, BREATHE, MILLSTONE, PAIN *n.*, RISK *v.*, SAVE *v.*, SCRUFF, STICK *v.*, WRING
■ ***verb*** (usually **be necking**) [I] (*old-fashioned, informal*) when two people **are necking**, they are kissing each other in a sexual way

neck·er·chief /ˈnekətʃiːf; *NAmE* -kər-/ *noun* a square of cloth that you wear around your neck

neck·lace /ˈnekləs/ *noun, verb*
■ ***noun*** a piece of jewellery consisting of a chain, string of BEADS, etc. worn around the neck: *a diamond necklace* ➲ VISUAL VOCAB page V53
■ ***verb*** **~ sb** to kill sb by putting a burning car tyre around their neck ▸ **neck·lacing** *noun* [U]

neck·line /ˈneklaɪn/ *noun* the edge of a piece of clothing, especially a woman's, which fits around or below the neck: *a dress with a* ***low/round/plunging neckline***

neck·tie /ˈnektaɪ/ *noun* (*old-fashioned* or *NAmE*) = TIE

necro·man·cer /ˈnekrəʊmænsə(r); *NAmE* ˈnekroʊ-/ *noun* a person who claims to communicate by magic with people who are dead

necro·mancy /ˈnekrəʊmænsi; *NAmE* ˈnekroʊ-/ *noun* [U] **1** the practice of claiming to communicate by magic with the dead in order to learn about the future **2** the use of magic powers, especially evil ones

necro·philia /ˌnekrəˈfɪliə/ *noun* [U] sexual interest in dead bodies ▸ **necro·phil·iac** *noun*

ne·crop·olis /nəˈkrɒpəlɪs; *NAmE* -ˈkrɑːp-/ *noun* (*pl.* **ne·crop·olises** /-lɪsɪz/) a CEMETERY (= place where dead people are buried), especially a large one in an ancient city

nec·ropsy /ˈnekrɒpsi; *NAmE* ˈnekrɑːpsi/ *noun* (*pl.* **-ies**) (*NAmE*) an official examination of a dead body (especially that of an animal) in order to discover the cause of death **SYN** **autopsy**

ne·cro·sis /neˈkrəʊsɪs; *NAmE* -ˈkroʊ-/ *noun* [U] (*medical*) the death of most or all of the cells in an organ or TISSUE caused by injury, disease, or a loss of blood supply

nec·tar /ˈnektə(r)/ *noun* [U] **1** a sweet liquid that is produced by flowers and collected by BEES for making HONEY: (*figurative*) *On such a hot day, even water was nectar* (= very good). **2** the thick juice of some fruits as a drink: *peach nectar*

N

nec·tar·ine /ˈnektəriːn/ *noun* a round red and yellow fruit, like a PEACH with smooth skin

née /neɪ/ *adj.* (from *French*) a word used after a married woman's name to introduce the family name that she had when she was born: *Jane Smith, née Brown*

need 🔑 /niːd/ *verb, modal verb, noun*
■ ***verb*** **1** 🔑 to require sth/sb because they are essential or very important, not just because you would like to have them: **~ sth/sb** *Do you need any help?* ◇ *It's here if you need it.* ◇ *Don't go—I might need you.* ◇ *They* ***badly needed*** *a change.* ◇ *Food aid is urgently needed.* ◇ *What do you need your own computer for? You can use ours.* ◇ *I don't need your comments, thank you.* ◇ **~ to do sth** *I need to get some sleep.* ◇ *He needs to win this game to stay in the match.* ◇ *You don't need to leave yet, do you?* ◇ *This shirt needs to be washed.* ◇ **~ doing sth** *This shirt needs washing.* ➲ SYNONYMS at REASON **2** 🔑 **~ to do sth** used to show what you should or have to do: *All you need to do is complete this form.* ◇ *I didn't need to go to the bank after all—Mary lent me the money.* ➲ note at MODAL
IDM **need (to have) your ˈhead examined** (*informal*) to be crazy
■ ***modal verb*** 🔑 (*negative* **need not**, *short form* **needn't** /ˈniːdnt/) used to state that sth is/was not necessary or that only very little is/was necessary; used to ask if sth is/was necessary: **~ (not) do sth** *You needn't bother asking Rick—I know he's too busy.* ◇ *I* ***need hardly*** *tell you* (= you must already know) *that the work is dangerous.* ◇ *If she wants anything, she* ***need only*** *ask.* ◇ ***All you need*** *bring are sheets.* ◇ **~ (not) have done sth** *You needn't have worried* (= it was not necessary for you to worry, but you did) *—it all turned out fine.* ◇ ***Need you*** *have paid so much?*
■ ***noun*** **1** 🔑 [sing., U] a situation when sth is necessary or must be done: *to* ***satisfy/meet/identify a need*** ◇ **~ (for sth)** *There is an urgent need for qualified teachers.* ◇ *We will contact you again if the need arises.* ◇ *The house is* ***in need of*** *a thorough clean.* ◇ **~ (for sb/sth) to do sth** *There is* ***no need*** *for you to get up early tomorrow.* ◇ *I* ***had no need to*** *open the letter—I knew what it would say.* ◇ *There's no need to cry* (= stop crying). **2** 🔑 [C, U] a strong feeling that you want sb/sth or must have sth: *to fulfil an emotional need* ◇ *She felt the need to talk to someone.* ◇ *I'm* ***in need of*** *some fresh air.* ◇ *She* ***had no*** *more* ***need of*** *me.* **3** 🔑 [C, usually pl.] the things that sb requires in order to live in a comfortable way or achieve what they want: *financial needs* ◇ *a programme to* ***suit*** *your individual* ***needs*** ◇ *to* ***meet*** *children's special educational* ***needs*** **4** 🔑 [U] the state of not having enough food, money or support **SYN** **hardship**: *The charity aims to provide assistance to people* ***in need.*** ◇ *He helped me in my* ***hour of need.*** ➲ see also NEEDY
IDM **if need ˈbe** if necessary: *There's always food in the freezer if need be.* ➲ more at CRYING *adj.*, FRIEND

Grammar Point

need

- There are two separate verbs **need**.
- **Need** as a main verb has the question form **do you need?**, the negative **you don't need** and the past forms **needed**, **did you need?** and **didn't need**. It has two meanings: 1. to require something or to think that something is necessary: *Do you need any help?* ◇ *I needed to get some sleep.* 2. to have to or to be obliged to do sth: *Will we need to show our passports?*
- **Need** as a modal verb has **need** for all forms of the present tense, **need you?** as the question form and **need not (needn't)** as the negative. The past is **need have, needn't have**. It is used to say that something is or is not necessary: *Need I pay the whole amount now?*

ˈneed-blind *adj.* (*US*) (of a university's or college's policy of choosing which people to offer places on a course of study) depending only on sb's academic ability, without considering their ability to pay for it: *a need-blind admissions policy*

need·ful /ˈniːdfl/ *adj.* (*old-fashioned*) necessary

nee·dle 🔑 /ˈniːdl/ *noun, verb*
■ ***noun*** [C]
▸ FOR SEWING **1** 🔑 a small thin piece of steel that you use for sewing, with a point at one end and a hole for the thread at the other: *a* ***needle and thread*** ◇ *the eye* (= hole) *of a needle* ➲ VISUAL VOCAB page V35 ➲ see also PINS AND NEEDLES
▸ FOR KNITTING **2** 🔑 a long thin piece of plastic or metal with a point at one end that you use for knitting. You usually use two together: *knitting needles* ➲ VISUAL VOCAB page V35
▸ FOR DRUGS **3** 🔑 a very thin, pointed piece of steel used on the end of a SYRINGE for putting a drug into sb's body, or for taking blood out of it: *a hypodermic needle*
▸ ON INSTRUMENT **4** 🔑 a thin piece of metal on a scientific instrument that moves to point to the correct measurement or direction: *The compass needle was pointing north.*
▸ ON PINE TREE **5** [usually pl.] the thin, hard, pointed leaf of a PINE tree ➲ VISUAL VOCAB page V8
▸ ON RECORD PLAYER **6** the very small pointed piece of metal that touches a record that is being played in order to produce the sound **SYN** **stylus**
IDM **a needle in a ˈhaystack** a thing that is almost impossible to find: *Searching for one man in this city is like looking for a needle in a haystack.*
■ ***verb*** **~ sb** (*informal*) to deliberately annoy sb, especially by criticizing them continuously **SYN** **antagonize**: *Don't let her needle you.*

needle·cord /ˈniːdlkɔːd; *NAmE* -kɔːrd/ *noun* [U] (*BrE*) a type of fine CORDUROY

needle·point /ˈniːdlpɔɪnt/ *noun* [U] a type of decorative sewing in which you use very small STITCHES to make a picture on strong cloth

need·less /ˈniːdləs/ *adj.* **needless** death or suffering is not necessary because it could have been avoided **SYN** **unnecessary**: *needless suffering* ◇ *Banning smoking would save needless deaths.* ▸ **need·less·ly** *adv.*: *Many soldiers died needlessly.* ◇ *The process was needlessly slow.*

IDM ˌ**needless to** ˈ**say** used to emphasize that the information you are giving is obvious: *The problem, needless to say, is the cost involved.*

needle·woman /ˈniːdlwʊmən/ *noun* (*pl.* **-women** /-wɪmɪn/) a woman who sews well

needle·work /ˈniːdlwɜːk; *NAmE* -wɜːrk/ *noun* [U] things that are sewn by hand, especially for decoration; the activity of making things by sewing

needn't /ˈniːdnt/ *short form* need not

needs /niːdz/ *adv.* (*old use*) in a way that cannot be avoided: *We must needs depart.*

IDM **needs** ˈ**must** (**when the Devil drives**) (*saying*) in certain situations it is necessary for you to do sth that you do not like or enjoy

need-to-ˈ**know** *adj.*

IDM **on a** ˌ**need-to-**ˈ**know basis** with people being told only the things they need to know when they need to know them, and no more than that: *Information will be released strictly on a need-to-know basis.*

needy /ˈniːdi/ *adj.* (**need·ier, needi·est**) **1** (of people) not having enough money, food, clothes, etc. ➲ SYNONYMS at POOR **2 the needy** *noun* [pl.] people who do not have enough money, food, etc. **3** (of people) not confident, and needing a lot of love and emotional support from other people

neep /niːp/ *noun* (*ScotE, informal*) a SWEDE (= a large round yellow root vegetable): *neeps and tatties*

ne'er /neə(r); *NAmE* ner/ *adv.* (*literary*) = NEVER

ˈ**ne'er-do-well** *noun* (*old-fashioned*) a useless or lazy person

ne·fari·ous /nɪˈfeəriəs; *NAmE* -ˈfer-/ *adj.* (*formal*) criminal; immoral: *nefarious activities*

neg. *abbr.* NEGATIVE

neg·ate AW /nɪˈɡeɪt/ *verb* (*formal*) **1 ~ sth** to stop sth from having any effect SYN **nullify**: *Alcohol negates the effects of the drug.* **2 ~ sth** to state that sth does not exist

neg·ation /nɪˈɡeɪʃn/ *noun* (*formal*) **1** [C, usually sing., U] the exact opposite of sth; the act of causing sth not to exist or to become its opposite: *This political system was the negation of democracy.* **2** [U] disagreement or refusal: *She shook her head in negation.*

nega·tive 🔑 AW /ˈneɡətɪv/ *adj., noun, verb*

■ ***adj.***

▸ BAD **1** 🔑 bad or harmful: *The crisis had a* ***negative effect on*** *trade.* ◇ *The whole experience was definitely more positive than negative.* OPP **positive**

▸ NOT HOPEFUL **2** 🔑 considering only the bad side of sth/sb; lacking enthusiasm or hope: *Scientists have a fairly* ***negative attitude*** *to the theory.* ◇ *'He probably won't show up.' 'Don't be so negative.'* OPP **positive**

▸ NO **3** 🔑 expressing the answer 'no': *His response was negative.* ◇ *They received a negative reply.* OPP **affirmative**

▸ GRAMMAR **4** 🔑 containing a word such as 'no', 'not', 'never', etc: *a* ***negative form/sentence***

▸ SCIENTIFIC TEST **5** 🔑 (*abbr.* **neg.**) not showing any evidence of a particular substance or medical condition: *Her pregnancy test was negative.* OPP **positive**

▸ ELECTRICITY **6** (*technical*) containing or producing the type of electricity that is carried by an ELECTRON: *a* ***negative charge/current*** ◇ *the negative terminal of a battery* OPP **positive**

▸ NUMBER/QUANTITY **7** less than zero: *a negative trade balance* OPP **positive**

▸ **nega·tive·ly** AW *adv.*: *to react negatively to stress* ◇ *to respond negatively* ◇ *negatively charged electrons*

■ ***noun***

▸ NO **1** a word or statement that means 'no'; a refusal or DENIAL: (*formal*) *She answered* ***in the negative*** (= said 'no'). OPP **affirmative**

▸ IN PHOTOGRAPHY **2** a developed film showing the dark areas of an actual scene as light and the light areas as dark ➲ compare POSITIVE

▸ IN SCIENTIFIC TEST **3** the result of a test or an experiment that shows that a substance or condition is not present: *The percentage of* ***false negatives*** *generated by the cancer test is of great concern.* OPP **positive**

■ ***verb*** (*formal*) **1 ~ sth** to refuse to agree to a proposal or a request **2 ~ sth** to prove that sth is not true

ˌ**negative** ˈ**equity** *noun* [U] the situation in which the value of sb's house is less than the amount of money that is still owed to a MORTGAGE company, such as a bank

nega·tiv·ity /ˌneɡəˈtɪvəti/ (also **nega·tiv·ism** /ˈneɡətɪvɪzəm/) *noun* [U] (*formal*) a tendency to consider only the bad side of sth/sb; a lack of enthusiasm or hope

neg·lect /nɪˈɡlekt/ *verb, noun*

■ ***verb*** **1 ~ sb/sth** to fail to take care of sb/sth: *She denies neglecting her baby.* ◇ *The buildings had been neglected for years.* **2 ~ sth** to not give enough attention to sth: *Dance has been neglected by television.* ◇ *She has neglected her studies.* **3 ~ to do sth** (*formal*) to fail or forget to do sth that you ought to do SYN **omit**: *You neglected to mention the name of your previous employer.* ➲ see also NEGLIGENCE

■ ***noun*** [U] **~ (of sth/sb)** the fact of not giving enough care or attention to sth/sb; the state of not receiving enough care or attention: *The law imposes penalties for the neglect of children.* ◇ *The buildings are crumbling from* ***years of neglect.*** ◇ *The place smelled of decay and neglect.*

neg·lect·ed /nɪˈɡlektɪd/ *adj.* not receiving enough care or attention: *neglected children* ◇ *a neglected area of research*

neg·lect·ful /nɪˈɡlektfl/ *adj.* (*formal*) not giving enough care or attention to sb/sth: *neglectful parents* ◇ **~ of sth/sb** *She became neglectful of her appearance.*

neg·ligee (also **neg·ligée**) /ˈneɡlɪʒeɪ; *NAmE* ˌneɡlɪˈʒeɪ/ *noun* a woman's DRESSING GOWN made of very thin cloth

neg·li·gence /ˈneɡlɪdʒəns/ *noun* [U] (*law* or *formal*) the failure to give sb/sth enough care or attention: *The accident was caused by negligence on the part of the driver.* ◇ *The doctor was sued for medical negligence.*

neg·li·gent /ˈneɡlɪdʒənt/ *adj.* **1** (*law* or *formal*) failing to give sb/sth enough care or attention, especially when this has serious results: *The school had been negligent in not informing the child's parents about the incident.* ◇ *grossly negligent* **2** (*literary*) (of a person or their manner) relaxed; not formal or awkward SYN **nonchalant**: *He waved his hand in a negligent gesture.* ▸ **neg·li·gent·ly** *adv.*: *The defendant drove negligently and hit a lamp post.* ◇ *She was leaning negligently against the wall.*

neg·li·gible /ˈneɡlɪdʒəbl/ *adj.* of very little importance or size and not worth considering SYN **insignificant**: *The cost was negligible.* ◇ *a negligible amount*

ne·go·ti·able /nɪˈɡəʊʃiəbl; *NAmE* -ˈɡoʊ-/ *adj.* **1** that you can discuss or change before you make an agreement or a decision: *The terms of employment are negotiable.* ◇ *The price was not negotiable.* **2** (*business*) that you can exchange for money or give to another person in exchange for money OPP **non-negotiable**

ne·go·ti·ate /nɪˈɡəʊʃieɪt; *NAmE* -ˈɡoʊ-/ *verb* **1** [I] **~ (with sb) (for/about sth)** to try to reach an agreement by formal discussion: *The government will not negotiate with terrorists.* ◇ *We have been negotiating for more pay.* ◇ *a strong negotiating position* ◇ *negotiating skills* **2** [T] **~ sth** to arrange or agree sth by formal discussion: *to* ***negotiate a deal/contract/treaty/settlement*** ◇ *We successfully negotiated the release of the hostages.* **3** [T] **~ sth** (*formal*) to successfully get over or past a difficult part on a path or route: *The climbers had to negotiate a steep rock face.*

the neˈ**gotiating table** *noun* [sing.] (used mainly in newspapers) a formal discussion to try and reach an agreement: *We want to get all the parties back to the negotiating table.*

ne·go·ti·ation /nɪˌɡəʊʃiˈeɪʃn; *NAmE* -ˌɡoʊʃi-/ *noun* [C, usually pl., U] formal discussion between people who are trying to reach an agreement: ***peace/trade/wage, etc. negotiations*** ◇ *They begin another* ***round of negotiations*** *today.* ◇ *to* ***enter into/open/conduct negotiations*** *with sb* ◇ *The rent is a* ***matter for negotiation*** *between the landlord and the tenant.* ◇ *A contract is prepared* ***in negotiation with*** *our clients.* ◇ *The issue is still* ***under negotiation.*** ◇ *The price*

N

is generally **open to negotiation**. ➲ COLLOCATIONS at INTERNATIONAL

ne·go·ti·ator /nɪˈɡəʊʃieɪtə(r); *NAmE* -ˈɡoʊʃi-/ *noun* a person who is involved in formal political or financial discussions, especially because it is their job

Ne·gress /ˈniːɡres/ *noun* (*old-fashioned*, often *offensive*) a Negro woman or girl

neg·ri·tude /ˈneɡrɪtjuːd; *NAmE* -tuːd; *NAmE* also ˈniː-/ *noun* [U] (*formal*) the quality or fact of being of black African origin

Negro /ˈniːɡrəʊ; *NAmE* -ɡroʊ/ *noun* (*pl.* -oes) (*old-fashioned*, often *offensive*) a member of a race of people with dark skin who originally came from Africa

ˌNegro ˈspiritual *noun* = SPIRITUAL

neigh /neɪ/ *verb* [I] when a horse **neighs** it makes a long high sound ▸ **neigh** *noun*

neigh·bour 🔑 (*especially US* **neigh·bor**) /ˈneɪbə(r)/ *noun*
1 🔑 a person who lives next to you or near you: *We've had a lot of support from all our* ***friends and neighbours***. ◇ *Our* ***next-door neighbours*** *are very noisy.* **2** 🔑 a country that is next to or near another country: *Britain's nearest neighbour is France.* **3** a person or thing that is standing or located next to another person or thing: *Stand quietly, children, and try not to talk to your neighbour.* ◇ *The tree fell slowly, its branches caught in those of its neighbours.* **4** (*literary*) any other human: *We should all love our neighbours.*

neigh·bour·hood 🔑 (*especially US* **neigh·bor·hood**) /ˈneɪbəhʊd; *NAmE* ˈneɪbər-/ *noun*
1 🔑 a district or an area of a town; the people who live there: *We grew up in the same neighbourhood.* ◇ *a poor/quiet/residential neighbourhood* ◇ *Manhattan is divided into distinct neighborhoods.* ◇ *the neighbourhood police* ◇ *He shouted so loudly that the whole neighbourhood could hear him.* **2** 🔑 the area that you are in or the area near a particular place SYN **vicinity**: *We searched the surrounding neighbourhood for the missing boy.* ◇ *Houses* ***in the neighbourhood of*** *Paris are extremely expensive.*
IDM **in the neighbourhood of** (of a number or an amount) approximately; not exactly: *It cost in the neighbourhood of $500.*

ˌneighbourhood ˈwatch (*especially US* **ˌneighborhood ˈwatch**) *noun* [U] an arrangement by which a group of people in an area watch each other's houses regularly as a way of preventing crime

neigh·bour·ing (*especially US* **neigh·bor·ing**) /ˈneɪbərɪŋ/ *adj.* [only before noun] located or living near or next to a place or person: *a neighbouring house* ◇ *neighbouring towns* ◇ *a neighbouring farmer*

neigh·bour·ly (*especially US* **neigh·bor·ly**) /ˈneɪbəli; *NAmE* -bərli/ *adj.* **1** involving people, countries, etc. that live or are located near each other: *the importance of good neighbourly relations between the two states* ◇ *neighbourly help* ◇ *a neighbourly dispute* **2** friendly and helpful SYN **kind**: *It was a neighbourly gesture of theirs.* ▸ **neigh·bour·li·ness** (*especially US* **neighbor·li·ness**) *noun* [U]: *good neighbourliness* ◇ *a sense of community and neighbourliness*

nei·ther 🔑 /ˈnaɪðə(r); ˈniːðə(r)/ *det., pron., adv.*
■ ***det., pron.*** 🔑 not one nor the other of two things or people: *Neither answer is correct.* ◇ ***Neither of them*** *has/have a car.* ◇ *They produced two reports,* ***neither of which*** *contained any useful suggestions.* ◇ *'Which do you like?' 'Neither. I think they're both ugly.'*
■ ***adv.*** **1** 🔑 used to show that a negative statement is also true of sb/sth else: *He didn't remember and* ***neither did I***. ◇ *I hadn't been to New York before and* ***neither had Jane***. ◇ *'I can't understand a word of it.'* ***'Neither can I.'*** ◇ (*informal*) *'I don't know.'* ***'Me neither.'*** **2** 🔑 **neither… nor…** used to show that a negative statement is true of two things: *I neither knew nor cared what had happened to him.* ◇ *Their house is neither big nor small.* ◇ *Neither the TV nor the video actually work/works.*

Grammar Point

neither / either

- After **neither** and **either** you use a singular verb: *Neither candidate was selected for the job.*
- **Neither of** and **either of** are followed by a plural noun or pronoun and a singular or plural verb. A plural verb is more informal: *Neither of my parents speaks/speak a foreign language.*
- When **neither… nor…** or **either… or…** are used with two singular nouns, the verb can be singular or plural. A plural verb is more informal.

nel·son /ˈnelsn/ *noun* a move in which a WRESTLER stands behind his/her opponent, puts one or both arms underneath the opponent's arm(s) and holds the back of the opponent's neck. When done with one arm it is called a **half nelson**, and with both arms a **full nelson**.

nema·tode /ˈnemətəʊd; *NAmE* -toʊd/ (also **ˌnematode ˈworm**) *noun* a WORM with a thin, tube-shaped body that is not divided into sections

nem·esis /ˈneməsɪs/ *noun* [U, sing.] (*formal*) punishment or defeat that is deserved and cannot be avoided

neo- /ˈniːəʊ; *NAmE* ˈniːoʊ/ *combining form* (in adjectives and nouns) new; in a later form: *neo-Georgian* ◇ *neo-fascist*

neo·clas·sic·al /ˌniːəʊˈklæsɪkl; *NAmE* ˌniːoʊ-/ *adj.* [usually before noun] used to describe art and ARCHITECTURE that is based on the style of ancient Greece or Rome, or music, literature, etc. that uses traditional ideas or styles

neo·co·lo·nial·ism /ˌniːəʊkəˈləʊniəlɪzəm; *NAmE* ˌniːoʊkəˈloʊ-/ *noun* [U] (*disapproving*) the use of economic or political pressure by powerful countries to control or influence other countries

neo·con·ser·va·tive /ˌniːəʊkənˈsɜːvətɪv; *NAmE* ˌniːoʊkənˈsɜːrvətɪv/ *adj.* (*politics*) relating to political, economic, religious, etc. beliefs that return to traditional conservative views in a slightly changed form ▸ **neo·con·ser·va·tive** (also **neo·con**) *noun*

neo·cor·tex /ˌniːəʊˈkɔːteks; *NAmE* ˌniːoʊˈkɔːrteks/ *noun* (*anatomy*) part of the brain that controls sight and hearing

neo·dym·ium /ˌniːəʊˈdɪmiəm; *NAmE* ˌniːoʊ-/ *noun* [U] (*symb.* **Nd**) a chemical element. Neodymium is a silver-white metal.

neo·liberal /ˌniːəʊˈlɪbərəl; *NAmE* ˌniːoʊ-/ *adj.* [usually before noun] (*politics*) relating to a type of LIBERALISM that believes in a global free market, without government regulation, with businesses and industry controlled and run for profit by private owners

Neo·lith·ic /ˌniːəˈlɪθɪk/ *adj.* of the later part of the STONE AGE: *Neolithic stone axes* ◇ *Neolithic settlements*

neolo·gism /niˈɒlədʒɪzəm; *NAmE* -ˈɑːl-/ *noun* (*formal*) a new word or expression or a new meaning of a word

neon /ˈniːɒn; *NAmE* ˈniːɑːn/ *noun* [U] (*symb.* **Ne**) a chemical element. Neon is a gas that does not react with anything and that shines with a bright light when electricity is passed through it: ***neon lights/signs***

neo·natal /ˌniːəʊˈneɪtl; *NAmE* ˌniːoʊ-/ *adj.* (*technical*) connected with a child that has just been born: *the hospital's neonatal unit* ◇ *neonatal care*

neo·nate /ˈniːəʊneɪt; *NAmE* ˈniːoʊ-/ *noun* (*medical*) a baby that has recently been born, especially within the last four weeks

neo·phyte /ˈniːəfaɪt/ *noun* (*formal*) **1** a person who has recently started an activity: *The site gives neophytes the chance to learn from experts.* **2** a person who has recently changed to a new religion **3** a person who has recently become a priest or recently entered a religious order

neo·prene /ˈniːəpriːn/ *noun* [U] an artificial material which looks like rubber, used for making WETSUITS

NEPAD /ˈniːpæd/ *abbr.* (*SAfrE*) New Partnership for Africa's Development (= a plan decided by governments in Africa to help the continent's economy)

nephew 0‑ᵀ /ˈnefjuː; ˈnevjuː/ *noun* the son of your brother or sister; the son of your husband's or wife's brother or sister ➲ compare NIECE

ne plus ultra /ˌneɪ plʊs ˈʊltrɑː; *NAmE* ˈʊltrə/ *noun* (from *Latin, formal*) the perfect example of sth

nepo·tism /ˈnepətɪzəm/ *noun* [U] (*disapproving*) giving unfair advantages to your own family if you are in a position of power, especially by giving them jobs

Nep·tune /ˈneptjuːn; *NAmE* also -tuːn/ *noun* a planet in the SOLAR SYSTEM that is 8th in order of distance from the sun

nep·tun·ium /nepˈtjuːniəm; *NAmE* also -ˈtuːn-/ *noun* [U] (*symb.* **Np**) a chemical element. Neptunium is a RADIOACTIVE metal.

nerd /nɜːd; *NAmE* nɜːrd/ *noun* (*informal, disapproving*) **1** a person who is boring, stupid and not fashionable **2** a person who is very interested in computers SYN **geek** ▸ **nerdy** *adj.*

nerve 0‑ᵀ /nɜːv; *NAmE* nɜːrv/ *noun, verb*

■ ***noun*** **1** 0‑ᵀ [C] any of the long threads that carry messages between the brain and parts of the body, enabling you to move, feel pain, etc: *the optic nerve ◇ nerve cells ◇ nerve endings ◇ Every nerve in her body was tense.* ➲ VISUAL VOCAB page V48 **2** 0‑ᵀ **nerves** [pl.] feelings of worry or anxiety: *Even after years as a singer, he still suffers from nerves before a performance. ◇ I need something to **calm/steady my nerves**. ◇ Everyone's **nerves were on edge*** (= everyone felt TENSE). ◇ *He **lives on his nerves*** (= is always worried). **3** [U] the courage to do sth difficult or dangerous SYN **guts**: *It took a lot of nerve to take the company to court. ◇ I was going to have a go at parachuting but **lost my nerve** at the last minute. ◇ He **kept his nerve** to win the final set 6–4.* **4** [sing., U] (*informal*) a way of behaving that other people think is rude or not appropriate SYN **cheek**: *I don't know how you **have the nerve** to show your face after what you said! ◇ He's **got a nerve** asking us for money! ◇ 'Then she demanded to see the manager!' '**What a nerve!**'*

IDM **be a bag/bundle of ˈnerves** (*informal*) to be very nervous **get on sb's ˈnerves** (*informal*) to annoy sb **have nerves of steel** to be able to remain calm in a difficult or dangerous situation **hit/touch a (raw/sensitive) ˈnerve** to mention a subject that makes sb feel angry, upset, embarrassed, etc: *You touched a raw nerve when you mentioned his first wife.* ➲ more at BRASS, STRAIN *v.*, WAR *n.*

■ ***verb*** **~ yourself for sth/to do sth** to give yourself the courage or strength to do sth: *He nerved himself to ask her out.*

ˈnerve centre (*BrE*) (*NAmE* **ˈnerve center**) *noun* the place from which an activity or organization is controlled and instructions are sent out

ˈnerve gas *noun* a poisonous gas used in war that attacks your CENTRAL NERVOUS SYSTEM

nerve·less /ˈnɜːvləs; *NAmE* ˈnɜːrv-/ *adj.* **1** having no strength or feeling: *The knife fell from her nerveless fingers.* **2** having no fear: *She is a nerveless rider.* OPP **nervous**

ˈnerve-racking (also **ˈnerve-wracking**) *adj.* making you feel very nervous and worried

ner·vous 0‑ᵀ /ˈnɜːvəs; *NAmE* ˈnɜːrvəs/ *adj.*

1 0‑ᵀ anxious about sth or afraid of sth: **~ (about/of sth)** *Consumers are very nervous about the future. ◇ The horse may be nervous of cars.* ◇ **~ (about/of doing sth)** *He had been nervous about inviting us. ◇ I felt really nervous before the interview. ◇ a **nervous glance/smile/voice*** (= one that shows that you feel anxious) ◇ *By the time the police arrived, I was a **nervous wreck**.* OPP **confident** ➲ SYNONYMS at WORRIED **2** 0‑ᵀ easily worried or frightened: *She was a thin, nervous girl. ◇ He's not the nervous type. ◇ She was **of a nervous disposition**.* **3** 0‑ᵀ connected with the body's nerves and often affecting you mentally or emotionally: *a **nervous condition/disorder/disease** ◇ She was in a state of **nervous exhaustion**.* IDM see SHADOW *n.* ▸ **ner·vous·ly** 0‑ᵀ *adv.*: *She smiled nervously.* **ner·vous·ness** *noun* [U]: *He tried to hide his nervousness.*

ˌnervous ˈbreakdown (also **break·down**) *noun* a period of mental illness in which sb becomes very depressed, anxious and tired, and cannot deal with normal life: *to have a nervous breakdown*

Synonyms

nervous

neurotic • on edge • jittery

These words all describe people who are easily frightened or are behaving in a frightened way.

nervous easily worried or frightened: *She was **of a nervous disposition**.* NOTE See also the entry for **worried**.

neurotic not behaving in a reasonable, calm way, because you are worried about sth: *She became neurotic about keeping the house clean.*

on edge nervous or bad-tempered: *She was always on edge before an interview.*

jittery (*informal*) anxious and nervous: *All this talk of job losses was making him jittery.*

PATTERNS

- a nervous/neurotic **man/woman/girl**
- to **feel** nervous/on edge/jittery
- **a bit** nervous/on edge/jittery

ˈnervous system *noun* the system of all the nerves in the body ➲ see also CENTRAL NERVOUS SYSTEM

nervy /ˈnɜːvi; *NAmE* ˈnɜːrvi/ *adj.* (*informal*) **1** (*BrE*) anxious and nervous **2** (*NAmE*) brave and confident in a way that might offend other people, or show a lack of respect

-ness *suffix* (in nouns) the quality, state or character of: *dryness ◇ blindness ◇ silliness*

nest 0‑ᵀ /nest/ *noun, verb*

■ ***noun*** **1** 0‑ᵀ [C] a hollow place or structure that a bird makes or chooses for laying its eggs in and sheltering its young ➲ VISUAL VOCAB page V10 **2** 0‑ᵀ [C] a place where insects or other small creatures live and produce their young **3** [sing.] a secret place which is full of bad people and their activities: *a nest of thieves* **4** [sing.] the home, thought of as the safe place where parents bring up their children: *to **leave the nest*** (= leave your parents' home) ➲ see also EMPTY NEST **5** [C, usually sing.] a group or set of similar things that are made to fit inside each other: *a nest of tables* IDM see FEATHER *v.*, FLY *v.*, HORNET, MARE

■ ***verb*** **1** [I] to make and use a nest: *Thousands of seabirds are nesting on the cliffs.* **2** [T] **~ sth** (*technical*) to put types of information together, or inside each other, so that they form a single unit

ˈnest box (also **ˈnesting box**) *noun* a box provided for a bird to make its nest in

ˈnest egg *noun* (*informal*) a sum of money that you save to use in the future

nes·tle /ˈnesl/ *verb* **1** [I] **+ adv./prep.** to sit or lie down in a warm or soft place: *He hugged her and she nestled against his chest.* **2** [T] **~ sb/sth + adv./prep.** to put or hold sb/sth in a comfortable position in a warm or soft place: *He nestled the baby in his arms.* **3** [I] **+ adv./prep.** to be located in a position that is protected, sheltered or partly hidden: *The little town nestles snugly at the foot of the hill.*

nest·ling /ˈnestlɪŋ/ *noun* a bird that is too young to leave the nest

net 0‑ᵀ /net/ *noun, adj., verb*

■ ***noun*** **1** 0‑ᵀ [U] a type of material that is made of string, thread or wire twisted or tied together, with small spaces in between: *net curtains* ➲ see also FISHNET, NETTING **2** 0‑ᵀ [C] (especially in compounds) a piece of net used for a particular purpose, such as catching fish or covering sth: *fishing nets ◇ a mosquito net* (= used to protect you from MOSQUITOES) ➲ see also HAIRNET, SAFETY NET **3 the net** [sing.] (in sports) the frame covered in net that forms the goal: *to kick the ball **into the back of the net*** **4 the net** [sing.] (in TENNIS, etc.) the piece of net between the two players that the ball goes over ➲ VISUAL VOCAB page

N

V37 **5** 🗝 **the Net** (also **the net**) (*informal*) = THE INTERNET IDM see CAST *v.*, SLIP *v.*, SPREAD *v.*

■ ***adj.*** (*BrE* also **nett**) **1** [usually before noun] a **net** amount of money is the amount that remains when nothing more is to be taken away: *a **net profit** of £500* ◇ ***net income/earnings*** (= after tax has been paid) ➲ compare GROSS **2** [only before noun] the **net** weight of sth is the weight without its container or the material it is wrapped in: *450 gms net weight* ➲ compare GROSS **3** [only before noun] final, after all the important facts have been included: *The **net result** is that small shopkeepers are being forced out of business.* ◇ *Canada is now a substantial net importer of medicines* (= it imports more than it exports). ◇ *a net gain* ▸ **net** *adv.*: *a salary of $50 000 net* ◇ *Interest on the investment will be paid net* (= tax will already have been taken away). ➲ compare GROSS

■ ***verb*** (-tt-) **1** **~ sth** to earn an amount of money as a profit after you have paid tax on it: *The sale of paintings netted £17 000.* **2** **~ sth** to catch sth, especially fish, in a net **3** **~ sb/sth** to catch sb or obtain sth in a skilful way: *A swoop by customs officers netted a large quantity of drugs.* **4** **~ sth** (*especially BrE*) to kick or hit a ball into the goal SYN **score**: *He has netted 21 goals so far this season.* **5** **~ sth** to cover sth with a net or nets

net·ball /'netbɔ:l/ *noun* [U] a game played by two teams of seven players, especially women or girls. Players score by throwing a ball through a high net hanging from a ring on a post.

net·book /'netbʊk/ *noun* a small LAPTOP computer, designed especially for using the Internet and email ➲ compare NOTEBOOK, SUBNOTEBOOK

ˌnet 'curtain (*BrE*) (*NAmE* **cur·tain**) *noun* a very thin curtain that you hang at a window, which allows light to enter but stops people outside from being able to see inside

N

nether /'neðə(r)/ *adj.* [only before noun] (*literary* or *humorous*) lower: *a person's nether regions* (= their GENITALS)

the neth·er·world /'neðəwɜ:ld; *NAmE* 'neðərwɜ:rld/ *noun* [sing.] (*literary*) the world of the dead SYN **hell**

neti·quette /'netɪket/ *noun* [U] (*informal, humorous*) the rules of correct or polite behaviour among people using the Internet

neti·zen /'netɪzn/ *noun* (*informal, humorous*) a person who uses the Internet a lot

'Net surfer *noun* = SURFER (2)

nett *adj.* (*BrE*) = NET

net·ting /'netɪŋ/ *noun* [U] material that is made of string, thread or wire twisted or tied together, with spaces in between: *wire netting*

net·tle /'netl/ *noun, verb*

■ ***noun*** (also **'stinging nettle**) a wild plant with leaves that have pointed edges, are covered in fine hairs and sting if you touch them ➲ VISUAL VOCAB page V9 IDM see GRASP *v.*

■ ***verb*** [usually passive] **~ sb** | **it nettles sb that...** (*informal, especially BrE*) to make sb slightly angry SYN **annoy**: *My remarks clearly nettled her.*

nettle·rash /'netlræʃ/ *noun* [U] = URTICARIA

net·tle·some /'netlsəm/ *adj.* (*especially NAmE*) causing trouble or difficulty

net·work 🗝 AW /'netwɜ:k; *NAmE* -wɜ:rk/ *noun, verb*

■ ***noun*** **1** 🗝 a complicated system of roads, lines, tubes, nerves, etc. that cross each other and are connected to each other: *a **rail/road/canal network*** ◇ *a network of veins* **2** 🗝 a closely connected group of people, companies, etc. that exchange information, etc: *a **communications/distribution network*** ◇ *a network of friends* **3** 🗝 (*computing*) a number of computers and other devices that are connected together so that equipment and information can be shared: *The office network allows users to share files and software, and to use a central printer.* ➲ see also LAN, WAN **4** 🗝 a group of radio or television stations in different places that are connected and that broadcast the same programmes at the same time: *the four big US television networks* IDM see OLD BOY

■ ***verb*** **1** [T] **~ sth** (*computing*) to connect a number of computers and other devices together so that equipment and information can be shared **2** [T] **~ sth** to broadcast a television or radio programme on stations in several different areas at the same time **3** [I] to try to meet and talk to people who may be useful to you in your work: *Conferences are a good place to network.*

net·work·ing /'netwɜ:kɪŋ; *NAmE* -wɜ:rk-/ *noun* [U] a system of trying to meet and talk to other people who may be useful to you in your work

neur·al /'njʊərəl; *NAmE* 'nʊrəl/ *adj.* (*technical*) connected with a nerve or the NERVOUS SYSTEM: *neural processes*

neur·al·gia /njʊə'rældʒə; *NAmE* nʊ'r-/ *noun* [U] (*medical*) a sharp pain felt along a nerve, especially in the head or face ▸ **neur·al·gic** /njʊə'rældʒɪk; *NAmE* nʊ'r-/ *adj.*

ˌneural 'network (also **ˌneural 'net**) *noun* (*computing*) a system with a structure which is similar to the human brain and nervous system

neur·as·the·nia /ˌnjʊərəs'θi:niə; *NAmE* ˌnʊrəs-/ *noun* [U] (*old-fashioned*) a condition in which sb feels tired and depressed over a long period of time

neuro- /'njʊərəʊ; *NAmE* 'nʊroʊ/ *combining form* (in nouns, adjectives and adverbs) connected with the nerves: *neuroscience* ◇ *a neurosurgeon*

neuro·lin·guis·tic pro·gram·ming /ˌnjʊərəʊlɪŋˌgwɪstɪk 'prəʊgræmɪŋ; *NAmE* ˌnʊroʊlɪŋˌgwɪstɪk 'proʊgræmɪŋ/ (*abbr.* **NLP**) *noun* [U] (*psychology*) a technique that people use to help themselves or others think in a more positive way, and which uses neurolinguistics as its basis

neuro·lin·guis·tics /ˌnjʊərəʊlɪŋ'gwɪstɪks; *NAmE* ˌnʊroʊ-/ *noun* [U] (*psychology*) the study of the way the human brain processes language

neuro·logic·al /ˌnjʊərə'lɒdʒɪkl; *NAmE* ˌnʊrə'lɑ:dʒ-/ *adj.* relating to nerves or to the science of NEUROLOGY: *neurological damage*

neurolo·gist /njʊə'rɒlədʒɪst; *NAmE* nʊ'rɑ:l-/ *noun* a doctor who studies and treats diseases of the nerves

neurol·ogy /njʊə'rɒlədʒi; *NAmE* nʊ'rɑ:l-/ *noun* [U] the scientific study of nerves and their diseases

neuron /'njʊərɒn; *NAmE* 'nʊrɑ:n/ (also **neur·one** /'njʊərəʊn; *NAmE* 'nʊroʊn/ especially in *BrE*) *noun* (*biology*) a cell that carries information within the brain and between the brain and other parts of the body; a nerve cell ➲ see also MOTOR NEURON DISEASE

neuro·physi·ology /ˌnjʊərəʊfɪzi'ɒlədʒi; *NAmE* ˌnʊroʊ-fɪzi'ɑ:lədʒi/ *noun* [U] the scientific study of the normal functions of the NERVOUS SYSTEM

neuro·science /'njʊərəʊsaɪəns; *NAmE* 'nʊroʊ-/ *noun* [U] the science that deals with the structure and function of the brain and the NERVOUS SYSTEM ▸ **neuro·scientist** /-saɪəntɪst/ *noun*

neur·osis /njʊə'rəʊsɪs; *NAmE* nʊ'roʊ-/ *noun* [C, U] (*pl.* **neur·oses** /-əʊsi:z; *NAmE* -oʊ-/) **1** (*medical*) a mental illness in which a person suffers strong feelings of fear and worry **2** any strong fear or worry SYN **anxiety**

neuro·sur·gery /'njʊərəʊsɜ:dʒəri; *NAmE* 'nʊroʊsɜ:rdʒə-ri/ *noun* [U] medical operations performed on the nervous system, especially the brain

neur·ot·ic /njʊə'rɒtɪk; *NAmE* nʊ'rɑ:-/ *adj., noun*

■ ***adj.*** **1** caused by or suffering from neurosis: *neurotic obsessions* ➲ note at MENTALLY ILL **2** not behaving in a reasonable, calm way, because you are worried about sth: *She became neurotic about keeping the house clean.* ◇ *a brilliant but neurotic actor* ➲ SYNONYMS at NERVOUS ▸ **neur·ot·ic·al·ly** /-kli/ *adv.*

■ ***noun*** a neurotic person

neuro·toxin /ˌnjʊərəʊ'tɒksɪn; *NAmE* ˌnʊroʊ'tɑ:ksɪn/ *noun* (*technical*) a poison that affects the NERVOUS SYSTEM

neuro·trans·mit·ter /ˈnjʊərəʊtrænzmɪtə(r); *NAmE* ˈnʊroʊ-/ *noun* (*biology*) a chemical that carries messages from nerve cells to other nerve cells or muscles

neu·ter /ˈnjuːtə(r); *NAmE* ˈnuːtər/ *adj.*, *verb*
■ ***adj.*** (*grammar*) (in some languages) belonging to a class of nouns, pronouns, adjectives or verbs whose GENDER is not FEMININE or MASCULINE: *The Polish word for 'window' is neuter.*
■ ***verb* 1 ~ sth** to remove part of the sex organs of an animal so that it cannot produce young: *Has your cat been neutered?* **2 ~ sth** (*disapproving*) to prevent sth from having the effect that it ought to have

neu·tral AW /ˈnjuːtrəl; *NAmE* ˈnuː-/ *adj.*, *noun*
■ ***adj.***
▸ IN DISAGREEMENT/CONTEST **1** not supporting or helping either side in a disagreement, competition, etc. SYN **impartial, unbiased**: *Journalists are supposed to be politically neutral.* ◇ *I didn't take my father's or my mother's side; I tried to* ***remain neutral****.*
▸ IN WAR **2** not belonging to any of the countries that are involved in a war; not supporting any of the countries involved in a war: ***neutral territory/waters*** ◇ *Switzerland was neutral during the war.*
▸ WITHOUT STRONG FEELING **3** deliberately not expressing any strong feeling: *'So you told her?' he said in a neutral tone of voice.*
▸ COLOUR **4** not very bright or strong, such as grey or light brown: *a neutral colour scheme* ◇ *neutral tones*
▸ CHEMISTRY **5** neither acid nor ALKALINE
▸ ELECTRICAL **6** (*abbr.* N) having neither a positive nor a negative electrical charge: *the neutral wire in a plug*
▶ **neu·tral·ly** /-rəli/ *adv.*
IDM **on neutral ground/territory** in a place that has no connection with either of the people or sides who are meeting and so does not give an advantage to either of them: *We decided to meet on neutral ground.*
■ ***noun***
▸ IN VEHICLE **1** [U] the position of the gears of a vehicle in which no power is carried from the engine to the wheels: *to leave the car* ***in neutral***
▸ IN DISAGREEMENT/WAR **2** [C] a person or country that does not support either side in a disagreement, competition or war
▸ COLOUR **3** [C] a colour that is not bright or strong, such as grey or light brown: *The room was decorated in neutrals.*

neu·tral·ist /ˈnjuːtrəlɪst; *NAmE* ˈnuː-/ *noun* (*especially NAmE*) a person who does not support either side in a war ▶ **neu·tral·ist** *adj.*: *a neutralist state*

neu·tral·ity AW /njuːˈtræləti; *NAmE* nuː-/ *noun* [U] the state of not supporting either side in a disagreement, competition or war

neu·tral·ize (*BrE* also **-ise**) AW /ˈnjuːtrəlaɪz; *NAmE* ˈnuː-/ *verb* **1 ~ sth** to stop sth from having any effect: *The latest figures should neutralize the fears of inflation.* **2 ~ sth** (*chemistry*) to make a substance NEUTRAL (5) **3 ~ sth** to make a country or an area NEUTRAL (2) ▶ **neu·tral·iza·tion, -isa·tion** AW /ˌnjuːtrəlaɪˈzeɪʃn; *NAmE* ˌnuːtrələˈz-/ *noun* [U]

ˈneutral zone *noun* **1** (in ICE HOCKEY) an area that covers the central part of the RINK, between two blue lines **2** (in AMERICAN FOOTBALL) an imaginary area between the teams where no player except the CENTRE is allowed to step until play has started

neu·trino /njuːˈtriːnəʊ; *NAmE* nuːˈtriːnoʊ/ *noun* (*pl.* -os) (*physics*) an extremely small PARTICLE that has no electrical charge, and which rarely reacts with other matter

neu·tron /ˈnjuːtrɒn; *NAmE* ˈnuːtrɑːn/ *noun* (*physics*) a very small piece of matter (= a substance) that carries no electric charge and that forms part of the NUCLEUS (= central part) of an atom ➲ see also ELECTRON, PROTON

ˈneutron bomb *noun* a bomb that can kill people by giving out neutrons, but does not cause a lot of damage to buildings

never 0-w /ˈnevə(r)/ *adv.*, *exclamation*
■ ***adv.* 1** 0-w not at any time; not on any occasion: *You never help me.* ◇ *He has never been abroad.* ◇ *'Would you vote for him?' 'Never.'* ◇ *'I work for a company called Orion Technology.' 'Never heard of them.'* ◇ ***Never in all my life*** *have I seen such a horrible thing.* ◇ ***Never ever*** *tell anyone your password.* **2** 0-w used to emphasize a negative statement instead of 'not': *I* ***never knew*** (= didn't know until now) *you had a twin sister.* ◇ (*especially BrE*) *Someone might find out, and that* ***would never do*** (= that is not acceptable). ◇ *He* ***never so much as*** *smiled* (= did not smile even once). ◇ (*especially BrE*) *'I told my boss exactly what I thought of her.' 'You never did!'* (= 'Surely you didn't!') ◇ (*BrE, slang*) *'You took my bike.' 'No, I never.'* ◇ (*old-fashioned* or *humorous*) ***Never fear*** (= Do not worry), *everything will be all right.*
IDM **on the ˌnever-ˈnever** (*BrE, informal*) on HIRE PURCHASE (= by making payments over a long period): *to buy a new car on the never-never* **Well, I never (did)!** (*old-fashioned*) used to express surprise or disapproval
■ ***exclamation*** (*informal*) used to show that you are very surprised about sth because you do not believe it is possible: *'I got the job.' 'Never!'* IDM see MIND *v.*

ˌnever-ˈending *adj.* seeming to last for ever SYN **endless, interminable**: *Housework is a never-ending task.*

never·more /ˌnevəˈmɔː(r); *NAmE* ˌnevərˈm-/ *adv.* (*old use*) never again

ˌnever-ˈnever land *noun* [sing.] an imaginary place where everything is wonderful

never·the·less 0-w AW /ˌnevəðəˈles; *NAmE* -vərðə-/ *adv.*
despite sth that you have just mentioned SYN **nonetheless**: *There is little chance that we will succeed in changing the law. Nevertheless, it is important that we try.* ◇ *Our defeat was expected but it is disappointing nevertheless.*

Language Bank

nevertheless

Conceding a point and making a counter-argument

- **While** the film is undoubtedly too long, it is **nevertheless** an intriguing piece of cinema.
- **It can be argued that** the movie is too long. It is **nonetheless** an intriguing piece of cinema.
- The film is undoubtedly too long. **Still**, it is an intriguing piece of cinema.
- **Of course**, huge chunks of the book have been sacrificed in order to make a two-hour movie, **but** it is **nevertheless** a successful piece of storytelling.
- Critics are wrong to argue that the film's plot is too complicated. **Certainly** there are a couple of major twists, **but** audiences will have no difficulty following them.
- **It is true that** you cannot make a good movie without a good script, **but it is equally true** that a talented director can make a good script into an excellent film.
- **It remains to be seen whether** these two movies herald a new era of westerns, **but there is no doubt that** they represent welcome additions to the genre.

➲ Language Banks at ARGUE, HOWEVER, IMPERSONAL, OPINION

new 0-w /njuː; *NAmE* nuː/ *adj.* (newer, new·est)
▸ NOT EXISTING BEFORE **1** 0-w not existing before; recently made, invented, introduced, etc: *Have you read her new novel?* ◇ *new ways of doing things* ◇ *This idea isn't new.* ◇ *The latest model has over 100 new features.* ➲ see also BRAND-NEW OPP **old** **2 the new** *noun* [U] something that is new: *It was a good mix of the old and the new.*
▸ RECENTLY BOUGHT **3** 0-w recently bought: *Let me show you my new dress.*
▸ NOT USED BEFORE **4** 0-w not used or owned by anyone before: *A second-hand car costs a fraction of a new one.*
▸ DIFFERENT **5** 0-w different from the previous one: *I like your new hairstyle.* ◇ *When do you start your new job?* ◇ *He's made a lot of new friends.* OPP **old**

N

▸ NOT FAMILIAR **6** already existing but not seen, experienced, etc. before; not familiar: *This is a new experience for me.* ◇ *I'd like to learn a new language.* ◇ *the discovery of a new star* ◇ **~ to sb** *Our system is probably new to you.*
▸ RECENTLY ARRIVED **7** **~ (to sth)** not yet familiar with sth because you have only just started, arrived, etc: *I should tell you, I'm completely new to this kind of work.* ◇ *I am new to the town.* ◇ *a* ***new arrival/recruit*** ◇ *You're new here, aren't you?*
▸ NEW- **8** used in compounds to describe sth that has recently happened: *He was enjoying his new-found freedom.*
▸ MODERN **9** (usually with *the*) modern; of the latest type: *the new morality* ◇ *They called themselves the New Romantics.*
▸ JUST BEGINNING **10** [usually before noun] just beginning or beginning again: *a new day* ◇ *It was a new era in the history of our country.* ◇ *She went to Australia to start a new life.*
▸ WITH FRESH ENERGY **11** having fresh energy, courage or health: *Since he changed jobs he's looked like a new man.*
▸ RECENTLY PRODUCED **12** only recently produced or developed: *The new buds are appearing on the trees now.* ◇ *new potatoes* (= ones dug from the soil early in the season) ▸ **new·ness** *noun* [U] ➲ see also NEWLY

IDM ˌ**break new ˈground** to make a new discovery or do sth that has not been done before ➲ see also GROUND-BREAKING **(as) ˌgood as ˈnew | like ˈnew** in very good condition, as it was when it was new: *I've had your coat cleaned—it's as good as new now.* **... is the new ...** (*BrE, informal*) used to say that sth has become very fashionable and can be thought of as replacing sth else: *Brown is the new black.* ◇ *Comedy is the new rock and roll.* ◇ *Fifty is the new forty.* **a new ˈbroom** (*BrE*, often *disapproving*) a person who has just started to work for an organization, department, etc, especially in a senior job, and who is likely to make a lot of changes: *Well, you know what they say—****A new broom sweeps clean.*** **a/the ˌnew kid on the ˈblock** (*informal*) a person who is new to a place, an organization, etc: *Despite his six years in politics, he was still regarded by many as the new kid on the block.* **a new one on ˈme** (*informal*) used to say that you have not heard a particular idea, piece of information, joke, etc. before: *'Have you come across this before?' 'No, it's a new one on me.'* **turn over a new ˈleaf** to change your way of life to become a better, more responsible person **what's ˈnew?** (*informal*) used as a friendly GREETING: *Hi! What's new?* ➲ more at BLOOD, BRAVE *adj.*, BREATHE, COMPLEXION, TEACH

N

ˌ**New ˈAge** *adj.* connected with a way of life that rejects modern Western values and is based on spiritual ideas and beliefs, ASTROLOGY, etc: *a New Age festival* ◇ ***New Age travellers*** (= people in Britain who reject the values of modern society and travel from place to place, living in their vehicles) ▸ ˌ**New ˈAge** *noun* [U]

new·bie /ˈnjuːbi; *NAmE* ˈnuːbi/ *noun* (*informal*) a person who is new and has little experience in doing sth, especially in using computers SYN **novice**

new·born /ˈnjuːbɔːn; *NAmE* ˈnuːbɔːrn/ *adj.* [only before noun] recently born: *a newborn baby*

ˌ**new ˈbroom** *noun* (*BrE*) a person who has just started to work for an organization, especially in a senior job, and who is likely to make a lot of changes

ˈ**new-build** *noun* [C, U] (*BrE*) a building, ship or aircraft that has been built very recently or that is to be built soon; buildings, etc. of this type: *new-build properties/apartments*

New·cas·tle /ˈnjuːkɑːsl; *NAmE* ˈnuːkæsl/ *noun* [U]
IDM see COAL

new·comer /ˈnjuːkʌmə(r); *NAmE* ˈnuː-/ *noun* **~ (to sth)** a person who has only recently arrived in a place or started an activity

newel post /ˈnjuːəl pəʊst; *NAmE* ˈnuːəl poʊst/ (also **newel**) *noun* a post at the top or bottom of a set of stairs

ˌ**New ˈEngland** *noun* an area in the north-eastern US that includes the states of Maine, New Hampshire, Vermont, Massachusetts, Rhode Island and Connecticut

new·fan·gled /ˌnjuːˈfæŋgld; *NAmE* ˌnuːˈf-/ *adj.* [usually before noun] (*disapproving*) used to describe sth that has recently been invented or introduced, but that you do not like because it is not what you are used to, or is too complicated

new·fie /ˈnjuːfi; *NAmE* ˈnuːfi/ *noun* (*CanE, informal*) a person from Newfoundland in Canada

ˌ**new-ˈfound** *adj.* [only before noun] recently discovered or achieved: *How is she handling her new-found fame?* ◇ *his new-found freedom/confidence/enthusiasm*

New·found·land Time /njuːˈfaʊndlənd taɪm; *NAmE* nuːˈf-/ *noun* [U] (*CanE*) the standard time system that is used in an area which includes the island of Newfoundland

ˌ**New ˈLabour** *noun* [sing.+ sing./pl. v.] (in Britain) the modern Labour Party which moved away from the political left in the 1990s in order to appeal to more people

newly /ˈnjuːli; *NAmE* ˈnuːli/ *adv.* (usually before a past participle) recently: *a newly qualified doctor* ◇ *a newly created job* ◇ *a newly independent republic*

ˈ**newly-wed** *noun* [usually pl.] a person who has recently got married ▸ ˈ**newly-wed** *adj.*

ˌ**new ˈman** *noun* (*BrE*) a man who shares the work in the home that is traditionally done by women, such as cleaning, cooking and taking care of children. New men are considered sensitive and not aggressive.

ˌ**new ˈmedia** *noun* [pl.] new information and entertainment technologies, such as the Internet, CD-ROMs and DIGITAL TELEVISION

ˌ**new ˈmoon** *noun* **1** the moon when it looks like a thin curved shape (= a CRESCENT) **2** the time of the month when the moon has this shape ➲ compare FULL MOON, HALF-MOON

the ˌNew ˈRight *noun* [sing.] (in the US) politicians and political groups who support conservative social and political policies and religious ideas based on Christian FUNDAMENTALISM

news /njuːz; *NAmE* nuːz/ *noun* [U]
1 new information about sth that has happened recently: *What's the latest news?* ◇ *Have you heard the news? Pat's leaving!* ◇ *That's great news.* ◇ *Tell me all your news.* ◇ *Have you had any* ***news of*** *Patrick?* ◇ *Any news on the deal?* ◇ *Messengers brought* ***news that*** *the battle had been lost.* ◇ *Do you want the* ***good news*** *or the* ***bad news*** *first?* ◇ *a* ***piece/bit of news*** ◇ (*informal*) *It's* ***news to me*** (= I haven't heard it before). **2** reports of recent events that appear in newspapers or on television or radio: ***national/international news*** ◇ *a* ***news story/item/report*** ◇ *News of a serious road accident is just coming in.* ◇ ***breaking news*** (= news that is arriving about events that have just happened) ◇ *She is always* ***in the news.*** ◇ *The wedding was* ***front-page news.*** **3** **the news** a regular television or radio broadcast of the latest news: *to* ***listen to/watch the news*** ◇ *Can you put the news on?* ◇ *I saw it* ***on the news.*** ◇ *the nine o'clock news* **4** a person, thing or event that is considered to be interesting enough to be reported as news: *Pop stars are always news.* ➲ see also NEWSY

IDM **be bad ˈnews (for sb/sth)** to be likely to cause problems: *Central heating is bad news for indoor plants.* **break the ˈnews (to sb)** to be the first to tell sb some bad news **be good news (for sb/sth)** to be likely to be helpful or give an advantage: *The cut in interest rates is good news for homeowners.* ˌ**no news is ˈgood news** (*saying*) if there were bad news we would hear it, so as we have heard nothing, it is likely that nothing bad has happened

ˈ**news agency** (also ˈ**press agency**) *noun* an organization that collects news and supplies it to newspapers and television and radio companies

news·agent /ˈnjuːzeɪdʒənt; *NAmE* ˈnuːz-/ (*BrE*) (*US* **news·deal·er**) *noun* **1** a person who owns or works in a shop selling newspapers and magazines, and often sweets/candy and cigarettes **2** **news·agent's** (*pl.* newsagents) (*BrE* also ˈ**paper shop**) a shop/store that sells newspapers, magazines, sweets/candy, etc: *I'll go to the newsagent's on my way home.*

news·cast /ˈnju:zkɑ:st; *NAmE* ˈnu:zkæst/ *noun* (*especially NAmE*) a news programme on radio or television

news·cast·er /ˈnju:zkɑ:stə(r); *NAmE* ˈnu:zkæstər/ (*BrE* also **news·read·er**) *noun* a person who reads the news on television or radio

ˈ**news conference** *noun* (*especially NAmE*) = PRESS CONFERENCE

news·deal·er /ˈnju:zdi:lə(r); *NAmE* ˈnu:z-/ (*US*) (*BrE* **news·agent**) *noun* **1** a person who owns or works in a shop selling newspapers and magazines, and often sweets/candy and cigarettes **2** (*BrE* also ˈ**paper shop**) a shop/store that sells newspapers, magazines, sweets/candy, etc. ➲ see also NEWS-STAND

ˈ**news desk** *noun* the department of a newspaper office or a radio or television station where news is received and prepared for printing or broadcasting: *She works on the news desk.*

news·flash /ˈnju:zflæʃ; *NAmE* ˈnu:z-/ (also **flash**) *noun* (*especially BrE*) a short item of important news that is broadcast on radio or television, often interrupting a programme

news·gather·ing /ˈnju:zgæðərɪŋ; *NAmE* ˈnu:z-/ *noun* [U] the process of doing research on news items, especially ones that will be broadcast on television or printed in a newspaper ▸ **news·gather·er** /ˈnju:zgæðərə(r); *NAmE* ˈnu:z-/ *noun*

news·group /ˈnju:zgru:p; *NAmE* ˈnu:z-/ *noun* a place in a computer network, especially the Internet, where people can discuss a particular subject and exchange information about it

news·let·ter /ˈnju:zletə(r); *NAmE* ˈnu:z-/ *noun* a printed report containing news of the activities of a club or organization that is sent regularly to all its members

news·man /ˈnju:zmæn; *NAmE* ˈnu:z-/, **news·woman** /ˈnju:zwʊmən; *NAmE* ˈnu:z-/ *noun* (*pl.* **-men** /-men/, **-women** /-wɪmɪn/) a journalist who works for a newspaper or a television or radio station: *a crowd of reporters and TV newsmen*

news·paper 🔑 /ˈnju:zpeɪpə(r); *NAmE* ˈnu:z-/ *noun* **1** 🔑 [C] a set of large printed sheets of paper containing news, articles, advertisements, etc. and published every day or every week: *a* ***daily/weekly newspaper*** ◇ *a* ***local/national newspaper*** ◇ *an* ***online newspaper*** ◇ *a* ***newspaper article*** ◇ *I read about it* ***in the newspaper.*** ◇ *a* ***newspaper cutting*** ◇ *She works for the local newspaper* (= the company that produces it). ◇ *newspaper proprietors* ➲ see also PAPER **2** [U] paper taken from old newspapers: *Wrap all your glasses in newspaper.*

news·paper·man /ˈnju:zpeɪpəmæn; *NAmE* ˈnu:zpeɪpərmæn/, **news·paper·woman** /ˈnju:zpeɪpəwʊmən; *NAmE* ˈnu:zpeɪpər-/ *noun* (*pl.* **-men** /-men/, **-women** /-wɪmɪn/) a journalist who works for a newspaper

new·speak /ˈnju:spi:k; *NAmE* ˈnu:-/ *noun* [U] language that is not clear or honest, for example the language that is used in political PROPAGANDA

news·print /ˈnju:zprɪnt; *NAmE* ˈnu:z-/ *noun* [U] the cheap paper that newspapers are printed on

news·read·er /ˈnju:zri:də(r); *NAmE* ˈnu:z-/ *noun* (*BrE*) = NEWSCASTER

news·reel /ˈnju:zri:l; *NAmE* ˈnu:z-/ *noun* a short film of news that was shown in the past in cinemas/movie theaters

news·room /ˈnju:zru:m; -rʊm; *NAmE* ˈnu:z-/ *noun* the room at a newspaper office or a radio or television station where news is received and prepared for printing or broadcasting

ˈ**news-sheet** *noun* a small newspaper with only a few pages

ˈ**news-stand** (*US* ˈ**newsstand**) *noun* a place on the street, at a station, etc. where you can buy newspapers and magazines

ˈ**news ticker** (also **ticker**) *noun* a line of text containing news which passes across the screen of a computer or television

news·wire /ˈnju:zwaɪə(r); *NAmE* ˈnu:z-/ *noun* a service that provides the latest news, for example using the Internet

news·worthy /ˈnju:zwɜ:ði; *NAmE* ˈnu:zwɜ:rði/ *adj.* interesting and important enough to be reported as news

newsy /ˈnju:zi; *NAmE* ˈnu:zi/ *adj.* (*informal*) full of interesting and entertaining news: *a newsy letter*

newt /nju:t; *NAmE* nu:t/ *noun* a small animal with short legs, a long tail and cold blood, that lives both in water and on land (= is an AMPHIBIAN) IDM see PISSED

the ˌNew ˈTestament *noun* [sing.] the second part of the Bible, that describes the life and teachings of Jesus Christ ➲ compare THE OLD TESTAMENT

new·ton /ˈnju:tən; *NAmE* ˈnu:-/ *noun* (*abbr.* **N**) (*physics*) a unit of force. One newton is equal to the force that would give a mass of one kilogram an ACCELERATION (= an increase in speed) of one metre per second per second.

ˈ**new town** *noun* one of the complete towns that were planned and built in Britain after 1946

ˌ**new ˌvariant CJˈD** *noun* [U] a disease similar to CREUTZFELDT-JAKOB DISEASE (= a brain disease in humans that causes death) that is thought to be connected with BSE

ˌ**new ˈwave** *noun* [U, sing.] **1** a group of people who together introduce new styles and ideas in art, music, cinema, etc: *one of the most exciting directors of the Australian new wave* ◇ *new wave films* **2** a style of rock music popular in the 1970s

the ˌNew ˈWorld *noun* [sing.] a way of referring to N, Central and S America, used especially in the past ➲ compare THE OLD WORLD

ˌ**new ˈyear** (also ˌ**New ˈYear**) *noun* [U, sing.] the beginning of the year: *Happy New Year!* ◇ *We're going to Germany for Christmas and New Year.* ◇ *I'll see you in the new year.* ➲ see also RESOLUTION

ˌ**New Year's ˈDay** (*NAmE* also ˈ**New Year's**) *noun* [U] 1 January

ˌ**New Year's ˈEve** (*NAmE* also ˈ**New Year's**) *noun* [U] 31 December, especially the evening of that day

Which Word?

next / nearest

- **(The) next** means 'after this/that one' in time or in a series of events, places or people: *When is your next appointment?* ◇ *Turn left at the next traffic lights.* ◇ *Who's next?* **(The) nearest** means 'closest' in space: *Where's the nearest supermarket?*
- Notice the difference between the prepositions **nearest to** and **next to**: *Janet's sitting nearest to the window* (= of all the people in the room). ◇ *Sarah's sitting next to the window* (= right beside it). In informal *BrE* **nearest** can be used instead of **nearest to**: *Who's sitting nearest the door?*

next 🔑 /nekst/ *adj., adv., noun*

▪ ***adj.*** [only before noun] **1** 🔑 (usually with *the*) coming straight after sb/sth in time, order or space: *The next train to Baltimore is at ten.* ◇ *The next six months will be the hardest.* ◇ *the next chapter* ◇ *Who's next?* ◇ *the woman in the next room* ◇ *I fainted and* ***the next thing I knew*** *I was in the hospital.* ◇ (*informal*) *Round here, you leave school at sixteen and* ***next thing you know,*** *you're married with three kids.* **2** 🔑 (used without *the*) **~ Monday, week, summer, year, etc.** the Monday, week, etc. immediately following: *Next Thursday is 12 April.* ◇ ***Next time*** *I'll bring a book.*
IDM **the ˈnext man, woman, person, etc.** the average

N

person: *I can enjoy a joke* **as well as the next man**, *but this is going too far.* ➲ more at DAY, LUCK *n.*
■ ***adv.*** **1** 🗝 after sth else; then; afterwards: *What happened next?* ◇ *Next, I heard the sound of voices.* ➲ LANGUAGE BANK at FIRST, PROCESS **2** 🗝 **~ best, biggest, most important, etc...** (**after/to sb/sth**) following in the order mentioned: *Jo was the next oldest after Martin.* ◇ ***The next best thing*** *to flying is gliding.* **3** used in questions to express surprise or confusion: *You're going bungee jumping?* ***Whatever next?***
■ ***noun*** 🗝 (usually **the next**) [sing.] a person or thing that is next: *One moment he wasn't there, the next he was.* ◇ *the week* ***after next***

ˌnext ˈdoor *adv., adj., noun*
■ ***adv.*** in the next room, house or building: *The cat is from the house next door.* ◇ *The manager's office is just next door.* ◇ *We live* **next door to** *the bank.* ▶ **ˌnext-ˈdoor** *adj.* [only before noun]: *our next-door neighbours* ◇ *the next-door house*
■ ***noun*** [U+sing./pl. v.] (*BrE, informal*) the people who live in the house or flat/apartment next to yours: *Is that next door's dog?*

ˌnext of ˈkin *noun* [C, U] (*pl.* **next of kin**) your closest living relative or relatives: *I'm her next of kin.* ◇ *Her next of kin have been informed.* ◇ *The form must be signed by next of kin.*

ˈnext to 🗝 *prep.*
1 🗝 in or into a position right beside sb/sth: *We sat next to each other.* ➲ note at NEXT **2** following in order or importance after sb/sth: *Next to skiing my favourite sport is skating.* **3** almost: *Charles knew* ***next to nothing*** *about farming.* ◇ *The horse came* ***next to last*** (= the one before the last one) *in the race.* **4** in comparison with sb/sth: *Next to her I felt like a fraud.*

nexus /ˈneksəs/ *noun* [sing.] (*formal*) a complicated series of connections between different things

Nez Percé /ˌnez ˈpɜːs; *NAmE* ˈpɜːrs/ *noun* (*pl.* **Nez Percé** or **Nez Percés**) a member of a Native American people, many of whom now live in the US state of Idaho ORIGIN From the French for 'pierced nose'.

NFC /ˌen ef ˈsiː/ *abbr.* **the NFC** (in the US) the National Football Conference (one of the two groups of teams in the National Football League)

NFL /ˌen ef ˈel/ *abbr.* (in the US) National Football League (the US organization for professional AMERICAN FOOTBALL with two groups of teams, the National Football Conference and the American Football Conference)

NGO /ˌen dʒiː ˈəʊ; *NAmE* ˈoʊ/ *abbr.* non-governmental organization (a charity, association, etc. that is independent of government and business)

ngoma /əŋˈɡəʊmə; *NAmE* -ˈɡoʊ-/ *noun* **1** [C] a traditional drum from southern or eastern Africa **2** [C, U] (*EAfrE*) a celebration or performance that involves dancing, singing and playing drums

NHS /ˌen eɪtʃ ˈes/ *noun* [sing.] the abbreviation for 'National Health Service' (the public health service in Britain that provides medical treatment and is paid for by taxes): *an NHS hospital* ◇ *I had the operation done* ***on the NHS*** (= paid for by the NHS).

NI *abbr.* (in Britain) NATIONAL INSURANCE

nia·cin /ˈnaɪəsɪn/ (also **ˌnico·tin·ic ˈacid**) *noun* [U] a VITAMIN of the B group that is found in foods such as milk and meat

nib /nɪb/ *noun* the metal point of a pen ➲ VISUAL VOCAB page V56

nib·ble /ˈnɪbl/ *verb, noun*
■ ***verb*** **1** [T, I] to take small bites of sth, especially food: **~ sth** *We sat drinking wine and nibbling olives.* ◇ *He nibbled her ear playfully.* ◇ **~ (at/on sth)** *She took some cake from the tray and nibbled at it.* **2** [I] **~ (at sth)** to show a slight interest in an offer, idea, etc: *He nibbled at the idea, but would not make a definite decision.*
PHR V **ˌnibble aˈway at sth** to take away small amounts of sth, so that the total amount is gradually reduced SYN **erode**: *Inflation is nibbling away at spending power.*
■ ***noun*** **1** [C] a small bite of sth **2 nibbles** [pl.] small things to eat with a drink before a meal or at a party

nibs /nɪbz/ *noun*
IDM **his nibs** (*old-fashioned, BrE, informal*) used to refer to a man who is, or thinks he is, more important than other people

nice 🗝 /naɪs/ *adj.* (**nicer, nicest**)
▸ PLEASANT/ATTRACTIVE **1** 🗝 pleasant, enjoyable or attractive: *a nice day/smile/place* ◇ *nice weather* ◇ *Did you* ***have a nice time?*** ◇ *You look very nice.* ◇ *'Do you want to come, too?' 'Yes,* ***that would be nice.****'* ◇ *The nicest thing about her is that she never criticizes us.* ◇ **~ (to do sth)** ***Nice to meet you!*** (= a friendly GREETING when you meet sb for the first time) ◇ **~ (doing sth)** ***It's been nice meeting you.*** ◇ **~ (that...)** ***It's nice that*** *you can come with us.* ◇ ***It would be nice if*** *he moved to London.* ◇ *We all had the flu last week —it wasn't very nice.* ◇ ***It's nice to know that*** *somebody appreciates what I do.* **2** 🗝 used before adjectives or adverbs to emphasize how pleasant sth is: *a nice hot bath* ◇ *a nice long walk* ◇ *It was nice and warm yesterday.* ◇ *Everyone arrived nice and early.* HELP **Nice and** with another adjective cannot be used before a noun: ~~*a nice and quiet place*~~.
▸ KIND/FRIENDLY **3** 🗝 kind; friendly: *Our new neighbours are very nice.* ◇ *He's a really nice guy.* ◇ **~ to sb** *Be nice to me. I'm not feeling well.* ◇ **~ of sb (to do sth)** *It was nice of them to invite us.* ◇ **~ about sth** *I complained to the manager and he was very nice about it.* ◇ *I asked him* ***in the nicest possible way*** *to put his cigarette out.* OPP **nasty**
▸ NOT NICE **4** (*ironic*) bad or unpleasant: *That's a nice thing to say!* ◇ *That's a nice way to speak to your mother!*
▸ SMALL DETAILS **5** (*formal*) involving a very small detail or difference SYN **subtle**: *a nice point of law* (= one that is difficult to decide)
▶ **nice·ness** *noun* [U]: *In some professions, niceness does not get you very far.*
IDM **as ˌnice as ˈpie** (*informal*) very kind and friendly, especially when you are not expecting it **have a nice ˈday!** (*informal, especially NAmE*) a friendly way of saying goodbye, especially to customers **ˈnice one!** (*BrE, informal*) used to show you are pleased when sth good has happened or sb has said sth amusing: *You got the job? Nice one!* **nice ˈwork!** (*informal, especially BrE*) used to show you are pleased when sb has done sth well: *You did a good job today. Nice work, James!* **nice work if you can ˈget it** (*informal*) used when you wish that you had sb's success or good luck and think they have achieved it with little effort ➲ more at MR

Vocabulary Building

Nice and very nice

Instead of saying that something is **nice** or **very nice**, try to use more precise and interesting adjectives to describe things:

- **pleasant/perfect/beautiful** weather
- a **cosy**/a **comfortable**/an **attractive** room
- a **pleasant**/an **interesting**/an **enjoyable** experience
- **expensive/fashionable/smart** clothes
- a **kind**/a **charming**/an **interesting** man
- The party was **fun**.

In conversation you can also use **great**, **wonderful**, **lovely** and (in *BrE*) **brilliant**: *The party was great.* ◇ *We had a brilliant weekend.*

➲ note at GOOD

ˌnice-ˈlooking *adj.* attractive: *What a nice-looking young man!*

nice·ly 🗝 /ˈnaɪsli/ *adv.*
1 🗝 in an attractive or acceptable way; well: *The room was nicely furnished.* ◇ *The plants are* ***coming along nicely*** (= growing well). **2** 🗝 in a kind, friendly or polite way: *If you ask her nicely she might say yes.* **3** (*formal*) carefully;

N

exactly: *His novels nicely describe life in Britain between the wars.*

IDM **do 'nicely** **1** to be making good progress: *Her new business is doing very nicely.* **2** to be acceptable: *Tomorrow at ten will do nicely* (= will be a good time).

ni·cety /'naɪsəti/ *noun* (*pl.* **-ies**) (*formal*) **1** [C, usually pl.] the small details or points of difference, especially concerning the correct way of behaving or of doing things **2** [U] (*formal*) the quality of being very detailed or careful about sth SYN **precision**: *the nicety of his argument*

niche /ni:ʃ; nɪtʃ; *NAmE* nɪtʃ; ni:ʃ/ *noun* **1** a comfortable or suitable role, job, way of life, etc: *He eventually found his niche in sports journalism.* **2** (*business*) an opportunity to sell a particular product to a particular group of people: *They spotted a niche in the market, with no serious competition.* ◇ *a niche market* ◇ *the development of* ***niche marketing*** (= aiming products at particular groups) **3** a small hollow place, especially in a wall to contain a statue, etc, or in the side of a hill SYN **nook** **4** (*biology*) a position or role taken by a kind of living thing within its community. Different living things may occupy the same niche in different places, for example ANTELOPES in Africa and KANGAROOS in Australia.

nick /nɪk/ *noun, verb*

■ ***noun*** **1 the nick** [sing.] (*BrE, slang*) a prison or a police station: *He'll end up in the nick.* **2** a small cut in the edge or surface of sth

IDM **in good, etc. 'nick** (*BrE, informal*) in good, etc. condition or health **in the ˌnick of 'time** (*informal*) at the very last moment; just in time before sth bad happens

■ ***verb*** **1** [T] **~ sth/yourself** to make a small cut in sth: *He nicked himself while shaving.* **2** [T] **~ sth (from sb/sth)** (*BrE, informal*) to steal sth SYN **pinch**: *Who nicked my pen?* **3** [T] **~ sb (for sth)** (*BrE, informal*) to arrest sb for committing a crime: *You're nicked!* **4** [I] **+ adv./prep.** (*AustralE, NZE, informal*) to go somewhere quickly

nickel /'nɪkl/ *noun* **1** [U] (*symb.* **Ni**) a chemical element. Nickel is a hard silver-white metal used in making some types of steel and other ALLOYS. **2** [C] a coin of the US and Canada worth 5 cents

ˌnickel-and-'dime *adj., verb*

■ ***adj.*** (*NAmE, informal*) involving only a small amount of money; not important

■ ***verb*** **~ sth/sb** (*NAmE*) to spend or save very small amounts of money; to charge small amounts of money for lots of extra items: *Set the money aside so you don't nickel-and-dime it away.* ◇ *She's careful not to nickel-and-dime clients for extra charges.*

nicker /'nɪkə(r)/ *noun* (*pl.* **nicker**) (*BrE, slang*) a pound (in money)

nick·name /'nɪkneɪm/ *noun, verb*

■ ***noun*** an informal, often humorous, name for a person that is connected with their real name, their personality or appearance, or with sth they have done

■ ***verb*** [often passive] **~ sb/sth + noun** to give a nickname to sb/sth: *She was nicknamed 'The Ice Queen'.*

nico·tine /'nɪkəti:n/ *noun* [U] a poisonous substance in TOBACCO that people become ADDICTED to, so that it is difficult to stop smoking

nico·tin·ic acid /ˌnɪkətɪnɪk 'æsɪd/ *noun* [U] = NIACIN

niece 0-w /ni:s/ *noun*
the daughter of your brother or sister; the daughter of your husband's or wife's brother or sister ➲ compare NEPHEW

nifty /'nɪfti/ *adj.* (*informal*) **1** skilful and accurate: *There's some nifty guitar work on his latest CD.* **2** practical; working well SYN **handy**: *a nifty little gadget for slicing cucumbers*

nig·gard·ly /'nɪgədli; *NAmE* -gərd-/ *adj.* (*formal, disapproving*) **1** unwilling to be generous with money, time, etc. SYN **mean** **2** (of a gift or an amount of money) not worth much and given unwillingly SYN **miserly**

nig·ger /'nɪgə(r)/ *noun* (*taboo, slang*) a very offensive word for a black person

nig·gle /'nɪgl/ *noun, verb*

■ ***noun*** **1** (*BrE*) a small criticism or complaint **2** a slight feeling, such as worry, doubt, etc. that does not go away: *a niggle of doubt* **3** a slight pain: *He gets the occasional niggle in his right shoulder.*

■ ***verb*** **1** [I, T] to irritate or annoy sb slightly; to make sb slightly worried SYN **bother**: **~ (at sb)** *A doubt niggled at her.* ◇ **it niggles sb that...** (*BrE*) *It niggled him that she had not phoned back.* ◇ **~ sb** (*BrE*) *Something was niggling her.* **2** [I] **~ (about/over sth)** | **~ (at sb) (for sth)** (*BrE*) to argue about sth unimportant; to criticize sb for sth that is not important SYN **quibble**

nig·gling /'nɪglɪŋ/ (also *less frequent* **nig·gly** /-li/) *adj.* **1** used to describe a slight feeling of worry or pain that does not go away: *She had niggling doubts about their relationship.* ◇ *a series of niggling injuries* **2** not important SYN **petty**: *niggling details*

nigh /naɪ/ *adv.* **1 ~ on** (*old-fashioned*) almost; nearly: *They've lived in that house for nigh on 30 years.* ➲ see also WELL-NIGH **2** (*old use* or *literary*) near: *Winter was drawing nigh.*

night 0-w /naɪt/ *noun* [U, C]

1 0-w the time between one day and the next when it is dark, when people usually sleep: *These animals only come out* ***at night.*** ◇ *They sleep by day and hunt* ***by night.*** ◇ *The accident happened on Friday night.* ◇ ***on the night of*** *10 January/January 10* ◇ *Did you hear the storm* ***last night?*** ◇ *I lay awake* ***all night.*** ◇ *Where did you* ***spend the night?*** ◇ *You're welcome to* ***stay the night*** *here.* ◇ *What is he doing calling* ***at this time of night?*** ◇ *You'll feel better after you've had* ***a good night's sleep.*** ◇ *The trip was for ten nights.* ◇ *The hotel costs €65 per person* ***per night.*** ◇ *the* ***night train/boat/flight*** ◇ ***Night fell*** (= it became dark). **2** 0-w the evening until you go to bed: *Let's go out* ***on Saturday night.*** ◇ *Bill's parents came for dinner* ***last night.*** ◇ *She doesn't like to walk home* ***late at night.*** ◇ *I saw her in town* ***the other night*** (= a few nights ago). ◇ *I'm working late* ***tomorrow night.*** ➲ see also GOODNIGHT **3** an evening when a special event happens: *the* ***first/opening night*** (= of a play, film/movie, etc.) ◇ *a karaoke night* ◇ ***an Irish/a Scottish, etc. night*** (= with Irish/Scottish music, entertainment, etc.) ➲ see also STAG NIGHT ▶ **nights** *adv.*: (*especially NAmE*) *He can't get used to working nights* (= at night).

IDM **have an early/a late 'night** to go to bed earlier or later than usual: *I've had a lot of late nights recently.* **have a good/bad 'night** to sleep well/badly during the night **have a night on the 'tiles** (*BrE, informal*) to stay out late enjoying yourself **ˌnight and 'day** | **ˌday and 'night** all the time; continuously: *The machines are kept running night and day.* **night 'night** used by children or to children, to mean 'Good night': *'Night night, sleep tight!'* **a night 'out** an evening that you spend enjoying yourself away from home: *They enjoy a night out occasionally.* ➲ more at ALL RIGHT *adj.*, DANCE *v.*, DEAD *n.*, MORNING, SPEND *v.*, STILL *n.*, THING

night·cap /'naɪtkæp/ *noun* **1** a drink, usually containing alcohol, taken before going to bed **2** (in the past) a soft cap worn in bed

night·clothes /'naɪtkləʊðz; *NAmE* -kloʊðz/ *noun* [pl.] clothes that you wear in bed

night·club /'naɪtklʌb/ *noun* a place that is open late in the evening where people can go to dance, drink, etc.

'night depository (*US*) (*BrE* **'night safe**) *noun* a SAFE in the outside wall of a bank where money, etc. can be left when the bank is closed

night·dress /'naɪtdres/ (*BrE*) (*NAmE* or *old-fashioned* **night·gown**) (also *informal* **nightie** *BrE, NAmE*) *noun* a long loose piece of clothing like a thin dress, worn by a woman or girl in bed ➲ **VISUAL VOCAB** page V51

'night duty *noun* [U] work that people have to do at night, for example in a hospital: *to be on night duty*

night·fall /'naɪtfɔ:l/ *noun* [U] (*formal* or *literary*) the time in the evening when it becomes dark SYN **dusk**

night·gown /'naɪtgaʊn/ *noun* (*NAmE* or *old-fashioned*) = NIGHTDRESS

nightie /ˈnaɪti/ *noun* (*informal*) = NIGHTDRESS

night·in·gale /ˈnaɪtɪŋɡeɪl/ *noun* a small brown bird, the male of which has a beautiful song

night·jar /ˈnaɪtdʒɑː(r)/ *noun* a brown bird with a long tail and a rough unpleasant cry, that is active mainly at night

night·life /ˈnaɪtlaɪf/ *noun* [U] entertainment that is available in the evening and at night ➲ COLLOCATIONS at TOWN

ˈnight light *noun* a light or CANDLE that is left on at night

ˈnight-long *adj.* [only before noun] lasting all night

night·ly /ˈnaɪtli/ *adj.* happening every night: *a nightly news bulletin* ▸ **night·ly** *adv.*

night·mare /ˈnaɪtmeə(r); *NAmE* -mer/ *noun* **1** a dream that is very frightening or unpleasant: *He still has nightmares about the accident.* **2 ~** (**for sb**) an experience that is very frightening and unpleasant, or very difficult to deal with: *The trip turned into a nightmare when they both got sick.* ◇ (*informal*) *Nobody knows what's going on—**it's a nightmare**!* ◇ (*informal*) *Filling in all those forms was a nightmare.* ◇ *Losing a child is most people's **worst nightmare**.* ◇ *If it goes ahead, it will be the **nightmare scenario*** (= the worst thing that could happen). ◇ *a nightmare situation* ▸ **night·mar·ish** /ˈnaɪtmeərɪʃ; *NAmE* -mer-/ *adj.*: *nightmarish living conditions*

ˈnight owl *noun* (*informal*) a person who enjoys staying up late at night

ˈnight safe (*BrE*) (*US* **ˈnight depository**) *noun* a SAFE in the outside wall of a bank where money, etc. can be left when the bank is closed

ˈnight school *noun* [U, C] (*old-fashioned*) classes for adults, held in the evening

night·shirt /ˈnaɪtʃɜːt; *NAmE* -ʃɜːrt/ *noun* a long loose shirt worn in bed

night·spot /ˈnaɪtspɒt; *NAmE* -spɑːt/ *noun* (*informal*) a place people go to for entertainment at night SYN **nightclub**

night·stand /ˈnaɪtstænd/ (also ˈ**night table**) (both *NAmE*) *noun* = BEDSIDE TABLE

night·stick /ˈnaɪtstɪk/ *noun* (*NAmE*) = TRUNCHEON

ˈnight-time *noun* [U] the time when it is dark: *This area can be very noisy **at night-time**.*

night·watch·man /naɪtˈwɒtʃmən; *NAmE* -ˈwɑːtʃ-/ *noun* (*pl.* **-men** /-mən/) a man whose job is to guard a building such as a factory at night

night·wear /ˈnaɪtweə(r); *NAmE* -wer/ *noun* [U] a word used by shops/stores for clothes that are worn in bed

ni·hil·ism /ˈnaɪɪlɪzəm/ *noun* [U] (*philosophy*) the belief that nothing has any value, especially that religious and moral principles have no value ▸ **ni·hil·is·tic** /ˌnaɪɪˈlɪstɪk/ *adj.*: *Her latest play is a nihilistic vision of the world of the future.*

ni·hil·ist /ˈnaɪɪlɪst/ *noun* a person who believes in nihilism

the Nikkei index /ˈnɪkeɪ ɪndeks/ (also **the ˈNikkei average**) *noun* [sing.] a figure that shows the relative price of shares on the Tokyo Stock Exchange

nil /nɪl/ *noun* [U] **1** (*especially BrE*) the number 0, especially as the score in some games SYN **zero**: *Newcastle beat Leeds four nil/by four goals to nil.* **2** nothing: *The doctors rated her chances as nil* (= there were no chances).

nim·ble /ˈnɪmbl/ *adj.* (**nim·bler** /ˈnɪmblə(r)/, **nim·blest** /ˈnɪmblɪst/) **1** able to move quickly and easily SYN **agile**: *You need nimble fingers for that job.* ◇ *She was extremely nimble on her feet.* **2** (of the mind) able to think and understand quickly ▸ **nim·bly** /ˈnɪmbli/ *adv.*

nim·bus /ˈnɪmbəs/ *noun* (*technical*) **1** [C, usually sing., U] a large grey rain cloud **2** [C, usually sing.] a circle of light

nimby /ˈnɪmbi/ *noun* (*pl.* **-ies**) (*disapproving, humorous*) a person who claims to be in favour of a new development or project, but objects if it is too near their home and will disturb them in some way ORIGIN Formed from the first letters of 'not in my back yard'.

nin·com·poop /ˈnɪŋkəmpuːp/ *noun* (*old-fashioned, informal*) a stupid person

nine 0‑ᴡ /naɪn/ *number* 9 HELP There are examples of how to use numbers at the entry for **five**.

IDM **have nine ˈlives** (especially of a cat) to be very lucky in dangerous situations **a ˌnine days' ˈwonder** a person or thing that makes people excited for a short time but does not last very long **ˌnine times out of ˈten** almost every time: *I'm always emailing her, but nine times out of ten she doesn't reply.* **ˌnine to ˈfive** the normal working hours in an office: *I work nine to five.* ◇ *a nine-to-five job* **the ˌwhole ˌnine ˈyards** (*informal, especially NAmE*) everything, or a situation which includes everything: *When Dan cooks dinner he always goes the whole nine yards, with three courses and a choice of dessert.* ➲ more at DRESSED, POSSESSION

nine·pins /ˈnaɪnpɪnz/ *noun*

IDM **ˌgo down, ˌdrop, etc. like ˈninepins** (*BrE, informal*) to fall down or become ill/sick in great numbers

nine·teen 0‑ᴡ /ˌnaɪnˈtiːn/ *number* 19 ▸ **nine·teenth** 0‑ᴡ /ˌnaɪnˈtiːnθ/ *ordinal number, noun* HELP There are examples of how to use ordinal numbers at the entry for **fifth**.

IDM **talk, etc. nineteen to the ˈdozen** (*BrE, informal*) to talk, etc. without stopping: *She was chatting away, nineteen to the dozen.*

ninety 0‑ᴡ /ˈnaɪnti/
1 0‑ᴡ *number* 90 **2** *noun* **the nineties** [pl.] numbers, years or temperatures from 90 to 99: *The temperature must be in the nineties today.* ▸ **nine·ti·eth** 0‑ᴡ /ˈnaɪntiəθ/ *ordinal number, noun* HELP There are examples of how to use ordinal numbers at the entry for **fifth**.

IDM **in your nineties** between the ages of 90 and 99 **ˌninety-nine ˌtimes out of a ˈhundred** almost always

ning-nong /ˈnɪŋ nɒŋ; *NAmE* nɑːŋ/ (also **nong**) *noun* (*AustralE, NZE, informal*) a stupid person

ninja /ˈnɪndʒə/ *noun* (*pl.* **ninjas** or **ninja**) (from *Japanese*) a person trained in traditional Japanese skills of fighting and moving quietly

ninny /ˈnɪni/ *noun* (*pl.* **-ies**) (*old-fashioned, informal*) a stupid person

ninth 0‑ᴡ /naɪnθ/ *ordinal number, noun*
▪ ***ordinal number*** 0‑ᴡ 9th HELP There are examples of how to use ordinal numbers at the entry for **fifth**.
▪ ***noun*** 0‑ᴡ each of nine equal parts of sth

nio·bium /naɪˈəʊbiəm; *NAmE* -ˈoʊ-/ *noun* [U] (*symb.* **Nb**) a chemical element. Niobium is a silver-grey metal used in steel ALLOYS.

nip /nɪp/ *verb, noun*
▪ ***verb*** (**-pp-**) **1** [T, I] to give sb/sth a quick painful bite or PINCH: **~ sth** *He winced as the dog nipped his ankle.* ◇ **~ (at sth)** *She nipped at my arm.* **2** [I, T] (of cold, wind, etc.) to harm or damage sth: **~ (at sth)** *The icy wind nipped at our faces.* ◇ **~ sth** *growing shoots nipped by frost* **3** [I] + **adv./prep.** (*BrE, informal*) to go somewhere quickly and/or for only a short time SYN **pop**: *He's just nipped out to the bank.* ◇ *A car nipped in* (= got in quickly) *ahead of me.*

IDM **nip sth in the ˈbud** to stop sth when it has just begun because you can see that problems will come from it

PHR V **ˌnip sth↔ˈoff** to remove a part of sth with your finger or with a tool

▪ ***noun*** **1** the act of giving sb a small bite or PINCH (= squeezing their skin between your finger and thumb) **2** (*informal*) a feeling of cold: *There was a real **nip in the air**.* ➲ see also NIPPY **3** (*informal*) a small drink of strong alcohol

ˌnip and ˈtuck *adj., adv., noun*
▪ ***adj., adv.*** (*especially NAmE*) = NECK AND NECK: *The presidential contest is nip and tuck.*
▪ ***noun*** (*informal*) a medical operation in which skin is removed or made tighter to make sb look younger or more attractive, especially a FACELIFT

nip·per /ˈnɪpə(r)/ *noun* (*informal*) a small child

nip·ple /ˈnɪpl/ *noun* **1** either of the two small round dark parts on a person's chest. Babies can suck milk from their mother's breasts through the nipples. ⊃ VISUAL VOCAB page V48 **2** (*NAmE*) (*BrE* **teat**) the rubber part at the end of a baby's bottle that the baby sucks in order to get milk, etc. from the bottle **3** a small metal, plastic or rubber object that is shaped like a nipple with a small hole in the end, especially one that is used as part of a machine to direct oil, etc. into a particular place: *a grease nipple*

nippy /ˈnɪpi/ *adj.* **1** (*BrE*) able to move quickly and easily: *a nippy little sports car* **2** (*informal*) (of the weather) cold

niqab /nɪˈkɑːb/ *noun* a piece of cloth that covers the face but not usually the eyes, worn in public by some Muslim women

nir·vana /nɪəˈvɑːnə; *NAmE* nɪrˈv-/ *noun* [U] (in the religion of Buddhism) the state of peace and happiness that a person achieves after giving up all personal desires

Nis·sen hut /ˈnɪsn hʌt/ (*BrE*) (*NAmE* **Quonset hut™**) *noun* a shelter made of metal with curved walls and roof

nit /nɪt/ *noun* **1** the egg or young form of a LOUSE (= a small insect that lives in human hair) **2** (*BrE, informal*) a stupid person

ˈnit-picking *noun* [U] (*informal, disapproving*) the habit of finding small mistakes in sb's work or paying too much attention to small details that are not important ▸ **ˈnit-picker** *noun* **ˈnit-picking** *adj.*

ni·trate /ˈnaɪtreɪt/ *noun* [U, C] (*chemistry*) a COMPOUND containing NITROGEN and OXYGEN. There are several different nitrates and they are used especially to make soil better for growing crops: *We need to cut nitrate levels in water.*

ni·tric acid /ˌnaɪtrɪk ˈæsɪd/ *noun* [U] (*chemistry*) (*symb.* HNO_3) a powerful clear acid that can destroy most substances and is used to make EXPLOSIVES and other chemical products

ni·trify /ˈnaɪtrɪfaɪ/ *verb* (**ni·tri·fies, ni·tri·fy·ing, ni·tri·fied, ni·tri·fied**) **~ sth** (*chemistry*) to change a substance into a COMPOUND that contains NITROGEN ⊃ see also NITRATE

ni·trite /ˈnaɪtraɪt/ *noun* [U, C] (*chemistry*) a COMPOUND containing NITROGEN and OXYGEN. There are several different nitrites.

ni·tro·gen /ˈnaɪtrədʒən/ *noun* [U] (*symb.* **N**) a chemical element. Nitrogen is a gas that is found in large quantities in the earth's atmosphere. ▸ **ni·tro·gen·ous** /naɪˈtrɒdʒənəs; *NAmE* -ˈtrɑːdʒ-/ *adj.*

ˈnitrogen cycle *noun* [C, U] the processes by which nitrogen is passed from one part of the environment to another, for example when plants decay

ˌnitrogen diˈoxide *noun* [U] (*chemistry*) a brown poisonous gas. Nitrogen dioxide is formed when some metals are dissolved in NITRIC ACID.

nitro·gly·cer·ine /ˌnaɪtrəʊˈɡlɪsəriːn; -rɪn; *NAmE* ˌnaɪtroʊˈɡlɪsərən/ (*especially BrE*) (*US* usually **nitro·gly·cerin** /-rɪn; *NAmE* -rən/) *noun* [U] a powerful liquid EXPLOSIVE

ni·trous oxide /ˌnaɪtrəs ˈɒksaɪd; *NAmE* ˈɑːk-/ (also *informal* **ˈlaughing gas**) *noun* [U] a gas used especially in the past by dentists to prevent you from feeling pain

the nitty-gritty /ˌnɪti ˈɡrɪti/ *noun* [sing.] (*informal*) the basic or most important details of an issue or a situation: *Time ran out before we could* ***get down to the real nitty-gritty.***

nit·wit /ˈnɪtwɪt/ *noun* (*informal*) a stupid person

nix /nɪks/ *verb, noun*

■ ***verb* ~ sth** (*NAmE, informal*) to prevent sth from happening by saying 'no' to it

■ ***noun*** [U] (*NAmE, informal*) nothing

NLP /ˌen el ˈpiː/ *abbr.* **1** NEUROLINGUISTIC PROGRAMMING **2** NATURAL LANGUAGE PROCESSING

No. *abbr.* **1** (also **no.**) (*pl.* **Nos, nos**) number: *Room No. 145* **2** (*NAmE*) north; northern

no ⊶ /nəʊ; *NAmE* noʊ/ *exclamation, det., adv., noun*

■ ***exclamation*** **1** ⊶ used to give a negative reply or statement: *Just say yes or no.* ◇ *'Are you ready?' 'No, I'm not.'* ◇ *Sorry, the answer's no.* ◇ *'Another drink?' 'No, thanks.'* ◇ *It's about 70—no, I'm wrong—80 kilometres from Rome.* ◇ *No! Don't touch it! It's hot.* ◇ *'It was Tony.' 'No, you're wrong. It was Ted.'* ◇ *'It's not very good, is it?' 'No, you're right, it isn't* (= I agree).*'* **2** ⊶ used to express shock or surprise at what sb has said: *'She's had an accident.' 'Oh, no!'* ◇ *'I'm leaving!' 'No!'*

IDM **not take no for an answer** to refuse to accept that sb does not want sth, will not do sth, etc: *You're coming and I won't take no for an answer!* ⊃ more at YES *exclam.*

■ ***det.*** **1** ⊶ not one; not any; not a: *No student is to leave the room.* ◇ *There were no letters this morning.* ◇ *There's no bread left.* ◇ *No two days are the same.* ⊃ see also NO ONE **2** ⊶ used, for example on notices, to say that sth is not allowed: *No smoking!* **3** ⊶ **there's ~ doing sth** used to say that it is impossible to do sth: *There's no telling what will happen next.* **4** ⊶ used to express the opposite of what is mentioned: *She's no fool* (= she's intelligent). ◇ *It was no easy matter* (= it was difficult).

■ ***adv.*** used before adjectives and adverbs to mean 'not': *She's feeling no better this morning.* ◇ *Reply by no later than 21 July.*

■ ***noun*** (*pl.* **noes** /nəʊz; *NAmE* noʊz/) **1** an answer that shows you do not agree with an idea, a statement, etc; a person who says 'no': *Can't you give me a straight yes or no?* ◇ *When we took a vote there were nine yesses and 3 noes.* ◇ *I'll put you down as a no.* **2 the noes** [pl.] the total number of people voting 'no' in a formal debate, for example in a parliament: *The noes have it* (= more people have voted against sth than for it). OPP **ayes**

Noah's ark /ˌnəʊəz ˈɑːk; *NAmE* ˌnoʊəz ˈɑːrk/ *noun* = ARK

nob /nɒb; *NAmE* nɑːb/ *noun* (*old-fashioned, BrE, informal*) a person who has a high social position; a member of the upper class

ˌno-ˈball *noun* (in CRICKET) a ball that is BOWLED (= thrown) in a way that is not allowed and which means that a RUN (= a point) is given to the other team

nob·ble /ˈnɒbl; *NAmE* ˈnɑːbl/ *verb* (*BrE, informal*) **1 ~ sth** to prevent a horse from winning a race, for example by giving it drugs **2 ~ sb** to persuade sb to do what you want, especially illegally, by offering them money: *his attempts to nobble the jury* **3 ~ sb** to prevent sb from achieving what they want SYN **thwart** **4 ~ sb** to catch sb or get their attention, especially when they are unwilling: *He was nobbled by the press who wanted details of the affair.* ▸ **nob·bling** *noun* [U]

no·bel·ium /nəʊˈbiːliəm; -ˈbel-; *NAmE* noʊ-/ *noun* [U] (*symb.* **No**) a chemical element. Nobelium is a RADIOACTIVE metal that does not exist naturally and is produced from CURIUM.

Nobel Prize /nəʊˌbel ˈpraɪz; *NAmE* noʊ-/ *noun* one of six international prizes given each year for excellent work in physics, chemistry, medicine, literature, ECONOMICS and work towards world peace

no·bil·ity /nəʊˈbɪləti; *NAmE* noʊ-/ *noun* **1 the nobility** [sing.+ sing./pl. v.] people of high social position who have titles such as that of DUKE or DUCHESS SYN **the aristocracy** **2** [U] (*formal*) the quality of being noble in character

noble /ˈnəʊbl; *NAmE* ˈnoʊbl/ *adj., noun*

■ ***adj.*** (**no·bler** /ˈnəʊblə(r); *NAmE* ˈnoʊ-/, **nob·lest** /ˈnəʊblɪst; *NAmE* ˈnoʊ-/) **1** having fine personal qualities that people admire, such as courage, HONESTY and care for others: *a noble leader* ◇ *noble ideals* ◇ *He died for a noble cause.* ⊃ compare IGNOBLE **2** very impressive in size or quality SYN **splendid**: *a noble building* **3** belonging to a family of high social rank (= belonging to the nobility) SYN **aristocratic**: *a man of noble birth* ▸ **nobly** /ˈnəʊbli; *NAmE* ˈnoʊbli/ *adv.*: *She bore the disappointment nobly.* ◇ *to be nobly born*

■ ***noun*** a person who comes from a family of high social rank; a member of the nobility SYN **aristocrat**

ˌnoble ˈgas (also **ˌinert ˈgas**, **ˈrare gas**) *noun* (*chemistry*) any of a group of gases that do not react with other chem-

N

icals. ARGON, HELIUM, KRYPTON and NEON are noble gases.

noble·man /ˈnəʊblmən; *NAmE* ˈnoʊbl-/, **noble·woman** /ˈnəʊblwʊmən; *NAmE* ˈnoʊbl-/ *nouns* (*pl.* **-men** /-mən/, **-women** /-wɪmɪn/) a person from a family of high social rank; a member of the NOBILITY **SYN aristocrat**

ˌnoble ˈsavage *noun* a word used in the past to refer in a positive way to a person or people who did not live in an advanced human society: *The book contrasts modern civilization with the ideal of the noble savage who lived in harmony with nature.*

no·blesse ob·lige /nəʊˌbles əˈbliːʒ; *NAmE* noʊ-/ *noun* [U] (from *French*) the idea that people who have special advantages of wealth, etc. should help other people who do not have these advantages

no·body 🗝 /ˈnəʊbədi; *NAmE* ˈnoʊ-/ *pron.*, *noun*
■ ***pron.*** 🗝 = NO ONE: *Nobody knew what to say.* **HELP Nobody** is more common than **no one** in spoken English. **OPP somebody**
■ ***noun*** (*pl.* **-ies**) a person who has no importance or influence **SYN nonentity**: *She rose from being a nobody to become a superstar.* ➲ compare SOMEONE

ˌno-ˈbrain·er *noun* (*informal*) a decision or a problem that you do not need to think about much because it is obvious what you should do

ˌno-ˈclaims bonus (also **ˌno-ˈclaim bonus**, **ˌno-ˈclaim(s) discount**) *noun* (all *BrE*) a reduction in the cost of your insurance because you made no claims in the previous year

noc·tur·nal /nɒkˈtɜːnl; *NAmE* nɑːkˈtɜːrnl/ *adj.* **1** (of animals) active at night **OPP diurnal** **2** (*formal*) happening during the night: *a nocturnal visit*

N

noc·turne /ˈnɒktɜːn; *NAmE* ˈnɑːktɜːrn/ *noun* a short piece of music in a romantic style, especially for the piano

Nod /nɒd; *NAmE* nɑːd/ *noun* [U] **IDM** see LAND *n.*

nod /nɒd; *NAmE* nɑːd/ *verb*, *noun*
■ ***verb*** (**-dd-**) **1** [I, T] if you **nod**, **nod** your head or your head **nods**, you move your head up and down to show agreement, understanding, etc: *I asked him if he would help me and he nodded.* ◇ *Her head nodded in agreement.* ◇ **~ sth** *He nodded his head sympathetically.* ◇ *She nodded approval.* **2** [I, T] to move your head down and up once to say hello to sb or to give them a sign to do sth: **~ (to/at sb)** *The president nodded to the crowd as he passed in the motorcade.* ◇ **~ to/at sb to do sth** *She nodded at him to begin speaking* ◇ **~ sth (to/at sb)** *to nod a greeting* **3** [I] **+ adv./prep.** to move your head in the direction of sb/sth to show that you are talking about them/it: *I asked where Steve was and she nodded in the direction of the kitchen.* **4** [I] to let your head fall forward when you are sleeping in a chair: *He sat nodding in front of the fire.*
IDM have a nodding acˈquaintance with sb/sth to only know sb/sth slightly
PHR V ˌnod ˈoff (*informal*) to fall asleep for a short time while you are sitting in a chair
■ ***noun*** a small quick movement of the head down and up again: *to give a* ***nod of approval/agreement/encouragement***
IDM get the ˈnod (*informal*) to be chosen for sth; to be given permission or approval to do sth: *He got the nod from the team manager* (= he was chosen for the team). **give sb/sth the ˈnod** (*informal*) **1** to give permission for sth; to agree to sth: *We've been given the nod to expand the business.* ◇ *I hope he'll give the nod to the plan.* **2** to choose sb for sth **a ˌnod and a ˈwink | a ˌnod is as good as a ˈwink** used to say that a suggestion or a HINT will be understood, without anything more being said: *Everything could be done by a nod and a wink.* **on the ˈnod** (*BrE, informal*) if a proposal is accepted **on the nod**, it is accepted without any discussion

nod·dle /ˈnɒdl; *NAmE* ˈnɑːdl/ (*NAmE* usually **noo·dle**) *noun* (*old-fashioned, slang*) your head; your brain

node /nəʊd; *NAmE* noʊd/ *noun* **1** (*biology*) a place on the STEM of a plant from which a branch or leaf grows **2** (*biology*) a small swelling on a root or branch **3** (*technical, computing*) a point at which two lines or systems meet or cross: *a network node* **4** (*anatomy*) a small hard mass of TISSUE, especially near a joint in the human body: *a lymph node* ▸ **nodal** *adj.*

nod·ule /ˈnɒdjuːl; *NAmE* ˈnɑːdʒuːl/ *noun* a small round lump or swelling, especially on a plant

Noel /nəʊˈel; *NAmE* noʊ-/ *noun* [C, U] a word for 'Christmas' used especially in songs or on cards: *Joyful Noel*

noes *pl.* of NO

ˌno-ˈfault *adj.* [only before noun] (*law*) (*especially NAmE*) not involving a decision as to who is to blame for sth: *no-fault insurance* (= in which the insurance company pays for damage, etc. without asking whose fault it was)

ˌno-ˈfly zone *noun* an area above a country where planes from other countries are not allowed to fly

ˌno-ˈfrills *adj.* [only before noun] (especially of a service or product) including only the basic features, without anything that is unnecessary, especially things added to make sth more attractive or comfortable: *a no-frills airline*

ˌno-ˈgo area *noun* (*especially BrE*) an area, especially in a city, which is dangerous for people to enter, or that the police or army do not enter, often because it is controlled by a violent group: (*figurative*) *Some clubs are no-go areas for people over 30.* ◇ (*figurative*) *This subject is definitely a no-go area* (= we must not discuss it).

ˈno-good *adj.* [only before noun] (*slang*) (of a person) bad or useless

Noh (also **No**) /nəʊ; *NAmE* noʊ/ *noun* [U] traditional Japanese theatre in which songs, dance, and MIME are performed by people wearing MASKS

ˌno-ˈhoper *noun* (*informal*) a person or an animal that is considered useless or very unlikely to be successful

noise 🗝 /nɔɪz/ *noun*
1 🗝 [C, U] a sound, especially when it is loud, unpleasant or disturbing: *a rattling noise* ◇ *What's that noise?* ◇ *Don't* ***make a noise***. ◇ *They were making too much noise.* ◇ *I was woken by the noise of a car starting up.* ◇ *We had to shout above the noise of the traffic.* ◇ *to reduce* ***noise levels*** **2** [U] (*technical*) extra electrical or electronic signals that are not part of the signal that is being broadcast or TRANSMITTED and which may damage it **3** [U] information that is not wanted and that can make it difficult for the important or useful information to be seen clearly: *There is some noise in the data which needs to be reduced.*
IDM make a ˈnoise (about sth) (*informal*) to complain loudly **make ˈnoises (about sth)** (*informal*) **1** to talk in an indirect way about sth that you think you might do: *The company has been making noises about closing several factories.* **2** to complain about sth **make soothing, encouraging, reassuring, etc. noises** to make remarks of the kind mentioned, even when that is not what you really think: *He made all the right noises at the meeting yesterday* (= said what people wanted to hear). ➲ more at BIG *adj.*

Which Word?

noise / sound

- **Noise** is usually loud and unpleasant. It can be countable or uncountable: *Try not to make so much noise.* ◇ *What a terrible noise!*
- **Sound** is a countable noun and means something that you hear: *All she could hear was the sound of the waves.* You do not use words like *much* or *a lot of* with **sound**.

noise·less /ˈnɔɪzləs/ *adj.* (*formal*) making little or no noise **SYN silent**: *He moved with noiseless steps.* ▸ **noise·less·ly** *adv.*

ˌnoises ˈoff *noun* [pl.] **1** (in theatre) sounds made off the stage, intended to be heard by the audience **2** (*humorous*) noise in the background which interrupts you

noi·some /ˈnɔɪsəm/ *adj.* (*formal*) extremely unpleasant or offensive: *noisome smells*

noisy 🔑 /ˈnɔɪzi/ *adj.* (**nois·ier**, **noisi·est**) **1** 🔑 making a lot of noise: *noisy children/traffic/crowds* ◇ *a noisy protest* (= when people shout) ◇ *The engine is very noisy at high speed.* **2** 🔑 full of noise: *a noisy classroom* ▸ **nois·ily** 🔑 /-ɪli/ *adv.*: *The children were playing noisily upstairs.*

nomad /ˈnəʊmæd; *NAmE* ˈnoʊ-/ *noun* a member of a community that moves with its animals from place to place ▸ **no·mad·ic** /nəʊˈmædɪk; *NAmE* noʊ-/ *adj.*: *nomadic tribes* ◇ *the nomadic life of a foreign correspondent*

ˈno-man's-land *noun* [U, sing.] an area of land between the borders of two countries or between two armies, that is not controlled by either

nom de guerre /ˌnɒm də ˈgeə(r); *NAmE* ˌnɑːm də ˈger/ *noun* (*pl.* **noms de guerre** /ˌnɒm də ˈgeə(r); *NAmE* ˌnɑːm də ˈger/) (from *French*, *formal*) a false name that is used, for example, by sb who belongs to a military organization that is not official

nom de plume /ˌnɒm də ˈpluːm; *NAmE* ˌnɑːm/ *noun* (*pl.* **noms de plume** /ˌnɒm də ˈpluːm; *NAmE* ˌnɑːm/) (from *French*) a name used by a writer instead of their real name **SYN** **pen-name, pseudonym**

no·men·clat·ure /nəˈmenklətʃə(r); *NAmE* ˈnoʊmənkleɪtʃər/ *noun* [U, C] (*formal*) a system of naming things, especially in a branch of science

nom·in·al /ˈnɒmɪnl; *NAmE* ˈnɑːm-/ *adj.* **1** being sth in name only, and not in reality: *the nominal leader of the party* ◇ *He remained in nominal control of the business for another ten years.* **2** (of a sum of money) very small and much less than the normal cost or change **SYN** **token**: *We only pay a nominal rent.* **3** (*grammar*) connected with a noun or nouns ▸ **nom·in·al·ly** /-nəli/ *adv.*: *He was nominally in charge of the company.*

nom·in·al·ize /ˈnɒmɪnəlaɪz; *NAmE* ˈnɑːm-/ *verb* **~ sth** (*grammar*) to form a noun from a verb or adjective, for example 'truth' from 'true'

nom·in·ate /ˈnɒmɪneɪt; *NAmE* ˈnɑːm-/ *verb* **1** to formally suggest that sb should be chosen for an important role, prize, position, etc. **SYN** **propose**: **~ sb (for sth)** *She has been nominated for the presidency.* ◇ **~ sb (as) sth** | **~ sb + noun** *He was nominated (as) best actor.* ◇ **~ sb to do sth** *I nominated Paul to take on the role of treasurer.* **2** to choose sb to do a particular job **SYN** **appoint**: **~ sb (to/as sth)** *I have been nominated to the committee.* ◇ **~ sb to do sth** *She was nominated to speak on our behalf.* **3 ~ sth (as sth)** to choose a time, date or title for sth **SYN** **select**: *1 December has been nominated as the day of the election.*

nom·in·ation /ˌnɒmɪˈneɪʃn; *NAmE* ˌnɑːm-/ *noun* [U, C] the act of suggesting or choosing sb as a candidate in an election, or for a job or an award; the fact of being suggested for this: *Membership of the club is by nomination only.* ◇ *He won the nomination as Democratic candidate for the presidency.* ◇ *They opposed her nomination to the post of Deputy Director.* ◇ *He has had nine Oscar nominations.*

nom·ina·tive /ˈnɒmɪnətɪv; *NAmE* ˈnɑːm-/ (also **sub·ject·ive**) *noun* (*grammar*) (in some languages) the form of a noun, a pronoun or an adjective when it is the subject of a verb ➲ compare ABLATIVE, ACCUSATIVE, DATIVE, GENITIVE, VOCATIVE ▸ **nom·ina·tive** *adj.*: *nominative pronouns*

nom·inee /ˌnɒmɪˈniː; *NAmE* ˌnɑːm-/ *noun* **1** a person who has been formally suggested for a job, a prize, etc: *a presidential nominee* ◇ *an Oscar nominee* **2** (*business*) a person in whose name money is invested in a company, etc.

non- 🔑 /nɒn; *NAmE* nɑːn/ *prefix* (in nouns, adjectives and adverbs) not: *nonsense* ◇ *non-fiction* ◇ *non-alcoholic* ◇ *non-profit-making* ◇ *non-committally* **HELP** Most compounds with **non** are written with a hyphen in *BrE* but are written as one word with no hyphen in *NAmE*.

nona·gen·ar·ian /ˌnɒnədʒəˈneəriən; ˌnəʊn-; *NAmE* ˌnɑːnədʒəˈner-; ˌnoʊn-/ *noun* a person who is between 90 and 99 years old ▸ **nona·gen·ar·ian** *adj.*

ˌnon-agˈgres·sion *noun* [U] (often used as an adjective) a relationship between two countries that have agreed not to attack each other: *a policy of non-aggression* ◇ *a* ***non-aggression pact/treaty***

ˌnon-alcoˈhol·ic *adj.* (of a drink) not containing any alcohol: *a non-alcoholic drink* ◇ *Can I have something non-alcoholic?*

ˌnon-aˈligned *adj.* not providing support for or receiving support from any of the powerful countries in the world ▸ **ˌnon-aˈlignment** *noun* [U]: *a policy of non-alignment*

ˌnon-alphaˈbet·ic (also **ˌnon-alphaˈbetical**) *adj.* not being one of the letters of the alphabet ➲ compare ALPHABETIC

ˌnon-apˈpear·ance *noun* [U] (*formal*) failure to be in a place where people expect to see you

ˌnon-atˈtend·ance *noun* [U] failure to go to a place at a time or for an event where you are expected

ˌnon-biodeˈgrad·able *adj.* a substance or chemical that is **non-biodegradable** cannot be changed to a harmless natural state by the action of bacteria, and may therefore damage the environment **OPP** **biodegradable**

nonce /nɒns; *NAmE* nɑːns/ *adj.* a **nonce** word or expression is one that is invented for one particular occasion

non·cha·lant /ˈnɒnʃələnt; *NAmE* ˌnɑːnʃəˈlɑːnt/ *adj.* behaving in a calm and relaxed way; giving the impression that you are not feeling any anxiety **SYN** **casual**: *to* ***appear/look/sound nonchalant*** ◇ *'It'll be fine,' she replied, with a nonchalant shrug.* ▸ **non·cha·lance** /-ləns; *NAmE* -ˈlɑːns/ *noun* [U]: *an air of nonchalance* **non·cha·lant·ly** *adv.*: *He was leaning nonchalantly against the wall.*

ˌnon-ˈcitizen *noun* (*NAmE*) = ALIEN (1)

ˌnon-ˈcombat·ant *noun* **1** a member of the armed forces who does not actually fight in a war, for example an army doctor **2** in a war, a person who is not a member of the armed forces **SYN** **civilian** ➲ compare COMBATANT

ˌnon-commis·sioned ˈofficer *noun* (*abbr.* **NCO**) a soldier in the army, etc. who has a rank such as SERGEANT or CORPORAL, but not a high rank ➲ compare COMMISSIONED OFFICER

ˌnon-coˈmmit·tal *adj.* not giving an opinion; not showing which side of an argument you agree with: *a* ***non-committal reply/tone*** ◇ *The doctor was non-committal about when I could drive again.* ➲ see also COMMIT (5) ▸ **non-com·mit·tal·ly** *adv.*

ˌnon-comˈpli·ance *noun* [U] **~ (with sth)** the fact of failing or refusing to obey a rule: *There are penalties for non-compliance with the fire regulations.* **OPP** **compliance**

ˌnon ˌcompos ˈmentis (also **ˌnon ˈcompos**) *adj.* (*formal*) not in a normal mental state **OPP** **compos mentis**

non·con·form·ist **AW** /ˌnɒnkənˈfɔːmɪst; *NAmE* ˌnɑːnkənˈfɔːrm-/ *noun* **1** **Nonconformist** (in England and Wales) a member of a Protestant Church that does not follow the beliefs and practices of the Church of England **2** a person who does not follow normal ways of thinking or behaving ▸ **non·con·form·ist**, **Non·con·form·ist** *adj.*

non·con·form·ity **AW** /ˌnɒnkənˈfɔːmɪti; *NAmE* ˌnɑːnkənˈfɔːrm-/ (also **non·con·form·ism** /ˌnɒnkənˈfɔːmɪzəm; *NAmE* ˌnɑːnkənˈfɔːrm-/) *noun* [U] **1** the fact of not following normal ways of thinking and behaving **2** **Nonconformity** the beliefs and practices of Nonconformist Churches

ˌnon-ˈcontact sport *noun* a sport in which players do not have physical contact with each other **OPP** **contact sport**

ˌnon-conˈtribu·tory *adj.* (of an insurance or pension plan) paid for by the employer and not the employee **OPP** **contributory**

ˌnon-contro·ˈver·sial *adj.* not causing, or not likely to cause, any disagreement **OPP** **controversial** **HELP** This is not as strong as **uncontroversial**, which is more common.

ˌnon-coˌopeˈr·ation *noun* [U] refusal to help a person in authority by doing what they have asked you to do, especially as a form of protest: *A strike is unlikely, but some forms of non-cooperation are being considered.*

ˌnon-ˈcount *adj.* (*grammar*) = UNCOUNTABLE

ˌnon-cuˈstod·ial *adj.* [only before noun] (*law*) **1** (of a punishment) that does not involve a period of time in prison: *a* ***non-custodial sentence/penalty*** **2** (of a parent) not having CUSTODY of a child OPP **custodial**

ˌnon-ˈdairy *adj.* [only before noun] not made with milk or cream: *a non-dairy whipped topping*

ˌnon-deˈfining *adj.* = NON-RESTRICTIVE

non·de·script /ˈnɒndɪskrɪpt; *NAmE* ˈnɑːn-/ *adj.* (*disapproving*) having no interesting or unusual features or qualities SYN **dull**

none 🔑 /nʌn/ *pron., adv.*

■ ***pron.*** 🔑 **~** (**of sb/sth**) not one of a group of people or things; not any: *None of these pens works/work.* ◇ *We have three sons but none of them lives/live nearby.* ◇ *We saw several houses but none we really liked.* ◇ *Tickets for Friday? Sorry we've got none left.* ◇ *He told me all the news but none of it was very exciting.* ◇ *'Is there any more milk?' 'No,* ***none at all****.'* ◇ (*formal*) *Everybody liked him but none* (= nobody) *more than I.*

IDM **ˈnone but** (*literary*) only: *None but he knew the truth.* **none ˈother than** used to emphasize who or what sb/sth is, when this is surprising: *Her first customer was none other than Mrs Obama.* **have/want none of sth** to refuse to accept sth: *I offered to pay but he was having none of it.* **ˌnone the ˈless** = NONETHELESS

■ ***adv.*** **1** used with *the* and a comparative to mean 'not at all': *She told me what it meant at great length but I'm afraid I'm* ***none the wiser****.* ◇ *He seems* ***none the worse*** *for the experience.* **2** used with *too* and an adjective or adverb to mean 'not at all' or 'not very': *She was looking none too pleased.*

Grammar Point

none of

- When you use **none of** with an uncountable noun, the verb is in the singular: *None of the work was done.*
- When you use **none of** with a plural noun or pronoun, or a singular noun referring to a group of people or things, you can use either a singular or a plural verb. The singular form is used in a formal style in *BrE*: *None of the trains is/are going to London.* ◇ *None of her family has/have been to college.*

non·en·tity /nɒˈnentəti; *NAmE* nɑːˈn-/ *noun* (*pl.* **-ies**) (*disapproving*) a person without any special qualities, who has not achieved anything important SYN **nobody**

ˌnon-esˈsential *adj.* [usually before noun] not completely necessary ➲ compare ESSENTIAL HELP This is not as strong as **inessential** and is more common. **Inessential** can suggest disapproval. ▶ **ˌnon-esˈsential** *noun* [usually pl.]: *I have no money for non-essentials.*

nonet /nəʊˈnet; nɒˈnet; *NAmE* noʊˈnet/ *noun* **1** [C+sing./pl. v.] a group of nine people or things, especially nine musicians **2** [C] a piece of music for nine singers or musicians

none·the·less AW /ˌnʌnðəˈles/ (also **ˌnone the ˈless**) *adv.* (*formal*) despite this fact SYN **nevertheless**: *The book is too long but, nonetheless, informative and entertaining.* ◇ *The problems are not serious. Nonetheless, we shall need to tackle them soon.* ➲ LANGUAGE BANK at NEVERTHELESS

ˌnon-eˈvent *noun* (*informal*) an event that was expected to be interesting, exciting and popular but is in fact very disappointing SYN **anticlimax**

ˌnon-exˈecutive *adj.* [only before noun] (*BrE, business*) a **non-executive** director of a company can give advice at a high level but does not have the power to make decisions about the company

ˌnon-eˈxistent *adj.* not existing; not real: *a non-existent problem* ◇ *'How's your social life?' 'Non-existent, I'm afraid.'* ◇ *Hospital beds were scarce and medicines were* ***practically non-existent****.* ➲ compare EXISTENT ▶ **ˌnon-eˈxistence** *noun* [U]

ˌnon-ˈfiction *noun* [U] books, articles or texts about real facts, people and events: *I prefer reading non-fiction.* ◇ *the non-fiction section of the library* OPP **fiction**

ˌnon-ˈfinite *adj.* (*grammar*) a **non-finite** verb form or clause does not show a particular tense, PERSON OR NUMBER OPP **finite**

ˌnon-ˈflammable *adj.* not likely to burn easily: *non-flammable nightwear* OPP **flammable**

nong /nɒŋ; *NAmE* nɑːŋ; nɔːŋ/ *noun* (*AustralE, NZE, informal*) = NING-NONG

ˌnon-ˈgradable *adj.* (*grammar*) (of an adjective) that cannot be used in the comparative and superlative forms, or be used with words like 'very' and 'less' OPP **gradable**

ˌnon-ˈhuman *adj.* not human: *similarities between human and non-human animals* ➲ compare HUMAN, INHUMAN

ˌnon-iˌdentical ˈtwin *adj.* = FRATERNAL TWIN

ˌnon-interˈven·tion (also **ˌnon-interˈfer·ence**) *noun* [U] the policy or practice of not becoming involved in other people's disagreements, especially those of foreign countries ▶ **ˌnon-interˈven·tion·ism** *noun* [U] **ˌnon-interˈven·tion·ist** *adj.*

ˌnon-inˈvasive *adj.* (of medical treatment) not involving cutting into the body

ˌnon-ˈissue *noun* a subject of little or no importance

ˌnon-ˈlinear *adj.* (*technical*) that does not develop from one thing to another in a single smooth series of stages OPP **linear**

ˌnon-maˈlignant *adj.* (of a TUMOUR) not caused by cancer and not likely to be dangerous SYN **benign** OPP **malignant**

ˌnon-ˈnative *adj.* **1** (of animals, plants, etc.) not existing naturally in a place but coming from somewhere else **2** a **non-native** speaker of a language is one who has not spoken it from the time they first learnt to talk OPP **native**

ˌnon-neˈgoti·able *adj.* **1** that cannot be discussed or changed **2** (of a cheque, etc.) that cannot be changed for money by anyone except the person whose name is on it OPP **negotiable**

ˈno-no *noun* [sing.] (*informal*) a thing or a way of behaving that is not acceptable in a particular situation

ˌnon-obˈservance *noun* [U] (*formal*) the failure to keep or to obey a rule, custom, etc. OPP **observance**

ˌno-ˈnonsense *adj.* [only before noun] simple and direct; only paying attention to important and necessary things

non·par·eil /ˌnɒnpəˈreɪl; *NAmE* ˌnɑːnpəˈrel/ *noun* [sing.] (*formal*) a person or thing that is better than others in a particular area

ˌnon-partiˈsan *adj.* [usually before noun] not supporting the ideas of one particular political party or group of people strongly OPP **partisan**

ˌnon-ˈpayment *noun* [U] (*formal*) failure to pay a debt, a tax, rent, etc.

ˌnon-ˈperson *noun* (*pl.* **ˌnon-ˈpersons**) a person who is thought not to be important, or who is ignored

non·plussed (*US* also **non·plused**) /ˌnɒnˈplʌst; *NAmE* ˌnɑːn-/ *adj.* so surprised and confused that you do not know what to do or say SYN **dumbfounded**

ˌnon-preˈscrip·tion *adj.* (of drugs) that you can buy directly without a special form from a doctor

ˌnon-proˈfes·sion·al *adj.* **1** having a job that does not need a high level of education or special training; connected with a job of this kind: *training for non-professional staff* **2** doing sth as a hobby rather than as a paid job: *non-professional actors* ➲ compare PROFESSIONAL, UNPROFESSIONAL ➲ see also AMATEUR

ˌnon-ˈprofit (*BrE* also **ˌnon-ˈprofit-making**) *adj.* (of an organization) without the aim of making a profit: *an independent non-profit organization* ◇ *The centre is run on a non-profit basis.* ◇ *The charity is non-profit-making.*

ˌnon-proˌlifeˈr·ation *noun* [U] a limit to the increase in the number of nuclear and chemical weapons that are produced

ˌnon-proˈpri·etary *adj.* not made by or belonging to a particular company: *non-proprietary medicines* OPP **proprietary**

ˌnon-reˈfund·able (also **ˌnon-reˈturnable**) *adj.* (of a sum of money) that cannot be returned: *a non-refundable deposit* ◇ *a non-refundable ticket* (= you cannot return it and get your money back)

ˌnon-reˈnewable *adj.* **1** (of natural resources such as gas or oil) that cannot be replaced after use **2** that cannot be continued or repeated for a further period of time after it has ended: *a non-renewable contract* OPP **renewable**

ˌnon-ˈresident *adj.*, *noun*

■ ***adj.*** (*formal*) **1** (of a person or company) not living or located permanently in a particular place or country **2** not living in the place where you work or in a house that you own **3** not staying at a particular hotel: *Non-resident guests are welcome to use the hotel swimming pool.*

■ ***noun*** **1** a person who does not live permanently in a particular country **2** a person not staying at a particular hotel

ˌnon-resiˈdent·ial *adj.* **1** that is not used for people to live in **2** that does not require you to live in the place where you work or study: *a non-residential course*

ˌnon-reˈstric·tive (also **ˌnon-deˈfining**) *adj.* (*grammar*) (of RELATIVE CLAUSES) giving extra information about a noun phrase, inside commas in writing or in a particular INTONATION in speech. In 'My brother, who lives in France, is coming to Rome with us', the part between the commas is a non-restrictive relative clause. ⇨ compare RESTRICTIVE

ˌnon-reˈturn·able *adj.* **1** = NON-REFUNDABLE **2** that you cannot give back, for example to a shop/store, to be used again; that will not be given back to you: *non-returnable bottles* ◇ *a non-returnable deposit* OPP **returnable**

ˌnon-scienˈti·fic *adj.* not involving or connected with science or scientific methods ⇨ compare SCIENTIFIC, UNSCIENTIFIC

non·sense 🔑 /ˈnɒnsns; *NAmE* ˈnɑːnsens; -sns/ *noun*

1 🔑 [U, C] ideas, statements or beliefs that you think are ridiculous or not true SYN **rubbish**: *Reports that he has resigned are nonsense.* ◇ *You're* ***talking nonsense!*** ◇ *'I won't go.' 'Nonsense! You must go!'* ◇ ***It's nonsense to*** *say they don't care.* ◇ *The idea is an economic nonsense.* **2** 🔑 [U] silly or unacceptable behaviour: *The new teacher won't stand for any nonsense.* ⇨ see also NO-NONSENSE **3** 🔑 [U] spoken or written words that have no meaning or make no sense: *a book of children's nonsense poems* ◇ *Most of the translation he did for me was complete nonsense.*

IDM **make (a) ˈnonsense of sth** to reduce the value of sth by a lot; to make sth seem ridiculous: *If people can bribe police officers, it makes a complete nonsense of the legal system.* ⇨ more at STUFF *n.*

ˈnonsense word *noun* a word with no meaning

non·sens·ical /nɒnˈsensɪkl; *NAmE* nɑːn-/ *adj.* ridiculous; with no meaning SYN **absurd**

non sequi·tur /ˌnɒn ˈsekwɪtə(r); *NAmE* ˌnɑːn/ *noun* (from *Latin*, *formal*) a statement that does not seem to follow what has just been said in any natural or logical way

ˌnon-ˈslip *adj.* that helps to prevent sb/sth from slipping; that does not slip: *a non-slip bath mat*

ˌnon-ˈsmoker *noun* a person who does not smoke OPP **smoker**

ˌnon-ˈsmoking (also **ˌno-ˈsmoking**) *adj.* [usually before noun] **1** (of a place) where people are not allowed to smoke: *a non-smoking area in a restaurant* **2** (of a person) who does not smoke: *She's a non-smoking, non-drinking fitness fanatic.* ▶ **ˌnon-ˈsmoking** (also **ˌno-ˈsmoking**) *noun* [U]: *Non-smoking is now the norm in most workplaces.*

ˌnon-speˈcif·ic *adj.* [usually before noun] **1** not definite or clearly defined; general: *The candidate's speech was non-specific.* **2** (*medical*) (of pain, a disease, etc.) with more than one possible cause

ˌnon-speˌcific ureˈthritis *noun* [U] (*abbr.* NSU) (*medical*) a condition in which the URETHRA becomes sore and swollen. It is often caused by an infection caught by having sex.

ˌnon-ˈstandard *adj.* **1** (of language) not considered correct by most educated people: *non-standard dialects* ◇ *non-standard English* ⇨ compare STANDARD **2** not the usual size, type, etc: *The paper was of non-standard size.*

ˌnon-ˈstarter *noun* (*informal*) a thing or a person that has no chance of success: *As a business proposition, it's a non-starter.*

ˌnon-ˈstick *adj.* [usually before noun] (of a pan or a surface) covered with a substance that prevents food from sticking to it

ˌnon-ˈstop *adj.* **1** (of a train, a journey, etc.) without any stops SYN **direct**: *a non-stop flight to Tokyo* ◇ *a non-stop train/service* **2** without any pauses or stops SYN **continuous**: *non-stop entertainment/work* ▶ **ˌnon-ˈstop** *adv.*: *We flew non-stop from Paris to Chicago.* ◇ *It rained non-stop all week.*

ˌnon-traˈditional AW *adj.* not following the usual methods, practices, etc. in a particular area of activity: *students from non-traditional backgrounds* OPP **traditional**

ˌnon-ˈU *adj.* (*old-fashioned*, *informal*) (of language or social behaviour) not considered socially acceptable among the upper classes ORIGIN From the abbreviation **U** for 'upper class'.

ˌnon-ˈunion (also *less frequent* **ˌnon-ˈunionized, -ised**) *adj.* [usually before noun] **1** not belonging to a TRADE/LABOR UNION: ***non-union labour/workers*** **2** (of a business, company, etc.) not accepting TRADE/LABOR UNIONS or employing TRADE/LABOR UNIONS members

ˌnon-vegeˈtar·ian (also *informal* **ˌnon-ˈveg**) *noun* (*IndE*) a person who eats meat, fish, eggs, etc: *They ordered a non-veg meal.*

ˌnon-ˈverbal *adj.* [usually before noun] not involving words or speech: *non-verbal communication*

ˌnon-ˈvintage *adj.* (of wine) not made only from GRAPES grown in a particular place in a particular year OPP **vintage**

ˌnon-ˈviolence *noun* [U] the policy of using peaceful methods, not force, to bring about political or social change

ˌnon-ˈviolent *adj.* **1** using peaceful methods, not force, to bring about political or social change: *non-violent resistance* ◇ *a non-violent protest* **2** not involving force, or injury to sb: *non-violent crimes*

ˌnon-ˈwhite *noun* a person who is not a member of a race of people who have white skin ▶ **ˌnon-ˈwhite** *adj.*

noo·dle /ˈnuːdl/ *noun* **1** [usually pl.] a long thin strip of PASTA, used especially in Chinese and Italian cooking: *chicken noodle soup* ◇ *Would you prefer rice or noodles?* **2** [C] (*old-fashioned*, *NAmE*, *slang*) = NODDLE

nook /nʊk/ *noun* a small quiet place or corner that is sheltered or hidden from other people: *a shady nook in the garden* ◇ *dark woods full of secret* ***nooks and crannies***

IDM **every ˌnook and ˈcranny** (*informal*) every part of a place; every aspect of a situation

nooky (also **nookie**) /ˈnʊki/ *noun* [U] (*slang*) sexual activity

noon /nuːn/ *noun* [U] 12 o'clock in the middle of the day SYN **midday**: *We should be there by noon.* ◇ *The conference opens at 12 noon on Saturday.* ◇ *the noon deadline for the end of hostilities* ◇ *I'm leaving on the noon train.* ◇ *the glaring light of* ***high noon*** IDM see MORNING

N

noon·day /ˈnuːndeɪ/ *adj.* [only before noun] (*old-fashioned* or *literary*) happening or appearing at noon: *the noonday sun*

ˈno one O→ (also **no·body**) *pron.*
not anyone; no person: *No one was at home.* ◇ *There was no one else around.* ◇ *We were told to speak to no one.* HELP **No one** is much more common than **nobody** in written English.

noon·tide /ˈnuːntaɪd/ *noun* [U] (*literary*) around 12 o'clock in the middle of the day

noose /nuːs/ *noun* a circle that is tied in one end of a rope with a knot that allows the circle to get smaller as the other end of the rope is pulled: *a hangman's noose* ◇ (*figurative*) *His debts were a noose around his neck.*

nope /nəʊp; *NAmE* noʊp/ *exclamation* (*informal*) used to say 'no': *'Have you seen my pen?' 'Nope.'*

ˈno place *adv.* (*informal, especially NAmE*) = NOWHERE: *I have no place else to go.*

nor O→ /nɔː(r)/ *conj., adv.*
1 O→ **neither... nor...** | **not... nor...** and not: *She seemed neither surprised nor worried.* ◇ *He wasn't there on Monday. Nor on Tuesday, for that matter.* ◇ (*formal*) *Not a building nor a tree was left standing.* **2** O→ used before a positive verb to agree with sth negative that has just been said: *She doesn't like them and nor does Jeff.* ◇ *'I'm not going.' 'Nor am I.'*

Nor·dic /ˈnɔːdɪk; *NAmE* ˈnɔːrdɪk/ *adj.* **1** of or connected with the countries of Scandinavia, Finland and Iceland **2** typical of a member of a European race of people who are tall and have blue eyes and blonde hair

ˌNordic ˈwalking *noun* [U] the sport of walking with special poles attached to your wrist

N

norm AW /nɔːm; *NAmE* nɔːrm/ *noun, verb*
▪ ***noun*** **1** (often **the norm**) [sing.] a situation or a pattern of behaviour that is usual or expected SYN **rule**: *a departure from the norm* ◇ *Older parents seem to be the norm rather than the exception nowadays.* **2 norms** [pl.] standards of behaviour that are typical of or accepted within a particular group or society: ***social/cultural norms*** ➲ COLLOCATIONS at RACE **3** [C] a required or agreed standard, amount, etc: *detailed education norms for children of particular ages*
▪ ***verb*** **~ sth** to adjust sth so that it is of the required standard; to establish a required or agreed standard for sth: *You can use the information to norm the test.* ◇ *to norm the practice of trading on the Internet*

nor·mal O→ AW /ˈnɔːml; *NAmE* ˈnɔːrml/ *adj., noun*
▪ ***adj.*** **1** O→ typical, usual or ordinary; what you would expect: ***quite/perfectly*** (= completely) ***normal*** ◇ *Her temperature is normal.* ◇ ***It's normal to*** *feel tired after such a long trip.* ◇ *Divorce is complicated enough* ***in normal circumstances****, but this situation is even worse.* ◇ ***Under normal circumstances****, I would say 'yes'.* ◇ *He should be able to* ***lead a*** *perfectly* ***normal life.*** ◇ ***In the normal course of events*** *I wouldn't go to that part of town.* ◇ *We are open during normal office hours.* **2** O→ not suffering from any mental DISORDER: *People who commit such crimes aren't normal.* OPP **abnormal** IDM see PER
▪ ***noun*** O→ [U] the usual or average state, level or standard: ***above/below normal*** ◇ *Things soon returned* ***to normal.***

ˌnormal distriˈbution *noun* (*statistics*) the usual way in which a particular feature varies among a large number of things or people, represented on a GRAPH by a line that rises to a high SYMMETRICAL curve in the middle ➲ compare BELL CURVE

nor·mal·ity AW /nɔːˈmæləti; *NAmE* nɔːrˈm-/ (also **nor·malcy** /ˈnɔːmlsi; *NAmE* ˈnɔːrm-/ especially in *NAmE*) *noun* [U] a situation where everything is normal or as you would expect it to be: *They are hoping for a* ***return to normality*** *now that the war is over.*

nor·mal·ize (*BrE* also **-ise**) AW /ˈnɔːməlaɪz; *NAmE* ˈnɔːrm-/ *verb* [T, I] **~ (sth)** (*formal*) to fit or make sth fit a normal pattern or condition: *a lotion to normalize oily skin* ◇ *The two countries agreed to* ***normalize relations*** (= return to a normal, friendly relationship, for example after a disagreement or war). ◇ *It took time until the political situation had normalized.* ▸ **nor·mal·iza·tion, -isa·tion** AW /ˌnɔːməlaɪˈzeɪʃn; *NAmE* ˌnɔːrmələˈz-/ *noun* [U]: *the normalization of relations*

nor·mal·ly O→ AW /ˈnɔːməli; *NAmE* ˈnɔːrm-/ *adv.*
1 O→ usually; in normal circumstances: *I'm not normally allowed to stay out late.* ◇ *It's normally much warmer than this in July.* ◇ *It normally takes 20 minutes to get there.* **2** O→ in the usual or ordinary way: *Her heart is beating normally.* ◇ *Just try to behave normally.*

Nor·man /ˈnɔːmən; *NAmE* ˈnɔːrm-/ *adj.* **1** used to describe the style of ARCHITECTURE in Britain in the 11th and 12th centuries that developed from the ROMANESQUE style: *a Norman church/castle* **2** connected with the Normans (= the people from northern Europe who defeated the English in 1066 and then ruled the country): *the Norman Conquest*

nor·ma·tive /ˈnɔːmətɪv; *NAmE* ˈnɔːrm-/ *adj.* (*formal*) describing or setting standards or rules of behaviour: *a normative approach*

Norse /nɔːs; *NAmE* nɔːrs/ *noun* [U] the Norwegian language, especially in an ancient form, or the Scandinavian language group

north O→ /nɔːθ; *NAmE* nɔːrθ/ *noun, adj., adv.*
▪ ***noun*** [U, sing.] (*abbr.* **N, No.**) **1** O→ (usually **the north**) the direction that is on your left when you watch the sun rise; one of the four main points of the COMPASS: *Which way is north?* ◇ *cold winds coming from the north* ◇ *Mount Kenya is* ***to the north of*** (= further north than) *Nairobi.* ➲ picture at COMPASS ➲ compare EAST, SOUTH, WEST ➲ see also MAGNETIC NORTH, TRUE NORTH **2** O→ **the north, the North** the northern part of a country, a region or the world: *birds migrating from the north* ◇ *Houses are less expensive in the North* (= of England) *than in the South.* **3 the North** the NE states of the US which fought against the South in the American Civil War **4 the North** the richer and more developed countries of the world, especially in Europe and N America
▪ ***adj.*** [only before noun] **1** O→ (*abbr.* **N, No.**) in or towards the north: *North London* ◇ *the north bank of the river* **2** O→ a **north wind** blows from the north ➲ compare NORTHERLY
▪ ***adv.*** O→ **1** towards the north: *The house faces north.* **2 ~ of sth** nearer to the north than sth: *They live ten miles north of Boston.* **3 ~ of sth** (*finance*)or *NAmE, informal*) more or higher than sth: *The estimated value is north of $5.4 billion.* OPP **south**
IDM **up ˈnorth** (*informal*) to or in the north of a country, especially England: *They've gone to live up north.*

ˌNorth Aˈmerica *noun* [U] the continent consisting of Canada, the United States, Mexico, the countries of Central America and Greenland

the ˌNorth Atˌlantic ˈDrift *noun* [sing.] (*technical*) a current of warm water in the Atlantic Ocean, that has the effect of making the climate of NW Europe warmer

north·bound /ˈnɔːθbaʊnd; *NAmE* ˈnɔːrθ-/ *adj.* travelling or leading towards the north: *northbound traffic* ◇ *the northbound carriageway of the motorway*

ˈnorth-country *adj.* [only before noun] connected with the northern part of a country or region: *a north-country accent*

ˌnorth-ˈeast *noun* (usually **the north-east**) [sing.] (*abbr.* **NE**) the direction or region at an equal distance between north and east ➲ picture at COMPASS ▸ **ˌnorth-ˈeast** *adv.*, *adj.*

ˌnorth-ˈeaster·ly *adj.* **1** [only before noun] in or towards the north-east: *travelling in a north-easterly direction* **2** [usually before noun] (of winds) blowing from the north-east

ˌnorth-ˈeastern *adj.* [only before noun] (*abbr.* **NE**) connected with the north-east

ˌnorth-ˈeastwards (also **ˌnorth-ˈeastward**) *adv.* towards the north-east ▸ **ˌnorth-ˈeastward** *adj.*

north·er·ly /ˈnɔːðəli; *NAmE* ˈnɔːrðərli/ *adj., noun*

■ ***adj.* 1** [only before noun] in or towards the north: *travelling in a northerly direction* **2** [usually before noun] (of winds) blowing from the north: *a northerly breeze* ➲ compare NORTH

■ ***noun*** (*pl.* -ies) a wind that blows from the north

north·ern 🔑 /ˈnɔːðən; *NAmE* ˈnɔːrðərn/ (also **Northern**) *adj.* [usually before noun] (*abbr.* N, No.) located in the north or facing north; connected with or typical of the north part of the world or a region: *the northern slopes of the mountains* ◇ *northern Scotland* ◇ *a northern accent*

north·ern·er /ˈnɔːðənə(r); *NAmE* ˈnɔːrðən-/ *noun* a person who comes from or lives in the northern part of a country

the ˌNorthern ˌIreland Asˈsembly *noun* [sing.] **1** the regional government of Northern Ireland from 1973 to 1986 **2** the parliament of Northern Ireland that was first elected in 1998

the ˌNorthern ˈLights *noun* [pl.] (also **aur·ora bor·ealis**) bands of coloured light, mainly green and red, that are sometimes seen in the sky at night in the most northern countries of the world

north·ern·most /ˈnɔːðənməʊst; *NAmE* ˈnɔːrðərnmoʊst/ *adj.* [usually before noun] furthest north: *the northernmost city in the world*

ˌnorth-north-ˈeast *noun* [sing.] (*abbr.* NNE) the direction at an equal distance between north and north-east ▶ **ˌnorth-north-ˈeast** *adv.*

ˌnorth-north-ˈwest *noun* [sing.] (*abbr.* NNW) the direction at an equal distance between north and north-west ▶ **ˌnorth-north-ˈwest** *adv.*

the ˌNorth ˈPole *noun* [sing.] the point on the surface of the earth that is furthest north ➲ VISUAL VOCAB page V59

the ˌNorth ˈSea *noun* [sing.] the part of the Atlantic Ocean that is next to the east coast of Britain

the ˌNorth-South Diˈvide *noun* [sing.] (*BrE*) the economic and social differences between the north of England and the richer south

north·wards /ˈnɔːθwədz; *NAmE* ˈnɔːrθwərdz/ (also **north·ward**) *adv.* towards the north: *to go/look/turn northwards* ▶ **north·ward** *adj.*: *in a northward direction*

ˌnorth-ˈwest *noun* (usually **the north-west**) [sing.] (*abbr.* NW) the direction or region at an equal distance between north and west ➲ picture at COMPASS ▶ **ˌnorth-ˈwest** *adv., adj.*

ˌnorth-ˈwester·ly *adj.* **1** [only before noun] in or towards the north-west **2** (of winds) blowing from the north-west

ˌnorth-ˈwestern *adj.* [only before noun] (*abbr.* NW) connected with the north-west

ˌnorth-ˈwestwards (also **ˌnorth-ˈwestward**) *adv.* towards the north-west ▶ **ˌnorth-ˈwestward** *adj.*

ˌNorway ˈlobster *noun* = LANGOUSTINE

ˌNorway ˈrat *noun* = BROWN RAT

nose 🔑 /nəʊz; *NAmE* noʊz/ *noun, verb*

■ ***noun* 1** 🔑 [C] the part of the face that sticks out above the mouth, used for breathing and smelling things: *He broke his nose in the fight.* ◇ *She wrinkled her nose in disgust.* ◇ *He* ***blew his nose*** (= cleared it by blowing strongly into a HANDKERCHIEF). ◇ *a* ***blocked/runny nose*** ◇ *Stop* ***picking your nose!*** (= removing dirt from it with your finger) ➲ COLLOCATIONS at PHYSICAL ➲ VISUAL VOCAB page V48 ➲ see also NASAL, PARSON'S NOSE, ROMAN NOSE **2 -nosed** (in adjectives) having the type of nose mentioned: *red-nosed* ◇ *large-nosed* ➲ see also HARD-NOSED, TOFFEE-NOSED **3** [C] the front part of a plane, SPACECRAFT, etc. ➲ VISUAL VOCAB page V43 **4** [sing.] **a ~ for sth** a special ability for finding or recognizing sth SYN **instinct**: *As a journalist, she has always had a nose for a good story.* **5** [sing.] a sense of smell: *a dog with a good nose* **6** [sing.] (of wine) a characteristic smell SYN **bouquet**

IDM **cut off your nose to spite your ˈface** (*informal*) to do sth when you are angry that is meant to harm sb else but which also harms you **get up sb's ˈnose** (*BrE, informal*) to annoy sb **have your nose in ˈsth** (*informal*) to be reading sth and giving it all your attention **have a nose ˈround** (*BrE, informal*) to look around a place; to look for sth in a place **keep your ˈnose clean** (*informal*) to avoid doing anything wrong or illegal: *Since leaving prison, he's managed to keep his nose clean.* **keep your nose out of sth** to try not to become involved in things that do not concern you **keep your nose to the ˈgrindstone** (*informal*) to work hard for a long period of time without stopping **look down your ˈnose at sb/sth** (*informal, especially BrE*) to behave in a way that suggests that you think that you are better than sb or that sth is not good enough for you SYN **look down on ˌnose to ˈtail** (*BrE*) if cars, etc. are **nose to tail**, they are moving slowly in a long line with little space between them **on the ˈnose** (*informal, especially NAmE*) exactly: *The budget should hit the $136 billion target on the nose.* **poke/stick your nose into ˈsth** (*informal*) to try to become involved in sth that does not concern you **put sb's ˈnose out of joint** (*informal*) to upset or annoy sb, especially by not giving them enough attention **turn your ˈnose up at sth** (*informal*) to refuse sth, especially because you do not think that it is good enough for you **under sb's ˈnose** (*informal*) **1** if sth is **under sb's nose**, it is very close to them but they cannot see it: *I searched everywhere for the letter and it was under my nose all the time!* **2** if sth happens **under sb's nose**, they do not notice it even though it is not being done secretly: *The police didn't know the drugs ring was operating right under their noses.* **with your nose in the air** (*informal*) in a way that is unfriendly and suggests that you think that you are better than other people ➲ more at FOLLOW, LEAD[1] *v.*, PAY *v.*, PLAIN *adj.*, POWDER *v.*, RUB *v.*, SKIN *n.*, THUMB *v.*

■ ***verb* 1** [I, T] to move forward slowly and carefully: **+ adv./prep.** *The plane nosed down through the thick clouds.* ◇ **~ your way + adv./prep.** *The taxi nosed its way back into the traffic.* **2** [I] **+ adv./prep.** (of an animal) to search for sth or push sth with its nose: *Dogs nosed around in piles of refuse.*

PHR V **ˌnose aˈbout/aˈround** (**for sth**) to look for sth, especially information about sb SYN **poke about/around**: *We found a man nosing around in our backyard.* **ˌnose sth↔ˈout** (*informal*) to discover information about sb/sth by searching for it: *Reporters nosed out all the details of the affair.*

nose·bag /ˈnəʊzbæg; *NAmE* ˈnoʊz-/ (*BrE*) (*NAmE* **feedbag**) *noun* a bag containing food for a horse, that you hang from its head

nose·band /ˈnəʊzbænd; *NAmE* ˈnoʊz-/ *noun* a leather band that passes over a horse's nose and under its chin and is part of its BRIDLE

nose·bleed /ˈnəʊzbliːd; *NAmE* ˈnoʊz-/ *noun* a flow of blood that comes from the nose

ˈnose cone *noun* the pointed front end of a ROCKET, an aircraft, etc.

nose·dive /ˈnəʊzdaɪv; *NAmE* ˈnoʊz-/ *noun, verb*

■ ***noun*** [sing.] **1** a sudden steep fall or drop; a situation where sth suddenly becomes worse or begins to fail: *Oil prices* ***took a nosedive*** *in the crisis.* ◇ *These policies have sent the construction industry into an abrupt nosedive.* **2** the sudden sharp fall of an aircraft towards the ground with its front part pointing down

■ ***verb* 1** [I] (of prices, costs, etc.) to fall suddenly SYN **plummet**: *Building costs have nosedived.* **2** [I] (of an aircraft) to fall suddenly with the front part pointing towards the ground

nose·gay /ˈnəʊzgeɪ; *NAmE* ˈnoʊz-/ *noun* (*old-fashioned*) a small bunch of flowers

ˈnose job *noun* (*informal*) a medical operation on the nose to improve its shape

ˈnose ring *noun* **1** a ring that is put in an animal's nose for leading it **2** a ring worn in the nose as a piece of jewellery

nosey = NOSY

nosh /nɒʃ; *NAmE* nɑːʃ/ *noun, verb*

■ ***noun* 1** [U, sing.] (*old-fashioned, BrE, slang*) food; a meal: *She*

N

likes her nosh. ◇ *Did you have a good nosh?* **2** [C] (*especially NAmE*) a small meal that you eat quickly between main meals

■ ***verb*** [I, T] **~** (**sth**) (*informal*) to eat

ˌno-ˈshow *noun* (*informal*) a person who is expected to be somewhere and does not come; a situation where this happens

ˈnosh-up *noun* (*slang, especially BrE*) a large meal: *We went for a nosh-up at that new restaurant in town.*

ˌno-ˈsmoking *adj.* = NON-SMOKING

nos·tal·gia /nɒˈstældʒə; *NAmE* nəˈs-; nɑːˈs-/ *noun* [U] a feeling of sadness mixed with pleasure and affection when you think of happy times in the past: *a **sense/wave/pang of nostalgia*** ◇ *She is filled with nostalgia for her own college days.* ▶ **nos·tal·gic** /nɒˈstældʒɪk; *NAmE* nəˈs-; nɑːˈs-/ *adj.*: *nostalgic memories* ◇ *I feel quite nostalgic for the place where I grew up.* **nos·tal·gic·al·ly** /-kli/ *adv.*: *to look back nostalgically to your childhood*

nos·tril /ˈnɒstrəl; *NAmE* ˈnɑːs-/ *noun* either of the two openings at the end of the nose that you breathe through ➲ VISUAL VOCAB page V48

nos·trum /ˈnɒstrəm; *NAmE* ˈnɑːs-/ *noun* **1** (*formal, disapproving*) an idea that is intended to solve a problem but that will probably not succeed **2** (*old-fashioned*) a medicine that is not made in a scientific way, and that is not effective

nosy (also **nosey**) /ˈnəʊzi; *NAmE* ˈnoʊzi/ *adj.* (*informal, disapproving*) too interested in things that do not concern you, especially other people's affairs SYN **inquisitive**: *nosy neighbours* ◇ *Don't be so nosy—it's none of your business.* ▶ **nosi·ly** *adv.* **nosi·ness** *noun* [U]

ˌnosy ˈparker *noun* (*BrE, informal*, becoming *old-fashioned*) a person who is too interested in other people's affairs

N

not 0➡ /nɒt; *NAmE* nɑːt/ *adv.*

1 0➡ used to form the negative of the verbs *be*, *do* and *have* and modal verbs like *can* or *must* and often reduced to *n't*: *She did not/didn't see him.* ◇ *It's not/It isn't raining.* ◇ *I can't see from here.* ◇ *He must not go.* ◇ *Don't you eat meat?* ◇ *It's cold, isn't it?* **2** 0➡ used to give the following word or phrase a negative meaning, or to reply in the negative: *He warned me not to be late.* ◇ *I was sorry not to have seen them.* ◇ *Not everybody agrees.* ◇ *'Who's next?' 'Not me.'* ◇ *'What did you do at school?' '**Not a lot**.'* ◇ *It's not easy being a parent* (= it's difficult). **3** 0➡ used after *hope*, *expect*, *believe*, etc. to give a negative reply: *'Will she be there?' 'I hope not.'* ◇ *'Is it ready?' 'I'm afraid not.'* ◇ (*formal*) *'Does he know?' 'I believe not.'* **4** 0➡ **or ~** used to show a negative possibility: *I don't know if he's telling the truth or not.* **5** 0➡ used to say that you do not want sth or will not allow sth: *'Some more?' 'Not for me, thanks.'* ◇ *'Can I throw this out?' 'Certainly not.'*

IDM **not a...** | **not one...** 0➡ used for emphasis to mean 'no thing or person': *He didn't speak to me—not one word.* **ˌnot at ˈall** 0➡ used to politely accept thanks or to agree to sth: *'Thanks a lot.' 'Not at all.'* ◇ *'Will it bother you if I smoke?' 'Not at all.'* **not only... (but) also...** 0➡ used to emphasize that sth else is also true: *She not only wrote the text but also selected the illustrations.* **ˈnot that** used to state that you are not suggesting sth: *She hasn't written—not that she said she would.*

not·able /ˈnəʊtəbl; *NAmE* ˈnoʊ-/ *adj., noun*

■ ***adj.*** (rather *formal*) deserving to be noticed or to receive attention; important SYN **striking**: *a **notable success/achievement/example*** ◇ *His eyes are his most **notable feature**.* ◇ **~** (**for sth**) *The town is notable for its ancient harbour.* ◇ ***With a few notable exceptions**, everyone gave something.*

■ ***noun*** [usually pl.] (*formal*) a famous or important person: *All the usual local notables were there.*

not·ably /ˈnəʊtəbli; *NAmE* ˈnoʊ-/ *adv.* **1** used for giving a good or the most important example of sth SYN **especially**: *The house had many drawbacks, most notably its price.* **2** to a great degree SYN **remarkably**: *This has not been a notably successful project.*

no·tar·ize (*BrE* also **-ise**) /ˈnəʊtəraɪz; *NAmE* ˈnoʊ-/ *verb* **~ sth** (*law*) if a document is **notarized**, it is given legal status by a NOTARY

no·tary /ˈnəʊtəri; *NAmE* ˈnoʊ-/ *noun* (*pl.* **-ies**) (also *technical* **ˌnotary ˈpublic** *pl.* **ˌnotaries ˈpublic**) a person, especially a lawyer, with official authority to be a witness when sb signs a document and to make this document valid in law

no·ta·tion /nəʊˈteɪʃn; *NAmE* noʊ-/ *noun* [U, C] a system of signs or symbols used to represent information, especially in mathematics, science and music ➲ picture at MUSIC

notch /nɒtʃ; *NAmE* nɑːtʃ/ *noun, verb*

■ ***noun*** **1** a level on a scale, often marking quality or achievement: *The quality of the food here has dropped a notch recently.* ➲ see also TOP-NOTCH **2** a V-shape or a circle cut in an edge or a surface, sometimes used to keep a record of sth: *For each day he spent on the island, he cut a new notch in his stick.* ◇ *She tightened her belt an extra notch.*

■ ***verb*** **1 ~ sth** (**up**) (*informal*) to achieve sth such as a win or a high score: *The team has notched up 20 goals already this season.* **2 ~ sth** to make a small V-shaped cut in an edge or a surface

note 0➡ /nəʊt; *NAmE* noʊt/ *noun, verb*

■ ***noun***

▸ TO REMIND YOU **1** 0➡ [C] a short piece of writing to help you remember sth: *Please **make a note** of the dates.* ◇ *She **made a mental note*** (= decided that she must remember) *to ask Alan about it.*

▸ SHORT LETTER **2** 0➡ [C] a short informal letter: *Just a quick note to say thank you for a wonderful evening.* ◇ *She left a note for Ben on the kitchen table.* ◇ *a suicide note*

▸ IN BOOK **3** 0➡ [C] a short comment on a word or passage in a book: *a new edition of 'Hamlet', with explanatory notes* ◇ *See note 3, page 259.* ➲ see also FOOTNOTE

▸ INFORMATION **4** 0➡ **notes** [pl.] information that you write down when sb is speaking, or when you are reading a book, etc: *He sat **taking notes** of everything that was said.* ◇ *Can I borrow your **lecture notes**?* ◇ *Patients' **medical notes** have gone missing.* **5** 0➡ [C, usually pl.] information about a performance, an actor's career, a piece of music, etc. printed in a special book or on a CD case, record cover, etc: *The sleeve notes include a short biography of the performers on this recording.*

▸ MONEY **6** 0➡ (also **bank·note**) (both *especially BrE*) (*NAmE* usually **bill**) [C] a piece of paper money: *a £5 note* ◇ *We only exchange notes and traveller's cheques.* ➲ picture at MONEY

▸ IN MUSIC **7** 0➡ [C] a single sound of a particular length and PITCH (= how high or low a sound is), made by the voice or a musical instrument; the written or printed sign for a musical note: *He played the first few notes of the tune.* ◇ ***high/low notes*** ➲ picture at MUSIC

▸ QUALITY **8** [sing.] **~** (**of sth**) a particular quality in sth, for example in sb's voice or the atmosphere at an event SYN **air**: *There was a note of amusement in his voice.* ◇ ***On a more serious note*** (= speaking more seriously)... ◇ ***On a slightly different note*** (= changing the subject slightly), *let's talk about...*

▸ OFFICIAL DOCUMENT **9** [C] an official document with a particular purpose: *a sick note from your doctor* ◇ *The buyer has to sign a delivery note as proof of receipt.* ➲ see also CREDIT NOTE, PROMISSORY NOTE **10** [C] (*technical*) an official letter from the representative of one government to another: *an exchange of diplomatic notes*

IDM **of ˈnote** of importance or of great interest: *a scientist of note* ◇ *The museum contains nothing of great note.* **hit/strike the right/wrong ˈnote** (*especially BrE*) to do, say or write sth that is suitable/not suitable for a particular occasion **sound/strike a ˈnote** (**of ˈsth**) to express feelings or opinions of a particular kind: *She sounded a note of warning in her speech.* **take ˈnote** (**of sth**) to pay attention to sth and be sure to remember it: *Take note of what he says.* ➲ more at COMPARE *v.*

■ ***verb*** (rather *formal*) **1** 0➡ to notice or pay careful attention to sth: **~ sth** *Note the fine early Baroque altar inside the chapel.* ◇ **~ (that)...** *Please note (that) the office will be closed on Monday.* ◇ **~ how, where, etc...** *Note how these animals sometimes walk with their tails up in the air.* ◇ **it is noted** that... *It should be noted that dissertations submitted late will not be accepted.* ➲ SYNONYMS at NOTICE ➲ LANGUAGE BANK at EMPHASIS **2 ~ sth | ~ that... | ~ how, where, etc ... | it is noted that...** to mention sth because it is important or interesting: *It is worth noting that the most successful companies had the lowest prices.* ➲ SYNONYMS at COMMENT ➲ LANGUAGE BANK at ARGUE

PHR V **ˌnote sth↔ˈdown** to write down sth important so that you will not forget it SYN **jot down**

note·book /ˈnəʊtbʊk; *NAmE* ˈnoʊt-/ *noun* **1** a small book of plain paper for writing notes in **2** (*NAmE*) (*BrE* ˈ**exercise book**) a small book for students to write their work in ➲ VISUAL VOCAB page V56 **3** (also ˌ**notebook comˈputer**) a small computer that can work with a battery and be easily carried SYN **laptop** ➲ compare DESKTOP COMPUTER, NETBOOK, SUBNOTEBOOK

note·card /ˈnəʊtkɑːd; *NAmE* ˈnoʊtkɑːrd/ *noun* **1** a small folded card, sometimes with a picture on the front, that you use for writing a short letter on ➲ see also NOTELET **2** (*especially NAmE*) a card on which notes are written, for example by sb to use when making a speech

noted /ˈnəʊtɪd; *NAmE* ˈnoʊt-/ *adj.* well known because of a special skill or feature SYN **famous**: *a noted dancer* ◇ **~ for sth** *He is not noted for his sense of humour.* ◇ **~ as sth** *The lake is noted as a home to many birds.*

note·let /ˈnəʊtlət; *NAmE* ˈnoʊt-/ *noun* (*BrE*) a small folded sheet of paper or card with a picture on the front that you use for writing a short letter on

No. 10 = NUMBER TEN

note·pad /ˈnəʊtpæd; *NAmE* ˈnoʊt-/ *noun* sheets of paper that are held together at the top and used for writing notes on: *a notepad by the phone for messages* ➲ VISUAL VOCAB page V56

note·paper /ˈnəʊtpeɪpə(r); *NAmE* ˈnoʊt-/ (also ˈ**writing paper**) *noun* [U] paper for writing letters on

note·worthy /ˈnəʊtwɜːði; *NAmE* ˈnoʊtwɜːrði/ *adj.* deserving to be noticed or to receive attention because it is unusual, important or interesting SYN **significant**

ʼnother /ˈnʌðə(r)/ *adj.* (*non-standard*) = ANOTHER: *Now that's a whole ʼnother question.*

noth·ing /ˈnʌθɪŋ/ *pron.*
1 not anything; no single thing: *There was nothing in her bag.* ◇ *There's nothing you can do to help.* ◇ *The doctor said there was nothing wrong with me.* ◇ ***Nothing else** matters to him apart from his job.* ◇ *It cost us nothing to go in.* ◇ (*BrE*) *He's five foot nothing* (= exactly five feet tall). **2** something that is not at all important or interesting: *'What's that in your pocket?' 'Oh, nothing.'* ◇ *We did nothing at the weekend.*

IDM **be ˈnothing to sb** to be a person for whom sb has no feelings: *I used to love her but she's nothing to me any more.* **be/have nothing to do with sb/sth** to have no connection with sb/sth: *Get out! It's nothing to do with you* (= you have no right to know about it). ◇ *That has nothing to do with what we're discussing.* **for ˈnothing 1** without payment SYN **free**: *She's always trying to get **something for nothing**.* **2** with no reward or result: *All that preparation was for nothing because the visit was cancelled.* **have nothing on sb** (*informal*) **1** to have much less of a particular quality than sb/sth: *I'm quite a fast worker, but I've got nothing on her!* **2** (of the police, etc.) to have no information that could show sb to be guilty of sth **not for ˈnothing** for a very good reason: *Not for nothing was he called the king of rock and roll.* ˈ**nothing but** only; no more/less than: *Nothing but a miracle can save her now.* ◇ *I want nothing but the best for my children.* ˈ**nothing if not** extremely; very: *The trip was nothing if not varied.* ˈ**nothing less than** used to emphasize how great or extreme sth is: *It was nothing less than a disaster.* **nothing ˈlike** (*informal*) **1** not at all like: *It looks nothing like a horse.* **2** not nearly; not at all: *I had nothing like enough time to answer all the questions.* ˌ**nothing ˈmuch** not a great amount of sth; nothing of great value or importance: *There's nothing much in the fridge.* ◇ *I got up late and did nothing much all day.* (**there's**) ˌ**nothing ˈto it** (it's) very easy: *You'll soon learn. There's nothing to it really.* **there is/was nothing** (**else**) ˈ**for it** (**but to do sth**) there is no other action to take except the one mentioned: *There was nothing else for it but to resign.* **there is/was nothing in sth** something is/was not true: *There was a rumour she was going to resign, but there was nothing in it.* **there's nothing like sth** used to say that you enjoy sth very much: *There's nothing like a brisk walk on a cold day!* ➲ more at ALL *det.*, STOP *v.*, SWEET *adj.*

noth·ing·ness /ˈnʌθɪŋnəs/ *noun* [U] a situation where nothing exists; the state of not existing

Synonyms

notice

note • detect • observe • witness

These words all mean to see sth, especially when you pay careful attention to it.

notice to see, hear or become aware of sb/sth; to pay attention to sb/sth: *The first thing I noticed about the room was the smell.*

note (*rather formal*) to notice or pay careful attention to sth: *Please note (that) the office will be closed on Monday.* NOTE This word is very common in business English: *Note that the prices are inclusive of VAT.*

detect to discover or notice sth, especially sth that is not easy to see, hear, etc: *The tests are designed to detect the disease early.*

observe (*formal*) to see or notice sb/sth: *Have you observed any changes lately?* ◇ *The police observed a man enter the bank.*

witness (*rather formal*) to see sth happen: *Police have appealed for anyone who witnessed the incident to contact them.*

PATTERNS
- to notice/note/detect/observe **that/how/what/where/who...**
- to notice/observe/witness **sth happen/sb do sth**

no·tice /ˈnəʊtɪs; *NAmE* ˈnoʊ-/ *noun, verb*

■ ***noun***

▸ PAYING ATTENTION **1** [U] the fact of sb paying attention to sb/sth or knowing about sth: ***Don't take any notice of** what you read in the papers.* ◇ ***Take no notice** of what he says.* ◇ *These protests have really made the government **sit up and take notice*** (= realize the importance of the situation). ◇ *It was Susan who **brought** the problem **to my notice*** (= told me about it). ◇ *Normally, the letter would not have **come to my notice*** (= I would not have known about it). ◇ (*formal*) *It will not have **escaped your notice** that there have been some major changes in the company.*

▸ GIVING INFORMATION **2** [C] a sheet of paper giving written or printed information, usually put in a public place: *There was a notice on the board saying the class had been cancelled.* **3** [C] a board or sign giving information, an instruction or a warning: *a notice saying 'Keep off the Grass'*

▸ ANNOUNCING STH **4** [C] a small advertisement or ANNOUNCEMENT in a newspaper or magazine: *notices of births, marriages and deaths* **5** [C] a short ANNOUNCEMENT made at the beginning or end of a meeting, a church service, etc: *There are just two notices this week.*

▸ WARNING **6** [U] information or a warning given in advance of sth that is going to happen: *You must give **one month's notice**.* ◇ *Prices may be altered without notice.* ◇ *The bar is closed **until further notice*** (= until you are told that it is open again). ◇ *You are welcome to come and stay as long as you give us plenty of notice.*

▸ WHEN LEAVING JOB/HOUSE **7** [U] a formal letter or statement saying that you will or must leave your job or house at the end of a particular period of time: *He has **handed in his notice**.* ◇ *They **gave** her two weeks' **notice**.*

▸ REVIEW OF BOOK/PLAY **8** [C] a short article in a newspaper or magazine, giving an opinion about a book, play, etc.

N

IDM **at short 'notice | at a moment's 'notice** not long in advance; without warning or time for preparation: *This was the best room we could get at such short notice.* ◇ *You must be ready to leave at a moment's notice.* **on short 'notice** (*NAmE*) = AT SHORT NOTICE

■ ***verb*** (not usually used in the progressive tenses)

▸ SEE/HEAR **1** [I, T] to see or hear sb/sth; to become aware of sb/sth: *People were making fun of him but he didn't seem to notice.* ◇ **~ sb/sth** *The first thing I noticed about the room was the smell.* ◇ **~ (that)...** *I couldn't help noticing (that) she was wearing a wig.* ◇ **~ how, what, etc...** *Did you notice how Rachel kept looking at her watch?* ◇ **~ sb/sth do sth** *I noticed them come in.* ◇ **~ sb/sth doing sth** *I didn't notice him leaving.*

▸ PAY ATTENTION **2** [T] **~ sb/sth** to pay attention to sb/sth: *She wears those strange clothes just to get herself noticed.*

no·tice·able /'nəʊtɪsəbl; *NAmE* 'noʊ-/ *adj.* easy to see or notice; clear or definite: *a noticeable improvement* ◇ **~ in sb/sth** *This effect is particularly noticeable in younger patients.* ◇ **~ that...** *It was noticeable that none of the family were present.* ▸ **no·tice·ably** /-əbli/ *adv.*: *Her hand was shaking noticeably.* ◇ *Marks were noticeably higher for girls than for boys.*

no·tice·board /'nəʊtɪsbɔːd; *NAmE* 'noʊtɪsbɔːrd/ (*BrE*) (*NAmE* '**bulletin board**) (also **board** *BrE, NAmE*) *noun* a board for putting notices on ➲ VISUAL VOCAB page V56

no·ti·fi·able /'nəʊtɪfaɪəbl; *NAmE* 'noʊ-/ *adj.* [usually before noun] (*formal*) (of a disease or a crime) so dangerous or serious that it must by law be reported officially to the authorities

no·ti·fi·ca·tion /ˌnəʊtɪfɪ'keɪʃn; *NAmE* ˌnoʊ-/ *noun* [U, C] (*formal*) the act of giving or receiving official information about sth: ***advance/prior notification*** (= telling sb in advance about sth) ◇ *written notification* ◇ *You should receive (a) notification of our decision in the next week.*

N

no·tify /'nəʊtɪfaɪ; *NAmE* 'noʊ-/ *verb* (**no·ti·fies, no·ti·fy·ing, no·ti·fied, no·ti·fied**) (*formal*) to formally or officially tell sb about sth SYN **inform**: **~ sb** *Competition winners will be notified by post.* ◇ **~ sb of sth** *The police must be notified of the date of the demonstration.* ◇ **~ sth to sb** *The date of the demonstration must be notified to the police.* ◇ **~ sb that...** *Members have been notified that there will be a small increase in the fee.*

no·tion AW /'nəʊʃn; *NAmE* 'noʊʃn/ *noun* an idea, a belief or an understanding of sth: **~ (of sth)** *a political system based on the notions of equality and liberty* ◇ *She had only a vague notion of what might happen.* ◇ **~ (that...)** *I have to reject the notion that greed can be a good thing.*

no·tion·al /'nəʊʃənl; *NAmE* 'noʊ-/ *adj.* (*formal*) based on a guess, estimate or theory; not existing in reality ▸ **no·tion·al·ly** /'nəʊʃənəli; *NAmE* 'noʊ-/ *adv.*

no·tori·ety /ˌnəʊtə'raɪəti; *NAmE* ˌnoʊ-/ *noun* [U, sing.] fame for being bad in some way: **~ (for sth)** *She achieved notoriety for her affair with the senator.* ◇ **~ (as sth)** *He gained a certain notoriety as a gambler.*

no·tori·ous /nəʊ'tɔːriəs; *NAmE* noʊ-/ *adj.* well known for being bad: *a notorious criminal* ◇ **~ for sth/for doing sth** *The country is notorious for its appalling prison conditions.* ◇ **~ as sth** *The bar has become notorious as a meeting-place for drug dealers.* ▸ **no·tori·ous·ly** *adv.*: *Mountain weather is notoriously difficult to predict.*

not·with·stand·ing AW /ˌnɒtwɪθ'stændɪŋ; -wɪð-; *NAmE* ˌnɑːt-/ *prep., adv.*

■ ***prep.*** (*formal*) (also used following the noun it refers to) without being affected by sth; despite sth: *Notwithstanding some major financial problems, the school has had a successful year.* ◇ *The bad weather notwithstanding, the event was a great success.*

■ ***adv.*** (*formal*) despite this SYN **however, nevertheless**: *Notwithstanding, the problem is a significant one.*

nou·gat /'nuːgɑː; *NAmE* 'nuːgət/ *noun* [U] a hard sweet/candy that has to be chewed a lot, often containing nuts, CHERRIES, etc. and pink or white in colour

nought /nɔːt/ *noun* **1** [C, U] (*BrE*) (also **zero** *NAmE, BrE*) the figure 0: *A million is written with six noughts.* ◇ *nought point one* (= written 0.1) ◇ *I give the programme nought out of ten for humour.* **2** (also **naught**) [U] (*literary*) used in particular phrases to mean 'nothing': *All our efforts have* ***come to nought*** (= have not been successful).

the Nought·ies /'nɔːtiz/ *noun* [pl.] (*BrE*) the years from 2000 to 2009

ˌnoughts and 'crosses (*BrE*) (*NAmE* **ˌtic-tac-'toe**) *noun* [U] a simple game in which two players take turns to write Os or Xs in a set of nine squares. The first player to complete a row of three Os or three Xs is the winner. ➲ VISUAL VOCAB page V33

noun /naʊn/ *noun* (*grammar*) (*abbr.* **n.**) a word that refers to a person, (such as *Ann* or *doctor*), a place (such as *Paris* or *city*) or a thing, a quality or an activity (such as *plant*, *sorrow* or *tennis*) ➲ see also ABSTRACT NOUN, COMMON NOUN, PROPER NOUN

'noun phrase *noun* (*grammar*) a word or group of words in a sentence that behaves in the same way as a noun, that is as a subject, an object, a COMPLEMENT, or as the object of a preposition: *In the sentence 'I spoke to the driver of the car', 'the driver of the car' is a noun phrase.*

nour·ish /'nʌrɪʃ; *NAmE* 'nɜːrɪʃ/ *verb* **1 ~ sb/sth** to keep a person, an animal or a plant alive and healthy with food, etc: *All the children were well nourished and in good physical condition.* **2 ~ sth** (*formal*) to allow a feeling, an idea, etc. to develop or grow stronger: *By investing in education, we nourish the talents of our children.* ▸ **nour·ish·ing** *adj.*: *nourishing food*

nour·ish·ment /'nʌrɪʃmənt; *NAmE* 'nɜːr-/ *noun* [U] (*formal* or *technical*) food that is needed to stay alive, grow and stay healthy: *Can plants obtain adequate nourishment from such poor soil?* ◇ (*figurative*) *As a child, she was starved of intellectual nourishment.*

nous /naʊs/ *noun* [U] (*BrE, informal*) intelligence and the ability to think and act in a practical way SYN **common sense**

nou·veau riche /ˌnuːvəʊ 'riːʃ; *NAmE* ˌnuːvoʊ/ *noun* (*pl.* **nou·veaux riches** /ˌnuːvəʊ 'riːʃ; *NAmE* ˌnuːvoʊ/ or **the nou·veau riche**) (from *French*, *disapproving*) a person who has recently become rich and likes to show how rich they are in a very obvious way ▸ **nou·veau riche** *adj.*

nou·velle cuis·ine /ˌnuːvel kwɪ'ziːn/ *noun* [U] (from *French*) a modern style of cooking that avoids heavy foods and serves small amounts of different dishes arranged in an attractive way on the plate

nova /'nəʊvə; *NAmE* 'noʊvə/ *noun* (*pl.* **novae** /-viː/ or **novas**) (*astronomy*) a star that suddenly becomes much brighter for a short period ➲ compare SUPERNOVA

novel /'nɒvl; *NAmE* 'nɑːvl/ *noun, adj.*

■ ***noun*** a story long enough to fill a complete book, in which the characters and events are usually imaginary: *to write/publish/read a novel* ◇ ***detective/historical/romantic novels*** ◇ *the novels of Jane Austen* ➲ COLLOCATIONS at LITERATURE

■ ***adj.*** (often *approving*) different from anything known before; new, interesting and often seeming slightly strange: *a novel feature*

nov·el·ette /ˌnɒvə'let; *NAmE* ˌnɑːv-/ *noun* a short novel, especially a romantic novel that is considered to be badly written

nov·el·ist /'nɒvəlɪst; *NAmE* 'nɑːv-/ *noun* a person who writes novels: *a romantic/historical novelist* ➲ COLLOCATIONS at LITERATURE

nov·el·is·tic /ˌnɒvə'lɪstɪk; *NAmE* ˌnɑːv-/ *adj.* (*formal*) typical of or used in novels

nov·ella /nə'velə/ *noun* a short novel

nov·elty /'nɒvlti; *NAmE* 'nɑːv-/ *noun, adj.*

■ ***noun*** (*pl.* **-ies**) **1** [U] the quality of being new, different and interesting: *It was fun working there at first but* ***the novelty soon wore off*** (= it became boring). ◇ *There's a certain* ***novelty value*** *in this approach.* **2** [C] a thing, person or situation that is interesting because it is new, unusual or has not been known before: *Electric cars are still something of a novelty.* **3** [C] a small cheap object sold as a toy or a decorative object

■ ***adj.*** [only before noun] different and unusual; intended to be amusing and to catch people's attention: *a novelty teapot*

No·vem·ber 🗝 /nəʊ'vembə(r); *NAmE* noʊ-/ *noun* [U, C] (*abbr.* **Nov.**)
the 11th month of the year, between October and December HELP To see how **November** is used, look at the examples at **April**.

nov·ice /'nɒvɪs; *NAmE* 'nɑːv-/ *noun* **1** a person who is new and has little experience in a skill, job or situation: *I'm a complete novice at skiing.* ◇ *computer software for novices/the novice user* **2** a person who has joined a religious group and is preparing to become a MONK or a NUN **3** a horse that has not yet won an important race

novi·ti·ate (also **novi·ci·ate**) /nəʊ'vɪʃiət; *NAmE* noʊ-/ *noun* (*formal*) a period of being a novice (2)

novo·caine /'nəʊvəkeɪn; *NAmE* 'noʊ-/ *noun* [U] (*medical*) = PROCAINE

now 🗝 /naʊ/ *adv., conj.*
■ ***adv.*** **1** 🗝 (at) the present time: *Where are you living now?* ◇ *It's been two weeks now since she called.* ◇ *It's too late now.* ◇ ***From now on*** *I'll be more careful.* ◇ *He'll be home* ***by now.*** ◇ *I've lived at home* ***up till now.*** ◇ *That's all* ***for now.*** **2** 🗝 at or from this moment, but not before: *Start writing now.* ◇ *I am now ready to answer your questions.* **3** 🗝 (*informal*) used to show that you are annoyed about sth: *Now they want to tax food!* ◇ *What do you want now?* ◇ *It's broken. Now I'll have to get a new one.* **4** 🗝 used to get sb's attention before changing the subject or asking them to do sth: *Now, listen to what she's saying.* ◇ *Now, the next point is quite complex.* ◇ *Now come and sit down.* ◇ *Now let me think...*
IDM (**every**) **now and a'gain/'then** 🗝 from time to time; occasionally: *Every now and again she checked to see if he was still asleep.* **now for 'sb/'sth** used when turning to a fresh activity or subject: *And now for some travel news.* **,now, 'now** (also **,now 'then**) used to show in a mild way that you do not approve of sth: *Now then, that's enough noise.* **now... now...** at one time... at another time...: *Her moods kept changing—now happy, now sad.* (**it's**) **,now or 'never** this is the only opportunity sb will have to do sth **'now then 1** = NOW, NOW **2** used when making a suggestion or an offer: *Now then, who wants to come for a walk?* **'now what?** (*informal*) **1** (also **what is it 'now?**) used when you are annoyed because sb is always asking questions or interrupting you: *'Yes, but Dad...' 'Now what?'* **2** used to say that you do not know what to do next in a particular situation
■ ***conj.*** 🗝 **~ (that)...** because the thing mentioned is happening or has just happened: *Now that the kids have left home we've got a lot of extra space.*

now·adays /'naʊədeɪz/ *adv.* at the present time, in contrast with the past: *Nowadays most kids prefer watching TV to reading.*

no·where 🗝 /'nəʊweə(r); *NAmE* 'noʊwer/ (also **'no place** especially in *NAmE*) *adv.*
not in or to any place: *This animal is found in Australia, and nowhere else.* ◇ *There was nowhere for me to sit.* ◇ *'Where are you going this weekend?' 'Nowhere special.'* ◇ *Nowhere is the effect of government policy more apparent than in agriculture.*
IDM **get/go 'nowhere | get sb 'nowhere** to make no progress or have no success; to not enable sb to make progress or have success: *We discussed it all morning but got nowhere.* ◇ *Talking to him will get you nowhere.* **nowhere to be 'found/'seen | nowhere in 'sight** impossible for anyone to find or see: *The children were nowhere to be seen.* ◇ *A peace settlement is nowhere in sight* (= is not likely in the near future). ➲ more at LEAD[1] *v.*, MIDDLE *n.*, NEAR *adv.*

,no-'win *adj.* [only before noun] (of a situation, policy, etc.) that will end badly whatever you decide to do: *We are considering the options available to us in this no-win situation.*

'now-now *adv.* (*SAfrE, informal*) **1** within a short period of time: *I'll be with you now-now.* **2** a short time ago: *She left now-now.*

nowt /naʊt/ *pron.* (*BrE, dialect, informal*) nothing: *There's nowt wrong with it.*

nox·ious /'nɒkʃəs; *NAmE* 'nɑːk-/ *adj.* (*formal*) poisonous or harmful: *noxious fumes*

noz·zle /'nɒzl; *NAmE* 'nɑːzl/ *noun* a narrow piece that is attached to the end of a pipe or tube to direct the stream of liquid, air or gas passing through

nr *abbr.* (*BrE*) near (used, for example, in the address of a small village): *Howden, nr Goole*

NRA /,en ɑːr 'eɪ/ *abbr.* National Rifle Association (a US organization that supports the right of citizens to own a gun)

NRI /,en ɑːr 'aɪ/ *abbr.* (*IndE*) Non-Resident Indian (a person of Indian origin who is working somewhere else but who keeps links with India)

ns *abbr.* NANOSECOND(S)

NST /,en es 'tiː/ *abbr.* (*CanE*) Newfoundland Standard Time

NSU /,en es 'juː/ *abbr.* NON-SPECIFIC URETHRITIS

nth /enθ/ *adj.* [only before noun] (*informal*) used when you are stating that sth is the last in a long series and emphasizing how often sth has happened: *It's the nth time I've explained it to you.*
IDM **to the nth 'degree** extremely; to an extreme degree

NTSC /,en tiː es 'siː/ *noun* [U] (*technical*) a television broadcasting system that is used in N America and Japan ➲ compare PAL, SECAM

nu /njuː/ *noun* the 13th letter of the Greek alphabet (Ν, ν)

nu·ance /'njuːɑːns; *NAmE* 'nuː-/ *noun* [C, U] a very slight difference in meaning, sound, colour or sb's feelings that is not usually very obvious: *He watched her face intently to catch every nuance of expression.*

nub /nʌb/ *noun* [sing.] **the ~ (of sth)** the central or essential point of a situation, problem, etc: ***The nub of the matter*** *is that business is declining.*

nu·bile /'njuːbaɪl; *NAmE* 'nuː-; 'nuːbl/ *adj.* (of a girl or young woman) sexually attractive

nu·buck /'njuːbʌk; *NAmE* 'nuː-/ *noun* [U] a type of leather that has been rubbed on one side to make it feel soft like SUEDE

N

nu·clear 🗝 AW /'njuːkliə(r); *NAmE* 'nuː-/ *adj.* [usually before noun]
1 🗝 using, producing or resulting from nuclear energy: *a nuclear power station* ◇ *the nuclear industry* ◇ *nuclear-powered submarines* **2** 🗝 connected with weapons that use nuclear energy: *a* ***nuclear weapon/bomb/missile*** ◇ *a* ***nuclear explosion/attack/war*** ◇ *the country's* ***nuclear capability*** (= the fact that it has nuclear weapons) ◇ ***nuclear capacity*** (= the number of nuclear weapons a country has) **3** (*physics*) of the NUCLEUS (= central part) of an atom: *nuclear particles* ◇ *a nuclear reaction*

,nuclear 'energy (also **,nuclear 'power**) *noun* [U] a powerful form of energy produced by converting matter into energy splitting the NUCLEI (= central parts) of atoms. It is used to produce electricity.

,nuclear 'family *noun* (*technical*) a family that consists of father, mother and children, when it is thought of as a unit in society ➲ compare EXTENDED FAMILY

,nuclear 'fission *noun* [U] = FISSION

,nuclear-'free *adj.* [usually before noun] (of a country or a region) not having or allowing nuclear energy, weapons or materials: *a nuclear-free zone*

,nuclear 'fuel *noun* [U] a substance that can be used as a source of NUCLEAR ENERGY because it is capable of NUCLEAR FISSION

,nuclear 'fusion *noun* [U] = FUSION

'nuclear option *noun* (*politics*) the most extreme possible response to a particular situation: *Currency controls would be the nuclear option.*

,nuclear 'physics *noun* [U] the area of physics which deals with the NUCLEUS of atoms and with nuclear energy ▸ **,nuclear 'physicist** *noun*

,nuclear 'power *noun* [U] = NUCLEAR ENERGY

,nuclear re'actor *noun* = REACTOR

,nuclear 'waste *noun* [U] waste material which is RADIOACTIVE, especially used fuel from nuclear power stations

ˌ**nuclear ˈwinter** *noun* a period without light, heat or growth which scientists believe would follow a nuclear war

nu·cle·ic acid /njuːˌkliːɪk ˈæsɪd; -ˌkleɪɪk; *NAmE* nuː-/ *noun* [U] (*chemistry*) either of two acids, DNA and RNA, that are present in all living cells

nu·cleus /ˈnjuːkliəs; *NAmE* ˈnuː-/ *noun* (*pl.* **nu·clei** /-kliaɪ/) **1** (*physics*) the part of an atom that contains most of its mass and that carries a positive electric charge ➲ see also NEUTRON, PROTON **2** (*biology*) the central part of some cells, containing the GENETIC material **3** the central part of sth around which other parts are located or collected: *These paintings will form the nucleus of a new collection.*

nude /njuːd; *NAmE* nuːd/ *adj., noun*
■ ***adj.*** **1** (especially of a human figure in art) not wearing any clothes SYN **naked**: *a nude model* ◇ *He asked me to pose nude for him.* **2** involving people who are naked: *a nude photograph* ◇ *Are there any nude scenes in the movie?* **3** (*NAmE*) (of TIGHTS/PANTYHOSE, etc.) skin-coloured
■ ***noun*** a work of art consisting of a naked human figure; a naked human figure in art: *a bronze nude by Rodin* ◇ *a reclining nude*
IDM **in the ˈnude** not wearing any clothes SYN **naked**: *She refuses to be photographed in the nude.*

nudge /nʌdʒ/ *verb, noun*
■ ***verb*** **1** [T] **~ sb/sth** to push sb gently, especially with your elbow, in order to get their attention: *He nudged me and whispered, 'Look who's just come in.'* **2** [T] **~ sb/sth + adv./prep.** to push sb/sth gently or gradually in a particular direction: *He nudged the ball past the goalie and into the net.* ◇ *She nudged me out of the way.* ◇ (*figurative*) *He nudged the conversation towards the subject of money.* ◇ (*figurative*) *She tried to nudge him into changing his mind* (= persuade him to do it). **3** [T, I] **~ (sth) + adv./prep.** to move forward by pushing with your elbow: *He* ***nudged his way*** *through the crowd.* **4** [T] **~ sth (+ adv./prep.)** to reach or make sth reach a particular level: *Inflation is nudging 20%.* ◇ *This afternoon's sunshine could nudge the temperature above freezing.*
■ ***noun*** a slight push, usually with the elbow: *She gave me a gentle nudge in the ribs to tell me to shut up.* ◇ (*figurative*) *He can work hard but he needs a nudge now and then.*
IDM ˌ**nudge ˈnudge, ˌwink ˈwink | a ˌnudge and a ˈwink** used to suggest sth to do with sex without actually saying it: *They've been spending a lot of time together, nudge nudge, wink wink.*

nudie /ˈnjuːdi; *NAmE* ˈnuː-/ *adj.* (*informal*) showing or including people wearing no clothes: *nudie photographs*

nud·ism /ˈnjuːdɪzəm; *NAmE* ˈnuː-/ (also **na·tur·ism** especially in *BrE*) *noun* [U] the practice of not wearing any clothes because you believe this is more natural and healthy

nud·ist /ˈnjuːdɪst; *NAmE* ˈnuː-/ (also **na·tur·ist** especially in *BrE*) *noun* a person who does not wear any clothes because they believe this is more natural and healthy: *a* ***nudist beach/camp***

nud·ity /ˈnjuːdəti; *NAmE* ˈnuː-/ *noun* [U] the state of being naked: *The committee claimed that there was too much nudity on television.*

nuf·fin /ˈnʌfɪn/ (also **nuf·fink** /ˈnʌfɪŋk/) *pron.* (*BrE, informal*) nothing

nu·ga·tory /ˈnjuːgətəri; *NAmE* ˈnuːgətɔːri/ *adj.* (*formal*) having no purpose or value SYN **worthless**

nug·get /ˈnʌgɪt/ *noun* **1** a small lump of a valuable metal or mineral, especially gold, that is found in the earth **2** a small round piece of some types of food: *chicken nuggets* **3** a small thing such as an idea or a fact that people think of as valuable SYN **snippet**: *a useful nugget of information*

nuis·ance /ˈnjuːsns; *NAmE* ˈnuː-/ *noun* **1** [C, usually sing.] a thing, person or situation that is annoying or causes trouble or problems: *I don't want to* ***be a nuisance*** *so tell me if you want to be alone.* ◇ *I hope you're not* ***making a nuisance of yourself.*** ◇ ***It's a nuisance*** *having to go back tomorrow.* ◇ *What a nuisance!* **2** [C, U] (*law*) behaviour by sb that annoys other people and that a court can order the person to stop: *He was charged with causing a public nuisance.*

ˈ**nuisance value** *noun* [U] (*BrE*) a quality that makes sth useful because it causes problems for your opponents

nuke /njuːk; *NAmE* usually nuːk/ *verb, noun* (*informal*)
■ ***verb*** **~ sth** to attack a place with nuclear weapons
■ ***noun*** a nuclear weapon

null /nʌl/ *adj.* (*technical*) having the value zero: *a null result*
IDM ˌ**null and ˈvoid** (*law*) (of an election, agreement, etc.) having no legal force; not valid: *The contract was declared null and void.*

ˈ**null hypothesis** *noun* (*statistics*) the idea that an experiment that is done using two groups of people will show the same results for each group

nul·lify /ˈnʌlɪfaɪ/ *verb* (**nul·li·fies, nul·li·fy·ing, nul·li·fied, nul·li·fied**) (*formal*) **1 ~ sth** to make sth such as an agreement or order lose its legal force SYN **invalidate**: *Judges were unwilling to nullify government decisions.* **2 ~ sth** to make sth lose its effect or power SYN **negate**: *An unhealthy diet will nullify the effects of training.*

null·ity /ˈnʌləti/ *noun* [sing.] (*formal* or *law*) the fact of sth, for example a marriage, having no legal force or no longer being valid; something which is no longer valid

numb /nʌm/ *adj., verb*
■ ***adj.*** **1** if a part of your body is **numb**, you cannot feel anything in it, for example because of cold: *to* ***be/go numb*** ◇ *numb with cold* ◇ *I've just been to the dentist and my face is still numb.* **2** unable to feel, think or react in the normal way: *He felt numb with shock.* ➲ see also NUMBING ▸ **numb·ly** *adv.*: *Her life would never be the same again, she realized numbly.* **numb·ness** *noun* [U]: *pain and numbness in my fingers* ◇ *He was still in a state of numbness and shock from the accident.*
■ ***verb*** **1 ~ sth** to make a part of your body unable to feel anything, for example because of cold: *His fingers were numbed with the cold.* **2 ~ sb** to make sb unable to feel, think or react in a normal way, for example because of an emotional shock SYN **stun**: *We sat there in silence, numbed by the shock of her death.*

num·ber 🔑 /ˈnʌmbə(r)/ *noun, verb*
■ ***noun***
▸ WORD/SYMBOL **1** 🔑 [C] a word or symbol that represents an amount or a quantity SYN **figure**: *Think of a number and multiply it by two.* ◇ *a* ***high/low number*** ◇ ***even numbers*** (= 2, 4, 6, etc.) ◇ ***odd numbers*** (= 1, 3, 5, etc.) ◇ *You owe me 27 dollars? Make it 30, that's a good* ***round number.*** ➲ see also CARDINAL NUMBER, ORDINAL, PRIME NUMBER, WHOLE NUMBER
▸ POSITION IN SERIES **2** 🔑 [C] (*abbr.* **No.**) (*symb.* **#**) used before a figure to show the position of sth in a series: *They live at number 26.* ◇ *The song reached number 5 in the charts.*
▸ TELEPHONE, ETC. **3** 🔑 [C] (often in compounds) a number used to identify sth or communicate by telephone, FAX, etc: *My phone number is 266998.* ◇ *I'm sorry, I think you have the* ***wrong number*** (= wrong telephone number). ◇ *What is your account number, please?* ➲ see also BOX NUMBER, E-NUMBER, PIN, REGISTRATION NUMBER, SERIAL NUMBER
▸ QUANTITY **4** 🔑 [C] **~ (of sb/sth)** a quantity of people or things: *A large number of people have applied for the job.* ◇ *The number of homeless people has increased dramatically.* ◇ *Huge numbers of* (= very many) *animals have died.* ◇ ***A number of*** (= some) *problems have arisen.* ◇ *I could give you* ***any number of*** (= a lot of) *reasons for not going.* ◇ *We were eight* ***in number*** (= there were eight of us). ◇ *Nurses are leaving the profession in increasing numbers.* ◇ ***Sheer weight of numbers*** (= the large number of soldiers) *secured them the victory.* ◇ *staff/student numbers* HELP A plural verb is needed after **a/an (large, small, etc.) number of...**
▸ GROUP OF PEOPLE **5** [sing.] (*formal*) a group or quantity of people: *one of our number* (= one of us) ◇ *The prime minister is elected by MPs from among their number.*
▸ MAGAZINE **6** [C] (*BrE*) the version of a magazine, etc. published on a particular day, in a particular month, etc. SYN **issue**: *the October number of 'Vogue'* ➲ see also BACK NUMBER

▸ SONG/DANCE **7** [C] a song or dance, especially one of several in a performance: *They sang a slow romantic number.*
▸ THING ADMIRED **8** [sing.] (*informal*) (following one or more adjectives) a thing, such as a dress or a car, that is admired: *She was wearing a black velvet number.*
▸ GRAMMAR **9** [U] the form of a word, showing whether one or more than one person or thing is being talked about: *The word 'men' is plural in number.* ◇ *The subject of a sentence and its verb must agree in number.*
IDM **by 'numbers** following a set of simple instructions identified by numbers: *painting by numbers* **by the 'numbers** (*NAmE*) following closely the accepted rules for doing sth **have (got) sb's 'number** (*informal*) to know what sb is really like and what they plan to do: *He thinks he can fool me but I've got his number.* **your 'number is up** (*informal*) the time has come when you will die or lose everything **'numbers game** a way of considering an activity, etc. that is concerned only with the number of people doing sth, things achieved, etc, not with who or what they are: *MPs were playing the numbers game as the crucial vote drew closer.* ➲ more at CUSHY, OPPOSITE *adj.*, SAFETY, WEIGHT *n.*
■ ***verb***
▸ MAKE A SERIES **1** [T] to give a number to sth as part of a series or list: **~ sth** *All the seats in the stadium are numbered.* ◇ *I couldn't work out the numbering system for the hotel rooms.* ◇ **~ sth from... to...** *Number the car's features from 1 to 10 according to importance.* ◇ **~ sth + noun** *The doors were numbered 2, 4, 6 and 8.*
▸ MAKE STH AS TOTAL **2** [I] **+ noun** to make a particular number when added together SYN **add up to sth**: *The crowd numbered more than a thousand.* ◇ *We numbered 20* (= there were 20 of us in the group).
▸ INCLUDE **3** [T, I] (*formal*) to include sb/sth in a particular group; to be included in a particular group: **~ sb/sth among sth** *I number her among my closest friends.* ◇ **~ among sth** *He numbers among the best classical actors in Britain.* IDM see DAY

'number crunching *noun* [U] (*informal*) the process of calculating numbers, especially when a large amount of data is involved and the data is processed in a short space of time

numbered *adj.* having a number to show that it is part of a series or list: *The players all wear numbered shirts.* IDM see DAY

num·ber·less /'nʌmbələs; *NAmE* -bərl-/ *adj.* (*literary*) too many to be counted SYN **innumerable**

ˌnumber 'one *noun, adj.* (*informal*)
■ ***noun*** **1** [U] the most important or best person or thing: *We're number one in the used car business.* **2** [U, C] the pop song or record that has sold the most copies in a particular week: *The new album went straight to number one.* ◇ *She's had three number ones.* **3** [U] yourself: ***Looking after number one*** *is all she thinks about.* **4** [sing.] (*informal*) an expression used especially by children or when speaking to children to talk about passing liquid waste from the body: *It's only a number one.* ➲ compare NUMBER TWO
■ ***adj.*** most important or best: *the world's number one athlete* ◇ *the number one priority*

'number plate (*BrE*) (*NAmE* **'license plate**) *noun* a metal or plastic plate on the front and back of a vehicle that shows its REGISTRATION NUMBER

ˌNumber 'Ten (also **No. 10**) *noun* [U+sing./pl. v.] 10 Downing Street, London, the official home of the British prime minister, often used to refer to the government: *Number Ten had nothing to say on the matter.*

ˌnumber 'two *noun* [sing.] (*informal*) an expression used especially by children or when speaking to children to talk about passing solid waste from the body: *Mum, I need a number two.* ➲ compare NUMBER ONE

numb·ing /'nʌmɪŋ/ *adj.* (of an experience or a situation) making you unable to feel anything: *numbing cold/fear* ◇ *Watching television had a numbing effect on his mind.*

numb·skull (also **num·skull**) /'nʌmskʌl/ *noun* (*informal*) a stupid person

nu·mer·acy /'nju:mərəsi; *NAmE* 'nu:-/ *noun* [U] a good basic knowledge of mathematics; the ability to understand and work with numbers: *standards of literacy and numeracy* ▸ **nu·mer·ate** /'nju:mərət; *NAmE* 'nu:-/ *adj.*: *All students should be numerate and literate when they leave school.* OPP **innumerate**

nu·meral /'nju:mərəl; *NAmE* 'nu:-/ *noun* a sign or symbol that represents a number ➲ see also ARABIC NUMERAL, ROMAN NUMERAL

nu·mer·ator /'nju:məreɪtə(r); *NAmE* 'nu:-/ *noun* (*mathematics*) the number above the line in a FRACTION, for example 3 in the FRACTION ¾ ➲ compare DENOMINATOR

nu·mer·ic·al /nju:'merɪkl; *NAmE* nu:-/ (also *less frequent* **nu·mer·ic** /-ɪk/) *adj.* relating to numbers; expressed in numbers: *numerical data* ◇ *The results are expressed in descending* ***numerical order.*** ▸ **nu·mer·ic·al·ly** /-kli/ *adv.*: *to express the results numerically*

nu·mer·ology /ˌnju:mə'rɒlədʒi; *NAmE* ˌnu:mə'rɑ:lədʒi/ *noun* [U] the use of numbers to try to tell sb what will happen in the future ▸ **nu·mero·logic·al** /ˌnju:mərə'lɒdʒɪkl; *NAmE* ˌnu:mərə'lɑ:dʒɪkl/ *adj.*

nu·mer·ous /'nju:mərəs; *NAmE* 'nu:-/ *adj.* (*formal*) existing in large numbers SYN **many**: *He has been late on numerous occasions.* ◇ *The advantages of this system are too numerous to mention.*

nu·min·ous /'nju:mɪnəs; *NAmE* 'nu:-/ *adj.* (*formal*) having a strong religious and spiritual quality that makes you feel that God is present

nu·mis·mat·ics /ˌnju:mɪz'mætɪks; *NAmE* ˌnu:-/ *noun* [U] the study of coins and MEDALS ▸ **nu·mis·mat·ic** *adj.*

nu·mis·ma·tist /nju:'mɪzmətɪst; *NAmE* nu:-/ *noun* a person who collects or studies coins or MEDALS

numpty /'nʌmpti/ (*pl.* -ies) *noun* (*ScotE, informal*) a stupid person

num·skull = NUMBSKULL

nun /nʌn/ *noun* a member of a religious community of women who promise to serve God all their lives and often live together in a CONVENT ➲ compare MONK

nun·cio /'nʌnsiəʊ; *NAmE* -sioʊ/ *noun* (*pl.* -os) a representative of the POPE (= the leader of the Roman Catholic Church) in a foreign country: *a papal nuncio*

nun·nery /'nʌnəri/ *noun* (*pl.* -ies) (*old-fashioned* or *literary*) = CONVENT

nup·tial /'nʌpʃl/ *adj.* [only before noun] (*formal*) connected with marriage or a wedding: *nuptial bliss* ◇ *a nuptial mass*

nup·tials /'nʌpʃlz/ *noun* [pl.] (*old-fashioned*) a wedding

nurse 0- /nɜ:s; *NAmE* nɜ:rs/ *noun, verb*
■ ***noun*** **1** 0- a person whose job is to take care of sick or injured people, usually in a hospital: *a qualified/registered nurse* ◇ *student nurses* ◇ *a male nurse* ◇ *a dental nurse* (= one who helps a dentist) ◇ *a psychiatric nurse* (= one who works in a hospital for people with mental illnesses) ◇ *Nurse Bennett* ◇ *Nurse, come quickly!* ➲ see also CHARGE NURSE, DISTRICT NURSE, PRACTICAL NURSE, REGISTERED NURSE, STAFF NURSE ➲ note at GENDER **2** (also **nurse·maid**) (*old-fashioned*) (in the past) a woman or girl whose job was to take care of babies or small children in their own homes ➲ see also NURSERY NURSE, WET NURSE
■ ***verb*** **1** [T] **~ sb** to care for sb who is ill/sick or injured: *He worked in a hospital for ten years nursing cancer patients.* ◇ *She* ***nursed*** *her daughter* ***back to health.*** **2** [T] **~ sth** to take care of an injury or illness: *Several weeks after the match, he was still nursing a shoulder injury.* ◇ *You'd better go to bed and nurse that cold.* ◇ (*figurative*) *She was nursing her hurt pride.* ➲ COLLOCATIONS at ILL **3** [T] **~ sth** (*formal*) to have a strong feeling or idea in your mind for a long time SYN **harbour**: *to* ***nurse*** *an* ***ambition/a grievance/a grudge*** ◇ *She had been nursing a secret desire to see him again.* **4** [T] **~ sth** to give special care or attention to sb/sth: *to nurse tender young plants* **5** [T] **~ sb/sth** to hold sb/sth carefully in your arms or close to your body: *He sat nursing his cup of coffee.* **6** [I, T] (of a woman or female animal) to feed a baby with milk from the breast SYN **suckle**: *a* ***nursing mother*** ◇ **~ sb/sth** *The lioness is still nursing her cubs.* ➲ compare BREASTFEED **7** [I] (of a baby) to suck milk from its mother's breast SYN **suckle**

N

nurse·maid /ˈnɜːsmeɪd; *NAmE* ˈnɜːrs-/ *noun* (*old-fashioned*) = NURSE (2)

ˌ**nurse pracˈtitioner** *noun* a nurse who is trained to do many of the tasks usually done by a doctor

nur·sery /ˈnɜːsəri; *NAmE* ˈnɜːrs-/ *noun, adj.*
- ***noun*** (*pl.* -ies) **1** = DAY NURSERY **2** = NURSERY SCHOOL: *Her youngest child is **at nursery** now.* **3** (*NAmE* or *old-fashioned*) a room in a house where a baby sleeps **4** (*old-fashioned*) a room in a house where young children can play **5** a place where young plants and trees are grown for sale or for planting somewhere else
- ***adj.*** [only before noun] (*BrE*) connected with the education of children from 2 to 5 years old: *nursery education* ◇ *a nursery teacher*

nur·sery·man /ˈnɜːsərimən; *NAmE* ˈnɜːrs-/ *noun* (*pl.* -men /-mən/) a person who owns or works in a nursery (5)

ˈ**nursery nurse** *noun* (*BrE*) a person whose job involves taking care of small children in a DAY NURSERY

ˈ**nursery rhyme** *noun* a simple traditional poem or song for children

ˈ**nursery school** *noun* a school for children between the ages of about two and five SYN **preschool** ➲ compare KINDERGARTEN, PLAYGROUP

ˈ**nursery slope** (*BrE*) (*NAmE* ˈ**bunny slope**) *noun* [usually pl.] a slope that is not very steep and is used by people who are learning to SKI

nurs·ing /ˈnɜːsɪŋ; *NAmE* ˈnɜːrs-/ *noun* [U] the job or skill of caring for people who are sick or injured: *a career in nursing* ◇ *nursing care* ◇ *the nursing profession*

ˈ**nursing home** *noun* a small private hospital, especially one where old people live and are cared for

nur·ture /ˈnɜːtʃə(r); *NAmE* ˈnɜːrtʃ-/ *verb, noun*
- ***verb*** (*formal*) **1** **~ sb/sth** to care for and protect sb/sth while they are growing and developing: *These delicate plants need careful nurturing.* ◇ *children nurtured by loving parents* **2** **~ sth** to help sb/sth to develop and be successful SYN **foster**: *It's important to nurture a good working relationship.* **3** **~ sth** to have a feeling, an idea, a plan, etc. for a long time and encourage it to develop: *She secretly nurtured a hope of becoming famous.*
- ***noun*** [U] (*formal*) care, encouragement and support given to sb/sth while they are growing

nut 0‑ /nʌt/ *noun, verb*
- ***noun*** **1** 0‑ (often in compounds) a small hard fruit with a very hard shell that grows on some trees: *to **crack a nut*** (= open it) ◇ *a Brazil nut* ◇ *a hazelnut* ◇ *nuts and raisins* ➲ VISUAL VOCAB page V8, V28 ➲ see also MONKEY NUT **2** a small piece of metal with a hole through the centre that is screwed onto a BOLT to hold pieces of wood, machinery, etc. together: *to tighten a nut* ◇ *a wheel nut* ➲ VISUAL VOCAB page V17 **3** (*BrE, slang*) a person's head or brain **4** (*BrE* also **nut·ter**) (*informal*) a strange or crazy person: *He's a complete nut, if you ask me.* ➲ see also NUTS, NUTTY **5** (*informal*) (in compounds) a person who is extremely interested in a particular subject, activity, etc: *a **fitness/tennis/computer, etc. nut*** **6** **nuts** [pl.] (*slang*) a man's TESTICLES

IDM **do your ˈnut** (*BrE, informal*) to become very angry **a hard/tough ˈnut** (*informal*) a person who is difficult to deal with or to influence **a hard/tough ˈnut** (**to ˈcrack**) a difficult problem or situation to deal with **the ˌnuts and ˈbolts** (**of sth**) (*informal*) the basic practical details of a subject or an activity ˌ**off your ˈnut** (*BrE, informal*) crazy ➲ more at SLEDGEHAMMER
- ***verb*** (-tt-) **~ sb** (*BrE, informal*) to deliberately hit sb hard with your head

PHR V ˌ**nut sth ˈout** (*AustralE, NZE, informal*) to calculate sth or find the answer to sth: *I'm going to have to nut it out on a piece of paper.*

ˌ**nut-ˈbrown** *adj.* dark brown in colour: *nut-brown hair*

nut·case /ˈnʌtkeɪs/ *noun* (*informal*) a crazy person

nut·crack·er /ˈnʌtkrækə(r)/ *noun* (*BrE* also **nut·crack·ers** [pl.]) a tool for cracking open the shells of nuts ➲ VISUAL VOCAB page V23

ˌ**nut ˈcutlet** *noun* nuts, bread and HERBS mixed together and cooked in a shape like a piece of meat

nut·meg /ˈnʌtmeg/ *noun* [U, C] the hard seed of a tropical tree originally from SE Asia, used in cooking as a spice, especially to give flavour to cakes and sauces: *freshly grated nutmeg* ➲ VISUAL VOCAB page V28

nutra·ceut·ical /ˌnjuːtrəˈsuːtɪkl/ *noun* = FUNCTIONAL FOOD

nu·tri·ent /ˈnjuːtriənt; *NAmE* ˈnuː-/ *noun* (*technical*) a substance that is needed to keep a living thing alive and to help it to grow: *a lack of **essential nutrients*** ◇ *Plants draw minerals and other nutrients from the soil.* ◇ *children suffering from a serious **nutrient deficiency*** ➲ COLLOCATIONS at DIET, LIFE

nu·tri·tion /njuˈtrɪʃn; *NAmE* nu-/ *noun* [U] the process by which living things receive the food necessary for them to grow and be healthy: *advice on diet and nutrition* ◇ *to study food science and nutrition* ➲ COLLOCATIONS at DIET ➲ compare MALNUTRITION ▸ **nu·tri·tion·al** /-ʃənl/ (also *less frequent* **nu·tri·tive**) *adj.*: *the nutritional value of milk* **nu·tri·tion·al·ly** /-ʃənəli/ *adv.*: *a nutritionally balanced menu*

nu·tri·tion·ist /njuˈtrɪʃənɪst; *NAmE* nu-/ *noun* a person who is an expert on the relationship between food and health ➲ see also DIETITIAN

nu·tri·tious /njuˈtrɪʃəs; *NAmE* nu-/ *adj.* (*approving*) (of food) very good for you; containing many of the substances which help the body to grow SYN **nourishing**: *tasty and nutritious meals*

nuts /nʌts/ *adj.* [not before noun] (*informal*) **1** crazy: *My friends think I'm nuts for saying yes.* ◇ *That phone ringing all the time is **driving me nuts!*** ➲ SYNONYMS at MAD **2** **~ about sb/sth** very much in love with sb; very enthusiastic about sth: *He's absolutely nuts about her.* IDM see SOUP *n.*

nut·shell /ˈnʌtʃel/ *noun*

IDM (**put sth**) **in a nutshell** (to say or express sth) in a very clear way, using few words: *To put it in a nutshell, we're bankrupt.*

nut·ter /ˈnʌtə(r)/ *noun* (*BrE, informal*) = NUT (4)

nutty /ˈnʌti/ *adj.* (**nut·tier, nut·ti·est**) **1** tasting of or containing nuts: *a nutty taste* **2** (*informal*) slightly crazy: *She's got some nutty friends.* ◇ *He's **as nutty as a fruitcake*** (= completely crazy).

nuz·zle /ˈnʌzl/ *verb* [T, I] to touch or rub sb/sth with the nose or mouth, especially to show affection: **~ sb/sth** *She nuzzled his ear.* ◇ **+ adv./prep.** *The child nuzzled up against his mother.*

NVQ /ˌen viː ˈkjuː/ *noun* the abbreviation for 'National Vocational Qualification' (a British qualification that shows that you have reached a particular standard in the work that you do): *NVQ Level 3 in Catering*

NW *abbr.* north-west; north-western: *NW Australia*

NY *abbr.* New York

NYC *abbr.* New York City

nylon /ˈnaɪlɒn; *NAmE* -lɑːn/ *noun* **1** [U] a very strong artificial material, used for making clothes, rope, brushes, etc: *a nylon fishing line* ◇ *This material is 45% nylon.* **2** **nylons** [pl.] (*old-fashioned*) women's STOCKINGS or TIGHTS/PANTYHOSE made of nylon

nymph /nɪmf/ *noun* **1** (in ancient Greek and Roman stories) a spirit of nature in the form of a young woman, that lives in rivers, woods, etc. **2** (*biology*) a young insect that has a body form which compares with that of the adult: *a dragonfly nymph*

nymph·et /ˈnɪmfet; nɪmˈfet/ *noun* a young girl who is very sexually attractive

nym·pho·maniac /ˌnɪmfəˈmeɪniæk/ (also *informal* **nym·pho** /ˈnɪmfəʊ; *NAmE* -foʊ/ *pl.* -os) *noun* (*disapproving*) a woman who has, or wants to have, sex very often ▸ **nym·pho·mania** *noun* [U]

NYSE /ˌen waɪ es ˈiː/ *abbr.* New York Stock Exchange

NZ (*BrE*) (also **N.Z.** *NAmE, BrE*) *abbr.* New Zealand

Oo

O /əʊ; *NAmE* oʊ/ *noun, exclamation, symbol*
■ ***noun*** (also **o**) (*pl.* Os, O's, o's /əʊz; *NAmE* oʊz/) **1** [C, U] the 15th letter of the English alphabet: *'Orange' begins with (an) O/'O'.* **2** used to mean 'zero' when saying telephone numbers, etc.: *My number is six o double three* (= 6033). ➲ see also O GRADE, O LEVEL
■ ***exclamation*** (especially *literary*) = OH
■ ***symbol*** the symbol for the chemical element Oxygen

o' /ə/ *prep.* used in written English to represent an informal way of saying *of*: *a couple o' times*

oaf /əʊf; *NAmE* oʊf/ *noun* a stupid, unpleasant or awkward person, especially a man: *Mind that cup, you clumsy oaf!* ▸ **oaf·ish** *adj.*

oak /əʊk; *NAmE* oʊk/ *noun* **1** [C, U] (also **'oak tree** [C]) a large tree that produces small nuts called ACORNS. Oaks are common in northern countries and can live to be hundreds of years old: *a gnarled old oak tree* ◇ *forests of oak and pine* ➲ VISUAL VOCAB page V8 ➲ see also POISON OAK **2** [U] the hard wood of the oak tree: *oak beams* ◇ *This table is made of solid oak.*
IDM **great/tall ˌoaks from little acorns ˈgrow** (*saying*) something large and successful often begins in a very small way

oaken /ˈəʊkən; *NAmE* ˈoʊkən/ *adj.* [only before noun] (*literary*) made of oak

oakum /ˈəʊkəm; *NAmE* ˈoʊkəm/ *noun* [U] a material obtained by pulling old rope to pieces, a job done in the past by prisoners

OAP /ˌəʊ eɪ ˈpiː; *NAmE* ˌoʊ/ *noun* (*BrE*, becoming *old-fashioned*) the abbreviation for OLD-AGE PENSIONER

oar /ɔː(r)/ *noun* a long pole with a flat blade at one end that is used for ROWING a boat: *He pulled as hard as he could on the oars.* ➲ VISUAL VOCAB page V44 ➲ compare PADDLE
IDM **put/stick your ˈoar in** (*BrE, informal*) to give your opinion, advice, etc. without being asked and when it is probably not wanted SYN **interfere**

oar·lock /ˈɔːlɒk; *NAmE* ˈɔːrlɑːk/ (*NAmE*) (*BrE* **row·lock**) *noun* a device fixed to the side of a boat for holding an OAR

oars·man /ˈɔːzmən; *NAmE* ˈɔːrz-/, **oars·woman** /ˈɔːzwʊmən; *NAmE* ˈɔːrz-/ *noun* (*pl.* -men /-mən/, -women /-wɪmɪn/) a person who ROWS a boat, especially as a member of a CREW (= team)

OAS /ˌəʊ eɪ ˈes; *NAmE* ˌoʊ/ *abbr.* (*CanE*) OLD AGE SECURITY

oasis /əʊˈeɪsɪs; *NAmE* oʊ-/ *noun* (*pl.* oases /-siːz/) **1** an area in the desert where there is water and where plants grow **2** a pleasant place or period of time in the middle of sth unpleasant or difficult SYN **haven**: *an oasis of calm* ◇ *a green oasis in the heart of the city*

oast house /ˈəʊst haʊs; *NAmE* ˈoʊst/ *noun* (*especially BrE*) a building made of bricks with a round roof that was built to contain an oven used for drying HOPS

oat /əʊt; *NAmE* oʊt/ *adj.* [only before noun] made from or containing OATS: *oat cakes* ◇ *oat bran* ➲ see also OATMEAL

oat·cake /ˈəʊtkeɪk; *NAmE* ˈoʊt-/ *noun* a Scottish biscuit made with oats, which is not sweet

oater /ˈəʊtə(r); *NAmE* ˈoʊtər/ *noun* (*NAmE, informal*) a film/movie about life in the western US in the 19th century

oath /əʊθ; *NAmE* oʊθ/ *noun* (*pl.* **oaths** /əʊðz; *NAmE* oʊðz/) **1** a formal promise to do sth or a formal statement that sth is true: *to* ***take/swear an oath*** *of allegiance* ◇ *Before giving evidence, witnesses in court have to* ***take the oath*** (= promise to tell the truth). ➲ COLLOCATIONS at VOTE **2** (*old-fashioned*) an offensive word or phrase used to express anger, surprise, etc; a swear word: *She heard the sound of breaking glass, followed by a muttered oath.*
IDM **on/under ˈoath** (*law*) having made a formal promise to tell the truth in court: *Is she prepared to give evidence on oath?* ◇ *The judge reminded the witness that he was still under oath.*

oat·meal /ˈəʊtmiːl; *NAmE* ˈoʊt-/ *noun* [U] **1** flour made from crushed oats, used to make biscuits/cookies, PORRIDGE, etc. **2** (*NAmE*) = PORRIDGE **3** a pale brown colour ▸ **oat·meal** *adj.*: *an oatmeal carpet*

oats /əʊts; *NAmE* oʊts/ *noun* [pl.] grain grown in cool countries as food for animals and for making flour, PORRIDGE/OATMEAL, etc. ➲ VISUAL VOCAB page V28 ➲ see also OAT
IDM see SOW *v.*

ob·bli·gato (*NAmE* also **ob·li·gato**) /ˌɒblɪˈɡɑːtəʊ; *NAmE* ˌɑːblɪˈɡɑːtoʊ/ *noun* (*pl.* -os) (*music*) (from *Italian*) an important part for an instrument in a piece of music which cannot be left out

ob·dur·ate /ˈɒbdjərət; *NAmE* ˈɑːbdər-/ *adj.* (*formal*, usually *disapproving*) refusing to change your mind or your actions in any way SYN **stubborn** ▸ **ob·dur·acy** /ˈɒbdjərəsi; *NAmE* ˈɑːbdər-/ *noun* [U] **ob·dur·ate·ly** *adv.*

OBE /ˌəʊ biː ˈiː; *NAmE* ˌoʊ/ *noun* the abbreviation for 'Officer of the Order of the British Empire' (an award given in Britain for a special achievement): *She was made an OBE.* ◇ *Matthew Silk OBE*

obedi·ent /əˈbiːdiənt/ *adj.* doing what you are told to do; willing to obey: *an obedient child* ◇ **~ to sb/sth** *He was always obedient to his father's wishes.* OPP **disobedient** ▸ **obedi·ence** /-əns/ *noun* [U]: ***blind/complete/unquestioning/total obedience*** ◇ **~ to sb/sth** *He has acted* ***in obedience*** *to the law.* **obedi·ent·ly** *adv.*
IDM **your obedient servant** (*old use*) used to end a formal letter

obei·sance /əʊˈbeɪsns; *NAmE* oʊˈbiːsns/ *noun* (*formal*) **1** [U] respect for sb/sth or willingness to obey sb **2** [C] the act of bending your head or the upper part of your body in order to show respect for sb/sth

ob·el·isk /ˈɒbəlɪsk; *NAmE* ˈɑːb-; ˈoʊb-/ *noun* a tall pointed stone column with four sides, put up in memory of a person or an event ➲ VISUAL VOCAB page V12

obese /əʊˈbiːs; *NAmE* oʊ-/ *adj.* (*formal* or *medical*) (of people) very fat, in a way that is not healthy ➲ COLLOCATIONS at DIET ▸ **obes·ity** /əʊˈbiːsəti; *NAmE* oʊ-/ *noun* [U]: *Obesity can increase the risk of heart disease.*

obey 🔑 /əˈbeɪ/ *verb*
[T, I] **~ (sb/sth)** to do what you are told or expected to do: *to* ***obey a command/an order/rules/the law*** ◇ *He had always obeyed his parents without question.* ◇ *'Sit down!' Meekly, she obeyed.* OPP **disobey**

ob·fus·cate /ˈɒbfʌskeɪt; *NAmE* ˈɑːb-/ *verb* [I, T] **~ (sth)** (*formal*) to make sth less clear and more difficult to understand, usually deliberately SYN **obscure** ▸ **ob·fus·ca·tion** *noun* [U, C]

ob-gyn /ˈəʊ biː ˌdʒiː waɪ ˈen; *NAmE* ˈoʊ/ *noun* (*NAmE, informal*) **1** [U] the branches of medicine concerned with the birth of children (=OBSTETRICS) and the diseases of women (=GYNAECOLOGY) **2** [C] a doctor who is trained in this type of medicine

obi /ˈəʊbi; *NAmE* ˈoʊ-/ *noun* (from *Japanese*) a wide piece of cloth worn around the waist of a Japanese KIMONO

ob·itu·ary /əˈbɪtʃuəri; *NAmE* oʊˈbɪtʃueri/ *noun* (*pl.* -ies) an article about sb's life and achievements, that is printed in a newspaper soon after they have died

ob·ject 🔑 *noun, verb*
■ ***noun*** /ˈɒbdʒɪkt; *NAmE* ˈɑːbdʒekt; -dʒɪkt/ **1** 🔑 a thing that can be seen and touched, but is not alive: *everyday objects such as cups and saucers* ◇ *Glass and plastic objects lined the shelves.* ➲ see also UFO **2** **~ of desire, study, attention, etc.** a person or thing that sb DESIRES, studies, pays attention to, etc. ➲ see also SEX OBJECT **3** 🔑 an aim or a purpose: *Her sole object in life is to become a travel writer.* ◇ *The object is to educate people about road safety.* ◇ *If you're late, you'll defeat the whole* ***object of the exercise.*** ➲ SYNONYMS at TARGET **4** (*grammar*) a noun, noun phrase or pronoun that refers to a person or thing that is affected by the action of the verb (called the DIRECT OBJECT), or that the

action is done to or for (called the INDIRECT OBJECT) ➲ compare SUBJECT (5)

IDM **expense, money, etc. is no 'object** used to say that you are willing to spend a lot of money: *He always travels first class—expense is no object.*

■ ***verb*** /əb'dʒekt/ **1** 0‑ᵣ [I] to say that you disagree with, disapprove of or oppose sth: **~ (to sb/sth)** *Many local people object to the building of the new airport.* ◇ *If nobody objects, we'll postpone the meeting till next week.* ◇ **~ to doing sth/to sb doing sth** *I really object to being charged for parking.* **2** [T] **~ that...** | **+ speech** to give sth as a reason for opposing sth SYN **protest**: *He objected that the police had arrested him without sufficient evidence.* ➲ SYNONYMS at COMPLAIN

Vocabulary Building

Objects you can use

It is useful to know some general words to help you describe objects, especially if you do not know the name of a particular object.

- A **device** is something that has been designed to do a particular job: *There is a new device for cars that warns drivers of traffic jams ahead.*
- A **gadget** is a small object that does something useful, but is not really necessary: *His kitchen is full of gadgets he never uses.*
- An **instrument** is used especially for delicate or scientific work: *'What do you call the instrument that measures temperature?' 'A thermometer.'*
- A **tool** is something that you use for making and repairing things: *'Have you got one of those tools for turning screws?' 'Do you mean a screwdriver?'*
- A **machine** has moving parts and is used for a particular job. It usually stands on its own: *'What's a blender?' 'It's an electric machine for mixing soft food or liquid.'*
- An **appliance** is a large machine that you use in the house, such as a washing machine.
- **Equipment** means all the things you need for a particular activity: *climbing equipment.*
- **Apparatus** means all the tools, machines or equipment that you need for something: *firefighters wearing breathing apparatus.*

'object code (also **'object language**) *noun* [U] (*computing*) the language into which a program is translated using a COMPILER or an ASSEMBLER

ob·ject·ifi·ca·tion /əbˌdʒektɪfɪ'keɪʃn/ *noun* [U] (*formal*) the act of treating people as if they are objects, without rights or feelings of their own

ob·ject·ify /əb'dʒektɪfaɪ/ *verb* (**ob·ject·ifies, ob·ject·ify·ing, ob·ject·ified, ob·ject·ified**) **~ sb/sth** (*formal*) to treat sb/sth as an object: *magazines that objectify women*

ob·jec·tion /əb'dʒekʃn/ *noun* **~ (to sth/to doing sth)** | **~ (that...)** a reason why you do not like or are opposed to sth; a statement about this: *I* ***have no objection*** *to him coming to stay.* ◇ *I'd like to come too, if you* ***have no objection.*** ◇ *The main objection to the plan was that it would cost too much.* ◇ *to* ***raise an objection*** *to sth* ◇ *No objections were raised at the time.* ◇ *The proposal will go ahead despite strong objections from the public.*

ob·jec·tion·able /əb'dʒekʃənəbl/ *adj.* (*formal*) unpleasant or offensive: *objectionable people/odours* ◇ *Why are you being so objectionable today?*

ob·ject·ive 0‑ᵣ AW /əb'dʒektɪv/ *noun, adj.*

■ ***noun*** **1** 0‑ᵣ something that you are trying to achieve SYN **goal**: *the* ***main/primary/principal objective*** ◇ *to* ***meet/achieve*** *your* ***objectives*** ◇ *You must set realistic* ***aims and objectives*** *for yourself.* ◇ *The main objective of this meeting is to give more information on our plans.* ➲ SYNONYMS at TARGET **2** (also **ob͵jective 'lens**) (*technical*) the LENS in a TELESCOPE or MICROSCOPE that is nearest to the object being looked at ➲ VISUAL VOCAB page V57

■ ***adj.*** **1** 0‑ᵣ not influenced by personal feelings or opinions; considering only facts SYN **unbiased**: *an* ***objective analysis/assessment/report*** ◇ *objective criteria* ◇ *I find it difficult to be objective where he's concerned.* OPP **subjective** **2** (*philosophy*) existing outside the mind; based on facts that can be proved: *objective reality* OPP **subjective** **3** [only before noun] (*grammar*) the **objective** case is the one which is used for the object of a sentence ▸ **ob·ject·ive·ly** AW *adv.*: *Looked at objectively, the situation is not too bad.* ◇ *Can these effects be objectively measured?* **ob·ject·iv·ity** AW /ˌɒbdʒek'tɪvəti; NAmE ˌɑːb-/ *noun* [U]: *There was a lack of objectivity in the way the candidates were judged.* ◇ *scientific objectivity* OPP **subjectivity**

'object language *noun* **1** [C] (*linguistics*) = TARGET LANGUAGE (1) **2** [U] (*computing*) = OBJECT CODE

'object lesson *noun* [usually sing.] a practical example of what you should or should not do in a particular situation

ob·ject·or /əb'dʒektə(r)/ *noun* **~ (to sth)** a person who objects to sth: *There were no objectors to the plan.* ➲ see also CONSCIENTIOUS OBJECTOR

objet d'art /ˌɒbʒeɪ 'dɑː; NAmE ˌɔːbdʒeɪ 'dɑːr/ *noun* (*pl.* **ob·jets d'art** /ˌɒbʒeɪ 'dɑː; NAmE ˌɔːbdʒeɪ 'dɑːr/) (from *French*) a small artistic object, used for decoration

ob·li·gated /'ɒblɪgeɪtɪd; NAmE 'ɑːb-/ *adj.* **~ (to do sth)** (*NAmE* or *BrE, formal*) having a moral or legal duty to do sth SYN **obliged**: *He felt obligated to help.*

ob·li·ga·tion /ˌɒblɪ'geɪʃn; NAmE ˌɑːb-/ *noun* **1** [U] **~ (to do sth)** the state of being forced to do sth because it is your duty, or because of a law, etc: *You are* ***under no obligation*** *to buy anything.* ◇ *She did not feel* ***under any obligation*** *to tell him the truth.* ◇ *I don't want people coming to see me out of a* ***sense of obligation.*** ◇ *We will send you an estimate for the work* ***without obligation*** (= you do not have to accept it). **2** [C] something which you must do because you have promised, because of a law, etc. SYN **commitment**: *to fulfil your* ***legal/professional/financial obligations*** ◇ *They reminded him of his contractual obligations.* ◇ **~ to do sth** *We have a* ***moral obligation*** *to protect the environment.*

ob·li·gato = OBBLIGATO

ob·liga·tory /ə'blɪgətri; NAmE -tɔːri/ *adj.* **1 ~ (for sb) (to do sth)** (*formal*) that you must do because of the law, rules, etc. SYN **compulsory**: *It is obligatory for all employees to wear protective clothing.* OPP **optional** **2** (often *humorous*) that you do because you always do it, or other people in the same situation always do it: *In the mid 60s he took the almost obligatory trip to India.*

ob·lige /ə'blaɪdʒ/ *verb* (*formal*) **1** [T, usually passive] **~ sb to do sth** to force sb to do sth, by law, because it is a duty, etc: *Parents are obliged by law to send their children to school.* ◇ *I* ***felt obliged*** *to ask them to dinner.* ◇ *He suffered a serious injury that obliged him to give up work.* **2** [I, T] to help sb by doing what they ask or what you know they want: *Call me if you need any help—I'd be* ***happy to oblige.*** ◇ **~ sb (with sth)** *Would you oblige me with some information?* ◇ **~ sb (by doing sth)** *Oblige me by keeping your suspicions to yourself.*

ob·liged /ə'blaɪdʒd/ *adj.* [not before noun] **~ (to sb) (for sth/for doing sth)** (*formal*) used when you are expressing thanks or asking politely for sth, to show that you are grateful to sb: *I'm* ***much obliged*** *to you for helping us.* ◇ *I'd be obliged if you would keep this to yourself.*

ob·li·ging /ə'blaɪdʒɪŋ/ *adj.* (*formal*) very willing to help SYN **helpful**: *They were very obliging and offered to wait for us.* ▸ **ob·li·ging·ly** *adv.*

ob·lique /ə'bliːk/ *adj., noun*

■ ***adj.*** **1** not expressed or done in a direct way SYN **indirect**: *an* ***oblique reference/approach/comment*** **2** (of a line) sloping at an angle **3 ~ angle** an angle that is not an angle of 90° ▸ **ob·lique·ly** *adv.*: *He referred only obliquely to their recent problems.* ◇ *Always cut stems obliquely to enable flowers to absorb more water.*

■ ***noun*** (*BrE*) = SLASH (3)

ob·lit·er·ate /ə'blɪtəreɪt/ *verb* [often passive] **~ sth** to remove all signs of sth, either by destroying or covering it

O

completely: *The building was completely obliterated by the bomb.* ◇ *The snow had obliterated their footprints.* ◇ *Everything that happened that night was obliterated from his memory.* ▶ **ob·lit·er·ation** /əˌblɪtəˈreɪʃn/ *noun* [U]

ob·liv·ion /əˈblɪviən/ *noun* [U] **1** a state in which you are not aware of what is happening around you, usually because you are unconscious or asleep: *He often drinks himself into oblivion.* ◇ *Sam longed for the oblivion of sleep.* **2** the state in which sb/sth has been forgotten and is no longer famous or important SYN **obscurity**: *An unexpected victory saved him from political oblivion.* ◇ *Most of his inventions have been consigned to oblivion.* **3** a state in which sth has been completely destroyed: *Hundreds of homes were bombed into oblivion during the first weeks of the war.*

ob·livi·ous /əˈblɪviəs/ *adj.* [not usually before noun] not aware of sth: **~ (of sth)** *He drove off, oblivious of the damage he had caused.* ◇ **~ (to sth)** *You eventually become oblivious to the noise.* ▶ **ob·livi·ous·ly** *adv.*

ob·long /ˈɒblɒŋ; *NAmE* ˈɑːblɔːŋ; ˈɑːblɑːŋ/ *adj.* **1** an **oblong** shape has four straight sides, two of which are longer than the other two, and four angles of 90° **2** (*NAmE*) used to describe any shape that is longer than it is wide: *an oblong melon* ▶ **ob·long** *noun*: *a tiny oblong of glass in the roof* ➲ see also RECTANGLE

ob·lo·quy /ˈɒbləkwi; *NAmE* ˈɑːb-/ *noun* [U] (*formal*) **1** strong public criticism **2** loss of respect and honour

ob·nox·ious /əbˈnɒkʃəs; *NAmE* -ˈnɑːk-/ *adj.* extremely unpleasant, especially in a way that offends people SYN **offensive**: *obnoxious behaviour* ◇ *a thoroughly obnoxious little man* ◇ *obnoxious odours* ▶ **ob·nox·ious·ly** *adv.*

o.b.o. *abbr.* (*NAmE*) or best offer (used in small advertisements to show that sth may be sold at a lower price than the price that has been asked): *$800 o.b.o.* ➲ see also O.N.O.

oboe /ˈəʊbəʊ; *NAmE* ˈoʊboʊ/ *noun* a musical instrument of the WOODWIND group. It is shaped like a pipe and has a double REED at the top that you blow into. ➲ VISUAL VOCAB page V30

obo·ist /ˈəʊbəʊɪst; *NAmE* ˈoʊboʊɪst/ *noun* a person who plays the oboe

ob·scene /əbˈsiːn/ *adj.* **1** connected with sex in a way that most people find offensive: *obscene gestures/language/books* ◇ *an obscene phone call* (= in which sb says obscene things) **2** extremely large in size or amount in a way that most people find unacceptable and offensive SYN **outrageous**: *He earns an obscene amount of money.* ◇ *It's obscene to spend so much on food when millions are starving.* ▶ **ob·scene·ly** *adv.*: *to behave obscenely* ◇ *obscenely rich*

ob·scen·ity /əbˈsenəti/ *noun* (*pl.* -ies) **1** [U] obscene language or behaviour: *The editors are being prosecuted for obscenity.* ◇ *the laws on obscenity* **2** [C, usually pl.] an obscene word or act: *She screamed a string of obscenities at the judge.*

ob·scur·ant·ism /ˌɒbskjuˈræntɪzəm; *NAmE* ɑːbˈskjʊr-/ *noun* [U] (*formal*) the practice of deliberately preventing sb from understanding or discovering sth ▶ **ob·scur·ant·ist** *adj.*

ob·scure /əbˈskjʊə(r); *NAmE* əbˈskjʊr/ *adj., verb*

■ ***adj.*** **1** not well known SYN **unknown**: *an obscure German poet* ◇ *He was born around 1650 but his origins remain obscure.* **2** difficult to understand: *I found her lecture very obscure.* ◇ ***For some obscure reason**, he failed to turn up.* ▶ **ob·scure·ly** *adv.*: *They were making her feel obscurely worried* (= for reasons that were difficult to understand).

■ ***verb*** **~ sth** to make it difficult to see, hear or understand sth: *The view was obscured by fog.* ◇ *We mustn't let these minor details obscure the main issue.*

ob·scur·ity /əbˈskjʊərəti; *NAmE* -ˈskjʊr-/ *noun* (*pl.* -ies) **1** [U] the state in which sb/sth is not well known or has been forgotten: *The actress was only 17 when she was plucked from obscurity and made a star.* ◇ *He spent most of his life working in obscurity.* **2** [U, C, usually pl.] the quality of being difficult to understand; something that is difficult to understand: *The course teaches students to avoid ambiguity and obscurity of expression.* ◇ *a speech full of obscurities* **3** [U] (*literary*) the state of being dark SYN **darkness**

ob·se·quies /ˈɒbsəkwiz; *NAmE* ˈɑːb-/ *noun* [pl.] (*formal*) funeral ceremonies: *state obsequies*

ob·se·qui·ous /əbˈsiːkwiəs/ *adj.* (*formal, disapproving*) trying too hard to please sb, especially sb who is important SYN **servile**: *an obsequious manner* ▶ **ob·se·qui·ous·ly** *adv.*: *smiling obsequiously* **ob·se·qui·ous·ness** *noun* [U]

ob·serv·able /əbˈzɜːvəbl; *NAmE* -ˈzɜːrv-/ *adj.* that can be seen or noticed: *observable differences* ◇ *Similar trends are observable in mainland Europe.* ▶ **ob·serv·ably** /əbˈzɜːvəbli; *NAmE* -ˈzɜːrv-/ *adv.*

ob·ser·vance /əbˈzɜːvəns; *NAmE* -ˈzɜːrv-/ *noun* **1** [U, sing.] the practice of obeying a law, celebrating a festival or behaving according to a particular custom: **~ (of sth)** *observance of the law* ◇ *a strict observance of the Sabbath* OPP **non-observance** **2** [C, usually pl.] an act performed as part of a religious or traditional ceremony: *religious observances*

ob·ser·vant /əbˈzɜːvənt; *NAmE* -ˈzɜːrv-/ *adj.* **1** good at noticing things around you SYN **sharp-eyed**: *Observant walkers may see red deer along this stretch of the road.* ◇ *How very observant of you!* **2** (*formal*) careful to obey religious laws and customs

ob·ser·va·tion 🔑 /ˌɒbzəˈveɪʃn; *NAmE* ˌɑːbzərˈv-/ *noun*

1 🔑 [U, C] the act of watching sb/sth carefully for a period of time, especially to learn sth: *Most information was collected by direct observation of the animals' behaviour.* ◇ *results based on scientific observations* ◇ *We managed to escape observation* (= we were not seen). ◇ *The suspect is being kept **under observation*** (= watched closely by the police). ◇ *She has outstanding **powers of observation*** (= the ability to notice things around her). ◇ *an **observation post/tower*** (= a place from where sb, especially an enemy, can be watched) ➲ COLLOCATIONS at SCIENTIFIC **2** 🔑 [C] **~ (about/on sth)** (*formal*) a comment, especially based on sth you have seen, heard or read SYN **remark**: *He began by making a few general observations about the report.* ◇ *She has some interesting observations on possible future developments.* ➲ note at DECLARATION ▶ **ob·ser·va·tion·al** *adj.*

ˌobserˈvation car *noun* a coach/car on a train with large windows, designed to give passengers a good view of the passing landscape

ob·ser·va·tory /əbˈzɜːvətri; *NAmE* əbˈzɜːrvətɔːri/ *noun* (*pl.* -ies) a special building from which scientists watch the stars, the weather, etc.

ob·serve 🔑 /əbˈzɜːv; *NAmE* əbˈzɜːrv/ *verb* [T]

1 🔑 (*formal*) to see or notice sb/sth: **~ sb/sth** *Have you observed any changes lately?* ◇ *All the characters in the novel are closely observed* (= seem like people in real life). ◇ **~ sb/sth do sth** *The police observed a man enter the bank.* ◇ **~ sb/sth doing sth** *They observed him entering the bank.* ◇ **~ that ...** *She observed that all the chairs were already occupied.* ◇ **be observed to do sth** *He was observed to follow her closely.* HELP This pattern is only used in the passive. ➲ SYNONYMS at COMMENT, NOTICE **2** 🔑 [T, I] (*formal*) to watch sb/sth carefully, especially to learn more about them SYN **monitor**: **~ (sb/sth)** *I felt he was observing everything I did.* ◇ *The patients were observed over a period of several months.* ◇ *He observes keenly, but says little.* ◇ **~ how, what, etc...** *They observed how the parts of the machine fitted together.* ➲ SYNONYMS at LOOK **3** [T] **~ that...** | **+ speech** (*formal*) to make a remark SYN **comment**: *She observed that it was getting late.* **4** [T] **~ sth** to obey rules, laws, etc: *Will the rebels observe the ceasefire?* ◇ *The crowd **observed a minute's silence*** (= were silent for one minute) *in memory of those who had died.* **5** [T] **~ sth** (*formal*) to celebrate festivals, birthdays, etc: *Do they observe Christmas?*

ob·ser·ver /əbˈzɜːvə(r); *NAmE* -ˈzɜːrv-/ *noun* **1** a person who watches sb/sth: *According to observers, the plane exploded shortly after take-off.* ◇ ***To the casual observer*** (= somebody who does not pay much attention), *the system appears confusing.* ➲ SYNONYMS at WITNESS **2** a person who attends a meeting, lesson, etc. to listen and watch

O

but not to take part: *A team of British officials were sent as observers to the conference.* **3** a person who watches and studies particular events, situations, etc. and is therefore considered to be an expert on them: *a royal observer*

ob·sess /əb'ses/ *verb* **1** [T, usually passive] **~ sb** to completely fill your mind so that you cannot think of anything else, in a way that is not normal: *He's obsessed by computers.* ◇ *She's completely obsessed with him.* ◇ *The need to produce the most exciting newspaper story obsesses most journalists.* **2** [I] **~** (**about sth**) to be always talking or worrying about a particular thing, especially when this annoys other people: *I think you should try to stop obsessing about food.*

ob·ses·sion /əb'seʃn/ *noun* **1** [U] the state in which a person's mind is completely filled with thoughts of one particular thing or person in a way that is not normal: *Her fear of flying is bordering on obsession.* ◇ **~ with sb/sth** *The media's obsession with the young prince continues.* **2** [C] **~** (**with sb**) a person or thing that sb thinks about too much: *Fitness has become an obsession with him.*

ob·ses·sion·al /əb'seʃənl/ *adj.* thinking too much about one particular person or thing, in a way that is not normal: *She is obsessional about cleanliness.* ◇ *obsessional behaviour* ▶ **ob·ses·sion·al·ly** *adv.*

ob·ses·sive /əb'sesɪv/ *adj., noun*
- ***adj.*** thinking too much about one particular person or thing, in a way that is not normal: *He's becoming more and more obsessive about punctuality.* ◇ *an obsessive attention to detail* ▶ **ob·ses·sive·ly** *adv.*: *obsessively jealous* ◇ *He worries obsessively about his appearance.*
- ***noun*** (*psychology*) a person whose mind is filled with thoughts of one particular thing or person so that they cannot think of anything else

ob,sessive com'pulsive disorder *noun* [U] (*abbr.* OCD) a mental DISORDER in which sb feels they have to repeat certain actions or activities to get rid of fears or unpleasant thoughts

ob·sid·ian /əb'sɪdiən/ *noun* [U] a type of dark rock that looks like glass and comes from VOLCANOES

ob·so·les·cence /ˌɒbsə'lesns; *NAmE* ˌɑːb-/ *noun* [U] (*formal*) the state of becoming old-fashioned and no longer useful: *products with* ***built-in/planned obsolescence*** (= designed not to last long so that people will have to buy new ones) ▶ **ob·so·les·cent** /ˌɒbsə'lesnt; *NAmE* ˌɑːb-/ *adj.*

ob·so·lete /'ɒbsəliːt; *NAmE* ˌɑːbsə'liːt/ *adj.* no longer used because sth new has been invented SYN **out of date**: *obsolete technology* ◇ *With technological changes many traditional skills have become obsolete.*

obs·tacle /'ɒbstəkl; *NAmE* 'ɑːb-/ *noun* **1 ~** (**to sth/to doing sth**) a situation, an event, etc. that makes it difficult for you to do or achieve sth SYN **hindrance**: *A lack of qualifications can be a major obstacle to finding a job.* ◇ *So far, we have managed to overcome all the obstacles that have been placed in our path.* **2** an object that is in your way and that makes it difficult for you to move forward: *The area was full of streams and bogs and other natural obstacles.* **3** (in SHOWJUMPING) a fence, etc. for a horse to jump over

'obstacle course *noun* **1** a series of objects that people taking part in a race have to climb over, under, through, etc. **2** a series of difficulties that people have to deal with in order to achieve a particular aim **3** (*NAmE*) (*BrE* **as'sault course**) an area of land with many objects that are difficult to climb, jump over or go through, which is used, especially by soldiers, for improving physical skills and strength

'obstacle race *noun* a race in which the people taking part have to climb over, under, through, etc. various objects

ob·stet·ri·cian /ˌɒbstə'trɪʃn; *NAmE* ˌɑːb-/ *noun* a doctor who is trained in obstetrics

ob·stet·rics /əb'stetrɪks/ *noun* [U] the branch of medicine concerned with the birth of children ▶ **ob·stet·ric** /əb'stetrɪk/ *adj.*: *obstetric medicine*

ob·stin·ate /'ɒbstɪnət; *NAmE* 'ɑːb-/ *adj.* **1** (often *disapproving*) refusing to change your opinions, way of behaving, etc. when other people try to persuade you to; behaviour that shows this SYN **stubborn**: *He can be very obstinate when he wants to be!* ◇ *her obstinate refusal to comply with their request* **2** [usually before noun] difficult to get rid of or deal with SYN **stubborn**: *the obstinate problem of unemployment* ◇ *an obstinate stain* ▶ **ob·stin·acy** /'ɒbstɪnəsi; *NAmE* 'ɑːb-/ *noun* [U]: *an act of sheer obstinacy* **ob·stin·ate·ly** *adv.*: *He obstinately refused to consider the future.*

ob·strep·er·ous /əb'strepərəs/ *adj.* (*formal* or *humorous*) noisy and difficult to control

ob·struct /əb'strʌkt/ *verb* (*formal*) **1 ~ sth** to block a road, an entrance, a passage, etc. so that sb/sth cannot get through, see past, etc: *You can't park here, you're obstructing my driveway.* ◇ *First check that the accident victim doesn't have an obstructed airway.* ◇ *The pillar obstructed our view of the stage.* **2 ~ sb/sth** to prevent sb/sth from doing sth or making progress, especially when this is done deliberately SYN **hinder**: *They were charged with obstructing the police in the course of their duty.* ◇ *terrorists attempting to obstruct the peace process*

IDM **ob,struct 'justice** (*NAmE*) (*BrE* **per,vert the course of 'justice**) (*law*) to tell a lie or to do sth in order to prevent the police, etc. from finding out the truth about a crime

ob·struc·tion /əb'strʌkʃn/ *noun* **1** [U, C] the fact of trying to prevent sth/sb from making progress: *the obstruction of justice* ◇ *He was arrested for obstruction of a police officer in the execution of his duty.* **2** [U, C] the fact of blocking a road, an entrance, a passage, etc: *obstruction of the factory gates* ◇ *The abandoned car was causing an obstruction.* **3** [C] something that blocks a road, an entrance, etc: *It is my job to make sure that all pathways are clear of obstructions.* **4** [C, U] (*medical*) something that blocks a passage or tube in your body; a medical condition resulting from this SYN **blockage**: *He had an operation to remove an obstruction in his throat.* ◇ ***bowel/intestinal obstruction*** **5** [U] (*sport*) the offence of unfairly preventing a player of the other team from moving to get the ball

ob·struc·tion·ism /əb'strʌkʃənɪzəm/ *noun* [U] (*formal*) the practice of trying to prevent a parliament or committee from making progress, passing laws, etc. ▶ **ob·struc·tion·ist** /-ɪst/ *noun, adj.*

ob·struct·ive /əb'strʌktɪv/ *adj.* **1** trying to prevent sb/sth from making progress: *Of course she can do it. She's just being deliberately obstructive.* ➲ compare CONSTRUCTIVE **2** [only before noun] (*medical*) connected with a passage, tube, etc. in your body that has become blocked: *obstructive lung disease*

ob·tain 0-w AW /əb'teɪn/ *verb* (*formal*)
1 0-w [T] **~ sth** to get sth, especially by making an effort: *to obtain advice/information/permission* ◇ *I finally managed to obtain a copy of the report.* ◇ *To obtain the overall score, add up the totals in each column.* **2** [I] (not used in the progressive tenses) (of rules, systems, customs, etc.) to exist SYN **apply**: *These conditions no longer obtain.*

ob·tain·able AW /əb'teɪnəbl/ *adj.* [not usually before noun] that can be obtained SYN **available**: *Full details are obtainable from any post office.*

ob·trude /əb'truːd/ *verb* [I, T] **~** (**sth/yourself**) (**on/upon sb**) (*formal*) to become or make sth/yourself noticed, especially in a way that is not wanted: *Music from the next room obtruded upon his thoughts.*

ob·tru·sive /əb'truːsɪv/ *adj.* noticeable in an unpleasant way: *The sofa would be less obtrusive in a paler colour.* ◇ *They tried to ensure that their presence was not too obtrusive.* ▶ **ob·tru·sive·ly** *adv.*

ob·tuse /əb'tjuːs; *NAmE* -'tuːs/ *adj.* (*formal, disapproving*) slow or unwilling to understand sth: *Are you being deliberately obtuse?* ▶ **ob·tuse·ness** *noun* [U]

ob,tuse 'angle *noun* an angle between 90° and 180° ➲ VISUAL VOCAB page V58 ➲ compare ACUTE ANGLE, REFLEX ANGLE, RIGHT ANGLE

ob·verse /'ɒbvɜːs; *NAmE* 'ɑːbvɜːrs/ *noun* (usually **the obverse**) [sing.] **1** (*formal*) the opposite of sth: *The obverse of* *love is hate.* **2** (*technical*) the side of a coin or MEDAL that has the head or main design on it

ob·vi·ate /ˈɒbvieɪt; *NAmE* ˈɑːb-/ *verb* **~ sth** (*formal*) to remove a problem or the need for sth **SYN** **preclude**: *This new evidence* ***obviates the need for*** *any further enquiries.*

ob·vi·ous 🔑 **AW** /ˈɒbviəs; *NAmE* ˈɑːb-/ *adj.*
1 🔑 **~ (to sb) (that...)** easy to see or understand **SYN** **clear**: *It was obvious to everyone that the child had been badly treated.* ◇ *It's obvious from what she said that something is wrong.* ◇ *I know you don't like her but try not to make it so obvious.* ◇ *He agreed with obvious pleasure.* ◇ ***For obvious reasons,*** *I'd prefer not to give my name.* ◇ *The reasons for this decision were* ***not immediately obvious.*** ➲ SYNONYMS at CLEAR **2** 🔑 that most people would think of or agree to: *She was the obvious choice for the job.* ◇ *There's no obvious solution to the problem.* ◇ *This seemed the most obvious thing to do.* **3** 🔑 (*disapproving*) not interesting, new or showing imagination; unnecessary because it is clear to everyone: *The ending was pretty obvious.* ◇ *I may be* ***stating the obvious*** *but without more money the project cannot survive.* ▸ **ob·vi·ous·ness** *noun* [U]

ob·vi·ous·ly 🔑 **AW** /ˈɒbviəsli; *NAmE* ˈɑːb-/ *adv.*
1 🔑 used when giving information that you expect other people to know already or agree with **SYN** **clearly**: *Obviously, we don't want to spend too much money.* ◇ *Diet and exercise are obviously important.* **2** 🔑 used to say that a particular situation or fact is easy to see or understand: *He was obviously drunk.* ◇ *They're obviously not coming.* ◇ *'I didn't realise it was a formal occasion.' 'Obviously!'* (= I can see by the way you are dressed)

oca·rina /ˌɒkəˈriːnə; *NAmE* ˌɑːk-/ *noun* a small egg-shaped musical instrument that you blow into, with holes for the fingers

oc·ca·sion 🔑 /əˈkeɪʒn/ *noun, verb*
■ ***noun*** **1** 🔑 [C] a particular time when sth happens: *on this/that occasion* ◇ *I've met him on several occasions.* ◇ *I can remember very few* ***occasions when*** *he had to cancel because of ill health.* ◇ *They have been seen together on two* ***separate occasions.*** ◇ *On one occasion, she called me in the middle of the night.* ◇ *He used the occasion to announce further tax cuts.* **2** 🔑 [C] a special event, ceremony or celebration: *a great/memorable/happy occasion* ◇ *Turn every meal into* ***a special occasion.*** ◇ *They* ***marked the occasion*** (= celebrated it) *with an open-air concert.* ◇ *Their wedding turned out to be quite an occasion.* ◇ *He was presented with the watch* ***on the occasion of*** *his retirement.* **3** 🔑 [sing.] **~ (for sth/doing sth)** a suitable time for sth: *It should have been an occasion for rejoicing, but she could not feel any real joy.* ◇ *I'll speak to him about it* ***if the occasion arises*** (= if I get a chance). **4** [U, sing.] (*formal*) a reason or cause: **~ (to do sth)** *I've had no occasion to visit him recently.* ◇ **~ (of/for sth)** *Her death was the occasion of mass riots.* ◇ *I'm willing to go to court over this* ***if the occasion arises*** (= if it becomes necessary).
IDM **on ocˈcasion(s)** 🔑 sometimes but not often: *He has been known on occasion to lose his temper.* ➲ more at SENSE *n.*
■ ***verb*** (*formal*) to cause sth: **~ sth** *The flight delay was occasioned by the need for a further security check.* ◇ **~ sb sth** *The decision occasioned us much anxiety.*

oc·ca·sion·al /əˈkeɪʒənl/ *adj.* [only before noun] happening or done sometimes but not often: *He works for us on an occasional basis.* ◇ *I enjoy the occasional glass of wine.* ◇ *He spent five years in Paris, with occasional visits to Italy.* ◇ *an occasional smoker* (= a person who smokes, but not often)

oc·ca·sion·al·ly 🔑 /əˈkeɪʒnəli/ *adv.*
sometimes but not often: *We occasionally meet for a drink after work.* ◇ *This type of allergy can very occasionally be fatal.*

ocˈcasional table *noun* (*BrE*) a small light table that is easy to move, used for different things at different times ➲ VISUAL VOCAB page V18

the Oc·ci·dent /ˈɒksɪdənt; *NAmE* ˈɑːk-/ *noun* [sing.] (*formal*) the western part of the world, especially Europe and America ➲ compare ORIENT ▸ **oc·ci·den·tal** /ˌɒksɪˈdentl; *NAmE* ˌɑːk-/ *adj.*

Oc·ci·tan /ˈɒksɪtən; *NAmE* ˈɑːksɪtæn/ *noun* [U] the traditional language of southern France

oc·clude /əˈkluːd/ *verb* **~ sth** (*technical*) to cover or block sth: *an occluded artery* ▸ **oc·clu·sion** /əˈkluːʒn/ *noun* [U]

oc·cult /əˈkʌlt; *BrE* also ˈɒkʌlt/ *adj.* **1** [only before noun] connected with magic powers and things that cannot be explained by reason or science **SYN** **supernatural**: *occult practices* **2 the occult** *noun* [sing.] everything connected with occult practices, etc: *He's interested in witchcraft and the occult.*

oc·cultist /əˈkʌltɪst; ˈɒkʌltɪst; *NAmE* ˈɑːk-/ *noun* a person who is involved in the occult

oc·cu·pancy **AW** /ˈɒkjəpənsi; *NAmE* ˈɑːk-/ *noun* [U] (*formal*) the act of living in or using a building, room, piece of land, etc: *Prices are based on full occupancy of an apartment.* ◇ *to be in sole occupancy*

oc·cu·pant **AW** /ˈɒkjəpənt; *NAmE* ˈɑːk-/ *noun* **1** a person who lives or works in a particular house, room, building, etc: *All outstanding bills will be paid by the previous occupants.* **2** a person who is in a vehicle, seat, etc. at a particular time: *The car was badly damaged but the occupants were unhurt.*

oc·cu·pa·tion **AW** /ˌɒkjuˈpeɪʃn; *NAmE* ˌɑːk-/ *noun* **1** [C] a job or profession: *Please state your name, age and occupation below.* ➲ SYNONYMS at WORK **2** [C] the way in which you spend your time, especially when you are not working: *Her main occupation seems to be shopping.* **3** [U] the act of moving into a country, town, etc. and taking control of it using military force; the period of time during which a country, town, etc. is controlled in this way: *the Roman occupation of Britain* ◇ *The zones* ***under occupation*** *contained major industrial areas.* ◇ *occupation forces* **4** [U] (*formal*) the act of living in or using a building, room, piece of land, etc: *The offices will be ready for occupation in June.* ◇ *The following applies only to tenants in occupation after January 1 2010.* ◇ *The level of* ***owner occupation*** (= people owning their homes) *has increased rapidly in the last 30 years.*

oc·cu·pa·tion·al **AW** /ˌɒkjuˈpeɪʃənl; *NAmE* ˌɑːk-/ *adj.* [only before noun] connected with a person's job or profession: *occupational health* ◇ *an* ***occupational risk/hazard*** ◇ *an occupational pension scheme* ▸ **oc·cu·pa·tion·al·ly** *adv.*: *occupationally induced disease*

ˌoccuˌpational ˈtherapist *noun* a person whose job is to help people get better after illness or injury by giving them special activities to do

ˌoccuˌpational ˈtherapy *noun* [U] the work of an occupational therapist

oc·cu·pied 🔑 **AW** /ˈɒkjupaɪd; *NAmE* ˈɑːk-/ *adj.*
1 🔑 [not before noun] being used by sb: *Only half of the rooms are occupied at the moment.* ➲ see also OWNER-OCCUPIED **2** 🔑 [not before noun] busy: **~ (doing sth/in doing sth/in sth)** *He's fully occupied looking after three small children.* ◇ **~ (with sth/with doing sth)** *Only half her time is occupied with politics.* ◇ *The most important thing is to* ***keep yourself occupied.*** **3** 🔑 (of a country, etc.) controlled by people from another country, etc, using military force: *He spent his childhood in occupied Europe.* **OPP** **unoccupied**

oc·cu·pier **AW** /ˈɒkjupaɪə(r); *NAmE* ˈɑːk-/ *noun* **1 ~ (of sth)** (*formal*) a person who lives in or uses a building, room, piece of land, etc. **SYN** **occupant**: *The letter was addressed to the occupier of the house.* ➲ see also OWNER-OCCUPIER **2** [usually pl.] a member of an army that is occupying a foreign country, etc.

oc·cupy 🔑 **AW** /ˈɒkjupaɪ; *NAmE* ˈɑːk-/ *verb* (**oc·cu·pies, oc·cu·py·ing, oc·cu·pied, oc·cu·pied**)
1 🔑 **~ sth** to fill or use a space, an area or an amount of time **SYN** **take up**: *The bed seemed to occupy most of the room.* ◇ *How much memory does the program occupy?* ◇ *Administrative work occupies half of my time.* **2** 🔑 **~ sth** (*formal*) to live or work in a room, house or building: *He occupies an office on the 12th floor.* **3** 🔑 **~ sth** to enter a

O

place in a large group and take control of it, especially by military force: *The capital has been occupied by the rebel army.* ◇ *Protesting students occupied the TV station.* **4** to fill your time or keep you busy doing sth: **~ sb/sth/yourself** *a game that will occupy the kids for hours* ◇ *Problems at work continued* **to occupy his mind** *for some time.* ◇ **~ sb/sth/yourself with sb/sth** *She occupied herself with routine office tasks.* ◇ **~ sb/sth/yourself (in) doing sth** *She occupied herself doing routine office tasks.* **5 ~ sth** to have an official job or position SYN **hold**: *The president occupies the position for four years.*

occur AW /ə'kɜː(r)/ *verb* (-rr-)
1 [I] (*formal*) to happen: *When exactly did the incident occur?* ◇ *Something unexpected occurred.* **2** [I] **+ adv./prep.** to exist or be found somewhere: *Sugar occurs naturally in fruit.*
PHR V **oc'cur to sb** (of an idea or a thought) to come into your mind: *The idea occurred to him in a dream.* ◇ **~ that...** *It didn't occur to him that his wife was having an affair.* ◇ **~ to do sth** *It didn't occur to her to ask for help.*

oc·cur·rence AW /ə'kʌrəns; *NAmE* ə'kɜːr-/ *noun* (*formal*) **1** [C] something that happens or exists: *a **common/everyday/frequent/regular occurrence*** ◇ *Vandalism used to be a **rare occurrence** here.* ◇ *The program counts the number of occurrences of any word, within the text.* **2** [U] **~ (of sth)** the fact of sth happening or existing: *a link between the occurrence of skin cancer and the use of computer monitors*

OCD /ˌəʊ siː 'diː; *NAmE* ˌoʊ/ *abbr.* OBSESSIVE COMPULSIVE DISORDER

ocean /'əʊʃn; *NAmE* 'oʊʃn/ *noun*
1 (usually **the ocean**) [sing.] (*especially NAmE*) the mass of salt water that covers most of the earth's surface: *the depths of the ocean* ◇ *People were swimming in the ocean despite the hurricane warning.* ◇ *The plane hit the ocean several miles offshore.* ◇ *Our beach house is just a couple of miles from the ocean.* ◇ *an ocean liner* ◇ *Ocean levels are rising.* **2** (usually **Ocean**) [C] one of the five large areas that the ocean is divided into: *the **Antarctic/Arctic/Atlantic/Indian/Pacific Ocean*** ➲ note at SEA ➲ VISUAL VOCAB page V4
IDM **an ocean of sth** (*BrE* also **oceans of sth**) (*informal*) a large amount of sth ➲ more at DROP *n.*

ocean·arium /ˌəʊʃə'neəriəm; *NAmE* ˌoʊʃə'neriəm/ *noun* an extremely large container in which fish and other sea creatures are kept to be seen by the public or to be studied by scientists ➲ see also AQUARIUM

ocean·front /'əʊʃnfrʌnt; *NAmE* 'oʊ-/ *adj.* (*NAmE*) located on land near the ocean: *an oceanfront hotel*

'ocean-going *adj.* [only before noun] (of ships) made for crossing the sea or ocean, not for journeys along the coast or up rivers

Ocea·nia /ˌəʊsi'ɑːniə; -ʃi-; *NAmE* ˌoʊʃi-/ *noun* [U] a large region of the world consisting of the Pacific islands and the seas around them

ocean·ic /ˌəʊʃi'ænɪk; *NAmE* ˌoʊʃi-/ *adj.* [usually before noun] (*technical*) connected with the ocean: *oceanic fish*

ocean·og·raphy /ˌəʊʃə'nɒgrəfi; *NAmE* ˌoʊʃə'nɑːg-/ *noun* [U] the scientific study of the ocean ▶ **ocean·og·raph·er** *noun*

ˌocean 'trench *noun* = TRENCH (3)

oce·lot /'ɒsəlɒt; *NAmE* 'ɑːsəlɑːt; 'oʊs-/ *noun* a wild animal of the cat family, that has yellow fur with black lines and spots, found in Central and S America

och /ɒk; ɒx; *NAmE* ɑːk; ɑːx/ *exclamation* (*ScotE, IrishE*) used to express the fact that you are surprised, sorry, etc.: *Och, aye* (= Oh, yes).

oche /'ɒki; *NAmE* 'ɑːki/ *noun* [sing.] the line which players must stand behind in the game of DARTS

ochre (*US* also **ocher**) /'əʊkə(r); *NAmE* 'oʊ-/ *noun* [U] **1** a type of red or yellow earth used in some paints and DYES **2** the red or yellow colour of ochre

ocker /'ɒkə(r); *NAmE* 'ɑːk-/ *noun* (*AustralE, informal*) a rude or aggressive Australian man ▶ **ocker** *adj.*

o'clock /ə'klɒk; *NAmE* ə'klɑːk/ *adv.*
used with the numbers 1 to 12 when telling the time, to mean an exact hour: *He left between five and six o'clock.* ◇ *at/after/before eleven o'clock*

OCR *abbr.* (*computing*) OPTICAL CHARACTER RECOGNITION

octa·gon /'ɒktəgən; *NAmE* 'ɑːktəgɑːn/ *noun* (*geometry*) a flat shape with eight straight sides and eight angles ➲ VISUAL VOCAB page V58 ▶ **oc·tag·on·al** /ɒk'tægənl; *NAmE* ɑːk't-/ *adj.*: *an octagonal coin*

oc·tane /'ɒkteɪn; *NAmE* 'ɑːk-/ *noun* a chemical substance in petrol/gas, used as a way of measuring its quality: *high-octane fuel*

oct·ave /'ɒktɪv; *NAmE* 'ɑːk-/ *noun* (*music*) the difference (the INTERVAL) between the first and last notes in a series of eight notes on a SCALE: *to play an octave higher* ◇ *Orbison's vocal range spanned three octaves.*

oc·tavo /ɒk'teɪvəʊ; -'tɑːv-; *NAmE* ɑːk-; -voʊ/ *noun* (*pl.* -os) (*technical*) a size of a book page that is made by folding each sheet of paper into eight LEAVES (= 16 pages)

octet /ɒk'tet; *NAmE* ɑːk-/ *noun* **1** [C+sing./pl. v.] a group of eight singers or musicians **2** [C] a piece of music for eight singers or musicians

octo- /'ɒktəʊ-; *NAmE* 'ɑːktoʊ-/ (also **oct-**) *combining form* (in nouns, adjectives and adverbs) eight; having eight: *octagon*

Oc·to·ber /ɒk'təʊbə(r); *NAmE* ɑːk'toʊ-/ *noun* [U, C] (*abbr.* **Oct.**)
the 10th month of the year, between September and November HELP To see how **October** is used, look at the examples at **April**.

oc·to·gen·ar·ian /ˌɒktədʒə'neəriən; *NAmE* ˌɑːktədʒə'ner-/ *noun* a person between 80 and 89 years old

octo·pus /'ɒktəpəs; *NAmE* 'ɑːk-/ *noun* [C, U] (*pl.* **octopuses**) a sea creature with a soft round body and eight long arms, that is sometimes used for food

'octopus trousers (*BrE*) (*NAmE* **'octopus pants**) *noun* [pl.] trousers/pants which have many strips of material hanging from them

octo·syl·lable /'ɒktəʊsɪləbl; *NAmE* 'ɑːktoʊ-/ *noun* (*technical*) a line of poetry consisting of eight syllables ▶ **octo·syl·lab·ic** /ˌɒktəʊsɪ'læbɪk; *NAmE* 'ɑːktoʊ-/ *adj.*

ocu·lar /'ɒkjələ(r); *NAmE* 'ɑːk-/ *adj.* [only before noun] **1** (*technical*) connected with the eyes: *ocular muscles* **2** (*formal*) that can be seen: *ocular proof*

ocu·list /'ɒkjəlɪst; *NAmE* 'ɑːk-/ *noun* (*old-fashioned*) a doctor who examines and treats people's eyes

OD /ˌəʊ 'diː; *NAmE* ˌoʊ/ *verb* (**OD's, OD'ing, OD'd, OD'd**) [I] **~ (on sth)** (*informal*) = OVERDOSE

odd AW /ɒd; *NAmE* ɑːd/ *adj.* (**odder, oddest**)
▸ STRANGE **1** strange or unusual: *They're very odd people.* ◇ *There's something odd about that man.* ◇ *It's **most odd that*** (= very odd that) *she hasn't written.* ◇ *The **odd thing** was that he didn't recognize me.* ◇ *She had the oddest feeling that he was avoiding her.* ➲ compare PECULIAR
▸ ODD- **2** (in compounds) strange or unusual in the way mentioned: *an odd-looking house* ◇ *an odd-sounding name*
▸ NOT REGULAR/OFTEN **3 the odd** [only before noun] (no comparative or superlative) happening or appearing occasionally; not very regular or frequent SYN **occasional**: *He makes the odd mistake—nothing too serious.*
▸ VARIOUS **4** [only before noun] (no comparative or superlative) of no particular type or size; various: *decorations made of odd scraps of paper*
▸ NOT MATCHING **5** [usually before noun] (no comparative or superlative) not with the pair or set that it belongs to; not matching: *You're wearing odd socks!*
▸ NUMBERS **6** (no comparative or superlative) (of numbers) that cannot be divided exactly by the number two: *1, 3, 5 and 7 are odd numbers.* OPP **even**
▸ AVAILABLE **7** [only before noun] available; that sb can use

SYN **spare**: *Could I see you when you've got an **odd moment**?*

▸ APPROXIMATELY **8** (no comparative or superlative; usually placed immediately after a number) approximately or a little more than the number mentioned: *How old is she—seventy odd?* ◇ *He's worked there for twenty-odd years.*

▶ **odd·ness** *noun* [U]: *the oddness of her appearance* ◇ *His oddness frightened her.*

IDM **the odd man/one 'out** a person or thing that is different from others or does not fit easily into a group or set: *At school he was always the odd man out.* ◇ *Dog, cat, horse, shoe—which is the odd one out?* ➲ more at FISH *n.*

odd·ball /'ɒdbɔːl; *NAmE* 'ɑːd-/ *noun* (*informal*) a person who behaves in a strange or unusual way ▶ **odd·ball** *adj.*: *oddball characters*

odd·ity /'ɒdəti; *NAmE* 'ɑːd-/ *noun* (*pl.* **-ies**) **1** [C] a person or thing that is strange or unusual: *The book deals with some of the oddities of grammar and spelling.* **2** [U] the quality of being strange or unusual: *She suddenly realized the oddity of her remark and blushed.*

ˌodd-'job man *noun* (*especially BrE*) a person paid to do odd jobs

ˌodd 'jobs *noun* [pl.] small jobs of various types: *to do odd jobs around the house*

oddly 🔑 /'ɒdli; *NAmE* 'ɑːd-/ *adv.*
1 🔑 in a strange or unusual way **SYN** **strangely**: *She's been behaving very oddly lately.* ◇ *oddly coloured clothes* ◇ *He looked at her in a way she found oddly disturbing.* **2** 🔑 used to show that sth is surprising **SYN** **surprisingly**: *She felt, oddly, that they had been happier when they had no money.* ◇ ***Oddly enough**, the most expensive tickets sold fastest.*

odd·ments /'ɒdmәntz; *NAmE* 'ɑːd-/ *noun* [pl.] (*especially BrE*) **1** small pieces of cloth, wood, etc. that are left after a larger piece has been used to make sth **SYN** **remnants** **2** small items that are not valuable or are not part of a larger set **SYN** **bits and pieces**

odds **AW** /ɒdz; *NAmE* ɑːdz/ *noun* [pl.] **1** (usually **the odds**) the degree to which sth is likely to happen: ***The odds are** very much **in our favour*** (= we are likely to succeed). ◇ ***The odds** are heavily **against him*** (= he is not likely to succeed). ◇ ***The odds are that*** (= it is likely that) *she'll win.* ◇ ***What are the odds*** (= how likely is it) *he won't turn up?* **2** something that makes it seem impossible to do or achieve sth: *They secured a victory in the face of overwhelming odds.* ◇ ***Against all (the) odds**, he made a full recovery.* **3** (in betting) the connection between two numbers that shows how much money sb will receive if they win a bet: *odds of ten to one* (= ten times the amount of money that has been bet by sb will be paid to them if they win) ◇ *They are offering **long/short odds*** (= the prize money will be high/low because there is a high/low risk of losing) *on the defending champion.* ◇ (*figurative*) *I'll **lay odds** on him getting the job* (= I'm sure he will get it).

IDM **be at 'odds (with sth)** to be different from sth, when the two things should be the same **SYN** **conflict**: *These findings are at odds with what is going on in the rest of the country.* **be at 'odds (with sb) (over/on sth)** to disagree with sb about sth: *He's always at odds with his father over politics.* **it makes no 'odds** (*informal, especially BrE*) used to say that sth is not important: *It makes no odds to me whether you go or stay.* **over the 'odds** (*BrE, informal*) more money than you would normally expect: *Many collectors are willing to pay over the odds for early examples of his work.* ➲ more at STACKED

ˌodds and 'ends (*BrE* also **ˌodds and 'sods**) *noun* [pl.] (*informal*) small items that are not valuable or are not part of a larger set: *She spent the day sorting through a box full of odds and ends.* ◇ *I've got a few odds and ends* (= small jobs) *to do before leaving.*

ˌodds-'on *adj.* very likely to happen, win, etc: *the **odds-on favourite*** (= the person, horse, etc. that is most likely to succeed, to win a race, etc.) ◇ ***It's odds-on that** he'll be late.* ◇ *Arazi is odds-on to win the Kentucky Derby.*

ode /әʊd; *NAmE* oʊd/ *noun* a poem that speaks to a person or thing or celebrates a special event: *Keats's 'Ode to a Nightingale'*

odi·ous /'әʊdiәs; *NAmE* 'oʊ-/ *adj.* (*formal*) extremely unpleasant **SYN** **horrible**: *What an odious man!*

odium /'әʊdiәm; *NAmE* 'oʊ-/ *noun* [U] (*formal*) a feeling of hatred that a lot of people have towards sb, because of sth they have done

odom·eter /әʊ'dɒmɪtә(r); *NAmE* oʊ'dɑːm-/ (*NAmE*) (*BrE* **mil·om·eter, mile·ometer**) (also *informal* **the clock** *US, BrE*) *noun* an instrument in a vehicle that measures the number of miles it has travelled ➲ VISUAL VOCAB page V42

odon·tol·ogy /ˌәʊdɒn'tɒlәdʒi; ˌɒd-; *NAmE* ˌoʊdɑːn'tɑːlәdʒi/ *noun* [U] the scientific study of the diseases and structure of teeth ▶ **odon·tolo·gist** /ˌәʊdɒn'tɒlәdʒɪst; ˌɒd-; *NAmE* ˌoʊdɑːn'tɑːlәdʒɪst/ *noun*

odor·ous /'әʊdәrәs; *NAmE* 'oʊ-/ *adj.* (*literary* or *technical*) having a smell: *odorous gases*

odour (*especially US* **odor**) /'әʊdә(r); *NAmE* 'oʊ-/ *noun* [C, U] (*formal*) a smell, especially one that is unpleasant: *a **foul/musty/pungent, etc. odour*** ◇ *the stale odour of cigarette smoke* ◇ (*figurative*) *the odour of suspicion* ➲ see also BODY ODOUR

IDM **be in good/bad 'odour (with sb)** (*formal*) to have/not have sb's approval and support

odour·less (*especially US* **odor·less**) /'әʊdәlәs; *NAmE* 'oʊdәrlәs/ *adj.* without a smell: *an odourless liquid*

odys·sey /'ɒdәsi; *NAmE* 'ɑːd-/ *noun* [sing.] (*literary*) a long journey full of experiences **ORIGIN** From the **Odyssey**, a Greek poem that is said to have been written by Homer, about the adventures of **Odysseus**. After a battle in Troy Odysseus had to spend ten years travelling before he could return home.

OECD /ˌәʊ iː siː 'diː; *NAmE* ˌoʊ/ *abbr.* Organization for Economic Cooperation and Development (an organization of industrial countries that encourages trade and economic growth)

the OED /ˌәʊ iː 'diː; *NAmE* ˌoʊ/ *abbr.* the Oxford English Dictionary (the largest dictionary of the English language, which was first published in Britain in 1928)

oe·dema (*BrE*) (*NAmE* **edema**) /ɪ'diːmә/ *noun* [U] (*medical*) a condition in which liquid collects in the spaces inside the body and makes it swell

Oedi·pal /'iːdɪpl; *US* usually 'ed-/ *adj.* [usually before noun] connected with an Oedipus complex

Oedi·pus com·plex /'iːdɪpәs kɒmpleks; *NAmE* 'iːdɪpәs kɑːm-; *US* usually 'edɪpәs kɑːm-/ *noun* [sing.] (*psychology*) feelings of sexual desire that a boy has for his mother and the jealous feelings towards his father that this causes ➲ compare ELECTRA COMPLEX **ORIGIN** From the Greek story of **Oedipus**, whose father Laius had been told by the oracle that his son would kill him. Laius left Oedipus on a mountain to die, but a shepherd rescued him. Oedipus returned home many years later but did not recognize his parents. He killed his father and married his mother Jocasta.

o'er /ɔː(r)/ *adv., prep.* (*old use*) over

oe·sopha·gus (*BrE*) (*NAmE* **esopha·gus**) /i'sɒfәgәs; *NAmE* i'sɑː-/ *noun* (*pl.* **-pha·guses** or **-ph·agi** /-gaɪ/) (*anatomy*) the tube through which food passes from the mouth to the stomach **SYN** **gullet** ➲ VISUAL VOCAB page V48

oes·tro·gen (*BrE*) (*NAmE* **es·tro·gen**) /'iːstrәdʒәn; *NAmE* 'es-/ *noun* [U] a HORMONE produced in women's OVARIES that causes them to develop the physical and sexual features that are characteristic of females and that causes them to prepare their body to have babies ➲ compare PROGESTERONE, TESTOSTERONE

oes·trus (*BrE*) (*NAmE* **es·trus**) /'iːstrәs; *NAmE* 'estrәs/ *noun* [U] (*technical*) a period of time in which a female animal is ready to have sex

oeuvre /'ɜːvrә/ *noun* [sing.] (from *French, formal*) all the works of a writer, artist, etc: *Picasso's oeuvre*

O

of 0-ᵂ /əv; *strong form* ɒv; *NAmE* ʌv/ *prep.*
1 0-ᵂ belonging to sb; relating to sb: *a friend of mine* ◇ *the love of a mother for her child* ◇ *the role of the teacher* ◇ *Can't you throw out that old bike of Tommy's?* ◇ *the paintings of Monet* HELP When you are talking about everything someone has painted, written, etc, use **of**. When you are referring to one or more examples of somebody's work, use **by**: *a painting by Monet* **2** 0-ᵂ belonging to sth; being part of sth; relating to sth: *the lid of the box* ◇ *the director of the company* ◇ *a member of the team* ◇ *the result of the debate* **3** 0-ᵂ coming from a particular background or living in a place: *a woman of Italian descent* ◇ *the people of Wales* **4** 0-ᵂ concerning or showing sb/sth: *a story of passion* ◇ *a photo of my dog* ◇ *a map of India* **5** 0-ᵂ used to say what sb/sth is, consists of, or contains: *the city of Dublin* ◇ *the issue of housing* ◇ *a crowd of people* ◇ *a glass of milk* **6** 0-ᵂ used with measurements and expressions of time, age, etc.: *2 kilos of potatoes* ◇ *an increase of 2%* ◇ *a girl of 12* ◇ *the fourth of July* ◇ *the year of his birth* ◇ (*old-fashioned*) *We would often have a walk of an evening.* **7** 0-ᵂ used to show sb/sth belongs to a group, often after *some, a few*, etc.: *some of his friends* ◇ *a few of the problems* ◇ *the most famous of all the stars* **8** 0-ᵂ used to show the position of sth/sb in space or time: *just north of Detroit* ◇ *at the time of the revolution* ◇ (*NAmE*) *at a quarter of eleven tonight* (= 10.45 p.m.) **9** 0-ᵂ used after nouns formed from verbs. The noun after 'of' can be either the object or the subject of the action.: *the arrival of the police* (= they arrive) ◇ *criticism of the police* (= they are criticized) ◇ *fear of the dark* ◇ *the howling of the wind* **10** 0-ᵂ used after some verbs before mentioning sb/sth involved in the action: *to deprive sb of sth* ◇ *He was cleared of all blame.* ◇ *Think of a number, any number.* **11** 0-ᵂ used after some adjectives before mentioning sb/sth that a feeling relates to: *to be proud of sth* **12** 0-ᵂ used to give your opinion of sb's behaviour: *It was kind of you to offer.* **13** used when one noun describes a second one: *Where's that idiot of a boy?* (= the boy that you think is stupid)
IDM **of 'all** used before a noun to say that sth is very surprising: *I'm surprised that you of all people should say that.* **of all the...** used to express anger: *Of all the nerve!*

O

off 0-ᵂ /ɒf; *NAmE* ɔːf; ɑːf/ *adv., prep., adj., noun, verb*
■ ***adv.*** HELP For the special uses of **off** in phrasal verbs, look at the entries for the verbs. For example **come off** is in the phrasal verb section at **come**. **1** 0-ᵂ away from a place; at a distance in space or time: *I called him but he ran off.* ◇ *Sarah's off in India somewhere.* ◇ *I must be off soon* (= leave). ◇ *Off you go!* ◇ *Summer's not far off now.* ◇ *A solution is still some way off.* **2** 0-ᵂ used to say that sth has been removed: *He's had his beard shaved off.* ◇ *Take your coat off.* ◇ *Don't leave the toothpaste with the top off.* **3** starting a race: *They're off* (= the race has begun). **4** 0-ᵂ no longer going to happen; cancelled: *The wedding is off.* **5** 0-ᵂ not connected or functioning: *The water is off.* ◇ *Make sure the TV is off.* **6** (*especially BrE*) (of an item on a menu) no longer available or being served: *Sorry, the duck is off.* **7** 0-ᵂ away from work or duty: *She's off today.* ◇ *I've got three days off next week.* ◇ *How many days did you **take off**?* ◇ *I need some **time off**.* **8** 0-ᵂ taken from the price: *shoes with $20 off* ◇ *All shirts have/are 10% off.* **9** behind or at the sides of the stage in a theatre SYN **offstage**
IDM **be well/better/badly, etc. 'off** 0-ᵂ used to say how much money sb has: *Families will be better off under the new law* (= will have more money). ◇ *They are both comfortably off* (= have enough money to be able to buy what they want without worrying too much about the cost). **be better/worse off (doing sth)** 0-ᵂ to be in a better or worse situation: *She's better off without him.* ◇ *The weather was so bad we'd have been better off staying at home.* ◇ *We can't be any worse off than we are already.* **be ˌoff for 'sth** (*informal*) to have a particular amount of sth: *How are we off for coffee* (= how much do we have)? ➲ see also BADLY OFF **ˌoff and 'on/ˌon and 'off** from time to time; now and again: *It rained on and off all day.*
■ ***prep.*** HELP For the special uses of **off** in phrasal verbs, look at the entries for the verbs. For example **take sth off sth** is in the phrasal verb section at **take**. **1** 0-ᵂ down or away from a place or at a distance in space or time: *I fell off the ladder.* ◇ *Keep off the grass!* ◇ *an island off the coast of Spain* ◇ *They were still 100 metres off the summit.* ◇ *Scientists are still a long way off finding a cure.* ◇ *We're getting right off the subject.* **2** 0-ᵂ leading away from sth, for example a road or room: *We live off Main Street.* ◇ *There's a bathroom off the main bedroom.* **3** 0-ᵂ used to say that sth has been removed: *You need to take the top off the bottle first!* ◇ *I want about an inch off the back of my hair.* **4** 0-ᵂ away from work or duty: *He's had ten days off school.* **5** 0-ᵂ away from a price: *They knocked £500 off the car.* **6 off of** (*non-standard* or *NAmE, informal*) off; from: *I got it off of my brother.* **7** not wanting or liking sth that you usually eat or use: *I'm off* (= not drinking) *alcohol for a week.* ◇ *He's finally off drugs* (= he no longer takes them).
■ ***adj.*** [not before noun] **1** (of food) no longer fresh enough to eat or drink: *This fish has gone off.* ◇ *The milk smells off.* ◇ *It's off.* **2 ~ (with sb)** (*informal, especially BrE*) not polite or friendly: *He was a bit off with me this morning.* **3** (*informal, especially BrE*) not acceptable: *It's a bit off expecting us to work on Sunday.*
■ ***noun*** [sing.] **the off** the start of a race: *They're ready for the off.*
■ ***verb* ~ sb** (*informal, especially NAmE*) to kill sb

off- /ɒf; *NAmE* ɔːf; ɑːf/ *prefix* (in nouns, adjectives, verbs and adverbs) not on; away from: *offstage* ◇ *offload*

ˌoff-'air *adj.* (in radio and television) not being broadcast: *off-air recording* OPP **on-air** ▶ **ˌoff-'air** *adv.*: *to record off-air*

offal /'ɒfl; *NAmE* 'ɔːfl; 'ɑːfl/ *noun* [U] (*US* also **va'riety meats** [pl.]) the inside parts of an animal, such as the heart and LIVER, cooked and eaten as food

off·beat /ˌɒf'biːt; *NAmE* ˌɔːf-; ˌɑːf-/ *adj.* [usually before noun] (*informal*) different from what most people expect SYN **unconventional**: *offbeat humour* ◇ *an offbeat approach to interviewing*

ˌoff-'Broadway *adj.* (*NAmE*) **1** (of a theatre) not on Broadway, New York's main theatre district **2** (of a play) unusual in some way and often by a new writer ➲ compare FRINGE THEATRE

ˌoff-'centre (*especially US* **ˌoff-'center**) *adv., adj.* not exactly in the centre of sth

'off chance *noun*
IDM **do sth on the 'off chance** to do sth even though you think that there is only a small possibility of it being successful: *She scanned the crowd on the off chance of seeing someone she knew.* ◇ *I called in at the office on the off chance that you would still be there.*

ˌoff 'colour (*especially US* **ˌoff 'color**) *adj.* **1** [not before noun] (*BrE, informal*) not in good health; looking or feeling ill/sick **2** [usually before noun] (*especially NAmE*) an **off-colour** joke is one that people think is rude, usually because it is about sex

off·cut /'ɒfkʌt; *NAmE* 'ɔːf-; 'ɑːf-/ *noun* (*especially BrE*) a piece of wood, paper, etc. that remains after the main piece has been cut

'off day *noun* (*informal*) a day when you do not do things as well as usual

ˌoff-'duty *adj.* not at work: *an off-duty policeman*

of·fence 0-ᵂ (*especially US* **of·fense**) /ə'fens/ *noun*
1 0-ᵂ [C] **~ (against sb/sth)** an illegal act SYN **crime**: ***a criminal/serious/minor/sexual, etc. offence*** ◇ ***a first offence*** (= the first time that sb has been found guilty of a crime) ◇ ***a capital offence*** (= one for which sb may be punished by death) ◇ *He was not aware that he had **committed an offence**.* ◇ *an **offence against society/humanity/the state*** ◇ *New legislation makes it an offence to carry guns.* **2** 0-ᵂ [U] the act of upsetting or insulting sb: *I'm sure he **meant no offence** when he said that.* ◇ *The photo may **cause offence** to some people.* ◇ *No one will **take offence*** (= feel upset or insulted) *if you leave early.* ◇ *Don't be so quick to **take offence**.*
IDM **no of'fence** (*informal*) used to say that you do not mean to upset or insult sb by sth you say or do: *No offence, but I'd really like to be on my own.*

of·fend 🔑 /əˈfend/ *verb*
1 🔑 [T, often passive, I] **~ (sb)** to make sb feel upset because of sth you say or do that is rude or embarrassing: *They'll be offended if you don't go to their wedding.* ◇ *Neil did not mean to offend anybody with his joke .* ◇ *A TV interviewer must be careful not to offend.* **2** [T] **~ sb/sth** to seem unpleasant to sb: *The smell from the farm offended some people.* ◇ *an ugly building that* ***offends the eye*** **3** [I] (*formal*) to commit a crime or crimes: *He started offending at the age of 16.* **4** [I] **~ (against sb/sth)** (*formal*) to be against what people believe is morally right: *comments that offend against people's religious beliefs* ▸ **of·fend·ed** *adj.*: *Alice looked rather offended.*

of·fend·er /əˈfendə(r)/ *noun* **1** (rather *formal*) a person who commits a crime: *a* ***persistent/serious/violent, etc. offender*** ◇ *a young offender institution* ➲ see also FIRST OFFENDER, SEX OFFENDER **2** a person or thing that does sth wrong: *When it comes to pollution, the chemical industry is a major offender.*

of·fend·ing /əˈfendɪŋ/ *adj.* [only before noun] **1** causing you to feel annoyed or upset; causing problems: *The offending paragraph was deleted.* ◇ *The traffic jam soon cleared once the offending vehicle had been removed.* **2** guilty of a crime: *The offending driver received a large fine.*

of·fense 🔑 *noun* (*NAmE*)
1 🔑 /əˈfens/ [C] = OFFENCE: *to commit an offense* ◇ *The new law makes it a criminal offense to drink alcohol in public places.* ◇ *a minor/serious offense* ◇ *She pleaded guilty to five traffic offenses.* **2** 🔑 /ˈɒfens; *NAmE* ˈɔːf-; ˈɑːf-/ [sing.+ sing./pl. v., U] (*BrE* **at·tack** [sing.]) (*sport*) the members of a team whose main aim is to score points against the other team; a method of attack: *The Redskins' offense is stronger than their defense.* ◇ *He played offense for the Chicago Bulls.* ➲ compare DEFENCE

of·fen·sive 🔑 /əˈfensɪv/ *adj., noun*
▪ ***adj.*** **1** 🔑 rude in a way that causes you to feel upset, insulted or annoyed: *offensive remarks* ◇ *The programme contains language which some viewers may find offensive.* ◇ **~ to sb** *His comments were deeply offensive to a large number of single mothers.* OPP **inoffensive** **2** (*formal*) extremely unpleasant SYN **obnoxious**: *an offensive smell* ➲ SYNONYMS at DISGUSTING **3** [only before noun] connected with the act of attacking sb/sth: *an offensive war* ◇ *offensive action* ◇ *He was charged with carrying an* ***offensive weapon***. ➲ compare DEFENSIVE **4** (*NAmE, sport*) connected with the team that has control of the ball; connected with the act of scoring points: *offensive play* ➲ compare DEFENSIVE ▸ **of·fen·sive·ly** *adv.* **of·fen·sive·ness** *noun* [U]
▪ ***noun*** **1** a military operation in which large numbers of soldiers, etc. attack another country SYN **strike**: *an air offensive* ◇ *They* ***launched the offensive*** *on January 10.* **2** a series of actions aimed at achieving sth in a way that attracts a lot of attention SYN **campaign**: *The government has launched a new offensive against crime.* ◇ *a sales offensive* ◇ *The public seems unconvinced by their latest* ***charm offensive*** (= their attempt to make people like them).
IDM **be on the ofˈfensive** to be attacking sb/sth rather than waiting for them to attack you **go on (to) the ofˈfensive | take the ofˈfensive** to start attacking sb/sth before they start attacking you

offer 🔑 /ˈɒfə(r); *NAmE* ˈɔːf-; ˈɑːf-/ *verb, noun*
▪ ***verb*** **1** 🔑 [T, I] to say that you are willing to do sth for sb or give sth to sb: **~ (sth)** *Josie had offered her services as a guide* ◇ *He offered some useful advice.* ◇ *I don't think they need help, but I think I should offer anyway.* ◇ **~ sth (to sb) (for sth)** *He offered $4 000 for the car.* ◇ *They decided to offer the job to Jo.* ◇ **~ sb sth** *They decided to offer Jo the job.* ◇ *I gratefully took the cup of coffee she offered me.* ◇ *Taylor offered him 500 dollars to do the work.* ◇ **~ to do sth** *The kids offered to do the dishes.* ◇ **+ speech** *'I'll do it,' she offered.* **2** 🔑 [T] **~ sth** to make sth available or to provide the opportunity for sth: *The hotel offers excellent facilities for families.* ◇ *The job didn't offer any prospects for promotion.* ◇ *He did not offer any explanation for his behaviour.* **3** [T] **~ sth/sb (up) (to sb)** (*formal*) to give sth to God: *We offered up our prayers for the men's safe return.*
IDM **have sth to offer** to have sth available that sb wants: *Oxford has a lot to offer visitors in the way of entertainment.* ◇ *a young man with a great deal to offer* (= who is intelligent, has many skills, etc.) **offer your ˈhand** (*formal*) to hold out your hand for sb to shake
▪ ***noun*** **1** 🔑 an act of saying that you are willing to do sth for sb or give sth to sb: **~ (of sth)** *Thank you for your kind offer of help.* ◇ *to* ***accept/refuse/decline an offer*** ◇ *I took him up on his offer of a loan.* ◇ *You can't just turn down offers of work like that.* ◇ *an offer of marriage* ◇ **~ to do sth** *I accepted her offer to pay.* **2** 🔑 **~ (for sth)** an amount of money that sb is willing to pay for sth: *I've had an offer of $2 500 for the car.* ◇ *They've decided to accept our original offer.* ◇ *The offer has been withdrawn.* ◇ *They made me an offer I couldn't refuse.* ◇ *The original price was £3 000, but I'm* ***open to offers*** (= willing to consider offers that are less than that). ➲ see also O.N.O. **3** 🔑 a reduction in the normal price of sth, usually for a short period of time: *This* ***special offer*** *is valid until the end of the month.* ◇ *See next week's issue for details of more* ***free offers***. ◇ *They have an offer on beer at the moment.*
IDM **on ˈoffer 1** that can be bought, used, etc: *The following is a list of courses currently on offer.* ◇ *Prizes worth more than £20 000 are on offer.* **2** (*especially BrE*) on sale at a lower price than normal for a short period of time: *Italian wines are on (special) offer this week.* **under ˈoffer** (*BrE*) if a house or other building is **under offer**, sb has agreed to buy it at a particular price

of·fer·ing /ˈɒfərɪŋ; *NAmE* ˈɔːf-; ˈɑːf-/ *noun* **1** something that is produced for other people to use, watch, enjoy, etc: *the latest offering from the Canadian-born writer* **2** something that is given to a god as part of religious worship ➲ see also BURNT OFFERING, PEACE OFFERING

of·fer·tory /ˈɒfətri; *NAmE* ˈɔːfərtɔːri; ˈɑːf-/ *noun* (*pl.* -ies) **1** the offering of bread and wine to God at a church service **2** an offering or a collection of money during a church service

ˌoff-ˈgrid *adj.* = OFF-THE-GRID

off·hand /ˌɒfˈhænd; *NAmE* ˌɔːf-; ˌɑːf-/ *adj., adv.*
▪ ***adj.*** (*disapproving*) not showing much interest in sb/sth: *an offhand manner* ◇ *He was very offhand with me.* ▸ **off·hand·ed·ly** /ˌɒfˈhændɪdli; *NAmE* ˌɔːf-; ˌɑːf-/ *adv.*: *He spoke offhandedly, making it clear I had no say in the matter.*
▪ ***adv.*** without being able to check sth or think about it: *I don't know offhand how much we made last year.*

of·fice 🔑 /ˈɒfɪs; *NAmE* ˈɔːf-; ˈɑːf-/ *noun*
▸ ROOM/BUILDING **1** 🔑 [C] a room, set of rooms or building where people work, usually sitting at desks: *The company is moving to new offices on the other side of town.* ◇ *Are you going to the office today?* ◇ *an* ***office job*** ◇ ***office workers*** ➲ COLLOCATIONS at JOB ➲ VISUAL VOCAB page V56 ➲ see also BACK OFFICE, HEAD OFFICE **2** 🔑 [C] a room in which a particular person works, usually at a desk: *Some people have to share an office.* ◇ *Come into my office.* **3** [C] (*NAmE*) (*BrE* **sur·gery**) a place where a doctor, dentist or VET sees patients: *a* ***doctor's/dentist's office*** **4** 🔑 [C] (often in compounds) a room or building used for a particular purpose, especially to provide information or a service: *the local tourist office* ◇ *a ticket office* ➲ see also BOX OFFICE, REGISTRY OFFICE
▸ GOVERNMENT DEPARTMENT **5 Office** [C] used in the names of some British government departments: *the Foreign Office* ◇ *the Home Office*
▸ IMPORTANT POSITION **6** 🔑 [U, C] an important position of authority, especially in government; the work and duties connected with this: *She* ***held office*** *as a cabinet minister for ten years.* ◇ *How long has he been* ***in office***? ◇ *The party has been* ***out of office*** (= has not formed a government) *for many years.* ◇ *The present government* ***took office*** *in 2009.* ◇ *to* ***seek/run for office*** ◇ (*BrE*) *to* ***stand for office*** ◇ *the office of treasurer* ➲ COLLOCATIONS at VOTE
IDM **through sb's good ˈoffices** (*formal*) with sb's help

ˈoffice block (*BrE*) (also **ˈoffice building** *NAmE, BrE*) *noun* a large building that contains offices, usually belonging to more than one company ➲ VISUAL VOCAB page V3

O

ˈoffice boy, **ˈoffice girl** *noun* (*old-fashioned*) a young person employed to do simple tasks in an office

ˈoffice-holder (also **ˈoffice-bearer**) *noun* a person who is in a position of authority, especially in the government or a government organization

ˈoffice hours *noun* [pl.] the time when people in offices are normally working: *Our telephone lines are open during normal office hours.*

of·fi·cer /ˈɒfɪsə(r); *NAmE* ˈɔːf-; ˈɑːf-/ *noun* **1** a person who is in a position of authority in the armed forces: ***army/airforce/naval, etc. officers*** ◇ *a* ***commissioned/non-commissioned officer*** ◇ *The matter was passed on to me, as your* ***commanding officer.*** ➲ see also FLYING OFFICER, PETTY OFFICER, PILOT OFFICER, WARRANT OFFICER **2** (often in compounds) a person who is in a position of authority in the government or a large organization: *an environmental health officer* ◇ *a customs/prison/welfare officer* ◇ *officers of state* (= ministers in the government) ➲ see also CHIEF EXECUTIVE OFFICER, MEDICAL OFFICER, PRESS OFFICER, PROBATION OFFICER, RETURNING OFFICER **3** (often used as a form of address) = POLICE OFFICER: *the officer in charge of the case* ◇ *the investigating officer* ◇ *Yes, officer, I saw what happened.* **4** (*NAmE*) a title for a police officer: *Officer Dibble*

ˈoffice worker *noun* a person who works in the offices of a business or company

of·fi·cial /əˈfɪʃl/ *adj., noun*

■ ***adj.*** **1** [only before noun] connected with the job of sb who is in a position of authority: *official responsibilities* ◇ *the Prime Minister's official residence* ◇ *He attended in his official capacity as mayor.* ◇ *This was her first official engagement.* ◇ *He made an official visit to Tokyo in March.* **2** [usually before noun] agreed to, said, done, etc. by sb who is in a position of authority: *an official announcement/decision/statement* ◇ *according to official statistics/figures* ◇ *An official inquiry has been launched into the cause of the accident.* ◇ *The country's official language is Spanish.* ◇ *I intend to lodge an official complaint* (= to complain to sb in authority). ◇ *The news is not yet official.* **3** [only before noun] that is told to the public but may not be true: *I only knew the official version of events.* ◇ *The official story has always been that they are just good friends.* **4** [only before noun] formal and attended by people in authority: *an official function/reception* ◇ *The official opening is planned for October.* OPP **unofficial**

■ ***noun*** (often in compounds) a person who is in a position of authority in a large organization: *a bank/company/court/government official* ◇ *a senior official in the State Department*

of·fi·cial·dom /əˈfɪʃldəm/ *noun* [U] (*disapproving*) people who are in positions of authority in large organizations when they seem to be more interested in following rules than in being helpful

of·fi·cial·ese /əˌfɪʃəˈliːz/ *noun* [U] (*disapproving*) language used in official documents that is thought by many people to be too complicated and difficult to understand

of·fi·cial·ly /əˈfɪʃəli/ *adv.* **1** publicly and by sb who is in a position of authority: *The library will be officially opened by the local MP.* ◇ *We haven't yet been told officially about the closure.* ◇ *The college is not an officially recognized English language school.* **2** according to a particular set of rules, laws, etc: *Many of those living on the streets are not officially homeless.* ◇ *I'm not officially supposed to be here.* **3** according to information that has been told to the public but that may not be true: *Officially, he resigned because of bad health.* OPP **unofficially**

ofˌficial reˈceiver *noun* (*law*) (*BrE*) = RECEIVER

ofˌficial ˈsecret *noun* (in Britain) a piece of information known only to the government and its employees, which it is illegal for them to tell anyone under the Official Secrets Act

the Ofˌficial ˈSecrets Act *noun* (in Britain) a law that prevents people giving information if the government wants it to remain secret

of·fi·ci·ate /əˈfɪʃieɪt/ *verb* **1** [I, T] **~ (at sth)** | **~ sth** to act as an official in charge of sth, especially a sports event: *A referee from a neutral country will officiate (at) the game.* **2** [I] **~ (at sth)** (*formal*) to do the official duties at a public or religious ceremony

of·fi·cious /əˈfɪʃəs/ *adj.* (*disapproving*) too ready to tell people what to do or to use the power you have to give orders SYN **self-important**: *a nasty officious little man* ▸ **of·fi·cious·ly** *adv.*: *'You can't park here,' he said officiously.* **of·fi·cious·ness** *noun* [U]

off·ing /ˈɒfɪŋ; *NAmE* ˈɔːf-; ˈɑːf-/ *noun* IDM **in the offing** (*informal*) likely to appear or happen soon: *I hear there are more staff changes in the offing.*

ˌoff-ˈkey *adj.* **1** (of a voice or a musical instrument) not in tune **2** not suitable or correct in a particular situation SYN **inappropriate**: *Some of his remarks were very off-key.* ▸ **ˌoff-ˈkey** *adv.*: *to sing off-key*

ˈoff-licence (*BrE*) (*US* **ˈliquor store**, **ˈpackage store**) *noun* a shop that sells alcoholic drinks in bottles and cans to take away

ˌoff-ˈlimits *adj.* **1 ~ (to sb)** (of a place) where people are not allowed to go: *The site is off-limits to the general public.* **2** not allowed to be discussed: *The subject was ruled off-limits.*

off·line /ˌɒfˈlaɪn; *NAmE* ˌɔːf-; ˌɑːf-/ *adj.* (*computing*) not directly controlled by or connected to a computer or to the Internet: *For offline orders, call this number.* ▸ **off·line** *adv.*: *How do I write an email offline?* ➲ see also ONLINE

off·load /ˌɒfˈləʊd; *NAmE* ˌɔːfˈloʊd; ˌɑːf-/ *verb* to get rid of sth/sb that you do not need or want by passing it/them to sb else: **~ sth/sb** *They should stop offloading waste from oil tankers into the sea.* ◇ **~ sth/sb on/onto sb** *It's nice to have someone you can offload your problems onto.*

ˌoff-ˈpeak *adj.* [only before noun] happening or used at a time that is less popular or busy, and therefore cheaper: *off-peak electricity/travel* ▸ **ˌoff-ˈpeak** *adv.*: *Phone calls cost 20c per unit off-peak.* ➲ compare PEAK

ˌoff-ˈpiste *adj.* away from the tracks of firm snow that have been prepared for SKIING on: *off-piste skiing* ▸ **ˌoff-ˈpiste** *adv.*: *We enjoy skiing off-piste.*

off·print /ˈɒfprɪnt; *NAmE* ˈɔːf-; ˈɑːf-/ *noun* a separate printed copy of an article that first appeared as part of a newspaper, magazine, etc.

ˈoff-putting *adj.* (*informal, especially BrE*) not pleasant, in a way that prevents you from liking sb/sth: *I find his manner very off-putting.*

ˈoff-ramp *noun* (*NAmE, SAfrE*) a road used for driving off a major road such as an INTERSTATE ➲ compare ON-RAMP

ˈoff-road *adj.* [usually before noun] not on the public road: *an* ***off-road vehicle*** (= one for driving on rough ground)

ˌoff-ˈroader *noun* **1** a vehicle which is driven across rough ground as a sport **2** a person who drives a vehicle across rough ground as a sport ▸ **ˌoff-ˈroading** *noun* [U]

ˌoff-ˈscreen *adj.* [only before noun] in real life, not in a film/movie: *They were off-screen lovers.* ▸ **ˌoff-ˈscreen** *adv.*: *She looks totally different off-screen.* ➲ compare ON-SCREEN

ˈoff season *noun* [sing.] **1** the time of the year that is less busy in business and travel SYN **low season** **2** (*NAmE*) (*BrE* **close season**) (*sport*) the time during the summer when teams do not play important games ▸ **ˌoff-ˈseason** *adj.* [only before noun]: *off-season prices* **ˌoff-ˈseason** *adv.*: *We prefer to travel off-season.*

off·set AW /ˈɒfset; *NAmE* ˈɔːf-; ˈɑːf-/ *verb, adj.*

■ ***verb*** (**off·set·ting, off·set, off·set**) to use one cost, payment or situation in order to cancel or reduce the effect of another: **~ sth** *Prices have risen in order to offset the increased cost of materials.* ◇ **~ sth against sth** (*BrE*) *What expenses can you* ***offset against tax?***

■ ***adj.*** [only before noun] used to describe a method of printing in which ink is put onto a metal plate, then onto a rubber surface and only then onto the paper ➲ see also CARBON OFFSET

off·shoot /ˈɒfʃuːt; NAmE ˈɔːf-; ˈɑːf-/ *noun* **1** a thing that develops from sth, especially a small organization that develops from a larger one **2** (*technical*) a new STEM that grows on a plant

off·shore /ˌɒfˈʃɔː(r); NAmE ˌɔːf-; ˌɑːf-/ *adj.* [usually before noun] **1** happening or existing in the sea, not far from the land: *offshore drilling* ◇ *an offshore island* **2** (of winds) blowing from the land towards the sea: *offshore breezes* **3** (*business*) (of money, companies, etc.) kept or located in a country that has more generous tax laws than other places: *offshore investments* ▸ **off·shore** *adv.*: *a ship anchored offshore* ◇ *profits earned offshore* ➲ compare INSHORE, ONSHORE

off·shor·ing /ˌɒfˈʃɔːrɪŋ; NAmE ˌɔːf-; ˌɑːf-/ *noun* [U] the practice of a company in one country arranging for people in another country to do work for it: *the offshoring of call-centre jobs to India* ▸ **off·shore** *verb* **~ sth**

off·side *adj., noun*

■ ***adj.*** /ˌɒfˈsaɪd; NAmE ˌɔːf-; ˌɑːf-/ **1** (*US* also **off·sides**) in some sports, for example football (SOCCER) and HOCKEY, a player is **offside** if he or she is in a position, usually ahead of the ball, that is not allowed: *He was offside when he scored.* ◇ *the offside rule* OPP **onside** **2** (*BrE*) on the side of a vehicle that is furthest from the edge of the road: *the offside mirror* OPP **nearside**

■ ***noun*** [U] **1** /ˌɒfˈsaɪd; NAmE ˌɔːf-; ˌɑːf-/ (*US* also **off·sides**) the fact of being offside in a game such as football (SOCCER) or HOCKEY: *The goal was disallowed for offside.* **2** /ˈɒfsaɪd; NAmE ˈɔːf-; ˈɑːf-/ (*BrE*) the side of a vehicle that is furthest from the edge of the road: *The offside was damaged.* OPP **nearside**

off·sider /ɒfˈsaɪdə(r); NAmE ɔːf-; ɑːf-/ *noun* (*AustralE, NZE, informal*) a person who works with or helps sb else

off·spring /ˈɒfsprɪŋ; NAmE ˈɔːf-; ˈɑːf-/ *noun* (*pl.* **off·spring**) (*formal* or *humorous*) **1** a child of a particular person or couple: *the problems parents have with their teenage offspring* ◇ *to* ***produce/raise offspring*** **2** the young of an animal or plant

off·stage /ˌɒfˈsteɪdʒ; NAmE ˌɔːf-; ˌɑːf-/ *adj.* **1** not on the stage in a theatre; not where the audience can see: *offstage sound effects* **2** happening to an actor in real life, not on the stage: *The stars were having an offstage relationship.* ▸ **off·stage** *adv.*: *The hero dies offstage.* OPP **onstage**

ˈoff-street *adj.* [usually before noun] not on the public road: *an apartment with* ***off-street parking*** OPP **on-street**

ˌoff-the-ˈcuff ➲ CUFF *n.* HELP You will also find other compounds beginning **off-the-** at the entry for the last word in the compound.

ˌoff-the-ˈgrid (also **ˌoff-ˈgrid**) *adj.* (*especially NAmE*) not using the public supplies of electricity, gas, water, etc: *an off-the-grid house, independent of traditional utility services* ➲ see also GRID

ˌoff-the-ˈshelf *adj.* [only before noun] (of a product) that can be bought immediately and does not have to be specially designed or ordered: *off-the-shelf software packages* ➲ see also SHELF

ˌoff-ˈwhite *adj.* very pale yellowish-white in colour ▸ **ˌoff-ˈwhite** *noun* [U]

ˈoff year *noun* (*US*) a year in which there are no important elections, especially no election for president ▸ **ˈoff-year** *adj.*

OFSTED /ˈɒfsted; NAmE ˈɔːf-/ *abbr.* the Office for Standards in Education (a British government department that is responsible for checking that standards in schools are acceptable)

oft /ɒft; NAmE ɔːft; ɑːft/ *adv.* (*old use*) often

oft- /ɒft; NAmE ɔːft; ɑːft/ *prefix* (in adjectives) often: *an oft-repeated claim*

often 🔑 /ˈɒfn; ˈɒftən; NAmE ˈɔːfn; ˈɔːftən; ˈɑːf-/ *adv.*
1 🔑 many times SYN **frequently**: *We often go there.* ◇ *I've often wondered what happened to him.* ◇ ***How often*** *do you go to the theatre?* ◇ *I see her quite often.* ◇ *Try to exercise as often as possible.* ◇ *We should meet for lunch more often.* ◇ ***It is not often that*** *you get such an opportunity.* **2** 🔑 in many cases SYN **commonly**: *Old houses are often damp.* ◇ *People are often afraid of things they don't understand.* ◇ ***All too often*** *the animals die through neglect.*
IDM **as ˌoften as ˈnot | more ˌoften than ˈnot** usually; in a way that is typical of sb/sth: *As often as not, he's late for work.* **ˌevery so ˈoften** occasionally; sometimes ➲ more at ONCE *adv.*

often·times /ˈɒfntaɪmz; ˈɒftən-; NAmE ˈɔːfn-; ˈɔːftən-; ˈɑːf-/ *adv.* (*old use* or *NAmE*) often

ogham (also **ogam**) /ˈɒgəm; NAmE ˈɑːg-/ *noun* [U] an ancient British and Irish alphabet of twenty characters

ogle /ˈəʊgl; NAmE ˈoʊgl/ *verb* [T, I] **~ (sb)** to look hard at sb in an offensive way, usually showing sexual interest: *He was not in the habit of ogling women.*

ˈO grade (also **ˈordinary grade**) *noun* [C, U] (in Scotland in the past) an exam in a particular subject, at a lower level than HIGHERS, usually taken at the age of 16. In 1988 it was replaced by the STANDARD GRADE.

ogre /ˈəʊgə(r); NAmE ˈoʊ-/ *noun* **1** (in stories) a cruel and frightening giant who eats people **2** a very frightening person: *My boss is a real ogre.*

ogress /ˈəʊgres; NAmE ˈoʊ-/ *noun* a female ogre

oh 🔑 (also especially *literary* **O**) /əʊ; NAmE oʊ/ *exclamation*
1 🔑 used when you are reacting to sth that has been said, especially if you did not know it before: *'I saw Ben yesterday.' 'Oh yes, how is he?'* ◇ *'Emma has a new job.' 'Oh, has she?'* **2** 🔑 used to express surprise, fear, joy, etc.: *Oh, how wonderful!* ◇ *Oh no, I've broken it!* **3** 🔑 used to attract sb's attention: *Oh, Sue! Could you help me a moment?* **4** 🔑 used when you are thinking of what to say next: *I've been in this job for, oh, about six years.*

ohm /əʊm; NAmE oʊm/ *noun* (*physics*) a unit for measuring electrical RESISTANCE

ohm·meter /ˈəʊmmiːtə(r); NAmE ˈoʊm-/ *noun* (*physics*) a device for measuring electrical RESISTANCE

oho /əʊˈhəʊ; NAmE oʊˈhoʊ/ *exclamation* used for showing that you are surprised in a happy way, or that you recognize sb/sth

ˈoh-oh *exclamation* = UH-OH

OHP /ˌəʊ eɪtʃ ˈpiː; NAmE ˌoʊ eɪtʃ ˈpiː/ *noun* the abbreviation for OVERHEAD PROJECTOR: *Will you be using an OHP?*

ˈoh-so *adv.* (*informal*) extremely: *their oh-so ordinary lives*

OHT /ˌəʊ eɪtʃ ˈtiː; NAmE ˌoʊ eɪtʃ ˈtiː/ *noun* the abbreviation for 'overhead transparency' (a transparent plastic sheet that you can write or print sth on and show on a screen using an OVERHEAD PROJECTOR)

oi (also **oy**) /ɔɪ/ *exclamation* (*BrE, informal*) used to attract sb's attention, especially in an angry way: *Oi, you! What do you think you're doing?*

-oid *suffix* (in adjectives and nouns) similar to: *humanoid* ◇ *rhomboid*

oik /ɔɪk/ *noun* (*BrE, slang*) an offensive way of referring to a person that you consider rude or stupid, especially a person of a lower social class

oil 🔑 /ɔɪl/ *noun, verb*

■ ***noun*** **1** 🔑 [U] a thick liquid that is found in rock underground SYN **petroleum**: *drilling for oil* **2** 🔑 [U] a form of PETROLEUM that is used as fuel and to make parts of machines move smoothly: *engine oil* ◇ *an* ***oil lamp/heater*** ◇ *Put some oil in the car.* **3** 🔑 [U, C] a smooth thick liquid that is made from plants or animals and is used in cooking: *olive oil* ◇ *vegetable oils* **4** [U, C] a smooth thick liquid that is made from plants, minerals, etc. and is used on the skin or hair: *lavender bath oil* ◇ *suntan oil* ➲ see also ESSENTIAL OIL **5** [U] (also **oils** [pl.]) coloured paint containing oil used by artists: *a painting done* ***in oils*** ◇ *landscapes in oil* ➲ COLLOCATIONS at ART ➲ see also OIL PAINT **6** [C] = OIL PAINTING: *Among the more important Turner oils was*

O

'Venus and Adonis'. ➲ see also OILY, CASTOR OIL, COD LIVER OIL, LINSEED OIL IDM see BURN v., POUR

■ **verb ~ sth** to put oil onto or into sth, for example a machine, in order to protect it or make it work smoothly: *He oiled his bike and pumped up the tyres.*

IDM **oil the 'wheels** (*BrE*) (*NAmE* **grease the 'wheels**) to help sth to happen easily and without problems, especially in business or politics

'oil-bearing *adj.* [only before noun] producing or containing oil

oil·can /'ɔɪlkæn/ *noun* a metal container for oil, especially one with a long thin SPOUT, used for putting oil onto machine parts

oil·cloth /'ɔɪlklɒθ; *NAmE* -klɔːθ/ *noun* [U] a type of cotton cloth that is covered on one side with a layer of oil so that water cannot pass through it, used especially in the past for covering tables

'oil colour (*especially US* **'oil color**) *noun* [C, U] = OIL PAINT

oiled /ɔɪld/ *adj.* **well ~** (*BrE, informal*) drunk

oil·field /'ɔɪlfiːld/ *noun* an area where oil is found in the ground or under the sea

,oil-'fired *adj.* (of a heating system, etc.) burning oil as fuel

oil·man /'ɔɪlmæn/ *noun* (*pl.* **-men** /-men/) a man who owns an oil company or works in the oil industry

'oil paint (also **'oil colour**) *noun* [C, U] a type of paint that contains oil

'oil painting *noun* **1** (also **oil**) [C] a picture painted in OIL PAINT **2** [U] the art of painting in OIL PAINT

IDM **be no 'oil painting** (*BrE, humorous*) used when you are saying that a person is not attractive to look at

'oil pan *noun* (*NAmE*) = SUMP

'oil rig (also **'oil platform**) *noun* a large structure with equipment for getting oil from under the ground or under the sea ➲ VISUAL VOCAB page V13

,oilseed 'rape *noun* [U] = RAPE (2)

oil·skin /'ɔɪlskɪn/ *noun* **1** [U] a type of cotton cloth that has had oil put on it in a special process so that water cannot pass through it, used for making WATERPROOF clothing **2** [C] a coat or jacket made of oilskin **3 oilskins** [pl.] a set of clothes made of oilskin, worn especially by sailors

'oil slick *noun* = SLICK

'oil tanker *noun* a large ship with containers for carrying oil

'oil well (also **well**) *noun* a hole made in the ground to obtain oil

oily /'ɔɪli/ *adj.* (**oil·ier, oili·est**) **1** containing or covered with oil: *oily fish* ◇ *an oily rag* **2** feeling, tasting, smelling or looking like oil: *an oily substance* **3** (*disapproving*) (of a person or their behaviour) trying to be too polite, in a way that is annoying: *an oily smile* SYN **obsequious** ▸ **oiliness** *noun* [U]

oink /ɔɪŋk/ *exclamation, noun* used to represent the sound a pig makes

oint·ment /'ɔɪntmənt/ *noun* [U, C] a smooth substance that you rub on the skin to heal a wound or sore place SYN **cream**: *antiseptic ointment* IDM see FLY *n.*

OJ /'əʊ dʒeɪ; *NAmE* 'oʊ/ *noun* [U] (*NAmE, informal*) the abbreviation for 'orange juice'

Ojibwa /əʊ'dʒɪbwɑː; *NAmE* oʊ-/ (*pl.* **Ojibwa** or **Ojib·was**) *noun* a member of a Native American people, many of whom live in the US states of Michigan, Wisconsin and Minnesota and in Ontario in Canada

OK 0- (also **okay**) /əʊ'keɪ; *NAmE* oʊ-/ *exclamation, adj., adv., noun, verb*

■ ***exclamation*** (*informal*) **1** 0- yes; all right: *'Shall we go for a walk?' 'OK.'* **2** 0- used to attract sb's attention or to introduce a comment: *Okay, let's go.* **3** 0- used to check that sb agrees with you or understands you: *The meeting's at 2, OK?* ◇ *I'll do it my way, OK?* **4** 0- used to stop people arguing with you or criticizing you: *OK, so I was wrong. I'm sorry.*

■ ***adj., adv.*** (*informal*) **1** 0- safe and well; in a calm or happy state: *Are you OK?* ➲ SYNONYMS at WELL **2** 0- **~ (for sb) (to do sth)** all right; acceptable; in an acceptable way: *Is it OK if I leave now?* ◇ *Is it OK for me to come too?* ◇ *Does my hair look okay?* ◇ *I think I did OK in the exam.* ◇ *Whatever you decide, it's* ***okay by me.*** ◇ *an okay movie*

■ ***noun*** [sing.] (*informal*) permission SYN **go ahead**: *I'm still waiting for the boss to give me the OK.*

■ ***verb*** (**OK's, OK'ing, OK'd, OK'd**) **~ sth** (*informal*) to officially agree to sth or allow it to happen: *She filled in an expenses claim and her manager OK'd it.* SYN **approve**

okapi /əʊ'kɑːpi; *NAmE* oʊ-/ *noun* an African animal that belongs to the same family as the GIRAFFE, but is smaller with a dark body and white lines across its legs

oke /əʊk; *NAmE* oʊk/ (also **ou**) *noun* (*SAfrE, informal*) a man or a boy: *He's quite a big oke.*

okey-doke /ˌəʊki 'dəʊk; *NAmE* ˌoʊki 'doʊk/ (also **okey-dokey** /ˌəʊki 'dəʊki; *NAmE* ˌoʊki 'doʊki/) *exclamation* (*BrE, informal*) used to express agreement SYN **OK**

okra /'əʊkrə; 'ɒkrə; *NAmE* 'oʊkrə/ (also **bhindi**) *noun* [U] (also **ˌladies' 'fingers**) the green seed cases of the okra plant, eaten as a vegetable ➲ VISUAL VOCAB page V27

Synonyms

old

elderly • aged • long-lived • mature

These words all describe sb/sth that has lived for a long time or that usually lives for a long time.

old having lived for a long time; no longer young: *She's getting old—she's 75 next year.*

elderly (*rather formal*) used as a polite word for 'old': *She is very busy caring for two elderly relatives.*

aged (*formal*) very old: *Having aged relatives to stay in your house can be quite stressful.*

long-lived having a long life; lasting for a long time: *Everyone in my family is exceptionally long-lived.*

mature used as a polite or humorous way of saying that sb is no longer young: *clothes for the mature woman*

PATTERNS

- a(n) old/elderly/aged/long-lived/mature **man/woman**
- a(n) old/elderly/aged/mature **gentleman/lady/couple**

old 0- /əʊld; *NAmE* oʊld/ *adj.* (**old·er, old·est**)

▸ AGE **1** 0- **be... years, months, etc. ~** of a particular age: *The baby was only a few hours old.* ◇ *In those days most people left school when they were only fifteen years old.* ◇ *At thirty years old, he was already earning £40 000 a year.* ◇ *two fourteen-year-old boys* ◇ *a class for five-year-olds* (= children who are five) ◇ *I didn't think she was* ***old enough*** *for the responsibility.* ◇ ***How old*** *is this building?* ◇ *He's the oldest player in the team.* ◇ *She's much older than me.*

▸ NOT YOUNG **2** 0- having lived for a long time; no longer young: *to* ***get/grow old*** ◇ *The old man lay propped up on cushions.* ◇ *She was a woman grown* ***old before her time*** (= who looked older than she was). OPP **young 3 the old** *noun* [pl.] old people: *The old feel the cold more than the young.*

▸ NOT NEW **4** 0- having existed or been used for a long time: *old habits* ◇ *He always gives the* ***same old*** *excuses.* ◇ *This carpet's getting pretty old now.* OPP **new 5** 0- [only before noun] former; belonging to past times or a past time in your life: *Things were different in* ***the old days.*** ◇ *I went back to visit my old school.* ◇ *Old and Middle English* **6** 0- [only before noun] used to refer to sth that has been replaced by sth else: *We had more room in our old house.* OPP **new 7** 0- [only before noun] known for a long time: *She's an old friend of mine* (= I have known her for a long time). ◇ *We're old rivals.* ➲ compare RECENT

▸ GOOD OLD/POOR OLD **8** [only before noun] (*informal*) used to show affection or a lack of respect: ***Good old*** *Dad!* ◇ *You* ***poor old*** *thing!* ◇ *I hate her, the silly old cow!*

IDM **'any old how** (*informal*) in a careless or untidy way: *The books were piled up all over the floor any old how.* **'any old...** (*informal*) any item of the type mentioned (used when it is not important which particular item is chosen): *Any old room would have done.* **as old as the 'hills** very old; ancient **for 'old times' sake** if you do sth **for old times' sake**, you do it because it is connected with sth good that happened to you in the past **the 'good/'bad old days** an earlier period of time in your life or in history that is seen as better/worse than the present: *That was in the bad old days of rampant inflation.* **of 'old** (*formal* or *literary*) in or since past times: *in days of old* ◇ *We know him of old* (= we have known him for a long time). **old 'boy, 'chap, 'man, etc.** (*old-fashioned, BrE, informal*) used by older men of the middle and upper classes as a friendly way of addressing another man **old enough to be sb's 'father/'mother** (*disapproving*) very much older than sb (especially used to suggest that a romantic or sexual relationship between the two people is not appropriate) **old enough to know 'better** old enough to behave in a more sensible way than you actually did **(have) an old head on young 'shoulders** used to describe a young person who acts in a more sensible way than you would expect for a person of their age **the (ˌsame) old 'story** what usually happens: *It's the same old story of a badly managed project with inadequate funding.* **an old 'wives' tale** (*disapproving*) an old idea or belief that has been proved not to be scientific **one of the 'old school** an old-fashioned person who likes to do things as they were done in the past ➲ see also OLD SCHOOL ➲ more at CHIP *n.*, FOOL *n.*, GRAND *adj.*, HEAVE-HO, HIGH *adj.*, MONEY, RIPE, SETTLE *v.*, TEACH, TOUGH *adj.*, TRICK *n.*

Which Word?

older / elder

- The usual comparative and superlative forms of **old** are **older** and **oldest**: *My brother is older than me.* ◇ *The palace is the oldest building in the city.* In *BrE* you can also use **elder** and **eldest** when comparing the ages of people, especially members of the same family, although these words are not common in speech now. As adjectives they are only used before a noun and you cannot say 'elder than': *my older/elder sister* ◇ *the elder/older of their two children* ◇ *I'm the eldest/oldest in the family.*

ˌold 'age *noun* [U] the time of your life when you are old: *Old age can bring many problems.* ◇ *He lived alone* ***in his old age.*** ➲ COLLOCATIONS at AGE

ˌold-age 'pension *noun* (*BrE*) a regular income paid by the state to people above a particular age

ˌold-age 'pensioner *noun* (*abbr.* OAP) (*BrE*, becoming *old-fashioned*) a person who receives an old-age pension ➲ see also SENIOR CITIZEN

ˌold age se'curity *noun* [U] (*abbr.* OAS) (*CanE*) a regular income paid by the government to people above the age of 65

the Old Bai·ley /ˌəʊld 'beɪli; *NAmE* ˌoʊld/ *noun* [sing.] the main criminal court in London

ˌold 'bat *noun* (*BrE, informal, disapproving*) a silly or annoying old person

the ˌOld 'Bill *noun* [sing.] (*BrE, informal*) the police

old boy *noun* **1 'old boy** (*BrE*) a man who used to be a student at a particular school, usually a private one **2 ˌold 'boy** (*informal, especially BrE*) an old man: *The old boy next door has died.* ➲ see also OLD GIRL

IDM **the ˌold 'boy network** (*BrE, informal*) the practice of men who went to the same school using their influence to help each other at work or socially

ˌold 'buffer *noun* (*BrE, old-fashioned*) = BUFFER (4)

the 'old country *noun* [sing.] the country where you were born, especially when you have left it to live somewhere else

ˌold 'dear *noun* (*BrE, informal*) an old woman

olde /əʊld; 'əʊldi; *NAmE* oʊld; 'oʊldi/ *adj.* [only before noun] (*old use*) a way of spelling 'old' that was used in the past and is now sometimes used in names and advertisements to give the impression that sth is traditional: *a pub that tries to recreate the flavour of olde England*

olden /'əʊldən; *NAmE* 'oʊldən/ *adj.* [only before noun] existing a long time ago in the past: *What was life like* ***in the olden days****, Gran?*

ˌOld 'English (also **ˌAnglo-'Saxon**) *noun* [U] the English language before about 1150, which is very different from modern English

ˌOld ˌEnglish 'sheepdog *noun* a very large dog with very long grey and white hair

ˌold-e'stablished *adj.* [only before noun] that has existed for a long time

olde worlde /ˌəʊldi 'wɜːldi; *NAmE* ˌoʊldi 'wɜːrldi/ *adj.* [usually before noun] (*BrE, humorous*) (of a place or its atmosphere) trying deliberately to seem old-fashioned: *the olde worlde atmosphere of the tea room with its log fire*

ˌold-'fashioned 🔑 *adj.* (sometimes *disapproving*) **1** 🔑 not modern; no longer fashionable SYN **dated**: *old-fashioned clothes/styles/methods/equipment* ➲ compare FASHIONABLE **2** 🔑 (of a person) believing in old or traditional ways; having traditional ideas: *My parents are old-fashioned about relationships and marriage.*

ˌold 'flame *noun* a former lover: *She met an old flame at the party.*

old girl *noun* **1 'old girl** (*BrE*) a woman who used to be a student at a particular school, usually a private one **2 ˌold 'girl** (*informal, especially BrE*) an old woman: *The old girl next door has died.*

ˌOld 'Glory *noun* (*NAmE*) a name for the flag of the US

the ˌold 'guard *noun* [sing.+ sing./pl. v.] the original members of a group or an organization, who are often against change

ˌold 'hand *noun* ~ (**at sth/at doing sth**) a person with a lot of experience and skill in a particular activity: *She's an old hand at dealing with the press.*

ˌold 'hat *noun* [U] something that is old-fashioned and no longer interesting: *Today's hits rapidly become old hat.*

oldie /'əʊldi; *NAmE* 'oʊldi/ *noun* (*informal*) an old person or thing ➲ see also GOLDEN OLDIE

old·ish /'əʊldɪʃ; *NAmE* 'oʊldɪʃ/ *adj.* fairly old

ˌold 'lady *noun* (*informal*) a person's wife or mother

ˌold 'lag *noun* (*BrE, informal*) a person who has been in prison many times

ˌold 'maid *noun* (*old-fashioned, disapproving*) a woman who has never married and is now no longer young

ˌold 'man *noun* (*informal*) a person's husband or father

ˌold 'master *noun* **1** a famous painter, especially of the 13th–17th centuries in Europe **2** a picture painted by an old master

ˌOld 'Nick *noun* (*old-fashioned, humorous*) the DEVIL

ˌold 'people's home (*BrE*) (also **re'tirement home** *NAmE, BrE*) *noun* a place where old people live and are cared for

'old school *adj.* old-fashioned or traditional

ˌold school 'tie *noun* (*BrE*) **1** [C] a tie worn by former students of a particular school, especially a private one **2 the old school tie** [sing.] used to refer to the fact of men who went to the same private school using their influence to help each other at work or socially, and to the traditional attitudes they share

ˌold 'stager *noun* (*informal*) a person who has great experience in a particular activity

old·ster /'əʊldstə(r); *NAmE* 'oʊld-/ *noun* (*informal*) an old person

ˈold-style *adj.* [only before noun] typical of past fashions or times: *an old-style dress shop* ◇ *old-style politics*

the ˌOld ˈTestament *noun* [sing.] the first part of the Bible, that tells the history of the Jews, their beliefs and their relationship with God before the birth of Christ ➲ compare THE NEW TESTAMENT

ˈold-time *adj.* [only before noun] typical of the past: *old-time dancing*

ˌold-ˈtimer *noun* **1** a person who has been connected with a club or an organization, or who has lived in a place, for a long time SYN **veteran** **2** (*NAmE*) an old man

ˌold ˈwoman *noun* **1** (*informal, especially BrE*) a person's wife or mother **2** (*BrE, disapproving*) a man who worries too much about things that are not important

the ˌOld ˈWorld *noun* [sing.] Europe, Asia and Africa ➲ compare THE NEW WORLD

ˈold-world *adj.* [only before noun] (*approving*) belonging to past times; not modern: *an old-world hotel with character and charm*

ole /əʊl; *NAmE* oʊl/ *adj.* used in written English to represent how some people say the word 'old': *My ole man used to work there.*

olé /əʊˈleɪ; *NAmE* oʊ-/ *exclamation* (from *Spanish, informal*) used for showing approval or happiness

ole·agin·ous /ˌəʊliˈædʒɪnəs; *NAmE* ˌoʊ-/ *adj.* (*formal*) covered in oil or GREASE or containing a lot of oil or grease

ole·an·der /ˌəʊliˈændə(r); *NAmE* ˌoʊli-/ *noun* [C, U] a Mediterranean bush or tree with white, pink or red flowers and long pointed thick leaves

Ol·es·tra™ /ɒˈlestrə; *NAmE* oʊˈl-/ *noun* [U] a substance which is used instead of fat in some foods

ˈO level (also **ˈordinary level**) *noun* [C, U] (in England and Wales in the past) an exam in a particular subject, at a lower level than A LEVEL, usually taken at the age of 16. In 1988 it was replaced by the GCSE: *O level French* ◇ *She took six subjects at O level.* ◇ *He's got an O level in Russian.* ➲ compare GCSE

ol·fac·tory /ɒlˈfæktəri; *NAmE* ɑːl-; oʊl-/ *adj.* [only before noun] (*technical*) connected with the sense of smell: ***olfactory cells/nerves/organs***

oli·garch /ˈɒlɪɡɑːk; *NAmE* ˈɑːləɡɑːrk/ *noun* **1** a member of an oligarchy **2** an extremely rich and powerful person, especially a Russian who became rich in business after the end of the former Soviet Union

oli·garchy /ˈɒlɪɡɑːki; *NAmE* ˈɑːləɡɑːrki/ *noun* (*pl.* -ies) **1** [U] a form of government in which only a small group of people hold all the power **2** [C+sing./pl. v.] the people who hold power in an oligarchy **3** [C] a country governed by an oligarchy

olive /ˈɒlɪv; *NAmE* ˈɑːlɪv/ *noun, adj.*

▪ ***noun*** **1** [C] a small green or black fruit with a strong taste, used in cooking and for its oil **2** (also **ˈolive tree**) [C] a tree on which olives grow: *olive groves* **3** (also **ˌolive ˈgreen**) [U] a yellowish-green colour

▪ ***adj.*** **1** (also **ˌolive-ˈgreen**) yellowish-green in colour **2** (of skin) yellowish-brown in colour: *an olive complexion*

ˈolive branch *noun* [usually sing.] a symbol of peace; sth you say or do to show that you wish to make peace with sb: *Management is* ***holding out an olive branch*** *to the strikers.*

ˌolive ˈdrab *noun* [U] a dull green colour, used in some military uniforms

ˌolive ˈoil *noun* [U] oil produced from OLIVES, used in cooking and on salad ➲ see also EXTRA VIRGIN

ollie /ˈɒli; *NAmE* ˈɑːli/ *noun* (in SKATEBOARDING) a jump that is done by pushing one foot down hard on the back of the board

ology /ˈɒlədʒi; *NAmE* ˈɑːl-/ *noun* (*pl.* -ies) (*informal, humorous*) a subject of study: *They come here with their ologies knowing nothing about life.*

-ology, -logy *combining form* (in nouns) **1** a subject of study: *sociology* ◇ *genealogy* **2** a characteristic of speech or writing: *phraseology* ◇ *trilogy* ▶ **-ological, -logical** (also **-ologic, -logic**) (in adjectives): *pathological* **-ologist, -logist** (in nouns): *biologist*

Olym·piad /əˈlɪmpiæd/ *noun* **1** an occasion when the modern Olympic games are held: *The 26th Olympiad took place in Atlanta, Georgia.* **2** an international competition in a particular subject, especially a science: *the 14th International Physics Olympiad*

Olym·pian /əˈlɪmpiən/ *adj.* (*formal*) like a god; powerful and impressive

Olym·pic /əˈlɪmpɪk/ *adj.* [only before noun] connected with the Olympic Games: *an Olympic athlete/medallist*

the Oˌlympic ˈGames (also **the Olym·pics**) *noun* [pl.] an international sports festival held every four years in a different country: *the Beijing Olympics, held in 2008*

om·buds·man /ˈɒmbʊdzmən; -mæn; *NAmE* ˈɑːm-/ *noun* (*pl.* -men /-mən; -men/) an official whose job is to examine and report on complaints made by ordinary people about companies, the government or public authorities

omega /ˈəʊmɪɡə; *NAmE* oʊˈmeɡə/ *noun* the last letter of the Greek alphabet (Ω, ω)

ˌOmega-ˈ3 /ˌəʊmɪɡəˈθriː; *NAmE* oʊˌmeɪɡə/ (also **ˌOmega-3 fatty ˈacid**) *noun* any of a group of acids, found mainly in fish oils, that many people think are important for human health

om·elette (*NAmE* also **om·elet**) /ˈɒmlət; *NAmE* ˈɑːm-/ *noun* a hot dish of eggs mixed together and fried, often with cheese, meat, vegetables, etc. added: *a cheese and mushroom omelette*

IDM **you can't make an ˌomelette without breaking ˈeggs** (*saying*) you cannot achieve sth important without causing a few small problems

omen /ˈəʊmən; *NAmE* ˈoʊ-/ *noun* a sign of what is going to happen in the future SYN **portent**: ***a good/bad omen*** ◇ *an* ***omen of death/disaster*** ◇ **~ for sth** *The omens for their future success are not good.*

omi·cron /əʊˈmaɪkrɒn; *NAmE* ˈɑːməkrɑːn/ *noun* the 15th letter of the Greek alphabet (O, o)

om·in·ous /ˈɒmɪnəs; *NAmE* ˈɑːm-/ *adj.* suggesting that sth bad is going to happen in the future SYN **foreboding**: *There were ominous dark clouds gathering overhead.* ◇ *She picked up the phone but there was an ominous silence at the other end.* ▶ **om·in·ous·ly** *adv.*

omis·sion /əˈmɪʃn/ *noun* (*formal*) **1** [U] **~ (from sth)** the act of not including sb/sth or not doing sth; the fact of not being included/done: *Everyone was surprised at her omission from the squad.* ◇ *The play was shortened by the omission of two scenes.* ◇ *sins of omission* (= not doing things that should be done) **2** [C] a thing that has not been included or done: *There were a number of errors and omissions in the article.*

omit /əˈmɪt/ *verb* (-tt-) (*formal*) **1** to not include sth/sb, either deliberately or because you have forgotten it/them SYN **leave out**: **~ sth/sb** *If you are a student, you can omit questions 16–18.* ◇ **~ sth/sb from sth** *People were surprised that Smith was omitted from the team.* **2 ~ to do sth** to not do or fail to do sth: *She omitted to mention that they were staying the night.*

omni- /ˈɒmnɪ-; *NAmE* ˈɑːm-/ *combining form* (in nouns, adjectives and adverbs) of all things; in all ways or places: *omnivore* ◇ *omnipresent*

omni·bus /ˈɒmnɪbəs; *NAmE* ˈɑːm-/ *noun, adj.*

▪ ***noun*** **1** (*BrE*) a television or radio programme that combines several recent programmes in a series: *the 90-minute Sunday omnibus edition* **2** a large book that contains a number of books, for example novels by the same author **3** (*old-fashioned*) a bus

▪ ***adj.*** (*NAmE*) including many things or different types of thing: *an omnibus law*

omni·dir·ec·tion·al /ˌɒmnɪdəˈrekʃənl; -dɪˈr-; -daɪˈr-; *NAmE* ˌɑːmnɪ-/ *adj.* (*technical*) receiving or sending signals in all directions: *an omnidirectional microphone*

om·nipo·tent /ɒmˈnɪpətənt; *NAmE* ɑːm-/ *adj.* (*formal*) having total power; able to do anything: *an omnipotent God* ▶ **om·nipo·tence** /-təns/ *noun* [U]: *the omnipotence of God*

omni·pres·ent /ˌɒmnɪˈpreznt; *NAmE* ˌɑːm-/ *adj.* (*formal*) present everywhere: *These days the media are omnipresent.* ▶ **omni·pres·ence** /ˌɒmnɪˈprezns; *NAmE* ˌɑːm-/ *noun* [U]

om·nis·ci·ent /ɒmˈnɪsiənt; *NAmE* ɑːm-/ *adj.* (*formal*) knowing everything: *The novel has an omniscient narrator.* ▶ **om·nis·ci·ence** /-siəns/ *noun* [U]

omni·vore /ˈɒmnɪvɔː(r); *NAmE* ˈɑːm-/ *noun* an animal or a person that eats all types of food, especially both plants and meat ⇨ compare CARNIVORE, HERBIVORE, INSECTIVORE

om·niv·or·ous /ɒmˈnɪvərəs; *NAmE* ɑːm-/ *adj.* **1** (*technical*) eating all types of food, especially both plants and meat ⇨ compare CARNIVOROUS, HERBIVOROUS **2** (*formal*) having wide interests in a particular area or activity: *She has always been an omnivorous reader.*

on 🔑 /ɒn; *NAmE* ɑːn; ɔːn/ *prep., adv.*

■ ***prep.*** HELP For the special uses of **on** in phrasal verbs, look at the entries for the verbs. For example **turn on sb** is in the phrasal verb section at **turn**. **1** 🔑 in or into a position covering, touching or forming part of a surface: *a picture on a wall* ◇ *There's a mark on your skirt.* ◇ *the diagram on page 5* ◇ *Put it down on the table.* ◇ *He had been hit on the head.* ◇ *She climbed on to the bed.* HELP This could also be written: *onto the bed* **2** 🔑 supported by sb/sth: *She was standing on one foot.* ◇ *Try lying on your back.* ◇ *Hang your coat on that hook.* **3** 🔑 used to show a means of transport: *He was on the plane from New York.* ◇ *to travel on the bus/tube/coach* ◇ *I came on my bike.* ◇ *a woman on horseback* **4** 🔑 used to show a day or date: *He came on Sunday.* ◇ *We meet on Tuesdays.* ◇ *on May the first/the first of May* ◇ *on the evening of May the first* ◇ *on one occasion* ◇ *on your birthday* **5** 🔑 immediately after sth: *On arriving home I discovered they had gone.* ◇ *Please report to reception on arrival.* ◇ *There was a letter waiting for him on his return.* **6** 🔑 about sth/sb: *a book on South Africa* ◇ *She tested us on irregular verbs.* **7** being carried by sb; in the possession of sb: *Have you got any money on you?* **8** 🔑 used to show that sb belongs to a group or an organization: *to be on the committee/staff/jury/panel* ◇ *Whose side are you on* (= which of two or more different views do you support)? **9** 🔑 eating or drinking sth; using a drug or a medicine regularly: *He lived on a diet of junk food.* ◇ *The doctor put me on antibiotics.* **10** 🔑 used to show direction: *on the left/right* ◇ *He turned his back on us.* **11** 🔑 at or near a place: *a town on the coast* ◇ *a house on the Thames* ◇ *We lived on an estate.* **12** 🔑 used to show the basis or reason for sth: *a story based on fact* ◇ *On their advice I applied for the job.* **13** 🔑 paid for by sth: *to live on a pension/a student grant* ◇ *to be on a low wage* ◇ *You can't feed a family on £50 a week.* ◇ *Drinks are* **on me** (= I am paying). **14** 🔑 by means of sth; using sth: *She played a tune on her guitar.* ◇ *The information is available on the Internet.* ◇ *We spoke on the phone.* ◇ *What's on TV?* ◇ *The programme's on Channel 4.* **15** 🔑 used with some nouns or adjectives to say who or what is affected by sth: *a ban on smoking* ◇ *He's hard on his kids.* ◇ *Go easy on the mayo!* (= do not take / give me too much) **16** compared with sb/sth: *Sales are up on last year.* **17** 🔑 used to describe an activity or a state: *to be on business/holiday/vacation* ◇ *The book is currently on loan.* **18** 🔑 used when giving a telephone number: *You can get me on 020 7946 0887.* ◇ *She's on extension 2401.*

■ ***adv.*** HELP For the special uses of **on** in phrasal verbs, look at the entries for the verbs. For example **get on** is in the phrasal verb section at **get**. **1** 🔑 used to show that sth continues: *He worked on without a break.* ◇ *If you like a good story, read on.* **2** 🔑 used to show that sb/sth moves or is sent forward: *She stopped for a moment, then walked on.* ◇ *Keep straight on for the beach.* ◇ *From then on he never trusted her again.* ◇ *Please send the letter on to my new address.* **3** 🔑 on sb's body; being worn: *Put your coat on.* ◇ *I didn't have my glasses on.* ◇ *What did she have on* (= what was she wearing)? **4** 🔑 covering, touching or forming part of sth: *Make sure the lid is on.* **5** 🔑 connected or operating; being used: *The lights were all on.* ◇ *The TV is always on in their house.* ◇ *We were without electricity for three hours but it's on again now.* **6** 🔑 happening: *There was a war on at the time.* ◇ *What's on at the movies?* ◇ *The band are on* (= performing) *in ten minutes.* **7** 🔑 planned to take place in the future: *The game is still on* (= it has not been cancelled). ◇ *I don't think we've got anything on this weekend.* ◇ *I'm sorry we can't come—we've* **got a lot on**. **8** 🔑 on duty; working: *I'm on now till 8 tomorrow morning.* **9** 🔑 in or into a vehicle: *The bus stopped and four people got on.* ◇ *They hurried on to the plane.* ⇨ see also ONTO

IDM **be ˈon about sth** (*informal*) to talk about sth; to mean sth: *I didn't know what he was on about. It didn't make sense.* **be/go/keep ˈon about sth** (*informal, disapproving*) to talk in a boring or complaining way about sth: *Stop keeping on about it!* **be/go/keep ˈon at sb** (**to do sth**) (*informal, disapproving*) to keep asking or telling sb sth so that they become annoyed or tired: *He was on at me again to lend him money.* **be ˈon for sth** (*informal*) to want to do sth: *Is anyone on for a drink after work?* **it isn't ˈon** (*informal*) used to say that sth is not acceptable **ˌon and ˈon** without stopping; continuously: *She went on and on about her trip.* **what are you, etc. ˈon?** (*informal*) used when you are very surprised at sb's behaviour and are suggesting that they are acting in a similar way to sb using drugs **you're ˈon** (*informal*) used when you are accepting a bet ⇨ more at OFF *adv.*

ˌon-ˈair *adj.* (in radio and television) being broadcast: *She explains how she deals with on-air technical problems.* OPP **off-air** ▶ **ˌon-ˈair** *adv.*

onan·ism /ˈəʊnənɪzəm; *NAmE* ˈoʊ-/ *noun* [U] (*formal*) **1** = MASTURBATION **2** = COITUS INTERRUPTUS

ˌon-ˈboard *adj.* [only before noun] **1** on a ship, aircraft or vehicle: *an on-board motor* **2** (*computing*) relating to, or controlled by, part of the main CIRCUIT BOARD: *a PC with on-board sound*

ˌon-ˈcall [only before noun] (*especially NAmE*) (of a doctor, police officer, etc.) available for work if necessary, especially in an emergency: *on-call doctors* ⇨ see also CALL *n.*

O

once 🔑 /wʌns/ *adv., conj.*

■ ***adv.*** **1** 🔑 on one occasion only; one time: *I've only been there once.* ◇ *He cleans his car* **once a** *week.* ◇ *She only sees her parents* **once every** *six months.* ◇ (*informal*) *He only did it* **the once**. **2** 🔑 at some time in the past: *I once met your mother.* ◇ *He once lived in Zambia.* ◇ *This book was famous once, but nobody reads it today.* **3** used in negative sentences and questions, and after *if* to mean 'ever' or 'at all': *He never once offered to help.* ◇ *If she once decides to do something, you won't change her mind.*

IDM **ˌall at ˈonce 1** 🔑 suddenly: *All at once she lost her temper.* **2** 🔑 all together; at the same time SYN **simultaneously**: *I can't do everything all at once—you'll have to be patient.* **at ˈonce 1** 🔑 immediately; without delay: *Come here at once!* **2** at the same time SYN **simultaneously**: *Don't all speak at once!* ◇ *I can't do two things at once.* (**just**) **for ˈonce** | **just this ˈonce** (*informal*) on this occasion (which is in contrast to what happens usually): *Just for once he arrived on time.* ◇ *Can't you be nice to each other just this once?* **going ˈonce, going ˈtwice, ˈsold** (*especially NAmE*) (*BrE* also **ˌgoing, ˌgoing, ˈgone**) said by an AUCTIONEER to show that an item has been sold **once aˈgain** | **once ˈmore** 🔑 one more time; another time: *Once again the train was late.* ◇ *Let me hear it just once more.* **once a…, always a…** used to say that sb cannot change: *Once an actor, always an actor.* **once and for ˈall** now and for the last time; finally or completely: *We need to settle this once and for all.* **ˌonce ˈbitten, ˌtwice ˈshy** (*saying*) after an unpleasant experience you are careful to avoid sth similar **once in a blue ˈmoon** (*informal*) very rarely (**every**) **ˌonce in a ˈwhile** occasionally **ˌonce or ˈtwice** 🔑 a few times: *I don't know her well, I've only met her once or twice.* **ˌonce too ˈoften** used to say that sb has done sth wrong or stupid again, and this time they will suffer because of it: *You've tried that trick once too often.* **ˌonce upon a ˈtime** used, especially at the beginning of stories, to mean 'a long time in the past': *Once upon a time there was a beautiful princess.*

■ ***conj.*** 0ᵥ as soon as; when: *We didn't know how we would cope once the money had gone.* ◇ *The water is fine once you're in!*

ˈonce-over *noun*

IDM **give sb/sth a/the ˈonce-over** (*informal*) **1** to look at sb/sth quickly to see what they or it are like **2** to clean sth quickly: *She gave the room a quick once-over before the guests arrived.*

on·col·ogy /ɒŋˈkɒlədʒi; *NAmE* ɑnˈkɑːl-/ *noun* [U] the scientific study of and treatment of TUMOURS in the body ▸ **on·colo·gist** /ɒŋˈkɒlədʒɪst; *NAmE* ɑːnˈkɑːl-/ *noun*

on·com·ing /ˈɒnkʌmɪŋ; *NAmE* ˈɑːn-; ˈɔːn-/ *adj.* [only before noun] coming towards you SYN **approaching**: *Always walk facing the oncoming traffic.*

ˈon-deˈmand *adj.* [only before noun] done or happening whenever sb asks: *The new network promises lightning-fast access to on-demand video.* ➲ see also DEMAND *n.*, PRINT ON DEMAND

one 0ᵥ /wʌn/ *number, det., pron.*

■ ***number, det.*** **1** 0ᵥ the number 1: *Do you want one or two?* ◇ *There's only room for one person.* ◇ *One more, please!* ◇ *a one-bedroomed apartment* ◇ *I'll see you at one* (= one o'clock). **2** 0ᵥ used in formal language or for emphasis before *hundred, thousand*, etc, or before a unit of measurement: *It cost one hundred and fifty pounds.* ◇ *He lost by less than one second.* **3** 0ᵥ used for emphasis to mean 'a single' or 'just one': *There's only one thing we can do.* **4** 0ᵥ a person or thing, especially when they are part of a group: *One of my friends lives in Brighton.* ◇ *One place I'd really like to visit is Bali.* **5** 0ᵥ used for emphasis to mean 'the only one' or 'the most important one': *He's the one person I can trust.* ◇ *Her one concern was for the health of her baby.* ◇ *It's the one thing I can't stand about him.* **6** 0ᵥ used when you are talking about a time in the past or the future, without actually saying which one: *I saw her one afternoon last week.* ◇ ***One day*** (= at some time in the future) *you'll understand.* **7** 0ᵥ the same: *They all went off in one direction.* **8** (*informal, especially NAmE*) used for emphasis instead of *a* or *an*: *That was one hell of a game!* ◇ *She's one snappy dresser.* **9** used with a person's name to show that the speaker does not know the person SYN **a certain**: *He worked as an assistant to one Mr Ming.*

IDM **as ˈone** (*formal*) in agreement; all together: *We spoke as one on this matter.* **(be) at ˈone (with sb/sth)** (*formal*) to feel that you completely agree with sb/sth, or that you are part of sth: *a place where you can feel at one with nature* **for ˈone** used to emphasize that a particular person does sth and that you believe other people do too: *I, for one, would prefer to postpone the meeting.* **get sth in ˈone** to understand or guess sth immediately **get one ˈover (on) sb/sth** (*informal*) to get an advantage over sb/sth: *I'm not going to let them get one over on me!* **go one ˈbetter (than sb/sth)** to do sth better than sb else or than you have done before SYN **outdo**: *She did well this year and next year she hopes to go one better.* **in ˈone** used to say that sb/sth has different roles, contains different things or is used for different purposes: *She's a mother and company director in one.* ◇ *It's a public relations office, a press office and a private office* ***all in one.*** ➲ see also ALL-IN-ONE **ˌone after aˈnother/the ˈother** first one person or thing, and then another, and then another, up to any number or amount: *The bills kept coming in, one after another.* **ˌone and ˈall** (*old-fashioned, informal*) everyone: *Happy New Year to one and all!* **ˌone and ˈonly** used to emphasize that sb is famous: *Here he is, the one and only Van Morrison!* **ˌone and the ˈsame** used for emphasis to mean 'the same': *I never realized Ruth Rendell and Barbara Vine were one and the same* (= the same person using two different names). **ˌone by ˈone** 0ᵥ separately and in order: *I went through the items on the list one by one.* **ˌone or ˈtwo** 0ᵥ a few: *We've had one or two problems—nothing serious.* **ˌone ˈup (on sb)** having an advantage over sb **when you've seen, heard, etc. ˈone, you've seen, heard, etc. them ˈall** (*saying*) used to say that all types of the things mentioned are very similar: *I don't like science fiction novels much. When you've read one, you've read them all.* ➲ more at ALL *pron.*, MINORITY, SQUARE *n.*

■ ***pron.*** **1** 0ᵥ used to avoid repeating a noun, when you are referring to sb/sth that has already been mentioned, or that the person you are speaking to knows about: *I'd like an ice cream. Are you having one, too?* ◇ *Our car's always breaking down. But we're getting a new one soon.* ◇ *She was wearing her new dress, the red one.* ◇ *My favourite band? Oh, that's a hard one* (= a hard question). ◇ *What made you choose the one rather than the other?* ◇ (*BrE*) *How about those ones over there?* **2** 0ᵥ used when you are identifying the person or thing you are talking about: *Our house is the one next to the school.* ◇ *The students who are most successful are usually the ones who come to all the classes.* **3** 0ᵥ **~ of** a person or thing belonging to a particular group: *It's a present for one of my children.* ◇ *We think of you as one of the family.* **4** 0ᵥ a person of the type mentioned: *10 o'clock is too late for the* ***little ones.*** ◇ *He ached to be home with his* ***loved ones.*** ◇ **~ to do sth** *She was never one to criticize.* **5** 0ᵥ (*formal*) used to mean 'people in general' or 'I', when the speaker is referring to himself or herself: *One should never criticize if one is not sure of one's facts.* ◇ *One gets the impression that they disapprove.* HELP This use of **one** is very formal and now sounds old-fashioned. It is much more usual to use **you** for 'people in general' and **I** when you are talking about yourself. **6 a ˈone** (*old-fashioned, especially BrE*) a person whose behaviour is amusing or surprising: *Oh, you are a one!* **7 the ~ about sth** the joke: *Have you heard the one about the Englishman, the Irishman and the Scotsman?*

IDM **be (a) one for (doing) sth** to be a person who enjoys sth, or who does sth often or well: *I've never been a great one for fish and chips.*

Grammar Point

one / ones

One/ones is used to avoid repeating a countable noun, but there are some times when you should not use it, especially in formal speech or writing:

- After a possessive (*my, your, Mary's*, etc.), *some, any, both* or a number, unless it is used with an adjective: *'Did you get any postcards?' 'Yes, I bought four nice ones.'* ◇ ~~*I bought four ones.*~~
- It can be left out after superlatives, *this, that, these, those, either, neither, another, which*, etc: *'Here are the designs. Which (one) do you prefer?' 'I think that (one) looks the most original.'*
- *These ones* and *those ones* are not used in *NAmE*, and are unusual in *BrE*: *Do you prefer these designs or those?*
- It is never used to replace uncountable nouns and is unusual with abstract countable nouns: *The Scottish legal system is not the same as the English system*, is better than *...as the English one.*

ˌone aˈnother 0ᵥ *pron.*
one another is used when you are saying that each member of a group does sth to or for the other people in the group: *We all try and help one another.* ◇ *I think we've learned a lot about one another in this session.*

ˌone-armed ˈbandit *noun* = SLOT MACHINE

ˌone-horse ˈtown *noun* (*informal*) a small town with not many interesting things to do or places to go to

ˌone-ˈliner *noun* (*informal*) a short joke or funny remark: *He came out with some good one-liners.*

ˌone-ˈman *adj.* [only before noun] done or controlled by one person only; suitable for one person: *a* ***one-man show/business*** ◇ *a one-man tent* ➲ see also ONE-WOMAN

ˌone-man ˈband *noun* a street musician who plays several instruments at the same time: (*figurative*) *He runs the business as a one-man band* (= one person does everything).

one·ness /ˈwʌnnəs/ *noun* [U] (*formal*) the state of being completely united with sb/sth, or of being in complete agreement with sb: *a sense of oneness with the natural world*

ˌone-night ˈstand *noun* (*informal*) a sexual relationship that lasts for a single night; a person that sb has this relationship with: *I wanted it to be more than a one-night stand.* ◇ *For her I was just a one-night stand.*

ˌone-ˈoff *adj., noun*
■ ***adj.*** (*BrE*) (*NAmE* ˈ**one-shot**) [only before noun] made or happening only once and not regularly: *a one-off payment*
■ ***noun*** (*BrE*) a thing that is made or that happens only once and not regularly: *It was just a one-off; it won't happen again.*

ˌone-on-ˈone *adj.* [usually before noun] (*NAmE*) = ONE-TO-ONE

ˌone-parent ˈfamily (also **ˌlone-parent ˈfamily**) *noun* a family in which the children live with one parent rather than two ➲ see also SINGLE PARENT

ˈone-piece *adj.* [only before noun] (especially of clothes) consisting of one piece, not separate parts: *a one-piece swimsuit*

oner·ous /ˈəʊnərəs; *NAmE* ˈɑːn-; ˈoʊ-/ *adj.* (*formal*) needing great effort; causing trouble or worry SYN **taxing**: *an* ***onerous duty/task/responsibility***

one's /wʌnz/ *det.* the possessive form of *one*: *One tries one's best.*

one·self /wʌnˈself/ *pron.* (*formal*) **1** (the reflexive form of *one*) used as the object of a verb or preposition when 'one' is the subject of the verb or is understood as the subject: *One has to ask oneself what the purpose of the exercise is.* ◇ *One cannot choose freedom for oneself without choosing it for others.* ◇ *It is difficult to make oneself concentrate for long periods.* **2** used to emphasize *one*: *One likes to do it oneself.* HELP **One** and **oneself** are very formal words and now sound old-fashioned. It is much more usual to use **you** and **yourself** for referring to people in general and **I** and **myself** when the speaker is referring to himself or herself.
IDM **be oneˈself** to be in a normal state of body and mind, not influenced by other people: *One needs space to be oneself.* **(all) by oneˈself** **1** alone; without anyone else **2** without help **(all) to oneˈself** not shared with anyone

ˈone-shot (*NAmE*) (*BrE* **ˌone-ˈoff**) *adj.* [only before noun] made or happening only once and not regularly

ˌone-ˈsided *adj.* **1** (*disapproving*) (of an argument, opinion, etc.) showing only one side of the situation; not balanced SYN **biased**: *The press were accused of presenting a very one-sided picture of the issue.* **2** (of a competition or a relationship) involving people who have different abilities; involving one person more than another: *a totally one-sided match* ◇ *a one-sided conversation* (= in which one person talks most of the time)

Onesie™ /ˈwʌnzi/ *noun* (*NAmE*) a piece of clothing for babies that covers the top half of the body and sometimes also the legs. It fastens between the legs. ➲ compare BABYGRO

ˌone-size-fits-ˈall *adj.* [only before noun] designed to be suitable for a wide range of situations or needs: *a one-size-fits-all monetary policy*

ˌone-ˈstar *adj.* [usually before noun] **1** having one star in a system that measures quality. The highest standard is usually represented by four or five stars: *a one-star hotel* **2** (*NAmE*) having the fifth-highest military rank, and wearing uniform which has one star on it: *a one-star general*

ˈone-stop *adj.* in which you can buy or do everything you want in one place: *Our agency is a one-stop shop for all your travel needs.*

ˈone-time *adj.* [only before noun] **1** former: *her one-time best friend, Anna* **2** not to be repeated SYN **one-off**: *a one-time fee of $500*

ˌone-to-ˈone (*especially BrE*) (*NAmE* usually **ˌone-on-ˈone**) *adj.* [usually before noun] **1** between two people only: *a one-to-one meeting* **2** matching sth else in an exact way: *There is no one-to-one correspondence between sounds and letters.* ▸ **ˌone-to-ˈone** *adv.*: *He teaches one-to-one.*

ˌone-track ˈmind *noun* [usually sing.] if sb has a **one-track mind**, they can only think about one subject (often used to refer to sb thinking about sex)

ˌone-trick ˈpony *noun* (becoming *old-fashioned, disapproving*) a performer who is only famous for one song, etc; a person or business that is only good at doing one thing: *This comedian is no one-trick pony.*

one-upmanship /wʌnˈʌpmənʃɪp/ *noun* [U] (*disapproving*) the skill of getting an advantage over other people

ˌone-ˈway *adj.* [usually before noun] **1** moving or allowing movement in only one direction: *one-way traffic* ◇ *a one-way street* ◇ *a one-way valve* **2** (*especially NAmE*) (*BrE* also **sin·gle**) a **one-way** ticket, etc. can be used for travelling to a place but not back again ➲ compare RETURN *n.* (7) **3** operating in only one direction: *Theirs was a one-way relationship* (= one person made all the effort). ◇ *They observed the prisoners through a* ***one-way mirror*** (= a mirror that allows a person standing behind it to see through it).

ˌone-ˈwoman *adj.* [only before noun] done or controlled by one woman only: *a one-woman show*

ˌon-ˈfield *adj.* at or on a sports field: *on-field medical treatment*

on·going AW /ˈɒngəʊɪŋ; *NAmE* ˈɑːngoʊ-; ˈɔːn-/ *adj.* [usually before noun] continuing to exist or develop: *an ongoing debate/discussion/process* ◇ *The police investigation is ongoing.*

onion 0-w /ˈʌnjən/ *noun* [C, U]
a round vegetable with many layers inside each other and a brown, red or white skin. Onions have a strong smell and flavour: *Chop the onions finely.* ◇ *French onion soup* ➲ VISUAL VOCAB page V27

ˌonion-skin ˈpaper *noun* [U] very thin smooth writing paper

on·line /ˌɒnˈlaɪn; *NAmE* ˌɑːn-; ˌɔːn-/ *adj.* controlled by or connected to a computer or to the Internet: *Online shopping is both cheap and convenient.* ◇ *an online database* ▸ **on·line** *adv.*: *The majority of small businesses now do their banking online.* ➲ COLLOCATIONS at EMAIL ➲ see also BE, COME, ETC. ON LINE at LINE *n.*

on·look·er /ˈɒnlʊkə(r); *NAmE* ˈɑːn-; ˈɔːn-/ *noun* a person who watches sth that is happening but is not involved in it SYN **bystander**: *A crowd of onlookers gathered at the scene of the crash.* ➲ SYNONYMS at WITNESS

only 0-w /ˈəʊnli; *NAmE* ˈoʊnli/ *adj., adv., conj.*
■ ***adj.*** [only before noun] **1** 0-w used to say that no other or others of the same group exist or are there: *She's their only daughter.* ◇ *We were the only people there.* ◇ *His only answer was a grunt.* **2** 0-w used to say that sb/sth is the best and you would not choose any other: *She's the only person for the job.*
IDM **the only thing ˈis...** 0-w (*informal*) used before mentioning a worry or problem you have with sth: *I'd love to come—the only thing is I might be late.* ➲ more at NAME *n.*, ONE *det.*
■ ***adv.*** **1** 0-w nobody or nothing except: *There are only a limited number of tickets available.* ◇ *The bar is for* ***members only.*** ◇ ***You only have to*** *look at her to see she doesn't eat enough.* ◇ *Only five people turned up.* **2** 0-w in no other situation, place, etc: *I agreed, but only because I was frightened.* ◇ *Children are admitted only if accompanied by an adult.* HELP In formal written English **only**, or **only if** and its clause, can be placed first in the sentence. In the second part of the sentence, **be, do, have**, etc. come before the subject and the main part of the verb: ***Only*** *in Paris* ***do*** *you find bars like this.* ◇ ***Only if*** *these conditions are fulfilled* ***can*** *the application proceed to the next stage.* **3** 0-w no more important, interesting, serious, etc. than: *It was only a suggestion.* ◇ *Don't blame me, I'm only the messenger!* ◇ *He was only teasing you.* **4** 0-w no more than; no longer than: *She's only 21 and she runs her own business.* ◇ *It only took a few seconds.* ◇ *It took only a few seconds.* **5** 0-w not until: *We only*

O

got here yesterday. ◇ (*formal*) ***Only then did** she realize the stress he was under.* HELP When **only** begins a sentence **be, do, have**, etc. come before the subject and the main part of the verb. **6** 0-w used to say that sb can do no more than what is mentioned, although this is probably not enough: *We can only guess what happened.* ◇ *He could only watch helplessly as the car plunged into the ravine.* ◇ *I **only hope** that she never finds out.* **7** 0-w used to say that sth will have a bad effect: *If you do that, it will only make matters worse.* ◇ *Trying to reason with him only enrages him even more.* **8 ~ to do sth** used to mention sth that happens immediately afterwards, especially sth that causes surprise, disappointment, etc.: *She turned up the driveway, only to find her way blocked.*

IDM **not only... but (also)...** 0-w both... and...: *He not only read the book, but also remembered what he had read.* ➲ LANGUAGE BANK at ADDITION **only 'just 1** not long ago/before: *We've only just arrived.* **2** almost not: *He only just caught the train.* ◇ *I can afford it, but only just.* **only too ...** very: *I was only too pleased to help.* ◇ *Children can be difficult as we know only too well.* **you're only young 'once** (*saying*) young people should enjoy themselves as much as possible, because they will have to work and worry later in their lives ➲ more at EYE *n.*, IF *conj.*

■ ***conj.*** (*informal*) except that; but: *I'd love to come, only I have to work.* ◇ *It tastes like chicken, only stronger.*

,only 'child *noun* a child who has no brothers or sisters: *I'm an only child.*

o.n.o. *abbr.* (*BrE*) or near/nearest offer (used in small advertisements to show that sth may be sold at a lower price than the price that has been asked): *Guitar £200 o.n.o.* ➲ see also O.B.O.

,on-'off *adj.* [only before noun] **1** (of a switch) having the positions 'on' and 'off': *an on-off switch* **2** (of a relationship) interrupted by periods when the relationship is not continuing

ono·mas·tics /ˌɒnəˈmæstɪks; *NAmE* ˌɑːnə-/ *noun* [U] the study of the history and origin of names, especially names of people

ono·mato·poeia /ˌɒnəˌmætəˈpiːə; *NAmE* ˌɑːn-/ *noun* [U] (*technical*) the fact of words containing sounds similar to the noises they describe, for example *hiss*; the use of words like this in a piece of writing ▸ **ono·mato·poe·ic** /-ˈpiːɪk/ *adj.*: *Bang and pop are onomatopoeic words.*

'on-ramp *noun* (*NAmE, SAfrE*) a road used for driving onto a major road such as an INTERSTATE ➲ compare OFF-RAMP

on·rush /ˈɒnrʌʃ; *NAmE* ˈɑːn-; ˈɔːn-/ *noun* [sing.] a strong movement forward; the sudden development of sth

,on-'screen *adj.* [only before noun] **1** appearing or written on the screen of a computer, television or cinema/movie theater: *on-screen courtroom dramas* ◇ *on-screen messages* **2** connected with the imaginary story of a film/movie and not with real life: *His on-screen father is also his father in real life.* ➲ compare OFF-SCREEN ▸ **,on-'screen** *adv.*

onset /ˈɒnset; *NAmE* ˈɑːn-; ˈɔːn-/ *noun* [sing.] the beginning of sth, especially sth unpleasant: *the onset of disease/old age/winter*

on·shore /ˈɒnʃɔː(r); *NAmE* ˈɑːn-; ˈɔːn-/ *adj.* [usually before noun] **1** on the land rather than at sea: *an onshore oil field* **2** (of wind) blowing from the sea towards the land ▸ **on·shore** *adv.* ➲ compare OFFSHORE

on·side /ˌɒnˈsaɪd; *NAmE* ˌɑːn-; ˌɔːn-/ *adj.* (in football (SOCCER), HOCKEY, etc.) in a position on the field where you are allowed to play the ball ▸ **on·side** *adv.* OPP **offside**

IDM **get/keep sb on'side** (*BrE*) to get/keep sb's support: *The party needs to keep the major national newspapers onside if it's going to win the next election.*

on·slaught /ˈɒnslɔːt; *NAmE* ˈɑːn-; ˈɔːn-/ *noun* [C, usually sing.] a strong or violent attack: **~ (against/on sb/sth)** *the enemy onslaught on our military forces* ◇ **~ (of sth)** *The town survives the onslaught of tourists every summer.* ◇ *an onslaught of abuse*

on·stage /ˌɒnˈsteɪdʒ; *NAmE* ˌɑːn-; ˌɔːn-/ *adj.* on the stage in a theatre; in front of an audience: *onstage fights* ▸ **on·stage** *adv.* OPP **offstage**

,on-'street *adj.* [only before noun] (of parking facilities) located at the side of a public road rather than in a garage, a drive, etc. OPP **off-street**

onto 0-w /ˈɒntə; *before vowels* ˈɒntu; *NAmE* ˈɑːn-; ˈɔːn-/ (also **on to**) *prep.*
1 0-w used with verbs to express movement on or to a particular place or position: *Move the books onto the second shelf.* ◇ *She stepped down from the train onto the platform.* **2** 0-w used to show that sth faces in a particular direction: *The window looked out onto the terrace.*

PHR V **be 'onto sb 1** (*informal*) to know about what sb has done wrong: *She knew the police would be onto them.* **2** to be talking to sb, usually in order to ask or tell them sth: *They've been onto me for ages to get a job.* **be 'onto sth** to know about sth or be in a situation that could lead to a good result for you: *Scientists believe they are onto something big.* ◇ *She's onto a good thing with that new job.*

ontol·ogy /ɒnˈtɒlədʒi; *NAmE* ɑːnˈtɑːl-/ *noun* **1** [U] a branch of philosophy that deals with the nature of existence **2** [C] (*computing*) a list of concepts and categories in a subject area that shows the relationships between them: *a guide to creating a marketing ontology* ▸ **onto·logic·al** /ˌɒntəˈlɒdʒɪkl; *NAmE* ˌɑːntəˈlɑːdʒ-/ *adj.*

onus /ˈəʊnəs; *NAmE* ˈoʊnəs/ *noun* (usually **the onus**) [sing.] (*formal*) the responsibility for sth: *The **onus is on** employers to follow health and safety laws.*

on·ward /ˈɒnwəd; *NAmE* ˈɑːnwərd; ˈɔːn-/ *adj.* [only before noun] (*formal*) continuing or moving forward: *Ticket prices include your flight and onward rail journey.*

on·wards /ˈɒnwədz; *NAmE* ˈɑːnwərdz; ˈɔːn-/ (*especially BrE*) (*NAmE* usually **on·ward** /ˈɒnwəd; *NAmE* ˈɑːnwərd; ˈɔːn-/) *adv.* **1 from... onwards** continuing from a particular time: *They lived there from the 1980s onwards.* ◇ *The pool is open from 7 a.m. onwards.* **2** (*formal*) forward: *We drove onwards towards the coast.*

onyx /ˈɒnɪks; *NAmE* ˈɑːn-/ *noun* [U] a type of stone that has layers of different colours in it, usually used for decorative objects

oo·dles /ˈuːdlz/ *noun* [pl.] **~ (of sth)** (*old-fashioned, informal*) a large amount of sth SYN **loads**

oo-er /ˌuːˈɜː(r)/ *exclamation* (*humorous*) used for expressing surprise, especially about sth sexual

ooh /uː/ *exclamation* used for expressing surprise, happiness or pain

oom·pah /ˈʊmpɑː; ˈuːm-/ (also **'oompah-pah**) *noun* (*informal*) used to refer to the sound produced by a group of BRASS instruments: *an oompah band*

oomph /ʊmf/ *noun* [U] (*informal*) energy; a special good quality: *a styling product to give your hair more oomph*

oops /ʊps; uːps/ *exclamation* **1** used when sb has almost had an accident, broken sth, etc.: *Oops! I almost spilled the wine.* **2** used when you have done sth embarrassing, said sth rude by accident, told a secret, etc.: *Oops, I shouldn't have said that.*

oops-a-daisy /ˈʊpsə deɪzi; ˈʌpsə/ *exclamation* = UPSY-DAISY

ooze /uːz/ *verb, noun*

■ ***verb* 1** [I, T] if a thick liquid **oozes** from a place, or if sth **oozes** a thick liquid, the liquid flows from the place slowly: **~ from/out of/through sth** | **~ out** *Blood oozed out of the wound.* ◇ **~ with sth** *an ugly swelling oozing with pus* ◇ **~ sth** *The wound was oozing blood.* ◇ *a plate of toast oozing butter* **2** [T, I] if sb/sth **oozes** a particular characteristic, quality, etc, they show it strongly SYN **exude**: **~ sth** *She walked into the party oozing confidence.* ◇ **~ with sth** *His voice oozed with sex appeal.*

■ ***noun* 1** [U] very soft mud, especially at the bottom of a lake or river **2** [sing.] the very slow flow of a thick liquid ▸ **oozy** *adj.*

op /ɒp; *NAmE* ɑːp/ *noun* (*BrE, informal*) = OPERATION (1): *I'm going in for my op on Monday.*

Op. (also **op.**) *abbr.* OPUS: *Webern's Five Pieces, Op. 10*

opa·city /əʊˈpæsəti; *NAmE* oʊ-/ *noun* [U] **1** (*technical*) the fact of being difficult to see through; the fact of being OPAQUE **2** (*formal*) the fact of being difficult to understand; the fact of being OPAQUE **OPP transparency**

opal /ˈəʊpl; *NAmE* ˈoʊpl/ *noun* [C, U] a white or almost clear SEMI-PRECIOUS STONE in which changes of colour are seen, used in jewellery: *an opal ring*

opal·es·cent /ˌəʊpəˈlesnt; *NAmE* ˌoʊpə-/ *adj.* (*formal* or *literary*) changing colour like an opal

opaque /əʊˈpeɪk; *NAmE* oʊ-/ *adj.* **1** (of glass, liquid, etc.) not clear enough to see through or allow light through: *opaque glass* ◇ *opaque tights* **2** (of speech or writing) difficult to understand; not clear **SYN impenetrable**: *The jargon in his talk was opaque to me.* **OPP transparent**

ˈ**op art** *noun* [U] a style of modern art that uses patterns and colours in a way that makes the images seem to move as you look at them

op. cit. *abbr.* used in formal writing to refer to a book or an article that has already been mentioned

op·code /ˈɒpkəʊd; *NAmE* ɑːpkoʊd/ *noun* = OPERATION CODE

OPEC /ˈəʊpek; *NAmE* ˈoʊ-/ *abbr.* Organization of Petroleum Exporting Countries (an organization of countries that produce and sell oil)

ˈ**op-ed** (also **op-ˈed page**) *noun* (*NAmE*) the page in a newspaper opposite the EDITORIAL page that contains comment on the news and articles on particular subjects

open 🔑 /ˈəʊpən; *NAmE* ˈoʊ-/ *adj., verb, noun*

■ ***adj.***

▸ NOT CLOSED **1** 🔑 allowing things or people to go through: *A wasp flew in the open window.* ◇ *She had left the door* **wide open**. **OPP closed** **2** 🔑 (of sb's eyes, mouth, etc.) with EYELIDS or lips apart: *She had difficulty keeping her eyes open* (= because she was very tired). ◇ *He was breathing through his open mouth.* **OPP closed** **3** 🔑 spread out; with the edges apart: *The flowers are all open now.* ◇ *The book lay open on the table.* **OPP closed** **4** 🔑 not blocked by anything: *The pass is* **kept open** *all the year.* **OPP closed**

▸ NOT FASTENED **5** 🔑 not fastened or covered, so that things can easily come out or be put in: *Leave the envelope open.* ◇ *The bag burst open and everything fell out.* **6** 🔑 (of clothes) not fastened: *Her coat was open.*

▸ NOT ENCLOSED **7** 🔑 not surrounded by anything; not confined: **open country** (= without forests, buildings, etc.) ◇ *a city with a lot of parks and* **open spaces** ◇ *driving along the* **open road** (= part of a road in the country, where you can drive fast)

▸ NOT COVERED **8** 🔑 with no cover or roof on: *an open drain* ◇ *people working in* **the open air** (= not in a building) ◇ *The hall of the old house was open to the sky.* ◇ *an open wound* (= with no skin covering it) ◇ (*NAmE*) *an open flame* **HELP** In British English this is called a *naked flame*.

▸ FOR CUSTOMERS/VISITORS **9** 🔑 [not usually before noun] if a shop/store, bank, business, etc. is **open**, it is ready for business and will admit customers or visitors: *Is the museum open on Sundays?* ◇ *The new store will be open in the spring.* ◇ *The house had been* **thrown open** *to the public.* ◇ *I declare this festival open.* **OPP closed**

▸ OF COMPETITION/BUILDING **10** if a competition, etc. is **open**, anyone can enter it **SYN public**: *an open debate/championship/scholarship* ◇ *She was tried in* **open court** (= the public could go and listen to the trial). ◇ *The debate was* **thrown open** *to the audience.* **11** 🔑 [not before noun] **~ to sb** if a competition, building, etc. is **open** to particular people, those people can enter it: *The competition is open to young people under the age of 18.* ◇ *The house is not open to the public.* **OPP closed**

▸ AVAILABLE **12** 🔑 [not before noun] **~ (to sb)** to be available and ready to use: *What options are open to us?* ◇ *Is the offer still open?* ◇ *I want to keep my Swiss bank account open.* **OPP closed**

▸ NOT PROTECTED **13** 🔑 **~ (to sth)** likely to suffer sth such as criticism, injury, etc. **SYN vulnerable**: *The system is open to abuse.* ◇ *He has* **laid himself wide open** *to political attack.*

▸ NOT HIDDEN **14** 🔑 known to everyone; not kept hidden: *an open quarrel* ◇ *open government* ◇ *their open display of affection* ◇ *His eyes showed open admiration as he looked at her.*

▸ PERSON'S CHARACTER **15** 🔑 honest; not keeping thoughts and feelings hidden **SYN frank**: *She was always open with her parents.* ◇ *He was quite open about his reasons for leaving.* ➲ SYNONYMS at HONEST **16** 🔑 **~ to sth** (of a person) willing to listen to and think about new ideas: *I'm open to suggestions for what you would like to do in our classes.*

▸ NOT YET DECIDED **17 ~ (to sth)** not yet finally decided or settled: *The race is still* **wide open** (= anyone could win). ◇ *The price is not open to negotiation.* ◇ *Some phrases in the contract are open to interpretation.* ◇ *Which route is better remains* **an open question** (= it is not decided). ◇ *In an interview try to ask* **open questions** (= to which the answer is not just 'yes' or 'no').

▸ CLOTH **18** with wide spaces between the threads: *an open weave*

▸ PHONETICS **19** (also **low**) (of a vowel) produced by opening the mouth wide ➲ compare CLOSE²

IDM be an ˌopen ˈsecret if sth is **an open secret**, many people know about it, although it is supposed to be a secret **have/keep an ˌopen ˈmind (about/on sth)** to be willing to listen to or accept new ideas or suggestions **keep your ˈears/ˈeyes open (for sth)** to be quick to notice or hear things **an ˌopen ˈbook** if you describe sb or their life as **an open book**, you mean that you can easily understand them and know everything about them **an ˌopen inviˈtation (to sb) 1** an invitation to sb to visit you at any time **2** if sth is **an open invitation** to criminals, etc, it encourages them to commit a crime by making it easier: *Leaving your camera on the seat in the car is an open invitation to thieves.* **with ˌopen ˈarms** if you welcome sb **with open arms**, you are extremely happy and pleased to see them ➲ more at BURST *v.*, DOOR, EYE *n.*, MARKET *n.*, OPTION

■ ***verb***

▸ DOOR/WINDOW/LID **1** 🔑 [T] **~ sth** to move a door, window, lid, etc. so that it is no longer closed: *Mr Chen opened the car door for his wife.* **OPP close** **2** 🔑 [I] to move or be moved so that it is no longer closed: *The door opened and Alan walked in.* **OPP close**

▸ CONTAINER/PACKAGE **3** 🔑 [T] **~ sth** to remove the lid, undo the FASTENING, etc. of a container, etc. in order to see or get what is inside: *Shall I open another bottle?* ◇ *He opened the letter and read it.*

▸ EYES **4** 🔑 [T, I] **~ (sth)** if you **open** your eyes or your eyes **open**, you move your EYELIDS upwards so that you can see **OPP close**

▸ MOUTH **5** 🔑 [T, I] **~ (sth)** if you **open** your mouth or your mouth **opens**, you move your lips, for example in order to speak: *He hardly ever opens his mouth* (= speaks).

▸ BOOK **6** 🔑 [T] **~ sth** to turn the cover or the pages of a book so that it is no longer closed: *Open your books at page 25.* **OPP close**

▸ SPREAD OUT **7** 🔑 [I, T] to spread out or UNFOLD; to spread sth out or UNFOLD it: *What if the parachute doesn't open?* ◇ *The flowers are starting to open.* ◇ **~ sth** *Open the map on the table.* ◇ *He opened his arms wide to embrace her.*

▸ BORDER/ROAD **8** 🔑 [T] **~ sth** to make it possible for people, cars, goods, etc. to pass through a place: *When did the country open its borders?* ◇ *The road will be opened again in a few hours after police have cleared it.* **OPP close**

▸ FOR CUSTOMERS/VISITORS **9** 🔑 [I, T] (of a shop/store, business, etc.) to start business for the day; to start business for the first time: *What time does the bank open?* ◇ **~ sth** *The company* **opened its doors** *for business a month ago.* **OPP close** **10** 🔑 [I] to be ready for people to go to: *The new hospital opens on July 1st.* ◇ *When does the play open?* **OPP close**

▸ START STH **11** 🔑 [T] to start an activity or event: **~ sth** *You need just one pound to* **open a bank account** *with us.* ◇ *The police have opened an investigation into the death.* ◇ *Troops*

O

opened fire on (= started shooting) *the crowds.* ◇ **~ sth with sth** *They will open the new season with a performance of 'Carmen'.* ➲ SYNONYMS at START **12** [I] **~ (with sth)** (of a story, film/movie, etc.) to start in a particular way: *The story opens with a murder.*

▸ WITH CEREMONY **13** [T] **~ sth** to perform a ceremony showing that a building can start being used: *The bridge was opened by the Queen.*

▸ COMPUTING **14** [T, I] **~ (sth)** to start a computer program or file so that you can use it on the screen

IDM **open 'doors for sb** to provide opportunities for sb to do sth and be successful **open your/sb's 'eyes (to sth)** to realize or make sb realize the truth about sth: *Travelling really opens your eyes to other cultures.* **open your/sb's mind to sth** to become or make sb aware of new ideas or experiences **open the way for sb/sth (to do sth)** to make it possible for sb to do sth or for sth to happen ➲ more at HEART, HEAVEN

PHR V **'open into/onto sth** to lead to another room, area or place **,open 'out** to become bigger or wider: *The street opened out into a small square.* **,open 'out (to sb)** (*BrE*) = OPEN UP (TO SB) **,open 'up 1** to begin shooting: *Anti-aircraft guns opened up.* **2** (often used in orders) to open a door, container, etc: *Open up or we'll break the door down!* **,open 'up (to sb)** (*BrE* also **,open 'out (to sb)**) to talk about what you feel and think; to become less shy and more willing to communicate: *It helps to discuss your problems but I find it hard to open up.* **,open sth↔'up | ,open 'up 1** to become or make sth possible, available or able to be reached: *The railway opened up the east of the country.* ◇ *Exciting possibilities were opening up for her in the new job.* **2** to begin business for the day; to start a new business: *I open up the store for the day at around 8.30.* OPP **close up 3** to start a new business: *There's a new Thai restaurant opening up in town.* OPP **close down 4** to develop or start to happen or exist; to develop or start sth: *A division has opened up between the two ministers over the issue.* ◇ *Scott opened up a 3-point lead in the first game.* **5** to appear and become wider; to make sth wider when it is narrow or closed: *The wound opened up and started bleeding.* ◇ *The operation will open up the blocked passages around his heart.* OPP **close up ,open sth↔'up** to make sth open that is shut, locked, etc: *She laid the book flat and opened it up.*

■ ***noun* the open** [sing.]

▸ OUTDOORS **1** outdoors; the countryside: *Children need to play out **in the open**.*

▸ NOT HIDDEN **2** not hidden or secret: *Government officials do not want these comments **in the open**.* ◇ *They intend to **bring** their complaints **out into the open**.*

the ,open 'air *noun* [sing.] a place outside rather than in a building: *He likes to cook in the open air.*

,open-'air *adj.* [only before noun] happening or existing outside rather than inside a building: *an open-air swimming pool*

,open-and-shut 'case *noun* a legal case or other matter that is easy to decide or solve: *The murder was an open-and-shut case.*

,open 'bar *noun* [U, C] an occasion when all the drinks at a party or other event have been paid for by sb else or are included in the ticket price

open·cast /'əʊpənkɑːst; *NAmE* 'oʊpənkæst/ (*BrE*) (*NAmE* **,open-'pit**) *adj.* [usually before noun] in **opencast** mines coal is taken out of the ground near the surface ➲ see also STRIP MINING

'open day (*BrE*) (*NAmE* **,open 'house**) *noun* a day when people can visit a school, an organization, etc. and see the work that is done there

,open 'door *noun, adj.*

■ ***noun*** [sing.] a situation that allows sth to happen, or that allows people to go to a place or get information without restrictions: *The government's policy is **an open door to** disaster.* ◇ *An insecure computer system is an open door to criminals.*

■ ***adj.* ,open-'door** [only before noun] **1** (of a policy, system, principle, etc.) allowing people or goods freedom to come into a country; allowing people to go to a place or get information without restrictions: *the country's **open-door policy** for refugees* **2** a policy within a company or other organization designed to allow people to freely communicate with the people in charge: *We operate an **open-door policy** here, and are always willing to listen to our students' suggestions.*

,open-'ended *adj.* without any limits, aims or dates fixed in advance: *an open-ended discussion* ◇ *The contract is open-ended.*

open·er /'əʊpnə(r); *NAmE* 'oʊ-/ *noun* **1** (usually in compounds) a tool that is used to open things: *a can opener* ◇ *a bottle-opener* ➲ see also EYE-OPENER **2** the first in a series of things such as sports games; the first action in an event, a game, etc: *They won the opener 4–2.* ◇ *Jones scored the opener.* ◇ *a good conversation opener* **3** (in CRICKET) either of the two BATSMEN who start play

IDM **for 'openers** (*informal, especially NAmE*) as a beginning or first part of a process SYN **for starters**

,open-faced 'sandwich (also **,open-face 'sandwich**) *noun* (*NAmE*) a slice of bread with meat, cheese, etc. on top but without a second slice of bread to cover this

,open-'handed *adj.* **1** generous and giving willingly: *an open-handed host* **2** using the flat part of the hand: *an open-handed blow*

,open-'hearted *adj.* kind and friendly

,open-heart 'surgery *noun* [U] a medical operation on the heart, during which the patient's blood is kept flowing by a machine

,open 'house *noun* **1** [U, sing.] a place or a time at which visitors are welcome: *It's always open house at their place.* **2** (*NAmE*) (*BrE* **'open day**) [C] a day when people can visit a school, an organization, etc. and see the work that is done there **3** [C] (*NAmE*) a time when people who are interested in buying a particular house or apartment can look around it

open·ing /'əʊpnɪŋ; *NAmE* 'oʊ-/ *noun, adj.*

■ ***noun* 1** [C] a space or hole that sb/sth can pass through: *We could see the stars through an opening in the roof.* **2** [C, usually sing.] the beginning or first part of sth: *The movie has an exciting opening.* OPP **ending 3** [C, usually sing.] a ceremony to celebrate the start of a public event or the first time a new building, road, etc. is used: *the opening of the Olympic Games* ◇ *the official opening of the new hospital* **4** [C, U] the act or process of making sth open or of becoming open: *the opening of a flower* ◇ *the opening of the new play* ◇ *Late opening of supermarkets is common in Britain now.* OPP **closing 5** [C] a job that is available SYN **vacancy**: *There are several openings in the sales department.* **6** [C] a good opportunity for sb: *Winning the competition was the opening she needed for her career.* **7** [C] part of a piece of clothing that is made to open and close so that it can be put on easily: *The skirt has a side opening.*

■ ***adj.*** [only before noun] first; beginning: *his opening remarks* ◇ *the opening chapter of the book* OPP **closing**

'opening hours *noun* [pl.] the time during which a shop/store, bank, etc. is open for business

,opening 'night *noun* [usually sing.] the first night that, for example, a play is performed or a film/movie is shown to the public

'opening time *noun* [U] (*BrE*) the time when pubs can legally open and begin to serve drinks OPP **closing time**

,opening 'up *noun* [sing.] **1** the process of removing restrictions and making sth such as land or jobs available to more people: *the opening up of new opportunities for women in business* **2** the process of making sth ready for use: *the opening up of a new stretch of highway*

,open-'jaw *adj.* [only before noun] (of a plane ticket or FARE) allowing sb to fly to one place and fly back from another place

,open 'letter *noun* a letter of complaint or protest to an important person or group that is printed in a newspaper so that the public can read it

ˌ**open ˈline** *noun, adj.*
▪ ***noun*** a telephone communication in which conversations can be heard or recorded by others
▪ ***adj.*** ˌ**open-ˈline** [only before noun] relating to a radio or television programme that the public can take part in by telephone: *an open-line radio show*

open·ly 0-ᴛ /ˈəʊpənli; *NAmE* ˈoʊ-/ *adv.* without hiding any feelings, opinions or information: *Can you talk openly about sex with your parents?* ◇ *The men in prison would never cry openly* (= so that other people could see).

ˌ**open ˈmarket** *noun* [sing.] a situation in which companies can trade without restrictions, and prices depend on the amount of goods and the number of people buying them: *to buy/sell/trade* ***on the open market***

ˌ**open ˈmike** *noun* [U] an occasion in a club when anyone can sing, play music or tell jokes: *open-mike night*

ˌ**open-ˈminded** *adj.* willing to listen to, think about or accept different ideas OPP **narrow-minded** ▸ ˌ**open-ˈminded·ness** *noun* [U]

ˌ**open-ˈmouthed** *adj.* with your mouth open because you are surprised or shocked

ˌ**open-ˈnecked** (also ˌ**open-ˈneck**) *adj.* (of a shirt) worn without a tie and with the top button undone

open·ness /ˈəʊpənnəs; *NAmE* ˈoʊ-/ *noun* [U] **1** the quality of being honest and not hiding information or feelings **2** the quality of being able to think about, accept or listen to different ideas or people **3** the quality of not being confined or covered

ˌ**open-ˈpit** (*NAmE*) (*BrE* **open·cast**) *adj.* [usually before noun] in **open-pit** mines coal is taken out of the ground near the surface ➲ see also STRIP MINING

ˌ**open-ˈplan** *adj.* an **open-plan** building or area does not have inside walls dividing it up into rooms: *an open-plan office*

ˌ**open ˈprison** (*BrE*) (*NAmE* ˌ**minimum seˈcurity prison**) *noun* a prison in which prisoners have more freedom than in ordinary prisons

ˌ**open ˈsandwich** *noun* a SANDWICH which is served on a plate with no top piece of bread

ˈ**open season** *noun* [sing.] **1** ~ (**for sth**) the time in the year when it is legal to hunt and kill particular animals or birds, or to catch fish, for sport OPP **close season** **2** ~ **for/on sb/sth** a time when there are no restrictions on criticizing particular groups of people or treating them unfairly: *It seems to be open season on teachers now.*

ˌ**open ˈsesame** *noun* [sing.] an easy way to gain or achieve sth that is usually very difficult to get: *Academic success is not always an open sesame to a well-paid job.* ORIGIN From the fairy tale *Ali Baba and the Forty Thieves*, in which the magic words **open sesame** had to be said to open the cave where the thieves kept their treasure.

ˌ**open ˈslather** *noun* [U] (*AustralE, disapproving*) freedom to act without restrictions or limits: *The changes will give developers open slather.*

ˌ**open-ˈsource** *adj.* (*computing*) used to describe software for which the original SOURCE CODE is made available to anyone

ˈ**open syllable** *noun* (*phonetics*) a syllable which does not end with a consonant, for example *so*

ˌ**open-ˈtoed** *adj.* (of shoes) not covering the toes: *open-toed sandals*

ˌ**open-ˈtop** (also ˌ**open-ˈtopped**) *adj.* (*BrE*) (of a vehicle) having no roof

ˌ**open ˈverdict** *noun* an official decision in a British court stating that the exact cause of a person's death is not known

opera /ˈɒprə; *NAmE* ˈɑːprə/ *noun* **1** [C, U] a dramatic work in which all or most of the words are sung to music; works of this type as an art form or entertainment: *Puccini's operas* ◇ *to go to the opera* ◇ *an opera singer* ◇ ***light/grand opera*** ➲ see also SOAP OPERA **2** [C] a company that performs opera; a building in which operas are performed: *the Vienna State Opera* ▸ **op·er·at·ic** /ˌɒpəˈrætɪk; *NAmE* ˌɑːp-/ *adj.*: *operatic arias/composers*

op·er·able /ˈɒpərəbl; *NAmE* ˈɑːp-/ *adj.* **1** that functions; that can be used: *When will the single currency be operable?* **2** (of a medical condition) that can be treated by an operation OPP **inoperable**

ˈ**opera glasses** *noun* [pl.] small BINOCULARS that people use in a theatre to see the actors or singers on the stage

ˈ**opera house** *noun* a theatre where operas are performed

op·er·and /ˈɒpərænd; *NAmE* ˈɑːp-/ *noun* (*mathematics*) the number on which an operation is to be done

op·er·ate 0-ᴛ /ˈɒpəreɪt; *NAmE* ˈɑːp-/ *verb*
▸ MACHINE **1** 0-ᴛ [I] + **adv./prep.** to work in a particular way SYN **function**: *Most domestic freezers operate at below −18 °C.* ◇ *Solar panels can only operate in sunlight.* ◇ (*figurative*) *Some people can only operate well under pressure.* **2** 0-ᴛ [T] ~ **sth** to use or control a machine or make it work: *What skills are needed to operate this machinery?*
▸ SYSTEM/PROCESS/SERVICE **3** 0-ᴛ [I, T] to be used or working; to use sth or make it work: *A new late-night service is now operating.* ◇ *The regulation operates in favour of married couples.* ◇ ~ **sth** *The airline operates flights to 25 countries.* ◇ *France operates a system of subsidized loans to dairy farmers.*
▸ OF BUSINESS/ORGANIZATION **4** [I] + **adv./prep.** to work in a particular way or from a particular place: *They plan to operate from a new office in Edinburgh.* ◇ *Illegal drinking clubs continue to operate in the city.*
▸ MEDICAL **5** 0-ᴛ [I] to cut open sb's body in order to remove a part that has a disease or to repair a part that is damaged: *The doctors operated last night.* ◇ ~ (**on sb**) (**for sth**) *We will have to operate on his eyes.*
▸ OF SOLDIERS **6** [I] (+ **adv./prep.**) to be involved in military activities in a place: *Troops are operating from bases in the north.*

ˈ**operating system** *noun* a set of programs that controls the way a computer works and runs other programs

ˈ**operating table** *noun* a special table that you lie on to have a medical operation in a hospital: *The patient died* ***on the operating table*** (= during an operation).

ˈ**operating theatre** (also **theatre**) (both *BrE*) (*NAmE* ˈ**operating room**) *noun* a room in a hospital used for medical operations

op·er·ation 0-ᴛ /ˌɒpəˈreɪʃn; *NAmE* ˌɑːp-/ *noun*
▸ MEDICAL **1** 0-ᴛ (also *BrE informal* **op**) [C] the process of cutting open a part of a person's body in order to remove or repair a damaged part: *Will I need to* ***have an operation?*** ◇ *He underwent a three-hour heart operation.* ◇ ~ (**on sb/sth**) (**to do sth**) *an operation on her lung to remove a tumour* ◇ ~ (**on sb/sth**) (**for sth**) *Doctors* ***performed an*** *emergency* ***operation*** *for appendicitis last night.* ➲ COLLOCATIONS at ILL
▸ ORGANIZED ACTIVITY **2** 0-ᴛ [C] an organized activity that involves several people doing different things: *a security operation* ◇ *The police have launched a major operation against drug suppliers.* ◇ *the UN peacekeeping operations*
▸ BUSINESS **3** 0-ᴛ [C, usually pl.] a business or company involving many parts: *a huge multinational operation* **4** 0-ᴛ [C] the activity or work done in an area of business or industry: *the firm's banking operations overseas*
▸ COMPUTER **5** 0-ᴛ [C, U] an act performed by a machine, especially a computer: *The whole operation is performed in less than three seconds.*
▸ MACHINE/SYSTEM **6** 0-ᴛ [U] the way that parts of a machine or a system work; the process of making sth work: *Regular servicing guarantees the smooth operation of the engine.* ◇ *Operation of the device is extremely simple.*
▸ MILITARY ACTIVITY **7** [C, usually pl.] military activity: *He was the officer in charge of operations.*
▸ MATHEMATICS **8** [C] a process in which a number or quantity is changed by adding, multiplying, etc.
IDM **in opeˈration** working, being used or having an effect: *The system has been in operation for six months.* ◇ *Tem-*

O

porary traffic controls are in operation on New Road. **come into ope'ration** to start working; to start having an effect SYN **come into force**: *The new rules come into operation from next week.* **put sth into ope'ration** to make sth start working; to start using sth: *It's time to put our plan into operation.*

op·er·ation·al /ˌɒpəˈreɪʃənl; *NAmE* ˌɑːp-/ *adj.* **1** [usually before noun] connected with the way in which a business, machine, system, etc. works: *operational activities/costs/difficulties* **2** [not usually before noun] ready to be used: *The new airport is now **fully operational**.* **3** [only before noun] connected with a military operation: *operational headquarters* ▶ **op·er·ation·al·ly** *adv.*

ˌoperational ˈresearch (also **ˈoperations research**) *noun* [U] (*technical*) the study of how businesses are organized, in order to make them more efficient

ˌopeˈration code (also **op·code**) *noun* [U, C] (*computing*) an instruction written in MACHINE CODE which relates to a particular task

opeˈrations room *noun* a room from which military or police activities are controlled

op·era·tive /ˈɒpərətɪv; *NAmE* ˈɑːpərətɪv; -reɪt-/ *noun, adj.*

■ ***noun*** **1** (*technical*) a worker, especially one who works with their hands: *a factory operative* ◇ ***skilled/unskilled operatives*** **2** (*especially NAmE*) a person who does secret work, especially for a government organization: *an intelligence operative*

■ ***adj.*** **1** [not usually before noun] ready to be used; in use SYN **functional**: *This law becomes operative immediately.* ◇ *The station will be **fully operative** again in January.* **2** [only before noun] (*medical*) connected with a medical operation: *operative treatment* ➲ see also POST-OPERATIVE

IDM **the operative word** used to emphasize that a particular word or phrase is the most important one in a sentence: *I was in love with her—'was' being the operative word.*

O

op·er·ator /ˈɒpəreɪtə(r); *NAmE* ˈɑːp-/ *noun* **1** (often in compounds) a person who operates equipment or a machine: *a computer/machine operator* **2** (*BrE* also **tel·eph·on·ist**) a person who works on the telephone SWITCHBOARD of a large company or organization, especially at a TELEPHONE EXCHANGE **3** (often in compounds) a person or company that runs a particular business: *a tour operator* ◇ *a bus operator* **4** (*informal*, especially *disapproving*) a person who is skilful at getting what they want, especially when this involves behaving in a dishonest way: *a **smooth/slick/shrewd operator*** **5** (*mathematics*) a symbol or function which represents an operation in mathematics

op·er·etta /ˌɒpəˈretə; *NAmE* ˌɑːpə-/ *noun* a short OPERA, usually with a humorous subject

oph·thal·mic /ɒfˈθælmɪk; *NAmE* ɑːf-/ *adj.* (*medical*) connected with the eye: *ophthalmic surgery*

ophˌthalmic opˈtician *noun* (*BrE*) = OPTICIAN

oph·thal·molo·gist /ˌɒfθælˈmɒlədʒɪst; *NAmE* ˌɑːfθælˈmɑːl-/ *noun* a doctor who studies and treats the diseases of the eye

oph·thal·mol·ogy /ˌɒfθælˈmɒlədʒi; *NAmE* ˌɑːfθælˈmɑːl-/ *noun* [U] the scientific study of the eye and its diseases

opi·ate /ˈəʊpiət; *NAmE* ˈoʊ-/ *noun* (*formal*) a drug derived from OPIUM. Opiates are used in medicine to reduce severe pain.

opine /əʊˈpaɪn; *NAmE* oʊ-/ *verb* **~ that…** (*formal*) to express a particular opinion: *He opined that Prague was the most beautiful city in Europe.*

opin·ion 0‑ᴡ /əˈpɪnjən/ *noun*

1 0‑ᴡ [C] your feelings or thoughts about sb/sth, rather than a fact SYN **view**: **~ (about/of/on sb/sth)** *We were invited to **give our opinions** about how the work should be done.* ◇ *I've recently changed my opinion of her.* ◇ ***Everyone had an opinion** on the subject.* ◇ **~ (that…)** *The chairman **expressed the opinion** that job losses were inevitable.* ◇ *He has very strong political opinions.* ◇ ***In my opinion**, it's a very sound investment.* ◇ (*formal*) *It is our opinion that he should resign.* ◇ *If you want my opinion, I think you'd be crazy not to accept.* ➲ LANGUAGE BANK at ACCORDING TO **2** 0‑ᴡ [U] the beliefs or views of a group of people: *legal/medical/political opinion* (= the beliefs of people working in the legal, etc. profession) ◇ *There is **a difference of opinion*** (= people disagree) *as to the merits of the plan.* ◇ ***Opinion is divided*** (= people disagree) *on the issue.* ◇ *There is a wide body of opinion that supports this proposal.* ◇ *Which is the better is a **matter of opinion*** (= people have different opinions about it). ➲ see also PUBLIC OPINION **3** 0‑ᴡ [C] advice from a professional person: *They called in a psychologist to give an independent opinion.* ◇ *I'd like a **second opinion*** (= advice from another person) *before I make a decision.*

IDM **be of the opinion that…** (*formal*) to believe or think that… **have a good, bad, high, low, etc. opinion of sb/sth** to think that sb/sth is good, bad, etc: *The boss has a very high opinion of her.* ➲ more at CONSIDER

Language Bank

opinion

Giving your personal opinion

- **In my opinion**, everyone should have some understanding of science.
- Everyone should, **in my opinion**, have some understanding of science.
- **It seems to me that** many people in this country have a poor understanding of science.
- This is, **in my view**, the result of a failure of the scientific community to get its message across.
- Another reason why so many people have such a poor understanding of science is, **I believe**, the lack of adequate funding for science in schools.
- Smith argues that science is separate from culture. **My own view is that** science belongs with literature, art, philosophy and religion as an integral part of our culture.
- **In this writer's opinion**, the more the public know about science, the less they will fear and distrust it.

➲ Synonyms at THINK
➲ Language Banks at ACCORDING TO, ARGUE, IMPERSONAL, NEVERTHELESS, PERHAPS

opin·ion·ated /əˈpɪnjəneɪtɪd/ (also **ˌself-oˈpinion·ated**) *adj.* (*disapproving*) having very strong opinions that you are not willing to change

oˈpinion poll *noun* = POLL

opium /ˈəʊpiəm; *NAmE* ˈoʊ-/ *noun* [U] a powerful drug made from the juice of a type of POPPY (= a kind of flower), used in the past in medicines to reduce pain and help people sleep. Some people take opium illegally for pleasure and can become ADDICTED to it.

opos·sum /əˈpɒsəm; *NAmE* əˈpɑːs-/ (*AustralE, NZE* or *NAmE informal* **pos·sum**) *noun* a small American or Australian animal that lives in trees and carries its young in a POUCH (= a pocket of skin on the front of the mother's body)

op·pon·ent 0‑ᴡ /əˈpəʊnənt; *NAmE* əˈpoʊ-/ *noun*

1 0‑ᴡ a person that you are playing or fighting against in a game, competition, argument, etc. SYN **adversary**: *a political opponent* ◇ *a **dangerous/worthy/formidable opponent*** ◇ *The team's opponents are unbeaten so far this season.* **2** 0‑ᴡ **~ (of sth)** a person who is against sth and tries to change or stop it: *opponents of abortion* ◇ *opponents of the regime*

op·por·tune /ˈɒpətjuːn; *NAmE* ˌɑːpərˈtuːn/ *adj.* (*formal*) **1** (of a time) suitable for doing a particular thing, so that it is likely to be successful SYN **favourable**: *The offer could not have come at a more opportune moment.* **2** (of an action or event) done or happening at the right time to be successful: *an opportune remark* OPP **inopportune** ▶ **op·por·tune·ly** *adv.*

op·por·tun·ism /ˌɒpəˈtjuːnɪzəm; *NAmE* ˌɑːpərˈtuː-/ *noun* [U] (*disapproving*) the practice of using situations unfairly to gain advantage for yourself without thinking about how your actions will affect other people

op·por·tun·ist /ˌɒpəˈtjuːnɪst; *NAmE* ˌɑːpərˈtuː-/ (also **op·por·tun·is·tic**) *adj.* [usually before noun] (often *disapproving*) making use of an opportunity, especially to get an advantage for yourself; not done in a planned way: *an opportunist crime* ▸ **op·por·tun·ist** *noun*: *80% of burglaries are committed by casual opportunists.*

op·por·tun·is·tic /ˌɒpətjuːˈnɪstɪk; *NAmE* ˌɑːpərtuːˈn-/ *adj.* **1** (*disapproving*) = OPPORTUNIST **2** [only before noun] (*medical*) harmful to people whose IMMUNE SYSTEM has been made weak by disease or drugs: *an opportunistic infection*

op·por·tun·ity 🔑 /ˌɒpəˈtjuːnəti; *NAmE* ˌɑːpərˈtuː-/ *noun* [C, U] (*pl.* -ies) a time when a particular situation makes it possible to do or achieve sth SYN **chance**: **~ (to do sth)** *You'll have the opportunity to ask any questions at the end.* ◇ **~ (for sth/for doing sth)** *There was no opportunity for further discussion.* ◇ **~ (of doing sth)** *At least give him the opportunity of explaining what happened.* ◇ *Our company promotes* ***equal opportunities*** *for women* (= women are given the same jobs, pay, etc. as men). ◇ ***career/employment/job opportunities*** ◇ *I'd like to* ***take this opportunity*** *to thank my colleagues for their support.* ◇ *He is rude to me* ***at every opportunity*** (= whenever possible). ◇ *They intend to close the school* ***at the earliest opportunity*** (= as soon as possible). ◇ *a* ***window of opportunity*** (= a period of time when the circumstances are right for doing sth) ➲ see also PHOTO OPPORTUNITY

oppor'tunity shop (also **'op shop**) *noun* (*AustralE, NZE*) a shop/store that sells clothes and other goods given by people to raise money for a charity SYN **charity shop, thrift store**

op·pose 🔑 /əˈpəʊz; *NAmE* əˈpoʊz/ *verb* **1** 🔑 to disagree strongly with sb's plan, policy, etc. and try to change it or prevent it from succeeding: **~ sb/sth** *This party would bitterly oppose the re-introduction of the death penalty.* ◇ *He threw all those that opposed him into prison.* ◇ **~ (sb/sth) doing sth** *I would oppose changing the law.* ➲ compare PROPOSE **2 ~ sb** to compete with sb in a contest: *He intends to oppose the prime minister in the leadership election.*

op·posed 🔑 /əˈpəʊzd; *NAmE* əˈpoʊzd/ *adj.* [not usually before noun] **~ (to sth) 1** 🔑 (of a person) disagreeing strongly with sth and trying to stop it: *She remained bitterly opposed to the idea of moving abroad.* ◇ *They are totally opposed to abortion.* **2** 🔑 (of ideas, opinions, etc.) very different from sth: *Our views are* ***diametrically opposed*** *on this issue.*
IDM **as opposed to** 🔑 (*formal*) used to make a contrast between two things: *200 attended, as opposed to 300 the previous year.* ◇ *This exercise develops suppleness as opposed to* (= rather than) *strength.*

op·pos·ing 🔑 /əˈpəʊzɪŋ; *NAmE* əˈpoʊzɪŋ/ *adj.* [only before noun] **1** 🔑 (of teams, armies, forces, etc.) playing, fighting, working, etc. against each other: *a player from the opposing side* ◇ *It is time for opposing factions to unite and work towards a common goal.* **2** 🔑 (of attitudes, views, etc.) very different from each other

op·pos·ite 🔑 /ˈɒpəzɪt; -sɪt; *NAmE* ˈɑːpəzət/ *adj., adv., noun, prep.*
■ ***adj.* 1** 🔑 [only before noun] on the other side of a particular area from sb/sth and usually facing them: *Answers are given on the opposite page.* ◇ *We live further down on the opposite side of the road.* ◇ *It's not easy having a relationship when you live at opposite ends of the country.* **2** 🔑 (used after the noun) facing the speaker or sb/sth that has been mentioned: *I could see smoke coming from the windows of the house directly opposite.* ◇ *He sat down in the chair opposite.* **3** 🔑 [usually before noun] as different as possible from sth: *I watched them leave and then drove off in the opposite direction.* ◇ *She tried calming him down but it seemed to be having the opposite effect.* ◇ *students at opposite ends of the ability range* ▸ **op·pos·ite** 🔑 *adv.*: *There's a newly married couple living opposite* (= on the other side of the road). ◇ *See opposite* (= on the opposite page) *for further details.*
IDM **your ˌopposite 'number** (*informal*) a person who does the same job as you in another organization: *The Foreign Secretary is currently having talks with his opposite number in the White House.* **the ˌopposite 'sex** the other sex: *He found it difficult to talk to members of the opposite sex.* ➲ more at PULL *v.*
■ ***noun*** 🔑 a person or thing that is as different as possible from sb/sth else: *Hot and cold are opposites.* ◇ *What is* ***the opposite of*** *heavy?* ◇ *I thought she would be small and blonde but she's* ***the complete opposite.*** ◇ *Exactly the opposite is true.* ◇ *'Is it better now?'* ***'Quite the opposite,*** *I'm afraid.'*
IDM **ˌopposites at'tract** used to say that people who are very different are often attracted to each other
■ ***prep.* 1** 🔑 on the other side of a particular area from sb/sth, and usually facing them: *I sat opposite him during the meal* (= on the other side of the table). ◇ *The bank is opposite the supermarket* (= on the other side of the road). ◇ *Write your address opposite* (= next to) *your name.* **2** acting in a film/movie or play as the partner of sb: *She starred opposite Tom Hanks.*

op·pos·ition 🔑 /ˌɒpəˈzɪʃn; *NAmE* ˌɑːpə-/ *noun* **1** 🔑 [U] **~ (to sb/sth)** the act of strongly disagreeing with sb/sth, especially with the aim of preventing sth from happening: *Delegates expressed* ***strong opposition*** *to the plans.* ◇ *The army* ***met with fierce opposition*** *in every town.* ◇ *He spent five years in prison for his opposition to the regime.* ◇ ***opposition forces*** (= people who are arguing, fighting, etc. with another group) **2** 🔑 **the opposition** [sing.+ sing./pl. v.] the people you are competing against in business, a competition, a game, etc: *He's gone to work for the opposition.* ◇ *The opposition is/are mounting a strong challenge to our business.* ◇ *Liverpool couldn't match the opposition in the final and lost 2–0.* **3** 🔑 **the Opposition** (*NAmE* **the opposition**) [sing.+ sing./pl. v.] the main political party that is opposed to the government; the political parties that are in a parliament but are not part of the government: *the* ***leader of the Opposition*** ◇ ***Opposition MPs/parties*** ◇ *the Opposition spokesman on education* **4** [U, C] (*formal*) the state of being as different as possible; two things that are as different as possible: *the opposition between good and evil* ◇ *His poetry is full of oppositions and contrasts.* ▸ **op·pos·ition·al** /-ʃənl/ *adj.* [usually before noun]: (*formal*) *oppositional groups/tactics*
IDM **in oppo'sition** (of a political party) forming part of a parliament but not part of the government **in oppo'sition to sb/sth 1** 🔑 disagreeing strongly with sb/sth, especially with the aim of preventing sth from happening: *Protest marches were held in opposition to the proposed law.* **2** contrasting two people or things that are very different: *Leisure is often defined in opposition to work.*

op·press /əˈpres/ *verb* **1 ~ sb** to treat sb in a cruel and unfair way, especially by not giving them the same freedom, rights, etc. as other people: *The regime is accused of oppressing religious minorities.* **2 ~ sb** to make sb only able to think about sad or worrying things: *The gloomy atmosphere in the office oppressed her.* SYN **weigh down** ▸ **op·pres·sion** /əˈpreʃn/ *noun* [U]: *victims of oppression*

op·pressed /əˈprest/ *adj.* **1** treated in a cruel and unfair way and not given the same freedom, rights, etc. as other people: *oppressed minorities* **2 the oppressed** *noun* [pl.] people who are oppressed

op·pres·sive /əˈpresɪv/ *adj.* **1** treating people in a cruel and unfair way and not giving them the same freedom, rights, etc. as other people: *oppressive laws* ◇ *an oppressive regime* **2** (of the weather) extremely hot and unpleasant and lacking fresh air SYN **stifling**: *oppressive heat* **3** making you feel unhappy and anxious SYN **stifling**: *an oppressive relationship* ▸ **op·pres·sive·ly** *adv.*: *to behave oppressively* ◇ *oppressively hot* ◇ *He suffered from an oppressively dominant mother.*

O

op·press·or /əˈpresə(r)/ *noun* a person or group of people that treats sb in a cruel and unfair way, especially by not giving them the same rights, etc. as other people

op·pro·brium /əˈprəʊbriəm; *NAmE* əˈproʊ-/ *noun* [U] (*formal*) severe criticism of a person, country, etc. by a large group of people ▸ **op·pro·bri·ous** /əˈprəʊbriəs; *NAmE* əˈproʊ-/ *adj.*: *an opprobrious remark*

ˈop shop *noun* (*AustralE, NZE*) = OPPORTUNITY SHOP

opt /ɒpt; *NAmE* ɑːpt/ *verb* [I, T] to choose to take or not to take a particular course of action: **~ for/against sth** *After graduating she opted for a career in music.* ◇ **~ to do sth** *Many workers opted to leave their jobs rather than take a pay cut.* ➲ SYNONYMS at CHOOSE
PHR V **ˌopt ˈin (to sth)** to choose to be part of a system or an agreement **ˌopt ˈout (of sth)** **1** to choose not to take part in sth: *Employees may opt out of the company's pension plan.* **2** (of a school or hospital in Britain) to choose not to be under the control of the local authority ➲ related noun OPT-OUT

optic /ˈɒptɪk; *NAmE* ˈɑːp-/ *adj., noun*
- ***adj.*** [usually before noun] (*technical*) connected with the eye or the sense of sight: *the optic nerve* (= from the eye to the brain)
- ***noun*** a device for measuring amounts of strong alcoholic drinks in a bar

op·tic·al /ˈɒptɪkl; *NAmE* ˈɑːp-/ *adj.* [usually before noun] **1** connected with the sense of sight or the relationship between light and sight: *optical effects* **2** used to help you see sth more clearly: *optical aids* ◇ *optical instruments such as microscopes and telescopes* **3** (*computing*) using light for reading or storing information: *optical storage* ◇ *an optical disk* ▸ **op·tic·al·ly** /-kli/ *adv.*

ˌoptical ˈcharacter recognition *noun* [U] (*abbr.* OCR) (*computing*) the process of using light to record printed information onto disks for use in a computer system

ˌoptical ˈfibre (*BrE*) (*NAmE* **ˌoptical ˈfiber**) *noun* [C, U] a thin glass thread through which light can be TRANSMITTED (= sent)

O

ˌoptical ilˈlusion *noun* something that tricks your eyes and makes you think that you can see sth that is not there, or makes you see sth as different from what it really is

optical illusions

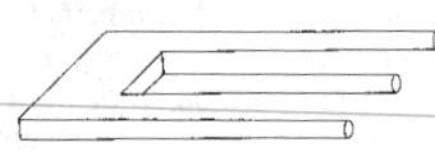

Are there two prongs or three?

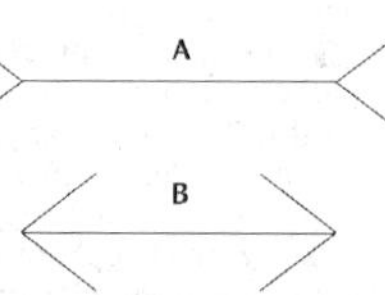

Horizontal line A and horizontal line B are of equal length, but horizontal line A appears to be longer.

op·ti·cian /ɒpˈtɪʃn; *NAmE* ɑːp-/ *noun* **1** (also **oph·ˌthalmic opˈtician**) (both *BrE*) (also **op·tom·etrist** *NAmE, BrE*) a person whose job is to examine people's eyes and to recommend and sell glasses **2** **op·ti·cian's** (*pl.* **op·ti·cians**) the shop/store where an optician works: *to go to the optician's* **3** a person who makes LENSES, glasses, etc.

op·tics /ˈɒptɪks; *NAmE* ˈɑːp-/ *noun* [U] the scientific study of sight and light ➲ see also FIBRE OPTICS

op·ti·mal /ˈɒptɪməl; *NAmE* ˈɑːp-/ *adj.* = OPTIMUM ▸ **op·ti·mal·ly** *adv.*

op·ti·mism /ˈɒptɪmɪzəm; *NAmE* ˈɑːp-/ *noun* [U] **~ (about/for sth)** a feeling that good things will happen and that sth will be successful; the tendency to have this feeling: *optimism about/for the future* ◇ *We may now look forward* **with optimism**. ◇ *a mood of* **cautious optimism** ◇ *There are very real grounds for optimism.* OPP **pessimism**

op·ti·mist /ˈɒptɪmɪst; *NAmE* ˈɑːp-/ *noun* a person who always expects good things to happen or things to be successful OPP **pessimist**

op·ti·mis·tic /ˌɒptɪˈmɪstɪk; *NAmE* ˌɑːp-/ *adj.* expecting good things to happen or sth to be successful; showing this feeling SYN **positive**: **~ (about sth)** *She's not very optimistic about the outcome of the talks.* ◇ **~ (that...)** *They are cautiously optimistic that the reforms will take place.* ◇ *We are now taking a more optimistic view.* ◇ *in an optimistic mood* ◇ *I think you're being a little* **over-optimistic**. OPP **pessimistic** ▸ **op·ti·mis·tic·al·ly** /-kli/ *adv.*

op·ti·mize (*BrE* also **-ise**) /ˈɒptɪmaɪz; *NAmE* ˈɑːp-/ *verb* **~ sth** to make sth as good as it can be; to use sth in the best possible way: *to optimize the use of resources*

op·ti·mum /ˈɒptɪməm; *NAmE* ˈɑːp-/ *adj.* [only before noun] **1** (also **op·ti·mal**) the best possible; producing the best possible results: *optimum growth* ◇ *the optimum use of resources* ◇ *the optimum conditions for effective learning* **2 the optimum** *noun* [sing.] the best possible result, set of conditions, etc. SYN **ideal**

Synonyms

option

choice • alternative • possibility

These are all words for sth that you choose to do in a particular situation.

option something that you can choose to have or do; the freedom to choose what you do: *As I see it, we have two options...* ◇ *Students have the option of studying abroad in their second year.* NOTE **Option** is also the word used in computing for one of the choices you can make when using a computer program: *Choose the 'Cut' option from the Edit menu.*

choice the freedom to choose what you do; something that you can choose to have or do: *If I had the choice, I would stop working tomorrow.* ◇ *There is a wide range of choices open to you.*

alternative something that you can choose to have or do out of two or more possibilities: *You can be paid in cash weekly or by cheque monthly: those are the two alternatives.*

OPTION, CHOICE OR ALTERNATIVE?

Choice is slightly less formal than **option** and **alternative** is slightly more formal. **Choice** is most often used for 'the freedom to choose', although you can sometimes also use **option** (but not usually **alternative**): *If I had the choice/option, I would...* ◇ ~~*If I had the alternative, I would...*~~ ◇ *parental choice in education* ◇ ~~*parental option/alternative in education*~~. Things that you can choose are **options**, **choices** or **alternatives**. However, **alternative** is more frequently used to talk about choosing between two things rather than several.

possibility one of the different things that you can do in a particular situation: *We need to explore a wide range of possibilities.* ◇ *The possibilities are endless.* NOTE **Possibility** can be used in a similar way to **option**, **choice** and **alternative**, but the emphasis here is less on the need to make a choice, and more on what is available.

PATTERNS
- **with/without** the option/choice/possibility **of** sth
- a(n) **good/acceptable/reasonable/possible** option/choice/alternative
- the **only** option/choice/alternative/possibility **open to** sb
- to **have** a/an/the option/choice **of doing sth**
- to **have no** option/choice/alternative **but to** do sth)
- a **number/range of** options/choices/alternatives/possibilities

op·tion 0➛ AW /ˈɒpʃn; *NAmE* ˈɑːp-/ *noun, verb*
- ***noun*** **1** 0➛ [C, U] something that you can choose to have or do; the freedom to choose what you do: *As I see it, we have two options...* ◇ *There are various options open to you.* ◇ *Going to college was not an option for me.* ◇ *I had* **no option but to** (= I had to) *ask him to leave.* ◇ **~ (of doing sth)** *Students have the option of studying abroad in their second year.* ◇ **~ (to do sth)** *A savings plan that gives you the option*

to vary your monthly payments. ◇ *This particular model comes with a wide range of options* (= things you can choose to have when buying sth but which you will have to pay extra for). **2** [C] a subject that a student can choose to study, but that they do not have to do: *The course offers options in design and computing.* **3** [C] the right to buy or sell sth at some time in the future: **~ (on sth)** *We have an option on the house.* ◇ *He has promised me first option on his car* (= the opportunity to buy it before anyone else). ◇ **~ (to do sth)** *The property is for rent with an option to buy at any time.* ◇ *share options* (= the right to buy shares in a company) **4** [C] (*computing*) one of the choices you can make when using a computer program: *Choose the 'Cut' option from the Edit menu.*

IDM **keep/leave your 'options open** to avoid making a decision now so that you still have a choice in the future **the ˌsoft/ˌeasy 'option** (often *disapproving*) a choice which is thought to be easier because it involves less effort, difficulty, etc: *They are anxious that the new course should not be seen as a soft option.* ◇ *He decided to* ***take the easy option*** *and give them what they wanted.*

■ ***verb*** **~ sth** to buy or sell the right to own or use sth, at some time in the future: *The novel has been optioned for the screen by his production company.*

op·tion·al AW /ˈɒpʃənl; *NAmE* ˈɑːp-/ *adj.* that you can choose to do or have if you want to: *Certain courses are compulsory; others are optional.* ◇ *This model comes with a number of* ***optional extras*** (= things you can choose to have but which you will have to pay extra for).

op·tom·etrist /ɒpˈtɒmətrɪst; *NAmE* ɑːpˈtɑːm-/ (*BrE* also **op·ti·cian**, **ophˌthalmic opˈtician**) *noun* a person whose job is to examine people's eyes and to recommend and sell glasses

op·tom·etry /ɒpˈtɒmətri; *NAmE* ɑːpˈtɑːm-/ *noun* [U] the job of measuring how well people can see and checking their eyes for disease

ˈopt-out *noun* (often used as an adjective) **1** (in Britain) the action of a school or hospital that decides to manage its own money and is therefore no longer controlled by a LOCAL AUTHORITY or similar organization **2** the act of choosing not to be involved in an agreement: *an opt-out clause* ◇ *MPs hoped to reverse Britain's opt-out from the treaty.*

opu·lent /ˈɒpjələnt; *NAmE* ˈɑːp-/ *adj.* (*formal*) **1** made or decorated using expensive materials SYN **luxurious** **2** (of people) extremely rich SYN **wealthy** ▸ **opu·lence** /-ləns/ *noun* [U] **opu·lent·ly** *adv.*

opus /ˈəʊpəs; *NAmE* ˈoʊ-/ *noun* (*pl.* **opera** /ˈɒpərə; *NAmE* ˈɑːp-/) [usually sing.] **1** (*abbr.* **op.**) a piece of music written by a famous COMPOSER and usually followed by a number that shows when it was written: *Beethoven's Opus 18* **2** (*formal*) an important piece of literature, etc, especially one that is on a large scale SYN **work** ➲ see also MAGNUM OPUS

or /ɔː(r)/ *conj.*
1 used to introduce another possibility: *Is your sister older or younger than you?* ◇ *Are you coming or not?* ◇ *Is it a boy or a girl?* ◇ *It can be black, white or grey.* ➲ compare EITHER… OR… **2** used in negative sentences when mentioning two or more things: *He can't read or write.* ◇ *There are people without homes, jobs or family.* ➲ compare NEITHER… NOR… **3** (also **or else**) used to warn or advise sb that sth bad could happen; otherwise: *Turn the heat down or it'll burn.* **4** used between two numbers to show approximately how many: *There were six or seven of us there.* **5** used to introduce a word or phrase that explains or means the same as another: *geology, or the science of the earth's crust* ◇ *It weighs a kilo, or just over two pounds.* **6** used to say why sth must be true: *He must like her, or he wouldn't keep calling her.* **7** used to introduce a contrasting idea: *He was lying—or was he?*

IDM **or so** about: *It'll cost €100 or so.* **or somebody/something/somewhere** | **somebody/something/somewhere or other** (*informal*) used when you are not exactly sure about a person, thing or place: *He's a factory supervisor or something.* ◇ *'Who said so?' 'Oh, somebody or other. I can't remember who it was.'*

-or *suffix* (in nouns) a person or thing that: *actor* ➲ compare -EE, -ER

or·acle /ˈɒrəkl; *NAmE* ˈɔːr-/ *noun* [C] **1** (in ancient Greece) a place where people could go to ask the gods for advice or information about the future; the priest or PRIESTESS through whom the gods were thought to give their message: *They consulted the oracle at Delphi.* **2** (in ancient Greece) the advice or information that the gods gave, which often had a hidden meaning **3** [usually sing.] a person or book that gives valuable advice or information: *My sister's the oracle on investment matters.*

or·acu·lar /əˈrækjələ(r)/ *adj.* (*formal* or *humorous*) of or like an oracle; with a hidden meaning

oral /ˈɔːrəl/ *adj., noun*

■ ***adj.*** **1** [usually before noun] spoken rather than written: *a test of both oral and written French* ◇ *oral evidence* ◇ *He was interested in* ***oral history*** (= history that is collected from interviews with people who have personal knowledge of past events). ➲ SYNONYMS at SPOKEN ➲ compare VERBAL **2** [only before noun] connected with the mouth: *oral hygiene* ◇ *oral sex* (= using the mouth to STIMULATE sb's sex organs) **3** (*phonetics*) (of a speech sound) produced without the air in the nose VIBRATING ➲ compare NASAL ▸ **or·al·ly** /ˈɔːrəli/ *adv.*: *Answers can be written or presented orally on tape.* ◇ *Not to be taken orally* (= a warning on some medicines to show that they must not be swallowed).

■ ***noun*** **1** (*especially BrE*) a spoken exam, especially in a foreign language: *a French oral* ◇ *He failed the oral.* **2** (*NAmE*) a spoken exam in a university

ˌoral ˈhistory *noun* [U] the collection and study of historical information using sound recordings of interviews with people who remember past events

oral·ism /ˈɔːrəlɪzəm/ *noun* [U] the system of teaching deaf people to communicate using speech and LIP-READING ▸ **oral·ist** /-ɪst/ *adj.*

or·ange /ˈɒrɪndʒ; *NAmE* ˈɔːr-; ˈɑːr-/ *noun, adj.*

■ ***noun*** [C, U] **1** a round CITRUS fruit with thick reddish-yellow skin and a lot of sweet juice: *orange peel* ◇ *an orange tree* ◇ *freshly squeezed orange juice* ◇ *orange groves* (= groups of orange trees) ◇ *orange blossom* ➲ VISUAL VOCAB page V26 ➲ see also BLOOD ORANGE **2** (*BrE*) orange juice, or a drink made from or tasting of oranges: *Would you like some orange?* ◇ *A vodka and orange, please.* **3** a bright reddish-yellow colour IDM see APPLE *n.*

■ ***adj.*** **1** bright reddish-yellow in colour: *yellow and orange flames* **2 Orange** related to or belonging to a Protestant political group which believes that Northern Ireland should remain part of the UK: *an Orange march*

or·ange·ade /ˌɒrɪndʒˈeɪd; *NAmE* ˌɔːr-; ˌɑːr-/ *noun* **1** [U] a sweet drink with an orange flavour. In Britain it always has bubbles in it; in the US it can be with or without bubbles. **2** [C] a glass of orangeade ➲ compare LEMONADE

Or·ange·man /ˈɒrɪndʒmən; *NAmE* ˈɔːr-; ˈɑːr-/ *noun* (*pl.* **-men** /-mən/) a member of the Orange Order, a Protestant political organization that wants Northern Ireland to remain part of the United Kingdom

or·an·gery /ˈɒrɪndʒəri; *NAmE* ˈɔːr-; ˈɑːr-/ *noun* (*pl.* **-ies**) a glass building where orange trees are grown

ˌorange ˈsquash *noun* (*BrE*) **1** [U] a thick sweet liquid made with orange juice and sugar; a drink made from this with water added: *a bottle of orange squash* **2** [C] a glass of orange squash: *Two orange squashes, please.*

orang-utan /ɔːˌræŋ uːˈtæn; əˈræŋ uːtæn; *NAmE* əˈræŋ ətæn/ *noun* a large APE (= an animal like a large MONKEY with no tail) with long arms and reddish hair, that lives in Borneo and Sumatra ORIGIN From Malay *orang utan/hutan*, meaning 'person of the forest'.

ora·tion /ɔːˈreɪʃn/ *noun* (*formal*) a formal speech made on a public occasion, especially as part of a ceremony

ora·tor /ˈɒrətə(r); *NAmE* ˈɔːr-; ˈɑːr-/ *noun* (*formal*) a person who makes formal speeches in public or is good at public speaking: *a fine political orator*

O

ora·tor·ic·al /ˌɒrəˈtɒrɪkl; *NAmE* ˌɔːrəˈtɔːr-/ *adj.* (*formal, sometimes disapproving*) connected with the art of public speaking: *oratorical skills*

ora·torio /ˌɒrəˈtɔːriəʊ; *NAmE* ˌɔːrəˈtɔːrioʊ; ˌɑːrə-/ *noun* (*pl.* -os) a long piece of music for singers and an ORCHESTRA, usually based on a story from the Bible ➲ compare CANTATA

ora·tory /ˈɒrətri; *NAmE* ˈɔːrətɔːri; ˈɑːr-/ *noun* (*pl.* -ies) **1** [U] the skill of making powerful and effective speeches in public SYN **rhetoric** **2** [C] a room or small building that is used for private prayer or worship

orb /ɔːb; *NAmE* ɔːrb/ *noun* **1** (*literary*) an object shaped like a ball, especially the sun or moon **2** a gold ball with a cross on top, carried by a king or queen at formal ceremonies as a symbol of power ➲ compare SCEPTRE

orbit /ˈɔːbɪt; *NAmE* ˈɔːrbɪt/ *noun, verb*

■ ***noun*** **1** [C, U] a curved path followed by a planet or an object as it moves around another planet, star, moon, etc: *the earth's orbit around the sun* ◇ *a space station **in orbit** round the moon* ◇ *A new satellite has been **put into orbit** around the earth.* **2** [sing.] an area that a particular person, organization, etc. deals with or is able to influence: *to **come/fall/be within sb's orbit***

■ ***verb*** [T, I] **~ (around) sth** to move in an orbit (= a curved path) around a much larger object, especially a planet, star, etc: *The earth takes a year to orbit the sun.*

or·bit·al /ˈɔːbɪtl; *NAmE* ˈɔːrb-/ *adj., noun*

■ ***adj.*** [only before noun] **1** connected with the orbit of a planet or object in space **2** (*BrE*) (of a road) built around the edge of a town or city to reduce the amount of traffic travelling through the centre

■ ***noun*** (*BrE*) a very large RING ROAD, especially if it is a MOTORWAY: *the M25 London orbital*

or·bit·er /ˈɔːbɪtə(r); *NAmE* ˈɔːrb-/ *noun* a SPACECRAFT designed to move around a planet or moon rather than to land on it

O

orca /ˈɔːkə; *NAmE* ˈɔːrkə/ *noun* = KILLER WHALE

Or·ca·dian /ɔːˈkeɪdiən; ɔːrˈk-/ *noun* a person from the islands of Orkney in Scotland ▶ **Or·ca·dian** *adj.*

orch·ard /ˈɔːtʃəd; *NAmE* ˈɔːrtʃərd/ *noun* a piece of land, normally separated from the surrounding area, in which fruit trees are grown ➲ VISUAL VOCAB page V2

or·ches·tra /ˈɔːkɪstrə; *NAmE* ˈɔːrk-/ *noun* **1** [C+sing./pl. v.] a large group of people who play various musical instruments together, led by a CONDUCTOR: *She plays the flute in the school orchestra.* ◇ *the Scottish Symphony Orchestra* ➲ see also CHAMBER ORCHESTRA, SYMPHONY ORCHESTRA **2 the orchestra** [sing.] (*NAmE*) (*BrE* **the ˈorchestra stalls, the stalls**) the seats that are nearest to the stage in a theatre

or·ches·tral /ɔːˈkestrəl; *NAmE* ɔːrˈk-/ *adj.* connected with an orchestra: *orchestral music*

ˈorchestra pit (also **pit**) *noun* the place in a theatre just in front of the stage where the orchestra sits and plays for an OPERA, a BALLET, etc.

or·ches·trate /ˈɔːkɪstreɪt; *NAmE* ˈɔːrk-/ *verb* **1 ~ sth** to arrange a piece of music in parts so that it can be played by an orchestra **2 ~ sth** to organize a complicated plan or event very carefully or secretly SYN **stage-manage**: *a carefully orchestrated publicity campaign* ▶ **or·ches·tra·tion** /ˌɔːkɪˈstreɪʃn; *NAmE* ˌɔːrk-/ *noun* [C, U]

or·chid /ˈɔːkɪd; *NAmE* ˈɔːrkɪd/ *noun* a plant with brightly coloured flowers of unusual shapes. There are many different types of orchid and some of them are very rare. ➲ VISUAL VOCAB page V9

or·dain /ɔːˈdeɪn; *NAmE* ɔːrˈd-/ *verb* **1 ~ sb (as sth) | ~ sb + noun** to make sb a priest, minister or RABBI: *He was ordained (as) a priest last year.* ➲ see also ORDINATION **2 ~ sth | ~ that...** (*formal*) (of God, the law or FATE) to order or command sth; to decide sth in advance: *Fate had ordained that they would never meet again.*

or·deal /ɔːˈdiːl; ˈɔːdiːl; *NAmE* ɔːrˈd-/ *noun* [usually sing.] **~ (of sth/of doing sth)** a difficult or unpleasant experience: *They are to be spared the ordeal of giving evidence in court.* ◇ *The hostages spoke openly about the terrible ordeal they had been through.* ◇ *The interview was less of an ordeal than she'd expected.*

order 🔑 /ˈɔːdə(r); *NAmE* ˈɔːrd-/ *noun, verb*

■ ***noun***

▸ ARRANGEMENT **1** 🔑 [U, C] the way in which people or things are placed or arranged in relation to each other: *The names are listed **in alphabetical order**.* ◇ ***in chronological/numerical order*** ◇ *arranged **in order of** priority/importance/size* ◇ *The results, ranked **in descending/ascending order**, are as follows:* ◇ *All the procedures must be done in the correct order.* ◇ *Let's take the problems in a different order.* **2** 🔑 [U] the state of being carefully and neatly arranged: *It was time she **put** her life **in order**.* ◇ *The house had been kept in good order.* ◇ *Get your ideas into some sort of order before beginning to write.* ◇ *It is one of the functions of art to bring order out of chaos.* OPP **disorder**

▸ CONTROLLED STATE **3** 🔑 [U] the state that exists when people obey laws, rules or authority: *The army has been sent in to maintain order in the capital.* ◇ *Some teachers find it difficult to **keep** their classes **in order**.* ◇ *The police are trying to restore public order.* ◇ *The argument continued until the chairman **called** them both **to order*** (= ordered them to obey the formal rules of the meeting). ➲ compare DISORDER (2) ➲ see also POINT OF ORDER

▸ INSTRUCTIONS **4** 🔑 [C] something that sb is told to do by sb in authority: **~ (for sb/sth to do sth)** *He **gave orders** for the work to be started.* ◇ **~ (to do sth)** *The general **gave the order** to advance.* ◇ *I'm **under orders** not to let anyone in.* ◇ *She **takes orders** only from the president.* ◇ *Dogs can be trained to **obey orders**.* ◇ (*informal*) *No sugar for me—**doctor's orders**.* ◇ *Interest rates can be controlled **by order of** the central bank.*

▸ GOODS **5** 🔑 [C, U] **~ (for sth)** a request to make or supply goods: *I would like to **place an order** for ten copies of this book.* ◇ *an order form* ◇ *The machine parts are still **on order*** (= they have been ordered but have not yet been received) ◇ *These items can be made **to order*** (= produced especially for a particular customer) ➲ see also MAIL ORDER **6** [C] goods supplied in response to a particular order that sb has placed: *The stationery order has arrived.*

▸ FOOD/DRINKS **7** 🔑 [C] a request for food or drinks in a restaurant, bar, etc; the food or drinks that you ask for: *May I **take your order**?* ◇ ***Last orders** at the bar now please!* (= because the bar is going to close) ◇ *an order for steak and fries* ◇ *a **side order*** (= for example, vegetables or salad that you eat with your main dish) ➲ COLLOCATIONS at RESTAURANT

▸ MONEY **8** [C] a formal written instruction for sb to be paid money or to do sth ➲ see also BANKER'S ORDER, COURT ORDER, MONEY ORDER, POSTAL ORDER, STANDING ORDER

▸ SYSTEM **9** [C, usually sing.] (*formal*) the way that a society, the world, etc. is arranged, with its system of rules and customs: *a change in the political and social order* ◇ *the natural order of things* ◇ *He was seen as a threat to **the established order**.* ◇ *A **new order** seems to be emerging.*

▸ SOCIAL CLASS **10** [C, usually pl.] (*disapproving* or *humorous*) a social class: *the lower orders*

▸ BIOLOGY **11** [C] a group into which animals, plants, etc. that have similar characteristics are divided, smaller than a CLASS and larger than a FAMILY: *the order of primates* ➲ compare GENUS

▸ RELIGIOUS COMMUNITY **12** [C+sing./pl. v.] a group of people living in a religious community, especially MONKS or NUNS: *religious orders* ◇ *the Benedictine order*

▸ SPECIAL HONOUR **13** [C+sing./pl. v.] a group of people who have been given a special honour by a queen, king, president, etc: *The Order of the Garter is an ancient order of chivalry.* **14** [C] a BADGE or RIBBON worn by members of an order who have been given a special honour

▸ SECRET SOCIETY **15** [C+sing./pl. v.] a secret society whose members meet for special ceremonies: *the Ancient Order of Druids*

IDM **be in/take (holy) ˈorders** to be/become a priest **in ˈorder 1** 🔑 (of an official document) that can be used because it is all correct and legal SYN **valid**: *Is your work permit in order?* **2** (*formal*) as it should be: *Is everything in order, sir?* **3** if sth is **in order**, it is a suitable thing to do or say on a particular occasion: *I think a drink would be in order.* **in 'order (to do sth)** (*formal*) allowed according to the rules of a meeting, etc: *Is it in order to speak now?* **in order that** (*formal*) so that sth can happen: *All those concerned must work together in order that agreement can be reached on this issue.* **in order to do sth** with the purpose or intention of doing or achieving sth: *She arrived early in order to get a good seat.* ◇ *In order to get a complete picture, further information is needed.* ➲ LANGUAGE BANK at PROCESS **in running/working 'order** (especially of machines) working well: *The engine is now in perfect working order.* **of a high order | of the highest/first order** of a high quality or degree; of the highest quality or greatest degree: *The job requires diplomatic skills of a high order.* ◇ *She was a snob of the first order.* **of/in the order of sth** (*BrE*) (*NAmE* **on the order of**) (*formal*) about sth; approximately sth: *She earns something in the order of £80 000 a year.* **the ˌorder of the 'day** common, popular or suitable at a particular time or for a particular occasion: *Pessimism seems to be the order of the day.* **Order! Order!** used to remind people to obey the rules of a formal meeting or debate **ˌout of 'order 1** (of a machine, etc.) not working correctly: *The phone is out of order.* **2** not arranged correctly or neatly: *I checked the files and some of the papers were out of order.* **3** (*BrE*) (*NAmE* **ˌout of 'line**) (*informal*) behaving in a way that is not acceptable or right: *You were well out of order taking it without asking.* **4** (*formal*) not allowed by the rules of a formal meeting or debate: *His objection was ruled out of order.* ➲ more at CALL *v.*, HOUSE *n.*, LAW, MARCH *v.*, PECK *v.*, SHORT *n.*, STARTER, TALL

Synonyms

order

tell • instruct • direct • command

These words all mean to use your position of authority to say to sb that they must do sth.

order to use your position of authority to tell sb to do sth: *The company was ordered to pay compensation to its former employee.* ◇ *'Come here at once!' she ordered.*

tell to say to sb that they must or should do sth: *He was told to sit down and wait.* ◇ *Don't tell me what to do!*

instruct (*rather formal*) to tell sb to do sth, especially in a formal or official way: *The letter instructed him to report to headquarters immediately.*

direct (*formal*) to give an official order: *The judge directed the jury to return a verdict of not guilty.*

command to use your position of authority to tell sb to do sth: *He commanded his men to retreat.*

ORDER OR COMMAND?

Order is a more general word than **command** and can be used about anyone in a position of authority, such as a parent, teacher or government telling sb to do sth. **Command** is slightly stronger than **order** and is the normal word to use about an army officer giving orders, or in any context where it is normal to give orders without any discussion about them. It is less likely to be used about a parent or teacher.

PATTERNS

- to order/tell/instruct/direct/command sb **to do sth**
- to order/instruct/direct/command **that...**
- to **do** sth **as** ordered/told/instructed/directed/commanded

■ ***verb***

▸ GIVE INSTRUCTIONS **1** [T] to use your position of authority to tell sb to do sth or say that sth must happen: **~ sb to do sth** *The company was ordered to pay compensation to its former employees.* ◇ *The officer ordered them to fire.* ◇ **~ sb + adv./prep.** *They were ordered out of the class for fighting.* ◇ **~ sth** *The government has ordered an investigation into the accident.* ◇ **~ that...** *They ordered that for every tree cut down two more be planted.* ◇ (*BrE* also) *They ordered that for every tree cut down two more should be planted.* ◇ **~ (sb) + speech** *'Sit down and be quiet,' she ordered.*

▸ GOODS/SERVICE **2** [T] to ask for goods to be made or supplied; to ask for a service to be provided: **~ sth (from sb)** *These boots can be ordered direct from the manufacturer.* ◇ **~ sb sth** *Shall I order you a taxi?* ◇ **~ sth for sb** *Shall I order a taxi for you?*

▸ FOOD/DRINK **3** [T, I] to ask for sth to eat or drink in a restaurant, bar, etc: **~ (sth)** *I ordered a beer and a sandwich.* ◇ *Have you ordered yet?* ◇ **~ sb/yourself sth** *He ordered himself a double whisky.* ◇ **~ (sth) (for sb)** *Will you order for me while I make a phone call?*

▸ ORGANIZE/ARRANGE **4** [T] **~ sth** (*formal*) to organize or arrange sth: *I need time to order my thoughts* ➲ see also ORDERED, DISORDERED IDM see DOCTOR *n.*

PHR V **ˌorder sb a'bout/a'round** (*disapproving*) to keep telling sb what to do in a way that is annoying or unpleasant

'order book *noun* a record kept by a business of the products it has agreed to supply to its customers, often used to show how well the business is doing: *We have a full order book for the coming year.*

or·dered /ˈɔːdəd; *NAmE* ˈɔːrdərd/ *adj.* [usually before noun] carefully arranged or organized SYN **orderly**: *an ordered existence* ◇ *a well-ordered society* OPP **disordered**

'order form *noun* a document filled in by customers when ordering goods

order·ing /ˈɔːdərɪŋ; *NAmE* ˈɔːrdər-/ *noun* [C, U] the way in which sth is ordered or arranged; the act of putting sth into an order SYN **arrangement**: *Many possible orderings may exist.* ◇ *the successful ordering of complex data*

or·der·ly /ˈɔːdəli; *NAmE* ˈɔːrdərli/ *adj.*, *noun*

■ ***adj.*** **1** arranged or organized in a neat, careful and logical way SYN **tidy**: *a calm and orderly life* ◇ *vegetables planted in orderly rows* **2** behaving well; peaceful: *an orderly demonstration* OPP **disorderly** ▸ **or·der·li·ness** /ˈɔːdəlinəs; *NAmE* ˈɔːrdər-/ *noun* [U]

■ ***noun*** (*pl.* -ies) **1** a person who works in a hospital, usually doing jobs that do not need any special training **2** a soldier who does jobs that do not need any special training

ˌorder of 'magnitude *noun* (*mathematics*) a level in a system of ordering things by size or amount, where each level is higher by a FACTOR of ten: *The actual measurement is two orders of magnitude* (= a hundred times) *greater than we expected.* ◇ (*figurative*) *The problem is of the same order of magnitude for all concerned.*

'Order Paper *noun* (*BrE*) a list of the subjects to be discussed by Parliament on a particular day

or·din·al /ˈɔːdɪnl; *NAmE* ˈɔːrdənl/ (also **ˌordinal 'number**) *noun* a number that refers to the position of sth in a series, for example 'first', 'second', etc. ➲ compare CARDINAL ▸ **or·din·al** *adj.*

or·din·ance /ˈɔːdɪnəns; *NAmE* ˈɔːrd-/ *noun* [C, U] (*formal*) an order or a rule made by a government or sb in a position of authority

or·din·and /ˈɔːdɪnænd; *NAmE* ˈɔːrd-/ *noun* a person who is preparing to become a priest, minister or RABBI

or·din·ar·ily /ˈɔːdnrəli; *NAmE* ˌɔːrdnˈerəli/ *adv.* **1** in a normal way SYN **normally**: *To the untrained eye, the children were behaving ordinarily.* **2** used to say what normally happens in a particular situation, especially because sth different is happening this time SYN **usually**: *Ordinarily, she wouldn't have bothered arguing with him.* ◇ *We do not ordinarily carry out this type of work.*

or·din·ary /ˈɔːdnri; *NAmE* ˈɔːrdneri/ *adj.*

1 [usually before noun] not unusual or different in any way: *an ordinary sort of day* ◇ *in the ordinary course of events* ◇ *ordinary people like you and me* ◇ *This was no ordinary meeting.* **2** (*disapproving*) having no unusual or interesting features: *The meal was very ordinary.* ➲ compare EXTRAORDINARY ▸ **or·din·ari·ness** *noun* [U]

O

IDM **in the ordinary way** (*BrE*) used to say what normally happens in a particular situation: *In the ordinary way, she's not a nervous person.* **out of the 'ordinary** unusual or different: *I'm looking for something a little more out of the ordinary.*

'ordinary grade *noun* = O GRADE

'ordinary level *noun* = O LEVEL

ˌordinary 'seaman *noun* (*abbr.* OS) a sailor of the lowest rank in the British navy

ˌordinary 'share *noun* a fixed unit of a company's capital. People who own ordinary shares have voting rights in the company.

or·din·ate /'ɔːdɪnət; *NAmE* 'ɔːrd-/ *noun* (*mathematics*) the COORDINATE that gives the distance along the vertical AXIS ➲ compare ABSCISSA

or·din·ation /ˌɔːdɪ'neɪʃn; *NAmE* ˌɔːrdn'eɪʃn/ *noun* [U, C] the act or ceremony of making sb a priest, minister or RABBI ➲ see also ORDAIN

ord·nance /'ɔːdnəns; *NAmE* 'ɔːrd-/ *noun* [U] **1** large guns on wheels SYN **artillery** **2** military supplies and materials: *an ordnance depot*

ˌOrdnance 'Survey map *noun* a very detailed map of an area of Britain or Ireland, prepared by an organization called the **Ordnance Survey**, which is supported by the government

ord·ure /'ɔːdjʊə(r); *NAmE* 'ɔːrdʒər/ *noun* [U] (*formal*) solid waste from the body of a person or an animal SYN **faeces**

ore /ɔː(r)/ *noun* [U, C] rock, earth, etc. from which metal can be obtained: *iron ore*

ore·gano /ˌɒrɪ'gɑːnəʊ; *NAmE* ə'regənoʊ/ *noun* [U] a plant with leaves that have a sweet smell and are used in cooking as a HERB ➲ VISUAL VOCAB page V28

organ 0➡ /'ɔːgən; *NAmE* 'ɔːrgən/ *noun*
1 0➡ a part of the body that has a particular purpose, such as the heart or the brain; part of a plant with a particular purpose: *the **internal organs*** ◇ *the **sense organs*** (= the eyes, ears, nose, etc.) ◇ *the **sexual/reproductive organs*** ◇ *an **organ transplant/donor*** ➲ COLLOCATIONS at ILL ➲ VISUAL VOCAB page V48 **2** (especially *humorous*) a PENIS: *the male organ* **3** 0➡ (also **'pipe organ**) a large musical instrument with keys like a piano. Sounds are produced by air forced through pipes: *She plays the organ in church.* ◇ *organ music* ➲ compare HARMONIUM **4** a musical instrument similar to a pipe organ, but without pipes: *an electric organ* ➲ see also BARREL ORGAN, MOUTH ORGAN **5** (*formal*) an official organization that is part of a larger organization and has a special purpose: *the organs of government* **6** (*formal*) a newspaper or magazine that gives information about a particular group or organization; a means of communicating the views of a particular group: *The People's Daily is the official organ of the Chinese Communist Party.*

or·gan·die (*NAmE* also **or·gandy**) /'ɔːgəndi; *NAmE* 'ɔːrg-/ *noun* [U] a type of thin cotton cloth that is slightly stiff, used especially for making formal dresses

'organ-grinder *noun* a person who plays a BARREL ORGAN (= a large musical instrument played by turning a handle): (*humorous*) *He's only the **organ-grinder's monkey*** (= an unimportant person who does what he is told to do).

or·gan·ic /ɔː'gænɪk; *NAmE* ɔːr'g-/ *adj.* [usually before noun] **1** (of food, farming methods, etc.) produced or practised without using artificial chemicals: ***organic cheese/vegetables/wine, etc.*** ◇ *an **organic farmer/gardener*** ◇ ***organic farming/horticulture*** ➲ VISUAL VOCAB page V7 **2** produced by or from living things: *Improve the soil by adding **organic matter**.* ◇ ***organic compounds*** OPP **inorganic** **3** (*technical*) connected with the organs of the body: *organic disease* **4** (*formal*) consisting of different parts that are all connected to each other: *the view of society as an organic whole* **5** (*formal*) happening in a slow and natural way, rather than suddenly: *the organic growth of foreign markets* ▶ **or·gan·ic·al·ly** /-kli/ *adv.*: *organically grown fruit* ◇ *The cardboard disintegrates organically.* ◇ *Doctors could find nothing organically wrong with her.* ◇ *The organization should be allowed to develop organically.*

orˌganic 'chemistry *noun* [U] the branch of chemistry that deals with substances that contain CARBON ➲ compare INORGANIC CHEMISTRY

or·gan·ism /'ɔːgənɪzəm; *NAmE* 'ɔːrg-/ *noun* **1** (*biology* or *formal*) a living thing, especially one that is extremely small ➲ see also MICRO-ORGANISM **2** (*formal*) a system consisting of parts that depend on each other: *the social organism* (= society)

or·gan·ist /'ɔːgənɪst; *NAmE* 'ɔːrg-/ *noun* a person who plays the organ

or·gan·iza·tion 0➡ (*BrE* also **-isa·tion**) /ˌɔːgənaɪ'zeɪʃn; *NAmE* ˌɔːrgənə'z-/ *noun*
1 0➡ [C] a group of people who form a business, club, etc. together in order to achieve a particular aim: *to work for a business/political/voluntary organization* ◇ *the World Health Organization* ◇ *He's the president of a large international organization.* **2** 0➡ [U] the act of making arrangements or preparations for sth SYN **planning**: *I leave most of the organization of these conferences to my assistant.* **3** 0➡ [U] the way in which the different parts of sth are arranged SYN **structure**: *The report studies the organization of labour within the company.* **4** 0➡ [U] the quality of being arranged in a neat, careful and logical way: *She is highly intelligent but her work lacks organization.* ▶ **or·gan·iza·tion·al, -isa·tion·al** /-ʃənl/ *adj.*: *organizational skills* ◇ *organizational change* **or·gan·iza·tion·al·ly, -isa·tion·al·ly** *adv.*

ˌorgani'zation chart (also **or·gano·gram**) *noun* a diagram of the structure of an organization, especially a large business, showing the relationships between all the jobs in it

or·gan·ize 0➡ (*BrE* also **-ise**) /'ɔːgənaɪz; *NAmE* 'ɔːrg-/ *verb*
1 0➡ [T] **~ sth** to arrange for sth to happen or to be provided: *to organize a meeting/party/trip* ◇ *I'll invite people if you can organize food and drinks.* **2** 0➡ [T] **~ sth** to arrange sth or the parts of sth into a particular order or structure: *Modern computers can organize large amounts of data very quickly.* ◇ *You should try and organize your time better.* ◇ *We do not fully understand how the brain is organized.* **3** [T] **~ yourself/sb** to plan your/sb's work and activities in an efficient way: *I'm sure you don't need me to organize you.* **4** [T, I] **~ (sb/yourself)** (**into sth**) to form a group of people with a shared aim, especially a union or political party: *the right of workers to organize themselves into unions* ➲ see also DISORGANIZED ▶ **or·gan·izer, -iser** *noun*: *the organizers of the festival* ➲ see also PERSONAL ORGANIZER

or·gan·ized 0➡ (*BrE* also **-ised**) /'ɔːgənaɪzd; *NAmE* 'ɔːrg-/ *adj.*
1 0➡ [only before noun] involving large numbers of people who work together to do sth in a way that has been carefully planned: *an organized body of workers* ◇ ***organized religion*** (= traditional religion followed by large numbers of people who obey a fixed set of rules) ◇ ***organized crime*** (= committed by professional criminals working in large groups) ➲ compare UNORGANIZED **2** 0➡ arranged or planned in the way mentioned: *a carefully organized campaign* ◇ *a well-organized office* ➲ compare DISORGANIZED **3** 0➡ (of a person) able to plan your work, life, etc. well and in an efficient way: *a very organized person* ◇ *Isn't it time you started to get organized?* ➲ compare DISORGANIZED

'organ loft *noun* a place where there is an organ high above the ground in a church or concert hall

or·gano·gram (also **or·gani·gram**) /ɔː'gænəgræm; *NAmE* ɔːr'g-/ *noun* (*business*) = ORGANIZATION CHART

or·gano·phos·phate /ˌɔːgənəʊ'fɒsfeɪt; ɔːˌgænəʊ-; *NAmE* ˌɔːrgənoʊ'fɑːsfeɪt; ɔːrˌgænoʊ-/ *noun* a chemical containing CARBON and PHOSPHORUS

or·ganza /ɔː'gænzə; *NAmE* ɔːr'g-/ *noun* [U] a type of thin stiff transparent cloth, used for making formal dresses

or·gasm /ˈɔːɡæzəm; NAmE ˈɔːrɡ-/ *noun* [U, C] the moment during sexual activity when feelings of sexual pleasure are at their strongest: *to achieve/reach orgasm* ◇ *to have an orgasm*

or·gas·mic /ɔːˈɡæzmɪk; NAmE ɔːrˈɡ-/ *adj.* [only before noun] connected with or like an ORGASM

or·gi·as·tic /ˌɔːdʒiˈæstɪk; NAmE ˌɔːrdʒ-/ *adj.* [usually before noun] (*formal*) typical of an orgy

orgy /ˈɔːdʒi; NAmE ˈɔːrdʒi/ *noun* (*pl.* **-ies**) **1** a party at which there is a lot of eating, drinking and sexual activity: *a drunken orgy* **2 ~ (of sth)** (*disapproving*) an extreme amount of a particular activity: *The rebels went on an orgy of killing.*

oriel /ˈɔːriəl/ *noun* (*architecture*) a part of a building, like a small room with windows, that sticks out from a wall above the ground: *an oriel window*

Ori·ent /ˈɔːriənt/ **the Orient** *noun* [sing.] (*literary*) the eastern part of the world, especially China and Japan ➲ compare OCCIDENT

ori·ent AW /ˈɔːrient/ (*BrE* also **orien·tate**) *verb* **1** [usually passive] **~ sb/sth (to/towards sb/sth)** to direct sb/sth towards sth; to make or adapt sb/sth for a particular purpose: *Our students are oriented towards science subjects.* ◇ *policies oriented to the needs of working mothers* ◇ *We run a commercially oriented operation.* ◇ *profit-orientated organizations* ◇ *Neither of them is politically oriented* (= interested in politics). **2 ~ yourself** to find your position in relation to your surroundings: *The mountaineers found it hard to orient themselves in the fog.* **3 ~ yourself** to make yourself familiar with a new situation: *It took him some time to orient himself in his new school.* ➲ compare DISORIENTATE

Orien·tal /ˌɔːriˈentl/ *noun* (*old-fashioned*, often *offensive*) a person from China, Japan or other countries in E Asia

orien·tal /ˌɔːriˈentl/ *adj.* connected with or typical of the eastern part of the world, especially China and Japan, and the people who live there: *oriental languages*

orien·tal·ist /ˌɔːriˈentəlɪst/ *noun* a person who studies the languages, arts, etc. of ORIENTAL countries

orien·tate AW /ˈɔːriənteɪt/ *verb* (*BrE*) = ORIENT

orien·ta·tion AW /ˌɔːriənˈteɪʃn/ *noun* **1** [U, C] the type of aims or interests that a person or an organization has; the act of directing your aims towards a particular thing: *The course is essentially theoretical in orientation.* ◇ **~ to/towards sth** *Companies have been forced into a greater orientation to the market.* **2** [U, C] a person's basic beliefs or feelings about a particular subject: ***religious/political orientation*** ◇ *a person's **sexual orientation*** (= whether they are attracted to men, women or both) **3** [U] training or information that you are given before starting a new job, course, etc: *an orientation course* **4** [C] (*technical*) the direction in which an object faces: *The orientation of the planet's orbit is changing continuously.*

orien·teer·ing /ˌɔːriənˈtɪərɪŋ; NAmE -ˈtɪr-/ *noun* [U] the sport of following a route across country on foot, as quickly as possible, using a map and COMPASS ➲ VISUAL VOCAB page V34

ori·fice /ˈɒrɪfɪs; NAmE ˈɔːr-/ *noun* (*formal* or *humorous*) a hole or opening, especially one in the body: *the nasal orifice*

ori·gami /ˌɒrɪˈɡɑːmi; NAmE ˌɔːr-/ *noun* [U] the Japanese art of folding paper into attractive shapes

ori·gin 🔑 /ˈɒrɪdʒɪn; NAmE ˈɔːr-/ *noun* [C, U] (also **origins** [pl.])
1 🔑 the point from which sth starts; the cause of sth: *the origins of life on earth* ◇ *Most coughs are viral **in origin*** (= caused by a virus). ◇ *The origin of the word remains obscure.* ◇ *This particular custom **has its origins in** Wales.* **2** 🔑 a person's social and family background: *She has risen from humble origins to immense wealth.* ◇ *children of various ethnic origins* ◇ *people of German origin* ◇ *a person's country **of origin*** (= where they were born)

ori·gin·al 🔑 /əˈrɪdʒənl/ *adj., noun*
▪***adj.* 1** 🔑 [only before noun] existing at the beginning of a particular period, process or activity: *The room still has many of its original features.* ◇ *I think you should go back to your original plan.* **2** 🔑 new and interesting in a way that is different from anything that has existed before; able to produce new and interesting ideas: *an original idea* ◇ *That's not a very original suggestion.* ◇ *an original thinker* **3** 🔑 [usually before noun] painted, written, etc. by the artist rather than copied: *an original painting by local artist Graham Tovey* ◇ *The original manuscript has been lost.* ◇ *Only original documents* (= not photocopies) *will be accepted as proof of status.*
▪***noun* 1** 🔑 a document, work of art, etc. produced for the first time, from which copies are later made: *This painting is a copy; the original is in Madrid.* ◇ *Send out the photocopies and keep the original.* **2** (*formal*) a person who thinks, behaves, dresses, etc. in an unusual way
IDM **in the oˈriginal** in the language in which a book, etc. was first written, before being translated: *I studied Italian so that I would be able to read Dante in the original.*

ori·gin·al·ity /əˌrɪdʒəˈnæləti/ *noun* [U] the quality of being new and interesting in a way that is different from anything that has existed before: *This latest collection lacks style and originality.*

ori·gin·al·ly 🔑 /əˈrɪdʒənəli/ *adv.*
used to describe the situation that existed at the beginning of a particular period or activity, especially before sth was changed: *The school was originally very small.* ◇ *She comes originally from York.* ◇ *Originally, we had intended to go to Italy, but then we won the trip to Greece.*

oˌriginal ˈsin *noun* [U] (in Christianity) the tendency to be evil that is believed to be present in everyone from birth

ori·gin·ate /əˈrɪdʒɪneɪt/ *verb* (*formal*) **1** [I] (**+ adv./prep.**) to happen or appear for the first time in a particular place or situation: *The disease is thought to have originated in the tropics.* **2** [T] **~ sth** to create sth new: *Locke originated this theory in the 17th century.* ▸ **ori·gin·ator** *noun*

ori·ole /ˈɔːriəʊl; NAmE -oʊl/ *noun* **1** a N American bird: the male is black and orange and the female is yellow-green **2** a European bird, the male of which is bright yellow with black wings

Oriya /ɒˈriːjə; NAmE ɔːˈr-/ *noun* [U] a language spoken in Orissa in eastern India

or·molu /ˈɔːməluː; NAmE ˈɔːrm-/ *noun* [U] a gold metal made of a mixture of other metals, used to decorate furniture, make decorative objects, etc.

or·na·ment *noun, verb*
▪***noun*** /ˈɔːnəmənt; NAmE ˈɔːrn-/ **1** [C] (*especially BrE*) an object that is used as decoration in a room, garden/yard, etc. rather than for a particular purpose: *a china/glass ornament* ◇ (*BrE, NAmE*) *Christmas tree ornaments* ➲ VISUAL VOCAB page V18 **2** [C] (*formal*) an object that is worn as jewellery **3** [U] (*formal*) the use of objects, designs, etc. as decoration: *The clock is simply for ornament; it doesn't work any more.* **4 ~ to sth** (*NAmE*) a person or thing whose good qualities improve sth: *The building is an ornament to the city.* **5 ornaments** [pl.] (*music*) features that are added when playing individual notes to make them more beautiful or interesting
▪***verb*** /ˈɔːnəment; NAmE ˈɔːrn-/ [usually passive] **~ sth** (*formal*) to add decoration to sth SYN **decorate**: *a room richly ornamented with carving*

or·na·men·tal /ˌɔːnəˈmentl; NAmE ˌɔːrn-/ *adj.* used as decoration rather than for a practical purpose SYN **decorative**: *an ornamental fountain* ◇ *The chimney pots are purely ornamental.*

or·na·men·ta·tion /ˌɔːnəmenˈteɪʃn; NAmE ˌɔːrn-/ *noun* [U] the use of objects, designs, etc. to decorate sth

or·nate /ɔːˈneɪt; NAmE ɔːrˈn-/ *adj.* covered with a lot of decoration, especially when this involves very small or complicated designs: *a mirror in an ornate gold frame* ▸ **or·nate·ly** *adv.*: *ornately carved chairs*

or·nery /ˈɔːnəri; NAmE ˈɔːrn-/ *adj.* (*NAmE, informal*) bad-tempered and difficult to deal with

O

or·ni·tholo·gist /ˌɔːnɪ'θɒlədʒɪst; *NAmE* ˌɔːrnɪ'θɑːl-/ *noun* a person who studies birds ➲ compare BIRD-WATCHER

or·ni·thol·ogy /ˌɔːnɪ'θɒlədʒi; *NAmE* ˌɔːrnɪ'θɑːl-/ *noun* [U] the scientific study of birds ▶ **or·ni·tho·logic·al** /ˌɔːnɪθə'lɒdʒɪkl; *NAmE* ˌɔːrnɪθə'lɑːdʒ-/ *adj.*

or·ogeny /ɒ'rɒdʒəni; *NAmE* ɔː'rɑːdʒ-/ *noun* [U] (*geology*) a process in which the outer layer of the earth is folded to form mountains

oro·graph·ic /ˌɒrə'græfɪk; *NAmE* ˌɔːrə'græfɪk/ *adj.* (*geology*) connected with mountains, especially with their position and shape

oro·tund /'ɒrətʌnd; *NAmE* 'ɔːrə-/ *adj.* (*formal*) (of the voice or the way something is said) using full and impressive sounds and language ▶ **oro·tund·ity** /ˌɒrə'tʌndɪti; *NAmE* ˌɔːrə-/ *noun* [U]

orphan /'ɔːfn; *NAmE* 'ɔːrfn/ *noun, verb*

- ***noun*** a child whose parents are dead: *He was an orphan and lived with his uncle.* ◇ *orphan boys/girls*
- ***verb*** [usually passive] **~ sb** to make a child an orphan: *She was orphaned in the war.*

or·phan·age /'ɔːfənɪdʒ; *NAmE* 'ɔːrf-/ *noun* a home for children whose parents are dead

ortho- /'ɔːθəʊ; *NAmE* 'ɔːrθoʊ/ *combining form* (in nouns, adjectives and adverbs) correct; standard: *orthodox* ◇ *orthography*

ortho·don·tics /ˌɔːθə'dɒntɪks; *NAmE* ˌɔːrθə'dɑːn-/ *noun* [U] the treatment of problems concerning the position of the teeth and JAWS ▶ **ortho·don·tic** *adj.*: *orthodontic treatment*

ortho·don·tist /ˌɔːθə'dɒntɪst; *NAmE* ˌɔːrθə'dɑːn-/ *noun* a dentist who treats problems concerning the position of the teeth and JAWS

ortho·dox /'ɔːθədɒks; *NAmE* 'ɔːrθədɑːks/ *adj.* **1** (especially of beliefs or behaviour) generally accepted or approved of; following generally accepted beliefs SYN **traditional**: *orthodox medicine* OPP **unorthodox** ➲ compare HETERODOX **2** following closely the traditional beliefs and practices of a religion: *an orthodox Jew* **3 Orthodox** belonging to or connected with the Orthodox Church

the ˌOrthodox 'Church (also **the ˌEastern ˌOrthodox 'Church**) *noun* [sing.] a branch of the Christian Church in eastern Europe and Greece

ortho·doxy /'ɔːθədɒksi; *NAmE* 'ɔːrθədɑːksi/ *noun* (*pl.* -ies) **1** [C, U] (*formal*) an idea or view that is generally accepted: *an economist arguing against the current financial orthodoxy* **2** [U, C, usually pl.] the traditional beliefs or practices of a religion, etc. **3 Orthodoxy** [U] the Orthodox Church, its beliefs and practices

orth·og·raphy /ɔː'θɒgrəfi; *NAmE* ɔːr'θɑːg-/ *noun* [U] (*formal*) the system of spelling in a language ▶ **or·tho·graph·ic** /ˌɔːθə'græfɪk; *NAmE* ˌɔːrθ-/ *adj.*

ortho·paed·ics (*especially US* **ortho·ped·ics**) /ˌɔːθə'piːdɪks; *NAmE* ˌɔːrθə-/ *noun* [U] the branch of medicine concerned with injuries and diseases of the bones or muscles ▶ **ortho·paed·ic** (*especially US* **ortho·ped·ic**) *adj.*: *an orthopaedic surgeon/hospital*

Or·well·ian /ɔː'weliən; *NAmE* ɔːr'w-/ *adj.* used to describe a political system in which a government tries to have complete control over people's behaviour and thoughts ORIGIN From the name of the English writer George Orwell, whose novel *Nineteen Eighty-Four* describes a government that has total control over the people.

-ory *suffix* **1** (in adjectives) that does...; involving the action concerned: *explanatory* **2** (in nouns) a place for: *observatory*

oryx /'ɒrɪks; *NAmE* 'ɔːr-/ *noun* a large ANTELOPE with long straight horns

OS /ˌəʊ 'es; *NAmE* ˌoʊ/ *abbr.* **1** (*computing*) OPERATING SYSTEM **2** ORDINARY SEAMAN

Oscar™ /'ɒskə(r); *NAmE* 'ɑːs-/ *noun* = ACADEMY AWARD: *The movie was nominated for an Oscar.* ◇ *an* ***Oscar nomination/winner***

os·cil·late /'ɒsɪleɪt; *NAmE* 'ɑːs-/ *verb* **1** [I] **~ (between A and B)** (*formal*) to keep changing from one extreme of feeling or behaviour to another, and back again SYN **swing**: *Her moods oscillated between depression and elation.* **2** [I] (*physics*) to keep moving from one position to another and back again: *Watch how the needle on the dial oscillates.* **3** [I] (*physics*) (of an electric current, radio waves, etc.) to change in strength or direction at regular intervals

os·cil·la·tion /ˌɒsɪ'leɪʃn; *NAmE* ˌɑːs-/ *noun* (*formal*) **1** [U, sing.] a regular movement between one position and another or between one amount and another: *the oscillation of the compass needle* ◇ **~ between A and B** *the economy's continual oscillation between growth and recession* **2** [C] **~ (between A and B)** | **~ (of sth) (against sth)** a single movement from one position to another of sth that is oscillating: *the oscillations of the pound against foreign currency* **3** [U, C] **~ (between A and B)** a repeated change between different feelings, types of behaviour or ideas: *his oscillation, as a teenager, between science and art*

os·cil·la·tor /'ɒsɪleɪtə(r); *NAmE* 'ɑːs-/ *noun* (*physics*) a piece of equipment for producing OSCILLATING electric currents

os·cil·lo·scope /ə'sɪləskəʊp; *NAmE* -skoʊp/ *noun* (*physics*) a piece of equipment that shows changes in electrical current as waves in a line on a screen

osier /'əʊziə(r); *NAmE* 'oʊʒər/ *noun* a type of WILLOW tree, with thin branches that bend easily and are used for making BASKETS

os·mium /'ɒzmiəm; *NAmE* 'ɑːzmiəm/ *noun* [U] (*symb.* **Os**) a chemical element. Osmium is a hard silver-white metal.

os·mo·sis /ɒz'məʊsɪs; *NAmE* ɑːz'moʊ-/ *noun* [U] **1** (*biology* or *chemistry*) the gradual passing of a liquid through a MEMBRANE (= a thin layer of material) as a result of there being different amounts of dissolved substances on either side of the membrane: *Water passes into the roots of a plant by osmosis.* **2** the gradual process of learning or being influenced by sth, as a result of being in close contact with it ▶ **os·mot·ic** /ɒz'mɒtɪk; *NAmE* ɑːz'mɑːtɪk/ *adj.*: *osmotic pressure*

os·prey /'ɒspreɪ; *NAmE* 'ɑːs-/ *noun* a large BIRD OF PREY (= a bird that kills other creatures for food) that eats fish

os·se·ous /'ɒsiəs; *NAmE* 'ɑːs-/ *adj.* (*technical*) made of or turned into bone

os·sify /'ɒsɪfaɪ; *NAmE* 'ɑːs-/ *verb* [usually passive] (**os·si·fies, os·si·fy·ing, os·si·fied, os·si·fied**) (*formal, disapproving*) **1** [I, T, usually passive] **~ (sth)** to become or make sth fixed and unable to change: *an ossified political system* **2** [I, T, usually passive] **~ (sth)** (*technical*) to become or make sth hard like bone ▶ **os·si·fi·ca·tion** *noun* [U] (*formal*)

os·ten·sible /ɒ'stensəbl; *NAmE* ɑː'st-/ *adj.* [only before noun] (*formal*) seeming or stated to be real or true, when this is perhaps not the case SYN **apparent**: *The ostensible reason for his absence was illness.* ▶ **os·ten·sibly** /-əbli/ *adv.*: *Troops were sent in, ostensibly to protect the civilian population.*

os·ten·ta·tion /ˌɒsten'teɪʃn; *NAmE* ˌɑːs-/ *noun* [U] (*disapproving*) an exaggerated display of wealth, knowledge or skill that is made in order to impress people

os·ten·ta·tious /ˌɒsten'teɪʃəs; *NAmE* ˌɑːs-/ *adj.* **1** (*disapproving*) expensive or noticeable in a way that is intended to impress people SYN **showy** **2** (*disapproving*) behaving in a way that is meant to impress people by showing how rich, important, etc. you are **3** (of an action) done in a very obvious way so that people will notice it: *He gave an ostentatious yawn.* ▶ **os·ten·ta·tious·ly** *adv.*: *ostentatiously dressed*

osteo- /'ɒstiəʊ; *NAmE* 'ɑːstioʊ-/ *combining form* (in nouns and adjectives) connected with bones: *osteopath*

osteo·arth·ritis /ˌɒstiəʊɑː'θraɪtɪs; *NAmE* ˌɑːstioʊɑːr'θ-/ *noun* [U] (*medical*) a disease that causes painful swelling and permanent damage in the joints of the body, especially the hips, knees and thumbs

osteo·path /ˈɒstiəpæθ; *NAmE* ˈɑːs-/ *noun* a person whose job involves treating some diseases and physical problems by pressing and moving the bones and muscles ➲ compare CHIROPRACTOR

oste·op·athy /ˌɒstiˈɒpəθi; *NAmE* ˌɑːstiˈɑːp-/ *noun* [U] the treatment of some diseases and physical problems by pressing and moving the bones and muscles ▸ **osteo·path·ic** /ˌɒstiəˈpæθɪk; *NAmE* ˌɑːs-/ *adj.*

osteo·por·osis /ˌɒstiəʊpəˈrəʊsɪs; *NAmE* ˌɑːstioʊpəˈroʊ-/ (also ˌ**brittle** ˈ**bone disease**) *noun* [U] (*medical*) a condition in which the bones become weak and are easily broken, usually when people get older or because they do not eat enough of certain substances

ost·ler /ˈɒslə(r); *NAmE* ˈɑːs-/ (*NAmE* also **host·ler**) *noun* (in the past) a man who took care of guests' horses at an INN

os·tra·cism /ˈɒstrəsɪzəm; *NAmE* ˈɑːs-/ *noun* [U] (*formal*) the act of deliberately not including sb in a group or activity; the state of not being included

os·tra·cize (*BrE* also **-ise**) /ˈɒstrəsaɪz; *NAmE* ˈɑːs-/ *verb* **~ sb** (*formal*) to refuse to let sb be a member of a social group; to refuse to meet or talk to sb **SYN shun**: *He was ostracized by his colleagues for refusing to support the strike.*

os·trich /ˈɒstrɪtʃ; *NAmE* ˈɑːs-; ˈɔːs-/ *noun* **1** a very large African bird with a long neck and long legs, that cannot fly but can run very fast **2** (*informal*) a person who prefers to ignore problems rather than try and deal with them

OTC /ˌəʊ tiː ˈsiː; *NAmE* ˌoʊ/ *abbr.* = OVER-THE-COUNTER: *OTC medicines and food supplements* ◇ *OTC trading of securities*

other 🔑 /ˈʌðə(r)/ *adj., pron.*
1 🔑 used to refer to people or things that are additional or different to people or things that have been mentioned or are known about: *Mr Harris and Mrs Bate and three other teachers were there.* ◇ *Are there any other questions?* ◇ *I can't see you now—**some other time**, maybe.* ◇ *Two buildings were destroyed and many others damaged in the blast.* ◇ *This option is preferable to any other.* ◇ ***Some** designs **are better than others**.* ➲ compare ANOTHER **2** 🔑 **the, my, your, etc. ~** used to refer to the second of two people or things: *My other sister is a doctor.* ◇ *One son went to live in Australia and **the other one** was killed in a car crash.* ◇ *He raised one arm and then the other.* ◇ *You must ask **one or other** of your parents.* **3** 🔑 **the, my, your, etc. ~** used to refer to the remaining people or things in a group: *I'll wear my other shoes—these are dirty.* ◇ *'I like this one.' 'What about **the other ones**?'* ◇ *I went swimming while the others played tennis.* **4** 🔑 **the other...** used to refer to a place, direction, etc. that is the opposite to where you are, are going, etc.: *I work on the other side of town.* ◇ *He crashed into a car coming the other way.* ◇ *He found me, not **the other way round/around**.* Most idioms containing **other** are at the entries for the nouns and verbs in the idioms, for example **in other words** is at **word**.
IDM **the** ˌ**other** ˈ**day/**ˈ**morning/**ˈ**evening/**ˈ**week** 🔑 recently: *I saw Jack the other day.* **other than** (usually used in negative sentences) **1** 🔑 except: *I don't know any French people other than you.* ◇ *We're going away in June but **other than that** I'll be here all summer.* **2** (*formal*) different or in a different way from; not: *I have never known him to behave other than selfishly.*

ˌ**other** ˈ**half** (also ˌ**better** ˈ**half**) *noun* (*informal, humorous*) the person that you are married to, or your boyfriend or girlfriend

other·ness /ˈʌðənəs; *NAmE* ˈʌðərnəs/ *noun* [U] (*formal*) the quality of being different or strange: *the otherness of an alien culture*

other·wise 🔑 /ˈʌðəwaɪz; *NAmE* ˈʌðərwaɪz/ *adv.*
1 🔑 used to state what the result would be if sth did not happen or if the situation were different: *My parents lent me the money. Otherwise, I couldn't have afforded the trip.* ◇ *Shut the window, otherwise it'll get too cold in here.* ◇ *We're committed to the project. We wouldn't be here otherwise.* **2** apart from that: *There was some music playing upstairs. Otherwise the house was silent.* ◇ *He was slightly bruised but otherwise unhurt.* **3** in a different way to the way mentioned; differently: *Bismarck, **otherwise known as** 'the Iron Chancellor'* ◇ *It is not permitted to sell or otherwise distribute copies of past examination papers.* ◇ *You know what this is about. Why **pretend otherwise** (= that you do not)?* ◇ *I wanted to see him but he was **otherwise engaged** (= doing sth else).*
IDM **or otherwise** used to refer to sth that is different from or the opposite of what has just been mentioned: *It was necessary to discover the truth or otherwise of these statements.* ◇ *We insure against all damage, accidental or otherwise.* ➲ more at KNOW *v.*

ˌ**other** ˈ**woman** *noun* [usually sing.] a woman with whom a man is having a sexual relationship, although he already has a wife or partner

ˌ**other-**ˈ**worldly** *adj.* concerned with spiritual thoughts and ideas rather than with ordinary life ▸ ˌ**other-**ˈ**worldli·ness** *noun* [U]

oti·ose /ˈəʊtiəʊs; *NAmE* ˈoʊʃioʊs/ *adj.* (*formal*) having no useful purpose **SYN unnecessary**: *an otiose round of meetings*

ot·itis /əʊˈtaɪtɪs; *NAmE* oʊ-/ *noun* [U] (*medical*) a painful swelling of the ear, caused by an infection

OTT /ˌəʊ tiː ˈtiː; *NAmE* ˌoʊ/ *adj.* (*BrE, informal*) = OVER THE TOP at TOP: *Her make-up was a bit OTT.*

otter /ˈɒtə(r); *NAmE* ˈɑːtər/ *noun* a small animal that has four WEBBED feet (= with skin between the toes), a tail and thick brown fur. Otters live in rivers and eat fish. ➲ **VISUAL VOCAB** page V10

otto /ˈɒtəʊ; *NAmE* ˈɑːtoʊ/ *noun* (*NAmE*) = ATTAR

ot·to·man /ˈɒtəmən; *NAmE* ˈɑːt-/ *noun* a piece of furniture like a large box with a soft top, used for storing things in and sitting on

OU /ˌəʊ ˈjuː; *NAmE* ˌoʊ/ *abbr.* (in Britain) Open University

ou /əʊ; *NAmE* oʊ/ *noun* (*pl.* os or ouens /ˈəʊənz; *NAmE* ˈoʊ-/) (*SAfrE*) = OKE

ouch /aʊtʃ/ *exclamation* used to express sudden pain: *Ouch! That hurt!*

oud /uːd/ *noun* a musical instrument similar to a LUTE played mainly in Arab countries

ought to 🔑 /ˈɔːt tə; *before vowels and finally* ˈɔːt tu/ *modal verb* (*negative* **ought not to**, *short form* (*especially BrE* **oughtn't to**)
1 🔑 used to say what is the right thing to do: *They ought to apologize.* ◇ *'Ought I to write to say thank you?' 'Yes, I think you ought (to).'* ◇ *They ought to have apologized (= but they didn't).* ◇ *Such things ought not to be allowed.* ◇ *He oughtn't to have been driving so fast.* ➲ note at SHOULD **2** 🔑 used to say what you expect or would like to happen: *Children ought to be able to read by the age of 7.* ◇ *Nurses ought to earn more.* **3** 🔑 used to say what you advise or recommend: *We ought to be leaving now.* ◇ *This is delicious. You ought to try some.* ◇ *You ought to have come to the meeting. It was interesting.* **4** 🔑 used to say what has probably happened or is probably true: *If he started out at nine, he ought to be here by now.* ◇ *That ought to be enough food for the four of us.* ◇ *Oughtn't the water to have boiled by now?* ➲ note at MODAL

Ouija board™ /ˈwiːdʒə bɔːd; *NAmE* bɔːrd/ *noun* a board marked with letters of the alphabet and other signs, used in SEANCES to receive messages said to come from people who are dead

ounce /aʊns/ *noun* **1** [C] (*abbr.* oz) a unit for measuring weight, 1/16 of a pound, equal to 28.35 grams ➲ see also FLUID OUNCE **2** [sing.] **~ of sth** (*informal*) (used especially with negatives) a very small quantity of sth: *There's not an ounce of truth in her story.* **IDM** see PREVENTION

our 🔑 /ɑː(r); ˈaʊə(r)/ *det.* (the possessive form of *we*)
1 🔑 belonging to us; connected with us: *our daughter/dog/house* ◇ *We showed them some of our photos.* ◇ *Our main export is rice.* ◇ *And now, over to our Rome correspond-*

O

ent... **2 Our** used to refer to or address God or a holy person: *Our Father* (= God) ◇ *Our Lady* (= the Virgin Mary)

ours 0‒ /ɑːz; ˈaʊəz; *NAmE* ɑːrz; ˈaʊərz/ *pron.*
1 0‒ the one or ones that belong to us: *Their house is very similar to ours, but ours is bigger.* ◇ *No, those are Ellie's kids. Ours are upstairs.* ◇ *He's a friend of ours.* **2** (*BrE, informal*) our home: *Do you fancy coming to ours for Sunday dinner?*

our·selves 0‒ /ɑːˈselvz; ˌaʊəˈs-; *NAmE* ɑːrˈs-; ˌaʊərˈs-/ *pron.*
1 0‒ the reflexive form of *we*; used when you and another person or other people together cause and are affected by an action: *We shouldn't blame ourselves for what happened.* ◇ *Let's just relax and enjoy ourselves.* ◇ *We'd like to see it for ourselves.* **2** 0‒ used to emphasize *we* or *us*; sometimes used instead of these words: *We've often thought of going there ourselves.* ◇ *The only people there were ourselves.*
IDM **(all) by ourˈselves 1** alone; without anyone else **2** without help **(all) to ourˈselves** for us alone; not shared with anyone: *We had the pool all to ourselves.*

-ous *suffix* (in adjectives) having the nature or quality of: *poisonous* ◇ *mountainous* ▸ **-ously** (in adverbs): *gloriously* **-ousness** (in nouns): *spaciousness*

oust /aʊst/ *verb* to force sb out of a job or position of power, especially in order to take their place: **~ sb (as sth)** *He was ousted as chairman.* ◇ **~ sb (from sth)** *The rebels finally managed to oust the government from power.*

oust·er /ˈaʊstə(r)/ *noun* (*NAmE*) the act of removing sb from a position of authority in order to put sb else in their place; the fact of being removed in this way: *the president's ouster by the military*

out 0‒ /aʊt/ *adv., prep., noun, adj., verb*
■ ***adv., prep.*** HELP For the special uses of **out** in phrasal verbs, look at the entries for the verbs. For example **burst out** is in the phrasal verb section at **burst**. **1** 0‒ **~ (of sth)** away from the inside of a place or thing: *She ran out into the corridor.* ◇ *She shook the bag and some coins fell out.* ◇ *I got out of bed.* ◇ *He opened the box and* ***out jumped*** *a frog.* ◇ ***Out you go!*** (= used to order sb to leave a room) ◇ (*informal*) *He ran out the door.* **2** 0‒ **~ (of sth)** (of people) away from or not at home or their place of work: *I called Liz but she was out.* ◇ *Let's go out this evening* (= for example to a restaurant or club). ◇ *We haven't had a* ***night out*** *for weeks.* ◇ *Mr Green is out of town this week.* **3** 0‒ **~ (of sth)** away from the edge of a place: *The boy dashed out into the road.* ◇ *Don't lean out of the window.* **4** 0‒ **~ (of sth)** a long or a particular distance away from a place or from land: *She's working out in Australia.* ◇ *He lives right out in the country.* ◇ *The boats are all out at sea.* ◇ *The ship sank ten miles out of Stockholm.* **5** 0‒ **~ (of sth)** used to show that sth/sb is removed from a place, job, etc.: *This detergent is good for getting stains out.* ◇ *We want this government out.* ◇ *He got thrown out of the restaurant.* **6** 0‒ **~ of sth/sb** used to show that sth comes from or is obtained from sth/sb: *He drank his beer out of the bottle.* ◇ *a statue made out of bronze* ◇ *a romance straight out of a fairy tale* ◇ *I paid for the damage out of my savings.* ◇ *We'll get the truth out of her.* **7** 0‒ **~ of sth** used to show that sb/sth does not have any of sth: *We're out of milk.* ◇ *He's been* ***out of work*** *for six months.* ◇ *You're* ***out of luck***—*she left ten minutes ago.* **8** 0‒ **~ of sth** used to show that sb/sth is not or no longer in a particular state or condition: *Try and stay out of trouble.* ◇ *I watched the car until it was* ***out of sight***. **9** 0‒ **~ (of sth)** used to show that sb is no longer involved in sth: *It was an awful job and I'm glad to be out of it.* ◇ *He gets out of the army in a few weeks.* ◇ *They'll be out* (= of prison) *on bail in no time.* ◇ *Brown goes on to the semi-finals but Lee is out.* **10 ~ of sth** used to show the reason why sth is done: *I asked out of curiosity.* ◇ *She did it out of spite.* **11** 0‒ **~ of sth** from a particular number or set: *You scored six out of ten.* ◇ *Two out of three people think the President should resign.* **12** 0‒ (of a book, etc.) not in the library; borrowed by sb else: *The book you wanted is out on loan.* **13** 0‒ (of the TIDE) at or towards its lowest point on land: *I like walking on the wet sand when the tide is out.* **14** 0‒ if the sun, moon or stars are or come **out**, they can be seen from the earth and are not hidden by clouds **15** (of flowers) fully open: *There should be some snowdrops out by now.* **16** 0‒ available to everyone; known to everyone: *When does her new book come out?* ◇ ***Word*** *always* ***gets out*** (= people find out about things) *no matter how careful you are.* ◇ ***Out with it!*** (= say what you know) **17** 0‒ clearly and loudly so that people can hear: *to* ***call/cry/shout out*** ◇ *Read it* ***out loud***. ◇ *Nobody* ***spoke out*** *in his defence.* **18** (*informal*) having told other people that you are HOMOSEXUAL: *I had been out since I was 17.* **19** (in CRICKET, BASEBALL, etc.) if a team or team member is **out**, it is no longer their turn with the BAT: *The West Indies were* ***all out for*** *364* (= after scoring 364 RUNS in CRICKET). **20** (in TENNIS, etc.) if the ball is **out**, it landed outside the line: *The umpire said the ball was out.* **21** 0‒ **~ (in sth)** not correct or exact; wrong: *I was slightly out in my calculations.* ◇ *Your guess was a long way out* (= completely wrong). ◇ *The estimate was* ***out by*** *more than $100.* **22** not possible or not allowed: *Swimming is out until the weather gets warmer.* **23** not fashionable: *Black is out this year.* **24** 0‒ (of fire, lights or burning materials) not or no longer burning or lit: *Suddenly all the lights went out.* ◇ *The fire had burnt itself out.* **25** at an end: *It was summer and school was out.* ◇ *She was to regret her words* ***before the day was out***. **26** unconscious: *He was out for more than an hour and came round in the hospital.* ◇ *She was knocked* ***out cold***. **27** (*BrE, informal*) on strike **28** to the end; completely: ***Hear me out*** *before you say anything.* ◇ *We left them to* ***fight it out*** (= settle a disagreement by fighting or arguing). ➲ see also ALL-OUT
IDM **be out for sth/to do sth** to be trying to get or do sth: *I'm not out for revenge.* ◇ *She's* ***out for what she can get*** (= trying to get something for herself). ◇ *The company is out to capture the Canadian market.* **ˌout and aˈbout** (*BrE*) **1** able to go outside again after an illness **2** travelling around a place: *We've been out and about talking to people all over the country.* **ˈout of here** (*informal*) going or leaving: *As soon as I get my money I'm out of here!* **ˈout of it** (*informal*) **1** sad because you are not included in sth: *We've only just moved here so we feel a little out of it.* **2** not aware of what is happening, usually because of drinking too much alcohol, or taking drugs
■ ***noun*** [sing.] a way of avoiding having to do sth: *She was desperately looking for an out.* IDM see IN *n.*
■ ***adj.*** (*informal*) having told other people that you are HOMOSEXUAL: *an out gay man*
■ ***verb*** **~ sb** to say publicly that sb is HOMOSEXUAL, especially when they would prefer to keep the fact a secret: *He is the latest politician to be outed by gay activists.*

out- /aʊt/ *prefix* **1** (in verbs) greater, better, further, longer, etc: *outnumber* ◇ *outwit* ◇ *outgrow* ◇ *outlive* **2** (in nouns and adjectives) outside; OUTWARD; away from: *outbuildings* ◇ *outpatient* ◇ *outlying* ◇ *outgoing*

out·age /ˈaʊtɪdʒ/ *noun* (*NAmE*) a period of time when the supply of electricity, etc. is not working: *a power outage*

ˌout-and-ˈout *adj.* [only before noun] in every way SYN **complete**: *What she said was an out-and-out lie.*

out·back /ˈaʊtbæk/ *noun* **the outback** [sing.] the area of Australia that is a long way from the coast and the towns, where few people live

out·bid /ˌaʊtˈbɪd/ *verb* (**out·bid·ding, out·bid, out·bid**) **~ sb (for sth)** to offer more money than sb else in order to buy sth, for example at an AUCTION

out·board /ˈaʊtbɔːd; *NAmE* -bɔːrd/ *adj.* (*technical*) on, towards or near the outside of a ship or an aircraft

ˌoutboard ˈmotor (also **ˌoutboard ˈengine, outboard**) *noun* an engine that you can fix to the back of a small boat

out·bound /ˈaʊtbaʊnd/ *adj.* (*formal*) travelling from a place rather than arriving in it: ***outbound flights/passengers*** OPP **inbound**

ˈout box (*US*) (*BrE* **ˈout tray**) *noun* (in an office) a container on your desk for letters or documents that are waiting to be sent out or passed to sb else ➲ compare IN TRAY ➲ VISUAL VOCAB Page V56

out·box /ˈaʊtbɒks; *NAmE* -bɑːks/ *noun* (*computing*) the place on a computer where new email messages that you write are stored before you send them

out·break /ˈaʊtbreɪk/ *noun* the sudden start of sth unpleasant, especially violence or a disease: *the outbreak of war* ◇ *an outbreak of typhoid* ◇ *Outbreaks of rain are expected in the afternoon.* ➲ COLLOCATIONS at ILL

out·build·ing /ˈaʊtbɪldɪŋ/ *noun* [usually pl.] a building such as a SHED or STABLE that is built near to, but separate from, a main building

out·burst /ˈaʊtbɜːst; *NAmE* -bɜːrst/ *noun* **1** a sudden strong expression of an emotion: *an outburst of anger* ◇ *She was alarmed by his violent outburst.* **2** a sudden increase in a particular activity or attitude: *an outburst of racism*

out·cast /ˈaʊtkɑːst; *NAmE* -kæst/ *noun* a person who is not accepted by other people and who sometimes has to leave their home and friends: *People with the disease were often treated as social outcasts.* ▶ **out·cast** *adj.*

out·class /ˌaʊtˈklɑːs; *NAmE* -ˈklæs/ *verb* [often passive] **~ sb/sth** to be much better than sb you are competing against: *Kennedy was outclassed 0–6 0–6 in the final.*

out·come AW /ˈaʊtkʌm/ *noun* the result or effect of an action or event: *We are waiting to hear the final outcome of the negotiations.* ◇ *These costs are payable whatever the outcome of the case.* ◇ *We are confident of a successful outcome.* ◇ *Four possible outcomes have been identified.* ➲ SYNONYMS at RESULT

out·crop /ˈaʊtkrɒp; *NAmE* -krɑːp/ *noun* a large mass of rock that stands above the surface of the ground

out·cry /ˈaʊtkraɪ/ *noun* [C, U] (*pl.* -ies) **~ (at/over/against sth)** a reaction of anger or strong protest shown by people in public: *an outcry over the proposed change* ◇ *The new tax provoked a* ***public outcry****.* ◇ *There was outcry at the judge's statement.*

out·dated /ˌaʊtˈdeɪtɪd/ *adj.* no longer useful because of being old-fashioned: *outdated equipment* ◇ *These figures are now outdated.* ➲ compare OUT OF DATE

out·dis·tance /ˌaʊtˈdɪstəns/ *verb* **~ sb/sth** to leave sb/sth behind by going faster, further, etc; to be better than sb/sth SYN **outstrip**

outdo /ˌaʊtˈduː/ *verb* (**out·does** /-ˈdʌz/, **out·did** /-ˈdɪd/, **out·done** /-ˈdʌn/) **~ sb/sth** to do more or better than sb else SYN **beat**: *Sometimes small firms can outdo big business when it comes to customer care.* ◇ ***Not to be outdone*** (= not wanting to let sb else do better)*, she tried again.*

out·door 0‑ᴡ /ˈaʊtdɔː(r)/ *adj.* [only before noun] used, happening or located outside rather than in a building: ***outdoor clothing/activities*** ◇ *an outdoor swimming pool* ◇ *I'm not really the* ***outdoor type*** (= I prefer indoor activities). OPP **indoor**

out·doors 0‑ᴡ /ˌaʊtˈdɔːz; *NAmE* -ˈdɔːrz/ *adv., noun*

- ***adv.*** 0‑ᴡ outside, rather than in a building: *The rain prevented them from eating outdoors.* OPP **indoors**
- ***noun*** **the outdoors** [sing.] the countryside, away from buildings and busy places: *They both have a love of the outdoors.* ◇ *Come to Canada and enjoy* ***the great outdoors****.* ➲ COLLOCATIONS at TOWN

outer 0‑ᴡ /ˈaʊtə(r)/ *adj.* [only before noun] **1** 0‑ᴡ on the outside of sth SYN **external**: *the outer layers of the skin* **2** 0‑ᴡ furthest from the inside or centre of sth: *I walked along the outer edge of the track.* ◇ *the outer suburbs of the city* ◇ *Outer London/Mongolia* ◇ (*figurative*) *to explore the outer* (= most extreme) *limits of human experience* OPP **inner**

ˈ**outer belt** (*US*) (*BrE* ˈ**ring road**) *noun* a road that is built around a city or town to reduce traffic in the centre

outer·most /ˈaʊtəməʊst; *NAmE* ˈaʊtərmoʊst/ *adj.* [only before noun] furthest from the inside or centre: *the outermost planet* ◇ *He fired and hit the outermost ring of the target.* OPP **innermost**

ˌ**outer** ˈ**space** *noun* [U] = SPACE (5): *radio waves from outer space*

outer·wear /ˈaʊtəweə(r); *NAmE* ˈaʊtərwer/ *noun* [U] clothes such as coats, hats, etc. that you wear outside

out·face /ˌaʊtˈfeɪs/ *verb* **~ sb** (*formal*) to defeat an enemy or opponent by being brave and remaining confident

out·fall /ˈaʊtfɔːl/ *noun* (*technical*) the place where a river, pipe, etc. flows out into the sea: *a sewage outfall*

out·field /ˈaʊtfiːld/ *noun, adv.*

- ***noun*** [sing.] the outer part of the field in BASEBALL, CRICKET and some other sports ➲ compare INFIELD
- ***adv.*** in or to the outfield

out·field·er /ˈaʊtfiːldə(r)/ *noun* (in CRICKET and BASEBALL) a player in the outfield

out·fit /ˈaʊtfɪt/ *noun, verb*

- ***noun*** **1** [C] a set of clothes that you wear together, especially for a particular occasion or purpose: *She was wearing an expensive new outfit.* ◇ *a wedding outfit* ◇ *a cowboy/Superman outfit* (= one that you wear for fun in order to look like the type of person mentioned) **2** [C+sing./pl. v.] (*informal*) a group of people working together as an organization, business, team, etc: *a market research outfit* ◇ *This was the fourth album by the top rock outfit.* **3** [C] a set of equipment that you need for a particular purpose: *a bicycle repair outfit*
- ***verb*** (-tt-) [often passive] **~ sth/sb (with sth)** (*especially NAmE*) to provide sb/sth with equipment or clothes for a special purpose SYN **equip**: *The ship was outfitted with a 12-bed hospital.*

out·fit·ter (also **out·fit·ters**) /ˈaʊtfɪtə(r)/ *noun* **1** (*old-fashioned, BrE*) a shop/store that sells men's clothes or school uniforms **2** (*NAmE*) a shop/store that sells equipment for camping and other outdoor activities

out·flank /ˌaʊtˈflæŋk/ *verb* **1 ~ sb/sth** to move around the side of an enemy or opponent, especially in order to attack them from behind **2 ~ sb/sth** to gain an advantage over sb, especially by doing sth unexpected SYN **outmanoeuvre**

out·flow /ˈaʊtfləʊ; *NAmE* -floʊ/ *noun* [usually sing.] **~ (of sth/sb) (from sth)** the movement of a large amount of money, liquid, people, etc. out of a place: *There was a capital outflow of $22 billion in 2008.* ◇ *a steady outflow of oil from the tank* ◇ *the outflow of refugees* OPP **inflow**

out·fox /ˌaʊtˈfɒks; *NAmE* -ˈfɑːks/ *verb* **~ sb** to gain an advantage over sb by being more clever than they are SYN **outwit**

out·going /ˈaʊtgəʊɪŋ; *NAmE* -goʊ-/ *adj.* **1** liking to meet other people, enjoying their company and being friendly towards them SYN **sociable**: *an outgoing personality* **2** [only before noun] leaving the position of responsibility mentioned: *the* ***outgoing president/government*** OPP **incoming** **3** [only before noun] going away from a particular place rather than arriving in it: *This telephone should be used for outgoing calls.* ◇ ***outgoing flights/passengers*** ◇ *the outgoing tide* OPP **incoming**

out·goings /ˈaʊtgəʊɪŋz; *NAmE* -goʊ-/ *noun* [pl.] (*BrE*) the amount of money that a person or a business has to spend regularly, for example every month SYN **expenditure**: ***low/high outgoings*** ◇ *Write down your* ***incomings and outgoings****.*

ˈ**out-group** *noun* the people who do not belong to a particular IN-GROUP in a society

out·grow /ˌaʊtˈgrəʊ; *NAmE* -ˈgroʊ/ *verb* (**out·grew** /-ˈgruː/, **out·grown** /-ˈgrəʊn; *NAmE* -ˈgroʊn/) **1 ~ sth** to grow too big to be able to wear or fit into sth SYN **grow out of**: *She's already outgrown her school uniform.* ◇ *The company has outgrown its offices.* **2 ~ sb** to grow taller, larger or more quickly than another person: *He's already outgrown his older brother.* **3 ~ sth** to stop doing sth or lose interest in sth as you become older SYN **grow out of**: *He's outgrown his passion for rock music.*

out·growth /ˈaʊtgrəʊθ; *NAmE* -groʊθ/ *noun* **1** (*technical*) a thing that grows out of sth else: *The eye first appears as a cup-shaped outgrowth from the brain.* **2** (*formal*) a natural

O

development or result of sth: *The law was an outgrowth of the 2008 presidential election.*

out·gun /ˌaʊtˈɡʌn/ *verb* (-nn-) [often passive] **~ sb/sth** to have greater military strength than sb: (*figurative*) *The England team was completely outgunned.*

out·house /ˈaʊthaʊs/ *noun* **1** (*BrE*) a small building, such as a SHED, outside a main building **2** (*especially NAmE*) a toilet in a small building of its own

out·ing /ˈaʊtɪŋ/ *noun* **1** [C] **~ (to…)** a trip that you go on for pleasure or education, usually with a group of people and lasting no more than one day SYN **excursion**: *We went **on an outing** to London.* ◇ *a family outing* ➲ SYNONYMS at TRIP **2** [C] (*sport*) (*informal*) an occasion when sb takes part in a competition **3** [U, C] the practice of naming people as HOMOSEXUALS in public, when they do not want anyone to know

out·land·ish /aʊtˈlændɪʃ/ *adj.* (usually *disapproving*) strange or extremely unusual SYN **bizarre**: *outlandish costumes/ideas* ▸ **out·land·ish·ly** *adv.*

out·last /ˌaʊtˈlɑːst; *NAmE* -ˈlæst/ *verb* **~ sb/sth** to continue to exist or take part in an activity for a longer time than sb/sth: *He can outlast anyone on the dance floor.*

out·law /ˈaʊtlɔː/ *verb, noun*

■ ***verb*** **1 ~ sth** to make sth illegal SYN **ban**: *plans to outlaw the carrying of knives* ◇ *the outlawed nationalist party* **2 ~ sb** (in the past) to make sb an outlaw

■ ***noun*** (used especially about people in the past) a person who has done sth illegal and is hiding to avoid being caught; a person who is not protected by the law: *Robin Hood, the world's most famous outlaw*

out·lay /ˈaʊtleɪ/ *noun* [C, U] **~ (on sth)** the money that you have to spend in order to start a new project: *The business quickly repaid the initial outlay on advertising.* ◇ *a massive **financial/capital outlay*** ➲ SYNONYMS at COSTS

out·let /ˈaʊtlet/ *noun* **1 ~ (for sth)** a way of expressing or making good use of strong feelings, ideas or energy: *She needed to find an outlet for her many talents and interests.* ◇ *Sport became the perfect outlet for his aggression.* **2** (*business*) a shop/store or an organization that sells goods made by a particular company or of a particular type: *The business has 34 retail outlets in this state alone.* **3** (*especially NAmE*) a shop/store that sells goods of a particular make at reduced prices: *the Nike outlet in the outlet mall* **4** a pipe or hole through which liquid or gas can flow out: *a sewage outlet* ◇ *an outlet pipe* OPP **inlet** **5** (also **re·cep·tacle**) (both *NAmE*) (*BrE* **socket**, ˈ**power point**) a device in a wall that you put a plug into in order to connect electrical equipment to the power supply of a building ➲ picture at PLUG

out·line 0‑w /ˈaʊtlaɪn/ *verb, noun*

■ ***verb*** **1** 0‑w **~ sth (to sb)** | **~ what, how, etc…** to give a description of the main facts or points involved in sth SYN **sketch**: *We outlined our proposals to the committee.* **2** 0‑w [usually passive] **~ sth (against sth)** to show or mark the outer edge of sth: *They saw the huge building outlined against the sky.*

■ ***noun*** [C, U] **1** 0‑w a description of the main facts or points involved in sth: *This is a brief outline of the events.* ◇ *You should draw up a plan or outline for the essay.* ◇ *The book describes **in outline** the main findings of the research.* ◇ *an **outline agreement/proposal*** **2** 0‑w the line that goes around the edge of sth, showing its main shape but not the details: *At last we could see the dim outline of an island.* ◇ *an **outline map/sketch*** ◇ *She drew the figures **in outline**.*

out·live /ˌaʊtˈlɪv/ *verb* **1 ~ sb** to live longer than sb: *He outlived his wife by three years.* **2 ~ sth** to continue to exist after sth else has ended or disappeared: *The machine had **outlived its usefulness*** (= was no longer useful).

out·look /ˈaʊtlʊk/ *noun* [usually sing.] **1 ~ (on sth)** the attitude to life and the world of a particular person, group or culture: *He had a practical outlook on life.* ◇ *Most Western societies are liberal **in outlook**.* **2 ~ (for sth)** the probable future for sb/sth; what is likely to happen SYN **prospect**: *The outlook for jobs is bleak.* ◇ *the country's economic outlook* ◇ *The outlook* (= the probable weather) *for the weekend is dry and sunny.* **3** (*formal*) a view from a particular place: *The house has a pleasant outlook over the valley.*

out·ly·ing /ˈaʊtlaɪɪŋ/ *adj.* [only before noun] far away from the cities of a country or from the main part of a place: *outlying areas*

out·man·oeuvre (*especially US* **out·ma·neu·ver**) /ˌaʊtməˈnuːvə(r)/ *verb* **~ sb/sth** to do better than an opponent by acting in a way that is cleverer or more skilful: *The president has so far managed to outmanoeuvre his critics.*

out·moded /ˌaʊtˈməʊdɪd; *NAmE* -ˈmoʊd-/ *adj.* (*disapproving*) no longer fashionable or useful: *an outmoded attitude*

out·num·ber /ˌaʊtˈnʌmbə(r)/ *verb* **~ sb/sth** to be greater in number than sb/sth: *The demonstrators were heavily outnumbered by the police.* ◇ *In this profession, women outnumber men by two to one* (= there are twice as many women as men).

ˌ**out-of-ˌbody exˈperience** *noun* a feeling of being outside your own body, especially when you feel that you are watching yourself from a distance

ˌ**out of ˈdate** *adj.* **1** old-fashioned or without the most recent information and therefore no longer useful: *These figures are very out of date.* ◇ *Suddenly she felt old and out of date.* ◇ *an out-of-date map* ◇ *out-of-date technology* ➲ compare OUTDATED **2** no longer valid: *an out-of-date driving licence* ➲ see also UP TO DATE

ˈ**out-of-pocket** *adj.* **~ expenses/costs/expenditure/spending** small business expenses that you pay yourself, with your employer paying you back later: *On business trips she has some travel and other out-of-pocket expenses.* ➲ compare POCKET *n.*

ˌ**out-of-ˈstate** *adj.* [only before noun] (*US*) coming from or happening in a different state: *out-of-state license plates*

ˌ**out-of-the-ˈway** *adj.* far from a town or city: *a little out-of-the-way place on the coast*

ˌ**out-of-ˈtown** *adj.* [only before noun] **1** located away from the centre of a town or city: *out-of-town superstores* **2** coming from or happening in a different place: *an out-of-town guest* ◇ *an out-of-town performance*

ˌ**out-of-ˈwork** *adj.* [only before noun] unemployed: *an out-of-work actor*

out·pace /ˌaʊtˈpeɪs/ *verb* **~ sb/sth** to go, rise, improve, etc. faster than sb/sth SYN **outstrip**: *He easily outpaced the other runners.* ◇ *Demand is outpacing production.*

out·pa·tient /ˈaʊtpeɪʃnt/ *noun* a person who goes to a hospital for treatment but does not stay there: *an outpatient clinic* ➲ compare INPATIENT

out·per·form /ˌaʊtpəˈfɔːm; *NAmE* -pərˈfɔːrm/ *verb* **~ sb/sth** to achieve better results than sb/sth ▸ **out·per·form·ance** *noun* [U]

out·place·ment /ˈaʊtpleɪsmənt/ *noun* [U] (*business*) the process of helping people to find new jobs after they have been made unemployed

out·play /ˌaʊtˈpleɪ/ *verb* **~ sb** to play much better than sb you are competing against: *We were totally outplayed and lost 106–74.*

out·point /ˌaʊtˈpɔɪnt/ *verb* **~ sb** (especially in boxing) to defeat sb by scoring more points

out·post /ˈaʊtpəʊst; *NAmE* -poʊst/ *noun* **1** a small military camp away from the main army, used for watching an enemy's movements, etc. **2** a small town or group of buildings in a lonely part of a country: *a remote outpost* ◇ *the last outpost of civilization*

out·pour·ing /ˈaʊtpɔːrɪŋ/ *noun* **1** [usually pl.] a strong and sudden expression of feeling: *spontaneous outpourings of praise* **2** a large amount of sth produced in a short time: *a remarkable outpouring of new ideas*

out·put 0‑w AW /ˈaʊtpʊt/ *noun, verb*

■ ***noun*** [U, sing.] **1** 0‑w the amount of sth that a person, a machine or an organization produces: *Manufacturing output has increased by 8%.* **2** (*computing*) the information, results, etc. produced by a computer: *data output* ◇ *an output* *device* ➲ compare INPUT **3** the power, energy, etc. produced by a piece of equipment: *an output of 100 watts* **4** a place where energy, power, information, etc. leaves a system: *Connect a cable to the output.*

■ ***verb*** (**out·put·ting, out·put, out·put**) **~ sth** (*computing*) to supply or produce information, results, etc: *Computers can now output data much more quickly.* ➲ compare INPUT

out·rage /ˈaʊtreɪdʒ/ *noun, verb*

■ ***noun*** **1** [U] a strong feeling of shock and anger: *The judge's remarks caused public outrage.* ◇ *Environmentalists have expressed outrage at the ruling.* **2** [C] an act or event that is violent, cruel or very wrong and that shocks people or makes them very angry SYN **atrocity**: *No one has yet claimed responsibility for this latest bomb outrage.*

■ ***verb*** [often passive] **~ sb** to make sb very shocked and angry: *He was outraged at the way he had been treated.*

out·ra·geous /aʊtˈreɪdʒəs/ *adj.* **1** very shocking and unacceptable SYN **scandalous**: *outrageous behaviour* ◇ *'That's outrageous!' he protested.* **2** very unusual and slightly shocking: *She says the most outrageous things sometimes.* ◇ *outrageous clothes* ▶ **out·ra·geous·ly** *adv.*: *an outrageously expensive meal* ◇ *They behaved outrageously.*

out·ran *past tense* of OUTRUN

out·rank /ˌaʊtˈræŋk/ *verb* **~ sb** to be of higher rank, quality, etc. than sb

outré /ˈuːtreɪ; *NAmE* uːˈtreɪ/ *adj.* (from *French, formal*) very unusual and slightly shocking

out·reach /ˈaʊtriːtʃ/ *noun* [U] the activity of an organization that provides a service or advice to people in the community, especially those who cannot or are unlikely to come to an office, a hospital, etc. for help: *an outreach and education programme* ◇ *outreach workers* ◇ *efforts to expand the outreach to black voters*

out·rider /ˈaʊtraɪdə(r)/ *noun* a person who rides a motorcycle or a horse in front of or beside the vehicle of an important person in order to give protection

out·rig·ger /ˈaʊtrɪɡə(r)/ *noun* a wooden structure that is fixed to the side of a boat or ship in order to keep it steady in the water; a boat fitted with such a structure

out·right /ˈaʊtraɪt/ *adj., adv.*

■ ***adj.*** [only before noun] **1** complete and total: *an outright ban/rejection/victory* ◇ *She was the outright winner.* ◇ *No one party is expected to gain an outright majority.* **2** open and direct: *There was outright opposition to the plan.*

■ ***adv.*** **1** in a direct way and without trying to hide anything: *Why don't you ask him outright if it's true?* ◇ *She couldn't help herself and she laughed outright.* **2** clearly and completely: *Neither candidate won outright.* ◇ *The group rejects outright any negotiations with the government.* **3** not gradually; immediately: *Most of the crash victims were **killed outright**.* ◇ *We had saved enough money to buy the house outright.*

out·run /ˌaʊtˈrʌn/ *verb* (**out·run·ning, out·ran** /-ˈræn/, **out·run**) **1 ~ sb/sth** to run faster or further than sb/sth: *He couldn't outrun his pursuers.* **2 ~ sth** to develop faster than sth SYN **outstrip**: *Demand for the new model is outrunning supply.*

out·sell /ˌaʊtˈsel/ *verb* (**out·sold, out·sold** /-ˈsəʊld; *NAmE* -ˈsoʊld/) **~ sb/sth** to sell more or to be sold in larger quantities than sb/sth: *We are now outselling all our competitors.* ◇ *This year the newspaper has outsold its main rival.*

out·set /ˈaʊtset/ *noun*

IDM **at/from the ˈoutset (of sth)** at/from the beginning of sth: *I made it clear right from the outset that I disapproved.*

out·shine /ˌaʊtˈʃaɪn/ *verb* (**out·shone, out·shone** /-ˈʃɒn; *NAmE* -ˈʃoʊn/) **~ sb/sth** to be more impressive than sb/sth; to be better than sb/sth

out·side 🔑 *noun, adj., prep., adv.*

■ ***noun*** /ˌaʊtˈsaɪd/ (usually **the outside**) **1** 🔑 [C, usually sing.] the outer side or surface of sth SYN **exterior**: *The outside of the house needs painting.* ◇ *You can't open the door from the outside.* **2** 🔑 [sing.] the area that is near or around a building, etc: *I walked around the outside of the building.* ◇ *I didn't go into the temple—I only saw it from the outside.* **3** 🔑 [sing.] the part of a road nearest to the middle: *Always overtake **on the outside**.* **4** [sing.] the part of a curving road or track furthest from the inner or shorter side of the curve OPP **the inside**

IDM **at the outside** at the most; as a maximum: *There was room for 20 people at the outside.* **on the outside 1** used to describe how sb appears or seems: *On the outside she seems calm, but I know she's worried.* **2** not in prison: *Life on the outside took some getting used to again.*

■ ***adj.*** /ˈaʊtsaɪd/ [only before noun] **1** 🔑 of, on or facing the outer side SYN **external**: *The outside walls are damp.* **2** 🔑 not located in the main building; going out of the main building SYN **external**: *an outside toilet* ◇ *You have to pay to make outside calls.* ◇ *I can't get an outside line.* **3** 🔑 not included in or connected with your group, organization, country, etc: *We plan to use an outside firm of consultants.* ◇ *She has a lot of **outside interests*** (= not connected with her work). ◇ *They felt cut off from the **outside world*** (= from other people and from other things that were happening). **4** used to say that sth is very unlikely: *They have only an **outside chance** of winning.* ◇ *150 is an outside estimate* (= it is very likely to be less).

■ ***prep.*** /ˌaʊtˈsaɪd/ (also **out·side of** especially in *NAmE*) **1** 🔑 on or to a place on the outside of sth: *You can park your car outside our house.* OPP **inside 2** 🔑 away from or not in a particular place: *It's the biggest theme park outside the United States.* ◇ *We live in a small village **just outside** Leeds.* **3** 🔑 not part of sth: *The matter is outside my area of responsibility.* ◇ *You may do as you wish outside working hours.* OPP **within 4 outside of** apart from: *There was nothing they could do, outside of hoping things would get better.*

■ ***adv.*** /ˌaʊtˈsaɪd/ **1** 🔑 not in a room, building or container but on or to the outside of it: *I'm seeing a patient—please wait outside.* ◇ *The house is painted green outside.* **2** 🔑 not inside a building: *It's warm enough to eat outside.* ◇ *Go outside and see if it's raining.* OPP **inside**

ˌoutside ˈbroadcast *noun* (*BrE*) a programme filmed or recorded away from the main studio

ˌoutside ˈlane (*BrE*) (*NAmE* **ˌpassing ˈlane**) *noun* the part of a major road such as a MOTORWAY or INTERSTATE nearest the middle of the road, where vehicles drive fastest and can go past vehicles ahead

out·sider /ˌaʊtˈsaɪdə(r)/ *noun* **1** a person who is not accepted as a member of a society, group, etc: *Here she felt she would always be an outsider.* **2** a person who is not part of a particular organization or profession: *They have decided to hire outsiders for some of the key positions.* ◇ *To an outsider it may appear to be a glamorous job.* **3** a person or an animal taking part in a race or competition that is not expected to win: *The race was won by a 20–1 outsider.* ◇ *To everyone's surprise, the post went to **a rank outsider*** (= a complete outsider).

out·size /ˈaʊtsaɪz/ (also **out·sized** /ˈaʊtsaɪzd/) *adj.* [usually before noun] **1** larger than the usual size: *an outsize desk* **2** designed for large people: *outsize clothes*

out·skirts /ˈaʊtskɜːts; *NAmE* -skɜːrts/ *noun* [pl.] the parts of a town or city that are furthest from the centre: *They live **on the outskirts** of Milan.*

out·smart /ˌaʊtˈsmɑːt; *NAmE* -ˈsmɑːrt/ *verb* **~ sb** to gain an advantage over sb by acting in a clever way SYN **outwit**: *She always managed to outsmart her political rivals.*

out·source /ˈaʊtsɔːs; *NAmE* -sɔːrs/ *verb* [T, I] **~ (sth)** (*business*) to arrange for sb outside a company to do work or provide goods for that company: *We outsource all our computing work.* ▶ **out·sourc·ing** *noun* [U]

out·spoken /aʊtˈspəʊkən; *NAmE* -ˈspoʊkən/ *adj.* saying exactly what you think, even if this shocks or offends people SYN **blunt**: *an outspoken opponent of the leader* ◇ *outspoken comments* ◇ **~ in sth** *She was outspoken in her criticism of the plan.* ➲ SYNONYMS at HONEST ▶ **out·spoken·ly** *adv.* **out·spoken·ness** *noun* [U]

out·spread /ˌaʊtˈspred/ *adj.* (*formal*) spread out completely: *The bird soared high, with outspread wings.*

O

out·stand·ing 🔑 /aʊtˈstændɪŋ/ *adj.* **1** 🔑 extremely good; excellent: *an outstanding player/achievement/success* ◇ *an area of* ***outstanding natural beauty*** ➲ SYNONYMS at EXCELLENT **2** 🔑 [usually before noun] very obvious or important SYN **prominent**: *the outstanding features of the landscape* **3** (of payment, work, problems, etc.) not yet paid, done, solved, etc: *She has outstanding debts of over £500.* ◇ *A lot of work is still outstanding.*

out·stand·ing·ly /aʊtˈstændɪŋli/ *adv.* **1** used to emphasize the good quality of sth SYN **remarkably**: *outstandingly successful* **2** extremely well: *He performed well but not outstandingly.*

out·stay /ˌaʊtˈsteɪ/ *verb* IDM see WELCOME *n.*

out·stretched /ˌaʊtˈstretʃt/ *adj.* (of parts of the body) stretched or spread out as far as possible: *He ran towards her* ***with arms outstretched/with outstretched arms***.

out·strip /ˌaʊtˈstrɪp/ *verb* (-pp-) **1** **~ sth** to become larger, more important, etc. than sb/sth: *Demand is outstripping supply.* **2** **~ sth** to be faster, better or more successful than sb you are competing against SYN **surpass**: *Their latest computer outstrips all its rivals.* **3** **~ sb** to run faster than sb in a race so that you pass them

outta (also **outa**) /ˈaʊtə/ *prep.* used for writing the way 'out of' is sometimes pronounced in informal speech: *I'm outta here!* (= I'm leaving now.)

ˈout-take *noun* a piece of a film that is removed before the film/movie is shown, for example because it contains a mistake

ˈout-there *adj.* (*NAmE, informal*) (of people) different, confident, having strong opinions, and attracting attention to yourself; (of ideas) different from what most people consider normal, but exciting: *Wow, this is such an out-there character. This role is definitely going to be cool.* ◇ *It may be totally out-there but I think it could work.*

O

ˈout tray (*BrE*) (*US* **ˈout box**) *noun* (in an office) a container on your desk for letters or documents that are waiting to be sent out or passed to sb else ➲ compare IN TRAY ➲ VISUAL VOCAB page V56

out·vote /ˌaʊtˈvəʊt; *NAmE* -ˈvoʊt/ *verb* [usually passive] **~ sb/sth** to defeat sb/sth by winning a larger number of votes SYN **vote sb/sth down**: *His proposal was outvoted by 10 votes to 8.*

out·ward /ˈaʊtwəd; *NAmE* -wərd/ *adj.* [only before noun] **1** connected with the way people or things seem to be rather than with what is actually true: *Mark showed no outward signs of distress.* ◇ *She simply observes the outward forms of religion.* ◇ ***To all outward appearances*** (= as far as it was possible to judge from the outside) *they were perfectly happy.* OPP **inward** **2** going away from a particular place, especially one that you are going to return to: *the* ***outward voyage/journey*** **3** away from the centre or a particular point: *outward movement* ◇ ***outward investment*** (= in other countries) ◇ *Managers need to become more* ***outward-looking*** (= more open to new ideas). OPP **inward**

ˌoutward ˈbound *adj.* going away from home or a particular place

the ˌOutward ˌBound ˈTrust [sing.] (also **ˌOutward ˈBound™** [U]) *noun* an international organization that provides training in outdoor activities including sports for young people

out·ward·ly /ˈaʊtwədli; *NAmE* -wərd-/ *adv.* on the surface; in appearance: *Though badly frightened, she remained outwardly composed.* ◇ *Outwardly, the couple seemed perfectly happy.* OPP **inwardly**

out·wards /ˈaʊtwədz; *NAmE* -wərdz/ (*BrE*) (also **outward** *NAmE, BrE*) *adv.* **~ (from sth)** towards the outside; away from the centre or from a particular point: *The door opens outwards.* ◇ *Factories were spreading outwards from the old heart of the town.* OPP **inwards**

out·weigh /ˌaʊtˈweɪ/ *verb* **~ sth** to be greater or more important than sth: *The advantages* ***far outweigh*** *the disadvantages.*

out·wit /ˌaʊtˈwɪt/ *verb* (-tt-) **~ sb/sth** to defeat sb/sth or gain an advantage over them by doing sth clever SYN **outsmart**: *Somehow he always manages to outwit his opponents.*

out·with /ˌaʊtˈwɪθ/ *prep.* (*ScotE*) outside of sth; not within sth

out·work /ˈaʊtwɜːk; *NAmE* -wɜːrk/ *noun* [U] (*business*) (*BrE*) work that is done by people at home ▶ **out·work·er** *noun*

out·work·ing /ˈaʊtwɜːkɪŋ; *NAmE* -wɜːrk-/ *noun* [U] (*business*) (*BrE*) the activity of doing work away from the office or factory that provides the work

out·worn /ˈaʊtwɔːn; *NAmE* -wɔːrn/ *adj.* [usually before noun] old-fashioned and no longer useful SYN **obsolete**: *outworn institutions* ➲ compare WORN OUT

ouzo /ˈuːzəʊ; *NAmE* ˈuːzoʊ/ *noun* [U] a strong alcoholic drink from Greece, made from ANISEED and usually drunk with water

ova *pl.* of OVUM

oval /ˈəʊvl; *NAmE* ˈoʊvl/ *adj., noun*
■ ***adj.*** shaped like an egg: *an oval face*
■ ***noun*** **1** an oval shape **2** (*AustralE*) a ground for Australian Rules football

the ˌOval ˈOffice *noun* [sing.] **1** the office of the US President in the White House **2** a way of referring to the US President and the part of the government that is controlled by the President: *Congress is waiting to see how the Oval Office will react.*

ovary /ˈəʊvəri; *NAmE* ˈoʊ-/ *noun* (*pl.* -ies) **1** either of the two organs in a woman's body that produce eggs; a similar organ in female animals, birds and fish **2** the part of a plant that produces seeds ➲ VISUAL VOCAB page V9 ▶ **ovar·ian** /əʊˈveəriən; *NAmE* oʊˈver-/ *adj.* [only before noun]: *ovarian cancer*

ova·tion /əʊˈveɪʃn; *NAmE* oʊ-/ *noun* enthusiastic clapping by an audience as a sign of their approval: *to give sb a* ***huge/rapturous/rousing ovation*** ◇ *The soloist got a ten-minute* ***standing ovation*** (= in which people stand up from their seats).

oven 🔑 /ˈʌvn/ *noun* the part of a cooker/stove shaped like a box with a door on the front, in which food is cooked or heated: *Take the cake out of the oven.* ◇ *a gas/an electric oven* ◇ *a* ***cool/hot/moderate oven*** ◇ *Open a window, it's* ***like an oven*** *in here!* ➲ VISUAL VOCAB pages V22, V24 ➲ compare MICROWAVE IDM see BUN

ˈoven glove (also **ˈoven mitt**) *noun* a glove made of thick material, used for holding hot dishes from an oven ➲ VISUAL VOCAB page V22

oven·proof /ˈʌvnpruːf/ *adj.* suitable for use in a hot oven: *an ovenproof dish*

ˌoven-ˈready *adj.* [usually before noun] (of food) bought already prepared and ready for cooking

oven·ware /ˈʌvnweə(r); *NAmE* -wer/ *noun* [U] dishes that can be used for cooking food in an oven

over 🔑 /ˈəʊvə(r); *NAmE* ˈoʊ-/ *adv., prep., noun*
■ ***adv.*** HELP For the special uses of **over** in phrasal verbs, look at the entries for the verbs. For example **take sth over** is in the phrasal verb section at **take**. **1** 🔑 downwards and away from a vertical position: *Try not to knock that vase over.* ◇ *The wind must have blown it over.* **2** 🔑 from one side to another side: *She turned over onto her front.* ◇ *The car skidded off the road and rolled over and over.* **3** 🔑 across a street, an open space, etc: *I stopped and crossed over.* ◇ *He rowed us over to the other side of the lake.* ◇ *They have gone over to France.* ◇ *This is my aunt who's over from Canada.* ◇ *I went over* (= across the room) *and asked her name.* ◇ *Put it down* ***over there***. **4** 🔑 so as to cover sb/sth completely: *The lake was frozen over.* ◇ *Cover her over with a blanket.* **5** 🔑 above; more: *children of 14 and over* ◇ *You get an A grade for scores of 75 and over.* **6** 🔑 remaining; not used or needed: *If there's any food left over, put it in the*

fridge. **7** 🔑 again: *He repeated it several times over until he could remember it.* ◇ (*NAmE*) *It's all wrong—you'll have to do it over.* **8** 🔑 ended: *By the time we arrived the meeting was over.* ◇ *Thank goodness that's over!* ◇ *I was glad when it was* ***over and done with.*** **9** 🔑 used to talk about sb/sth changing position: *He's gone over to the enemy* (= joined them). ◇ *Please change the wheels over* (= for example, put the front wheels at the back). ◇ *Let's ask some friends over* (= to our home). ◇ *Hand over the money!* **10** used when communicating by radio: *Message received. Over* (= it is your turn to speak). ◇ *Message understood.* ***Over and out.***

IDM (**all**) **over a'gain** 🔑 a second time from the beginning: *He did the work so badly that I had to do it all over again myself.* **over against sth** in contrast with sth **ˌover and 'over** (**a'gain**) many times; repeatedly: *I've told you over and over again not to do that.* **ˌover to 'you** used to say that it is sb's turn to do sth

■ ***prep.*** **HELP** For the special uses of **over** in phrasal verbs, look at the entries for the verbs. For example **get over sth** is in the phrasal verb section at **get**. **1** 🔑 resting on the surface of sb/sth and partly or completely covering them/it: *She put a blanket over the sleeping child.* ◇ *He wore an overcoat over his suit.* ◇ *She put her hand over her mouth to stop herself from screaming.* **2** 🔑 in or to a position higher than but not touching sb/sth; above sb/sth: *They held a large umbrella over her.* ◇ *The balcony juts out over the street.* ◇ *There was a lamp hanging over the table.* **3** 🔑 from one side of sth to the other; across sth: *a bridge over the river* ◇ *They ran over the grass.* ◇ *They had a wonderful view over the park.* **4** 🔑 on the far or opposite side of sth: *He lives over the road.* **5** 🔑 so as to cross sth and be on the other side: *She climbed over the wall.* **6** 🔑 falling from or down from a place: *The car had toppled over the cliff.* ◇ *He didn't dare look over the edge.* **7** 🔑 **all ~** in or on all or most parts of sth: *Snow is falling all over the country.* ◇ *They've travelled all over the world.* ◇ *There were papers lying around* ***all over the place.*** **8** 🔑 more than a particular time, amount, cost, etc: *over 3 million copies sold* ◇ *She stayed in Lagos for over a month.* ◇ *He's over sixty.* **9** 🔑 used to show that sb has control or authority: *She has only the director over her.* ◇ *He ruled over a great empire.* ◇ *She has editorial control over what is included.* **10** 🔑 during sth: *We'll discuss it over lunch.* ◇ *Over the next few days they got to know the town well.* ◇ *She has not changed much over the years.* ◇ *He built up the business over a period of ten years.* ◇ *We're away over* (= until after) *the New Year.* **11** 🔑 past a particular difficult stage or situation: *We're over the worst of the recession.* ◇ *It took her ages to get over her illness.* **12** 🔑 because of or concerning sth; about sth: *an argument over money* ◇ *a disagreement over the best way to proceed* **13** 🔑 using sth; by means of sth: *We heard it over the radio.* ◇ *She wouldn't tell me over the phone.* **14** louder than sth: *I couldn't hear what he said over the noise of the traffic.* ➲ note at ABOVE

IDM **ˌover and a'bove** in addition to sth: *There are other factors over and above those we have discussed.*

■ ***noun*** (in CRICKET) a series of six balls BOWLED by the same person

over- /'əʊvə(r); *NAmE* 'oʊ-/ *prefix* (in nouns, verbs, adjectives and adverbs) **1** more than usual; too much: *overproduction* ◇ *overload* ◇ *over-optimistic* ◇ *overconfident* ◇ *overanxious* **2** completely: *overjoyed* **3** upper; outer; extra: *overcoat* ◇ *overtime* **4** over; above: *overcast* ◇ *overhang*

over·achieve /ˌəʊvərə'tʃiːv; *NAmE* ˌoʊ-/ *verb* **1** [I] to do better than expected in your studies or work **2** [I] to try too hard to be successful in your work ▸ **over·achiever** *noun*

over·act /ˌəʊvər'ækt; *NAmE* ˌoʊ-/ *verb* [I, T] **~** (**sth**) (*disapproving*) to behave in a way that is exaggerated and not natural, especially when you are acting a part in a play

over·active /ˌəʊvər'æktɪv; *NAmE* ˌoʊvər-/ *adj.* [usually before noun] **1** (of an organ or part of the body) causing harm by doing sth too much: *an overactive thyroid* **2** (of sb's imagination) too active, especially so that they imagine things that are not true: *She suffers from an overactive imagination.*

over·age /ˌəʊvər'eɪdʒ; *NAmE* ˌoʊ-/ *adj.* too old to be allowed to do a particular thing

over·all 🔑 **AW** *adj., adv., noun*

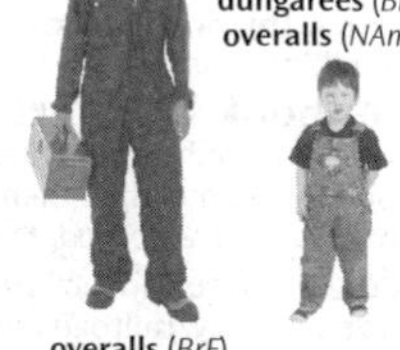

■ ***adj.*** 🔑 /ˌəʊvər'ɔːl; *NAmE* ˌoʊ-/ [only before noun] including all the things or people that are involved in a particular situation; general: *the person with* ***overall responsibility*** *for the project* ◇ *There will be winners in each of three age groups, and one* ***overall winner.*** ◇ *an* ***overall improvement*** *in standards of living* (= affecting everyone) ◇ *When she finished painting, she stepped back to admire the* ***overall effect.***

■ ***adv.*** /ˌəʊvər'ɔːl; *NAmE* ˌoʊ-/ **1** 🔑 including everything or everyone; in total: *The company will invest $1.6m overall in new equipment.* **2** 🔑 generally; when you consider everything: *Overall, this is a very useful book.* ➲ LANGUAGE BANK at CONCLUSION

■ ***noun*** /'əʊvərɔːl; *NAmE* 'oʊ-/ **1** (*BrE*) [C] a loose coat worn over other clothes to protect them from dirt, etc: *The lab assistant was wearing a white overall.* **2 overalls** (*BrE*) (*NAmE* **cov·er·alls**) [pl.] a loose piece of clothing like a shirt and trousers/pants in one piece, made of heavy cloth and usually worn over other clothing by workers doing dirty work: *The mechanic was wearing a pair of blue overalls.* ➲ compare BOILER SUIT **3 overalls** (also **'bib overalls**) (both *NAmE*) (*BrE* **dun·garees**) [pl.] a piece of clothing that consists of trousers/pants with an extra piece of cloth covering the chest, held up by strips of cloth over the shoulders

ˌoverall ma'jority *noun* [usually sing.] **1** more votes in an election or vote than all the other people or parties together **2** the difference between the number of members that the government has in a parliament and the number that all the other political parties have together: *a huge 101-seat overall majority*

over·am·bi·tious /ˌəʊvəræm'bɪʃəs; *NAmE* ˌoʊ-/ *adj.* **1** (of a person) too determined to be successful, rich, powerful, etc. **2** (of a plan, task, etc.) unsuccessful or likely to be unsuccessful because of needing too much effort, money or time: *Her plans were overambitious.*

over·arch·ing /ˌəʊvər'ɑːtʃɪŋ; *NAmE* ˌoʊvər'ɑːrtʃɪŋ/ *adj.* [usually before noun] (*formal*) very important, because it includes or influences many things

over·arm /'əʊvərɑːm; *NAmE* 'oʊvərɑːrm/ (*especially BrE*) (also **over·hand** especially in *NAmE*) *adv.* if you throw a ball **overarm**, you throw it with your arm swung backwards and then lifted high above your shoulder ▸ **over·arm** (*especially BrE*) (also **over·hand** especially in *NAmE*) *adj.*: *an overarm throw* ➲ compare UNDERARM

over·ate *past tense* of OVEREAT

over·awe /ˌəʊvər'ɔː; *NAmE* ˌoʊ-/ *verb* [usually passive] **~ sb** to impress sb so much that they feel nervous or frightened ▸ **over·awed** *adj.*

over·bal·ance /ˌəʊvə'bæləns; *NAmE* ˌoʊvər'b-/ *verb* [I, T] **~** (**sb/sth**) (*especially BrE*) to lose your balance and fall; to make sb/sth lose their balance and fall: *He overbalanced and fell into the water.*

over·bear·ing /ˌəʊvə'beərɪŋ; *NAmE* ˌoʊvər'ber-/ *adj.* (*disapproving*) trying to control other people in an unpleasant way **SYN** **domineering**: *an overbearing manner*

over·bite /'əʊvəbaɪt; *NAmE* 'oʊvərb-/ *noun* [usually sing.] (*technical*) a condition in which a person or animal's upper JAW is too far forward in relation to their lower JAW

over·blown /ˌəʊvə'bləʊn; *NAmE* ˌoʊvər'bloʊn/ *adj.* **1** that is made to seem larger, more impressive or more important than it really is **SYN** **exaggerated** **2** (of flowers) past the best, most beautiful stage

O

over·board /ˈəʊvəbɔːd; NAmE ˈoʊvərbɔːrd/ *adv.* over the side of a boat or a ship into the water: *to **fall/jump overboard*** ◇ *Huge waves washed him overboard.*
IDM **go ˈoverboard** (*informal*) to be too excited or enthusiastic about sth or about doing sth: *Don't go overboard on fitness.* **throw sb/sth ˈoverboard** to get rid of sb/sth that you think is useless

over·book /ˌəʊvəˈbʊk; NAmE ˌoʊvərˈbʊk/ *verb* [T, I] **~ (sth)** to sell more tickets on a plane or reserve more rooms in a hotel than there are places available: *The flight was heavily overbooked.* ➲ compare DOUBLE-BOOK

over·bridge /ˈəʊvəbrɪdʒ; NAmE ˈoʊvərb-/ *noun* a bridge over a railway/railroad or road

over·bur·den /ˌəʊvəˈbɜːdn; NAmE ˌoʊvərˈbɜːrdn/ *verb* [usually passive] **~ sb/sth (with sth)** to give sb/sth more work, worry, etc. than they can deal with

over·came *past tense of* OVERCOME

over·cap·acity /ˌəʊvəkəˈpæsəti; NAmE ˌoʊvərkə-/ *noun* [U, sing.] (*business*) the situation in which an industry or a factory cannot sell as much as it is designed to produce

over·cast /ˌəʊvəˈkɑːst; NAmE ˌoʊvərˈkæst/ *adj.* covered with clouds; dull: *an **overcast sky/day*** ◇ *Today it will be dull and overcast.*

over·cau·tious /ˌəʊvəˈkɔːʃəs; NAmE ˌoʊvərˈk-/ *adj.* too careful

over·charge /ˌəʊvəˈtʃɑːdʒ; NAmE ˌoʊvərˈtʃɑːrdʒ/ *verb* [T, I] **~ (sb) (for sth)** to make sb pay too much for sth: *Make sure they don't overcharge you for the drinks.* ◇ *We were overcharged by £5.* OPP **undercharge**

over·coat /ˈəʊvəkəʊt; NAmE ˈoʊvərkoʊt/ *noun* a long warm coat worn in cold weather ➲ VISUAL VOCAB page V50

over·come 0-w /ˌəʊvəˈkʌm; NAmE ˌoʊvərˈkʌm/ *verb* (over·came /-ˈkeɪm/, over·come)
1 0-w **~ sth** to succeed in dealing with or controlling a problem that has been preventing you from achieving sth: *She overcame injury to win the Olympic gold medal.* ◇ *The two parties managed to overcome their differences on the issue.* **2** 0-w **~ sb/sth** to defeat sb: *In the final game Sweden easily overcame France.* **3** 0-w [usually passive] **~ sb** to be extremely strongly affected by sth SYN **overwhelm**: *Her parents were overcome with grief at the funeral.* ◇ *The dead woman had been overcome by smoke.*

over·com·pen·sate /ˌəʊvəˈkɒmpenseɪt; NAmE ˌoʊvərˈkɑːm-/ *verb* [I] **~ (for sth) (by doing sth)** to do too much when trying to correct a problem and so cause a different problem: *She overcompensated for her shyness by talking too much and laughing too loud.*

over·con·fi·dent /ˌəʊvəˈkɒnfɪdənt; NAmE ˌoʊvərˈkɑːn-/ *adj.* too confident

over·cook /ˌəʊvəˈkʊk; NAmE ˌoʊvərˈkʊk/ *verb* **~ sth** to cook food for too long

over·crit·ic·al /ˌəʊvəˈkrɪtɪkl; NAmE ˌoʊvərˈk-/ *adj.* too critical

over·crowd·ed /ˌəʊvəˈkraʊdɪd; NAmE ˌoʊvərˈk-/ *adj.* (of a place) with too many people or things in it: *overcrowded cities/prisons* ◇ *Too many poor people are living in **overcrowded conditions**.*

over·crowd·ing /ˌəʊvəˈkraʊdɪŋ; NAmE ˌoʊvərˈk-/ *noun* [U] the situation when there are too many people or things in one place

over·de·veloped /ˌəʊvədɪˈveləpt; NAmE ˌoʊvərd-/ *adj.* that has grown too large: *overdeveloped muscles* ◇ *an overdeveloped sense of humour* ▸ **over·de·velop** *verb* **~ sth** **over·devel·op·ment** *noun* [U]

over·do /ˌəʊvəˈduː; NAmE ˌoʊvərˈduː/ *verb* (over·does /-ˈdʌz/, over·did /-ˈdɪd/, over·done /-ˈdʌn/) **1 ~ sth** to do sth too much; to exaggerate sth: *She really overdid the sympathy* (= and so did not seem sincere). **2 ~ sth** to use too much of sth: *Don't overdo the salt in the food.* ◇ *Use illustrations where appropriate but don't **overdo it**.* **3** [usually passive] **~ sth** to cook sth for too long: *The fish was overdone and very dry.*
IDM **overˈdo it/things** to work, study, etc. too hard or for too long: *He's been overdoing things recently.* ◇ *I overdid it in the gym and hurt my back.*

over·dog /ˈəʊvədɒg; NAmE ˈoʊvərdɔːg/ *noun* (*disapproving*) a person, organization or country that is successful or in a stronger position than others, especially when they seem to have an unfair advantage: *political leaders who support the interests of the overdog* OPP **underdog**

over·dose /ˈəʊvədəʊs; NAmE ˈoʊvərdoʊs/ *noun, verb*
■ ***noun*** too much of a drug taken at one time: *a **drug/drugs overdose*** ◇ *She took a massive overdose of sleeping pills.*
■ ***verb*** (also *informal* **OD**) [I] **~ (on sth)** to take too much of a drug at one time, so that it is dangerous: *He had overdosed on heroin.* ◇ (*figurative*) *I had overdosed on sun.*

over·draft /ˈəʊvədrɑːft; NAmE ˈoʊvərdræft/ *noun* the amount of money that you owe to a bank when you have spent more money than is in your bank account; an arrangement that allows you to do this: *to **run up/pay off an overdraft*** ➲ COLLOCATIONS at FINANCE

over·draw /ˌəʊvəˈdrɔː; NAmE ˌoʊvərˈdrɔː/ *verb* (over·drew /-ˈdruː/, over·drawn /-ˈdrɔːn/) [T, I] **~ (sth)** (*especially BrE*) to take out more money from a bank account than it contains: *Customers who overdraw their accounts will be charged a fee.*

over·drawn /ˌəʊvəˈdrɔːn; NAmE ˌoʊvərˈd-/ *adj.* **1** [not usually before noun] (of a person) having taken more money out of your bank account than you have in it: *I'm overdrawn by £100.* **2** (of a bank account) with more money taken out than was paid in or left in: *an overdrawn account* ◇ *Your account is £200 overdrawn.*

over·dressed /ˌəʊvəˈdrest; NAmE ˌoʊvərˈd-/ *adj.* (usually *disapproving*) wearing clothes that are too formal or too elegant for a particular occasion

over·drive /ˈəʊvədraɪv; NAmE ˈoʊvərd-/ *noun* [U] an extra high gear in a vehicle, that you use when you are driving at high speeds: *to be in overdrive*
IDM **go into ˈoverdrive** to start being very active and working very hard: *As the wedding approached, the whole family went into overdrive.*

over·dub /ˌəʊvəˈdʌb; NAmE ˌoʊvərˈd-/ *verb* (-bb-) **~ sb** to record new sounds over the sounds on an original recording so that both can be heard

over·due /ˌəʊvəˈdjuː; NAmE ˌoʊvərˈduː/ *adj.* **1** not paid, done, returned, etc. by the required or expected time: *an overdue payment/library book* ◇ *The rent is now overdue.* ◇ *Her baby is two weeks overdue.* ◇ *This car is overdue for a service.* **2** that should have happened or been done before now: *overdue reforms* ◇ *A book like this is **long overdue**.*

ˌover ˈeasy *adj.* (*NAmE*) (of fried eggs) turned over when almost cooked and fried for a short time on the other side

over·eat /ˌəʊvərˈiːt; NAmE ˌoʊ-/ *verb* (over·ate /-ˈet; NAmE -ˈeɪt/, over·eaten /-ˈiːtn/) [I] to eat more than you need or more than is healthy ▸ **over·eat·ing** *noun* [U]: *She went through periods of compulsive overeating.*

ˌover-ˈegg *verb*
IDM **ˌover-egg the ˈpudding** used to say that you think sb has done more than is necessary, or has added unnecessary details to make sth seem better or worse than it really is: *If you're telling lies, keep it simple—never over-egg the pudding.*

over·empha·sis /ˌəʊvərˈemfəsɪs; NAmE ˌoʊ-/ *noun* [U, sing.] **~ (on sth)** too much emphasis or importance: *an overemphasis on curing illness rather than preventing it* ▸ **over·empha·size, -ise** /ˌəʊvərˈemfəsaɪz; NAmE ˌoʊ-/ *verb*: **~ sth** *The importance of preparation **cannot be overemphasized**.*

over·esti·mate AW *verb, noun*
■ ***verb*** /ˌəʊvərˈestɪmeɪt; NAmE ˌoʊ-/ **~ sth** to estimate sth to be larger, better, more important, etc. than it really is: *They overestimated his ability when they promoted him.* ◇ *The importance of these findings **cannot be overestimated*** (= is very great). OPP **underestimate** ▸ **over·esti·mation** *noun* [U, C]
■ ***noun*** /ˌəʊvərˈestɪmət; NAmE ˌoʊ-/ [usually sing.] an estimate

O

about the size, cost, etc. of sth that is too high OPP **underestimate**

over·ex·cited /ˌəʊvərɪk'saɪtɪd; *NAmE* ˌoʊ-/ *adj.* too excited and not behaving in a calm or sensible way: *Don't get the children overexcited just before bedtime.*

over·ex·pose /ˌəʊvərɪk'spəʊz; *NAmE* ˌoʊvərɪk'spoʊz/ *verb* [usually passive] **1 ~ sth** to affect the quality of a photograph or film by allowing too much light to enter the camera OPP **underexpose 2 ~ sb/sth** to allow sb/sth to be seen too much on television, in the newspapers, etc: *The club is careful not to let the younger players be overexposed, and rarely allows them to be interviewed.* ▸ **over·ex·pos·ure** /ˌəʊvərɪk'spəʊʒə(r); *NAmE* ˌoʊvərɪk'spoʊ-/ *noun* [U]

over·ex·tend·ed /ˌəʊvərɪk'stendɪd; *NAmE* ˌoʊ-/ *adj.* [not usually before noun] involved in more work or activities, or spending more money, than you can manage without problems ▸ **over·ex·tend** *verb*: **~ yourself** *They should not overextend themselves on the mortgage.*

over·feed /'əʊvəfiːd; *NAmE* 'oʊvərfiːd/ *verb* (**over·fed, over·fed** /'əʊvəfed; *NAmE* 'oʊvərfed/) **~ sb/sth** to give sb/sth too much food ▸ **over·fed** *adj.* OPP **underfed**

over·fish·ing /ˌəʊvə'fɪʃɪŋ; *NAmE* ˌoʊvər'f-/ *noun* [U] the process of taking so many fish from the sea, a river, etc. that the number of fish in it becomes very low

over·flow *verb, noun*

■ ***verb*** /ˌəʊvə'fləʊ; *NAmE* ˌoʊvər'floʊ/ **1** [I, T] to be so full that the contents go over the sides: *The bath is overflowing* ◇ **~ with sth** *Plates overflowed with party food.* ◇ (*figurative*) *Her heart overflowed with love.* ◇ **~ sth** *The river overflowed its banks.* **2** [I] **~ (with sth)** (of a place) to have too many people in it: *The streets were overflowing with the crowds.* ◇ *The hospitals are* ***filled to overflowing*** (= with patients). **3** [I, T] **~ (into sth)** | **~ (sth)** to spread beyond the limits of a place or container that is too full: *The meeting overflowed into the street.*

■ ***noun*** /'əʊvəfləʊ; *NAmE* 'oʊvərfloʊ/ **1** [U, sing.] a number of people or things that do not fit into the space available: *A new office block was built to accommodate the overflow of staff.* ◇ *an overflow car park* **2** [U, sing.] the action of liquid flowing out of a container, etc. that is already full; the liquid that flows out: *an overflow of water from the lake* ◇ (*figurative*) *an overflow of powerful emotions* **3** (also **'overflow pipe**) [C] a pipe that allows extra liquid to escape **4** [C, usually sing.] (*computing*) a fault that happens because a number or data item (for example, the result of a calculation) is too large for the computer to represent it exactly

over·fly /ˌəʊvə'flaɪ; *NAmE* ˌoʊvər'f-/ *verb* (**over·flies, over·fly·ing, over·flew** /-'fluː/, **over·flown** /-'fləʊn; *NAmE* -'floʊn/) [T, I] **~ (sth)** to fly over a place: *We overflew the war zone, taking photographs.* ◇ *the noise from overflying planes* ▸ **over·flight** *noun*

over·fond /ˌəʊvə'fɒnd; *NAmE* ˌoʊvər'fɑːnd/ *adj.* **~ of sb/sth** liking sb/sth too much

over·gar·ment /'əʊvəgɑːmənt; *NAmE* 'oʊvərgɑːrm-/ *noun* (*formal*) an item of clothing that is worn over other clothes

over·gen·er·al·ize (*BrE* also **-ise**) /ˌəʊvə'dʒenrəlaɪz; *NAmE* ˌoʊvər'dʒ-/ *verb* [I] to make a statement that is not accurate because it is too general ▸ **over·gen·er·al·iza·tion, -isa·tion** /ˌəʊvəˌdʒenrəlaɪ'zeɪʃn; *NAmE* ˌoʊvərˌdʒenrələ'zeɪʃn/ *noun* [C, U]

over·gen·er·ous /ˌəʊvə'dʒenərəs; *NAmE* ˌoʊvər'dʒ-/ *adj.* **~ (with sth)** giving too much of sth: *She is not overgenerous with praise.*

over·graze /ˌəʊvə'greɪz; *NAmE* ˌoʊvər'g-/ *verb* **~ sth** if land is **overgrazed**, it is damaged by having too many animals feeding on it

over·ground /'əʊvəgraʊnd; *NAmE* 'oʊvərg-/ *adv.* (*BrE*) on or above the surface of the ground, rather than under it: *The new railway line will run overground.* ▸ **overground** *adj.*: *overground trains* ➲ compare UNDERGROUND

over·grown /ˌəʊvə'grəʊn; *NAmE* ˌoʊvər'groʊn/ *adj.* **1** (of gardens, etc.) covered with plants that have been allowed to grow wild and have not been controlled: *an overgrown path* ◇ **~ with sth** *The garden's completely overgrown with weeds.* **2** (often *disapproving*) that has grown too large: *an overgrown village* ◇ *They act like a pair of overgrown children* (= they are adults but they behave like children).

over·growth /'əʊvəgrəʊθ; *NAmE* 'oʊvərgroʊθ/ *noun* [U, sing.] (*technical*) too much growth of sth, especially sth that grows on or over sth else

over·hand /'əʊvəhænd; *NAmE* 'oʊvərh-/ *adj., adv.* (*especially NAmE*) = OVERARM

over·hang *verb, noun*

■ ***verb*** /ˌəʊvə'hæŋ; *NAmE* ˌoʊvər'h-/ (**over·hung, over·hung** /-'hʌŋ/) [T, I] **~ (sth)** to stick out over and above sth else: *His big fat belly overhung his belt.* ◇ *The path was cool and dark with overhanging trees.*

■ ***noun*** /'əʊvəhæŋ; *NAmE* 'oʊvərh-/ **1** the part of sth that sticks out over and above sth else: *The roof has an overhang to protect the walls from the rain.* **2** the amount by which sth hangs over and above sth else **3** [usually sing.] (*business*) (*especially NAmE*) the state of being extra to what is required; the things that are extra: *attempts to reduce the overhang of unsold goods*

over·hasty /ˌəʊvə'heɪsti; *NAmE* ˌoʊvər'h-/ *adj.* done too soon or doing sth too soon, especially without enough thought: *an overhasty decision* ◇ *We were overhasty in making the choice.*

over·haul *noun, verb*

■ ***noun*** /'əʊvəhɔːl; *NAmE* 'oʊvərh-/ an examination of a machine or system, including doing repairs on it or making changes to it: *a* ***complete/major overhaul*** ◇ *A radical overhaul of the tax system is necessary.*

■ ***verb*** /ˌəʊvə'hɔːl; *NAmE* ˌoʊvər-/ **1 ~ sth** to examine every part of a machine, system, etc. and make any necessary changes or repairs: *The engine has been completely overhauled.* **2 ~ sb** to come from behind a person you are competing against in a race and go past them SYN **overtake**: *He managed to overhaul the leader on the final lap.*

over·head *adv., adj., noun*

■ ***adv.*** /ˌəʊvə'hed; *NAmE* ˌoʊvər'hed/ above your head; in the sky: *Planes flew overhead constantly.* ◇ *Thunder boomed in the sky overhead.*

■ ***adj.*** /'əʊvəhed; *NAmE* 'oʊvərhed/ **1** above your head; raised above the ground: *overhead power lines* **2** [only before noun] connected with the general costs of running a business or an organization, for example paying for rent or electricity: *overhead costs*

■ ***noun*** [U] (*especially NAmE*) = OVERHEADS

ˌoverhead pro'jector *noun* (*abbr.* **OHP**) a piece of equipment that projects an image onto a wall or screen so that many people can see it ➲ compare DATA PROJECTOR, SLIDE PROJECTOR

over·heads /'əʊvəhedz; *NAmE* 'oʊvərh-/ *noun* [pl.] (*especially BrE*) (also **over·head** [U] (especially in *NAmE*)) regular costs that you have when you are running a business or an organization, such as rent, electricity, wages, etc. ➲ SYNONYMS at COSTS

over·hear /ˌəʊvə'hɪə(r); *NAmE* ˌoʊvər'hɪr/ *verb* (**overheard, over·heard** /-'hɜːd; *NAmE* -'hɜːrd/) to hear, especially by accident, a conversation in which you are not involved: **~ sb/sth** *We talked quietly so as not to be overheard.* ◇ *I overheard a conversation between two boys on the bus.* ◇ **~ sb doing sth** *We overheard them arguing.* ◇ **~ sb do sth** *I overheard him say he was going to France.* ➲ compare EAVESDROP

over·heat /ˌəʊvə'hiːt; *NAmE* ˌoʊvər'h-/ *verb* **1** [I, T] to become or to make sth become too hot: *The engine is overheating.* ◇ **~ sth** *It's vital not to overheat the liquid.* **2** [I] (of a country's economy) to be too active, with rising prices ▸ **over·heat·ing** *noun* [U]

over·heated /ˌəʊvə'hiːtɪd; *NAmE* ˌoʊvər'h-/ *adj.* **1** too hot: *Don't sleep in an overheated room.* **2** too interested or excited: *the figment of an overheated imagination* **3** (of a

O

country's economy) too active in a way that may cause problems

over·hung *past tense* of OVERHANG

over·in·dulge /ˌəʊvərɪnˈdʌldʒ; *NAmE* ˌoʊ-/ *verb* **1** [I] **~ (in sth)** to have too much of sth nice, especially food or drink **2** [T] **~ sb** to give sb more than is good for them: *His mother overindulged him.*

over·in·flated /ˌəʊvərɪnˈfleɪtɪd; *NAmE* ˌoʊ-/ *adj.* **1** (of a price or value) too high: *overinflated house prices* **2** made to seem better, worse, more important, etc. than it really is SYN **exaggerated** **3** filled with too much air: *Overinflated tyres burst more easily.*

over·joyed /ˌəʊvəˈdʒɔɪd; *NAmE* ˌoʊvərˈdʒ-/ *adj.* [not before noun] extremely happy or pleased SYN **delighted**: **~ (at sth)** *He was overjoyed at my success.* ◇ **~ (to do sth)** *We were overjoyed to hear their good news.* ◇ **~ (that...)** *She was overjoyed that her article had been published.*

over·kill /ˈəʊvəkɪl; *NAmE* ˈoʊvərkɪl/ *noun* [U] (*disapproving*) too much of sth that reduces the effect it has: *There is a danger of overkill if you plan everything too carefully.*

over·laid *past tense, past part.* of OVERLAY

over·land /ˈəʊvəlænd; *NAmE* ˈoʊvərl-/ *adj.* across the land; by land, not by sea or by air: *an overland route* ▸ **over·land** *adv.*: *to travel overland*

over·lap AW *verb, noun*

■ **verb** /ˌəʊvəˈlæp; *NAmE* ˌoʊvərˈlæp/ (-pp-) **1** [T, I] **~ (sth)** if one thing **overlaps** another, or the two things **overlap**, part of one thing covers part of the other: *A fish's scales overlap each other* ◇ *The floor was protected with overlapping sheets of newspaper.* **2** [T] **~ sth** to make two or more things overlap: *You will need to overlap the pieces of wood slightly.* **3** [I, T] **~ (sth)** if two events **overlap** or **overlap** each other, the second one starts before the first one has finished **4** [I, T] to cover part of the same area of interest, knowledge, responsibility, etc: *Our jobs overlap slightly, which sometimes causes difficulties.* ◇ **~ (with) sth** *The language of science overlaps with that of everyday life.*

O

■ **noun** /ˈəʊvəlæp; *NAmE* ˈoʊvərlæp/ **1** [C, U] **~ (between sth and sth)** a shared area of interest, knowledge, responsibility, etc: *There is (a) considerable overlap between the two subjects.* **2** [C, U] the amount by which one thing covers another thing: *an overlap of 5 cm on each roof tile* **3** [U, sing.] a period of time in which two events or activities happen together: *There will be an overlap of a week while John teaches Ann the job.*

over·lay *verb, noun*

■ **verb** /ˌəʊvəˈleɪ; *NAmE* ˌoʊvərˈleɪ/ (**over·laid**, **over·laid** /-ˈleɪd/) [usually passive] **1 ~ sth (with sth)** (*technical*) to put sth on top of a surface so as to cover it completely; to lie on top of a surface: *wood overlaid with gold* **2 ~ sth (with sth)** (*literary*) to add sth, especially a feeling or quality, to sth else so that it seems to cover it: *The place was overlaid with memories of his childhood.*

■ **noun** /ˈəʊvəleɪ; *NAmE* ˈoʊvərleɪ/ **1** a transparent sheet with drawings, figures, etc. on it that can be placed on top of another sheet in order to change it: *An overlay showing population can be placed on top of the map.* **2** a thing that is laid on top of or covers sth else: *an overlay of fibreglass insulation*

over·leaf /ˌəʊvəˈliːf; *NAmE* ˌoʊvərˈliːf/ *adv.* on the other side of the page of a book, etc: *Complete the form overleaf.* ◇ *The changes are explained in detail overleaf.*

over·lie /ˌəʊvəˈlaɪ; *NAmE* ˌoʊvərˈlaɪ/ *verb* (**over·ly·ing**, **over·lay** /-ˈleɪ/, **over·lain** /-ˈleɪn/) [I, T] **~ (sth)** (*technical*) to lie over sth: *overlying rock*

over·load *verb, noun*

■ **verb** /ˌəʊvəˈləʊd; *NAmE* ˌoʊvərˈloʊd/ [often passive] **1 ~ sth** to put too great a load on sth: *an overloaded truck* **2 ~ sb (with sth)** to give sb too much of sth: *He's overloaded with responsibilities.* ◇ *Don't overload the students with information.* **3 ~ sth** to put too great a demand on a computer, an electrical system, etc. causing it to fail

■ **noun** /ˈəʊvələʊd; *NAmE* ˈoʊvərloʊd/ [U, sing.] too much of sth: *In these days of technological change we all suffer from* ***information overload.***

over·long /ˌəʊvəˈlɒŋ; *NAmE* ˌoʊvərˈlɔːŋ; ˌoʊvərˈlɑːŋ/ (*BrE*) (*NAmE* ˈ**overly long**) *adj.* too long: *an overlong agenda*

over·look /ˌəʊvəˈlʊk; *NAmE* ˌoʊvərˈlʊk/ *verb* **1 ~ sth** to fail to see or notice sth SYN **miss**: *He seems to have overlooked one important fact.* **2 ~ sth** to see sth wrong or bad but decide to ignore it SYN **turn a blind eye to**: *We could not afford to overlook such a serious offence.* **3 ~ sth** if a building, etc. **overlooks** a place, you can see that place from the building: *a restaurant overlooking the lake* ◇ *Our back yard is overlooked by several houses.* **4 ~ sb (for sth)** to not consider sb for a job or position, even though they might be suitable SYN **pass over**: *She's been overlooked for promotion several times.*

over·lord /ˈəʊvəlɔːd; *NAmE* ˈoʊvərlɔːrd/ *noun* (especially in the past) a person who has power over many other people: *feudal overlords*

over·ly /ˈəʊvəli; *NAmE* ˈoʊvərli/ *adv.* (before an adjective) too; very SYN **excessively**: *I'm not overly fond of pasta.* ◇ *We think you are being overly optimistic.*

over·manned /ˌəʊvəˈmænd; *NAmE* ˌoʊvərˈm-/ *adj.* (of a company, office, etc.) having more workers than are needed SYN **overstaffed** OPP **undermanned** ▸ **over·man·ning** /ˌəʊvəˈmænɪŋ; *NAmE* ˌoʊvərˈm-/ *noun* [U]: *the problems of overmanning in industry*

over·much /ˌəʊvəˈmʌtʃ; *NAmE* ˌoʊvərˈm-/ (*BrE*) (*NAmE* ˈ**overly much**) *adv.* (especially with a negative verb) too much; very much: *She didn't worry overmuch about it.* ▸ **over·much** *adj.*

over·night *adv., adj.*

■ **adv.** /ˌəʊvəˈnaɪt; *NAmE* ˌoʊvərˈn-/ **1** during or for the night: *We* ***stayed overnight*** *in London after the theatre.* **2** suddenly or quickly: *Don't expect it to improve overnight.*

■ **adj.** /ˈəʊvənaɪt; *NAmE* ˈoʊvərn-/ [only before noun] **1** happening during the night; for a night: *an overnight flight* ◇ *overnight accommodation* ◇ *She took only* ***an overnight bag*** (= containing the things needed for a night spent away from home). **2** happening suddenly or quickly: *The play was an overnight success.*

ˌover-optiˈmis·tic *adj.* **1** too confident that sth will be successful: *I'm not over-optimistic about my chances of getting the job.* **2** showing more confidence that sth will be successful than is justified by later events: *The sales forecasts turned out to be over-optimistic.*

over·pass /ˈəʊvəpɑːs; *NAmE* ˈoʊvərpæs/ (*NAmE*) (*BrE* **flyover**) *noun* a bridge that carries one road over another one ➲ compare UNDERPASS

over·pay /ˌəʊvəˈpeɪ; *NAmE* ˌoʊvərˈpeɪ/ *verb* (**over·paid**, **over·paid** /-ˈpeɪd/) [usually passive] **~ sb** to pay sb too much; to pay sb more than their work is worth OPP **underpay** ▸ **over·pay·ment** /-ˈpeɪmənt/ *noun* [C, U]

over·play /ˌəʊvəˈpleɪ; *NAmE* ˌoʊvərˈp-/ *verb* **~ sth** to give too much importance to sth OPP **underplay**

IDM **overplay your ˈhand** to spoil your chance of success by judging your position to be stronger than it really is

over·popu·lated /ˌəʊvəˈpɒpjuleɪtɪd; *NAmE* ˌoʊvərˈpɑːp-/ *adj.* (of a country or city) with too many people living in it ▸ **over·popu·la·tion** /ˌəʊvəˌpɒpjuˈleɪʃn; *NAmE* ˌoʊvərˌpɑːp-/ *noun* [U]: *the problems of overpopulation*

over·power /ˌəʊvəˈpaʊə(r); *NAmE* ˌoʊvərˈp-/ *verb* **1 ~ sb** to defeat or gain control over sb completely by using greater strength: *Police finally managed to overpower the gunman.* **2 ~ sb/sth** to be so strong or great that it affects or disturbs sb/sth seriously SYN **overwhelm**: *Her beauty overpowered him.* ◇ *The flavour of the garlic overpowered the meat.*

over·power·ing /ˌəʊvəˈpaʊərɪŋ; *NAmE* ˌoʊvərˈp-/ *adj.* very strong or powerful: *an overpowering smell of fish* ◇ *an overpowering personality* ◇ *The heat was overpowering.* ▸ **over·power·ing·ly** *adv.*

over·priced /ˌəʊvəˈpraɪst; *NAmE* ˌoʊvərˈp-/ *adj.* too expensive; costing more than it is worth ➲ SYNONYMS at EXPENSIVE

over·print /ˌəʊvəˈprɪnt; *NAmE* ˌoʊvərˈp-/ *verb* **~ A (on B)** | **~ B with A** to print sth on a document, etc. that already has printing on it

over·pro·duce /ˌəʊvəprəˈdjuːs; *NAmE* ˌoʊvərprəˈduːs/ *verb* [T, I] **~ (sth)** to produce more of sth than is wanted or needed ▸ **over·pro·duc·tion** /ˌəʊvəprəˈdʌkʃn; *NAmE* ˌoʊvərp-/ *noun* [U]

over·pro·tect·ive /ˌəʊvəprəˈtektɪv; *NAmE* ˌoʊvərp-/ *adj.* too anxious to protect sb from being hurt, in a way that restricts their freedom: *overprotective parents*

over·quali·fied /ˌəʊvəˈkwɒlɪfaɪd; *NAmE* ˌoʊvərˈkwɔːl-/ *adj.* having more experience or training than is necessary for a particular job, so that people do not want to employ you

over·ran *past tense* of OVERRUN

over·rate /ˌəʊvəˈreɪt; *NAmE* ˌoʊvərˈr-/ *verb* [usually passive] **~ sb/sth** to have too high an opinion of sb/sth; to put too high a value on sb/sth: *In my opinion, Hirst's work has been vastly overrated.* **OPP** **underrate**

over·reach /ˌəʊvəˈriːtʃ; *NAmE* ˌoʊvərˈr-/ *verb* [T, I] **~ (yourself)** to fail by trying to achieve more than is possible: *In making these promises, the company had clearly overreached itself.*

over·react /ˌəʊvəriˈækt; *NAmE* ˌoʊ-/ *verb* [I] **~ (to sth)** to react too strongly, especially to sth unpleasant ▸ **over·reac·tion** /-ˈækʃn/ *noun* [sing., U]

over·ride /ˌəʊvəˈraɪd; *NAmE* ˌoʊvərˈr-/ *verb* (**over·rode** /-ˈrəʊd; *NAmE* -ˈroʊd/, **over·rid·den** /-ˈrɪdn/) **1 ~ sth** to use your authority to reject sb's decision, order, etc. **SYN** **overrule**: *The chairman overrode the committee's objections and signed the agreement.* **2 ~ sth** to be more important than sth: *Considerations of safety override all other concerns.* **3 ~ sth** to stop a process that happens automatically and control it yourself: *A special code is needed to override the time lock.*

over·rid·ing /ˌəʊvəˈraɪdɪŋ; *NAmE* ˌoʊvərˈr-/ *adj.* [only before noun] more important than anything else in a particular situation: *the* ***overriding factor/consideration/concern*** ◇ *Their overriding aim was to keep costs low.*

over·ripe /ˌəʊvəˈraɪp; *NAmE* ˌoʊvərˈr-/ *adj.* too RIPE: *overripe fruit*

over·rule /ˌəʊvəˈruːl; *NAmE* ˌoʊvərˈr-/ *verb* [often passive] **~ sb/sth** to change a decision or reject an idea from a position of greater power **SYN** **override**: *to overrule a decision/an objection* ◇ *The verdict was overruled by the Supreme Court.*

over·run /ˌəʊvəˈrʌn; *NAmE* ˌoʊ-/ *verb* (**over·ran** /-ˈræn/, **over·run**) **1** [T, often passive] **~ sth** (especially of sth bad or not wanted) to fill or spread over an area quickly, especially in large numbers: *The house was completely overrun with mice.* ◇ *Enemy soldiers had overrun the island.* **2** [I, T] to take more time or money than was intended: *Her lectures never overrun.* ◇ **~ sth** *You've overrun your time by 10 minutes.* ▸ **over·run** /ˈəʊvərʌn; *NAmE* ˈoʊ-/ *noun*: *a cost overrun*

over·seas **AW** /ˌəʊvəˈsiːz; *NAmE* ˌoʊvərˈs-/ *adj., adv.*
■ ***adj.*** connected with foreign countries, especially those separated from your country by the sea or ocean: *overseas development/markets/trade* ◇ *overseas students/visitors* ➲ compare HOME
■ ***adv.*** to or in a foreign country, especially those separated from your country by the sea or ocean **SYN** **abroad**: *to* ***live/work/go overseas*** ◇ *The product is sold both at home and overseas.*

over·see /ˌəʊvəˈsiː; *NAmE* ˌoʊvərˈsiː/ *verb* (**over·saw** /-ˈsɔː/, **over·seen** /-ˈsiːn/) **~ sb/sth** to watch sb/sth and make sure that a job or an activity is done correctly **SYN** **supervise**

over·seer /ˈəʊvəsɪə(r); *NAmE* ˈoʊvərsɪr/ *noun* **1** (*old-fashioned*) a person whose job is to make sure that other workers do their work **2** a person or an organization that is responsible for making sure that a system is working as it should

over·sell /ˌəʊvəˈsel; *NAmE* ˌoʊvərˈsel/ *verb* (**over·sold**, **over·sold** /ˌəʊvəˈsəʊld; *NAmE* ˌoʊvərˈsoʊld/) [often passive] **1 ~ sb/sth/yourself** to say that sb/sth is better than they really are: *He has a tendency to oversell himself.* **2 ~ sth** (*business*) to sell too much or more of sth than is available: *The seats on the plane were oversold.*

over·sen·si·tive /ˌəʊvəˈsensɪtɪv; *NAmE* ˌoʊvərˈs-/ *adj.* too easily upset or offended

over·sexed /ˌəʊvəˈsekst; *NAmE* ˌoʊvərˈs-/ *adj.* having stronger sexual desire than is usual

over·shadow /ˌəʊvəˈʃædəʊ; *NAmE* ˌoʊvərˈʃædoʊ/ *verb* [often passive] **1 ~ sb/sth** to make sb/sth seem less important, or successful: *He had always been overshadowed by his elder sister.* **2 ~ sth** to make an event less enjoyable than it should be **SYN** **cloud**: *News of the accident overshadowed the day's events.* **3 ~ sth** to throw a shadow over sth: *The garden is overshadowed by tall trees.*

over·shoe /ˈəʊvəʃuː; *NAmE* ˈoʊvərʃuː/ *noun* a shoe worn over another shoe, especially in wet weather or to protect a floor

over·shoot /ˌəʊvəˈʃuːt; *NAmE* ˌoʊvərˈʃ-/ *verb* (**over·shot**, **over·shot** /-ˈʃɒt; *NAmE* -ˈʃɑːt/) **1** [T, I] to go further than the place you intended to stop or turn: **~ sth** *The aircraft overshot the runway.* ◇ **~ (sth) (by sth)** *She had overshot by 20 metres.* **2** [T] **~ sth (by sth)** to do more or to spend more money than you originally planned: *The department may overshoot its cash limit this year.*

over·sight /ˈəʊvəsaɪt; *NAmE* ˈoʊvərs-/ *noun* **1** [C, U] the fact of making a mistake because you forget to do sth or you do not notice sth: *I didn't mean to leave her name off the list; it was an oversight.* **2** [U] (*formal*) the state of being in charge of sb/sth: *The committee has oversight of finance and general policy.*

over·sim·plify /ˌəʊvəˈsɪmplɪfaɪ; *NAmE* ˌoʊvərˈs-/ *verb* (**over·sim·pli·fies**, **over·sim·pli·fy·ing**, **over·sim·pli·fied**, **over·sim·pli·fied**) [T, I] **~ (sth)** to describe a situation, a problem, etc. in a way that is too simple and ignores some of the facts: *It's easy to oversimplify the issues involved.* ◇ *an oversimplified view of human nature* ▸ **over·sim·pli·fi·ca·tion** /ˌəʊvəˌsɪmplɪfɪˈkeɪʃn; *NAmE* ˌoʊvərˌs-/ *noun* [C, usually sing., U]: *This is a gross oversimplification of the facts.* ➲ compare SIMPLIFICATION

over·sized /ˈəʊvəsaɪzd; *NAmE* ˈoʊvərs-/ (also *less frequent* **over·size** /-saɪz/) *adj.* bigger than the normal size; too big

over·sleep /ˌəʊvəˈsliːp; *NAmE* ˌoʊvərˈs-/ *verb* (**over·slept**, **over·slept** /-ˈslept/) [I] to sleep longer than you intended: *I overslept and missed the bus.*

over·spend /ˌəʊvəˈspend; *NAmE* ˌoʊvərˈs-/ *verb* (**over·spent**, **over·spent** /-ˈspent/) [I, T] to spend too much money or more than you planned: **~ (on sth)** *The company has overspent on marketing.* ◇ **~ sth** *Many departments have overspent their budgets this year.* ▸ **over·spend** /ˈəʊvəspend; *NAmE* ˈoʊvərs-/ *noun* [sing.]: (*BrE*) *a £1 million overspend* **over·spent** /ˌəʊvəˈspent; *NAmE* ˌoʊvərs-/ *adj.*: *The organization is heavily overspent.*

over·spill /ˈəʊvəspɪl; *NAmE* ˈoʊvərs-/ *noun* [U, sing.] (*BrE*) people who move out of a city because it is too crowded to an area where there is more space: *New towns were designed to house London's overspill.*

over·staffed /ˌəʊvəˈstɑːft; *NAmE* ˌoʊvərˈstæft/ *adj.* (of a company, office, etc.) having more workers than are needed **SYN** **overmanned** **OPP** **understaffed**

over·state /ˌəʊvəˈsteɪt; *NAmE* ˌoʊvərˈs-/ *verb* **~ sth** to say sth in a way that makes it seem more important than it really is **SYN** **exaggerate**: *He tends to* ***overstate his case*** *when talking politics.* ◇ *The seriousness of the crime* ***cannot be overstated.*** **OPP** **understate** ▸ **over·state·ment** /ˈəʊvəsteɪtmənt; *NAmE* ˈoʊvərs-/ *noun* [C, U]: *It is not an overstatement to say a crisis is imminent.*

over·stay /ˌəʊvəˈsteɪ; *NAmE* ˌoʊvərˈs-/ *verb* **~ sth** to stay longer than the length of time you are expected or allowed to stay: *They overstayed their visa.* **IDM** see WELCOME *n.*

over·step /ˌəʊvəˈstep; *NAmE* ˌoʊvərˈs-/ *verb* (-pp-) **~ sth** to go beyond what is normal or allowed: *to overstep your authority* ◇ *He tends to* ***overstep the boundaries of*** *good taste.*

IDM **overstep the 'mark/'line** to behave in a way that people think is not acceptable

over·stock /ˌəʊvəˈstɒk; NAmE ˌoʊvərˈstɑːk/ *verb* **1** [T, I] **~ (sth)** to buy or make more of sth than you need or can sell **2** [T, I] **~ (sth)** to put too many animals in a place where there is not enough room or food for them

over·stretch /ˌəʊvəˈstretʃ; NAmE ˌoʊvərˈs-/ *verb* **~ sb/sth/yourself** (*especially BrE*) to do more than you are capable of; to make sb/sth do more than they are capable of: *This will overstretch the prison service's resources.* ◇ *Credit cards can tempt you to overstretch yourself* (= spend more money than you can afford). ▶ **over·stretched** *adj.*: *overstretched muscles* ◇ *overstretched services*

over·sub·scribed /ˌəʊvəsəbˈskraɪbd; NAmE ˌoʊvərs-/ *adj.* if an activity, service, etc. is **oversubscribed**, there are fewer places, tickets, etc. than the number of people who are asking for them

overt /əʊˈvɜːt; ˈəʊvɜːt; NAmE oʊˈvɜːrt; ˈoʊvɜːrt/ *adj.* [usually before noun] (*formal*) done in an open way and not secretly: *There was little overt support for the project.* ➲ compare COVERT ▶ **overt·ly** *adv.*: *overtly political activities*

over·take /ˌəʊvəˈteɪk; NAmE ˌoʊvərˈt-/ *verb* (**over·took** /-ˈtʊk/, **over·taken** /-ˈteɪkən/) **1** [T, I] **~ (sb/sth)** (*especially BrE*) to go past a moving vehicle or person ahead of you because you are going faster than they are: *He pulled out to overtake a truck.* ◇ *It's dangerous to overtake on a bend.* **2** [T] **~ sb/sth** to become greater in number, amount or importance than sth else SYN **outstrip**: *Nuclear energy may overtake oil as the main fuel.* ◇ *We mustn't let ourselves be overtaken by our competitors.* **3** [T, often passive] **~ sb/sth** if sth unpleasant **overtakes** a person, it unexpectedly starts to happen and to affect them: *The climbers were overtaken by bad weather.* ◇ *Sudden panic overtook her.* ◇ *Our original plan was* ***overtaken by events*** (= the situation changed very rapidly) *and we had to make a new one.*

O

over·tax /ˌəʊvəˈtæks; NAmE ˌoʊvərˈt-/ *verb* **1 ~ sb/sth/yourself** to do more than you are able or want to do; to make sb/sth do more than they are able or want to do: *to overtax your strength* ◇ *Take it easy. Don't overtax yourself.* **2 ~ sb/sth** to make a person or an organization pay too much tax

ˌover-the-ˈcounter *adj.* [only before noun] **1** (of drugs and medicines) that can be obtained without a PRESCRIPTION (= a written order from a doctor) **2** (*business*) (*NAmE*) (of stocks and shares) not appearing in an official STOCK EXCHANGE list

over·throw *verb, noun*

■ ***verb*** /ˌəʊvəˈθrəʊ; NAmE ˌoʊvərˈθroʊ/ (**over·threw** /-ˈθruː/, **over·thrown** /-ˈθrəʊn; NAmE -ˈθroʊn/) **~ sb/sth** to remove a leader or a government from a position of power by force: *The president was overthrown in a military coup.*

■ ***noun*** /ˈəʊvəθrəʊ; NAmE ˈoʊvərθroʊ/ [usually sing.] the act of taking power by force from a leader or government

over·time /ˈəʊvətaɪm; NAmE ˈoʊvərt-/ *noun* [U] **1** time that you spend working at your job after you have worked the normal hours: *to* ***do/work overtime*** ◇ ***overtime pay/earnings/hours*** ◇ *The union announced a ban on overtime.* ➲ COLLOCATIONS at JOB **2** the money sb earns for doing overtime: *They pay $150 a day plus overtime.* **3** (*NAmE*) (*BrE* **ˌextra ˈtime**) (*sport*) a set period of time that is added to the end of a sports game, etc, if there is no winner at the end of the normal period

IDM **be working ˈovertime** (*informal*) to be very active or too active: *There was nothing to worry about. It was just her imagination working overtime.*

over·tired /ˌəʊvəˈtaɪəd; NAmE ˌoʊvərˈtaɪərd/ *adj.* extremely tired, so that you become irritated easily

over·tone /ˈəʊvətəʊn; NAmE ˈoʊvərtoʊn/ *noun* [usually pl.] an attitude or an emotion that is suggested and is not expressed in a direct way: *There were political overtones to the point he was making.* ➲ compare UNDERTONE

over·took *past tense of* OVERTAKE

over·train /ˌəʊvəˈtreɪn; NAmE ˌoʊvərˈt-/ *verb* [I] (of an ATHLETE) to train too hard or for too long

over·ture /ˈəʊvətʃʊə(r); -tjʊə(r); NAmE ˈoʊvərtʃər; -tʃʊr/ *noun* **1** a piece of music written as an introduction to an OPERA or a BALLET: *Prokofiev's overture to 'Romeo and Juliet'* **2** [usually pl.] **~ (to sb)** a suggestion or an action by which sb tries to make friends, start a business relationship, have discussions, etc. with sb else: *He began* ***making overtures to*** *a number of merchant banks.*

over·turn /ˌəʊvəˈtɜːn; NAmE ˌoʊvərˈtɜːrn/ *verb* **1** [I, T] if sth **overturns**, or if sb **overturns** it, it turns upside down or on its side: *The car skidded and overturned.* ◇ **~ sth** *He stood up quickly, overturning his chair.* **2** [T] **~ sth** to officially decide that a legal decision, etc. is not correct, and to make it no longer valid: *to* ***overturn a decision/conviction/verdict*** ◇ *His sentence was overturned by the appeal court.*

over·use /ˌəʊvəˈjuːz; NAmE ˌoʊvərˈj-/ *verb* **~ sth** to use sth too much or too often: *'Nice' is a very overused word.* ▶ **over·use** /ˌəʊvəˈjuːs; NAmE ˌoʊvərˈj-/ *noun* [U, sing.]

over·value /ˌəʊvəˈvæljuː; NAmE ˌoʊvərˈv-/ *verb* [often passive] **~ sth** to put too high a value on sth: *Intelligence cannot be overvalued.* ◇ (*business*) *overvalued currencies/stocks*

over·view /ˈəʊvəvjuː; NAmE ˈoʊvərv-/ *noun* a general description or an outline of sth SYN **survey**, **10 000-foot view**, **helicopter view** ➲ LANGUAGE BANK at ABOUT

over·ween·ing /ˌəʊvəˈwiːnɪŋ; NAmE ˌoʊvərˈw-/ *adj.* [only before noun] (*formal, disapproving*) showing too much confidence or pride SYN **arrogant**

over·weight /ˌəʊvəˈweɪt; NAmE ˌoʊvərˈw-/ *adj.* **1** (of people) too heavy and fat: *She was only a few pounds overweight.* OPP **underweight** ➲ COLLOCATIONS at DIET **2** above an allowed weight: *overweight baggage*

over·whelm /ˌəʊvəˈwelm; NAmE ˌoʊvərˈw-/ *verb* [often passive] **1 ~ sb** to have such a strong emotional effect on sb that it is difficult for them to resist or know how to react SYN **overcome**: *She was overwhelmed by feelings of guilt.* ◇ *The beauty of the landscape overwhelmed me.* **2 ~ sb** to defeat sb completely SYN **overpower**: *The army was overwhelmed by the rebels.* **3 ~ sb** to be so bad or so great that a person cannot deal with it; to give too much of a thing to a person: *We were overwhelmed by requests for information.* **4 ~ sb/sth** (*literary*) (of water) to cover sb/sth completely SYN **flood**

over·whelm·ing /ˌəʊvəˈwelmɪŋ; NAmE ˌoʊvərˈw-/ *adj.* very great or very strong; so powerful that you cannot resist it or decide how to react: *The evidence against him was overwhelming.* ◇ *The* ***overwhelming majority*** *of those present were in favour of the plan.* ◇ *an* ***overwhelming sense of*** *loss* ◇ *She had the almost overwhelming desire to tell him the truth.* ◇ *You may find it somewhat overwhelming at first.* ▶ **over·whelm·ing·ly** *adv.*: *They voted overwhelmingly against the proposal.*

over·winter /ˌəʊvəˈwɪntə(r); NAmE ˌoʊvərˈw-/ *verb* [I, T] **~ (sth)** (of animals, birds and plants) to spend the winter months in a place; to stay alive or to keep sth alive during the winter ➲ compare WINTER

over·work /ˌəʊvəˈwɜːk; NAmE ˌoʊvərˈwɜːrk/ *verb, noun*

■ ***verb*** [I, T] to work too hard; to make a person or an animal work too hard: *You look tired. Have you been overworking?* ◇ **~ sb/sth** *She overworks her staff.*

■ ***noun*** [U] the fact of working too hard: *His illness was brought on by money worries and overwork.*

over·worked /ˌəʊvəˈwɜːkt; NAmE ˌoʊvərˈwɜːrkt/ *adj.* **1** made to work too hard or too much: *overworked nurses* **2** (of words or phrases) used too often so that the meaning or effect has become weaker

over·write /ˌəʊvəˈraɪt; NAmE ˌoʊvərˈr-/ *verb* (**over·wrote** /-ˈrəʊt; NAmE -ˈroʊt/, **over·writ·ten** /-ˈrɪtn/) **~ sth** (*computing*) to replace information on the screen or in a file by putting new information over it

over·wrought /ˌəʊvəˈrɔːt; NAmE ˌoʊvərˈr-/ *adj.* very worried and upset; excited in a nervous way SYN **distraught**

over·zeal·ous /ˌəʊvəˈzeləs; *NAmE* ˌoʊvərˈz-/ *adj.* showing too much energy or enthusiasm: *An overzealous fan ran onto the stage during the concert.*

ovi·duct /ˈəʊvɪdʌkt; *NAmE* ˈoʊ-/ *noun* (*anatomy*) either of the tubes that carry eggs from the OVARIES in women and female animals

ovine /ˈəʊvaɪn; *NAmE* ˈoʊ-/ *adj.* (*technical*) relating to sheep

ovip·ar·ous /əʊˈvɪpərəs; *NAmE* oʊ-/ *adj.* (*biology*) (of an animal) producing eggs rather than live babies ➲ compare OVOVIVIPAROUS, VIVIPAROUS

ovoid /ˈəʊvɔɪd; *NAmE* ˈoʊ-/ *adj.* (*formal*) shaped like an egg ▸ **ovoid** *noun*

ovo·vi·vip·ar·ous /ˌəʊvəʊvɪˈvɪpərəs; *NAmE* ˌoʊvoʊ-/ *adj.* (*biology*) (of an animal) producing babies by means of eggs that are HATCHED inside the body of the parent, like some snakes ➲ compare OVIPAROUS, VIVIPAROUS

ovu·late /ˈɒvjuleɪt; *NAmE* ˈɑːv-/ *verb* [I] (of a woman or a female animal) to produce an egg (called an OVUM), from the OVARY ▸ **ovu·la·tion** /ˌɒvjuˈleɪʃn; *NAmE* ˌɑːv-/ *noun* [U]: *methods of predicting ovulation*

ovule /ˈɒvjuːl; ˈəʊ-; *NAmE* ˈoʊ-/ *noun* (*biology*) the part of the OVARY of a plant containing the female cell, which becomes the seed when it is FERTILIZED ➲ **VISUAL VOCAB** page V9

ovum /ˈəʊvəm; *NAmE* ˈoʊ-/ *noun* (*pl.* ova /ˈəʊvə; *NAmE* ˈoʊvə/) (*biology*) a female cell of an animal or a plant that can develop into a young animal or plant when FERTILIZED

ow /aʊ/ *exclamation* used to express sudden pain: *Ow! That hurt!*

owe 🔑 /əʊ; *NAmE* oʊ/ *verb* (not used in the progressive tenses)
1 🔑 to have to pay sb for sth that you have already received or return money that you have borrowed: **~ sb sth** *She still owes her father £3 000.* ◇ (*figurative*) *I'm still owed three days' leave.* ◇ **~ sb sth for sth** *How much do I owe you for the groceries?* ◇ **~ sth** (**to sb**) (**for sth**) *She still owes £3 000 to her father* ◇ *The country owes billions of dollars to foreign creditors.* **2** 🔑 to feel that you ought to do sth for sb or give them sth, especially because they have done sth for you: **~ sth to sb** *I owe a debt of gratitude to all my family.* ◇ *You* **owe it to** *your staff to be honest with them.* ◇ **~ sb sth** *You owe me a favour!* ◇ *Thanks for sticking up for me—***I owe you one** (= I owe you a favour). ◇ *I think you owe us an explanation.* ◇ *I think we're owed an apology.* **HELP** The passive is not used in this meaning except with a person as the subject: ~~*An apology is owed to us.*~~ **3** to exist or be successful because of the help or influence of sb/sth: **~ sth to sb/sth** *He owes his success to hard work.* ◇ *The play owes much to French tragedy.* ◇ *I owe everything to him.* ◇ **~ sb sth** *I owe him everything.* ◇ *I knew that I owed the surgeon my life.* **4 ~ allegiance/loyalty/obedience** (**to sb**) (*formal*) to have to obey or be loyal to sb who is in a position of authority or power

owing /ˈəʊɪŋ; *NAmE* ˈoʊɪŋ/ *adj.* [not before noun] money that is **owing** has not been paid yet: *£100 is still owing on the loan.*

ˈowing to *prep.* because of: *The game was cancelled owing to torrential rain.*

owl /aʊl/ *noun* a BIRD OF PREY (= a bird that kills other creatures for food) with large round eyes, that hunts at night. Owls are traditionally thought to be wise: *An owl hooted nearby.* ➲ see also BARN OWL, NIGHT OWL, TAWNY OWL

owlet /ˈaʊlət/ *noun* a young OWL

owl·ish /ˈaʊlɪʃ/ *adj.* looking like an owl, especially because you are wearing round glasses, and therefore seeming serious and intelligent ▸ **owl·ish·ly** *adv.*: *She blinked at them owlishly.*

own 🔑 /əʊn; *NAmE* oʊn/ *adj., pron., verb*
■ ***adj., pron.*** **1** 🔑 used to emphasize that sth belongs to or is connected with sb: *It was her own idea.* ◇ *I saw it with my own eyes* (= I didn't hear about it from somebody else). ◇ *Is the car your own?* ◇ *Your day off is your own* (= you can spend it as you wish). ◇ *Our children are grown up and have children* **of their own.** ◇ **For reasons of his own** (= particular reasons that perhaps only he knew about), *he refused to join the club.* ◇ *The accident happened* **through no fault of her own.** ◇ *He wants to come into the business* **on his own terms.** ◇ *I need a room* **of my own.** ◇ *I have my* **very own** *room at last.* **HELP** **Own** cannot be used after an article: *I need my own room.* ◇ ~~*I need an own room.*~~ ◇ *It's good to have your own room.* ◇ ~~*It's good to have the own room.*~~ **2** 🔑 done or produced by and for yourself: *She makes all her own clothes.* ◇ *He has to cook his own meals.*
IDM **come into your/its ˈown** to have the opportunity to show how good or useful you are or sth is: *When the traffic's this bad, a bicycle really comes into its own.* **get your ˈown back** (**on sb**) (*informal*) to do sth to sb in return for harm they have done to you; to get REVENGE: *I'll get my own back on him one day, I swear!* **hold your ˈown** (**against sb/sth**) (**in sth**) to remain in a strong position when sb is attacking you, competing with you, etc: *Business isn't good but we're managing to hold our own.* ◇ *She can hold her own against anybody in an argument.* ◇ *The patient is holding her own although she is still very sick.* (**all**) **on your ˈown 1** 🔑 alone; without anyone else: *I'm all on my own today.* ◇ *She lives on her own.* **2** 🔑 without help: *He did it on his own.* ➲ more at DEVIL, MIND *n.*, SAKE[1], SOUND *n.*
■ ***verb*** (not used in the progressive tenses) **1** 🔑 [T] **~ sth** to have sth that belongs to you, especially because you have bought it: *Do you own your house or do you rent it?* ◇ *I don't own anything of any value.* ◇ *Most of the apartments are privately owned.* ◇ *an American-owned company* **2** [I, T] (*old-fashioned*) to admit that sth is true: **~ to sth/to doing sth** *He owned to a feeling of guilt.* ◇ **~** (**that**)... *She owned (that) she had been present.*
IDM **ˌbehave/ˌact as if you ˈown the place | think you ˈown the place** (*disapproving*) to behave in a very confident way that annoys other people, for example by telling them what to do
PHR V **ˌown ˈup** (**to sth/to doing sth**) 🔑 to admit that you are responsible for sth bad or wrong **SYN** **confess**: *I'm still waiting for someone to own up to the breakages.*

ˌown-ˈbrand (also **ˌown-ˈlabel**) (both *BrE*) (*US* **ˈstore-brand**) *adj.* used to describe goods that are marked with the name of the shop/store in which they are sold rather than with the name of the company that produced them

owner 🔑 /ˈəʊnə(r); *NAmE* ˈoʊ-/ *noun*
a person who owns sth: *a dog/factory owner* ◇ *The painting has been returned to its* **rightful owner.** ◇ *He's now the* **proud owner** *of a cottage in Wales.* ➲ see also HOMEOWNER, LANDOWNER

ˌowner-ˈoccupied *adj.* (of a house, etc.) lived in by the owner rather than rented to sb else

ˌowner-ˈoccupier *noun* a person who owns the house, flat/apartment, etc. that they live in

own·er·ship /ˈəʊnəʃɪp; *NAmE* ˈoʊnərʃɪp/ *noun* [U] the fact of owning sth: *a growth in home ownership* ◇ *Ownership of the land is currently being disputed.* ◇ *to be in* **joint/private/public ownership** ◇ *The restaurant is under new ownership.*

ˌown ˈgoal *noun* [usually sing.] (*BrE*) **1** (in football (SOCCER)) a goal that is scored by mistake by a player against his or her own team **2** something that you do that achieves the opposite of what you wanted and that brings you a disadvantage

ˌown-ˈlabel *adj.* (*BrE*) = OWN-BRAND

owt /aʊt/ *pron.* (*BrE, dialect, informal*) anything: *I didn't say owt.*

ox /ɒks; *NAmE* ɑːks/ *noun* (*pl.* **oxen** /ˈɒksn; *NAmE* ˈɑːksn/) **1** a BULL (= a male cow) that has been CASTRATED (= had part of its sex organs removed), used, especially in the past, for pulling farm equipment, etc. ➲ compare BULLOCK, STEER **2** (*old-fashioned*) any cow or BULL on a farm ➲ see also CATTLE

O

oxbow

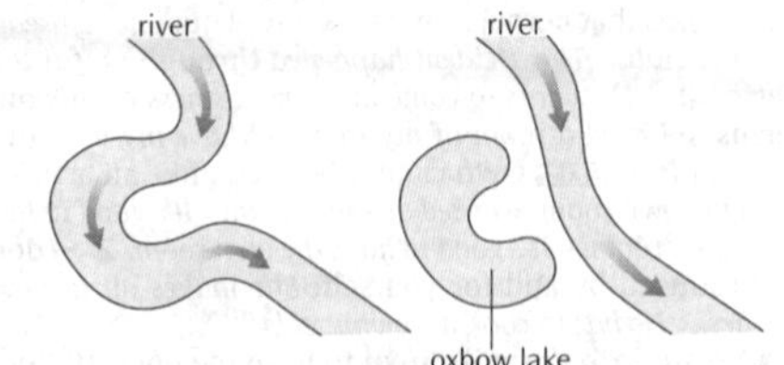

oxbow /'ɒksbəʊ; *NAmE* 'ɑːksboʊ/ *noun* (*technical*) a bend in a river that almost forms a full circle; a lake that forms when this bend is separated from the river

Ox·bridge /'ɒksbrɪdʒ; *NAmE* 'ɑːks-/ *noun* [U] the universities of Oxford and Cambridge, when they are thought of together: *an Oxbridge education* ➲ compare IVY LEAGUE, RED-BRICK

ox·ford /'ɒksfəd; *NAmE* 'ɑːksfərd/ *noun* **1 oxfords** [pl.] (*especially NAmE*) leather shoes that fasten with LACES ➲ compare LACE-UP ➲ **VISUAL VOCAB** page V52 **2** [U] = OXFORD CLOTH: *an oxford shirt*

ˌoxford 'cloth (also **ox·ford**) *noun* [U] (*NAmE*) a type of heavy cotton cloth used mainly for making shirts

oxi·dant /'ɒksɪdənt; *NAmE* 'ɑːks-/ *noun* (*chemistry*) a substance that makes another substance combine with oxygen

oxide /'ɒksaɪd; *NAmE* 'ɑːk-/ *noun* [U, C] (*chemistry*) a COMPOUND of OXYGEN and another chemical element: *iron oxide* ◇ *an oxide of tin*

oxi·dize (*BrE* also **-ise**) /'ɒksɪdaɪz; *NAmE* 'ɑːk-/ *verb* [T, I] **~ (sth)** (*chemistry*) to remove one or more ELECTRONS from a substance, or to combine or to make sth combine with OXYGEN, especially when this causes metal to become covered with RUST ▸ **oxi·da·tion** /ˌɒksɪ'deɪʃn; *NAmE* ˌɑːk-/ *noun* [U] ➲ compare REDUCE, REDUCTION

Oxon /'ɒksɒn; *NAmE* 'ɑːksɑːn/ *abbr.* (used after degree titles) of Oxford University: *Alice Tolley MA (Oxon)*

Oxon·ian /ɒk'səʊniən; *NAmE* ɑːk'soʊ-/ *adj.* (*formal* or *humorous*) relating to Oxford in England, or to Oxford University

ox·tail /'ɒksteɪl; *NAmE* 'ɑːks-/ *noun* [U, C] meat from the tail of a cow, used especially for making soup: *oxtail soup*

oxter /'ɒkstə(r); *NAmE* 'ɑːks-/ *noun* (*BrE, dialect, informal*) a person's ARMPIT

oxy·acet·yl·ene /ˌɒksiə'setəliːn; *NAmE* ˌɑːk-/ *adj.* connected with a mixture of oxygen and ACETYLENE gas which produces a very hot flame, used especially for cutting or joining metal: *an oxyacetylene torch*

oxy·gen /'ɒksɪdʒən; *NAmE* 'ɑːk-/ *noun* [U] (*symb.* O) a chemical element. Oxygen is a gas that is present in air and water and is necessary for people, animals and plants to live.

oxy·gen·ate /'ɒksɪdʒəneɪt; *NAmE* 'ɑːk-/ *verb* **~ sth** (*technical*) to supply sth with oxygen ▸ **oxy·gen·ation** *noun* [U]

oxy·gen·ator /'ɒksɪdʒəneɪtə(r); *NAmE* 'ɑːks-/ *noun* **1** (*medical*) a device for putting oxygen into the blood **2** a water plant that puts oxygen into the water around it

'oxygen bar *noun* a place where you can pay to breathe pure oxygen in order to improve your health and help you relax

'oxygen mask *noun* a device placed over the nose and mouth through which a person can breathe OXYGEN, for example in an aircraft or a hospital

'oxygen tent *noun* (*medical*) a structure like a tent which can be used to increase sb's supply of oxygen and help them to breathe

oxy·moron /ˌɒksɪ'mɔːrɒn; *NAmE* ˌɑːksɪ'mɔːrɑːn/ *noun* (*technical*) a phrase that combines two words that seem to be the opposite of each other, for example *a deafening silence*

oy *exclamation* = OI

oyez (also **oyes**) /əʊ'jeɪ; *NAmE* oʊ-/ *exclamation* used by a TOWN CRIER or an officer in court to tell people to be quiet and pay attention

oys·ter /'ɔɪstə(r)/ *noun* a large flat SHELLFISH. Some types of oyster can be eaten and others produce shiny white JEWELS called PEARLS: *Oyster beds, on the mudflats, are a form of fish farming.* ➲ picture at SHELLFISH **IDM** see WORLD

oys·ter·catch·er /'ɔɪstəkætʃə(r); *NAmE* 'ɔɪstərk-/ *noun* a black bird with long legs and a long red beak that lives near the coast and feeds on SHELLFISH

'oyster mushroom *noun* a type of wide, flat FUNGUS that grows on trees and that you can eat

oy vey /ˌɔɪ 'veɪ/ *exclamation* used for showing disappointment or sadness (mainly by Yiddish speakers or Jewish people)

Oz /ɒz; *NAmE* ɑːz/ *noun* [U] (*BrE, AustralE, NZE, informal*) Australia

oz *abbr.* OUNCE(S): *4oz sugar*

ozone /'əʊzəʊn; *NAmE* 'oʊzoʊn/ *noun* [U] **1** (*chemistry*) a poisonous gas with a strong smell that is a form of OXYGEN **2** (*BrE, informal*) air near the sea that smells fresh and pure

ˌozone-'friend·ly *adj.* not containing substances that will damage the OZONE LAYER

'ozone hole *noun* an area in the ozone layer where the amount of OZONE has been very much reduced so that harmful RADIATION from the sun can pass through it

'ozone layer *noun* [sing.] a layer of OZONE high above the earth's surface that helps to protect the earth from harmful RADIATION from the sun ➲ **COLLOCATIONS** at ENVIRONMENT

Oz·zie = AUSSIE

O

Pp

P (also **p**) /piː/ *noun* [C, U] (*pl.* **Ps, P's, p's** /piːz/) the 16th letter of the English alphabet: *'Pizza' begins with (a) P/'P'.* **IDM** see MIND *v.*

p (also **p.**) *abbr.* **1** (*pl.* **pp.**) page: *See p.34 and pp.63-72.* **2** PENNY, PENCE: *a 30p stamp* **3** (*music*) quietly (from Italian 'piano') ➲ see also P. AND P., P. AND H.

PA /ˌpiː ˈeɪ/ *abbr.* **1** PUBLIC ADDRESS (SYSTEM): *Announcements were made over the PA.* **2** (*especially BrE*) PERSONAL ASSISTANT: *She's the Managing Director's PA.*

Pa *abbr.* PASCAL

pa /pɑː/ *noun* (*old-fashioned, informal*) father: *I used to know your pa.*

p.a. *abbr.* per year (from Latin 'per annum'): *an increase of 3% p.a.*

paan (also **pan**) /pɑːn/ *noun* [U, C] (*IndE*) a BETEL leaf, usually folded into a shape with three sides and filled with spices for eating

PAC /ˌpiː eɪ ˈsiː/ *abbr.* POLITICAL ACTION COMMITTEE

pace[1] 🗝 /peɪs/ *noun, verb* ➲ see also PACE[2]
■ ***noun*** **1** 🗝 [sing., U] the speed at which sb/sth walks, runs or moves: *to set off* ***at a steady/gentle/leisurely pace*** ◇ *Congestion frequently reduces traffic to* ***walking pace.*** ◇ *The ball* ***gathered pace*** *as it rolled down the hill.* ◇ *The runners have noticeably quickened their pace.* **2** 🗝 [sing., U] **~ (of sth)** the speed at which sth happens: *It is difficult to keep up with the rapid pace of change.* ◇ *We encourage all students to work* ***at their own pace*** (= as fast or as slow as they can). ◇ *I prefer the relaxed* ***pace of life*** *in the country.* ◇ *Rumours of corruption and scandal* ***gathered pace*** (= increased in number). **3** 🗝 [C] an act of stepping once when walking or running; the distance travelled when doing this **SYN step**: *She took two paces forward.* **4** [U] the fact of sth happening, changing, etc. quickly: *He gave up his job in advertising because he couldn't* ***stand the pace.*** ◇ *The novel lacks pace* (= it develops too slowly). ➲ see also PACY
IDM **go through your 'paces | show your 'paces** to perform a particular activity in order to show other people what you are capable of doing **keep 'pace (with sb/sth)** to move, increase, change, etc. at the same speed as sb/sth: *She found it hard to keep pace with him as he strode off.* ◇ *Until now, wage increases have always kept pace with inflation.* **off the 'pace** (in sport) behind the leader or the leading group in a race or a competition: *Tiger Woods is still three shots off the pace* (= in GOLF). **put sb/sth through their/its 'paces** to give sb/sth a number of tasks to perform in order to see what they are capable of doing **set the 'pace 1** to do sth at a particular speed or to a particular standard so that other people are then forced to copy it if they want to be successful: *The company is no longer setting the pace in the home computer market.* **2** (in a race) to run faster than the other people taking part, at a speed that they then try to copy ➲ more at FORCE *v.*, SNAIL
■ ***verb*** **1** [I, T] to walk up and down in a small area many times, especially because you are feeling nervous or angry: **+ adv./prep.** *She* ***paced up and down*** *outside the room.* ◇ **~ sth** *Ted paced the floor restlessly.* **2** [T] **~ sth** to set the speed at which sth happens or develops: *He paced his game skilfully.* **3** [T] **~ yourself** to find the right speed or rhythm for your work or an activity so that you have enough energy to do what you have to do: *He'll have to learn to pace himself in this job.*
PHR V **ˌpace sth↔'off/'out** to measure the size of sth by walking across it with regular steps

pace[2] /ˈpɑːkeɪ; ˈpɑːtʃeɪ; ˈpeɪsi/ *prep.* (from *Latin, formal*) used before a person's name to express polite disagreement with what they have said: *The evidence suggests, pace Professor Jones, that...* (= Professor Jones has a different opinion). ➲ see also PACE[1]

ˌpace 'bowler *noun* = FAST BOWLER

pace·maker /ˈpeɪsmeɪkə(r)/ *noun* **1** an electronic device that is put inside a person's body to help their heart beat regularly **2** (also **pace·setter** especially in *NAmE*) a person or an animal that begins a race quickly so that the other people taking part will try to copy the speed and run a fast race: (*figurative*) *The big banks have been the pacesetters in developing the system.* **3** (also **pace·setter** especially in *NAmE*) a person or team that is winning in a sports competition: *The local club are now only one point off the pacemakers.*

pace·man /ˈpeɪsmæn/ *noun* (*pl.* **-men** /-men/) = FAST BOWLER

pace·setter /ˈpeɪssetə(r)/ *noun* (*especially NAmE*) = PACEMAKER

pacey = PACY

pa·chinko /pəˈtʃɪŋkəʊ; *NAmE* -koʊ/ *noun* [U] (from *Japanese*) a Japanese form of PINBALL, in which you can win prizes

pachy·derm /ˈpækidɜːm; *NAmE* -dɜːrm/ *noun* (*technical*) a type of animal with a very thick skin, for example, an ELEPHANT

pa·cif·ic /pəˈsɪfɪk/ *adj.* [usually before noun] (*literary*) peaceful or loving peace

Paˌcific 'Daylight Time *noun* [U] (*abbr.* **PDT**) the time used in summer in the western parts of Canada and the US that is nine hours earlier than GMT

the Paˌcific 'Rim *noun* [sing.] the countries around the Pacific Ocean, especially the countries of eastern Asia, considered as an economic group

Paˌcific 'Standard Time *noun* [U] (*abbr.* **PST**) the time used in winter in the western parts of Canada and the US that is eight hours earlier than GMT

Pa'cific time *noun* [U] the standard time on the west coast of the US and Canada

paci·fier /ˈpæsɪfaɪə(r)/ (*NAmE*) (*BrE* **dummy**) *noun* a specially shaped rubber or plastic object for a baby to suck

paci·fism /ˈpæsɪfɪzəm/ *noun* [U] the belief that war and violence are always wrong

paci·fist /ˈpæsɪfɪst/ *noun* a person who believes in pacifism and who refuses to fight in a war ➲ compare CONSCIENTIOUS OBJECTOR ▸ **paci·fist** *adj.* [usually before noun]: *pacifist beliefs*

pacify /ˈpæsɪfaɪ/ *verb* (**paci·fies, paci·fy·ing, paci·fied**) **1 ~ sb** to make sb who is angry or upset become calm and quiet **SYN placate**: *The baby could not be pacified.* ◇ *The speech was designed to pacify the irate crowd.* **2 ~ sth** to bring peace to an area where there is fighting or a war ▸ **paci·fi·ca·tion** /ˌpæsɪfɪˈkeɪʃn/ *noun* [U]

pack 🗝 /pæk/ *verb, noun*
■ ***verb***
▸ PUT INTO CONTAINER **1** 🗝 [I, T] to put clothes, etc. into a bag in preparation for a trip away from home: *I haven't packed yet.* ◇ **~ sth** *I haven't packed my suitcase yet.* ◇ *He packed a bag with a few things and was off.* ◇ *He packed a few things into a bag.* ◇ *Did you pack the camera?* ◇ **~ sb sth** *I've packed you some food for the journey.* **2** 🗝 [T] **~ sth (up) (in/into sth)** to put sth into a container so that it can be stored, transported or sold: *The pottery was packed in boxes and shipped to the US.* ◇ *I carefully packed up the gifts.* **OPP unpack**
▸ PROTECT **3** 🗝 [T] **~ sth (in/with sth)** to protect sth that breaks easily by surrounding it with soft material: *The paintings were carefully packed in newspaper.*
▸ PRESERVE FOOD **4** 🗝 [T] **~ sth (in sth)** to preserve food in a particular substance: *fish packed in ice*
▸ FILL **5** 🗝 [I, T] to fill sth with a lot of people or things: **+ adv./prep.** *We all packed together into one car.* ◇ **~ sth (with sth)** *Fans packed the hall to see the band.* ➲ see also PACKED, PACKED OUT
▸ SNOW/SOIL **6** [T] **~ sth (down)** to press sth such as snow or soil to form a thick hard mass: *Pack the earth down around the plant.* ◇ *a patch of packed snow*
▸ CARRY GUN **7** [T, I] **~ (sth)** (*NAmE, informal*) to carry a gun: *to pack a gun* ◇ *Is he packing?*

▸ STORM **8** [T] **~ sth** to have sth: *A storm packing 75 mph winds swept across the area last night.*

IDM **pack a (powerful, real, etc.) 'punch** (*informal*) **1** (of a BOXER) to be capable of hitting sb very hard **2** to have a powerful effect on sb: *The advertising campaign packs quite a punch.* **pack your 'bags** (*informal*) to leave a person or place permanently, especially after a disagreement ➲ more at SEND

PHR V **,pack a'way** to be capable of being folded up small when it is not being used: *The tent packs away in a small bag.* **,pack sth↔a'way** to put sth in a box, etc. when you have finished using it: *We packed away the summer clothes.* **,pack sb↔'in** [no passive] (of plays, performers, etc.) to attract a lot of people to see it/them: *The show is still **packing them in**.* **,pack sth↔'in** (*informal*) to stop doing sth SYN **give up**: *She decided to pack in her job.* ◇ (*especially BrE*) ***Pack it in*** (= stop behaving badly or annoying me), *you two!* **,pack sb/sth 'in/'into sth 1** to do a lot of things in a limited period of time: *You seem to have packed a lot into your life!* **2** to put a lot of things or people into a limited space SYN **cram in**: *They've managed to pack a lot of information into a very small book.* **,pack 'into sth** to go somewhere in large numbers so that all available space is filled SYN **cram**: *Over 80 000 fans packed into the stadium to watch the final.* ➲ see also PACK (5) **,pack sb↔'off (to...)** (*informal*) to send sb somewhere, especially because you do not want them with you: *My parents always packed me off to bed early.* **,pack sth↔'out** (of shows, performers, etc.) to attract enough people to completely fill a theatre, etc: *The band can still pack out concert halls.* ➲ see also PACKED OUT **,pack 'up** (*informal, especially BrE*) (of a machine) to stop working: *The TV's packed up again.* **,pack 'up** | **,pack sth↔'up 1** 🔑 to put your possessions into a bag, etc. before leaving a place: *Are you packing up already? It's only 4 o'clock.* ◇ *We arrived just as the musicians were packing up their instruments.* **2** (*BrE, informal*) to stop doing sth, especially a job SYN **give up**: *What made you pack up a good job like that?* ➲ see also PACK (2)

■ ***noun***

▸ CONTAINER **1** 🔑 [C] (*especially NAmE*) a container, usually made of paper, that holds a number of the same thing or an amount of sth, ready to be sold: *a pack of cigarettes/gum* ◇ *You can buy the envelopes in packs of ten.* ➲ VISUAL VOCAB page V29 ➲ compare PACKAGE, PACKET ➲ see also FLAT-PACK, SIX-PACK

▸ SET **2** 🔑 [C] a set of different things that are supplied together for a particular purpose: *Send for your free information pack today.*

▸ THINGS TIED FOR CARRYING **3** [C] a number of things that are wrapped or tied together, especially for carrying: *donkeys carrying packs of wool* ◇ (*figurative*) *Everything she told us is **a pack of lies*** (= a story that is completely false).

▸ LARGE BAG **4** [C] a large bag that you carry on your back: *We passed a group of walkers, carrying huge packs.* ➲ see also BACKPACK, FANNY PACK

▸ OF ANIMALS **5** [C+sing./pl. v.] a group of animals that hunt together or are kept for hunting: *packs of savage dogs* ◇ *wolves hunting in packs* ◇ *a pack of hounds*

▸ OF PEOPLE **6** [C+sing./pl. v.] a group of similar people or things, especially one that you do not like or approve of: *We avoided a pack of journalists waiting outside.* ◇ *He's the leader of the pack.* **7** [C+sing./pl. v.] all the people who are behind the leaders in a race, competition, etc: *measures aimed at keeping the company ahead of the pack*

▸ OF CARDS **8** (*BrE*) (also **deck** *NAmE, BrE*) [C] a complete set of 52 PLAYING CARDS: *a pack of cards* ➲ VISUAL VOCAB page V32

▸ OF CUBS/BROWNIES **9** [C+sing./pl. v.] an organized group of CUBS/CUB SCOUTS or BROWNIES: *to join a Brownie pack*

▸ FOR WOUND **10** [C] a hot or cold piece of soft material that absorbs liquid, used for treating a wound ➲ see also FACE PACK, ICE PACK, MUD PACK IDM see JOKER

pack·age 🔑 /'pækɪdʒ/ *noun, verb*

■ ***noun* 1** 🔑 (*especially NAmE*) = PARCEL: *A large package has arrived for you.* ➲ compare PACK **2** 🔑 (*NAmE*) a box, bag, etc. in which things are wrapped or packed; the contents of a box etc: *Check the list of ingredients on the side of the package.* ◇ *a package of hamburger buns* ➲ VISUAL VOCAB page V29 ➲ compare PACKET **3** (also **'package deal**) a set of items or ideas that must be bought or accepted together: *a benefits package* ◇ *an aid package* ◇ *a package of measures to help small businesses* **4** (also **'software package**) (*computing*) a set of related programs for a particular type of task, sold and used as a single unit: *The system came with a database software package.*

■ ***verb*** [often passive] **1** 🔑 to put sth into a box, bag, etc. to be sold or transported: **~ sth** *packaged food/goods* ◇ *We package our products in recyclable materials.* ◇ **~ sth up** *The orders were already packaged up, ready to be sent.* **2 ~ sb/sth (as sth)** to present sb/sth in a particular way: *an attempt to package news as entertainment*

'package store *noun* (*US*) = LIQUOR STORE

'package tour (*BrE* also **'package holiday**) *noun* a holiday/vacation that is organized by a company at a fixed price and that includes the cost of travel, hotels, etc.

pack·aging 🔑 /'pækɪdʒɪŋ/ *noun* [U]

1 🔑 materials used to wrap or protect goods that are sold in shops/stores: *Attractive packaging can help to sell products.* ➲ VISUAL VOCAB page V29 **2** the process of wrapping goods: *His company offers a flexible packaging service for the food industry.*

'pack animal *noun* an animal used for carrying loads, for example a horse

packed /pækt/ *adj.* **1** extremely full of people SYN **crowded**: *The restaurant was packed.* ◇ *The show played to **packed houses*** (= large audiences). **2** containing a lot of a particular thing: **~ with sth** *The book is packed with information.* ◇ **~ -packed** *an information-packed book* **3 tightly ~** pressed closely together: *The birds' nests are lined with tightly packed leaves.* **4** [not before noun] (*informal*) having put everything you need into cases, boxes, etc. before you go somewhere: *I'm all packed and ready to go.*

,packed 'lunch *noun* (*BrE*) a meal of SANDWICHES, fruit, etc. that is prepared at home and eaten at school, work, etc. ➲ compare BAG LUNCH, BOX LUNCH

,packed 'out *adj.* [not before noun] (*informal, especially BrE*) completely full of people or things: *Opera houses are packed out wherever she sings.*

pack·er /'pækə(r)/ *noun* a person, machine or company that puts food, goods, etc. into containers to be sold or sent to sb

packet 🔑 /'pækɪt/ *noun*

1 🔑 (*BrE*) a small paper or cardboard container in which goods are packed for selling: *a packet of biscuits/cigarettes/crisps* ➲ VISUAL VOCAB page V29 ➲ compare PACK *n.* (1), PACKAGE ➲ see also PAY PACKET **2** 🔑 a small object wrapped in paper or put into a thick envelope so that it can be sent by mail, carried easily or given as a present: *A packet of photographs arrived with the mail.* **3** (*NAmE*) (*BrE* **sa·chet**) a closed plastic or paper package that contains a very small amount of liquid or a powder: *a packet of instant cocoa mix* ➲ VISUAL VOCAB page V29 **4** [sing.] (*BrE, informal*) a large amount of money: *That car must have cost a packet.* **5** (*computing*) a piece of information that forms part of a message sent through a computer network **6** (*NAmE*) a set of documents that are supplied together for a particular purpose: *a training packet*

'packet switching *noun* [U] (*computing*) a process in which data is separated into parts before being sent, and then joined together after it arrives

pack·horse /'pækhɔːs; *NAmE* -hɔːrs/ *noun* a horse that is used to carry heavy loads

'pack ice *noun* [U] a large mass of ice floating in the sea, formed from smaller pieces that have frozen together

pack·ing /'pækɪŋ/ *noun* [U] **1** the act of putting your possessions, clothes, etc. into bags or boxes in order to take or send them somewhere: *Have you finished your packing?* **2** material used for wrapping around delicate objects in order to protect them, especially before sending them somewhere: (*BrE*) *The price includes **postage and packing**.*

ˈ**packing case** *noun* (*BrE*) a large strong box for packing or transporting goods in

ˈ**pack rat** *noun* **1** (*NAmE*) a person who collects and stores things that they do not really need **2** a small N American animal like a mouse that collects small sticks, etc. in its hole

pact /pækt/ *noun* ~ (**between A and B**) | ~ (**with sb**) (**to do sth**) a formal agreement between two or more people, groups or countries, especially one in which they agree to help each other: *a non-aggression pact* ◇ *They have* ***made a pact*** *with each other not to speak about their differences in public.* ◇ *a* ***suicide pact*** (= an agreement by two or more people to kill themselves at the same time)

pacy (also **pacey**) /ˈpeɪsi/ *adj.* (*BrE, informal*) **1** (of a book, film/movie, etc.) having a story that develops quickly **2** able to run quickly SYN **fast**: *a pacy winger who can also score goals*

pad /pæd/ *noun, verb*

■ ***noun***

▸ OF SOFT MATERIAL **1** a thick piece of soft material that is used, for example, for absorbing liquid, cleaning or protecting sth: *medicated cleansing pads for sensitive skin* ◇ *sanitary pads* (= that a woman uses during her PERIOD) ➲ see also SHOULDER PAD

▸ OF PAPER **2** a number of pieces of paper for writing or drawing on, that are fastened together at one edge: *a* ***sketch/writing pad*** ➲ see also NOTEPAD, SCRATCH PAD

▸ OF ANIMAL'S FOOT **3** the soft part under the foot of a cat, dog, etc.

▸ FOR CLEANING **4** a small piece of rough material used for cleaning pans, surfaces, etc: *a scouring pad*

▸ FOR SPACECRAFT/HELICOPTER **5** a flat surface where a SPACECRAFT or a HELICOPTER takes off and lands ➲ see also HELIPAD, LAUNCH PAD

▸ FOR PROTECTION **6** [usually pl.] a piece of thick material that you wear in some sports, for example football and CRICKET, to protect your legs, elbows, etc. ➲ VISUAL VOCAB page V36

▸ OF WATER PLANTS **7** the large flat leaf of some water plants, especially the WATER LILY: *floating lily pads*

▸ FLAT/APARTMENT **8** [usually sing.] (*old-fashioned, informal*) the place where sb lives, especially a flat/apartment ➲ see also INK-PAD, KEYPAD

■ ***verb*** (-dd-)

▸ ADD SOFT MATERIAL **1** [T, often passive] ~ **sth** (**with sth**) to put a layer of soft material in or on sth in order to protect it, make it thicker or change its shape: *All the sharp corners were padded with foam.* ◇ *a padded jacket* ◇ *a* ***padded envelope*** (= for sending delicate objects)

▸ WALK QUIETLY **2** [I] + **adv./prep.** to walk with quiet steps: *She padded across the room to the window.*

▸ BILLS **3** [T] ~ **sth** (*NAmE*) to dishonestly add items to bills to obtain more money: *to* ***pad bills/expense accounts***

PHR V ˌ**pad sth**↔ˈ**out 1** to put soft material into a piece of clothing in order to change its shape **2** to make sth such as an article, seem longer or more impressive by adding things that are unnecessary: *The report was padded out with extracts from previous documents.*

ˌ**padded** ˈ**cell** *noun* a room in a hospital for mentally ill people, with soft walls to prevent violent patients from injuring themselves

pad·ding /ˈpædɪŋ/ *noun* [U] **1** soft material that is placed inside sth to make it more comfortable or to change its shape **2** words that are used to make a speech, piece of writing, etc. longer, but that do not contain any interesting information

pad·dle /ˈpædl/ *noun, verb*

■ ***noun*** **1** [C] a short pole with a flat wide part at one or both ends, that you hold in both hands and use for moving a small boat, especially a CANOE, through water ➲ VISUAL VOCAB page V45 ➲ compare OAR **2** [C] a tool or part of a machine shaped like a paddle, especially one used for mixing food **3 a paddle** [sing.] (*BrE*) an act or period of walking in shallow water with no shoes or socks: *Let's go for a paddle.* ➲ see also DOG-PADDLE **4** [C] (*NAmE*) a BAT used for playing TABLE TENNIS **5** [C] (*NAmE*) a piece of wood with a handle, used for hitting children as a punishment IDM see CREEK

■ ***verb*** **1** [I, T] to move a small boat through water using a paddle: (+ **adv./prep.**) *We paddled downstream for about a mile.* ◇ ~ **sth** (+ **adv./prep.**) *We paddled the canoe along the coast.* **2** (*BrE*) (*NAmE* **wade**) [I] to walk or stand with no shoes or socks in shallow water in the sea, a lake, etc: *The children have* ***gone paddling***. **3** [I] to swim with short movements of your hands or feet up and down **4** [T] ~ **sb/sth** (*NAmE*) to hit a child with a flat piece of wood as a punishment

ˈ**paddle steamer** (*BrE*) (also **paddle·boat** *NAmE, BrE*) *noun* an old-fashioned type of boat driven by steam and moved forward by a large wheel or wheels at the side ➲ VISUAL VOCAB page V44

ˈ**paddling pool** (*BrE*) (*NAmE* ˈ**wading pool**) *noun* a shallow swimming pool for children to play in, especially a small plastic one that you fill with water

pad·dock /ˈpædək/ *noun* **1** a small field in which horses are kept **2** (in horse racing or motor racing) an area where horses or cars are taken before a race and shown to the public **3** (*AustralE, NZE*) any field or area of land that has fences around it

Paddy /ˈpædi/ *noun* (*pl.* -ies) (*informal*) an offensive word for a person from Ireland

paddy /ˈpædi/ *noun* (*pl.* -ies) **1** (also ˈ**paddy field**) a field in which rice is grown: *a rice paddy* **2** [usually sing.] (*BrE, informal*) a state of being angry or in a bad mood SYN **temper**: *The news put him in a bit of a paddy.*

ˈ**paddy wagon** *noun* (*informal, NAmE*) = PATROL WAGON

pad·kos /ˈpʌtkɒs; *NAmE* -kɑːs/ *noun* [U] (*SAfrE*) food that you take with you to eat while on a journey

pad·lock /ˈpædlɒk; *NAmE* -lɑːk/ *noun, verb*

■ ***noun*** a type of lock that is used to fasten two things together or to fasten one thing to another. Padlocks are used with chains on gates, etc.

■ ***verb*** to lock sth with a padlock: ~ **sth to sth** *She always padlocked her bike to the railings.* ◇ ~ **sth** *The doors were padlocked.*

padlock

padre /ˈpɑːdreɪ/ *noun* (often used as a form of address) a priest, or other Christian minister, especially in the armed forces ➲ compare CHAPLAIN

paean /ˈpiːən/ *noun* (*literary*) a song of praise or victory

paed- (*BrE*) (*NAmE* **ped-**) /piːd-/ *combining form* (in nouns and adjectives) connected with children: *paediatrician*

paed·er·ast, paed·er·asty *nouns* (*BrE*) = PEDERAST, PEDERASTY

paedi·at·ri·cian (*BrE*) (*NAmE* **pedi·at·ri·cian**) /ˌpiːdiəˈtrɪʃn/ *noun* a doctor who studies and treats the diseases of children

paedi·at·rics (*BrE*) (*NAmE* **pedi·at·rics**) /ˌpiːdiˈætrɪks/ *noun* [U] the branch of medicine concerned with children and their diseases ▸ **paedi·at·ric** (*BrE*) (*NAmE* **pedi-**) *adj.*: *paediatric surgery*

paedo·phile (*BrE*) (*NAmE* **pedo-**) /ˈpiːdəʊfaɪl; *NAmE* -doʊ-/ *noun* a person who is sexually attracted to children

paedo·philia (*BrE*) (*NAmE* **pedo-**) /ˌpiːdəˈfɪliə/ *noun* [U] the condition of being sexually attracted to children; sexual activity with children

pa·ella /paɪˈelə/ *noun* [U, C] a Spanish dish of rice, chicken, fish and vegetables, cooked and served in a large shallow pan

pagan /ˈpeɪɡən/ *noun* (often *disapproving*) **1** a person who holds religious beliefs that are not part of any of the world's main religions **2** used in the past by Christians to describe a person who did not believe in Christianity ▸ **pagan** *adj.*: *a pagan festival* **pa·gan·ism** /ˈpeɪɡənɪzəm/ *noun* [U]

page 0‑ᵯ /peɪdʒ/ *noun, verb*
■ ***noun*** **1** 0‑ᵯ (*abbr.* p) one side or both sides of a sheet of paper in a book, magazine, etc: *Turn to page 64.* ◇ *Someone has torn a page out of this book.* ◇ *a* ***blank/new page*** ◇ *the* ***sports/financial pages*** *of the newspaper* ◇ *on the* ***opposite/facing page*** ◇ ***over the page*** (= on the next page) ➲ see also FRONT PAGE, FULL-PAGE, YELLOW PAGES **2** 0‑ᵯ a section of data or information that can be shown on a computer screen at any one time ➲ see also HOME PAGE **3** (*literary*) an important event or period of history: *a glorious page of Arab history* **4** (*especially NAmE*) = PAGEBOY **5** (*NAmE*) a student who works as an assistant to a member of the US Congress **6** (in the Middle Ages) a boy or young man who worked for a KNIGHT while training to be a knight himself
IDM **on the same 'page** (*especially NAmE*) if two or more people or groups are **on the same page**, they agree about what they are trying to achieve **turn the 'page** to begin doing things in a different way and thinking in a more positive way after a period of difficulties ➲ more at PRINT *v.*
■ ***verb*** **1 ~ sb** to call sb's name over a PUBLIC ADDRESS SYSTEM in order to find them and give them a message: *Why don't you have him paged at the airport?* **2 ~ sb** to contact sb by sending a message to their PAGER: *Page Dr Green immediately.*
PHR V **,page 'through sth** (*NAmE*) to quickly turn the pages of a book, magazine, etc. and look at them without reading them carefully or in detail SYN **flick through sth, leaf through sth**

pa·geant /'pædʒənt/ *noun* **1** a public entertainment in which people dress in historical COSTUMES and give performances of scenes from history **2** (*NAmE*) a competition for young women in which their beauty, personal qualities and skills are judged: *a beauty pageant* ➲ compare BEAUTY CONTEST **3 ~** (**of sth**) (*literary*) something that is considered as a series of interesting and different events: *life's rich pageant*

pa·geant·ry /'pædʒəntri/ *noun* [U] impressive and exciting events and ceremonies involving a lot of people wearing special clothes: *the pageantry of royal occasions*

P

page·boy /'peɪdʒbɔɪ/ *noun* **1** (also **page** especially in *NAmE*) a small boy who helps or follows a BRIDE during a marriage ceremony ➲ compare BRIDESMAID **2** (also **page**) (*old-fashioned*) a boy or young man, usually in uniform, employed in a hotel to open doors, deliver messages for people, etc. **3** a HAIRSTYLE for women in which the hair is shoulder-length and turned under at the ends

pager /'peɪdʒə(r)/ *noun* a small electronic device that you carry around with you and that shows a message or lets you know when sb is trying to contact you, for example by making a sound ➲ see also BEEPER, BLEEPER

,page-'three girl *noun* (*BrE*) a naked or partly naked young woman whose picture is printed in a newspaper ORIGIN From page three of the *Sun* newspaper, where one of these pictures is or was printed every day.

'page-turner *noun* (*informal*) a book that is very exciting

'page view *noun* [C, sing.] (*business*) one visit to a single page on a website: *a surge in page views*

pa·gin·ate /'pædʒɪneɪt/ *verb* **~ sth** (*technical*) to give a number to each page of a book, piece of writing, etc.

pa·gin·ation /,pædʒɪ'neɪʃn/ *noun* [U] (*technical*) the process of giving a page number to each page of a book; the page numbers given

pa·goda /pə'gəʊdə; *NAmE* -'goʊ-/ *noun* a TEMPLE (= religious building) in S or E Asia in the form of a tall tower with several levels, each of which has its own roof that extends beyond the walls ➲ VISUAL VOCAB page V13

pah /pɑː/ *exclamation* used to represent the sound that people make when they disagree with sth or disapprove of sth strongly

paid /peɪd/ *adj.* [usually before noun] **1** (of work, etc.) for which people receive money: *Neither of them is currently in paid employment.* ◇ *a well-paid job* **2** (of a person) receiving money for doing work: *Men still outnumber women in the paid workforce.* ◇ *a poorly paid teacher* OPP **unpaid**
IDM **put 'paid to sth** (*informal*) to stop or destroy sth, especially what sb plans or wants to do

'paid-up *adj.* [only before noun] **1** having paid all the money necessary to be a member of a club or an organization: *a fully paid-up member* **2** (*BrE, informal*) strongly supporting sb/sth: *a fully paid-up environmental campaigner*

pail /peɪl/, **pail·ful** /'peɪlfʊl/ *noun* (*NAmE* or *old-fashioned*) = BUCKET, BUCKETFUL

pain 0‑ᵯ /peɪn/ *noun, verb*
■ ***noun*** ➲ see also PAINS **1** 0‑ᵯ [U, C] the feelings that you have in your body when you have been hurt or when you are ill/sick: *a cry of pain* ◇ *She was clearly* ***in*** *a lot of* ***pain***. ◇ *He felt a sharp pain in his knee.* ◇ *patients suffering from acute back pain* ◇ ***stomach/chest pains*** ◇ *You get more* ***aches and pains*** *as you get older.* ◇ *The booklet contains information on* ***pain relief*** *during labour.* ◇ *This cream should help to* ***relieve the pain***. ➲ see also GROWING PAINS **2** 0‑ᵯ [U, C] mental or emotional suffering: *the pain of separation* ◇ *I never meant to cause her pain.* ◇ *the* ***pleasures and pains*** *of growing old* **3** [C] (*informal*) a person or thing that is very annoying: *She can be a real pain when she's in a bad mood.* ◇ ***It's a pain*** *having to go all that way for just one meeting.*
IDM **no ,pain, no 'gain** (*saying*) used to say that you need to suffer if you want to achieve sth **on/under pain of sth** (*formal*) with the threat of having sth done to you as a punishment if you do not obey: *They were required to cut pollution levels, on pain of a £10 000 fine if they disobeyed.* **a pain in the 'neck** (*BrE* also **a pain in the 'arse/'backside**) (*NAmE* also **a pain in the 'ass/'butt**) (*informal*) a person or thing that is very annoying
■ ***verb*** (not used in the progressive tenses) (*formal*) to cause sb pain or make them unhappy SYN **hurt**: **~ sb** *She was deeply pained by the accusation.* ◇ (*old use*) *The wound still pained him occasionally.* ◇ **it pains sb to do sth** *It pains me to see you like this.* ◇ **it pains sb that...** *It pained him that she would not acknowledge him.*

'pain barrier *noun* [usually sing.] the moment at which sb doing hard physical activity feels the greatest pain, after which the pain becomes less: *He broke through the pain barrier at 25 kilometres and went on to win his first marathon.*

pained /peɪnd/ *adj.* showing that sb is feeling annoyed or upset: *a* ***pained expression/voice***

pain·ful 0‑ᵯ /'peɪnfl/ *adj.*
1 0‑ᵯ causing you pain: *Is your back still painful?* ◇ *a painful death* ◇ *My ankle is still too painful to walk on.* **2** 0‑ᵯ **~** (**for sb**) (**to do sth**) | **~** (**doing sth**) causing you to feel upset or embarrassed: *a* ***painful experience/memory*** ◇ *Their efforts were painful to watch.* **3** 0‑ᵯ unpleasant or difficult to do SYN **trying**: *Applying for jobs can be a long and painful process.*

pain·ful·ly /'peɪnfəli/ *adv.* **1** extremely, and in a way that makes you feel annoyed, upset, etc: *Their son was* ***painfully*** *shy.* ◇ *The dog was* ***painfully*** *thin.* ◇ *He was* ***painfully aware*** *of his lack of experience.* ◇ *Progress has been* ***painfully slow***. **2** in a way that causes you physical or emotional pain: *He banged his knee painfully against the desk.* **3** with a lot of effort and difficulty: *painfully acquired experience*

pain·kill·er /'peɪnkɪlə(r)/ *noun* a drug that reduces pain: *She's on* (= taking) *painkillers.* ▸ **pain·kill·ing** *adj.* [only before noun]: ***painkilling drugs/injections***

pain·less /'peɪnləs/ *adj.* **1** causing you no pain: *a painless death* ◇ *The treatment is painless.* **2** not unpleasant or difficult to do: *The interview was relatively painless.* ▸ **pain·less·ly** *adv.*

pains /peɪnz/ *noun* [pl.]
IDM **be at pains to do sth** to put a lot of effort into doing sth correctly: *She was at great pains to stress the advantages of the new system.* **for your 'pains** (*especially BrE*, often *ironic*) as payment, reward or thanks for sth you have done: *I told her what I thought and got a mouthful of abuse*

Synonyms

painful

sore • raw • inflamed • excruciating • burning • itchy

These words all describe sth that causes you physical pain.

painful causing you physical pain. NOTE **Painful** can describe a part of the body, illness, injury, treatment or death: *Is your knee still painful? ◇ a series of painful injections ◇ a slow and painful death*

sore (of a part of the body) painful and often red, especially because of infection or because a muscle has been used too much: *a sore throat ◇ Their feet were sore after hours of walking.*

raw (of a part of the body) red and painful, for example because of an infection or because the skin has been damaged: *The skin on her feet had been rubbed raw.*

inflamed (of a part of the body) painful, red and hot because of an infection or injury: *The wound had become inflamed.*

excruciating extremely painful. NOTE **Excruciating** can describe feelings, treatments or death but not parts of the body: ~~*an excruciating throat/back/knee*~~.

burning painful and giving a feeling of being very hot: *She felt a burning sensation in her throat.*

itchy giving an uncomfortable feeling on your skin that makes you want to scratch; having this feeling: *an itchy rash ◇ I feel itchy all over.*

PATTERNS
- sore/inflamed/itchy **eyes**
- raw/inflamed/itchy **skin**
- a painful/an excruciating **death**
- a painful/burning **sensation**
- excruciating/burning **pain**

for my pains! **take (great) pains (to do sth) | go to great pains (to do sth)** to put a lot of effort into doing sth: *The couple went to great pains to keep their plans secret.* **take (great) pains with/over sth** to do sth very carefully: *He always takes great pains with his lectures.*

pains·tak·ing /ˈpeɪnzteɪkɪŋ/ *adj.* [usually before noun] needing a lot of care, effort and attention to detail SYN **thorough**: *painstaking research ◇ The event had been planned with painstaking attention to detail.* ▸ **pains·tak·ing·ly** *adv.*

paint 🔑 /peɪnt/ *noun, verb*
■ ***noun* 1** 🔑 [U] a liquid that is put on surfaces to give them a particular colour; a layer of this liquid when it has dried on a surface: *white paint ◇* ***gloss/matt/acrylic paint*** *◇ The woodwork has recently been given a fresh* ***coat of paint****. ◇* ***Wet paint!*** (= used as a sign) *◇ The paint is starting to peel off.* ➲ see also GREASEPAINT, OIL PAINT, WARPAINT **2** 🔑 **paints** [pl.] tubes or blocks of paint used for painting pictures: *oil paints*
■ ***verb* 1** 🔑 [T, I] **~ sth (with sth)** to cover a surface or object with paint: **~ (sth)** *We've had the house painted. ◇ Paint the shed with weather-resistant paint. ◇ a brightly painted barge ◇* **~ sth + adj./noun** *The walls were painted yellow.* ➲ COLLOCATIONS at DECORATE **2** 🔑 [T, I] to make a picture or design using paints: **~ sth/sb** *to paint portraits ◇ A friend painted the children for me* (= painted a picture of the children). *◇* **~ sth on sth** *Slogans had been painted on the walls. ◇* **~ (in sth)** *She paints in oils. ◇ My mother paints well.* ➲ COLLOCATIONS at ART **3** [T] to give a particular impression of sb/sth SYN **portray**: **~ sb/sth as sth** *The article paints them as a bunch of petty criminals. ◇* **~ sb/sth in...** *The documentary painted her in a bad light.* **4** [T] **~ sth** to put coloured make-up on your nails, lips, etc.
IDM **paint a (grim, gloomy, rosy, etc.) ˈpicture of sb/sth** to describe sb/sth in a particular way; to give a particular impression of sb/sth: *The report paints a vivid picture of life in the city. ◇ Journalists paint a grim picture of conditions in the camps.* **paint the town ˈred** (*informal*) to go to a lot of different bars, clubs, etc. and enjoy yourself **paint sth with a ˌbroad ˈbrush** to describe sth in a general way, ignoring the details ➲ more at BLACK *adj.*
PHR V **ˌpaint sth↔ˈout** to cover part of a picture, sign, etc. with another layer of paint **ˌpaint ˈover sth** to cover sth with a layer of paint: *We painted over the dirty marks on the wall.*

paint·ball /ˈpeɪntbɔːl/ *noun* [U] a game in which people shoot balls of paint at each other

paint·box /ˈpeɪntbɒks; *NAmE* -bɑːks/ *noun* a box containing a set of paints

paint·brush /ˈpeɪntbrʌʃ/ *noun* a brush that is used for painting ➲ VISUAL VOCAB page V17

ˌpaint-by-ˈnumbers *adj.* [only before noun] **1** (of pictures) having sections with different numbers showing which colours should be used to fill them in **2** (*disapproving*) used to describe sth that is produced without using the imagination: *He accused the government of relying on paint-by-numbers policies.*

ˈpaint chip *noun* **1** a small piece of paint that has broken off sth or the small area where the paint has come off **2** (*NAmE*) a strip of card with samples of paint in different colours, provided in shops/stores to help customers decide what paint to buy

paint·er 🔑 /ˈpeɪntə(r)/ *noun*
1 🔑 a person whose job is painting buildings, walls, etc: *He works as a painter and decorator.* **2** 🔑 an artist who paints pictures: *a famous painter ◇ a* ***portrait/landscape painter*** **3** a rope fastened to the front of a boat, used for tying it to a post, ship, etc.

paint·er·ly /ˈpeɪntəli; *NAmE* -ərli/ *adj.* typical of artists or painting SYN **artistic**

paint·ing 🔑 /ˈpeɪntɪŋ/ *noun*
1 🔑 [C] a picture that has been painted: *a collection of paintings by American artists ◇ cave paintings* ➲ SYNONYMS at PICTURE ➲ COLLOCATIONS at ART ➲ see also OIL PAINTING **2** 🔑 [U] the act or art of using paint to produce pictures: *Her hobbies include music and painting.* ➲ VISUAL VOCAB page V35 **3** 🔑 [U] the act of putting paint onto the surface of objects, walls, etc: *painting and decorating*

ˈpaint stripper *noun* [U] a liquid used to remove old paint from surfaces

paint·work /ˈpeɪntwɜːk; *NAmE* -wɜːrk/ *noun* [U] (*especially BrE*) the layer of paint on the surface of a door, wall, car, etc: *The paintwork is beginning to peel.*

pair 🔑 /peə(r); *NAmE* per/ *noun, verb*
■ ***noun***
▸ TWO THINGS THE SAME **1** 🔑 [C] two things of the same type, especially when they are used or worn together: *a* ***pair of gloves/shoes/earrings, etc.*** *◇ a huge pair of eyes ◇ The vase is one of a* ***matching pair****.*
▸ TWO PARTS JOINED **2** 🔑 [C] an object consisting of two parts that are joined together: *a* ***pair of trousers/pants/jeans, etc.*** *◇ a* ***pair of glasses/binoculars/scissors, etc.*** HELP A plural verb is sometimes used with **pair** in the singular in senses 1 and 2. In informal *NAmE* some people use **pair** as a plural form: *three pair of shoes*. This is not considered correct in written English.
▸ TWO PEOPLE **3** 🔑 [C+sing./pl. v.] two people who are doing sth together or who have a particular relationship: *Get pairs of students to act out the dialogue in front of the class. ◇ Get the students to do the exercise as* ***pair work*** (= two students work together). *◇ (informal) I've had enough of the pair of you!* HELP In *BrE* a plural verb is usually used: *A pair of children were kicking a ball about. ◇ The pair are planning a trip to India together.*
▸ TWO ANIMALS/BIRDS **4** [C+sing./pl. v.] two animals or birds of the same type that are breeding together: *a breeding pair ◇ a pair of swans*
▸ TWO HORSES **5** [C] two horses working together to pull a CARRIAGE: *a carriage and pair* ➲ see also AU PAIR
IDM **a pair of ˈhands** (*informal*) a person who can do, or is doing, a job: *We need an extra pair of hands if we're going to finish on time. ◇ Colleagues regard him as a* ***safe pair of***

P

hands (= sb who can be relied on to do a job well). **in 'pairs** ⊶ in groups of two objects or people: *Students worked in pairs on the project.* **I've only got one pair of 'hands** (*informal*) used to say that you are too busy to do anything else ➲ more at SAFE *adj.*

■ ***verb***

▸ MAKE GROUPS OF TWO **1** [T, usually passive] to put people or things into groups of two: **~ A with B** *Each blind student was paired with a sighted student.* ◇ **~ A (and B) (together)** *All the shoes on the floor were neatly paired.*

▸ OF ANIMALS/BIRDS **2** [I] (*technical*) to come together in order to breed: *Many of the species pair for life.*

PHR V ˌ**pair 'off (with sb)** | ˌ**pair sb↔'off (with sb)** to come together, especially in order to have a romantic relationship; to bring two people together for this purpose: *It seemed that all her friends were pairing off.* ◇ *He's always trying to pair me off with his cousin.* ˌ**pair 'up (with sb)** | ˌ**pair sb↔'up (with sb)** to come together or to bring two people together to work, play a game, etc.

pair·ing /ˈpeərɪŋ; *NAmE* ˈper-/ *noun* **1** [C] two people or things that work together or are placed together; the act of placing them together: *Tonight they take on a Chinese pairing in their bid to reach the final tomorrow.* **2** [U] (in the British Parliament) the practice of an MP agreeing with an MP of a different party that neither of them will vote in a debate so that they do not need to attend the debate

paisa /ˈpaɪsɑː; -sə/ *noun* (*pl.* **paise** /-seɪ; -sə/) a coin of India, Pakistan and Nepal. There are one hundred paise in a RUPEE.

pais·ley /ˈpeɪzli/ *noun* [U] a detailed pattern of curved shapes that look like feathers, used especially on cloth: *a paisley tie*

Pai·ute /ˈpaɪuːt/ *noun* (*pl.* **Pai·ute** or **Pai·utes**) a member of a Native American people many of whom live in the south-western US

pa·ja·mas (*NAmE*) (*BrE, CanE* **py·ja·mas**) /pəˈdʒɑːməz; *NAmE* -ˈdʒæm-/ *noun* [pl.] a loose jacket and pants/trousers worn in bed ➲ VISUAL VOCAB page V51

pak choi /ˌpæk ˈtʃɔɪ/ (*BrE*) (*NAmE* ˌ**bok 'choy**) *noun* [U] a type of CHINESE CABBAGE with long dark green leaves and thick white STEMS

Pak·eha /ˈpɑːkɪhɑː/ *noun* (*NZE*) a white person from New Zealand (that is, not a Maori)

Paki /ˈpæki/ *noun* (*BrE, informal, taboo*) a very offensive word for a person from Pakistan, especially one living in Britain. The word is often also used for people from India or Bangladesh.

pa·kora /pəˈkɔːrə/ *noun* a flat piece of spicy S Asian food consisting of meat or vegetables fried in BATTER

PAL /pæl/ *noun* [U] a television broadcasting system that is used in most of Europe ➲ compare NTSC, SECAM

pal /pæl/ *noun, verb*

■ ***noun* 1** (*informal*, becoming *old-fashioned*) a friend: *We've been pals for years.* ➲ see also PEN PAL **2** (*informal*) used to address a man in an unfriendly way: *If I were you, pal, I'd stay away from her!* ▸ **pally** *adj.*: *I got very pally* (= friendly) *with him.*

■ ***verb*** (-ll-)

PHR V ˌ**pal a'round (with sb)** (*informal, especially NAmE*) to do things with sb as a friend: *I palled around with him and his sister at school.* ˌ**pal 'up (with sb)** (*BrE*) (*NAmE* ˌ**buddy 'up (to/with sb)**) (*informal*) to become sb's friend: *They palled up while they were at college.*

pal·ace ⊶ /ˈpæləs/ *noun*

1 ⊶ [C] the official home of a king, queen, president, etc: *Buckingham Palace* ◇ *the royal/presidential palace* ➲ VISUAL VOCAB page V13 **2** (often **the Palace**) [sing.] the people who live in a palace, especially the British royal family: *The Palace last night refused to comment on the reports.* ◇ *a Palace spokesman* **3** [C] any large impressive house: *The Old Town has a whole collection of churches, palaces and mosques.* **4** [C] (*old-fashioned*) (sometimes used in the names of buildings) a large public building, such as a hotel or cinema/movie theater: *the Strand Palace Hotel*

ˌ**palace 'coup** (also ˌ**palace revo'lution**) *noun* a situation in which a ruler or leader has their power taken away from them by sb within the same party, etc.

palaeo- (*especially BrE*) (*NAmE* usually **paleo-**) /ˈpæliəʊ; ˈpeɪl-; *NAmE* -ioʊ/ *combining form* (in nouns, adjectives and adverbs) connected with ancient times

palae·og·raphy (*BrE*) (*NAmE* **pale·og·raphy**) /ˌpæliˈɒɡrəfi; ˌpeɪl-; *NAmE* -ˈɑːɡ-/ *noun* [U] the study of ancient writing systems ▸ **palae·og·rapher** (also **pale·og·rapher**) /ˌpæliˈɒɡrəfə(r); ˌpeɪl-; *NAmE* -ˈɑːɡ-/ *noun*

Palaeo·lith·ic (*especially BrE*) (*NAmE* usually **Paleo-**) /ˌpæliəˈlɪθɪk; ˌpeɪl-/ *adj.* from or connected with the early part of the Stone Age

palae·on·tolo·gist (*especially BrE*) (*NAmE* usually **paleo-**) /ˌpæliɒnˈtɒlədʒɪst; ˌpeɪl-; *NAmE* ˌpeɪliɑːnˈtɑːl-/ *noun* a person who studies FOSSILS

palae·on·tology (*especially BrE*) (*NAmE* usually **paleo-**) /ˌpæliɒnˈtɒlədʒi; ˌpeɪl-; *NAmE* ˌpeɪliɑːnˈtɑːl-/ *noun* [U] the study of FOSSILS (= the remains of animals or plants in rocks) as a guide to the history of life on earth

pal·ais /ˈpæleɪ/ (also ˌ**palais de 'danse** /ˌpæleɪ də ˈdɑːns/) *noun* (*BrE*) (in the past) a large public building used for dancing; a dance hall

pal·at·able /ˈpælətəbl/ *adj.* **1** (of food or drink) having a pleasant or acceptable taste **2 ~ (to sb)** pleasant or acceptable to sb: *Some of the dialogue has been changed to make it more palatable to an American audience.* OPP **unpalatable**

pal·atal /ˈpælətl/ *noun* (*phonetics*) a speech sound made by placing the tongue against or near the hard PALATE of the mouth, for example /j/ at the beginning of *yes* ▸ **pal·atal** *adj.*

pal·at·al·ize (*BrE* also **-ise**) /ˈpælətəlaɪz/ *verb* **~ sth** (*phonetics*) to make a speech sound by putting your tongue against or near your hard PALATE ▸ **pal·at·al·iz·ation, -is·ation** /ˌpælətəlaɪˈzeɪʃn/ *noun* [U]

pal·ate /ˈpælət/ *noun* **1** the top part of the inside of the mouth: *the* ***hard/soft palate*** (= the hard/soft part at the front/back of the palate) ➲ see also CLEFT PALATE **2** [usually sing.] the ability to recognize and/or enjoy good food and drink: *a menu to tempt even the most* ***jaded palate***

pa·la·tial /pəˈleɪʃl/ *adj.* [usually before noun] (of a room or building) very large and impressive, like a palace SYN **splendid**

pa·lat·in·ate /pəˈlætɪnət/ *noun* **1** [C] the area ruled by a Count Palatine (= a ruler with the power of a king or queen) **2 the Palatinate** [sing.] the land of the German Empire that was ruled over by the Count Palatine of the Rhine

pal·at·ine /ˈpælətaɪn/ *adj.* [only before noun] **1** (of an official, etc. in the past) having the power in a particular area that a king or queen usually has **2** (of an area of land) ruled over by sb who has the power of a king or queen

pa·la·ver /pəˈlɑːvə(r); *NAmE* also -ˈlæv-/ *noun* (*informal*) **1** [U, sing.] (*BrE*) a lot of unnecessary activity, excitement or trouble, especially caused by sth that is unimportant SYN **fuss**: *What's all the palaver about?* ◇ *What a palaver it is, trying to get a new visa!* **2** [U] (*NAmE*) talk that does not have any meaning; nonsense: *He's talking palaver.*

pa·lazzo pants /pəˈlætsəʊ pænts; *NAmE* pəˈlɑːtsoʊ/ *noun* [pl.] women's trousers/pants with wide loose legs

pale ⊶ /peɪl/ *adj., verb, noun*

■ ***adj.*** (**paler, pal·est**) **1** ⊶ (of a person, their face, etc.) having skin that is almost white; having skin that is whiter than usual because of illness, a strong emotion, etc: *a pale complexion* ◇ *pale with fear* ◇ *to* ***go/turn pale*** ◇ *You look pale. Are you OK?* ◇ *The ordeal left her looking* ***pale and drawn.*** **2** ⊶ light in colour; containing a lot of white: *pale blue eyes* ◇ *a paler shade of green* ◇ *a pale sky* OPP **dark, deep 3** ⊶ (of light) not strong or bright: *the cold pale light of dawn* ➲ see also PALLID, PALLOR ▸ **pale·ly** /ˈpeɪlli/ *adv.*: *Mark stared palely* (= with a pale face) *at his plate.* **pale·ness** *noun* [U]

■ ***verb*** [I] **~ (at sth)** to become paler than usual: *She* (= her

face) *paled visibly at the sight of the police car.* ◇ *The blue of the sky paled to a light grey.*
IDM **ˈpale beside/next to sth** | **ˈpale in/by comparison (with/to sth)** | **ˈpale into insignificance** to seem less important when compared with sth else: *Last year's riots pale in comparison with this latest outburst of violence.*
■ ***noun***
IDM **beˌyond the ˈpale** considered by most people to be unacceptable or unreasonable: *His remarks were clearly beyond the pale.*

pale·face /ˈpeɪlfeɪs/ *noun* (used in film/movies, etc.) a name for a white person, said to have been used by Native Americans

paleo- (*NAmE*) = PALAEO-

pal·ette /ˈpælət/ *noun* **1** a thin board with a hole in it for the thumb to go through, used by an artist for mixing colours on when painting ➲ VISUAL VOCAB page V35 **2** [usually sing.] (*technical*) the colours used by a particular artist: *Greens and browns are typical of Ribera's palette.*

ˈpalette knife *noun* a knife with a blade that bends easily and has a round end, used by artists and in cooking ➲ VISUAL VOCAB page V23

pali·mony /ˈpælɪməni/ *noun* [U] (*informal, especially NAmE*) money that a court orders sb to pay regularly to a former partner when they have lived together without being married ➲ compare ALIMONY

pal·imp·sest /ˈpælɪmpsest/ *noun* **1** an ancient document from which some or all of the original text has been removed and replaced by a new text **2** (*formal*) something that has many different layers of meaning or detail

pal·in·drome /ˈpælɪndrəʊm; *NAmE* -droʊm/ *noun* a word or phrase that reads the same backwards as forwards, for example *madam* or *nurses run*

pal·ing /ˈpeɪlɪŋ/ *noun* [C, usually pl., U] a metal or wooden post that is pointed at the top; a fence made of these posts

pal·is·ade /ˌpælɪˈseɪd/ *noun* **1** a fence made of strong wooden or metal posts that are pointed at the top, especially used to protect a building in the past **2 palisades** [pl.] (*US*) a line of high steep CLIFFS, especially along a river or by the sea or ocean

pall /pɔːl/ *noun, verb*
■ ***noun*** **1** [usually sing.] **~ of sth** a thick dark cloud of sth: *a **pall of smoke/dust*** ◇ (*figurative*) *News of her death **cast a pall** over the event.* **2** a cloth spread over a COFFIN (= a box used for burying a dead person in)
■ ***verb*** [I] (not used in the progressive tenses) **~ (on sb)** to become less interesting to sb over a period of time because they have done or seen it too much: *Even the impressive scenery began to pall on me after a few hundred miles.*

pal·la·dium /pəˈleɪdiəm/ *noun* [U] (*symb.* **Pd**) a chemical element. Palladium is a rare silver-white metal that looks like PLATINUM.

ˈpall-bearer *noun* a person who walks beside or helps to carry the COFFIN at a funeral

pal·let /ˈpælət/ *noun* **1** a heavy wooden or metal base that can be used for moving or storing goods **2** a cloth bag filled with STRAW, used for sleeping on

pal·li·asse /ˈpæliæs; *NAmE* pælˈjæs/ *noun* a cloth bag filled with STRAW, used for sleeping on SYN **pallet**

pal·li·ate /ˈpælieɪt/ *verb* **~ sth** (*formal*) to make a disease or an illness less painful or unpleasant without curing it

pal·lia·tive /ˈpæliətɪv/ *noun* **1** (*medical*) a medicine or medical treatment that reduces pain without curing its cause **2** (*formal*, usually *disapproving*) an action, a decision, etc. that is designed to make a difficult situation seem better without actually solving the cause of the problems ▸ **pal·lia·tive** *adj.* [usually before noun]: *palliative treatment* ◇ *short-term palliative measures*

pal·lid /ˈpælɪd/ *adj.* **1** (of a person, their face, etc.) pale, especially because of illness: *a pallid complexion* **2** (of colours or light) not strong or bright, and therefore not attractive: *a pallid sky*

pal·lor /ˈpælə(r)/ *noun* [U] pale colouring of the face, especially because of illness or fear: *Her cheeks had an unhealthy pallor.*

pally /ˈpæli/ *adj.* ➲ PAL

palm /pɑːm/ *noun, verb*
■ ***noun*** **1** the inner surface of the hand between the wrist and the fingers: *He held the bird gently in **the palm of his hand**.* ◇ *sweaty palms* ◇ *to **read sb's palm*** (= to say what you think will happen to sb by looking at the lines on their palm) ➲ VISUAL VOCAB page V48 **2** (also **ˈpalm tree**) a straight tree with a mass of long leaves at the top, growing in tropical countries. There are several types of palm tree, some of which produce fruit: *a date palm* ◇ *a coconut palm* ◇ ***palm leaves/fronds/groves*** ➲ VISUAL VOCAB page V8
IDM **have sb in the ˌpalm of your ˈhand** to have complete control or influence over sb ➲ more at CROSS *v.*, GREASE *v.*
■ ***verb*** **~ sth** to hide a coin, card, etc. in your hand, especially when performing a trick
PHR V **ˌpalm sb↔ˈoff (with sth)** (*informal*) to persuade sb to believe an excuse or an explanation that is not true, in order to stop them asking questions or complaining **ˌpalm sth↔ˈoff (on/onto sb)** | **ˌpalm sb↔ˈoff (with sth)** (*informal*) to persuade sb to accept sth that has no value or that you do not want, especially by tricking them: *She's always palming the worst jobs off on her assistant.* ◇ *Make sure he doesn't try to palm you off with faulty goods.* **ˌpalm sth ˈoff as sth** (*informal*) to tell sb that sth is better than it is, especially in order to sell it: *They were trying to palm the table off as a genuine antique.*

Palm·cord·er™ /ˈpɑːmkɔːdə(r); *NAmE* -kɔːrd-/ *noun* a small CAMCORDER (= video camera that records pictures and sound) that can be held in the PALM of one hand

pal·metto /pælˈmetəʊ; *NAmE* -toʊ/ *noun* (*pl.* **-os**) a small PALM tree that grows in the south-eastern US

palm·ist /ˈpɑːmɪst/ *noun* a person who claims to be able to tell what a person is like and what will happen to them in the future, by looking at the lines on the PALM of their hand

palm·is·try /ˈpɑːmɪstri/ *noun* [U] the art of telling what a person is like and what will happen to them by looking at the lines on the PALM of their hand

ˈpalm oil *noun* [U] oil obtained from the fruit of some types of PALM tree, used in cooking and in making soap, CANDLES, etc.

ˌPalm ˈSunday *noun* [U, C] (in the Christian Church) the Sunday before Easter

palm·top /ˈpɑːmtɒp; *NAmE* -tɑːp/ *noun* a small computer that can be held in the PALM of one hand

palmy /ˈpɑːmi/ *adj.* (**palm·ier**, **palmi·est**) used to describe a time in the past when life was good: *That's a picture of me in my palmier days.*

palo·mino /ˌpæləˈmiːnəʊ; *NAmE* -noʊ/ *noun* (*pl.* **-os**) a horse that is a cream or gold colour with a white MANE and tail

palp·able /ˈpælpəbl/ *adj.* that is easily noticed by the mind or the senses: *a **palpable sense** of relief* ◇ *The tension in the room was almost palpable.* ▸ **palp·ably** /-əbli/ *adv.*: *It was palpably clear what she really meant.*

pal·pate /pælˈpeɪt/ *verb* **~ sth** (*medical*) to examine part of the body by touching it ▸ **pal·pa·tion** *noun* [U]

pal·pi·tate /ˈpælpɪteɪt/ *verb* [I] (of the heart) to beat rapidly and/or in an IRREGULAR way especially because of fear or excitement

pal·pi·ta·tions /ˌpælpɪˈteɪʃnz/ *noun* [pl.] a physical condition in which your heart beats very quickly and in an IRREGULAR way: *Just the thought of flying gives me palpitations* (= makes me very nervous).

palsy /ˈpɔːlzi/ *noun* [U] (*old-fashioned*) PARALYSIS (= loss of control or feeling in part or most of the body), especially when the arms and legs shake without control ➲ see also CEREBRAL PALSY ▸ **pal·sied** /ˈpɔːlzid/ *adj.*

pal·try /ˈpɔːltri/ *adj.* [usually before noun] **1** (of an amount) too small to be considered as important or useful SYN **meagre**: *This account offers a paltry 1% return on your*

P

investment. ◇ *a paltry sum* **2** having no value or useful qualities: *a paltry gesture*

pam·pas /ˈpæmpəs; *NAmE* also -pəz/ *noun* (usually **the pampas**) [sing.+ sing./pl. v.] the large area of land in S America that has few trees and is covered in grass

ˈ**pampas grass** *noun* [U] a type of tall grass from S America that is often grown in gardens/yards for its long silver-white flowers that look like feathers

pam·per /ˈpæmpə(r)/ *verb* **~ sb** (sometimes *disapproving*) to take care of sb very well and make them feel as comfortable as possible SYN **cosset**: *Pamper yourself with our new range of beauty treatments.* ◇ *a spoilt and pampered child*

pamph·let /ˈpæmflət/ *noun* a very thin book with a paper cover, containing information about a particular subject SYN **leaflet**

pamph·let·eer /ˌpæmfləˈtɪə(r); *NAmE* -ˈtɪr/ *noun* a person who writes pamphlets on particular subjects

pan[1] /pæn/ *noun, verb*

■ ***noun*** **1** a container, usually made of metal, with a handle or handles, used for cooking food in: *pots and pans* ◇ *a large stainless steel pan* ➲ see also FRYING PAN, SAUCEPAN **2** the amount contained in a pan: *a pan of boiling water* **3** (*NAmE*) (*BrE* **tin**) a metal container used for cooking food in: *a cake pan* ➲ VISUAL VOCAB page V24 **4** either of the dishes on a pair of SCALES that you put things into in order to weigh them **5** (*BrE*) the bowl of a toilet ➲ see also BEDPAN, DUSTPAN, SKIDPAN, WARMING PAN

IDM **go down the ˈpan** (*BrE, informal*) to be wasted or spoiled: *That's another brilliant idea down the pan.* ➲ more at FLASH *n.*

■ ***verb*** (-nn-) **1** [T, usually passive] **~ sth** (*informal*) to severely criticize sth such as a play or a film/movie SYN **slate** **2** [I, T] if a television or video camera **pans** somewhere, or a person **pans** or **pans a camera**, the camera moves in a particular direction, to follow an object or to film a wide area: **+ adv./prep.** *The camera panned back to the audience.* ◇ **~ sth + adv./prep.** *He panned the camera along the row of faces.* **3** [I, T] **~ (for) sth** to wash soil or small stones in a pan to find gold or other valuable minerals: *panning for gold*

PHR V ˌ**pan ˈout** (*informal*) (of events or a situation) to develop in a particular way: *I'm happy with the way things have panned out.*

pan[2] = PAAN

pan- /pæn/ *combining form* (in adjectives and nouns) including all of sth; connected with the whole of sth: *pan-African* ◇ *pandemic*

pana·cea /ˌpænəˈsiːə/ *noun* **~ (for sth)** something that will solve all the problems of a particular situation

pan·ache /pəˈnæʃ; pæˈn-; *NAmE* also -ˈnɑːʃ/ *noun* [U] the quality of being able to do things in a confident and elegant way that other people find attractive SYN **flair, style**

pan·ama /ˈpænəmɑː/ (also ˌ**panama ˈhat**) *noun* a man's hat made from fine STRAW ➲ VISUAL VOCAB page V53

pana·tella (*BrE*) (*NAmE* **pana·tela**) /ˌpænəˈtelə/ *noun* a long thin CIGAR

pan·cake /ˈpænkeɪk/ *noun* **1** [C] a thin flat round cake made from a mixture of flour, eggs and milk that is fried on both sides, usually eaten hot for breakfast in the US, and in Britain either as a DESSERT with sugar, jam, etc. or as a main course with meat, cheese, etc. **2** [U] thick make-up for the face, used especially in the theatre IDM see FLAT *adj.*

ˈ**Pancake Day** *noun* (*informal*) the day before the beginning of Lent, when people traditionally eat PANCAKES ➲ compare SHROVE TUESDAY

ˈ**pancake race** *noun* a traditional race in Britain on Pancake Day, in which each runner keeps throwing a PANCAKE into the air from a pan

pan·chay·at /pʌnˈtʃaɪjət/ *noun* (in some S Asian countries) **1** a village council **2** the official organization that governs local areas in the country, outside large towns

pan·creas /ˈpæŋkriəs/ *noun* an organ near the stomach that produces INSULIN and a liquid that helps the body to DIGEST food ➲ VISUAL VOCAB page V48 ▶ **pan·cre·at·ic** /ˌpæŋkriˈætɪk/ *adj.* [only before noun]

panda /ˈpændə/ *noun* **1** (also ˌ**giant ˈpanda**) a large black and white animal like a BEAR, that lives in China and is very rare **2** (also ˌ**red ˈpanda**) an Asian animal like a RACCOON, with reddish-brown fur and a long thick tail

ˈ**panda car** *noun* (*old-fashioned, BrE, informal*) a small police car

pan·dem·ic /pænˈdemɪk/ *noun* a disease that spreads over a whole country or the whole world ▶ **pan·dem·ic** *adj.*: *a pandemic disease* ➲ compare ENDEMIC, EPIDEMIC

pan·de·mon·ium /ˌpændəˈməʊniəm; *NAmE* -ˈmoʊ-/ *noun* [U] a situation in which there is a lot of noise, activity and confusion, especially because people are feeling angry or frightened SYN **chaos**: *Pandemonium broke out when the news was announced.*

pan·der /ˈpændə(r)/ *verb*

PHR V ˈ**pander to sth/sb** (*disapproving*) to do what sb wants, or try to please them, especially when this is not acceptable or reasonable: *to pander to sb's wishes* ◇ *The speech was pandering to racial prejudice.*

p. and h. (also **p. & h.**) /ˌpiː ənd ˈeɪtʃ/ *abbr.* (*NAmE*) postage and handling ➲ compare P. AND P.

pan·dit /ˈpændɪt/ (also **pun·dit**) *noun* **1** a Hindu priest or wise man **2** (*IndE*) a teacher **3** (*IndE*) a skilled musician

Pandora's box /pænˌdɔːrəz ˈbɒks; *NAmE* ˈbɑːks/ *noun* [sing., U] a process that, if started, will cause many problems that cannot be solved: *This court case could* ***open a Pandora's box*** *of similar claims.* ORIGIN From the Greek myth in which **Pandora** was created by the god Zeus and sent to the earth with a box containing many evils. When she opened the box, the evils came out and infected the earth.

pan·dowdy /pænˈdaʊdi/ *noun* (*pl.* **-ies**) [C, U] (*US*) a sweet dish of apples and spices covered with a mixture of butter, milk and eggs, that is baked

p. and p. (also **p. & p.**) /ˌpiː ən ˈpiː/ *abbr.* (*BrE*) postage and packing (= the cost of packing sth and sending it by post): *Add £2 for p. and p.* ➲ compare P. AND H., S AND H

pane /peɪn/ *noun* a single sheet of glass in a window: *a pane of glass* ◇ *a windowpane*

pan·eer (also **panir**) /pæˈnɪə(r); *NAmE* -ˈnɪr/ *noun* [U] a type of soft cheese used in Asian cooking

pan·egyr·ic /ˌpænəˈdʒɪrɪk/ *noun* (*formal*) a speech or piece of writing praising sb/sth

panel AW /ˈpænl/ *noun, verb*

■ ***noun*** **1** [C] a square or RECTANGULAR piece of wood, glass or metal that forms part of a larger surface such as a door or wall: *One of the glass panels in the front door was cracked.* ➲ VISUAL VOCAB page V21 ➲ see also SOLAR PANEL **2** [C] a piece of metal that forms part of the outer frame of a vehicle **3** [C] a piece of cloth that forms part of a piece of clothing: *The trousers have double thickness knee panels for extra protection.* **4** [C+sing./pl. v.] a group of specialists who give their advice or opinion about sth; a group of people who discuss topics of interest on television or radio: *an advisory panel* ◇ *a panel of experts* ◇ *We have two politicians on tonight's panel.* ◇ *a panel discussion* **5** (also ˈ**jury panel**) [C] (both *especially NAmE*) = JURY **6** [C] a flat board in a vehicle or on a piece of machinery where the controls and instruments are fixed: *an* ***instrument panel*** ◇ *a* ***control/display panel***

■ ***verb*** (-ll-, *especially US* -l-) [usually passive] **~ sth** to cover or decorate a surface with flat strips of wood, glass, etc: *The walls were panelled in oak.* ◇ *a* ***glass-/wood-panelled*** *door*

ˈ**panel beater** *noun* (*BrE*) a person whose job is to remove the DENTS from the outer frame of a vehicle that has been in an accident

ˈ**panel game** *noun* (*BrE*) a game in which a team of people try to answer questions correctly, especially on television or radio

pan·el·ling AW (*especially US* **pan·el·ing**) /ˈpænəlɪŋ/ *noun* [U] square or RECTANGULAR pieces of wood used to cover and decorate walls, ceilings, etc.

pan·el·list (*especially US* **pan·el·ist**) /ˈpænəlɪst/ *noun* a person who is a member of a panel answering questions during a discussion, for example on radio or television

ˈpanel van (*AustralE, NZE, SAfrE*) (*NAmE* **ˈpanel truck**) *noun* a small van/truck, especially one without windows at the sides or seats for passengers

ˈpan-fry *verb* (**pan-fries, pan-frying, pan-fried, pan-fried**) **~ sth** to fry food in a pan in shallow fat: *pan-fried chicken*

pang /pæŋ/ *noun* a sudden strong feeling of physical or emotional pain: ***hunger pangs/pangs of hunger*** ◇ *a sudden **pang of jealousy***

panga /ˈpæŋɡə/ *noun* (*EAfrE, SAfrE*) a large heavy knife that is used for cutting grass or small sticks or for removing WEEDS

Pan·gaea /pænˈdʒiːə/ *noun* [sing.] (*geology*) an extremely large area of land which existed millions of years ago, made up of all the present continents

pan·go·lin /ˈpæŋɡəlɪn; *BrE* also pæŋˈɡəʊlɪn/ (also ˌ**scaly ˈanteater**) *noun* a small animal from Africa or Asia that eats insects, and has a long nose, tongue and tail, and hard SCALES on its body

pan·han·dler /ˈpænhændlə(r)/ *noun* (*NAmE, informal*) a person who asks other people for money in the street ▶ **pan·han·dle** *verb* [I]

panic /ˈpænɪk/ *noun, verb*

■ ***noun*** [U, C, usually sing.] **1** a sudden feeling of great fear that cannot be controlled and prevents you from thinking clearly: *a moment of panic* ◇ *They were in a state of panic.* ◇ *Office workers fled **in panic** as the fire took hold.* ◇ *There's no point **getting into a panic** about the exams.* ◇ *a **panic attack*** (= a condition in which you suddenly feel very anxious, causing your heart to beat faster, etc.) ◇ *a panic decision* (= one that is made when you are in a state of panic) ➲ SYNONYMS at FEAR **2** a situation in which people are made to feel very anxious, causing them to act quickly and without thinking carefully: *News of the losses caused (a) panic among investors.* ◇ *Careful planning at this stage will help to avoid a last-minute panic.* ◇ ***There's no panic*** (= we do not need to rush), *we've got plenty of time.* ◇ ***panic buying/selling*** (= the act of buying/selling things quickly and without thinking carefully because you are afraid that a particular situation will become worse)

IDM **ˈpanic stations** (*BrE, informal*) a situation in which people feel anxious and there is a lot of confused activity, especially because there is a lot to do in a short period of time

■ ***verb*** (**-ck-**) [I, T] to suddenly feel frightened so that you cannot think clearly and you say or do sth stupid, dangerous, etc; to make sb do this: *I panicked when I saw smoke coming out of the engine.* ◇ **~ sb/sth** *The gunfire panicked the horses.*

PHR V **ˈpanic sb into doing sth** [usually passive] to make sb act too quickly because they are afraid of sth

ˈpanic button *noun* a button that sb working in a bank, etc. can press to call for help if they are in danger

IDM **press/push the ˈpanic button** (*BrE*) to react in a sudden or extreme way to sth unexpected that has frightened you

pan·icky /ˈpænɪki/ *adj.* (*informal*) anxious about sth; feeling or showing panic SYN **hysterical**

ˈpanic room (also **ˈsafe room**) *noun* a room in a home or an office building where people can go to avoid a dangerous situation

ˈpanic-stricken *adj.* extremely anxious about sth, in a way that prevents you from thinking clearly SYN **hysterical**

pa·nini /pəˈniːni/ (also **pa·nino** /pəˈniːnəʊ; *NAmE* -noʊ/) *noun* (*pl.* **pa·nini** or **pa·ninis**) a sandwich made with Italian bread, usually toasted

panir = PANEER

pan·nier /ˈpæniə(r)/ *noun* each of a pair of bags or boxes carried on either side of the back wheel of a bicycle or motorcycle; each of a pair of BASKETS carried on either side of its back by a horse or DONKEY

pan·oply /ˈpænəpli/ *noun* [sing., U] (*formal*) a large and impressive number or collection of sth SYN **array**

pan·or·ama /ˌpænəˈrɑːmə; *NAmE* -ˈræmə/ *noun* **1** a view of a wide area of land SYN **vista**: *There is a superb panorama of the mountains from the hotel.* ➲ SYNONYMS at VIEW **2** a description, study or set of pictures that presents all the different aspects or stages of a particular subject, event, etc. ▶ **pan·or·am·ic** /ˌpænəˈræmɪk/ *adj.* [usually before noun]: *a panoramic view over the valley*

ˈpan pipes *noun* [pl.] (*BrE*) (*NAmE* **ˈpan·pipe** [C]) a musical instrument made of a row of pipes of different lengths that you play by blowing across the open ends

pansy /ˈpænzi/ *noun* (*pl.* **-ies**) **1** a small garden plant with brightly coloured flowers **2** (*taboo, slang*) an offensive word for a HOMOSEXUAL man

pant /pænt/ *verb* [I, T] (**+ speech**) to breathe quickly with short breaths, usually with your mouth open, because you have been doing some physical exercise, or because it is very hot: *She finished the race panting heavily.* ◇ *She could hear him panting up the stairs* (= running up and breathing quickly). ◇ *He found her **panting for breath** at the top of the hill.* ▶ **pant** *noun* [usually pl.]: *His breath came in short pants.* ➲ see also PANTS IDM see PUFF *v.*

PHR V **ˈpant for/after sb/sth** to want sth/sb very much: *The end of the novel leaves you panting for more.*

pan·ta·loons /ˌpæntəˈluːnz/ *noun* [pl.] **1** women's loose trousers/pants with wide legs that fit tightly at the ankles **2** (in the past) men's tight trousers/pants fastened at the foot

pan·tech·nicon /pænˈteknɪkən/ *noun* (*old-fashioned, BrE*) = REMOVAL VAN

pan·the·ism /ˈpænθiɪzəm/ *noun* [U] **1** the belief that God is present in all natural things **2** belief in many or all gods ▶ **pan·the·ist** /-θiɪst/ *noun* **pan·the·ist·ic** /ˌpænθiˈɪstɪk/ *adj.*

pan·theon /ˈpænθiən; *NAmE* -θiɑːn/ *noun* **1** (*technical*) all the gods of a nation or people: *the ancient Egyptian pantheon* **2** (*formal*) a group of people who are famous within a particular area of activity **3** a TEMPLE (= religious building) built in honour of all the gods of a nation; a building in which famous dead people of a nation are buried or HONOURED

pan·ther /ˈpænθə(r)/ *noun* **1** a black LEOPARD (= a large wild animal of the cat family) **2** (*NAmE*) = PUMA

pantie girdle *noun* = PANTY GIRDLE

pan·ties /ˈpæntiz/ (*especially NAmE*) (*BrE* also **knick·ers**) *noun* [pl.] a piece of women's underwear that covers the body from the waist to the tops of the legs

pan·tile /ˈpæntaɪl/ *noun* a curved TILE used for roofs

panto /ˈpæntəʊ; *NAmE* -toʊ/ *noun* (*pl.* **-os** /-təʊz; *NAmE* -toʊz/) (*BrE, informal*) = PANTOMIME

panto·graph /ˈpæntəɡrɑːf; *NAmE* -ɡræf/ *noun* a device used for copying a drawing in a bigger or smaller size

panto·mime /ˈpæntəmaɪm/ *noun* **1** (also *BrE informal* **panto**) [C, U] (in Britain) a type of play with music, dancing and jokes, that is based on a FAIRY TALE and is usually performed at Christmas **2** [U, C, usually sing.] the use of movement and the expression of your face to communicate sth or to tell a story SYN **mime** **3** [C, usually sing.] (*BrE*) a ridiculous situation, usually with a lot of confusion SYN **farce**

ˌ**pantomime ˈdame** (also **dame**) *noun* (*BrE*) a female character in a PANTOMIME (1), that is usually played by a man

ˌ**pantomime ˈhorse** *noun* (*BrE*) a character in a PANTOMIME (1) that is supposed to be a horse, played by two people in a special COSTUME

pan·try /ˈpæntri/ *noun* (*pl.* **-ies**) a cupboard/closet or small room in a house, used for storing food SYN **larder**

P

pants 0‑w /pænts/ *noun* [pl.]
1 0‑w (*BrE*) UNDERPANTS or KNICKERS: *a pair of pants* **2** 0‑w (*especially NAmE*) trousers: *a new pair of pants* ◇ *ski pants* ➲ VISUAL VOCAB page V50 ➲ see also CARGO PANTS **3** (*BrE, slang*) (also used as an adjective) something you think is of poor quality SYN **rubbish**: *Their new CD is absolute pants!* ◇ *Do we have to watch this pants programme?*
IDM **bore, scare, etc. the 'pants off sb** (*informal*) to make sb extremely bored, frightened, etc. ➲ more at ANT, CATCH *v.*, SEAT *n.*, WEAR *v.*, WET *v.*

pant·suit /'pæntsu:t; *BrE* also -sju:t/ (*NAmE*) (*BrE* **'trouser suit**) *noun* a woman's suit of jacket and trousers/ pants

pant·sula /ˌpænt'su:lə/ *noun* [U] a style of South African dancing in which each person takes a turn to perform dance movements in front of a group of other dancers who are in a circle

panty girdle (also **pantie girdle**) /'pænti gɜ:dl; *NAmE* gɜ:rdl/ *noun* a tight piece of women's underwear that combines KNICKERS/PANTIES and a GIRDLE

panty·hose /'pæntihəʊz; *NAmE* -hoʊz/ (*NAmE*) (*BrE* **tights**) *noun* [pl.] a piece of clothing made of very thin cloth that fits closely over a woman's hips, legs and feet ➲ compare STOCKING

pap /pæp/ *noun* [U] **1** (*disapproving*) books, magazines, television programmes, etc. that have no real value **2** soft or almost liquid food eaten by babies or people who are ill/sick **3** (*SAfrE*) PORRIDGE made with flour from CORN (MAIZE)

papa /pə'pɑ:; *NAmE* 'pɑ:pə/ *noun* (*BrE, old-fashioned* or *NAmE*) used to talk about or to address your father

pap·acy /'peɪpəsi/ *noun* **1 the papacy** [sing.] the position or the authority of the POPE **2** [C, usually sing.] the period of time when a particular POPE is in power

papal /'peɪpl/ *adj.* [only before noun] connected with the POPE: *papal authority* ◇ *a papal visit to Mexico*

pap·ar·azzo /ˌpæpə'rætsəʊ; *NAmE* -'rætsoʊ/ *noun* (*pl.* **pap·ar·azzi** /-tsi/) [usually pl.] a photographer who follows famous people around in order to get interesting photographs of them to sell to a newspaper

pa·paya /pə'paɪə/ (*BrE* also **paw·paw**) *noun* a tropical fruit with yellow and green skin, sweet orange or red flesh and round black seeds ➲ VISUAL VOCAB page V26

paper 0‑w /'peɪpə(r)/ *noun, verb*
■ ***noun***
▸ FOR WRITING/WRAPPING **1** 0‑w [U] (often in compounds) the thin material that you write and draw on and that is also used for wrapping and packing things: ***a piece/sheet of paper*** ◇ *a package wrapped in brown paper* ◇ *recycled paper* ◇ *She wrote her name and address on* ***a slip*** (= a small piece) ***of paper.*** ◇ *Experience is more important for this job than* ***paper qualifications*** (= that exist on paper, but may not have any real value). ◇ ***paper losses/profits*** (= that are shown in accounts but which may not exist in reality) ◇ *This journal is available in paper and electronic form.* ➲ see also NOTEPAPER, WRAPPING PAPER, WRITING PAPER
▸ NEWSPAPER **2** 0‑w [C] a newspaper: *a* ***local/national paper*** ◇ *a* ***daily/evening/Sunday paper*** ◇ *I read about it* ***in the paper.*** ◇ *Have you seen today's paper?* ◇ ***The papers*** (= newspapers in general) *soon got hold of the story.*
▸ DOCUMENTS **3** 0‑w **papers** [pl.] pieces of paper with writing on them, such as letters, pieces of work or private documents: *His desk was covered with books and papers.* **4** 0‑w **papers** [pl.] official documents that prove your identity, give you permission to do sth, etc: ***divorce/identification papers*** ➲ see also WALKING PAPERS, WORKING PAPER
▸ EXAM **5** [C] (*BrE*) a set of exam questions on a particular subject; the answers that people write to the questions: *The Geography paper was hard.* ◇ *She spent the evening marking exam papers.*
▸ ARTICLE **6** [C] an academic article about a particular subject that is written by and for specialists: *a recent paper in the Journal of Medicine* ◇ *She was invited to* ***give a paper*** (= a talk) *on the results of her research.* ➲ COLLOCATIONS at SCIENTIFIC ➲ see also GREEN PAPER, ORDER PAPER, POSITION PAPER, WHITE PAPER, WORKING PAPER (1) **7** [C] (*NAmE*) a piece of written work done by a student: *Your grade will be based on four papers and a final exam.* ➲ see also TERM PAPER
▸ ON WALLS **8** [C, U] paper that you use to cover and decorate the walls of a room: *The room was damp and the paper was peeling off.* HELP There are many other compounds ending in **paper**. You will find them at their place in the alphabet.
IDM **on paper 1** 0‑w when you put sth **on paper**, you write it down **2** judged from written information only, but not proved in practice: *The idea* ***looks good on paper.*** ➲ more at PEN *n.*, WORTH *adj.*
■ ***verb*** **~ sth** to decorate the walls of a room by covering them with WALLPAPER
PHR V **ˌpaper 'over sth 1** to cover a wall with WALLPAPER in order to hide sth SYN **wallpaper**: *The previous owners had obviously papered over any damp patches.* **2** to try to hide a problem or disagreement in a way that is temporary and not likely to be successful: *The government is trying to* ***paper over the cracks*** *in the cabinet.* ◇ *We can't just paper over the problem.*

paper·back /'peɪpəbæk; *NAmE* -pərb-/ *noun* [C, U] a book that has a thick paper cover: *a cheap paperback* ◇ *When is it coming out* ***in paperback?*** ◇ *a* ***paperback book/edition*** ➲ compare HARDBACK

'paper boy, 'paper girl *noun* a boy or girl who delivers newspapers to people's houses

pa·per·chase /'peɪpətʃeɪs; *NAmE* -pərtʃ-/ *noun* **1** (*BrE*) a game in which one runner drops pieces of paper for the other runners to follow **2** (*NAmE, informal*) the fact of producing too much work on paper

'paper clip *noun* a piece of bent wire or plastic that is designed to hold loose sheets of paper together ➲ VISUAL VOCAB page V56

'paper cutter (*US*) (*BrE* **guil·lo·tine**) *noun* [C] a device with a long blade for cutting paper

paper·knife /'peɪpənaɪf; *NAmE* 'peɪpər-/ *noun* (*pl.* **-knives**) (*especially BrE*) (*NAmE* usually **'letter opener**) a knife used for opening envelopes

paper·less /'peɪpələs; *NAmE* -pərləs/ *adj.* using computers, telephones, etc. rather than paper to exchange information: *the paperless office* ◇ *a system of paperless business transactions*

ˌpaper 'money *noun* [U] money that is made of paper, not coins SYN **notes**

ˌpaper 'plate *noun* a cardboard plate that can be thrown away after it is used

'paper-pusher *noun* (*disapproving*) a person who does unimportant office work as their job

'paper round (*BrE*) (*NAmE* **'paper route**) *noun* the job of delivering newspapers to houses; the route taken when doing this

'paper shop *noun* (*BrE*) = NEWSAGENT

ˌpaper-'thin *adj.* (of objects) very thin and delicate: *paper-thin slices of meat* ➲ compare WAFER-THIN

ˌpaper 'tiger *noun* a person, a country or a situation that seems or claims to be powerful or dangerous but is not really

ˌpaper 'towel *noun* **1** [C] a thick sheet of paper that you use to dry your hands or to absorb water **2** [U] (*NAmE*) (*BrE* **'kitchen paper, 'kitchen roll, 'kitchen towel**) thick paper on a roll, used for cleaning up liquid, food, etc. ➲ VISUAL VOCAB page V22

'paper trail *noun* (*informal, especially NAmE*) a series of documents that provide evidence of what you have done or what has happened: *He was a shrewd lawyer with a talent for uncovering paper trails of fraud.*

paper·weight /'peɪpəweɪt; *NAmE* -pərw-/ *noun* a small heavy object that you put on top of loose papers to keep them in place

P

paper·work /ˈpeɪpəwɜːk; *NAmE* ˈpeɪpərwɜːrk/ *noun* [U] **1** the written work that is part of a job, such as filling in forms or writing letters and reports: *We're trying to cut down on the amount of paperwork involved.* **2** all the documents that you need for sth, such as a court case or buying a house: *How quickly can you prepare the paperwork?*

pa·pery /ˈpeɪpəri/ *adj.* like paper; thin and dry

pa·pier mâché /ˌpæpieɪ ˈmæʃeɪ; *NAmE* ˌpeɪpər məˈʃeɪ; ˌpæpjeɪ/ *noun* [U] (from *French*) paper mixed with glue or flour and water, that is used to make decorative objects

pap·il·loma /ˌpæpɪˈləʊmə; *NAmE* -ˈloʊ-/ *noun* (*medical*) a small lump like a WART that grows on the skin and is usually harmless

pap·ist /ˈpeɪpɪst/ *noun* (*taboo*) an offensive word for a Roman Catholic, used by some Protestants ▶ **pap·ist** *adj.*

pa·poose /pəˈpuːs/ *noun* a type of bag that can be used for carrying a baby in, on your back or in front of you

pap·rika /pəˈpriːkə; *BrE* also ˈpæprɪkə/ *noun* [U] a red powder made from a type of PEPPER, used in cooking as a spice ➲ VISUAL VOCAB page V28

ˈPap smear (*NAmE*) (*BrE* **ˈsmear test, smear, ˌcervical ˈsmear**) *noun* a medical test in which a very small amount of TISSUE from a woman's CERVIX is removed and examined for cancer cells

pa·pyrus /pəˈpaɪrəs/ *noun* (*pl.* **pa·pyri** /pəˈpaɪriː/) **1** [U] a tall plant with thick STEMS that grows in water **2** [U] paper made from the STEMS of the papyrus plant, used in ancient Egypt for writing and drawing on **3** [C] a document or piece of paper made of papyrus

par /pɑː(r)/ *noun* [U] **1** (in GOLF) the number of strokes a good player should need to complete a course or to hit the ball into a particular hole: *a par five hole* ◇ *Par for the course is 72.* **2** (also **ˈpar value**) (*business*) the value that a share in a company had originally: *to be redeemed* ***at par*** IDM **below/under ˈpar** less well, good, etc. than is usual or expected: *Teaching in some subjects has been well below par.* **be ˌpar for the ˈcourse** (*disapproving*) to be just what you would expect to happen or expect sb to do in a particular situation SYN **the norm**: *Starting early and working long hours is par for the course in this job.* **on a par with sb/sth** as good, bad, important, etc. as sb/sth else **up to ˈpar** as good as usual or as good as it should be SYN **up to scratch**

par. (also **para.**) *abbr.* (in writing) paragraph: *See par. 3.*

para /ˈpærə/ *noun* (*informal*) = PARATROOPER

para- /ˈpærə/ *prefix* (in nouns and adjectives) **1** beyond: *paranormal* **2** similar to but not official or not fully qualified: *paramilitary* ◇ *a paramedic*

par·able /ˈpærəbl/ *noun* a short story that teaches a moral or spiritual lesson, especially one of those told by Jesus as recorded in the Bible

para·bola /pəˈræbələ/ *noun* (*geometry*) a curve like the path of an object thrown into the air and falling back to earth ➲ VISUAL VOCAB page V58 ▶ **para·bol·ic** /ˌpærəˈbɒlɪk; *NAmE* -ˈbɑːlɪk/ *adj.*: *parabolic curves*

para·ceta·mol /ˌpærəˈsiːtəmɒl; -ˈset-; *NAmE* -mɑːl/ (*BrE*) (*NAmE* **acet·amino·phen**) *noun* [U, C] (*pl.* **para·ceta·mol** or **para·ceta·mols**) a drug used to reduce pain and fever: *Do you have any paracetamol?* ◇ *Take two paracetamol(s) and try to sleep.*

para·chute /ˈpærəʃuːt/ *noun, verb*

■ ***noun*** (also *informal* **chute**) a device that is attached to people or objects to make them fall slowly and safely when they are dropped from an aircraft. It consists of a large piece of thin cloth that opens out in the air to form an umbrella shape: *Planes dropped supplies by parachute.* ◇ *a* ***parachute drop/jump*** ◇ *a parachute regiment*

■ ***verb*** **1** [I] (+ **adv./prep.**) to jump from an aircraft using a parachute: *The pilot was able to parachute to safety.* ◇ *She regularly* ***goes parachuting.*** **2** [T] **~ sb/sth + adv./prep.** to drop sb/sth from an aircraft by parachute

para·chut·ist /ˈpærəʃuːtɪst/ *noun* a person who jumps from a plane using a parachute

para·clin·ical /ˌpærəˈklɪnɪkl/ *adj.* (*technical*) related to the parts of medicine, especially laboratory sciences, that are not directly involved in the care of patients

par·ade /pəˈreɪd/ *noun, verb*

■ ***noun***

▸ PUBLIC CELEBRATION **1** [C] a public celebration of a special day or event, usually with bands in the streets and decorated vehicles SYN **procession**: *the Lord Mayor's parade* ◇ *St Patrick's Day parade in New York*

▸ OF SOLDIERS **2** [C, U] a formal occasion when soldiers march or stand in lines so that they can be examined by their officers or other important people: *a military parade* ◇ *They stood as straight as soldiers* ***on parade.*** ◇ (*figurative*) *The latest software will be on parade at the exhibition.* ➲ see also IDENTIFICATION PARADE

▸ SERIES **3** [C] a series of things or people: *Each generation passes through a similar parade of events.*

▸ WEALTH/KNOWLEDGE **4** [C, usually sing.] **~ of wealth, knowledge, etc.** (often *disapproving*) an obvious display of sth, particularly in order to impress other people

▸ ROW OF SHOPS **5** [C] (*especially BrE*) (often in names) a street with a row of small shops: *a shopping parade* IDM see RAIN *v.*

■ ***verb***

▸ WALK TO CELEBRATE/PROTEST **1** [I] (+ **adv./prep.**) to walk somewhere in a formal group of people, in order to celebrate or protest about sth: *The victorious team will parade through the city tomorrow morning.*

▸ SHOW IN PUBLIC **2** [I] + **adv./prep.** to walk around in a way that makes other people notice you: *People were parading up and down showing off their finest clothes.* **3** [T] **~ sb/sth + adv./prep.** to show sb/sth in public so that people can see them/it: *The trophy was paraded around the stadium.* ◇ *The prisoners were paraded in front of the crowd.* ◇ (*figurative*) *He is not one to parade his achievements.*

▸ OF SOLDIERS **4** [I, T] to come together, or to bring soldiers together, in order to march in front of other people: **+ adv./prep.** *The crowds applauded as the guards paraded past.* ◇ **~ sb + adv./prep.** *The colonel paraded his men before the Queen.*

▸ PRETEND **5** [I, T] to pretend to be, or to make sb/sth seem to be, good or important when they are not: **~ as sth** *myth parading as fact* ◇ **~ sb/sth/yourself as sth** *He paraded himself as a loyal supporter of the party.*

paˈrade ground *noun* a place where soldiers gather to march or to be INSPECTED by an officer or an important visitor

para·digm AW /ˈpærədaɪm/ *noun* **1** (*technical* or *formal*) a typical example or pattern of sth: *a paradigm for students to copy* ◇ *The war was a paradigm of the destructive side of human nature.* **2** (*grammar*) a set of all the different forms of a word: *verb paradigms* ▶ **para·dig·mat·ic** /ˌpærədɪgˈmætɪk/ *adj.*

ˈparadigm shift *noun* a great and important change in the way sth is done or thought about

para·dise /ˈpærədaɪs/ *noun* **1** (often **Paradise**) [U] (in some religions) a perfect place where people are said to go when they die SYN **heaven**: *The ancient Egyptians saw paradise as an idealized version of their own lives.* **2** [C] a place that is extremely beautiful and that seems perfect, like heaven: *a tropical paradise* **3** [C] a perfect place for a particular activity or kind of person: *The area is a birdwatcher's paradise.* **4** [U] a state of perfect happiness SYN **bliss**: *Being alone is his idea of paradise.* **5 Paradise** [U] (in the Bible) the garden of Eden, where Adam and Eve lived

para·dox /ˈpærədɒks; *NAmE* -dɑːks/ *noun* **1** [C] a person, thing or situation that has two opposite features and therefore seems strange: *He was a paradox—a loner who loved to chat to strangers.* ◇ *It is a curious paradox that professional comedians often have unhappy personal lives.* **2** [C, U] a statement containing two opposite ideas that make it seem impossible or unlikely, although it is probably true; the use of this in writing: *'More haste, less speed' is a well-known paradox.* ◇ *It's a work full of paradox and*

P

ambiguity. ▶ **para·dox·ical** /ˌpærəˈdɒksɪkl; *NAmE* -ˈdɑːks-/ *adj.*: *It is paradoxical that some of the poorest people live in some of the richest areas of the country.* **para·dox·ic·al·ly** /-kli/ *adv.*: *Paradoxically, the less she ate, the fatter she got.*

par·af·fin /ˈpærəfɪn/ (also ˈ**paraffin oil**) (both *BrE*) (*NAmE* **kero·sene**) *noun* [U] a type of oil obtained from PETROLEUM and used as a fuel for heat and light: *a **paraffin heater/lamp/stove***

ˈ**paraffin wax** *noun* [U] a soft white substance that is made from PETROLEUM or coal, and is used especially for making CANDLES

para·glider /ˈpærəglaɪdə(r)/ *noun* **1** a structure consisting of a big thin piece of cloth like a PARACHUTE, and a HARNESS which is attached to a person when they jump from a plane or a high place in the sport of PARAGLIDING **2** a person who does paragliding

para·glid·ing /ˈpærəglaɪdɪŋ/ *noun* [U] a sport in which you wear a special structure like a PARACHUTE, jump from a plane or a high place and are carried along by the wind before coming down to earth: *to go paragliding* ➲ VISUAL VOCAB page V40

para·gon /ˈpærəgən; *NAmE* -gɑːn/ *noun* a person who is perfect or who is a perfect example of a particular good quality: *I make no claim to be a paragon.* ◇ *He wasn't the **paragon of virtue** she had expected.*

para·graph AW /ˈpærəgrɑːf; *NAmE* -græf/ *noun* (*abbr.* par., para.) a section of a piece of writing, usually consisting of several sentences dealing with a single subject. The first sentence of a paragraph starts on a new line: *an **opening/introductory paragraph*** ◇ *Write a paragraph on each of the topics given below.* ◇ *See paragraph 15 of the handbook.*

para·graph·ing AW /ˈpærəgrɑːfɪŋ; *NAmE* -græf-/ *noun* [U] the way that a piece of writing is divided into paragraphs

para·keet (also **parra·keet**) /ˈpærəkiːt/ *noun* a small bird of the PARROT family, usually with a long tail

para·legal /ˌpærəˈliːgl/ *noun* (*especially NAmE*) a person who is trained to help a lawyer ▶ **para·legal** *adj.*

para·lin·guis·tic /ˌpærəlɪŋˈgwɪstɪk/ *adj.* (*linguistics*) relating to communication through ways other than words, for example tone of voice, expressions on your face and actions

par·all·ax /ˈpærəlæks/ *noun* [U] (*technical*) the effect by which the position or direction of an object appears to change when the object is seen from different positions

par·al·lel 🔑 AW /ˈpærəlel/ *adj., noun, verb*

■ ***adj.*** **1** 🔑 two or more lines that are **parallel** to each other are the same distance apart at every point: *parallel lines* ◇ **~ to/with sth** *The road and the canal are parallel to each other.* **2** very similar or taking place at the same time: *a parallel case* ◇ *parallel trends* **3** (*computing*) involving several computer operations at the same time: *parallel processing* ▶ **par·al·lel** *adv.*: *The road and the canal **run parallel** to each other.* ◇ *The plane flew parallel to the coast.*

■ ***noun*** **1** [C, U] a person, a situation, an event, etc. that is very similar to another, especially one in a different place or time SYN **equivalent**: *These ideas have parallels in Freud's thought too.* ◇ *This is an achievement **without parallel** in modern times.* ◇ *This tradition **has no parallel** in our culture.* **2** [C, usually pl.] similar features: *There are interesting parallels between the 1960s and the late 1990s.* ◇ *It is possible to **draw a parallel between*** (= find similar features in) *their experience and ours.* **3** (also ˌ**parallel of ˈlatitude**) [C] an imaginary line around the earth that is always the same distance from the EQUATOR; this line on a map: *the 49th parallel*

IDM **in ˈparallel (with sth/sb)** with and at the same time as sth/sb else: *The new degree and the existing certificate courses would run in parallel.*

■ ***verb*** **1 ~ sth** to be similar to sth; to happen at the same time as sth: *Their legal system parallels our own.* ◇ *The rise in unemployment is paralleled by an increase in petty crime.* **2 ~ sth** to be as good as sth SYN **equal**: *a level of achievement that has never been paralleled* ➲ compare UNPARALLELED

ˌ**parallel ˈbars** *noun* [pl.] two bars on posts that are used for doing GYMNASTIC exercises ➲ VISUAL VOCAB page V37

ˌ**parallel ˈimports** *noun* [pl.] (*economics*) goods that are imported into a country without the permission of the company that produced them, and sold at a lower price than the company sells them at

par·al·lel·ism /ˈpærəlelɪzəm/ *noun* [U, C] (*formal*) the state of being similar; a similar feature: *I think he exaggerates the parallelism between the two cases.*

par·al·lelo·gram /ˌpærəˈleləgræm/ *noun* (*geometry*) a flat shape with four straight sides, the opposite sides being parallel and equal to each other

ˈ**parallel port** *noun* (*computing*) a point on a computer where you connect a device such as a printer that sends or receives more than one piece of data at a time

ˌ**parallel ˈprocessing** *noun* [U] (*computing*) the division of a process into different parts, which are performed at the same time by different PROCESSORS in a computer

ˌ**parallel ˈruler** *noun* a device for drawing lines that are always the same distance apart, consisting of two connected rulers

the Para·lym·pics /ˌpærəˈlɪmpɪks/ *noun* [pl.] an international ATHLETICS competition for people who are disabled

para·lyse (*BrE*) (*NAmE* **para·lyze**) /ˈpærəlaɪz/ *verb* [often passive] **1 ~ sb** to make sb unable to feel or move all or part of their body: *The accident left him **paralysed from the waist down**.* ◇ (*figurative*) *paralysing heat* ◇ (*figurative*) *She stood there, paralysed with fear.* **2 ~ sth** to prevent sth from functioning normally: *The airport is still paralysed by the strike.*

par·aly·sis /pəˈræləsɪs/ *noun* (*pl.* **par·aly·ses** /-siːz/) **1** [U, C] a loss of control of, and sometimes feeling in, part or most of the body, caused by disease or an injury to the nerves: *paralysis of both legs* **2** [U] a total inability to move, act, function, etc: *The strike caused total paralysis in the city.*

para·lyt·ic /ˌpærəˈlɪtɪk/ *adj.* **1** [not before noun] (*BrE, informal*) very drunk **2** [usually before noun] (*formal*) suffering from PARALYSIS; making sb unable to move: *a paralytic illness* ◇ *paralytic fear*

para·med·ic /ˌpærəˈmedɪk/ *noun* a person whose job is to help people who are sick or injured, but who is not a doctor or a nurse: *Paramedics treated the injured at the roadside.* ➲ compare AMBULANCE WORKER ▶ **para·med·ic·al** /-ɪkl/ *adj.*: *paramedical staff*

par·am·eter AW /pəˈræmɪtə(r)/ *noun* [usually pl.] (*formal*) something that decides or limits the way in which sth can be done: *to **set/define the parameters*** ◇ *We had to work within the parameters that had already been established.*

para·mili·tary /ˌpærəˈmɪlətri; *NAmE* -teri/ *adj., noun*

■ ***adj.*** [usually before noun] **1** a **paramilitary** organization is an illegal group that is organized like an army: *a right-wing paramilitary group* **2** helping the official army of a country: *paramilitary police, such as the CRS in France*

■ ***noun*** [usually pl.] (*pl.* -ies) **1** a member of an illegal paramilitary group or organization **2** a member of an organization that helps the official army of a country

para·mount /ˈpærəmaʊnt/ *adj.* **1** more important than anything else: *This matter is **of paramount importance**.* ◇ *Safety is paramount.* ➲ LANGUAGE BANK at VITAL **2** (*formal*) having the highest position or the greatest power: *China's paramount leader* ▶ **para·mount·cy** /-maʊntsi/ *noun* [U]

par·amour /ˈpærəmʊə(r); *NAmE* -mʊr/ *noun* (*old-fashioned* or *literary*) a person that sb is having a romantic or sexual relationship with SYN **lover**

para·noia /ˌpærəˈnɔɪə/ *noun* [U] **1** (*medical*) a mental illness in which a person may wrongly believe that other people are trying to harm them, that they are sb very important, etc. **2** (*informal*) fear or suspicion of other people when there is no evidence or reason for this

para·noid /ˈpærənɔɪd/ *adj., noun*

■ ***adj.*** (also *less frequent* **para·noiac** /ˌpærəˈnɔɪɪk; -ˈnɔɪæk/) **1** afraid or suspicious of other people and believing that they are trying to harm you, in a way that is not reasonable: *She's getting really paranoid about what other people say about her.* ⊃ SYNONYMS at AFRAID **2** suffering from a mental illness in which you wrongly believe that other people are trying to harm you or that you are very important: *paranoid delusions* ◇ *paranoid schizophrenia* ◇ *a paranoid killer*

■ ***noun*** (also **para·noiac** /ˌpærəˈnɔɪɪk; -ˈnɔɪæk/) a person who suffers from paranoia

para·nor·mal /ˌpærəˈnɔːml; *NAmE* -ˈnɔːrml/ *adj.*

■ ***adj.*** **1** that cannot be explained by science or reason and that seems to involve mysterious forces SYN **supernatural** **2 the paranormal** *noun* [sing.] events or subjects that are paranormal SYN **the supernatural**

para·pet /ˈpærəpɪt; -pet/ *noun* a low wall along the edge of a bridge, a roof, etc. to stop people from falling: (*figurative*) *He was not prepared to* ***put his head above the parapet*** *and say what he really thought* (= he did not want to risk doing it).

para·pher·na·lia /ˌpærəfəˈneɪliə; *NAmE* also -fərˈn-/ *noun* [U] a large number of objects or personal possessions, especially the equipment that you need for a particular activity: *skiing paraphernalia* ◇ *an electric kettle and all the paraphernalia for making tea and coffee*

para·phrase /ˈpærəfreɪz/ *verb, noun*

■ ***verb*** [T, I] **~ (sth)** to express what sb has said or written using different words, especially in order to make it easier to understand: *Try to paraphrase the question before you answer it.*

■ ***noun*** a statement that expresses sth that sb has written or said using different words, especially in order to make it easier to understand

para·ple·gia /ˌpærəˈpliːdʒə/ *noun* [U] PARALYSIS (= loss of control or feeling) in the legs and lower body

para·ple·gic /ˌpærəˈpliːdʒɪk/ *noun* a person who suffers from paraplegia ▸ **para·ple·gic** *adj.*

para·psych·ology /ˌpærəsaɪˈkɒlədʒi; *NAmE* -ˈkɑːl-/ *noun* [U] the study of mental powers that seem to exist but that cannot be explained by scientific knowledge

para·quat /ˈpærəkwɒt; *NAmE* -kwɑːt/ *noun* [U] an extremely poisonous liquid used to kill plants that are growing where they are not wanted

para·sail·ing /ˈpærəseɪlɪŋ/ *noun* [U] the sport of being pulled up into the air behind a boat while wearing a special PARACHUTE

par·as·cend·ing /ˈpærəsendɪŋ/ *noun* [U] (*BrE*) a sport in which you wear a PARACHUTE and are pulled along behind a boat, car, etc. so that you rise up into the air: *to go parascending*

para·site /ˈpærəsaɪt/ *noun* **1** a small animal or plant that lives on or inside another animal or plant and gets its food from it **2** (*disapproving*) a person who always relies on or benefits from other people and gives nothing back

para·sit·ic /ˌpærəˈsɪtɪk/ (also *less frequent* **para·sit·ical** /ˌpærəˈsɪtɪkl/) *adj.* **1** caused by a parasite: *a* ***parasitic disease/infection*** **2** living on another animal or plant and getting its food from it: *a parasitic mite* **3** (*disapproving*) (of a person) always relying on or benefiting from other people and giving nothing back ▸ **para·sit·ic·al·ly** /-kli/ *adv.*

para·sol /ˈpærəsɒl; *NAmE* -sɔːl; -sɑːl/ *noun* **1** a type of light umbrella that women in the past carried to protect themselves from the sun **2** a large umbrella that is used for example on beaches or outside restaurants to protect people from hot sun ⊃ VISUAL VOCAB page V16 ⊃ compare SUNSHADE

para·statal /ˌpærəˈsteɪtl/ *adj.* (*technical*) (of an organization) having some political power and serving the state

para·taxis /ˌpærəˈtæksɪs/ *noun* [U] (*grammar*) the placing of clauses and phrases one after the other, without words to link them or show their relationship ⊃ compare HYPOTAXIS

par·atha /pəˈrɑːtə/ *noun* a type of S Asian bread made without YEAST, usually fried on a GRIDDLE

para·troop·er /ˈpærətruːpə(r)/ (also *informal* **para**) *noun* a member of the paratroops

para·troops /ˈpærətruːps/ *noun* [pl.] soldiers who are trained to jump from planes using a PARACHUTE ▸ **para·troop** *adj.* [only before noun]: *a paratroop regiment*

par·boil /ˈpɑːbɔɪl; *NAmE* ˈpɑːrb-/ *verb* **~ sth** to boil food, especially vegetables, until it is partly cooked

par·cel /ˈpɑːsl; *NAmE* ˈpɑːrsl/ *noun, verb*

■ ***noun*** **1** (*especially BrE*) (*NAmE* usually **pack·age**) something that is wrapped in paper or put into a thick envelope so that it can be sent by mail, carried easily, or given as a present: *There's a parcel and some letters for you.* ◇ *She was carrying a parcel of books under her arm.* ◇ *The prisoners were allowed food parcels.* **2** a piece of land: *50 five-acre parcels have already been sold.* **3** (*especially BrE*) a small amount of food that is wrapped in sth, usually pastry, before it is cooked: *filo pastry parcels* IDM see PART *n.*

■ ***verb*** (*especially BrE*) (-ll-, *especially US* -l-) **~ sth (up)** to wrap sth up and make it into a parcel: *She parcelled up the books to send.*

PHR V **ˌparcel sth↔ˈout** to divide sth into parts or between several people: *The land was parcelled out into small lots.*

ˈparcel bomb *noun* (*BrE*) a bomb that is sent to sb in a package and that explodes when the package is opened

parch /pɑːtʃ; *NAmE* pɑːrtʃ/ *verb* **~ sth** (especially of hot weather) to make an area of land very dry

parched /pɑːtʃt; *NAmE* pɑːrtʃt/ *adj.* **1** very dry, especially because the weather is hot: *dry parched land* ◇ *soil parched by drought* ◇ *She licked her parched lips.* **2** (*informal*) very thirsty: *Let's get a drink—I'm parched.*

ˌparched ˈrice *noun* [U] rice that has been pressed flat and dried, used in Asian cooking

Par·cheesi™ /pɑːˈtʃiːzi; *NAmE* pɑːrˈtʃ-/ *noun* [U] (*NAmE*) a simple game played with DICE and COUNTERS on a special board, similar to the British game, LUDO

parch·ment /ˈpɑːtʃmənt; *NAmE* ˈpɑːrtʃ-/ *noun* **1** [U] material made from the skin of a sheep or GOAT, used in the past for writing on: *parchment scrolls* **2** [U] a thick yellowish type of paper **3** [C] a document written on a piece of parchment

pard·ner /ˈpɑːdnə(r); *NAmE* ˈpɑːrd-/ *noun* (*NAmE, informal, non-standard*) a way of saying or writing 'partner' in informal speech

par·don /ˈpɑːdn; *NAmE* ˈpɑːrdn/ *exclamation, noun, verb*

■ ***exclamation*** **1** (also **ˌpardon ˈme** especially in *NAmE*) used to ask sb to repeat sth because you did not hear it or did not understand it: *'You're very quiet today.' 'Pardon?' 'I said you're very quiet today.'* **2** (also **ˌpardon ˈme**) used by some people to say 'sorry' when they have accidentally made a rude noise, or said or done sth wrong

■ ***noun*** **1** (also *law*) (also *BrE* **ˌfree ˈpardon**) [C] an official decision not to punish sb for a crime, or to say that sb is not guilty of a crime: *to* ***ask/grant/receive a pardon*** ◇ *a* ***royal/presidential pardon*** **2** [U] (*formal*) **~ (for sth)** the action of forgiving sb for sth SYN **forgiveness**: *He asked her pardon for having deceived her.* IDM see BEG

■ ***verb*** (not usually used in the progressive tenses) **1 ~ sb** to officially allow sb who has been found guilty of a crime to leave prison and/or avoid punishment: *She was pardoned after serving ten years of a life sentence.* **2** to forgive sb for sth they have said or done (used in many expressions when you want to be polite) SYN **excuse**: **~ sth** *Pardon my ignorance, but what is a 'duplex'?* ◇ *The place was,* ***if you'll pardon the expression****, a dump.* ◇ **~ sb (for sth/for doing sth)** (*BrE*) *You could be pardoned for thinking* (= it is easy to understand why people think) *that education is not the government's priority.* ◇ *Pardon me for interrupting you.* ◇ **~ sb doing sth** *Pardon my asking, but is that your husband?*

P

IDM ˌpardon ˈme (*informal*) **1** (*especially NAmE*) used to ask sb to repeat sth because you did not hear it or do not understand it **2** used by some people to say 'sorry' when they have accidentally made a rude noise or done sth wrong ➲ see also I BEG YOUR PARDON ˌ**pardon me for** ˈ**doing sth** used to show that you are upset or offended by the way that sb has spoken to you: *'Oh, just shut up!' 'Well, pardon me for breathing!'* ➲ more at FRENCH *n.*

par·don·able /ˈpɑːdnəbl; *NAmE* ˈpɑːrdn-/ *adj.* that can be forgiven or excused SYN **excusable** OPP **unpardonable**

pare /peə(r); *NAmE* per/ *verb* **1** to remove the thin outer layer of sth, especially of fruit: **~ sth** *She pared the apple.* ◇ **~ sth from sth** *First, pare the rind from the lemon.* ◇ **~ sth off/away** *He pared away the excess glue with a razor blade.* ➲ see also PARING KNIFE **2 ~ sth (back/down)** to gradually reduce the size or amount: *The training budget has been pared back to a minimum.* ◇ *The workforce has been* ***pared to the bone*** (= reduced to the lowest possible level). **3 ~ sth** (*especially BrE*) to cut away the edges of sth, especially your nails, in order to make them smooth and neat ➲ see also PARINGS

par·ent 🔑 /ˈpeərənt; *NAmE* ˈper-/ *noun*
1 🔑 [usually pl.] a person's father or mother: *He's still living with his parents.* ◇ *her adoptive parents* ◇ *Sue and Ben have recently become parents.* ➲ see also ONE-PARENT FAMILY, SINGLE PARENT, STEP-PARENT **2** an animal or a plant which produces other animals or plants: *the parent bird/tree* **3** (often used as an adjective) an organization that produces and owns or controls smaller organizations of the same type: *a parent bank and its subsidiaries* ◇ *the parent company*

par·ent·age /ˈpeərəntɪdʒ; *NAmE* ˈper-/ *noun* [U] the origin of a person's parents and who they are: *a young American of German parentage* ◇ *Nothing is known about her parentage and background.*

par·en·tal /pəˈrentl/ *adj.* [usually before noun] connected with a parent or parents: *parental responsibility/rights* ◇ *parental choice in education* ◇ *the parental home*

paˌrental conˈtrols *noun* [pl.] (also **paˌrental ˈlock** [C]) a feature that is offered in some computer, mobile/cell phone and DIGITAL television services, that enables parents or other adults to control children's access to material that is not suitable for them ▶ **parental control** *adj.* [only before noun]: *parental control software*

paˌrental ˈleave *noun* [U] time when a parent is allowed to be away from work to care for a child: *paid/unpaid parental leave* ◇ *fathers who take parental leave* ➲ see also MATERNITY LEAVE, PATERNITY LEAVE

par·en·thesis /pəˈrenθəsɪs/ *noun* (*pl.* **par·en·theses** /-əsiːz/) **1** a word, sentence, etc. that is added to a speech or piece of writing, especially in order to give extra information. In writing, it is separated from the rest of the text using brackets, commas or DASHES. **2** (*formal* or *NAmE*) (*BrE* **bracket**, ˈ**round bracket**) [usually pl.] either of a pair of marks, ( ) placed around extra information in a piece of writing or part of a problem in mathematics: *Irregular forms are given* ***in parentheses***.

par·en·thet·ical /ˌpærənˈθetɪkl/ (also **par·en·thet·ic** /-ɪk/) *adj.* [usually before noun] (*formal*) given as extra information in a speech or piece of writing: *parenthetical remarks* ▶ **par·en·thet·ic·al·ly** /-kli/ *adv.*

par·ent·hood /ˈpeərənthʊd; *NAmE* ˈper-/ *noun* [U] the state of being a parent: *the* ***responsibilities/joys of parenthood***

par·ent·ing /ˈpeərəntɪŋ; *NAmE* ˈper-/ *noun* [U] the process of caring for your child or children: ***good/poor parenting*** ◇ ***parenting skills*** ➲ COLLOCATIONS at CHILD

par·en·tis ➲ IN LOCO PARENTIS

ˈ**parents-in-law** *noun* [pl.] the parents of your husband or wife ➲ see also IN-LAWS

ˌ**parent-ˈteacher association** *noun* = PTA

par excellence /ˌpɑːr ˈeksəlɑːns; *NAmE* ˌeksəˈlɑːns/ *adj.* (from *French*) (only used after the noun it describes) better than all the others of the same kind; a very good example of sth: *She turned out to be an organizer par excellence.* ▶ **par excellence** *adv.*: *Chemistry was par excellence the laboratory science of the early nineteenth century.*

par·iah /pəˈraɪə/ *noun* a person who is not acceptable to society and is avoided by everyone SYN **outcast**

ˈ**paring knife** *noun* a small sharp knife, used especially for cutting and PEELING fruit ➲ see also PARE ➲ VISUAL VOCAB page V23

par·ings /ˈpeərɪŋz; *NAmE* ˈper-/ *noun* [pl.] thin pieces that have been cut off sth: *cheese parings* ➲ see also PARE

par·ish /ˈpærɪʃ/ *noun* **1** [C] an area that has its own church and that a priest is responsible for: *a* ***parish church/priest*** ◇ *He is vicar of a large rural parish.* **2** [C] (in England) a small country area that has its own elected local government: *the parish council* **3** [C+sing./pl. v.] the people living in a particular area, especially those who go to church

par·ish·ad /ˈpʌrɪʃʌd/ *noun* (*IndE*) a council

ˌ**parish ˈclerk** *noun* an official who organizes the affairs of a church in a particular area

pa·rish·ion·er /pəˈrɪʃənə(r)/ *noun* a person living in a parish, especially one who goes to church regularly

ˌ**parish-ˈpump** *adj.* [only before noun] (*BrE, disapproving*) connected with local affairs only (and therefore not thought of as being very important) SYN **parochial**: *parish-pump politics*

ˌ**parish ˈregister** *noun* a book that has a list of all the BAPTISMS, marriages and funerals that have taken place at a particular PARISH church

par·ity /ˈpærəti/ *noun* (*pl.* -ies) **1** [U] **~ (with sb/sth)** | **~ (between A and B)** (*formal*) the state of being equal, especially the state of having equal pay or status: *Prison officers are demanding pay parity with the police force.* **2** [U, C] (*finance*) the fact of the units of money of two different countries being equal: *to achieve parity with the dollar*

park 🔑 /pɑːk; *NAmE* pɑːrk/ *noun, verb*
■ ***noun* 1** 🔑 [C] an area of public land in a town or a city where people go to walk, play and relax: *Hyde Park* ◇ *We went for a walk in the park.* ◇ *a park bench* **2** 🔑 [C] (in compounds) an area of land used for a particular purpose: *a business/science park* ◇ *a wildlife park* ➲ see also AMUSEMENT PARK, CAR PARK, NATIONAL PARK, RETAIL PARK, SAFARI PARK, THEME PARK **3** [C] (in Britain) an area of land, usually with fields and trees, attached to a large country house **4** [C] (*NAmE*) a piece of land for playing sports, especially BASEBALL ➲ see also BALLPARK **5 the park** [sing.] (*BrE*) a football (SOCCER) or RUGBY field: *the fastest man on the park* IDM see WALK *n.*
■ ***verb* 1** 🔑 [I, T] **~ (sth)** to leave a vehicle that you are driving in a particular place for a period of time: *You can't park here.* ◇ *You can't park the car here.* ◇ *He's parked very badly.* ◇ *a badly parked truck* ◇ *A red van was parked in front of the house.* ◇ *a parked car* ◇ (*informal, figurative*) *Just park your bags in the hall until your room is ready.* ➲ see also DOUBLE-PARK **2** [T] **~ yourself + adv./prep.** (*informal*) to sit or stand in a particular place for a period of time: *She parked herself on the edge of the bed.* **3** [T] **~ sth** (*business*) (*informal*) to decide to leave an idea or issue to be dealt with or considered at a later meeting: *Let's park that until our next meeting.*

PHR V ˌ**park ˈup** | ˌ**park sth↔ˈup** (*especially BrE* or *AustralE*) to find a place where you can park your vehicle: *There was a police car parked up outside the warehouse.* ◇ *I couldn't* ***get parked up*** *anywhere near the restaurant.*

parka /ˈpɑːkə; *NAmE* ˈpɑːrkə/ *noun* a very warm jacket or coat with a HOOD that often has fur inside

park·ade /pɑːˈkeɪd; *NAmE* pɑːrˈk-/ *noun* (*CanE*) a parking garage for many cars

ˌ**park and ˈride** *noun* a system designed to reduce traffic in towns in which people park their cars on the edge of a town and then take a special bus or train to the town centre; the area where people park their cars before taking the bus: *Use the park and ride.* ◇ *I've left my car in the park and ride.* ◇ *a park-and-ride service*

par·kin /ˈpɑːkɪn; *NAmE* ˈpɑːrkɪn/ *noun* [U] (*BrE*) a dark brown sticky cake made with OATMEAL and TREACLE, flavoured with GINGER

park·ing /ˈpɑːkɪŋ; *NAmE* ˈpɑːrk-/ *noun* [U] **1** the act of stopping a vehicle at a place and leaving it there for a period of time: *There is no parking here between 9 a.m. and 6 p.m.* ◇ *I managed to find a* ***parking space.*** ◇ *a parking fine* (= for parking illegally) **2** a space or an area for leaving vehicles: *The hotel is centrally situated with ample free parking.*

ˈparking brake *noun* (*NAmE*) = HANDBRAKE

ˈparking garage (*NAmE*) (*BrE* **ˌmulti-storey ˈcar park, ˌmulti-ˈstorey**) *noun* a large building with several floors for parking cars in

ˈparking lot *noun* (*NAmE*) an area where people can leave their cars ➲ compare CAR PARK

ˈparking meter (also **meter**) *noun* a machine beside the road that you put money into when you park your car next to it ➲ VISUAL VOCAB page V2

ˈparking ticket (also **ticket**) *noun* an official notice that is put on your car when you have parked illegally, ordering you to pay money

Par·kin·son's dis·ease /ˈpɑːkɪnsnz dɪziːz; *NAmE* ˈpɑːrk-/ (also **par·kin·son·ism** /ˈpɑːkɪnsənɪzəm; *NAmE* ˈpɑːrk-/) *noun* [U] a disease of the nervous system that gets worse over a period of time and causes the muscles to become weak and the arms and legs to shake

ˈParkinson's law *noun* [U] (*humorous*) the idea that work will always take as long as the time available for it

park·land /ˈpɑːklænd; *NAmE* ˈpɑːrk-/ *noun* [U] open land with grass and trees, for example around a large house in the country

par·kour /pɑːˈkʊə(r); *NAmE* pɑːrˈkʊr/ *noun* [U] the sport of moving through a city by running, jumping and climbing under, around and through things ➲ compare FREE RUNNING **ORIGIN** From French *parcours du combatant*, a type of military training. ➲ VISUAL VOCAB page V40

park·way /ˈpɑːkweɪ; *NAmE* ˈpɑːrk-/ *noun* (*NAmE*) a wide road with trees and grass along the sides or middle

parky /ˈpɑːki; *NAmE* ˈpɑːrki/ *adj.* (*BrE, informal, old-fashioned* or *humorous*) (of the weather) cold

par·lance /ˈpɑːləns; *NAmE* ˈpɑːrl-/ *noun* [U] (*formal*) a particular way of using words or expressing yourself, for example one used by a particular group: *in* ***common/legal/modern parlance*** ◇ *A Munro, in climbing parlance, is a Scottish mountain exceeding 3 000 feet.*

par·lay /ˈpɑːleɪ; *NAmE* ˈpɑːrleɪ/ *verb*

PHR V **ˈparlay sth into sth** (*NAmE*) to use or develop sth such as money or a skill to make it more successful or worth more: *She hopes to parlay her success as a model into an acting career.*

par·ley /ˈpɑːli; *NAmE* ˈpɑːrli/ *noun, verb*

- ***noun*** (*old-fashioned*) a discussion between enemies or people who disagree, in order to try and find a way of solving a problem
- ***verb*** [I] **~ (with sb)** (*old-fashioned*) to discuss sth with sb in order to solve a disagreement

par·lia·ment 0‒ /ˈpɑːləmənt; *NAmE* ˈpɑːrl-/ *noun* **1** 0‒ [C, sing.+ sing./pl. v.] the group of people who are elected to make and change the laws of a country: *The German parliament is called the 'Bundestag'.* ➲ COLLOCATIONS at POLITICS **2** 0‒ **Parliament** [U+sing./pl. v.] the parliament of the United Kingdom, consisting of the House of Commons and the House of Lords: *a Member of Parliament* ◇ *The issue was debated* ***in Parliament.*** ◇ *an Act of Parliament* ◇ *to win* ***a seat in Parliament*** ◇ *to* ***be elected to Parliament*** **3** (also **Parliament**) [C, U] a particular period during which a parliament is working; Parliament as it exists between one GENERAL ELECTION and the next: *We are now into the second half of the parliament.* ◇ *to dissolve Parliament* (= formally end its activities) *and call an election* ➲ see also HOUSES OF PARLIAMENT, HUNG

par·lia·men·tar·ian /ˌpɑːləmənˈteəriən; *NAmE* ˌpɑːrləmənˈter-/ *noun* a member of a parliament, especially one with a lot of skill and experience

par·lia·men·tary /ˌpɑːləˈmentri; *NAmE* ˌpɑːrl-/ *adj.* [usually before noun] connected with a parliament; having a parliament: *parliamentary elections* ◇ *a parliamentary democracy* ➲ compare UNPARLIAMENTARY

ˌparliamentary private ˈsecretary *noun* = PPS

ˌparliamentary ˈprivilege *noun* [U] the special right of Members of Parliament to speak freely in Parliament, especially about another person, without risking legal action: *He made the allegation under the protection of parliamentary privilege.*

ˌparliamentary ˈsecretary *noun* a Member of Parliament who works in a government department below the minister ➲ compare PARLIAMENTARY PRIVATE SECRETARY, PARLIAMENTARY UNDERSECRETARY

parliaˌmentary ˌunderˈsecretary *noun* (in the UK) a Member of Parliament in a government department, below a minister in rank

par·lour (*especially US* **par·lor**) /ˈpɑːlə(r); *NAmE* ˈpɑːrl-/ *noun* **1** (*old-fashioned*) a room in a private house for sitting in, entertaining visitors, etc. **2** (in compounds) (*especially NAmE*) a shop/store that provides particular goods or services: *a beauty/an ice-cream parlour* ➲ see also FUNERAL PARLOUR, MASSAGE PARLOUR

ˈparlour game (*especially US* **ˈparlor game**) *noun* a game played in the home, especially a word game or guessing game

par·lour·maid (*especially US* **par·lor·maid**) /ˈpɑːləmeɪd; *NAmE* ˈpɑːrlərmeɪd/ *noun* (*old use*) a female servant who was employed in the past to serve food at the dinner table

par·lous /ˈpɑːləs; *NAmE* ˈpɑːrləs/ *adj.* (*formal*) (of a situation) very bad and very uncertain; dangerous **SYN** **perilous**

Parma vio·let /ˌpɑːmə ˈvaɪələt; *NAmE* ˌpɑːrmə/ *noun* a strong-smelling plant with light purple flowers

Par·mesan /ˈpɑːmɪzæn; ˌpɑːmɪˈzæn; *NAmE* ˈpɑːrməzɑːn; -zæn/ (also **ˌParmesan ˈcheese**) *noun* [U] a type of very hard Italian cheese that is usually GRATED and eaten on Italian food

pa·ro·chial /pəˈrəʊkiəl; *NAmE* -ˈroʊ-/ *adj.* **1** [usually before noun] (*formal*) connected with a church PARISH: *parochial schools* ◇ *a member of the parochial church council* **2** (*disapproving*) only concerned with small issues that happen in your local area and not interested in more important things ▸ **pa·ro·chial·ism** /-ɪzəm/ *noun* [U]: *the parochialism of a small community*

parochial school *noun* (*NAmE*) a private school supported by a particular Christian church ➲ compare FAITH SCHOOL

par·od·ist /ˈpærədɪst/ *noun* a person who writes parodies

par·ody /ˈpærədi/ *noun, verb*

- ***noun*** (*pl.* **-ies**) **~ (of sth)** **1** [C, U] a piece of writing, music, acting, etc. that deliberately copies the style of sb/sth in order to be amusing: *a parody of a horror film* **2** [C] (*disapproving*) something that is such a bad or unfair example of sth that it seems ridiculous **SYN** **travesty**: *The trial was a parody of justice.*
- ***verb*** (**par·odies, par·ody·ing, par·odied, par·odied**) **~ sb/sth** to copy the style of sb/sth in an exaggerated way, especially in order to make people laugh **SYN** **lampoon**

par·ole /pəˈrəʊl; *NAmE* pəˈroʊl/ *noun, verb*

- ***noun*** [U] **1** permission that is given to a prisoner to leave prison before the end of their SENTENCE on condition that they behave well: *to be eligible for parole* ◇ *She was released* ***on parole.*** ➲ COLLOCATIONS at JUSTICE **2** (*linguistics*) language considered as the words individual people use, rather than as the communication system of a particular community ➲ compare LANGUE
- ***verb*** [usually passive] **~ sb** to give a prisoner permission to leave prison before the end of their SENTENCE on condition that they behave well: *She was paroled after two years.*

P

par·ox·ysm /ˈpærəksɪzəm/ *noun* ~ **(of sth)** **1** a sudden strong feeling or expression of an emotion that cannot be controlled: *paroxysms of hate* ◇ *a paroxysm of laughter* **2** (*medical*) a sudden short attack of pain, causing physical shaking that cannot be controlled

par·quet /ˈpɑːkeɪ; *NAmE* pɑːrˈkeɪ/ *noun* [U] a floor covering made of flat pieces of wood fixed together in a pattern: *parquet flooring* ➲ compare WOODBLOCK

parra·keet ➲ PARAKEET

parri·cide /ˈpærɪsaɪd/ *noun* [U, C] (*formal*) the crime of killing your father, mother or a close relative; a person who is guilty of this crime ➲ compare FRATRICIDE, MATRICIDE, PATRICIDE

par·rot /ˈpærət/ *noun, verb*
■ ***noun*** a tropical bird with a curved beak. There are several types of parrot, most of which have bright feathers. Some are kept as pets and can be trained to copy human speech. IDM see SICK *adj.*
■ ***verb*** ~ **sb/sth** (*disapproving*) to repeat what sb else has said without thinking about what it means

ˈ**parrot-fashion** *adv.* (*BrE, disapproving*) if sb learns or repeats sth **parrot-fashion**, they do it without thinking about it or understanding what it means

parry /ˈpæri/ *verb* (**par·ries, parry·ing, par·ried, par·ried**) **1** [T, I] ~ **(sth)** to defend yourself against sb who is attacking you by pushing their arm, weapon, etc. to one side SYN **deflect**: *He parried a blow to his head.* ◇ *The shot was parried by the goalie.* **2** [T] ~ **sth** | + **speech** to avoid having to answer a difficult question, criticism, etc, especially by replying in the same way SYN **fend off**: *She parried all questions about their relationship.* ▶ **parry** *noun* (*pl.* **-ies**)

parse /pɑːz; *NAmE* pɑːrs/ *verb* ~ **sth** (*grammar*) to divide a sentence into parts and describe the grammar of each word or part

Par·see (also **Parsi**) /ˌpɑːˈsiː; ˈpɑːsiː; *NAmE* ˌpɑːrˈsiː; ˈpɑːrsiː/ *noun* a member of a religious group whose ANCESTORS originally came from Persia and whose religion is Zoroastrianism

P

par·si·mo·ni·ous /ˌpɑːsɪˈməʊniəs; *NAmE* ˌpɑːrsəˈmoʊ-/ *adj.* (*formal*) extremely unwilling to spend money SYN **mean** ▶ **par·si·mo·ni·ous·ly** *adv.*

par·si·mony /ˈpɑːsɪməni; *NAmE* ˈpɑːrsəmoʊni/ *noun* [U] (*formal*) the fact of being extremely unwilling to spend money SYN **meanness**

pars·ley /ˈpɑːsli; *NAmE* ˈpɑːrsli/ *noun* [U] a plant with curly green leaves that are used in cooking as a HERB and to decorate food: *fish with parsley sauce* ➲ VISUAL VOCAB page V28 ➲ see also COW PARSLEY

pars·nip /ˈpɑːsnɪp; *NAmE* ˈpɑːrs-/ *noun* [C, U] a long pale yellow root vegetable ➲ VISUAL VOCAB page V27

par·son /ˈpɑːsn; *NAmE* ˈpɑːrsn/ *noun* **1** (*old-fashioned*) an Anglican VICAR or PARISH priest **2** (*informal*) a Protestant CLERGYMAN

par·son·age /ˈpɑːsənɪdʒ; *NAmE* ˈpɑːrs-/ *noun* a parson's house

ˌ**parson's** ˈ**nose** (*NAmE* also ˌ**pope's** ˈ**nose**) *noun* the piece of flesh at the tail end of a cooked bird, usually a chicken

part O→ /pɑːt; *NAmE* pɑːrt/ *noun, verb, adv.*
■ ***noun***
▸ SOME **1** O→ [U] ~ **of sth** some but not all of a thing: *We spent part of the time in the museum.* ◇ *Part of the building was destroyed in the fire.* ◇ *Voters are given* ***only part of the story*** (= only some of the information). ◇ ***Part of me*** *feels sorry for him* (= I feel partly, but not entirely, sorry for him).
▸ PIECE **2** O→ [C] a section, piece or feature of sth: *The early part of her life was spent in Paris.* ◇ *The novel is good* ***in parts.*** ◇ *We've done the difficult part of the job.* ◇ *The procedure can be divided into two parts.* ◇ *The worst part was having to wait three hours in the rain.*
▸ MEMBER **3** O→ [U] a member of sth; a person or thing that, together with others, makes up a single unit: *You need to be able to work as part of a team.*
▸ OF MACHINE **4** O→ [C] a piece of a machine or structure: *aircraft parts* ◇ *the working parts of the machinery* ◇ ***spare parts***
▸ OF BODY/PLANT **5** O→ [C] a separate piece or area of a human or animal body or of a plant: *the parts of the body* ➲ see also PRIVATE PARTS
▸ REGION/AREA **6** O→ [C] an area or a region of the world, a country, a town, etc: *the northern part of the country* ◇ *a plant that grows in many parts of the world* ◇ *Which part of Japan do you come from?* ◇ *Come and visit us if you're ever in our part of the world.* **7 parts** [pl.] (*old-fashioned, informal*) a region or an area: *She's not from these parts.* ◇ *He's just arrived back from foreign parts.*
▸ OF BOOK/SERIES **8** O→ [C] (*abbr.* **pt**) a section of a book, television series, etc, especially one that is published or broadcast separately: *an encyclopedia published in 25 weekly parts* ◇ *Henry IV, Part II* ◇ *The final part will be shown next Sunday evening.*
▸ FOR ACTOR **9** O→ [C] a role played by an actor in a play, film/movie, etc; the words spoken by an actor in a particular role: *She was very good in the part.* ◇ *Have you learned your part yet?* ◇ (*figurative*) *He's always* ***playing a part*** (= pretending to be sth that he is not).
▸ INVOLVEMENT **10** [C, usually sing., U] the way in which sb/sth is involved in an action or situation: *He* ***had no part in*** *the decision.*
▸ IN MUSIC **11** [C] music for a particular voice or instrument in a group singing or playing together: *the clarinet part* ◇ *four-part harmony*
▸ EQUAL PORTION **12** [C] a unit of measurement that allows you to compare the different amounts of substances in sth: *Add three parts wine to one part water.*
▸ IN HAIR **13** (*NAmE*) (*BrE* **part·ing**) [C] a line on a person's head where the hair is divided with a COMB ➲ VISUAL VOCAB page V49
IDM **the best/better part of sth** most of sth, especially a period of time; more than half of sth: *The journey took her the better part of an hour.* **for the** ˈ**most part** O→ mostly; usually: *The contributors are, for the most part, professional scientists.* ➲ LANGUAGE BANK at GENERALLY **for** ˈ**my,** ˈ**his,** ˈ**their, etc. part** speaking for myself, etc. SYN **personally** **have a part to** ˈ**play (in sth)** to be able to help sth: *We all have a part to play in the fight against crime.* **have/play a** ˈ**part (in sth)** to be involved in sth: *She plays an active part in local politics.* **have/play/take/want no** ˈ**part in/of sth** to not be involved or refuse to be involved in sth, especially because you disapprove of it: *I want no part of this sordid business.* **in** ˈ**part** O→ partly; to some extent: *Her success was due in part to luck.* **look/dress the** ˈ**part** to have an appearance or wear clothes suitable for a particular job, role or position **a man/woman of (many)** ˈ**parts** a person with many skills **on the part of sb/on sb's part** made or done by sb: *It was an error on my part.* **part and parcel of sth** an essential part of sth: *Keeping the accounts is part and parcel of my job.* **part of the** ˈ**furniture** a person or thing that you are so used to seeing that you no longer notice them: *I worked there so long that I became part of the furniture.* **take sth in good** ˈ**part** (*BrE*) to accept sth slightly unpleasant without complaining or being offended **take** ˈ**part (in sth)** O→ to be involved in sth SYN **participate**: *to take part in a discussion/demonstration/fight/celebration* ◇ *How many countries took part in the last Olympic Games?* **take sb's** ˈ**part** (*BrE*) to support sb, for example in an argument SYN **side with**: *His mother always takes his part.* ➲ more at DISCRETION, LARGE, SUM *n.*
■ ***verb***
▸ LEAVE SB **1** [I] (*formal*) if a person **parts** from another person, or two people **part**, they leave each other: *We parted at the airport.* ◇ *I hate to part on such bad terms.* ◇ ~ **from sb** *He has recently parted from his wife* (= they have started to live apart). ➲ see also PARTING *adj.*
▸ KEEP APART **2** [T, often passive] ~ **sb (from sb)** (*formal*) to prevent sb from being with sb else: *I hate being parted from the children.* ◇ *The puppies were parted from their mother at birth.*
▸ MOVE AWAY **3** [I, T] if two things or parts of things **part** or you **part** them, they move away from each other: *The*

crowd parted in front of them. ◇ The elevator doors parted and out stepped the President. ◇ **~ sth** *Her lips were slightly parted.* ◇ *She parted the curtains a little and looked out.*

▸ HAIR **4** [T] **~ sth** to divide your hair into two sections with a COMB, creating a line that goes from the back of your head to the front: *He parts his hair in the middle.* ➲ see also PARTING *n.*

IDM **part 'company (with/from sb)** **1** to leave sb; to end a relationship with sb: *This is where we part company* (= go in different directions). ◇ *The band have parted company with their manager.* ◇ *The band and their manager have parted company.* **2** to disagree with sb about sth: *Weber parted company with Marx on a number of important issues.* ➲ more at FOOL *n.*

PHR V **'part with sth** to give sth to sb else, especially sth that you would prefer to keep: *Make sure you read the contract before parting with any money.*

■ ***adv.*** (often in compounds) consisting of two things; to some extent but not completely: *She's part French, part English.* ◇ *His feelings were part anger, part relief.* ◇ *The course is part funded by the European Commission.* ◇ *He is part owner of a farm in France.*

par·take /pɑː'teɪk; *NAmE* pɑːr't-/ *verb* (**par·took** /-'tʊk/, **par·taken** /-'teɪkən/) (*formal*) **1** [I] **~ (of sth)** (*old-fashioned* or *humorous*) to eat or drink sth especially sth that is offered to you: *Would you care to partake of some refreshment?* **2** [I] **~ (in sth)** (*old-fashioned*) to take part in an activity: *They preferred not to partake in the social life of the town.*

PHR V **par'take of sth** (*formal*) to have some of a particular quality: *His work partakes of the aesthetic fashions of his time.*

par·terre /pɑː'teə(r); *NAmE* pɑːr'ter/ *noun* (from *French*) **1** a flat area in a garden, with plants arranged in a formal design **2** (*especially NAmE*) the lower level in a theatre where the audience sits, especially the area underneath the BALCONY

,part ex'change *noun* [U] (*BrE*) a way of buying sth, such as a car, in which you give the old one as part of the payment for a more expensive one: *We'll take your car* ***in part-exchange.*** ▸ **,part-ex'change** *verb* **~ sth**

par·theno·gen·esis /,pɑːθənəʊ'dʒenɪsɪs; *NAmE* ,pɑːrθənoʊ-/ *noun* [U] (*biology*) the process of producing new plants or animals from an OVUM that has not been FERTILIZED ▸ **par·theno·gen·et·ic** /,pɑːθənəʊdʒə'netɪk; *NAmE* ,pɑːrθənoʊ-/ *adj.*: *parthenogenetic species* **par·theno·gen·et·ic·ally** /-kli/ *adj.*: *These organisms reproduce parthenogenetically.*

par·tial /'pɑːʃl; *NAmE* 'pɑːrʃl/ *adj.* **1** not complete or whole: *It was only a partial solution to the problem.* ◇ *a partial eclipse of the sun* **2** [not before noun] **~ to sb/sth** (*old-fashioned*) liking sb/sth very much: *I'm not partial to mushrooms.* **3** [not usually before noun] **~ (towards sb/sth)** (*disapproving*) showing or feeling too much support for one person, team, idea, etc, in a way that is unfair SYN **biased** OPP **impartial**

par·ti·al·ity /,pɑːʃi'æləti; *NAmE* ,pɑːrʃ-/ *noun* (*formal*) **1** [U] (*disapproving*) the unfair support of one person, team, idea, etc. SYN **bias** OPP **impartiality** **2** [sing.] **~ for sth/sb** a feeling of liking sth/sb very much SYN **fondness**: *She has a partiality for exotic flowers.*

par·tial·ly /'pɑːʃəli; *NAmE* 'pɑːrʃ-/ *adv.* partly; not completely: *The road was partially blocked by a fallen tree.* ◇ *a society for the blind and* ***partially sighted*** (= people who can see very little). ➲ note at PARTLY

par·tici·pant AW /pɑː'tɪsɪpənt; *NAmE* pɑːr't-/ *noun* **~ (in sth)** a person who is taking part in an activity or event: *He has been an active participant in the discussion.*

par·tici·pate AW /pɑː'tɪsɪpeɪt; *NAmE* pɑːr't-/ *verb* [I] **~ (in sth)** (rather *formal*) to take part in or become involved in an activity: *She didn't participate in the discussion.* ◇ *We encourage students to participate fully in the running of the college.* ◇ *Details of the competition are available at all participating stores.*

par·tici·pa·tion AW /pɑː,tɪsɪ'peɪʃn; *NAmE* pɑːr,t-/ *noun* [U] the act of taking part in an activity or event: *a show with lots of* ***audience participation*** ◇ **~ in sth** *A back injury prevented active participation in any sports for a while.*

par·tici·pa·tory AW /pɑː,tɪsɪ'peɪtəri; *NAmE* pɑːr'tɪsəpətɔːri/ *adj.* [usually before noun] allowing everyone in a society, business, etc. to give their opinions and to help make decisions: *Participatory democracy is a fundamental principle of cooperative businesses.*

par·ti·ciple /pɑː'tɪsɪpl; *NAmE* pɑːr't-/ *noun* (*grammar*) (in English) a word formed from a verb, ending in *-ing* (= the PRESENT PARTICIPLE) or *-ed, -en*, etc. (= the PAST PARTICIPLE) ▸ **par·ti·ci·pial** /,pɑːtɪ'sɪpiəl; *NAmE* ,pɑːrt-/ *adj.*

par·ticle /'pɑːtɪkl; *NAmE* 'pɑːrt-/ *noun* **1** a very small piece of sth: *particles of dust* ◇ *dust particles* ◇ *There was* ***not a particle of*** *evidence* (= no evidence at all) *to support the case.* **2** (*physics*) a very small piece of matter, such as an ELECTRON or PROTON, that is part of an atom ➲ see also ALPHA PARTICLE, ELEMENTARY PARTICLE **3** (*grammar*) an adverb or a preposition that can combine with a verb to make a phrasal verb: *In 'She tore up the letter', the word 'up' is a particle.* ➲ see also ADVERBIAL PARTICLE

'particle physics *noun* [U] the scientific study of very small pieces of matter that are parts of an atom

par·ticu·lar 🔑 /pə'tɪkjələ(r); *NAmE* pər't-/ *adj.*, *noun*

■ ***adj.*** **1** 🔑 [only before noun] used to emphasize that you are referring to one individual person, thing or type of thing and not others SYN **specific**: *There is one particular patient I'd like you to see.* ◇ *Is there a particular type of book he enjoys?* **2** 🔑 [only before noun] greater than usual; special: *We must pay particular attention to this point.* ◇ *These documents are of particular interest.* **3** **~ (about/over sth)** very definite about what you like and careful about what you choose SYN **fussy**: *She's very particular about her clothes.*

IDM **in par'ticular** **1** 🔑 especially or particularly: *He loves science fiction in particular.* ➲ LANGUAGE BANK at EMPHASIS **2** 🔑 special or specific: *Peter was lying on the sofa doing* ***nothing in particular.*** ◇ *Is there* ***anything in particular*** *you'd like for dinner?* ◇ *She directed the question at* ***no one in particular.***

■ ***noun*** (*formal*) **1** [usually pl.] a fact or detail, especially one that is officially written down: *The police officer took down all the particulars of the burglary.* ◇ *The nurse asked me for my particulars* (= personal details such as your name, address, etc.). ◇ *The new contract will be the same in every particular as the old one.* **2** **particulars** [pl.] written information and details about a property, business, job, etc: *Application forms and further particulars are available from the Personnel Office.*

par·ticu·lar·ity /pə,tɪkju'lærəti; *NAmE* pər't-/ *noun* (*pl.* **-ies**) (*formal*) **1** [U] the quality of being individual or unique: *the particularity of each human being* **2** [U] attention to detail; being exact **3** **particularities** [pl.] the special features or details of sth

par·ticu·lar·ize (*BrE* also **-ise**) /pə'tɪkjələraɪz; *NAmE* pər't-/ *verb* [I, T] **~ (sth)** (*formal*) to give details of sth, especially one by one; to give particular examples of sth

par·ticu·lar·ly 🔑 /pə'tɪkjələli; *NAmE* pər'tɪkjələrli/ *adv.*
especially; more than usual or more than others: *particularly good/important/useful* ◇ *Traffic is bad, particularly in the city centre.* ◇ *I enjoyed the play, particularly the second half.* ◇ *The lecture was* ***not particularly*** (= not very) *interesting.* ◇ *'Did you enjoy it?' 'No,* ***not particularly*** (= not very much).'

par·ticu·late /pɑː'tɪkjələt; -leɪt; *NAmE* pɑːr't-/ *adj.*, *noun* (*chemistry*)

■ ***adj.*** relating to, or in the form of, PARTICLES: *particulate pollution*

■ ***noun*** **particulates** [pl.] matter in the form of PARTICLES

part·ing /'pɑːtɪŋ; *NAmE* 'pɑːrt-/ *noun*, *adj.*

■ ***noun*** **1** [U, C] the act or occasion of leaving a person or place: *the moment of parting* ◇ *We had a tearful parting at the airport.* **2** (*BrE*) (*NAmE* **part**) [C] a line on a person's

P

head where the hair is divided with a COMB: *a side/centre parting* ➲ VISUAL VOCAB page V49 **3** [U, C] the act or result of dividing sth into parts: *the parting of the clouds*
IDM **a/the ˌparting of the ˈways** a point at which two people or groups of people decide to separate
■ *adj.* [only before noun] said or done by sb as they leave: *a parting kiss* ◇ *His parting words were 'I love you.'*
IDM **ˌparting ˈshot** a final remark, especially an unkind one, that sb makes as they leave

par·ti·san /ˌpɑːtɪˈzæn; ˈpɑːtɪzæn; NAmE ˈpɑːrtəzn/ *adj., noun*
■ *adj.* (often *disapproving*) showing too much support for one person, group or idea, especially without considering it carefully SYN **one-sided**: *Most newspapers are politically partisan.*
■ *noun* **1** a person who strongly supports a particular leader, group or idea SYN **follower** **2** a member of an armed group that is fighting secretly against enemy soldiers who have taken control of its country ▶ **par·ti·san·ship** /-ʃɪp/ *noun* [U]

par·ti·tion /pɑːˈtɪʃn; NAmE pɑːrˈt-/ *noun, verb*
■ *noun* **1** [C] a wall or screen that separates one part of a room from another: *a glass partition* ◇ *partition walls* ➲ VISUAL VOCAB page V56 **2** [U] the division of one country into two or more countries: *the partition of Germany after the war*
■ *verb* [often passive] to divide sth into parts: **~ sth** *to partition a country* ◇ **~ sth into sth** *The room is partitioned into three sections.*
PHR V **parˌtition sth↔ˈoff** to separate one area, one part of a room, etc. from another with a wall or screen

par·ti·tive /ˈpɑːtətɪv; NAmE ˈpɑːrt-/ *noun* (*grammar*) a word or phrase that shows a part or quantity of sth: *In 'a spoonful of sugar', the word 'spoonful' is a partitive.* ▶ **par·ti·tive** *adj.*

part·ly 🔑 /ˈpɑːtli; NAmE ˈpɑːrt-/ *adv.*
to some extent; not completely: *Some people are unwilling to attend the classes* ***partly because*** *of the cost involved.* ◇ *He was only partly responsible for the accident.*

P

Which Word?

partly / partially

■ **Partly** and **partially** both mean 'not completely': *The road is partly/partially finished.* **Partly** is especially used to talk about the reason for something, often followed by *because* or *due to*: *I didn't enjoy the trip very much, partly because of the weather.* **Partially** should be used when you are talking about physical conditions: *His mother is partially blind.*

part·ner 🔑 AW /ˈpɑːtnə(r); NAmE ˈpɑːrt-/ *noun, verb*
■ *noun* **1** 🔑 the person that you are married to or having a sexual relationship with: *Come to the New Year disco and bring your partner!* ◇ *a marriage partner* ➲ COLLOCATIONS at MARRIAGE **2** 🔑 one of the people who owns a business and shares the profits, etc: *a partner in a law firm* ◇ ***a junior/senior partner*** **3** 🔑 a person that you are doing an activity with, such as dancing or playing a game: ***a dancing/tennis, etc. partner*** ➲ see also SPARRING PARTNER **4** 🔑 a country or an organization that has an agreement with another country: *a trading partner* ➲ see also SLEEPING PARTNER
■ *verb* **~ sb** to be sb's partner in a dance, game, etc: *Gerry offered to partner me at tennis.*

part·ner·ship 🔑 AW /ˈpɑːtnəʃɪp; NAmE ˈpɑːrtnərʃɪp/ *noun*
1 🔑 [U] the state of being a partner in business: *to* ***be in/to go into partnership*** ◇ **~ with sb/sth** *He developed his own program* ***in partnership*** *with an American expert.* **2** 🔑 [C, U] a relationship between two people, organizations, etc; the state of having this relationship: *Marriage should be an equal partnership.* ◇ **~ with sb/sth** *the school's partnership with parents* ◇ **~ between A and B** *a partnership between the United States and Europe* **3** 🔑 [C] a business owned by two or more people who share the profits: *a junior member of the partnership*

ˌpart of ˈspeech *noun* (*grammar*) one of the classes into which words are divided according to their grammar, such as noun, verb, adjective, etc. SYN **word class**

par·took *past tense of* PARTAKE

par·tridge /ˈpɑːtrɪdʒ; NAmE ˈpɑːrt-/ *noun* [C, U] (*pl.* **par·tridges** or **par·tridge**) a brown bird with a round body and a short tail, that people hunt for sport or food; the meat of this bird

ˌpart-ˈtime *adj.* (*abbr.* **PT**) for part of the day or week in which people work: *She's looking for a part-time job.* ◇ *to study on a part-time basis* ◇ *part-time workers* ◇ *I'm only part-time at the moment.* ▶ **ˌpart-ˈtime** *adv.*: *Liz works part-time from 10 till 2.* ➲ compare FULL-TIME

ˌpart-ˈtimer *noun* a person who works part-time

par·tur·ition /ˌpɑːtjʊˈrɪʃn; NAmE ˌpɑːrt-/ *noun* [U] (*technical*) the act of giving birth

ˈpart-way *adv.* some of the way: *They were part-way through the speeches when he arrived.*

ˈpart-work *noun* (*BrE*) a book that is published in several parts that people can collect over a period of time

party 🔑 /ˈpɑːti; NAmE ˈpɑːrti/ *noun, verb*
■ *noun* (*pl.* **-ies**) **1** 🔑 (also **Party**) [C+sing./pl. v.] a political organization that you can vote for in elections and whose members have the same aims and ideas: *the Democratic and Republican Parties in the United States* ◇ *She belongs to the Labour Party.* ◇ *the* ***ruling/opposition party*** ◇ *the* ***party leader/manifesto/policy*** ➲ COLLOCATIONS at POLITICS **2** 🔑 [C] (especially in compounds) a social occasion, often in a person's home, at which people eat, drink, talk, dance and enjoy themselves: ***a birthday/dinner/garden, etc.*** *party* ◇ *to* ***give/have/throw a party*** ◇ *Did you* ***go to the party?*** ◇ *party games* ➲ see also HEN PARTY, HOUSE PARTY, STAG PARTY **3** 🔑 [C+sing./pl. v.] a group of people who are doing sth together such as travelling or visiting somewhere: *The school is taking a party of 40 children to France.* ◇ *The theatre gives a 10% discount to parties of more than ten.* ➲ see also SEARCH PARTY, WORKING PARTY **4** [C] (*formal*) one of the people or groups of people involved in a legal agreement or argument: *the* ***guilty/innocent party*** ◇ *The contract can be terminated by either party with three months' notice.* ➲ see also INJURED PARTY, THIRD PARTY
IDM **be (a) party to sth** (*formal*) to be involved in an agreement or action: *to be party to a decision* ◇ *He refused to be a party to any violence.* **ˌbring sth to the ˈparty/ˈtable** to contribute sth useful to a discussion, project, etc: *What Hislop brought to the party was real commitment and energy.*
■ *verb* (**par·ties**, **party·ing**, **par·tied**, **par·tied**) [I] (*informal*) to enjoy yourself, especially by eating, drinking alcohol and dancing: *They were out partying every night.*

ˌparty ˈfavors (also **favors**) (both *NAmE*) *noun* [pl.] small gifts that are often given to children at a party

ˈparty-goer *noun* a person who enjoys going to parties or who is a guest at a particular party

ˌparty ˈline *noun* [usually sing.] the official opinions and policies of a political party, which members are expected to support IDM see TOE *v.*

ˈparty piece *noun* (*BrE, informal*) a thing that sb does to entertain people, especially at parties, for example singing a song

ˌparty poˈlitical *adj.* [only before noun] (*especially BrE*) made by or relating to a political party: *a party political broadcast*

ˌparty ˈpolitics *noun* [U+sing./pl. v.] political activity that involves political parties: *The President should stand above party politics.* ◇ *Many people think that party politics should not enter into local government.*

party-pooper /ˈpɑːti puːpə(r); NAmE ˈpɑːrti puːpər/ *noun* (*informal*) a person who does not want to take part in an enjoyable activity and spoils the fun for other people

ˌparty ˈspirit *noun* [U] the sort of mood in which you can enjoy a party and have fun

ˌparty ˈwall *noun* a wall that divides two buildings or rooms and belongs to both owners

par·venu /ˈpɑːvənjuː; *NAmE* ˈpɑːrvənuː/ *noun* (*pl.* **-us**) (*formal, disapproving*) a person from a low social or economic position who has suddenly become rich or powerful

pas·cal /ˈpæskl/ *noun* **1** (*abbr.* **Pa**) the standard unit for measuring pressure **2 Pascal**, **PASCAL** a language used for writing programs for computer systems

pas·chal /ˈpɑːskl; *NAmE* ˈpæskl/ *adj.* (*formal*) **1** relating to Easter **2** relating to the Jewish Passover

pas de deux /ˌpɑː də ˈdɜː/ *noun* (*pl.* **pas de deux** /ˌpɑː də ˈdɜː/) (from *French*) a dance, often part of a BALLET, that is performed by two people

pash·mi·na /pæʃˈmiːnə/ *noun* a long piece of cloth made of fine soft wool from a type of GOAT and worn by a woman around the shoulders

Pashto /ˈpæʃtəʊ; *NAmE* -toʊ/ *noun* [U] the official language of Afghanistan, also spoken in northern Pakistan

pass 0‑ /pɑːs; *NAmE* pæs/ *verb, noun*

■ *verb*

▸ MOVE **1** 0‑ [I, T] to move past or to the other side of sb/sth: *Several people were passing but nobody offered to help.* ◇ *I hailed a passing taxi.* ◇ *The road was so narrow that cars were unable to pass.* ◇ **~ sb/sth** *to pass a barrier/sentry/checkpoint* ◇ *You'll pass a bank on the way to the train station.* ◇ *She passed me in the street without even saying hello.* ◇ (*especially NAmE*) *There was a truck behind that was trying to pass me.* HELP The usual word in British English in the last example is **overtake**. **2** 0‑ [I] **+ adv./prep.** to go or move in the direction mentioned: *The procession passed slowly along the street.* ◇ *A plane passed low overhead.* **3** [T] **~ sth + adv./prep.** to make sth move in the direction or into the position mentioned: *He passed the rope around the post three times to secure it.*

▸ GIVE **4** 0‑ [T] to give sth to sb by putting it into their hands or in a place where they can easily reach it: **~ sth (to sb)** *Pass the salt, please.* ◇ *Pass that book over.* ◇ **~ sb sth** *Pass me over that book.*

▸ BALL **5** 0‑ [T, I] (in ball games) to kick, hit or throw the ball to a player of your own side: **~ sth (to sb)** *He passed the ball to Rooney.* ◇ **~ (to sb)** *Why do they keep passing back to the goalie?*

▸ AFTER DEATH **6** [I] **~ to sb** to be given to another person after first belonging to sb else, especially after the first person has died: *On his death, the title passed to his eldest son.*

▸ BECOME GREATER **7** 0‑ [T] **~ sth** (of an amount) to become greater than a particular total SYN **exceed**: *Unemployment has now* **passed the** *three million* **mark**.

▸ CHANGE **8** [I] **~ from sth to/into sth** to change from one state or condition to another: *She had passed from childhood to early womanhood.*

▸ TIME **9** 0‑ [I] when time **passes**, it goes by: *Six months passed and we still had no news of them.* ◇ *We grew more anxious* **with every passing day**. **10** 0‑ [T] **~ sth** to spend time, especially when you are bored or waiting for sth: *We sang songs to* **pass the time**. ◇ *How did you pass the evening?*

▸ END **11** 0‑ [I] to come to an end; to be over: *They waited for the storm to pass.*

▸ TEST/EXAM **12** 0‑ [I, T] to achieve the required standard in an exam, a test, etc: *I'm not really expecting to pass first time.* ◇ **~ sth** *She hasn't passed her driving test yet.* OPP **fail** **13** [T] **~ sb** to test sb and decide that they are good enough, according to an agreed standard: *The examiners passed all the candidates.* OPP **fail**

▸ LAW/PROPOSAL **14** 0‑ [T] **~ sth** to accept a proposal, law, etc. by voting: *The bill was passed by 360 votes to 280.*

▸ HAPPEN **15** [I] to be allowed: *I don't like it, but I'll* **let it pass** (= will not object). ◇ *Her remarks passed without comment* (= people ignored them). **16** [I] to happen; to be said or done: **~ (between A and B)** *They'll never be friends again after all that has passed between them.* ◇ **+ adj.** *His departure* **passed unnoticed**.

▸ NOT KNOW **17** [I] **~ (on sth)** to say that you do not know the answer to a question, especially during a QUIZ: *'What's the capital of Peru?' 'I'll have to pass on that one.'* ◇ *'Who wrote 'Catch-22'?' 'Pass* (= I don't know).*'*

▸ NOT WANT **18** [I] **~ (on sth)** to say that you do not want sth that is offered to you: *Thanks. I'm going to pass on dessert, if you don't mind.*

▸ SAY/STATE STH **19** [T] **~ sth (on sb/sth)** to say or state sth, especially officially: *The court waited in silence for the judge to* **pass sentence**. ◇ *It's not for me to* **pass judgement** *on your behaviour.* ◇ *The man smiled at the girl and passed a friendly remark.*

▸ BELIEF/UNDERSTANDING **20** [T] **~ belief, understanding, etc.** (*formal*) to go beyond the limits of what you can believe, understand, etc: *It passes belief* (= is impossible to believe) *that she could do such a thing.*

▸ IN CARD GAMES **21** [I] to refuse to play a card or make a BID when it is your turn

▸ FROM THE BODY **22** [T] **~ sth** to send sth out from the body as or with waste matter: *If you're passing blood you ought to see a doctor.*

IDM **ˌcome to ˈpass** (*old use*) to happen **not pass your ˈlips** **1** if words do **not pass your lips**, you say nothing **2** if food or drink does **not pass your lips**, you eat or drink nothing **pass the ˈhat round/around** (*informal*) to collect money from a number of people, for example to buy a present for sb **pass ˈmuster** to be accepted as of a good enough standard **pass the time of ˈday (with sb)** to say hello to sb and have a short conversation with them **pass ˈwater** (*formal*) to URINATE

PHR V **ˌpass sth↔aˈround/ˈround** 0‑ (*BrE*) to give sth to another person, who gives it to sb else, etc. until everyone has seen it: *Can you pass these pictures around for everyone to look at, please?* **ˈpass as sb/sth** = PASS FOR/AS SB/STH **ˌpass aˈway** **1** 0‑ (also **ˌpass ˈon**) to die. People say 'pass away' to avoid saying 'die': *His mother passed away last year.* **2** to stop existing: *civilizations that have passed away* **ˌpass ˈby (sb/sth)** 0‑ to go past: *The procession passed right by my front door.* **ˌpass sb/sth ˈby** to happen without affecting sb/sth: *She feels that life is passing her by* (= that she is not enjoying the opportunities and pleasures of life). **ˌpass sth↔ˈdown** [often passive] to give or teach sth to your children or people younger than you, who will then give or teach it to those who live after them, and so on SYN **hand down** **ˈpass for/as sb/sth** to be accepted as sb/sth: *He speaks the language so well he could easily pass for a German.* ◇ *We had some wine—or what passes for wine in that area.* **ˈpass into sth** to become a part of sth: *Many foreign words have passed into the English language.* **ˌpass ˈoff** (*BrE*) (of an event) to take place and be completed in a particular way: *The demonstration passed off peacefully.* **ˌpass sb/yourself/sth ˈoff as sb/sth** to pretend that sb/sth is sth they are not: *He escaped by passing himself off as a guard.* **ˌpass ˈon** = PASS AWAY **ˌpass sth↔ˈon (to sb)** 0‑ to give sth to sb else, especially after receiving it or using it yourself: *Pass the book on to me when you've finished with it.* ◇ *I passed your message on to my mother.* ◇ *Much of the discount is pocketed by retailers instead of being passed on to customers.* **ˌpass ˈout** 0‑ to become unconscious SYN **faint** **ˌpass ˈout (of sth)** (*BrE*) to leave a military college after finishing a course of training: *a passing-out ceremony* **ˌpass sb↔ˈover** to not consider sb for promotion in a job, especially when they deserve it or think that they deserve it: *He was passed over in favour of a younger man.* **ˌpass ˈover sth** to ignore or avoid sth SYN **overlook**: *They chose to pass over her rude remarks.* **ˌpass ˈthrough...** 0‑ to go through a town, etc, stopping there for a short time but not staying: *We were passing through, so we thought we'd come and say hello.* **ˌpass sth↔ˈup** (*informal*) to choose not to make use of a chance, an opportunity, etc: *Imagine passing up an offer like that!*

■ *noun*

▸ IN EXAM **1** (*especially BrE*) a successful result in an exam: *She got a pass in French.* ◇ *12 passes and 3 fails* ◇ *Two A-level passes are needed for this course.* ◇ *The* **pass mark** *is 50%.* ◇ *The school has a 90%* **pass rate** (= 90% of students pass their exams).

P

▸ OFFICIAL DOCUMENT **2** an official document or ticket that shows that you have the right to enter or leave a place, to travel on a bus or train, etc: *a boarding pass* (= for a plane) ◇ *There is no admittance without a security pass.* ➲ see also BUS PASS
▸ OF BALL **3** (in some sports) an act of hitting or throwing the ball to another player in your team: *a long pass to Rooney* ◇ *a back pass to the goalkeeper*
▸ THROUGH MOUNTAINS **4** a road or way over or through mountains: *a mountain pass* ➲ VISUAL VOCAB page V5
▸ MOVING PAST/OVER **5** an act of going or moving past or over sth: *The helicopter made several passes over the village before landing.*
▸ STAGE IN PROCESS **6** a stage in a process, especially one that involves separating things from a larger group: *In the first pass all the addresses are loaded into the database.*
IDM **come to such a 'pass | come to a pretty 'pass** (*old-fashioned* or *humorous*) to reach a sad or difficult state **make a pass at sb** (*informal*) to try to start a sexual relationship with sb

pass·able /'pɑːsəbl; *NAmE* 'pæs-/ *adj.* **1** fairly good but not excellent SYN **satisfactory** **2** [not usually before noun] if a road or a river is **passable**, it is not blocked and you can travel along or across it OPP **impassable**

pass·ably /'pɑːsəbli; *NAmE* 'pæs-/ *adv.* in a way that is acceptable or good enough SYN **reasonably**: *He speaks passably good French.*

pas·sage 0‑ /'pæsɪdʒ/ *noun*
▸ LONG NARROW WAY **1** 0‑ (also **pas·sage·way** /'pæsɪdʒweɪ/) [C] a long narrow area with walls on either side that connects one room or place with another SYN **corridor**: *a secret underground passage* ◇ *A dark narrow passage led to the main hall.*
▸ IN THE BODY **2** [C] a tube in the body through which air, liquid, etc. passes: *blocked nasal passages* ➲ see also BACK PASSAGE
▸ SECTION FROM BOOK **3** 0‑ [C] a short section from a book, piece of music, etc. SYN **excerpt**, **extract**: *Read the following passage and answer the questions below.* ➲ COLLOCATIONS at LITERATURE
▸ OF TIME **4** [sing.] **the ~ of time** (*literary*) the process of time passing: *Her confidence grew with the passage of time.*
▸ OF BILL IN PARLIAMENT **5** [sing.] the process of discussing a BILL in a parliament so that it can become law: *The bill is now guaranteed an easy passage through the House of Representatives.*
▸ JOURNEY BY SHIP **6** [sing.] a journey from one place to another by ship: *Her grandfather had* ***worked his passage*** (= worked on a ship to pay for the journey) *to America.*
▸ GOING THROUGH **7** [sing.] **a ~ (through sth)** a way through sth: *The officers forced a passage through the crowd.* **8** [U] (*formal*) the action of going across, through or past sth: *Large trees may obstruct the passage of light.* **9** [U, C, usually sing.] the permission to travel across a particular area of land: *We were promised (a) safe passage through the occupied territory.* ➲ see also BIRD OF PASSAGE, RITE OF PASSAGE

pas·sant ➲ EN PASSANT

pass·book /'pɑːsbʊk; *NAmE* 'pæs-/ *noun* a small book containing a record of the money you put into and take out of an account at a BUILDING SOCIETY or a bank

passé /'pæseɪ; 'pɑːs-; *NAmE* pæ'seɪ/ *adj.* [not usually before noun] (from *French, disapproving*) no longer fashionable SYN **outmoded**

pas·sen·ger 0‑ /'pæsɪndʒə(r)/ *noun*
1 0‑ a person who is travelling in a car, bus, train, plane or ship and who is not driving it or working on it: *a passenger train* (= carrying passengers, not goods) **2** (*informal, disapproving, especially BrE*) a member of a group or team who does not do as much work as the others: *The firm cannot afford to carry passengers.*

'passenger seat *noun* the seat in a car which is next to the driver's seat ➲ VISUAL VOCAB page V42

ˌpasser-'by *noun* (*pl.* **passers-by**) a person who is going past sb/sth by chance, especially when sth unexpected happens: *Police asked passers-by if they had seen the accident.* ➲ SYNONYMS at WITNESS

ˌpass-'fail *adj.* (*US*) connected with a grading system for school classes, etc. in which a student passes or fails rather than receiving a grade as a letter (for example, A or B) ▸ **ˌpass-'fail** *adv.*: *to take a class pass-fail*

pas·sim /'pæsɪm/ *adv.* (from *Latin*) used in the notes to a book or an article to show that a particular name or subject appears in several places in it

pass·ing 0‑ /'pɑːsɪŋ; *NAmE* 'pæs-/ *noun, adj.*
■ ***noun*** [U] **1** 0‑ **the ~ of time/the years** the process of time going by **2** (*formal*) the fact of sth ending or of sb dying: *When the government is finally brought down, no one will mourn its passing.* ◇ *the passing of the old year* (= on New Year's Eve) ◇ *Many will mourn her passing* (= her death, when you do not want to say this directly). **3** 0‑ **the ~ of sth** the act of making sth become a law: *the passing of a resolution/law*
IDM **in passing** done or said while you are giving your attention to sth else SYN **casually**: *He only mentioned it in passing and didn't give any details.*
■ ***adj.*** [only before noun] **1** 0‑ lasting only for a short period of time and then disappearing SYN **brief**: *a passing phase/thought/interest* ◇ *He makes only a* ***passing reference*** *to the theory in his book* (= it is not the main subject of his book). ◇ *She* ***bears*** *more than* ***a passing resemblance to*** (= looks very like) *your sister.* **2** 0‑ going past: *I love him more with each passing day.* ◇ *the noise of passing cars* **3 ~ grade/mark** (*NAmE*) a grade/mark that achieves the required standard in an exam, a test, etc.

'passing lane (*NAmE*) (*BrE* **ˌoutside 'lane**) *noun* the part of a major road such as a MOTORWAY or INTERSTATE nearest the middle of the road, where vehicles drive fastest and can go past vehicles ahead

'passing shot *noun* (in TENNIS) a shot which goes past your opponent, and which he or she cannot reach

pas·sion /'pæʃn/ *noun* **1** [C, U] a very strong feeling of love, hatred, anger, enthusiasm, etc: *He's a man of violent passions.* ◇ *a* ***crime of passion*** ◇ *She argued her case with considerable passion.* ◇ ***Passions were running high*** (= people were angry and emotional) *at the meeting.* **2** [sing.] (*formal*) a state of being very angry SYN **rage**: *She* ***flies into a passion*** *if anyone even mentions his name.* **3** [U] **~ (for sb)** a very strong feeling of sexual love: *His passion for her made him blind to everything else.* **4** [C] **~ (for sth)** a very strong feeling of liking sth; a hobby, an activity, etc. that you like very much: *The English have a passion for gardens.* ◇ *Music is a passion with him.* **5 the Passion** [sing.] (in Christianity) the suffering and death of Jesus Christ

pas·sion·ate /'pæʃənət/ *adj.* **1** having or showing strong feelings of sexual love or of anger, etc: *to have a passionate nature* **2** having or showing strong feelings of enthusiasm for sth or belief in sth: *a passionate interest in music* ◇ *a passionate defender of civil liberties* ▸ **pas·sion·ate·ly** *adv.*: *He took her in his arms and kissed her passionately.* ◇ *They are all passionately interested in environmental issues.*

'passion flower *noun* a tropical climbing plant with large brightly coloured flowers

'passion fruit *noun* [C, U] (*pl.* **passion fruit**) a small tropical fruit with a thick purple skin and many seeds inside, produced by some types of passion flower ➲ VISUAL VOCAB page V26

pas·sion·less /'pæʃnləs/ *adj.* without emotion or enthusiasm

'Passion play *noun* a play about the suffering and death of Jesus Christ

pas·sive AW /'pæsɪv/ *adj., noun*
■ ***adj.*** **1** accepting what happens or what people do without trying to change anything or oppose them: *He played a passive role in the relationship.* ◇ *a passive observer of events* **2** (*grammar*) connected with the form of a verb used when the subject is affected by the action of the verb, for ex-

ample *He was bitten by a dog.* is a passive sentence ➲ compare ACTIVE ▸ **pas·sive·ly** AW *adv.*

▪ **noun** (also ˌ**passive ˈvoice**) [sing.] (*grammar*) the form of a verb used when the subject is affected by the action of the verb ➲ compare ACTIVE

ˌ**passive-agˈgressive** *adj.* being angry without expressing your anger openly, but resisting people in authority by refusing to do what they want or to accept responsibility for your actions: *He exhibited passive-aggressive tendencies.*

ˌ**passive reˈsistance** *noun* [U] a way of opposing a government or an enemy by peaceful means, often by refusing to obey laws or orders

ˌ**passive ˈsmoking** *noun* [U] the act of breathing in smoke from other people's cigarettes

pas·siv·ity AW /pæˈsɪvəti/ *noun* [U] the state of accepting what happens without reacting or trying to fight against it

pas·siv·ize (*BrE* also **-ise**) /ˈpæsɪvaɪz/ *verb* **~ sth** (*grammar*) to put a verb into the passive form

ˈ**pass key** *noun* = MASTER KEY

Pass·over /ˈpɑːsəʊvə(r); *NAmE* ˈpæsoʊ-/ *noun* [U, C] the Jewish religious festival and holiday in memory of the escape of the Jews from Egypt

pass·port 🗝 /ˈpɑːspɔːt; *NAmE* ˈpæspɔːrt/ *noun* **1** 🗝 an official document that identifies you as a citizen of a particular country, and that you may have to show when you enter or leave a country: *a valid passport* ◇ *a South African passport* ◇ *I was stopped as I went through* **passport control** (= where passports are checked). ◇ *a passport photo* **2** 🗝 **~ to sth** a thing that makes sth possible or enables you to achieve sth SYN **key**: *The only passport to success is hard work.*

pass·word /ˈpɑːswɜːd; *NAmE* ˈpæswɜːrd/ *noun* **1** a secret word or phrase that you need to know in order to be allowed into a place **2** (*computing*) a series of letters or numbers that you must type into a computer or computer system in order to be able to use it: *Enter a username and password to get into the system.*

past 🗝 /pɑːst; *NAmE* pæst/ *adj., noun, prep., adv.*

▪ **adj. 1** 🗝 gone by in time: *in past years/centuries/ages* ◇ *in times past* ◇ *The time for discussion is past.* **2** 🗝 [only before noun] gone by recently; just ended: *I haven't seen much of her in the past few weeks.* ◇ *The past month has been really busy at work.* **3** 🗝 [only before noun] belonging to an earlier time: *past events* ◇ *From past experience I'd say he'd probably forgotten the time.* ◇ ***past and present students** of the college* ◇ *Let's forget about who was more to blame—it's all* ***past history.*** **4** [only before noun] (*grammar*) connected with the form of a verb used to express actions in the past

▪ **noun 1** 🗝 **the past** [sing.] the time that has gone by; things that happened in an earlier time: *I used to go there often in the past.* ◇ *the* ***recent/distant past*** ◇ *She looked back on the past without regret.* ◇ *Writing letters seems to be* ***a thing of the past.*** **2** 🗝 [C] a person's past life or career: *We don't know anything about his past.* ◇ *They say she has a 'past'* (= bad things in her past life that she wishes to keep secret). **3 the past** [sing.] (*grammar*) = PAST TENSE IDM see BLAST *n.*, DISTANT, LIVE[1]

▪ **prep. 1** 🗝 (*NAmE* also **after**) later than sth: *half past two* ◇ *ten (minutes) past six* ◇ *There's a bus at twenty minutes past the hour* (= at 1.20, 2.20, etc.). ◇ *We arrived at two o'clock and left at ten past* (= ten minutes past two). ◇ *It was past midnight when we got home.* **2** 🗝 on or to the other side of sb/sth: *We live in the house just past the church.* ◇ *He hurried past them without stopping.* ◇ *He just walked* ***straight past us!*** **3** 🗝 above or further than a particular point or stage: *Unemployment is now past the 3 million mark.* ◇ *The flowers are past their best.* ◇ *He's past his prime.* ◇ *She's long past retirement age.* ◇ *Honestly, I'm* ***past caring*** *what happens* (= I can no longer be bothered to care).
IDM ˈ**past it** (*BrE, informal*) too old to do what you used to be able to do; too old to be used for its normal function: *In some sports you're past it by the age of 25.* ◇ *That coat is looking decidedly past it.*

▪ **adv. 1** 🗝 from one side of sth to the other: *I called out to him as he ran past.* **2** 🗝 used to describe time passing SYN **by**: *A week went past and nothing had changed.*

pasta /ˈpæstə; *NAmE* ˈpɑːstə/ *noun* [U] an Italian food made from flour, water and sometimes eggs, formed into different shapes and usually served with a sauce. It is hard when dry and soft when cooked.

paste /peɪst/ *noun, verb*

▪ **noun 1** [sing.] a soft wet mixture, usually made of a powder and a liquid: *She mixed the flour and water to a smooth paste.* **2** [C] (especially in compounds) a smooth mixture of crushed meat, fish, etc. that is spread on bread or used in cooking **3** [U] a type of glue that is used for sticking paper to things: *wallpaper paste* **4** [U] a substance like glass, that is used for making artificial JEWELS, for example diamonds

▪ **verb 1** [T] **~ sth + adv./prep.** to stick sth to sth else using glue or paste: *He pasted the pictures into his scrapbook.* ◇ *Paste the two pieces together.* ◇ *Paste down the edges.* **2** [T] **~ sth** to make sth by sticking pieces of paper together: *The children were busy cutting and pasting paper hats.* **3** [T, I] **~ (sth)** (*computing*) to copy or move text into a document from another place or another document: *This function allows you to* ***cut and paste*** *text.* ◇ *It's quicker to cut and paste than to retype.*

paste·board /ˈpeɪstbɔːd; *NAmE* -bɔːrd/ *noun* [U] a type of thin board made by sticking sheets of paper together

pas·tel /ˈpæstl; *NAmE* pæˈstel/ *noun* **1** [U] soft coloured CHALK, used for drawing pictures: *drawings in pastel* **2 pastels** [pl.] small sticks of CHALK: *a box of pastels* **3** [C] a picture drawn with pastels ➲ COLLOCATIONS at ART **4** [C] a pale delicate colour: *The whole house was painted in soft pastels.*

pas·tern /ˈpæstən; *NAmE* -tərn/ *noun* (*anatomy*) the part of a horse's foot between the FETLOCK and the HOOF

pas·teur·ize (*BrE* also **-ise**) /ˈpɑːstʃəraɪz; *NAmE* ˈpæs-/ *verb* **~ sth** to heat a liquid, especially milk, to a particular temperature and then cool it, in order to kill harmful bacteria ▸ **pas·teur·iza·tion**, **-isa·tion** /ˌpɑːstʃəraɪˈzeɪʃn; *NAmE* ˌpæstʃərəˈzeɪʃn/ *noun* [U]

pas·tiche /pæˈstiːʃ/ *noun* **1** [C] a work of art, piece of writing, etc. that is created by deliberately copying the style of sb/sth else: *a pastiche of the classic detective story* **2** [C] a work of art, etc. that consists of a variety of different styles **3** [U] the art of creating a pastiche

pas·tille /ˈpæstəl; *NAmE* pæˈstiːl/ *noun* (*especially BrE*) a small sweet/candy that you suck, especially one that is flavoured with fruit or that contains medicine for a sore throat: *fruit pastilles* ◇ *throat pastilles*

pas·time /ˈpɑːstaɪm; *NAmE* ˈpæs-/ *noun* something that you enjoy doing when you are not working SYN **hobby** ➲ SYNONYMS at INTEREST

past·ing /ˈpeɪstɪŋ/ *noun* [sing.] (*especially BrE*) **1** a heavy defeat in a game or competition **2** an instance of being hit very hard as a punishment SYN **thrashing**

pas·tis /pæˈstiːs/ *noun* [U, C] (*pl.* **pas·tis**) (from *French*) a strong alcoholic drink usually drunk before a meal, that has the flavour of ANISEED

ˌ**past ˈmaster** *noun* **~ (at sth/at doing sth)** a person who is very good at sth because they have a lot of experience in it SYN **expert**: *She's a past master at getting what she wants.*

pas·tor /ˈpɑːstə(r); *NAmE* ˈpæs-/ *noun* a minister in charge of a Christian church or group, especially in some NONCONFORMIST churches

pas·tor·al /ˈpɑːstərəl; *NAmE* ˈpæs-/ *adj.* **1** relating to the work of a priest or teacher in giving help and advice on personal matters, not just those connected with religion or education: *pastoral care* **2** showing country life or the countryside, especially in a romantic way: *a pastoral scene/poem/symphony* **3** relating to the farming of animals: *agricultural and pastoral practices*

P

pas·tor·al·ism /ˈpɑːstərəlɪzəm; *NAmE* ˈpæs-/ *noun* [U] a way of keeping animals such as CATTLE, sheep, etc. that involves moving them from place to place to find water and food ▶ **pas·tor·al·ist** *noun, adj.*

ˌpast ˈparticiple *noun* (*grammar*) the form of a verb that in English ends in *-ed*, *-en*, etc. and is used with the verb *have* to form PERFECT tenses such as *I have eaten*, with the verb *be* to form passive sentences such as *It was destroyed*, or sometimes as an adjective as in *an upset stomach* ➲ compare PRESENT PARTICIPLE

the ˌpast ˈperfect (also **the ˌpast ˌperfect ˈtense**, **the plu·per·fect**) *noun* [sing.] (*grammar*) the form of a verb that expresses an action completed before a particular point in the past, formed in English with *had* and the past participle

pas·trami /pæˈstrɑːmi/ *noun* [U] cold spicy smoked beef

pas·try /ˈpeɪstri/ *noun* (*pl.* **-ies**) **1** [U] a mixture of flour, fat and water or milk that is rolled out flat and baked as a base or covering for PIES, etc. ➲ see also CHOUX PASTRY, FILO PASTRY, PUFF PASTRY, SHORTCRUST PASTRY **2** [C] a small cake made using pastry ➲ see also DANISH PASTRY

ˈpastry cook *noun* a professional cook whose main job is to make pastry, cakes, etc.

the ˌpast ˈtense (also **the past**) *noun* [sing.] (*grammar*) the form of a verb used to describe actions in the past: *The past tense of 'take' is 'took'.*

pas·tur·age /ˈpɑːstʃərɪdʒ; *NAmE* ˈpæs-/ *noun* [U] (*technical*) land covered with grass for animals to eat

pas·ture /ˈpɑːstʃə(r); *NAmE* ˈpæs-/ *noun, verb*
■ *noun* **1** [U, C] land covered with grass that is suitable for feeding animals on: *an area of permanent/rough/rich pasture* ◇ *high mountain pastures* ◇ *The cattle were put* **out to pasture.** ➲ VISUAL VOCAB page V2 **2 pastures** [pl.] the circumstances of your life, work, etc: *I felt we were off to* **greener pastures** (= a better way of life). ◇ (*BrE*) *She decided it was time to move on to* **pastures new** (= a new job, place to live, etc.).
■ *verb* **~ sth** to put animals in a field to feed on grass

pas·ture·land /ˈpɑːstʃəlænd; *NAmE* ˈpæstʃərl-/ *noun* [U, pl.] (also **pas·tur·age** [U]) land where animals can feed on grass

pasty¹ /ˈpæsti/ *noun* (*pl.* **-ies**) (*BrE*) a small PIE containing meat and vegetables ➲ see also CORNISH PASTY

pasty² /ˈpeɪsti/ *adj.* pale and not looking healthy SYN **pallid**: *a* **pasty face/complexion**

pat /pæt/ *verb, noun, adj., adv.*
■ *verb* (-tt-) to touch sb/sth gently several times with your hand flat, especially as a sign of affection: **~ sth** *She patted the dog on the head.* ◇ *He patted his sister's hand consolingly.* ◇ **~ sth + adj.** *Pat your face dry with a soft towel.*
IDM **pat sb/yourself on the ˈback** (*informal*) to praise sb or yourself for doing sth well
■ *noun* **1** [usually sing.] a gentle friendly touch with your open hand or with a flat object: *a pat on the head* ◇ *He gave her knee an affectionate pat.* **2 ~ of butter** a small, soft, flat lump of butter ➲ see also COWPAT
IDM **a ˌpat on the ˈback (for sth/for doing sth)** (*informal*) praise or approval for sth that you have done well: *He deserves a pat on the back for all his hard work.*
■ *adj.* (usually *disapproving*) (of an answer, a comment, etc.) too quick, easy or simple; not seeming natural or realistic SYN **glib**: *The ending of the novel is a little too pat to be convincing.* ◇ *There are no pat answers to these questions.*
■ *adv.*
IDM **have/know sth off ˈpat** (*BrE*) (*NAmE* **have/know sth down ˈpat**) to know sth perfectly so that you can repeat it at any time without having to think about it: *He had all the answers off pat.* **stand ˈpat** (*especially NAmE*) to refuse to change your mind about a decision you have made or an opinion you have

patch /pætʃ/ *noun, verb*
■ *noun*
▸ SMALL AREA **1** a small area of sth, especially one which is different from the area around it: *a black dog with a white patch on its back* ◇ *a bald patch on the top of his head* ◇ *damp patches on the wall* ◇ *patches of dense fog*
▸ PIECE OF MATERIAL **2** a small piece of material that is used to cover a hole in sth or to make a weak area stronger, or as decoration: *I sewed patches on the knees of my jeans.* **3** a piece of material that you wear over an eye, usually because the eye is damaged: *He had a black patch over one eye.* ➲ see also EYEPATCH **4** (*NAmE*) (*BrE* **badge**) a piece of material that you sew onto clothes as part of a uniform **5** a piece of material that people can wear on their skin to help them to stop smoking: *nicotine patches*
▸ PIECE/AREA OF LAND **6** a small piece of land, especially one used for growing vegetables or fruit: *a vegetable patch* ➲ VISUAL VOCAB page V16 **7** (*BrE, informal*) an area that sb works in, knows well or comes from: *He knows every house in his patch.* ◇ *She has had a lot of success in her* **home patch.**
▸ DIFFICULT TIME **8** (*informal, especially BrE*) a period of time of the type mentioned, usually a difficult or unhappy one: *to go through a* **bad/difficult/sticky patch** ➲ see also PURPLE PATCH
▸ IN COMPUTING **9** a small piece of code (= instructions that a computer can understand) which can be added to a computer program to improve it or to correct a fault: *Follow the instructions below to download and install the patch.*
IDM **be not a ˈpatch on sb/sth** (*informal, especially BrE*) to be much less good, attractive, etc. than sb/sth else

Synonyms

patch

dot • mark • spot

These are all words for a small part on a surface that is a different colour from the rest.

patch an area of sth, especially one which is different from the area around it: *a white dog with a black patch on its head* ◇ *patches of dense fog*

dot a small round mark on sth, especially one that is printed: *The letters 'i' and 'j' have dots over them.* ◇ *The island is a small green dot on the map.*

mark a noticeable area of colour on the body of a person or animal: *The horse had a white mark on its head.*

spot a small round area that is a different colour or feels different from the surface it is on: *Which has spots, a leopard or a tiger?*

PATTERNS
- a patch/dot/mark/spot **on** sth
- **with** patches/dots/marks/spots
- a **blue/black/red, etc.** patch/dot/mark/spot

■ *verb* **~ sth (with sth)** to cover a hole or a worn place, especially in clothes, with a piece of cloth or other material SYN **mend**: *patched jeans* ◇ *to patch a hole in the roof*
PHR V **ˌpatch sb/sth ˈthrough (to sb/sth)** to connect telephone or electronic equipment temporarily: *She was patched through to London on the satellite link.* **ˌpatch sth↔toˈgether** to make sth from several different parts, especially in a quick careless way: *They hope to be able to patch together a temporary settlement.* **ˌpatch sth/sb↔ˈup** (rather *informal*) **1** to repair sth, especially in a temporary way by adding a new piece of material or a patch: *Just to patch the boat up will cost £10 000.* **2** to treat sb's injuries, especially quickly or temporarily: *The doctor will soon patch you up.* **3** to try to stop arguing with sb and be friends again: *They've managed to patch up their differences.* ◇ *Have you tried* **patching things up** *with her?* **4** to agree on sth, especially after long discussions and even though the agreement is not exactly what everyone wants: *They managed to patch up a deal.*

patch·ouli /ˈpætʃʊli; pəˈtʃuːli/ *noun* [U] a PERFUME made with oil from the leaves of a SE Asian bush

patch·work /ˈpætʃwɜːk; *NAmE* -wɜːrk/ *noun* **1** [U] a type of NEEDLEWORK in which small pieces of cloth of different colours or designs are sewn together: *a patchwork quilt*

➲ compare CRAZY QUILT ➲ VISUAL VOCAB page V20 **2** [sing.] a thing that is made up of many different pieces or parts: *a patchwork of different styles and cultures* ◇ *From the plane, the landscape was just a patchwork of fields.*

patchy /ˈpætʃi/ *adj.* **1** existing or happening in some places and not others SYN **uneven**: *patchy fog* ◇ *The grass was dry and patchy.* **2** (*NAmE* also **spotty**) not complete; good in some parts, but not in others: *a patchy knowledge of Spanish* ◇ *It was a patchy performance.* ▶ **patch·ily** *adv.* **patchi·ness** *noun* [U]

pate /peɪt/ *noun* (*old use* or *humorous*) the top part of the head, especially when there is no hair on it: *The sun beat down on his bald pate.*

pâté /ˈpæteɪ; *NAmE* pɑːˈteɪ/ *noun* [U] a soft mixture of very finely chopped meat or fish, served cold and used for spreading on bread, etc.

pâté de foie gras /ˌpæteɪ də fwʌ ˈɡrɑː; *NAmE* pɑːˌteɪ/ (also ˌ**foie** ˈ**gras**) *noun* [U] (from *French*) an expensive type of pâté made from the LIVER of a GOOSE

pa·tel·la /pəˈtelə/ *noun* (*pl.* **pa·tel·lae** /-liː/) (*anatomy*) the KNEECAP ➲ VISUAL VOCAB page V48

pa·tent *noun, adj., verb*

■ ***noun*** /ˈpætnt; *BrE* also ˈpeɪtnt/ [C, U] an official right to be the only person to make, use or sell a product or an invention; a document that proves this: *to **apply for/obtain a patent** on an invention* ◇ *The device was protected **by patent**.*

■ ***adj.*** /ˈpeɪtnt; *NAmE* also ˈpætnt/ [only before noun] **1** connected with a patent: *patent applications/laws* ◇ *the US Patent Office* **2** (of a product) made or sold by a particular company: *patent medicines* **3** (*formal*) used to emphasize that sth bad is very clear and obvious SYN **blatant**: *It was a patent lie.*

■ ***verb*** /ˈpætnt; *BrE* also ˈpeɪtnt/ **~ sth** to obtain a patent for an invention or a process

pa·tent·ee /ˌpætənˈtiː; *BrE* also ˌpeɪt-/ *noun* a person or an organization that holds the patent for sth

patent leather /ˌpeɪtnt ˈleðə(r); *NAmE* usually ˈpætnt/ *noun* [U] a type of leather with a hard shiny surface, used especially for making shoes and bags

pa·tent·ly /ˈpeɪtəntli; ˈpætəntli; *NAmE* ˈpæt-/ *adv.* (*formal*) without doubt SYN **clearly**: *Her explanation was patently ridiculous.* ◇ *It was **patently obvious** that she was lying.*

pater /ˈpeɪtə(r)/ *noun* (*old-fashioned, BrE*) father

pater·famil·ias /ˌpeɪtəfəˈmɪliæs; *NAmE* ˌpætərf-/ *noun* [sing.] (*formal* or *humorous*) the man who is the head of a family

pa·ter·nal /pəˈtɜːnl; *NAmE* -ˈtɜːrnl/ *adj.* **1** connected with being a father; typical of a kind father: *paternal love* ◇ *He gave me a piece of paternal advice.* **2** related through the father's side of the family: *my paternal grandmother* (= my father's mother) ▶ **pa·ter·nal·ly** *adv.*: *He smiled paternally at them.* ➲ compare MATERNAL

pa·ter·nal·ism /pəˈtɜːnəlɪzəm; *NAmE* -ˈtɜːrn-/ *noun* [U] (sometimes *disapproving*) the system in which a government or an employer protects the people who are governed or employed by providing them with what they need, but does not give them any responsibility or freedom of choice ▶ **pa·ter·nal·is·tic** /pəˌtɜːnəˈlɪstɪk; *NAmE* -ˌtɜːrn-/ (also **pa·ter·nal·ist**) *adj.*: *a paternalistic employer*

pa·ter·nity /pəˈtɜːnəti; *NAmE* -ˈtɜːrn-/ *noun* [U] the fact of being the father of a child: *He refused to admit paternity of the child.* ➲ compare MATERNITY

paˈternity leave *noun* [U] time that the father of a new baby is allowed to have away from work ➲ COLLOCATIONS at CHILD ➲ see also MATERNITY LEAVE, PARENTAL LEAVE

paˈternity suit (also **paˈternity case**) *noun* a court case that is intended to prove who a child's father is, especially so that he can be ordered to give the child financial support

path 🔑 /pɑːθ; *NAmE* pæθ/ (*pl.* **paths** /pɑːðz; *NAmE* pæðz/) (also **path·way**) *noun*
1 🔑 a way or track that is built or is made by the action of people walking: *a concrete path* ◇ *the **garden path*** ◇ *Follow **the path** through the woods.* ◇ *to walk along a path* ◇ *The **path led** up a steep hill.* ◇ *a **coastal path*** ➲ see also FOOTPATH **2** 🔑 [usually sing.] a line along which sb/sth moves; the space in front of sb/sth as they move SYN **way**: *He threw himself **into the path of** an oncoming vehicle.* ◇ *The avalanche forced its way down the mountain, crushing everything **in its path**.* ◇ *Three men blocked her path.* ➲ see also FLIGHT PATH **3** 🔑 a plan of action or a way of achieving sth: *a career path* ◇ *the path to success* IDM see BEAT *v.*, CROSS *v.*, LEAD[1] *v.*, PRIMROSE, SMOOTH *v.*

path·et·ic /pəˈθetɪk/ *adj.* **1** making you feel pity or sadness SYN **pitiful**: *a pathetic and lonely old man* ◇ *The starving children were a pathetic sight.* **2** (*informal, disapproving*) weak and not successful SYN **feeble**: *a pathetic excuse* ◇ *She made a pathetic attempt to smile.* ◇ *You're pathetic!* ▶ **path·et·ic·al·ly** /-kli/ *adv.*: *He cried pathetically.* ◇ *a pathetically shy woman*

paˌthetic ˈfallacy *noun* [U, sing.] (in art and literature) the act of describing animals and things as having human feelings

path·find·er /ˈpɑːθfaɪndə(r); *NAmE* ˈpæθ-/ *noun* **1** a person, group or thing that goes before others and shows the way over unknown land **2** a person, group or thing that finds a new way of doing sth SYN **trailblazer**: *The company is a pathfinder in computer technology.*

patho- /ˈpæθəʊ; *NAmE* -θoʊ/ *combining form* (in nouns, adjectives and adverbs) connected with disease: *pathogenesis* (= the development of a disease) ◇ *pathophysiology*

patho·gen /ˈpæθədʒən/ *noun* (*technical*) a thing that causes disease ▶ **patho·gen·ic** /-ˈdʒenɪk/ *adj.*

patho·gen·esis /ˌpæθəˈdʒenɪsɪs/ *noun* (*medical*) the way in which a disease develops

patho·logic·al /ˌpæθəˈlɒdʒɪkl; *NAmE* -ˈlɑːdʒ-/ *adj.* **1** not reasonable or sensible; impossible to control: *pathological fear/hatred/violence* ◇ *a **pathological liar*** (= a person who cannot stop telling lies) **2** caused by, or connected with, disease or illness: *pathological depression* **3** (*technical*) connected with PATHOLOGY ▶ **patho·logic·al·ly** /-kli/ *adv.*: *pathologically jealous*

path·olo·gist /pəˈθɒlədʒɪst; *NAmE* -ˈθɑːl-/ *noun* a doctor who studies pathology and examines dead bodies to find out the cause of death ➲ compare MEDICAL EXAMINER

path·ology /pəˈθɒlədʒi; *NAmE* -ˈθɑːl-/ *noun* **1** [U] (*medical*) the scientific study of diseases **2** [C] an aspect of sb's behaviour that is extreme and unreasonable and that they cannot control

pathos /ˈpeɪθɒs; *NAmE* -θɑːs; -θɔːs/ *noun* [U] (in writing, speech and plays) the power of a performance, description, etc. to produce feelings of sadness and sympathy

path·way /ˈpɑːθweɪ; *NAmE* ˈpæθ-/ *noun* = PATH

pa·tience 🔑 /ˈpeɪʃns/ *noun* [U]
1 🔑 **~ (with sb/sth)** the ability to stay calm and accept a delay or sth annoying without complaining: *She **has little patience with*** (= will not accept or consider) *such views.* ◇ *People have **lost patience with*** (= have become annoyed about) *the slow pace of reform.* ◇ *I have run out of patience with her.* ◇ *My patience is wearing thin.* ◇ *Teaching children with special needs requires patience and understanding.* **2** 🔑 the ability to spend a lot of time doing sth difficult that needs a lot of attention and effort: *It takes time and patience to photograph wildlife.* ◇ *I don't **have the patience to** do jigsaw puzzles.* **3** (*BrE*) (*NAmE* **soli·taire**) a card game for only one player IDM see JOB, TRY *v.*

pa·tient 🔑 /ˈpeɪʃnt/ *noun, adj.*

■ ***noun*** **1** 🔑 a person who is receiving medical treatment, especially in a hospital: *cancer patients* **2** 🔑 a person who receives treatment from a particular doctor, dentist, etc: *He's one of Dr Shaw's patients.* **3** (*grammar*) the person or thing that is affected by the action of the verb. In the sentence 'I started the car', the patient is *car*. ➲ compare AGENT

■ ***adj.*** 🔑 **~ (with sb/sth)** able to wait for a long time or accept annoying behaviour or difficulties without becoming

P

angry: *She's very patient with young children.* ◇ *You'll just have to be patient and wait till I'm finished.* ▶ **pa·tient·ly** *adv.*: *She sat patiently waiting for her turn.*

pat·ina /ˈpætɪnə; *NAmE* pəˈtiːnə/ *noun* [usually sing.] **1** a green, black or brown layer that forms on the surface of some metals **2** a thin layer that forms on other materials; the shiny surface that develops on wood or leather when it is polished: (*figurative*) *He looked relaxed and elegant and had the patina of success.*

pat·in·ation /ˌpætɪˈneɪʃn/ *noun* [U, C] (*technical*) a shiny layer on the surface of metal, wood, etc; the process of covering sth with a shiny layer

patio /ˈpætiəʊ; *NAmE* -oʊ/ *noun* (*pl.* **-os**) a flat hard area outside, and usually behind, a house where people can sit: *Let's have lunch out* ***on the patio.*** ➲ VISUAL VOCAB page V16

ˌpatio ˈdoor *noun* [usually pl.] (*especially BrE*) a large glass sliding door that leads to a garden or BALCONY

pa·tis·serie /pəˈtiːsəri/ *noun* (from *French*) **1** [C] a shop/store that sells cakes, etc. **2** [U] (also **pa·tis·series** [pl.]) (*formal*) cakes

Pat Malone /ˌpæt məˈləʊn; *NAmE* -loʊn/ *noun*

IDM **on your Pat Maˈlone** (*AustralE, NZE, informal*) alone; without anybody else

pat·ois /ˈpætwɑː/ *noun* (*pl.* **pat·ois** /-twɑːz/) a form of a language, spoken by people in a particular area, that is different from the standard language of the country

patri·arch /ˈpeɪtriɑːk; *NAmE* -ɑːrk/ *noun* **1** the male head of a family or community ➲ compare MATRIARCH **2** an old man that people have a lot of respect for **3 Patri·arch** the title of a most senior BISHOP (= a senior priest) in the Orthodox or Roman Catholic Church

patri·arch·al /ˌpeɪtriˈɑːkl; *NAmE* -ˈɑːrkl/ *adj.* **1** ruled or controlled by men; giving power and importance only to men: *a patriarchal society* **2** connected with a patriarch ➲ compare MATRIARCHAL

patri·arch·ate /ˈpeɪtriɑːkət; *NAmE* -ɑːrk-/ *noun* (*formal*) **1** the title, position or period of office of a patriarch (3) **2** the area governed by a patriarch (3)

patri·archy /ˈpeɪtriɑːki; *NAmE* -ɑːrki/ *noun* [C, U] (*pl.* **-ies**) a society, system or country that is ruled or controlled by men ➲ compare MATRIARCHY

pa·tri·cian /pəˈtrɪʃn/ *adj.* (*formal*) connected with or typical of the highest social class SYN **aristocratic** ▶ **pa·tri·cian** *noun* ➲ compare PLEBEIAN

patri·cide /ˈpætrɪsaɪd/ *noun* [U, C] (*formal*) the crime of killing your father; a person who is guilty of this crime ➲ compare FRATRICIDE, MATRICIDE, PARRICIDE

patri·lin·eal /ˌpætrɪˈlɪniəl/ *adj.* (*formal*) used to describe the relationship between father and child that continues in a family with each generation, or sth that is based on this relationship: *In that society, inheritance of land is patrilineal* (= the children get the land that their father owned). ➲ compare MATRILINEAL

patri·mony /ˈpætrɪməni; *NAmE* -moʊni/ *noun* [sing.] (*formal*) **1** property that is given to sb when their father dies SYN **inheritance** **2** the works of art and TREASURES of a nation, church, etc. SYN **heritage**

pat·riot /ˈpeɪtriət; *BrE* also ˈpæt-/ *noun* a person who loves their country and who is ready to defend it against an enemy

pat·ri·ot·ic /ˌpeɪtriˈɒtɪk; ˌpæt-; *NAmE* ˌpeɪtriˈɑːtɪk/ *adj.* having or expressing a great love of your country: *a patriotic man who served his country well* ◇ *patriotic songs* ▶ **pat·ri·ot·ic·al·ly** *adv.* /-kli/

pat·ri·ot·ism /ˈpeɪtriətɪzəm; *BrE* also ˈpæt-/ *noun* [U] love of your country and willingness to defend it

pa·trol /pəˈtrəʊl; *NAmE* pəˈtroʊl/ *verb, noun*

■ ***verb*** (**-ll-**) **1** [T, I] **~ (sth)** to go around an area or a building at regular times to check that it is safe and that there is no trouble: *Troops patrolled the border day and night.* ◇ *Guards can be seen patrolling everywhere.* **2** [T] **~ sth** to drive or walk around a particular area, especially in a threatening way: *Gangs of youths patrol the streets at night.*

■ ***noun*** **1** [C, U] the act of going to different parts of a building, an area, etc. to make sure that there is no trouble or crime: *Security guards make regular patrols at night.* ◇ *a police car* ***on patrol*** **2** [C] a group of soldiers, vehicles, etc. that patrol an area: *a naval/police patrol* ◇ *a patrol car/boat* **3** [C] a group of about six BOY SCOUTS or GIRL GUIDES/SCOUTS that forms part of a larger group

pa·trol·man /pəˈtrəʊlmən; *NAmE* -ˈtroʊ-/, **pa·trol·woman** /pəˈtrəʊlwʊmən; *NAmE* -ˈtroʊ-/ *noun* (*pl.* **-men** /-mən/, **-women** /-wɪmɪn/) **1** (in the US) a police officer who walks or drives around an area to make sure that there is no trouble or crime: *Patrolman Don Lilly* **2** (in Britain) an official of an association for car owners who goes to give help to drivers who have a problem with their cars

paˈtrol wagon (also *informal* **ˈpaddy wagon**) (both *NAmE*) *noun* a police van for transporting prisoners in

pat·ron /ˈpeɪtrən/ *noun* **1** a person who gives money and support to artists and writers: *Frederick the Great was the patron of many artists.* **2** a famous person who supports an organization such as a charity and whose name is used in the advertisements, etc. for the organization **3** (*formal*) a person who uses a particular shop/store, restaurant, etc: *Patrons are requested not to smoke.*

pat·ron·age /ˈpætrənɪdʒ; ˈpeɪt-/ *noun* [U] **1** the support, especially financial, that is given to a person or an organization by a patron: *Patronage of the arts comes from businesses and private individuals.* **2** the system by which an important person gives help or a job to sb in return for their support **3** (*especially NAmE*) the support that a person gives a shop/store, restaurant, etc. by spending money there

pat·ron·ess /ˌpeɪtrənˈes/ *noun* a female PATRON (1) ➲ note at GENDER

pat·ron·ize (*BrE* also **-ise**) /ˈpætrənaɪz; *NAmE* ˈpeɪt-/ *verb* **1** [T, I] **~ (sb)** (*disapproving*) to treat sb in a way that seems friendly, but which shows that you think that they are not very intelligent, experienced, etc: *Some television programmes tend to patronize children.* **2** [T] **~ sth** (*formal*) to be a regular customer of a shop/store, restaurant, etc: *The club is patronized by students and locals alike.* **3** [T] **~ sb/sth** to help a particular person, organization or activity by giving them money: *She patronizes many contemporary British artists.*

pat·ron·iz·ing (*BrE* also **-is·ing**) /ˈpætrənaɪzɪŋ; *NAmE* ˈpeɪtrənaɪzɪŋ/ *adj.* (*disapproving*) showing that you feel better, or more intelligent than sb else SYN **superior**: *a patronizing smile* ◇ *I was only trying to explain; I didn't want to sound patronizing.* ▶ **pat·ron·iz·ing·ly, -is·ing·ly** *adv.*: *He patted her hand patronizingly.*

ˌpatron ˈsaint *noun* a Christian SAINT who is believed to protect a particular place or group of people: *St Patrick, Ireland's patron saint* ◇ *St Christopher, patron saint of travellers*

patro·nym·ic /ˌpætrəˈnɪmɪk/ *noun* (*technical*) a name formed from the name of your father or a male ANCESTOR, especially by adding sth to the beginning or end of their name ➲ compare MATRONYMIC

patsy /ˈpætsi/ *noun* (*pl.* **-ies**) (*informal, especially NAmE*) a weak person who is easily cheated or tricked, or who is forced to take the blame for sth that sb else has done wrong

pat·ter /ˈpætə(r)/ *noun, verb*

■ ***noun*** **1** [sing.] the sound that is made by sth repeatedly hitting a surface quickly and lightly: *the* ***patter of feet/footsteps*** ◇ *the patter of rain on the roof* **2** [U, sing.] fast continuous talk by sb who is trying to sell you sth or entertain you: *sales patter*

IDM **the patter of tiny feet** (*informal* or *humorous*) a way of referring to children when sb wants, or is going to have, a baby: *We can't wait to hear the patter of tiny feet.*

■ ***verb*** **1** [I] **+ adv./prep.** to make quick, light sounds as a surface is being hit several times: *Rain pattered against the window.* **2** [I] **+ adv./prep.** to walk with light steps in a particular direction: *I heard her feet pattering along the corridor.*

pat·tern 0→ /ˈpætn; *NAmE* -tərn/ *noun, verb*

■ ***noun* 1** 0→ the regular way in which sth happens or is done: ***changing patterns*** *of behaviour* ◇ *an irregular sleeping pattern* ◇ *The murders all seem to* ***follow a*** (***similar***) ***pattern*** (= happen in the same way). **2** 0→ [usually sing.] an excellent example to copy: *This system* ***sets the pattern*** *for others to follow.* **3** 0→ a regular arrangement of lines, shapes, colours, etc. as a design on material, carpets, etc: *a pattern of diamonds and squares* ◇ *a shirt with a floral pattern* **4** 0→ a design, set of instructions or shape to cut around that you use in order to make sth: *a knitting pattern* ◇ *She bought a dress pattern and some material.* **5** a small piece of material, paper, etc. that helps you choose the design of sth SYN **sample**: *wallpaper patterns*

■ ***verb* 1 ~ sth** to form a regular arrangement of lines or shapes on sth: *Frost patterned the window.* ◇ *a landscape patterned by vineyards* **2 ~ sth** (*technical*) to cause a particular type of behaviour to develop: *Adult behaviour is often patterned by childhood experiences.*

PHR V **ˈpattern sth on sth** (*BrE*) (*NAmE* **ˈpattern sth after sth**) [usually passive] to use sth as a model for sth; to copy sth: *a new approach patterned on Japanese ideas*

pat·terned /ˈpætənd; *NAmE* -tərnd/ *adj.* decorated with a pattern: *patterned wallpaper* ◇ **~ with sth** *cups patterned with yellow flowers* ➲ VISUAL VOCAB page V50

pat·tern·ing /ˈpætənɪŋ; *NAmE* -tərn-/ *noun* [U] **1** (*technical*) the forming of fixed ways of behaving by copying or repeating sth: *cultural patterning* ◇ *the patterning of husband-wife roles* **2** the arrangement of shapes or colours to make patterns: *a red fish with black patterning*

patty /ˈpæti/ *noun* (*pl.* -ies) (*especially NAmE*) finely chopped meat, fish, etc. formed into a small round flat shape: *a hamburger patty*

pau·city /ˈpɔːsəti/ *noun* [sing.] **~** (**of sth**) (*formal*) a small amount of sth; less than enough of sth: *a paucity of information*

paunch /pɔːntʃ/ *noun* a fat stomach on a man ▸ **paunchy** *adj.*

pau·per /ˈpɔːpə(r)/ *noun* (*old use*) a very poor person

pause 0→ /pɔːz/ *verb, noun*

■ ***verb* 1** 0→ [I] to stop talking or doing sth for a short time before continuing: *Anita paused for a moment, then said: 'All right'.* ◇ *The woman spoke almost without* ***pausing for breath*** (= very quickly). ◇ *I paused at the door and looked back.* ◇ ***Pausing only to*** *pull on a sweater, he ran out of the house.* **2** 0→ [T] **~ sth** to stop a tape, CD, etc. for a short time using the pause button: *She paused the DVD and went to answer the phone.*

■ ***noun* 1** 0→ [C] **~** (**in sth**) a period of time during which sb stops talking or stops what they are doing: *There was a long pause before she answered.* ◇ *David waited for a pause in the conversation so he could ask his question.* ◇ *After a brief pause, they continued climbing.* ◇ *The rain fell* ***without pause.*** **2** [C] (*especially BrE*) (also **fer·mata** especially in *NAmE*) (*music*) a sign (⌒) over a note or a REST to show that it should be longer than usual **3** [U] (also **ˈpause button**) a control that allows you to stop a TAPE RECORDER, CD player, etc. for a short time: *Press pause to stop the tape.*

IDM **give** (**sb**) **ˈpause** (*BrE* also **give** (**sb**) **pause for ˈthought**) (*formal*) to make sb think seriously about sth or hesitate before doing sth ➲ more at PREGNANT

pav·ane /pəˈvæn; -ˈvɑːn/ (also **pavan** /ˈpævən/) *noun* a slow dance popular in the 16th and 17th centuries; a piece of music for this dance

pave /peɪv/ *verb* [often passive] **~ sth** (**with sth**) to cover a surface with flat stones or bricks: *a paved area near the back door*

IDM **ˌpave the ˈway** (**for sb/sth**) to create a situation in which sb will be able to do sth or sth can happen: *This decision paved the way for changes in employment rights for women.* ➲ more at ROAD, STREET

pave·ment /ˈpeɪvmənt/ *noun* **1** [C] (*BrE*) (*NAmE* **sidewalk**) a flat part at the side of a road for people to walk on: *a pavement cafe* ➲ VISUAL VOCAB page V3 **2** [C, U] (*BrE*) any area of flat stones on the ground: *a mosaic pavement* **3** [U] (*NAmE*) the surface of a road: *Two cars skidded on the icy pavement.*

ˈpavement artist (*BrE*) (*NAmE* **ˈsidewalk artist**) *noun* an artist who draws pictures in CHALK on the PAVEMENT/SIDEWALK, hoping to get money from people who pass

pa·vil·ion /pəˈvɪliən/ *noun* **1** a temporary building used at public events and exhibitions: *the US pavilion at the Trade Fair* **2** (*BrE*) a building next to a sports ground, used by players and people watching the game: *a cricket pavilion* **3** (*NAmE*) a large building used for sports or entertainment: *the Pauley Pavilion, home of the university's basketball team* **4** a building that is meant to be more beautiful than useful, built as a shelter in a park or used for concerts and dances: *his first show at the Winter Gardens Pavilion, Blackpool*

pav·ing /ˈpeɪvɪŋ/ *noun* [U] **1** a surface of flat stones or material like stone on the ground: *Weeds grew through the cracks in the paving.* ➲ see also CRAZY PAVING **2** the stones or material that are used to make a flat surface on the ground: *We'll use concrete paving.*

ˈpaving stone *noun* a flat, usually square, piece of stone that is used to make a hard surface for walking on SYN **flagstone**

pav·lova /pævˈləʊvə; *NAmE* -ˈloʊ-/ *noun* a cold DESSERT (= sweet dish) made of MERINGUE, cream and fruit

Pav·lov·ian /pævˈləʊviən; *NAmE* -ˈloʊ-/ *adj.* (of an animal's or human's reaction) happening in response to a particular STIMULUS: *Her yawn was a Pavlovian response to my yawn.* ORIGIN From the name of the Russian scientist, I P Pavlov, who carried out experiments on dogs, showing how they could be conditioned to react to certain stimuli.

paw /pɔː/ *noun, verb*

■ ***noun* 1** the foot of an animal that has CLAWS or nails ➲ VISUAL VOCAB page V10 **2** (*informal*) a person's hand: *Take your filthy paws off me!*

■ ***verb* 1** [I, T] (of an animal) to scratch or touch sth repeatedly with a paw: **~ at sth** *The dog pawed at my sleeve.* ◇ **~ sth** *The stallion pawed the ground impatiently.* **2** [T] **~ sb** (sometimes *humorous*) to touch sb in a rough sexual way that they find offensive

pawn /pɔːn/ *noun, verb*

■ ***noun* 1** a CHESS piece of the smallest size and least value. Each player has eight pawns at the start of a game. ➲ VISUAL VOCAB page V33 **2** a person or group whose actions are controlled by more powerful people: *The hostages are being used as political pawns.*

IDM **in pawn** if sth is **in pawn**, it has been pawned: *All her jewellery was in pawn.*

■ ***verb* ~ sth** to leave an object with a pawnbroker in exchange for money. The object is returned to the owner if he or she pays back the money within an agreed period of time. If not, it can be sold.

pawn·broker /ˈpɔːnbrəʊkə(r); *NAmE* -broʊ-/ *noun* a person who lends money in exchange for articles left with them. If the money is not paid back by a particular time, the pawnbroker can sell the article.

Paw·nee /ˈpɔːniː/ *noun* (*pl.* **Paw·nee** or **Paw·nees**) a member of a Native American people, many of whom live in the US state of Oklahoma

pawn·shop /ˈpɔːnʃɒp; *NAmE* -ʃɑːp/ *noun* a pawnbroker's shop/store

paw·paw /ˈpɔːpɔː/ *noun* (*BrE*) = PAPAYA

pay 0→ /peɪ/ *verb, noun*

■ ***verb*** (**paid, paid** /peɪd/) **1** 0→ [I, T] to give sb money for work, goods, services, etc: **~** (**for sth**) *I'll pay for the tickets.* ◇ *Are you* ***paying in cash*** *or* ***by credit card?*** ◇ *My company* ***pays well*** (= pays high salaries). ◇ **~ for sb to do sth** *Her parents paid for her to go to Canada.* ◇ **~ sth** *to* ***pay cash*** ◇ **~ sth for sth** *She pays £200 a week for this apartment.* ◇ **~ sb** (**for sth**) *Would you mind paying the taxi driver?* ◇ **~ sb sth** *He still hasn't* ***paid*** *me* ***the money*** *he owes me.* ◇ *I'm paid $100 a day.* ◇ **~ sb/sth to do sth** *I don't pay you to*

P

sit around all day doing nothing! ➲ see also LOW-PAID, PRE-PAY, WELL PAID **2** ⊶ [T] to give sb money that you owe them: **~ sth** *to pay a bill/debt/fine/ransom, etc.* ◇ **~ sth to sb** *Membership fees should be paid to the secretary.* ◇ **~ sb sth** *Have you paid him the rent yet?* **3** ⊶ [I] (of a business, etc.) to produce a profit: *It's hard to make farming pay.* **4** ⊶ [I, T] to result in some advantage or profit for sb: *Crime doesn't pay.* ◇ **it pays to do sth** *It pays to keep up to date with your work.* ◇ **it pays sb to do sth** *It would probably pay you to hire an accountant.* **5** ⊶ [I] to suffer or be punished for your beliefs or actions: **~ (for sth)** *You'll pay for that remark!* ◇ **~ (with sth)** *Many people paid with their lives* (= they died). **6** ⊶ [T] used with some nouns to show that you are giving or doing the thing mentioned: **~ sth** *I didn't* ***pay attention*** *to what she was saying.* ◇ *The director* ***paid tribute to*** *all she had done for the charity.* ◇ *I'll* ***pay a call on*** (= visit) *my friends.* ◇ **~ sb sth** *I'll pay you a call when I'm in town.* ◇ *He's always* ***paying me compliments.***

IDM **the 'devil/'hell to pay** (*informal*) a lot of trouble: *There'll be hell to pay when he finds out.* **he who pays the piper calls the 'tune** (*saying*) the person who provides the money for sth can also control how it is spent **pay 'court to sb** (*old-fashioned*) to treat sb with great respect in order to gain favour with them **pay 'dividends** to produce great advantages or profits: *Exercising regularly will pay dividends in the end.* **ˌpay for it'self** (of a new system, sth you have bought, etc.) to save as much money as it cost: *The rail pass will pay for itself after about two trips.* **pay good 'money for sth** used to emphasize that sth cost(s) a lot of money, especially if the money is wasted: *I paid good money for this jacket, and now look at it—it's ruined!* **pay its 'way** (of a business, etc.) to make enough money to pay what it costs to keep it going: *The bridge is still not paying its way.* **pay the 'penalty (for sth/for doing sth) | pay a/the 'price (for sth/for doing sth)** to suffer because of bad luck, a mistake or sth you have done: *He looked terrible this morning. I think he's paying the penalty for all those late nights.* ◇ *They're now paying the price for past mistakes.* **pay your re'spects (to sb)** (*formal*) to visit sb or to send a message of good wishes as a sign of respect for them: *Many came to* ***pay their last respects*** (= by attending sb's funeral). **pay through the 'nose (for sth)** (*informal*) to pay too much money for sth **pay your 'way** to pay for everything yourself without having to rely on anyone else's money **you pays your ˌmoney and you takes your 'choice** (*informal, especially BrE*) used for saying that there is very little difference between two or more things that you can choose ➲ more at ARM *n.*, HEED *n.*, ROB

PHR V **ˌpay sb 'back (sth) | ˌpay sth↔'back (to sb)** ⊶ to return money that you borrowed from sb SYN **repay**: *I'll pay you back next week.* ◇ *You can pay back the loan over a period of three years.* ◇ *Did he ever pay you back that $100 he owes you?* **ˌpay sb 'back (for sth)** ⊶ to punish sb for making you or sb else suffer: *I'll pay him back for making me look like a fool in front of everyone.* ➲ related noun PAYBACK **ˌpay sth↔'down** (*NAmE*) to reduce an amount of money that you owe by paying some of it: *She used the money to pay down her mortgage.* **ˌpay sth↔'in | ˌpay sth 'into sth** to put money into a bank account: *I paid in a cheque this morning.* ◇ *I'd like to pay some money into my account.* **ˌpay 'off** (*informal*) (of a plan or an action, especially one that involves risk) to be successful and bring good results: *The gamble paid off.* **ˌpay sb↔'off 1** to pay sb what they have earned and tell them to leave their job: *The crew were paid off as soon as the ship docked.* **2** (*informal*) to give sb money to prevent them from doing sth or talking about sth illegal or dishonest that you have done: *All the witnesses had been paid off.* ➲ related noun PAY-OFF **ˌpay sth↔'off** to finish paying money owed for sth: *We paid off our mortgage after fifteen years.* **ˌpay sth↔'out 1** ⊶ to pay a large sum of money for sth: *I had to pay out £500 to get my car repaired.* ➲ related noun PAYOUT **2** to pass a length of rope through your hands **ˌpay 'up** ⊶ to pay all the money that you owe to sb, especially when you do not want to or when the payment is late: *I had a hard time getting him to pay up.*

■ ***noun*** ⊶ [U] the money that sb gets for doing regular work: *Her job is hard work, but the pay is good.* ◇ *a* ***pay increase*** ◇ (*BrE*) *a* ***pay rise*** ◇ (*NAmE*) *a* ***pay raise*** ◇ *a 3%* ***pay offer*** ◇ *holiday pay* ◇ *to make a* ***pay claim*** (= to officially ask for an increase in pay) ➲ SYNONYMS at INCOME ➲ see also SICK PAY

IDM **in the pay of sb/sth** (usually *disapproving*) working for sb or for an organization, often secretly

pay·able /ˈpeɪəbl/ *adj.* [not before noun] **1** that must be paid or can be paid: *A 10% deposit is payable in advance.* ◇ *The price is payable in monthly instalments.* **2** when a cheque, etc. is made **payable to** sb, their name is written on it and they can then pay it into their bank account

ˌpay and dis'play *noun* [U] (*BrE*) a system of car parking in which you buy a ticket from a machine for a period of time and put it in the window of the car

ˌpay as you 'earn *noun* [U] = PAYE ➲ compare WITHHOLDING TAX

ˌpay-as-you-'go *adj.* connected with a system of paying for a service just before you use it rather than paying for it later: *pay-as-you-go phones*

pay·back /ˈpeɪbæk/ *noun* [C, U] **1** the money that you receive back on money that you have invested (especially when this is equal to the amount that you invested to start with); the time that it takes to get your money back: *a 10-year payback* **2** the advantage or reward that sb receives for sth they have done; the act of paying sth back: *His victory was seen as payback for all the hard work he'd put in during training.* ◇ (*informal*) *It's* ***payback time!*** (= a person will have to suffer for what they have done)

'pay bed *noun* (in the UK) a bed for private patients that they pay to use in a free public hospital

'pay channel *noun* a television channel that you must pay for separately in order to watch it

'pay cheque (*BrE*) (*US* **pay·check** /ˈpeɪtʃek/) *noun* **1** the cheque that you are given when your wages are paid to you **2** (*especially NAmE*) a way of referring to the amount of money that you earn: *a huge paycheck*

pay·day /ˈpeɪdeɪ/ *noun* [U, C] the day on which you get your wages or salary: *Friday is payday.*

'pay dirt *noun* [U] (*especially NAmE*) earth that contains valuable minerals or metal such as gold

IDM **hit/strike 'pay dirt** (*informal*) to suddenly be in a successful situation, especially one that makes you rich

PAYE /ˌpiː eɪ waɪ ˈiː/ *abbr.* pay as you earn (a British system of paying income tax in which money is taken from your wages by your employer and paid to the government)

payee /ˌpeɪˈiː/ *noun* (*technical*) a person that money or a cheque is paid to

'pay envelope (*NAmE*) (*BrE* **'pay packet**, **'wage packet**) *noun* an envelope containing your wages; the amount a person earns

payer /ˈpeɪə(r)/ *noun* a person who pays or who has to pay for sth: *mortgage payers* ◇ *The company are not very good payers* (= they are slow to pay their bills, or they do not pay their employees well).

ˌpay-for-per'formance *adj.* [only before noun] (*NAmE*) paying more or less money depending on how well a person does their job: *There has been an increase in pay-for-performance plans all over the US.* ➲ compare PERFORMANCE (3), PERFORMANCE-RELATED

ˌpaying 'guest *noun* a person who pays to live in sb's house with them, usually for a short time

pay·load /ˈpeɪləʊd; *NAmE* -loʊd/ *noun* (*technical*) **1** the passengers and goods on a ship or an aircraft for which payment is received **2** the goods that a vehicle, for example a lorry/truck, is carrying; the amount it is carrying **3** the EXPLOSIVE power of a bomb or a MISSILE **4** the equipment carried by a SPACECRAFT or SATELLITE

pay·mas·ter /ˈpeɪmɑːstə(r); *NAmE* -mæs-/ *noun* **1** (usually *disapproving*) a person or group of people that pays another person or organization and therefore can control their actions **2** an official who pays the wages in the army, a factory, etc.

P

pay·ment /ˈpeɪmənt/ *noun*
1 [U] ~ (**for sth**) the act of paying sb/sth or of being paid: ***payment in instalments/in advance/by cheque/in cash*** ◇ *There will be a penalty for late payment of bills.* **2** [C] ~ (**for sth**) a sum of money paid or expected to be paid: *a* ***cash payment*** ◇ *They are finding it difficult to* ***meet the payments*** *on their car.* ◇ *He agreed to make ten* ***monthly payments*** *of £50.* ➲ COLLOCATIONS at FINANCE ➲ see also BALANCE OF PAYMENTS, DOWN PAYMENT **3** [U, sing.] ~ (**for sth**) a reward or an act of thanks for sth you have done SYN **recompense**: *We'd like you to accept this gift* ***in payment for*** *your kindness.* ◇ *Is this all the payment I get for my efforts?*
IDM **on payment of sth** when sth has been paid: *Entry is only allowed on payment of the full registration fee.*

Synonyms

payment

premium • contribution • subscription • repayment • deposit • instalment

These are all words for an amount of money that you pay or are expected to pay, or for the act of paying.

payment an amount of money that you pay or are expected to pay; the act of paying: *ten monthly payments of $50* ◇ *payment in advance*

premium an amount of money that you pay once or regularly for an insurance policy; an extra payment added to the basic rate; a higher amount of money than usual: *an insurance premium* ◇ *a premium for express delivery*

contribution a sum of money that you pay regularly to your employer or the governmentin order to pay for benefits such as health insurance, a pension, etc: *You can increase your monthly contributions to the pension plan.*

subscription an amount of money you pay in advance to receive regular copies of a newspaper or magazine or to receive a service: *a subscription to 'Newsweek'*

repayment (*BrE*) an amount of money that you pay regularly to a bank, etc. until you have returned all the money that you owe; the act of paying this money: *the repayments on the loan*

deposit an amount of money that you pay as the first part of a larger payment: *We've put down a 5% deposit on the house.*

instalment one of a number of payments that you make regularly over a period of time until you have paid for sth: *We paid for the car by/in instalments.*

PATTERNS

- (a/an) **annual/monthly/regular** payment/premium/contributions/subscription/repayment/deposit/instalment
- payment/repayment **in full**
- to **pay** a(n) premium/contribution/subscription/deposit/instalment
- to **make** (a) payment/repayment/deposit
- to **meet/keep up (with)** (the) payment(s)/the premiums/(the) repayment(s)/the instalments

ˈpay-off *noun* (*informal*) **1** a payment of money to sb so that they will not cause you any trouble or to make them keep a secret SYN **bribe** **2** a payment of money to sb to persuade them to leave their job **3** an advantage or a reward from sth you have done

pay·ola /peɪˈəʊlə; *NAmE* -ˈoʊlə/ *noun* [U] (*NAmE, informal*) the practice of giving or taking payments for doing sth illegal, especially for illegally influencing the sales of a particular product SYN **bribery**

pay·out /ˈpeɪaʊt/ *noun* a large amount of money that is given to sb: *an insurance payout* ◇ *a lottery payout*

ˈpay packet (also **ˈwage packet**) (both *BrE*) (*NAmE* **ˈpay envelope**) *noun* an envelope containing your wages; the amount a person earns

ˌpay-per-ˈview *noun* [U] a system of television broadcasting in which you pay an extra sum of money to watch a particular programme, such as a film/movie or a sports event

pay·phone /ˈpeɪfəʊn; *NAmE* -foʊn/ *noun* a telephone, usually in a public place, that is operated using coins or a card

pay·roll /ˈpeɪrəʊl; *NAmE* -roʊl/ *noun* **1** a list of people employed by a company showing the amount of money to be paid to each of them: *We have 500 people* ***on the payroll.*** **2** [usually sing.] the total amount paid in wages by a company

pay·slip /ˈpeɪslɪp/ *noun* (*BrE*) a piece of paper given to an employee that shows how much money they have been paid and how much has been taken away for tax, etc.

ˌpay TˈV (also **ˈpay television**) *noun* [U] a system of television broadcasting in which you pay extra money to watch particular television programmes or channels

PBS /ˌpiː biː ˈes/ *abbr.* the Public Broadcasting Service (an organization in the US that broadcasts television programmes to local stations that do not show advertisements)

PC /ˌpiː ˈsiː/ *abbr.* **1** personal computer (a small computer that is designed for one person to use at work or at home) ➲ VISUAL VOCAB pages V54, V56 **2** (*BrE*) Police Constable (a police officer of the lowest rank): *PC Tom March* ➲ see also WPC **3** POLITICALLY CORRECT

PCB /ˌpiː siː ˈbiː/ *abbr.* printed circuit board

ˌPˈC card *noun* (*computing*) a plastic card with a PRINTED CIRCUIT on it that can be put into a computer to allow it to work with other devices

PCP /ˌpiː siː ˈpiː/ *abbr.* **1** PRIMARY CARE PHYSICIAN **2** PRIMARY CARE PROVIDER

PC Plod /ˌpiː siː ˈplɒd; *NAmE* ˈplɑːd/ *noun* (*BrE, informal, humorous*) a junior police officer

PCSO /ˌpiː siː es ˈəʊ; *NAmE* ˈoʊ/ *abbr.* (in England and Wales) police community support officer (a person who is not a police officer but works in an area to help the work of the police)

PDA /ˌpiː diː ˈeɪ/ *noun* the abbreviation for 'personal digital assistant' (a very small computer that is used for storing personal information and creating documents, and that may include other functions such as telephone, FAX, connection to the Internet, etc.) ➲ VISUAL VOCAB page V54

PDF /ˌpiː diː ˈef/ (also **ˌPDˈF file**) *noun* (*computing*) the abbreviation for 'Portable Document Format' (a type of computer file that can contain words or pictures. It can be read using any system, can be sent from one computer to another, and will look the same on any computer.): *I'll send it to you as a PDF.*

p.d.q. /ˌpiː diː ˈkjuː/ *abbr.* pretty damn/damned quick (= very fast): *Make sure you get here p.d.q.*

PDT /ˌpiː diː ˈtiː/ *abbr.* PACIFIC DAYLIGHT TIME

PE (*BrE*) (*US* **P.E.**) /ˌpiː ˈiː/ *noun* [U] the abbreviation for 'physical education' (sport and exercise that is taught in schools): *a PE class*

pea /piː/ *noun* a small round green seed, eaten as a vegetable. Several peas grow together inside a long thin POD on a climbing plant also called a pea: *frozen peas* ◇ *pea soup* ➲ VISUAL VOCAB page V27 ➲ see also CHICKPEA, MUSHY PEAS, SPLIT PEA, SWEET PEA

peace /piːs/ *noun*
1 [U, sing.] a situation or a period of time in which there is no war or violence in a country or an area: *war and peace* ◇ ***peace talks/negotiations*** ◇ *The negotiators are trying to* ***make peace*** *between the warring factions.* ◇ *A UN force has been sent to* ***keep the peace*** (= to prevent people from fighting). ◇ *After years of war, the people long for a lasting peace.* ◇ *the Peace of Utrecht, 1713* (= the agreement ending the war) ◇ *The two communities live together* ***in peace.*** ◇ *The countries have been* ***at peace*** *for more than a century.* ◇ *the*

P

peace movement (= that tries to prevent war by protesting, persuading politicians, etc.) ➲ COLLOCATIONS at WAR **2** 🔑 [U] the state of being calm or quiet: *She lay back and enjoyed the peace of the summer evening.* ◇ *I would work better if I had some* **peace and quiet**. ◇ *He just wants to be* **left in peace** (= not to be disturbed). ◇ *I need to check that she is all right, just for my own* **peace of mind** (= so that I do not have to worry). ◇ *He never felt really* **at peace** *with himself.* **3** 🔑 [U] the state of living in friendship with sb without arguing: *They simply can't seem to live in peace with each other.* ◇ *She felt* **at peace with** *the world.* ➲ see also BREACH, JUSTICE OF THE PEACE

IDM ˌ**hold your ˈpeace/ˈtongue** (*old-fashioned*) to say nothing although you would like to give your opinion **make (your) peace with sb** to end an argument with sb, usually by saying you are sorry ➲ more at WICKED *n.*

Which Word?

peace / peacefulness

- The noun **peace** can be used to talk about a peaceful state or situation: *world peace* ◇ *I just need some peace and quiet.* **Peacefulness** is not a common word. It means 'the quality of being peaceful'.

peace·able /ˈpiːsəbl/ *adj.* **1** not involving or causing argument or violence SYN **peaceful**: *A peaceable settlement has been reached.* **2** not liking to argue; wishing to live in peace with others SYN **peaceful, calm**: *a peaceable character* ▶ **peace·ably** /-əbli/ *adv.*

the ˈPeace Corps *noun* [sing.] a US organization that sends young Americans to work in other countries without pay in order to create international friendship

ˈpeace dividend *noun* [usually sing.] money previously spent on weapons and the defence of a country and now available to be used for other things because of a reduction in a country's military forces

peace·ful 🔑 /ˈpiːsfl/ *adj.*

1 🔑 not involving a war, violence or argument: *a* **peaceful** *protest/demonstration/solution* ◇ *They hope for a* **peaceful settlement** *of the dispute.* **2** 🔑 quiet and calm; not worried or disturbed in any way SYN **tranquil**: *a peaceful atmosphere* ◇ *peaceful sleep* ◇ *It's so peaceful out here in the country.* ◇ *He had a peaceful life.* **3** 🔑 trying to create peace or to live in peace; not liking violence or disagreement SYN **peaceable**: *a peaceful society* ◇ *The aims of the organization are wholly peaceful.* ▶ **peace·ful·ly** /-fəli/ *adv.*: *The siege has ended peacefully.* ◇ *The baby slept peacefully.* **peace·ful·ness** *noun* [U] ➲ note at PEACE

peace·keep·er /ˈpiːskiːpə(r)/ *noun* **1** a member of a military force who has been sent to help stop people fighting in a place where war or violence is likely **2** a person who tries to stop people arguing or fighting: *She's the peacekeeper in that family.*

peace·keep·ing /ˈpiːskiːpɪŋ/ *adj.* [only before noun] intended to help stop people fighting and prevent war or violence in a place where this is likely: *peacekeeping operations* ◇ *a United Nations peacekeeping force* ➲ COLLOCATIONS at WAR

ˈpeace-loving *adj.* preferring to live in peace and to avoid arguments and fighting SYN **peaceable**

peace·maker /ˈpiːsmeɪkə(r)/ *noun* a person who tries to persuade people or countries to stop arguing or fighting and to make peace

peace·nik /ˈpiːsnɪk/ *noun* (*informal*, sometimes *disapproving*) a PACIFIST (= sb who believes war and violence are always wrong and refuses to fight)

ˈpeace offering *noun* a present given to sb to show that you are sorry for sth or want to make peace after an argument

ˈpeace pipe *noun* a TOBACCO pipe offered and smoked as a symbol of peace by Native Americans

ˈpeace process *noun* [usually sing.] a series of talks and agreements designed to end war or violence between two groups

peace·time /ˈpiːstaɪm/ *noun* [U] a period of time when a country is not at war ➲ compare WARTIME

peach /piːtʃ/ *noun, adj.*

■ *noun* **1** [C] a round fruit with soft red and yellow skin, yellow flesh and a large rough seed inside: *a peach tree* ➲ VISUAL VOCAB page V26 ➲ compare NECTARINE **2** [sing.] ~ (**of a...**) (*old-fashioned, informal*) a particularly good or attractive person or thing **3** [U] a pinkish-orange colour

■ *adj.* pinkish-orange in colour

peach Melba /ˌpiːtʃ ˈmelbə/ *noun* [U, C] a cold DESSERT (= a sweet dish) made from half a PEACH, ice cream and RASPBERRY sauce

peachy /ˈpiːtʃi/ *adj.* **1** like a peach in colour or appearance: *pale peachy skin* **2** (*NAmE, informal*) fine; very nice: *Everything is just peachy.*

ˈpea coat (also **ˈpea jacket**) *noun* (*NAmE*) a type of thick short coat

pea·cock /ˈpiːkɒk; *NAmE* -kɑːk/ *noun* a large male bird with long blue and green tail feathers that it can spread out like a fan: *as proud as a peacock* ➲ see also PEAHEN

ˌ**peacock ˈblue** *adj.* deep greenish-blue in colour ▶ ˌ**peacock ˈblue** *noun* [U]

pea·fowl /ˈpiːfaʊl/ *noun* (*pl.* **pea·fowl**) a large PHEASANT found mainly in Asia. The male is called a PEACOCK and the female is called a PEAHEN.

ˌ**pea-ˈgreen** *adj.* bright green in colour, like PEAS

pea·hen /ˈpiːhen/ *noun* a large brown bird, the female of the peacock

peak 🔑 /piːk/ *noun, verb, adj.*

■ *noun* **1** 🔑 [usually sing.] the point when sb/sth is best, most successful, strongest, etc. SYN **height**: *Traffic* **reaches its peak** *between 8 and 9 in the morning.* ◇ *She's* **at the peak of** *her career.* ◇ *the* **peaks and troughs** *of married life* ➲ compare OFF-PEAK **2** 🔑 the pointed top of a mountain; a mountain with a pointed top: *a* **mountain peak** ◇ **snow-capped/jagged peaks** ◇ *The climbers made camp halfway up the peak.* ➲ VISUAL VOCAB page V5 **3** any narrow and pointed shape, edge, etc: *Whisk the egg whites into stiff peaks.* **4** (*BrE*) (*NAmE* **bill, visor**) the stiff front part of a cap that sticks out above your eyes ➲ VISUAL VOCAB page V53

■ *verb* [I] to reach the highest point or value: *Oil production peaked in the early 1980s.* ◇ *Unemployment peaked at 17%.* ◇ *an athlete who peaks* (= produces his or her best performance) *at just the right time*

■ *adj.* [only before noun] used to describe the highest level of sth, or a time when the greatest number of people are doing sth or using sth: *It was a time of* **peak demand** *for the product.* ◇ *March is one of the* **peak periods** *for our business.* ◇ *The athletes are all in* **peak condition**. ◇ *We need extra help during the* **peak season**. ➲ compare OFF-PEAK

peaked /piːkt/ *adj.* **1** having a PEAK *n.* (4) **2** (*NAmE*) (*BrE* **peaky**) ill/sick or pale

ˌ**peak ˈoil** *noun* [U] the point in time when world oil production reaches its highest rate, after which it goes into permanent decline

ˌ**peak ˈrate** *noun* the busiest time, which is therefore charged at the highest rate: *peak-rate phone calls*

ˈpeak time (also ˌ**peak ˈviewing time**) *noun* (*BrE*) = PRIME TIME

peaky /ˈpiːki/ (*BrE, informal*) (*NAmE* **peaked**) *adj.* ill/sick or pale: *You're looking a little peaky. Are you OK?*

peal /piːl/ *noun, verb*

■ *noun* **1** ~ (**of sth**) a loud sound or series of sounds: *She burst into peals of laughter.* **2** the loud ringing sound of a bell: *a peal of bells rang out* **3** a set of bells that all have different notes; a musical pattern that can be rung on a set of bells

■ *verb* **1** [I] ~ (**out**) (of bells) to ring loudly: *The bells of the city began to peal out.* **2** [I] ~ (**with sth**) to suddenly laugh loudly: *Ellen pealed with laughter.*

pea·nut /ˈpiːnʌt/ *noun* **1** (*BrE* also **ground·nut**) [C] a nut that grows underground in a thin shell: *a packet of salted peanuts* ◇ *peanut oil* ➲ VISUAL VOCAB page V28 **2 peanuts** [pl.] (*informal*) a very small amount of money: *He gets paid peanuts for doing that job.*

ˌpeanut ˈbutter *noun* [U] a thick soft substance made from very finely chopped PEANUTS, usually eaten spread on bread: (*NAmE*) *a peanut butter and jelly sandwich*

pear /peə(r); *NAmE* per/ *noun* a yellow or green fruit that is narrow at the top and wide at the bottom: *a pear tree* ➲ see also PRICKLY PEAR

pearl /pɜːl; *NAmE* pɜːrl/ *noun* **1** [C] a small hard shiny white ball that forms inside the shell of an OYSTER and is of great value as a JEWEL: *a string of pearls* ◇ *a pearl necklace* ◇ *She was wearing her pearls* (= a NECKLACE of pearls). ➲ VISUAL VOCAB page V53 ➲ see also SEED PEARL **2** [C] a copy of a pearl that is made artificially **3** [U] = MOTHER-OF-PEARL: *pearl buttons* **4** [C, usually sing.] a thing that looks like a pearl in shape or colour: *pearls of dew on the grass* **5** [C] a thing that is very highly valued: *She is a pearl among women.*
IDM **cast, throw, etc. pearls before ˈswine** to give or offer valuable things to people who do not understand their value **a ˌpearl of ˈwisdom** (usually *ironic*) a wise remark: *Thank you for those pearls of wisdom.*

ˌpearl ˈbarley *noun* [U] smooth grains of BARLEY, which are added to soups and other dishes

pearly /ˈpɜːli; *NAmE* ˈpɜːrli/ *adj.* of or like a pearl: *pearly white teeth*

the ˌPearly ˈGates *noun* [pl.] (*humorous*) the gates of heaven

ˈpear-shaped *adj.* **1** shaped like a pear **2** a **pear-shaped** person is wider around their waist and hips than around the top part of their body
IDM **go ˈpear-shaped** (*BrE, informal*) if things **go pear-shaped**, they go wrong

peas·ant /ˈpeznt/ *noun* **1** (especially in the past, or in poorer countries) a farmer who owns or rents a small piece of land: *peasant farmers* **2** (*informal, disapproving*) a person who is rude, behaves badly, or has little education SYN **lout**

peas·ant·ry /ˈpezntri/ *noun* [sing.+ sing./pl. v.] all the peasants in a region or country: *the local peasantry*

pease pudding /ˌpiːz ˈpʊdɪŋ/ *noun* [U] (*BrE*) a hot dish made from dried PEAS that are left in water and then boiled until they form a soft mass, usually served with HAM OR PORK

ˈpea-shooter *noun* (*BrE*) a small tube that children use to blow small objects such as dried PEAS at sb/sth, in order to hit them or it

pea-souper /ˌpiː ˈsuːpə(r)/ *noun* (*old-fashioned, BrE, informal*) a very thick yellowish FOG

peat /piːt/ *noun* [U] a soft black or brown substance formed from decaying plants just under the surface of the ground, especially in cool wet areas. It is burned as a fuel or used to improve garden soil: *peat bogs* ▸ **peaty** *adj.*: *peaty soils*

peb·ble /ˈpebl/ *noun* a smooth, round stone that is found in or near water ➲ VISUAL VOCAB page V4

ˈpebble-dash *noun* [U] (*BrE*) CEMENT mixed with small stones used for covering the outside walls of houses

pebbly /ˈpebli/ *adj.* covered with pebbles: *a pebbly beach*

pecan /ˈpiːkən; pɪˈkæn; *NAmE* pɪˈkɑːn/ *noun* the nut of the American **pecan tree** with a smooth pinkish-brown shell ➲ VISUAL VOCAB page V28

pecca·dillo /ˌpekəˈdɪləʊ; *NAmE* -ˈdɪloʊ/ *noun* (*pl.* **-oes** or **-os**) a small unimportant thing that sb does wrong

pec·cary /ˈpekəri/ (*pl.* **-ies**) *noun* an animal like a pig, which lives in the southern US, Mexico and Central and S America

peck /pek/ *verb, noun*
▪ *verb* **1** [I, T] (of birds) to move the beak forward quickly and hit or bite sth: **~ (at sth)** *A robin was pecking at crumbs on the ground.* ◇ **~ sth** *A bird had pecked a hole in the sack.* ◇ **~ sth out** *Vultures had pecked out the dead goat's eyes.* **2** [T] (*informal*) to kiss sb lightly and quickly: **~ sb on sth** *He pecked her on the cheek as he went out.* ◇ **~ sth** *She pecked his cheek.*
IDM **a/the ˈpecking order** (*informal*, often *humorous*) the order of importance in relation to one another among the members of a group SYN **hierarchy**: *New Zealand is at the top of the pecking order of rugby nations.*
PHR V **ˈpeck at sth** to eat only a very small amount of a meal because you are not hungry SYN **pick at**
▪ *noun* **1** (*informal*) a quick kiss: *He gave her a friendly peck on the cheek.* **2** an act of pecking sb/sth: *The budgerigar gave a quick peck at the seed.*

peck·er /ˈpekə(r)/ *noun* (*slang, especially NAmE*) a PENIS
IDM **ˌkeep your ˈpecker up** (*BrE, informal*) to remain cheerful despite difficulties

peck·ish /ˈpekɪʃ/ *adj.* (*BrE, informal*) slightly hungry

pecs /peks/ *noun* [pl.] (*informal*) = PECTORALS

pec·tin /ˈpektɪn/ *noun* [U] (*chemistry*) a substance similar to sugar that forms in fruit that is ready to eat, and is used to make jam/jelly firm as it is cooked

pec·toral /ˈpektərəl/ *adj., noun*
▪ *adj.* (*anatomy*) relating to or connected with the chest or breast: *pectoral muscles*
▪ *noun* **pectorals** (also *informal* **pecs**) [pl.] the muscles of the chest

pe·cu·liar /pɪˈkjuːliə(r)/ *adj.* **1** (*BrE* or rather *formal, NAmE*) strange or unusual, especially in a way that is unpleasant or worrying SYN **odd**: *a peculiar smell/taste* ◇ *There was something peculiar in the way he smiled.* ◇ *I had a peculiar feeling we'd met before.* ◇ ***For some peculiar reason**, she refused to come inside.* ➲ compare ODD **2 ~ (to sb/sth)** belonging or relating to one particular place, situation, person, etc, and not to others: *a humour that is peculiar to American sitcoms* ◇ *a species of bird peculiar to Asia* ◇ *He has his own peculiar style which you'll soon get used to.* ◇ *the peculiar properties of mercury* **3** (*BrE, informal*) slightly ill/sick IDM see FUNNY

pe·cu·li·ar·ity /pɪˌkjuːliˈærəti/ *noun* (*pl.* **-ies**) **1** [C] a strange or unusual feature or habit: *a physical peculiarity* **2** [C] a feature that only belongs to one particular person, thing, place, etc. SYN **characteristic**: *the cultural peculiarities of the English* **3** [U] the quality of being strange or unusual

pe·cu·li·ar·ly /pɪˈkjuːliəli; *NAmE* -ərli/ *adv.* **1** very; more than usually SYN **particularly, especially**: *These plants are peculiarly prone to disease.* **2** in a way that relates to or is especially typical of one particular person, thing, place, etc. SYN **uniquely**: *He seemed to believe that it was a peculiarly British problem.* **3** in a strange or unusual way

pe·cu·ni·ary /pɪˈkjuːniəri; *NAmE* -ieri/ *adj.* (*formal*) relating to or connected with money: *pecuniary advantage*

ped- (*NAmE*) (*BrE* **paed-**) /piːd-/ *combining form* (in nouns and adjectives) connected with children

peda·gogic /ˌpedəˈgɒdʒɪk; *NAmE* -ˈgɑːdʒ-/ (also **peda·gogic·al** /-ɪkl/) *adj.* (*formal*) concerning teaching methods: *pedagogic principles* ▸ **peda·gogic·al·ly** /ˌpedəˈgɒdʒɪkli; *NAmE* -ˈgɑːdʒ-/ *adv.*

peda·gogue /ˈpedəgɒg; *NAmE* -gɑːg/ *noun* (*old use* or *formal*) a teacher; a person who likes to teach people things, especially because they think they know more than other people

peda·gogy /ˈpedəgɒdʒi; *NAmE* -gɑːdʒ-/ *noun* [U] (*technical*) the study of teaching methods

pedal /ˈpedl/ *noun, verb*
▪ *noun* **1** a flat bar on a machine such as a bicycle, car, etc. that you push down with your foot in order to make parts of the machine move or work: *I couldn't reach the pedals on her bike.* ◇ *She pressed her foot down sharply on the brake pedal.* ➲ VISUAL VOCAB page V41 **2** a bar on a musical instrument such as a piano or an organ that you push with your foot in order to control the sound ➲ VISUAL VOCAB page V31

P

■ *verb* (-ll-, *US* also -l-) **1** [I, T] to ride a bicycle somewhere: **+ adv./prep.** *I saw her pedalling along the towpath.* ◇ *He jumped on his bike and pedalled off.* ◇ **~ sth + adv./prep.** *She pedalled her bicycle up the track.* **2** [I, T] to turn or press the pedals on a bicycle or other machine: (**+ adv./prep.**) *You'll have to pedal hard up this hill.* ◇ **~ sth** *She had been pedalling her exercise bike all morning.* ➲ see also BACK-PEDAL, SOFT-PEDAL

'pedal bin *noun* (*BrE*) a container for rubbish, usually in a kitchen, with a lid that opens when a pedal is pressed

ped·alo /'pedələʊ; *NAmE* -loʊ/ *noun* (*pl.* -oes or -os) (*BrE*) a small pleasure boat that you move through the water by pushing PEDALS with your feet

'pedal pushers *noun* [pl.] (*BrE*) women's trousers/pants that reach just below the knee

ped·ant /'pednt/ *noun* (*disapproving*) a person who is too concerned with small details or rules especially when learning or teaching

pe·dan·tic /pɪ'dæntɪk/ *adj.* (*disapproving*) too worried about small details or rules ▶ **pe·dan·tic·al·ly** /-kli/ *adv.*

ped·ant·ry /'pedntri/ *noun* [U] (*disapproving*) too much attention to small details or rules

ped·dle /'pedl/ *verb* **1 ~ sth** to try to sell goods by going from house to house or from place to place: *He worked as a door-to-door salesman peddling cloths and brushes.* ◇ *to peddle illegal drugs* **2 ~ sth** to spread an idea or story in order to get people to accept it: *to peddle malicious gossip* ◇ *This line* (= publicly stated opinion) *is being peddled by all the government spokesmen.*

ped·dler /'pedlə(r)/ *noun* **1** (also **'drug peddler**) (both *BrE*) a person who sells illegal drugs **2** (*NAmE*) (*BrE* **ped·lar**) a person who in the past travelled from place to place trying to sell small objects

ped·er·ast (*BrE* also **paed·er·ast**) /'pedəræst/ *noun* (*formal*) a man who has sex with a boy ▶ **ped·er·asty** (*BrE* also **paed·er·asty**) /'pedəræsti/ *noun* [U]

ped·es·tal /'pedɪstl/ *noun* the base that a column, statue, etc. rests on: *a pedestal basin* (= a WASHBASIN supported by a column) ◇ *I replaced the vase carefully on its pedestal* ➲ VISUAL VOCAB page V12

IDM **to put/place sb on a 'pedestal** to admire sb so much that you do not see their faults ➲ more at KNOCK *v.*

ped·es·trian /pə'destriən/ *noun, adj.*

■ *noun* a person walking in the street and not travelling in a vehicle ➲ compare MOTORIST

■ *adj.* **1** [only before noun] used by or for the use of pedestrians; connected with pedestrians: *pedestrian areas* ◇ *Pedestrian accidents are down by 5%.* **2** without any imagination or excitement; dull SYN **unimaginative**

pe,destrian 'crossing (*BrE*) (*NAmE* **cross·walk**) *noun* a part of a road where vehicles must stop to allow people to cross ➲ VISUAL VOCAB page V2 ➲ see also ZEBRA CROSSING

ped·es·tri·an·ize (*BrE* also **-ise**) /pə'destriənaɪz/ *verb* **~ sth** to make a street or part of a town into an area that is only for people who are walking, not for vehicles ▶ **ped·es·tri·an·iza·tion, -isa·tion** /pə'destriənaɪ'zeɪʃn/ *noun* [U]

pe,destrian 'precinct (*BrE*) (*NAmE* **pe,destrian 'mall**) *noun* a part of a town, especially a shopping area, that vehicles are not allowed to enter ➲ VISUAL VOCAB page V2

pedi·at·ri·cian (*NAmE*) (*BrE* **paedi·at·ri·cian**) /,piːdiə'trɪʃn/ *noun* a doctor who studies and treats the diseases of children

pedi·at·rics (*NAmE*) (*BrE* **paedi·at·rics**) /,piːdi'ætrɪks/ *noun* [U] the branch of medicine concerned with children and their diseases ▶ **pedi·at·ric** (*NAmE*) (*BrE* **paedi-**) *adj.*

pedi·cure /'pedɪkjʊə(r); *NAmE* -kjʊr/ *noun* [C, U] care and treatment of the feet and TOENAILS ➲ compare MANICURE

pedi·gree /'pedɪgriː/ *noun, adj.*

■ *noun* **1** [C] knowledge of or an official record of the animals from which an animal has been bred: *dogs with good pedigrees* (= their ANCESTORS are known and of the same breed) **2** [C, U] a person's family history or the background of sth, especially when this is impressive: *She was proud of her long pedigree.* ◇ *The product has a pedigree going back to the last century.*

■ *adj.* (*BrE*) (*NAmE* **pedi·greed**) [only before noun] (of an animal) coming from a family of the same breed that has been officially recorded for a long time and is thought to be of a good quality: *pedigree sheep*

pedi·ment /'pedɪmənt/ *noun* (*architecture*) the part in the shape of a triangle above the entrance of a building in the ancient Greek style

ped·lar (*BrE*) (*NAmE* **ped·dler**) /'pedlə(r)/ *noun* a person who in the past travelled from place to place trying to sell small objects

ped·ometer /pe'dɒmɪtə(r); *NAmE* -'dɑːm-/ *noun* an instrument for measuring how far you have walked

pedo·phile (*NAmE*) (*BrE* **paedo-**) /'piːdəʊfaɪl; *NAmE* -doʊ-/ *noun* a person who is sexually attracted to children

pedo·philia (*NAmE*) (*BrE* **paedo-**) *noun* [U] the condition of being sexually attracted to children; sexual activity with children

pee /piː/ *verb, noun*

■ *verb* (**peed, peed**) [I] (*informal*) to pass waste liquid from your body SYN **urinate**: *I need to pee.*

■ *noun* (*informal*) **1** [sing.] an act of passing liquid waste from your body: (*BrE*) *to go for a pee* ◇ *to have a pee* ◇ (*NAmE*) *to take a pee* **2** [U] liquid waste passed from your body; URINE

peek /piːk/ *verb* **1** [I] to look at sth quickly and secretly because you should not be looking at it SYN **peep**: *No peeking!* ◇ **+ adv./prep.** *She peeked at the audience from behind the curtain.* ◇ *I couldn't resist peeking in the drawer.* **2** [I] **~ out/over/through, etc.** to be just visible: *Her feet peeked out from the end of the blanket.* ▶ **peek** *noun* [sing.]: *I took a quick peek inside.*

peek·aboo /,piːkə'buː/ (*BrE* also **'peep-bo**) *noun* [U] a simple game played to amuse young children, in which you keep hiding your face and then showing it again, saying 'Peekaboo!' or 'Peep-bo!'

peel /piːl/ *verb, noun*

■ *verb* **1** [T] **~ sth** to take the skin off fruit, vegetables, etc: *to peel an orange/a banana* ◇ *Have you peeled the potatoes?* ➲ COLLOCATIONS at COOKING **2** [T, I] **~ (sth) away/off/back** to remove a layer, covering, etc. from the surface of sth; to come off the surface of sth: *Carefully peel away the lining paper.* ◇ *The label will peel off if you soak it in water.* **3** [I] **~ (off)** (of a covering) to come off in strips or small pieces: *The wallpaper was beginning to peel.* **4** [I] (of a surface) to lose strips or small pieces of its covering: *Put on some cream to stop your nose from peeling.* ◇ *The walls have begun to peel.* IDM see EYE *n.*

PHR V **,peel 'off** to leave a group of vehicles, aircraft, etc. and turn to one side: *The leading car in the motorcade peeled off to the right.* **,peel 'off | ,peel (sth)↔'off** (*informal*) to remove some or all of your clothes: *You look hot—why don't you peel off?* ◇ *He peeled off his shirt.* **,peel 'out** (*NAmE, informal*) to leave quickly and in a noisy way, especially in a car, on a motorcycle, etc.

■ *noun* **1** [U, C] the thick skin of some fruits and vegetables: *orange/lemon peel* ◇ (*NAmE* also) *an orange/a lemon peel* ➲ VISUAL VOCAB page V26 ➲ compare RIND, SKIN, ZEST **2 peels** [pl.] (*NAmE*) = PEELINGS

peel·er /'piːlə(r)/ *noun* (usually in compounds) a special type of knife for taking the skin off fruit and vegetables: *a potato peeler* ➲ VISUAL VOCAB page V23

peel·ings /'piːlɪŋz/ (*NAmE* also **peels**) *noun* [pl.] the skin of fruit or vegetables that has been removed

peep /piːp/ *verb, noun*

■ *verb* **1** [I] (**+ adv./prep.**) to look quickly and secretly at sth, especially through a small opening: *We caught her peeping through the keyhole.* ◇ *Could I just peep inside?* ◇ *He was peeping at her through his fingers.* **2** [I] **+ adv./prep.** to be just visible: *The tower peeped above the trees.* ◇ *The sun peeped out from behind the clouds.* **3** [I, T] **~ (sth)** to make a short high sound; to make sth make this sound.

■ ***noun*** **1** [C, usually sing.] a quick or secret look at sth: *Dave **took a quick peep** at the last page.* **2** [sing.] (*informal*) something that sb says or a sound that sb makes: *We did **not hear a peep out of** the baby all night.* **3** [C] a short high sound like the one made by a young bird or by a whistle **4** (also **peep ˈpeep**) [C] (*BrE*) a word for the sound of a car's horn, used especially by children

peep-bo /ˈpiːpbəʊ; ˈpiːpəʊ; *NAmE* -boʊ; -poʊ/ *noun* [U] (*BrE*) = PEEKABOO

peep·hole /ˈpiːphəʊl; *NAmE* -hoʊl/ *noun* a small opening in a wall, door, etc. that you can look through

ˌPeeping ˈTom *noun* (*disapproving*) a person who likes to watch people secretly when they are taking off their clothes **SYN** **voyeur**

ˈpeep show *noun* **1** a series of moving pictures in a box that you look at through a small opening **2** a type of show in which sb pays to watch a woman take off her clothes in a small room

peer /pɪə(r); *NAmE* pɪr/ *noun, verb*

■ ***noun*** **1** [usually pl.] a person who is the same age or who has the same social status as you: *She enjoys the respect of her peers.* ◇ *Children are worried about failing in front of their peers.* ◇ ***Peer pressure** is strong among young people* (= they want to be like other people of the same age). **2** (in Britain) a member of the NOBILITY ➲ see also LIFE PEER, PEERESS

■ ***verb*** [I] (+ **adv./prep.**) to look closely or carefully at sth, especially when you cannot see it clearly: *We peered into the shadows.* ◇ *He went to the window and peered out.* ◇ *She kept peering over her shoulder.* ◇ *He peered closely at the photograph.* ➲ **SYNONYMS** at STARE

peer·age /ˈpɪərɪdʒ; *NAmE* ˈpɪr-/ *noun* **1** [sing.] all the peers (2) as a group: *a member of the peerage* **2** [C] the rank of a peer (2) or peeress

peer·ess /ˈpɪəres; *NAmE* ˈpɪrəs/ *noun* a female PEER (2)

ˈpeer group *noun* a group of people of the same age or social status: *She gets on well with her peer group.* ◇ *peer-group pressure*

peer·less /ˈpɪələs; *NAmE* ˈpɪrləs/ *adj.* better than all others of its kind **SYN** **unsurpassed**: *a peerless performance*

ˌpeer reˈview *noun* [U, C] a judgement on a piece of scientific or other professional work by others working in the same area: *All research proposals are subject to peer review before selection.* ▸ **ˌpeer-reˈviewed** *adj.*: *peer-reviewed journals*

ˌpeer-to-ˈpeer *adj.* [only before noun] (*computing*) (of a computer system) in which each computer can act as a SERVER for the others, allowing data to be shared without the need for a central server ➲ compare CLIENT-SERVER

peeve /piːv/ *noun*

IDM **sb's pet ˈpeeve** (*NAmE*) (*BrE* **sb's pet ˈhate**) something that you particularly dislike

peeved /piːvd/ *adj.* **~ (about sth)** (*informal*) annoyed: *He sounded peeved about not being told.*

peev·ish /ˈpiːvɪʃ/ *adj.* easily annoyed by unimportant things; bad-tempered **SYN** **irritable** ▸ **peev·ish·ly** *adv.*

pee·wit /ˈpiːwɪt/ *noun* = LAPWING

peg /peg/ *noun, verb*

■ ***noun*** **1** a short piece of wood, metal or plastic used for holding things together, hanging things on, marking a position, etc: *There's a peg near the door to hang your coat on.* **2** (also **ˈtent peg**) a small pointed piece of wood or metal that you attach to the ropes of a tent and push into the ground in order to hold the tent in place **3** (also **ˈclothes peg**) (both *BrE*) (*NAmE* **clothes·pin**) a piece of wood or plastic used for attaching wet clothes to a clothes line **4** (also **ˈtuning peg**) a wooden, metal or plastic screw used for making the strings of a musical instrument tighter or looser ➲ **VISUAL VOCAB** page V30

IDM **ˌoff the ˈpeg** (*BrE*) (*NAmE* **ˌoff the ˈrack**) (of clothes) made to a standard average size and not made especially to fit you: *He buys his clothes off the peg.* ◇ *off-the-peg fashions* **ˌbring/ˌtake sb ˈdown a peg (or two)** to make sb realize that they are not as good, important, etc. as they think they are: *He needed to be taken down a peg or two.* **a peg to ˈhang sth on** something that gives you an excuse or opportunity to discuss or explain sth ➲ more at SQUARE *adj.*

■ ***verb*** (-gg-) **1** to fasten sth with pegs: **~ sth (out) + adv./prep.** *All their wet clothes were pegged out on the line.* ◇ **~ sth to sth** *She was busy pegging her tent to the ground.* **2** [usually passive] to fix or keep prices, wages, etc. at a particular level: **~ sth (at sth)** *Pay increases will be pegged at 5%.* ◇ **~ sth (to sth)** *Loan repayments are pegged to your income.* **3 ~ sb as sth** (*NAmE, informal*) to think of sb in a particular way: *She pegged him as a big spender.* **IDM** see LEVEL *adj.*

PHR V **ˌpeg aˈway (at sth)** (*informal, especially BrE*) to continue working hard at sth or trying to achieve sth difficult **ˌpeg sb/sth↔ˈback** (especially in sport) to stop sb/sth from winning or increasing the amount by which they are ahead: *Each time we scored we were pegged back minutes later.* **ˌpeg ˈout** (*BrE, informal*) to die

pegs

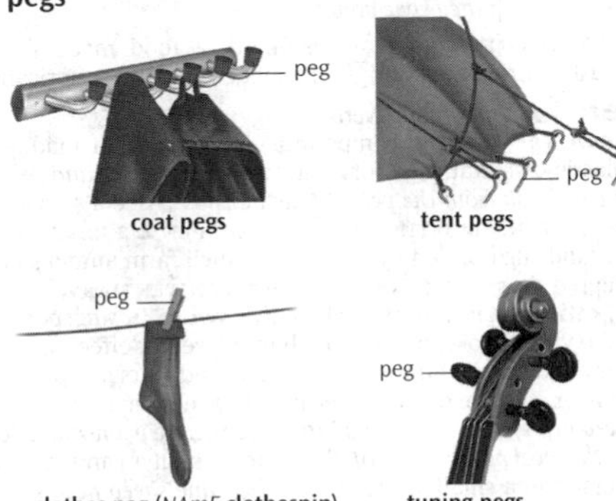

coat pegs — tent pegs — clothes peg (*NAmE* clothespin) — tuning pegs

ˈpeg leg *noun* (*informal*) an artificial leg, especially one made of wood

pe·jora·tive /pɪˈdʒɒrətɪv; *NAmE* -ˈdʒɔːr-; -ˈdʒɑːr-/ *adj.* (*formal*) a word or remark that is **pejorative** expresses disapproval or criticism **SYN** **derogatory**: *I'm using the word 'academic' here in a pejorative sense.* ▸ **pe·jora·tive·ly** *adv.*

Pe·kin·ese (also **Pe·king·ese**) /ˌpiːkɪˈniːz/ *noun* (*pl.* **Pe·kin·ese** or **Pe·kin·eses**) a very small dog with long soft hair, short legs and a flat nose

pe·la·gic /pəˈlædʒɪk/ *adj.* (*technical*) connected with, or living in, the parts of the sea that are far from land

peli·can /ˈpelɪkən/ *noun* a large bird that lives near water, with a bag of skin under its long beak for storing food

ˌpelican ˈcrossing *noun* (in Britain) a place on a road where you can stop the traffic and cross by operating a set of TRAFFIC LIGHTS

pel·lagra /pəˈlægrə/ *noun* [U] a disease caused by a lack of good food, that causes the skin to crack and may lead to mental illness

pel·let /ˈpelɪt/ *noun* **1** a small hard ball of any substance, often of soft material that has become hard: *food pellets for chickens* **2** a very small metal ball that is fired from a gun

pell-mell /ˌpelˈmel/ *adv.* (*old-fashioned*) very quickly and in a way that is not controlled

pel·lu·cid /pəˈluːsɪd/ *adj.* (*literary*) extremely clear **SYN** **transparent**

Pel·man·ism /ˈpelmənɪzəm/ *noun* [U] a game in which players must remember cards or other objects that they have seen

P

pel·met /ˈpelmɪt/ (also **val·ance** especially in *NAmE*) *noun* a strip of wood or cloth above a window that hides the curtain rail

pe·lota /pəˈlɒtə; -ˈləʊ-; *NAmE* -ˈloʊ-/ *noun* **1** [U] a game from Spain in which players hit a ball against a wall using a kind of BASKET attached to their hand **2** [C] the ball used in the game of pelota

the pelo·ton /ˈpelətɒn; *NAmE* -tɑːn/ *noun* [sing.] (from *French*) the main group of riders in a bicycle race

pelt /pelt/ *verb, noun*
■ ***verb*** **1** [T] **~ sb (with sth)** to attack sb by throwing things at them: *The children pelted him with snowballs.* **2** [I] **~ (down)** (of rain) to fall very heavily **3** [I] **+ adv./prep.** (*informal*) to run somewhere very fast SYN **dash**: *We pelted down the hill after the car.*
■ ***noun*** the skin of an animal, especially with the fur or hair still on it
IDM **(at) full ˈpelt/ˈtilt** as fast as possible

ˌpelvic ˈfloor *noun* (*anatomy*) the muscles at the base of the ABDOMEN, attached to the pelvis

pel·vis /ˈpelvɪs/ *noun* the wide curved set of bones at the bottom of the body that the legs and SPINE are connected to ➲ VISUAL VOCAB page V48 ▸ **pel·vic** /ˈpelvɪk/ *adj.* [only before noun]: *the pelvic bones*

pem·mican /ˈpemɪkən/ *noun* [U] a food made from crushed dried meat, originally made by Native Americans

pen 0→ /pen/ *noun, verb*
■ ***noun*** **1** 0→ (often in compounds) an instrument made of plastic or metal used for writing with ink: *pen and ink* ◇ *a new book from the pen of Martin Amis* ➲ see also BALLPOINT PEN, FELT-TIP PEN, FOUNTAIN PEN **2** a small piece of land surrounded by a fence in which farm animals are kept: *a sheep pen* **3** (*NAmE, slang*) = PENITENTIARY
IDM **the ˌpen is ˌmightier than the ˈsword** (*saying*) people who write books, poems, etc. have a greater effect on history and human affairs than soldiers and wars **put pen to ˈpaper** to write or start to write sth ➲ more at SLIP *n.*
■ ***verb*** (-nn-) **1 ~ sth** (*formal*) to write sth: *He penned a letter to the local paper.* **2 ~ sb/sth (in/up)** to shut an animal or a person in a small space: *At clipping time sheep need to be penned.* ◇ *The whole family were penned up in one room for a month.*

penal /ˈpiːnl/ *adj.* [usually before noun] **1** connected with or used for punishment, especially by law: *penal reforms* ◇ *the **penal system*** ◇ *Criminals could at one time be sentenced to **penal servitude*** (= prison with hard physical work). ◇ *a **penal colony*** (= a place where criminals were sent as a punishment in the past) **2** that can be punished by law: *a penal offence* **3** very severe: *penal rates of interest*

ˈpenal code *noun* a system of laws connected with crime and punishment

pen·al·ize (*BrE* also **-ise**) /ˈpiːnəlaɪz/ *verb* **1 ~ sb (for sth)** to punish sb for breaking a rule or law by making them suffer a disadvantage: *You will be penalized for poor spelling.* **2** to punish sb for breaking a rule in a sport or game by giving an advantage to their opponent: **~ sb (for sth)** *He was penalized for time-wasting.* ◇ **~ sth** *Foul play will be severely penalized.* **3 ~ sb** to put sb at a disadvantage by treating them unfairly: *The new law appears to penalize the poorest members of society.*

pen·alty /ˈpenəlti/ *noun* (*pl.* -ies) **1** a punishment for breaking a law, rule or contract: *to impose a penalty* ◇ *Assault **carries a** maximum **penalty** of seven years' imprisonment.* ◇ **~ (for sth)** *The penalty for travelling without a ticket is £200.* ◇ *Contractors who fall behind schedule incur heavy financial penalties.* ◇ *a penalty clause in a contract* ◇ *You can withdraw money from the account at any time **without penalty**.* ➲ see also DEATH PENALTY **2 ~ (of sth)** a disadvantage suffered as a result of sth: *One of the penalties of fame is loss of privacy.* **3** (in sports and games) a disadvantage given to a player or a team when they break a rule: *He incurred a ten-second penalty in the first round.* **4** (in football (SOCCER) and some other similar sports) a chance to score a goal or point without any defending players, except the GOALKEEPER, trying to stop it; the goal or point that is given if it is successful. This chance is given because the other team has broken the rules: *Two minutes later Ford equalized with a penalty.* ◇ *We **were awarded a penalty** after a late tackle.* ◇ *I volunteered to **take the penalty*** (= be the person who tries to score the goal/point) ◇ *He **missed a penalty** in the last minute of the game.* IDM see PAY *v.*

ˈpenalty area (*BrE* also **ˈpenalty box, area**) *noun* (in football (SOCCER)) the area in front of the goal. If the defending team breaks the rules within this area, the other team is given a penalty.

ˈpenalty box *noun* **1** (*BrE*) = PENALTY AREA **2** (in ICE HOCKEY) an area next to the ice where a player who has broken the rules must wait for a short time

ˈpenalty kick (*BrE* also **ˈspot kick**) *noun* a kick that is taken as a PENALTY in the game of football (SOCCER)

ˈpenalty point *noun* (*BrE*) a note on sb's DRIVING LICENCE showing they have committed an offence while driving

ˌpenalty ˈshoot-out *noun* (in football (SOCCER)) a way of deciding the winner when both teams have the same score at the end of a game. Each team is given a number of chances to kick the ball into the goal and the team that scores the most goals wins.

pen·ance /ˈpenəns/ *noun* **1** [C, usually sing., U] (especially in particular religions) an act that you give yourself to do, or that a priest gives you to do in order to show that you are sorry for sth you have done wrong: *an act of penance* ◇ **~ for sth** *to do penance for your sins* ➲ COLLOCATIONS at RELIGION **2** [sing.] something that you have to do even though you do not like doing it: *She regards living in New York as a penance; she hates big cities.*

ˌpen-and-ˈink *adj.* [usually before noun] drawn with a pen: *pen-and-ink drawings*

pence /pens/ (*BrE*) (*abbr.* **p**) *pl.* of PENNY

pen·chant /ˈpɒ̃ʃɒ̃; *NAmE* ˈpentʃənt/ *noun* **~ for sth** a special liking for sth SYN **fondness**: *She **has a penchant for** champagne.*

pen·cil 0→ /ˈpensl/ *noun, verb*
■ ***noun*** 0→ [C, U] a narrow piece of wood, or a metal or plastic case, containing a black or coloured substance, used for drawing or writing: *a pencil drawing* ◇ *I'll get a pencil and paper.* ◇ *She scribbled a note **in pencil**.* ◇ *coloured pencils* ➲ VISUAL VOCAB page V56 ➲ see also EYEBROW PENCIL, PROPELLING PENCIL
■ ***verb*** (-ll-, *especially US* -l-) **~ sth** to write, draw or mark sth with a pencil: *a pencilled portrait* ◇ *A previous owner had pencilled 'First Edition' inside the book's cover.*
PHR V **ˌpencil sth/sb↔ˈin** to write down sb's name or details of an arrangement with them that you know might have to be changed later: *We've pencilled in a meeting for Tuesday afternoon.* ◇ *Shall I pencil you in for Friday?* (= for a meeting)

ˈpencil case *noun* a small bag, etc. for holding pencils and pens ➲ VISUAL VOCAB page V57

ˈpencil-pusher *noun* (*NAmE*) = PEN-PUSHER

ˈpencil sharpener *noun* a small device with a blade inside, used for making pencils sharp ➲ VISUAL VOCAB page V56

ˈpencil skirt *noun* (*BrE*) a narrow straight skirt

pen·dant /ˈpendənt/ *noun* a piece of jewellery that you wear around your neck on a chain ➲ VISUAL VOCAB page V53

pend·ing /ˈpendɪŋ/ *prep., adj.*
■ ***prep.*** (*formal*) while waiting for sth to happen; until sth happens: *He was released on bail pending further inquiries.*
■ ***adj.*** (*formal*) **1** waiting to be decided or settled: *Nine cases are still pending.* ◇ *a **pending file/tray*** (= where you put letters, etc. you are going to deal with soon) **2** going to happen soon SYN **imminent**: *An election is pending in Italy.* ◇ *his pending departure*

ˈpen drive *noun* = FLASH DRIVE

P

pen·du·lous /ˈpendjələs; *NAmE* -dʒələs/ *adj.* (*formal*) hanging down loosely and swinging from side to side

pen·du·lum /ˈpendjələm; *NAmE* -dʒələm/ *noun* a long straight part with a weight at the end that moves regularly from side to side to control the movement of a clock: (*figurative*) *In education, the pendulum has swung back to traditional teaching methods.* ◇ *the pendulum of public opinion* ➲ picture at CLOCK

pene·trable /ˈpenɪtrəbl/ *adj.* (*formal*) that allows sth to be pushed into or through it; that can have a way made through it: *soil that is easily penetrable with a fork* **OPP** **impenetrable**

pene·trate /ˈpenətreɪt/ *verb* **1** [T, I] to go into or through sth: **~ sth** *The knife had penetrated his chest.* ◇ *The sun's radiation penetrates the skin.* ◇ (*figurative*) *The war penetrates every area of the nation's life.* ◇ **~ into/through/to sth** *These fine particles penetrate deep into the lungs.* **2** [T, I] to succeed in entering or joining an organization, a group, etc. especially when this is difficult to do: **~ sth** *They had penetrated airport security.* ◇ *The party has been penetrated by extremists.* ◇ *This year the company has been trying to penetrate new markets* (= to start selling their products there). ◇ **~ into sth** *The troops had penetrated deep into enemy lines.* **3** [T] **~ sth** to see or show a way into or through sth: *Our eyes could not penetrate the darkness.* ◇ *The flashlights barely penetrated the gloom.* **4** [T] **~ sth** to understand or discover sth that is difficult to understand or is hidden: *Science can penetrate many of nature's mysteries.* **5** [I, T] to be understood or realized by sb: *I was at the door before his words penetrated.* ◇ **~ sth** *None of my advice seems to have penetrated his thick skull* (= he has not listened to any of it). **6** [T] **~ sb/sth** (of a man) to put the PENIS into the VAGINA or ANUS of a sexual partner

pene·trat·ing /ˈpenɪtreɪtɪŋ/ *adj.* **1** (of sb's eyes or the way they look at you) making you feel uncomfortable because the person seems to know what you are thinking: *penetrating blue eyes* ◇ *a* ***penetrating gaze/look/stare*** **2** (of a sound or voice) loud and hard **SYN** **piercing**: *Her voice was shrill and penetrating.* **3** showing that you have understood sth quickly and completely: *a* ***penetrating comment/criticism/question*** **4** spreading deeply or widely: *a penetrating smell* ◇ *the* ***penetrating cold/damp***

pene·tra·tion /ˌpenɪˈtreɪʃn/ *noun* [U] **1** the act or process of making a way into or through sth: *The floor is sealed to prevent water penetration.* ◇ *the company's successful penetration of overseas markets* **2** the act of a man putting his PENIS into his partner's VAGINA or ANUS

pene·tra·tive /ˈpenɪtrətɪv; *NAmE* -treɪtɪv/ *adj.* **1** (of sexual activity) involving putting the PENIS into sb's VAGINA or ANUS: *penetrative sex* **2** able to make a way into or through sth: *penetrative weapons* **3** deep and thorough: *a penetrative survey*

pen·friend /ˈpenfrend/ (*BrE*) (also **ˈpen pal** *NAmE, BrE*) *noun* a person that you make friends with by writing letters, often sb you have never met

pen·guin /ˈpeŋɡwɪn/ *noun* a black and white bird that lives in the Antarctic. Penguins cannot fly but use their wings for swimming. There are several types of penguin, some of them very large but some of them quite small.

peni·cil·lin /ˌpenɪˈsɪlɪn/ *noun* [U] a substance obtained from MOULD, used as a drug to treat or prevent infections caused by bacteria; a type of ANTIBIOTIC

pen·ile /ˈpiːnaɪl/ *adj.* [only before noun] (*technical*) relating to the PENIS

pen·in·sula /pəˈnɪnsjələ; *NAmE* -sələ/ *noun* an area of land that is almost surrounded by water but is joined to a larger piece of land: *the Iberian peninsula* (= Spain and Portugal)

pen·in·su·lar /pəˈnɪnsjələ(r); *NAmE* -sələr/ *adj.* on or connected with a peninsula: *peninsular Spanish* (= that is spoken in Spain, not in Latin America)

penis /ˈpiːnɪs/ *noun* the organ on the body of a man or male animal that is used for URINATING and sex

peni·tence /ˈpenɪtəns/ *noun* [U] a feeling of being sorry because you have done sth wrong

peni·tent /ˈpenɪtənt/ *adj., noun*
- ***adj.*** feeling or showing that you are sorry for having done sth wrong **SYN** **remorseful**
- ***noun*** a person who shows that they are sorry for doing sth wrong, especially a religious person who wants God to forgive them

peni·ten·tial /ˌpenɪˈtenʃl/ *adj.* (*formal*) showing that you are sorry for having done sth wrong

peni·ten·tiary /ˌpenɪˈtenʃəri/ *noun* (*pl.* **-ies**) (also *slang* **pen**) (both *NAmE*) a prison

penknife

pen·knife /ˈpennaɪf/ *noun* (*pl.* **-knives** /-naɪvz/) (also **pock·et·knife** especially in *NAmE*) a small knife with one or more blades that fold down into the handle ➲ VISUAL VOCAB page V17

pen·man·ship /ˈpenmənʃɪp/ *noun* [U] (*formal*) the art of writing by hand; skill in doing this

ˈpen-name *noun* a name used by a writer instead of their real name **SYN** **nom de plume** ➲ compare PSEUDONYM

pen·nant /ˈpenənt/ *noun* **1** a long narrow pointed flag, for example one used on a ship to give signals **2** (in the US) a flag given to the winning team in a sports league, especially in BASEBALL

pen·ni·less /ˈpeniləs/ *adj.* having no money; very poor **SYN** **destitute** ➲ SYNONYMS at POOR

penn'orth /ˈpenəθ; *NAmE* -nərθ/ *noun* [usually sing.] (*old-fashioned, BrE*) = PENNYWORTH

Penn·syl·va·nia Dutch /ˌpensɪlveɪniə ˈdʌtʃ/ *noun* **1 the Pennsylvania Dutch** [pl.] a group of people originally from Germany and Switzerland who settled in Pennsylvania in the 17th and 18th centuries **2** [U] a type of German mixed with English spoken by the Pennsylvania Dutch

penny 🔑 /ˈpeni/ *noun* (*pl.* **pen·nies** or **pence**) **HELP** In senses 1 and 2, **pennies** is used to refer to the coins, and **pence** to refer to an amount of money. In sense 3, the plural is **pennies**. **1** 🔑 (*abbr.* **p**) a small British coin and unit of money. There are 100 pence in one pound (£1): *He had a few pennies in his pocket.* ◇ *That will be 45 pence, please.* ◇ *They cost 20p each.* **2** (*abbr.* **d**) a British coin in use until 1971. There were twelve pennies in one SHILLING. **3** 🔑 (*NAmE*) a cent
IDM **ˌevery ˈpenny** all of the money: *We collected £700 and every penny went to charity.* **ˌin for a ˈpenny, ˌin for a ˈpound** (*BrE, saying*) used to say that since you have started to do sth, it is worth spending as much time or money as you need to in order to complete it **not a ˈpenny** no money at all: *It didn't cost a penny.* **the ˈpenny drops** (*informal, especially BrE*) used to say that sb has finally understood or realized sth that they had not understood or realized before **a ˌpenny for your ˈthoughts | a penny for them** (*saying*) used to ask sb what they are thinking about **turn up like a bad ˈpenny** (*informal*) (of a person) to appear when they are not welcome or not wanted, especially when this happens regularly **ˌtwo/ˌten a ˈpenny** (*BrE*) (*NAmE* **a ˌdime a ˈdozen**) very common and therefore not valuable ➲ more at PINCH *v.*, PRETTY *adj.*, SPEND *v.*

ˌpenny ˈblack *noun* an old British stamp worth one penny, first used in 1840. It was the first stamp in the world that could be stuck to an envelope.

ˌpenny-ˈfarthing *noun* (*BrE*) an early type of bicycle with a very large front wheel and a very small back wheel

ˈpenny-pinching *adj.* (*disapproving*) unwilling to spend money **SYN** **mean** ▸ **ˈpenny-pinching** *noun* [U]

ˌpenny ˈwhistle *noun* = TIN WHISTLE

penny·worth /ˈpeniwɜːθ; *NAmE* -wɜːrθ/ *noun* [sing.] (*old-fashioned, BrE*) as much as you can buy with a penny; a small amount of sth
IDM **put in your two ˈpennyworth** (also **put in your two ˈpenn'orth**) (both *BrE*) (*NAmE* **put in your two ˈcents'**

worth) (*informal*) to give your opinion about sth, even if other people do not want to hear it

pen·ology /piːˈnɒlədʒi; pɪ-; *NAmE* -ˈnɑːl-/ *noun* [U] the scientific study of the punishment of criminals and the operation of prisons ▸ **pen·olo·gist** /piːˈnɒlədʒɪst; pɪ-; *NAmE* -ˈnɑːl-/ *noun*

ˈ**pen pal** (*especially NAmE*) (*BrE* also **pen·friend**) *noun* a person that you make friends with by writing letters, often sb you have never met

ˈ**pen-pusher** (*especially BrE*) (*NAmE* usually ˈ**pencil-pusher**) *noun* (*informal, disapproving*) a person with a boring job, especially in an office, that involves a lot of writing

pen·sion[1] /ˈpenʃn/ *noun, verb* ➲ see also PENSION[2]

■ ***noun*** an amount of money paid regularly by a government or company to sb who is considered to be too old or too ill/sick to work: *to receive* ***an old-age/a retirement pension*** ◇ *a* ***disability/widow's pension*** ◇ *a* ***state pension*** ◇ *to live* ***on a pension*** ◇ *to take out a* ***personal/private pension*** ◇ *a* ***pension fund*** ➲ COLLOCATIONS at AGE, FINANCE

■ ***verb***

PHRV ˌ**pension sb ˈoff** (*especially BrE*) [usually passive] to allow or force sb to retire and to pay them a pension: *He was pensioned off and his job given to a younger man.* ◇ (*informal, figurative*) *That car of yours should have been pensioned off years ago.*

pen·sion[2] /ˈpɒ̃sjɒ̃; *NAmE* pɑːnsiˈoʊn/ *noun* (from *French*) a small, usually cheap, hotel in some European countries, especially France ➲ see also PENSION[1]

pen·sion·able /ˈpenʃənəbl/ *adj.* giving sb the right to receive a pension: *people of pensionable age* ◇ *pensionable pay*

pen·sion·er /ˈpenʃənə(r)/ *noun* (*especially BrE*) a person who is receiving a pension, especially from the government: *an old-age pensioner* ➲ see also OAP, SENIOR CITIZEN

ˈ**pension plan** (*BrE* usually ˈ**pension scheme**) (*NAmE* also **reˈtirement plan**) *noun* a system in which you, and usually your employer, pay money regularly into a fund while you are employed. You are then paid a PENSION when you retire.

pen·sive /ˈpensɪv/ *adj.* thinking deeply about sth, especially because you are sad or worried: *a pensive mood* ◇ *to look pensive* ▸ **pen·sive·ly** *adv.*

penta- /ˈpentə/ *combining form* (in nouns, adjectives and adverbs) five; having five: *pentagon* ◇ *pentathlon*

penta·gon /ˈpentəgən; *NAmE* -gɑːn/ *noun* **1** [C] (*geometry*) a flat shape with five straight sides and five angles ➲ VISUAL VOCAB page V58 **2** **the Pentagon** [sing.] the building near Washington DC that is the HEADQUARTERS of the US Department of Defense and the military leaders: *a spokesman for the Pentagon*

pen·tagon·al /penˈtægənl/ *adj.* (*geometry*) having five sides

penta·gram /ˈpentəgræm/ *noun* a flat shape of a star with five points, formed by five straight lines. Pentagrams are often used as magic symbols.

pen·tam·eter /penˈtæmɪtə(r)/ *noun* [C, U] (*technical*) a line of poetry with five stressed syllables; the rhythm of poetry with five stressed syllables to a line

pent·ath·lon /penˈtæθlən/ *noun* a sporting event in which people compete in five different sports (running, riding, swimming, shooting and FENCING) ➲ compare BIATHLON, DECATHLON, HEPTATHLON, TETRATHLON, TRIATHLON

penta·tonic /ˌpentəˈtɒnɪk; *NAmE* -ˈtɑːn-/ *adj.* (*music*) related to or based on a SCALE of five notes

Pente·cost /ˈpentɪkɒst; *NAmE* -kɔːst; -kɑːst/ *noun* [U, C] **1** (*BrE* also ˌ**Whit ˈSunday**) (in the Christian Church) the 7th Sunday after Easter when Christians celebrate the Holy Spirit coming to the APOSTLES **2** = SHAVUOTH

Pente·cos·tal /ˌpentɪˈkɒstl; *NAmE* -ˈkɔːs-; -ˈkɑːs-/ *adj.* connected with a group of Christian Churches that emphasize the gifts of the Holy Spirit, such as the power to heal the sick ▸ **Pente·cos·talist** *noun*

pent·house /ˈpenthaʊs/ *noun* an expensive and comfortable flat/apartment or set of rooms at the top of a tall building

pent-up /ˌpent ˈʌp/ *adj.* **1** (of feelings, energy, etc.) that cannot be expressed or released: *pent-up frustration/energy* **2** having feelings that you cannot express: *She was too pent-up to speak.*

pen·ul·ti·mate /penˈʌltɪmət/ *adj.* [only before noun] immediately before the last one SYN **last but one**: *the penultimate chapter/day/stage*

pen·um·bra /pəˈnʌmbrə/ *noun* (*technical*) **1** an area of shadow which is between fully dark and fully light **2** (*astronomy*) the shadow made by the earth or the moon during a PARTIAL ECLIPSE ➲ compare UMBRA

pen·uri·ous /pəˈnjʊəriəs; *NAmE* -ˈnʊr-/ *adj.* (*formal*) very poor SYN **destitute, penniless**

pen·ury /ˈpenjəri/ *noun* [U] (*formal*) the state of being very poor SYN **poverty**

peon /ˈpiːən/ *noun* **1** a worker on a farm in Latin America **2** (*NAmE, humorous*) a person with a hard or boring job that is not well paid and not considered important

peony /ˈpiːəni/ *noun* (*pl.* **-ies**) a garden plant with large round white, pink or red flowers

people /ˈpiːpl/ *noun, verb*

■ ***noun*** **1** [pl.] persons; men, women and children: *At least ten people were killed in the crash.* ◇ *There were a lot of people at the party.* ◇ *Many young people are out of work.* **2** [pl.] persons in general or everyone: *He doesn't care what people think of him.* ◇ *She tends to annoy people.* HELP Use **everyone** or **everybody** instead of 'all people'. **3** [C] all the persons who live in a particular place or belong to a particular country, race, etc: *the French people* ◇ *the native peoples of Siberia* ➲ see also TOWNSPEOPLE **4** **the people** [pl.] the ordinary men and women of a country rather than those who govern or have a special position in society: *the life of the common people* ◇ *It was felt that the government was no longer in touch with the people.* ➲ see also LITTLE PEOPLE **5** [pl.] men and women who work in a particular type of job or are involved in a particular area of activity: *a meeting with business people and bankers* ◇ *These garments are intended for professional sports people.* **6** [pl.] (*literary*) the men, women and children that a person leads: *The king urged his people to prepare for war.* **7** [pl.] the men and women who work for you or support you: *I've had my people watching the house for a few days.* **8** [pl.] (*BrE, informal*) guests or friends: *I'm having people to dinner this evening.* **9** [pl.] (*old-fashioned*) the men, women and children that you are closely related to, especially your parents, grandparents, etc: *She's spending the holidays with her people.* ➲ see also BOAT PEOPLE, STREET PEOPLE, TRADESPEOPLE

IDM **of ˈall people** when you say **of all people**, you are emphasizing that sb is the person you would most or least expect to do sth: *She of all people should know the answer to that.* **people (who live) in glass houses shouldn't throw ˈstones** (*saying*) you should not criticize other people, because they will easily find ways of criticizing you ➲ more at MAN *n.*, THING

■ ***verb*** [usually passive] **~ sth (with sth)** to live in a place or fill it with people: *The town was peopled largely by workers from the car factory and their families.* ◇ *The ballroom was peopled with guests.*

ˈ**people carrier** (also ˈ**people mover**) (both *BrE*) (*NAmE, BrE* **mini·van, Mini Van™**) *noun* a large car, like a van, designed to carry up to eight people ➲ VISUAL VOCAB page V42

ˈ**people person** *noun* (*informal*) a person who enjoys, and is good at, being with and talking to other people

Pe·oria /piˈɔːriə/ *noun* a small city in the US state of Illinois. The opinions of the people who live there are considered to be typical of opinions in the whole of the US: *Ask yourself what the folks in Peoria will think of it.*

pep /pep/ *verb, noun*
■ ***verb*** (-pp-)
PHR V ˌ**pep sb/sth**↔'**up** (*informal*) to make sb/sth more interesting or full of energy **SYN** **liven up**: *Pep up meals by adding more unusual spices.* ◇ *A walk in the fresh air will pep you up.*
■ ***noun*** [U] energy and enthusiasm

pep·per 0-ᴛ /'pepə(r)/ *noun, verb*
■ ***noun*** **1** 0-ᴛ [U] a powder made from dried BERRIES (called PEPPERCORNS), used to give a hot flavour to food: *Season with* ***salt and pepper*** ◇ *freshly* ***ground pepper*** ➲ see also BLACK PEPPER, CAYENNE, WHITE PEPPER **2** (*BrE*) (also ˌ**sweet** '**pepper** *BrE, NAmE*) (*NAmE* '**bell pepper**) [C, U] a hollow fruit, usually red, green or yellow, eaten as a vegetable either raw or cooked ➲ VISUAL VOCAB page V27
■ ***verb*** **~ sth** to put pepper on food: *peppered steak* ◇ *Salt and pepper the potatoes.*
PHR V '**pepper sb/sth with sth** [usually passive] to hit sb/sth with a series of small objects, especially bullets **SYN** **spray** '**pepper sth with sth** [often passive] to include large numbers of sth in sth: *He peppered his speech with jokes.*

ˌ**pepper-and-'salt** (also ˌ**salt-and-'pepper**) *adj.* (especially of hair) having two colours that are mixed together, especially a dark colour and a light one

pep·per·corn /'pepəkɔːn; *NAmE* -pərkɔːrn/ *noun* a dried BERRY from a tropical plant, that is crushed to make pepper ➲ VISUAL VOCAB page V28

ˌ**peppercorn 'rent** *noun* (*BrE*) a very low rent

pep·per·mint /'pepəmɪnt; *NAmE* -pərm-/ *noun* **1** [U] a type of MINT (= a plant used to give flavour to food that produces an oil with a strong flavour) ➲ compare SPEARMINT **2** [C] a sweet/candy flavoured with peppermint oil

pep·per·oni /ˌpepə'rəʊni; *NAmE* -'roʊ-/ *noun* [U] a type of spicy SAUSAGE: *a pepperoni pizza*

'**pepper pot** (*especially BrE*) (*NAmE* usually '**pepper shaker**) *noun* a small container with holes in the top, used for putting pepper on food ➲ VISUAL VOCAB page V19

pep·pery /'pepəri/ *adj.* **1** tasting of pepper **2** bad-tempered: *a peppery old man*

'**pep pill** *noun* (*informal*) a pill containing a drug that gives you more energy or makes you happy for a short time

peppy /'pepi/ *adj.* (**pep·pier**, **pep·pi·est**) (*informal, especially NAmE*) lively and full of energy or enthusiasm: *a peppy advertising jingle*

'**pep rally** *noun* (*NAmE, informal*) a meeting of school students before a sports event to encourage support for the team: (*figurative*) *The Democrats held a pep rally on Capitol Hill yesterday.*

pep·sin /'pepsɪn/ *noun* [U] (*biology*) a substance in the stomach that breaks down PROTEINS in the process of DIGESTION

'**pep talk** *noun* (*informal*) a short speech intended to encourage sb to work harder, try to win, have more confidence, etc.

pep·tic ulcer /ˌpeptɪk 'ʌlsə(r)/ *noun* an ULCER in the DIGESTIVE SYSTEM, especially in the stomach

pep·tide /'peptaɪd/ *noun* (*chemistry*) a chemical consisting of two or more AMINO ACIDS joined together

per 0-ᴛ /pə(r); *strong form* pɜː(r)/ *prep.* used to express the cost or amount of sth for each person, number used, distance travelled, etc.: *Rooms cost £50 per person, per night.* ◇ *60 miles per hour*
IDM **as per sth** following sth that has been decided: *The work was carried out as per instructions.* **as per** '**normal**/'**usual** (*informal*) in the way that is normal or usual; as often happens: *Everyone blamed me as per usual.*

per·am·bu·la·tion /pəˌræmbju'leɪʃn/ *noun* [C] (*formal* or *humorous*) a slow walk or journey around a place, especially one made for pleasure ▸ **per·am·bu·late** *verb* /pə'ræmbjuleɪt/ [I, T] **~** (**sth**)

per·am·bul·ator /pə'ræmbjuleɪtə(r)/ *noun* **1** (*technical*) a device consisting of a wheel on a long handle, which is pushed along the ground to measure distances **2** (*old-fashioned, BrE*) = PRAM

per annum /pər 'ænəm/ *adv.* (*abbr.* **p.a.**) (from *Latin*) for each year: *earning £30 000 per annum*

per·cale /pə'keɪl; *NAmE* pər'keɪl/ *noun* [U] a type of cotton or POLYESTER cloth used for making sheets

per cap·ita /pə 'kæpɪtə; *NAmE* pər/ *adj.* (from *Latin*) for each person: *Per capita income rose sharply last year.* ▸ **per cap·ita** *adv.*: *average earnings per capita*

per·ceive **AW** /pə'siːv; *NAmE* pər's-/ *verb* (*formal*) **1** to notice or become aware of sth: **~ sth** *I perceived a change in his behaviour.* ◇ **~ that...** *She perceived that all was not well.* ◇ **~ sb/sth to be/have sth** *The patient was perceived to have difficulty in breathing.* **HELP** This pattern is usually used in the passive. **2** to understand or think of sb/sth in a particular way **SYN** **see**: **~ sb/sth/yourself** (**as sth**) *This discovery was perceived as a major breakthrough.* ◇ *She did not perceive herself as disabled.* ◇ **~ sb/sth to be/have sth** *They were widely perceived to have been unlucky.* **HELP** This pattern is usually used in the passive.

> **WORD FAMILY**
> **perceive** *verb*
> **perception** *noun*
> **perceptive** *adj.*
> **perceptible** *adj.* (≠ imperceptible)

per cent 0-ᴛ (*especially BrE*) (*NAmE* usually **per·cent**) /pə 'sent; *NAmE* pər 'sent/ (*symb.* %) *noun, adj., adv.*
■ ***noun*** 0-ᴛ (*pl.* **per cent**, **per·cent**) one part in every hundred: *Poor families spend about 80 to 90 per cent of their income on food.* ◇ *It is often stated that we use only 10 per cent of our brain.* ◇ *What per cent of the population is/are overweight?*
■ ***adj.***, ***adv.*** 0-ᴛ by, in or for every hundred: *a 15 per cent rise in price* ◇ *House prices rose five per cent last year.*

> **Grammar Point**
>
> **expressing percentages**
>
> - Percentages (= numbers of per cent) are written in words as *twenty-five per cent* and in figures as *25%*.
> - If a percentage is used with an uncountable or a singular noun the verb is generally singular: *90% of the land is cultivated.*
> - If the noun is singular but represents a group of people, the verb is singular in *NAmE* but in *BrE* it may be singular or plural: *Eighty per cent of the work force* ***is/are*** *against the strike.*
> - If the noun is plural, the verb is plural: *65% of children* ***play*** *computer games.*

per·cent·age **AW** /pə'sentɪdʒ; *NAmE* pər's-/ *noun* **1** [C+sing./pl. v.] the number, amount, rate of sth, expressed as if it is part of a total which is 100; a part or share of a whole: *What percentage of the population is/are overweight?* ◇ *A high percentage of the female staff are part-time workers.* ◇ *Interest rates are expected to rise by one* ***percentage point*** (= one per cent). ◇ *The figure is* ***expressed as a percentage.*** ◇ *The results were analysed* ***in percentage terms.*** **2** [C, usually sing.] a share of the profits of sth: *He gets a percentage for every car sold.*

per·cent·ile /pə'sentaɪl; *NAmE* pər's-/ *noun* (*technical*) one of the 100 equal groups that a larger group of people can be divided into, according to their place on a scale measuring a particular value: *Overall these students rank in the 21st percentile on the tests—that is, they did worse than 79 per cent of all children taking the test.*

per·cep·tible /pə'septəbl; *NAmE* pər's-/ *adj.* **1** (*formal*) great enough for you to notice it **SYN** **noticeable**: *a perceptible change/increase/decline/impact* ◇ *The price increase has had no perceptible effect on sales.* ◇ *Her foreign accent was* ***barely perceptible.*** **2** (*technical*) that you can notice or feel with your senses: *the perceptible world*

P

OPP **imperceptible** ▸ **per·cep·tibly** /-əbli/ *adv.*: *Income per head rose perceptibly.* ◇ *It was perceptibly colder.*

per·cep·tion AW /pə'sepʃn; *NAmE* pər's-/ *noun* **1** [U] (*technical* or *formal*) the way you notice things, especially with the senses: *our perception of reality* ◇ *visual perception* ➲ see also EXTRASENSORY PERCEPTION **2** [U] (*formal*) the ability to understand the true nature of sth SYN **insight**: *She showed great perception in her assessment of the family situation.* **3** [U, C] (*formal*) an idea, a belief or an image you have as a result of how you see or understand sth: *a campaign to change public perception of the police* ◇ **~ that...** *There is a general public perception that standards in schools are falling.*

per·cep·tive /pə'septɪv; *NAmE* pər's-/ *adj.* **1** (*approving*) having or showing the ability to see or understand things quickly, especially things that are not obvious: *a* **highly perceptive** *comment* ◇ *It was very perceptive of you to notice that.* **2** (*technical* or *formal*) connected with seeing, hearing and understanding: *our innate perceptive abilities* ▸ **per·cep·tive·ly** *adv.* **per·cep·tive·ness** *noun* [U]

per·cep·tual /pə'septʃuəl; *NAmE* pər's-/ *adj.* [only before noun] (*technical*) relating to the ability to PERCEIVE things or the process of PERCEIVING: *perceptual skills*

perch /pɜːtʃ; *NAmE* pɜːrtʃ/ *verb, noun*
■ ***verb*** **1** [I] **~ (on sth)** (of a bird) to land and stay on a branch, etc: *A robin was perching on the fence.* **2** [I, T] (*informal*) to sit or to make sb sit on sth, especially on the edge of it: **~ (on sth)** *We perched on a couple of high stools at the bar.* ◇ **~ sb/yourself (on sth)** *She perched herself on the edge of the bed.* ➲ SYNONYMS at SIT **3** [I] **~ (on sth)** to be placed on the top or the edge of sth: *The hotel perched precariously on a steep hillside.*
■ ***noun*** **1** a place where a bird rests, especially a branch or bar for this purpose, for example in a bird's CAGE **2** a high seat or position: *He watched the game from his precarious perch on top of the wall.* **3** (*pl.* **perch**) a FRESHWATER fish that is sometimes used for food IDM see KNOCK *v.*

per·chance /pə'tʃɑːns; *NAmE* pər'tʃæns/ *adv.* (*old use*) perhaps

perched /pɜːtʃt; *NAmE* pɜːrtʃt/ *adj.* **~ on, etc. sth 1** (especially of a bird) sitting or resting on sth: *There was a bird perched on the roof.* **2** placed in a high and/or dangerous position: *a hotel perched high on the cliffs*

per·cipi·ent /pə'sɪpiənt; *NAmE* pər's-/ *adj.* (*formal*) having or showing the ability to understand things, especially things that are not obvious SYN **perceptive**

per·co·late /'pɜːkəleɪt; *NAmE* 'pɜːrk-/ *verb* **1** [I] (+ **adv./prep.**) (of a liquid, gas, etc.) to move gradually through a surface that has very small holes or spaces in it: *Water had percolated down through the rocks.* **2** [I] to gradually become known or spread through a group or society: *It had percolated through to us that something interesting was about to happen.* **3** [T, I] **~ (sth)** to make coffee in a percolator; to be made in this way ▸ **per·co·la·tion** /ˌpɜːkə'leɪʃn; *NAmE* ˌpɜːrk-/ *noun* [U]

per·co·la·tor /'pɜːkəleɪtə(r); *NAmE* 'pɜːrk-/ *noun* a pot for making coffee, in which boiling water is forced up a central tube and then comes down again through the coffee

per·cus·sion /pə'kʌʃn; *NAmE* pər'k-/ *noun* **1** [U] musical instruments that you play by hitting them with your hand or with a stick, for example drums: *percussion instruments* ◇ *The track features Joey Langton* **on percussion**. ➲ VISUAL VOCAB page V30 **2 the percussion** [sing.] (also **per'cussion section** [C]) the players of percussion instruments in an ORCHESTRA ➲ compare BRASS, STRINGS, WOODWIND

per·cus·sion·ist /pə'kʌʃənɪst; *NAmE* pər'k-/ *noun* a person who plays percussion instruments

per·cus·sive /pə'kʌsɪv; *NAmE* pər'k-/ *adj.* (*technical*) connected with sounds made by hitting things, especially PERCUSSION instruments

per·cu·tan·eous /ˌpɜːkjuː'teɪniəs; *NAmE* ˌpɜːrk-/ *adj.* (*medical*) made or done through the skin: *a percutaneous injection*

per diem /ˌpɜː 'diːem; *NAmE* ˌpɜːr/ *adj., noun* (from Latin, especially *NAmE*)
■ ***adj.*** [only before noun] (of money) for each day: *a per diem allowance* ▸ **per diem** *adv.*: *He agreed to pay at specified rates per diem.*
■ ***noun*** [U, C] money paid, for example to employees, for things they need to buy every day: *He will get $14 000 a year in per diem to help with the higher costs of living in Washington.*

per·di·tion /pɜː'dɪʃn; *NAmE* pɜːr'd-/ *noun* [U] (*formal*) punishment that lasts for ever after death

pere·grin·ation /ˌperəgrɪ'neɪʃn/ *noun* [usually pl.] (*literary* or *humorous*) a journey, especially a long slow one

pere·grine /'perɪgrɪn/ (also ˌ**peregrine 'falcon**) *noun* a grey and white BIRD OF PREY (= a bird that kills other creatures for food) that can be trained to hunt for sport

per·emp·tor·ily /pə'remptrəli/ *adv.* (*formal, disapproving*) in a way that allows no discussion or refusal: *She peremptorily rejected the request.*

per·emp·tory /pə'remptəri/ *adj.* (*formal, disapproving*) (especially of sb's manner or behaviour) expecting to be obeyed immediately and without question or refusal: *a peremptory summons* ◇ *The letter was peremptory in tone.*

per·en·nial /pə'reniəl/ *adj., noun*
■ ***adj.*** **1** continuing for a very long time; happening again and again: *the perennial problem of water shortage* ◇ *that perennial favourite, hamburgers* **2** (of plants) living for two years or more ▸ **per·en·ni·al·ly** /-niəli/ *adv.*: *a perennially popular subject*
■ ***noun*** any plant that lives for more than two years ➲ compare ANNUAL, BIENNIAL

per·fect 0-w *adj., verb, noun*
■ ***adj.*** /'pɜːfɪkt; *NAmE* 'pɜːrf-/ **1** 0-w having everything that is necessary; complete and without faults or weaknesses: *in perfect condition* ◇ *a perfect set of teeth* ◇ *Well I'm sorry—but* **nobody's perfect** (= used when sb has criticized you). **2** 0-w completely correct; exact and accurate: *She speaks perfect English.* ◇ *a* **perfect copy/fit/match** ◇ *What* **perfect timing!** ➲ see also WORD-PERFECT **3** 0-w the best of its kind: *a* **perfect example** *of the painter's early style* ◇ *the* **perfect crime** (= one in which the criminal is never discovered) **4** 0-w excellent; very good: *The weather was perfect.* ➲ SYNONYMS at EXCELLENT **5** 0-w **~ for sb/sth** exactly right for sb/sth SYN **ideal**: *It was a perfect day for a picnic.* ◇ *She's the perfect candidate for the job.* ◇ *'Will 2.30 be OK for you?' 'Perfect, thanks.'* **6** [only before noun] total; complete: *I don't know him—he's a perfect stranger.* **7** (*grammar*) connected with the form of a verb that consists of part of the verb *have* with the past participle of the main verb, used to express actions completed by the present or a particular point in the past or future: *'I have eaten' is the present perfect tense of the verb 'to eat', 'I had eaten' is the past perfect and 'I will have eaten' is the future perfect.* ➲ see also FUTURE PERFECT, PAST PERFECT, PRESENT PERFECT IDM see PRACTICE, WORLD
■ ***verb*** /pə'fekt; *NAmE* pər'f-/ **~ sth** to make sth perfect or as good as you can: *As a musician, she has spent years perfecting her technique.*
■ ***noun*** /'pɜːfɪkt; *NAmE* 'pɜːrf-/ **the perfect** (also **the ˌper·fect 'tense**) [sing.] (*grammar*) the form of a verb that expresses actions completed by the present or a particular point in the past or future, formed in English with part of the verb *have* and the past participle of the main verb ➲ see also FUTURE PERFECT, PAST PERFECT, PRESENT PERFECT

per·fec·tion /pə'fekʃn; *NAmE* pər'f-/ *noun* [U, sing.] **1** the state of being perfect: *physical perfection* ◇ *The fish was cooked* **to perfection**. ◇ *The novel achieves a perfection of form that is quite new.* ◇ *His performance was perfection* (= sth perfect). **2** the act of making sth perfect by doing the final improvements: *They have been working on the perfection of the new model.* IDM see COUNSEL *n.*

per·fec·tion·ist /pə'fekʃənɪst; *NAmE* pər'f-/ *noun* (sometimes *disapproving*) a person who likes to do things perfectly and is not satisfied with anything less ▸ **per·fec·tion·ism** /pəˈfekʃənɪzəm; *NAmE* pərˈf-/ *noun* [U]

per·fect·ly 🗝 /ˈpɜːfɪktli; *NAmE* ˈpɜːrf-/ *adv.* **1** 🗝 completely: *It's perfectly normal to feel like this.* ◇ *It's perfectly good as it is* (= it doesn't need changing). ◇ *You* ***know perfectly well*** *what I mean.* ◇ *To be* ***perfectly honest****, I didn't want to go anyway.* ◇ *He stood perfectly still until the danger had passed.* ◇ *'Do you understand?' 'Perfectly.'* ◇ (*old-fashioned*) *How perfectly awful!* **2** 🗝 in a perfect way: *The TV works perfectly now.* ◇ *It fits perfectly.*

ˌperfect ˈpitch *noun* [U] (*music*) the ability to identify or sing a musical note correctly without the help of an instrument

ˌperfect ˈstorm *noun* [sing.] (*especially NAmE*) an occasion when several bad things happen at the same time, creating a situation that could not be worse

per·fidi·ous /pəˈfɪdiəs; *NAmE* pərˈf-/ *adj.* (*literary*) that cannot be trusted **SYN** **treacherous**

per·fidy /ˈpɜːfədi; *NAmE* ˈpɜːrf-/ *noun* [U] (*literary*) unfair treatment of sb who trusts you **SYN** **treachery**

per·for·ate /ˈpɜːfəreɪt; *NAmE* ˈpɜːrf-/ *verb* **~ sth** to make a hole or holes through sth: *The explosion perforated his eardrum.* ◇ *a perforated line* (= a row of small holes in paper, made so that a part can be torn off easily)

per·for·ation /ˌpɜːfəˈreɪʃn; *NAmE* ˌpɜːrf-/ *noun* **1** [C, usually pl.] a small hole in a surface, often one of a series of small holes: *Tear the sheet of stamps along the perforations.* **2** [U] (*medical*) the process of splitting or tearing in such a way that a hole is left: *Excessive pressure can lead to perforation of the stomach wall.*

per·force /pəˈfɔːs; *NAmE* pərˈfɔːrs/ *adv.* (*old use* or *formal*) because it is necessary or cannot be avoided **SYN** **necessarily**

per·form 🗝 /pəˈfɔːm; *NAmE* pərˈfɔːrm/ *verb* **1** 🗝 [T] **~ sth** to do sth, such as a piece of work, task or duty **SYN** **carry out**: *to perform an experiment/a miracle/a ceremony* ◇ *She performs an important role in our organization.* ◇ *This operation has never been performed in this country.* ◇ *A computer can perform many tasks at once.* **2** 🗝 [T, I] **~ (sth)** to entertain an audience by playing a piece of music, acting in a play, etc: *to perform somersaults/magic tricks* ◇ *The play was first performed in 2007.* ◇ *I'd like to hear it performed live.* ◇ *to perform on the flute* ◇ *I'm looking forward to seeing you perform.* **3** 🗝 [I] **~ (well/badly/poorly)** to work or function well or badly: *The engine seems to be performing well.* ◇ *The company has been performing poorly over the past year.* **IDM** see MIRACLE

per·form·ance 🗝 /pəˈfɔːməns; *NAmE* pərˈfɔːrm-/ *noun* **1** 🗝 [C] the act of performing a play, concert or some other form of entertainment: *The performance starts at seven.* ◇ *an evening performance* ◇ *a performance of Ravel's String Quartet* ◇ *a series of performances by the Kirov Ballet* ◇ *one of the band's rare* ***live performances*** ➲ COLLOCATIONS at MUSIC **2** 🗝 [C] the way a person performs in a play, concert, etc: *She* ***gave the*** *greatest* ***performance*** *of her career.* ◇ *an Oscar-winning performance from Kate Winslet* ➲ COLLOCATIONS at CINEMA **3** 🗝 [U, C] how well or badly you do sth; how well or badly sth works: *the country's economic performance* ◇ *It was an impressive performance by the French team.* ◇ *The new management techniques aim to improve performance.* ◇ *He criticized the recent poor performance of the company.* ◇ ***high-performance*** (= very powerful) *cars* ◇ ***performance indicators*** (= things that show how well or badly sth is working) ➲ compare PAY-FOR-PERFORMANCE, PERFORMANCE-RELATED **4** [U, sing.] (*formal*) the act or process of performing a task, an action, etc: *She has shown enthusiasm in the performance of her duties.* ◇ *He did not want* ***a repeat performance*** *of the humiliating defeat he had suffered.* **5** [sing.] (*informal, especially BrE*) an act that involves a lot of effort or trouble, sometimes when it is not necessary **SYN** **carry-on**: *It's such a performance getting the children off to school in the morning.*

perˈformance art *noun* [U] an art form in which an artist gives a performance, rather than producing a physical work of art

perˈformance-enhancing *adj.* [only before noun] (of a substance, especially a drug) that people take so that they will be more successful in a sports competition: *steroids and other performance-enhancing drugs*

perˌformance-reˈlated *adj.* [only before noun] depending on how well a person does their job: *Is there any evidence that* ***performance-related pay*** *actually improves performance?* ➲ compare PAY-FOR-PERFORMANCE, PERFORMANCE (3)

per·forma·tive /pəˈfɔːmətɪv; *NAmE* pərˈfɔːrm-/ *adj.* (*grammar*) when sb uses a performative word or expression, for example 'I promise' or 'I apologize', they are also doing sth (promising or apologizing) ➲ see also CONSTATIVE

per·form·er 🗝 /pəˈfɔːmə(r); *NAmE* pərˈfɔːrm-/ *noun* **1** 🗝 a person who performs for an audience in a show, concert, etc: *a brilliant/polished/seasoned performer* **2** a person or thing that behaves or works in the way mentioned: *He was a poor performer at school and left with no qualifications.* ◇ *VW is the* ***star performer*** *of the motor industry this year.*

the perˌforming ˈarts *noun* [pl.] arts such as music, dance and drama which are performed for an audience

per·fume /ˈpɜːfjuːm; *NAmE* pərˈfjuːm/ *noun, verb*

■ ***noun*** [C, U] **1** a liquid, often made from flowers, that you put on your skin to make yourself smell nice: *a bottle of expensive perfume* ◇ *We stock a wide range of perfumes.* ◇ *the perfume counter of the store* ◇ *She was wearing too much perfume.* **2** a pleasant, often sweet, smell **SYN** **scent**: *the heady perfume of the roses*

■ ***verb*** [often passive] **1 ~ sth (with sth)** (*literary*) (especially of flowers) to make the air in a place smell pleasant **SYN** **scent**: *The garden was perfumed with the smell of roses.* **2 ~ sth (with sth)** to put perfume in or on sth: *She perfumed her bath with fragrant oils.* ▸ **per·fumed** *adj.*: *perfumed soap*

per·fumery /pəˈfjuːməri; *NAmE* pərˈf-/ *noun* (*pl.* -ies) **1** [C] a place where perfumes are made and/or sold **2** [U] the process of making perfume

per·func·tory /pəˈfʌŋktəri; *NAmE* pərˈf-/ *adj.* (*formal*) (of an action) done as a duty or habit, without real interest, attention or feeling: *a perfunctory nod/smile* ◇ *They only made a perfunctory effort.* ▸ **per·func·tor·ily** /-trəli/ *adv.*: *to nod/smile perfunctorily*

per·gola /ˈpɜːɡələ; *NAmE* ˈpɜːrɡ-/ *noun* an ARCH in a garden/yard with a frame for plants to grow over and through ➲ VISUAL VOCAB page V16

Language Bank

perhaps

Making an opinion sound less definite

- Most cybercrime involves traditional crimes, such as theft and fraud, being committed in new ways. Phishing is **perhaps/possibly/probably** the best-known example of this.
- It **seems/appears** that the more personal data which organizations collect, the more opportunity there is for this data to be lost or stolen.
- **It seems clear that** introducing national ID cards would do little to prevent identity theft.
- **It could be argued that** the introduction of national ID cards might actually make identity theft easier.
- **It is possible that/It may be that** the only way to protect ourselves against DNA identity theft is to avoid the creation of national DNA databases.

➲ Language Banks at IMPERSONAL, OPINION

P

per·haps 0-▾ /pə'hæps; præps; *NAmE* pər'h-/ *adv.* **1** 0-▾ possibly **SYN maybe**: *'Are you going to come?' 'Perhaps. I'll see how I feel.'* ◇ *Perhaps he's forgotten.* **2** 0-▾ used when you want to make a statement or opinion less definite: *This is perhaps his best novel to date.* **3** 0-▾ used when making a rough estimate: *a change which could affect perhaps 20% of the population* **4** 0-▾ used when you agree or accept sth unwillingly, or do not want to say strongly that you disapprove: *'You could do it yourself.' 'Yeah, perhaps.'* **5** 0-▾ used when making a polite request, offer or suggestion: *Perhaps it would be better if you came back tomorrow.* ◇ *I think perhaps you've had enough to drink tonight.*

per·igee /'perɪdʒiː/ *noun* (*astronomy*) the point in the ORBIT of the moon, a planet or other object in space when it is nearest the planet, for example the earth, around which it turns ➲ compare APOGEE

peril /'perəl/ *noun* (*formal* or *literary*) **1** [U] serious danger: *The country's economy is now in grave peril.* **2** [C, usually pl.] **~ (of sth)** the fact of sth being dangerous or harmful: *a warning about the perils of drug abuse*

IDM **do sth at your (own) 'peril** used to warn sb that if they do sth, it may be dangerous or cause them problems

per·il·ous /'perələs/ *adj.* (*formal* or *literary*) very dangerous **SYN hazardous** ▸ **per·il·ous·ly** *adv.*: *We came **perilously close** to disaster.*

per·im·eter /pə'rɪmɪtə(r)/ *noun* **1** the outside edge of an area of land: *Guards patrol the perimeter of the estate.* ◇ *a **perimeter fence/track/wall*** **2** (*mathematics*) the total length of the outside edge of an area or a shape ➲ compare CIRCUMFERENCE

peri·natal /ˌperɪ'neɪtl/ *adj.* (*technical*) at or around the time of birth: *perinatal care* ◇ *perinatal mortality*

peri·neum /ˌperɪ'niːəm/ *noun* (*pl.* **peri·nea** /-'niːə/) (*anatomy*) the area between the ANUS and the SCROTUM or VULVA

period 0-▾ **AW** /'pɪəriəd; *NAmE* 'pɪr-/ *noun, adv., adj.*

■ ***noun***

▸ LENGTH OF TIME **1** 0-▾ a particular length of time: *a period of consultation/mourning/uncertainty* ◇ *The factory will be closed down over a 2-year period/a period of two years.* ◇ *This compares with a 4% increase for the same period last year.* ◇ *This offer is available for a **limited period** only.* ◇ *All these changes happened over **a period of time**.* ◇ *The aim is to reduce traffic at **peak periods**.* ◇ *You can have it for a **trial period*** (= in order to test it). ➲ see also COOLING-OFF PERIOD **2** 0-▾ a length of time in the life of a particular person or in the history of a particular country: *Which period of history would you most like to have lived in?* ◇ *the post-war period* ◇ *Like Picasso, she too had a blue period.* ◇ *Most teenagers go through a period of rebelling.* **3** (*geology*) a length of time which is a division of an ERA. A period is divided into EPOCHS: *the Jurassic period*

▸ LESSON **4** any of the parts that a day is divided into at a school, college, etc. for study: *'What do you have next period?' 'French.'* ◇ *a **free/study period*** (= for private study)

▸ WOMAN **5** the flow of blood each month from the body of a woman who is not pregnant: *period pains* ◇ *monthly periods* ◇ *When did you last **have a period**?* ➲ compare MENSTRUATION

▸ PUNCTUATION **6** (*NAmE*) (*BrE* **ˌfull 'stop**) the mark (.) used at the end of a sentence and in some abbreviations, for example *e.g.*

■ ***adv.*** (*especially NAmE*) (*BrE* also **ˌfull 'stop**) (*informal*) used at the end of a sentence to emphasize that there is nothing more to say about a subject: *The answer is no, period!*

■ ***adj.*** [only before noun] having a style typical of a particular time in history: *period costumes/furniture*

peri·od·ic **AW** /ˌpɪəri'ɒdɪk; *NAmE* ˌpɪri'ɑːdɪk/ (also *less frequent* **peri·od·ical** /-kl/) *adj.* [usually before noun] happening fairly often and regularly: *Periodic checks are carried out on the equipment.* ▸ **peri·od·ic·al·ly** **AW** /-kli/ *adv.*: *Mailing lists are updated periodically.*

peri·od·ical **AW** /ˌpɪəri'ɒdɪkl; *NAmE* ˌpɪri'ɑːd-/ *noun* a magazine that is published every week, month, etc, especially one that is concerned with an academic subject

the ˌperiodic 'table *noun* [sing.] (*chemistry*) a list of all the chemical elements, arranged according to their ATOMIC NUMBER

peri·odon·tal /ˌperiə'dɒntl; *NAmE* -'dɑːn-/ *adj.* (*medical*) related to or affecting the parts of the mouth that surround and support the teeth

peri·odon·titis /ˌperiədɒn'taɪtɪs; *NAmE* -dɑːn-/ (*BrE* also **pyor·rhoea**) (*NAmE* also **pyor·rhea**) *noun* [U] (*medical*) a condition in which the area around the teeth becomes sore and swollen, which may make the teeth fall out

'period piece *noun* **1** a play, film/movie, etc. that is set in a particular period of history **2** a decorative object, piece of furniture, etc. that was made during a particular period of history and is typical of that period

peri·pat·et·ic /ˌperipə'tetɪk/ *adj.* (*formal*) going from place to place, for example in order to work: *a peripatetic music teacher*

per·iph·eral /pə'rɪfərəl/ *adj., noun*

■ ***adj.*** **1** (*formal*) not as important as the main aim, part, etc. of sth: *peripheral information* ◇ **~ to sth** *Fund-raising is peripheral to their main activities.* **2** (*technical*) connected with the outer edge of a particular area: *the peripheral nervous system* ◇ *peripheral vision* **3** (*computing*) (of equipment) connected to a computer: *a peripheral device* ▸ **per·iph·er·al·ly** /pə'rɪfərəli/ *adv.*

■ ***noun*** (*computing*) a piece of equipment that is connected to a computer: *monitors, printers and other peripherals*

per·iph·ery /pə'rɪfəri/ *noun* [usually sing.] (*pl.* **-ies**) (*formal*) **1** the outer edge of a particular area: *industrial development **on the periphery of** the town* ◇ *The condition makes it difficult for patients to see objects at the periphery of their vision.* **2** the less important part of sth, for example of a particular activity or of a social or political group: *minor parties **on the periphery of** American politics*

peri·phrasis /pə'rɪfrəsɪs/ *noun* [U] **1** (*technical*) the use of an indirect way of speaking or writing **2** (*grammar*) the use of separate words to express a GRAMMATICAL relationship, instead of verb endings, etc. ▸ **peri·phras·tic** /ˌperɪ'fræstɪk/ *adj.*

peri·scope /'perɪskəʊp; *NAmE* -skoʊp/ *noun* a device like a long tube, containing mirrors which enable the user to see over the top of sth, used especially in a SUBMARINE (= a ship that can operate underwater) to see above the surface of the sea

per·ish /'perɪʃ/ *verb* **1** [I] (*formal* or *literary*) (of people or animals) to die, especially in a sudden violent way: *A family of four perished in the fire.* **2** [I] (*formal*) to be lost or destroyed: *Early buildings were made of wood and have perished.* **3** [I, T] **~ (sth)** (*BrE*) if a material such as rubber **perishes** or **is perished**, it becomes damaged, weaker or full of holes

IDM **ˌperish the 'thought** (*informal* or *humorous*) used to say that you find a suggestion unacceptable or that you hope that sth will never happen: *Me get married? Perish the thought!*

per·ish·able /'perɪʃəbl/ *adj.* (especially of food) likely to decay or go bad quickly: ***perishable goods/foods***

per·ish·ables /'perɪʃəblz/ *noun* [pl.] (*technical*) types of food that decay or go bad quickly

per·ished /'perɪʃt/ *adj.* [not before noun] (*BrE, informal*) (of a person) very cold: *We were perished.*

per·ish·er /'perɪʃə(r)/ *noun* (*old-fashioned, BrE, informal*) a child, especially one who behaves badly

per·ish·ing /'perɪʃɪŋ/ *adj.* (*BrE, informal*) **1** extremely cold **SYN freezing**: *It's perishing outside!* ◇ *I'm perishing!* **2** [only before noun] (*old-fashioned*) used to show that you are annoyed about sth: *I've had enough of this perishing job!*

peri·stal·sis /ˌperɪ'stælsɪs/ *noun* [U] (*biology*) the wave-like movements of the INTESTINE, etc. caused when the muscles contract and relax

peri·ton·eum /ˌperɪtəˈniːəm/ *noun* (*pl.* **peri·ton·eums** or **peri·ton·ea** /-ˈniːə/) (*anatomy*) the MEMBRANE (= very thin layer of TISSUE) on the inside of the ABDOMEN that covers the stomach and other organs

peri·ton·itis /ˌperɪtəˈnaɪtɪs/ *noun* [U] (*medical*) a serious condition in which the inside wall of the body becomes swollen and infected

peri·win·kle /ˈperiwɪŋkl/ *noun* **1** [C, U] a small plant that grows along the ground **2** (*BrE* also **win·kle**) [C] a small SHELLFISH, like a SNAIL, that can be eaten

per·jure /ˈpɜːdʒə(r); *NAmE* ˈpɜːrdʒ-/ *verb* **~ yourself** (*law*) to tell a lie in court after you have sworn to tell the truth ▶ **per·jurer** /ˈpɜːdʒərə(r); *NAmE* ˈpɜːrdʒ-/ *noun*

per·jury /ˈpɜːdʒəri; *NAmE* ˈpɜːrdʒ-/ *noun* [U] (*law*) the crime of telling a lie in court

perk /pɜːk; *NAmE* pɜːrk/ *noun, verb*

▪ ***noun*** (also *formal* **per·quis·ite**) [usually pl.] something you receive as well as your wages for doing a particular job: *Perks offered by the firm include a car and free health insurance.* ◇ (*figurative*) *Not having to get up early is just one of the perks of being retired.*

▪ ***verb***

PHR V ˌ**perk ˈup** | ˌ**perk sb↔ˈup** (*informal*) to become or to make sb become more cheerful or lively, especially after they have been ill/sick or sad **SYN** **brighten**: *He soon perked up when his friends arrived.* ˌ**perk ˈup** | ˌ**perk sth↔ˈup** (*informal*) to increase, or to make sth increase in value, etc: *Share prices had perked up slightly by close of trading.* ˌ**perk sth↔ˈup** (*informal*) to make sth more interesting, more attractive, etc. **SYN** **liven up**: *ideas for perking up bland food*

perky /ˈpɜːki; *NAmE* ˈpɜːrki/ *adj.* (**perk·ier**, **perki·est**) (*informal*) cheerful and full of energy ▶ **perki·ness** *noun* [U]

perm /pɜːm; *NAmE* pɜːrm/ *noun, verb*

▪ ***noun*** a way of changing the style of your hair by using chemicals to create curls that last for several months: *to have a perm*

▪ ***verb*** **~ sth** to give sb's hair a perm: *to have your hair permed* ◇ *a shampoo for permed hair* ➲ **VISUAL VOCAB** page V49

perma·frost /ˈpɜːməfrɒst; *NAmE* ˈpɜːrməfrɔːst; ˈpɜːrməfrɑːst/ *noun* [U] (*technical*) a layer of soil that is permanently frozen, in very cold regions of the world

per·man·ence /ˈpɜːmənəns; *NAmE* ˈpɜːrm-/ (also *less frequent* **per·man·ency** /-nənsi/) *noun* [U] the state of lasting for a long time or for all time in the future: *The spoken word is immediate but lacks permanence.* ◇ *We no longer talk of the permanence of marriage.*

per·man·ent 🔑 /ˈpɜːmənənt; *NAmE* ˈpɜːrm-/ *adj., noun*

▪ ***adj.*** 🔑 lasting for a long time or for all time in the future; existing all the time: *a permanent job* ◇ *permanent staff* ◇ *They are now living together on a permanent basis.* ◇ *The accident has not done any permanent damage.* ◇ *a permanent fixture* (= a person or an object that is always in a particular place) **OPP** **impermanent**, **temporary** ▶ **per·man·ent·ly** 🔑 *adv.*: *The stroke left his right side permanently damaged.* ◇ *She had decided to settle permanently in France.*

▪ ***noun*** (*old-fashioned*, *NAmE*) = PERM

ˌ**Permanent ˈResident Card** *noun* an official card that shows that sb from another country is allowed to live and work in Canada

ˌ**Permanent ˈUndersecretary** (also ˌ**Permanent ˈSecretary**) *noun* (in Britain) a person of high rank in the CIVIL SERVICE, who advises a SECRETARY OF STATE ➲ compare UNDERSECRETARY

ˌ**permanent ˈwave** *noun* (*old-fashioned*) = PERM

perma·tan /ˈpɜːmətæn; *NAmE* ˈpɜːrmə-/ *noun* (*BrE*, *informal*, *humorous*) the brown skin colour that a person with pale skin gets from being in the sun, when they have this skin colour all year

per·me·able /ˈpɜːmiəbl; *NAmE* ˈpɜːrm-/ *adj.* **~ (to sth)** (*technical*) allowing a liquid or gas to pass through: *The skin of amphibians is permeable to water.* ◇ *permeable rocks* **OPP** **impermeable** ▶ **per·mea·bil·ity** /ˌpɜːmiəˈbɪləti; *NAmE* ˌpɜːrm-/ *noun* [U]

per·me·ate /ˈpɜːmieɪt; *NAmE* ˈpɜːrm-/ *verb* (*formal*) **1** [T, I] (of a liquid, gas, etc.) to spread to every part of an object or a place: **~ sth** *The smell of leather permeated the room.* ◇ **+ adv./prep.** *rainwater permeating through the ground* **2** [T, I] (of an idea, an influence, a feeling, etc.) to affect every part of sth: **~ sth** *a belief that permeates all levels of society* ◇ **+ adv./prep.** *Dissatisfaction among the managers soon permeated down to members of the workforce.* ▶ **per·me·ation** /ˌpɜːmiˈeɪʃn; *NAmE* ˌpɜːrm-/ *noun* [U] (*formal*)

per·mis·sible /pəˈmɪsəbl; *NAmE* pərˈm-/ *adj.* (*formal*) acceptable according to the law or a particular set of rules: *permissible levels of nitrates in water* ◇ **~ (for sb) (to do sth)** *It is not permissible for employers to discriminate on grounds of age.*

per·mis·sion 🔑 /pəˈmɪʃn; *NAmE* pərˈm-/ *noun*

1 🔑 [U] the act of allowing sb to do sth, especially when this is done by sb in a position of authority: **~ (for sth)** *You must **ask permission** for all major expenditure.* ◇ **~ (for sb/sth) (to do sth)** *The school has been refused permission to expand.* ◇ *No official **permission** has been **given** for the event to take place.* ◇ *She took the car **without permission**.* ◇ *poems reprinted **by kind permission of** the author* ◇ (*formal*) *With your permission, I'd like to say a few words.* **2** [C, usually pl.] an official written statement allowing sb to do sth: *The publisher is responsible for obtaining the necessary permissions to reproduce illustrations.* ➲ see also PLANNING PERMISSION

per·mis·sive /pəˈmɪsɪv; *NAmE* pərˈm-/ *adj.* allowing or showing a freedom of behaviour that many people do not approve of, especially in sexual matters: *permissive attitudes* ◇ *permissive parents* (= who allow their children a lot of freedom) ▶ **per·mis·sive·ness** *noun* [U]

the perˌmissive soˈciety *noun* [sing.] (often *disapproving*) the changes towards greater freedom in attitudes and behaviour that happened in many countries in the 1960s and 1970s, especially the greater freedom in sexual matters

P

per·mit 🔑 *verb, noun*

▪ ***verb*** /pəˈmɪt; *NAmE* pərˈm-/ (**-tt-**) (*formal*) **1** 🔑 [T] to allow sb to do sth or to allow sth to happen: **~ sth** *Radios are not permitted in the library.* ◇ *There are fines for exceeding permitted levels of noise pollution.* ◇ **~ sb/yourself sth** *We were not permitted any contact with each other.* ◇ *Jim permitted himself a wry smile.* ◇ **~ sb/yourself to do sth** *Visitors are not permitted to take photographs.* ◇ *She would not permit herself to look at them.* ◇ (*formal*) *Permit me to offer you some advice.* **2** 🔑 [I, T] to make sth possible: *We hope to visit the cathedral, if time permits.* ◇ *I'll come tomorrow, **weather permitting*** (= if the weather is fine). ◇ **~ sth** *The password permits access to all files on the hard disk.* ◇ **~ sb/sth to do sth** *Cash machines permit you to withdraw money at any time.*

▪ ***noun*** /ˈpɜːmɪt; *NAmE* ˈpɜːrmɪt/ an official document that gives sb the right to do sth, especially for a limited period of time: *a **fishing/residence/parking, etc. permit*** ◇ *to **apply for a permit*** ◇ *to **issue a permit*** ➲ see also WORK PERMIT

per·mu·ta·tion /ˌpɜːmjuˈteɪʃn; *NAmE* ˌpɜːrm-/ *noun* [usually pl.] any of the different ways in which a set of things can be ordered: *The possible permutations of x, y and z are xyz, xzy, yxz, yzx, zxy and zyx.*

per·ni·cious /pəˈnɪʃəs; *NAmE* pərˈn-/ *adj.* (*formal*) having a very harmful effect on sb/sth, especially in a way that is gradual and not easily noticed

per·nick·ety /pəˈnɪkəti; *NAmE* pərˈn-/ (*especially BrE*) (*NAmE* usually **per·snick·ety**) *adj.* (*informal*, *disapproving*) worrying too much about unimportant details; showing this **SYN** **fussy**

per·or·ation /ˌperəˈreɪʃn/ *noun* (*formal*) **1** the final part of a speech in which the speaker gives a summary of the main points **2** (*disapproving*) a long speech that is not very interesting

per·ox·ide /pəˈrɒksaɪd; *NAmE* -ˈrɑːk-/ (also ˌ**hydrogen peˈroxide**) *noun* [U] a clear liquid used to kill bacteria and to BLEACH hair (= make it lighter): *a woman with peroxide blonde hair*

per·pen·dicu·lar /ˌpɜːpənˈdɪkjələ(r); *NAmE* ˌpɜːrp-/ *adj., noun*

■ ***adj.* 1 ~ (to sth)** (*technical*) forming an angle of 90° with another line or surface; vertical and going straight up: *Are the lines perpendicular to each other?* ◇ *The staircase was almost perpendicular* (= very steep). **2 Perpendicular** (*architecture*) connected with a style of ARCHITECTURE common in England in the 14th and 15th centuries, that makes use of vertical lines and wide ARCHES

■ ***noun* the perpendicular** [sing.] a line, position or direction that is exactly perpendicular: *The wall is a little out of the perpendicular.*

per·pet·rate /ˈpɜːpətreɪt; *NAmE* ˈpɜːrp-/ *verb* (*formal*) to commit a crime or do sth wrong or evil: **~ sth** *to* ***perpetrate a crime/fraud/massacre*** ◇ **~ sth against/upon/on sb** *violence perpetrated against women and children* ▸ **per·pet·ra·tion** /ˌpɜːpəˈtreɪʃn; *NAmE* ˌpɜːrp-/ *noun* [U]

per·pet·ra·tor /ˈpɜːpətreɪtə(r); *NAmE* ˈpɜːrp-/ *noun* a person who commits a crime or does sth that is wrong or evil: *the perpetrators of the crime*

per·pet·ual /pəˈpetʃuəl; *NAmE* pərˈp-/ *adj.* **1** [usually before noun] continuing for a long period of time without interruption SYN **continuous**: *the perpetual noise of traffic* ◇ *We lived for years in a perpetual state of fear.* **2** [usually before noun] frequently repeated, in a way that is annoying SYN **continual**: *How can I work with these perpetual interruptions?* **3** [only before noun] (of a job or position) lasting for the whole of sb's life: *He was elected perpetual president.* ◇ (*humorous*) *She's a perpetual student.* ▸ **per·petu·al·ly** /-tʃuəli/ *adv.*

perˌpetual ˈmotion *noun* [U] a state in which sth moves continuously without stopping, or appears to do so: *We're all in a state of* ***perpetual motion*** *in this office* (= we're always moving around or changing things).

per·petu·ate /pəˈpetʃueɪt; *NAmE* pərˈp-/ *verb* **~ sth** (*formal*) to make sth such as a bad situation, a belief, etc. continue for a long time: *to perpetuate injustice* ◇ *This system perpetuated itself for several centuries.* ◇ *Comics tend to perpetuate the myth that 'boys don't cry'.* ▸ **per·petu·ation** /pəˌpetʃuˈeɪʃn; *NAmE* pərˌp-/ *noun* [U]

per·petu·ity /ˌpɜːpəˈtjuːəti; *NAmE* ˌpɜːrpəˈtuː-/ *noun* [U] IDM **in perpetuity** (*formal*) for all time in the future SYN **forever**: *They do not own the land in perpetuity.*

per·plex /pəˈpleks; *NAmE* pərˈp-/ *verb* [usually passive] **~ sb | it perplexes sb that...** if sth **perplexes** you, it makes you confused or worried because you do not understand it SYN **puzzle**: *They were perplexed by her response.* ▸ **per·plex·ing** *adj.*: *a perplexing problem*

per·plexed /pəˈplekst; *NAmE* pərˈp-/ *adj.* confused and anxious because you are unable to understand sth; showing this: *a perplexed expression* ◇ *She looked perplexed.* ▸ **per·plex·ed·ly** /-ɪdli/ *adv.*

per·plex·ity /pəˈpleksəti; *NAmE* pərˈp-/ *noun* (*pl.* -ies) (*formal*) **1** [U] the state of feeling confused and anxious because you do not understand sth SYN **confusion**: *Most of them just stared at her in perplexity.* **2** [C, usually pl.] something that is difficult to understand: *the perplexities of life*

per·quis·ite /ˈpɜːkwɪzɪt; *NAmE* ˈpɜːrk-/ *noun* (*formal*) **1** [usually pl.] = PERK **2 ~ (of sb)** something to which sb has a special right because of their social position: *Politics used to be the perquisite of the property-owning classes.*

perry /ˈperi/ *noun* [U] a slightly sweet alcoholic drink made from the juice of PEARS ➲ compare CIDER

per se /ˌpɜː ˈseɪ; *NAmE* ˌpɜːr/ *adv.* (from *Latin*) used meaning 'by itself' to show that you are referring to sth on its own, rather than in connection with other things: *The drug is not harmful per se, but is dangerous when taken with alcohol.*

per·se·cute /ˈpɜːsɪkjuːt; *NAmE* ˈpɜːrs-/ *verb* [often passive] **1 ~ sb (for sth)** to treat sb in a cruel and unfair way, especially because of their race, religion or political beliefs: *Throughout history, people have been persecuted for their religious beliefs.* ◇ *persecuted minorities* **2 ~ sb** to deliberately annoy sb all the time and make their life unpleasant SYN **harass**: *Why are the media persecuting him like this?* ▸ **per·se·cu·tion** /ˌpɜːsɪˈkjuːʃn; *NAmE* ˌpɜːrs-/ *noun* [U, C]: *the victims of religious persecution* ➲ COLLOCATIONS at RACE

perseˈcution complex *noun* a type of mental illness in which sb believes that other people are trying to harm them

per·se·cu·tor /ˈpɜːsɪkjuːtə(r); *NAmE* ˈpɜːrs-/ *noun* a person who treats another person or group of people in a cruel and unfair way

per·se·ver·ance /ˌpɜːsɪˈvɪərəns; *NAmE* ˌpɜːrsəˈvɪr-/ *noun* [U] (*approving*) the quality of continuing to try to achieve a particular aim despite difficulties: *They showed great perseverance in the face of difficulty.* ◇ *The only way to improve is through hard work and dogged perseverance.*

per·se·vere /ˌpɜːsɪˈvɪə(r); *NAmE* ˌpɜːrsəˈvɪr/ *verb* [I] (*approving*) to continue trying to do or achieve sth despite difficulties: **~ (in sth/in doing sth)** *Despite a number of setbacks, they persevered in their attempts to fly around the world in a balloon.* ◇ **~ (with sth/sb)** *She persevered with her violin lessons.* ◇ *You have to persevere with difficult students.*

per·se·ver·ing /ˌpɜːsɪˈvɪərɪŋ; *NAmE* ˌpɜːrsəˈvɪrɪŋ/ *adj.* [usually before noun] (*approving*) showing determination to achieve a particular aim despite difficulties

Per·sian /ˈpɜːʃn; -ʒn; *NAmE* ˈpɜːrʒn/ *noun* **1** [C] a person from ancient Persia, or modern Persia, now called Iran **2** (also **Farsi**) [U] the official language of Iran **3** [C] = PERSIAN CAT ▸ **Per·sian** *adj.*

ˌ**Persian ˈcarpet** (also ˌ**Persian ˈrug**) *noun* a carpet of traditional design from the Near East, made by hand from silk or wool

ˌ**Persian ˈcat** (also **Per·sian**) *noun* a breed of cat with long hair, short legs and a round flat face

per·si·flage /ˈpɜːsɪflɑːʒ; *NAmE* ˈpɜːrs-/ *noun* [U] (*formal*) comments and jokes in which people laugh at each other in a fairly unkind but not serious way

per·sim·mon /pəˈsɪmən; *NAmE* pərˈs-/ *noun* a sweet tropical fruit that looks like a large orange tomato ➲ VISUAL VOCAB page V26 ➲ see also SHARON FRUIT

per·sist AW /pəˈsɪst; *NAmE* pərˈs-/ *verb* **1** [I, T] to continue to do sth despite difficulties or opposition, in a way that can seem unreasonable: **~ (in doing sth)** *Why do you persist in blaming yourself for what happened?* ◇ **~ (in sth)** *She persisted in her search for the truth.* ◇ **~ (with sth)** *He persisted with his questioning.* ◇ **+ speech** *'So, did you agree or not?' he persisted.* **2** [I] to continue to exist: *If the symptoms persist, consult your doctor.*

per·sist·ence AW /pəˈsɪstəns; *NAmE* pərˈs-/ *noun* [U] **1** the fact of continuing to try to do sth despite difficulties, especially when other people are against you and think that you are being annoying or unreasonable: *His persistence was finally rewarded when the insurance company agreed to pay for the damage.* ◇ *It was her sheer persistence that wore them down in the end.* **2** the state of continuing to exist for a long period of time: *the persistence of unemployment in the 1970s and 1980s*

per·sist·ent AW /pəˈsɪstənt; *NAmE* pərˈs-/ *adj.* **1** determined to do sth despite difficulties, especially when other people are against you and think that you are being annoying or unreasonable: *How do you deal with persistent salesmen who won't take no for an answer?* ◇ *a* ***persistent offender*** (= a person who continues to commit crimes after they have been caught and punished) **2** continuing for a long period of time without interruption, or repeated frequently, especially in a way that is annoying and cannot be stopped SYN **unrelenting**: *persistent rain* ◇ *a persistent cough* ▸ **per·sist·ent·ly** AW *adv.*: *They have persistently denied claims of illegal dealing.* ◇ *persistently high interest rates*

per,sistent ,vegetative 'state *noun* (*medical*) a condition in which a person's body is kept working by medical means but the person shows no sign of brain activity

per·snick·ety /pə'snɪkəti; *NAmE* pər's-/ *adj.* (*NAmE*) = PERNICKETY

per·son /'pɜːsn; *NAmE* 'pɜːrsn/ *noun* (*pl.* **people** /'piːpl/ or, especially in formal use, **per·sons**)
1 a human as an individual: *What sort of person would do a thing like that?* ◇ *He's a fascinating person.* ◇ *What is she like as a person?* ◇ *He's just the person we need for the job.* ◇ *I had a letter from the people who used to live next door.* ◇ *I'm not really a city person* (= I don't really like cities). ➲ see also PEOPLE PERSON HELP Use **everyone** or **everybody** instead of 'all people'. **2** (*formal* or *disapproving*) a human, especially one who is not identified: *A certain person* (= somebody that I do not wish to name) *told me about it.* ◇ *The price is $40 per person.* ◇ *This vehicle is licensed to carry 4 persons.* (= in a notice) ◇ (*law*) *The verdict was murder by a person or persons unknown.* ➲ see also VIP **3** **-person** (in compounds) a person working in the area of business mentioned; a person concerned with the thing mentioned: *a salesperson* ◇ *a spokesperson* **4** (*grammar*) any of the three classes of personal pronouns. The **first person** (*I/we*) refers to the person(s) speaking; the **second person** (*you*) refers to the person(s) spoken to; the **third person** (*he/she/it/they*) refers to the person(s) or thing(s) spoken about.
IDM **about/on your 'person** if you have or carry sth **about/on your person**, you carry it about with you, for example in your pocket **in 'person** if you do sth **in person**, you go somewhere and do it yourself, instead of doing it by letter, asking sb else to do it, etc. **in the person of sb** (*formal*) in the form or shape of sb: *Help arrived in the person of his mother.* ➲ more at RESPECTER

per·sona /pə'səʊnə; *NAmE* pər'soʊnə/ *noun* (*pl.* **per·son·ae** /-niː; -naɪ/ or **per·so·nas**) (*formal*) the aspects of a person's character that they show to other people, especially when their real character is different: *His public persona is quite different from the family man described in the book.* ➲ see also DRAMATIS PERSONAE

per·son·able /'pɜːsənəbl; *NAmE* 'pɜːrs-/ *adj.* (of a person) attractive to other people because of having a pleasant appearance and character

per·son·age /'pɜːsənɪdʒ; *NAmE* 'pɜːrs-/ *noun* (*formal*) an important or famous person: *a royal personage*

per·son·al /'pɜːsənl; *NAmE* 'pɜːrs-/ *adj.*
▸ YOUR OWN **1** [only before noun] your own; not belonging to or connected with anyone else: ***personal effects/belongings/possessions*** ◇ ***personal details*** (= your name, age, etc.) ◇ *Of course, this is just a personal opinion.* ◇ *Coogan has run a* ***personal best*** *of just under four minutes.* ◇ *The novel is written from* ***personal experience.*** ◇ *Use stencils to add a few* ***personal touches*** *to walls and furniture.* ◇ *All hire cars are for* ***personal use*** *only.*
▸ FEELINGS/CHARACTER/RELATIONSHIPS **2** [only before noun] connected with individual people, especially their feelings, characters and relationships: *Having good* ***personal relationships*** *is the most important thing for me.* ◇ *He was popular as much for his personal qualities as for his management skills.*
▸ NOT OFFICIAL **3** not connected with a person's job or official position: *The letter was marked 'Personal'.* ◇ *I'd like to talk to you about a personal matter.* ◇ *I try not to let work interfere with my* ***personal life.*** ◇ *She's a personal friend of mine* (= not just somebody I know because of my job).
▸ DONE BY PERSON **4** [only before noun] done by a particular person rather than by sb who is acting for them: *The President made a personal appearance at the event.* ◇ *I shall give the matter my personal attention.*
▸ DONE FOR PERSON **5** [only before noun] made or done for a particular person rather than for a large group of people or people in general: *We offer a* ***personal service*** *to all our customers.* ◇ *a* ***personal pension plan*** (= a pension organized by a private company for one particular person)
▸ OFFENSIVE **6** referring to a particular person's character, appearance, opinions, etc. in a way that is offensive: *Try to avoid making personal remarks.* ◇ *There's no need to get personal!* ◇ ***Nothing personal*** (= I do not wish to offend you), *but I do have to go now.*
▸ CONNECTED WITH BODY **7** [only before noun] connected with a person's body: ***personal cleanliness/hygiene***

'personal ad *noun* a private advertisement in a newspaper, etc, especially from sb who is looking for a romantic or sexual partner

,personal al'lowance (*BrE*) (*NAmE* **,personal ex'emption**) *noun* the amount of money you are allowed to earn each year before you have to pay INCOME TAX

,personal as'sistant *noun* (*abbr.* **PA**) a person who works as a secretary or an assistant for one person

'personal column *noun* a part of a newspaper or magazine for private messages or small advertisements

,personal com'puter *noun* (*abbr.* **PC**) a small computer that is designed for one person to use at work or at home ➲ compare MAINFRAME, MICROCOMPUTER, MINICOMPUTER

'personal day *noun* (*NAmE*) a day that you take off work for personal reasons, but not because you are ill/sick or on holiday/vacation ➲ compare DUVET DAY

,personal ,digital as'sistant *noun* = PDA

,personal ex'emption (*NAmE*) (*BrE* **,personal al'lowance**) *noun* the amount of money you are allowed to earn each year before you have to pay INCOME TAX

,personal infor'mation manager *noun* (*abbr.* **PIM**) a computer program in which you write names, addresses, things that you have to do, etc.

,personal 'injury *noun* [U] (*law*) physical injury, rather than damage to property or to sb's reputation

per·son·al·ity /,pɜːsə'næləti; *NAmE* ,pɜːrs-/ *noun* (*pl.* -ies)
1 [C, U] the various aspects of a person's character that combine to make them different from other people: *His wife has a strong personality.* ◇ *The children all have very different personalities.* ◇ *He maintained order by sheer force of personality.* ◇ *There are likely to be tensions and* ***personality clashes*** *in any social group.* **2** [U] the qualities of a person's character that make them interesting and attractive: *We need someone with lots of personality to head the project.* **3** [C] a famous person, especially one who works in entertainment or sport SYN **celebrity**: *personalities from the world of music* ◇ *a* ***TV/sports personality*** **4** [C] a person whose strong character makes them noticeable: *Their son is a real personality.* **5** [U] the qualities of a place or thing that make it interesting and different SYN **character**: *The problem with many modern buildings is that they lack personality.*

perso'nality cult *noun* (*disapproving*) a situation in which people are encouraged to show extreme love and admiration for a famous person, especially a political leader

perso'nality disorder *noun* (*technical*) a serious mental condition in which sb's behaviour makes it difficult for them to have normal relationships with other people or a normal role in society

per·son·al·ize (*BrE* also **-ise**) /'pɜːsənəlaɪz; *NAmE* 'pɜːrs-/ *verb* **1** [usually passive] **~ sth** to mark sth in some way to show that it belongs to a particular person: *All the towels were personalized with their initials.* **2 ~ sth** to design or change sth so that it is suitable for the needs of a particular person: *All our courses are personalized to the needs of the individual.* **3 ~ sth** to refer to particular people when discussing a general subject: *The mass media tends to personalize politics.* ▸ **per·son·al·ized, -ised** *adj.*: *a highly personalized service* ◇ (*BrE*) *a personalized number plate* (= on a car)

per·son·al·ly /'pɜːsənəli; *NAmE* 'pɜːrs-/ *adv.*
1 used to show that you are giving your own opinion about sth: *Personally, I prefer the second option.* ◇ *'Is it worth the effort?' 'Speaking personally, yes.'* **2** by a particular person rather than by sb acting for them: *All letters*

P

will be answered personally. ◇ *Do you know him personally* (= have you met him, rather than just knowing about him from other people)? **3** ⊶ in a way that is connected with one particular person rather than a group of people SYN **individually**: *He was personally criticized by inspectors for his incompetence.* ◇ *You will be held personally responsible for any loss or breakage.* **4** ⊶ in a way that is intended to be offensive: *I'm sure she didn't mean it personally.* **5** ⊶ in a way that is connected with sb's personal life rather than with their job or official position: *Have you had any dealings with any of the suspects, either personally or professionally?*
IDM **take sth 'personally** to be offended by sth: *I'm afraid he took your remarks personally.*

ˌpersonal 'organizer (*BrE* also **-iser**) *noun* a small file with loose sheets of paper in which you write down information, addresses, what you have arranged to do, etc; a very small computer for the same purpose ➲ see also FILOFAX

ˌpersonal 'pronoun *noun* (*grammar*) any of the pronouns *I, you, he, she, it, we, they, me, him, her, us, them*

ˌpersonal 'shopper *noun* a person whose job is to help sb else buy things, either by going with them around a shop/store or by doing their shopping for them

ˌpersonal 'space *noun* [U] the space directly around where you are standing or sitting: *He leaned towards her and she stiffened at this invasion of her personal space.*

ˌpersonal 'stereo *noun* a small CD or CASSETTE player with HEADPHONES that you carry with you and use while you are moving around

ˌpersonal 'trainer *noun* a person who is paid by sb to help them exercise, especially by deciding what types of exercise are best for them

persona non grata /pɜːˌsəʊnə nɒn 'ɡrɑːtə; nəʊn; *NAmE* pɜːrˌsoʊnə nɑːn/ *noun* [U] (from *Latin*) a person who is not welcome in a particular place because of sth they have said or done, especially one who is told to leave a country by the government

P

per·soni·fi·ca·tion /pəˌsɒnɪfɪ'keɪʃn; *NAmE* pərˌsɑːn-/ *noun* **1** [C, usually sing.] **~ of sth** a person who has a lot of a particular quality or characteristic SYN **epitome**: *She was the personification of elegance.* **2** [U, C] the practice of representing objects, qualities, etc. as humans, in art and literature; an object, quality, etc. that is represented in this way: *the personification of autumn in Keats's poem*

per·son·ify /pə'sɒnɪfaɪ; *NAmE* pər'sɑːn-/ *verb* (**per·soni·fies**, **per·soni·fy·ing**, **per·soni·fied**, **per·soni·fied**) **1 ~ sth** to be an example of a quality or characteristic, or to have a lot of it SYN **typify**: *These children personify all that is wrong with the education system.* ◇ *He is kindness personified.* **2** [usually passive] **~ sth** (**as sb**) to show or think of an object, quality, etc. as a person: *The river was personified as a goddess.*

per·son·nel /ˌpɜːsə'nel; *NAmE* ˌpɜːrs-/ *noun* **1** [pl.] the people who work for an organization or one of the armed forces: *skilled personnel* ◇ ***sales/technical/medical/security/military, etc. personnel*** **2** [U+sing./pl. v.] the department in a company that deals with employing and training people SYN **human resources**: *the **personnel department/manager*** ◇ *She works in personnel.* ◇ *Personnel is/are currently reviewing pay scales.*

ˌperson'nel carrier *noun* a military vehicle for carrying soldiers

ˌperson-to-'person *adj.* [usually before noun] **1** happening between two or more people who deal directly with each other rather than through another person: *Technical support is offered on a person-to-person basis.* **2** (*especially NAmE*) (of a telephone call) made by calling the OPERATOR (= a person who works at a telephone exchange) and asking to speak to a particular person. If that person is not available, the call does not have to be paid for: *a person-to-person call*

per·spec·tive AW /pə'spektɪv; *NAmE* pər's-/ *noun* **1** [C] a particular attitude towards sth; a way of thinking about sth SYN **viewpoint**: *a global perspective* ◇ *Try to see the issue **from** a different **perspective**.* ◇ *a report that looks at the education system **from the perspective of** deaf people* ◇ **~ on sth** *His experience abroad provides a wider perspective on the problem.* **2** [U] the ability to think about problems and decisions in a reasonable way without exaggerating their importance: *She was aware that she was losing all sense of perspective.* ◇ *Try to **keep** these issues **in perspective**.* ◇ *Talking to others can often help to **put** your own problems **into perspective**.* ◇ *It is important not to let things **get out of perspective**.* **3** [U] the art of creating an effect of depth and distance in a picture by representing people and things that are far away as being smaller than those that are nearer the front: *We learnt how to draw buildings **in perspective**.* ◇ *The tree on the left is **out of perspective**.* **4** [C] (*formal*) a view, especially one in which you can see far into the distance: *a perspective of the whole valley*

Per·spex™ /'pɜːspeks; *NAmE* 'pɜːrs-/ (*BrE*) (*NAmE* **Plexiglas™**) *noun* [U] a strong transparent plastic material that is often used instead of glass

per·spi·ca·cious /ˌpɜːspɪ'keɪʃəs; *NAmE* ˌpɜːrs-/ *adj.* (*formal*) able to understand sb/sth quickly and accurately; showing this: *a perspicacious remark* ▸ **per·spi·ca·city** /ˌpɜːspɪ'kæsəti; *NAmE* ˌpɜːrs-/ *noun* [U]

per·spir·ation /ˌpɜːspə'reɪʃn; *NAmE* ˌpɜːrs-/ *noun* [U] **1** drops of liquid that form on your skin when you are hot SYN **sweat**: *Beads of perspiration stood out on his forehead.* ◇ *Her skin was damp with perspiration.* **2** the act of perspiring: *Perspiration cools the skin in hot weather.*

per·spire /pə'spaɪə(r); *NAmE* pər's-/ *verb* [I] (*formal*) to produce sweat on your body SYN **sweat**

per·suade ⊶ /pə'sweɪd; *NAmE* pər's-/ *verb* **1** ⊶ to make sb do sth by giving them good reasons for doing it: **~ sb to do sth** *Try to persuade him to come.* ◇ **~ sb** *Please try and persuade her.* ◇ *She's always easily persuaded.* ◇ *I'm sure he'll come with a bit of persuading.* ◇ **~ sb into sth/into doing sth** *I allowed myself to be persuaded into entering the competition.* **2** ⊶ to make sb believe that sth is true SYN **convince**: **~ sb/yourself that...** *It will be difficult to persuade them that there's no other choice.* ◇ *She had persuaded herself that life was not worth living.* ◇ **~ sb** *No one was persuaded by his arguments.* ◇ **~ sb of sth** (*formal*) *I am still not fully persuaded of the plan's merits.*

Which Word?

persuade / convince

- The main meaning of **persuade** is to make someone agree to do something by giving them good reasons for doing it: *I tried to persuade her to see a doctor.* The main meaning of **convince** is to make someone believe that something is true: *He convinced me he was right.*
- It is quite common, however, for each of these words to be used with both meanings, especially for **convince** to be used as a synonym for **persuade**: *I persuaded/convinced her to see a doctor.* Some speakers of *BrE* think that this is not correct.

per·sua·sion /pə'sweɪʒn; *NAmE* pər's-/ *noun* **1** [U] the act of persuading sb to do sth or to believe sth: *It didn't take much persuasion to get her to tell us where he was.* ◇ *After a little gentle persuasion, he agreed to come.* ◇ *She has great powers of persuasion.* **2** [C, U] a particular set of beliefs, especially about religion or politics: *politicians of all persuasions* ◇ *every shade of religious persuasion*

per·sua·sive /pə'sweɪsɪv; *NAmE* pər's-/ *adj.* able to persuade sb to do or believe sth: *persuasive arguments* ◇ *He can be very persuasive.* ▸ **per·sua·sive·ly** *adv.*: *They argue persuasively in favour of a total ban on handguns.* **per·sua·sive·ness** *noun* [U]

pert /pɜːt; *NAmE* pɜːrt/ *adj.* **1** (especially of a girl or young woman) showing a lack of respect, especially in a cheerful and amusing way SYN **impudent**: *a pert reply* **2** (of a part of the body) small, firm and attractive: *a pert nose* ◇ *pert features* ▶ **pert·ly** *adv.*

per·tain /pəˈteɪn; *NAmE* pərˈt-/ *verb* [I] (*formal*) to exist or to apply in a particular situation or at a particular time: *Living conditions are vastly different from those pertaining in their country of origin.* ◇ *Those laws no longer pertain.*
PHRV **perˈtain to sth/sb** (*formal*) to be connected with sth/sb: *the laws pertaining to adoption*

per·tin·acious /ˌpɜːtɪˈneɪʃəs; *NAmE* ˌpɜːrtnˈeɪ-/ *adj.* (*formal*) determined to achieve a particular aim despite difficulties or opposition ▶ **per·tin·acity** /ˌpɜːtɪˈnæsəti; *NAmE* ˌpɜːrtnˈæ-/ *noun* [U]

per·tin·ent /ˈpɜːtɪnənt; *NAmE* ˈpɜːrtnənt/ *adj.* (*formal*) appropriate to a particular situation **SYN** **relevant**: *a **pertinent question/fact*** ◇ **~ to sth** *Please keep your comments pertinent to the topic under discussion.* ▶ **per·tin·ent·ly** *adv.* **per·tin·ence** /-əns/ *noun* [U]

per·turb /pəˈtɜːb; *NAmE* pərˈtɜːrb/ *verb* **~ sb** (*formal*) to make sb worried or anxious **SYN** **alarm**: *Her sudden appearance did not seem to perturb him in the least.* ▶ **per·turbed** /-ˈtɜːbd; *NAmE* -ˈtɜːrbd/ *adj.*: *a perturbed young man* ◇ **~ at/about sth** *She didn't seem perturbed at the change of plan.* **OPP** **unperturbed**

per·turb·ation /ˌpɜːtəˈbeɪʃn; *NAmE* ˌpɜːrtərˈb-/ *noun* **1** [U] (*formal*) the state of feeling anxious about sth that has happened **SYN** **alarm** **2** [C, U] (*technical*) a small change in the quality, behaviour or movement of sth: *temperature perturbations*

per·use /pəˈruːz/ *verb* **~ sth** (*formal* or *humorous*) to read sth, especially in a careful way: *A copy of the report is available for you to peruse at your leisure.* ▶ **per·usal** /pəˈruːzl/ *noun* [U, sing.]: *The agreement was signed after careful perusal.*

perv (also **perve**) /pɜːv; *NAmE* pɜːrv/ *noun* (*informal*) **1** = PERVERT **2** (*AustralE, NZE*) a look at sb/sth that shows sexual interest in them or it, in an unpleasant way

per·vade /pəˈveɪd; *NAmE* pərˈv-/ *verb* **~ sth** (*formal*) to spread through and be noticeable in every part of sth **SYN** **permeate**: *a pervading mood of fear* ◇ *the sadness that pervades most of her novels* ◇ *The entire house was pervaded by a sour smell.*

per·va·sive /pəˈveɪsɪv; *NAmE* pərˈv-/ *adj.* existing in all parts of a place or thing; spreading gradually to affect all parts of a place or thing: *a pervasive smell of damp* ◇ *A sense of social change is pervasive in her novels.* ▶ **per·va·sive·ly** *adv.* **per·va·sive·ness** *noun* [U]

per·verse /pəˈvɜːs; *NAmE* pərˈvɜːrs/ *adj.* showing deliberate determination to behave in a way that most people think is wrong, unacceptable or unreasonable: *a perverse decision* (= one that most people do not expect and think is wrong) ◇ *She finds a perverse pleasure in upsetting her parents.* ◇ *Do you really mean that or are you just being **deliberately perverse**?* ▶ **per·verse·ly** *adv.*: *She seemed perversely proud of her criminal record.* **per·vers·ity** *noun* [U]: *He refused to attend out of sheer perversity.*

per·ver·sion /pəˈvɜːʃn; *NAmE* pərˈvɜːrʒn/ *noun* [U, C] **1** behaviour that most people think is not normal or acceptable, especially when it is connected with sex; an example of this type of behaviour: *sexual perversion* ◇ *sadomasochistic perversions* **2** the act of changing sth that is good or right into sth that is bad or wrong; the result of this: *the perversion of justice* ◇ *Her account was a perversion of the truth.*

per·vert *verb, noun*
■ ***verb*** /pəˈvɜːt; *NAmE* pərˈvɜːrt/ **1 ~ sth** to change a system, process, etc. in a bad way so that it is not what it used to be or what it should be: *Some scientific discoveries have been perverted to create weapons of destruction.* **2 ~ sb/sth** to affect sb in a way that makes them act or think in an immoral or unacceptable way **SYN** **corrupt**: *Some people believe that television can pervert the minds of children.*
IDM **perˌvert the course of ˈjustice** (*BrE*) (*NAmE* **obˈstruct justice**) (*law*) to tell a lie or to do sth in order to prevent the police, etc. from finding out the truth about a crime
■ ***noun*** /ˈpɜːvɜːt; *NAmE* ˈpɜːrvɜːrt/ (also *informal* **perv**) a person whose sexual behaviour is not thought to be normal or acceptable by most people **SYN** **deviant**: *a sexual pervert*

per·verted /pəˈvɜːtɪd; *NAmE* pərˈvɜːr-/ *adj.* not thought to be normal or acceptable by most people: *sexual acts, normal and perverted* ◇ *She was having difficulty following his perverted logic.* ◇ *They clearly take a perverted delight in watching others suffer.*

pe·seta /pəˈseɪtə/ *noun* the former unit of money in Spain (replaced in 2002 by the euro)

pesky /ˈpeski/ *adj.* [only before noun] (*informal, especially NAmE*) annoying: *pesky insects*

peso /ˈpeɪsəʊ; *NAmE* -soʊ/ *noun* (*pl.* **-os**) the unit of money in many Latin American countries and the Philippines

pes·sary /ˈpesəri/ *noun* (*pl.* **-ies**) **1** a small piece of solid medicine that is placed inside a woman's VAGINA and left to dissolve, used to cure an infection or to prevent her from becoming pregnant ➲ see also SUPPOSITORY **2** a device that is placed inside a woman's VAGINA to support the WOMB

pes·sim·ism /ˈpesɪmɪzəm/ *noun* [U] **~ (about/over sth)** a feeling that bad things will happen and that sth will not be successful; the tendency to have this feeling: *There is a mood of pessimism in the company about future job prospects.* **OPP** **optimism**

pes·sim·ist /ˈpesɪmɪst/ *noun* a person who always expects bad things to happen: *You don't have to be a pessimist to realize that we're in trouble.* **OPP** **optimist**

pes·sim·is·tic /ˌpesɪˈmɪstɪk/ *adj.* **~ (about sth)** expecting bad things to happen or sth not to be successful; showing this: *They appeared surprisingly pessimistic about their chances of winning.* ◇ *a pessimistic view of life* ◇ *I think you're being far too pessimistic.* **OPP** **optimistic** ▶ **pes·sim·is·tic·al·ly** /-kli/ *adv.*

pest /pest/ *noun* **1** an insect or animal that destroys plants, food, etc: *pest control* ◇ ***insect/plant/garden pests*** **2** (*informal*) an annoying person or thing: *That child is being a real pest.*

pes·ter /ˈpestə(r)/ *verb* [T, I] to annoy sb, especially by asking them sth many times **SYN** **badger**: **~ sb for sth** *Journalists pestered neighbours for information.* ◇ **~ sb with sth** *He has been pestering her with phone calls for over a week.* ◇ **~ sb/sth** *The horses were continually pestered by flies.* ◇ **~ (sb to do sth)** *The kids kept pestering me to read to them.*

ˈpester power *noun* [U] (*informal*) the ability that children have to make their parents buy things, by repeatedly asking them until they agree

pesti·cide /ˈpestɪsaɪd/ *noun* [C, U] a chemical used for killing pests, especially insects: *vegetables grown without the use of pesticides* ◇ *crops sprayed with pesticide* ➲ see also HERBICIDE, INSECTICIDE

pesti·lence /ˈpestɪləns/ *noun* [U, sing.] (*old use* or *literary*) any infectious disease that spreads quickly and kills a lot of people

pesti·len·tial /ˌpestɪˈlenʃl/ *adj.* **1** [only before noun] (*literary*) extremely annoying **2** (*old use*) connected with or causing a pestilence

pes·tle /ˈpesl/ *noun* a small heavy tool with a round end used for crushing things in a special bowl called a MORTAR ➲ **VISUAL VOCAB** pages V23, V57

pesto /ˈpestəʊ; *NAmE* ˈpestoʊ/ *noun* [U] an Italian sauce made of BASIL leaves, PINE NUTS, cheese and oil

PET *noun* [U] **1** /ˌpiː iː ˈtiː/ the abbreviation for 'polyethylene terephthalate' (an artificial substance used to make materials for packaging food, including plastic drinks bottles) **2** /pet/ (*medical*) the abbreviation for 'positron emission tomography' (a process that produces an image of your brain or of another part inside your body): *a PET scan* **3** /pet/ the abbreviation for 'Preliminary English Test' (a British test, set by the University of Cambridge, that measures a person's ability to speak and write English as a foreign language at an INTERMEDIATE level)

P

pet 0‑π /pet/ *noun, verb, adj.*

■ ***noun* 1** 0‑π an animal, a bird, etc. that you have at home for pleasure, rather than one that is kept for work or food: *Do you have any pets?* ◇ *a **pet dog/hamster, etc.*** ◇ *a **family/domestic pet*** ◇ ***pet food*** ◇ *a **pet shop*** (= where animals are sold as pets) **2** (usually *disapproving*) a person who is given special attention by sb, especially in a way that seems unfair to other people SYN **favourite**: *She's the **teacher's pet**.* **3** (*BrE, informal*) used when speaking to sb to show affection or to be friendly: *What's wrong, pet?* ◇ *Be a pet* (= be kind) *and post this letter for me.*

■ ***verb*** (-tt-) **1** [T] **~ sb/sth** (*especially NAmE*) to touch or move your hand gently over an animal or a child in a kind and loving way **2** [I] (*informal*) (of two people) to kiss and touch each other in a sexual way ⊃ see also PETTING

■ ***adj.*** [only before noun] that you are very interested in: *his **pet subject/theory/project, etc.*** ⊃ see also PET NAME

IDM **sb's pet 'hate** (*BrE*) (*NAmE* **sb's pet 'peeve**) something that you particularly dislike

petal /'petl/ *noun* a delicate coloured part of a flower. The head of a flower is usually made up of several petals around a central part. ⊃ VISUAL VOCAB page V9

pe·tard /pə'tɑːd; *NAmE* pə'tɑːrd/ *noun* IDM see HOIST *v.*

Peter /'piːtə(r)/ *noun* IDM see ROB

peter /'piːtə(r)/ *verb*

PHR V ˌ**peter 'out** to gradually become smaller, quieter, etc. and then end: *The campaign petered out for lack of support.* ◇ *The road petered out into a dirt track.*

ˌ**Peter 'Pan** *noun* a person who looks unusually young for their age, or who behaves in a way that would be more appropriate for sb younger ORIGIN From a story by J M Barrie about a boy with magic powers who never grew up.

'**Peters projection** *noun* [sing.] a map of the world on which the relative size, but not the shape of countries is more accurate than on more traditional maps ⊃ compare MERCATOR PROJECTION

peth·id·ine /'peθədiːn/ *noun* [U] a drug used to reduce severe pain, especially for women giving birth

petit bourgeois /ˌpeti 'bʊəʒwɑː; *NAmE* 'bʊrʒ-/ (also ˌ**petty 'bourgeois**) *noun* (*pl.* **petits/petty bourgeois**) (*disapproving*) a member of the lower middle class in society, especially one who thinks that money, work and social position are very important ▶ ˌ**petit 'bourgeois** (also ˌ**petty 'bourgeois**) *adj.* [usually before noun]

pe·tite /pə'tiːt/ *adj.* (*approving*) (of a girl, woman or her figure) small and thin: *a petite blonde*

the peˌtite ˌbourgeoi'sie (also ˌ**petty ˌbourgeoi'sie**) *noun* [sing.] the lower middle class in society

petit four /ˌpeti 'fɔː(r)/ *noun* [usually pl.] (*pl.* **petits fours** /ˌpeti 'fɔː(r)/) (from *French*) a very small decorated cake or biscuit/cookie that is served with coffee or tea

pe·ti·tion /pə'tɪʃn/ *noun, verb*

■ ***noun* 1 ~ (against/for sth)** a written document signed by a large number of people that asks sb in a position of authority to do or change sth: *a petition against experiments on animals* ◇ *The workers are getting up* (= starting) *a petition for tighter safety standards.* **2** (*law*) an official document asking a court to take a particular course of action **3** (*formal*) a formal prayer to God or request to sb in authority

■ ***verb* 1** [I, T] to make a formal request to sb in authority, especially by sending them a petition: **~ for/against sth** *Local residents have successfully petitioned against the siting of a prison in their area.* ◇ **~ sb/sth (for sth)** *The group intends to petition Parliament for reform of the law.* ◇ **~ sb/sth to do sth** *Parents petitioned the school to review its admission policy.* **2** [I, T] **~ (sb) (for sth)** | **~ sb/sth to do sth** to formally ask for sth in court: *to petition for divorce*

pe·ti·tion·er /pə'tɪʃənə(r)/ *noun* **1** a person who organizes or signs a petition **2** (*law*) a person who asks a court to take a particular course of action **3** (*formal*) a person who makes a formal request to sb in authority

petit mal /ˌpeti 'mæl/ *noun* [U] a form of EPILEPSY that is not very serious, in which sb becomes unconscious only for very short periods

'**pet name** *noun* a name you use for sb instead of their real name, as a sign of affection

pet·rel /'petrəl/ *noun* a black and white bird that can fly over the sea a long way from land

Petri dish /'petri dɪʃ; 'piːtri/ *noun* a shallow covered dish used for growing bacteria, etc. in ⊃ VISUAL VOCAB page V57

petri·fied /'petrɪfaɪd/ *adj.* **1** extremely frightened SYN **terrified**: *a petrified expression* ◇ **~ (of sth)** *I'm petrified of snakes.* ◇ *They were petrified with fear* (= so frightened that they were unable to move or think). ◇ **~ (that...)** *She was petrified that the police would burst in at any moment.* **2** [only before noun] **petrified** trees, insects, etc. have died and been changed into stone over a very long period of time: *a petrified forest*

pet·rify /'petrɪfaɪ/ *verb* (**petri·fies, petri·fy·ing, petri·fied, petri·fied**) **1** [T] **~ sb** to make sb feel extremely frightened SYN **terrify 2** [I, T] **~ (sth)** to change or to make sth change into a substance like stone

petro- /'petrəʊ; *NAmE* 'petroʊ/ *combining form* (in nouns, adjectives and adverbs) **1** connected with rocks: *petrology* **2** connected with petrol/gas: *petrochemical*

petro·chem·ical /ˌpetrəʊ'kemɪkl; *NAmE* ˌpetroʊ-/ *noun* any chemical substance obtained from PETROLEUM oil or natural gas: *the petrochemical industry*

petro·dol·lar /'petrəʊdɒlə(r); *NAmE* 'petroʊdɑːlər/ *noun* a unit of money that is used for calculating the money earned by countries that produce and sell oil

pet·rol 0‑π /'petrəl/ (*BrE*) (*NAmE* **gas, gas·oline**) *noun* [U]

a liquid obtained from PETROLEUM, used as fuel in car engines, etc: *to **fill** a car **up with petrol*** ◇ *to **run out of petrol*** ◇ *the **petrol tank** of a car* ◇ *an increase in petrol prices* ◇ ***leaded/unleaded petrol*** ⊃ compare DIESEL

ˌ**petrol 'blue** *adj.* a deep greenish blue in colour: *petrol-blue eyes* ▶ ˌ**petrol 'blue** *noun* [U]

'**petrol bomb** *noun* (*BrE*) = MOLOTOV COCKTAIL

'**petrol bunk** *noun* (*IndE*) a petrol station

pet·rol·eum /pə'trəʊliəm; *NAmE* -'troʊ-/ *noun* [U] mineral oil that is found under the ground or the sea and is used to produce petrol/gas, PARAFFIN, DIESEL oil, etc.

peˌtroleum 'jelly (*NAmE* also **pet·rol·atum** /ˌpetrə'leɪtəm/) *noun* [U] a soft clear substance obtained from petroleum, used to heal injuries on the skin or to make machine parts move together more smoothly SYN **Vaseline**

pet·rology /pə'trɒlədʒi; *NAmE* -'trɑːl-/ *noun* [U] the scientific study of how rocks are made and what they are made of

'**petrol station** (*BrE*) (*NAmE* '**gas station**) (also '**filling station**, '**service station** *NAmE, BrE*) *noun* a place at the side of a road where you take your car to buy petrol/gas, oil, etc.

petti·coat /'petɪkəʊt; *NAmE* -koʊt/ *noun* (*old-fashioned*) a piece of women's underwear like a thin dress or skirt, worn under a dress or skirt SYN **slip**

petti·fog·ging /'petɪfɒgɪŋ; *NAmE* -fɔːg-; -fɑːg-/ *adj.* [only before noun] (*old-fashioned*) paying too much attention to unimportant details; concerned with unimportant things SYN **petty**

pet·ting /'petɪŋ/ *noun* [U] the activity of kissing and touching sb, especially in a sexual way: *heavy petting* (= sexual activity which avoids PENETRATION)

'**petting zoo** *noun* (*NAmE*) a zoo with animals that children can touch

pet·tish /'petɪʃ/ *adj.* behaving in a bad-tempered or unreasonable way, especially because you cannot have or do what you want ▶ **pet·tish·ly** *adv.*

petty /'peti/ *adj.* (usually *disapproving*) **1** [usually before noun] small and unimportant SYN **minor**: *petty squabbles*

◇ ***petty crime/theft*** (= that is not very serious) ◇ *a **petty criminal/thief*** ◇ *a **petty bureaucrat/official*** (= who does not have much power or authority, although they might pretend to) **2** caring too much about small and unimportant matters, especially when this is unkind to other people **SYN small-minded**: *How could you be so petty?* ▸ **pettiness** *noun* [U]

ˌpetty ˈbourgeois *noun, adj.* = PETIT BOURGEOIS

the ˌpetty ˌbourgeoiˈsie *noun* [sing.] = PETITE BOURGEOISIE

ˌpetty ˈcash *noun* [U] a small amount of money kept in an office for small payments

ˌpetty ˈofficer *noun (abbr.* **PO**) a sailor of middle rank in the navy

petu·lant /ˈpetjulənt; *NAmE* ˈpetʃə-/ *adj.* bad-tempered and unreasonable, especially because you cannot do or have what you want ▸ **petu·lant·ly** *adv.* **petu·lance** /-əns/ *noun* [U]

pe·tu·nia /pəˈtjuːniə; *NAmE* -ˈtuː-/ *noun* a garden plant with white, pink, purple or red flowers

pew /pjuː/ *noun* a long wooden seat in a church
IDM ˌtake a ˈpew! (*BrE, informal, humorous*) used to tell sb to sit down

pew·ter /ˈpjuːtə(r)/ *noun* [U] a grey metal made by mixing tin with LEAD, used especially in the past for making cups, dishes, etc; objects made from pewter

pey·ote /peɪˈəʊti; *NAmE* -ˈoʊ-/ *noun* **1** (also **mes·cal**) [C, U] a small, blue-green CACTUS that contains a powerful drug that affects people's minds **2** [U] the drug that comes from this plant

PG /ˌpiː ˈdʒiː/ *abbr.* (*BrE*) parental guidance. A film that has the label 'PG' is not suitable for children to watch without an adult.

PGCE /ˌpiː dʒiː siː ˈiː/ *noun* the abbreviation for 'Postgraduate Certificate in Education' (a British teaching qualification taken by people who have a university degree)

pH /ˌpiː ˈeɪtʃ/ *noun* [sing.] (*chemistry*) a measurement of the level of acid or ALKALI in a SOLUTION or substance. In the pH range of 0 to 14 a reading of below 7 shows an acid and of above 7 shows an alkali: *a pH of 7.5* ◇ *to test the pH level of the soil*

phago·cyte /ˈfæɡəsaɪt/ *noun* (*biology*) a type of cell present in the body that is able to absorb bacteria and other small cells

phal·anx /ˈfælæŋks/ *noun* (*formal*) a group of people or things standing very close together

phal·lic /ˈfælɪk/ *adj.* of or like a phallus: *phallic symbols*

phal·locen·tric /ˌfæləʊˈsentrɪk; *NAmE* -loʊˈs-/ *adj.* (*formal*) related to men, male power, or the phallus as a symbol of male power ▸ **phal·locen·trism** /ˌfæləʊˈsentrɪzəm; *NAmE* -loʊˈs-/ *noun* [U]

phal·lus /ˈfæləs/ *noun* **1** (*technical*) the male sexual organ, especially when it is ERECT (= stiff) **2** a model or an image of the male sexual organ that represents power and FERTILITY

phan·tasm /ˈfæntæzəm/ *noun* (*formal*) a thing seen in the imagination **SYN illusion**

phan·tas·ma·goria /ˌfæntæzməˈɡɒriə; *NAmE* -ˈɡɔːr-/ *noun* [sing.] (*formal*) a changing scene of real or imagined figures, for example as seen in a dream or created as an effect in a film/movie ▸ **phan·tas·ma·gor·ical** /-ˈɡɒrɪkl; *NAmE* -ˈɡɔːr-/ *adj.*

phan·tasy *noun* [C, U] (*old use*) = FANTASY

phantom /ˈfæntəm/ *noun, adj.*
▪ ***noun*** **1** a GHOST: *the phantom of his dead father* **2** a thing that exists only in your imagination
▪ ***adj.*** [only before noun] **1** like a GHOST: *a phantom horseman* **2** existing only in your imagination: *phantom profits* ◇ *phantom illnesses* ◇ *a **phantom pregnancy*** (= a condition in which a woman seems to be pregnant but in fact is not)

phar·aoh /ˈfeərəʊ; *NAmE* ˈferoʊ/ *noun* a ruler of ancient Egypt

Phari·see /ˈfærɪsiː/ *noun* **1** a member of an ancient Jewish group who followed religious laws and teaching very strictly **2** (*disapproving*) a person who is very proud of the fact that they have high religious and moral standards, but who does not care enough about other people **SYN hypocrite**

pharma·ceut·ical /ˌfɑːməˈsuːtɪkl; -ˈsjuː-; *NAmE* ˌfɑːrmə-ˈsuː-/ *adj., noun*
▪ ***adj.*** [only before noun] connected with making and selling drugs and medicines: *pharmaceutical products* ◇ *the pharmaceutical industry*
▪ ***noun*** [usually pl.] (*technical*) a drug or medicine: *the development of new pharmaceuticals* ◇ *the pharmaceuticals industry*

pharma·cist /ˈfɑːməsɪst; *NAmE* ˈfɑːrm-/ *noun* **1** (*NAmE* also **drug·gist**) a person whose job is to prepare medicines and sell or give them to the public in a shop/store or in a hospital: *We had to wait for the pharmacist to make up her prescription.* ➲ compare CHEMIST **2 pharmacist's** (*pl.* **pharma·cists**) (*BrE*) a shop that sells medicines: *They sell vitamin supplements at the pharmacist's.* ➲ compare CHEMIST ➲ see also PHARMACY

pharma·colo·gist /ˌfɑːməˈkɒlədʒɪst; *NAmE* ˌfɑːrmə-ˈkɑːl-/ *noun* a scientist who studies pharmacology

pharma·col·ogy /ˌfɑːməˈkɒlədʒi; *NAmE* ˌfɑːrməˈkɑːl-/ *noun* [U] the scientific study of drugs and their use in medicine ▸ **pharma·co·logic·al** /ˌfɑːməkəˈlɒdʒɪkl; *NAmE* ˌfɑːrməkəˈlɑːdʒ-/ *adj.*: *pharmacological research*

pharma·co·poeia (*NAmE* also **pharma·co·peia**) /ˌfɑːməkəˈpiːə; *NAmE* ˌfɑːrmə-/ *noun* (*technical*) an official book containing a list of medicines and drugs and instructions for their use

phar·macy /ˈfɑːməsi; *NAmE* ˈfɑːrm-/ *noun* (*pl.* -ies) **1** [C] a shop/store, or part of one, that sells medicines and drugs ➲ compare CHEMIST, DRUGSTORE **2** [C] a place in a hospital where medicines are prepared ➲ see also DISPENSARY **3** [U] the study of how to prepare medicines and drugs

pharm·ing /ˈfɑːmɪŋ; *NAmE* ˈfɑːrmɪŋ/ *noun* [U] **1 pharming™** the process of changing the GENES of an animal or a plant so that it produces large quantities of a substance, especially for use in medicine **ORIGIN** from 'farming' and 'pharmaceutical' **2** the practice of secretly changing computer files or software so that visitors to a popular website are sent to a different website instead, without their knowledge, where their personal details are stolen and used to steal money from them ➲ compare PHISHING

pha·ryn·geal *adj.* /fəˈrɪndʒiəl; ˌfærɪnˈdʒiːəl/ *adj., noun*
▪ ***adj.*** (*medical*) relating to the pharynx
▪ ***noun*** (also **phaˌryngeal ˈconsonant**) (*phonetics*) a speech sound produced by the root of the tongue using the PHARYNX

pha·ryn·gitis *adj.* /ˌfærɪnˈdʒaɪtɪs/ *noun* [U] (*medical*) a condition in which the throat is red and sore

phar·ynx /ˈfærɪŋks/ *noun* (*pl.* **pha·ryn·ges** /fəˈrɪndʒiːz/) (*anatomy*) the soft area at the top of the throat where the passages to the nose and mouth connect with the throat ➲ VISUAL VOCAB page V48

phase 🔑 **AW** /feɪz/ *noun, verb*
▪ ***noun*** **1** 🔑 a stage in a process of change or development: *during the first/next/last phase* ◇ *the **initial/final phase** of the project* ◇ *a **critical/decisive phase*** ◇ *the **design phase*** ◇ *His anxiety about the work was just **a passing phase**.* ◇ *She's going through a **difficult phase**.* ◇ *The wedding marked the beginning of a **new phase** in Emma's life.* **2** each of the shapes of the moon as we see it from the earth at different times of the month
IDM in phase/out of phase (with sth) (*BrE*) working/not working together in the right way: *The traffic lights were out of phase.*
▪ ***verb*** [usually passive] **~ sth** to arrange to do sth gradually in stages over a period of time: *the phased withdrawal of*

troops from the area ◇ Closure of the hospitals was phased over a three-year period.

PHR V ˌphase sth↔ˈin to introduce or start using sth gradually in stages over a period of time: *The new tax will be phased in over two years.* ˌphase sth↔ˈout to stop using sth gradually in stages over a period of time: *Subsidies to farmers will be phased out by next year.*

phat /fæt/ *adj.* (*slang, especially NAmE*) very good

phat·ic *adj.* /ˈfætɪk/ *adj.* (*linguistics*) relating to language used for social purposes rather than to give information or ask questions: *phatic communication*

PhD (also **Ph.D.** especially in *NAmE*) /ˌpiː eɪtʃ ˈdiː/ *noun* the abbreviation for 'Doctor of Philosophy' (a university degree of a very high level that is given to sb who has done research in a particular subject): *to* ***be/have/do a PhD*** ◇ *Anne Thomas, PhD* ➲ COLLOCATIONS at EDUCATION

phea·sant /ˈfeznt/ *noun* [C, U] (*pl.* **phea·sants** or **phea·sant**) a large bird with a long tail, the male of which is brightly coloured. People sometimes shoot pheasants for sport or food. Meat from this bird is also called pheasant: (*BrE*) *to shoot pheasant* ◇ (*NAmE*) *to hunt pheasant* ◇ *roast pheasant* ➲ VISUAL VOCAB page V10

phe·nol /ˈfiːnɒl; *NAmE* -nɔːl; -nɑːl/ *noun* [U] (*chemistry*) a poisonous white chemical. When dissolved in water it is used as an ANTISEPTIC and DISINFECTANT, usually called CARBOLIC ACID.

phen·ology /fəˈnɒlədʒi; *NAmE* -ˈnɑːl-/ *noun* [U] the study of patterns of events in nature, especially in the weather and in the behaviour of plants and animals

phe·nom /fəˈnɒm; ˈfiːnɒm; *NAmE* -nɑːm/ *noun* (*NAmE, informal*) a person or thing that is very successful or impressive **SYN** **phenomenon**

phe·nom·enal **AW** /fəˈnɒmɪnl; *NAmE* -ˈnɑːm-/ *adj.* very great or impressive **SYN** **extraordinary**: *The product has been a phenomenal success.*

phe·nom·en·al·ly /fəˈnɒmɪnəli; *NAmE* -ˈnɑːm-/ *adv.* **1** in a very great or impressive way **SYN** **extraordinarily**: *This product has been phenomenally successful* **2** extremely; very: *phenomenally bad weather*

phe·nom·en·ology /fɪˌnɒmɪˈnɒlədʒi; *NAmE* -ˌnɑːməˈnɑːl-/ *noun* [U] the branch of philosophy that deals with what you see, hear, feel, etc. in contrast to what may actually be real or true about the world ▸ **phe·nom·eno·logic·al** /fɪˌnɒmɪnəˈlɒdʒɪkl; *NAmE* -ˌnɑːmənəˈlɑːdʒ-/ *adj.*

phe·nom·enon **AW** /fəˈnɒmɪnən; *NAmE* fəˈnɑːm-/ *noun* (*pl.* **phe·nom·ena** /-ɪnə/) **1** a fact or an event in nature or society, especially one that is not fully understood: ***cultural/natural/social phenomena*** ◇ *Globalization is a phenomenon of the 21st century.* **2** (*pl.* **phe·nom·enons** in *NAmE*) a person or thing that is very successful or impressive

phe·no·type /ˈfiːnətaɪp/ *adj., noun* (*biology*) the set of characteristics of a living thing, resulting from its combination of GENES and the effect of its environment ➲ compare GENOTYPE

phero·mone /ˈferəməʊn; *NAmE* -moʊn/ *noun* (*biology*) a substance produced by an animal as a chemical signal, often to attract another animal of the same SPECIES

phew /fjuː/ *exclamation* a sound that people make to show that they are hot, tired, or happy that sth bad has finished or did not happen: *Phew, it's hot in here!* ◇ *Phew, I'm glad that's all over.* ➲ compare WHEW

phi /faɪ/ *noun* the 21st letter of the Greek alphabet (Φ, φ)

phial /ˈfaɪəl/ (also **vial** especially in *NAmE*) *noun* (*formal*) a small glass container, for medicine or PERFUME

ˌPhi ˌBeta ˈKappa *noun* (in the US) a society for college and university students who are very successful in their studies

phil·an·der·er /fɪˈlændərə(r)/ *noun* (*old-fashioned, disapproving*) a man who has sexual relationships with many different women

phil·an·dering /fɪˈlændərɪŋ/ *noun* [U] (*old-fashioned, disapproving*) (of a man) the fact of having sexual relationships with many different women **SYN** **womanizing** ▸ **phil·an·dering** *adj.* [only before noun]

phil·an·throp·ist /fɪˈlænθrəpɪst/ *noun* a rich person who helps the poor and those in need, especially by giving money

phil·an·thropy /fɪˈlænθrəpi/ *noun* [U] the practice of helping the poor and those in need, especially by giving money ▸ **phil·an·throp·ic** /ˌfɪlənˈθrɒpɪk; *NAmE* -ˈθrɑːp-/ *adj.*: *philanthropic work* **phil·an·throp·ic·al·ly** /ˌfɪlənˈθrɒpɪkli; *NAmE* -ˈθrɑːp-/ *adv.*

phila·tel·ist /fɪˈlætəlɪst/ *noun* (*technical*) a person who collects or studies stamps

phil·ately /fɪˈlætəli/ *noun* [U] (*technical*) the collection and study of stamps ▸ **phila·tel·ic** /ˌfɪləˈtelɪk/ *adj.*

-phile *combining form* (in nouns and adjectives) liking a particular thing; a person who likes a particular thing: *Anglophile* ◇ *bibliophile* ➲ compare -PHOBE

phil·har·mon·ic /ˌfɪlɑːˈmɒnɪk; *NAmE* ˌfɪlərˈmɑːnɪk/ *adj.* used in the names of ORCHESTRAS, music societies, etc.: *the Berlin Philharmonic (Orchestra)*

-philia *combining form* (in nouns) love of sth, especially connected with a sexual attraction that is not considered normal: *paedophilia* ➲ compare -PHOBIA

phil·is·tine /ˈfɪlɪstaɪn; *NAmE* -stiːn/ *noun* (*disapproving*) a person who does not like or understand art, literature, music, etc. ▸ **phil·is·tine** *adj.*: *philistine attitudes* **phil·is·tin·ism** /-tɪnɪzəm/ *noun* [U]: *the philistinism of the tabloid press*

Phil·lips /ˈfɪlɪps/ *adj.* (of a screw or SCREWDRIVER) with a cross-shaped part for turning ➲ compare FLATHEAD, SLOTTED

philo- /ˈfɪləʊ; *NAmE* ˈfɪloʊ/ (also **phil-**) *combining form* (in nouns, adjectives, verbs and adverbs) liking: *philanthropy*

phil·olo·gist /fɪˈlɒlədʒɪst; *NAmE* -ˈlɑːl-/ *noun* a person who studies philology

phil·ology /fɪˈlɒlədʒi; *NAmE* -ˈlɑːl-/ *noun* [U] the scientific study of the development of language or of a particular language ▸ **phil·olo·gic·al** /ˌfɪləˈlɒdʒɪkl; *NAmE* -ˈlɑːdʒ-/ *adj.*

phil·oso·pher **AW** /fəˈlɒsəfə(r); *NAmE* -ˈlɑːs-/ *noun* **1** a person who studies or writes about philosophy: *the Greek philosopher Aristotle* **2** a person who thinks deeply about things: *He seems to be a bit of a philosopher.*

the phiˌlosopher's ˈstone *noun* [sing.] an imaginary substance that, in the past, people believed could change any metal into gold or silver, or could make people live for ever

philo·soph·ical **AW** /ˌfɪləˈsɒfɪkl; *NAmE* -ˈsɑːf-/ (also **philo·soph·ic** /-ˈsɒfɪk; *NAmE* -ˈsɑːfɪk/) *adj.* **1** connected with philosophy: *the philosophical writings of Kant* ◇ *philosophic debate* **2 ~ (about sth)** (*approving*) having a calm attitude towards a difficult or disappointing situation **SYN** **stoical**: *He was philosophical about losing and said that he'd be back next year to try again.* ▸ **philo·soph·ic·al·ly** **AW** /-kli/ *adv.*: *This kind of evidence is philosophically unconvincing.* ◇ *She took the bad news philosophically.*

philo·so·phize (*BrE* also **-ise**) **AW** /fəˈlɒsəfaɪz; *NAmE* -ˈlɑːs-/ *verb* [I] **~ (about/on sth)** to talk about sth in a serious way, especially when other people think this is boring: *He spent the evening philosophizing on the meaning of life.* ▸ **phil·oso·phiz·ing, -is·ing** **AW** *noun* [U]

phil·oso·phy 🔑 **AW** /fəˈlɒsəfi; *NAmE* -ˈlɑːs-/ *noun* **1** 🔑 [U] the study of the nature and meaning of the universe and of human life: *moral philosophy* ◇ *the philosophy of science* ◇ *a professor of philosophy* ◇ *a degree in philosophy* **2** 🔑 [C] a particular set or system of beliefs resulting from the search for knowledge about life and the universe: *the philosophy of Jung* **3** 🔑 [C] a set of beliefs or an attitude to

P

life that guides sb's behaviour: *Her philosophy of life is to take every opportunity that presents itself.*

phil·tre (*especially US* **phil·ter**) /'fɪltə(r)/ *noun* (*literary*) a magic drink that is supposed to make people fall in love

phish·ing /'fɪʃɪŋ/ *noun* [U] the activity of tricking people by getting them to give their identity, bank account numbers, etc. over the Internet or by email, and then using these to steal money from them ➲ compare PHARMING (2)

phle·bitis /flə'baɪtɪs/ *noun* [U] (*medical*) a condition in which the walls of a VEIN become sore and swollen

phle·bot·omy /flə'bɒtəmi; *NAmE* -'bɑːt-/ *noun* [C, U] (*pl.* -ies) (*medical*) the opening of a VEIN in order to remove blood or put another liquid in

phlegm /flem/ *noun* [U] **1** the thick substance that forms in the nose and throat, especially when you have a cold **2** the ability to remain calm in a situation that is difficult or upsetting

phleg·mat·ic /fleg'mætɪk/ *adj.* not easily made angry or upset SYN **calm**: *a phlegmatic temperament* ▸ **phleg·mat·ic·al·ly** /-kli/ *adv.*

phloem /'fləʊem; *NAmE* 'floʊ-/ *noun* [U] (*biology*) the material in a plant containing very small tubes that carry sugars produced in the leaves around the plant ➲ compare XYLEM

phlox /flɒks; *NAmE* flɑːks/ *noun* **1** a tall garden plant with groups of white, blue or red flowers with a sweet smell **2** a low, spreading plant with small white, blue or pink flowers

-phobe *combining form* (in nouns) a person who dislikes a particular thing or particular people: *Anglophobe* ◇ *xenophobe* ➲ compare -PHILE

pho·bia /'fəʊbiə; *NAmE* 'foʊ-/ *noun* **1** a strong unreasonable fear of sth: *He* ***has a phobia about*** *flying.* **2 -phobia** (in nouns) a strong unreasonable fear or hatred of a particular thing: *claustrophobia* ◇ *xenophobia* ➲ compare -PHILIA

pho·bic /'fəʊbɪk; *NAmE* 'foʊ-/ *noun* **1** a person who has a strong unreasonable fear or hatred of sth: *cat phobics* **2 -phobic** (in adjectives) having a strong unreasonable fear or hatred of a particular thing: *claustrophobic* ◇ *xenophobic* ▸ **pho·bic** *adj.*: *phobic anxiety*

phoe·nix /'fiːnɪks/ *noun* (in stories) a magic bird that lives for several hundred years before burning itself and then being born again from its ASHES: *to rise like a phoenix from the ashes* (= to be powerful or successful again)

British/American

phone / call / ring

Verbs

- In *BrE*, **to phone, to ring** and **to call** are the usual ways of saying **to telephone**. In *NAmE* the most common word is **call**, but **phone** is also used. Speakers of *NAmE* do not say **ring**. **Telephone** is very formal and is used mainly in *BrE*.

Nouns

- You can use **call** or **phone call** (more formal) in both *BrE* and *NAmE*: *Were there any phone calls for me?* ◇ *How do I make a local call?* The idiom **give sb a call** is also common: *I'll give you a call tonight.* In informal *BrE* you could also say: *I'll give you a ring tonight.*

phone 0-m /fəʊn; *NAmE* foʊn/ *noun, verb*

■ *noun* **1** 0-m [U, C] a system for talking to sb else over long distances using wires or radio; a machine used for this; a telephone: *I have to* ***make a phone call.*** ◇ *The* ***phone rang*** *and Pat answered it.* ◇ *They like to do business* ***by phone/over the phone.*** ◇ *His phone must be switched off.* ◇ *I hadn't got my phone with me.* ◇ *a phone bill* ➲ see also CAR PHONE, CELL PHONE, CELLULAR PHONE, ENTRYPHONE, MOBILE PHONE, PAYPHONE, TELEPHONE **2** 0-m [C] the part of a phone that you hold in your hand and speak into; a telephone: *to* ***pick up the phone*** ◇ *to* ***put the phone down*** ◇ *He left the phone off the hook as he didn't want to be disturbed.* ➲ see also ANSWERPHONE, TELEPHONE **3 -phone** (in nouns) an instrument that uses or makes sound: *dictaphone* ◇ *xylophone* **4 -phone** (in adjectives and nouns) speaking a particular language; a person who does this: *anglophone* ◇ *francophone* **5** (*phonetics*) a sound made in speech, especially when not considered as part of the sound system of a particular language ➲ compare PHONEME

IDM **be on the 'phone 1** to be using the telephone: *He's been on the phone to Kate for more than an hour.* **2** (*BrE*) to have a telephone in your home or place of work: *They're not on the phone at the holiday cottage.*

■ *verb* 0-m (*especially BrE*) (*BrE* also **,phone 'up**) [I, T] to make a telephone call to sb SYN **call**: *I was just phoning up for a chat.* ◇ *He phoned to invite me out for dinner.* ◇ *Someone phone for an ambulance!* ◇ *Could you* ***phone back*** *later?* ◇ *He* ***phoned home****, but there was no reply.* ◇ **~ sb/sth** *Don't forget to phone New York.* ◇ *For reservations, phone 020 281 3964.* ◇ *Phone them up and find out when they are coming.*

PHR V **,phone 'in** (*especially BrE*) **1** to make a telephone call to the place where you work: **+ adj.** *Three people have* ***phoned in sick*** *already this morning.* **2** to make a telephone call to a radio or television station: *Listeners are invited to phone in with their comments.* ➲ related noun PHONE-IN **,phone sth↔'in** (*especially BrE*) to make a telephone call to the place where you work in order to give sb some information: *I need you to phone the story in before five.*

Collocations

Phones

Making and receiving phone calls

- the phone/telephone **rings**
- **answer/pick up/hang up** the phone/telephone
- **lift/pick up/hold/replace** the receiver
- **dial** a (phone/extension/wrong) number/an area code
- **call sb/talk (to sb)/speak (to sb)** on the phone/telephone; from home/work/the office
- **make/get/receive** a phone call
- **take** the phone **off the hook** (= remove the receiver so that the phone does not ring)
- the line is (*BrE*) **engaged**/(*especially NAmE*) **busy**
- the phones have been (*NAmE*) **ringing off the hook** (= ringing frequently)
- **put sb through/get through** to the person you want to speak to
- **put sb** on hold (= so that they must wait for the person they want to speak to)
- **call from/use** a landline

Mobile/cell phones

- **be/talk** on a (*both BrE*) mobile phone/mobile/(*especially NAmE*) cell phone/(*informal, especially NAmE*) cell
- **use/answer/call (sb on)/get a message on** your mobile phone/mobile/cell phone/cell
- **switch/turn on/off** your mobile phone/mobile/cell phone/cell
- **charge/recharge** your mobile phone/mobile/cell phone/cell
- a mobile/cell phone **is on/is off/rings/goes off**
- (*BrE*) **top up** your mobile (phone)
- **send/receive** a text (message)/an SMS (message)/a fax
- **insert/remove/change** a SIM card

'phone book *noun* = TELEPHONE DIRECTORY

'phone booth (also **'telephone booth**) *noun* a place that is partly separated from the surrounding area, containing a public telephone, in a hotel, restaurant, in the street, etc.

ˈphone box (also **ˈtelephone box**, **ˈtelephone kiosk**, **ˈcall box**) (all *BrE*) *noun* a small unit with walls and a roof, containing a public telephone, in the street, etc.

ˈphone call *noun* = CALL

phone·card /ˈfəʊnkɑːd; *NAmE* ˈfoʊnkɑːrd/ *noun* (*NAmE* also **ˈcalling card**) **1** a plastic card that you can use in some public telephones instead of money **2** (*NAmE*) a card with a number on it that you use in order to pay to make a call from any phone. The cost of the call is charged to your account and you pay it later.

ˈphone-in (*BrE*) (*NAmE* **ˈcall-in**) *noun* a radio or television programme in which people can telephone and make comments or ask questions about a particular subject

phon·eme /ˈfəʊniːm; *NAmE* ˈfoʊ-/ *noun* (*phonetics*) any one of the set of smallest units of speech in a language that distinguish one word from another. In English, the /s/ in *sip* and the /z/ in *zip* represent two different phonemes. ▸ **phon·em·ic** /fəˈniːmɪk/ *adj.*

ˈphone number *noun* = TELEPHONE NUMBER

ˈphone tapping *noun* = TELEPHONE TAPPING

phon·et·ic /fəˈnetɪk/ *adj.* **1** using special symbols to represent each different speech sound: *the International Phonetic Alphabet* ◇ *a phonetic symbol/transcription* **2** (of a spelling or spelling system) that closely matches the sounds represented: *Spanish spelling is phonetic, unlike English spelling.* **3** connected with the sounds of human speech ▸ **phon·et·ic·al·ly** /-kli/ *adv.*

phon·et·ics /fəˈnetɪks/ *noun* [U] the study of speech sounds and how they are produced ▸ **phon·et·ician** /ˌfəʊnəˈtɪʃn; ˌfɒn-; *NAmE* ˌfoʊn-; ˌfɑːn-/ *noun*

pho·ney (also **phony** especially in *NAmE*) /ˈfəʊni; *NAmE* ˈfoʊni/ *adj.*, *noun*

■ ***adj.*** (**pho·nier**, **pho·ni·est**) (*informal, disapproving*) not real or true; false, and trying to trick people SYN **fake**: *She spoke with a phoney Russian accent.*

■ ***noun*** (*pl.* -neys or -nies) (*informal*) a person who is not honest or sincere; a thing that is not real or true

ˌphoney ˈwar *noun* [sing.] (*BrE*) a period of time when two groups are officially at war but not actually fighting

phon·ic /ˈfɒnɪk; *NAmE* ˈfɑːnɪk/ *adj.* **1** (*technical*) relating to sound; relating to sounds made in speech **2 -phonic** (in adjectives) connected with an instrument that uses or makes sound: *telephonic*

phon·ics /ˈfɒnɪks; *NAmE* ˈfɑːn-/ *noun* [U] a method of teaching people to read based on the sounds that letters represent

phono- /ˈfəʊnəʊ; *NAmE* ˈfoʊnoʊ-/ (also **phon-**) *combining form* (in nouns, adjectives and adverbs) connected with sound or sounds: *phonetic*

phono·graph /ˈfəʊnəgrɑːf; *NAmE* ˈfoʊnəgræf/ *noun* (*old-fashioned*) = RECORD PLAYER

phon·ology /fəˈnɒlədʒi; *NAmE* -ˈnɑːl-/ *noun* [U] (*linguistics*) the speech sounds of a particular language; the study of these sounds ▸ **phono·logic·al** /ˌfəʊnəˈlɒdʒɪkl; ˌfɒn-; *NAmE* ˌfoʊnəˈlɑːdʒ-; ˌfɑːn-/ *adj.*: *phonological analysis* **phon·olo·gist** /fəˈnɒlədʒɪst; *NAmE* fəˈnɑːl-/ *noun*

phony (*especially NAmE*) = PHONEY

phooey /ˈfuːi/ *exclamation* used when you think sb/sth is wrong or silly ▸ **phooey** *noun* [U]: *It's all phooey!*

phos·gene /ˈfɒzdʒiːn; *NAmE* ˈfɑːz-/ *noun* [U] a poisonous gas that was used as a CHEMICAL WEAPON during the First World War

phos·phate /ˈfɒsfeɪt; *NAmE* ˈfɑːs-/ *noun* [C, U] (*chemistry*) any COMPOUND containing phosphorus, used in industry or for helping plants to grow: *phosphate-free washing powder*

phos·phor·es·cent /ˌfɒsfəˈresnt; *NAmE* ˌfɑːs-/ *adj.* (*technical*) **1** producing a faint light in the dark ➲ compare FLUORESCENT **2** producing light without heat or with so little heat that it cannot be felt ▸ **phos·phor·es·cence** /-sns/ *noun* [U]

phosphoric acid /fɒsˌfɒrɪk ˈæsɪd; *NAmE* fɑːsˌfɔːrɪk/ *noun* [U] an acid used in FERTILIZERS and in the production of DETERGENTS and food

phos·phorus /ˈfɒsfərəs; *NAmE* ˈfɑːs-/ *noun* [U] (*symb.* P) a chemical element. Phosphorus is found in several different forms, including as a poisonous, pale yellow substance that shines in the dark and starts to burn as soon as it is placed in air.

phot·ic /ˈfəʊtɪk; *NAmE* ˈfoʊ-/ *adj.* (*technical*) **1** relating to, or caused by, light **2** relating to the part of the ocean which receives enough light for plants to grow: *the photic zone*

photo O-w /ˈfəʊtəʊ; *NAmE* ˈfoʊtoʊ/ *noun* (*pl.* -os) = PHOTOGRAPH: *a **colour/black-and-white photo*** ◇ *a **passport photo*** ◇ ***a photo album*** (= a book for keeping your photos in) ◇ *I'll **take a photo** of you.* HELP The usual phrase in *NAmE* is **take a picture.** ➲ SYNONYMS at PHOTOGRAPH

photo- /ˈfəʊtəʊ; *NAmE* ˈfoʊtoʊ/ *combining form* (in nouns, adjectives, verbs and adverbs) **1** connected with light: *photosynthesis* **2** connected with photography: *photogenic*

ˈphoto booth *noun* a small structure with walls and a roof where you can put money in a machine and get a photograph of yourself in a few minutes

photo·call /ˈfəʊtəʊkɔːl; *NAmE* ˈfoʊtoʊ-/ *noun* a time that is arranged in advance when newspaper photographers are invited to take photographs of sb: *The president joined the team for a photocall.*

photo·cell /ˈfəʊtəʊsel; *NAmE* ˈfoʊtoʊ-/ *noun* = PHOTOELECTRIC CELL

photo·chem·ical /ˌfəʊtəʊˈkemɪkl; *NAmE* ˌfoʊtoʊ-/ *adj.* (*chemistry*) caused by or relating to the chemical action of light: *photochemical smog*

photo·copier /ˈfəʊtəʊkɒpiə(r); *NAmE* ˈfoʊtoʊkɑːp-/ (also **copier** especially in *NAmE*) *noun* a machine that makes copies of documents, etc. by photographing them ➲ VISUAL VOCAB page V56

photo·copy O-w /ˈfəʊtəʊkɒpi; *NAmE* ˈfoʊtoʊkɑːpi/ *noun*, *verb*

■ ***noun*** O-w (also **copy**) (*pl.* -ies) a copy of a document, etc. made by the action of light on a specially treated surface: *Make as many photocopies as you need.*

■ ***verb*** (**photo·cop·ies**, **photo·copy·ing**, **photo·cop·ied**, **photo·cop·ied**) (also **copy** especially in *BrE*) **1** O-w [T, I] **~ (sth)** to make a photocopy of sth: *a photocopied letter* ◇ *Can you get these photocopied for me by 5 o'clock?* ◇ *I seem to have spent most of the day photocopying.* **2** [I] **~ well/badly** (of printed material) to produce a good/bad photocopy: *The comments in pencil haven't photocopied very well.*

photo·elec·tric /ˌfəʊtəʊɪˈlektrɪk; *NAmE* ˌfoʊtoʊ-/ *adj.* using an electric current that is controlled by light

ˌphotoelectric ˈcell (also **photo·cell**) *noun* an electric device that uses a stream of light. When the stream is broken it shows that sb/sth is present, and can be used to control alarms, machinery, etc.

ˌphoto ˈfinish *noun* [usually sing.] the end of a race in which the leading runners or horses are so close together that only a photograph of them passing the finishing line can show which is the winner

photo·fit /ˈfəʊtəʊfɪt; *NAmE* ˈfoʊtoʊfɪt/ *noun* (*BrE*) a picture of a person who is wanted by the police, made by putting together photographs of different features of faces from information that is given by sb who has seen the person ➲ compare E-FIT, IDENTIKIT

photo·gen·ic /ˌfəʊtəʊˈdʒenɪk; *NAmE* ˌfoʊtoʊ-/ *adj.* looking attractive in photographs: *I'm not very photogenic.*

photo·graph O-w /ˈfəʊtəgrɑːf; *NAmE* ˈfoʊtəgræf/ *noun*, *verb*

■ ***noun*** O-w (also **photo**) a picture that is made by using a camera that has a film sensitive to light inside it: ***aerial/satellite photographs*** ◇ *colour photographs* ◇ *Please enclose a recent passport-sized photograph of yourself.* ◇ *I spent*

P

the day **taking photographs** of the city. **HELP** The usual phrase in *NAmE* is **take pictures**.

■ ***verb* 1** [T] to take a photograph of sb/sth: **~ sb/sth** *He has photographed some of the world's most beautiful women.* ◇ *a beautifully photographed book* (= with good photographs in it) ◇ **~ sb/sth + adj.** *She refused to be photographed nude.* ◇ **~ sb/sth doing sth** *They were photographed playing with their children.* **2** [I] **~ well, badly, etc.** to look or not look attractive in photographs: *Some people just don't photograph well.*

Synonyms

photograph

picture • photo • shot • snapshot/snap • print

These are all words for a picture that has been made using a camera.

photograph a picture that has been made using a camera: *a photograph of the house* ◇ *Can I take a photograph?*

picture a photograph: *We had our picture taken in front of the hotel.*

photo a photograph: *a passport photo*

PHOTOGRAPH, PICTURE OR PHOTO?

Photograph is slightly more formal and **photo** is slightly less formal. **Picture** is used especially in the context of photographs in newspapers, magazines and books.

shot a photograph: *I tried to get a shot of him in the water.* **NOTE** **Shot** often places more emphasis on the process of taking the photograph, rather than the finished picture.

snapshot/snap an informal photograph that is taken quickly, and not by a professional photographer: *holiday snaps*

print a copy of a photograph that is produced from film or from a digital camera: *a set of prints*

PATTERNS

- a **colour** photograph/picture/photo/snap/print
- to **take** a photograph/picture/photo/shot/snapshot

pho·tog·raph·er /fə'tɒgrəfə(r); *NAmE* fə'tɑːg-/ *noun* a person who takes photographs, especially as a job: *a **wildlife/fashion/portrait photographer***

photo·graph·ic /ˌfəʊtə'græfɪk; *NAmE* ˌfoʊ-/ *adj.* connected with photographs or photography: *photographic equipment/film/images* ◇ *They produced a photographic record of the event.* ◇ *His paintings are almost photographic in detail.* ▸ **photo·graph·ic·al·ly** /-kli/ *adv.*

ˌphotographic 'memory *noun* [usually sing.] the ability to remember things accurately and in great detail after seeing them

pho·tog·raphy /fə'tɒgrəfi; *NAmE* fə'tɑːg-/ *noun* [U] the art, process or job of taking photographs or filming sth: ***colour/flash/aerial, etc. photography*** ◇ *fashion **photography** by David Burn* ◇ *Her hobbies include hiking and photography.* ◇ *the **director of photography*** (= the person who is in charge of the actual filming of a film/movie, programme, etc.) ◇ *Did you see the film about Antarctica? The photography was superb!* ➲ VISUAL VOCAB page V35

photo·jour·nal·ism /ˌfəʊtəʊ'dʒɜːnəlɪzəm; *NAmE* ˌfoʊtoʊ'dʒɜːrn-/ *noun* [U] the work of giving news using mainly photographs, especially in a magazine

photo·mon·tage /ˌfəʊtəʊmɒn'tɑːʒ; *NAmE* ˌfoʊtoʊmɑːn'tɑːʒ/ *noun* [C, U] a picture which is made up of different photographs put together; the technique of producing these pictures

pho·ton /'fəʊtɒn; *NAmE* 'foʊtɑːn/ *noun* (*physics*) a unit of ELECTROMAGNETIC energy

'photo opportunity *noun* an occasion when a famous person arranges to be photographed doing sth that will impress the public

photo·real·ism /ˌfəʊtəʊ'riːəlɪzəm; -'rɪəl-; *NAmE* ˌfoʊtoʊ'riːəlɪzəm/ *noun* [U] an artistic style that represents a subject in an accurate and detailed way, like a photograph

photo·recep·tor /'fəʊtəʊrɪseptə(r); *NAmE* 'foʊtoʊ-/ *noun* (*biology*) a cell or an organ that is sensitive to light

photo·sensi·tive /ˌfəʊtəʊ'sensətɪv; *NAmE* ˌfoʊtoʊ-/ *adj.* (*technical*) reacting to light, for example by changing colour or producing an electrical signal

'photo shoot *noun* an occasion when a photographer takes pictures of sb, for example a famous person, fashion model, etc. for use in a magazine, etc: *I **went on a photo shoot** to Rio with him.*

photo·shop /'fəʊtəʊʃɒp; *NAmE* 'foʊtoʊʃɑːp/ (also **Photoshop**) *verb* (-pp-) **~ sth** to change a picture or photograph using a computer: *I'm sure this picture has been photoshopped.*

photo·stat /'fəʊtəstæt; *NAmE* 'foʊ-/ *noun* a photocopy or a machine that produces them

photo·syn·thesis /ˌfəʊtəʊ'sɪnθəsɪs; *NAmE* ˌfoʊtoʊ-/ *noun* [U] (*biology*) the process by which green plants turn CARBON DIOXIDE and water into food using energy obtained from light from the sun ➲ COLLOCATIONS at LIFE

photo·syn·the·size (*BrE* also **-ise**) /ˌfəʊtəʊ'sɪnθəsaɪz; *NAmE* ˌfoʊtoʊ-/ *verb* [I, T] **~ (sth)** (*biology*) (of plants) to make food by means of PHOTOSYNTHESIS

photo·trop·ism /ˌfəʊtəʊ'trəʊpɪzəm; *NAmE* ˌfoʊtoʊ'troʊ-/ *noun* [U] (*biology*) the action of a plant turning towards or away from light ▸ **photo·trop·ic** /-'trɒpɪk; *NAmE* -'trɑːpɪk/ *adj.*

phrasal /'freɪzl/ *adj.* of or connected with a phrase

ˌphrasal 'verb *noun* (*grammar*) a verb combined with an adverb or a preposition, or sometimes both, to give a new meaning, for example *go in for*, *win over* and *see to*

phrase /freɪz/ *noun, verb*

■ ***noun* 1** (*grammar*) a group of words without a FINITE verb, especially one that forms part of a sentence. 'the green car' and 'on Friday morning' are phrases. ➲ SYNONYMS at WORD ➲ see also NOUN PHRASE **2** a group of words which have a particular meaning when used together: *a memorable phrase* ◇ *She was, in her own favourite phrase, 'a woman without a past'.* ➲ see also CATCHPHRASE **3** (*music*) a short series of notes that form a unit within a longer passage in a piece of music **IDM** see COIN *v.*, TURN *n.*

■ ***verb* 1** [T] to say or write sth in a particular way: **~ sth (+ adv./prep.)** *a carefully phrased remark* ◇ *I agree with what he says, but I'd have phrased it differently.* ◇ **~ sth as sth** *Her order was phrased as a suggestion.* **2** [I, T] **~ (sth)** to divide a piece of music into small groups of notes; to play or sing these in a particular way, especially in an effective way

'phrase book *noun* a book containing lists of common expressions translated into another language, especially for people visiting a foreign country

phrase·ology /ˌfreɪzi'ɒlədʒi; *NAmE* -'ɑːlə-/ *noun* [U] (*formal*) the particular way in which words and phrases are arranged when saying or writing sth

phras·ing /'freɪzɪŋ/ *noun* [U] **1** the words used to express sth: *The phrasing of the report is ambiguous.* **2** (*music*) the way in which a musician or singer divides a piece of music into phrases by pausing in suitable places

phreak·ing /'friːkɪŋ/ *noun* [U] (*informal, especially NAmE*) the act of getting into a communications system illegally, usually in order to make telephone calls without paying ▸ **phreak·er** *noun*

phren·ology /frə'nɒlədʒi; *NAmE* -'nɑːl-/ *noun* [U] the study of the shape of the human head, which some people

P

think is a guide to a person's character ▸ **phren·olo·gist** /frəˈnɒlədʒɪst; *NAmE* -ˈnɑːl-/ *noun*

phwoah (also **phwoor, phwoar**) /ˈfwɔːə/ *exclamation* (*BrE, informal*) used when you find sth or sb very impressive and attractive, especially in a sexual way

phylum /ˈfaɪləm/ *noun* (*pl.* **phyla** /-lə/) (*biology*) a group into which animals, plants, etc. are divided, smaller than a KINGDOM and larger than a CLASS ➲ compare GENUS

phys·ic·al 🔑 AW /ˈfɪzɪkl/ *adj., noun*

■ ***adj.***

▸ THE BODY **1** 🔑 [usually before noun] connected with a person's body rather than their mind: *physical fitness* ◇ *physical appearance* ◇ *The ordeal has affected both her mental and physical health.* ◇ *He tends to avoid all physical contact.*

▸ REAL THINGS **2** 🔑 [only before noun] connected with things that actually exist or are present and can be seen, felt, etc. rather than things that only exist in a person's mind: *the **physical world/universe/environment*** ◇ *the **physical properties*** (= the colour, weight, shape, etc.) *of copper*

▸ NATURE/SCIENCE **3** 🔑 [only before noun] according to the laws of nature: *It is a physical impossibility to be in two places at once.* **4** 🔑 [only before noun] connected with the scientific study of forces such as heat, light, sound, etc. and how they affect objects: *physical laws*

▸ SEX **5** 🔑 involving sex: *physical love* ◇ *They are having a physical relationship.*

▸ PERSON **6** (*informal*) (of a person) liking to touch other people a lot: *She's not very physical.*

▸ VIOLENT **7** (*informal*) violent (used to avoid saying this in a direct way): *Are you going to cooperate or do we have to get physical?*

■ ***noun*** (also ˌ**physical examiˈnation**) a medical examination of a person's body, for example, to check that they are fit enough to do a particular job

ˌ**physical eduˈcation** *noun* = PE

ˌ**physical geˈography** *noun* [U] **1** the scientific study of the natural features on the surface of the earth, for example mountains and rivers **2** the way in which the natural features of a place are arranged: *the physical geography of Scotland*

P

phys·ic·al·ity /ˌfɪzɪˈkæləti/ *noun* [U] (*formal*) the quality of being physical rather than emotional or spiritual

phys·ic·al·ly 🔑 AW /ˈfɪzɪkli/ *adv.*

1 🔑 in a way that is connected with a person's body rather than their mind: *mentally and physically handicapped* ◇ *physically and emotionally exhausted* ◇ *I felt physically sick before the exam.* ◇ *I don't find him physically attractive.* ◇ *They were physically prevented from entering the building.* **2** 🔑 according to the laws of nature or what is probable: *It's physically impossible to finish by the end of the week.*

ˌ**physical ˈscience** *noun* [U] (also **the physical sciences** [pl.]) the areas of science concerned with studying natural forces and things that are not alive, for example physics and chemistry ➲ compare LIFE SCIENCES

ˌ**physical ˈtherapist** (*US*) (*BrE* **physio·ther·ap·ist**, *informal* **physio**) *noun* a person whose job is to give patients physical therapy

ˌ**physical ˈtherapy** (*US*) (*BrE* **physio·ther·apy**, *informal* **physio**) *noun* [U] the treatment of disease, injury or weakness in the joints or muscles by exercises, MASSAGE and the use of light and heat

ˌ**physical ˈtraining** *noun* = PT

phys·ician /fɪˈzɪʃn/ *noun* (*especially NAmE*) a doctor, especially one who is a specialist in general medicine and not SURGERY ➲ compare SURGEON HELP This word is now old-fashioned in *BrE*. **Doctor** or **GP** is used instead.

physi·cist /ˈfɪzɪsɪst/ *noun* a scientist who studies physics: *a nuclear physicist*

phys·ics 🔑 /ˈfɪzɪks/ *noun* [U]

the scientific study of matter and energy and the relationships between them, including the study of forces, heat, light, sound, electricity and the structure of atoms: *a degree in physics* ◇ ***particle/nuclear/theoretical physics*** ◇ *the laws of physics* ◇ *a school physics department* ◇ *to study the physics of the electron* ➲ see also ASTROPHYSICS, GEOPHYSICS

Collocations

Physical appearance

■ A person may be described as **having**:

Eyes
- (bright) blue/green/(dark/light) brown/hazel **eyes**
- deep-set/sunken/bulging/protruding **eyes**
- small/beady/sparkling/twinkling/(*informal*) shifty **eyes**
- piercing/penetrating/steely **eyes**
- bloodshot/watery/puffy **eyes**
- bushy/thick/dark/raised/arched **eyebrows**
- long/dark/thick/curly/false **eyelashes/lashes**

Face
- a flat/bulbous/pointed/sharp/snub **nose**
- a straight/a hooked/a Roman/(*formal*) an aquiline **nose**
- full/thick/thin/pouty **lips**
- dry/chapped/cracked **lips**
- flushed/rosy/red/ruddy/pale **cheeks**
- soft/chubby/sunken **cheeks**
- white/perfect/crooked/protruding **teeth**
- a large/high/broad/wide/sloping **forehead**
- a strong/weak/pointed/double **chin**
- a long/full/bushy/wispy/goatee **beard**
- a long/thin/bushy/droopy/handlebar/pencil **moustache**/(*especially US*) **mustache**

Hair and skin
- pale/fair/olive/dark/tanned **skin**
- dry/oily/smooth/rough/leathery/wrinkled **skin**
- a dark/pale/light/sallow/ruddy/olive/swarthy/clear **complexion**
- deep/fine/little/facial **wrinkles**
- blonde/blond/fair/(light/dark) brown/(jet-)black/auburn/red/(*BrE*) ginger/grey **hair**
- straight/curly/wavy/frizzy/spiky **hair**
- thick/thin/fine/bushy/thinning **hair**
- dyed/bleached/soft/silky/dry/greasy/shiny **hair**
- long/short/shoulder-length/cropped **hair**
- a bald/balding/shaved **head**
- a receding **hairline**
- a bald **patch/spot**
- a side/centre/(*US*) center (*BrE*) **parting**/(*NAmE*) **part**

Body
- a long/short/thick/slender/(*disapproving*) scrawny **neck**
- broad/narrow/sloping/rounded/hunched **shoulders**
- a bare/broad/muscular/small/large **chest**
- a flat/swollen/bulging **stomach**
- a small/tiny/narrow/slim/slender/28-inch **waist**
- big/wide/narrow/slim **hips**
- a straight/bent/arched/broad/hairy **back**
- thin/slender/muscular **arms**
- big/large/small/manicured/calloused/gloved **hands**
- long/short/fat/slender/delicate/bony **fingers**
- long/muscular/hairy/shapely/(*both informal, often disapproving*) skinny/spindly **legs**
- muscular/chubby/(*informal, disapproving*) flabby **thighs**
- big/little/small/dainty/wide/narrow/bare **feet**
- a good/a slim/a slender/an hourglass **figure**
- **be of** slim/medium/average/large/athletic/stocky **build**

physio /ˈfɪziəʊ; *NAmE* ˈfɪzioʊ/ *noun* (*pl.* -os) (*BrE, informal*) **1** [U] = PHYSIOTHERAPY **2** [C] = PHYSIOTHERAPIST

physio- /ˈfɪziəʊ; *NAmE* ˈfɪzioʊ/ *combining form* (in nouns, adjectives and adverbs) **1** connected with nature **2** connected with PHYSIOLOGY

physi·ognomy /ˌfɪziˈɒnəmi; *NAmE* -ˈɑːnə-/ *noun* (*pl.* -ies) (*formal*) the shape and features of a person's face

physi·olo·gist /ˌfɪziˈɒlədʒɪst; *NAmE* -ˈɑːlə-/ *noun* a scientist who studies physiology

physi·ology /ˌfɪziˈɒlədʒi; *NAmE* -ˈɑːlə-/ *noun* **1** [U] the scientific study of the normal functions of living things: *the department of anatomy and physiology* **2** [U, sing.] the way in which a particular living thing functions: *plant physiology* ◇ *the physiology of the horse* ▸ **physio·logic·al** /ˌfɪziəˈlɒdʒɪkl; *NAmE* -ˈlɑːdʒ-/ *adj.*: *the physiological effect of space travel* **physio·lo·gic·al·ly** /-ɪkli/ *adv.*

physio·ther·ap·ist /ˌfɪziəʊˈθerəpɪst; *NAmE* ˌfɪzioʊ-/ (also *informal* **physio**) (both *BrE*) (*US* ˌ**physical** ˈ**therapist**) *noun* a person whose job is to give patients physiotherapy

physio·ther·apy /ˌfɪziəʊˈθerəpi; *NAmE* ˌfɪzioʊ-/ (also *informal* **physio**) (both *BrE*) (*US* ˌ**physical** ˈ**therapy**) *noun* [U] the treatment of disease, injury or weakness in the joints or muscles by exercises, MASSAGE and the use of light and heat ➲ COLLOCATIONS at INJURY

phys·ique /fɪˈziːk/ *noun* [C, U] the size and shape of a person's body SYN **build**: *He has the physique of a rugby player.* ◇ *a powerful physique*

pi /paɪ/ *noun* **1** (*geometry*) the symbol π used to show the RATIO of the CIRCUMFERENCE of (= distance around) a circle to its DIAMETER (= distance across), that is about 3.14159 **2** the 16th letter of the Greek alphabet (Π, π)

pi·an·is·simo /ˌpiəˈnɪsɪməʊ; *NAmE* -moʊ/ *adv.* (*abbr.* **pp**) (*music*) played or sung very quietly OPP **fortissimo** ▸ **pi·an·is·simo** *adj.*

pi·an·ist /ˈpɪənɪst/ *noun* a person who plays the piano: *a concert pianist* ◇ *a jazz pianist*

piano 🔑 *noun, adv.*
- *noun* 🔑 /piˈænəʊ; *NAmE* -noʊ/ (*pl.* -os) (also *old-fashioned, formal* **pi·ano·forte** /piˌænəʊˈfɔːti; *NAmE* piˌænoʊˈfɔːr-/) a large musical instrument played by pressing the black and white keys on the keyboard. The sound is produced by small HAMMERS hitting the metal strings inside the piano: *to play the piano* ◇ *playing jazz* ***on the piano*** ◇ *piano music* ◇ *a* ***piano teacher/lesson*** ◇ *Ravel's piano concerto in G* ➲ see also GRAND PIANO, THUMB PIANO, UPRIGHT PIANO
- *adv.* /ˈpjɑːnəʊ; *NAmE* -noʊ/ (*abbr.* **p**) (*music*) played or sung quietly OPP **forte** ▸ **piano** *adj.*

piˌano acˈcordion *noun* a type of ACCORDION that you press buttons and keys on to produce the different notes

Pi·an·ola™ /ˌpiəˈnəʊlə; *NAmE* -ˈnoʊ-/ *noun* a piano that plays automatically by means of a PIANO ROLL SYN **player piano**

piˈano roll *noun* a roll of paper full of very small holes that controls the movement of the keys in a PLAYER PIANO

pi·azza /piˈætsə; *NAmE* piˈɑːzə/ *noun* a public square, especially in an Italian town

pi·broch /ˈpiːbrɒk; -brɒx; *NAmE* -brɑːk; -brɑːx/ *noun* [C, U] a piece of music played on the BAGPIPES, especially at military occasions or funerals; music of this type

pic /pɪk/ *noun* (*informal*) a picture

pica /ˈpaɪkə/ *noun* (*technical*) a unit for measuring the size of printed letters and the length of a line of printed text

pi·can·te /pɪˈkɑːnteɪ/ *adj.* (from *Spanish, NAmE*) (of food) hot and spicy: *tortilla chips dipped in a picante sauce*

pic·ar·esque /ˌpɪkəˈresk/ *adj.* (*formal*) connected with literature that describes the adventures of a person who is sometimes dishonest but easy to like: *a picaresque novel*

Pic·ca·dilly Cir·cus /ˌpɪkədɪli ˈsɜːkəs; *NAmE* ˈsɜːrkəs/ *noun* (*BrE*) used to describe a place that is very busy or crowded: *It's been like Piccadilly Circus in this house all morning.* ORIGIN From the name of a busy area in the centre of London where several large roads meet and where there is always a lot of traffic. ➲ compare GRAND CENTRAL STATION

pic·ca·ninny (also **picka·ninny**) /ˌpɪkəˈnɪni/ *noun* (*pl.* -ies) (*old-fashioned*) an offensive word for a small black child

pic·colo /ˈpɪkələʊ; *NAmE* -loʊ/ *noun* (*pl.* -os) a musical instrument of the WOODWIND group, like a small FLUTE that plays high notes ➲ VISUAL VOCAB page V30

pick 🔑 /pɪk/ *verb, noun*
- *verb* **1** 🔑 [T] (rather *informal*) to choose sb/sth from a group of people or things: **~ sb/sth** *Pick a number from one to twenty.* ◇ *She picked the best cake for herself.* ◇ *He* ***picked his words*** *carefully.* ◇ *Have I picked a bad time to talk to you?* ◇ **~ sb/sth to do sth** *He has been picked to play in this week's game.* ➲ SYNONYMS at CHOOSE ➲ see also HAND-PICKED **2** 🔑 [T] **~ sth** to take flowers, fruit, etc. from the plant or the tree where they are growing: *to pick grapes* ◇ *flowers freshly picked from the garden* ◇ *to go blackberry picking* **3** 🔑 [T] to pull or remove sth or small pieces of sth from sth else, especially with your fingers: **~ sth + adv./prep.** *She picked bits of fluff from his sweater.* ◇ *He picked the nuts off the top of the cake.* ◇ **~ sth** *to* ***pick your nose*** (= put your finger inside your nose to remove dried MUCUS) ◇ *to* ***pick your teeth*** (= use a small sharp piece of wood to remove pieces of food from your teeth) ◇ **~ sth + adj.** *The dogs picked the bones clean* (= ate all the meat from the bones). **4** [I, T] **~ (sth)** (*NAmE*) = PLUCK (3)

IDM ˌ**pick and** ˈ**choose** to choose only those things that you like or want very much: *You have to take any job you can get—you can't pick and choose.* **pick sb's** ˈ**brains** (*informal*) to ask sb a lot of questions about sth because they know more about the subject than you do **pick a** ˈ**fight/** ˈ**quarrel (with sb)** to deliberately start a fight or an argument with sb **pick** ˈ**holes in sth** to find the weak points in sth such as a plan, suggestion, etc: *It was easy to pick holes in his arguments.* **pick a** ˈ**lock** to open a lock without a key, using sth such as a piece of wire **pick sb's** ˈ**pocket** to steal sth from sb's pocket without them noticing ➲ related noun PICKPOCKET **pick up the** ˈ**bill,** ˈ**tab, etc. (for sth)** (*informal*) to pay for sth: *The company picked up the tab for his hotel room.* ◇ *The government will continue to pick up college fees for some students.* **pick up the** ˈ**pieces** to return or to help sb return to a normal situation, particularly after a shock or a disaster: *You cannot live your children's lives for them; you can only be there to pick up the pieces when things go wrong.* **pick up** ˈ**speed** to go faster **pick up the** ˈ**threads** to return to an earlier situation or way of life after an interruption **pick your** ˈ**way (across, along, among, over, through sth)** to walk carefully, choosing the safest, driest, etc. place to put your feet: *She picked her way delicately over the rough ground.* **pick a** ˈ**winner** **1** to choose a horse, etc. that you think is most likely to win a race **2** (*informal*) to make a very good choice ➲ more at BONE *n.*, PIECE *n.*, SHRED *n.*

PHR V ˈ**pick at sth** **1** to eat food slowly, taking small amounts or bites because you are not hungry **2** to pull or touch sth several times: *He tried to undo the knot by picking at it with his fingers.*

ˌ**pick sb↔**ˈ**off** (*informal*) to aim carefully at a person, an animal or an aircraft, especially one of a group, and then shoot them: *Snipers were picking off innocent civilians.*

ˌ**pick sth↔**ˈ**off** to remove sth from sth such as a tree, a plant, etc: *Pick off all the dead leaves.*

ˈ**pick on sb/sth** **1** to treat sb unfairly, by blaming, criticizing or punishing them: *She was picked on by the other girls because of her size.* **2** to choose sb/sth: *He picked on two of her statements which he said were untrue.*

ˌ**pick sb/sth↔**ˈ**out** **1** to choose sb/sth carefully from a group of people or things SYN **select**: *She was picked out from dozens of applicants for the job.* ◇ *He picked out the ripest peach for me.* **2** to recognize sb/sth from among other people or things: *See if you can pick me out in this photo.* ˌ**pick sth↔**ˈ**out** **1** to play a tune on a musical instrument slowly without using written music: *He picked out the tune on the piano with one finger.* **2** to discover or

P

recognize sth after careful study: *Read the play again and pick out the major themes.* **3** to make sth easy to see or hear: *a sign painted cream, with the lettering picked out in black*

ˌ**pick sth↔ˈover** | ˌ**pick ˈthrough sth** to examine a group of things carefully, especially to choose the ones you want: *Pick over the lentils and remove any little stones.* ◇ *I picked through the facts of the case.*

ˌ**pick ˈup 1** to get better, stronger, etc; to improve: *Trade usually picks up in the spring.* ◇ *The wind is picking up now.* ◇ *Sales have picked up 14% this year.* ➲ related noun PICK-UP **2** (*informal*) to start again; to continue: *Let's* **pick up where we left off** *yesterday.* **3** (*informal, especially NAmE*) to put things away and make things neat, especially for sb else: *All I seem to do is cook, wash and pick up after the kids.* ˌ**pick ˈup** | ˌ**pick sth ˈup** to answer a phone: *The phone rang and rang and nobody picked up.* ˌ**pick sb↔ˈup 1** 🔑 to go somewhere in your car and collect sb who is waiting for you SYN **collect**: *I'll pick you up at five.* **2** to allow sb to get into your vehicle and take them somewhere: *The bus picks up passengers outside the airport.* **3** to rescue sb from the sea or from a dangerous place, especially one that is difficult to reach: *A lifeboat picked up survivors.* **4** (*informal*, often *disapproving*) to start talking to sb you do not know because you want to have a sexual relationship with them: *He goes to clubs to pick up girls.* ➲ related noun PICKUP **5** (*informal*) (of the police) to arrest sb: *He was picked up by police and taken to the station for questioning.* **6** to make sb feel better: *Try this—it will pick you up.* ➲ related noun PICK-ME-UP ˌ**pick sb/sth↔ˈup 1** 🔑 to take hold of sb/sth and lift them/it up: *She went over to the crying child and picked her up.* **2** 🔑 to receive an electronic signal, sound or picture: *We were able to pick up the BBC World Service.* ˌ**pick sth↔ˈup 1** 🔑 to get information or a skill by chance rather than by making a deliberate effort: *to pick up bad habits* ◇ *Here's a tip I picked up from my mother.* ◇ *She picked up Spanish when she was living in Mexico.* **2** to identify or recognize sth: *Scientists can now pick up early signs of the disease.* **3** 🔑 to collect sth from a place: *I picked up my coat from the cleaners.* ➲ related noun PICKUP **4** (*informal*) to buy sth, especially cheaply or by chance: *We managed to pick up a few bargains at the auction.* **5** (*informal*) to get or obtain sth: *I seem to have picked up a terrible cold from somewhere.* ◇ *I picked up £30 in tips today.* **6** to find and follow a route: *to pick up the scent of an animal* ◇ *We can pick up the motorway in a few miles.* **7** to return to an earlier subject or situation in order to continue it SYN **take up**: *He picks up this theme again in later chapters of the book.* **8** to notice sth that is not very obvious; to see sth that you are looking for: *I picked up the faint sound of a car in the distance.* **9** (*especially NAmE*) to put things away neatly: *Will you pick up all your toys?* **10** (*NAmE*) to put things away and make a room neat: *to pick up a room* ˌ**pick ˈup on sth 1** to notice sth and perhaps react to it: *She failed to pick up on the humour in his remark.* **2** to return to a point that has already been mentioned or discussed: *If I could just pick up on a question you raised earlier.* ˌ**pick sb ˈup on sth** to mention sth that sb has said or done that you think is wrong: *I knew he would pick me up on that slip sooner or later.* ˌ**pick yourself ˈup** to stand up again after you have fallen: *He just picked himself up and went on running.* ◇ (*figurative*) *She didn't waste time feeling sorry for herself—she just picked herself up and carried on.*

▪ ***noun* 1** [sing.] (rather *informal*) an act of choosing sth: ***Take your pick*** (= choose). ◇ *The winner gets first pick of the prizes.* **2** [C] (*informal*) a person or thing that is chosen: *She was his pick for best actress.* ➲ **SYNONYMS** at CHOICE **3** [sing.] **the ~ of sth** (rather *informal*) the best thing or things in a group: *We're reviewing the pick of this month's new books.* ◇ *I think we got* **the pick of the bunch** (= the best in the group). **4** [C] = PICKAXE: *picks and shovels* **5** [C] (*informal*) = PLECTRUM ➲ see also ICE PICK, TOOTHPICK IDM see BUNCH *n.*

ˈ**pick-and-mix** *adj.* (*BrE*) used to describe a way of putting sth together by choosing things from among a large variety of different items: *a pick-and-mix programme of study*

picka·ninny = PICCANINNY

pick·axe (*NAmE* also **pick·ax**) /ˈpɪkæks/ (also **pick**) *noun* a large heavy tool that has a curved metal bar with sharp ends fixed at the centre to a wooden handle. It is used for breaking rocks or hard ground. ➲ picture at AXE

pick·er /ˈpɪkə(r)/ *noun* a person or machine that picks flowers, vegetables, etc: *cotton pickers*

picket /ˈpɪkɪt/ *noun, verb*

▪ ***noun* 1** a person or group of people who stand outside the entrance to a building in order to protest about sth, especially in order to stop people from entering a factory, etc. during a strike; an occasion at which this happens: *Five pickets were arrested by police.* ◇ *I was on picket duty at the time.* ◇ *a mass picket of the factory* ➲ see also FLYING PICKET, PICKETER **2** a soldier or group of soldiers guarding a military base **3** a pointed piece of wood that is fixed in the ground, especially as part of a fence: *a picket fence*

▪ ***verb*** [T, I] **~ (sth)** to stand outside somewhere such as your place of work to protest about sth or to try and persuade people to join a strike: *200 workers were picketing the factory.* ◇ *Striking workers picketed outside the gates.*

pick·et·er /ˈpɪkɪtə(r)/ *noun* (*NAmE*) a person who takes part in a picket

picket·ing /ˈpɪkɪtɪŋ/ *noun* [U] the activity of standing outside the entrance to a building in order to protest about sth and stop people from entering the building: *mass picketing of the factory*

ˈ**picket line** *noun* a line or group of PICKETS (1): *Fire crews refused to cross the picket line.*

pick·ings /ˈpɪkɪŋz/ *noun* [pl.] something, especially money, that can be obtained from a particular situation in an easy or a dishonest way: *There were only* ***slim pickings*** *to be made at the fair.* ◇ *There are* ***rich pickings*** *to be had by investing in this sort of company.* ◇ *The strike affecting the country's largest airline is producing* ***easy pickings*** *for smaller companies.*

pickle /ˈpɪkl/ *noun, verb*

▪ ***noun* 1** [C, usually pl.] (*BrE*) a vegetable that has been preserved in VINEGAR or salt water and has a strong flavour, served cold with meat, salads, etc. **2** [U] (*BrE*) a cold thick spicy sauce made from fruit and vegetables that have been boiled, often sold in JARS and served with meat, cheese, etc. **3** (*NAmE*) (*BrE* **gher·kin**) [U, C] a small CUCUMBER that has been preserved in VINEGAR before being eaten IDM **in a ˈpickle** (*informal*) in a difficult or unpleasant situation

▪ ***verb*** **~ sth** to preserve food in VINEGAR or salt water

pickled /ˈpɪkld/ *adj.* **1** (of food) preserved in VINEGAR: *pickled cabbage/herring/onions* **2** (*old-fashioned, informal*) drunk

ˈ**pick-me-up** *noun* (*informal*) something that makes you feel better, happier, healthier, etc, especially medicine or an alcoholic drink: (*figurative*) *This deal would offer the best possible pick-me-up to the town's ailing economy.*

pick·off /ˈpɪkɒf; *NAmE* -ɔːf; -ɑːf/ *noun* (*NAmE*) (in BASEBALL) a situation in which a player running to a BASE is out because a FIELDER or the PITCHER suddenly throws the ball to that base

pick·pocket /ˈpɪkpɒkɪt; *NAmE* -pɑːkɪt/ *noun* a person who steals money, etc. from other people's pockets, especially in crowded places

pick·up /ˈpɪkʌp/ *noun, adj.*

▪ ***noun* 1** (also ˈ**pickup truck**) [C] a vehicle with low sides and no roof at the back used, for example, by farmers ➲ **VISUAL VOCAB** page V46 **2** [C] a person sb meets for the first time, for example in a bar, with whom they start a sexual relationship: *casual pickups* **3** [C] **~ (in sth)** an improvement: *a pickup in the housing market* **4** [U, C] an occasion when sb/sth is collected: *Goods are delivered not later than noon on the day after pickup.* **5** [C] the part of a record player or musical instrument that changes electrical signals into sound, or sound into electrical signals **6** [U] (*NAmE*) a vehicle's ability to ACCELERATE (= increase in speed)

■ *adj.* [only before noun] (*NAmE*) (of a sports game) often not planned in advance and that anyone who wants to can join in: *A group of kids started a pickup game of basketball on the street outside.*

picky /ˈpɪki/ *adj.* (*informal*) (of a person) liking only particular things and difficult to please SYN **fussy**

ˌ**pick-your-ˈown** *adj.* [only before noun] (of fruit or vegetables) picked by the customer on the farm where they are grown: *pick-your-own strawberries*

pic·nic /ˈpɪknɪk/ *noun, verb*

■ ***noun*** **1** an occasion when people pack a meal and take it to eat outdoors, especially in the countryside: *It's a nice day. Let's* ***go for a picnic.*** ◇ *We* ***had a picnic*** *beside the river.* **2** the meal, usually consisting of SANDWICHES, salad and fruit, etc. that you take with you when you go on a picnic: *Let's eat our picnic by the lake.* ◇ *a picnic lunch* ◇ *a picnic basket*

IDM **be no ˈpicnic** (*informal*) to be difficult and cause a lot of problems: *Bringing up a family when you're unemployed is no picnic.*

■ ***verb*** (-ck-) [I] to have a picnic: *No picnicking allowed* (= on a sign)

pic·nick·er /ˈpɪknɪkə(r)/ *noun* a person who is having a picnic

pico- /ˈpiːkəʊ-; ˈpaɪkəʊ-; *NAmE* -koʊ-/ *combining form* (in nouns; used in units of measurement) 10^{-12}; one million millionth

picto·gram /ˈpɪktəɡræm/ *noun* **1** a picture representing a word or phrase **2** a diagram that uses pictures to represent amounts or numbers of a particular thing

pic·tor·ial /pɪkˈtɔːriəl/ *adj.* [usually before noun] **1** using or containing pictures: *a* ***pictorial account/record*** *of the expedition* **2** connected with pictures: *pictorial traditions* ▶ **pic·tori·al·ly** /-əli/ *adv.*

pic·ture 0-w /ˈpɪktʃə(r)/ *noun, verb*

■ ***noun***

▸ PAINTING/DRAWING **1** 0-w [C] a painting or drawing, etc. that shows a scene, a person or thing: *A picture of flowers hung on the wall.* ◇ *The children were* ***drawing pictures*** *of their pets.* ◇ *She wanted a famous artist to* ***paint her picture*** (= a picture of herself). ◇ *a book with lots of pictures in it*

▸ PHOTOGRAPH **2** 0-w [C] a photograph: *We had our* ***picture taken*** *in front of the hotel.* ◇ *The picture shows the couple together on their yacht.* ◇ *Have you got any pictures of your trip?* ➲ SYNONYMS at PHOTOGRAPH

▸ ON TV **3** 0-w [C] an image on a television screen: *harrowing television pictures of the famine* ◇ *satellite pictures* ◇ *The picture isn't very clear tonight.*

▸ DESCRIPTION **4** 0-w [C, usually sing.] a description that gives you an idea in your mind of what sth is like: *The writer paints a gloomy picture of the economy.* ◇ *The police are trying* ***to build up a picture*** *of what happened.*

▸ MENTAL IMAGE **5** 0-w [C, usually sing.] a mental image or memory of sth: *I have a vivid picture of my grandfather smiling down at me when I was very small.*

▸ GENERAL SITUATION **6** **the picture** [sing.] the general situation concerning sb/sth: *Just a few years ago the picture was very different.* ◇ *The overall picture for farming is encouraging.*

▸ MOVIES **7** [C] a film/movie: *The movie won nine Academy Awards, including Best Picture.* ◇ (*especially NAmE*) *I believe her husband's* ***in pictures*** (= he acts in movies or works in the movie industry). ➲ see also MOTION PICTURE **8** **the pictures** [pl.] (*old-fashioned, informal*) the cinema/the movies: *Shall we go to the pictures tonight?*

IDM **be/look a ˈpicture** to look very beautiful or special **be the picture of ˈhealth, ˈguilt, ˈmisery, etc.** (*informal*) to look extremely healthy, guilty, unhappy, etc. **get the ˈpicture** (*informal*) to understand a situation, especially one that sb is describing to you: *'I pretended that I hadn't heard.' 'I get the picture.'* **in/out of the ˈpicture** (*informal*) involved/not involved in a situation: *Morris is likely to win, with Jones out of the picture now.* **put/keep sb in the ˈpicture** (*informal*) to give sb the information they need in order to understand a situation: *Just to put you in the picture—there have been a number of changes here recently.* ➲ more at BIG *adj.*, PAINT *v.*, PRETTY *adj.*

■ ***verb***

▸ IMAGINE **1** to imagine sb/sth; to create an image of sb/sth in your mind: **~ sb/sth** *I can still picture the house I grew up in.* ◇ **~ sb/sth as sth** *We found it hard to picture him as the father of teenage sons.* ◇ **~ sb/sth doing sth** *When he did not come home she pictured him lying dead on the roadside somewhere.* ◇ **~ what, how, etc...** *I tried to picture what it would be like to live alone.*

▸ DESCRIBE **2** [often passive] **~ sb/sth as sth** to describe or present sb/sth in a particular way SYN **portray**: *Before the trial Liz had been pictured as a frail woman dominated by her husband.*

▸ SHOW IN PHOTOGRAPH **3** [usually passive] to show sb/sth in a photograph or picture: **~ sb/sth (+ adv./prep/adj.)** *She is pictured here with her parents.* ◇ **~ sb/sth doing sth** *The team is pictured setting off on their European tour.*

Synonyms

picture

painting • drawing • portrait • print • sketch

These are all words for a scene, person or thing that has been represented on paper by drawing, painting, etc.

picture a scene, person or thing that has been represented on paper using a pencil, a pen or paint: *The children were drawing pictures of their pets.*

painting a picture that has been made using paint: *a collection of paintings by American artists*

drawing a picture that has been made using a pencil or pen, not paint: *a pencil/charcoal drawing*

portrait a painting, drawing or photograph of a person, especially of the head and shoulders: *Vermeer's 'Portrait of the artist in his studio'* ◇ *a self-portrait* (= a painting that you do of yourself)

print a picture that has been copied from a painting using photography: *a Renoir print*

sketch a simple picture that is drawn quickly and does not have many details: *I usually do a few very rough sketches before I start on a painting.*

PATTERNS

- to **draw** a picture/portrait/sketch
- to **paint** a picture/portrait
- to **make** a painting/drawing/portrait/print/sketch
- to **do** a painting/drawing/portrait/sketch

ˈ**picture book** *noun* a book with a lot of pictures, especially one for children

ˈ**picture messaging** *noun* [U] a system of sending images from one mobile/cell phone to another SYN **EMS**

ˌ**picture-ˈperfect** *adj.* (*NAmE*) exactly right in appearance or in the way things are done

ˌ**picture ˈpostcard** *noun* (*old-fashioned*) a POSTCARD with a picture on one side

ˌ**picture-ˈpostcard** *adj.* [only before noun] (*especially BrE*) (of places) very pretty: *a picture-postcard village*

ˈ**picture rail** *noun* a narrow strip of wood attached to the walls of a room below the ceiling and used for hanging pictures from

pic·tur·esque /ˌpɪktʃəˈresk/ *adj.* **1** (of a place, building, scene, etc.) pretty, especially in a way that looks old-fashioned SYN **quaint**: *a picturesque cottage/setting/village* **2** (of language) producing strong mental images by using unusual words: *a picturesque description of life at sea* ▶ **pic·tur·esque·ly** *adv.*: *The inn is picturesquely situated on the banks of the river.*

ˈ**picture window** *noun* a very large window made of a single piece of glass

pic·tur·ize (*BrE* also **-ise**) /ˈpɪktʃəraɪz/ *verb* **~ sth** (*IndE*) to adapt a story or play as a film/movie; to create a film

P

SEQUENCE to accompany a song: *The novel has been picturized twice.* ▶ **pic·tur·iza·tion, -isa·tion** /ˌpɪktʃəraɪˈzeɪʃn/ *noun* [C, U]: *It was one of the few song picturizations that created magic with both music and visuals.*

pid·dle /ˈpɪdl/ *verb* [I] (*old-fashioned, informal*) to URINATE

pid·dling /ˈpɪdlɪŋ/ *adj.* [only before noun] (*informal, disapproving*) small and unimportant SYN **trivial**

pidgin /ˈpɪdʒɪn/ *noun* [U] **1** a simple form of a language, especially English, Portuguese or Dutch, with a limited number of words, that are used together with words from a local language. It is used when people who do not speak the same language need to talk to each other. **2 Pidgin** = TOK PISIN **3 ~ English, French, Japanese, etc.** a way of speaking a language that uses simple words and forms, used when a person does not speak the language well, or when he or she is talking to sb who does not speak the language well: *I tried to get my message across in my pidgin Italian.*

pi-dog = PYE-DOG

pie /paɪ/ *noun* [C, U] **1** fruit baked in a dish with PASTRY on the bottom, sides and top: *a slice of apple pie* ◇ *Help yourself to some more pie.* ◇ *a pie dish* ➲ see also CUSTARD PIE **2** (*especially BrE*) meat, vegetables, etc. baked in a dish with PASTRY on the bottom, sides and top: *a steak and kidney pie* ➲ see also MINCE PIE, PORK PIE, SHEPHERD'S PIE

IDM **a ˌpiece/ˌslice/ˌshare of the ˈpie** a share of sth such as money, profits, etc. **ˌpie in the ˈsky** (*informal*) an event that sb talks about that seems very unlikely to happen: *This talk of moving to Australia is all just pie in the sky.* ➲ more at AMERICAN *adj.*, EASY *adj.*, EAT, FINGER *n.*, NICE

pie·bald /ˈpaɪbɔːld/ *adj.* (of a horse) with areas on it of two colours, usually black and white ➲ compare SKEWBALD

piece 0‑ /piːs/ *noun, verb*

■ ***noun***

▸ SEPARATE AMOUNT **1** 0‑ [C] **~ (of sth)** (used especially with *of* and uncountable nouns) an amount of sth that has been cut or separated from the rest of it; a standard amount of sth: *a piece of string/wood* ◇ *She wrote something on a small piece of paper.* ◇ *a large piece of land* ◇ *a piece of cake/cheese/meat* ◇ *He cut the pizza into bite-sized pieces.* ◇ *I've got a piece of grit in my eye.*

▸ PART **2** 0‑ [C, usually pl.] one of the bits or parts that sth breaks into: *There were tiny pieces of glass all over the road.* ◇ *The boat had been smashed* ***to pieces*** *on the rocks.* ◇ *The vase lay* ***in pieces*** *on the floor.* **3** 0‑ [C] one of the parts that sth is made of: *He* ***took*** *the clock* ***to pieces***. ◇ *a missing piece of the puzzle* ◇ *The bridge was taken down* ***piece by piece***. ◇ *a 500-piece jigsaw* ➲ see also ONE-PIECE, TWO-PIECE, THREE-PIECE

▸ SINGLE ITEM **4** 0‑ [C] (used especially with *of* and uncountable nouns) a single item of a particular type, especially one that forms part of a set: *a piece of clothing/furniture/luggage* ◇ *a piece of equipment/machinery* ◇ *a 28-piece dinner service* **5** 0‑ [C] **~ of sth** used with many uncountable nouns to describe a single example or an amount of sth: *a* ***piece of advice/information/news*** ◇ *an interesting piece of research* ◇ *Isn't that a* ***piece of luck?*** **6** 0‑ [C] **~ (of sth)** a single item of writing, art, music, etc. that sb has produced or created: *a* ***piece of art/music/poetry, etc.*** ◇ *They performed pieces by Bach and Handel.* ◇ (*formal*) *They have some beautiful pieces* (= works of art, etc.) *in their home.* ➲ see also MASTERPIECE, MUSEUM PIECE, PARTY PIECE, PERIOD PIECE, SHOWPIECE

▸ NEWS ARTICLE **7** [C] an article in a newspaper or magazine or a broadcast on television or radio: *Did you see her piece about the Internet in the paper today?* ➲ see also SET PIECE

▸ COIN **8** [C] a coin of the value mentioned: *a 50p piece* ◇ *a five-cent piece*

▸ IN CHESS, ETC. **9** [C] one of the small figures or objects that you move around in games such as CHESS

▸ SHARE OF STH **10** [sing.] **~ of sth** (*especially NAmE*) a part or share of sth: *companies seeking a piece of the market*

▸ GUN **11** [C] (*NAmE, slang*) a gun

▸ DISTANCE **12 a piece** [sing.] (*old-fashioned, NAmE, informal*) a short distance: *She lives down the road a piece from here.* HELP You will find other compounds ending in **piece** at their place in the alphabet.

IDM **a/some ˌpiece of ˈwork** (*NAmE, informal*) used to express the fact that you admire sb or find them amusing, often when they have done sth that surprises you: *You're some piece of work, Jack, do you know that?* **fall to ˈpieces** 0‑ **1** 0‑ (usually used in the progressive tenses) (of things) to become very old and in bad condition because of long use SYN **fall apart**: *Our car is falling to pieces, we've had it so long.* **2** 0‑ (of a person, an organization, a plan, etc.) to stop working; to be destroyed: *He's worried the business will fall to pieces without him.* **give sb a piece of your ˈmind** (*informal*) to tell sb that you disapprove of their behaviour or are angry with them **go to ˈpieces** (*informal*) (of a person) to be so upset or afraid that you cannot manage to live or work normally **(all) in one ˈpiece** (*informal*) safe; not damaged or hurt, especially after a journey or dangerous experience: *They were lucky to get home in one piece.* **(all) of a ˈpiece** (*formal*) **1** all the same or similar: *The houses are all of a piece.* **2** all at the same time: *The house was built all of a piece in 1754.* **pick/pull/tear sb/sth to ˈpieces/ˈshreds** (*informal*) to criticize sb, or their work or ideas, very severely **a ˌpiece of ˈcake** (*informal*) a thing that is very easy to do **a ˌpiece of ˈpiss** (*BrE, taboo, slang*) a thing that is very easy to do ➲ more at ACTION, BIT, LONG *adj.*, NASTY, PICK *v.*, PIE, SAY *v.*, VILLAIN

■ ***verb***

PHR V **ˌpiece sth↔toˈgether 1** to understand a story, situation, etc. by taking all the facts and details about it and putting them together: *Police are trying to piece together the last hours of her life.* **2** to put all the separate parts of sth together to make a complete whole SYN **assemble**: *to piece together a jigsaw*

Vocabulary Building

Pieces

If you want to talk about a small amount or one example of something that is normally an uncountable noun, there is a range of words you can use. You must choose the right one to go with the substance you are talking about.

- **Piece** and (*BrE, informal*) **bit** are very general words and can be used with most uncountable nouns: *a piece of paper / wood / string / cake / fruit / meat / work / research / advice* ◇ *a bit of paper / work / chocolate / luck.*
- A **slice** is a thin flat piece: *a slice of bread / cake / salami / cheese / pie / apple* ◇ (*figurative*) *a slice of life*
- A **chunk** is a thick, solid piece: *a chunk of cheese / bread / rock* ◇ *a chunk of land* (= a fairly large piece)
- A **lump** is a piece of something solid without any particular shape: *a lump of coal / rock / mud*
- A **fragment** is a very small piece of something that is broken or damaged: *fragments of glass* ◇ (*figurative*) *fragments of conversation.* It can also be used with countable nouns to mean a small part of something: *a fragment of the story.*
- A **speck** is a tiny piece of powder: *a speck of dust / dirt.* You can also say: *a speck of light*
- **Drop** is used with liquids: *a drop of water / rain / blood / milk / whisky*
- A **pinch** is as much as you can hold between your finger and thumb: *a pinch of salt / cinnamon*
- A **portion** is enough for one person: *a portion of chicken*

pièce de ré·sist·ance /ˌpjes də reˈzɪstɒ̃s; *NAmE* -stɑːns/ *noun* [usually sing.] (*pl.* **pièces de ré·sist·ance** /ˌpjes də reˈzɪstɒ̃s; *NAmE* ˌreziːˈstɑːns/) (from *French*) the most important or impressive part of a group or series of things

piece·meal /ˈpiːsmiːl/ *adj.* [usually before noun] (often *disapproving*) done or happening gradually at different times and often in different ways, rather than carefully planned at the beginning: *a piecemeal approach to dealing with the problem* ◇ *piecemeal changes* ▶ **piece·meal** *adv.*: *The reforms were implemented piecemeal.*

ˌ**piece of ˈeight** *noun* (*pl.* ˌpieces of ˈeight) an old Spanish coin

ˈ**piece rate** *noun* an amount of money paid for each thing or amount of sth that a worker produces

piece·work /ˈpiːswɜːk; *NAmE* -wɜːrk/ *noun* [U] work that is paid for by the amount done and not by the hours worked ▶ **piece·work·er** *noun*

ˈ**pie chart** *noun* a diagram consisting of a circle that is divided into sections to show the size of particular amounts in relation to the whole ➲ LANGUAGE BANK at ILLUSTRATE, PROCESS ➲ WRITING TUTOR page WT16

pied /paɪd/ *adj.* (especially of birds) of two or more different colours, especially black and white

pied-à-terre /ˌpjeɪd ɑː ˈteə(r); *NAmE* ˈter/ *noun* (*pl.* pieds-à-terre /ˌpjeɪd ɑː/) (from *French*) a small flat/apartment, usually in a town, that you do not live in as your main home but keep for use when necessary

pie-dog = PYE-DOG

ˌ**Pied ˈPiper** *noun* a person who persuades a lot of other people to follow them or do sth with them ORIGIN From the old German story of the Pied Piper of Hamelin, who made first rats and later children follow him by playing beautiful music on his pipe.

ˌ**pie-ˈeyed** *adj.* (*informal*) very drunk

pier /pɪə(r); *NAmE* pɪr/ *noun* **1** a long structure built in the sea and joined to the land at one end, often with places of entertainment on it ➲ VISUAL VOCAB page V4 **2** a long low structure built in a lake, river or the sea and joined to the land at one end, used by boats to allow passengers to get on and off SYN **landing stage** **3** (*technical*) a large strong piece of wood, metal or stone that is used to support a roof, wall, bridge, etc.

pierce /pɪəs; *NAmE* pɪrs/ *verb* **1** [T, I] to make a small hole in sth, or to go through sth, with a sharp object: **~ sth** *The arrow pierced his shoulder.* ◇ *He pierced another hole in his belt with his knife.* ◇ *to* ***have your ears/nose, etc. pierced*** (= to have a small hole made in your ears/nose, etc. so that you can wear jewellery there) ◇ **~ sb** (*figurative*) *She was pierced to the heart with guilt.* ◇ **~ through sth** *The knife pierced through his coat.* **2** [T, I] **~ (through) sth** (*literary*) (of light, sound, etc.) to be suddenly seen or heard: *Sirens pierced the silence of the night.* ◇ *Shafts of sunlight pierced the heavy mist.* **3** [T, I] **~ (through) sth** to force a way through a barrier SYN **penetrate**: *They failed to pierce the Liverpool defence.*

pier·cing /ˈpɪəsɪŋ; *NAmE* ˈpɪrsɪŋ/ *adj., noun*

■ ***adj.*** **1** [usually before noun] (of eyes or the way they look at sb) seeming to notice things about another person that would not normally be noticed, especially in a way that makes that person feel anxious or embarrassed: *She looked at me with piercing blue eyes.* ◇ *a piercing look* **2** [usually before noun] (of sounds) very high, loud and unpleasant SYN **shrill**: *a piercing shriek* ◇ *She has such a* ***piercing voice.*** **3** [only before noun] (of feelings) affecting you very strongly, especially in a way that causes you pain: *piercing sadness* **4** (of the wind or cold) very strong and feeling as if it can pass through your clothes and skin **5** [only before noun] sharp and able to make a hole in sth: *The animal is covered in long piercing spines.* ▶ **pier·cing·ly** *adv.*: *His eyes were piercingly blue.* ◇ *The weather remained piercingly cold.*

■ ***noun*** **1** [U] = BODY PIERCING **2** [C] the hole that is made in your ear, nose or some other part of your body so that you can wear jewellery there: *She has a tongue piercing.*

Pier·rot /ˈpɪərəʊ; ˈpjerəʊ; *NAmE* ˈpɪəroʊ/ *noun* a male character in traditional French plays, with a sad white face and a pointed hat

pietà /pjerˈtɑː/ *noun* (*art*) a picture or SCULPTURE of the Virgin Mary holding the dead body of Christ

piety /ˈpaɪəti/ *noun* [U] the state of having or showing a deep respect for sb/sth, especially for God and religion; the state of being PIOUS OPP **impiety**

pif·fle /ˈpɪfl/ *noun* [U] (*old-fashioned, informal*) nonsense SYN **rubbish**

pif·fling /ˈpɪflɪŋ/ *adj.* (*informal, disapproving*) small and unimportant: *piffling amounts*

pig 🔑 /pɪg/ *noun, verb*

■ ***noun*** **1** 🔑 (also **hog** especially in *NAmE*) an animal with pink, black or brown skin, short legs, a broad nose and a short tail which curls round itself. Pigs are kept on farms for their meat (called PORK) or live in the wild: *a pig farmer* ◇ *Pigs were grunting and squealing in the yard.* ➲ see also BOAR, PIGLET, SOW, SWINE, GUINEA PIG **2** (*informal, disapproving*) an unpleasant or offensive person; a person who is dirty or GREEDY: *Arrogant pig!* ◇ *Don't be such a pig!* ◇ *The greedy pig's eaten all the biscuits!* ◇ *She* ***made a pig of herself*** *with the ice cream* (= ate too much). ◇ *He's a real* ***male chauvinist pig*** (= a man who does not think women are equal to men). **3** (*slang*) an offensive word for a police officer

IDM **make a ˈpig's ear (out) of sth** (*BrE, informal*) to do sth badly; to make a mess of sth **(buy) a pig in a ˈpoke** if you **buy a pig in a poke**, you buy sth without seeing it or knowing if it is good enough **a pig of a sth** (*BrE, informal*) a difficult or unpleasant thing or task: *I've had a pig of a day.* **pigs might ˈfly** (*BrE*) (*NAmE* **when pigs ˈfly**) (*ironic, saying*) used to show that you do not believe sth will ever happen: *'With a bit of luck, we'll be finished by the end of the year.' 'Yes, and pigs might fly!'*

■ ***verb*** (-gg-) (*BrE, informal*) to eat too much of sth: **~ sth** *I had a whole box of chocolates and pigged the lot!* ◇ **~ yourself (on sth)** *Don't give me cakes—I'll just pig myself.*

PHR V ˌ**pig ˈout (on sth)** (*informal*) to eat too much food: *They pigged out on pizza.*

pi·geon /ˈpɪdʒɪn/ *noun* a fat grey and white bird with short legs. Pigeons are common in cities and also live in woods and fields where people shoot them for sport or food: *the sound of pigeons cooing* ➲ compare DOVE ➲ see also CARRIER PIGEON, CLAY PIGEON, HOMING PIGEON, WOOD PIGEON

IDM **be sb's pigeon** (*old-fashioned, BrE*) to be sb's responsibility or business ➲ more at CAT

pi·geon·hole /ˈpɪdʒɪnhəʊl; *NAmE* -hoʊl/ *noun, verb*

■ ***noun*** one of a set of small boxes that are fixed on a wall and open at the front, used for putting letters, messages, etc. in; one of a similar set of boxes that are part of a desk, used for keeping papers, documents, etc. in: *If you can't come, leave a note in my pigeonhole.*

■ ***verb*** **1 ~ sb (as sth)** to decide that sb belongs to a particular group or type without thinking deeply enough about it and considering what other qualities they might have SYN **categorize, label**: *He has been pigeonholed as a children's writer.* **2 ~ sth** to decide to deal with sth later or to forget it SYN **shelve**: *Plans for a new school have been pigeonholed.*

ˌ**pigeon-ˈtoed** *adj.* having feet that point towards each other and not straight forward

pig·gery /ˈpɪgəri/ *noun* (*pl.* -ies) a place where pigs are kept or bred

piggy /ˈpɪgi/ *noun, adj.*

■ ***noun*** (*pl.* -ies) a child's word for a pig

■ ***adj.*** [only before noun] (*informal, disapproving*) (of a person's eyes) like those of a pig

pig·gy·back /ˈpɪgibæk/ *noun, verb*

■ ***noun*** a ride on sb's back, while he or she is walking: *Give me a piggyback, Daddy!* ◇ *a piggyback ride* ▶ **pig·gy·back** *adv.*: *to ride piggyback*

■ ***verb***

PHR V ˈ**piggyback on sb/sth** to use sth that already exists as a support for your own work; to use a larger organization, etc. for your own advantage

ˈ**piggy bank** *noun* a container in the shape of a pig, with a narrow opening in the top for putting coins in, used by children to save money ➲ compare MONEY BOX

P

ˌpiggy in the ˈmiddle (also **ˌpig in the ˈmiddle**) (both *BrE*) (*NAmE* **ˌmonkey in the ˈmiddle**) *noun* **1** a children's game where two people throw a ball to each other over the head of another person who tries to catch it **2** a person who is caught between two people or groups who are fighting or arguing

ˌpig-ˈheaded *adj.* unwilling to change your opinion about sth, in a way that other people think is annoying and unreasonable SYN **obstinate, stubborn** ▸ **ˌpig-ˈheaded·ness** *noun* [U]

ˌpig-ˈignorant *adj.* (*informal*) very stupid or badly educated

ˈpig iron *noun* [U] a form of iron that is not pure

pig·let /ˈpɪɡlət/ *noun* a young pig

pig·ment /ˈpɪɡmənt/ *noun* [U, C] **1** a substance that exists naturally in people, animals and plants and gives their skin, leaves, etc. a particular colour **2** a coloured powder that is mixed with a liquid to produce paint, etc.

pig·men·ta·tion /ˌpɪɡmenˈteɪʃn/ *noun* [U] the presence of pigments in skin, hair, leaves, etc. that causes them to be a particular colour

pig·ment·ed /pɪɡˈmentɪd/ *adj.* (especially of skin) having a natural colour

pigmy *noun, adj.* = PYGMY

pig·skin /ˈpɪɡskɪn/ *noun* **1** [U] leather made from the skin of a pig **2** [sing.] (*NAmE, informal*) the ball used in AMERICAN FOOTBALL

pig·sty /ˈpɪɡstaɪ/ (also **sty**) *noun* (*pl.* -ies) (*NAmE* also **ˈpig·pen** /ˈpɪɡpen/) **1** [C] a small building or a confined area where pigs are kept **2** [sing.] (*informal*) a very dirty or untidy place

pig·swill /ˈpɪɡswɪl/ *noun* [U] = SWILL

pig·tail /ˈpɪɡteɪl/ (*BrE*) (also **braid** *NAmE, BrE*) *noun* hair that is tied together into one or two bunches and twisted into a PLAIT or PLAITS, worn either at the back of the head or one on each side of the head: *She wore her hair **in pigtails**.* ➲ VISUAL VOCAB page V49 ➲ compare PONYTAIL

pike /paɪk/ *noun, verb*

■ *noun* **1** (*pl.* **pike**) a large FRESHWATER fish with very sharp teeth **2** a weapon with a sharp blade on a long wooden handle, used in the past by soldiers on foot **3** (*NAmE*) = TURNPIKE **4** (*dialect*) a pointed top of a hill in the north of England

IDM **come down the ˈpike** (*NAmE, informal*) to happen; to become noticeable: *We're hearing a lot about new inventions coming down the pike.*

■ *verb* (*AustralE, NZE, informal*)

PHR V **ˌpike ˈout** to decide not to do sth that you had agreed to do **ˈpike on sb** to fail to help or support sb as they had hoped or expected

pike·staff /ˈpaɪkstɑːf; *NAmE* -stæf/ *noun* IDM see PLAIN *adj.*

pikey /ˈpaɪki/ *noun* (*BrE, informal, offensive*) **1** a name for a GYPSY **2** a person who is poor and not educated: *He referred to them as dirty pikey scum.*

pilaf (also **pilaff**) /ˈpiːlæf; *NAmE* pɪˈlɑːf/ (also **pilau** /ˈpiːlaʊ/) *noun* [U, C] a hot spicy Eastern dish of rice and vegetables and often pieces of meat or fish

pi·las·ter /pɪˈlæstə(r)/ *noun* (*technical*) a flat column that sticks out from the wall of a building, used as decoration

Pi·la·tes /pɪˈlɑːtiːz/ *noun* [U] a system of stretching and pushing exercises using special equipment, which help make your muscles stronger and make you able to bend parts of your body more easily

pil·chard /ˈpɪltʃəd; *NAmE* -tʃərd/ *noun* a small sea fish that is used for food

pile 🔑 /paɪl/ *noun, verb*

■ *noun* ➲ see also PILES **1** 🔑 [C] a number of things that have been placed on top of each other: *a pile of books/clothes/bricks* ◇ *He arranged the documents in neat piles.* ◇ *She looked in horror at the mounting pile of letters on her desk.* **2** 🔑 [C] a mass of sth that is high in the middle and wider at the bottom than at the top SYN **heap**: *a pile of sand* ◇ *piles of dirty washing* **3** 🔑 [C, usually pl.] **~ of sth** (*informal*) a lot of sth: *I have got piles of work to do.* ◇ *He walked out leaving a pile of debts behind him.* **4** [U, sing.] the short threads, pieces of wool, etc. that form the soft surface of carpets and some types of cloth such as VELVET: *a deep-pile carpet* **5** [C] a large wooden, metal or stone post that is fixed into the ground and used to support a building, bridge, etc. **6** [C] (*formal* or *humorous*) a large impressive building

IDM **(at the) bottom/top of the ˈpile** in the least/most important position in a group of people or things **make a/your ˈpile** (*informal*) to make a lot of money

■ *verb* **1** 🔑 [T] to put things one on top of another; to form a pile: **~ sth** *She **piled** the boxes **one on top of the other**.* ◇ *The clothes were **piled high** on the chair.* ◇ **~ sth up** *Snow was piled up against the door.* **2** 🔑 [T] to put sth on/into sth; to load sth with sth: **~ A with B** *The sofa was **piled high** with cushions.* ◇ *He piled his plate with as much food as he could.* ◇ **~ B on(to) A** *He piled as much food as he could onto his plate.* ◇ **~ B in(to) A** *She piled everything into her suitcase.* ➲ see also STOCKPILE **3** [I] **+ adv./prep.** (*informal*) (of a number of people) to go somewhere quickly without order or control: *The coach finally arrived and we all piled on.*

IDM **pile on the ˈagony/ˈgloom** (*informal, especially BrE*) to make an unpleasant situation worse: *Bosses piled on the agony with threats of more job losses.*

PHR V **ˌpile ˈon** (especially of a person's weight) to increase quickly: *The weight just piled on while I was abroad.* **ˌpile sth↔ˈon 1** to make sth increase rapidly: *The team piled on the points in the first half of the game.* ◇ *I've been piling on the pounds* (= I have put on weight) *recently.* **2** to express a feeling in a much stronger way than is necessary: *Don't pile on the drama!* ◇ *Things aren't really that bad—she does tend to **pile it on**.* **3** to give sb more or too much of sth: *The German team **piled on the pressure** in the last 15 minutes.* **ˌpile sth ˈon(to) sb** to give sb a lot of sth to do, carry, etc: *He felt his boss was piling too much work on him.* **ˌpile ˈup** 🔑 to become larger in quantity or amount SYN **accumulate**: *Work always piles up at the end of the year.*

pile·driver /ˈpaɪldraɪvə(r)/ *noun* **1** (*BrE, informal*) a very heavy kick or blow **2** a machine for forcing heavy posts into the ground

piles /paɪlz/ *noun* [pl.] painful swollen VEINS at or near the ANUS SYN **haemorrhoids**

ˈpile-up *noun* a road accident involving several vehicles crashing into each other: *Three people died in a multiple pile-up in freezing fog.*

pil·fer /ˈpɪlfə(r)/ *verb* [I, T] to steal things of little value or in small quantities, especially from the place where you work: **~ (from sb/sth)** *He was caught pilfering.* ◇ **~ sth (from sb/sth)** *She regularly pilfered stamps from work.* ▸ **pil·fer·age** /ˈpɪlfərɪdʒ/ *noun* [U]: (*formal*) *pilferage of goods* **pil·fer·er** *noun*: *Certain types of goods are preferred by pilferers.* **pil·fering** *noun* [U]: *We know that pilfering goes on.*

pil·grim /ˈpɪlɡrɪm/ *noun* **1** a person who travels to a holy place for religious reasons: *Muslim pilgrims on their way to Mecca* ◇ *Christian pilgrims visiting Lourdes* **2 Pilgrim** a member of the group of English people (the **Pilgrim Fathers**) who sailed to America on the ship *The Mayflower* in 1620 and started a COLONY in Massachusetts

pil·grim·age /ˈpɪlɡrɪmɪdʒ/ *noun* [C, U] **1** a journey to a holy place for religious reasons: *to **go on/make a pilgrimage*** ➲ COLLOCATIONS at RELIGION **2** a journey to a place that is connected with sb/sth that you admire or respect: *His grave has become a **place of pilgrimage**.*

pill 🔑 /pɪl/ *noun, verb*

■ *noun* **1** 🔑 [C] a small flat round piece of medicine that you swallow without chewing it: *a vitamin pill* ➲ see also PEP PILL, SLEEPING PILL **2 the pill** or **the Pill** [sing.] a pill that some women take to prevent them becoming pregnant: *the contraceptive pill* ◇ *to be/go **on the pill*** ➲ see also MORNING-AFTER PILL **3** [C] (*NAmE*) an annoying person

IDM **sugar/sweeten the pill** to do sth that makes an unpleasant situation seem less unpleasant SYN **sugar-coat** ➲ more at BITTER *adj.*

▪ ***verb*** [I] (of a piece of clothing, especially one made of wool) to become covered in very small balls of FIBRE

pil·lage /ˈpɪlɪdʒ/ *verb* [I, T] to steal things from a place or region, especially in a war, using violence SYN **plunder**: *The rebels went looting and pillaging.* ◇ **~ sth** *The town had been pillaged and burned.* ◇ **~ sth from sth** *Works of art were pillaged from churches and museums.* ▶ **pil·lage** *noun* [U]: *They brought back horrific accounts of murder and pillage.* **pil·la·ger** *noun* ➲ compare LOOT, PLUNDER

pil·lar /ˈpɪlə(r)/ *noun* **1** a large round stone, metal or wooden post that is used to support a bridge, the roof of a building, etc, especially when it is also decorative **2** a large round stone, metal or wooden post that is built to remind people of a famous person or event SYN **column** **3 ~ of sth** a mass of sth that is shaped like a pillar: *a* ***pillar of smoke/rock*** **4 ~ of sth** a strong supporter of sth; an important member of sth: *a pillar of the Church* ◇ *a pillar of society* **5 ~ of sth** a person who has a lot of a particular quality: *She is a* ***pillar of strength*** *in a crisis.* **6** a basic part or feature of a system, organization, belief, etc: *the central pillar of this theory*

IDM **be driven, pushed, etc. from ˌpillar to ˈpost** to be forced to go from one person or situation to another without achieving anything

ˈpillar box *noun* (*old-fashioned, BrE*) a tall red metal box in the street, used for putting letters in which are being sent by post ➲ compare LETTER BOX, POSTBOX

ˌpillar-box ˈred *adj.* (*BrE*) very bright red in colour ▶ **ˌpillar-box ˈred** *noun* [U]

pil·lared /ˈpɪləd; *NAmE* -ərd/ *adj.* [only before noun] (of a building or part of a building) having PILLARS

pill·box /ˈpɪlbɒks; *NAmE* -bɑːks/ *noun* a small shelter for soldiers, often partly underground, from which a gun can be fired

pil·lion /ˈpɪliən/ *noun* a seat for a passenger behind the driver of a motorcycle: *a* ***pillion passenger/seat*** ▶ **pil·lion** *adv.*: *to ride pillion*

pil·lock /ˈpɪlək/ *noun* (*BrE, slang*) a stupid person

pil·lory /ˈpɪləri/ *verb, noun*

▪ ***verb*** (**pil·lor·ies, pil·lory·ing, pil·lor·ied, pil·lor·ied**) [often passive] **~ sb** to criticize sb strongly in public: *He was regularly pilloried by the press for his radical ideas.*

▪ ***noun*** (*pl.* -ies) a wooden frame, with holes for the head and hands, which people were locked into in the past as a punishment ➲ compare STOCKS (9)

pil·low /ˈpɪləʊ; *NAmE* -loʊ/ *noun, verb*

▪ ***noun*** **1** a square or RECTANGULAR piece of cloth filled with soft material, used to rest your head on in bed: *She lay back against the pillows.* ◇ ***pillow talk*** (= conversations in bed between lovers) ◇ *He lay back on the grass using his backpack as a pillow.* ➲ VISUAL VOCAB page V20 **2** (*NAmE*) = CUSHION

▪ ***verb*** **~ sth** (**+ adv./prep.**) (*literary*) to rest sth, especially your head, on an object: *She lay on the grass, her head pillowed on her arms.*

pil·low·case /ˈpɪləʊkeɪs; *NAmE* -loʊ-/ (also **ˈpil·low·slip** /ˈpɪləʊslɪp; *NAmE* -loʊ-/) *noun* a cloth cover for a PILLOW, that can be removed ➲ VISUAL VOCAB page V20

pilot 🔑 /ˈpaɪlət/ *noun, verb, adj.*

▪ ***noun*** **1** 🔑 a person who operates the controls of an aircraft, especially as a job: *an airline pilot* ◇ *a fighter pilot* ◇ *The accident was caused by pilot error.* ➲ see also AUTOMATIC PILOT, AUTOPILOT, CO-PILOT, TEST PILOT **2** a person with special knowledge of a difficult area of water, for example, the entrance to a HARBOUR, whose job is to guide ships through it **3** a single television programme that is made in order to find out whether people will like it and want to watch further programmes **4** = PILOT LIGHT

▪ ***verb*** **1 ~ sth** to fly an aircraft or guide a ship; to act as a pilot: *The plane was piloted by the instructor.* ◇ *The captain piloted the boat into a mooring.* **2 ~ sth** (**through sth**) to guide sb/sth somewhere, especially through a complicated place or system: *She piloted a bill on the rights of part-time workers through parliament.* **3 ~ sth** to test a new product, idea, etc. with a few people or in a small area before it is introduced everywhere

▪ ***adj.*** [only before noun] done on a small scale in order to see if sth is successful enough to do on a large scale: *a* ***pilot project/study/survey*** ◇ *a* ***pilot episode*** (= of a radio or television series)

ˈpilot light (also **pilot**) *noun* a small flame that burns all the time, for example on a gas BOILER, and lights a larger flame when the gas is turned on

ˈpilot officer *noun* (*abbr.* **PO**) an officer of the lowest rank in the British AIR FORCE

ˈpilot whale *noun* a small WHALE that lives in warm seas

Pils /pɪlz; pɪls/ (also **Pilsner** /ˈpɪlznə(r); ˈpɪls-/) *noun* [U] a type of strong light-coloured beer originally made in what is now the Czech Republic

PIM /ˌpiː aɪ ˈem; pɪm/ *abbr.* PERSONAL INFORMATION MANAGER

Pima /ˈpiːmə/ *noun* (*pl.* **Pima** or **Pimas**) *noun* a member of a Native American people, many of whom live in the US state of Arizona

pi·mento /pɪˈmentəʊ; *NAmE* -toʊ/ *noun* (*pl.* **-os**) a small red PEPPER with a mild taste

pimp /pɪmp/ *noun, verb*

▪ ***noun*** a man who controls PROSTITUTES and lives on the money that they earn

▪ ***verb*** **1** [I] **~ (for sb)** to get customers for a PROSTITUTE **2** [T] (*informal*) to add things to sth to make it look or sound better, especially by making it more individual: **~ sth** *Pimp your car with stylish custom wheels!* ◇ **~ sth up** *I would love to pimp the songs up.*

pim·per·nel /ˈpɪmpənel; *NAmE* -pərnel/ *noun* a small wild plant with red, white or blue flowers

pim·ple /ˈpɪmpl/ *noun* a small raised red spot on the skin ➲ compare SPOT ➲ see also GOOSE PIMPLES ▶ **pim·ply** /ˈpɪmpli/ *adj.*: *pimply skin* ◇ *a pimply youth*

PIN /pɪn/ (also **ˈPIN number**) *noun* the abbreviation for 'personal identification number' (a number given to you, for example by a bank, so that you can use a plastic card to take out money from a cash machine) ➲ see also CHIP AND PIN

pin 🔑 /pɪn/ *noun, verb*

▪ ***noun***

▸ FOR FASTENING/JOINING **1** 🔑 a short thin piece of stiff wire with a sharp point at one end and a round head at the other, used especially for fastening together pieces of cloth when sewing ➲ see also BOBBY PIN, DRAWING PIN, HAIRPIN, LINCHPIN, PINS AND NEEDLES, SAFETY PIN

▸ JEWELLERY **2** a short thin piece of stiff wire with a sharp point at one end and an item of decoration at the other, worn as jewellery: *a diamond pin* ➲ see also TIEPIN **3** (*especially NAmE*) = BROOCH

▸ BADGE **4** (*especially NAmE*) a type of BADGE that is fastened with a pin at the back: *He supports the group and wears its pin on his lapel.*

▸ MEDICAL **5** a piece of steel used to support a bone in your body when it has been broken

▸ ELECTRICAL **6** one of the metal parts that stick out of an electric plug and fit into a SOCKET: *a 2-pin plug* ➲ picture at PLUG

▸ IN GAMES **7** a wooden or plastic object that is shaped like a bottle and that players try to knock down in games such as BOWLING ➲ VISUAL VOCAB page V34 ➲ see also NINEPINS, TENPIN

▸ IN GOLF **8** a stick with a flag on top of it, placed in a hole so that players can see where they are aiming for

▸ LEGS **9 pins** [pl.] (*informal*) a person's legs

▸ ON SMALL BOMB **10** a small piece of metal on a HAND GRENADE that stops it from exploding and is pulled out just before the HAND GRENADE is thrown ➲ see also LINCHPIN

IDM **for two ˈpins** (*old-fashioned, BrE*) used to say that you

P

would like to do sth, even though you know that it would not be sensible: *I'd kill him for two pins.* ➲ more at HEAR

■ ***verb*** (-nn-)

▸ FASTEN/JOIN **1** ~ **sth + adv./prep.** to attach sth onto another thing or fasten things together with a pin, etc: *She pinned the badge onto her jacket.* ◇ *A message had been pinned to the noticeboard.* ◇ *Pin all the pieces of material together.* ◇ *She always wears her hair pinned back.*

▸ PREVENT MOVEMENT **2** ~ **sb/sth + adv./prep.** to make sb unable to move by holding them or pressing them against sth: *They pinned him against a wall and stole his wallet.* ◇ *He grabbed her arms and pinned them to her sides.* ◇ *They found him pinned under the wreckage of the car.*

IDM **ˌpin (all) your ˈhopes on sb/sth** | **ˌpin your ˈfaith on sb/sth** to rely on sb/sth completely for success or help: *The company is pinning its hopes on the new project.*

PHR V **ˌpin sb↔ˈdown 1** to make sb unable to move by holding them firmly: *Two men pinned him down until the police arrived.* **2** to find sb and make them answer a question or tell you sth you need to know: *I need the up-to-date sales figures but I can never pin him down at the office.* **ˌpin sb↔ˈdown (to sth/doing sth)** to make sb make a decision or say clearly what they think or what they intend to do: *It's difficult to pin her down to fixing a date for a meeting.* **ˌpin sth↔ˈdown** to explain or understand sth exactly: *The cause of the disease is difficult to pin down precisely.* **ˈpin sth on sb** to make sb be blamed for sth, especially for sth they did not do: *No one would admit responsibility. They all tried to* **pin the blame on** *someone else.* ◇ *You can't pin this one on me—I wasn't even there!*

pina co·lada /ˌpiːnə kəˈlɑːdə/ *noun* [C, U] an alcoholic drink made by mixing RUM with PINEAPPLE juice and COCONUT

pina·fore /ˈpɪnəfɔː(r)/ *noun* **1** (also **ˈpinafore dress**) (both *especially BrE*) (*NAmE* usually **jumper**) a loose dress with no sleeves, usually worn over a BLOUSE or sweater **2** (*old-fashioned*) (also *informal* **pinny**) (both *BrE*) a long loose piece of clothing without sleeves, worn by women over the front of their clothes to keep them clean, for example when cooking ➲ compare APRON **3** a loose piece of clothing like a dress without sleeves, worn by children over their clothes to keep them clean, or by young girls over a dress

P

pi·ña·ta (also **pi·na·ta**) /pɪnˈjɑːtə/ *noun* (from Spanish) (in Spanish-speaking communities in the US) a brightly decorated figure, filled with toys and sweets/candy, which children try to hit with a stick with their eyes covered in order to break it open, as a party game

pin·ball /ˈpɪnbɔːl/ *noun* [U] a game played on a **pinball machine**, in which the player sends a small metal ball up a sloping board and scores points as it BOUNCES off objects. The player tries to prevent the ball from reaching the bottom of the machine by pressing two buttons at the side.

pin·board /ˈpɪnbɔːd; *NAmE* -bɔːrd/ *noun* (*BrE*) a board made of CORK that is fixed to an indoor wall, on which you can display messages, notices, etc.

pince-nez /ˌpæ̃s ˈneɪ/ *noun* (*pl.* **pince-nez**) (from *French*) a pair of glasses, worn in the past, with a spring that fits on the nose, instead of parts at the sides that fit over the ears

pin·cer /ˈpɪnsə(r)/ *noun* **1 pincers** [pl.] a tool made of two crossed pieces of metal, used for holding things firmly and pulling things, for example nails out of wood: *a pair of pincers* **2** [C] one of a pair of curved CLAWS of some types of animal, for example CRABS and LOBSTERS ➲ VISUAL VOCAB page V11

ˈpincer movement *noun* [usually sing.] a military attack in which an army attacks the enemy from two sides at the same time

pinch /pɪntʃ/ *verb, noun*

■ ***verb***

▸ WITH THUMB AND FINGER **1** [T] ~ **sb/sth/yourself** to take a piece of sb's skin between your thumb and first finger and squeeze hard, especially to hurt the person: *My sister's always pinching me and it really hurts.* ◇ *He pinched the baby's cheek playfully.* ◇ (*figurative*) *She had to pinch herself to make sure she was not dreaming.* **2** [T] ~ **sth (+ adv./prep.)** to hold sth tightly between the thumb and finger or between two things that are pressed together: *Pinch the nostrils together between your thumb and finger to stop the bleeding.* ◇ *a pinched nerve in the neck*

▸ OF A SHOE **3** [I, T] ~ **(sb/sth)** if sth such as a shoe **pinches** part of your body, it hurts you because it is too tight: *These new shoes pinch.*

▸ STEAL **4** [T] ~ **sth (from sb/sth)** (*BrE, informal*) to steal sth, especially sth small and not very valuable SYN **nick**: *Who's pinched my pen?*

▸ COST TOO MUCH **5** [T] ~ **sb/sth** to cost a person or an organization a lot of money or more than they can spend: *Higher interest rates are already pinching the housing industry.*

▸ ARREST **6** [T] ~ **sb** (*old-fashioned, BrE, informal*) to arrest sb: *I was pinched for dangerous driving.*

IDM **pinch ˈpennies** (*informal*) to try to spend as little money as possible

PHR V **ˌpinch sth↔ˈoff/ˈout** to remove sth by pressing your fingers together and pulling

■ ***noun***

▸ WITH THUMB AND FINGER **1** an act of squeezing a part of sb's skin tightly between your thumb and finger, especially in order to hurt them: *She gave him a pinch on the arm to wake him up.*

▸ SMALL AMOUNT **2** the amount of sth that you can hold between your finger and thumb: *a pinch of salt*

IDM **at a ˈpinch** (*BrE*) (*NAmE* **in a ˈpinch**) used to say that sth could be done or used in a particular situation if it is really necessary: *We can get six people round this table at a pinch.* **take sth with a pinch of ˈsalt** to be careful about believing that sth is completely true ➲ more at FEEL *v.*

pinched /pɪntʃt/ *adj.* (of a person's face) pale and thin, especially because of illness, cold or worry

ˈpinch-hit *verb* (*NAmE*) **1** [I] (in BASEBALL) to hit the ball for another player **2** [I] ~ **(for sb)** (*informal*) to do sth for sb else who is suddenly unable to do it

ˈpinch run *verb* [I] (in BASEBALL) to take the place of a player who is on a BASE: *Gordon pinch ran for Gomez.*

pin·cush·ion /ˈpɪnkʊʃn/ *noun* a small thick PAD made of cloth, used for sticking pins in when they are not being used

pine /paɪn/ *noun, verb*

■ ***noun* 1** [C, U] (also **ˈpine tree** [C]) an EVERGREEN forest tree with leaves like needles: *pine forests* ◇ *pine needles* ◇ *a Scots pine* **2** (also **pine·wood**) [U] the pale soft wood of the pine tree, used in making furniture, etc: *a pine table*

■ ***verb*** [I] to become very sad because sb has died or gone away: *She pined for months after he'd gone.*

PHR V **ˌpine aˈway** to become very sick and weak because you miss sb/sth very much: *After his wife died, he just pined away.* **ˈpine for sb/sth** to want or miss sb/sth very much: *She was pining for the mountains of her native country.*

pin·eal /paɪˈniːəl/ (also **piˈneal gland**) *noun* (*anatomy*) a small organ in the brain that releases a HORMONE

pine·apple /ˈpaɪnæpl/ *noun* [C, U] a large tropical fruit with thick rough skin, sweet yellow flesh with a lot of juice and stiff leaves on top: *fresh pineapple* ◇ *a tin of pineapple chunks* ◇ *pineapple juice* ➲ VISUAL VOCAB page V26

IDM see ROUGH *adj.*

ˈpine cone *noun* the hard dry fruit of the PINE tree

ˈpine marten *noun* a small wild animal with a long body, short legs and sharp teeth. Pine martens live in forests and eat smaller animals.

ˈpine nut (*BrE* also **ˈpine kernel**) *noun* the white seed of some PINE trees, used in cooking

pine·wood /ˈpaɪnwʊd/ *noun* = PINE (2)

ping /pɪŋ/ *noun, verb*

■ ***noun*** a short high sound made when a hard object hits sth that is made of metal or glass

■ ***verb* 1** [I, T] ~ **(sth)** to make a short, high ringing sound; to make sth produce this sound **2** (*NAmE*) (*BrE* **pink**) [I] (of a car engine) to make knocking sounds because the fuel is not burning correctly **3** [T] ~ **sth** to test whether an Internet connection is working by sending a signal to a computer and waiting for a reply **4** [T] **~ sth (to sb)** (*informal*) to send an email or TEXT MESSAGE to sb: *I'll ping it to you later.*

ping·er /ˈpɪŋə(r)/ *noun* a device that makes a series of short high sounds, for example on a cooker/stove to tell you that the cooking time has ended

ˈping-pong (*BrE, informal*) (*NAmE* **ˈPing-Pong™**) *noun* [U] a game played like TENNIS with BATS and a small plastic ball on a table with a net across it

pin·head /ˈpɪnhed/ *noun* the very small flat surface at one end of a pin

pin·hole /ˈpɪnhəʊl; *NAmE* -hoʊl/ *noun* a very small hole, especially one made by a pin

pin·ion /ˈpɪnjən/ *verb* **~ sb/sth + adv./prep.** to hold or tie sb, especially by their arms, so that they cannot move: *His arms were pinioned to his sides.* ◇ *They were pinioned against the wall.*

pink 🔑 /pɪŋk/ *adj., noun, verb*

■ ***adj.*** **1** 🔑 pale red in colour: *pale pink roses* ◇ *She went bright pink with embarrassment.* **2** [only before noun] (*BrE*) connected with HOMOSEXUAL people: *the* ***pink pound*** (= money spent by HOMOSEXUALS as an influence in the economy) **3** (*politics*) (*informal, disapproving*) having or showing slightly LEFT-WING political views ➲ compare RED *adj.* ▶ **pink·ness** *noun* [U] IDM see TICKLE *v.*

■ ***noun*** **1** 🔑 [U, C] the colour that is produced when you mix red and white together: *She was dressed in pink.* ◇ *The bedroom was decorated in pale pinks.* **2** [C] a garden plant with pink, red or white flowers that have a sweet smell

IDM **in the ˈpink** (*old-fashioned, informal*) in good health

■ ***verb*** (*BrE*) (*NAmE* **ping**) [I] (of a car engine) to make knocking sounds because the fuel is not burning correctly

ˌpink-ˈcollar *adj.* [only before noun] (*especially NAmE*) connected with low-paid jobs done mainly by women, for example in offices and restaurants: *pink-collar workers* ➲ compare BLUE-COLLAR, WHITE-COLLAR

ˌpink ˈgin *noun* **1** [U] an alcoholic drink made from GIN mixed with ANGOSTURA that gives it a bitter flavour **2** [C] a glass of pink gin

ˈpink·ing shears *noun* [pl.] special scissors used for cutting cloth so that it will not FRAY at the edges

pink·ish /ˈpɪŋkɪʃ/ *adj.* fairly pink in colour

pinko /ˈpɪŋkəʊ; *NAmE* -koʊ/ *noun* (*pl.* **-os** or **-oes**) **1** (*NAmE, informal, disapproving*) a COMMUNIST or a SOCIALIST **2** (*BrE, informal*) a person who is slightly LEFT-WING in their ideas, but not very ➲ compare RED *n.* (3) ▶ **pinko** *adj.*

ˌpink ˈslip *noun* (*NAmE, informal*) a letter given to sb to say that they must leave their job

pinky (also **pinkie**) /ˈpɪŋki/ *noun* (*pl.* **-ies**) (*NAmE, ScotE*) the smallest finger of the hand: *a pinky ring* (= worn on the smallest finger) SYN **little finger**

ˈpin money *noun* [U] a small amount of money that you earn, especially when this is used to buy things that you want rather than things that you need

pin·na·cle /ˈpɪnəkl/ *noun* **1** [usually sing.] **~ of sth** the most important or successful part of sth: *the pinnacle of her career* **2** a small pointed stone decoration built on the roof of a building **3** a high pointed piece of rock, especially at the top of a mountain

pinny /ˈpɪni/ *noun* (*pl.* **-ies**) (*BrE, informal*) = PINAFORE

Pinoc·chio /pɪˈnəʊkiəʊ; *NAmE* -ˈnoʊkioʊ/ *noun* a character in a children's story who changes from a wooden figure into a boy. Whenever he tells a lie, his nose grows longer: *Cartoons showed the Minister as a long-nosed Pinocchio.*

pin·point /ˈpɪnpɔɪnt/ *verb, adj., noun*

■ ***verb*** **1 ~ sth** to find and show the exact position of sb/sth or the exact time that sth happened: *He was able to pinpoint on the map the site of the medieval village.* **2 ~ sth** to be able to give the exact reason for sth or to describe sth exactly: *The report pinpointed the areas most in need of help.*

■ ***adj.*** if sth is done with **pinpoint accuracy**, it is done exactly and in exactly the right position: *The pilots bombed strategic targets with pinpoint accuracy.*

■ ***noun*** a very small area of sth, especially light

pin·prick /ˈpɪnprɪk/ *noun* **1** a very small area of sth, especially light: *His eyes narrowed to two small pinpricks.* **2** a very small hole in sth, especially one that has been made by a pin **3** something that annoys you even though it is small and unimportant

ˌpins and ˈneedles *noun* [U] an uncomfortable feeling in a part of your body, caused when a normal flow of blood returns after it has been partly blocked, especially because you have been sitting or lying in an awkward position: *to have pins and needles*

IDM **be on ˌpins and ˈneedles** (*NAmE*) = BE ON TENTERHOOKS

pin·stripe /ˈpɪnstraɪp/ *noun* **1** [C] one of the white vertical lines printed on dark cloth that is used especially for making business suits **2** [U, C] dark cloth with white vertical lines printed on it; a suit made from this cloth: *a pinstripe suit* ▶ **pin·striped** *adj.* [only before noun]: *a pinstriped suit* ◇ *a pinstriped official* (= who is wearing a pinstriped suit)

pint 🔑 /paɪnt/ *noun*

1 🔑 (*abbr.* **pt**) a unit for measuring liquids and some dry goods. There are 8 pints in a gallon, equal to 0.568 of a litre in the UK and some other countries, and 0.473 of a litre in the US: *a* ***pint of beer/milk*** ◇ *We'd better get a couple of extra pints* (= of milk) *tomorrow.* ◇ *Add half a pint of cream.* **2** 🔑 (*BrE*) a pint of beer (especially in a pub): *Do you want to* ***go for a pint*** *later?*

pinta /ˈpaɪntə/ *noun* (*old-fashioned, BrE, informal*) a pint of milk

pinto /ˈpɪntəʊ; *NAmE* -toʊ/ *adj.* (*NAmE*) (of a horse) with areas on it of two colours, usually black and white SYN **piebald** ▶ **pinto** *noun* (*pl.* **-os**)

ˈpinto bean *noun* a type of curved BEAN with coloured marks on the skin

ˌpint ˈpot *noun* a beer glass, often with a handle, that holds one pint IDM see QUART

ˈpint-sized *adj.* (*informal*) (of people) very small

ˈpin-up *noun* **1** a picture of an attractive person, especially one who is not wearing many clothes, that is put on a wall for people to look at **2** a person who appears in a pin-up

pin·wheel /ˈpɪnwiːl/ *noun* (*NAmE*) **1** (*BrE* **wind·mill**) a toy with curved plastic parts that form the shape of a flower which turns round on the end of a stick when you blow on it **2** = CATHERINE WHEEL

Pin·yin /pɪnˈjɪn/ *noun* [U] the standard system of ROMAN spelling in Chinese

pi·on·eer /ˌpaɪəˈnɪə(r); *NAmE* -ˈnɪr/ *noun, verb*

■ ***noun*** **1 ~ (in/of sth)** a person who is the first to study and develop a particular area of knowledge, culture, etc. that other people then continue to develop SYN **trailblazer**: *a pioneer in the field of microsurgery* ◇ *a computer pioneer* ◇ *a pioneer aviator* ◇ *a pioneer design* (= one that introduces new ideas, methods, etc.) **2** one of the first people to go to a particular area in order to live and work there: *the pioneer spirit*

■ ***verb*** **~ sth** when sb **pioneers** sth, they are one of the first people to do, discover or use sth new: *a new technique pioneered by surgeons in a London hospital*

pi·on·eer·ing /ˌpaɪəˈnɪərɪŋ; *NAmE* -ˈnɪr-/ *adj.* [usually before noun] introducing ideas and methods that have never been used before: *pioneering work on infant mortality* ◇ *the pioneering days of radio*

pious /ˈpaɪəs/ *adj.* **1** having or showing a deep respect for God and religion SYN **devout**: *pious acts* OPP **impious** ➲ see also PIETY **2** (*disapproving*) pretending to be religious, moral or good in order to impress other people SYN **sanctimonious**: *pious sentiments* **3 ~ hope** something that you want to happen but is unlikely to be

P

achieved: *Such reforms seem likely to remain little more than pious hopes.* ▸ **pi·ous·ly** *adv.*

pip /pɪp/ *noun, verb*

■ ***noun*** **1** (*especially BrE*) (*NAmE* usually **seed**) the small hard seed that is found in some types of fruit: *an* ***apple/orange pip*** ➲ VISUAL VOCAB page V26 **2 the pips** [pl.] (*old-fashioned, BrE*) a series of short high sounds, especially those used when giving the exact time on the radio **3** (*NAmE*) one of the dots showing the value on DICE and DOMINOES; one of the marks showing the value and SUIT of a PLAYING CARD

■ ***verb*** (-pp-) **~ sb** (*BrE, informal*) to beat sb in a race, competition, etc. by only a small amount or at the last moment: *She pipped her rival for the gold medal.* ◇ *He was* ***pipped at/to the post*** *for the top award.*

pipes

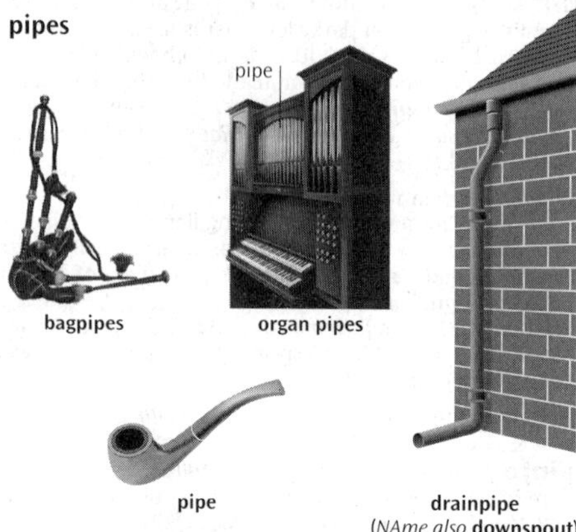

bagpipes

organ pipes

pipe

drainpipe (*NAme also* **downspout**)

pipe 🔑 /paɪp/ *noun, verb*

■ ***noun*** **1** 🔑 [C, U] a tube through which liquids and gases can flow: *hot and cold water pipes* ◇ *lead/plastic pipes* ◇ *a leaking gas pipe* ◇ *Copper pipe is sold in lengths.* ◇ *a* ***burst pipe*** ➲ COLLOCATIONS at DECORATE ➲ see also DRAINPIPE, EXHAUST, WASTE PIPE, WINDPIPE **2** 🔑 [C] a narrow tube with a bowl at one end, used for smoking TOBACCO: *to smoke a pipe* ◇ *He puffed on his pipe.* ◇ *pipe tobacco* **3** [C] a musical instrument in the shape of a tube, played by blowing ➲ see also PAN PIPES **4** [C] any of the tubes from which sound is produced in an organ **5 pipes** [pl.] = BAGPIPES

■ ***verb*** **1** [T] **~ sth (+ adv./prep.)** to send water, gas, oil, etc. through a pipe from one place to another: *to pipe oil across the desert* ◇ *Water is piped from the reservoir to the city.* **2** [T] **~ sth (+ adv./prep.)** [usually passive] to send sounds or signals through a wire or cable from one place to another: *The speech was piped over a public address system.* **3** [T, I] **~ (sb)** to play music on a pipe or the BAGPIPES, especially to welcome sb who has arrived: *Passengers were piped aboard ship at the start of the cruise.* ◇ *a prize for piping and drumming* **4** [I, T] (**+ speech**) to speak or sing in a high voice or with a high sound: *Outside a robin piped.* **5** [T] **~ sth (on sth)** to decorate food, especially a cake, with thin lines of ICING, etc. by squeezing it out of a special bag or tube: *The cake had 'Happy Birthday' piped on it.*

PHR V **ˌpipe ˈdown** (*informal*) used especially in orders, to tell sb to stop talking or to be less noisy **ˌpipe ˈup (with sth)** (*informal*) to begin to speak: *The person next to me piped up with a silly comment.* ◇ **+ speech** *'I know the answer,' piped up a voice at the back of the room.*

ˈpipe band *noun* a marching band consisting of BAGPIPES and drums

ˈpipe cleaner *noun* a short piece of wire, covered with soft material, used for cleaning inside a TOBACCO pipe

ˌpiped ˈmusic *noun* [U] (*BrE*) recorded music that is played continuously in shops, restaurants, etc.

ˈpipe dream *noun* a hope or plan that is impossible to achieve or not practical

pipe·line /ˈpaɪplaɪn/ *noun* a series of pipes that are usually underground and are used for carrying oil, gas, etc. over long distances

IDM **in the ˈpipeline** something that is **in the pipeline** is being discussed, planned or prepared and will happen or exist soon

ˈpipe organ *noun* = ORGAN

piper /ˈpaɪpə(r)/ *noun* a person who plays music on a pipe or the BAGPIPES IDM see PAY *v.*

pip·ette /pɪˈpet; *NAmE* paɪˈp-/ *noun* (*technical*) a narrow tube used in a laboratory for measuring or transferring small amounts of liquids ➲ VISUAL VOCAB page V57

pipe·work /ˈpaɪpwɜːk; *NAmE* -wɜːrk/ *noun* [U] the pipes used for carrying oil, gas or water around a machine, building, etc.

pip·ing /ˈpaɪpɪŋ/ *noun, adj.*

■ ***noun*** [U] **1** a pipe or pipes of the type or length mentioned: *ten metres of lead piping* **2** a folded strip of cloth, often with a length of string inside, used to decorate a piece of clothing, a CUSHION, etc: *a uniform with gold piping* **3** lines of cream or ICING/FROSTING as decoration on a cake **4** the sound of a pipe or pipes being played

■ ***adj.*** (of a person's voice) high

ˌpiping ˈhot *adj.* (of liquids or food) very hot

pipit /ˈpɪpɪt/ *noun* (often in compounds) a small brown bird with a pleasant song: *a meadow/rock/tree pipit*

pip·squeak /ˈpɪpskwiːk/ *noun* (*old-fashioned, informal*) a person that you think is unimportant or does not deserve respect because they are small or young

pi·quancy /ˈpiːkənsi/ *noun* [U] the quality of being piquant: *The tart flavour of the cranberries adds piquancy.* ◇ *The situation has an added piquancy since the two men are also rivals in love.*

pi·quant /ˈpiːkənt/ *adj.* **1** having a pleasantly strong or spicy taste **2** exciting and interesting

pique /piːk/ *noun, verb*

■ ***noun*** [U] (*formal*) annoyed or bitter feelings that you have, usually because your pride has been hurt: *When he realized nobody was listening to him, he left in a* ***fit of pique***.

■ ***verb*** **~ sb/sth** (*formal*) to make sb annoyed or upset SYN **wound** ▸ **piqued** *adj.* [not before noun]: *She couldn't help feeling a little piqued by his lack of interest.*

IDM **ˌpique sb's ˈinterest, curiˈosity, etc.** (*especially NAmE*) to make sb very interested in sth

piqué /ˈpiːkeɪ/ *noun* [U] a type of stiff cloth with a raised pattern

pir·acy /ˈpaɪrəsi/ *noun* [U] **1** the crime of attacking ships at sea in order to steal from them **2** the act of making illegal copies of DVDs, computer programs, books, etc, in order to sell them: *software piracy* ➲ see also PIRATE

pi·ranha /pɪˈrɑːnə/ *noun* a small S American FRESHWATER fish that attacks and eats live animals

pir·ate /ˈpaɪrət/ *noun, verb*

■ ***noun*** **1** (especially in the past) a person on a ship who attacks other ships at sea in order to steal from them: *a pirate ship* **2** (often used as an adjective) a person who makes illegal copies of DVDs, computer programs, books, etc, in order to sell them: *a pirate edition* ◇ *software pirates* **3** (often used as an adjective) a person or an organization that broadcasts illegally: *a pirate radio station* ➲ see also PIRACY ▸ **pir·at·ical** /ˌpaɪˈrætɪkl/ *adj.*

■ ***verb*** **~ sth** to copy and use or sell sb's work or a product without permission and without having the right to do so: *pirated computer games*

piri-piri /ˌpɪri ˈpɪri/ *noun* [U] a type of spicy sauce made from CHILLIES

pirou·ette /ˌpɪruˈet/ *noun* a fast turn or spin that a person, especially a BALLET dancer, makes on one foot ▸ **pirou·ette** *verb* [I]: *She pirouetted across the stage.*

pisca·tor·ial /ˌpɪskəˈtɔːriəl/ (also **pisca·tory** /ˈpɪskətəri; *NAmE* -tɔːri/) *adj.* (*formal*) relating to fishing or to FISHERMEN

Pis·ces /ˈpaɪsiːz/ *noun* **1** [U] the 12th sign of the ZODIAC, the Fishes **2** [sing.] a person born when the sun is in this sign, that is between 20 February and 20 March ▸ **Pis·cean** /ˈpaɪsiən/ *noun, adj.*

pis·cine /ˈpɪsaɪn; ˈpaɪsiːn/ *adj.* (*formal* or *technical*) of or related to fish

piss /pɪs/ *verb, noun* (*taboo, slang*)
■ *verb* [I] to URINATE HELP A more polite way of expressing this is **go to the toilet/loo** (*BrE*), **go to the bathroom** (*NAmE*) or simply **go** (*NAmE, BrE*).
IDM **ˈpiss yourself** (**laughing**) to laugh very hard
PHR V **ˌpiss aˈbout/aˈround** (*BrE*) to waste time by behaving in a silly way HELP A more polite, informal way of saying this is **mess about** (*BrE*) or **mess around** (*NAmE, BrE*). **ˌpiss sb aˈbout/aˈround** (*BrE*) to treat sb in a way that is deliberately not helpful to them or wastes their time HELP A more polite, informal way of saying this is **mess sb about/around**. **ˈpiss down** (*BrE*) to rain heavily **ˌpiss ˈoff** (*especially BrE*) (usually used in orders) to go away: *Why don't you just piss off and leave me alone?* **ˌpiss sb↔ˈoff** to make sb annoyed or bored: *Her attitude really pisses me off.*
■ *noun* **1** [U] = URINE **2** [sing.] an act of URINATING: *to go for a piss*
IDM **be on the ˈpiss** (*BrE*) to be out at a pub, club, etc. and drinking a large amount of alcohol **take the ˈpiss** (**out of sb/sth**) (*BrE*) to make fun of sb, especially by copying them or laughing at them for reasons they do not understand ➲ more at PIECE *n.*

ˈpiss artist *noun* (*BrE, taboo, slang*) **1** a person who drinks too much alcohol SYN **alcoholic 2** a person who behaves in a stupid way

pissed /pɪst/ *adj.* **1** (*BrE, taboo, slang*) drunk **2** (*NAmE, slang*) (also **ˌpissed ˈoff** *BrE, NAmE*) very angry or annoyed: *I'm pissed off with the way they've treated me.*
IDM (**as**) **pissed as a ˈnewt** (*BrE*) very drunk

ˌpiss-ˈpoor *adj.* (*taboo, slang*) **1** of a very low standard: *That band really was piss-poor.* **2** not having enough money for basic needs

piss·pot /ˈpɪspɒt; *NAmE* -pɑːt/ *noun* (*slang, offensive*) = CHAMBER POT

ˈpiss-take *noun* (*BrE, taboo, slang*) a joke that is intended to make sb/sth seem ridiculous

ˈpiss-up *noun* (*BrE, taboo, slang*) an occasion when a large amount of alcohol is drunk HELP A more polite, informal word for this is **booze-up**.

pis·ta·chio /pɪˈstæʃiəʊ; -ˈstɑːʃiəʊ; *NAmE* -ʃioʊ/ *noun* (*pl.* -os) **1** (also **piˈstachio nut**) [C] the small green nut of an Asian tree ➲ VISUAL VOCAB page V28 **2** [U] a pale green colour

piste /piːst/ *noun* a track of firm snow prepared for SKIING on ➲ see also OFF-PISTE

pis·til /ˈpɪstɪl/ *noun* (*biology*) the female organs of a flower, which receive the POLLEN and produce seeds

pis·tol /ˈpɪstl/ *noun* a small gun that you can hold and fire with one hand: *an automatic pistol* ◇ *a starting pistol* (= used to signal the start of a race) ➲ see also WATER PISTOL

ˈpistol-whip *verb* **~ sb** to hit sb with the BUTT of a pistol many times

pis·ton /ˈpɪstən/ *noun* a part of an engine that consists of a short CYLINDER that fits inside a tube and moves up and down or backwards and forwards to make other parts of the engine move

piston

pit /pɪt/ *noun, verb*
■ *noun*
▸ DEEP HOLE **1** [C] a large deep hole in the ground: *We dug a deep pit in the yard.* ◇ *The body had been dumped in a pit.* **2** [C] (especially in compounds) a deep hole in the ground from which minerals are dug out: *a chalk/gravel pit*
▸ MINE **3** [C] = COAL MINE: *pit closures* ◇ (*BrE*) *He went down the pit* (= started work as a MINER) *when he left school.*
▸ IN SKIN **4** [C] a small shallow hole in the surface of sth, especially a mark left on the surface of the skin by some disease, such as CHICKENPOX ➲ see also PITTED
▸ IN FRUIT **5** [C] (*especially NAmE*) = STONE (5): *a peach pit*
▸ IN MOTOR RACING **6 the pits** [pl.] (*BrE*) (*NAmE* **the pit** [C]) a place near the track where cars can stop for fuel, new tyres, etc. during a race ➲ see also PIT STOP
▸ IN THEATRE **7** [C] = ORCHESTRA PIT
▸ PART OF BODY **8** [C] (*NAmE, informal*) = ARMPIT
▸ IN BUSINESS **9** [C] (*NAmE*) the area of a STOCK EXCHANGE where a particular product is traded: *the corn pit* ➲ compare FLOOR (6) ➲ see also SANDPIT
IDM **be the ˈpits** (*informal*) to be very bad or the worst example of sth **the pit of your/the ˈstomach** the bottom of the stomach where people say they feel strong feelings, especially fear: *He had a sudden sinking feeling in the pit of his stomach.* ➲ more at BOTTOMLESS
■ *verb* (-tt-) [usually passive]
▸ MAKE HOLES **1 ~ sth** to make marks or holes on the surface of sth: *The surface of the moon is pitted with craters.* ◇ *Smallpox scars had pitted his face.*
▸ FRUIT **2** (*BrE* also **stone**) **~ sth** to remove the stone from the inside of a fruit: *pitted olives*
PHR V **ˈpit sb/sth against sth** to test sb or their strength, intelligence, etc. in a struggle or contest against sb/sth else: *Lawyers and accountants felt that they were being pitted against each other.* ◇ *a chance to* **pit your wits** *against the world champions* (= in a test of your intelligence)

pita, **ˈpita bread** *noun* [U] (*NAmE*) = PITTA

pit-a-pat /ˌpɪtəˈpæt/ (also **ˈpitter-patter**) *adv.* with quick light steps or beats: *Her heart went pit-a-pat.* ▸ **pit-a-pat** (also **pitter-patter**) *noun* [sing.]: *I could hear the pit-a-pat of feet in the corridor.*

ˌpit ˌbull ˈterrier (also **ˈpit bull**) *noun* a small strong aggressive dog, sometimes used in dog fights where people bet on which dog will win

pitch 🔑 /pɪtʃ/ *noun, verb*
■ *noun*
▸ FOR SPORT **1** 🔑 (*BrE*) (also **field** *NAmE, BrE*) [C] an area of ground specially prepared and marked for playing a sports game: *a* **football/cricket/rugby pitch** ◇ *The rugby tour was a disaster both on and off the pitch.*
▸ OF SOUND **2** 🔑 [sing., U] how high or low a sound is, especially a musical note: *A basic sense of rhythm and pitch is essential in a music teacher.* ➲ see also PERFECT PITCH
▸ DEGREE/STRENGTH **3** [sing., U] the degree or strength of a feeling or activity; the highest point of sth: *a frenetic pitch of activity* ◇ *Speculation has reached such a pitch that a decision will have to be made immediately.* ➲ see also FEVER PITCH
▸ TO SELL STH **4** [C, usually sing.] talk or arguments used by a person trying to sell things or persuade people to do sth: *an aggressive* **sales pitch** ◇ *the candidate's campaign pitch* ◇ *Each company was given ten minutes to* **make its pitch**.
▸ IN BASEBALL **5** [C] an act of throwing the ball; the way in which it is thrown ➲ SYNONYMS at THROW
▸ BLACK SUBSTANCE **6** [U] a black sticky substance made from oil or coal, used on roofs or the wooden boards of a ship to stop water from coming through
▸ IN STREET/MARKET **7** [C] (*BrE*) a place in a street or market where sb sells things, or where a street entertainer usually performs
▸ OF SHIP/AIRCRAFT **8** [U] (*technical*) the movement of a ship up and down in the water or of an aircraft in the air ➲ compare ROLL *n.* (5)
▸ OF ROOF **9** [sing., U] (*technical*) the degree to which a roof slopes
IDM **make a ˈpitch for sb/sth** | **make a ˈpitch to sb** to make a determined effort to get sth or to persuade sb of sth ➲ more at QUEER *v.*
■ *verb*
▸ THROW **1** [T] **~ sb/sth + adv./prep.** to throw sb/sth with force: *The explosion pitched her violently into the air.* ◇ (*fig-*

P

urative) The new government has already been pitched into a crisis.
▸ IN SPORTS **2** [I, T] **~ (sth)** (in BASEBALL) to throw the ball to the person who is BATTING ➲ VISUAL VOCAB page V36 **3** [I, T] **~ (sth) + adv./prep.** (of the ball in the games of CRICKET or GOLF) to hit the ground; to make the ball hit the ground: *The ball pitched a yard short.* **4** [T, I] **~ (sth)** (in GOLF) to hit the ball in a high curve
▸ FALL **5** [I] **+ adv./prep.** to fall heavily in a particular direction: *With a cry she pitched forward.*
▸ OF SHIP/AIRCRAFT **6** [I] to move up and down on the water or in the air: *The sea was rough and the ship pitched and rolled all night.*
▸ SET LEVEL **7** [T] to set sth at a particular level: **~ sth (+ adv./prep./adj.)** *They have pitched their prices too high.* ◇ **~ sth (at sth)** *The test was pitched at too low a level for the students.*
▸ TRY TO SELL **8** [T] to aim or direct a product or service at a particular group of people: **~ sth (at sb)** *The new software is being pitched at banks.* ◇ **~ sth (as sth)** *Orange juice is to be pitched as an athlete's drink.* **9** [T, I] to try to persuade sb to buy sth, to give you sth or to make a business deal with you: **~ sth** *Representatives went to Japan to pitch the company's newest products.* ◇ **~ (for sth)** *We were pitching against a much larger company for the contract.*
▸ SOUND/MUSIC **10** [T] **~ sth + adj.** to produce a sound or piece of music at a particular level: *You pitched that note a little flat.* ◇ *The song was pitched too low for my voice.* ➲ see also HIGH-PITCHED, LOW-PITCHED
▸ TENT **11** [T] **~ sth** to set up a tent or a camp for a short time: *We could* ***pitch our tent*** *in that field.* ◇ *They* ***pitched camp*** *for the night near the river.* ➲ see also PITCHED
IDM ˌ**pitch a 'story/'line/'yarn (to sb)** (*informal*) to tell sb a story or make an excuse that is not true
PHR V ˌ**pitch 'in (with sb/sth)** (*informal*) to join in and help with an activity, by doing some of the work or by giving money, advice, etc: *Everyone pitched in with the work.* ◇ *Local companies pitched in with building materials and labour.* ˌ**pitch sth↔'in** to give a particular amount of money in order to help with sth: *We all pitched in $10 to buy her a gift.* ˌ**pitch 'into sb** (*informal*) to attack or criticize sb: *She started pitching into me as soon as I arrived.* ˌ**pitch 'into sth** (*informal*) to start an activity with enthusiasm: **~ doing sth** *I rolled up my sleeves and pitched into cleaning the kitchen.* ˌ**pitch 'up** (*BrE, informal*) to arrive somewhere, especially late or without planning **SYN turn up**: *You can't just pitch up and expect to get in without a ticket.*

ˌ**pitch and 'putt** *noun* [U] (*BrE*) GOLF played on a very small course

ˌ**pitch-'black** *adj.* completely black or dark

ˌ**pitch-'dark** *adj.* completely dark

pitched /pɪtʃt/ *adj.* (of a roof) sloping; not flat

ˌ**pitched 'battle** *noun* **1** a fight that involves a large number of people: *The demonstration escalated into a pitched battle with the police.* **2** a military battle fought with soldiers arranged in prepared positions

pitch·er /ˈpɪtʃə(r)/ *noun* **1** (*NAmE*) (*BrE* **jug**) a container with a handle and a LIP, for holding and pouring liquids: *a pitcher of water* **2** (*BrE*) a large CLAY container with a small opening and one or two handles, used, especially in the past, for holding liquids ➲ picture at JUG **3** (in BASEBALL) the player who throws the ball to the BATTER ➲ VISUAL VOCAB page V36

pitch·fork /ˈpɪtʃfɔːk; *NAmE* -fɔːrk/ *noun* a farm tool in the shape of a large fork with a long handle and two or three sharp metal points, used especially for lifting and moving HAY (= dried grass), etc.

ˈ**pitch invasion** *noun* (*BrE*) an occasion when a crowd of people who are watching a sports game run onto the field, for example to celebrate sth or protest about sth

pitch·out /ˈpɪtʃaʊt/ *noun* **1** (in BASEBALL) a BALL deliberately thrown so that it is too far away to hit so that the CATCHER can throw it to get a player out who is running between BASES **2** (in AMERICAN FOOTBALL) a ball thrown sideways

pit·eous /ˈpɪtiəs/ *adj.* [usually before noun] (*literary*) deserving pity or causing you to feel pity: *a piteous cry/sight* ▸ **pit·eous·ly** *adv.* **SYN pathetic**

pit·fall /ˈpɪtfɔːl/ *noun* a danger or difficulty, especially one that is hidden or not obvious at first: *the potential pitfalls of buying a house*

pith /pɪθ/ *noun* [U] **1** a soft dry white substance inside the skin of oranges and some other fruits ➲ VISUAL VOCAB page V26 **2** the essential or most important part of sth: *the pith of her argument*

pit·head /ˈpɪthed/ *noun* the entrance to a coal mine and the offices, machinery, etc. in the area around it

ˈ**pith helmet** *noun* a light hard hat worn to give protection from the sun in very hot countries

pithy /ˈpɪθi/ *adj.* (*approving*) (**pith·ier**, **pithi·est**) (of a comment, piece of writing, etc.) short but expressed well and full of meaning ▸ **pith·ily** /-ɪli/ *adv.*: *pithily expressed*

piti·able /ˈpɪtiəbl/ *adj.* (*formal*) **1** deserving pity or causing you to feel pity: *The refugees were in a pitiable state.* **2** not deserving respect: *a pitiable lack of talent* ▸ **piti·ably** /-əbli/ *adv.*

piti·ful /ˈpɪtɪfl/ *adj.* **1** deserving pity or causing you to feel pity **SYN pathetic**: *The horse was a* ***pitiful sight*** (= because it was very thin or sick). **2** not deserving respect **SYN poor**: *a pitiful effort/excuse/performance* ▸ **piti·fully** /-fəli/ *adv.*: *The dog was whining pitifully.* ◇ *She was pitifully thin.* ◇ *The fee is pitifully low.*

piti·less /ˈpɪtiləs/ *adj.* **1** showing no pity; cruel **SYN callous**: *a pitiless killer/tyrant* **2** very cruel or severe, and never ending **SYN relentless**: *a scorching, pitiless sun* ▸ **piti·less·ly** *adv.*

piton /ˈpiːtɒn; *NAmE* -tɑːn/ *noun* a short pointed piece of metal used in rock-climbing. The piton is fixed into the rock and has a rope attached to it through a ring at the other end.

ˈ**pit pony** *noun* a small horse that was used in the past for moving coal in a mine

ˈ**pit prop** *noun* a large piece of wood used to support the roof of part of a coal mine from which coal has been removed

ˈ**pit stop** *noun* **1** (in motor racing) an occasion when a car stops during a race for more fuel, etc. **2** (*NAmE, informal*) a short stop during a long trip for a rest, a meal, etc.

pitta (*BrE*) (*NAmE* **pita**) /ˈpiːtə; *BrE* also ˈpɪtə/ (also ˈ**pitta bread**, ˈ**pita bread**) *noun* [U, C] a type of flat bread in the shape of an OVAL that can be split open and filled

pit·tance /ˈpɪtns/ *noun* [usually sing.] a very small amount of money that sb receives, for example as a wage, and that is hardly enough to live on: *to pay sb a pittance* ◇ *to work for a pittance*

pit·ted /ˈpɪtɪd/ *adj.* **1** having small marks or holes in the surface **2** (of fruit) having had the large hard seed (= the PIT) removed: *pitted olives*

pitter-patter /ˈpɪtə pætə(r)/ *adv., noun* = PIT-A-PAT

pi·tu·it·ary /pɪˈtjuːɪtəri; *NAmE* -ˈtuːəteri/ (also **piˈtuitary gland**) *noun* a small organ at the base of the brain that produces HORMONES that influence growth and sexual development

pity 🔑 /ˈpɪti/ *noun, verb*

■ ***noun* 1** 🔑 [U] **~ (for sb/sth)** a feeling of sympathy and sadness caused by the suffering and troubles of others: *I could only feel pity for what they were enduring.* ◇ *a* ***look/feeling/surge of pity*** ◇ *I* ***took pity on*** *her and lent her the money.* ◇ (*formal*) *I beg you to* ***have pity on*** *him.* ◇ *I don't want your pity.* **2** 🔑 [sing.] used to show that you are disappointed about sth **SYN shame**: **a ~ (that...)** ***It's a pity*** *that you can't stay longer.* ◇ *'I've lost it!' 'Oh,* ***what a pity.****'* ◇ *What a pity that she didn't tell me earlier.* ◇ **a ~ (to do sth)** *It* ***seems a pity*** *to waste this food.* ◇ *This dress is really nice. Pity it's so*

WORD FAMILY
pity *noun, verb*
pitiful *adj.*
pitiless *adj.*
pitiable *adj.*
piteous *adj.*

P

expensive. ◇ Oh, **that's a pity.** ◇ It would be **a great pity** if you gave up now.

IDM **more's the 'pity** (*BrE, informal*) unfortunately: *'Was the bicycle insured?' 'No, more's the pity!'*

■ **verb** (**pit·ies, pity·ing, pit·ied, pit·ied**) (not used in the progressive tenses) to feel sorry for sb because of their situation; to feel pity for sb: **~ sb** *He pitied people who were stuck in dead-end jobs.* ◇ *Compulsive gamblers are more* **to be pitied** *than condemned.* ◇ **~ sb doing sth** *I pity her having to work such long hours.*

pity·ing /'pɪtiɪŋ/ *adj.* [usually before noun] showing pity for sb, often in a way that shows that you think you are better than them: *a* **pitying look/smile** ▸ **pity·ing·ly** *adv.*

pivot /'pɪvət/ *noun, verb*

■ **noun 1** the central point, pin or column on which sth turns or balances **2** the central or most important person or thing: *West Africa was the pivot of the cocoa trade.* ◇ *The pivot on which the old system turned had disappeared.*

■ **verb** [I, T] **~ (sth)** (**+ adv./prep.**) to turn or balance on a central point (= a pivot); to make sth do this: *Windows that pivot from a central point are easy to clean.* ◇ *She pivoted around and walked out.*

PHR V **'pivot on/around sth** (of an argument, a theory, etc.) to depend completely on sth SYN **hinge on**

piv·otal /'pɪvətl/ *adj.* of great importance because other things depend on it: *a pivotal role in European affairs*

pixel /'pɪksl/ *noun* (*computing*) any of the small individual areas on a computer screen, which together form the whole display

pix·el·ate (also **pix·el·late**) /'pɪksəleɪt/ *verb* **1 ~ sth** to divide an image into PIXELS **2 ~ sth** to show an image on television as a small number of large PIXELS, especially in order to hide sb's identity

pixie /'pɪksi/ *noun* (in stories) a creature like a small person with pointed ears, who has magic powers

pizza /'piːtsə/ *noun* [C, U] an Italian dish consisting of a flat round bread base with cheese, tomatoes, vegetables, meat, etc. on top: *a ham and mushroom pizza* ◇ *Is there any pizza left?*

pizz·azz /pɪ'zæz/ *noun* [U] (*informal*) a lively and exciting quality or style SYN **flair**: *We need someone with youth, glamour and pizzazz.*

piz·zeria /ˌpiːtsə'riːə/ (*NAmE* also **'pizza parlor**) *noun* a restaurant that serves mainly pizzas

pizzi·cato /ˌpɪtsɪ'kɑːtəʊ; *NAmE* -toʊ/ *adj., adv.* (*music*) played using the fingers instead of a BOW to pull at the strings of a musical instrument such as a VIOLIN

Pl. *abbr.* (used in written addresses) PLACE: *Grosvenor Pl.*

pl. *abbr.* (in writing) plural

plac·ard /'plækɑːd; *NAmE* -kɑːrd/ *noun* a large written or printed notice that is put in a public place or carried on a stick in a march: *They were carrying placards and banners demanding that he resign.*

pla·cate /plə'keɪt; *NAmE* 'pleɪkeɪt/ *verb* **~ sb** to make sb feel less angry about sth SYN **pacify**: *a placating smile* ◇ *The concessions did little to placate the students.*

pla·ca·tory /plə'keɪtəri; *NAmE* 'pleɪkətɔːri/ *adj.* (*formal*) designed to make sb feel less angry by showing that you are willing to satisfy or please them: *a* **placatory remark/smile/gesture**

place 0-w /pleɪs/ *noun, verb*

■ **noun**

▸ POSITION/POINT/AREA **1** 0-w [C] a particular position, point or area: *Is this the place where it happened?* ◇ *This would be a good place for a picnic.* ◇ *I can't be in two places at once.*

▸ CITY/TOWN/BUILDING **2** 0-w [C] a particular city, town, building, etc: *I can't remember all the places we visited in Thailand.* ◇ *I used to live in York and I'm still fond of the place.* ◇ *The police searched the place.* ◇ *We were looking for a* **place to eat.** ◇ *Let's get out of this place!* **3** 0-w [C] (especially in compounds or phrases) a building or an area of land used for a particular purpose: *a* **meeting place** ◇ *The town has many excellent* **eating places.** ◇ (*formal*) *churches and other* **places of worship** ◇ *He can usually be contacted at his* **place of work.** ➲ see also RESTING PLACE

Synonyms

place

site • **area** • **position** • **point** • **location** • **scene** • **spot** • **venue**

These are all words for a particular area or part of an area, especially one used for a particular purpose or where sb/sth is situated or happens.

place a particular point, area, city, town, building, etc, especially one used for a particular purpose or where a particular thing happens: *This would be a good place for a picnic.*

site the place where sth, especially a building, is or will be situated; a place where sth happened or that is used for a particular purpose: *They've chosen a site for the new school.*

area a part of a room, building or particular space that is used for a special purpose; a particular place on an object: *the hotel reception area* ◇ *Move the cursor to a blank area on the screen.*

position the place where a person or thing is situated; the place where sb/sth is meant to be: *From his position at the top of the hill, he could see the harbour.* NOTE The **position** of sb/sth is often temporary: the place where sb/sth is at a particular time.

point a particular place within an area, where sth happens or is supposed to happen: *the point at which the river divides*

location a place where sth happens or exists, especially a place that is not named or not known: *The company is moving to a new location.*

scene a place where sth happens, especially sth unpleasant: *the scene of the accident*

spot a particular point or area, especially one that has a particular character or where sth particular happens: *The lake is one of the local* **beauty spots**.

venue the place where people meet for an organized event such as a performance or sports event.

PATTERNS

- **at** a place/site/position/point/location/scene/spot/venue
- **in** a(n) place/area/position/location/venue
- the place/site/point/location/spot/venue **where...**
- the **right** place/site/position/location/spot/venue
- a **central** site/position/location/venue
- the/sb's/sth's **exact/precise** place/site/position/point/location/spot

▸ AREA ON SURFACE **4** 0-w [C] a particular area on a surface, especially on a person's body: *He broke his arm in three places.* ◇ *The paint was peeling off the wall* **in places**.

▸ IN BOOK/SPEECH, ETC. **5** 0-w [C] a point in a book, speech, piece of music, etc, especially one that sb has reached at a particular time: *She had marked her place with a bookmark.* ◇ *Excuse me, I seem to have* **lost my place.**

▸ SEAT **6** 0-w [C] a position, seat, etc, especially one that is available for or being used by a person or vehicle: *Come and sit here—I've* **saved you a place.** ◇ *I don't want to* **lose my place** *in the line.* ◇ *Would you like to* **change places** *with me so you can see better?* ◇ *I've* **set a place** *for you at the table.*

▸ ROLE/IMPORTANCE **7** [sing.] **~ (in sth)** the role or importance of sb/sth in a particular situation, usually in relation to others: *He is assured of his place in history.* ◇ *Accurate reporting* **takes second place** *to lurid detail.* ◇ *My father believed that people should* **know their place** (= behave according to their social position). ◇ *It's* **not your place** (= your role) *to give advice.* ◇ *Anecdotes* **have no place in** (= are not acceptable in) *an academic essay.*

▸ AT UNIVERSITY/SCHOOL **8** 0-w [C] an opportunity to take part

P

in sth, especially to study at a school or university or on a course: *She's been offered a place at Bath to study Business.* ◇ *There are very few places left on the course.*

▸ IN SPORTS TEAM **9** [C] the position of being a member of a sports team: *She has* ***won a place*** *in the Olympic team.* ◇ *He* ***lost his place*** *in the first team.*

▸ CORRECT POSITION **10** 🔑 [C] the natural or correct position for sth: *Is there a place on the form to put your address?* ◇ *Put it back in its place when you've finished with it.*

▸ SAFE AREA **11** [C] (usually with a negative) a suitable or safe area for sb to be: *These streets are* ***no place for*** *a child to be out alone at night.*

▸ HOME **12** 🔑 [sing.] (*informal*) a house or flat/apartment; a person's home: *What about dinner at* ***my place****?* ◇ *I'm fed up with living with my parents, so I'm looking for* ***a place of my own***.

▸ IN RACE/COMPETITION **13** 🔑 [C, usually sing.] a position among the winners of a race or competition: *He finished in third place.*

▸ MATHEMATICS **14** [C] the position of a figure after a DECIMAL POINT: *The number is correct to three decimal places.*

▸ STREET/SQUARE **15 Place** [sing.] (*abbr.* **Pl.**) used as part of a name for a short street or square: *66 Portland Place*

IDM **all ˈover the place** (*BrE* also **all ˈover the shop**) (*US* also **all ˈover the lot**) (*informal*) **1** everywhere: *New restaurants are appearing all over the place.* **2** not neat or tidy; not well organized: *Your calculations are all over the place* (= completely wrong). **change/swap ˈplaces (with sb)** (usually used in negative sentences) to be in sb else's situation: *I'm perfectly happy—I wouldn't change places with anyone.* **fall/slot into ˈplace** if sth complicated or difficult to understand **falls** or **slots into place**, it becomes organized or clear in your mind **give ˈplace to sb/sth** (*formal*) to be replaced by sb/sth SYN **give way to**: *Houses and factories gave place to open fields as the train gathered speed.* **be ˈgoing places** (*informal*) to be getting more and more successful in your life or career: *a young architect who's really going places* **if ˌI was/were in ˈyour place** used to introduce a piece of advice you are giving to sb: *If I were in your place, I'd resign immediately.* **in the ˈfirst place** used at the end of a sentence to talk about why sth was done or whether it should have been done or not: *I still don't understand why you chose that name in the first place.* ◇ *I should never have taken that job in the first place.* **in the ˈfirst, ˈsecond, etc. place** used at the beginning of a sentence to introduce the different points you are making in an argument: *Well, in the first place he has all the right qualifications.* **in ˈmy, ˈyour, etc. place** in my, your, etc. situation: *I wouldn't like to be in your place.* **in ˈplace 1** 🔑 (also **into ˈplace**) in the correct position; ready for sth: *Carefully lay each slab in place.* ◇ *The receiver had already clicked into place.* **2** 🔑 working or ready to work: *All the arrangements are now in place for their visit.* **3** (*NAmE*) = ON THE SPOT **in place of sb/sth | in sb's/sth's ˈplace** 🔑 instead of sb/sth: *You can use milk in place of cream in this recipe.* ◇ *He was unable to come to the ceremony, but he sent his son to accept the award in his place.* **out of ˈplace 1** 🔑 not in the correct place: *Some of these files seem to be out of place.* **2** 🔑 not suitable for a particular situation: *Her remarks were out of place.* ◇ *I felt completely out of place among all these successful people.* **a place in the ˈsun** a position in which you are comfortable or have an advantage over other people **put yourself in sb else's/sb's ˈplace** to imagine that you are in sb else's situation: *Of course I was upset—just put yourself in my place.* **put sb in their ˈplace** to make sb feel stupid or embarrassed for showing too much confidence: *At first she tried to take charge of the meeting but I soon put her in her place.* **take ˈplace** 🔑 to happen, especially after previously being arranged or planned: *The film festival takes place in October.* ◇ *We may never discover what took place that night.* **take sb's/sth's ˈplace | take the place of sb/sth** 🔑 to replace sb/sth: *She couldn't attend the meeting so her assistant took her place.* ◇ *Computers have taken the place of typewriters in most offices.* **take your ˈplace 1** to go to the physical position that is necessary for an activity: *Take your places for dinner.* **2** to take or accept the status in society that is correct or that you deserve ➲ more at HAIR, HEART, LIGHTNING *n.*, OWN *v.*, PRIDE *n.*, ROCK *n.*

■ ***verb***

▸ IN POSITION **1** 🔑 [T] **~ sth + adv./prep.** to put sth in a particular place, especially when you do it carefully or deliberately: *He placed his hand on her shoulder.* ◇ *A bomb had been placed under the seat.* ◇ *The parking areas in the town are few, but strategically placed.*

▸ IN SITUATION **2** [T] **~ sb/yourself + adv./prep.** (more formal than *put*) to put sb/yourself in a particular situation: *to place sb in command* ◇ *She was placed in the care of an uncle.* ◇ *His resignation placed us in a difficult position.* ◇ *The job places great demands on me.*

▸ ATTITUDE **3** 🔑 [T] **~ sth on sth/doing sth** used to express the attitude sb has towards sb/sth: *Great emphasis is placed on education.* ◇ *They place a high value on punctuality.*

▸ RECOGNIZE **4** [T] **~ sb/sth** (usually used in negative sentences) to recognize sb/sth and be able to identify them/it: *I've seen her before but I just can't place her.* ◇ *His accent was impossible to place.*

▸ BET/ORDER/ADVERTISEMENT **5** 🔑 [T] **~ sth** to give instructions about sth or make a request for sth to happen: *to place a bet/an order* ◇ *We placed an advertisement for a cleaner in the local paper.*

▸ FIND HOME/JOB **6** [T] to find a suitable home, job, etc. for sb: **~ sb (with sb/sth)** *The children were placed with foster parents.* ◇ **~ sb (in sth)** *The agency placed about 2 000 secretaries last year.*

▸ GIVE RANK **7** [T] **~ sb/sth + adv./prep.** to decide that sb/sth has a particular position or rank compared with other people or things: *I would place her among the top five tennis players in the world.* ◇ *Nursing attracts people who place relationships high on their list of priorities.*

▸ IN RACE **8** [T, I] used to describe a person, a team, a horse, etc. finishing in a particular position in a race: **~ sb/sth + adj.** *He was placed fifth in last Saturday's race.* ◇ **~ (sth)** (*BrE*) *My horse has been placed several times* (= it was among the first three or four to finish the race). ◇ (*NAmE*) *His horse placed in the last race* (= it was among the first three to finish the race, usually in second place).

IDM **be well, ideally, uniquely, better, etc. placed for sth/to do sth 1** to be in a good, very good, etc. position or have a good, etc. opportunity to do sth: *Engineering graduates are well placed for a wide range of jobs.* ◇ *The company is ideally placed to take advantage of the new legislation.* **2** to be located in a pleasant or convenient place: *The hotel is well placed for restaurants, bars and clubs.* ➲ more at PEDESTAL, PREMIUM *n.*, RECORD *n.*

pla·cebo /pləˈsiːbəʊ; *NAmE* -boʊ/ *noun* (*pl.* **-os**) a substance that has no physical effects, given to patients who do not need medicine but think that they do, or used when testing new drugs: *the* ***placebo effect*** (= the effect of taking a placebo and feeling better)

ˈplace card *noun* a small card with a person's name on it, placed on a table to show where they are to sit

place·hold·er /ˈpleɪshəʊldə(r); *NAmE* -hoʊld-/ *noun* **1** (*technical*) a symbol or piece of text which replaces sth that is missing **2** (*linguistics*) an item which is necessary in a sentence, but does not have real meaning, for example the word 'it' in 'It's a pity she left.'

ˈplace kick *noun* (in RUGBY and AMERICAN FOOTBALL) a kick made by putting the ball on the ground first

place·man /ˈpleɪsmən/ *noun* (*pl.* **-men** /-mən/) (*BrE, disapproving*) a person who is given an official position as a reward for supporting a politician or government

ˈplace mat *noun* a MAT on a table on which a person's plate is put ➲ VISUAL VOCAB page V19

place·ment /ˈpleɪsmənt/ *noun* **1** [U] the act of finding sb a suitable job or place to live: *a job placement service* ◇ *placement with a foster family* **2** (also **ˈwork placement**) [U, C] (*BrE*) a job, often as part of a course of study, where you get some experience of a particular kind of work: *The third year is spent* ***on placement*** *in selected companies.* ◇ *The course includes a placement in Year 3.* ➲ compare INTERNSHIP, WORK EXPERIENCE **3** [U] the act of placing sth somewhere: *This procedure ensures correct placement*

P

of the catheter. ➲ see also ADVANCED PLACEMENT, PRODUCT PLACEMENT

ˈ**placement test** *noun* a test which is designed to find the appropriate level for students in a course or programme of study

ˈ**place name** *noun* a name of a town or other place

pla·centa /pləˈsentə/ (usually **the placenta**) *noun* (*anatomy*) the material that comes out of a woman or female animal's body after a baby has been born, and which was necessary to feed and protect the baby SYN **afterbirth**

pla·cen·tal /pləˈsentl/ *adj.* [usually before noun] **1** (*medical*) of or related to the PLACENTA **2** (*biology*) having a PLACENTA: *placental mammals*

ˈ**place setting** *noun* a set or an arrangement of knives, forks and spoons, and/or plates and dishes for one person

pla·cid /ˈplæsɪd/ *adj.* **1** (of a person or an animal) not easily excited or irritated: *a placid baby/horse* OPP **high-spirited** **2** calm and peaceful, with very little movement SYN **tranquil**: *the placid waters of the lake* ▸ **pla·cid·ity** /pləˈsɪdəti/ *noun* [U] **pla·cid·ly** *adv.*

pla·cing /ˈpleɪsɪŋ/ *noun* the position of sb/sth in a race or a competition or in a list arranged in order of success: *He needs a high placing in today's qualifier to reach the final.*

pla·giar·ism /ˈpleɪdʒərɪzəm/ *noun* [U, C] (*disapproving*) an act of plagiarizing sth; sth that has been plagiarized: *There were accusations of plagiarism.* ◇ *a text full of plagiarisms* ➲ WRITING TUTOR page WT11 ▸ **pla·giar·ist** /ˈpleɪdʒərɪst/ *noun*

pla·giar·ize (*BrE* also **-ise**) /ˈpleɪdʒəraɪz/ *verb* [T, I] **~ (sth)** (*disapproving*) to copy another person's ideas, words or work and pretend that they are your own: *He was accused of plagiarizing his colleague's results.*

plague /pleɪɡ/ *noun, verb*

■ ***noun*** **1** (also **the plague**) [U] = BUBONIC PLAGUE: *an outbreak of plague* **2** [C] any infectious disease that kills a lot of people SYN **epidemic**: *the plague of AIDS* **3** [C] **~ of sth** large numbers of an animal or insect that come into an area and cause great damage: *a **plague of locusts/rats, etc.*** IDM see AVOID

■ ***verb*** **1 ~ sb/sth (with sth)** to cause pain or trouble to sb/sth over a period of time SYN **trouble**: *to **be plagued by** doubt* ◇ *Financial problems are plaguing the company.* ◇ *The team has been plagued by injury this season.* **2 ~ sb (with sth)** to annoy sb or create problems, especially by asking for sth, demanding attention, etc. SYN **hound**: *Rock stars have to get used to being plagued by autograph hunters.*

plaice /pleɪs/ *noun* [C, U] (*pl.* **plaice**) a flat sea fish that is used for food

plaid /plæd/ *noun* **1** [U] a type of thick cloth with a pattern of lines and squares of different colours and widths, especially a TARTAN pattern ➲ VISUAL VOCAB page V50 **2** [C] a long piece of plaid made of wool, worn over the shoulders as part of the Scottish national dress

Plaid Cymru /ˌplaɪd ˈkʌmriː/ *noun* [U+sing./pl. v.] (*WelshE*) a Welsh political party that wants Wales to be an independent state

plain 0━ /pleɪn/ *adj., noun, adv.*

■ ***adj.*** (**plain·er**, **plain·est**) **1** 0━ easy to see or understand SYN **clear**: *He **made it plain that** we should leave.* ◇ *She made her annoyance plain.* ◇ *The facts were **plain to see**.* ◇ *It was a rip-off, **plain and simple**.* ➲ SYNONYMS at CLEAR **2** 0━ not trying to trick anyone; honest and direct: ***The plain fact is** that nobody really knows.* ◇ *a politician with a reputation for **plain speaking*** **3** 0━ not decorated or complicated; simple: *a plain but elegant dress* ◇ *plain food* ◇ *The interior of the church was plain and simple.* ◇ *plain yogurt* (= without sugar or fruit) ➲ compare FANCY **4** 0━ without marks or a pattern on it: *covers in plain or printed cotton* ◇ *Write on plain paper* (= without lines). **5** [only before noun] used to emphasize that sth is very ordinary, not special in any way SYN **everyday**: *You don't need any special skills for this job, just plain common sense.* **6** (especially of a woman) not beautiful or attractive **7** describing a simple STITCH used in knitting ▸ **plain·ness** *noun* [U]

IDM **be plain ˈsailing** (*US* also **be clear ˈsailing**) to be simple and free from trouble **in plain ˈEnglish** simply and clearly expressed, without using technical language (**as**) **plain as a ˈpikestaff** | (**as**) **plain as ˈday** | (**as**) **plain as the nose on your ˈface** very obvious

■ ***noun*** (also **plains** [pl.]) a large area of flat land: *the flat coastal plain of Thassos* ◇ *the Great Plains* ➲ see also FLOODPLAIN

■ ***adv.*** (*informal*) used to emphasize how bad, stupid, etc. sth is: *plain stupid/wrong*

Synonyms

plain

simple • stark • bare • unequivocal

These words all describe statements, often about sth unpleasant, that are very clear, not trying to hide anything, and not using more words than necessary.

plain used for talking about a fact that other people may not like to hear; honest and direct in way that other people may not like: *The plain fact is that nobody really knows.*

simple [only before noun] used for talking about a fact that other people may not like to hear; very obvious and not complicated by anything else: *The simple truth is that we just can't afford it.*

PLAIN OR SIMPLE?

When it is being used to emphasize facts that other people may not like to hear, **plain** is usually used in the expression *the plain fact/truth is that...* **Simple** can be used in this way too, but it can also be used in a wider variety of structures and collocations (such as *reason* and *matter*): *The problem was due to the simple fact that...* ◇ ~~*The problem was due to the plain fact that...*~~ ◇ ~~*for the plain reason that...*~~ ◇ ~~*It's a plain matter of...*~~ Expressions with **simple** often suggest impatience with other people's behaviour.

stark (*rather formal*) used for describing an unpleasant fact or difference that is very obvious: *The stark truth is that there is not enough money left.* NOTE The *simple/plain truth* may be sth that some people do not want to hear, but it may be good for them to hear it anyway. The *stark truth* is sth particularly unpleasant and has no good side to it at all.

bare [only before noun] the most basic or simple, with nothing extra: *She gave me only the bare facts of the case.*

unequivocal (*formal*) expressing your opinion or intention very clearly and firmly: *The reply was an unequivocal 'no'.*

PATTERNS

- the plain/simple/stark/bare/unequivocal **truth**
- a(n) plain/simple/stark/bare/unequivocal **fact/statement**
- a(n) plain/simple/unequivocal **answer**

plain·chant /ˈpleɪntʃɑːnt; *NAmE* -tʃænt/ *noun* [U] = PLAINSONG

ˌ**plain ˈchocolate** *noun* [U] (*BrE*) = DARK CHOCOLATE

ˌ**plain ˈclothes** *noun* [pl.] ordinary clothes, not uniform, when worn by police officers on duty: *officers **in plain clothes*** ▸ ˌ**plain-ˈclothes** *adj.* [only before noun]: *plain-clothes police officers*

ˌ**plain ˈflour** (*BrE*) (*NAmE* ˌ**all-purpose ˈflour**) *noun* [U] flour that does not contain BAKING POWDER ➲ compare SELF-RAISING FLOUR

plain·ly /ˈpleɪnli/ *adv.* **1** in a way that is easy to see, hear, understand or believe SYN **clearly**: *The sea was plainly visible in the distance.* ◇ *The lease plainly states that all damage must be paid for.* ◇ *She had no right to interfere in what was plainly a family matter.* ◇ *Plainly* (= obviously) *something was wrong.* **2** using simple words to say sth in a direct and honest way: *To put it plainly, he's a crook.* **3** in a simple way, without decoration: *She was plainly dressed and wore no make-up.*

plain·song /ˈpleɪnsɒŋ; *NAmE* -sɔːŋ; -sɑːŋ/ (also **plain·chant**) *noun* [U] a type of church music for voices alone, used since the Middle Ages

plaint /pleɪnt/ *noun* **1** (*BrE, law*) a complaint made against sb in court **2** (*literary*) a sad cry or sound

ˈ**plain text** *noun* [U] (*technical*) data that is stored in the form of ASCII (= a standard code used so that data can be moved between computers that use different programs). Plain text cannot be FORMATTED (= displayed in a particular way on the screen).

plain·tiff /ˈpleɪntɪf/ (*BrE less frequent* **com·plain·ant**) *noun* (*law*) a person who makes a formal complaint against sb in court ➲ compare DEFENDANT

plaint·ive /ˈpleɪntɪv/ *adj.* sounding sad, especially in a weak complaining way SYN **mournful**: *a* ***plaintive cry/voice*** ▸ **plaint·ive·ly** *adv.*

plait /plæt/ (*BrE*) (also **braid** *NAmE, BrE*) *noun, verb*

■ *noun* a long piece of sth, especially hair, that is divided into three parts and twisted together: *She wore her hair* ***in plaits.*** ➲ VISUAL VOCAB page V49

■ *verb* **~ sth** to twist three or more long pieces of hair, rope, etc. together to make one long piece

plan 🔑 /plæn/ *noun, verb*

■ *noun*

▸ INTENTION **1** 🔑 something that you intend to do or achieve: **~ (for sth)** *Do you have any plans for the summer?* ◇ **~ (to do sth)** *There are no plans to build new offices.* ◇ *Your* ***best plan*** (= the best thing to do) *would be to go by car.* ◇ *There's been* ***a change of plan.*** ◇ *We can't change our plans now.* ➲ SYNONYMS at PURPOSE

▸ ARRANGEMENT **2** 🔑 a set of things to do in order to achieve sth, especially one that has been considered in detail in advance: **~ (for sth)** *Both sides agreed to a detailed plan for keeping the peace.* ◇ **~ (to do sth)** *The government has announced plans to create one million new training places.* ◇ *a* ***development/business/peace, etc. plan*** ◇ *a five-point plan* ◇ *a three-year plan* ◇ *We need to* ***make plans*** *for the future.* ◇ *a* ***plan of action/campaign*** ◇ *Let's hope everything will* ***go according to plan.*** ➲ see also MASTER PLAN

▸ MAP **3** 🔑 a detailed map of a building, town, etc: *a plan of the museum* ◇ *a street plan of the city*

▸ DRAWING **4** 🔑 [usually pl.] **~ (for/of sth)** (*technical*) a detailed drawing of a machine, building, etc. that shows its size, shape and measurements: *The architect is* ***drawing up plans*** *for the new offices.* ➲ compare ELEVATION (4), GROUND PLAN **5** 🔑 a diagram that shows how sth will be arranged: *a* ***seating plan*** (= showing where each person will sit, for example at a dinner) ◇ *a* ***floor plan*** (= showing how furniture is arranged)

▸ MONEY **6** 🔑 (especially in compounds) a way of investing money for the future: *a savings plan*

IDM ˌ**make a ˈplan** (*SAfrE*) to think of sth you can do to solve a problem or make sth happen: *It's going to be difficult to find the time but I'll make a plan.* ➲ more at SOUND *v.*

■ *verb* (-nn-)

▸ MAKE ARRANGEMENTS **1** 🔑 [T, I] to make detailed arrangements for sth you want to do in the future: **~ sth** *to plan a trip* ◇ *Everything* ***went*** *exactly* ***as planned.*** ◇ *We planned the day down to the last detail.* ◇ **~ sth for sth** *A meeting has been planned for early next year.* ◇ **~ (for sth)** *to plan for the future* ◇ **~ how, what, etc…** *I've been planning how I'm going to spend the day.* ◇ **~ that…** *They planned that the two routes would connect.*

▸ INTEND/EXPECT **2** 🔑 [I, T] to intend or expect to do sth: **~ on sth/on doing sth** *We hadn't planned on going anywhere this evening.* ◇ **~ to do sth** *They plan to arrive some time after three.* ◇ **~ sth** *We're planning a trip to France in the spring—are you interested?*

▸ DESIGN **3** 🔑 [T] **~ sth** to make a design or an outline for sth: *to plan an essay/a garden* ◇ *a well-planned campaign*

PHR V ˌ**plan sth↔ˈout** to plan carefully and in detail sth that you are going to do in the future: *Plan out your route before you go.* ◇ *She has her career all planned out.*

Plan ˈA *noun* [sing.] the thing or things sb intends to do if everything happens as they expect

pla·nar /ˈpleɪnə(r)/ *adj.* (*technical*) of or related to a flat surface

Plan ˈB *noun* [sing.] the thing or things sb intends to do if their first plan is not successful: *If Plan A fails, go to Plan B.*

plane 🔑 /pleɪn/ *noun, adj., verb*

■ *noun* **1** 🔑 (*BrE* also **aero·plane**) (also **air·plane** especially in *NAmE*) a flying vehicle with wings and one or more engines: *She left* ***by plane*** *for Berlin.* ◇ *a* ***plane crash*** ◇ *I* ***caught the*** *next* ***plane*** *to Dublin.* ◇ *The* ***plane took off*** *an hour late.* ◇ *The* ***plane landed*** *at Geneva.* ➲ COLLOCATIONS at TRAVEL ➲ VISUAL VOCAB page V43 **2** (*geometry*) any flat or level surface, or an imaginary flat surface through or joining material objects: *the* ***horizontal/vertical plane*** **3** a level of thought, existence or development: *to reach a higher plane of achievement* **4** a tool with a blade set in a flat surface, used for making the surface of wood smooth by shaving very thin layers off it ➲ VISUAL VOCAB page V17

■ *adj.* [only before noun] (*technical*) completely flat; level: *a plane surface*

■ *verb* **1** [T] to make a piece of wood smoother or flatter with a PLANE *n.* (4): **~ sth** *Plane the surface down first.* ◇ **~ sth + adj.** *Then plane the wood smooth.* **2** [I] (of a bird) to fly without moving the wings, especially high up in the air **3** [I] (of a boat, etc.) to move quickly across water, only just touching the surface

plane·load /ˈpleɪnləʊd; *NAmE* -loʊd/ *noun* the number of people or the amount of goods that can be carried in a plane: *two planeloads of refugees*

planer /ˈpleɪnə(r)/ *noun* an electric tool for making wooden surfaces smooth

planet 🔑 /ˈplænɪt/ *noun*

1 🔑 [C] a large round object in space that moves around a star (such as the sun) and receives light from it: *the planets of our solar system* ◇ *the planet Earth/Venus/Mars* **2** 🔑 **the planet** [sing.] used to mean 'the world', especially when talking about the environment: *the battle to save the planet*

IDM **to be on another ˈplanet | what ˈplanet is sb on?** (*informal, humorous*) used to suggest that sb's ideas are not realistic or practical: *He thinks being a father is easy. What planet is he on?*

plan·et·arium /ˌplænɪˈteəriəm; *NAmE* -ˈter-/ *noun* (*pl.* -iums) a building with a curved ceiling to represent the sky at night, with moving images of the planets and stars, used to educate and entertain people

plan·et·ary /ˈplænətri; *NAmE* -teri/ *adj.* [only before noun] (*technical*) relating to a planet or planets: *a planetary system*

ˈ**plane tree** *noun* a tree with spreading branches and broad leaves, that is often found in towns in northern countries

plan·gent /ˈplændʒənt/ *adj.* **1** (*formal*) (of sounds) loud, with a strong beat **2** (*literary*) (of sounds or images) expressing sadness SYN **plaintive**: *the plangent sound of the harpsichord*

plank /plæŋk/ *noun* **1** a long narrow flat piece of wood that is used for making floors, etc: *a plank of wood* ◇ *a wooden plank* **2** a main point in the policy of an organization, especially a political party: *The* ***central plank*** *of the bill was rural development.* IDM see THICK *adj.*, WALK *v.*

plank·ing /ˈplæŋkɪŋ/ *noun* [U] planks used to make a floor, etc.

plank·ton /ˈplæŋktən/ *noun* [U+sing./pl. v.] the very small forms of plant and animal life that live in water

ˌ**planned eˈconomy** (also **comˌmand eˈconomy**) *noun* an economy in which production, prices and incomes are decided and fixed by the central government

plan·ner /ˈplænə(r)/ *noun* **1** (also ˌ**town ˈplanner**) a person whose job is to plan the growth and development of a town **2** a person who makes plans for a particular area of activity: *curriculum planners* **3** a book, chart, computer program, etc. that contains dates and is used for recording information, arranging meetings, etc: *a journey planner* ◇ *a wall planner* ➲ VISUAL VOCAB page V56

plan·ning 0‑ /ˈplænɪŋ/ *noun* [U] **1** 0‑ the act or process of making plans for sth: *financial planning* ➲ see also FAMILY PLANNING **2** = TOWN PLANNING

ˈplanning permission *noun* [U] (*BrE*) official permission to build a new building or change one that already exists

plant 0‑ /plɑːnt; *NAmE* plænt/ *noun, verb*

■ ***noun***

▸ LIVING THING **1** 0‑ [C] a living thing that grows in the earth and usually has a STEM, leaves and roots, especially one that is smaller than a tree or bush: *All plants need light and water.* ◇ ***flowering/garden/indoor plants*** ◇ *a tomato/potato plant* ◇ *the animal and plant life of the area* ➲ COLLOCATIONS at LIFE ➲ VISUAL VOCAB page V9 ➲ see also BEDDING PLANT, HOUSE PLANT, POT PLANT, RUBBER PLANT

▸ FACTORY **2** 0‑ [C] a factory or place where power is produced or an industrial process takes place: *a nuclear reprocessing plant* ◇ *Japanese car plants* ◇ *a chemical plant* ➲ see also SEWAGE PLANT ➲ SYNONYMS at FACTORY

▸ MACHINERY **3** [U] the large machinery that is used in industrial processes: *The company has been investing in new plant and equipment.*

▸ STH ILLEGAL **4** [C, usually sing.] (*informal*) something that sb has deliberately placed among another person's clothes or possessions in order to make them appear guilty of a crime

▸ PERSON **5** [C] a person who joins a group of criminals or enemies in order to get and secretly report information about their activities

■ ***verb***

▸ SEEDS/PLANTS **1** 0‑ **~ sth** to put plants, seeds, etc. in the ground to grow: *to plant and harvest rice* ◇ *Plant these shrubs in full sun.* **2** 0‑ to cover or supply a garden/yard, area of land, etc. with plants: **~ sth** *a densely planted orange grove* ◇ **~ sth with sth** *The field had been ploughed and planted with corn.*

▸ PUT IN POSITION **3** **~ sth/yourself + adv./prep.** to place sth or yourself firmly in a particular place or position: *They planted a flag on the summit.* ◇ *He planted himself squarely in front of us.*

▸ BOMB **4** **~ sth** (**+ adv./prep.**) to hide sth such as a bomb in a place where it will not be found

▸ STH ILLEGAL **5** **~ sth** (**on sb**) to hide sth, especially sth illegal, in sb's clothing, possessions, etc. so that when it is found it will look as though they committed a crime: *He claims that the drugs were planted on him.*

▸ PERSON **6** **~ sb** (**in sth**) to send sb to join a group, etc, especially in order to make secret reports on its members

▸ THOUGHT/IDEA **7** **~ sth** (**in sth**) to make sb think or believe sth, especially without them realizing that you gave them the idea: *He planted the first seeds of doubt in my mind.*

PHR V **ˌplant sth↔ˈout** to put plants in the ground so that they have enough room to grow

plan·tain /ˈplæntɪn/ *noun* **1** [C, U] a fruit like a large BANANA, but less sweet, that is cooked and eaten as a vegetable **2** [C] a wild plant with small green flowers and broad flat leaves that spread out close to the ground

plan·tar /ˈplæntə(r)/ *adj.* [only before noun] (*anatomy*) of or related to the bottom of the foot

ˌplantar ˈwart (*NAmE*) (*BrE* **ver·ruca**) *noun* a small hard lump like a WART on the bottom of the foot, which can be easily spread from person to person

plan·ta·tion /plɑːnˈteɪʃn; *NAmE* plæn-/ *noun* **1** a large area of land, especially in a hot country, where crops such as coffee, sugar, rubber, etc. are grown: *a banana plantation* **2** a large area of land that is planted with trees to produce wood: *conifer/forestry plantations*

plant·er /ˈplɑːntə(r); *NAmE* ˈplæn-/ *noun* **1** an attractive container to grow a plant in ➲ VISUAL VOCAB page V16 **2** a person who owns or manages a PLANTATION in a tropical country: *a tea planter* **3** a machine that plants seeds, etc.

plant·ing /ˈplɑːntɪŋ; *NAmE* ˈplæn-/ *noun* [U, C] an act of planting sth; sth that has just been planted: *The Tree Council promotes tree planting.* ◇ *These bushes are fairly recent plantings.*

ˈplant pot *noun* a container for growing plants in ➲ VISUAL VOCAB page V18

plants·man /ˈplɑːntsmən; *NAmE* ˈplænts-/, **plants·woman** /ˈplɑːntswʊmən; *NAmE* ˈplænts-/ *noun* (*pl.* **-men** /-mən/, **-women** /-wɪmɪn/) an expert in garden plants and GARDENING

plaque /plæk; *BrE* also plɑːk/ *noun* **1** [C] a flat piece of stone, metal, etc, usually with a name and dates on, attached to a wall in memory of a person or an event **2** [U] a soft substance that forms on teeth and encourages the growth of harmful bacteria ➲ compare SCALE

plasma /ˈplæzmə/ (also **plasm** /ˈplæzəm/) *noun* [U] **1** (*biology* or *medical*) the clear liquid part of blood, in which the blood cells, etc. float **2** (*physics*) a gas that contains approximately equal numbers of positive and negative electric charges and is present in the sun and most stars

ˌplasma ˈscreen *noun* a type of television or computer screen that is larger and thinner than most screens and produces a very clear image

ˌplasma TˈV *noun* a television set with a plasma screen

plas·ter /ˈplɑːstə(r); *NAmE* ˈplæs-/ *noun, verb*

■ ***noun*** **1** [U] a substance made of LIME, water and sand, that is put on walls and ceilings to give them a smooth hard surface: *an old house with crumbling plaster and a leaking roof* **2** (also *less frequent* **ˌplaster of ˈParis**) [U] a white powder that is mixed with water and becomes very hard when it dries, used especially for making copies of statues or holding broken bones in place: *a plaster bust of Julius Caesar* ◇ (*BrE*) *She broke her leg a month ago and it's still* ***in plaster***. **3** (also **ˈsticking plaster**) (both *BrE*) (also **ˈBand-Aid™** *NAmE, BrE*) [C, U] material that can be stuck to the skin to protect a small wound or cut; a piece of this ➲ COLLOCATIONS at INJURY

■ ***verb*** **1** **~ sth** to cover a wall, etc. with plaster ➲ COLLOCATIONS at DECORATE **2** **~ sb/sth/yourself in/with sth** to cover sb/sth with a wet or sticky substance: *She plastered herself in suntan lotion.* ◇ *We were plastered from head to foot with mud.* **3** **~ sth + adv./prep.** to make your hair flat and stick to your head: *His wet hair was plastered to his head.* **4** **~ sth + adv./prep.** to completely cover a surface with pictures or POSTERS: *Her bedroom wall was plastered with photos of him.* ◇ *She had photos of him plastered all over her bedroom wall.* ◇ *The next day their picture was plastered all over the newspapers.*

PHR V **ˌplaster ˈover sth** to cover sth such as a crack or an old wall with plaster

plas·ter·board /ˈplɑːstəbɔːd; *NAmE* ˈplæstərbɔːrd/ (*NAmE* also **ˈdry wall**) *noun* [U] a building material made of sheets of cardboard with plaster between them, used for inside walls and ceilings

ˈplaster cast *noun* **1** (also **cast**) a case made of PLASTER OF PARIS that covers a broken bone and protects it **2** a copy of sth, made from PLASTER OF PARIS: *They took a plaster cast of the teeth for identification purposes.*

plas·tered /ˈplɑːstəd; *NAmE* ˈplæstərd/ *adj.* [not before noun] (*informal*) drunk: *to be/get plastered*

plas·terer /ˈplɑːstərə(r); *NAmE* ˈplæs-/ *noun* a person whose job is to put plaster on walls and ceilings

plaster of Paris /ˌplɑːstər əv ˈpærɪs; *NAmE* ˌplæs-/ *noun* [U] = PLASTER (2)

ˌplaster ˈsaint *noun* a person who tries to appear to have no moral faults or weaknesses, especially when this appearance is false

plas·ter·work /ˈplɑːstəwɜːk; *NAmE* ˈplæstərwɜːrk/ *noun* [U] the dry PLASTER on ceilings when it has been formed into shapes and patterns for decoration

plas·tic 0‑ /ˈplæstɪk/ *noun, adj.*

■ ***noun*** **1** 0‑ [U, C, usually pl.] a light strong material that is produced by chemical processes and can be formed into

P

shapes when heated. There are many different types of plastic, used to make different objects and FABRICS: *The pipes should be* ***made of plastic.*** ◇ *a sheet of clear plastic* ◇ *the plastic industry* **2 plastics** [U] the science of making plastics **3** [U] (*informal*) a way of talking about CREDIT CARDS: *Do they take plastic?*

■ ***adj.*** **1** made of plastic: *a plastic bag/cup/toy* **2** (of a material or substance) easily formed into different shapes SYN **malleable**: *Clay is a plastic substance.* **3** (*disapproving*) that seems artificial; false; not real or sincere SYN **false**: *TV game show hosts with their banal remarks and plastic smiles*

ˌplastic ˈarts *noun* [pl.] (*technical*) art forms that involve making models or representing things so that they seem solid: *The plastic arts include sculpture, pottery and painting.*

ˌplastic ˈbullet *noun* a bullet made of plastic, that is intended to injure but not to kill people

ˌplastic exˈplosive *noun* [U, C] an EXPLOSIVE that is used to make bombs

Plas·ti·cine™ /ˈplæstəsiːn/ *noun* [U] (*BrE*) a soft substance like CLAY that is made in different colours, used especially by children for making models

plas·ti·city /plæˈstɪsəti/ *noun* [U] (*technical*) the quality of being easily made into different shapes

plas·ti·cize (*BrE* also **-ise**) /ˈplæstɪsaɪz/ *verb* **~ sth** (*technical*) to add sth to a substance so that it becomes easy to bend and form into different shapes

ˌplastic ˈsurgeon *noun* a doctor who is qualified to perform plastic surgery

ˌplastic ˈsurgery *noun* [U] medical operations to repair injury to a person's skin, or to improve a person's appearance

ˈplastic wrap (also **Saran Wrap™**) (both *NAmE*) (*BrE* **ˈcling film**) *noun* [U] a thin transparent plastic material that sticks to a surface and to itself, used especially for wrapping food

plate /pleɪt/ *noun, verb*

■ ***noun***

▸ FOOD **1** [C] a flat, usually round, dish that you put food on: *sandwiches on a plate* ◇ *a pile of dirty plates* ◇ *dinner plates* ➲ VISUAL VOCAB page V19 **2** [C] the amount of food that you can put on a plate: *a plate of sandwiches* ◇ *two large plates of pasta* ➲ compare PLATEFUL **3** [C] (*especially NAmE*) a whole main course of a meal, served on one plate: *Try the seafood plate.*

▸ FOR STRENGTH **4** [C] a thin flat piece of metal, used especially to join or make sth stronger: *The tanks were mainly constructed of steel plates.* ◇ *She had a metal plate inserted in her arm.*

▸ FOR INFORMATION **5** [C] a flat piece of metal with some information on it, for example sb's name: *A brass plate beside the door said 'Dr Alan Tate'.* ➲ see also NAMEPLATE

▸ ON VEHICLE **6** [usually pl.] the pieces of metal or plastic at the front and back of a vehicle with numbers and letters on it ➲ see also L-PLATE, LICENSE PLATE, NUMBER PLATE

▸ SILVER/GOLD **7** [U] ordinary metal that is covered with a thin layer of silver or gold: *The cutlery is plate, not solid silver.* ➲ see also GOLD PLATE, SILVER PLATE, TINPLATE **8** [U] dishes, bowls, etc. that are made of silver or gold

▸ ON ANIMAL **9** [C] (*biology*) one of the thin flat pieces of horn or bone that cover and protect an animal: *the armadillo's protective shell of bony plates*

▸ GEOLOGY **10** [C] one of the very large pieces of rock that form the earth's surface and move slowly: *the Pacific plate* ◇ *Earthquakes are caused by two* ***tectonic plates*** *bumping into each other.* ➲ see also PLATE TECTONICS

▸ PRINTING/PHOTOGRAPHY **11** [C] a photograph that is used as a picture in a book, especially one that is printed on a separate page on high quality paper: *The book includes 55 colour plates.* ◇ *See plate 4.* **12** [C] a sheet of metal, plastic, etc. that has been treated so that words or pictures can be printed from it: *a printing plate* **13** [C] a thin sheet of glass, metal, etc. that is covered with chemicals so that it reacts to light and can form an image, used in larger or older cameras

▸ IN MOUTH **14** [C] a thin piece of plastic with wire or artificial teeth attached to it which fits inside your mouth in order to make your teeth straight ➲ compare BRACE, DENTURES

▸ IN BASEBALL **15** [sing.] (*NAmE*) = HOME PLATE

▸ IN CHURCH **16** (usually **the plate**) [sing.] a flat dish that is used to collect money from people in a church ➲ see also BOOKPLATE, BREASTPLATE, FOOTPLATE, HOTPLATE

IDM **have enough/a lot/too much on your ˈplate** (*informal*) to have a lot of work or problems, etc. to deal with ➲ more at HAND *v.*, STEP *v.*

■ ***verb*** [usually passive] **1 ~ sth (with sth)** to cover a metal with a thin layer of another metal, especially gold or silver: *a silver ring plated with gold* ➲ see also GOLD-PLATED, SILVER PLATE **2 ~ sth (with sth)** to cover sth with sheets of metal or another hard substance: *The walls of the vault were plated with steel.* ➲ see also ARMOUR-PLATED

plat·eau /ˈplætəʊ; *NAmE* plæˈtoʊ/ *noun, verb*

■ ***noun*** (*pl.* **plat·eaux** or **plat·eaus** /-təʊz; *NAmE* -ˈtoʊz/) **1** an area of flat land that is higher than the land around it ➲ VISUAL VOCAB page V4 **2** a time of little or no change after a period of growth or progress: *Inflation has reached a plateau.*

■ ***verb*** [I] **~ (out)** to stay at a steady level after a period of growth or progress: *Unemployment has at last plateaued out.*

plate·ful /ˈpleɪtfʊl/ *noun* the amount that a plate holds: *She ate three platefuls of spaghetti.* ➲ compare PLATE

ˌplate ˈglass *noun* [U] very clear glass of good quality, made in thick sheets, used for doors, windows of shops/stores, etc.

plate·lay·er /ˈpleɪtleɪə(r)/ *noun* (*BrE*) a person whose job is to lay and repair railway tracks

plate·let /ˈpleɪtlət/ *noun* a very small part of a cell in the blood, shaped like a disc. Platelets help to CLOT the blood from a cut or wound.

ˌplate tecˈtonics *noun* [U] (*geology*) the movements of the large sheets of rock (called PLATES) that form the earth's surface; the scientific study of these movements

British/American

platform / track

- In British stations the platforms, where passengers get on and off trains, have numbers: *The Edinburgh train is waiting at platform 4.*
- In stations in the USA, it is the track that the train travels along that has a number: *The train for Chicago is on track 9.*

plat·form /ˈplætfɔːm; *NAmE* -fɔːrm/ *noun*

▸ AT TRAIN STATION **1** the raised flat area beside the track at a train station where you get on or off the train: (*BrE*) *What platform does it go from?* ◇ (*BrE*) *The train now standing at platform 1 is for Leeds.* ➲ compare TRACK ➲ VISUAL VOCAB page V47

▸ FOR PERFORMERS **2** a flat surface raised above the level of the ground or floor, used by public speakers or performers so that the audience can see them SYN **rostrum**: *Coming onto the platform now is tonight's conductor, Jane Glover.* ◇ *Representatives of both parties shared a platform* (= they spoke at the same meeting).

▸ RAISED SURFACE **3** a raised level surface, for example one that equipment stands on or is operated from: *an* ***oil/gas platform*** ◇ *a* ***launch platform*** (= for SPACECRAFT) ◇ *a* ***viewing platform*** *giving stunning views over the valley*

▸ POLITICS/OPINIONS **4** [usually sing.] the aims of a political party and the things that they say they will do if they are elected to power: *They are campaigning on an anti-immigration platform.* **5** an opportunity or a place for sb to express their opinions publicly or make progress in a particular area: *She used the newspaper column as a platform for her feminist views.*

▸ COMPUTING **6** the type of computer system or the software that is used: *an IBM platform* ◇ *a multimedia platform*
▸ SHOES **7** a type of shoe with a high, thick SOLE; the sole on such a shoe: *platform shoes* ➲ VISUAL VOCAB page V52
▸ ON BUS **8** (*BrE*) the open part at the back of a DOUBLE-DECKER bus where you get on or off

'platform game (also **plat·form·er** /'plætfɔːmə(r); *NAmE* -fɔːrm-/) *noun* a computer game in which the player controls a character who jumps and climbs between platforms at different positions on the screen

plat·ing /'pleɪtɪŋ/ *noun* [U] **1** a thin covering of a metal, especially silver or gold, on another metal **2** a layer of coverings, especially of metal plates: *armour plating*

plat·inum /'plætɪnəm/ *noun* [U] (*symb.* Pt) a chemical element. Platinum is a silver-grey PRECIOUS METAL, used in making expensive jewellery and in industry.

,platinum 'blonde *noun* (*informal*) a woman whose hair is a very pale silver colour, especially because it has been coloured with chemicals; this colour of hair ▸ **,platinum 'blonde** *adj.*

,platinum 'disc *noun* a platinum record in a frame, given to a singer, etc. who has sold a very high number of records

plati·tude /'plætɪtjuːd; *NAmE* -tuːd/ *noun* (*disapproving*) a comment or statement that has been made very often before and is therefore not interesting ▸ **plati·tud·in·ous** /,plætɪ'tjuːdɪnəs; *NAmE* -'tuːdənəs/ *adj.* (*formal*)

pla·ton·ic /plə'tɒnɪk; *NAmE* -'tɑːn-/ *adj.* (of a relationship) friendly but not involving sex: *platonic love* ◇ *Their relationship is strictly platonic.*

Pla·ton·ism /'pleɪtənɪzəm/ *noun* [U] (*philosophy*) the ideas of the ancient Greek PHILOSOPHER Plato and those who followed him ▸ **Pla·ton·ist** /'pleɪtənɪst/ *adj.*, *noun*

pla·toon /plə'tuːn/ *noun* a small group of soldiers that is part of a COMPANY and commanded by a LIEUTENANT

plat·ter /'plætə(r)/ *noun* a large plate that is used for serving food: *a silver platter* ◇ *I'll have the fish platter* (= several types of fish and other food served on a large plate). IDM see SILVER *n.*

platy·pus /'plætɪpəs/ (also **,duck-billed 'platypus**) *noun* an Australian animal that is covered in fur and has a beak like a DUCK, WEBBED feet (= with skin between the toes) and a flat tail. Platypuses lay eggs but give milk to their young.

plau·dits /'plɔːdɪts/ *noun* [usually pl.] (*formal*) praise and approval: *His work* ***won him plaudits*** *from the critics.*

plaus·ible /'plɔːzəbl/ *adj.* **1** (of an excuse or explanation) reasonable and likely to be true: *Her story sounded perfectly plausible.* ◇ *The only plausible explanation is that he forgot.* OPP **implausible 2** (*disapproving*) (of a person) good at sounding honest and sincere, especially when trying to trick people: *She was a plausible liar.* ▸ **plausi·bil·ity** /,plɔːzə'bɪləti/ *noun* [U] **plaus·ibly** /-əbli/ *adv.*: *He argued very plausibly that the claims were true.*

play 0→ /pleɪ/ *verb*, *noun*
■ *verb*
▸ OF CHILDREN **1** 0→ [I, T] to do things for pleasure, as children do; to enjoy yourself, rather than work: *You'll have to play inside today.* ◇ *There's a time to work and a time to play.* ◇ **~ with sb/sth** *A group of kids were playing with a ball in the street.* ◇ *I haven't got anybody to play with!* ◇ **~ sth** *Let's play a different game.* ➲ SYNONYMS at ENTERTAINMENT **2** 0→ [T, no passive, I] to pretend to be or do sth for fun: **~ sth** *Let's play pirates.* ◇ **~ at doing sth** *They were playing at being cowboys.*
▸ TRICK **3** 0→ [T] **~ a trick/tricks (on sb)** to trick sb for fun
▸ SPORTS/GAMES **4** 0→ [T, I] **~ (sth) (with/against sb)** to be involved in a game; to compete against sb in a game: **~ sth** *to* ***play football/chess/cards, etc.*** ◇ **~ sb** *France are playing Wales tomorrow.* ◇ **~ sb at sth** *Have you played her at squash yet?* ◇ **~ for sb** *He plays for Cleveland.* ◇ **~ against sb** *France are playing against Wales on Saturday.* ◇ **+ adv./prep.** *Evans played very well.* **5** [I] to take a particular position in a sports team: **+ adv./prep.** *Who's playing on the wing?* ◇ **+ noun** *I've never played right back before.* **6** [T] **~ sb (+ adv./prep.)** to include sb in a sports team: *I think we should play Matt on the wing.* **7** [T] **~ sth** to make contact with the ball and hit or kick it in the way mentioned: *She played the ball and ran forward.* ◇ *He played a backhand volley.* **8** [T] **~ sth** (in CHESS) to move a piece in CHESS, etc: *She played her bishop.* **9** [T, I] **~ (sth)** (in card games) to put a card face upwards on the table, showing its value: *to play your ace/a trump* ◇ *He played out of turn!*
▸ MUSIC **10** 0→ [T, I] **~ (sth) (on sth)** to perform on a musical instrument; to perform music: **~ (sth)** *to* ***play the piano/violin/flute, etc.*** ◇ *In the distance a band was playing.* ◇ **~ sth (on sth)** *He played a tune on his harmonica.* ◇ **~ sth to sb** *Play that new piece to us.* ◇ **~ sb sth** *Play us that new piece.* **11** 0→ [T, I] to make a tape, CD, etc. produce sound: **~ sth (for sb)** *Play their new CD for me, please.* ◇ **~ (sb sth)** *Play me their new CD, please.* ◇ *My favourite song was playing on the radio.* ◇ *For some reason this CD won't play.*
▸ DVD/VIDEO **12** [I, T] (of a DVD or video) to start working; to make a DVD or video start working: *This DVD won't play on my computer.* ◇ **~ sth** *Click below to play videos.*
▸ ACT/PERFORM **13** 0→ [T] **~ sth** to act in a play, film/movie, etc; to act the role of sb: *The part of Elizabeth was played by Cate Blanchett.* ◇ *He had always wanted to play Othello.* **14** 0→ [I] to pretend to be sth that you are not: **+ adj.** *I decided it was safer to* ***play dead.*** ◇ **+ noun** *She enjoys playing the wronged wife.* **15** [I] **~ (to sb)** to be performed: *A production of 'Carmen' was playing to packed houses.*
▸ HAVE EFFECT **16** [T] **~ a part/role (in sth)** to have an effect on sth: *The media played an important part in the last election.*
▸ SITUATION **17** [T] **~ sth + adv./prep.** to deal with a situation in the way mentioned: *He played the situation carefully for maximum advantage.*
▸ OF LIGHT/A SMILE **18** [I] **+ adv./prep.** to move or appear quickly and lightly, often changing direction or shape: *Sunlight played on the surface of the lake.*
▸ OF FOUNTAIN **19** [I] when a FOUNTAIN **plays**, it produces a steady stream of water
IDM Most idioms containing **play** are at the entries for the nouns and adjectives in the idioms, for example **play the game** is at **game**. **have money, time, etc. to 'play with** (*informal*) to have plenty of money, time, etc. for doing sth **what is sb 'playing at?** used to ask in an angry way about what sb is doing: *What do you think you are playing at?* **'play with yourself** (*informal*) to MASTURBATE
PHR V **,play a'bout/a'round (with sb/sth) 1** 0→ to behave or treat sth in a careless way: *Don't play around with my tools!* **2** (*informal*) to have a sexual relationship with sb, usually with sb who is not your usual partner: *Her husband is always playing around.* **,play a'long (with sb/sth)** to pretend to agree with sb/sth: *I decided to play along with her idea.* **'play at sth/at doing sth** (often *disapproving*) to do sth without being serious about it or putting much effort into it **play a'way (from home)** (*BrE*) **1** (of a sports team) to play a match at the opponent's ground or STADIUM **2** (of a person who is married or who has a regular sexual partner) to have a secret sexual relationship with sb else **,play sth↔'back (to sb)** to play music, film, etc. that has been recorded on a tape, video, etc: *Play that last section back to me again.* ➲ related noun PLAYBACK **,play sth↔'down** to try to make sth seem less important than it is SYN **downplay** OPP **play up ,play A 'off against B** (*BrE*) (*NAmE* **'play A off B**) to put two people or groups in competition with each other, especially in order to get an advantage for yourself: *She played her two rivals off against each other and got the job herself.* ➲ related noun PLAY-OFF **,play 'on** (*sport*) to continue to play; to start playing again: *The home team claimed a penalty but the referee told them to play on.* **'play on/upon sth** to take advantage of sb's feelings, etc. SYN **exploit**: *Advertisements often play on people's fears.* **,play sth↔'out** when an event **is played out**, it happens SYN **enact**: *Their love affair was played out against the backdrop of war.* **,play yourself/itself 'out** to become weak and no longer useful or important **,play 'up | ,play sb 'up** (*informal, especially BrE*) to cause sb problems or pain: *The kids have been playing up all day.* ◇ *My shoulder is playing me up today.* **,play sth↔'up** to try

P

to make sth seem more important than it is **SYN overplay** **OPP play down** **'play with sb/sth** to treat sb who is emotionally attached to you in a way that is not serious and which can hurt their feelings: *She tends to play with men's emotions.* ◇ *She realized that Patrick was merely playing with her.* **'play with sth 1** 0-ᵣ to keep touching or moving sth: *She was playing with her hair.* ◇ *Stop playing with your food!* **2** to use things in different ways to produce an interesting or humorous effect, or to see what effect they have: *In this poem Fitch plays with words which sound alike.* ◇ *The composer plays with the exotic sounds of Japanese instruments.*

■ ***noun***

▸ CHILDREN **1** 0-ᵣ [U] things that people, especially children, do for pleasure rather than as work: *the happy sounds of children* ***at play*** ◇ *the importance of learning through play* ◇ *a play area*

▸ IN THEATRE **2** 0-ᵣ [C] a piece of writing performed by actors in a theatre or on television or radio: *to* ***put on*** (= perform) *a play* ◇ *a play by Shakespeare* ◇ *a radio play* ➲ see also MYSTERY PLAY, PASSION PLAY

▸ IN SPORT **3** [U] the playing of a game: *Rain stopped play.* ◇ *There was some excellent play in yesterday's match.* ➲ see also FAIR PLAY, FOUL PLAY **4** [C] (*NAmE*) an action or move in a game: *a defensive play*

▸ IN ROPE **5** [U] the possibility of free and easy movement: *We need more play in the rope.*

▸ ACTIVITY/INFLUENCE **6** [U] the activity or operation of sth; the influence of sth on sth else: *the free play of market forces* ◇ *The financial crisis has* ***brought*** *new factors* ***into play.*** ◇ *Personal feelings should not* ***come into play*** *when you are making business decisions.*

▸ OF LIGHT/A SMILE **7** [U] (*literary*) a light, quick movement that keeps changing: *the play of sunlight on water*

IDM **have a 'play (with sth)** to spend time playing with a toy, game, etc: *I had a play with the new computer game.* **in/out of 'play** (*sport*) (of a ball) inside/outside the area allowed by the rules of the game: *She just managed to keep the ball in play.* **make a 'play for sb/sth** to try to obtain sth; to do things that are intended to produce a particular result: *She was making a play for the sales manager's job.* **make great/much 'play of sth** to emphasize the importance of a particular fact: *He made great play of the fact that his uncle was a duke.* **a play on 'words** the humorous use of a word or phrase that can have two different meanings **SYN pun** ➲ more at CALL *v.*, CHILD, STATE *n.*, WORK *n.*

play·able /ˈpleɪəbl/ *adj.* **1** (of a piece of music or a computer game) easy to play **2** (of a sports field) in a good condition and suitable for playing on **OPP unplayable**

'play-acting *noun* [U] behaviour that seems to be honest and sincere when in fact the person is pretending ▸ **'play-act** *verb* [I]: *He thought she was play-acting but in fact she had really hurt herself.*

play·back /ˈpleɪbæk/ *noun* [U, C, usually sing.] the act of playing music, showing a film/movie or listening to a telephone message that has been recorded before; a recording that you listen to or watch again

play·bill /ˈpleɪbɪl/ *noun* **1** a printed notice advertising a play **2** (*NAmE*) a theatre programme

play·boy /ˈpleɪbɔɪ/ *noun* a rich man who spends his time enjoying himself

ˌplay-by-'play *noun* [usually sing.] (*NAmE*) a report on what is happening in a sports game, given as the game is being played

ˌplayed 'out *adj.* [not before noun] (*informal*) no longer having any influence or effect

play·er 0-ᵣ /ˈpleɪə(r)/ *noun*
1 0-ᵣ a person who takes part in a game or sport: *a* ***tennis/rugby/chess, etc. player*** ◇ *a game for four players* ◇ *a midfield player* **2** a company or person involved in a particular area of business or politics: *The company has emerged as a* ***major player*** *in the London property market.* ➲ see also TEAM PLAYER **3** 0-ᵣ (in compounds) a machine for reproducing sound or pictures that have been recorded on CDs, etc: *a* ***CD/DVD/cassette/record player*** **4** 0-ᵣ (usually in compounds) a person who plays a musical instrument: *a trumpet player* **5** (*old-fashioned*) (especially in names) an actor: *Phoenix Players present 'Romeo and Juliet'.*

'player piano *noun* a piano that plays automatically by means of a PIANO ROLL **SYN Pianola**

play·ful /ˈpleɪfl/ *adj.* **1** full of fun; wanting to play: *a playful puppy* **2** (of a remark, an action, etc.) made or done in fun; not serious **SYN light-hearted**: *He gave her a playful punch on the arm.* ▸ **play·ful·ly** /-fəli/ *adv.* **play·ful·ness** *noun* [U]

play·goer /ˈpleɪgəʊə(r); *NAmE* -goʊər/ *noun* = THEATRE-GOER

play·ground /ˈpleɪgraʊnd/ *noun* **1** an outdoor area where children can play, especially at a school or in a park ➲ VISUAL VOCAB page V57 ➲ compare SCHOOLYARD ➲ see also ADVENTURE PLAYGROUND **2** a place where a particular type of people go to enjoy themselves: *The resort is a playground of the rich and famous.*

play·group /ˈpleɪgruːp/ (also **play·school**) (both *BrE*) *noun* [C, U] a place where children who are below school age go regularly to play together and to learn through playing ➲ compare NURSERY SCHOOL

play·house /ˈpleɪhaʊs/ *noun* **1** used in names of theatres: *the Liverpool Playhouse* **2** (*BrE* also **'Wendy house**) a model of a house large enough for children to play in

play·ing /ˈpleɪɪŋ/ *noun* **1** [U] the way in which sb plays sth, especially a musical instrument: *The orchestral playing is superb.* **2** [C] the act of playing a piece of music: *repeated playings of the National Anthem*

'playing card (also **card**) *noun* any one of a set of 52 cards with numbers and pictures printed on one side, which are used to play various card games: (*BrE*) *a pack of (playing) cards* ◇ (*NAmE*) *a deck of (playing) cards* ➲ VISUAL VOCAB page V32

'playing field *noun* a large area of grass, usually with lines marked on it, where people play sports and games: *the school playing fields* **IDM** see LEVEL *adj.*

play·let /ˈpleɪlət/ *noun* a short play

play·list /ˈpleɪlɪst/ *noun* a list of all the songs and pieces of music that are played by a radio station or on a radio programme

play·maker /ˈpleɪmeɪkə(r)/ *noun* a player in a team game who starts attacks or brings other players on the same side into a position in which they could score

play·mate /ˈpleɪmeɪt/ *noun* a friend with whom a child plays

'play-off *noun* a match/game, or a series of them, between two players or teams with equal points or scores to decide who the winner is: *They lost to Chicago in the play-offs.*

play·pen /ˈpleɪpen/ *noun* a frame with wooden bars or NETTING that surrounds a small area in which a baby or small child can play safely

play·room /ˈpleɪruːm; -rʊm/ *noun* a room in a house for children to play in

play·scheme /ˈpleɪskiːm/ *noun* (*BrE*) a project that provides organized activities for children, especially during school holidays

play·school /ˈpleɪskuːl/ *noun* (*BrE*) = PLAYGROUP

play·suit /ˈpleɪsuːt; *BrE* also -sjuːt/ *noun* **1** a piece of clothing for babies or small children that covers the body, arms and legs **2** (*BrE*) a set of clothes that children wear for fun so that they look like a particular person: *a Spiderman playsuit* **3** a piece of women's underwear that covers the upper body to the tops of the legs

play·thing /ˈpleɪθɪŋ/ *noun* **1** a person or thing that you treat like a toy, without really caring about them or it: *She was an intelligent woman who refused to be a rich man's plaything.* **2** (*old-fashioned*) a toy: *The teddy bear was his favourite plaything.*

play·time /ˈpleɪtaɪm/ *noun* [U, C] **1** (*especially BrE*) a time at school when teaching stops for a short time and children can play **2** a time for playing and having fun: *With so much homework to do, her playtime is now very limited.*

play·wright /ˈpleɪraɪt/ *noun* a person who writes plays for the theatre, television or radio **SYN dramatist** ➲ compare SCREENWRITER, SCRIPTWRITER

plaza /ˈplɑːzə; *NAmE* ˈplæzə/ *noun* (*especially NAmE*) **1** a public outdoor square especially in a town where Spanish is spoken **2** a small shopping centre, sometimes also with offices: *a downtown shopping plaza*

plc /ˌpiː el ˈsiː/ (also **PLC**) *abbr.* (*BrE*) public limited company (used after the name of a company or business): *Lloyd's Bank plc*

plea /pliː/ *noun* **1** (*formal*) an urgent emotional request: **~ (for sth)** *She made an impassioned plea for help.* ◇ **~ (to sb) (to do sth)** *a plea to industries to stop pollution* ◇ *He refused to listen to her tearful pleas.* **2** (*law*) a statement made by sb or for sb who is accused of a crime: *a **plea of guilty/not guilty*** ◇ *to **enter a** guilty **plea*** **3 ~ of sth** (*law*) a reason given to a court for doing or not doing sth: *He was charged with murder, but got off on a plea of insanity.*

ˈplea-bargain·ing *noun* [U] (*law*) an arrangement in court by which a person admits to being guilty of a smaller crime in the hope of receiving less severe punishment for a more serious crime ➲ compare COP A PLEA at COP *v.*, TURN KING'S/QUEEN'S EVIDENCE at EVIDENCE ▶ **ˈplea bargain** *noun*: *He reached a plea bargain with the authorities.*

plead /pliːd/ *verb* (**pleaded, pleaded**, *NAmE* also **pled, pled** /pled/) **1** [I, T] to ask sb for sth in a very strong and serious way **SYN beg**: **~ (with sb) (to do sth)** *She pleaded with him not to go.* ◇ **~ (with sb) (for sth)** *I was forced to plead for my child's life.* ◇ *pleading eyes* ◇ **~ to do sth** *He pleaded to be allowed to see his mother one more time.* ◇ **+ speech** *'Do something!' she pleaded.* **2** [I, T, no passive] to state in court that you are guilty or not guilty of a crime: (**+ adj.**) *to **plead guilty/not guilty*** ◇ *How do you plead?* (= said by the judge at the start of the trial) ◇ **~ sth** *He advised his client to plead insanity* (= say that he/she was mentally ill and therefore not responsible for his/her actions). **3** [T] **~ sth** to present a case to a court: *They hired a top lawyer to plead their case.* **4** [T, no passive] **~ sth (for sth)** | **~ that...** to give sth as an explanation or excuse for sth: *He pleaded family problems for his lack of concentration.* **5** [T, I] to argue in support of sb/sth: **~ sth** *She appeared on television to plead the cause of political prisoners everywhere.* ◇ **~ for sb/sth** *The United Nations has pleaded for a halt to the bombing.*

plead·ing /ˈpliːdɪŋ/ *noun* **1** [C, U] an act of asking for sth that you want very much, in an emotional way: *He refused to give in to her pleadings.* **2** [C, usually pl.] (*law*) a formal statement of sb's case in court ➲ see also SPECIAL PLEADING

plead·ing·ly /ˈpliːdɪŋli/ *adv.* in an emotional way that shows that you want sth very much but are not certain that sb will give it to you: *He looked pleadingly at her.*

pleas·ant 🗝 /ˈpleznt/ *adj.* (**pleas·ant·er, pleas·ant·est**) **HELP more pleasant** and **most pleasant** are more common
1 🗝 enjoyable, pleasing or attractive: *a pleasant climate/evening/place* ◇ *What a pleasant surprise!* ◇ *to live in pleasant surroundings* ◇ *music that is pleasant to the ear* ◇ *a pleasant environment to work in* ◇ ***It was pleasant to** be alone again.* **2** 🗝 friendly and polite: *a pleasant young man* ◇ *a pleasant smile/voice/manner* ◇ **~ to sb** *Please try to be pleasant to our guests.* **OPP unpleasant** ▶ **pleas·ant·ly** 🗝 *adv.*: *a pleasantly cool room* ◇ *I was pleasantly surprised by my exam results.* ◇ *'Can I help you?' he asked pleasantly.* **pleas·ant·ness** *noun* [U]: *She remembered the pleasantness of the evening.*

pleas·ant·ry /ˈplezntri/ *noun* [C, usually pl., U] (*pl.* **-ies**) (*formal*) a friendly remark made in order to be polite: *After exchanging the usual pleasantries, they got down to serious discussion.*

please 🗝 /pliːz/ *exclamation, verb*
■ ***exclamation* 1** 🗝 used as a polite way of asking for sth or telling sb to do sth: *Please sit down.* ◇ *Two coffees, please.* ◇ *Quiet please!* ◇ *Please could I leave early today?* **2** 🗝 used to add force to a request or statement: *Please don't leave me here alone.* ◇ *Please, please don't forget.* ◇ *Please, I don't understand what I have to do.* **3** 🗝 used as a polite way of accepting sth: *'Would you like some help?' 'Yes, please.'* ◇ *'Coffee?' 'Please.'* **4 Please!** (*informal*, often *humorous*) used to ask sb to stop behaving badly: *Children, please! I'm trying to work.* ◇ *John! Please!* **5 Please/P-lease** /pəˈliːz/ used when you are replying to sb who has said sth that you think is stupid: *Oh, please! You cannot be serious.*
■ ***verb* 1** 🗝 [T, I] **~ (sb)** | **it pleases sb to do sth** to make sb happy: *You can't please everybody.* ◇ *He's a difficult man to please.* ◇ ***There's** just **no pleasing some people*** (= some people are impossible to please). ◇ *I did it to please my parents.* ◇ *She's always very eager to please.* **OPP displease** **2** [I] often used after *as* or *what, where*, etc. to mean 'to want', 'to choose' or 'to like' to do sth: *You may stay as long as you please.* ◇ *She always does exactly as she pleases.* ◇ *I'm free now to live wherever I please.*
IDM if you ˈplease 1 (*old-fashioned, formal*) used when politely asking sb to do sth: *Take a seat, if you please.* **2** (*old-fashioned, especially BrE*) used to say that you are annoyed or surprised at sb's actions: *And now, if you please, he wants me to rewrite the whole thing!* **ˌplease the ˈeye** to be very attractive to look at **ˌplease ˈGod** used to say that you very much hope or wish that sth will happen: *Please God, don't let him be dead.* **ˌplease yourˈself** (*informal*) used to tell sb that you are annoyed with them and do not care what they do: *'I don't think I'll bother finishing this.' 'Please yourself.'* **ˌplease yourˈself** | **ˌdo as you ˈplease** to be able to do whatever you like: *There were no children to cook for, so we could just please ourselves.*

pleased 🗝 /pliːzd/ *adj.*
1 🗝 feeling happy about sth: **~ (with sb/sth)** *She was very pleased with her exam results.* ◇ *The boss should be pleased with you.* ◇ **~ (that...)** *I'm really pleased that you're feeling better.* ◇ **~ (to hear, know, etc. sth)** *I'm pleased to hear about your news.* ◇ *You're coming? I'm so pleased.* ◇ *He did not look too pleased when I told him.* ➲ SYNONYMS at GLAD **2** 🗝 **~ to do sth** happy or willing to do sth: *We are always pleased to be able to help.* ◇ *I was **pleased to hear** you've been promoted.* ◇ *Aren't you pleased to see me?* ◇ (*especially BrE*) ***Pleased to meet you*** (= said when you are introduced to sb). ◇ *Thank you for your invitation, which I am very pleased to accept.* ◇ *I am pleased to inform you that the book you ordered has arrived.*
IDM (as) ˌpleased as ˈPunch (*BrE*) very pleased **far from ˈpleased** | **none too ˈpleased** not pleased; angry: *She was none too pleased at having to do it all again.* **only too ˈpleased (to do sth)** very happy or willing to do sth: *We're only too pleased to help.* **ˈpleased with yourself** (often *disapproving*) too proud of sth you have done: *He was looking very pleased with himself.*

pleas·ing 🗝 /ˈpliːzɪŋ/ *adj.*
that gives you pleasure or satisfaction: *a pleasing design* ◇ **~ to sb/sth** *The new building was **pleasing to the eye**.* ➲ SYNONYMS at SATISFYING ▶ **pleas·ing·ly** *adv.*: *She had a pleasingly direct manner.*

pleas·ur·able /ˈpleʒərəbl/ *adj.* (*formal*) giving pleasure **SYN enjoyable**: *a pleasurable experience* ◇ *We do everything we can to make your trip pleasurable.*

pleas·ur·ably /ˈpleʒərəbli/ *adv.* with pleasure: *He sipped his coffee pleasurably.*

pleas·ure 🗝 /ˈpleʒə(r)/ *noun*
1 🗝 [U] a state of feeling or being happy or satisfied **SYN enjoyment**: *to read **for pleasure*** ◇ **~ (in sth/in doing sth)** *He **takes** no **pleasure** in his work.* ◇ **~ (of sth/of doing sth)** *She **had the pleasure of** seeing him look surprised.* ◇ (*formal*) *We request the pleasure of your company at the marriage of our daughter Lisa.* ◇ ***It gives me great pleasure** to introduce our guest speaker.* ➲ SYNONYMS at FUN **2** 🗝 [U] the activity of enjoying yourself, especially in contrast to working: *Are you in Paris on business or pleasure?* ➲ SYNONYMS at ENTERTAINMENT **3** 🗝 [C] a thing that makes you happy or satisfied: *the pleasure and pains of*

P

everyday life ◇ *the simple pleasures of the countryside* ◇ ***It's a pleasure*** *to meet you.* ◇ *'Thanks for doing that.'* ***'It's a pleasure.'*** ➲ compare DISPLEASURE

IDM **at your/sb's 'pleasure** (*formal*) as you want; as sb else wants: *The land can be sold at the owner's pleasure.* **my 'pleasure** used as a polite way of replying when sb thanks you for doing sth, to show that you were happy to do it **with 'pleasure** ⚷ used as a polite way of accepting or agreeing to sth: *'May I sit here?' 'Yes, with pleasure.'*

Synonyms

pleasure

delight • joy • privilege • treat • honour

These are all words for things that make you happy or bring you enjoyment.

pleasure a thing that brings you enjoyment or satisfaction: *the pleasures and pains of everyday life* ◇ ***It's been a pleasure*** *meeting you.*

delight a thing or person that brings you great enjoyment or satisfaction: *the delights of living in the country*

joy a thing or person that brings you great enjoyment or happiness: *the joys and sorrows of childhood*

PLEASURE, DELIGHT OR JOY?

A **delight** or **joy** is greater than a **pleasure**; a person, especially a child, can be a **delight** or **joy**, but not a **pleasure**; **joys** are often contrasted with **sorrows**, but **delights** are not.

privilege (*rather formal*) something that you are proud and lucky to have the opportunity to do: *It was a great privilege to hear her sing.*

treat (*informal*) a thing that sb enjoyed or is likely to enjoy very much: *You've never been to this area before? Then you're* ***in for a real treat.***

honour/honor (*formal*) something that you are very pleased or proud to do because people are showing you great respect: *It was a great honour to be invited here today.*

PATTERNS

- the pleasures/delights/joys **of** sth
- **It's a great** pleasure/joy **to me that...**
- **It's a** pleasure/delight/joy/privilege/treat/honour **to do sth**
- **It's a** pleasure/delight/joy **to see/find...**
- a pleasure/delight/joy **to behold/watch**
- a **real** pleasure/delight/joy/privilege/treat
- a **great** pleasure/joy/privilege/honour
- a **rare** joy/privilege/treat/honour

'pleasure boat (also **'pleasure craft**) *noun* a boat used for short pleasure trips

pleat /pliːt/ *noun* a permanent fold in a piece of cloth, made by sewing the top or side of the fold

pleat·ed /'pliːtɪd/ *adj.* having pleats: *a pleated skirt*

plea·ther /'pleðə(r)/ *noun* [U] a plastic material that looks like leather: *a pleather jacket* ORIGIN from 'plastic' and 'leather'

pleb /pleb/ *noun* (*disapproving*) an ordinary person, especially one who is poor or not well educated

plebe /pliːb/ *noun* (*US, informal*) a first-year student at a military or NAVAL college in the US

ple·beian /plə'biːən/ *adj., noun*

▪ ***adj.*** **1** connected with ordinary people or people of the lower social classes **2** (*disapproving*) lacking in culture or education: *plebeian tastes*

▪ ***noun*** (usually *disapproving*) a person from a lower social class (used originally in ancient Rome) ➲ compare PATRICIAN

pleb·is·cite /'plebɪsɪt; -saɪt/ *noun* **~** (**on sth**) (*politics*) a vote by the people of a country or a region on an issue that is very important SYN **referendum**: *to* ***hold a plebiscite*** *on the country's future system of government*

plebs /plebz/ *noun* (usually **the plebs**) [pl.] (*informal*) an offensive way of referring to ordinary people, especially those of the lower social classes

plec·trum /'plektrəm/ *noun* (*pl.* **plec·trums** or **plec·tra** /-trə/) (also *informal* **pick**) a small piece of metal, plastic, etc. used for PLUCKING the strings of a GUITAR or similar instrument

pled (*US*) *past tense, past part.* of PLEAD

pledge /pledʒ/ *noun, verb*

▪ ***noun*** **1** a serious promise SYN **commitment**: **~** (**of sth**) *a pledge of support* ◇ **~** (**to do sth** *Will the government* ***honour*** *its election* ***pledge*** *not to raise taxes?* ◇ **~** (**that...**) *Management has* ***given a pledge*** *that there will be no job losses this year.* **2** a sum of money or sth valuable that you leave with sb to prove that you will do sth or pay back money that you owe

IDM **sign/take the 'pledge** (*old-fashioned*) to make a promise never to drink alcohol

▪ ***verb*** **1** [T] to formally promise to give or do sth: **~ sth** *Japan has pledged $100 million in humanitarian aid.* ◇ *The government* ***pledged their support*** *for the plan.* ◇ **~ sth to sb/sth** *We all had to* ***pledge allegiance*** *to the flag* (= state that we are loyal to our country). ◇ **~ to do sth** *The group has pledged to continue campaigning.* ◇ **~** (**that**)... *The group has pledged that they will continue campaigning.* **2** [T] to make sb or yourself formally promise to do sth SYN **swear**: **~ sb/yourself** (**to sth**) *They were all pledged to secrecy.* ◇ **~ sb/yourself to do sth** *The government has pledged itself to root out corruption.* **3** [T] **~ sth** to leave sth with sb as a pledge (2) **4** [I, T] (*NAmE*) to promise to become a junior member of a FRATERNITY or SORORITY: *Do you think you'll pledge this semester?* ◇ **~ sth** *My brother pledged Sigma Nu.*

the ˌPledge of Al'legiance *noun* [sing.] a formal promise to be loyal to the US, which Americans make standing in front of the flag with their right hand on their heart

plen·ary /'pliːnəri/ *adj., noun*

▪ ***adj.*** [only before noun] (*formal*) **1** (of meetings, etc.) to be attended by everyone who has the right to attend: *The new committee holds its first* ***plenary session*** *this week.* **2** without any limit; complete: *The Council has plenary powers to administer the agreement.*

▪ ***noun*** (*pl.* **-ies**) a plenary meeting

pleni·po·ten·tiary /ˌplenɪpə'tenʃəri; *NAmE* also -ʃieri/ *noun* (*pl.* **-ies**) (*technical*) a person who has full powers to take action, make decisions, etc. on behalf of their government, especially in a foreign country ▸ **pleni·po·ten·tiary** *adj.*: *plenipotentiary powers*

pleni·tude /'plenɪtjuːd; *NAmE* -tuːd/ *noun* [sing., U] (*formal*) a large amount of sth SYN **abundance**

plent·eous /'plentiəs/ *adj.* (*literary*) = PLENTIFUL

plen·ti·ful /'plentɪfl/ (also **plent·eous**) *adj.* available or existing in large amounts or numbers SYN **abundant**: *a* ***plentiful supply*** *of food* ◇ *In those days jobs were plentiful.* ▸ **plen·ti·ful·ly** /-fəli/ *adv.*: *Evidence is plentifully available.* ◇ *She kept them plentifully supplied with gossip.*

plenty ⚷ /'plenti/ *pron., adv., noun, det.*

▪ ***pron.*** ⚷ **~** (**of sth**) a large amount; as much or as many as you need: *plenty of eggs/money/time* ◇ *'Do we need more milk?' 'No, there's plenty in the fridge.'* ◇ *They always gave us plenty to eat.* ◇ *We had plenty to talk about.* ➲ note at MANY, MUCH

▪ ***adv.*** **1** ⚷ **~ more** (**of**) (**sth**) a lot: *We have plenty more of them in the warehouse.* ◇ *There's plenty more paper if you need it.* **2 ~ big, long, etc. enough** (**to do sth**) (*informal*) more than big, long, etc. enough: *The rope was plenty long enough to reach the ground.* **3** (*NAmE*) a lot; very: *We talked plenty about our kids.* ◇ *You can be married and still be plenty lonely.* IDM see FISH *n.*

▪ ***noun*** [U] (*formal*) a situation in which there is a large sup-

P

ply of food, money, etc: *Everyone is happier **in times of plenty**.* ◇ *We had food and drink **in plenty**.*
■ ***det.*** (*NAmE* or *informal*) a lot of: *There's plenty room for all of you!*

ple·num /ˈpliːnəm/ *noun* a meeting attended by all the members of a committee, etc; a PLENARY meeting

ple·on·asm /ˈpliːənæzəm/ *noun* [U, C] (*technical*) the use of more words than are necessary to express a meaning. For example, 'see with your eyes' is a pleonasm because the same meaning can be expressed using 'see'. ▶ **ple·on·as·tic** /ˌpliːəˈnæstɪk/ *adj.*

pleth·ora /ˈpleθərə/ *noun* [sing.] (*formal*) an amount that is greater than is needed or can be used SYN **excess**

pleura /ˈplʊərə; *NAmE* ˈplʊrə/ *noun* (*pl.* **pleurae** /-riː/) (*anatomy*) one of the two MEMBRANES that surround the lungs

pleur·isy /ˈplʊərəsi; *NAmE* ˈplʊr-/ *noun* [U] a serious illness that affects the inner covering of the chest and lungs, causing severe pain in the chest or sides

Plexi·glas™ /ˈpleksiglɑːs; *NAmE* -glæs/ (*NAmE*) (*BrE* **Per·spex™**) *noun* [U] a strong transparent plastic material that is often used instead of glass

plexus ➲ SOLAR PLEXUS

pli·able /ˈplaɪəbl/ *adj.* **1** easy to bend without breaking SYN **flexible 2** (of people) easy to influence or control SYN **impressionable**

pli·ant /ˈplaɪənt/ *adj.* **1** (of a person or their body) soft and giving way to sb, especially in a sexual way: *her pliant body* ◇ *She lay pliant in his arms.* **2** (sometimes *disapproving*) willing to accept change; easy to influence or control: *He was deposed and replaced by a more pliant successor.* ▶ **pli·ancy** /ˈplaɪənsi/ *noun* [U] **pli·ant·ly** *adv.*

pli·ers /ˈplaɪəz; *NAmE* -ərz/ *noun* [pl.] a metal tool with handles, used for holding things firmly and twisting and cutting wire: *a pair of pliers* ➲ VISUAL VOCAB page V17

plight /plaɪt/ *noun, verb*
■ ***noun*** [sing.] a difficult and sad situation: *the plight of the homeless* ◇ *The African elephant is in a desperate plight.*
■ ***verb***
IDM **plight your ˈtroth** (*old use* or *humorous*) to make a promise to a person saying that you will marry them; to marry sb

plim·soll /ˈplɪmsəl/ (also **pump**) (both *BrE*) (also **ˈgym shoe** *BrE, NAmE*) *noun* a light simple sports shoe made of CANVAS (= strong cotton cloth) with a rubber SOLE: *a pair of plimsolls*

ˈPlimsoll line (also **ˈload line**) *noun* a line on the side of a ship showing the highest point that the water can safely reach when the ship is loaded

plinth /plɪnθ/ *noun* a block of stone on which a column or statue stands ➲ VISUAL VOCAB page V12

plod /plɒd; *NAmE* plɑːd/ *verb* (**-dd-**) [I, T] to walk slowly with heavy steps, especially because you are tired SYN **trudge**: **+ adv./prep.** *Our horses plodded down the muddy track.* ◇ *We plodded on through the rain.* ◇ **~ your way + adv./prep.** *I watched her plodding her way across the field.* ▶ **plod** *noun* [sing.]
PHR V **ˌplod aˈlong/ˈon** to make very slow progress, especially with difficult or boring work SYN **slog**

plod·der /ˈplɒdə(r); *NAmE* ˈplɑːd-/ *noun* a person who works slowly and steadily but without imagination

plod·ding /ˈplɒdɪŋ; *NAmE* ˈplɑːd-/ *adj.* working or doing sth slowly and steadily, especially in a way that other people think is boring

plonk /plɒŋk; *NAmE* plɑːŋk/ *verb, noun*
■ ***verb*** (*especially BrE*) (*NAmE* usually **plunk**) (*informal*) **1 ~ sth + adv./prep.** to put sth down on sth, especially noisily or carelessly: *He plonked the books down on the table.* ◇ *Just plonk your bag anywhere.* **2 ~ yourself (down)** to sit down heavily or carelessly: *He just plonked himself down and turned on the TV.*
■ ***noun*** (*informal, especially BrE*) **1** [U] cheap wine that is not of good quality **2** [C, usually sing.] a low sound like that of sth heavy falling and hitting a surface: *She sat down with a plonk.*

plonk·er /ˈplɒŋkə(r); *NAmE* ˈplɑːŋk-/ *noun* (*BrE, slang*) a stupid person

plop /plɒp; *NAmE* plɑːp/ *noun, verb*
■ ***noun*** [usually sing.] a short sound like that of a small object dropping into water
■ ***verb*** (**-pp-**) **1** [I] **+ adv./prep.** to fall, making a plop: *The frog plopped back into the water.* ◇ *A tear plopped down onto the page she was reading.* **2** [T] **~ sth + adv./prep.** to drop sth into sth, especially a liquid, so that it makes a plop: *Can you just plop some ice in my drink?* **3** [T, I] **~ (yourself) (down)** to sit or lie down heavily or in a relaxed way

plo·sive /ˈpləʊsɪv; *NAmE* ˈploʊ-/ *noun* (*phonetics*) a speech sound made by stopping the flow of air coming out of the mouth and then suddenly releasing it, for example /t/ and /p/ in *top* ▶ **plo·sive** *adj.*

plot 🔑 /plɒt; *NAmE* plɑːt/ *noun, verb*
■ ***noun*** **1** 🔑 [C, U] the series of events that form the story of a novel, play, film/movie, etc: *a conventional plot about love and marriage* ◇ *The book is well organized in terms of plot.* ➲ COLLOCATIONS at LITERATURE **2** 🔑 [C] **~ (to do sth)** a secret plan made by a group of people to do sth wrong or illegal SYN **conspiracy 3** 🔑 [C] a small piece of land that is used or intended for a special purpose: *She bought a small plot of land to build a house on.* ◇ *a vegetable plot* ➲ SYNONYMS at LAND
IDM **ˌlose the ˈplot** (*BrE, informal*) to lose your ability to understand or deal with what is happening **the plot ˈthickens** used to say that a situation is becoming more complicated and difficult to understand
■ ***verb*** (**-tt-**) **1** 🔑 [I, T] to make a secret plan to harm sb, especially a government or its leader SYN **conspire**: **~ (with sb) (against sb)** *They were accused of plotting against the state.* ◇ **~ sth** *Military officers were suspected of plotting a coup.* ◇ **~ to do sth** *They were plotting to overthrow the government.* **2** [T] **~ sth (on sth)** to mark sth on a map, for example the position or course of sth: *The earthquake centres had been plotted on a world map.* **3** [T] **~ sth (on sth)** to make a diagram or chart from some information: *We carefully plotted each patient's response to the drug on a chart.* **4** [T] **~ sth (on sth)** to mark points on a GRAPH and draw a line or curve connecting them: *First, plot the temperature curve on the graph.* **5** [T] **~ sth** to write the plot of a novel, play, etc: *a tightly-plotted thriller*

plot·ter /ˈplɒtə(r); *NAmE* ˈplɑːtər/ *noun* **1** a person who makes a secret plan to harm sb SYN **conspirator 2** a device that turns data from a computer into a GRAPH, usually on paper

plough (*NAmE* **plow**) /plaʊ/ *noun, verb*
■ ***noun*** **1** [C] a large piece of farming equipment with one or several curved blades, pulled by a TRACTOR or by animals. It is used for digging and turning over soil, especially before seeds are planted. ➲ see also SNOWPLOUGH **2 the Plough** (*BrE*) (*NAmE* **the ˌBig ˈDipper**) [sing.] a group of seven bright stars that can only be seen from the northern half of the world
IDM **under the ˈplough** (*BrE, formal*) (of land) used for growing crops, not for keeping animals on SYN **arable**
■ ***verb*** [T, I] **~ (sth)** to dig and turn over a field or other area of land with a plough: *ploughed fields* ➲ COLLOCATIONS at FARMING
IDM **ˌplough a lonely, your own, etc, ˈfurrow** (*literary*) to do things that other people do not do, or be interested in things that other people are not interested in
PHR V **ˌplough sth↔ˈback (in/into sth)** | **ˌplough sth↔back ˈin 1** to turn over growing crops, grass, etc. with a plough and mix them into the soil to improve its quality **2** to put money made as profit back into a business in order to improve it: *The money was all ploughed back into the company.* **ˈplough into sb/sth** (especially of a vehicle or its driver) to crash violently into sth, especially because you are driving too fast or not paying enough attention: *A truck ploughed into the back of the bus.* **ˌplough sth ˈinto sth** to invest a large amount of money in a company or project: *The government has ploughed more than $20 billion into building new schools.* **ˌplough**

P

ˈon (**with sth**) to continue doing sth that is difficult or boring: *No one was listening to her, but she* ***ploughed on regardless.*** ˌ**plough** (**your way**) ˈ**through sth 1** to force a way through sth: *She ploughed her way through the waiting crowds.* **2** (of a vehicle or an aircraft) to go violently through sth, out of control: *The plane ploughed through the trees.* **3** to make slow progress through sth difficult or boring, especially a book, a report, etc: *I had to plough through dozens of legal documents* . ˌ**plough sth↔ˈup 1** to turn over a field or other area of land with a plough to change it from grass, for example, to land for growing crops **2** to break up the surface of the ground by walking or driving across it again and again: *The paths get all ploughed up by motorbikes.*

plough·man (*NAmE* **plow·man**) /ˈplaʊmən/ *noun* (*pl.* -men /-mən/) a man whose job is guiding a plough, especially one pulled by animals

ˌ**ploughman's ˈlunch** (also ˈ**ploughman's**) *noun* (*BrE*) a cold meal of bread, cheese, PICKLE and salad, often served in pubs

plough·share (*NAmE* **plow·share**) /ˈplaʊʃeə(r); *NAmE* -ʃer/ (*NAmE* also **share**) *noun* the broad curved blade of a PLOUGH IDM see SWORD

plover /ˈplʌvə(r)/ *noun* a bird with long legs and a short tail that lives on wet ground

plow, plow·man, plow·share (*NAmE*) = PLOUGH, PLOUGHMAN, PLOUGHSHARE

ploy /plɔɪ/ *noun* words or actions that are carefully planned to get an advantage over sb else SYN **manoeuvre**: *a clever marketing ploy* ◇ **~ to do sth** *It was all a ploy to distract attention from his real aims.*

pluck /plʌk/ *verb, noun*

■ ***verb***

▸ HAIR **1** [T] **~ sth** (**out**) to pull out hairs with your fingers or with TWEEZERS: *She plucked out a grey hair.* ◇ *expertly plucked eyebrows*

▸ CHICKEN, ETC. **2** [T] **~ sth** to pull the feathers off a dead bird, for example a chicken, in order to prepare it for cooking

P

▸ MUSICAL INSTRUMENT **3** (*NAmE* also **pick**) [T, I] **~** (**at**) **sth** to play a musical instrument, especially a GUITAR, by pulling the strings with your fingers: *to pluck the strings of a violin* ◇ *He took the guitar and plucked at the strings.*

▸ REMOVE SB/STH **4** [T] **~ sb** (**from sth**) (**to sth**) to remove sb from a place or situation, especially one that is unpleasant or dangerous: *Police plucked a drowning girl from the river yesterday.* ◇ *Survivors of the wreck were* ***plucked to safety*** *by a helicopter.* ◇ *She was plucked from obscurity to instant stardom.* **5** [T] **~ sth** (**from sth**) to take hold of sth and remove it by pulling it: *He plucked the wallet from the man's grasp.*

▸ FRUIT/FLOWER **6** [T] **~ sth** (**from sth**) (*old-fashioned* or *literary*) to pick a fruit, flower, etc. from where it is growing: *I plucked an orange from the tree.*

IDM **pluck sth out of the ˈair** to say a name, number, etc. without thinking about it, especially in answer to a question: *I just plucked a figure out of the air and said: 'Would £1000 seem reasonable to you?'* **pluck up** (**the**) ˈ**courage** (**to do sth**) to make yourself do sth even though you are afraid to do it: *I finally plucked up the courage to ask her for a date.*

PHR V ˈ**pluck at sth** to hold sth with the fingers and pull it gently, especially more than once SYN **tug**: *The child kept plucking at his mother's sleeve.* ◇ (*figurative*) *The wind plucked at my jacket.*

■ ***noun*** [U] (*informal*) courage and determination: *It takes a lot of pluck to do what she did.*

plucky /ˈplʌki/ *adj.* (*informal*) (**pluck·ier, plucki·est**) having a lot of courage and determination SYN **brave** ▸ **pluck·ily** *adv.*

plug /plʌg/ *noun, verb*

■ ***noun***

▸ ELECTRICAL EQUIPMENT **1** a small plastic object with two or three metal pins, that connects a piece of electrical equipment to the main supply of electricity: *a three-pin plug* ◇ *I'll have to* ***change the plug*** *on my hairdryer.* **2** (*informal, especially BrE*) a small opening in a wall, by which you connect a piece of electrical equipment to the main supply of electricity SYN **socket**: *Can I use this plug for my iron?* **3** a small object that connects a wire from one piece of electrical equipment to an opening in another: *the plug from the computer to the printer*

▸ IN ENGINE **4** = SPARK PLUG

▸ IN BATH/SINK **5** a thick round piece of plastic, rubber or metal that you put in the hole in a bath/BATHTUB or a SINK to stop the water flowing out: *She* ***pulled out the plug*** *and let the water drain away.* ➲ SYNONYMS at LID ➲ VISUAL VOCAB page V21

▸ IN HOLE **6** a round piece of material that fits into a hole and blocks it: *She took the plug of cotton wool from her ear.* ➲ see also EARPLUG **7** (*NAmE*) = STOPPER ➲ SYNONYMS at LID

▸ FOR SCREW **8** a small plastic tube that you put into a hole in a wall so that it will hold a screw

▸ FOR BOOK/MOVIE **9** (*informal*) praise or attention that sb gives to a new book, film/movie, etc. in order to encourage people to buy or see it: *He managed to get in a plug for his new book.* IDM see PULL *v.*

plugs

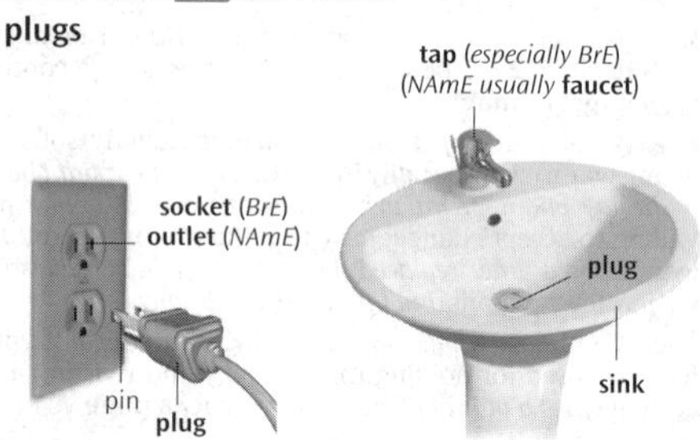

■ ***verb*** (-gg-)

▸ FILL HOLE **1 ~ sth** (**up**) to fill a hole with a substance or piece of material that fits tightly into it: *He plugged the hole in the pipe with an old rag.*

▸ PROVIDE STH MISSING **2 ~ sth** to provide sth that has been missing from a particular situation and is needed in order to improve it: *A cheaper range of products was introduced to* ***plug the gap*** *at the lower end of the market.*

▸ BOOK/MOVIE **3 ~ sth** (*informal*) to give praise or attention to a new book, film/movie, etc. in order to encourage people to buy it or see it SYN **promote**: *She came on the show to plug her latest album.*

▸ SHOOT **4 ~ sb** (*old-fashioned, NAmE, informal*) to shoot sb

PHR V ˌ**plug aˈway** (**at sth**) to continue working hard at sth, especially sth that you find difficult ˌ**plug sth↔ˈin** | ˌ**plug sth ˈinto sth** to connect a piece of electrical equipment to the main supply of electricity or to another piece of electrical equipment: *Is the printer plugged in?* OPP **unplug** ˌ**plug sth ˈinto sth 1** = TO PLUG STH IN **2** to connect a computer to a computer system: *All our computers are plugged into the main network.* ˌ**plug ˈinto sth 1** (of a piece of electrical equipment) to be able to be connected to the main supply of electricity or to another piece of electrical equipment: *The DVD player plugs into the back of the television.* **2** to become involved with a particular activity or group of people: *The company has doubled its profits since plugging into lucrative overseas markets.*

ˌ**Plug and ˈPlay** *noun* [U] (*computing*) a system that makes it possible for a piece of equipment, such as a printer, to be connected to a computer and to work immediately, without the user needing to do anything ▸ ˌ**plug-and-ˈplay** *adj.*: *plug-and-play peripherals*

plug·hole /ˈplʌghəʊl; *NAmE* -hoʊl/ (*BrE*) (*US* **drain**) *noun* a hole in a bath/BATHTUB, SINK, etc. where the water flows away and into which a plug fits ➲ VISUAL VOCAB page V21

IDM (**go**) **down the ˈplughole** (*BrE*) = (GO) DOWN THE DRAIN at DRAIN *n.*

ˈ**plug-in** *adj.*, *noun*
■ ***adj.*** [only before noun] **1** able to be connected using a plug: *a plug-in kettle* **2** (*computing*) able to be added to a computer system so that it can do more things: *a plug-in graphics card*
■ ***noun*** **1** (*computing*) a piece of computer software that can be added to a system so that it can do more things **2** (*CanE*) a connection to an electricity supply in a garage, etc. so that you can use an electric HEATER to warm the engine of a car, so that it starts more easily

ˌ**plug-ˈugly** *adj.* (*informal*) very ugly

plum /plʌm/ *noun*, *adj.*
■ ***noun*** **1** [C] a soft round fruit with smooth red or purple skin, sweet flesh and a large flat seed inside: *a plum tree* **2** [U, C] a dark reddish-purple colour
■ ***adj.*** [only before noun] (of a job, etc.) considered very good and worth having: *She's landed a plum job at the BBC.*

plum·age /ˈplu:mɪdʒ/ *noun* [U] the feathers covering a bird's body

plumb /plʌm/ *verb*, *adv.*
■ ***verb*** **~ sth** (*literary*) to try to understand or succeed in understanding sth mysterious SYN **fathom**: *She spent her life plumbing the mysteries of the human psyche.*
IDM **plumb the depths of sth** to be or to experience an extreme example of sth unpleasant: *His latest novel plumbs the depths of horror and violence.* ◇ *The team's poor performances* ***plumbed new depths*** *last night when they lost 10-2.*
PHR V ˌ**plumb sth↔ˈin** (*especially BrE*) to connect a WASHING MACHINE, toilet, etc. to the water supply in a building
■ ***adv.*** **1** (used before prepositions) exactly: *He was standing plumb in the middle of the road.* **2** (*old-fashioned, NAmE, informal*) completely: *He's plumb crazy.*

plumb·er /ˈplʌmə(r)/ *noun* a person whose job is to fit and repair things such as water pipes, toilets, etc.

plumb·ing /ˈplʌmɪŋ/ *noun* [U] **1** the system of pipes, etc. that supply water to a building ➲ **COLLOCATIONS** at DECORATE **2** the work of a plumber

ˈ**plumb line** *noun* a piece of thick string with a weight attached to one end, used to find the depth of water or to test whether a wall, etc. is straight

plume /plu:m/ *noun* **1** a cloud of sth that rises and curves upwards in the air: *a plume of smoke* **2** a large feather: *a black hat with an ostrich plume* **3** a group of feathers or long thin pieces of material tied together and often used as a decoration ➲ see also NOM DE PLUME

plumed /ˈplu:md/ *adj.* having or decorated with a plume or plumes: *a plumed helmet*

plum·met /ˈplʌmɪt/ *verb* [I] to fall suddenly and quickly from a high level or position SYN **plunge**: *Share prices plummeted to an all-time low.* ◇ *Her spirits plummeted at the thought of meeting him again.* ◇ *The jet plummeted into a row of houses.*

plummy /ˈplʌmi/ *adj.* **1** (*BrE, informal*, usually *disapproving*) (of a voice) having a sound that is typical of upper-class English people: *a plummy accent* **2** like a PLUM in colour, taste, etc.

plump /plʌmp/ *adj.*, *verb*
■ ***adj.*** (**plump·er**, **plump·est**) **1** having a soft, round body; slightly fat: *a short, plump woman* ◇ *a plump face* **2** looking soft, full and attractive to use or eat: *plump cushions* ◇ *plump tomatoes* ▶ **plump·ness** *noun* [U]
■ ***verb*** **~ sth** (**up**) to make sth larger, softer and rounder: *He leaned forward while the nurse plumped up his pillows.*
PHR V ˈ**plump for sb/sth** (*informal*) to choose sb/sth from a number of people or things, especially after thinking carefully

ˌ**plum ˈpudding** *noun* [U, C] (*old-fashioned, BrE*) = CHRISTMAS PUDDING

ˌ**plum toˈmato** *noun* an Italian tomato that is long and thin, rather than round

plun·der /ˈplʌndə(r)/ *verb*, *noun*
■ ***verb*** [I, T] to steal things from a place, especially using force during a time of war SYN **loot**: *The troops crossed the country, plundering and looting as they went.* ◇ **~ sth** (**of sth**) *The abbey had been plundered of its valuables.* ◇ **~ sth** (**from sth**) *Only a small amount of the money that he plundered from his companies has been recovered.* ➲ compare PILLAGE ▶ **plun·der·er** *noun*
■ ***noun*** [U] **1** the act of plundering **2** things that have been stolen, especially during a war, etc. ➲ compare PILLAGE

plunge /plʌndʒ/ *verb*, *noun*
■ ***verb*** **1** [I, T] to move or make sb/sth move suddenly forwards and/or downwards: **+ adv./prep.** *She lost her balance and plunged 100 feet to her death.* ◇ **~ sb/sth + adv./prep.** *The earthquake plunged entire towns over the edge of the cliffs.* **2** [I] (of prices, temperatures, etc.) to decrease suddenly and quickly SYN **plummet**: *Stock markets plunged at the news of the coup.* **3** [I] **+ adv./prep.** (of a road, surface, etc.) to slope down steeply: *The track plunged down into the valley.* **4** [I] to move up and down suddenly and violently: *The horse plunged and reared.* ◇ (*figurative*) *His heart plunged* (= because of a strong emotion).
PHR V ˌ**plunge ˈin** | ˌ**plunge ˈinto sth** **1** to jump into sth, especially with force: *The pool was declared open and eager swimmers plunged in.* **2** to start doing sth in an enthusiastic way, especially without thinking carefully about what you are doing: *She was about to plunge into her story when the phone rang.* ◇ *He's always plunging in at the deep end* (= becoming involved in difficult situations without being well enough prepared). ˌ**plunge sth ˈin** | ˌ**plunge sth ˈinto sth** to push sth quickly and with force into sth else: *She plunged the knife deep into his chest.* ˌ**plunge ˈinto sth** **1** = PLUNGE IN **2** to experience sth unpleasant: *The country plunged deeper into recession.* ˌ**plunge sb/sth ˈinto sth** to make sb/sth experience sth unpleasant: *The news plunged them into deep depression.* ◇ *There was a flash of lightning and the house was* ***plunged into darkness***.
■ ***noun*** [usually sing.] **1** a sudden movement downwards or away from sth SYN **drop**: *The calm water ends there and the river begins a headlong plunge.* **2 ~** (**in sth**) a sudden decrease in an amount or the value of sth SYN **drop**: *a dramatic plunge in profits* **3 ~ into sth** the act of becoming involved in a situation or activity: *The company is planning a deeper plunge into the commercial market.* **4** an act of jumping or DIVING into water; a quick swim: *He took the plunge into the deep end.* ◇ *She went for a plunge.*
IDM **take the ˈplunge** (*informal*) to decide to do sth important or difficult, especially after thinking about it for a long time

ˈ**plunge pool** *noun* a small deep artificial pool filled with cold water, especially one that you jump into in order to get cooler after a SAUNA

plun·ger /ˈplʌndʒə(r)/ *noun* **1** a part of a piece of equipment that can be pushed down ➲ **VISUAL VOCAB** page V22 **2** a piece of equipment used for clearing kitchen and bathroom pipes, that consists of a rubber cup fixed to a handle

plun·ging /ˈplʌndʒɪŋ/ *adj.* [only before noun] (of a dress, BLOUSE, etc.) cut in a deep V shape at the front: *a plunging neckline*

plunk /plʌŋk/ *verb* (*informal*) **1 ~ sth + adv./prep.** (*NAmE*) = PLONK: *He plunked the package down on the desk.* **2 ~ sth** to play a GUITAR, a keyboard, etc. with your fingers and produce a rough unpleasant sound ▶ **plunk** *noun*: *the plunk, plunk of the banjo*
PHR V ˈ**plunk down sth** to pay money for sth, especially a large amount

plu·per·fect /ˌplu:ˈpɜ:fɪkt; *NAmE* -ˈpɜ:rf-/ *noun* (*grammar*) = PAST PERFECT

plural /ˈplʊərəl; *NAmE* ˈplʊrəl/ *noun*, *adj.*
■ ***noun*** (*grammar*) (*abbr.* **pl.**) a form of a noun or verb that refers to more than one person or thing: *The plural of 'child' is 'children'.* ◇ *The verb should be* ***in the plural***. ➲ compare SINGULAR
■ ***adj.*** **1** (*grammar*) (*abbr.* **pl.**) connected with or having the plural form: *Most plural nouns in English end in 's'.* **2** relating to more than one: *a plural society* (= one with more than one RACIAL, religious, etc. group)

P

plur·al·ism /ˈplʊərəlɪzəm; *NAmE* ˈplʊr-/ *noun* [U] (*formal*) **1** the existence of many different groups of people in one society, for example people of different races or of different political or religious beliefs: *cultural pluralism* **2** the belief that it is possible and good for different groups of people to live together in peace in one society **3** (usually *disapproving*) the fact of having more than one job or position at the same time, especially in the Church

plur·al·ist /ˈplʊərəlɪst; *NAmE* ˈplʊr-/ *adj., noun*
- *adj.* (also **plur·al·is·tic** /ˌplʊərəˈlɪstɪk; *NAmE* ˌplʊr-/) **1** (of a society) having many different groups of people and different political parties in it: *a pluralist democracy* **2** (*philosophy*) not based on a single set of principles or beliefs: *a pluralist approach to politics*
- *noun* **1** a person who believes that it is possible and good for different groups of people to live together in peace in our society **2** a person who has more than one job or position at the same time, especially in the Church

plur·al·ity /plʊəˈræləti; *NAmE* plʊˈr-/ *noun* (*pl.* -ies) **1** [C, usually sing.] (*formal*) a large number: *a plurality of influences* **2** [C, usually sing.] (*politics*) (*US*) the number of votes given to one person, political party, etc. when this number is less than 50% but more than any other single person, etc. receives: *In order to be elected, a candidate needs only a plurality of the votes cast.* ➲ compare MAJORITY **3** [U] (*grammar*) the state of being plural

plur·al·ize (*BrE* also **-ise**) /ˈplʊərəlaɪz; *NAmE* ˈplʊrə-/ *verb* **~ sth** to make a word plural ▸ **plur·al·iza·tion** /ˌplʊərəlaɪˈzeɪʃn; *NAmE* ˌplʊrələˈzeɪʃn/ *noun* [U]

plus[1] 🔑 AW /plʌs/ *prep., noun, adj., conj.*
- *prep.* **1** 🔑 used when the two numbers or amounts mentioned are being added together: *Two plus five is seven.* ◊ *The cost is £22, plus £1 for postage.* **2** 🔑 as well as sth/sb; and also: *We have to fit five of us plus all our gear in the car.* OPP **minus**

IDM **plus or ˈminus** used when the number mentioned may actually be more or less by a particular amount SYN **give or take**: *The margin of error was plus or minus three percentage points.*
- *noun* **1** (*informal*) an advantage; a good thing: *Knowledge of French is a plus in her job.* ◊ *There were a lot of pluses in the performance.* **2** (also ˈ**plus sign**) the symbol (+), used in mathematics: *He put a plus instead of a minus.* OPP **minus**
- *adj.* **1** used after a number to show that the real number or amount is more than the one mentioned: *The work will cost £10 000 plus.* **2** 🔑 above zero: *The temperature is plus four degrees.* OPP **minus** **3** 🔑 [only before noun] used to describe an aspect of sth that you consider to be a good thing: *One of the hotel's **plus points** is that it is very central.* ◊ ***On the plus side**, all the staff are enthusiastic.* OPP **minus** **4** [not before noun] (used in a system of marks/grades) slightly higher than the mark/grade A, B, etc: *I got B plus (B+) in the test.* OPP **minus**
- *conj.* 🔑 (*informal*) used to add more information SYN **furthermore**: *I've got too much on at work. Plus my father is not well.*

plus[2] /pluː/

IDM **plus ça change** /ˌpluː sæ ˈʃɒ̃ʒ; *NAmE* -sɑː ˈʃɑːnʒ/ (*saying*, from *French*) used as a way of saying that people and situations never really change over time, although they may appear to

ˌplus ˈfours *noun* [pl.] (*BrE*) wide loose trousers/pants that end just below the knees, where they fit closely, and that used to be worn, for example, by men playing GOLF: *a pair of plus fours*

plush /plʌʃ/ *noun, adj.*
- *noun* [U] a type of silk or cotton cloth with a thick soft surface made of a mass of threads: *red plush armchairs*
- *adj.* (*informal*) very comfortable; expensive and of good quality SYN **luxurious**: *a plush hotel*

ˌplus-ˈminus *adv.* (*SAfrE*) (used when you are giving a figure that is not exact) approximately: *'How many people were there?' 'Plus-minus thirty.'*

Pluto /ˈpluːtəʊ; *NAmE* -toʊ/ *noun* one of a number of round objects in space that are not as large as planets but which go around the sun. In August 2006, the International Astronomical Union declared that Pluto should be called a DWARF PLANET because it is smaller and has different characteristics from the other planets in our SOLAR SYSTEM; in 2008 it declared that DWARF PLANETS further from the sun than Neptune could also be called plutoids.

plu·toc·racy /pluːˈtɒkrəsi; *NAmE* -ˈtɑːk-/ *noun* (*pl.* -ies) **1** [U] government by the richest people of a country **2** [C] a country governed by the richest people in it

plu·to·crat /ˈpluːtəkræt/ *noun* (often *disapproving*) a person who is powerful because of their wealth

plu·toid /ˈpluːtɔɪd/ *noun* any DWARF PLANET that is further from the sun than the planet Neptune

plu·to·nium /pluːˈtəʊniəm; *NAmE* -ˈtoʊ-/ *noun* [U] (*symb.* Pu) a chemical element. Plutonium is RADIOACTIVE and is used in nuclear weapons and in producing nuclear energy.

ply /plaɪ/ *verb, noun*
- *verb* (**plies, ply·ing, plied, plied**) **1** [I, T] (*literary* or *IndE*) (of ships, buses, etc.) to travel regularly along a particular route or between two particular places: **+ adv./prep.** *Ferries ply across a narrow strait to the island.* ◊ *Buses ply regularly to and from these places.* ◊ **~ sth** *canals plied by gondolas and steam boats* **2** [T] **~ sth** (*formal*) to use a tool, especially in a skilful way: *The tailor delicately plied his needle.*

IDM **ply your ˈtrade** to do your work or business **ply for ˈhire/ˈtrade/ˈbusiness** (*BrE*) to look for customers, passengers, etc. in order to do business: *taxis plying for hire outside the theatre*

PHR V **ˈply sb with sth** **1** to keep giving sb large amounts of sth, especially food and/or drink **2** to keep asking sb questions: *He plied me with questions from the moment he arrived.*
- *noun* [U] (especially in compounds) a measurement of wool, rope, wood, etc. that tells you how thick it is: *four-ply knitting yarn*

Ply·mouth Breth·ren /ˌplɪməθ ˈbreðrən/ *noun* [pl.] a strict Protestant group started in England around 1830

ply·wood /ˈplaɪwʊd/ *noun* [U] board made by sticking thin layers of wood on top of each other: *plywood furniture*

PM /ˌpiː ˈem/ *noun* (*informal, especially BrE*) the abbreviation for 'prime minister': *an interview with the PM*

p.m. 🔑 (*NAmE* also **P.M.**) /ˌpiː ˈem/ *abbr.* after 12 o'clock NOON (from Latin 'post meridiem'): *The appointment is at 3 p.m.* ➲ compare A.M.

PMP /ˌpiː em ˈpiː/ *noun* the abbreviation for 'portable media player' (a piece of equipment that stores and plays sound and pictures)

PMS /ˌpiː em ˈes:/ (*BrE*) (also **PMT** /ˌpiː em ˈtiː/ *NAmE, BrE*) *noun* [U] physical and emotional problems such as pain and feeling depressed that many women experience before their PERIOD (= flow of blood) each month. PMS/PMT are abbreviations for 'premenstrual syndrome/tension'. ➲ see also PREMENSTRUAL

pneu·mat·ic /njuːˈmætɪk; *NAmE* nuː-/ *adj.* [usually before noun] **1** filled with air: *a pneumatic tyre* **2** worked by air under pressure: *pneumatic tools*

pneuˌmatic ˈdrill (*BrE*) (*NAmE* **jack·ham·mer**) *noun* a large powerful tool, worked by air pressure, used especially for breaking up road surfaces

pneu·mo·nia /njuːˈməʊniə; *NAmE* nuːˈmoʊ-/ *noun* [U] a serious illness affecting one or both lungs that makes breathing difficult

PO /ˌpiː ˈəʊ; *NAmE* ˈoʊ/ *abbr.* **1** POST OFFICE ➲ see also PO BOX **2** POSTAL ORDER

poach /pəʊtʃ; *NAmE* poʊtʃ/ *verb* **1** [T] **~ sth** to cook food, especially fish, gently in a small amount of liquid: *poached salmon* **2** [T] **~ sth** to cook an egg gently in nearly boiling water after removing its shell **3** [T, I] **~ (sth)** to illegally hunt birds, animals or fish on sb else's property or without permission: *The elephants are poached for their tusks.* **4** [T, I] **~ (sb/sth) (from sb/sth)** to take and use sb/sth that belongs to sb/sth else, especially in a secret, dishonest or unfair way: *The company poached the contract from their main rivals.* ◇ *Several of our employees have been poached by a rival firm.* ◇ *I hope I'm not* **poaching on your territory** (= doing sth that is actually your responsibility).

poach·er /ˈpəʊtʃə(r); *NAmE* ˈpoʊtʃ-/ *noun* **1** a person who illegally hunts birds, animals or fish on sb's else's property **2** a special pan for POACHING eggs **3** (also ˈ**goal poacher**) (especially in football (SOCCER)) a player who waits near the opposite team's goal in order to try to score if they get the ball

IDM **poacher turned ˈgamekeeper** (*especially BrE*) a person who has changed from one situation or attitude to the opposite one, especially sb who used to oppose people in authority but is now in a position of authority

ˌPˈO box (also ˈ**post office box**) *noun* used as a kind of address, so that mail can be sent to a post office where it is kept until it is collected: *Radio Netherlands, PO Box 222, Hilversum*

pocked /pɒkt; *NAmE* pɑːkt/ *adj.* having holes or hollow marks on the surface SYN **pitted**

pocket 0- /ˈpɒkɪt; *NAmE* ˈpɑːk-/ *noun, verb*

■ ***noun***

▸ IN CLOTHING **1** 0- a small piece of material like a small bag sewn into or onto a piece of clothing so that you can carry things in it: *a coat pocket* ◇ *I put the note in my pocket.* ◇ ***Turn out your pockets*** (= empty your pockets). ◇ *Take your hands out of your pockets!* ◇ *a pocket dictionary* (= one that is small enough to fit in your pocket) ➲ VISUAL VOCAB page V51

▸ SMALL CONTAINER **2** 0- a small bag or container fastened to sth so that you can put things in it, for example, in a car door or in a bag: *Information about safety procedures is in the pocket in front of you* (= on a plane).

▸ MONEY **3** [usually sing.] used to talk about the amount of money that you have to spend: *We have holidays to* ***suit every pocket.*** ◇ *He had no intention of paying for the meal* ***out of his own pocket.*** ◇ *The Foundation is reputed to have very* ***deep pockets*** (= to have a lot of money).

▸ SMALL GROUP/AREA **4** a small group or area that is different from its surroundings: *There are still a few isolated pockets of resistance to the new regime.* ◇ *a pocket of air* ➲ see also AIR POCKET

▸ IN BILLIARDS, ETC. **5** any of the holes or nets around the edges of the table used in the games of BILLIARDS, POOL or SNOOKER, which you have to hit the ball into ➲ VISUAL VOCAB page V34

IDM **be in sb's ˈpocket** to be controlled or strongly influenced by sb **be/live in each other's ˈpockets** (*BrE*) if two people are **in each other's pockets**, they are too close to each other or spend too much time with each other **have sb in your ˈpocket** to have influence or power over sb, for example, a police officer or a politician, especially by threatening them or by offering them money **have sth in your ˈpocket** to be certain to win sth **ˌin/ˌout of ˈpocket** (*especially BrE*) having gained/lost money as a result of sth: *That one mistake left him thousands of pounds out of pocket.* ➲ compare OUT-OF-POCKET ➲ more at BURN *v.*, DIP *v.*, HAND *n.*, LINE *v.*, PICK *v.*

■ ***verb***

▸ PUT INTO POCKET **1** **~ sth** to put sth into your pocket: *She paid for the drink and pocketed the change without counting it.*

▸ MONEY **2** **~ sth** to take or keep sth, especially an amount of money, that does not belong to you: *He regularly charges passengers more than the normal fare and pockets the difference.* **3** **~ sth** to earn or win an amount of money: *Last year, she pocketed over $1 million in advertising contracts.*

▸ IN BILLIARDS, ETC. **4** **~ sth** (in the games of BILLIARDS, POOL and SNOOKER) to hit a ball into a POCKET *n.* (5) SYN **pot**

pock·et·book /ˈpɒkɪtbʊk; *NAmE* ˈpɑːk-/ *noun* **1** (*NAmE*) used to refer to the financial situation of a person or country. (In the past it was a small flat case for carrying papers or money.): *Many foreign goods are too expensive for American pocketbooks.* ◇ *The increase is likely to hit the pocketbooks of consumers.* **2** (*especially BrE*) a small book for writing in SYN **notebook** **3** (*old-fashioned*, *NAmE*) = HANDBAG

pock·et·ful /ˈpɒkɪtfʊl; *NAmE* ˈpɑːk-/ *noun* the amount a pocket holds: *a pocketful of coins*

pock·et·knife /ˈpɒkɪtnaɪf; *NAmE* ˈpɑːk-/ *noun* (*especially NAmE*) = PENKNIFE

ˈpocket money *noun* [U] **1** (*especially BrE*) (also **allowance** especially in *NAmE*) a small amount of money that parents give their children, usually every week or every month **2** a small amount of money that you can spend on things you need or want ➲ compare SPENDING MONEY

ˈpocket-sized (also ˈ**pocket-size**) *adj.* small enough to fit into your pocket or to be carried easily

ˌpocket ˈveto *noun* (in the US) a method by which the President can stop a new law from being introduced by not signing it and keeping it until a session of Congress has finished

pock·mark /ˈpɒkmɑːk; *NAmE* ˈpɑːkmɑːrk/ *noun* a hollow mark on the skin, often caused by disease or infection

ˈpock-marked *adj.* covered with hollow marks or holes: *a pock-marked face* ◇ *The district is pock-marked with caves.*

pod /pɒd; *NAmE* pɑːd/ *noun* **1** a long thin case filled with seeds that develops from the flowers of some plants, especially PEAS and BEANS: *a pea pod* ◇ *a vanilla pod* ➲ VISUAL VOCAB pages V27, V28 **2** a long narrow container that is hung under an aircraft and used to carry fuel, equipment, weapons, etc. **3** part of a SPACECRAFT or a boat that can be separated from the main part **4** [C] a small group of sea animals, such as DOLPHINS or WHALES, swimming together: *a pod of adult dolphins*

pod·cast /ˈpɒdkɑːst; *NAmE* ˈpɑːdkæst/ *noun* a recording of a radio broadcast or a video that can be taken from the Internet: *To listen to the podcast, click on the link below.* ➲ COLLOCATIONS at EMAIL ▸ **pod·caster** *noun*: *The US has an estimated 60 million podcasters.* **pod·cast·ing** *noun* [U]: *Podcasting could turn into an audio form of blogging.*

podgy /ˈpɒdʒi; *NAmE* ˈpɑːdʒi/ (*BrE*) (also **pudgy** *NAmE, BrE*) *adj.* (*informal*, usually *disapproving*) slightly fat: *podgy arms*

po·dia·trist /pəˈdaɪətrɪst/ *noun* (*especially NAmE*) = CHIROPODIST

po·dia·try /pəˈdaɪətri/ *noun* [U] (*especially NAmE*) = CHIROPODY

po·dium /ˈpəʊdiəm; *NAmE* ˈpoʊ-/ *noun* **1** a small platform that a person stands on when giving a speech or CONDUCTING an ORCHESTRA, etc. SYN **rostrum** **2** (*NAmE*) = LECTERN

Po·dunk /ˈpəʊdʌŋk; *NAmE* ˈpoʊ-/ *adj.* (*US, informal*) (of a town) small, dull and not important ORIGIN From a place name of southern New England.

poem 0- /ˈpəʊɪm; *NAmE* ˈpoʊəm/ *noun* a piece of writing in which the words are chosen for their sound and the images they suggest, not just for their obvious meanings. The words are arranged in separate lines, usually with a repeated rhythm, and often the lines RHYME at the end. ➲ COLLOCATIONS at LITERATURE

poesy /ˈpəʊəzi; -si; *NAmE* ˈpoʊ-/ *noun* [U] (*literary*) poetry

poet /ˈpəʊɪt; *NAmE* ˈpoʊət/ *noun* a person who writes poems

poet·ess /ˌpəʊɪˈtes; *NAmE* ˌpoʊəˈtes/ *noun* (*old-fashioned*) a woman who writes poems

poet·ic /pəʊˈetɪk; *NAmE* poʊ-/ (also *less frequent* **poet·ical** /-ɪkl/) *adj.* **1** [only before noun] connected with poetry; being poetry: *poetic language* ◇ *Byron's Poetical Works* **2** (*approving*) like or suggesting poetry, especially because it shows imagination and deep feeling SYN **lyrical**: *There is a poetic quality to her playing.* IDM see LICENCE ▸ **poet·ic·al·ly** /-kli/ *adv.*

poˌetic ˈjustice *noun* [U] a situation in which sth bad happens to sb, and you think that this is what they deserve

poˌetic ˈlicence (*NAmE* **poˌetic ˈlicense**) *noun* [U] the freedom to change facts, the normal rules of language,

P

etc. in a special piece of writing or speech in order to achieve a particular effect

poet·ics /pəʊˈetɪks; *NAmE* poʊ-/ *noun* [U] **1** the art of writing poetry **2** the study of poetry, literature, etc.

ˌPoet ˈLaureate *noun* **1** (especially in Britain) a person who has been officially chosen to write poetry for the country's important occasions **2** (*especially NAmE*) a person whose poetry is considered to be the best, or most typical of their country or region.

poet·ry 🗝 /ˈpəʊətri; *NAmE* ˈpoʊ-/ *noun* **1** 🗝 [U] a collection of poems; poems in general SYN **verse**: ***epic/lyric/pastoral, etc. poetry*** ◇ *Maya Angelou's poetry* ◇ *a poetry reading* ➲ COLLOCATIONS at LITERATURE ➲ compare PROSE **2** [U, sing.] (*approving*) a beautiful and elegant quality: *There was poetry in all her gestures.*

po-faced /ˈpəʊ feɪst; *NAmE* ˈpoʊ/ *adj.* (*BrE, informal, disapproving*) looking very serious and as though you do not approve of sb/sth

pogo stick /ˈpəʊgəʊ stɪk; *NAmE* ˈpoʊgoʊ/ *noun* a pole with a bar to stand on and a spring at the bottom, that you jump around on for fun

pog·rom /ˈpɒgrəm; *NAmE* ˈpoʊg-/ *noun* the organized killing of large numbers of people, because of their race or religion (originally the killing of Jews in Russia)

poign·ant /ˈpɔɪnjənt/ *adj.* having a strong effect on your feelings, especially in a way that makes you feel sad SYN **moving**: *a* ***poignant image/moment/memory, etc.*** ◇ *Her face was a* ***poignant reminder*** *of the passing of time.* ▶ **poign·ancy** /-jənsi/ *noun* [U]: *the poignancy of parting and separation* ◇ *Of particular poignancy was the photograph of their son with his sisters, taken the day before he died.* **poign·ant·ly** /-jəntli/ *adv.*

poin·set·tia /ˌpɔɪnˈsetiə/ *noun* a tropical plant with large red or pink leaves that grow to look like flowers, often grown indoors in pots

point 🗝 /pɔɪnt/ *noun, verb*

■ ***noun***

▸ OPINION/FACT **1** 🗝 [C] a thing that sb says or writes giving their opinion or stating a fact: *She* ***made*** *several interesting* ***points*** *in the article.* ◇ *I* ***take your point*** (= understand and accept what you are saying). ◇ *He's just saying that to* ***prove a point*** (= to show his idea is right). ◇ *OK, you've* ***made your point!*** ➲ see also TALKING POINT

▸ MAIN IDEA **2** 🗝 [C] (usually **the point**) the main or most important idea in sth that is said or done: ***The point is*** *you shouldn't have to wait so long to see a doctor.* ◇ *I wish he would* ***get to the point*** (= say it quickly). ◇ *I'll* ***come straight to the point:*** *we need more money.* ◇ *Do you* ***see my point*** (= understand)? ◇ *I think I* ***missed the point*** (= did not understand). ◇ *You* ***have a point*** (= your idea is right) —*it would be better to wait till this evening.* ◇ *'There won't be anywhere to park.' 'Oh,* ***that's a*** (***good***) ***point.***' (= I had not thought of that) ◇ *It just isn't true. That's* ***the whole point*** (= the only important fact). ◇ *'He's been married before.' '****That's beside the point****'* (= not important). ◇ *I know it won't cost very much but* ***that's not the point*** (= not the important thing).

▸ PURPOSE **3** 🗝 [U, sing.] the purpose or aim of sth: *What's the point of all this violence?* ◇ *There's* ***no point*** *in getting angry.* ◇ *I* ***don't see the point of*** *doing it all again.* ◇ *The point of the lesson is to compare the two countries.* ➲ SYNONYMS at PURPOSE

▸ DETAIL **4** 🗝 [C] a particular detail or fact: *Here are the* ***main points*** *of the news.* ◇ *Can you explain that point again?*

▸ QUALITY **5** 🗝 [C] a particular quality or feature that sb/sth has: *Tact is not one of her* ***strong points.*** ◇ *Read the manual to learn the program's* ***finer points*** (= small details). ◇ *Living in Scotland* ***has its good points*** *but the weather is not one of them.* ◇ *One of the hotel's* ***plus points*** (= good features) *is that it is very central.* ➲ see also SELLING POINT

▸ TIME **6** 🗝 [C] a particular time or stage of development: *The climber was* ***at/on the point of*** *death when they found him.* ◇ *We were* ***on the point of*** *giving up.* ◇ *Many people suffer from mental illness* ***at some point*** *in their lives.* ◇ *We had* ***reached the point*** *when there was no money left.* ◇ ***At this point in time*** *we just have to wait.* ◇ ***At this point*** *I don't care what you decide to do.* ➲ see also HIGH POINT, LOW POINT, SATURATION POINT, STARTING POINT, STICKING POINT, TURNING POINT

▸ PLACE **7** 🗝 [C] a particular place or area: *I'll wait for you at the meeting point in the arrivals hall.* ◇ *the point at which the river divides* ◇ *Draw a line from point A to point B.* ◇ *No parking beyond this point.* ➲ SYNONYMS at PLACE ➲ see also FOCAL POINT, JUMPING-OFF POINT, THREE-POINT TURN, VANISHING POINT, VANTAGE POINT

▸ DIRECTION **8** [C] one of the marks of direction around a COMPASS: *the points of the compass* (= N, S, E, W, etc.)

▸ IN COMPETITION **9** 🗝 [C] (*abbr.* **pt**) an individual unit that adds to a score in a game or sports competition: *to* ***win/lose a point*** ◇ *Australia finished 20 points ahead.* ◇ *They won* ***on points*** (= by scoring more points rather than by completely defeating their opponents). ➲ see also BROWNIE POINT, MATCH POINT

▸ MEASUREMENT **10** [C] a mark or unit on a scale of measurement: *The party's share of the vote fell by ten percentage points.* ➲ see also BOILING POINT, FREEZING POINT, MELTING POINT

▸ SHARP END **11** 🗝 [C] the sharp thin end of sth: *the point of a pencil/knife/pin* ➲ VISUAL VOCAB page V23 ➲ see also BALLPOINT, GUNPOINT, KNIFEPOINT

▸ LAND **12** [C] (also **Point**) a narrow piece of land that stretches into the sea: *The ship sailed around the point.* ◇ *Pagoda Point*

▸ PUNCTUATION **13** [C] a small dot used in writing, especially the dot that separates a whole number from the part that comes after it: *two point six* (2.6) ◇ *a decimal point* ◇ *We broadcast on ninety-five point nine* (95.9) *FM.* ➲ see also BULLET POINT, FULL STOP

▸ OF LIGHT/COLOUR **14** [C] a very small dot of light or colour: *The stars were points of light in the sky.*

▸ FOR ELECTRICITY **15** [C] (*BrE*) a place in a wall, etc. where a piece of equipment can be connected to electricity: *a* ***power/shaver/telephone point***

▸ IN BALLET **16 points** [pl.] = POINTE

▸ ON RAILWAY TRACK **17 points** [pl.] (*BrE*) (*NAmE* **switch** [C]) a piece of track at a place where a railway/railroad line divides that can be moved to allow a train to change tracks

▸ SIZE OF LETTERS **18** [U] a unit of measurement for the size of letters in printing or on a computer screen, etc: *Change the text to 10 point.*

IDM **if/when it comes to the ˈpoint** used when you have to decide sth or say what you really think: *When it comes to the point, he always changes his mind.* **in point of ˈfact** used to say what is true in a situation: *In point of fact, she is their adopted daughter.* **make a ˈpoint of doing sth** to be or make sure you do sth because it is important or necessary: *I made a point of closing all the windows before leaving the house.* **ˌmore to the ˈpoint** used to say that sth is more important than sth else: *I couldn't do the job—I've never been to Spain and, more to the point, I don't speak Spanish.* **on point** (*NAmE*) appropriate or relevant to the situation: *The quotation was directly on point.* ◇ *Let's stay on point.* **ˌpoint of ˈcontact** a place where you go or a person that you speak to when you are dealing with an organization: *The receptionist is the first point of contact most people have with the clinic.* **a ˌpoint of deˈparture 1** a place where a journey starts **2** (*formal*) an idea, a theory or an event that is used to start a discussion, an activity, etc. **a ˌpoint of ˈhonour** a thing that sb considers to be very important for their honour or reputation **the ˌpoint of ˌno reˈturn** the time when you must continue with what you have decided to do, because it is not possible to get back to an earlier situation **ˌpoint ˈtaken** used to say that you accept that sb else is right when they have disagreed with you or criticized you: *Point taken. Let's drop the subject.* **to the ˈpoint** expressed in a simple, clear way without any extra information or feelings SYN **pertinent**: *The letter was short and to the point.* **to the ˈpoint of (doing) sth** to a degree that can be described as sth: *He was rude to the point of being aggressive.* **up to a (certain) ˈpoint** to some extent; to some degree but not completely: *I agree with you up to a point.* ➲ more at BELABOUR, CASE *n.*, FINE *adj.*, LABOUR *v.*, MOOT *adj.*, SCORE *v.*, SORE *adj.*, STRETCH *v.*

■ *verb*
▸ SHOW WITH FINGER **1** 🔑 [I, T, no passive] to stretch out your finger or sth held in your hand towards sb/sth in order to show sb where a person or thing is: **~ (at/to/towards sb/sth)** *'What's your name?' he asked, pointing at the child with his pen.* ◇ *He pointed to the spot where the house used to stand.* ◇ *She pointed in my direction.* ◇ *It's rude to point!* ◇ **~ sth** *She pointed her finger in my direction.*
▸ AIM **2** 🔑 [T] **~ sth (at sb/sth)** to aim sth at sb/sth: *He pointed the gun at her head.*
▸ FACE DIRECTION **3** 🔑 [I] **+ adv./prep.** to face in or be directed towards a particular direction: *The telescope was pointing in the wrong direction.* ◇ *The signpost pointed straight ahead.* ◇ *A compass needle points north.*
▸ LEAD TO **4** [I, T] to lead to or suggest a particular development or logical argument: **+ adv./prep.** *The evidence seems to point in that direction.* ◇ **~ the way + adv./prep.** *The fans are looking to the new players to point the way to victory.*
▸ SHOW THE WAY **5** [T] to show sb which way to go: **~ sb + adv./prep.** *I wonder if you could point me in the right direction for the bus station.* ◇ **~ the way + adv./prep.** *A series of yellow arrows pointed the way to reception.*
▸ WALL **6** [T] **~ sth** to put MORTAR between the bricks of a wall

IDM **point a/the 'finger (at sb)** to accuse sb of doing sth: *The article points an accusing finger at the authorities.*

PHR V **,point sb/sth↔'out (to sb)** 🔑 to stretch your finger out towards sb/sth in order to show sb which person or thing you are referring to: *I'll point him out to you next time he comes in.* **,point 'out (to sb)** | **,point sth↔'out (to sb)** 🔑 to mention sth in order to give sb information about it or make them notice it: *She tried in vain to point out to him the unfairness of his actions.* ◇ *He pointed out the dangers of driving alone.* ◇ **~ that...** *I should point out that not one of these paintings is original.* ◇ **+ speech** *'It's not very far,' she pointed out.* ➲ LANGUAGE BANK at ARGUE **'point to sth 1** to mention sth that you think is important and/or the reason why a particular situation exists: *The board of directors pointed to falling productivity to justify their decision.* **2** to suggest that sth is true or likely: *All the signs point to a successful year ahead.* **,point sth↔'up** (*formal*) to emphasize sth so that it becomes more noticeable SYN **highlight**: *The conference merely pointed up divisions in the party.*

,point-and-'click *adj.* [usually before noun] (*computing*) able to be used with a mouse

,point-and-'shoot *adj.* (of a camera) easy to use, without a person needing to adjust controls on it

,point-'blank *adj.* [only before noun] **1** (of a shot) fired with the gun touching or very close to the person or thing it is aimed at: *The officer was shot dead **at point-blank range**.* **2** (of sth that is said) very definite and direct and not very polite SYN **blunt**: *a point-blank refusal* ▸ **,point-'blank** *adv.*: *She fired point-blank at his chest.* ◇ *He refused point-blank to be photographed.*

'point duty *noun* [U] (*BrE*) the job of controlling traffic that is done by a police officer standing in the middle of the road: *to be on point duty*

pointe /pwæ̃t/ *noun* [U] (also **pointes** /pwæ̃t/, **points** [pl.]) the hard tops of the toes of a kind of shoe that a BALLET dancer balances on

point·ed 🔑 /'pɔɪntɪd/ *adj.*
1 🔑 having a sharp end: *a pointed chin* ◇ *pointed teeth* ◇ *a pointed instrument* ➲ see also POINTY **2** aimed in a clear and often critical way against a particular person or their behaviour: *a **pointed comment/remark*** ◇ *His words were a pointed reminder of her position.*

point·ed·ly /'pɔɪntɪdli/ *adv.* in a way that is clearly intended to show what you mean or to express criticism: *She yawned and looked pointedly at her watch.*

point·er /'pɔɪntə(r)/ *noun* **1** (*informal*) a piece of advice: *Here are some pointers on how to go about the writing task.* **2 ~ (to sth)** a sign that sth exists; a sign that shows how sth may develop in the future: *The surge in car sales was regarded as an encouraging pointer to an improvement in the economy.* **3** a thin strip of metal that points to the numbers on a DIAL on a piece of equipment for measuring sth **4** a stick used to point to things on a map or picture on a wall **5** (*computing*) a small symbol, for example an arrow, that marks a point on a computer screen **6** a large dog used in hunting, trained to stand still with its nose pointing towards the birds that are being hunted

'pointer finger *noun* (*NAmE*) a child's word for the INDEX FINGER

'point guard *noun* (in BASKETBALL) the player who directs the team's attacking players

poin·til·lism /'pɔɪntɪlɪzəm; 'pwænt-/ *noun* [U] a style of painting that was developed in France in the late 19th century in which very small dots of colour are used to build up the picture ▸ **poin·til·list** /-lɪst/ *adj.* **poin·til·list** *noun*: *Seurat, the French pointillist*

point·ing /'pɔɪntɪŋ/ *noun* [U] (*BrE*) the MORTAR that is put in the spaces between the bricks or stones in a wall; the method of filling in the spaces with MORTAR

'pointing device *noun* (*computing*) a mouse or other device which allows you to move the CURSOR on a computer screen

point·less /'pɔɪntləs/ *adj.* having no purpose; not worth doing: *We searched until we knew it would be pointless to continue.* ▸ **point·less·ly** *adv.*: *He argued pointlessly with his parents.* **point·less·ness** *noun* [U]: *the pointlessness of war*

'point man *noun* a soldier who goes in front of the others to look for danger: (*figurative, NAmE*) *the President's point man on education* (= the person who is responsible for it)

,point of 'order *noun* (*pl.* **points of order**) (*formal*) a question about whether the rules of behaviour in a formal discussion or meeting are being followed correctly

,point of 'reference *noun* (*pl.* **points of reference**) something that you already know that helps you understand a situation or explain sth to sb

,point of 'sale *noun* [usually sing.] the place where a product is sold: *More information on healthy foods should be provided **at the point of sale**.*

,point of 'use *noun* [usually sing.] the place where a product or a service is actually used: *Medical care is still free **at the point of use**.*

,point of 'view *noun* (*pl.* **points of view**) **1** the particular attitude or opinion that sb has about sth: *Why can't you ever see my point of view?* ◇ *There are a number of different points of view on this issue.* ◇ ***From my point of view*** (= as far as I was concerned), *the party was a complete success.* **2** a particular way of considering or judging a situation SYN **angle**: *These statistics are important from an ecological point of view.* ◇ *The book is written from the father's point of view.*

,point-to-'point *noun* (*BrE*) a race on horses that goes over a marked course across fields and has fences or walls for the horses to jump over

pointy /'pɔɪnti/ *adj.* (*informal*) with a point at one end SYN **pointed**: *pointy ears* ◇ (*humorous*) *Don't try to argue when you find yourself at the **pointy end** of a knife* (= when sb is threatening you with a knife).

poise /pɔɪz/ *noun, verb*
■ *noun* [U] **1** a calm and confident manner with control of your feelings or behaviour **2** the ability to move or stand in an elegant way with good control of your body
■ *verb* [I, T] to be or hold sth steady in a particular position, especially above sth else: **+ adv./prep.** *The hawk poised in mid-air ready to swoop.* ◇ **~ sth/yourself to do sth** *He was poising himself to launch a final attack.* ◇ **~ sth/yourself + adv./prep.** *She poised the javelin in her hand before the throw.*

poised /pɔɪzd/ *adj.* **1** [not before noun] in a position that is completely still but is ready to move at any moment: **~ (on, above, over, etc. sth)** *Tina was tense, her hand poised over the telephone.* ◇ *He stopped writing and looked at me, pen poised.* ◇ **~ to do sth** *The cat crouched in the grass, poised to jump.* **2** [not before noun] **~ (in, on, above, etc. sth)** in a position that is balanced but likely to change

P

in one direction or another: *The cup was poised on the edge of the chair.* ◇ (*figurative*) *The world stood poised between peace and war.* **3** [not before noun] completely ready for sth or to do sth SYN **set**: **~ for sth** *The economy is poised for recovery.* ◇ **~ to do sth** *Kate is poised to become the highest-paid supermodel in the fashion world.* **4** having a calm and confident manner and in control of your feelings and behaviour SYN **assured**: *He is a remarkably poised young man.*

poi·son 🔑 /ˈpɔɪzn/ *noun, verb*
■ ***noun*** [C, U] **1** 🔑 a substance that causes death or harm if it is swallowed or absorbed into the body: *Some mushrooms contain a deadly poison.* ◇ *How did he die? Was it poison?* ◇ *The dog was killed by rat poison* (= poison intended to kill RATS). ◇ *to hunt with poison arrows* ◇ *bombs containing poison gas* **2** an idea, a feeling, etc. that is extremely harmful: *the poison of racial hatred*
IDM **what's your ˈpoison?** (*informal, humorous*) used to ask sb what alcoholic drink they would like ➲ more at MAN *n.*
■ ***verb*** **1** 🔑 **~ sb/yourself** (**with sth**) to harm or kill a person or an animal by giving them poison **2** 🔑 **~ sth** to put poison in or on sth: *a poisoned arrow* ◇ *Someone had been poisoning his food.* ◇ *Large sections of the river have been poisoned by toxic waste from factories.* **3** **~ sth** to have a bad effect on sth: *His comment served only to poison the atmosphere still further.* ◇ *She succeeded in* ***poisoning their minds*** *against me.*
IDM **a poisoned ˈchalice** (*especially BrE*) a thing that seems attractive when it is given to sb but which soon becomes unpleasant

poi·son·er /ˈpɔɪzənə(r)/ *noun* a person who murders sb by using poison

poi·son·ing /ˈpɔɪzənɪŋ/ *noun* [U, C] **1** the fact or state of having swallowed or absorbed poison: *a series of deaths caused by carbon monoxide poisoning* ◇ *At least 10 000 children are involved in accidental poisonings every year.* **2** the act of killing or harming sb/sth by giving them poison: *The police suspected poisoning.* ◇ *The rats were controlled by poisoning.* ➲ see also BLOOD POISONING, FOOD POISONING

P

ˌpoison ˈivy *noun* [U] a N American climbing plant that causes painful spots on the skin when you touch it

ˌpoison ˈoak *noun* [U] a N American bush that causes painful spots on the skin when you touch it

poi·son·ous 🔑 /ˈpɔɪzənəs/ *adj.*
1 🔑 causing death or illness if swallowed or absorbed into the body SYN **toxic**: *poisonous chemicals/plants* ◇ *This gas is highly poisonous.* ◇ *The leaves of certain trees are poisonous to cattle.* **2** 🔑 (of animals and insects) producing a poison that can cause death or illness if the animal or insect bites you SYN **venomous**: *poisonous snakes* **3** extremely unpleasant or unfriendly: *the poisonous atmosphere in the office*

ˌpoison ˈpen letter *noun* an unpleasant letter that is not signed and is intended to upset the person who receives it

ˌpoison ˈpill *noun* (*informal, business*) a form of defence used by a company to prevent, or to reduce the effect of, a TAKEOVER BID that they do not want, for example by selling some of their important possessions

poke /pəʊk; *NAmE* poʊk/ *verb, noun*
■ ***verb*** **1** [T] to quickly push your fingers or another object into sb/sth SYN **prod**: **~ sb/sth with sth** *She poked him in the ribs with her elbow.* ◇ **~ sth into sth** *She poked her elbow into his ribs.* ◇ **~ sb/sth** *I'm sick of being poked and prodded by doctors.* ◇ *She got up and poked the fire* (= to make it burn more strongly). **2** [T] **~ sth + adv./prep.** to push sth somewhere or move it in a particular direction with a small quick movement: *He poked his head around the corner to check that nobody was coming.* ◇ *Someone had poked a message under the door.* ◇ *Don't poke her eye out with that stick!* **3** [I] **+ adv./prep.** if an object is **poking out of, through, etc.** sth, you can see a part of it that is no longer covered by sth else: *The end of the cable was left poking out of the wall.* ◇ *Clumps of grass poked up through the snow.* **4** [T] **~ a hole in sth** (**with sth**) to make a hole in sth by pushing your finger or another object into it: *The kids poked holes in the ice with sticks.* **5** [T] **~ sb** (*taboo, slang*) (of a man) to have sex with sb
IDM **poke ˈfun at sb/sth** to say unkind things about sb/sth in order to make other people laugh at them SYN **ridicule**: *Her novels poke fun at the upper class.* ➲ more at NOSE *n.*
PHR V **ˌpoke aˈbout/aˈround** (*informal*) to look for sth, especially sth that is hidden among other things that you have to move: *The police spent the day poking around in his office but found nothing.* ◇ (*figurative*) *We've had journalists poking around and asking a lot of questions.* **ˈpoke at sth** to push a pointed object, your finger, etc. at sth repeatedly with small quick movements: *He poked at the spaghetti with a fork.*
■ ***noun*** **1** [C, usually sing.] the action of quickly pushing your fingers or another object into sb/sth: *to give the fire a poke* ◇ *He gave me a poke in the ribs to wake me up.* **2** [U] (*BrE*) power in a car: *I prefer something with a bit more poke.*
IDM **have a ˌpoke aˈround** (*informal*) to look carefully around a place to see what you can find; to try to find out information about sb/sth **take a ˈpoke at sb/sth** (*old-fashioned, NAmE, informal*) to make an unkind remark about sb/sth; to laugh at sb/sth ➲ more at PIG *n.*

poker /ˈpəʊkə(r); *NAmE* ˈpoʊ-/ *noun* **1** [U] a card game for two or more people, in which the players bet on the values of the cards they hold **2** [C] a metal stick for moving or breaking up coal in a fire ➲ VISUAL VOCAB page V18

ˈpoker-faced *adj.* (*informal*) with an expression on your face that does not show what you are thinking or feeling ▸ **ˈpoker face** *noun*: *He maintained a poker face.*

poky /ˈpəʊki; *NAmE* ˈpoʊki/ *adj.* (*informal*) (**poki·er, poki·est**) **1** (of a room or a building) too small; without much space SYN **cramped**: *a poky little room* **2** (also **pokey**) (both *NAmE*) extremely slow and annoying

pol /pɒl; *NAmE* pɑːl/ *noun* (*NAmE, informal*) = POLITICIAN

Po·lack /ˈpəʊlæk; *NAmE* ˈpoʊ-/ *noun* (*taboo, slang, especially NAmE*) an offensive word for a person from Poland, or a person of Polish origin

polar /ˈpəʊlə(r); *NAmE* ˈpoʊ-/ *adj.* [only before noun] **1** connected with, or near the North or South Pole: *the polar regions* ◇ *polar explorers* **2** (*technical*) connected with the POLES (= the positive and negative ends) of a MAGNET: *polar attraction* **3** (*formal*) used to describe sth that is the complete opposite of sth else: *The parents' position is often the polar opposite of the child's.*

ˈpolar bear *noun* a white BEAR that lives near the North Pole

po·lar·ity /pəˈlærəti/ *noun* [U] **1** **~ (between A and B)** (*formal*) the situation when two tendencies, opinions, etc. oppose each other: *the growing polarity between the left and right wings of the party* **2** [U, C] (*physics*) the condition of having two POLES with opposite qualities

po·lar·ize (*BrE* also **-ise**) /ˈpəʊləraɪz; *NAmE* ˈpoʊ-/ *verb* **1** [I, T] to separate or make people separate into two groups with completely opposite opinions: *Public opinion has polarized on this issue.* ◇ **~ sth** *The issue has polarized public opinion.* **2** [T] **~ sth** (*physics*) to make waves of light, etc. VIBRATE in a single direction **3** [T] **~ sth** (*physics*) to give polarity to sth: *to polarize a magnet* ▸ **po·lar·iza·tion, -isa·tion** /ˌpəʊləraɪˈzeɪʃn; *NAmE* ˌpoʊlərəˈz-/ *noun* [U, C]

Po·lar·oid™ /ˈpəʊlərɔɪd; *NAmE* ˈpoʊ-/ *noun* **1** [C] (also **ˌPolaroid ˈcamera**) a camera that can produce a photograph within a few seconds **2** [C] a photograph that has been taken with a Polaroid camera **3** [U] a transparent substance that is put on SUNGLASSES and car windows to make the sun seem less bright: *Polaroid sunglasses* **4** **Polaroids** [pl.] (also **ˌPolaroid ˈsunglasses**) SUNGLASSES that have a layer of Polaroid on them

pole 🔑 /pəʊl; *NAmE* poʊl/ *noun, verb*
■ ***noun*** **1** 🔑 a long thin straight piece of wood or metal, especially one with the end placed in the ground, used as a support: *a tent pole* ◇ *a ski pole* ◇ *a curtain pole* ➲ VISUAL VOCAB pages V18, V39, V45 ➲ see also BARGEPOLE,

FLAGPOLE, TELEGRAPH POLE, TOTEM POLE **2** either of the two points at the opposite ends of the line on which the earth or any other planet turns: *the North/South Pole* **3** (*physics*) either of the two ends of a MAGNET, or the positive or negative points of an electric battery **4** either of two opposite or contrasting extremes: *Their opinions were at opposite poles of the debate.*

IDM **be 'poles apart** to be widely separated; to have no interests that you share **up the 'pole** (*old-fashioned, BrE, informal*) crazy ➲ more at GREASY, TOUCH *v.*

■ **verb** [T, I] **~ (sth) + adv.prep.** to move a boat by pushing on the bottom of a river, etc. with a pole

pole·axe (*BrE*) (*US* **pole·ax**) /ˈpəʊlæks; *NAmE* ˈpoʊl-/ *verb* **1 ~ sb** to hit sb very hard so that they fall down and cannot stand up again **2** [usually passive] **~ sb** to surprise or shock you so much that you do not know what to say or do SYN **dumbfound**

pole·cat /ˈpəʊlkæt; *NAmE* ˈpoʊl-/ *noun* **1** a small European wild animal with a long thin body, dark brown fur and a strong unpleasant smell **2** (*NAmE*) = SKUNK

ˈpole dancing *noun* [U] sexually exciting dancing that is performed in a bar or club, with the dancer moving his or her body around a long pole ▸ **ˈpole dancer** *noun*

po·lem·ic /pəˈlemɪk/ *noun* (*formal*) **1** [C] a speech or a piece of writing that argues very strongly for or against sth/sb **2** [U] (also **polemics** [pl.]) the practice or skill of arguing strongly for or against sth/sb: *Her speech was memorable for its polemic rather than its substance.*

po·lem·ic·al /pəˈlemɪkl/ (also *less frequent* **po·lem·ic**) *adj.* (*formal*) involving strong arguments for or against sth, often in opposition to the opinion of others

po·lemi·cist /pəˈlemɪsɪst/ *noun* (*formal*) a person who makes skilful use of POLEMIC

po·lenta /pəˈlentə/ *noun* [U] **1** a yellow food made with MAIZE (CORN) flour, used in Italian cooking **2** the flour used to make polenta

ˈpole position *noun* [U, C] the leading position at the start of a race involving cars or bicycles

the ˈPole Star *noun* [sing.] the star that is above the North Pole in the sky

the ˈpole vault *noun* [sing.] a sporting event in which people try to jump over a high bar, using a long pole to push themselves off the ground ➲ VISUAL VOCAB page V38 ▸ **ˈpole-vaulter** *noun* **ˈpole-vaulting** *noun* [U]

po·lice /pəˈliːs/ *noun, verb*

■ **noun** (often **the police**) [pl.] an official organization whose job is to make people obey the law and to prevent and solve crime; the people who work for this organization: *A man was arrested by the police and held for questioning.* ◇ *Get out of the house or **I'll call the police**.* ◇ *Police suspect a local gang.* ◇ *a **police car*** ◇ *Hundreds of police in riot gear struggled to control the violence.* ➲ see also KITCHEN POLICE, SECRET POLICE

■ **verb 1 ~ sth** (of the police, army, etc.) to go around a particular area to make sure that nobody is breaking the law there: *The border will be policed by UN officials.* **2 ~ sth** (of a committee, etc.) to make sure that a particular set of rules is obeyed SYN **monitor**: *The profession is policed by its own regulatory body.*

poˈlice commissioner *noun* (*especially NAmE*) = COMMISSIONER

poˌlice ˈconstable (also **constable**) *noun* (*abbr.* PC) (in Britain and some other countries) a police officer of the lowest rank: *Police Constable Jordan*

poˈlice department *noun* (in the US) the police organization of a particular city

poˈlice dog *noun* a dog that is trained to find or attack suspected criminals

poˈlice force *noun* the police organization of a country, district or town

po·lice·man /pəˈliːsmən/ *noun* (*pl.* **-men** /-mən/) a male police officer ➲ note at GENDER

poˈlice officer (also **officer**) *noun* a member of the police

poˈlice state *noun* (*disapproving*) a country where people's freedom, especially to travel and to express political opinions, is controlled by the government, with the help of the police

poˈlice station (*NAmE* also **ˈstation house**) *noun* the office of a local police force: *The suspect was taken to the nearest police station for questioning.*

po·lice·wo·man /pəˈliːswʊmən/ *noun* (*pl.* **-women** /-wɪmɪn/) a female police officer ➲ note at GENDER

po·licing /pəˈliːsɪŋ/ *noun* [U] **1** the activity of keeping order in a place with police: *community policing* **2** the activity of controlling an industry, an activity, etc. to make sure that people obey the rules

pol·icy AW /ˈpɒləsi; *NAmE* ˈpɑːl-/ *noun* (*pl.* **-ies**)
1 [C, U] **~ (on sth)** a plan of action agreed or chosen by a political party, a business, etc: *the present government's policy on education* ◇ *The company has **adopted a firm policy** on shoplifting.* ◇ *We have tried to **pursue a policy** of neutrality.* ◇ *US **foreign/domestic policy*** ◇ *They have had a significant **change in policy** on paternity leave.* ◇ *a policy document* ➲ COLLOCATIONS at POLITICS **2** [C, U] (*formal*) a principle that you believe in that influences how you behave; a way in which you usually behave: *She is following her usual policy of ignoring all offers of help.* ◇ (*saying*) *Honesty is the best policy.* **3** [C] a written statement of a contract of insurance: *Check the terms of the policy before you sign.*

pol·icy·hold·er /ˈpɒləsihəʊldə(r); *NAmE* ˈpɑːləsihoʊl-/ *noun* (*formal*) a person or group that holds an insurance policy

polio /ˈpəʊliəʊ; *NAmE* ˈpoʊlioʊ/ (also *formal* **polio·my·el·itis** /ˌpəʊliəʊˌmaɪəˈlaɪtɪs; *NAmE* ˌpoʊlioʊ-/) *noun* [U] an infectious disease that affects the central nervous system and can cause temporary or permanent PARALYSIS (= loss of control or feeling in part or most of the body)

pol·ish /ˈpɒlɪʃ; *NAmE* ˈpɑːl-/ *noun, verb*

■ **noun 1** [U, C] a substance used when rubbing a surface to make it smooth and shiny: ***furniture/floor/shoe/silver polish*** ◇ *wax polish* ➲ see also FRENCH POLISH, NAIL POLISH ➲ VISUAL VOCAB page V49 **2** [sing.] an act of polishing sth: *I give it a polish now and again.* **3** [sing.] the shiny appearance of sth after it has been polished SYN **lustre, sheen 4** [U] a high quality of performance achieved with great skill SYN **brilliance**: *She played the cello with the polish of a much older musician.* **5** [U] high standards of behaviour; being polite SYN **refinement** IDM see SPIT *n.*

■ **verb 1** [T, I] to make sth smooth and shiny by rubbing it: **~ (sth)** *Polish shoes regularly to protect the leather.* ◇ **~ sth (up) (with sth)** *He polished his glasses with a handkerchief.* ➲ see also FRENCH POLISH **2** [T] to make changes to sth in order to improve it: **~ sth** *The statement was carefully polished and checked before release.* ◇ **~ sth up** *The hotel has polished up its act (= improved its service) since last year.*

PHR V **ˌpolish sb↔ˈoff** (*informal, especially NAmE*) to kill sb **ˌpolish sth↔ˈoff** (*informal*) to finish sth, especially food, quickly: *He polished off the remains of the apple pie.*

pol·ished /ˈpɒlɪʃt; *NAmE* ˈpɑːl-/ *adj.* **1** shiny as a result of polishing SYN **gleaming 2** elegant, confident and/or highly skilled SYN **fine**

pol·ish·er /ˈpɒlɪʃə(r); *NAmE* ˈpɑːl-/ *noun* a machine for polishing sth: *a floor polisher*

pol·it·buro /ˈpɒlɪtbjʊərəʊ; *NAmE* ˈpɑːlɪtbjʊroʊ/ *noun* (*pl.* **-os**) the most important committee of a Communist party, with the power to decide on policy

po·lite /pəˈlaɪt/ *adj.* (**po·liter, po·litest**) HELP **more polite** and **most polite** are also common
1 having or showing good manners and respect for the feelings of others SYN **courteous**: *Please be polite to our guests.* ◇ *We were all too polite to object.* OPP **impolite**
2 socially correct but not always sincere: *I don't know how to make **polite conversation**.* ◇ *The performance was greeted with polite applause.* **3** [only before noun] from a class of society that believes it is better than others: *'Bum'*

P

is not a word we use in polite company. ▸ **po·lite·ly** ⊶ *adv.* **po·lite·ness** *noun* [U]

poli·tesse /ˌpɒlɪˈtes; *NAmE* ˌpɑːl-/ *noun* [U] (from *French, literary*) formal POLITENESS

pol·it·ic /ˈpɒlətɪk; *NAmE* ˈpɑːl-/ *adj.* (*formal*) (of actions) based on good judgement SYN **prudent, wise**: *It seemed politic to say nothing.* ➲ see also BODY POLITIC

pol·it·ical ⊶ /pəˈlɪtɪkl/ *adj.*
1 ⊶ connected with the state, government or public affairs: *a monarch without political power* ◇ *He was a* ***political prisoner*** (= one who was put in prison because he was thought to be harmful to the state). **2** ⊶ connected with the different groups working in politics, especially their policies and the competition between them: *a political debate/party/leader* ◇ *What are your political sympathies?* **3** (of people) interested in or active in politics: *She became very political at university.* ◇ *I'm not a* ***political animal*** (= person who is interested in politics). **4** concerned with power, status, etc. within an organization, rather than with matters of principle: *I suspect that he was dismissed for political reasons.* ➲ see also POLITICALLY

poˌlitical ˈaction committee *noun* (*abbr.* PAC) (in the US) a group of people who collect money to support the candidates and policies that will help them achieve their political and social aims

poˌlitical aˈsylum *noun* [U] (*formal*) = ASYLUM

poˌlitical corˈrectness *noun* [U] (sometimes *disapproving*) the principle of avoiding language and behaviour that may offend particular groups of people

poˌlitical eˈconomy *noun* [U] the study of how nations organize the production and use of wealth

poˌlitical geˈography *noun* [U] the way in which the world is divided into different countries, especially as a subject of study

pol·it·ic·al·ly ⊶ /pəˈlɪtɪkli/ *adv.*
in a way that is connected with politics: *a politically sensitive issue* ◇ *politically motivated crimes* ◇ *It makes sense politically as well as economically.*

P

poˌlitically corˈrect *adj.* (*abbr.* PC) used to describe language or behaviour that deliberately tries to avoid offending particular groups of people

poˌlitically incorˈrect *adj.* failing to avoid language or behaviour that may offend particular groups of people

poˌlitical ˈscience (also **pol·it·ics**) *noun* [U] the study of government and politics

poˌlitical ˈscientist *noun* an expert in political science

pol·it·ician ⊶ /ˌpɒləˈtɪʃn; *NAmE* ˌpɑːl-/ *noun*
1 ⊶ (also *NAmE informal* **pol**) a person whose job is concerned with politics, especially as an elected member of parliament, etc. **2** (*disapproving*) a person who is good at using different situations in an organization to try to get power or advantage for himself or herself

pol·iti·cize (*BrE* also **-ise**) /pəˈlɪtɪsaɪz/ *verb* [often passive]
1 **~ sth** to make sth a political issue: *the highly politicized issue of unemployment* **2** **~ sb/sth** to make sb/sth become more involved in politics: *The rural population has become increasingly politicized in recent years.* ▸ **pol·iti·ciza·tion, -isa·tion** /pəˌlɪtɪsaɪˈzeɪʃn/ *noun* [U]: *the politicization of education*

pol·it·ick·ing /ˈpɒlətɪkɪŋ; *NAmE* ˈpɑːl-/ *noun* [U] (often *disapproving*) political activity, especially to win support for yourself

pol·it·ico /pəˈlɪtɪkəʊ; *NAmE* -koʊ/ *noun* (*pl.* -os) (*informal, disapproving*) a politician; a person who is active in politics

pol·it·ics ⊶ /ˈpɒlətɪks; *NAmE* ˈpɑːl-/ *noun*
1 ⊶ [U+sing./pl. v.] the activities involved in getting and using power in public life, and being able to influence decisions that affect a country or a society: *party politics* ◇ *local politics* ◇ *He's thinking of* ***going into politics*** (= trying to become a Member of Parliament, Congress, etc.) ◇ *a major figure in British politics* **2** ⊶ [U+sing./pl. v.] (*disapproving*) matters concerned with getting or using power within a particular group or organization: *I don't want to get involved in office politics.* ◇ *the internal politics of the legal profession* ◇ *sexual politics* (= concerning relationships of power between the sexes) **3** ⊶ [pl.] a person's political views or beliefs: *His politics are extreme.* **4** [U] = POLITICAL SCIENCE: *a degree in Politics* **5** [sing.] a system

Collocations

Politics

Power

- **create/form/be the leader of** a political party
- **gain/take/win/lose/regain** control of Congress
- **start/spark/lead/be on the brink of** a revolution
- **be engaged/locked in** an internal power struggle
- **lead/form** a rival/breakaway faction
- **seize/take** control of the government/power
- **bring down/overthrow/topple** the government/president/regime
- **abolish/overthrow/restore** the monarchy
- **establish/install** a military dictatorship/a stable government
- **be forced/removed/driven from** office/power
- **resign/step down as** party leader/an MP/president/prime minister
- **enter/retire from/return to** political life

Political debate

- **spark/provoke** a heated/hot/intense/lively debate
- **engage in/participate in/contribute to** (the) political/public debate (on/over sth)
- **get involved in/feel excluded from** the political process
- **launch/start/lead/spearhead** a campaign/movement
- **join/be linked with** the peace/anti-war/feminist/civil rights movement
- **criticize/speak out against/challenge/support** the government
- **lobby/put pressure on** the government (to do sth)
- **come under fire/pressure from** opposition parties

Policy

- **call for/demand/propose/push for/advocate** democratic/political/land reform(s)
- **formulate/implement** domestic economic policy
- **change/influence/shape/have an impact on** government/economic/public policy
- **be consistent with/be in line with/go against/be opposed to** government policy
- **reform/restructure/modernize** the tax system
- **privatize/improve/deliver/make cuts in** public services
- **invest (heavily) in/spend sth on** schools/education/public services/(the) infrastructure
- **nationalize** the banks/the oil industry
- **promise/propose/deliver/give** ($80 billion in/significant/substantial/massive) tax cuts
- a/the budget is **approved/**(*especially NAmE*) **passed** by parliament/congress

Making laws

- **have a majority in/have seats in** Parliament/Congress/the Senate
- **propose/sponsor** a bill/legislation/a resolution
- **introduce/bring in/draw up/draft/adopt/pass** a bill/a law/legislation/measures
- **amend/repeal** an act/a law/legislation
- **veto/vote against/oppose** a bill/legislation/a measure/a proposal/a resolution
- **get/require/be decided by** a majority vote

➲ more collocations at ECONOMY, VOTING

of political beliefs; a state of political affairs: *A politics of the future has to engage with new ideas.*

pol·ity /ˈpɒləti; *NAmE* ˈpɑːl-/ *noun* (*pl.* -ies) (*technical*) **1** [C] a society as a political unit **2** [U] the form or process of government

polka /ˈpɒlkə; *NAmE* ˈpoʊlkə/ *noun* a fast dance for two people together that was popular in the 19th century; a piece of music for this dance

ˈ**polka dot** *noun* one of many dots that together form a pattern, especially on cloth: *a polka-dot tie* ➲ VISUAL VOCAB page V50 ➲ compare SPOT

poll /pəʊl; *NAmE* poʊl/ *noun, verb*

■ ***noun* 1** (also oˈ**pinion poll**) [C] the process of questioning people who are representative of a larger group in order to get information about the general opinion **SYN** **survey**: *to* ***carry out/conduct*** *a poll* ◇ *A recent poll suggests some surprising changes in public opinion.* **2** [C] (also **the polls** [pl.]) the process of voting at an election; the process of counting the votes: *The final result of the poll will be known tomorrow.* ◇ *Thursday is traditionally the day when Britain* ***goes to the polls*** (= when elections are held). ◇ *Polls close* (= voting ends) *at 9 p.m.* ➲ SYNONYMS at ELECTION **3** [sing.] the number of votes given in an election **SYN** **ballot**: *Labour is ahead in the poll.* ◇ *They gained 20% of the poll.* ➲ see also DEED POLL, EXIT POLL, STRAW POLL

■ ***verb* 1** [T, I] to receive a particular number of votes in an election: **~ sth** *They polled 39% of the vote in the last election.* ◇ **+ adv./prep.** *The Republicans have polled well* (= received many votes) *in recent elections.* **2** [T, usually passive] **~ sb** to ask a large number of members of the public what they think about sth **SYN** **survey**: *Over 50% of those polled were against the proposed military action.*

pol·lard /ˈpɒləd; -lɑːd; *NAmE* ˈpɑːlərd/ *verb* [usually passive] **~ sth** (*technical*) to cut off the branches at the top of a tree so that the lower branches will grow more thickly

pol·len /ˈpɒlən; *NAmE* ˈpɑːlən/ *noun* [U] fine powder, usually yellow, that is formed in flowers and carried to other flowers of the same kind by the wind or by insects, to make those flowers produce seeds ➲ COLLOCATIONS at LIFE

ˈ**pollen count** *noun* [usually sing.] a number that shows the amount of pollen in the air, used to warn people whose health is affected by it

ˈ**pollen tube** *noun* (*biology*) a tube that grows when pollen lands on the STIGMA (= a part of the female organ) of a flower to carry the male cell to the OVULE (= the part that contains the female cell)

pol·lin·ate /ˈpɒləneɪt; *NAmE* ˈpɑːl-/ *verb* **~ sth** to put POLLEN into a flower or plant so that it produces seeds: *flowers pollinated by bees/the wind* ▶ **pol·lin·ation** /ˌpɒləˈneɪʃn; *NAmE* ˌpɑːl-/ *noun* [U]

poll·ing /ˈpəʊlɪŋ; *NAmE* ˈpoʊ-/ *noun* [U] **1** the activity of voting: *Polling has been heavy since 8 a.m.* **2** the act of asking questions as part of an opinion POLL

ˈ**polling booth** (*especially BrE*) (*NAmE* usually ˈ**voting booth**) *noun* a small place in a POLLING STATION, separated from the surrounding area, where people vote by marking a card, etc.

ˈ**polling day** *noun* [U, C] (*BrE*) a day on which people vote in an election: *a week before polling day*

ˈ**polling station** (*especially BrE*) (*NAmE* usually ˈ**polling place**) *noun* a building where people go to vote in an election ➲ COLLOCATIONS at VOTE

polli·wog (also **polly·wog**) /ˈpɒliwɒg; *NAmE* ˈpɑːliwɑːg/ *noun* (*NAmE*) = TADPOLE

poll·ster /ˈpəʊlstə(r); *NAmE* ˈpoʊl-/ *noun* a person who makes or asks the questions in an OPINION POLL

ˈ**poll tax** *noun* a tax that must be paid at the same rate by every person or every adult in a particular area

pol·lu·tant /pəˈluːtənt/ *noun* (*formal*) a substance that pollutes sth, especially air and water

pol·lute /pəˈluːt/ *verb* to add dirty or harmful substances to land, air, water, etc. so that it is no longer pleasant or safe to use: **~ sth** *the exhaust fumes that are polluting our cities* ◇ **~ sth by/with sth** *The river has been polluted with toxic waste from local factories.* ◇ (*figurative*) *a society polluted by racism* ➲ COLLOCATIONS at ENVIRONMENT

pol·luter /pəˈluːtə(r)/ *noun* a person, company, country, etc. that causes pollution

pol·lu·tion 🗝 /pəˈluːʃn/ *noun* [U]

1 🗝 the process of making air, water, soil, etc. dirty; the state of being dirty: ***air/water pollution*** ◇ *to reduce levels of environmental pollution* ➲ COLLOCATIONS at ENVIRONMENT **2** 🗝 substances that make air, water, soil, etc. dirty: *beaches covered with pollution* **3 noise/light ~** harmful or annoying levels of noise, or of artificial light at night

Polly·anna /ˌpɒliˈænə; *NAmE* ˈpɑːl-/ *noun* [usually sing.] a person who is always cheerful and expects only good things to happen **ORIGIN** From the name of a character created by the US writer of children's stories, Eleanor Hodgman Porter.

polly·wog = POLLIWOG

polo /ˈpəʊləʊ; *NAmE* ˈpoʊloʊ/ *noun* [U] a game in which two teams of players riding on horses try to hit a ball into a goal using long wooden hammers (called MALLETS) ➲ VISUAL VOCAB page V38 ➲ see also WATER POLO

pol·on·aise /ˌpɒləˈneɪz; *NAmE* ˌpɑːl-/ *noun* a slow Polish dance that was popular in the 19th century; a piece of music for this dance

ˈ**polo neck** (*BrE*) (*NAmE* **turtle·neck**) *noun* a high round COLLAR made when the neck of a piece of clothing is folded over; a piece of clothing with a polo neck: *a polo-neck sweater* ◇ *You can wear a polo neck with that jacket.* ➲ VISUAL VOCAB page V51

po·lo·nium /pəˈləʊniəm; *NAmE* -ˈloʊ-/ *noun* [U] (*symb.* Po) a chemical element. Polonium is a RADIOACTIVE metal that is present in nature when URANIUM decays.

ˈ**polo shirt** *noun* an informal shirt with short sleeves, a COLLAR and a few buttons at the neck ➲ VISUAL VOCAB page V51

pol·ter·geist /ˈpəʊltəgaɪst; ˈpɒl-; *NAmE* ˈpoʊltərg-/ *noun* a GHOST that makes loud noises and throws objects

pol·troon /pɒlˈtruːn; *NAmE* pɑːlˈt-/ *noun* (*old use, disapproving*) a COWARD (= a person who lacks courage)

P

poly /ˈpɒli; *NAmE* ˈpɑːli/ *noun* (*pl.* polys) (*BrE, informal*) = POLYTECHNIC

poly- /ˈpɒli; *NAmE* ˈpɑːli/ *combining form* (in nouns, adjectives and adverbs) many: *polygamy* ◇ *polyphonic*

poly·an·dry /ˌpɒliˈændri; *NAmE* ˌpɑːl-/ *noun* [U] (*technical*) the custom of having more than one husband at the same time ➲ compare POLYGAMY ▶ **poly·an·drous** /ˌpɒliˈændrəs; *NAmE* ˌpɑːl-/ *adj.*

poly·an·thus /ˌpɒliˈænθəs; *NAmE* ˌpɑːl-/ *noun* [C, U] a small garden plant with round brightly coloured flowers, several of which grow at the end of each STEM

poly·car·bon·ate /ˌpɒliˈkɑːbənət; *NAmE* ˌpɑːliˈkɑːrb-/ *noun* [U, C] (*technical*) a very strong transparent plastic used, for example, in windows and LENSES

poly·clinic /ˈpɒliklɪnɪk; *NAmE* ˈpɑːl-/ *noun* (*BrE*) a medical centre that is not part of a hospital, where both general doctors and specialists work

poly·es·ter /ˌpɒliˈestə(r); *NAmE* ˌpɑːli-; ˈpɑːliestər/ *noun* [U] a strong material made of FIBRES (called polyesters) which are produced by chemical processes, often mixed with other materials and used especially for making clothes: *a cotton and polyester shirt*

poly·ethyl·ene /ˌpɒliˈeθəliːn; *NAmE* ˌpɑːl-/ (*NAmE*) (*BrE* **poly·thene**) *noun* [U] a strong thin plastic material, used especially for making bags or for wrapping things in

pol·yg·amy /pəˈlɪgəmi/ *noun* [U] (*technical*) the custom of having more than one wife at the same time ➲ compare POLYANDRY ▶ **pol·yg·am·ist** /pəˈlɪgəmɪst/ *noun* **pol·yg·am·ous** /pəˈlɪgəməs/ *adj.*: *a polygamous marriage/society*

poly·glot /ˈpɒliglɒt; *NAmE* ˈpɑːliglɑːt/ *adj.* (*formal*) knowing, using or written in more than one language **SYN multilingual**: *a polyglot nation* ▶ **poly·glot** *noun*

poly·gon /ˈpɒlɪgən; *NAmE* ˈpɑːligɑːn/ *noun* (*geometry*) a flat shape with at least three straight sides and angles, and usually five or more ➲ VISUAL VOCAB page V58 ▶ **pol·yg·on·al** /pəˈlɪgənl/ *adj.*

poly·graph /ˈpɒligræf; *NAmE* ˈpɑːli-; *BrE* also -grɑːf/ *noun* (*technical*) (*formal*) = LIE DETECTOR

poly·he·dron /ˌpɒliˈhiːdrən; -ˈhed-; *NAmE* ˌpɑːli-/ *noun* (*pl.* **poly·he·dra** /-ˈhiːdrə; -ˈhed-/ or **poly·he·drons**) (*geometry*) a solid shape with many flat sides, usually more than six ▶ **poly·he·dral** *adj.*

poly·math /ˈpɒlimæθ; *NAmE* ˈpɑːl-/ *noun* (*formal, approving*) a person who knows a lot about many different subjects

poly·mer /ˈpɒlɪmə(r); *NAmE* ˈpɑːl-/ *noun* (*chemistry*) a natural or artificial substance consisting of large MOLECULES (= groups of atoms) that are made from combinations of small simple MOLECULES

poly·mer·ize (*BrE* also **-ise**) /ˈpɒlɪməraɪz; *NAmE* ˈpɑːli-/ *verb* [I, T] **~ (sth)** (*chemistry*) to combine, or to make units of a chemical combine, to make a POLYMER: *The substance polymerizes to form a hard plastic.* ▶ **poly·mer·iza·tion** /ˌpɒlɪməraɪˈzeɪʃn; *NAmE* ˌpɑːli-/ *noun* [U]

poly·morph·ous /ˌpɒliˈmɔːfəs; *NAmE* ˌpɑːliˈmɔːrfəs/ (also **poly·morph·ic** /-fɪk/) *adj.* (*formal* or *technical*) having or passing through many stages of development

polyp /ˈpɒlɪp; *NAmE* ˈpɑːlɪp/ *noun* **1** (*medical*) a small lump that grows inside the body, especially in the nose, that is caused by disease but is usually harmless **2** a small and very simple sea creature with a body shaped like a tube

pol·yph·ony /pəˈlɪfəni/ *noun* [U] (*music*) the combination of several different patterns of musical notes sung together to form a single piece of music **SYN counterpoint** ▶ **poly·phon·ic** /ˌpɒliˈfɒnɪk; *NAmE* ˌpɑːliˈfɑːnɪk/ *adj.*

poly·pro·pyl·ene /ˌpɒliˈprəʊpəliːn; *NAmE* ˌpɑːliˈproʊ-/ *noun* [U] a strong plastic often used for objects such as toys or chairs that are made in a MOULD

poly·sem·ous /ˌpɒliˈsiːməs; *NAmE* ˌpɑːl-/ *adj.* (*linguistics*) (of a word) having more than one meaning

poly·semy /pəˈlɪsɪmi/ *noun* [U] (*linguistics*) the fact of having more than one meaning

poly·styr·ene /ˌpɒliˈstaɪriːn; *NAmE* ˌpɑːl-/ (also **Styro·foam™** especially in *NAmE*) *noun* [U] a very light soft plastic that is usually white, used especially for making containers that prevent heat loss: *polystyrene cups*

poly·syl·lable /ˈpɒlisɪləbl; *NAmE* ˈpɑːl-/ *noun* (*technical*) a word of several (usually more than three) syllables ▶ **poly·syl·lab·ic** /ˌpɒlisɪˈlæbɪk; *NAmE* ˌpɑːl-/ *adj.*

poly·tech·nic /ˌpɒliˈteknɪk; *NAmE* ˌpɑːl-/ (also *BrE informal* **poly**) *noun* (in Britain in the past) a college for higher education, especially in scientific and technical subjects. Most polytechnics are now called, and have the same status as, universities.

poly·the·ism /ˈpɒliθiɪzəm; *NAmE* ˈpɑːl-/ *noun* [U] the belief that there is more than one god ➲ compare MONOTHEISM ▶ **poly·the·is·tic** /ˌpɒliθiˈɪstɪk; *NAmE* ˌpɑːl-/ *adj.*

poly·thene /ˈpɒlɪθiːn; *NAmE* ˈpɑːl-/ (*BrE*) (*NAmE* **poly·ethyl·ene**) *noun* [U] a strong thin plastic material, used especially for making bags or for wrapping things in: *a polythene bag*

poly·tun·nel /ˈpɒlitʌnl; *NAmE* ˈpɑːl-/ *noun* a long low structure covered with plastic, used for growing seeds or young plants outdoors ➲ VISUAL VOCAB page V2

poly·un·sat·ur·ated fat /ˌpɒliʌnˌsætʃəreɪtɪd ˈfæt; *NAmE* ˌpɑːl-/ *noun* [C, U] a type of fat found, for example, in seeds and vegetable oils, which does not encourage the harmful development of CHOLESTEROL: *foods that are high in polyunsaturated fats* ➲ see also MONOUNSATURATED FAT, SATURATED FAT, TRANS-FATTY ACID, UNSATURATED FAT ▶ **poly·un·sat·ur·ates** /ˌpɒliʌnˈsætʃərəts; *NAmE* ˌpɑːl-/ *noun* [pl.]: *foods that are high in polyunsaturates* (=polyunsaturated fats)

poly·ur·eth·ane /ˌpɒliˈjʊərəθeɪn; *NAmE* ˌpɑːliˈjʊr-/ *noun* [U] (*technical*) a type of plastic material used in making paints, glues, etc.

poly·va·lent /ˌpɒliˈveɪlənt; *NAmE* ˌpɑːl-/ *adj.* **1** (*chemistry*) having a VALENCY of 3 or more **2** (*formal*) having many different functions or forms: *polyvalent managerial skills* ▶ **poly·va·lence** /ˌpɒliˈveɪləns; *NAmE* ˌpɑːl-/ *noun* [U]

pom /pɒm; *NAmE* pɑːm/ *noun* = POMMY

Poma™ /ˈpəʊmə; *NAmE* ˈpoʊmə/ *noun* (*BrE*) = BUTTON LIFT

pom·ade /pəˈmeɪd; -ˈmɑːd/ *noun* (*old-fashioned*) [U, C] a liquid that is put on the hair to make it look shiny and smell nice

po·man·der /pəˈmændə(r); *NAmE* ˈpoʊmændər/ *noun* a round container filled with dried flowers, leaves, etc. that is used to give a pleasant smell to rooms or clothes

pom·egran·ate /ˈpɒmɪgrænɪt; *NAmE* ˈpɑːm-/ *noun* a round fruit with thick smooth skin and red flesh full of large seeds ➲ VISUAL VOCAB page V26

pom·elo /ˈpɒmələʊ; *NAmE* ˈpɑːməloʊ/ (also **pum·melo**) *noun* (*pl.* -os) a large CITRUS fruit that has thick yellow skin and that tastes similar to a GRAPEFRUIT, but sweeter

pom·mel /ˈpɒml; *NAmE* ˈpɑːml/ *noun* **1** the higher front part of a SADDLE on a horse **2** the round part on the end of the handle of a SWORD

ˈpommel horse *noun* a large object on four legs with two handles on top, which GYMNASTS put their hands on and swing their body and legs around

pommy /ˈpɒmi; *NAmE* ˈpɑːmi/ *noun* (*pl.* -ies) (also **pom**) (*AustralE, NZE, informal*, often *disapproving*) a British person

pomp /pɒmp; *NAmE* pɑːmp/ *noun* [U] the impressive clothes, decorations, music, etc. and traditional customs that are part of an official occasion or ceremony: *all the pomp and ceremony of a royal wedding*

IDM **ˌpomp and ˈcircumstance** formal and impressive ceremony

pom·pom /ˈpɒmpɒm; *NAmE* ˈpɑːmpɑːm/ (also **pom·pon** /ˈpɒmpɒn; *NAmE* ˈpɑːmpɑːn/) *noun* **1** a small ball made of wool, used for decoration, especially on a hat **SYN bobble** ➲ VISUAL VOCAB page V53 **2** (especially in the US) a large round bunch of strips of plastic, tied to a handle, used by CHEERLEADERS

pom·pous /ˈpɒmpəs; *NAmE* ˈpɑːm-/ *adj.* (*disapproving*) showing that you think you are more important than other people, especially by using long and formal words **SYN pretentious**: *a pompous official* ▶ **pom·pos·ity** /pɒmˈpɒsəti; *NAmE* pɑːmˈpɑːs-/ *noun* [U]: *The prince's manner was informal, without a trace of pomposity.* **pom·pous·ly** *adv.*

ponce /pɒns; *NAmE* pɑːns/ *noun, verb*

■ ***noun*** (*BrE, informal*) **1** a man who controls one or several PROSTITUTES and the money that they earn **SYN pimp** **2** an offensive word for a man whose appearance and behaviour seem similar to a woman's, or who is thought to be HOMOSEXUAL

■ ***verb***

PHR V **ˌponce aˈbout/aˈround** (usually used in the progressive tenses) (*BrE, informal*) to waste time when you are doing sth so that you achieve nothing; to do silly things in a way that looks ridiculous

poncey (also **poncy**) /ˈpɒnsi; *NAmE* ˈpɑːnsi/ *adj.* (*BrE, disapproving, informal*) trying to be impressive in a way that is silly and not natural: *I don't want to go to some poncey restaurant—I just want something to eat!*

pon·cho /ˈpɒntʃəʊ; *NAmE* ˈpɑːntʃoʊ/ *noun* (*pl.* -os) a type of coat without sleeves, made from one large piece of cloth with a hole in the middle for the head to go through

pond /pɒnd; *NAmE* pɑːnd/ *noun* a small area of still water, especially one that is artificial: *a fish pond* ➲ VISUAL VOCAB pages V2, V16

IDM **across the ˈpond** (*informal*) on the other side of the Atlantic Ocean from Britain/the US ➲ more at BIG *adj.*

pon·der /ˈpɒndə(r); *NAmE* ˈpɑːn-/ *verb* [I, T] (*formal*) to think about sth carefully for a period of time SYN **consider**: **~ (about/on/over sth)** *She pondered over his words.* ◇ *They were left to ponder on the implications of the announcement.* ◇ **~ sth** *The senator pondered the question for a moment.* ◇ **~ whether, what, etc...** *They are pondering whether the money could be better used elsewhere.* ◇ **+ speech** *'I wonder why,' she pondered aloud.*

pon·der·ous /ˈpɒndərəs; *NAmE* ˈpɑːn-/ *adj.* (*formal*) **1** (*disapproving*) (of speech and writing) too slow and careful; serious and boring SYN **tedious 2** moving slowly and heavily; able to move only slowly SYN **laboured**: *She watched the cow's ponderous progress.* ▸ **pon·der·ous·ly** *adv.* **pon·der·ous·ness** *noun* [U]

ˈ**pond skater** (*BrE*) (*NAmE* ˈ**water strider**) *noun* an insect that moves quickly across the surface of water

pone /pəʊn; *NAmE* poʊn/ *noun* [U] (*US*) = CORN PONE

pong /pɒŋ; *NAmE* pɔːŋ; pɑːŋ/ *noun* (*BrE, informal*) a strong unpleasant smell ▸ **pong** *verb* [I]: *That cheese pongs!*

pon·tiff /ˈpɒntɪf; *NAmE* ˈpɑːn-/ *noun* (*formal*) the POPE (= the leader of the Roman Catholic Church)

pon·tif·ic·al /pɒnˈtɪfɪkl; *NAmE* pɑːn-/ *adj.* (*formal*) connected with a POPE

pon·tifi·cate *verb, noun*
■ ***verb*** /pɒnˈtɪfɪkeɪt; *NAmE* pɑːn-/ [I] **~ (about/on sth)** (*disapproving*) to give your opinions about sth in a way that shows that you think you are right
■ ***noun*** /pɒnˈtɪfɪkət; *NAmE* pɑːn-/ the official position or period in office of a POPE

pon·toon /pɒnˈtuːn; *NAmE* pɑːn-/ *noun* **1** [C] a temporary floating platform built across several boats or hollow structures, especially one used for tying boats to **2** [C] a boat or hollow structure that is one of several used to support a floating platform or bridge: *a pontoon bridge* **3** [U] (*BrE*) = BLACKJACK

pony /ˈpəʊni; *NAmE* ˈpoʊni/ *noun, verb*
■ ***noun*** (*pl.* -ies) **1** a type of small horse ➲ see also SHETLAND PONY **2** (*BrE, slang*) £25 IDM see DOG *n.*, SHANK
■ ***verb*** (**po·nies, pony·ing, po·nied, po·nied**)
PHR V ˌ**pony** ˈ**up sth** (*NAmE, informal*) to pay money for sth: *Each guest had to pony up $40 for the meal.*

pony·tail /ˈpəʊniteɪl; *NAmE* ˈpoʊ-/ *noun* a bunch of hair tied at the back of the head so that it hangs like a horse's tail ➲ VISUAL VOCAB page V49 ➲ compare PIGTAIL

ˈ**pony-trekking** *noun* [U] (*BrE*) the activity of riding PONIES in the countryside for pleasure: *to go pony-trekking*

Ponzi scheme /ˈpɒnzi skiːm; *NAmE* ˈpɑːnzi/ *noun* a plan for making money that involves encouraging people to invest by offering them a high rate of interest and using their money to pay earlier INVESTORS. When there are not enough new INVESTORS, people who have recently invested lose their money. ORIGIN From Charles Ponzi, who organized the first scheme of this kind in the US in 1919.

poo (also **pooh**) /puː/ (both *BrE*) *noun* [U, C] (also **poop** *NAmE, BrE*) a child's word for the solid waste that is passed through the BOWELS SYN **faeces**: *dog poo* ◇ *I want to do a poo!* ▸ **poo** (also **pooh**) *verb* [I]

pooch /puːtʃ/ *noun* (*informal, especially NAmE*) a dog

poo·dle /ˈpuːdl/ *noun* **1** a dog with thick curly hair that is sometimes cut into special shapes **2** (*BrE, informal*) a person who is too willing to do what sb else tells them to do

poof /pʊf/ *noun, exclamation*
■ ***noun*** (also **poof·ter** /ˈpʊftə(r)/) (*BrE, taboo, slang*) an offensive word for a HOMOSEXUAL man
■ ***exclamation*** used when talking about sth disappearing suddenly: *He walked through—and vanished. Poof! Like that.*

pooh /puː/ *exclamation, noun, verb*
■ ***exclamation*** (*especially BrE*) **1** used to express disgust at a bad smell: *It stinks! Pooh!* **2** used to say that you think sb's idea, suggestion, etc. is not very good or that you do not believe what sb has said: *'I might lose my job for this.' 'Oh, pooh, nobody will care.'*
■ ***noun, verb*** = POO

ˌ**pooh-**ˈ**pooh** *verb* **~ sth** (*informal*) to say that a suggestion, an idea, etc. is not true or not worth thinking about

pool 🔑 /puːl/ *noun, verb*
■ ***noun***
▸ FOR SWIMMING **1** 🔑 [C] = SWIMMING POOL: *Does the hotel have a pool?* ◇ *relaxing by the pool* ➲ see also PLUNGE POOL
▸ OF WATER **2** 🔑 [C] a small area of still water, especially one that has formed naturally: *freshwater pools* ◇ *a rock pool* (= between rocks by the sea)
▸ OF LIQUID/LIGHT **3** 🔑 [C] **~ (of sth)** a small amount of liquid or light lying on a surface: *The body was lying in a pool of blood.* ◇ *a pool of light*
▸ GROUP OF THINGS/PEOPLE **4** [C] **~ (of sth)** a supply of things or money that is shared by a group of people and can be used when needed: *a pool of cars used by the firm's sales force* ◇ *a pool car* **5** [C] **~ (of sth)** a group of people available for work when needed: *a pool of cheap labour*
▸ GAME **6** [U] a game for two people played with 16 balls on a table, often in pubs and bars. Players use CUES (= long sticks) to try to hit the balls into pockets at the edge of the table: *a pool table* ◇ *to shoot* (= play) *pool* ➲ VISUAL VOCAB page V34 ➲ compare BILLIARDS, SNOOKER
▸ FOOTBALL **7 the pools** [pl.] = FOOTBALL POOLS: *He does the pools every week.* ◇ *a pools winner* ➲ see also GENE POOL
■ ***verb*** **~ sth** to collect money, information, etc. from different people so that it can be used by all of them: *The students work individually, then pool their ideas in groups of six.* ◇ *Police forces across the country are pooling resources in order to solve this crime.*

pool·room /ˈpuːlruːm; -rʊm/ *noun* (*NAmE*) **1** a place for playing a game of POOL **2** a BETTING SHOP

pool·side /ˈpuːlsaɪd/ *noun* [sing.] the area around a swimming pool: *lazing at the poolside* ◇ *a poolside bar*

poop /puːp/ *noun, verb*
■ ***noun* 1** (also ˈ**poop deck**) [C] the raised part at the back end of a ship ➲ compare STERN **2** [U] (*especially NAmE*) (*BrE* also **poo**) (*informal*) a child's word for the solid waste that is passed through the BOWELS: *dog poop on the sidewalk* **3** [U] (*old-fashioned, informal, especially NAmE*) information about sth, especially the most recent news
■ ***verb*** (*NAmE, informal*) **1** [I] to pass solid waste from the BOWELS: *The dog just pooped in the kitchen!* **2** [T] **~ sb (out)** to make sb very tired
PHR V ˌ**poop** ˈ**out** to stop working or functioning

pooped /puːpt/ (also ˌ**pooped** ˈ**out**) *adj.* [not before noun] (*informal, especially NAmE*) very tired

pooper scoop·er /ˈpuːpə skuːpə(r)/ (also ˈ**poop scoop**) *noun* (*informal*) a tool used by dog owners for removing their dogs' solid waste from the streets, parks, etc.

poor 🔑 /pɔː(r); pʊə(r); *NAmE* pɔːr; pʊr/ *adj.* (**poor·er, poor·est**)
▸ HAVING LITTLE MONEY **1** 🔑 having very little money; not having enough money for basic needs: *They were too poor to buy shoes for the kids.* ◇ *We aim to help the poorest families.* ◇ *It's among the poorer countries of the world.* OPP **rich 2 the poor** *noun* [pl.] people who have very little money: *They provided food and shelter for the poor.* OPP **the rich**
▸ UNFORTUNATE **3** 🔑 [only before noun] deserving pity and sympathy: *Have you heard about* **poor old** *Harry? His wife's left him.* ◇ *It's hungry—the poor little thing.* ◇ *'I have stacks of homework to do.' 'Oh,* **you poor thing**.*'*
▸ NOT GOOD **4** 🔑 not good; of a quality that is low or lower than expected: *the party's poor performance in the election* ◇ *to be in poor health* ◇ *It was raining heavily and visibility was poor.* ◇ *poor food/light/soil* ◇ *to have a poor opinion of sb* (= to not think well of sb) **5** 🔑 (of a person) not good or skilled at sth: *a poor swimmer* ◇ *a poor judge of character* ◇ *She's a good teacher but a poor manager.* ◇ *a poor sailor* (= sb who easily gets sick at sea)
▸ HAVING LITTLE OF STH **6** 🔑 **~ in sth** having very small amounts of sth: *a country poor in natural resources* ◇ *soil poor in nutrients* OPP **rich**
IDM **be/come a poor second, third, etc.** (*especially BrE*)

P

to finish a long way behind the winner in a race, competition, etc. **the ˌpoor man's ˈsb/ˈsth** a person or thing that is similar to but of a lower quality than a particular famous person or thing: *Sparkling white wine is the poor man's champagne.* ➲ more at ACCOUNT *n.*

Synonyms

poor

disadvantaged • needy • impoverished • deprived • penniless • hard up

These words all describe sb who has very little or no money and therefore cannot satisfy their basic needs.

poor having very little money; not having enough money for basic needs: *They were too poor to buy shoes for the kids.*

disadvantaged having less money and fewer opportunities than most people in society: *socially disadvantaged sections of the community*

needy poor: *It's a charity that provides help for needy children.*

impoverished (*journalism*) poor: *Thousands of impoverished peasants are desperate to move to the cities.*

deprived [usually before noun] without enough food, education, and all the things that are necessary for people to live a happy and comfortable life

POOR, NEEDY, IMPOVERISHED OR DEPRIVED?

Poor is the most general of these words and can be used to describe yourself, another individual person, people as a group, or a country or an area. **Needy** is mostly used to describe people considered as a group: it is not used to talk about yourself or individual people: *poor/needy children/families* ◇ ~~*They were too needy to buy shoes for the kids.*~~ **Impoverished** is used, especially in journalism, to talk about poor countries and the people who live there. To talk about poor areas in rich countries, use **deprived**.

penniless (*literary*) having no money; very poor: *He died penniless in Paris.*

hard up (*informal*) having very little money, especially for a short period of time: *I was always hard up as a student.*

PATTERNS

- poor/disadvantaged/needy/impoverished/deprived/penniless/hard-up **people/families**
- poor/disadvantaged/needy/impoverished/deprived **areas**
- poor/disadvantaged/impoverished **countries**
- a(n) poor/disadvantaged/impoverished/deprived **background**

poor·house /ˈpɔːhaʊs; ˈpʊə-; *NAmE* ˈpʊr-; ˈpɔːr-/ (*BrE* also **work·house**) *noun* (in Britain in the past) a building where very poor people were sent to live and given work to do

the ˈPoor Law *noun* a group of laws used in Britain in the past to control the help that was given to poor people

poor·ly /ˈpɔːli; ˈpʊəli; *NAmE* ˈpʊrli; ˈpɔːrli/ *adv., adj.*

■ ***adv.*** in a way that is not good enough **SYN** **badly**: *a poorly attended meeting* (= at which there are not many people) ◇ *poorly designed* ◇ *The job is relatively poorly paid.* ◇ *Our candidate **fared poorly** in the election* (= did not get many votes).

■ ***adj.*** [not usually before noun] (*BrE, informal*) ill/sick: *She felt poorly.*

poor·ness /ˈpɔːnəs; ˈpʊənəs; *NAmE* ˈpɔːrnəs; ˈpʊrnəs/ *noun* [U] the state of lacking a good quality or feature: *The poorness of the land makes farming impossible.*

ˌpoor reˈlation *noun* something that is not treated with as much respect as other similar things because it is not thought to be as good, important or successful: *The short story is often considered to be a poor relation to the novel.*

poo·tle /ˈpuːtl/ *verb* [I] + **adv./prep.** (*BrE, informal*) to move or travel without any hurry: *She pootled along in her old car.*

pop 🔑 /pɒp; *NAmE* pɑːp/ *noun, verb, adj., adv.*

■ ***noun***

▸ MUSIC **1** 🔑 (also ˈ**pop music**) [U] popular music of the sort that has been popular since the 1950s, usually with a strong rhythm and simple tunes, often contrasted with rock, SOUL and other forms of popular music: *rock, pop and soul* ➲ COLLOCATIONS at MUSIC

▸ SOUND **2** 🔑 [C] a short sharp EXPLOSIVE sound: *The cork came out of the bottle with a loud pop.*

▸ DRINK **3** [U] (*old-fashioned, informal*) a sweet FIZZY drink (= with bubbles) that is not alcoholic

▸ FATHER **4** [sing.] (*informal, especially NAmE*) used as a word for 'father', especially as a form of address: *Hi, Pop!*

IDM **have/take a ˈpop (at sb)** (*BrE, informal*) to attack sb physically or in words **...a pop** (*informal, especially NAmE*) costing a particular amount for each one: *We can charge $50 a pop.*

■ ***verb*** (-pp-)

▸ MAKE SOUND **1** 🔑 [I, T] **~ (sth)** to make a short EXPLOSIVE sound; to cause sth to make this sound: *the sound of corks popping* **2** [T, I] **~ (sth)** to burst, or make sth burst, with a short EXPLOSIVE sound: *She jumped as someone popped a balloon behind her.*

▸ GO QUICKLY **3** 🔑 [I] + **adv./prep.** (*BrE, informal*) to go somewhere quickly, suddenly or for a short time: *I'll pop over and see you this evening.* ◇ *Why don't you pop in* (= visit us) *for a drink next time you're in the area?*

▸ PUT QUICKLY **4** [T] **~ sth/sb + adv./prep.** (*informal, especially BrE*) to put sth/sb somewhere quickly, suddenly or for a short time: *He popped his head around the door and said hello.* ◇ *I'll pop the books in* (= deliver them) *on my way home.* ◇ *Pop your bag on here.*

▸ APPEAR SUDDENLY **5** [I] + **adv./prep.** to suddenly appear, especially when not expected: *The window opened and a dog's head popped out.* ◇ *An idea suddenly popped into his head.* ◇ (*computing*) *The menu pops up when you click twice on the mouse.*

▸ OF EARS **6** [I] if your ears **pop** when you are going up or down in a plane, etc, the pressure in them suddenly changes

▸ OF EYES **7** [I] if your eyes **pop** or **pop out**, they suddenly open fully because you are surprised or excited: *Her eyes nearly popped out of her head when she saw them.*

▸ TAKE DRUGS **8** [T] **~ sth** (*informal*) to take a lot of a drug, regularly: *She's been popping pills for months.* **9** [T] **~ the hood** (*NAmE*) to open the HOOD/BONNET of a car

IDM **pop your ˈclogs** (*BrE, humorous*) to die **pop the ˈquestion** (*informal*) to ask sb to marry you

PHR V **ˌpop ˈoff** (*informal*) to die **ˌpop sth↔ˈon** (*BrE, informal*) **1** to put on a piece of clothing: *I'll just pop on a sweater and meet you outside.* **2** to turn on a piece of electrical equipment

■ ***adj.*** [only before noun]

▸ MUSIC/STYLE **1** connected with modern popular music: *a **pop song** ◇ a **pop band/group** ◇ a **pop star** ◇ a **pop concert*** **2** made in a modern popular style: *pop culture*

■ ***adv.***

IDM **go ˈpop** to burst or explode with a sudden short sound: *The balloon went pop.*

pop. *abbr.* population: *pop. 200 000*

ˈpop art (also **Pop Art**) *noun* [U] a style of art, developed in the 1960s, that was based on popular culture and used material such as advertisements, film/movie images, etc.

pop·corn /ˈpɒpkɔːn; *NAmE* ˈpɑːpkɔːrn/ *noun* [U] a type of food made from grains of MAIZE (CORN) that are heated until they burst, forming light whitish balls that are then covered with salt or sugar

pope /pəʊp; *NAmE* poʊp/ (often **the Pope**) *noun* the leader of the Roman Catholic Church, who is also the Bishop of Rome: *the election of a new pope* ◇ *Pope Benedict* ◇ *a visit from the Pope* ➲ see also PAPACY, PAPAL

IDM **Is the Pope a 'Catholic?** (*humorous*) used to say that there is no doubt that sth is true: *'Will they arrive late?' 'Is the Pope a Catholic?'*

popery /ˈpəʊpəri; *NAmE* ˈpoʊ-/ *noun* [U] (*taboo*) an offensive way of referring to Roman Catholicism

ˌpope's ˈnose *noun* (*NAmE*) = PARSON'S NOSE

ˈpop-eyed *adj.* (*informal*) having eyes that are wide open, especially because you are very surprised, excited or frightened

pop·gun /ˈpɒpgʌn; *NAmE* ˈpɑːp-/ *noun* a toy gun that fires small objects such as CORKS and makes a short sharp noise

pop·ish /ˈpəʊpɪʃ; *NAmE* ˈpoʊ-/ *adj.* [usually before noun] (*taboo, offensive*) used by some people to describe sb/sth that is connected with Roman Catholicism

pop·lar /ˈpɒplə(r); *NAmE* ˈpɑːp-/ *noun* a tall straight tree with soft wood

pop·lin /ˈpɒplɪn; *NAmE* ˈpɑːp-/ *noun* [U] a type of strong cotton cloth used for making clothes

ˈpop music *noun* = POP

pop·over /ˈpɒpəʊvə(r); *NAmE* ˈpɑːpoʊvər/ *noun* (*NAmE*) a type of food made from a mixture of eggs, milk and flour which rises to form a hollow shell when it is baked

poppa /ˈpɒpə; *NAmE* ˈpɑːpə/ *noun* (*NAmE, informal*) used by children to talk about or to address their father ➲ see also PAPA, POP

pop·pa·dom /ˈpɒpədəm; *NAmE* ˈpɑːp-/ *noun* a type of thin round crisp S Asian bread that is fried in oil and often served with CURRY

pop·per /ˈpɒpə(r); *NAmE* ˈpɑːp-/ *noun* (*BrE*) = PRESS STUD

pop·pers /ˈpɒpəz; *NAmE* ˈpɑːpərz/ *noun* [pl.] (*informal*) = AMYL NITRITE

pop·pet /ˈpɒpɪt; *NAmE* ˈpɑːp-/ *noun* (*BrE, informal*) used to talk to or about sb you like or love, especially a child

ˌpop psyˈchology *noun* [U] the use by ordinary people of simple or fashionable ideas from PSYCHOLOGY in order to understand or explain people's feelings and emotional problems

poppy /ˈpɒpi; *NAmE* ˈpɑːpi/ *noun* (*pl.* **-ies**) a wild or garden plant, with a large delicate flower that is usually red, and small black seeds. OPIUM is obtained from one type of poppy: *poppy fields/seeds* ➲ VISUAL VOCAB page V9

poppy·cock /ˈpɒpikɒk; *NAmE* ˈpɑːpikɑːk/ *noun* [U] (*old-fashioned, informal*) nonsense

ˈpop quiz *noun* (*NAmE*) a short test that is given to students without any warning

Pop·sicle™ /ˈpɒpsɪkl; *NAmE* ˈpɑːp-/ (*NAmE*) (*BrE* **ˌice ˈlolly**, *informal* **lolly**) *noun* a piece of ice flavoured with fruit, served on a stick

pop·sock /ˈpɒpsɒk; *NAmE* ˈpɑːpsɑːk/ *noun* a short STOCKING that covers the foot and the lower part of the leg to the ankle or knee

pop·tas·tic /pɒpˈtæstɪk; *NAmE* pɑːp-/ *adj.* (*informal, especially BrE*) very good: *She's the most poptastic pop star of the lot.*

popu·lace /ˈpɒpjələs; *NAmE* ˈpɑːp-/ (usually **the populace**) *noun* [sing.+ sing./pl. v.] (*formal*) all the ordinary people of a particular country or area: *He had the support of large sections of the local populace.* ◇ *The populace at large is/are opposed to sudden change.*

popu·lar 🔑 /ˈpɒpjələ(r); *NAmE* ˈpɑːp-/ *adj.* **1** 🔑 liked or enjoyed by a large number of people: *a **hugely/immensely popular** singer* ◇ *This is one of our most popular designs.* ◇ *Skiing has become very popular recently.* ◇ **~ (with sb)** *These policies are unlikely to **prove popular** with middle-class voters.* ◇ *I'm not very popular with my parents* (= they are annoyed with me) *at the moment.* ◇ (*ironic*) *'Our dog got into the neighbour's garden again!' 'You'll be popular.'* **OPP** **unpopular** **2** 🔑 [only before noun] (sometimes *disapproving*) suited to the taste and knowledge of ordinary people: ***popular music/culture/fiction*** ◇ *the popular press* **3** 🔑 [only before noun] (of ideas, beliefs and opinions) shared by a large number of people: *a popular misconception* ◇ ***Contrary to popular belief**, women cause fewer road accidents than men.* ◇ ***Popular opinion** was divided on the issue.* ◇ *By **popular demand**, the tour has been extended by two weeks.* **4** [only before noun] connected with the ordinary people of a country: *The party still has widespread popular support.*

ˌpopular etyˈmology *noun* = FOLK ETYMOLOGY

ˌpopular ˈfront *noun* a political group or party that has SOCIALIST aims

popu·lar·ity /ˌpɒpjuˈlærəti; *NAmE* ˌpɑːp-/ *noun* [U] the state of being liked, enjoyed or supported by a large number of people: *the increasing popularity of cycling* ◇ *Her novels have **gained in popularity** over recent years.* ◇ **~ with/among sb** *to **win/lose popularity** with the students*

popu·lar·ize (*BrE* also **-ise**) /ˈpɒpjələraɪz; *NAmE* ˈpɑːp-/ *verb* **1** **~ sb/sth** to make a lot of people know about sth and enjoy it: *The programme did much to popularize little-known writers.* **2** **~ sth** to make a difficult subject easier to understand for ordinary people: *He spent his life popularizing natural history.* ▸ **popu·lar·iza·tion, -isa·tion** /ˌpɒpjələraɪˈzeɪʃn; *NAmE* ˌpɑːpjələrəˈz-/ *noun* [U]

popu·lar·ly /ˈpɒpjələli; *NAmE* ˈpɑːpjələrli/ *adv.* **1** by a large number of people **SYN** **commonly**: *a popularly held belief* ◇ *the UN Conference on Environment and Development, popularly known as the 'Earth Summit'* **2** by the ordinary people of a country **SYN** **democratically**: *a popularly elected government*

popu·late /ˈpɒpjuleɪt; *NAmE* ˈpɑːp-/ *verb* **1** [often passive] **~ sth** to live in an area and form its population **SYN** **inhabit**: *a **heavily/densely/sparsely/thinly populated** country* ◇ *The island is populated largely by sheep.* ◇ (*figurative*) *the amazing characters that populate her novels* **2** **~ sth** to move people or animals to an area to live there: *The French began to populate the island in the 15th century.* **3** **~ sth** (*computing*) to add data to a document

popu·la·tion 🔑 /ˌpɒpjuˈleɪʃn; *NAmE* ˌpɑːp-/ *noun* **1** 🔑 [C+sing./pl. v., U] all the people who live in a particular area, city or country; the total number of people who live there: *One third of the world's population consumes/consume two thirds of the world's resources.* ◇ *The entire population of the town was at the meeting.* ◇ *countries with ageing populations* ◇ *Muslims make up 55% of the population.* ◇ *an increase in population* ◇ *areas of **dense/sparse population*** (= where many/not many people live) ◇ *The population is increasing at about 6% per year.* ◇ *Japan has a population of nearly 130 million.* **2** 🔑 [C+sing./pl. v.] a particular group of people or animals living in a particular area: *the **adult/working/rural, etc. population** of the country*

popuˈlation explosion *noun* a sudden large increase in the number of people in an area

popu·lism /ˈpɒpjəlɪzəm; *NAmE* ˈpɑːp-/ *noun* [U] a type of politics that claims to represent the opinions and wishes of ordinary people ▸ **popu·list** /-ɪst/ *noun*: *a party of populists* **popu·list** *adj.* [usually before noun]: *a populist leader*

popu·lous /ˈpɒpjələs; *NAmE* ˈpɑːp-/ *adj.* (*formal*) where a large number of people live: *one of America's most populous states*

ˈpop-up *adj.* [only before noun] **1** (of a book, etc.) containing a picture that stands up when the pages are opened: *a pop-up birthday card* **2** (of an electric TOASTER) that pushes the bread quickly upwards when it is ready **3** (of a computer menu, etc.) that can be brought to the screen quickly while you are working on another document: *a **pop-up menu/window***

por·cel·ain /ˈpɔːsəlɪn; *NAmE* ˈpɔːrs-/ *noun* [U, C] a hard white shiny substance made by baking CLAY and used for making delicate cups, plates and decorative objects; objects that are made of this: *a porcelain figure*

porch /pɔːtʃ; *NAmE* pɔːrtʃ/ *noun* **1** a small area at the entrance to a building, such as a house or a church, that is

P

covered by a roof and often has walls ➲ VISUALVOCAB page V15 **2** (*NAmE*) = VERANDA

por·cine /ˈpɔːsaɪn; *NAmE* ˈpɔːrs-/ *adj.* (*formal*) like a pig; connected with pigs

por·cu·pine /ˈpɔːkjupaɪn; *NAmE* ˈpɔːrk-/ *noun* an animal covered with long stiff parts like needles (called QUILLS), which it can raise to protect itself when it is attacked

pore /pɔː(r)/ *noun, verb*

▪ ***noun*** one of the very small holes in your skin that sweat can pass through; one of the similar small holes in the surface of a plant or a rock ➲ see also POROUS

▪ ***verb***

PHR V **ˈpore over sth** to look at or read sth very carefully SYN **examine**: *His lawyers are poring over the small print in the contract.*

pork /pɔːk; *NAmE* pɔːrk/ *noun* [U] meat from a pig that has not been CURED (= preserved using salt or smoke): *roast pork* ◇ *pork chops* ◇ *a leg of pork* ➲ compare BACON, GAMMON, HAM (1)

ˈpork barrel *noun* [U] (*NAmE, slang*) local projects that are given a lot of government money in order to win votes; the money that is used

porker /ˈpɔːkə(r); *NAmE* ˈpɔːrk-/ *noun* a pig that is made fat and used as food

ˌpork ˈpie *noun* [C, U] (*BrE*) a small PIE filled with PORK and usually eaten cold

ˌpork ˈscratchings (*BrE*) (*US* **ˈpork rinds**) *noun* [pl.] crisp pieces of pig skin that are fried and eaten cold, often sold in bags as a SNACK

porky /ˈpɔːki; *NAmE* ˈpɔːrki/ *noun, adj.*

▪ ***noun*** (*pl.* **-ies**) (also **ˌporky ˈpie**) (*BrE, slang*) a statement that is not true; a lie: *to tell porkies*

▪ ***adj.*** (*informal, disapproving*) (of people) fat

porn /pɔːn; *NAmE* pɔːrn/ *noun* [U] (*informal*) = PORNOGRAPHY ➲ see also HARD PORN, SOFT PORN

porno /ˈpɔːnəʊ; *NAmE* ˈpɔːrnoʊ/ *adj.* [usually before noun] (*informal*) = PORNOGRAPHIC: *a porno movie*

P

porn·og·raph·er /pɔːˈnɒɡrəfə(r); *NAmE* pɔːrˈnɑːɡ-/ *noun* (*disapproving*) a person who produces or sells pornography

porno·graph·ic /ˌpɔːnəˈɡræfɪk; *NAmE* ˌpɔːrn-/ (also *informal* **porno**) *adj.* [usually before noun] (*disapproving*) intended to make people feel sexually excited by showing naked people or sexual acts, usually in a way that many other people find offensive: *pornographic movies/magazines*

porn·og·raphy /pɔːˈnɒɡrəfi; *NAmE* pɔːrˈnɑːɡ-/ (also *informal* **porn**) *noun* [U] (*disapproving*) books, magazines, DVDs, etc. that describe or show naked people and sexual acts in order to make people feel sexually excited, especially in a way that many other people find offensive: *child pornography*

por·os·ity /pɔːˈrɒsəti; *NAmE* -ˈrɑːs-/ *noun* [U] (*technical*) the quality or state of being porous

por·ous /ˈpɔːrəs/ *adj.* having many small holes that allow water or air to pass through slowly: *porous material/rocks/surfaces*

por·phy·ria /pɔːˈfɪriə; *NAmE* pɔːrˈf-/ *noun* [U] (*medical*) a disease of the blood that causes mental problems and makes the skin sensitive to light

por·poise /ˈpɔːpəs; *NAmE* ˈpɔːrpəs/ *noun* a sea animal that looks like a large fish with a pointed mouth. Porpoises are similar to DOLPHINS but smaller.

por·ridge /ˈpɒrɪdʒ; *NAmE* ˈpɔːr-/ *noun* [U] **1** (*especially BrE*) (*NAmE* usually **oat·meal**) a type of soft thick white food made by boiling OATS in milk or water, eaten hot, especially for breakfast **2** (*EAfrE*) a type of thick drink made by boiling flour with water

port 0⊸ /pɔːt; *NAmE* pɔːrt/ *noun, verb*

▪ ***noun*** **1** 0⊸ [C] a town or city with a HARBOUR, especially one where ships load and unload goods: *fishing ports* ◇ *Rotterdam is a major port.* **2** 0⊸ [C, U] (*abbr.* **Pt.**) a place where ships load and unload goods or shelter from storms: *a naval port* ◇ *The ship spent four days **in port**.* ◇ *They reached port at last.* ◇ ***port of entry*** (= a place where people or goods can enter a country) ➲ see also AIRPORT, FREE PORT, HELIPORT, SEAPORT **3** (also **port ˈwine**) [U] a strong sweet wine, usually dark red, that is made in Portugal. It is usually drunk at the end of a meal. **4** [C] a glass of port **5** [U] the side of a ship or aircraft that is on the left when you are facing forward: *the port side* ➲ compare STARBOARD **6** [C] (*computing*) a place on a computer where you can attach another piece of equipment, often using a cable: *the modem port* ➲ VISUAL VOCAB page V54

IDM **any port in a ˈstorm** (*saying*) if you are in great trouble, you take any help that is offered

▪ ***verb*** **1 ~ sth (to sth)** (*computing*) to copy software from one system or machine to another **2 ~ sth (to sth)** to continue to use the same number when you change from one phone company to another: *how to port your number to a new mobile phone*

port·able /ˈpɔːtəbl; *NAmE* ˈpɔːrt-/ *adj., noun*

▪ ***adj.*** that is easy to carry or to move: *a portable TV* ◇ (*figurative*) *a portable loan/pension* (= that can be moved if you change banks, jobs, etc.) ◇ *portable software* ▶ **port·ab·il·ity** /ˌpɔːtəˈbɪləti; *NAmE* ˌpɔːrt-/ *noun* [U]: *The new light cover increases this model's portability.*

▪ ***noun*** a small type of machine that is easy to carry, especially a computer or a television

port·age /ˈpɔːtɪdʒ; *NAmE* ˈpɔːrt-/ *noun* [U] the act of carrying boats or goods between two rivers

Porta-john™ /ˈpɔːtə dʒɒn; *NAmE* ˈpɔːrtə dʒɑːn/ *noun* = PORTAPOTTY

Porta·kabin™ /ˈpɔːtəkæbɪn; *NAmE* ˈpɔːrt-/ *noun* (*BrE*) a small building that can be moved from place to place by a vehicle, designed to be used as a temporary office, etc.

por·tal /ˈpɔːtl; *NAmE* ˈpɔːrtl/ *noun* **1** [usually pl.] (*formal* or *literary*) a large, impressive gate or entrance to a building **2** (*computing*) a website that is used as a point of entry to the Internet, where information has been collected that will be useful to a person interested in particular kinds of things: *a business/news/shopping portal*

Porta·loo™ /ˈpɔːtəluː; *NAmE* ˈpɔːrt-/ (*BrE*) (*NAmE* **porta-potty, Porta-john™**) *noun* (*pl.* **-oos**) a toilet inside a small light building that can be moved from place to place

ˈportal vein (also **hepatic ˈportal vein**) *noun* (*anatomy*) a VEIN that takes blood from the stomach and other organs near the stomach to the LIVER

porta·potty (also **Porta Potti™**) /ˈpɔːtə pɒti; *NAmE* ˈpɔːrtəpɑːti/ *noun* (*pl.* **-ies**) **1** (*NAmE*) (*BrE* **Portaloo™**) (*NAmE* also **Porta-john™**) a toilet inside a small light building that can be moved from place to place **2** (*BrE*) a toilet that you can take with you when you are travelling

port·cul·lis /pɔːtˈkʌlɪs; *NAmE* pɔːrt-/ *noun* a strong, heavy iron gate that can be raised or let down at the entrance to a castle

por·tend /pɔːˈtend; *NAmE* pɔːrˈt-/ *verb* **~ sth** (*formal*) to be a sign or warning of sth that is going to happen in the future, especially sth bad or unpleasant SYN **foreshadow**

por·tent /ˈpɔːtent; *NAmE* ˈpɔːrt-/ *noun* (*literary*) a sign or warning of sth that is going to happen in the future, especially when it is sth unpleasant SYN **omen**

por·tent·ous /pɔːˈtentəs; *NAmE* pɔːrˈt-/ *adj.* **1** (*literary*) important as a sign or a warning of sth that is going to happen in the future, especially when it is sth unpleasant: *a portentous sign* **2** (*formal, disapproving*) very serious and intended to impress people SYN **pompous**: *a portentous remark* ▶ **por·tent·ous·ly** *adv.* **por·tent·ous·ness** *noun* [U]

por·ter /ˈpɔːtə(r); *NAmE* ˈpɔːrt-/ *noun* **1** a person whose job is carrying people's bags and other loads, especially at a train station, an airport or in a hotel ➲ see also KITCHEN PORTER **2** (*BrE*) a person whose job is to move patients from one place to another in a hospital **3** (*BrE*) a person whose job is to be in charge of the entrance to a hotel, large building, college, etc: *the night porter* ◇ *The hotel porter will get you a taxi.* ➲ compare DOORMAN **4** (*NAmE*) a person whose job is helping passengers on a train, especially in a SLEEPING CAR

port·folio /pɔːtˈfəʊliəʊ; *NAmE* pɔːrtˈfoʊlioʊ/ *noun* (*pl.* -os) **1** a thin flat case used for carrying documents, drawings, etc. **2** a collection of photographs, drawings, etc. that you use as an example of your work, especially when applying for a job **3** (*finance*) a set of shares owned by a particular person or organization: *an* ***investment/share portfolio*** **4** (*formal, especially BrE*) the particular area of responsibility of a government minister: *the defence portfolio* ◇ *She resigned her portfolio.* ◇ *He was asked to join as a* ***minister without portfolio*** (= one without responsibility for a particular government department). **5** the range of products or services offered by a particular company or organization: *a portfolio of wines*

port·hole /ˈpɔːthəʊl; *NAmE* ˈpɔːrthoʊl/ *noun* a round window in the side of a ship or an aircraft

por·tico /ˈpɔːtɪkəʊ; *NAmE* ˈpɔːrtɪkoʊ/ *noun* (*pl.* -oes or -os) (*formal*) a roof that is supported by columns, especially one that forms the entrance to a large building ➲ VISUAL VOCAB page V12

por·tion AW /ˈpɔːʃn; *NAmE* ˈpɔːrʃn/ *noun, verb*

■ ***noun*** **1** one part of sth larger: *a* ***substantial/significant portion*** *of the population* ◇ *Only a small portion of the budget is spent on books.* ◇ *The central portion of the bridge collapsed.* **2** an amount of food that is large enough for one person: *a generous portion of meat* ◇ *She cut the cake into six small portions.* **3** [usually sing.] a part of sth that is shared with other people SYN **share**: *You must accept a portion of the blame for this crisis.*

■ ***verb*** to divide sth into parts or portions: **~ sth** *The factory portions and packs over 12 000 meals a day.* ◇ **~ sth out** *Land was portioned out among the clans.*

port·ly /ˈpɔːtli; *NAmE* ˈpɔːrt-/ *adj.* [usually before noun] (especially of an older man) rather fat SYN **stout**

port·man·teau /pɔːtˈmæntəʊ; *NAmE* pɔːrtˈmæntoʊ/ *noun, adj.*

■ ***noun*** (*pl.* **portmanteaus** or **portmanteaux**) (*old-fashioned*) a large heavy suitcase that opens into two parts

■ ***adj.*** [only before noun] consisting of a number of different items that are combined into a single thing: *a portmanteau course* ◇ *'Depression' is a portmanteau condition.*

port'manteau word *noun* a word that is invented by combining the beginning of one word and the end of another and keeping the meaning of each. For example *motel* is a portmanteau word that is a combination of *motor* and *hotel*.

ˌport of ˈcall *noun* (*pl.* **ports of call**) **1** a port where a ship stops during a journey **2** (*informal*) a place where you go or stop for a short time, especially when you are going to several places: *My first port of call in town was the bank.*

por·trait /ˈpɔːtreɪt; -trət; *NAmE* ˈpɔːrtrət/ *noun, adj.*

■ ***noun*** **1** a painting, drawing or photograph of a person, especially of the head and shoulders: *He had his portrait painted in uniform.* ◇ *a full-length portrait* ◇ *a portrait painter* ➲ SYNONYMS at PICTURE ➲ COLLOCATIONS at ART ➲ see also SELF-PORTRAIT **2** a detailed description of sb/sth SYN **depiction**: *a portrait of life at the French court*

■ ***adj.*** (*computing*) (of a page of a document) printed so that the top of the page is one of the shorter sides ➲ compare LANDSCAPE

por·trait·ist /ˈpɔːtreɪtɪst; -trət-; *NAmE* ˈpɔːrtrət-/ *noun* a person who makes portraits

por·trait·ure /ˈpɔːtrətʃə(r); *NAmE* ˈpɔːrt-/ *noun* [U] the art of making portraits; the portraits that are made

por·tray /pɔːˈtreɪ; *NAmE* pɔːrˈt-/ *verb* **1 ~ sb/sth** to show sb/sth in a picture; to describe sb/sth in a piece of writing SYN **depict** **2 ~ sb/sth (as sb/sth)** to describe or show sb/sth in a particular way, especially when this does not give a complete or accurate impression of what they are like SYN **represent**: *Throughout the trial, he portrayed himself as the victim.* **3 ~ sb/sth** to act a particular role in a film/movie or play SYN **play**: *Her father will be portrayed by Sean Connery.*

por·tray·al /pɔːˈtreɪəl; *NAmE* pɔːrˈt-/ *noun* [C, U] the act of showing or describing sb/sth in a picture, play, book, etc; a particular way in which this is done: *The article examines the portrayal of gay men in the media.* ◇ *He is best known for his chilling portrayal of Hannibal Lecter.*

Por·tu·guese /ˌpɔːtʃuˈɡiːz; *NAmE* ˌpɔːrt-/ *adj., noun*

■ ***adj.*** from or connected with Portugal

■ ***noun*** **1** [C] (*pl.* **Por·tu·guese**) a person from Portugal **2** [U] the language used in Portugal and Brazil and some other countries

pose 0-w AW /pəʊz; *NAmE* poʊz/ *verb, noun*

■ ***verb*** **1** 0-w [T] **~ sth** to create a threat, problem, etc. that has to be dealt with: *to* ***pose a threat/challenge/danger/risk*** ◇ *The task poses no special* ***problems.*** **2** [T] **~ a question** (*formal*) to ask a question, especially one that needs serious thought **3** 0-w [I] **~ (for sb/sth)** to sit or stand in a particular position in order to be painted, drawn or photographed: *The delegates posed for a group photograph.* **4** 0-w [I] **~ as sb** to pretend to be sb in order to trick other people: *The gang entered the building posing as workmen.* **5** [I] (usually used in the progressive tenses) (*disapproving*) to dress or behave in a way that is intended to impress other people: *I saw him out posing in his new sports car.*

■ ***noun*** **1** 0-w a particular position in which sb stands, sits, etc, especially in order to be painted, drawn or photographed: *He adopted a relaxed pose for the camera.* **2** 0-w (*disapproving*) a way of behaving that is not sincere and is only intended to impress other people SYN **affectation** IDM see STRIKE *v.*

poser /ˈpəʊzə(r); *NAmE* ˈpoʊ-/ *noun* **1** (*informal*) a difficult question or problem SYN **puzzler** **2** (also **pos·eur**) (*disapproving*) a person who behaves or dresses in a way that is intended to impress other people and is not sincere

pos·eur /pəʊˈzɜː(r); *NAmE* poʊ-/ *noun* = POSER (2)

posey /ˈpəʊzi; *NAmE* ˈpoʊzi/ *adj.* (*informal*) trying to impress other people, especially in a way that is silly or not natural

posh /pɒʃ; *NAmE* pɑːʃ/ *adj.* (**posh·er**, **posh·est**) (*informal*) **1** elegant and expensive: *a posh hotel* ◇ *You look very posh in your new suit.* **2** (*BrE*, sometimes *disapproving*) typical of or used by people who belong to a high social class SYN **stylish**: *a* ***posh accent/voice*** ◇ *They live in the posh part of town.* ◇ *They pay for their children to go to a posh school.* ▸ **posh** *adv.*: (*BrE*) *to talk posh*

posho /ˈpɒʃəʊ; *NAmE* ˈpɑːʃoʊ/ *noun* **1** [C] (*pl.* -os) (*BrE, informal, disapproving*) a person from a high social class **2** [U] (*EAfrE*) a type of flour made from MAIZE (CORN): *a posho mill*

ˈposing pouch *noun* (*BrE*) an item of men's clothing that covers only the GENITALS

posit /ˈpɒzɪt; *NAmE* ˈpɑːz-/ *verb* **~ sth | ~ that...** (*formal*) to suggest or accept that sth is true so that it can be used as the basis for an argument or discussion SYN **postulate**: *Most religions posit the existence of life after death.*

pos·ition 0-w /pəˈzɪʃn/ *noun, verb*

■ ***noun***

▸ PLACE **1** 0-w [C] the place where sb/sth is located: *From his position on the cliff top, he had a good view of the harbour.* ◇ *Where would be the best position for the lights?* ➲ SYNONYMS at PLACE **2** 0-w [U] the place where sb/sth is meant to be; the correct place: *Is everybody* ***in position?*** ◇ *He took up his position by the door.*

▸ WAY SB/STH IS PLACED **3** 0-w [C, U] the way in which sb is sitting or standing, or the way in which sth is arranged: *a* ***sitting/kneeling/lying position*** ◇ *Keep the box in an upright position.* ◇ *Make sure that you are working in a comfortable position.* ◇ *My arms were aching so I shifted (my) position slightly.* ➲ see also MISSIONARY POSITION

▸ SITUATION **4** 0-w [C, usually sing.] the situation that sb is in, especially when it affects what they can and cannot do: *to be in a* ***position of power/strength/authority*** ◇ *What would you do in my position?* ◇ *This put him and his colleagues in a difficult position.* ◇ *The company's financial position is not certain.* ◇ **~ to do sth** *I'm afraid I am* ***not in a position*** *to help you.* ➲ note at SITUATION

P

▸ OPINION **5** [C] **~ (on sth)** an opinion on or an attitude towards a particular subject: *to* ***declare/reconsider/shift/change your position*** ◇ *the party's position on education reforms* ◇ *She has made her position very clear.* ◇ *My parents always* ***took the position*** *that early nights meant healthy children.*
▸ LEVEL OF IMPORTANCE **6** [C, U] a person or organization's level of importance when compared with others: *the position of women in society* ◇ *the company's dominant position in the world market* ◇ *Wealth and position* (= high social status) *were not important to her.*
▸ JOB **7** [C] (*formal*) a job SYN **post**: *He held a senior position in a large company.* ◇ *I should like to apply for the position of Sales Director.* ➲ SYNONYMS at JOB
▸ IN RACE/COMPETITION **8** [C] a place in a race, competition, or test, when compared to others: *United's 3–0 win moved them up to third position.*
▸ IN SPORT **9** [C] the place where sb plays and the responsibilities they have in some team games: *What position does he play?*
▸ IN WAR **10** [C, usually pl.] a place where a group of people involved in fighting have put men and guns: *They attacked the enemy positions at dawn.*
■ *verb* **~ sth (+ adv./prep.)** to put sb/sth in a particular position SYN **place**: *Large television screens were positioned at either end of the stadium.* ◇ *She quickly positioned herself behind the desk.* ◇ *The company is now well positioned to compete in foreign markets.* ▸ **pos·ition·ing** *noun* [U]

pos·ition·al /pəˈzɪʃənəl/ *adj.* [only before noun] (*technical* or *sport*) connected with the position of sb/sth: *The team has made some positional changes because two players are injured.*

poˈsition paper *noun* a written report from an organization or a government department that explains or recommends a particular course of action

posi·tive AW /ˈpɒzətɪv; *NAmE* ˈpɑːz-/ *adj., noun*
■ *adj.*
▸ CONFIDENT **1** thinking about what is good in a situation; feeling confident and sure that sth good will happen: *a* ***positive attitude/outlook*** ◇ *the power of positive thought* ◇ **~ (about sth)** *She tried to be more positive about her new job.* ◇ ***On the positive side****, profits have increased.* ◇ *The report ended on a positive note.* OPP **negative**
▸ EFFECTIVE/USEFUL **2** directed at dealing with sth or producing a successful result: *We must take* ***positive steps*** *to deal with the problem.* ◇ *It will require* ***positive action*** *by all in the industry.* OPP **negative 3** expressing agreement or support: *We've had a very positive response to the idea.* OPP **negative 4** good or useful: *to make a positive contribution to a discussion* ◇ *His family have been a very positive influence on him.* ◇ *Overseas investment has had a positive effect on exports.* OPP **negative**
▸ SURE/DEFINITE **5** [not before noun] (of a person) completely sure that sth is correct or true: **~ (about sth)** *I can't be positive about what time it happened.* ◇ **~ (that...)** *She was positive that he had been there.* ◇ *'Are you sure?' 'Positive.'* ➲ SYNONYMS at SURE **6** [only before noun] (*informal*) complete and definite SYN **absolute**: *He has a positive genius for upsetting people.* ◇ *It was a positive miracle that we survived.* **7** giving clear and definite proof or information SYN **conclusive**: *We have no positive evidence that she was involved.* ◇ (*formal*) *This is* ***proof positive*** *that he stole the money.*
▸ SCIENTIFIC TEST **8** showing clear evidence that a particular substance or medical condition is present: *a positive pregnancy test* ◇ *The athlete* ***tested positive*** *for steroids.* ◇ *to be HIV positive* OPP **negative**
▸ NUMBER/QUANTITY **9** greater than zero OPP **negative**
▸ ELECTRICITY **10** (*technical*) containing or producing the type of electricity that is carried by a PROTON: *a* ***positive charge*** ◇ *the* ***positive terminal*** *of a battery* OPP **negative**
■ *noun*
▸ GOOD QUALITY **1** [C, U] a good or useful quality or aspect: *Take your weaknesses and translate them into positives.*
▸ IN PHOTOGRAPHY **2** [C] (*technical*) a developed film showing light and dark areas and colours as they actually were, especially one printed from a NEGATIVE
▸ RESULT OF TEST **3** [C] the result of a test or an experiment that shows that a substance or condition is present OPP **negative**

ˌpositive disˌcriminˈation (*BrE*) (also **afˌfirmative ˈaction** *NAmE, BrE*) *noun* [U] the practice or policy of making sure that a particular number of jobs, etc. are given to people from groups that are often treated unfairly because of their race, sex, etc. ➲ COLLOCATIONS at RACE ➲ compare REVERSE DISCRIMINATION

posi·tive·ly AW /ˈpɒzətɪvli; *NAmE* ˈpɑːz-/ *adv.* **1** used to emphasize the truth of a statement, especially when this is surprising or when it contrasts with a previous statement: *The instructions were not just confusing, they were positively misleading.* **2** in a way that shows you are thinking of the good things about a situation, not the bad: *Very few of those interviewed spoke positively about their childhood.* ◇ *Thinking positively is one way of dealing with stress.* OPP **negatively 3** in a way that shows you approve of or agree with sth/sb: *Investors reacted positively to news of the takeover.* OPP **negatively 4** in a way that leaves no possibility of doubt SYN **conclusively**: *Her attacker has now been positively identified by police.* **5** (*technical*) in a way that contains or produces the type of electricity that is opposite to that carried by an ELECTRON: *positively charged protons* OPP **negatively**

ˌpositive ˈvetting *noun* [U, C] (*BrE*) the process of checking everything about a person's background and character when they apply for a job in which they will have to deal with secret information, especially in the CIVIL SERVICE

posi·tiv·ism /ˈpɒzətɪvɪzəm; *NAmE* ˈpɑːz-/ *noun* [U] a system of philosophy based on things that can be seen or proved, rather than on ideas ▸ **posi·tiv·ist** /-vɪst/ *noun* **posi·tiv·ist** *adj.*: *a positivist approach*

posi·tron /ˈpɒzɪtrɒn; *NAmE* ˈpɑːzɪtrɑːn/ *noun* (*physics*) a PARTICLE in an atom which has the same mass as an ELECTRON and an equal but positive charge

poss /pɒs; *NAmE* pɑːs/ *adj.* [not before noun] (*BrE, informal*) possible: *I'll be there* ***if poss****.* ◇ *as soon* ***as poss***

posse /ˈpɒsi; *NAmE* ˈpɑːsi/ *noun* **1** (*informal*) a group of people who are similar in some way, or who spend time together: *a little posse of helpers* **2** (in the US in the past) a group of people who were brought together by a SHERIFF (= an officer of the law) in order to help him catch a criminal **3** (*informal*) a group of young men involved in crime connected with drugs

pos·sess /pəˈzes/ *verb* (not used in the progressive tenses)
1 **~ sth** (*formal*) to have or own sth: *He was charged with possessing a shotgun without a licence.* ◇ *The gallery possesses a number of the artist's early works.* **2** **~ sth** (*formal*) to have a particular quality or feature: *I'm afraid he doesn't possess a sense of humour.* **3** [usually passive] **~ sb** (*literary*) (of a feeling, an emotion, etc.) to have a powerful effect on sb and control the way that they think, behave, etc. **4** **~ sb to do sth** (used in negative sentences and questions) to make sb do sth that seems strange or unreasonable: *What possessed him to say such a thing?*

pos·sessed /pəˈzest/ *adj.* [not before noun] **~ (by sth)** (of a person or their mind) controlled by an evil spirit: *She has convinced herself that she is possessed by the devil.*
IDM **be possessed of sth** (*formal*) to have a particular quality or feature: *She was possessed of exceptional powers of concentration.* **like a man/woman posˈsessed | like one posˈsessed** with a lot of force or energy: *He flew out of the room like a man possessed.*

pos·ses·sion /pəˈzeʃn/ *noun*
▸ HAVING/OWNING **1** [U] (*formal*) the state of having or owning sth: *The manuscript is just one of the treasures* ***in their possession****.* ◇ *The gang was caught* ***in possession of*** *stolen goods.* ◇ *The possession of a passport is essential for foreign travel.* ◇ *On her father's death, she* ***came into possession of*** (= received) *a vast fortune.* ◇ *You cannot legally* ***take possession of*** *the property* (= start using it after buying it) *until three weeks after the contract is signed.* ➲ see

also VACANT POSSESSION **2** 0-w [C, usually pl.] something that you own or have with you at a particular time SYN **belongings**: *personal possessions* ◇ *The ring is one of her most treasured possessions.* ➲ SYNONYMS at THING
▸ IN SPORT **3** [U] the state of having control of the ball: *to* ***win/get/lose possession*** *of the ball*
▸ LAW **4** [U] the state of having illegal drugs or weapons with you at a particular time: *She was charged with possession.*
▸ COUNTRY **5** [C] (*formal*) a country that is controlled or governed by another country
▸ BY EVIL SPIRIT **6** [U] the situation when sb's mind is believed to be controlled by the DEVIL or by an evil spirit
IDM **possession is nine tenths of the 'law** (*saying*) if you already have or control sth, it is difficult for sb else to take it away from you, even if they have the legal right to it ➲ more at FIELD *n.*

pos·ses·sive /pəˈzesɪv/ *adj., noun*
■ *adj.* **1 ~ (of/about sb/sth)** demanding total attention or love; not wanting sb to be independent: *Some parents are too possessive of their children.* **2 ~ (of/about sth)** not liking to lend things or share things with others: *Jimmy's very possessive about his toys.* **3** [usually before noun] (*grammar*) showing that sth belongs to sb/sth: *possessive pronouns* (= yours, theirs, etc.) ▸ **pos·ses·sive·ly** *adv.*: *'That's mine!' she said possessively.* **pos·ses·sive·ness** *noun* [U]: *I couldn't stand his jealousy and possessiveness.*
■ *noun* (*grammar*) **1** [C] an adjective, a pronoun or a form of a word that expresses the fact that sth belongs to sb/sth: *'Ours' and 'their' are possessives.* **2 the possessive** *noun* [sing.] the special form of a word that expresses belonging ➲ compare GENITIVE

pos·ses·sor /pəˈzesə(r)/ *noun* (*formal* or *humorous*) a person who owns or has sth SYN **owner**: *He is now* ***the proud possessor*** *of a driving licence.*

pos·set /ˈpɒsɪt; *NAmE* ˈpɑːs-/
■ *noun* in the past, a drink made with hot milk and beer or wine
■ *verb* (*BrE*) (-tt-, *NAmE* also -t-) [I] if a baby **possets**, milk comes back up from its stomach and out through its mouth

pos·si·bil·ity 0-w /ˌpɒsəˈbɪləti; *NAmE* ˌpɑːs-/ *noun* (*pl.* -ies)
1 0-w [U, C] the fact that sth might exist or happen, but is not certain to: **~ (that...)** *There is now no possibility that she will make a full recovery.* ◇ **~ (of sth/of doing sth)** *He refused to rule out the possibility of a tax increase.* ◇ *It is not* ***beyond the bounds of possibility*** *that we'll all meet again one day.* ◇ *Bankruptcy is a real possibility if sales don't improve.* ◇ *What had seemed impossible now seemed a* ***distinct possibility.*** OPP **impossibility** **2** 0-w [C, usually pl.] one of the different things that you can do in a particular situation: *to* ***explore/consider/investigate*** *a wide range of* ***possibilities*** ◇ *to* ***exhaust*** *all* ***the possibilities*** ◇ *Selling the house is just one possibility that is open to us.* ◇ ***The possibilities are endless.*** ➲ SYNONYMS at OPTION **3** 0-w [C, usually pl.] something that gives you a chance to achieve sth SYN **opportunity**: *The course offers a range of exciting possibilities for developing your skills.* **4 possibilities** [pl.] if sth **has possibilities**, it can be improved or made successful SYN **potential**: *The house is in a bad state of repair but it has possibilities.*

pos·sible 0-w /ˈpɒsəbl; *NAmE* ˈpɑːs-/ *adj., noun*
■ *adj.* **1** 0-w [not usually before noun] that can be done or achieved: ***It is possible to*** *get there by bus.* ◇ ***Would it be possible for*** *me to leave a message for her?* ◇ *This wouldn't have been possible without you.* ◇ *Try to avoid losing your temper* ***if at all possible*** (= if you can). ◇ *Use public transport* ***whenever possible*** (= when you can). ◇ *It's just not* ***physically possible*** *to finish all this by the end of the week.* ◇ *We spent every possible moment on the beach.* OPP **impossible** **2** 0-w that might exist or happen but is not certain to: *a possible future president* ◇ *the possible side effects of the drug* ◇ *Frost is possible, although unlikely, at this time of year.* ◇ *It's just possible that I gave them the wrong directions.* ◇ *With the possible exception of the Beatles, no other band has become so successful so quickly.* ➲ LANGUAGE BANK at PERHAPS **3** 0-w reasonable or acceptable in a particular situation: *There are several possible explanations.* **4** used after adjectives to emphasize that sth is the best, worst, etc. of its type: *It was the* ***best possible*** *surprise anyone could have given me.* ◇ *Don't leave your packing until the* ***last possible*** *moment.*
IDM **as quickly, much, soon, etc. as 'possible** 0-w as quickly, much, soon, etc. as you can: *We will get your order to you as soon as possible.* ➲ more at WORLD, WORST *n.*
■ *noun* a person or thing that is suitable for a particular job, purpose, etc. and might be chosen: *Out of all the people interviewed, there are only five possibles.*

pos·sibly 0-w /ˈpɒsəbli; *NAmE* ˈpɑːs-/ *adv.*
1 0-w used to say that sth might exist, happen or be true, but you are not certain SYN **perhaps**: *It was possibly their worst performance ever.* ◇ *She found it difficult to get on with her, possibly because of the difference in their ages.* ◇ *'Will you be around next week?' 'Possibly.'* ➲ LANGUAGE BANK at PERHAPS **2** 0-w used to emphasize that you are surprised, annoyed, etc. about sth: *You can't possibly mean that!* **3** 0-w used to ask sb politely to do sth: *Could you possibly open that window?* **4** 0-w used to say that sb will do or has done as much as they can in order to make sth happen: *I will come as soon as I possibly can.* ◇ *They tried everything they possibly could to improve the situation.* **5** used with negatives, especially 'can't' and 'couldn't', to say strongly that you cannot do sth or that sth cannot or could not happen or be done: *I can't possibly tell you that!* ◇ *You can't possibly carry all those bags.* ◇ *'Let me buy it for you.' 'That's very kind of you, but I couldn't possibly* (= accept).*'*

pos·sum /ˈpɒsəm; *NAmE* ˈpɑːsəm/ *noun* (*AustralE, NZE* or *NAmE, informal*) = OPOSSUM
IDM **play 'possum** (*informal*) to pretend to be asleep or not aware of sth, in order to trick sb

post 0-w /pəʊst; *NAmE* poʊst/ *noun, verb*
■ *noun*
▸ LETTERS **1** 0-w (*BrE*) (also **mail** *NAmE, BrE*) [U] the official system used for sending and delivering letters, packages, etc: *I'll send the original to you* ***by post.*** ◇ *I'll put the information* ***in the post*** *to you tomorrow.* ◇ *My application* ***got lost in the post.*** **2** 0-w (*BrE*) (also **mail** *NAmE, BrE*) [U] letters, packages, etc. that are sent and delivered: *There was a lot of post this morning.* ◇ *Have you opened your post yet?* **3** 0-w (*BrE*) [U, sing.] an occasion during the day when letters, etc. are collected or delivered: *to* ***catch/miss the post*** ◇ *The parcel came in this morning's post.* ◇ *Payment should be sent* ***by return of post*** (= immediately).
▸ JOB **4** 0-w [C] a job, especially an important one in a large organization SYN **position**: *an academic/government post* ◇ *to* ***take up a post*** ◇ *to* ***resign*** (***from***) ***a post*** ◇ *We will be creating 15 new posts next year.* ◇ *The company has been unable to* ***fill the post.*** ◇ *He has* ***held the post*** *for three years.* ➲ SYNONYMS at JOB **5** (*especially NAmE*) (*BrE* usually **posting**) an act of sending sb to a particular place to do their job, especially for a limited period of time: *an overseas post*
▸ FOR SOLDIER/GUARD **6** 0-w [C] the place where sb, especially a soldier, does their job: *a* ***police/customs/military post*** ◇ *an observation post* ◇ *The guards were ordered not to leave their posts.* ➲ see also THE LAST POST, STAGING POST, TRADING POST
▸ WOOD/METAL **7** [C] (often in compounds) a piece of wood or metal that is set in the ground in a vertical position, especially to support sth or to mark a point: *corner posts* (= that mark the corners of a sports field) ➲ see also BEDPOST, GATEPOST, LAMP POST, SIGNPOST
▸ END OF RACE **8 the post** [sing.] the place where a race finishes, especially in horse racing ➲ see also FIRST-PAST-THE-POST, WINNING POST
▸ FOOTBALL **9** [C, usually sing.] = GOALPOST: *The ball hit the post and bounced in.*
▸ INTERNET **10** (also **post·ing**) [C] (*computing*) a message sent to a discussion group on the Internet; a piece of writing that forms part of a BLOG: *The forum does not allow posts from non-members.* IDM see DEAF, PILLAR

P

British/American

post / mail

Nouns

- In *BrE* the official system used for sending and delivering letters, parcels/packages, etc. is usually called the **post**. In *NAmE* it is usually called the **mail**: *I'll put an application form in the post/mail for you today.* ◇ *Send your fee by post/mail to this address.* **Mail** is sometimes used in *BrE* in such expressions as *the Royal Mail*. **Post** occurs in *NAmE* in such expressions as *the US Postal Service*.
- In *BrE* **post** is also used to mean the letters, parcels/packages, etc. that are delivered to you. **Mail** is the usual word in *NAmE* and is sometimes also used in *BrE*: *Was there any post/mail this morning?* ◇ *I sat down to open my post/mail.*

Verbs

- Compare: *I'll post the letter when I go out.* (*BrE*) and *I'll mail the letter when I go out.* (*NAmE*)

Compounds

- Note these words: **postman** (*BrE*), **mailman/mail carrier** (both *NAmE*); **postbox** (*BrE*), **mailbox** (*NAmE*) Some compounds are used in both *BrE* and *NAmE*: **post office**, **postcard**, **mail order**.

■ ***verb***
▸ LETTERS **1** (*BrE*) (*NAmE* **mail**) [T] to send a letter, etc. to sb by post/mail: **~ sth (off) (to sb)** *Have you posted off your order yet?* ◇ *Is it OK if I post the cheque to you next week?* ◇ **~ sb sth** *Is it OK if I post you the cheque next week?* ➲ compare MAIL **2** (*BrE*) (*NAmE* **mail**) [T] **~ sth** to put a letter, etc. into a POSTBOX: *Could you post this letter for me?*
▸ STH THROUGH HOLE **3** [T] **~ sth + adv./prep.** to put sth through a hole into a container: *Let yourself out and post the keys through the letter box.*
▸ SB FOR JOB **4** [T, usually passive] **~ sb + adv./prep.** to send sb to a place for a period of time as part of their job: *She's been posted to Washington for two years.* ◇ *Most of our employees get posted abroad at some stage.*
▸ SOLDIER/GUARD **5** [T] **~ sb + adv./prep.** to put sb, especially a soldier, in a particular place so that they can guard a building or area: *Guards have been posted along the border.*
▸ PUBLIC NOTICE **6** [T, often passive] **~ sth + adv./prep.** to put a notice, etc. in a public place so that people can see it SYN **display**: *A copy of the letter was posted on the noticeboard.*
▸ GIVE INFORMATION **7** [T] (*especially NAmE*) to announce sth publicly or officially, especially financial information or a warning: **~ sth** *The company posted a $1.1 billion loss.* ◇ *A snow warning was posted for Ohio.* ◇ **~ sb/sth + adj.** *The aircraft and its crew were **posted missing**.* **8** [T, I] to put information or pictures on a website: **~ sth (on sth)** *The results will be posted on the Internet.* ◇ **~ (on sth)** *The photos have been provided by fans who post on the message board.*
▸ PAY MONEY TO COURT **9** [T] **~ bail/(a) bond** (*especially NAmE*) to pay money to a court so that a person accused of a crime can go free until their trial: *She was released after posting $100 cash bond and her driver's license.*
IDM **keep sb 'posted (about/on sth)** to regularly give sb the most recent information about sth and how it is developing

post- /pəʊst; *NAmE* poʊst/ *prefix* (in nouns, verbs and adjectives) after: *a postgraduate* ◇ *a post-Impressionist* ◇ *the post-1945 period* ➲ compare ANTE-, PRE-

post·age /'pəʊstɪdʒ; *NAmE* 'poʊ-/ *noun* [U] the cost of sending a letter, etc. by post: *an increase in postage rates* ◇ *How much was the postage on that letter?* ◇ (*BrE*) *All prices include **postage and packing**.* ◇ (*NAmE*) *All prices include **postage and handling**.*

'postage meter *noun* (*NAmE*) = FRANKING MACHINE

'postage stamp *noun* (*formal*) = STAMP

pos·tal /'pəʊstl; *NAmE* 'poʊstl/ *adj.* [only before noun] **1** connected with the official system for sending and delivering letters, etc: *your full **postal address*** ◇ *the **postal service/system*** ◇ *postal charges* **2** (*especially BrE*) involving things that are sent by post: *postal bookings*
IDM **go 'postal** (*informal, especially NAmE*) to become very angry: *He went postal when he found out.*

'postal ballot *noun* (*BrE*) a system of voting on a particular issue in which everyone sends their vote by post

'postal code *noun* (*BrE, CanE*) = POSTCODE

'postal order (*BrE*) (also **'money order** *NAmE, BrE*) *noun* (*abbr.* **PO**) an official document that you can buy at a bank or a post office and send to sb so that they can exchange it for money

'postal service *noun* **1** a system of collecting and delivering letters, etc: *a good postal service* **2 the Postal Service** (*US*) (*BrE* **the 'Post Office**) the national organization in many countries that is responsible for collecting and delivering letters, etc.

'postal vote (*BrE*) (*US* **,absentee 'ballot**) *noun* a vote in an election that you can send when you cannot be present

post·bag /'pəʊstbæg; *NAmE* 'poʊst-/ *noun* (*BrE*) **1** (also **mail·bag** *NAmE, BrE*) [usually sing.] all the letters, emails, etc. received by a newspaper, a TV station, a website, or an important person at a particular time or about a particular subject: *We had a huge postbag on the subject from our readers.* **2** = MAILBAG (1)

post·box /'pəʊstbɒks; *NAmE* 'poʊstbɑːks/ (also **'letter box**) (both *BrE*) (*NAmE* **mail·box**) *noun* a public box, for example in the street, that you put letters into when you send them ➲ picture at LETTER BOX ➲ VISUAL VOCAB page V2 ➲ compare PILLAR BOX

post·card /'pəʊstkɑːd; *NAmE* 'poʊstkɑːrd/ (also **card**) *noun* a card used for sending messages by post without an envelope, especially one that has a picture on one side: *colourful postcards of California* ◇ *Send us a postcard from Venice!* ◇ *Send your answers on a postcard to the above address.* ➲ see also PICTURE POSTCARD

post·code /'pəʊstkəʊd; *NAmE* 'poʊstkoʊd/ (also **'postal code**) (*BrE, CanE*) (*US* **'zip code**) *noun* a group of letters and/or numbers that are used as part of an address so that post/mail can be separated into groups and delivered more quickly

,postcode 'lottery *noun* [sing.] (*BrE*) a situation in which the amount or type of medical treatment that is provided to people depends on the particular area of the country they live in

post-coital /,pəʊst 'kɔɪtl; 'kəʊɪtl; *NAmE* ,poʊst; 'koʊɪtl/ *adj.* [usually before noun] happening or done after SEXUAL INTERCOURSE

,post-'date *verb* **1 ~ sth** to write a date on a cheque that is later than the actual date so that the cheque cannot be CASHED (= exchanged for money) until that date ➲ compare BACKDATE **2 ~ sth** to happen, exist or be made at a later date than sth else in the past OPP **predate**

post·doc·tor·al /,pəʊst'dɒktərəl; *NAmE* ,poʊst'dɑːk-/ *adj.* [usually before noun] connected with advanced research or study that is done after a PHD has been completed

pos·ter /'pəʊstə(r); *NAmE* 'poʊ-/ *noun* **1** a large notice, often with a picture on it, that is put in a public place to advertise sth SYN **placard**: *election posters* ◇ *a poster campaign* (= an attempt to educate people about sth by using posters) **2** a large picture that is printed on paper and put on a wall as decoration: *posters of her favourite pop stars* ➲ VISUAL VOCAB page V57 **3** a person who posts a message on a MESSAGE BOARD (= a place on a website where people can read or write messages)

'poster child (also **'poster boy**, **'poster girl**) *noun* (*especially NAmE*) **1** a child with a particular illness or other problem whose picture appears on a poster advertising an organization that helps children with that illness or problem **2** (often *humorous*) a person who is seen as representing a particular quality or activity: *He is the poster child for incompetent government.*

poste rest·ante /ˌpəʊst ˈrestɑːnt; *NAmE* ˌpoʊst reˈst-/ (*BrE*) (*NAmE* ˌ**general deˈlivery**) *noun* [U] an arrangement in which a post office keeps a person's mail until they go to collect it, used especially when sb is travelling

pos·ter·ior /pɒˈstɪəriə(r); *NAmE* pɑːˈstɪr-/ *adj.*, *noun*
- *adj.* [only before noun] (*technical*) located behind sth or at the back of sth **OPP anterior**
- *noun* (*humorous*) the part of your body that you sit on; your bottom

pos·teri·ori ➲ A POSTERIORI

pos·ter·ity /pɒˈsterəti; *NAmE* pɑːˈs-/ *noun* [U] (*formal*) all the people who will live in the future: *Their music has been* ***preserved for posterity.*** ◇ *Posterity will remember him as a great man.*

ˈ**poster paint** *noun* [U, C] a thick paint used especially for children's paintings

ˌ**post exˈchange** *noun* = PX

ˌ**post-ˈfree** *adj.* [only before noun] (*BrE*) used to describe sth that you can send by post without having to pay anything ▶ ˌ**post-ˈfree** *adv.*: *Information will be sent post-free to any interested readers.*

post·grad /ˈpəʊstgræd; *NAmE* ˈpoʊst-/ *noun* (*informal*) a POSTGRADUATE

post·gradu·ate /ˌpəʊstˈgrædʒuət; *NAmE* ˌpoʊst-/ (also *informal* **post·grad**) *noun* (*especially BrE*) a person who already holds a first degree and who is doing advanced study or research; a GRADUATE student: *postgraduate students* ◇ *a postgraduate course* ➲ note at STUDENT

ˌ**post-ˈhaste** *adv.* (*literary*) as quickly as you can: *to depart post-haste*

post hoc /ˌpəʊst ˈhɒk; *NAmE* ˌpoʊst ˈhɑːk/ *adj.* (from *Latin*, *formal*) (of an argument, etc.) happening after the event, especially when one event is the cause of another: *a post hoc explanation* ▶ **post hoc** *adv.*

post·hu·mous /ˈpɒstjʊməs; *NAmE* ˈpɑːstʃəməs/ *adj.* [usually before noun] happening, done, published, etc. after a person has died: *a posthumous award for bravery* ▶ **post·hu·mous·ly** *adv.*

post·ie /ˈpəʊsti; *NAmE* ˈpoʊ-/ *noun* (*BrE, informal*) = POSTMAN

ˌ**post-in·ˈdus·trial** *adj.* [only before noun] (of a place or society) no longer relying on heavy industry (= the production of steel, large machinery, etc.)

post·ing /ˈpəʊstɪŋ; *NAmE* ˈpoʊ-/ *noun* **1** (*especially BrE*) (*NAmE* usually **post**) an act of sending sb to a particular place to do their job, especially for a limited period of time: *an overseas posting* **2** = POST *n.* (10)

ˈ**Post-it™** (also ˈ**Post-it note**) *noun* a small piece of coloured, sticky paper that you use for writing a note on, and that can be easily removed ➲ VISUAL VOCAB page V56

post·man /ˈpəʊstmən; *NAmE* ˈpoʊst-/, **post·woman** /ˈpəʊstwʊmən; *NAmE* ˈpoʊst-/ *noun* (*pl.* **-men** /-mən/, **-women** /-wɪmɪn/) (also *informal* **post·ie**) (*especially BrE*) a person whose job is to collect and deliver letters, etc. ➲ see also MAILMAN ➲ note at GENDER

ˌ**postman's ˈknock** (*BrE*) (*NAmE* ˈ**post office**) *noun* [U] a children's game in which imaginary letters are exchanged for kisses

post·mark /ˈpəʊstmɑːk; *NAmE* ˈpoʊstmɑːrk/ *noun* an official mark placed over the stamp on a letter, etc. that shows when and where it was posted and makes it impossible to use the stamp again ▶ **post·mark** *verb* [usually passive]: **~ sth** *The card was postmarked Tokyo 9th March.*

post·mas·ter /ˈpəʊstmɑːstə(r); *NAmE* ˈpoʊstmæstər/, **post·mist·ress** /ˈpəʊstmɪstrəs; *NAmE* ˈpoʊst-/ *noun* a person who is in charge of a post office

post·mod·ern /ˌpəʊstˈmɒdn; *NAmE* ˌpoʊstˈmɑːdərn/ *adj.* connected with or influenced by postmodernism

post·mod·ern·ism /ˌpəʊstˈmɒdənɪzəm; *NAmE* ˌpoʊstˈmɑːdərn-/ *noun* [U] a style and movement in art, ARCHITECTURE, literature, etc. in the late 20th century that reacts against modern styles, for example by mixing features from traditional and modern styles ➲ compare MODERNISM ▶ **post·mod·ern·ist** *noun*, *adj.* [usually before noun]

post·modi·fier /ˌpəʊstˈmɒdɪfaɪə(r); *NAmE* ˌpoʊstˈmɑːd-/ *noun* (*grammar*) a word or group of words that describes a noun phrase or restricts its meaning in some way, and is placed after it: *In 'the house on the corner', 'on the corner' is a postmodifier.* ➲ compare MODIFIER, PREMODIFIER

post-mortem /ˌpəʊst ˈmɔːtəm; *NAmE* ˌpoʊst ˈmɔːrtəm/ *noun* **1** (also **post-ˌmortem examiˈnation**) a medical examination of the body of a dead person in order to find out how they died **SYN autopsy**: *to* ***do/conduct/carry out a post-mortem*** ◇ **~ on sb** *The post-mortem on the child revealed that she had been poisoned.* **2 ~** (**on sth**) a discussion or an examination of an event after it has happened, especially in order to find out why it failed: *to hold a post-mortem on the party's election defeat*

post-natal /ˌpəʊst ˈneɪtl; *NAmE* ˌpoʊst/ (*BrE*) (*NAmE* **post-partum**) *adj.* [only before noun] connected with the period after the birth of a child: *post-natal care* ➲ compare ANTENATAL, PRENATAL

ˌ**post-ˌnatal deˈpression** (*BrE*) (*NAmE* ˌ**post-ˌpartum deˈpression**) *noun* [U] a medical condition in which a woman feels very sad and anxious in the period after her baby is born

ˈ**post office** 🔑 *noun*
1 🔑 [C] a place where you can buy stamps, send letters, etc: *Where's the main post office?* ◇ *You can buy your stamps at the post office.* ◇ *a post office counter* **2** 🔑 **the ˈPost Office** [sing.] (*abbr.* **PO**) the national organization in many countries that is responsible for collecting and delivering letters, etc: *He works for the Post Office.* **3** (*NAmE*) (*BrE* ˌ**postman's ˈknock**) [U] a children's game in which imaginary letters are exchanged for kisses

ˈ**post office box** *noun* = PO BOX

ˌ**post-ˈop·era·tive** *adj.* [only before noun] (*medical*) connected with the period after a medical operation: *post-operative complications/pain/care*

ˌ**post-ˈpaid** *adj.* [only before noun] that you can send free because the charge has already been paid: *a post-paid envelope* ▶ ˌ**post-ˈpaid** *adv.*

post-partum /ˌpəʊst ˈpɑːtəm; *NAmE* ˌpoʊst ˈpɑːrtəm/ (*NAmE*) (*BrE* **post-natal**) *adj.* [only before noun] connected with the period after the birth of a child ➲ compare ANTENATAL, PRENATAL

ˌ**post-ˌpartum deˈpression** (*NAmE*) (*BrE* ˌ**post-ˌnatal deˈpression**) *noun* [U] a medical condition in which a woman feels very sad and anxious in the period after her baby is born

post·pone /pəˈspəʊn; *NAmE* poʊˈspoʊn/ *verb* to arrange for an event, etc. to take place at a later time or date **SYN put off**: **~ sth** *The game has already been postponed three times.* ◇ **~ sth to/until sth** *We'll have to postpone the meeting until next week.* ◇ **~ doing sth** *It was an unpopular decision to postpone building the new hospital.* ➲ compare CANCEL ▶ **post·pone·ment** *noun* [U, C]: *Riots led to the postponement of local elections.*

post·pos·ition /ˌpəʊstpəˈzɪʃn; *NAmE* ˌpoʊst-/ *noun* (*grammar*) a word or part of a word that comes after the word it relates to, for example '-ish' in 'greenish' ▶ **post·pos·ition·al** /-ʃənl/ *adj.*

post·pran·dial /ˌpəʊstˈprændiəl; *NAmE* ˌpoʊst-/ *adj.* [usually before noun] (*formal* or *humorous*) happening immediately after a meal

ˌ**post-proˈduc·tion** *adj.* [usually before noun] **post-production** work on music or on films/movies is done after recording or filming: *post-production editing* ▶ ˌ**post-proˈduc·tion** *noun* [U]: *The movie is now in post-production and will be released next month.*

ˈ**post room** *noun* (*BrE*) the department of a company that deals with sending and receiving mail

post·script /ˈpəʊstskrɪpt; *NAmE* ˈpoʊst-/ *noun* **1** (*abbr.* PS) **~ (to sth)** an extra message that you add at the end of a letter after your signature **2 ~ (to sth)** extra facts or information about a story, an event, etc. that are added after it has finished

ˌpost-ˈsync (also **ˌpost-ˈsynch**) *verb* **~ sth** (*technical*) to add sound to a film/movie after it has been filmed

ˌpost-ˌtraumatic ˈstress disorder *noun* [U] (*medical*) a medical condition in which a person suffers mental and emotional problems resulting from an experience that shocked them very much

pos·tu·late *verb, noun*
- *verb* /ˈpɒstjuleɪt; *NAmE* ˈpɑːstʃəl-/ **~ sth** | **~ that...** (*formal*) to suggest or accept that sth is true so that it can be used as the basis for a theory, etc. SYN **posit**: *They postulated a 500-year lifespan for a plastic container.*
- *noun* /ˈpɒstjʊlət; *NAmE* ˈpɑːstʃəl-/ (*formal*) a statement that is accepted as true, that forms the basis of a theory, etc.

pos·tural /ˈpɒstʃərəl; *NAmE* ˈpɑːs-/ *adj.* (*formal*) connected with the way you hold your body when sitting or standing

pos·ture /ˈpɒstʃə(r); *NAmE* ˈpɑːs-/ *noun, verb*
- *noun* **1** [U, C] the position in which you hold your body when standing or sitting: *a comfortable/relaxed posture* ◇ ***upright/sitting/supine postures*** ◇ ***Good posture** is essential when working at the computer.* ◇ *Back pains can be the result of **bad posture**.* **2** [C, usually sing.] your attitude to a particular situation or the way in which you deal with it: *The government has adopted an aggressive posture on immigration.*
- *verb* [I] **~ (as sth)** (*formal*) to pretend to be sth that you are not by saying and doing things in order to impress or trick people

pos·tur·ing /ˈpɒstʃərɪŋ; *NAmE* ˈpɑːs-/ *noun* [U, C] (*disapproving*) behaviour that is not natural or sincere but is intended to attract attention or to have a particular effect

P

post·viral syn·drome /ˌpəʊstˈvaɪrəl sɪndrəʊm; *NAmE* ˌpoʊstˈvaɪrəl sɪndroʊm/ (also **ˌpostˌviral faˈtigue syndrome**) *noun* [U] a condition that follows a VIRAL infection, in which sb feels extremely weak and tired, and which can last for a long time

ˌpost-ˈwar *adj.* [usually before noun] existing, happening or made in the period after a war, especially the Second World War: *the post-war years*

post·woman ➲ POSTMAN

posy /ˈpəʊzi; *NAmE* ˈpoʊzi/ *noun* (*pl.* -ies) a small bunch of flowers

pot 0‑w /pɒt; *NAmE* pɑːt/ *noun, verb*
- *noun*
- ▸ FOR COOKING **1** 0‑w [C] a deep round container used for cooking things in: *pots and pans*
- ▸ CONTAINER **2** 0‑w [C] (*especially BrE*) a container made of glass, CLAY or plastic, used for storing food in: *a pot of jam* ◇ *a yogurt pot* ➲ VISUAL VOCAB page V29 **3** 0‑w [C] (especially in compounds) a container of various kinds, made for a particular purpose: *a coffee pot* ◇ *a pepper pot* ◇ *a teapot* ◇ *Is there any more tea in the pot?* ➲ VISUAL VOCAB page V22 ➲ see also CHAMBER POT, CHIMNEY POT, FLOWERPOT, LOBSTER POT, MELTING POT, POTTED **4** 0‑w [C] the amount contained in a pot: *They drank a pot of coffee.* **5** [C] a bowl, etc. that is made by a POTTER
- ▸ MONEY **6 the pot** [sing.] (*especially NAmE*) the total amount of money that is bet in a card game **7 the pot** [sing.] (*especially NAmE*) all the money given by a group of people in order to do sth together, for example to buy food ➲ see also KITTY
- ▸ DRUG **8** [U] (*informal*) = MARIJUANA: *pot smoking*
- ▸ SHOT **9** [C] = POTSHOT: *He took a pot at the neighbour's cat with his air rifle.*
- ▸ IN BILLIARDS, ETC. **10** [C] (in the game of BILLIARDS, POOL or SNOOKER) the act of hitting a ball into one of the pockets around the edge of the table
- ▸ STOMACH **11** [C] (*informal*) = POT BELLY

IDM **go to ˈpot** (*informal*) to be spoiled because people are not working hard or taking care of things: *Her handwriting's gone to pot since she started using a computer all the time.* **the pot calling the kettle ˈblack** (*saying, informal*) used to say that you should not criticize sb for a fault that you have yourself **ˌpot ˈluck** when you take **pot luck**, you choose sth or go somewhere without knowing very much about it, but hope that it will be good, pleasant, etc: *It's pot luck whether you get good advice or not.* ◇ *You're welcome to stay to supper, but you'll have to take pot luck* (= eat whatever is available). ➲ see also POTLUCK **ˈpots of money** (*BrE, informal*) a very large amount of money ➲ more at GOLD *n.*, MELTING POT, QUART, WATCH *v.*

- *verb* (-tt-)
- ▸ PLANT **1 ~ sth** to put a plant into a FLOWERPOT filled with soil
- ▸ IN BILLIARDS, ETC. **2 ~ sth** (in the games of BILLIARDS, POOL and SNOOKER) to hit a ball into one of the pockets (= holes at the corners and edges of the table) SYN **pocket**: *He potted the black to take a 7–3 lead.*
- ▸ SHOOT **3 ~ sth** to kill an animal or a bird by shooting it ➲ see also POTTED

pot·able /ˈpəʊtəbl; *NAmE* ˈpoʊ-/ *adj.* (*formal*) (of water) safe to drink

pot·ash /ˈpɒtæʃ; *NAmE* ˈpɑːt-/ *noun* [U] a chemical containing potassium, used to improve soil for farming and in making soap

po·tas·sium /pəˈtæsiəm/ *noun* [U] (*symb.* K) a chemical element. Potassium is a soft silver-white metal that exists mainly in COMPOUNDS which are used in industry and farming.

po·tato 0‑w /pəˈteɪtəʊ; *NAmE* -toʊ/ *noun* [C, U] (*pl.* -oes) a round white vegetable with a brown or red skin that grows underground as the root of a plant also called a potato: *Will you peel the potatoes for me?* ◇ ***roast/boiled/baked/fried potatoes*** ➲ VISUAL VOCAB page V27 ➲ see also COUCH POTATO, HOT POTATO, JACKET, MASHED POTATO, MEAT AND POTATOES, MEAT-AND-POTATOES, SMALL POTATOES, SWEET POTATO

poˌtato ˈcrisp (*BrE*), **poˈtato chip** (*NAmE*) *noun* = CRISP, CHIP

poˈtato masher *noun* a kitchen UTENSIL (= tool) for MASHING potatoes ➲ VISUAL VOCAB pages V23, V25

ˌpot-ˈbellied *adj.* (of people and animals) having a large stomach that sticks out ▸ **ˌpot ˈbelly** (also *informal* **pot**) *noun*

pot·boil·er /ˈpɒtbɔɪlə(r); *NAmE* ˈpɑːt-/ *noun* (*disapproving*) a book, a play, etc. that is produced only to earn money quickly

ˈpot-bound (also **ˈroot-bound**) *adj.* (of a plant) having roots that fill the flower pot, with no more room for them to grow

ˈpot cheese *noun* [U] (*US*) a type of soft white cheese with lumps in it

po·teen (also **po·theen**) /pəˈtiːn; pəˈtʃiːn/ *noun* [U] (*IrishE*) strong alcoholic drink made illegally, usually from potatoes

po·tency /ˈpəʊtnsi; *NAmE* ˈpoʊ-/ *noun* (*pl.* -ies) **1** [U, C] the power that sb/sth has to affect your body or mind: *the potency of desire* ◇ *If you keep a medicine too long, it may lose its potency.* **2** [U] the ability of a man to have sex

po·tent /ˈpəʊtnt; *NAmE* ˈpoʊ-/ *adj.* **1** having a strong effect on your body or mind: *a potent drug* ◇ *a very potent alcoholic brew* ◇ *a potent argument* **2** powerful: *a potent force* ➲ see also IMPOTENT ▸ **po·tent·ly** *adv.*

po·ten·tate /ˈpəʊtnteɪt; *NAmE* ˈpoʊ-/ *noun* (*literary*, often *disapproving*) a ruler who has a lot of power, especially when this is not restricted by a parliament, etc.

po·ten·tial 0‑w AW /pəˈtenʃl/ *adj., noun*
- *adj.* 0‑w [only before noun] that can develop into sth or be developed in the future SYN **possible**: *potential customers* ◇ *a potential source of conflict* ◇ *a potential prime minister* ◇

First we need to identify actual and potential problems. ▸ **po·ten·tial·ly** 🔑 AW /-ʃəli/ *adv.*: *a potentially dangerous situation*

■ ***noun*** **1** 🔑 [U] the possibility of sth happening or being developed or used: **~** (**for**) *the potential for change* ◇ **~** (**for doing sth**) *The European marketplace offers excellent potential for increasing sales.* **2** 🔑 [U] qualities that exist and can be developed SYN **promise**: *All children should be encouraged to* ***realize their full potential.*** ◇ *She has great potential as an artist.* ◇ *He has the potential to become a world-class musician.* ◇ *The house has a lot of potential.* **3** [U, C] (*physics*) the difference in VOLTAGE between two points in an electric field or CIRCUIT

po,tential 'energy *noun* [U] (*physics*) the form of energy that an object gains as it is lifted

po·ten·ti·al·ity /pəˌtenʃiˈæləti/ *noun* (*pl.* -ies) (*formal*) a power or a quality that exists and is capable of being developed: *We often underestimate our potentialities.*

po·tenti·om·eter /pəˌtenʃiˈɒmɪtə(r); *NAmE* -ˈɑːm-/ *noun* **1** a device for measuring differences in electrical POTENTIAL **2** a device for varying electrical RESISTANCE, used, for example, in volume controls

po·theen = POTEEN

pot·hole /ˈpɒthəʊl; *NAmE* ˈpɑːthoʊl/ *noun* **1** a large rough hole in the surface of a road that is formed by traffic and bad weather **2** a deep hole that is formed in rock, especially by the action of water

pot·hol·ing /ˈpɒthəʊlɪŋ; *NAmE* ˈpɑːthoʊlɪŋ/ (*BrE*) *noun* [U] = CAVING: *to go potholing* ▸ **pot·holer** *noun* = CAVER

po·tion /ˈpəʊʃn; *NAmE* ˈpoʊʃn/ *noun* (*literary*) a drink of medicine or poison; a liquid with magic powers: *a* ***magic/love potion*** ◇ (*humorous*) *I've tried all sorts of drugs, creams, pills and potions.*

potjie /ˈpɔɪki/ *noun* (*SAfrE*) **1** a round pot, usually with three legs, that is made from CAST IRON and used for cooking food slowly over a fire **2** a meal that is prepared in a pot like this: *a chicken potjie*

'pot liquor *noun* [U] (*especially US*) the liquid in which meat, fish, or vegetables have been cooked

pot·luck /pɒtˈlʌk; *NAmE* pɑːt-/ *noun* (*NAmE*) a meal to which each guest brings some food, which is then shared out among the guests

'pot plant *noun* (*BrE*) = HOUSE PLANT

pot·pourri /ˌpəʊpʊˈriː; *NAmE* ˌpoʊ/ *noun* (from *French*) **1** [U, C] a mixture of dried flowers and leaves used for making a room smell pleasant **2** [sing.] a mixture of various things that were not originally intended to form a group: *a potpourri of tunes*

'pot roast *noun* a piece of meat cooked with vegetables in a pot ▸ **'pot-roast** *verb* **~ sth**

pot·shot /ˈpɒtʃɒt; *NAmE* ˈpɑːtʃɑːt/ (also **pot**) *noun* (*informal*) a shot that sb fires without aiming carefully: *Somebody* ***took a potshot at*** *him as he drove past.* ◇ (*figurative*) *The newspapers* ***took*** *constant* ***potshots at*** (= criticized) *the president.*

pot·tage /ˈpɒtɪdʒ; *NAmE* ˈpɑːt-/ *noun* [U] (*old use*) soup or STEW

pot·ted /ˈpɒtɪd; *NAmE* ˈpɑːt-/ *adj.* [only before noun] **1** planted in a pot: *potted plants* **2** (*BrE*) (of a book, or a story) in a short simple form: *a potted history of England* **3** (*BrE*) **potted** meat or fish has been cooked and preserved in a small container

pot·ter /ˈpɒtə(r); *NAmE* ˈpɑːt-/ *verb, noun*

■ ***verb*** (*BrE*) (*NAmE* **putt·er**) [I] **+ adv./prep.** to do things or move without hurrying, especially when you are doing sth that you enjoy and that is not important: *I spent the day pottering around the house.*

■ ***noun*** a person who makes CLAY pots by hand

,potter's 'wheel *noun* a piece of equipment with a flat disc that goes around, on which potters put wet CLAY in order to shape it into pots ➲ VISUAL VOCAB page V35

pot·tery /ˈpɒtəri; *NAmE* ˈpɑːt-/ *noun* (*pl.* -ies) **1** [U] pots, dishes, etc. made with CLAY that is baked in an oven, especially when they are made by hand: *Roman pottery* ◇ *a piece of pottery* **2** [U] the CLAY that some dishes and pots are made of: *a jug made of blue-glazed pottery* **3** [U] the skill of making pots and dishes from CLAY, especially by hand: *a pottery class* ➲ VISUAL VOCAB page V35 **4** [C] a place where CLAY pots and dishes are made

'potting compost *noun* [U] good quality soil, used for growing plants in flower pots

'potting shed *noun* (*BrE*) a small building where seeds and young plants are grown in pots before they are planted outside

potto /ˈpɒtəʊ; *NAmE* ˈpɑːtoʊ/ *noun* (*pl.* -os) an animal like a MONKEY with a pointed face, found in tropical W Africa

potty /ˈpɒti; *NAmE* ˈpɑːti/ *adj., noun*

■ ***adj.*** (*BrE, informal*, becoming *old-fashioned*) (**pot·tier, pot·ti·est**) **1** crazy: *The kids are driving me potty!* **2 ~ about sb/sth** liking sb/sth a lot

■ ***noun*** (*pl.* -ies) (*informal*) a bowl that very young children use when they are too small to use a toilet ➲ compare CHAMBER POT

,potty-'mouthed *adj.* (*informal, especially NAmE*) using rude, offensive language: *a potty-mouthed comedian*

'potty-train *verb* **~ sb** to teach a small child to use a potty or toilet ▸ **'potty-trained** *adj.* **'potty-training** *noun* [U]

pouch /paʊtʃ/ *noun* **1** a small bag, usually made of leather, and often carried in a pocket or attached to a belt: *a tobacco pouch* ◇ *She kept her money in a pouch around her neck.* **2** a large bag for carrying letters, especially official ones ➲ see also DIPLOMATIC POUCH **3** a pocket of skin on the stomach of some female MARSUPIAL animals, such as KANGAROOS, in which they carry their young ➲ VISUAL VOCAB page V10 **4** a pocket of skin in the cheeks of some animals, such as HAMSTERS, in which they store food

pouffe (also **pouf**) /puːf/ (both *BrE*) (*NAmE* **has·sock**) *noun* a large thick CUSHION used as a seat or for resting your feet on

poult·ice /ˈpəʊltɪs; *NAmE* ˈpoʊ-/ *noun* a soft substance spread on a cloth, sometimes heated, and put on the skin to reduce pain or swelling

poult·ry /ˈpəʊltri; *NAmE* ˈpoʊ-/ *noun* **1** [pl.] chickens, DUCKS and GEESE, kept for their meat or eggs: *to keep poultry* ◇ *poultry farming* ➲ VISUAL VOCAB page V10 **2** [U] meat from chickens, DUCKS and GEESE: *Eat plenty of fish and poultry.*

pounce /paʊns/ *verb* [I] to move suddenly forwards in order to attack or catch sb/sth: *The lion crouched ready to pounce.* ◇ **~ on/upon sb/sth** *The muggers pounced on her as she got out of the car.* ◇ *Rooney pounced on the loose ball and scored.*

PHR V **'pounce on/upon sth** to quickly notice sth that sb has said or done, especially in order to criticize it SYN **seize on/upon**: *His comments were pounced upon by the press.*

pound 🔑 /paʊnd/ *noun, verb*

■ ***noun***

▸ MONEY **1** 🔑 [C] (also *technical* **,pound 'sterling**) (*symb.* £) the unit of money in the UK, worth 100 pence: *a ten-pound note* ◇ *a pound coin* ◇ *I've spent £25 on food today.* ◇ *What would you do if you won a million pounds?* ➲ see also STERLING **2** 🔑 [C] the unit of money of several other countries **3 the pound** [sing.] (*finance*) the value of the British pound compared with the value of the money of other countries: *the* ***strength/weakness of the pound*** (*against other currencies*) ◇ *The pound closed slightly down at $1.534.*

▸ WEIGHT **4** 🔑 [C] (*abbr.* **lb**) a unit for measuring weight, equal to 0.454 of a kilogram: *half a pound of butter* ◇ *They cost two dollars* ***a pound.*** ◇ *I've lost six and a half pounds since I started my diet.*

▸ FOR CARS **5** [C] a place where vehicles that have been parked illegally are kept until their owners pay to get them back

▸ FOR DOGS **6** [C] a place where dogs that have been found in

P

the street without their owners are kept until their owners claim them

IDM (have, get, want, etc.) **your pound of 'flesh** the full amount that sb owes you, even if this will cause them trouble or suffering ORIGIN From Shakespeare's *Merchant of Venice*, in which the moneylender Shylock demanded a pound of flesh from Antonio's body if he could not pay back the money he borrowed. ➲ more at PENNY, PREVENTION

■ *verb*

▸ HIT **1** [I, T] to hit sth/sb hard many times, especially in a way that makes a lot of noise SYN **hammer**: **~ at/against/on sth** *Heavy rain pounded on the roof.* ◇ *Someone was pounding at the door.* ◇ **~ away (at/against/on sth)** *The factory's machinery pounded away day and night.* ◇ **~ sb/sth (with sth)** *She pounded him with her fists.* ➲ SYNONYMS at BEAT

▸ WALK NOISILY **2** [I] **+ adv./prep.** to move with noisy steps: *She pounded along the corridor after him.*

▸ OF HEART/BLOOD **3** [I] to beat quickly and loudly: *Her heart was pounding with excitement.* ◇ *The blood was pounding* (= making a beating noise) *in his ears.* ◇ *Her head began to pound.* ◇ *a pounding headache*

▸ BREAK INTO PIECES **4** [T] **~ sth (to/into sth)** to hit sth many times in order to break it into smaller pieces: *The seeds were pounded to a fine powder.*

▸ ATTACK WITH BOMBS **5** [T] **~ sth** to attack an area with a large number of bombs over a period of time: *The area is still being pounded by rebel guns.*

▸ OF MUSIC **6** [I] **~ (out)** to be played loudly: *Rock music was pounding out from the jukebox.*

PHR V ˌ**pound sth↔'out** to play music loudly on a musical instrument: *to pound out a tune on the piano*

pound·age /'paʊndɪdʒ/ *noun* [U] **1** (*technical*) a charge that is made for every pound in weight of sth, or for every £1 in value **2** (*informal*) weight: *to carry extra poundage*

'pound cake (*NAmE*) (*BrE* **Ma'deira cake**) *noun* [C, U] a plain yellow cake made with eggs, fat, flour and sugar

pound·er /'paʊndə(r)/ *noun* (in compounds) **1** something that weighs the number of pounds mentioned: *a three-pounder* (= a fish, for example, that weighs 3lb) **2** a gun that fires a SHELL that weighs the number of pounds mentioned: *an eighteen-pounder*

pound·ing /'paʊndɪŋ/ *noun* [usually sing.] **1** a very loud repeated noise, such as the sound of sth hitting sth else hard; the sound or the feeling of your heart beating strongly: *We were awoken by a pounding at the door.* ◇ *There was a pounding in his head.* **2** an occasion when sth is hit hard or attacked and severely damaged SYN **battering**: *The boat* ***took a pounding*** *in the gale.* ◇ (*figurative*) *The team* ***took a pounding*** (= were badly defeated).

'pound sign *noun* **1** the symbol (£) that represents a pound in British money **2** (*NAmE*) (*BrE* **hash**, **'hash sign**) the symbol (#), especially one on a telephone

pour 0- /pɔː(r)/ *verb*

1 0- [T] **~ sth (+ adv./prep.)** to make a liquid or other substance flow from a container in a continuous stream, especially by holding the container at an angle: *Pour the sauce over the pasta.* ◇ *Although I poured it carefully, I still managed to spill some.* **2** 0- [I] **+ adv./prep.** (of liquid, smoke, light, etc.) to flow quickly in a continuous stream: *Tears poured down his cheeks.* ◇ *Thick black smoke was pouring out of the roof.* **3** 0- [T, I] to serve a drink by letting it flow from a container into a cup or glass: **~ (sth)** *Will you pour the coffee?* ◇ *Shall I pour?* ◇ **~ sth out** *I was in the kitchen, pouring out drinks.* ◇ **~ sth for sb** *I've poured a cup of tea for you.* ◇ **~ sb sth** *I've poured you a cup of tea.* **4** 0- [I, T] when rain **pours** down or when **it's pouring (with) rain**, rain is falling heavily: **~ (down)** *The rain continued to pour down.* ◇ *It's pouring outside.* ◇ (*BrE*) **~ with rain** *It's pouring with rain.* ◇ (*NAmE*) **~ (down) rain** *It's pouring rain outside.* **5** 0- [I] **+ adv./prep.** to come or go somewhere continuously in large numbers SYN **flood**: *Letters of complaint continue to pour in.* ◇ *Commuters came pouring out of the station.*

IDM **pour oil on troubled 'water(s)** to try to settle a disagreement or argument ➲ more at COLD *adj.*, HEART, RAIN *v.*, SCORN *n.*

PHR V ˌ**pour sth 'into sth** to provide a large amount of money for sth: *The government has poured millions into the education system.* ˌ**pour 'out** when feelings or sb's words **pour out** they are expressed, usually after they have been kept hidden for some time: *The whole story then came pouring out.* ˌ**pour sth↔'out** to express your feelings or give an account of sth, especially after keeping them or it secret or hidden: *She poured out her troubles to me over a cup of coffee.* ➲ related noun OUTPOURING

pout /paʊt/ *verb* [I, T] **~ (sth)** | **+ speech** if you **pout**, **pout** your lips or if your lips **pout**, you push out your lips, to show you are annoyed or to look sexually attractive: *He pouted angrily.* ◇ *Her lips pouted invitingly.* ◇ *models pouting their lips for the camera* ▸ **pout** *noun*: *Her lips were set in a pout of annoyance.* **pouty** *adj.*: *pouty lips*

pout·ine /puː'tiːn/ *noun* [U] (*CanE*) a dish of FRENCH FRIES with melted cheese on top, served with a sauce (usually GRAVY)

pov·erty /'pɒvəti; *NAmE* 'pɑːvərti/ *noun* **1** [U] the state of being poor: *conditions of* ***abject/extreme poverty*** ◇ *to* ***alleviate/relieve poverty*** ◇ *Many elderly people live* ***in poverty***. ➲ COLLOCATIONS at INTERNATIONAL **2** [U, sing.] a lack of sth; poor quality: *There is a poverty of colour in her work.*

the 'poverty line (also **the 'poverty level** especially in *US*) *noun* [sing.] the official level of income that is necessary to be able to buy the basic things you need such as food and clothes and to pay for somewhere to live: *A third of the population is living* ***at*** *or* ***below the poverty line***.

'poverty-stricken *adj.* extremely poor; with very little money

'poverty trap *noun* [usually sing.] a situation in which a person stays poor even when they get a job because the money they receive from the government is reduced

POW /ˌpiː əʊ 'dʌbljuː; *NAmE* oʊ/ *noun* the abbreviation for PRISONER OF WAR: *a POW camp*

pow /paʊ/ *exclamation* used to express the sound of an explosion, a gun firing or sb hitting sb else

pow·der 0- /'paʊdə(r)/ *noun, verb*

■ *noun* **1** 0- [U, C] a dry mass of very small fine pieces or grains: *chilli powder* ◇ *lumps of chalk crushed to (a) fine white powder* ◇ *The snow was like powder.* ◇ *A wide range of cleaning fluids and powders is available.* ◇ *The mustard is sold in* ***powder form***. ➲ see also BAKING POWDER, CURRY POWDER, SOAP POWDER, TALCUM POWDER, WASHING POWDER **2** [U] a very fine, soft, dry substance that you can put on your face to make it look smooth and dry ➲ VISUAL VOCAB page V49 **3** [U] = GUNPOWDER

IDM **keep your 'powder dry** (*old-fashioned*) to remain ready for a possible emergency **take a 'powder** (*NAmE, informal*) to leave suddenly; to run away

■ *verb* **~ sth** to put powder on sth: *She powdered her face and put on her lipstick.*

IDM **powder your 'nose** (*old-fashioned*) a polite way of referring to the fact that a woman is going to the toilet/bathroom: *I'm just going to powder my nose.*

ˌ**powder 'blue** *adj.* very pale blue in colour ▸ ˌ**powder 'blue** *noun* [U]

pow·dered /'paʊdəd; *NAmE* -dərd/ *adj.* **1** (of a substance that is naturally liquid) dried and made into powder: *powdered milk* **2** crushed and made into a powder: *powdered chalk* **3** covered with powder: *her powdered cheeks*

ˌ**powdered 'milk** *noun* [U] = MILK POWDER

'powdered sugar *noun* [U] (*US*) = CONFECTIONER'S SUGAR

'powder keg *noun* a dangerous situation that may suddenly become very violent

'powder puff *noun* a round thick piece of soft material that you use for putting powder on your face

'powder room *noun* **1** a polite word for a women's toilet/bathroom in a public building **2** (*NAmE*) a small room in a house containing a WASHBASIN and a toilet, usually for guests to use SYN **half-bath**

pow·dery /ˈpaʊdəri/ *adj.* like powder; covered with powder: *a light fall of powdery snow* ◇ *powdery cheeks*

power 0ᵚ /ˈpaʊə(r)/ *noun, verb*

■ ***noun***

▸ CONTROL **1** 0ᵚ [U] the ability to control people or things: **~ (over sb/sth)** *The aim is to give people more power over their own lives.* ◇ **~ (to do sth)** *He has the power to make things very unpleasant for us.* ◇ *to have sb* ***in your power*** (= to be able to do what you like with sb) **2** 0ᵚ [U] political control of a country or an area: *to* ***take/seize/lose power*** ◇ *The present regime has been* ***in power*** *for two years.* ◇ *The party* ***came to power*** *at the last election.* ◇ *They are hoping to return to power.* ◇ *a* ***power struggle*** *between rival factions within the party* ➲ COLLOCATIONS at POLITICS ➲ see also BALANCE OF POWER

▸ ABILITY **3** 0ᵚ [U] (in people) the ability or opportunity to do sth: *It is not* ***within my power*** (= I am unable or not in a position) *to help you.* ◇ *I will* ***do everything in my power*** *to help you.* **4** 0ᵚ [U] (also **powers** [pl.]) a particular ability of the body or mind: *He had lost the power of speech.* ◇ *The drug may affect your powers of concentration.* ◇ *He had to use all his powers of persuasion.* **5 powers** [pl.] all the abilities of a person's body or mind: *At 26, he is* ***at the height of his powers*** *and ranked fourth in the world.*

▸ AUTHORITY **6** 0ᵚ [U, C, usually pl.] the right or authority of a person or group to do sth: **~ (to do sth)** *The Secretary of State has the power to approve the proposals.* ◇ *The powers of the police must be clearly defined.* ◇ **~ (of sth)** *The president has the power of veto over all new legislation.* ➲ see also POWER OF ATTORNEY

▸ COUNTRY **7** 0ᵚ [C] a country with a lot of influence in world affairs, or with great military strength: *world powers* ◇ *an* ***allied/enemy power*** ➲ see also SUPERPOWER

▸ INFLUENCE **8** 0ᵚ [U] (in compounds) strength or influence in a particular area of activity: *economic power* ◇ ***air/sea power*** (= military strength in the air/ at sea) ◇ *purchasing power* **9** 0ᵚ [U] the influence of a particular thing or group within society: *the power of the media* ◇ *parent power*

▸ ENERGY **10** [U] the strength or energy contained in sth: *The ship was helpless against the power of the storm.* ◇ *It was a performance of great power.* ➲ see also FIREPOWER, STAYING POWER **11** [U] physical strength used in action; physical strength that sb possesses and might use: *He hit the ball with as much power as he could.* ◇ *the sheer physical power of the man* **12** 0ᵚ [U] energy that can be collected and used to operate a machine, to make electricity, etc: ***nuclear/wind/solar power*** ◇ *engine power* ➲ see also HORSEPOWER

▸ ELECTRICITY **13** 0ᵚ [U] the public supply of electricity: *They've switched off the power.* ◇ *a power failure*

▸ MATHEMATICS **14** [C, usually sing.] the number of times that an amount is to be multiplied by itself: *4* ***to the power of*** *3 is* 4^3 (= 4 × 4 × 4 = 64).

▸ OF LENS **15** [U] the amount by which a LENS can make objects appear larger: *the power of a microscope/telescope*

▸ GOOD/EVIL SPIRIT **16** [C] a good or evil spirit that controls the lives of others: *the powers of darkness* (= the forces of evil)

IDM **do sb a ˈpower of good** (*old-fashioned, informal*) to be very good for sb's physical or mental health **more power to sb's ˈelbow** (*old-fashioned, BrE, informal*) used to express support or encouragement for sb to do sth **the (real) power behind the ˈthrone** the person who really controls an organization, a country, etc. in contrast to the person who is legally in charge **the ˌpowers that ˈbe** (often *ironic*) the people who control an organization, a country, etc. ➲ more at CORRIDOR, SWEEP *v.*

■ ***verb***

▸ SUPPLY ENERGY **1** [T, usually passive] **~ sth** to supply a machine or vehicle with the energy that makes it work: *The aircraft is powered by a jet engine.*

▸ MOVE QUICKLY **2** [I, T] to move or move sth very quickly and with great power in a particular direction: **+ adv./prep.** *He powered through the water.* ◇ **~ sth + adv./prep.** *She* ***powered her way*** *into the lead.* ◇ *He powered his header past the goalie.*

PHR V **ˌpower ˈdown** | **ˌpower sth↔ˈdown** to stop a machine, especially a computer, by turning off the electricity supply: *We were told to power down at 9.45.* ◇ *Log off or power down your system.* OPP **power sth up** ➲ related noun POWER-DOWN **ˌpower sth↔ˈup** to prepare a machine to start working by supplying it with electricity, etc. OPP **power sth down**

ˌpower-assisted ˈsteering *noun* [U] (*BrE*) = POWER STEERING

ˈpower base *noun* the area or the people that provide the main support for a politician or a political party

power·boat /ˈpaʊəbəʊt; *NAmE* ˈpaʊərboʊt/ *noun* a fast boat with a powerful engine that is used especially for racing

ˈpower breakfast *noun* a meeting that business people have early in the morning while they eat breakfast

ˈpower broker *noun* a person who has a strong influence on who has political power in an area

ˈpower cut (*BrE*) (*NAmE* **ˈpower outage**) *noun* an interruption in the supply of electricity; a period of time when this happens

ˈpower-down (also **power·down**) *noun* [C, U] a time when a machine or system stops working: *a power-down of the whole building* ◇ *The internal clock and date were not stored after power-down.*

ˈpower dressing *noun* [U] a style of dressing in which people in business wear formal and expensive clothes to emphasize how important they and their jobs are

powered /ˈpaʊəd; *NAmE* ˈpaʊərd/ *adj.* (usually in compounds) operated by a form of energy such as electricity or by the type of energy mentioned: *a powered wheelchair* ◇ *a solar-powered calculator* ➲ see also HIGH-POWERED

power·ful 0ᵚ /ˈpaʊəfl; *NAmE* ˈpaʊərfl/ *adj.* **1** 0ᵚ (of people) being able to control and influence people and events SYN **influential**: *an* ***immensely powerful*** *organization* ◇ *a rich and powerful man* ◇ *Only the intervention of powerful friends obtained her release.* **2** 0ᵚ having great power or force; very effective: *powerful weapons* ◇ *a powerful engine* ◇ *a powerful voice* **3** 0ᵚ having a strong effect on your mind or body: *a powerful image/drug/speech* **4** 0ᵚ (of a person or an animal) physically strong SYN **muscular**: *a powerful body* ◇ *a powerful athlete* ▸ **power·ful·ly** /-fəli/ *adv.*: *a powerfully emotive song* ◇ *He is powerfully built* (= he has a large strong body). ◇ *She argued powerfully for reform.*

power·house /ˈpaʊəhaʊs; *NAmE* ˈpaʊərh-/ *noun* **1** a group or an organization that has a lot of power: *China has been described as an 'emerging economic powerhouse'.* **2** a person who is very strong and full of energy

power·less /ˈpaʊələs; *NAmE* ˈpaʊərləs/ *adj.* **1** without power to control or to influence sb/sth SYN **helpless**: *powerless minorities* ◇ *When the enemy attacked, we were completely powerless against them.* **2 ~ to do sth** completely unable to do sth: *I saw what was happening, but I was powerless to help.* ▸ **power·less·ness** *noun* [U]: *a* ***feeling/sense of powerlessness***

power·lift·ing /ˈpaʊəlɪftɪŋ; *NAmE* ˈpaʊər-/ *noun* [U] the sport of lifting weights in three different ways, in a set order ▸ **power·lift·er** *noun*

ˈpower line *noun* a thick wire that carries electricity: *overhead power lines*

ˈpower nap *noun* a short sleep that sb has during the day in order to get back their energy ▸ **ˈpower-nap** *verb* [I] (-pp-)

ˌpower of atˈtorney *noun* [U, C] (*pl.* **powers of attorney**) (*law*) the right to act as the representative of sb in business or financial matters; a document that gives sb this right

ˈpower outage (*NAmE*) (*BrE* **ˈpower cut**) *noun* an interruption in the supply of electricity; a period of time when this happens

ˈpower plant (*BrE* also **ˈpower station**) *noun* a building or group of buildings where electricity is produced

P

ˈ**power play** *noun* [U] **1** (in ICE HOCKEY) a situation in which one team has more players than another because a player is off the ice as a punishment **2** a way of behaving that shows or increases a person's power, especially in a relationship: *political power play*

ˈ**power point** *noun* (*BrE*) = SOCKET (1)

ˈ**power politics** *noun* [U+sing./pl. v.] a situation in which a country tries to achieve its aims by using or threatening to use its military or economic power against another country

ˈ**power-sharing** *noun* [U] a policy or system in which different groups or political parties share responsibility for making decisions, taking political action, etc.

ˈ**power shower** *noun* (*BrE*) a shower that has an electric PUMP to make the water come out fast

ˈ**power station** (*BrE*) (also ˈ**power plant** *NAmE, BrE*) *noun* a building or group of buildings where electricity is produced: *a coal-fired power station* ◇ *a nuclear power station*

ˈ**power steering** (*BrE* also ˌ**power-assisted** ˈ**steering**) *noun* [U] (in a vehicle) a system that uses power from the engine to help the driver change direction

ˈ**power-up** *noun* **1** [U] the moment when a machine is switched on and starts working: *Does the computer beep on power-up?* **2** [C] in computer games, an advantage that a character can get if a player wins a certain number of points, for example more strength

ˈ**power user** *noun* (*computing*) a user who needs computer products that are fastest and have the most features

ˈ**power walking** *noun* [U] the activity of walking very quickly as a form of exercise

pow·wow /ˈpaʊwaʊ/ *noun* **1** a meeting of Native Americans **2** (*informal* or *humorous*) a meeting for discussion

pox /pɒks; *NAmE* pɑːks/ *noun* **the pox** [sing.] (*old use*) **1** an infectious disease spread by sexual contact SYN **syphilis** **2** = SMALLPOX

poxy /ˈpɒksi; *NAmE* ˈpɑːksi/ *adj.* [only before noun] (*BrE, informal*) if sb describes sth as **poxy**, they think it has little value or importance

P

pp *abbr.* **1 pp.** pages: *See pp. 100–117.* **2** (also **p.p.**) (*especially BrE*) used in front of a person's name when sb signs a business letter on his/her behalf: *pp Chris Baker* (= from Chris Baker, but signed by sb else because Chris Baker is away) **3** (*music*) very quietly (from Italian 'pianissimo')

ppi /ˌpiː piː ˈaɪ/ *abbr.* (*computing*) pixels per inch (a measure of the quality of images)

PPS /ˌpiː piː ˈes/ *noun* the abbreviation for 'Parliamentary Private Secretary' (a Member of Parliament in Britain who is given the job of helping a minister)

PPV /ˌpiː piː ˈviː/ *abbr.* PAY-PER-VIEW

PR /ˌpiː ˈɑː(r)/ *noun* [U] **1** the abbreviation for PUBLIC RELATIONS: *a **PR department/agency/campaign*** ◇ *The article is very good PR for the theatre.* **2** the abbreviation for PROPORTIONAL REPRESENTATION

prac·tic·able /ˈpræktɪkəbl/ *adj.* (*formal*) able to be done; likely to be successful SYN **feasible, workable**: *at the earliest practicable opportunity* ◇ *as soon as (is) practicable* ◇ *The only practicable alternative is to postpone the meeting.* ◇ *Employers should provide a safe working environment, as far as is reasonably practicable.* ➲ compare IMPRACTICABLE ▸ **prac·tic·abil·ity** /ˌpræktɪkəˈbɪləti/ *noun* [U]: *We were doubtful about the practicability of the plan.* **prac·tic·ably** /-əbli/ *adv.*: *Please reply as soon as is practicably possible.*

prac·tical 🔑 /ˈpræktɪkl/ *adj., noun*

■ *adj.*

▸ CONNECTED WITH REAL THINGS **1** 🔑 connected with real situations rather than with ideas or theories: *to have gained **practical experience** of the work* ◇ ***practical advice/help/support*** ◇ *practical problems* ◇ *There are some obvious practical applications of the research.* ◇ ***In practical terms,*** *it means spending less.* ◇ *From a practical point of view, it isn't a good place to live.* ➲ compare THEORETICAL

▸ LIKELY TO WORK **2** 🔑 (of an idea, a method or a course of action) right or sensible; likely to be successful SYN **workable**: *It wouldn't be practical for us to go all that way just for the weekend.* OPP **impractical**

▸ USEFUL **3** 🔑 (of things) useful or suitable: *a practical little car, ideal for the city* OPP **impractical**

▸ SENSIBLE **4** 🔑 (of a person) sensible and realistic: *Let's be practical and work out the cost first.* OPP **impractical**

▸ GOOD AT MAKING THINGS **5** 🔑 (of a person) good at making or repairing things SYN **handy**: *Bob's very practical. He does all the odd jobs around the house.*

▸ ALMOST TOTAL **6** [only before noun] almost complete or total SYN **virtual**: *She married a practical stranger.*

IDM **for (all)** ˈ**practical purposes** used when you are stating what the reality of a situation is: *There's still another ten minutes of the game to go, but for practical purposes it's already over.*

■ *noun* (*BrE, informal*) a lesson or an exam in science or technology in which students have to do or make things, not just read or write about them

prac·ti·cal·ity /ˌpræktɪˈkæləti/ *noun* **1** [U] the quality of being suitable, or likely to be successful SYN **feasibility**: *I have doubts about the practicality of their proposal.* **2** [U] the quality of being sensible and realistic: *I was impressed by her practicality.* **3 practicalities** [pl.] the real facts and circumstances rather than ideas or theories: *It sounds like a good idea; let's look at the practicalities and work out the costs.*

ˌ**practical** ˈ**joke** *noun* a trick that is played on sb to make them look stupid and to make other people laugh ▸ ˌ**practical** ˈ**joker** *noun*

prac·tic·al·ly 🔑 /ˈpræktɪkli/ *adv.*

1 🔑 almost; very nearly SYN **virtually**: *The theatre was practically empty.* ◇ *I meet famous people practically every day.* ◇ *My essay is practically finished now.* ◇ *There's practically no difference between the two options.* ➲ SYNONYMS at ALMOST **2** 🔑 in a realistic or sensible way; in real situations: *Practically speaking, we can't afford it.* ◇ *It sounds like a good idea, but I don't think it will work practically.* ➲ compare THEORETICALLY

ˌ**practical** ˈ**nurse** *noun* (*NAmE*) a nurse with practical experience but less training than a REGISTERED NURSE

prac·tice 🔑 /ˈpræktɪs/ *noun, verb*

■ *noun*

▸ ACTION NOT IDEAS **1** 🔑 [U] action rather than ideas: *the **theory and practice** of teaching* ◇ *She's determined to **put** her new ideas **into practice**.*

▸ WAY OF DOING STH **2** 🔑 [U, C] a way of doing sth that is the usual or expected way in a particular organization or situation: ***common/current/standard practice*** ◇ *guidelines for **good practice*** ◇ *a review of pay and **working practices*** ◇ *religious practices* ➲ see also BEST PRACTICE, CODE OF PRACTICE, RESTRICTIVE PRACTICES, SHARP PRACTICE

▸ HABIT/CUSTOM **3** [C] a thing that is done regularly; a habit or a custom: *the German practice of giving workers a say in how their company is run* ◇ *It is his practice to read several books a week.*

▸ FOR IMPROVING SKILL **4** 🔑 [U, C] doing an activity or training regularly so that you can improve your skill; the time you spend doing this: *conversation practice* ◇ *It takes a lot of practice to play the violin well.* ◇ *There's a basketball practice every Friday evening.* ◇ *She does an hour's piano practice every day.* ➲ see also TEACHING PRACTICE

▸ OF DOCTOR/LAWYER **5** [U, C] the work or the business of some professional people such as doctors, dentists and lawyers; the place where they work: *the practice of medicine* ◇ *Students should have prior experience of veterinary practice.* ◇ *My solicitor is no longer in practice.* ◇ *a successful **medical/dental/law practice*** ➲ see also GENERAL PRACTICE, GROUP PRACTICE, PRIVATE PRACTICE

IDM **in** ˈ**practice** 🔑 in reality: *Prisoners have legal rights, but in practice these rights are not always respected.* **be/get/**ˌ**out of** ˈ**practice** to be/become less good at doing sth than you were because you have not spent time doing it recently: *Don't ask me to speak French! I'm out of practice.* ˌ**practice makes** ˈ**perfect** (*saying*) a way of encouraging people by telling them that if you do an activity regularly and try to improve your skill, you will become very good at it

■ **verb** (especially US) = PRACTISE: *to practice the piano every day* ◇ *The team is practicing for their big game on Friday.* ◇ *They practiced the dance until it was perfect.* ◇ *She's practicing medicine in Philadelphia.*

prac·tise (especially US **prac·tice**) /ˈpræktɪs/ *verb*
1 [I, T] to do an activity or train regularly so that you can improve your skill: *You need to practise every day.* ◇ **~ for sth** *She's practising for her piano exam.* ◇ **~ sth** *I've been practising my serve for weeks.* ◇ **~ (sth) on sb/sth** *He usually wants to practise his English on me.* ◇ **~ doing sth** *Practise reversing the car into the garage.* **2** [T] **~ sth** (*formal*) to do sth regularly as part of your normal behaviour: *to practise self-restraint/safe sex* ◇ *Do you still practise your religion?* **3** [I, T] to work as a doctor, lawyer, etc: *There are over 50 000 solicitors practising in England and Wales.* ◇ **~ as sth** *She practised as a barrister for many years.* ◇ **~ sth** *He was banned from practising medicine.*
IDM **ˌpractise what you ˈpreach** to do the things yourself that you tell other people to do

prac·tised (especially US **-ticed**) /ˈpræktɪst/ *adj.* good at doing sth because you have been doing it regularly: *She's only 18 but she's already a practised composer.* ◇ *It took* ***a practised eye*** *to spot the difference.* ◇ **~ in sth** *He has good ideas but he isn't practised in the art of marketing.*

prac·tis·ing (especially US **-ticing**) /ˈpræktɪsɪŋ/ *adj.* [only before noun] taking an active part in a particular religion, profession, etc: *a practising Christian/teacher*

prac·ti·tion·er AW /prækˈtɪʃənə(r)/ *noun* **1** (*technical*) a person who works in a profession, especially medicine or law: *dental practitioners* ◇ *a qualified practitioner* ➲ see also GENERAL PRACTITIONER **2** (*formal*) a person who regularly does a particular activity, especially one that requires skill: *one of the greatest practitioners of science fiction*

prae·sid·ium (especially BrE) = PRESIDIUM

prag·mat·ic /prægˈmætɪk/ *adj.* solving problems in a practical and sensible way rather than by having fixed ideas or theories SYN **realistic**: *a pragmatic approach to management problems* ▶ **prag·mat·ic·al·ly** /-kli/ *adv.*

prag·mat·ics /prægˈmætɪks/ *noun* [U] (*linguistics*) the study of the way in which language is used to express what sb really means in particular situations, especially when the actual words used may appear to mean sth different

prag·ma·tism /ˈprægmətɪzəm/ *noun* [U] (*formal*) thinking about solving problems in a practical and sensible way rather than by having fixed ideas and theories ▶ **prag·ma·tist** /-tɪst/ *noun*

prairie /ˈpreəri; NAmE ˈpreri/ *noun* [C, U] a flat wide area of land in N America and Canada, without many trees and originally covered with grass

ˈprairie dog *noun* a small brown N American animal of the SQUIRREL family that lives in holes on the prairies

ˌprairie ˈoyster *noun* **1** a drink containing raw egg, used as a treatment for a HANGOVER (= the bad feeling sb has the day after drinking too much alcohol) **2** **prairie oysters** [pl.] (*especially NAmE*) a dish consisting of cooked TESTICLES from a young cow

ˈprairie wolf *noun* = COYOTE

praise /preɪz/ *noun, verb*
■ **noun** [U] **1** (also *less frequent* **praises** [pl.]) words that show approval of or admiration for sb/sth: *His teachers are* ***full of praise for*** *the progress he's making.* ◇ *She wrote poems* ***in praise of*** *freedom.* ◇ *His latest movie has* ***won high praise*** *from the critics.* ◇ *We have* ***nothing but praise*** *for the way they handled the investigation.* ◇ *The team coach singled out two players for special praise.* ◇ *She left with their praises ringing in her ears.* ◇ *They always* ***sing his praises*** (= praise him very highly). **2** the expression of worship to God: ***hymns/songs of praise*** ◇ *Praise be (to God)!* (= expressing belief or joy) IDM see DAMN *v.*
■ **verb 1** to express your approval or admiration for sb/sth SYN **compliment**: **~ sb/sth** *She praised his cooking.* ◇ **~ sb/sth for sth/for doing sth** *He praised his team for their performance.* ◇ **~ sb/sth as sth** *Critics praised the work as highly original.* **2** **~ sb** to express your thanks to or your respect for God: *Praise the Lord.* ◇ *Allah be praised.*
IDM **praise sb/sth to the ˈskies** to praise sb/sth a lot

praise·worthy /ˈpreɪzwɜːði; NAmE -wɜːrði/ *adj.* (*formal*) deserving praise SYN **commendable**: *a praiseworthy achievement*

pra·line /ˈprɑːliːn; ˈpreɪliːn/ *noun* [U] a sweet substance made of nuts and boiled sugar, often used to fill chocolates

pram /præm/ (*BrE*) (*NAmE* **ˈbaby carriage**) *noun* a small vehicle on four wheels for a baby to go out in, pushed by a person on foot ➲ picture at PUSHCHAIR

prana /ˈprɑːnə/ *noun* [U] (in Hindu philosophy) the force that keeps all life in existence

prance /prɑːns; NAmE præns/ *verb* **1** [I] **+ adv./prep.** to move quickly with exaggerated steps so that people will look at you: *The lead singer was prancing around with the microphone.* **2** [I] (of a horse) to move with high steps

prang /præŋ/ *verb* **~ sth** (*BrE, informal*) to damage a vehicle in an accident ▶ **prang** *noun*

prank /præŋk/ *noun* a trick that is played on sb as a joke: *a childish prank* ▶ **prank·ster** /ˈpræŋkstə(r)/ *noun*: *Student pranksters have done considerable damage to the school buildings.*

praseo·dym·ium /ˌpreɪziəʊˈdɪmiəm; NAmE -zioʊ-/ *noun* [U] (*symb.* **Pr**) a chemical element. Praseodymium is a soft silver-white metal used in ALLOYS and to colour glass.

prat /præt/ *noun* (*BrE, informal*) a stupid person

prate /preɪt/ *verb* [I] **~ (on) (about sth)** (*old-fashioned, disapproving*) to talk too much in a stupid or boring way

prat·fall /ˈprætfɔːl/ *noun* (*especially NAmE*) **1** an embarrassing mistake **2** a fall on your bottom

prat·tle /ˈprætl/ *verb* [I] **~ (on/away) (about sb/sth)** (*old-fashioned, often disapproving*) to talk a lot about unimportant things: *She prattled on about her children all evening.* ▶ **prat·tle** *noun* [U]

prawn /prɔːn/ *noun* [C, U] (*especially BrE*) (*NAmE* usually **shrimp**) a SHELLFISH with ten legs and a long tail, that can be eaten. Prawns turn pink when cooked. ➲ VISUAL VOCAB page V11

ˌprawn ˈcracker *noun* (*BrE*) a small piece of food made from rice flour with a PRAWN flavour, that is fried until it is crisp

praxis /ˈpræksɪs/ *noun* [U] (*philosophy*) a way of doing sth; the use of a theory or a belief in a practical way

pray /preɪ/ *verb, adv.*
■ **verb 1** [I, T] to speak to God, especially to give thanks or ask for help: *They knelt down and prayed.* ◇ **~ for sb/sth** *I'll pray for you.* ◇ *to pray for peace* ◇ **~ to sb (for sb/sth)** *She prayed to God for an end to her sufferings.* ◇ **~ (that)...** *We prayed (that) she would recover from her illness.* ◇ **~ to do sth** *He prayed to be forgiven.* ◇ **+ speech** *'Please God don't let it happen,' she prayed.* **2** [I, T] to hope very much that sth will happen: **~ (for sth)** *We're praying for good weather on Saturday.* ◇ **~ that...** *I prayed that nobody would notice my mistake.*
■ **adv.** (*old use* or *ironic*) used to mean 'please' when you are asking a question or telling sb to do sth: *What, pray, is the meaning of this?* ◇ *Pray continue.*

pray·er /preə(r); NAmE prer/ *noun*
1 [C] **~ (for sb/sth)** words that you say to God giving thanks or asking for help: *to say your prayers* ◇ *prayers for the sick* ◇ *He arrived at that very moment, as if* ***in answer to her prayer.*** ◇ *Their* ***prayers were answered*** *and the child was found safe and well.* ➲ COLLOCATIONS at RELIGION **2** [C] a fixed form of words that you can say when you speak to God: *It was a prayer she had learnt as a child.* ➲ see also THE LORD'S PRAYER **3** [U] the act or habit of praying: *They knelt in prayer.* ◇ *We believe in the power of prayer.*

P

4 prayers [pl.] a religious meeting that takes place regularly in which people say prayers **5** [C, usually sing.] a thing that you hope for very much: *My prayer is that one day he will walk again.* IDM see WING *n.*

IDM **not have a ˈprayer (of doing sth)** to have no chance of succeeding (in doing sth)

ˈprayer book *noun* a book that contains prayers, for use in religious services

ˈprayer meeting *noun* a religious meeting when people say prayers to God

ˈprayer rug (also **ˈprayer mat**) *noun* a small carpet on which Muslims rest their knees when they are saying prayers

ˈprayer wheel *noun* (in Tibetan Buddhism) an object that is turned as a way of saying a prayer or MEDITATING

ˌpraying ˈmantis (also **mantis**) *noun* a large green insect that eats other insects. The female praying mantis often eats the male.

pre- /priː/ *prefix* (in verbs, nouns and adjectives) before: *preheat* ◇ *precaution* ◇ *pre-war* ◇ *preseason training* (= before a sports season starts) ➲ compare ANTE-, POST-

preach /priːtʃ/ *verb* **1** [I, T] to give a religious talk in a public place, especially in a church during a service: *She preached to the congregation about forgiveness.* ◇ **~ sth** *The minister preached a sermon on the parable of the lost sheep.* **2** [T, I] to tell people about a particular religion, way of life, system, etc. in order to persuade them to accept it: **~ sth** *to preach the word of God* ◇ *He preached the virtues of capitalism to us.* ◇ **~ (about sth)** *She preached about the benefits of a healthy lifestyle.* ➲ COLLOCATIONS at RELIGION **3** [I] (*disapproving*) to give sb advice on moral standards, behaviour, etc, especially in a way that they find annoying or boring: *I'm sorry, I didn't mean to preach.* ◇ **~ at sb** *You're preaching at me again!*

IDM **preach to the conˈverted** to speak to people in support of views that they already hold ➲ more at PRACTISE

preach·er /ˈpriːtʃə(r)/ *noun* a person, often a member of the CLERGY, who gives religious talks and often performs religious ceremonies, for example in a church: *a preacher famous for her inspiring sermons* ◇ *a* ***lay preacher*** (= who is not a priest, etc. but who has been trained to give religious talks)

preachy /ˈpriːtʃi/ *adj.* (*informal, disapproving*) trying to give advice or to persuade people to accept an opinion on what is right and wrong

pre·amble /priˈæmbl; ˈpriːæmbl/ *noun* [C, U] (*formal*) an introduction to a book or a written document; an introduction to sth you say: *The aims of the treaty are stated in its preamble.* ◇ *She gave him the bad news* ***without preamble.***

pre·ar·ranged /ˌpriːəˈreɪndʒd/ *adj.* planned or arranged in advance SYN **predetermined**

ˌpre-ˈbook *verb* [I, T] (*BrE*) to arrange to have sth such as a room, table, seat, or ticket in advance: *You are advised to pre-book.* ◇ **~ sth** *Accommodation is cheaper if you pre-book it.*

pre·but·tal /ˈpriːbʌtl/ *noun* [C, U] (*informal*) a statement saying or proving that a criticism is false or unfair before the criticism has actually been made

pre·can·cer·ous /ˌpriːˈkænsərəs/ *adj.* (*medical*) that will develop into cancer if not treated: *precancerous cells*

pre·car·ious /prɪˈkeəriəs; *NAmE* -ˈker-/ *adj.* **1** (of a situation) not safe or certain; dangerous: *He earned a precarious living as an artist.* ◇ *The museum is in a financially precarious position.* **2** likely to fall or cause sb to fall: *That ladder looks very precarious.* ◇ *The path down to the beach is very precarious in wet weather.* ▸ **pre·car·ious·ly** *adv.*: *The economy is precariously close to recession.* ◇ *He balanced the glass precariously on the arm of his chair.* **pre·car·ious·ness** *noun* [U]

pre·cast /ˌpriːˈkɑːst; *NAmE* -ˈkæst/ *adj.* (of some building materials) made into blocks ready to use: *precast concrete slabs*

pre·cau·tion /prɪˈkɔːʃn/ *noun* [usually pl.] **1 ~ (against sth)** something that is done in advance in order to prevent problems or to avoid danger: *safety precautions* ◇ *precautions against fire* ◇ *You must* ***take all reasonable precautions*** *to protect yourself and your family.* ◇ *I'll keep the letter* ***as a precaution.*** **2 precautions** [pl.] a way of referring to CONTRACEPTION: *We didn't* ***take any precautions*** *and I got pregnant.* ▸ **pre·cau·tion·ary** /prɪˈkɔːʃənəri; *NAmE* -neri/ *adj.*: *He was kept in the hospital overnight* ***as a precautionary measure.***

pre·cede AW /prɪˈsiːd/ *verb* (*formal*) **1** [T, I] **~ (sb/sth)** to happen before sth or come before sth/sb in order: *the years preceding the war* ◇ *His resignation was preceded by weeks of speculation.* ◇ *She preceded me in the job.* ◇ *See the preceding chapter.* **2** [T] **~ sb + adv./prep.** to go in front of sb: *She preceded him out of the room.*

PHR V **preˈcede sth with sth** to do or say sth to introduce sth else: *She preceded her speech with a vote of thanks to the committee.*

pre·ce·dence AW /ˈpresɪdəns/ *noun* [U] **~ (over sb/sth)** the condition of being more important than sb else and therefore coming or being dealt with first SYN **priority**: *She had to learn that her wishes did not* ***take precedence over*** *other people's needs.* ◇ *The speakers came on to the platform* ***in order of precedence*** (= the most important one first).

pre·ce·dent AW /ˈpresɪdənt/ *noun* **1** [C, U] an official action or decision that has happened in the past and that is seen as an example or a rule to be followed in a similar situation later: *The ruling* ***set a precedent*** *for future libel cases.* **2** [C, U] a similar action or event that happened earlier: *historical precedents* ◇ *There is no precedent for a disaster of this scale.* ◇ *Such protests are* ***without precedent*** *in recent history.* **3** [U] the way that things have always been done SYN **tradition**: *to break with precedent* (= to do sth in a different way) ➲ see also UNPRECEDENTED

pre·cept /ˈpriːsept/ *noun* [C, U] (*formal*) a rule about how to behave or what to think SYN **principle**

pre·cinct /ˈpriːsɪŋkt/ *noun* **1** (*BrE*) a commercial area in a town where cars cannot go: *a* ***pedestrian/shopping precinct*** **2** (*NAmE*) one of the parts into which a town or city is divided in order to organize elections **3** (*NAmE*) a part of a city that has its own police station; the police station in this area: *Detective Hennessy of the 44th precinct* ◇ *The murder occurred just a block from the precinct.* **4** [usually pl.] (*formal*) the area around a place or a building, sometimes surrounded by a wall: *the* ***cathedral/college precincts*** ◇ *within the precincts of the castle*

pre·cious /ˈpreʃəs/ *adj., adv.*

- ***adj.*** **1** rare and worth a lot of money: *a precious vase* ◇ *The crown was set with precious jewels—diamonds, rubies and emeralds.* ➲ see also PRECIOUS METAL, PRECIOUS STONE ➲ SYNONYMS at VALUABLE **2** valuable or important and not to be wasted: *Clean water is a precious commodity in that part of the world.* ◇ *You're wasting precious time!* **3** loved or valued very much SYN **treasured**: ***precious memories/possessions*** **4** [only before noun] (*informal*) used to show you are angry that another person thinks sth is very important: *I didn't touch your precious car!* **5** (*disapproving*) (especially of people and their behaviour) very formal, exaggerated and not natural in what you say and do SYN **affected** ▸ **pre·cious·ness** *noun* [U]: *the preciousness of an old friendship* ◇ *His writings reveal an unattractive preciousness of style.* ➲ see also PRECIOSITY
- ***adv.*** (*informal*) **~ little/few** used to emphasize the fact that there is very little of sth or that there are very few of sth: *There's precious little to do in this town.*

ˌprecious ˈmetal *noun* [C, U] a very valuable metal such as gold or silver

ˌprecious ˈstone (also **stone**) *noun* a rare valuable stone, such as a diamond, that is used in jewellery ➲ see also SEMI-PRECIOUS

preci·pice /ˈpresəpɪs/ *noun* a very steep side of a high CLIFF, mountain or rock ➲ VISUAL VOCAB page V5: (*figura-*

tive) The country was now ***on the edge of a precipice*** (= very close to disaster). ➲ see also PRECIPITOUS

pre·cipi·tate *verb, adj., noun*

■ ***verb*** /prɪˈsɪpɪteɪt/ (*formal*) **1 ~ sth** to make sth, especially sth bad, happen suddenly or sooner than it should SYN **bring on, spark off**: *His resignation precipitated a leadership crisis.* **2 ~ sb/sth into sth** to suddenly force sb/sth into a particular state or condition: *The assassination of the president precipitated the country into war.*

■ ***adj.*** /prɪˈsɪpɪtət/ (*formal*) (of an action or a decision) happening very quickly or suddenly and usually without enough care and thought ▶ **pre·cipi·tate·ly** *adv.*: *to act precipitately*

■ ***noun*** /prɪˈsɪpɪteɪt/ (*chemistry*) a solid substance that has been separated from a liquid in a chemical process

pre·cipi·ta·tion /prɪˌsɪpɪˈteɪʃn/ *noun* **1** [U] (*technical*) rain, snow, etc. that falls; the amount of this that falls: *an increase in annual precipitation* **2** [U, C] (*chemistry*) a chemical process in which solid material is separated from a liquid

pre·cipit·ous /prɪˈsɪpɪtəs/ *adj.* (*formal*) **1** very steep, high and often dangerous SYN **sheer**: *precipitous cliffs* ◇ *a precipitous drop at the side of the road* **2** sudden and great SYN **abrupt**: *a precipitous decline in exports* **3** done very quickly, without enough thought or care SYN **hasty**: *a precipitous action* ▶ **pre·cipit·ous·ly** *adv.*: *The land dropped precipitously down to the rocky shore.* ◇ *The dollar plunged precipitously.* ◇ *We don't want to act precipitously.* ➲ see also PRECIPICE

pre·cis /ˈpreɪsiː; *NAmE* preɪˈsiː/ *noun* [C, U] (*pl.* **pre·cis** /-siːz/) a short version of a speech or a piece of writing that gives the main points or ideas SYN **summary**: *to* ***write/give/make a precis*** *of a report* ▶ **pre·cis** *verb* (**pre·cises** /-siːz/, **pre·cis·ing** /-siːɪŋ/, **pre·cised**, **pre·cised** /-siːd/): **~ sth** *to precis a scientific report*

pre·cise 🔑 AW /prɪˈsaɪs/ *adj.*

1 🔑 clear and accurate SYN **exact**: *precise details/instructions/measurements* ◇ *Can you give a more precise definition of the word?* ◇ *I can be reasonably precise about the time of the incident.* **2** 🔑 [only before noun] used to emphasize that sth happens at a particular time or in a particular way: *We were just talking about her when,* ***at that precise moment****, she walked in.* ◇ *Doctors found it hard to establish the precise nature of her illness.* **3** 🔑 taking care to be exact and accurate, especially about small details SYN **meticulous**: *a skilled and precise worker* ◇ *small, precise movements* ◇ (*disapproving*) *She's rather prim and precise.*

IDM **to be (more) preˈcise** used to show that you are giving more detailed and accurate information about sth you have just mentioned: *The shelf is about a metre long—well, 98cm, to be precise.*

pre·cise·ly 🔑 AW /prɪˈsaɪsli/ *adv.*

1 🔑 exactly: *They look precisely the same to me.* ◇ *That's precisely what I meant.* ◇ *It's not clear precisely how the accident happened.* ◇ *The meeting starts at 2 o'clock precisely.* **2** 🔑 accurately; carefully: *to describe sth precisely* ◇ *She pronounced the word very slowly and precisely.* **3** 🔑 used to emphasize that sth is very true or obvious: *It's* ***precisely because*** *I care about you that I don't like you staying out late.* **4** used to emphasize that you agree with a statement, especially because you think it is obvious or is similar to what you have just said: *'It's not that easy, is it?' 'No, precisely.'*

IDM **more preˈcisely** used to show that you are giving more detailed and accurate information about sth you have just mentioned: *The problem is due to discipline, or, more precisely, the lack of discipline, in schools.* ➲ LANGUAGE BANK at I.E.

pre·ci·sion AW /prɪˈsɪʒn/ *noun* [U] the quality of being exact, accurate and careful SYN **accuracy**: *done with mathematical precision* ◇ *Historians can't estimate the date* ***with any (degree of) precision****.* ◇ *He chose his words* ***with precision****.* ◇ ***precision instruments/tools***

pre·clude /prɪˈkluːd/ *verb* (*formal*) to prevent sth from happening or sb from doing sth; to make sth impossible: **~ sth** *Lack of time precludes any further discussion.* ◇ **~ sb from doing sth** *My lack of interest in the subject precluded me from gaining much enjoyment out of it.* ◇ **~ (sb) doing sth** *His religious beliefs precluded him/his serving in the army.*

pre·co·cious /prɪˈkəʊʃəs; *NAmE* -ˈkoʊ-/ *adj.* (sometimes *disapproving*) (of a child) having developed particular abilities and ways of behaving at a much younger age than usual: *a precocious child who started her acting career at the age of 5* ◇ *sexually precocious* ◇ *From an early age she displayed a precocious talent for music.* ▶ **pre·co·cious·ly** *adv.*: *a precociously talented child* **pre·co·city** /prɪˈkɒsəti; *NAmE* -ˈkɑːs-/ (also **pre·co·cious·ness**) *noun* [U]: *his unusual precocity*

pre·cog·ni·tion /ˌpriːkɒɡˈnɪʃn; *NAmE* -kɑːɡ-/ *noun* [U] (*formal*) the knowledge that sth will happen in the future, which sb has because of a dream or a sudden feeling

pre-Columbian /ˌpriː kəˈlʌmbiən/ *adj.* connected with N and S America and their cultures before the arrival of Columbus in 1492

pre·con·ceived /ˌpriːkənˈsiːvd/ *adj.* [only before noun] (of ideas, opinions, etc.) formed before you have enough information or experience of sth: *Before I started the job, I had no preconceived notions of what it would be like.*

pre·con·cep·tion /ˌpriːkənˈsepʃn/ *noun* [C, usually pl., U] an idea or opinion that is formed before you have enough information or experience SYN **assumption**: *a book that will challenge your preconceptions about rural life* ➲ compare MISCONCEPTION

pre·con·di·tion /ˌpriːkənˈdɪʃn/ *noun* **~ (for/of sth)** something that must happen or exist before sth else can exist or be done SYN **prerequisite**: *A ceasefire is an essential precondition for negotiation.*

pre·con·scious /ˌpriːˈkɒnʃəs; *NAmE* -ˈkɑːn-/ *adj.* (*psychology*) associated with a part of the mind from which memories and thoughts that have not been REPRESSED can be brought to the surface

pre·cooked /ˌpriːˈkʊkt/ *adj.* (of food) prepared and partly cooked in advance so that it can be quickly heated and eaten later

pre·cur·sor /priːˈkɜːsə(r); *NAmE* -ˈkɜːrs-/ *noun* **~ (of/to sth)** (*formal*) a person or thing that comes before sb/sth similar and that leads to or influences its development SYN **forerunner**

P

ˌpre-ˈcut *adj.* cut in advance and ready to use

pre·date /ˌpriːˈdeɪt/ (also **ante·date**) *verb* **~ sth** to be built or formed, or to happen, at an earlier date than sth else in the past: *Few of the town's fine buildings predate the earthquake of 1755.* OPP **post-date**

pre·da·tion /prɪˈdeɪʃn/ *noun* [U] (*technical*) the act of an animal killing and eating other animals

preda·tor /ˈpredətə(r)/ *noun* [C, U] **1** an animal that kills and eats other animals: *Some animals have no natural predators.* **2** (*disapproving*) a person or an organization that uses weaker people for their own advantage: *to protect domestic industry from foreign predators*

preda·tory /ˈpredətri; *NAmE* -tɔːri/ *adj.* **1** (*technical*) (of animals) living by killing and eating other animals **2** (of people) using weaker people for their own financial or sexual advantage: *a predatory insurance salesman* ◇ *a predatory look*

ˌpredatory ˈpricing *noun* [U] (*business*) the fact of a business company selling its goods at such a low price that other companies can no longer compete and have to stop selling similar goods

pre·de·cease /ˌpriːdɪˈsiːs/ *verb* **~ sb** (*law*) to die before sb: *His wife predeceased him.*

pre·de·ces·sor /ˈpriːdɪsesə(r); *NAmE* ˈpredəs-/ *noun* **1** a person who did a job before sb else: *The new president reversed many of the policies of his predecessor.* **2** a thing, such as a machine, that has been followed or replaced by sth else ➲ compare SUCCESSOR

pre·des·tin·ation /ˌpriːdestɪˈneɪʃn/ *noun* [U] the theory or the belief that everything that happens has been decided or planned in advance by God or by FATE and that humans cannot change it

pre·des·tined /ˌpriːˈdestɪnd/ *adj.* **~ (to do sth)** (*formal*) already decided or planned by God or by FATE: *It seems she was predestined to be famous.*

pre·de·ter·mine /ˌpriːdɪˈtɜːmɪn; *NAmE* -ˈtɜːrm-/ *verb* **~ sth** (*formal*) to decide sth in advance so that it does not happen by chance: *The sex of the embryo is predetermined at fertilization.* ▶ **pre·de·ter·mined** *adj.*: *An alarm sounds when the temperature reaches a predetermined level.*

pre·de·ter·miner /ˌpriːdɪˈtɜːmɪnə(r); *NAmE* -ˈtɜːrm-/ *noun* (*grammar*) a word that can be used before a determiner, such as *all* in *all the students* or *twice* in *twice the price*

pre·dica·ment /prɪˈdɪkəmənt/ *noun* a difficult or unpleasant situation, especially one where it is difficult to know what to do **SYN quandary**: *the club's financial predicament* ◇ *I'm in a terrible predicament.*

predi·cate *noun, verb*

- ***noun*** /ˈpredɪkət/ (*grammar*) a part of a sentence containing a verb that makes a statement about the subject of the verb, such as *went home* in *John went home.* ➲ compare OBJECT *n.* (5)
- ***verb*** /ˈpredɪkeɪt/ (*formal*) **1** [usually passive] **~ sth on/upon sth** to base sth on a particular belief, idea or principle: *Democracy is predicated upon the rule of law.* **2 ~ that...** | **~ sth** to state that sth is true: *The article predicates that the market collapse was caused by weakness of the dollar.*

pre·dica·tive /prɪˈdɪkətɪv; *NAmE* ˈpredɪkeɪtɪv/ *adj.* (*grammar*) (of an adjective) coming after a verb such as *be, become, get, seem, look*. Many adjectives, for example *old* can be either predicative as in *The man is very old*, or ATTRIBUTIVE as in *an old man*. Some, like *asleep*, can only be predicative. ▶ **pre·dica·tive·ly** *adv.*

pre·dict 0-w AW /prɪˈdɪkt/ *verb* to say that sth will happen in the future **SYN forecast**: **~ sth** *a reliable method of predicting earthquakes* ◇ *Nobody could predict the outcome.* ◇ **~ what, whether, etc...** *It is impossible to predict what will happen.* ◇ **~ (that)...** *She predicted (that) the election result would be close.* ◇ **it is predicted that...** *It was predicted that inflation would continue to fall.* ◇ **sb/sth is predicted to do sth** *The trial is predicted to last for months.* ➲ LANGUAGE BANK at EXPECT

pre·dict·able AW /prɪˈdɪktəbl/ *adj.* **1** if sth is **predictable**, you know in advance that it will happen or what it will be like: *a predictable result* ◇ *The ending of the book was entirely predictable.* ◇ *In March and April, the weather is much less predictable.* **2** (often *disapproving*) behaving or happening in a way that you would expect and therefore boring: *He's very nice, but I find him rather dull and predictable.* ▶ **pre·dict·abil·ity** AW /prɪˌdɪktəˈbɪləti/ *noun* [U] **pre·dict·ably** AW /-əbli/ *adv.*: *Prices were predictably high.* ◇ *Predictably, the new regulations proved unpopular.*

pre·dic·tion AW /prɪˈdɪkʃn/ *noun* [C, U] a statement that says what you think will happen; the act of making such a statement: *Not many people agree with the government's prediction that the economy will improve.* ◇ *The results of the experiment confirmed our predictions.* ◇ *Skilled readers make use of context and prediction.* ◇ *It's difficult to make accurate predictions about the effects on the environment.* ➲ COLLOCATIONS at SCIENTIFIC ➲ LANGUAGE BANK at EXPECT

pre·dict·ive /prɪˈdɪktɪv/ *adj.* [usually before noun] **1** (*formal*) connected with the ability to show what will happen in the future: *the predictive power of science* **2** (of a computer program) allowing you to enter text on a computer or a mobile/cell phone more quickly by using the first few letters of each word to predict what you want to say: ***predictive text input*** ◇ ***predictive messaging***

pre·dic·tor /prɪˈdɪktə(r)/ *noun* (*formal*) something that can show what will happen in the future: *Cholesterol level is not a strong predictor of heart disease in women.*

pre·digest·ed /ˌpriːdaɪˈdʒestɪd/ *adj.* (of information) put in a simple form that is easy to understand

pre·di·lec·tion /ˌpriːdɪˈlekʃn; *NAmE* ˌpredlˈek-/ *noun* [usually sing.] **~ (for sth)** (*formal*) if you **have a predilection for** sth, you like it very much **SYN liking, preference**

pre·dis·pose /ˌpriːdɪˈspəʊz; *NAmE* -ˈspoʊz/ *verb* (*formal*) **1** to influence sb so that they are likely to think or behave in a particular way: **~ sb to sth** *He believes that some people are predisposed to criminal behaviour.* ◇ **~ sb to do sth** *Her good mood predisposed her to enjoy the play.* **2 ~ sb to sth** to make it likely that you will suffer from a particular illness: *Stress can predispose people to heart attacks.*

pre·dis·pos·ition /ˌpriːdɪspəˈzɪʃn/ *noun* [C, U] **~ (to/towards sth)** | **~ (to do sth)** (*formal*) a condition that makes sb/sth likely to behave in a particular way or to suffer from a particular disease: *a genetic predisposition to liver disease*

pre·dom·in·ance AW /prɪˈdɒmɪnəns; *NAmE* -ˈdɑːm-/ *noun* **1** [sing.] the situation of being greater in number or amount than other things or people **SYN preponderance**: *a predominance of female teachers in elementary schools* **2** [U] the state of having more power or influence than others **SYN dominance**

pre·dom·in·ant AW /prɪˈdɒmɪnənt; *NAmE* -ˈdɑːm-/ *adj.* **1** most obvious or noticeable: *a predominant feature* ◇ *Yellow is the predominant colour this spring in the fashion world.* **2** having more power or influence than others **SYN dominant**: *a predominant culture*

pre·dom·in·ant·ly AW /prɪˈdɒmɪnəntli; *NAmE* -ˈdɑːm-/ (also *less frequent* **pre·dom·in·ate·ly** /prɪˈdɒmɪnətli; *NAmE* -ˈdɑːm-/) *adv.* mostly; mainly: *She works in a predominantly male environment.* ➲ LANGUAGE BANK at GENERALLY

pre·dom·in·ate AW /prɪˈdɒmɪneɪt; *NAmE* -ˈdɑːm-/ *verb* **1** [I] to be greater in amount or number than sth/sb else in a place, group, etc: *a colour scheme in which red predominates* ◇ *Women predominated in the audience.* **2** [I] **~ (over sb/sth)** to have the most influence or importance: *Private interest was not allowed to predominate over the public good.*

ˌpre-eˈclamp·sia *noun* [U] (*medical*) a condition in which a pregnant woman has high BLOOD PRESSURE, which can become serious if it is not treated

pree·mie /ˈpriːmi/ *noun* (*NAmE, informal*) a PREMATURE baby

ˌpre-ˈeminent *adj.* (*formal*) more important, more successful or of a higher standard than others **SYN outstanding**: *Dickens was pre-eminent among English writers of his day.* ▶ **ˌpre-ˈeminence** *noun* [U]: *to achieve pre-eminence in public life*

ˌpre-ˈeminent·ly *adv.* to a very great degree; especially

pre-empt /priˈempt/ *verb* **1 ~ sth** to prevent sth from happening by taking action to stop it: *A good training course will pre-empt many problems.* **2 ~ sb/sth** to do or say sth before sb else does: *She was just about to apologize when he pre-empted her.* **3 ~ sth** (*NAmE*) to replace a planned programme on the television: *The scheduled programme will be pre-empted by a special news bulletin.*

pre-emption /priˈempʃn/ *noun* [U] (*business*) the opportunity given to one person or group to buy goods, shares, etc: *Existing shareholders will have pre-emption rights.*

pre-emptive /priˈemptɪv/ *adj.* [usually before noun] done to stop sb taking action, especially action that will be harmful to yourself: *a **pre-emptive attack/strike** on the military base*

preen /priːn/ *verb* **1** [T, I] **~ (yourself)** (usually *disapproving*) to spend a lot of time making yourself look attractive and then admiring your appearance: *Will you stop preening yourself in front of the mirror?* **2** [T] **~ yourself (on sth)** (usually *disapproving*) to feel very pleased with yourself about sth and show other people how pleased you are **3** [I, T] **~ (itself)** (of a bird) to clean itself or make its feathers smooth with its beak

ˌ**pre-eˈxist** *verb* [I] to exist from an earlier time: *a pre-existing medical condition* ▸ ˌ**pre-eˈxistent** *adj.*

pre·fab /ˈpriːfæb/ *noun* (*informal*) a prefabricated building: *prefabs built after the war*

pre·fab·ri·cated /ˌpriːˈfæbrɪkeɪtɪd/ *adj.* (especially of a building) made in sections that can be put together later ▸ **pre·fab·ri·ca·tion** /ˌpriːfæbrɪˈkeɪʃn/ *noun* [U]

pref·ace /ˈprefəs/ *noun, verb*
▪ ***noun*** an introduction to a book, especially one that explains the author's aims ➲ compare FOREWORD
▪ ***verb*** **1** **~ sth (with sth)** to provide a book or other piece of writing with a preface: *He prefaced the diaries with a short account of how they were discovered.* **2** **~ sth by/with sth** | **~ sth by doing sth** (*formal*) to say sth before you start making a speech, answering a question, etc: *I must preface my remarks with an apology.*

prefa·tory /ˈprefətri; *NAmE* -tɔːri/ *adj.* [only before noun] (*formal*) acting as a PREFACE or an introduction to sth: *a prefatory note*

pre·fect /ˈpriːfekt/ *noun* **1** (in some British schools) an older student with some authority over younger students and some other responsibilities and advantages **2** (also **Prefect**) an officer responsible for an area of local government in some countries, for example France, Italy and Japan

pre·fec·ture /ˈpriːfektʃə(r)/ *noun* an area of local government in some countries, for example France, Italy and Japan

pre·fer 🔑 /prɪˈfɜː(r)/ *verb* (-rr-) (not used in the progressive tenses)
to like one thing or person better than another; to choose one thing rather than sth else because you like it better: **~ sth** *'Coffee or tea?' 'I'd prefer tea, thanks.'* ◇ *I much prefer jazz to rock music.* ◇ *I* ***would prefer it if*** *you didn't tell anyone.* ◇ *A local firm is* ***to be preferred.*** ◇ **~ sth + adj.** *I prefer my coffee black.* ◇ **~ to do sth** *The donor prefers to remain anonymous.* ◇ *I prefer not to think about it.* ◇ **~ sb/sth to do sth** *Would you prefer me to stay?* ◇ **~ doing sth** *I prefer playing in defence.* ◇ **~ that...** (*formal*) *I would prefer that you did not mention my name.* IDM see CHARGE *n.*

pref·er·able /ˈprefrəbl/ *adj.* more attractive or more suitable; to be preferred to sth: **~ (to sth)** *Anything was preferable to the tense atmosphere at home.* ◇ **~ (to doing sth)** *He finds country life* ***infinitely preferable*** *to living in the city.* ◇ **~ (to do sth)** *It would be preferable to employ two people, not one.* ▸ **pref·er·ably** /ˈprefrəbli/ *adv.*: *We're looking for a new house, preferably one near the school.*

pref·er·ence 🔑 /ˈprefrəns/ *noun*
1 🔑 [U, sing.] **~ (for sb/sth)** a greater interest in or desire for sb/sth than sb/sth else: *It's a matter of* ***personal preference.*** ◇ *Many people* ***expressed a strong preference*** *for the original plan.* ◇ *I can't say that I have any particular preference.* ◇ *Let's make a list of possible speakers,* ***in order of preference.*** **2** 🔑 [C] a thing that is liked better or best: *a study of consumer preferences* ➲ SYNONYMS at CHOICE
IDM **give (a) preference to sb/sth** to treat sb/sth in a way that gives them an advantage over other people or things: *Preference will be given to graduates of this university.* **in preference to sb/sth** 🔑 rather than sb/sth: *She was chosen in preference to her sister.*

pref·er·en·tial /ˌprefəˈrenʃl/ *adj.* [only before noun] giving an advantage to a particular person or group: *Don't expect to get* ***preferential treatment.*** ▸ **pref·er·en·tial·ly** /-ʃəli/ *adv.*

pre·fer·ment /prɪˈfɜːmənt; *NAmE* ˈfɜːrm-/ *noun* [U] (*formal*) the fact of being given a more important job or a higher rank SYN **promotion**

pre·fig·ure /ˌpriːˈfɪɡə(r); *NAmE* -ɡjər/ *verb* **~ sth** (*formal*) to suggest or show sth that will happen in the future

pre·fix /ˈpriːfɪks/ *noun, verb*
▪ ***noun*** **1** (*grammar*) a letter or group of letters added to the beginning of a word to change its meaning, such as *un-* in *unhappy* and *pre-* in *preheat* ➲ compare AFFIX, SUFFIX **2** a word, letter or number that is put before another: *Car insurance policies have the prefix MC (for motor car).* **3** (*old-fashioned*) a title such as *Dr* or *Mrs* used before a person's name
▪ ***verb*** to add letters or numbers to the beginning of a word or number: **~ A to B** *American members have the letters US prefixed to their code numbers.* ◇ **~ B with A** *Their code numbers are prefixed with US.*

preg·gers /ˈpreɡəz; *NAmE* -ɡərz/ *adj.* [not before noun] (*BrE, informal*) pregnant

preg·nancy /ˈpreɡnənsi/ *noun* [U, C] (*pl.* -ies) the state of being pregnant: *Many women experience sickness* ***during pregnancy.*** ◇ *a* ***pregnancy test*** ◇ ***unplanned/unwanted pregnancies*** ◇ *the increase in teenage pregnancies* ➲ COLLOCATIONS at CHILD

preg·nant 🔑 /ˈpreɡnənt/ *adj.*
1 🔑 (of a woman or female animal) having a baby or young animal developing inside her/its body: *My wife is pregnant.* ◇ *I was pregnant with our third child at the time.* ◇ *a* ***heavily pregnant*** *woman* (= one whose baby is nearly ready to be born) ◇ *to* ***get/become pregnant*** ◇ *He got his girlfriend pregnant and they're getting married.* ◇ *She's six months pregnant.* ➲ COLLOCATIONS at CHILD **2** **~ with sth** (*formal*) full of a quality or feeling: *Her silences were pregnant with criticism.*
IDM **a pregnant ˈpause/ˈsilence** an occasion when nobody speaks, although people are aware that there are feelings or thoughts to express

pre·heat /ˌpriːˈhiːt/ *verb* **~ sth** to heat an oven to a particular temperature before you put food in it to cook

pre·hen·sile /prɪˈhensaɪl; *NAmE* -sl/ *adj.* (*technical*) (of a part of an animal's body) able to hold things: *the monkey's prehensile tail* ➲ VISUAL VOCAB page V10

pre·his·toric /ˌpriːhɪˈstɒrɪk; *NAmE* -ˈstɔːr-/ *adj.* connected with the time in history before information was written down: *in prehistoric times* ◇ *prehistoric man/remains/animals/burial sites*

pre·his·tory /ˌpriːˈhɪstri/ *noun* **1** [U] the period of time in history before information was written down **2** [sing.] the earliest stages of the development of sth: *the prehistory of capitalism*

ˌ**pre-inˈstall** *verb* = PRELOAD

pre·judge /ˌpriːˈdʒʌdʒ/ *verb* **~ sth** (*formal*) to make a judgement about a situation before you have all the necessary information: *They took care not to* ***prejudge the issue.***

preju·dice /ˈpredʒudɪs/ *noun, verb*
▪ ***noun*** [U, C] an unreasonable dislike of or preference for a person, group, custom, etc, especially when it is based on their race, religion, sex, etc: *a victim of* ***racial prejudice*** ◇ *Their decision was based on ignorance and prejudice.* ◇ **~ against sb/sth** *There is little prejudice against workers from other EU states.* ◇ **~ in favour of sb/sth** *I must admit to a prejudice in favour of British universities.* ➲ COLLOCATIONS at RACE
IDM **without ˈprejudice (to sth)** (*law*) without affecting any other legal matter: *They agreed to pay compensation without prejudice* (= without admitting GUILT).
▪ ***verb*** **1** **~ sb (against sb/sth)** to influence sb so that they have an unfair or unreasonable opinion about sb/sth SYN **bias**: *The prosecution lawyers have been trying to prejudice the jury against her.* **2** **~ sth** (*formal*) to have a harmful effect on sth: *Any delay will prejudice the child's welfare.*

preju·diced /ˈpredʒədɪst/ *adj.* having an unreasonable dislike of or preference for sb/sth, especially based on their race, religion, sex, etc: *Few people will admit to being racially prejudiced.* ◇ **~ (against/in favour of sb/sth)** *They are prejudiced against older applicants.* ◇ (*humorous*) *I think it's an excellent article, but then I'm prejudiced—I wrote it.*

preju·di·cial /ˌpredʒuˈdɪʃl/ *adj.* **~ (to sth)** (*formal*) harming or likely to harm sb/sth SYN **damaging**: *developments prejudicial to the company's future*

prel·ate /ˈprelət/ *noun* (*formal*) a priest of high rank in the Christian Church, such as a BISHOP or CARDINAL

P

pre·lim·in·ary AW /prɪˈlɪmɪnəri; *NAmE* -neri/ *adj., noun*

■ ***adj.*** happening before a more important action or event SYN **initial**: *After a few preliminary remarks he announced the winners.* ◇ *preliminary results/findings/enquiries* ◇ *the preliminary rounds of the contest* ◇ **~ to sth** *pilot studies preliminary to a full-scale study*

■ ***noun*** (*pl.* -ies) **~ (to sth)** a **preliminary** is an action or event that is done in preparation for sth: *Research will be needed as a preliminary to taking a decision.* ◇ *I'll skip the usual preliminaries and come straight to the point.* ◇ *England was lucky to get through the preliminaries* (= the preliminary stages in a sports competition).

pre·load /ˌpriː ˈləʊd; *NAmE* -ˈloʊd/ (also ˌ**pre-inˈstall**) *verb* **~ sth** to load sth in advance: *The PC comes with office software preloaded.* ▸ **pre·load** *noun*

prel·ude /ˈpreljuːd/ *noun* **1** a short piece of music, especially an introduction to a longer piece **2** **~ (to sth)** an action or event that happens before another more important one and forms an introduction to it

pre·mar·ital /ˌpriːˈmærɪtl/ *adj.* [only before noun] happening before marriage: *premarital sex*

pre·ma·ture /ˈpremətʃə(r); *NAmE* ˌpriːməˈtʃʊr; -ˈtʊr/ *adj.* **1** happening before the normal or expected time: *his premature death at the age of 37* **2** (of a birth or a baby) happening or being born before the normal length of PREGNANCY has been completed: *The baby was four weeks premature.* ◇ *a premature birth after only thirty weeks* **3** happening or made too soon: *a premature conclusion/decision/judgement* ◇ ***It is premature*** *to talk about success at this stage.* ▸ **pre·ma·ture·ly** *adv.*: *The child was born prematurely.* ◇ *Her hair became prematurely white.*

ˈ**pre-med** *noun* (*informal*) **1** [U] (*especially NAmE*) a course or set of classes that students take in preparation for medical school **2** [C] (*especially NAmE*) a student who is taking classes in preparation for medical school **3** [U] = PREMEDICATION

pre·medi·ca·tion /ˌpriːˌmedɪˈkeɪʃn/ (also *informal* **pre-med**) *noun* [U] drugs given to sb in preparation for an operation or other medical treatment

P

pre·medi·tated /ˌpriːˈmedɪteɪtɪd/ *adj.* (of a crime or bad action) planned in advance: *a premeditated attack* ◇ *The killing had not been premeditated.* OPP **unpremeditated** ▸ **pre·medi·ta·tion** /ˌpriːˌmedɪˈteɪʃn/ *noun* [U]

pre·men·strual /ˌpriːˈmenstruəl/ *adj.* happening or experienced before MENSTRUATION: *Many women suffer from* ***premenstrual tension/syndrome****, causing headaches and depression.* ➲ see also PMS

prem·ier /ˈpremiə(r); *NAmE* prɪˈmɪr; -ˈmjɪr/ *adj., noun*

■ ***adj.*** [only before noun] most important, famous or successful: *one of the country's premier chefs* ◇ (*BrE, sport*) *the Premier League/Division*

■ ***noun*** **1** used especially in newspapers, etc. to mean 'prime minister' **2** (in Canada) the first minister of a PROVINCE or TERRITORY

premi·ere /ˈpremieə(r); *NAmE* prɪˈmɪr; -ˈmjɪr/ *noun, verb*

■ ***noun*** the first public performance of a film/movie or play: *the* ***world premiere*** *of his new play* ◇ *The movie will have its premiere in July.*

■ ***verb*** [T, I] **~ (sth)** to perform a play or piece of music or show a film/movie to an audience for the first time; to be performed or shown to an audience for the first time: *The play was premiered at the Birmingham Rep in 2008.* ◇ *His new movie premieres in New York this week.*

prem·ier·ship /ˈpremiəʃɪp; *NAmE* prɪˈmɪrʃɪp; -ˈmjɪr-/ *noun* [sing.] **1** the period or position of being prime minister: *during Gordon Brown's premiership* **2** (often **the Premiership**) the football (SOCCER) league in England and Wales which has the best teams in it

prem·ise (*BrE* also *less frequent* **prem·iss**) /ˈpremɪs/ *noun* (*formal*) a statement or an idea that forms the basis for a reasonable line of argument: *the basic premise of her argument* ◇ *a false premise* ◇ *His reasoning is based on the premise that all people are equally capable of good and evil.*

prem·ised /ˈpremɪst/ *adj.* **~ on/upon sth** (*formal*) based on a particular idea or belief that is considered to be true: *Traditional economic analysis is premised on the assumption that more is better.*

prem·ises 🔑 /ˈpremɪsɪz/ *noun* [pl.] the building and land near to it that a business owns or uses: ***business/commercial/industrial premises*** ◇ *No alcohol may be consumed* ***on the premises****.* ◇ *Police were called to escort her* ***off the premises****.* ➲ SYNONYMS at BUILDING

pre·mium /ˈpriːmiəm/ *noun, adj.*

■ ***noun*** **1** an amount of money that you pay once or regularly for an insurance policy: *a monthly premium of £6.25* ➲ SYNONYMS at PAYMENT **2** an extra payment added to the basic rate: *You have to pay a high premium for express delivery.* ◇ *A premium of 10% is paid out after 20 years.*

IDM **at a ˈpremium** **1** if sth is **at a premium**, there is little of it available and it is difficult to get: *Space is at a premium in a one-bedroomed apartment.* **2** at a higher than normal price: *Shares are selling at a premium.* **put/place/set a premium on sb/sth** to think that sb/sth is particularly important or valuable

■ ***adj.*** [only before noun] very high (and higher than usual); of high quality: *premium prices/products*

pre·modi·fier /ˌpriːˈmɒdɪfaɪə(r); *NAmE* -ˈmɑːd-/ *noun* (*grammar*) a word, especially an adjective or a noun, that is placed before a noun and describes it or restricts its meaning in some way: *In 'a loud noise', the adjective 'loud' is a premodifier.* ➲ compare MODIFIER, POSTMODIFIER

pre·mon·ition /ˌpriːməˈnɪʃn; ˌprem-/ *noun* a feeling that sth is going to happen, especially sth unpleasant: **~ (of sth)** *a premonition of disaster* ◇ **~ (that...)** *He had a premonition that he would never see her again.* ▸ **pre·moni·tory** /prɪˈmɒnɪtəri; *NAmE* -ˈmɑːnɪtɔːri/ *adj.*: (*formal*) *a premonitory dream*

pre·natal /ˌpriːˈneɪtl/ (*especially NAmE*) (*BrE* also **antenatal**) *adj.* relating to the medical care given to pregnant women ➲ compare POST-NATAL

pre·nup·tial agreement /priːˌnʌpʃl əˈgriːmənt/ (also *informal* **pre·nup** /ˈpriːnʌp/) *noun* an agreement made by a couple before they get married in which they say how their money and property is to be divided if they get divorced

pre·occu·pa·tion /priˌɒkjuˈpeɪʃn; *NAmE* -ˌɑːk-/ *noun* **1** [U, C] **~ (with sth)** a state of thinking about sth continuously; sth that you think about frequently or for a long time SYN **obsession**: *She found his preoccupation with money irritating.* ◇ *His current preoccupation is the appointment of the new manager.* **2** [U] a mood created by thinking or worrying about sth and ignoring everything else: *She spoke slowly, in a state of preoccupation.*

pre·occu·pied /priˈɒkjupaɪd; *NAmE* -ˈɑːk-/ *adj.* **~ (with sth)** thinking and/or worrying continuously about sth so that you do not pay attention to other things: *He was too preoccupied with his own thoughts to notice anything wrong.*

pre·occupy /priˈɒkjupaɪ; *NAmE* -ˈɑːk-/ *verb* (**pre·occu·pies, pre·occu·py·ing, pre·occu·pied, pre·occu·pied**) **~ sb** if sth is **preoccupying** you, you think or worry about it very often or all the time

pre·or·dained /ˌpriːɔːˈdeɪnd; *NAmE* -ɔːrˈd-/ *adj.* (*formal*) already decided or planned by God or by FATE SYN **predestined**: *Is everything we do preordained?* ◇ **~ to do sth** *They seemed preordained to meet.*

ˌ**pre-ˈowned** *adj.* (*NAmE*) not new; owned by sb else before

prep /prep/ *noun, verb*

■ ***noun*** [U] (*BrE*) (in some private schools) school work that is done at the end of the day after lessons

■ ***verb*** (-pp-) **1** [T, I] (*NAmE, informal*) to prepare (sth): **~ sth** *Prep the vegetables in advance.* ◇ **~ (for sth)** *They're prepping for college.* **2** [T] **~ sb** (*technical*) to prepare sb for a medical operation

ˌ**pre-ˈpacked** (also ˌ**pre-ˈpackaged**) *adj.* (of goods, especially food) put into packages before being sent to shops/stores to be sold: *pre-packed sandwiches*

pre·paid /ˌpriːˈpeɪd/ (*BrE* also ˌ**pre-ˈpay**) *adj.* paid for in advance: *a prepaid mobile phone* ◇ *A prepaid envelope is enclosed* (= so you do not have to pay the cost of sending a letter).

prep·ar·ation 🔑 /ˌprepəˈreɪʃn/ *noun*
1 🔑 [U] **~ (for sth)** the act or process of getting ready for sth or making sth ready: *Preparation for the party started early.* ◇ *food preparation* ◇ *Careful preparation for the exam is essential.* ◇ *The third book in the series is currently* ***in preparation.*** ◇ *The team has been training hard* ***in preparation for*** *the big game.* **2** 🔑 [C, usually pl.] things that you do to get ready for sth or make sth ready: **~ (for sth)** *The country is* ***making preparations*** *for war.* ◇ *Was going to college a good preparation for your career?* ◇ **~ (to do sth)** *We made preparations to move to new offices.* ◇ *wedding preparations* **3** [C] a substance that has been specially prepared for use as a medicine, COSMETIC, etc: *a pharmaceutical preparation* ◇ *preparations for the hair and skin*

pre·para·tory /prɪˈpærətri; *NAmE* -tɔːri/ *adj.* (*formal*) done in order to prepare for sth: *preparatory meetings* ◇ *Security checks had been carried out* ***preparatory to*** (= to prepare for) *the President's visit.*

preˈparatory school (also ˈ**prep school**) *noun* **1** (in Britain) a private school for children between the ages of 7 and 13 ➲ compare PUBLIC SCHOOL **2** (in the US) a school, usually a private one, that prepares students for college

pre·pare 🔑 /prɪˈpeə(r); *NAmE* -ˈper/ *verb*
1 🔑 [T] to make sth or sb ready to be used or to do sth: **~ sth/sb** *to prepare a report* ◇ **~ sth/sb for sb/sth** *A hotel room is being prepared for them.* ◇ *The college prepares students for a career in business.* **2** 🔑 [I, T] to make yourself ready to do sth or for sth that you expect to happen: *I had no time to prepare.* ◇ **~ for sth** *The whole class is working hard preparing for the exams.* ◇ **~ yourself (for sth)** *The police are preparing themselves for trouble at the demonstration.* ◇ **~ to do sth** *I was preparing to leave.* ◇ **~ yourself to do sth** *The troops prepared themselves to go into battle.* **3** 🔑 [T] **~ sth** to make food ready to be eaten: *He was in the kitchen preparing lunch.* **4** [T] **~ sth (from sth)** to make a medicine or chemical substance, for example by mixing other substances together: *remedies prepared from herbal extracts*
IDM **prepare the ˈground (for sth)** to make it possible or easier for sth to be achieved: *The committee will prepare the ground for next month's meeting.*

pre·pared 🔑 /prɪˈpeəd; *NAmE* -ˈperd/ *adj.*
1 🔑 [not before noun] **~ (for sth)** ready and able to deal with sth: *I was not prepared for all the problems it caused.* ◇ *We'll be better prepared next time.* ◇ *When they set out they were well prepared.* **OPP** **unprepared** ➲ see also ILL-PREPARED **2** 🔑 **~ to do sth** willing to do sth: *We are not prepared to accept these conditions.* ◇ *How much are you prepared to pay?* **OPP** **unwilling** **3** 🔑 done, made, written, etc. in advance: *The police officer read out a prepared statement.*

pre·pared·ness /prɪˈpeərɪdnəs; *NAmE* -ˈperd-/ *noun* [U] **~ (to do sth)** (*formal*) the state of being ready or willing to do sth: *I was surprised by his preparedness to break the law.* ◇ *The troops are in a state of preparedness.*

ˌ**pre-ˈpay** *adj.* (*BrE*) = PREPAID: *pre-pay phones*

pre·pay·ment /ˌpriːˈpeɪmənt/ *noun* [U] payment in advance: *a prepayment plan*

pre·pon·der·ance /prɪˈpɒndərəns; *NAmE* -ˈpɑːn-/ *noun* [sing.] if there is a **preponderance** of one type of people or things in a group, there are more of them than others **SYN** **predominance**

pre·pon·der·ant /prɪˈpɒndərənt; *NAmE* -ˈpɑːn-/ *adj.* [usually before noun] (*formal*) larger in number or more important than other people or things in a group ▶ **pre·pon·der·ant·ly** *adv.*

pre·pone /priːˈpəʊn; *NAmE* -ˈpoʊn/ *verb* **~ sth** (*IndE, informal*) to move sth to an earlier time than was originally planned

prep·os·ition /ˌprepəˈzɪʃn/ *noun* (*grammar*) a word or group of words, such as *in, from, to, out of* and *on behalf of*, used before a noun or pronoun to show place, position, time or method ▶ **prep·os·ition·al** /-ʃənl/ *adj.*: *a prepositional phrase* (= a preposition and the noun following it, for example *at night* or *after breakfast*)

pre·pos·sess·ing /ˌpriːpəˈzesɪŋ/ *adj.* (especially after a negative) (*formal*) attractive in appearance **SYN** **appealing**: *He was not a prepossessing sight.* ➲ compare UNPREPOSSESSING

pre·pos·ter·ous /prɪˈpɒstərəs; *NAmE* -ˈpɑːs-/ *adj.* (*formal*) **1** completely unreasonable, especially in a way that is shocking or annoying **SYN** **outrageous**: *These claims are absolutely preposterous!* **2** unusual in a silly or shocking way **SYN** **outrageous**: *The band were famous for their preposterous clothes and haircuts.* ▶ **pre·pos·ter·ous·ly** *adv.*: *a preposterously expensive bottle of wine*

prep·py (also **prep·pie**) /ˈprepi/ *noun* (*pl.* **-ies**) (*NAmE, informal*) a young person who goes or went to an expensive private school and who dresses and acts in a way that is thought to be typical of such a school ▶ **prep·py** (also **prep·pie**) *adj.*: *a preppy image* ◇ *preppy clothes*

pre·pran·dial /ˌpriːˈprændiəl/ *adj.* [only before noun] (*formal* or *humorous*) happening immediately before a meal: *a preprandial drink*

ˌ**pre-proˈduc·tion** *adj.* [usually before noun] done before the process of producing sth, especially a film/movie, begins: *the pre-production script* ▶ ˌ**pre-proˈduc·tion** *adv.* ˌ**pre-proˈduc·tion** *noun* [U]

ˈ**prep school** *noun* = PREPARATORY SCHOOL

ˌ**pre-ˈqualify·ing** *adj.* [only before noun] relating to a competition or game in which teams or players take part to decide if they are good enough to be in another competition: *players who fail at the pre-qualifying stage* ▶ ˌ**pre-ˈqualifier** *noun*

pre·quel /ˈpriːkwəl/ *noun* a book or a film/movie about events that happened before those in a popular book or film/movie: *Fans waited for years for the first Star Wars prequel.* ➲ compare SEQUEL

Pre-Raphael·ite /ˌpriː ˈræfəlaɪt/ *noun, adj.*
■ ***noun*** a member of a group of British 19th century artists who painted in a style similar to Italian artists of the 14th and 15th centuries, before the time of Raphael
■ ***adj.*** **1** connected with or in the style of the Pre-Raphaelites: *Pre-Raphaelite paintings* **2** (especially of a woman) looking like a person in a painting by one of the Pre-Raphaelites, for example with pale skin and long thick dark red hair

ˌ**pre-reˈcord** *verb* **~ sth** to record music, a television programme, etc. in advance, so that it can be broadcast or used later

pre·regis·ter /ˌpriːˈredʒɪstə(r)/ *verb* [I] **~ (for sth)** (*especially NAmE*) to register for sth before the usual time or before sth starts ▶ **pre·regis·tra·tion** /ˌpriːredʒɪˈstreɪʃn/ *noun* [U]

pre·requis·ite /ˌpriːˈrekwəzɪt/ *noun* [usually sing.] **~ (for/of/to sth)** (*formal*) something that must exist or happen before sth else can happen or be done **SYN** **precondition**: *A degree is an essential prerequisite for employment at this level.* ➲ compare REQUISITE ▶ **pre·requis·ite** *adj.* [only before noun]: *prerequisite knowledge*

pre·roga·tive /prɪˈrɒɡətɪv; *NAmE* -ˈrɑːɡ-/ *noun* (*formal*) a right or advantage belonging to a particular person or group because of their importance or social position: *In many countries education is still the prerogative of the rich.* ◇ *the* ***royal prerogative*** (= the special rights of a king or queen)

P

pres·age /ˈpresɪdʒ; prɪˈseɪdʒ/ *verb* **~ sth** (*literary*) to be a warning or sign that sth will happen, usually sth unpleasant ▸ **pre·sage** /ˈpresɪdʒ/ *noun*: *the first presages of winter*

Pres·by·ter·ian /ˌprezbɪˈtɪəriən; *NAmE* -ˈtɪr-/ *noun* a member of a branch of the Christian Protestant Church that is the national Church of Scotland and one of the largest Churches in the US. It is governed by ELDERS who are all equal in rank. ▸ **Pres·by·ter·ian** *adj.* **Pres·by·ter·ian·ism** /ˌprezbɪˈtɪəriənɪzəm; *NAmE* -ˈtɪr-/ *noun* [U]

pres·by·tery /ˈprezbɪtri; *NAmE* -teri/ *noun* (*pl.* -ies) **1** a local council of the Presbyterian Church **2** a house where a Roman Catholic priest lives **3** part of a church, near the east end, beyond the CHOIR

pre·school /ˈpriːskuːl/ *noun* a school for children between the ages of about two and five SYN **nursery school**

pres·ci·ent /ˈpresiənt/ *adj.* (*formal*) knowing or appearing to know about things before they happen ▸ **pres·ci·ence** /-əns/ *noun* [U]

pre·scribe /prɪˈskraɪb/ *verb* **1** (of a doctor) to tell sb to take a particular medicine or have a particular treatment; to write a PRESCRIPTION for a particular medicine, etc: **~ sth** *Valium is usually prescribed to treat anxiety.* ◇ **~ (sb) sth (for sth)** *He may be able to prescribe you something for that cough.* **2** (of a person or an organization with authority) to say what should be done or how sth should be done SYN **stipulate**: **~ sth** *The prescribed form must be completed and returned to this office.* ◇ **~ that...** *Police regulations prescribe that an officer's number must be clearly visible.* ◇ **~ which, what, etc...** *The syllabus prescribes precisely which books should be studied.*

pre·scrip·tion /prɪˈskrɪpʃn/ *noun* **1** [C] **~ (for sth)** an official piece of paper on which a doctor writes the type of medicine you should have, and which enables you to get it from a chemist's shop/drugstore: *The doctor gave me a prescription for antibiotics.* ◇ (*BrE*) *Antibiotics are only available* ***on prescription.*** ◇ (*NAmE*) *Antibiotics are only available* ***by prescription.*** ◇ *They are not available without a prescription.* ◇ ***prescription drugs/medication(s)*** **2** [C] medicine that your doctor has ordered for you: *The pharmacist will make up your prescription.* ◇ *a* ***prescription charge*** (= in Britain, the money you must pay for a medicine your doctor has ordered for you) **3** [U] the act of prescribing medicine: *The prescription of drugs is a doctor's responsibility.* **4** [C] **~ (for sth)** (*formal*) a plan or a suggestion for making sth happen or for improving it: *a prescription for happiness*

pre·scrip·tive /prɪˈskrɪptɪv/ *adj.* **1** (*formal*) telling people what should be done: *prescriptive methods of teaching* **2** (*linguistics*) telling people how a language should be used, rather than describing how it is used OPP **descriptive** **3** (*technical*) (of rights and institutions) made legal or acceptable because they have existed for a long time: *prescriptive powers*

pre·select /ˌpriːsɪˈlekt/ *verb* **~ sth** to choose sth in advance so it is ready to be used: *You can preselect programmes you want to watch, and program your VCR to record them.*

pre·sell /ˌpriːˈsel/ *verb* (**pre·sold, pre·sold** /ˌpriːˈsəʊld; *NAmE* -ˈsoʊld/) **1 ~ sth** to help sell a product, service, etc, especially one that is not yet available, by using advertising and other techniques to attract consumers' attention: *Putting a trial version on your website is a great way of preselling your product.* **2 ~ sth** to sell sth in advance of when it is available: *These farmers presell their crops.*

pres·ence 🔑 /ˈprezns/ *noun*
1 🔑 [U] (of a person) the fact of being in a particular place: *He hardly seemed to notice my presence.* ◇ *Her presence during the crisis had a calming effect.* ◇ (*formal*) *Your presence is requested at the meeting.* OPP **absence** **2** 🔑 [U] (of a thing or a substance) the fact of being in a particular place or thing: *The test can identify the presence of abnormalities in the unborn child.* OPP **absence** **3** [sing.] a group of people, especially soldiers, who have been sent to a place to deal with a particular situation: *The government is maintaining a heavy police presence in the area.* ◇ *a military presence* **4** [C, usually sing.] (*literary*) a person or spirit that you cannot see but that you feel is near: *She felt a presence behind her.* **5** [U] (*approving*) the quality of making a strong impression on other people by the way you talk or behave: *a man of great presence*
IDM **in the ˈpresence of sb | in sb's ˈpresence** with sb in the same place: *The document was signed in the presence of two witnesses.* ◇ *She asked them not to discuss the matter in her presence.* **in the ˈpresence of sth** when sth exists in a particular place: *Litmus paper turns red in the presence of an acid.* **make your presence ˈfelt** to do sth to make people very aware of the fact that you are there; to have a strong influence on a group of people or a situation

ˌpresence of ˈmind *noun* [U] the ability to react quickly and stay calm in a difficult or dangerous situation: *The boy* ***had the presence of mind to*** *turn off the gas.*

pres·ent 🔑 *adj., noun, verb*
■ ***adj.*** /ˈpreznt/ **1** 🔑 [only before noun] existing or happening now: *in the present situation* ◇ *the present owner of the house* ◇ *a list of all club members,* ***past and present*** ◇ *We do not have any more information* ***at the present time.*** ◇ *A few brief comments are sufficient* ***for present purposes.*** ➲ note at ACTUAL ➲ see also THE PRESENT DAY **2** 🔑 [not before noun] **~ (at sth)** (of a person) being in a particular place: *There were 200 people present at the meeting.* OPP **absent** **3** 🔑 [not before noun] **~ (in sth)** (of a thing or a substance) existing in a particular place or thing: *Levels of pollution present in the atmosphere are increasing.* ◇ *Analysis showed that traces of arsenic were present in the body.* OPP **absent**
IDM **all ˌpresent and corˈrect** (*BrE*) (*NAmE* **all present and acˈcounted for**) used to say that all the things or people who should be there are now there **present company exˈcepted** (*informal*) used after being rude or critical about sb to say that the people you are talking to are not included in the criticism
■ ***noun*** /ˈpreznt/ **1** 🔑 a thing that you give to sb as a gift: ***birthday/Christmas/wedding, etc. presents*** ◇ *What can I get him for a birthday present?* **2** 🔑 (usually **the present**) [sing.] the time now: *You've got to forget the past and start living in the present.* ◇ *I'm sorry he's out* ***at present*** (= now). **3 the present** [sing.] (*grammar*) = THE PRESENT TENSE
IDM see MOMENT, TIME *n.*
■ ***verb*** /prɪˈzent/
▸ GIVE **1** 🔑 to give sth to sb, especially formally at a ceremony: **~ sth** *The local MP will start the race and present the prizes.* ◇ **~ sb with sth** *On his retirement, colleagues presented him with a set of golf clubs.* ◇ **~ sth to sb** *The sword was presented by the family to the museum.*
▸ STH TO BE CONSIDERED **2** 🔑 to show or offer sth for other people to look at or consider: **~ sth (to sb)** *The committee will present its final report to Parliament in June.* ◇ **~ sth (for sth)** *Eight options were presented for consideration.* ◇ *Are you presenting a paper at the conference?*
▸ STH IN PARTICULAR WAY **3** 🔑 to show or describe sth/sb in a particular way: **~ sth** *The company has decided it must present a more modern image.* ◇ *It is essential that we present a united front* (= show that we all agree). ◇ **~ yourself + adv./prep.** *You need to present yourself better.* ◇ **~ sth/sb/yourself as sth** *He likes to present himself as a radical politician.* ◇ *The article presents these proposals as misguided.*
▸ SB WITH PROBLEM **4** to cause sth to happen or be experienced: **~ sb with sth** *Your request shouldn't present us with any problems.* ◇ **~ sth** *Use of these chemicals may present a fire risk.*
▸ ITSELF **5** (of an opportunity, a solution, etc.) to suddenly happen or become available SYN **arise**: **~ itself** *One major problem did present itself, though.* ◇ *As soon as the opportunity presented itself, she would get another job.* ◇ **~ itself to sb** *Thankfully, a solution presented itself to him surprisingly soon.*
▸ RADIO/TV PROGRAMME **6 ~ sth** (*BrE*) to appear in a radio or television programme and introduce the different items in it: *She used to present a gardening programme on TV.*
▸ PLAY/BROADCAST **7 ~ sth** to produce a show, play, broad-

P

cast, etc. for the public: *Compass Theatre Company presents a new production of 'King Lear'.*
▸ INTRODUCE SB **8 ~ sb (to sb)** (*formal*) to introduce sb formally, especially to sb of higher rank or status: *May I present my fiancé to you?*
▸ YOURSELF **9 ~ yourself at, for, in, etc.** (*formal*) to officially appear somewhere: *You will be asked to present yourself for interview.* ◇ *She was ordered to present herself in court on 20 May.*
▸ EXPRESS STH **10 ~ sth (to sb)** (*formal*) to offer or express sth in speech or writing: *Please allow me to present my apologies.*
▸ CHEQUE/BILL **11 ~ sth** to give sb a cheque or bill that they should pay: *A cheque presented by Mr Jackson was returned by the bank.* ◇ *The builders presented a bill for several hundred pounds.*
IDM **pre,sent 'arms** (of soldiers) to hold a RIFLE vertical in front of the body as a mark of respect

pre·sent·able /prɪ'zentəbl/ *adj.* **1** looking clean and attractive and suitable to be seen in public: *I must go and* ***make myself presentable*** *before the guests arrive.* **2** acceptable: *You're going to have to do a lot more work on this essay before it's presentable.*

pre·sen·ta·tion 0-w /ˌprezn'teɪʃn; *NAmE* ˌpriːzen-/ *noun*
1 0-w [U] the act of showing sth or of giving sth to sb: *The trial was adjourned following the presentation of new evidence to the court.* ◇ *The presentation of prizes began after the speeches.* ◇ *The Mayor will* ***make the presentation*** (= hand over the gift) *herself.* ◇ *Members will be admitted* ***on presentation of*** *a membership card.* **2** 0-w [U] the way in which sth is offered, shown, explained, etc. to others: *Improving the product's presentation* (= the way it is wrapped, advertised, etc.) *should increase sales.* ◇ *I admire the clear, logical presentation of her arguments.* **3** 0-w [C] a meeting at which sth, especially a new product or idea, or piece of work, is shown to a group of people: *The sales manager will* ***give a presentation*** *on the new products.* ➲ WRITING TUTOR page WT12 **4** [C] the series of computer SLIDES (= images) that accompany the talk when sb gives a presentation at a meeting: *I've put my presentation on a memory stick.* ➲ WRITING TUTOR page WT12 **5** [C] a ceremony or formal occasion during which a gift or prize is given **6** [C] a performance of a play, etc. in a theatre **7** [C, U] (*medical*) the position in which a baby is lying in the mother's body just before birth

pre·sen·ta·tion·al /ˌprezn'teɪʃənl; *NAmE* ˌpriːzen-/ *adj.* [only before noun] connected with the act of showing, explaining or offering sth to other people, especially a new product, a policy or a performance: *a course on developing presentational skills*

the ,present 'day *noun* [sing.] the situation that exists in the world now, rather than in the past or the future: *a study of European drama, from Ibsen* ***to the present day***
▸ **,present-'day** *adj.* [only before noun]: *present-day fashions* ◇ *present-day America*

pre·sent·ee·ism /ˌprezn'tiːɪzəm/ *noun* [U] (*BrE*) the practice of spending more time at your work than you need to according to your contract

pre·sent·er /prɪ'zentə(r)/ *noun* **1** (*BrE*) a person who introduces the different sections of a radio or television programme: *a TV presenter* ➲ see also ANNOUNCER, HOST **2** a person who makes a speech or talks to an audience about a particular subject: *conference presenters* **3** (*NAmE*) a person who gives sb a prize at a ceremony

pre·sen·ti·ment /prɪ'zentɪmənt/ *noun* (*formal*) a feeling that sth is going to happen, especially sth unpleasant SYN **foreboding**: *a presentiment of disaster*

pres·ent·ly /'prezntli/ *adv.* **1** (*especially NAmE*) at the time you are speaking or writing; now SYN **currently**: *The crime is presently being investigated by the police.* ◇ *These are the courses presently available.* HELP In this meaning **presently** usually comes before the verb, adjective or noun that it refers to. **2** used to show that sth happened after a short time: *Presently, the door opened again and three men stepped out.* HELP In this meaning **presently** usually comes at the beginning of a sentence. **3** used to show that sth will happen soon SYN **shortly**: *She'll be here presently.* HELP In this meaning **presently** usually comes at the end of a sentence.

British / American

presently

- In both *BrE* and *NAmE*, **presently** can mean 'soon' or 'after a short time': *I'll be with you presently.* In *NAmE* the usual meaning of **presently** is 'at the present time' or 'now': *She is presently living in Milan.* ◇ *There is presently no cure for the disease.* This use is becoming more accepted in *BrE*, but **at present** or **currently** are usually used.

,present 'participle *noun* (*grammar*) the form of the verb that in English ends in *-ing* and is used with the verb *to be* to form progressive tenses such as *I was running* or sometimes as an adjective as in *running water* ➲ compare PAST PARTICIPLE

the ,present 'perfect *noun* [sing.] (*grammar*) the form of a verb that expresses an action done in a time period up to the present, formed in English with the present tense of *have* and the past participle of the verb, as in *I have eaten*

,present 'tense (also **the present**) *noun* [usually sing.] (*grammar*) the form of a verb that expresses an action that is happening now or at the time of speaking

pre·ser·va·tion /ˌprezə'veɪʃn; *NAmE* -zər'v-/ *noun* [U] **1** the act of keeping sth in its original state or in good condition: *building/environmental/food preservation* ◇ *a preservation group/society* **2** the act of making sure that sth is kept: *The central issue in the strike was the preservation of jobs.* **3** the degree to which sth has not been changed or damaged by age, weather, etc: *The paintings were in an excellent state of preservation.* ➲ see also SELF-PRESERVATION

pre·ser·va·tion·ist /ˌprezə'veɪʃənɪst; *NAmE* -zər'v-/ *noun* a person who works to keep old buildings or areas of the countryside in their original condition and to prevent them from being destroyed

preser'vation order *noun* (in Britain) a document that makes it illegal to change or destroy a building, a tree or part of the countryside, because of its beauty or historical interest

pre·ser·va·tive /prɪ'zɜːvətɪv; *NAmE* -'zɜːrv-/ *noun* [C, U] a substance used to prevent food or wood from decaying: *The juice contains no artificial preservatives.* ◇ *(a) wood preservative* ➲ COLLOCATIONS at DIET ▸ **pre·ser·va·tive** *adj.* [only before noun]

pre·serve 0-w /prɪ'zɜːv; *NAmE* -'zɜːrv/ *verb, noun*
■ *verb* **1** 0-w **~ sth** to keep a particular quality, feature, etc; to make sure that sth is kept: *He was anxious to preserve his reputation.* ◇ *Efforts to preserve the peace have failed.* **2** 0-w [often passive] to keep sth in its original state in good condition: **~ sth/sb** *a perfectly preserved 14th century house* ◇ (*humorous*) *Is he really 60? He's remarkably* ***well preserved.*** ◇ **~ sth + adj.** *This vase has been preserved intact.* **3** 0-w **~ sth** to prevent sth, especially food, from decaying by treating it in a particular way: *olives preserved in brine* ◇ *Wax polish preserves wood and leather.* **4** 0-w **~ sb/sth (from sth)** to keep sb/sth alive, or safe from harm or danger SYN **save**: *The society was set up to preserve endangered species from extinction.* ➲ compare CONSERVE
■ *noun* **1** [sing.] **~ (of sb)** an activity, a job, an interest, etc. that is thought to be suitable for one particular person or group of people: *Football is no longer the preserve of men.* ◇ *in the days when nursing was a female preserve* **2** [C, usually pl., U] a type of jam made by boiling fruit with a large amount of sugar **3** [C, usually pl., U] (*especially BrE*) a type of PICKLE made by cooking vegetables with salt or VINEGAR **4** [C] (*NAmE*) = RESERVE (2) **5** [C] an area of private

P

land or water where animals and fish are kept for people to hunt

pre·server /prɪˈzɜːvə(r); *NAmE* -ˈzɜːrv-/ *noun* **1** [C] a person who makes sure that a particular situation does not change: *The police are the preservers of law and order.* **2** [C, U] a substance used to prevent wood from decaying ➲ see also LIFE PRESERVER

pre·set /ˌpriːˈset/ *verb* (**pre·setting**, **pre·set**, **pre·set**) **1** to set the controls of a piece of electrical equipment so that it will start to work at a particular time: **~ sth to do sth** *You can preset the radiators to come on when you need them to.* ◇ **~ sth** *to preset TV channels/radio stations* (= to set the controls so that particular channels are selected when you press particular buttons) **2** [usually passive] **~ sth** to decide sth in advance: *They kept to the preset route.*

pre·side /prɪˈzaɪd/ *verb* [I] (*formal*) to lead or be in charge of a meeting, ceremony, etc: *the presiding judge* ◇ **~ at/over sth** *They asked if I would preside at the committee meeting.* ◇ (*figurative*) *The party presided over one of the worst economic declines in the country's history* (= it was in power when the decline happened).

presi·dency /ˈprezɪdənsi/ *noun* [usually sing.] (*pl.* -ies) the job of being president of a country or an organization; the period of time sb holds this job: *the current holder of the EU presidency* ◇ *He was a White House official during the Bush presidency.*

presi·dent 🔑 /ˈprezɪdənt/ *noun*
1 🔑 (also **President**) the leader of a REPUBLIC, especially the US: *Several presidents attended the funeral.* ◇ *the President of the United States* ◇ *President Obama is due to visit the country next month.* ◇ *Do you have any comment, Mr President?* ➲ COLLOCATIONS at POLITICS **2** 🔑 (also **President**) the person in charge of some organizations, clubs, colleges, etc: *to be made president of the students' union* **3** 🔑 (*especially NAmE*) the person in charge of a bank or a commercial organization: *the bank president* ◇ *the president of Columbia Pictures* ▶ **presi·den·tial** /ˌpreziˈdenʃl/ *adj.*: *a presidential campaign/candidate/election* ◇ *a presidential system of government*

P

ˌpresident-eˈlect *noun* (*pl.* **presidents-elect**) a person who has been elected to be president but who has not yet begun the job

Presiˌdential ˌMedal of ˈFreedom *noun* a MEDAL in the US that is the highest award a person can be given during a time of peace

ˈPresidents' Day *noun* (in the US) a legal holiday on the third Monday in February, in memory of the birthdays of George Washington and Abraham Lincoln

pre·sid·ium (also **prae·sid·ium** especially in *BrE*) /prɪˈsɪdiəm/ *noun* a permanent committee that makes important decisions as part of a government or large political organization, especially in COMMUNIST countries

press 🔑 /pres/ *noun, verb*
■ ***noun***
▸ NEWSPAPERS **1** 🔑 (often **the Press**) [sing.+ sing./pl. v.] newspapers and magazines: *the **local/national/foreign press*** ◇ *the **popular/tabloid press*** (= smaller newspapers with a lot of pictures and stories of famous people) ◇ *The story was reported **in the press** and on television.* ◇ *the **music/sporting press*** (= newspapers and magazines about music/sport) ◇ *Unlike the American, the British press operates on a national scale.* ◇ *the **freedom of the Press/press freedom*** (= the freedom to report any events and express opinions) ◇ *The event is bound to attract wide **press coverage*** (= it will be written about in many newspapers). ➲ see also GUTTER PRESS **2** 🔑 **the press**, **the Press** [sing.+ sing./pl. v.] the journalists and photographers who work for newspapers and magazines: *The Press was/were not allowed to attend the trial.* **3** [sing., U] the type or amount of reports that newspapers write about sb/sth: *The airline has **had a bad press** recently* (= journalists have written unpleasant things about it).
▸ PUBLISHING/PRINTING **4** [C, U] a machine for printing books, newspapers, etc; the process of printing them: *We were able to watch the books rolling off the presses.* ◇ *These prices are correct at the time of **going to press**.* ◇ *a story that is **hot off the press*** (= has just appeared in the newspapers) ➲ see also PRINTING PRESS, STOP PRESS **5** [C] a business that prints and publishes books: *Oxford University Press*
▸ EQUIPMENT FOR PRESSING **6** [C] (especially in compounds) a piece of equipment that is used for creating pressure on things, to make them flat or to get liquid from them: *a trouser press* ◇ *a garlic press* ➲ VISUAL VOCAB page V23
▸ ACT OF PUSHING **7** [C, usually sing.] an act of pushing sth with your hand or with a tool that you are holding: *He gave the bell another press.* ◇ *Those shirts need a press* (= with an iron).
▸ CROWD **8** [sing.] a large number of people or things competing for space or movement SYN **throng**: *the press of bodies all moving the same way*
▸ CUPBOARD **9** [C] (*IrishE, ScotE*) a large cupboard, usually with shelves, for holding clothes, books, etc.
■ ***verb***
▸ PUSH/SQUEEZE **1** 🔑 [T, I] to push sth closely and firmly against sth; to be pushed in this way: **~ sth/sb/yourself against sth** *She pressed her face against the window.* ◇ **~ sth to sth** *He pressed a handkerchief to his nose.* ◇ **~ sth together** *She pressed her lips together.* ◇ **~ against sth** *His body was pressing against hers.* **2** 🔑 [T, I] to push or squeeze part of a device, etc. in order to make it work: **~ sth** *to **press a button/switch/key*** ◇ **~ sth + adj.** *He pressed the lid firmly shut.* ◇ (**+ adv./prep.**) *Press here to open.* ◇ *She pressed down hard on the gas pedal.* ➲ picture at SQUEEZE **3** [T] **~ sth into/onto sth** to put sth in a place by pushing it firmly: *He pressed a coin into her hand and moved on.* **4** [T] **~ sth** to squeeze sb's hand or arm, especially as a sign of affection **5** [I] **+ adv./prep.** (of people in a crowd) to move in the direction mentioned by pushing: *The photographers pressed around the royal visitors.* ◇ (*figurative*) *A host of unwelcome thoughts were pressing in on him.*
▸ TRY TO PERSUADE **6** [T] to make strong efforts to persuade or force sb to do sth SYN **push**, **urge**: **~ sb** *If **pressed**, he will admit that he knew about the affair.* ◇ **~ sb for sth** *The bank is pressing us for repayment of the loan.* ◇ **~ sb to do sth** *They are pressing us to make a quick decision.* ◇ **~ sb into sth/into doing sth** *Don't let yourself be pressed into doing something you don't like.*
▸ POINT/CLAIM/CASE **7** [T] **~ sth** to express or repeat sth with force: *I don't want to **press the point**, but you do owe me $200.* ◇ *She is still **pressing her claim** for compensation.* ◇ *They were determined to **press their case** at the highest level.*
▸ MAKE FLAT/SMOOTH **8** [T] to make sth flat or smooth by using force or putting sth heavy on top: **~ sth** *pressed flowers* (= pressed between the pages of a book) ◇ **~ sth + adj.** *Press the soil flat with the back of a spade.* **9** [T] **~ sth** to make clothes smooth using a hot iron SYN **iron**: *My suit needs pressing.*
▸ FRUIT/VEGETABLES **10** [T] **~ sth** to squeeze the juice out of fruit or vegetables by using force or weight
▸ METAL **11** [T] to make sth from a material, using pressure: **~ sth** *to press a CD* ◇ **~ sth from/out of sth** *The car bodies are pressed out of sheets of metal.*
IDM **ˌpress (the) ˈflesh** (*informal*) (of a famous person or politician) to say hello to people by shaking hands **ˌpress sth ˈhome** to get as much advantage as possible from a situation by attacking or arguing in a determined way: *to press home an attack/an argument/a point* ◇ *Simon saw she was hesitating and pressed home his advantage.* **ˌpress sb/sth into ˈservice** to use sb/sth for a purpose that they were not trained or intended for because there is nobody or nothing else available: *Every type of boat was pressed into service to rescue passengers from the sinking ferry.* ➲ more at BUTTON *n.*, CHARGE *n.*, PANIC BUTTON
PHR V **ˌpress aˈhead/ˈon (with sth)** to continue doing sth in a determined way; to hurry forward: *The company is pressing ahead with its plans for a new warehouse.* ◇ *'Shall we stay here for the night?' 'No, let's press on.'* **ˈpress for sth** to keep asking for sth SYN **demand**, **push for**: *They continued to press for a change in the law.* **ˈpress sth on sb** to

try to make sb accept sth, especially food or drink, although they may not want it: *She kept pressing cake on us.*

ˈpress agency *noun* = NEWS AGENCY

ˈpress agent (also *NAmE informal* **flack**) *noun* a person whose job is to supply information and advertising material about a particular actor, musician, theatre, etc. to newspapers, radio or television

ˈpress box *noun* a special area or a room at a sports ground where sports journalists sit

ˈpress conference (*especially BrE*) (*NAmE* usually **ˈnews conference**) *noun* a meeting at which sb talks to a group of journalists in order to answer their questions or to make an official statement: *to **hold/give a press conference***

ˈpress corps *noun* (*pl.* press corps) a group of journalists who work in or go to a particular place to report on an event

ˈpress cutting (*BrE*) (also **ˈpress clipping** *NAmE, BrE*) *noun* = CUTTING

pressed /prest/ *adj.* **1** [not before noun] **~** (**for sth**) not having enough of sth, especially time or money: *I'm really pressed for cash at the moment.* ➲ see also HARD-PRESSED **2** made flat using force or a heavy object: *pictures made with pressed flowers* ◇ *neatly pressed trousers*

ˈpress gallery *noun* an area in a parliament building or a court for journalists to sit in

ˈpress gang *noun* a group of people who were employed in the past to force men to join the army or navy

ˈpress-gang *verb* **~ sb** (**into sth/into doing sth**) (*informal*) to force sb to do sth that they do not want to do

pres·sie *noun* = PREZZIE

press·ing /ˈpresɪŋ/ *adj., noun*

■ ***adj.*** [usually before noun] **1** needing to be dealt with immediately SYN **urgent**: *I'm afraid I have some pressing business to attend to.* **2** difficult to refuse or to ignore: *a pressing invitation*

■ ***noun*** an object, especially a record, made by using pressure or weight to shape a piece of metal, plastic, etc; a number of such objects that are made at one time: *The initial pressing of the group's album has already sold out.*

press·man /ˈpresmæn/ *noun* (*pl.* **-men** /-men/) (*BrE, informal*) a journalist

ˈpress office *noun* the office of a large organization, political party or government department that answers questions from journalists and provides them with information

ˈpress officer *noun* a person who is in charge of or works for a press office

ˈpress release *noun* an official statement made to journalists by a large organization, a political party or a government department

ˈpress secretary *noun* a person who works for a politician or a political organization and gives information about them to journalists, the newspapers, etc.

ˈpress stud (also **pop·per**) (both *BrE*) (*NAmE* **snap**) *noun* a type of button used for fastening clothes, consisting of two metal or plastic sections that can be pressed together ➲ VISUAL VOCAB page V51

ˈpress-up (*BrE*) (also **ˈpush-up** *NAmE, BrE*) *noun* [usually pl.] an exercise in which you lie on your stomach and raise your body off the ground by pressing down on your hands until your arms are straight ➲ VISUAL VOCAB page V35

pres·sure 🔑 /ˈpreʃə(r)/ *noun, verb*

■ ***noun***

▸ WHEN STH PRESSES **1** 🔑 [U] the force or weight with which sth presses against sth else: *The nurse applied pressure to his arm to stop the bleeding.* ◇ *The barriers gave way under the pressure of the crowd.*

▸ OF GAS/LIQUID **2** 🔑 [U, C] the force produced by a particular amount of gas or liquid in a confined space or container; the amount of this: ***air/water pressure*** ◇ *Check the **tyre pressure*** (= the amount of air in a tyre) *regularly.* ➲ see also BLOOD PRESSURE

▸ OF ATMOSPHERE **3** 🔑 [U] the force of the atmosphere on the earth's surface: *A band of **high/low pressure** is moving across the country.* ➲ see also ATMOSPHERIC

▸ PERSUASION/FORCE **4** 🔑 [U] the act of trying to persuade or to force sb to do sth: **~** (**for sth**) *The pressure for change continued to mount.* ◇ **~** (**on sb**) (**to do sth**) *There is a great deal of pressure on young people to conform.* ◇ *The government eventually bowed to **popular pressure*** (= they agreed to do what people were trying to get them to do). ◇ *Teenagers may find it difficult to resist **peer pressure**.*

▸ STRESS **5** 🔑 [U] (also **pressures** [pl.]) difficulties and feelings of anxiety that are caused by the need to achieve or to behave in a particular way: *She was unable to attend because of the pressure of work.* ◇ *You need to be able to handle pressure in this job.* ◇ *How can anyone enjoy the pressures of city life?*

IDM **put ˈpressure on sb** (**to do sth**) to force or to try to persuade sb to do sth **under ˈpressure** **1** 🔑 if a liquid or a gas is kept **under pressure**, it is forced into a container so that when the container is opened, the liquid or gas escapes quickly **2** 🔑 being forced to do sth: *The director is under increasing pressure to resign.* **3** 🔑 made to feel anxious about sth you have to do: *The team performs well under pressure.*

■ ***verb*** [often passive] (*especially NAmE*) (*BrE* also **pres·sur·ize**) **~ sb** (**into sth/into doing sth**) | **~ sb to do sth** to persuade sb to do sth, especially by making them feel that they have to or should do it: *Don't let yourself be pressured into making a hasty decision.*

Synonyms

pressure

stress • tension • strain

These are all words for the feelings of anxiety caused by the problems in sb's life.

pressure difficulties and feelings of anxiety that are caused by the need to achieve sth or to behave in a particular way: *She was unable to attend because of the pressures of work.*

stress pressure or anxiety caused by the problems in sb's life: *stress-related illnesses*

PRESSURE OR STRESS?

It is common to say that sb *is suffering from stress*, while **pressure** may be the thing that causes **stress**.

tension a feeling of anxiety and stress that makes it impossible to relax: *nervous tension*

strain pressure on sb/sth because they have too much to do or manage; the problems, worry or anxiety that this produces: *I found it a strain looking after four children.*

PATTERNS

- to be **under** pressure/stress/strain
- **considerable** pressure/stress/tension/strain
- to **cause** stress/tension/strain
- to **cope with** the pressure/stress/tension/strain
- to **relieve/release** the pressure/stress/tension/strain
- to be **suffering from** stress/tension

ˈpressure cooker *noun* **1** a strong metal pot with a tight lid, that cooks food quickly by steam under high pressure **2** a situation that is difficult or dangerous because people are likely to become anxious or violent

ˈpressure group *noun* a group of people who try to influence the government and ordinary people's opinions in order to achieve the action they want, for example a change in a law: *the environmental pressure group 'Greenpeace'* ➲ compare ADVOCACY GROUP ➲ see also INTEREST GROUP

ˈpressure hose *noun* a long tube that is strong enough for liquid to pass through it at high pressure

ˈpressure point *noun* **1** a place on the surface of the body that is sensitive to pressure, for example where an artery can be pressed against a bone to stop the loss of

P

blood **2** a place or situation where there is likely to be trouble

ˈ**pressure suit** *noun* a suit which can be filled with air, used to protect the person wearing it from low air pressure, for example while flying a plane very high in the atmosphere

ˈ**pressure washer** *noun* a machine that cleans things by spraying them with water under high pressure

pres·sur·ize (*BrE* also **-ise**) /ˈpreʃəraɪz/ *verb* **1** (*BrE*) (also **pres·sure** *NAmE, BrE*) [often passive] to persuade sb to do sth, especially by making them feel that they have to or should do it: **~ sb (into sth/into doing sth)** *She was pressurized into accepting the job.* ◇ **~ sb to do sth** *He felt that he was being pressurized to resign.* **2** [usually passive] **~ sth** to keep the air pressure in a SUBMARINE, an aircraft, etc. the same as it is on earth ▸ **pres·sur·iza·tion, -isa·tion** /ˌpreʃəraɪˈzeɪʃn; *NAmE* -rəˈz-/ *noun* [U]

pres·tige /preˈstiːʒ/ *noun, adj.*

■ ***noun*** [U] the respect and admiration that sb/sth has because of their social position, or what they have done SYN **status**: *personal prestige* ◇ *There is a lot of prestige attached to owning a car like this.* ◇ *jobs with low prestige*

■ ***adj.*** [only before noun] **1** that brings respect and admiration; important: *a prestige job* **2** admired and respected because it looks important and expensive SYN **luxury**: *a prestige car*

pres·ti·gious /preˈstɪdʒəs/ *adj.* [usually before noun] respected and admired as very important or of very high quality: *a prestigious award* ◇ *a prestigious university*

presto /ˈprestəʊ; *NAmE* ˈprestoʊ/ *exclamation, adv., adj., noun*

■ ***exclamation*** (*NAmE*) (*BrE* ˌ**hey** ˈ**presto**) **1** something that people say when they have just done sth so quickly and easily that it seems to have been done by magic **2** something that people say just before they finish a magic trick

■ ***adv., adj.*** (used as an instruction in a piece of music) very quickly

■ ***noun*** (*pl.* -os) a piece of music that should be performed very quickly

P

pre·sum·ably 0‑w AW /prɪˈzjuːməbli; *NAmE* -ˈzuː-/ *adv.*
used to say that you think that sth is probably true: *Presumably this is where the accident happened.* ◇ *You'll be taking the car, presumably?* ◇ *I couldn't concentrate, presumably because I was so tired.*

pre·sume AW /prɪˈzjuːm; *NAmE* -ˈzuːm/ *verb* **1** [I, T] to suppose that sth is true, although you do not have actual proof SYN **assume**: *They are very expensive, I presume?* ◇ *'Is he still abroad?' '**I presume so.**'* ◇ **~ (that)...** *I presumed (that) he understood the rules.* ◇ **it is presumed that...** *Little is known of the youngest son; it is presumed that he died young.* ◇ **~ sb/sth to be/have sth** *I presumed him to be her husband.* **2** [T] to accept that sth is true until it is shown not to be true, especially in court: **~ sb/sth + adj.** *Twelve passengers are missing, **presumed dead**.* ◇ *In English law, a person is **presumed innocent** until proved guilty.* ◇ **~ sth** *We must presume innocence until we have proof of guilt.* ◇ **~ sb/sth to be/have sth** *We must presume them to be innocent until we have proof of guilt.* **3** [T] **~ sth** (*formal*) to accept sth as true or existing and to act on that basis: *The course seems to presume some previous knowledge of the subject.* **4** [I] **~ to do sth** (*formal*) to behave in a way that shows a lack of respect by doing sth that you have no right to do: *I wouldn't presume to tell you how to run your own business.*

PHR V **preˈsume on/upon sb/sth** (*formal*) to make use of sb's friendship by asking them for more than you should: **~ to do sth** *I felt it would be presuming on our personal relationship to keep asking her for help.*

pre·sump·tion AW /prɪˈzʌmpʃn/ *noun* **1** [C] something that is thought to be true or probable: *There is a general presumption that the doctor knows best.* **2** [U] (*formal*) behaviour that is too confident and shows a lack of respect for other people **3** [U, C] (*law*) the act of supposing that sth is true, although it has not yet been proved or is not certain: *Everyone is entitled to the presumption of innocence until they are proved to be guilty.*

pre·sump·tive /prɪˈzʌmptɪv/ *adj.* [usually before noun] (*formal* or *technical*) likely to be true, based on the facts that are available ➲ see also HEIR PRESUMPTIVE

pre·sump·tu·ous AW /prɪˈzʌmptʃuəs/ *adj.* [not usually before noun] too confident, in a way that shows a lack of respect for other people

pre·sup·pose /ˌpriːsəˈpəʊz; *NAmE* -ˈpoʊz/ *verb* (*formal*) **1 ~ sth** to accept sth as true or existing and act on that basis, before it has been proved to be true SYN **presume**: *Teachers sometimes presuppose a fairly high level of knowledge by the students.* **2 ~ that...** | **~ sth** to depend on sth in order to exist or be true SYN **assume**: *His argument presupposes that it does not matter who is in power.*

pre·sup·pos·ition /ˌpriːsʌpəˈzɪʃn/ *noun* [C, U] (*formal*) something that you believe to be true and use as the beginning of an argument even though it has not been proved; the act of believing it is true SYN **assumption**: *theories based on presupposition and coincidence*

ˌ**pre-ˈtax** *adj.* [only before noun] before the tax has been taken away: ***pre-tax profits/losses/income***

ˌ**pre-ˈteach** *verb* **~ sth** to teach sth, especially new words, to students before a test or exercise

ˌ**pre-ˈteen** *noun* a young person of about 11 or 12 years of age ▸ ˌ**pre-ˈteen** *adj.* [usually before noun]: *the pre-teen years*

pre·tence (*BrE*) (*NAmE* **pre·tense**) /prɪˈtens; *NAmE* ˈpriːtens/ *noun* **1** [U, sing.] the act of behaving in a particular way, in order to make other people believe sth that is not true: *Their friendliness was only pretence.* ◇ **~ of doing sth** *By the end of the evening she had abandoned all pretence of being interested.* ◇ **~ of sth** *He made no pretence of great musical knowledge.* ◇ **~ that...** *She was unable to **keep up the pretence** that she loved him.* **2** [U, C, usually sing.] (*formal* or *literary*) a claim that you have a particular quality or skill: **~ (to sth)** *a woman with some pretence to beauty* ◇ **~ (to doing sth)** *I **make no pretence to** being an expert on the subject.* IDM see FALSE

pre·tend 0‑w /prɪˈtend/ *verb, adj.*

■ ***verb*** **1** 0‑w [I, T] to behave in a particular way, in order to make other people believe sth that is not true: *I'm tired of having to pretend all the time.* ◇ *Of course I was wrong; it would be hypocritical to **pretend otherwise**.* ◇ **~ (to sb) (that...)** *He pretended to his family that everything was fine.* ◇ *We pretended (that) nothing had happened.* ◇ **~ to do sth** *He pretended not to notice.* ◇ *She didn't love him, though she **pretended to**.* ◇ **~ sth** (*formal*) *She pretended an interest she did not feel.* **2** 0‑w [I, T] (especially of children) to imagine that sth is true as part of a game: *They didn't have any real money so they had to pretend.* ◇ **~ (that)...** *Let's pretend (that) we're astronauts.* **3** [I, T] (usually used in negative sentences and questions) to claim to be, do or have sth, especially when this is not true: **~ to sth** *I can't pretend to any great musical talent.* ◇ **~ (that)...** *I don't pretend (that) I know much about the subject, but...* ◇ **~ to be/do/have sth** *The book doesn't pretend to be a great work of literature.*

■ ***adj.*** [usually before noun] (*informal*) (often used by children) not real, imaginary: *pretend cakes*

pre·tend·er /prɪˈtendə(r)/ *noun* **~ (to sth)** a person who claims they have a right to a particular title even though other people disagree with them

pre·tense (*NAmE*) = PRETENCE

pre·ten·sion /prɪˈtenʃn/ *noun* [C, usually pl., U] **1** the act of trying to appear more important, intelligent, etc. than you are in order to impress other people: *intellectual pretensions* ◇ *The play mocks the pretensions of the new middle class.* ◇ *He spoke without pretension.* **2** a claim to be or to do sth: **~ (to sth/to doing sth)** *a building with no pretensions to architectural merit* ◇ **~ (to do sth)** *The movie makes no pretension to reproduce life.*

pre·ten·tious /prɪˈtenʃəs/ *adj.* (*disapproving*) trying to appear important, intelligent, etc. in order to impress other people; trying to be sth that you are not, in order to impress: *That's a pretentious name for a dog!* ◇ *It was just an ordinary house—nothing pretentious.* ◇ *He's so pretentious!*

⮊ compare UNPRETENTIOUS ▸ **pre·ten·tious·ly** *adv.* **pre·ten·tious·ness** *noun* [U]

the pret·er·ite (*NAmE* also **pret·erit**) /ˈpretərət/ *noun* [sing.] (*grammar*) a form of a verb that expresses the past

pre·term /ˌpriːˈtɜːm; *NAmE* -ˈtɜːrm/ *adj.* born or happening after a short PREGNANCY, especially one that is less than 37 weeks: *caring for low birthweight and preterm babies* ◇ *a preterm birth/delivery* ▸ **preterm** *adv.*: *Babies born preterm are at greater risk of needing hospitalization.*

pre·ter·nat·ural /ˌpriːtəˈnætʃrəl; *NAmE* -tərˈn-/ *adj.* [only before noun] (*formal*) that does not seem natural; that cannot be explained by natural laws ▸ **pre·ter·nat·ur·al·ly** *adv.*: *The city was preternaturally quiet.*

pre·test /ˈpriːtest/ *noun* a test that you take to find out how much you already know or can do before learning or doing sth ▸ **pre·test** *verb* **~ sb**

pre·text /ˈpriːtekst/ *noun* **~ (for sth/for doing sth)** | **~ (to do sth)** a false reason that you give for doing sth, usually sth bad, in order to hide the real reason; an excuse: *The incident was used as a pretext for intervention in the area.* ◇ *He left the party early* ***on the pretext of*** *having work to do.* ⮊ SYNONYMS at REASON

pret·tify /ˈprɪtifaɪ/ *verb* (**pret·ti·fies, pret·ti·fy·ing, pret·ti·fied, pret·ti·fied**) **~ sth** (usually *disapproving*) to try to make sth pretty, often with the result that it looks worse or false

pretty 0⇀ /ˈprɪti/ *adv., adj.*

▪ ***adv.*** (with adjectives and adverbs) (rather *informal*) **1** 0⇀ to some extent; fairly: *I'm pretty sure I'll be going.* ◇ *The game was pretty good.* ◇ *It's pretty hard to explain.* ◇ *I'm going to have to find a new apartment pretty soon.* ⮊ note at QUITE **2** 0⇀ very: *That performance was pretty impressive.* ◇ *Things are looking pretty good!*

IDM **pretty ˈmuch/ˈwell** (*BrE* also **pretty ˈnearly**) (*NAmE* also **pretty ˈnear**) (*informal*) almost; almost completely: *One dog looks pretty much like another to me.* ⮊ more at SIT

▪ ***adj.*** (**pret·tier, pret·ti·est**) **1** 0⇀ (especially of a woman, or a girl) attractive without being very beautiful: *a pretty face* ◇ *a pretty little girl* ◇ *You look so pretty in that dress!* ⮊ SYNONYMS at BEAUTIFUL **2** 0⇀ (of places or things) attractive and pleasant to look at or to listen to without being large, beautiful or impressive: *pretty clothes* ◇ *a pretty garden* ◇ *a pretty name* ▸ **pret·tily** /ˈprɪtɪli/ *adv.*: (*especially BrE*) *She laughed prettily.* ◇ *The rooms are simply but prettily furnished.* **pret·ti·ness** *noun* [U]: *the prettiness of youth*

IDM **as ˌpretty as a ˈpicture** (*old-fashioned*) very pretty **not just a pretty ˈface** (*humorous*) used to emphasize that you have particular skills or qualities: *'I didn't know you could play the piano.' 'I'm not just a pretty face, you know!'* **ˌnot a pretty ˈsight** (*humorous*) not pleasant to look at: *You should have seen him in his swimming trunks—not a pretty sight!* **a pretty ˈpenny** (*old-fashioned*) a lot of money ⮊ more at PASS *n.*

pret·zel /ˈpretsl/ *noun* a crisp salty biscuit in the shape of a knot or stick, often served with drinks at a party

pre·vail /prɪˈveɪl/ *verb* (*formal*) **1** [I] **~ (in/among sth)** to exist or be very common at a particular time or in a particular place: *We were horrified at the conditions prevailing in local prisons.* ◇ *Those beliefs still prevail among certain social groups.* **2** [I] **~ (against/over sth)** (of ideas, opinions, etc.) to be accepted, especially after a struggle or an argument SYN **triumph**: *Justice will prevail over tyranny.* ◇ *Fortunately, common sense prevailed.* **3** [I] **~ (against/over sb)** to defeat an opponent, especially after a long struggle

PHR V **preˈvail on/upon sb to do sth** to persuade sb to do sth: *I'm sure he could be prevailed upon to give a talk.*

pre·vail·ing /prɪˈveɪlɪŋ/ *adj.* [only before noun] **1** existing or most common at a particular time SYN **current, predominant**: *the prevailing economic conditions* ◇ *the attitude towards science prevailing at the time* ◇ *The prevailing view seems to be that they will find her guilty.* **2** the **prevailing wind** in an area is the one that blows over it most frequently

preva·lent /ˈprevələnt/ *adj.* **~ (among sb)** | **~ (in sb/sth)** (*formal*) that exists or is very common at a particular time or in a particular place SYN **common, widespread**: *a prevalent view* ◇ *These prejudices are particularly prevalent among people living in the North.* ▸ **preva·lence** /-əns/ *noun* [U]

pre·vari·cate /prɪˈværɪkeɪt/ *verb* [I, T] (**+ speech**) (*formal*) to avoid giving a direct answer to a question in order to hide the truth SYN **beat about the bush**: *Stop prevaricating and come to the point.* ▸ **pre·vari·ca·tion** /prɪˌværɪˈkeɪʃn/ *noun* [U, C]

pre·vent 0⇀ /prɪˈvent/ *verb* to stop sb from doing sth; to stop sth from happening: **~ sth/sb** *The accident could have been prevented.* ◇ **~ sb/sth from doing sth** *He is prevented by law from holding a licence.* ◇ *Nothing would prevent him from speaking out against injustice.* ◇ **~ (sb/sth) doing sth** (*BrE*) *Nothing would prevent him/his speaking out against injustice.* ▸ **pre·vent·able** /prɪˈventəbl/ *adj.*: *preventable diseases/accidents*

pre·ven·tion /prɪˈvenʃn/ *noun* [U] the act of stopping sth bad from happening: ***accident/crime prevention*** ◇ *the prevention of disease* ◇ *a fire prevention officer*

IDM **preˌvention is better than ˈcure** (*BrE*) (*US* **an ounce of preˌvention is better than a pound of ˈcure**) (*saying*) it is better to stop sth bad from happening rather than try to deal with the problems after it has happened

pre·vent·ive /prɪˈventɪv/ (also **pre·venta·tive** /prɪˈventətɪv/) *adj.* [only before noun] intended to try to stop sth that causes problems or difficulties from happening: *preventive medicine* ◇ *The police were able to take preventive action and avoid a possible riot.* ⮊ compare CURATIVE

pre·ver·bal /ˌpriːˈvɜːbl; *NAmE* -ˈvɜːrbl/ *adj.* [usually before noun] (*technical*) connected with the time before a child learns to speak: *preverbal communication*

pre·view /ˈpriːvjuː/ *noun, verb*

▪ ***noun*** **1** an occasion at which you can see a film/movie, a show, etc. before it is shown to the general public: *a press preview* (= for journalists only) ◇ *a special preview of our winter fashion collection* ⮊ see also SNEAK PREVIEW **2** a description in a newspaper or a magazine that tells you about a film/movie, a television programme, etc. before it is shown to the public: *Turn to page 12 for a preview of next week's programmes.* **3** (*NAmE*) = TRAILER *n.* (4)

▪ ***verb*** **1 ~ sth** to see a film/movie, a television programme, etc. before it is shown to the general public and write an account of it for a newspaper or magazine: *The exhibition was previewed in last week's issue.* **2 ~ sth** (*especially NAmE*) to give sb a short account of sth that is going to happen, be studied, etc: *The professor previewed the course for us.*

pre·vi·ous 0⇀ AW /ˈpriːviəs/ *adj.* [only before noun] **1** 0⇀ happening or existing before the event or object that you are talking about SYN **prior**: *No previous experience is necessary for this job.* ◇ *The car has only had one previous owner.* ◇ *She is his daughter from a previous marriage.* ◇ *I was unable to attend because of a previous engagement.* ◇ *The judge will take into consideration any previous convictions.* **2** 0⇀ immediately before the time you are talking about SYN **preceding**: *I couldn't believe it when I heard the news. I'd only seen him the previous day.* ▸ **pre·vi·ous·ly** 0⇀ AW *adv.*: *The building had previously been used as a hotel.* ◇ *I had visited them three days previously.* **pre·vi·ous to** *prep.*: *Previous to this, she'd always been well.*

ˌpre-ˈwar *adj.* [usually before noun] happening or existing before a war, especially before the Second World War: *the pre-war years* ◇ *pre-war Britain*

ˌpre-ˈwash *verb, noun*

▪ ***verb*** **1 ~ sth** to wash cloth before it is used, or clothing before it is sold **2 ~ sth** to give clothing an extra wash before the main wash, especially in a machine

▪ ***noun*** **ˈpre-wash 1** [C] an extra wash before the main wash **2** [U] a substance which is applied to clothing before washing, in order to make it cleaner

prey /preɪ/ *noun, verb*

▪ ***noun*** [U, sing.] **1** an animal, a bird, etc. that is hunted,

P

killed and eaten by another: *The lion will often stalk its prey for hours.* ◇ **birds of prey** (= birds that kill for food) ➲ COLLOCATIONS at LIFE **2** a person who is harmed or tricked by sb, especially for dishonest purposes: *Elderly people are* ***easy prey*** *for dishonest salesmen.*

IDM **be/fall 'prey to sth** (*formal*) **1** (of an animal) to be killed and eaten by another animal or bird **2** (of a person) to be harmed or affected by sth bad

■ ***verb***

IDM **prey on sb's 'mind** (of a thought, problem, etc.) to make sb think and worry about it all the time

PHR V **'prey on/upon sb/sth 1** (of an animal or a bird) to hunt and kill another animal for food **2** to harm sb who is weaker than you, or make use of them in a dishonest way to get what you want: *Bogus social workers have been preying on old people living alone.*

prez /prez/ *noun* (*slang*) = PRESIDENT

prez·zie (also **pres·sie**) /'prezi/ *noun* (*BrE, informal*) a present that you give sb, for example for their birthday

pri·ap·ic /,praɪ'æpɪk; *NAmE* also -'eɪp-/ *adj.* **1** (*formal*) connected with or like a PENIS **2** (*formal*) connected with male sexual activity **3** (*medical*) having a PENIS which is always ERECT (= stiff)

pri·ap·ism /'praɪəpɪzəm/ *noun* [U] (*medical*) a condition in which a man's PENIS remains ERECT (= stiff)

price 0→ /praɪs/ *noun, verb*

■ ***noun* 1** 0→ [C, U] the amount of money that you have to pay for sth: *Boat for sale, price £2 000* ◇ *house/retail/oil/share prices* ◇ *to charge a* ***high/reasonable/low price*** *for sth* ◇ *The price of cigarettes is set to rise again.* ◇ *He managed to get a good price for the car.* ◇ ***rising/falling prices*** ◇ *Can you* ***give me a price*** *for the work* (= tell me how much you will charge)? ◇ *I'm only buying it if it's the* ***right price*** (= a price that I think is reasonable). ◇ *Children over five must pay* (*the*) ***full price*** *for the ticket.* ◇ *How much are these? They don't have a price on them.* ◇ *It's amazing how much computers have come down* ***in price*** *over the past few years.* ◇ ***price rises/increases/cuts*** ◇ *a price list* ➲ see also ASKING PRICE, COST PRICE, CUT-PRICE, HALF-PRICE, MARKET PRICE, LIST PRICE, PURCHASE PRICE, SELLING PRICE **2** 0→ [sing.] the unpleasant things that you must do or experience in order to achieve sth or as a result of achieving sth: **~ (of sth)** *Criticism is part of the price of leadership.* ◇ **~ (for sth/for doing sth)** *Loneliness is* ***a high price to pay*** *for independence in your old age.* ◇ *Giving up his job was* ***a small price to pay*** *for his children's happiness.* **3** [C] (in horse racing) the numbers that tell you how much money you will receive if the horse that you bet on wins the race SYN **odds**: *Six to one is a good price for that horse.* ➲ see also STARTING PRICE

IDM **at 'any price** whatever the cost or the difficulties may be: *We want peace at any price.* **at a 'price 1** costing a lot of money: *You can buy strawberries all year round, but at a price.* **2** involving sth unpleasant: *He'll help you—at a price!* **beyond 'price** (*formal* or *literary*) extremely valuable or important **everyone has their 'price** (*saying*) you can persuade anyone to do sth by giving them more money or sth that they want **not at 'any price** used to say that no amount of money would persuade you to do or to sell sth: *I wouldn't work for her again—not at any price!* **a 'price on sb's head** an amount of money that is offered for capturing or killing sb **put a 'price on sth** to say how much money sth valuable is worth: *They haven't yet put a price on the business.* ◇ *You can't put a price on that sort of loyalty.* **'what price…?** (*BrE, informal*) **1** used to say that you think that sth you have achieved may not be worth all the problems and difficulties it causes: *What price fame and fortune?* **2** used to say that sth seems unlikely: *What price England winning the World Cup?* ➲ more at CHEAP *adj.*, PAY *v.*

■ ***verb* 1** [usually passive] to fix the price of sth at a particular level: **~ sth + adv./prep.** *a reasonably priced house* ◇ *These goods are priced too high.* ◇ **~ sth at sth** *The tickets are priced at $100 each.* **2 ~ sth (up)** to write or stick tickets on goods to show how much they cost **3 ~ sth** to compare the prices of different types of the same thing: *We priced various models before buying this one.*

IDM **price yourself/sth out of the 'market** to charge such a high price for your goods, services, etc. that nobody wants to buy them

Synonyms

price

cost • value • expense • worth

These words all refer to the amount of money that you have to pay for sth.

price the amount of money that you have to pay for an item or service: *house prices* ◇ *How much are these? They don't have a price on them.* ◇ *I can't afford it* ***at that price.***

cost the amount of money that you need in order to buy, make or do sth: *A new computer system has been installed at a cost of £80 000.*

value how much sth is worth in money or other goods for which it can be exchanged: *The winner will receive a prize* ***to the value of*** *£1 000.* NOTE Especially in British English, **value** can also mean how much sth is worth compared with its price: *This restaurant is excellent value* (= is worth the money it costs).

PRICE, COST OR VALUE?

The **price** is what sb asks you to pay for an item or service: *to ask/charge a high price* ◇ ~~*to ask/charge a high cost/value*~~. Obtaining or achieving sth may have a **cost**; the **value** of sth is how much other people would be willing to pay for it: *house prices* ◇ *the cost of moving house* ◇ *The house now has a market value of one million pounds.*

expense the money that you spend on sth; sth that makes you spend money: *The garden was transformed* ***at great expense.*** ◇ *Running a car is a big expense.*

worth the financial value of sb/sth: *He has a personal net worth of $10 million.* NOTE Worth is more often used to mean the practical or moral value of sth.

PATTERNS

- the **high** price/cost/value
- the **real/true** price/cost/value/worth
- to **put/set** a price/value **on** sth
- to **increase/reduce** the price/cost/value/expense
- to **raise/double/lower** the price/cost/value
- to **cut** the price/cost

'price controls *noun* [pl.] (*economics*) restrictions that a government puts on the price of goods at particular times, such as when there is not enough of sth, when there is a war, etc.

'price-fixing *noun* [U] the practice of companies agreeing not to sell goods below a particular price

'price index *noun* = RETAIL PRICE INDEX

price·less /'praɪsləs/ *adj.* **1** extremely valuable or important: *a priceless collection of antiques* ◇ *priceless information* ➲ SYNONYMS at VALUABLE **2** (*informal*) extremely amusing: *You should have seen his face—it was priceless!*

'price tag *noun* a label on sth that shows how much you must pay: (*figurative*) *There is a £2 million price tag on the team's star player.* ➲ picture at LABEL

'price war *noun* a situation in which companies or shops/stores keep reducing the prices of their products and services in order to attract customers away from their COMPETITORS

pricey /'praɪsi/ *adj.* (**prici·er, prici·est**) (*informal*) expensive ➲ SYNONYMS at EXPENSIVE

pri·cing /'praɪsɪŋ/ *noun* [U] the act of deciding how much to charge for sth: *competitive pricing* ◇ *pricing policy* ➲ see also ROAD PRICING

prick /prɪk/ *verb, noun*

■ ***verb* 1** [T] to make a very small hole in sth with a sharp point: **~ sth** *He pricked the balloon and burst it.* ◇ **~ sth with**

P

sth *Prick holes in the paper with a pin.* **2** [T] **~ sth** (**on sth**) to make a small hole in the skin so that it hurts or blood comes out: *She pricked her finger on a needle.* **3** [I, T] to make sb feel a slight pain as if they were being pricked: *He felt a pricking sensation in his throat.* ◇ **~ sth** *Tears pricked her eyes.*

IDM **prick your 'conscience | your 'conscience pricks you** to make you feel guilty about sth; to feel guilty about sth: *Her conscience pricked her as she lied to her sister.* **prick (up) your 'ears 1** (of an animal, especially a horse or dog) to raise the ears **2** (also **your 'ears prick up**) (of a person) to listen carefully, especially because you have just heard sth interesting: *Her ears pricked up at the sound of his name.*

■ ***noun*** **1** (*taboo, slang*) a PENIS **2** (*taboo, slang*) an offensive word for a stupid or unpleasant man: *Don't be such a prick!* **3** an act of making a very small hole in sth with a sharp point: *I'm going to give your finger a little prick with this needle.* **4** a slight pain caused by a sharp point or sth that feels like a sharp point: *You will feel a tiny prick in your arm.* ◇ (*figurative*) *He could feel the hot prick of tears in his eyes.*

prickle /ˈprɪkl/ *verb, noun*
■ ***verb*** **1** [T, I] **~ (sth)** to give sb an unpleasant feeling on their skin, as if a lot of small sharp points are pushing into it: *The rough cloth prickled my skin.* ◇ *His moustache prickled when he kissed me.* **2** [I] **~ (with sth)** (of skin, eyes, etc.) to sting or feel strange and unpleasant because you are frightened, angry, excited, etc: *Her eyes prickled with tears.* ◇ *The hairs on the back of my neck prickled when I heard the door open.* ◇ (*figurative*) *He prickled* (= became angry) *at the suggestion that it had been his fault.*
■ ***noun*** **1** a small sharp part on the STEM or leaf of a plant or on the skin of some animals: *a cactus covered in prickles* **2** a slight stinging feeling on the skin: *a prickle of fear/excitement*

prick·ly /ˈprɪkli/ *adj.* (**prick·lier, prick·li·est**) **1** covered with prickles: *a prickly bush* **2** causing you to feel as if your skin is touching sth that is covered with prickles: *a prickly feeling* **3** (*informal*) (of a person) easily annoyed or offended SYN **touchy 4** (of a decision, an issue, etc.) difficult to deal with because people have very different ideas about it SYN **thorny**: *Let's move on to the prickly subject of taxation reform.*

ˌprickly ˈheat *noun* [U] a skin condition, common in hot countries, that causes small red spots that ITCH

ˌprickly ˈpear *noun* **1** a type of CACTUS with PRICKLES (= sharp parts like needles), and yellow flowers **2** the reddish fruit of the prickly pear that is shaped like a PEAR and can be eaten

ˈprick-teaser (also **ˈprick-tease**) *noun* (*taboo, slang*) = COCK-TEASER

pride 0➡ /praɪd/ *noun, verb*
■ ***noun***
▸ PLEASURE/SATISFACTION **1** 0➡ [U, sing.] a feeling of pleasure or satisfaction that you get when you or people who are connected with you have done sth well or own sth that other people admire: *The sight of her son graduating filled her with pride.* ◇ **~ (in sth)** *I* ***take*** (***a***) ***pride in*** *my work.* ◇ **~ (in doing sth)** *We take great pride in offering the best service in town.* ◇ *I looked* ***with pride*** *at what I had achieved.* ◇ *Success in sport is a source of national pride.* ➲ SYNONYMS at SATISFACTION **2** [sing.] **the ~ of sth** a person or thing that gives people a feeling of pleasure or satisfaction: *The new sports stadium is the pride of the town.*
▸ RESPECT FOR YOURSELF **3** 0➡ [U] the feeling of respect that you have for yourself: *Pride would not allow him to accept the money.* ◇ *Her pride was hurt.* ◇ *Losing his job was a real* ***blow to his pride.*** ◇ *It's time to* ***swallow your pride*** (= hide your feelings of pride) *and ask for your job back.* **4** 0➡ [U] (*disapproving*) the feeling that you are better or more important than other people: *Male pride forced him to suffer in silence.* ➲ see also PROUD
▸ LIONS **5** [C+sing./pl. v.] a group of LIONS

IDM **sb's pride and 'joy** a person or thing that causes sb to feel great pleasure or satisfaction **pride comes/goes before a 'fall** (*saying*) if you have too high an opinion of yourself or your abilities, sth will happen to make you look stupid **pride of 'place** the position in which sth is most easily seen, that is given to the most important thing in a particular group
■ ***verb***
PHR V **'pride yourself on sth/on doing sth** [no passive] to be proud of sth: *She had always prided herself on her appearance.*

priest 0➡ /priːst/ *noun*
1 0➡ a person who is qualified to perform religious duties and ceremonies in the Roman Catholic, Anglican and Orthodox Churches: *a parish priest* ◇ *the ordination of women priests* ➲ compare CHAPLAIN, CLERGYMAN, MINISTER, VICAR **2** 0➡ (*feminine* **priest·ess** /ˈpriːstes/) a person who performs religious ceremonies in some religions that are not Christian

priest·hood /ˈpriːsthʊd/ *noun* **1 the priesthood** [sing.] the job or position of being a priest: *to enter the priesthood* (= to become a priest) ➲ COLLOCATIONS at RELIGION **2** all the priests of a particular religion or country

priest·ly /ˈpriːstli/ *adj.* [usually before noun] connected with a priest; like a priest

ˈpriest's hole *noun* a secret space in a house where Catholic priests hid in the past at times when Catholicism was against the law in England

prig /prɪg/ *noun* (*disapproving*) a person who behaves in a morally correct way and who shows that they disapprove of what other people do ▸ **prig·gish** *adj.* **prig·gish·ness** *noun* [U]

prim /prɪm/ *adj.* (**prim·mer, prim·mest**) (*disapproving*) **1** (of a person) always behaving in a careful and formal way, and easily shocked by anything that is rude: *You can't tell her that joke—she's much too* ***prim and proper.*** **2** formal and neat SYN **demure**: *a prim suit with a high-necked collar* ▸ **prim·ly** *adv.*: *'You're not supposed to say that,' she said primly.*

prima ballerina /ˌpriːmə ˌbæləˈriːnə/ *noun* the main woman dancer in a BALLET company

pri·macy AW /ˈpraɪməsi/ *noun* (*pl.* -ies) (*formal*) **1** [U] the fact of being the most important person or thing: *a belief in the primacy of the family* **2** [C] the position of an ARCHBISHOP

prima donna /ˌpriːmə ˈdɒnə; *NAmE* ˈdɑːnə/ *noun* **1** the main woman singer in an OPERA performance or an OPERA company **2** (*disapproving*) a person who thinks they are very important because they are good at sth, and who behaves badly when they do not get what they want

prim·aeval *adj.* = PRIMEVAL

prima facie /ˌpraɪmə ˈfeɪʃi/ *adj.* [only before noun] (*from Latin, law*) based on what at first seems to be true, although it may be proved false later: *prima facie evidence* ▸ **prima facie** *adv.*: *Prima facie, there is a strong case against him.*

primal /ˈpraɪml/ *adj.* [only before noun] (*formal*) connected with the earliest origins of life; very basic SYN **primeval**: *the primal hunter-gatherer* ◇ *a primal urge/fear*

pri·mar·ily 0➡ AW /praɪˈmerəli; *BrE* also ˈpraɪmərəli/ *adv.*
mainly SYN **chiefly**: *a course designed primarily for specialists* ◇ *The problem is not primarily a financial one.*

pri·mary 0➡ AW /ˈpraɪməri; *NAmE* -meri/ *adj., noun*
■ ***adj.*** **1** 0➡ [usually before noun] main; most important; basic SYN **prime**: *The primary aim of this course is to improve your spoken English.* ◇ *Our primary concern must be the children.* ◇ *Good health care is of primary importance.* **2** 0➡ [usually before noun] (*formal* or *technical*) developing or happening first; earliest: *primary causes* ◇ *The disease is still in its primary stage.* **3** 0➡ [only before noun] (*especially BrE*) connected with the education of children between the ages of about five and eleven: *primary teachers* ➲ compare ELEMENTARY, SECONDARY, TERTIARY
■ ***noun*** (*pl.* -ies) (also **ˌprimary eˈlection**) (in the US) an election in which people in a particular area vote to choose

P

a candidate for a future important election: *the Illinois primary* ◇ *the presidential primaries*

ˌprimary ˈcare (also **ˌprimary ˈhealth care**) *noun* [U] the medical treatment that you receive first when you are ill/sick, for example from your family doctor

primary ˌcare phyˈsician *noun* (*abbr.* PCP) (*especially NAmE*) a doctor who provides primary care

primary ˌcare proˈvider *noun* (*abbr.* PCP) a company or organization that provides primary care

ˌprimary ˈcolour (*especially US* **ˌprimary ˈcolor**) *noun* one of the three colours, red, yellow and blue, that can be mixed together to make all other colours

ˌprimary ˈhealth care *noun* = PRIMARY CARE

ˈprimary industry *noun* [U, C] (*economics*) the section of industry that provides RAW MATERIALS to be made into goods, for example farming and MINING ➲ compare SECONDARY INDUSTRY, TERTIARY INDUSTRY

ˈprimary school *noun* **1** (*BrE*) a school for children between the ages of 5 and 11 **2** (*old-fashioned, NAmE*) = ELEMENTARY SCHOOL ➲ compare SECONDARY SCHOOL

ˈprimary source *noun* a document, etc. that contains information obtained by research or observation, not taken from other books, etc. ➲ compare SECONDARY SOURCE

ˌprimary ˈstress *noun* [C, U] (*phonetics*) the strongest stress that is put on a syllable in a word or a phrase when it is spoken ➲ compare SECONDARY STRESS

pri·mate *noun* **1** /ˈpraɪmeɪt/ any animal that belongs to the group of MAMMALS that includes humans, APES and MONKEYS ➲ VISUAL VOCAB page V10 **2** /ˈpraɪmət; -meɪt/ an ARCHBISHOP (= a priest of very high rank in the Christian Church): *the Primate of all England* (= the Archbishop of Canterbury)

prime AW /praɪm/ *adj., noun, verb*

■ *adj.* [only before noun] **1** main; most important; basic: *My prime concern is to protect my property.* ◇ *Winning is not the prime objective in this sport.* ◇ *The care of the environment is of prime importance.* ◇ *He's the police's* **prime suspect** *in this case.* ➲ SYNONYMS at MAIN **2** of the best quality; excellent: *prime (cuts of) beef* ◇ *The store has a prime position in the mall.* **3** a **prime example** of sth is one that is typical of it: *The building is a prime example of 1960s architecture.* **4** most likely to be chosen for sth; most suitable: *The house is isolated and a prime target for burglars.* ◇ *He's a prime candidate for promotion.*

■ *noun* [sing.] the time in your life when you are strongest or most successful: *a young woman in her prime* ◇ *He was barely 30 and* **in the prime of (his) life**. ◇ *These flowers are long* **past their prime**.

■ *verb* **1** to prepare sb for a situation so that they know what to do, especially by giving them special information SYN **brief**: **~ sb (with sth)** *They had been primed with good advice.* ◇ **~ sb (for sth)** *She was ready and primed for action.* ◇ **~ sb to do sth** *He had primed his friends to give the journalists as little information as possible.* **2 ~ sth** to make sth ready for use or action: *The bomb was primed, ready to explode.* **3 ~ sth** to prepare wood, metal, etc. for painting by covering it with a special paint that helps the next layer of paint to stay on

IDM **prime the ˈpump** to encourage the growth of a new or weak business or industry by putting money into it

ˈprime cost (also **ˈfirst cost**) *noun* [C, U] (*business*) the cost of sth calculated by adding the cost of materials used to make it and the cost of paying sb to make it, but not including costs that are connected with running a business, such as rent and electricity

ˌprime ˈminister 0‑w (also **ˌPrime ˈMinister**) *noun* (*abbr.* PM) the main minister and leader of the government in some countries

ˌprime ˈmover *noun* a person or thing that starts sth and has an important influence on its development

ˌprime ˈnumber *noun* (*mathematics*) a number that can be divided exactly only by itself and 1, for example 7, 17 and 41

primer /ˈpraɪmə(r)/ *noun* **1** [U, C] a type of paint that is put on wood, metal, etc. before it is painted to help the paint to stay on the surface **2** [C] /ˈpraɪmə(r); *NAmE* ˈprɪmər/ (*NAmE*) a book that contains basic instructions: *The President doesn't need a primer on national security.* **3** [C] /ˈpraɪmə(r); *NAmE* ˈprɪmər/ (*old-fashioned*) a book for teaching children how to read, or containing basic facts about a school subject

ˈprime rate *noun* (in the US) the lowest rate of interest at which business customers can borrow money from banks ➲ compare BASE RATE

ˈprime time (*BrE* also **ˈpeak time, ˌpeak ˈviewing time**) *noun* [U] the time when the greatest number of people are watching television or listening to the radio: *prime-time television*

pri·meval (also **prim·aeval**) /praɪˈmiːvl/ *adj.* [usually before noun] **1** from the earliest period of the history of the world, very ancient: *primeval forests* **2** (*formal*) (of a feeling, or a desire) very strong and not based on reason, as if from the earliest period of human life: *primeval urges*

primi·tive /ˈprɪmətɪv/ *adj., noun*

■ *adj.* **1** [usually before noun] belonging to a very simple society with no industry, etc: *primitive tribes* ◇ *primitive beliefs* **2** [usually before noun] belonging to an early stage in the development of humans or animals: *primitive man* **3** very simple and old-fashioned, especially when sth is also not convenient and comfortable SYN **crude**: *The methods of communication used during the war were primitive by today's standards.* ◇ *The facilities on the campsite were very primitive.* **4** [usually before noun] (of a feeling or a desire) very strong and not based on reason, as if from the earliest period of human life: *a primitive instinct* ▶ **primi·tive·ly** *adv.* **primi·tive·ness** *noun* [U]

■ *noun* **1** an artist of the period before the Renaissance; an example of work from this period **2** an artist who paints in a very simple style like a child; an example of the work of such an artist

primi·tiv·ism /ˈprɪmɪtɪvɪzəm/ *noun* [U] a belief that simple forms and ideas are the most valuable, expressed as a philosophy or in art or literature

primo·geni·ture /ˌpraɪməʊˈdʒenɪtʃə(r); *NAmE* -moʊ-/ *noun* [U] **1** (*formal*) the fact of being the first child born in a family **2** (*law*) the system in which the oldest son in a family receives all the property when his father dies

prim·or·dial /praɪˈmɔːdiəl; *NAmE* -ˈmɔːrdiəl/ *adj.* [usually before noun] (*formal*) **1** existing at or from the beginning of the world SYN **primeval** **2** (of a feeling or a desire) very basic SYN **primeval**: *primordial impulses*

primp /prɪmp/ *verb* [I, T] **~ (sth/yourself)** (often *disapproving*) to make yourself look attractive by arranging your hair, putting on make-up, etc.

prim·rose /ˈprɪmrəʊz; *NAmE* -roʊz/ *noun* **1** [C] a small wild plant that produces pale yellow flowers in spring ➲ VISUAL VOCAB page V9 **2** (also **ˌprimrose ˈyellow**) [U] a pale yellow colour ▶ **prim·rose** (also **ˌprimrose ˈyellow**) *adj.*

IDM **the primrose ˈpath** (*literary*) an easy life that is full of pleasure but that causes you harm in the end

prim·ula /ˈprɪmjələ/ *noun* a type of primrose that is often grown in gardens/yards

Pri·mus™ /ˈpraɪməs/ (also **ˈPrimus stove**) *noun* a small cooker/stove that you can move around that burns oil. It is used especially by people who are camping.

prince 0‑w /prɪns/ *noun*

1 0‑w a male member of a royal family who is not king, especially the son or grandson of the king or queen: *the royal princes* ◇ *the Prince of Wales* **2** 0‑w the male ruler of a small country or state that has a royal family; a male member of this family, especially the son or grandson of the ruler: *Prince Albert of Monaco* **3** (in some European countries) a NOBLEMAN **4 ~ of/among sth** (*literary*) a man who is

P

thought to be one of the best in a particular field: *the prince of comedy*

ˌPrince ˈCharming *noun* [sing.] (usually *humorous*) a man who seems to be a perfect boyfriend or husband because he is very attractive, kind, etc. ORIGIN From the hero of some European fairy tales, for example *Cinderella* and *Sleeping Beauty*.

ˌprince ˈconsort *noun* a title sometimes given to the husband of a queen who is himself a prince: *Prince Albert, the Prince Consort*

prince·ling /ˈprɪnslɪŋ/ *noun* (usually *disapproving*) a prince who rules a small or unimportant country

prince·ly /ˈprɪnsli/ *adj.* [usually before noun] **1** (usually *ironic*) if you say that an amount of money is **princely**, you are usually saying the opposite and that it is not very large: *I bought a bike for* ***the princely sum of*** *£20!* **2** (*old-fashioned, formal*) very grand; generous: *princely buildings* ◇ *a princely gift* **3** connected with a prince; like a prince

the ˌPrince of ˈDarkness *noun* a name for the DEVIL

the ˌPrince of ˈPeace *noun* a name for Jesus Christ

prin·cess 🔑 /ˌprɪnˈses; ˈprɪnses/ *noun*
1 🔑 a female member of a royal family who is not a queen, especially the daughter or granddaughter of the king or queen: *the royal princesses* ◇ *Princess Anne* **2** 🔑 the wife of a prince: *the Princess of Wales* ◇ *Princess Michael of Kent* **3** (*disapproving*) a young woman who has always been given everything that she wants, and who thinks that she is better than other people **4** (*BrE, informal*) used as a form of address by a man to a girl or young woman: *Is something the matter, princess?*

ˌprincess ˈroyal *noun* a title often given to the oldest daughter of a British king or queen

prin·ci·pal AW /ˈprɪnsəpl/ *adj., noun*
■ ***adj.*** [only before noun] most important; main: *The principal reason for this omission is lack of time.* ◇ *New roads will link the principal cities of the area.* ➲ SYNONYMS at MAIN
■ ***noun*** **1** (*BrE*) the person who is in charge of a college or a university: *Peter Brown, principal of St John's College* ➲ see also DEAN **2** (*NAmE*) (*BrE* **ˌhead ˈteacher**) a teacher who is in charge of a school: *Principal Ray Smith* **3** [usually sing.] (*finance*) an amount of money that you lend to sb or invest to earn interest **4** the person who has the most important part in a play, an OPERA, etc. **5** (*technical*) a person that you are representing, especially in business or law

ˌprincipal ˈboy *noun* (*BrE*) the main male role in a PANTOMIME, usually played by a woman

prin·ci·pal·ity /ˌprɪnsɪˈpæləti/ *noun* (*pl.* -ies) **1** [C] a country that is ruled by a prince: *the principality of Monaco* **2 the Principality** [sing.] (*BrE*) Wales

prin·ci·pal·ly AW /ˈprɪnsəpli/ *adv.* mainly SYN **chiefly**: *The book is aimed principally at beginners.* ◇ *No new power stations have been built, principally because of the cost.*

ˌprincipal ˈparts *noun* [pl.] (*grammar*) the forms of a verb from which all the other forms can be made. In English these are the infinitive (for example *swim*), the past tense (*swam*) and the past participle (*swum*).

prin·ciple 🔑 AW /ˈprɪnsəpl/ *noun*
1 🔑 [C, usually pl., U] a moral rule or a strong belief that influences your actions: *He has high moral principles.* ◇ *I refuse to lie about it;* ***it's against my principles.*** ◇ ***Stick to your principles*** *and tell him you won't do it.* ◇ *She refuses to allow her family to help her as* ***a matter of principle.*** ◇ *He doesn't invest in the arms industry* ***on principle.*** **2** 🔑 [C] a law, a rule or a theory that sth is based on: *the principles and practice of writing reports* ◇ *The principle behind it is very simple.* ◇ *There are three fundamental principles of teamwork.* ◇ *Discussing all these details will get us nowhere; we must get back to* ***first principles*** (= the most basic rules). **3** 🔑 [C] a belief that is accepted as a reason for acting or thinking in a particular way: *the principle that free education should be available for all children* **4** 🔑 [sing.] a general or scientific law that explains how sth works or why sth happens: *the principle that heat rises*
IDM **in ˈprinciple 1** 🔑 if something can be done **in principle**, there is no good reason why it should not be done although it has not yet been done and there may be some difficulties: *In principle there is nothing that a human can do that a machine might not be able to do one day.* **2** 🔑 in general but not in detail: *They have agreed to the proposal in principle but we still have to negotiate the terms.*

prin·cipled AW /ˈprɪnsəpld/ *adj.* **1** having strong beliefs about what is right and wrong; based on strong beliefs: *a principled woman* ◇ *to take a principled stand against abortion* OPP **unprincipled 2** based on rules or truths: *a principled approach to language teaching*

print 🔑 /prɪnt/ *verb, noun*
■ ***verb***
▸ LETTERS/PICTURES **1** 🔑 [T, I] **~ (sth)** to produce letters, pictures, etc. on paper using a machine that puts ink on the surface: *Do you want your address printed at the top of the letter?* ◇ *I'm printing a copy of the document for you.* ◇ *Each card is printed with a different message.* ◇ (*computing*) *Click on the icon when you want to print.*
▸ BOOKS/NEWSPAPERS **2** 🔑 [T] **~ sth** to produce books, newspapers, etc. by printing them in large quantities: *They printed 30 000 copies of the book.*
▸ PUBLISH **3** 🔑 [T] **~ sth** to publish sth in printed form: *The photo was printed in all the national newspapers.*
▸ PHOTOGRAPH **4** 🔑 [T] **~ sth** to produce a photograph from a film: *I'm having the pictures developed and printed.*
▸ WRITE **5** [I, T] to write without joining the letters together: *In some countries children learn to print when they first go to school.* ◇ **~ sth** *Print your name and address clearly in the space provided.*
▸ MAKE MARK **6** [T] **~ sth (in/on sth)** to make a mark on a soft surface by pressing: *The tracks of the large animal were clearly printed in the sand.* ◇ (*figurative*) *The memory of that day was indelibly printed on his brain.*
▸ MAKE DESIGN **7** [T] to make a design on a surface or cloth by pressing a surface against it which has been coloured with ink or DYE: *They had printed their own design on the T-shirt.*
IDM **the ˌprinted ˈword/ˈpage** what is published in books, newspapers, etc: *the power of the printed word* ➲ more at LICENCE *n.*, WORTH *adj.*
PHR V **ˌprint sth↔ˈoff/ˈout** 🔑 to produce a document or information from a computer in printed form ➲ related noun PRINTOUT
■ ***noun***
▸ LETTERS/NUMBERS **1** 🔑 [U] letters, words, numbers, etc. that have been printed onto paper: *in* ***large/small/bold print*** ◇ *The print quality of the new laser printer is superb.* ➲ see also THE SMALL PRINT
▸ NEWSPAPERS/BOOKS **2** [U] used to refer to the business of producing newspapers, magazines and books: *the print media* ◇ *print unions*
▸ MARK **3** [C, usually pl.] a mark left by your finger, foot, etc. on the surface of sth: *His prints were found on the gun.* ➲ see also FINGERPRINT, FOOTPRINT
▸ PICTURE **4** 🔑 [C] a picture that is cut into wood or metal then covered with ink and printed onto paper; a picture that is copied from a painting using photography: *a framed set of prints* ➲ SYNONYMS at PICTURE ➲ COLLOCATIONS at ART
▸ PHOTOGRAPH **5** 🔑 [C] a photograph produced from film: *How many sets of prints would you like?* ◇ *a colour print* ➲ SYNONYMS at PHOTOGRAPH
▸ CLOTH **6** [U, C] cotton cloth that has a pattern printed on it; this pattern: *a cotton print dress* ◇ *a floral print* ➲ see also BLUEPRINT
IDM **get into ˈprint** to be published: *By the time this gets into print, they'll already have left the country.* **in print 1** (of a book) still available from the company that publishes it **2** (of a person's work) printed in a book, newspaper, etc: *It was the first time he had seen his name in print.* **ˌout of ˈprint** (of a book) no longer available from the company that publishes it

print·able /ˈprɪntəbl/ *adj.* (usually used with a negative) suitable to be repeated in writing and read by people: *His comment when he heard the news was not printable* (= was very rude). OPP **unprintable**

P

ˌprinted ˈcircuit *noun* a CIRCUIT for electricity that uses thin strips of metal instead of wires to carry the current

print·er 🔑 /ˈprɪntə(r)/ *noun*
1 🔑 a machine for printing text on paper, especially one connected to a computer: *a* ***colour/laser printer*** ⇨ VISUAL VOCAB page V56 **2** 🔑 a person or a company whose job is printing books, etc. **3** 🔑 **printer's** (*pl.* printers) a place where books, etc. are printed

print·ing 🔑 /ˈprɪntɪŋ/ *noun*
1 🔑 [U] the act of producing letters, pictures, patterns, etc. on sth by pressing a surface covered with ink against it: *the invention of printing* ◇ *the printing trade* ◇ *colour printing* **2** [C] the act of printing a number of copies of a book at one time: *The book is in its sixth printing.* **3** [U] a type of writing when you write all the letters separately and do not join them together

ˈprinting press *noun* a machine that produces books, newspapers, etc. by pressing a surface covered in ink onto paper

print·maker /ˈprɪntmeɪkə(r)/ *noun* an artist who prints pictures or designs

ˌprint on deˈmand *noun* (*abbr.* POD) [U] a system of printing books only when a customer wants one: *The titles are available through print on demand.* ◇ *This is a print-on-demand title.*

print·out /ˈprɪntaʊt/ *noun* [U, C] a page or set of pages containing information in printed form from a computer: *a printout of text downloaded from the Internet* ⇨ VISUAL VOCAB page V56 ⇨ compare READ-OUT

ˈprint run *noun* (*technical*) the number of copies of a book, magazine, etc. printed at one time

print·works /ˈprɪntwɜːks; *NAmE* -wɜːrks/ *noun* (*pl.* print·works) (*BrE*) a factory where patterns are printed on cloth

prion /ˈpriːɒn; *NAmE* -ɑːn/ *noun* (*biology*) a very small unit of PROTEIN that is believed to be the cause of brain diseases such as BSE, CJD and SCRAPIE

P

prior 🔑 AW /ˈpraɪə(r)/ *adj., noun*
■ ***adj.*** [only before noun] (*formal*) **1** 🔑 happening or existing before sth else or before a particular time: *Although not essential, some* ***prior knowledge*** *of statistics is desirable.* ◇ *This information must not be disclosed without* ***prior written consent****.* ◇ *Visits are by* ***prior arrangement****.* ◇ *Please give us* ***prior notice*** *if you need an evening meal.* ◇ *She will be unable to attend because of a* ***prior engagement****.* **2** 🔑 already existing and therefore more important: *They have a* ***prior claim*** *to the property.* **3** 🔑 **ˈprior to** before sth: *during the week prior to the meeting*
■ ***noun*** (*feminine* pri·or·ess /ˈpraɪərəs; *BrE* also ˌpraɪəˈres/) **1** a person who is in charge of a group of MONKS or NUNS living in a PRIORY **2** (in an ABBEY) a person next in rank below an ABBOT or ABBESS

pri·ori ⇨ A PRIORI

pri·ori·tize (*BrE* also **-ise**) AW /praɪˈɒrətaɪz; *NAmE* -ˈɔːr-/ *verb* **1** [T, I] **~ (sth)** to put tasks, problems, etc. in order of importance, so that you can deal with the most important first: *You should make a list of all the jobs you have to do and prioritize them.* **2** [T] **~ sth** (*formal*) to treat sth as being more important than other things: *The organization was formed to prioritize the needs of older people.* ▸ **pri·ori·tiza·tion, -isa·tion** AW /praɪˌɒrətaɪˈzeɪʃn; *NAmE* -ˌɔːrətəˈz-/ *noun* [U]

pri·or·ity 🔑 AW /praɪˈɒrəti; *NAmE* -ˈɔːr-/ *noun* (*pl.* -ies)
1 🔑 [C] something that you think is more important than other things and should be dealt with first: *a* ***high/low priority*** ◇ *Education is a* ***top priority****.* ◇ *Our* ***first priority*** *is to improve standards.* ◇ *Financial security was high on his* ***list of priorities****.* ◇ *You need to* ***get your priorities right*** (= decide what is important to you). ◇ (*NAmE*) *You need to* ***get your priorities straight****.* **2** 🔑 [U] **~ (over sth)** the most important place among various things that have to be done or among a group of people SYN **precedence**: *Club members will be* ***given priority****.* ◇ *The search for a new vaccine will* ***take priority over*** *all other medical research.* ◇ *Priority cases, such as homeless families, get dealt with first.* **3** [U] (*BrE*) the right of a vehicle to go before other traffic at a particular place on a road SYN **right of way**: *Buses have priority at this junction.*

pri·ory /ˈpraɪəri/ *noun* (*pl.* -ies) a building where a community of MONKS or NUNS lives, which is smaller and less important than an ABBEY

prise (*especially BrE*) (*US* **prize**) /praɪz/ (also **pry** especially in *NAmE*) *verb* to use force to separate sth from sth else: **~ sth + adv./prep.** *He prised her fingers from the bag and took it from her.* ◇ **~ sth + adj.** *She used a knife to prise open the lid.*
PHR V **ˌprise sth↔ˈout (of sb)** | **ˈprise sth from sb** to force sb to give you information about sb/sth

prism /ˈprɪzəm/ *noun* **1** (*geometry*) a solid figure with ends that are parallel and of the same size and shape, and with sides whose opposite edges are equal and parallel ⇨ VISUAL VOCAB page V58 **2** a transparent glass or plastic object, often with ends in the shape of a triangle, which separates light that passes through it into the colours of the RAINBOW

pris·mat·ic /prɪzˈmætɪk/ *adj.* **1** (*technical*) using or containing a prism; in the shape of a prism **2** (*literary*) (of colours) formed by a prism; very bright and clear

prison 🔑 /ˈprɪzn/ *noun*
1 🔑 [C, U] a building where people are kept as a punishment for a crime they have committed, or while they are waiting for trial SYN **jail**: *He was* ***sent to prison*** *for five years.* ◇ *She is* ***in prison****, awaiting trial.* ◇ *to* ***be released from prison*** ◇ *a* ***maximum-security prison*** ◇ *the* ***prison population*** (= the total number of prisoners in a country) ◇ *the problem of overcrowding in prisons* ◇ *Ten prison officers and three inmates needed hospital treatment following the riot.* ⇨ COLLOCATIONS at JUSTICE ⇨ note at SCHOOL **2** 🔑 [U] the system of keeping people in prisons: *the* ***prison service/system*** ◇ *The government insists that 'prison works' and plans to introduce a tougher sentencing policy for people convicted of violent crime.* **3** [C] a place or situation from which sb cannot escape: *His hospital room had become a prison.*

ˈprison camp *noun* a guarded camp where prisoners, especially prisoners of war or political prisoners, are kept

pris·on·er 🔑 /ˈprɪznə(r)/ *noun*
1 🔑 a person who is kept in prison as a punishment, or while they are waiting for trial: *The number of prisoners serving life sentences has fallen.* ◇ *They are demanding the release of all* ***political prisoners****.* **2** 🔑 a person who has been captured, for example by an enemy, and is being kept somewhere: *He was* ***taken prisoner*** *by rebel soldiers.* ◇ *They are* ***holding*** *her* ***prisoner*** *and demanding a large ransom.* ◇ (*figurative*) *She is afraid to go out and has become a virtual prisoner in her own home.*

ˌprisoner of ˈconscience *noun* (*pl.* prisoners of conscience) a person who is kept in prison because of his or her political or religious beliefs

ˌprisoner of ˈwar *noun* (*pl.* prisoners of war) (*abbr.* POW) a person, usually a member of the armed forces, who is captured by the enemy during a war and kept in a prison camp until the war has finished

ˌprison ˈvisitor *noun* (in Britain) a person who visits people in prison in order to help them, and who does not get paid for doing so

prissy /ˈprɪsi/ *adj.* (*informal, disapproving*) too careful to always behave correctly and appearing easily shocked by rude behaviour, etc. SYN **prudish**

pris·tine /ˈprɪstiːn/ *adj.* **1** fresh and clean, as if new SYN **immaculate**: *The car is* ***in pristine condition****.* **2** not developed or changed in any way; left in its original condition SYN **unspoiled**: *pristine, pollution-free beaches*

pri·thee /ˈprɪðiː/ *exclamation* (*old use*) used when asking sb politely to do sth

priv·acy /ˈprɪvəsi; *NAmE* ˈpraɪv-/ *noun* [U] **1** the state of being alone and not watched or disturbed by other people: *She was longing for some peace and privacy.* ◊ *I value my privacy.* ◊ *He read the letter later* ***in the privacy of*** *his own room.* **2** the state of being free from the attention of the public: *freedom of speech and the* ***right to privacy***

pri·vate /ˈpraɪvət/ *adj., noun*

■ ***adj.***

▸ NOT PUBLIC **1** [usually before noun] belonging to or for the use of a particular person or group; not for public use: *The sign said, 'Private property. Keep out.'* ◊ *Those are my father's private papers.* ◊ *The hotel has 110 bedrooms, all with private bathrooms.*

▸ CONVERSATION/MEETING **2** intended for or involving a particular person or group of people, not for people in general or for others to know about: *a private conversation* ◊ *They were sharing a private joke.* ◊ *Senior defence officials held private talks.*

▸ FEELINGS/INFORMATION **3** that you do not want other people to know about SYN **secret**: *her private thoughts and feelings*

▸ NOT OWNED/RUN BY STATE **4** [usually before noun] owned or managed by an individual person or an independent company rather than by the state: ***private banks*** ◊ *a programme to return many of the state companies to* ***private ownership*** OPP **public** **5** [only before noun] working or acting for yourself rather than for the state or for a group or company, especially in health or education: *private doctors* ◊ (*BrE*) *If I can afford it, I think I'll* ***go private*** (= pay for medical care rather than use the government service).

▸ NOT WORK **6** [usually before noun] not connected with your work or official position: *a politician's* ***private life***

▸ QUIET **7** where you are not likely to be disturbed; quiet: *Let's go somewhere a bit more private.* OPP **public**

▸ PERSON **8** [usually before noun] not wanting to share thoughts and feelings with other people: *He's a very private person.*

▸ LESSONS **9** [usually before noun] given by a teacher, etc. to one person or a small group of people for payment: *She gives private English lessons at weekends.*

▸ MONEY **10** that you receive from property or other sources but do not have to earn: *He has a private income.*

▸ **pri·vate·ly** *adv.*: *Can we speak privately?* ◊ *In public he supported the official policy, but privately he was sure it would fail.* ◊ *a privately owned company* ◊ *Their children were educated privately.* ◊ *She smiled, but privately she was furious.*

■ ***noun*** **1** [C] (*abbr.* Pte) (*BrE*) a soldier of the lowest rank in the army: *Private (John) Smith* **2** **privates** [pl.] (*informal*) = PRIVATE PARTS

IDM **in ˈprivate** with nobody else present: *Is there somewhere we can discuss this in private?* ➲ compare IN PUBLIC

ˌprivate ˈcompany (also **ˌprivate ˌlimited ˈcompany**) *noun* (*business*) a business that may not offer its shares for sale to the public ➲ compare PUBLIC COMPANY, PLC

ˌprivate deˈtective (also **ˌprivate inˈvestigator**) (also *informal* **ˌprivate ˈeye**) *noun* a DETECTIVE who is not in the police, but who can be employed to find out information, find a missing person, follow sb, etc.

ˌprivate ˈenterprise *noun* [U] the economic system in which industry or business is owned by independent companies or private people and is not controlled by the government ➲ compare FREE ENTERPRISE

ˌprivate ˈequity *noun* [U] (*finance*) investment made in a company, usually a small one, whose shares are not bought and sold by the public

pri·vat·eer /ˌpraɪvəˈtɪə(r); *NAmE* -ˈtɪr/ *noun* a ship used in the past for attacking and stealing from other ships

ˌprivate ˈlaw *noun* [U] (*law*) the part of the law that concerns individual people and their property

ˌprivate ˈmember *noun* (in the British political system) a member of parliament who is not a minister in the government

ˌprivate ˈmember's bill *noun* (in the British political system) a law that is suggested by a member of parliament who is not a minister in the government and that is not part of the government's plans

ˌprivate ˈparts (also *informal* **pri·vates**) *noun* [pl.] a polite way of referring to the sexual organs without saying their names

ˌprivate ˈpatient *noun* (in Britain) a person who is treated by a doctor outside the National Health Service and who pays for their treatment

ˌprivate ˈpractice *noun* **1** [U] (of a profession) the fact of working on your own or in a small independent company rather than as an employee of the government or a large company: *Most solicitors in England and Wales are* ***in private practice.*** **2** [U, C] (in Britain) the fact of providing medical care outside the National Health Service, which people must pay for; a place providing this care

ˌprivate ˈschool (also **indeˌpendent ˈschool**) *noun* a school that receives no money from the government and where the education of the students is paid for by their parents ➲ compare PUBLIC SCHOOL, STATE SCHOOL

ˌprivate ˈsecretary *noun* **1** a secretary whose job is to deal with the more important and personal affairs of a business person **2** a CIVIL SERVANT who acts as an assistant to a senior government official

the ˌprivate ˈsector *noun* [sing.] the part of the economy of a country that is not under the direct control of the government ➲ COLLOCATIONS at ECONOMY ➲ compare THE PUBLIC SECTOR

ˌprivate ˈsoldier *noun* a soldier of the lowest rank

ˌprivate ˈview (also **ˌprivate ˈviewing**) *noun* an occasion when a few people are invited to look at an exhibition of paintings before it is open to the public

pri·va·tion /praɪˈveɪʃn/ *noun* [C, usually pl., U] (*formal*) a lack of the basic things that people need for living SYN **hardship**: *the privations of poverty* ◊ *They endured years of suffering and privation.*

pri·vat·ize (*BrE* also **-ise**) /ˈpraɪvətaɪz/ *verb* **~ sth** to sell a business or an industry so that it is no longer owned by the government SYN **denationalize** OPP **nationalize** ▸ **pri·vat·iza·tion, -isa·tion** /ˌpraɪvətaɪˈzeɪʃn; *NAmE* -təˈz-/ *noun* [U]: *There were fears that privatization would lead to job losses.*

privet /ˈprɪvɪt/ *noun* [U] a bush with small dark green leaves that remain on the bush and stay green all year, often used for garden HEDGES: *a privet hedge*

priv·il·ege /ˈprɪvəlɪdʒ/ *noun, verb*

■ ***noun*** **1** [C] a special right or advantage that a particular person or group of people has: *Education should be a universal right and not a privilege.* ◊ *You can enjoy all the benefits and privileges of club membership.* **2** [U] (*disapproving*) the rights and advantages that rich and powerful people in a society have: *As a member of the nobility, his life had been one of wealth and privilege.* **3** [sing.] something that you are proud and lucky to have the opportunity to do SYN **honour**: *I hope to have the privilege of working with them again.* ◊ *It was a great privilege to hear her sing.* ➲ SYNONYMS at PLEASURE **4** [C, U] (*technical*) a special right to do or say things without being punished: *parliamentary privilege* (= the special right of members of parliament to say particular things without risking legal action)

■ ***verb*** **~ sb/sth** (*formal*) to give sb/sth special rights or advantages that others do not have SYN **favour**: *education policies that privilege the children of wealthy parents*

priv·il·eged /ˈprɪvəlɪdʒd/ *adj.* **1** (sometimes *disapproving*) having special rights or advantages that most people do not have: *Those in authority were in a privileged position.* ◊ *She comes from a privileged background.* ◊ *In those days, only* ***a privileged few*** *had the vote.* **2** [not before noun] having an opportunity to do sth that makes you feel proud SYN **honoured**: *We are privileged to welcome you as our speaker this evening.* **3** (*law*) (of information) known only to a few people and legally protected so that it does not have to be made public SYN **confidential**

P

privy /ˈprɪvi/ *adj., noun*
■ **adj.** (*formal*) **~ to sth** allowed to know about sth secret: *She was not privy to any information contained in the letters.*
■ **noun** (*pl.* -ies) (*old-fashioned*) a toilet, especially an outdoor one

the ˌPrivy ˈCouncil *noun* [sing.+ sing./pl. v.] (in Britain) a group of people who advise the king or queen on political affairs ▸ **ˌPrivy ˈCouncillor** *noun*

the ˌprivy ˈpurse *noun* [sing.] (in Britain) an amount of money that the government gives to the king or queen to pay his or her private expenses plus some official expenses

prize 🔑 /praɪz/ *noun, adj., verb*
■ **noun 1** 🔑 an award that is given to a person who wins a competition, race, etc. or who does very good work: *She was awarded the Nobel Peace prize.* ◇ *He* **won first prize** *in the woodwind section.* ◇ *There are* **no prizes for guessing** (= it is very easy to guess) *who she was with.* ◇ *I won £500 in* **prize money.** ◇ *Win a car in our grand* **prize draw!** ➲ see also CONSOLATION PRIZE **2** something very important or valuable that is difficult to achieve or obtain: *World peace is the greatest prize of all.*
■ **adj.** [only before noun] **1** (especially of an animal, a flower or a vegetable) good enough to win a prize in a competition: *prize cattle* **2** being a very good example of its kind: *a prize student* ◇ *He's a* **prize specimen** *of the human race!* ◇ (*informal*) *She's a* **prize idiot** (= very silly).
■ **verb 1** [usually passive] to value sth highly SYN **treasure**: **~ sth** *an era when honesty was prized above all other virtues* ◇ **~ sth for sth** *Oil of cedarwood is* **highly prized** *for its use in perfumery.* **2** (*NAmE*) = PRISE

prized /praɪzd/ *adj.* [only before noun] very valuable to sb: *I lost some of my most* **prized possessions** *in the fire.*

prize·fight /ˈpraɪzfaɪt/ *noun* a BOXING competition that is fought for money ▸ **prize·fight·er** *noun* **prize·fight·ing** *noun* [U]

ˈprize-giving *noun* (*BrE*) a ceremony at which prizes are given to people who have done very good work

prize·win·ner /ˈpraɪzwɪnə(r)/ *noun* a person who has won a prize ▸ **prize·win·ning** *adj.* [only before noun]: *a prizewinning story*

P

pro /prəʊ; *NAmE* proʊ/ *noun, adj., prep.*
■ **noun** (*pl.* **pros**) (*informal*) a person who works as a professional, especially in a sport: *a golf pro* ◇ *He handled the situation like an* **old pro** (= sb who has a lot of experience).
IDM **the ˌpros and ˈcons** the advantages and disadvantages of sth: *We weighed up the pros and cons.*
■ **adj.** (*especially NAmE*) (in sport) professional: *a pro wrestler* ◇ *pro football* ◇ *a young boxer who's just* **turned pro**
■ **prep.** (*informal*) if sb is **pro** sb/sth, they are in favour of or support that person or thing: *He has always been pro the environment.* ➲ compare ANTI

pro- /prəʊ; *NAmE* proʊ/ *prefix* (in adjectives) in favour of; supporting: *pro-democracy* ➲ compare ANTI-

pro·active /ˌprəʊˈæktɪv; *NAmE* ˌproʊ-/ *adj.* (of a person or policy) controlling a situation by making things happen rather than waiting for things to happen and then reacting to them ➲ compare REACTIVE ▸ **pro·active·ly** *adv.*

ˌpro-ˈam *adj.* [only before noun] (in sport) involving both professional and AMATEUR players: *a pro-am golf tournament* ▸ **ˌpro-ˈam** *noun*: *to play in a pro-am*

prob·abil·ist·ic /ˌprɒbəbɪˈlɪstɪk; *NAmE* ˌprɑːb-/ *adj.* [usually before noun] (*technical*) (of methods, arguments, etc.) based on the idea that, as we cannot be certain about things, we can base our beliefs or actions on what is probable

prob·abil·ity /ˌprɒbəˈbɪləti; *NAmE* ˌprɑːb-/ *noun* (*pl.* -ies) **1** [U, C] how likely sth is to happen SYN **likelihood**: *The probability is that prices will rise rapidly.* ◇ *There seemed to be a high probability of success.* **2** [C] a thing that is likely to happen: *A fall in interest rates is a* **strong probability** *in the present economic climate.* ◇ *It now seems a probability rather than just a possibility.* **3** [C, U] (*mathematics*) a RATIO showing the chances that a particular thing will happen: *There is a 60% probability that the population will be infected with the disease.*
IDM **in ˌall probaˈbility...** it is very likely that: *In all probability he failed to understand the consequences of his actions.* ➲ more at BALANCE *n.*

prob·able 🔑 /ˈprɒbəbl; *NAmE* ˈprɑːb-/ *adj., noun*
■ **adj.** 🔑 likely to happen, to exist or to be true: *the probable cause/explanation/outcome* ◇ **highly/quite/most probable** ◇ **It is probable that** *the disease has a genetic element.* ➲ compare IMPROBABLE
■ **noun ~** (**for sth**) (*especially BrE*) a person or an animal that is likely to win a race or to be chosen for a team

prob·ably 🔑 /ˈprɒbəbli; *NAmE* ˈprɑːb-/ *adv.* used to say that sth is likely to happen or to be true: *You're probably right.* ◇ *It'll probably be OK.* ◇ *It was the best known and probably the most popular of her songs.* ◇ *'Is he going to be there?' 'Probably.'* ◇ *'Do we need the car?'* **'Probably not.'** ◇ *As you probably know, I'm going to be changing jobs soon.* ◇ *The two cases are* **most probably** *connected.* ➲ LANGUAGE BANK at PERHAPS

pro·bate /ˈprəʊbeɪt; *NAmE* ˈproʊ-/ *noun, verb*
■ **noun** [U] (*law*) the official process of proving that a WILL (= a legal document that says what is to happen to a person's property when they die) is valid
■ **verb ~ sth** (*NAmE, law*) to prove that a WILL is valid

pro·ba·tion /prəˈbeɪʃn; *NAmE* proʊ-/ *noun* [U] **1** (*law*) a system that allows a person who has committed a crime not to go to prison if they behave well and if they see an official (called a PROBATION OFFICER) regularly for a fixed period of time: *The prisoner was put* **on probation.** ◇ *He was given two years' probation.* **2** a time of training and testing when you start a new job to see if you are suitable for the work: *a period of probation* **3** (*NAmE*) a fixed period of time during which a student who has behaved badly or not worked hard must improve their work or their behaviour ▸ **pro·ba·tion·ary** /prəˈbeɪʃnri; *NAmE* proʊˈbeɪʃəneri/ *adj.*: *a probationary period* ◇ *young probationary teachers*

pro·ba·tion·er /prəˈbeɪʃnə(r); *NAmE* proʊ-/ *noun* **1** a person who is new in a job and is being watched to see if they are suitable **2** a person who is seeing a PROBATION OFFICER because of having committed a crime

proˈbation officer *noun* a person whose job is to check on people who are on probation and help them

probe /prəʊb; *NAmE* proʊb/ *verb, noun*
■ **verb 1** [I, T] to ask questions in order to find out secret or hidden information about sb/sth SYN **investigate**: **~** (**into sth**) *He didn't like the media probing into his past.* ◇ **~ sth** *a TV programme that probed government scandals in the 1990s* ◇ **+ speech** *'Then what happened?' he probed.* **2** [T] **~ sth** to touch, examine or look for sth, especially with a long thin instrument: *The doctor probed the wound for signs of infection.* ◇ *Searchlights probed the night sky.*
■ **noun 1 ~** (**into sth**) (used especially in newspapers) a thorough and careful investigation of sth: *a police probe into the financial affairs of the company* **2** (also **ˈspace probe**) a SPACECRAFT without people on board which obtains information and sends it back to earth **3** (*technical*) a long thin metal tool used by doctors for examining inside the body **4** (*technical*) a small device put inside sth and used by scientists to test sth or record information

prob·ing /ˈprəʊbɪŋ; *NAmE* ˈproʊ-/ *adj.* **1** intended to discover the truth: *They asked a lot of* **probing questions.** **2** examining sb/sth closely: *She looked away from his dark probing eyes.* ▸ **prob·ing** *noun*: *the journalist's unwanted probings*

pro·biot·ic /ˌprəʊbaɪˈɒtɪk; *NAmE* ˌproʊbaɪˈɑːtɪk/ *adj.* [only before noun] encouraging the growth of bacteria that have a good effect on the body: *probiotic products/yogurt/cheese*

prob·ity /ˈprəʊbəti; *NAmE* ˈproʊ-/ *noun* [U] (*formal*) the quality of being completely honest: *financial probity*

prob·lem 🔑 /ˈprɒbləm; *NAmE* ˈprɑːb-/ *noun, adj.*
■ **noun 1** 🔑 a thing that is difficult to deal with or to understand: **big/major/serious problems** ◇ **health/family, etc.**

problems ◇ ***financial/practical/technical problems*** ◇ *to* ***address/tackle/solve a problem*** ◇ *(especially NAmE) to* ***fix a problem*** ◇ *the problem of drug abuse* ◇ *If he chooses Mary it's bound to* ***cause problems.*** ◇ *Let me know if you have any problems.* ◇ *Most students* ***face the problem*** *of funding themselves while they are studying.* ◇ *The problem first arose in 2008.* ◇ *Unemployment is a very real problem for graduates now.* ◇ *It's a nice table!* ***The only problem is*** (***that***) *it's too big for our room.* ◇ *Stop worrying about their marriage—it isn't your problem.* ◇ *There's no history of heart problems* (= disease connected with the heart) *in our family.* ◇ *the magazine's* ***problem page*** (= containing letters about readers' problems and advice about how to solve them) **2** a question that can be answered by using logical thought or mathematics: *mathematical problems* ◇ *to find the answer to the problem*

IDM **have a 'problem with sth** to disagree with or object to sth: *I have no problem with you working at home tomorrow.* ◇ (*informal*) *We are going to do this my way.* ***Do you have a problem with that?*** (= showing that you are impatient with the person that you are speaking to) **no 'problem** (*informal*) **1** (also **not a 'problem**) used to show that you are happy to help sb or that sth will be easy to do: *'Can I pay by credit card?' 'Yes, no problem.'* **2** used after sb has thanked you or said they are sorry for sth: *'Thanks for the ride.' 'No problem.'* **ˌit's/ˌthat's not 'my problem** (*informal*) used to show that you do not care about sb else's difficulties **that's 'her/'his/'their/'your problem** (*informal*) used to show that you think a person should deal with their own difficulties **what's your problem?** (*informal*) used to show that you think sb is being unreasonable: *What's your problem?—I only asked if you could help me for ten minutes.*

■ ***adj.*** [only before noun] causing problems for other people: *She was a* ***problem child,*** *always in trouble with the police.*

prob·lem·at·ic /ˌprɒbləˈmætɪk; *NAmE* ˌprɑːb-/ (also *less frequent* **prob·lem·at·ical** /-ɪkl/) *adj.* difficult to deal with or to understand; full of problems; not certain to be successful **OPP** **unproblematic**

'problem-solving *noun* [U] the act of finding ways of dealing with problems

pro bono /ˌprəʊ ˈbəʊnəʊ; *NAmE* ˌproʊ ˈboʊnoʊ/ *adj.* [only before noun] (from *Latin*) (especially of legal work) done without asking for payment ▸ **pro bono** *adv.*

pro·bos·cis /prəˈbɒsɪs; *NAmE* -ˈbɑːs-; *NAmE* also -ˈbɑːskɪs/ *noun* (*pl.* **pro·bos·ces** /-siːz/, **pro·bos·cises**) (*technical*) **1** the long FLEXIBLE nose of some animals, such as an ELEPHANT **2** the long thin mouth, like a tube, of some insects **3** (*humorous*) a large human nose

probs /prɒbz; *NAmE* prɑːbz/ *noun* [pl.]

IDM **no 'probs** (*informal*) used to mean 'there is no problem': *I can let you have it by next week. No probs.*

pro·caine /ˈprəʊkeɪn; *NAmE* ˈproʊ-/ (also **novo·caine**) *noun* [U] (*medical*) a substance used to stop sb from feeling pain in a particular part of their body, especially by a dentist

pro·ced·ure **AW** /prəˈsiːdʒə(r)/ *noun*
1 [C, U] ~ (**for sth**) a way of doing sth, especially the usual or correct way: *maintenance procedures* ◇ ***emergency/safety/disciplinary procedures*** ◇ *to follow* ***normal/standard/accepted procedure*** ◇ *Making a complaint is quite a simple procedure.* **2** [U] the official or formal order or way of doing sth, especially in business, law or politics: ***court/legal/parliamentary procedure*** **3** [C] (*medical*) a medical operation: *to perform a routine surgical procedure* ▸ **pro·ced·ural** **AW** /prəˈsiːdʒərəl/ *adj.*: (*formal*) *procedural rules*

pro·ceed **AW** /prəˈsiːd; *NAmE* proʊ-/ *verb*
1 [I] ~ (**with sth**) to continue doing sth that has already been started; to continue being done: *We're not sure whether we still want to proceed with the sale.* ◇ *Work is proceeding slowly.* **2** [I] **~ to do sth** to do sth next, after having done sth else first **SYN** **go on**: *He outlined his plans and then proceeded to explain them in more detail.* ◇ (*humorous*) *Having said she wasn't hungry, she then proceeded to order a three-course meal.* **3** [I] **+ adv./prep.** (*formal*) to move or travel in a particular direction: *The marchers proceeded slowly along the street.* ◇ *Passengers for Rome should proceed to Gate 32 for boarding.*

PHR V **pro'ceed against sb** (*law*) to start a court case against sb **pro'ceed from sth** (*formal*) to be caused by or be the result of sth

pro·ceed·ing **AW** /prəˈsiːdɪŋ/ *noun* (*formal*) **1** [C, usually pl.] ~ (**against sb**) (**for sth**) the process of using a court to settle a disagreement or to deal with a complaint: ***bankruptcy/divorce/extradition, etc. proceedings*** ◇ *to bring* ***legal proceedings*** *against sb* **2** **proceedings** [pl.] an event or a series of actions: *The Mayor will open the proceedings at the City Hall tomorrow.* ◇ *We watched the proceedings from the balcony.* **3** **proceedings** [pl.] the official written report of a meeting, etc.

pro·ceeds **AW** /ˈprəʊsiːdz; *NAmE* ˈproʊ-/ *noun* [pl.] **~** (**of/from sth**) the money that you receive when you sell sth or organize a performance, etc; profits: *She sold her car and bought a piano with the proceeds.* ◇ *The proceeds of the concert will go to charity.*

Language Bank

process

Describing a process

- This diagram **illustrates the process of** paper-making. / This diagram **shows how** paper is made.
- **First/First of all**, logs are delivered to a paper mill, where the bark is removed and the wood is cut into small chips.
- **Next/Second**, the wood chips are pulped, either using chemicals or in a pulping machine.
- Pulping breaks down the internal structure of the wood and **enables/allows** the natural oils **to** be removed.
- **Once/After** the wood has been pulped, the pulp is bleached **in order to** remove impurities. /...is bleached **so that** impurities **can** be removed.
- **The next stage is to** feed the pulp into the paper machine, where it is mixed with water **and then** poured onto a wire conveyor belt.
- As the pulp travels along the conveyor belt, the water drains away. **This causes** the solid material **to** sink to the bottom, forming a layer of paper.
- **At this point** the new paper is still wet, **so** it is passed between large heated rollers, which press out the remaining water and **simultaneously** dry the paper. / ...dry the paper **at the same time**.
- **The final stage is to** wind the paper onto large rolls. / **Finally**, the paper is wound onto large rolls.

➲ notes at FIRSTLY, LASTLY
➲ Language Banks at CONCLUSION, FIRST

pro·cess[1] **AW** /ˈprəʊses; *NAmE* ˈprɑːses; ˈproʊ-/ *noun, verb* ➲ see also PROCESS[2]

■ ***noun*** **1** a series of things that are done in order to achieve a particular result: *a consultation process* ◇ *to begin the difficult process of reforming the education system* ◇ *I'm afraid getting things changed will be a slow process.* ◇ *mental processes* ◇ *Coming off the drug was a long and painful* (= difficult) *process for him.* ◇ *Find which food you are allergic to by* ***a process of elimination.*** ◇ *We're* ***in the process of*** *selling our house.* ◇ *I was moving some furniture and I twisted my ankle* ***in the process*** (= while I was doing it). ➲ see also PEACE PROCESS **2** a series of things that happen, especially ones that result in natural changes: *the ageing process* ◇ *It's a normal part of the* ***learning process.*** **3** a method of doing or making sth, especially one that is used in industry: *manufacturing processes*

■ ***verb*** **1** **~ sth** to treat raw material, food, etc. in order to change it, preserve it, etc: *Most of the food we buy is processed in some way.* ◇ *processed cheese* ◇ *a sewage processing plant* **2** **~ sth** to deal officially with a document, request,

P

etc: *It will take a week for your application to be processed.* **3** **~ sth** (*computing*) to perform a series of operations on data in a computer ▸ **pro·cess·ing** AW *noun* [U]: *the food processing industry* ➲ see also DATA PROCESSING, WORD PROCESSING

pro·cess² /prəˈses/ *verb* [I] **+ adv./prep.** (*formal*) to walk or move along slowly in, or as if in, a procession ➲ see also PROCESS¹

pro·ces·sion /prəˈseʃn/ *noun* **1** [C, U] a line of people or vehicles that move along slowly, especially as part of a ceremony; the act of moving in this way: *a funeral procession* ◇ *a torchlight procession* ◇ *The procession made its way down the hill.* ◇ *Groups of unemployed people from all over the country marched* ***in procession*** *to the capital.* **2** [C] a number of people who come one after the other: *A procession of waiters appeared bearing trays of food.*

pro·ces·sion·al /prəˈseʃənl/ *adj.* [only before noun] used in a procession, especially a religious one; connected with a procession

pro·ces·sor /ˈprəʊsesə(r); *NAmE* ˈprɑː-; ˈproʊ-/ *noun* **1** a machine or person that processes things **2** (*computing*) a part of a computer that controls all the other parts of the system SYN **central processing unit** ➲ see also FOOD PROCESSOR, MICROPROCESSOR, WORD PROCESSOR

ˌpro-ˈchoice *adj.* believing that a pregnant woman should be able to choose to have an ABORTION if she wants ➲ compare ANTI-CHOICE, PRO-LIFE

pro·claim /prəˈkleɪm/ *verb* (*formal*) **1** to publicly and officially tell people about sth important SYN **declare**: **~ sth** *The president proclaimed a state of emergency.* ◇ **~ that...** *The charter proclaimed that all states would have their own government.* ◇ **~ sb/sth/yourself + noun** *He proclaimed himself emperor.* ◇ **~ sb/sth/yourself to be/have sth** *Steve checked the battery and proclaimed it to be dead.* ◇ **~ how, what, etc...** *The senator proclaimed how shocked he was at the news.* ◇ **+ speech** *'We will succeed,' she proclaimed.* **2** to show sth clearly; to be a sign of sth: **~ sth** *This building, more than any other, proclaims the character of the town.* ◇ **~ sb/sth + noun** *His accent proclaimed him a Scot.* ◇ **~ sb/sth to be/have sth** *His accent proclaimed him to be a Scot.*

P

proc·lama·tion /ˌprɒkləˈmeɪʃn; *NAmE* ˌprɑːk-/ *noun* [C, U] an official statement about sth important that is made to the public; the act of making an official statement

pro·cliv·ity /prəˈklɪvəti/ *noun* (*pl.* -ies) **~ (for sth/for doing sth)** (*formal*) a natural tendency to do sth or to feel sth, often sth bad SYN **propensity**: *his sexual/criminal proclivities* ◇ *the government's proclivity for spending money*

pro·cras·tin·ate /prəʊˈkræstɪneɪt; *NAmE* proʊ-/ *verb* [I] (*formal, disapproving*) to delay doing sth that you should do, usually because you do not want to do it ▸ **pro·cras·tin·ation** /prəʊˌkræstɪˈneɪʃn; *NAmE* proʊ-/ *noun* [U]

pro·cre·ate /ˈprəʊkrieɪt; *NAmE* ˈproʊ-/ *verb* [I, T] **~ (sth)** (*formal*) to produce children or baby animals SYN **reproduce** ▸ **pro·cre·ation** /ˌprəʊkriˈeɪʃn; *NAmE* ˌproʊ-/ *noun* [U]: *They believe that sex is primarily for procreation.*

Pro·crus·tean /ˌprəʊˈkrʌstiən; *NAmE* ˌproʊ-/ *adj.* (of a system, a set of rules, etc.) treating all people or things as if they are the same, without considering individual differences and in a way that is too strict and unreasonable ORIGIN From the Greek story of **Procrustes**, a robber who forced people to lie on a bed and made them fit it by stretching their bodies or cutting off part of their legs.

proc·tor /ˈprɒktə(r); *NAmE* ˈprɑːk-/ (*NAmE*) (*BrE* **in·vigi·la·tor**) *noun* a person who watches people while they are taking an exam to make sure that they have everything they need, that they keep to the rules, etc. ▸ **proc·tor** (*NAmE*) (*BrE* **in·vigi·late**) *verb* [T, I] **~ (sth)**

proc·ur·ator fis·cal /ˌprɒkjureɪtə ˈfɪskl; *NAmE* ˌprɑːkjəreɪtər/ *noun* (*pl.* **proc·ur·ators fis·cal**) (in Scotland) a public official whose job is to decide whether people who are suspected of a crime should be brought to trial

pro·cure /prəˈkjʊə(r); *NAmE* -ˈkjʊr/ *verb* **1** [T] (*formal*) to obtain sth, especially with difficulty: **~ sth (for sb/sth)** *She managed to procure a ticket for the concert.* ◇ *They procured a copy of the report for us.* ◇ **~ sb sth** *They procured us a copy of the report.* **2** [T, I] **~ (sb)** to provide a PROSTITUTE for sb: *He was accused of procuring under-age girls.*

pro·cure·ment /prəˈkjʊəmənt; *NAmE* -ˈkjʊrm-/ *noun* [U] (*formal*) the process of obtaining supplies of sth, especially for a government or an organization

prod /prɒd; *NAmE* prɑːd/ *verb, noun*

■ ***verb*** (**-dd-**) **1** [T, I] to push sb/sth with your finger or with a pointed object SYN **poke**: **~ sb/sth (+ adv./prep.)** *She prodded him in the ribs to wake him up.* ◇ **~ at sb/sth** *He prodded at his breakfast with a fork.* **2** [T] **~ sb (into sth/into doing sth)** to try to make sb do sth, especially when they are unwilling: *She finally prodded him into action.*

■ ***noun*** **1** the act of pushing sb with your finger or with a pointed object SYN **dig**: *She gave him a sharp prod with her umbrella.* **2** (*informal*) an act of encouraging sb or of reminding sb to do sth: *If they haven't replied by next week, you'll have to call them and* ***give them a prod.*** **3** an instrument like a stick that is used for prodding animals **4** **Prod** (also **Prod·die** /ˈprɒdi; *NAmE* ˈprɑːdi/) (*informal*) an offensive word for a Protestant

prod·ding /ˈprɒdɪŋ; *NAmE* ˈprɑːd-/ *noun* [U] encouragement to do sth: *He needed no prodding.*

prod·igal /ˈprɒdɪgl; *NAmE* ˈprɑːd-/ *adj.* (*formal, disapproving*) too willing to spend money or waste time, energy or materials SYN **extravagant** ▸ **prod·ig·al·ity** /ˌprɒdɪˈgæləti; *NAmE* ˌprɑːd-/ *noun* [U]

IDM **the/a ˌprodigal (ˈson)** a person who leaves home and wastes their money and time on a life of pleasure, but who later is sorry about this and returns home

pro·di·gious /prəˈdɪdʒəs/ *adj.* [usually before noun] (*formal*) very large or powerful and causing surprise or admiration SYN **colossal**, **enormous**: *a prodigious achievement/memory/talent* ◇ *DVDs can store* ***prodigious amounts*** *of information.* ▸ **pro·di·gious·ly** *adv.*: *a prodigiously talented musician*

prod·igy /ˈprɒdədʒi; *NAmE* ˈprɑːd-/ *noun* (*pl.* -ies) a young person who is unusually intelligent or skilful for their age: ***a child/an infant prodigy*** ◇ *a musical prodigy*

pro·duce ⚷ *verb, noun*

WORD FAMILY
produce *verb*
producer *noun*
production *noun*
productive *adj.* (≠ unproductive)
productively *adv.*
product *noun*
produce *noun*

■ ***verb*** /prəˈdjuːs; *NAmE* -ˈduːs/

▸ GOODS **1** ⚷ **~ sth** to make things to be sold, especially in large quantities SYN **manufacture**: *a factory that produces microchips* ➲ SYNONYMS at MAKE, PRODUCT ➲ see also MASS-PRODUCE

▸ MAKE NATURALLY **2** ⚷ **~ sth** to grow or make sth as part of a natural process; to have a baby or young animal: *The region produces over 50% of the country's wheat.* ◇ *Our cat produced kittens last week.* ◇ *Her duty was to produce an heir to the throne.*

▸ CREATE WITH SKILL **3** ⚷ **~ sth** to create sth, especially when skill is needed: *She produced a delicious meal out of a few leftovers.*

▸ RESULT/EFFECT **4** ⚷ **~ sth** to cause a particular result or effect SYN **bring about**: *A phone call to the manager produced the result she wanted.* ◇ *The drug produces a feeling of excitement.*

▸ SHOW/BRING OUT **5** **~ sth (from/out of sth)** to show sth or make sth appear from somewhere: *He produced a letter from his pocket.* ◇ *At the meeting the finance director produced the figures for the previous year.*

▸ PERSON **6** **~ sb** if a town, country, etc. **produces** sb with a particular skill or quality, the person comes from that town, country, etc: *He is the greatest athlete this country has ever produced.*

▸ MOVIE/PLAY **7** **~ sth** to be in charge of preparing a film/movie, play, etc. for the public to see: *She produced a TV series about adopted children.*

■ ***noun*** /ˈprɒdjuːs; *NAmE* ˈprɑːduːs; ˈproʊ-/ [U] things that have been made or grown, especially things connected with farming: *farm produce* ◇ *The shop sells only fresh local produce.* ◇ *It says on the label 'Produce of France'.*

pro·du·cer 0-ᴡ /prəˈdjuːsə(r); *NAmE* -ˈduː-/ *noun* **1** 0-ᴡ a person, a company or a country that grows or makes food, goods or materials: *French wine producers* ◇ *Libya is a major oil producer.* ➲ compare CONSUMER **2** 0-ᴡ a person who is in charge of the practical and financial aspects of making a film/movie or a play: *Hollywood screenwriters, actors and producers* ➲ compare DIRECTOR (2) **3** a person or company that arranges for sb to make a programme for radio or television, or a record, CD, etc: *an independent television producer*

prod·uct 0-ᴡ /ˈprɒdʌkt; *NAmE* ˈprɑːd-/ *noun* **1** 0-ᴡ [C, U] a thing that is grown or produced, usually for sale: ***dairy/meat/pharmaceutical, etc. products*** ◇ *investment in **product development*** ◇ *to **launch a new product** on to the market* ◇ (*business*) *We need new product to sell* (= a new range of products). ➲ COLLOCATIONS at BUSINESS ➲ see also END PRODUCT, GROSS NATIONAL PRODUCT **2** 0-ᴡ [C] a thing produced during a natural, chemical or industrial process: *the products of the reaction* ➲ see also BY-PRODUCT, WASTE PRODUCT **3** [C] **~ of sth** a person or thing that is the result of sth: *The child is the product of a broken home.* **4** [C, U] a cream, jelly or liquid that you put on your hair or skin to make it look better: *This product can be used on wet or dry hair.* **5** (*mathematics*) [C] a quantity obtained by multiplying one number by another: *The product of 21 and 16 is 336.*

Synonyms

product

goods • commodity • merchandise • produce

These are all words for things that are produced to be sold.

product a thing that is produced or grown, usually to be sold: *to create/develop/launch a new product*

goods things that are produced to be sold: *cotton/leather goods* ◇ *electrical goods*

commodity (*economics*) a product or raw material that can be bought and sold, especially between countries: *rice, flour and other basic commodities*

merchandise [U] goods that are bought or sold; things that you can buy that are connected with or advertise a particular event or organization: *official Olympic merchandise*

GOODS OR MERCHANDISE?

Choose **goods** if the emphasis is on what the product is made of or what it is for: *leather/household goods*. Choose **merchandise** if the emphasis is less on the product itself and more on its brand or the fact of buying/selling it.

produce [U] things that have been grown or made, especially things connected with farming: *We sell only fresh local produce.*

PATTERNS

- **consumer/industrial** products/goods/commodities
- **household** products/goods
- **farm** products/produce
- **luxury** products/goods/commodities
- to **sell/market** a product/goods/a commodity/merchandise/produce
- to **export** a product/goods/a commodity/merchandise
- to **buy/purchase** a product/goods/a commodity/merchandise/produce

pro·duc·tion 0-ᴡ /prəˈdʌkʃn/ *noun* **1** 0-ᴡ [U] the process of growing or making food, goods or materials, especially large quantities: ***wheat/oil/car, etc. production*** ◇ *land available for **food production*** ◇ *The new model will be **in production** by the end of the year.* ◇ *Production of the new aircraft will start next year.* ◇ *The car **went out of production** in 2007.* ◇ *production costs* ◇ *a production process* ➲ see also MASS PRODUCTION **2** 0-ᴡ [U] the quantity of goods that is produced: ***a decline/an increase in production*** ◇ *It is important not to let **production levels** fall.* **3** 0-ᴡ [U] the act or process of making sth naturally: *drugs to stimulate the body's production of hormones* **4** 0-ᴡ [C, U] a film/movie, a play or a broadcast that is prepared for the public; the act of preparing a film or a play, etc: *a new production of 'King Lear'* ◇ *He wants a career in film production.*

IDM **on production of sth** (*formal*) when you show sth: *Discounts only on production of your student ID card.*

proˈduction line (also **asˈsembly line**) *noun* a line of workers and machines in a factory, along which a product passes, having parts made, put together or checked at each stage until the product is finished: *Cars are checked as they come off the production line.*

proˈduction number *noun* a scene in a musical play or a film/movie where a lot of people sing and dance

pro·duct·ive /prəˈdʌktɪv/ *adj.* **1** making goods or growing crops, especially in large quantities: ***highly productive*** *farming land* ◇ *productive workers* OPP **unproductive** **2** doing or achieving a lot SYN **fruitful**: *a productive meeting* ◇ *My time spent in the library was very productive.* ➲ compare COUNTERPRODUCTIVE **3 ~ of sth** (*formal*) resulting in sth or causing sth: *a play productive of the strongest emotions* ▸ **pro·duct·ive·ly** *adv.*: *to use land more productively* ◇ *It's important to spend your time productively.*

prod·uct·iv·ity /ˌprɒdʌkˈtɪvəti; *NAmE* ˌprɑːd-; ˌproʊd-/ *noun* [U] the rate at which a worker, a company or a country produces goods, and the amount produced, compared with how much time, work and money is needed to produce them: ***high/improved/increased productivity*** ◇ *Wage rates depend on levels of productivity.*

ˌproduct ˈplacement *noun* [U, C] the use of particular products in films/movies or television programmes in order to advertise them

Prof. *abbr.* (in writing) PROFESSOR: *Prof. Mike Harrison*

prof /prɒf; *NAmE* prɑːf/ *noun* (*informal*) = PROFESSOR: *a college prof*

pro·fane /prəˈfeɪn/ *adj., verb*

■ ***adj.*** **1** (*formal*) having or showing a lack of respect for God or holy things: *profane language* **2** (*technical*) not connected with religion or holy things SYN **secular**: *songs of sacred and profane love*

■ ***verb* ~ sth** (*formal*) to treat sth holy with a lack of respect

pro·fan·ity /prəˈfænəti; *NAmE* also proʊˈf-/ *noun* (*pl.* -ies) (*formal*) **1** [U] behaviour that shows a lack of respect for God or holy things **2** [C, usually pl.] swear words, or religious words used in a way that shows a lack of respect for God or holy things: *He uttered a stream of profanities.*

pro·fess /prəˈfes/ *verb* (*formal*) **1** to claim that sth is true or correct, especially when it is not: **~ sth** *She still professes her innocence.* ◇ **~ to be/have sth** *I don't profess to be an expert in this subject.* **2** to state openly that you have a particular belief, feeling, etc. SYN **declare**: **~ sth** *He professed his admiration for their work.* ◇ **~ yourself + adj.** *She professed herself satisfied with the progress so far.* **3 ~ sth** to belong to a particular religion: *to profess Christianity/Islam/Judaism*

pro·fessed /prəˈfest/ *adj.* [only before noun] (*formal*) **1** used to describe a belief or a position that sb has publicly made known: *a professed Christian/anarchist* **2** used to describe a feeling or an attitude that sb says they have but which may not be sincere: *These, at least, were their professed reasons for pulling out of the deal.*

pro·fes·sion 0-ᴡ /prəˈfeʃn/ *noun* **1** 0-ᴡ [C] a type of job that needs special training or skill, especially one that needs a high level of education: *the **medical/legal/teaching, etc. profession*** ◇ *to **enter/go into/join a profession*** ◇ (*BrE*) *the **caring professions*** (= that involve looking after people) ◇ *He was an electrician **by profession**.* ◇ *She was at the very top of her profession.* ➲ SYNONYMS at WORK ➲ COLLOCATIONS at JOB **2** 0-ᴡ **the profession** [sing.+ sing./pl. v.] all the people who work in a particular type of profession: *The legal profession has/have always resisted change.* **3 the professions** [pl.] the

P

traditional jobs that need a high level of education and training, such as being a doctor or a lawyer: *employment in industry and the professions* **4** [C] **~ of sth** a statement about what you believe, feel or think about sth, that is sometimes made publicly SYN **declaration**: *a profession of faith*

pro·fes·sion·al 0-w AW /prəˈfeʃənl/ *adj., noun*
■ ***adj.*** **1** 0-w [only before noun] connected with a job that needs special training or skill, especially one that needs a high level of education: *professional qualifications/skills* ◇ *professional standards/practice* ◇ *an opportunity for professional development* ◇ *If it's a legal matter you need* ***to seek professional advice.*** **2** 0-w (of people) having a job which needs special training and a high level of education: *Most of the people on the course were professional women.* **3** 0-w showing that sb is well trained and extremely skilled SYN **competent**: *He dealt with the problem in a highly professional way.* OPP **amateur** **4** 0-w suitable or appropriate for sb working in a particular profession: ***professional conduct/misconduct*** OPP **unprofessional** **5** 0-w doing sth as a paid job rather than as a hobby: *a professional golfer* ◇ *After he won the amateur championship he* ***turned professional.*** OPP **amateur** **6** 0-w (of sport) done as a paid job rather than as a hobby: *the world of professional football* OPP **amateur** ➲ compare NON-PROFESSIONAL
■ ***noun*** **1** 0-w a person who does a job that needs special training and a high level of education: *the terms that doctors and other health professionals use* **2** 0-w (also *informal* **pro**) a person who does a sport or other activity as a paid job rather than as a hobby: *a top golf professional* OPP **amateur** **3** 0-w (also *informal* **pro**) a person who has a lot of skill and experience: *This was clearly a job for a real professional.* OPP **amateur**

pro,fessional de'velopment day *noun* (*especially CanE*) a day on which classes at schools are cancelled so that teachers can get further training in their subjects

pro,fessional 'foul *noun* (*BrE*) (in sport, especially football (SOCCER)) a rule that sb breaks deliberately so that their team can gain an advantage, especially to prevent a player from the other team from scoring a goal

P

pro·fes·sion·al·ism AW /prəˈfeʃənəlɪzəm/ *noun* [U] **1** the high standard that you expect from a person who is well trained in a particular job: *We were impressed by the professionalism of the staff.* **2** great skill and ability: *the power and professionalism of her performance* **3** the practice of using professional players in sport: *Increased professionalism has changed the game radically.*

pro·fes·sion·al·ize (*BrE* also **-ise**) /prəˈfeʃənəlaɪz/ *verb* [usually passive] **~ sth** to make an activity more professional, for example by paying people who take part in it ▸ **pro·fes·sion·al·iza·tion, -isa·tion** /prə,feʃənəlaɪˈzeɪʃn/ *noun* [U]: *the increasing professionalization of sports*

pro·fes·sion·al·ly AW /prəˈfeʃənəli/ *adv.* **1** in a way that is connected with a person's job or training: *You need a complete change, both professionally and personally.* **2** in a way that shows skill and experience: *The product has been marketed very professionally.* **3** by a person who has the right skills and qualifications: *The burglar alarm should be professionally installed.* **4** as a paid job, not as a hobby: *After the injury, he never played professionally again.*

pro·fes·sor 0-w /prəˈfesə(r)/ (also *informal* **prof**) *noun* (*abbr.* **Prof.**)
1 0-w (*especially BrE*) (*NAmE* **'full professor**) a university teacher of the highest rank: *Professor (Ann) Williams* ◇ *a chemistry professor* ◇ *to be appointed Professor of French at Cambridge* ◇ *He was made (a) professor at the age of 40.* HELP **Full professor** is used to describe a rank of university teacher, and not as a title. **2** 0-w (*NAmE*) a teacher at a university or college ➲ compare ASSISTANT PROFESSOR, ASSOCIATE PROFESSOR

pro·fes·sor·ial /,prɒfəˈsɔːriəl; *NAmE* ,prɑːf-/ *adj.* connected with a professor; like a professor: *professorial duties* ◇ *His tone was almost professorial.*

pro·fes·sor·ship /prəˈfesəʃɪp; *NAmE* -sərʃ-/ *noun* the rank or position of a university professor: *a visiting professorship* ◇ *She was appointed to a professorship in Economics at Princeton.*

prof·fer /ˈprɒfə(r); *NAmE* ˈprɑːf-/ *verb* (*formal*) **1** **~ sth (to sb)** | **~ sb sth** to offer sth to sb, by holding it out to them: *'Try this,' she said, proffering a plate.* **2** to offer sth such as advice or an explanation: **~ sth (to sb)** *What advice would you proffer to someone starting up in business?* ◇ **~ sb sth** *What advice would you proffer her?* ◇ **~ itself** *A solution proffered itself.*

pro·fi·cient /prəˈfɪʃnt/ *adj.* able to do sth well because of training and practice: *I'm a reasonably proficient driver.* ◇ **~ in sth/in doing sth** *She's proficient in several languages.* ◇ **~ at sth/at doing sth** *He's proficient at his job.* ▸ **pro·fi·ciency** /-nsi/ *noun* [U]: *to develop proficiency* ◇ *a certificate of language proficiency* ◇ **~ in sth/in doing sth** *a high level of oral proficiency in English*

pro·file /ˈprəʊfaɪl; *NAmE* ˈproʊ-/ *noun, verb*
■ ***noun*** **1** the outline of a person's face when you look from the side, not the front: *his strong profile* ◇ *a picture of the president* ***in profile*** **2** a description of sb/sth that gives useful information: *a* ***job/employee profile*** ◇ *We first build up a detailed profile of our customers and their requirements.* ◇ *You can update your Facebook profile* (= your description of yourself on a SOCIAL NETWORKING website). **3** the general impression that sb/sth gives to the public and the amount of attention they receive: *The deal will certainly raise the company's international profile.* **4** the edge or outline of sth that you see against a background: *the profile of the tower against the sky*
IDM **a ,high/,low 'profile** the amount of attention sb/sth has from the public: *This issue has had a high profile in recent months.* ◇ *I advised her to* ***keep a low profile*** *for the next few days* (= not to attract attention).
■ ***verb*** **~ sb/sth** to give or write a description of sb/sth that gives the most important information: *His career is profiled in this month's journal.*

pro·fil·ing /ˈprəʊfaɪlɪŋ; *NAmE* ˈproʊ-/ *noun* [U] the act of collecting useful information about sb/sth so that you can give a description of them or it: *customer profiling* ◇ *offender profiling* ➲ see also RACIAL PROFILING ▸ **pro·fil·er** /ˈprəʊfaɪlə(r); *NAmE* ˈproʊ-/ *noun*

profit 0-w /ˈprɒfɪt; *NAmE* ˈprɑːfɪt/ *noun, verb*
■ ***noun*** **1** 0-w [C, U] the money that you make in business or by selling things, especially after paying the costs involved: *a rise/an increase/a drop/a fall in profits* ◇ **~ (on sth)** *The company* ***made a*** *healthy* ***profit*** *on the deal.* ◇ **~ (from sth)** *Profit from exports rose 7.3%* ◇ ***Net profit*** (= after you have paid costs and tax) *was up 16.1%.* ◇ *The sale generated* ***record profits.*** ◇ *We should be able to sell the house* ***at a profit.*** ◇ *The agency is voluntary and not run* ***for profit.*** OPP **loss** ➲ COLLOCATIONS at BUSINESS **2** [U] (*formal*) the advantage that you get from doing sth: *Future lawyers could study this text with profit.*
■ ***verb*** [I, T] (*formal*) to get sth useful from a situation; to be useful to sb or give them an advantage: **~ (from sth)** *Farmers are profiting from the new legislation.* ◇ **~ (by sth)** *We tried to profit by our mistakes* (= learn from them). ◇ **~ sth** *Many local people believe the development will profit them.*

prof·it·able /ˈprɒfɪtəbl; *NAmE* ˈprɑːf-/ *adj.* **1** that makes or is likely to make money: *a highly profitable business* ◇ *It is usually more profitable to sell direct to the public.* ➲ SYNONYMS at SUCCESSFUL **2** that gives sb an advantage or a useful result SYN **rewarding**: *She spent a profitable afternoon in the library.* ▸ **prof·it·abil·ity** /,prɒfɪtəˈbɪləti; *NAmE* ,prɑːf-/ *noun* [U]: *to increase profitability* **prof·it·ably** /-əbli/ *adv.*: *to run a business profitably* ◇ *He spent the weekend profitably.*

,profit and 'loss account *noun* (*business*) a list that shows the amount of money that a company has earned and the total profit or loss that it has made in a particular period of time

prof·it·eer·ing /,prɒfɪˈtɪərɪŋ; *NAmE* ,prɑːfəˈtɪr-/ *noun* [U] (*disapproving*) the act of making a lot of money in an unfair way, for example by asking very high prices for things that are hard to get ▶ **prof·it·eer** *noun*

pro·fit·er·ole /prəˈfɪtərəʊl; *NAmE* -roʊl/ (*especially BrE*) (*NAmE* usually ˌ**cream ˈpuff**) *noun* a small cake in the shape of a ball, made of light PASTRY, filled with cream and usually with chocolate on top

prof·it·less /ˈprɒfɪtləs; *NAmE* ˈprɑːf-/ *adj.* (*formal*) producing no PROFIT or useful result

ˈ**profit-making** *adj.* [usually before noun] (of a company or a business) that makes or will make a profit

ˈ**profit margin** (also **margin**) *noun* (*business*) the difference between the cost of buying or producing sth and the price that it is sold for

ˈ**profit-sharing** *noun* [U] the system of dividing all or some of a company's profits among its employees

ˈ**profit-taking** *noun* [U] (*business*) the sale of shares in companies whose value has increased

prof·li·gate /ˈprɒflɪɡət; *NAmE* ˈprɑːf-/ *adj.* (*formal, disapproving*) using money, time, materials, etc. in a careless way SYN **wasteful**: *profligate spending* ▶ **prof·li·gacy** /ˈprɒflɪɡəsi; *NAmE* ˈprɑːf-/ *noun* [U]

ˈ**pro-form** *noun* (*grammar*) a word that depends on another part of the sentence or text for its meaning, for example 'her' in 'I like Ruth but I don't love her.'

pro forma /ˌprəʊ ˈfɔːmə; *NAmE* ˌproʊ ˈfɔːrmə/ *adj.* (from *Latin*) [usually before noun] **1** (especially of a document) prepared in order to show the usual way of doing sth or to provide a standard method: *a pro forma letter* ◇ *pro forma instructions* **2** (of a document) sent in advance: *a pro forma invoice* (= a document that gives details of the goods being sent to a customer) **3** done because it is part of the usual way of doing sth, although it has no real meaning: *a pro forma debate* ▶ **pro forma** *noun*: *I enclose a pro forma for you to complete, sign and return.*

pro·found /prəˈfaʊnd/ *adj.* **1** very great; felt or experienced very strongly: *profound changes in the earth's climate* ◇ *My father's death had a profound effect on us all.* **2** showing great knowledge or understanding: *profound insights* ◇ *a profound book* **3** needing a lot of study or thought: *profound questions about life and death* **4** (*medical*) very serious; complete: *profound disability*

pro·found·ly /prəˈfaʊndli/ *adv.* **1** in a way that has a very great effect on sb/sth: *We are profoundly affected by what happens to us in childhood.* **2** (*medical*) very seriously; completely: *profoundly deaf*

pro·fund·ity /prəˈfʌndəti/ *noun* (*pl.* -ies) (*formal*) **1** [U] the quality of understanding or dealing with a subject at a very serious level SYN **depth**: *He lacked profundity and analytical precision.* **2** [U] the quality of being very great, serious or powerful: *the profundity of her misery* **3** [C, usually pl.] something that sb says that shows great understanding: *His profundities were lost on the young audience.*

pro·fuse /prəˈfjuːs/ *adj.* produced in large amounts: *profuse apologies/thanks* ◇ *profuse bleeding* ▶ **pro·fuse·ly** *adv.*: *to bleed profusely* ◇ *to apologize profusely*

pro·fu·sion /prəˈfjuːʒn/ *noun* [sing.+ sing./pl. v., U] (*formal* or *literary*) a very large quantity of sth SYN **abundance**: *a profusion of colours* ◇ *Roses grew* ***in profusion*** *against the old wall.*

pro·geni·tor /prəʊˈdʒenɪtə(r); *NAmE* proʊ-/ *noun* (*formal*) **1** a person or thing from the past that a person, animal or plant that is alive now is related to SYN **ancestor**: *He was the progenitor of a family of distinguished actors.* **2** a person who starts an idea or a development: *the progenitors of modern art*

pro·geny /ˈprɒdʒəni; *NAmE* ˈprɑːdʒ-/ *noun* [pl.] (*formal* or *humorous*) a person's children; the young of animals and plants: *He was surrounded by his numerous progeny.*

pro·ges·ter·one /prəˈdʒestərəʊn; *NAmE* -roʊn/ *noun* [U] a HORMONE produced in the bodies of women and female animals which prepares the body to become pregnant and is also used in CONTRACEPTION ➲ compare OESTROGEN, TESTOSTERONE

prog·no·sis /prɒɡˈnəʊsɪs; *NAmE* prɑːɡˈnoʊ-/ *noun* (*pl.* **prog·no·ses** /-siːz/) **1** (*medical*) an opinion, based on medical experience, of the likely development of a disease or an illness **2** (*formal*) a judgement about how sth is likely to develop in the future SYN **forecast**: *The prognosis is for more people to work part-time in the future.* ▶ **prog·nos·tic** /prɒɡˈnɒstɪk; *NAmE* prɑːɡˈnɑːs-/ *adj.*

prog·nos·ti·ca·tion /prɒɡˌnɒstɪˈkeɪʃn; *NAmE* prɑːɡˌnɑːs-/ *noun* (*formal*) a thing that sb says will happen in the future: *gloomy prognostications*

pro·gram 0‑w /ˈprəʊɡræm; *NAmE* ˈproʊ-/ *noun, verb*

■ ***noun*** **1** 0‑w (*computing*) a set of instructions in CODE that control the operations or functions of a computer: *Load the program into the computer.* **2** 0‑w (*NAmE*) = PROGRAMME: *an intense training program* ◇ *the university's graduate programs* ◇ *a TV program*

■ ***verb*** (-mm-, *NAmE* also -m-) **1** 0‑w [I, T] (*computing*) to give a computer, etc. a set of instructions to make it perform a particular task: *In this class, students will learn how to program.* ◇ **~ sth (to do sth)** *The computer is programmed to warn users before information is deleted.* ➲ compare PROGRAMME **2** 0‑w (*NAmE*) = PROGRAMME

pro·gram·mable /ˈprəʊɡræməbl; prəʊˈɡræm-; *NAmE* ˈproʊ-; proʊˈɡ-/ *adj.* (of a computer or electrical device) able to accept instructions that control how it operates or functions

pro·gram·mat·ic /ˌprəʊɡrəˈmætɪk; *NAmE* ˌproʊ-/ *adj.* [usually before noun] (*formal*) connected with, suggesting or following a plan: *programmatic reforms*

pro·gramme 0‑w (*BrE*) (*NAmE* **pro·gram**) /ˈprəʊɡræm; *NAmE* ˈproʊ-/ *noun, verb*

■ ***noun***

▸ PLAN **1** 0‑w a plan of things that will be done or included in the development of sth: *to launch a research programme* ◇ *a training programme for new staff* ◇ *a programme of economic reform*

▸ ON TV/RADIO **2** 0‑w something that people watch on television or listen to on the radio: *a news programme* ◇ *Did you see that programme on India last night?* ➲ COLLOCATIONS at TELEVISION

▸ FOR PLAY/CONCERT **3** 0‑w a thin book or a piece of paper that gives you information about a play, a concert, etc: *a theatre programme*

▸ ORDER OF EVENTS **4** 0‑w an organized order of performances or events SYN **line-up**: *an exciting musical programme* ◇ *a week-long programme of lectures* ◇ *What's the programme for* (= what are we going to do) *tomorrow?*

▸ COURSE OF STUDY **5** (*NAmE*) a course of study: *a school programme* ➲ note at COURSE

▸ OF MACHINE **6** a series of actions done by a machine, such as a WASHING MACHINE: *Select a cool programme for woollen clothes.*

IDM **get with the ˈprogramme** (*BrE*) (*NAmE* **get with the ˈprogram**) (*informal*) (usually in orders) used to tell sb that they should change their attitude and do what they are supposed to be doing

■ ***verb*** [usually passive]

▸ PLAN **1** 0‑w **~ sth (for sth)** to plan for sth to happen, especially as part of a series of planned events: *The final section of road is programmed for completion next month.*

▸ PERSON/ANIMAL **2** 0‑w **~ sb/sth to do sth** to make a person, an animal, etc. behave in a particular way, so that it happens automatically: *Human beings are genetically programmed to learn certain kinds of language.*

▸ MACHINE **3** **~ sth (to do sth)** to give a machine instructions to do a particular task: *She programmed the VCR to come on at eight.*

ˌ**programmed ˈlearning** *noun* [U] a method of study in which a subject is divided into very small parts and the student must be successful in one part before he or she can go on to the next

pro·gram·mer /ˈprəʊɡræmə(r); *NAmE* ˈproʊ-/ *noun* a person whose job is writing programs for computers

P

pro·gram·ming /ˈprəʊɡræmɪŋ; *NAmE* ˈproʊ-/ *noun* [U] **1** the process of writing and testing programs for computers: *a high-level programming language* **2** the planning of which television or radio programmes to broadcast: *politically balanced programming*

pro·gress 🗝 *noun, verb*

■ ***noun*** /ˈprəʊɡres; *NAmE* ˈprɑːɡ-; -ɡrəs/ [U] **1** 🗝 the process of improving or developing, or of getting nearer to achieving or completing sth: *to* ***make progress*** ◇ ***slow/steady/rapid/good progress*** ◇ *We have made great progress in controlling inflation.* ◇ ***economic/scientific/technical progress*** ◇ *They asked for* ***a progress report*** *on the project.* **2** movement forwards or towards a place: *She watched his slow progress down the steep slope.* ◇ *There wasn't much traffic so we made good progress.*

IDM **in progress** 🗝 (*formal*) happening at this time: *Work on the new offices is now in progress.* ◇ *Please be quiet—examination in progress.*

■ ***verb*** /prəˈɡres/ **1** 🗝 [I] to improve or develop over a period of time; to make progress SYN **advance**: *The course allows students to progress at their own speed.* ◇ *Work on the new road is progressing slowly.* **2** 🗝 [I] **+ adv./prep.** (*formal*) to move forward: *The line of traffic progressed slowly through the town.* ◇ (*figurative*) *Cases can take months to progress through the courts.* **3** [I] to go forward in time SYN **go on**: *The weather became colder as the day progressed.*

PHR V **proˈgress to sth** to move on from doing one thing to doing sth else: *She started off playing the recorder and then progressed to the clarinet.*

pro·gres·sion /prəˈɡreʃn/ *noun* **1** [U, C] the process of developing gradually from one stage or state to another: *opportunities for career progression* ◇ *the rapid progression of the disease* ◇ **~ (from sth) (to sth)** *a natural progression from childhood to adolescence* **2** [C] a number of things that come in a series ➲ see also ARITHMETIC PROGRESSION, GEOMETRIC PROGRESSION

pro·gres·sive /prəˈɡresɪv/ *adj., noun*

■ ***adj.*** **1** in favour of new ideas, modern methods and change: *progressive schools* OPP **retrogressive** **2** happening or developing steadily: *a progressive reduction in the size of the workforce* ◇ *a progressive muscular disease* **3** (also **con·tinu·ous**) (*grammar*) connected with the form of a verb (for example *I am waiting* or *It is raining*) that is made from a part of *be* and the present participle. Progressive forms are used to express an action that continues for a period of time. ▶ **pro·gres·siv·ism** *noun* [U]: *political progressivism*

■ ***noun*** [usually pl.] a person who is in favour of new ideas, modern methods and change: *political battles between progressives and conservatives*

pro·gres·sive·ly /prəˈɡresɪvli/ *adv.* (often with a comparative) steadily and continuously: *The situation was becoming progressively more difficult.* ◇ *The pain got progressively worse.*

prog rock /ˌprɒɡ ˈrɒk; *NAmE* ˌprɑːɡ ˈrɑːk/ (also **proˌgressive ˈrock**) *noun* [U] a style of rock music that includes elements of other kinds of music, including JAZZ

pro·hibit AW /prəˈhɪbɪt; *NAmE* also proʊˈh-/ *verb* (*formal*) **1** [often passive] to stop sth from being done or used especially by law SYN **forbid**: **~ sth** *a law prohibiting the sale of alcohol* ◇ **~ sb from doing sth** *Soviet citizens were prohibited from travelling abroad.* ◇ **~ (sb) doing sth** *The policy prohibits smoking on school grounds.* **2 ~ sth / sb from doing sth** to make sth impossible to do SYN **prevent**: *The high cost of equipment prohibits many people from taking up this sport.*

pro·hib·ition AW /ˌprəʊɪˈbɪʃn; *NAmE* ˌproʊəˈb-/ *noun* **1** [U] (*formal*) the act of stopping sth being done or used, especially by law: *the prohibition of smoking in public areas* **2** [C] **~ (against/on sth)** (*formal*) a law or a rule that stops sth being done or used: *a prohibition against selling alcohol to people under the age of 18* **3 Prohibition** [U] (in the US) the period of time from 1920 to 1933 when it was illegal to make and sell alcoholic drinks

pro·hib·ition·ist /ˌprəʊɪˈbɪʃənɪst; *NAmE* ˌproʊəˈb-/ *noun* a person who supports the act of making sth illegal, especially the sale of alcoholic drinks

pro·hibi·tive AW /prəˈhɪbətɪv; *NAmE* also proʊˈh-/ *adj.* **1** (of a price or a cost) so high that it prevents people from buying sth or doing sth SYN **exorbitant**: *prohibitive costs* ◇ *The price of property in the city is prohibitive.* **2** preventing people from doing sth by law: *prohibitive legislation* **3** (*NAmE*) (of a person taking part in an election or a competition) extremely likely to win: *Miami began the day a prohibitive Super Bowl favorite.* ▶ **pro·hibi·tive·ly** *adv.*: *Car insurance can be prohibitively expensive for young drivers.*

pro·ject 🗝 AW *noun, verb*

■ ***noun*** /ˈprɒdʒekt; *NAmE* ˈprɑːdʒ-/

▸ PLANNED WORK **1** 🗝 a planned piece of work that is designed to find information about sth, to produce sth new, or to improve sth: *a research project* ◇ *a building project* ◇ *to set up a project to computerize the library system*

▸ SCHOOL/COLLEGE WORK **2** 🗝 a piece of work involving careful study of a subject over a period of time, done by school or college students: *a history project* ◇ *The final term will be devoted to project work.*

▸ SET OF AIMS/ACTIVITIES **3** a set of aims, ideas or activities that sb is interested in or wants to bring to people's attention: *The party attempted to assemble its aims into a focussed political project.*

▸ HOUSING **4** (*NAmE*) = HOUSING PROJECT: *Going into the projects alone is dangerous.*

■ ***verb*** /prəˈdʒekt/

▸ PLAN **1** 🗝 [T, usually passive] **~ sth** to plan an activity, a project etc. for a time in the future: *The next edition of the book is projected for publication in March.* ◇ *The projected housing development will go ahead next year.*

▸ ESTIMATE **2** 🗝 [T, usually passive] to estimate what the size, cost or amount of sth will be in the future based on what is happening now SYN **forecast**: **~ sth** *A growth rate of 4% is projected for next year.* ◇ **~ sth to do sth** *The unemployment rate has been projected to fall.* HELP This pattern is usually used in the passive.: **it is projected that...** *It is projected that the unemployment rate will fall.*

▸ LIGHT/IMAGE **3** 🗝 [T] **~ sth (on/onto sth)** to make light, an image, etc. fall onto a flat surface or screen: *Images are projected onto the retina of the eye.*

▸ STICK OUT **4** [I] **+ adv./prep.** to stick out beyond an edge or a surface SYN **protrude**: *a building with balconies projecting out over the street*

▸ PRESENT YOURSELF **5** [T] to present sb/sth/yourself to other people in a particular way, especially one that gives a good impression: **~ sth** *They sought advice on how to project a more positive image of their company.* ◇ *She projects an air of calm self-confidence.* ◇ **~ sb/sth/yourself (as sb/sth)** *He projected himself as a man worth listening to.*

▸ SEND/THROW UP OR AWAY **6** [T] **~ sth/sb (+ adv./prep.)** to send or throw sth up or away from yourself: *Actors must learn to project their voices.* ◇ (*figurative*) *the powerful men who would project him into the White House*

PHR V **proˈject sth onto sb** (*psychology*) to imagine that other people have the same feelings, problems, etc. as you, especially when this is not true

pro·ject·ile /prəˈdʒektaɪl; *NAmE* -tl/ *noun, adj.*

■ ***noun*** (*formal* or *technical*) **1** an object, such as a bullet, that is fired from a gun or other weapon **2** any object that is thrown as a weapon

■ ***adj.*** (*formal* or *technical*) very fast and with a lot of force: *projectile motion* ◇ *The virus causes projectile* (= sudden and violent) *vomiting.*

pro·jec·tion AW /prəˈdʒekʃn/ *noun*

▸ ESTIMATE **1** [C] an estimate or a statement of what figures, amounts, or events will be in the future, or what they were in the past, based on what is happening now: *to make* ***forward/backward projections*** *of population figures* ◇ *Sales have exceeded our projections.*

▸ OF IMAGE **2** [U, C] the act of putting an image of sth onto a surface; an image that is shown in this way: *the projection of three-dimensional images on a computer screen* ◇ *laser projections*

P

▸ OF SOLID SHAPE **3** [C] (*technical*) a solid shape or object as represented on a flat surface: *map projections*
▸ STH THAT STICKS OUT **4** [C] something that sticks out from a surface: *tiny projections on the cell*
▸ OF VOICE/SOUND **5** [U] the act of making your voice, a sound, etc. AUDIBLE (= able to be heard) at a distance: *voice projection*
▸ PSYCHOLOGY **6** [U] the act of imagining that sb else is thinking the same as you and is reacting in the same way
▸ OF THOUGHTS/FEELINGS **7** [C, U] the act of giving a form and structure to inner thoughts and feelings: *The idea of God is a projection of humans' need to have something greater than themselves.*

pro·jec·tion·ist /prə'dʒekʃənɪst/ *noun* a person whose job is to show films/movies by operating a PROJECTOR

pro·ject·or /prə'dʒektə(r)/ *noun* a piece of equipment for projecting photographs, films/movies or computer SLIDES onto a screen ➲ see also DATA PROJECTOR ➲ VISUAL VOCAB pages V56, V57 ➲ see also OVERHEAD PROJECTOR, SLIDE PROJECTOR

pro·lapse /'prəʊlæps; *NAmE* 'proʊ-/ *noun* (*medical*) a condition in which an organ of the body has slipped forward or down from its normal position

prole /prəʊl; *NAmE* proʊl/ *noun* (*old-fashioned, BrE, informal*) an offensive word for a WORKING CLASS person

pro·le·tar·ian /ˌprəʊlə'teəriən; *NAmE* ˌproʊlə'ter-/ *adj.* connected with ordinary people who earn money by working, especially those who do not own any property ➲ compare BOURGEOIS ▸ **pro·le·tar·ian** *noun*

the pro·le·tar·iat /ˌprəʊlə'teəriət; *NAmE* ˌproʊlə'ter-/ *noun* [sing.+ sing./pl. v.] (*technical*) (used especially when talking about the past) the class of ordinary people who earn money by working, especially those who do not own any property ➲ compare BOURGEOISIE

ˌpro-'life *adj.* [usually before noun] opposed to ABORTION: *the pro-life movement* ◇ *a pro-life campaigner* ➲ compare PRO-CHOICE

pro·lif·er·ate /prə'lɪfəreɪt/ *verb* [I] to increase rapidly in number or amount SYN **multiply**: *Books and articles on the subject have proliferated over the last year.*

pro·lif·er·ation /prəˌlɪfə'reɪʃn/ *noun* [U, sing.] the sudden increase in the number or amount of sth; a large number of a particular thing: *attempts to prevent cancer cell proliferation* ◇ *a proliferation of personal computers*

pro·lif·ic /prə'lɪfɪk/ *adj.* **1** (of an artist, a writer, etc.) producing many works, etc: *a prolific author* ◇ *a prolific goal-scorer* ◇ *one of the most prolific periods in her career* **2** (of plants, animals, etc.) producing a lot of fruit, flowers, young, etc. **3** able to produce enough food, etc. to keep many animals and plants alive: *prolific rivers* **4** existing in large numbers: *a pop star with a prolific following of teenage fans* ▸ **pro·lif·ic·al·ly** *adv.*: *to write prolifically* ◇ *animals that breed prolifically*

pro·lix /'prəʊlɪks; *NAmE* 'proʊ-/ *adj.* (*formal*) (of writing, a speech, etc.) using too many words and therefore boring ▸ **pro·lix·ity** /prəʊ'lɪksəti; *NAmE* proʊ-/ *noun* [U]

pro·logue /'prəʊlɒg; *NAmE* 'proʊlɔːg; -lɑːg/ *noun* a speech, etc. at the beginning of a play, book, or film/movie that introduces it ➲ compare EPILOGUE

pro·long /prə'lɒŋ; *NAmE* -'lɔːŋ; -'lɑːŋ/ *verb* **~ sth** to make sth last longer SYN **extend**: *The operation could prolong his life by two or three years.* ◇ *Don't* ***prolong the agony*** (= of not knowing sth) *—just tell us who won!*

pro·longa·tion /ˌprəʊlɒŋ'geɪʃn; *NAmE* ˌproʊlɔːŋ-/ *noun* [U, sing.] (*formal*) the act of making sth last longer: *the artificial prolongation of human life*

pro·longed /prə'lɒŋd; *NAmE* -'lɔːŋd; -'lɑːŋd/ *adj.* continuing for a long time: *a prolonged illness* ◇ *a prolonged period of dry weather*

prom /prɒm; *NAmE* prɑːm/ *noun* **1** (especially in the US) a formal dance, especially one that is held at a HIGH SCHOOL: *the senior prom* **2** (*BrE, informal*, becoming *old-fashioned*) = PROMENADE *n.* (1): *to walk along the prom* **3** (*BrE*) = PROMENADE CONCERT: *the last night of the proms*

prom·en·ade /ˌprɒmə'nɑːd; *NAmE* ˌprɑːmə'neɪd/ *noun, verb*
■ ***noun*** **1** (also *informal* **prom**) (both *BrE*, becoming *old-fashioned*) a public place for walking, usually a wide path beside the sea ➲ VISUAL VOCAB page V4 **2** (*old-fashioned*) a walk that you take for pleasure or exercise, especially by the sea, in a public park, etc.
■ ***verb*** [I] (*old-fashioned*) to walk up and down in a relaxed way, by the sea, in a public park, etc.

ˌpromenade 'concert (also *informal* **prom**) (both *BrE*) *noun* a concert at which many of the audience stand up or sit on the floor

Pro·me·thean /prə'miːθiən/ *adj.* doing things in an individual and original way and showing no respect for authority and rules ORIGIN From the Greek myth in which **Prometheus**, a Titan, stole fire from the gods and gave it to humans.

pro·me·thium /prə'miːθiəm/ *noun* [U] (*symb.* **Pm**) a chemical element. Promethium is a RADIOACTIVE metal that was first produced artificially in a nuclear REACTOR and is found in small amounts in nature.

prom·in·ence /'prɒmɪnəns; *NAmE* 'prɑːm-/ *noun* [U, sing.] the state of being important, well known or noticeable: *a young actor who has recently risen to prominence* ◇ *The newspapers have given undue prominence to the story.* ◇ *She has achieved a prominence she hardly deserves.*

prom·in·ent /'prɒmɪnənt; *NAmE* 'prɑːm-/ *adj.* **1** important or well known: *a prominent politician* ◇ *He* ***played a prominent part*** *in the campaign.* ◇ *She was prominent in the fashion industry.* **2** easily seen SYN **noticeable**: *The church tower was a prominent feature in the landscape.* ◇ *The story was given a prominent position on the front page.* **3** sticking out from sth: *a prominent nose* ◇ *prominent cheekbones* ▸ **prom·in·ent·ly** *adv.*: *The photographs were prominently displayed on her desk.* ◇ *Problems of family relationships feature prominently in her novels.*

pro·mis·cu·ous /prə'mɪskjuəs/ *adj.* (*disapproving*) **1** having many sexual partners: *promiscuous behaviour* ◇ *a promiscuous lifestyle* ◇ *to be sexually promiscuous* **2** (*formal*) taken from a wide range of sources, especially without careful thought: *promiscuous reading* ◇ *a stylistically promiscuous piece of music* ▸ **prom·is·cu·ity** /ˌprɒmɪs'kjuːəti; *NAmE* ˌprɑːməs-/ *noun* [U]: *sexual promiscuity* **prom·is·cu·ous·ly** *adv.*

P

prom·ise 0⊷ /'prɒmɪs; *NAmE* 'prɑːm-/ *verb, noun*
■ ***verb*** **1** 0⊷ [I, T] to tell sb that you will definitely do or not do sth, or that sth will definitely happen: **~** (**to do sth**) *The college principal promised to look into the matter.* ◇ *'Promise not to tell anyone!' 'I promise.'* ◇ *They arrived at 7.30* ***as they had promised.*** ◇ **~ sth** *The government has promised a full investigation into the disaster.* ◇ *I'll see what I can do but* ***I can't promise anything.*** ◇ **~** (**that**)... *The brochure promised (that) the local food would be superb.* ◇ **~ sb** (**that**)... *You promised me (that) you'd be home early tonight.* ◇ **~ sth to sb** *He promised the money to his grandchildren.* ◇ **~ sb sth** *He promised his grandchildren the money.* ◇ **~ yourself sth** *I've promised myself some fun when the exams are over.* ◇ **~** (**sb**) **+ speech** *'I'll be back soon,' she promised.* **2** [T] to make sth seem likely to happen; to show signs of sth: **it promises to be sth** *It promises to be an exciting few days.* ◇ **~ sth** *There were dark clouds overhead promising rain.*
IDM **I** (**can**) **'promise you** (*informal*) used as a way of encouraging or warning sb about sth: *I can promise you, you'll have a wonderful time.* ◇ *If you don't take my advice, you'll regret it, I promise you.* **promise** (**sb**) **the 'earth/'moon/'world** (*informal*) to make promises that will be impossible to keep
■ ***noun*** **1** 0⊷ [C] a statement that tells sb that you will definitely do or not do sth: *to* ***make/keep/break a promise*** ◇ **~** (**to do sth**) *She kept her promise to visit her aunt regularly.* ◇ **~** (**of sth**) *The government failed to keep its promise of lower taxes.* ◇ **~** (**that...**) *Do I have your promise that you*

won't tell anyone about this? ◇ *You haven't gone back on your promise, have you?* IDM see LICK *n.* **2** [U] a sign that sb/sth will be successful SYN **potential**: *Her work* ***shows*** *great* ***promise***. ◇ *He failed to fulfil his* ***early promise***. ◇ *Their future was* ***full of promise***. **3** [U, sing.] **~ of sth** a sign, or a reason for hope that sth may happen, especially sth good: *The day dawned bright and clear, with the promise of warm, sunny weather.*

the ˌPromised ˈLand *noun* [sing.] a place or situation where you expect to be happy, safe, etc.

prom·is·ing /ˈprɒmɪsɪŋ; *NAmE* ˈprɑːm-/ *adj.* showing signs of being good or successful: *He was voted the most promising new actor for his part in the movie.* ◇ *The weather doesn't look very promising.* ▸ **prom·is·ing·ly** *adv.*: *The day began promisingly with bright sunshine.*

prom·is·sory note /ˈprɒmɪsəri nəʊt; *NAmE* ˈprɑːm-; noʊt/ *noun* (*technical*) a signed document containing a promise to pay a stated amount of money before a particular date

promo /ˈprəʊməʊ; *NAmE* ˈproʊmoʊ/ *adj.* [only before noun] (*informal*) connected with advertising (=PROMOTING) sb/sth, especially a new pop record: *a promo video* ▸ **promo** *noun* (*pl.* -os): *to make pop promos*

prom·on·tory /ˈprɒməntri; *NAmE* ˈprɑːməntɔːri/ *noun* (*pl.* -ies) a long narrow area of high land that goes out into the sea SYN **headland** ➲ VISUAL VOCAB page V4

pro·mote AW /prəˈməʊt; *NAmE* -ˈmoʊt/ *verb* **1** **~ sth** to help sth to happen or develop SYN **encourage**: *policies to promote economic growth* ◇ *a campaign to promote awareness of environmental issues* **2** to help sell a product, service, etc. or make it more popular by advertising it or offering it at a special price: **~ sth** *The band has gone on tour to promote their new album.* ◇ **~ sth as sth** *The area is being promoted as a tourist destination.* **3** [often passive] to move sb to a higher rank or more senior job: **~ sb** *She worked hard and was soon promoted.* ◇ **~ sb (from sth) (to sth)** *He has been promoted to sergeant.* OPP **demote** **4** **~ sth (from sth) (to sth)** to move a sports team from playing with one group of teams to playing in a better group: *They were promoted to the First Division last season.* OPP **relegate**

pro·moter AW /prəˈməʊtə(r); *NAmE* -ˈmoʊ-/ *noun* **1** a person or company that organizes or provides money for an artistic performance or a sporting event **2** **~ of sth** a person who tries to persuade others about the value or importance of sth SYN **champion**: *She became a leading promoter of European integration.*

pro·mo·tion AW /prəˈməʊʃn; *NAmE* -ˈmoʊʃn/ *noun*
1 [U, C] **~ (to sth)** a move to a more important job or rank in a company or an organization: *Her promotion to Sales Manager took everyone by surprise.* ◇ *The new job is a promotion for him.* ◇ *a job with excellent* ***promotion prospects*** ➲ COLLOCATIONS at JOB **2** [U] **~ (to sth)** a move by a sports team from playing in one group of teams to playing in a better group: *the team's promotion to the First Division* OPP **relegation** **3** [U, C] activities done in order to increase the sales of a product or service; a set of advertisements for a particular product or service: *Her job is mainly concerned with sales and promotion.* ◇ *We are doing a special promotion of Chilean wines.* ➲ see also CROSS-PROMOTION ➲ SYNONYMS at ADVERTISEMENT **4** [U] **~ of sth** (*formal*) activity that encourages people to believe in the value or importance of sth, or that helps sth to succeed: *a society for the promotion of religious tolerance*

pro·mo·tion·al /prəˈməʊʃənl; *NAmE* -ˈmoʊ-/ *adj.* connected with advertising: *promotional material*

prompt /prɒmpt; *NAmE* prɑːmpt/ *adj., verb, noun, adv.*
■ ***adj.*** **1** done without delay SYN **immediate**: *Prompt action was required as the fire spread.* ◇ *Prompt payment of the invoice would be appreciated.* **2** [not before noun] (of a person) acting without delay; arriving at the right time SYN **punctual**: *Please be prompt when attending these meetings.* ▸ **prompt·ness** *noun* [U]
■ ***verb*** **1** [T] to make sb decide to do sth; to cause sth to happen SYN **provoke**: **~ sth** *The discovery of the bomb prompted an increase in security.* ◇ *His speech prompted an angry outburst from a man in the crowd.* ◇ **~ sb to do sth** *The thought of her daughter's wedding day prompted her to lose some weight.* **2** [T] to encourage sb to speak by asking them questions or suggesting words that they could say: **~ sb** *She was too nervous to speak and had to be prompted.* ◇ **~ sb to do sth** (*computing*) *The program will prompt you to enter data where required.* ◇ **~ (sb) + speech** *'And then what happened?' he prompted.* **3** [T, I] **~ (sb)** to follow the text of a play and remind the actors what the words are if they forget their lines
■ ***noun*** **1** a word or words said to an actor, to remind them what to say next when they have forgotten **2** (*computing*) a sign on a computer screen that shows that the computer has finished doing sth and is ready for more instructions
■ ***adv.*** exactly at the time mentioned: *The meeting will begin at ten o'clock prompt.*

prompt·er /ˈprɒmptə(r); *NAmE* ˈprɑːm-/ *noun* a person who prompts actors in a play

prompt·ing /ˈprɒmptɪŋ; *NAmE* ˈprɑːm-/ *noun* [U] (also **promptings** [pl.]) an act of persuading sb to do sth: *He wrote the letter without further prompting.* ◇ *Never again would she listen to the promptings of her heart.*

prompt·ly /ˈprɒmptli; *NAmE* ˈprɑːm-/ *adv.*
1 without delay: *She deals with all the correspondence promptly and efficiently.* **2** exactly at the correct time or at the time mentioned SYN **punctually**: *They arrived promptly at two o'clock.* **3** (always used before the verb) immediately: *She read the letter and promptly burst into tears.*

pro·mul·gate /ˈprɒmlgeɪt; *NAmE* ˈprɑːm-/ *verb* (*formal*) **1** [usually passive] **~ sth** to spread an idea, a belief, etc. among many people **2** **~ sth** to announce a new law or system officially or publicly ▸ **pro·mul·ga·tion** /ˌprɒmlˈgeɪʃn; *NAmE* ˌprɑːm-/ *noun* [U]

prone /prəʊn; *NAmE* proʊn/ *adj.* **1** likely to suffer from sth or to do sth bad SYN **liable**: **~ to sth** *prone to injury* ◇ *Working without a break makes you more prone to error.* ◇ **~ to do sth** *Tired drivers were found to be particularly prone to ignore warning signs.* **2** **-prone** (in adjectives) likely to suffer or do the thing mentioned: *error-prone* ◇ *injury-prone* ➲ see also ACCIDENT-PRONE **3** (*formal*) lying flat with the front of your body touching the ground SYN **prostrate**: *The victim lay prone without moving.* ◇ *He was found lying in a prone position.* ➲ compare SUPINE ▸ **prone·ness** /ˈprəʊnnəs; *NAmE* ˈproʊn-/ *noun* [U]: *proneness to depression*

prong /prɒŋ; *NAmE* prɔːŋ/ *noun* **1** each of the two or more long pointed parts of a fork ➲ VISUAL VOCAB page V19 **2** each of the separate parts of an attack, argument, etc, that move towards a place, subject, etc. from different positions **3** **-pronged** (in adjectives) having the number or type of prongs mentioned: *a two-pronged fork* ◇ *a three-pronged attack*

pro·nom·inal /prəʊˈnɒmɪnl; *NAmE* proʊˈnɑːm-/ *adj.* (*grammar*) relating to a pronoun

pro·noun /ˈprəʊnaʊn; *NAmE* ˈproʊ-/ *noun* (*grammar*) a word that is used instead of a noun or noun phrase, for example *he, it, hers, me, them*, etc: *demonstrative/interrogative/possessive/relative pronouns* ➲ see also PERSONAL PRONOUN

pro·nounce /prəˈnaʊns/ *verb*
1 **~ sth** to make the sound of a word or letter in a particular way: *Very few people can pronounce my name correctly.* ◇ *The 'b' in lamb is not pronounced.* ➲ see also PRONUNCIATION, UNPRONOUNCEABLE **2** (*formal*) to say or give sth formally, officially or publicly: **~ sth** *to pronounce an opinion* ◇ *The judge will* ***pronounce sentence*** *today.* ◇ **~ sb/sth + noun** *She pronounced him the winner of the competition.* ◇ *I now pro-*

> **WORD FAMILY**
> **pronounce** *verb*
> **pronunciation** *noun*
> **unpronounceable** *adj.*
> **mispronounce** *verb*

nounce you man and wife (= in a marriage ceremony). ◇ **~ sb/sth + adj.** *She was pronounced dead on arrival at the hospital.* ◇ **~ sb/sth to be/have sth** *He pronounced the country to be in a state of war.* ◇ **~ that...** *She pronounced that an error had been made.* ◇ **+ speech** *'It's pneumonia,' he pronounced gravely.*

PHR V **pro'nounce for/against sb** (*law*) to give a judgement in court for or against sb: *The judge pronounced for* (= in favour of) *the defendant.* **pro'nounce on/upon sth** (*formal*) to state your opinion on sth, or give a decision about sth: *The minister will pronounce on further security measures later today.*

pro·nounce·able /prəˈnaʊnsəbl/ *adj.* (of sounds or words) that can be pronounced OPP **unpronounceable**

pro·nounced /prəˈnaʊnst/ *adj.* very noticeable, obvious or strongly expressed SYN **definite**: *He walked with a pronounced limp.* ◇ *She has very pronounced views on art.*

pro·nounce·ment /prəˈnaʊnsmənt/ *noun* **~ (on sth)** (*formal*) a formal public statement

pronto /ˈprɒntəʊ; *NAmE* ˈprɑːntoʊ/ *adv.* (*informal*) quickly; immediately: *I expect to see you back here, pronto!*

pro·nun·ci·ation 🔑 /prəˌnʌnsiˈeɪʃn/ *noun* **1** 🔑 [U, C] the way in which a language or a particular word or sound is pronounced: *a guide to English pronunciation* ◇ *There is more than one pronunciation of 'garage'.* **2** 🔑 [sing.] the way in which a particular person pronounces the words of a language: *Your pronunciation is excellent.*

proof 🔑 /pruːf/ *noun, adj., verb*

■ ***noun*** **1** 🔑 [U, C] information, documents, etc. that show that sth is true SYN **evidence**: ***positive/conclusive proof*** ◇ **~ of sth** *Can you provide any* ***proof of identity****?* ◇ *Keep the receipt as* ***proof of purchase****.* ◇ *These results are a further proof of his outstanding ability.* ◇ **~ that...** *There is no proof that the knife belonged to her.* **2** [U] the process of testing whether sth is true or a fact: *Is the claim capable of proof?* ➲ see also BURDEN OF PROOF **3** [C] (*mathematics*) a way of proving that a statement is true or that what you have calculated is correct **4** [C, usually pl.] a copy of printed material which is produced so that mistakes can be corrected: *She was checking the proofs of her latest novel.* **5** [U] a standard used to measure the strength of alcoholic drinks

IDM **the proof of the 'pudding (is in the 'eating)** (*saying*) you can only judge if sth is good or bad when you have tried it ➲ more at LIVING *adj.*

■ ***adj.*** **1 ~ against sth** (*formal*) that can resist the damaging or harmful effects of sth: *The sea wall was not proof against the strength of the waves.* **2** (in compounds) that can resist or protect against the thing mentioned: ***rainproof/windproof*** *clothing* ◇ *The car has childproof locks on the rear doors.* ◇ *an inflation-proof pension plan*

■ ***verb*** **1 ~ sth** to put a special substance on sth, especially cloth, to protect it against water, fire, etc: *proofed canvas* **2 ~ sth** to produce a test copy of a piece of printed work so that mistakes can be corrected: *colour proofing*

proof·read /ˈpruːfriːd/ *verb* (**proof·read, proof·read** /-red/) [T, I] **~ (sth)** to read and correct a piece of written or printed work: *Has this document been proofread?* ▸ **proof·read·er** *noun*: *to work as a proofreader for a publishing company*

prop /prɒp; *NAmE* prɑːp/ *noun, verb*

■ ***noun*** **1** a piece of wood, metal, etc. used to support sth or keep it in position: *Rescuers used props to stop the roof of the tunnel collapsing.* ◇ *a pit prop* (= one used in a coal mine) **2** a person or thing that gives help or support to sb/sth that is weak **3** [usually pl.] a small object used by actors during the performance of a play or in a film/movie: *He is responsible for all the stage props and lighting.* **4** (also **'prop forward**) (in RUGBY) a player on either side of the front row of a SCRUM

IDM **give props to sb** (*informal*) used to say that people should appreciate what sb has done because it is good: *I gotta give props to the bass player.* ORIGIN **Props** here means 'proper respect or recognition'.

■ ***verb*** (-pp-) to support an object by leaning it against sth, or putting sth under it etc; to support a person in the same way: **~ sth/sb/yourself (up) (against sth)** *He propped his bike against the wall.* ◇ *She propped herself up on one elbow.* ◇ *He lay propped against the pillows.* ◇ **~ sth + adj.** *The door was propped open.*

PHR V **ˌprop sth↔'up 1** to prevent sth from falling by putting sth under it to support it SYN **shore up 2** (often *disapproving*) to help sth that is having difficulties: *The government was accused of propping up declining industries.*

propa·ganda /ˌprɒpəˈɡændə; *NAmE* ˌprɑːpə-/ *noun* [U] (usually *disapproving*) ideas or statements that may be false or exaggerated and that are used in order to gain support for a political leader, party, etc: *enemy propaganda* ◇ *a propaganda campaign*

propa·gand·ist /ˌprɒpəˈɡændɪst; *NAmE* ˌprɑːpə-/ *noun* (*formal*, usually *disapproving*) a person who creates or spreads propaganda ▸ **propa·gand·ist** *adj.* [only before noun]: *a propagandist organization*

propa·gand·ize (*BrE* also **-ise**) /ˌprɒpəˈɡændaɪz; *NAmE* ˌprɑːpə-/ *verb* [I, T] **~ (sb/sth)** (*formal, disapproving*) to spread PROPAGANDA; to influence people using PROPAGANDA

propa·gate /ˈprɒpəɡeɪt; *NAmE* ˈprɑːp-/ *verb* **1** [T] **~ sth** (*formal*) to spread an idea, a belief or a piece of information among many people: *Television advertising propagates a false image of the ideal family.* **2** [T, I] **~ (sth)** (*technical*) to produce new plants from a parent plant: *The plant can be propagated from seed.* ◇ *Plants won't propagate in these conditions.* ▸ **propa·ga·tion** /ˌprɒpəˈɡeɪʃn; *NAmE* ˌprɑːp-/ *noun* [U]

prop·aga·tor /ˈprɒpəɡeɪtə(r); *NAmE* ˈprɑːp-/ *noun* a box for propagating plants in

pro·pane /ˈprəʊpeɪn; *NAmE* ˈproʊ-/ *noun* [U] a gas found in natural gas and PETROLEUM and used as a fuel for cooking and heating: *a propane gas cylinder*

pro·pel /prəˈpel/ *verb* (-ll-) [often passive] **1 ~ sth (+ adv./prep.)** to move, drive or push sth forward or in a particular direction: *mechanically propelled vehicles* ◇ *He succeeded in propelling the ball across the line.* **2 ~ sb + adv./prep.** to force sb to move in a particular direction or to get into a particular situation: *He was grabbed from behind and propelled through the door.* ◇ *Fury propelled her into action.* ➲ see also PROPULSION

pro·pel·lant /prəˈpelənt/ *noun* [C, U] **1** a gas that forces out the contents of an AEROSOL **2** a thing or substance that propels sth, for example the fuel that fires a ROCKET

pro·pel·ler /prəˈpelə(r)/ *noun* a device with two or more blades that turn quickly and cause a ship or an aircraft to move forward ➲ VISUAL VOCAB page V43

proˌpelling 'pencil *noun* a pencil with a LEAD that can be moved down for writing by turning or pushing the top of the pencil

pro·pen·sity /prəˈpensəti/ *noun* (*pl.* -ies) (*formal*) a tendency to a particular kind of behaviour SYN **inclination**: **~ (for sth/for doing sth)** *He showed a propensity for violence.* ◇ **~ (to do sth)** *She has a propensity to exaggerate.*

proper 🔑 /ˈprɒpə(r); *NAmE* ˈprɑːp-/ *adj.* **1** 🔑 [only before noun] (*especially BrE*) right, appropriate or correct; according to the rules: *We should have had a proper discussion before voting.* ◇ *Please follow the proper procedures for dealing with complaints.* ◇ *Nothing is in its proper place.* **2** 🔑 [only before noun] (*BrE, informal*) that you consider to be real and of a good enough standard: *Eat some proper food, not just toast and jam!* ◇ *When are you going to get a proper job?* **3** socially and morally acceptable: *It is* ***right and proper*** *that parents take responsibility for their children's attendance at school.* ◇ *The development was planned without proper regard to the interests of local people.* ◇ *He is always perfectly proper in his behaviour.* OPP **improper** ➲ see also PROPRIETY **4** [after noun] according to the most exact meaning of the word: *The celebrations proper always begin on the last stroke of midnight.* **5** [only before noun] (*BrE, informal*) complete: *We're in a proper mess now.* **6 ~ to sth** (*formal*) belonging to a particular type of thing; natural in a particular situ-

P

ation or place: *They should be treated with the dignity proper to all individuals created by God.*

IDM ˌ**good and 'proper** (*BrE, informal*) completely; thoroughly: *That's messed things up good and proper.*

ˌ**proper 'fraction** *noun* (*mathematics*) a FRACTION that is less than one, with the bottom number greater than the top number, for example ¼ or ⅝

prop·er·ly 0‑π /'prɒpəli; *NAmE* 'prɑːpərli/ *adv.* **1** 0‑π (*especially BrE*) in a way that is correct and/or appropriate: *How much money do we need to do the job properly?* ◇ *The television isn't working properly.* ◇ *Make sure the letter is properly addressed.* **2** 0‑π in a way that is socially or morally acceptable: *You acted perfectly properly in approaching me first.* ◇ *When will these kids learn to behave properly?* OPP **improperly** **3** really; in fact: *He had usurped powers that properly belonged to parliament.* ◇ *The subject is not, **properly speaking** (= really), a science.*

ˌ**proper 'noun** (also ˌ**proper 'name**) *noun* (*grammar*) a word that is the name of a person, a place, an institution, etc. and is written with a capital letter, for example *Tom, Mrs Jones, Rome, Texas, the Rhine, the White House* ➲ compare ABSTRACT NOUN, COMMON NOUN

prop·er·tied /'prɒpətid; *NAmE* 'prɑːpərtid/ *adj.* [only before noun] (*formal*) owning property, especially land

prop·erty 0‑π /'prɒpəti; *NAmE* 'prɑːpərti/ *noun* (*pl.* -ies) **1** 0‑π [U] a thing or things that are owned by sb; a possession or possessions: *This building is government property.* ◇ *Be careful not to damage other people's property.* ➲ see also INTELLECTUAL PROPERTY, LOST PROPERTY, PUBLIC PROPERTY ➲ SYNONYMS at THING **2** 0‑π [U] land and buildings: *The price of property has risen enormously.* ◇ *property prices* ◇ *a property developer* ➲ SYNONYMS at BUILDING **3** 0‑π [C] a building or buildings and the surrounding land: *There are a lot of empty properties in the area.* ➲ SYNONYMS at BUILDING ➲ COLLOCATIONS at HOUSE **4** [C, usually pl.] (*formal*) a quality or characteristic that sth has: *Compare the physical properties of the two substances.* ◇ *a plant with medicinal properties*

P

proph·ecy /'prɒfəsi; *NAmE* 'prɑːf-/ *noun* (*pl.* -ies) **1** [C] a statement that sth will happen in the future, especially one made by sb with religious or magic powers: *to fulfil a prophecy* (= make it come true) **2** [U] (*formal*) the power of being able to say what will happen in the future: *She was believed to have the gift of prophecy.*

proph·esy /'prɒfəsaɪ; *NAmE* 'prɑːf-/ *verb* (**proph·es·ies, proph·esy·ing, proph·es·ied, proph·es·ied**) to say what will happen in the future (done in the past using religious or magic powers): **~ sth** *to prophesy war* ◇ **~ that...** *She prophesied that she would win a gold medal.* ◇ **+ speech** *'It will end in disaster,' he prophesied.*

prophet /'prɒfɪt; *NAmE* 'prɑːf-/ *noun* **1** [C] (in the Christian, Jewish and Muslim religions) a person sent by God to teach the people and give them messages from God **2 the Prophet** [sing.] Muhammad, who founded the religion of Islam **3** [C] a person who claims to know what will happen in the future **4** [C] **~ (of sth)** a person who teaches or supports a new idea, theory, etc: *William Morris was one of the early prophets of socialism.* **5 the Prophets** [pl.] the name used for some books of the Old Testament and the Hebrew Bible IDM see DOOM *n.*

proph·et·ess /'prɒfɪtes; ˌprɒfɪ'tes; *NAmE* 'prɑːfətəs/ *noun* a woman who is a prophet (1, 3, 4)

proph·et·ic /prə'fetɪk/ *adj.* (*formal*) **1** correctly stating or showing what will happen in the future: *Many of his warnings proved prophetic.* **2** like or connected with a prophet or prophets: *the prophetic books of the Old Testament* ▶ **proph·et·ic·al·ly** /prə'fetɪkli/ *adv.*

prophy·lac·tic /ˌprɒfɪ'læktɪk; *NAmE* ˌproʊfə'læktɪk/ *adj., noun*

■ **adj.** (*medical*) done or used in order to prevent a disease: *prophylactic treatment* ▶ **prophy·lac·tic·al·ly** /-kli/ *adv.*

■ **noun 1** (*medical*) a medicine, device or course of action that prevents disease **2** (*NAmE, formal*) = CONDOM

prophy·laxis /ˌprɒfɪ'læksɪs; *NAmE* ˌprɑːf-/ *noun* [U] (*medical*) action that is taken in order to prevent disease

pro·pin·quity /prə'pɪŋkwəti/ *noun* [U] (*formal*) the state of being near in space or time SYN **proximity**

pro·piti·ate /prə'pɪʃieɪt/ *verb* **~ sb** (*formal*) to stop sb from being angry by trying to please them SYN **placate**: *Sacrifices were made to propitiate the gods.* ▶ **pro·piti·ation** /prəˌpɪʃi'eɪʃn/ *noun* [U]

pro·piti·atory /prə'pɪʃiətri; *NAmE* -tɔːri/ *adj.* (*formal*) intended to win back the friendship and approval of an angry or aggressive person: *She saw the flowers as a propitiatory offering.*

pro·pi·tious /prə'pɪʃəs/ *adj.* **~ (for sth/sb)** (*formal*) likely to produce a successful result: *It was not a propitious time to start a new business.*

pro·pon·ent /prə'pəʊnənt; *NAmE* -'poʊ-/ *noun* **~ (of sth)** (*formal*) a person who supports an idea or course of action SYN **advocate**

pro·por·tion 0‑π AW /prə'pɔːʃn; *NAmE* -'pɔːrʃn/ *noun*

▸ PART OF WHOLE **1** 0‑π [C+sing./pl. v.] a part or share of a whole: *Water covers a large proportion of the earth's surface.* ◇ *Loam is a soil with roughly equal proportions of clay, sand and silt.* ◇ *The proportion of regular smokers increases with age.* ◇ *A higher proportion of Americans go on to higher education than is the case in Britain.*

▸ RELATIONSHIP **2** 0‑π [U] **~ (of sth to sth)** the relationship of one thing to another in size, amount, etc. SYN **ratio**: *The proportion of men to women in the college has changed dramatically over the years.* ◇ *The basic ingredients are limestone and clay in the proportion 2:1.* ◇ *The room is very long **in proportion to** (= relative to) its width.* **3** 0‑π [U, C, usually pl.] the correct relationship in size, degree, importance, etc. between one thing and another or between the parts of a whole: *You haven't drawn the figures in the foreground **in proportion**.* ◇ *The head is **out of proportion with** the body.* ◇ *an impressive building with fine proportions* ◇ *Always try to keep a **sense of proportion** (= of the relative importance of different things).*

▸ SIZE/SHAPE **4 proportions** [pl.] the measurements of sth; its size and shape: *This method divides the task into more manageable proportions.* ◇ *a food shortage that could soon **reach crisis proportions*** ◇ *a room of fairly generous proportions*

▸ MATHEMATICS **5** [U] the equal relationship between two pairs of numbers, as in the statement '4 is to 8 as 6 is to 12'

IDM ˌ**keep sth in pro'portion** to react to sth in a sensible way and not think it is worse or more serious than it really is **out of (all) pro'portion (to sth)** larger, more serious, etc. in relation to sth than is necessary or appropriate: *They earn salaries out of all proportion to their ability.* ◇ *The media have blown the incident up out of all proportion.*

Language Bank

proportion

Describing fractions and proportions

- According to this pie chart, **a third of** students' leisure time is spent watching TV.
- **One in five** hours is/are spent socializing.
- Socializing **accounts for/makes up/comprises** about 20% of leisure time.
- Students spend **twice as much** time playing computer games as doing sport.
- **Three times as many** hours are spent playing computer games as reading.
- The figure for playing computer games is **three times higher than** the figure for reading.
- **The largest proportion of** time is spent playing computer games.

➲ note at HALF

➲ Synonyms at CONSIST

➲ Language Banks at EXPECT, FALL, ILLUSTRATE, INCREASE

Grammar Point

proportion

- If **proportion** is used with an uncountable or a singular noun, the verb is generally singular: *A proportion of the land* **is** *used for agriculture.*
- If **the proportion of** is used with a plural countable noun, or a singular noun that represents a group of people, the verb is usually singular, but with **a (large, small, etc.) proportion of** a plural verb is often used, especially in *BrE*: *The proportion of small cars on America's roads* **is** *increasing.* ◇ *A high proportion of five-year-olds* **have** *teeth in poor condition.*

pro·por·tion·al AW /prəˈpɔːʃənl; *NAmE* -ˈpɔːrʃ-/ *adj.* **~ (to sth)** of an appropriate size, amount or degree in comparison with sth: *Salary is proportional to years of experience.* ◇ *to be* ***directly/inversely proportional*** *to sth* ▸ **pro·por·tion·al·ly** AW *adv.*: *Families with children spend proportionally less per person than families without children.*

pro·por·tion·al·ity /prəˌpɔːʃəˈnæləti; *NAmE* -pɔːrʃ-/ *noun* [U] (*formal*) the principle that an action, a punishment, etc. should not be more severe than is necessary

proˌportional ˌrepresenˈtation *noun* [U] (*abbr.* PR) a system that gives each party in an election a number of seats in relation to the number of votes its candidates receive ➲ compare FIRST-PAST-THE-POST

pro·por·tion·ate AW /prəˈpɔːʃənət; *NAmE* -ˈpɔːrʃ-/ *adj.* **~ (to sth)** (*formal*) increasing or decreasing in size, amount or degree according to changes in sth else SYN **proportional**: *The number of accidents is proportionate to the increased volume of traffic.* ➲ compare DISPROPORTIONATE ▸ **pro·por·tion·ate·ly** AW *adv.*: *Prices have risen but wages have not risen proportionately.*

pro·por·tioned /prəˈpɔːʃənd; *NAmE* -ˈpɔːrʃ-/ *adj.* (used especially after an adverb) having parts that relate in size to other parts in the way that is described: *a well-proportioned living room* ◇ *She was tall and perfectly proportioned.*

pro·posal 🔑 /prəˈpəʊzl; *NAmE* -ˈpoʊzl/ *noun* **1** 🔑 [C, U] a formal suggestion or plan; the act of making a suggestion: *to* ***submit/consider/accept/reject a proposal*** ◇ **~ to do sth** *a proposal to build more office accommodation* ◇ **~ that...** *His proposal that the system should be changed was rejected.* ◇ **~ for sth** *They judged that the time was right for the proposal of new terms for the trade agreement.* **2** 🔑 [C] an act of formally asking sb to marry you

pro·pose 🔑 /prəˈpəʊz; *NAmE* -ˈpoʊz/ *verb*
▸ SUGGEST PLAN **1** 🔑 [T] (*formal*) to suggest a plan, an idea, etc. for people to think about and decide on: **~ sth** *The government proposed changes to the voting system.* ◇ *What would you propose?* ◇ **~ that...** *She proposed that the book be banned.* ◇ (*BrE* also) *She proposed that the book should be banned.* ◇ **it is proposed that...** *It was proposed that the president be elected for a period of two years.* ◇ **~ doing sth** *He proposed changing the name of the company.* ◇ **it is proposed to do sth** *It was proposed to pay the money from public funds.*
▸ INTEND **2** 🔑 [T] (*formal*) to intend to do sth: **~ to do sth** *What do you propose to do now?* ◇ **~ doing sth** *How do you propose getting home?*
▸ MARRIAGE **3** 🔑 [I, T] to ask sb to marry you: *He was afraid that if he proposed she might refuse.* ◇ **~ to sb** *She proposed to me!* ◇ **~ sth (to sb)** *to propose marriage*
▸ AT FORMAL MEETING **4** [T] to suggest sth at a formal meeting and ask people to vote on it: **~ sb (for/as sth)** *I propose Tom Ellis for chairman.* ◇ **~ sth** *to* ***propose a motion*** (= to be the main speaker in support of an idea at a formal debate) ➲ compare OPPOSE, SECOND
▸ SUGGEST EXPLANATION **5** [T] **~ sth** (*formal*) to suggest an explanation of sth for people to consider SYN **propound**: *She proposed a possible solution to the mystery.*
IDM **propose a ˈtoast (to sb)** | **propose sb's ˈhealth** to ask people to wish sb health, happiness and success by raising their glasses and drinking: *I'd like to propose a toast to the bride and groom.*

pro·poser /prəˈpəʊzə(r); *NAmE* -ˈpoʊz-/ *noun* a person who formally suggests sth at a meeting ➲ compare SECONDER

prop·os·ition /ˌprɒpəˈzɪʃn; *NAmE* ˌprɑːp-/ *noun, verb*
■ ***noun*** **1** an idea or a plan of action that is suggested, especially in business: *I'd like to put a business proposition to you.* ◇ *He was trying to make it look like an* ***attractive proposition.*** **2** a thing that you intend to do; a problem or task to be dealt with SYN **matter**: *Getting a work permit in the UK is not always a simple proposition.* **3** (also **Proposition**) (in the US) a suggested change to the law that people can vote on: *How did you vote on Proposition 8?* **4** (*formal*) a statement that expresses an opinion: *Her assessment is based on the proposition that power corrupts.* **5** (*mathematics*) a statement of a THEOREM, and an explanation of how it can be proved ▸ **prop·os·ition·al** *adj.*
■ ***verb*** **~ sb** to say in a direct way to sb that you would like to have sex with them: *She was propositioned by a strange man in the bar.*

pro·pound /prəˈpaʊnd/ *verb* **~ sth** (*formal*) to suggest an idea or explanation of sth for people to consider SYN **propose, put forward**: *the theory of natural selection, first propounded by Charles Darwin*

pro·pri·etary /prəˈpraɪətri; *NAmE* -teri/ *adj.* [usually before noun] **1** (of goods) made and sold by a particular company and protected by a REGISTERED TRADEMARK: *a proprietary medicine* ◇ *proprietary brands* ◇ *a proprietary name* **2** relating to an owner or to the fact of owning sth: *The company has a proprietary right to the property.*

pro·pri·etor /prəˈpraɪətə(r)/ *noun* (*formal*) the owner of a business, a hotel, etc: *newspaper proprietors* ▸ **pro·pri·etor·ship** /prəˈpraɪətəʃɪp; *NAmE* -tərʃ-/ *noun* [U] ➲ see also PROPRIETRESS

pro·pri·etor·ial /prəˌpraɪəˈtɔːriəl/ *adj.* (*formal*) relating to an owner or to the fact of owning sth: *proprietorial rights* ◇ *He laid a proprietorial hand on her arm* (= as if he owned her). ▸ **pro·pri·etor·ial·ly** *adv.*

pro·pri·etress /prəˈpraɪətres/ *noun* (*old-fashioned*) a woman who owns a business, hotel, etc. ➲ see also PROPRIETOR ➲ note at GENDER

pro·pri·ety /prəˈpraɪəti/ *noun* (*formal*) **1** [U] moral and social behaviour that is considered to be correct and acceptable: *Nobody questioned the propriety of her being there alone.* OPP **impropriety 2 the proprieties** [pl.] the rules of correct behaviour SYN **etiquette**: *They were careful to observe the proprieties.*

pro·pul·sion /prəˈpʌlʃn/ *noun* [U] (*technical*) the force that drives sth forward: ***wind/steam/jet propulsion*** ➲ see also PROPEL ▸ **pro·pul·sive** /prəˈpʌlsɪv/ *adj.*

pro rata /ˌprəʊ ˈrɑːtə; *NAmE* ˌproʊ/ *adj.* (from *Latin*, *formal*) (of a payment or share of sth) calculated according to how much of sth has been used, the amount of work done, etc. SYN **proportionate**: *If costs go up, there will be a pro rata increase in prices.* ▸ **pro rata** *adv.*: *Prices will increase pro rata.*

pro·sa·ic /prəˈzeɪɪk/ *adj.* (usually *disapproving*) **1** ordinary and not showing any imagination SYN **unimaginative**: *a prosaic style* **2** dull; not romantic SYN **mundane**: *the prosaic side of life* ▸ **pro·saic·al·ly** /-kli/ *adv.*

pro·scen·ium /prəˈsiːniəm/ *noun* the part of the stage in a theatre that is in front of the curtain: *a traditional theatre with a* ***proscenium arch*** (= one that forms a frame for the stage where the curtain is opened)

pro·scribe /prəˈskraɪb; *NAmE* proʊˈs-/ *verb* **~ sth** (*formal*) to say officially that sth is banned: *proscribed organizations* ▸ **pro·scrip·tion** /prəˈskrɪpʃn; *NAmE* proʊˈs-/ *noun* [U, C]

prose /prəʊz; *NAmE* proʊz/ *noun* [U] writing that is not poetry: *the author's clear elegant prose* (= style of writing)

pros·ecute /ˈprɒsɪkjuːt; *NAmE* ˈprɑːs-/ *verb* **1** [T, I] **~ (sb/sth) (for sth/doing sth)** to officially charge sb with a crime in court: *The company was prosecuted for breaching the*

P

Health and Safety Act. ◇ *Trespassers will be prosecuted* (= a notice telling people to keep out of a particular area). ◇ *The police decided not to prosecute.* **2** [I, T] **~ (sb)** to be a lawyer in a court case for a person or an organization that is charging sb with a crime: *the* ***prosecuting counsel/lawyer/attorney*** ◇ *James Spencer, prosecuting, claimed that the witness was lying.* **3** [T] **~ sth** (*formal*) to continue taking part in or doing sth: *They had overwhelming public support to prosecute the war.*

pros·ecu·tion /ˌprɒsɪˈkjuːʃn; *NAmE* ˌprɑːs-/ *noun* **1** [U, C] the process of trying to prove in court that sb is guilty of a crime (= of prosecuting them); the process of being officially charged with a crime in court: *Prosecution for a first minor offence rarely leads to imprisonment.* ◇ *He threatened to bring a private prosecution against the doctor.* ➲ COLLOCATIONS at JUSTICE **2 the prosecution** [sing. + sing./pl. v.] a person or an organization that prosecutes sb in court, together with the lawyers, etc: *He was a* ***witness for the prosecution.*** ◇ *The prosecution has/have failed to prove its/their case.* ◇ *defence and prosecution* ◇ *a prosecution lawyer* **3** [U] (*formal*) the act of making sth happen or continue

pros·ecu·tor /ˈprɒsɪkjuːtə(r); *NAmE* ˈprɑːs-/ *noun* **1** a public official who charges sb officially with a crime and prosecutes them in court: *the* ***public/state prosecutor*** **2** a lawyer who leads the case against a DEFENDANT in court

pros·elyt·ize (*BrE* also **-ise**) /ˈprɒsələtaɪz; *NAmE* ˈprɑːs-/ *verb* [I] (*formal*, often *disapproving*) to try to persuade other people to accept your beliefs, especially about religion or politics

ˈprose poem *noun* a piece of writing that uses the language and ideas associated with poetry, but is not in VERSE form

ˈpro shop *noun* a shop/store at a GOLF club that sells or repairs golf equipment, usually run by a professional player who works at that club

pros·ody /ˈprɒsədi; *NAmE* ˈprɑːs-/ *noun* [U] **1** (*technical*) the patterns of sounds and rhythms in poetry; the study of this **2** (*phonetics*) the part of PHONETICS which is concerned with stress and INTONATION as opposed to individual speech sounds ▸ **pro·sodic** /prəʊˈsɒdɪk; *NAmE* prəˈsɑːdɪk/ *adj.*

pro·spect 🔑 AW *noun, verb*
■ ***noun*** /ˈprɒspekt; *NAmE* ˈprɑːs-/ **1** 🔑 [U, sing.] the possibility that sth will happen: **~ (of sth/of doing sth)** *There is no immediate prospect of peace.* ◇ *A place in the semi-finals is* ***in prospect*** (= likely to happen). ◇ **~ (that…)** *There's a reasonable prospect that his debts will be paid.* **2** 🔑 [sing.] an idea of what might or will happen in the future: *an exciting prospect* ◇ *Travelling alone around the world is a daunting prospect.* ◇ **~ (of sth/of doing sth)** *The prospect of becoming a father filled him with alarm.* **3** 🔑 **prospects** [pl.] the chances of being successful: *good* ***job/employment/career prospects*** ◇ *At 25 he was an unemployed musician with no prospects.* ◇ **~ for sth** *Long-term prospects for the economy have improved.* ◇ **~ of sth** *What are the prospects of promotion in this job?* **4** [C] **~ (for sth)** a person who is likely to be successful in a competition: *She is one of Canada's best prospects for a gold medal.* **5** [C] (*formal*) a wide view of an area of land, etc: *a delightful prospect of the lake*
■ ***verb*** /prəˈspekt; *NAmE* ˈprɑːspekt/ [I] **~ (for sth)** to search an area for gold, minerals, oil, etc: *Thousands moved to the area to prospect for gold.* ◇ (*figurative*) *to prospect for new clients*

pro·spect·ive AW /prəˈspektɪv/ *adj.* [usually before noun] **1** expected to do sth or to become sth SYN **potential**: *a prospective buyer* **2** expected to happen soon SYN **forthcoming**: *They are worried about prospective changes in the law.*

pro·spect·or /prəˈspektə(r); *NAmE* ˈprɑːspektər/ *noun* a person who searches an area for gold, minerals, oil, etc.

pro·spec·tus /prəˈspektəs/ *noun* **1** a book or printed document that gives information about a school, college, etc. in order to advertise it **2** (*business*) a document that gives information about a company's shares before they are offered for sale

pros·per /ˈprɒspə(r); *NAmE* ˈprɑːs-/ *verb* [I] to develop in a successful way; to be successful, especially in making money SYN **thrive**

pros·per·ity /prɒˈsperəti; *NAmE* prɑːˈs-/ *noun* [U] the state of being successful, especially in making money SYN **affluence**: *Our future prosperity depends on economic growth.* ◇ *The country is enjoying a period of* ***peace and prosperity.***

pros·per·ous /ˈprɒspərəs; *NAmE* ˈprɑːs-/ *adj.* (*formal*) rich and successful SYN **affluent**: *prosperous countries* ➲ SYNONYMS at RICH

pro·state /ˈprɒsteɪt; *NAmE* ˈprɑːs-/ (also **ˈprostate gland**) *noun* a small organ in men, near the BLADDER, that produces a liquid in which SPERM is carried

pros·thesis /prɒsˈθiːsɪs; *NAmE* prɑːs-/ *noun* (*pl.* **prostheses** /-ˈθiːsiːz/) (*medical*) an artificial part of the body, for example a leg, an eye or a tooth ▸ **pros·thet·ic** /prɒsˈθetɪk; *NAmE* prɑːs-/ *adj.*: *a prosthetic arm*

pros·thet·ics /prɒsˈθetɪks; *NAmE* prɑːs-/ *noun* **1** [pl.] artificial parts of the body **2** [U] the activity of making or attaching artificial body parts

pros·ti·tute /ˈprɒstɪtjuːt; *NAmE* ˈprɑːstətuːt/ *noun, verb*
■ ***noun*** a person who has sex for money
■ ***verb*** **1 ~ sth/yourself** to use your skills, abilities, etc. to do sth that earns you money but that other people do not respect because you are capable of doing sth better: *Many felt he was prostituting his talents by writing Hollywood scripts.* **2 ~ yourself** to work as a prostitute

pros·ti·tu·tion /ˌprɒstɪˈtjuːʃn; *NAmE* ˌprɑːstəˈtuːʃn/ *noun* [U] **1** the work of a prostitute: *Many women were forced into prostitution.* ◇ *child prostitution* **2 ~ of sth** (*formal*) the use of your abilities on sth of little value

pros·trate *adj., verb*
■ ***adj.*** /ˈprɒstreɪt; *NAmE* ˈprɑːs-/ (*formal*) **1** lying on the ground and facing downwards: *They fell prostrate in worship.* ◇ *He stumbled over Luke's prostrate body.* **2 ~ (with sth)** so shocked, upset, etc. that you cannot do anything: *She was* ***prostrate with grief*** *after her son's death.*
■ ***verb*** /prɒˈstreɪt; *NAmE* ˈprɑːstreɪt/ **1 ~ yourself** to lie on your front with your face looking downwards, especially as an act of worship **2** [usually passive] **~ sb** to make sb feel weak, shocked, and unable to do anything SYN **overcome**: *He was expecting to find her prostrated by the tragedy.* ◇ *For months he was* ***prostrated with grief.***

pros·tra·tion /prɒˈstreɪʃn; *NAmE* prɑːˈs-/ *noun* [U] (*formal*) **1** extreme physical weakness: *a state of prostration brought on by the heat* **2** the action of lying with your face downwards, especially in worship

prot·ac·tin·ium /ˌprəʊtækˈtɪniəm; *NAmE* ˌproʊ-/ *noun* [U] (*symb.* Pa) a chemical element. Protactinium is a RADIOACTIVE metal found naturally when URANIUM decays.

prot·ag·on·ist /prəˈtæɡənɪst/ *noun* (*formal*) **1** the main character in a play, film/movie or book ➲ compare HERO **2** one of the main people in a real event, especially a competition, battle or struggle **3** an active supporter of a policy or movement, especially one that is trying to change sth SYN **champion**: *a leading protagonist of the conservation movement*

pro·tea /ˈprəʊtiə; *NAmE* ˈproʊ-/ *noun* **1** a type of bush found in South Africa with large flowers with thick orange or pink outer leaves **2** the flower itself, which is one of South Africa's national symbols

pro·tean /ˈprəʊtiən; prəʊˈtiːən; *NAmE* ˈproʊ-; proʊˈt-/ *adj.* (*literary*) able to change quickly and easily: *a protean character*

pro·te·ase /ˈprəʊtieɪz; *NAmE* ˈproʊ-/ *noun* (*biology*) a substance in the body that breaks down PROTEINS and PEPTIDES

pro·tect 0‑ᵚ /prəˈtekt/ *verb*
1 0‑ᵚ [T, I] to make sure that sb/sth is not harmed, injured, damaged, etc: **~ sb/sth/yourself (against/from sth)** *Troops have been sent to protect aid workers against attack.* ◇ *They huddled together to protect themselves from the wind.* ◇ *Each company is fighting to protect its own commercial interests.* ◇ **~ (against/from sth)** *a paint that helps protect against rust* **2** 0‑ᵚ [T, usually passive] **~ sth** to introduce laws that make it illegal to kill, harm or damage a particular animal, area of land, building, etc: *a protected area/species* **3** [T, usually passive] **~ sth** to help an industry in your own country by taxing goods from other countries so that there is less competition: *protected markets* **4** [T, I] **~ (sb/sth) (against sth)** to provide sb/sth with insurance against fire, injury, damage, etc: *Many policies do not protect you against personal injury.*

pro·tec·tion 0‑ᵚ /prəˈtekʃn/ *noun*
1 0‑ᵚ [U] **~ (for/of sb/sth) (against/from sth)** the act of protecting sb/sth; the state of being protected: *Wear clothes that provide adequate protection against the wind and rain.* ◇ *He asked to be put* ***under*** *police* ***protection.*** ◇ *the conservation and protection of the environment* ◇ ***data protection*** *laws* **2** 0‑ᵚ [C] **~ (against sth)** a thing that protects sb/sth against sth: *They wore the charm as a protection against evil spirits.* **3** [U] **~ (against sth)** insurance against fire, injury, damage, etc: *Our policy offers complete protection against fire and theft.* **4** [U] the system of helping an industry in your own country by taxing foreign goods: *The government is ready to introduce protection for the car industry.* **5** [U] the system of paying criminals so that they will not attack your business or property: *to pay* ***protection money*** ◇ *to run a* ***protection racket***

pro·tec·tion·ism /prəˈtekʃənɪzəm/ *noun* [U] the principle or practice of protecting a country's own industry by taxing foreign goods ▸ **pro·tec·tion·ist** /-ʃənɪst/ *adj.*: *protectionist policies*

pro·tect·ive /prəˈtektɪv/ *adj.* **1** [only before noun] providing or intended to provide protection: *Workers should wear full* ***protective clothing.*** ◇ *a protective layer of varnish* ◇ *a protective barrier against the sun's rays* **2** having or showing a wish to protect sb/sth: **~ (towards sb/sth)** *She had been fiercely protective towards him as a teenager.* ◇ **~ (of sb/sth)** *He was extremely protective of his role as advisor.* ◇ *He put a protective arm around her shoulders.* ◇ *Parents can easily become over-protective of their children* (= want to protect them too much). **3** intended to give an advantage to your own country's industry: *protective tariffs* ▸ **pro·tect·ive·ly** *adv.*: *She clutched her bag protectively.* **pro·tect·ive·ness** *noun* [U]

proˌtective ˈcustody *noun* [U] the state of being kept in prison for your own safety

pro·tect·or /prəˈtektə(r)/ *noun* a person, an organization or a thing that protects sb/sth: *I regarded him as my friend and protector.* ◇ *the company's image as a protector of the environment* ◇ *Hard hats and ear protectors are provided.*

pro·tect·or·ate /prəˈtektərət/ *noun* **1** [C] a country that is controlled and protected by a more powerful country ➲ compare COLONY **2** [U] the state or period of being controlled and protected by another country

pro·tégé (*feminine* **pro·té·gée**) /ˈprɒtəʒeɪ; *NAmE* ˈproʊt-/ *noun* (from *French*) a young person who is helped in their career and personal development by a more experienced person: *a protégé of the great violinist Yehudi Menuhin*

pro·tein /ˈprəʊtiːn; *NAmE* ˈproʊ-/ *noun* [C, U] a natural substance found in meat, eggs, fish, some vegetables, etc. There are many different proteins and they are an essential part of what humans and animals eat to help them grow and stay healthy: *essential proteins and vitamins* ◇ *protein deficiency* ◇ *Peas, beans and lentils are a good source of vegetable protein.*

pro tem /ˌprəʊ ˈtem; *NAmE* ˌproʊ/ *adv.* (from *Latin*) for now, but not for a long time SYN **temporarily**: *A new manager will be appointed pro tem.* ▸ **pro tem** *adj.*: *A pro tem committee was formed from existing members.*

pro·test 0‑ᵚ *noun, verb*
■ ***noun*** 0‑ᵚ /ˈprəʊtest; *NAmE* ˈproʊ-/ [U, C] the expression of strong disagreement with or opposition to sth; a statement or an action that shows this: *The director resigned* ***in protest*** *at the decision.* ◇ *The announcement* ***raised a storm of protest.*** ◇ *a protest march* ◇ *She accepted the charge* ***without protest.*** ◇ **~ (against sth)** *The workers staged a protest against the proposed changes in their contracts.* ◇ *The building work will go ahead, despite protests from local residents.* ◇ *The riot began as a peaceful protest.*
IDM **under ˈprotest** unwillingly and after expressing disagreement: *She wrote a letter of apology but only under protest.*
■ ***verb*** /prəˈtest; *NAmE* also ˈproʊ-/ **1** 0‑ᵚ [I, T] to say or do sth to show that you disagree with or disapprove of sth, especially publicly: **~ (about/against/at sth)** *Students took to the streets to protest against the decision.* ◇ *The victim's widow protested at the leniency of the sentence.* ◇ *There's no use protesting, I won't change my mind.* ◇ **~ sth** (*NAmE*) *They fully intend to protest the decision.* ➲ SYNONYMS at COMPLAIN **2** [T] to say firmly that sth is true, especially when you have been accused of sth or when other people do not believe you: **~ sth** *She has always* ***protested her innocence.*** ◇ **~ that...** *He protested that the journey was too far by car.* ◇ **+ speech** *'That's not what you said earlier!' Jane protested.*

Prot·est·ant /ˈprɒtɪstənt; *NAmE* ˈprɑːt-/ *noun* a member of a part of the Western Christian Church that separated from the Roman Catholic Church in the 16th century: *He's a Protestant.* ▸ **Prot·est·ant** *adj.*: *The majority of the population is Protestant.* ◇ *a Protestant church/country* **Prot·est·ant·ism** /ˈprɒtɪstəntɪzəm; *NAmE* ˈprɑːt-/ *noun* [U]

ˌProtestant ˈethic (also **ˌProtestant ˈwork ethic**) *noun* [sing.] the idea that a person has a duty to work hard and spend their time and money in a careful, responsible way, sometimes thought to be typical of Protestants

pro·test·ation /ˌprɒtəˈsteɪʃn; *NAmE* ˌprɑːt-/ *noun* [C, U] (*formal*) a strong statement that sth is true, especially when other people do not believe you: *She repeated her protestation of innocence.* ◇ *Despite his protestation to the contrary, he was extremely tired.*

pro·test·er /prəˈtestə(r)/ *noun* a person who makes a public protest SYN **demonstrator**: *Thousands of protesters marched through the city.*

proto- /ˈprəʊtəʊ; *NAmE* ˈproʊtoʊ/ *combining form* (in nouns and adjectives) original; from which others develop: *prototype* ◇ *proto-modernist painters*

proto·col AW /ˈprəʊtəkɒl; *NAmE* ˈproʊtəkɔːl; -kɑːl/ *noun* **1** [U] a system of fixed rules and formal behaviour used at official meetings, usually between governments: *a breach of protocol* ◇ *the protocol of diplomatic visits* **2** [C] (*technical*) the first or original version of an agreement, especially a TREATY between countries, etc; an extra part added to an agreement or TREATY: *the first Geneva Protocol* ◇ *It is set out in a legally binding protocol which forms part of the treaty.* **3** [C] (*computing*) a set of rules that control the way data is sent between computers **4** [C] (*technical*) a plan for performing a scientific experiment or medical treatment

ˌProto-ˌIndo-ˌEuroˈpean *noun* [U] the ancient language on which all Indo-European languages are thought to be based. There are no written records of Proto-Indo-European, but experts have tried to construct it from the evidence of modern languages.

pro·ton /ˈprəʊtɒn; *NAmE* ˈproʊtɑːn/ *noun* (*physics*) a very small piece of matter (= a substance) with a positive electric charge that forms part of the NUCLEUS (= central part) of an atom ➲ see also ELECTRON, NEUTRON

proto·plasm /ˈprəʊtəplæzəm; *NAmE* ˈproʊ-/ *noun* [U] (*biology*) a clear substance like jelly which forms the living part of an animal or plant cell ➲ compare CYTOPLASM

P

proto·type /ˈprəʊtətaɪp; *NAmE* ˈproʊ-/ *noun* **~ (for/of sth)** the first design of sth from which other forms are copied or developed: *the prototype of the modern bicycle* ▶ **proto·typ·ical** /ˌprəʊtəˈtɪpɪkl; *NAmE* ˌproʊ-/ *adj.*

proto·zoan /ˌprəʊtəˈzəʊən; *NAmE* ˌproʊtəˈzoʊən/ *noun* (*pl.* **proto·zoans** or **proto·zoa** /-ˈzəʊə; *NAmE* -ˈzoʊə/) (*biology*) a very small living thing, usually with only one cell, that can only be seen under a MICROSCOPE ▶ **proto·zoan** *adj.*

pro·tract·ed /prəˈtræktɪd; *NAmE* also proʊˈt-/ *adj.* (*formal*) lasting longer than expected or longer than usual SYN **prolonged**: ***protracted delays/disputes/negotiations***

pro·tract·or /prəˈtræktə(r); *NAmE* also proʊˈt-/ *noun* an instrument for measuring and drawing angles, usually made from a half circle of clear plastic with degrees (0° to 180°) marked on it ➲ VISUAL VOCAB page V57

pro·trude /prəˈtruːd; *NAmE* proʊ-/ *verb* [I] (*formal*) to stick out from a place or a surface: *protruding teeth* ◇ **~ from sth** *He hung his coat on a nail protruding from the wall.*

pro·tru·sion /prəˈtruːʒn; *NAmE* proʊˈt-/ *noun* [C, U] (*formal*) a thing that sticks out from a place or surface; the fact of doing this: *a protrusion on the rock face*

pro·tu·ber·ance /prəˈtjuːbərəns; *NAmE* proʊˈtuː-/ *noun* (*formal*) a round part that sticks out from a surface SYN **bulge**

pro·tu·ber·ant /prəˈtjuːbərənt; *NAmE* proʊˈtuː-/ *adj.* (*formal*) curving or swelling out from a surface SYN **bulging**: *protuberant eyes*

proud 🔑 /praʊd/ *adj.*, *adv.*

■ ***adj.*** (**proud·er**, **proud·est**)

▸ PLEASED **1** 🔑 feeling pleased and satisfied about sth that you own or have done, or are connected with: *proud parents* ◇ *the* ***proud owner*** *of a new car* ◇ **~ of sb/sth/yourself** *Your achievements are* ***something to be proud of.*** ◇ *He was proud of himself for not giving up.* ◇ **~ to be/have sth** *I feel very proud to be a part of the team.* ◇ **~ that...** *She was proud that her daughter had so much talent.* ➲ see also HOUSE-PROUD ➲ SYNONYMS at GLAD **2** 🔑 [only before noun] causing sb to feel pride: *This is the proudest moment of my life.* ◇ *The car had been his* ***proudest possession.***

▸ FEELING TOO IMPORTANT **3** 🔑 (*disapproving*) feeling that you are better and more important than other people SYN **arrogant**: *She was too proud to admit she could be wrong.*

▸ HAVING SELF-RESPECT **4** 🔑 having respect for yourself and not wanting to lose the respect of others: *They were a proud and independent people.* ◇ *Don't be too proud to ask for help.*

▸ BEAUTIFUL/TALL **5** (*literary*) beautiful, tall and impressive: *The sunflowers stretched tall and proud to the sun.* ➲ see also PRIDE

■ ***adv.***

IDM **do sb ˈproud** (*old-fashioned*, *BrE*) to treat sb very well by giving them a lot of good food, entertainment, etc. **do yourself/sb ˈproud** to do sth that makes you proud of yourself or that makes other people proud of you

proud·ly 🔑 /ˈpraʊdli/ *adv.*

1 🔑 in a way that shows that sb is proud of sth: *She proudly displayed her prize.* **2** (*literary*) in a way that is large and impressive: *The Matterhorn rose proudly in the background.*

prov·able /ˈpruːvəbl/ *adj.* that can be shown to be true SYN **verifiable**

prove 🔑 /pruːv/ *verb* (**proved**, **proved** or **proved**, **proven** /ˈpruːvn/ (especially in *NAmE*)) HELP In *BrE* **proved** is the more common form. Look also at **proven**.

> **WORD FAMILY**
> **prove** *verb* (≠ disprove)
> **proof** *noun*
> **proven** *adj.* (≠ unproven)

▸ SHOW STH IS TRUE **1** 🔑 [T] to use facts, evidence, etc. to show that sth is true: **~ sth** *They hope this new evidence will prove her innocence.* ◇ *'I know you're lying.' 'Prove it!'* ◇ *He felt he needed to* ***prove his point*** (= show other people that he was right). ◇ *Are you just doing this to* ***prove a point?*** ◇ ***What are you trying to prove?*** ◇ *I certainly* ***don't have anything to prove***—*my record speaks for itself.* ◇ **~ sth to sb** *Just give me a chance and I'll prove it to you.* ◇ **~ (that)...** *This proves (that) I was right.* ◇ **~ sb/sth/yourself + adj./noun** *She was determined to prove everyone wrong.* ◇ *In this country, you are innocent until proved guilty.* ◇ **~ sb/sth/yourself to be/have sth** *You've just proved yourself to be a liar.* ◇ **~ what, how, etc...** *This just proves what I have been saying for some time.* ◇ **it is proved that...** ***Can it be proved that*** *he did commit these offences?* OPP **disprove** ➲ LANGUAGE BANK at EVIDENCE ➲ see also PROOF

▸ BE **2** 🔑 *linking verb* if sth **proves** dangerous, expensive, etc. or if it **proves to be** dangerous, etc, you discover that it is dangerous, etc. over a period of time SYN **turn out**: **+ adj.** *The opposition proved too strong for him.* ◇ **+ noun** *Shares in the industry proved a poor investment.* ◇ **~ to be sth** *The promotion proved to be a turning point in his career.*

▸ YOURSELF **3** 🔑 [T] **~ yourself (to sb)** to show other people how good you are at doing sth or that you are capable of doing sth: *He constantly feels he has to prove himself to others.* **4** [T] **~ yourself + adj/noun | ~ yourself to be sth** to show other people that you are a particular type of person or that you have a particular quality: *He proved himself determined to succeed.*

▸ OF BREAD **5** [I] to swell before being baked because of the action of YEAST SYN **rise** IDM see EXCEPTION

proven /ˈpruːvn; ˈprəʊvn; *NAmE* ˈproʊ-/ *adj.* [only before noun] tested and shown to be true: *a student of proven ability* ◇ *It is a proven fact that fluoride strengthens growing teeth.* ➲ see also PROVE *v.* OPP **unproven**

IDM **not ˈproven** (in Scottish law) a VERDICT (= decision) at a trial that there is not enough evidence to show that sb is guilty or innocent, and that they must be set free

prov·en·ance /ˈprɒvənəns; *NAmE* ˈprɑːv-/ *noun* [U, C] (*technical*) the place that sth originally came from SYN **origin**: *All the furniture is of English provenance.* ◇ *There's no proof about the provenance of the painting* (= whether it is genuine or not).

ˈpro-verb *noun* (*grammar*) a verb that depends on another verb for its meaning for example 'do' in 'she likes chocolate and so do I.'

prov·erb /ˈprɒvɜːb; *NAmE* ˈprɑːvɜːrb/ *noun* a well-known phrase or sentence that gives advice or says sth that is generally true, for example 'Waste not, want not'.

pro·verb·ial /prəˈvɜːbiəl; *NAmE* -ˈvɜːrb-/ *adj.* **1** [only before noun] used to show that you are referring to a particular proverb or well-known phrase: *Let's not count our proverbial chickens.* **2** [not usually before noun] well known and talked about by a lot of people SYN **famous**: *Their hospitality is proverbial.* ▶ **pro·verbi·al·ly** /-biəli/ *adv.*

pro·vide 🔑 /prəˈvaɪd/ *verb*

1 🔑 to give sth to sb or make it available for them to use SYN **supply**: **~ sth** *The hospital has a commitment to provide the best possible medical care.* ◇ *The report was not expected to provide any answers.* ◇ *Please answer questions in the space provided.* ◇ **~ sth for sb** *We are here to provide a service for the public.* ◇ **~ sb with sth** *We are here to provide the public with a service.* **2 ~ that...** (*formal*) (of a law or rule) to state that sth will or must happen SYN **stipulate**: *The final section provides that any work produced for the company is thereafter owned by the company.* ➲ see also PROVISION

PHR V **proˈvide against sth** (*formal*) to make preparations to deal with sth bad or unpleasant that might happen in the future **proˈvide for sb** to give sb the things that they need to live, such as food, money and clothing **proˈvide for sth** (*formal*) **1** to make preparations to deal with sth that might happen in the future **2** (of a law, rule, etc.) to make it possible for sth to be done: *The legislation provides for the detention of suspected terrorists for up to seven days.*

pro·vided 🔑 /prəˈvaɪdɪd/ (also **pro·vid·ing**) *conj.* **~ (that)...** used to say what must happen or be done to make it possible for sth else to happen SYN **if**: *We'll buy everything you produce, provided of course the price is right.*

◇ *Provided that you have the money in your account, you can withdraw up to £100 a day.*

provi·dence /ˈprɒvɪdəns; *NAmE* ˈprɑːv-/ (also **Provi·dence**) *noun* [U] (*formal*) God, or a force that some people believe controls our lives and the things that happen to us, usually in a way that protects us SYN **fate**: *to trust in divine providence* IDM see TEMPT

provi·dent /ˈprɒvɪdənt; *NAmE* ˈprɑːv-/ *adj.* (*formal*) careful in planning for the future, especially by saving money SYN **prudent** OPP **improvident**

provi·den·tial /ˌprɒvɪˈdenʃl; *NAmE* ˌprɑːv-/ *adj.* (*formal*) lucky because it happens at the right time, but without being planned SYN **timely** ▸ **provi·den·tial·ly** /-ʃəli/ *adv.*

pro·vider /prəˈvaɪdə(r)/ *noun* a person or an organization that supplies sb with sth they need or want: *training providers* ◇ *We are one of the largest providers of employment in the area.* ◇ *The eldest son is the family's sole provider* (= the only person who earns money). ➲ see also SERVICE PROVIDER

pro·vid·ing 🗝 /prəˈvaɪdɪŋ/ *conj.* = PROVIDED

prov·ince /ˈprɒvɪns; *NAmE* ˈprɑːv-/ *noun* **1** [C] one of the areas that some countries are divided into with its own local government: *the provinces of Canada* **2 the provinces** [pl.] (*BrE*) all the parts of a country except the capital city: *The show will tour the provinces after it closes in London.* ◇ *a shy young man from the provinces* **3** [sing.] (*formal*) a person's particular area of knowledge, interest or responsibility: *Such decisions are normally the province of higher management.* ◇ *I'm afraid the matter is* ***outside my province*** (= I cannot or need not deal with it).

pro·vin·cial /prəˈvɪnʃl/ *adj., noun*

■ ***adj.*** **1** [only before noun] connected with one of the large areas that some countries are divided into, with its own local government: ***provincial assemblies/elections*** **2** [only before noun] (sometimes *disapproving*) connected with the parts of a country that do not include the capital city: *a provincial town* **3** (*disapproving*) unwilling to consider new or different ideas or things SYN **narrow-minded** ▸ **pro·vin·cial·ly** /-ʃəli/ *adv.*

■ ***noun*** (often *disapproving*) a person who lives in or comes from a part of the country that is not near the capital city

pro·vin·cial·ism /prəˈvɪnʃlɪzəm/ *noun* [U] (*disapproving*) the attitude of people who are unwilling to consider new or different ideas or things

ˈproving ground *noun* a place where sth such as a new machine, vehicle or weapon can be tested: *It's an ideal proving ground for the new car.* ◇ (*figurative*) *The club is the proving ground for young boxers.*

pro·vi·sion /prəˈvɪʒn/ *noun, verb*

■ ***noun*** **1** [U, C, usually sing.] the act of supplying sb with sth that they need or want; sth that is supplied: *housing provision* ◇ *The government is responsible for the provision of health care.* ◇ *There is no provision for anyone to sit down here.* ◇ *The provision of specialist teachers is being increased.* **2** [U, C] **~ for sb/sth** preparations that you make for sth that might or will happen in the future: *He had already* ***made provisions for*** (= planned for the financial future of) *his wife and children before the accident.* ◇ *You should* ***make provision for*** *things going wrong.* **3 provisions** [pl.] supplies of food and drink, especially for a long journey **4** [C] a condition or an arrangement in a legal document: *Under the provisions of the lease, the tenant is responsible for repairs.* ➲ see also PROVIDE

■ ***verb*** [often passive] **~ sb/sth** (**with sth**) (*formal*) to supply sb/sth with enough of sth, especially food, to last for a particular period of time

pro·vi·sion·al /prəˈvɪʒənl/ *adj.* **1** arranged for the present time only and likely to be changed in the future SYN **temporary**: *a provisional government* ◇ *provisional arrangements* **2** arranged, but not yet definite: *The booking is only provisional.* ▸ **pro·vi·sion·al·ly** /-nəli/ *adv.*: *The meeting has been provisionally arranged for Friday.*

proˌvisional ˈlicence (*BrE*) (*NAmE* **ˈlearner's permit**) *noun* an official document that you must have when you start to learn to drive

pro·viso /prəˈvaɪzəʊ; *NAmE* -zoʊ/ *noun* (*pl.* -os) (*formal*) a condition that must be accepted before an agreement can be made SYN **provision**: *Their participation is subject to a number of important provisos.* ◇ *He agreed to their visit* ***with the proviso that*** *they should stay no longer than one week.*

pro·voca·teur /prəˌvɒkəˈtɜː(r); *NAmE* -ˌvɑːkə-/ *noun* = AGENT PROVOCATEUR

provo·ca·tion /ˌprɒvəˈkeɪʃn; *NAmE* ˌprɑːv-/ *noun* [U, C] the act of doing or saying sth deliberately in order to make sb angry or upset; something that is done or said to cause this: *He reacted violently only* ***under provocation.*** ◇ *The terrorists can strike at any time* ***without provocation.*** ◇ *She bursts into tears* ***at the slightest provocation.*** ◇ *So far the police have refused to respond to their provocations.*

pro·voca·tive /prəˈvɒkətɪv; *NAmE* -ˈvɑːkə-/ *adj.* **1** intended to make people angry or upset; intended to make people argue about sth: *a provocative remark* ◇ *He doesn't really mean that—he's just being deliberately provocative.* **2** intended to make sb sexually excited: *a provocative smile* ▸ **pro·voca·tive·ly** *adv.*

pro·voke /prəˈvəʊk; *NAmE* -ˈvoʊk/ *verb* **1 ~ sth** to cause a particular reaction or have a particular effect: *The announcement provoked a storm of protest.* ◇ *The article was intended to provoke discussion.* ◇ *Dairy products may provoke allergic reactions in some people.* **2 ~ sb** (**into sth/into doing sth**) | **~ sb to do sth** to say or do sth that you know will annoy sb so that they react in an angry way SYN **goad**: *The lawyer claimed his client was provoked into acts of violence by the defendant.* ◇ *Be careful what you say—he's easily provoked.*

prov·ost /ˈprɒvəst; *NAmE* ˈproʊvoʊst/ (also **Provost**) *noun* **1** (in Britain) the person in charge of a college at some universities **2** (in the US) a senior member of the staff who organize the affairs of some universities **3** (in Scotland) the head of a council in some towns, cities and districts ➲ compare MAYOR **4** the head of a group of priests belonging to a particular CATHEDRAL

prow /praʊ/ *noun* (*formal* or *literary*) the pointed front part of a ship or boat

prow·ess /ˈpraʊəs/ *noun* [U] (*formal*) great skill at doing sth: *academic/sporting prowess*

prowl /praʊl/ *verb, noun*

■ ***verb*** **1** [I, T] (+ **adv./prep.**) | **~ sth** (of an animal) to move quietly and carefully around an area, especially when hunting: *The tiger prowled through the undergrowth.* **2** [I, T] (+ **adv./prep.**) | **~ sth** to move quietly and carefully around an area, especially with the intention of committing a crime: *A man was seen prowling around outside the factory just before the fire started.* **3** [T, I] **~ sth** | (+ **adv./prep.**) to walk around a room, an area, etc, especially because you are bored, anxious, etc, and cannot relax: *He prowled the empty rooms of the house at night.*

■ ***noun***

IDM (**be/go**) **on the ˈprowl** (of an animal or a person) moving quietly and carefully, hunting or looking for sth: *There was a fox on the prowl near the chickens.* ◇ *an intruder on the prowl*

prowl·er /ˈpraʊlə(r)/ *noun* a person who follows sb or who moves around quietly outside their house, especially at night, in order to frighten them, harm them or steal sth from them

prox·imal /ˈprɒksɪməl; *NAmE* ˈprɑːk-/ *adj.* (*anatomy*) located towards the centre of the body

prox·im·ate /ˈprɒksɪmət; *NAmE* ˈprɑːk-/ *adj.* [usually before noun] (*technical*) nearest in time, order, etc. to sth

prox·im·ity /prɒkˈsɪməti; *NAmE* prɑːk-/ *noun* [U] **~ (of sb/sth)** (**to sb/sth**) (*formal*) the state of being near sb/sth in distance or time: *a house* ***in the proximity of*** (= near) *the motorway* ◇ *The proximity of the college to London makes it very popular.* ◇ *The area has a number of schools* ***in close proximity*** *to each other.* ◇ *the death of two members of her family in close proximity*

P

proxy /ˈprɒksi; *NAmE* ˈprɑːksi/ *noun* (*pl.* -ies) **1** [U] the authority that you give to sb to do sth for you, when you cannot do it yourself: *You can vote either in person or* ***by proxy***. ◇ ***a proxy vote*** **2** [C, U] a person who has been given the authority to represent sb else: *Your proxy will need to sign the form on your behalf.* ◇ *They were like proxy parents to me.* ◇ **~ for sb** *She is acting as proxy for her husband.* **3** [C] **~ for sth** (*formal* or *technical*) something that you use to represent sth else that you are trying to measure or calculate: *The number of patients on a doctor's list was seen as a good proxy for assessing how hard they work.*

Pro·zac™ /ˈprəʊzæk; *NAmE* ˈproʊ-/ *noun* [C, U] a drug used to treat the illness of DEPRESSION: *She's been* ***on Prozac*** *for two years.*

prude /pruːd/ *noun* (*disapproving*) a person that you think is too easily shocked by things connected with sex

pru·dent /ˈpruːdnt/ *adj.* (*formal*) sensible and careful when you make judgements and decisions; avoiding unnecessary risks: *a prudent businessman* ◇ *a prudent decision/investment* ◇ *It might be more prudent to get a second opinion before going ahead.* OPP **imprudent** ▸ **pru·dence** /-dns/ *noun* [U] (*formal*) ➲ SYNONYMS at CARE **pru·dent·ly** *adv.*

prud·ery /ˈpruːdəri/ *noun* [U] (*formal, disapproving*) the attitude or behaviour of people who seem very easily shocked by things connected with sex

prud·ish /ˈpruːdɪʃ/ *adj.* (*disapproving*) very easily shocked by things connected with sex SYN **strait-laced** ▸ **prud·ish·ness** *noun* [U]

prune /pruːn/ *noun, verb*

■ ***noun*** a dried PLUM that is often eaten cooked: *stewed prunes*

■ ***verb*** **1** to cut off some of the branches from a tree, bush, etc. so that it will grow better and stronger: **~ sth** *When should you prune apple trees?* ◇ *He pruned the longer branches off the tree.* ◇ **~ sth back** *The hedge needs pruning back.* **2** **~ sth (back)** to make sth smaller by removing parts; to cut out parts of sth: *Staff numbers have been pruned back to 175.* ◇ *Prune out any unnecessary details.* ▸ **prun·ing** *noun* [U]: *All roses require annual pruning.* ◇ *The company would benefit from a little pruning here and there.*

pruri·ent /ˈprʊəriənt; *NAmE* ˈprʊr-/ *adj.* (*formal, disapproving*) having or showing too much interest in things connected with sex ▸ **pruri·ence** /-əns/ *noun* [U]

Prus·sian blue /ˌprʌʃn ˈbluː/ *noun* [U] a deep blue colour used in paints

pry /praɪ/ *verb* (**pries, pry·ing, pried, pried** /praɪd/) **1** [I] **~ (into sth)** to try to find out information about other people's private lives in a way that is annoying or rude: *I'm sick of you prying into my personal life!* ◇ *I'm sorry. I didn't mean to pry.* ◇ *She tried to keep the children away from* ***the prying eyes*** *of the world's media.* **2** (*especially NAmE*) = PRISE

PS /ˌpiː ˈes/ *noun* something written at the end of a letter to introduce some more information or sth that you have forgotten. PS is the abbreviation for 'postscript'.: *PS Could you send me your fax number again?* ◇ *She added a PS asking me to water the plants.*

psalm /sɑːm/ *noun* a song, poem or prayer that praises God, especially one in the Bible: *the Book of Psalms*

psal·ter /ˈsɔːltə(r)/ *noun* a book containing a collection of songs and poems, (called PSALMS), with their music, that is used in a church

PSAT /ˌpiː es eɪ ˈtiː/ *noun* (in the US) the abbreviation for 'Preliminary Scholastic Aptitude Test' (a test taken by HIGH SCHOOL students in order to prepare for the SAT)

pseph·ology /siˈfɒlədʒi; *NAmE* -ˈfɑːl-/ *noun* [U] the study of how people vote in elections ▸ **pseph·olo·gist** /siˈfɒlədʒɪst; *NAmE* -ˈfɑːl-/ *noun*

pseud /suːd; *BrE* also sjuːd/ *noun* (*BrE, informal, disapproving*) a person who pretends to know a lot about a particular subject in order to impress other people ▸ **pseud** *adj.*

pseudo- /ˈsuːdəʊ; ˈsjuː-; *NAmE* ˈsuːdoʊ/ *combining form* (in nouns, adjectives and adverbs) not genuine; false or pretended: *pseudo-intellectual* ◇ *pseudo-science*

pseudo·nym /ˈsuːdənɪm; *BrE* also ˈsjuː-/ *noun* a name used by sb, especially a writer, instead of their real name: *She writes* ***under a pseudonym***. ➲ compare PEN-NAME ▸ **pseud·onym·ous** /suːˈdɒnɪməs; sjuː-; *NAmE* suːˈdɑːn-/ *adj.*

PSHE /ˌpiː es eɪtʃ ˈiː/ *noun* [U] the abbreviation for 'personal, social and health education' (a subject taught in British schools that deals with a person's emotional and social development and discusses such issues as health, sex, drugs and relationships with other people) HELP In secondary schools the subject also includes 'economic education' that deals with managing personal finances.

psi /psaɪ; saɪ/ *noun* the 23rd letter of the Greek alphabet (Ψ, ψ)

p.s.i. /ˌpiː es ˈaɪ/ *abbr.* pounds per square inch (used for giving the pressure of tyres, etc.)

psit·ta·cosis /ˌsɪtəˈkəʊsɪs; *NAmE* -ˈkoʊ-/ *noun* [U] (*medical*) a disease of birds, especially PARROTS, which causes PNEUMONIA (= a disease of the lungs) in humans

psor·ia·sis /səˈraɪəsɪs/ *noun* [U] (*medical*) a skin disease that causes rough red areas where the skin comes off in small pieces

psst /pst/ *exclamation* the way of writing the sound people say when they want to attract sb's attention quietly: *Psst! Let's get out now before they see us!*

PST /ˌpiː es ˈtiː/ *abbr.* **1** PACIFIC STANDARD TIME **2** provincial sales tax (a tax that is added to the price of goods in some parts of Canada)

psych /saɪk/ *verb*

PHR V **ˌpsych sb↔ˈout (of sth)** (*informal*) to make an opponent feel less confident by saying or doing things that make you seem better, stronger, etc. than them **ˌpsych sb/yourself ˈup (for sth)** (*informal*) to prepare sb/yourself mentally for sth difficult or unpleasant: *I'd got myself all psyched up for the interview and then it was called off at the last minute.* ➲ see also PSYCHED

psy·che /ˈsaɪki/ *noun* (*formal*) the mind; your deepest feelings and attitudes: *the human psyche* ◇ *She knew, at some deep level of her psyche, that what she was doing was wrong.*

psyched /saɪkt/ *adj.* [not before noun] (*informal, especially NAmE*) excited, especially about sth that is going to happen

psy·che·delia /ˌsaɪkəˈdiːliə/ *noun* [U] music, art, fashion, etc. that is created as a result of the effects of psychedelic drugs

psy·che·del·ic /ˌsaɪkəˈdelɪk/ *adj.* [usually before noun] **1** (of drugs) causing the user to see and hear things that are not there or that do not exist (= to HALLUCINATE) **2** (of art, music, clothes, etc.) having bright colours, strange sounds, etc. like those that are experienced when taking psychedelic drugs

psy·chi·at·ric /ˌsaɪkiˈætrɪk/ *adj.* relating to PSYCHIATRY or to mental illness: *a psychiatric hospital/nurse* ◇ *psychiatric treatment* ◇ *psychiatric disorders* ➲ compare MENTAL

psych·iatrist /saɪˈkaɪətrɪst/ *noun* a doctor who studies and treats mental illnesses

psych·iatry /saɪˈkaɪətri/ *noun* [U] the study and treatment of mental illness

psy·chic /ˈsaɪkɪk/ *adj., noun*

■ ***adj.*** **1** (also *less frequent* **psych·ical** /ˈsaɪkɪkl/) connected with strange powers of the mind and not able to be explained by natural laws SYN **paranormal**: *psychic energy/forces/phenomena/powers* ◇ *psychic healing* **2** (of a person) seeming to have strange mental powers and to be able to do things that are not possible according to natural laws: *She claims to be psychic and helps people to contact the dead.* ◇ *How am I supposed to know—I'm not psychic!* **3** (also *less frequent* **psych·ical**) (*formal*) connected with the mind rather than the body ▸ **psych·ic·al·ly** /-kli/ *adv.*

■ *noun* a person who claims to have strange mental powers so that they can do things that are not possible according to natural laws, such as predicting the future and speaking to dead people

psy·cho /ˈsaɪkəʊ; *NAmE* -koʊ/ *noun* (*pl.* -os) (*informal*) a person who is mentally ill and who behaves in a very strange violent way ▸ **psy·cho** *adj.*

psycho- /ˈsaɪkəʊ; *NAmE* -koʊ/ (also **psych-**) *combining form* (in nouns, adjectives and adverbs) connected with the mind: *psychology* ◇ *psychiatric*

psy·cho·active /ˌsaɪkəʊˈæktɪv; *NAmE* -koʊ-/ *adj.* (*technical*) (of a drug) affecting the mind

psy·cho·ana·lyse (*BrE*) (*NAmE* **-yze**) /ˌsaɪkəʊˈænəlaɪz; *NAmE* -koʊ-/ (also **ana·lyse, ana·lyze**) *verb* ~ **sb** to treat or study sb using psychoanalysis

psy·cho·analy·sis /ˌsaɪkəʊəˈnæləsɪs; *NAmE* -koʊə-/ (also **an·aly·sis**) *noun* [U] a method of treating sb who is mentally ill by asking them to talk about past experiences and feelings in order to try to find explanations for their present problems ▸ **psy·cho·ana·lyt·ic** /ˌsaɪkəʊˌænəˈlɪtɪk; *NAmE* -koʊ-/ *adj.* [only before noun]: *a psychoanalytic approach* **psy·cho·ana·lyt·ic·al·ly** /-ɪkli/ *adv.*

psy·cho·ana·lyst /ˌsaɪkəʊˈænəlɪst; *NAmE* -koʊ-/ (also **ana·lyst**) *noun* a person who treats patients using psychoanalysis

psy·cho·bab·ble /ˈsaɪkəʊbæbl; *NAmE* -koʊ-/ *noun* [U] (*informal, disapproving*) the language that people use when they talk about feelings and emotional problems, that sounds very scientific, but really has little meaning

psy·cho·drama /ˈsaɪkəʊdrɑːmə; *NAmE* -koʊ-/ *noun* **1** a way of treating people who are mentally ill by encouraging them to act events from their past to help them understand their feelings **2** a play or film/movie that makes the minds and feelings of the characters more important than the events

psy·cho·kin·esis /ˌsaɪkəʊkɪˈniːsɪs; -kaɪˈn-; *NAmE* -koʊ-/ *noun* [U] the act of moving an object by using the power of the mind

psy·cho·lin·guis·tics /ˌsaɪkəʊlɪŋˈgwɪstɪks; *NAmE* -koʊ-/ *noun* [U] the study of how the mind processes and produces language ▸ **psy·cho·lin·guis·tic** /ˌsaɪkəʊlɪŋˈgwɪstɪk; *NAmE* -koʊ-/ *adj.*

psy·cho·logic·al AW /ˌsaɪkəˈlɒdʒɪkl; *NAmE* -ˈlɑːdʒ-/ *adj.* **1** [usually before noun] connected with a person's mind and the way in which it works: *the psychological development of children* ◇ *Abuse can lead to both psychological and emotional problems.* ◇ *Her symptoms are more psychological than physical* (= imaginary rather than real). ◇ *Victory in the last game gave them* ***a psychological advantage*** *over their opponents.* ◇ *a psychological novel* (= one that examines the minds of the characters) **2** [only before noun] connected with the study of PSYCHOLOGY: *psychological research* ▸ **psy·cho·logic·al·ly** AW /-kli/ *adv.*: *psychologically harmful* ◇ *Psychologically, the defeat was devastating.*

IDM **the ˌpsychological ˈmoment** the best time to do sth in order for it to be successful

ˌpsychological ˈwarfare *noun* [U] things that are said and done in order to make an opponent believe that they cannot win a war, a competition, etc.

psych·olo·gist AW /saɪˈkɒlədʒɪst; *NAmE* -ˈkɑːl-/ *noun* a scientist who studies and is trained in psychology: *an educational psychologist* ◇ *a clinical psychologist* (= one who treats people with mental DISORDERS or problems)

psych·ology AW /saɪˈkɒlədʒi; *NAmE* -ˈkɑːl-/ *noun* **1** [U] the scientific study of the mind and how it influences behaviour: ***social/educational/child psychology*** ➲ compare POP PSYCHOLOGY **2** [sing.] the kind of mind that sb has that makes them think or behave in a particular way: *the psychology of small boys* **3** [sing.] how the mind influences behaviour in a particular area of life: *the psychology of interpersonal relationships*

psy·cho·met·ric /ˌsaɪkəˈmetrɪk/ *adj.* [only before noun] (*technical*) used for measuring mental abilities and processes: *psychometric testing*

psy·cho·path /ˈsaɪkəpæθ/ *noun* a person suffering from a serious mental illness that causes them to behave in a violent way towards other people ▸ **psy·cho·path·ic** /ˌsaɪkəˈpæθɪk/ *adj.*: *a psychopathic disorder/killer*

psy·cho·path·ology /ˌsaɪkəʊpəˈθɒlədʒi; *NAmE* -koʊpəˈθɑːl-/ *noun* **1** [U] the scientific study of mental DISORDERS **2** [C] a DISORDER that affects sb's mind or their behaviour

psych·osis /saɪˈkəʊsɪs; *NAmE* -ˈkoʊ-/ *noun* [C, U] (*pl.* **psych·oses** /-siːz/) a serious mental illness that affects the whole personality ➲ see also PSYCHOTIC

psy·cho·somat·ic /ˌsaɪkəʊsəˈmætɪk; *NAmE* -koʊ-/ *adj.* **1** (of an illness) caused by mental problems, such as stress and worry, rather than physical problems **2** (*technical*) connected with the relationship between the mind and the body

psy·cho·ther·apy /ˌsaɪkəʊˈθerəpi; *NAmE* -koʊ-/ (also **ther·apy**) *noun* [U] the treatment of mental illness by discussing sb's problems with them rather than by giving them drugs ▸ **psy·cho·ther·ap·ist** /-pɪst/ (also **ther·ap·ist**) *noun*

psych·ot·ic /saɪˈkɒtɪk; *NAmE* -ˈkɑːt-/ *noun* (*medical*) a person suffering from severe mental illness ▸ **psych·ot·ic** *adj.*: *a psychotic disorder/illness* ◇ *a psychotic patient* ➲ see also PSYCHOSIS ➲ note at MENTALLY ILL

psy·cho·trop·ic /ˌsaɪkəˈtrəʊpɪk; *NAmE* -ˈtroʊpɪk/ *adj.* [usually before noun] (*medical*) relating to drugs or substances that affect a person's mental state: *psychotropic medication/drugs*

PT /ˌpiː ˈtiː/ *abbr.* **1** (*BrE*) physical training (sport and physical exercise that is taught in schools, in the army, etc.) **2** (also **P/T**) (in writing) PART-TIME: *The course is 1 year FT, 2 years PT.*

pt (also **pt.** especially in *NAmE*) *abbr.* **1** part: *Shakespeare's Henry IV Pt 2* **2** pint **3** point: *The winner scored 10 pts.* **4** **Pt.** (especially on a map) port: *Pt. Moresby*

PTA /ˌpiː tiː ˈeɪ/ *noun* the abbreviation for 'parent-teacher association' (a group run by parents and teachers in a school that organizes social events and helps the school in different ways)

ptar·migan /ˈtɑːmɪgən; *NAmE* ˈtɑːrm-/ *noun* a type of GROUSE (= a bird with a fat body and feathers on its legs), found in mountain areas and in Arctic regions

Pte *abbr.* (*BrE*) (in writing) PRIVATE: *Pte Jim Hill*

ptero·dac·tyl /ˌterəˈdæktɪl/ *noun* a flying REPTILE that lived millions of years ago

PTO /ˌpiː tiː ˈəʊ; *NAmE* ˈoʊ/ *abbr.* (*BrE*) please turn over (written at the bottom of a page to show that there is more on the other side)

Pty *abbr.* proprietary (used in the names of some companies in Australia and South Africa): *Computer Software Packages Pty Ltd*

pub 0-w /pʌb/ (also *formal* **ˌpublic ˈhouse**) (both *BrE*) *noun*
a building where people go to drink and meet their friends. Pubs serve alcoholic and other drinks, and often also food: *They've gone down the pub for a drink.* ◇ *a pub lunch* ◇ *the landlord of the local pub* ➲ VISUAL VOCAB page V13

ˈpub crawl *noun* (*BrE, informal*) a visit to several pubs, going straight from one to the next, drinking at each of them

pube /pjuːb/ *noun* [usually pl.] (*informal*) a pubic hair

pu·berty /ˈpjuːbəti; *NAmE* -bərti/ *noun* [U] the period of a person's life during which their sexual organs develop and they become capable of having children: *to reach puberty* ➲ COLLOCATIONS at AGE ➲ see also ADOLESCENCE

pubes /ˈpjuːbiːz/ *noun* (*pl.* **pubes**) the lower front part of the body, above the legs, covered by hair in adults

P

pu·bes·cent /pjuːˈbesnt/ *adj.* [usually before noun] (*formal*) in the period of a person's life when they are changing physically from a child to an adult

pubic /ˈpjuːbɪk/ *adj.* [only before noun] connected with the part of a person's body near their sexual organs: *pubic hair* ◇ *the pubic bone*

pubis /ˈpjuːbɪs/ *noun* (*pl.* **pubes** /-biːz/) one of the two bones that form the sides of the PELVIS

pub·lic /ˈpʌblɪk/ *adj., noun*

■ ***adj.***

▸ OF ORDINARY PEOPLE **1** [only before noun] connected with ordinary people in society in general: *The campaign is designed to increase public awareness of the issues.* ◇ *Levels of waste from the factory may be a danger to public health.* ◇ *Why would the closure of hospitals be* ***in the public interest*** (= useful to ordinary people)? ◇ *The government had to bow to public pressure.*

▸ FOR EVERYONE **2** [only before noun] provided, especially by the government, for the use of people in general: *a public education system* ◇ *a public library* OPP **private**

▸ OF GOVERNMENT **3** [only before noun] connected with the government and the services it provides: ***public money/spending/funding/expenditure*** ◇ *He spent much of his career in* ***public office*** (= working in the government). ◇ (*BrE*) *the* ***public purse*** (= the money that the government can spend) ◇ *The rail industry is no longer in* ***public ownership*** (= controlled by the government). OPP **private**

▸ SEEN/HEARD BY PEOPLE **4** known to people in general: *a* ***public figure*** (= a person who is well known because they are often on the television, radio, etc.) ◇ *Details of the government report have not yet been* ***made public***. ◇ *She entered* ***public life*** (= started a job in which she became known to the public) *at the age of 25.* **5** open to people in general; intended to be seen or heard by people in general: *a public apology* ◇ *The painting will be put on* ***public display*** *next week.* ◇ *This may be the band's last* ***public appearance*** *together.*

▸ PLACE **6** where there are a lot of people who can see and hear you: *Let's go somewhere a little less public.* OPP **private**

▸ **pub·lic·ly** /-kli/ *adv.*: *a publicly owned company* ◇ *He later publicly apologized for his comments.* ◇ *This information is not publicly available.*

IDM **go ˈpublic 1** to tell people about sth that is a secret **2** (of a company) to start selling shares on the STOCK EXCHANGE **in the public ˈeye** well known to many people through newspapers and television: *She doesn't want her children growing up in the public eye.* ➲ more at KNOWLEDGE

■ ***noun*** [sing.+ sing./pl. v.]

▸ ORDINARY PEOPLE **1** **the public** ordinary people in society in general: *The palace is now* ***open to the public***. ◇ *There have been many complaints from* ***members of the public***. ◇ *The public has/have a right to know what is contained in the report.* ➲ see also THE GENERAL PUBLIC

▸ GROUP OF PEOPLE **2** a group of people who share a particular interest or who are involved in the same activity: *the theatre-going public* ◇ *She knows how to keep her public* (= for example, the people who buy her books) *satisfied.*

IDM **in ˈpublic** when other people, especially people you do not know, are present: *She doesn't like to be seen in public without her make-up on.* ➲ compare IN PRIVATE ➲ more at WASH *v.*

ˌpublic ˈaccess *noun* [U] **1** the right of people in general to go into particular buildings or areas of land or to obtain particular information: *public access to the countryside* **2** (in the US and some other countries) the right of people in general to use television or radio channels to present their own programmes: *a public access channel*

ˌpublic adˈdress system *noun* (*abbr.* PA system) an electronic system that uses MICROPHONES and LOUDSPEAKERS to make music, voices, etc. louder so that they can be heard by everyone in a particular place or building

ˌpublic afˈfairs *noun* [pl.] issues and questions about social, economic, political or business activities, etc. that affect ordinary people in general

pub·lican /ˈpʌblɪkən/ *noun* **1** (*BrE, formal*) a person who owns or manages a pub **2** (*AustralE, NZE*) a person who owns or manages a hotel

pub·li·ca·tion AW /ˌpʌblɪˈkeɪʃn/ *noun*
1 [U, C] the act of printing a book, a magazine, etc. and making it available to the public; a book, a magazine, etc. that has been published: *the publication date* ◇ *the publication of his first novel* ◇ *specialist publications* **2** [U] the act of printing sth in a newspaper, report, etc. so that the public knows about it: *a delay in the publication of the exam results* ◇ *The newspaper continues to defend its publication of the photographs.*

ˌpublic ˈbar *noun* (in Britain) a bar in a pub with simple or less comfortable furniture than the other bars ➲ compare LOUNGE BAR

ˌpublic ˈcompany (also **ˌpublic ˌlimited ˈcompany**) (both *BrE*) (*NAmE* **ˌpublic corpoˈration**) *noun* (*abbr.* plc, PLC) a company that sells shares in itself to the public

ˌpublic conˈvenience *noun* (*BrE, formal*) a public building containing toilets that are provided for anyone to use

ˌpublic corpoˈration *noun* **1** (*NAmE*) (*BrE* **ˌpublic ˈcompany, ˌpublic ˌlimited ˈcompany**) a company that sells shares in itself to the public **2** (*BrE*) an organization that is owned by the government and that provides a national service

ˌpublic deˈfender *noun* (*law*) (in the US) a lawyer who is paid by the government to defend people in court if they cannot pay for a lawyer themselves

ˌpublic ˈdomain *noun* [sing.] something that is in the **public domain** is available for everyone to use or to discuss and is not secret: *The information has been placed in the public domain.* ◇ *public domain software*

ˌpublic ˈenemy *noun* a person who has done, or is believed to have done, a very bad thing, especially sth that is harmful to society: *public enemy number one* (= the person or thing that is most frightening or that is most hated)

ˌpublic ˈholiday *noun* a day on which most of the shops/stores, businesses and schools in a country are closed, often to celebrate a particular event ➲ compare BANK HOLIDAY

ˌpublic ˈhouse *noun* (*BrE, formal*) = PUB

ˌpublic ˈhousing *noun* [U] (in the US) houses and flats/apartments that are built by the government for people who do not have enough money to pay for private accommodation

pub·li·cist /ˈpʌblɪsɪst/ *noun* a person whose job is to make sth known to the public, for example a new product, actor, etc.

pub·li·city /pʌbˈlɪsəti/ *noun* [U]
1 the attention that is given to sb/sth by newspapers, television, etc: ***good/bad/adverse publicity*** ◇ *There has been a great deal of publicity surrounding his disappearance.* ◇ *The trial took place amid* ***a blaze of*** (= a lot of) ***publicity***. **2** the business of attracting the attention of the public to sth/sb; the things that are done to attract attention: *She works in publicity.* ◇ *There has been a lot of advance publicity for her new film.* ◇ *publicity material* ◇ *a* ***publicity campaign*** ◇ *The band dressed up as the Beatles as a* ***publicity stunt***. ➲ SYNONYMS at ADVERTISEMENT

pub·li·cize (*BrE* also **-ise**) /ˈpʌblɪsaɪz/ *verb* **~ sth** to make sth known to the public; to advertise sth: *They flew to Europe to publicize the plight of the refugees.* ◇ *a* ***much/highly/widely publicized*** *speech* (= that has received a lot of attention on television, in newspapers, etc.) ◇ *He was in London publicizing his new biography of Kennedy.*

ˌpublic ˌlimited ˈcompany *noun* (*BrE*) (*abbr.* plc) = PUBLIC COMPANY

ˌpublic ˈnuisance *noun* **1** [sing., U] (*law*) an illegal act that causes harm to people in general: *He was charged with committing (a) public nuisance.* **2** [C, usually sing.] (*informal*) a person or thing that annoys a lot of people

ˌpublic oˈpinion *noun* [U] the opinions that people in society have about an issue: *The media has a powerful influence on public opinion.*

ˌpublic ˈproperty *noun* [U] **1** (*law*) land, buildings, etc. that are owned by the government and can be used by everyone **2** a person or thing that everyone has a right to know about: *Sophie became public property when she married into the royal family.*

ˌpublic ˈprosecutor *noun* (*BrE*) a lawyer who works for the government and tries to prove people guilty in court ➲ see also DISTRICT ATTORNEY

ˌpublic reˈlations *noun* **1** [U] (*abbr.* **PR**) the business of giving the public information about a particular organization or person in order to create a good impression: *She works in public relations.* ◇ *a public relations exercise* **2** [pl.] the state of the relationship between an organization and the public: *Sponsoring the local team is good for public relations.*

ˌpublic ˈschool *noun* [C, U] **1** (in Britain, especially in England) a private school for young people between the ages of 13 and 18, whose parents pay for their education. The students often live at the school while they are studying: *He was educated at (a) public school.* ➲ compare PREPARATORY SCHOOL, PRIVATE SCHOOL **2** **ˈpublic school** (in the US, Australia, Scotland and other countries) a free local school paid for by the government ➲ compare STATE SCHOOL

the ˌpublic ˈsector *noun* [sing.] (*economics*) the part of the economy of a country that is owned or controlled by the government ➲ compare THE PRIVATE SECTOR

ˌpublic ˈservant *noun* a person who is employed by the state or in local government or who is an elected representative: *pay increases for public servants* ◇ *a long and outstanding career as a public servant*

ˌpublic ˈservice *noun* **1** [C] a service such as transport or health care that a government or an official organization provides for people in general in a particular society: *to improve public services in the area* ◇ *a public service broadcast* **2** [C, U] something that is done to help people rather than to make a profit: *to perform a public service* **3** [U] the government and government departments: *to work in public service* ◇ *public service workers*

ˌpublic ˈservice broadcasting *noun* [U] radio and television programmes broadcast by organizations such as the BBC in Britain that are independent of government but are financed by public money

ˌpublic-ˈspirit·ed *adj.* willing to do things that will help other people in society: *a public-spirited act* ◇ *That was very public-spirited of you.* ▶ **ˌpublic ˈspirit** *noun* [U]

ˌpublic ˈtelevision *noun* [U] (*NAmE*) a television service that shows mainly EDUCATIONAL programmes and is paid for by the government, the public and some companies

ˌpublic ˈtransport (*BrE*) (*NAmE* **ˌpublic transporˈtation**) *noun* [U] the system of buses, trains, etc. provided by the government or by companies, which people use to travel from one place to another: *to* ***travel on/by public transport*** ◇ *Most of us use public transport to get to work.* ➲ COLLOCATIONS at TOWN ➲ VISUAL VOCAB page V7

ˌpublic uˈtility *noun* (*formal*) a private company that must obey government rules, that supplies essential services such as gas, water and electricity to the public

ˌpublic ˈworks *noun* [pl.] building work, such as that of hospitals, schools and roads, that is paid for by the government

pub·lish 0‑w AW /ˈpʌblɪʃ/ *verb*
1 0‑w [T] **~ sth** to produce a book, magazine, CD-ROM, etc. and sell it to the public: *The first edition was published in 2007.* ◇ *He works for a company that publishes reference books.* ◇ *Most of our titles are also published on CD-ROM.* **2** 0‑w [T] **~ sth** to print a letter, an article, etc. in a newspaper or magazine: *Pictures of the suspect were published in all the daily papers.* **3** 0‑w [T] **~ sth** to make sth available to the public on the Internet: *The report will be published on the Internet.* **4** 0‑w [T, I] **~ (sth)** (of an author) to have your work printed and sold to the public: *She hasn't published anything for years.* ◇ *University teachers are under pressure to publish.* **5** [T] **~ sth** (*formal*) to make official information known to the public SYN **release**: *The findings of the committee will be published on Friday.*

pub·lish·er AW /ˈpʌblɪʃə(r)/ *noun* a person or company that prepares and prints books, magazines, newspapers or electronic products and makes them available to the public

pub·lish·ing 0‑w AW /ˈpʌblɪʃɪŋ/ *noun* [U] the profession or business of preparing and printing books, magazines, CD-ROMs, etc. and selling or making them available to the public: *a publishing house* (= company) ➲ see also DESKTOP PUBLISHING

puce /pjuːs/ *adj.* reddish-purple in colour: *His face was puce with rage.* ▶ **puce** *noun* [U]

puck /pʌk/ *noun* **1** a hard flat rubber disc that is used as a ball in ICE HOCKEY ➲ VISUAL VOCAB page V36 **2** (*computing*) a pointing device that looks like a computer mouse and is used to control the movement of the CURSOR on a computer screen

puck·er /ˈpʌkə(r)/ *verb* [I, T] **~ (sth) (up)** to form or to make sth form small folds or lines: *His* ***face puckered****, and he was ready to cry.* ◇ *She puckered her lips.* ◇ *puckered fabric*

puck·ish /ˈpʌkɪʃ/ *adj.* [usually before noun] (*literary*) enjoying playing tricks on other people SYN **mischievous**

pud /pʊd/ *noun* (*BrE, informal*) = PUDDING

pud·ding /ˈpʊdɪŋ/ (*BrE informal* **pud**) *noun* [U, C] **1** (*BrE*) a sweet dish eaten at the end of a meal: *What's for pudding?* ◇ *I haven't made a pudding today.* SYN **afters, dessert, sweet** **2** (*BrE*) a hot sweet dish, often like a cake, made from flour, fat and eggs with fruit, jam, etc. in or on it: *treacle pudding* ◇ *bread and butter pudding* (= made with bread, butter and milk) ➲ see also CHRISTMAS PUDDING, RICE PUDDING, SPONGE PUDDING, SUMMER PUDDING **3** (*BrE*) a hot dish like a PIE with soft PASTRY made from flour, fat and eggs and usually filled with meat: *a steak and kidney pudding* **4** (*especially NAmE*) a cold DESSERT (= a sweet dish) like cream flavoured with fruit, chocolate, etc: *chocolate pudding* ➲ see also BLACK PUDDING, YORKSHIRE PUDDING IDM see OVER-EGG, PROOF

ˈpudding basin *noun* (*BrE*) a deep round bowl that is used for mixing food or for cooking puddings in

pud·dle /ˈpʌdl/ *noun* a small amount of water or other liquid, especially rain, that has collected in one place on the ground

pu·denda /pjuːˈdendə/ *noun* [pl.] (*old-fashioned, formal*) the sexual organs that are outside the body, especially those of a woman

pudgy /ˈpʌdʒi/ (*BrE* also **podgy**) *adj.* (*informal*, usually *disapproving*) slightly fat

Pue·blo /ˈpwebləʊ; *NAmE* -loʊ/ *noun* (*pl.* **Pue·blo** or **Pue·blos**) *noun* a member of a group of Native American people who live in the US states of Arizona and New Mexico

pue·blo /ˈpwebləʊ; *NAmE* -bloʊ/ *noun* (*pl.* -os) (from *Spanish*) a town or village in Latin America or the south-western US, especially one with traditional buildings

pu·er·ile /ˈpjʊəraɪl; *NAmE* ˈpjʊrəl/ *adj.* (*disapproving*) silly; suitable for a child rather than an adult SYN **childish**

puff /pʌf/ *verb, noun*
■ ***verb*** **1** [I, T] to smoke a cigarette, pipe, etc: **~ (at/on sth)** *He puffed (away) on his pipe.* ◇ **~ sth** *I sat puffing my cigar.* **2** [T, I] to make smoke or steam blow out in clouds; to blow out in clouds: **~ sth (out)** *Chimneys were puffing out clouds of smoke.* ◇ **~ (out)** *Steam puffed out.* **3** [I, T] **(+ speech)** (*informal*) to breathe loudly and quickly, especially after you have been running SYN **gasp**: *I was starting to puff a little from the climb.* ➲ see also PUFFED, PUFFED OUT **4** [I] **+ adv./prep.** to move in a particular direction, sending out small clouds of smoke or steam: *The train puffed into the station.*
IDM **be puffed up with ˈpride, etc.** to be too full of pride, etc. **ˌpuff and ˈpant** (also **ˌpuff and ˈblow**, *informal*) to

P

breathe quickly and loudly through your mouth after physical effort ➲ more at HUFF *v.*

PHR V ˌ**puff sth↔ˈout** to make sth bigger and rounder, especially by filling it with air: *She puffed out her cheeks.* ˌ**puff ˈup** | ˌ**puff sth↔ˈup** to swell or to make sth swell: *Her cheeks puffed up.* ◇ *The frog puffed itself up.*

■ ***noun*** **1** [C] an act of breathing in sth such as smoke from a cigarette, or drugs: *He had a few puffs at the cigar.* ◇ *Take two puffs from the inhaler every four hours.* **2** [C] a small amount of air, smoke, etc. that is blown from somewhere: *a puff of wind* ◇ *Puffs of white smoke came from the chimney.* ◇ *Any chance of success seemed to vanish in a puff of smoke* (= to disappear quickly). **3** [C] a hollow piece of light PASTRY that is filled with cream, jam, etc. ➲ see also CREAM PUFF **4** (*NAmE* also ˈ**puff piece**) [C] (*informal*, usually *disapproving*) a piece of writing or speech that praises sb/sth too much **5** [U] (*informal, especially BrE*) breath: *The hill was very steep and I soon* ***ran out of puff.*** ➲ see also POWDER PUFF

puff·ball /ˈpʌfbɔːl/ *noun* a FUNGUS with a round brown head, that bursts when it is ready to release its seeds

puffed /pʌft/ (also ˌ**puffed ˈout**) *adj.* [not before noun] (*BrE, informal*) breathing quickly and with difficulty because you have been having a lot of physical exercise

puff·er /ˈpʌfə(r)/ *noun* **1** (*informal*) = INHALER **2** = PUFFERFISH

puff·er·fish /ˈpʌfəfɪʃ; *NAmE* -fərf-/ *noun* (*pl.* **puffer·fish** or **puffer·fishes**) (also **puff·er**) a poisonous fish that lives in warm seas and fills with air when it is in danger

puf·fin /ˈpʌfɪn/ *noun* a black and white bird with a large, brightly coloured beak that lives near the sea, common in the N Atlantic ➲ VISUAL VOCAB page V10

ˌ**puff ˈpastry** *noun* [U] a type of light PASTRY that forms many thin layers when baked, used for making PIES, cakes, etc.

ˈ**puff piece** *noun* (*NAmE*) = PUFF (4)

ˌ**puff ˈsleeve** (also ˌ**puffed ˈsleeve**) *noun* a type of sleeve on a piece of clothing that fits close to the body at the shoulder and the lower edge and is wider in the middle, forming a round shape

P

puffy /ˈpʌfi/ *adj.* (**puff·ier, puffi·est**) **1** (of eyes, faces, etc.) looking swollen (= larger, rounder, etc. than usual): *Her eyes were puffy from crying.* **2** (of clouds, etc.) looking soft, round and white ▶ **puf·fi·ness** *noun* [U]

pug /pʌg/ *noun* a small dog with short hair and a wide flat face with deep folds of skin

pu·gil·ist /ˈpjuːdʒɪlɪst/ *noun* (*old-fashioned*) a BOXER ▶ **pu·gil·ism** /-lɪzəm/ *noun* [U] **pu·gil·is·tic** /ˌpjuːdʒɪˈlɪstɪk/ *adj.*

pug·na·cious /pʌgˈneɪʃəs/ *adj.* (*formal*) having a strong desire to argue or fight with other people SYN **bellicose** ▶ **pug·na·cious·ly** *adv.* **pug·na·city** /pʌgˈnæsəti/ *noun* [U]

puis·sance /ˈpwiːsɒ̃s; *NAmE* ˈpwɪsəns/ *noun* **1 Puis·sance** [sing.] a competition in SHOWJUMPING to test a horse's ability to jump high fences **2** [U] (*literary*) great power or influence

puja /ˈpuːdʒɑː/ *noun* **1** a Hindu ceremony of worship **2** an OFFERING (= a gift that is given to a god) at the ceremony

pu·jari /puːˈdʒɑːri/ *noun* a Hindu priest

puke /pjuːk/ *verb* [I, T] **~ (sth) (up)** (*informal*) to VOMIT: *The baby puked all over me this morning.* ◇ *That guy makes me puke!* (= makes me angry) ◇ *I puked up my dinner.* ▶ **puke** *noun* [U]: *to be covered in puke*

pukka /ˈpʌkə/ *adj.* (*BrE*) **1** (*old-fashioned*) genuine; not a copy; appropriate in a particular social situation **2** (*informal*) of very good quality

pul·chri·tude /ˈpʌlkrɪtjuːd; *NAmE* also -tuːd/ *noun* [U] (*literary*) beauty

Pul·it·zer Prize /ˈpʊlɪtzə(r); *NAmE* also ˈpjuːl-/ *noun* [C, usually sing.] in the US, one of 13 prizes that are given each year for excellent work in literature, music, or JOURNALISM

pull 🔑 /pʊl/ *verb, noun*

■ ***verb***

▸ MOVE/REMOVE STH **1** 🔑 [I, T] to hold sth firmly and use force in order to move it or try to move it towards yourself: *You push and I'll pull.* ◇ *Don't pull so hard or the handle will come off.* ◇ **~ at/on sth** *I pulled on the rope to see if it was secure.* ◇ **~ sth** *Stop pulling her hair!* ◇ **~ sb/sth + adv./prep.** *She pulled him gently towards her.* ◇ **~ sth + adj.** *Pull the door shut.* **2** 🔑 [T] **~ sth (+ adv./prep.)** to remove sth from a place by pulling: *Pull the plug out.* ◇ *She pulled off her boots.* ◇ *He pulled a gun on me* (= took out a gun and aimed it at me). **3** 🔑 [T] **~ sb/sth + adv./prep.** to move sb/sth in a particular direction by pulling: *Pull your chair nearer the table.* ◇ *He pulled on his sweater.* ◇ *She took his arm and pulled him along.* **4** 🔑 [T] **~ sth** to hold or be attached to sth and move it along behind you: *In this area oxen are used to pull carts.*

▸ BODY **5** 🔑 [I, T] to move your body or a part of your body in a particular direction, especially using force: **+ adv./prep.** *He tried to kiss her but she pulled away.* ◇ **~ sth/yourself + adv./prep.** *The dog snapped at her and she quickly pulled back her hand.* ◇ **~ sth/yourself + adj.** *John* ***pulled*** *himself* ***free*** *and ran off.*

▸ CURTAINS **6** 🔑 [T] **~ sth** to open or close curtains, etc. SYN **draw**: *Pull the curtains—it's dark outside.*

▸ MUSCLE **7** 🔑 [T] **~ sth** to damage a muscle, etc. by using too much force: *to* ***pull a muscle/ligament/tendon*** ➲ SYNONYMS at INJURE

▸ SWITCH **8** 🔑 [T] **~ sth** to move a switch, etc. towards yourself or down in order to operate a machine or piece of equipment: *Pull the lever to start the motor.* ◇ *Don't pull the trigger!*

▸ VEHICLE/ENGINE **9** [I, T] **~ (sth) to the right/the left/one side** to move or make a vehicle move sideways: *The wheel is pulling to the left.* ◇ *She pulled the car to the right to avoid the dog.* **10** [I] (of an engine) to work hard and use a lot of power: *The old car pulled hard as we drove slowly up the hill.*

▸ BOAT **11** [I, T] **~ (sth) (+ adv./prep.)** to use OARS to move a boat along: *They pulled towards the shore.*

▸ CROWD/SUPPORT **12** [T] **~ sb/sth (in)** to attract the interest or support of sb/sth: *They pulled in huge crowds on their latest tour.*

▸ ATTRACT SEXUALLY **13** [T, I] **~ (sb)** (*BrE, informal*) to attract sb sexually: *He can still pull the girls.* ◇ *She's hoping to pull tonight.*

▸ TRICK/CRIME **14** [T] **~ sth** (*informal*) to succeed in playing a trick on sb, committing a crime, etc: *He's pulling some sort of trick on you.*

▸ CANCEL **15** [T] **~ sth** (*informal*) to cancel an event; to stop showing an advertisement, etc: *The gig was pulled at the last moment.*

IDM **pull a ˈfast one (on sb)** (*slang*) to trick sb **pull in different/opposite diˈrections** to have different aims that cannot be achieved together without causing problems **pull sb's ˈleg** (*informal*) to play a joke on sb, usually by making them believe sth that is not true **pull the ˈother one (—it's got ˈbells on)** (*BrE, informal*) used to show that you do not believe what sb has just said **pull out all the ˈstops** (*informal*) to make the greatest effort possible to achieve sth **pull the ˈplug on sb/sth** (*informal*) to put an end to sb's project, a plan, etc. **pull your ˈpunches** (*informal*) (usually used in negative sentences) to express sth less strongly than you are able to, for example to avoid upsetting or shocking sb: *Her articles certainly don't pull any punches.* **pull sth/a ˌrabbit out of the ˈhat** (*informal*) to suddenly produce sth as a solution to a problem **pull ˈrank (on sb)** to make use of your place or status in society or at work to make sb do what you want **pull the rug (out) from under sb's ˈfeet** (*informal*) to take help or support away from sb suddenly **pull your ˈsocks up** (*BrE, informal*) to try to improve your performance, work, behaviour, etc: *You're going to have to pull your socks up.* **pull ˈstrings (for sb)** (*NAmE* also **pull ˈwires**) (*informal*) to use your influence in order to get an advantage for sb **pull the ˈstrings** to control events or the actions of other people ˌ**pull up ˈstakes** (*NAmE*) (*BrE* ˌ**up ˈsticks**) to suddenly move from your house and go to live somewhere else **pull your**

'**weight** to work as hard as everyone else in a job, an activity, etc. **pull the 'wool over sb's eyes** (*informal*) to try to trick sb; to hide your real actions or intentions from sb ➲ more at BOOTSTRAP, FACE *n.*, HORN, PIECE *n.*, SHRED *n.*
PHR V ˌ**pull a'head** (**of sb/sth**) to move in front of sb/sth: *The cyclists were together until the bend, when Tyler pulled ahead.* ˌ**pull sb/sth a'part** to separate people or animals that are fighting ˌ**pull sth a'part** 🔑 to separate sth into pieces by pulling different parts of it in different directions '**pull at sth** = PULL ON STH ˌ**pull a'way** (**from sth**) (of a vehicle) to start moving: *They waved as the bus pulled away.* ˌ**pull 'back** **1** (of an army) to move back from a place **SYN** **withdraw** **2** to decide not to do sth that you were intending to do, because of possible problems **SYN** **withdraw**: *Their sponsors pulled back at the last minute.* ˌ**pull sb↔'back** to make an army move back from a place ˌ**pull 'back** | ˌ**pull sth↔'back** (*sport*) to improve a team's position in a game: *Rangers pulled back to 4–3.* ◇ *They pulled back a goal just before half-time.* ˌ**pull sb 'down** (*especially US*) to make sb less happy, healthy or successful ˌ**pull sth↔'down** **1** 🔑 to destroy a building completely **SYN** **demolish** **2** = PULL STH IN ˌ**pull sb↔'in** (*informal*) to bring sb to a police station in order to ask them questions about a crime ˌ**pull sth↔'in/'down** (*informal*) to earn the large amount of money mentioned **SYN** **make**: *I reckon she's pulling in over $100 000.* ˌ**pull 'in** (**to sth**) 🔑 **1** (of a train) to enter a station and stop **2** (*BrE*) (of a vehicle or its driver) to move to the side of the road or to the place mentioned and stop: *The police car signalled to us to pull in.* ˌ**pull 'off** | ˌ**pull 'off sth** 🔑 (of a vehicle or its driver) to leave the road in order to stop for a short time ˌ**pull sth↔'off** (*informal*) to succeed in doing sth difficult: *We pulled off the deal.* ◇ *I never thought you'd pull it off.* '**pull on/at sth** to take long deep breaths from a cigarette, etc. ˌ**pull 'out** 🔑 (of a vehicle or its driver) to move away from the side of the road, etc: *A car suddenly pulled out in front of me.* ˌ**pull 'out** (**of sth**) **1** 🔑 (of a train) to leave a station **2** 🔑 to move away from sth or stop being involved in it **SYN** **withdraw**: *The project became so expensive that we had to pull out.* ˌ**pull sb/sth 'out** (**of sth**) 🔑 to make sb/sth move away from sth or stop being involved in it **SYN** **withdraw**: *They are pulling their troops out of the war zone.* ➲ related noun PULL-OUT ˌ**pull 'over** 🔑 (of a vehicle or its driver) to move to the side of the road in order to stop or let sth pass ˌ**pull sb/sth↔'over** 🔑 (of the police) to make a driver or vehicle move to the side of the road ˌ**pull 'through** | ˌ**pull 'through sth** **1** 🔑 to get better after a serious illness, operation, etc: *The doctors think she will pull through.* **2** to succeed in doing sth very difficult: *It's going to be tough but we'll pull through it together.* ˌ**pull sb 'through** | ˌ**pull sb 'through sth** **1** to help sb get better after a serious illness, operation, etc. **2** to help sb succeed in doing sth very difficult: *I relied on my instincts to pull me through.* ˌ**pull to'gether** to act, work, etc. together with other people in an organized way and without fighting ˌ**pull yourself to'gether** 🔑 to take control of your feelings and behave in a calm way: *Stop crying and pull yourself together!* ˌ**pull 'up** 🔑 (of a vehicle or its driver) to stop: *He pulled up at the traffic lights.* ˌ**pull sb 'up** (*BrE, informal*) to criticize sb for sth that they have done wrong ■ *noun*
▸ TRYING TO MOVE STH **1** 🔑 [C] an act of trying to make sth move by holding it firmly and bringing it towards you: *I gave the door a sharp pull and it opened.*
▸ PHYSICAL FORCE **2** 🔑 [sing.] **the ~** (**of sth**) a strong physical force that makes sth move in a particular direction: *the earth's gravitational pull*
▸ ATTRACTION **3** 🔑 [C, usually sing.] **the ~** (**of sth**) the fact of sth attracting you or having a strong effect on you: *The magnetic pull of the city was hard to resist.*
▸ INFLUENCE **4** [U] (*informal*) power and influence over other people: *people who have a lot of pull with the media*
▸ ON CIGARETTE/DRINK **5** [C] **~** (**at/on sth**) an act of taking a deep breath of smoke from a cigarette, etc. or a deep drink of sth: *She* ***took a long pull*** *on her cigarette.*
▸ WALK UP HILL **6** [C, usually sing.] (*BrE*) a difficult walk up a steep hill: *It's* ***a long pull*** *up to the summit.*
▸ MUSCLE INJURY **7** [C] an injury to a muscle caused by using too much force
▸ HANDLE/ROPE **8** [C] (especially in compounds) something such as a handle or rope that you use to pull sth: *a* ***bell/door pull*** ➲ see also RING PULL
IDM **on the 'pull** (*BrE, slang*) (of a person) trying to find a sexual partner

Synonyms

pull

drag • draw • haul • tow • tug

These words all mean to move sth in a particular direction, especially towards or behind you.

pull to hold sth and move it in a particular direction; to hold or be attached to a vehicle and move it along behind you: *Pull the chair nearer the table.* ◇ *They use oxen to pull their carts.*

drag to pull sb/sth in a particular direction or behind you, usually along the ground, and especially with effort: *The sack is too heavy to lift—you'll have to drag it.*

draw (*formal*) to move sb/sth by pulling them/it gently; to pull a vehicle such as a carriage: *I drew my chair closer to the fire.* ◇ *a* ***horse-drawn*** *carriage*

haul to pull sb/sth to a particular place with a lot of effort: *Fishermen were hauling in their nets.*

DRAG OR HAUL?

You usually **drag** sth behind you along the ground; you usually **haul** sth towards you, often upwards towards you. **Dragging** sth often needs effort, but **hauling** sth always does.

tow to pull a car, boat or light plane behind another vehicle, using a rope or chain: *Our car was towed away by the police.*

tug to pull sb/sth hard in a particular direction: *She tried to escape but he tugged her back.*

PATTERNS

- to pull/drag/draw/haul/tow/tug sb/sth **along/down/towards** sth
- to pull/drag/draw/haul/tow sb/sth **behind you**
- to pull/drag/draw/haul a **cart/sledge**
- to pull/draw a **coach/carriage**
- to pull/haul/tow a **truck**
- **horses** pull/draw/haul sth
- **dogs** pull/drag/haul sth

pull·back /ˈpʊlbæk/ *noun* **1** an act of taking soldiers away from an area **2** a time when prices are reduced, or when fewer people want to buy sth

'**pull date** (*US*) (*BrE* '**sell-by date**) *noun* the date printed on food packages, etc. after which the food must not be sold

'**pull-down** *adj.* **1** designed to be used by being pulled down: *a pull-down bed* **2 ~ menu** (*computing*) a list of possible choices that appears on a computer screen below a menu title ➲ VISUAL VOCAB page V55

ˌ**pulled 'pork** *noun* [U] meat from a pig that is cooked very slowly, often with smoke, until it is so soft you can pull it into small pieces with your hands

pul·let /ˈpʊlɪt/ *noun* a young chicken, especially one that is less than one year old

pul·ley /ˈpʊli/ *noun* a wheel or set of wheels over which a rope or chain is pulled in order to lift or lower heavy objects: *a system of ropes and pulleys* ➲ picture at BLOCK AND TACKLE

'**pulling power** (*BrE*) (*NAmE* '**drawing power**) *noun* [U] the ability of sb/sth to attract people

Pull·man /ˈpʊlmən/ *noun* (*pl.* **Pull·mans**) a type of very comfortable coach/car on a train

P

ˈpull-out *noun, adj.*
■ ***noun*** **1** a part of a magazine, newspaper, etc. that can be taken out easily and kept separately: *an eight-page pull-out on health* ◇ *a pull-out guide* **2** an act of taking an army away from a particular place; an act of taking an organization out of a system
■ ***adj.*** [only before noun] (*especially NAmE*) a **pull-out** bed, couch, etc. can be kept hidden when not in use and pulled out when it is needed

pull·over /ˈpʊləʊvə(r); *NAmE* -oʊ-/ *noun* (*especially BrE*) a knitted piece of clothing made of wool or cotton for the upper part of the body, with long sleeves and no buttons **SYN** **jumper, sweater**

ˈpull tab (also **tab**) (both *NAmE*) (*BrE* **ˈring pull**) *noun* a small piece of metal with a ring attached which is pulled to open cans of food, drink, etc. ➲ VISUAL VOCAB page V29

pul·lu·late /ˈpʌljuleɪt/ *verb* (*formal*) **1** [I] to breed or spread quickly **2** [I] to be full of life or activity ▸ **pul·lu·lat·ing** *adj.*: *a pullulating mass of people*

ˈpull-up (also **ˈchin-up** especially in *NAmE*) *noun* [usually pl.] an exercise in which you hold onto a high bar above your head and pull yourself up towards it

pul·mon·ary /ˈpʌlmənəri; *NAmE* -neri/ *adj.* [only before noun] (*medical*) connected with the lungs

pulp /pʌlp/ *noun, verb, adj.*
■ ***noun*** **1** [sing., U] a soft wet substance that is made especially by crushing sth: *Cook the fruit gently until it forms a pulp.* ◇ *His face had been* ***beaten to a pulp*** (= very badly beaten). **2** [U] a soft substance that is made by crushing wood, cloth or other material and then used to make paper: ***paper/wood pulp*** **3** [U] the soft part inside some fruit and vegetables **SYN** **flesh** ▸ **pulpy** *adj.*: *Cook the fruit slowly until soft and pulpy.*
■ ***verb*** **~ sth** to crush or beat sth so that it becomes soft and wet: *Unsold copies of the novel had to be pulped.* ◇ *pulped fruit*
■ ***adj.*** [only before noun] (of books, magazines, etc.) badly written and often intended to shock people: *pulp fiction*

P

pul·pit /ˈpʊlpɪt/ *noun* a small platform in a church that is like a box and is high above the ground, where a priest, etc. stands to speak to the people

pul·sar /ˈpʌlsɑː(r)/ *noun* (*astronomy*) a star that cannot be seen but that sends out regular rapid radio signals ➲ compare QUASAR

pul·sate /pʌlˈseɪt; *NAmE* ˈpʌlseɪt/ *verb* **1** [I] to make strong regular movements or sounds: *pulsating rhythms* ◇ *a pulsating headache* ◇ *Lights were pulsating in the sky.* **2** [I] to be full of excitement or energy **SYN** **buzz**: *a pulsating game* ◇ **~ with sth** *The streets were pulsating with life.* ▸ **pul·sa·tion** /pʌlˈseɪʃn/ *noun* [C, U]

pulse /pʌls/ *noun, verb*
■ ***noun*** **1** [usually sing.] the regular beat of blood as it is sent around the body, that can be felt in different places, especially on the inside part of the wrist; the number of times the blood beats in a minute: *a* ***strong/weak pulse*** ◇ *an abnormally high pulse rate* ◇ *The doctor* ***took/felt my pulse.*** ◇ *Fear sent her* ***pulse racing*** (= made it beat very quickly). **2** a strong regular beat in music **SYN** **rhythm**: *the throbbing pulse of the drums* **3** a single short increase in the amount of light, sound or electricity produced by a machine, etc: *pulse waves* ◇ *sound pulses* **4** **pulses** [pl.] the seeds of some plants that are eaten as food, such as PEAS and LENTILS **IDM** see FINGER *n.*
■ ***verb*** **1** [I] to move, beat or flow with strong regular movements or sounds **SYN** **throb**: *A vein pulsed in his temple.* ◇ *the pulsing rhythm of the music* **2** [I] **~ (with sth)** to be full of a feeling such as excitement or energy **SYN** **buzz**: *The auditorium pulsed with excitement.*

pul·ver·ize (*BrE* also **-ise**) /ˈpʌlvəraɪz/ *verb* **1 ~ sth** (*formal*) to crush sth into a fine powder **2 ~ sb/sth** (*informal, especially BrE*) to defeat or destroy sb/sth completely **SYN** **crush**: *We pulverized the opposition.*

puma /ˈpjuːmə; *NAmE* ˈpuːmə/ (*especially BrE*) (*NAmE* usually **cou·gar**) (*NAmE* also **ˈmountain lion, pan·ther**) *noun* a large American wild animal of the cat family, with yellowish-brown or greyish fur

pum·ice /ˈpʌmɪs/ (also **ˈpumice stone**) *noun* [U] a type of grey stone that comes from VOLCANOES and is very light in weight. It is used in powder form for cleaning and polishing, and in pieces for rubbing on the skin to make it softer.

pum·mel /ˈpʌml/ *verb* (-ll-, *US* -l-) [T, I] to keep hitting sb/sth hard, especially with your FISTS (= tightly closed hands): **~ sb/sth (with sth)** *He pummelled the pillow with his fists.* ◇ (*figurative*) *She pummelled* (= strongly criticized) *her opponents.* ◇ **~ (at sth)** *Her fists pummelled at his chest.*

pum·melo /ˈpʌmələʊ; *NAmE* -loʊ/ *noun* = POMELO

pump /pʌmp/ *noun, verb*
■ ***noun*** **1** a machine that is used to force liquid, gas or air into or out of sth: *She washed her face at the pump in front of the inn.* ◇ (*BrE*) *a petrol pump* ◇ (*NAmE*) *a gas pump* ◇ *a* ***foot/hand pump*** (= that you work by using your foot or hand) ◇ *a bicycle pump* ➲ VISUAL VOCAB pages V20, V41 ➲ see also STOMACH PUMP **2** (*BrE*) = PLIMSOLL **3** (*especially NAmE*) (*BrE* **ˈcourt shoe**) a woman's formal shoe that is plain and does not cover the top part of the foot ➲ VISUAL VOCAB page V52 **4** (*BrE*) a woman's light soft flat shoe worn for dancing or exercise; a similar style of shoe worn as a fashion item: *ballet pumps* ➲ VISUAL VOCAB page V52 **IDM** see HAND *n.*, PRIME *v.*
■ ***verb*** **1** [T, I] to make water, air, gas, etc. flow in a particular direction by using a pump or sth that works like a pump: **~ (sth) (+ adv./prep.)** *The engine is used for pumping water out of the mine.* ◇ *The heart pumps blood around the body.* ◇ **~ sth + adj.** *The lake had been pumped dry.* **2** [I] **+ adv./prep.** (of a liquid) to flow in a particular direction as if it is being forced by a pump: *Blood was pumping out of his wound.* **3** [T] **~ sth (+ adv./prep.)** to move sth quickly up and down or in and out: *He kept pumping my hand up and down.* ◇ *I pumped the handle like crazy.* **4** [I] to move quickly up and down or in and out: *She sprinted for the line, legs pumping.* ◇ *My heart was pumping with excitement.* **5** [T] **~ sb (for sth)** (*informal*) to try to get information from sb by asking them a lot of questions: *See if you can pump him for more details.*
IDM **pump ˈbullets, ˈshots, etc. into sb** to fire a lot of bullets into sb **pump sb full of sth** to fill sb with sth, especially drugs: *They pumped her full of painkillers.* **pump ˈiron** (*informal*) to do exercises in which you lift heavy weights in order to make your muscles stronger **pump sb's ˈstomach** to remove the contents of sb's stomach using a pump, because they have swallowed sth harmful
PHR V **ˌpump sth ˈinto sth** | **ˌpump sth ˈin** to put a lot of money into sth: *He pumped all his savings into the business.* **ˌpump sth ˈinto sb** to force a lot of sth into sb: *It's difficult to pump facts and figures into tired students.* **ˌpump sth↔ˈout** (*informal*) to produce sth in large amounts: *loudspeakers pumping out rock music* ◇ *Our cars pump out thousands of tonnes of poisonous fumes every year.* **ˌpump sb↔ˈup** [usually passive] to make sb feel more excited or determined **ˌpump sth↔ˈup** **1** to fill a tyre, etc. with air using a pump **2** (*informal*) to increase the amount, value or volume of sth: *Interest rates were pumped up last week.*

ˈpump-action *adj.* [only before noun] (of a gun or other device) worked by quickly pulling or pressing part of it in and out or up and down: *a pump-action shotgun* ◇ *a pump-action spray*

pum·per·nickel /ˈpʌmpənɪkl; *NAmE* -pərn-/ *noun* [U] (from *German*) a type of heavy dark brown bread made from RYE, originally from Germany and often sold in slices

pump·kin /ˈpʌmpkɪn/ *noun* [U, C] a large round vegetable with thick orange skin. The seeds can be dried and eaten and the soft flesh can be cooked as a vegetable or in sweet PIES: *Pumpkin pie is a traditional American dish served on Thanksgiving.* ➲ VISUAL VOCAB page V27

ˈpump-priming *noun* [U] the act of investing money to encourage growth in an industry or a business, especially by a government

ˈ**pump room** *noun* (especially in the past) the room at a SPA where people go to drink the special water

pun /pʌn/ *noun, verb*

▪ ***noun*** **~ (on sth)** the clever or humorous use of a word that has more than one meaning, or of words that have different meanings but sound the same: *We're banking on them lending us the money—no pun intended!* ➲ compare WORDPLAY

▪ ***verb*** (-nn-) [I] to make a pun

Punch /pʌntʃ/ *noun* IDM see PLEASED

punch 🔑 /pʌntʃ/ *verb, noun*

▪ ***verb*** **1** 🔑 to hit sb/sth hard with your FIST (= closed hand): **~ sb/sth** *He was kicked and punched as he lay on the ground.* ◇ *He was* ***punching the air*** *in triumph.* ◇ **~ sb/sth in/on sth** *She punched him on the nose.* **2** to make a hole in sth with a PUNCH *n.* (3) or some other sharp object: **~ sth** *to punch a time card* ◇ **~ sth in/through sth** *The machine punches a row of holes in the metal sheet.* **3 ~ sth** to press buttons or keys on a computer, telephone, etc. in order to operate it: *I punched the button to summon the elevator.* ▸ **punch·er** *noun*: *He's one of boxing's strongest punchers.*

IDM ˌ**punch above your** ˈ**weight** to be or try to be more successful than others in doing sth that normally requires more skill, experience, money, etc. than you have: *This player seems to be able to constantly punch above his weight.*

PHR V ˌ**punch** ˈ**in/**ˈ**out** (*NAmE*) to record the time you arrive at/leave work by putting a card into a special machine ➲ see also CLOCK IN/ON, CLOCK OUT/OFF ˌ**punch sth↔**ˈ**in** | ˌ**punch sth** ˈ**into sth** to put information into a computer by pressing the keys: *He punched in the security code.* ˌ**punch sb** ˈ**out** (*NAmE, informal*) to hit sb so hard that they fall down ˌ**punch sth↔**ˈ**out 1** to press a combination of buttons or keys on a computer, telephone, etc: *He picked up the telephone and punched out his friend's number.* **2** to make a hole in sth or knock sth out by hitting it very hard: *I felt as if all my teeth had been punched out.* **3** to cut sth from paper, wood, metal, etc. with a special tool

▪ ***noun*** **1** 🔑 [C] a hard hit made with the FIST (= closed hand): *a punch in the face* ◇ *Hill* ***threw a punch*** *at the police officer.* ◇ *a knockout punch* ◇ *He shot out his right arm and* ***landed a punch*** *on Lorrimer's nose.* **2** [U] the power to interest people: *It's a well-constructed crime story, told with speed and punch.* **3** [C] a tool or machine for cutting holes in paper, leather or metal: *a hole punch* ➲ VISUAL VOCAB page V56 **4** [U] a hot or cold drink made by mixing water, fruit juice, spices, and usually wine or another alcoholic drink IDM see BEAT *V.*, PACK *V.*, PULL *V.*, ROLL *V.*

Punch and Judy show /ˌpʌntʃ ən ˈdʒuːdi ʃəʊ; *NAmE* ʃoʊ/ *noun* (in Britain) a traditional type of entertainment for children in which PUPPETS are used to tell stories about Punch, who is always fighting with his wife Judy

punch·bag /ˈpʌntʃbæg/ (*BrE*) (*NAmE* ˈ**punching bag**) *noun* a heavy leather bag, hung on a rope, which is punched, especially by BOXERS as part of training, or as a form of exercise

punch·ball /ˈpʌntʃbɔːl/ *noun* a heavy leather ball, fixed on a spring, which is punched, especially by BOXERS as a part of training, or as a form of exercise

punch·bowl /ˈpʌntʃbəʊl; *NAmE* -boʊl/ *noun* a bowl used for serving PUNCH *n.* (4)

punch·card /ˈpʌntʃkɑːd; *NAmE* -kɑːrd/ (also ˌ**punched** ˈ**card**) *noun* a card on which, in the past, information was recorded as lines of holes and used for giving instructions, etc. to computers and other machines

ˈ**punch-drunk** (also ˌ**slap-**ˈ**happy** especially in *NAmE*) *adj.* **1** (of a BOXER) confused as a result of being punched on the head many times **2** unable to think clearly; in a confused state

ˈ**punching bag** (*NAmE*) (*BrE* **punch·bag**) *noun* a heavy leather bag, hung on a rope, which is punched, especially by BOXERS as part of training, or as a form of exercise

punch·line /ˈpʌntʃlaɪn/ (also *NAmE informal* ˈ**tag line**) *noun* the last few words of a joke that make it funny

ˈ**punch-up** *noun* (*BrE, informal*) a physical fight SYN **brawl**

punchy /ˈpʌntʃi/ *adj.* (**punch·ier**, **punchi·est**) (of a speech, song, etc.) having a strong effect because it expresses sth clearly in only a few words

punc·tili·ous /pʌŋkˈtɪliəs/ *adj.* (*formal*) very careful to behave correctly or to perform your duties exactly as you should: *a punctilious host* ▸ **punc·tili·ous·ly** *adv.* **punc·tili·ous·ness** *noun* [U]

punc·tual /ˈpʌŋktʃuəl/ *adj.* happening or doing sth at the arranged or correct time; not late: *She has been reliable and punctual.* ◇ *a punctual start at 9 o'clock* ▸ **punc·tu·al·ity** /ˌpʌŋktʃuˈæləti/ *noun* [U] **punc·tu·al·ly** /ˈpʌŋktʃuəli/ *adv.*: *They always pay punctually.*

punc·tu·ate /ˈpʌŋktʃueɪt/ *verb* **1** [T, often passive] **~ sth (with sth)** to interrupt sth at intervals: *Her speech was punctuated by bursts of applause.* **2** [I, T] **~ (sth)** to divide writing into sentences and phrases by using special marks, for example commas, question marks, etc.

punc·tu·ation /ˌpʌŋktʃuˈeɪʃn/ *noun* [U] the marks used in writing that divide sentences and phrases; the system of using these marks

ˌ**punctu**ˈ**ation mark** *noun* a sign or mark used in writing to divide sentences and phrases

punc·ture /ˈpʌŋktʃə(r)/ *noun, verb*

▪ ***noun*** **1** (*BrE*) a small hole in a tyre made by a sharp point: *I had a puncture on the way and arrived late.* ➲ see also FLAT *n.* (6) **2** a small hole, especially in the skin, made by a sharp point

▪ ***verb*** **1** [T, I] **~ (sth)** to make a small hole in sth; to get a small hole: *to puncture a tyre* ◇ *She was taken to the hospital with broken ribs and a punctured lung.* ◇ *One of the front tyres had punctured.* **2** [T] **~ sth** to suddenly make sb feel less confident, proud, etc: *to puncture sb's confidence*

pun·dit /ˈpʌndɪt/ *noun* **1** a person who knows a lot about a particular subject and who often talks about it in public SYN **expert 2** = PANDIT

pun·gent /ˈpʌndʒənt/ *adj.* **1** having a strong taste or smell: *the pungent smell of burning rubber* ➲ SYNONYMS at BITTER **2** direct and having a strong effect: *pungent criticism* ▸ **pun·gency** /-nsi/ *noun* [U] **pung·ent·ly** *adv.*

pun·ish 🔑 /ˈpʌnɪʃ/ *verb*

1 🔑 to make sb suffer because they have broken the law or done sth wrong: **~ sb** *Those responsible for this crime will be severely punished.* ◇ *My parents used to punish me by not letting me watch TV.* ◇ **~ sb for sth/for doing sth** *He was punished for refusing to answer their questions.* **2 ~ sth (by/with sth)** to set the punishment for a particular crime: *In those days murder was always punished with the death penalty.* **3 ~ yourself (for sth)** to blame yourself for sth that has happened

pun·ish·able /ˈpʌnɪʃəbl/ *adj.* **~ (by/with sth)** (of a crime) that can be punished, especially by law: *a crime punishable by/with imprisonment* ◇ *Giving false information to the police is a punishable offence.*

pun·ish·ing /ˈpʌnɪʃɪŋ/ *adj.* [usually before noun] long and difficult and making you work hard so you become very tired: *The President has a punishing schedule for the next six months.*

pun·ish·ment 🔑 /ˈpʌnɪʃmənt/ *noun*

1 🔑 [U, C] an act or a way of punishing sb: *to* ***inflict/impose/mete out punishment*** ◇ **~ (for sth)** *What is the punishment for murder?* ◇ *There is little evidence that harsher punishments deter any better than more lenient ones.* ◇ *The punishment should fit the crime.* ◇ *He was sent to his room* ***as a punishment***. ➲ see also CAPITAL PUNISHMENT, CORPORAL PUNISHMENT **2** [U] rough treatment: *The carpet by the door takes the most punishment.*

pu·ni·tive /ˈpjuːnətɪv/ *adj.* [usually before noun] (*formal*) **1** intended as punishment: *There are calls for more* ***punitive measures*** *against people who drink and drive.* ◇ (*NAmE*) *He was awarded* ***punitive damages*** (= in a court of law). **2** very severe and that people find very difficult to pay: *punitive taxes* ▸ **pu·ni·tive·ly** *adv.*

P

Pun·jabi /pʊn'dʒɑːbi/ *noun* **1** [C] a person from the Punjab area in NW India and Pakistan **2** [U] the language of people from the Punjab ▸ **Pun·jabi** *adj.*

punk /pʌŋk/ *noun* **1** (also ˌ**punk 'rock**) [U] a type of loud and aggressive rock music popular in the late 1970s and early 1980s: *a punk band* **2** (also ˌ**punk 'rocker**) [C] a person who likes punk music and dresses like a punk musician, for example by wearing metal chains, leather clothes and having brightly coloured hair: *a punk haircut* **3** [C] (*informal, especially NAmE*) a young man or boy who behaves in a rude or violent way SYN **lout**

pun·kah /'pʌŋkə; -kɑː/ *noun* **1** (*IndE*) an electric fan **2** (in India in the past) a large cloth fan that hung from the ceiling and that was moved by pulling a string

pun·net /'pʌnɪt/ *noun* (*BrE*) a small box or BASKET that soft fruit is often sold in ➲ VISUAL VOCAB page V29

pun·ster /'pʌnstə(r)/ *noun* a person who often makes PUNS

punt[1] /pʌnt/ *noun, verb* ➲ see also PUNT[2]

■ ***noun*** **1** a long shallow boat with a flat bottom and square ends which is moved by pushing the end of a long pole against the bottom of a river ➲ VISUAL VOCAB page V45 **2** (*BrE, informal*) a bet: *The investment is little more than a punt.* **3** (in RUGBY or AMERICAN FOOTBALL) a long kick made after dropping the ball from your hands

■ ***verb*** **1** [I, T] **~ (sth) (+ adv./prep.)** to travel in a punt, especially for pleasure: *We spent the day punting on the river.* ◇ *to go punting* **2** [T] **~ sth (+ adv./prep.)** to kick a ball hard so that it goes a long way, sometimes after it has dropped from your hands and before it reaches the ground

punt[2] /pʊnt/ *noun* the former unit of money in the Republic of Ireland (replaced in 2002 by the euro) ➲ see also PUNT[1]

punt·er /'pʌntə(r)/ *noun* (*BrE, informal*) **1** a person who buys or uses a particular product or service SYN **customer**: *It's important to keep the punters happy.* **2** a person who gambles on the result of a horse race

puny /'pjuːni/ *adj.* (**puni·er, puni·est**) (*disapproving*) **1** small and weak SYN **feeble**: *The lamb was a puny little thing.* **2** not very impressive: *They laughed at my puny efforts.*

P

pup /pʌp/ *noun* **1** = PUPPY **2** a young animal of various SPECIES (= types): *a seal pup*

IDM **sell sb/buy a pup** (*old-fashioned, BrE, informal*) to sell sb or be sold sth that has no value or is worth much less than the price paid

pupa /'pjuːpə/ *noun* (*pl.* **pupae** /'pjuːpiː/) an insect in the stage of development between a LARVA and an adult insect ➲ compare CHRYSALIS ▸ **pupal** /'pjuːpəl/ *adj.* [usually before noun]

pu·pate /pjuː'peɪt; *NAmE* 'pjuːpeɪt/ *verb* [I] (*biology*) to develop into a pupa

pupil 0➛ /'pjuːpl/ *noun*

1 0➛ (*especially BrE*, becoming *old-fashioned*) a person who is being taught, especially a child in a school: *How many pupils does the school have?* ◇ *She now teaches only private pupils.* ➲ SYNONYMS at STUDENT **2** 0➛ a person who is taught artistic, musical, etc. skills by an expert: *The painting is by a pupil of Rembrandt.* **3** the small round black area at the centre of the eye: *Her pupils were dilated.* ➲ VISUAL VOCAB page V48 ➲ compare IRIS

pu·pil·lage (*especially US* **pu·pil·age**) /'pjuːpɪlɪdʒ/ *noun* [U, C, sing.] **1** (*formal*) a period during which you are a student, especially when you are being taught by a particular person **2** (*BrE*) a period during which a lawyer trains to become a BARRISTER by studying with a qualified barrister; the system which allows this training

pup·pet /'pʌpɪt/ *noun* **1** a model of a person or an animal that can be made to move, for example by pulling strings attached to parts of its body or by putting your hand inside it. A puppet with strings is also called a MARIONETTE: *a hand puppet* ◇ *a puppet show* ➲ see also GLOVE PUPPET **2** (usually *disapproving*) a person or group whose actions are controlled by another: *The occupying forces set up a **puppet government**.*

pup·pet·eer /ˌpʌpɪ'tɪə(r); *NAmE* -'tɪr/ *noun* a person who performs with puppets

pup·pet·ry /'pʌpɪtri/ *noun* [U] the art and skill of making and using puppets

puppy /'pʌpi/ *noun* (*pl.* **-ies**) (also **pup**) **1** a young dog: *a litter of puppies* ◇ *a Labrador puppy* **2** (*old-fashioned, informal*) a proud or rude young man

'puppy fat (*BrE*) (*NAmE* **'baby fat**) *noun* [U] fat on a child's body that disappears as the child grows older

'puppy love *noun* [U] feelings of love that a young person has for sb else and that adults do not think is very serious

'pup tent *noun* (*NAmE*) a small tent for two people

pur·chase 0➛ AW /'pɜːtʃəs; *NAmE* 'pɜːrtʃəs/ *noun, verb*

■ ***noun*** (*formal*) **1** 0➛ [U, C] the act or process of buying sth: *to **make a purchase** (= buy sth)* ◇ *Keep your receipt as **proof of purchase**.* ◇ *The company has just announced its £27 million purchase of Park Hotel.* ➲ COLLOCATIONS at SHOPPING ➲ see also HIRE PURCHASE **2** 0➛ [C] something that you have bought: *major purchases, such as a new car* ◇ *If you are not satisfied with your purchase we will give you a full refund.* **3** [U, sing.] (*technical*) a firm hold on sth with the hands or feet, for example when you are climbing SYN **grip**: *She tried to get a purchase on the slippery rock.*

■ ***verb*** 0➛ **~ sth (from sb)** (*formal*) to buy sth: *The equipment can be purchased from your local supplier.* ◇ *They purchased the land for $1 million.* ◇ *(figurative) Victory was purchased* (= achieved) *at too great a price.*

'purchase price *noun* [usually sing.] (*formal*) the price that is paid for sth you buy

pur·chaser AW /'pɜːtʃəsə(r); *NAmE* 'pɜːrtʃ-/ *noun* (*formal*) a person who buys sth ➲ compare BUYER

pur·chas·ing AW /'pɜːtʃəsɪŋ; *NAmE* 'pɜːrtʃ-/ *noun* [U] (*business*) the activity of buying things, especially for a company

'purchasing power *noun* [U] **1** money that people have available to buy goods with **2** the amount that a unit of money can buy: *the peso's purchasing power*

pur·dah /'pɜːdə; *NAmE* 'pɜːrdə/ *noun* [U] the system in some Muslim societies by which women live in a separate part of a house or cover their faces so that men do not see them: *to be **in purdah*** ◇ *He kept his daughters in virtual purdah.*

pure 0➛ /pjʊə(r); *NAmE* pjʊr/ *adj.* (**purer** /'pjʊərə(r); *NAmE* 'pjʊr-/, **purest** /'pjʊərɪst; *NAmE* 'pjʊr-/)

▸ NOT MIXED **1** 0➛ [usually before noun] not mixed with anything else; with nothing added: ***pure gold/silk, etc.*** ◇ *These shirts are **100% pure** cotton.* ◇ *Classical dance **in its purest form** requires symmetry and balance.* ◇ *One movie is classified as pure art, the other as entertainment.*

▸ CLEAN **2** 0➛ clean and not containing any harmful substances: *a bottle of pure water* ◇ *The air was sweet and pure.* OPP **impure**

▸ COMPLETE **3** 0➛ [only before noun] complete and total: *They met by pure chance.* ◇ *She laughed with pure joy.*

▸ COLOUR/SOUND/LIGHT **4** 0➛ very clear; perfect: *beaches of pure white sand* ◇ *a pure voice*

▸ MORALLY GOOD **5** without evil thoughts or actions, especially sexual ones; morally good: *to lead a pure life* ◇ *His motives were pure.* ◇ (*literary*) *to be pure in body and mind* OPP **impure**

▸ SUBJECT YOU STUDY **6** [only before noun] concerned with increasing knowledge of the subject rather than with using knowledge in practical ways: *pure mathematics* ◇ *technology as opposed to pure science subjects* ➲ compare APPLIED

▸ BREED/RACE **7** not mixed with any other breed or race, etc: *These cattle are one of the purest breeds in Britain.* ➲ see also PURE-BRED ➲ see also PURIFY, PURITY

IDM ˌ**pure and 'simple** used after the noun that it refers to in order to emphasize that there is nothing but the thing you have just mentioned involved in sth: *It's laziness, pure and simple.*

'pure-bred *adj.* (of an animal) born from parents of the same breed, not from a mix of two or more breeds

purée /ˈpjʊəreɪ; *NAmE* pjʊˈreɪ/ *noun, verb*
■ ***noun*** [U, C] food in the form of a thick liquid made by crushing fruit or cooked vegetables in a small amount of water: *apple purée*
■ ***verb*** (**pur·éed, pur·éed**) **~ sth** to make food into a purée

pure·ly 0→ /ˈpjʊəli; *NAmE* ˈpjʊrli/ *adv.* only; completely: *I saw the letter purely by chance.* ◇ *The charity is run on a purely voluntary basis.* ◇ *She took the job* ***purely and simply*** *for the money.*

pur·ga·tive /ˈpɜːɡətɪv; *NAmE* ˈpɜːrɡ-/ *noun* a substance, especially a medicine, that causes your BOWELS to empty ▸ **pur·ga·tive** *adj.*

pur·ga·tory /ˈpɜːɡətri; *NAmE* ˈpɜːrɡətɔːri/ *noun* [U] **1** (usually **Purgatory**) (in Roman Catholic teaching) a place or state in which the souls of dead people suffer for the bad things they did when they were living, so that they can become pure enough to go to heaven **2** (*informal, humorous*) any place or state of suffering SYN **hell**: *Getting up at four o'clock every morning is sheer purgatory.*

purge /pɜːdʒ; *NAmE* pɜːrdʒ/ *verb, noun*
■ ***verb*** **1** to remove people from an organization, often violently, because their opinions or activities are unacceptable to the people in power: **~ sth** (**of sb**) *His first act as leader was to purge the party of extremists.* ◇ **~ sb** (**from sth**) *He purged extremists from the party.* **2** (*formal*) to make yourself/sb/sth pure, healthy or clean by getting rid of bad thoughts or feelings: **~ yourself/sb/sth** (**of sth**) *We need to purge our sport of racism.* ◇ **~ sth** (**from sth**) *Nothing could purge the guilt from her mind.*
■ ***noun*** the act of removing people, often violently, from an organization because their views are unacceptable to the people who have power

puri·fier /ˈpjʊərɪfaɪə(r); *NAmE* ˈpjʊr-/ *noun* a device that removes substances that are dirty, harmful or not wanted: *an* ***air/water purifier***

pur·ify /ˈpjʊərɪfaɪ; *NAmE* ˈpjʊr-/ *verb* (**puri·fies, puri·fy·ing, puri·fied, puri·fied**) **1 ~ sth** to make sth pure by removing substances that are dirty, harmful or not wanted: *One tablet will purify a litre of water* **2 ~ sb/sth/yourself** to make sb pure by removing evil from their souls: *Hindus purify themselves by bathing in the river Ganges.* **3 ~ sth** (**from sth**) (*technical*) to take a pure form of a substance out of another substance that contains it ▸ **puri·fi·ca·tion** /ˌpjʊərɪfɪˈkeɪʃn; *NAmE* ˌpjʊr-/ *noun* [U]: *a water purification plant*

Pu·rim /ˈpʊərɪm; pʊˈriːm; *NAmE* ˈpʊr-/ *noun* [U] a Jewish festival that is celebrated in the spring

pur·ist /ˈpjʊərɪst; *NAmE* ˈpjʊr-/ *noun* a person who thinks things should be done in the traditional way and who has strong opinions on what is correct in language, art, etc. ▸ **pur·ism** /ˈpjʊərɪzəm; *NAmE* ˈpjʊr-/ *noun* [U]

pur·itan /ˈpjʊərɪtən; *NAmE* ˈpjʊr-/ *noun, adj.*
■ ***noun*** **1** (usually *disapproving*) a person who has very strict moral attitudes and who thinks that pleasure is bad **2 Puritan** a member of a Protestant group of Christians in England in the 16th and 17th centuries who wanted to worship God in a simple way
■ ***adj.*** **1 Puritan** connected with the Puritans and their beliefs **2** = PURITANICAL

pur·it·an·ical /ˌpjʊərɪˈtænɪkl; *NAmE* ˌpjʊr-/ (also **pur·itan**) *adj.* (usually *disapproving*) having very strict moral attitudes: *Their parents had a puritanical streak and didn't approve of dancing.*

pur·itan·ism /ˈpjʊərɪtənɪzəm; *NAmE* ˈpjʊr-/ *noun* [U] **1 Puritanism** the beliefs and practices of the Puritans **2** very strict moral attitudes

pur·ity /ˈpjʊərəti; *NAmE* ˈpjʊr-/ *noun* [U] the state or quality of being pure: *The purity of the water is tested regularly.* ◇ *spiritual purity* OPP **impurity**

purl /pɜːl; *NAmE* pɜːrl/ *noun* [U] a STITCH used in knitting ▸ **purl** *verb* [I]

pur·lieus /ˈpɜːljuːz; *NAmE* ˈpɜːrluːz/ *noun* [pl.] (*literary*) the area near or surrounding a place

pur·loin /pɜːˈlɔɪn; ˈpɜːlɔɪn; *NAmE* pɜːrˈl-; ˈpɜːrl-/ *verb* **~ sth** (**from sb/sth**) (*formal* or *humorous*) to steal sth or use it without permission

pur·ple 0→ /ˈpɜːpl; *NAmE* ˈpɜːrpl/ *adj.* **1** 0→ having the colour of blue and red mixed together: *a purple flower* ◇ *His face was purple with rage.* **2 ~ prose/passage** writing or a piece of writing that is too grand in style ▸ **pur·ple** 0→ *noun* [U, C]: *She was dressed in purple.*

ˌPurple ˈHeart *noun* a MEDAL given to a member of the armed forces of the US who has been wounded in battle

ˈpurple patch *noun* (*BrE*) a period of success or good luck

purp·lish /ˈpɜːpəlɪʃ; *NAmE* ˈpɜːrp-/ *adj.* similar to purple in colour: *purplish lips*

pur·port *verb, noun*
■ ***verb*** /pəˈpɔːt; *NAmE* pərˈpɔːrt/ **~ to be/have sth** (*formal*) to claim to be sth or to have done sth, when this may not be true SYN **profess**: *The book does not purport to be a complete history of the period.*
■ ***noun*** /ˈpɜːpɔːt; *NAmE* ˈpɜːrpɔːrt/ [sing.] **the ~ of sth** (*formal*) the general meaning of sth

pur·ported /pəˈpɔːtɪd; *NAmE* pərˈpɔːrt-/ *adj.* [only before noun] (*formal*) that has been stated to have happened or to be true, when this might not be the case: *the scene of the purported crime* ▸ **pur·port·ed·ly** *adv.*: *a letter purportedly written by Mozart*

pur·pose 0→ /ˈpɜːpəs; *NAmE* ˈpɜːrpəs/ *noun* **1** 0→ [C] the intention, aim or function of sth; the thing that sth is supposed to achieve: *Our campaign's main purpose is to raise money.* ◇ *The purpose of the book is to provide a complete guide to the university.* ◇ *A meeting was called* ***for the purpose of*** *appointing a new treasurer.* ◇ *The experiments* ***serve no useful purpose*** (= are not useful). ◇ *The building is used for religious purposes.* **2** 0→ **purposes** [pl.] what is needed in a particular situation: *These gifts count as income for tax purposes.* ◇ ***For the purposes of*** *this study, the three groups have been combined.* **3** 0→ [C, U] meaning that is important and valuable to you: *Volunteer work gives her life* (***a sense of***) ***purpose.*** **4** [U] the ability to plan sth and work successfully to achieve it SYN **determination**: *He has enormous confidence and* ***strength of purpose.*** ➲ see also CROSS PURPOSES
IDM **on ˈpurpose** 0→ not by accident; deliberately: *He did it on purpose, knowing it would annoy her.* **to little/no ˈpurpose** (*formal*) with little/no useful effect or result ➲ more at INTENT *n.*, PRACTICAL *adj.* ➲ note on p. 1234

ˌpurpose-ˈbuilt *adj.* (*BrE*) designed and built for a particular purpose

pur·pose·ful /ˈpɜːpəsfl; *NAmE* ˈpɜːrp-/ *adj.* having a useful purpose; acting with a clear aim and with determination: *Purposeful work is an important part of the regime for young offenders.* ◇ *She looked purposeful and determined.* ▸ **pur·pose·ful·ly** /-fəli/ *adv.* **pur·pose·ful·ness** *noun* [U]

pur·pose·less /ˈpɜːpəsləs; *NAmE* ˈpɜːrp-/ *adj.* having no meaning, use or clear aim SYN **meaningless, pointless**: *purposeless destruction*

pur·pose·ly /ˈpɜːpəsli; *NAmE* ˈpɜːrp-/ *adv.* on purpose; deliberately: *He sat down, purposely avoiding her gaze.*

pur·pos·ive /ˈpɜːpəsɪv; *NAmE* ˈpɜːrp-/ *adj.* (*formal*) having a clear and definite purpose SYN **purposeful**

purr /pɜː(r)/ *verb* **1** [I] when a cat **purrs**, it makes a low continuous sound in the throat, especially when it is happy or comfortable **2** [I] (of a machine or vehicle) to make a low continuous sound; to move making such a sound: *a purring engine* ◇ *The car purred away.* **3** [I, T] (**+ speech**) to speak in a low and gentle voice, for example to show you are happy or satisfied, or because you want to attract sb or get them to do sth: *He was purring with satisfaction.* ▸ **purr** (also **pur·ring**) *noun* [sing.]: *the purr of a cat/a car engine*

purse /pɜːs; *NAmE* pɜːrs/ *noun, verb*

Synonyms

purpose

aim • intention • plan • point • idea

These are all words for talking about what sb/sth intends to do or achieve.

purpose what sth is supposed to achieve; what sb is trying to achieve: *Our campaign's main purpose is to raise money.*

aim what sb is trying to achieve; what sth is supposed to achieve: *She went to London with the aim of finding a job.* ◇ *Our main aim is to increase sales in Europe.*

PURPOSE OR AIM?

Your **purpose** for doing something is your reason for doing it; your **aim** is what you want to achieve. **Aim** can suggest that you are only trying to achieve sth; **purpose** gives a stronger sense of achievement being certain. **Aim** can be *sb's aim* or *the aim of sth*. **Purpose** is more usually *the purpose of sth*: you can talk about *sb's purpose* but that is more formal.

intention what you intend to do: *I have no intention of going to the wedding.* ◇ *She's full of **good intentions** but they rarely work out.*

plan what you intend to do or achieve: *There are no plans to build new offices.*

INTENTION OR PLAN?

Your **intentions** are what you want to do, especially in the near future; your **plans** are what you have decided or arranged to do, often, but not always, in the longer term.

point (*rather informal*) the purpose or aim of sth: ***What's the point** of all this violence?* ◇ *The point of the lesson is to compare the two countries.*

idea (*rather informal*) the purpose of sth; sb's aim: *The whole idea of going was so that we could meet her new boyfriend.* ◇ ***What's the idea** behind this?*

POINT OR IDEA?

Point is a more negative word than **idea.** If you say *What's the point...?* you are suggesting that there is no point; if you say *What's the idea...?* you are genuinely asking a question. **Point**, but not **idea**, is used to talk about things you feel annoyed or unhappy about: ~~*There's no idea in...*~~ ◇ ~~*I don't see the idea of...*~~.

PATTERNS

- **with** the purpose/aim/intention/idea **of** doing sth
- sb's intention/plan **to do sth**
- to **have** a(n) purpose/aim/intention/plan/point
- to **achieve/fulfil** a(n) purpose/aim

■ ***noun*** **1** [C] (*especially BrE*) a small bag made of leather, plastic, etc. for carrying coins and often also paper money, cards, etc, used especially by women: *I took a coin out of my purse and gave it to the child.* ➲ VISUAL VOCAB page V52 ➲ compare CHANGE PURSE, WALLET **2** [C] (*NAmE*) = HANDBAG **3** [sing.] the amount of money that is available to a person, an organization or a government to spend: *We have holidays to suit every purse.* ◇ *Should spending on the arts be met out of the **public purse*** (= from government money)? **4** [C] (*sport*) a sum of money given as a prize in a BOXING match IDM see SILK

■ ***verb*** **~ your lips** to form your lips into a small tight round shape, for example to show disapproval

pur·ser /ˈpɜːsə(r); *NAmE* ˈpɜːrs-/ *noun* an officer on a ship who is responsible for taking care of the passengers, and for the accounts

the ˈpurse strings *noun* [pl.] a way of referring to money and how it is controlled or spent: *Who **holds the purse strings** in your house?* ◇ *The government will have to **tighten the purse strings*** (= spend less).

pur·su·ance /pəˈsjuːəns; *NAmE* pərˈsuː-/ *noun*
IDM **in pursuance of sth** (*formal* or *law*) in order to do sth; in the process of doing sth: *They may need to borrow money in pursuance of their legal action.*

pur·su·ant /pəˈsjuːənt; *NAmE* pərˈsuː-/ *adj.* **~ to sth** (*formal* or *law*) according to or following sth, especially a rule or law SYN **in accordance with**

pur·sue 🔑 AW /pəˈsjuː; *NAmE* pərˈsuː/ *verb* (*formal*) **1** 🔑 **~ sth** to do sth or try to achieve sth over a period of time: *to **pursue a goal/an aim/an objective*** ◇ *We intend to pursue this policy with determination.* ◇ *She wishes to pursue a medical career.* **2** 🔑 **~ sth** | **+ speech** to continue to discuss, find out about or be involved in sth: *to pursue legal action* ◇ *We have decided not to pursue the matter.* **3** 🔑 **~ sb/sth** to follow or chase sb/sth, especially in order to catch them: *She left the theatre, hotly pursued by the press.* ◇ *Police pursued the car at high speed.*

pur·suer /pəˈsjuːə(r); *NAmE* pərˈsuː-/ *noun* a person who is following or chasing sb

pur·suit AW /pəˈsjuːt; *NAmE* pərˈsuːt/ *noun* **1** [U] **~ of sth** the act of looking for or trying to find sth: *the **pursuit of happiness/knowledge/profit*** ◇ *She travelled the world **in pursuit of** her dreams.* **2** [U] the act of following or chasing sb: *We drove away with two police cars **in pursuit*** (= following). ◇ *I galloped off on my horse with Rosie **in hot pursuit*** (= following quickly behind). **3** [C, usually pl.] something that you give your time and energy to, that you do as a hobby SYN **hobby, pastime**: ***outdoor/leisure/artistic pursuits***

puru·lent /ˈpjʊərələnt; *NAmE* ˈpjʊr-/ *adj.* (*medical*) containing or producing PUS: *a purulent discharge from the wound*

pur·vey /pəˈveɪ; *NAmE* pərˈveɪ/ *verb* **~ sth** (*formal*) to supply food, services or information to people

pur·vey·or /pəˈveɪə(r); *NAmE* pərˈv-/ *noun* (*formal*) a person or company that supplies sth

pur·view /ˈpɜːvjuː; *NAmE* ˈpɜːrv-/ *noun* [U]
IDM **within/outside the purview of sth** (*formal*) within the limits of what a person, an organization, etc. is responsible for; dealt with by a document, law, etc.

pus /pʌs/ *noun* [U] a thick yellowish or greenish liquid that is produced in an infected wound

push 🔑 /pʊʃ/ *verb, noun*

■ ***verb***

▸ USING HANDS/ARMS/BODY **1** 🔑 [I, T] to use your hands, arms or body in order to make sb/sth move forward or away from you; to move part of your body into a particular position: *We pushed and pushed but the piano wouldn't move.* ◇ *Push hard when I tell you to.* ◇ *You push and I'll pull.* ◇ **~ at sth** *She pushed at the door but it wouldn't budge.* ◇ **~ sth** *He walked slowly up the hill pushing his bike.* ◇ **~ sb/sth + adv./prep.** *She pushed the cup towards me.* ◇ *He pushed his chair back and stood up.* ◇ *He tried to kiss her but she pushed him away.* ◇ *She pushed her face towards him.* ◇ **~ sth + adj.** *I pushed the door open.* **2** 🔑 [I, T] to use force to move past sb/sth using your hands, arms, etc: *People were **pushing and shoving** to get to the front.* ◇ **+ adv./prep.** *The fans pushed against the barrier.* ◇ **~ your way + adv./prep.** *Try and push your way through the crowd.*

▸ AFFECT STH **3** 🔑 [T] **~ sth + adv./prep.** to affect sth so that it reaches a particular level or state: *This development could push the country into recession.* ◇ *The rise in interest rates will push prices up.*

▸ SWITCH/BUTTON **4** 🔑 [T] **~ sth** to press a switch, button, etc, for example in order to make a machine start working: *I pushed the button for the top floor.*

▸ PERSUADE **5** 🔑 [T] to persuade or encourage sb to do sth that they may not want to do: **~ sb (into sth/into doing sth)** *My teacher pushed me into entering the competition.* ◇ **~ sb to do sth** *No one pushed you to take the job, did they?*

▸ WORK HARD **6** 🔑 [T] **~ sb/yourself** to make sb work hard: *The music teacher really pushes her pupils.* ◇ *Lucy should push herself a little harder.*

▸ PUT PRESSURE ON SB **7** [T] **~ sb (+ adv./prep.)** (*informal*) to put pressure on sb and make them angry or upset: *Her* parents are very tolerant, but sometimes she pushes them too far.

- NEW IDEA/PRODUCT **8** [T] **~ sth** (*informal*) to try hard to persuade people to accept or agree with a new idea, buy a new product, etc: *The interview gave him a chance to push his latest movie.* ◇ *She didn't want to* ***push the point*** *any further at that moment.*
- SELL DRUGS **9** [T] **~ sth** (*informal*) to sell illegal drugs
- OF ARMY **10** [I] **+ adv./prep.** to move forward quickly through an area: *The army pushed (on) towards the capital.*

IDM **be ˌpushing ˈ40, ˈ50, etc.** (*informal*) to be nearly 40, 50, etc. years old **be ˌpushing up (the) ˈdaisies** (*old-fashioned, humorous*) to be dead and in a grave **push the ˈboat out** (*BrE, informal*) to spend a lot of money on enjoying yourself or celebrating sth SYN **splash out** **ˈpush the envelope** (*informal*) to go beyond the limits of what is allowed or thought to be possible: *He is a performer who consistently pushes the envelope of TV comedy.* **push your ˈluck | ˈpush it/things** (*informal*) to take a risk because you have successfully avoided problems in the past: *You didn't get caught last time, but don't push your luck!* **push sth to the back of your ˈmind** to try to forget about sth unpleasant: *I tried to push the thought to the back of my mind.* ➲ more at BUTTON *n.*, PANIC BUTTON

PHR V **ˌpush sb aˈbout/aˈround** 🔑 to give orders to sb in a rude or unpleasant way **ˌpush aˈhead/ˈforward (with sth)** 🔑 to continue with a plan in a determined way: *The government is pushing ahead with its electoral reforms.* **ˌpush sth↔ˈaside** to avoid thinking about sth: *He pushed aside the feelings of fear.* **ˌpush sth ˈback** to make the time or date of a meeting, etc. later than originally planned: *The start of the game was pushed back from 2 p.m. to 4 p.m.* **ˈpush for sth | ˈpush sb for sth** to repeatedly ask for sth or try to make sth happen because you think it is very important: *The pressure group is pushing for a ban on GM foods.* ◇ *I'm going to have to push you for an answer.* **ˌpush ˈforward** to continue moving or travelling somewhere, especially when it is a long distance or difficult **ˌpush yourself/sb ˈforward** to make other people think about and notice you or sb else: *She had to push herself forward to get a promotion.* **ˌpush ˈin** (*BrE*) (*NAmE* **ˌcut ˈin**) to go in front of other people who are waiting **ˌpush ˈoff 1** (*BrE, informal*) used to tell sb rudely to go away: *Hey, what are you doing? Push off!* **2** to move away from land in a boat, or from the side of a swimming pool, etc. **ˌpush ˈon** to continue with a journey or an activity: *We rested for a while then pushed on to the next camp.* **ˌpush sb↔ˈout** to make sb leave a place or an organization **ˌpush sb/sth↔ˈout** to make sth less important than it was; to replace sth **ˌpush sth↔ˈout** to produce sth in large quantities: *factories pushing out cheap cotton shirts* **ˌpush sb/sth ˈover** to make sb/sth fall to the ground by pushing them: *Sam pushed me over in the playground.* ➲ see also PUSHOVER **ˌpush sth↔ˈthrough** to get a new law or plan officially accepted: *The government is pushing the changes through before the election.*

■ ***noun***

- USING HANDS/ARMS/BODY **1** 🔑 an act of pushing sth/sb: *She gave him a gentle push.* ◇ *The car won't start. Can you give it a push?* ◇ ***At the push of a button*** (= very easily) *he could get a whole list of names.*
- OF ARMY **2** 🔑 a large and determined military attack: *a final push against the enemy* ◇ (*figurative*) *The firm has begun a major push into the European market.*
- EFFORT **3** 🔑 **~ for sth** a determined effort to achieve sth: *The push for reform started in 2007.* **4** 🔑 encouragement to do sth: *He wants to open his own business, but needs a push in the right direction to get him started.*

IDM **at a ˈpush** (*BrE, informal*) used to say that sth is possible, but only with difficulty: *We can provide accommodation for six people at a push.* **give sb/get the ˈpush 1** (*BrE, informal*) to dismiss sb/to be dismissed from your job SYN **be fired/ fire sb**: *They gave him the push after only six weeks.* **2** (*BrE, informal*) to end a romantic relationship with sb; to be told that a romantic relationship with sb is over: *He was devastated when his girlfriend gave him the push.* **when ˌpush comes to ˈshove** (*informal*) when there is no other choice; when everything else has failed

push·back /ˈpʊʃbæk/ *noun* [U] (*especially NAmE*) opposition or resistance to a plan, an idea or a change: *The plan was abandoned because the pushback from the military was so strong.*

push·bike /ˈpʊʃbaɪk/ *noun* (*old-fashioned, BrE*) a bicycle

ˈpush-button *adj.* [only before noun] operated by pressing buttons with your fingers: *a push-button phone* ▸ **ˈpush-button** *noun*

pushchair (*BrE*)
stroller (*NAmE*)

pram (*BrE*)
baby carriage (*NAmE*)

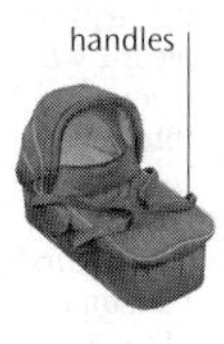

carrycot (*BrE*)

push·chair /ˈpʊʃtʃeə(r); *NAmE* -tʃer/ (*BrE*) (*NAmE* **stroll·er**) *noun* a small folding seat on wheels in which a small child sits and is pushed along ➲ compare BUGGY

pushed /pʊʃt/ *adj.* [not before noun] (*informal*) **1 ~ (to do sth)** having difficulty doing sth: *You'll be* ***hard pushed*** *to finish this today.* **2 ~ for sth** not having enough of sth: *to* ***be pushed for money/time*** **3** busy: *I know you're pushed, but can you make tomorrow's meeting?*

push·er /ˈpʊʃə(r)/ *noun* (*informal*) a person who sells illegal drugs: *drug pushers* ➲ see also PAPER-PUSHER, PEN-PUSHER

push·over /ˈpʊʃəʊvə(r); *NAmE* -oʊ-/ *noun* (*informal*) **1** a thing that is easy to do or win: *The game will be a pushover.* **2** a person who is easy to persuade or influence: *I don't think she'll agree—she's no pushover.*

push·pin /ˈpʊʃpɪn/ *noun* (*NAmE*) a type of DRAWING PIN with a coloured plastic head that is not flat ➲ VISUAL VOCAB page V56

ˈpush poll *noun* (*politics*) a way of trying to influence the way people vote by giving them information, often sth bad about an opposing candidate, while seeming to be asking their opinion ▸ **ˈpush polling** *noun* [U]: *allegations of push polling*

ˈpush-start *verb* **~ sth** (*especially BrE*) to push a vehicle in order to make the engine start ▸ **ˈpush-start** *noun* ➲ see also KICK-START

ˈpush technology *noun* [U] (*computing*) a service that allows Internet users to keep receiving the particular type of information that they describe by completing a form

ˈpush-up (*especially NAmE*) (*BrE* also **ˈpress-up**) *noun* [usually pl.] an exercise in which you lie on your stomach and raise your body off the ground by pressing down on your hands until your arms are straight ➲ VISUAL VOCAB page V35

pushy /ˈpʊʃi/ *adj.* (**push·ier, pushi·est**) (*informal, disapproving*) trying hard to get what you want, especially in a way that seems rude: *a pushy salesman* ▸ **pushi·ness** *noun* [U]

pu·sil·lan·im·ous /ˌpjuːsɪˈlænɪməs/ *adj.* (*formal*) frightened to take risks SYN **cowardly**

puss /pʊs/ *noun* **1** (*especially BrE*) used when you are calling or talking to a cat **2** (*informal, especially NAmE*) a person's face or mouth

pussy /ˈpʊsi/ *noun* (*pl.* -ies) **1** a child's word for a cat **2** (*taboo, slang*) the female sexual organs, especially the VULVA

pussy·cat /ˈpʊsikæt/ *noun* (*informal*) **1** a child's word for a cat **2** a person who is kind and friendly, especially when you would not expect them to be like this: *He's just a pussycat really, once you get to know him.*

P

pussy·foot /ˈpʊsifʊt/ *verb* [I] **~ (about/around)** (*informal*, usually *disapproving*) to be careful or anxious about expressing your opinion in case you upset sb

ˈpussy willow *noun* a small tree with flowers in spring that are like soft fur

pus·tule /ˈpʌstjuːl; *NAmE* -tʃuːl/ *noun* (*formal* or *medical*) a spot on the skin containing PUS

put 0-ᵥ /pʊt/ *verb* (**put·ting, put, put**)

▸ IN PLACE/POSITION **1** 0-ᵥ **~ sth + adv./prep.** to move sth into a particular place or position: *Put the cases down there, please.* ◇ *Did you put sugar in my coffee?* ◇ *Put your hand up if you need more paper.* **2** 0-ᵥ **~ sth + adv./prep.** to move sth into a particular place or position using force: *He put his fist through a glass door.* **3** 0-ᵥ **~ sb/sth + adv./prep.** to cause sb/sth to go to a particular place: *Her family put her into a nursing home.* ◇ *It was the year the Americans put a man on the moon.*

▸ ATTACH **4** 0-ᵥ **~ sth + adv./prep.** to attach or fix sth to sth else: *We had to put new locks on all the doors.*

▸ WRITE **5** 0-ᵥ **~ sth (+ adv./prep.)** to write sth or make a mark on sth: *Put your name here.* ◇ *Friday at 11? I'll put it in my diary.* ◇ *I couldn't read what she had put.*

▸ INTO STATE/CONDITION **6** 0-ᵥ **~ sb/sth + adv./prep.** to bring sb/sth into the state or condition mentioned: *I was put in charge of the office.* ◇ *The incident put her in a bad mood.* ◇ ***Put yourself in my position.*** *What would you have done?* ◇ *I tried to* ***put the matter into perspective.*** ◇ *Don't go* ***putting yourself at risk.*** ◇ *It was time to* ***put*** *their suggestion* ***into practice.*** ◇ *This new injury will* ***put him out of action*** *for several weeks.*

▸ AFFECT SB/STH **7** 0-ᵥ **~ sth on/onto/to sth** to make sb/sth feel sth or be affected by sth: *Her new job has put a great strain on her.* ◇ *They* ***put pressure on*** *her to resign.* ◇ *It's time you* ***put a stop to*** *this childish behaviour.*

▸ GIVE VALUE/RANK **8 ~ sth on sth** to give or attach a particular level of importance, trust, value, etc. to sth: *Our company puts the emphasis on quality.* ◇ *He put a limit on the amount we could spend.* **9 ~ sb/sth + adv./prep.** to consider sb/sth to belong to the class or level mentioned: *I'd put her in the top rank of modern novelists.*

P

▸ EXPRESS **10** 0-ᵥ **~ sth + adv./prep.** to express or state sth in a particular way: *She put it very tactfully.* ◇ ***Put simply,*** *we accept their offer or go bankrupt.* ◇ *I was,* ***to put it mildly,*** *annoyed* (= I was extremely angry). ◇ *He was too trusting—or,* ***to put it another way,*** *he had no head for business.* ◇ *The meat was—****how shall I put it?****—a little overdone.* ◇ *As T.S. Eliot puts it...* ◇ *She had never tried to* ***put*** *this feeling* ***into words.*** ◇ *Can you help me put this letter into good English, please?*

▸ IN SPORT **11 ~ sth** to throw the SHOT

IDM Most idioms containing **put** are at the entries for the nouns and adjectives in the idioms, for example **put your foot in it** is at **foot**. **put it aˈbout** (*BrE, informal*) to have many sexual partners **I wouldn't put it ˈpast sb (to do sth)** (*informal*) used to say that you think sb is capable of doing sth wrong, illegal, etc. **put it to sb that...** to suggest sth to sb to see if they can argue against it: *I put it to you that you are the only person who had a motive for the crime.* **put one ˈover on sb** (*informal*) to persuade sb to believe sth that is not true: *Don't try to put one over on me!* **put sb ˈthrough it** (*informal, especially BrE*) to force sb to experience sth difficult or unpleasant: *They really put me through it* (= asked me difficult questions) *at the interview.* **put toˈgether** used when comparing or contrasting sb/sth with a group of other people or things to mean 'combined' or 'in total': *Your department spent more last year than all the others put together.* **ˌput up or ˈshut up** (*especially BrE*) used to tell sb to stop just talking about sth and actually do it, show it, etc.

PHR V **ˌput sth↔aˈbout** (*BrE, informal*) to tell a lot of people news, information, etc. that may be false: **put it about that** *... Someone's been putting it about that you plan to resign.*

ˈput sth above sth = PUT STH BEFORE STH

ˌput yourself/sth↔aˈcross/ˈover (to sb) to communicate your ideas, feelings, etc. successfully to sb: *She's not very good at putting her views across.*

ˌput sth↔aˈside 1 to ignore or forget sth, usually a feeling or difference of opinion SYN **disregard**: *They decided to put aside their differences.* **2** to save sth or keep it available to use: *We put some money aside every month for our retirement.* ◇ *I put aside half an hour every day to write my diary.*

ˈput sb/sth at sth to calculate sb/sth to be a particular age, weight, amount, etc: *The damage to the building is put at over $1 million.*

ˌput sb↔aˈway [often passive] (*informal*) to send sb to prison, to a mental hospital, etc. **ˌput sth↔aˈway 1** 0-ᵥ to put sth in the place where it is kept because you have finished using it: *I'm just going to put the car away* (= in the garage). **2** to save money to spend later: *She has a few thousand dollars put away for her retirement.* **3** (*informal*) to eat or drink large quantities of sth: *He must have put away a bottle of whisky last night.*

ˌput sth↔ˈback 1 0-ᵥ to return sth to its usual place or to the place where it was before it was moved: *If you use something, put it back!* **2** 0-ᵥ to move sth to a later time or date SYN **postpone**: *The meeting has been put back to next week.* **3** to cause sth to be delayed: *Poor trading figures put back our plans for expansion.* **4** to move the hands of a clock so that they show the correct earlier time: *Remember to put your clocks back tonight* (= because the time has officially changed).

ˈput sth before/above sth to treat sth as more important than sth else

ˌput sth beˈhind you to try to forget about an unpleasant experience and think about the future

ˌput sth↔ˈby (*especially BrE*) (also **ˌput sth↔aˈside**) to save money for a particular purpose: *I'm putting by part of my wages every week to buy a bike.*

ˌput ˈdown (of an aircraft or its pilot) to land: *He put down in a field.* **ˌput sb↔ˈdown** (*informal*) to make sb look or feel stupid, especially in front of other people ➲ related noun PUT-DOWN **ˌput sth↔ˈdown 1** 0-ᵥ to stop holding sth and place it on a table, shelf, etc: *Put that knife down before you hurt somebody!* ◇ *It's a great book.* ***I couldn't put it down.*** ◇ (*BrE*) *She put the phone down on me* (= ended the call before I had finished speaking). ➲ see also UNPUTDOWNABLE **2** to write sth; to make a note of sth: *The meeting's on the 22nd. Put it down in your diary.* **3** to pay part of the cost of sth: *We put a 5% deposit down on the house.* **4** to stop sth by force SYN **crush**: *to put down a rebellion* ◇ *The military government is determined to put down all opposition.* **5** [often passive] to kill an animal, usually by giving it a drug, because it is old or sick: *We had to have our cat put down.* **6** (*BrE*) to put a baby to bed: *Can you be quiet—I've just put the baby down.* **7** to present sth formally for discussion by a parliament or committee SYN **table**: *to* ***put down a motion/an amendment*** **ˌput sb ˈdown as sth** to consider or judge sb to be a particular type of person: *I'd put them both down as retired teachers.* **ˌput sb ˈdown for sth** to put sb's name on a list, etc. for sth: *Put me down for three tickets for Saturday.* ◇ *They've put their son down for the local school.* **ˈput sth down to sth** to consider that sth is caused by sth SYN **attribute**: *What do you put her success down to?*

ˌput sth↔ˈforth (*formal*) = PUT STH OUT (9)

ˌput yourself/sb↔ˈforward to suggest yourself/sb as a candidate for a job or position: *Can I put you/your name forward for club secretary?* **ˌput sth↔ˈforward 1** 0-ᵥ to move sth to an earlier time or date: *We've put the wedding forward by one week.* **2** to move the hands of a clock to the correct later time: *Remember to put your clocks forward tonight* (= because the time has officially changed). **3** 0-ᵥ to suggest sth for discussion: *to put forward a suggestion*

ˌput sb↔ˈin to elect a political party to govern a country: *Who will the voters put in this time?* **ˌput sth↔ˈin 1** 0-ᵥ to fix equipment or furniture into position so that it can be used SYN **install**: *We're having a new shower put in.* **2** to include sth in a letter, story, etc. **3** to interrupt another speaker in order to say sth: *Could I put in a word?* ◇ **+ speech** *'But what about us?' he put in.* **4** to officially make a claim, request, etc: *The company has put in a claim for damages.* **5 ~ a (...) performance** to give a performance of sth, especially one of a particular kind: *All the actors put in great performances.* **6** (also ˈ**put sth into sth**) to spend a lot of time or make a lot of effort doing sth: *She often puts in twelve hours' work a day.* ◇ **~ doing sth** *He's putting a lot of work into improving his French.* ➲ related noun INPUT **7** (also ˈ**put sth into sth**) to use or give money: **~ doing sth** *He's put all his savings into buying that house.* ˌ**put ˈin (at...)** | ˈ**put into...** (of a boat or its sailors) to enter a port: *They put in at Lagos for repairs.* OPP **put out (to.../from...)** ˌ**put ˈin for sth** (*especially BrE*) to officially ask for sth: *Are you going to put in for that job?* ˌ**put yourself/sb/sth ˈin for sth** to enter yourself/sb/sth for a competition

ˌ**put sth ˈinto sth 1** to add a quality to sth: *He put as much feeling into his voice as he could.* **2** = PUT STH IN (6), (7)

ˌ**put sb↔ˈoff 1** to cancel a meeting or an arrangement that you have made with sb: *It's too late to put them off now.* **2** 🔑 to make sb dislike sb/sth or not trust them/it: *She's very clever but her manner does tend to put people off.* ◇ *Don't be put off by how it looks—it tastes delicious.* ➲ see also OFF-PUTTING **3** 🔑 (also ˌ**put sb ˈoff sth**) to disturb sb who is trying to give all their attention to sth that they are doing: *Don't put me off when I'm trying to concentrate.* ◇ *The sudden noise put her off her game.* **4** (*BrE*) (of a vehicle or its driver) to stop in order to allow sb to leave: *I asked the bus driver to put me off at the station.* ˌ**put sb ˈoff sth/sb** 🔑 to make sb lose interest in or enthusiasm for sth/sb: *He was put off science by bad teaching.* ◇ **~ doing sth** *The accident put her off driving for life.* ˌ**put sth↔ˈoff** 🔑 to change sth to a later time or date SYN **postpone, delay**: *We've had to put off our wedding until September.* ◇ **~ doing sth** *He keeps putting off going to the dentist.*

ˌ**put sb ˈon** to give sb the telephone so that they can talk to the person at the other end: *Hi, Dad—can you put Nicky on?* ˌ**put sth↔ˈon 1** 🔑 to dress yourself in sth: *Hurry up! Put your coat on!* OPP **take off 2** 🔑 to apply sth to your skin, face, etc: *She's just putting on her make-up.* **3** 🔑 to switch on a piece of equipment: *I'll put the kettle on for tea.* ◇ *She put on the brakes suddenly.* **4** 🔑 to make a tape, CD, DVD, etc. begin to play: *Do you mind if I put some music on?* ◇ *He put some jazz on the stereo.* **5** 🔑 to become heavier, especially by the amount mentioned SYN **gain**: *She looks like she's* ***put on weight.*** ◇ *He must have put on several kilos.* **6** (*BrE*) to provide sth specially: *The city is putting on extra buses during the summer.* **7** to produce or present a play, a show, etc: *The local drama club is putting on 'Macbeth'.* **8** to pretend to have a particular feeling, quality, way of speaking, etc: *He put on an American accent.* ◇ *I don't think she was hurt. She was just* ***putting it on.*** ˌ**put sth ˈon sth 1** to add an amount of money or a tax to the cost of sth: *The government has put ten pence on the price of twenty cigarettes.* **2** to bet money on sth: *I've never put money on a horse.* ◇ *I put £5 on him to win.*

ˌ**put sb ˈonto sb/sth 1** to tell the police, etc. about where a criminal is or about a crime: *What first put the police onto the scam?* **2** to tell sb about sb/sth that they may like or find useful: *Who put you onto this restaurant—it's great!*

ˌ**put ˈout (for sb)** (*NAmE, slang*) to agree to have sex with sb

ˌ**put yourself ˈout (for sb)** (*informal*) to make a special effort to do sth for sb: *Please don't put yourself out on my account.* ˌ**put sb ˈout 1** to cause sb trouble, extra work, etc. SYN **inconvenience**: *I hope our arriving late didn't put them out.* **2 be put out** to be upset or offended: *He looked really put out.* **3** to make sb unconscious: *These pills should put him out for a few hours.* ˌ**put sth↔ˈout 1** 🔑 to take sth out of your house and leave it, for example for sb to collect: (*BrE*) *to put the rubbish out* ◇ (*NAmE*) *to put the garbage/trash out* **2** 🔑 to place sth where it will be noticed and used: *Have you put out clean towels for the guests?* **3** 🔑 to stop sth from burning or shining: *to put out a candle/cigarette/light* ◇ *Firefighters soon put the fire out.* **4** to produce sth, especially for sale: *The factory puts out 500 new cars a week.* ➲ related noun OUTPUT **5** to publish or broadcast sth: *Police have put out a description of the man they wish to question.* **6** to give a job or task to a worker who is not your employee or to a company that is not part of your own group or organization: *A lot of the work is put out to freelancers.* **7** to make a figure, result, etc. wrong: *The rise in interest rates put our estimates out by several thousands.* **8** to push a bone out of its normal position SYN **dislocate**: *She fell off her horse and put her shoulder out.* **9** (also *formal* ˌ**put sth↔ˈforth**) to develop or produce new leaves, SHOOTS, etc. ˌ**put ˈout (to.../from...)** (of a boat or its sailors) to leave a port: *to put out to sea* ◇ *We put out from Liverpool.* OPP **put in (at...)**

ˌ**put yourself/sth ˈover (to sb)** = PUT YOURSELF/STH ACROSS (TO SB)

ˌ**put sth↔ˈthrough** to continue with and complete a plan, programme, etc: *We managed to put the deal through.* ˌ**put sb ˈthrough sth 1** to make sb experience sth very difficult or unpleasant: *You have put your family through a lot recently.* **2** to arrange or pay for sb to attend a school, college, etc: *He put all his children through college.* ˌ**put sb/sth ˈthrough (to sb/...)** 🔑 to connect sb by telephone: *Could you put me through to the manager, please?*

ˈ**put sb to sth** to cause sb trouble, difficulty, etc: *I hope we're not putting you to too much trouble.* ˈ**put sth to sb 1** to offer a suggestion to sb so that they can accept or reject it: *Your proposal will be put to the board of directors.* **2** to ask sb a question: *The audience is now invited to put questions to the speaker.*

ˌ**put sth↔toˈgether** 🔑 to make or prepare sth by fitting or collecting parts together: *to put together a model plane/an essay/a meal* ◇ *I think we can put together a very strong case for the defence.*

ˈ**put sth towards sth** to give money to pay part of the cost of sth: *Here's $100 to put towards your ski trip.*

ˌ**put ˈup sth 1** to show a particular level of skill, determination, etc. in a fight or contest: *They surrendered without putting up much of a fight.* ◇ *The team put up a great performance* (= played very well). **2** to suggest an idea, etc. for other people to discuss: *to* ***put up an argument/a case/a proposal*** ˌ**put sb↔ˈup 1** 🔑 to let sb stay at your home: *We can put you up for the night.* **2** to suggest or present sb as a candidate for a job or position: *The Green Party hopes to put up more candidates in the next election.* ˌ**put sth↔ˈup 1** 🔑 to raise sth or put it in a higher position: *to put up a flag* ◇ *She's put her hair up.* **2** 🔑 to build sth or place sth somewhere: *to put up a building/fence/memorial/tent* ➲ SYNONYMS at BUILD **3** 🔑 to fix sth in a place where it will be seen SYN **display**: *to put up a notice* **4** 🔑 to raise or increase sth: *They've put up the rent by £20 a month.* **5** to provide or lend money: *A local businessman has put up the £500 000 needed to save the club.* ˌ**put ˈup (at...)** (*especially BrE*) to stay somewhere for the night: *We put up at a motel.* ˌ**put ˈup for sth** | ˌ**put yourself ˈup for sth** to offer yourself as a candidate for a job or position: *She is putting up for election to the committee.* ˌ**put sb ˈup to sth** (*informal*) to encourage or persuade sb to do sth wrong or stupid: *Some of the older boys must have put him up to it.* ˌ**put ˈup with sb/sth** 🔑 to accept sb/sth that is annoying, unpleasant, etc. without complaining SYN **tolerate**: *I don't know how she puts up with him.* ◇ *I'm not going to put up with their smoking any longer.*

pu·ta·tive /ˈpjuːtətɪv/ *adj.* [only before noun] (*formal* or *law*) believed to be the person or thing mentioned SYN **presumed**: *the putative father of this child*

ˈ**put-down** *noun* (*informal*) a remark or criticism that is intended to make sb look or feel stupid

ˈ**put-on** *noun* [usually sing.] (*NAmE*) something that is done to trick or cheat people

pu·tong·hua /puːˈtʊŋhwɑː/ *noun* [U] the standard spoken form of modern Chinese, based on the form spoken in Beijing ➲ compare MANDARIN

pu·tre·fac·tion /ˌpjuːtrɪˈfækʃn/ *noun* [U] (*formal*) the process of decaying, especially that of a dead body

pu·trefy /ˈpjuːtrɪfaɪ/ *verb* (**pu·tre·fies, pu·tre·fy·ing, pu·tre·fied, pu·tre·fied**) [I] (*formal*) to decay and smell very bad SYN **rot**

pu·trid /ˈpjuːtrɪd/ *adj.* **1** (of dead animals or plants) decaying and therefore smelling very bad SYN **foul**: *the putrid smell of rotten meat* **2** (*informal*) very unpleasant: *a putrid pink colour*

P

putsch /pʊtʃ/ *noun* (from *German*) a sudden attempt to remove a government by force

putt /pʌt/ *verb* [I, T] **~ (sth)** (in GOLF) to hit the ball gently when it is on the short grass near the hole, so that it rolls across the ground a short distance into or towards the hole ▸ **putt** *noun*

put·ter /ˈpʌtə(r)/ *verb, noun*
▪ *verb* **1** [I] (*BrE*) (of a boat or vehicle) to make a repeated low sound as it moves slowly: *the puttering of the engine as it reduced speed* **2** (*NAmE*) (*BrE* **pot·ter**) [I] (**+ adv./prep.**) to do things or move without hurrying, especially when you are doing sth that you enjoy and that is not important: *I spent the morning puttering around the house.*
▪ *noun* (in the game of GOLF) the type of CLUB that is used for putting (= hitting the ball short distances)

ˈputting green *noun* a small GOLF COURSE on an area of smooth short grass where people can practise PUTTING

putty /ˈpʌti/ *noun* [U] a soft sticky substance that becomes hard when it is dry and that is used for fixing glass into window frames
IDM **(like) putty in sb's ˈhands** easily controlled or influenced by another person: *She'll persuade him. He's like putty in her hands.*

ˌput-up ˈjob *noun* [usually sing.] (*BrE, informal*) a plan or an event that has been arranged secretly in order to trick or cheat sb

ˈput-upon *adj.* treated in an unfair way by sb because they take advantage of your kindness or willingness to do things: *his much put-upon wife*

putz /pʌts/ *verb, noun*
▪ [I] **~ around** (*NAmE, informal*) to waste time not doing anything useful or important
▪ *noun* (*NAmE, informal*) a stupid person

puz·zle /ˈpʌzl/ *noun, verb*
▪ *noun* **1** a game, etc. that you have to think about carefully in order to answer it or do it: *a crossword puzzle* ◇ *a book of puzzles for children* ➲ VISUAL VOCAB page V33 **2** (*especially NAmE*) = JIGSAW **3** [usually sing.] something that is difficult to understand or explain SYN **mystery**
▪ *verb* **~ sb** to make sb feel confused because they do not understand sth SYN **baffle**: *What puzzles me is why he left the country without telling anyone.* ▸ **puz·zling** /ˈpʌzlɪŋ/ *adj.*: *one of the most puzzling aspects of the crime*
PHR V **ˈpuzzle over/about sth** to think hard about sth in order to understand or explain it **ˌpuzzle sth↔ˈout** to find the answer to a difficult or confusing problem by thinking carefully SYN **work out**: **~ why, what, etc...** *He was trying to puzzle out why he had been brought to the house.*

puz·zled /ˈpʌzld/ *adj.* unable to understand sth or the reason for sth SYN **baffled**: *She had a* ***puzzled look*** *on her face.* ◇ *Scientists are puzzled as to why the whale had swum to the shore.* ◇ *He looked puzzled so I repeated the question.*

puzzle·ment /ˈpʌzlmənt/ *noun* [U] (*formal*) a feeling of being confused because you do not understand sth: *She frowned in puzzlement.*

puz·zler /ˈpʌzlə(r)/ *noun* (*informal*) something that makes you feel confused SYN **poser**

PVC /ˌpiː viː ˈsiː/ *noun* [U] a strong plastic material used for a wide variety of products, such as clothing, pipes, floor coverings, etc.

PVR /ˌpiː viː ˈɑː(r)/ *noun* (*BrE*) a device that records video onto a hard disk or other memory device, using digital technology (the abbreviation for 'personal video recorder') SYN **DVR**

p.w. *abbr.* (*BrE*) per week: *Rent is £100 p.w.*

PX /ˌpiː ˈeks/ (*pl.* PXs /ˌpiː ˈeksɪz/) *noun* post exchange (a shop/store at a US military base that sells food, clothes and other things)

pye-dog (also **pie-dog, pi-dog**) /ˈpaɪ dɒg; *NAmE* dɔːg/ (also **paˈriah dog**) *noun* (especially in Asia) a dog that has no owner or home and is of no particular breed

pygmy (also **pigmy**) /ˈpɪgmi/ *noun, adj.*
▪ *noun* (*pl.* **-ies**) **1 Pygmy** a member of a race of very short people living in parts of Africa and SE Asia **2** (*disapproving*) a very small person or thing or one that is weak in some way: *He regarded them as intellectual pygmies.*
▪ *adj.* [only before noun] used to describe a plant or SPECIES (= type) of animal that is much smaller than other similar kinds: *a pygmy shrew*

py·jama /pəˈdʒɑːmə; *NAmE* -ˈdʒæm-/ *noun* loose trousers/pants tied at the waist and worn by men or women in some Asian countries: *He was dressed in a pyjama and kurta, ideal for a summer evening.*

py·ja·mas (*especially US* **pa·ja·mas**) /pəˈdʒɑːməz; *NAmE* -ˈdʒæm-/ *noun* [pl.] a loose jacket and trousers/pants worn in bed: *a pair of pyjamas* ➲ VISUAL VOCAB page V51 ▸ **py·jama** (*especially US* **pa·jama**) *adj.* [only before noun]: *pyjama bottoms* IDM see CAT

pylon /ˈpaɪlən; *NAmE* also -lɑːn/ *noun* a tall metal structure that is used for carrying electricity wires high above the ground

pyra·mid /ˈpɪrəmɪd/ *noun* **1** a large building with a square or TRIANGULAR base and sloping sides that meet in a point at the top. The ancient Egyptians built stone pyramids as places to bury their kings and queens. ➲ VISUAL VOCAB page V13 **2** (*geometry*) a solid shape with a square or TRIANGULAR base and sloping sides that meet in a point at the top ➲ VISUAL VOCAB page V58 **3** an object or a pile of things that has the shape of a pyramid: *a pyramid of cans in a shop window* **4** an organization or a system in which there are fewer people at each level as you get near the top: *a management pyramid* ▸ **pyr·am·idal** /ˈpɪrəmɪdl/ *adj.*

ˌpyramid ˈselling *noun* [U] a way of selling things in which sb buys the right to sell a company's goods and then sells the goods to other people. These other people sell the goods again to others.

pyre /ˈpaɪə(r)/ *noun* a large pile of wood on which a dead body is placed and burned in a funeral ceremony

pyr·eth·rum /paɪˈriːθrəm/ *noun* **1** [C] a type of flower grown especially in Kenya **2** [U] a substance made from this flower and used for killing insects

Pyrex™ /ˈpaɪreks/ *noun* [U] a type of hard glass that does not break at high temperatures, and is often used to make dishes for cooking food in

pyr·ites /paɪˈraɪtiːz; *NAmE* pəˈr-/ *noun* [U] a shiny yellow mineral that is made up of SULPHUR and a metal such as iron: ***iron/copper pyrites***

pyro·mania /ˌpaɪrəʊˈmeɪniə; *NAmE* ˌpaɪroʊ-/ *noun* [U] (*technical*) a mental illness that causes a strong desire to set fire to things

pyro·maniac /ˌpaɪrəʊˈmeɪniæk; *NAmE* ˌpaɪroʊ-/ *noun* **1** (*technical*) a person who suffers from pyromania **2** (*informal, humorous*) a person who enjoys making or watching fires

pyro·tech·nics /ˌpaɪrəˈteknɪks/ *noun* **1** [U+sing./pl. v.] (*technical*) FIREWORKS or a display of FIREWORKS **2** [pl.] (*formal*) a clever and complicated display of skill, for example by a musician, writer or speaker: *guitar pyrotechnics* ▸ **pyro·tech·nic** *adj.* [usually before noun]

Pyr·rhic vic·tory /ˌpɪrɪk ˈvɪktəri/ *noun* a victory that is not worth winning because the winner has suffered or lost so much in winning it ORIGIN From **Pyrrhus**, the king of Epirus who defeated the Romans in 279BC but lost many of his own men.

Py·thag·oras' the·orem /paɪˈθægərəsɪz θɪərəm; *NAmE* θiːə-; θɪr-/ (*NAmE* **Py·thag·orean the·orem** /paɪˌθægəˈriːən θɪərəm; *NAmE* also pə-; θiːə-; θɪr-/) *noun* (*geometry*) the rule that, in a RIGHT-ANGLED TRIANGLE/RIGHT TRIANGLE, the SQUARE *n.* (4) of the HYPOTENUSE (= the side opposite the right angle) is equal to the squares of the other two sides added together

py·thon /ˈpaɪθən; *NAmE* -θɑːn/ *noun* a large tropical snake that kills animals for food by winding its long body around them and crushing them

Qq

Q /kjuː/ *noun, abbr.*

■ ***noun*** (also **q**) [C, U] (*pl.* Qs, Q's, q's /kjuːz/) the 17th letter of the English alphabet: *'Queen' begins with (a) Q/'Q'.* ➲ see also Q-TIP

■ ***abbr.*** question IDM see MIND *v.*

Qa·ba·lah = KABBALAH

QC /ˌkjuː ˈsiː/ *noun* (in Britain) the highest level of BARRISTER, who can speak for the government in court. QC is the abbreviation for 'Queen's Counsel' and is used when there is a queen in Britain. ➲ compare KC

QED (*BrE*) (also **Q.E.D.** *US, BrE*) /ˌkjuː iː ˈdiː/ *abbr.* that is what I wanted to prove and I have proved it (from Latin 'quod erat demonstrandum')

qib·lah (also **qibla, kibla**) /ˈkɪblə/ *noun* [sing.] the direction of the Kaaba (the holy building at Mecca), towards which Muslims turn when they are PRAYING

qt *abbr.* (in writing) QUART

ˈQ-tip™ *noun* (*NAmE*) = COTTON BUD

qua /kweɪ; kwɑː/ *prep.* (from *Latin, formal*) as sth; in the role of sth: *The soldier acted qua soldier, not as a human being.* ➲ see also SINE QUA NON

quack /kwæk/ *noun, verb*

■ ***noun*** **1** the sound that a DUCK makes **2** (*informal, disapproving*) a person who dishonestly claims to have medical knowledge or skills: *quack doctors* ◇ *I've got a check-up with the quack* (= the doctor) *next week.*

■ ***verb*** [I] when a DUCK **quacks**, it makes the noise that is typical of ducks

quack·ery /ˈkwækəri/ *noun* [U] the methods or behaviour of sb who pretends to have medical knowledge

quad /kwɒd; *NAmE* kwɑːd/ *noun* **1** = QUADRANGLE **2** = QUADRUPLET ➲ see also QUADS

ˈquad bike (*BrE*) (*NAmE* **ˌfour-ˈwheeler**) *noun* a motorcycle with four large wheels, used for riding over rough ground, often for fun ➲ VISUAL VOCAB page V41 ➲ see also ATV

quad·ran·gle /ˈkwɒdræŋɡl; *NAmE* ˈkwɑːd-/ *noun* (*formal*) (also rather *informal* **quad**) an open square area that has buildings all around it, especially in a school or college

quad·ran·gu·lar /kwɒˈdræŋɡjələ(r); *NAmE* kwɑːˈd-/ *adj.* **1** (*geometry*) (of a shape) having four sides and flat rather than solid **2** (of a sporting competition) involving four teams or individuals who each compete against all the others

quad·rant /ˈkwɒdrənt; *NAmE* ˈkwɑːd-/ *noun* **1** (*geometry*) a quarter of a circle or of its CIRCUMFERENCE (= the distance around it) ➲ VISUAL VOCAB page V58 **2** an instrument for measuring angles, especially to check your position at sea or to look at stars

quadra·phon·ic (also **quadro·phon·ic**) /ˌkwɒdrəˈfɒnɪk; *NAmE* ˌkwɑːdrəˈfɑːn-/ *adj.* (of a system of recording or broadcasting sound) coming from four different SPEAKERS at the same time ➲ compare MONO, STEREO

quad·rat·ic /kwɒˈdrætɪk; *NAmE* kwɑːˈd-/ *adj.* (*mathematics*) involving an unknown quantity that is multiplied by itself once only: *a quadratic equation*

quadri- /ˈkwɒdrɪ-; *NAmE* ˈkwɑːd-/ (also **quadr-**) *combining form* (in nouns, adjectives and adverbs) four; having four: *quadrilateral* ◇ *quadruplet*

quad·ri·ceps /ˈkwɒdrɪseps; *NAmE* ˈkwɑːd-/ *noun* (*pl.* quad·ri·ceps) (also *informal* **quads**) (*anatomy*) the large muscle at the front of the THIGH

quad·ri·lat·eral /ˌkwɒdrɪˈlætərəl; *NAmE* ˌkwɑːd-/ *noun* (*geometry*) a flat shape with four straight sides ➲ VISUAL VOCAB page V58 ▶ **quad·ri·lat·eral** *adj.*

quad·rille /kwəˈdrɪl/ *noun* a dance for four or more couples in a square, popular in the past

quad·ril·lion /kwɒˈdrɪljən; *NAmE* kwɑːˈd-/ *number* the number 10^{15}, or 1 followed by 15 zeros

quadri·ple·gic /ˌkwɒdrɪˈpliːdʒɪk; *NAmE* ˌkwɑːd-/ *noun* a person who is permanently unable to use their arms and legs ▶ **quadri·ple·gic** *adj.* **quadri·ple·gia** /ˌkwɒdrɪˈpliːdʒə; *NAmE* ˌkwɑːd-/ *noun* [U]

quadro·phon·ic *adj.* = QUADRAPHONIC

quad·ru·ped /ˈkwɒdruped; *NAmE* ˈkwɑːd-/ *noun* (*technical*) any creature with four feet ➲ compare BIPED

quad·ru·ple *verb, adj., det.*

■ ***verb*** /kwɒˈdruːpl; *NAmE* kwɑːˈd-/ [I, T] **~ (sth)** to become four times bigger; to make sth four times bigger: *Sales have quadrupled in the last five years.*

■ ***adj.*** [only before noun], ***det.*** /ˈkwɒdrʊpl; *NAmE* kwɑːˈdruːpl/ **1** consisting of four parts, people or groups: *a quadruple alliance* **2** being four times as much or as many: *a quadruple whisky* ◇ *This year we produced quadruple the amount produced in 2008.*

quad·ru·plet /ˈkwɒdrʊplət; kwɒˈdruːplət; *NAmE* kwɑːˈ-/ (also **quad**) *noun* one of four children born at the same time to the same mother

quads /kwɒdz/ *noun* [pl.] (*informal*) = QUADRICEPS

quaff /kwɒf; *NAmE* kwæf; kwɑːf/ *verb* **~ sth** (*old-fashioned* or *literary*) to drink a large amount of sth quickly

quag·mire /ˈkwæɡmaɪə(r); *BrE* also ˈkwɒɡ-/ *noun* **1** an area of soft wet ground SYN **bog** **2** a difficult or dangerous situation SYN **morass**

quail /kweɪl/ *noun, verb*

■ ***noun*** [C, U] (*pl.* **quails** or **quail**) a small brown bird, whose meat and eggs are used for food; the meat of this bird

■ ***verb*** [I] **~ (at/before sb/sth)** (*literary*) to feel frightened or to show that you are frightened

quaint /kweɪnt/ *adj.* attractive in an unusual or old-fashioned way: *quaint old customs* ◇ *a quaint seaside village* ▶ **quaint·ly** *adv.* **quaint·ness** *noun* [U]

quake /kweɪk/ *verb, noun*

■ ***verb*** **1** [I] **~ (with sth)** (of a person) to shake because you are very frightened or nervous SYN **tremble**: *Quaking with fear, Polly slowly opened the door.* **2** [I] (of the earth or a building) to move or shake violently: *The ground quaked as the bomb exploded.*

■ ***noun*** (*informal*) = EARTHQUAKE

Quaker /ˈkweɪkə(r)/ *noun* a member of the Society of Friends, a Christian religious group that meets without any formal ceremony and is strongly opposed to violence and war ▶ **Quaker** *adj.*: *a Quaker school*

quali·fi·ca·tion 🔑 /ˌkwɒlɪfɪˈkeɪʃn; *NAmE* ˌkwɑːl-/ *noun*

1 🔑 [C, usually pl.] (*BrE*) an exam that you have passed or a course of study that you have successfully completed: ***academic/educational/professional/vocational qualifications*** ◇ *a* ***nursing/teaching, etc. qualification*** ◇ *He left school with no* ***formal qualifications.*** ◇ *to* ***acquire/gain/get/obtain/have/hold qualifications*** ◇ *In this job, experience counts for more than* ***paper qualifications.*** ➲ COLLOCATIONS at EDUCATION **2** 🔑 [C] a skill or type of experience that you need for a particular job or activity: *Previous teaching experience is a necessary qualification for this job.* **3** [C, U] information that you add to a statement to limit the effect that it has or the way it is applied SYN **proviso**: *I accept his theories, but not without certain qualifications.* ◇ *The plan was approved without qualification.* **4** [U] the fact of passing an exam, completing a course of training or reaching the standard necessary to do a job or take part in a competition: *Nurses in training should be given a guarantee of employment following qualification.* ◇ *A victory in this game will earn them qualification for the World Cup.*

quali·fied 🔑 /ˈkwɒlɪfaɪd; *NAmE* ˈkwɑːl-/ *adj.*

1 🔑 having passed the exams or completed the training that are necessary in order to do a particular job; having the experience to do a particular job: *a* ***qualified accountant/teacher, etc.*** ◇ *to be* ***highly/suitably/fully qualified*** ◇ **~ for sth** *She's extremely* ***well qualified*** *for the job.*

2 0‑m [not before noun] ~ (**to do sth**) having the practical knowledge or skills to do sth: *I don't know much about it, so I don't feel qualified to comment.* **3** [usually before noun] (of approval, support, etc.) limited in some way: *The plan was given only qualified support.* ◇ *The project was only a* ***qualified success***.

quali·fier /ˈkwɒlɪfaɪə(r); *NAmE* ˈkwɑːl-/ *noun* **1** a person or team that has defeated others in order to enter a particular competition **2** a game or match that a person or team has to win in order to enter a particular competition: *a World Cup qualifier* **3** (*grammar*) a word, especially an adjective or adverb, that describes another word in a particular way: *In 'the open door', 'open' is a qualifier, describing the door.*

quali·fy 0‑m /ˈkwɒlɪfaɪ; *NAmE* ˈkwɑːl-/ *verb* (**quali·fies, quali·fy·ing, quali·fied, quali·fied**)

▸ FOR JOB **1** 0‑m [I] to reach the standard of ability or knowledge needed to do a particular job, for example by completing a course of study or passing exams: *How long does it take to qualify?* ◇ **~ as sth** *He qualified as a doctor last year.*

▸ GIVE SKILLS/KNOWLEDGE **2** 0‑m [T] to give sb the skills and knowledge they need to do sth: **~ sb** (**for sth**) *This training course will qualify you for a better job.* ◇ **~ sb to do sth** *The test qualifies you to drive heavy vehicles.*

▸ HAVE/GIVE RIGHT **3** 0‑m [I, T] to have or give sb the right to do sth: **~** (**for sth**) *If you live in the area, you qualify for a parking permit.* ◇ *To qualify, you must have lived in this country for at least three years.* ◇ **~ sb** (**for sth**) *Paying a fee doesn't automatically qualify you for membership.*

▸ FOR COMPETITION **4** 0‑m [I] to be of a high enough standard to enter a competition; to defeat another person or team in order to enter or continue in a competition: *He failed to qualify.* ◇ **~ for sth** *They qualified for the World Cup.*

▸ FIT DESCRIPTION **5** [I, T] to have the right qualities to be described as a particular thing: **~** (**as sth**) *Do you think this dress qualifies as evening wear?* ◇ **~ sth** (**as sth**) *It's an old building, but that doesn't qualify it as an ancient monument!*

▸ STATEMENT **6** [T] **~ sth** | **~ what...** to add sth to a previous statement to make the meaning less strong or less general: *I want to qualify what I said earlier—I didn't mean he couldn't do the job, only that he would need supervision.*

▸ GRAMMAR **7** [T] **~ sth** (of a word) to describe another word in a particular way: *In 'the open door', 'open' is an adjective qualifying 'door'.*

Q

quali·ta·tive AW /ˈkwɒlɪtətɪv; *NAmE* ˈkwɑːləteɪt-/ *adj.* [usually before noun] connected with how good sth is, rather than with how much of it there is: ***qualitative analysis/research*** ◇ *There are qualitative differences between the two products.* ➲ compare QUANTITATIVE ▸ **quali·ta·tive·ly** AW *adv.*: *qualitatively different*

qual·ity 0‑m /ˈkwɒləti; *NAmE* ˈkwɑːl-/ *noun, adj.*

■ *noun* (*pl.* -ies) **1** 0‑m [U, C] the standard of sth when it is compared to other things like it; how good or bad sth is: *to* ***be of good/poor/top quality*** ◇ *goods of a* ***high quality*** ◇ *high-quality goods* ◇ *a decline in water quality* ◇ *When costs are cut product quality suffers.* ◇ *Their* ***quality of life*** *improved dramatically when they moved to France.* **2** 0‑m [U] a high standard SYN **excellence**: *contemporary writers* ***of quality*** ◇ *We aim to provide quality at reasonable prices.* **3** 0‑m [C] a thing that is part of a person's character, especially sth good: ***personal qualities*** *such as honesty and generosity* ◇ *to have* ***leadership qualities*** **4** [C, U] a feature of sth, especially one that makes it different from sth else: *the special quality of light and shade in her paintings* **5** [C] (*BrE*) = QUALITY NEWSPAPER

■ *adj.* **1** [only before noun] used especially by people trying to sell goods or services to say that sth is of a high quality: *We specialize in quality furniture.* ◇ *quality service at a competitive price* **2** (*BrE, slang*) very good: *'What was the film like?' 'Quality!'*

ˈ**quality assurance** *noun* [U] the practice of managing the way goods are produced or services are provided to make sure they are kept at a high standard

ˈ**quality control** *noun* [U] the practice of checking goods as they are being produced, to make sure that they are of a high standard

ˌ**quality ˈnewspaper** (also *less frequent* **qual·ity**) *noun* (*BrE*) a newspaper that is intended for people who are intelligent and educated ➲ compare TABLOID (2)

ˈ**quality time** *noun* [U] time spent giving your full attention to sb, especially to your children after work

qualm /kwɑːm; kwɔːm/ *noun* [usually pl.] **~** (**about sth**) a feeling of doubt or worry about whether what you are doing is right SYN **misgiving**: *He had been working very hard so he had* ***no qualms about*** *taking a few days off.*

quan·dary /ˈkwɒndəri; *NAmE* ˈkwɑːn-/ *noun* [usually sing.] (*pl.* -ies) the state of not being able to decide what to do in a difficult situation SYN **dilemma**: *George was* ***in a quandary****—should he go or shouldn't he?*

quango /ˈkwæŋgəʊ; *NAmE* -goʊ/ *noun* (*pl.* -os) (often *disapproving*) (in Britain) an organization dealing with public matters, started by the government, but working independently and with its own legal powers

quanta *pl.* of QUANTUM

quan·ti·fier /ˈkwɒntɪfaɪə(r); *NAmE* ˈkwɑːn-/ *noun* (*grammar*) a determiner or pronoun that expresses quantity, for example 'all' or 'both'

quan·tify /ˈkwɒntɪfaɪ; *NAmE* ˈkwɑːn-/ *verb* (**quan·ti·fies, quan·ti·fy·ing, quan·ti·fied, quan·ti·fied**) **~ sth** to describe or express sth as an amount or a number: *The risks to health are impossible to quantify.* ▸ **quan·ti·fi·able** *adj.*: *quantifiable data* **quan·ti·fi·ca·tion** /ˌkwɒntɪfɪˈkeɪʃn; *NAmE* ˌkwɑːn-/ *noun* [U]

quan·ti·ta·tive /ˈkwɒntɪtətɪv; *NAmE* ˈkwɑːnteɪt-/ *adj.* connected with the amount or number of sth rather than with how good it is: ***quantitative analysis/research*** ◇ *There is no difference between the two in quantitative terms.* ➲ compare QUALITATIVE ▸ **quan·ti·ta·tive·ly** *adv.*

quan·tity 0‑m /ˈkwɒntəti; *NAmE* ˈkwɑːn-/ *noun* (*pl.* -ies)

1 0‑m [C, U] an amount or a number of sth: *a* ***large/small quantity*** *of sth* ◇ ***enormous/vast/huge quantities*** *of food* ◇ *a product that is cheap to produce* ***in large quantities*** ◇ *Is it available in sufficient quantity?* **2** 0‑m [U] the measurement of sth by saying how much of it there is: *The data is limited in terms of both quality and quantity.* **3** 0‑m [C, U] a large amount or number of sth: *The police found a quantity of drugs at his home.* ◇ *It's cheaper to buy goods* ***in quantity***. ◇ *I was overwhelmed by the sheer quantity of information available.* IDM see UNKNOWN

ˈ**quantity surveyor** *noun* (*BrE*) a person whose job is to calculate the quantity of materials needed for building sth, how much it will cost and how long it will take

quan·tum /ˈkwɒntəm; *NAmE* ˈkwɑːn-/ *noun* (*pl.* **quanta** /-tə/) (*physics*) a very small quantity of ELECTROMAGNETIC energy

ˌ**quantum ˈleap** (also *less frequent* ˌ**quantum ˈjump**) *noun* a sudden, great and important change, improvement or development

ˌ**quantum meˈchanics** *noun* [U] (*physics*) the branch of MECHANICS that deals with movement and force in pieces of matter smaller than atoms

ˈ**quantum theory** *noun* [U] (*physics*) a theory based on the idea that energy exists in units that cannot be divided

quar·an·tine /ˈkwɒrəntiːn; *NAmE* ˈkwɔːr-/ *noun, verb*

■ *noun* [U] a period of time when an animal or a person that has or may have a disease is kept away from others in order to prevent the disease from spreading: *The dog was kept* ***in quarantine*** *for six months.* ◇ *quarantine regulations*

■ *verb* **~ sth/sb** to put an animal or a person into quarantine

quark /kwɑːk; *NAmE* kwɑːrk/ *noun* **1** [C] (*physics*) a very small part of matter (= a substance). There are several types of quark and it is thought that PROTONS, NEUTRONS, etc. are formed from them. **2** [U] a type of soft cheese from central Europe, similar to CURD CHEESE

quar·rel /ˈkwɒrəl; *NAmE* ˈkwɔːr-; ˈkwɑːr-/ *noun, verb*
■ ***noun*** **1** [C] **~ (with sb/between A and B) (about/over sth)** an angry argument or disagreement between people, often about a personal matter: *a family quarrel* ◇ *He did not mention the quarrel with his wife.* ◇ *They had a quarrel about money.* ◇ *Were you at any time aware of a quarrel between the two of them?* **2** [U] **~ (with sb/sth)** (especially in negative sentences) a reason for complaining about sb/sth or for disagreeing with sb/sth: *We **have no quarrel with** his methods.* IDM see PICK *v.*
■ ***verb*** (-ll-, *US* -l-) [I] to have an angry argument or disagreement: *My sister and I used to quarrel all the time.* ◇ **~ (with sb) (about/over sth)** *She quarrelled with her brother over their father's will.*
PHR V **ˈquarrel with sb/sth** to disagree with sb/sth: *Nobody could quarrel with your conclusions.*

quar·rel·some /ˈkwɒrəlsəm; *NAmE* ˈkwɔːr-; ˈkwɑːr-/ *adj.* (of a person) liking to argue with other people SYN **argumentative**

quarry /ˈkwɒri; *NAmE* ˈkwɔːri; ˈkwɑːri/ *noun, verb*
■ ***noun*** (*pl.* -ies) **1** [C] a place where large amounts of stone, etc. are dug out of the ground: *a slate quarry* ◇ *the site of a disused quarry* ➲ compare MINE *n.* (1) **2** [sing.] an animal or a person that is being hunted or followed SYN **prey**: *The hunters lost sight of their quarry in the forest.* ◇ *The photographers pursued their quarry through the streets.*
■ ***verb*** (**quar·ries, quarry·ing, quar·ried, quar·ried**) [T, I] to take stone, etc. out of a quarry: **~ sth (from/out of sth)** *The local rock is quarried from the hillside.* ◇ **~ (for) sth** *The area is being quarried for limestone.* ► **quarry·ing** *noun* [U]: *There has been quarrying in the area for centuries.*

ˈquarry tile *noun* a floor TILE made from stone that has not been GLAZED

quart /kwɔːt; *NAmE* kwɔːrt/ *noun* (*abbr.* qt) a unit for measuring liquids, equal to 2 pints or about 1.14 litres in the UK and Canada, and 0.94 of a litre in the US
IDM **put a quart into a pint ˈpot** (*BrE*) to put sth into a space that is too small for it

quar·ter 0-w /ˈkwɔːtə(r); *NAmE* ˈkwɔːrt-/ *noun, verb*
■ ***noun***
► 1 OF 4 PARTS **1** 0-w (also **fourth** especially in *NAmE*) [C] one of four equal parts of sth: *a quarter of a mile* ◇ *The programme lasted an hour and a quarter.* ◇ *Cut the apple into quarters.* ◇ *The theatre was about three quarters full.* ➲ note at HALF
► 15 MINUTES **2** 0-w [C] a period of 15 minutes either before or after every hour: *It's (a) quarter to four now—I'll meet you at (a) quarter past.* ◇ (*NAmE* also) *It's quarter of four now—I'll meet you at quarter after.*
► 3 MONTHS **3** [C] a period of three months, used especially as a period for which bills are paid or a company's income is calculated
► PART OF TOWN **4** [C, usually sing.] a district or part of a town: *the Latin quarter* ◇ *the historic quarter of the city*
► PERSON/GROUP **5** [C] a person or group of people, especially as a source of help, information or a reaction: *Support for the plan came from an unexpected quarter.* ◇ *The news was greeted with dismay **in some quarters**.*
► 25 CENTS **6** [C] a coin of the US and Canada worth 25 cents
► ROOMS TO LIVE IN **7 quarters** [pl.] rooms that are provided for soldiers, servants, etc. to live in: *We were moved to more comfortable **living quarters**.* ◇ ***married quarters***
► OF MOON **8** [C] the period of time twice a month when we can see a quarter of the moon: *The moon is in its first quarter.*
► IN SPORT **9** [C] one of the four periods of time into which a game of AMERICAN FOOTBALL is divided
► WEIGHT **10** [C] (*BrE*) a unit for measuring weight, a quarter of a pound; 4 OUNCES **11** [C] a unit for measuring weight, 28 pounds in the UK or 25 pounds in the US; a quarter of a HUNDREDWEIGHT
► PITY **12** [U] (*old-fashioned* or *literary*) pity that sb shows towards an enemy or opponent who is in their power SYN **mercy**: *His rivals knew that they could expect no quarter from such a ruthless adversary.* IDM see CLOSE[2] *adj.*
■ ***verb***
► DIVIDE INTO 4 **1 ~ sth** to cut or divide sth into four parts: *She peeled and quartered an apple.*
► PROVIDE ROOMS **2 ~ sb (+ adv./prep.)** (*formal*) to provide sb with a place to eat and sleep: *The soldiers were quartered in the town.*

quar·ter·back /ˈkwɔːtəbæk; *NAmE* ˈkwɔːrtərbæk/ *noun, verb*
■ ***noun*** (in AMERICAN FOOTBALL) the player who directs the team's attacking play and passes the ball to other players at the start of each attack
■ ***verb*** **1** [I] (in AMERICAN FOOTBALL) to play as a quarterback **2** [T] **~ sth** to direct or organize sth

ˈquarter day *noun* (*BrE, technical*) the first day of a QUARTER (= a period of three months) on which payments must be made, for example at the STOCK EXCHANGE

quar·ter·deck /ˈkwɔːtədek; *NAmE* ˈkwɔːrtərdek/ *noun* a part of the upper level of a ship, at the back, that is used mainly by officers

ˌquarter-ˈfinal *noun* (in sports or competitions) one of the four games or matches to decide the players or teams for the SEMI-FINALS of a competition

ˈQuarter Horse *noun* (*NAmE*) a small breed of horse that can run very fast over short distances

quar·ter·ly /ˈkwɔːtəli; *NAmE* ˈkwɔːrtərli/ *adj., adv., noun*
■ ***adj.*** produced or happening every three months: *a quarterly meeting of the board* ► **quar·ter·ly** *adv.*: *to pay the rent quarterly*
■ ***noun*** (*pl.* -ies) a magazine, etc. published four times a year

quar·ter·mas·ter /ˈkwɔːtəmɑːstə(r); *NAmE* ˈkwɔːrtərmæs-/ *noun* an officer in the army who is in charge of providing food, uniforms and accommodation

ˈquarter note (*NAmE*) (*BrE* **crot·chet**) *noun* (*music*) a note that lasts half as long as a MINIM/HALF NOTE ➲ picture at MUSIC

ˈquarter sessions *noun* [pl.] (in England, in the past) a court with limited powers that was held every three months

ˈquarter-tone *noun* (*music*) a quarter of a TONE on a musical SCALE, for example half of the INTERVAL (= the difference) between the notes E and F

quar·tet /kwɔːˈtet; *NAmE* kwɔːrˈtet/ *noun* **1** [C+sing./pl. v.] a group of four musicians or singers who play or sing together: *the Amadeus Quartet* **2** [C] a piece of music for four musicians or singers: *a Beethoven string quartet* **3** [C+sing./pl. v.] a set of four people or things: *the last in a quartet of novels*

quar·tile /ˈkwɔːtaɪl; *NAmE* ˈkwɔːrt-; -tl/ *noun* (*statistics*) one of four equal groups into which a set of things can be divided according to the DISTRIBUTION of a particular VARIABLE: *women in the fourth quartile of height* (= the shortest 25% of women) ➲ compare QUINTILE

quarto /ˈkwɔːtəʊ; *NAmE* ˈkwɔːrtoʊ/ *noun* (*pl.* -os) (*technical*) **1** [U] a size of page made by folding a standard sheet of paper twice to make eight pages **2** [C] a book with pages in quarto size

quartz /kwɔːts; *NAmE* kwɔːrts/ *noun* [U] a hard mineral, often in CRYSTAL form, that is used to make very accurate clocks and watches

qua·sar /ˈkweɪzɑː(r)/ *noun* (*astronomy*) a large object like a star, that is far away and that shines very brightly and occasionally sends out strong radio signals ➲ compare PULSAR

quash /kwɒʃ; *NAmE* kwɔːʃ; kwɑːʃ/ *verb* **1 ~ sth** (*BrE, law*) to officially say that a decision made by a court is no longer valid or correct SYN **overturn**: *His conviction was later quashed by the Court of Appeal.* **2 ~ sth** to take action to stop sth from continuing SYN **suppress**: *The rumours were quickly quashed.*

quasi- /ˈkweɪzaɪ; -saɪ; ˈkwɑːzi/ *combining form* (in adjectives and nouns) **1** that appears to be sth but is not really so: *a quasi-scientific explanation* **2** partly; almost: *a quasi-official body*

quat·er·cen·ten·ary /ˌkwætəsen'tiːnəri; *NAmE* -tərsen'teneri/ *noun* (*pl.* -ies) a 400th anniversary: *to celebrate the quatercentenary of Shakespeare's birth*

quat·rain /'kwɒtreɪn; *NAmE* 'kwɑːt-/ *noun* (*technical*) a poem or VERSE of a poem that has four lines

qua·ver /'kweɪvə(r)/ *verb, noun*
■ **verb** [I, T] (+ **speech**) if sb's voice **quavers**, it is unsteady, usually because the person is nervous or afraid: *'I'm not safe here, am I?' she asked in a quavering voice.* ▶ **qua·very** /'kweɪvəri/ *adj.*: *a quavery voice*
■ **noun 1** (*BrE*) (*NAmE* ˈ**eighth note**) (*music*) a note that lasts half as long as a CROTCHET/QUARTER NOTE ➲ picture at MUSIC **2** [usually sing.] a shaking sound in sb's voice

quay /kiː/ *noun* a platform in a HARBOUR where boats come in to load, etc: *A crowd was waiting on the quay.* ➲ VISUAL VOCAB page V5

quay·side /'kiːsaɪd/ *noun* [usually sing.] a quay and the area near it: *crowds waiting* ***on/at the quayside*** *to welcome them*

queasy /'kwiːzi/ *adj.* **1** feeling sick; wanting to VOMIT SYN **nauseous 2** slightly nervous or worried about sth ▶ **queas·ily** *adv.* **queasi·ness** *noun* [U]

Que·chua /'ketʃwə/ *noun* [U] a language originally spoken by the Quechua people of S America, now spoken in Peru, Bolivia, Chile, Colombia and Ecuador

queen 🔑 /kwiːn/ *noun*
▸ FEMALE RULER **1** 🔑 the female ruler of an independent state that has a royal family: *to* ***be crowned queen*** ◇ *kings and queens* ◇ *the Queen of Norway* ◇ *Queen Victoria* **2** 🔑 (also ˌ**queen** ˈ**consort**) the wife of a king
▸ BEST IN GROUP **3 ~** (**of sth**) a woman, place or thing that is thought to be one of the best in a particular group or area: *the queen of fashion* ◇ *a movie queen* ◇ *Venice, queen of the Adriatic*
▸ AT FESTIVAL **4** a woman or girl chosen to perform official duties at a festival or celebration: *a carnival queen* ◇ *a May queen* (= at a festival to celebrate the coming of spring) ◇ *a homecoming queen* ➲ see also BEAUTY QUEEN
▸ IN CHESS **5** the most powerful piece used in the game of CHESS that can move any number of squares in any direction ➲ VISUAL VOCAB page V33
▸ IN CARDS **6** a PLAYING CARD with the picture of a queen on it ➲ VISUAL VOCAB page V32
▸ INSECT **7** a large female insect that lays eggs for the whole group: *a queen bee*
▸ HOMOSEXUAL **8** (*informal, taboo*) an offensive word for a male HOMOSEXUAL who behaves like a woman IDM see ENGLISH, EVIDENCE, UNCROWNED

ˌ**queen** ˈ**bee** *noun* **1** a female BEE that produces eggs for the whole group of bees in a HIVE ➲ compare DRONE, WORKER **2** a woman who behaves as if she is the most important person in a particular place or group

queen·ly /'kwiːnli/ *adj.* of, like or suitable for a queen

ˌ**queen** ˈ**mother** *noun* a title given to the wife of a king who has died and who is the mother of the new king or queen: *Queen Elizabeth, the Queen Mother*

ˌ**Queen's** ˈ**Bench** (also ˌ**Queen's** ˈ**Bench Division**) *noun* [sing.] part of the UK High Court

Queens·berry Rules /ˌkwiːnzbəri 'ruːlz; *NAmE* -beri/ *noun* [pl.] **1** the standard rules of BOXING **2** the rules of polite and acceptable behaviour

ˌ**Queen's** ˈ**Counsel** *noun* = QC

the ˌ**Queen's** ˈ**English** *noun* [U] (*old-fashioned*) the English language as written and spoken correctly by educated people in the UK HELP 'The Queen's English' is used when the United Kingdom has a queen, and 'the King's English' when it has a king.

ˌ**Queen's** ˈ**evidence** *noun* [U] (*BrE*) if a criminal **turns Queen's evidence**, he or she gives evidence against the people who committed a crime with him or her

ˈ**queen-size** (also ˈ**queen-sized**) *adj.* (*NAmE*) (of beds, sheets, etc.) larger than a standard size but not as big as KING-SIZE

the ˌ**Queen's** ˈ**Speech** *noun* [sing.] in the UK, a statement read by the Queen at the start of a new Parliament, which contains details of the government's plans

queer /kwɪə(r); *NAmE* kwɪr/ *adj., noun, verb*
■ **adj.** (**queer·er, queer·est**) **1** (*old-fashioned*) strange or unusual SYN **odd**: *His face was a queer pink colour.* **2** (*taboo, slang*) an offensive way of describing a HOMOSEXUAL, especially a man, which is, however, also used by some homosexuals about themselves IDM see FISH *n.*
■ **noun** (*taboo, slang*) an offensive word for a HOMOSEXUAL, especially a man, which is, however, also used by some homosexuals about themselves
■ **verb**
IDM **queer sb's** ˈ**pitch** | **queer the** ˈ**pitch** (**for sb**) (*BrE, informal*) to spoil sb's plans or their chances of getting sth

queer·ly /'kwɪəli; *NAmE* 'kwɪrli/ *adv.* in a strange or unusual way: *He looked at me queerly.*

quell /kwel/ *verb* (*formal*) **1 ~ sth/sb** to stop sth such as violent behaviour or protests: *Extra police were called in to quell the disturbances.* ◇ (*figurative*) *She started to giggle, but Bob quelled her with a look.* **2 ~ sth** to stop or reduce strong or unpleasant feelings SYN **calm**: *to quell your fears*

quench /kwentʃ/ *verb* **1 ~ your thirst** to drink so that you no longer feel thirsty SYN **slake 2 ~ sth** (*formal*) to stop a fire from burning SYN **extinguish**: *Firemen tried to quench the flames raging through the building.*

queru·lous /'kwerələs; -rjə-/ *adj.* (*formal, disapproving*) complaining; showing that you are annoyed SYN **peevish** ▶ **queru·lous·ly** *adv.*

query /'kwɪəri; *NAmE* 'kwɪri/ *noun, verb*
■ **noun** (*pl.* -ies) **1** a question, especially one asking for information or expressing a doubt about sth: *Our assistants will be happy to answer your queries.* ◇ *If you have a query about your insurance policy, contact our helpline.* **2** a question mark to show that sth has not been finished or decided: *Put a query against Jack's name—I'm not sure if he's coming.*
■ **verb** (**quer·ies, query·ing, quer·ied, quer·ied**) **1 ~ sth** | **~ what, whether, etc...** to express doubt about whether sth is correct or not: *We queried the bill as it seemed far too high.* ◇ *I'm not in a position to query their decision.* **2 + speech** to ask a question: *'Who will be leading the team?' queried Simon.*

ˈ**query language** *noun* [C, U] (*computing*) a system of words and symbols that you type in order to ask a computer to give you information

quest /kwest/ *noun, verb*
■ **noun ~** (**for sth**) (*formal* or *literary*) a long search for sth, especially for some quality such as happiness: *the quest for happiness/knowledge/truth* ◇ *He set off* ***in quest of*** *adventure.*
■ **verb** [I] **~** (**for sth**) (*formal* or *literary*) to search for sth that is difficult to find

ques·tion 🔑 /'kwestʃən/ *noun, verb*
■ **noun 1** 🔑 [C] a sentence, phrase or word that asks for information: *to* ***ask/answer a question*** ◇ ***The question is,*** *how much are they going to pay you?* ◇ (*formal*) ***The question arises*** *as to whether or not he knew of the situation.* ◇ *The key question of what caused the leak remains unanswered.* ◇ (*formal*) *He* ***put a question to*** *the minister about the recent reforms.* ◇ *I hope the police don't ask any* ***awkward questions.*** ◇ *In an interview try to ask* ***open questions*** *that don't just need 'Yes' or 'No' as an answer.* **2** 🔑 [C] a task or request for information that is intended to test your knowledge or understanding, for example in an exam or a competition: *Question 3 was very difficult.* ◇ *In the exam there's sure to be* ***a question on*** *energy.* **3** 🔑 [C] **~** (**of sth**) a matter or topic that needs to be discussed or dealt with: *Let's look at the question of security.* ◇ *The question which needs to be addressed is one of funding.* ◇ *Which route is better remains* ***an open question*** (= it is not decided). **4** [U] doubt or confusion about sth: *Her honesty is* ***beyond question.*** ◇ *His suitability for the job is* ***open to question.*** ◇ *Her version of events was accepted* ***without question.***

IDM **bring/throw sth into ˈquestion** to cause sth to become a matter for doubt and discussion: *This case brings into question the whole purpose of the law.* **come into ˈquestion** to become a matter for doubt and discussion **ˌgood ˈquestion!** (*informal*) used to show that you do not know the answer to a question: *'How much is all this going to cost?' 'Good question!'* **in ˈquestion 1** 🔑 that is being discussed: *On the day in question we were in Cardiff.* **2** 🔑 in doubt; uncertain: *The future of public transport is not in question.* **just/merely/only a question of (sth/doing sth)** 🔑 used to say that sth is not difficult to predict, explain, do, etc.: *It's merely a question of time before the business collapses.* ◇ *It's just a question of deciding what you really want.* **out of the ˈquestion** 🔑 impossible or not allowed and therefore not worth discussing: *Another trip abroad this year is out of the question.* **there is/was no question of (sth happening/sb doing sth)** 🔑 there is/was no possibility of sth: *There was no question of his/him cancelling the trip so near the departure date.* ➲ more at BEG, CALL *v.*, MOOT *adj.*, POP *v.*

■ ***verb* 1** 🔑 **~ sb (about/on sth)** | **+ speech** to ask sb questions about sth, especially officially: *She was arrested and questioned about the fire.* ◇ *The students were questioned on the books they had been studying.* ◇ *Over half of those questioned said they rarely took any exercise.* **2** 🔑 to have or express doubts or suspicions about sth: **~ sth** *I just accepted what he told me. I never thought to question it.* ◇ *No one has ever questioned her judgement.* ◇ **~ whether, what, etc...** *He questioned whether the accident was solely the truck driver's fault.*

ques·tion·able /ˈkwestʃənəbl/ *adj.* **1** that you have doubts about because you think it is not accurate or correct SYN **debatable**: *The conclusions that they come to are highly questionable.* ◇ ***It is questionable whether*** *this is a good way of solving the problem.* **2** likely to be dishonest or morally wrong SYN **suspect**: *Her motives for helping are questionable.* ▸ **ques·tion·ably** /-əbli/ *adv.*

ques·tion·er /ˈkwestʃənə(r)/ *noun* a person who asks questions, especially in a broadcast programme or a public debate

ques·tion·ing /ˈkwestʃənɪŋ/ *noun, adj.*

■ ***noun*** [U] the activity of asking sb questions: *He was taken to the police station for questioning.* ◇ *They faced some hostile questioning over the cost of the project.*

■ ***adj.*** showing that you need information, or that you have doubts: *a questioning look* ◇ *She raised a questioning eyebrow.* ▸ **ques·tion·ing·ly** *adv.*

ˈquestion mark *noun* the mark (?) used in writing after a question

IDM **a ˈquestion mark over/against sth** used to say that sth is not certain: *There's still a big question mark hanging over his future with the team.*

ˈquestion master (also **quiz·master**) *noun* (both *BrE*) a person who asks the questions in a QUIZ, especially on television or the radio

ques·tion·naire /ˌkwestʃəˈneə(r); *NAmE* -ˈner/ *noun* **~ (on/about sth)** a written list of questions that are answered by a number of people so that information can be collected from the answers: *to complete a questionnaire* ◇ (*BrE*) *to fill in a questionnaire* ◇ (*especially NAmE*) *to fill out a questionnaire*

ˈquestion tag (also **ˈtag question**) *noun* (*grammar*) a phrase such as *isn't it?* or *don't you?* that you add to the end of a statement in order to turn it into a question or check that the statement is correct, as in *You like mushrooms, don't you?*

queue /kjuː/ *noun, verb*

■ ***noun* 1** (*BrE*) (*NAmE* **line**) a line of people, cars, etc. waiting for sth or to do sth: *the bus queue* ◇ *I had to join a queue for the toilets.* ◇ *How long were you* ***in the queue****?* ◇ *There was a queue of traffic waiting to turn right.* ➲ COLLOCATIONS at SHOPPING **2** (*computing*) a list of items of data stored in a particular order **IDM** see JUMP *v.*

■ ***verb*** (**queu·ing** or **queue·ing**) **1** [I] (*BrE*) **~ (up) (for sth)** to wait in a line of people, vehicles, etc. in order to do sth, get sth or go somewhere: *We had to queue up for an hour for the tickets.* ◇ *Queue here for taxis.* **2** [T, I] **~ (sth)** (*computing*) to add tasks to other tasks so that they are ready to be done in order; to come together to be done in order: *The system queues the jobs before they are processed.*

PHR V **be ˌqueuing ˈup (for sth/to do sth)** if people are said to be **queuing up** for sth or to do sth, a lot of them want to have it or do it: *Italian football clubs are queuing up to sign the young star.*

ˈqueue-jumping *noun* [U] (*BrE*) a situation in which a person moves to the front of a queue to get served before other people who have been waiting longer

quib·ble /ˈkwɪbl/ *verb, noun*

■ ***verb*** [I] **~ (about/over sth)** to argue or complain about a small matter or an unimportant detail: *It isn't worth quibbling over such a small amount.*

■ ***noun*** a small complaint or criticism, especially one that is not important: *minor quibbles*

quiche /kiːʃ/ *noun* [C, U] an open PIE filled with a mixture of eggs and milk with meat, vegetables, cheese, etc. ➲ compare FLAN, TART

quick 🔑 /kwɪk/ *adj., adv., noun*

■ ***adj.*** (**quick·er, quick·est**) **1** 🔑 done with speed; taking or lasting a short time: *She gave him a quick glance.* ◇ *These cakes are very quick and easy to make.* ◇ *Would you like a quick drink?* ◇ *The doctor said she'd make a quick recovery.* ◇ *It's quicker by train.* ◇ *Are you sure this is the quickest way?* ◇ *Have you finished already? That was quick!* ◇ *His quick thinking saved her life.* ◇ *He fired three shots* ***in quick succession****.* ➲ see also DOUBLE QUICK **2** 🔑 moving or doing sth fast: *a quick learner* ◇ **~ (to do sth)** *The kids were quick to learn.* ◇ *She was quick* (= too quick) *to point out the mistakes I'd made.* ◇ *Her quick hands suddenly stopped moving.* ◇ *Try to* ***be quick****! We're late already.* ◇ *Once again, his* ***quick wits*** (= quick thinking) *got him out of an awkward situation.* ◇ (*NAmE, informal*) *He's a* ***quick study*** (= he learns quickly). **3** 🔑 [only before noun] happening very soon or without delay: *We need to make a quick decision.* ◇ *The company wants quick results.* ➲ SYNONYMS at FAST

IDM **to have a quick ˈtemper** to become angry easily **ˌquick and ˈdirty** (*informal*) used to describe sth that is usually complicated, but is being done quickly and simply in this case: *Read our quick-and-dirty guide to creating a website.* ➲ more at BUCK *n.*, DRAW *n.*, MARK *n.*, UPTAKE

■ ***adv.*** (**quick·er, quick·est**) **1** quickly; fast: *Come as quick as you can!* ◇ *Let's see who can get there quickest.* ◇ *It's another of his schemes to* ***get rich quick****.* **2** **quick-** (in adjectives) doing the thing mentioned quickly: *quick-thinking* ◇ *quick-growing*

IDM **(as) quick as a ˈflash** very quickly: *Quick as a flash she was at his side.*

■ ***noun*** **the quick** [sing.] the soft, sensitive flesh that is under your nails: *She has bitten her nails down to the quick.*

IDM **cut sb to the ˈquick** to upset sb very much by doing or saying sth unkind

Which Word?

quick / quickly / fast

- **Quickly** is the usual adverb from **quick**: *I quickly realized that I was on the wrong train.* ◇ *My heart started to beat more quickly.*
- **Quick** is sometimes used as an adverb in very informal language, especially as an exclamation: *Come on! Quick! They'll see us!* **Quicker** is used more often: *My heart started to beat much quicker.* ◇ *The quicker I get you away from here, the better.*
- **Fast** is more often used when you are talking about the speed that somebody or something moves at: *How fast can a cheetah run?* ◇ *Can't you drive any faster?* ◇ ~~*You're driving too quickly.*~~ There is no word **fastly**.

quick·en /ˈkwɪkən/ *verb* (*formal*) **1** [I, T] to become quicker or make sth quicker: *She felt her heartbeat quicken as he approached.* ◇ **~ sth** *He quickened his pace to catch up with*

Q

them. **2** [I, T] **~ (sth)** to become more active; to make sth more active: *His interest quickened as he heard more about the plan.*

ˌquick-ˈfire *adj.* [only before noun] (of a series of things) done or said very fast, one after the other: *a series of quick-fire questions*

quickie /ˈkwɪki/ *noun* (*informal*) **1** a thing that only takes a short time: *I've got a question—it's just a quickie.* ◇ *a quickie divorce* **2** a sexual act that takes a very short time

quick·lime /ˈkwɪklaɪm/ *noun* [U] = LIME (1)

quick·ly 0‑ /ˈkwɪkli/ *adv.*
1 0‑ fast: *She walked quickly away.* ◇ *We'll repair it as quickly as possible.* ◇ *The last few weeks have* **gone quickly** (= the time seems to have passed quickly). **2** 0‑ soon; after a short time: *He replied to my letter very quickly.* ◇ *It quickly became clear that she was dying.* ➲ note at QUICK, SOON

quick·ness /ˈkwɪknəs/ *noun* [U] the quality of being fast, especially at thinking, etc: *She was known for the quickness of her wit.* ◇ *He amazes me with his quickness and eagerness to learn.*

ˈquick one *noun* (*BrE, informal*) a drink, usually an alcoholic one, taken quickly

quick·sand /ˈkwɪksænd/ *noun* [U] (also **quicksands** [pl.]) **1** deep wet sand that you sink into if you walk on it **2** a situation that is dangerous or difficult to escape from

quick·sil·ver /ˈkwɪksɪlvə(r)/ *noun, adj.*
■ ***noun*** [U] (*old use*) = MERCURY
■ ***adj.*** [only before noun] (*literary*) changing or moving very quickly: *his quicksilver temperament*

quick·step /ˈkwɪkstep/ *noun* a dance for two people together, with a lot of fast steps; a piece of music for this dance

ˌquick-ˈtempered *adj.* likely to become angry very quickly: *a quick-tempered woman*

ˌquick-ˈwitted *adj.* able to think quickly; intelligent: *a quick-witted student/response* OPP **slow-witted**

quid /kwɪd/ *noun* (*pl.* **quid**) (*BrE, informal*) one pound in money: *Can you lend me five quid?*
IDM **not the full ˈquid** (*AustralE, NZE, informal*) not very intelligent **quids ˈin** in a position of having made a profit, especially a good profit

Q

quid pro quo /ˌkwɪd prəʊ ˈkwəʊ; *NAmE* proʊ ˈkwoʊ/ *noun* [sing.] (from *Latin*) a thing given in return for sth else

qui·es·cent /kwiˈesnt/ *adj.* **1** (*formal*) quiet; not active **2** (*medical*) (of a disease, etc.) not developing, especially when this is probably only a temporary state SYN **dormant** ▸ **qui·es·cence** /‑sns/ *noun* [U]

quiet 0‑ /ˈkwaɪət/ *adj., noun, verb*
■ ***adj.*** (**quiet·er, quiet·est**) **1** 0‑ making very little noise: *her quiet voice* ◇ *a quieter, more efficient engine* ◇ *Could you keep the kids quiet while I'm on the phone?* ◇ *He* **went** *very* **quiet** (= did not say much) *so I knew he was upset.* ◇ ***'Be quiet,'*** *said the teacher.* ◇ *She crept downstairs* (**as**) **quiet as a mouse**. **2** 0‑ without many people or much noise or activity: *a quiet street* ◇ *They lead a quiet life.* ◇ *Business is usually quieter at this time of year.* ◇ *They had a quiet wedding.* **3** 0‑ not disturbed; peaceful: *to have a quiet drink* ◇ *I was looking forward to a quiet evening at home.* **4** 0‑ (of a person) tending not to talk very much: *She was quiet and shy.* **5** (of a feeling or an attitude) definite but not expressed in an obvious way: *He had an air of quiet authority.* ▸ **quiet·ly** 0‑ *adv.*: *to speak/move quietly* ◇ *I spent a few hours quietly relaxing.* ◇ *He is* **quietly confident** *that they can succeed* (= he is confident, but he is not talking about it too much). ◇ *a* **quietly-spoken** *woman* **quiet·ness** *noun* [U]: *the quietness of the countryside* ◇ *His quietness worried her.*
IDM **keep quiet about sth** | **keep sth quiet** 0‑ to say nothing about sth; to keep sth secret: *I've decided to resign but I'd rather you kept quiet about it.*
■ ***noun*** [U] the state of being calm and without much noise: *the quiet of his own room* ◇ *the quiet of the early morning* ◇ *I go to the library for a little* **peace and quiet**.
IDM **on the ˈquiet** without telling anyone SYN **secretly**
■ ***verb*** [I, T] (*especially NAmE*) to become calmer or less noisy; to make sb/sth calmer or less noisy SYN **calm (sb) down**: **~ (down)** *The demonstrators quieted down when the police arrived.* ◇ **~ sb/sth (down)** *He's very good at quieting the kids.*

quiet·en /ˈkwaɪətn/ *verb* [I, T] **~ (sb/sth) (down)** (*BrE*) to become calmer or less noisy; to make sb/sth calmer or less noisy: *The chatter of voices gradually quietened.* ◇ *Things seem to have quietened down a bit this afternoon* (= we are not so busy, etc.).

quiet·ism /ˈkwaɪətɪzəm/ *noun* [U] (*formal*) an attitude to life which makes you calmly accept things as they are rather than try to change them ▸ **quiet·ist** /‑ɪst/ *noun, adj.*

quiet·ude /ˈkwaɪətjuːd; *NAmE* ‑tuːd/ *noun* [U] (*literary*) the state of being still and quiet SYN **calm**

quie·tus /kwaɪˈiːtəs/ *noun* [C, U] (*literary*) **1** death, or sth that causes death, considered as a welcome end to life **2** something that makes a person or situation calm

quiff /kwɪf/ *noun* (*especially BrE*) a piece of hair at the front of the head that is brushed upwards and backwards

quill /kwɪl/ *noun* **1** (also **ˈquill feather**) a large feather from the wing or tail of a bird **2** (also **ˌquill ˈpen**) a pen made from a quill feather **3** one of the long sharp stiff SPINES on a PORCUPINE

quilt /kwɪlt/ *noun* **1** a decorative cover for a bed, made of two layers with soft material between them: *a patchwork quilt* ➲ VISUAL VOCAB page V20 **2** (*BrE*) = DUVET ➲ compare COMFORTER

quilt·ed /ˈkwɪltɪd/ *adj.* (of clothes, etc.) made of two layers of cloth with soft material between them, held in place by lines of STITCHES: *a quilted jacket*

quilt·ing /ˈkwɪltɪŋ/ *noun* [U] the work of making a QUILT; cloth that is used for this

quin /kwɪn/ *noun* (*BrE, informal*) = QUINTUPLET

quince /kwɪns/ *noun* a hard bitter yellow fruit used for making jam, etc. It grows on a tree, also called a quince: *quince jelly* ◇ *a flowering quince*

quin·cen·ten·ary /ˌkwɪnsenˈtiːnəri; *NAmE* ‑senˈteneri/ *noun* (*pl.* **‑ies**) a 500th anniversary: *the quincentenary of Columbus's voyage to America*

quin·ine /kwɪˈniːn; ˈkwɪniːn; *NAmE* also ˈkwaɪnaɪn/ *noun* [U] a drug made from the BARK of a S American tree, used in the past to treat MALARIA

qui·noa /ˈkiːnwɑː; *BrE* also kiˈnəʊə; *NAmE* also kiˈnoʊə/ *noun* [U] a South American plant, grown for its seeds, used as food and to make alcoholic drinks; the seeds of the quinoa plant

quint /kwɪnt/ *noun* (*NAmE, informal*) = QUINTUPLET

quint·es·sence /kwɪnˈtesns/ *noun* [sing.] **the ~ of sth** (*formal*) **1** the perfect example of sth: *It was the quintessence of an English manor house.* **2** the most important features of sth SYN **essence**: *a painting that captures the quintessence of Viennese elegance* ▸ **quint·es·sen·tial** /ˌkwɪntɪˈsenʃl/ *adj.*: *He was the quintessential tough guy.* **quint·es·sen·tial·ly** /‑ʃəli/ *adv.*

quin·tet /kwɪnˈtet/ *noun* **1** [C+sing./pl. v.] a group of five musicians or singers who play or sing together: *the Miles Davis Quintet* **2** [C] a piece of music for five musicians or singers: *a string quintet*

quin·tile /ˈkwɪntaɪl/ *noun* (*statistics*) one of five equal groups into which a set of things can be divided according to the DISTRIBUTION of a particular VARIABLE: *men in the first quintile of weight* (= the heaviest 20% of men) ➲ compare QUARTILE

quin·tu·ple /ˈkwɪntjʊpl; kwɪnˈtjuːpl; *NAmE* also ‑ˈtuːpl/ *adj., det., verb*
■ ***adj.*** [only before noun], ***det.*** **1** consisting of five parts, people, or groups **2** being five times as much or as many
■ ***verb*** [I, T] **~ (sth)** to become five times bigger; to make sth five times bigger: *Sales have quintupled over the past few years.*

quin·tu·plet /ˈkwɪntʊplət; kwɪnˈtjuːplət; -ˈtʌpl-/ (also *BrE informal* **quin**) (also *NAmE informal* **quint**) *noun* one of five children born at the same time to the same mother

quip /kwɪp/ *noun, verb*
■ *noun* a quick and clever remark: *to make a quip*
■ *verb* (-pp-) + **speech** to make a quick and clever remark

quire /ˈkwaɪə(r)/ *noun* (*old-fashioned*) four sheets of paper folded to make eight LEAVES (= 16 pages)

quirk /kwɜːk; *NAmE* kwɜːrk/ *noun, verb*
■ *noun* **1** an aspect of sb's personality or behaviour that is a little strange SYN **peculiarity** **2** a strange thing that happens, especially by accident: *By a strange* **quirk of fate** *they had booked into the same hotel.* ▸ **quirky** *adj.*: *a quirky sense of humour*
■ *verb* [T, I] ~ (**sth**) (*especially NAmE*) to twist your mouth or eyebrows suddenly; (of your mouth or eyebrows) to move in this way: *David quirked an eyebrow and smirked slightly.* ◇ *Her lips quirked suddenly.*

quis·ling /ˈkwɪzlɪŋ/ *noun* (*disapproving*) a person who helps an enemy that has taken control of his or her country SYN **collaborator**

quit 🔑 /kwɪt/ *verb* (**quit·ting, quit, quit**) (*BrE* also **quit·ting, quit·ted, quit·ted**)
1 🔑 [I, T] (*informal*) to leave your job, school, etc: *If I don't get more money I'll quit.* ◇ ~ **as sth** *He has decided to quit as manager of the team.* ◇ ~ **sth** *He quit the show last year because of bad health.* ◇ (*NAmE*) *She quit school at 16.* **2** 🔑 [T, I] (*informal, especially NAmE*) to stop doing sth: ~ **doing sth** *I've quit smoking.* ◇ ~ (**sth**) *Just quit it!* ◇ *We only just started. We're not going to quit now.* **3** [T, I] ~ (**sth**) to leave the place where you live: *We decided it was time to quit the city.* ◇ *The landlord gave them all* **notice to quit**. **4** 🔑 [I, T] ~ (**sth**) to close a computer program or application

Which Word?

quite / fairly / rather / pretty

Look at these examples:
- *The exam was fairly difficult.*
- *The exam was quite difficult.*
- *The exam was rather difficult.*
- **Quite** is a little stronger than **fairly**, and **rather** is a little stronger than **quite**. **Rather** is not very common in *NAmE*; **pretty** has the same meaning and this is used in informal *BrE* too: *The exam was pretty difficult.*
- In *BrE* **quite** has two meanings: *I feel quite tired today* (= fairly tired). With adjectives that describe an extreme state ('non-gradable' adjectives) it means 'completely' or 'absolutely': *I feel quite exhausted.* With some adjectives, both meanings are possible. The speaker's stress and intonation will show you which is meant: *Your essay is 'quite good* (= fairly good — it could be better); *Your essay is quite 'good* (= very good, especially when this is unexpected).
- In *NAmE* **quite** usually means something like 'very', not 'fairly' or 'rather'. **Pretty** is used instead for this sense.

quite 🔑 /kwaɪt/ *adv.*
1 🔑 (*BrE*) (not used with a negative) to some degree SYN **fairly, pretty**: *quite big/good/cold/warm/interesting* ◇ *He plays quite well.* ◇ *I* **quite like** *opera.* HELP When **quite** is used with an adjective before a noun, it comes before *a* or *an*. You can say: *It's quite a small house* or: *Their house is quite small* but not ~~*It's a quite small house.*~~ **2** 🔑 (*BrE*) to the greatest possible degree SYN **completely, absolutely, entirely**: *quite delicious/amazing/empty/perfect* ◇ *This is quite a different problem.* ◇ *I'm* **quite happy** *to wait for you here.* ◇ *Flying is* **quite the best** *way to travel.* ◇ *It wasn't quite as simple as I thought it would be.* ◇ **Quite frankly**, *I don't blame you.* ◇ *I've had* **quite enough** *of your tantrums.* ◇ *Are you* **quite sure**? ◇ *I* **quite agree**. ◇ *I don't quite know what to do next.* ◇ **Quite apart from** *all the work, he had financial problems.* ◇ *The theatre was* **not quite** (= was almost) *full.* ◇ *It's like being in the Alps, but not quite.* ◇ *'I almost think she prefers animals to people.'* **'Quite right too,'** *said Bill.* ◇ *'I'm sorry to be so difficult.'* **'That's quite all right.'** **3** 🔑 to a great degree; very; really: *You'll be quite comfortable here.* ◇ *I can see it quite clearly.* ◇ (*NAmE*) *'You've no intention of coming back?' 'I'm quite sorry, but no, I have not.'* **4** (also *formal* **quite so**) (*BrE*) used to agree with sb or show that you understand them: *'He's bound to feel shaken after his accident.' 'Quite.'*
IDM **ˈquite a/the sth** (also *informal* **ˈquite some sth**) used to show that a person or thing is particularly impressive or unusual in some way: *She's quite a beauty.* ◇ *We found it quite a change when we moved to London.* ◇ *He's quite the little gentleman, isn't he?* ◇ *It must be quite some car.* **quite a ˈlot (of sth)** 🔑 (also *BrE informal* **quite a ˈbit**) a large number or amount of sth: *They drank quite a lot of wine.* **ˈquite some sth** **1** a large amount of sth: *She hasn't been seen for quite some time.* **2** (*informal*) = QUITE A/THE STH ➲ more at CONTRARY, FEW *pron.*

quits /kwɪts/ *adj.*
IDM **be quits (with sb)** (*informal*) when two people **are quits**, they do not owe each other anything, especially money: *I'll give you £5 and then we're quits.* ➲ more at CALL *v.*, DOUBLE *n.*

quit·ter /ˈkwɪtə(r)/ *noun* (often *disapproving*) a person who gives up easily and does not finish a task they have started

quiver /ˈkwɪvə(r)/ *verb, noun*
■ *verb* [I] to shake slightly; to make a slight movement SYN **tremble**: *Her lip quivered and then she started to cry.*
■ *noun* **1** an emotion that has an effect on your body; a slight movement in part of your body: *He felt a quiver of excitement run through him.* ◇ *Jane couldn't help the quiver in her voice.* **2** a case for carrying arrows

qui vive /ˌkiː ˈviːv/ *noun*
IDM **on the qui ˈvive** paying close attention to a situation, in case sth happens: *He's always on the qui vive for a business opportunity.*

quix·ot·ic /kwɪkˈsɒtɪk; *NAmE* -ˈsɑːtɪk/ *adj.* (*formal*) having or involving ideas or plans that show imagination but are usually not practical ORIGIN From the character Don Quixote in the novel by Miguel de Cervantes, whose adventures are a result of him trying to achieve or obtain things that are impossible.

Q

quiz /kwɪz/ *noun, verb*
■ *noun* (*pl.* **quiz·zes**) **1** a competition or game in which people try to answer questions to test their knowledge: *a general knowledge quiz* ◇ *a television quiz show* **2** (*especially NAmE*) an informal test given to students: *a reading comprehension quiz* ➲ see also POP QUIZ ➲ note at EXAM
■ *verb* (-zz-) **1** to ask sb a lot of questions about sth in order to get information from them SYN **question**: ~ **sb (about sb/sth)** *Four men are being quizzed by police about the murder.* ◇ ~ **sb (on/over sth)** *We were quizzed on our views about education.* **2** ~ **sb** (*NAmE*) to give students an informal test: *You will be quizzed on chapter 6 tomorrow.*

quiz·master /ˈkwɪzmɑːstə(r); *NAmE* -mæs-/ *noun* = QUESTION MASTER

quiz·zical /ˈkwɪzɪkl/ *adj.* (of an expression) showing that you are slightly surprised or amused: *a quizzical expression* ▸ **quiz·zi·cal·ly** /-kli/ *adv.*: *She looked at him quizzically.*

quoit /kɔɪt; kwɔɪt/ *noun* **1** [C] a ring that is thrown onto a small post in the game of quoits **2** **quoits** [U] a game in which rings are thrown onto a small post

Quonset hut™ /ˈkwɒnset hʌt; *NAmE* ˈkwɑːn-/ (*NAmE*) (*BrE* **Nis·sen hut**) *noun* a shelter made of metal with curved walls and roof

quor·ate /ˈkwɔːrət; -ət/ *adj.* (*BrE, technical*) a meeting that is **quorate** has enough people present for them to make official decisions by voting OPP **inquorate**

Quorn™ /kwɔːn; *NAmE* kwɔːrn/ *noun* [U] a substance made from a type of FUNGUS, used in cooking instead of meat

quorum /ˈkwɔːrəm/ *noun* [sing.] the smallest number of people who must be at a meeting before it can begin or decisions can be made

quota /ˈkwəʊtə; *NAmE* ˈkwoʊtə/ *noun* **1** [C] the limited number or amount of people or things that is officially allowed: *to introduce a strict import quota on grain* ◇ *a quota system for accepting refugees* **2** [C] an amount of sth that sb expects or needs to have or achieve: *I'm going home now—I've done my quota of work for the day.* **3** [sing.] (*politics*) a fixed number of votes that a candidate needs in order to be elected: *He was 76 votes short of the quota.*

quot·able /ˈkwəʊtəbl; *NAmE* ˈkwoʊ-/ *adj.* (of a statement) interesting or amusing and worth repeating

quota·tion AW /kwəʊˈteɪʃn; *NAmE* kwoʊ-/ *noun* **1** (rather *formal*) (also rather *informal* **quote**) [C] a group of words or a short piece of writing taken from a book, play, speech, etc. and repeated because it is interesting or useful: *The book began with a quotation from Goethe.* ◇ *a dictionary of quotations* ➲ see also MISQUOTATION **2** [U] the act of repeating sth interesting or useful that another person has written or said: *The writer illustrates his point by quotation from a number of sources.* **3** [C] (rather *formal*) (also rather *informal* **quote**) a statement of how much money a particular piece of work will cost SYN **estimate**: *You need to get a written quotation before they start work.* **4** [C] (*finance*) a statement of the current value of goods or shares: *the latest quotations from the Stock Exchange*

quoˈtation marks (also **quotes**, ˈ**speech marks**) (*BrE* also **in·vert·ed commas**) *noun* [pl.] a pair of marks (' ') or (" ") placed around a word, sentence, etc. to show that it is what sb said or wrote, that it is a title or that you are using it in an unusual way

quote 🔑 AW /kwəʊt; *NAmE* kwoʊt/ *verb, noun*

■ ***verb***

▸ REPEAT EXACT WORDS **1** 🔑 [T, I] to repeat the exact words that another person has said or written: **~ sth (from sb/sth)** *He quoted a passage from the minister's speech.* ◇ *to quote Shakespeare* ◇ *Quote this reference number in all correspondence.* ◇ **~ (sb) (as doing sth)** *The President was* ***quoted*** *in the press* ***as saying*** *that he disagreed with the decision.* ◇ *'It will all be gone tomorrow.'* ***'Can I quote you on that?'*** ◇ ***Don't quote me on this*** (= this is not an official statement), *but I think he is going to resign.* ◇ *She said, and I quote, 'Life is meaningless without love.'* ◇ **+ speech** *'The man who is tired of London is tired of life,' he quoted.* ➲ see also MISQUOTE

▸ GIVE EXAMPLE **2** [T] **~ (sb) sth** to mention an example of sth to support what you are saying: *Can you quote me an instance of when this happened?* ➲ SYNONYMS at MENTION

▸ GIVE PRICE **3** [T, I] **~ (sb) (sth) (for sth/for doing sth)** to tell a customer how much money you will charge them for a job, service or product: *They quoted us £300 for installing a shower unit.* **4** [T] **~ sth (at sth)** (*finance*) to give a market price for shares, gold or foreign money: *Yesterday the pound was quoted at $1.8285, unchanged from Monday.* **5** [T] **~ sth** (*finance*) to give the prices for a business company's shares on a STOCK EXCHANGE: *Several football clubs are now quoted on the Stock Exchange.*

IDM ˈ**quote (... ˈunquote)** (*informal*) used to show the beginning (and end) of a word, phrase, etc. that has been said or written by sb else: *It was quote, 'the hardest decision of my life', unquote, and one that he lived to regret.*

■ ***noun*** (rather *informal*)

▸ EXACT WORDS **1** = QUOTATION (1): *The essay was full of quotes.*

▸ PRICE **2** = QUOTATION (3): *Their quote for the job was way too high.*

▸ PUNCTUATION **3 quotes** [pl.] = QUOTATION MARKS: *If you take text from other sources, place it* ***in quotes.***

quoth /kwəʊθ; *NAmE* kwoʊθ/ *verb* **+ speech** (*old use* or *humorous*) used meaning 'said' before 'I', 'he' or 'she'

quo·tid·ian /kwɒˈtɪdiən; kwəʊˈt-; *NAmE* kwoʊ-/ *adj.* (*formal*) ordinary; typical of what happens every day SYN **day to day**

quo·tient /ˈkwəʊʃnt; *NAmE* ˈkwoʊ-/ *noun* (*mathematics*) a number which is the result when one number is divided by another ➲ see also INTELLIGENCE QUOTIENT

Qur'an = KORAN

q.v. /ˌkjuː ˈviː/ *abbr.* used in books to tell a reader that there is more information in another part of the book (from Latin 'quod vide')

QWERTY /ˈkwɜːti; *NAmE* ˈkwɜːrti/ *adj.* [usually before noun] (of a keyboard on a computer or TYPEWRITER) with the keys arranged in the usual way with Q, W, E, R, T and Y on the left of the top row of letters

Rr

R /ɑː(r)/ *noun, abbr.*
■ ***noun*** (also **r**) [C, U] (*pl.* Rs, R's, r's /ɑːz; *NAmE* ɑːrz/) the 18th letter of the English alphabet: *'Rose' begins with (an) R/'R'.* **IDM** see THREE
■ ***abbr.*** **1** (*BrE*) Queen; King (from Latin 'Regina'; 'Rex'): *Elizabeth R.* **2 R.** (especially on maps) River: *R. Trent* **3** (also **R.** especially in *NAmE*) (in politics in the US) REPUBLICAN **4** (*BrE*) Royal: *the RAC* (= Royal Automobile Club) **5** (*NAmE*) the abbreviation for 'restricted' (a label for a film/movie that is not suitable for people under the age of 17 to see without an adult present) **6** ROENTGEN ➲ see also R & B, R & D

rabbi /ˈræbaɪ/ *noun* a Jewish religious leader or a teacher of Jewish law: *the Chief Rabbi* (= the leader of Jewish communities in a particular country) ◇ *Rabbi Sacks*

rab·bin·ical /rəˈbɪnɪkl/ (also **rab·bin·ic**) *adj.* connected with rabbis or Jewish law or teaching

rab·bit /ˈræbɪt/ *noun, verb*
■ ***noun*** **1** [C] a small animal with soft fur, long ears and a short tail. Rabbits live in holes in the ground or are kept as pets or for food: *a rabbit hutch* ➲ compare HARE **2** [U] meat from a rabbit **IDM** see PULL *v.*
■ ***verb*** [I] **go rabbiting** to hunt or shoot rabbits
PHR V ˌ**rabbit ˈon** (**about sb/sth**) (*BrE, informal, disapproving*) to talk continuously about things that are not important or interesting **SYN** chatter

rabbit

hare

ˈ**rabbit warren** (also **war·ren**) *noun* **1** a system of holes and underground tunnels where wild rabbits live **2** (*disapproving*) a building or part of a city with many narrow passages or streets

rab·ble /ˈræbl/ *noun* [sing.+ sing./pl. v.] (*disapproving*) **1** a large group of noisy people who are or may become violent **SYN** **mob**: *a drunken rabble* **2 the rabble** ordinary people or people who are considered to have a low social position **SYN** **the masses**: *a speech that appealed to the rabble*

ˈ**rabble-rouser** *noun* a person who makes speeches to crowds of people intending to make them angry or excited, especially for political aims ▸ ˈ**rabble-rousing** *adj.* ˈ**rabble-rousing** *noun* [U]

Rabe·lais·ian /ˌræbəˈleɪziən; -ˈleɪʒn/ *adj.* dealing with sex and the human body in a rude but humorous way **ORIGIN** From the French writer François Rabelais, whose works dealt with sex and the body in this way.

rabid /ˈræbɪd; ˈreɪb-/ *adj.* **1** [usually before noun] (*disapproving*) (of a type of person) having very strong feelings about sth and acting in an unacceptable way: *rabid right-wing fanatics* ◇ *the rabid tabloid press* **2** [usually before noun] (*disapproving*) (of feelings or opinions) violent or extreme: *rabid speculation* **3** suffering from rabies: *a rabid dog* ▸ **rabid·ly** *adv.*

ra·bies /ˈreɪbiːz/ *noun* [U] a disease of dogs and other animals that causes MADNESS and death. Infected animals can pass the disease to humans by biting them.

RAC /ˌɑːr eɪ ˈsiː/ *abbr.* Royal Automobile Club (a British organization which provides services for car owners)

rac·coon (also **ra·coon**) /rəˈkuːn; *NAmE* ræ-/ *noun* **1** [C] a small N American animal with greyish-brown fur, black marks on its face and a thick tail **2** [U] the fur of the raccoon

race 🔑 /reɪs/ *noun, verb*
■ ***noun***
▸ COMPETITION **1** 🔑 [C] **~ (between A and B)** | **~ (against sb)** a competition between people, animals, vehicles, etc. to see which one is the faster or fastest: *a race between the two best runners of the club* ◇ *Who* ***won the race?*** ◇ *He's already in training for the big race against Bailey.* ◇ *Their horse came third in the race last year.* ◇ *a* ***boat/horse/road,***

Collocations

Race and immigration

Prejudice and racism

- **experience/encounter** racism/discrimination/prejudice/anti-semitism
- **face/suffer** persecution/discrimination
- **fear/escape from/flee** racial/political/religious persecution
- **constitute/be a form of** racial/race discrimination
- **reflect/reveal/show/have** a racial/cultural bias
- **be biased/be prejudiced against** (*especially BrE*) black people/(*both especially NAmE*) people of color/African Americans/Asians/Africans/Indians, etc.
- **discriminate against** minority groups/minorities
- **perpetuate/conform to/fit/defy** a common/popular/traditional/negative stereotype
- **overcome/be blinded by** deep-seated/racial/(*especially NAmE*) race prejudice
- **entrench/perpetuate** racist attitudes
- **hurl/shout** (*especially BrE*) racist abuse; (*especially NAmE*) a racist/racial/ethnic slur
- **challenge/confront** racism/discrimination/prejudice
- **combat/fight (against)/tackle** blatant/overt/covert/subtle/institutional/systemic racism

Race and society

- **damage/improve** (*especially BrE*) race relations
- **practise/**(*especially US*) **practice** (racial/religious) tolerance/segregation
- **bridge/break down/transcend** cultural/racial barriers
- **encourage/promote** social integration
- **outlaw/end** discrimination/slavery/segregation
- **promote/embrace/celebrate** cultural diversity
- **conform to/challenge/violate** (accepted/established/prevailing/dominant) social/cultural norms
- **live in** a multicultural society
- **attack/criticize** multiculturalism
- **fight for/struggle for/promote** racial equality
- **perpetuate/reinforce** economic and social inequality
- **introduce/be for/be against** (*BrE*) positive discrimination/(*especially NAmE*) affirmative action
- **support/be active in/play a leading role in** the civil rights movement

Immigration

- **control/restrict/limit/encourage** immigration
- **attract/draw** a wave of immigrants
- **assist/welcome** refugees
- **house/shelter** refugees and asylum seekers
- **smuggle** illegal immigrants into the UK
- **deport/repatriate** illegal immigrants/failed asylum seekers
- **assimilate/integrate** new immigrants
- **employ/hire** migrant workers
- **exploit/rely on** (cheap/illegal) immigrant labour/(*especially US*) labor
- **apply for/gain/obtain/be granted/be denied** (full) citizenship
- **have/hold** dual citizenship

etc. **race** ◇ *a five-kilometre race* ◇ *Shall we* **have a race** *to the end of the beach?* ➲ see also DRAG RACE, HORSE RACE **2** ⚷ [sing.] a situation in which a number of people, groups, organizations, etc. are competing, especially for political power or to achieve sth first: **~ (for sth)** *the race for the presidency* ◇ **~ (to do sth)** ***The race is on*** (= has begun) *to find a cure for the disease.* ➲ see also RAT RACE
▸ FOR HORSES **3 the races** [pl.] a series of horse races that happen at one place on a particular day: *to go to the races*
▸ PEOPLE **4** ⚷ [C, U] one of the main groups that humans can be divided into according to their physical differences, for example the colour of their skin: *the* ***Caucasian/Mongolian, etc. race*** ◇ *people of* ***mixed race*** ◇ *This custom is found in people of all races throughout the world.* ◇ *legislation against discrimination on the grounds of race or sex* **5** [C] a group of people who share the same language, history, culture, etc: *the Nordic races* ◇ *He admired Canadians as a hardy and determined race.* ➲ see also HUMAN RACE
▸ ANIMALS/PLANTS **6** [C] a breed or type of animal or plant: *a race of cattle*
IDM **a ˌrace against ˈtime/the ˈclock** a situation in which you have to do sth or finish sth very fast before it is too late ➲ more at HORSE *n.*
■ *verb*
▸ COMPETE **1** ⚷ [I, T] to compete against sb/sth to see who can go faster or the fastest, do sth first, etc; to take part in a race or races: **~ (against sb/sth)** *Who will he be racing against in the next round?* ◇ *They raced to a thrilling victory in the relay.* ◇ *She'll be racing for the senior team next year.* ◇ **~ sb/sth** *We raced each other back to the car.* ◇ **~ to do sth** *Television companies are racing to be the first to screen his life story.* **2** [T] **~ sth** to make an animal or a vehicle compete in a race: *to race dogs/horses/pigeons* ◇ *to race motorbikes*
▸ MOVE FAST **3** ⚷ [I, T] to move very fast; to move sb/sth very fast: **+ adv./prep.** *He raced up the stairs.* ◇ *The days seemed to race past.* ◇ **~ sb/sth + adv./prep.** *The injured man was raced to the hospital.* ◇ *She raced her car through the narrow streets of the town.*
▸ OF HEART/MIND/THOUGHTS **4** [I] to function very quickly because you are afraid, excited, etc: *My mind raced as I tried to work out what was happening.* ◇ *She took a deep breath to calm her racing pulse.*
▸ OF ENGINE **5** [I] to run too fast: *The truck came to rest against a tree, its engine racing.*

ˈrace car (*NAmE*) (*BrE* **ˈracing car**) *noun* a car that has been specially designed for motor racing

ˈrace card *noun*
IDM **play the ˈrace card** (*disapproving*) to criticize people who belong to different races in a way that is meant to make other people feel opposed to them and to gain you a political advantage, especially during an election

race·card /ˈreɪskɑːd; *NAmE* -kɑːrd/ *noun* (*BrE*) a list of all the horse races at a particular event

race·course /ˈreɪskɔːs; *NAmE* -kɔːrs/ (*BrE*) (*NAmE* **race·track**) *noun* a track where horses race and the buildings, etc. that are connected with it ➲ VISUAL VOCAB page V38

race·goer /ˈreɪsɡəʊə(r); *NAmE* -ɡoʊ-/ *noun* (*BrE*) a person who goes to horse races

race·horse /ˈreɪshɔːs; *NAmE* -hɔːrs/ *noun* a horse that is bred and trained to run in races ➲ VISUAL VOCAB page V38

ˈrace meeting *noun* (*BrE*) a series of races, especially for horses, held at one course over one day or several days

racer /ˈreɪsə(r)/ *noun* **1** a person or an animal that competes in races: *Italy's champion downhill racer* **2** a car, boat, etc. designed for racing: *an ocean racer*

ˌrace reˈlations *noun* [pl.] the relationships between people of different races who live in the same community

ˈrace riot *noun* violent behaviour between people of different races living in the same community

race·track /ˈreɪstræk/ *noun* **1** a track for races between runners, cars, bicycles, etc: *You can't cross the road—it's like a racetrack.* **2** (*NAmE*) (*BrE* **race·course**) a track where horses race and the buildings, etc. that are connected with it ➲ VISUAL VOCAB page V38

race·way /ˈreɪsweɪ/ *noun* (*NAmE*) a track for racing cars or horses

ra·cial /ˈreɪʃl/ *adj.* **1** [only before noun] happening or existing between people of different races: ***racial hatred/prejudice/tension/violence*** ◇ *racial equality* ◇ *They have pledged to end* ***racial discrimination*** *in areas such as employment.* **2** [usually before noun] connected with a person's race: *racial minorities* ◇ *a person's* ***racial origin*** ▸ **ra·cial·ly** /-ʃəli/ *adv.*: *The attacks were not racially motivated.* ◇ *racially mixed schools*

ra·cial·ism /ˈreɪʃəlɪzəm/ *noun* [U] (*old-fashioned, BrE*) = RACISM

ra·cial·ist /ˈreɪʃəlɪst/ *noun, adj.* (*old-fashioned, BrE*) = RACIST

ˌracial ˈprofiling *noun* [U] (*NAmE*) the fact of police officers, etc. suspecting that sb has committed a crime based on the colour of their skin or their race rather than on any evidence

ra·cing ⚷ /ˈreɪsɪŋ/ *noun* [U]
1 ⚷ (also **ˈhorse racing**) the sport of racing horses: *a racing stable* ➲ see also FLAT RACING **2** ⚷ (usually in compounds) any sport that involves competing in races: ***motor/yacht/greyhound, etc. racing*** ◇ *a racing driver* ➲ see also DRAG RACING

ˈracing car (*BrE*) (*NAmE* **ˈrace car**) *noun* a car that has been specially designed for motor racing

ˌracing ˈcertainty *noun* (*BrE, informal*) a thing that is certain to happen: *It's a racing certainty that the vote will go against him .*

ra·cism /ˈreɪsɪzəm/ *noun* [U] (*disapproving*) **1** the unfair treatment of people who belong to a different race; violent behaviour towards them: *a victim of racism* ◇ *ugly outbreaks of racism* ➲ COLLOCATIONS at RACE **2** the belief that some races of people are better than others: *irrational racism* ▸ **ra·cist** /ˈreɪsɪst/ *noun*: *He's a racist.* **ra·cist** *adj.*: *racist thugs* ◇ *racist attitudes/attacks/remarks*

racks

plate rack

wine rack

vegetable rack

toast rack

magazine rack

luggage rack

roof rack (also luggage rack especially *NAmE*)

rack /ræk/ *noun, verb*
■ *noun* **1** (often in compounds) a piece of equipment, usually made of metal or wooden bars, that is used for holding things or for hanging things on: *a* ***vegetable/wine/plate/toast rack*** ◇ *I looked through a rack of clothes at the back of the shop.* ➲ VISUAL VOCAB pages V18, V57 ➲ see also LUGGAGE RACK, ROOF RACK **2** (usually **the rack**) an instrument of TORTURE, used in the past for punishing and hurting people. Their arms and legs were tied to the wooden frame and then pulled in opposite directions, stretching the body. **3 ~ of lamb/pork** a particular piece of meat that includes the front RIBS and is cooked in the oven **4** a part

of a machine that consists of a bar with parts that a wheel or gear can fit into

IDM **go to ˌrack and ˈruin** to get into a bad condition: *They let the house go to rack and ruin.* **ˌoff the ˈrack** (*NAmE*) (*BrE* **ˌoff the ˈpeg**) (of clothes) made to a standard average size and not made especially to fit you **on the ˈrack** feeling extreme pressure, anxiety or pain

■ *verb* (also *less frequent* **wrack**) [often passive] **~ sb/sth** to make sb suffer great physical or mental pain: *to be racked with/by guilt* ◇ *Her face was racked with pain.* ◇ *Violent sobs racked her whole body.* ◇ (*BrE*) *a racking cough*

IDM **rack your ˈbrain(s)** to think very hard or for a long time about sth: *She racked her brains, trying to remember exactly what she had said.*

PHR V **ˌrack ˈup sth** (*especially NAmE*) to collect sth, such as profits or losses in a business, or points in a competition: *The company racked up $200 million in losses in two years.* ◇ *In ten years of boxing he racked up a record 176 wins.*

racket /ˈrækɪt/ *noun* **1** [sing.] (*informal*) a loud unpleasant noise SYN **din**: *Stop making that terrible racket!* **2** [C] (*informal*) a dishonest or illegal way of getting money: *a* ***protection/extortion/drugs, etc. racket*** **3** (also **racquet**) [C] a piece of sports equipment used for hitting the ball, etc. in the games of TENNIS, SQUASH or BADMINTON. It has an OVAL frame, with strings stretched across and down it. ➲ VISUAL VOCAB page V37 ➲ compare BAT **4 rackets, racquets** [U] a game for two or four people, similar to SQUASH, played with rackets and a small hard ball in a COURT with four walls

rack·et·eer /ˌrækəˈtɪə(r); *NAmE* -ˈtɪr/ *noun* (*disapproving*) a person who makes money through dishonest or illegal activities ▸ **rack·et·eer·ing** *noun* [U]

ˈrack rate *noun* (*especially NAmE*) the standard price of a hotel room

ra·con·teur /ˌrækɒnˈtɜː(r); *NAmE* -kɑːn-/ *noun* a person who is good at telling stories in an interesting and amusing way

ra·coon = RACCOON

rac·quet = RACKET ➲ VISUAL VOCAB page V37

rac·quet·ball /ˈrækɪtbɔːl/ *noun* [U] a game played especially in the US by two or four players on a COURT with four walls, using RACKETS and a small hollow rubber ball

racy /ˈreɪsi/ *adj.* (**raci·er**, **raci·est**) having a style that is exciting and amusing, sometimes in a way that is connected with sex: *a racy novel*

rad /ræd/ *adj.*, *noun*

■ *adj.* (*old-fashioned, slang, especially NAmE*) very good

■ *noun* (*physics*) a unit for measuring the effect of RADIATION

radar /ˈreɪdɑː(r)/ *noun* [U] a system that uses radio waves to find the position and movement of objects, for example planes and ships, when they cannot be seen: *They located the ship by radar.* ◇ *a radar screen* ➲ compare SONAR

IDM **below/under the ˈradar** used to say that people are not aware of sth: *Experts say a lot of corporate crime stays under the radar.* **on/off the ˈradar screen** used to say that people's attention is on or not on sth: *The issue of terrorism is back on the radar screen.* ➲ more at BUBBLE *v.*

ˈradar trap *noun* (*BrE*) = SPEED TRAP

rad·dled /ˈrædld/ *adj.* (*BrE*) (of a person, their face, etc.) looking very tired SYN **worn**

ra·dial /ˈreɪdiəl/ *adj.*, *noun*

■ *adj.* having a pattern of lines, etc. that go out from a central point towards the edge of a circle: *the radial pattern of public transport facilities* ▸ **ra·di·al·ly** /-iəli/ *adv.*

■ *noun* (*BrE* also **ˌradial ˈtyre**) (*NAmE* also **ˌradial ˈtire**) a car tyre with strong parts inside that point away from the outside part and make the tyre stronger and safer

ra·dian /ˈreɪdiən/ *noun* (*geometry*) a unit used to measure an angle, equal to the angle at the centre of a circle whose ARC is the same length as the circle's RADIUS

ra·di·ance /ˈreɪdiəns/ *noun* [U] **1** a special bright quality that shows in sb's face, for example because they are very happy or healthy **2** warm light shining from sth

ra·di·ant /ˈreɪdiənt/ *adj.* **1** showing great happiness, love or health: *a radiant smile* ◇ *The bride looked radiant.* ◇ **~ with sth** *She was radiant with health.* **2** giving a warm bright light: *The sun was radiant in a clear blue sky.* **3** [only before noun] (*technical*) sent out in RAYS from a central point: *the* ***radiant heat/energy*** *of the sun* ▸ **ra·di·ant·ly** *adv.*: *radiantly happy* ◇ *He smiled radiantly.*

ra·di·ate /ˈreɪdieɪt/ *verb* **1** [T, I] **~ (sth)** | **~ (from sb)** if a person **radiates** a particular quality or emotion, or if it **radiates** from them, people can see it very clearly: *He radiated self-confidence and optimism.* **2** [I, T] **~ (from sth)** | **~ (sth)** if sth **radiates** heat, light or energy or heat, etc. **radiates** from it, the heat is sent out in all directions SYN **give (sth) off**: *Heat radiates from the stove.* **3** [I] **+ adv./prep.** (of lines, etc.) to spread out in all directions from a central point: *Five roads radiate from the square.* ◇ *The pain started in my stomach and radiated all over my body.*

ra·di·ation /ˌreɪdiˈeɪʃn/ *noun* **1** [U, C] powerful and very dangerous RAYS that are sent out from RADIOACTIVE substances: *high* ***levels/doses of radiation*** *that damage cells* ◇ *the link between exposure to radiation and childhood cancer* ◇ *a radiation leak from a nuclear power station* ◇ *radiation sickness* ◇ *the radiations emitted by radium* **2** [U] heat, energy, etc. that is sent out in the form of RAYS: *ultraviolet radiation* ◇ *electromagnetic radiation from power lines* **3** (also **ˌradiˈation therapy**) [U] the treatment of cancer and other diseases using radiation ➲ compare CHEMOTHERAPY, RADIOTHERAPY

ra·di·ator /ˈreɪdieɪtə(r)/ *noun* **1** a hollow metal device for heating rooms. Radiators are usually connected by pipes through which hot water is sent: *a central heating system with a radiator in each room* ➲ VISUAL VOCAB page V18 **2** a device for cooling the engine of a vehicle or an aircraft

rad·ical AW /ˈrædɪkl/ *adj.*, *noun*

■ *adj.* [usually before noun] **1** concerning the most basic and important parts of sth; thorough and complete SYN **far-reaching**: *the need for* ***radical changes*** *in education* ◇ *demands for radical reform of the law* ◇ *radical differences between the sexes* **2** new, different and likely to have a great effect: *radical ideas* ◇ *a radical solution to the problem* ◇ *radical proposals* **3** in favour of thorough and complete political or social change: *the radical wing of the party* ◇ *radical politicians/students/writers* **4** (*old-fashioned, NAmE, slang*) very good ▸ **rad·ic·al·ly** AW /-kli/ *adv.*: *The new methods are radically different from the old.* ◇ *Attitudes have changed radically.*

■ *noun* **1** a person with radical opinions: *political radicals* **2** (*chemistry*) a group of atoms that behave as a single unit in a number of COMPOUNDS ➲ see also FREE RADICAL

ˌradical ˈchic *noun* [U] fashionable LEFT-WING views; the people, behaviour and way of life connected with these views

rad·ic·al·ism /ˈrædɪkəlɪzəm/ *noun* [U] belief in RADICAL ideas and principles

rad·ic·al·ize (*BrE* also **-ise**) /ˈrædɪkəlaɪz/ *verb* **~ sb/sth** to make people more willing to consider new and different policies, ideas, etc; to make people more RADICAL in their political opinions: *Recent events have radicalized opinion on educational matters.*

rad·icchio /ræˈdiːkiəʊ; *NAmE* -kioʊ/ *noun* [U] a type of CHICORY (= a leaf vegetable) with dark red leaves

radii *pl.* of RADIUS

radio 0-w /ˈreɪdiəʊ; *NAmE* -oʊ/ *noun*, *verb*

■ *noun* **1** 0-w (often **the radio**) [U, sing.] the activity of broadcasting programmes for people to listen to; the programmes that are broadcast: *The interview was broadcast* ***on radio*** *and television.* ◇ *The play was written specially for radio.* ◇ *I* ***listen to the radio*** *on the way to work.* ◇ *Did you hear the interview with him* ***on the radio****?* ◇ ***local/national radio*** ◇ *a* ***radio programme/station*** **2** 0-w [C] a piece of equipment used for listening to programmes that are

R

broadcast to the public: *to* ***turn the radio on/off*** ◇ *a car radio* ◇ *a radio cassette player* ➲ see also CLOCK RADIO **3** [U] the process of sending and receiving messages through the air using ELECTROMAGNETIC waves: *He was unable to contact Blake* ***by radio.*** ◇ *to keep in* ***radio contact*** ◇ ***radio signals/waves*** **4** [C] a piece of equipment, for example on ships or planes, for sending and receiving radio signals: *to hear a gale warning on/over the ship's radio*

■ ***verb*** (**ra·dio·ing, ra·dioed, ra·dioed**) [I, T] **~ (sth)** | **~ that...** to send a message to sb by radio: *The police officer radioed for help.* ◇ *The warning was radioed to headquarters.*

radio- /ˈreɪdiəʊ; *NAmE* -oʊ/ *combining form* (in nouns, adjectives and adverbs) **1** connected with radio waves or broadcasting: *radio-controlled* **2** connected with RADIOACTIVITY: *radiotherapy*

radio·active /ˌreɪdiəʊˈæktɪv; *NAmE* -oʊˈæk-/ *adj.* sending out harmful RADIATION caused when the NUCLEI (= central parts) of atoms are broken up ▸ **radio·activ·ity** /ˌreɪdiəʊækˈtɪvəti; *NAmE* -oʊæk-/ *noun* [U]: *the study of radioactivity* ◇ *a rise in the level of radioactivity*

ˌradio aˈstronomy *noun* [U] the part of ASTRONOMY that studies radio waves sent out by objects in space

ˈradio button *noun* (*computing*) a small circle that you click on in order to make a particular choice. The radio button is then marked with a dot to show that it has been selected.

radio·car·bon /ˌreɪdiəʊˈkɑːbən; *NAmE* -oʊˈkɑːrb-/ *noun* [U] (*technical*) a RADIOACTIVE form of CARBON that is present in the materials of which living things are formed, used in CARBON DATING: *radiocarbon analysis*

ˌradiocarbon ˈdating *noun* [U] (*formal*) = CARBON DATING

radio·chem·is·try /ˌreɪdiəʊˈkemɪstri; *NAmE* -oʊˈk-/ *noun* [U] the area of chemistry which is concerned with RADIOACTIVE substances ▸ **radio·chem·ical** /ˌreɪdiəʊˈkemɪkl; *NAmE* -oʊˈk-/ *adj.*

ˌradio-conˈtrolled *adj.* controlled from a distance by radio signals

radi·og·raph·er /ˌreɪdiˈɒɡrəfə(r); *NAmE* -ˈɑːɡ-/ *noun* a person working in a hospital whose job is to take X-RAY photographs or to use X-RAYS to treat some illnesses, such as cancer

radi·og·raphy /ˌreɪdiˈɒɡrəfi; *NAmE* -ˈɑːɡ-/ *noun* [U] the process or job of taking X-RAY photographs

radio·iso·tope /ˌreɪdiəʊˈaɪsətəʊp; *NAmE* ˌreɪdioʊˈaɪsətoʊp/ *noun* (*chemistry*) a form of a chemical element which sends out RADIATION

radi·olo·gist /ˌreɪdiˈɒlədʒɪst; *NAmE* -ˈɑːlə-/ *noun* a doctor who is trained in radiology

radi·ology /ˌreɪdiˈɒlədʒi; *NAmE* -ˈɑːlə-/ *noun* [U] the study and use of different types of RADIATION in medicine, for example to treat diseases

radio·met·ric /ˌreɪdiəʊˈmetrɪk; *NAmE* -dioʊ-/ *adj.* relating to a measurement of RADIOACTIVITY ▸ **radio·met·ric·ally** /-ɪkli/ *adv.*: *These rocks have been dated radiometrically at two billion years old.*

ˌradio-ˈtelephone *noun* a telephone that works by sending and receiving radio signals, used especially in cars, boats, etc.

ˌradio ˈtelescope *noun* a piece of equipment that receives radio waves from space and is used for finding stars and the position of SPACECRAFT, etc.

radio·ther·apy /ˌreɪdiəʊˈθerəpi; *NAmE* -oʊˈθe-/ *noun* [U] the treatment of disease by RADIATION: *a course of radiotherapy* ➲ compare CHEMOTHERAPY ▸ **radio·thera·pist** *noun*

ˈradio wave *noun* a low-energy ELECTROMAGNETIC wave, especially when used for long-distance communication

rad·ish /ˈrædɪʃ/ *noun* [C, U] a small crisp red or white root vegetable with a strong taste, eaten raw in salads: *a bunch of radishes* ➲ VISUAL VOCAB page V27

ra·dium /ˈreɪdiəm/ *noun* [U] (*symb.* **Ra**) a chemical element. Radium is a white RADIOACTIVE metal used in the treatment of diseases such as cancer.

ra·dius /ˈreɪdiəs/ *noun* (*pl.* **radii** /ˈreɪdiaɪ/) **1** a straight line between the centre of a circle and any point on its outer edge; the length of this line ➲ VISUAL VOCAB page V58 ➲ compare DIAMETER **2** a round area that covers the distance mentioned from a central point: *They deliver to within a 5-mile radius of the store.* **3** (*anatomy*) the shorter bone of the two bones in the lower part of the arm between the elbow and the wrist, on the same side as the thumb ➲ VISUAL VOCAB page V48 ➲ see also ULNA

radon /ˈreɪdɒn; *NAmE* -dɑːn/ *noun* [U] (*symb.* **Rn**) a chemical element. Radon is a RADIOACTIVE gas used in the treatment of diseases such as cancer.

RAF /ˌɑːr eɪ ˈef; *or, in informal use,* ræf/ *abbr.* Royal Air Force (the British AIR FORCE): *He was an RAF pilot.*

Raf·fer·ty's rules /ˈræfətiz ruːlz; *NAmE* -fərt-/ *noun* [pl.] (*AustralE, NZE, informal*) no rules at all

raf·fia /ˈræfiə/ *noun* [U] soft material that looks like string and is made from the leaves of a type of PALM tree, used for making BASKETS, MATS, etc. or for tying things

raff·ish /ˈræfɪʃ/ *adj.* (of sb's behaviour, clothes, etc.) not very acceptable according to some social standards, but interesting and attractive

raf·fle /ˈræfl/ *noun, verb*

■ ***noun*** a way of making money for a particular project or organization. People buy tickets with numbers on them and some of these numbers are later chosen to win prizes. ➲ compare LOTTERY

■ ***verb*** **~ sth** to give sth as a prize in a raffle

raft /rɑːft; *NAmE* ræft/ *noun* **1** a flat structure made of pieces of wood tied together and used as a boat or floating platform **2** a small boat made of rubber or plastic that is filled with air: *an inflatable raft* **3** [usually sing.] **~ of sth** (*informal*) a large number or amount of sth: *a whole raft of new proposals*

raft·er /ˈrɑːftə(r); *NAmE* ˈræf-/ *noun* [C, usually pl.] one of the sloping pieces of wood that support a roof

raft·ing /ˈrɑːftɪŋ; *NAmE* ˈræft-/ *noun* [U] the sport or activity of travelling down a river on a RAFT: *We went* ***white-water rafting*** *on the Colorado River.* ➲ VISUAL VOCAB page V40

rag /ræɡ/ *noun, verb*

■ ***noun*** **1** [C, U] a piece of old, often torn, cloth used especially for cleaning things ➲ see also GLAD RAGS **2** [C] (*informal*, usually *disapproving*) a newspaper that you believe to be of low quality: *the local rag* **3** [C] a piece of RAGTIME music **4** (*BrE*) [U, C] an event or a series of events organized by students each year to raise money for charity: *rag week*

IDM **in ˈrags** wearing very old torn clothes: *The children were dressed in rags.* **(from) ˌrags to ˈriches** from being extremely poor to being very rich: *a rags-to-riches story* ◇ *Hers was a classic tale of rags to riches.* **ˌlose your ˈrag** (*BrE, informal*) to get angry ➲ more at RED *adj.*

■ ***verb*** (**-gg-**) **~ sb (about sth)** (*old-fashioned, BrE*) to laugh at and/or play tricks on sb SYN **tease**

PHR V **ˈrag on sb** (*NAmE, informal*) to complain to sb about their behaviour, work, etc.

raga /ˈrɑːɡə/ *noun* a traditional pattern of notes used in Indian music; a piece of music based on one of these patterns

raga·muf·fin (also **ragga·muf·fin**) /ˈræɡəmʌfɪn/ *noun* **1** [C] a person, usually a child, who is wearing old clothes that are torn and dirty **2** [C] (*especially BrE*) a person who likes or performs RAGGA music **3** [U] = RAGGA

ˌrag-and-ˈbone man *noun* (*BrE*) (especially in the past) a man who travels around buying things that people no longer want and selling them to other people

rag·bag /ˈræɡbæɡ/ *noun* [sing.] a collection of things that appear to have little connection with each other: *a ragbag of ideas*

R

ˌrag ˈdoll *noun* a soft DOLL made from pieces of cloth ➲ VISUAL VOCAB page V32

rage /reɪdʒ/ *noun, verb*
■ ***noun*** **1** [U, C] a feeling of violent anger that is difficult to control: *His face was dark with rage.* ◇ *to* ***be shaking/trembling/speechless with rage*** ◇ *Sue stormed out of the room* ***in a rage.*** ◇ *He* ***flies into a rage*** *if you even mention the subject.* **2** [U] (in compounds) anger and violent behaviour caused by a particular situation: *a case of trolley rage in the supermarket* ➲ see also ROAD RAGE
IDM **be all the ˈrage** (*informal*) to be very popular and fashionable
■ ***verb*** **1** [I, T] to show that you are very angry about sth or with sb, especially by shouting **SYN** **rail**: **~ (at/against/about sb/sth)** *He raged against the injustice of it all.* ◇ **+ speech** *'That's unfair!' she raged.* **2** [I] **~ (on)** (of a storm, a battle, an argument, etc.) to continue in a violent way: *The riots raged for three days.* ◇ *The blizzard was still raging outside.* **3** [I] (**+ adv./prep.**) (of an illness, a fire, etc.) to spread very quickly: *Forest fires were raging out of control.* ◇ *A flu epidemic raged through Europe.* **4** [I] (*AustralE, NZE, slang*) to go out and enjoy yourself

ragga /ˈrægə/ (also **ragga·muf·fin, raga·muf·fin**) *noun* [U] a type of dance music from the West Indies that contains features of REGGAE and HIP HOP

ragga·muf·fin = RAGAMUFFIN

rag·ged /ˈrægɪd/ *adj.* **1** (of clothes) old and torn **SYN** **shabby** **2** (of people) wearing old or torn clothes: *ragged children* **3** having an outline, an edge or a surface that is not straight or even: *ragged clouds* ◇ *a ragged coastline* **4** not smooth or controlled: *I could hear the sound of his ragged breathing.* ◇ *Their performance was still very ragged.* **5** (*informal*) very tired, especially after physical effort ▸ **rag·ged·ly** *adv.*: *raggedly dressed* ◇ *She was breathing raggedly.* **rag·ged·ness** *noun* [U]
IDM **ˌrun sb ˈragged** (*informal*) to make sb do a lot of work or make a big effort so that they become tired

ra·ging /ˈreɪdʒɪŋ/ *adj.* [only before noun] **1** (of feelings or emotions) very strong: *a raging appetite/thirst* ◇ *raging jealousy* **2** (of natural forces) very powerful: *a raging storm* ◇ *The stream had become a raging torrent.* ◇ *The building was now a raging inferno.* **3** (of a pain or an illness) very strong or painful: *a raging headache* **4** very serious and causing strong feelings: *His speech has provoked a raging debate.*

rag·lan /ˈræglən/ *adj.* [only before noun] **1** (of a sleeve) sewn to the front and back of a coat, sweater, etc. in a line that slopes down from the neck to under the arm **2** (of a coat, sweater, etc.) having raglan sleeves

ra·gout /ræˈɡuː; ˈræɡuː/ *noun* [C, U] (from *French*) a hot dish of meat and vegetables boiled together with various spices

rag·tag /ˈrægtæg/ *adj.* [usually before noun] (*informal*) (of a group of people or an organization) not well organized; giving a bad impression: *a ragtag band of rebels*

rag·time /ˈrægtaɪm/ *noun* [U] an early form of JAZZ, especially for the piano, first played by African American musicians in the early 1900s

the ˈrag trade *noun* [sing.] (*old-fashioned, informal*) the business of designing, making and selling clothes

rag·weed /ˈrægwiːd/ *noun* [U] a N American plant with small green flowers that contain a lot of POLLEN, which causes HAY FEVER in some people

rag·wort /ˈrægwɜːt; *NAmE* -wɜːrt/ *noun* [U] a wild plant with yellow flowers, poisonous to cows and horses

raid /reɪd/ *noun, verb*
■ ***noun*** **1 ~ (on sth)** a short surprise attack on an enemy by soldiers, ships or aircraft: *They carried out a bombing raid on enemy bases.* ➲ COLLOCATIONS at WAR ➲ see also AIR RAID **2 ~ (on sth)** a surprise visit by the police looking for criminals or for illegal goods or drugs: *They were arrested during a* ***dawn raid.*** **3 ~ (on sth)** an attack on a building, etc. in order to commit a crime: *an armed bank raid* ➲ see also RAM-RAIDING
■ ***verb*** **1 ~ sth** (of police) to visit a person or place without warning to look for criminals, illegal goods, drugs, etc. **2 ~ sth** (of soldiers, fighting planes, etc.) to attack a place without warning: *Villages along the border are regularly raided.* ◇ *a* ***raiding party*** (= a group of soldiers, etc. that attack a place) **3 ~ sth** to enter a place, usually using force, and steal from it **SYN** **plunder, ransack**: *Many treasures were lost when the tombs were raided in the last century.* ◇ (*humorous*) *I caught him raiding the fridge again* (= taking food from it).

raid·er /ˈreɪdə(r)/ *noun* a person who makes a criminal raid on a place: ***armed/masked raiders***

rail 🔑 /reɪl/ *noun, verb*
■ ***noun*** **1** 🔑 [C] a wooden or metal bar placed around sth as a barrier or to provide support: *She leaned on the ship's rail and gazed out to sea.* ➲ see also GUARD RAIL, HANDRAIL **2** 🔑 [C] a bar fixed to the wall for hanging things on: *a picture/curtain/towel rail* ➲ VISUAL VOCAB page V20 **3** 🔑 [C, usually pl.] each of the two metal bars that form the track that trains run on ➲ VISUAL VOCAB page V47 **4** 🔑 [U] (often before another noun) railways/railroads as a means of transport: *to travel* ***by rail*** ◇ *rail travel/services/fares* ◇ *a rail link/network*
IDM **get back on the ˈrails** (*informal*) to become successful again after a period of failure, or to begin functioning normally again **go off the ˈrails** (*informal*) **1** to start behaving in a strange or unacceptable manner, for example, drinking a lot or taking drugs **2** to lose control and stop functioning correctly: *The company has gone badly off the rails in recent years.* ➲ more at JUMP *v.*
■ ***verb*** [I, T] **~ (at/against sth/sb)** | **+ speech** (*formal*) to complain about sth/sb in a very angry way **SYN** **rage**: *She railed against the injustice of it all.*
PHR V **ˌrail sth ˈin/ˈoff** to separate an area or object from others by placing rails around it

rail·car /ˈreɪlkɑː(r)/ *noun* = CAR (2)

rail·card /ˈreɪlkɑːd; *NAmE* -kɑːrd/ *noun* (*BrE*) a card that allows sb to travel by train at a reduced price

rail·head /ˈreɪlhed/ *noun* (*technical*) the point at which a railway/railroad ends

rail·ing /ˈreɪlɪŋ/ *noun* [C, usually pl.] a fence made of vertical metal bars; one of these bars: *iron railings* ◇ *I chained my bike to the park railings.* ◇ *She leaned out over the railing.* ➲ VISUAL VOCAB page V2

rail·lery /ˈreɪləri/ *noun* [U] (*formal*) friendly joking about a person

rail·man /ˈreɪlmən/ *noun* (*pl.* **-men** /-mən/) (*BrE*) = RAILWAYMAN

rail·road 🔑 /ˈreɪlrəʊd; *NAmE* -roʊd/ *noun, verb*
■ ***noun*** (*NAmE*) (*BrE* **rail·way**) **1** 🔑 (*BrE* also **ˈrailway line**) a track with rails on which trains run: *railroad tracks* **2** 🔑 a system of tracks, together with the trains that run on them, and the organization and people needed to operate them: *This town got a lot bigger when the railroad came in the 1860s.*
■ ***verb*** **1 ~ sb (into sth/into doing sth)** to force sb to do sth before they have had enough time to decide whether or not they want to do it **SYN** **bulldoze** **2 ~ sth (through/through sth)** to make a group of people accept a decision, law, etc. quickly by putting pressure on them: *The bill was railroaded through the House.* **3 ~ sb** (*NAmE*) to decide that sb is guilty of a crime, without giving them a fair trial

ˈrailroad crossing (*NAmE*) (*BrE* **ˌlevel ˈcrossing**) *noun* a place where a road crosses a railway/railroad line

rail·road·er /ˈreɪlrəʊdə(r); *NAmE* -roʊd-/ (*NAmE*) (*BrE* **rail·way·man, rail·man**) *noun* a person who works for a rail company

rail·way 🔑 /ˈreɪlweɪ/ (*BrE*) (*NAmE* **rail·road**) *noun* **1** 🔑 (*BrE* also **ˈrailway line**) a track with rails on which trains run: *The railway is still under construction.* ◇ *a disused railway* **2** 🔑 a system of tracks, together with the trains that run on them, and the organization and people needed to operate them: *Her father worked on the railways.* ◇ *a* ***railway station/worker/company*** ◇ *the Midland Railway* ◇ *a model railway*

R

rail·way·man /ˈreɪlweɪmən/ *noun* (*pl.* -men /-mən/) (also **rail·man**) (both *BrE*) (*NAmE* **rail·road·er**) a person who works for a rail company

rai·ment /ˈreɪmənt/ *noun* [U] (*old use*) clothing

rain 0‑ /reɪn/ *noun, verb*

■ *noun* **1** 0‑ [U, sing.] water that falls from the sky in separate drops: *There will be rain in all parts tomorrow.* ◇ *Rain is forecast for the weekend.* ◇ *Don't go out* **in the rain.** ◇ *It's* **pouring with rain** (= raining very hard). ◇ ***heavy/torrential/driving rain*** ◇ *The rain poured down.* ◇ ***It looks like rain*** (= as if it is going to rain). ◇ *A light rain began to fall.* ◇ *I think I felt a drop of rain.* ➲ COLLOCATIONS at WEATHER ➲ see also ACID RAIN, RAINY **2** **the rains** [pl.] the season of heavy continuous rain in tropical countries: *The rains come in September.* **3** [sing.] **~ of sth** a large number of things falling from the sky at the same time: *a* ***rain of arrows/stones***

IDM **come ˌrain, come ˈshine** | **(come) ˌrain or ˈshine** whether there is rain or sun; whatever happens: *He goes jogging every morning, rain or shine.* ➲ more at RIGHT *adj.*

■ *verb* **1** 0‑ [I] when **it rains**, water falls from the sky in drops: *Is it raining?* ◇ *It had been raining hard all night.* ◇ *It hardly rained at all last summer.* ◇ *It started to rain.* **2** [I, T] to fall or to make sth fall on sb/sth in large quantities: **~ (down) (on sb/sth)** *Bombs rained (down) on the city's streets.* ◇ *Falling debris rained on us from above.* ◇ *He covered his face as the blows rained down on him* (= he was hit repeatedly). ◇ **~ sth (down) (on sb/sth)** *The volcano erupted, raining hot ash over a wide area.*

IDM **be raining cats and ˈdogs** (*informal*) to be raining heavily **it never rains but it ˈpours** (*BrE*) (*NAmE* **when it rains, it ˈpours**) (*saying*) used to say that when one bad thing happens to you, other bad things happen soon after **ˌrain on sb's ˈparade** (*NAmE, informal*) to spoil sth for sb

PHR V **be ˌrained ˈoff** (*BrE*) (*NAmE* **be ˌrained ˈout**) (of an event) to be cancelled or to have to stop because it is raining: *The game has been rained off again.*

Vocabulary Building

Rain and storms

Rain

- **Drizzle** is fine light rain.
- A **shower** is a short period of rain.
- A **downpour** or a **cloudburst** is a heavy fall of rain that often starts suddenly.
- When it is raining very hard you can say that it is **pouring**. In informal *BrE* you can also say that it is **bucketing down** or **chucking it down**. You can also say: **The heavens opened.**

Storms

- A **cyclone** and a **typhoon** are types of violent tropical storms with very strong winds.
- A **hurricane** has very strong winds and is usually at sea.
- A **monsoon** is a period of very heavy rain in particular countries, or the wind that brings this rain.
- A **squall** is a sudden strong, violent wind, usually in a rain or snow storm.
- A **tornado** (or *informal* **twister**) has very strong winds which move in a circle, often with a long narrow cloud.
- A **whirlwind** moves very fast in a spinning movement and causes a lot of damage.
- A **blizzard** is a snow storm with very strong winds.
- **Tempest** is used mainly in literary language to describe a violent storm.

ˈrain barrel (*NAmE*) (*BrE* **ˈwater butt**) *noun* a large BARREL for collecting rain as it flows off a roof ➲ VISUAL VOCAB page V16

rain·bow /ˈreɪnbəʊ; *NAmE* -boʊ/ *noun* a curved band of different colours that appears in the sky when the sun shines through rain: *all the colours of the rainbow*

ˌrainbow coaˈlition *noun* a political group formed by different parties who agree to work together, especially one that includes one or more very small parties

ˌrainbow ˈnation *noun* [usually sing.] (*approving*) a name used to describe the people of South Africa because of their many races and cultures

ˌrainbow ˈtrout *noun* [C, U] type of TROUT (= a fish that is often eaten as food, and often caught in the sport of fishing)

ˈrain check *noun* (*especially NAmE*) a ticket that can be used later if a game, show, etc. is cancelled because of rain

IDM **take a rain check (on sth)** (*informal, especially NAmE*) to refuse an offer or invitation but say that you might accept it later: *'Are you coming for a drink?' 'Can I take a rain check?—I must get this finished tonight.'*

rain·coat /ˈreɪnkəʊt; *NAmE* -koʊt/ *noun* a long light coat that keeps you dry in the rain ➲ VISUAL VOCAB page V50

ˈrain date *noun* (*NAmE*) an alternative date when an event will take place if it has to be cancelled on the original date because of rain: *July 15 is our annual fun day (rain date July 22).*

rain·drop /ˈreɪndrɒp; *NAmE* -drɑːp/ *noun* a single drop of rain

rain·fall /ˈreɪnfɔːl/ *noun* [U, sing.] the total amount of rain that falls in a particular area in a particular amount of time; an occasion when rain falls: *There has been below average rainfall this month.* ◇ *an average annual rainfall of 10 cm*

rain·for·est /ˈreɪnfɒrɪst; *NAmE* -fɔːr-; -fɑːr-/ *noun* [C, U] a thick forest in tropical parts of the world that have a lot of rain: *the Amazon rainforest* ➲ compare CLOUD FOREST

rain·maker /ˈreɪnmeɪkə(r)/ *noun* **1** (*especially NAmE, business*) a person who makes a business grow and become successful **2** a person who is believed to have the power to make rain fall, especially among Native Americans

rain·out /ˈreɪnaʊt/ *noun* (*NAmE*) an occasion when bad weather prevents an event from starting or finishing

rain·proof /ˈreɪnpruːf/ *adj.* that can keep rain out: *a rainproof jacket*

rain·storm /ˈreɪnstɔːm; *NAmE* -stɔːrm/ *noun* a heavy fall of rain

rain·water /ˈreɪnwɔːtə(r); *NAmE* also -wɑːtər/ *noun* [U] water that has fallen as rain: *a barrel for collecting rainwater*

rainy /ˈreɪni/ *adj.* (**rain·ier**, **rain·iest**) having or bringing a lot of rain: *a rainy day* ◇ *the rainy season* ◇ *the rainiest place in Britain*

IDM **save, keep, etc. sth for a ˌrainy ˈday** to save sth, especially money, for a time when you will really need it

raise 0‑ /reɪz/ *verb, noun*

■ *verb*

▸ MOVE UPWARDS **1** 0‑ **~ sth** to lift or move sth to a higher level: *She raised the gun and fired.* ◇ *He raised a hand in greeting.* ◇ *She raised her eyes from her work.* OPP **lower** ➲ note at RISE **2** 0‑ **~ sth/sb/yourself (+ adv./prep.)** to move sth/sb/yourself to a vertical position: *Somehow we managed to raise her to her feet.* ◇ *He raised himself up on one elbow.* OPP **lower**

▸ INCREASE **3** 0‑ **~ sth (to sth)** to increase the amount or level of sth: *to* ***raise salaries/prices/taxes*** ◇ *They raised their offer to $500.* ◇ *How can we raise standards in schools?* ◇ *Don't tell her about the job until you know for sure—we don't want to* ***raise her hopes*** (= make her hope too much). ◇ *I've never heard him even* ***raise his voice*** (= speak louder because he was angry).

▸ COLLECT MONEY/PEOPLE **4** 0‑ **~ sth** to bring or collect money or people together; to manage to get or form sth: *to raise a loan* ◇ *We are* ***raising money*** *for charity.* ◇ *He set about* ***raising an army.*** ➲ see also FUND-RAISER

▸ MENTION SUBJECT **5** 0‑ **~ sth** to mention sth for people to discuss or sb to deal with SYN **broach**: *The book* ***raises***

many important **questions**. ◇ *I'm glad you* ***raised the subject*** *of money.*
▸ CAUSE **6 ~ sth** to cause or produce sth; to make sth appear: *to raise doubts in people's minds* ◇ *The plans for the new development have raised angry protests from local residents.* ◇ *It wasn't an easy audience but he* ***raised a laugh*** *with his joke.* ◇ *It had been a difficult day but she managed to* ***raise a smile.*** ◇ *The horses' hooves raised a cloud of dust.* ➲ see also CURTAIN-RAISER, FIRE-RAISER
▸ CHILD/ANIMAL **7** 🗝 (*especially NAmE*) to care for a child or young animal until it is able to take care of itself: **~ sb/sth** *They were both raised in the South.* ◇ *kids raised on a diet of hamburgers* ◇ **~ sb/sth as sth** | **~ sb/sth + noun** *They raised her (as) a Catholic.* ◇ *I was* ***born and raised*** *a city boy.* ➲ compare BRING UP
▸ FARM ANIMALS/CROPS **8 ~ sth** to breed particular farm animals; to grow particular crops: *to raise cattle/corn*
▸ END STH **9 ~ sth** to end a restriction on sb/sth: *to* ***raise a blockade/a ban/an embargo/a siege***
▸ ON RADIO/PHONE **10 ~ sb** to contact sb and speak to them by radio or telephone: *We managed to raise him on his mobile phone.*
▸ DEAD PERSON **11 ~ sb (from sth)** to make sb who has died come to life again SYN **resurrect**: *Christians believe that God raised Jesus from the dead.*
▸ IN CARD GAMES **12 ~ sb sth** to make a higher bet than another player in a card game: *I'll raise you another hundred dollars.*
▸ MATHEMATICS **13 ~ sth to the power of sth** to multiply an amount by itself a particular number of times: *3 raised to the power of 3 is 27* (= 3 × 3 × 3).
IDM **raise a/your 'hand against/to sb** to hit or threaten to hit sb **raise the 'bar** to set a new, higher standard of quality or performance: *The factory has raised the bar on productivity, food safety and quality.* OPP **lower the bar** ➲ compare SET THE BAR at BAR *n.* **raise your 'eyebrows (at sth)** [often passive] to show that you disapprove of or are surprised by sth: *Eyebrows were raised when he arrived without his wife.* **raise your 'glass (to sb)** to hold up your glass and wish sb happiness, good luck, etc. before you drink **raise 'hell** (*informal*) to protest angrily, especially in a way that causes trouble for sb **raise the 'roof** to produce or make sb produce a lot of noise in a building, for example by shouting or CHEERING **raise sb's 'spirits** to make sb feel more cheerful or brave SYN **cheer sb up** ➲ more at ANTE, HACKLES, LIFT *v.*, SIGHT *n.*, TEMPERATURE
PHR V **'raise sth to sb/sth** to build or place a statue, etc. somewhere in honour or memory of sb/sth: *The town raised a memorial to those killed in the war.*
■ ***noun*** 🗝 (*NAmE*) (*BrE* **rise**) an increase in the money you are paid for the work you do

raised /reɪzd/ *adj.* **1** higher than the area around: *a raised platform* **2** at a higher level than normal: *the sound of raised voices* ◇ *Smokers often have raised blood pressure.*

rai·sin /'reɪzn/ *noun* a dried GRAPE, used in cakes, etc.

rais·ing /'reɪzɪŋ/ *noun* [U, sing.] the act of raising sth: *consciousness raising* ◇ *a raising of standards in schools* ➲ see also FUND-RAISING

rai·son d'être /ˌreɪzɒ̃ 'detrə; *NAmE* ˌreɪzoːn/ *noun* [sing.] (from *French*) the most important reason for sb's/sth's existence: *Work seems to be her sole raison d'être.*

raita /'raɪtə/ *noun* [U] a S Asian dish of finely chopped raw vegetables mixed with YOGURT

the Raj /rɑːdʒ; rɑːʒ/ *noun* [sing.] British rule in India before 1947

raja (also **rajah**) /'rɑːdʒə/ *noun* an Indian king or prince who ruled over a state in the past

rake /reɪk/ *noun, verb*
■ ***noun*** **1** [C] a garden tool with a long handle and a row of metal points at the end, used for gathering fallen leaves and making soil smooth ➲ VISUAL VOCAB page V16 **2** [C] (*old-fashioned*) a man, especially a rich and fashionable one, who is thought to have low moral standards, for example because he drinks or gambles a lot or has sex with a lot of women **3** [sing.] (*technical*) the amount by which sth, especially the stage in a theatre, slopes
■ ***verb*** **1** [T, I] to pull a rake over a surface in order to make it level or to remove sth: **~ (sth) (+ adv./prep.)** *The leaves had been raked into a pile.* ◇ (*figurative*) *She raked a comb through her hair.* ◇ **~ sth + adj.** *First rake the soil smooth.* **2** [T] **~ sth (with sth)** to point a camera, light, gun, etc. at sb/sth and move it slowly from one side to the other: *They raked the streets with machine-gun fire.* ◇ *Searchlights raked the grounds.* **3** [I] **+ adv./prep.** to search a place carefully for sth: *She raked around in her bag for her keys.* **4** [T, I] **~ (sth)** to scratch the surface of sth with a sharp object, especially your nails
IDM **rake sb over the 'coals** (*NAmE*) (*BrE* **haul sb over the 'coals**) to criticize sb severely because they have done sth wrong
PHR V **ˌrake 'in sth** (*informal*) to earn a lot of money, especially when it is done easily: *The movie raked in more than $300 million.* ◇ *She's been* ***raking it in*** *since she started her new job.* **ˌrake 'over sth** (*informal, disapproving*) to examine sth that happened in the past in great detail and keep talking about it, when it should be forgotten: *She had no desire to rake over the past.* **ˌrake sth↔'up** (*informal, disapproving*) to mention sth unpleasant that happened in the past and that other people would like to forget

raked /reɪkt/ *adj.* (*technical*) placed on a slope: *raked seating*

'rake-off *noun* (*informal*) a share of profits, especially from dishonest or illegal activity

raki /'rɑːki; rə'kiː/ *noun* [U, C] a strong alcoholic drink from eastern Europe and the Middle East

rak·ish /'reɪkɪʃ/ *adj.* **1** (of a man) acting like a RAKE (= in an immoral, etc. way) SYN **dissolute** **2** if you wear a hat at a **rakish angle**, it is not straight on your head and it makes you look relaxed and confident SYN **jaunty** ▸ **rak·ish·ly** *adv.*

rally /'ræli/ *noun, verb*
■ ***noun*** **1** [C] a large public meeting, especially one held to support a particular idea or political party: *to* ***attend/hold a rally*** ◇ *a* ***peace/protest, etc. rally*** ◇ *a* ***mass rally*** *in support of the strike* ➲ see also PEP RALLY **2** [C] (*BrE*) a race for cars, motorcycles, etc. over public roads: *the Monte Carlo rally* ◇ *rally driving* **3** [C] (in TENNIS and similar sports) a series of hits of the ball before a point is scored **4** [sing.] (in sport or on the Stock Exchange) an act of returning to a strong position after a period of difficulty or weakness SYN **recovery**: *After a furious late rally, they finally scored.* ◇ *a rally in shares on the stock market*
■ ***verb*** (**ral·lies, rally·ing, ral·lied, ral·lied**) **1** [I, T] to come together or bring people together in order to help or support sb/sth: **~ (around/behind/to sb/sth)** *The cabinet rallied behind the Prime Minister.* ◇ *Many national newspapers rallied to his support.* ◇ **~ sb/sth (around/behind/to sb/sth)** *They have rallied a great deal of support for their campaign.* **2** [I] to become healthier, stronger, etc. after a period of illness, weakness, etc. SYN **recover**: *He never really rallied after the operation.* ◇ *The champion rallied to win the second set 6–3.* **3** [I] (*finance*) (especially of share prices or a country's money) to increase in value after falling in value SYN **recover**: *The company's shares had rallied slightly by the close of trading.* ◇ *The pound rallied against the dollar.*
PHR V **ˌrally 'round/a'round** | **ˌrally 'round/a'round sb** (of a group of people) to work together in order to help sb who is in a difficult or unpleasant situation

rally·cross /'rælikrɒs; *NAmE* -krɔːs; -krɑːs/ *noun* [U] a form of motor racing in which cars are driven both over rough ground and on roads ➲ compare AUTOCROSS

'rallying cry *noun* a phrase or an idea that is used to encourage people to support sb/sth

'rallying point *noun* a person, a group, an event, etc. that makes people come together in support of sth

RAM /ræm/ *noun* [U] the abbreviation for 'random-access memory' (computer memory in which data can be changed or removed and can be looked at in any order): *256 megabytes of RAM*

ram /ræm/ *verb, noun*
■ ***verb*** (-mm-) **1 ~ sth** (of a vehicle, a ship, etc.) to drive into

R

or hit another vehicle, ship, etc. with force, sometimes deliberately: *Two passengers were injured when their taxi was rammed from behind by a bus.* **2 ~ sth + adv./prep.** to push sth somewhere with force: *She rammed the key into the lock.* ◇ (*figurative*) *The spending cuts had been rammed through Congress.*

IDM ˌ**ram sth↔ˈhome** (*especially BrE*) to emphasize an idea, argument, etc. very strongly to make sure people listen to it ➲ more at THROAT

PHR V ˌ**ram ˈinto sth** | ˌ**ram sth ˈinto sth** to hit against sth or to make sth hit against sth with force: *He rammed his truck into the back of the one in front.*

■ ***noun*** **1** a male sheep ➲ compare EWE **2** a part in a machine that is used for hitting sth very hard or for lifting or moving things: *hydraulic rams* ➲ see also BATTERING RAM

Ram·adan /ˈræmədæn; ˌræməˈdæn/ *noun* [U, C] the 9th month of the Muslim year, when Muslims do not eat or drink between SUNRISE and SUNSET

ram·ble /ˈræmbl/ *verb, noun*

■ ***verb*** **1** [I] **+ adv./prep.** (*especially BrE*) to walk for pleasure, especially in the countryside: *We spent the summer rambling in Ireland.* **2** [I] to talk about sb/sth in a confused way, especially for a long time: *He had lost track of what he was saying and began to ramble.* ◇ **~** (**on**) (**about sb/sth**) *What is she rambling on about now?* **3** [I] (**+ adv./prep.**) (of plants) to grow in many different directions, especially over other plants or objects: *Climbing plants rambled over the front of the house.* ➲ see also RAMBLING

■ ***noun*** **1** (*especially BrE*) a long walk for pleasure: *to go for a ramble in the country* **2** a long confused speech or piece of writing: *She went into a long ramble about the evils of television.*

ram·bler /ˈræmblə(r)/ *noun* **1** (*especially BrE*) a person who walks in the countryside for pleasure, especially as part of an organized group **2** a plant, especially a ROSE, that grows up walls, fences, etc.

ram·bling /ˈræmblɪŋ/ *adj., noun*

■ ***adj.*** **1** (of a building) spreading in various directions with no particular pattern SYN **sprawling** **2** (of a speech or piece of writing) very long and confused SYN **incoherent**: *a rambling letter* **3** (of a plant) growing or climbing in all directions, for example up a wall: *a rambling rose*

■ ***noun*** **1** [U] (*BrE*) the activity of walking for pleasure in the countryside **2 ramblings** [pl.] speech or writing that continues for a long time without saying much and seems very confused: *the ramblings of a madman*

Rambo /ˈræmbəʊ; *NAmE* -boʊ/ *noun* (*informal*) a very strong and aggressive man ORIGIN From the name of the main character in David Morrell's novel *First Blood*, which was made popular in three films/movies in the 1980s.

ram·bunc·tious /ræmˈbʌŋkʃəs/ *adj.* (*informal, especially NAmE*) = RUMBUSTIOUS

ram·bu·tan /ræmˈbuːtn/ *noun* a red tropical fruit with soft pointed parts on its skin and a slightly sour taste

ram·ekin /ˈræməkɪn/ *noun* a small dish for baking and serving food for one person ➲ VISUAL VOCAB page V23

ram·ifi·ca·tion /ˌræmɪfɪˈkeɪʃn/ *noun* [usually pl.] one of the large number of complicated and unexpected results that follow an action or a decision SYN **complication**: *These changes are bound to have widespread social ramifications.*

ramp /ræmp/ *noun, verb*

■ ***noun*** **1** a slope that joins two parts of a road, path, building, etc. when one is higher than the other: *Ramps should be provided for wheelchair users.* **2** (*NAmE*) (*BrE* **ˈslip road**) a road used for driving onto or off a major road such as a MOTORWAY or INTERSTATE: *a freeway exit ramp* ➲ see also OFF-RAMP, ON-RAMP **3** a slope or set of steps that can be moved, used for loading a vehicle or getting on or off a plane: *a loading ramp* **4** (*IndE*) the long stage that models walk on during a fashion show SYN **catwalk, runway**

■ ***verb***

PHR V ˌ**ramp sth↔ˈup** to make sth increase in amount

ram·page *noun, verb*

■ ***noun*** /ˈræmpeɪdʒ/ [usually sing.] a sudden period of wild and violent behaviour, often causing damage and destruction: *Gangs of youths* ***went on the rampage*** *in the city yesterday.*

■ ***verb*** /ræmˈpeɪdʒ; ˈræmpeɪdʒ/ [I] **+ adv./prep.** (of people or animals) to move through a place in a group, usually breaking things and causing damage SYN **run amok**: *a herd of rampaging elephants*

ram·pant /ˈræmpənt/ *adj.* **1** (of sth bad) existing or spreading everywhere in a way that cannot be controlled SYN **unchecked**: *rampant inflation* ◇ *Unemployment is now rampant in most of Europe.* **2** (of plants) growing thickly and very fast in a way that cannot be controlled ▶ **ram·pant·ly** *adv.*

ram·part /ˈræmpɑːt; *NAmE* -pɑːrt/ *noun* [usually pl.] a high wide wall of stone or earth with a path on top, built around a castle, town, etc. to defend it

ˈ**ram-raiding** *noun* [U] (*BrE*) the crime of driving a vehicle into a shop/store window in order to steal goods ▶ ˈ**ram-raid** *noun* ˈ**ram-raid** *verb* **~ sth** ˈ**ram-raider** *noun*

ram·rod /ˈræmrɒd; *NAmE* -rɑːd/ *noun* a long straight piece of iron used in the past to push EXPLOSIVE into a gun

IDM ˌ**ramrod ˈstraight** | (**as**) **straight as a ˈramrod** (of a person) with a very straight back and looking serious and formal

ram·shackle /ˈræmʃækl/ *adj.* **1** (of buildings, vehicles, furniture, etc.) in a very bad condition and needing repair SYN **tumbledown** **2** (of an organization or a system) badly organized or designed and not likely to last very long SYN **rickety**

ran *past tense of* RUN

ranch /rɑːntʃ; *NAmE* ræntʃ/ *noun* a large farm, especially in N America or Australia, where cows, horses, sheep, etc. are bred: *a* ***cattle/sheep ranch*** ◇ ***ranch hands*** (= the people who work on a ranch) ➲ see also DUDE RANCH

ranch·er /ˈrɑːntʃə(r); *NAmE* ˈræntʃər/ *noun* a person who owns, manages or works on a ranch: *a cattle rancher*

ˈ**ranch house** *noun* **1** a house on a ranch **2** (*NAmE*) a house built all on one level, that is very wide but not very deep from front to back and has a roof that is not very steep ➲ compare BUNGALOW ➲ VISUAL VOCAB page V14

ranch·ing /ˈrɑːntʃɪŋ; *NAmE* ˈræntʃɪŋ/ *noun* [U] the activity of running a RANCH: ***cattle/sheep ranching***

ran·cid /ˈrænsɪd/ *adj.* if food containing fat is **rancid**, it tastes or smells unpleasant because it is no longer fresh

ran·cour (*US* **ran·cor**) /ˈræŋkə(r)/ *noun* [U] (*formal*) feelings of hatred and a desire to hurt other people, especially because you think that sb has done sth unfair to you SYN **bitterness**: *She learned to accept criticism* ***without rancour.*** ▶ **ran·cor·ous** /ˈræŋkərəs/ *adj.*: *a rancorous legal battle*

rand /rænd; *in South Africa, commonly* rɑːnt/ *noun* (*pl.* **rand**) **1** [C] the unit of money in the Republic of South Africa **2 the Rand** [sing.] (in South Africa) a large area around Johannesburg where gold is mined and where there are many cities and towns

R & B /ˌɑːr ən ˈbiː/ *abbr.* RHYTHM AND BLUES

R & D /ˌɑːr ən ˈdiː/ *abbr.* RESEARCH AND DEVELOPMENT

ran·dom AW /ˈrændəm/ *adj., noun*

■ ***adj.*** **1** [usually before noun] done, chosen, etc. without sb deciding in advance what is going to happen, or without any regular pattern: *the random killing of innocent people* ◇ *a* ***random sample/selection*** (= in which each thing has an equal chance of being chosen) ◇ *The information is processed in a random order.* ◇ (*informal*) *He grabbed a pair of random jeans and an old red shirt.* ◇ *She dodged the random items that were on the concrete floor.* **2** [only before noun] (*informal*) (especially of a person) not known or not identified: *Some random guy gave me a hundred bucks.* **3** (*informal*) a thing or person that is **random** is strange and does not make sense, often in a way that amuses or interests you: *Mom, you are so random!* ◇ *The humour is great because it's just so random and unhinged from reality.*

▸ **ran·dom·ly** AW *adv.*: *The winning numbers are randomly selected by computer.* ◇ *My phone seems to switch itself off randomly.* **ran·dom·ness** AW *noun* [U]: *It introduced an element of randomness into the situation.*

■ ***noun***

IDM **at ˈrandom** without deciding in advance what is going to happen, or without any regular pattern: *She opened the book at random* (= not at any particular page) *and started reading.* ◇ *The terrorists fired into the crowd at random.* ◇ *Names were chosen at random from a list.*

ˌrandom ˈaccess *noun* [U] (*computing*) the ability in a computer to go straight to data items without having to read through items stored previously

ˌrandom-ˌaccess ˈmemory *noun* [U] (*computing*) = RAM

ran·dom·ize (*BrE* also **-ise**) /ˈrændəmaɪz/ *verb* **~ sth** (*technical*) to use a method in an experiment, a piece of research, etc. that gives every item an equal chance of being considered; to put things in a RANDOM order

R & R /ˌɑːr ən ˈɑː(r)/ *abbr.* **1** rest and recreation (doing things for enjoyment rather than working) **2** (*medical*) rescue and resuscitation

randy /ˈrændi/ *adj.* (**ran·dier**, **ran·di·est**) (*BrE, informal*) sexually excited: *to feel/get randy*

ranee = RANI

rang *past tense* of RING

range AW /reɪndʒ/ *noun, verb*

■ ***noun***

▸ VARIETY **1** [C, usually sing.] **~ (of sth)** a variety of things of a particular type: *The hotel offers **a wide range of** facilities.* ◇ *There is **a full range of** activities for children.*

▸ LIMITS **2** [C, usually sing.] the limits between which sth varies: *Most of the students are in the 17-20 **age range**.* ◇ *There will be an increase **in the range of** 0 to 3 per cent.* ◇ *It's difficult to find a house in our **price range*** (= that we can afford). ◇ *This was **outside the range of** his experience.*

▸ OF PRODUCTS **3** [C] a set of products of a particular type: *our new range of hair products* ➲ see also MID-RANGE, TOP OF THE RANGE

▸ DISTANCE **4** [C, U] the distance over which sth can be seen or heard: *The child was now out of her **range of vision*** (= not near enough for her to see). **5** [C, U] the distance over which a gun or other weapon can hit things: *These missiles have a range of 300 miles.* ➲ see also CLOSE-RANGE, LONG-RANGE, SHORT-RANGE **6** [C] the distance that a vehicle will travel before it needs more fuel

▸ OF MOUNTAINS **7** [C] a line or group of mountains or hills: *the great mountain range of the Alps* ➲ VISUAL VOCAB page V4

▸ FOR SHOOTING **8** [C] an area of land where people can practise shooting or where bombs, etc. can be tested: *a shooting range* ➲ see also DRIVING RANGE, RIFLE RANGE

▸ OVEN **9** [C] a large piece of equipment that can burn various fuels and is kept hot all the time, used for cooking, especially in the past **10** (*NAmE*) = STOVE: *Cook the meat on a low heat on top of the range.*

▸ FOR COWS **11 the range** [sing.] (*NAmE*) a large open area for keeping cows, etc. ➲ see also FREE-RANGE

IDM **in/within ˈrange (of sth)** near enough to be reached, seen or heard: *He shouted angrily at anyone within range.* **out of ˈrange (of sth)** too far away to be reached, seen or heard: *The cat stayed well out of range of the children.*

■ ***verb***

▸ VARY **1** [I] to vary between two particular amounts, sizes, etc, including others between them: **~ from A to B** *to **range in size/length/price** from A to B* ◇ *Accommodation ranges from tourist class to luxury hotels.* ◇ **~ between A and B** *Estimates of the damage range between $1 million and $5 million.* **2** [I] to include a variety of different things in addition to those mentioned: **~ from A to B** *She has had a number of different jobs, ranging from chef to swimming instructor.* ◇ **+ adv./prep.** *The conversation ranged widely* (= covered a lot of different topics). ➲ see also WIDE-RANGING

▸ ARRANGE **3** [T, usually passive] **~ sb/sth/yourself + adv./prep.** (*formal*) to arrange people or things in a particular position or order: *The delegates ranged themselves around the table.* ◇ *Spectators were ranged along the whole route of the procession.*

▸ MOVE AROUND **4** [I, T] to move around an area: **+ adv./prep.** *He ranges far and wide in search of inspiration for his paintings.* ◇ **~ sth** *Her eyes ranged the room.*

PHR V **ˌrange yourself/sb aˈgainst/ˈwith sb/sth** [usually passive] to join with other people to oppose or support sb/sth: *The whole family seemed ranged against him.* **ˈrange over sth** to include a variety of different subjects: *His lecture ranged over a number of topics.*

range·find·er /ˈreɪndʒfaɪndə(r)/ *noun* an instrument for estimating how far away an object is, used with a camera or gun

ran·ger /ˈreɪndʒə(r)/ *noun* **1** a person whose job is to take care of a park, a forest or an area of countryside **2 Ranger (Guide)** a girl who belongs to the part of the Guide Association in Britain for girls between the ages of 14 and 19 **3 Ranger** (*US*) a soldier who is trained to make quick attacks in enemy areas ➲ compare COMMANDO

rangy /ˈreɪndʒi/ *adj.* (of a person or an animal) having long thin arms and/or legs

rani (also **ranee**) /ˈrɑːniː; rɑːˈniː/ *noun* an Indian queen; the wife of a RAJA

rank /ræŋk/ *noun, verb, adj.*

■ ***noun***

▸ POSITION IN ORGANIZATION/ARMY, ETC. **1** [U, C] the position, especially a high position, that sb has in a particular organization, society, etc: *She was not used to mixing with people of high social rank.* ◇ *He **rose through the ranks** to become managing director.* ◇ *Within months she was elevated to ministerial rank.* ➲ see also RANKING **2** [C, U] the position that sb has in the army, navy, police, etc: *He was soon promoted to the rank of captain.* ◇ *officers of **junior/senior rank*** ◇ *a campaign to attract more women into the military ranks* ◇ *officers, and **other ranks*** (= people who are not officers) ◇ *The colonel was stripped of his rank* (= was given a lower position, especially as a punishment). **3 the ranks** [pl.] the position of ordinary soldiers rather than officers: *He served in the ranks for most of the war.* ◇ *He **rose from the ranks*** (= from being an ordinary soldier) *to become a warrant officer.*

▸ QUALITY **4** [sing.] the degree to which sb/sth is of high quality: *a painter **of the first rank*** ◇ *Britain is no longer **in the front rank of** world powers.* ◇ *The findings are arranged **in rank order** according to performance.*

▸ MEMBERS OF GROUP **5 the ranks** [pl.] the members of a particular group or organization: *We have a number of international players in our ranks.* ◇ *At 50, he was forced to **join the ranks of** the unemployed.* ◇ *There were serious divisions within the party's own ranks.*

▸ LINE/ROW **6** [C] a line or row of soldiers, police, etc. standing next to each other: *They watched as ranks of marching infantry passed the window.* **7** [C] a line or row of people or things: *massed ranks of spectators* ◇ *The trees grew **in serried ranks*** (= very closely together). ➲ see also TAXI RANK

IDM **break ˈranks 1** (of soldiers, police, etc.) to fail to remain in line **2** (of the members of a group) to refuse to support the group or the organization of which they are members ➲ more at CLOSE[1] *v.*, PULL *v.*

■ ***verb*** (not used in the progressive tenses)

▸ GIVE POSITION **1** [T, I] to give sb/sth a particular position on a scale according to quality, importance, success, etc; to have a position of this kind: **~ sb/sth (+ adv./prep.)** *The tasks have been ranked in order of difficulty.* ◇ *She is currently the highest ranked player in the world.* ◇ ***top-ranked** players* ◇ **~ sb/sth as sth** *Voters regularly rank education as being more important than defence.* ◇ **~ (sb/sth) + adj.** *At the height of her career she ranked second in the world.* ◇ **~ sb/sth + noun** *The university is ranked number one in the country for engineering.* ◇ **~ as sth** *It certainly doesn't rank as his greatest win.* ◇ **(+ adv./prep.)** *The restaurant ranks among the finest in town.* ◇ *This must rank with*

R

(= be as good as) *the greatest movies ever made.* ◇ (*NAmE*) *You just don't rank* (= you're not good enough).
▸ PUT IN LINE/ROW **2** [T, usually passive] **~ sth** to arrange objects in a line or row
■ ***adj.*** **1** having a strong unpleasant smell: *The house was full of the rank smell of urine.* **2** [only before noun] used to emphasize a particular quality, state, etc.: *an example of rank stupidity* ◇ *The winning horse was a **rank outsider**.* **3** (of plants, etc.) growing too thickly

the ˌrank and ˈfile *noun* [sing.+ sing./pl. v.] **1** the ordinary soldiers who are not officers **2** the ordinary members of an organization: *the rank and file of the workforce* ◇ *rank-and-file members*

ˈrank correlation *noun* [U] (*statistics*) a method for finding to what extent two sets of numbers, each arranged in order, are connected or have an effect on each other

rank·ing /ˈræŋkɪŋ/ *noun, adj.*
■ ***noun*** **1** the position of sb/sth on a scale that shows how good or important they are in relation to other similar people or things, especially in sport: *He has improved his ranking this season from 67th to 30th.* ◇ *She has retained her No.1 world ranking.* **2 the rankings** [pl.] an official list showing the best players of a particular sport in order of how successful they are
■ ***adj.*** **1** (*especially NAmE*) having a high or the highest rank in an organization, etc: *a ranking diplomat* ◇ *He was the **ranking officer*** (= the most senior officer present at a particular time). **2** (in compounds) having the particular rank mentioned: *high-ranking/low-ranking police officers* ◇ *a top-ranking player*

ran·kle /ˈræŋkl/ *verb* [I, T] if sth such as an event or a remark **rankles**, it makes you feel angry or upset for a long time: **~ (sb)** *Her comments still rankled.* ◇ **~ with sb** *His decision to sell the land still rankled with her.*

ran·sack /ˈrænsæk/ *verb* **~ sth (for sth)** to make a place untidy, causing damage, because you are looking for sth SYN **turn upside down**: *The house had been ransacked by burglars.*

ran·som /ˈrænsəm/ *noun, verb*
■ ***noun*** [C, U] money that is paid to sb so that they will set free a person who is being kept as a prisoner by them: *The kidnappers demanded a ransom of £50 000 from his family.* ◇ *a **ransom demand/note*** ◇ *ransom money* ◇ *They are refusing to pay ransom for her release.*
IDM **hold sb to ˈransom 1** to keep sb as a prisoner and demand that other people pay you an amount of money before you set them free **2** (*disapproving*) to take action that puts sb in a very difficult situation in order to force them to do what you want ➲ more at KING
■ ***verb*** **~ sb** to pay money to sb so that they will set free the person that they are keeping as a prisoner: *The kidnapped children were all ransomed and returned home unharmed.*

rant /rænt/ *verb* [I, T] **~ (on) (about sth)** | **~ at sb** | **+ speech** (*disapproving*) to speak or complain about sth in a loud and/or angry way ▸ **rant** *noun*
IDM **ˌrant and ˈrave** (*disapproving*) to show that you are angry by shouting or complaining loudly for a long time

rant·ings /ˈræntɪŋz/ *noun* [pl.] loud or angry comments or speeches that continue for a long time

rap /ræp/ *noun, verb*
■ ***noun*** **1** [C] a quick sharp hit or knock: *There was a sharp rap on the door.* **2** [U] a type of popular music with a fast strong rhythm and words which are spoken fast, not sung: *a **rap song/artist*** **3** [C] a rap song **4** [C] (*NAmE, informal*) a criminal CONVICTION (= the fact of being found guilty of a crime): *a police **rap sheet*** (= a record of the crimes sb has committed) **5** [sing.] (*NAmE, informal*) an unfair judgement on sth or sb: *He denounced the criticisms as 'just one **bum rap** after another.'* ◇ *Wolves **get a bad rap**, says a woman who owns three.*
IDM **(give sb/get) a rap on/over/across the ˈknuckles** (*informal*) (to give sb/receive) strong criticism for sth: *We got a rap over the knuckles for being late.* **take the ˈrap (for sb/sth)** (*informal*) to be blamed or punished, especially for sth you have not done SYN **take the blame**: *She was prepared to take the rap for the shoplifting, though it had been her sister's idea.* ➲ more at BEAT *v.*
■ ***verb*** (-pp-) **1** [I, T] to hit a hard object or surface several times quickly, making a noise: **(+ adv./prep.)** *She rapped angrily on the door.* ◇ **~ sth (+ adv./prep.)** *He rapped the table with his pen.* **2** [T] **~ sth (out)** | **+ speech** to say sth suddenly and quickly in a loud, angry way: *He walked through the store, rapping out orders to his staff.* **3** [T] **~ sb/sth (for sth/for doing sth)** (used mainly in newspapers) to criticize sb severely, usually publicly: *Some of the teachers were rapped for poor performance.* **4** [I, T] **~ (sth)** (*music*) to say the words of a rap ➲ see also RAPPER
IDM **ˌrap sb on/over the ˈknuckles** | **rap sb's ˈknuckles** to criticize sb for sth

ra·pa·cious /rəˈpeɪʃəs/ *adj.* (*formal, disapproving*) wanting more money or goods than you need or have a right to SYN **grasping** ▸ **ra·pa·cious·ly** *adv.* **rap·acity** /rəˈpæsəti/ *noun* [U]: *the rapacity of landowners seeking greater profit*

rape /reɪp/ *verb, noun*
■ ***verb*** **~ sb** to force sb to have sex with you when they do not want to by threatening them or using violence ➲ see also RAPIST
■ ***noun*** **1** [U, C] the crime of forcing sb to have sex with you, especially using violence: *He was charged with rape.* ◇ *a rape victim* ◇ *an increase in the number of reported rapes* ➲ see also DATE RAPE, RAPIST **2** [sing.] **~ (of sth)** (*literary*) the act of destroying or spoiling an area in a way that seems unnecessary **3** (also **ˌoilseed ˈrape**) [U] a plant with bright yellow flowers, grown as food for farm animals and for its seeds that are used to make oil

rape·seed /ˈreɪpsiːd/ [U] seeds of the rape plant, used mainly for cooking oil ➲ see also CANOLA

rapid 0‑ /ˈræpɪd/ *adj.*
1 0‑ [usually before noun] happening in a short period of time: ***rapid change/expansion/growth*** ◇ *a **rapid rise/decline** in sales* ◇ *The patient made a **rapid recovery**.* **2** 0‑ done or happening very quickly: *a **rapid pulse/heartbeat*** ◇ *The guard fired four shots in rapid succession.* ◇ *The disease is spreading at a rapid rate.* ➲ SYNONYMS at FAST ▸ **rap·id·ity** /rəˈpɪdəti/ *noun* [U]: *the rapidity of economic growth* ◇ *The disease is spreading with alarming rapidity.* **rap·id·ly** 0‑ *adv.*: *a rapidly growing economy* ◇ *Crime figures are rising rapidly.*

ˌrapid-ˈfire *adj.* [only before noun] **1** (of questions, comments, etc.) spoken very quickly, one after the other **2** (of a gun) able to shoot bullets very quickly, one after the other

ˌrapid-reˈsponse *adj.* [only before noun] having the necessary training and equipment to be able to act quickly when there is an emergency such as an accident, an attack or a natural disaster: *a UN rapid-response unit* ◇ *rapid-response systems for early detection of the virus*

rapids /ˈræpɪdz/ *noun* [pl.] part of a river where the water flows very fast, usually over rocks: *to **shoot the rapids*** (= to travel quickly over them in a boat)

ˌrapid ˈtransit *noun* [U] (*especially NAmE*) the system of fast public transport in cities, especially the SUBWAY ➲ see also TRANSIT (3)

ra·pier /ˈreɪpiə(r)/ *noun* a long thin light SWORD that has two sharp edges: (*figurative*) *rapier wit* (= very quick and sharp)

rap·ist /ˈreɪpɪst/ *noun* a person who forces sb to have sex when they do not want to (=RAPES them)

rap·pel /ræˈpel/ (*NAmE*) (*BrE* **ab·seil**) *verb* (-ll-) [I] **~ (down, off, etc. sth)** to go down a steep CLIFF or rock while attached to a rope, pushing against the slope or rock with your feet ➲ VISUAL VOCAB page V40 ▸ **rap·pel** (*NAmE*) (*BrE* **ab·seil**) *noun*

rap·per /ˈræpə(r)/ *noun* a person who speaks the words of a RAP song

rap·port /ræˈpɔː(r)/ *noun* [sing., U] **~ (with sb)** | **~ (between A and B)** a friendly relationship in which people understand each other very well: *She understood the importance of establishing a close rapport with clients.*

rap·por·teur /ˌræpɔːˈtɜː(r); *NAmE* -pɔːrˈt-/ *noun* (from *French, technical*) a person officially chosen by an organization to investigate a problem and report on it: *the UN special rapporteur on human rights*

rap·proche·ment /ræˈprɒʃmɒ̃; ræˈprəʊʃmɒ̃; *NAmE* ˌræprouʃˈmɑːn; -prɑːʃ-/ *noun* [sing., U] (from *French, formal*) a situation in which the relationship between two countries or groups of people becomes more friendly after a period during which they were enemies: **~ (with sb)** *policies aimed at bringing about a rapprochement with China* ◇ **~ (between A and B)** *There now seems little chance of rapprochement between the warring factions.*

rapt /ræpt/ *adj.* so interested in one particular thing that you are not aware of anything else: *a rapt audience* ◇ *She listened to the speaker with rapt attention.* ▶ **rapt·ly** *adv.*

rap·tor /ˈræptə(r)/ *noun* (*technical*) any BIRD OF PREY (= a bird that kills other creatures for food)

rap·ture /ˈræptʃə(r)/ *noun* [U] (*formal*) a feeling of extreme pleasure and happiness SYN **delight**: *Charles listened with rapture to her singing.* ◇ *The children gazed at her in rapture.*
IDM **be in, go into, etc. ˈraptures (about/over sb/sth)** to feel or express extreme pleasure or enthusiasm for sb/sth: *The critics went into raptures about her performance.* ◇ *The last minute goal sent the fans into raptures.*

rap·tur·ous /ˈræptʃərəs/ *adj.* [usually before noun] expressing extreme pleasure or enthusiasm for sb/sth SYN **ecstatic**: *rapturous applause* ➲ SYNONYMS at EXCITED ▶ **rap·tur·ous·ly** *adv.*

rare 0➡ /reə(r); *NAmE* rer/ *adj.* (**rarer**, **rar·est**)
1 0➡ not done, seen, happening, etc. very often: *a rare disease/occurrence/sight* ◇ **~ (for sb/sth to do sth)** *It's extremely rare for it to be this hot in April.* ◇ **~ (to do sth)** ***It is rare** to find such loyalty these days.* ◇ ***On the rare occasions when** they met he hardly even dared speak to her.* ◇ *It was a rare* (= very great) *honour to be made a fellow of the college.* **2** 0➡ existing only in small numbers and therefore valuable or interesting: *a rare book/coin/stamp* ◇ *a rare breed/plant* ◇ *This species is extremely rare.* **3** (of meat) cooked for only a short time so that the inside is still red ➲ compare WELL DONE ➲ see also RARITY

rare·bit /ˈreəbɪt; *NAmE* ˈrerbɪt/ *noun* = WELSH RAREBIT

rar·efied /ˈreərɪfaɪd; *NAmE* ˈrerəf-/ *adj.* [usually before noun] **1** (often *disapproving*) understood or experienced by only a very small group of people who share a particular area of knowledge or activity: *the rarefied atmosphere of academic life* **2** (of air) containing less OXYGEN than usual

ˈrare gas *noun* (*chemistry*) = NOBLE GAS

rare·ly 0➡ /ˈreəli; *NAmE* ˈrerli/ *adv.*
not very often: *She is rarely seen in public nowadays.* ◇ *We rarely agree on what to do.* ◇ *a rarely-performed play* ◇ (*formal*) *Rarely has a debate attracted so much media attention.*

rar·ing /ˈreərɪŋ; *NAmE* ˈrer-/ *adj.* **~ to do sth** (*informal*) very enthusiastic about starting to do sth: *The new recruits arrived early, all dressed up and **raring to go*** (= to start). ◇ *She is raring to get back to work after her operation.*

rar·ity /ˈreərəti; *NAmE* ˈrer-/ *noun* (*pl.* **-ies**) **1** [C] a person or thing that is unusual and is therefore often valuable or interesting: *Women are still something of a rarity in senior positions in business.* ◇ *His collection of plants contains many rarities.* **2** (also *less frequent* **rare·ness**) [U] the quality of being rare: *The value of antiques will depend on their condition and rarity.*

ras·cal /ˈrɑːskl; *NAmE* ˈræskl/ *noun* **1** (*humorous*) a person, especially a child or man, who shows a lack of respect for other people and enjoys playing tricks on them: *Come here, you little rascal!* **2** (*old-fashioned*) a dishonest man ▶ **ras·cal·ly** *adj.* (*old-fashioned*)

rash /ræʃ/ *noun, adj.*
■ ***noun*** **1** [C, usually sing.] an area of red spots on a person's skin, caused by an illness or a reaction to sth: *I woke up covered in a rash.* ◇ *I **come out in a rash*** (= a rash appears on my skin) *if I eat chocolate.* ◇ *The sun **brought her out in*** (= caused) *an itchy rash.* ◇ *a **heat rash*** (= caused by heat) ➲ compare SPOT **2** [sing.] **~ (of sth)** a lot of sth; a series of unpleasant things that happen over a short period of time SYN **spate**: *a rash of movies about life in prison* ◇ *There has been a rash of burglaries in the area over the last month.*
■ ***adj.*** (of people or their actions) doing sth that may not be sensible without first thinking about the possible results; done in this way SYN **impulsive**, **reckless**: *a rash young man* ◇ **~ (to do sth)** *It would be rash to assume that everyone will agree with you on this.* ◇ *Think twice before doing anything rash.* ◇ *This is what happens when you make rash decisions.* ▶ **rash·ly** *adv.*: *She had rashly promised to lend him the money.* **rash·ness** *noun* [U]: *He bitterly regretted his rashness.*

rasher /ˈræʃə(r)/ *noun* (*especially BrE*) a thin slice of BACON (= meat from the back or sides of a pig)

rasp /rɑːsp; *NAmE* ræsp/ *noun, verb*
■ ***noun*** **1** [sing.] a rough unpleasant sound **2** [C] a metal tool with a long blade covered with rows of sharp points, used for making rough surfaces smooth
■ ***verb*** **1** [T, I] to say sth in a rough unpleasant voice SYN **croak**: **+ speech** *'Where have you been?' she rasped.* ◇ **~ (sth) (out)** *He rasped out some instructions.* **2** [I] to make a rough unpleasant sound SYN **grate**: *a rasping **cough/voice*** **3** [T] **~ sth** to rub a surface with a rasp or with sth rough that works or feels like a rasp: *The wind rasped his face.*

rasp·berry /ˈrɑːzbəri; *NAmE* ˈræzberi/ *noun* (*pl.* **-ies**) **1** a small dark red soft fruit that grows on bushes: *raspberry jam* ➲ VISUAL VOCAB page V26 **2** (*NAmE* also **ˌBronx ˈcheer**) (*informal*) a rude sound made by sticking out the tongue and blowing: *to blow a raspberry at sb*

raspy /ˈrɑːspi; *NAmE* ˈræspi/ *adj.* (of sb's voice) having a rough sound, as if the person has a sore throat SYN **croaky**

Ras·ta·far·ian /ˌræstəˈfeəriən; *NAmE* -ˈfer-/ (also *informal* **Rasta**) *noun* a member of a Jamaican religious group which worships the former Emperor of Ethiopia, Haile Selassie, and which believes that black people will one day return to Africa. Rastafarians often wear DREADLOCKS and have other distinguishing patterns of behaviour and dress. ▶ **Ras·ta·far·ian** (also *informal* **Rasta**) *adj.* **Ras·ta·far·ian·ism** *noun* [U]

ras·ter·ize (*BrE* also **-ise**) /ˈræstəraɪz/ (also **rip**) *verb* **~ sth** (*computing*) to change text or images into a form in which they can be printed

rat /ræt/ *noun, verb*
■ ***noun*** **1** a small animal with a long tail, that looks like a large mouse, usually considered a PEST (= an animal which is disliked because it destroys food or spreads disease): *rat poison* ➲ compare RUG RAT **2** (*informal, disapproving*) an unpleasant person, especially one who is not loyal or who tricks sb IDM see SINK *v.*, SMELL *v.*
■ ***verb*** (**-tt-**)
PHR V **ˈrat on sb** (*NAmE* also **rat sb out (to sb)**) (*informal, disapproving*) to tell sb in authority about sth wrong that sb else has done: *Where I come from, you don't rat on your friends.* **ˈrat on sth** (*BrE, informal*) to not do sth that you have agreed or promised to do SYN **renege**: *The government is accused of ratting on its promises to the unemployed.* **rat sb↔out (to sb)** (*especially NAmE, informal, disapproving*) = RAT ON SB: *Someone ratted us out to the police.*

rata ➲ PRO RATA

ˈrat-arsed *adj.* (*BrE, slang*) extremely drunk

ˌrat-a-tat-ˈtat *noun* [sing.] = RAT-TAT

rata·touille /ˌrætəˈtuːi; -ˈtwiː/ *noun* [U, C] a dish of onions, PEPPERS, AUBERGINES/EGGPLANTS, COURGETTES/ZUCCHINI and tomatoes cooked together

rat·bag /ˈrætbæg/ *noun* (*BrE, slang*) an unpleasant or disgusting person

ratchet /ˈrætʃɪt/ *noun, verb*
■ ***noun*** a wheel or bar with teeth along the edge and a metal piece that fits between the teeth, allowing movement in one direction only

R

■ ***verb***

PHR V ˌ**ratchet** (**sth**)↔ˈ**up** to increase, or make sth increase, repeatedly and by small amounts: *Overuse of credit cards has ratcheted up consumer debt to unacceptable levels.*

rate 🔑 /reɪt/ *noun, verb*

■ ***noun*** **1** 🔑 [C] a measurement of the speed at which sth happens: *Most people walk at an average rate of 5 kilometres an hour.* ◇ *The number of reported crimes is increasing at an alarming rate.* ◇ *Figures published today show another fall in the rate of inflation.* ◇ *At the rate you work, you'll never finish!* **2** 🔑 [C] a measurement of the number of times sth happens or exists during a particular period: *Local businesses are closing* ***at a/the rate of*** *three a year.* ◇ *a* ***high/low/rising rate*** *of unemployment* ◇ *the annual* ***crime/divorce rate*** ◇ *His pulse rate dropped suddenly.* ◇ *a high* ***success/failure rate*** ➲ see also BIRTH RATE, DEATH RATE **3** [C] a fixed amount of money that is charged or paid for sth: ***advertising/insurance/postal, etc. rates*** ◇ *a* ***low/high*** *hourly* ***rate of pay*** ◇ *We offer special* ***reduced rates*** *for students.* ◇ *a* ***fixed-rate*** *mortgage* (= one in which the amount of money paid back each month is fixed for a particular period) ◇ *the basic rate of tax* (= the lowest amount that is paid by everyone) ◇ ***exchange/interest rates*** ◇ ***rates of exchange/interest*** ➲ see also BASE RATE, FLAT RATE, RACK RATE **4 rates** [pl.] (in Britain) a tax paid by businesses to a local authority for land and buildings that they use and in the past also paid by anyone who owned a house ➲ SYNONYMS at TAX ➲ see also FIRST-RATE, SECOND-RATE, THIRD-RATE

IDM **at ˈany rate** (*informal*) **1** used to say that a particular fact is true despite what has happened in the past or what may happen in the future: *Well, that's one good piece of news at any rate.* ◇ *I may be away on business next week but at any rate I'll be back by Friday.* **2** used to show that you are being more accurate about sth that you have just said: *He said he'll be coming tomorrow. At any rate, I think that's what he said.* **3** used to show that what you have just said is not as important as what you are going to say: *There were maybe 60 or 70 people there. At any rate, the room was packed.* **at a rate of ˈknots** (*BrE, informal*) very quickly **at ˈthis/ˈthat rate** (*informal*) used to say what will happen if a particular situation continues to develop in the same way: *At this rate, we'll soon be bankrupt.* ➲ more at GOING *adj.*

■ ***verb*** (not used in the progressive tenses) **1** 🔑 [T, I] **~ sb/sth (as) sth** | **~ as sth** to have or think that sb/sth has a particular level of quality, value, etc: **~ sb/sth (+ adv./prep.)** *The university is* ***highly rated*** *for its research.* ◇ *They rated him highly as a colleague.* ◇ **~ sb/sth + adj.** *Voters continue to rate education high on their list of priorities.* ◇ **~ sb/sth (as) sth** | **~ sb/sth + noun** *The show was rated (as) a success by critics and audiences.* ◇ **~ as sth** *The match rated as one of their worst defeats.* ◇ **+ adj.** *I'm afraid our needs do not rate very high with this administration.* **2** [T] **~ sth** (*informal*) to think that sb/sth is good: *What did you think of the movie? I didn't rate it myself.* **3** 🔑 [T, usually passive] to place sb/sth in a particular position on a scale in relation to similar people or things **SYN** **rank**: **~ sb/sth (+ adv./prep.)** *The schools were rated according to their exam results.* ◇ *a top-rated programme* ◇ **~ sb/sth + noun** *She is currently rated number two in the world.* **4** [T] **~ sth** to be good, important, etc. enough to be treated in a particular way **SYN** **merit**: *The incident didn't even* ***rate a mention*** *in the press.* **5** [T, usually passive] **~ sth** (**+ noun**) to state that a film/movie or video is suitable for a particular audience ➲ see also X-RATED, ZERO-RATED

ˈ**rate cap** *noun* (in the US) a limit placed on the amount of interest banks, etc. may charge

rate·pay·er /ˈreɪtpeɪə(r)/ *noun* (in Britain in the past) a person who paid taxes to the local authority on the buildings and land they owned

Synonyms

rate

charge • fee • rent • fine • fare • toll • rental

These are all words for an amount of money that is charged or paid for sth.

rate a fixed amount of money that is asked or paid for sth: *a low hourly rate of pay* ◇ *interest rates*

charge an amount of money that is asked for goods or services: *an admission charge*

fee (*rather formal*) an amount of money that you have to pay for professional advice or services, to go to a school or college, or to join an organization: *legal fees* ◇ *an annual membership fee*

rent an amount of money that you regularly have to pay for use of a building or room. **NOTE** In American English, **rent** can be used to mean **rental**: *The weekly rent on the car was over $300.*

fine a sum of money that must be paid as punishment for breaking a law or rule: *a parking fine*

fare the money that you pay to travel by bus, plane, taxi, etc.

toll an amount of money that you have to pay to use a particular road or bridge.

rental an amount of money that you have to pay to use sth for a particular period of time.

RENT OR RENTAL?

In British English **rent** is only money paid to use a building or room: for other items use **rental**. In American English **rent** can be used for both, but **rental** is still more common for other items.

PATTERNS

- (a) rate/charge/fee/rent/fine/fare/toll/rental **for** sth
- (a) rate/charge/fee/rent/toll/rental **on** sth
- **at** a rate/charge/fee/rent/fare/rental of...
- **for** a charge/fee
- to **pay** (a) rate/charge/fee/rent/fine/fare/toll/rental
- to **charge** (a) rate/fee/rent/fare/toll/rental

ra·ther 🔑 /ˈrɑːðə(r); *NAmE* ˈræðər/ *adv., exclamation*

■ ***adv.*** **1** 🔑 used to mean 'fairly' or 'to some degree', often when you are expressing slight criticism, disappointment or surprise: *The instructions were rather complicated.* ◇ *She fell and hurt her leg rather badly.* ◇ *I didn't fail the exam; in fact I did rather well!* ◇ *It was a rather difficult question.* ◇ *It was* ***rather a*** *difficult question.* ◇ *He looks rather like his father.* ◇ *The patient has responded to the treatment rather better than expected.* ◇ *He was conscious that he was talking* ***rather too*** *much.* ➲ note at QUITE **2** used with a verb to make a statement sound less strong: *I rather suspect we're making a mistake.* ◇ *We were rather hoping you'd be able to do it by Friday.* **3** 🔑 used to correct sth you have said, or to give more accurate information: *She worked as a secretary, or rather, a personal assistant.* ◇ *In the end he had to walk—or rather run—to the office.* ➲ LANGUAGE BANK at I.E. **4** 🔑 used to introduce an idea that is different or opposite to the idea that you have stated previously: *The walls were not white, but rather a sort of dirty grey.*

IDM **rather you, him, etc. than ˈme** (*informal*) used for saying that you would not like to do sth that another person is going to do: *'I'm going climbing tomorrow.' 'Rather you than me!'* **rather than** 🔑 instead of sb/sth: *I think I'll have a cold drink rather than coffee.* ◇ *Why didn't you ask for help, rather than trying to do it on your own?* **would rather... (than)** 🔑 (usually reduced to *'d rather*) would prefer to: *She'd rather die than give a speech.* ◇ *'Do you want to come with us?' 'No, I'd rather not.'* ◇ *Would you rather walk or take the bus?* ◇ *'Do you mind if I smoke?' 'Well, I'd rather you didn't.'*

■ ***exclamation*** /*also* ˌrɑːˈðɜː(r)/ (*old-fashioned, BrE*) used to agree with sb's suggestion: *'How about a trip to the beach?' 'Rather!'*

rat·ify /ˈrætɪfaɪ/ *verb* (**rati·fies, rati·fy·ing, rati·fied, rati·fied**) **~ sth** to make an agreement officially valid by voting for or signing it: *The treaty was ratified by all the member states.* ▸ **rati·fi·ca·tion** /ˌrætɪfɪˈkeɪʃn/ *noun* [U]

rat·ing /ˈreɪtɪŋ/ *noun* **1** [C] a measurement of how good, popular, important, etc. sb/sth is, especially in relation to other people or things: *The poll gave a popular approval rating of 39% for the President.* ◇ *Education has been given a high-priority rating by the new administration.* ➲ see also CREDIT RATING **2 the ratings** [pl.] a set of figures that show how many people watch or listen to a particular television or radio programme, used to show how popular a programme is: *The show has gone up in the ratings.* ➲ COLLOCATIONS at TELEVISION **3** [C] a number or letter that shows which groups of people a particular film/movie is suitable for: *The film was given a 15 rating by British censors.* ◇ *The movie carries an R rating.* **4** [C] (*BrE*) a sailor in the navy who is not an officer

ratio AW /ˈreɪʃiəʊ; *NAmE* -oʊ/ *noun* (*pl.* -os) **~ (of A to B)** the relationship between two groups of people or things that is represented by two numbers showing how much larger one group is than the other: *What is the ratio of men to women in the department?* ◇ *The school has a very high teacher-student ratio.* ◇ *The ratio of applications to available places currently stands at 100:1.*

rati·ocin·ation /ˌrætiˌɒsɪˈneɪʃn; *NAmE* ˌreɪʃioʊ-/ *noun* [U] (*formal*) the process of thinking or arguing about sth in a logical way

ra·tion /ˈræʃn/ *noun, verb*

■ ***noun* 1** [C] a fixed amount of food, fuel, etc. that you are officially allowed to have when there is not enough for everyone to have as much as they want, for example during a war: *the weekly butter ration* **2 rations** [pl.] a fixed amount of food given regularly to a soldier or to sb who is in a place where there is not much food available: *We're* ***on short rations*** (= allowed less than usual) *until fresh supplies arrive.* ◇ *Once these latest rations run out, the country will again face hunger and starvation.* **3** [sing.] **~ (of sth)** an amount of sth that is thought to be normal or fair: *As part of the diet, allow yourself a small daily ration of sugar.* ◇ *I've had my ration of problems for one day—you deal with it!*

■ ***verb*** [often passive] to limit the amount of sth that sb is allowed to have, especially because there is not enough of it available: **~ sth** *Eggs were rationed during the war.* ◇ **~ sb to sth** *The villagers are rationed to two litres of water a day.* ➲ see also RATIONING

ra·tion·al AW /ˈræʃnəl/ *adj.* **1** (of behaviour, ideas, etc.) based on reason rather than emotions: *a rational argument/choice/decision* ◇ *rational analysis/thought* ◇ *There is no rational explanation for his actions.* **2** (of a person) able to think clearly and make decisions based on reason rather than emotions SYN **reasonable**: *No rational person would ever behave like that.* OPP **irrational** ▸ **ra·tion·al·ity** AW /ˌræʃəˈnæləti/ *noun* [U]: *the rationality of his argument* **ra·tion·al·ly** AW /ˈræʃnəli/ *adv.*: *to act/behave/think rationally* ◇ *She argued her case calmly and rationally.*

ra·tion·ale /ˌræʃəˈnɑːl; *NAmE* -ˈnæl/ *noun* **~ (behind/for/of sth)** (*formal*) the principles or reasons which explain a particular decision, course of action, belief, etc. SYN **reason**: *What is the rationale behind these new exams?*

ra·tion·al·ism AW /ˈræʃnəlɪzəm/ *noun* [U] (*philosophy*) the belief that all behaviour, opinions, etc. should be based on reason rather than on emotions or religious beliefs

ra·tion·al·ist /ˈræʃnəlɪst/ *noun* a person who believes in rationalism ▸ **ra·tion·al·ist** (also **ra·tion·al·is·tic** /ˌræʃnəˈlɪstɪk/) *adj.* [usually before noun]: *a rationalistic position*

ra·tion·al·ize (*BrE* also **-ise**) AW /ˈræʃnəlaɪz/ *verb* **1** [T, I] **~ (sth)** to find or try to find a logical reason to explain why sb thinks, behaves, etc. in a way that is difficult to understand: *an attempt to rationalize his violent behaviour* **2** [T, I] **~ (sth)** (*BrE*) to make changes to a business, system, etc. in order to make it more efficient, especially by spending less money: *Twenty workers lost their jobs when the department was rationalized.* ➲ SYNONYMS at CUT ▸ **ra·tion·al·iza·tion, -isa·tion** AW /ˌræʃnəlaɪˈzeɪʃn; *NAmE* -ləˈz-/ *noun* [U, C]: *No amount of rationalization could justify his actions.* ◇ *a need for rationalization of the industry*

ˈrational number *noun* (*mathematics*) a number that can be expressed as the RATIO of two whole numbers

ra·tion·ing /ˈræʃənɪŋ/ *noun* [U] the policy of limiting the amount of food, fuel, etc. that people are allowed to have when there is not enough for everyone to have as much as they want

ˈrat pack *noun* [sing.+ sing./pl. v.] (*BrE*, *disapproving*) journalists and photographers who follow famous people around in a way which makes their lives unpleasant

the ˈrat race *noun* [sing.] (*disapproving*) the way of life of people living and working in a large city where people compete in an aggressive way with each other in order to be more successful, earn more money, etc. ➲ COLLOCATIONS at TOWN

ˈrat run *noun* (*BrE*, *informal*) a small road, especially one with houses on it, used by drivers during busy times when the main roads are full of traffic

rats /ræts/ *exclamation* (*informal*) used to show that you are annoyed about sth: *Rats! I forgot my glasses.*

rat·tan /ræˈtæn/ *noun* [U] a SE Asian climbing plant with long thin strong STEMS used especially for making furniture: *a rattan chair*

ˌrat-ˈtat (also **ˌrat-a-tat-ˈtat**) *noun* [sing.] the sound of knocking, especially on a door

rat·tle /ˈrætl/ *verb, noun*

■ ***verb*** (*informal*) **1** [I, T] **~ (sth)** to make a series of short loud sounds when hitting against sth hard; to make sth do this: *Every time a bus went past, the windows rattled.* **2** [I] **+ adv./prep.** (of a vehicle) to make a series of short loud sounds as it moves somewhere: *A convoy of trucks rattled by.* **3** [T] **~ sb** to make sb nervous or frightened SYN **unnerve**: *He was clearly rattled by the question.* ➲ see also SABRE-RATTLING

IDM **ˌrattle sb's ˈcage** (*informal*) to annoy sb: *Who's rattled his cage?*

PHR V **ˌrattle aˈround | ˌrattle aˈround sth** (*informal*) to be living, working, etc. in a room or building that is too big: *She spent the last few years alone, rattling around the old family home.* **ˌrattle sth↔ˈoff** to say sth from memory without having to think too hard: *She can rattle off the names of all the presidents of the US.* **ˌrattle ˈon (about sth)** (*informal*) to talk continuously about sth that is not important or interesting, especially in an annoying way

■ ***noun* 1** (also **rat·tling**) [usually sing.] a series of short loud sounds made when hard objects hit against each other: *the rattle of gunfire* ◇ *From the kitchen came a rattling of cups and saucers.* ➲ see also DEATH RATTLE **2** a baby's toy that makes a series of short loud sounds when it is shaken **3** (*BrE*) a wooden object that is held in one hand and makes a series of short loud sounds when you spin it round, used, for example, by people watching a sports game

rattle·snake /ˈrætlsneɪk/ (also *informal* **rat·tler** /ˈrætlə(r)/) *noun* a poisonous American snake that makes a noise like a rattle with its tail when it is angry or afraid

rat·tling /ˈrætlɪŋ/ *adv.* **~ good** (*old-fashioned*, *BrE*) very good: *This book is a rattling good read.*

ratty /ˈræti/ *adj.* **1** (*BrE*, *informal*) becoming angry very easily SYN **grumpy, irritable**: *He gets ratty if he doesn't get enough sleep.* **2** (*NAmE*, *informal*) in bad condition SYN **shabby**: *long ratty hair* ◇ *a ratty old pair of jeans* **3** looking like a RAT

rau·cous /ˈrɔːkəs/ *adj.* sounding loud and rough: *raucous laughter* ◇ *a raucous voice* ◇ *a group of raucous young men* ▸ **rau·cous·ly** *adv.* **rau·cous·ness** *noun* [U]

raunchy /ˈrɔːntʃi/ *adj.* (*informal*) **1** intended to be sexually exciting SYN **sexy**: *a raunchy magazine* ◇ *Their stage act is a little too raunchy for television.* **2** (*NAmE*) looking dirty and untidy: *a raunchy old man*

R

rav·age /ˈrævɪdʒ/ *verb* [usually passive] **~ sth** to damage sth badly SYN **devastate**: *a country ravaged by civil war*

rav·ages /ˈrævɪdʒɪz/ *noun* [pl.] **the ~ of sth** (*formal*) the destruction caused by sth: *the ravages of war* ◇ *Her looks had not survived **the ravages of time**.*

rave /reɪv/ *verb, noun*

■ ***verb*** **1** [I, T] **~ (about sb/sth)** | **+ speech** to talk or write about sth in a very enthusiastic way: *The critics raved about his performance in 'Hamlet'.* **2** [I, T] **~ (at sb)** | **+ speech** to shout in a loud and emotional way at sb because you are angry with them: *She was shouting and raving at them.* **3** [I, T] **~ (at sb)** | **+ speech** to talk or shout in a way that is not logical or sensible: *He wandered the streets raving at passers-by.* IDM see RANT

■ ***noun*** **1** (in Britain) a large party, held outside or in an empty building, at which people dance to fast electronic music and often take illegal drugs: *an all-night rave* **2** (*NAmE*) = RAVE REVIEW

ravel /ˈrævl/ *verb* (-ll-, *US* -l-) **~ sth** to make a situation or problem more complicated

PHR V **ravel sth↔out** to open sth which has become twisted or which contains knots SYN **unravel**: (*figurative*) *He was trying to ravel out the complicated series of events that had led to this situation.*

raven /ˈreɪvn/ *noun, adj.*

■ ***noun*** a large bird of the CROW family, with shiny black feathers and a rough unpleasant cry

■ ***adj.*** [only before noun] (*literary*) (of hair) shiny and black: *raven-haired*

raven·ing /ˈrævənɪŋ/ *adj.* (*literary*) (especially of animals) aggressive and hungry: *He says the media are ravening wolves.*

rav·en·ous /ˈrævənəs/ *adj.* **1** (of a person or an animal) extremely hungry SYN **starving**: *What's for lunch? I'm absolutely ravenous.* **2** [only before noun] (of HUNGER) very great: *a ravenous appetite* ▶ **rav·en·ous·ly** *adv.*

raver /ˈreɪvə(r)/ *noun* (*BrE, informal*) **1** (often *humorous*) a person who likes going out and who has an exciting social life **2** a person who goes to RAVES

ˌrave reˈview (*NAmE* also **rave**) *noun* an article in a newspaper or magazine that is very enthusiastic about a particular film/movie, book, etc.

ˈrave-up *noun* (*old-fashioned, BrE, informal*) a lively party or celebration

R

rav·ine /rəˈviːn/ *noun* a deep, very narrow valley with steep sides ➲ VISUAL VOCAB page V4

rav·ing /ˈreɪvɪŋ/ *adj., adv.*

■ ***adj.*** [only before noun] **1** (of a person) talking or behaving in a way that shows they are crazy: *The man's a raving lunatic.* **2** used to emphasize a particular state or quality: *She's no raving beauty.*

■ ***adv.***

IDM (**stark**) **raving ˈmad/ˈbonkers** (*informal*) completely crazy

rav·ings /ˈreɪvɪŋz/ *noun* [pl.] words that have no meaning, spoken by sb who is crazy: *He dismissed her words as the ravings of a hysterical woman.*

ravi·oli /ˌræviˈəʊli; *NAmE* -ˈoʊli/ *noun* [U] PASTA in the shape of small squares filled with meat, cheese, etc, usually served with a sauce

rav·ish /ˈrævɪʃ/ *verb* (*literary*) **1 ~ sb** (of a man) to force a woman to have sex SYN **rape** **2** [usually passive] **~ sb** to give sb great pleasure

rav·ish·ing /ˈrævɪʃɪŋ/ *adj.* extremely beautiful SYN **gorgeous**: *a ravishing blonde* ▶ **rav·ish·ing·ly** *adv.*: *ravishingly beautiful*

raw 0‑w /rɔː/ *adj., noun*

■ ***adj.***

▸ FOOD **1** 0‑w not cooked: *raw meat* ◇ *These fish are often eaten raw.*

▸ MATERIALS **2** [usually before noun] in its natural state; not yet changed, used or made into sth else: *raw sugar*

▸ INFORMATION **3** [usually before noun] not yet organized into a form in which it can be easily used or understood: *This information is only **raw data** and will need further analysis.*

▸ EMOTIONS/QUALITIES **4** [usually before noun] powerful and natural; not controlled or trained: *songs full of raw emotion* ◇ *He started with nothing but raw talent and determination.*

▸ PART OF BODY **5** red and painful because the skin has been damaged: *There were raw patches on her feet where the shoes had rubbed.* ➲ SYNONYMS at PAINFUL

▸ PERSON **6** [usually before noun] new to a job or an activity and therefore without experience or skill: *a raw beginner* ◇ *raw recruits* (= for example, in the army)

▸ WEATHER **7** very cold: *a raw north wind* ◇ *It had been a wet raw winter.*

▸ DESCRIPTION **8** honest, direct and sometimes shocking: *a raw portrayal of working-class life* ◇ (*NAmE*) *raw language* (= containing many sexual details)

▶ **raw·ness** *noun* [U]

IDM **a raw ˈdeal** the fact of sb being treated unfairly: *Older workers often get a raw deal.*

■ ***noun***

IDM **catch/touch sb on the ˈraw** (*BrE*) to upset sb by reminding them of sth they are particularly sensitive about **in the ˈraw** **1** in a way that does not hide the unpleasant aspects of sth: *He spent a couple of months on the streets to experience life in the raw.* **2** (*especially NAmE*) with no clothes on SYN **naked** ➲ more at NERVE *n.*

raw·hide /ˈrɔːhaɪd/ *noun* [U] natural leather that has not had any special treatment

Rawl·plug™ /ˈrɔːlplʌg/ *noun* (also **ˈwall plug**) (both *BrE*) (*NAmE* **ˈwall anchor**) a small plastic tube, closed at one end, that you put into a wall to hold a screw

ˌraw maˈterial *noun* [C, U] a basic material that is used to make a product: *We have had problems with the supply of raw materials to the factory.* ◇ *These trees provide the raw material for high-quality paper.* ◇ (*figurative*) *The writer uses her childhood as raw material for this novel.*

ray /reɪ/ *noun* **1** a narrow line of light, heat or other energy: *the sun's rays* ◇ *ultraviolet rays* ◇ *The windows were shining in the reflected rays of the setting sun.* ➲ see also COSMIC RAYS, GAMMA RAYS, X-RAY **2 ~ of sth** a small amount of sth good or of sth that you are hoping for SYN **glimmer**: *There was just one small **ray of hope**.* **3** a sea fish with a large broad flat body and a long tail, that is used for food **4** (also **re**) (*music*) the second note of a MAJOR SCALE

IDM **a ˌray of ˈsunshine** (*informal*) a person or thing that makes life brighter or more cheerful **catch/get/grab some ˈrays** (*informal*) to sit or lie in the sun, especially in order to get a SUNTAN

ˈray gun *noun* (in SCIENCE FICTION stories) a gun that kills or injures people by sending out harmful rays

rayon /ˈreɪɒn; *NAmE* -ɑːn/ *noun* [U] a FIBRE made from CELLULOSE; a smooth material made from this, used for making clothes

raze /reɪz/ *verb* [usually passive] **~ sth** to completely destroy a building, town, etc. so that nothing is left: *The village was **razed to the ground**.*

razor /ˈreɪzə(r)/ *noun* an instrument that is used for shaving: *an electric razor* ◇ *a **cut-throat/safety/disposable razor*** ➲ VISUAL VOCAB page V21 ➲ compare SHAVER

IDM **be on the ˈrazor's edge** | **be on a ˈrazor edge** to be in a difficult situation where any mistake may be very dangerous

razor·bill /ˈreɪzəbɪl; *NAmE* -zərb-/ *noun* a black and white bird with a beak that looks like an old-fashioned RAZOR, found in the N Atlantic and the Baltic Sea

ˈrazor blade *noun* a thin sharp piece of metal that is used in a razor, especially one that can be thrown away when it is no longer sharp ➲ picture at BLADE

ˌrazor-ˈsharp *adj.* **1** extremely sharp: *razor-sharp teeth* **2** showing that sb is extremely intelligent: *a razor-sharp mind*

ˌrazor-ˈthin *adj.* (*NAmE*) (of a victory in an election, etc.) won by a very small number of votes

ˈ**razor wire** *noun* [U] strong wire with sharp blades sticking out, placed on top of walls and around areas of land to keep people out

razz /ræz/ *verb* **~ sb** (*old-fashioned, NAmE, informal*) to TEASE sb by saying or doing things to make people laugh at them

raz·zle /ˈræzl/ *noun*

IDM **be/go (out) on the razzle** (*BrE, informal*) to go out drinking, dancing and enjoying yourself

razz·ma·tazz /ˌræzməˈtæz/ (also **raz·za·ma·tazz** /ˌræzəməˈtæz/) (also ˌ**razzle-ˈdazzle**) *noun* [U] (*informal*) a lot of noisy exciting activity that is intended to attract people's attention: *The documentary focuses on the razzmatazz of an American political campaign.*

RC /ˌɑː ˈsiː; *NAmE* ˌɑːr/ *abbr.* ROMAN CATHOLIC

RCMP /ˌɑː siː em ˈpiː; *NAmE* ˌɑːr/ *abbr.* Royal Canadian Mounted Police (the national police force of Canada)

Rd (also **Rd.** especially in *NAmE*) *abbr.* (used in written addresses) Road: *12 Ashton Rd*

RDA /ˌɑː diː ˈeɪ; *NAmE* ˌɑːr/ *abbr.* recommended daily allowance (the amount of a chemical, for example a VITAMIN or a mineral, which you should have every day)

RE /ˌɑːr ˈiː/ *noun* [U] the abbreviation for religious education (a school subject in which students learn about different religions): *an RE teacher*

re¹ /reɪ/ = RAY (4)

re² /riː/ *prep.* used at the beginning of a business letter, etc. to introduce the subject that it is about; used on an email that you are sending as a reply: *Re your letter of 1 September… ◇ Re: travel expenses*

re- 🔑 /riː/ *prefix*
(in verbs and related nouns, adjectives and adverbs) again: *reapply ◇ reincarnation ◇ reassuring*

reach 🔑 /riːtʃ/ *verb, noun*

■ ***verb***

▸ ARRIVE **1** 🔑 [T] **~ sth/sb** to arrive at the place that you have been travelling to: *They didn't reach the border until after dark. ◇ I hope this letter reaches you.* **2** 🔑 [T] **~ sb** to come to sb's attention: *The rumours eventually reached the President.*

▸ LEVEL/SPEED/STAGE **3** 🔑 [T] **~ sth** to increase to a particular level, speed, etc. over a period of time: *The conflict has now reached a new level of intensity. ◇ Daytime temperatures can reach 40°C.* **4** 🔑 [T] **~ sth** to arrive at a particular point or stage of sth after a period of time: *He first reached the finals in 2008. ◇ The negotiations have reached deadlock.*

▸ ACHIEVE AIM **5** 🔑 [T] **~ sth** to achieve a particular aim SYN **arrive at**: *to **reach a conclusion/decision/verdict/compromise** ◇ Politicians again failed to **reach an agreement**.* ➲ see also FAR-REACHING

▸ WITH HAND/ARM **6** 🔑 [I, T] to stretch your hand towards sth in order to touch it, pick it up, etc: **+ adv./prep.** *She reached inside her bag for a pen.* ◇ **~ sth + adv./prep.** *He reached out his hand to touch her.* **7** 🔑 [I, T] to be able to stretch your hand far enough in order to touch sth, pick sth up, etc: (**+ adv./prep.**) *'Grab the end of the rope.' 'I can't reach that far!'* ◇ **~ sth** *Can you reach the light switch from where you're sitting?* **8** [T] to stretch your hand out or up in order to get sth for sb: **~ sth (down) for sb** *Can you reach that box down for me?* ◇ **~ sb (down) sth** *Can you reach me down that box?*

▸ BE LONG ENOUGH **9** 🔑 [I, T] to be big enough, long enough, etc. to arrive at a particular point: **+ adv./prep.** *The carpet only reached halfway across the room.* ◇ **~ sth** *Is the cable long enough to reach the socket?*

▸ CONTACT SB **10** [T] **~ sb** to communicate with sb, especially by telephone: *Do you know where I can reach him?*

▸ BE SEEN/HEARD BY SB **11** [T] **~ sb** to be seen or heard by sb: *Through television and radio we are able to reach a wider audience.*

IDM **reach for the** ˈ**stars** to try to be successful at sth that is difficult ➲ more at EAR

PHR V ˌ**reach** ˈ**out to sb** to show sb that you are interested in them and/or want to help them: *The church needs to find new ways of reaching out to young people.*

■ ***noun***

▸ OF ARMS **1** [sing., U] the distance over which you can stretch your arms to touch sth; the distance over which a particular object can be used to touch sth else: *As a boxer, his long reach gives him a significant advantage. ◇ The shot was well **beyond the reach of** the goalkeeper. ◇ Cleaning fluids should be kept **out of the reach of** children. ◇ He lashed out angrily, hitting anyone **within his reach**. ◇ Use shears with a long reach for cutting high hedges.*

▸ OF POWER/INFLUENCE **2** [sing., U] the limit to which sb/sth has the power or influence to do sth: *Such matters are **beyond the reach of** the law. ◇ Victory is now **out of her reach**. ◇ The basic model is priced well **within the reach of** most people. ◇ The company has now overtaken IBM in terms of size and reach.*

▸ OF RIVER **3** [C, usually pl.] a straight section of water between two bends on a river: *the **upper/lower reaches** of the Nile* (= the part that is furthest from/nearest to the sea)

▸ PLACE FAR FROM CENTRE **4 reaches** [pl.] **the outer, further, etc. ~ of sth** the parts of an area or a place that are a long way from the centre: *the outer reaches of space ◇* (*figurative*) *an exploration of the deepest reaches of the human mind*

▸ SECTIONS OF ORGANIZATION **5 reaches** [pl.] **the higher, lower, etc. ~ of sth** the higher, etc. sections of an organization, a system, etc: *There are still few women in the upper reaches of the civil service. ◇ Many clubs in the lower reaches of the league are in financial difficulty.*

IDM **within (easy)** ˈ**reach (of sth)** close to sth: *The house is within easy reach of schools and sports facilities.*

reach·able /ˈriːtʃəbl/ *adj.* [not before noun] that is possible to reach: *The farm is only reachable by car.*

re·acquaint /ˌriːəˈkweɪnt/ *verb* **~ sb/yourself with sth** to let sb/yourself find out about sth again or get used to sth again: *I'll need to reacquaint myself with this program—it's a long time since I've used it.*

react 🔑 AW /riˈækt/ *verb*
1 🔑 [I] **~ (to sth) (by doing sth)** to change or behave in a particular way as a result of or in response to sth: *Local residents have reacted angrily to the news. ◇ I nudged her but she didn't react. ◇ You never know how he is going to react. ◇ The market reacted by falling a further two points.* **2** 🔑 [I] (**+ adv./prep.**) to become ill/sick after eating, breathing, etc. a particular substance: *People can react badly to certain food additives.* **3** [I] **~ (with sth)** | **~ (together)** (*chemistry*) (of substances) to experience a chemical change when coming into contact with another substance: *Iron reacts with water and air to produce rust.*

PHR V **reˌact aˈgainst sb/sth** to show dislike or opposition in response to sth, especially by deliberately doing the opposite of what sb wants you to do: *He reacted strongly against the artistic conventions of his time.*

react·ance /riˈæktəns/ *noun* [U, C] (*physics*) (*symb.* X) the opposition of a piece of electrical equipment, etc. to the flow of an ALTERNATING CURRENT ➲ compare RESISTANCE

react·ant /riˈæktənt/ *noun* (*chemistry*) a substance that takes part in and is changed by a chemical reaction

re·ac·tion 🔑 AW /riˈækʃn/ *noun*

▸ TO EVENT/SITUATION **1** 🔑 [C, U] **~ (to sb/sth)** what you do, say or think as a result of sth that has happened: *What was his reaction to the news? ◇ My **immediate reaction** was one of shock. ◇ A spokesman said the changes were not **in reaction to** the company's recent losses. ◇ There has been a **mixed reaction** to her appointment as director. ◇ The decision provoked an angry reaction from local residents. ◇ I tried shaking him but there was no reaction.*

▸ CHANGE IN ATTITUDES **2** 🔑 [C, usually sing., U] **~ (against sth)** a change in people's attitudes or behaviour caused by disapproval of the attitudes, etc. of the past: *The return to traditional family values is a reaction against the permissiveness of recent decades.*

▸ TO DRUGS **3** 🔑 [C, U] a response by the body, usually a bad one, to a drug, chemical substance, etc: *to have an **allergic reaction** to a drug*

R

▸ TO DANGER **4** ⊶ **reactions** [pl.] the ability to move quickly in response to sth, especially if in danger: *a skilled driver with quick reactions*
▸ SCIENCE **5** ⊶ [C, U] (*chemistry*) a chemical change produced by two or more substances acting on each other: *a **chemical/nuclear reaction*** ➲ see also CHAIN REACTION **6** [U, C] (*physics*) a force shown by sth in response to another force, which is of equal strength and acts in the opposite direction
▸ AGAINST PROGRESS **7** [U] opposition to social or political progress or change: *The forces of reaction made change difficult.*

re·ac·tion·ary AW /ri'ækʃənri; *NAmE* -neri/ *noun* (*pl.* -ies) (*disapproving*) a person who is opposed to political or social change ▸ **re·ac·tion·ary** *adj.*: *a reactionary government*

re·acti·vate AW /ri'æktɪveɪt/ *verb* **~ sth** to make sth start working or happening again after a period of time ▸ **re·acti·va·tion** AW /ri,æktɪ'veɪʃn/ *noun* [U]

re·act·ive AW /ri'æktɪv/ *adj.* **1** (*formal*) showing a reaction or response: *The police presented a reactive rather than preventive strategy against crime.* ➲ compare PROACTIVE **2** (*chemistry*) tending to show chemical change when mixed with another substance: *highly reactive substances*

re·activ·ity /,ri:æk'tɪvɪti/ *adj.* (*chemistry*) the degree to which sth reacts, or is likely to react: *Oxygen has high reactivity.*

re·act·or AW /ri'æktə(r)/ (also **,nuclear re'actor**) *noun* a large structure used for the controlled production of nuclear energy

read ⊶ *verb* /ri:d/ *noun* /ri:d/ *adj.* /red/
▪ ***verb*** /ri:d/ (**read**, **read** /red/)
▸ WORDS/SYMBOLS **1** ⊶ [I, T] (not used in the progressive tenses) to look at and understand the meaning of written or printed words or symbols: *She's still learning to read.* ◇ *Some children can read and write before they go to school.* ◇ **~ sth** *I can't read your writing.* ◇ *Can you read music?* ◇ *I'm trying to read the map.* **2** ⊶ [I, T] to go through written or printed words, etc. in silence or speaking them to other people: *I'm going to go to bed and read.* ◇ **~ to sb/yourself** *He liked reading to his grandchildren.* ◇ **~ sth** *to read a book/a magazine/the newspaper* ◇ *Have you read any Steinbeck* (= novels by him)? ◇ *He read the poem aloud.* ◇ **~ sth to sb/yourself** *Go on—read it to us.* ◇ **~ sb sth** *She read us a story.* ➲ see also PROOFREAD
▸ DISCOVER BY READING **3** ⊶ [I, T] (not used in the progressive tenses) to discover or find out about sb/sth by reading: **~ about/of sth** *I read about the accident in the local paper.* ◇ **~ that...** *I read that he had resigned.* ◇ **~ sth** *Don't believe everything you read in the papers.*
▸ SB'S MIND/THOUGHTS **4** [T] **~ sb's mind/thoughts** to guess what sb else is thinking
▸ SB'S LIPS **5** [T] **~ sb's lips** to look at the movements of sb's lips to learn what they are saying ➲ see also LIP-READ
▸ UNDERSTAND **6** [T] to understand sth in a particular way SYN **interpret**: **~ sth** *How do you read the present situation?* ◇ **~ sth as sth** *Silence must not always be read as consent.*
▸ OF A PIECE OF WRITING **7** [T] **+ speech** to have sth written on it; to be written in a particular way: *The sign read 'No admittance'.* ◇ *I've changed the last paragraph. It now reads as follows...* **8** [I] **+ adv./prep.** to give a particular impression when read: *Generally, the article reads very well.* ◇ *The poem reads like* (= sounds as if it is) *a translation.*
▸ MEASURING INSTRUMENT **9** [T] **~ sth** (of measuring instruments) to show a particular weight, pressure, etc: *What does the thermometer read?* **10** [T] **~ sth** to get information from a measuring instrument: *A man came to read the gas meter.*
▸ HEAR **11** [T] **~ sb** to hear and understand sb speaking on a radio set: *'Do you read me?' 'I'm reading you loud and clear.'*
▸ REPLACE WORD **12** [T] **~ A for B** | **~ B as A** to replace one word, etc. with another when correcting a text: *For 'madam' in line 3 read 'madman'.*
▸ SUBJECT AT UNIVERSITY **13** [T, I] (*BrE*, rather *old-fashioned*) to study a subject, especially at a university: **~ sth** *I read English at Oxford.* ◇ **~ for sth** *She's reading for a law degree.*
▸ COMPUTING **14** [T] (of a computer or the person using it) to take information from a disk: **~ sth** *My computer can't read the CD-ROM you sent.* ◇ **~ sth into sth** *to read a file into a computer*
IDM **,read between the 'lines** to look for or discover a meaning in sth that is not openly stated: *Reading between the lines, I think Clare needs money.* **,read sb like a 'book** to understand easily what sb is thinking or feeling **,read my 'lips** (*informal*) used to tell sb to listen carefully to what you are saying: *Read my lips: no new taxes* (= I promise there will be no new taxes). **,read (sb) the 'Riot Act** (*BrE*) to tell sb with force that they must not do sth ORIGIN From an Act of Parliament passed in 1715 to prevent riots. It made it illegal for a group of twelve or more people to refuse to split up if they were ordered to do so and part of the Act was read to them. **,take it/sth as 'read** (*BrE*) to accept sth without discussing it: *Can we take it as read that you want the job?*
PHR V **,read sth↔'back** to read a message, etc. to others in order to check that it is correct **,read sth 'into sth** to think that sth means more than it really does: *Don't read too much into what she says.* **,read 'on** to continue reading: *That's the story so far. Now read on...* **,read sth↔'out** ⊶ to read sth using your voice, especially to other people **,read sth↔'over/'through** ⊶ to read sth carefully from beginning to end to look for mistakes or check details **,read sth↔'up** | **,read 'up on sb/sth** to read a lot about a subject: *I'll need to read up on the case before the meeting.*
▪ ***noun*** /ri:d/ [sing.] (*informal*) **1** (*especially BrE*) an act or a period of reading sth: *I was having a quiet read when the phone rang.* **2 a good, interesting, etc. ~** a book, an article, etc. that is good, etc: *His thrillers are always a gripping read.*
▪ ***adj.*** /red/ (used after an adverb) (of a person) having knowledge that has been gained from reading books, etc: *She's very widely read in law.* ➲ see also WELL READ

read·able /'ri:dəbl/ *adj.* **1** (of a book, an article, etc.) that is easy, interesting and enjoyable to read **2** (of written or printed words) clear and easy to read SYN **legible** ➲ see also MACHINE-READABLE ▸ **read·abil·ity** /,ri:də'bɪləti/ *noun* [U]

re·address /,ri:ə'dres/ *verb* **~ sth** to change the address written on an envelope because the person the letter is for does not live at the address it has been delivered to

read·er ⊶ /'ri:də(r)/ *noun*
1 ⊶ a person who reads, especially one who reads a lot or in a particular way: *an avid reader of science fiction* ◇ *a **fast/slow reader*** ◇ *The reader is left to draw his or her own conclusions.* ➲ COLLOCATIONS at LITERATURE **2** ⊶ a person who reads a particular newspaper, magazine, etc: *readers' letters* ◇ *Are you a 'Times' reader?* **3** an easy book that is intended to help people learn to read their own or a foreign language: *a series of graded English readers* **4** (usually **Reader**) a senior teacher at a British university just below the rank of a professor: *She is Reader in Music at Edinburgh.* **5** (*computing*) an electronic device that reads data stored in one form and changes it into another form so that a computer can perform operations on it **6** (*technical*) a machine that produces on a screen a large image of a text stored on a MICROFICHE or MICROFILM ➲ see also MIND-READER, NEWSREADER

read·er·ship /'ri:dəʃɪp; *NAmE* -dərʃ-/ *noun* **1** [usually sing.] the number or type of people who read a particular newspaper, magazine, etc: *a readership of around 10 000* ◇ *In its new format, the magazine hopes to attract a much wider readership.* **2** (usually **Readership**) **~ (in sth)** (*BrE*) the position of a READER at a university

read·ily /'redɪli/ *adv.* **1** quickly and without difficulty SYN **freely**: *All ingredients are **readily available** from your local store.* **2** in a way that shows you do not object to sth SYN **willingly**: *Most people readily accept the need for laws.*

'read-in *noun* **1** [U, C] (*computing*) the entry of data into a computer or onto a disk **2** [C] (*NAmE*) an organized event when people come to a place to read books together

readi·ness /ˈredinəs/ *noun* **1** [U] **~ (for sth)** the state of being ready or prepared for sth: *Everyone has doubts about their readiness for parenthood.* **2** [U, sing.] **~ (of sb) (to do sth)** the state of being willing to do sth: *Over half the people interviewed expressed their readiness to die for their country.*

read·ing 0-w /ˈriːdɪŋ/ *noun*
▸ ACTIVITY **1** 0-w [U] the activity of sb who reads: *My hobbies include reading and painting.* ◇ *He needs more help with his reading.* ◇ *Are you any good at map reading?* ◇ ***reading glasses*** (= worn when reading) ◇ *a* ***reading lamp/light*** (= one that can be moved to shine light onto sth that you are reading) **2** [sing.] an act of reading sth: *A closer* (= more detailed) *reading of the text reveals just how desperate he was feeling.*
▸ BOOKS/ARTICLES **3** 0-w [U] books, articles, etc. that are intended to be read: ***reading matter/material*** ◇ *a series of* ***reading books*** *for children* ◇ *a* ***reading list*** (= a list of books, etc. that students are expected to read for a particular subject) ◇ ***further reading*** (= at the end of a book, a list of other books that give more information about the same subject) ◇ *The report makes for interesting reading* (= it is interesting to read) ◇ *The article is not exactly* ***light reading*** (= it is not easy to read).
▸ WAY OF UNDERSTANDING **4** [C] **~ (of sth)** the particular way in which you understand a book, situation, etc. SYN **interpretation**: *a literal reading of the text* ◇ *My own reading of events is less optimistic.*
▸ MEASUREMENT **5** 0-w [C] the amount or number shown on an instrument used for measuring sth: *Meter readings are taken every three months.*
▸ EVENT **6** [C] an event at which sth is read to an audience for entertainment; a piece of literature that is read at such an event: *a poetry reading* ◇ *The evening ended with a reading from her latest novel.*
▸ FROM BIBLE **7** [C] a short section from the Bible that is read to people as part of a religious service: *The reading today is from the Book of Daniel.*
▸ IN PARLIAMENT **8** [C] one of the stages during which a BILL (= a proposal for a new law) must be discussed and accepted by a parliament before it can become law

ˈreading age *noun* a person's ability to read, measured by comparing it with the average ability of children of a particular age: *a 30-year-old man with a reading age of eight*

ˈreading group *noun* = BOOK GROUP

ˈreading room *noun* a room in a library, club, etc. where people can read or study

re·adjust AW /ˌriːəˈdʒʌst/ *verb* **1** [I] to get used to a changed or new situation: *Children are highly adaptable—they just need time to readjust.* ◇ **~ to sth/doing sth** *Once again he had to readjust to living alone.* **2** [T] **~ sth** to change or move sth slightly: *She got out of the car and readjusted her dress.* ▸ **re·adjust·ment** AW *noun* [C, U]: *He has made a number of readjustments to his technique.* ◇ *a painful period of readjustment*

re·admit /ˌriːədˈmɪt/ *verb* (-tt-) [often passive] **1 ~ sb (to sth)** to allow sb to join a group, an organization or an institution again **2 ~ sb (to sth)** to take sb into a hospital again after they had been allowed to leave: *He was readmitted only a week after being discharged.* ▸ **re·admis·sion** /ˌriːədˈmɪʃn/ *noun* [U, C] **~ (to sth)**

ˌread-only ˈmemory *noun* [U] (*computing*) = ROM

ˈread-out *noun* (*computing*) a display of information on a computer screen ➲ compare PRINTOUT

ˈread-through *noun* an occasion when the words of a play are spoken by members of a theatre group, before they begin practising acting it

ˌre-ˈadvertise *verb* [T, I] **~ (sth)** to advertise sth again, especially a job

ready 0-w /ˈredi/ *adj., verb, adv., noun*
■ ***adj.*** (read·ier, readi·est)
▸ PREPARED/AVAILABLE **1** 0-w [not before noun] fully prepared for what you are going to do: *Are you nearly ready?* ◇ *'Shall we go?' 'I'm* ***ready when you are****!'* ◇ **~ for sth** *I'm just getting the kids* ***ready*** *for school.* ◇ *I was twenty years old and* ***ready for anything.*** ◇ **~ to do sth** *Right, we're ready to go.* ◇ *Volunteers were* ***ready and waiting*** *to pack the food in boxes.* **2** 0-w [not before noun] completed and available to be used: *Come on, dinner's ready!* ◇ *The new building should be ready by 2015.* ◇ **~ for sth** *Can you help me* ***get*** *everything* ***ready*** *for the party?* ◇ **~ to do sth** *The contract will be ready to sign in two weeks.* **3** available to be used easily and immediately: *All the relevant records are easily available* ***ready to hand.*** ◇ *a ready supply of wood* ◇ *a ready source of income* ➲ see also READILY, READINESS, ROUGH-AND-READY
▸ WILLING **4** [not before noun] willing and quick to do or give sth: **~ for sth** *I was very angry and ready for a fight.* ◇ **~ with sth** *She's always ready with advice.* ◇ **~ to do sth** *He's always ready to help his friends.* ◇ *Don't be so ready to believe the worst about people.*
▸ LIKELY TO DO STH **5 ~ to do sth** likely to do sth very soon SYN **on the point of**: *She looked ready to collapse at any minute.*
▸ NEEDING STH **6 ~ for sth** needing sth as soon as possible: *Right, I'm ready for bed.* ◇ *After the long walk, we were all ready for a drink.*
▸ QUICK/CLEVER **7** [only before noun] quick and clever: *She has great charm and a ready wit.*
IDM **make ˈready (for sth)** (*formal*) to prepare: *to make ready for the President's visit* **ready, steady, ˈgo!** (*BrE*) (also **(get) ready, (get) set, ˈgo** *NAmE, BrE*) what you say to tell people to start a race **ˌready to ˈroll** (*informal*) ready to start
■ ***verb*** (read·ies, ready·ing, read·ied, read·ied) **~ sb/yourself/sth (for sth)** | **~ sb/yourself/sth (to do sth)** (*formal*) to prepare sb/yourself/sth for sth: *Western companies were readying themselves for the challenge from Eastern markets.*
■ ***adv.*** (used before a past participle, especially in compounds) already done: *ready-cooked meals* ◇ *The concrete was ready mixed.*
■ ***noun* the ready** [sing.] (also **read·ies** [pl.]) (*BrE, informal*) money that you can use immediately
IDM **at the ˈready** available to be used immediately: *We all had our cameras at the ready.*

ˌready-ˈmade *adj.* **1** prepared in advance so that you can eat or use it immediately: *ready-made pastry* **2** (*old-fashioned*) (especially of clothes) made in standard sizes, not to the measurements of a particular customer: *a ready-made suit* **3** already provided for you so you do not need to produce or think about it yourself: *When he married her he also took on a ready-made family.*

ˌready ˈmeal *noun* (*BrE*) a meal that you buy already prepared and which only needs to be heated before you eat it

ˌready-ˈmixed *adj.* already mixed and ready to use: *ready-mixed concrete*

ˌready ˈmoney (also **ˌready ˈcash**) *noun* [U] (*informal*) money in the form of coins and notes that you can spend immediately

ˌready-to-ˈwear *adj.* (of clothes) made in standard sizes, not to the measurements of a particular customer

re·affirm /ˌriːəˈfɜːm; *NAmE* -ˈfɜːrm/ *verb* **~ sth** to state sth again in order to emphasize that it is still true ▸ **re·affirm·ation** /ˌriːˌæfəˈmeɪʃn; *NAmE* -fərˈm-/ *noun* [C, U]

re·affor·estation /ˌriːəˌfɒrɪˈsteɪʃn; *NAmE* -ˌfɔːr-/ *noun* [U] (*BrE, technical*) = REFORESTATION

re·agent /riˈeɪdʒənt/ *noun* (*chemistry*) a substance used to cause a chemical reaction, especially in order to find out if another substance is present

real 0-w /ˈriːəl; *BrE* usually rɪəl/ *adj., adv.*
■ ***adj.***
▸ EXISTING/NOT IMAGINED **1** 0-w actually existing or happening and not imagined or pretended: *It wasn't a ghost; it was a real person.* ◇ *pictures of animals, both real and mythological* ◇ *In the movies guns kill people instantly, but it's not like that* ***in real life.*** ◇ *Politicians seem to be out of touch with* ***the real world.*** ◇ *The growth of violent crime is a very real problem.* ◇ *There's no real possibility of them changing their minds.* ◇ *We have a real chance of success.*
▸ TRUE/GENUINE **2** 0-w genuine and not false or artificial: *Are*

R

those *real flowers?* ◇ *real leather* **3** 🔑 [only before noun] actual or true, rather than what appears to be true: *Tell me the real reason.* ◇ *Bono's real name is Paul Hewson.* ◇ *See the real Africa on one of our walking safaris.* ◇ *I couldn't resist the opportunity to meet a* ***real live*** *celebrity.* **4** 🔑 [only before noun] having all the important qualities that it should have to deserve to be called what it is called: *She never had any real friends at school.* ◇ *his first real kiss* ◇ *I had no real interest in politics.* ◇ *He was making a real effort to be nice to her.* ◇ *She has not shown any real regret for what she did.*
▸ FOR EMPHASIS **5** 🔑 [only before noun] used to emphasize a state or quality: *He looks a real idiot.* ◇ *This accident could have produced a real tragedy.* ◇ *Her next play was a real contrast.*
▸ MONEY/INCOME **6** [only before noun] when the effect of such things as price rises on the power of money to buy things is included in the sums: *Real wage costs have risen by 10% in the past year.* ◇ *This represents a reduction of 5%* ***in real terms.***
IDM **for 'real** genuine or serious: *This is not a fire drill—it's for real.* ◇ (*NAmE*) *He managed to convince voters that he was for real.* **get 'real!** (*informal*) used to tell sb that they are behaving in a stupid or unreasonable way **keep it 'real** (*informal*) to act in an honest and natural way **the ,real 'thing** (*informal*) the genuine thing: *Are you sure it's the real thing* (= love), *not just infatuation?* ➲ more at McCoy, POWER *n.*
■ ***adv.*** (*NAmE, ScotE, informal*) very: *That tastes real good.* ◇ *He's a real nice guy.* ◇ *I'm real sorry.*

,real 'ale *noun* [U, C] (*BrE*) a type of beer that is made and stored in the traditional way

'real estate *noun* [U] (*especially NAmE*) **1** (also **realty**) property in the form of land or buildings: *My father sold real estate.* ➲ COLLOCATIONS at HOUSE **2** the business of selling houses or land for building: *to work in real estate*

'real estate agent (also **Real·tor™**) (both *NAmE*) (*BrE* **e'state agent**) *noun* a person whose job is to sell houses and land for people

realia /reɪ'ɑːliə; ri'eɪliə/ *noun* [U] ordinary objects used in a class for teaching purposes

re·align /,riːə'laɪn/ *verb* **1 ~ sth** to change the position or direction of sth slightly: *The road was realigned to improve visibility.* **2 ~ sth** to make changes to sth in order to adapt it to a new situation: *The company has been forced to realign its operations in the area.* **3 ~ yourself (with sb/sth)** to change your opinions, policies, etc. so that they are the same as those of another person, group, etc: *The rebel MPs have realigned themselves with the opposition party.* ▸ **re·align·ment** *noun* [U, C]: **~ (of sth)** *the realignment of personal goals* ◇ *political realignments*

real·ism /'riːəlɪzəm; *BrE* also 'rɪəl-/ *noun* [U] **1** a way of seeing, accepting and dealing with situations as they really are without being influenced by your emotions or false hopes: *There was a new mood of realism among the leaders at the peace talks.* **2** (of novels, paintings, films/movies, etc.) the quality of being very like real life **3** (also **Realism**) a style in art or literature that shows things and people as they are in real life ➲ compare IDEALISM, ROMANTICISM

real·ist /'riːəlɪst; *BrE* also 'rɪə-/ *noun* **1** a person who accepts and deals with a situation as it really is and does not try to pretend that it is different: *I'm a realist—I know you can't change people overnight.* **2** a writer, painter, etc. whose work represents things as they are in real life

real·is·tic 🔑 /,riːə'lɪstɪk; *BrE* also ,rɪə-/ *adj.*
1 🔑 accepting in a sensible way what it is actually possible to do or achieve in a particular situation: *a realistic assessment* ◇ *We have to* ***be realistic*** *about our chances of winning.* ◇ *It is not realistic to expect people to spend so much money.* **2** 🔑 sensible and appropriate; possible to achieve SYN **feasible, viable**: *We must set realistic goals.* ◇ *a realistic target* ◇ *to pay a realistic salary* **3** 🔑 representing things as they are in real life: *a realistic drawing* ◇ *We try to make these training courses as realistic as possible.* OPP **unrealistic**

real·is·tic·al·ly /,riːə'lɪstɪkli; *BrE* also ,rɪə-/ *adv.* **1** used to say what you think can actually be achieved in a particular situation: *Realistically, there is little prospect of a ceasefire.* **2** in a way that shows sb accepts in a sensible way what it is actually possible to do or achieve: *How many can you realistically hope to sell?* ◇ *Kate spoke realistically about the task ahead.* **3** in a way that represents things as they are in real life: *a fireplace with realistically glowing coals*

real·ity 🔑 /ri'æləti/ *noun* (*pl.* -ies)
1 🔑 [U] the true situation and the problems that actually exist in life, in contrast to how you would like life to be: *She refuses to* ***face reality.*** ◇ *You're* ***out of touch with reality.*** ◇ *The reality is that there is not enough money to pay for this project.* **2** 🔑 [C] a thing that is actually experienced or seen, in contrast to what people might imagine: *the* ***harsh realities of*** *life* ◇ *This decision reflects the realities of the political situation.* ◇ *Will time travel ever* ***become a reality?*** **3** [U] **~ television/TV/shows/series/contestants** television/shows, etc. that use real people (not actors) in real situations, presented as entertainment: *a reality TV star* ◇ *the reality show 'Big Brother'*
IDM **in re'ality** 🔑 used to say that a situation is different from what has just been said or from what people believe: *Outwardly she seemed confident but in reality she felt extremely nervous.* ➲ see also VIRTUAL REALITY

re'ality check *noun* [usually sing.] (*informal*) an occasion when you are reminded of how things are in the real world, rather than how you would like things to be

re,ality T'V *noun* [U] television shows that are based on real people (not actors) in real situations, presented as entertainment

real·iz·able (*BrE* also **-is·able**) /'riːəlaɪzəbl; *BrE* also 'rɪə-/ *adj.* **1** possible to achieve or make happen SYN **achievable**: *realizable objectives* **2** that can be sold and turned into money: *realizable assets*

real·iza·tion (*BrE* also **-isa·tion**) /,riːəlaɪ'zeɪʃn; ,rɪəl-; *NAmE* ,riːələ'z-/ *noun* **1** [U, sing.] the process of becoming aware of sth SYN **awareness**: **~ (of sth)** *the sudden realization of what she had done* ◇ **~ (that...)** *There is a growing realization that changes must be made.* **2** [U] **~ (of sth)** the process of achieving a particular aim, etc. SYN **achievement**: *It was the realization of his greatest ambition.* **3** [U] **~ of your assets** (*formal*) the act of selling sth that you own, such as property, in order to get the money that you need for sth **4** [U, C] **~ (of sth)** (*formal*) the act of producing a sound, play, design, etc; or the thing that is produced

real·ize 🔑 (*BrE* also **-ise**) /'riːəlaɪz; *BrE* also 'rɪəl-/ *verb*
▸ BE/BECOME AWARE **1** 🔑 [T, I] (not used in the progressive tenses) to understand or become aware of a particular fact or situation: **~ (that)...** *I didn't realize (that) you were so unhappy.* ◇ *The moment I saw her, I realized something was wrong.* ◇ **~ how, what, etc...** *I don't think you realize how important this is to her.* ◇ **~ (sth)** *I hope you realize the seriousness of this crime.* ◇ *Only later did she realize her mistake.* ◇ *The situation was more complicated than they had at first realized.* ◇ *They managed to leave without any of us realizing.* ◇ **it is realized that...** *There was a cheer when it was realized that everyone was safely back.*
▸ ACHIEVE STH **2** 🔑 [T] **~ sth** to achieve sth important that you very much want to do: *She never realized her ambition of becoming a professional singer.* ◇ *We try to help all students* ***realize their full potential*** (= be as successful as they are able to be).
▸ HAPPEN **3** [T, usually passive] **~ sth** if sb's fears **are realized**, the things that they are afraid will happen, do happen: *His worst fears were realized when he saw that the door had been forced open.*
▸ SELL **4** [T] **~ your assets** (*formal*) to sell things that you own, for example property, in order to get the money that you need for sth SYN **convert** **5** [T] **~ sth** (*formal*) (of goods, etc.) to be sold for a particular amount of money SYN **make**: *The paintings realized $2 million at auction.*
▸ MAKE STH REAL **6** [T] **~ sth** (*formal*) to produce sth that can

R

be seen or heard, based on written information or instructions: *The stage designs have been beautifully realized.*

ˌreal-ˈlife *adj.* [only before noun] actually happening or existing in life, not in books, stories or films/movies: *a novel based on real-life events* ◇ *a real-life Romeo and Juliet* OPP **fictional**

re·allo·cate /ˌriːˈæləkeɪt/ *verb* **~ sth (to sb/sth)** to change the way money or materials are shared between different people, groups, projects, etc. SYN **redistribute** ▸ **re·allo·ca·tion** /ˌriːˌæləˈkeɪʃn/ *noun* [U]

real·ly 🔑 /ˈriːəli; *BrE* also ˈrɪəli/ *adv.*
1 🔑 used to say what is actually the fact or the truth about sth: *What do you really think about it?* ◇ *Tell me what really happened.* ◇ *They are not really my aunt and uncle.* ◇ *I can't believe I am really going to meet the princess.* **2** 🔑 used to emphasize sth you are saying or an opinion you are giving: *I want to help, I really do.* ◇ *Now I really must go.* ◇ *I really don't mind.* ◇ *He really likes you.* ◇ *I* **really and truly** *am in love this time.* **3** 🔑 used to emphasize an adjective or adverb: *a really hot fire* ◇ *I'm really sorry.* **4** 🔑 used, often in negative sentences, to reduce the force of sth you are saying: *I don't really agree with that.* ◇ *It doesn't really matter.* ◇ *'Did you enjoy the book?' '***Not really***'* (= 'no' or 'not very much'). HELP The position of **really** can change the meaning of the sentence. **I don't really know** means that you are not sure about something; **I really don't know** emphasizes that you do not know. (Look at sense 2.) **5** 🔑 used in questions and negative sentences when you want sb to say 'no': *Do you really expect me to believe that?* ◇ *I don't really need to go, do I?* **6** 🔑 used to express interest in or surprise at what sb is saying: *'We're going to Japan next month.' 'Oh, really?'* ◇ *'She's resigned.' 'Really? Are you sure?'* **7** used to show that you disapprove of sth sb has done: *Really, you could have told us before.*

realm /relm/ *noun* **1** an area of activity, interest, or knowledge: *in the realm of literature* ◇ *At the end of the speech he seemed to be moving* **into the realms of** *fantasy.* **2** (*formal*) a country ruled by a king or queen SYN **kingdom**: *the defence of the realm*
IDM **beyond/within the realms of possibility** not possible/possible: *A successful outcome is not beyond the realms of possibility.*

ˌreal ˈnumber *noun* (*mathematics*) any number that is not an IMAGINARY NUMBER ➲ compare COMPLEX NUMBER

real·poli·tik /reɪˈɑːlpɒlɪtiːk; *NAmE* -pɑːl-/ *noun* [U] (from *German*) a system of politics that is based on the actual situation and needs of a country or political party rather than on moral principles

ˈreal tennis (*BrE*) (*NAmE* **ˈcourt tennis**) (*AustralE* **ˈroyal tennis**) *noun* [U] an old form of tennis played inside a building with a hard ball

ˌreal ˈtime *noun* [U] (*computing*) the fact that there is only a very short time between a computer system receiving information and dealing with it: *To make the training realistic the simulation operates* **in real time**. ◇ *real-time missile guidance systems*

real·tone /ˈriːəltəʊn; *BrE* usually ˈrɪəl-; *NAmE* -toʊn/ *noun* (*BrE*) a part of a song or other recording that is used as the sound a MOBILE/CELL PHONE makes when it rings: *Get the top realtones from the best artists delivered instantly to your mobile.*

Real·tor™ (also **real·tor**) /ˈriːəltə(r)/ *noun* (*NAmE*) = REAL ESTATE AGENT

realty /ˈriːəlti/ *noun* [U] (*especially NAmE*) = REAL ESTATE

ˈreal-world *adj.* existing in the real world and not specially invented for a particular purpose: *Teachers need to prepare their students to deal with real-world situations outside the classroom.*

ream /riːm/ *noun, verb*
■ *noun* **1 reams** [pl.] (*informal*) a large quantity of writing: *She wrote reams in the exam.* **2** [C] (*technical*) 500 sheets of paper
■ *verb* **~ sb** (*NAmE, informal*) to treat sb unfairly or cheat them: *We got reamed on that deal.*
PHR V **ˌream sb↔ˈout** (*NAmE, informal*) to criticize sb strongly because they have done sth wrong

re·ani·mate /riːˈænɪmeɪt/ *verb* **~ sb/sth** (*formal*) to give sb/sth new life or energy

reap /riːp/ *verb* **1** [T] **~ sth** to obtain sth, especially sth good, as a direct result of sth that you have done: *They are now reaping the rewards of all their hard work.* **2** [I, T] **~ (sth)** to cut and collect a crop, especially WHEAT, from a field SYN **harvest**
IDM **reap a/the ˈharvest** (*BrE*) to benefit or suffer as a direct result of sth that you have done **you ˌreap what you ˈsow** (*saying*) you have to deal with the bad effects or results of sth that you originally started

reap·er /ˈriːpə(r)/ *noun* a person or a machine that cuts and collects crops on a farm ➲ see also THE GRIM REAPER

re·appear /ˌriːəˈpɪə(r); *NAmE* -ˈpɪr/ *verb* [I] to appear again after not being heard of or seen for a period of time: *She went upstairs and did not reappear until morning.* ▸ **re·appear·ance** /-rəns/ *noun* [U, sing.]

re·apply /ˌriːəˈplaɪ/ *verb* (**re·applies, re·apply·ing, re·applied, re·applied**) **1** [T] **~ sth** to put another layer of a substance on a surface: *Sunblock should be reapplied every hour.* **2** [I] **~ (for sth)** to make another formal request for sth: *Previous applicants for the post need not reapply.* **3** [T] **~ sth** to use sth again, especially in a different situation: *Students are taught a number of skills that can be reapplied throughout their studies.*

re·appoint /ˌriːəˈpɔɪnt/ *verb* **~ sb (as) sth | ~ sb + noun | ~ sb (to sth)** to give sb the job that they used to have in the past: *After the trial he was reappointed (as) treasurer.* ▸ **re·appoint·ment** *noun* [U]

re·appraisal /ˌriːəˈpreɪzl/ *noun* [C, usually sing., U] the act of examining sth again to see if it needs to be changed SYN **reassessment**

re·appraise /ˌriːəˈpreɪz/ *verb* **~ sth/sb** (*formal*) to think again about the value or nature of sth/sb to see if your opinion about it/them should be changed SYN **reassess**

rear 🔑 /rɪə(r); *NAmE* rɪr/ *noun, adj., verb*
■ *noun* **1** 🔑 (usually **the rear**) [sing.] the back part of sth: *A trailer was attached to the rear of the truck.* ◇ *There are toilets at both* **front and rear** *of the plane.* ◇ *A high gate blocks the only entrance* **to the rear**. ➲ note at BACK **2** (also **ˌrear ˈend**) [C, usually sing.] (*informal*) the part of the body that you sit on SYN **bottom**: *a kick in the rear*
IDM **ˌbring up the ˈrear** to be at the back of a line of people, or last in a race
■ *adj.* 🔑 [only before noun] at or near the back of sth: *front and rear windows* ◇ *the rear entrance of the building*
■ *verb* **1** [T] **~ sb/sth** [often passive] to care for young children or animals until they are fully grown SYN **bring sb up, raise**: *She reared a family of five on her own.* **2** [T] **~ sth** to breed or keep animals or birds, for example on a farm: *to rear cattle* **3** [I] **~ (up)** (of an animal, especially a horse) to raise itself on its back legs, with the front legs in the air: *The horse reared, throwing its rider.* **4** [I] **~ (up)** (of sth large) to seem to lean over you, especially in a threatening way: *The great bulk of the building reared up against the night sky.*
IDM **sth rears its (ugly) ˈhead** if sth unpleasant **rears its head** or **rears its ugly head**, it appears or happens
PHR V **ˈrear sb/sth on sth** [usually passive] to give a person or an animal a particular type of food, entertainment, etc. while they are young: *I was the son of sailors and reared on stories of the sea.*

ˌrear ˈadmiral *noun* an officer of very high rank in the navy: *Rear Admiral Baines*

ˈrear-end *verb* **~ sth/sb** (*informal, especially NAmE*) (of a vehicle or driver) to drive into the back of another vehicle

rear·guard /ˈrɪəɡɑːd; *NAmE* ˈrɪrɡɑːrd/ *noun* (usually **the rearguard**) [sing.+ sing./pl. v.] a group of soldiers that protect the back part of an army especially when the army is RETREATING after it has been defeated OPP **vanguard**

R

ˌ**rearguard ˈaction** *noun* [usually sing.] a struggle to change or stop sth even when it is not likely that you will succeed: *They have been* ***fighting a rearguard action*** *for two years to stop their house being demolished.*

rear·ing /ˈrɪərɪŋ; *NAmE* ˈrɪrɪŋ/ *noun* [U] **1** the process of caring for children as they grow up, teaching them how to behave as members of society **2** the process of breeding animals or birds and caring for them as they grow: *livestock rearing*

rearm /riˈɑːm; *NAmE* -ˈɑːrm/ *verb* [I, T] to obtain, or supply sb with, new or better weapons, armies, etc: *The country was forbidden to rearm under the terms of the treaty.* ◇ **~ sb** *Rebel troops were being rearmed.* ▶ **re·arma·ment** /riˈɑːməmənt; *NAmE* -ˈɑːrm-/ *noun* [U]

rear·most /ˈrɪəməʊst; *NAmE* ˈrɪrmoʊst/ *adj.* (*formal*) furthest back: *the rearmost section of the aircraft*

re·arrange /ˌriːəˈreɪndʒ/ *verb* **1 ~ sth** to change the position or order of things; to change your position: *We've rearranged the furniture in the bedroom.* ◇ *She rearranged herself in another pose.* **2 ~ sth** to change the time, date or place of an event SYN **reschedule**: *Can we rearrange the meeting for next Tuesday at 2?* ▶ **re·arrange·ment** *noun* [C, U]

ˌ**rear-view ˈmirror** *noun* a mirror in which a driver can see the traffic behind ➲ VISUAL VOCAB page V42

rear·ward /ˈrɪəwəd; *NAmE* ˈrɪrwərd/ *adj.* (*formal*) at or near the back of sth: *rearward seats*

ˌ**rear-wheel ˈdrive** *noun* [U] a system in which power from the engine is sent to the back wheels of a vehicle ➲ compare FRONT-WHEEL DRIVE

rea·son 🔑 /ˈriːzn/ *noun, verb*

■ ***noun*** **1** 🔑 [C] a cause or an explanation for sth that has happened or that sb has done: **~ (why…)** *I'd like to know the reason why you're so late.* ◇ *Give me* ***one good reason*** *why I should help you.* ◇ **~ (that…)** *We aren't going for the* ***simple reason*** *that we can't afford it.* ◇ **~ (for sth)** *She gave no reasons for her decision.* ◇ **~ (for doing sth)** *I have no particular reason for doubting him.* ◇ *He said no but he didn't* ***give a reason.*** ◇ ***For some reason*** (= one that I don't know or don't understand) *we all have to come in early tomorrow.* ◇ *The man attacked me* ***for no apparent reason.*** ◇ *She resigned for* ***personal reasons.*** ◇ ***For reasons of*** *security the door is always kept locked.* ◇ *He wants to keep them all in his office* ***for reasons best known to himself.*** ◇ *people who,* ***for whatever reason,*** *are unable to support themselves* ◇ *'Why do you want to know?'* ***'No reason'*** (= I do not want to say why). ◇ *'Why did she do that?' 'She must* ***have her reasons'*** (= secret reasons which she does not want to tell). ◇ (*formal*) *He was excused* ***by reason of*** (= because of) *his age.* ➲ LANGUAGE BANK at THEREFORE **2** 🔑 [U] a fact that makes it right or fair to do sth: **~ (to do sth)** *They have reason to believe that he is lying.* ◇ *We* ***have every reason*** (= have very good reasons) *to feel optimistic.* ◇ **~ (why…)** *There is no reason why we should agree to this.* ◇ **~ (for sth/for doing sth)** *This result gives us* ***all the more reason*** *for optimism.* ◇ *She complained,* ***with reason*** (= rightly), *that she had been underpaid.* **3** 🔑 [U] the power of the mind to think in a logical way, to understand and have opinions, etc: *Only human beings are capable of reason* (= of thinking in a logical way, etc.). ◇ *to lose your reason* (= become mentally ill) **4** 🔑 [U] what is possible, practical or right: *I can't get her to* ***listen to reason.*** ◇ *Why can't they* ***see reason?*** ◇ *to be open to reason* (= to be willing to accept sensible advice) ◇ *He's looking for a job and he's willing to do anything* ***within reason.***

IDM **it ˌstands to ˈreason** (*informal*) it must be clear to any sensible person who thinks about it: *It stands to reason that they'll leave if you don't pay them enough.* ➲ more at RHYME *n.*

■ ***verb*** **1** [T, I] **~ (that…)** | **+ speech** to form a judgement about a situation by considering the facts and using your power to think in a logical way: *She reasoned that she must have left her bag on the train.* ◇ *They couldn't fire him, he reasoned. He was the only one who knew how the system worked.* **2** [I] to use your power to think and understand: *the human ability to reason*

PHR V ˌ**reason sth ˈout** to try and find the answer to a problem by using your power to think in a logical way SYN **figure out** ˈ**reason with sb** to talk to sb in order to persuade them to be more sensible: *I tried to reason with him, but he wouldn't listen.*

Synonyms

reason

explanation • grounds • basis • excuse • motive • justification • pretext

These are all words for a cause or an explanation for sth that has happened or that sb has done.

reason a cause or an explanation for sth that has happened or that sb has done; a fact that makes it right or fair to do sth: *He said no but he didn't give a reason.*

explanation a statement, fact or situation that tells you why sth has happened; a reason given for sth: *The most likely explanation is that his plane was delayed.* ◇ *She left the room abruptly without explanation.*

grounds (*rather formal*) a good or true reason for saying, doing or believing sth: *You have no grounds for complaint.*

basis (*rather formal*) the reason why people take a particular action: *On what basis will this decision be made?*

excuse a reason, either true or invented, that you give to explain or defend your behaviour; a good reason that you give for doing sth that you want to do for other reasons: *Late again! What's your excuse this time?* ◇ *It gave me an excuse to take the car.*

motive a reason that explains sb's behaviour: *There seemed to be no motive for the murder.*

justification (*rather formal*) a good reason why sth exists or is done: *I can see no possible justification for any further tax increases.*

GROUNDS OR JUSTIFICATION?

Justification is used to talk about finding or understanding reasons for actions, or trying to explain why it is a good idea to do sth. It is often used with words like *little, no, some, every, without,* and *not any.* **Grounds** is used more for talking about reasons that already exist, or that have already been decided, for example by law: *moral/economic grounds.*

pretext (*rather formal*) a false reason that you give for doing sth, usually sth bad, in order to hide the real reason: *He left the party early on the pretext of having to work.*

PATTERNS

- (a/an) reason/explanation/grounds/basis/excuse/motive/justification/pretext **for** sth
- the reason/motive **behind** sth
- **on the** grounds/basis/pretext **of/that…**
- (a) **good/valid** reason/explanation/grounds/excuse/motive/justification

rea·son·able 🔑 /ˈriːznəbl/ *adj.*

1 🔑 **~ (to do sth)** fair, practical and sensible: ***It is reasonable*** *to assume that he knew beforehand that this would happen.* ◇ ***Be reasonable!*** *We can't work late every night.* ◇ *Any reasonable person would have done exactly as you did.* ◇ *The prosecution has to prove* ***beyond reasonable doubt*** *that he is guilty of murder.* OPP **unreasonable** **2** 🔑 acceptable and appropriate in a particular situation: *He made us a reasonable offer for the car.* ◇ *You must submit your claim within a reasonable time.* **3** 🔑 (of prices) not too expensive SYN **fair**: *We sell good quality food at reasonable prices.* ➲ SYNONYMS at CHEAP **4** 🔑 [usually before noun] fairly good, but not very good SYN **average**: *a reasonable standard of living* ◇ *The hotel was reasonable, I suppose* (= but not excellent). ▶ **rea·son·able·ness** *noun* [U]

rea·son·ably 0‑ /ˈriːznəbli/ *adv.*
1 0‑ to a degree that is fairly good but not very good: *The instructions are reasonably straightforward.* ◇ *She seems reasonably happy in her new job.* **2** 0‑ in a logical and sensible way: *We tried to discuss the matter calmly and reasonably.* **3** 0‑ in a fair way: *He couldn't reasonably be expected to pay back the loan all at once.* ◇ *The apartments are* ***reasonably priced*** (= not too expensive).

rea·soned /ˈriːzənd/ *adj.* [only before noun] (of an argument, opinion, etc.) presented in a logical way that shows careful thought

rea·son·ing /ˈriːzənɪŋ/ *noun* [U] the process of thinking about things in a logical way; opinions and ideas that are based on logical thinking: *What is* ***the reasoning behind*** *this decision?* ◇ *This* ***line of reasoning*** *is faulty.*

re·assem·ble /ˌriːəˈsembl/ *verb* **1** [T] **~ sth** to fit the parts of sth together again after it has been taken apart: *We had to take the table apart and reassemble it upstairs.* **2** [I] to meet together again as a group after a break: *The class reassembled after lunch.*

re·assert /ˌriːəˈsɜːt; *NAmE* -ˈsɜːrt/ *verb* **1 ~ sth** to make other people recognize again your right or authority to do sth, after a period when this has been in doubt: *She found it necessary to reassert her position.* **2 ~ itself** to start to have an effect again, after a period of not having any effect: *He thought about giving up his job, but then common sense reasserted itself.* **3** to state again, clearly and firmly, that sth is true: **~ that...** *He reasserted that all parties should be involved in the talks.* ◇ **~ sth** *Traditional values have been reasserted.* ▶ **re·asser·tion** *noun* [sing., U]

re·assess AW /ˌriːəˈses/ *verb* **~ sth** to think again about sth to decide if you need to change your opinion of it SYN **reappraise** ▶ **re·assess·ment** AW *noun* [U, C]

re·assign AW /ˌriːəˈsaɪn/ *verb* [often passive] **1 ~ sb (to sth)** to give sb a different duty, position, or responsibility: *After his election defeat he was reassigned to the diplomatic service.* **2 ~ sth (to sb/sth)** to give sth to a different person or organization; to change the status of sth: *The case was reassigned to a different court.* ▶ **re·assign·ment** *noun* [U]

re·assur·ance /ˌriːəˈʃʊərəns; -ˈʃɔːr-; *NAmE* -ˈʃʊr-/ *noun* **1** [U] **~ (that...)** the fact of giving advice or help that takes away a person's fears or doubts: *to* ***give/provide/offer reassurance*** **2** [C] **~ (that...)** something that is said or done to take away a person's fears or doubts: *We have been given reassurances that the water is safe to drink.*

re·assure /ˌriːəˈʃʊə(r); -ˈʃɔː(r); *NAmE* -ˈʃʊr/ *verb* to say or do sth that makes sb less frightened or worried SYN **set sb's mind at rest**: **~ sb (about sth)** *They tried to reassure her, but she still felt anxious.* ◇ **~ sb that...** *The doctor reassured him that there was nothing seriously wrong.*

re·assur·ing /ˌriːəˈʃʊərɪŋ; -ˈʃɔːr-; *NAmE* -ˈʃʊr-/ *adj.* making you feel less worried or uncertain about sth: *a reassuring smile* ◇ ***It's reassuring (to know) that*** *we've got the money if necessary.* ▶ **re·assur·ing·ly** *adv.*

re·awaken /ˌriːəˈweɪkən/ *verb* **~ sth** to make you feel a particular emotion again or to make you remember sth again SYN **rekindle**: *The place reawakened childhood memories.*

re·bar·ba·tive /rɪˈbɑːbətɪv; *NAmE* -ˈbɑːrb-/ *adj.* (*formal*) not attractive SYN **objectionable**

re·bate /ˈriːbeɪt/ *noun* **1** an amount of money that is paid back to you because you have paid too much: *a tax rebate* **2** an amount of money that is taken away from the cost of sth, before you pay for it SYN **discount**: *Buyers are offered a cash rebate.*

rebel *noun, verb*
■ ***noun*** /ˈrebl/ **1** a person who fights against the government of their country: *rebel forces* ◇ *Armed rebels advanced towards the capital.* **2** a person who opposes sb in authority over them within an organization, a political party, etc. **3** a person who does not like to obey rules or who does not accept normal standards of behaviour, dress, etc: *I've always been the rebel of the family.*
■ ***verb*** /rɪˈbel/ (-ll-) [I] **~ (against sb/sth)** to fight against or refuse to obey an authority, for example a government, a system, your parents, etc: *He later rebelled against his strict religious upbringing.* ◇ *Most teenagers find something to rebel against.*

re·bel·lion /rɪˈbeljən/ *noun* **~ (against sb/sth) 1** [U, C] an attempt by some of the people in a country to change their government, using violence SYN **uprising**: *The north of the country rose in rebellion against the government.* ◇ *The army put down the rebellion.* ➲ COLLOCATIONS at WAR **2** [U, C] opposition to authority within an organization, a political party, etc: (*a*) *back-bench rebellion* **3** [U] opposition to authority; being unwilling to obey rules or accept normal standards of behaviour, dress, etc: *teenage rebellion*

re·bel·li·ous /rɪˈbeljəs/ *adj.* **1** unwilling to obey rules or accept normal standards of behaviour, dress, etc: *rebellious teenagers* ◇ *He has always had* ***a rebellious streak***. **2** opposed to the government of a country; opposed to those in authority within an organization: *rebellious cities/factions* ▶ **re·bel·li·ous·ly** *adv.*: *'I don't care!' she said rebelliously.* **re·bel·li·ous·ness** *noun* [U]

re·birth /ˌriːˈbɜːθ; *NAmE* -ˈbɜːrθ/ *noun* [U, sing.] **1** a period of new life, growth or activity: *the seasonal cycle of death and rebirth* **2** a spiritual change when a person's faith becomes stronger or they convert to another religion

re·birth·ing /ˌriːˈbɜːθɪŋ; *NAmE* -ˈbɜːrθ-/ *noun* [U] a type of PSYCHOTHERAPY that involves reproducing the experience of being born using controlled breathing

re·boot /ˌriːˈbuːt/ *verb* [T, I] **~ (sth)** (*computing*) if you **reboot** a computer or it **reboots**, you switch it off and then start it again immediately

re·born /ˌriːˈbɔːn; *NAmE* -ˈbɔːrn/ *verb, adj.*
■ ***verb be reborn*** (used only in the passive without *by*) **1** to become active or popular again **2** to be born again: *If you were reborn as an animal, which animal would you be?*
■ ***adj.*** **1** having become active again: *a reborn version of social democracy* **2** having experienced a complete spiritual change: *reborn evangelical Christians* ➲ see also BORN-AGAIN

re·bound *verb, noun*
■ ***verb*** /rɪˈbaʊnd/ **1** [I] **~ (from/off sth)** to BOUNCE back after hitting sth: *The ball rebounded from the goalpost and Podolski headed it in.* **2** [I] **~ (on sb)** (*formal*) if sth that you do **rebounds** on you, it has an unpleasant effect on you, especially when the effect was intended for sb else SYN **backfire 3** [I] (*business*) (of prices, etc.) to rise again after they have fallen SYN **bounce back**
■ ***noun*** /ˈriːbaʊnd/ **1** (*sport*) a ball that hits sth and BOUNCES back **2** (in BASKETBALL) the act of catching the ball after a player has thrown it at the BASKET and has not scored a point **3** (*business*) a positive reaction that happens after sth negative
IDM **on the ˈrebound** while you are sad and confused, especially after a relationship has ended

re·brand /ˌriːˈbrænd/ *verb* **~ sth/yourself** to change the image of a company or an organization or one of its products or services, for example by changing its name or by advertising it in a different way: *In the 1990s the Labour Party rebranded itself as New Labour.* ▶ **re·brand·ing** *noun* [sing., U]: *a rebranding exercise* ◇ *a £5 million rebranding*

re·buff /rɪˈbʌf/ *noun* (*formal*) an unkind refusal of a friendly offer, request or suggestion SYN **rejection**: *Her offer of help was met with a sharp rebuff.* ▶ **re·buff** *verb*: **~ sth** *They rebuffed her request for help.*

re·build /ˌriːˈbɪld/ *verb* (**re·built**, **re·built** /ˌriːˈbɪlt/) **1 ~ sth** to build or put sth together again: *After the earthquake, the people set about rebuilding their homes.* ◇ *He rebuilt the engine using parts from cars that had been scrapped.* **2 ~ sth** to make sth/sb complete and strong again: *When she lost her job, she had to* ***rebuild her life*** *completely.* ◇ *attempts to rebuild the shattered post-war economy*

re·buke /rɪˈbjuːk/ *verb* [often passive] **~ sb (for sth/for doing sth)** (*formal*) to speak severely to sb because they

R

have done sth wrong SYN **reprimand**: *The company was publicly rebuked for having neglected safety procedures.* ▸ **re·buke** *noun* [C, U]: *He was silenced by her stinging rebuke.*

rebus

to be or not to be

rebus /ˈriːbəs/ *noun* a combination of pictures and letters which represent a word or phrase whose meaning has to be guessed

rebut /rɪˈbʌt/ *verb* (-tt-) **~ sth** (*formal*) to say or prove that a statement or criticism is false SYN **refute** ▸ **re·but·tal** /-tl/ *noun* [C, U]: *The accusations met with a firm rebuttal.*

re·cal·ci·trant /rɪˈkælsɪtrənt/ *adj.* (*formal*) unwilling to obey rules or follow instructions; difficult to control ▸ **re·cal·ci·trance** /-əns/ *noun* [U]

re·call 🔑 *verb, noun*

■ ***verb*** /rɪˈkɔːl/ **1** 🔑 [T, I] (*formal*) (not used in the progressive tenses) to remember sth SYN **recollect**: **~ sth** *She could not recall his name.* ◇ (**+ adv./prep.**) *If I recall correctly, he lives in Luton.* ◇ **~ (sb/sth) doing sth** *I can't recall meeting her before.* ◇ **~ that...** *He recalled that she always came home late on Wednesdays.* ◇ **~ what, when, etc...** *Can you recall exactly what happened?* ◇ **+ speech** *'It was on a Thursday in March,' he recalled.* **2** [T] **~ sth** (not used in the progressive tenses) to make sb think of sth SYN **evoke**: *The poem recalls Eliot's 'The Waste Land'.* **3** [T] to order sb to return: **~ sb** *Both countries recalled their ambassadors.* ◇ **~ sb to sth** *He was recalled to military duty.* ◇ *They have both been recalled to the Welsh squad* (= selected as members of the team after a time when they were not selected). **4** [T] **~ sth** to ask for sth to be returned, often because there is sth wrong with it: *The company has recalled all the faulty hairdryers.*

■ ***noun*** /rɪˈkɔːl; ˈriːkɔːl/ **1** [U] the ability to remember sth that you have learned or sth that has happened in the past: *She has amazing powers of recall.* ◇ *to have **instant recall*** (= to be able to remember sth immediately) ◇ *to have **total recall*** (= to be able to remember all the details of sth) **2** [sing.] an official order or request for sb/sth to return, or for sth to be given back: *Thomas's recall to the Welsh team*

IDM **beyond reˈcall** impossible to bring back to the original state; impossible to remember

R

re·cant /rɪˈkænt/ *verb* [T, I] **~ (sth)** (*formal*) to say, often publicly, that you no longer have the same belief or opinion that you had before ▸ **re·can·ta·tion** /ˌriːkænˈteɪʃn/ *noun* [C, U]

recap /ˈriːkæp/ *verb, noun*

■ ***verb*** (-pp-) [I, T] **~ (on sth)** | **~ sth** | **~ what, where, etc...** = RECAPITULATE: *Let me just recap on what we've decided so far.*

■ ***noun*** = RECAPITULATION

re·cap·itu·late /ˌriːkəˈpɪtʃuleɪt/ *verb* (*formal*) (also **recap**) [I, T] **~ (on sth)** | **~ sth** | **~ what, where, etc...** to repeat or give a summary of what has already been said, decided, etc: *To recapitulate briefly, the three main points are these...* ▸ **re·cap·itu·la·tion** /ˌriːkəpɪtʃuˈleɪʃn/ *noun* [C, U] (*formal*) (also **recap**)

re·cap·ture /ˌriːˈkæptʃə(r)/ *verb* **1 ~ sth** to win back a place, position, etc. that was previously taken from you by an enemy or a rival: *Government troops soon recaptured the island.* **2 ~ sb/sth** to catch a person or an animal that has escaped **3 ~ sth** to bring back a feeling or repeat an experience that you had in the past: *He was trying to recapture the happiness of his youth.* ▸ **re·cap·ture** *noun* [U]: *the recapture of towns occupied by the rebels*

re·cast /ˌriːˈkɑːst; *NAmE* -ˈkæst/ *verb* (**re·cast**, **re·cast**) **1 ~ sth (as sth)** to change sth by organizing or presenting it in a different way: *She recast her lecture as a radio talk.* **2 ~ sb (as sth)** to change the actors or the role of a particular actor in a play, etc.

recce /ˈreki/ *noun* (*BrE, informal*) = RECONNAISSANCE: *to do a quick recce of an area*

re·cede /rɪˈsiːd/ *verb* **1** [I] to move gradually away from sb or away from a previous position: *The sound of the truck receded into the distance.* ◇ *She watched his receding figure.* **2** [I] (especially of a problem, feeling or quality) to become gradually weaker or smaller: *The prospect of bankruptcy has now receded* (= it is less likely). ◇ *The pain was receding slightly.* **3** [I] (of hair) to stop growing at the front of the head: *a middle-aged man with **receding hair/a receding hairline*** ⊃ VISUAL VOCAB page V49 **4** [I] **a ~ chin** a chin that slopes backwards towards the neck

re·ceipt 🔑 /rɪˈsiːt/ *noun*

1 🔑 (*NAmE* also **ˈsales slip**) [C] **~ (for sth)** a piece of paper that shows that goods or services have been paid for: *Can I have a receipt, please?* ◇ *to make out* (= write) *a receipt* ⊃ COLLOCATIONS at SHOPPING **2** [U] **~ (of sth)** (*formal*) the act of receiving sth: *to acknowledge receipt of a letter* ◇ *The goods will be dispatched **on receipt of** an order form.* ◇ *Are you **in receipt of** any state benefits?* **3 receipts** [pl.] (*business*) money that a business, bank or government receives: ***net/gross receipts***

re·ceiv·able /rɪˈsiːvəbl/ *adj.* (*business*) (usually following a noun) (of bills, accounts, etc.) for which money has not yet been received: *accounts receivable*

re·ceiv·ables /rɪˈsiːvəblz/ *noun* [pl.] (*business*) money that is owed to a business

re·ceive 🔑 /rɪˈsiːv/ *verb*

▸ GET/ACCEPT **1** 🔑 [T] (rather *formal*) to get or accept sth that is sent or given to you: **~ sth** *to receive a letter/present/phone call* ◇ *to receive information/payment/thanks* ◇ **~ sth from sb/sth** *He received an award for bravery from the police service.*

▸ TREATMENT/INJURY **2** 🔑 [T] to experience or be given a particular type of treatment or an injury: **~ sth from sb** *We received a warm welcome from our hosts.* ◇ **~ sth** *Emergency cases will receive professional attention immediately.* ◇ *to receive severe injuries*

▸ REACT TO STH **3** 🔑 [T, usually passive] to react to sth new, in a particular way: **~ sth + adv./prep.** *The play was **well received** by the critics.* ◇ **~ sth with sth** *The statistics were received with concern.*

▸ GUESTS **4** [T, often passive] **~ sb (with sth)** | **~ sb (as sth)** (*formal*) to welcome or entertain a guest, especially formally: *He was received as an honoured guest at the White House.*

▸ AS MEMBER OF STH **5** [T] **~ sb (into sth)** (*formal*) to officially recognize and accept sb as a member of a group: *Three young people were received into the Church at Easter.*

▸ TV/RADIO **6** [T] **~ sth** to change broadcast signals into sounds or pictures on a television, radio, etc: *to receive programmes via satellite* **7** [T] **~ sth/sb** to be able to hear a radio message that is being sent by sb: *I'm receiving you loud and clear.*

▸ STOLEN GOODS **8** [T, I] **~ (sth)** (*especially BrE*) to buy or accept goods that you know have been stolen

▸ IN SPORT **9** [I, T] **~ (sth)** (in TENNIS, etc.) to be the player that the SERVER hits the ball to: *She won the toss and chose to receive.*

IDM **be at/on the reˈceiving end (of sth)** (*informal*) to be the person that an action, etc. is directed at, especially an unpleasant one: *She found herself on the receiving end of a great deal of criticism.*

re·ceived /rɪˈsiːvd/ *adj.* [only before noun] (*formal*) accepted by most people as being correct: *The **received wisdom** is that they cannot win.* IDM see WISDOM

reˌceived pronunciˈation *noun* [U] = RP

re·ceiver /rɪˈsiːvə(r)/ *noun* **1** the part of a telephone that you hold close to your mouth and ear: *to **pick up/lift/put down/replace the receiver*** ⊃ COLLOCATIONS at PHONE ⊃ compare HANDSET **2** a piece of radio or television equipment that changes broadcast signals into sound or pictures: *a satellite receiver* ➲ compare TRANSMITTER **3** (*BrE* also **of,ficial re'ceiver**) (*law*) a person who is chosen by a court to be in charge of a company that is BANKRUPT: *to call in the receivers* **4** a person who receives sth: *Molly's more of a giver than a receiver.* **5** a person who buys or accepts stolen goods, knowing that they have been stolen **6** (in AMERICAN FOOTBALL) a player who plays in a position in which the ball can be caught when it is being passed forward

re·ceiv·er·ship /rɪ'si:vəʃɪp; *NAmE* -vərʃ-/ *noun* [U] (*law*) the state of a business being controlled by an official receiver because it has no money

re·cent 🔑 /'ri:snt/ *adj.* [usually before noun] that happened or began only a short time ago: *a recent development/discovery/event* ◇ *his most recent visit to Poland* ◇ *There have been many changes* ***in recent years***.

re·cent·ly 🔑 /'ri:sntli/ *adv.* not long ago: *We received a letter from him recently.* ◇ *Until recently they were living in York.* ◇ *I haven't seen them recently* (= it is some time since I saw them). ◇ *Have you used it recently* (= in the recent past)?

re·cep·tacle /rɪ'septəkl/ *noun* **1** ~ (**for sth**) (*formal*) a container for putting sth in: (*figurative*) *The seas have been used as a receptacle for a range of industrial toxins.* **2** (*NAmE*) = OUTLET (5)

re·cep·tion 🔑 /rɪ'sepʃn/ *noun* **1** 🔑 [U] (*especially BrE*) the area inside the entrance of a hotel, an office building, etc. where guests or visitors go first when they arrive: *the reception area* ◇ *We arranged to meet* ***in reception*** *at 6.30.* ◇ *You can leave a message* ***with reception***. ◇ (*NAmE, BrE*) *the reception desk* ➲ compare FRONT DESK **2** 🔑 [C] a formal social occasion to welcome sb or celebrate sth: *a wedding reception* **3** 🔑 [sing.] the type of welcome that is given to sb/sth: *Her latest album has met with a* ***mixed reception*** *from fans.* ◇ *Delegates gave him a* ***warm reception*** *as he called for more spending on education.* **4** 🔑 [U] the quality of radio and television signals that are broadcast: ***good/bad reception*** ◇ *There was very poor reception on my phone.* **5** [U] the act of receiving or welcoming sb: *the reception of refugees from the war zone*

re'ception centre (*NAmE* **re'ception center**) *noun* **1** a place where people can get information or advice: *The museum is building a new reception centre for visitors.* **2** a place where people, for example those without a home, can get help and temporary accommodation: *a reception centre for refugees*

re'ception class *noun* (in Britain) the first class at school for children aged 4 or 5

re·cep·tion·ist /rɪ'sepʃənɪst/ *noun* a person whose job is to deal with people arriving at or telephoning a hotel, an office building, a doctor's SURGERY, etc.

re'ception room *noun* (*BrE*) (used especially when advertising houses for sale) a room in a house where people can sit, for example a living room or DINING ROOM

re·cep·tive /rɪ'septɪv/ *adj.* ~ (**to sth**) willing to listen to or to accept new ideas or suggestions **SYN** **responsive**: *She was always receptive to new ideas.* ◇ *He gave an impressive speech to a receptive audience.* ▶ **re·cep·tive·ness**, **re·cep·tiv·ity** /,ri:sep'tɪvəti/ *noun* [U]: *receptivity to change*

re·cep·tor /rɪ'septə(r)/ *noun* (*biology*) a sense organ or nerve ending in the body that reacts to changes such as heat or cold and makes the body react in a particular way

re·cess *noun, verb*

■ ***noun*** /rɪ'ses; 'ri:ses/ **1** [C, U] a period of time during the year when the members of a parliament, committee, etc. do not meet **2** [C] a short break in a trial in court: *The judge called a short recess.* **3** (*NAmE*) (*BrE* **break**, **'break time**) [U] a period of time between lessons at school **4** [C] a part of a wall that is set further back than the rest of the wall, forming a space **SYN** **alcove**: *a recess for books* **5** [C, usually pl.] the part of a place that is furthest from the light and hard to see or get to: *He stared into the dark recesses of the room.* ◇ (*figurative*) *The doubt was still there, in the deep recesses of her mind.*

■ ***verb*** /rɪ'ses/ [often passive] **1** [T, I] ~ (**sth**) (*NAmE*) to take or to order a recess: *The hearing was recessed for the weekend.*

2 [T] ~ **sth** (**in/into sth**) to put sth in a position that is set back into a wall, etc: *recessed shelves*

re·ces·sion /rɪ'seʃn/ *noun* **1** [C, U] a difficult time for the economy of a country, when there is less trade and industrial activity than usual and more people are unemployed: *the impact of the current recession on manufacturing* ◇ *The economy is* ***in deep recession***. ◇ *policies to pull the country out of recession* ➲ COLLOCATIONS at ECONOMY **2** [U] (*formal*) the movement backwards of sth from a previous position: *the gradual recession of the floodwater*

re·ces·sion·ary /rɪ'seʃnri; *NAmE* -neri/ *adj.* [only before noun] connected with a recession or likely to cause one

re·ces·sive /rɪ'sesɪv/ *adj.* (*biology*) a **recessive** physical characteristic only appears in a child if it has two GENES for this characteristic, one from each parent. It does not appear if a DOMINANT gene is also present.

re·charge /,ri:'tʃɑ:dʒ; *NAmE* -'tʃɑ:rdʒ/ *verb* **1** [T, I] ~ (**sth**) to fill a battery with electrical power; to be filled with electrical power: *He plugged his razor in to recharge it.* ◇ *The drill takes about three hours to recharge.* **2** [I] (*informal*) to get back your strength and energy by resting for a time: *We needed the break in order to recharge.* ▶ **re·charge·able** *adj.*: *rechargeable batteries*

IDM **recharge your 'batteries** to get back your strength and energy by resting for a while

re·cher·ché /rə'ʃeəʃeɪ; *NAmE* ,rəʃer'ʃeɪ/ *adj.* (from *French, formal*, usually *disapproving*) unusual and not easy to understand, chosen in order to impress people

re·cid·iv·ist /rɪ'sɪdɪvɪst/ *noun* (*formal*) a person who continues to commit crimes, and seems unable to stop, even after being punished ▶ **re·cid·iv·ism** /-ɪzəm/ *noun* [U]

re·cipe /'resəpi/ *noun* **1** ~ (**for sth**) a set of instructions that tells you how to cook sth and the INGREDIENTS (= items of food) you need for it: *a recipe for chicken soup* ◇ *vegetarian recipes* ◇ *a recipe book* ➲ COLLOCATIONS at COOKING **2** ~ **for sth** a method or an idea that seems likely to have a particular result **SYN** **formula**: *His plans are* ***a recipe for disaster***. ◇ *What's her recipe for success?*

re·cipi·ent /rɪ'sɪpiənt/ *noun* (*formal*) a person who receives sth: *recipients of awards*

re·cip·ro·cal /rɪ'sɪprəkl/ *adj.* involving two people or groups who agree to help each other or behave in the same way to each other: *The two colleges have a reciprocal arrangement whereby students from one college can attend classes at the other.* ▶ **re·cip·ro·cal·ly** /-kli/ *adv.*

re'ciprocal verb *noun* (*grammar*) a verb that expresses the idea of an action that is done by two or more people or things to each other, for example 'kiss' in the sentence 'Paul and Claire kissed.'

re·cip·ro·cate /rɪ'sɪprəkeɪt/ *verb* **1** [T, I] to behave or feel towards sb in the same way as they behave or feel towards you: ~ **sth** (**with sth**) *Her passion for him was not reciprocated.* ◇ *He smiled but his smile was not reciprocated.* ◇ ~ (**with sth**) *I wasn't sure whether to laugh or to reciprocate with a remark of my own.* **2** [I] (*technical*) to move backwards and forwards in a straight line: *a reciprocating action* ▶ **re·cip·ro·ca·tion** /rɪ,sɪprə'keɪʃn/ *noun* [U]

reci·procity /,resɪ'prɒsəti; *NAmE* -'prɑ:s-/ *noun* [U] (*formal*) a situation in which two people, countries, etc. provide the same help or advantages to each other

re·cital /rɪ'saɪtl/ *noun* **1** a public performance of music or poetry, usually given by one person or a small group: *to give a piano recital* ➲ COLLOCATIONS at MUSIC **2** a spoken description of a series of events, etc. that is often long and boring

reci·ta·tion /,resɪ'teɪʃn/ *noun* **1** [C, U] an act of saying a piece of poetry or literature that you have learned to an audience **2** [C] an act of talking or writing about a series of things: *She continued her recitation of the week's events.*

reci·ta·tive /,resɪtə'ti:v/ *noun* [C, U] (*music*) a passage in an OPERA or ORATORIO that is sung in the rhythm of ordinary speech with many words on the same note

R

re·cite /rɪˈsaɪt/ *verb* **1** [T, I] **~ (sth) (to sb)** | **~ what...** | **+ speech** to say a poem, piece of literature, etc. that you have learned, especially to an audience: *Each child had to recite a poem to the class.* **2** [T] **~ sth (to sb)** | **~ what...** | **+ speech** to say a list or series of things: *They recited all their grievances to me.* ◇ *She could recite a list of all the kings and queens.*

reck·less /ˈrekləs/ *adj.* showing a lack of care about danger and the possible results of your actions SYN **rash**: *He showed **a reckless disregard for** his own safety.* ◇ *She was a good rider, but reckless.* ◇ *He had always been reckless with money.* ◇ *to cause death by **reckless driving*** ▸ **reck·less·ly** *adv.*: *He admitted driving recklessly.* **reck·less·ness** *noun* [U]

reckon O-w /ˈrekən/ *verb*
1 O-w [T, I] **~ (that)...** (*informal, especially BrE*) to think sth or have an opinion about sth: *I reckon (that) I'm going to get that job.* ◇ *He'll be famous one day.* ***What do you reckon*** (= do you agree)? ◇ *It's worth a lot of money, I reckon.* ◇ *'They'll never find out.' 'You reckon?'* (= I think you may be wrong about that) ➲ SYNONYMS at THINK **2** O-w **be reckoned** [T] (not used in the progressive tenses) to be generally considered to be sth: **~ to be/have sth** *Children are reckoned to be more sophisticated nowadays.* ◇ **+ noun/adj.** *It was generally reckoned a success.* **3** [T] **~ to do sth** (*BrE, informal*) to expect to do sth: *We reckon to finish by ten.* **4** [T] to calculate an amount, a number, etc: **~ sth (at sth)** *The age of the earth is reckoned at about 4 600 million years.* ◇ **~ (that)...** *They reckon (that) their profits are down by at least 20%.* ◇ **be reckoned to do sth** *The journey was reckoned to take about two hours.* IDM see NAME *n.*
PHR V ˈ**reckon on sth** O-w to expect sth to happen or to rely on sth happening: *They hadn't reckoned on a rebellion.* ◇ **~ doing sth** *We'd reckoned on having good weather.* ˌ**reckon sth↔ˈup** (*especially BrE*) to calculate the total amount or number of sth: *He reckoned up the cost of everything in his mind.* ˈ**reckon with sb/sth 1** [usually passive] to consider or treat sb/sth as a serious opponent, problem, etc: *They were already a political force **to be reckoned with**.* **2** (usually used in negative sentences) to consider sth as a possible problem that you should be prepared for SYN **take sth into account**: **~ doing sth** *I didn't reckon with getting caught up in so much traffic.* ˈ**reckon without sb/sth** (*especially BrE*) to not consider sb/sth as a possible problem that you should be prepared for SYN **not take sth into account**: *They had reckoned without the determination of the opposition.*

R

reck·on·ing /ˈrekənɪŋ/ *noun* **1** [U, C] the act of calculating sth, especially in a way that is not very exact: ***By my reckoning** you still owe me £5.* **2** [C, usually sing., U] a time when sb's actions will be judged to be right or wrong and they may be punished: *In the **final reckoning** truth is rewarded.* ◇ *Officials concerned with environmental policy predict that **a day of reckoning** will come.*
IDM **in/into/out of the ˈreckoning** (*especially BrE*) (especially in sport) among/not among those who are likely to win or be successful

re·claim /rɪˈkleɪm/ *verb* **1** to get sth back or to ask to have it back after it has been lost, taken away, etc: **~ sth** *You'll have to go to the police station to reclaim your wallet.* ◇ **~ sth from sb/sth** *The team reclaimed the title from their rivals.* ➲ see also BAGGAGE RECLAIM **2 ~ sth (from sth)** to make land that is naturally too wet or too dry suitable to be built on, farmed, etc: *The site for the airport will be reclaimed from the swamp.* ◇ *reclaimed marshland* **3** [usually passive] **~ sth** if a piece of land **is reclaimed by** desert, forest, etc, it turns back into desert, etc. after being used for farming or building **4 ~ sth (from sth)** to obtain materials from waste products so that they can be used again ➲ see also RECYCLE **5 ~ sb (from sth)** to rescue sb from a bad or criminal way of life ▸ **rec·lam·ation** /ˌrekləˈmeɪʃn/ *noun* [U]: *land reclamation*

re·clas·sify /ˌriːˈklæsɪfaɪ/ *verb* (**re·clas·si·fies, re·clas·si·fy·ing, re·clas·si·fied, re·clas·si·fied**) **~ sth** to put sth in a different class or category: *The drug is to be reclassified after trials showed it to be more harmful than previously thought.*

re·cline /rɪˈklaɪn/ *verb* **1** [I] **~ (against/in/on sth)** (*formal*) to sit or lie in a relaxed way, with your body leaning backwards: *She was reclining on a sofa.* ◇ *a reclining figure* (= for example in a painting) **2** [I, T] **~ (sth)** when a seat **reclines** or when you **recline** a seat, the back of it moves into a comfortable sloping position: *a reclining chair*

re·cliner /rɪˈklaɪnə(r)/ (also **reˈcliner chair**) *noun* (*especially NAmE*) a soft comfortable chair with a back that can be pushed back at an angle so that you can lean back in it ➲ VISUAL VOCAB page V18

re·cluse /rɪˈkluːs; *NAmE* ˈrekluːs/ *noun* a person who lives alone and likes to avoid other people: *to lead the life of a recluse* ▸ **re·clu·sive** /rɪˈkluːsɪv/ *adj.*: *a reclusive millionaire*

rec·og·ni·tion O-w /ˌrekəgˈnɪʃn/ *noun*
1 O-w [U] the act of remembering who sb is when you see them, or of identifying what sth is: *He glanced briefly towards her but there was no sign of recognition.* ◇ *the automatic recognition of handwriting and printed text by computer* **2** O-w [sing., U] **~ (that...)** the act of accepting that sth exists, is true or is official: *a growing recognition that older people have potential too* ◇ *There is a general recognition of the urgent need for reform.* ◇ *to seek **international/official/formal recognition** as a sovereign state* **3** O-w [U] **~ (for sth)** public praise and reward for sb's work or actions: *She gained only minimal recognition for her work.* ◇ *He received the award **in recognition of** his success over the past year.*
IDM **to change, alter, etc. beyond/out of (all) recogˈnition** to change so much that you can hardly recognize it: *The town has changed beyond recognition since I was last here.*

rec·og·niz·able (*BrE* also **-is·able**) /ˈrekəgnaɪzəbl; ˌrekəgˈnaɪzəbl/ *adj.* **~ (as sth/sb)** easy to know or identify: *The building was easily recognizable as a prison.* ◇ *After so many years she was still instantly recognizable.* OPP **unrecognizable** ▸ **rec·og·niz·ably, -is·ably** /-əbli/ *adv.*

rec·og·niz·ance (*BrE* also **-sance**) /rɪˈkɒgnɪzəns; *NAmE* -ˈkɑːg-/ *noun* [U] (*law*) a promise by sb who is accused of a crime to appear in court on a particular date; a sum of money paid as a guarantee of this promise

rec·og·nize O-w (*BrE* also **-ise**) /ˈrekəgnaɪz/ *verb* (not used in the progressive tenses)
1 O-w to know who sb is or what sth is when you see or hear them, because you have seen or heard them or it before: **~ sb/sth** *I recognized him as soon as he came in the room.* ◇ *Do you recognize this tune?* ◇ **~ sb/sth by/from sth** *I recognized her by her red hair.* ➲ SYNONYMS at IDENTIFY **2** O-w to admit or to be aware that sth exists or is true SYN **acknowledge**: **~ sth** *They recognized the need to take the problem seriously.* ◇ **~ sth as sth** *Drugs were not recognized as a problem then.* ◇ **~ how, what, etc...** *Nobody recognized how urgent the situation was.* ◇ **~ that...** *We recognized that the task was not straightforward.* ◇ **it is recognized that...** *It was recognized that this solution could only be temporary.* ◇ **~ sb/sth to be/have sth** *Drugs were not recognized to be a problem then.* ➲ SYNONYMS at ADMIT **3** O-w to accept and approve of sb/sth officially: **~ sb/sth (as sth)** *recognized qualifications* ◇ *The UK has refused to recognize the new regime.* ◇ **be recognized to be/have sth** *He is recognized to be their natural leader.* **4** O-w **be recognized (as sth)** to be thought of as very good or important by people in general: *The book is now recognized as a classic.* ◇ *She's a recognized authority on the subject.* **5 ~ sb/sth** to give sb official thanks for sth that they have done or achieved: *His services to the state were recognized with the award of a knighthood.*

re·coil *verb, noun*
■ ***verb*** /rɪˈkɔɪl/ **1** [I] to move your body quickly away from sb/sth because you find them or it frightening or unpleasant SYN **flinch**: **~ (from sb/sth)** *She recoiled from his touch.* ◇ **~ (at sth)** *He **recoiled in horror** at the sight of the corpse.* **2** [I] **~ (from sth/from doing sth)** | **~ (at sth)** to react to an idea or a situation with strong dislike or fear SYN **shrink**: *She recoiled from the idea of betraying her own*

brother. **3** [I] (of a gun) to move suddenly backwards when you fire it

■ ***noun*** /ˈriːkɔɪl/ [U, sing.] a sudden movement backwards, especially of a gun when it is fired

rec·ol·lect /ˌrekəˈlekt/ *verb* [T, I] (not used in the progressive tenses) (rather *formal*) to remember sth, especially by making an effort to remember it **SYN recall**: **~ (sth)** *She could no longer recollect the details of the letter.* ◇ *As far as I can recollect, she wasn't there on that occasion.* ◇ **~ what, how, etc...** *I don't recollect what he said.* ◇ **~ that...** *I recollect that we were all gathered in the kitchen.* ◇ **~ (sb/sth) doing sth** *I recollect him/his saying that it was dangerous.* ◇ **+ speech** *'It was just before the war,' she recollected.*

rec·ol·lec·tion /ˌrekəˈlekʃn/ *noun* (*formal*) **1** [U] the ability to remember sth; the act of remembering sth **SYN memory**: **~ (of doing sth)** *I have no* ***recollection of*** *meeting her before.* ◇ **~ (of sth)** *My recollection of events differs from his.* ◇ ***To the best of my recollection*** (= if I remember correctly) *I was not present at that meeting.* **2** [C] a thing that you remember from the past **SYN memory**: *to have a* ***clear/vivid/dim/vague recollection*** *of sth*

re·com·mence AW /ˌriːkəˈmens/ *verb* [I, T] (*formal*) to begin again; to start doing sth again: *Work on the bridge will recommence next month.* ◇ **~ (doing) sth** *The two countries agreed to recommence talks the following week.*

Synonyms

recommend

advise • **advocate** • **urge**

These words all mean to tell sb what you think they should do in a particular situation.

recommend to tell sb what you think they should do in a particular situation; to say what you think the price or level of sth should be: *We'd recommend you to book your flight early.* ◇ *a recommended price of $50*

advise to tell sb what you think they should do in a particular situation: *I'd advise you not to tell him.*

RECOMMEND OR ADVISE?

Advise is a stronger word than **recommend** and is often used when the person giving the advice is in a position of authority: *Police are advising fans without tickets to stay away.* ◇ ~~*Police are recommending fans without tickets to stay away.*~~ *I advise you...* can suggest that you know better than the person you are advising: this may cause offence if they are your equal or senior to you. *I recommend...* mainly suggests that you are trying to be helpful and is less likely to cause offence. **Recommend** is often used with more positive advice to tell sb about possible benefits and **advise** with more negative advice to warn sb about possible dangers: ~~*He advised reading the book before seeing the movie.*~~ ◇ ~~*I would recommend against going out on your own.*~~

advocate (*formal*) to support or recommend sth publicly: *The group does not advocate the use of violence.*

urge (*formal*) to recommend sth strongly: *The situation is dangerous and the UN is urging caution.*

PATTERNS

- to recommend/advise/advocate/urge **that...**
- **It is** recommended/advised/advocated/urged **that...**
- to recommend/advise/urge **sb to do sth**
- to recommend/advise/advocate **doing sth**
- to **strongly** recommend/advise/advocate sb/sth

rec·om·mend 0-w /ˌrekəˈmend/ *verb*
1 0-w to tell sb that sth is good or useful, or that sb would be suitable for a particular job, etc: **~ sb/sth** *Can you recommend a good hotel?* ◇ **~ sb/sth (to sb) (for/as sth)** *I recommend the book to all my students.* ◇ *She was recommended for the post by a colleague.* ◇ *The hotel's new restaurant comes* ***highly recommended*** (= a lot of people have praised it). **2** 0-w to advise a particular course of action; to advise sb to do sth: **~ sth** *The report recommended a 10% pay increase.* ◇ *It is dangerous to exceed the recommended dose.* ◇ *a recommended price of $50* ◇ **~ (that)...** *I recommend (that) he see a lawyer.* ◇ (*BrE* also) *I recommend (that) he should see a lawyer.* ◇ **it is recommended that...** *It is strongly recommended that the machines should be checked every year.* ◇ **~ sb to do sth** *We'd recommend you to book your flight early.* ◇ **~ (sb) doing sth** *He recommended reading the book before seeing the movie.* ◇ **~ how, what, etc...** *Can you recommend how much we should charge?* **3 ~ sb/sth (to sb)** to make sb/sth seem attractive or good **SYN commend**: *This system has* ***much to recommend it.***

rec·om·men·da·tion /ˌrekəmenˈdeɪʃn/ *noun* **1** [C] an official suggestion about the best thing to do: *to accept/reject a recommendation* ◇ **~ (to sb) (for/on/about sth)** *The committee* ***made recommendations*** *to the board on teachers' pay and conditions.* ◇ *I had the operation* ***on the recommendation of*** *my doctor.* **2** [U, C] the act of telling sb that sth is good or useful or that sb would be suitable for a particular job, etc: *We chose the hotel* ***on their recommendation*** (= because they recommended it). ◇ *It's best to find a builder through* ***personal recommendation.*** ◇ *Here's a list of my top CD recommendations.* **3** [C] (*especially NAmE*) a formal letter or statement that sb would be suitable for a particular job, etc. **SYN testimonial**

rec·om·pense /ˈrekəmpens/ *noun, verb*

■ ***noun*** [U] **~ (for sth/sb)** (*formal*) something, usually money, that you are given because you have suffered in some way, or as a payment for sth: *There must be adequate recompense for workers who lose their jobs.* ◇ *I received $1 000* ***in recompense*** *for loss of earnings.*

■ ***verb*** **~ sb (for sth)** (*formal*) to do sth for sb or give them a payment for sth that they have suffered **SYN compensate**: *There was no attempt to recompense the miners for the loss of their jobs.*

recon /rɪˈkɒn; *NAmE* rɪˈkɑːn/ *noun* [C, U] (*US, informal*) = RECONNAISSANCE

rec·on·cile /ˈrekənsaɪl/ *verb* (*formal*) **1 ~ sth (with sth)** to find an acceptable way of dealing with two or more ideas, needs, etc. that seem to be opposed to each other: *an attempt to reconcile the need for industrial development with concern for the environment* ◇ *It was hard to reconcile his career ambitions with the needs of his children.* **2** [usually passive] to make people become friends again after an argument or a disagreement: **~ sb** *The pair were reconciled after Jackson made a public apology.* ◇ **~ sb with sb** *He has recently been reconciled with his wife.* **3 ~ sb/yourself (to sth)** to make sb/yourself accept an unpleasant situation because it is not possible to change it **SYN resign yourself to**: *He could not reconcile himself to the prospect of losing her.* ▶ **rec·on·cil·able** /ˌrekənˈsaɪləbl/ *adj.*

rec·on·cili·ation /ˌrekənsɪliˈeɪʃn/ *noun* **1** [sing., U] **~ (between A and B)** | **~ (with sb)** an end to a disagreement and the start of a good relationship again: *Their change of policy brought about a reconciliation with Britain.* **2** [U] **~ (between A and B)** | **~ (with sth)** the process of making it possible for two different ideas, facts, etc. to exist together without being opposed to each other: *the reconciliation between environment and development*

rec·on·dite /ˈrekəndaɪt/ *adj.* (*formal*) not known about or understood by many people **SYN obscure**

re·con·di·tion /ˌriːkənˈdɪʃn/ *verb* [often passive] **~ sth** to repair a machine so that it is in good condition and works well **SYN overhaul**

re·con·fig·ure /ˌriːkənˈfɪɡə(r); *NAmE* -ˈfɪɡjər/ *verb* **~ sth** to make changes to the way that sth is arranged to work, especially computer equipment or a program: *You may need to reconfigure the firewall if you add a new machine to your network.*

re·con·firm /ˌriːkənˈfɜːm; *NAmE* -ˈfɜːrm/ *verb* **~ sth** to check again that sth is definitely correct or as previously arranged: *You have to reconfirm your flight 24 hours before travelling.*

R

re·con·nais·sance /rɪˈkɒnɪsns; *NAmE* -ˈkɑːn-/ (also *BrE informal* **recce**) (also *US informal* **recon**) *noun* [C, U] the activity of getting information about an area for military purposes, using soldiers, planes, etc: *to make an aerial reconnaissance of the island* ◇ *Time spent on reconnaissance is seldom wasted.* ◇ *a reconnaissance aircraft/mission/satellite* ➲ COLLOCATIONS at WAR

re·con·nect /ˌriːkəˈnekt/ *verb* [T, I] to connect sth again; to connect to sth again: **~ sth (to sth)** *I replaced the taps and reconnected the water supply.* ◇ **~ (to sth)** *Once you have removed the virus it is safe to reconnect to the Internet.*

rec·on·noitre (*especially US* **-ter**) /ˌrekəˈnɔɪtə(r); *NAmE* also ˌriːkə-/ *verb* [I, T] **~ (sth)** to get information about an area, especially for military purposes, by using soldiers, planes, etc.

re·con·quer /ˌriːˈkɒŋkə(r); *NAmE* -ˈkɑːŋ-/ *verb* **~ sth** to take control again of a country or city by force, after having lost it

re·con·sider /ˌriːkənˈsɪdə(r)/ *verb* [T, I] **~ (sth)** | **~ what, how, etc...** to think about sth again, especially because you might want to change a previous decision or opinion: *to* ***reconsider your decision/position*** ◇ *Recent information may persuade the board to reconsider.* ▸ **re·con·sid·er·ation** /ˌriːkənˌsɪdəˈreɪʃn/ *noun* [U, sing.]

re·con·sti·tute /ˌriːˈkɒnstɪtjuːt; *NAmE* -ˈkɑːnstətuːt/ *verb* **1 ~ sth/itself (as sth)** (*formal*) to form an organization or a group again in a different way: *The group reconstituted itself as a political party.* **2** [usually passive] **~ sth** to bring dried food, etc. back to its original form by adding water ▸ **re·con·sti·tu·tion** /ˌriːˌkɒnstɪˈtjuːʃn; *NAmE* -ˌkɑːnstəˈtuːʃn/ *noun* [U]

re·con·struct AW /ˌriːkənˈstrʌkt/ *verb* **1 ~ sth (from sth)** to build or make sth again that has been damaged or that no longer exists: *They have tried to reconstruct the settlement as it would have been in Iron Age times.* **2 ~ sth** to be able to describe or show exactly how a past event happened, using the information you have gathered: *Investigators are trying to reconstruct the circumstances of the crash.*

re·con·struc·tion AW /ˌriːkənˈstrʌkʃn/ *noun* **1** [U] the process of changing or improving the condition of sth or the way it works; the process of putting sth back into the state it was in before: *the post-war reconstruction of Germany* ◇ *a reconstruction period* **2** [U] the activity of building again sth that has been damaged or destroyed: *the reconstruction of the sea walls* **3** [C] a copy of sth that no longer exists: *The doorway is a 19th century reconstruction of Norman work.* **4** [C] a short film showing events that are known to have happened in order to try and get more information or better understanding, especially about a crime: *Last night police staged a reconstruction of the incident.* **5 Reconstruction** [U] (in the US) the period after the Civil War when the southern states returned to the US and laws were passed that gave rights to African Americans

re·con·struct·ive /ˌriːkənˈstrʌktɪv/ *adj.* [only before noun] (of medical treatment) that involves RECONSTRUCTING part of a person's body because it has been badly damaged or because the person wants to change its shape: *reconstructive surgery*

re·con·vene /ˌriːkənˈviːn/ *verb* [I, T] **~ (sth)** if a meeting, parliament, etc. **reconvenes** or if sb **reconvenes** it, it meets again after a break

re·cord 🔑 *noun, verb*

■ ***noun*** /ˈrekɔːd; *NAmE* ˈrekərd/

▸ WRITTEN ACCOUNT **1** 🔑 [C] **~ (of sth)** a written account of sth that is kept so that it can be looked at and used in the future: *You should* ***keep a record*** *of your expenses.* ◇ ***medical/dental records*** ◇ *Last summer was the wettest* ***on record***. ◇ *It was the worst flood* ***since records began***.

▸ MUSIC **2** 🔑 [C] a thin round piece of plastic on which music, etc. is recorded: *to* ***play a record*** ◇ *a* ***record collection*** ➲ see also VINYL (2) **3** [C] a piece or collection of music released as a record, or on CD, the Internet, etc: *a* ***record company*** (= one which produces and sells records) ◇ *During her career Billie Holiday made over 100 records.* ◇ *His new record is available on CD or as a download.* ➲ COLLOCATIONS at MUSIC ➲ see also ALBUM (2)

▸ HIGHEST/BEST **4** 🔑 [C] the best result or the highest or lowest level that has ever been reached, especially in sport: *She* ***holds the world record*** *for the 100 metres.* ◇ *to* ***break the record*** (= to achieve a better result than there has ever been before) ◇ *to* ***set a new record*** ◇ *There was a* ***record number*** *of candidates for the post.* ◇ *I got to work in* ***record time***. ◇ *record profits* ◇ *Unemployment has reached a* ***record high*** (= the highest level ever).

▸ OF SB/STH'S PAST **5** 🔑 [sing.] **~ (on sth)** the facts that are known about sb/sth's past behaviour, character, achievements, etc: *The report criticizes the government's record on housing.* ◇ *The airline has a good* ***safety record***. ◇ *He has an impressive record of achievement.* ➲ see also TRACK RECORD

▸ OF CRIMES **6** (also ˌ**criminal** ˈ**record**) [C] the fact of having committed crimes in the past: *Does he have a record?*

IDM **(just) for the ˈrecord 1** used to show that you want what you are saying to be officially written down and remembered **2** used to emphasize a point that you are making, so that the person you are speaking to takes notice: *And, for the record, he would be the last person I'd ask.* ˌ**off the ˈrecord** if you tell sb sth **off the record**, it is not yet official and you do not want them to repeat it publicly **put/place sth on (the) ˈrecord** | **be/go on (the) ˈrecord (as saying...)** to say sth publicly or officially so that it may be written down and repeated: *He didn't want to go on the record as either praising or criticizing the proposal.* **put/set the ˈrecord straight** to give people the correct information about sth in order to make it clear that what they previously believed was in fact wrong ➲ more at MATTER *n.*

■ ***verb*** /rɪˈkɔːd; *NAmE* rɪˈkɔːrd/

▸ KEEP ACCOUNT **1** 🔑 [T] to keep a permanent account of facts or events by writing them down, filming them, storing them in a computer, etc: **~ sth** *Her childhood is recorded in the diaries of those years.* ◇ *You should record all your expenses during your trip.* ◇ **~ how, what, etc...** *His job is to record how politicians vote on major issues.* ◇ **~ that...** *She recorded in her diary that they crossed the Equator on 15 June.* ◇ **it is recorded that...** *It is recorded that, by the year 630, four hundred monks were attached to the monastery.*

▸ MAKE COPY **2** 🔑 [T, I] to make a copy of music, a film/movie, etc. by storing it on tape or a disc so that you can listen to or watch it again: **~ (sth)** *Did you remember to record that programme for me?* ◇ *a recorded concert* ◇ *Tell me when the tape starts recording.* ◇ **~ sb/sth doing sth** *He recorded the class rehearsing before the performance.*

▸ MUSIC **3** 🔑 [T, I] **~ (sth)** to perform music so that it can be copied onto and kept on tape: *The band is back in the US recording their new album.*

▸ MAKE OFFICIAL STATEMENT **4** [T] **~ sth** | **~ that...** to make an official or legal statement about sth: *The coroner recorded a verdict of accidental death.*

▸ OF MEASURING INSTRUMENT **5** [T] **~ sth** | **~ what, how, etc ...** to show a particular measurement or amount: *The thermometer recorded a temperature of 40°C.*

ˈ**record-breaker** *noun* a person or thing that achieves a better result or higher level than has ever been achieved before ▸ ˈ**record-breaking** *adj.* [only before noun]: *a record-breaking jump*

reˌcorded deˈlivery (*BrE*) (*NAmE* ˌ**certified** ˈ**mail**) *noun* [U] a method of sending a letter or package in which the person sending it gets an official note to say it has been posted and the person receiving it must sign a form when it is delivered: *I'd like to send this (by) recorded delivery.* ➲ compare REGISTERED MAIL

re·cord·er /rɪˈkɔːdə(r); *NAmE* -ˈkɔːrd-/ *noun* **1** (in compounds) a machine for recording sound or pictures or both: *a* ***tape/cassette/video/DVD recorder*** ➲ see also FLIGHT RECORDER **2** a musical instrument in the shape of a pipe that you blow into, with holes that you cover with your fingers ➲ VISUAL VOCAB page V30 **3** a judge in a court in some parts of Britain and the US **4** a person who keeps a record of events or facts

R

ˈ**record holder** *noun* a person who has achieved the best result that has ever been achieved in a sport

re·cord·ing 0➡ /rɪˈkɔːdɪŋ; *NAmE* -ˈkɔːrd-/ *noun* **1** 0➡ [C] sound or pictures that have been recorded on CD, DVD, video, etc: *a video recording of the wedding* **2** 0➡ [U] the process of making a record, film/movie, radio or television show, etc: *during the recording of the show* ◇ ***recording equipment*** ◇ *a* ***recording studio*** ◇ *the* ***recording industry*** (= the industry that records and sells music) **3** 0➡ [U] the process or act of writing down and storing information for official purposes: *the recording of financial transactions*

re·cord·ist /rɪˈkɔːdɪst; *NAmE* -ˈkɔːrd-/ *noun* a person whose job is making sound recordings, especially in a recording studio

ˈ**record player** *noun* a piece of equipment for playing records in order to listen to the music, etc. on them

re·count[1] /rɪˈkaʊnt/ *verb* (*formal*) to tell sb about sth, especially sth that you have experienced: **~ sth** (**to sb**) *She was asked to recount the details of the conversation to the court.* ◇ **~ what, how, etc...** *They recounted what had happened during those years.* ◇ **+ speech** *'It was before the war,' he recounted.*

re·count[2] /ˌriːˈkaʊnt/ *verb* **~ sth** to count sth again, especially votes ▶ **re·count** /ˈriːkaʊnt/ *noun*: *The defeated candidate demanded a recount.*

re·coup /rɪˈkuːp/ *verb* **~ sth** (*formal*) to get back an amount of money that you have spent or lost SYN **recover**: *We hope to recoup our initial investment in the first year.*

re·course /rɪˈkɔːs; *NAmE* ˈriːkɔːrs/ *noun* [U] (*formal*) the fact of having to, or being able to, use sth that can provide help in a difficult situation: *Your only recourse is legal action.* ◇ *She made a complete recovery* ***without recourse to*** *surgery.* ◇ *The government, when necessary,* ***has recourse to*** *the armed forces.*

re·cover 0➡ AW /rɪˈkʌvə(r)/ *verb*

▸ FROM ILLNESS **1** 0➡ [I] **~** (**from sth**) to get well again after being ill/sick, hurt, etc: *He's still recovering from his operation.*

▸ FROM STH UNPLEASANT **2** 0➡ [I] **~** (**from sth**) to return to a normal state after an unpleasant or unusual experience or a period of difficulty: *It can take many years to recover from the death of a loved one.* ◇ *The economy is at last beginning to recover.*

▸ MONEY **3** 0➡ [T] **~ sth** (**from sb/sth**) to get back the same amount of money that you have spent or that is owed to you SYN **recoup**: *He is unlikely to ever recover his legal costs.*

▸ STH LOST/STOLEN **4** 0➡ [T] to get back or find sth that was lost, stolen or missing: **~ sth** *The police eventually recovered the stolen paintings.* ◇ **~ sth from sb/sth** *Six bodies were recovered from the wreckage.*

▸ POSITION/STATUS **5** 0➡ [T] **~ sth** to win back a position, level, status, etc. that has been lost SYN **regain**: *The team recovered its lead in the second half.*

▸ SENSES/EMOTIONS **6** 0➡ [T] to get back the use of your senses, control of your emotions, etc. SYN **regain**: **~ sth** *It took her a few minutes to* ***recover consciousness.*** ◇ *to recover your sight* ◇ **~ yourself** *She seemed upset but quickly recovered herself.*

▶ **re·covered** AW *adj.* [not before noun]: *She is now fully recovered from her injuries.*

re-cover /ˌriː ˈkʌvə(r)/ *verb* **~ sth** to put a new cover on sth

re·cov·er·able AW /rɪˈkʌvərəbl/ *adj.* **1** that you can get back after it has been spent or lost: *Travel expenses will be recoverable from the company.* **2** that can be obtained from the ground: *recoverable oil reserves*

re·cov·ery AW /rɪˈkʌvəri/ *noun* (*pl.* -ies) **1** [U, C, usually sing.] **~** (**from sth**) the process of becoming well again after an illness or injury: *My father has* ***made a full recovery*** *from the operation.* ◇ *to make* ***a remarkable/quick/speedy/slow, etc. recovery*** ◇ *She is* ***on the road to*** (= making progress towards) ***recovery.*** **2** [U, C, usually sing.] **~** (**in sth**) the process of improving or becoming stronger again: *The government is forecasting an* ***economic recovery.*** ◇ *a recovery in consumer spending* ◇ *The economy is showing signs of recovery.* **3** [U] **~** (**of sth**) the action or process of getting sth back that has been lost or stolen: *There is a reward for information leading to the recovery of the missing diamonds.* **4** [U] (also **reˈcovery room** [C]) the room in a hospital where patients are kept immediately after an operation

reˈcovery position *noun* [sing.] a position lying on the side, with the arms and legs carefully placed, that helps a person who is not conscious to breathe

rec·re·ant /ˈrekriənt/ *adj.* (*literary*) not brave SYN **cowardly**

re·create AW /ˌriːkriˈeɪt/ *verb* **~ sth** to make sth that existed in the past exist or seem to exist again: *The movie recreates the glamour of 1940s Hollywood.* ▶ **re·cre·ation** /-ˈeɪʃn/ *noun* [C, U]: *The writer attempts a recreation of the sights and sounds of his childhood.*

rec·re·ation /ˌrekriˈeɪʃn/ *noun* **1** [U] the fact of people doing things for enjoyment, when they are not working: *the need to improve facilities for leisure and recreation* ◇ *the increasing use of land for recreation* **2** [C] (*BrE*) a particular activity that sb does when they are not working SYN **hobby, pastime**: *His recreations include golf, football and shooting.* ➲ SYNONYMS at ENTERTAINMENT

rec·re·ation·al /ˌrekriˈeɪʃənl/ *adj.* connected with activities that people do for enjoyment when they are not working: *recreational activities/facilities* ◇ *These areas are set aside for public recreational use.*

recreˈational vehicle (*NAmE*) (*BrE* **camp·er**, ˈ**camper van**) (also **motor·home** *NAmE, BrE*) *noun* (*abbr.* RV) a large vehicle designed for people to live and sleep in when they are travelling ➲ VISUAL VOCAB page V47

recreˈation ground *noun* (*BrE*) an area of land used by the public for sports and games

recreˈation room (also *NAmE informal* ˈ**rec room**) *noun* **1** a room in a school, a hospital, an office building, etc. in which people can relax, play games, etc. **2** (*NAmE*) a room in a private house used for games, entertainment, etc.

re·crim·in·ation /rɪˌkrɪmɪˈneɪʃn/ *noun* [C, usually pl., U] an angry statement that sb makes accusing sb else of sth, especially in response to a similar statement from them: *bitter recriminations* ◇ *We spent the rest of the evening in mutual recrimination.* ▶ **re·crim·in·atory** /rɪˈkrɪmɪnətri; *NAmE* -tɔːri/ *adj.*

rec room /ˈrek ruːm; *NAmE* rʊm/ *noun* (*NAmE, informal*) = RECREATION ROOM

re·cru·desce /ˌriːkruːˈdes/ *verb* [I] (*formal*) to happen again SYN **recur** ▶ **re·cru·des·cence** /ˌriːkruːˈdesns/ *noun* [U] **re·cru·des·cent** /ˌriːkruːˈdesnt/ *adj.*

re·cruit /rɪˈkruːt/ *verb, noun*

■ *verb* **1** [T, I] **~** (**sb**) (**to sth**) | **~ sb to do sth** to find new people to join a company, an organization, the armed forces, etc: *The police are trying to recruit more officers from ethnic minorities.* ◇ *They recruited several new members to the club.* ◇ *He's responsible for recruiting at all levels.* ➲ COLLOCATIONS at JOB **2** [T] **~ sb to do sth** to persuade sb to do sth, especially to help you: *We were recruited to help peel the vegetables.* **3** [T] **~ sth** to form a new army, team, etc. by persuading new people to join it: *to recruit a task force* ▶ **re·cruit·er** *noun* **re·cruit·ment** *noun* [U]: *the recruitment of new members* ◇ *a recruitment drive*

■ *noun* **1** a person who has recently joined the armed forces or the police: *the training of new recruits* ◇ *He spoke of us scornfully as* ***raw recruits*** (= people without training or experience). **2** a person who joins an organization, a company, etc: *attempts to attract new recruits to the nursing profession*

rec·tal /ˈrektəl/ *adj.* (*anatomy*) relating to the RECTUM

rect·angle /ˈrektæŋgl/ *noun* a flat shape with four straight sides, two of which are longer than the other

R

two, and four angles of 90° ➲ VISUAL VOCAB page V58 ▸ **rect·angu·lar** /rekˈtæŋɡjələ(r)/ *adj.*

rect·ify /ˈrektɪfaɪ/ *verb* (**rec·ti·fies**, **rec·ti·fy·ing**, **rec·ti·fied**, **rec·ti·fied**) **~ sth** (*formal*) to put right sth that is wrong SYN **correct**: *to rectify a fault* ◇ *We must take steps to rectify the situation.* ▸ **rec·ti·fi·able** /ˌrektɪˈfaɪəbl/ *adj.*: *The damage will be easily rectifiable.* **rec·ti·fi·ca·tion** /ˌrektɪfɪˈkeɪʃn/ *noun* [U]

rec·ti·lin·ear /ˌrektɪˈlɪniə(r)/ *adj.* (*technical*) **1** in a straight line: *rectilinear motion* **2** having straight lines: *rectilinear forms*

rec·ti·tude /ˈrektɪtjuːd; *NAmE* -tuːd/ *noun* [U] (*formal*) the quality of thinking or behaving in a correct and honest way SYN **uprightness**

recto /ˈrektəʊ; *NAmE* -toʊ/ *noun* (*pl.* **-os**) (*technical*) the page on the right side of an open book OPP **verso**

rec·tor /ˈrektə(r)/ *noun* **1** an Anglican priest who is in charge of a particular area, (called a PARISH). In the past a rector received an income directly from this area. ➲ compare VICAR **2** (in Britain) the head of certain universities, colleges or schools

rec·tory /ˈrektəri/ *noun* (*pl.* **-ies**) *noun* a house where the rector of a church lives, or lived in the past

rec·tum /ˈrektəm/ *noun* (*pl.* **rec·tums** or **recta** /ˈrektə/) (*anatomy*) the end section of the tube where food waste collects before leaving the body through the ANUS ➲ VISUAL VOCAB page V48

re·cum·bent /rɪˈkʌmbənt/ *adj.* [usually before noun] (*formal*) (of a person's body or position) lying down SYN **reclining**

re·cu·per·ate /rɪˈkuːpəreɪt/ *verb* (*formal*) **1** [I] **~ (from sth)** to get back your health, strength or energy after being ill/sick, tired, injured, etc. SYN **recover**: *He's still recuperating from his operation.* **2** [T] **~ sth** to get back money that you have spent or lost SYN **recoup**, **recover**: *He hoped to recuperate at least some of his losses.* ▸ **re·cu·per·ation** /rɪˌkuːpəˈreɪʃn/ *noun* [U]: *It was a period of rest and recuperation.*

re·cu·pera·tive /rɪˈkuːpərətɪv/ *adj.* (*formal*) helping you to get better after you have been ill/sick, very tired, etc.

recur /rɪˈkɜː(r)/ *verb* (**-rr-**) [I] to happen again or a number of times: *This theme recurs several times throughout the book.* ◇ *a* ***recurring illness/problem/nightmare, etc.***

R

re·cur·rence /rɪˈkʌrəns; *NAmE* -ˈkɜːr-/ *noun* [C, usually sing., U] if there is **a recurrence of** sth, it happens again: *attempts to prevent a recurrence of the problem*

re·cur·rent /rɪˈkʌrənt; *NAmE* -ˈkɜːr-/ *adj.* that happens again and again: *recurrent infections* ◇ *Poverty is a* ***recurrent theme*** *in her novels.*

re·cur·sion /rɪˈkɜːʃn; *NAmE* -ˈkɜːrʃn/ *noun* [U] (*mathematics*) the process of repeating a FUNCTION, each time applying it to the result of the previous stage

re·cur·sive /rɪˈkɜːsɪv; *NAmE* -ˈkɜːrs-/ *adj.* (*technical*) involving a process that is applied repeatedly

re·cus·ant /ˈrekjʊzənt; *NAmE* rəˈkjuːzənt/ *noun* (*formal*) a person who refuses to do what a rule or person in authority says they should do ▸ **re·cus·ancy** /ˈrekjʊzənsi/ *noun* [U]

re·cyc·lable /ˌriːˈsaɪkləbl/ *adj.* able to be RECYCLED

re·cycle /ˌriːˈsaɪkl/ *verb* **1 ~ sth** to treat things that have already been used so that they can be used again: *Denmark recycles nearly 85% of its paper.* ◇ *recycled paper* ➲ COLLOCATIONS at ENVIRONMENT **2 ~ sth** to use the same ideas, methods, jokes, etc. again: *He recycled all his old jokes.* ▸ **re·cyc·ling** *noun* [U]: *the recycling of glass* ◇ *a recycling plant*

red 0-w /red/ *adj., noun*

■ ***adj.*** (**red·der**, **red·dest**) **1** 0-w having the colour of blood or fire: *a red car* ◇ *The lights* (= traffic lights) *changed to red before I could get across.* **2** (of the eyes) BLOODSHOT (= with thin lines of blood in them) or surrounded by red or very pink skin: *Her eyes were red from crying.* **3** 0-w (of the face) bright red or pink, especially because you are angry, embarrassed or ashamed: *He stammered something and went very red in the face.* ◇ (*BrE*) *She went* ***red as a beetroot.*** ◇ (*NAmE*) *She went* ***red as a beet.*** **4** 0-w (of hair or an animal's fur) reddish-brown in colour: *a red-haired girl* ◇ *red deer* ➲ see also REDHEAD **5** (*informal, politics*) (sometimes *disapproving*) having very LEFT-WING political opinions ➲ compare PINK **6** (*politics*) (of an area in the US) having more people who vote for the REPUBLICAN candidate than the DEMOCRATIC one: *red states/counties* OPP **blue** ▸ **red·ness** *noun* [U, sing.]: *You may notice redness and swelling after the injection.*

IDM **red in ˌtooth and ˈclaw** involving opposition or competition that is violent and without pity: *nature, red in tooth and claw* **a red rag to a ˈbull** (*BrE*) (*NAmE* **like waving a red flag in front of a ˈbull**) something that is likely to make sb very angry ➲ more at PAINT *v.*

■ ***noun*** **1** 0-w [C, U] the colour of blood or fire: *She often wears red.* ◇ *the reds and browns of the woods in the fall* (= of the leaves) ◇ *I've marked the corrections in red* (= in red ink). ◇ *The traffic lights were on red.* **2** [U, C] red wine: *Would you prefer red or white?* ◇ *an Italian red* **3** [C] (*informal, disapproving, politics*) a person with very LEFT-WING political opinions ➲ compare PINKO

IDM **be in the ˈred** (*informal*) to owe money to your bank because you have spent more than you have in your account: *The company has plunged $37 million into the red.* ➲ compare BE IN THE BLACK **see ˈred** (*informal*) to become very angry

re·dact /rɪˈdækt/ *verb* **~ sth (from sth)** to remove information from a document because you do not want the public to see it: *All sensitive personal information has been redacted from the public documents.* ▸ **re·dac·tion** /rɪˈdækʃn/ *noun* [C, U]

ˌred ˈadmiral *noun* a BUTTERFLY (= a flying insect with large brightly coloured wings) that has black wings with bright red marks on them

ˌred aˈlert *noun* [U, sing.] a situation in which you are prepared for sth dangerous to happen; a warning of this: *Following the bomb blast, local hospitals have been* ***put on red alert.***

ˌred ˈblood cell (also **ˈred cell**) (also *biology* **eryth·ro·cyte**) *noun* any of the red-coloured cells in the blood, that carry OXYGEN

ˌred-ˈblooded *adj.* [usually before noun] (*informal*) full of strength and energy, often sexual energy SYN **virile**: *red-blooded young males*

ˌred ˈbox *noun* (*BrE*) a box used by a government minister to hold official documents

red·breast /ˈredbrest/ *noun* (*literary*) a ROBIN

ˈred-brick *adj.* [usually before noun] **1** (of buildings, walls, etc.) built with bricks of a reddish-brown colour: *red-brick cottages* **2** (becoming *old-fashioned*) (of universities in Britain) built in the late 19th or early 20th century, in contrast to older universities, such as Oxford and Cambridge ➲ compare OXBRIDGE

red·cap /ˈredkæp/ *noun* **1** (*BrE*) a member of the MILITARY POLICE **2** (*NAmE*) a railway/railroad PORTER

ˌred ˈcard *noun* (in football (SOCCER)) a card shown by the REFEREE to a player who has broken the rules of the game and is not allowed to play for the rest of the game ➲ compare YELLOW CARD

ˌred ˈcarpet (usually **the red carpet**) *noun* [sing.] a strip of red carpet laid on the ground for an important visitor to walk on when he or she arrives: *I didn't expect to be given* ***the red carpet treatment!***

ˈred cell *noun* = RED BLOOD CELL

ˌred ˈcent *noun* [sing.] (*NAmE*) (especially after a negative) a very small amount of money: *I didn't get a red cent for all my work.*

red·coat /ˈredkəʊt; *NAmE* -koʊt/ *noun* **1** a British soldier in the past **2** (in Britain) a worker at a HOLIDAY CAMP who entertains and helps guests

the ˌRed ˈCrescent *noun* [sing.] the name used by national branches in Muslim countries of the International Movement of the Red Cross and the Red Crescent, an organization that takes care of people suffering because of war or natural disasters

the ˌRed ˈCross *noun* [sing.] an international organization that takes care of people suffering because of war or natural disasters. Its full name is the International Movement of the Red Cross and the Red Crescent.

red·cur·rant /ˌredˈkʌrənt; ˈredkʌrənt; *NAmE* -kɜːr-/ *noun* a very small red BERRY that grows in bunches on a bush and can be eaten: *redcurrant jelly* ◇ *a redcurrant bush*

ˌred ˈdeer *noun* (*pl.* **red deer**) a DEER with large ANTLERS (= horns shaped like branches), which has a reddish-brown coat in summer

red·den /ˈredn/ *verb* [I, T] **~ (sth)** to become red; to make sth red: *The sky was reddening.* ◇ *He could feel his face reddening with embarrassment.* ◇ *He stared at her and she reddened.*

red·dish /ˈredɪʃ/ *adj.* fairly red in colour

ˌred ˈdwarf *noun* (*astronomy*) a small, old star that is not very hot

re·dec·or·ate /ˌriːˈdekəreɪt/ *verb* [I, T] to put new paint and/or paper on the walls of a room or house: *We've just redecorated.* ◇ **~ sth** *The house has been fully redecorated.* ▸ **re·dec·or·ation** /ˌriːˌdekəˈreɪʃn/ *noun* [U]

re·deem /rɪˈdiːm/ *verb* **1** **~ sb/sth** to make sb/sth seem less bad SYN **compensate for**: *The excellent acting wasn't enough to redeem a weak plot.* ◇ *The only* ***redeeming feature*** *of the job* (= good thing about it) *is the salary.* ➲ SYNONYMS at SAVE **2** **~ yourself** to do sth to improve the opinion that people have of you, especially after you have done sth bad: *He has a chance to redeem himself after last week's mistakes.* **3** **~ sb** (in Christianity) to save sb from the power of evil: *Jesus Christ came to redeem us from sin.* **4** **~ sth** to pay the full sum of money that you owe sb; to pay a debt: *to* ***redeem a loan/mortgage*** **5** **~ sth** to exchange sth such as shares or VOUCHERS for money or goods: *This voucher can be redeemed at any of our branches.* **6** **~ sth** to get back a valuable object from sb by paying them back the money you borrowed from them in exchange for the object: *He was able to redeem his watch from the pawnshop.* **7** **~ a pledge/promise** (*formal*) to do what you have promised that you will do

re·deem·able /rɪˈdiːməbl/ *adj.* **~ (against sth)** that can be exchanged for money or goods: *These vouchers are redeemable against any future purchase.*

the Re·deem·er /rɪˈdiːmə(r)/ *noun* [sing.] (*literary*) Jesus Christ

re·define AW /ˌriːdɪˈfaɪn/ *verb* to change the nature or limits of sth; to make people consider sth in a new way: **~ sth** *The new constitution redefined the powers of the president.* ◇ **~ what, how, etc...** *We need to redefine what we mean by democracy.* ▸ **re·def·in·ition** /ˌriːdefɪˈnɪʃn/ *noun* [U, C]

re·demp·tion /rɪˈdempʃn/ *noun* [U] **1** (*formal*) the act of saving or state of being saved from the power of evil; the act of REDEEMING: *the redemption of the world from sin* **2** (*finance*) the act of exchanging shares for money (= of REDEEMING them)

IDM **beyond/past reˈdemption** too bad to be saved or improved

re·demp·tive /rɪˈdemptɪv/ *adj.* (*formal*) that saves you from the power of evil: *the redemptive power of love*

re·deploy /ˌriːdɪˈplɔɪ/ *verb* to move sb/sth to a new position or job: **~ sb/sth** *Our troops are to be redeployed elsewhere.* ◇ **~ sb/sth to sth** *Most of the employees will be redeployed to other parts of the company.* ▸ **re·deploy·ment** *noun* [U]: *the redeployment of staff/resources*

re·design /ˌriːdɪˈzaɪn/ *verb* **~ sth** to design sth again, in a different way ▸ **re·design** *noun* [U, C]

re·develop /ˌriːdɪˈveləp/ *verb* [T, I] **~ (sth)** to change an area by building new roads, houses, factories, etc: *The city has plans to redevelop the site.* ▸ **re·devel·op·ment** *noun* [U]: *inner-city redevelopment*

ˈred-eye *noun* **1** (also **ˌred-eye ˈflight**) [C] (*informal, especially NAmE*) a flight in a plane at night, on which you cannot get enough sleep: *We took the red-eye to Boston.* **2** [U] the appearance of having red eyes that people sometimes have in photographs taken using flash

ˌred-ˈfaced *adj.* with a red face, especially because you are embarrassed or angry

ˌred ˈflag *noun* **1** a flag used to warn people of danger **2** a red flag as a symbol of revolution or COMMUNISM

ˌred ˈgiant *noun* (*astronomy*) a large star towards the end of its life that is relatively cool and gives out a reddish light

ˌred-ˈhanded *adj.* IDM see CATCH *v.*

red·head /ˈredhed/ *noun* (sometimes *offensive*) a person who has red hair ➲ compare BLONDE, BRUNETTE ▸ **ˌred-ˈheaded** *adj.*: *a red-headed girl*

ˌred ˈherring *noun* an unimportant fact, idea, event, etc. that takes people's attention away from the important ones ORIGIN From the custom of using the smell of a smoked, dried herring (which was red) to train dogs to hunt.

ˌred-ˈhot *adj.* **1** (of metal or sth burning) so hot that it looks red: *Red-hot coals glowed in the fire.* **2** showing strong feeling: *her red-hot anger* **3** (*informal*) new, exciting and of great interest to people: *a red-hot issue* **4** used to describe the person, animal or team that is considered almost certain to win a race, etc.: *The race was won by the* ***red-hot favourite***.

re·dial /ˈriːdaɪəl/ *verb, noun*

■ ***verb*** (-ll-, *NAmE* -l-) **1** [I, T] **~ (sth)** to call a telephone number again by pressing all of the individual numbers again **2** [I] to call a telephone number again, using the button that automatically calls the last number that was called

■ ***noun*** **1** [U] the ability to redial a telephone number automatically **2** (also **ˈredial button**) [sing.] the button that automatically calls the last number that was called

redid *past tense* of REDO

ˌRed ˈIndian (also **red·skin**) *noun* (*old-fashioned, taboo*) a very offensive word for a Native American

re·dir·ect /ˌriːdəˈrekt; -dɪ-; -daɪ-/ *verb* **1** **~ sth (to sth)** to use sth, for example money, in a different way or for a different purpose: *Resources are being redirected to this important new project.* **2** **~ sth (to sth)** to send sth to a different address or in a different direction: *Enquiries on this matter are being redirected to the press office.* ◇ *Make sure you get your mail redirected to your new address.* ▸ **re·dir·ec·tion** *noun* [sing., U]: *a sudden redirection of economic policy* ◇ *the redirection of mail*

re·dis·cover /ˌriːdɪˈskʌvə(r)/ *verb* **~ sth** to find again sth that had been forgotten or lost ▸ **re·dis·cov·ery** /ˌriːdɪˈskʌvəri/ *noun* [U, C] (*pl.* -ies)

re·dis·trib·ute AW /ˌriːdɪˈstrɪbjuːt; ˌriːˈdɪs-/ *verb* **~ sth (from sb/sth) (to sb/sth)** to share sth out among people in a different way: *Wealth needs to be redistributed from the rich to the poor.* ▸ **re·dis·tri·bu·tion** AW /ˌriːdɪstrɪˈbjuːʃn/ *noun* [U, sing.]: *the redistribution of wealth* **re·dis·tribu·tive** /ˌriːdɪˈstrɪbjətɪv/ *adj.*

re·dis·trict /ˌriːˈdɪstrɪkt/ *verb* [T, I] **~ (sth)** (*US*) to change the official borders between districts

ˌred-ˈletter day *noun* an important day, or a day that you will remember, because of sth good that happened then ORIGIN From the custom of using red ink to mark holidays and festivals on a calendar.

ˌred ˈlight *noun* a signal telling the driver of a vehicle to stop: *to go through a red light* (= not stop at one)

ˌred-ˈlight district *noun* a part of a town where there are many PROSTITUTES

red ˈline *noun* an issue or a demand that one person or group refuses to change their opinion about during a dis-

R

agreement or NEGOTIATIONS: *The issue of sovereignty is a red line that cannot be crossed.*

ˌred ˈmeat *noun* [U] meat that is dark brown in colour when it has been cooked, such as beef and LAMB ➲ compare WHITE MEAT

red·neck /ˈrednek/ *noun* (*informal*) an offensive word for a person who lives in a country area of the US, has little education and has strong conservative political opinions

redo /ˌriːˈduː/ *verb* (**re·does** /-ˈdʌz/, **redid** /-ˈdɪd/, **re·done** /-ˈdʌn/) **~ sth** to do sth again or in a different way: *A whole day's work had to be redone.* ◇ *We've just redone the bathroom* (= decorated it again).

redo·lent /ˈredələnt/ *adj.* [not before noun] **~ of/with sth** (*literary*) **1** making you think of the thing mentioned: *an atmosphere redolent of the sea and ships* **2** smelling strongly of the thing mentioned: *a kitchen redolent with the smell of baking* ▶ **redo·lence** /-əns/ *noun* [U]

re·double /ˌriːˈdʌbl/ *verb* **~ sth** to increase sth or make it stronger: *The leading banks are expected to* ***redouble their efforts*** *to keep the value of the dollar down.* ◇ *redoubled enthusiasm*

re·doubt /rɪˈdaʊt/ *noun* **1** (*literary*) a place or situation in which sb/sth is protected when they are being attacked or threatened **2** a small building from which soldiers can fight and defend themselves

re·doubt·able /rɪˈdaʊtəbl/ *adj.* (*formal*) if a person is **redoubtable**, they have very strong qualities that make you respect them and perhaps feel afraid of them SYN **formidable**

re·dound /rɪˈdaʊnd/ *verb*

PHR V **reˈdound to sth** (*formal*) to improve the impression that people have of you: *Their defeat redounds to the glory of those whom they attacked.*

ˌred ˈpanda *noun* = PANDA (2)

ˌred ˈpepper *noun* **1** [C, U] a hollow red fruit that is eaten, raw or cooked, as a vegetable **2** [U] (*especially NAmE*) = CAYENNE

re·draft AW /ˌriːˈdrɑːft; *NAmE* -ˈdræft/ *verb* **~ sth** to write an article, a letter, etc. again in order to improve it or make changes ▶ **ˈre·draft** *noun*

re·draw /ˌriːˈdrɔː/ *verb* (**re·drew** /-ˈdruː/, **re·drawn** /-ˈdrɔːn/) **~ sth** to make changes to sth such as the borders of a country or region, a plan, an arrangement, etc: *After the war the map of Europe was redrawn.* ◇ *to* ***redraw the boundaries*** *between male and female roles in the home*

R

re·dress *verb, noun*

■ *verb* /rɪˈdres/ **~ sth** (*formal*) to correct sth that is unfair or wrong SYN **put right**: *to redress an injustice*

IDM **redress the ˈbalance** to make a situation equal or fair again

■ *noun* /rɪˈdres; ˈriːdres/ [U] **~ (for/against sth)** (*formal*) payment, etc. that you should get for sth wrong that has happened to you or harm that you have suffered SYN **compensation**: *to seek legal redress for unfair dismissal* ◇ *to have little prospect of redress*

red·skin /ˈredskɪn/ *noun* (*old-fashioned, taboo, offensive*) = RED INDIAN

ˌred ˈtape *noun* [U] (*disapproving*) official rules that seem more complicated than necessary and prevent things from being done quickly ORIGIN From the custom of tying up official documents with red or pink tape.

ˈred-top *noun* (*BrE, informal*) a British TABLOID newspaper, whose name is in red at the top of the front page

re·duce 0-w /rɪˈdjuːs; *NAmE* -ˈduːs/ *verb*

1 0-w [T] to make sth less or smaller in size, quantity, price, etc: **~ sth** *Reduce speed now* (= on a sign). ◇ *Giving up smoking reduces the risk of heart disease.* ◇ **~ sth by sth** *Costs have been reduced by 20% over the past year.* ◇ **~ sth (from sth) (to sth)** *The number of employees was reduced from 40 to 25.* ◇ *The skirt was reduced to £10 in the sale.* **2** [T, I] **~ (sth)** if you **reduce** a liquid or a liquid **reduces**, you boil it so that it becomes less in quantity **3** [I] (*NAmE, informal*) to lose weight by limiting the amount and type of food that you eat: *a reducing plan* **4** [T] **~ sth** (*chemistry*) to add one or more ELECTRONS to a substance or to remove OXYGEN from a substance ➲ compare OXIDIZE

IDM **reˌduced ˈcircumstances** the state of being poorer than you were before. People say 'living in reduced circumstances' to avoid saying 'poor'.

PHR V **reˈduce sb/sth (from sth) to sth/to doing sth** [usually passive] to force sb/sth into a particular state or condition, usually a worse one: *a beautiful building reduced to rubble* ◇ *She was* ***reduced to tears*** *by their criticisms.* ◇ *They were reduced to begging in the streets.* **reˈduce sth to sth** to change sth to a more general or more simple form: *We can reduce the problem to two main issues.*

re·du·cible /rɪˈdjuːsəbl; *NAmE* -ˈduːs-/ *adj.* **~ to sth** (*formal*) that can be described or considered simply as sth: *The problem is not reducible to one of money.*

re·duc·tio ad ab·sur·dum /rɪˌdʌktiəʊ æd æbˈsɜːdəm; *NAmE* rɪˌdʌktioʊ æd æbˈsɜːrdəm/ *noun* [U, C] (*philosophy*) (from *Latin*) a method of proving that sth is not true by showing that its result is not logical or sensible

re·duc·tion 0-w /rɪˈdʌkʃn/ *noun*

1 0-w [C, U] **~ (in sth)** an act of making sth less or smaller; the state of being made less or smaller: *a 33% reduction in the number of hospital beds available* ◇ *There has been some reduction in unemployment.* ◇ *a* ***slight/significant/substantial/drastic reduction*** *in costs* **2** 0-w [C] an amount of money by which sth is made cheaper: *There are reductions for children sharing a room with two adults.* **3** [C] a copy of a photograph, map, picture, etc. that is made smaller than the original one OPP **enlargement** **4** [U, C] (*chemistry*) the fact of adding one or more ELECTRONS to a substance or of removing OXYGEN from a substance ➲ compare OXIDATION

re·duc·tion·ism /rɪˈdʌkʃənɪzəm/ *noun* [U] (*formal*, often *disapproving*) the belief that complicated things can be explained by considering them as a combination of simple parts ▶ **re·duc·tion·ist** /-ɪst/ *adj., noun*

re·duc·tive /rɪˈdʌktɪv/ *adj.* (*formal*, often *disapproving*) that tries to explain sth complicated by considering it as a combination of simple parts

re·dun·dancy /rɪˈdʌndənsi/ *noun* (*pl.* **-ies**) **1** [U, C, usually pl.] (*BrE*) the situation when sb has to leave their job because there is no more work available for them: *Thousands of factory workers are facing redundancy.* ◇ *to accept/take* ***voluntary redundancy*** (= to offer to leave your job) ◇ *the threat of* ***compulsory redundancies*** ◇ *redundancy payments* ➲ COLLOCATIONS at UNEMPLOYMENT ➲ see also LAY-OFF **2** [U] (*formal* or *technical*) the state of not being necessary or useful: *Natural language is characterized by redundancy* (= words are used that are not really necessary for sb to understand the meaning).

re·dun·dant /rɪˈdʌndənt/ *adj.* **1** (*BrE*) (of a person) without a job because there is no more work available for you in a company: *to be* ***made redundant*** *from your job* ◇ *redundant employees* ➲ COLLOCATIONS at UNEMPLOYMENT **2** not needed or useful: *The picture has too much redundant detail.* ▶ **re·dun·dant·ly** *adv.*

re·du·pli·cate /ˌriːˈdjuːplɪkeɪt; *NAmE* -ˈduː-/ *verb* [I, T] **~ (sth/itself)** to make a copy of sth in order to form another of the same kind: *These cells are able to reduplicate themselves.*

ˌred ˈwine *noun* **1** [U, C] wine that gets its red colour from the skins of the GRAPES **2** [C] a glass of red wine ➲ compare ROSÉ, WHITE WINE

red·wood /ˈredwʊd/ *noun* **1** [C] a very tall type of tree that grows especially in California and Oregon: *giant redwoods* **2** [U] the reddish wood of the redwood tree

ˈred zone *noun* [sing.] (in AMERICAN FOOTBALL) the area within 20 YARDS of a team's GOAL LINE

ˌre-ˈecho *verb* [I, T] to be repeated many times; to repeat sth many times: *Their shouts re-echoed through the darkness.* ◇ *Her words re-echoed in his mind.* ◇ **~ sth** *He has constantly re-echoed the main theme of his acceptance speech: 'We want to be proud again!'.*

reed /riːd/ *noun* **1** a tall plant like grass with a hollow STEM that grows in or near water: *reed beds* (= where they grow) ➲ VISUAL VOCAB pages V3, V9 **2** a small thin piece of CANE, metal or plastic in some musical instruments such as the OBOE or the CLARINET that moves very quickly when air is blown over it, producing a sound ➲ VISUAL VOCAB page V30

ˌre-'educate *verb* **~ sb** to teach sb to think or behave in a new or different way ▸ **ˌre-edu'cation** *noun* [U]

reedy /'riːdi/ *adj.* [usually before noun] **1** (of a voice or sound) high and not very pleasant **2** full of reeds: *reedy river banks*

reef /riːf/ *noun, verb*
■ **noun 1** a long line of rocks or sand near the surface of the sea: *a coral reef* ➲ VISUAL VOCAB page V5 **2** a part of a sail that can be tied or rolled up to make the sail smaller in a strong wind
■ **verb ~ sth** (*technical*) to make a sail smaller by tying or rolling up part of it

reef·er /'riːfə(r)/ *noun* **1** (also **'reefer jacket**) a short thick jacket made of wool, usually dark blue, with two rows of buttons **2** (*old-fashioned, slang*) a cigarette containing MARIJUANA

'reef knot (*especially BrE*) (*NAmE* usually **'square knot**) *noun* a type of double knot that will not come undone easily

reek /riːk/ *verb, noun*
■ **verb 1** [I] **~ (of sth)** to smell very strongly of sth unpleasant: *His breath reeked of tobacco.* **2** [I] **~ (of sth)** (*disapproving*) to suggest very strongly that sth unpleasant or suspicious is involved in a situation: *Her denials reeked of hypocrisy.*
■ **noun** [sing.] a strong unpleasant smell SYN **stench**

reel /riːl/ *noun, verb*
■ **noun 1** (*especially BrE*) (also **spool** especially in *NAmE*) a round object around which you wind such things as thread, wire or film; a reel together with the film, wire, thread, etc. that is wound around it: *a cotton reel* ◇ *a reel on a fishing rod* ◇ *reels of magnetic tape* ◇ *a new reel of film* ◇ *The hero was killed in the final reel* (= in the final part of the film/movie). ➲ VISUAL VOCAB page V35 **2** a fast Scottish, Irish or American dance, usually for two or four couples; a piece of music for this dance
■ **verb 1** [I] (**+ adv./prep.**) to move in a very unsteady way, for example because you are drunk or have been hit SYN **stagger**: *I punched him on the chin, sending him reeling backwards.* **2** [I] **~ (at/from/with sth)** to feel very shocked or upset about sth: *I was still reeling from the shock.* **3** [I] to seem to be spinning around and around: *When he opened his eyes, the room was reeling.*
PHR V **ˌreel sth↔'in/'out** to wind sth on/off a reel: *I slowly reeled the fish in.* **ˌreel sth↔'off** to say or repeat sth quickly without having to stop or think about it: *She immediately reeled off several names.*

ˌre-e'lect *verb* **~ sb (to sth)** to elect sb again: **~ sb (to sth)** *She was re-elected to parliament.* ◇ **~ sb (as) sth | ~ sb + noun** *The committee voted to re-elect him (as) chairman.* ▸ **ˌre-e'lection** *noun* [U]: (*BrE*) *to stand for re-election* ◇ (*NAmE*) *to run for re-election*

ˌre-e'merge *verb* [I] to appear somewhere again: *The cancer may re-emerge years later.*

ˌre-e'nact *verb* **~ sth** to repeat the actions of a past event: *Members of the English Civil War Society will re-enact the battle.* ▸ **ˌre-e'nactment** *noun*

ˌre-'enter *verb* [T, I] **~ (sth)** to return to a place or to an area of activity that you used to be in

ˌre-'entry *noun* [U] **~ (into sth) 1** the act of returning to a place or an area of activity that you used to be in: *She feared she would not be granted re-entry into Britain.* ◇ *a re-entry programme for nurses* (= for nurses returning to work after a long time doing sth else) **2** the return of a SPACECRAFT into the earth's atmosphere

ˌre-e'valuate AW *verb* **~ sth** to think about sth again, especially in order to form a new opinion about it ▸ **ˌre-evalu'ation** AW *noun* [C, U]

reeve /riːv/ *noun* a law officer in England in the past

ˌre-e'xamine *verb* **~ sth** to examine or think about sth again, especially because you may need to change your opinion SYN **reassess**: *All the evidence needs to be re-examined.* ▸ **ˌre-e'xamin·ation** *noun* [U, sing.]

ref /ref/ *noun, verb* (*informal*)
■ **noun** = REFEREE: *The game's not over till the ref blows the whistle.*
■ **verb** (-ff-) **~ sth** = REFEREE: *The game was badly reffed.*

ref. /ref/ *abbr.* reference (used especially in business as a way of identifying sth such as a document): *our ref.: 3498*

re·fec·tory /rɪ'fektri/ *noun* (*pl.* -ies) a large room in which meals are served, especially in a religious institution and in some schools and colleges in Britain

refer 🔑 /rɪ'fɜː(r)/ *verb* (-rr-)
PHR V **re'fer to sb/sth (as sth)** 🔑 to mention or speak about sb/sth: *The victims were not referred to by name.* ◇ *Her mother never referred to him again.* ◇ *You know who I'm referring to.* ◇ *She always referred to Ben as 'that nice man'.* ◇ *I promised not to refer to the matter again.* ➲ SYNONYMS at MENTION **re'fer to sb/sth 1** 🔑 to describe or be connected to sb/sth: *The star refers to items which are intended for the advanced learner.* ◇ *The term 'Arts' usually refers to humanities and social sciences.* ◇ *This paragraph refers to the events of last year.* ➲ LANGUAGE BANK at DEFINE **2** 🔑 to look at sth or ask a person for information SYN **consult**: *You may refer to your notes if you want.* ◇ *to refer to a dictionary* **re'fer sb/sth to sb/sth** to send sb/sth to sb/sth for help, advice or a decision: *My doctor referred me to a specialist.* ◇ *The case was referred to the Court of Appeal.* ◇ (*formal*) *May I refer you to my letter of 14 May?*

re·fer·able /rɪ'fɜːrəbl; 'refrəbl/ *adj.* **~ to sth** (*formal*) that can be related to sth else: *These symptoms may be referable to virus infection rather than parasites.*

ref·er·ee /ˌrefə'riː/ *noun, verb*
■ **noun 1** (also *informal* **ref**) the official who controls the game in some sports: *He was sent off for arguing with the referee.* ➲ compare UMPIRE **2** (*BrE*) a person who gives information about your character and ability, usually in a letter, for example when you are applying for a job **3** a person who is asked to settle a disagreement: *to act as a referee between the parties involved* **4** a person who reads and checks the quality of a technical article before it is published
■ **verb 1** (also *informal* **ref**) [I, T] to act as the referee in a game: *a refereeing decision* ◇ **~ sth** *Who refereed the final?* **2** [T] **~ sth** to read and check the quality of a technical article before it is published

referee's assistant *noun* = ASSISTANT REFEREE

ref·er·ence 🔑 /'refrəns/ *noun, verb*
■ **noun**
▸ MENTIONING SB/STH **1** 🔑 [C, U] **~ (to sb/sth)** a thing you say or write that mentions sb/sth else; the act of mentioning sb/sth: *The book is full of references to growing up in India.* ◇ *She **made** no **reference to** her illness but only to her future plans.* ◇ *the President's **passing reference to*** (= brief mention of) *the end of the war*
▸ LOOKING FOR INFORMATION **2** 🔑 [U] the act of looking at sth for information: *Keep the list of numbers near the phone for easy reference.* ◇ *I wrote down the name of the hotel **for future reference*** (= because it might be useful in the future). ◇ *The library contains many popular **works of reference*** (= reference books).
▸ ASKING FOR ADVICE **3** [U] **~ (to sb/sth)** (*formal*) the act of asking sb for help or advice: *The emergency nurse can treat minor injuries without reference to a doctor.*
▸ NUMBER/WORD/SYMBOL **4** 🔑 [C] (*abbr.* **ref.**) a number, word or symbol that shows where sth is on a map, or where you can find a piece of information: *The map reference is Y4.* ◇ *Please quote your **reference number** when making an enquiry.*
▸ FOR NEW JOB **5** 🔑 [C] a letter written by sb who knows you, giving information about your character and abilities, especially to a new employer: *We will **take up references** after the interview.* **6** [C] a person who agrees to write a

R

reference, for you, for example when you are applying for a job SYN **referee**: *My previous boss will act as a reference for me.*
‣ IN BOOK **7** [C] a note in a book that tells you where a particular piece of information comes from: *There is a list of references at the end of each chapter.* ➲ WRITING TUTOR page WT11 ➲ see also CROSS REFERENCE, FRAME OF REFERENCE, TERMS OF REFERENCE
IDM **in/with reference to** (*formal*) used to say what you are talking or writing about: *With reference to your letter of July 22…*
■ **verb** ~ **sth** (*formal*) to refer to sth; to provide a book, etc. with references: *Each chapter is referenced, citing literature up to 2008.*

'reference book *noun* a book that contains facts and information, that you look at when you need to find out sth particular

'reference library *noun* a library containing books that can be read in the library but cannot be borrowed ➲ compare LENDING LIBRARY

'reference point *noun* a standard by which sth can be judged or compared

ref·er·en·dum /ˌrefəˈrendəm/ *noun* (*pl.* **ref·er·en·dums** or **ref·er·enda**) [C, U] ~ (**on sth**) an occasion when all the people of a country can vote on an important issue: *Switzerland decided to **hold a referendum** on joining the EU.* ◇ *The changes were approved by referendum.* ➲ COLLOCATIONS at VOTE ➲ note at ELECTION

re·fer·ral /rɪˈfɜːrəl/ *noun* [U, C] ~ (**to sb/sth**) the act of sending sb who needs professional help to a person or place that can provide it: *illnesses requiring referral to hospitals* ◇ *to make a referral*

re·fill *verb, noun*
■ **verb** /ˌriːˈfɪl/ ~ **sth** (**with sth**) to fill sth again: *He refilled her glass.* ▸ **re·fill·able** /ˌriːˈfɪləbl/ *adj.*: *a refillable gas cylinder*
■ **noun** /ˈriːfɪl/ **1** another drink of the same type: *Would you like a refill?* **2** an amount of sth, sold in a cheap container, that you use to fill up a more expensive container that is now empty

re·fi·nance /ˌriːˈfaɪnæns/ *verb* [T, I] ~ (**sth**) (*finance*) to borrow money in order to pay a debt

re·fine AW /rɪˈfaɪn/ *verb* **1** ~ **sth** to make a substance pure by taking other substances out of it: *the process of refining oil/sugar* **2** ~ **sth** to improve sth by making small changes to it

R

re·fined AW /rɪˈfaɪnd/ *adj.* **1** [usually before noun] (of a substance) made pure by having other substances taken out of it: *refined sugar* **2** (of a person) polite, well educated and able to judge the quality of things; having the sort of manners that are considered typical of a high social class SYN **cultured, genteel** OPP **unrefined**

re·fine·ment AW /rɪˈfaɪnmənt/ *noun* **1** [C] a small change to sth that improves it SYN **enhancement**: *This particular model has a further refinement.* **2** [C] ~ **of sth** a thing that is an improvement on an earlier, similar thing: *The new plan is a refinement of the one before.* **3** [U] the process of improving sth or of making sth pure: *the refinement of industrial techniques* ◇ *the refinement of uranium* **4** [U] the quality of being polite and well educated and able to judge the quality of things; the state of having the sort of manners that are considered typical of a high social class SYN **gentility**: *a person of considerable refinement* ◇ *an atmosphere of refinement*

re·finer /rɪˈfaɪnə(r)/ *noun* a person or company that refines substances such as sugar or oil: *oil refiners*

re·finery /rɪˈfaɪnəri/ *noun* (*pl.* -ies) a factory where a substance such as oil is REFINED (= made pure)

refit /ˌriːˈfɪt/ *verb* (-tt-) ~ **sth** to repair or fit new parts, equipment, etc. to sth: *He spent £70 000 refitting his yacht.* ▸ **refit** /ˈriːfɪt/ *noun*: *The ship has undergone a complete refit.*

re·flate /ˌriːˈfleɪt/ *verb* [T, I] ~ (**sth**) (*economics*) to increase the amount of money that is used in a country, usually in order to increase the demand for goods ➲ compare DEFLATE, INFLATE ▸ **re·fla·tion** /ˌriːˈfleɪʃn/ *noun* [U] **re·fla·tion·ary** /ˌriːˈfleɪʃnri; *NAmE* -neri/ *adj.*: *reflationary policies*

re·flect /rɪˈflekt/ *verb*
1 [T, usually passive] ~ **sb/sth** (**in sth**) to show the image of sb/sth on the surface of sth such as a mirror, water or glass: *His face was reflected in the mirror.* ◇ *She could see herself reflected in his eyes.* **2** [T] ~ **sth** to throw back light, heat, sound, etc. from a surface: *The windows reflected the bright afternoon sunlight.* ◇ *When the sun's rays hit the earth, a lot of the heat is reflected back into space.* **3** [T] ~ **sth** to show or be a sign of the nature of sth or of sb's attitude or feeling: *Our newspaper aims to reflect the views of the local community.* **4** [I, T] to think carefully and deeply about sth: *Before I decide, I need time to reflect.* ◇ ~ **on/upon sth** *She was left to reflect on the implications of her decision.* ◇ ~ **that…** *On the way home he reflected that the interview had gone well.* ◇ ~ **how, what, etc…** *She reflected how different it could have been.* ◇ + **speech** *'It could all have been so different,' she reflected.*
IDM **reflect well, badly, etc. on sb/sth** to make sb/sth appear to be good, bad, etc. to other people: *This incident reflects badly on everyone involved.*

re·flect·ance /rɪˈflektəns/ *noun* [U, C] (*physics*) a measure of how much light is reflected off a surface, considered as a part of the total light that shines onto it

reˌflected 'glory *noun* [U] (*disapproving*) admiration or praise that is given to sb, not because of sth that they have done, but because of sth that sb connected with them has done: *She basked in the reflected glory of her daughter's success.*

re·flec·tion (*BrE* also *old-fashioned* **re·flex·ion**) /rɪˈflekʃn/ *noun* **1** [C] an image in a mirror, on a shiny surface, on water, etc: *He admired his reflection in the mirror.* **2** [U] the action or process of sending back light, heat, sound, etc. from a surface **3** [C] a sign that shows the state or nature of sth: *Your clothes are often a reflection of your personality.* ◇ *The increase in crime is **a sad reflection on*** (= shows sth bad about) *our society today.* **4** [U] careful thought about sth, sometimes over a long period of time: *She decided **on reflection** to accept his offer after all.* ◇ *A week off would give him time for reflection.* **5** [C, usually pl.] your written or spoken thoughts about a particular subject or topic: *a book of her reflections on childhood* **6** [C] an account or a description of sth: *The article is an accurate reflection of events that day.* IDM see MATURE *adj.*

re·flect·ive /rɪˈflektɪv/ *adj.* **1** (*formal*) thinking deeply about things SYN **thoughtful**: *a quiet and reflective man* **2 reflective** surfaces send back light or heat: *reflective car number plates* ◇ *On dark nights children should wear reflective clothing.* **3** ~ **of sth** typical of a particular situation or thing; showing the state or nature of sth: *His abilities are not reflective of the team as a whole.* ◇ *Everything you do or say is reflective of your personality.* ▸ **re·flect·ive·ly** *adv.*: *She sipped her wine reflectively.*

re·flect·ivity /ˌriːflekˈtɪvɪti; rɪˌflek-/ *noun* [U] (*physics*) the degree to which a material reflects light or RADIATION

re·flect·or /rɪˈflektə(r)/ *noun* **1** a surface that reflects light **2** a small piece of special glass or plastic that is put on a bicycle, or on clothing, so that it can be seen at night when light shines on it ➲ VISUAL VOCAB page V41

re·flex /ˈriːfleks/ *noun* an action or a movement of your body that happens naturally in response to sth and that you cannot control; sth that you do without thinking: *The doctor tested her reflexes.* ◇ *to have **quick/slow reflexes*** ◇ *a **reflex response/reaction*** ◇ *Only the goalkeeper's reflexes* (= his ability to react quickly) *stopped the ball from going in.* ◇ *Almost as a **reflex action**, I grab my pen as the phone rings.*

ˌreflex 'angle *noun* an angle of more than 180° ➲ VISUAL VOCAB page V58 ➲ compare ACUTE ANGLE, OBTUSE ANGLE, RIGHT ANGLE

re·flex·ion (*BrE*) = REFLECTION

re·flex·ive /rɪˈfleksɪv/ *adj.* a **reflexive** word or form of a word shows that the action of the verb affects the person who performs the action: *In 'He cut himself', 'cut' is a reflexive verb and 'himself' is a reflexive pronoun.*

re·flex·ology /ˌriːfleks'ɒlədʒi; *NAmE* ˌriːfleks'ɑːl-/ *noun* [U] a type of alternative treatment in which sb's feet are rubbed in a particular way in order to heal other parts of their body or to make them feel mentally relaxed ▸ **re·flex·olo·gist** *noun*

re·float /ˌriː'fləʊt; *NAmE* -'floʊt/ *verb* **~ sth** to make a boat or ship float again, for example after it has become stuck on the bottom in shallow water

re·flow /'riːfləʊ; *NAmE* -floʊ/ *noun* [U] (*technical*) **1** a method of joining metals together by heating and melting SOLDER (= a soft metal mixture) **2** the fact of changing text on a computer screen so that it takes more or less space

re·focus AW /ˌriː'fəʊkəs; *NAmE* -'foʊ-/ *verb* **1** [I, T] to give attention, effort, etc. to sth new or different: **~ (on/upon sb/sth)** *Policy must refocus on people instead of places.* ◇ **~ sth (on/upon sb/sth)** *We need to refocus attention on the real issues facing this country.* **2** [I, T] (of your eyes, a camera, etc.) to adapt or be adjusted again so that things can be seen clearly; to adjust sth again so that you can see things clearly

re·for·est·ation /ˌriːfɒrɪ'steɪʃn; *NAmE* -fɔːr-; -fɑːr-/ (*BrE* also **re·affor·est·ation**) *noun* [U] (*technical*) the act of planting new trees in an area where there used to be a forest ➲ VISUAL VOCAB page V7 ➲ compare DEFORESTATION

re·form 0-w /rɪ'fɔːm; *NAmE* rɪ'fɔːrm/ *verb, noun*

■ *verb* **1** 0-w [T] **~ sth** to improve a system, an organization, a law, etc. by making changes to it: *proposals to reform the social security system* ◇ *The law needs to be reformed.* **2** 0-w [I, T] to improve your behaviour; to make sb do this: *He has promised to reform.* ◇ **~ sb** *She thought she could reform him.* ▸ **re·formed** *adj.*: *a reformed character*

■ *noun* 0-w [U, C] change that is made to a social system, an organization, etc. in order to improve or correct it: *a government committed to reform* ◇ ***economic/electoral/constitutional, etc. reform*** ◇ *the reform of the educational system* ◇ *reforms in education* ◇ ***far-reaching/major/sweeping reforms***

ˌre-'form *verb* [I, T] to form again or form sth again, especially into a different group or pattern: *The band is re-forming after 23 years.* ◇ **~ sth** *The party has recently been re-formed.*

re·format /ˌriː'fɔːmæt; *NAmE* -'fɔːr-/ *verb* (-tt-) **~ sth** (*computing*) to give a new FORMAT to a computer disk

ref·or·ma·tion /ˌrefə'meɪʃn; *NAmE* -fər'm-/ *noun* **1** [U] (*formal*) the act of improving or changing sb/sth **2 the Reformation** [sing.] new ideas in religion in 16th century Europe that led to attempts to reform the Roman Catholic Church and to the forming of the Protestant Churches; the period of time when these changes were taking place

re·forma·tory /rɪ'fɔːmətri; *NAmE* rɪ'fɔːrmətɔːri/ *noun* (*pl.* -ies) (also **re'form school**) (*NAmE*) (*old-fashioned* in British English) a type of school that young criminals are sent to instead of prison

Re'formed Church *noun* [sing.] a church that has accepted the principles of the REFORMATION, especially a Calvinist one

re·form·er /rɪ'fɔːmə(r); *NAmE* -'fɔːrm-/ *noun* a person who works to achieve political or social change

re·form·ist /rɪ'fɔːmɪst; *NAmE* -'fɔːrm-/ *adj.* wanting or trying to change political or social situations ▸ **re·form·ist** *noun*

re·for·mu·late AW /ˌriː'fɔːmjuleɪt; *NAmE* -'fɔːrm-/ *verb* **1 ~ sth** to create or prepare sth again: *It is never too late to reformulate your goals.* **2 ~ sth** to say or express sth in a different way: *Let me try to reformulate the problem.* ▸ **re·for·mu·la·tion** AW /ˌriːˌfɔːmju'leɪʃn; *NAmE* -'fɔːrm-/ *noun* [U, C]

re·fract /rɪ'frækt/ *verb* **~ sth** (*physics*) (of water, air, glass, etc.) to make light change direction when it goes through at an angle: *Light is refracted when passed through a prism.* ▸ **re·frac·tion** /rɪ'frækʃn/ *noun* [U]

re·fract·ive /rɪ'fræktɪv/ *adj.* (*physics*) causing, caused by or relating to refraction

reˌfractive 'index *noun* (*physics*) a measurement of how much an object or a substance refracts light

re·fract·om·eter /ˌrɪfræk'tɒmɪtə(r); *NAmE* -'tɑːm-/ *noun* (*physics*) an instrument for measuring a refractive index

re·fract·or /rɪ'fræktə(r)/ *noun* (*physics*) something such as a LENS which REFRACTS light (= causes it to change direction)

re·frac·tory /rɪ'fræktəri/ *adj.* **1** (*formal*) (of a person) difficult to control; behaving badly **2** (*medical*) (of a disease or medical condition) difficult to treat or cure

re·frain /rɪ'freɪn/ *verb, noun*

■ *verb* [I] (*formal*) to stop yourself from doing sth, especially sth that you want to do SYN **desist from**: **~ (from sth)** *Please refrain from smoking.* ◇ **~ (from doing sth)** *He has refrained from criticizing the government in public.*

■ *noun* **1** a comment or complaint that is often repeated: *Complaints about poor food in schools have become a familiar refrain.* **2** the part of a song or a poem that is repeated after each VERSE SYN **chorus**

re·fresh /rɪ'freʃ/ *verb* **1** [T] **~ sb/yourself** to make sb feel less tired or less hot: *The long sleep had refreshed her.* ◇ *He refreshed himself with a cool shower.* **2** [T] **~ sth** (*informal, especially NAmE*) to fill sb's glass or cup again: *Let me refresh your glass.* **3** [T] **~ your/sb's memory** to remind yourself/sb of sth, especially with the help of sth that can be seen or heard SYN **jog**: *He had to refresh his memory by looking at his notes.* **4** [T, I] **~ (sth)** (*computing*) to get the most recent information, for example on an Internet page, by clicking on a button on the screen: *Click here to refresh this document.* ◇ *The page refreshes automatically.*

re'fresher course (also **re·fresh·er** especially in *NAmE*) *noun* a short period of training to improve your skills or to teach you about new ideas and developments in your job

re·fresh·ing /rɪ'freʃɪŋ/ *adj.* **1** pleasantly new or different: *It **made a refreshing change** to be taken seriously for once.* **2** making you feel less tired or hot: *a **refreshing drink/shower*** ▸ **re·fresh·ing·ly** *adv.*: *refreshingly different* ◇ *The house was refreshingly cool inside.*

re·fresh·ment /rɪ'freʃmənt/ *noun* **1 refreshments** [pl.] drinks and small amounts of food that are provided or sold to people in a public place or at a public event: *Light refreshments will be served during the break.* **2** [U] (*formal*) food and drink: *In York we had a short stop for refreshment.* ◇ *Can we offer you some refreshment?* ◇ *a **refreshment room/kiosk/tent*** ◇ (*humorous*) ***liquid refreshment*** (= alcoholic drink) **3** [U] (*formal*) the fact of making sb feel stronger or less tired or hot: *a place to rest and find refreshment for mind and body*

refried beans /ˌriːfraɪd 'biːnz/ *noun* [pl.] BEANS that have been boiled and fried in advance and are heated again when needed, used especially in Mexican cooking

re·friger·ate /rɪ'frɪdʒəreɪt/ *verb* **~ sth** (*formal*) to make food, etc. cold in order to keep it fresh or preserve it: *Once opened, this product should be kept refrigerated.* ◇ *a **refrigerated lorry/truck*** ▸ **re·friger·ation** /rɪˌfrɪdʒə'reɪʃn/ *noun* [U]: *Keep all meat products under refrigeration.*

re·friger·ator 0-w /rɪ'frɪdʒəreɪtə(r)/ *noun* (*formal* or *NAmE*) = FRIDGE: *This dessert can be served straight from the refrigerator.* ➲ VISUAL VOCAB page V22

re·fuel /ˌriː'fjuːəl/ *verb* (-ll-, *US* -l-) [T, I] **~ (sth)** to fill sth, especially a plane, with fuel in order to continue a journey; to be filled with fuel: *to refuel a plane* ◇ *The planes needed to refuel before the next mission.* ◇ *a refuelling stop*

ref·uge /'refjuːdʒ/ *noun* **1** [U] shelter or protection from danger, trouble, etc: *A further 300 people have **taken refuge** in the US embassy.* ◇ **~ (from sb/sth)** *They were forced to **seek refuge** from the fighting.* ◇ *a place of refuge* ◇ *As the*

R

situation at home got worse she increasingly took refuge in her work. **2** [C] **~ (from sb/sth)** a place, person or thing that provides shelter or protection for sb/sth: *He regarded the room as a refuge from the outside world.* ◇ *a wetland refuge for birds* **3** [C] a building that provides a temporary home for people in need of shelter or protection from sb/sth: *a women's refuge* ◇ *a refuge for the homeless* **4** (*BrE*) = TRAFFIC ISLAND

refu·gee /ˌrefjuˈdʒiː/ *noun* a person who has been forced to leave their country or home, because there is a war or for political, religious or social reasons: *a steady flow of refugees from the war zone* ◇ ***political/economic refugees*** ◇ *a **refugee camp*** ➲ COLLOCATIONS at RACE, WAR

re·ful·gent /rɪˈfʌldʒənt/ *adj.* (*formal*) very bright

re·fund *noun, verb*

■ ***noun*** /ˈriːfʌnd/ a sum of money that is paid back to you, especially because you paid too much or because you returned goods to a shop/store: *a tax refund* ◇ *to **claim/demand/receive a refund*** ◇ *If there is a delay of 12 hours or more, you will receive a **full refund** of the price of your trip.* ➲ COLLOCATIONS at SHOPPING

■ ***verb*** /rɪˈfʌnd/ to give sb their money back, especially because they have paid too much or because they are not satisfied with sth they bought SYN **reimburse**: **~ sth** *Tickets cannot be exchanged or money refunded.* ◇ **~ sth to sb** *We will refund your money to you in full if you are not entirely satisfied.* ◇ **~ sb sth** *We will refund you your money in full.* ▸ **re·fund·able** *adj.*: *a refundable deposit* ◇ *Tickets are not refundable.*

re·fur·bish /ˌriːˈfɜːbɪʃ; *NAmE* -ˈfɜːrb-/ *verb* **~ sth** to clean and decorate a room, building, etc. in order to make it more attractive, more useful, etc. ➲ COLLOCATIONS at DECORATE ▸ **re·fur·bish·ment** *noun* [U, C]: *The hotel is closed for refurbishment.*

re·fusal 🔑 /rɪˈfjuːzl/ *noun* [U, C] an act of saying or showing that you will not do, give or accept sth: **~ (of sth)** *the refusal of a request/an invitation/an offer* ◇ *a **blunt/flat/curt refusal*** ◇ **~ to do sth** *His refusal to discuss the matter is very annoying.* ➲ see also FIRST REFUSAL

re·fuse[1] 🔑 /rɪˈfjuːz/ *verb*
1 🔑 [I, T] to say that you will not do sth that sb has asked you to do: *Go on, ask her; she can hardly refuse.* ◇ **~ to do sth** *He **flatly refused** to discuss the matter.* ◇ *She refused to accept that there was a problem.* **2** 🔑 [T] **~ sth** to say that you do not want sth that has been offered to you SYN **turn down**: *I politely refused their invitation.* ◇ *The job offer was simply too good to refuse.* **3** 🔑 [T] to say that you will not allow sth; to say that you will not give or allow sb sth that they want or need SYN **deny**: **~ sth** *The bank refused his demand for a full refund.* ◇ *The authorities refused permission for the new housing development.* ◇ **~ sb sth** *They refused him a visa.* ◇ *She would never refuse her kids anything.*

re·fuse[2] /ˈrefjuːs/ *noun* [U] (*formal*) waste material that has been thrown away SYN **rubbish/garbage**: ***domestic/household refuse*** ◇ *the city refuse dump* ◇ ***refuse collection/disposal*** ➲ note at RUBBISH

ˈ**refuse collector** (*BrE*) (*NAmE* ˈ**garbage collector**) *noun* (*formal*) = DUSTMAN

re·fuse·nik /rɪˈfjuːznɪk/ *noun* a person who refuses to obey an order or law as a protest

re·fute /rɪˈfjuːt/ *verb* (*formal*) **1 ~ sth** to prove that sth is wrong SYN **rebut**: *to **refute an argument/a theory, etc.*** **2 ~ sth** to say that sth is not true or fair SYN **deny**: *She refutes any suggestion that she behaved unprofessionally.* ▸ **re·fut·able** /-əbl/ *adj.* **refu·ta·tion** /ˌrefjuˈteɪʃn/ *noun* [C, U]: *a refutation of previously held views*

reg /redʒ/ *abbr.* (*BrE, informal*) REGISTRATION: *a V reg car* (= a car with 'V' in its REGISTRATION NUMBER, showing the year that it was registered)

re·gain /rɪˈɡeɪn/ *verb* **1 ~ sth** to get back sth you no longer have, especially an ability or a quality: *I struggled to regain some dignity.* ◇ *The party has regained control of the region.* ◇ *She paused on the edge, trying to **regain her balance**.* ◇ *He did not **regain consciousness*** (= wake up after being unconscious) *for several days.* **2 ~ sth** (*literary*) to get back to a place that you have left: *They finally managed to regain the beach.*

regal /ˈriːɡl/ *adj.* typical of a king or queen, and therefore impressive: *regal power* ◇ *the regal splendour of the palace* ◇ *She dismissed him with a regal gesture.* ➲ compare ROYAL ▸ **re·gal·ly** /-ɡəli/ *adv.*

re·gale /rɪˈɡeɪl/ *verb*
PHR V **reˈgale sb with sth** to amuse or entertain sb with stories, jokes, etc: *He regaled us with tales of his days as a jazz pianist.*

re·galia /rɪˈɡeɪliə/ *noun* [U] the special clothes that are worn or objects that are carried at official ceremonies

Synonyms

regard

call • find • consider • see • view

These words all mean to think about sb/sth in a particular way.

regard to think of sb/sth in a particular way: *He seemed to regard the whole thing as a joke.*

call to say that sb/sth has particular qualities or characteristics: *I wouldn't call German an easy language.*

find to have a particular feeling or opinion about sth: *You may find your illness hard to accept.*

consider to think of sb/sth in a particular way: *Who do you consider (to be) responsible for the accident?*

REGARD OR CONSIDER?

These two words have the same meaning, but they are used in different patterns and structures. In this meaning **consider** must be used with a complement or clause: you can *consider sb/sth to be sth* or *consider sb/sth as sth*, although very often the *to be* or *as* is left out: *He considers himself an expert.* ◇ *They are considered a high-risk group.* You can also *consider that sb/sth is sth* and again, the *that* can be left out. **Regard** is used in a narrower range of structures. The most frequent structure is *regard sb/sth as sth*; the *as* cannot be left out: ~~*I regard him a close friend.*~~ You cannot ~~*regard sb/sth to be sth*~~ or ~~*regard that sb/sth is sth*~~. However, **regard** (but not **consider** in this meaning) can also be used without a noun or adjective complement but with just an object and adverb (*sb/sth is highly regarded*) or adverbial phrase (*regard sb/sth with suspicion/jealousy/admiration*).

see to have an opinion of sth: *Try to see things from her point of view.*

view to think of sb/sth in a particular way: *How do you view your position within the company?* NOTE **View** has the same meaning as **regard** and **consider** but is slightly less frequent and slightly less formal. The main structures are *view sb/sth as sb/sth* (you cannot leave out the *as*) and *view sb/sth with sth*.

PATTERNS

- to regard/consider/see/view sb/sth **as** sth
- to regard/consider/see/view sb/sth **from** a particular point of view
- to find/consider sb/sth **to be** sth
- **generally/usually** regarded/considered/seen/viewed as sth
- to regard/consider/view sb/sth **favourably/unfavourably**

re·gard 🔑 /rɪˈɡɑːd; *NAmE* rɪˈɡɑːrd/ *verb, noun*
■ ***verb*** **1** 🔑 to think about sb/sth in a particular way: **~ sb/sth (+ adv./prep.)** *Her work is very highly regarded.* ◇ **~ sb/sth/yourself as sth** *Capital punishment was regarded as inhuman and immoral.* ◇ *He regards himself as a patriot.* ◇ *She is **widely regarded** as the current leader's natural successor.* **2** 🔑 **~ sb/sth (+ adv./prep.)** (*formal*) to look at sb/sth, es-

R

pecially in a particular way SYN **contemplate**: *He regarded us suspiciously.*

IDM **as regards sb/sth** (*formal*) concerning or in connection with sb/sth: *I have little information as regards her fitness for the post.* ◇ *As regards the first point in your letter…*

■ ***noun* 1** [U] (*formal*) attention to or thought and care for sb/sth: **~ for sb/sth** *to do sth with **scant/little/no regard for sb/sth*** ◇ *to **have/pay/show little regard** for other people's property* ◇ **~ to sb/sth** *He was driving **without regard to** speed limits.* ◇ *Social services should **pay proper regard** to the needs of inner-city areas.* **2** [U] (*formal*) respect or admiration for sb: *He **held her in high regard*** (= had a good opinion of her). ◇ **~ for sb/sth** *I had great regard for his abilities.* **3 regards** [pl.] used to send good wishes to sb at the end of a letter, or when asking sb to give your good wishes to another person who is not present: *With kind regards, Yours…* ◇ *Give your brother my regards when you see him.*

IDM **have re'gard to sth** (*law*) to remember and think carefully about sth: *It is always necessary to have regard to the terms of the contract.* **in this/that re'gard** (*formal*) concerning what has just been mentioned: *I have nothing further to say in this regard.* **in/with regard to sb/sth** (*formal*) concerning sb/sth: *a country's laws in regard to human rights* ◇ *The company's position with regard to overtime is made clear in their contracts.* ➲ more at AS *conj.*

re·gard·ing /rɪ'ɡɑːdɪŋ; *NAmE* -'ɡɑːrd-/ *prep.* concerning sb/sth; about sb/sth: *She has said nothing regarding your request.* ◇ *Call me if you have any problems regarding your work.*

re·gard·less /rɪ'ɡɑːdləs; *NAmE* -'ɡɑːrd-/ *adv.* paying no attention, even if the situation is bad or there are difficulties: *The weather was terrible but we **carried on regardless**.*

re'gardless of *prep.* paying no attention to sth/sb; treating sth/sb as not being important: *The club welcomes all new members regardless of age.* ◇ *He went ahead and did it, regardless of the consequences.* ◇ *The amount will be paid to everyone regardless of whether they have children or not.*

re·gatta /rɪ'ɡætə/ *noun* a sporting event in which races between ROWING BOATS or SAILING BOATS are held

Re·gency /'riːdʒənsi/ *adj.* [usually before noun] of or in the style of the period 1811–20 in Britain, when George, Prince of Wales, was REGENT (= ruled the country in place of the king, his father): *Regency architecture*

re·gency /'riːdʒənsi/ *noun* (*pl.* **-ies**) a period of government by a REGENT (= a person who rules a country in place of the king or queen)

re·gen·er·ate /rɪ'dʒenəreɪt/ *verb* **1** [T] **~ sth** to make an area, institution, etc. develop and grow strong again: *The money will be used to regenerate the commercial heart of the town.* **2** [I, T] (*biology*) to grow again; to make sth grow again: *Once destroyed, brain cells do not regenerate.* ◇ **~ sth/itself** *If the woodland is left alone, it will regenerate itself in a few years.* ► **re·gen·er·ation** /rɪˌdʒenə'reɪʃn/ *noun* [U]: *economic regeneration* ◇ *the regeneration of cells in the body* **re·gen·era·tive** /rɪ'dʒenərətɪv/ *adj.*: *the regenerative powers of nature*

re·gent /'riːdʒənt/ (also **Regent**) *noun* a person who rules a country because the king or queen is too young, old, ill/sick, etc: *to act as regent* ► **re·gent** (also **Regent**) *adj.* [after noun]: *the Prince Regent*

reg·gae /'reɡeɪ/ *noun* [U] a type of popular music with strong rhythms, developed in Jamaica in the 1960s

reggo = REGO

regi·cide /'redʒɪsaɪd/ *noun* [U, C] (*formal*) the crime of killing a king or queen; a person who is guilty of this crime

re·gime AW /reɪ'ʒiːm/ *noun* **1** a method or system of government, especially one that has not been elected in a fair way: *a **fascist/totalitarian/military, etc. regime*** ◇ *an **oppressive/brutal regime*** ➲ COLLOCATIONS at POLITICS **2** a method or system of organizing or managing sth: *Our tax regime is one of the most favourable in Europe.* **3** = REGIMEN: *a dietary regime*

regi·men /'redʒɪmən/ (also **re·gime**) *noun* (*medical* or *formal*) a set of rules about food and exercise or medical treatment that you follow in order to stay healthy or to improve your health

regi·ment /'redʒɪmənt/ *noun* [C+sing./pl. v.] **1** a large group of soldiers that is commanded by a COLONEL **2** (*formal*) a large number of people or things

regi·men·tal /ˌredʒɪ'mentl/ *adj.* [only before noun] connected with a particular regiment of soldiers: *a regimental flag* ◇ *regimental headquarters*

regi·ment·ed /'redʒɪmentɪd/ *adj.* (*disapproving*) **1** involving strict discipline and/or organization: *The school imposes a very regimented lifestyle on its students.* **2** arranged in strict groups, patterns, etc: *regimented lines of trees* ► **regi·men·ta·tion** /ˌredʒɪmen'teɪʃn/ *noun* [U]: *She rebelled against the regimentation of school life.*

Re·gina /rɪ'dʒaɪnə/ *noun* [U] (*BrE*, *formal*, from *Latin*) a word meaning 'queen', used, for example, in the titles of legal cases which are brought by the state when there is a queen in Britain: *Regina v Jones* ➲ compare REX

re·gion AW /'riːdʒən/ *noun*
1 [C] a large area of land, usually without exact limits or borders: *the **Arctic/tropical/desert, etc. regions*** ◇ *one of the most densely populated regions of North America* **2** [C] one of the areas that a country is divided into, that has its own customs and/or its own government: *the Basque region of Spain* **3 the regions** [pl.] (*BrE*) all of a country except the capital city **4** [C] a part of the body, usually one that has a particular character or problem: *pains in the abdominal region*

IDM **in the region of** used when you are giving a number, price, etc. to show that it is not exact SYN **approximately**: *He earns somewhere in the region of €50 000.*

re·gion·al AW /'riːdʒənl/ *adj.* [usually before noun] of or relating to a region: *regional variations in pronunciation* ◇ *the conflict between regional and national interests* ◇ *regional councils/elections/newspapers* ► **re·gion·al·ly** AW /-nəli/ *adv.*: *regionally based television companies*

re·gion·al·ism /'riːdʒənəlɪzəm/ *noun* **1** [C] a feature of a language that exists in a particular part of a country, and is not part of the standard language **2** [U] the desire of the people who live in a particular region of a country to have more political and economic independence

regis·ter AW /'redʒɪstə(r)/ *verb, noun*

■ ***verb***

▸ PUT NAME ON LIST **1** [T, I] to record your/sb's/sth's name on an official list: **~ sth** *to **register a birth/marriage/death*** ◇ *to **register a company/trademark*** ◇ **~ sth in sth** *The ship was registered in Panama.* ◇ **~ sb + adj.** | **~ (sb) as sth** *She is officially registered (as) disabled.* ◇ **~ (with sb/sth)** *to register with a doctor* ◇ **~ (at/for sth)** *to register at a hotel*

▸ GIVE OPINION PUBLICLY **2** [T] **~ sth** (*formal*) to make your opinion known officially or publicly: *China has registered a protest over foreign intervention.*

▸ ON MEASURING INSTRUMENT **3** [I] (**+ noun**) if a measuring instrument **registers** an amount or sth **registers** an amount on a measuring instrument, the instrument shows or records that amount: *The thermometer registered 32°C.* ◇ *The earthquake registered 3 on the Richter scale.* ◇ *The stock exchange has registered huge losses this week.*

▸ SHOW FEELING **4** [T, no passive, I] **~ (sth)** (*formal*) to show or express a feeling: *Her face registered disapproval.* ◇ *Shock registered on everyone's face.*

▸ NOTICE STH **5** [T, no passive, I] (often used in negative sentences) **~ (sth)** to notice sth and remember it; to be noticed: *He barely registered our presence.* ◇ *I told her my name, but it obviously didn't register.*

▸ LETTER/PACKAGE **6** [T, usually passive] **~ sth** to send sth by mail, paying extra money to protect it against loss or damage: *Can I register this, please?* ◇ *a registered letter*

■ ***noun***

▸ LIST OF NAMES **1** [C] an official list or record of names,

R

items, etc; a book that contains such a list: *a **parish register*** (= of births, marriages and deaths) ◇ *to be on the **electoral register/register of voters*** ◇ *Could you sign the **hotel register** please, sir?* ◇ (*BrE*) *The teacher **called the register*** (= checked who was present at school).
▸ OF VOICE/INSTRUMENT **2** [C] the range, or part of a range, of a human voice or a musical instrument: *in the **upper/middle/lower register***
▸ OF WRITING/SPEECH **3** [C, U] (*linguistics*) the level and style of a piece of writing or speech, that is usually appropriate to the situation that it is used in: *The essay suddenly switches from a formal to an informal register.*
▸ FOR HOT/COLD AIR **4** [C] (*NAmE*) an opening, with a cover that you can have open or shut, that allows hot or cold air from a heating or cooling system into a room ➲ compare VENT
▸ MACHINE **5** [C] (*NAmE*) = CASH REGISTER

ˌregistered ˈmail (*BrE* also **ˌregistered ˈpost**) *noun* [U] a method of sending a letter or package in which the person sending it can claim money if it arrives late or is lost or damaged ➲ compare RECORDED DELIVERY

ˌregistered ˈnurse *noun* (*abbr.* RN) **1** (*NAmE*) a nurse who has a degree in NURSING and who has passed an exam to be allowed to work in a particular state **2** (*BrE*) a nurse who has an official qualification

ˌregistered ˈtrademark *noun* (*symb.* ®) the sign or name of a product, etc. that is officially recorded and protected so that nobody else can use it

ˈregister office *noun* the official way of referring to a REGISTRY OFFICE

regis·trar /ˌredʒɪˈstrɑː(r); ˈredʒɪstrɑː(r)/ *noun* **1** a person whose job is to keep official records, especially of births, marriages and deaths **2** the senior officer who organizes the affairs of a college or university **3** a doctor working in a British hospital who is training to become a specialist in a particular area of medicine: *a paediatric registrar* ➲ compare CONSULTANT, RESIDENT

regis·tra·tion AW /ˌredʒɪˈstreɪʃn/ *noun* **1** [U, C] the act of making an official record of sth/sb: *the registration of letters and parcels* ◇ *the registration of students for a course* ◇ *registration fees* ◇ *vehicle registrations* ◇ *the registration of a child's birth* **2** [U, C] a document showing that an official record has been made of sth ➲ compare LOGBOOK **3** [C] (*BrE*) = REGISTRATION NUMBER **4** [U] (*BrE*) the time when a teacher looks at the list of students on the class register and checks that the students are present

R

regiˈstration number (also **regis·tra·tion**) (both *BrE*) (*NAmE* **ˈlicense (plate) number**) *noun* the series of letters and numbers that are shown on a NUMBER PLATE at the front and back of a vehicle to identify it

regis·try /ˈredʒɪstri/ *noun* (*pl.* -ies) a place where registers are kept

ˈregistry office (also **ˈregister office**) *noun* (in Britain) a place where CIVIL marriages (= that do not involve a religious ceremony) are performed and where records of births, marriages and deaths are made: *to get married in/at a registry office*

rego (also **reggo**) /ˈredʒəʊ; *NAmE* -oʊ/ *noun* (*pl.* -os) (*AustralE, NZE, informal*) a REGISTRATION for a car, etc.

re·gress /rɪˈɡres/ *verb* [I] **~ (to sth)** (*formal*, usually *disapproving*) to return to an earlier or less advanced form or way of behaving

re·gres·sion /rɪˈɡreʃn/ *noun* [U, C] **~ (to sth)** the process of going back to an earlier or less advanced form or state

re·gres·sive /rɪˈɡresɪv/ *adj.* **1** becoming or making sth less advanced: *The policy has been condemned as a regressive step.* **2** (*technical*) (of taxes) having less effect on the rich than on the poor

re·gret 🔑 /rɪˈɡret/ *verb, noun*
■ *verb* (-tt-) **1** 🔑 to feel sorry about sth you have done or about sth that you have not been able to do: **~ sth** *If you don't do it now, **you'll** only **regret it**.* ◇ *The decision could be one he **lives to regret**.* ◇ *'I've had a wonderful life,' she said, 'I don't regret a thing.'* ◇ **~ doing sth** *He **bitterly regretted** ever having mentioned it.* ◇ **~ what, how, etc...** *I **deeply regret** what I said.* ◇ **~ that...** *I regret that I never got to meet him in person.* **2** 🔑 (*formal*) used to say in a polite or formal way that you are sorry or sad about a situation: **~ sth** *The airline regrets any inconvenience.* ◇ **~ that...** *I regret that I am unable to accept your kind invitation.* ◇ **~ to do sth** *We regret to inform you that your application has not been successful.* ◇ **it is regretted that...** ***It is to be regretted that*** *so many young people leave school without qualifications.*
■ ***noun*** 🔑 [U, C] a feeling of sadness or disappointment that you have because of sth that has happened or sth that you have done or not done: *It is **with great regret** that I accept your resignation.* ◇ *She **expressed her regret at** the decision.* ◇ *a **pang/twinge of regret*** ◇ ***I have no regrets** about leaving Newcastle* (= I do not feel sorry about it). ◇ *What is your greatest regret* (= the thing that you are most sorry about doing or not doing)? ◇ *He gave up teaching in 2009, **much to the regret of** his students.*

re·gret·ful /rɪˈɡretfl/ *adj.* feeling or showing sadness or disappointment because of sth that has happened or sth that you have done or not done SYN **rueful**: *a regretful look*

re·gret·ful·ly /rɪˈɡretfəli/ *adv.* **1** in a way that shows you are sad or disappointed about sth: *'I'm afraid not,' he said regretfully.* ◇ *Emma shook her head regretfully.* **2** used to show that you are sorry that sth is the case and you wish the situation were different SYN **regrettably**: *Regretfully, mounting costs have forced the museum to close.*

Which Word?

regretfully / regrettably

- **Regretfully** and **regrettably** can both be used as sentence adverbs to show that you are sorry about something and wish the situation were different: *Regretfully, some jobs will be lost.* ◇ *Regrettably, some jobs will be lost.*
- **Regretfully** can also be used to mean 'in a way that shows you are sad or disappointed about something': *He sighed regretfully.*

re·gret·table /rɪˈɡretəbl/ *adj.* **~ (that...)** (*formal*) that you are sorry about and wish had not happened: ***It is regrettable that*** *the police were not informed sooner.* ◇ *The loss of jobs is highly regrettable.* ▸ **re·gret·tably** /-əbli/ *adv.*: *Regrettably, crime has been increasing in this area.*

re·group /ˌriːˈɡruːp/ *verb* **1** [T, I] **~ (sth) (for sth)** to arrange the way people or soldiers work together in a new way, especially in order to continue fighting or attacking sb: *They regrouped their forces and renewed the attack.* ◇ *After its election defeat, the party needs to regroup.* **2** [I] (of a person) to return to a normal state after an unpleasant experience or a period of difficulty, and become ready to make an effort again with new enthusiasm or strength: *Summer is a time to relax, regroup and catch up on all those things you've been putting off all year.*

regu·lar 🔑 /ˈreɡjələ(r)/ *adj., noun*
■ ***adj.***
▸ FOLLOWING PATTERN **1** 🔑 following a pattern, especially with the same time and space in between each thing and the next: *regular breathing* ◇ *a **regular pulse/heartbeat*** ◇ *A light flashed **at regular intervals**.* ◇ *There is a regular bus service to the airport.* ◇ ***regular meetings/visits*** ◇ *The equipment is checked **on a regular basis**.* OPP **irregular**
▸ FREQUENT **2** 🔑 done or happening often: *Do you take regular exercise?* ◇ *Domestic violence is a regular occurrence in some families.* OPP **irregular** **3** 🔑 [only before noun] (of people) doing the same thing or going to the same place often: *our regular customers* ◇ *regular offenders* (= against the law) ◇ *He was a regular visitor to her house.*
▸ USUAL **4** 🔑 [only before noun] usual: *I couldn't see my regular doctor today.* ◇ *On Monday he would have to return to his*

regular duties. ◇ *It's important to follow the regular procedure.*

▸ EVEN **5** having an even shape: *a face with regular features* ◇ *a regular geometric pattern* OPP **irregular**

▸ PERMANENT **6** lasting or happening over a long period: *a regular income* ◇ *She couldn't find any regular employment.*

▸ STANDARD SIZE **7** (*especially NAmE*) of a standard size: *Regular or large fries?*

▸ ORDINARY **8** [only before noun] (*especially NAmE*) ordinary; without any special or extra features: *Do you want regular or diet cola?* ◇ (*approving*) *He's just a regular guy who loves his dog.*

▸ SOLDIER **9** [only before noun] belonging to or connected with the permanent armed forces or police force of a country: *a **regular army/soldier*** OPP **irregular**

▸ GRAMMAR **10** (especially of verbs or nouns) changing their form in the same way as most other verbs and nouns: *The past participle of regular verbs ends in '-ed'.* OPP **irregular**

▸ FOR EMPHASIS **11** (*informal*) used for emphasis to show that sb/sth is an exact or clear example of the thing mentioned: *The whole thing was a regular disaster.*

IDM **(as) regular as 'clockwork** very regularly; happening at the same time in the same way: *He is home by six every day, regular as clockwork.*

■ ***noun***

▸ CUSTOMER **1** a customer who often goes to a particular shop/store, pub, restaurant, etc: *He's one of our regulars.*

▸ MEMBER OF TEAM **2** a person who often plays in a particular team, takes part in a particular television show, etc: *We are missing six first-team regulars because of injury.*

▸ SOLDIER **3** a professional soldier who belongs to a country's permanent army

re·gu·lar·ity /ˌregjuˈlærəti/ *noun* **1** [U] the fact that the same thing happens again and again, and usually with the same length of time between each time it happens: *Aircraft passed overhead **with monotonous regularity**.* **2** [U] the fact that sth is arranged in an even way or in an organized pattern: *the striking regularity of her features* **3** [C] a thing that has a pattern to it: *They had observed regularities in the behaviour of the animals.* ➲ compare IRREGULARITY

regu·lar·ize (*BrE* also **-ise**) /ˈregjələraɪz/ *verb* **~ sth** to make a situation that already exists legal or official: *Illegal immigrants were given the opportunity to regularize their position.*

regu·lar·ly /ˈregjələli; *NAmE* -lərli/ *adv.* **1** at regular intervals or times: *We meet regularly to discuss the progress of the project.* **2** often: *I go there quite regularly.* **3** in an even or balanced way: *The plants were spaced regularly, about 50 cm apart.*

regu·late AW /ˈregjuleɪt/ *verb* **1** [T, I] **~ (sth)** to control sth by means of rules: *The activities of credit companies are regulated by law.* ◇ *It is up to the regulating authority to put the measures into effect.* **2** [T] **~ sth** to control the speed, pressure, temperature, etc. in a machine or system: *This valve regulates the flow of water.*

regu·la·tion AW /ˌregjuˈleɪʃn/ *noun, adj.*

■ ***noun* 1** [C, usually pl.] an official rule made by a government or some other authority: *too many **rules and regulations*** ◇ ***fire/safety/building, etc. regulations*** ◇ *to comply with the regulations* ◇ ***Under the** new **regulations** spending on office equipment will be strictly controlled.* ◇ *the strict regulations governing the sale of weapons* **2** [U] controlling sth by means of rules: *the voluntary regulation of the press*

■ ***adj.*** [only before noun] that must be worn or used according to the official rules: *in regulation uniform*

regu·la·tor AW /ˈregjuleɪtə(r)/ *noun* **1** a person or an organization that officially controls an area of business or industry and makes sure that it is operating fairly **2** a device that automatically controls sth such as speed, temperature or pressure

regu·la·tory AW /ˈregjələtəri; *NAmE* -tɔːri/ *adj.* [usually before noun] having the power to control an area of business or industry and make sure that it is operating fairly: ***regulatory bodies/authorities/agencies***

re·gur·gi·tate /rɪˈɡɜːdʒɪteɪt; *NAmE* -ˈɡɜːrdʒ-/ *verb* **1 ~ sth** (*formal*) to bring food that has been swallowed back up into the mouth again **2 ~ sth** (*disapproving*) to repeat sth you have heard or read without really thinking about it or understanding it ▸ **re·gur·gi·ta·tion** /rɪˌɡɜːdʒɪˈteɪʃn; *NAmE* -ˌɡɜːrdʒ-/ *noun* [U]

rehab /ˈriːhæb/ *noun* [U] (*especially NAmE*) the process of helping to cure sb who has a problem with drugs or alcohol: *to go into rehab* ◇ *a rehab clinic*

re·habili·tate /ˌriːəˈbɪlɪteɪt/ *verb* **1 ~ sb** to help sb to have a normal, useful life again after they have been very ill/sick or in prison for a long time: *a unit for rehabilitating drug addicts* **2 ~ sb (as sth)** to begin to consider that sb is good or acceptable after a long period during which they were considered bad or unacceptable: *He played a major role in rehabilitating Magritte as an artist.* **3 ~ sth** to return a building or an area to its previous good condition ▸ **re·habili·ta·tion** /ˌriːəˌbɪlɪˈteɪʃn/ *noun* [U]: *a drug rehabilitation centre* ◇ *the rehabilitation of the steel industry*

re·hash /ˌriːˈhæʃ/ *verb* **~ sth** (*disapproving*) to arrange ideas, pieces of writing or pieces of film into a new form but without any great change or improvement: *He just rehashes songs from the 60s.* ▸ **re·hash** /ˈriːhæʃ/ *noun* [sing.]: (*disapproving*) *The movie is just a rehash of the best TV episodes.*

re·hear /ˌriːˈhɪə(r); *NAmE* -ˈhɪr/ *verb* (**re·heard**, **re·heard** /ˌriːˈhɜːd; *NAmE* -ˈhɜːrd/) **~ sth** (*law*) to hear or consider again a case in court

re·hear·ing /ˌriːˈhɪərɪŋ; *NAmE* -ˈhɪr-/ *noun* (*law*) an opportunity for a case to be heard or considered again in court

re·hearsal /rɪˈhɜːsl; *NAmE* rɪˈhɜːrsl/ *noun* **1** [C, U] time that is spent practising a play or piece of music in preparation for a public performance: *to **have a rehearsal*** ◇ *We only had six days of rehearsal.* ◇ *Our new production of 'Hamlet' is currently **in rehearsal**.* ◇ *a rehearsal room* ➲ see also DRESS REHEARSAL **2** [C, usually sing.] **~ (for sth)** an experience or event that helps to prepare you for sth that is going to happen in the future: *These training exercises are designed to be a rehearsal for the invasion.* **3** [C, usually sing.] **~ of sth** (*formal*) the act of repeating sth that has been said before: *We listened to his lengthy rehearsal of the arguments.*

re·hearse /rɪˈhɜːs; *NAmE* rɪˈhɜːrs/ *verb* **1** [I, T] to practise or make people practise a play, piece of music, etc. in preparation for a public performance: **~ (for sth)** *We were given only two weeks to rehearse.* ◇ **~ sth/sb** *Today, we'll just be rehearsing the final scene.* ◇ *The actors were poorly rehearsed.* **2** [T] **~ sth** to prepare in your mind or practise privately what you are going to do or say to sb: *She walked along rehearsing her excuse for being late.* **3** [T] **~ sth** (*formal*, usually *disapproving*) to repeat ideas or opinions that have often been expressed before

re·heat /ˌriːˈhiːt/ *verb* **~ sth** to heat cooked food again after it has been left to go cold

re·home /ˌriːˈhəʊm; *NAmE* -ˈhoʊm/ *verb* **~ sth** to find a new owner for a pet, especially a dog or cat, usually after caring for it for a time: *The organization rescues stray dogs and rehomes them.*

re·house /ˌriːˈhaʊz/ *verb* **~ sb** to provide sb with a different home to live in: *Thousands of earthquake victims are still waiting to be rehoused.*

reign /reɪn/ *noun, verb*

■ ***noun* 1** the period during which a king, queen, EMPEROR, etc. rules: ***in/during the reign** of Charles II* **2** the period during which sb is in charge of an organization, a team, etc.

■ ***verb* 1** [I] to rule as king, queen, EMPEROR, etc: *the reigning monarch* ◇ *Queen Victoria reigned from 1837 to 1901.* ◇ **~ over sb/sth** *Herod reigned over Palestine at that time.* **2** [I] **~ (over sb/sth)** to be the best or most important in a particular situation or area of skill: *the reigning champion* ◇ *In the field of classical music, he still **reigns supreme**.* **3** [I]

R

(*literary*) (of an idea, a feeling or an atmosphere) to be the most obvious feature of a place or moment: *At last* ***silence reigned*** (= there was complete silence).

re·ig·nite /ˌriːɪɡˈnaɪt/ *verb* [I, T] to start burning again; to make sth start burning again: *The oven burners reignite automatically if blown out.* ◇ **~ sth** *You may need to reignite the pilot light.* ◇ (*figurative*) *Their passion was reignited by a romantic trip to Venice.*

ˌreign of ˈterror *noun* (*pl.* **reigns of terror**) a period during which there is a lot of violence and many people are killed by the ruler or people in power

reiki /ˈreɪki/ *noun* [U] (from *Japanese*) a method of healing based on the idea that energy can be directed into a person's body by touch

re·im·burse /ˌriːɪmˈbɜːs; *NAmE* -ˈbɜːrs/ *verb* (*formal*) to pay back money to sb which they have spent or lost: **~ sth** *We will reimburse any expenses incurred.* ◇ **~ sb (for sth)** *You will be reimbursed for any loss or damage caused by our company.* ▶ **re·im·burse·ment** *noun* [U]

rein /reɪn/ *noun, verb*

■ ***noun*** **1** [C, usually pl.] a long narrow leather band that is attached to a metal bar in a horse's mouth (= a BIT) and is held by the rider in order to control the horse: *She pulled gently on the reins.* **2 reins** [pl.] (*BrE*) strips of leather, etc. worn by a small child and held by an adult in order to stop the child from walking off and getting lost **3 the reins** [pl.] the state of being in control or the leader of sth: *It was time to* ***hand over the reins*** *of power* (= to give control to sb else). ◇ *The vice-president was forced to* ***take up the reins*** *of office.*

IDM **give/allow sb/sth free/full ˈrein | give/allow free/full ˈrein to sth** to give sb complete freedom of action; to allow a feeling to be expressed freely: *The designer was given free rein.* ◇ *The script allows full rein to her larger-than-life acting style.* ➲ more at TIGHT

■ ***verb***

PHR V **ˌrein sb/sth↔ˈback | ˌrein sth↔ˈin 1** to start to control sb/sth more strictly SYN **check**: *We need to rein back public spending.* ◇ *She kept her emotions tightly reined in.* **2** to stop a horse or make it go more slowly by pulling back the reins

re·incar·nate /ˌriːɪnˈkɑːneɪt; *NAmE* -ˈkɑːrn-/ *verb* [often passive, T, I] **~ (sb/sth) (in/as sb/sth)** to be born again in another body after you have died; to make sb be born again in this way: *They believe humans are reincarnated in animal form.*

R

re·incar·na·tion /ˌriːɪnkɑːˈneɪʃn; *NAmE* -kɑːrˈn-/ *noun* **1** [U] the belief that after sb's death their soul lives again in a new body ➲ COLLOCATIONS at RELIGION **2** [C, usually sing.] a person or an animal whose body contains the soul of a dead person

rein·deer /ˈreɪndɪə(r); *NAmE* -dɪr/ *noun* (*pl.* **rein·deer** or **rein·deers**) a large DEER with long ANTLERS (= horns shaped like branches), that lives in cold northern regions: *herds of reindeer*

re·inforce AW /ˌriːɪnˈfɔːs; *NAmE* -ˈfɔːrs/ *verb* **1 ~ sth** to make a feeling, an idea, etc. stronger: *Such jokes tend to reinforce racial stereotypes.* ◇ *The climate of political confusion has only reinforced the country's economic decline.* ◇ *Success in the talks will reinforce his reputation as an international statesman.* **2 ~ sth** to make a structure or material stronger, especially by adding another material to it: *All buildings are now reinforced to withstand earthquakes.* ◇ *reinforced steel* **3 ~ sth** to send more people or equipment in order to make an army, etc. stronger: *The UN has undertaken to reinforce its military presence along the borders.*

ˌreinforced ˈconcrete *noun* [U] concrete with metal bars or wires inside to make it stronger

re·inforce·ment AW /ˌriːɪnˈfɔːsmənt; *NAmE* -ˈfɔːrs-/ *noun* **1 reinforcements** [pl.] extra soldiers or police officers who are sent to a place because more are needed: *to send in reinforcements* **2** [U, sing.] the act of making sth stronger, especially a feeling or an idea

re·instate /ˌriːɪnˈsteɪt/ *verb* **1 ~ sb/sth (in/as sth)** to give back a job or position that had been taken away from sb: *He was reinstated in his post.* **2 ~ sth (in/as sth)** to return sth to its previous position or status SYN **restore**: *There have been repeated calls to reinstate the death penalty.* ▶ **re·instate·ment** *noun* [U]

re·insur·ance /ˌriːɪnˈʃʊərəns; -ˈʃɔːr-; *NAmE* -ˈʃʊr-/ *noun* [U] (*finance*) the practice of one insurance company buying insurance from another company against any losses that result from claims that are made against it

re·inter·pret AW /ˌriːɪnˈtɜːprɪt; *NAmE* -ˈtɜːrp-/ *verb* **~ sth** to interpret sth in a new or different way ▶ **re·inter·pret·ation** AW /ˌriːɪnˌtɜːprɪˈteɪʃn; *NAmE* -ˌtɜːrp-/ *noun* [C, U]

re·intro·duce /ˌriːɪntrəˈdjuːs; *NAmE* -ˈduːs/ *verb* **1 ~ sth** to start to use sth again SYN **bring back**: *to reintroduce the death penalty* ◇ *plans to reintroduce trams to the city* **2 ~ sth** to put a type of animal, bird or plant back into a region where it once lived ▶ **re·intro·duc·tion** *noun* [U, C]

re·invent /ˌriːɪnˈvent/ *verb* **~ sth/yourself (as sth)** to present yourself/sth in a new form or with a new image: *The former wild man of rock has reinvented himself as a respectable family man.*

IDM **reinvent the wheel** to waste time creating sth that already exists and works well

re·invest AW /ˌriːɪnˈvest/ *verb* [T, I] **~ (sth)** to put profits that have been made on an investment back into the same investment or into a new one ▶ **re·invest·ment** AW *noun* [U, C]

re·in·vig·or·ate /ˌriːɪnˈvɪɡəreɪt/ *verb* **~ sth/sb** to give new energy or strength to sth/sb: *We need to reinvigorate the economy of the area.* ◇ *I felt reinvigorated after a rest and a shower.*

re·issue /ˌriːˈɪʃuː/ *verb, noun*

■ ***verb*** **~ sth (as sth)** to publish or produce again a book, record, etc. that has not been available for some time: *old jazz recordings reissued on CD* ◇ *The novel was reissued in paperback.*

■ ***noun*** an old book or record that has been published or produced again after not being available for some time

re·iter·ate /riˈɪtəreɪt/ *verb* (*formal*) to repeat sth that you have already said, especially to emphasize it: **~ sth** *to reiterate an argument/a demand/an offer* ◇ **~ that…** *Let me reiterate that we are fully committed to this policy.* ◇ **+ speech** *'I said "money",' he reiterated.* ▶ **re·iter·ation** /riˌɪtəˈreɪʃn/ *noun* [sing.]: *a reiteration of her previous statement*

re·ject 0-w AW *verb, noun*

■ ***verb*** /rɪˈdʒekt/

▸ ARGUMENT/IDEA/PLAN **1** 0-w **~ sth** to refuse to accept or consider sth: *to reject an argument/a claim/a decision/an offer/a suggestion* ◇ *The prime minister rejected any idea of reforming the system.* ◇ *The proposal was* ***firmly rejected.*** ◇ *All our suggestions were* ***rejected out of hand.***

▸ SB FOR JOB **2** 0-w **~ sb** to refuse to accept sb for a job, position, etc: *Please reject the following candidates…* ◇ *I've been rejected by all the universities I applied to.*

▸ NOT USE/PUBLISH **3** 0-w **~ sth** to decide not to use, sell, publish, etc. sth because its quality is not good enough: *Imperfect articles are rejected by our quality control.*

▸ NEW ORGAN **4** 0-w **~ sth** (of the body) to not accept a new organ after a TRANSPLANT operation, by producing substances that attack the organ

▸ NOT LOVE **5** 0-w **~ sb/sth** to fail to give a person or an animal enough care or affection: *The lioness rejected the smallest cub, which died.* ◇ *When her husband left home she felt rejected and useless.*

▶ **re·jec·tion** AW /rɪˈdʒekʃn/ *noun* [U, C]: *Her proposal met with unanimous rejection.* ◇ *a rejection letter* (= a letter in which you are told, for example, that you have not been accepted for a job) ◇ *painful feelings of rejection*

■ ***noun*** /ˈriːdʒekt/

▸ STH THAT CANNOT BE USED **1** something that cannot be used or sold because there is sth wrong with it

▸ PERSON **2** a person who has not been accepted as a member of a team, society, etc: *one of society's rejects*

rejig /ˌriːˈdʒɪɡ/ *verb* (-gg-) (*BrE*) (*US* **rejig·ger** /ˌriːˈdʒɪɡə(r)/) **~ sth** (*informal*) to make changes to sth; to arrange sth in a different way

re·joice /rɪˈdʒɔɪs/ *verb* [I, T] (*formal*) to express great happiness about sth: *When the war ended, people finally had cause to rejoice.* ◇ **~ at/in/over sth** *The motor industry is rejoicing at the cut in car tax.* ◇ **~ to do sth** *They rejoiced to see their son well again.* ◇ **~ that...** *I rejoice that justice has prevailed.*
IDM **rejoice in the name of...** (*BrE, humorous*) to have a name that sounds funny: *He rejoiced in the name of Owen Owen.*

re·joi·cing /rɪˈdʒɔɪsɪŋ/ *noun* [U] (also **rejoicings** [pl.]) the happy celebration of sth: *a time of great rejoicing*

re·join¹ /ˌriːˈdʒɔɪn/ *verb* [T, I] **~ (sb/sth)** to join sb/sth again after leaving them: *to rejoin a club* ◇ *She turned off her phone and rejoined them at the table.* ◇ *The path goes through a wood before rejoining the main road.*

re·join² /rɪˈdʒɔɪn/ *verb* **+ speech** | **~ that...** (*formal*) to say sth as an answer, especially sth quick, critical or amusing SYN **retort**: *'You're wrong!' she rejoined.*

re·join·der /rɪˈdʒɔɪndə(r)/ *noun* [usually sing.] (*formal*) a reply, especially a quick, critical or amusing one SYN **retort**

re·ju·ven·ate /rɪˈdʒuːvəneɪt/ *verb* **~ sb/sth** to make sb/sth look or feel younger or more lively ▶ **re·ju·ven·ation** /rɪˌdʒuːvəˈneɪʃn/ *noun* [U, sing.]

re·kin·dle /ˌriːˈkɪndl/ *verb* **~ sth** (*formal*) to make sth become active again SYN **reawaken**: *to rekindle feelings/hopes*

re·laid *past tense, past part.* of RELAY

re·lapse *noun, verb*
- ***noun*** /rɪˈlæps; ˈriːlæps/ [C, U] the fact of becoming ill/sick again after making an improvement: *to* ***have/suffer a relapse*** ◇ *a risk of relapse*
- ***verb*** /rɪˈlæps/ [I] **~ (into sth)** to go back into a previous condition or into a worse state after making an improvement: *They relapsed into silence.* ◇ *He relapsed into his old bad habits.* ◇ *Two days after leaving the hospital she relapsed into a coma.*

re·late 0‒ /rɪˈleɪt/ *verb*
1 0‒ show or make a connection between two or more things SYN **connect**: **~ sth** *I found it difficult to relate the two ideas in my mind.* ◇ **~ A to B** *In the future, pay increases will be related to productivity.* **2** 0‒ (*formal*) to give a spoken or written report of sth; to tell a story: **~ sth** *She relates her childhood experiences in the first chapters.* ◇ **~ sth to sb** *He related the facts of the case to journalists.* ◇ **~ how, what, etc...** *She related how he had run away from home as a boy.* ◇ **~ that...** *The story relates that an angel appeared and told him to sing.*
PHR V **reˈlate to sth/sb 1** 0‒ to be connected with sth/sb; to refer to sth/sb: *We shall discuss the problem as it relates to our specific case.* ◇ *The second paragraph relates to the situation in Scotland.* **2** 0‒ to be able to understand and have sympathy with sb/sth SYN **empathize with**: *Many adults can't relate to children.* ◇ *Our product needs an image that people can relate to.*

re·lated 0‒ /rɪˈleɪtɪd/ *adj.*
1 0‒ **~ (to sth/sb)** connected with sth/sb in some way: *Much of the crime in this area is related to drug abuse.* ◇ *These problems are* ***closely related.*** ◇ *a* ***related issue/question*** ◇ *a stress-related illness* **2** 0‒ **~ (to sth/sb)** in the same family: *Are you related to Margaret?* ◇ *We're distantly related.* **3** 0‒ **~ (to sth)** belonging to the same group: *related languages* ◇ *The llama is related to the camel.* OPP **unrelated** ▶ **re·lated·ness** *noun* [U]

re·la·tion 0‒ /rɪˈleɪʃn/ *noun*
1 0‒ **relations** [pl.] the way in which two people, groups or countries behave towards each other or deal with each other: ***diplomatic/international/foreign relations*** ◇ *US-Chinese relations* ◇ *teacher-pupil relations* ◇ **~ (with sb/sth)** *Relations with neighbouring countries are under strain at present.* ◇ **~ (between A and B)** *We seek to improve relations between our two countries.* ◇ (*formal*) *to have* ***sexual relations*** (= to have sex) ➲ COLLOCATIONS at INTERNATIONAL ➲ see also INDUSTRIAL RELATIONS, PUBLIC RELATIONS, RACE RELATIONS **2** 0‒ [U, C] the way in which two or more things are connected: **~ between A and B** *the relation between rainfall and crop yields* ◇ **~ to sth** *the relation of the farmer to the land* ◇ *The fee they are offering* ***bears no relation to*** *the amount of work involved.* ◇ (*formal*) *I have some comments to make* ***in relation to*** (= concerning) *this matter.* ◇ *Its brain is small* ***in relation to*** (= compared with) *its body.* **3** 0‒ [C] a person who is in the same family as sb else SYN **relative**: *a* ***close/near/distant relation*** *of mine* ◇ *a relation by marriage* ◇ *a party for friends and relations* ◇ *He's called Brady too, but we're* ***no relation*** (= not related). ◇ *Is he any relation to you?* ➲ see also BLOOD RELATION, POOR RELATION

re·la·tion·al /rɪˈleɪʃənl/ *adj.* (*formal* or *technical*) existing or considered in relation to sth else

reˌlational ˈdatabase *noun* (*computing*) a DATABASE that recognizes relationships between different pieces of information

re·la·tion·ship 0‒ /rɪˈleɪʃnʃɪp/ *noun*
1 0‒ [C] the way in which two people, groups or countries behave towards each other or deal with each other: **~ (between A and B)** *The relationship between the police and the local community has improved.* ◇ **~ (with sb)** *She has a very* ***close relationship*** *with her sister.* ◇ *I have established a good* ***working relationship*** *with my boss.* ◇ *a master-servant relationship* ➲ see also LOVE-HATE RELATIONSHIP **2** 0‒ [C] **~ (between A and B)** | **~ (with sb)** a loving and/or sexual friendship between two people: *Their affair did not develop into a lasting relationship.* ◇ *She's had a series of miserable relationships.* ◇ *Are you* ***in a relationship****?* **3** 0‒ [C, U] the way in which two or more things are connected: **~ (between A and B)** *the relationship between mental and physical health* ◇ **~ (to sth)** *This comment* ***bore no relationship to*** *the subject of our conversation.* ◇ *People alter their voices* ***in relationship to*** *background noise.* **4** 0‒ [C, U] the way in which a person is related to sb else in a family: *a father-son relationship* ◇ **~ between A and B** *I'm not sure of the exact relationship between them—I think they're cousins.*

rela·tive 0‒ /ˈrelətɪv/ *adj., noun*
- ***adj.* 1** 0‒ considered and judged by being compared with sth else: *the* ***relative merits*** *of the two plans* **2** 0‒ **~ (to sth)** considered according to its position or connection with sth else: *the position of the sun relative to the earth* **3** 0‒ [only before noun] that exists or that has a particular quality only when compared with sth else SYN **comparative**: *They now live in relative comfort* (= compared with how they lived before). ◇ *Given the failure of the previous plan, this turned out to be a relative success.* ◇ ***It's all relative*** *though, isn't it? We never had any money when I was a kid and $500 was a fortune to us.* ➲ compare ABSOLUTE **4 ~ to sth** (*formal*) having a connection with sth; referring to sth: *the facts relative to the case* **5** (*grammar*) referring to an earlier noun, sentence or part of a sentence: *In 'the man who came', 'who' is a* ***relative pronoun*** *and 'who came' is a* ***relative clause.***
- ***noun* 1** 0‒ a person who is in the same family as sb else SYN **relation**: *a* ***close/distant relative*** ◇ *her friends and relatives* **2** 0‒ a thing that belongs to the same group as sth else: *The ibex is a distant relative of the mountain goat.*

ˌrelative atomic ˈmass (also **aˌtomic ˈmass, aˌtomic ˈweight**) *noun* (*chemistry*) the average MASS of all the naturally occurring atoms of a chemical element

ˌrelative ˈdensity (also **speˌcific ˈgravity**) *noun* [U] (*chemistry*) the mass of a substance divided by the mass of the same volume of water or air

rela·tive·ly 0‒ /ˈrelətɪvli/ *adv.*
to a fairly large degree, especially in comparison to sth else: *I found the test relatively easy.* ◇ *We had relatively few applications for the job.* ◇ *Lack of exercise is also a risk factor for heart disease but it's relatively small when compared with the others.*
IDM **ˈrelatively speaking** used when you are comparing

R

sth with all similar things: *Relatively speaking, these jobs provide good salaries.*

rela·tiv·ism /ˈrelətɪvɪzəm/ *noun* [U] (*formal*) the belief that truth is not always and generally valid, but can be judged only in relation to other things, such as your personal situation ▸ **rela·tiv·ist** *adj.*: *a relativist view* **rela·tiv·ist** *noun*

rela·tiv·ity /ˌreləˈtɪvəti/ *noun* [U] **1** (*physics*) Einstein's theory of the universe based on the principle that all movement is relative and that time is a fourth DIMENSION related to space **2** (*formal*) the state of being relative and only able to be judged when compared with sth else

re·launch /ˌriːˈlɔːntʃ/ *verb* **~ sth** to start or present sth again in a new or different way, especially a product for sale ▸ **re·launch** /ˈriːlɔːntʃ/ *noun*

relax 0‑w AW /rɪˈlæks/ *verb*
1 0‑w [I] to rest while you are doing sth enjoyable, especially after work or effort SYN **unwind**: *Just relax and enjoy the movie.* ◇ *I'm going to spend the weekend just relaxing.* ◇ **~ with sth** *When I get home from work I like to relax with the newspaper.* **2** 0‑w [I, T] **~ (sb)** to become or make sb become calmer and less worried: *I'll only relax when I know you're safe.* ◇ *Relax! Everything will be OK.* **3** 0‑w [I, T] to become or make sth become less tight or stiff: *Allow your muscles to relax completely.* ◇ **~ sth** *The massage relaxed my tense back muscles.* ◇ *He* ***relaxed his grip*** *on her arm.* ◇ (*figurative*) *The dictator refuses to relax his grip on power.* **4** 0‑w [T] **~ sth** to allow rules, laws, etc. to become less strict: *The council has relaxed the ban on dogs in city parks.* **5** [T] **~ sth** to allow your attention or effort to become weaker: *You cannot afford to relax your concentration for a moment.*

re·lax·ant /rɪˈlæksənt/ *noun* (*medical*) a drug that is used to make the body relax: *a muscle relaxant*

re·lax·ation AW /ˌriːlækˈseɪʃn/ *noun* **1** [U] ways of resting and enjoying yourself; time spent resting and enjoying yourself: *I go hill-walking for relaxation.* ◇ *a few days of relaxation* ◇ *relaxation techniques* ⊃ SYNONYMS at ENTERTAINMENT **2** [C] something pleasant you do in order to rest, especially after you have been working: *Fishing is his favourite relaxation.* **3** [U, C, usually sing.] the act of making a rule or some form of control less strict or severe: *the relaxation of foreign currency controls* ◇ *a relaxation of travel restrictions*

re·laxed 0‑w AW /rɪˈlækst/ *adj.*
1 0‑w **~ (about sth)** (of a person) calm and not anxious or worried: *He appeared relaxed and confident before the match.* ◇ *She had a very relaxed manner.* **2** 0‑w (of a place) calm and informal: *a family-run hotel with a* ***relaxed atmosphere*** **3** 0‑w **~ (about sth)** not caring too much about discipline or making people follow rules SYN **laid-back**: *I take a fairly* ***relaxed attitude*** *towards what the kids wear to school.*

re·lax·ing 0‑w AW /rɪˈlæksɪŋ/ *adj.*
helping you to rest and become less anxious: *a relaxing evening with friends*

relay *verb, noun*
■ **verb** /ˈriːleɪ; rɪˈleɪ/ **1 ~ sth (to sb)** to receive and send on information, news, etc. to sb: *He relayed the message to his boss.* ◇ *Instructions were relayed to him by phone.* **2 ~ sth (to sb)** to broadcast television or radio signals: *The game was relayed by satellite to audiences all over the world.*
■ **noun** /ˈriːleɪ/ **1** (also **ˈrelay race**) a race between teams in which each member of the team runs or swims one section of the race: *the 4 × 100m relay* ◇ *a relay team* ◇ *the sprint relay* **2** a fresh set of people or animals that take the place of others that are tired or have finished a period of work: *Rescuers worked* ***in relays*** *to save the trapped miners.* **3** an electronic device that receives radio or television signals and sends them on again with greater strength: *a relay station*

re·lease 0‑w AW /rɪˈliːs/ *verb, noun*
■ **verb**
▸ SET SB/STH FREE **1** 0‑w to let sb/sth come out of a place where they have been kept or trapped: **~ sb/sth** *to* ***release a prisoner/hostage*** ◇ **~ sb/sth from sth** *Firefighters took two hours to release the driver from the wreckage.*
▸ STOP HOLDING STH **2** 0‑w **~ sth** to stop holding sth or stop it from being held so that it can move, fly, fall, etc. freely SYN **let go, let loose**: *He refused to release her arm.* ◇ *10 000 balloons were released at the ceremony.* ◇ *Intense heat is released in the reaction.*
▸ FEELINGS **3** 0‑w **~ sth** to express feelings such as anger or worry in order to get rid of them: *She burst into tears, releasing all her pent-up emotions.*
▸ FREE SB FROM DUTY **4** to free sb from a duty, responsibility, contract, etc: **~ sb** *The club is releasing some of its older players.* ◇ **~ sb from sth** *The new law released employers from their obligation to recognize unions.*
▸ PART OF MACHINE **5** 0‑w **~ sth** to remove sth from a fixed position, allowing sth else to move or function: *to* ***release the clutch/handbrake/switch, etc.***
▸ MAKE LESS TIGHT **6 ~ sth** to make sth less tight: *You need to release the tension in these shoulder muscles.*
▸ MAKE AVAILABLE **7** 0‑w **~ sth** to make sth available to the public: *Police have released no further details about the accident.* ◇ *to release a movie/book/CD* ◇ *new products released onto the market* **8 ~ sth** to make sth available that had previously been restricted: *The new building programme will go ahead as soon as the government releases the funds.*
■ **noun**
▸ SETTING SB/STH FREE **1** 0‑w [U, sing.] **~ (of sb) (from sth)** the act of setting a person or an animal free; the state of being set free: *The government has been working to secure the release of the hostages.* ◇ *She can expect an early release from prison.*
▸ MAKING STH AVAILABLE **2** 0‑w [U, sing.] the act of making sth available to the public: *The new software is planned for release in April.* ◇ *The movie* ***goes on*** *general* ***release*** (= will be widely shown in cinemas/movie theaters) *next week.* **3** 0‑w [C] a thing that is made available to the public, especially a new CD or film/movie: *the latest new releases*
▸ OF GAS/CHEMICAL **4** 0‑w [U, C] the act of letting a gas, chemical, etc. come out of the container where it has been safely held: *the release of carbon dioxide into the atmosphere* ◇ *to monitor radiation releases*
▸ FROM UNPLEASANT FEELING **5** [U, sing.] the feeling that you are free from pain, anxiety or some other unpleasant feeling: *a sense of release after the exam* ◇ *I think her death was a merciful release.* ⊃ see also PRESS RELEASE

rele·gate /ˈrelɪɡeɪt/ *verb* **1 ~ sb/sth (to sth)** to give sb a lower or less important position, rank, etc. than before: *She was then relegated to the role of assistant.* ◇ *He relegated the incident to the back of his mind.* **2** [usually passive] **~ sth** (*especially BrE*) to move a sports team, especially a football (SOCCER) team, to a lower position within an official league OPP **promote** ▸ **rele·ga·tion** /ˌrelɪˈɡeɪʃn/ *noun* [U]: *teams threatened with relegation*

re·lent /rɪˈlent/ *verb* (*formal*) **1** [I] to finally agree to sth after refusing SYN **give in**: *'Well, just for a little while then,' she said, finally relenting.* **2** [I] to become less determined, strong, etc: *After two days the rain relented.* ◇ *The police will not relent in their fight against crime.*

re·lent·less /rɪˈlentləs/ *adj.* **1** not stopping or getting less strong SYN **unrelenting**: *her* ***relentless pursuit of*** *perfection* ◇ *The sun was relentless.* **2** refusing to give up or be less strict or severe: *a relentless enemy* ▸ **re·lent·less·ly** *adv.*

rele·vant 0‑w AW /ˈreləvənt/ *adj.*
1 0‑w closely connected with the subject you are discussing or the situation you are thinking about: *a relevant suggestion/question/point* ◇ *Do you have the relevant experience?* ◇ **~ to sth/sb** *These comments are not directly relevant to this inquiry.* OPP **irrelevant** **2** 0‑w **~ (to sth/sb)** having ideas that are valuable and useful to people in their lives and work: *Her novel is still relevant today.* ▸ **rele·vance** AW /-əns/ *noun* [U]: *I don't see the relevance of your question.* ◇ *What he said has no direct relevance to the matter in hand.* ◇ *a classic play of contemporary relevance* **rele·vant·ly** *adv.*: *The applicant has experience in teaching and, more relevantly, in industry.*

R

re·li·able AW /rɪˈlaɪəbl/ *adj.* **1** that can be trusted to do sth well; that you can rely on SYN **dependable**: *We are looking for someone who is reliable and hard-working.* ◇ *a reliable friend* ◇ *My car's not as reliable as it used to be.* **2** that is likely to be correct or true: *Our information comes from a reliable source.* ◇ *a reliable witness* OPP **unreliable** ▸ **re·li·abil·ity** AW /rɪˌlaɪəˈbɪləti/ *noun* [U]: *The incident cast doubt on her motives and reliability.* ◇ *The reliability of these results has been questioned.* **re·li·ably** AW /-əbli/ *adv.*: *I am* ***reliably informed*** (= told by sb who knows the facts) *that the company is being sold.*

re·li·ance AW /rɪˈlaɪəns/ *noun* [U, sing.] **~ (on/upon sb/sth)** the state of needing sb/sth in order to survive, be successful, etc; the fact of being able to rely on sb/sth SYN **dependence**: *Heavy reliance on one client is risky when you are building up a business.* ◇ *Such learning methods encourage too great a reliance upon the teacher.* ◇ *The study programme concentrates more on group work and* ***places*** *less* ***reliance on*** (= depends less on) *lectures.* ◇ *I wouldn't* ***place*** *too much* ***reliance on*** (= trust) *these figures.*

re·li·ant AW /rɪˈlaɪənt/ *adj.* **~ on/upon sb/sth** needing sb/sth in order to survive, be successful, etc. SYN **dependent**: *The hostel is heavily reliant upon charity.* ➲ see also SELF-RELIANT

relic /ˈrelɪk/ *noun* **1 ~ (of/from sth)** an object, a tradition, a system, etc. that has survived from the past: *The building stands as the last remaining relic of the town's cotton industry.* ◇ *Videotapes may already seem like relics of a bygone era.* **2** a part of the body or clothing of a holy person, or sth that they owned, that is kept after their death and respected as a religious object: *holy relics*

re·lief 🔑 /rɪˈliːf/ *noun*
▸ REMOVAL OF ANXIETY/PAIN **1** 🔑 [U, sing.] the feeling of happiness that you have when sth unpleasant stops or does not happen: *a sense of relief* ◇ *We all* ***breathed a sigh of relief*** *when he left.* ◇ *She sighed with relief.* ◇ *Much* ***to my relief*** *the car was not damaged.* ◇ *News of their safety came as a great relief.* ◇ *It was a relief to be able to talk to someone about it.* ◇ ***What a relief!*** **2** 🔑 [U] **~ (from/of sth)** the act of removing or reducing pain, anxiety, etc: *modern methods of* ***pain relief*** ◇ *the relief of suffering*
▸ HELP **3** 🔑 [U] food, money, medicine, etc. that is given to help people in places where there has been a war or natural disaster SYN **aid**: ***famine relief*** ◇ ***a relief agency/organization/worker*** **4** 🔑 [U] (*especially NAmE*) financial help given by the government to people who need it
▸ ON TAX **5** [U] = TAX RELIEF: *relief on mortgage interest payments*
▸ STH DIFFERENT **6** 🔑 [U, sing.] something that is interesting or enjoyable that replaces sth boring, difficult or unpleasant for a short period of time: *a few moments of* ***light relief*** *in an otherwise dull performance* ◇ *There was little* ***comic relief*** *in his speech.* ◇ **~ from sth** *The calm of the countryside came as a welcome relief from the hustle and bustle of city life.*
▸ WORKERS **7** [C+sing./pl. v.] (often used as an adjective) a person or group of people that replaces another when they have finished working for the day or when they are sick: *The next crew relief comes on duty at 9 o'clock.* ◇ *relief drivers*
▸ FROM ENEMY **8** [sing.] **~ of…** the act of freeing a town, etc. from an enemy army that has surrounded it
▸ IN ART **9** [U, C] a way of decorating wood, stone, etc. by cutting designs into the surface of it so that some parts stick out more than others; a design that is made in this way: *The column was decorated* ***in high relief*** (= with designs that stick out a lot) *with scenes from Greek mythology.* ◇ *The bronze doors are covered with sculpted reliefs.* ➲ VISUAL VOCAB page V12
▸ MAKING STH NOTICEABLE **10** [U] the effect of colours, light, etc. that makes an object more noticeable than others around it: *The snow-capped mountain stood out* ***in sharp relief*** *against the blue sky.* **11** [U] the quality of a particular situation, problem, etc. that makes it more noticeable than before: *Their differences have been* ***thrown into sharp relief*** *by the present crisis.*

reˈlief map *noun* a map that uses various colours, etc. to show the different heights of hills, valleys, etc.

reˈlief road *noun* (*BrE*) a road that vehicles can use to avoid an area of heavy traffic, especially a road built for this purpose

re·lieve /rɪˈliːv/ *verb* **1 ~ sth** to remove or reduce an unpleasant feeling or pain: *to relieve the symptoms of a cold* ◇ *to* ***relieve anxiety/guilt/stress*** ◇ *Being able to tell the truth at last seemed to relieve her.* **2 ~ sth** to make a problem less serious SYN **alleviate**: *efforts to relieve poverty* ◇ *to relieve traffic congestion* **3 ~ sth** to make sth less boring, especially by introducing sth different: *We played cards to relieve the boredom of the long wait.* ◇ *The black and white pattern is relieved by tiny coloured flowers.* **4 ~ sb** to replace sb who is on duty: *to relieve a sentry* ◇ *You'll be relieved at six o'clock.* **5 ~ sth** to free a town, etc. from an enemy army that has surrounded it **6 ~ yourself** a polite way of referring to going to the toilet: *I had to relieve myself behind a bush.*

PHR V **reˈlieve sb of sth 1** to help sb by taking sth heavy or difficult from them: *Let me relieve you of some of your bags.* ◇ *The new secretary will relieve us of some of the paperwork.* **2** (*informal, ironic*) to steal sth from sb: *A boy with a knife relieved him of his wallet.* **3** to dismiss sb from a job, position, etc: *General Beale was relieved of his command.*

re·lieved /rɪˈliːvd/ *adj.* feeling happy because sth unpleasant has stopped or has not happened; showing this: *She sounded relieved.* ◇ **~ (to see, hear, find, etc. sth)** *You'll be relieved to know your jobs are safe.* ◇ **~ (that…)** *I'm just relieved that nobody was hurt.* ◇ *They exchanged relieved glances.* ➲ SYNONYMS at GLAD

re·li·gion 🔑 /rɪˈlɪdʒən/ *noun*
1 🔑 [U] the belief in the existence of a god or gods, and the activities that are connected with the worship of them: *Is there always a conflict between science and religion?* **2** 🔑 [C] one of the systems of faith that are based on the belief in the existence of a particular god or gods: *the Jewish religion* ◇ *Christianity, Islam and other world religions* ◇ *The law states that everyone has the right to practise their own religion.* **3** [sing.] a particular interest or influence that is very important in your life: *For him, football is an absolute religion.*

IDM **get reˈligion** (*informal, disapproving*) to suddenly become interested in religion ➲ note on page 1288

re·ligi·os·ity /rɪˌlɪdʒiˈɒsəti; *NAmE* -ˈɑːsəti/ *noun* [U] (*formal*, sometimes *disapproving*) the state of being religious or too religious

re·li·gious 🔑 /rɪˈlɪdʒəs/ *adj.*
1 🔑 [only before noun] connected with religion or with a particular religion: ***religious beliefs/faith*** ◇ ***religious education*** (= education about religion) ◇ ***religious instruction*** (= instruction in a particular religion) ◇ *religious groups* ◇ *objects which have a religious significance* **2** 🔑 (of a person) believing strongly in the existence of a god or gods SYN **devout**: *His wife is very religious.* ▸ **re·li·gious·ness** *noun* [U]

re·li·gious·ly /rɪˈlɪdʒəsli/ *adv.* **1** very carefully or regularly: *She followed the instructions religiously.* **2** in a way that is connected with religion: *Were you brought up religiously?*

re·lin·quish /rɪˈlɪŋkwɪʃ/ *verb* (*formal*) to stop having sth, especially when this happens unwillingly SYN **give up**: **~ sth** *He was forced to relinquish control of the company.* ◇ *They had relinquished all hope that she was alive.* ◇ **~ sth to sb** *She relinquished possession of the house to her sister.*

reli·quary /ˈrelɪkwəri; *NAmE* -kweri/ *noun* (*pl.* -ies) a container in which a RELIC of a holy person is kept

rel·ish /ˈrelɪʃ/ *verb, noun*
■ ***verb*** to get great pleasure from sth; to want very much to do or have sth SYN **enjoy**: **~ sth** *to relish a fight/challenge/debate* ◇ *to relish the idea/thought of sth* ◇ ***I don't relish the prospect*** *of getting up early tomorrow.* ◇ **~ (sb/sth) doing sth** *Nobody relishes cleaning the oven.*
■ ***noun*** **1** [U] great enjoyment or pleasure: *She savoured the moment* ***with obvious relish.*** **2** [U, C] a cold thick spicy

R

Collocations

Religion

Being religious

- **believe in** God/Christ/Allah/free will/predestination/heaven and hell/an afterlife/reincarnation
- **be/become** a believer/an atheist/an agnostic/a Christian/Muslim/Hindu/Buddhist, etc.
- **convert to/practise/**(*especially US*) **practice** a religion/Buddhism/Catholicism/Christianity/Islam/Judaism, etc.
- **go to** church/(*NAmE*) temple (= the synagogue)
- **go to** the local church/mosque/synagogue/gurdwara
- **belong to** a church/a religious community
- **join/enter** the church/a convent/a monastery/a religious sect/the clergy/the priesthood
- **praise/worship/obey/serve/glorify** God

Celebrations and ritual

- **attend/hold/conduct/lead** a service
- **perform** a ceremony/a rite/a ritual/a baptism/the Hajj/a mitzvah
- **carry out/perform** a sacred/burial/funeral/fertility/purification rite
- **go on/make** a pilgrimage
- **celebrate** Christmas/Easter/Eid/Ramadan/Hanukkah/Passover/Diwali
- **observe/break** the Sabbath/a fast/Ramadan
- **deliver/preach/hear** a sermon
- **lead/address** the congregation
- **say/recite** a prayer/blessing

Religious texts and ideas

- **preach/proclaim/spread** the word of God/the Gospel/the message of Islam
- **study/follow** the dharma/the teachings of Buddha
- **read/study/understand/interpret** scripture/the Bible/the Koran/the gospel/the Torah
- **be based on/derive from** divine revelation
- **commit/consider sth** heresy/sacrilege

Religious belief and experience

- **seek/find/gain** enlightenment/wisdom
- **strengthen/lose** your faith
- **keep/practise/practice/abandon** the faith
- **save/purify/lose** your soul
- **obey/follow/keep/break/violate** a commandment/Islamic law/Jewish law
- **be/accept/do** God's will
- **receive/experience** divine grace
- **achieve/attain** enlightenment/salvation/nirvana
- **undergo** a conversion/rebirth/reincarnation
- **hear/answer** a prayer
- **commit/confess/forgive** a sin
- **do/perform** penance

sauce made from fruit and vegetables that have been boiled, that is served with meat, cheese, etc.

re·live /ˌriːˈlɪv/ *verb* **~ sth** to experience sth again, especially in your imagination: *He relives the horror of the crash every night in his dreams.*

rel·lie /ˈreli/ *noun* (*AustralE, NZE, informal*) a relative: *All the rellies will be at the party.*

re·load /ˌriːˈləʊd; *NAmE* -ˈloʊd/ *verb* **1** [I, T] **~ (sth)** to put more bullets into a gun, more film into a camera, etc. **2** [T] **~ sth** to put data or a program into the memory of a computer again **3** [T] **~ sth** to fill a container, vehicle, machine, etc. again

re·locate AW /ˌriːləʊˈkeɪt; *NAmE* ˌriːˈloʊkeɪt/ *verb* [I, T] (especially of a company or workers) to move or to move sb/sth to a new place to work or operate: *The firm may be forced to relocate from New York to Stanford.* ◇ **~ sth** *The company relocated its head office to Stanford.* ▸ **re·loca·tion** AW /ˌriːləʊˈkeɪʃn; *NAmE* ˌriːloʊ-/ *noun* [U]: *relocation costs*

re·luc·tant AW /rɪˈlʌktənt/ *adj.* hesitating before doing sth because you do not want to do it or because you are not sure that it is the right thing to do: *reluctant agreement* ◇ **~ (to do sth)** *She was reluctant to admit she was wrong.* ◇ *He finally gave a reluctant smile.* ◇ *a* ***reluctant hero*** (= a person who does not want to be called a hero) ▸ **re·luc·tance** AW /-əns/ *noun* [U, sing.]: **~ (to do sth)** *There is still some reluctance on the part of employers to become involved in this project.* ◇ *They finally agreed to our terms with a certain reluctance.* **re·luc·tant·ly** AW *adv.*: *We reluctantly agreed to go with her.*

rely 0‑w AW /rɪˈlaɪ/ *verb* (**re·lies, rely·ing, re·lied, re·lied**)

PHR V **re'ly on/upon sb/sth** **1** 0‑w to need or depend on sb/sth: *As babies, we rely entirely on others for food.* ◇ **~ to do sth** *These days we rely heavily on computers to organize our work.* ◇ **~ doing sth** *The industry relies on the price of raw materials remaining low.* **2** 0‑w to trust or have faith in sb/sth: *You should rely on your own judgement.* ◇ **~ to do sth** *You can rely on me to keep your secret.* ◇ *He can't be relied on to tell the truth.* ➲ SYNONYMS at TRUST

> **WORD FAMILY**
> **rely** *verb*
> **reliable** *adj.* (≠ unreliable)
> **reliably** *adv.*
> **reliability** *noun* (≠ unreliability)
> **reliance** *noun*

REM /ˌɑːr iː ˈem/ *abbr.* rapid eye movement (describes a period of sleep during which you dream and your eyes make many small movements)

re·made *past tense, past part.* of REMAKE

re·main 0‑w /rɪˈmeɪn/ *verb* (rather *formal*) (not usually in the progressive tenses)
1 0‑w *linking verb* to continue to be sth; to be still in the same state or condition: **+ adj.** *to remain silent/standing/seated/motionless* ◇ *Train fares are likely to remain unchanged.* ◇ ***It remains*** *true that sport is about competing well, not winning.* ◇ **+ noun** *In spite of their quarrel, they remain the best of friends.* ◇ *He will remain (as) manager of the club until the end of his contract.* **2** 0‑w [I] to still be present after the other parts have been removed, used, etc; to continue to exist: *Very little of the house remained after the fire.* ◇ *There were only ten minutes remaining.* **3** 0‑w [I] **~ (to do sth)** to still need to be done, said, or dealt with: *Much remains to be done.* ◇ ***It remains to be seen*** (= it will only be known later) *whether you are right.* ◇ ***There remained*** *one significant problem.* ◇ *Questions remain about the president's honesty.* ◇ *I feel sorry for her, but* **the fact remains** (**that**) *she lied to us.* ➲ LANGUAGE BANK at NEVERTHELESS **4** 0‑w [I] **+ adv./prep.** to stay in the same place; to not leave: *They remained in Mexico until June.* ◇ *The plane remained on the ground.* ◇ *She left, but I remained behind.* IDM see ALOOF

re·main·der /rɪˈmeɪndə(r)/ *noun, verb*

- ***noun*** **1** (usually **the remainder**) [sing.+ sing./pl. v.] the remaining people, things or time SYN **the rest**: *I kept some of his books and gave away the remainder.* HELP When **the remainder** refers to a plural noun, the verb is plural: *Most of our employees work in New York; the remainder are in London.* **2** [C, usually sing.] (*mathematics*) the numbers left after one number has been SUBTRACTED from another, or one number has been divided into another: *Divide 2 into 7, and the answer is 3, remainder 1.* **3** [C] a book that has been remaindered
- ***verb*** [I, T, usually passive] **~ (sth)** to sell books at a reduced price

re·main·ing 0‑w /rɪˈmeɪnɪŋ/ *adj.* [only before noun] still needing to be done or dealt with: *The remaining twenty patients were transferred to another hospital.* ◇ *Any remaining tickets for the concert will be sold on the door.* ➲ see also REMAIN

re·mains 0⸺ /rɪˈmeɪnz/ *noun* [pl.]
1 0⸺ **~ (of sth)** the parts of sth that are left after the other parts have been used, eaten, removed, etc: *She fed the remains of her lunch to the dog.* **2** 0⸺ the parts of ancient objects and buildings that have survived and are discovered in the present day: *prehistoric remains* ◇ *the remains of a Roman fort* **3** 0⸺ (*formal*) the body of a dead person or animal: *They had discovered* ***human remains.***

re·make *noun, verb*
■ ***noun*** /ˈriːmeɪk/ a new or different version of an old film/movie or song
■ ***verb*** /ˌriːˈmeɪk/ (**re·made, re·made** /-ˈmeɪd/) **~ sth** to make a new or different version of sth such as an old film/movie or song; to make sth again: *'The Seven Samurai' was remade in Hollywood as 'The Magnificent Seven'.*

re·mand /rɪˈmɑːnd; *NAmE* -ˈmænd/ *verb, noun*
■ ***verb*** [usually passive] **~ sb (+ adv./prep.)** to send sb away from a court to wait for their trial which will take place at a later date: *The two men were charged with burglary and* ***remanded in custody*** (= sent to prison until their trial). ◇ *She was* ***remanded on bail*** (= allowed to go free until the trial after leaving a sum of money with the court).
■ ***noun*** [U] (*BrE*) the process of keeping sb in prison while they are waiting for their trial: *He is currently being held* ***on remand.*** ◇ *a remand prisoner*

reˈmand centre *noun* (*BrE*) a place where young people are sent when they are accused of a crime and are waiting for their trial

re·mark 0⸺ /rɪˈmɑːk; *NAmE* -ˈmɑːrk/ *noun, verb*
■ ***noun*** **1** 0⸺ [C] something that you say or write which expresses an opinion, a thought, etc. about sb/sth SYN **comment**: *to* ***make a remark*** ◇ *He made a number of rude remarks about the food.* ◇ *What exactly did you mean by that last remark?* ➲ note at STATEMENT **2** [U] (*old-fashioned* or *formal*) the quality of being important or interesting enough to be noticed SYN **note**: *The exhibition contains nothing that is worthy of remark.*
■ ***verb*** 0⸺ [I, T] to say or write a comment about sth/sb SYN **comment**: **~ on/upon sth/sb** *The judges remarked on the high standard of entries for the competition.* ◇ **~ how** *... She remarked how tired I was looking.* ◇ **+ speech** *'It's much colder than yesterday,' he remarked casually.* ◇ **~ that** *... Critics remarked that the play was not original.* ◇ **be remarked on** *The similarities between the two have often been remarked on.* ➲ SYNONYMS at COMMENT

re·mark·able 0⸺ /rɪˈmɑːkəbl; *NAmE* -ˈmɑːrk-/ *adj.* unusual or surprising in a way that causes people to take notice SYN **astonishing**: *a remarkable achievement/career/talent* ◇ *She was a truly remarkable woman.* ◇ **~ for sth** *The area is remarkable for its scenery.* ◇ **~ that...** *It is remarkable that nobody noticed sooner.* OPP **unremarkable**
▸ **re·mark·ably** 0⸺ /-əbli/ *adv.*: *The car is in remarkably good condition for its age.* ◇ *Remarkably, nobody was killed.*

re·marry /ˌriːˈmæri/ *verb* (**re·mar·ries, re·marry·ing, re·mar·ried, re·mar·ried**) [I] to marry again after being divorced or after your husband or wife has died ▸ **re·mar·riage** /ˌriːˈmærɪdʒ/ *noun* [U, C]

re·mas·ter /ˌriːˈmɑːstə(r); *NAmE* -ˈmæs-/ *verb* **~ sth** to make a new MASTER copy of a recording in order to improve the sound quality: *All the tracks have been* ***digitally remastered*** *from the original tapes.*

re·match /ˈriːmætʃ/ *noun* [usually sing.] a match or game played again between the same people or teams, especially because neither side won the first match or game

re·medi·able /rɪˈmiːdiəbl/ *adj.* (*formal*) that can be solved or cured SYN **curable**: *remediable problems/diseases*

re·med·ial /rɪˈmiːdiəl/ *adj.* [only before noun] **1** aimed at solving a problem, especially when this involves correcting or improving sth that has been done wrong: *remedial treatment* (= for a medical problem) ◇ ***Remedial action*** *must be taken now.* **2** connected with school students who are slower at learning than others: *remedial education* ◇ *a remedial class*

re·me·di·ation /rɪˌmiːdiˈeɪʃn/ *noun* [U] (*NAmE*) the process of improving sth or correcting sth that is wrong, especially changing or stopping damage to the environment: *remediation of contaminated soil* ▸ **remediate** /rɪˈmiːdieɪt/ *verb*: **~ sth** (*NAmE*) *The problems need to be detected and remediated quickly.*

rem·edy /ˈremədi/ *noun, verb*
■ ***noun*** (*pl.* **-ies**) **1** a way of dealing with or improving an unpleasant or difficult situation SYN **solution**: **~ (for sth)** *There is no simple remedy for unemployment.* ◇ **~ (to sth)** *There are a number of possible remedies to this problem.* **2** a treatment or medicine to cure a disease or reduce pain that is not very serious: *a herbal remedy* ◇ **~ for sth** *an excellent home remedy for sore throats* **3** **~ (against sth)** (*law*) a way of dealing with a problem, using the processes of the law SYN **redress**: *Holding copyright provides the only legal remedy against unauthorized copying.*
■ ***verb*** (**rem·ed·ies, rem·edy·ing, rem·ed·ied, rem·ed·ied**) **~ sth** to correct or improve sth SYN **put right**: *to remedy a problem* ◇ *This situation is easily remedied.*

re·mem·ber 0⸺ /rɪˈmembə(r)/ *verb* (not usually used in the progressive tenses)
▸ SB/STH FROM THE PAST **1** 0⸺ [T, I] to have or keep an image in your memory of an event, a person, a place, etc. from the past: **~ (sb/sth)** *This is Carla. Do you remember her?* ◇ *I don't remember my first day at school.* ◇ *He still remembered her as the lively teenager he'd known years before.* ◇ ***As far as I can remember,*** *this is the third time we've met.* ◇ **~ doing sth** *Do you remember switching the lights off before we came out?* ◇ *I* ***vaguely remember*** *hearing him come in.* ◇ **~ sb/sth doing sth** *I can still vividly remember my grandfather teaching me to play cards.* ◇ (*formal*) *I can't remember his taking a single day off work.* ◇ **~ (that)...** *I remember (that) we used to go and see them most weekends.*
▸ FACT/INFORMATION **2** 0⸺ [T, I] to bring back to your mind a fact, piece of information, etc. that you knew: **~ (sth)** *I'm sorry—I can't remember your name.* ◇ *You were going to help me with this. Remember?* ◇ **~ how, what, etc...** *Can you remember how much money we spent?* ◇ **~ (that)...** *Remember that we're going out tonight.* **3** 0⸺ [T] to keep an important fact in your mind: **~ (that)...** *Remember (that) you may feel sleepy after taking the pills.* ◇ **it is remembered that...** ***It should be remembered that*** *the majority of accidents happen in the home.*
▸ STH YOU HAVE TO DO **4** 0⸺ [T] to not forget to do sth; to actually do what you have to do: **~ to do sth** *Remember to call me when you arrive!* ◇ **~ sth** *Did you remember your homework* (= to bring it)? HELP Notice the difference between **remember doing sth** and **remember to do sth**: *I remember posting the letter* means 'I have an image in my memory of doing it'; *I remembered to post the letter* means 'I didn't forget to do it.'
▸ IN PRAYERS **5** [T] **~ sb** to think about sb with respect, especially when saying a prayer SYN **commemorate**: *a church service to remember the war dead*
▸ GIVE PRESENT **6** [T] **~ sb/sth** to give money, a present, etc. to sb/sth: *My aunt always remembers my birthday* (= by sending a card or present). ◇ *His grandfather remembered him* (= left him money) *in his will.*
IDM **be reˈmembered for sth | be reˈmembered as sth** to be famous or known for a particular thing that you have done in the past: *He is best remembered as the man who brought jazz to England.*
PHR V **reˈmember me to sb** (*especially BrE*) used to ask sb to give your good wishes to sb else: *Remember me to your parents.*

re·mem·brance /rɪˈmembrəns/ *noun* **1** [U] the act or process of remembering an event in the past or a person who is dead: *A service was held* ***in remembrance of*** *local soldiers killed in the war.* ◇ *a remembrance service* ◇ (*formal*) *He smiled at the remembrance of their first kiss.* **2** [C] (*formal*) an object that causes you to remember sb/sth; a memory of sb/sth: *The cenotaph stands as a remembrance of those killed during the war.*

ReˌmembranceˈSunday (also **Reˈmembrance Day**) *noun* the Sunday nearest to the 11 November on which those killed in war, especially the wars of 1914–18

R

and 1939–45, are remembered in ceremonies and church services in Britain and some other countries ➲ see also MEMORIAL DAY, VETERANS DAY

re·mind 0→ /rɪˈmaɪnd/ *verb* **~ sb (about/of sth)** to help sb remember sth, especially sth important that they must do: **~ sb** *I'm sorry, I've forgotten your name. Can you remind me?* ◇ ***That*** (= what you have just said, done, etc.) ***reminds me****, I must get some cash.* ◇ *'You need to finish that essay.' '**Don't remind me*** (= I don't want to think about it)*.'* ◇ *'Don't forget the camera.' 'Remind me about it nearer the time.'* ◇ **~ sb to do sth** *Remind me to phone Alan before I go out.* ◇ **~ sb (that)...** *Passengers are reminded (that) no smoking is allowed on this train.* ◇ **~ sb what, how, etc...** *Can someone remind me what I should do next?* ◇ **~ sb + speech** *'You had an accident,' he reminded her.*

PHR V **reˈmind sb of sb/sth** 0→ if sb/sth **reminds** you of sb/sth else, they make you remember or think about the other person, place, thing, etc. because they are similar in some way: *You remind me of your father when you say that.* ◇ *That smell reminds me of France.*

re·mind·er /rɪˈmaɪndə(r)/ *noun* **1 ~ (of sb/sth) | ~ (that ...)** something that makes you think about or remember sb/sth, that you have forgotten or would like to forget: *The sheer size of the cathedral is a **constant reminder** of the power of religion.* ◇ *The incident **served as a** timely **reminder** of just how dangerous mountaineering can be.* **2** a letter or note informing sb that they have not done sth

rem·in·isce /ˌremɪˈnɪs/ *verb* [I] **~ (about sth/sb)** to think, talk or write about a happy time in your past: *We spent a happy evening reminiscing about the past.*

rem·in·is·cence /ˌremɪˈnɪsns/ *noun* **1** [C, usually pl.] a spoken or written description of sth that sb remembers about their past life SYN **memory**: *The book is a collection of his reminiscences about the actress.* ◇ *reminiscences of a wartime childhood* **2** [U] the act of remembering things that happened in the past SYN **recollection 3** [C, usually pl.] something that reminds you of sth similar: *Her music is full of reminiscences of African rhythms.*

rem·in·is·cent /ˌremɪˈnɪsnt/ *adj.* **1 ~ of sb/sth** reminding you of sb/sth: *The way he laughed was strongly reminiscent of his father.* **2** [only before noun] (*formal*) showing that you are thinking about the past, especially in a way that causes you pleasure: *a reminiscent smile*

re·miss /rɪˈmɪs/ *adj.* [not before noun] (*formal*) not giving sth enough care and attention SYN **negligent**: **~ (of sb) (to do sth)** *It was remiss of them not to inform us of these changes sooner.* ◇ **~ (in sth/in doing sth)** *She had clearly been remiss in her duty.*

re·mis·sion /rɪˈmɪʃn/ *noun* [U, C] **1** a period during which a serious illness improves for a time and the patient seems to get better: *The patient has been **in remission** for the past six months.* ◇ *The symptoms reappeared after only a short remission.* **2** (*BrE*) a reduction in the amount of time sb spends in prison, especially because they have behaved well **3** (*formal*) an act of reducing or cancelling the amount of money that sb has to pay: *New businesses may qualify for tax remission.* ◇ *There is a partial remission of fees for overseas students.*

remit *noun, verb*

■ ***noun*** /ˈriːmɪt; rɪˈmɪt/ [usually sing.] **~ (of sb/sth) | ~ (to do sth)** (*BrE*) the area of activity over which a particular person or group has authority, control or influence: *Such decisions are **outside the remit** of this committee.* ◇ *In future, staff recruitment will **fall within the remit** of the division manager.* ◇ *a remit to report on medical services*

■ ***verb*** /rɪˈmɪt/ (-tt-) (*formal*) **1** to send money, etc. to a person or place SYN **forward**: **~ sth** *to remit funds* ◇ **~ sth to sb** *Payment will be remitted to you in full.* **2 ~ sth** to cancel or free sb from a debt, duty, punishment, etc. SYN **cancel**: *to remit a fine* ◇ *to remit a prison sentence* ➲ see also UNREMITTING

PHR V **reˈmit sth to sb** [usually passive] (*law*) to send a matter to an authority so that a decision can be made: *The case was remitted to the Court of Appeal.*

re·mit·tance /rɪˈmɪtns/ *noun* **1** [C] (*formal*) a sum of money that is sent to sb in order to pay for sth: *Please return the completed form with your remittance.* **2** [U] the act of sending money to sb in order to pay for sth SYN **payment**: *Remittance can be made by cheque or credit card.*

remix /ˌriːˈmɪks/ *verb* **~ sth** to make a new version of a recorded piece of music by using a machine to arrange the separate parts of the recording in a different way, add new parts, etc. ▸ **remix** /ˈriːmɪks/ (also **mix**) *noun* **re·mixer** *noun*: *the skills of remixer Tom Moulton*

rem·nant /ˈremnənt/ *noun* **1** [usually pl.] a part of sth that is left after the other parts have been used, removed, destroyed, etc. SYN **remains**: *The woods are remnants of a huge forest which once covered the whole area.* **2** a small piece of cloth that is left when the rest has been sold

re·model /ˌriːˈmɒdl; *NAmE* -ˈmɑːdl/ *verb* (-ll-, *especially US* -l-) **~ sth** to change the structure or shape of sth

re·mold (*NAmE*) = REMOULD

rem·on·strance /rɪˈmɒnstrəns; *NAmE* -ˈmɑːn-/ *noun* [C, U] (*formal*) a protest or complaint

rem·on·strate /ˈremənstreɪt; *NAmE* rɪˈmɑːnstreɪt/ *verb* [I, T] **~ (with sb) (about sth) | + speech** (*formal*) to protest or complain about sth/sb: *They remonstrated with the official about the decision.*

re·morse /rɪˈmɔːs; *NAmE* rɪˈmɔːrs/ *noun* [U] the feeling of being extremely sorry for sth wrong or bad that you have done: *I felt guilty and full of remorse.* ◇ **~ for sth/for doing sth** *He was filled with remorse for not believing her.* ▸ **re·morse·ful** /-fl/ *adj.* **re·morse·ful·ly** /-fəli/ *adv.*

re·morse·less /rɪˈmɔːsləs; *NAmE* -ˈmɔːrs-/ *adj.* **1** (especially of an unpleasant situation) seeming to continue or become worse in a way that cannot be stopped SYN **relentless**: *the remorseless increase in crime* **2** cruel and having or showing no pity for other people SYN **merciless**: *a remorseless killer* ▸ **re·morse·less·ly** *adv.*

re·mort·gage /ˌriːˈmɔːɡɪdʒ; *NAmE* -ˈmɔːrɡ-/ *verb* [I, T] **~ (sth)** to arrange a second MORTGAGE on your house or apartment, or to increase or change your first one ▸ **re·mort·gage** *noun*

re·mote 0→ /rɪˈməʊt; *NAmE* rɪˈmoʊt/ *adj., noun*

■ ***adj.*** (re·moter, re·mot·est)

▸ PLACE **1** 0→ far away from places where other people live SYN **isolated**: *a remote beach* ◇ *one of the remotest areas of the world* ◇ **~ from sth** *The farmhouse is remote from any other buildings.*

▸ TIME **2** 0→ [only before noun] far away in time SYN **distant**: *in the **remote past/future*** ◇ *a **remote ancestor*** (= who lived a long time ago)

▸ RELATIVES **3** [only before noun] (of people) not closely related SYN **distant**: *a remote cousin*

▸ COMPUTER/SYSTEM **4** that you can connect to from far away, using an electronic link: *a **remote terminal/database***

▸ DIFFERENT **5 ~ (from sth)** very different from sth: *His theories are somewhat remote from reality.*

▸ NOT FRIENDLY **6** (of people or their behaviour) not very friendly or interested in other people SYN **aloof, distant**

▸ VERY SMALL **7** 0→ not very great SYN **slight**: *There is still a **remote chance** that they will find her alive.* ◇ *I don't have **the remotest idea** what you're talking about.*

▸ **re·mote·ness** *noun* [U]: *the geographical remoteness of the island* ◇ *His remoteness made her feel unloved.*

■ ***noun*** (*informal*) = REMOTE CONTROL

reˌmote ˈaccess *noun* [U] the use of a computer system, etc. that is in another place, that you can connect to when you are far away, using an electronic link

reˌmote conˈtrol *noun* **1** [U] the ability to operate a machine from a distance using radio or electrical signals: *It works **by remote control**.* ◇ *a remote-control camera* **2** (also *informal* **re·mote**, **zap·per**) [C] a device that allows you to operate a television, etc. from a distance: *I* *can't find the remote control.* ➲ VISUAL VOCAB page V18 ▸ **re,mote-con'trolled** *adj.*: *remote-controlled equipment*

re·mote·ly /rɪ'məʊtli; *NAmE* -'moʊt-/ *adv.* **1** (usually in negative sentences) to a very slight degree **SYN slightly**: *It wasn't even remotely funny* (= it wasn't at all funny). ◇ *The two incidents were only remotely connected.* **2** from a distance: *remotely operated* **3** far away from places where other people live: *The church is remotely situated on the north coast of the island.*

re,mote 'sensing *noun* [U] the use of SATELLITES to search for and collect information about the earth

re·mould (*especially US* **re·mold**) /,ri:'məʊld; *NAmE* -'moʊld/ *verb* **~ sth** (*formal*) to change sth such as an idea, a system, etc: *attempts to remould policy to make it more acceptable*

re·mount /,ri:'maʊnt/ *verb* **1** [I, T] **~ (sth)** to get on a horse, bicycle, etc. again after getting off it or falling off it **2** [T] **~ sth** to organize and begin sth a second time

re·mov·able AW /rɪ'mu:vəbl/ *adj.* [usually before noun] that can be taken off or out of sth **SYN detachable**

re·moval 🔑 AW /rɪ'mu:vl/ *noun* **1** 🔑 [U] **~ (of sb/sth)** the act of taking sb/sth away from a particular place: *Clearance of the site required the removal of a number of trees.* ◇ *the removal of a tumour* **2** 🔑 [U] **~ (of sth)** the act of getting rid of sth: *stain removal* ◇ *the removal of trade barriers* **3** 🔑 [U] **~ (of sb)** the act of dismissing sb from their job **SYN dismissal**: *events leading to the removal of the president from office* **4** 🔑 [C] (*BrE*) an act of taking furniture, etc. from one house to another: *house removals* ◇ *a* ***removal company/firm*** ◇ *When are the removal men coming?*

re'moval van (also **'furniture van**) (both *BrE*) (*NAmE* **'moving van**) *noun* a large van used for moving furniture from one house to another

re·move 🔑 AW /rɪ'mu:v/ *verb, noun*

■ *verb* **1** 🔑 to take sth/sb away from a place: **~ sth/sb** *Illegally parked vehicles will be removed.* ◇ **~ sth/sb from sth/sb** *He removed his hand from her shoulder.* ◇ *Three children were removed from the school for persistent bad behaviour.* **2** 🔑 **~ sth** to take off clothing, etc. from the body: *She removed her glasses and rubbed her eyes.* **3** 🔑 to get rid of sth unpleasant, dirty, etc; to make sth disappear: **~ sth** *She has had the tumour removed.* ◇ *to remove problems/obstacles/objections* ◇ **~ sth from sb/sth** *The news removed any doubts about the company's future.* **4** 🔑 **~ sb from sth** to dismiss sb from their position or job: *The elections removed the government from power.*

IDM **once, twice, etc. re'moved** (of a cousin) belonging to a different generation: *He's my cousin's son so he's my first cousin once removed.* **be far/further/furthest removed from sth** to be very different from sth; to not be connected with sth: *Many of these books are far removed from the reality of the children's lives.*

■ *noun* [C, U] (*formal*) an amount by which two things are separated: *Charlotte seemed to be living* ***at one remove*** *from reality.*

re·mover /rɪ'mu:və(r)/ *noun* **1** [U, C] (usually in compounds) a substance used for getting rid of marks, paint, etc: *nail varnish remover* ◇ *stain remover* ➲ see also STAPLE REMOVER **2** [usually pl.] (*BrE*) a person or company whose job is to take furniture, etc. from one house to another: *a firm of removers*

re·mu·ner·ate /rɪ'mju:nəreɪt/ *verb* [usually passive] **~ sb (for sth)** (*formal*) to pay sb for work that they have done

re·mu·ner·ation /rɪ,mju:nə'reɪʃn/ *noun* [U, C] (*formal*) an amount of money that is paid to sb for the work they have done

re·mu·nera·tive /rɪ'mju:nərətɪv/ *adj.* [usually before noun] (*formal*) paying a lot of money: *remunerative work*

REN /,ɑ:r i: 'en/ *abbr.* registered enrolled nurse

re·nais·sance /rɪ'neɪsns; *NAmE* 'renəsɑ:ns/ *noun* [sing.] **1 the Renaissance** the period in Europe during the 14th, 15th and 16th centuries when people became interested in the ideas and culture of ancient Greece and Rome and used these influences in their own art, literature, etc: *Renaissance art* **2** a situation when there is new interest in a particular subject, form of art, etc. after a period when it was not very popular **SYN revival**: *to experience a renaissance*

Re,naissance 'man *noun* a person who is good at a lot of things and has a lot of interests, especially writing and painting

renal /'ri:nl/ *adj.* [usually before noun] (*medical*) relating to or involving the KIDNEYS: *renal failure*

re·name /,ri:'neɪm/ *verb* to give sb/sth a new name: **~ sth** *to rename a street* ◇ **~ sth + noun** *Leningrad was renamed St Petersburg.*

re·nas·cence /rɪ'næsns; -'neɪ-/ *noun* [U, sing.] (*formal*) a situation in which there is new interest in a particular subject, form of art, etc. after a period when it was not very popular ▸ **re·nas·cent** /rɪ'næsnt; -'neɪ-/ *adj.*: *renascent fascism*

rend /rend/ *verb* (**rent, rent** /rent/) **~ sth** (*old use* or *literary*) to tear sth apart with force or violence: *They rent their clothes in grief.* ◇ (*figurative*) *a country rent in two by civil war* ◇ (*figurative*) *Loud screams rent the air.* ➲ see also HEART-RENDING

ren·der /'rendə(r)/ *verb*

▸ CAUSE SB/STH TO BE STH **1 ~ sb/sth + adj.** (*formal*) to cause sb/sth to be in a particular state or condition **SYN make**: *to render sth harmless/useless/ineffective* ◇ *Hundreds of people were rendered homeless by the earthquake.*

▸ GIVE HELP **2** (*formal*) to give sb sth, especially in return for sth or because it is expected: **~ sth to sb/sth** *They rendered assistance to the disaster victims.* ◇ *to render a service to sb* ◇ **~ sb sth** *to render sb a service* ◇ **~ sth** *It was payment* ***for services rendered.***

▸ PRESENT STH **3 ~ sth** (*formal*) to present sth, especially when it is done officially **SYN furnish**: *The committee was asked to render a report on the housing situation.*

▸ EXPRESS/PERFORM **4 ~ sth** (*formal*) to express or perform sth: *He stood up and rendered a beautiful version of 'Summertime'.* ◇ *The artist has rendered the stormy sea in dark greens and browns.*

▸ TRANSLATE **5** to express sth in a different language **SYN translate**: **~ sth (as sth)** *The Italian phrase can be rendered as 'I did my best'.* ◇ **~ sth (into sth)** *It's a concept that is difficult to render into English.*

▸ WALL **6 ~ sth** (*BrE, technical*) to cover a wall with a layer of PLASTER or CEMENT

▸ MELT **7 ~ sth (down)** to make fat liquid by heating it; to melt sth

ren·der·ing /'rendərɪŋ/ *noun* **1** [C] the performance of a piece of music, a role in a play, etc; the particular way in which sth is performed **SYN interpretation, rendition**: *her dramatic rendering of Lady Macbeth* **2** [C] a piece of writing that has been translated into a different language; the particular way in which it has been translated: *a faithful rendering of the original text* **3** [U, C] (*technical*) a layer of PLASTER or CEMENT that is put on a brick or stone wall in order to make it smooth

ren·dez·vous /'rɒndɪvu:; -deɪ-; *NAmE* 'rɑ:n-/ *noun, verb*

■ *noun* (*pl.* **ren·dez·vous** /-vu:z/) (from *French*) **1 ~ (with sb)** an arrangement to meet sb at a particular time and place **2** a place where people have arranged to meet **3** a bar, etc. that is a popular place for people to meet: *a lively Paris rendezvous*

■ *verb* (**ren·dez·voused** /-vu:d/, **ren·dez·voused**) [I] **~ (with sb)** (from *French*) to meet at a time and place that have been arranged in advance

ren·di·tion /ren'dɪʃn/ *noun* **1** [C] the performance of sth, especially a song or piece of music; the particular way in which it is performed **SYN interpretation** **2** (also **ex,traordinary ren'dition**) [U] (especially in the US) the practice of sending foreign suspects to be questioned in another country where the laws about the treatment of prisoners are less strict

rene·gade /'renɪgeɪd/ *noun* (*formal, disapproving*) **1** (often used as an adjective) a person who leaves one

R

political, religious, etc. group to join another that has very different views **2** a person who opposes and lives outside a group or society that they used to belong to SYN **outlaw**

re·nege /rɪˈniːg; rɪˈneɪg/ *verb* [I] **~ (on sth)** (*formal*) to break a promise, an agreement, etc. SYN **go back on**: *to* ***renege on a deal/debt/contract, etc.***

renew /rɪˈnjuː; *NAmE* -ˈnuː/ *verb* **1 ~ sth** to begin sth again after a pause or an interruption SYN **resume**: *The army renewed its assault on the capital.* ◇ *We have to renew our efforts to attract young players.* ◇ *The annual dinner is a chance to renew acquaintance with old friends.* **2 ~ sth** to make sth valid for a further period of time: *to* ***renew a licence/lease/subscription/contract, etc.*** ◇ *How do I go about renewing my passport?* ◇ *I'd like to renew these library books* (= arrange to borrow them for a further period of time). **3 ~ sth** to emphasize sth by saying or stating it again SYN **reiterate, repeat**: *to* ***renew an appeal/a request/a complaint, etc.*** ◇ *Community leaders have renewed calls for a peaceful settlement.* ◇ *The project is to go ahead following renewed promises of aid from the UN.* **4 ~ sth** to change sth that is old or damaged and replace it with sth new of the same kind: *The wiring in your house should be renewed every ten to fifteen years.*

re·new·able /rɪˈnjuːəbl; *NAmE* -ˈnuː-/ *adj.* **1** [usually before noun] (of energy and natural resources) that is replaced naturally or controlled carefully and can therefore be used without the risk of finishing it all: *renewable sources of energy such as wind and solar power* ➲ COLLOCATIONS at ENVIRONMENT **2** (of a contract, ticket, etc.) that can be made valid for a further period of time after it has finished: *a renewable lease* ◇ *The work permit is not renewable.* OPP **non-renewable**

re·new·ables /rɪˈnjuːəblz; *NAmE* -ˈnuː-/ *noun* [pl.] types of energy that can be replaced naturally such as energy produced from wind or water: *renewables such as hydroelectricity and solar energy* ◇ *investment in renewables* HELP **Renewables** are more commonly referred to as **renewable energy (sources)**. ➲ COLLOCATIONS at ENVIRONMENT

re·newal /rɪˈnjuːəl; *NAmE* -ˈnuːəl/ *noun* [U, C] **1 ~ (of sth)** a situation in which sth begins again after a pause or an interruption: *a renewal of interest in traditional teaching methods* **2** the act of making a contract, etc. valid for a further period of time after it has finished: *The lease comes* ***up for renewal*** *at the end of the month.* ◇ *the renewal date* **3** a situation in which sth is replaced, improved or made more successful: *economic renewal* ◇ ***urban renewal*** (= the act of improving the buildings, etc. in a particular area)

R

re·newed /rɪˈnjuːd; *NAmE* rɪˈnuːd/ *adj.* [usually before noun] happening again with increased interest or strength: *Renewed fighting has been reported on the border.* ◇ *with renewed enthusiasm*

ren·min·bi /ˈrenmɪnbi/ *noun* (*pl.* **ren·min·bi**) **1 the renminbi** [sing.] the money system of China **2** = YUAN

ren·net /ˈrenɪt/ *noun* [U] a substance that makes milk thick and sour and is used in making cheese

re·nounce /rɪˈnaʊns/ *verb* (*formal*) **1 ~ sth** to state officially that you are no longer going to keep a title, position, etc. SYN **give up**: *to* ***renounce a claim/title/privilege/right*** **2 ~ sth** to state publicly that you no longer have a particular belief or that you will no longer behave in a particular way: *to* ***renounce ideals/principles/beliefs, etc.*** ◇ *a joint declaration renouncing the use of violence* **3 ~ sb/sth** to state publicly that you no longer wish to have a connection with sb/sth because you disapprove of them SYN **disown**: *He had renounced his former associates.* ➲ see also RENUNCIATION

reno·vate /ˈrenəveɪt/ *verb* **~ sth** to repair and paint an old building, a piece of furniture, etc. so that it is in good condition again ➲ COLLOCATIONS at DECORATE ▸ **reno·va·tion** /ˌrenəˈveɪʃn/ *noun* [U, C, usually pl.]: *buildings in need of renovation* ◇ *There will be extensive renovations to the hospital.*

re·nown /rɪˈnaʊn/ *noun* [U] (*formal*) fame and respect because of sth you have done that people admire: *He* ***won renown as*** *a fair judge.* ◇ *a pianist* ***of some/international/great*** *renown*

re·nowned /rɪˈnaʊnd/ *adj.* famous and respected SYN **celebrated, noted**: *a renowned author* ◇ **~ as sth** *It is renowned as one of the region's best restaurants.* ◇ **~ for sth** *She is renowned for her patience.*

rent 0→ /rent/ *noun, verb* ➲ see also REND *v.*

▪ *noun* **1** 0→ [U, C] an amount of money that you regularly pay so that you can use a house, etc: *How much rent do you pay for this place?* ◇ *The landlord has put the rent up again.* ◇ *a month's rent in advance* ◇ *a* ***high/low/fair rent*** ◇ (*BrE*) *a rent book* (= used to record payments of rent) ➲ SYNONYMS at RATE ➲ COLLOCATIONS at HOUSE ➲ compare HIRE *n.* **2** [U, C] (*especially NAmE*) = RENTAL (1) **3** [C] (*formal*) a torn place in a piece of material or clothing IDM **for rent** 0→ (*especially NAmE*) (especially on printed signs) available to rent

▪ *verb* **1** 0→ [T, I] to regularly pay money to sb so that you can use sth that they own, such as a house, some land, a machine, etc: **~ (sth)** *to live in* ***rented accommodation/housing/property*** ◇ **~ sth from sb** *Who do you rent the land from?* **2** 0→ [T] to allow sb to use sth that you own such as a house or some land in exchange for regular payments: **~ sth (out) (to sb)** *He rents rooms in his house to students.* ◇ *The land is rented out to other farmers.* ◇ *She agreed to rent the room to me.* ◇ **~ sb sth** *She agreed to rent me the room.* **3** 0→ [T] **~ sth** (*especially NAmE*) to pay money to sb so that you can use sth for a short period of time: *We rented a car for the week and explored the area.* ◇ *Shall we rent a movie this evening?* ➲ compare HIRE *v.* (1) **4** [I] (*NAmE*) to be available for sb to use if they pay a particular amount of money: *The apartment rents for $500 a month.*

British / American

rent / hire / let

Verbs

- You can **hire** something for a short period of time (*BrE* only), but **rent** something for a longer period: *We can hire bikes for a day to explore the town.* ◇ *We don't own our TV, we rent it.*
- In *NAmE*, **rent** is always used. It is sometimes now used in *BrE* instead of **hire**, too.
- The owners of a thing can **hire it out** for a short period (*BrE*): *Do you hire out bikes?* Or they can **rent (out)/let (out)** a building, etc: *We rent out rooms in our house to students.*
- Outside a building you could see: *To let* (*BrE*) ◇ *For rent* (*especially NAmE*).
- To **hire** can also mean to employ somebody, especially in *NAmE*: *We hired a new secretary.*

➲ see also LEASE *v.*

Nouns

- The amount of money that you pay to rent something is **rent** or **rental** (more formal). When you hire something you pay a **hire charge** (*BrE*). On a sign outside a shop you might see: *Bikes for hire* (*BrE*).

➲ see also LET, LEASE, HIRE *n.*

ˈrent-a- *combining form* (*informal*, often *humorous*) (in nouns and adjectives) showing that the thing mentioned can be hired/rented: *rent-a-car* ◇ *rent-a-crowd*

ren·tal /ˈrentl/ *noun* **1** (also **rent** especially in *NAmE*) [U, C, usually sing.] the amount of money that you pay to use sth for a particular period of time: *Telephone charges include line rental.* ➲ SYNONYMS at RATE **2** [U] the act of renting sth or an arrangement to rent sth: *the world's largest car rental company* ◇ *DVD rental* ◇ (*especially NAmE*) *a rental car* ◇ *a minimum rental period of three months* ➲ compare HIRE **3** [C] (*especially NAmE*) a house, car, or piece of equipment that you can rent: *'Is this your own car?' 'No, it's a rental.'*

ˈrent boy *noun* (*BrE*) a young male PROSTITUTE

rent·ed 0‑ /ˈrentɪd/ *adj.* that you pay rent for: *a rented studio*

rent·er /ˈrentə(r)/ *noun* **1** a person who rents sth: *house buyers and renters* **2** (*NAmE*) a person or an organization that provides sth for people to rent: *the nation's biggest automobile renter*

ˌrent-ˈfree *adj.* for which no rent is paid: *rent-free housing* ▸ **ˌrent-ˈfree** *adv.*

ren·tier /ˈrɒntieɪ; *NAmE* ˈrɑːntjeɪ/ *noun* (*technical*) a person who lives from money earned from property and investments

re·nun·ci·ation /rɪˌnʌnsiˈeɪʃn/ *noun* (*formal*) **1** [U, C] an act of stating publicly that you no longer believe sth or that you are giving sth up: *the renunciation of violence* **2** [U] the act of rejecting physical pleasures, especially for religious reasons SYN **self-denial** ⮊ see also RENOUNCE

re·occur AW /ˌriːəˈkɜː(r)/ *verb* (-rr-) [I] to happen again or a number of times SYN **recur**

re·of·fend /ˌriːəˈfend/ *verb* [I] to commit a crime again: *Without help, many released prisoners will reoffend.* ▸ **re·of·fend·er** /ˌriːəˈfendə(r)/ *noun*

re·open /ˌriːˈəʊpən; *NAmE* -ˈoʊ-/ *verb* **1** [T, I] **~ (sth)** to open a shop/store, theatre, etc. again, or to be opened again, after being closed for a period of time: *The school was reopened just two weeks after the fire.* ◇ *The store will reopen at 9 a.m. on 2 January.* **2** [T, I] **~ (sth)** to deal with or begin sth again after a period of time; to start again after a period of time: *to reopen a discussion* ◇ *The police have decided to reopen the case.* ◇ *Management have agreed to reopen talks with the union.* ◇ *The trial reopened on 6 March.* ▸ **re·open·ing** /ˌriːˈəʊpənɪŋ; *NAmE* -ˈoʊ-/ *noun* [U, sing.]
IDM **reˌopen old ˈwounds** to remind sb of sth unpleasant that happened or existed in the past

re·order /ˌriːˈɔːdə(r); *NAmE* -ˈɔːrd-/ *verb* **1** [T, I] **~ (sth)** to ask sb to supply you with more of a product: *Please quote this reference number when reordering stock.* **2** [T] **~ sth** to change the order in which sth is arranged

re·organ·ize (*BrE* also **-ise**) /riˈɔːɡənaɪz; *NAmE* -ˈɔːrɡ-/ *verb* [T, I] **~ (sth)** to change the way in which sth is organized or done ▸ **re·organ·iza·tion, -isa·tion** /riˌɔːɡənaɪˈzeɪʃn; *NAmE* -ˌɔːrɡənəˈz-/ *noun* [U, C]: *the reorganization of the school system*

re·ori·ent AW /ˌriːˈɔːrient/ *verb* **1 ~ sb/sth (to/towards/away from sb/sth)** to change the focus or direction of sb/sth: *Other governments may reorient their foreign policies away from the United States.* **2 ~ yourself** to find your position again in relation to your surroundings ▸ **re·orien·ta·tion** AW /ˌriːɔːrienˈteɪʃn/ *noun* [U]

Rep. *abbr.* (in American politics) **1** REPRESENTATIVE **2** REPUBLICAN

rep /rep/ *noun* (*informal*) **1** [C] = SALES REPRESENTATIVE, REPRESENTATIVE **2** [C] a person who speaks officially for a group of people, especially at work: *a union rep* **3** [U] (*informal*) the abbreviation for REPERTORY

re·pack·age /ˌriːˈpækɪdʒ/ *verb* **1 ~ sth** to change the boxes, bags, etc. in which a product is sold **2 ~ sth** to present sth in a new way: *She earns more since she repackaged herself as a business consultant.*

re·paid *past tense, past part.* of REPAY

re·pair 0‑ /rɪˈpeə(r); *NAmE* -ˈper/ *verb, noun*
■ *verb* **1** 0‑ **~ sth** to restore sth that is broken, damaged or torn to good condition: *to repair a car/roof/road/television* ◇ *It's almost 15 years old. It isn't worth* **having it repaired.** **2** 0‑ **~ sth** to say or do sth in order to improve a bad or unpleasant situation SYN **put right**: *It was too late to repair the damage done to their relationship.* ▸ **re·pair·er** *noun*: *TV repairers*
PHR V **reˈpair to…** (*formal* or *humorous*) to go to a particular place
■ *noun* 0‑ [C, U] an act of repairing sth: *They agreed to pay the costs of any repairs.* ◇ *I took my bike in* **for repair.** ◇ *The building was* **in need of repair.** ◇ *a TV repair shop* ◇ *The car was damaged* **beyond repair** (= it was too badly damaged to be repaired). ◇ *The hotel is currently* **under repair** (= being repaired). ◇ *The bridge will remain closed until essential* **repair work** *has been carried out.*
IDM **in good, bad, etc. reˈpair | in a good, bad, etc. state of reˈpair** (*formal*) in good, etc. condition

re·pair·able /rɪˈpeərəbl; *NAmE* -ˈper-/ *adj.* [not usually before noun] that can be repaired OPP **irreparable**

re·pair·man /rɪˈpeəmæn; *NAmE* -ˈperm-/ *noun* (*pl.* **-men** /-men/) (also **re·pair·er** especially in *BrE*) a person whose job is to repair things: *a TV repairman*

rep·ar·ation /ˌrepəˈreɪʃn/ *noun* (*formal*) **1 reparations** [pl.] money that is paid by a country that has lost a war, for the damage, injuries, etc. that it has caused **2** [U] the act of giving sth to sb or doing sth for them in order to show that you are sorry for suffering that you have caused: *Offenders should be forced to* **make reparation to** *the community.*

rep·ar·tee /ˌrepɑːˈtiː; *NAmE* -ɑːrˈtiː/ *noun* [U] clever and amusing comments and replies that are made quickly

re·past /rɪˈpɑːst; *NAmE* -ˈpæst/ *noun* (*old-fashioned* or *formal*) a meal

re·pat·ri·ate /ˌriːˈpætrieɪt; *NAmE* -ˈpeɪt-/ *verb* **1 ~ sb** (*formal*) to send or bring sb back to their own country: *The refugees were forcibly repatriated.* **2 ~ sth** (*business*) to send money or profits back to your own country ▸ **re·pat·ri·ation** /ˌriːˌpætriˈeɪʃn; *NAmE* -ˌpeɪt-/ *noun* [U, C]: *the repatriation of immigrants/profits* ◇ *a voluntary repatriation programme*

repay /rɪˈpeɪ/ *verb* (**re·paid, re·paid** /rɪˈpeɪd/) **1** to pay back the money that you have borrowed from sb: **~ sth** *to* **repay a debt/loan/mortgage** ◇ *I'll repay the money I owe them next week.* ◇ **~ sth to sb** *The advance must be repaid to the publisher if the work is not completed on time.* ◇ **~ sb** *When are you going to repay them?* ◇ **~ sb sth** *I fully intend to repay them the money that they lent me.* **2** to give sth to sb or do sth for them in return for sth that they have done for you SYN **recompense**: **~ sb (for sth)** *How can I ever repay you for your generosity?* ◇ **~ sth (with sth)** *Their trust was repaid with fierce loyalty.* **3 ~ sth** (*BrE, formal*) if sth **repays** your attention, interest, study, etc, it is worth spending time to look at it, etc: *The report repays careful reading.*

re·pay·able /rɪˈpeɪəbl/ *adj.* that can or must be paid back: *The loan is repayable in monthly instalments.*

re·pay·ment /rɪˈpeɪmənt/ *noun* **1** [U] the act of paying back money that you have borrowed from a bank, etc: *The loan is due for repayment by the end of the year.* **2** [C, usually pl.] (*BrE*) a sum of money that you pay regularly to a bank, etc. until you have returned all the money that you owe: *We were unable to* **meet** (= pay) **the repayments** *on the loan.* ◇ *mortgage repayments* ⮊ SYNONYMS at PAYMENT ⮊ COLLOCATIONS at FINANCE

reˈpayment mortgage *noun* (*BrE*) a type of MORTGAGE in which you pay regular sums of money to the bank, etc. until you have returned all the money and interest that you owe ⮊ compare ENDOWMENT MORTGAGE

re·peal /rɪˈpiːl/ *verb* **~ sth** if a government or other group or person with authority **repeals** a law, that law is no longer valid ▸ **re·peal** *noun* [U]

re·peat 0‑ /rɪˈpiːt/ *verb, noun*
■ *verb*
▸ SAY/WRITE AGAIN **1** 0‑ [T] to say or write sth again or more than once: **~ sth** *to repeat a question* ◇ *I'm sorry—could you repeat that?* ◇ *She kept repeating his name softly over and over again.* ◇ *The opposition have been repeating their calls for the president's resignation.* ◇ **~ yourself** *Do say if I'm repeating myself* (= if I have already said this). ◇ **~ that** *… He's fond of repeating that the company's success is all down to him.*

WORD FAMILY
repeat *verb, noun*
repeatable *adj.* (≠ unrepeatable)
repeated *adj.*
repeatedly *adv.*
repetition *noun*
repetitive *adj.*
repetitious *adj.*

R

▸ DO AGAIN **2** [T, I] ~ (**sth**) to do or produce sth again or more than once: *to repeat a mistake/a process/an exercise* ◇ *The treatment should be repeated every two to three hours.* ◇ *They are hoping to repeat last year's victory.* ◇ *These offers are unlikely to be repeated.* ◇ *The programmes will be repeated next year.* ◇ *to* **repeat the class/year/grade** (= in a school, to take the class/year/grade again) ◇ *Lift and lower the right leg 20 times. Repeat with the left leg.*

▸ HAPPEN AGAIN **3** [T, I] ~ (**sth/itself**) to happen more than once in the same way: *History has a strange way of repeating itself.* ◇ *a repeating pattern/design*

▸ WHAT SB ELSE SAID **4** [T] to tell sb sth that you have heard or been told by sb else: ~ **sth to sb** *I don't want you to repeat a word of this to anyone.* ◇ ~ **sth** *The rumour has been widely repeated in the press.* **5** [T] to say sth that sb else has said, especially in order to learn it: ~ **sth (after sb)** *Listen and repeat each sentence after me.* ◇ ~ **what...** *Can you repeat what I've just said word for word?* ◇ + **speech** *'Are you really sure?' she repeated.*

▸ OF FOOD **6** [I] ~ (**on sb**) (*BrE, informal*) if food **repeats**, you can taste it for some time after you have eaten it: *Do you find that onions repeat on you?*

▸ FOR EMPHASIS **7** [I, T] used to emphasize sth that you have already said: *The claims are, I repeat, totally unfounded.* ◇ ~ **sth** *I am not, repeat not, travelling in the same car as him!*

■ ***noun*** **1** a television or radio programme that has been broadcast before: *'Is it a new series?' 'No, a repeat'.* **2** an event that is very similar to sth that happened before: *A repeat of the 1906 earthquake could kill up to 11 000 people.* ◇ *She didn't want a* **repeat performance** *of what had happened the night before.* ◇ (*business*) *a* **repeat order** (= for a further supply of the same goods) **3** (*music*) a passage that is repeated

re·peat·able /rɪˈpiːtəbl/ *adj.* [not usually before noun] **1** (of a comment, etc.) (usually in negative sentences) polite and not offensive: *His reply was not repeatable.* **2** that can be repeated OPP **unrepeatable**

re·peated /rɪˈpiːtɪd/ *adj.* [only before noun] happening, said or done many times: *repeated absences from work* ▸ **re·peat·ed·ly** *adv.*: *The victim had been stabbed repeatedly in the chest.*

re·peat·er /rɪˈpiːtə(r)/ *noun* (*technical*) a gun that you can fire several times without having to load it again

R

repel /rɪˈpel/ *verb* (-ll-) **1** [T] ~ **sb/sth** (*formal*) to successfully fight sb who is attacking you, your country, etc. and drive them away: *to* ***repel an attack/invasion/invader*** ◇ *Troops repelled an attempt to infiltrate the south of the island.* ◇ (*figurative*) *The reptile's prickly skin repels nearly all of its predators.* **2** [T] ~ **sth** to drive, push or keep sth away: *a cream that repels insects* ◇ *The fabric has been treated to repel water.* **3** [T] ~ **sb** (not used in the progressive tenses) to make sb feel horror or disgust SYN **disgust, repulse**: *I was repelled by the smell.* **4** [T, I] ~ (**sth**) (*technical*) if one thing **repels** another, or if two things **repel** each other, an electrical or MAGNETIC force pushes them apart: *Like poles repel each other.* OPP **attract** ➲ see also REPULSION, REPULSIVE

re·pel·lent /rɪˈpelənt/ *adj., noun*

■ ***adj.*** **1** ~ (**to sb**) (*formal*) very unpleasant; causing strong dislike SYN **repulsive**: *Their political ideas are repellent to most people.* **2** (in compounds) not letting a particular substance, especially water, pass through it: *water-repellent cloth*

■ ***noun*** [U, C] **1** a substance that is used for keeping insects away from you: (*an*) *insect repellent* **2** a substance that is used on cloth, stone, etc. to prevent water from passing through it: (*a*) *water repellent*

re·pent /rɪˈpent/ *verb* [I, T] (*formal*) to feel and show that you are sorry for sth bad or wrong that you have done: *God welcomes the sinner who repents.* ◇ ~ **of sth** *She had repented of what she had done.* ◇ ~ **sth** *He came to repent his hasty decision* (= wished he had not taken it).

re·pent·ance /rɪˈpentəns/ *noun* [U] ~ (**for sth**) (*formal*) the fact of showing that you are sorry for sth wrong that you have done SYN **contrition, remorse**: *He shows no sign of repentance.*

re·pent·ant /rɪˈpentənt/ *adj.* (*formal*) feeling or showing that you are sorry for sth wrong that you have done SYN **contrite, remorseful** OPP **unrepentant**

re·per·cus·sion /ˌriːpəˈkʌʃn; *NAmE* -pərˈk-/ *noun* [usually pl.] an indirect and usually bad result of an action or event that may happen some time afterwards SYN **consequence**: *The collapse of the company will* ***have repercussions*** *for the whole industry.* ➲ SYNONYMS at RESULT

rep·er·toire /ˈrepətwɑː(r); *NAmE* -pərt-/ *noun* **1** (also *formal* **rep·er·tory**) all the plays, songs, pieces of music, etc. that a performer knows and can perform: *a pianist with a wide repertoire* **2** all the things that a person is able to do: *a young child's growing verbal repertoire*

rep·er·tory /ˈrepətri; *NAmE* ˈrepərtɔːri/ *noun* **1** (also *informal* **rep**) [U] the type of work of a theatre company in which different plays are performed for short periods of time: *an actor in repertory* ◇ *a repertory company* **2** [C] (*formal*) = REPERTOIRE (1)

repe·ti·tion /ˌrepəˈtɪʃn/ *noun* **1** [U, C] the fact of doing or saying the same thing many times: *learning by repetition* **2** [C] a thing that has been done or said before: *We do not want to see a repetition of last year's tragic events.*

repe·ti·tious /ˌrepəˈtɪʃəs/ *adj.* (often *disapproving*) involving sth that is often repeated: *a long and repetitious speech* ▸ **repe·ti·tious·ly** *adv.* **repe·ti·tious·ness** *noun*

re·peti·tive /rɪˈpetətɪv/ *adj.* **1** saying or doing the same thing many times, so that it becomes boring SYN **monotonous**: *a repetitive task.* **2** repeated many times: *a repetitive pattern of behaviour* ▸ **re·peti·tive·ly** *adv.* **re·peti·tive·ness** *noun* [U]

re·phrase /ˌriːˈfreɪz/ *verb* ~ **sth** to say or write sth using different words in order to make the meaning clearer

re·place /rɪˈpleɪs/ *verb*

1 ~ **sth/sb** to be used instead of sth/sb else; to do sth instead of sb/sth else SYN **take over from**: *The new design will eventually replace all existing models.* ◇ *Teachers will never be replaced by computers in the classroom.* **2** to remove sb/sth and put another person or thing in their place: ~ **sb/sth** *He will be difficult to replace when he leaves.* ◇ ~ **sb/sth with/by sb/sth** *It is not a good idea to miss meals and replace them with snacks.* **3** ~ **sth** to change sth that is old, damaged, etc. for a similar thing that is newer or better: *All the old carpets need replacing.* ◇ *You'll be expected to replace any broken glasses.* **4** ~ **sth** (+ **adv./prep.**) to put sth back in the place where it was before: *I replaced the cup carefully in the saucer.* ◇ *to replace the handset* (= after using the telephone).

re·place·able /rɪˈpleɪsəbl/ *adj.* that can be replaced OPP **irreplaceable**

re·place·ment /rɪˈpleɪsmənt/ *noun* **1** [U] the act of replacing one thing with another, especially sth that is newer or better: *the replacement of worn car parts* ◇ *replacement windows* **2** [C] a thing that replaces sth, especially because the first thing is old, broken, etc: *a hip replacement* **3** [C] ~ (**for sb**) a person who replaces another person in an organization, especially in their job: *We need to find a replacement for Sue.*

re·play *noun, verb*

■ ***noun*** /ˈriːpleɪ/ **1** (*sport*) a game that is played again because neither side won in the previous game **2** the playing again of a short section of a film/movie, tape, etc. especially to look at or listen to sth more carefully: *We watched a replay of the wedding on DVD.* ➲ see also ACTION REPLAY **3** (*informal*) something that is repeated or happens in exactly the same way as it did before: *This election will not be a replay of the last one.*

■ ***verb*** /ˌriːˈpleɪ/ **1** [usually passive] ~ **sth** to play a sports game again because neither team won the first game **2** ~ **sth** to play again sth that has been recorded on tape, film, etc: *The police replayed footage of the accident over and over again.* ◇ (*figurative*) *He replayed the scene in his mind.*

re·plen·ish /rɪˈplenɪʃ/ *verb* **~ sth (with sth)** (*formal*) to make sth full again by replacing what has been used SYN **top up**: *to replenish food and water supplies* ◇ *Allow me to replenish your glass.* ▶ **re·plen·ish·ment** *noun* [U]

re·plete /rɪˈpliːt/ *adj.* **1** [not before noun] **~ (with sth)** (*formal*) filled with sth; with a full supply of sth: *literature replete with drama and excitement* **2** (*old-fashioned* or *formal*) very full of food

rep·lica /ˈreplɪkə/ *noun* a very good or exact copy of sth: *a replica of the Eiffel Tower* ◇ *The weapon used in the raid was a replica.* ◇ *replica guns*

rep·li·cate /ˈreplɪkeɪt/ *verb* **1** [T] **~ sth** (*formal*) to copy sth exactly SYN **duplicate**: *Subsequent experiments failed to replicate these findings.* **2** [T, I] **~ (itself)** (*technical*) (of a virus or a MOLECULE) to produce exact copies of itself: *The drug prevents the virus from replicating itself.* ▶ **rep·li·ca·tion** /ˌreplɪˈkeɪʃn/ *noun* [U, C]

reply 0-π /rɪˈplaɪ/ *verb, noun*

■ ***verb*** (**re·plies, re·ply·ing, re·plied, re·plied**) **1** 0-π [I, T] to say or write sth as an answer to sb/sth: **~ (to sb/sth) (with sth)** *to reply to a question/an advertisement* ◇ *He never replied to any of my letters.* ◇ *She only replied with a smile.* ◇ **+ speech** *'I won't let you down,' he replied confidently.* ◇ **~ that...** *The senator replied that he was not in a position to comment.* ⊃ note at ANSWER **2** [I] **~ (to sth) (with sth)** to do sth as a reaction to sth that sb has said or done: *The terrorists replied to the government's statement with more violence.*

■ ***noun*** 0-π [C, U] an act of replying to sth/sb in speech, writing or by some action: *We had over 100 replies to our advertisement.* ◇ *I asked her what her name was but she* ***made no reply.*** ◇ (*formal*) *I am writing* ***in reply to*** *your letter of 16 March.* ◇ (*BrE*) ***a reply-paid envelope*** (= on which you do not have to put a stamp because it has already been paid for) ◇ (*BrE*) *Morocco scored four goals without reply to win the game.* ⊃ note at ANSWER

repo man /ˈriːpəʊ mæn; *NAmE* ˈriːpoʊ/ *noun* (*NAmE, informal*) a person whose job is to REPOSSESS (= take back) goods from people who still owe money for them and cannot pay

re·port 0-π /rɪˈpɔːt; *NAmE* rɪˈpɔːrt/ *verb, noun*

■ ***verb***

▸ GIVE INFORMATION **1** 0-π [T, I] to give people information about sth that you have heard, seen, done, etc: **~ sth (to sb)** *The crash happened seconds after the pilot reported engine trouble.* ◇ *Call me urgently if you have anything to report.* ◇ **~ (on sth) (to sb)** *The committee will report on its research next month.* ◇ **~ (sb/sth) doing sth** *The neighbours reported seeing him leave the building around noon.* ◇ **~ sb/sth + adj.** *The doctor reported the patient fully recovered.* ◇ **~ sb/sth as sth/as doing sth** *The house was reported as being in excellent condition.* ◇ **be reported to be/have sth** *The house was reported to be in excellent condition.* ◇ **~ (that)...** *Employers reported that graduates were deficient in writing and problem-solving skills.* ◇ **~ what, how, etc...** *She failed to report what had occurred.* ◇ **+ speech** *'The cabin's empty,' he reported back.*

▸ NEWS/STORY **2** 0-π [T, I] to present a written or spoken account of an event in a newspaper, on television, etc: **~ sth** *The stabbing was reported in the local press.* ◇ **it is reported that...** *It was reported that several people had been arrested.* ◇ **~ that...** *The TV news reported that several people had been arrested.* ◇ **~ (on sth)** *She reports on royal stories for the BBC.* **3** 0-π **be reported** [T] used to show that sth has been stated, and you do not know if it is true or not: **~ to do sth** *She is reported to earn over $10 million a year.* ◇ **~ as doing sth** *The President is reported as saying that he needs a break.* ◇ **it is reported that...** ***It was reported that*** *changes were being considered.*

▸ CRIME/ACCIDENT, ETC. **4** 0-π [T] to tell a person in authority about a crime, an accident, an illness, etc. or about sth bad that sb has done: **~ sth (to sb)** *Have you reported the accident to the police yet?* ◇ *a decrease in the number of reported cases of AIDS* ◇ **~ sb (to sb) (for sth/for doing sth)** *He's already been reported twice for arriving late.* ◇ **~ sb/sth + adj.** *She has reported her daughter missing.*

▸ ARRIVE **5** 0-π [I] **~ (to sb/sth) (for sth)** to tell sb that you have arrived, for example for work or for a meeting with sb: *You should report for duty at 9.30 a.m.* ◇ *All visitors must report to the reception desk on arrival.*

PHR V **reˌport ˈback** to return to a place, especially in order to work again: *Take an hour for lunch and report back at 2.* **reˌport ˈback (on sth) (to sb)** to give sb information about sth that they have asked you to find out about: *Find out as much as you can about him and report back to me.* ◇ *One person in the group should be prepared to report back to the class on your discussion.* ◇ **~ that...** *They reported back that no laws had actually been broken.* **reˈport to sb** (not used in the progressive tenses) (*business*) if you **report to** a particular manager in an organization that you work for, they are officially responsible for your work and tell you what to do

■ ***noun***

▸ OF NEWS **1** 0-π **~ (on/of sth)** a written or spoken account of an event, especially one that is published or broadcast: *Are these newspaper reports true?* ◇ *a weather report*

▸ INFORMATION **2** 0-π **~ (on sth)** a spoken or written description of sth containing information that sb needs to have: *a police/medical report* ◇ *Can you give us a progress report?*

▸ OFFICIAL STUDY **3** 0-π **~ (on sth)** an official document written by a group of people who have examined a particular situation or problem: *The committee will publish their report on the health service in a few weeks.* ⊃ WRITING TUTOR page WT18

▸ STORY **4** 0-π a story or piece of information that may or may not be true: *I don't believe these reports of UFO sightings.* ◇ *There are unconfirmed reports of a shooting in the capital.*

▸ ON STUDENT'S WORK **5** (*BrE*) (*NAmE* **reˈport card**) a written statement about a student's work at school, college, etc: *a school report* ◇ *to get a* ***good/bad report***

▸ EMPLOYEE **6** (*BrE, business*) an employee whose work is the responsibility of a particular manager: *a weekly meeting with my direct reports*

▸ OF GUN **7** the sound of an explosion or of a gun being fired SYN **bang, blast**: *a loud report*

IDM **of bad/good reˈport** (*formal*) talked about by people in a bad/good way

Synonyms

report

story • account • version

These are all words for a written or spoken account of events.

report a written or spoken account of an event, especially one that is published or broadcast: *Are these newspaper reports true?*

story an account, often spoken, of what happened to sb or of how sth happened; a report of events in a newspaper, magazine or news broadcast: *It was many years before the full story was made public.* ◇ *the front-page story*

account a written or spoken description of sth that has happened: *She gave the police a full account of the incident.*

REPORT OR ACCOUNT?

A **report** is always of recent events, especially news. An **account** may be of recent or past events.

version a description of an event from the point of view of a particular person or group of people: *She gave us her version of what had happened that day.*

PATTERNS

- a report/story **about** sth
- a **brief/short** report/story/account
- a **full** report/story/account/version
- a **news** report/story
- **to give** a(n) report/account/version

R

re·por·tage /rɪˈpɔːtɪdʒ; ˌrepɔːˈtɑːʒ; *NAmE* rɪˈpɔːrt-; ˌrepɔːrˈt-/ *noun* [U] (*formal*) the reporting of news or the typical style in which this is done in newspapers, or on TV and radio

re·port·ed·ly /rɪˈpɔːtɪdli; *NAmE* -ˈpɔːrt-/ *adv.* according to what some people say: *The band have reportedly decided to split up.*

reˌported ˈquestion *noun* (*grammar*) = INDIRECT QUESTION

reˌported ˈspeech (also ˌ**indirect ˈspeech**) *noun* [U] (*grammar*) a report of what sb has said that does not use their exact words: *In reported speech, 'I'll come later' becomes 'He said he'd come later'.*

re·port·er /rɪˈpɔːtə(r); *NAmE* -ˈpɔːrt-/ *noun* a person who collects and reports news for newspapers, radio or television: *a reporter from the New York Times* ◇ *a crime reporter* ➲ compare JOURNALIST ➲ see also CUB REPORTER

re·port·ing /rɪˈpɔːtɪŋ; *NAmE* -ˈpɔːrt-/ *noun* [U] the presenting and writing about news on television and radio, and in newspapers: *accurate/balanced/objective reporting* ◇ (*BrE*) ***Reporting restrictions*** *on the trial have been lifted* (= it can now legally be reported).

re·pose /rɪˈpəʊz; *NAmE* rɪˈpoʊz/ *noun, verb*
- ***noun*** [U] (*literary*) a state of rest, sleep or feeling calm
- ***verb*** (*literary*) **1** [I] + **adv./prep.** (of an object) to be or be kept in a particular place **2** [I] + **adv./prep.** (of a person) to lie or rest in a particular place

re·posi·tory /rɪˈpɒzətri; *NAmE* rɪˈpɑːzətɔːri/ *noun* (*pl.* -ies) (*formal*) **1** a place where sth is stored in large quantities **2** a person or book that is full of information: *My father is a repository of family history.*

re·pos·sess /ˌriːpəˈzes/ *verb* [usually passive] **~ sth** to take back property or goods from sb who has arranged to buy them but who still owes money for them and cannot pay: (*BrE*) *First I lost my job, then my house was repossessed.* HELP In *NAmE*, when a bank takes possession of sb's house because they cannot afford to pay the money they owe on it, the usual word is **foreclose**, but **repossess** is used in other contexts. ➲ COLLOCATIONS at HOUSE ➲ compare FORECLOSE

re·pos·ses·sion /ˌriːpəˈzeʃn/ *noun* **1** [U, C] the act of repossessing property, goods, etc: *families threatened with repossession* ◇ *a repossession order* **2** [C] a house, car, etc. that has been repossessed: *Auctions are the best place for buying repossessions.*

R

rep·re·hen·sible /ˌreprɪˈhensəbl/ *adj.* (*formal*) morally wrong and deserving criticism SYN **deplorable**

rep·re·sent 0‑w /ˌreprɪˈzent/ *verb*
- ▸ ACT/SPEAK FOR SB **1** 0‑w [often passive] **~ sb/sth** to be a member of a group of people and act or speak on their behalf at an event, a meeting, etc: *The competition attracted over 500 contestants representing 8 different countries.* ◇ *Local businesses are well represented on the committee* (= there are a lot of people from them on the committee). ◇ *The President was represented at the ceremony by the Vice-President.* **2** 0‑w **~ sb/sth** to act or speak officially for sb and defend their interests: *The union represents over 200 000 teachers.* ◇ *The association was formed to* ***represent the interests of*** *women artists.* ◇ *Ms Dale is representing the defendant* (= is his/her lawyer) *in the case.*
- ▸ BE EQUAL TO **3** 0‑w *linking verb* + **noun** (not used in the progressive tenses) to be sth SYN **constitute**: *This contract represents 20% of the company's annual revenue.* ◇ *This decision represents a significant departure from previous policy.*
- ▸ BE EXAMPLE OF **4** 0‑w [no passive] **~ sth** to be an example or expression of sth SYN **be typical of**: *a project representing all that is good in the community* ◇ *Those comments do not represent the views of us all.*
- ▸ BE SYMBOL **5** 0‑w **~ sth** (not used in the progressive tenses) to be a symbol of sth SYN **symbolize**: *Each colour on the chart represents a different department.* ◇ *Wind direction is represented by arrows.*
- ▸ IN PICTURE **6** 0‑w **~ sb/sth** (**as sb/sth**) | **~ sb/sth doing sth** (*formal*) to show sb/sth, especially in a picture SYN **depict**: *The carvings represent a hunting scene.* ◇ *The results are represented in fig.3 below.*
- ▸ DESCRIBE **7** **~ sb** (**as sth**) (*formal*) to present or describe sb/sth in a particular way, especially when this may not be fair: *The king is represented as a villain in the play.* ◇ *The risks were represented as negligible.*
- ▸ MAKE FORMAL STATEMENT **8** **~ sth** (**to sb**) | **~ that...** (*formal*) to make a formal statement to sb in authority to make your opinions known or to protest: *They represented their concerns to the authorities.*

re-present /ˌriː prɪˈzent/ *verb* **~ sth** to give, show or send sth again, especially a cheque, bill, etc. that has not been paid

rep·re·sen·ta·tion /ˌreprɪzenˈteɪʃn/ *noun* **1** [U, C] the act of presenting sb/sth in a particular way; something that shows or describes sth SYN **portrayal**: *the negative representation of single mothers in the media* ◇ *The snake swallowing its tail is a representation of infinity.* **2** [U] the fact of having representatives who will speak or vote for you or on your behalf: *The green movement lacks effective representation in Parliament.* ◇ *The accused was not allowed legal representation.* ➲ see also PROPORTIONAL REPRESENTATION **3** **representations** [pl.] (*formal, especially BrE*) formal statements made to sb in authority, especially in order to make your opinions known or to protest: *We have* ***made representations to*** *the prime minister, but without success.*

rep·re·sen·ta·tion·al /ˌreprɪzenˈteɪʃnl/ *adj.* **1** (*technical*) (especially of a style of art or painting) trying to show things as they really are ➲ compare ABSTRACT **2** involving the act of representing sb/sth: *local representational democracy*

rep·re·sen·ta·tive 0‑w /ˌreprɪˈzentətɪv/ *noun, adj.*
- ***noun*** **~** (**of sb/sth**) **1** 0‑w a person who has been chosen to speak or vote for sb else or on behalf of a group: *a representative of the UN* ◇ *our elected representatives in government* ◇ *a union representative* ◇ *The committee includes representatives from industry.* **2** 0‑w (also *informal* **rep**) a person who works for a company and travels around selling its products: *a sales representative* ◇ *She's our representative in France.* **3** 0‑w a person chosen to take the place of sb else: *He was the Queen's representative at the ceremony.* **4** 0‑w a person who is typical of a particular group: *The singer is regarded as a representative of the youth of her generation.* **5** **Representative** (*abbr.* **Rep.**) (in the US) a member of the House of Representatives, the Lower House of Congress; a member of the House of Representatives in the lower house of a state parliament
- ***adj.*** **1** 0‑w **~** (**of sb/sth**) typical of a particular group of people: *Is a questionnaire answered by 500 people* ***truly representative*** *of the population as a whole?* **2** 0‑w [usually before noun] containing or including examples of all the different types of people or things in a large group: ***a representative sample*** *of teachers* **3** 0‑w **~** (**of sth**) able to be used as a typical example of sth: *The painting is not representative of his work of the period.* **4** (of a system of government, etc.) consisting of people who have been chosen to speak or vote on behalf of the rest of a group: *a representative democracy* OPP **unrepresentative**

re·press /rɪˈpres/ *verb* **1** **~ sth** to try not to have or show an emotion, a feeling, etc. SYN **control**: *to repress a smile* ◇ *He burst in, making no effort to repress his fury.* **2** [often passive] **~ sb/sth** to use political and/or military force to control a group of people and restrict their freedom SYN **put down, suppress**

re·pressed /rɪˈprest/ *adj.* **1** (of a person) having emotions or desires that are not allowed to be expressed **2** (of emotions) not expressed openly: *repressed anger*

re·pres·sion /rɪˈpreʃn/ *noun* [U] **1** the act of using force to control a group of people and restrict their freedom: *government repression* **2** the act of controlling strong emotions and desires and not allowing them to be expressed so that they no longer seem to exist: *sexual repression*

re·pres·sive /rɪˈpresɪv/ *adj.* **1** (of a system of government) controlling people by force and restricting their freedom SYN **dictatorial**, **tyrannical**: *a **repressive** regime/measure/law* **2** controlling emotions and desires and not allowing them to be expressed ▸ **re·pres·sive·ly** *adv.* **re·pres·sive·ness** *noun* [U]

re·prieve /rɪˈpriːv/ *verb, noun*

▪ ***verb*** [usually passive] (not usually used in the progressive tenses) **1 ~ sb** to officially cancel or delay a punishment for a prisoner who is CONDEMNED to death: *a reprieved murderer* **2 ~ sth** to officially cancel or delay plans to close sth or end sth: *70 jobs have been reprieved until next April.*

▪ ***noun*** [usually sing.] **1** an official order stopping a punishment, especially for a prisoner who is CONDEMNED to death SYN **stay of execution** **2** a delay before sth bad happens: *Campaigners have won a reprieve for the hospital threatened with closure.*

rep·ri·mand /ˈreprɪmɑːnd; *NAmE* -mænd/ *verb* **~ sb (for sth)** | **+ speech** (*formal*) to tell sb officially that you do not approve of them or their actions SYN **rebuke**: *The officers were severely reprimanded for their unprofessional behaviour.* ▸ **rep·ri·mand** *noun* [C, U]: *He received a severe reprimand for his behaviour.*

re·print *verb, noun*

▪ ***verb*** /ˌriːˈprɪnt/ [usually passive] **~ sth** to print more copies of a book, an article, etc. with few or no changes

▪ ***noun*** /ˈriːprɪnt/ **1** an act of printing more copies of a book because all the others have been sold **2** a book that has been reprinted

re·prisal /rɪˈpraɪzl/ *noun* [C, U] a violent or aggressive act towards sb because of sth bad that they have done towards you SYN **retaliation**: *They did not want to give evidence for fear of reprisals.* ◇ *They shot ten hostages **in reprisal for** the assassination of their leader.* ➲ COLLOCATIONS at WAR

re·prise /rɪˈpriːz/ *noun* [usually sing.] a repeated part of sth, especially a piece of music

repro /ˈriːprəʊ; *NAmE* -proʊ/ *adj., noun*

▪ ***adj.*** (*informal*) copied, especially from a style that was originally made in the past: *Victorian repro furniture*

▪ ***noun*** **1** [C, U] something that is copied from a style that was originally made in the past **2** [U] = REPROGRAPHICS

re·proach /rɪˈprəʊtʃ; *NAmE* -ˈproʊtʃ/ *noun, verb*

▪ ***noun*** (*formal*) **1** [U] blame or criticism for sth you have done: *His voice was full of reproach.* ◇ *The captain's behaviour is **above/beyond reproach*** (= you cannot criticize it). **2** [C] a word or remark expressing blame or criticism: *He listened to his wife's bitter reproaches.* **3** [U] a state of shame or loss of honour: *Her actions brought reproach upon herself.* **4** [sing.] **~ (to sb/sth)** a person or thing that brings shame on sb/sth SYN **discredit**: *Such living conditions are a reproach to our society.*

▪ ***verb*** (*formal*) **1 ~ sb (for sth/for doing sth)** | **~ sb (with sth/with doing sth)** | **~ (sb) + speech** to blame or criticize sb for sth that they have done or not done, because you are disappointed in them: *She was reproached by colleagues for leaking the story to the press.* **2 ~ yourself (for sth/for doing sth)** | **~ yourself (with sth)** to feel guilty about sth that you think you should have done in a different way: *He reproached himself for not telling her the truth.*

re·proach·ful /rɪˈprəʊtʃfl; *NAmE* -ˈproʊtʃ-/ *adj.* expressing blame or criticism: *a reproachful look* ▸ **re·proach·ful·ly** /-fəli/ *adv.*

rep·ro·bate /ˈreprəbeɪt/ *noun* (*formal* or *humorous*) a person who behaves in a way that society thinks is immoral ▸ **rep·ro·bate** *adj.* [only before noun]

re·pro·cess /riːˈprəʊses; *NAmE* riːˈprɑːses; -ˈproʊ-/ *verb* **~ sth** to treat waste material so that it can be used again: *All these countries reprocess nuclear fuel.*

re·pro·duce 0‑w /ˌriːprəˈdjuːs; *NAmE* -ˈduːs/ *verb* **1** 0‑w [T] **~ sth** to make a copy of a picture, piece of text, etc: *It is illegal to reproduce these worksheets without permission from the publisher.* ◇ *The photocopier reproduces colours very well.* **2** 0‑w [T] **~ sth** to produce sth again; to make sth happen again in the same way: *The atmosphere of the novel is successfully reproduced in the movie.* **3** 0‑w [I, T] if people, plants, animals, etc. **reproduce** or **reproduce themselves**, they produce young: *Most reptiles reproduce by laying eggs on land.* ◇ **~ itself** *cells reproducing themselves* (= making new ones) ▸ **re·pro·du·cible** /-əbl/ *adj.*

re·pro·duc·tion /ˌriːprəˈdʌkʃn/ *noun* **1** [U] the act or process of producing babies, young animals or plants: *sexual reproduction* **2** [U] the act or process of producing copies of a document, book, picture, etc: *Use a black pen on white paper to ensure good reproduction.* **3** [U] the process of recording sounds onto tapes, CDs, DVDs, etc: *Digital recording gives excellent sound reproduction.* **4** [C] a thing that has been reproduced, especially a copy of a work of art: *a catalogue with colour reproductions of the paintings for sale* ◇ *reproduction furniture* (= furniture made as a copy of an earlier style)

re·pro·duct·ive /ˌriːprəˈdʌktɪv/ *adj.* [only before noun] connected with reproducing babies, young animals or plants: *reproductive organs*

repro·graph·ics /ˌriːprəˈɡræfɪks/ (also *informal* **repro**) *noun* [U] (*technical*) the science and practice of copying documents and pictures for publishing, etc.

re·proof /rɪˈpruːf/ *noun* (*formal*) **1** [U] blame or disapproval: *His words were a mixture of pity and reproof.* **2** [C] a remark that expresses blame or disapproval SYN **rebuke**: *She received a mild reproof from the teacher.*

re·prove /rɪˈpruːv/ *verb* **~ sb (for sth/for doing sth)** | **~ (sb) + speech** (*formal*) to tell sb that you do not approve of sth that they have done SYN **rebuke**: *He reproved her for rushing away.* ▸ **re·prov·ing** *adj.* [usually before noun]: *a reproving glance* **re·prov·ing·ly** *adv.*

rep·tile /ˈreptaɪl; *NAmE* also -tl/ *noun* any animal that has cold blood and skin covered in SCALES, and that lays eggs. Snakes, CROCODILES and TORTOISES are all reptiles. ➲ VISUAL VOCAB page V11 ➲ compare AMPHIBIAN ▸ **rep·til·ian** /repˈtɪliən/ *adj.*: *our reptilian ancestors* ◇ (*figurative*) *He licked his lips in an unpleasantly reptilian way.*

re·pub·lic /rɪˈpʌblɪk/ *noun* a country that is governed by a president and politicians elected by the people and where there is no king or queen: *newly independent republics* ◇ *the Republic of Ireland* ➲ compare MONARCHY

re·pub·lic·an /rɪˈpʌblɪkən/ *noun, adj.*

▪ ***noun*** **1** a person who supports a form of government with a president and politicians elected by the people with no king or queen ➲ compare ROYALIST **2** **Republican** (*abbr.* **R**, **Rep.**) a member or supporter of the Republican Party of the US ➲ compare DEMOCRAT **3** **Republican** a person from Northern Ireland who believes that Northern Ireland should be part of the Republic of Ireland and not part of the United Kingdom ➲ compare LOYALIST

▪ ***adj.*** **1** connected with or like a republic; supporting the principles of a republic: *a republican government/movement* **2** (also **Republican**) (*abbr.* **R**, **Rep.**) connected with the Republican Party in the US **3** (also **Republican**) connected with or supporting the Republicans in Northern Ireland ▸ **re·pub·lic·an·ism** (also **Re·pub·lic·an·ism**) *noun* [U]: *a strong commitment to Republicanism*

the Reˈpublican Party *noun* [sing.] one of the two main political parties in the US, usually considered to support conservative views, and to want to limit the power of central government ➲ compare THE DEMOCRATIC PARTY

re·pudi·ate /rɪˈpjuːdieɪt/ *verb* (*formal*) **1 ~ sth** to refuse to accept sth SYN **reject**: *to repudiate a suggestion* **2 ~ sth** to say officially and/or publicly that sth is not true SYN **deny**: *to repudiate a report* **3 ~ sb** (*old-fashioned*) to refuse to be connected with sb any longer SYN **disown**: *He repudiated his first wife and married her sister.* ▸ **re·pudi·ation** /rɪˌpjuːdiˈeɪʃn/ *noun* [U]

re·pudi·atory /rɪˈpjuːdiətri; *NAmE* -tɔːri/ *adj.* (*law*) relating to a situation in which sb refuses to do sth that they are legally required to do

re·pug·nance /rɪˈpʌɡnəns/ *noun* [U] (*formal*) a strong feeling of dislike or disgust about sth SYN **repulsion**: *She was trying to overcome her physical repugnance for him.*

re·pug·nant /rɪˈpʌɡnənt/ *adj.* [not usually before noun] (*formal*) making you feel strong dislike or disgust SYN **repulsive**: *We found his suggestion absolutely repugnant.* ◇ **~ to sb** *The idea of eating meat was repugnant to her.*

re·pulse /rɪˈpʌls/ *verb* (*formal*) **1** [usually passive] **~ sb** to make sb feel disgust or strong dislike SYN **repel**: *I was repulsed by the horrible smell.* **2 ~ sb/sth** to fight sb who is attacking you and drive them away SYN **repel**: *to repulse **an attack/invasion/offensive*** **3 ~ sb/sth** to refuse to accept sb's help, attempts to be friendly, etc. SYN **reject**: *Each time I tried to help I was repulsed.* ◇ *She repulsed his advances.*

re·pul·sion /rɪˈpʌlʃn/ *noun* [U] **1** a feeling of very strong dislike of sth that you find extremely unpleasant **2** (*physics*) the force by which objects tend to push each other away: *the forces of attraction and repulsion* ➲ see also REPEL ➲ compare ATTRACTION

re·pul·sive /rɪˈpʌlsɪv/ *adj.* **1** causing a feeling of strong dislike; very unpleasant SYN **disgusting**: *a repulsive sight/smell/habit* ◇ *What a repulsive man!* ➲ SYNONYMS at DISGUSTING **2** (*physics*) causing repulsion (= a force that pushes away): *repulsive forces* ▶ **re·pul·sive·ly** *adv.*: *repulsively ugly*

re·pur·pose /ˌriːˈpɜːpəs; *NAmE* -ˈpɜːrp-/ *verb* **~ sth** to change sth slightly in order to make it suitable for a new purpose

rep·ut·able /ˈrepjətəbl/ *adj.* that people consider to be honest and to provide a good service SYN **respected**: *a reputable dealer/company/supplier* ➲ compare DISREPUTABLE

repu·ta·tion 0‑ /ˌrepjuˈteɪʃn/ *noun* [C, U] the opinion that people have about what sb/sth is like, based on what has happened in the past: *to **earn/establish/build a reputation*** ◇ *to have **a good/bad reputation*** ◇ **~ (as sth)** *She soon acquired a reputation as a first-class cook.* ◇ **~ (for sth/for doing sth)** *I'm aware of Mark's reputation for being late.* ◇ *to damage/ruin sb's reputation* ◇ *The weather in England is **living up to its reputation*** (= is exactly as expected).

re·pute /rɪˈpjuːt/ *noun* [U] (*formal*) the opinion that people have of sb/sth SYN **reputation**: *She is a writer of international repute.* ◇ *My parents were artists **of** (**some**) **repute*** (= having a very good reputation).

R

re·puted /rɪˈpjuːtɪd/ *adj.* [not usually before noun] generally thought to be sth or to have done sth, although this is not certain SYN **rumoured**: **~ (to be sth)** *He is reputed to be the best heart surgeon in the country.* ◇ **~ (to have done sth)** *The house is wrongly reputed to have been the poet's birthplace.* ◇ *She sold her share of the company for a reputed £7 million.* ▶ **re·puted·ly** *adv.*

re·quest 0‑ /rɪˈkwest/ *noun, verb*
- ***noun* ~ (for sth)** | **~ (that...)** **1** 0‑ the action of asking for sth formally and politely: *They made a request for further aid.* ◇ *He was there **at the request of his manager/at his manager's request*** (= because his manager had asked him to go). ◇ *The writer's name was withheld **by request*** (= because the writer asked for this to be done). ◇ *Catalogues are available **on request**.* **2** 0‑ a thing that you formally ask for: *My request was granted.* ◇ *a radio request programme* (= a programme of music, songs, etc. that people have asked for)
- ***verb*** 0‑ (*formal*) to ask for sth or ask sb to do sth in a polite or formal way: **~ sth (from sb)** *She requested permission to film at the White House.* ◇ *You can request a free copy of the leaflet.* ◇ **~ sb to do sth** *You are requested not to smoke in the restaurant.* ◇ **~ that...** *She requested that no one be told of her decision until the next meeting.* ◇ (*BrE* also) *She requested that no one should be told of her decision.* ◇ **+ speech** *'Please come with me,' he requested.*

reˈquest stop *noun* (*BrE*) a BUS STOP where buses stop only if sb signals to the driver that they want the bus to stop

re·quiem /ˈrekwiəm; -iem/ (also ˌ**requiem ˈmass**) *noun* **1** a Christian ceremony for a person who has recently died, at which people say prayers for his or her soul **2** a piece of music for this ceremony

re·quire 0‑ AW /rɪˈkwaɪə(r)/ *verb* (not usually used in the progressive tenses) (*formal*)
1 0‑ to need sth; to depend on sb/sth: **~ sth** *These pets require a lot of care and attention.* ◇ *This condition requires urgent treatment.* ◇ *Do you require anything else?* (= in a shop/store, for example) ◇ **~ sb/sth to do sth** *True marriage requires us to show trust and loyalty.* ◇ **~ that...** *The situation required that he be present.* ◇ (*BrE* also) *The situation required that he should be present.* ◇ **~ doing sth** *Lentils do not require soaking before cooking.* **2** 0‑ [often passive] to make sb do or have sth, especially because it is necessary according to a particular law or set of rules: **~ sth** *The wearing of seat belts is required by law.* ◇ *'Hamlet' is **required reading*** (= must be read) *for this course.* ◇ *Several students failed to reach the required standard.* ◇ **~ sth of sb** *What exactly is required of a receptionist* (= what are they expected to do)? ◇ **~ sb to do sth** *All candidates will be required to take a short test.* ◇ **~ that...** *We require that you comply with the following rules:...* ➲ SYNONYMS at DEMAND

re·quire·ment 0‑ AW /rɪˈkwaɪəmənt; *NAmE* -ˈkwaɪərm-/ *noun* (*formal*)
1 0‑ (usually **requirements**) [pl.] something that you need or want: *the basic requirements of life* ◇ *a software package to **meet your requirements*** ◇ *Our immediate requirement is extra staff.* ◇ *These goods are **surplus to requirements*** (= more than we need). **2** 0‑ something that you must have in order to do sth else: *to **meet/fulfil/satisfy the requirements*** ◇ *What is the minimum entrance requirement for this course?*

requis·ite /ˈrekwɪzɪt/ *adj., noun*
- ***adj.*** [only before noun] (*formal*) necessary for a particular purpose: *She lacks the requisite experience for the job.*
- ***noun*** (*formal*) something that you need for a particular purpose: *toilet requisites* (= soap, TOOTHPASTE, etc.) ◇ **~ for/of sth** *A university degree has become a requisite for entry into most professions.* ➲ compare PREREQUISITE

requi·si·tion /ˌrekwɪˈzɪʃn/ *noun, verb*
- ***noun*** [C, U] a formal, official written request or demand for sth: *the requisition of ships by the government* ◇ *a **requisition form/order***
- ***verb* ~ sth** to officially demand the use of a building, vehicle, etc, especially during a war or an emergency: *The school was requisitioned as a military hospital.*

re·quite /rɪˈkwaɪt/ *verb* **~ sth** (*formal*) to give sth such as love, kindness, a favour, etc. in return for what sb has given you: *requited love* ➲ compare UNREQUITED

ˌ**re-ˈroute** *verb* **~ sth** to change the route that a road, vehicle, telephone call, etc. normally follows

rerun *noun, verb*
- ***noun*** /ˈriːrʌn/ **1** a television programme that is shown again: *reruns of old TV shows* **2** an event, such as a race or competition, that is held again **3** something that is done in the same way as sth in the past: *We wanted to avoid a rerun of last year's disastrous trip.*
- ***verb*** /ˌriːˈrʌn/ (**re·run·ning**, **reran** /ˌriːˈræn/, **rerun**) **1 ~ sth** to show a film/movie, television programme, etc. again **2 ~ sth** to do sth again in a similar way: *to rerun an experiment* **3 ~ sth** to run a race again

re·sale /ˈriːseɪl; ˌriːˈseɪl/ *noun* [U] the sale to another person of sth that you have bought: *the resale value of a car*

re·sched·ule AW /ˌriːˈʃedjuːl; *NAmE* ˌriːˈskedʒuːl/ *verb* **1 ~ sth (for/to sth)** | **~ sth to do sth** to change the time at which sth has been arranged to happen, especially so that it takes place later: *The meeting has been rescheduled for next week.* **2 ~ sth** (*finance*) to arrange for sb to pay back money that they have borrowed at a later date than was originally agreed ▶ **re·sched·ul·ing** *noun* [U, sing.]

re·scind /rɪˈsɪnd/ *verb* **~ sth** (*formal*) to officially state that a law, contract, decision, etc. is no longer valid SYN **revoke**

re·scis·sion /rɪˈsɪʒn/ *noun* (*formal*) the act of cancelling or ending a law, an order, or an agreement

res·cue 0-w /ˈreskjuː/ *verb, noun*

■ ***verb*** 0-w to save sb/sth from a dangerous or harmful situation: **~ sb/sth from sth/sb** *He rescued a child from drowning.* ◇ *The house was rescued from demolition.* ◇ *You rescued me from an embarrassing situation.* ◇ **~ sb/sth** *They were eventually rescued by helicopter.* ◇ **~ sb/sth + adj.** *She had despaired of ever being rescued alive.* ➲ SYNONYMS at SAVE ▸ **res·cuer** *noun*

■ ***noun* 1** 0-w [U] the act of saving sb/sth from a dangerous or difficult situation; the fact of being saved: *We had given up hope of rescue.* ◇ *A wealthy benefactor* ***came to their rescue*** *with a generous donation.* ◇ *a* ***rescue attempt/operation*** ◇ *a* ***mountain rescue*** *team* ◇ ***rescue workers/boats/helicopters*** **2** 0-w [C] an occasion when sb/sth is saved from a dangerous or difficult situation: *Ten fishermen were saved in a daring sea rescue.*

re·search 0-w AW *noun, verb*

■ ***noun*** 0-w /rɪˈsɜːtʃ; ˈriːsɜːtʃ; *NAmE* -sɜːrtʃ/ [U] (also **re·searches** [pl.]) (especially in *BrE*) a careful study of a subject, especially in order to discover new facts or information about it: ***medical/historical/scientific, etc. research*** ◇ *to* ***do/conduct/undertake research*** ◇ **~ (into/on sth/sb)** *He has carried out extensive research into renewable energy sources.* ◇ *Recent research on deaf children has produced some interesting findings about their speech.* ◇ *What have their researches shown?* ◇ *a* ***research project/grant/student*** ◇ *I've done some research to find out the cheapest way of travelling there.* ➲ COLLOCATIONS at SCIENTIFIC ➲ see also MARKET RESEARCH, OPERATIONAL RESEARCH

■ ***verb*** 0-w /rɪˈsɜːtʃ; *NAmE* -ˈsɜːrtʃ/ [I, T] to study sth carefully and try to discover new facts about it: **~ (into/in/on sth)** *They're researching into ways of improving people's diet.* ◇ **~ sth** *to research a problem/topic/market* ◇ *She's in New York researching her new book* (= finding facts and information to put in it). ◇ **~ how, what, etc...** *We have to research how the product will actually be used.* ▸ **re·search·er** AW *noun*

reˌsearch and deˈvelopment *noun* [U] (*abbr.* R & D) (in industry, etc.) work that tries to find new products and processes or to improve existing ones

re·sect /rɪˈsekt/ *verb* **~ sth** (*medical*) to cut out part of an organ or a piece of TISSUE from the body ▸ **re·sec·tion** /rɪˈsekʃn/ *noun* [U, C]

re·sell /ˌriːˈsel/ *verb* (**re·sold, re·sold** /ˌriːˈsəʊld; *NAmE* -ˈsoʊld/) **~ sth** to sell sth that you have bought: *He resells the goods at a profit.*

re·sem·blance /rɪˈzembləns/ *noun* [C, U] the fact of being or looking similar to sb/sth SYN **likeness**: *a* ***striking/close/strong resemblance*** ◇ *family resemblances* ◇ **~ to sb/sth** *She* ***bears an uncanny resemblance*** *to Dido.* ◇ *The movie* ***bears little resemblance to*** *the original novel.* ◇ **~ between A and B** *The resemblance between the two signatures was remarkable.*

re·sem·ble /rɪˈzembl/ *verb* [no passive] (not used in the progressive tenses) **~ sb/sth** to look like or be similar to another person or thing: *She closely resembles her sister.* ◇ *So many hotels resemble each other.* ◇ *The plant resembles grass in appearance.*

re·sent /rɪˈzent/ *verb* to feel bitter or angry about sth, especially because you feel it is unfair: **~ sth/sb** *I deeply resented her criticism.* ◇ **~ doing sth** *He bitterly resents being treated like a child.* ◇ **~ sb doing sth** *She resented him making all the decisions.* ◇ (*formal*) *She resented his making all the decisions.*

re·sent·ful /rɪˈzentfl/ *adj.* feeling bitter or angry about sth that you think is unfair: *a resentful look* ◇ **~ of/at/about sth** *They seemed to be resentful of our presence there.* ◇ *She was resentful at having been left out of the team.* ▸ **re·sent·ful·ly** /-fəli/ *adv.*

re·sent·ment /rɪˈzentmənt/ *noun* [U, sing.] a feeling of anger or unhappiness about sth that you think is unfair: *to* ***feel/harbour/bear resentment towards/against*** *sb* ◇ *She could not conceal the deep resentment she felt at the way she had been treated.*

re·ser·va·tion 0-w /ˌrezəˈveɪʃn; *NAmE* -zərˈv-/ *noun* **1** 0-w [C] an arrangement for a seat on a plane or train, a room in a hotel, etc. to be kept for you: *I'll call the restaurant and* ***make a reservation.*** ◇ *We have a reservation in the name of Grant.* ➲ COLLOCATIONS at RESTAURANT ➲ compare BOOKING **2** 0-w [C, U] a feeling of doubt about a plan or an idea SYN **misgiving**: *I* ***have*** *serious* ***reservations*** *about his ability to do the job.* ◇ *They support the measures* ***without reservation*** (= completely). **3** (also **re·serve**) [C] an area of land in the US that is kept separate for Native Americans to live in **4** [U] = RESERVATION POLICY ➲ see also CENTRAL RESERVATION

reserˈvation policy (also **re·ser·va·tion**) *noun* [U] (in India) the policy of keeping a certain percentage of jobs or places in schools, colleges, etc. for people who are members of SCHEDULED CASTES, SCHEDULED TRIBES or other BACKWARD CLASSES

re·serve 0-w /rɪˈzɜːv; *NAmE* rɪˈzɜːrv/ *verb, noun*

■ ***verb* 1** 0-w to ask for a seat, table, room, etc. to be available for you or sb else at a future time SYN **book**: **~ sth for sb/sth** *I'd like to reserve a table for three for eight o'clock.* ◇ **~ sth** *I've reserved a room in the name of Jones.* ➲ compare BOOK **2** 0-w to keep sth for sb/sth, so that it cannot be used by any other person or for any other reason: **~ sth for sb/sth** *These seats are reserved for special guests.* ◇ **~ sth** *I'd prefer to* ***reserve*** (***my***) ***judgement*** (= not make a decision) *until I know all the facts.* **3 ~ sth** to have or keep a particular power: *The management* ***reserves the right*** *to refuse admission.* ◇ (*law*) ***All rights reserved*** (= nobody else can publish or copy this).

■ ***noun***

▸ SUPPLY **1** 0-w [C, usually pl.] a supply of sth that is available to be used in the future or when it is needed: *large oil and gas reserves* ◇ *He discovered unexpected reserves of strength.* ◇ *reserve funds*

▸ PROTECTED LAND **2** 0-w (*NAmE* also **pre·serve**) [C] a piece of land that is a protected area for animals, plants, etc: *a wildlife reserve* ➲ see also GAME RESERVE, NATURE RESERVE **3** [C] = RESERVATION (3)

▸ QUALITY/FEELING **4** 0-w [U] the quality that sb has when they do not talk easily to other people about their ideas, feelings, etc. SYN **reticence**: *She found it difficult to make friends because of her natural reserve.* **5** [U] (*formal*) a feeling that you do not want to accept or agree to sth, etc. until you are quite sure that it is all right to do so: *Any contract should be treated* ***with reserve*** *until it has been checked.* ◇ *She trusted him* ***without reserve*** (= completely).

▸ IN SPORT **6** [C] an extra player who plays in a team when one of the other players is injured or not available to play **7 the reserves** [pl.] a team that is below the level of the main team

▸ MILITARY FORCE **8 the reserve** [sing.] (also **the reserves** [pl.]) an extra military force, etc. that is not part of a country's regular forces, but is available to be used when needed: *the army reserve(s)* ◇ *the reserve police*

▸ PRICE **9** (also **reˈserve price**) [C] (*BrE*) the lowest price that sb will accept for sth, especially sth that is sold at an AUCTION

IDM **in reˈserve** available to be used in the future or when needed: *The money was being* ***kept in reserve*** *for their retirement.* ◇ *200 police officers were* ***held in reserve.***

re·served /rɪˈzɜːvd; *NAmE* rɪˈzɜːrvd/ *adj.* (of a person or their character) slow or unwilling to show feelings or express opinions SYN **shy** ➲ compare UNRESERVED

re·serv·ist /rɪˈzɜːvɪst; *NAmE* -ˈzɜːrv-/ *noun* a soldier, etc. who is a member of the RESERVES (= a military force that can be used in an emergency)

res·er·voir /ˈrezəvwɑː(r); *NAmE* ˈrezərv-/ *noun* **1** a natural or artificial lake where water is stored before it is taken by pipes to houses, etc. **2** (*formal*) a large amount of sth that is available to be used **3** (*technical*) a place in

R

an engine or a machine where a liquid is kept before it is used

reset /ˌriːˈset/ *verb* (re·set·ting, reset, reset) **1 ~ sth (to sth)** | **~ sth to do sth** to change a machine, an instrument or a control so that it gives a different time or number or is ready to use again: *You need to reset your watch to local time.* **2** [often passive] **~ sth** to place sth in the correct position again: *to reset a broken bone*

re·set·tle /ˌriːˈsetl/ *verb* **1** [T, I] **~ (sb)** to help people go and live in a new country or area; to go and live in a new country or area: *Many of the refugees were resettled in Britain and Canada.* **2** [T] **~ sth** to start to use an area again as a place to live: *The region was only resettled 200 years later.* **3** [I, T] **~ (yourself)** to make yourself comfortable in a new position: *The birds flew around and then resettled on the pond.* ▶ **re·set·tle·ment** *noun* [U]: *the resettlement of refugees* ◇ *a resettlement agency*

re·shape /ˌriːˈʃeɪp/ *verb* **~ sth** to change the shape or structure of sth

re·shuf·fle /ˌriːˈʃʌfl/ (also *less frequent* **shuf·fle**) *verb* [T, I] **~ (sth)** to change around the jobs that a group of people do, for example in a government: *The Prime Minister eventually decided against reshuffling the Cabinet.* ▶ **re·shuf·fle** /ˈriːʃʌfl/ *noun*: *a Cabinet reshuffle*

res·ide AW /rɪˈzaɪd/ *verb* [I] **+ adv./prep.** (*formal*) to live in a particular place: *He returned to Britain in 1939, having resided abroad for many years.*

PHR V **reˈside in sb/sth** to be in sb/sth; to be caused by sth: *The source of the problem resides in the fact that the currency is too strong.* **reˈside in/with sb/sth** (of a power, a right, etc.) to belong to sb/sth SYN **be vested in**: *The ultimate authority resides with the board of directors.*

resi·dence AW /ˈrezɪdəns/ *noun* (*formal*) **1** [C] a house, especially a large or impressive one: *a desirable family residence for sale* (= for example, in an advertisement) ◇ *10 Downing Street is the British Prime Minister's* ***official residence***. **2** [U] the state of living in a particular place: *They were not able to* ***take up residence*** *in their new home until the spring.* ◇ *Please state your occupation and* ***place of residence***. ◇ *The flag flies when the Queen is* ***in residence***. ➲ see also HALL OF RESIDENCE **3** (also **resi·dency**) [U] permission to live in a country that is not your own: *They have been denied residence in this country.* ◇ *a residence permit*

IDM **in ˈresidence** having an official position in a particular place such as a college or university: *a writer in residence*

resi·dency /ˈrezɪdənsi/ *noun* (*pl.* -ies) (*formal*) **1** [U] = RESIDENCE (3): *She has been granted permanent residency in Britain.* **2** [U, C] the period of time that an artist, a writer or a musician spends working for a particular institution **3** [U] the state of living in a particular place: *a residency requirement for students* **4** [U, C] (*especially NAmE*) the period of time when a doctor working in a hospital receives special advanced training **5** (also **resi·dence**) [C] the official house of sb such as an AMBASSADOR

resi·dent 0-w AW /ˈrezɪdənt/ *noun, adj.*

■ ***noun*** **1** 0-w a person who lives in a particular place or who has their home there: *a resident of the United States* ◇ *There were confrontations between local residents and the police.* **2** 0-w (*formal*) a person who is staying in a hotel: *The hotel restaurant is open to non-residents.* **3** a doctor working in a hospital in the US who is receiving special advanced training ➲ compare REGISTRAR

■ ***adj.*** 0-w living in a particular place: *the town's resident population* (= not tourists or visitors) ◇ *to be resident abroad/in the US* ◇ *Tom's our* ***resident expert*** (= our own expert) *on foreign movies.*

ˌresident ˈalien *noun* (*NAmE, law*) a person from another country who has permission to stay in the US

resi·den·tial AW /ˌrezɪˈdenʃl/ *adj.* [usually before noun] **1** (of an area of a town) suitable for living in; consisting of houses rather than factories or offices: *a quiet residential area* **2** (of a job, a course, etc.) requiring a person to live at a particular place; offering living accommodation: *a residential language course* ◇ *a residential home for the elderly* ◇ *residential care for children*

ˈresidents' association *noun* a group of people who live in a particular area and join together to discuss the problems of that area

re·sidual /rɪˈzɪdjuəl; *NAmE* -dʒu-/ *adj.* [only before noun] (*formal*) remaining at the end of a process SYN **outstanding**: *There are still a few residual problems with the computer program.*

re·sidu·ary /rɪˈzɪdjuəri; *NAmE* -dʒueri/ *adj.* **1** (*law*) remaining from the money and property left by a person who has died after all debts, gifts, etc. have been paid **2** (*technical*) remaining at the end of a process

resi·due /ˈrezɪdjuː; *NAmE* -duː/ *noun* **1** a small amount of sth that remains at the end of a process: *pesticide residues in fruit and vegetables* **2** (*law*) the part of the money, property, etc. of a person who has died that remains after all the debts, gifts, etc. have been paid: *The residue of the estate was divided equally among his children.*

re·siduum /rɪˈzɪdjuəm/ *noun* (*pl.* **re·sidua** /-djuə/) (*technical*) something that remains after a reaction or process has taken place

re·sign /rɪˈzaɪn/ *verb* [I, T] to officially tell sb that you are leaving your job, an organization, etc: **~ (as sth)** *He resigned as manager after eight years.* ◇ **~ (from sth)** *Two members resigned from the board in protest.* ◇ **~ sth** *My father resigned his directorship last year.*

PHR V **reˈsign yourself to sth** to accept sth unpleasant that cannot be changed or avoided: *She resigned herself to her fate.* ◇ **~ doing sth** *We had to resign ourselves to making a loss on the sale.*

res·ig·na·tion /ˌrezɪɡˈneɪʃn/ *noun* **1** [U, C] the act of giving up your job or position; the occasion when you do this: *a letter of resignation* ◇ *There were calls for her resignation from the board of directors.* ◇ *Further resignations are expected.* ➲ COLLOCATIONS at JOB **2** [C] a letter, for example to your employers, to say that you are giving up your job or position: *to* ***offer/hand in/tender your resignation*** ◇ *We haven't received his resignation yet.* **3** [U] patient willingness to accept a difficult or unpleasant situation that you cannot change: *They accepted their defeat with resignation.*

re·signed /rɪˈzaɪnd/ *adj.* being willing to calmly accept sth unpleasant or difficult that you cannot change: *a resigned sigh* ◇ **~ to sth/doing sth** *He was resigned to never seeing his birthplace again.* ▶ **re·sign·ed·ly** /-nɪdli/ *adv.*: *'I suppose you're right,' she said resignedly.*

re·sili·ence /rɪˈzɪliəns/ (also *less frequent* **re·sili·ency** /-nsi/) *noun* [U] **1** the ability of people or things to feel better quickly after sth unpleasant, such as shock, injury, etc. **2** the ability of a substance to return to its original shape after it has been bent, stretched or pressed

re·sili·ent /rɪˈzɪliənt/ *adj.* **1** able to feel better quickly after sth unpleasant such as shock, injury, etc: *He'll get over it—young people are amazingly resilient.* **2** (of a substance) returning to its original shape after being bent, stretched, or pressed ▶ **re·sili·ent·ly** *adv.*

resin /ˈrezɪn; *NAmE* ˈrezn/ *noun* [C, U] **1** a sticky substance that is produced by some trees and is used in making VARNISH, medicine, etc. **2** an artificial substance similar to resin, used in making plastics ▶ **res·in·ous** /ˈrezɪnəs; *NAmE* ˈrezənəs/ *adj.*: *the resinous scent of pine trees*

re·sist 0-w /rɪˈzɪst/ *verb*

1 0-w [T, I] to refuse to accept sth and try to stop it from happening SYN **oppose**: **~ (sth)** *to resist change* ◇ *They are determined to resist pressure to change the law.* ◇ **~ doing sth** *The bank strongly resisted cutting interest rates.* **2** 0-w [I, T] to fight back when attacked; to use force to stop sth from happening: *He tried to pin me down, but I resisted.* ◇ **~ sth** *She was charged with* ***resisting arrest***. **3** 0-w [T, I] (usually in negative sentences) to stop yourself from having sth you like or doing sth you very much want to do: **~ (sth)** *I finished the cake. I* ***couldn't resist it***. ◇ *I found the temptation to miss the class too hard to resist.* ◇ **~ doing sth** *He couldn't resist showing off his new car.* **4** 0-w [T] **~ sth** to not be harmed or damaged by sth: *A healthy diet should help your* *body resist infection.* ◇ *This new paint is designed to resist heat.*

re·sist·ance 🗝 /rɪˈzɪstəns/ *noun* **1** 🗝 [U, sing.] dislike of or opposition to a plan, an idea, etc; refusal to obey: *As with all new ideas it met with resistance.* ◇ **~ to sb/sth** *There has been a lot of resistance to this new law.* ◇ *Resistance to change has nearly destroyed the industry.* **2** 🗝 [U, sing.] the act of using force to oppose sb/sth: *armed resistance* ◇ *The defenders* ***put up a strong resistance.*** ◇ **~ to sb/sth** *The demonstrators* ***offered*** *little or no* ***resistance*** *to the police.* **3** 🗝 [U, sing.] **~ (to sth)** the power not to be affected by sth: *AIDS lowers the body's resistance to infection.* **4** [U, sing.] **~ (to sth)** a force that stops sth moving or makes it move more slowly: ***wind/air resistance*** (= in the design of planes or cars) **5** [U, C] (*physics*) (*symb.* R) the opposition of a substance or device to the flow of an electrical current ➲ compare REACTANCE **6** (often **the Resistance**) [sing.+ sing./pl. v.] a secret organization that resists the authorities, especially in a country that an enemy has control of: *resistance fighters* IDM see LINE *n.*

re·sist·ant /rɪˈzɪstənt/ *adj.* **1 ~ (to sth)** not affected by sth; able to resist sth: *plants that are resistant to disease* **2 ~ (to sth)** opposing sth and trying to stop it happening: *Elderly people are not always resistant to change.* **3 -resistant** (in adjectives) not damaged by the thing mentioned: *disease-resistant plants* ◇ *fire-resistant materials* ➲ see also HEAT-RESISTANT, WATER-RESISTANT

re·sist·er /rɪˈzɪstə(r)/ *noun* a person who resists sb/sth

re·sist·ible /rɪˈzɪstəbl/ *adj.* that can be resisted OPP **irresistible**

re·sist·ive /rɪˈzɪstɪv/ *adj.* **1** able to survive or cope with the action or effect of sth **2** (*physics*) relating to electrical resistance ▶ **re·sist·iv·ity** /ˌrɪzɪˈstɪvɪti/ *noun* [U, C]

re·sis·tor /rɪˈzɪstə(r)/ *noun* (*physics*) a device that has RESISTANCE to an electric current in a CIRCUIT

resit /ˌriːˈsɪt/ *verb* (**re·sit·ting, resat, resat** /ˌriːˈsæt/) (also **re·take**) [T, I] **~ (sth)** (*BrE*) to take an exam or a test again, usually after failing it the first time ▶ **resit** /ˈriːsɪt/ (also **re·take**) *noun*: *Students are only allowed one resit.*

re·size /ˌriːˈsaɪz/ *verb* **~ sth** to make sth bigger or smaller, especially an image on a computer screen

re·skill /ˌriːˈskɪl/ *verb* [I, T] **~ (sb)** to learn new skills so that you can do a new job; to teach sb new skills

reso·lute /ˈrezəluːt/ *adj.* having or showing great determination SYN **determined**: *resolute leadership* ◇ *He became even more resolute in his opposition to the plan.* OPP **irresolute** ▶ **reso·lute·ly** *adv.*: *They remain resolutely opposed to the idea.* **reso·lute·ness** *noun* [U]

reso·lution AW /ˌrezəˈluːʃn/ *noun* **1** [C] a formal statement of an opinion agreed on by a committee or a council, especially by means of a vote: *to* ***pass/adopt/carry a resolution*** **2** [U, sing.] the act of solving or settling a problem, disagreement, etc. SYN **settlement**: *The government is pressing for an early resolution of the dispute.* **3** [U] the quality of being resolute or determined SYN **resolve**: *The reforms owe a great deal to the resolution of one man.* **4** [C] **~ (to do sth)** a firm decision to do or not to do sth: *She* ***made a resolution*** *to visit her relatives more often.* ◇ *Have you made any* ***New Year's resolutions*** (= for example, to give up smoking from 1 January)? **5** [U, sing.] the power of a computer screen, printer, etc. to give a clear image, depending on the size of the dots that make up the image: *high-resolution graphics*

re·solve 🗝 AW /rɪˈzɒlv; *NAmE* rɪˈzɑːlv; rɪˈzɔːlv/ *verb, noun*

■ ***verb*** (*formal*) **1** 🗝 [T] **~ sth/itself** to find an acceptable solution to a problem or difficulty SYN **settle**: *to* ***resolve an issue/a dispute/a conflict/a crisis*** ◇ *Both sides met in order to try to resolve their differences.* **2** [T, I] to make a firm decision to do sth: **~ to do sth** *He resolved not to tell her the truth.* ◇ **~ (that)...** *She resolved (that) she would never see him again.* ◇ **~ on sth/on doing sth** *We had resolved on making an early start.* **3** [T] (of a committee, meeting, etc.) to reach a decision by means of a formal vote: **it is resolved that...** *It was resolved that the matter be referred to a higher authority.* ◇ **~ that...** *They resolved that the matter be referred to a higher authority.* ◇ **~ to do sth** *The Supreme Council resolved to resume control over the national press.* PHR V **re'solve into sth** | **re'solve sth into sth 1** to separate or to be separated into its parts: *to resolve a complex argument into its basic elements* **2** (of sth seen or heard at a distance) to gradually turn into a different form when it is seen or heard more clearly: *The orange light resolved itself into four lanterns.* **3** to gradually become or be understood as sth: *The discussion eventually resolved itself into two main issues.*

■ ***noun*** [U] (*formal*) strong determination to achieve sth SYN **resolution**: *The difficulties in her way merely strengthened her resolve.* ◇ **~ to do sth** *The government reiterated its resolve to uncover the truth.*

re·solved /rɪˈzɒlvd; *NAmE* rɪˈzɑːlvd; rɪˈzɔːlvd/ *adj.* [not before noun] **~ (to do sth)** (*formal*) determined: *I was resolved not to see him.*

res·on·ance /ˈrezənəns/ *noun* **1** [U] (*formal*) (of sound) the quality of being resonant: *Her voice had a strange and thrilling resonance.* **2** [C, U] (*technical*) the sound or other VIBRATION produced in an object by sound or VIBRATIONS of a similar FREQUENCY from another object **3** [U, C] (*formal*) (in a piece of writing, music, etc.) the power to bring images, feelings, etc. into the mind of the person reading or listening; the images, etc. produced in this way

res·on·ant /ˈrezənənt/ *adj.* **1** (*formal*) (of sound) deep, clear and continuing for a long time: *a deep resonant voice* **2** (*technical*) causing sounds to continue for a long time SYN **resounding**: *resonant frequencies* **3** (*literary*) having the power to bring images, feelings, memories, etc. into your mind: *a poem filled with resonant imagery* ▶ **res·on·ant·ly** *adv.*

res·on·ate /ˈrezəneɪt/ *verb* (*formal*) **1** [I] (of a voice, an instrument, etc.) to make a deep, clear sound that continues for a long time **2** [I] (of a place) to be filled with sound; to make a sound continue longer SYN **resound**: *a resonating chamber* ◇ **~ with sth** *The room resonated with the chatter of 100 people.* **3** [I] **~ (with sb/sth)** to remind sb of sth; to be similar to what sb thinks or believes: *These issues resonated with the voters.* PHR V **'resonate with sth** (*literary*) to be full of a particular quality or feeling: *She makes a simple story resonate with complex themes and emotions.*

res·on·ator /ˈrezəneɪtə(r)/ *noun* (*technical*) a device for making sound louder and stronger, especially in a musical instrument

R

re·sort 🗝 /rɪˈzɔːt; *NAmE* rɪˈzɔːrt/ *noun, verb*

■ ***noun*** **1** 🗝 [C] a place where a lot of people go on holiday/vacation: ***seaside/ski/mountain, etc. resorts*** ◇ (*BrE*) *a popular* ***holiday resort*** ◇ *the resort town of Byron Bay* ➲ COLLOCATIONS at TRAVEL **2** [U] **~ to sth** the act of using sth, especially sth bad or unpleasant, because nothing else is possible SYN **recourse**: *There are hopes that the conflict can be resolved* ***without resort to violence.*** **3** 🗝 **the first/last/final ~** the first or last course of action that you should or can take in a particular situation: *Strike action should be regarded* ***as a last resort,*** *when all attempts to negotiate have failed.* ◇ ***In the last resort*** (= in the end) *everyone must decide for themselves.*

■ ***verb***

PHR V **re'sort to sth** 🗝 to make use of sth, especially sth bad, as a means of achieving sth, often because there is no other possible solution SYN **have recourse to**: *They felt obliged to resort to violence.* ◇ **~ doing sth** *We may have to resort to using untrained staff.*

re·sound /rɪˈzaʊnd/ *verb* (*formal*) **1** [I] **~ (through sth)** (of a sound, voice, etc.) to fill a place with sound: *Laughter resounded through the house.* ◇ (*figurative*) *The tragedy resounded around the world.* **2** [I] **~ (with/to sth)** (of a place) to be filled with sound: *The street resounded to the thud of marching feet.*

re·sound·ing /rɪˈzaʊndɪŋ/ *adj.* [only before noun] **1** very great SYN **emphatic**: *a* ***resounding victory/win/defeat*** ◇

*The evening was **a resounding success**.* **2** (of a sound) very loud and continuing for a long time SYN **resonant** ▶ **re·sound·ing·ly** *adv.*

re·source 0‑ᵣ AW /rɪˈsɔːs; -ˈzɔːs; *NAmE* ˈriːsɔːrs; rɪˈsɔːrs/ *noun, verb*

■ ***noun*** **1** 0‑ᵣ [C, usually pl.] a supply of sth that a country, an organization or a person has and can use, especially to increase their wealth: *the exploitation of minerals and other **natural resources*** ◇ *We do not have the resources* (= money) *to update our computer software.* ◇ *We must make the most efficient use of the available financial resources.* ◇ *We agreed to **pool our resources*** (= so that everyone gives sth). ➲ COLLOCATIONS at ENVIRONMENT ➲ see also HUMAN RESOURCES **2** 0‑ᵣ [C] something that can be used to help achieve an aim, especially a book, equipment, etc. that provides information for teachers and students: *The database could be used as a teaching resource in colleges.* ◇ *Time is your most valuable resource, especially in examinations.* ◇ *resource books for teachers* **3 resources** [pl.] personal qualities such as courage and imagination that help you deal with difficult situations: *He has no inner resources and hates being alone.*

■ ***verb*** **~ sth** to provide sth with the money or equipment that is needed: *Schools in the area are still inadequately resourced.*

re·source·ful AW /rɪˈsɔːsfl; -ˈzɔːs-; *NAmE* -ˈsɔːrs-/ *adj.* (*approving*) good at finding ways of doing things and solving problems, etc. SYN **enterprising** ▶ **re·source·ful·ly** /-fəli/ *adv.* **re·source·ful·ness** *noun* [U]

re·spect 0‑ᵣ /rɪˈspekt/ *noun, verb*

■ ***noun*** **1** 0‑ᵣ [U, sing.] **~ (for sb/sth)** a feeling of admiration for sb/sth because of their good qualities or achievements: *I have the greatest respect for your brother.* ◇ *A two-minute silence was held as a **mark of respect**.* ◇ *A deep mutual respect and understanding developed between them.* ➲ see also SELF-RESPECT OPP **disrespect** **2** 0‑ᵣ [U, sing.] **~ (for sb/sth)** polite behaviour towards or care for sb/sth that you think is important: *to show a lack of respect for authority* ◇ *He has no respect for her feelings.* ◇ *Everyone has a right to be **treated with respect**.* OPP **disrespect** **3** 0‑ᵣ [C] a particular aspect or detail of sth: ***In this respect** we are very fortunate.* ◇ *There was one respect, however, in which they differed.*

IDM **in respect of sth** (*formal* or *business*) **1** concerning: *A writ was served on the firm in respect of their unpaid bill.* **2** in payment for sth: *money received in respect of overtime worked* **with reˈspect** | **with all due reˈspect** (*formal*) used when you are going to disagree, usually quite strongly, with sb: *With all due respect, the figures simply do not support you on this.* **with respect to sth** (*formal* or *business*) concerning: *The two groups were similar with respect to income and status.* ➲ more at DUE *adj.*, PAY *v.*

■ ***verb*** **1** 0‑ᵣ (not usually used in the progressive tenses) to have a very good opinion of sb/sth; to admire sb/sth: **~ sb/sth** *I respect Jack's opinion on most subjects.* ◇ *a much loved and **highly respected** teacher* ◇ **~ sb/sth for sth** *She had always been honest with me, and I respect her for that.* **2** 0‑ᵣ **~ sth** to be careful about sth; to make sure you do not do sth that sb would consider to be wrong: *to respect other people's property* ◇ *She promised to respect our wishes.* ◇ *He doesn't respect other people's right to privacy.* **3** 0‑ᵣ **~ sth** to agree not to break a law, principle, etc: *The new leader has promised to respect the constitution.*

re·spect·abil·ity /rɪˌspektəˈbɪləti/ *noun* [U] the fact of being considered socially acceptable

re·spect·able /rɪˈspektəbl/ *adj.* **1** considered by society to be acceptable, good or correct: *a highly respectable neighbourhood* ◇ *a respectable married man* ◇ *Go and make yourself look respectable.* OPP **disreputable** **2** fairly good; that there is not reason to be ashamed of SYN **acceptable**: *a perfectly respectable result* ▶ **re·spect·ably** *adv.*: *respectably dressed*

re·spect·er /rɪˈspektə(r)/ *noun*

IDM **be no respecter of ˈpersons** to treat everyone in the same way, without being influenced by their importance, wealth, etc.

re·spect·ful /rɪˈspektfl/ *adj.* showing or feeling respect: *The onlookers stood at a respectful distance.* ◇ *We were brought up to be respectful of authority.* OPP **disrespectful** ▶ **re·spect·ful·ly** /-fəli/ *adv.*: *He listened respectfully.*

re·spect·ing /rɪˈspektɪŋ/ *prep.* (*formal*) concerning SYN **with respect to**: *information respecting the child's whereabouts*

re·spect·ive /rɪˈspektɪv/ *adj.* [only before noun] belonging or relating separately to each of the people or things already mentioned: *They are each recognized specialists in their respective fields.* ◇ *the respective roles of men and women in society*

re·spect·ive·ly /rɪˈspektɪvli/ *adv.* in the same order as the people or things already mentioned: *Julie and Mark, aged 17 and 19 respectively*

res·pir·ation /ˌrespəˈreɪʃn/ *noun* [U] (*formal*) the act of breathing: *Blood pressure and respiration are also recorded.* ➲ see also ARTIFICIAL RESPIRATION

res·pir·ator /ˈrespəreɪtə(r)/ *noun* **1** a piece of equipment that makes it possible for sb to breathe over a long period when they are unable to do so naturally: *She was **put on a respirator**.* **2** a device worn over the nose and mouth to allow sb to breathe in a place where there is a lot of smoke, gas, etc.

re·spira·tory /rəˈspɪrətri; ˈrespərətri; *NAmE* ˈrespərətɔːri/ *adj.* connected with breathing: *the respiratory system* ◇ *respiratory diseases*

re·spire /rɪˈspaɪə(r)/ *verb* [I] (*technical*) to breathe

res·pir·om·eter /ˌrespɪˈrɒmɪtə(r); *NAmE* -ˈrɑːm-/ *noun* (*medical*) a piece of equipment for measuring how much air sb's lungs will hold

res·pite /ˈrespaɪt; *NAmE* ˈrespɪt/ *noun* [sing., U] **1 ~ (from sth)** a short break or escape from sth difficult or unpleasant: *The drug brought a brief respite from the pain.* ◇ *There was no respite from the suffocating heat.* ◇ *She continued to work without respite.* ◇ ***respite care*** (= temporary care arranged for old, mentally ill, etc. people so that the people who usually care for them can have a rest) ➲ SYNONYMS at REST **2** a short delay allowed before sth difficult or unpleasant must be done SYN **reprieve**: *His creditors agreed to give him a temporary respite.*

re·splen·dent /rɪˈsplendənt/ *adj.* **~ (in sth)** (*formal* or *literary*) brightly coloured in an impressive way: *He glimpsed Sonia, resplendent in a red dress.* ▶ **re·splen·dent·ly** *adv.*

re·spond 0‑ᵣ AW /rɪˈspɒnd; *NAmE* rɪˈspɑːnd/ *verb*
1 0‑ᵣ [I, T] (rather *formal*) to give a spoken or written answer to sb/sth SYN **reply**: *I asked him his name, but he didn't respond.* ◇ **~ (to sb/sth) (with sth)** *She never responded to my letter.* ◇ **+ speech** *'I'm not sure,' she responded.* ◇ **~ that** *... When asked about the company's future, the director responded that he remained optimistic.* ➲ note at ANSWER **2** 0‑ᵣ [I] **~ (to sth) (with sth/by doing sth)** to do sth as a reaction to sth that sb has said or done SYN **react**: *How did they respond to the news?* ◇ *The government responded by banning all future demonstrations.* **3** 0‑ᵣ [I] **~ (to sth/sb)** to react quickly or in the correct way to sth/sb: *The car responds very well to the controls.* ◇ *You can rely on him to respond to a challenge.* **4** [I] **~ (to sth)** to improve as a result of a particular kind of treatment: *The infection did not respond to the drugs.*

re·spond·ent AW /rɪˈspɒndənt; *NAmE* -ˈspɑːnd-/ *noun* **1** a person who answers questions, especially in a survey: *60% of the respondents agreed with the suggestion.* **2** (*law*) a person who is accused of sth

re·sponse 0‑ᵣ AW /rɪˈspɒns; *NAmE* rɪˈspɑːns/ *noun* **1** 0‑ᵣ [C, U] a spoken or written answer: *She made no response.* ◇ **~ to sb/sth** ***In response to** your enquiry...* ◇ *I received an encouraging response to my advertisement.* **2** 0‑ᵣ [C, U] a reaction to sth that has happened or been said: *The news provoked an angry response.* ◇ *a positive response* ◇ *I knocked on the door but there was no response.* ◇ **~ (to sb/sth)** *The product was developed **in response to** customer de-*

R

mand. ◇ *We sent out over 1 000 letters but the* ***response rate*** *has been low* (= few people replied). **3** [C, usually pl.] **~** (**to sb/sth**) a part of a church service that the people sing or speak as an answer to the part that the priest sings or speaks

res'ponse time *noun* the length of time that a person or system takes to react to sth: *The average response time to emergency calls was 9 minutes.*

re·spon·si·bil·ity 🔑 /rɪˌspɒnsəˈbɪləti; *NAmE* -ˌspɑːn-/ *noun* (*pl.* -ies)
1 🔑 [U, C] a duty to deal with or take care of sb/sth, so that you may be blamed if sth goes wrong: **~** (**for sth**) *We are recruiting a sales manager with responsibility for the European market.* ◇ **~** (**for doing sth**) *They have responsibility for ensuring that the rules are enforced.* ◇ **~** (**to do sth**) *It is their responsibility to ensure that the rules are enforced.* ◇ *parental rights and responsibilities* ◇ *to* ***take/assume*** *overall* ***responsibility*** *for personnel* ◇ *I don't feel ready* ***to take on*** *new* ***responsibilities.*** ◇ *to be in a* ***position of responsibility*** ◇ *I did it* ***on my own responsibility*** (= without being told to and being willing to take the blame if it had gone wrong). **2** 🔑 [U] **~** (**for sth**) blame for sth bad that has happened: *The bank refuses to* ***accept responsibility*** *for the mistake.* ◇ *Nobody has* ***claimed responsibility*** *for the bombing.* ➲ see also DIMINISHED RESPONSIBILITY **3** 🔑 [U, C] a duty to help or take care of sb because of your job, position, etc: **~** (**to/towards sb**) *She feels a strong* ***sense of responsibility*** *towards her employees.* ◇ **~** (**to do sth**) *I think we have a* ***moral responsibility*** *to help these countries.*

re·spon·sible 🔑 /rɪˈspɒnsəbl; *NAmE* -ˈspɑːn-/ *adj.*
▸ HAVING JOB/DUTY **1** 🔑 having the job or duty of doing sth or taking care of sb/sth, so that you may be blamed if sth goes wrong: **~** (**for doing sth**) *Mike is responsible for designing the entire project.* ◇ **~** (**for sb/sth**) *Even where parents no longer live together, they each continue to be responsible for their children.*
▸ CAUSING STH **2** 🔑 **~** (**for sth**) being able to be blamed for sth: *Who's responsible for this mess?* ◇ *Everything will be done to bring those responsible to justice.* ◇ *He is mentally ill and cannot* ***be held responsible*** *for his actions.* **3** 🔑 **~** (**for sth**) being the cause of sth: *Cigarette smoking is responsible for about 90% of deaths from lung cancer.*
▸ TO SB IN AUTHORITY **4** 🔑 **~ to sb/sth** to have to report to sb/sth with authority or in a higher position and explain to them what you have done: *The Council of Ministers is responsible to the Assembly.*
▸ RELIABLE **5** 🔑 (of people or their actions or behaviour) that you can trust and rely on SYN **conscientious**: *Clare has a mature and responsible attitude to work.* OPP **irresponsible**
▸ JOB **6** 🔑 [usually before noun] needing sb who can be trusted and relied on; involving important duties: *a* ***responsible job/position***

re·spon·sibly /rɪˈspɒnsəbli; *NAmE* -ˈspɑːn-/ *adv.* in a sensible way that shows you can be trusted: *to act responsibly* OPP **irresponsibly**

re·spon·sive AW /rɪˈspɒnsɪv; *NAmE* -ˈspɑːn-/ *adj.* **1** [not usually before noun] **~** (**to sb/sth**) reacting quickly and in a positive way: *Firms have to be responsive to consumer demand.* ◇ *a flu virus that is not responsive to treatment* **2** **~** (**to sb/sth**) reacting with interest or enthusiasm SYN **receptive**: *The club is responsive to new ideas.* ◇ *a responsive and enthusiastic audience* OPP **unresponsive** ▸ **re·spon·sive·ly** *adv.* **re·spon·sive·ness** AW *noun* [U]: *a lack of responsiveness to client needs*

re·spray /ˌriːˈspreɪ/ *verb* **~ sth** to change the colour of sth, especially a car, by painting it with a spray ▸ **re·spray** /ˈriːspreɪ/ *noun* [usually sing.]

rest 🔑 /rest/ *noun, verb*
■ ***noun***
▸ REMAINING PART/PEOPLE/THINGS **1** 🔑 [sing.] **the ~** (**of sth**) the remaining part of sth: *I'm not doing this job for the rest of my life.* ◇ *How would you like to spend the rest of the day?* ◇ *Take what you want and throw the rest away.* **2** 🔑 [pl.] **the ~** (**of sth**) the remaining people or things; the others: *Don't blame Alex. He's human, like the rest of us.* ◇ *The first question was difficult, but the rest were pretty easy.*
▸ PERIOD OF RELAXING **3** 🔑 [C, U] a period of relaxing, sleeping or doing nothing after a period of activity: *I had a good night's rest.* ◇ *We stopped for a well-earned rest.* ◇ **~** (**from sth**) *to* ***have/take a rest*** *from all your hard work* ◇ *Try to* ***get some rest****—you have a busy day tomorrow.* ◇ *There are no matches tomorrow, which is a* ***rest day****, but the tournament resumes on Monday.*
▸ SUPPORT **4** [C] (often in compounds) an object that is used to support or hold sth: *an armrest* (= for example on a seat or chair) ➲ VISUAL VOCAB page V30
▸ IN MUSIC **5** [C, U] a period of silence between notes; a sign that shows a rest between notes ➲ picture at MUSIC
IDM **and (all) the 'rest (of it)** (*informal*) used at the end of a list to mean everything else that you might expect to be on the list: *He wants a big house and an expensive car and all the rest of it.* **and the 'rest** (*informal*) used to say that the actual amount or number of sth is much higher than sb has stated: *'It cost 250 pounds...' 'And the rest, and the rest!'* **at 'rest 1** (*technical*) not moving: *At rest the insect looks like a dead leaf.* **2** dead and therefore free from trouble or anxiety. People say 'at rest' to avoid saying 'dead': *She now* ***lies at rest*** *in the churchyard.* **come to 'rest** to stop moving: *The car crashed through the barrier and came to rest in a field.* ◇ *His eyes came to rest on Clara's face.* **for the 'rest** (*BrE, formal*) apart from that; as far as other matters are concerned: *The book has some interesting passages about the author's childhood. For the rest, it is extremely dull.* **give it a 'rest** (*informal*) used to tell sb to stop talking about sth because they are annoying you **give sth a 'rest** (*informal*) to stop doing sth for a while **lay sb to 'rest** to bury sb. People say 'to lay sb to rest' to avoid saying 'to bury' sb: *George was laid to rest beside his parents.* **lay/put sth to 'rest** to stop sth by showing it is not true: *The announcement finally laid all the speculation about their future to rest.* **the rest is 'history** used when you are telling a story to say that you do not need to tell the end of it, because everyone knows it already ➲ more at MIND *n.*, WICKED *n.*

Synonyms

rest

break • respite • time out • breathing space

These are all words for a short period of time spent relaxing.

rest a period of relaxing, sleeping or doing nothing after a period of activity: *We stopped for a well-earned rest.*

break a short period of time when you stop what you are doing and rest or eat: *Let's* ***take a break.*** NOTE In British English **break** is a period of time between lessons at school. The North American English word is **recess**.

respite a short break from sth difficult or unpleasant: *The drug brought a brief respite from the pain.*

time out (*informal, especially NAmE*) time for resting or relaxing away from your usual work or studies: *Take time out to relax by the pool.*

breathing space a short rest in the middle of a period of mental or physical effort: *This delay gives the party a breathing space in which to sort out its policies.*

PATTERNS
- (a) rest/break/respite/time out **from** sth
- to **have/take** (a) rest/break/time out
- to **give sb** (a) rest/break/respite/breathing space

■ ***verb***
▸ RELAX **1** 🔑 [I, T] to relax, sleep or do nothing after a period of activity or illness; to not use a part of your body for some time: *The doctor told me to rest.* ◇ *I can* ***rest easy*** (= stop worrying) *knowing that she's safely home.* ◇ (*figurative*) *He* ***won't rest*** (= will never be satisfied) *until he finds her.* ◇ **~ sth** *Rest your eyes every half an hour.* ➲ see also RESTED
▸ SUPPORT **2** 🔑 [T, I] to support sth by putting it on or against sth; to be supported in this way: **~ sth + adv./prep.** *Rest*

R

your head on my shoulder. ◇ *He rested his chin in his hands.* ◇ **+ adv./prep.** *His chin rested on his hands.* ◇ *Their bikes were resting against the wall.*

▸ BE LEFT **3** [I] if you let a matter **rest**, you stop discussing it or dealing with it: *The matter cannot rest there—I intend to sue.*

▸ BE BURIED **4** [I] **+ adv./prep.** to be buried. People say 'rest' to avoid saying 'be buried': *She rests beside her husband in the local cemetery.* ◇ *May he* ***rest in peace.*** ➲ see also RIP

IDM **rest as'sured (that...)** (*formal*) used to emphasize that what you say is true or will definitely happen: *You may rest assured that we will do all we can to find him.* **ˌrest your 'case 1 I rest my case** (sometimes *humorous*) used to say that you do not need to say any more about sth because you think that you have proved your point **2** (*law*) used by lawyers in court to say that they have finished presenting their case: *The prosecution rests its case.* ➲ more at EASY *adj.*, GOD, LAUREL

PHR V **'rest on/upon sb/sth 1** to depend or rely on sb/sth: *All our hopes now rest on you.* **2** to look at sb/sth: *Her* ***eyes rested on*** *the piece of paper in my hand.* **'rest on sth** to be based on sth: *The whole argument rests on a false assumption.* **'rest with sb (to do sth)** (*formal*) if **it rests with sb to do sth**, it is their responsibility to do it: ***It rests with*** *management to justify their actions.* ◇ *The final decision rests with the doctors.*

'rest area, 'rest stop *noun* (*NAmE*) an area beside an important road where people can stop their cars to rest, eat food, etc. ➲ compare LAY-BY

re·start /ˌriːˈstɑːt; *NAmE* -ˈstɑːrt/ *verb* [I, T] **~ (sth)** to start again, or to make sth start again, after it has stopped: *to restart a game* ◇ *The doctors struggled to restart his heart.* ▸ **re·start** /ˈriːstɑːt; *NAmE* -stɑːrt/ *noun*

Collocations

Restaurants

Eating out

- **eat (lunch/dinner)/dine/meet** at/in a restaurant
- **go (out)/take sb (out)** for lunch/dinner/a meal
- **have** a meal with sb
- **make/have** a reservation (in/under the name of Yamada)
- **reserve**/(*especially BrE*) **book** a table for six
- **ask for/request** a table for two/a table by the window

In the restaurant

- **wait** to be seated
- **show sb** to their table
- **sit** in the corner/by the window/at the bar/at the counter
- **hand sb/give sb** the menu/wine list
- **open/read/study/peruse** the menu
- the restaurant **has** a three-course set menu/ a children's menu/an extensive wine list
- **taste/sample/try** the wine
- the waiter **takes** your order
- **order/choose/have** the soup of the day/one of the specials/the house (*BrE*) speciality/(*especially NAmE*) specialty
- **serve/finish** the first course/the starter/the main course/dessert/coffee
- **complain about** the food/the service/your meal
- **enjoy** your meal

Paying

- **pay/ask for** (*especially BrE*) the bill/(*NAmE*) the check
- **pay for/treat sb to** dinner/lunch/the meal
- service **is (not) included**
- **give sb/leave (sb)** a tip

re·state /ˌriːˈsteɪt/ *verb* **~ sth** (*formal*) to say sth again or in a different way, especially so that it is more clearly or strongly expressed ▸ **re·state·ment** *noun* [U]

res·taur·ant 🗝 /ˈrestrɒnt; *NAmE* -trɑːnt; -tərɑːnt/ *noun* a place where you can buy and eat a meal: *an Italian restaurant* ◇ *We had a meal in a restaurant.* ◇ *We went out to a restaurant to celebrate.* ◇ *a restaurant owner* ◇ *a self-service restaurant* ➲ compare CAFE

'restaurant car *noun* (*BrE*) = DINING CAR

res·taura·teur /ˌrestərəˈtɜː(r)/ *noun* (*formal*) a person who owns and manages a restaurant

'rest cure *noun* a period spent resting or relaxing in order to improve your physical or mental health

rest·ed /ˈrestɪd/ *adj.* feeling healthy and full of energy because you have had a rest: *I awoke feeling rested and refreshed.* ➲ see also REST

rest·ful /ˈrestfl/ *adj.* that makes you feel relaxed and peaceful SYN **calming**: *a hotel with a restful atmosphere*

'rest home *noun* a place where old or sick people are cared for

'rest house *noun* (in parts of Asia and Africa) a house or HUT that you can pay to stay in like a hotel room, especially in wild country

'resting place *noun* **1** a grave. People say 'resting place' to avoid saying 'grave': *her* ***final/last resting place*** **2** a place where you can rest

res·ti·tu·tion /ˌrestɪˈtjuːʃn; *NAmE* -ˈtuː-/ *noun* [U] **~ (of sth) (to sb/sth) 1** (*formal*) the act of giving back sth that was lost or stolen to its owner SYN **restoration 2** (*law*) payment, usually money, for some harm or wrong that sb has suffered

rest·ive /ˈrestɪv/ *adj.* (*formal*) unable to stay still, or unwilling to be controlled, especially because you feel bored or not satisfied ▸ **rest·ive·ness** *noun* [U]

rest·less /ˈrestləs/ *adj.* **1** unable to stay still or be happy where you are, because you are bored or need a change: *The audience was becoming restless.* ◇ *After five years in the job, he was beginning to feel restless.* **2** without real rest or sleep SYN **disturbed**: *a restless night* ▸ **rest·less·ly** *adv.*: *He moved restlessly from one foot to the other.* **rest·less·ness** *noun* [U]: *the restlessness of youth*

re·stock /ˌriːˈstɒk; *NAmE* -ˈstɑːk/ *verb* [T, I] **~ (sth) (with sth)** to fill sth with new or different things to replace those that have been used, sold, etc; to get a new supply of sth

res·tor·ation AW /ˌrestəˈreɪʃn/ *noun* **1** [U, C] the work of repairing and cleaning an old building, a painting, etc. so that its condition is as good as it originally was: *The palace is closed* ***for restoration.*** ◇ *restoration work* **2** [U, C] **~ of sth** the act of bringing back a system, a law, etc. that existed previously: *the restoration of democracy/the monarchy* **3** [U] **~ (of sth)** the act of returning sth to its correct place, condition or owner: *the restoration of the Elgin marbles to Greece* **4 the Restoration** [sing.] the time in Britain after 1660 when, following a period with no king or queen, Charles II became king: *Restoration comedy/poetry* (= written during and after this time)

re·stora·tive /rɪˈstɔːrətɪv/ *adj., noun*

- ***adj.* 1** (*formal*) making you feel strong and healthy again: *the restorative power of fresh air* **2** (*medical*) connected with treatment that repairs the body or a part of it: ***restorative dentistry/surgery***
- ***noun*** (*old-fashioned*) a thing that makes you feel better, stronger, etc.

re·store 🗝 AW /rɪˈstɔː(r)/ *verb*

1 🗝 **~ sth (to sb)** to bring back a situation or feeling that existed before: *The measures are intended to restore public confidence in the economy.* ◇ ***Order was*** *quickly* ***restored*** *after the riots.* ◇ *Such kindness restores your faith in human nature* (= makes you believe most people are kind). ◇ *The operation restored his sight* (= made him able to see again). **2** 🗝 **~ sb/sth to sth** to bring sb/sth back to a former condition, place or position: *He is now fully restored to health.* ◇ *We hope to* ***restore*** *the garden* ***to its former glory*** (= make it as beautiful as it used to be). **3** 🗝 **~ sth** to repair a building, work of art, piece of furniture, etc. so that it looks as good as it did originally: *Her job is restoring old paintings.* **4 ~ sth** to bring a law, tradition, way of working, etc. back into use SYN **reintroduce**: *to restore ancient traditions* ◇ *Some people argue that the death penalty should be restored.* **5 ~ sth** (**to sb/sth**) (*formal*) to give sth that was lost or stolen back to sb: *The police have now restored the painting to its rightful owner.*

re·storer /rɪˈstɔːrə(r)/ *noun* a person whose job is to repair old buildings, works of art, etc. so that they look as they did when new

re·strain AW /rɪˈstreɪn/ *verb* **1** to stop sb/sth from doing sth, especially by using physical force: **~ sb/sth** *The prisoner had to be restrained by the police.* ◇ *He placed a restraining hand on her arm.* ◇ **~ sb/sth from sth/from doing sth** *They have obtained an injunction restraining the company from selling the product.* **2** to stop yourself from feeling an emotion or doing sth that you would like to do: **~ sth** *John managed to restrain his anger.* ◇ **~ yourself** (**from sth/from doing sth**) *She had to restrain herself from crying out in pain.* **3 ~ sth** to stop sth that is growing or increasing from becoming too large SYN **keep under control**: *The government is taking steps to restrain inflation.*

re·strained AW /rɪˈstreɪnd/ *adj.* **1** showing calm control rather than emotion: *her restrained smile* **2** not too brightly coloured or decorated SYN **discreet**: *The costumes and lighting in the play were restrained.*

reˈstraining order *noun* **~** (**against sb**) (*especially NAmE*) an official order given by a judge which demands that sth must or must not be done. A restraining order does not require a trial in court but only lasts for a limited period of time. ➲ compare INJUNCTION

re·straint AW /rɪˈstreɪnt/ *noun* **1** [C, usually pl.] **~** (**on sb/sth**) a rule, a fact, an idea, etc. that limits or controls what people can do: *The government has imposed export restraints on some products.* ➲ SYNONYMS at LIMIT **2** [U] the act of controlling or limiting sth because it is necessary or sensible to do so: *wage restraint* **3** [U] the quality of behaving calmly and with control SYN **self-control**: *The police appealed to the crowd for restraint.* ◇ *He* ***exercised*** *considerable* ***restraint*** *in ignoring the insults.* **4** [U] (*formal*) the use of physical force to control sb who is behaving in a violent way: *the physical restraint of prisoners* **5** [C] (*formal*) a type of SEAT BELT or safety device: *Children must use an approved child restraint or adult seat belt.*

re·strict 0-w AW /rɪˈstrɪkt/ *verb* **1** 0-w to limit the size, amount or range of sth: **~ sth to sth** *Speed is restricted to 30 mph in towns.* ◇ *We restrict the number of students per class to 10.* ◇ **~ sth** *Fog severely restricted visibility.* ◇ *Having small children tends to restrict your freedom.* **2** 0-w **~ sth** to stop sb/sth from moving or acting freely SYN **impede**: *The long skirt restricted her movements.* **3** 0-w **~ sth** (**to sb**) to control sth with rules or laws: *Access to the club is restricted to members only.* **4 ~ yourself/sb** (**to sth/to doing sth**) to allow yourself or sb to have only a limited amount of sth or to do only a particular kind of activity: *I restrict myself to one cup of coffee a day.*

re·stricted 0-w AW /rɪˈstrɪktɪd/ *adj.* **1** 0-w limited or small in size or amount: *a restricted space* ◇ *a restricted range of foods* **2** 0-w limited in what you are able to do: *In those days women led fairly restricted lives.* ◇ *Her vision is restricted in one eye.* **3** 0-w controlled by rules or laws: *to allow children only restricted access to the Internet* ◇ (*BrE*) *a restricted area* (= controlled by laws about speed or parking) ◇ *The tournament is* ***restricted to*** *players under the age of 23.* **4** [usually before noun] (of a place) only open to people with special permission, especially because it is secret or dangerous: *to enter a restricted zone* **5** (*BrE*) officially secret and only available to people with special permission SYN **classified**: *a restricted document* OPP **unrestricted**

re·stric·tion 0-w AW /rɪˈstrɪkʃn/ *noun* **1** 0-w [C] a rule or law that limits what you can do or what can happen: ***import/speed/travel, etc. restrictions*** ◇ **~ on sth** *to* ***impose/place a restriction on sth*** ◇ *The government has agreed to* ***lift restrictions*** *on press freedom.* ➲ SYNONYMS at LIMIT **2** [U] the act of limiting or controlling sb/sth: *sports clothes that prevent any restriction of movement* **3** [C] a thing that limits the amount of freedom you have: *the restrictions of a prison*

re·strict·ive AW /rɪˈstrɪktɪv/ *adj.* **1** preventing people from doing what they want: *restrictive laws* **2** (also **defining**) (*grammar*) (of RELATIVE CLAUSES) explaining which particular person or thing you are talking about rather than giving extra information about them. In 'The books which are on the table are mine', 'which are on the table' is a restrictive relative clause. ➲ compare NON-RESTRICTIVE ▸ **re·strict·ive·ly** AW *adv.*

reˌstrictive ˈpractices *noun* [pl.] (*especially BrE*, often *disapproving*) agreements or ways of working that limit the freedom of workers or employers in order to prevent competition or to protect people's jobs

re·string /ˌriːˈstrɪŋ/ *verb* (**restrung**, **restrung** /ˌriːˈstrʌŋ/) **~ sth** to fit new strings on a musical instrument such as a GUITAR or VIOLIN, or on a sports RACKET

rest·room /ˈrestruːm; -rʊm/ *noun* (*NAmE*) a room with a toilet in a public place, such as a theatre or restaurant

re·struc·ture AW /ˌriːˈstrʌktʃə(r)/ *verb* [T, I] **~** (**sth**) to organize sth such as a system or a company in a new and different way ▸ **re·struc·tur·ing** AW *noun* [U, C, usually sing.]

Synonyms

result

consequence • outcome • repercussion

These are all words for a thing that is caused because of sth else.

result a thing that is caused or produced by sth else: *She died as a result of her injuries.* ◇ *This book is the result of 25 years of research.*

consequence (*rather formal*) a result of sth that has happened, especially a bad result: *This decision could have serious consequences for the industry.* NOTE **Consequences** is used most frequently to talk about possible negative results of an action. It is commonly used with such words as *adverse, dire, disastrous, fatal, harmful, negative, serious, tragic* and *unfortunate*. Even when there is no adjective, **consequences** often suggests negative results.

outcome the result of an action or process: *We are waiting to hear the final outcome of the negotiations.*

RESULT OR OUTCOME?

Result is often used to talk about things that are caused directly by sth else: *Aggression is often the result of fear.* **Outcome** is more often used to talk about what happens at the end of a process when the exact relation of cause and effect is less clear: ~~*Aggresssion is often the outcome of fear.*~~ **Result** is often used after an event to talk about what happened. **Outcome** is often used before an action or process to talk about what is likely to happen.

repercussion (*rather formal*) an indirect and usually bad result of an action or event that may happen some time afterwards.

PATTERNS

- to have consequences/repercussions **for** sb/sth
- **with** the result/consequence/outcome **that...**
- a(n)/the **possible** result/consequences/outcome/repercussions
- a(n)/the **likely/inevitable** result/consequences/outcome
- (a/an) **negative** results/consequences/outcome/repercussions
- (a/an) **far-reaching/serious** results/consequences/repercussions
- to **have** a result/consequences/an outcome/repercussions

R

re·sult 0→ /rɪˈzʌlt/ *noun, verb*

■ ***noun***

▸ CAUSED BY STH **1** 0→ [C, U] **~ (of sth)** a thing that is caused or produced because of sth else: *She died **as a result of** her injuries.* ◇ *The failure of the company was a direct result of bad management.* ◇ *He made one big mistake, and, as a result, lost his job.* ◇ *The farm was flooded, **with the result that** most of the harvest was lost.* ◇ *The **end result*** (= the final one) *of her hard work was a place at medical school.* ◇ *This book is the result of 25 years of research.* ➲ LANGUAGE BANK at BECAUSE OF, CONSEQUENTLY

▸ OF GAME/ELECTION **2** 0→ [C] **~ (of sth)** the final score or the name of the winner in a sports event, competition, election, etc: *They will announce the result of the vote tonight.* ◇ *the election results* ◇ *the football results* **3** [C, usually sing.] (*BrE, informal*) a victory or a success, especially in a game of football (SOCCER): *We badly need to **get a result** from this match.*

▸ OF EXAM **4** 0→ [C, usually pl.] (*BrE*) the mark/grade you get in an exam or in a number of exams: *Have you had your results yet?*

▸ OF TEST/RESEARCH **5** 0→ [C] **~ (of sth)** the information that you get from a scientific test or piece of research: *the result of an experiment* ➲ COLLOCATIONS at SCIENTIFIC

▸ SUCCESS **6** 0→ **results** [pl.] things that are achieved successfully: *The project is beginning to show results.* ◇ *a coach who knows how to get results from his players*

■ ***verb*** 0→ [I] **~ (from sth)** to happen because of sth else that happened first: *job losses resulting from changes in production* ◇ *When water levels rise, flooding results.* ◇ *It was a large explosion and the resulting damage was extensive.*

PHR V **reˈsult in sth** 0→ to make sth happen SYN **lead to**: *The cyclone has resulted in many thousands of deaths.* ◇ **~ sb/sth doing sth** *These policies resulted in many elderly people suffering hardship.* ➲ LANGUAGE BANK at CAUSE

re·sult·ant /rɪˈzʌltənt/ *adj.* [only before noun] (*formal*) caused by the thing that has just been mentioned: *the growing economic crisis and resultant unemployment*

re·sulta·tive /rɪˈzʌltətɪv/ *adj.* (*grammar*) (of verbs, conjunctions or clauses) expressing or relating to the result of an action

re·sume /rɪˈzjuːm; *NAmE* -ˈzuːm/ *verb* (*formal*) **1** [T, I] if you **resume** an activity, or if it **resumes**, it begins again or continues after an interruption: **~ (sth)** *to **resume talks/negotiations*** ◇ *She resumed her career after an interval of six years.* ◇ *The noise resumed, louder than before.* ◇ **~ doing sth** *He got back in the car and resumed driving.* **2** [T] **~ your seat/place/position** to go back to the seat or place that you had before

ré·sumé /ˈrezjumeɪ; *NAmE* ˈrezəmeɪ/ *noun* **1 ~ (of sth)** a short summary or account of sth: *a brief résumé of events so far* **2** (*NAmE*) (*BrE* **cur·ricu·lum vitae**) a written record of your education and the jobs you have done, that you send when you are applying for a job ➲ WRITING TUTOR page WT30

re·sump·tion /rɪˈzʌmpʃn/ *noun* [sing., U] **~ (of sth)** (*formal*) the act of beginning sth again after it has stopped: *We are hoping for an early resumption of peace talks.*

re·sup·ply /ˌriːsəˈplaɪ/ *verb* **~ sb (with sth)** to give sb new supplies of sth they need; to give sth to sb again in a different form ▸ **re·supply** *noun*

re·sur·face /ˌriːˈsɜːfɪs; *NAmE* -ˈsɜːrf-/ *verb* **1** [I] to come to the surface again after being underwater or under the ground: *The submarine resurfaced.* ◇ (*figurative*) *All the old hostilities resurfaced when they met again.* **2** [T] **~ sth** to put a new surface on a road, path, etc.

re·sur·gence /rɪˈsɜːdʒəns; *NAmE* -ˈsɜːrdʒ-/ *noun* [sing., U] the return and growth of an activity that had stopped

re·sur·gent /rɪˈsɜːdʒənt; *NAmE* -ˈsɜːrdʒ-/ *adj.* [usually before noun] (*formal*) becoming stronger or more popular again

res·ur·rect /ˌrezəˈrekt/ *verb* **1 ~ sth** to bring back into use sth, such as a belief, a practice, etc, that had disappeared or been forgotten SYN **revive 2 ~ sb** to bring a dead person back to life SYN **raise from the dead**

res·ur·rec·tion /ˌrezəˈrekʃn/ *noun* **1 the Resurrection** [sing.] (in the Christian religion) the time when Jesus Christ returned to life again after his death; the time when all dead people will become alive again, when the world ends **2** [U, sing.] a new beginning for sth which is old or which had disappeared or become weak

re·sus·ci·tate /rɪˈsʌsɪteɪt/ *verb* **~ sb/sth** to make sb start breathing again or become conscious again after they have almost died SYN **revive**: *He had a heart attack and all attempts to resuscitate him failed.* ◇ (*figurative*) *efforts to resuscitate the economy* ▸ **re·sus·ci·ta·tion** /rɪˌsʌsɪˈteɪʃn/ *noun* [U]: *frantic attempts at resuscitation* ➲ see also MOUTH-TO-MOUTH RESUSCITATION

re·tail[1] /ˈriːteɪl/ *noun, adv., verb* ➲ see also RETAIL[2] *verb*

■ ***noun*** [U] the selling of goods to the public, usually through shops/stores: *The recommended retail price is £9.99.* ◇ *department stores and other **retail outlets*** ◇ *the **retail trade*** ➲ compare WHOLESALE ▸ **re·tail** *adv.*: *to **buy/sell retail*** (= in a shop/store)

■ ***verb* 1** [T] **~ sth** to sell goods to the public, usually through shops/stores: *The firm manufactures and retails its own range of sportswear.* **2** [I] **~ at/for sth** (*business*) to be sold at a particular price: *The book retails at £14.95.*

re·tail[2] /rɪˈteɪl/ *verb* **~ sth (to sb)** (*formal*) to tell people about sth, especially about a person's behaviour or private life SYN **recount**: *She retailed the neighbours' activities with relish.* ➲ see also RETAIL[1]

re·tail·er /ˈriːteɪlə(r)/ *noun* a person or business that sells goods to the public

re·tail·ing /ˈriːteɪlɪŋ/ *noun* [U] the business of selling goods to the public, usually through shops/stores: *career opportunities in retailing* ➲ compare WHOLESALING

ˈretail park *noun* (*BrE*) an area containing a group of large shops/stores, located outside a town

ˌretail ˈprice index (also **ˈprice index**) *noun* [sing.] (*abbr.* **RPI**) (in Britain) a list of the prices of some ordinary goods and services which shows how much these prices change each month ➲ see also CONSUMER PRICE INDEX

ˌretail ˈtherapy *noun* [U] (usually *humorous*) the act of going shopping and buying things in order to make yourself feel more cheerful: *I was ready for a little retail therapy.* ➲ COLLOCATIONS at SHOPPING

re·tain 0→ AW /rɪˈteɪn/ *verb* (rather *formal*)

1 0→ **~ sth** to keep sth; to continue to have sth SYN **preserve**: *to retain your independence* ◇ *He struggled to retain control of the situation.* ◇ *The house retains much of its original charm.* ◇ *She retained her tennis title for the third year.* **2** 0→ **~ sth** to continue to hold or contain sth: *a soil that retains moisture* ◇ *This information is no longer retained within the computer's main memory.* ◇ (*figurative*) *She has a good memory and finds it easy to retain facts.* **3 ~ sb/sth** (*law*) if a member of the public **retains** sb such as a lawyer, he or she pays money regularly or in advance so the lawyer, etc. will do work for him or her: *a retaining fee* ◇ *to retain the services of a lawyer* ➲ see also RETENTION, RETENTIVE

re·tain·er AW /rɪˈteɪnə(r)/ *noun* **1** a sum of money that is paid to sb to make sure they will be available to do work when they are needed: *The agency will pay you a monthly retainer.* **2** (*BrE*) a small amount of rent that you pay for a room, etc. when you are not there in order to keep it available for your use **3** (*NAmE*) a device that keeps a person's teeth straight after they have had ORTHODONTIC treatment with BRACES **4** (*old-fashioned*) a servant, especially one who has been with a family for a long time

re·tain·ing /rɪˈteɪnɪŋ/ *adj.* [only before noun] (*technical*) intended to keep sth in the correct position: *a **retaining wall*** (= one that keeps the earth or water behind it in position)

re·take *verb, noun*

■ ***verb*** /ˌriːˈteɪk/ (**re·took** /-ˈtʊk/, **re·taken** /-ˈteɪkən/) **1 ~ sth** (especially of an army) to take control of sth such as a town

again: *Government forces moved in to retake the city.* ◇ (*figurative*) *Moore fought back to retake the lead later in the race.* **2** = RESIT
▪**noun** /ˈriːteɪk/ **1** the act of filming a scene in a film/movie again, because it was not right before **2** = RESIT

re·tali·ate /rɪˈtælieɪt/ *verb* [I] to do sth harmful to sb because they have harmed you first SYN **take revenge**: **~ (against sb/sth)** *to retaliate against an attack* ◇ **~ (by doing sth/with sth)** *The boy hit his sister, who retaliated by kicking him.* ▸ **re·tali·atory** /rɪˈtæliətri; *NAmE* -tɔːri/ *adj.*: *retaliatory action*

re·tali·ation /rɪˌtæliˈeɪʃn/ *noun* [U] **~ (against sb/sth) (for sth)** action that a person takes against sb who has harmed them in some way SYN **reprisal**: *retaliation against UN workers* ◇ *The shooting may have been* ***in retaliation for*** *the arrest of the terrorist suspects.*

re·tard *verb, noun*
▪**verb** /rɪˈtɑːd; *NAmE* rɪˈtɑːrd/ **~ sth** (*formal*) to make the development or progress of sth slower SYN **delay, slow down**: *The progression of the disease can be retarded by early surgery.* ▸ **re·tard·ation** /ˌriːtɑːˈdeɪʃn; *NAmE* ˌriːtɑːrˈd-/ *noun* [U]: *Many factors can lead to growth retardation in unborn babies.*
▪**noun** /ˈriːtɑːd; *NAmE* ˈriːtɑːrd/ (*taboo, slang*) an offensive way of describing sb who is not intelligent or who has not developed normally

re·tard·ed /rɪˈtɑːdɪd; *NAmE* -ˈtɑːrd-/ *adj.* (*old-fashioned, offensive*) less developed mentally than is normal for a particular age SYN **backward**

retch /retʃ/ *verb* [I] to make sounds and movements as if you are VOMITING although you do not actually do so: *The smell made her retch.*

re·tell /ˌriːˈtel/ *verb* (**re·told, re·told** /-ˈtəʊld; *NAmE* -ˈtoʊld/) **~ sth** to tell a story again, often in a different way

re·ten·tion AW /rɪˈtenʃn/ *noun* [U] (*formal*) **1** the action of keeping sth rather than losing it or stopping it: *The company needs to improve its training and retention of staff.* **2** the action of keeping liquid, heat, etc. inside sth rather than letting it escape: *Eating too much salt can cause fluid retention.* **3** the ability to remember things: *Visual material aids the retention of information.* ➲ see also RETAIN

re·ten·tive AW /rɪˈtentɪv/ *adj.* (of the memory) able to store facts and remember things easily ➲ see also RETAIN

re·test /ˌriːˈtest/ *verb* **~ sb/sth** to test sb/sth again: *Subjects were retested one month later.*

re·think /ˌriːˈθɪŋk/ *verb* (**re·thought, re·thought** /-ˈθɔːt/) [T, I] **~ (sth)** to think again about an idea, a course of action, etc, especially in order to change it: *to rethink a plan* ▸ **re·think** /ˈriːθɪŋk/ (also **re·think·ing**) *noun* [sing.]: *a* ***radical rethink*** *of company policy*

reti·cent /ˈretɪsnt/ *adj.* (*formal*) unwilling to tell people about things SYN **reserved, uncommunicative**: *She was shy and reticent.* ◇ **~ about sth** *He was extremely reticent about his personal life.* ▸ **reti·cence** /-sns/ *noun* [U]

re·ticu·la·ted /rɪˈtɪkjuleɪtɪd/ *adj.* (*technical*) built, arranged or marked like a net or network, with many small squares or sections

reti·cule /ˈretɪkjuːl/ *noun* (*old use* or *humorous*) a woman's small bag, usually made of cloth and with a string that can be pulled tight to close it

ret·ina /ˈretɪnə; *NAmE* ˈretənə/ *noun* (*pl.* **ret·inas** or **ret·inae** /-niː/) a layer of TISSUE at the back of the eye that is sensitive to light and sends signals to the brain about what is seen ➲ VISUAL VOCAB page V48 ▸ **ret·inal** /ˈretɪnl/ [usually before noun], *adj.*

ret·inue /ˈretɪnjuː; *NAmE* ˈretənuː/ *noun* [C+sing./pl. v.] a group of people who travel with an important person to provide help and support SYN **entourage**

re·tire 🔑 /rɪˈtaɪə(r)/ *verb*
▸ FROM JOB **1** 🔑 [I, T] to stop doing your job, especially because you have reached a particular age or because you are ill/sick; to tell sb they must stop doing their job: **~ (from sth)** *She was forced to retire early from teaching because of ill health.* ◇ *The company's official retiring age is 65.* ◇ **~ to sth** *My dream is to retire to a villa in France.* ◇ **~ as sth** *He has no plans to retire as editor of the magazine.* ◇ **~ sb** *She was retired on medical grounds.*
▸ IN SPORT **2** [I] to stop competing during a game, race, etc, usually because you are injured: **~ (from sth)** *She fell badly, spraining her ankle, and had to retire.* ◇ **+ adj.** *He retired hurt in the first five minutes of the game.*
▸ FROM/TO A PLACE **3** [I] (*formal*) to leave a place, especially to go somewhere quieter or more private: *The jury retired to consider the evidence.* ◇ **~ to sth** *After dinner he likes to retire to his study.*
▸ OF ARMY **4** [I] (*formal*) to move back from a battle in order to organize your soldiers in a different way
▸ GO TO BED **5** [I] (*literary*) to go to bed: *I retired late that evening.*
▸ IN BASEBALL **6** [T] **~ sb** to make a player or team have to stop their turn at BATTING: *He retired twelve batters in a row.*

re·tired 🔑 /rɪˈtaɪəd; *NAmE* rɪˈtaɪərd/ *adj.* having retired from work: *a retired doctor* ◇ *Dad is retired now.*

re·tir·ee /rɪˌtaɪəˈriː/ *noun* (*NAmE*) a person who has stopped working because of their age

re·tire·ment 🔑 /rɪˈtaɪəmənt; *NAmE* -ˈtaɪərm-/ *noun*
1 🔑 [U, C] the fact of stopping work because you have reached a particular age; the time when you do this: *At 60, he was now approaching retirement.* ◇ *Susan is going to* ***take early retirement*** (= retire before the usual age). ◇ *retirement age* ◇ *a retirement pension* ➲ COLLOCATIONS at JOB **2** 🔑 [U, sing.] the period of your life after you have stopped work at a particular age: *to provide for retirement* ◇ *We all wish you a long and happy retirement.* ◇ *Up to a third of one's life is now being spent* ***in retirement.*** ➲ COLLOCATIONS at AGE **3** 🔑 [U] **~ (from sth)** the act of stopping a particular type of work, especially in sport, politics, etc: *He announced his retirement from football.* ◇ *She* ***came out of retirement*** *to win two gold medals at the championships.*

reˈtirement home (*BrE* also **ˌold ˈpeople's home**) *noun* a place where old people live and are cared for

reˈtirement plan *noun* (*NAmE*) = PENSION PLAN

re·tir·ing /rɪˈtaɪərɪŋ/ *adj.* preferring not to spend time with other people SYN **shy**: *a quiet, retiring man*

re·told *past tense, past part.* of RETELL

re·tool /ˌriːˈtuːl/ *verb* **1** [T, I] **~ (sth)** to replace or change the machines or equipment in a factory so that it can produce new or better goods **2** [T] **~ sth** (*NAmE, informal*) to organize sth in a new or different way

re·tort /rɪˈtɔːt; *NAmE* rɪˈtɔːrt/ *verb, noun*
▪**verb** to reply quickly to a comment, in an angry, offended or humorous way: **+ speech** *'Don't be ridiculous!' Pat retorted angrily.* ◇ **~ that…** *Sam retorted that it was my fault as much as his.*
▪**noun 1** a quick, angry or humorous reply SYN **rejoinder, riposte**: *She bit back* (= stopped herself from making) *a sharp retort.* **2** a closed bottle with a long narrow bent SPOUT that is used in a laboratory for heating chemicals ➲ VISUAL VOCAB page V57

re·touch /ˌriːˈtʌtʃ/ *verb* **~ sth** to make small changes to a picture or photograph so that it looks better

re·trace /rɪˈtreɪs/ *verb* **1 ~ sth** to go back along exactly the same path or route that you have come along: *She turned around and began to* ***retrace her steps*** *towards the house.* **2 ~ sth** to make the same trip that sb else has made in the past: *They are hoping to retrace the epic voyage of Christopher Columbus.* **3 ~ sth** to find out what sb has done or where they have been: *Detectives are trying to retrace her movements on the night she disappeared.*

re·tract /rɪˈtrækt/ *verb* **1** [T] **~ sth** (*formal*) to say that sth you have said earlier is not true or correct or that you did not mean it: *He made a false confession which he later retracted.* ◇ *They tried to persuade me to retract my words.* **2** [T] **~ sth** (*formal*) to refuse to keep an agreement, a

R

promise, etc: *to retract an offer* **3** [I, T] (*technical*) to move back into the main part of sth; to pull sth back into the main part of sth: *The animal retracted into its shell.* ◇ **~ sth** *The undercarriage was fully retracted.*

re·tract·able /rɪˈtræktəbl/ *adj.* that can be moved or pulled back into the main part of sth: *a knife with a retractable blade*

re·trac·tion /rɪˈtrækʃn/ *noun* (*formal*) **1** [C] a statement saying that sth you previously said or wrote is not true: *He demanded a full retraction of the allegations against him.* **2** [U] (*technical*) the act of pulling sth back (= of RETRACTING it): *the retraction of a cat's claws*

re·train /ˌriːˈtreɪn/ *verb* [I, T] to learn, or to teach sb, a new type of work, a new skill, etc: **~ (sb) (as sth)** *She retrained as a teacher.* ◇ **~ sb to do sth** *Staff have been retrained to use the new technology.* ▸ **re·train·ing** *noun* [U]

re·tread /ˈriːtred/ *noun* **1** a tyre made by putting a new rubber surface on an old tyre **2** (*NAmE, disapproving*) a book, film/movie, song, etc. that contains ideas that have been used before

re·treat /rɪˈtriːt/ *verb, noun*

■ ***verb***

▸ FROM DANGER/DEFEAT **1** [I] to move away from a place or an enemy because you are in danger or because you have been defeated: *The army was forced to retreat after suffering heavy losses.* ◇ *We retreated back down the mountain.* **OPP advance**

▸ MOVE AWAY/BACK **2** [I] to move away or back **SYN recede**: *He watched her retreating figure.* ◇ *The flood waters slowly retreated.*

▸ CHANGE DECISION **3** [I] **+ adv./prep.** to change your mind about sth because of criticism or because a situation has become too difficult **SYN back off**: *The government had retreated from its pledge to reduce class sizes.*

▸ TO QUIET PLACE **4** [I] (**+ adv./prep.**) to escape to a place that is quieter or safer **SYN retire**: *Bored with the conversation, she retreated to her bedroom.* ◇ (*figurative*) *He retreated into a world of fantasy.*

▸ FINANCE **5** [I] **+ noun** to lose value: *Share prices retreated 45p to 538p.*

■ ***noun***

▸ FROM DANGER/DEFEAT **1** [C, usually sing., U] a movement away from a place or an enemy because of danger or defeat: *Napoleon's retreat from Moscow* ◇ *The army was* ***in full retreat*** (=retreating very quickly). ◇ *to* ***sound the retreat*** (= to give a loud signal for an army to move away) ➲ COLLOCATIONS at WAR

▸ ESCAPE **2** [C, usually sing., U] **~ (from/into sth)** an act of trying to escape from a particular situation to one that you think is safer or more pleasant **SYN escape**: *Is watching television a retreat from reality?*

▸ CHANGE OF DECISION **3** [C, usually sing.] an act of changing a decision because of criticism or because a situation has become too difficult: *The Senator made an embarrassing retreat from his earlier position.*

▸ QUIET PLACE **4** [C] a quiet, private place that you go to in order to get away from your usual life: *a country retreat* **5** [U, C] a period of time when sb stops their usual activities and goes to a quiet place for prayer and thought; an organized event when people can do this: *He went into retreat and tried to resolve the conflicts within himself.* ◇ *to go on a Buddhist retreat* **IDM** see BEAT *v.*

re·trench /rɪˈtrentʃ/ *verb* **1** [I] (*formal*) (of a business, government, etc.) to spend less money; to reduce costs **2** [T] **~ sb** (*AustralE, NZE, SAfrE*) to tell sb that they cannot continue working for you ➲ COLLOCATIONS at UNEMPLOYMENT ▸ **re·trench·ment** *noun* [U, C]: *a period of retrenchment*

re·trial /ˌriːˈtraɪəl; ˈriːtraɪəl/ *noun* [usually sing.] a new trial of a person whose criminal offence has already been judged once in court

ret·ri·bu·tion /ˌretrɪˈbjuːʃn/ *noun* [U] **~ (for sth)** (*formal*) severe punishment for sth seriously wrong that sb has done: *People are seeking retribution for the latest terrorist outrages.* ◇ *fear of divine retribution* (= punishment from God) ▸ **re·tribu·tive** /rɪˈtrɪbjətɪv/ *adj.* [usually before noun]: *retributive justice*

re·trieval /rɪˈtriːvl/ *noun* [U] **1** (*formal*) the process of getting sth back, especially from a place where it should not be **SYN recovery**: *The ship was buried, beyond retrieval, at the bottom of the sea.* ◇ (*figurative*) *By then the situation was* ***beyond retrieval*** (= impossible to put right). **2** (*computing*) the process of getting back information that is stored on a computer: *methods of* ***information retrieval***

re·trieve /rɪˈtriːv/ *verb* **1** (*formal*) to bring or get sth back, especially from a place where it should not be **SYN recover**: **~ sth from sb/sth** *She bent to retrieve her comb from the floor.* ◇ **~ sth** *The police have managed to retrieve some of the stolen money.* **2** (*computing*) to find and get back data or information that has been stored in the memory of a computer: **~ sth from sb/sth** *to retrieve information from the database* ◇ **~ sth** *The program allows you to retrieve items quickly by searching under a keyword.* **3 ~ sth** to make a bad situation better; to get back sth that was lost: *You can only* ***retrieve the situation*** *by apologizing.* ▸ **re·triev·able** /rɪˈtriːvəbl/ *adj.* **OPP irretrievable**

re·triever /rɪˈtriːvə(r)/ *noun* a large dog used in hunting to bring back birds that have been shot ➲ see also GOLDEN RETRIEVER

retro /ˈretrəʊ; *NAmE* -troʊ/ *adj.* using styles or fashions from the recent past: *the current Seventies retro trend*

retro- /ˈretrəʊ; *NAmE* -troʊ/ *prefix* (in nouns, adjectives and adverbs) back or backwards: *retrograde* ◇ *retrospectively*

retro·active /ˌretrəʊˈæktɪv; *NAmE* -troʊ-/ *adj.* (*formal*) = RETROSPECTIVE ▸ **retro·active·ly** *adv.*: *The ruling should be applied retroactively.*

retro·fit /ˈretrəʊfɪt; *NAmE* -troʊ-/ *verb* (-tt-) **~ sth** to put a new piece of equipment into a machine that did not have it when it was built; to provide a machine with a new part, etc: *Voice recorders were retrofitted into planes already in service.* ◇ *They retrofitted the plane with improved seating.* ▸ **retro·fit** *noun*

retro·flex /ˈretrəfleks/ *adj.* **1** (*medical*) (of a part of the body) turned backwards **2** (*phonetics*) (of a speech sound) produced with the end of the tongue turned up against the hard PALATE

retro·grade /ˈretrəgreɪd/ *adj.* (*formal, disapproving*) (of an action) making a situation worse or returning to how sth was in the past: *The closure of the factory is* ***a retrograde step.***

retro·gres·sive /ˌretrəˈgresɪv/ *adj.* (*formal, disapproving*) returning to old-fashioned ideas or methods instead of making progress **OPP progressive**

retro·spect /ˈretrəspekt/ *noun*

IDM in retrospect thinking about a past event or situation, often with a different opinion of it from the one you had at the time: *In retrospect, I think that I was wrong.* ◇ *The decision seems extremely odd, in retrospect.*

retro·spec·tion /ˌretrəˈspekʃn/ *noun* [U] (*formal*) thinking about past events or situations

retro·spect·ive /ˌretrəˈspektɪv/ *adj., noun*

■ ***adj.*** **1** thinking about or connected with sth that happened in the past **2** (also *less frequent, formal* **retroactive**) (of a new law or decision) intended to take effect from a particular date in the past rather than from the present date: *retrospective legislation* ◇ *retrospective pay awards* ▸ **retro·spect·ive·ly** *adv.*: *She wrote retrospectively about her childhood.* ◇ *The new rule will be applied retrospectively.*

■ ***noun*** a public exhibition of the work that an artist has done in the past, showing how his or her work has developed

retro·virus /ˈretrəʊvaɪrəs; *NAmE* ˈretroʊ-/ *noun* any of a group of viruses that includes HIV. Retroviruses multiply by making changes to DNA. ➲ see also ANTI-RETROVIRAL

retry /ˌriːˈtraɪ/ *verb* (**re·tries, re·try·ing, re·tried, re·tried**) **1** [T] **~ sb/sth** to examine a person or case again in court

2 [I] to make another attempt to do sth, especially on a computer

ret·sina /ret'si:nə/ *noun* [U, C] a type of red or white wine from Greece that is given a special flavour with RESIN (1)

re·turn /rɪ'tɜ:n; *NAmE* rɪ'tɜ:rn/ *verb, noun*

■ ***verb***

▸ COME/GO BACK **1** [I] to come or go back from one place to another: *I waited a long time for him to return.* ◇ **~ (to...) (from...)** *She's returning to Australia tomorrow after six months in Europe.* ◇ *I returned from work to find the house empty.* ◇ *When did she return home from the trip?*

▸ BRING/GIVE BACK **2** [T] to bring, give, put or send sth back to sb/sth: **~ sb/sth to sb/sth** *We had to return the hairdryer to the store because it was faulty.* ◇ *I must return some books to the library.* ◇ **~ sth** *Don't forget to return my pen!* ◇ **~ sb/sth + adj.** *I returned the letter unopened.*

▸ OF FEELING/QUALITY **3** [I] to come back again SYN **reappear, resurface**: *The following day the pain returned.* ◇ *Her suspicions returned when things started going missing again.*

▸ TO PREVIOUS SUBJECT/ACTIVITY **4** [I] **~ (to sth)** to start discussing a subject you were discussing earlier, or doing an activity you were doing earlier: *He returns to this topic later in the report.* ◇ *She looked up briefly then returned to her sewing.* ◇ *The doctor may allow her to* ***return to work*** *next week.*

▸ TO PREVIOUS STATE **5** [I] **~ to sth** to go back to a previous state: *Train services have* ***returned to normal*** *after the strike.*

▸ DO/GIVE THE SAME **6** [T] **~ sth** to do or give sth to sb because they have done or given the same to you first; to have the same feeling about sb that they have about you: *to return a favour/greeting/stare* ◇ *She phoned him several times but he was too busy to* ***return her call.*** ◇ *It's time we* ***returned their invitation*** (= invite them to sth as they invited us to sth first). ◇ *He did not return her love.* ◇ *'You were both wonderful!' 'So were you!' we said,* ***returning the compliment.*** ◇ *to* ***return fire*** (= to shoot at sb who is shooting at you)

▸ IN TENNIS **7** [T] **~ sth** to hit the ball back to your opponent during a game: *to return a service/shot*

▸ A VERDICT **8** [T] **~ a verdict** to give a decision about sth in court: *The jury returned a verdict of not guilty.*

▸ ELECT POLITICIAN **9** [T, usually passive] **~ sb (to sth)** | **~ sb (as sth)** (*BrE*) to elect sb to a political position

▸ PROFIT/LOSS **10** [T] **~ sth** (*business*) to give or produce a particular amount of money as a profit or loss: *to return a high rate of interest* ◇ *Last year the company returned a loss of £157 million.*

■ ***noun***

▸ COMING BACK **1** [sing.] **~ (to...) (from...)** the action of arriving in or coming back to a place that you were in before: *He was met by his brother* ***on his return*** *from Italy.* ◇ *I saw the play on its return to Broadway.* ◇ *on the* ***return flight/journey/trip***

▸ GIVING/SENDING BACK **2** [U, sing.] the action of giving, putting or sending sth/sb back: *We would appreciate the prompt return of books to the library.* ◇ *The judge ordered the return of the child to his mother.* ◇ *Write your* ***return address*** (= the address that a reply should be sent to) *on the back of the envelope.*

▸ OF FEELING/STATE **3** [sing.] **~ (of sth)** the situation when a feeling or state that has not been experienced for some time starts again SYN **reappearance**: *the return of spring* ◇ *a return of my doubts*

▸ TO PREVIOUS SITUATION/ACTIVITY **4** [sing.] **~ to sth** the action of going back to an activity or a situation that you used to do or be in: *his return to power* ◇ *They appealed for* ***a return to work*** (= after a strike).

▸ PROFIT **5** [U, C] the amount of profit that you get from sth SYN **earnings, yield**: *a high* ***rate of return*** *on capital* ◇ *farmers seeking to improve returns from their crops*

▸ OFFICIAL REPORT **6** [C] an official report or statement that gives particular information to the government or another body: *census returns* ◇ *election returns* (= the number of votes for each candidate in an election) ➲ see also TAX RETURN

▸ TICKET **7** [C] (*BrE*) = RETURN TICKET: *'Brighton, please.' 'Single or return?'* ◇ *A return is cheaper than two singles.* ◇ *the return fare to London* ➲ see also DAY RETURN **8** [C] a ticket for the theatre or a sports game that was bought by sb but is given back to be sold again

▸ ON COMPUTER **9** [U] (also **re'turn key** [C]) the button that you press on a computer when you reach the end of an instruction, or to begin a new line: *To exit this option, press return.*

▸ IN TENNIS **10** [C] (in TENNIS and some other sports) the action of hitting the ball, etc. back to your opponent: *a powerful* ***return of serve***

IDM **by re'turn (of 'post)** (*BrE*) using the next available post; as soon as possible: *Please reply by return of post.* **in re'turn (for sth) 1** as a way of thanking sb or paying them for sth they have done: *Can I buy you lunch in return for your help?* **2** as a response or reaction to sth: *I asked her opinion, but she just asked me a question in return.* ➲ more at HAPPY, POINT *n.*, SALE *n.*

Synonyms

return

come back • go back • get back • turn back

These words all mean to come or go back from one place to another.

return to come or go back from one place to another: *I waited a long time for him to return.* NOTE **Return** is slightly more formal than the other words in this group, and is used more often in writing or formal speech.

come back to return. NOTE **Come back** is usually used from the point of view of the person or place that sb returns to: *Come back and visit again soon!*

go back to return to the place you recently or originally came from or that you have been to before. NOTE **Go back** is usually used from the point of view of the person who is returning: *Do you ever want to go back to China?*

get back to arrive back somewhere, especially at your home or the place where you are staying: *What time did you get back last night?*

turn back to return the way that you came, especially because sth stops you from continuing: *The weather got so bad that we had to turn back.*

PATTERNS

- to return/come back/go back/get back **to/from/with** sth
- to return/come back/go back/get back/turn back **again**
- to return/come back/go back/get back **home/to work**
- to return/come back/get back **safely**

re·turn·able /rɪ'tɜ:nəbl; *NAmE* -'tɜ:rn-/ *adj.* **1** (*formal*) that can or must be given back after a period of time: *A returnable deposit is payable on arrival.* ◇ *The application form is returnable not later than 7th June.* **2** (of bottles and containers) that can be taken back to a shop/store in order to be used again OPP **non-returnable**

re·turn·ee /rɪˌtɜ:'ni:; *NAmE* rɪˌtɜ:r'ni:/ *noun* [usually pl.] (*especially NAmE*) a person who returns to their own country, after living in another country

re·turn·er /rɪ'tɜ:nə(r); *NAmE* -'tɜ:rn-/ *noun* (*BrE*) a person who goes back to work after not working for a long time

re'turning officer *noun* (*BrE*) an official in a particular area who is responsible for arranging an election and announcing the result

reˌturn 'match (also **reˌturn 'game**) *noun* (*especially BrE*) a second match or game between the same two players or teams

reˌturn 'ticket (also **re·turn**) (both *BrE*) (*NAmE* **ˌround-trip 'ticket**) *noun* a ticket for a journey to a place and back again

R

re͵turn ˈvisit *noun* a trip to a place that you have been to once before, or a trip to see sb who has already come to see you: *This hotel is worth a return visit.* ◇ *The US president* ***is making a return visit*** *to Moscow.*

re·unify /ˌriːˈjuːnɪfaɪ/ *verb* (**re·uni·fies**, **re·uni·fy·ing**, **re·uni·fied**, **re·uni·fied**) [often passive] **~ sth** to join together two or more regions or parts of a country so that they form a single political unit again ▸ **re·uni·fi·ca·tion** /ˌriːˌjuːnɪfɪˈkeɪʃn/ *noun* [U]: *the reunification of Germany*

re·union /ˌriːˈjuːniən/ *noun* **1** [C] a social occasion or party attended by a group of people who have not seen each other for a long time: *a family reunion* ◇ *the school's annual reunion* ◇ *a reunion of the class of '85* **2** [C, U] **~ (with sb)** | **~ (between A and B)** the act of people coming together after they have been apart for some time: *an emotional reunion between mother and son* ◇ *Christmas is a time of reunion.* **3** [U] the action of becoming a single group or organization again: *the reunion of the Church of England with the Church of Rome*

re·unite /ˌriːjuːˈnaɪt/ *verb* [T, I] **1** [usually passive] to bring two or more people together again after they have been separated for a long time; to come together again: **~ A with/and B** *Last night she was reunited with her children.* ◇ **~ (sb)** *The family was reunited after the war.* ◇ *There have been rumours that the band will reunite for a world tour.* **2 ~ (sth)** to join together again separate areas or separate groups within an organization, a political party, etc; to come together again: *As leader, his main aim is to reunite the party.*

re·us·able /ˌriːˈjuːzəbl/ *adj.* that can be used again: *reusable plastic bottles*

reuse /ˌriːˈjuːz/ *verb* **~ sth** to use sth again: *Please reuse your envelopes.* ▸ **reuse** /ˌriːˈjuːs/ *noun* [U]

Rev. (*BrE* also **Revd**) *abbr.* (used before a name) REVEREND: *Rev. Jesse Jackson*

rev /rev/ *verb, noun*

■ ***verb*** (**-vv-**) [T, I] **~ (sth) (up)** when you **rev** an engine or it **revs**, it runs quickly: *The taxi driver revved up his engine.* ◇ *I could hear the car revving outside.*

■ ***noun*** (*informal*) a complete turn of an engine, used when talking about an engine's speed SYN **revolution**: *4 000 revs per minute* ◇ *The needle on the rev counter soared.* ➲ **VISUAL VOCAB** page V42

re·value /ˌriːˈvæljuː/ *verb* **1** [T] **~ sth** to estimate the value of sth again, especially giving it a higher value **2** [T, I] **~ (sth)** to increase the value of the money of a country when it is exchanged for the money of another country: *The yen is to be revalued.* OPP **devalue** ▸ **re·valu·ation** /ˌriːvæljuˈeɪʃn/ *noun* [U, C, usually sing.]: *the revaluation of the pound*

re·vamp /ˌriːˈvæmp/ *verb* **~ sth** to make changes to the form of sth, usually to improve its appearance ▸ **re·vamp** /ˈriːvæmp/ *noun* [sing.]

re·vanch·ism /rɪˈvæntʃɪzəm; -ˈvænʃ-/ *noun* [U] a policy of attacking sb who has attacked you, especially by a country in order to get back land

re·veal 0-w AW /rɪˈviːl/ *verb*

1 0-w to make sth known to sb SYN **disclose**: **~ sth (to sb)** *to reveal a secret* ◇ *Details of the murder were revealed by the local paper.* ◇ **~ (that)...** *The report reveals (that) the company made a loss of £20 million last year.* ◇ **it is revealed that...** *It was revealed that important evidence had been suppressed.* ◇ **~ how, what, etc...** *Officers could not reveal how he died.* ◇ **~ sb/sth to be/have sth** *Salted peanuts were recently revealed to be the nation's favourite snack.* ➲ **LANGUAGE BANK** at EVIDENCE **2** 0-w to show sth that previously could not be seen SYN **display**: **~ sth** *He laughed, revealing a line of white teeth.* ◇ *The door opened to reveal a cosy little room.* ◇ **~ yourself** *She crouched in the dark, too frightened to reveal herself.* ➲ see also REVELATION, REVELATORY

re͵vealed reˈligion *noun* [U, C] religion that is based on a belief that God has shown himself

re·veal·ing AW /rɪˈviːlɪŋ/ *adj.* **1** giving you interesting information that you did not know before: *The document provided a revealing insight into the government's priorities.* ◇ *The answers the children gave were extremely revealing.* **2** (of clothes) allowing more of sb's body to be seen than usual: *a revealing blouse* ▸ **re·veal·ing·ly** *adv.*: *He spoke revealingly about his problems.*

re·veille /rɪˈvæli; *NAmE* ˈrevəli/ *noun* [U] a tune that is played to wake soldiers in the morning; the time when it is played

revel /ˈrevl/ *verb, noun*

■ ***verb*** (**-ll-**, *US* **-l-**) [I] to spend time enjoying yourself in a noisy, enthusiastic way SYN **make merry**

PHR V **ˈrevel in sth** to enjoy sth very much: *She was clearly revelling in all the attention.* ◇ **~ doing sth** *Some people seem to revel in annoying others.*

■ ***noun*** [usually pl.] (*literary*) noisy celebrations

reve·la·tion AW /ˌrevəˈleɪʃn/ *noun* **1** [C] **~ (about/concerning sth)** | **~ (that...)** a fact that people are made aware of, especially one that has been secret and is surprising SYN **disclosure**: ***startling/sensational revelations*** *about her private life* **2** [U] **~ (of sth)** the act of making people aware of sth that has been secret SYN **disclosure**: *The company's financial problems followed the revelation of a major fraud scandal.* **3** [C, U] something that is considered to be a sign or message from God ➲ **COLLOCATIONS** at RELIGION ➲ see also REVEAL

IDM **come as/be a revelation (to sb)** to be a completely new or surprising experience; to be different from what was expected

rev·ela·tory /ˌrevəˈleɪtəri; *NAmE* ˈrevələtɔːri/ *adj.* (*formal*) making people aware of sth that they did not know before: *a revelatory insight* ➲ see also REVEAL

rev·el·ler (*US* **rev·el·er**) /ˈrevələ(r)/ *noun* a person who is having fun in a noisy way, usually with a group of other people and often after drinking alcohol

rev·el·ry /ˈrevlri/ *noun* [U] (also **rev·el·ries** [pl.]) noisy fun, usually involving a lot of eating and drinking SYN **festivity, merrymaking**: *We could hear sounds of revelry from next door.* ◇ *New Year revelries*

re·venge /rɪˈvendʒ/ *noun, verb*

■ ***noun*** [U] **1** something that you do in order to make sb suffer because they have made you suffer: *He swore to* ***take (his) revenge on*** *his political enemies.* ◇ *She is* ***seeking revenge for*** *the murder of her husband.* ◇ *The bombing was* ***in revenge for*** *the assassination.* ◇ *an act of revenge* ◇ ***revenge attacks/killings*** **2** (*sport*) the defeat of a person or team that defeated you in a previous game: *The team wanted to get revenge for their defeat earlier in the season.*

■ ***verb***

PHR V **reˈvenge yourself on sb** | **be reˈvenged on sb** (*literary*) to punish or hurt sb because they have made you suffer: *She vowed to be revenged on them all.* ➲ note at AVENGE

rev·enue AW /ˈrevənjuː; *NAmE* -nuː/ *noun* [U] (also **rev·enues** [pl.]) the money that a government receives from taxes or that an organization, etc. receives from its business SYN **receipts**: *a shortfall in tax revenue* ◇ *a slump in oil revenues* ◇ *The company's annual revenues rose by 30%.* ➲ **COLLOCATIONS** at BUSINESS ➲ see also THE INLAND REVENUE

͵Revenue and ˈCustoms *noun* = HM REVENUE AND CUSTOMS

re·verb /ˈriːvɜːb; rɪˈvɜːb; *NAmE* -vɜːrb/ *noun* [U] a sound effect that can be adjusted by electronic means to give music more or less of an ECHO

re·ver·ber·ate /rɪˈvɜːbəreɪt; *NAmE* -ˈvɜːrb-/ *verb* **1** [I] (of a sound) to be repeated several times as it is reflected off different surfaces SYN **echo**: *Her voice reverberated around the hall.* **2** [I] **~ (with/to sth)** (of a place) to seem to shake because of a loud noise: *The hall reverberated with the sound of music and dancing.* **3** [I] (*formal*) to have a strong effect on people for a long time or over a large area: *Repercussions of the case continue to reverberate through the financial world.*

re·ver·ber·ation /rɪˌvɜːbəˈreɪʃn; *NAmE* -ˌvɜːrb-/ *noun* **1** [C, usually pl., U] a loud noise that continues for some time after it has been produced because of the surfaces around it SYN **echo** **2 reverberations** [pl.] the effects of sth that happens, especially unpleasant ones that spread among a large number of people SYN **repercussion**

re·vere /rɪˈvɪə(r); *NAmE* rɪˈvɪr/ *verb* [usually passive] **~ sb (as sth)** (*formal*) to feel great respect or admiration for sb/sth SYN **idolize**

rev·er·ence /ˈrevərəns/ *noun* [U] **~ (for sb/sth)** (*formal*) a feeling of great respect or admiration for sb/sth: *The poem conveys his deep reverence for nature.*

rev·er·end /ˈrevərənd/ *adj.* [only before noun] **Reverend** (*abbr.* Rev.) the title of a member of the clergy that is also sometimes used to talk to or about one: *the Reverend Charles Dodgson* ◇ *Good morning, Reverend.* ➲see also RIGHT REVEREND

ˌReverend ˈMother *noun* a title of respect used when talking to or about a MOTHER SUPERIOR (= the head of a female religious community)

rev·er·ent /ˈrevərənt/ *adj.* (*formal*) showing great respect and admiration SYN **respectful** ▶ **rev·er·ent·ly** *adv.*

rev·er·en·tial /ˌrevəˈrenʃl/ *adj.* (*formal*) full of respect or admiration: *His name was always mentioned in almost reverential tones.* ▶ **rev·er·en·tial·ly** /-ʃəli/ *adv.*: *She lowered her voice reverentially.*

rev·erie /ˈrevəri/ *noun* [C, U] (*formal*) a state of thinking about pleasant things, almost as though you are dreaming SYN **daydream**: *She was jolted out of her reverie as the door opened.*

re·vers /rɪˈvɪə(r); *NAmE* rɪˈvɪr/ *noun* (*pl.* re·vers /-ˈvɪəz; *NAmE* -ˈvɪrz/) (*technical*) the edge of a coat, jacket, etc. that is turned back so that you see the opposite side of it, especially at the LAPEL

re·ver·sal AW /rɪˈvɜːsl; *NAmE* rɪˈvɜːrsl/ *noun* **1** [C, U] **~ (of sth)** a change of sth so that it is the opposite of what it was: *a* ***complete/dramatic/sudden reversal*** *of policy* ◇ *the reversal of a decision* ◇ *The government suffered a total* ***reversal of fortune(s)*** *last week.* **2** [C] a change from being successful to having problems or being defeated: *the team's recent reversal* ◇ *The company's financial problems were only a temporary reversal.* **3** [C, U] an exchange of positions or functions between two or more people: *It's a complete* ***role reversal/reversal of roles*** (= for example when a husband cares for the house and children while the wife works).

re·verse 🔑 AW /rɪˈvɜːs; *NAmE* rɪˈvɜːrs/ *verb, noun, adj.*

■ *verb*

▸ CHANGE TO OPPOSITE **1** 🔑 [T] **~ sth** to change sth completely so that it is the opposite of what it was before: *to reverse a procedure/process/trend* ◇ *The government has failed to reverse the economic decline.* ◇ *It is sometimes possible to arrest or reverse the disease.* **2** 🔑 [T] **~ sth** to change a previous decision, law, etc. to the opposite one SYN **revoke**: *The Court of Appeal reversed the decision.* **3** 🔑 [T] **~ sth** to turn sth the opposite way around or change the order of sth around: *Writing is reversed in a mirror.* ◇ *You should reverse the order of these pages.*

▸ EXCHANGE TWO THINGS **4** 🔑 [T] **~ sth** to exchange the positions or functions of two things: *It felt as if we had reversed our roles of parent and child.* ◇ *She used to work for me, but our situations are now reversed.*

▸ YOURSELF **5** [T] **~ yourself (on sth)** (*NAmE*) to admit you were wrong or to stop having a particular position in an argument: *He has reversed himself on a dozen issues.*

▸ VEHICLE **6** 🔑 [I, T] (*especially BrE*) when a vehicle or its driver **reverses** or the driver **reverses** a vehicle, the vehicle goes backwards: *He reversed around the corner.* ◇ *She reversed into a parking space.* ◇ *Caution! This truck is reversing.* ◇ **~ sth** *Now reverse the car.* ➲compare BACK *v.*

▸ TELEPHONE CALL **7** [T] **~ (the) charges** (*BrE*) to make a telephone call that will be paid for by the person you are calling, not by you: *I want to reverse the charges, please.* ➲see also COLLECT *adj.*

■ *noun*

▸ OPPOSITE **1** 🔑 **the reverse** [sing.] the opposite of what has just been mentioned: *This problem is the reverse of the previous one.* ◇ *Although I expected to enjoy living in the country, in fact* ***the reverse is true.*** ◇ *In the south, the reverse applies.* ◇ *It wasn't easy to persuade her to come—* ***quite the reverse.***

▸ BACK **2** 🔑 **the reverse** [sing.] the back of a coin, piece of material, piece of paper, etc.

▸ IN VEHICLE **3** 🔑 (also **reˌverse ˈgear**) [U] the machinery in a vehicle used to make it move backwards: *Put the car* ***in/into reverse.***

▸ LOSS/DEFEAT **4** [C] (*formal*) a loss or defeat; a change from success to failure SYN **setback**: *Property values have suffered another reverse.* ◇ *a damaging political reverse*

IDM **in reˈverse** 🔑 in the opposite order or way SYN **backwards**: *The secret number is my phone number in reverse.* ◇ *We did a similar trip to you, but in reverse.* **go/put sth into reˈverse** to start to happen or to make sth happen in the opposite way: *In 2008 economic growth went into reverse.*

■ *adj.* [only before noun]

▸ OPPOSITE **1** 🔑 opposite to what has been mentioned: *to travel in the reverse direction* ◇ *The winners were announced* ***in reverse order*** (= the person in the lowest place was announced first). ◇ *The experiment had the reverse effect to what was intended.*

▸ BACK **2** opposite to the front: *Iron the garment on the reverse side.*

reˌverse-ˈcharge *adj.* a **reverse-charge** telephone call is paid for by the person who receives the call, not by the person who makes it ▶ **reˌverse-ˈcharge** *adv.*: *I didn't have any money so I had to call reverse-charge.*

reˌverse discrimiˈnation *noun* [U] (*disapproving*) the practice or policy of making sure that a particular number of jobs, etc. are given to people from groups that are often treated unfairly because of their race, sex, etc. HELP The term **reverse discrimination** is nearly always used in a disapproving way; to describe this policy in a way that is not necessarily disapproving use **positive discrimination** or **affirmative action**.

reˌverse engiˈneering *noun* [U] the copying of another company's product after examining it carefully to find out how it is made

re·vers·ible AW /rɪˈvɜːsəbl; *NAmE* -ˈvɜːrs-/ *adj.* **1** (of clothes, materials, etc.) that can be turned inside out and worn or used with either side showing: *a reversible jacket* **2** (of a process, an action or a disease) that can be changed so that sth returns to its original state or situation: *Is the trend towards privatization reversible?* ◇ *reversible kidney failure* OPP **irreversible** ▶ **re·vers·ibil·ity** /rɪˌvɜːsəˈbɪləti; *NAmE* -ˌvɜːrs-/ *noun* [U]

reˈversing light (*BrE*) (*NAmE* **ˈbackup light**) *noun* a white light at the back of a vehicle that comes on when the vehicle moves backwards

re·ver·sion /rɪˈvɜːʃn; *NAmE* rɪˈvɜːrʒn/ *noun* **1** [U, sing.] **~ (to sth)** (*formal*) the act or process of returning to a former state or condition: *a reversion to traditional farming methods* **2** [U, C] (*law*) the return of land or property to sb: *the reversion of Hong Kong to China* **3** (*NAmE, law*) = LEASEBACK

re·vert /rɪˈvɜːt; *NAmE* rɪˈvɜːrt/ *verb* [I] (**+ adv./prep.**) (*IndE, rather formal*) to reply: *Excellent openings—kindly revert with your updated CV.*

PHRV **reˈvert to sb/sth** (*law*) (of property, rights, etc.) to return to the original owner again ➲see also REVERSION **reˈvert to sth** (*formal*) **1** to return to a former state; to start doing sth again that you used to do in the past: *After her divorce she reverted to her maiden name.* ◇ *His manner seems to have reverted to normal.* ◇ *Try not to revert to your old eating habits.* **2** to return to an earlier topic or subject: *So, to revert to your earlier question…* ◇ *The conversation kept reverting to the events of March 6th.*

R

re·vet·ment /rɪˈvetmənt/ *noun* (*technical*) stones or other material used to make a wall stronger, hold back a bank of earth, etc.

re·view 🔑 /rɪˈvjuː/ *noun, verb*

▪ ***noun*** **1** 🔑 [U, C] an examination of sth, with the intention of changing it if necessary: *the government's review of its education policy* ◇ *The case is* ***subject to judicial review.*** ◇ *His parole application is* ***up for review*** *next week.* ◇ *The terms of the contract are* ***under review.*** ◇ *a* ***pay/salary review*** ◇ *a* ***review body/date/panel*** **2** 🔑 [C, U] a report in a newspaper or magazine, or on the Internet, television or radio, in which sb gives their opinion of a book, play, film/movie, etc; the act of writing this kind of report: *a book review* ◇ *the reviews (page) in the papers* ◇ ***good/bad/mixed/rave reviews*** *in the national press* ◇ *He submitted his latest novel for review.* ➲ COLLOCATIONS at LITERATURE ➲ WRITING TUTOR page WT20 **3** [C] a report on a subject or on a series of events: *a review of customer complaints* ◇ *to publish a review of recent cancer research* **4** [C] (*formal*) a ceremony that involves an official INSPECTION of soldiers, etc. by an important visitor **5** 🔑 [C] (*NAmE*) a lesson in which you look again at sth you have studied, especially in order to prepare for an exam

▪ ***verb*** **1** 🔑 **~ sth** to carefully examine or consider sth again, especially so that you can decide if it is necessary to make changes SYN **reassess**: *to review the evidence* ◇ *The government will review the situation later in the year.* ➲ SYNONYMS at EXAMINE **2** 🔑 **~ sth** to think about past events, for example to try to understand why they happened SYN **take stock of**: *to review your failures and triumphs* ◇ *She had been reviewing the previous week on her way home.* **3** 🔑 **~ sth** to write a report of a book, play, film/movie, etc. in which you give your opinion of it: *The play was reviewed in the national newspapers.* **4 ~ sb/sth** to make an official INSPECTION of a group of soldiers, etc. in a military ceremony **5** 🔑 **~ sth** (*especially NAmE*) to look again at sth you have studied, especially in order to prepare for an exam **6** 🔑 **~ sth** (*especially NAmE*) to check a piece of work to see if there are any mistakes

re·view·er /rɪˈvjuːə(r)/ *noun* **1** a person who writes reviews of books, films/movies or plays **2** a person who examines or considers sth carefully, for example to see if any changes need to be made

re·vile /rɪˈvaɪl/ *verb* [usually passive] **~ sb** (**for sth/for doing sth**) (*formal*) to criticize sb/sth in a way that shows how much you dislike them

re·vise 🔑 AW /rɪˈvaɪz/ *verb*

1 🔑 [T] **~ sth** to change your opinions or plans, for example because of sth you have learned: *I can see I will have to revise my opinions of his abilities now.* ◇ *The government may need to revise its policy in the light of this report.* **2** 🔑 [T] **~ sth** to change sth, such as a book or an estimate, in order to correct or improve it: *a revised edition of a textbook* ◇ *I'll prepare a revised estimate for you.* ◇ *We may have to revise this figure upwards.* **3** 🔑 [I, T] (*BrE*) to prepare for an exam by looking again at work that you have done: *I spent the weekend revising for my exam.* ◇ *I can't come out tonight. I have to revise.* ◇ **~ sth** *I'm revising Geography today.*

re·vi·sion 🔑 AW /rɪˈvɪʒn/ *noun*

1 🔑 [C] a change or set of changes to sth: *He made some minor revisions to the report before printing it out.* **2** 🔑 [U, C] the act of changing sth, or of examining sth with the intention of changing it: *a system in need of revision* ◇ *a revision of trading standards* **3** 🔑 [U] (*BrE*) the process of learning work for an exam: *Have you started your revision yet?* ➲ COLLOCATIONS at EDUCATION

re·vi·sion·ism /rɪˈvɪʒənɪzəm/ *noun* [U] (*politics*) (often *disapproving*) ideas that are different from, and want to change, the main ideas or practices of a political system, especially MARXISM ▸ **re·vi·sion·ist** /-ʒənɪst/ *noun*: *bourgeois revisionists* **re·vi·sion·ist** /-ʒənɪst/ *adj.*: *revisionist historians*

re·visit /ˌriːˈvɪzɪt/ *verb* **1 ~ sth** to visit a place again, especially after a long period of time **2 ~ sth** to return to an idea or a subject and discuss it again: *It's an idea that may be worth revisiting at a later date.*

re·vit·al·ize (*BrE* also **-ise**) /ˌriːˈvaɪtəlaɪz/ *verb* **~ sth** to make sth stronger, more active or more healthy: *measures to revitalize the inner cities* ▸ **re·vit·al·iza·tion, -isa·tion** /ˌriːˌvaɪtəlaɪˈzeɪʃn; *NAmE* -ləˈz-/ *noun* [U]: *the revitalization of the steel industry*

re·vival /rɪˈvaɪvl/ *noun* **1** [U, C] an improvement in the condition or strength of sth: *the revival of trade* ◇ *an economic revival* ◇ *a* ***revival of interest*** *in folk music* **2** [C, U] the process of sth becoming or being made popular or fashionable again: *a religious revival* ◇ *Jazz is enjoying a revival.* **3** [C] a new production of a play that has not been performed for some time: *a revival of Peter Shaffer's 'Equus'*

re·vival·ism /rɪˈvaɪvəlɪzəm/ *noun* [U] **1** the process of creating interest in sth again, especially religion **2** the practice of using ideas, designs, etc. from the past: *revivalism in architecture*

re·vival·ist /rɪˈvaɪvəlɪst/ *noun* a person who tries to make sth popular again ▸ **re·vival·ist** *adj.*: *revivalist movements* ◇ *a revivalist preacher*

re·vive /rɪˈvaɪv/ *verb* **1** [I, T] to become, or to make sb/sth become, conscious or healthy and strong again: *The flowers soon revived in water.* ◇ *The economy is beginning to revive.* ◇ **~ sb/sth** *The paramedics couldn't revive her.* ◇ *This movie is intended to revive her flagging career.* **2** [T] **~ sth** to make sth start being used or done again: *This quaint custom should be revived.* ◇ *She has been trying to revive the debate over equal pay.* **3** [T] **~ sth** to produce again a play, etc. that has not been performed for some time: *This 1930s musical is being revived at the National Theatre.* ➲ see also REVIVAL

re·viv·ify /ˌriːˈvɪvɪfaɪ/ *verb* (**re·vivi·fies, re·vivi·fy·ing, re·vivi·fied, re·vivi·fied**) **~ sth** (*formal*) to give new life or health to sth SYN **revitalize**

revo·ca·tion /ˌrevəˈkeɪʃn/ *noun* [U, C] (*formal*) the act of cancelling a law, etc: *the revocation of planning permission*

re·voke /rɪˈvəʊk; *NAmE* -ˈvoʊk/ *verb* **~ sth** (*formal*) to officially cancel sth so that it is no longer valid

re·volt /rɪˈvəʊlt; *NAmE* -ˈvoʊlt/ *noun, verb*

▪ ***noun*** [C, U] a protest against authority, especially that of a government, often involving violence; the action of protesting against authority SYN **uprising**: *the Peasants' Revolt of 1381* ◇ *to* ***lead/stage a revolt*** ◇ *The army quickly crushed the revolt.* ◇ *the biggest back-bench revolt this government has ever seen* ◇ *Attempts to negotiate peace ended in armed revolt.* ◇ (*formal*) *The people rose* ***in revolt.***

▪ ***verb*** **1** [I] to take violent action against the people in power SYN **rebel, rise up**: *The peasants threatened to revolt.* ◇ **~ against sb/sth** *Finally the people revolted against the military dictatorship.* ➲ COLLOCATIONS at WAR ➲ see also REVOLUTION **2** [I] **~** (**against sth**) to behave in a way that is the opposite of what sb expects of you, especially in protest SYN **rebel**: *Teenagers often revolt against parental discipline.* **3** [T] **~ sb** to make you feel horror or disgust SYN **disgust**: *All the violence in the movie revolted me.* ◇ *The way he ate his food revolted me.* ➲ see also REVULSION

re·volt·ing /rɪˈvəʊltɪŋ; *NAmE* -ˈvoʊlt-/ *adj.* extremely unpleasant SYN **disgusting**: *a revolting smell* ◇ *a revolting little man* ➲ SYNONYMS at DISGUSTING ▸ **re·volt·ing·ly** *adv.*: *She's revoltingly overweight.*

revo·lu·tion 🔑 AW /ˌrevəˈluːʃn/ *noun*

1 🔑 [C, U] an attempt, by a large number of people, to change the government of a country, especially by violent action: *a socialist revolution* ◇ *the outbreak of the French Revolution in 1789* ◇ *to start a revolution* ◇ *a country on the brink of revolution* ➲ COLLOCATIONS at POLITICS ➲ see also COUNTER-REVOLUTION, REVOLT **2** 🔑 [C] a great change in conditions, ways of working, beliefs, etc. that affects large numbers of people: *a* ***cultural/social/scientific, etc. revolution*** ◇ **~ in sth** *A revolution in information technology is taking place.* ➲ see also INDUSTRIAL REVOLUTION **3** [C, U] **~** (**around/on sth**) a complete CIRCULAR movement around a point, especially of one planet around another: *the revolution of the earth around the sun* ➲ see also REVOLVE **4** (also *informal* **rev**) [C] a CIRCULAR movement made by sth fixed to a central point, for example in a car engine: *rotating at 300* ***revolutions per minute***

revo·lu·tion·ary AW /ˌrevəˈluːʃənəri; *NAmE* -neri/ *adj., noun*

■ ***adj.*** **1** [usually before noun] connected with political revolution: *a revolutionary leader* ◇ *revolutionary uprisings* **2** involving a great or complete change: *a* ***revolutionary idea*** ◇ *a time of rapid and* ***revolutionary change***

■ ***noun*** (*pl.* -ies) a person who starts or supports a revolution, especially a political one: *socialist revolutionaries*

revo·lu·tion·ize (*BrE* also **-ise**) AW /ˌrevəˈluːʃənaɪz/ *verb* **~ sth** to completely change the way that sth is done: *Aerial photography has revolutionized the study of archaeology.*

re·volve /rɪˈvɒlv; *NAmE* rɪˈvɑːlv; rɪˈvɔːlv/ *verb* [I] to go in a circle around a central point: *The fan revolved slowly.* ◇ *The earth revolves on its axis.*

PHR V **reˈvolve around/round sth** to move around sth in a circle: *The earth revolves around the sun.* **reˈvolve around/round sb/sth** to have sb/sth as the main interest or subject: *His whole life revolves around surfing.* ◇ *She thinks that the world revolves around her.* ◇ *The discussion revolved around the question of changing the club's name.*

re·volver /rɪˈvɒlvə(r); *NAmE* -ˈvɑːl-; -ˈvɔːl-/ *noun* a small gun that has a container for bullets that turns around so that shots can be fired quickly without having to stop to put more bullets in

re·volv·ing /rɪˈvɒlvɪŋ; *NAmE* -ˈvɔːl-; -ˈvɑːl-/ *adj.* [usually before noun] able to turn in a circle: *a revolving chair* ◇ *The theatre has a revolving stage.*

ˌrevolving ˈdoor *noun* **1** a type of door in an entrance to a large building that turns around in a circle as people go through it **2** used to talk about a place or an organization that people enter and then leave again very quickly: *The company became a revolving-door workplace.*

revue /rɪˈvjuː/ *noun* [C, U] a show in a theatre, with songs, dances, jokes, short plays, etc, often about recent events

re·vul·sion /rɪˈvʌlʃn/ *noun* [U, sing.] **~ (at/against/from sth)** (*formal*) a strong feeling of disgust or horror SYN **repugnance**: *She felt a deep sense of revulsion at the violence.* ◇ *I started to feel a revulsion against their decadent lifestyle.* ◇ *Most people viewed the bombings* ***with revulsion.*** ➲ see also REVOLT

re·ward 🔑 /rɪˈwɔːd; *NAmE* rɪˈwɔːrd/ *noun, verb*

■ ***noun*** **1** 🔑 [C, U] a thing that you are given because you have done sth good, worked hard, etc: *a financial reward* ◇ **~ (for sth/for doing sth)** *a reward for good behaviour* ◇ *You deserve a reward for being so helpful.* ◇ *Winning the match was* ***just reward*** *for the effort the team had made.* ◇ *The company is now* ***reaping the rewards*** *of their investments.* **2** 🔑 [C] an amount of money that is offered to sb for helping the police to find a criminal or for finding sth that is lost: *A £100 reward has been offered for the return of the necklace.* IDM see VIRTUE

■ ***verb*** 🔑 [often passive] to give sth to sb because they have done sth good, worked hard, etc: **~ sb for sth** *She was rewarded for her efforts with a cash bonus.* ◇ **~ sb for doing sth** *He rewarded us handsomely* (= with a lot of money) *for helping him.* ◇ **~ sb with sth** *She started singing to the baby and was rewarded with a smile.* ◇ **~ sb/sth** *Our patience was finally rewarded.*

re·ward·ing /rɪˈwɔːdɪŋ; *NAmE* -ˈwɔːrd-/ *adj.* **1** (of an activity, etc.) worth doing; that makes you happy because you think it is useful or important: *a rewarding experience/job* ➲ SYNONYMS at SATISFYING **2** producing a lot of money SYN **profitable**: *Teaching is not very financially rewarding* (= is not very well paid). OPP **unrewarding**

re·wind /ˌriːˈwaɪnd/ *verb* (**re·wound, re·wound** /-ˈwaʊnd/) [T, I] **~ (sth)** to make a tape in a CASSETTE player, etc. go backwards

re·wire /ˌriːˈwaɪə(r)/ *verb* **~ sth** to put new electrical wires into a building or piece of equipment

re·word /ˌriːˈwɜːd; *NAmE* -ˈwɜːrd/ *verb* **~ sth** to write sth again using different words in order to make it clearer or more acceptable ▸ **re·word·ing** *noun* [C, U]

re·work /ˌriːˈwɜːk; *NAmE* -ˈwɜːrk/ *verb* **~ sth** to make changes to sth in order to improve it or make it more suitable ▸ **re·work·ing** *noun* [C, U]: *The movie is a reworking of the Frankenstein story.*

re·writ·able /ˌriːˈraɪtəbl/ *adj.* (*computing*) able to be used again for different data: *a rewritable CD*

re·write /ˌriːˈraɪt/ *verb* (**re·wrote** /-ˈrəʊt; *NAmE* -ˈroʊt/, **re·writ·ten** /-ˈrɪtn/) **~ sth** to write sth again in a different way, usually in order to improve it or because there is some new information: *I intend to rewrite the story for younger children.* ◇ *This essay will have to be completely rewritten.* ◇ *an attempt to* ***rewrite history*** (= to present historical events in a way that shows or proves what you want them to) ▸ **re·write** /ˈriːraɪt/ *noun*

Rex /reks/ *noun* [U] (*BrE, formal*, from *Latin*) a word meaning 'king', used, for example, in the titles of legal cases brought by the state when there is a king in Britain: *Rex v Jones* ➲ compare REGINA

RGN /ˌɑː dʒiː ˈen; *NAmE* ˌɑːr dʒiː ˈen/ *abbr.* (*BrE*) registered general nurse

r.h. *abbr.* (in writing) RIGHT HAND

rhap·sod·ize (*BrE* also **-ise**) /ˈræpsədaɪz/ *verb* [I, T] **~ (about/over sth)** | **+ speech** (*formal*) to talk or write with great enthusiasm about sth SYN **go into raptures about**

rhap·sody /ˈræpsədi/ *noun* (*pl.* -ies) **1** (often in titles) a piece of music that is full of feeling and is not regular in form: *Liszt's Hungarian Rhapsodies* **2** (*formal*) the expression of great enthusiasm or happiness in speech or writing ▸ **rhap·sodic** /ræpˈsɒdɪk; *NAmE* -ˈsɑːdɪk/ *adj.*

rhea /ˈriːə/ *noun* a large S American bird that does not fly

rheme /riːm/ *noun* (*linguistics*) the part of a sentence or clause that adds new information to what the reader or audience already knows ➲ compare THEME (5)

rhe·nium /ˈriːniəm/ *noun* [U] (*symb.* **Re**) a chemical element. Rhenium is a rare silver-white metal that exists naturally in the ORES of MOLYBDENUM and some other metals.

rhe·sus factor /ˈriːsəs fæktə(r)/ *noun* [sing.] (*medical*) a substance present in the red blood cells of around 85% of humans. Its presence (**rhesus positive**) or absence (**rhesus negative**) can be dangerous for babies when they are born and for people having BLOOD TRANSFUSIONS.

rhe·sus monkey /ˈriːsəs mʌŋki/ *noun* a small S Asian MONKEY, often used in scientific experiments

rhet·oric /ˈretərɪk/ *noun* [U] **1** (*formal*, often *disapproving*) speech or writing that is intended to influence people, but that is not completely honest or sincere: *the rhetoric of political slogans* ◇ *empty rhetoric* **2** (*formal*) the skill of using language in speech or writing in a special way that influences or entertains people SYN **eloquence, oratory**

rhet·oric·al /rɪˈtɒrɪkl; *NAmE* -ˈtɔːr-/ *adj.* **1** (of a question) asked only to make a statement or to produce an effect rather than to get an answer: *'Don't you care what I do?' he asked, but it was a* ***rhetorical question.*** **2** (*formal*, often *disapproving*) (of a speech or piece of writing) intended to influence people, but not completely honest or sincere **3** (*formal*) connected with the art of RHETORIC: *the use of rhetorical devices such as metaphor and irony* ▸ **rhet·oric·al·ly** /-kli/ *adv.*: *'Do you think I'm stupid?' she asked rhetorically.* ◇ *a rhetorically structured essay*

rhet·or·ician /ˌretəˈrɪʃn/ *noun* (*technical*) a person who is skilled in the art of formal rhetoric

rheuˌmatic ˈfever *noun* [U] a serious disease that causes fever with swelling and pain in the joints

rheuma·tism /ˈruːmətɪzəm/ *noun* [U] a disease that makes the muscles and joints painful, stiff and swollen ▸ **rheum·at·ic** /ruˈmætɪk/ *adj.*: *rheumatic pains*

R

rheuma·toid arth·ritis /ˌruːmətɔɪd ɑːˈθraɪtɪs; *NAmE* ɑːrˈθ-/ *noun* [U] (*medical*) a disease that gets worse over a period of time and causes painful swelling and permanent damage in the joints of the body, especially the fingers, wrists, feet and ankles

rheuma·tol·ogy /ˌruːməˈtɒlədʒi; *NAmE* -ˈtɑːl-/ *noun* [U] the study of the diseases of joints and muscles, such as RHEUMATISM and ARTHRITIS

rheumy /ˈruːmi/ *adj.* (of the eyes) containing a lot of water

rhine·stone /ˈraɪnstəʊn; *NAmE* -stoʊn/ *noun* a clear stone that is intended to look like a diamond, used in cheap jewellery

rhin·itis /raɪˈnaɪtɪs/ *noun* [U] (*medical*) a condition in which the inside of the nose becomes swollen and sore, caused by an infection or an ALLERGY

rhino /ˈraɪnəʊ; *NAmE* -noʊ/ *noun* (*pl.* -os) (*informal*) = RHINOCEROS: *black/white rhino* ◇ *rhino horn*

rhi·noceros /raɪˈnɒsərəs; *NAmE* -ˈnɑːs-/ *noun* (*pl.* rhi·noceros or rhi·nocer·oses) (also *informal* **rhino**) a large heavy animal with very thick skin and either one or two horns on its nose, that lives in Africa and Asia

rhi·zome /ˈraɪzəʊm; *NAmE* -zoʊm/ *noun* (*technical*) the thick STEM of some plants, such as IRIS and MINT, that grows along or under the ground and has roots and STEMS growing from it

rho /rəʊ; *NAmE* roʊ/ *noun* the 17th letter of the Greek alphabet (P, ρ)

Rhodes scholar /ˌrəʊdz ˈskɒlə(r); *NAmE* ˌroʊdz ˈskɑːl-/ *noun* a student from the US, Germany or the Commonwealth who is given a SCHOLARSHIP to study in Britain at Oxford University from a fund that was started by Cecil Rhodes in 1902

rho·dium /ˈrəʊdiəm; *NAmE* ˈroʊ-/ *noun* [U] (*symb.* Rh) a chemical element. Rhodium is a hard silver-white metal that is usually found with PLATINUM.

rhodo·den·dron /ˌrəʊdəˈdendrən; *NAmE* ˌroʊ-/ *noun* a bush with large red, purple, pink or white flowers

rhom·boid /ˈrɒmbɔɪd; *NAmE* ˈrɑːm-/ *noun* (*geometry*) a flat shape with four straight sides, with only the opposite sides and angles equal to each other ➲ VISUAL VOCAB page V58

rhom·bus /ˈrɒmbəs; *NAmE* ˈrɑːm-/ *noun* (*geometry*) a flat shape with four equal sides and four angles which are not 90° ➲ VISUAL VOCAB page V58

R

rho·tic /ˈrəʊtɪk; *NAmE* ˈroʊ-/ *adj.* (*phonetics*) (of an accent) pronouncing the /r/ after a vowel in words like *car*, *early*, etc. General American and Scottish accents are rhotic.

rhu·barb /ˈruːbɑːb; *NAmE* -bɑːrb/ *noun* [U] **1** the thick red STEMS of a garden plant, also called rhubarb, that are cooked and eaten as a fruit: *rhubarb pie* **2** a word that a group of actors repeat on stage to give the impression of a lot of people talking at the same time

rhumba = RUMBA

rhyme /raɪm/ *noun, verb*

■ ***noun*** **1** [C] a word that has the same sound or ends with the same sound as another word: *Can you think of a rhyme for 'beauty'?* **2** [C] a short poem in which the last word in the line has the same sound as the last word in another line, especially the next one: *children's rhymes and stories* ➲ see also NURSERY RHYME **3** [U] the use of words in a poem or song that have the same sound, especially at the ends of lines: *a poem written* ***in rhyme*** ◇ *the poet's use of rhyme*

IDM **there's no ˌrhyme or ˈreason to/for sth | without ˌrhyme or ˈreason** if there is **no rhyme or reason to sth** or it happens **without rhyme or reason**, it happens in a way that cannot be easily explained or understood

■ ***verb*** **1** [I] **~ (with sth)** if two words, syllables, etc. **rhyme**, or if one **rhymes** with the other, they have or end with the same sound: *'Though' rhymes with 'low'.* ◇ *'Tough' and 'through' don't rhyme.* ◇ *rhyming couplets* **2** [T] **~ sth (with sth)** to put words that sound the same together, for example when you are writing poetry: *You can rhyme 'girl' with 'curl'.* **3** [I] (of a poem) to have lines that end with the same sound: *I prefer poems that rhyme.*

ˈrhyming slang *noun* [U] a way of talking in which you use words or phrases that rhyme with the word you mean, instead of using that word. For example in COCKNEY rhyming slang 'apples and pears' means 'stairs'.

rhythm 🔑 /ˈrɪðəm/ *noun* [U, C]

1 🔑 a strong regular repeated pattern of sounds or movements: *to dance to the rhythm of the music* ◇ *music with* ***a fast/slow/steady rhythm*** ◇ *jazz rhythms* ◇ *He can't seem to play* ***in rhythm.*** ◇ *The boat rocked up and down* ***in rhythm with*** *the sea.* ◇ *the rhythm of her breathing* ◇ *a dancer with a* ***natural sense of rhythm*** (= the ability to move in time to a fixed beat) **2** a regular pattern of changes or events: *the rhythm of the seasons* ◇ ***biological/body rhythms*** ➲ see also BIORHYTHM

ˌrhythm and ˈblues *noun* [U] (*abbr.* R & B) a type of music that is a mixture of BLUES and JAZZ and has a strong rhythm

ˌrhythm guiˈtar *noun* [U] a GUITAR style that consists mainly of CHORDS played with a strong rhythm ➲ compare LEAD GUITAR

rhyth·mic /ˈrɪðmɪk/ (also *less frequent* **rhyth·mic·al** /ˈrɪðmɪkl/) *adj.* having a regular pattern of sounds, movements or events: *music with a fast, rhythmic beat* ◇ *the rhythmic ticking of the clock* ▶ **rhyth·mic·al·ly** /-kli/ *adv.*

the ˈrhythm method *noun* [sing.] a method of avoiding getting pregnant that involves a woman only having sex during the time of the month when she is unlikely to get pregnant

ˈrhythm section *noun* the part of a band that supplies the rhythm, usually consisting of drums, BASS, and sometimes piano

ria /ˈriːə/ *noun* (*technical*) a long narrow area of water formed when a river valley floods

rib /rɪb/ *noun, verb*

■ ***noun*** **1** [C] any of the curved bones that are connected to the SPINE and surround the chest: *a* ***broken/bruised/cracked rib*** ◇ *Stop* ***poking me in the ribs!*** ➲ VISUAL VOCAB page V48 ➲ see also RIBCAGE **2** [U, C] a piece of meat with one or more bones from the ribs of an animal ➲ see also SPARE RIB **3** [C] a curved piece of wood, metal or plastic that forms the frame of a boat, roof, etc. and makes it stronger **4** [U, C] a way of knitting that produces a pattern of vertical lines in which some are higher than others: *a rib cotton sweater* IDM see DIG *v.*

■ ***verb*** (-bb-) **~ sb (about/over sth)** (*old-fashioned, informal*) to laugh at sb and make jokes about them, but in a friendly way SYN **tease**

rib·ald /ˈrɪbld; ˈraɪbɔːld/ *adj.* (of language or behaviour) referring to sex in a rude but humorous way

rib·ald·ry /ˈrɪbldri; ˈraɪb-/ *noun* [U] language or behaviour that refers to sex in a rude but humorous way

ribbed /rɪbd/ *adj.* (especially of material for clothes) having raised lines: *a ribbed sweater*

rib·bing /ˈrɪbɪŋ/ *noun* [U] **1** a pattern of raised lines in knitting or on a surface **2** (*old-fashioned, informal*) the act of making fun of sb in a friendly way SYN **teasing**

rib·bon /ˈrɪbən/ *noun* **1** [U, C] a narrow strip of material, used to tie things or for decoration: *a present tied with yellow ribbon* ◇ *lengths of velvet ribbon* ◇ *She was wearing two blue silk ribbons in her hair.* ➲ picture at ROPE **2** [C] something that is long and narrow in shape: *The road was a ribbon of moonlight.* **3** [C] a ribbon in special colours, or tied in a special way, that is given to sb as a prize or as a military honour, or that is worn by sb to show that they belong to a particular political party ➲ compare ROSETTE **4** [C] a long strip of material containing ink that you put into TYPEWRITERS and some computer printers

IDM **cut/tear, etc. sth to ˈribbons** to cut/tear, etc. sth very badly

'ribbon development *noun* [C, U] (*BrE, technical*) houses that are built along a main road leading out of a village or town; the building of houses in this position

'ribbon lake *noun* (*technical*) a long narrow lake

rib·cage /ˈrɪbkeɪdʒ/ *noun* the structure of curved bones (called RIBS), that surrounds and protects the chest ➲ VISUAL VOCAB page V48

'rib-eye (also **,rib-eye 'steak**) *noun* a piece of beef which is cut from outside the RIBS

ribo·fla·vin /ˌraɪbəˈfleɪvɪn/ *noun* [U] a VITAMIN which is important for producing energy, found in milk, LIVER, eggs and green vegetables

'rib-tickler *noun* (*informal*) a funny joke or story ▶ **'rib-tickling** *adj.*

rice 🔑 /raɪs/ *noun* [U] short, narrow white or brown grain grown on wet land in hot countries as food; the plant that produces this grain: *a grain of rice* ◇ ***boiled/steamed/fried rice*** ◇ ***long-/short-grain rice*** ◇ ***brown rice*** (= without its outer covering removed) ◇ ***rice paddies*** (= rice fields) ➲ VISUAL VOCAB page V28

rice·paper /ˈraɪspeɪpə(r)/ *noun* [U] a type of very thin paper made from tropical plants, used as a base for some types of cake

,rice 'pudding *noun* [U, C] a DESSERT (= a sweet dish) made from rice cooked with milk and sugar

Synonyms

rich

wealthy • prosperous • affluent • well off • comfortable

These words all describe sb/sth that has a lot of money, property or valuable possessions.

rich (of a person) having a lot of money, property or valuable possessions; (of a country or city) producing a lot of wealth so that many of its people can live at a high standard

wealthy rich

RICH OR WEALTHY?

There is no real difference in meaning between these two words. Both are very frequent, but **rich** is more frequent and can be used in some fixed phrases where **wealthy** cannot: ~~*He's stinking/filthy wealthy.*~~ ◇ ~~*It's a favourite resort for the wealthy and famous.*~~

prosperous (*rather formal*) rich and successful.

affluent (*rather formal*) rich and with a good standard of living: *affluent Western countries*

PROSPEROUS OR AFFLUENT?

Both **prosperous** and **affluent** are used to talk about people and places. **Prosperous** is used much more than **affluent** to talk about times and periods. **Affluent** is often used to contrast rich people or societies with poor ones. Being **prosperous** is nearly always seen as a good thing: *It's good to see you looking so prosperous.* ◇ ~~*It's good to see you looking so affluent.*~~

well off (often used in negative sentences) rich: *His family is not very well off.* NOTE The opposite of **well off** is **badly off**, but this is not very frequent; it is more common to say that sb is *not well off*.

comfortable having enough money to buy what you want without worrying about the cost: *They're not millionaires, but they're certainly very comfortable.*

PATTERNS

- a(n) rich/wealthy/prosperous/affluent/well-off **family**
- a(n) rich/wealthy/prosperous/well-off **man/woman**
- a(n) rich/wealthy/prosperous/affluent **country/city**

rich 🔑 /rɪtʃ/ *adj.* (**rich·er, rich·est**)
▸ WITH A LOT OF MONEY **1** 🔑 having a lot of money or property: *one of the richest women in the world* ◇ *Nobody gets rich from writing nowadays.* ◇ (*slang*) *to be* ***filthy/stinking*** (= extremely) ***rich*** OPP **poor** **2 the rich** *noun* [pl.] people who have a lot of money or property: *It's a favourite resort for the rich and famous.* OPP **the poor** **3** 🔑 (of a country) producing a lot of wealth so that many of its people can live at a high standard: *the richest countries/economies/nations* OPP **poor**
▸ FULL OF VARIETY **4** 🔑 very interesting and full of variety: *the region's rich history and culture* ◇ *She leads a rich and varied life.*
▸ CONTAINING/PROVIDING STH **5** 🔑 **~ (in sth)** (often in compounds) containing or providing a large supply of sth: *Oranges are rich in vitamin C.* ◇ *The area is rich in wildlife.* ◇ *His novels are a rich source of material for the movie industry.* ◇ *iron-rich rocks* OPP **poor**
▸ FOOD **6** 🔑 containing a lot of fat, butter, eggs, etc. and making you feel full quickly: *a rich creamy sauce* ◇ *a rich chocolate cake*
▸ SOIL **7** containing the substances that make it good for growing plants in SYN **fertile**: *a rich well-drained soil* OPP **poor**
▸ COLOURS/SOUNDS **8** (of colours, sounds, smells and tastes) strong or deep; very beautiful or pleasing: *rich dark reds*
▸ EXPENSIVE **9** (*literary*) expensive and beautiful SYN **sumptuous**: *The rooms were decorated with rich fabrics.*
▸ CRITICISM **10** (*informal, especially BrE*) used to say that a criticism sb makes is surprising and not reasonable, because they have the same fault: *Me? Lazy? That's rich, coming from you!* ➲ compare RICHNESS IDM see STRIKE *v.*

riches /ˈrɪtʃɪz/ *noun* [pl.] large amounts of money and valuable or beautiful possessions: *a career that brought him fame and riches* ◇ *material riches* IDM see EMBARRASSMENT, RAG *n.*

rich·ly /ˈrɪtʃli/ *adv.* **1** in a beautiful and expensive manner: *a richly decorated room* **2** used to express the fact that sth has a pleasant strong colour, taste or smell: *a richly flavoured sauce* ◇ *The polished floor glowed richly.* **3** in a generous way: *She was richly rewarded for all her hard work.* **4** in a way that people think is right and good SYN **thoroughly**: ***richly deserved*** *success* ◇ *richly earned respect* **5** used to express the fact that the quality or thing mentioned is present in large amounts: *richly varied countryside* ◇ *a richly atmospheric novel*

rich·ness /ˈrɪtʃnəs/ *noun* [U] the state of being rich in sth, such as colour, minerals or interesting qualities: *The richness and variety of marine life.* ➲ compare WEALTH

R

the Rich·ter scale /ˈrɪktə skeɪl; *NAmE* ˈrɪktər/ *noun* [sing.] a system for measuring how strong an EARTHQUAKE is: *an earthquake measuring 7.3 on the Richter scale*

ricin /ˈraɪsɪn/ *noun* [U] a very poisonous substance obtained from the seeds of the CASTOR OIL plant

rick /rɪk/ *noun, verb*
■ ***noun*** a large pile of HAY or STRAW that is built in a regular shape and covered to protect it from rain
■ ***verb* ~ sth** (*BrE*) to injure a part of your body by twisting it suddenly SYN **sprain**

rick·ets /ˈrɪkɪts/ *noun* [U] a disease of children caused by a lack of good food that makes the bones become soft and badly formed, especially in the legs

rick·ety /ˈrɪkəti/ *adj.* not strong or well made; likely to break: *a rickety chair*

rick·shaw /ˈrɪkʃɔː/ *noun* a small light vehicle with two wheels used in some Asian countries to carry passengers. The rickshaw is pulled by sb walking or riding a bicycle.

rico·chet /ˈrɪkəʃeɪ; *BrE* also -ʃet/ *verb, noun*
■ ***verb*** (**rico·chet·ing** /ˈrɪkəʃeɪɪŋ/, **rico·cheted, rico·cheted** /ˈrɪkəʃeɪd/, *BrE* also **rico·chet·ting** /ˈrɪkəʃetɪŋ/, **rico·chet·ted, rico·chet·ted** /ˈrɪkəʃetɪd/) [I] **+ adv./prep.** (of a moving object) to hit a surface and come off it fast at a different angle: *The bullet ricocheted off a nearby wall.*
■ ***noun*** **1** [C] a ball, bullet or stone that ricochets: *A woman protester was killed by a ricochet (bullet).* **2** [U] the action of

ricocheting: *the ricochet of bricks and bottles off police riot shields*

ric·tus /ˈrɪktəs/ *noun* (*formal*) a wide twisted or smiling mouth that does not look natural or relaxed

rid 🔑 /rɪd/ *verb* (**rid·ding, rid, rid**)
IDM **be ˈrid of sb/sth** (*formal*) to be free of sb/sth that has been annoying you or that you do not want: *She wanted to be rid of her parents and their authority.* ◇ *I was glad to be rid of the car when I finally sold it.* ◇ (*BrE*) *He was a nuisance and we're all* **well rid of** *him* (= we'll be much better without him). **get ˈrid of sb/sth** 🔑 to make yourself free of sb/sth that is annoying you or that you do not want; to throw sth away: *Try and get rid of your visitors before I get there.* ◇ *The problem is getting rid of nuclear waste.* ◇ *I can't get rid of this headache.* ◇ *We got rid of all the old furniture.* ➲ more at WANT *v.*
PHR V **ˈrid sb/sth of sb/sth** (*formal*) to remove sth that is causing a problem from a place, group, etc: *Further measures will be taken to rid our streets of crime.* **ˈrid yourself of sb/sth** (*formal*) to make yourself free from sb/sth that is annoying you or causing you a problem: *to rid yourself of guilt* ◇ *He wanted to rid himself of the burden of the secret.*

rid·dance /ˈrɪdns/ *noun* [U]
IDM **good ˈriddance (to sb/sth)** an unkind way of saying that you are pleased that sb/sth has gone: *'Goodbye and good riddance!' she said to him angrily as he left.*

rid·den /ˈrɪdn/ *adj.* (usually in compounds) full of a particular unpleasant thing: *a disease-ridden slum* ◇ *a class-ridden society* ◇ *She was guilt-ridden at the way she had treated him.* ◇ *She was ridden with guilt.* ➲ see also RIDE *v.*

rid·dle /ˈrɪdl/ *noun, verb*
■ ***noun*** **1** a question that is difficult to understand, and that has a surprising answer, that you ask sb as a game: *Stop* ***talking in riddles*** (= saying things that are confusing)—*say what you mean.* ◇ *to solve the riddle of the Sphinx* **2** a mysterious event or situation that you cannot explain SYN **mystery**: *the riddle of how the baby died*
■ ***verb*** [usually passive] **~ sb/sth (with sth)** to make a lot of holes in sb/sth: *The car was* ***riddled with bullets***.
IDM **be ˈriddled with sth** to be full of sth, especially sth bad or unpleasant: *His body was riddled with cancer.* ◇ *Her typing was slow and riddled with mistakes.*

ride 🔑 /raɪd/ *verb, noun*
■ ***verb*** (**rode** /rəʊd; *NAmE* roʊd/, **rid·den** /ˈrɪdn/)
▸ HORSE **1** 🔑 [I, T] to sit on a horse, etc. and control it as it moves: *I learnt to ride as a child.* ◇ **+ adv./prep.** *They rode along narrow country lanes.* ◇ *He was riding on a large black horse.* ◇ **~ sth** *She had never ridden a horse before.* ◇ *He's ridden six winners so far this year* (= in horse racing). **2** 🔑 **go riding** (*BrE*) (*NAmE* **go ˈhorseback riding**) [I] to spend time riding a horse for pleasure: *How often do you go riding?*
▸ BICYCLE/MOTORCYCLE **3** 🔑 [T, I] to sit on and control a bicycle, motorcycle, etc: **~ sth (+ adv./prep.)** *The boys were riding their bikes around the streets.* ◇ *He rode a Harley Davidson.* ◇ (**+ adv./prep.**) *The ground there is too rough to ride over.*
▸ IN VEHICLE **4** 🔑 [I, T] to travel in a vehicle, especially as a passenger: (**+ adv./prep.**) *I walked back while the others rode in the car.* ◇ **~ sth (+ adv./prep.)** (*NAmE*) *to* ***ride the subway/an elevator, etc.*** ◇ *She rode the bus to school every day.*
▸ ON WATER/AIR **5** [I, T] to float or be supported on water or air: (**+ adv./prep.**) *We watched the balloon riding high above the fields.* ◇ **~ sth** *surfers riding the waves*
▸ GO THROUGH AREA **6** [T] **~ sth** to go through or over an area on a horse, bicycle, etc: *We rode the mountain trails.*
▸ CRITICIZE **7** [T] **~ sb** (*NAmE*) to criticize or TEASE sb in an annoying way: *Why is everybody riding me today?*
IDM **be riding for a ˈfall** to be doing sth that involves risks and that may end in disaster **be riding ˈhigh** to be successful or very confident **let sth ˈride** to decide to do nothing about a problem that you know you may have to deal with later **ride the crest of sth** to enjoy great success or support because of a particular situation or event: *The band is riding the crest of its last tour.* **ride ˈherd on sb/sth** (*NAmE, informal*) to keep watch or control over sb/sth: *police riding herd on crowds of youths on the streets* **ride ˈshotgun** (*NAmE, informal*) to ride in the front passenger seat of a car or truck **ride a/the wave of sth** to enjoy or be supported by the particular situation or quality mentioned: *Schools are riding a wave of renewed public interest.* ➲ more at WISH *n.*
PHR V **ˈride on sth** (usually used in the progressive tenses) to depend on sth: *My whole future is riding on this interview.* **ˌride sth↔ˈout** to manage to survive a difficult situation or time without having to make great changes **ˌride ˈup** (of clothing) to move gradually upwards, out of position: *Short skirts tend to ride up when you sit down.*
■ ***noun***
▸ IN VEHICLE **1** 🔑 a short journey in a vehicle, on a bicycle, etc: *a train ride through beautiful countryside* ◇ *It's a ten-minute bus ride from here to town.* ◇ *Steve* ***gave me a ride*** *on his motorbike.* ◇ *We* ***went for a ride*** *on our bikes.* ◇ *a bike ride* **2** 🔑 (*NAmE*) (*BrE* **lift**) a free ride in a car, etc. to a place you want to get to: *She hitched a ride to the station.* ◇ *We managed to get a ride into town when we missed the bus.* **3** 🔑 the kind of journey you make in a car, etc: *a* ***smooth/comfortable/bumpy, etc. ride*** ◇ (*figurative*) *The new legislation faces* ***a bumpy ride*** (= will meet with opposition and difficulties).
▸ ON HORSE **4** 🔑 a short journey on a horse, etc: *a pony ride* ◇ *The kids had a ride on an elephant at the zoo.* ◇ *He goes for a ride most mornings.*
▸ AT FUNFAIR **5** a large machine at a FUNFAIR or AMUSEMENT PARK that you ride on for fun or excitement; an occasion when you go on one of these: *The rides are free.* ◇ *a roller coaster ride*
IDM **come/go along for the ˈride** (*informal*) to join in an activity for pleasure but without being seriously interested in it **have a rough/an easy ˈride | give sb a rough/an easy ˈride** (*informal*) to experience/not experience difficulties when you are doing sth; to make things difficult/easy for sb: *He will be given a rough ride at the party conference.* **take sb for a ˈride** (*informal*) to cheat or trick sb: *It's not a pleasant feeling to discover you've been taken for a ride by someone you trusted.* ➲ more at FREE *adj.*

ˈride-off *noun* (*NAmE*) = JUMP-OFF

rider 🔑 /ˈraɪdə(r)/ *noun*
1 🔑 a person who rides a horse, bicycle or motorcycle: *Three riders* (= people riding horses) *were approaching.* ◇ *horses and their riders* ◇ *She's an experienced rider.* ◇ *a motorcycle dispatch rider* ➲ VISUAL VOCAB page V38 **2 ~ (to sth)** an extra piece of information that is added to an official document

ridge /rɪdʒ/ *noun, verb*
■ ***noun*** **1** a narrow area of high land along the top of a line of hills; a high pointed area near the top of a mountain: *walking along the ridge* ◇ *the north-east ridge of Mount Everest* ➲ VISUAL VOCAB page V4 **2** a raised line on the surface of sth; the point where two sloping surfaces join: *The ridges on the soles of my boots stopped me from slipping.* ◇ *the ridge of the roof* ➲ VISUAL VOCAB page V15 **3** [usually sing.] **~ (of high pressure)** (*technical*) a long narrow area of high pressure in the atmosphere ➲ compare TROUGH
■ ***verb*** [usually passive] **~ sth** to make narrow raised lines or areas on the surface of sth

ridged /rɪdʒd/ *adj.* (of an object or area) with raised lines on the surface

ˈridge tent (*BrE*) (also **ˈA-frame tent** *BrE, NAmE*) *noun* a tent which forms an upside-down V shape ➲ compare DOME TENT, FRAME TENT

ridi·cule /ˈrɪdɪkjuːl/ *noun, verb*
■ ***noun*** [U] unkind comments that make fun of sb/sth or make them look silly SYN **mockery**: *She is* ***an object of ridicule*** *in the tabloid newspapers.* ◇ *to* ***hold sb up to ridicule*** (= make fun of sb publicly)
■ ***verb*** **~ sb/sth** to make sb/sth look silly by laughing at them or it in an unkind way SYN **make fun of**

ri·dicu·lous 🔑 /rɪˈdɪkjələs/ *adj.*
very silly or unreasonable SYN **absurd, ludicrous**: *I look*

ridiculous in this hat. ◇ Don't be ridiculous! You can't pay £50 for a T-shirt! ▶ **ri·dicu·lous·ly** *adv.*: *The meal was ridiculously expensive.* **ri·dicu·lous·ness** *noun* [U] IDM see SUBLIME *n.*

rid·ing 0-w /ˈraɪdɪŋ/ *noun* **1** 0-w (*BrE* also ˈ**horse riding**) (*NAmE* also ˈ**horseback riding**) [U] the sport or activity of riding horses: *I'm taking riding lessons.* ◇ *riding boots* ◇ (*BrE*) *to* **go riding** ◇ (*NAmE*) *to* **go horseback riding** **2** **Riding** one of the three former parts of the English county of Yorkshire called the **East Riding**, the **North Riding** and the **West Riding** ORIGIN From an Anglo-Saxon word meaning 'one third'.

rife /raɪf/ *adj.* [not before noun] **1** if sth bad or unpleasant is **rife** in a place, it is very common there SYN **widespread**: *It is a country where corruption is rife.* ◇ *Rumours are rife that he is going to resign.* **2** ~ (**with sth**) full of sth bad or unpleasant: *Los Angeles is rife with gossip about the stars' private lives.*

riff /rɪf/ *noun* a short repeated pattern of notes in popular music or JAZZ

rif·fle /ˈrɪfl/ *verb* [I, T] to turn over papers or the pages of a book quickly and without reading them all SYN **leaf**: ~ **through sth** *He was riffling through the papers on his desk.* ◇ ~ **sth** *to riffle the pages of a book*

riff-raff /ˈrɪf ræf/ *noun* [U+sing./pl. v.] (*disapproving*) an insulting way of referring to people of low social class or people who are not considered socially acceptable

rifle /ˈraɪfl/ *noun, verb*

■***noun*** a gun with a long BARREL which you hold to your shoulder to fire

■***verb*** **1** [I, T] ~ (**through**) **sth** to search quickly through sth in order to find or steal sth: *She rifled through her clothes for something suitable to wear.* **2** [T] ~ **sth** to steal sth from somewhere: *His wallet had been rifled.* **3** [T] ~ **sth + adv./prep.** to kick a ball very hard and straight in a game of football (SOCCER)

rifle·man /ˈraɪflmən/ *noun* (*pl.* **-men** /-mən/) a soldier who carries a rifle

ˈ**rifle range** *noun* **1** [C] a place where people practise shooting with rifles **2** [U] the distance that a bullet from a rifle will travel

rift /rɪft/ *noun* **1** a serious disagreement between people that stops their relationship from continuing SYN **breach, division**: *The rift within the party deepened.* ◇ *Efforts to* **heal the rift** *between the two countries have failed.* ➲ COLLOCATIONS at INTERNATIONAL **2** a large crack or opening in the ground, rocks or clouds

ˈ**rift valley** *noun* a valley with steep sides formed when two parallel cracks develop in the earth's surface and the land between them sinks

rig /rɪɡ/ *verb, noun*

■***verb*** (**-gg-**) [usually passive] **1** ~ **sth** to arrange or influence sth in a dishonest way in order to get the result that you want SYN **fix**: *He said the election had been rigged.* ◇ *to rig the market* (= to cause an artificial rise or fall in prices, in order to make a profit) **2** ~ **sth** (**with sth**) to provide a ship or boat with ropes, sails, etc; to fit the sails, etc. in position **3** ~ **sth** (**up**) (**with sth**) to fit equipment somewhere, sometimes secretly: *The lights had been rigged (up) but not yet tested.* ◇ *The car had been rigged with about 300 lbs of explosive.*

PHR V ˌ**rig sb/sth/yourself**↔ˈ**out** (**in/with sth**) [often passive] (*old-fashioned*) to provide sb/sth with a particular kind of clothes or equipment: *I was accepted for the job and rigged out in a uniform.* ˌ**rig sth**↔ˈ**up** to make or to build sth quickly, using whatever materials are available: *We managed to rig up a shelter for the night.*

■***noun*** **1** (especially in compounds) a large piece of equipment that is used for taking oil or gas from the ground or the bottom of the sea: *an oil rig* **2** the way that the MASTS and sails on a boat, etc. are arranged **3** (*NAmE, informal*) a large lorry/truck **4** equipment that is used for a special purpose: *a CB radio rig*

rig·ging /ˈrɪɡɪŋ/ *noun* [U] **1** the ropes that support the MASTS and sails of a boat or ship **2** the act of influencing sth in a dishonest way in order to get the result that you want: *vote rigging*

right 0-w /raɪt/ *adj., adv., noun, verb, exclamation*

■***adj.***

▸ MORALLY GOOD **1** 0-w [not usually before noun] ~ (**to do sth**) morally good or acceptable; correct according to law or a person's duty: *You were quite right to criticize him.* ◇ *Is it ever right to kill?* ◇ *It seems* **only right** *to warn you of the risk.* ◇ *I hope we're doing* **the right thing**. OPP **wrong**

▸ TRUE/CORRECT **2** 0-w true or correct as a fact: *Did you get the answer right?* ◇ *'What's the* **right time***?' '10.37.'* ◇ *'David, isn't it?' 'Yes,* **that's right**.*'* ◇ (*informal*) *It was Monday you went to see Angie, right?* ◇ *Let me* **get this right** (= understand correctly) —*you want us to do an extra ten hours' work for no extra pay?* OPP **wrong** ➲ SYNONYMS at TRUE **3** 0-w correct for a particular situation or thing, or for a particular person: *Have you got the* **right money** (= the exact amount) *for the bus fare?* ◇ *Is this the right way to the beach?* ◇ *You're not holding it* **the right way up**. ◇ *Are you sure you've got that on* **the right way round***?* ◇ *Next time we'll* **get it right**. ◇ *He's the right man for the job.* ◇ *I'm glad you split up. She wasn't right for you.* ◇ *I was waiting for the right moment to ask him.* ◇ *She knows all the* **right people** (= important people, for example those who can help her career). ◇ *His success was down to being* **in the right place at the right time** (= being able to take opportunities when they came). OPP **wrong** **4** 0-w [not before noun] correct in your opinion or judgement: ~ (**about sth**) *She was right about Tom having no money.* ◇ ~ (**to do sth**) *You're right to be cautious.* ◇ *'It's not easy.' 'Yeah,* **you're right**.*'* ◇ ~ (**in doing sth**) **Am I right in thinking** *we've met before?* OPP **wrong**

▸ NORMAL **5** 0-w [not before noun] in a normal or good enough condition: *I don't feel quite right today* (= I feel ill/sick). ◇ *That sausage doesn't smell right.* ◇ *Things aren't right between her parents.* ◇ *If only I could have helped* **put** *matters* **right**. ◇ *He's* **not quite right in the head** (= not mentally normal). OPP **wrong**

▸ NOT LEFT **6** 0-w [only before noun] of, on or towards the side of the body that is towards the east when a person faces north: *my right eye* ◇ *Keep on the right side of the road.* ◇ *Take a right turn at the intersection.* ➲ see also RIGHT-WING OPP **left**

▸ COMPLETE **7** [only before noun] (*BrE, informal*, especially *disapproving*) used to emphasize sth bad: *You made a right mess of that!* ◇ *I felt a right idiot.* ➲ see also ALL RIGHT ▶ **right·ness** *noun* [U]: *the rightness* (= justice) *of their cause* ◇ *the rightness of his decision*

IDM ˌ**give your right** ˈ**arm for sth/to do sth** (*informal*) used to say that sb is willing to give up a lot in order to have or do sth that they really want: *I'd have given my right arm to have been there with them.* (**not**) **in your right** ˈ**mind** (not) mentally normal ➲ SYNONYMS at MAD (**as**) **right as** ˈ**rain** (*informal*) in excellent health or condition **right e**ˈ**nough** (*informal*) certainly; in a way that cannot be denied: *You heard me right enough* (= so don't pretend that you did not). **right** ˈ**on** (*informal*) used to express strong approval or encouragement ➲ see also RIGHT-ON ˌ**right side** ˈ**up** (*NAmE*) with the top part turned to the top; in the correct, normal position: *I dropped my toast, but luckily it fell right side up.* OPP **upside down** ˈ**she'll be right** (*AustralE, informal*) used to say that everything will be all right, even if there is a problem now ˌ**too** ˈ**right** (*BrE, informal*) used to say that there is no doubt about sth: *'We need to stick together.' 'Too right!'* ◇ *'I'll have to do it again.' 'Too right you will.'* ➲ more at BUTTON *v.*, FOOT *n.*, HEAD *n.*, HEART, IDEA, LEFT *adv.*, MIGHT *n.*, MR, NOTE *n.*, SIDE *n.*, TRACK *n.*

■***adv.***

▸ EXACTLY **1** 0-w exactly; directly: *Lee was standing* **right behind** *her.* ◇ *The wind was right in our faces.* ◇ *I'm* **right behind you** *on this one* (= I am supporting you). ◇ *The bus came right on time.*

▸ COMPLETELY **2** 0-w all the way; completely: *The car spun right off the track.* ◇ *I'm right out of ideas.* ◇ *She kept right on swimming until she reached the other side.*

R

▸ IMMEDIATELY **3** (*informal*) immediately; without delay: *I'll be right back.* ◇ *I'll be right with you* (= I am coming very soon).
▸ CORRECTLY **4** correctly: *You guessed right.* OPP **wrong**
▸ SATISFACTORILY **5** in the way that things should happen or are supposed to happen: *Nothing's going right for me today.* OPP **wrong**
▸ NOT LEFT **6** on or to the right side: *Turn right at the end of the street.* OPP **left**

IDM **,right and 'left** everywhere: *She owes money right and left.* **right a'way/'off** immediately; without delay: *I want it sent right away.* ◇ *I told him right off what I thought of him.* **,right, left and 'centre** = LEFT, RIGHT AND CENTRE at LEFT *adv.* **right 'now 1** at this moment: *He's not in the office right now.* **2** immediately: *Do it right now!* **right off the 'bat** (*informal, especially NAmE*) immediately; without delay: *We both liked each other right off the bat.* **see sb 'right** (*NAmE* also **do sb 'right**) (*informal*) to make sure that sb has all they need or want: *You needn't worry about money—I'll see you right.* ➲ more at ALLEY, HIT *v.*, SERVE *v.*, WORD *n.*

■ ***noun***
▸ STH MORALLY GOOD **1** [U, C] what is morally good or correct: *She doesn't understand the difference between right and wrong.* ◇ *You* **did right** *to tell me about it.* ◇ *They both had some right on their side.* ◇ *He wouldn't apologize. He knew he was* **in the right** (= had justice on his side). ◇ *It was difficult to establish* **the rights and wrongs** (= the true facts) *of the matter.* OPP **wrong**
▸ MORAL/LEGAL CLAIM **2** [C, U] a moral or legal claim to have or get sth or to behave in a particular way: **~ (to sth)** *Everyone has a right to a fair trial.* ◇ **~ (to do sth)** *You have* **no right** *to stop me from going in there.* ◇ **What gives you the right** *to do that?* ◇ *She* **had every right** *to be angry.* ◇ *You're quite* **within your rights** *to ask for your money back.* ◇ **By rights** (= if justice were done) *half the money should be mine.* ◇ *There is no right of appeal against the decision.* ◇ *Education is provided by the state* **as of right** (= everyone has a right to it). ◇ *The property belongs to her* **by right**. ◇ *They had fought hard for* **equal rights**. ➲ see also ANIMAL RIGHTS, CIVIL RIGHTS, HUMAN RIGHT
▸ FOR BOOK/MOVIE, ETC. **3** **rights** [pl.] the authority to perform, publish, film, etc. a particular work, event, etc: *He sold the rights for $2 million.* ◇ *all rights reserved* (= protected or kept for the owners of the book, film/movie, etc.)
▸ NOT LEFT SIDE **4** **the/sb's right** [sing.] the right side or direction: *Take the first street* **on the right**. ◇ *She seated me on her right.* OPP **left 5** [sing.] **the first, second, etc. ~** the first, second, etc. road on the right side: *Take the first right, then the second left.* OPP **left 6 a right** [sing.] a turn to the right: *to make a right* ◇ (*NAmE, informal*) *to hang a right* OPP **left**
▸ POLITICS **7** **the right ,the Right** [sing.+ sing./pl. v.] political groups that most strongly support the CAPITALIST system ➲ compare RIGHT WING: *The Right in British politics is represented by the Conservative Party.* OPP **left 8** **the right** [sing.+ sing./pl. v.] the part of a political party whose members are most conservative: *He's on the right of the Labour Party.* OPP **left**
▸ IN BOXING **9** [C] a blow that is made with your right hand OPP **left**

IDM **bang to 'rights** (*BrE*) (*NAmE* **dead to 'rights**) (*informal*) with definite proof of having committed a crime, so that you cannot claim to be innocent: *We've got you bang to rights handling stolen property.* **do 'right by sb** (*old-fashioned*) to treat sb fairly **in your own 'right** because of your personal qualifications or efforts, not because of your connection with sb else: *She sings with a rock band, but she's also a jazz musician in her own right.* **put/set sb/sth to 'rights** to correct sb/sth; to put things in their right places or right order: *It took me ages to put things to rights after the workmen had left.* ➲ more at WORLD, WRONG *n.*

■ ***verb***
▸ RETURN TO POSITION **1** **~ sb/sth/yourself** to return sb/sth/yourself to the normal, vertical position: *They learnt to right a capsized canoe.* ◇ *At last the plane* **righted itself** *and flew on.*
▸ CORRECT **2** **~ sth** to correct sth that is wrong or not in its normal state SYN **put right**: *Righting the economy will demand major cuts in expenditure.*

IDM **right a 'wrong** to do sth to correct an unfair situation or sth bad that you have done

■ ***exclamation*** (*BrE, informal*) **1** used to show that you accept a statement or an order: *'You may find it hurts a little at first.' 'Right.'* ◇ *'Barry's here.' 'Oh, right.'* ◇ *'I'll have a whisky and soda.'* **'Right you are**, *sir.'* **2** used to get sb's attention to say that you are ready to do sth, or to tell them to do sth: *Right! Let's get going.* **3** used to check that sb agrees with you or has understood you: *So that's twenty of each sort, right?* ◇ *And I didn't think any more of it, right, but Mum says I should see a doctor.* **4** (*ironic*) used to say that you do not believe sb or that you disagree with them: *'I won't be late tonight.'* **'Yeah, right.'**

Synonyms

right
correct

Both these words describe a belief, opinion, decision or method that is suitable or the best one for a particular situation.

right if sb is right to do or think sth, that is a good thing to do or think in that situation: *You're right to be cautious.* ◇ *You made the right decision.* ◇ *'It's not easy.' 'Yes, you're right.'*

correct (of a method, belief, opinion or decision) right and suitable in a particular situation: *What's the correct way to shut the machine down?* ◇ *I don't think she's correct to say he's incompetent.*

RIGHT OR CORRECT?

Correct is more formal than **right**. It is more often used for methods and **right** is more often used for beliefs, opinions and decisions.

PATTERNS

- right/correct **about** sb/sth
- right/correct **to do** sth
- right/correct **in thinking/believing/saying** sth
- the right/correct **decision/judgement/conclusion**
- the right/correct **way/method/approach**
- **absolutely/quite** right/correct

Which Word?

right / rightly

- **Right** and **rightly** can both be used as adverbs. In the sense 'correctly' or 'in the right way', **right** is the usual adverb. It is only used after verbs: *He did it right.* ◇ *Did I spell your name right?* **Rightly** cannot be used like this. In formal language **correctly** is used: *Is your name spelled correctly?*
- The usual meaning of **rightly** is 'for a good reason' and it comes before an adjective: *They are rightly proud of their children.* It can be used to mean 'correctly' before a verb or in particular phrases: *As you rightly say, we have a serious problem.* In *NAmE* **rightly** is not at all common.

'right angle *noun* an angle of 90°: *Place the table* **at right angles/at a right angle** *to the wall* ➲ VISUAL VOCAB page V58 ➲ compare ACUTE ANGLE, OBTUSE ANGLE, REFLEX ANGLE

'right-angled *adj.* having or consisting of a right angle

,right-angled 'triangle (*especially BrE*) (*NAmE* usually **,right 'triangle**) *noun* a triangle with a right angle ➲ VISUAL VOCAB page V58

ˌright ˈbrain *noun* [U, sing.] the right side of the human brain, that is thought to be used for creating new ideas and to be where emotions come from ➲ compare LEFT BRAIN

ˌright-ˈclick *verb* [T, I] **~ sth | ~ (on sth)** to choose a particular function or item on a computer screen, etc, by pressing the button on a mouse that is on the right side

right·eous /ˈraɪtʃəs/ *adj.* (*formal*) **1** morally right and good: *a righteous God* **2** that you think is morally acceptable or fair: ***righteous anger/indignation, etc.*** ➲ see also SELF-RIGHTEOUS ▶ **right·eous·ly** *adv.* **right·eous·ness** *noun* [U]

ˌright ˈfield *noun* [sing.] (in BASEBALL) the part of the field to the right of the BATTER

right·ful /ˈraɪtfl/ *adj.* [only before noun] (*formal*) that is correct, right or legal SYN **proper**: *The stolen car was returned to its* ***rightful owner.*** ▶ **right·ful·ly** /-fəli/ *adv.*: *She was only claiming what was rightfully hers.*

ˈright-hand *adj.* [only before noun] **1** on the right side of sth: *on the right-hand side of the road* ◇ *the top right-hand corner of the screen* **2** intended for use by your right hand: *a right-hand glove* OPP **left-hand**

ˌright-hand ˈdrive *adj.* (of a vehicle) with the driver's seat and STEERING WHEEL on the right side OPP **left-hand drive**

ˌright-ˈhanded *adj.* **1** a person who is **right-handed** uses their right hand for writing, using tools, etc. **2** a **right-handed** tool is designed to be used with the right hand OPP **left-handed** ▶ **ˌright-ˈhanded** *adv.*

ˌright-ˈhander *noun* **1** a person who uses their right hand for writing, using tools, etc. **2** a hit with the right hand OPP **left-hander**

ˌright-hand ˈman *noun* [sing.] a person who helps sb a lot and who they rely on, especially in an important job: *the President's right-hand man*

ˌRight ˈHonourable *adj.* [only before noun] (*abbr.* **Rt Hon**) **1 the Right Honourable...** a title of respect used when talking to or about a person of high social rank, especially a lord **2 the/my Right Honourable...** the title of respect used by Members of Parliament in Britain when talking to or about a senior Member of Parliament during a debate ➲ compare HONOURABLE

right·ist /ˈraɪtɪst/ *noun* a person who supports RIGHT-WING political parties and their ideas SYN **right-winger** OPP **leftist** ▶ **right·ist** *adj.*

right·ly 🔑 /ˈraɪtli/ *adv.*
1 🔑 for a good reason SYN **justifiably**: *The school was rightly proud of the excellent exam results.* ◇ *He was proud of his beautiful house,* ***and rightly so.*** ◇ ***Quite rightly,*** *the environment is of great concern.* **2** 🔑 in a correct or accurate way SYN **correctly**: ***Rightly or wrongly,*** *many older people are afraid of violence in the streets.* ◇ *As she rightly pointed out the illness can affect adults as well as children.* ◇ *I can't* ***rightly say*** *what happened.* ◇ ***I don't rightly know*** *where he's gone.* ◇ ***If I remember rightly,*** *there's a train at six o'clock.* ➲ note at RIGHT

ˌright-ˈminded (also **ˌright-ˈthinking**) *adj.* (of a person) having beliefs and opinions that most people approve of

right·most /ˈraɪtməʊst; *NAmE* -moʊst/ *adj.* [only before noun] furthest to the right

righto /ˈraɪtəʊ; *NAmE* -oʊ/ (also **righty-ho**) *exclamation* (*old-fashioned, BrE, informal*) used to show that you accept a statement or an order

ˌright of aˈbode *noun* [U] official permission that allows a person to live in a particular country

ˌright-of-ˈcentre *adj.* = CENTRE-RIGHT

ˌright of ˈway *noun* (*pl.* **ˌrights of ˈway**) **1** [U] (*especially BrE*) legal permission to go onto or through another person's land: *Private property—no right of way.* **2** [C] (*especially BrE*) a public path that goes through private land **3** [U] the right to drive across or into a road before another vehicle: *I had right of way at the junction.* ◇ *Whose right of way is it?*

ˌright-ˈon *adj.* (*BrE, informal*, sometimes *disapproving*) having political opinions or being aware of social issues that are fashionable and LEFT-WING: *right-on middle-class intellectuals*

ˌRight ˈReverend *adj.* [only before noun] (*abbr.* **Rt Revd**) a title of respect used when talking about a BISHOP (= a senior priest)

ˈrights issue *noun* (*business*) an offer to buy shares in a company at a cheaper price to people who already own some shares in it

right·size /ˈraɪtsaɪz/ *verb* [I, T] **~ (sth)** (*business*) to change the size of a company in order to reduce costs, especially by reducing the number of employees

ˌright-ˈthinking *adj.* = RIGHT-MINDED

ˌright ˈtriangle *noun* (*NAmE*) = RIGHT-ANGLED TRIANGLE

right·ward /ˈraɪtwəd; *NAmE* -wərd/ (also **right·wards** /ˈraɪtwədz; *NAmE* -wərdz/ especially in *BrE*) *adj.* **1** on or to the right: *a rightward movement* **2** towards more RIGHT-WING political ideas: *a rightward shift in voting patterns* ▶ **right·ward** (also **right·wards**) *adv.*

the ˌright ˈwing *noun* **1** [sing.+ sing./pl. v.] the part of a political party whose members are least in favour of social change: *He is on the right wing of the party.* **2** [C, U] an attacking player or a position on the right side of the field in a sports game OPP **left wing**

ˌright-ˈwing *adj.* strongly supporting the CAPITALIST system: *right-wing policies* OPP **left-wing**

ˌright-ˈwinger *noun* **1** a person on the right wing of a political party: *She is a prominent Tory right-winger.* **2** a person who plays on the right side of the field in a sports game OPP **left-winger**

righty-ho /ˈraɪtihəʊ; *NAmE* -hoʊ/ *exclamation* (*old-fashioned, BrE, informal*) = RIGHTO

rigid AW /ˈrɪdʒɪd/ *adj.* **1** (often *disapproving*) (of rules, methods, etc.) very strict and difficult to change SYN **inflexible**: *The curriculum was too narrow and too rigid.* ◇ *His rigid adherence to the rules made him unpopular.* **2** (of a person) not willing to change their ideas or behaviour SYN **inflexible**: *rigid attitudes* **3** (of an object or substance) stiff and difficult to move or bend: *a rigid support for the tent* ◇ *She sat upright, her body* ***rigid with fear.*** ◇ (*figurative*) *I was* ***bored rigid*** (= extremely bored). ▶ **ri·gid·ity** AW /rɪˈdʒɪdəti/ *noun* [U, C]: *the rigidity of the law on this issue* ◇ *the rigidity of the metal bar* **ri·gid·ly** AW *adv.*: *The speed limit must be rigidly enforced.* ◇ *She stared rigidly ahead.*

rig·mar·ole /ˈrɪgmərəʊl; *NAmE* -roʊl/ *noun* [U, sing.] **1** a long and complicated process that is annoying and seems unnecessary: *I couldn't face the whole rigmarole of getting a work permit again.* **2** a long and complicated story

rigor mor·tis /ˌrɪgə ˈmɔːtɪs; *NAmE* ˌrɪgər ˈmɔːrtɪs/ *noun* [U] the process by which the body becomes stiff after death

rig·or·ous /ˈrɪgərəs/ *adj.* **1** done carefully and with a lot of attention to detail SYN **thorough**: *a rigorous analysis* **2** demanding that particular rules, processes, etc. are strictly followed SYN **strict**: *The work failed to meet their rigorous standards.* ▶ **rig·or·ous·ly** *adv.*: *The country's press is rigorously controlled.*

rig·our (*especially US* **rigor**) /ˈrɪgə(r)/ *noun* **1** [U] the fact of being careful and paying great attention to detail: ***academic/intellectual/scientific, etc. rigour*** **2** [U] (*formal*) the fact of being strict or severe SYN **severity**: *This crime must be treated with the full rigour of the law.* **3 the rigours of sth** [pl.] the difficulties and unpleasant conditions of sth: *The plants were unable to withstand the rigours of a harsh winter.*

ˈrig-out *noun* (*BrE, informal*, often *disapproving*) a set of clothes worn together: *Where are you going in that rig-out?*

the Rig Veda /ˌrɪg ˈveɪdə; ˈviːdə/ *noun* [sing.] the oldest and most important of the Vedas (= Hindu holy texts)

R

rile /raɪl/ *verb* **~ sb** | **it riles sb that…** to annoy sb or make them angry SYN **anger**: *Nothing ever seemed to rile him.*
IDM **be/get (all) ˌriled ˈup** (*informal, especially NAmE*) to be or get very annoyed

Riley /ˈraɪli/ *noun* IDM see LIFE

rill /rɪl/ *noun* a shallow channel cut by water flowing over rock or soil

rim /rɪm/ *noun, verb*
■ ***noun* 1** the edge of sth in the shape of a circle: *He looked at them over the rim of his glass.* ◇ *The rims of her eyes were red with crying.* ◇ *spectacles with gold rims* ➲ picture at EDGE **2** the metal edge of a wheel onto which the tyre is fixed ➲ VISUAL VOCAB page V41 **3 -rimmed** *adj.* having a particular type of rim: *gold-rimmed spectacles* ◇ *red-rimmed eyes* (= for example, from crying) ➲ see also HORN-RIMMED
■ ***verb*** (**-mm-**) [often passive] **~ sth** (*formal*) to form an edge around sth

rime /raɪm/ *noun* [U] (*literary*) FROST

rim·less /ˈrɪmləs/ *adj.* [only before noun] (of glasses) having LENSES (= the transparent parts that you look through) that are not surrounded by frames

rind /raɪnd/ *noun* **1** [U] the thick outer skin of some types of fruit: *lemon rind* ➲ compare PEEL, SKIN, ZEST **2** [U, C] the thick outer skin of some foods such as BACON and some types of cheese

rings

diamond ring

key ring

boxing ring

gas ring (*especially BrE*) / burner

ring¹ ⁰ /rɪŋ/ *noun, verb* ➲ see also RING²
■ ***noun***
▸ JEWELLERY **1** ⁰ [C] a piece of jewellery that you wear on your finger, consisting of a round band of gold, silver, etc, sometimes decorated with PRECIOUS STONES: *a gold ring* ◇ *A diamond glittered on her* ***ring finger*** (= the finger next to the little finger, especially on the left hand). ➲ VISUAL VOCAB page V53 ➲ see also ENGAGEMENT RING, SIGNET RING, WEDDING RING
▸ CIRCLE **2** ⁰ [C] an object in the shape of a circle with a large hole in the middle: *a key ring* ◇ *curtain rings* ◇ *onion rings* ➲ VISUAL VOCAB page V39 **3** ⁰ [C] a round mark or shape: *She had dark rings a round her eyes from lack of sleep.* ◇ *The children sat on the floor in a ring.*
▸ FOR PERFORMANCE/COMPETITION **4** ⁰ [C] a confined area in which animals or people perform or compete, with seats a round the outside for the audience: *a boxing ring* ◇ *a circus ring* ➲ see also BULLRING
▸ FOR COOKING **5** [C] (*especially BrE*) a small flat place on a cooker/stove that is heated by gas or electricity and is used for cooking on SYN **burner**: *to turn off the gas ring*
▸ GROUP OF PEOPLE **6** [C] a group of people who are working together, especially in secret or illegally: *a spy ring* ◇ *a drugs ring*
IDM **run ˈrings a round/round sb** (*informal*) to be much better at doing sth than sb else ➲ more at HAT
■ ***verb*** (**ringed**, **ringed**)
▸ SURROUND **1** [often passive] **~ sb/sth (with sth)** to surround sb/sth: *Thousands of demonstrators ringed the building.*
▸ BIRD'S LEG **2 ~ sth** to put a metal ring a round a bird's leg so that it can be easily identified in the future
▸ DRAW CIRCLE **3 ~ sth** (*especially BrE*) to draw a circle a round sth SYN **circle**: *Ring the correct answer in pencil.*

ring² ⁰ /rɪŋ/ *verb, noun* ➲ see also RING¹
■ ***verb*** (**rang** /ræŋ/, **rung** /rʌŋ/)
▸ TELEPHONE **1** ⁰ (*BrE*) (also **call** *NAmE, BrE*) [T, I] to telephone sb/sth: **~ sb/sth up** *I'll ring you up later.* ◇ *He rang up the police station.* ◇ **~ sb/sth** *When is the best time to ring New York?* ◇ **~ (up)** *David rang up while you were out.* ◇ *He said he was ringing from London.* ◇ *I'm ringing about your advertisement in the paper.* ◇ *She rang to say she'd be late.* ◇ **~ for sth** *Could you ring for a cab?* ➲ note at PHONE **2** ⁰ [I] (of a telephone) to make a sound because sb is trying to telephone you: *Will you answer the telephone if it rings?*
▸ BELL **3** ⁰ [T, I] if you **ring** a bell or if a bell **rings**, it produces a sound: **~ (sth)** *Someone was ringing the doorbell.* ◇ *The church bells rang.* ◇ **~ for sb/sth** *Just ring for the nurse* (= attract the nurse's attention by ringing a bell) *if you need her.*
▸ WITH SOUND **4** [I] **~ (with sth)** (*literary*) to be full of a sound; to fill a place with sound SYN **resound**: *The house rang with children's laughter.* ◇ *Applause rang through the hall.*
▸ WITH QUALITY **5** [I] **~ (with sth)** to be full of a particular quality: *His words rang with pride.*
▸ OF EARS **6** [I] to be uncomfortable and be unable to hear clearly, usually because you have heard a loud noise, etc: *The music was so loud it made my ears ring.*
IDM **ring a ˈbell** (*informal*) to sound familiar to you, as though you have heard it before: *His name rings a bell but I can't think where we met.* **ring the ˈchanges (with sth)** (*BrE*) to make changes to sth in order to have greater variety: *Ring the changes with a new colour.* **ˌring in your ˈears/ˈhead** to make you feel that you can still hear sth: *His warning was still ringing in my ears.* **ˌring off the ˈhook** (usually used in the progressive tenses) (*NAmE*) (of a telephone) to ring many times: *The phone has been ringing off the hook with offers of help.* **ring ˈtrue/ˈhollow/ˈfalse** to give the impression of being sincere/true or not sincere/true: *It may seem a strange story but it rings true to me.* ➲ more at ALARM *n.*
PHR V **ˌring aˈround** = RING ROUND **ˌring ˈback** | **ˌring sb↔ˈback** ⁰ (*BrE*) to telephone sb again, for example because they were not there when you called earlier, or to return a call they made to you: *He isn't here now—could you ring back later?* ◇ *I'll ask Simon to ring you back when he gets in.* **ˌring ˈin** (*BrE*) to telephone a television or radio show, or the place where you work **ˌring ˈin sth** to ring bells to celebrate sth, especially the new year **ˌring ˈoff** (*BrE*) to put down the telephone because you have finished speaking: *He rang off before I could explain.* **ˌring ˈout** to be heard loudly and clearly: *A number of shots rang out.* **ˌring ˈround (sb/sth)** | **ˌring aˈround (sb/sth)** (*BrE*) to telephone a number of people in order to organize sth or to get some information, etc: *I rang round all the travel agents in the area.* **ˌring ˈthrough (to sb)** (*BrE*) to make a telephone call to sb, especially within the same building: *Reception just rang through to say my visitor has arrived.* **ˌring sth↔ˈup** to enter the cost of goods being bought in a shop/store on a CASH REGISTER by pressing the buttons; to make sales of a particular value: *She rang up all the items on the till.* ◇ *The company rang up sales of $166 million last year.*
■ ***noun***
▸ OF BELL **1** ⁰ [C] the sound that a bell makes; the act of ringing a bell: *There was a ring at the door.* ◇ *He gave a couple of loud rings on the doorbell.*
▸ SOUND **2** [sing.] a loud clear sound: *the ring of horse's hooves on the cobblestones*
▸ QUALITY **3** [sing.] **~ (of sth)** a particular quality that words, sounds, etc. have: *His explanation* ***has a ring of truth*** *about it.* ◇ *Her protestation of innocence* ***had a hollow ring to it*** (= did not sound sincere). ◇ *The story had a* ***familiar ring*** *to it* (= as if I had heard it before).
IDM **give sb a ˈring** ⁰ (*BrE, informal*) to make a telephone call to sb: *I'll give you a ring tomorrow.* ➲ note at PHONE ➲ more at BRASS

ring-a-ring o' roses /ˌrɪŋ ə rɪŋ ə ˈrəʊzɪz; *NAmE* ˈroʊzɪz/ (*BrE*) (*NAmE* **ring around the ˈrosy**) *noun* [U] a singing game played by children, in which the players hold hands and dance in a circle, falling down at the end of the song

ring·back /ˈrɪŋbæk/ (also **Callback™**) *noun* [U, C] a telephone service that you can use if you call sb and their telephone is being used, so that your telephone will ring when the line is free; a call made using this service

ˈring bearer *noun* (*NAmE*) a person, usually a boy, who carries the rings for the BRIDE and GROOM at a wedding

ˈring binder *noun* a file for holding papers, in which metal rings go through the edges of the pages, holding them in place ➲ VISUAL VOCAB page V56

ˈring circuit (also **ˈring main**) *noun* (*technical*) an arrangement of wires which supply electricity to several different places in a room or building

ringed /rɪŋd/ *adj.* [only before noun] **1** having a ring or rings on: *a ringed finger* **2** (especially of an animal or bird) having a mark or marks like a ring on it: *a ringed plover*

ringer /ˈrɪŋə(r)/ *noun* **1** = BELL-RINGER **2** (*NAmE*) a horse or person that takes part in a race illegally, for example by using a false name IDM see DEAD *adj.*

ring·ette /rɪŋˈet/ *noun* [U] a Canadian game similar to ICE HOCKEY, played with a straight stick and rubber ring, especially by women

ˈring-fence *verb* (*BrE*) **1** **~ sth** (*finance*) to protect a particular sum of money by putting restrictions on it so that it can only be used for a particular purpose **2** **~ sth** to protect sth by putting restrictions on it so that it can only be used by particular people or for a particular purpose: *All employees can access the parts of the Intranet that are not ring-fenced.* ▸ **ˈring fence** *noun*: *The government has promised to put a ring fence around funding for education.*

ˈring finger *noun* the finger next to the smallest one, especially on the left hand, on which a wedding ring is traditionally worn ➲ VISUAL VOCAB page V48

ring·ing /ˈrɪŋɪŋ/ *adj.*, *noun*

■ ***adj.*** [only before noun] **1** (of a sound) loud and clear **2** (of a statement, etc.) powerful and made with a lot of force: *a ringing endorsement of her leadership*

■ ***noun*** [sing., U] an act or a sound of ringing: *There was an unpleasant ringing in my ears.*

ring·lead·er /ˈrɪŋliːdə(r)/ *noun* (*disapproving*) a person who leads others in crime or in causing trouble

ring·let /ˈrɪŋlət/ *noun* [usually pl.] a long curl of hair hanging down from sb's head ➲ VISUAL VOCAB page V49

ˈring main *noun* (*technical*) **1** an arrangement of cables that allows electricity to be supplied to a series of places from either of two directions **2** = RING CIRCUIT **3** an arrangement of connected pipes that allows water, steam, etc. to enter and leave a system

ring·mas·ter /ˈrɪŋmɑːstə(r); *NAmE* -mæs-/ *noun* a person in charge of a CIRCUS performance

ˈring pull (*BrE*) (*NAmE* **ˈpull tab, tab**) *noun* a small piece of metal with a ring attached which is pulled to open cans of food, drink, etc. ➲ VISUAL VOCAB page V29

ˈring road (*BrE*) (*US* **ˈouter belt**) *noun* a road that is built around a city or town to reduce traffic in the centre

ring·side /ˈrɪŋsaɪd/ *noun* [U] the area closest to the space in which a BOXING match or CIRCUS takes place: *According to law, a doctor must be present at the ringside.* ◇ *a* ***ringside seat***

ring·tone /ˈrɪŋtəʊn; *NAmE* -toʊn/ *noun* the sound a telephone makes when sb is calling you. Ringtones are often short tunes, and the word is especially used to refer to the different sounds mobile phones/cell phones make when they ring.

ring·toss /ˈrɪŋtɒs; *NAmE* -tɔːs; -tɑːs/ (*NAmE*) (*BrE* **hoopla**) *noun* [U] a game in which players try to throw rings over objects in order to win them as prizes

ring·worm /ˈrɪŋwɜːm; *NAmE* -wɜːrm/ *noun* [U] an infectious skin disease that produces small round red areas

rink /rɪŋk/ *noun* **1** = ICE RINK **2** = SKATING RINK

rinky-dink /ˈrɪŋki dɪŋk/ *adj.* (*NAmE, informal*) of poor quality; cheap and/or old-fashioned: *a rinky-dink rhinestone necklace* ◇ *a rinky-dink little town*

rinse /rɪns/ *verb*, *noun*

■ ***verb*** **1** **~ sth** to wash sth with clean water only, not using soap: *Rinse the cooked pasta with boiling water.* **2** **~ sth** to remove the soap from sth with clean water after washing it ➲ SYNONYMS at CLEAN **3** **~ sth + adv./prep.** to remove dirt, etc. from sth by washing it with clean water: *She rinsed the mud from her hands.* ◇ *I wanted to rinse the taste out of my mouth.*

PHR V **ˌrinse sth↔ˈout** to make sth clean, especially a container, by washing it with water: *Rinse the cup out before use.*

■ ***noun*** **1** [C] an act of rinsing sth: *I gave the glass a rinse.* ◇ *Fabric conditioner is added during the final rinse.* **2** [C, U] a liquid that you put on your hair when it is wet in order to change its colour: *a blue rinse* **3** [C, U] a liquid used for cleaning the mouth and teeth

riot /ˈraɪət/ *noun*, *verb*

■ ***noun*** **1** [C] a situation in which a group of people behave in a violent way in a public place, often as a protest: *One prison guard was killed when a riot broke out in the jail.* ◇ ***food/race riots*** **2** [sing.] **~ of sth** (*formal*) a collection of a lot of different types of the same thing: *The garden was a* ***riot of colour.*** **3 a riot** [sing.] (*old-fashioned, informal*) a person or an event that is very amusing and enjoyable

IDM **run ˈriot** **1** (of people) to behave in a way that is violent and/or not under control SYN **rampage**: *They let their kids run riot.* **2** if your imagination, a feeling, etc. **runs riot**, you allow it to develop and continue without trying to control it **3** (of plants) to grow and spread quickly ➲ more at READ *v.*

■ ***verb*** [I] (of a crowd of people) to behave in a violent way in a public place, often as a protest ▸ **riot·er** *noun*: *Rioters set fire to parked cars.* **riot·ing** *noun* [U]: *Rioting broke out in the capital.*

ˈriot gear *noun* [U] the clothes and equipment used by the police when they are dealing with riots

riot·ous /ˈraɪətəs/ *adj.* [usually before noun] **1** (*formal* or *law*) noisy and/or violent, especially in a public place: *riotous behaviour* ◇ *The organizers of the march were charged with assault and* ***riotous assembly.*** **2** noisy, exciting and enjoyable in an uncontrolled way SYN **uproarious**: *a riotous party* ◇ *riotous laughter*

riot·ous·ly /ˈraɪətəsli/ *adv.* extremely: *riotously funny*

ˈriot police *noun* [pl.] police who are trained to deal with people RIOTING

ˈriot shield (also **shield**) *noun* a piece of equipment made from strong plastic, used by the police to protect themselves from angry crowds

RIP **1** (*BrE*) (also **R.I.P.** *US, BrE*) /ˌɑːr aɪ ˈpiː/ *abbr.* rest in peace (often written on graves) **2** *noun* (*computing*) = RASTER IMAGE PROCESSOR

rip /rɪp/ *verb*, *noun*

■ ***verb*** (-pp-) **1** [T, I] to tear sth or to become torn, often suddenly or violently: **~ (sth)** *I ripped my jeans on the fence.* ◇ *The flags had been ripped in two.* ◇ *I heard the tent rip.* ◇ **~ sth + adj.** *She* ***ripped the letter open.*** **2** [T] **~ sth + adv./prep.** to remove sth quickly or violently, often by pulling it: *He ripped off his tie.* ◇ *The carpet had been ripped from the stairs.* **3** [T] **~ sth** (*computing*) to copy sound or video files from a website or CD on to a computer **4** (*computing*) = RASTERIZE

IDM **let ˈrip (at sb)** (*informal*) to speak or do sth with great force, enthusiasm, etc. and without control: *When she gets angry with her boyfriend, she really lets rip at him.* ◇ *The group let rip with a single from their new album.* **let ˈrip | let sth ˈrip** (*informal*) **1** to go or allow sth such as a car to go as fast as possible: *Once on the open road, he let rip.* ◇ *Come on Steve—let her rip.* **2** to do sth or to allow sth to happen as fast as possible: *This would cause inflation to let rip again.* **rip sb/sth aˈpart/to ˈshreds/to ˈbits, etc.** to destroy sth; to criticize sb very strongly ➲ more at HEART, LIMB

PHR V **ˈrip at sth** to attack sth violently, usually by tearing or cutting it **ˌrip ˈinto sb (for/with sth)** to criticize sb and

R

tell them that you are very angry with them ˌ**rip ˈinto/ˈthrough sb/sth** to go very quickly and violently into or through sb/sth: *A bullet ripped into his shoulder.* ˌ**rip sb↔ˈoff** [usually passive] (*informal*) to cheat sb, by making them pay too much, by selling them sth of poor quality, etc: *Tourists complain of being ripped off by local cab drivers.* ➲ related noun RIP-OFF ˌ**rip sth↔ˈoff** (*informal*) to steal sth: *Thieves broke in and ripped off five computers.* ˌ**rip sth↔ˈup** to tear sth into small pieces: *He ripped up the letter and threw it in the fire.*

■ ***noun*** [usually sing.] **1** a long tear in cloth, paper, etc. **2** = RIP CURRENT

ri·par·ian /raɪˈpeəriən; *NAmE* -ˈper-/ *adj.* [usually before noun] **1** (*technical*) growing in, living in, or relating to areas of wet land near to a river or stream **2** (*law*) on, near or relating to the bank of a river

rip·cord /ˈrɪpkɔːd; *NAmE* -kɔːrd/ *noun* the string that you pull to open a PARACHUTE

ˌ**rip ˈcurrent** (also **rip**) *noun* a strong current of water that flows away from the coast

ripe /raɪp/ *adj.* (**riper**, **rip·est**) **1** (of fruit or crops) fully grown and ready to be eaten OPP **unripe** **2** (of cheese or wine) having a flavour that has fully developed SYN **mature** **3** (of a smell) strong and unpleasant **4** ~ (**for sth**) ready or suitable for sth to happen: *This land is ripe for development.* ◇ *The conditions were ripe for social change.* ◇ *Reforms were promised when **the time was ripe**.* ▸ **ripe·ness** *noun* [U]

IDM **a/the ripe old age** (**of**...) an age that is considered to be very old: *He lived to the ripe old age of 91.*

ripen /ˈraɪpən/ *verb* [I, T] ~ (**sth**) to become ripe; to make sth ripe

ˈ**rip-off** *noun* (*informal*) **1** [usually sing.] something that is not worth what you pay for it: *$70 for a T-shirt! What a rip-off!* **2** ~ (**of sth**) a copy of sth, especially one that is less expensive or not as good as the original thing: *The single is a rip-off of a 70s hit.*

ri·poste /rɪˈpɒst; *NAmE* rɪˈpoʊst/ *noun* (*formal*) **1** a quick and clever reply, especially to criticism SYN **retort**: *a witty riposte* **2** a course of action that takes place in response to sth that has happened: *The US delivered an early riposte to the air attack.* ▸ **ri·poste** *verb* + **speech**

rip·per /ˈrɪpə(r)/ *noun* (*informal*) a person who is very good at SNOWBOARDING

rip·ping /ˈrɪpɪŋ/ *adj.* (*BrE, old-fashioned*) wonderful

rip·ple /ˈrɪpl/ *noun, verb*

■ ***noun*** **1** a small wave on the surface of a liquid, especially water in a lake, etc: *The air was so still that there was hardly a ripple on the pond's surface.* **2** a thing that looks or moves like a small wave: *ripples of sand* **3** [usually sing.] ~ **of sth** a sound that gradually becomes louder and then quieter again: *a **ripple of applause/laughter*** **4** [usually sing.] ~ **of sth** a feeling that gradually spreads through a person or group of people: *A ripple of fear passed through him.* ◇ *The announcement sent a ripple of excitement through the crowd.*

■ ***verb*** **1** [I, T] to move or to make sth move in very small waves: *The sea rippled and sparkled.* ◇ *rippling muscles* ◇ ~ **sth** *The wind rippled the wheat in the fields.* **2** [I] + **adv./prep.** (of a feeling, etc.) to spread through a person or a group of people like a wave: *A gasp rippled through the crowd.*

ˈ**ripple effect** *noun* a situation in which an event or action has an effect on sth, which then has an effect on sth else: *His resignation will have a ripple effect on the whole department.*

ˈ**rip-roaring** *adj.* [only before noun] (*informal*) **1** noisy, exciting and/or full of activity: *a rip-roaring celebration* **2** ~ **drunk** extremely drunk **3** ~ **success** a great success

Rip Van Winkle /ˌrɪp væn ˈwɪŋkl/ *noun* a person who is surprised to find how much the world has changed over a period of time ORIGIN From the name of a character in a short story by the US writer Washington Irving. He sleeps for 20 years and wakes up to find that the world has completely changed.

rise 0‑ /raɪz/ *noun, verb*

■ ***noun***

▸ INCREASE **1** 0‑ [C] an increase in an amount, a number or a level: *The industry is feeling the effects of recent price rises.* ◇ ~ **in sth** *There has been a **sharp rise** in the number of people out of work.* ➲ LANGUAGE BANK at INCREASE **2** 0‑ [C] (*BrE*) (*NAmE* **raise**) an increase in the money you are paid for the work you do: *I'm going to ask for a rise.* ◇ *He criticized the huge pay rises awarded to industry bosses.*

▸ IN POWER/IMPORTANCE **3** 0‑ [sing.] ~ (**of sb/sth**) the act of becoming more important, successful, powerful, etc: *the rise of fascism in Europe* ◇ *the **rise and fall** of the British Empire* ◇ *her meteoric **rise to power***

▸ UPWARD MOVEMENT **4** 0‑ [sing.] an upward movement: *She watched the gentle **rise and fall** of his chest as he slept.*

▸ SLOPING LAND **5** [C] an area of land that slopes upwards SYN **slope**: *The church was built at the top of a small rise.* ➲ see also HIGH-RISE

IDM **get a rise out of sb** to make sb react in an angry way by saying sth that you know will annoy them, especially as a joke **give ˈrise to sth** (*formal*) to cause sth to happen or exist: *The novel's success gave rise to a number of sequels.*

■ ***verb*** (**rose** /rəʊz; *NAmE* roʊz/, **risen** /ˈrɪzn/)

▸ MOVE UPWARDS **1** 0‑ [I] (+ **adv./prep.**) to come or go upwards; to reach a higher level or position: *Smoke was rising from the chimney.* ◇ *The river has risen (by) several metres.*

▸ GET UP **2** 0‑ [I] (+ **adv./prep.**) (*formal*) to get up from a lying, sitting or KNEELING position SYN **get up**: *He was accustomed to rising (= getting out of bed) early.* ◇ *They rose from the table.* ◇ *She rose to her feet.* ➲ SYNONYMS at STAND

▸ OF SUN/MOON **3** 0‑ [I] when the sun, moon, etc. **rises**, it appears above the HORIZON: *The sun rises in the east.* OPP **set**

▸ END MEETING **4** [I] (*formal*) (of a group of people) to end a meeting SYN **adjourn**: *The House (= members of the House of Commons) rose at 10 p.m.*

▸ INCREASE **5** 0‑ [I] to increase in amount or number: *rising fuel bills* ◇ *The price of gas rose.* ◇ *Gas **rose in price**.* ◇ *Unemployment rose (by) 3%.* ◇ *Air pollution has risen above an acceptable level.* ➲ LANGUAGE BANK at INCREASE

▸ BECOME POWERFUL/IMPORTANT **6** 0‑ [I] (+ **adv./prep.**) to become more successful, important, powerful, etc: *a rising young politician* ◇ *She **rose to power** in the 70s.* ◇ *He rose to the rank of general.* ◇ *She **rose through the ranks** to become managing director.*

▸ OF SOUND **7** 0‑ [I] if a sound **rises**, it become louder and higher: *Her **voice rose** angrily.*

▸ OF WIND **8** 0‑ [I] if the wind **rises**, it begins to blow more strongly SYN **get up**

▸ OF FEELING **9** 0‑ [I] (*formal*) if a feeling **rises** inside you, it begins and gets stronger: *He felt anger rising inside him.* ◇ *Her **spirits rose** (= she felt happier) at the news.*

▸ OF YOUR COLOUR **10** [I] (*formal*) if your colour **rises**, your face becomes pink or red with embarrassment

▸ OF HAIR **11** [I] if hair **rises**, it stands vertical instead of lying flat: *The hair on the back of my neck rose when I heard the scream.*

▸ FIGHT **12** 0‑ [I] ~ (**up**) (**against sb/sth**) (*formal*) to begin to fight against your ruler or government or against a foreign army SYN **rebel**: *The peasants rose in revolt.* ◇ *He called on the people to rise up against the invaders.* ➲ related noun UPRISING

▸ BECOME VISIBLE **13** [I] (*formal*) to be or become visible above the surroundings: *Mountains rose in the distance.*

▸ OF LAND **14** 0‑ [I] if land **rises**, it slopes upwards: *The ground rose steeply all around.*

▸ OF BEGINNING OF RIVER **15** [I] + **adv./prep.** a river **rises** where it begins to flow: *The Thames rises in the Cotswold hills.*

▸ OF BREAD/CAKES **16** [I] when bread, cakes, etc. **rise**, they swell because of the action of YEAST or BAKING POWDER

▸ OF DEAD PERSON **17** [I] ~ (**from sth**) to come to life again: *to rise from the dead* ◇ (*figurative*) *Can a new party **rise from the ashes** of the old one?*

IDM ˌ**rise and ˈshine** (*old-fashioned*) usually used in orders to tell sb to get out of bed and be active ➲ more at GORGE *n.*, HACKLES, HEIGHT

PHR V **,rise a'bove sth 1** to not be affected or limited by problems, insults, etc: *She had the courage and determination to rise above her physical disability.* **2** to be wise enough or morally good enough not to do sth wrong or not to think the same as other people: *I try to rise above prejudice.* **3** to be of a higher standard than other things of a similar kind: *His work rarely rises above the mediocre.* **'rise to sth 1** to show that you are able to deal with an unexpected situation, problem, etc: *Luckily, my mother* ***rose to the occasion.*** ◇ *He was determined to* ***rise to the challenge.*** **2** to react when sb is deliberately trying to make you angry or get you interested in sth: *I refuse to rise to that sort of comment.* ◇ *As soon as I mentioned money he* ***rose to the bait.***

Which Word?

rise / raise

Verbs

- **Raise** is a verb that must have an object and **rise** is used without an object. When you **raise** something, you lift it to a higher position or increase it: *He raised his head from the pillow.* ◇ *We were forced to raise the price.* When people or things **rise**, they move from a lower to a higher position: *She rose from the chair.* ◇ *The helicopter rose into the air.* **Rise** can also mean 'to increase in number or quantity': *Costs are always rising.*

Nouns

- The noun **rise** means a movement upwards or an increase in an amount or quantity: *a rise in interest rates.* In *BrE* it can also be used to mean an increase in pay: *Should I ask my boss for a rise?* In *NAmE* this is a **raise**: *a three per cent pay raise.* **Rise** can also mean the process of becoming more powerful or important: *his dramatic rise to power.*

riser /'raɪzə(r)/ *noun* **1 early/late ~** a person who usually gets out of bed early/late in the morning **2** (*technical*) the vertical part between two steps in a set of stairs ➲ picture at STAIRCASE ➲ compare TREAD

ris·ible /'rɪzəbl/ *adj.* (*formal, disapproving*) deserving to be laughed at rather than taken seriously **SYN** **ludicrous, ridiculous**

ris·ing /'raɪzɪŋ/ *noun* a situation in which a group of people protest against, and try to get rid of, a government, a leader, etc. **SYN** **revolt, uprising**

,rising 'damp *noun* [U] (*BrE*) a condition in which water comes up from the ground into the walls of a building, causing damage

risk 0→ /rɪsk/ *noun, verb*

■ ***noun* 1** 0→ [C, U] the possibility of sth bad happening at some time in the future; a situation that could be dangerous or have a bad result: **~ (of sth/of doing sth)** *Smoking can increase the risk of developing heart disease.* ◇ *Patients should be made aware of the risks involved with this treatment.* ◇ **~ (that...)** *There is still a risk that the whole deal will fall through.* ◇ **~ (to sb/sth)** *The chemicals* ***pose little risk*** (= are not dangerous) *to human health.* ◇ *a* ***calculated risk*** (= one that you think is small compared with the possible benefits) ◇ *Any business venture contains an* ***element of risk.*** ◇ *We could probably trust her with the information but it's just not* ***worth the risk.*** **2** 0→ [C] **~ (to sth)** a person or thing that is likely to cause problems or danger at some time in the future: *The group was considered to be a risk to national security.* ◇ *a major* ***health/fire risk*** **3** [C] **a good/bad/poor ~** a person or business that a bank or an insurance company is willing/unwilling to lend money or sell insurance to because they are likely/unlikely to pay back the money etc: *With five previous claims, he's now a bad insurance risk.*

IDM **at 'risk (from/of sth)** 0→ in danger of sth unpleasant or harmful happening: *As with all diseases, certain groups will be more at risk than others.* ◇ *If we go to war, innocent lives will be* ***put at risk.*** **at the 'risk of doing sth** used to introduce sth that may sound stupid or may offend sb: *At the risk of showing my ignorance, how exactly does the Internet work?* **at risk to yourself/sb/sth** with the possibility of harming yourself/sb/sth: *He dived in to save the dog at considerable risk to his own life.* **do sth at your ,own 'risk** to do sth even though you have been warned about the possible dangers and will have to take responsibility for anything bad that happens: *Persons swimming beyond this point do so at their own risk* (= on a notice). ◇ *Valuables are left at their owner's risk* (= on a notice). **run a 'risk (of sth/of doing sth)** to be in a situation in which sth bad could happen to you: *People who are overweight run a risk of a heart attack or stroke.* **run the 'risk (of sth/of doing sth) | run 'risks** 0→ to be or put yourself in a situation in which sth bad could happen to you: *We don't want to run the risk of losing their business.* ◇ *Investment is all about running risks.* **take a 'risk | take 'risks** 0→ to do sth even though you know that sth bad could happen as a result: *That's a risk I'm not prepared to take.* ◇ *You have no right to take risks with other people's lives.*

■ ***verb* 1** 0→ **~ sth** to put sth valuable or important in a dangerous situation, in which it could be lost or damaged: *He risked his life to save her.* ◇ *She was risking her own and her children's health.* ◇ *He risked all his money on a game of cards.* **2** 0→ to do sth that may mean that you get into a situation which is unpleasant for you: **~ sth** *There was no choice. If they stayed there, they risked death.* ◇ **~ (sb/sth) doing sth** *They knew they risked being arrested.* **3** 0→ to do sth that you know is not really a good idea or may not succeed: **~ sth** *He risked a glance at her furious face.* ◇ *It was a difficult decision but we decided to* ***risk it.*** ◇ **~ doing sth** *We've been advised not to risk travelling in these conditions.*

IDM **risk ,life and 'limb | risk your 'neck** to risk being killed or injured in order to do sth

'risk assessment *noun* [C, U] (*business*) the act of identifying possible risks, calculating how likely they are to happen and estimating what effects they might have, especially in the context of a company taking responsibility for the safety of its employees or members of the public: *The employer has an obligation to carry out a risk assessment.*

'risk-averse *adj.* not willing to do sth if it is possible that sth bad could happen as a result: *We live in a risk-averse culture.* ◇ *In business you cannot be innovative and risk-averse at the same time.*

'risk-taking *noun* [U] the practice of doing things that involve risks in order to achieve sth

risky /'rɪski/ *adj.* (**risk·ier, riski·est**) **HELP** You can also use **more risky** and **most risky**.) involving the possibility of sth bad happening **SYN** **dangerous:** *Life as an aid worker can be a* ***risky business*** (= dangerous). ◇ *a risky investment* ◇ *It's far too risky to generalize from one set of results.* ▶ **risk·ily** /-ɪli/ *adv.* **riski·ness** /-ɪnəs/ *noun* [U]

ris·otto /rɪ'zɒtəʊ; *NAmE* rɪ'sɔːtoʊ; -'zɔː-/ *noun* (*pl.* **-os**) [C, U] an Italian dish of rice cooked with vegetables, meat, etc.

ris·qué /'rɪskeɪ; *NAmE* rɪ'skeɪ/ *adj.* a **risqué** performance, comment, joke, etc. is a little shocking, usually because it is about sex

ris·sole /'rɪsəʊl; *NAmE* -soʊl/ *noun* a small flat mass or ball of chopped meat that is fried. It is sometimes covered with BREADCRUMBS or, in the US, with PASTRY before it is cooked.

Rit·alin™ /'rɪtəlɪn/ *noun* a drug given to children who cannot keep quiet or still, to help them become calmer and concentrate better

rite /raɪt/ *noun* a ceremony performed by a particular group of people, often for religious purposes: *funeral rites* ◇ *initiation rites* (= performed when a new member joins a secret society) ➲ COLLOCATIONS at RELIGION ➲ see also THE LAST RITES

R

ˌ**rite of 'passage** *noun* a ceremony or an event that marks an important stage in sb's life

rit·ual /'rɪtʃuəl/ *noun, adj.*
- ***noun*** [C, U] **1** a series of actions that are always performed in the same way, especially as part of a religious ceremony: *religious rituals* ◇ *She objects to the ritual of organized religion.* ➲ COLLOCATIONS at RELIGION **2** something that is done regularly and always in the same way: *Sunday lunch with the in-laws has become something of a ritual.*
- ***adj.*** [only before noun] **1** done as part of a ritual or ceremony: *ritual chanting* **2** always done or said in the same way, especially when this is not sincere: *ritual expressions of sympathy* ▸ **ritu·al·ly** *adv.*: *The goat was ritually slaughtered.*

ritu·al·is·tic /ˌrɪtʃuə'lɪstɪk/ *adj.* [usually before noun] **1** connected with the rituals performed as part of a ceremony: *a ritualistic act of worship* **2** always done or said in the same way, especially when this is not sincere

ritu·al·ize (*BrE* also **-ise**) /'rɪtʃuəlaɪz/ *verb* [usually passive] **~ sth** (*formal*) to do sth in the same way or pattern every time: *ritualized expressions of grief*

ritzy /'rɪtsi/ *adj.* (*informal*) expensive and fashionable ORIGIN From the **Ritz**, the name of several very comfortable and expensive hotels in London and other cities.

rival 🔑 /'raɪvl/ *noun, adj., verb*
- ***noun*** 🔑 **~ (to sb/sth)** (**for sth**) a person, company, or thing that competes with another in sport, business, etc: *The two teams have always been rivals.* ◇ *The Japanese are our biggest economic rivals.* ◇ *This latest design* **has no rivals** (= it is easily the best design available). ▸ **rival** 🔑 *adj.* [only before noun]: *a* ***rival bid/claim/offer*** ◇ *fighting between rival groups* ◇ *He was shot by a member of a rival gang.*
- ***verb*** (-ll-, *NAmE* also -l-) **~ sb/sth** (**for/in sth**) to be as good, impressive, etc. as sb/sth else SYN **compare with**: *You will find scenery to rival anything you can see in the Alps.* ➲ see also UNRIVALLED

ri·val·ry /'raɪvlri/ *noun* [C, U] (*pl.* **-ries**) a state in which two people, companies, etc. are competing for the same thing: **~ (with sb/sth)** (**for sth**) *a fierce rivalry for world supremacy* ◇ **~ (between A and B)** (**for sth**) *There is a certain amount of friendly rivalry between the teams.* ◇ *political rivalries* ◇ *sibling rivalry* (= between brothers and sisters)

riven /'rɪvn/ *adj.* [not before noun] **~ (by/with sth)** (*formal*) **1** (of a group of people) divided because of disagreements, especially in a violent way: *a party riven by internal disputes* **2** (of an object) divided into two or more pieces

R

river 🔑 /'rɪvə(r)/ *noun*
1 🔑 (*abbr.* R.) a natural flow of water that continues in a long line across land to the sea/ocean: *the River Thames* ◇ *the Hudson River* ◇ *on the banks of the river* (= the ground at the side of a river) ◇ *to travel* ***up/down river*** (= in the opposite direction to/in the same direction as the way in which the river is flowing) ◇ *the mouth of the river* (= where it enters the sea/ocean) ◇ *Can we swim* ***in the river?*** ◇ *a boat on the river* ◇ *They have a house on the river* (= beside it). ➲ VISUAL VOCAB pages V3, V4 **2 ~** (**of sth**) a large amount of liquid that is flowing in a particular direction: *Rivers of molten lava flowed down the mountain.* IDM see SELL *v.*

river·bank /'rɪvəbæŋk; *NAmE* 'rɪvər-/ *noun* the ground at the side of a river: *on the riverbank* ➲ VISUAL VOCAB page V3

'**river bed** *noun* the area of ground over which a river usually flows: *a dried-up river bed*

'**river blindness** *noun* [U] (*medical*) a tropical skin disease caused by a PARASITE of certain flies that breed in rivers, which can also cause a person to become blind

river·front /'rɪvəfrʌnt; *NAmE* -vərf-/ *noun* (*especially NAmE*) an area of land next to a river with buildings, shops/stores, restaurants, etc. on it

river·ine /'rɪvəraɪn/ *adj.* [usually before noun] (*technical*) on, near, or relating to a river or the banks of a river

river·side /'rɪvəsaɪd; *NAmE* -vərs-/ *noun* [sing.] the ground along either side of a river: *a riverside path* ◇ *a walk by the riverside*

rivet /'rɪvɪt/ *noun, verb*
- ***noun*** a metal pin that is used to fasten two pieces of leather, metal, etc. together
- ***verb*** [usually passive] **1 ~ sb/sth** to hold sb's interest or attention so completely that they cannot look away or think of anything else: *I was absolutely riveted by her story.* ◇ *My eyes* ***were riveted on*** *the figure lying in the road.* **2 ~ sth** to fasten sth with rivets: *The steel plates were riveted together.*

IDM **be riveted to the spot/ground** to be so shocked or frightened that you cannot move

rivet·ing /'rɪvɪtɪŋ/ *adj.* (*approving*) so interesting or exciting that it holds your attention completely SYN **engrossing**

rivi·era /ˌrɪvi'eərə; *NAmE* -'erə/ *noun* (often **Riviera**) an area by the sea that is warm and popular for holidays, especially the Mediterranean coast of France: *the French Riviera*

rivu·let /'rɪvjələt/ *noun* (*formal*) a very small river; a small stream of water or other liquid

RM /ˌɑːr 'em/ *abbr.* (in Britain) Royal Marine ➲ see also MARINE

RN /ˌɑːr 'en/ *abbr.* **1** REGISTERED NURSE **2** (in Britain) Royal Navy

RNA /ˌɑːr en 'eɪ/ *noun* [U] (*chemistry*) a chemical present in all living cells; like DNA it is a type of NUCLEIC ACID

roach /rəʊtʃ; *NAmE* roʊtʃ/ *noun* **1** (*NAmE, informal*) = COCKROACH: *The apartments were infested with rats and roaches.* **2** (*pl.* **roach**) a small European FRESHWATER fish **3** (*slang*) the end part of a cigarette containing MARIJUANA

More About

roads

Roads and streets

- In a town or city, **street** is the most general word for a road with houses and buildings on one or both sides: *a street map of London.* **Street** is not used for roads between towns, but streets in towns are often called **Road**: *Oxford Street* ◇ *Mile End Road.* A **road map** of a country shows you the major routes between, around and through towns and cities.
- Other words used in the names of streets include: **Circle**, **Court**, **Crescent**, **Drive**, **Hill** and **Way**. **Avenue** suggests a wide street lined with trees. A **lane** is a narrow street between buildings or, in *BrE*, a narrow country road.

The high street

- **High street** is used in *BrE*, especially as a name, for the main street of a town, where most shops, banks, etc. are: *the record store in the High Street* ◇ *high street shops.* In *NAmE* **Main Street** is often used as a name for this street.

Larger roads

- British and American English use different words for the roads that connect towns and cities. **Motorways**, (for example, the M57) in *BrE*, **freeways**, **highways** or **interstates**, (for example State Route 347, Interstate 94, the Long Island Expressway) in *NAmE*, are large divided roads built for long-distance traffic to avoid towns.
- A **ring road** (*BrE*) / an **outer belt** (*NAmE*) is built around a city or town to reduce traffic in the centre. This can also be called a **beltway** in *NAmE*, especially when it refers to the road around Washington D.C. A **bypass** passes around a town or city rather than through the centre.

road 🔑 /rəʊd; *NAmE* roʊd/ *noun*
1 🔑 a hard surface built for vehicles to travel on: *a **main/major/minor road** ◇ a **country/mountain road** ◇ They live just **along/up/down the road*** (= further on the same road). ◇ *The house is on a very busy road.* ◇ *He was walking **along the road** when he was attacked.* ◇ *It takes about five hours **by road*** (= driving). ◇ *It would be better to transport the goods by rail rather than **by road**.* ◇ *Take the first road on the left and then follow the signs.* ◇ *We parked on a **side road**.* ◇ ***road accidents/safety/users*** **2** 🔑 **Road** (*abbr.* **Rd**) used in names of roads, especially in towns: *35 York Road* **3** the way to achieving sth: *to be **on the road to** recovery* ◇ *We have discussed privatization, but we would prefer not to **go down that** particular **road**.*
IDM **ˈany road** (*NEngE*) = ANYWAY **(further) along/down the ˈroad** at some time in the future: *There are certain to be more job losses further down the road.* **one for the ˈroad** (*informal*) a last alcoholic drink before you leave a party, etc. **on the ˈroad 1** travelling, especially for long distances or periods of time: *The band has been on the road for six months.* **2** (of a car) in good condition so that it can be legally driven: *It will cost about £500 to get the car back on the road.* **3** moving from place to place, and having no permanent home: *Life on the road can be very hard.* **the road to ˌhell is paved with good inˈtentions** (*saying*) it is not enough to intend to do good things; you must actually do them ➲ more at END *n.*, FURTHER *adv.*, HIT *v.*, RUBBER, SHOW *n.*

road·block /ˈrəʊdblɒk; *NAmE* ˈroʊdblɑːk/ *noun* **1** a barrier put across the road by the police or army so that they can stop and search vehicles **2** (*NAmE*) something that stops a plan from going ahead

ˈroad fund licence (also **ˈtax disc**) *noun* (in Britain) a small circle of paper that is put on the window of a vehicle or on a motorcycle to show that the owner has paid the tax that allows them to use the vehicle on public roads

ˈroad hog *noun* (*informal, disapproving*) a person who drives in a dangerous way without thinking about the safety of other road users

road·hold·ing /ˈrəʊdhəʊldɪŋ; *NAmE* ˈroʊdhoʊldɪŋ/ *noun* [U] the ability of a car to remain steady when it goes around a corner at a fast speed

road·house /ˈrəʊdhaʊs; *NAmE* ˈroʊd-/ *noun* (*old-fashioned, NAmE*) a restaurant or bar on a main road in the country

roadie /ˈrəʊdi; *NAmE* ˈroʊdi/ *noun* (*informal*) a person who works with a band of musicians on tour, and helps move and set up their equipment

road·kill /ˈrəʊdkɪl; *NAmE* ˈroʊd-/ *noun* **1** [U] an animal, or animals, that have been killed by a car on the road **2** [C, U] the killing of an animal by a car hitting it on the road

ˈroad map *noun* **1** a map that shows the roads of an area, especially one that is designed for a person who is driving a car **2** a set of instructions or suggestions about how to do sth or find out about sth

ˈroad movie *noun* a film/movie which is based on a journey made by the main character or characters

ˈroad pricing *noun* [U] the system of making drivers pay to use busy roads at certain times

ˈroad rage *noun* [U] a situation in which a driver becomes extremely angry or violent with the driver of another car because of the way they are driving

road·run·ner /ˈrəʊdrʌnə(r); *NAmE* ˈroʊd-/ *noun* a N American bird of the CUCKOO family, that lives in desert areas and can run very fast

ˈroad sense *noun* [U] the ability to behave in a safe way when driving, walking, etc. on roads

road·show /ˈrəʊdʃəʊ; *NAmE* ˈroʊdʃoʊ/ *noun* a travelling show arranged by a radio or television programme, or by a magazine, company or political party

road·side /ˈrəʊdsaɪd; *NAmE* ˈroʊd-/ *noun* [sing.] the edge of the road: *We parked by the roadside.* ◇ *a roadside cafe*

ˈroad sign *noun* a sign near a road giving information or instructions to drivers ➲ VISUAL VOCAB page V3

road·ster /ˈrəʊdstə(r); *NAmE* ˈroʊd-/ *noun* (*old-fashioned*) a car with no roof and two seats

ˈroad tax *noun* [U] (in Britain) a tax that sb who owns a car must pay to drive on the roads

ˈroad test *noun* **1** a test to see how a vehicle functions or what condition it is in **2** (*NAmE*) = DRIVING TEST

ˈroad-test *verb* **~ sth** to test a vehicle to see how it functions or what condition it is in

ˈroad train *noun* (*especially AustralE*) a large lorry/truck pulling one or more TRAILERS

ˈroad trip *noun* (*informal, especially NAmE*) a trip made in a car over a long distance

road·way /ˈrəʊdweɪ; *NAmE* ˈroʊd-/ *noun* [C, U] a road or the part of a road used by vehicles

road·works /ˈrəʊdwɜːks; *NAmE* ˈroʊdwɜːrks/ *noun* [pl.] (*BrE*) (*NAmE* **road·work** [U]) repairs that are being done to the road; an area where these repairs are being done

road·worthy /ˈrəʊdwɜːði; *NAmE* ˈroʊdwɜːrði/ *adj.* (of a vehicle) in a safe condition to drive ▸ **road·worthi·ness** *noun* [U]

roam /rəʊm; *NAmE* roʊm/ *verb* **1** [I, T] to walk or travel around an area without any definite aim or direction **SYN** **wander**: (+ **adv./prep.**) *The sheep are allowed to roam freely on this land.* ◇ **~ sth** *to **roam the countryside/the streets, etc.*** **2** [I, T] (of the eyes or hands) to move slowly over every part of sb/sth: **~ (over sth/sb)** *His gaze roamed over her.* ◇ **~ sth/sb** *Her eyes roamed the room.*

roam·ing /ˈrəʊmɪŋ; *NAmE* ˈroʊ-/ *noun* [U] using a mobile/cell phone by connecting to a different company's network, for example when you are in a different country: *international roaming charges*

roan /rəʊn; *NAmE* roʊn/ *noun* an animal, especially a horse, that has hair of two colours mixed together: *a strawberry roan* (= with a mixture of brown and grey hair that looks pink) ▸ **roan** *adj.* [only before noun]

roar /rɔː(r)/ *verb, noun*
■ ***verb* 1** [I] to make a very loud, deep sound: *We heard a lion roar.* ◇ *The gun roared deafeningly.* ◇ *The engine **roared to life*** (= started noisily). **2** [I, T] to shout sth very loudly: *The crowd roared.* ◇ **~ sth (out)** *The fans roared (out) their approval.* ◇ **+ speech** *'Stand back,' he roared.* **3** [I] to laugh very loudly: *He looked so funny, we all roared.* ◇ **~ with laughter** *It made them roar with laughter.* **4** [I] **+ adv./prep.** (of a vehicle or its rider/driver) to move very fast, making a lot of noise: *She put her foot down and the car roared away.* **5** [I] (of a fire) to burn brightly with a lot of flames, heat and noise **IDM** see VICTORY *n.*
■ ***noun* 1** a loud deep sound made by an animal, especially a LION, or by sb's voice: *His speech was greeted by a roar of applause.* ◇ *roars of laughter* **2** a loud continuous noise made by the wind or sea, or by a machine: *I could barely hear above the roar of traffic.*

roar·ing /ˈrɔːrɪŋ/ *adj.* [only before noun] **1** making a continuous loud deep noise: *All we could hear was the sound of roaring water.* **2** (of a fire) burning with a lot of flames and heat
IDM **do a ˈroaring trade (in sth)** (*informal*) to sell a lot of sth very quickly **ˌroaring ˈdrunk** extremely drunk and noisy **a ˌroaring sucˈcess** (*informal*) a very great success

the ˌroaring ˈforties *noun* [pl.] an area of rough ocean between LATITUDES 40° and 50° south

the ˌroaring ˈtwenties *noun* [pl.] the years from 1920 to 1929, considered as a time when people were confident and cheerful

roast /rəʊst; *NAmE* roʊst/ *verb, noun, adj.*
■ ***verb* 1** [T, I] **~ (sth)** to cook food, especially meat, without liquid in an oven or over a fire; to be cooked in this way: *to roast a chicken* ◇ *the smell of roasting meat* ➲ COLLOCATIONS at COOKING **2** [T, I] **~ (sth)** to cook nuts, BEANS, etc. in order to dry them and turn them brown; to be cooked in this way: *roasted chestnuts* **3** [T] **~ sb** (*informal* or *humorous*) to be very angry with sb; to criticize sb strongly **4** [I, T] **~ (sth)** (*informal*) to become or to make sth become very

hot in the sun or by a fire: *She could feel her skin beginning to roast.*

■ ***noun*** **1** (*BrE* also **joint**) a large piece of meat that is cooked whole in the oven: *the Sunday roast* **2** (*NAmE*) (often in compounds) a party that takes place in sb's garden/yard at which food is cooked over an open fire: *a hot dog roast* **3** (*NAmE*) an event, especially a meal, at which people celebrate sb's life by telling funny stories about them

■ ***adj.*** [only before noun] cooked in an oven or over a fire: *roast chicken*

roast·ing /'rəʊstɪŋ; *NAmE* 'roʊ-/ *adj., noun*

■ ***adj.*** **1** [only before noun] used for roasting meat, vegetables, etc: *a roasting dish* **2** (also ˌ**roasting 'hot**) so hot that you feel uncomfortable: *a roasting hot day*

■ ***noun*** [U, sing.] (*slang*) an occasion when a woman has sex with more than one man

IDM **give sb/get a 'roasting** to criticize sb or be criticized in an angry way

rob 0-w /rɒb; *NAmE* rɑːb/ *verb* (-bb-) **~ sb/sth (of sth)** to steal money or property from a person or place: *to* ***rob a bank*** ◇ *The tomb had been robbed of its treasures.* ➲ COLLOCATIONS at CRIME

IDM ˌ**rob sb 'blind** (*informal*) to cheat or trick sb so that they lose a lot of money ˌ**rob the 'cradle** (*NAmE, informal*) to have a sexual relationship with a much younger person **rob ˌPeter to pay 'Paul** (*saying*) to borrow money from one person to pay back what you owe to another person; to take money from one thing to use for sth else

PHR V **'rob sb/sth of sth** [often passive] to prevent sb having sth that they need or deserve SYN **deprive**: *A last-minute goal robbed the team of victory.* ◇ *He had been robbed of his dignity.*

rob·ber /'rɒbə(r); *NAmE* 'rɑːb-/ *noun* a person who steals from a person or place, especially using violence or threats: *a bank robber*

rob·bery /'rɒbəri; *NAmE* 'rɑːb-/ *noun* [U, C] (*pl.* -ies) the crime of stealing money or goods from a bank, shop/store, person, etc, especially using violence or threats: *armed robbery* (= using a gun, knife, etc.) ◇ *There has been a spate of robberies in the area recently.* ➲ COLLOCATIONS at CRIME ➲ compare BURGLARY, THEFT IDM see DAYLIGHT, HIGHWAY

robe /rəʊb; *NAmE* roʊb/ *noun, verb*

■ ***noun*** **1** a long loose outer piece of clothing, especially one worn as a sign of rank or office at a special ceremony: *coronation robes* ◇ *cardinals in scarlet robes* **2** = BATHROBE

■ ***verb*** [usually passive] **~ sb/yourself (in sth)** (*formal*) to dress sb/yourself in long loose clothes or in the way mentioned: *a robed choir* ◇ *The priests were robed in black.*

robin /'rɒbɪn; *NAmE* 'rɑːb-/ *noun* **1** a small brown European bird with a red breast **2** a grey American bird with a red breast, larger than a European robin ➲ see also ROUND ROBIN

ˌ**Robin 'Hood** *noun* a person who takes or steals money from rich people and gives it to poor people ORIGIN From the name of a character in traditional English stories who lived in a forest, robbing rich people and giving money to poor people.

robo·call /'rəʊbəʊkɔːl; *NAmE* 'roʊboʊ-/ *noun* (*NAmE, informal, disapproving*) a phone call from a company that is trying to sell you sth, using an automatic DIALLING system to call your number and a recorded message

robot /'rəʊbɒt; *NAmE* 'roʊbɑːt/ *noun* **1** a machine that can perform a complicated series of tasks automatically: *These cars are built by robots.* **2** (especially in stories) a machine that is made to look like a human and that can do some things that a human can do **3** (*SAfrE*) a TRAFFIC LIGHT: *Turn left at the first robot.*

ro·bot·ic /rəʊ'bɒtɪk; *NAmE* roʊ'bɑːtɪk/ *adj.* **1** connected with robots: *a robotic arm* **2** like a robot, making stiff movements, speaking without feeling or expression, etc.

ro·bot·ics /rəʊ'bɒtɪks; *NAmE* roʊ'bɑːt-/ *noun* [U] the science of designing and operating ROBOTS

ro·bust /rəʊ'bʌst; *NAmE* roʊ-/ *adj.* **1** strong and healthy: *She was almost 90, but still very robust.* **2** strong; able to survive being used a lot and not likely to break SYN **sturdy**: *a robust piece of equipment* **3** (of a system or an organization) strong and not likely to fail or become weak: *robust economic growth* **4** strong and full of determination; showing that you are sure about what you are doing or saying SYN **vigorous**: *It was a typically robust performance by the Foreign Secretary.* ▸ **ro·bust·ly** *adv.*: *The furniture was robustly constructed.* ◇ *They defended their policies robustly.* **ro·bust·ness** *noun* [U]

rock 0-w /rɒk; *NAmE* rɑːk/ *noun, verb*

■ ***noun***

▸ HARD MATERIAL **1** 0-w [U, C] the hard solid material that forms part of the surface of the earth and some other planets: *They drilled through several layers of rock to reach the oil.* ◇ *a cave with striking* ***rock formations*** (= shapes made naturally from rock) ◇ *The tunnel was blasted out of solid rock.* ◇ ***volcanic/igneous/sedimentary, etc. rocks*** **2** 0-w [C] a mass of rock standing above the earth's surface or in the sea/ocean: *the Rock of Gibraltar* ◇ *The ship crashed into the infamous Sker Point rocks and broke into three pieces.* ➲ VISUAL VOCAB page V5 **3** 0-w [C] a large single piece of rock: *They clambered over the rocks at the foot of the cliff.* ◇ *The sign said 'Danger: falling rocks'.*

▸ STONE **4** 0-w [C] (*NAmE*) a small stone: *Protesters pelted the soldiers with rocks.*

▸ MUSIC **5** 0-w (also **'rock music**) [U] a type of loud popular music, developed in the 1960s, with a strong beat played on electric GUITARS and drums: *punk rock* ◇ *a* ***rock band/star***

▸ SWEET/CANDY **6** (*BrE*) [U] a type of hard sweet/candy made in long sticks, often sold in places where people go on holiday/vacation by the sea/ocean: *a stick of Brighton rock*

▸ JEWEL **7** [C, usually pl.] (*NAmE, informal*) a PRECIOUS STONE, especially a diamond

▸ PERSON **8** [C, usually sing.] a person who is emotionally strong and who you can rely on: *He is my rock.*

IDM **(caught/stuck) between a ˌrock and a 'hard place** in a situation where you have to choose between two things, both of which are unpleasant **get your 'rocks off** (*slang*) **1** to have an ORGASM **2** to do sth that you really enjoy **on the 'rocks 1** a relationship or business that is **on the rocks** is having difficulties and is likely to fail soon: *Sue's marriage is on the rocks.* **2** (of drinks) served with pieces of ice but no water: *Scotch on the rocks* ➲ more at STEADY *adj.*

■ ***verb***

▸ MOVE GENTLY **1** [I, T] to move gently backwards and forwards or from side to side; to make sb/sth move in this way: (**+ adv./prep.**) *The boat* ***rocked from side to side*** *in the waves.* ◇ *She was* ***rocking backwards and forwards*** *in her seat.* ◇ **~ sb/sth (+ adv./prep.)** *He rocked the baby gently in his arms.*

▸ SHOCK **2** [T, often passive] **~ sb/sth** (rather *informal*) to shock sb/sth very much or make them afraid: *The country was rocked by a series of political scandals.* ◇ *The news rocked the world.*

▸ SHAKE **3** [I, T] to shake or to make sth shake violently: *The house rocked when the bomb exploded.* ◇ **~ sth** *The town was rocked by an earthquake.* ◇ (*figurative*) *The scandal rocked the government* (= made the situation difficult for it).

▸ DANCE **5** [I] (*old-fashioned*) to dance to rock music

▸ BE GOOD **5 sth rocks** [I] (*slang*) used to say that sth is very good: *Her new movie rocks!*

IDM **rock the 'boat** (*informal*) to do sth that upsets a situation and causes problems: *She was told to keep her mouth shut and not rock the boat.* ➲ more at FOUNDATION

rocka·billy /'rɒkəbɪli; *NAmE* 'rɑːk-/ *noun* [U] a type of American music that combines ROCK AND ROLL and country music

ˌ**rock and 'roll** (also ˌ**rock 'n' 'roll**) *noun* [U] a type of music popular in the 1950s with a strong beat and simple tunes

ˌ**rock 'bottom** *noun* [U] (*informal*) the lowest point or level that is possible: *Prices hit rock bottom.* ◇ *The marriage* *had reached rock bottom.* ▸ ˌ**rock-ˈbottom** *adj.*: *rock-bottom prices*

ˈ**rock cake** *noun* (*BrE*) a small cake that has a hard rough surface and contains dried fruit

ˌ**rock ˈcandy** *noun* [U] (*NAmE*) a type of hard sweet/candy made from sugar that is melted then allowed to form CRYSTALS

ˈ**rock climbing** *noun* [U] the sport or activity of climbing steep rock surfaces: *to go rock climbing*

ˈ**rock crystal** *noun* [U] a pure clear form of QUARTZ (= a hard mineral)

rock·er /ˈrɒkə(r); *NAmE* ˈrɑːk-/ *noun* **1** one of the two curved pieces of wood on the bottom of a rocking chair **2** (*especially NAmE*) = ROCKING CHAIR **3 Rocker** (*BrE*) a member of a group of young people in Britain, especially in the 1960s, who liked to wear leather jackets, ride motorcycles and listen to ROCK AND ROLL music ➲ compare MOD **4** a person who performs, dances to or enjoys rock music

IDM **be ˌoff your ˈrocker** (*informal*) to be crazy

ˈ**rocker switch** *noun* (*technical*) a type of electrical switch often used, for example, for lights or electrical SOCKETS, where you press one end down to switch it on, and the other end down to switch it off again

rock·ery /ˈrɒkəri; *NAmE* ˈrɑːk-/ *noun* (*pl.* -ies) (also ˈ**rock garden**) a garden or part of a garden consisting of an arrangement of large stones with plants growing among them

rocket /ˈrɒkɪt; *NAmE* ˈrɑːkɪt/ *noun, verb*

■ ***noun* 1** [C] a SPACECRAFT in the shape of a tube that is driven by a stream of gases let out behind it when fuel is burned inside: *a **space rocket** ◇ The **rocket was launched** in 2007. ◇ The idea **took off like a rocket*** (= it immediately became popular). **2** [C] a MISSILE (= a weapon that travels through the air) that carries a bomb and is driven by a stream of burning gases: *a rocket attack* **3** [C] a FIREWORK that goes high into the air and then explodes with coloured lights **4** [U] (*BrE*) (*NAmE* **aru·gula**) a plant with long green leaves that have a strong flavour and are eaten raw in salads

IDM **to give sb a ˈrocket | to get a ˈrocket** (*BrE, informal*) to speak angrily to sb because they have done sth wrong; to be spoken to angrily for this reason

■ ***verb* 1** [I] (+ **adv./prep.**) to increase very quickly and suddenly SYN **shoot up**: *rocketing prices ◇ Unemployment has rocketed up again. ◇ The total has rocketed from 376 to 532.* **2** [I] + **adv./prep.** to move very fast: *The car rocketed out of a side street.* **3** to achieve or to make sb/sth achieve a successful position very quickly: [I, T] **~ (sb/sth) to sth** *The band **rocketed to stardom** with their first single.* **4** [T] **~ sth** to attack a place with rockets

ˈ**rocket-fuelled** (*US* ˈ**rocket-fueled**) *adj.* [only before noun] happening, moving or increasing very fast: *There are already signs of rocket-fuelled growth.*

rock·et·ry /ˈrɒkɪtri; *NAmE* ˈrɑːk-/ *noun* [U] the area of science which deals with ROCKETS and with sending rockets into space; the use of rockets

ˈ**rocket science** *noun* [U]

IDM **it's not ˈrocket science** (*informal*) used to emphasize that sth is easy to do or understand SYN **brain surgery**: *Go on, you can do it. It's not exactly rocket science, is it?*

ˈ**rock face** *noun* a vertical surface of rock, especially on a mountain

rock·fall /ˈrɒkfɔːl; *NAmE* ˈrɑːk-/ *noun* the fact of rocks falling down; a pile of rocks that have fallen

ˈ**rock garden** *noun* = ROCKERY

ˌ**rock-ˈhard** *adj.* extremely hard or strong

ˈ**rocking chair** (also **rock·er** especially in *NAmE*) *noun* a chair with two curved pieces of wood under it that make it move backwards and forwards ➲ VISUAL VOCAB page V18

ˈ**rocking horse** *noun* a wooden horse for children that can be made to ROCK backwards and forwards ➲ VISUAL VOCAB page V32

ˈ**rock music** *noun* = ROCK

rock 'n' roll *noun* = ROCK AND ROLL

the Rock of Gibraltar /ˌrɒk əv dʒɪˈbrɔːltə(r); *NAmE* ˌrɑːk/ *noun* [sing.] a high CLIFF in southern Spain, at the south-western edge of the Mediterranean Sea, near the town and port of Gibraltar. When people say that sth is like the Rock of Gibraltar, they mean it is very safe or solid: *When I invested my money with the company I was told it was as safe as the Rock of Gibraltar.*

ˈ**rock pool** (*BrE*) (*NAmE* ˈ**tide pool**) *noun* a small amount of water that collects between the rocks by the sea/ocean ➲ VISUAL VOCAB page V5

ˈ**rock salt** *noun* [U] a kind of salt that comes from the ground

ˌ**rock ˈsolid** *adj.* **1** that you can trust not to change or to disappear: *The support for the party was rock solid.* **2** extremely hard and not likely to break

rocky /ˈrɒki; *NAmE* ˈrɑːki/ *adj.* (**rock·ier, rocki·est**) **1** made of rock; full of rocks: *a rocky coastline ◇ rocky soil* **2** difficult and not certain to continue or to be successful: *a rocky marriage*

the ˌRocky Mountain ˈStates *noun* [pl.] the eight US states in the area of the Rocky Mountains

ro·coco /rəˈkəʊkəʊ; *NAmE* rəˈkoʊkoʊ/ (also **Rococo**) *adj.* used to describe a style of ARCHITECTURE, furniture, etc. that has a lot of decoration, especially in the shape of curls; used to describe a style of literature or music that has a lot of detail and decoration. The rococo style was popular in the 18th century.

rod /rɒd; *NAmE* rɑːd/ *noun* **1** (often used in compounds) a long straight piece of wood, metal or glass ➲ VISUAL VOCAB pages V18, V57 ➲ see also LIGHTNING ROD **2** = FISHING ROD: *fishing with rod and line* **3** (also **the rod**) (*old-fashioned*) a stick that is used for hitting people as a punishment: *There used to be a saying: 'Spare the rod and spoil the child.'* **4** (*NAmE, slang*) a small gun

IDM **make a rod for your own ˈback** to do sth that will cause problems for you in the future ➲ more at BEAT *v.*, RULE *v.*

rode *past tense* of RIDE

ro·dent /ˈrəʊdnt; *NAmE* ˈroʊ-/ *noun* any small animal that belongs to a group of animals with strong sharp front teeth. Mice, RATS and RABBITS are all rodents. ➲ VISUAL VOCAB page V10

rodeo /ˈrəʊdiəʊ; rəʊˈdeɪəʊ; *NAmE* ˈroʊdioʊ; roʊˈdeɪoʊ/ *noun* (*pl.* -os) a public competition, especially in the US, in which people show their skill at riding wild horses and catching CATTLE with ropes

roe /rəʊ; *NAmE* roʊ/ *noun* **1** [U, C] the mass of eggs inside a female fish (**hard roe**) or the SPERM of a male fish (**soft roe**), used as food: *cod's roe* **2** = ROE DEER

ˈ**roe deer** *noun* (*pl.* **roe deer**) (also **roe**) a small European and Asian DEER

roent·gen·ium /ˌrɒntˈgiːniəm; *NAmE* ˌrent-/ *noun* [U] (*symb.* **Rg**) a chemical element. Roentgenium is a RADIOACTIVE element that is produced artificially and has no known use.

Roe v Wade /ˌrəʊ vɜːsəs ˈweɪd; *NAmE* ˌroʊ vɜːrsəs/ *noun* a legal case in the US Supreme Court that decided that ABORTION is allowed by the Constitution

roger /ˈrɒdʒə(r); *NAmE* ˈrɑːdʒ-/ *exclamation, verb*

■ ***exclamation*** people say **Roger!** in communication by radio to show that they have understood a message

■ ***verb* ~ sb** (*BrE, taboo, slang*) (of a man) to have sex with sb

rogue /rəʊg; *NAmE* roʊg/ *noun, adj.*

■ ***noun* 1** (*humorous*) a person who behaves badly, but in a harmless way SYN **scoundrel**: *He's a bit of a rogue, but very charming.* **2** (*old-fashioned*) a man who is dishonest and immoral SYN **rascal**: *a **rogues' gallery*** (= a collection of pictures of criminals)

■ ***adj.*** [only before noun] **1** (of an animal) living apart from the main group, and possibly dangerous **2** behaving in a

R

different way from other similar people or things, often causing damage: *a rogue gene* ◇ *a rogue police officer*

roguish /ˈrəʊɡɪʃ; *NAmE* ˈroʊ-/ *adj.* (usually *approving*) (of a person) pleasant and amusing but looking as if they might do sth wrong: *a roguish smile* ▸ **roguish·ly** *adv.*

Ro·hyp·nol™ /rəʊˈhɪpnɒl; *NAmE* roʊˈhɪpnɑːl/ *noun* [U] a drug that makes you want to sleep, and which can make you unable to remember what happens for a period after you take it

rois·ter·ing /ˈrɔɪstərɪŋ/ *adj.* (*old-fashioned*) having fun in a cheerful, noisy way

role 🔑 AW /rəʊl; *NAmE* roʊl/ *noun*
1 🔑 the function or position that sb has or is expected to have in an organization, in society or in a relationship: *the role of the teacher in the classroom* ◇ *She refused to take on the traditional woman's role.* ◇ *In many marriages there has been a complete* **role reversal** (= change of roles) *with the man staying at home and the woman going out to work.* **2** 🔑 an actor's part in a play, film/movie, etc: *It is one of the greatest roles she has played.* ◇ *Who is in the* **leading role** (= the most important one)? ➲ COLLOCATIONS at CINEMA **3** 🔑 the degree to which sb/sth is involved in a situation or an activity and the effect that they have on it: *the role of diet in preventing disease* ◇ *The media play a* **major role** *in influencing people's opinions.* ◇ *a* **key/vital role**

ˈrole model *noun* a person that you admire and try to copy

ˈrole-play *noun* a learning activity in which you behave in the way sb else would behave in a particular situation: *Role-play allows students to practise language in a safe situation.* ▸ **ˈrole-play** *verb* [I, T] **~ (sth)**

ˈrole-playing game *noun* a game in which players pretend to be imaginary characters who take part in adventures, especially in situations from FANTASY literature

rolls

toilet roll (*BrE*)
roll of toilet paper

bread rolls

roll of tape

roll 🔑 /rəʊl; *NAmE* roʊl/ *noun, verb*
■ ***noun***
▸ OF PAPER/CLOTH, ETC. **1** 🔑 [C] **~ (of sth)** a long piece of paper, cloth, film, etc. that has been wrapped around itself or a tube several times so that it forms the shape of a tube: *a roll of film* ◇ *Wallpaper is sold in rolls.* ➲ VISUAL VOCAB page V29 ➲ see also TOILET ROLL
▸ OF SWEETS/CANDY **2** 🔑 [C] **~ (of sth)** (*NAmE*) a paper tube wrapped around sweets/candy, etc: *a roll of mints* ➲ VISUAL VOCAB page V29
▸ BREAD **3** 🔑 (also ˌ**bread ˈroll**) [C] a small LOAF of bread for one person: *Soup and a roll: £3.50* ◇ *a* **chicken/cheese, etc. roll** (= filled with chicken/cheese, etc.) ➲ compare BUN ➲ see also SAUSAGE ROLL, SPRING ROLL, SWISS ROLL
▸ OF BODY **4** [sing.] an act of rolling the body over and over: *The kittens were enjoying a roll in the sunshine.* **5** [C] a physical exercise in which you roll your body on the ground, moving your back and legs over your head: *a* **forward/backward roll**
▸ OF SHIP/PLANE **6** [U] the act of moving from side to side so that one side is higher than the other ➲ compare PITCH *n.* (8)
▸ OF FAT **7** [C] an area of too much fat on your body, especially around your waist: *Rolls of fat hung over his belt.*
▸ LIST OF NAMES **8** [C] an official list of names: *the* **electoral roll** (= a list of all the people who can vote in an election) ◇ *The chairman* **called/took the roll** (= called out the names on a list to check that everyone was present). ➲ see also PAYROLL
▸ SOUND **9** [C] **~ (of sth)** a deep continuous sound: *the distant roll of thunder* ◇ *a drum roll*
▸ OF DICE **10** [C] an act of rolling a DICE: *The order of play is decided by the roll of a dice.*
▸ PHONETICS **11** = TRILL (3)

IDM **be on a ˈroll** (*informal*) to be experiencing a period of success at what you are doing: *Don't stop me now—I'm on a roll!* **a ˌroll in the ˈhay** (*informal*) an act of having sex with sb

■ ***verb***
▸ TURN OVER **1** 🔑 [I, T] to turn over and over and move in a particular direction; to make a round object do this: **+ adv./prep.** *The ball rolled down the hill.* ◇ *We watched the waves rolling onto the beach.* ◇ **~ sth + adv./prep.** *Delivery men were rolling barrels across the yard.* **2** 🔑 [I, T] to turn over and over or round and round while remaining in the same place; to make sth do this: (**+ adv./prep.**) *a dog rolling in the mud* ◇ *Her eyes rolled.* ◇ **~ sth (+ adv./prep.)** *She* **rolled her eyes** *upwards* (= to show surprise or disapproval). ◇ *He was rolling a pencil between his fingers.* **3** 🔑 [I, T] **~ (sb/sth) over (onto sth)** | **~ (sb/sth) (over) onto sth** to turn over to face a different direction; to make sb/sth do this: **~ over (onto sth)** *She rolled over to let the sun brown her back.* ◇ **~ onto sth** *He rolled onto his back.* ◇ **~ sb/sth (over) (onto sth)** *I rolled the baby over onto its stomach.* ◇ *to* **roll a dice/die** (= in a game) ◇ (*especially NAmE*) *She rolled her car in a 100 mph crash.*
▸ MOVE (AS IF) ON WHEELS **4** 🔑 [I, T] to move smoothly (on wheels or as if on wheels); to make sth do this: (**+ adv./prep.**) *The car began to roll back down the hill.* ◇ *The traffic rolled slowly forwards.* ◇ *Mist was rolling in from the sea.* ◇ **~ sth (+ adv./prep.)** *He rolled the trolley across the room.*
▸ MAKE BALL/TUBE **5** 🔑 [T, I] **~ (sth) (up) (into sth)** to make sth/yourself into the shape of a ball or tube: *I rolled the string into a ball.* ◇ *We rolled up the carpet.* ◇ *a rolled-up newspaper* ◇ *I always* **roll my own** (= make my own cigarettes). ◇ *The hedgehog rolled up into a ball.* ➲ compare UNROLL
▸ FOLD CLOTHING **6** 🔑 [T] to fold the edge of a piece of clothing, etc. over and over on itself to make it shorter: **~ sth up** *Roll up your sleeves.* ◇ **~ sth + adv./prep.** *She rolled her jeans to her knees.* ➲ VISUAL VOCAB page V50
▸ MAKE STH FLAT **7** [T] **~ sth (out)** to make sth flat by pushing sth heavy over it: *Roll the pastry on a floured surface.*
▸ WRAP UP **8** [T] **~ sb/sth/yourself (up) in sth** to wrap or cover sb/sth/yourself in sth: *Roll the meat in the breadcrumbs.* ◇ *He rolled himself up in the blanket.*
▸ OF SHIP/PLANE/WALK **9** [I, T] **~ (sth) (+ adv./prep.)** to move or make sth move from side to side: *He walked with a rolling gait.* ◇ *The ship was rolling heavily to and fro.* ➲ compare PITCH *v.* (6)
▸ MAKE SOUND **10** [I, T] to make a long continuous sound: *rolling drums* ◇ *Thunder rolled.* ◇ **~ sth** *to* **roll your r's** (= by letting your tongue VIBRATE with each 'r' sound)
▸ MACHINE **11** [I, T] when a machine **rolls** or sb **rolls** it, it operates: *They had to repeat the scene because the cameras weren't rolling.* ◇ **~ sth** *Roll the cameras!*

IDM **be ˈrolling in money/it** (*informal*) to have a lot of money **let's ˈroll** (*informal, especially NAmE*) used to suggest to a group of people that you should all start doing sth or going somewhere **rolled into ˈone** combined in one person or thing: *Banks are several businesses rolled into one.* ˌ**rolling in the ˈaisles** (*informal*) laughing a lot: *She soon had us rolling in the aisles.* **a rolling ˈstone gathers no ˈmoss** (*saying*) a person who moves from place to place, job to job, etc. does not have a lot of money, possessions or friends but is free from responsibilities **ˈroll on...!** (*BrE, informal*) used to say that you want sth to happen or arrive soon: *Roll on Friday!* **roll up your ˈsleeves** to prepare to work or fight **roll with the ˈpunches** to adapt yourself to a difficult situation ➲ more at BALL *n.*, GRAVE[1] *n.*, HEAD *n.*, READY *adj.*, TONGUE *n.*

PHR V ˌ**roll aˈround** (*BrE* also ˌ**roll aˈbout**) to be laughing so much that you can hardly control yourself ˌ**roll sth↔ˈback 1** to turn or force sth back or further away: *to roll back the frontiers of space* **2** (*NAmE*) to reduce prices, etc: *to roll back inflation* ˌ**roll sth↔ˈdown 1** to open sth by turning a handle: *He rolled down his car window and started shouting at them.* **2** to make a rolled piece of clothing, etc. hang or lie flat: *to roll down your sleeves* **ˌroll ˈin** (*informal*) **1** to arrive in great numbers or amounts: *Offers of help are still rolling in.* **2** to arrive late at a place, without seeming worried or sorry: *Steve rolled in around lunchtime.* **ˌroll sth↔ˈout 1** to make sth flat by pushing sth over it: *Roll out the pastry.* ➲ VISUAL VOCAB page V25 **2** to officially make a new product available or start a new political CAMPAIGN SYN **launch**: *The new model is to be rolled out in July.* ➲ related noun ROLL-OUT **ˌroll ˈover** (*informal*) to be easily defeated without even trying: *We can't expect them to just roll over for us.* **ˌroll sb↔ˈover** (*BrE, informal*) to defeat sb easily: *They rolled us over in the replay.* **ˌroll sth↔ˈover** (*technical*) to allow money that sb owes to be paid back at a later date: *The bank refused to roll over the debt.* ➲ related noun ROLLOVER **ˌroll ˈup** (*informal*) to arrive: *Bill finally rolled up two hours late.* ◇ *Roll up! Roll up!* (= used to invite people who are passing to form an audience) **ˌroll sth↔ˈup** to close sth by turning a handle: *She rolled up all the windows.*

roll·back /ˈrəʊlbæk; *NAmE* ˈroʊl-/ *noun* [sing., U] (*especially NAmE*) **1** a reduction in a price or in pay, to a past level **2** the act of changing a situation, law, etc. back to what it was before

ˈroll bar *noun* a metal bar over the top of a car without a roof, used to make the car stronger and to protect passengers if the car turns over

ˈroll-call *noun* [U, sing.] the reading of a list of names to a group of people to check who is there: *Roll-call will be at 7 a.m.* ◇ *The guest list reads like a roll-call of the nation's heroes.*

ˌrolled ˈgold *noun* [U] gold in the form of a thin layer that is rolled onto sth to cover it

ˌrolled ˈoats *noun* [pl.] OATS that have had their shells removed before being crushed, used especially for making PORRIDGE

roll·er /ˈrəʊlə(r); *NAmE* ˈroʊ-/ *noun* **1** a piece of wood, metal or plastic, shaped like a tube, that rolls over and over and is used in machines, for example to make sth flat, or to move sth: *the heavy steel rollers under the conveyor belt* **2** (often in compounds) a machine or piece of equipment with a part shaped like a tube so that it rolls backwards and forwards. It may be used for making sth flat, crushing or spreading sth: *Flatten the surface of the grass with a roller.* ◇ *a paint roller* ➲ VISUAL VOCAB page V17 ➲ see also STEAMROLLER **3** a piece of wood or metal, shaped like a tube, that is used for moving heavy objects: *We'll need to move the piano on rollers.* **4** a long, powerful wave in the sea/ocean: *Huge Atlantic rollers crashed onto the rocks.* **5** a small plastic tube that hair is rolled around to give it curls SYN **curler**: *heated rollers* ◇ *Her hair was* ***in rollers.*** ➲ see also HIGH ROLLER

roller·ball /ˈrəʊləbɔːl; *NAmE* ˈroʊlərb-/ *noun* **1** a type of BALLPOINT pen **2** = TRACKBALL

Roll·er·blade™ (*BrE*) (*NAmE* **Roller Blade™**) /ˈrəʊləbleɪd; *NAmE* ˈroʊlərb-/ *noun* = IN-LINE SKATE ➲ VISUAL VOCAB page V34 ▸ **Roll·er·blade** *verb* [I]

ˈroller blind *noun* a covering for a window made of a roll of cloth that is fixed at the top of the window and can be pulled up and down ➲ VISUAL VOCAB page V18

ˈroller coaster *noun* **1** a track at a FAIRGROUND that goes up and down very steep slopes and that people ride on in a small train for fun and excitement: *a roller-coaster ride* **2** a situation that keeps changing very quickly: *The last few weeks have been a real roller coaster.*

ˈroller skate (also **skate**) *noun, verb*
▪ ***noun*** a type of boot with two pairs of small wheels attached to the bottom: *a pair of roller skates*
▪ ***verb*** [I] to move over a hard surface wearing roller skates ▸ **ˈroller skating** (also **skat·ing**) *noun* [U]

ˈroller towel *noun* a long roll of towel, usually in a public toilet/bathroom, part of which hangs down for you to dry your hands on

rol·licking /ˈrɒlɪkɪŋ; *NAmE* ˈrɑːl-/ *adj., noun*
▪ ***adj.*** [only before noun] cheerful and often noisy SYN **exuberant**: *a rollicking comedy*
▪ ***noun*** (*BrE, informal*) angry criticism for sth bad sb has done: *He gave us both a rollicking.*

roll·ing /ˈrəʊlɪŋ; *NAmE* ˈroʊ-/ *adj.* [only before noun] **1** (of hills or countryside) having gentle slopes **2** done in regular stages or at regular intervals over a period of time: *a rolling programme of reform*

ˈrolling mill *noun* a machine or factory that produces flat sheets of metal

ˈrolling pin *noun* a wooden or glass kitchen UTENSIL (= a tool) in the shape of a tube, used for rolling PASTRY flat ➲ VISUAL VOCAB pages V23, V25

ˈrolling stock *noun* [U] the engines, trains, etc. that are used on a railway/railroad

roll·mop /ˈrəʊlmɒp; *NAmE* ˈroʊlmɑːp/ *noun* a piece of raw HERRING (= a type of fish) that is rolled up and preserved in VINEGAR, often sold in JARS

ˌroll of ˈhonour (*especially US* **ˈhonor roll**) *noun* [usually sing.] a list of people who are being praised officially for sth they have done

ˈroll-on *adj.* [only before noun] spread or put on the body using a ball that moves around in the top of a bottle or container: *a roll-on deodorant* ▸ **ˈroll-on** *noun*

ˌroll-ˌon ˌroll-ˈoff *adj.* [usually before noun] (*abbr.* **ˈro-ro**) (*BrE*) (of a ship) designed so that cars can be driven straight on and off: *a roll-on roll-off car ferry*

ˈroll-out *noun* an occasion when a company introduces or starts to use a new product

roll·over /ˈrəʊləʊvə(r); *NAmE* ˈroʊloʊvər/ *noun* **1** [U] (*technical*) the act of allowing money that is owed to be paid at a later date **2** [U, C] (*BrE*) a prize of money in a competition or LOTTERY in a particular week, that is added to the prize given in the following week if nobody wins it: *a rollover jackpot* **3** [U] (*especially NAmE*) the turning over of a vehicle during an accident

Rolls-Royce™ /ˌrəʊlz ˈrɔɪs; *NAmE* ˌroʊlz/ *noun* **1** (also *informal* **Rolls™**) a large, comfortable and expensive make of car made by a company in the UK **2 the ~ of sth** (*BrE*) something that is thought of as an example of the highest quality of a type of thing: *This is the Rolls-Royce of canoes.*

ˌroll-top ˈdesk *noun* a desk with a top that you roll back to open it

ˈroll-up *noun* (*BrE, informal*) a cigarette that you make yourself with TOBACCO and special paper

roly-poly /ˌrəʊli ˈpəʊli; *NAmE* ˌroʊli ˈpoʊli/ *adj., noun*
▪ ***adj.*** [only before noun] (*informal*) (of people) short, round and fat SYN **plump**
▪ ***noun*** (*pl.* **-ies**) (also **ˌroly-poly ˈpudding**) [U, C] (*BrE*) a hot DESSERT (= a sweet dish) made from SUET PASTRY spread with jam and rolled up

ROM /rɒm; *NAmE* rɑːm/ *noun* [U] the abbreviation for 'read-only memory' (computer memory that contains instructions or data that cannot be changed or removed) ➲ compare CD-ROM

the Roma /ˈrəʊmə; *NAmE* ˈroʊmə/ *noun* [pl.] the ROMANI people: *the Roma population of eastern Europe*

ro·maine /rəʊˈmeɪn; *NAmE* roʊ-/ (*NAmE*) (*BrE* **cos lettuce**) *noun* [C, U] a type of LETTUCE with long crisp leaves

ro·maji /ˈrəʊmədʒi; *NAmE* ˈroʊ-/ *noun* [U] (from *Japanese*) a system of writing Japanese that uses the ROMAN ALPHABET

Roman /ˈrəʊmən; *NAmE* ˈroʊ-/ *adj., noun*
▪ ***adj.*** **1** connected with ancient Rome or the Roman Empire: *a Roman road/temple/villa* ◇ *Roman Britain* **2** connected with the modern city of Rome **3** connected with the Roman Catholic Church **4 roman** roman type is ordinary printing type which does not lean forward: *Definitions in this dictionary are printed in roman type.* ➲ compare ITALIC

R

■ **noun 1** [C] a member of the ancient Roman REPUBLIC or empire **2** [C] a person from the modern city of Rome **3 roman** [U] the ordinary style of printing that uses small letters that do not lean forward ➲ compare ITALICS IDM see ROME

the ˌRoman ˈalphabet *noun* [sing.] the alphabet that is used in English and in most western European languages

ˌRoman ˈCatholic (also **Cath·olic**) *noun* (*abbr.* **RC**) a member of the part of the Christian Church that has the POPE as its leader ▸ **ˌRoman ˈCatholic** (also **Cath·olic**) *adj.* **ˌRoman Caˈtholicism** (also **Cath·oli·cism**) *noun* [U]

Ro·mance /rəʊˈmæns; ˈrəʊmæns; *NAmE* ˈroʊ-/ *adj.* [only before noun] **Romance** languages, such as French, Italian and Spanish, are languages that developed from Latin

ro·mance /rəʊˈmæns; ˈrəʊmæns; *NAmE* ˈroʊ-/ *noun, verb*

■ **noun 1** [C] an exciting, usually short, relationship between two people who are in love with each other: *a holiday romance* ◇ *They had a* ***whirlwind romance.*** **2** [U] love or the feeling of being in love: *Spring is here and romance is in the air.* ◇ *How can you put the romance back into your marriage?* ➲ COLLOCATIONS at MARRIAGE **3** [U] a feeling of excitement and adventure, especially connected to a particular place or activity: *the romance of travel* **4** [C] a story about a love affair: *She's a compulsive reader of romances.* **5** [C] a story of excitement and adventure, often set in the past: *medieval romances*

■ **verb 1** [I] to tell stories that are not true or to describe sth in a way that makes it seem more exciting or interesting than it really is **2** [T] **~ sb** to have or to try to have a romantic relationship with sb

Ro·man·esque /ˌrəʊməˈnesk; *NAmE* ˌroʊ-/ *adj.* used to describe a style of ARCHITECTURE that was popular in western Europe from the 10th to the 12th centuries and that had round ARCHES, thick walls and tall PILLARS ➲ see also NORMAN

Rom·ani (also **Rom·any**) /ˈrɒməni; ˈrəʊm-; *NAmE* ˈrɑːm-; ˈroʊm-/ *noun* (*pl.* **-ies**) **1** [C] a member of a race of people, originally from Asia, who traditionally travel around and live in CARAVANS ➲ see also ROMA, GYPSY **2** [U] the language of Romani people ▸ **Rom·ani** (also **Rom·any**) *adj.* [usually before noun]

ˌRoman ˈlaw *noun* the legal system of the ancient Romans, and the basis for CIVIL LAW in many countries

ˌRoman ˈnose *noun* a nose that curves out at the top

ˌRoman ˈnumeral *noun* one of the letters used by the ancient Romans to represent numbers and still used today, in some situations. In this system I = 1, V = 5, X = 10, L = 50, C = 100, D = 500, M = 1000 and these letters are used in combinations to form other numbers: *Henry VIII* ◇ *© BBC MMIX (2009)* ➲ picture at IDEOGRAM ➲ compare ARABIC NUMERAL

Romano- /rəˈmɑːnəʊ; *NAmE* -noʊ; roʊˈm-/ *combining form* (in nouns and adjectives) Roman: *Romano-British pottery*

ro·man·tic 🔑 /rəʊˈmæntɪk; *NAmE* roʊ-/ *adj., noun*

■ **adj. 1** 🔑 connected or concerned with love or a sexual relationship: *a romantic candlelit dinner* ◇ *romantic stories/fiction/comedy* ◇ *I'm not interested in a romantic relationship.* **2** 🔑 (of people) showing feelings of love: *Why don't you ever give me flowers? I wish you'd be more romantic.* **3** 🔑 beautiful in a way that makes you think of love or feel strong emotions: *romantic music* ◇ *romantic mountain scenery* **4** 🔑 having an attitude to life where imagination and the emotions are especially important; not looking at situations in a realistic way: *a romantic view of life* ◇ *When I was younger, I had romantic ideas of becoming a writer.* **5 Romantic** [usually before noun] used to describe literature, music or art, especially of the 19th century, that is concerned with strong feelings, imagination and a return to nature, rather than reason, order and INTELLECTUAL ideas: *the Romantic movement* ◇ *Keats is one of the greatest Romantic poets.* ▸ **ro·man·tic·al·ly** /-kli/ *adv.*: *to be romantically involved with sb* ◇ *Their names have been linked romantically.* ◇ *He talked romantically of the past and his youth.*

■ **noun 1** a person who is emotional and has a lot of imagination, and who has ideas and hopes that may not be realistic: *an incurable romantic* ◇ *He was a romantic at heart and longed for adventure.* **2 Romantic** a writer, a musician or an artist who writes, etc. in the style of Romanticism

ro·man·ti·cism /rəʊˈmæntɪsɪzəm; *NAmE* roʊ-/ *noun* [U] **1** (also **Romanticism**) a style and movement in art, music and literature in the late 18th and early 19th century, in which strong feelings, imagination and a return to nature were more important than reason, order and INTELLECTUAL ideas ➲ compare REALISM **2** the quality of seeing people, events and situations as more exciting and interesting than they really are **3** strong feelings of love; the fact of showing emotion, affection, etc.

ro·man·ti·cize (*BrE* also **-ise**) /rəʊˈmæntɪsaɪz; *NAmE* roʊ-/ *verb* [T, I] **~ (sth)** to make sth seem more attractive or interesting than it really is: *romanticizing the past* ◇ *a romanticized picture of parenthood*

Rome /rəʊm; *NAmE* roʊm/ *noun*

IDM **Rome wasn't built in a ˈday** (*saying*) used to say that a complicated task will take a long time and needs patience **when in ˈRome (do as the ˈRomans do)** (*saying*) used to say that when you are in a foreign country, or a situation you are not familiar with, you should behave in the way that the people around you behave

romeo /ˈrəʊmiəʊ; *NAmE* ˈroʊmioʊ/ (also **Romeo**) *noun* (*pl.* **-os**) (often *humorous*) a young male lover or a man who has sex with a lot of women ORIGIN From the name of the young hero of Shakespeare's play *Romeo and Juliet.*

romp /rɒmp; *NAmE* rɑːmp; rɔːmp/ *verb, noun*

■ **verb** [I] (+ **adv./prep.**) to play in a happy and noisy way: *kids romping around in the snow*

IDM **romp home/to victory** to easily win a race or competition: *Their horse romped home in the 2 o'clock race.* ◇ *The Dutch team romped to a 5–1 victory over Celtic.* IDM see VICTORY *n.*

PHR V **ˌromp aˈway/aˈhead** (*BrE, informal*) to increase, make progress or win quickly and easily **ˌromp ˈthrough (sth)** (*BrE, informal*) to do sth easily and quickly: *She romped through the exam questions.*

■ **noun** (often used in newspapers) (*informal*) **1** [C] an enjoyable sexual experience that is not serious: *politicians involved in sex romps with call girls* **2** [C] an amusing book, play or film/movie that is full of action or adventure **3** [sing.] an easy victory in a sports competition: *They won in a 5–1 romp.*

romp·ers /ˈrɒmpəz; *NAmE* ˈrɑːmpərz; ˈrɔːm-/ *noun* [pl.] (also ˈ**romper suit** [C]) (*old-fashioned*) a piece of clothing worn by a baby, that covers the body and legs

ron·davel /rɒnˈdɑːvl; *NAmE* rɑːn-/ *noun* (*SAfrE*) a round HUT with a pointed roof that is usually made from THATCH (= dried grass)

rondo /ˈrɒndəʊ; *NAmE* ˈrɑːndoʊ/ *noun* (*pl.* **-os**) a piece of music in which the main tune is repeated several times, sometimes forming part of a longer piece

roo /ruː/ *noun* (*informal*) = KANGAROO

rood screen /ˈruːd skriːn/ *noun* (*technical*) a wooden or stone structure in some churches that divides the part near the ALTAR from the rest of the church

roof 🔑 /ruːf/ *noun, verb*

■ **noun** (*pl.* **roofs**) **1** 🔑 the structure that covers or forms the top of a building or vehicle: *a* ***flat/sloping roof*** ◇ *a* ***thatched/slate, etc. roof*** ◇ *The corner of the classroom was damp where the roof had leaked.* ◇ *Tim climbed on to the garage roof.* ◇ *The roof of the car was not damaged in the accident.* ➲ see also SUNROOF ➲ VISUAL VOCAB page V15 **2 -roofed** (in adjectives) having the type of roof mentioned: *flat-roofed buildings* **3** the top of an underground space such as a tunnel or CAVE **4 ~ of your mouth** the top of the inside of your mouth

IDM **go through the ˈroof 1** (of prices, etc.) to rise or increase very quickly **2** (also **hit the 'roof**) (*informal*) to become very angry **have a 'roof over your head** to have somewhere to live **under one 'roof** | **under the same 'roof** in the same building or house: *There are various stores and restaurants all under one roof.* ◇ *I don't think I can live under the same roof as you any longer.* **under your 'roof** in your home: *I don't want her under my roof again.* ➲ more at HIT *v.*, RAISE *v.*

■ ***verb*** [often passive] to cover sth with a roof; to put a roof on a building: **~ sth (in/over)** *The shopping centre is not roofed over.* ◇ **~ sth with/in sth** *Their cottage was roofed with green slate.*

roof·er /'ru:fə(r)/ *noun* a person whose job is to repair or build roofs

'roof garden *noun* a garden on the flat roof of a building

roof·ing /'ru:fɪŋ/ *noun* [U] **1** material used for making or covering roofs **2** the process of building roofs

'roof rack (also **'luggage rack** especially in *NAmE*) *noun* a metal frame fixed to the roof of a car and used for carrying bags, cases and other large objects ➲ picture at RACK

roof·top /'ru:ftɒp; *NAmE* -tɑ:p/ *noun* the outside part of the roof of a building: *From the hill we looked out over the rooftops of Athens.* ◇ *The prisoners staged a rooftop protest.*

IDM **ˌshout, etc. sth from the 'rooftops** to talk about sth in a very public way: *He was in love and wanted to shout it from the rooftops.*

rooi·bos /'rɔɪbɒs; *NAmE* -bɔ:s/ *noun* [U] (*SAfrE*) a type of bush grown in South Africa whose leaves are dried and used to make tea: *rooibos tea*

rook /rʊk/ *noun* **1** a large black bird of the CROW family. Rooks build their nests in groups at the tops of trees. **2** = CASTLE (2)

rook·ery /'rʊkəri/ *noun* (*pl.* **-ies**) a group of trees with rooks' nests in them

rookie /'rʊki/ *noun* (*informal*) **1** (*especially NAmE*) a person who has just started a job or an activity and has very little experience **2** (*NAmE*) a member of a sports team in his or her first full year of playing that sport

room 0-w /ru:m; rʊm/ *noun, verb*

■ ***noun***

▸ IN BUILDING **1** 0-w [C] a part of a building that has its own walls, floor and ceiling and is usually used for a particular purpose: *He walked out of the room and slammed the door.* ◇ *They were in **the next room** and we could hear every word they said.* ◇ *a **dining/living/sitting room*** ◇ *They had to sit in the waiting room for an hour.* ◇ *I think Simon is in his room* (= bedroom). ◇ *I don't want to watch television. I'll be in **the other room*** (= a different room). HELP There are many compounds ending in **room**. You will find them at their place in the alphabet.

▸ -ROOMED/-ROOM **2** 0-w (in adjectives) having the number of rooms mentioned: *a three-roomed/three-room apartment*

▸ IN HOTEL **3** 0-w [C] a bedroom in a hotel, etc: *a **double/single room*** ◇ *I'd like to book a room with a view of the lake.* ◇ *She lets out rooms to students.* ➲ COLLOCATIONS at TRAVEL

▸ PLACE TO LIVE **4** **rooms** [pl.] (*old-fashioned, BrE*) a set of two or more rooms that you rent to live in SYN **lodgings**: *They lived in rooms in Kensington.*

▸ SPACE **5** 0-w [U] empty space that can be used for a particular purpose: **~ (for sb/sth)** *Is there enough room for me in the car?* ◇ *There's room for one more at the table.* ◇ *Do you have room for a computer on your desk?* ◇ *Yes, there's **plenty of room**.* ◇ *How can we **make room for** all the furniture?* ◇ *I'll move the table—it **takes up too much room**.* ◇ **~ (to do sth)** *Make sure you have plenty of room to sit comfortably.* ➲ see also ELBOW ROOM, HEADROOM, HOUSEROOM, LEGROOM, STANDING ROOM

▸ POSSIBILITY **6** [U] **~ for sth** the possibility of sth existing or happening; the opportunity to do sth: *He had to be certain. There could be **no room for doubt**.* ◇ *There's some **room for improvement** in your work* (= it is not as good as it could be). ◇ *It is important to give children room to think for themselves.*

▸ PEOPLE **7** [sing.] all the people in a room: *The whole room burst into applause.*

IDM **no room to swing a 'cat** (*informal*) when sb says **there's no room to swing a cat**, they mean that a room is very small and that there is not enough space ➲ more at ELEPHANT, MANOEUVRE *n.*, SMOKE *n.*

■ ***verb*** [I] **~ (with sb)** | **~ (together)** (*NAmE*) to rent a room somewhere; to share a rented room or flat/apartment with sb: *She and Nancy roomed together at college.*

room·er /'ru:mə(r); 'rʊm-/ *noun* (*NAmE*) a person who rents a room in sb's house

room·ful /'ru:mfʊl; 'rʊm-/ *noun* [sing.] a large number of people or things that are in a room: *He announced his resignation to a roomful of reporters.*

roomie /'ru:mi; 'rʊmi/ *noun* (*NAmE, informal*) = ROOMMATE

'rooming house *noun* (*NAmE*) a building where rooms with furniture can be rented for living in

roommate /'ru:mmeɪt; 'rʊm-/ *noun* (also *informal* **roomie**) **1** a person that you share a room with, especially at a college or university **2** (both *NAmE*) (*BrE* **flat·mate**) a person who shares a flat/apartment with one or more others

'room service *noun* [U] a service provided in a hotel, by which guests can order food and drink to be brought to their rooms: *He ordered coffee from room service.*

'room temperature *noun* [U] the normal temperature inside a building: *Serve the wine **at room temperature**.*

roomy /'ru:mi; 'rʊmi/ *adj.* (**room·ier**, **roomi·est**) (*approving*) having a lot of space inside SYN **spacious**: *a surprisingly roomy car* ▸ **roomi·ness** *noun* [U]

roost /ru:st/ *noun, verb*

■ ***noun*** a place where birds sleep IDM see RULE *v.*

■ ***verb*** [I] (of birds) to rest or go to sleep somewhere IDM see HOME *adv.*

roost·er /'ru:stə(r)/ (*especially NAmE*) (*BrE* also **cock**) *noun* an adult male chicken ➲ compare HEN

root 0-w /ru:t/ *noun, verb*

■ ***noun***

▸ OF PLANT **1** 0-w [C] the part of a plant that grows under the ground and absorbs water and minerals that it sends to the rest of the plant: *deep spreading roots* ◇ *I pulled the plant up **by** (= including) **the roots**.* ◇ *Tree roots can cause damage to buildings.* ◇ ***root crops/vegetables*** (= plants whose roots you can eat, such as carrots) ➲ COLLOCATIONS at LIFE ➲ VISUAL VOCAB pages V8, V9 ➲ see also GRASS ROOTS, TAPROOT

▸ OF HAIR/TOOTH/NAIL **2** 0-w [C] the part of a hair, tooth, nail or tongue that attaches it to the rest of the body: *hair that is blonde at the ends and dark at the roots*

▸ MAIN CAUSE OF PROBLEM **3** 0-w [C, usually sing.] the main cause of sth, such as a problem or difficult situation: *Money, or love of money, is said to be the root of all evil.* ◇ *We have to get to **the root of the problem**.* ◇ *What lies **at the root of** his troubles is a sense of insecurity.* ◇ *What would you say was the **root cause** of the problem?*

▸ ORIGIN **4** 0-w [C, usually pl.] the origin or basis of sth: *Flamenco has its roots in Arabic music.*

▸ CONNECTION WITH PLACE **5** 0-w **roots** [pl.] the feelings or connections that you have with a place because you have lived there or your family came from there: *I'm proud of my Italian roots.* ◇ *After 20 years in America, I still feel my roots are in England.*

▸ OF WORD **6** [C] (*linguistics*) the part of a word that has the main meaning and that its other forms are based on; a word that other words are formed from: *'Walk' is the root of 'walks', 'walked', 'walking' and 'walker'.*

▸ MATHEMATICS **7** [C] a quantity which, when multiplied by itself a particular number of times, produces another quantity ➲ see also CUBE ROOT, SQUARE ROOT

IDM **put down 'roots 1** (of a plant) to develop roots **2** to settle and live in one place: *After ten years travelling the world, she felt it was time to put down roots somewhere.* **ˌroot and 'branch** thoroughly and completely: *The government set out to destroy the organization root and branch.* ◇ *root-and-branch reforms* **take 'root 1** (of a plant) to de-

R

velop roots **2** (of an idea) to become accepted widely: *Fortunately, militarism failed to take root in Europe as a whole.*

■ ***verb***

▸ OF PLANTS **1** [I, T] **~ (sth)** to grow roots; to make or encourage a plant to grow roots

▸ SEARCH **2** [I] to search for sth by moving things or turning things over SYN **rummage**: **~ (about/around) for sth** *pigs rooting for food* ◇ *Who's been rooting around in my desk?* ◇ **~ (through sth) (for sth)** *'It must be here somewhere,' she said, rooting through the suitcase.*

▸ SEX **3** [I, T] **~ (sb)** (*AustralE, NZE, taboo, slang*) to have sex with sb

PHR V **'root for sb** [no passive] (usually used in the progressive tenses) (*informal*) to support or encourage sb in a sports competition or when they are in a difficult situation: *We're rooting for the Bulls.* ◇ *Good luck—I'm rooting for you!* **ˌroot sth/sb↔'out 1** to find the person or thing that is causing a problem and remove or get rid of them **2** to find sb/sth after searching for a long time **ˌroot sb to 'sth** to make sb unable to move because of fear, shock, etc: *Embarrassment* ***rooted her to the spot****.* **ˌroot sth↔'up** to dig or pull up a plant with its roots

'root beer *noun* **1** [U] a sweet FIZZY drink (= with bubbles), that does not contain alcohol, made from GINGER and the roots of other plants. It is drunk especially in the US. **2** [C] a bottle, can or glass of root beer

'root-bound *adj.* = POT-BOUND

'root canal *noun* the space inside the root of a tooth

'root directory *noun* (*computing*) a file that contains all the other files in a program, system, etc.

root·ed /ˈruːtɪd/ *adj.* **1 ~ in sth** developing from or being strongly influenced by sth: *His problems are deeply rooted in his childhood experiences.* **2** fixed in one place; not moving or changing: *She was rooted to her chair.* ◇ *Their life is rooted in Chicago now.* ◇ *Racism is still deeply rooted in our society.* ➲ see also DEEP-ROOTED **3** (*AustralE, slang*) extremely tired **4** (*AustralE, slang*) too old or broken to use

IDM **rooted to the 'spot** so frightened or shocked that you cannot move

root·er /ˈruːtə(r)/ *noun* (*NAmE, informal*) a person who supports a particular team or player SYN **supporter**

rootin'-tootin' /ˌruːtɪn ˈtuːtɪn/ *adj.* [only before noun] (*NAmE, informal*) enthusiastic, cheerful and lively

root·less /ˈruːtləs/ *adj.* having nowhere that you really think of as home, or as the place where you belong: *She had had a rootless childhood moving from town to town.* ▸ **root·less·ness** *noun* [U]

rootsy /ˈruːtsi/ *adj.* (*informal*) (of music) belonging to a particular tradition, and not changed from the original style

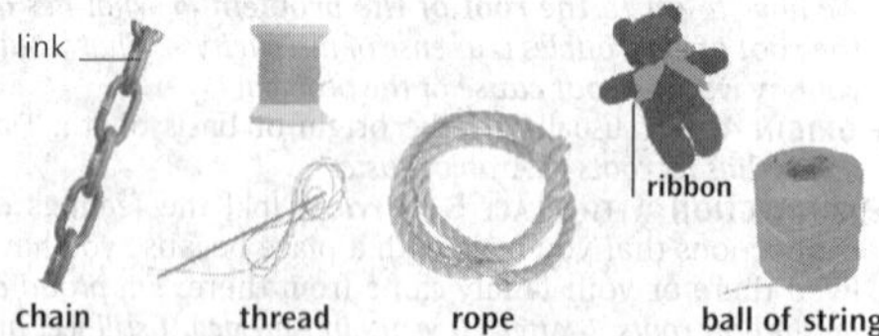

rope 0‑w /rəʊp; *NAmE* roʊp/ *noun, verb*

■ ***noun* 1** 0‑w [C, U] very strong thick string made by twisting thinner strings, wires, etc. together: *The rope broke and she fell 50 metres onto the rocks.* ◇ *We tied his hands together with rope.* ◇ *The anchor was attached to a length of rope.* ◇ *Coils of rope lay on the quayside.* ➲ see also JUMP ROPE, SKIPPING ROPE, TOW ROPE **2 the ropes** [pl.] the fence made of rope that is around the edge of the area where a BOXING or WRESTLING match takes place ➲ VISUAL VOCAB page V39 **3** [C] a number of similar things attached together by a string or thread: *a rope of pearls*

IDM **give sb enough 'rope** to allow sb freedom to do what they want, especially in the hope that they will make a mistake or look silly: *The question was vague, giving the interviewee* ***enough rope to hang herself****.* **on the 'ropes** (*informal*) very close to being defeated **show sb/know/learn the 'ropes** (*informal*) to show sb/know/learn how a particular job should be done ➲ more at END *n.*, MONEY

■ ***verb* 1** to tie one person or thing to another with a rope: **~ A and B together** *The thieves had roped the guard's feet together.* ◇ **~ A to B** *I roped the goat to a post.* **2 ~ sth** to tie sth with a rope so that it is held tightly and safely: *I closed and roped the trunk.* **3 ~ sth** (*especially NAmE*) to catch an animal by throwing a circle of rope around it SYN **lasso**

PHR V **ˌrope sb↔'in** | **ˌrope sb 'into sth** [usually passive] (*informal*) to persuade sb to join in an activity or to help to do sth, even when they do not want to: **~ to do sth** *Everyone was roped in to help with the show.* ◇ **~ doing sth** *Ben was roped into making coffee for the whole team.* **ˌrope sth↔'off** to separate an area from another one, using ropes, to stop people from entering it: *Police roped off the street to investigate the accident.*

ˌrope 'ladder *noun* a LADDER made of two long ropes connected by short pieces of wood or metal at regular intervals

ropy (also **ropey**) /ˈrəʊpi; *NAmE* ˈroʊpi/ *adj.* (*BrE, informal*) **1** not in good condition; of bad quality: *We spent the night in a ropy old tent.* **2** feeling slightly ill/sick

Roque·fort™ /ˈrɒkfɔː; *NAmE* ˈroʊkfərt/ *noun* [U] a type of soft French cheese with blue marks and a strong flavour

ro-ro /ˈrəʊ rəʊ; *NAmE* ˈroʊ roʊ/ *abbr.* (*BrE*) ROLL-ON ROLL-OFF

Rorschach test /ˈrɔːʃɑːk test; *NAmE* ˈrɔːrʃɑːk/ (also **'ink-blot test**) *noun* (*psychology*) a test in which people have to say what different shapes made by ink make them think of

rort /rɔːt; *NAmE* rɔːrt/ *noun* (*AustralE, NZE, informal*) a dishonest thing that sb does: *a tax rort* ▸ **rort** [T, I]: **~ (sth)** *He was an expert at rorting the system* (= getting the best out of it for himself without actually doing anything illegal).

ros·ary /ˈrəʊzəri; *NAmE* ˈroʊ-/ *noun* (*pl.* **-ies**) **1** [C] a string of BEADS that are used by some Roman Catholics for counting prayers as they say them **2 the Rosary** [sing.] the set of prayers said by Roman Catholics while counting rosary BEADS

rose /rəʊz; *NAmE* roʊz/ *noun, adj.* ➲ see also RISE *v.*

■ ***noun* 1** [C] a flower with a sweet smell that grows on a bush with THORNS (= sharp points) on its STEMS: *a bunch of red roses* ◇ *a* ***rose bush/garden*** ◇ *a* ***climbing/rambling rose*** ➲ VISUAL VOCAB page V9 **2** (also **ˌrose 'pink**) [U] a pink colour **3** [C] a piece of metal or plastic with small holes in it that is attached to the end of a pipe or WATERING CAN so that the water comes out in a fine spray when you are watering plants **4** = CEILING ROSE

IDM **be coming up 'roses** (*informal*) (of a situation) to be developing in a successful way **put 'roses in sb's cheeks** (*BrE, informal*) to make sb look healthy **a ˌrose by any other ˌname would smell as 'sweet** (*saying*) what is important is what people or things are, not what they are called ➲ more at BED *n.*, SMELL *v.*

■ ***adj.*** (also **ˌrose 'pink**) pink in colour

rosé /ˈrəʊzeɪ; *NAmE* roʊˈzeɪ/ *noun* [U, C] (from *French*) a light pink wine: *a bottle of rosé* ◇ *an excellent rosé* ➲ compare RED WINE, WHITE WINE

ros·eate /ˈrəʊziət; *NAmE* ˈroʊ-/ *adj.* [usually before noun] (*literary* or *technical*) pink in colour

rose·bud /ˈrəʊzbʌd; *NAmE* ˈroʊz-/ *noun* the flower of a ROSE before it is open

'rose-coloured (*especially US* **'rose-colored**) *adj.* **1** pink in colour **2** (also **'rose-tinted**) used to describe an idea or a way of looking at a situation as being better or more positive than it really is: *a rose-tinted vision of the world* ◇ *He tends to view the world* ***through rose-coloured spectacles****.*

'rose hip *noun* = HIP

rose·mary /ˈrəʊzməri; *NAmE* ˈroʊzmeri/ *noun* [U] a bush with small narrow leaves that smell sweet and are used in cooking as a HERB ➲ VISUAL VOCAB page V28

Rosetta Stone /rəʊˈzetə; *NAmE* roʊ-/ *noun* [sing.] something, especially a discovery, that helps people to understand or find an explanation for a mystery or area of knowledge that not much was known about ORIGIN From the name of an ancient stone with writing in three different languages on it that was found near Rosetta in Egypt in 1799. It has helped archaeologists to understand and translate many other ancient Egyptian texts.

ros·ette /rəʊˈzet; *NAmE* roʊ-/ *noun* **1** a round decoration made of RIBBON that is worn by supporters of a political party or sports team, or to show that sb has won a prize ➲ picture at MEDAL **2** a thing that has the shape of a ROSE: *The leaves formed a dark green rosette.*

ˈ**rose water** *noun* [U] a liquid with a sweet smell made from ROSES, used as a PERFUME or in cooking

ˌ**rose** ˈ**window** *noun* a decorative round window in a church, often with coloured glass (=STAINED GLASS) in it

rose·wood /ˈrəʊzwʊd; *NAmE* ˈroʊz-/ *noun* [U] the hard reddish-brown wood of a tropical tree, that has a pleasant smell and is used for making expensive furniture

Rosh Hash·ana (also **Rosh Hash·anah**) /ˌrɒʃ həˈʃɑːnə; *NAmE* ˌrɑːʃ/ *noun* [U] the Jewish New Year festival, held in September

rosin /ˈrɒzɪn; *NAmE* ˈrɑːzn/ *noun* [U] a substance that is used on the BOW of a musical instrument such as a VIOLIN so that it moves across the strings more easily ▶ **rosin** *verb* **~ sth**

ros·ter /ˈrɒstə(r); *NAmE* ˈrɑːs-; ˈrɔːs-/ *noun, verb*

- ***noun*** **1** a list of people's names and the jobs that they have to do at a particular time SYN **rota**: *a duty roster* **2** a list of the names of people who are available to do a job, play in a team, etc.
- ***verb*** **~ sb (to do sth)** (*BrE*) to put sb's name on a roster: *The driver was rostered for Sunday.*

ros·trum /ˈrɒstrəm; *NAmE* ˈrɑːs-; ˈrɔːs-/ *noun* (*pl.* **ros·trums** or **ros·tra** /-trə/) a small raised platform that a person stands on to make a speech, CONDUCT music, receive a prize, etc.

rosy /ˈrəʊzi; *NAmE* ˈroʊzi/ *adj.* (**rosi·er, rosi·est**) **1** pink and pleasant in appearance: *She had rosy cheeks.* **2** likely to be good or successful SYN **hopeful**: *The future is looking very rosy for our company.* ◇ *She* ***painted a rosy picture*** *of their life together in Italy* (= made it appear to be very good and perhaps better than it really was). IDM see GARDEN *n.*

rot /rɒt; *NAmE* rɑːt/ *verb, noun*

- ***verb*** (**-tt-**) [I, T] to decay, or make sth decay, naturally and gradually SYN **decompose**: *rotting leaves* ◇ **~ (away)** *The window frame had rotted away completely.* ◇ (*figurative*) *prisoners thrown in jail and* ***left to rot*** ◇ **~ sth** *Too much sugar will rot your teeth.* ➲ see also ROTTEN
- ***noun*** [U] **1** the process or state of decaying and falling apart: *The wood must not get damp as rot can quickly result.* ➲ see also DRY ROT, WET ROT **2 the rot** used to describe the fact that a situation is getting worse: ***The rot set in*** *last year when they reorganized the department.* ◇ *The team should manage to* ***stop the rot*** *if they play well this week.* **3** (*old-fashioned, BrE*) nonsense; silly things that sb says SYN **rubbish**: *Don't talk such rot!*

rota /ˈrəʊtə; *NAmE* ˈroʊtə/ *noun* (*BrE*) a list of jobs that need to be done and the people who will do them in turn SYN **roster**: *Dave organized a cleaning rota.*

ro·tary /ˈrəʊtəri; *NAmE* ˈroʊ-/ *adj., noun*

- ***adj.*** [only before noun] **1** (of a movement) moving in a circle around a central fixed point: *rotary motion* **2** (of a machine or piece of equipment) having parts that move in this way: *a rotary engine*
- ***noun*** (*pl.* **-ies**) (*NAmE*) = TRAFFIC CIRCLE

ˈ**Rotary club** *noun* a branch of an organization of business and professional people whose members meet for social reasons and to raise money for charity

ro·tate /rəʊˈteɪt; *NAmE* ˈroʊteɪt/ *verb* **1** [I, T] to move or turn around a central fixed point; to make sth do this: *Stay well away from the helicopter when its blades start to rotate.* ◇ **~ about/around sth** *winds rotating around the eye of a hurricane* ◇ **~ sth** *Rotate the wheel through 180 degrees.* **2** [I, T] if a job **rotates**, or if people **rotate** a job, they regularly change the job or regularly change who does the job: (**+ adv./prep.**) *The EU presidency rotates among the members.* ◇ *When I joined the company, I rotated around the different sections.* ◇ **~ sth** *We rotate the night shift so no one has to do it all the time.* ▶ **ro·tat·ing** *adj.* [only before noun]: *rotating parts* ◇ *a rotating presidency*

ro·ta·tion /rəʊˈteɪʃn; *NAmE* roʊ-/ *noun* **1** [U] the action of an object moving in a circle around a central fixed point: *the daily rotation of the earth on its axis* **2** [C] one complete movement in a circle around a fixed point: *This switch controls the number of rotations per minute.* **3** [U, C] the act of regularly changing the thing that is being used in a particular situation, or of changing the person who does a particular job: ***crop rotation/the rotation of crops*** (= changing the crop that is grown on an area of land in order to protect the soil) ◇ *Wheat, maize and sugar beet are planted* ***in rotation.*** ◇ *The committee is chaired by all the members* ***in rotation.*** ▶ **ro·ta·tion·al** /-ʃənl/ *adj.* [only before noun]

Ro·ta·va·tor™ (also **Ro·to·va·tor™**) /ˈrəʊtəveɪtə(r); *NAmE* ˈroʊ-/ *noun* (*BrE*) a machine with blades that turn and break up soil

ROTC /ˈrɒtsi; *NAmE* ˈrɑːt-/ *abbr.* (*US*) Reserve Officers' Training Corps (an organization for students in the US who are training to be military officers while they are studying)

rote /rəʊt; *NAmE* roʊt/ *noun* [U] (often used as an adjective) the process of learning sth by repeating it until you remember it rather than by understanding the meaning of it: *to learn* ***by rote*** ◇ *rote learning*

roti /ˈrəʊti; *NAmE* ˈroʊ-/ *noun* [U, C] **1** a type of S Asian bread that is cooked on a GRIDDLE **2** (*IndE*) bread of any kind

ro·tis·serie /rəʊˈtɪsəri; *NAmE* roʊ-/ *noun* (from *French*) a piece of equipment for cooking meat that turns it around on a long straight piece of metal (called a SPIT)

rotor /ˈrəʊtə(r); *NAmE* ˈroʊ-/ *noun* a part of a machine that turns around a central point: *rotor blades on a helicopter* ➲ VISUAL VOCAB page V43

Ro·to·va·tor = ROTAVATOR

rot·ten /ˈrɒtn; *NAmE* ˈrɑːtn/ *adj., adv.*

- ***adj.*** **1** (of food, wood, etc.) that has decayed and cannot be eaten or used: *the smell of rotten vegetables* ◇ *The fruit is starting to* ***go rotten.*** ◇ *rotten floorboards* **2** [usually before noun] (*informal*) very bad SYN **terrible**: *I've had a rotten day!* ◇ *What rotten luck!* ◇ *She's a rotten singer.* **3** [usually before noun] (*informal*) dishonest: *The organization is* ***rotten to the core.*** **4** [not before noun] (*informal*) looking or feeling ill/sick: *She felt rotten.* **5** [not before noun] (*informal*) feeling guilty about sth you have done: *I feel rotten about leaving them behind.* **6** [only before noun] (*informal*) used to emphasize that you are angry or upset about sth: *You can keep your rotten money!* ▶ **rot·ten·ness** *noun* [U]

IDM **a rotten** ˈ**apple** one bad person who has a bad effect on others in a group

- ***adv.*** (*informal*) to a large degree; very much: *She spoils the children rotten.* ◇ (*BrE*) *He fancies you (something) rotten.*

rot·ter /ˈrɒtə(r); *NAmE* ˈrɑːt-/ *noun* (*old-fashioned, BrE, informal*) a person who behaves badly towards other people

Rott·weiler /ˈrɒtwaɪlə(r); -vaɪ-; *NAmE* ˈrɑːtwaɪ-; ˈrɔːt-waɪ-/ *noun* a large dog that can be very aggressive

ro·tund /rəʊˈtʌnd; *NAmE* roʊ-/ *adj.* (*formal* or *humorous*) having a fat round body SYN **plump**: *the rotund figure of Mr Stevens* ▶ **ro·tund·ity** *noun* [U]

ro·tunda /rəʊˈtʌndə; *NAmE* roʊ-/ *noun* a round building or hall, especially one with a curved roof (= a DOME) ➲ VISUAL VOCAB page V12

rou·ble (*especially BrE*) (*NAmE* usually **ruble**) /ˈruːbl/ *noun* the unit of money in Russia

roué /ˈruːeɪ; *NAmE* ruːˈeɪ/ *noun* (*old-fashioned*) a man who drinks too much alcohol, uses illegal drugs, or is sexually immoral, especially a man who is fairly old

R

rouge /ruːʒ/ *noun* [U] (*old-fashioned*) a red powder used by women for giving colour to their cheeks ▶ **rouge** *verb* **~ sth**

rough 0━ /rʌf/ *adj., noun, verb, adv.*

■ ***adj.*** (**rough·er, rough·est**)

▸ NOT SMOOTH **1** 0━ having a surface that is not even or regular: *rough ground* ◇ *The skin on her hands was hard and rough.* ◇ *Trim rough edges with a sharp knife.* OPP **smooth**

▸ NOT EXACT **2** 0━ not exact; not including all details SYN **approximate**: *a* ***rough calculation/estimate*** *of the cost* ◇ *I've got a* ***rough idea*** *of where I want to go.* ◇ *There were about 20 people there,* ***at a rough guess****.* ◇ *a rough draft of a speech* ◇ *a rough sketch*

▸ VIOLENT **3** 0━ not gentle or careful; violent: *This watch is not designed for rough treatment.* ◇ *They complained of rough handling by the guards.* ◇ *rough kids* ◇ *Don't try any* ***rough stuff*** *with me!* **4** 0━ where there is a lot of violence or crime: *the roughest neighbourhood in the city*

▸ SEA **5** 0━ having large and dangerous waves: *It was too rough to sail that night.*

▸ WEATHER **6** wild and with storms

▸ DIFFICULT **7** 0━ difficult and unpleasant SYN **tough**: *He's had a really* ***rough time*** *recently* (= he's had a lot of problems). ◇ *We'll get someone in to do the rough work* (= the hard physical work).

▸ NOT WELL **8** (*BrE*) not feeling well: *You look rough—are you OK?* ◇ *I had a rough night* (= I didn't sleep well).

▸ PLAIN/BASIC **9** 0━ simply made and not finished in every detail; plain or basic: *rough wooden tables* ◇ *a rough track* ◇ (*BrE*) *rough paper for making notes on*

▸ NOT SMOOTH **10** not smooth or pleasant to taste, listen to, etc: *a rough wine/voice*

▶ **rough·ness** *noun* [U] ➲ see also ROUGHLY

IDM **a rough 'deal** the fact of being treated unfairly **rough 'edges** small parts of sth or of a person's character that are not yet as good as they should be: *The ballet still had some rough edges.* ◇ *He had a few rough edges knocked off at school.* **the ˌrough end of the 'pineapple** (*AustralE, informal*) a situation in which sb is treated badly or unfairly ➲ more at RIDE *n.*

■ ***noun***

▸ IN GOLF **1 the rough** [sing.] the part of a GOLF COURSE where the grass is long, making it more difficult to hit the ball ➲ compare FAIRWAY

▸ DRAWING/DESIGN **2** [C] (*technical*) the first version of a drawing or design that has been done quickly and without much detail

▸ VIOLENT PERSON **3** [C] (*old-fashioned, informal*) a violent person: *a gang of roughs*

IDM **in 'rough** (*especially BrE*) if you write or draw sth **in rough**, you make a first version of it, not worrying too much about mistakes or details **take the ˌrough with the 'smooth** to accept the unpleasant or difficult things that happen in life as well as the good things ➲ more at BIT

■ ***verb***

IDM **'rough it** (*informal*) to live in a way that is not very comfortable for a short time: *We can sleep on the beach. I don't mind roughing it for a night or two.*

PHR V **ˌrough sth↔'out** to draw or write sth without including all the details: *I've roughed out a few ideas.* **ˌrough sb↔'up** (*informal*) to hurt sb by hitting or kicking them: *He claimed that guards had roughed him up in prison.*

■ ***adv.*** using force or violence: *Do they always play this rough?*

IDM **live/sleep 'rough** (*BrE*) to live or sleep outdoors, usually because you have no home and no money: *young people sleeping rough on the streets*

rough·age /ˈrʌfɪdʒ/ *noun* [U] the part of food that helps to keep a person healthy by keeping the BOWELS working and moving other food quickly through the body SYN **fibre**

ˌrough-and-'ready *adj.* [usually before noun] **1** simple and prepared quickly but good enough for a particular situation: *a rough-and-ready guide to the education system* **2** (of a person) not very polite, educated or fashionable

ˌrough and 'tumble *noun* [U, sing.] **1 ~ (of sth)** a situation in which people compete with each other and are aggressive in order to get what they want: *the rough and tumble of politics* **2** noisy and slightly violent behaviour when children or animals are playing together

rough·cast /ˈrʌfkɑːst; *NAmE* -kæst/ *noun* [U] a type of PLASTER containing small stones that is used for covering the outside walls of buildings ▶ **rough·cast** *adj.*

'rough cut *noun* the first version of a film/movie, after the different scenes have been put together

'rough-cut *verb* **~ sth** to cut sth quickly, without paying attention to the exact size

ˌrough 'diamond (*BrE*) (*NAmE* **ˌdiamond in the 'rough**) *noun* a person who has many good qualities even though they do not seem to be very polite, educated, etc.

rough·en /ˈrʌfn/ *verb* [I, T] to become rough; to make sth rough: *His voice roughened with every word.* ◇ **~ sth** *Cold weather roughens your skin.*

ˌrough-'hewn *adj.* [only before noun] **1** (of stone, wood, etc.) cut in a way that leaves it with a rough surface: *rough-hewn walls* ◇ (*figurative*) *the rough-hewn features of his face* **2** (*formal*) (of a person or their behaviour) not very polite or educated

rough·house /ˈrʌfhaʊs; -haʊz/ *verb* [I, T] **~ (sb)** (*NAmE, informal*) to fight sb or play with sb roughly: *Quit roughhousing, you two!*

rough·ing /ˈrʌfɪŋ/ *noun* [U] (in ICE HOCKEY and AMERICAN FOOTBALL) an illegal use of force, for which a PENALTY may be given

ˌrough 'justice *noun* [U] **1** punishment that does not seem fair: *It was rough justice that they lost in the closing seconds of the game.* **2** treatment that is fair but not official or expected: *There was a certain amount of rough justice in his downfall.*

rough·ly 0━ /ˈrʌfli/ *adv.*

1 0━ approximately but not exactly: *Sales are up by roughly 10%.* ◇ *We live roughly halfway between here and the coast.* ◇ *They all left at roughly the same time.* ◇ ***Roughly speaking****, we receive about fifty letters a week on the subject.* **2** 0━ using force or not being careful and gentle: *He pushed her roughly out of the way.* ◇ *'What do you want?' she demanded roughly.* **3** 0━ in a way that does not leave a smooth surface: *roughly plastered walls*

rough·neck /ˈrʌfnek/ *noun* (*informal*) **1** (*especially NAmE*) a man who is noisy, rude and aggressive **2** a man who works on an OIL RIG

rough·shod /ˈrʌfʃɒd; *NAmE* -ʃɑːd/ *adv.*

IDM **ride, etc. 'roughshod over sb** (*especially BrE*) (*US* usually **run 'roughshod over sb**) to treat sb badly and not worry about their feelings

roul·ette /ruːˈlet/ *noun* [U] a gambling game in which a ball is dropped onto a moving wheel that has holes with numbers on it. Players bet on which hole the ball will be in when the wheel stops. ➲ see also RUSSIAN ROULETTE

round 0━ /raʊnd/ *adj., adv., prep., noun, verb*

■ ***adj.*** (**round·er, round·est**) **1** 0━ shaped like a circle or a ball: *a round plate* ◇ *These glasses suit people with round faces.* ◇ *The fruit are small and round.* ◇ *Rugby isn't played with a round ball.* ◇ *the discovery that the world is round* ◇ *The child was watching it all with big round eyes* (= showing interest). ◇ *a T-shirt with a round neck* ➲ see also ROUND-EYED, ROUND-TABLE **2** 0━ having a curved shape: *the round green hills of Donegal* ◇ *round brackets* (= in writing) ◇ *She had a small mouth and round pink cheeks.* **3** 0━ [only before noun] a **round** figure or amount is one that is given as a whole number, usually one ending in 0 or 5: *Make it a round figure—say forty dollars.* ◇ *Two thousand is a nice round number—put that down.* ◇ *Well,* ***in round figures*** (= not giving the exact figures) *we've spent twenty thousand so far.* ▶ **round·ness** *noun* [U]: *His face had lost its boyish roundness.*

■ ***adv.*** (*especially BrE*) (*NAmE* usually **around**) For the special uses of **round** in phrasal verbs, look at the verb entries. For

R

example, the meaning of **come round to sth** is given in the phrasal verb section of the entry for **come**. **1** 🔑 moving in a circle: *Everybody joins hands and dances round.* ◇ *How do you make the wheels go round?* ◇ *The children were spinning* ***round and round****.* ◇ (*figurative*) *The thought kept going round and round in her head.* **2** 🔑 measuring or marking the edge or outside of sth: *a young tree measuring only 18 inches round* ◇ *They've built a high fence* ***all round*** *to keep intruders out.* **3** 🔑 on all sides of sb/sth: *A large crowd had gathered round to watch.* **4** 🔑 at various places in an area: *People stood round waiting for something to happen.* **5** 🔑 in a circle or curve to face another way or the opposite way: *He turned the car round and drove back again.* ◇ *She looked round at the sound of his voice.* **6** 🔑 to the other side of sth: *We walked round to the back of the house.* ◇ *The road's blocked—you'll have to drive* ***the long way round****.* **7** 🔑 from one place, person, etc. to another: *They've moved all the furniture round.* ◇ *He went round interviewing people about local traditions.* ◇ *Pass the biscuits round.* ◇ *Have we* ***enough*** *cups* ***to go round****?* **8** 🔑 (*informal*) to or at a particular place, especially where sb lives: *I'll be round in an hour.* ◇ *We've invited the Frasers round this evening.* ➲ note at AROUND

IDM ˌ**round aˈbout 1** 🔑 approximately: *We're leaving round about ten.* ◇ *A new roof will cost round about £3 000.* **2** in the area near a place: *in Oxford and the villages round about* ➲ more at TIME

■ ***prep.*** (*especially BrE*) (*NAmE* usually **around**) **1** 🔑 in a circle: *the first woman to sail round the world* ◇ *The earth moves round the sun.* **2** 🔑 on, to or from the other side of sth: *Our house is round the next bend.* ◇ *There she is, coming round the corner.* ◇ *There must be* ***a way round*** *the problem.* **3** 🔑 on all sides of sb/sth; surrounding sb/sth: *She put her arms round him.* ◇ *He had a scarf round his neck.* ◇ *They were all sitting round the table.* **4** 🔑 in or to many parts of sth: *She looked all round the room.* **5** to fit in with particular people, ideas, etc: *He has to organize his life round the kids.* ➲ note at AROUND

IDM ˌ**round ˈhere** 🔑 near where you are now or where you live: *There are no decent schools round here.* ➲ more at MILLSTONE

■ ***noun***

‣ STAGE IN PROCESS **1** a set of events which form part of a longer process: *the next round of peace talks* ◇ *the final round of voting in the election*

‣ IN SPORT **2** a stage in a sports competition: *the qualifying rounds of the National Championships* ◇ *Hewitt was knocked out of the tournament in the third round.* **3** a stage in a BOXING or WRESTLING match: *The fight only lasted five rounds.* **4** a complete game of GOLF; a complete way around the course in some other sports, such as SHOW-JUMPING: *We played a round of golf.* ◇ *the first horse to jump a clear round*

‣ REGULAR ACTIVITIES/ROUTE **5** a regular series of activities: ***the daily round*** *of school life* ◇ *Her life is one long round of parties and fun.* **6** a regular route that sb takes when delivering or collecting sth; a regular series of visits that sb makes: *Dr Green was* ***on her*** *daily ward* ***rounds****.* ◇ (*BrE*) *a postman on his delivery round* ➲ see also MILK ROUND, PAPER ROUND

‣ DRINKS **7** a number of drinks bought by one person for all the others in a group: *a round of drinks* ◇ *It's my round* (= it is my turn to pay for the next set of drinks).

‣ BREAD **8** (*BrE*) a whole slice of bread; SANDWICHES made from two whole slices of bread: *Who's for another round of toast?* ◇ *two rounds of beef sandwiches*

‣ CIRCLE **9** a round object or piece of sth: *Cut the pastry into rounds.*

‣ OF APPLAUSE/CHEERS **10 ~ of applause/cheers** a short period during which people show their approval of sb/sth by clapping, etc: *There was a great round of applause when the dance ended.*

‣ SHOT **11** a single shot from a gun; a bullet for one shot: *They fired several rounds at the crowd.* ◇ *We only have three rounds of ammunition left.*

‣ SONG **12** (*music*) a song for two or more voices in which each sings the same tune but starts at a different time

IDM **do/go the ˈrounds (of sth) 1** (*BrE*) (*NAmE* **make the ˈrounds**) if news or a joke **does the rounds**, it is passed on quickly from one person to another **2** (*BrE*) (also **make the ˈrounds** *NAmE, BrE*) to go around from place to place, especially when looking for work or support for a political CAMPAIGN, etc. **in the ˈround 1** (of a work of art) made so that it can be seen from all sides: *an opportunity to see Canova's work in the round* **2** (of a theatre or play) with the people watching all around a central stage

■ ***verb*** **1** [T] **~ sth** to go around a corner of a building, a bend in the road, etc: *The boat rounded the tip of the island.* ◇ *We rounded the bend at high speed.* **2** [T, I] **~ (sth)** to make sth into a round shape; to form into a round shape: *She rounded her lips and whistled.* ◇ *His eyes rounded with horror.* **3** [T] **~ sth (up/down) (to sth)** to increase or decrease a number to the next highest or lowest whole number

PHR V ˌ**round sth↔ˈoff (with sth) 1** (*NAmE* also ˌ**round sth↔ˈout**) to finish an activity or complete sth in a good or suitable way: *She rounded off the tour with a concert at Carnegie Hall.* **2** to take the sharp or rough edges off sth: *You can round off the corners with sandpaper.* ˈ**round on sb** to suddenly speak angrily to sb and criticize or attack them SYN **turn on**: *He rounded on journalists, calling them 'a pack of vultures'.* ˌ**round sb/sth↔ˈup 1** to find and gather together people, animals or things: *I rounded up a few friends for a party.* ◇ *The cattle are rounded up in the evenings.* **2** if police or soldiers **round up** a group of people, they find them and arrest or capture them ➲ related noun ROUND-UP

roundabout (*BrE*)
merry-go-round (*NAmE*)

merry-go-round /
roundabout (*both BrE*)
carousel (*NAmE*)

round·about /ˈraʊndəbaʊt/ *noun, adj.*

■ ***noun*** (*BrE*) **1** (*NAmE* ˈ**traffic circle, ro·tary**) a place where two or more roads meet, forming a circle that all traffic must go around in the same direction: *At the roundabout, take the second exit.* ➲ see also MINI-ROUNDABOUT **2** (*NAmE* ˈ**merry-go-round**) a round platform for children to play on in a park, etc. that is pushed round while the children are sitting on it **3** (*BrE*) = MERRY-GO-ROUND-(1) IDM see SWING *n.*

■ ***adj.*** [usually before noun] not done or said using the shortest, simplest or most direct way possible: *It was a difficult and roundabout trip.* ◇ *He told us, in a very roundabout way, that he was thinking of leaving.*

ˈ**round bracket** *noun* (*BrE*) = BRACKET *n* (1)

round·ed 🔑 /ˈraʊndɪd/ *adj.* [usually before noun] **1** 🔑 having a round shape: *a surface with rounded edges* ◇ *rounded shoulders* **2** having a wide variety of qualities that combine to produce sth pleasant, complete and balanced: *a smooth rounded taste* ◇ *a fully rounded education* **3** (*phonetics*) (of a speech sound) produced with the lips in a narrow round position OPP **unrounded** ➲ see also WELL ROUNDED

roundel /ˈraʊndl/ *noun* (*technical*) a round design that is used as a decoration or to identify an aircraft

round·ers /ˈraʊndəz; *NAmE* -ərz/ *noun* [U] a British game played especially in schools by two teams using a BAT and ball. Each player tries to hit the ball and then run around the four sides of a square before the other team can return the ball. ➲ compare BASEBALL

ˌ**round-ˈeyed** *adj.* with eyes that are fully open because of surprise, fear, etc.

Round·head /ˈraʊndhed/ *noun* a person who supported Parliament against the King in the English Civil War (1642-49) ➲ compare CAVALIER

R

round·house /ˈraʊndhaʊs/ *noun* a punch where the arm moves around in a wide curve

ˈ**roundhouse kick** *noun* a move in KARATE and other MARTIAL ARTS, in which you turn on one foot as you make a high kick with the other

round·ing /ˈraʊndɪŋ/ *noun* [U] (*phonetics*) the fact of producing a speech sound with the lips in a rounded position

round·ly /ˈraʊndli/ *adv.* strongly or by a large number of people: *The report has been roundly criticized.* ◇ *They were roundly defeated* (= they lost by a large number of points).

ˌ**round ˈrobin** *noun* **1** (*sport*) a competition in which every player or team plays every other player or team **2** a letter that has been signed by a large number of people who wish to express their opinions about sth **3** something that is made, written, etc. by several people who each add a part one after another: *a round robin story* **4** a letter intended to be read by many people that is copied and sent to each one

ˌ**round-ˈshouldered** *adj.* with shoulders that are bent forward or sloping downwards

rounds·man /ˈraʊndzmən/ *noun* (*pl.* **-men** /-mən/) **1** (*NAmE* ˈ**route man**) a person who delivers things to people in a particular area **2** (*NAmE*) the police officer in charge of a group of officers that is moving around an area **3** (*AustralE*) a journalist who deals with a particular subject

ˌ**round-ˈtable** *adj.* [only before noun] (of discussions, meetings, etc.) at which everyone is equal and has the same rights: *round-table talks*

ˌ**round-the-ˈclock** (also aˌ**round-the-ˈclock**) *adj.* [only before noun] lasting or happening all day and night: *round-the-clock nursing care* ➲ see also CLOCK

ˌ**round ˈtrip** *noun* [C, U] a journey to a place and back again: *a 30-mile round trip to work* ◇ (*NAmE*) *It's 30 miles round trip to work.* ▸ ˌ**round-ˈtrip** *adj.*: (*NAmE*) *a round-trip ticket* ➲ see also RETURN TICKET

ˈ**round-up** *noun* [usually sing.] **1** a summary of the most important points of a particular subject, especially the news: *We'll be back after the break with a round-up of today's other stories.* **2** an act of bringing people or animals together in one place for a particular purpose

round·worm /ˈraʊndwɜːm; *NAmE* -wɜːrm/ *noun* a small WORM that lives in the INTESTINES of pigs, humans and some other animals

R

rouse /raʊz/ *verb* **1** (*formal*) to wake sb up, especially when they are sleeping deeply **~ sb from sleep/bed**: *The telephone roused me from my sleep at 6 a.m.* ◇ **~ sb** *Nicky roused her with a gentle nudge.* **2** to make sb want to start doing sth when they were not active or interested in doing it: **~ sb/yourself (to sth)** *A lot of people were roused to action by the appeal.* ◇ **~ sb/yourself to do sth** *Richard couldn't rouse himself to say anything in reply.* **3 ~ sth** (*formal*) to make sb feel a particular emotion: *to rouse sb's anger* ◇ *What* ***roused your suspicions*** (= what made you suspicious)? **4** [usually passive] **~ sb** to make sb angry, excited or full of emotion: *Chris is not easily roused.* ➲ see also AROUSE

rous·ing /ˈraʊzɪŋ/ *adj.* [usually before noun] **1** full of energy and enthusiasm: *a rousing cheer* ◇ *The team was given* ***a rousing reception*** *by the fans.* **2** intended to make other people feel enthusiastic about sth: *a rousing speech*

roust /raʊst/ *verb* **~ sb (from sth)** (*NAmE*) to disturb sb or make them move from a place

roust·about /ˈraʊstəbaʊt/ *noun* (*especially NAmE*) a man with no special skills who does temporary work, for example on an OIL RIG or in a CIRCUS SYN **casual labourer**

rout /raʊt/ *noun, verb*

▪ ***noun*** [sing.] a situation in which sb is defeated easily and completely in a battle or competition

IDM **put sb to ˈrout** (*literary*) to defeat sb easily and completely

▪ ***verb*** **~ sb** to defeat sb completely in a competition, a battle, etc: *The Buffalo Bills routed the Atlanta Falcons 41–14.*

route 🔑 AW /ruːt; *NAmE* also raʊt/ *noun, verb*

▪ ***noun*** **1** 🔑 a way that you follow to get from one place to another: *Which is the best route to take?* ◇ *Motorists are advised to find an alternative route.* ◇ *a coastal route* ◇ **~ (from A to B)** *the quickest route from Florence to Rome* ◇ *an* ***escape route*** ➲ see also EN ROUTE **2** 🔑 a fixed way along which a bus, train, etc. regularly travels or goods are regularly sent: *The house is not on a* ***bus route.*** ◇ ***shipping routes*** ◇ *a* ***cycle route*** (= a path that is only for CYCLISTS) **3** 🔑 **~ (to sth)** a particular way of achieving sth: *the route to success* **4** 🔑 used before the number of a main road in the US: *Route 66*

▪ ***verb*** (**rout·ing** or **route·ing**, **rout·ed**, **rout·ed**) **~ sb/sth (+ adv./prep.)** to send sb/sth by a particular route: *Satellites route data all over the globe.*

Route 128 /ˌruːt ˌwʌn twentiˈeɪt/ *noun* (in the US) an area in Massachusetts where there are many companies connected with the computer and ELECTRONICS industries ORIGIN From the name of an important road in the area.

ˈ**route man** (*NAmE*) (*BrE* **rounds·man**) *noun* a person who delivers things to people in a particular area

ˈ**route march** *noun* a long march for soldiers over a particular route, especially to improve their physical condition

ˌ**Route ˈOne** *noun* [U] (*BrE*) (in football (SOCCER)) kicking the ball a long way towards your opponent's end, used as a direct way of attacking, rather than passing the ball between players

router[1] /ˈruːtə(r); *NAmE* also ˈraʊt-/ *noun* (*computing*) a device which sends data to the appropriate parts of a computer network ➲ VISUAL VOCAB page V54

router[2] /ˈraʊtə(r)/ *noun* an electric tool which cuts shallow lines in surfaces

rou·tine 🔑 /ruːˈtiːn/ *noun, adj.*

▪ ***noun*** **1** 🔑 [C, U] the normal order and way in which you regularly do things: *We are trying to get the baby into a routine for feeding and sleeping.* ◇ *Make exercise a part of your* ***daily routine.*** ◇ *We clean and repair the machines* ***as a matter of routine.*** **2** 🔑 [U] (*disapproving*) a situation in which life is boring because things are always done in the same way: *She needed a* ***break from routine.*** **3** [C] a series of movements, jokes, etc. that are part of a performance: *a dance routine* **4** [C] (*computing*) a list of instructions that enable a computer to perform a particular task

▪ ***adj.*** [usually before noun] **1** 🔑 done or happening as a normal part of a particular job, situation or process: ***routine enquiries/questions/tests*** ◇ *The fault was discovered during a routine check.* **2** 🔑 not unusual or different in any way: *He died of a heart attack during a routine operation.* **3** 🔑 (*disapproving*) ordinary and boring SYN **dull, humdrum**: *a routine job* ◇ *This type of work rapidly becomes routine.* ▸ **rou·tine·ly** *adv.*: *Visitors are routinely checked as they enter the building.*

ˈ**routing number** (*US*) (*BrE* ˈ**sort code**) *noun* a number that is used to identify a particular bank

roux /ruː/ *noun* [C, U] (*pl.* **roux**) (from *French*) a mixture of fat and flour heated together until they form a solid mass, used for making sauces

rove /rəʊv; *NAmE* roʊv/ *verb* **1** [I, T] (*formal*) to travel from one place to another, often with no particular purpose SYN **roam**: **+ adv./prep.** *A quarter of a million refugees roved around the country.* ◇ **~ sth** *bands of thieves who roved the countryside* **2** [I] (**+ adv./prep.**) if sb's eyes **rove**, the person keeps looking in different directions

rover /ˈrəʊvə(r); *NAmE* ˈroʊ-/ *noun* (*literary*) a person who likes to travel a lot rather than live in one place

rov·ing /ˈrəʊvɪŋ; *NAmE* ˈroʊ-/ *adj.* [usually before noun] travelling from one place to another and not staying anywhere permanently: *a roving reporter for ABC news* ◇ *Patrick's roving lifestyle takes him between London and Los Angeles.*

IDM **have a roving ˈeye** (*old-fashioned*) to always be looking for the chance to have a new sexual relationship

row[1] 🔑 /rəʊ; *NAmE* roʊ/ *noun, verb* ➲ see also ROW[2]

▪ ***noun*** **1** 🔑 **~ (of sb/sth)** a number of people standing or sitting next to each other in a line; a number of objects arranged in a line: *a row of trees* ◇ *We sat* **in a row** *at the back of the room.* ◇ *The vegetables were planted in neat rows.* **2** a line of seats in a cinema/movie theater, etc: *Let's sit in the back row.* ◇ *Our seats are five rows from the front.* **3** a complete line of STITCHES in knitting or CROCHET ➲ VISUAL VOCAB page V35 **4 Row** used in the name of some roads: *Manor Row* **5** [usually sing.] an act of ROWING a boat; the period of time spent doing this: *We went for a row on the lake.* ➲ see also DEATH ROW, SKID ROW

IDM **in a 'row 1** if sth happens several times **in a row**, it happens in exactly the same way each time, and nothing different happens in the time between: *This is her third win in a row.* **2** if sth happens for several days, etc. **in a row**, it happens on each of those days: *Inflation has fallen for the third month in a row.* ➲ more at DUCK *n.*

■ *verb* **1** [I, T] to move a boat through water using OARS (= long wooden poles with flat ends): *We rowed around the island.* ◇ **~ sth** *Grace rowed the boat out to sea again.* **2** [T] **~ sb (+ adv./prep.)** to take sb somewhere in a boat with OARS: *The fisherman rowed us back to the shore.*

row² /raʊ/ *noun, verb* ➲ see also ROW¹

■ *noun* (*informal, especially BrE*) **1** [C] **~ (about/over sth)** a serious disagreement between people, organizations, etc. about sth: *A row has broken out over education.* **2** [C] a noisy argument between two or more people SYN **quarrel**: *She left him after a* **blazing row.** ◇ *family rows* ◇ *He* **had a row with** *his son.* **3** [sing.] a loud unpleasant noise SYN **din, racket**: *Who's making that row?*

■ *verb* [I] (*BrE, informal*) to have a noisy argument: *Mike and Sue are always rowing.* ◇ **~ (with sb) (about sb/sth)** *She had rowed with her parents about her boyfriend.*

rowan /'rəʊən; 'raʊən; *NAmE* 'roʊən; 'raʊən/ (also **'rowan tree**, **,mountain 'ash**) *noun* a small tree that has red BERRIES in the autumn/fall

row·boat /'rəʊbəʊt; *NAmE* 'roʊboʊt/ (*NAmE*) (*BrE* **'rowing boat**) *noun* a small open boat that you move using OARS ➲ VISUAL VOCAB page V44

rowdy /'raʊdi/ *adj.* (**row·dier, row·di·est**) (of people) making a lot of noise or likely to cause trouble SYN **disorderly**: *a rowdy crowd at the pub* ▶ **row·dily** *adv.* **row·di·ness** *noun* [U] **rowdy** *noun* (*pl.* -ies): *rowdies and troublemakers*

rowdy·ism /'raʊdiɪzəm/ *noun* [U] behaviour that is noisy and causes trouble

rower /'rəʊə(r); *NAmE* 'roʊ-/ *noun* a person who ROWS a boat

row house /'rəʊ haʊs; *NAmE* 'roʊ/ (also **'town house**) (both *NAmE*) (*BrE* **,terraced 'house**) *noun* a house that is one of a row of houses that are joined together on each side ➲ VISUAL VOCAB page V14

row·ing /'rəʊɪŋ; *NAmE* 'roʊɪŋ/ *noun* [U] the sport or activity of travelling in a boat using OARS: *to go rowing*

'rowing boat (*BrE*) (*NAmE* **row·boat**) *noun* a small open boat that you move using OARS ➲ VISUAL VOCAB page V44

'rowing machine *noun* a piece of sports equipment on which you make the same movements as sb who is ROWING a boat ➲ VISUAL VOCAB page V35

row·lock /'rɒlək; 'rəʊlɒk; *NAmE* 'rɑːl-; 'roʊlɑːk/ (*BrE*) (*NAmE* **oar·lock**) *noun* a device fixed to the side of a boat for holding an OAR

royal /'rɔɪəl/ *adj., noun*

■ *adj.* [only before noun] **1** connected with or belonging to the king or queen of a country: *the royal family* ◇ *the royal household* ➲ compare REGAL **2** (*abbr.* R) used in the names of organizations that serve or are supported by a king or queen: *the Royal Navy* ◇ *the Royal Society for the Protection of Birds* **3** impressive; suitable for a king or queen SYN **splendid**: *We were given a royal welcome.*

■ *noun* [usually pl.] (*informal*) a member of a royal family

the ,Royal A'cademy (also **the ,Royal Academy of 'Arts**) *noun* [sing.] a British organization whose members are famous artists. Its building in London contains an art school and space for exhibitions.

the ,royal as'sent *noun* [sing.] (in Britain) the signature of an Act of Parliament by the king or queen so that it becomes law

,royal 'blue *adj.* deep bright blue ▶ **,royal 'blue** *noun* [U]

,Royal Com'mission *noun* **~ (on/into sth)** | **~ (to do sth)** (in Britain) a group of people who are officially chosen to examine a particular law or subject and suggest any changes or new laws that should be introduced

,Royal 'Highness *noun* **His/Her/Your Royal Highness** a title of respect used when talking to or about a member of the royal family: *Their Royal Highnesses, the Duke and Duchess of Kent*

,royal 'icing *noun* [U] (*BrE*) a hard white covering for a fruit cake, made with sugar and the white part of eggs

roy·al·ist /'rɔɪəlɪst/ *noun* a person who believes that a country should have a king or queen SYN **monarchist** ➲ compare REPUBLICAN ▶ **roy·al·ist** *adj.*

,royal 'jelly *noun* [U] a substance that is produced by worker BEES and that is fed to a young queen bee: *health food products containing royal jelly*

roy·al·ly /'rɔɪəli/ *adv.* (*old-fashioned*) very well; in a very impressive way or to a great degree

the ,Royal 'Mail *noun* (in Britain) the service that collects and delivers letters

,royal 'tennis *noun* [U] (*AustralE*) = REAL TENNIS

roy·alty /'rɔɪəlti/ *noun* (*pl.* -ies) **1** [U] one or more members of a royal family: *The gala evening was attended by royalty and politicians.* ◇ *We were treated like royalty.* **2** [C, usually pl.] a sum of money that is paid to sb who has written a book, piece of music, etc. each time that it is sold or performed: *All royalties from the album will go to charity.* ◇ *She received £2 000* **in royalties.** **3** [C, usually pl.] a sum of money that is paid by an oil or mining company to the owner of the land that they are working on

,royal 'warrant *noun* [usually sing.] a king's or queen's permission for a company to supply goods to them and to advertise this fact on the company's products, etc.

the ,royal "we' *noun* [sing.] the use of 'we' instead of 'I' by a single person, as used traditionally by kings and queens in the past

roz·zer /'rɒzə(r); *NAmE* 'rɑːz-/ *noun* (*old-fashioned, BrE, informal*) a police officer

RP /,ɑː 'piː; *NAmE* ,ɑːr/ *noun* [U] the abbreviation for 'received pronunciation' (the standard form of British pronunciation, based on educated speech in southern England)

RPI /,ɑː piː 'aɪ; *NAmE* ,ɑːr/ *abbr.* RETAIL PRICE INDEX

rpm /,ɑː piː 'em; *NAmE* ,ɑːr/ *abbr.* revolutions per minute (a measurement of the speed of an engine or a record when it is playing)

RRP /,ɑːr ɑː 'piː; *NAmE* ,ɑːr ɑːr/ *abbr.* recommended retail price

RRSP /,ɑːr ɑːr es 'piː/ *abbr.* (*CanE*) registered retirement savings plan (a special type of savings plan in which you can save money without paying taxes on it until you stop working when you are older)

RSA /,ɑːr es 'eɪ/ *abbr.* (in the UK) Royal Society of Arts

RSI /,ɑːr es 'aɪ/ *noun* [U] the abbreviation for 'repetitive strain injury' or 'repetitive stress injury' (pain and swelling, especially in the arms and hands, caused by performing the same movement many times in a job or an activity)

RSPCA /,ɑːr es piː siː 'eɪ/ *abbr.* (in the UK) Royal Society for the Prevention of Cruelty to Animals

RSS /,ɑːr es 'es/ *abbr.* (*computing*) Really Simple Syndication (a standard system for the distribution of information, especially news, from an Internet publisher to Internet users)

RSVP (*BrE*) (also **R.S.V.P.** *US, BrE*) /,ɑːr es viː 'piː/ *abbr.* (written on invitations) please reply (from French 'répondez s'il vous plaît')

RTA /,ɑː tiː 'eɪ; *NAmE* ,ɑːr/ *abbr.* (*BrE*) road traffic accident

R

RTF /ˌɑː tiː ˈef; *NAmE* ˌɑːr/ *abbr.* (*computing*) rich text format (a type of file containing data that can be used with different programs or systems): *an RTF file*

Rt Hon *abbr.* (*BrE*) (in writing) RIGHT HONOURABLE

Rt Revd (also **Rt. Rev.**) *abbr.* (*BrE*) (in writing) RIGHT REVEREND

rub 0‑ /rʌb/ *verb, noun*

■ ***verb*** (**-bb-**) **1** 0‑ [T, I] to move your hand, or sth such as a cloth, backwards and forwards over a surface while pressing firmly: **~ sth** *She rubbed her chin thoughtfully.* ◇ **~ sth/ yourself with sth** *Rub the surface with sandpaper before painting.* ◇ **~ sth/yourself against sth** *The cat rubbed itself against my legs.* ◇ **~ at sth** *I rubbed at the stain on the cloth.* ◇ **~ against sth** *Animals had been rubbing against the trees.* ◇ **~ sth/yourself + adj.** *Rub the surface smooth.* **2** 0‑ [T, I] to press two surfaces against each other and move them backwards and forwards; to be pressed together and move in this way: **~ sth** (**together**) *She rubbed her hands in delight.* ◇ **~** (**together**) *It sounded like two pieces of wood rubbing together.* **3** 0‑ [I, T] (of a surface) to move backwards and forwards many times against sth while pressing it, especially causing pain or damage: *The back of my shoe is rubbing.* ◇ **~ on/against sth** *The wheel is rubbing on the mudguard.* ◇ **~ sth** (**+ adj.**) *The horse's neck was* ***rubbed raw*** (= until the skin came off) *where the rope had been.* **4** 0‑ [T] **~ sth + adv./prep.** to spread a liquid or other substance over a surface while pressing firmly: *She rubbed the lotion into her skin.*

IDM **rub sb's ˈnose in it** (*informal*) to keep reminding sb in an unkind way of their past mistakes **rub ˈsalt into the wound** | **rub ˈsalt into sb's wounds** to make a difficult experience even more difficult for sb **rub ˈshoulders with sb** (*NAmE* also **rub ˈelbows with sb**) to meet and spend time with a famous person, socially or as part of your job **rub sb up the wrong ˈway** (*BrE*) (*NAmE* **rub sb the wrong ˈway**) (*informal*) to make sb annoyed or angry, often without intending to, by doing or saying sth that offends them ➲ more at TWO

PHR V **ˌrub aˈlong** (**with sb/together**) (*BrE, informal*) (of two people) to live or work together in a friendly enough way **ˌrub sb/oneself/sth↔ˈdown** to rub the skin of a person, horse, etc. hard with sth to make it clean and dry **ˌrub sth↔ˈdown** to make sth smooth by rubbing it with a special material **ˌrub it ˈin** | **ˌrub sth ˈin** [no passive] to keep reminding sb of sth they feel embarrassed about and want to forget: *I know I was stupid; you don't have to* ***rub it in***. **ˌrub ˈoff** (**on/onto sb**) (of personal qualities, behaviour, opinions, etc.) to become part of a person's character as a result of that person spending time with sb who has those qualities, etc: *Her sense of fun has rubbed off on her children.* **ˌrub sth↔ˈoff** (**sth**) | **ˌrub ˈoff** to remove sth or to be removed by rubbing: *She rubbed off the dead skin.* ◇ *The gold colouring had begun to rub off.* ◇ (*BrE*) *If you write on the blackboard, rub it off at the end of the lesson.* **ˌrub sb↔ˈout** (*NAmE, slang*) to murder sb **ˌrub sth↔ˈout** (*BrE*) (also **erase** *NAmE, BrE*) to remove the marks made by a pencil, etc, using a RUBBER/ERASER: *to rub out a mistake*

■ ***noun*** **1** [C, usually sing.] an act of rubbing a surface: *She gave her knee a quick rub.* **2 the rub** [sing.] (*formal* or *humorous*) a problem or difficulty: *The hotel is in the middle of nowhere and* ***there lies the rub***. *We don't have a car.*

rub·ber 0‑ /ˈrʌbə(r)/ *noun*

1 0‑ [U] a strong substance that can be stretched and does not allow liquids to pass through it, used for making tyres, boots, etc. It is made from the liquid (=SAP) inside a tropical plant or is produced using chemicals: *a ball made of rubber* ◇ *a rubber tree* ➲ see also FOAM RUBBER, INDIA RUBBER **2** [C] (*BrE*) (also **eraser** *NAmE, BrE*) a small piece of rubber or a similar substance, used for removing pencil marks from paper; a piece of soft material used for removing CHALK marks from a BLACKBOARD ➲ VISUAL VOCAB page V56 **3** [C] (*old-fashioned, informal, especially NAmE*) = CONDOM **4** [C] (in some card games or sports) a competition consisting of a series of games or matches between the same teams or players

IDM **where the ˌrubber meets the ˈroad** (*NAmE*) the point at which sth is tested and you really find out whether it is successful or true: *Here's where the rubber meets the road: will consumers actually buy the product?* ➲ more at BURN *v.* ▸ **rub·ber** *adj.* [usually before noun]: *a rubber ball* ◇ *rubber gloves*

ˌrubber ˈband (*BrE* also **eˌlastic ˈband**) *noun* a thin round piece of rubber used for holding things together ➲ VISUAL VOCAB page V56

ˌrubber ˈboot (*NAmE*) (*BrE* **wel·ling·ton**, **ˌwellington ˈboot**, *informal* **welly**) *noun* one of a pair of long rubber boots, usually reaching almost up to the knee, that you wear to stop your feet getting wet ➲ VISUAL VOCAB page V52

ˌrubber ˈbullet *noun* a bullet made of rubber intended to injure but not to kill people, used by the army or police to control violent crowds

ˌrubber ˈdinghy (also **dinghy**) (*US* also **ˌrubber ˈraft**) *noun* a small boat made of rubber that is filled with air, used especially for rescuing people from ships and planes

rub·ber·ized (*BrE* also **-ised**) /ˈrʌbəraɪzd/ *adj.* [only before noun] covered with rubber: *rubberized cloth*

rub·ber·neck /ˈrʌbənek; *NAmE* -bərn-/ *verb* [I] (*informal, especially NAmE*) to turn to look at sth while you are driving past it ▸ **rub·ber·neck·er** *noun*

ˈrubber plant *noun* a plant with thick shiny green leaves, often grown indoors

ˌrubber ˈstamp *noun* **1** a small tool that you hold in your hand and use for printing the date, the name of an organization, etc. on a document ➲ VISUAL VOCAB page V56 **2** (*disapproving*) a person or group that automatically gives approval to the actions or decisions of others: *Parliament is seen as a rubber stamp for decisions made elsewhere.*

ˌrubber-ˈstamp *verb* **~ sth** (often *disapproving*) to give official approval to a law, plan, decision, etc, especially without considering it carefully

rub·bery /ˈrʌbəri/ *adj.* **1** looking or feeling like rubber: *The eggs were overcooked and rubbery.* **2** (of legs or knees) feeling weak and unable to support your weight

rub·bing /ˈrʌbɪŋ/ *noun* a copy of writing or a design on a piece of stone or metal that is made by placing a piece of paper over it and rubbing with CHALK, a pencil, etc. ➲ see also BRASS RUBBING

ˈrubbing alcohol (*NAmE*) (*BrE* **ˌsurgical ˈspirit**) *noun* [U] a clear liquid, consisting mainly of alcohol, used for cleaning wounds, etc.

British/American

rubbish / garbage / trash / refuse

- **Rubbish** is the usual word in *BrE* for the things that you throw away because you no longer want or need them. **Garbage** and **trash** are both used in *NAmE*. Inside the home, **garbage** tends to mean waste food and other wet material, while **trash** is paper, cardboard and dry material.
- In *BrE*, you put your **rubbish** in a **dustbin** in the street to be collected by the **dustmen**. In *NAmE*, your **garbage** and **trash** goes in a **garbage/trashcan** in the street and is collected by **garbage men/collectors**.
- **Refuse** is a formal word and is used in both *BrE* and *NAmE*. **Refuse collector** is the formal word for a dustman or garbage collector.

rub·bish 0‑ /ˈrʌbɪʃ/ *noun, verb*

■ ***noun*** [U] **1** 0‑ (*especially BrE*) things that you throw away because you no longer want or need them: *a* ***rubbish bag/ bin*** ◇ *a* ***rubbish dump/heap/tip*** ◇ *The streets were littered with rubbish.* ◇ ***garden/household rubbish*** ➲ COLLOCATIONS at ENVIRONMENT ➲ see also GARBAGE, TRASH **2** 0‑ (*BrE, informal*) (also used as an adjective) something that you think is of poor quality: *I thought the play was rubbish!* ◇ *Do we have to listen to this rubbish music?* **3** 0‑ (*BrE, informal*) comments, ideas, etc. that you think are stu-

pid or wrong SYN **nonsense**: *Rubbish! You're not fat.* ◇ *You're talking a load of rubbish.* ◇ *It's not rubbish—it's true!*
■ ***verb*** (*BrE, informal*) (*NAmE* **trash**) **~ sb/sth** to criticize sb/sth severely or treat them as though they are of no value

rub·bishy /'rʌbɪʃi/ *adj.* (*BrE, informal*) of very poor quality SYN **trashy**: *rubbishy old films*

rub·ble /'rʌbl/ *noun* [U] broken stones or bricks from a building or wall that has been destroyed or damaged: *The bomb* ***reduced*** *the houses* ***to rubble***.

'rub-down *noun* **1** the act of rubbing sb/sth with a cloth or special material, for example to make a person dry or to make sth dry, clean or smooth: *You may need to give the floor a rub-down with glasspaper.* **2** (*NAmE*) the act of rubbing and pressing a person's body with the hands to reduce pain in the muscles and joints SYN **massage**

Rube Goldberg /ˌru:b 'gəʊldbɜ:g; *NAmE* 'goʊldbɜ:rg/ (*NAmE*) (*BrE* **Heath Rob·in·son**) *adj.* [only before noun] (*humorous*) (of machines and devices) having a very complicated design, especially when used to perform a very simple task; not practical

ru·bella /ru:'belə/ *noun* [U] (*medical*) = GERMAN MEASLES

Ru·ben·esque /ˌru:bə'nesk/ *adj.* (of a woman) having a round body with large breasts and hips ORIGIN From the name of the Flemish painter Peter Paul Rubens, who often painted women with large, fairly fat bodies.

Ru·bi·con /'ru:bɪkən; *NAmE* -kɑ:n/ **the Rubicon** *noun* [sing.] the point at which a decision has been taken which can no longer be changed: *Today we* ***cross the Rubicon***. *There is no going back.* ORIGIN From the **Rubicon**, a stream which formed the border between Italy and Gaul. When Julius Caesar broke the law by crossing it with his army in 49BC, it led inevitably to war.

ru·bi·cund /'ru:bɪkənd/ *adj.* (*literary*) (of a person's face) having a healthy red colour SYN **ruddy**

ru·bid·ium /rʊ'bɪdiəm/ *noun* [U] (*symb.* **Rb**) a chemical element. Rubidium is a rare soft silver-coloured metal that reacts strongly with water and burns when it is brought into contact with air.

Rubik's Cube™ /'ru:bɪks kju:b/ *noun* a PUZZLE consisting of a plastic CUBE covered with coloured squares that you turn to make each side of the cube a different colour

ruble *noun* (*especially NAmE*) = ROUBLE

ru·bric /'ru:brɪk/ *noun* (*formal*) a title or set of instructions written in a book, an exam paper, etc.

ruby /'ru:bi/ *noun* (*pl.* -ies) **1** [C] a dark red PRECIOUS STONE: *a ruby ring* **2** [U] a dark red colour ▸ **ruby** *adj.*: *ruby lips*

ˌruby 'wedding (*BrE*) (*US* **ˌruby anni'versary**) (also **ˌruby 'wedding anniversary** *US, BrE*) *noun* the 40th anniversary of a wedding ➲ compare DIAMOND WEDDING, GOLDEN WEDDING, SILVER WEDDING

ruched /ru:ʃt/ *adj.* (of cloth, clothes, etc.) sewn so that they hang in folds: *ruched curtains*

ruck /rʌk/ *noun, verb*
■ ***noun*** **1** [C] (in RUGBY) a group of players who gather round the ball when it is lying on the ground and push each other in order to get the ball **2** [sing.] a group of people standing closely together or fighting **3 the ruck** [sing.] (*disapproving*) ordinary people or events: *She saw marriage to him as a way out of the ruck.*
■ ***verb*** [I] (in RUGBY) to take part in a ruck (1)
PHR V **ˌruck 'up | ˌruck sth↔'up** (of cloth) to form untidy folds; to make sth do this: *Your dress is rucked up at the back.*

ruck·sack /'rʌksæk/ (*BrE*) (also **back·pack** *NAmE, BrE*) *noun* a large bag, often supported on a light metal frame, carried on the back and used especially by people who go climbing or walking ➲ VISUAL VOCAB page V52

ruckus /'rʌkəs/ *noun* [sing.] (*informal, especially NAmE*) a situation in which there is a lot of noisy activity, confusion or argument SYN **commotion**

ruc·tions /'rʌkʃnz/ *noun* [pl.] (*especially BrE*) angry protests or arguments: *There'll be ructions if her father ever finds out.*

rud·der /'rʌdə(r)/ *noun* a piece of wood or metal at the back of a boat or an aircraft that is used for controlling its direction ➲ VISUAL VOCAB page V43

rud·der·less /'rʌdələs; *NAmE* -dərl-/ *adj.* (*formal*) with nobody in control; not knowing what to do

ruddy /'rʌdi/ *adj., adv.*
■ ***adj.*** **1** (of a person's face) looking red and healthy: *ruddy cheeks* ◇ *a ruddy complexion* **2** (*literary*) red in colour: *a ruddy sky* **3** [only before noun] (*BrE, informal*) a mild swear word that some people use to show that they are annoyed: *I can't get the ruddy car to start!*
■ ***adv.*** (*BrE, informal*) a mild swear word used by some people to emphasize what they are saying, especially when they are annoyed: *There was a ruddy great hole in the ceiling.*

Synonyms

rude

cheeky • insolent • disrespectful • impolite • impertinent • discourteous

These are all words for people showing a lack of respect for other people.

rude having or showing a lack of respect for other people and their feelings: *Why are you so rude to your mother?* ◇ *It's rude to speak when you're eating.*

cheeky (*BrEinformal*) (especially of children) rude in an amusing or an annoying way: *You cheeky monkey!* ◇ *a cheeky grin*

insolent (*rather formal*) very rude, especially to sb who is older or more important NOTE **Insolent** is used especially to talk about the behaviour of children towards adults.

disrespectful (*rather formal*) showing a lack of respect for sb/sth: *Some people said he had been disrespectful to the President in his last speech.*

impolite (*rather formal*) not behaving in a pleasant way that follows the rules of society: *Some people think it is impolite to ask someone's age.* NOTE **Impolite** is often used in the phrases *It seemed impolite* and *It would be impolite.*

impertinent (*rather formal*) not showing respect for sb who is older or more important NOTE **Impertinent** is often used by people such as parents and teachers when they are telling children that they are angry with them for being rude: *Don't be impertinent!*

discourteous (*formal*) having bad manners and not showing respect: *He didn't wish to appear discourteous.*

PATTERNS
- rude/cheeky/disrespectful/impolite/discourteous **to** sb
- rude/impolite/impertinent **to do sth**

rude 🔑 /ru:d/ *adj.* (**ruder, rud·est**)
1 🔑 having or showing a lack of respect for other people and their feelings SYN **impolite**: *a rude comment* ◇ **~ (to sb) (about sb/sth)** *The man was downright rude to us.* ◇ *Why are you so rude to your mother?* ◇ *She was very rude about my driving.* ◇ **~ (to do sth)** *It's rude to speak when you're eating.* **2** (*especially BrE*) (*NAmE* usually **crude**) connected with sex or the body in a way that people find offensive or embarrassing: *a rude gesture* ◇ *Someone made a rude noise.* ◇ *The joke is too rude to repeat.* **3** [only before noun] (*formal*) sudden, unpleasant and unexpected: *Those expecting good news will get a rude shock.* ◇ *If the players think they can win this match easily, they are in for* ***a rude awakening***. **4** (*literary*) made in a simple, basic way SYN **primitive**: *rude*

R

shacks ▸ **rude·ness** *noun* [U]: *She was critical to the point of rudeness.*

IDM **in rude 'health** (*old-fashioned, BrE*) looking or feeling very healthy

rude·ly 0-m /'ruːdli/ *adv.*
1 0-m in a way that shows a lack of respect for other people and their feelings: *They brushed rudely past us.* ◇ *'What do you want?' she asked rudely.* **2** in a way that is sudden, unpleasant and unexpected: *I was rudely awakened by the phone ringing.*

ru·di·men·tary /ˌruːdɪ'mentri/ *adj.* **1** (*formal*) dealing with only the most basic matters or ideas SYN **basic**: *They were given only rudimentary training in the job.* **2** (*formal or technical*) not highly or fully developed SYN **basic**: *Some dinosaurs had only rudimentary teeth.*

ru·di·ments /'ruːdɪmənts/ *noun* [pl.] **the ~ (of sth)** (*formal*) the most basic or essential facts of a particular subject, skill, etc. SYN **basics**

rue /ruː/ *verb* (**rue·ing** or **ruing, rued, rued**) **~ sth** (*old-fashioned* or *formal*) to feel bad about sth that happened or sth that you did because it had bad results SYN **regret**: *He **rued the day** they had bought such a large house.*

rue·ful /'ruːfl/ *adj.* feeling or showing that you are sad or sorry: *a rueful smile* ▸ **rue·ful·ly** /'ruːfəli/ *adv.*: *'So this is goodbye,' she said ruefully.*

ruff /rʌf/ *noun* **1** a ring of coloured or marked feathers or fur around the neck of a bird or an animal **2** a wide stiff white COLLAR with many folds in it, worn especially in the 16th and 17th centuries

ruf·fian /'rʌfiən/ *noun* (*old-fashioned*) a violent man, especially one who commits crimes SYN **thug**

ruf·fle /'rʌfl/ *verb, noun*
■ *verb* **1** to disturb the smooth surface of sth, so that it is not even: **~ sth** *She ruffled his hair affectionately.* ◇ **~ sth up** *The bird ruffled up its feathers.* **2** [often passive] **~ sb** to make sb annoyed, worried or upset SYN **fluster**: *She was obviously ruffled by his question.* ◇ *He never **gets ruffled**, even under pressure.*

IDM **ruffle sb's/a few 'feathers** (*informal*) to annoy or upset sb or a group of people: *The senator's speech ruffled a few feathers in the business world.* ➲ more at SMOOTH *v.*

■ *noun* [usually pl.] a strip of cloth that is sewn in folds and is used to decorate a piece of clothing at the neck or wrists SYN **frill**

R

ruf·fled /'rʌfld/ *adj.* decorated with ruffles SYN **frilled**: *a ruffled blouse*

rug /rʌg/ *noun* **1** a piece of thick material like a small carpet that is used for covering or decorating part of a floor: *a hearth rug* (= in front of a FIREPLACE) ➲ VISUAL VOCAB pages V18, V20 **2** (*BrE*) a piece of thick warm material, like a BLANKET, that is used for wrapping around your legs to keep warm **3** (*informal, especially NAmE*) = TOUPEE

IDM see PULL *v.*, SWEEP *v.*

rugby /'rʌgbi/ (sometimes **Rugby**) (also **ˌrugby 'foot·ball**) *noun* [U] a game played by two teams of 13 or 15 players, using an OVAL ball which may be kicked or carried. Teams try to put the ball over the other team's line. ➲ VISUAL VOCAB page V36 ORIGIN Named after Rugby school, where the game was first played.

ˌRugby 'League *noun* [U] a form of rugby, with 13 players in a team

ˌRugby 'Union (also *informal* **rug·ger** especially in *BrE*) *noun* [U] a form of rugby, with 15 players in a team

rug·ged /'rʌgɪd/ *adj.* **1** (of the landscape) not level or smooth and having rocks rather than plants or trees: *rugged cliffs* ◇ *They admired the rugged beauty of the coastline.* **2** [usually before noun] (*approving*) (of a man's face) having strong, attractive features **3** [usually before noun] (of a person) determined to succeed in a difficult situation, even if this means using force or upsetting other people: *a rugged individualist* **4** (of equipment, clothing, etc.) strong and designed to be used in difficult conditions: *A less rugged vehicle would never have made the trip.* ◇ *rugged outdoor clothing* ▸ **rug·ged·ly** *adv.*: *ruggedly handsome* **rug·ged·ness** *noun* [U]

rug·ger /'rʌgə(r)/ *noun* [U] (*informal, especially BrE*) = RUGBY UNION

'rugger-bugger *noun* (*BrE, informal*) an enthusiastic player or supporter of RUGBY, especially one who is noisy and aggressive

'rug rat *noun* (*NAmE, informal*) a child

ruin 0-m /'ruːɪn/ *verb, noun*
■ *verb* **1** 0-m **~ sth** to damage sth so badly that it loses all its value, pleasure, etc; to spoil sth SYN **wreck**: *The bad weather ruined our trip.* ◇ *That one mistake ruined his chances of getting the job.* ◇ *My new shoes **got ruined** in the mud.* **2** 0-m **~ sb/sth** to make sb/sth lose all their money, their position, etc: *If she loses the court case it will ruin her.* ◇ *The country was ruined by the war.*
■ *noun* **1** 0-m [U] the state or process of being destroyed or severely damaged: *A large number of churches **fell into ruin** after the revolution.* **2** 0-m [U] the fact of having no money, of having lost your job, position, etc: *The divorce ultimately led to his ruin.* ◇ *The bank stepped in to save the company from **financial ruin**.* **3** [sing.] something that causes a person, company, etc. to lose all their money, job, position, etc. SYN **downfall**: *Gambling was his ruin.* **4** 0-m [C] (also **ruins** [pl.]) the parts of a building that remain after it has been destroyed or severely damaged: *The old mill is now little more than a ruin.* ◇ *We visited the ruins of a Norman castle.* ◇ (*figurative*) *He was determined to build a new life out of the ruins of his career.*

IDM **in 'ruins** destroyed or severely damaged: *Years of fighting have left the area in ruins.* ◇ *The scandal left his reputation in ruins.* ➲ more at RACK *n.*

ruin·ation /ˌruːɪ'neɪʃn/ *noun* [U] (*formal*) the process of destroying sth/sb or being destroyed SYN **destruction**: *Urban development has led to the ruination of vast areas of countryside.*

ru·ined 0-m /'ruːɪnd/ *adj.* [only before noun] (of a building, town, etc.) destroyed or severely damaged so that only parts remain: *a ruined castle*

ruin·ous /'ruːɪnəs/ *adj.* (*formal*) **1** costing a lot of money and more than you can afford: *ruinous legal fees* **2** causing serious problems or damage SYN **devastating**: *The decision was to prove ruinous.* **3** (*formal*) (of a town, building, etc.) destroyed or severely damaged: *a ruinous chapel* ◇ *The buildings were in a ruinous state.* ▸ **ruin·ous·ly** *adv.*: *ruinously expensive*

rule 0-m /ruːl/ *noun, verb*
■ *noun*
▸ OF ACTIVITY/GAME **1** 0-m [C] a statement of what may, must or must not be done in a particular situation or when playing a game: *to **follow/obey/observe the rules*** ◇ *It's against all **rules and regulations**.* ◇ *to **break a rule*** (= not follow it) ◇ *This explains the rules under which the library operates.* ◇ *Without **unwritten rules** civilized life would be impossible.* ➲ see also GROUND RULE
▸ ADVICE **2** 0-m [C] a statement of what you are advised to do in a particular situation: *There are no **hard and fast rules** for planning healthy meals.* ◇ *The first rule is to make eye contact with your interviewer.* ➲ see also GOLDEN RULE
▸ HABIT/NORMALLY TRUE **3** [C, usually sing.] a habit; the normal state of things; what is true in most cases: *He makes it a rule never to borrow money.* ◇ *I go to bed early **as a rule**.* ◇ *Cold winters here are **the exception rather than the rule*** (= are rare). ◇ ***As a general rule** vegetable oils are better for you than animal fats.*
▸ OF SYSTEM **4** 0-m [C] a statement of what is possible according to a particular system, for example the grammar of a language: *the rules of grammar*
▸ GOVERNMENT/CONTROL **5** 0-m [U] the government of a country or control of a group of people by a particular person, group or system: ***under Communist/civilian/military, etc. rule*** ◇ ***majority rule*** (= government by the political party that most people have voted for) ◇ *The 1972 act imposed **direct rule** from Westminster.* ➲ see also HOME RULE
▸ MEASURING TOOL **6** [C] a measuring instrument with a straight edge ➲ see also SLIDE RULE

IDM **bend/stretch the 'rules** to change the rules to suit a particular person or situation **play by sb's (own) 'rules** if sb **plays by their own rules** or makes other people **play by their rules**, they set the conditions for doing business or having a relationship **play by the 'rules** to deal fairly and honestly with people **the rules of the 'game** the standards of behaviour that most people accept or that actually operate in a particular area of life or business **the rule of 'law** the condition in which all members of society, including its rulers, accept the authority of the law **a rule of 'thumb** a practical method of doing or measuring sth, usually based on past experience rather than on exact measurement **work to 'rule** to follow the rules of your job in a very strict way in order to cause delay, as a form of protest against your employer or your working conditions ➲ see also WORK-TO-RULE ➲ more at EXCEPTION

■ *verb*

▸ GOVERN/CONTROL **1** 🔑 [T, I] to control and have authority over a country, a group of people, etc: **~ sth** *At that time John ruled England.* ◇ (*figurative*) *Eighty million years ago, dinosaurs ruled the earth.* ◇ **~ (over sb/sth)** *Charles I ruled for eleven years.* ◇ *She once ruled over a vast empire.* ◇ (*figurative*) *After the revolution, anarchy ruled.* **2** 🔑 [T, often passive] **~ sth** (often *disapproving*) to be the main thing that influences and controls sb/sth: *The pursuit of money ruled his life.* ◇ *We live in a society where we are ruled by the clock.*

▸ GIVE OFFICIAL DECISION **3** [I, T] to give an official decision about sth SYN **pronounce**: **~ (on sth)** *The court will rule on the legality of the action.* ◇ **~ against/in favour of sb/sth** *The judge ruled against/in favour of the plaintiff.* ◇ **~ sb/sth + adj.** *The deal may be ruled illegal.* ◇ **~ sb/sth to be/have sth** *The deal was ruled to be illegal.* ◇ **~ that...** *The court ruled that the women were unfairly dismissed.* ◇ **it is ruled that...** *It was ruled that the women had been unfairly dismissed.*

▸ DRAW STRAIGHT LINE **4** [T] **~ sth** to draw a straight line using sth that has a firm straight edge: *Rule a line at the end of every piece of work.*

IDM **rule the 'roost** (*informal*) to be the most powerful member of a group **rule (sb/sth) with a rod of 'iron** to control a person or a group of people very severely ➲ more at COURT *n.*, DIVIDE *v.*, HEART

PHR V **,rule 'off | ,rule sth↔'off** to separate sth from the next section of writing by drawing a line underneath it **,rule sb/sth↔'out 1** 🔑 **~ (as sth)** to state that sth is not possible or that sb/sth is not suitable SYN **exclude**: *Police have not ruled out the possibility that the man was murdered.* ◇ *The proposed solution was ruled out as too expensive.* **2** to prevent sb from doing sth; to prevent sth from happening: *His age effectively ruled him out as a possible candidate.* **,rule sb 'out of sth** [usually passive] (in sport) to state that a player, runner, etc. will not be able to take part in a sporting event; to prevent a player from taking part: *He has been ruled out of the match with a knee injury.*

'rule book *noun* (usually **the rule book**) the set of rules that must be followed in a particular job, organization or game

ruled /ru:ld/ *adj.* **ruled** paper has lines printed across it

ruler 🔑 /'ru:lə(r)/ *noun*
1 🔑 a person who rules or governs **2** 🔑 a straight strip of wood, plastic or metal, marked in centimetres or inches, used for measuring or for drawing straight lines ➲ VISUAL VOCAB page V57

rul·ing /'ru:lɪŋ/ *noun, adj.*
■ ***noun*** **~ (on sth)** an official decision made by sb in a position of authority, especially a judge: *The court will make its ruling on the case next week.*
■ ***adj.*** [only before noun] having control over a particular group, country, etc: *the ruling party*

rum /rʌm/ *noun, adj.*
■ ***noun*** **1** [U, C] a strong alcoholic drink made from the juice of SUGAR CANE **2** [C] a glass of rum
■ ***adj.*** [usually before noun] (*old-fashioned, BrE, informal*) strange SYN **odd, peculiar**

rumba (also **rhumba**) /'rʌmbə/ *noun* a fast dance originally from Cuba; a piece of music for this dance

rum·ble /'rʌmbl/ *verb, noun*
■ ***verb*** **1** [I] to make a long deep sound or series of sounds: *The machine rumbled as it started up.* ◇ *thunder rumbling in the distance* ◇ *I'm so hungry my* ***stomach's rumbling.*** **2** [I] **+ adv./prep.** to move slowly and heavily, making a rumbling sound: *tanks rumbling through the streets* **3** [T] **~ sb** (*BrE, informal*) to discover the truth about sb or what they are trying to hide: *They knew they had been rumbled.* **4** [I] (*NAmE, informal*) (of a GANG of young people) to fight against another GANG

PHR V **,rumble 'on** (*especially BrE*) (of an argument, a disagreement, etc.) to continue slowly and steadily for a long time: *Discussions rumble on over the siting of the new airport.*

■ ***noun*** **1** [U, C] **~ (of sth)** a long deep sound or series of sounds: *the rumble of thunder* ◇ *Inside, the noise of the traffic was reduced to a distant rumble.* ◇ (*figurative*) *Although an agreement has been reached, rumbles of resentment can still be heard.* **2** [C] (*NAmE, informal*) a fight in the street between two or more GANGS (= groups of young people)

'rumble strip *noun* (*informal*) a series of raised strips across a road or along its edge that make a loud noise when a vehicle drives over them in order to warn the driver to go slower or that he or she is too close to the edge of the road

rum·bling /'rʌmblɪŋ/ *noun* **1** (also used as an adjective) a long deep sound or series of sounds: *the rumblings of thunder* ◇ *a rumbling noise* ◇ (*figurative*) *the rumblings of discontent* **2** [usually pl.] things that people are saying that may not be true SYN **rumour**: *There are rumblings that the election may have to be postponed.*

rum·bus·tious /rʌm'bʌstʃəs/ (*especially BrE*) (*NAmE* usually **ram·bunc·tious**) *adj.* [usually before noun] (*informal*) full of energy in a cheerful and noisy way SYN **boisterous**

ru·min·ant /'ru:mɪnənt/ *noun* (*technical*) any animal that brings back food from its stomach and chews it again. Cows and sheep are both ruminants. ▸ **ru·min·ant** *adj.*: *ruminant animals*

ru·min·ate /'ru:mɪneɪt/ *verb* [I, T] **~ (on/over/about sth) | + speech** (*formal*) to think deeply about sth SYN **ponder** ▸ **ru·min·ation** /,ru:mɪ'neɪʃn/ *noun* [C, U]

ru·mina·tive /'ru:mɪnətɪv; *NAmE* -neɪtɪv/ *adj.* (*formal*) tending to think deeply and carefully about things SYN **pensive, thoughtful**: *in a ruminative mood* ▸ **ru·mina·tive·ly** *adv.*

rum·mage /'rʌmɪdʒ/ *verb, noun*
■ ***verb*** [I] **+ adv./prep.** to move things around carelessly while searching for sth: *She was rummaging around in her bag for her keys.* ◇ *I rummaged through the contents of the box until I found the book I wanted.*
■ ***noun*** [sing.] the act of looking for sth among a group of other objects in a way that makes them untidy: *Have a rummage around in the drawer and see if you can find a pen.*

'rummage sale (*especially NAmE*) (*BrE* also **'jumble sale**) *noun* a sale of old or used clothes, etc. to make money for a church, school or other organization

rummy /'rʌmi/ *noun* [U] a simple card game in which players try to collect particular combinations of cards

ru·mour 🔑 (*especially US* **rumor**) /'ru:mə(r)/ *noun, verb*
■ ***noun*** 🔑 [C, U] a piece of information, or a story, that people talk about, but that may not be true: *to* ***start/spread a rumour*** ◇ **~ (of sth)** *There are widespread rumours of job losses.* ◇ **~ (about sth)** *Some malicious rumours are circulating about his past.* ◇ **~ (that...)** *I heard a rumour that they are getting married.* ◇ *Many of the stories are based on rumour.* ◇ ***Rumour has it*** (= people say) *that he was murdered.*
■ ***verb*** **be rumoured** to be reported as a rumour and possibly not true: **it is rumoured that...** *It's widely rumoured that she's getting promoted.* ◇ **~ to be/have sth** *He was ru-*

R

moured to be involved in the crime. ▸ **ru·moured** *adj.* [only before noun]: *He denied his father's rumoured love affair.*

rumour-monger (*especially US* **ru·mor·mon·ger**) /ˈruːmə mʌŋɡə(r); *NAmE* ˈruːmər/ *noun* a person who spreads rumours

rump /rʌmp/ *noun* **1** [C] the round area of flesh at the top of the back legs of an animal that has four legs **2** [U] (also ˌ**rump ˈsteak** [C, U]) a piece of good quality meat cut from the rump of a cow **3** [C, usually sing.] (*humorous*) the part of the body that you sit on SYN **backside 4** [sing.] (*BrE*) the small or unimportant part of a group or an organization that remains when most of its members have left

rum·ple /ˈrʌmpl/ *verb* **~ sth** to make sth untidy or not smooth and neat: *She rumpled his hair playfully.* ◇ *The bed was rumpled where he had slept.*

rum·pus /ˈrʌmpəs/ *noun* [usually sing.] (*informal*) a lot of noise that is made especially by people who are complaining about sth SYN **commotion**: *to cause a rumpus*

ˈ**rumpus room** *noun* (*NAmE, AustralE, NZE*) a room in a house for playing games in, sometimes in the BASEMENT

rumpy pumpy /ˌrʌmpi ˈpʌmpi/ *noun* [U] (*BrE, informal, humorous*) the physical activity of sex

run 0-w /rʌn/ *verb, noun*

■ ***verb*** (**running, ran** /ræn/, **run**)

▸ MOVE FAST ON FOOT **1** 0-w [I] to move using your legs, going faster than when you walk: *Can you run as fast as Mike?* ◇ *They turned and ran when they saw us coming.* ◇ *She* ***came running*** *to meet us.* ◇ *The dogs ran off as soon as we appeared.* HELP In spoken English **run** can be used with **and** plus another verb, instead of with **to** and the infinitive, especially to tell somebody to hurry and do something: *Run and get your swimsuits, kids.* ◇ *I ran and knocked on the nearest door.* **2** 0-w [T] **~ sth** to travel a particular distance by running: *Who was the first person to run a mile in under four minutes?* ➲ see also MILE **3** 0-w [I] (sometimes **go running**) to run as a sport: *She used to run when she was at college.* ◇ *I often go running before work.*

▸ RACE **4** 0-w [I, T] to take part in a race: **~ (in sth)** *He will be running in the 100 metres tonight.* ◇ *There are only five horses running in the first race.* ◇ **~ sth** *to run the marathon* ◇ *Holmes ran a fine race to take the gold medal.* ➲ see also RUNNER (1) **5** [T, often passive] **~ sth** to make a race take place: *The Derby will be run in spite of the bad weather.*

▸ HURRY **6** [I] **+ adv./prep.** to hurry from one place to another: *I've spent the whole day running around after the kids.* ➲ see also RAT RUN

▸ MANAGE **7** 0-w [T] **~ sth** to be in charge of a business, etc: *to run a hotel/store/language school* ◇ *He has no idea how to run a business.* ◇ *Stop trying to* ***run my life*** (= organize it) *for me.* ◇ *The shareholders want more say in how the company is run.* ◇ *a badly run company* ◇ *state-run industries* ➲ see also RUNNING *n.* (2)

▸ PROVIDE **8** [T] **~ sth** to make a service, course of study, etc. available to people SYN **organize**: *The college runs summer courses for foreign students.*

▸ VEHICLE/MACHINE **9** [T] **~ sth** (*BrE*) to own and use a vehicle or machine: *I can't afford to run a car on my salary.* **10** 0-w [I, T] to operate or function; to make sth do this: *Stan had the chainsaw running.* ◇ (*figurative*) *Her life had always run smoothly before.* ◇ **~ on sth** *Our van runs on* (= uses) *diesel.* ◇ **~ sth** *Could you run the engine for a moment?*

▸ BUSES/TRAINS **11** 0-w [I] (**+ adv./prep.**) to travel on a particular route: *Buses to Oxford run every half-hour.* ◇ *All the trains* ***are running late*** (= are leaving later than planned). **12** [T] **~ sth** (**+ adv./prep.**) to make buses, trains, etc. travel on a particular route: *They run extra trains during the rush hour.*

▸ DRIVE SB **13** [T] **~ sb + adv./prep.** (*informal*) to drive sb to a place in a car: *Shall I run you home?*

▸ MOVE SOMEWHERE **14** 0-w [I] **+ adv./prep.** to move, especially quickly, in a particular direction: *The car ran off the road into a ditch.* ◇ *A shiver ran down my spine.* ◇ *The sledge ran smoothly over the frozen snow.* ◇ *The old tramlines are still there but now no trams run on them.* **15** 0-w [T] **~ sth + adv./prep.** to move sth in a particular direction: *She ran her fingers nervously through her hair.* ◇ ***I ran my eyes over*** *the page.*

▸ LEAD/STRETCH **16** 0-w [I, T] to lead or stretch from one place to another; to make sth do this: **+ adv./prep.** *He had a scar running down his left cheek.* ◇ *The road runs parallel to the river.* ◇ **~ sth + adv./prep.** *We ran a cable from the lights to the stage.*

▸ CONTINUE FOR TIME **17** [I] **~ (for sth)** to continue for a particular period of time without stopping: *Her last musical ran for six months on Broadway.* ◇ *This debate will* ***run and run!*** **18** [I] **~ (for sth)** to operate or be valid for a particular period of time: *The permit runs for three months.* ◇ *The lease on my house only has a year left to run.*

▸ HAPPEN **19** 0-w [I] (usually used in the progressive tenses) to happen at the time mentioned: **+ adv./prep.** *Programmes are* ***running*** *a few minutes* ***behind schedule*** *this evening.* ◇ *The murderer was given three life sentences, to run concurrently.*

▸ GUNS, DRUGS, ETC. **20** [T] **~ sth** (**+ adv./prep.**) to bring or take sth into a country illegally and secretly SYN **smuggle** ➲ see also RUNNER

▸ OF STORY/ARGUMENT **21** [I, T] to have particular words, contents, etc: *Their argument ran something like this...* ◇ **+ speech** *'Ten shot dead by gunmen,' ran the newspaper headline.*

▸ LIQUID **22** 0-w [I] **+ adv./prep.** to flow: *The tears ran down her cheeks.* ◇ *Water was running all over the bathroom floor.* **23** [T] to make liquid flow: **~ sth** (**into sth**) *She ran hot water into the bucket.* ◇ *to* ***run the hot tap*** (= to turn it so that water flows from it) ◇ **~ sth for sb** *I'll* ***run a bath*** *for you.* ◇ **~ sb sth** *I'll* ***run you a bath.*** **24** 0-w [I] to send out a liquid: *Who left the tap running?* ◇ *Your nose is running* (=MUCUS is flowing from it). ◇ *The smoke makes my eyes run.* **25** [I] (usually used in the progressive tenses) **~ with sth** to be covered with a liquid: *His face was running with sweat.* ◇ *The bathroom floor was running with water.*

▸ OF COLOUR **26** [I] if the colour **runs** in a piece of clothing when it gets wet, it dissolves and may come out of the clothing into other things

▸ MELT **27** [I] (of a solid substance) to melt: *The wax began to run.* ➲ see also RUNNY

▸ BE/BECOME **28** 0-w [I] **+ adj.** to become different in a particular way, especially a bad way: *The river* ***ran dry*** (= stopped flowing) *during the drought.* ◇ *Supplies are* ***running low.*** ◇ *We've* ***run short*** *of milk.* ◇ *You've got your rivals* ***running scared.*** **29** [I] **~ at sth** to be at or near a particular level: *Inflation was running at 26%.*

▸ OF NEWSPAPER/MAGAZINE **30** [T] **~ sth** to print and publish an item or a story: *On advice from their lawyers they decided not to run the story.*

▸ A TEST/CHECK **31** [T] **~ a test/check** (**on sth**) to do a test/check on sth: *The doctors decided to run some more tests on the blood samples.*

▸ IN ELECTION **32** 0-w [I] to be a candidate in an election for a political position, especially in the US: *Bush ran a second time in 2004.* ◇ **~ for sb/sth** *to run for president* ◇ **~ in sth** *to run in the election* ➲ compare STAND *v.* (16)

▸ OF TIGHTS/STOCKINGS **33** [I] (*NAmE*) if TIGHTS or STOCKINGS **run**, a long thin hole appears in them SYN **ladder**

IDM Most idioms containing **run** are at the entries for the nouns and adjectives in the idioms, for example **run riot** is at **riot**. **come ˈrunning** to be pleased to do what sb wants: *She knew she had only to call and he would come running.* ˈ**run for it** (often used in orders) to run in order to escape from sb/sth ˌ**up and ˈrunning** working fully and correctly: *It will be a lot easier when we have the database up and running.* ➲ more at CLOSE² *adv.*, HIT *v.*

PHR V ˈ**run across sb/sth** to meet sb or find sth by chance

ˌ**run ˈafter sb** (*informal*) to try to have a romantic or sexual relationship with sb SYN **pursue**: *He's always running after younger women.* ˌ**run ˈafter sb/sth** 0-w to run to try to catch sb/sth SYN **pursue**

ˌ**run aˈlong** (*old-fashioned, informal*) used in orders to tell sb, especially a child, to go away

ˌ**run aˈround with sb** (*NAmE* also ˈ**run with sb**) (usually *disapproving*) to spend a lot of time with sb: *She's always running around with older men.*

ˈrun at sb [no passive] to run towards sb to attack or as if to attack them: *He ran at me with a knife.*

ˌrun aˈway (from sb/...) 🔑 to leave sb/a place suddenly; to escape from sb/a place: *He* ***ran away from home*** *at the age of thirteen.* ◇ *Looking at all the accusing faces, she felt a sudden urge to run away.* ➲ related noun RUNAWAY **ˌrun aˈway from sth** to try to avoid sth because you are shy, lack confidence, etc: *You can't just run away from the situation.* **ˌrun aˈway with you** if a feeling **runs away with you**, it gets out of your control: *Her imagination tends to run away with her.* **ˌrun aˈway/ˈoff with sb | ˌrun aˈway/ˈoff (together)** to leave home, your husband, wife, etc. in order to have a relationship with another person: *She ran away with her boss.* ◇ *She and her boss ran away together.*

ˌrun aˈway with sth 1 to win sth clearly or easily **2** to believe sth that is not true: *I don't want you to* ***run away with the impression*** *that all I do is have meetings all day.*

ˌrun back ˈover sth to discuss or consider sth again SYN **review**: *I'll run back over the procedure once again.*

ˌrun sth ˈby/ˈpast sb (*informal*) to show sb sth or tell sb about an idea in order to see their reaction to it

ˌrun ˈdown 1 to lose power or stop working: *The battery has run down.* **2** to gradually stop functioning or become smaller in size or number: *British manufacturing industry has been running down for years.* ➲ related noun RUN-DOWN **ˌrun sth↔ˈdown 1** to make sth lose power or stop working: *If you leave your headlights on you'll soon run down the battery.* **2** to make sth gradually stop functioning or become smaller in size or number: *The company is running down its sales force.* ➲ related noun RUNDOWN **ˌrun sb/sth↔ˈdown 1** (of a vehicle or its driver) to hit sb/sth and knock them/it to the ground **2** to criticize sb/sth in an unkind way: *He's always running her down in front of other people.* **3** to find sb/sth after a search

ˌrun sb↔ˈin (*old-fashioned, informal*) to arrest sb and take them to a police station **ˌrun sth↔ˈin** (*BrE*) (in the past) to prepare the engine of a new car for normal use by driving slowly and carefully: (*figurative*) *Whatever system you choose, it must be run in properly.*

ˌrun ˈinto sb (*informal*) to meet sb by chance: *Guess who I ran into today!* **ˈrun into sth 1** to enter an area of bad weather while travelling: *We ran into thick fog on the way home.* **2** to experience difficulties, etc: *Be careful not to run into debt.* ◇ *to* ***run into danger/trouble/difficulties*** **3** to reach a particular level or amount: *Her income runs into six figures* (= is more than £100 000, $100 000, etc.). **ˈrun into sb/sth** to crash into sb/sth: *The bus went out of control and ran into a line of people.* **ˈrun sth into sb/sth** to make a vehicle crash into sb/sth: *He ran his car into a tree.*

ˌrun ˈoff (*BrE*) (of a liquid) to flow out of a container **ˌrun sth↔ˈoff 1** to copy sth on a machine: *Could you run off twenty copies of the agenda?* **2** to cause a race to be run: *The heats of the 200 metres will be run off tomorrow.* **3** to make a liquid flow out of a container **ˌrun ˈoff with sb | ˌrun ˈoff (together)** = RUN AWAY WITH SB **ˌrun ˈoff with sth** to steal sth and take it away: *The treasurer had run off with the club's funds.*

ˌrun ˈon to continue without stopping; to continue longer than is necessary or expected: *The meeting will finish promptly—I don't want it to run on.* **ˈrun on sth** [no passive] if your thoughts, a discussion, etc. **run on** a subject, you think or talk a lot about that subject

ˌrun ˈout 1 🔑 if a supply of sth **runs out**, it is used up or finished: *Time is running out for the trapped miners.* **2** 🔑 if an agreement or a document **runs out**, it becomes no longer valid SYN **expire** **ˌrun ˈout (of sth)** 🔑 to use up or finish a supply of sth: *We ran out of fuel.* ◇ *Could I have a cigarette? I seem to have run out.* **ˌrun ˈout on sb** (*informal*) to leave sb that you live with, especially when they need your help **ˌrun sb↔ˈout** [often passive] (in CRICKET) to make a player stop BATTING by hitting the WICKET with the ball before the player has completed his or her run

ˌrun ˈover if a container or its contents **run over**, the contents come over the edge of the container SYN **overflow** **ˌrun sb/sth↔ˈover** 🔑 (of a vehicle or its driver) to knock a person or an animal down and drive over their body or a part of it: *Two children were run over and killed.* **ˌrun ˈover sth** to read through or practise sth quickly: *She ran over her notes before giving the lecture.*

ˌrun sth ˈpast sb = RUN STH BY/PAST SB: *Run that past me again.*

ˌrun sb↔ˈthrough (*literary*) to kill sb by sticking a knife, SWORD, etc. through them **ˌrun ˈthrough sth 1** 🔑 to discuss, repeat or read sth quickly: *He ran through the names on the list.* ◇ *Could we run through your proposals once again?* **2** [no passive] to pass quickly through sth: *An angry murmur ran through the crowd.* ◇ *Thoughts of revenge kept running through his mind.* **3** [no passive] to be present in every part of sth: *A deep melancholy runs through her poetry.* **4** to perform, act or practise sth: *Can we run through Scene 3 again, please?* ➲ related noun RUN-THROUGH **5** to use up or spend money carelessly: *She ran through the entire amount within two years.*

ˈrun to sth 1 to be of a particular size or amount: *The book runs to nearly 800 pages.* **2** (*especially BrE*) if you or your money will **not run to sth**, you do not have enough money for sth: *Our funds won't run to a trip abroad this year.*

ˌrun sth↔ˈup 1 to allow a bill, debt, etc. to reach a large total SYN **accumulate**: *How had he managed to run up so many debts?* **2** to make a piece of clothing quickly, especially by sewing: *to run up a blouse* **3** to raise sth, especially a flag **ˌrun ˈup against sth** to experience a difficulty: *The government is running up against considerable opposition to its tax reforms.*

ˈrun with sb = RUN AWAY WITH SB **ˈrun with sth** to accept or start to use a particular idea or method: *OK, let's run with Jan's suggestion.*

■ ***noun***

▸ ON FOOT **1** 🔑 [C] an act of running; a period of time spent running or the distance that sb runs: *I go for a run every morning.* ◇ *a five-mile run* ◇ *Catching sight of her he* ***broke into a run*** (= started running). ◇ *I decided* ***to make a run for it*** (= to escape by running). ◇ *She took the stairs* ***at a run.*** ➲ see also FUN RUN

▸ TRIP **2** [C] a trip by car, plane, boat, etc, especially a short one or one that is made regularly: *They took the car out for a run.* ➲ see also MILK RUN, RAT RUN, SCHOOL RUN

▸ OF SUCCESS/FAILURE **3** [C] a period of sth good or bad happening; a series of successes or failures SYN **spell**: *a* ***run of good/bad luck*** ◇ *Liverpool lost to Leeds, ending an unbeaten run of 18 games.*

▸ OF PLAY/MOVIE **4** [C] a series of performances of a play or film/movie: *The show had a record-breaking run in the London theatre.*

▸ OF PRODUCT **5** [C] the amount of a product that a company decides to make at one time: *The first* ***print run*** *of 6 000 copies sold out.*

▸ MONEY **6** [C, usually sing.] **~ on the dollar, pound, etc.** a situation when many people sell dollars, etc. and the value of the money falls

▸ SUDDEN DEMAND **7** [C, usually sing.] **~ on sth** a situation when many people suddenly want to buy sth: *a run on the band's latest CD*

▸ MONEY **8** [C, usually sing.] **~ on a bank** a situation when many people suddenly want to take their money out of a bank

▸ WAY THINGS HAPPEN **9** [sing.] **the ~ of sth** the way things usually happen; the way things seem to be happening on a particular occasion: *In* ***the normal run of things*** *the only exercise he gets is climbing in and out of taxis.* ◇ (*BrE*) *Wise scored in the 15th minute* ***against the run of play*** (= although the other team had seemed more likely to score).

▸ IN SPORTS **10** [C] a sloping track used in SKIING and some other sports: *a* ***ski/toboggan, etc. run*** **11** [C] a point scored in the game of CRICKET or BASEBALL: *Our team won by four runs.* ➲ see also HOME RUN

▸ IN ELECTION **12** [sing.] (*NAmE*) an act of trying to get elected to public office: *He made an unsuccessful run for governor in 2008.*

▸ FOR ANIMALS/BIRDS **13** [C] (often in compounds) a confined area in which animals or birds are kept as pets or on a farm: *a chicken run*

▸ IN MUSIC **14** [C] a series of notes sung or played quickly up or down the SCALE

▸ IN CARD GAMES **15** [C] a series of cards held by one player

R

▸ IN TIGHTS/STOCKINGS **16** [C] (*NAmE*) = LADDER
▸ ILLNESS **17 the runs** [pl.] (*informal*) = DIARRHOEA ➲ see also DRY RUN, DUMMY RUN, TRIAL RUN
IDM **the common, general, ordinary, usual run (of sth)** the average type of sth: *He was very different from the general run of movie stars.* **give sb/get/have the 'run of sth** to give sb/get/have permission to make full use of sth: *Her dogs have the run of the house.* **give sb a (good) run for their 'money** to make sb try very hard, using all their skill and effort, in order to beat you in a game or competition **on the 'run 1** trying to avoid being captured: *He's on the run from the police.* **2** (*informal*) continuously active and moving around: *I've been on the run all day and I'm exhausted.* ◇ *Here are some quick recipes for when you're eating on the run* (= in a hurry). ➲ more at LONG *adj.*, SHORT *adj.*

run·about /ˈrʌnəbaʊt/ *noun* (*BrE, informal*) a small car, especially one used for short journeys

run·around /ˈrʌnəraʊnd/ *noun*
IDM **give sb the 'runaround** (*informal*) to treat sb badly by not telling them the truth, or by not giving them the help or the information they need, and sending them somewhere else

run·away /ˈrʌnəweɪ/ *adj., noun*
■ ***adj.*** [only before noun] **1** (of a person) having left without telling anyone: *runaway children* **2** (of an animal or a vehicle) not under the control of its owner, rider or driver: *a runaway horse/car* **3** happening very easily or quickly, and not able to be controlled: *a runaway winner/victory* ◇ *the **runaway success** of her first play* ◇ *runaway inflation*
■ ***noun*** a person who has suddenly left or escaped from sb/sth, especially a child who has left home without telling anyone: *teenage runaways living on the streets*

run·down /ˈrʌndaʊn/ *noun* [usually sing.] **1 ~ (in/of sth)** (*BrE*) a reduction in the amount, size or activity of sth, especially a business: *a rundown of transport services* **2 ~ (on/of sth)** an explanation or a description of sth: *I can give you a brief rundown on each of the applicants.*

ˌrun-'down *adj.* **1** (of a building or place) in very bad condition; that has not been taken care of SYN **neglected**: *run-down inner-city areas* **2** (of a business, etc.) not as busy or as active as it used to be: *run-down transport services* **3** [not before noun] (of a person) tired or slightly ill/sick, especially from working hard: *to be run-down*

rune /ruːn/ *noun* **1** one of the letters in an alphabet that people in northern Europe used in ancient times and cut into wood or stone **2** a symbol that has a mysterious or magic meaning ▸ **runic** *adj.*: *runic inscriptions*

rung /rʌŋ/ *noun* one of the bars that forms a step in a LADDER: *He put his foot on the bottom rung to keep the ladder steady.* ◇ (*figurative*) *to get a foot on the bottom rung of the career ladder* ◇ *She was a few rungs above him on the social ladder.* ➲ VISUAL VOCAB page V17 ➲ see also RING *v.*

'run-in *noun* **1 ~ (with sb)** (*informal*) an argument or a fight: *The fiery player has had numerous run-ins with referees.* **2 ~ (to sth)** (*BrE*) = RUN-UP

run·nel /ˈrʌnl/ *noun* (*formal* or *literary*) a small stream or channel

run·ner 0‑ᵀ /ˈrʌnə(r)/ *noun*
1 0‑ᵀ a person or an animal that runs, especially one taking part in a race: ***a long-distance/cross-country/marathon, etc. runner*** ◇ *a list of runners* (= horses in a race) *and riders* ➲ see also FORERUNNER, FRONT RUNNER, ROADRUNNER **2** (especially in compounds) a person who takes goods illegally into or out of a place: *a drug runner* ➲ see also GUNRUNNER **3** a strip of metal, plastic or wood that sth slides on or can move along on: *the runners of a sledge* **4** a plant STEM that grows along the ground and puts down roots to form a new plant **5** a long narrow piece of cloth or carpet on a piece of furniture or on the floor **6** a person in a company or an organization whose job is to take messages, documents, etc. from one place to another **7** (*CanE*) a shoe that is used for running or doing other sport in
IDM **do a 'runner** (*BrE, informal*) to leave or run away from somewhere in a hurry, especially to avoid paying a bill or receiving a punishment

ˌrunner 'bean (also **ˌstring 'bean**) *noun* (both *BrE*) a type of BEAN which is a long flat green POD growing on a climbing plant also called a runner bean. The pods are cut up, cooked and eaten as a vegetable.

ˌrunner-'up *noun* (*pl.* **runners-up**) a person or team that finishes second in a race or competition; a person or team that has not finished first but that wins a prize: *Winner: Kay Hall. Runner-up: Chris Platts.* ◇ *They finished runners-up behind Sweden.* ◇ *The runners-up will all receive a £50 prize.*

run·ning 0‑ᵀ /ˈrʌnɪŋ/ *noun, adj.*
■ ***noun*** [U] **1** 0‑ᵀ the action or sport of running: *to **go running*** ◇ *running shoes* **2** 0‑ᵀ the activity of managing or operating sth: *the day-to-day running of a business* ◇ *the **running costs** of a car* (= for example of fuel, repairs, insurance) **3 -running** (in compounds) the activity of bringing sth such as drugs, guns, etc. into a country secretly and illegally: *drug-running*
IDM **in/out of the 'running (for sth)** (*informal*) having some/no chance of succeeding or achieving sth **make the 'running** (*BrE, informal*) to set the speed at which sth is done; to take the lead in doing sth
■ ***adj.*** **1** used after a number and a noun such as 'year' 'day' or 'time', to say that sth has happened in the same way several times, without a change: *She's won the championship three years running.* ◇ *It was the third day running that the train had been late.* ◇ *No party has won an election four times running.* **2 running water** is water that is flowing somewhere or water that is supplied to a building and available to be used through taps/faucets: *I can hear the sound of running water.* ◇ *a remote cottage without electricity or running water* **3** [only before noun] lasting a long time; continuous SYN **ongoing**: *For years he had fought a **running battle** with the authorities over the land.* ◇ *a running argument* ◇ *His old raincoat became a running joke* (= people kept laughing at it). ➲ see also LONG-RUNNING **4 -running** (in compounds) running or flowing in the way mentioned: *a fast-running river*
IDM **(go and) take a running 'jump** (*old-fashioned, informal*) used to tell sb in a rude way to go away ➲ more at ORDER *n.*

'running back *noun* (in AMERICAN FOOTBALL) an attacking player whose main job is to run forward carrying the ball

ˌrunning 'commentary *noun* a continuous description of an event, especially a sporting event, that sb gives as it happens: *to give a running commentary on the game*

'running dog *noun* **1** (*disapproving*) a person who follows a political system or set of beliefs without questioning them **2** a dog which has been bred to run, especially for racing or for pulling a SLEDGE across snow

ˌrunning 'head *noun* (*technical*) a title or word printed at the top of each page of a book

'running mate *noun* [usually sing.] (*politics*) (in the US) a person who is chosen by the candidate in an election, especially that for president, to support them and to have the next highest political position if they win: *The presidential nominee was advised to choose a woman as a running mate.*

'running order *noun* [sing.] the order of the items in a television programme or a show; the order that members of a team will play in

ˌrunning re'pairs *noun* [pl.] small things that you do to a piece of clothing, a vehicle, a machine, etc. to repair it or to keep it working

ˌrunning 'sore *noun* a small area on the body that is infected and has liquid (called PUS) coming out of it

'running time *noun* the amount of time that a film/movie, a journey, etc. lasts

ˌrunning 'total *noun* the total number or amount of things, money, etc. that changes as you add each new item

runny /ˈrʌni/ *adj.* (**run·nier, run·ni·est**) **1** (of your nose or eyes) producing a lot of liquid, for example when you have

R

a cold **2** having more liquid than is usual; not solid: *runny honey* ◇ *Omelettes should be runny in the middle.*

ˈrun-off *noun* **1** [C] a second vote or competition that is held to find a winner because two people taking part in the first competition got the same result **2** [U, C] rain, water or other liquid that runs off land into streams and rivers

ˌrun-of-the-ˈmill *adj.* (often *disapproving*) ordinary, with no special or interesting features

ˌrun-on ˈsentence *noun* two or more sentences or independent CLAUSES joined without the correct grammar

ˈrun-out *noun* (in CRICKET) a situation in which a player fails to complete a RUN before an opposing player hits the STUMPS with the ball, and so is OUT

runt /rʌnt/ *noun* **1** the smallest, weakest animal of the young that are born from the same mother at the same time: *the runt of the litter* **2** (*informal, disapproving*) a rude way of referring to a small, weak or unimportant person

ˈrun-through *noun* a practice for a performance of a play, show, etc. SYN **rehearsal**

ˈrun-time *noun* [U, C] (*computing*) **1** the amount of time that a program takes to perform a task **2** the time when a program is performing a task

ˈrun-up *noun* (*BrE*) **1** (also *less frequent* **ˈrun-in**) **~ (to sth)** a period of time leading up to an important event; the preparation for this: *an increase in spending in the run-up to Christmas* ◇ *during the run-up to the election* **2** the act of running or the distance you run, to gain speed before you jump a long distance, throw a ball, etc.

run·way /ˈrʌnweɪ/ *noun* **1** a long narrow strip of ground with a hard surface that an aircraft takes off from and lands on ➲ **COLLOCATIONS** at TRAVEL **2** (*NAmE*) = CATWALK

rupee /ruːˈpiː/ *noun* the unit of money in India, Pakistan and some other countries

rup·ture /ˈrʌptʃə(r)/ *noun, verb*

■ ***noun*** [C, U] **1** (*medical*) an injury in which sth inside the body breaks apart or bursts: *the rupture of a blood vessel* **2** a situation when sth breaks or bursts: *ruptures of oil and water pipelines* **3** (*informal*) a HERNIA of the ABDOMEN: *I nearly gave myself a rupture lifting that pile of books.* **4** (*formal*) the ending of agreement or of good relations between people, countries, etc: *a rupture in relations between the two countries* ◇ *Nothing could heal the rupture with his father.*

■ ***verb*** **1** [T, I] **~ (sth/yourself)** (*medical*) to burst or break apart sth inside the body; to be broken or burst apart: *a ruptured appendix* ◇ *He ruptured himself* (= got a HERNIA) *trying to lift the piano.* **2** [T, I] **~ (sth)** (*formal*) to make sth such as a container or a pipe break or burst; to be broken or burst: *The impact ruptured both fuel tanks.* ◇ *A pipe ruptured, leaking water all over the house.* **3** [T] **~ sth** (*formal*) to make an agreement or good relations between people or countries end: *the risk of rupturing North-South relations*

rural 0‑w /ˈrʊərəl; *NAmE* ˈrʊrəl/ *adj.* [usually before noun] connected with or like the countryside: *rural areas* ◇ *a rural economy* ◇ *rural America* ◇ *a rural way of life* ➲ compare URBAN

ˌrural ˈdean *noun* = DEAN

ˈrural route *noun* (*NAmE*) a route along which mail is delivered in rural areas

Ruri·ta·nian /ˌrʊərɪˈteɪniən; *NAmE* ˌrʊrəˈt-/ *adj.* (especially of stories) full of romantic adventure ORIGIN From **Ruritania**, the name of an imaginary country in central Europe in stories by Anthony Hope.

ruse /ruːz/ *noun* a way of doing sth or of getting sth by cheating sb SYN **trick**

rush 0‑w /rʌʃ/ *verb, noun*

■ ***verb***

▸ MOVE FAST **1** 0‑w [I, T] to move or to do sth with great speed, often too fast: *We've got plenty of time; there's no need to rush.* ◇ *the sound of rushing water* ◇ **+ adv./prep.** *Don't rush off, I haven't finished.* ◇ *I've been rushing around all day trying to get everything done.* ◇ *People rushed to buy shares in the company.* ◇ **~ sth** *We had to rush our meal.*

▸ TAKE/SEND QUICKLY **2** 0‑w [T] **~ sb/sth + adv./prep.** | **~ sb sth** to transport or send sb/sth somewhere with great speed: *Ambulances rushed the injured to the hospital.* ◇ *Relief supplies were rushed in.*

▸ DO STH TOO QUICKLY **3** 0‑w [I, T] to do sth or to make sb do sth without thinking about it carefully: **~ into sth/into doing sth** *We don't want to rush into having a baby.* ◇ **~ sb** *Don't rush me. I need time to think about it.* ◇ **~ sb into sth/into doing sth** *I'm not going to be rushed into anything.*

▸ ATTACK **4** [T] **~ sb/sth** to try to attack or capture sb/sth suddenly: *A group of prisoners rushed an officer and managed to break out.* ◇ *Fans rushed the stage after the concert.*

▸ IN AMERICAN FOOTBALL **5** [T] **~ sb** (*NAmE*) to run into sb who has the ball **6** [I] (*NAmE*) to move forward and gain ground by carrying the ball and not passing it

▸ IN AMERICAN COLLEGES **7** [T] **~ sb** (*NAmE*) to give a lot of attention to sb, especially to a student because you want them to join your FRATERNITY or SORORITY: *He is being rushed by Sigma Nu.* IDM see FOOL *n.*, FOOT *n.*

PHR V **ˌrush sth↔ˈout** to produce sth very quickly: *The editors rushed out an item on the crash for the late news.* **ˌrush sth↔ˈthrough** | **ˌrush sth ˈthrough sth** to deal with official business very quickly by making the usual process shorter than usual: *to rush a bill through Parliament*

■ ***noun***

▸ FAST MOVEMENT **1** 0‑w [sing.] a sudden strong movement: *Shoppers* ***made a rush for*** *the exits.* ◇ *She was trampled in the rush to get out.* ◇ *They listened to the rush of the sea below.* ◇ *The door blew open, letting in a rush of cold air.* ◇ *He had a* ***rush of blood to the head*** *and punched the man.*

▸ HURRY **2** 0‑w [sing., U] a situation in which you are in a hurry and need to do things quickly: *I can't stop—I'm* ***in a rush.*** ◇ ***What's the rush?*** ◇ *'I'll let you have the book back tomorrow.' '****There's no rush.****'* ◇ *The words came out* ***in a rush.*** ◇ *a* ***rush job*** (= one that has been done quickly)

▸ BUSY SITUATION **3** 0‑w [sing.] a situation in which people are very busy and there is a lot of activity: *The evening rush was just starting.* ◇ *the Christmas rush*

▸ OF FEELING **4** [sing.] **~ (of sth)** a sudden strong emotion or sign of strong emotion: *a sudden* ***rush of excitement/fear/anger*** **5** [sing.] a sudden feeling of extreme pleasure or excitement: *Parachuting will give you the rush of a lifetime.* ◇ *Users of the drug report experiencing a rush that lasts several minutes.*

▸ SUDDEN DEMAND **6** [sing.] **~ (on/for sth)** a sudden large demand for goods, etc: *There's been a rush on umbrellas this week.* ➲ see also GOLD RUSH

▸ PLANT **7** [C, usually pl.] a tall plant like grass that grows near water. Its long thin STEMS can be dried and used for making BASKETS, the seats of chairs, etc: *rush matting*

▸ OF FILM/MOVIE **8 rushes** [pl.] (*technical*) the first prints of a film/movie before they have been EDITED

▸ IN AMERICAN FOOTBALL **9** [C] an occasion when a player or players run towards a player on the other team who has the ball: *There was a rush on the quarterback.* **10** [C] an occasion when a player runs forward with the ball: *Johnson carried the ball an average of 6 yards per rush.*

▸ IN AMERICAN COLLEGES **11** [sing.] (*NAmE*) the time when parties are held for students who want to join a FRATERNITY or SORORITY: *rush week* ◇ *a rush party* IDM see BUM *n.*

rushed /rʌʃt/ *adj.* done too quickly or made to do sth too quickly SYN **hurried**: *It was a rushed decision made at the end of the meeting.* ◇ *Let's start work on it now so we're not too rushed at the end.* IDM see FOOT *n.*

ˈrush hour *noun* [C, usually sing., U] the time, usually twice a day, when the roads are full of traffic and trains are crowded because people are travelling to or from work: *the* ***morning/evening rush hour*** ◇ *Don't travel* ***at rush hour/in the rush hour.*** ◇ *rush-hour traffic* ➲ **COLLOCATIONS** at DRIVING

rusk /rʌsk/ *noun* (*especially BrE*) a hard crisp biscuit for babies to eat

R

rus·set /ˈrʌsɪt/ *adj.* reddish-brown in colour ▸ **rus·set** *noun* [U]: *leaves of russet and gold*

Rus·sian /ˈrʌʃn/ *adj., noun*
▪ ***adj.*** from or connected with Russia
▪ ***noun*** **1** [C] a person from Russia **2** [U] the language of Russia

ˌRussian ˈdoll *noun* one of a set of hollow painted figures which fit inside each other

ˌRussian rouˈlette *noun* [U] a dangerous game in which a person shoots at their own head with a gun that contains a bullet in only one of its chambers, so that the person does not know if the gun will fire or not: (*figurative*) *The airline was accused of playing Russian roulette with passenger safety.*

Russo- /ˈrʌsəʊ; *NAmE* ˈrʌsoʊ/ *combining form* (in nouns and adjectives) Russian: *Russo-Japanese relations*

rust /rʌst/ *noun, verb*
▪ ***noun*** [U] **1** a reddish-brown substance that is formed on some metals by the action of water and air: *pipes covered with rust* ◇ *rust spots* ◇ *a rust-coloured dress* ➲ see also RUSTY **2** a plant disease that causes reddish-brown spots; the FUNGUS that causes this disease
▪ ***verb*** [I, T] if metal **rusts** or sth **rusts** it, it becomes covered with rust SYN **corrodes**: *old rusting farming implements* ◇ *Brass doesn't rust.* ◇ **~ sth** *Water had got in and rusted the engine.* ▸ **rust·ed** *adj.*: *rusted iron* ➲ see also RUSTY
PHR V **ˌrust aˈway** to be gradually destroyed by rust

ˈrust belt *noun* (*especially US*) a region that used to have a lot of industry, but that has now decreased in importance and wealth, especially parts of the northern US where there were many factories that have now closed

rus·tic /ˈrʌstɪk/ *adj., noun*
▪ ***adj.*** **1** (*approving*) typical of the country or of country people; simple: *an old cottage full of rustic charm* **2** made very simply of rough wood: *a rustic garden seat* ◇ *a rustic fence* ▸ **rus·ti·city** /rʌˈstɪsəti/ *noun* [U]
▪ ***noun*** (*disapproving* or *humorous*) a person who lives in or comes from the country

rus·tle /ˈrʌsl/ *verb, noun*
▪ ***verb*** **1** [I, T] **~ (sth)** if sth dry and light **rustles** or you **rustle it**, it makes a sound like paper, leaves, etc. moving or rubbing together: *the sound of the trees rustling in the breeze* **2** [T] **~ sth** to steal farm animals
PHR V **ˌrustle sth↔ˈup (for sb)** (*informal*) to make or find sth quickly for sb and without planning: *I'm sure I can rustle you up a sandwich.* ◇ *She's trying to rustle up some funding for the project.*
▪ ***noun*** [sing.] a light dry sound like leaves or pieces of paper moving or rubbing against each other: *There was a rustle of paper as people turned the pages.* ◇ *I heard a faint rustle in the bushes.*

rust·ler /ˈrʌslə(r)/ *noun* a person who steals farm animals

rust·ling /ˈrʌslɪŋ/ *noun* **1** [U, C] the sound of light, dry things moving together: *the soft rustling of leaves* **2** [U] the act of stealing farm animals

rust·proof /ˈrʌstpruːf/ *adj.* **rustproof** metal has had a substance put on it so that it will not RUST

rusty /ˈrʌsti/ *adj.* (**rust·ier, rusti·est**) **1** covered with RUST: *rusty metal* ◇ *a rusty old car* **2** [not usually before noun] (*informal*) (of a sport, skill, etc.) not as good as it used to be, because you have not been practising: *My tennis is very rusty these days.* ◇ *I haven't played the piano for ages—I may be a little rusty.* ▸ **rusti·ness** *noun* [U]

rut /rʌt/ *noun* **1** [C] a deep track that a wheel makes in soft ground **2** [C] a boring way of life that does not change: *I gave up my job because I felt I was* ***stuck in a rut.*** ◇ *If you don't go out and meet new people, it's easy to* ***get into a rut.*** **3** [U] (also **the rut**) the time of year when male animals, especially DEER, become sexually active ➲ see also RUTTED, RUTTING

ru·ta·baga /ˌruːtəˈbeɪɡə/ (*NAmE*) (*BrE* **swede**) (*ScotE* **turnip**) *noun* [C, U] a large round yellow root vegetable ➲ VISUAL VOCAB page V27

ru·the·nium /ruːˈθiːniəm/ *noun* [U] (*symb.* **Ru**) a chemical element. Ruthenium is a hard silver-white metal that breaks easily and is found in PLATINUM ORES.

ruth·er·ford·ium /ˌrʌðəˈfɔːdiəm; *NAmE* ˌrʌðərˈfɔːrd-/ *noun* [U] (*symb.* **Rf**) a chemical element. Rutherfordium is RADIOACTIVE and does not exist in nature but is produced artificially when atoms COLLIDE (= crash into each other).

ruth·less /ˈruːθləs/ *adj.* (*disapproving*) (of people or their behaviour) hard and cruel; determined to get what you want and not caring if you hurt other people: *a ruthless dictator* ◇ *The way she behaved towards him was utterly ruthless.* ◇ *He has a ruthless determination to succeed.* ▸ **ruth·less·ly** *adv.* **ruth·less·ness** *noun* [U]

rut·ted /ˈrʌtɪd/ *adj.* (of a road or path) with deep tracks that have been made by wheels ➲ see also RUT (1)

rut·ting /ˈrʌtɪŋ/ *adj.* (of male animals, especially DEER) in a time of sexual activity: *rutting deer* ◇ *the rutting season* ➲ see also RUT (3)

RV /ˌɑː ˈviː; *NAmE* ˌɑːr/ (*NAmE*) (*BrE* **camp·er**, **ˈcamper van**) (also **motor·home** *NAmE, BrE*) *noun* a large vehicle designed for people to live and sleep in when they are travelling (the abbreviation for 'recreational vehicle')

Rx /ˌɑːr ˈeks/ *noun* (*NAmE*) **1** the written abbreviation for a doctor's PRESCRIPTION **2** a solution to a problem: *There's no Rx for unemployment.*

-ry ➲ -ERY

rye /raɪ/ *noun* [U] a plant that looks like BARLEY but that produces larger grain, grown as food for animals and for making flour and WHISKY; the grain of this plant: *rye bread* ◇ *rye whisky* ➲ VISUAL VOCAB page V28

rye·grass /ˈraɪɡrɑːs; *NAmE* -ɡræs/ *noun* [U] a type of grass which is grown as food for animals

Ss

S /es/ *noun, abbr., symbol*
■ ***noun*** (also **s**) [C, U] (*pl.* Ss, S's, s's /'esɪz/) the 19th letter of the English alphabet: *'Snow' begins with (an) S/'S'.* ➲ see also S-BEND
■ ***abbr.*** **1** (*pl.* SS) Saint **2** (especially for sizes of clothes) small **3** (*NAmE* also **So.**) south; southern: *S Yorkshire* **4** SIEMENS ➲ see also S AND H
■ ***symbol*** the symbol for ENTROPY

-'s /s; z/ *suffix, short form*
■ ***suffix*** (added to nouns) **1** belonging to: *the woman's hat* ◊ *Peter's desk* ◊ *children's clothes* **2** used to refer to sb's home or, in British English, a particular shop: *Shall we go to David's* (= David's house) *tonight?* ◊ (*BrE*) *I'll call in at the chemist's on my way home*
■ ***short form*** (*informal*) **1** used after *he*, *she* or *it* and *where*, *what*, *who* or *how* to mean 'is' or 'has': *She's still in the bath.* ◊ *What's he doing now?* ◊ *It's time to go now.* ◊ *Who's taken my pen?* ◊ *Where's he gone?* ◊ *It's gone wrong again.* **2** (used after *let* when making a suggestion that includes yourself and others) us: *Let's go out for lunch.*

-s' *suffix* (forming the end of plural nouns) belonging to: *the cats' tails* ◊ *their wives' jobs*

SA *abbr.* South Africa

saag (also **sag**) /sæg; *BrE* also sɑːg/ *noun* [U] (*IndE*) = SPINACH

sab·bath /'sæbəθ/ (often **the Sabbath**) *noun* [sing.] (in Judaism and Christianity) the holy day of the week that is used for resting and worshipping God. For Jews this day is Saturday and for Christians it is Sunday: *to* ***keep/break the Sabbath*** (= to obey/not obey the religious rules for this day)

sab·bat·ic·al /sə'bætɪkl/ *noun* [C, U] a period of time when sb, especially a teacher at a university, is allowed to stop their normal work in order to study or travel: *to take a year's sabbatical* ◊ *a* ***sabbatical term/year*** ◊ *He's* ***on sabbatical****.*

saber (*NAmE*) = SABRE

sable /'seɪbl/ *noun* **1** [C] a small animal from northern Asia with dark yellowish-brown fur **2** [U] the skin and fur of the sable, used for making expensive coats and artists' brushes

sabo·tage /'sæbətɑːʒ/ *noun, verb*
■ ***noun*** [U] **1** the act of doing deliberate damage to equipment, transport, machines, etc. to prevent an enemy from using them, or to protest about sth: *an act of* ***economic/military/industrial sabotage*** ◊ *Police investigating the train derailment have not ruled out sabotage.* **2** the act of deliberately spoiling sth in order to prevent it from being successful
■ ***verb*** **1 ~ sth** to damage or destroy sth deliberately to prevent an enemy from using it or to protest about sth: *The main electricity supply had been sabotaged by the rebels.* **2 ~ sth** to prevent sth from being successful or being achieved, especially deliberately: *Protesters failed to sabotage the peace talks.* ◊ *The rise in interest rates sabotaged any chance of the firm's recovery.*

sabo·teur /ˌsæbə'tɜː(r)/ *noun* a person who does deliberate damage to sth to prevent an enemy from using it, or to protest about sth: *Saboteurs blew up a small section of the track.* ◊ (*BrE*) ***hunt saboteurs*** (= people who try to stop people from hunting FOXES, etc.)

sabre (*especially US* **saber**) /'seɪbə(r)/ *noun* **1** a heavy SWORD with a curved blade **2** a light SWORD with a thin blade used in the sport of FENCING

'sabre-rattling (*especially US* **'saber-rattling**) *noun* [U] the act of trying to frighten sb by threatening to use force

sabre·tooth (*BrE*) (*US* **saber·tooth**) /'seɪbətuːθ; *NAmE* -bərt-/ (*BrE* also **ˌsabre-toothed 'tiger**) (*US* also **ˌsaber-toothed 'tiger**) *noun* a large animal of the cat family with two very long curved upper teeth, that lived thousands of years ago and is now EXTINCT

sac /sæk/ *noun* a part inside the body of a person, an animal or a plant, that is shaped like a bag, has thin skin around it, and contains liquid or air

sac·charin /'sækərɪn/ *noun* [U] a sweet chemical substance used instead of sugar, especially by people who are trying to lose weight

sac·char·ine (also *less frequent* **sac·char·in**) /'sækəriːn; -rɪn/ *adj.* (*disapproving*) (of people or things) too emotional in a way that seems exaggerated SYN **sentimental**: *a saccharine smile* ◊ *saccharine songs*

sacer·dotal /ˌsæsə'dəʊtl; *NAmE* -sər'doʊtl/ *adj.* (*formal*) connected with a priest or priests

sa·chet /'sæʃeɪ; *NAmE* sæ'ʃeɪ/ *noun* **1** (*BrE*) (*NAmE* **packet**) a closed plastic or paper package that contains a very small amount of liquid or a powder: *a sachet of sauce/sugar/shampoo* ➲ VISUAL VOCAB page V29 **2** a small bag containing dried HERBS or flowers that you put with your clothes to make them smell pleasant

sack 🔑 /sæk/ *noun, verb*
■ ***noun*** **1** 🔑 [C] a large bag with no handles, made of strong rough material or strong paper or plastic, used for storing and carrying, for example flour, coal, etc. **2** 🔑 [C] (*NAmE*) a strong paper bag for carrying shopping **3** 🔑 [C] the contents of a sack: *They got through a sack of potatoes.* ◊ (*NAmE*) *two sacks of groceries* **4** 🔑 **the sack** [sing.] (*BrE, informal*) being told by your employer that you can no longer continue working for a company, etc, usually because of sth that you have done wrong: *He* ***got the sack*** *for swearing.* ◊ *Her work was so poor that she was* ***given the sack****.* ◊ *Four hundred workers face the sack.* **5 the sack** [sing.] (*informal, especially NAmE*) a bed: *He caught them in the sack together.* **6** (usually **the sack**) [sing.] (*formal*) the act of stealing or destroying property in a captured town: *the sack of Rome* IDM see HIT *v.*
■ ***verb*** **1** 🔑 **~ sb** (*informal, especially BrE*) to dismiss sb from a job SYN **fire**: *She was sacked for refusing to work on Sundays.* ➲ COLLOCATIONS at UNEMPLOYMENT **2 ~ sth** (of an army, etc, especially in the past) to destroy things and steal property in a town or building: *Rome was sacked by the Goths in 410.* **3 ~ sb** (in AMERICAN FOOTBALL) to knock down the QUARTERBACK
PHR V **ˌsack 'out** (*NAmE, informal*) to go to sleep or to bed

sack·but /'sækbʌt/ *noun* a type of TROMBONE used in the RENAISSANCE period

sack·cloth /'sækklɒθ; *NAmE* -klɔːθ; -klɑːθ/ (also **sack·ing**) *noun* [U] a type of rough cloth made from JUTE, etc, used for making sacks
IDM **wear, put on, etc. ˌsackcloth and 'ashes** to behave in a way that shows that you are sorry for sth that you have done

sack·ful /'sækfʊl/ *noun* the amount contained in a SACK: *two sackfuls of flour*

sack·ing /'sækɪŋ/ *noun* **1** [C] an act of SACKING sb (= dismissing them from their job) **2** [U] = SACKCLOTH

'sack race *noun* a race in which the competitors jump forward inside a sack

sac·ra·ment /'sækrəmənt/ *noun* (in Christianity) **1** [C] an important religious ceremony such as marriage, BAPTISM or COMMUNION **2 the sacrament** [sing.] the bread and wine that are eaten and drunk during the service of COMMUNION ▶ **sac·ra·men·tal** /ˌsækrə'mentl/ *adj.* [usually before noun]: *sacramental wine*

sac·red /'seɪkrɪd/ *adj.* **1** connected with God or a god; considered to be holy: *a sacred image/shrine/temple* ◊ *sacred music* ◊ *Cows are sacred to Hindus.* **2** very important and treated with great respect SYN **sacrosanct**: *Human life must always be sacred.* ◊ *For journalists* ***nothing is sacred*** (= they write about anything). ▶ **sac·red·ness** *noun* [U] ➲ see also SANCTITY

ˌsacred ˈcow *noun* (*disapproving*) a custom, system, etc. that has existed for a long time and that many people think should not be questioned or criticized

sac·ri·fice /ˈsækrɪfaɪs/ *noun, verb*

■ ***noun*** **1** [C, U] the fact of giving up sth important or valuable to you in order to get or do sth that seems more important; sth that you give up in this way: *The makers of the product assured us that there had been no sacrifice of quality.* ◇ *Her parents* ***made sacrifices*** *so that she could have a good education.* ◇ *to make the* ***final/supreme sacrifice*** (= to die for your country, to save a friend, etc.) **2** [C, U] **~ (to sb)** the act of offering sth to a god, especially an animal that has been killed in a special way; an animal, etc. that is offered in this way: *They offered sacrifices to the gods.* ◇ *a human sacrifice* (= a person killed as a sacrifice)

■ ***verb*** **1** [T] to give up sth that is important or valuable to you in order to get or do sth that seems more important for yourself or for another person: **~ sth for sb/sth** *She sacrificed everything for her children.* ◇ *The designers have sacrificed speed for fuel economy.* ◇ **~ sth** *Would you sacrifice a football game to go out with a girl?* **2** [T, I] **~ (sb/sth)** to kill an animal or a person and offer it or them to a god, in order to please the god

sac·ri·fi·cial /ˌsækrɪˈfɪʃl/ *adj.* [usually before noun] offered as a sacrifice: *a sacrificial lamb*

sac·ri·lege /ˈsækrəlɪdʒ/ *noun* [U, sing.] an act of treating a holy thing or place without respect: (*figurative*) *It would be sacrilege to alter the composer's original markings.* ➲ COLLOCATIONS at RELIGION ▶ **sac·ri·le·gious** /ˌsækrəˈlɪdʒəs/ *adj.*

sac·ris·tan /ˈsækrɪstən/ *noun* a person whose job is to take care of the holy objects in a Christian church and to prepare the ALTAR for services

sac·risty /ˈsækrɪsti/ *noun* (*pl.* -ies) a room in a church where a priest prepares for a service by putting on special clothes and where various objects used in worship are kept SYN **vestry**

sacro·sanct /ˈsækrəʊsæŋkt; *NAmE* -kroʊ-/ *adj.* that is considered to be too important to change or question SYN **sacred**: *I'll work till late in the evening, but my weekends are sacrosanct.*

sac·rum /ˈseɪkrəm; ˈsæk-/ *noun* (*pl.* **sacra** /-krə/ or **sacrums**) (*anatomy*) a bone in the lower back, between the two hip bones of the PELVIS

SAD /sæd/ *abbr.* SEASONAL AFFECTIVE DISORDER

sad 0‑ᴿ /sæd/ *adj.* (**sad·der**, **sad·dest**)

▸ UNHAPPY **1** 0‑ᴿ unhappy or showing unhappiness: **~ (to do sth)** *We are very sad to hear that you are leaving.* ◇ **~ (that...)** *I was sad that she had to go.* ◇ **~ (about sth)** *I felt terribly sad about it.* ◇ *She looked sad and tired.* ◇ *He gave a slight, sad smile.* ◇ *The divorce left him* ***sadder and wiser*** (= having learned from the unpleasant experience). **2** 0‑ᴿ that makes you feel unhappy: *a sad story* ◇ **~ (to do sth)** ***It was sad to*** *see them go.* ◇ **~ (that...)** ***It is sad that*** *so many of his paintings have been lost.* ◇ *We had some sad news yesterday.* ◇ *He's a sad case—his wife died last year and he can't seem to manage without her.* ◇ ***Sad to say*** (= unfortunately) *the house has now been demolished.*

▸ UNACCEPTABLE **3** 0‑ᴿ unacceptable; deserving blame or criticism SYN **deplorable**: *a sad state of affairs* ◇ ***It's a sad fact that*** *many of those killed were children.*

▸ BORING **4** (*informal*) boring or not fashionable: *You sad old man.* ◇ *You'd have to be sad to wear a shirt like that.*

▸ IN POOR CONDITION **5** in poor condition: *The salad consisted of a few leaves of sad-looking lettuce.* ➲ see also SADLY, SADNESS

sad·den /ˈsædn/ *verb* [often passive] (*formal*) to make sb sad: **~ sb** *We were deeply saddened by the news of her death.* ◇ **~ sb to do sth** *Fans were saddened to see the former champion play so badly.* ◇ **it saddens sb that...** *It saddened her that people could be so cruel.*

sad·dle /ˈsædl/ *noun, verb*

■ ***noun*** **1** a leather seat for a rider on a horse: *She swung herself into the saddle.* **2** a seat on a bicycle or motorcycle ➲ VISUAL VOCAB page V41 **3** a piece of meat from the back of an animal

IDM **in the ˈsaddle 1** in a position of authority and control **2** riding a horse: *Three weeks after the accident he was back in the saddle.*

■ ***verb*** **~ sth** to put a saddle on a horse

PHR V **ˌsaddle ˈup** | **ˌsaddle sth↔ˈup** to put a saddle on a horse **ˈsaddle sb/yourself with sth** [often passive] to give sb/yourself an unpleasant responsibility, task, debt, etc: *I've been saddled with organizing the conference.* ◇ *The company was saddled with debts of £12 million.*

saddle·bag /ˈsædlbæg/ *noun* **1** one of a pair of bags put over the back of a horse **2** a bag attached to the back of a bicycle or motorcycle saddle

ˈsaddle horse *noun* **1** a frame on which saddles are cleaned or stored **2** (*NAmE*) a horse which is used only for riding

sad·dler /ˈsædlə(r)/ *noun* a person whose job is making, repairing and selling SADDLES and other leather goods

sad·dlery /ˈsædləri/ *noun* [U] SADDLES and leather goods for horses; the art of making these

ˈsaddle sore *adj.* feeling sore and stiff after riding a horse

ˈsaddle stitch *noun* a STITCH of thread or piece of wire put through the fold of a magazine, etc. to hold it together

saddo /ˈsædəʊ; *NAmE* -doʊ/ *noun* (*pl.* -os) (*BrE, informal*) a person that you think is boring or not fashionable: *a bunch of saddos who spend their lives playing computer games*

sadhu /ˈsɑːduː/ *noun* (*pl.* -us) a Hindu holy man, especially one who lives away from people and society

Sadie Haw·kins Day /ˌseɪdi ˈhɔːkɪnz deɪ/ *noun* (in the US) a day when there is a custom that women can invite men to a social event instead of waiting to be invited, especially to a **Sadie Hawkins Day** dance

sad·ism /ˈseɪdɪzəm/ *noun* [U] **1** enjoyment from watching or making sb suffer: *There's a streak of sadism in his nature.* **2** a need to hurt sb in order to get sexual pleasure ➲ compare MASOCHISM

sad·ist /ˈseɪdɪst/ *noun* a person who gets pleasure, especially sexual pleasure, from hurting other people ▶ **sad·is·tic** /səˈdɪstɪk/ *adj.*: *He took sadistic pleasure in taunting the boy.* **sad·is·tic·al·ly** /-kli/ *adv.*

sadly 0‑ᴿ /ˈsædli/ *adv.*

1 0‑ᴿ unfortunately: *Sadly, after eight years of marriage they had grown apart.* **2** 0‑ᴿ in a sad way: *She shook her head sadly.* **3** 0‑ᴿ very much and in a way that makes you sad: *She will be sadly missed.* ◇ *If you think I'm going to help you again, you're* ***sadly*** (= completely) ***mistaken.***

sad·ness 0‑ᴿ /ˈsædnəs/ *noun*

1 0‑ᴿ [U, sing.] the feeling of being sad: *memories tinged with sadness* ◇ *I felt a deep sadness.* **2** [C, usually pl.] something which makes you sad: *our joys and sadnesses*

sado·maso·chism /ˌseɪdəʊˈmæsəkɪzəm; *NAmE* -doʊ-/ *noun* [U] enjoyment from hurting sb and being hurt, especially during sexual activity ▶ **sado·maso·chist** /ˌseɪdəʊˈmæsəkɪst; *NAmE* -doʊ-/ *noun* **sado·maso·chis·tic** /ˌseɪdəʊˌmæsəˈkɪstɪk; *NAmE* -doʊ-/ *adj.*

sae /ˌes eɪ ˈiː/ *noun* (*BrE*) the abbreviation for 'stamped addressed envelope' or 'self-addressed envelope' (an envelope on which you have written your name and address and usually put a stamp so that sb else can use it to send sth to you): *Please enclose an sae for your test results.* ➲ compare SASE

sa·fari /səˈfɑːri/ *noun* [U, C] **1** a trip to see or hunt wild animals, especially in east or southern Africa: *to* ***be/go on safari*** **2** (*EAfrE*) a journey; a period of time spent travelling or when you are not at home or work: *I just got back from a month-long safari.* ◇ *It arrived while I was* ***on safari.***

saˈfari park *noun* a park in which wild animals move around freely and are watched by visitors from their cars

saˈfari suit *noun* a light-coloured suit worn by men in hot weather, especially one with pockets on the front of the jacket

safe 0‑w /seɪf/ *adj., noun*

■ ***adj.*** (safer, saf·est)

▸ PROTECTED **1** 0‑w [not before noun] protected from any danger or harm: *The children are quite safe here.* ◇ *She didn't **feel safe** on her own.* ◇ *Will the car be safe parked in the road?* ◇ **~ (from sb/sth)** *They aimed to make the country safe from terrorist attacks.* ◇ *Your secret is safe with me* (= I will not tell anyone else). ◇ *Here's your passport. Now **keep it safe**.* OPP **unsafe**

▸ WITHOUT PHYSICAL DANGER **2** 0‑w not likely to lead to any physical harm or danger: **~ (for sb) (to do sth)** *Is the water here safe to drink?* ◇ *The street is not safe for children to play in.* ◇ *It is one of the safest cars in the world.* ◇ *We watched the explosion **from a safe distance**.* ◇ *Builders were called in to **make** the building **safe**.* OPP **unsafe**

▸ NOT HARMED/LOST **3** 0‑w not harmed, damaged, lost, etc: *We were glad she let us know she was safe.* ◇ *The missing child was found **safe and well**.* ◇ *They turned up **safe and sound**.* ◇ *A reward was offered for the animal's **safe return**.*

▸ PLACE **4** 0‑w where sb/sth is not likely to be in danger or to be lost: *We all want to live in safer cities.* ◇ *Keep your passport in a safe place.* OPP **unsafe**

▸ WITHOUT RISK **5** 0‑w not involving much or any risk; not likely to be wrong or to upset sb: *a safe investment* ◇ *a safe subject for discussion* ◇ **~ (to do sth)** ***It's safe to assume (that)*** *there will always be a demand for new software.* ◇ *It would be safer to take more money with you in case of emergency.* ◇ (*disapproving*) *The show was well performed, but so safe and predictable.*

▸ PERSON **6** 0‑w [usually before noun] doing an activity in a careful way SYN **careful**: *a safe driver*

▸ LAW **7** based on good evidence: *a safe verdict* OPP **unsafe**

▸ APPROVING **8** (*BrE, informal*) used by young people to show that they approve of sb/sth: *I like him, he's safe.* ◇ *That kid's safe.* **9** (*BrE, informal*) used by young people as a way of accepting sth that is offered: *'You want some?' 'Yeah, safe.'* ➲ see also FAIL-SAFE

IDM ˌ**better** ˌ**safe than** ˈ**sorry** (*saying*) used to say that it is wiser to be too careful than to act too quickly and do sth you may later wish you had not **in safe** ˈ**hands** | **in the safe hands of sb** being taken care of well by sb: *I've left the kids in safe hands—with my parents.* ◇ *Their problem was in the safe hands of the experts.* **on the** ˈ**safe side** being especially careful; taking no risks: *I took some extra cash just to be on the safe side.* **play (it)** ˈ**safe** to be careful; to avoid risks **(as)** ˌ**safe as** ˈ**houses** (*BrE*) very safe **safe in the knowledge that** confident because you know that sth is true or will happen: *She went out safe in the knowledge that she looked fabulous.* **a safe pair of** ˈ**hands** (*especially BrE*) a person that you can trust to do a job well ➲ more at BET *n.*

■ ***noun*** a strong metal box or cupboard with a complicated lock, used for storing valuable things in, for example, money or jewellery

ˌ**safe** ˈ**conduct** (also ˌ**safe** ˈ**passage**) *noun* [U, C] official protection from being attacked, arrested, etc. when passing through an area; a document that promises this: *The guerrillas were promised safe conduct out of the country.*

ˈ**safe deposit box** (also ˈ**safety deposit box**) *noun* a metal box for storing valuable things, usually kept in a special room at a bank

safe·guard /ˈseɪfgɑːd; *NAmE* -gɑːrd/ *verb, noun*

■ ***verb*** [T, I] (*formal*) to protect sth/sb from loss, harm or damage; to keep sth/sb safe: **~ sth** *to safeguard a person's interests* ◇ *to safeguard jobs* ◇ **~ sth/sb against/from sth** *The new card will safeguard the company against fraud.* ◇ **~ against sth** *The leaflet explains how to safeguard against dangers in the home.*

■ ***noun*** **~ (against sth)** something that is designed to protect people from harm, risk or danger: *Stronger legal safeguards are needed to protect the consumer.*

ˌ**safe** ˈ**haven** *noun* a place where sb can go to be safe from danger or attack

ˈ**safe house** *noun* a house used by people who are hiding, for example by criminals hiding from the police, or by people who are being protected by the police from other people who may wish to harm them

ˌ**safe** ˈ**keeping** *noun* [U] **1** the fact of sth being in a safe place where it will not be lost or damaged: *She had put her watch in her pocket **for safe keeping**.* **2** the fact of sb/sth being taken care of by sb who can be trusted: *The documents are **in the safe keeping** of our lawyers.*

safe·ly 0‑w /ˈseɪfli/ *adv.*

1 0‑w without being harmed, damaged or lost: *The plane landed safely.* **2** 0‑w in a way that does not cause harm or that protects sb/sth from harm: *The bomb has been safely disposed of.* ◇ *The money is safely locked in a drawer.* **3** without much possibility of being wrong: *We can **safely say** that he will accept the job.* **4** without any possibility of the situation changing: *I thought the kids were safely tucked up in bed.* **5** without any problems being caused; with no risk: *These recommendations can safely be ignored.*

ˈ**safe mode** *noun* [U] (*computing*) a way of starting a computer that makes it easier to find a problem without the risk of losing data

ˌ**safe** ˈ**passage** *noun* [U, C] = SAFE CONDUCT

the ˈ**safe period** *noun* [sing.] the time just before and during a woman's PERIOD when she is unlikely to become pregnant

ˈ**safe room** *noun* = PANIC ROOM

ˌ**safe** ˈ**seat** *noun* (*BrE*) a CONSTITUENCY where a particular political party has a lot of support and is unlikely to be defeated in an election

ˌ**safe** ˈ**sex** *noun* [U] sexual activity in which people try to protect themselves from AIDS and other sexual diseases, for example by using a CONDOM

safety 0‑w /ˈseɪfti/ *noun* (*pl.* -ies)

1 0‑w [U] the state of being safe and protected from danger or harm: *a place where children can play **in safety*** ◇ *The police are concerned for the safety of the 12-year-old boy who has been missing for three days.* ◇ *He was kept in custody **for his own safety**.* **2** 0‑w [U] the state of not being dangerous: *I'm worried about the safety of the treatment.* ◇ *safety standards* ◇ *a local campaign to improve **road safety*** ◇ *The airline has an excellent **safety record**.* **3** 0‑w [U] a place where you are safe: *I managed to swim **to safety**.* ◇ *We watched the lions **from the safety of** the car.* ◇ *They reached safety seconds before the building was engulfed in flames.* **4** [C] (*NAmE*) = SAFETY CATCH **5** [C] (*NAmE*) (in AMERICAN FOOTBALL) a defending player who plays in a position far away from the other team

IDM ˌ**safety** ˈ**first** (*saying*) safety is the most important thing **there's** ˌ**safety in** ˈ**numbers** (*saying*) being in a group makes you safer and makes you feel more confident

ˈ**safety belt** *noun* = SEAT BELT

ˈ**safety catch** (*especially BrE*) (*NAmE* usually **safety**) *noun* a device that stops a gun from being fired or a machine from working by accident

ˈ**safety curtain** *noun* a curtain which can come down across the stage in a theatre, intended to stop a fire from spreading

ˈ**safety deposit box** *noun* = SAFE DEPOSIT BOX

ˈ**safety glass** *noun* [U] strong glass that does not break into sharp pieces

ˈ**safety island** *noun* (*US*) = TRAFFIC ISLAND

ˈ**safety lamp** *noun* a special lamp used by MINERS with a flame that does not cause underground gases to explode

ˈ**safety match** *noun* a type of match that will light only if it is rubbed against a specially prepared rough surface, often on the side of its box

ˈ**safety measure** *noun* something that you do in order to prevent sth bad or dangerous from happening

ˈ**safety net** *noun* **1** an arrangement that helps to prevent disaster if sth goes wrong: *a financial safety net* ◇ *people who have fallen through the safety net and ended up homeless on the streets* **2** a net placed underneath ACROBATS, etc. to catch them if they fall

ˈ**safety pin** *noun* a pin with a point bent back towards the head, that is covered when closed so that it cannot hurt you ➲ VISUAL VOCAB page V51

S

'safety razor *noun* a RAZOR with a cover over the blade to stop it from cutting the skin ⮊ compare CUT-THROAT RAZOR

'safety valve *noun* **1** a device that lets out steam or pressure in a machine when it becomes too great **2** a harmless way of letting out feelings of anger, excitement, etc: *Exercise is a good safety valve for the tension that builds up at work.*

saf·flower /'sæflaʊə(r)/ *noun* [C, U] a plant with orange flowers, whose seeds produce an oil which is used in cooking

saf·fron /'sæfrən/ *noun* [U] **1** a bright yellow powder made from CROCUS flowers, used in cooking to give colour to food ⮊ VISUAL VOCAB page V28 **2** a bright orange-yellow colour ▸ **saf·fron** *adj.*: *Buddhist monks in saffron robes*

SAG /ˌes eɪ 'dʒiː/ *abbr.* SCREEN ACTORS GUILD

sag[1] /sæg/ *verb* (-gg-) **1** [I] to hang or bend down in the middle, especially because of weight or pressure: *a sagging roof* ◇ *The tent began to sag under the weight of the rain.* ◇ *Your skin starts to sag as you get older.* **2** [I] to become weaker or fewer: *Their share of the vote sagged badly at the last election.* ▸ **sag** *noun* [U, C, usually sing.]: *Weight has caused the sag.* IDM see JAW *n.*

PHR V **ˌsag 'off | sag off sth** (*BrE, informal*) to stay away from school or work when you should be there, or leave before you should: *We sagged off school and wrote the song.*

sag[2] /sɑːg/ *noun* = SAAG

saga /'sɑːgə/ *noun* **1** a long traditional story about adventures and brave acts, especially one from Norway or Iceland **2** a long story about events over a period of many years: *a family saga* **3** a long series of events or adventures and/or a report about them: *The front page is devoted to the continuing saga of the hijack.* ◇ (*humorous*) *the saga of how I missed the plane*

sa·ga·cious /sə'geɪʃəs/ *adj.* (*formal*) showing good judgement and understanding SYN **wise** ▸ **sa·ga·city** /sə'gæsəti/ *noun* [U]

sage /seɪdʒ/ *noun, adj.*

■ *noun* **1** [U] a plant with flat, light green leaves that have a strong smell and are used in cooking as a HERB ⮊ VISUAL VOCAB page V28 **2** [C] (*formal*) a very wise person

■ *adj.* (*literary*) wise, especially because you have a lot of experience ▸ **sage·ly** *adv.*: *She nodded sagely.*

sage·brush /'seɪdʒbrʌʃ/ *noun* [U] a plant with leaves that smell sweet that grows in dry regions in the western US; an area of ground covered with sagebrush

S

saggy /'sægi/ *adj.* (sag·gier, sag·gi·est) (*informal*) no longer firm; hanging or sinking down in way that is not attractive

Sa·git·tar·ius /ˌsædʒɪ'teəriəs; *NAmE* -'ter-/ *noun* **1** [U] the 9th sign of the ZODIAC, the ARCHER **2** [sing.] a person born when the sun is in this sign, that is between 22 November and 20 December, approximately ▸ **Sa·git·tar·ian** *noun, adj.*

sago /'seɪgəʊ; *NAmE* -goʊ/ *noun* [U] hard white grains made from the soft inside of a type of PALM tree, often cooked with milk to make a DESSERT: *sago pudding*

sa·guaro /sə'gwɑːrəʊ; *NAmE* -roʊ/ *noun* (*pl.* -os) a very large CACTUS that grows in the southern US and Mexico

sahib /sɑːb; 'sɑːɪb/ *noun* used in India, especially in the past, to address a European man, especially one with some social or official status

said /sed/ **1** *past tense, past part.* of SAY **2** *adj.* [only before noun] (*formal* or *law*) = AFOREMENTIONED: *the said company*

sail 🔑 /seɪl/ *verb, noun*

■ *verb* **1** 🔑 [I, T] (of a boat or ship or the people on it) to travel on water using sails or an engine: (+ **adv./prep.**) *to sail into harbour* ◇ *The dinghy sailed smoothly across the lake.* ◇ *The ferry sails from Newhaven to Dieppe.* ◇ *one of the first people to sail around the world* ◇ **~ sth** *to sail the Atlantic* **2** 🔑 (also **go sailing**) [I, T] to control or travel on a boat with a sail, especially as a sport: *We spent the weekend sailing off the south coast.* ◇ *Do you* **go sailing** *often?* ◇ **~ sth** *She sails her own yacht.* **3** [I] (of a boat or ship or the people in it) to begin a journey on water: *We sail at 2 p.m. tomorrow.* ◇ **~ for sth** *He sailed for the West Indies from Portsmouth.* **4** [I] + **adv./prep.** to move quickly and smoothly in a particular direction; (of people) to move in a confident manner: *clouds sailing across the sky* ◇ *The ball sailed over the goalie's head.* ◇ *She sailed past, ignoring me completely.*

IDM **sail close to the 'wind** to take a risk by doing sth that is dangerous or that may be illegal

PHR V **ˌsail 'through (sth)** to pass an exam, a test, etc. without any difficulty

■ *noun* **1** 🔑 [C, U] a sheet of strong cloth which the wind blows against to make a boat or ship travel through the water: *As the boat moved down the river the wind began to fill the sails.* ◇ *a ship* **under sail** (= using sails) ◇ *in the days of sail* (= when ships all used sails) ◇ *She moved away like a ship* **in full sail** (= with all its sails spread out). **2** 🔑 [sing.] a trip in a boat or ship: *We went for a sail.* ◇ *a two-hour sail across the bay* **3** [C] a set of boards attached to the arm of a WINDMILL

IDM **set 'sail (from/for...)** (*formal*) to begin a trip by sea: *a liner setting sail from New York* ◇ *We set sail (for France) at high tide.* ⮊ more at TRIM *v.*, WIND[1] *n.*

sail·board /'seɪlbɔːd; *NAmE* -bɔːrd/ (also **board**) *noun* = WINDSURFER (1) ▸ **sail·board·er** *noun* **sail·board·ing** *noun* [U]

sail·boat /'seɪlbəʊt; *NAmE* -boʊt/ (*NAmE*) (*BrE* **'sailing boat**) *noun* a boat with sails ⮊ VISUAL VOCAB page V44

sail·cloth /'seɪlklɒθ; *NAmE* -klɔːθ; -klɑːθ/ *noun* [U] a type of strong cloth used for making sails

sail·ing 🔑 /'seɪlɪŋ/ *noun*

1 🔑 [U] the sport or activity of travelling in a boat with sails: *to go sailing* ◇ *a sailing club* **2** [C] one of the regular times that a ship leaves a port: *There are six sailings a day.*

IDM see CLEAR *adj.*, PLAIN *adj.*

'sailing boat (*BrE*) (*NAmE* **sail·boat**) *noun* a boat with sails ⮊ VISUAL VOCAB page V44

'sailing ship *noun* a ship with sails

sail·maker /'seɪlmeɪkə(r)/ *noun* a person whose job is to make or repair sails ▸ **sail·mak·ing** *noun* [U]

sail·or 🔑 /'seɪlə(r)/ *noun*

1 🔑 a person who works on a ship as a member of the CREW **2** 🔑 a person who sails a boat

IDM **a good/bad 'sailor** a person who rarely/often becomes sick at sea

'sailor suit *noun* a suit for a child made in the style of an old-fashioned sailor's uniform

saint /seɪnt; *or, in British use before names,* snt/ *noun* **1** (*abbr.* S, St) a person that the Christian Church recognizes as being very holy, because of the way they have lived or died: *St John* ◇ *St Valentine's Day* ◇ *The children were all named after saints.* ⮊ see also PATRON SAINT, ST BERNARD **2** a very good, kind or patient person: *She's a saint to go on living with that man.* ◇ *His behaviour would try* **the patience of a saint**. ▸ **saint·hood** *noun* [U]

saint·ed /'seɪntɪd/ *adj.* [usually before noun] (*old-fashioned* or *humorous*) considered or officially stated to be a saint: *And how is my sainted sister?*

saint·ly /'seɪntli/ *adj.* like a SAINT; very holy and good: *to lead a saintly life* ▸ **saint·li·ness** *noun* [U]

'saint's day *noun* (in the Christian Church) a day of the year when a particular SAINT is remembered and on which, in some countries, people who are named after that SAINT have celebrations

saith /seθ/ (*old use*) = SAYS

sake[1] /seɪk/ *noun* ⮊ see also SAKE[2]

IDM **for Christ's, God's, goodness', heaven's, pity's, etc. 'sake** used to emphasize that it is important to do sth or when you are annoyed about sth: *Do be careful, for goodness' sake.* ◇ *Oh, for heaven's sake!* ◇ *For pity's sake, help me!* HELP Some people find the use of **Christ**, **God** or **heaven** here offensive. **for sth's sake** because of the interest or value sth has, not because of the advantages it may bring: *I believe in education for its own sake.* ◇ *art for art's sake* **for the sake of sb/sth | for sb's/sth's sake** in order to help sb/sth or because you like sb/sth: *They stayed together for the sake of the children.* ◇ *You can do it. Please, for my sake.* ◇ *I hope you're right, for all our sakes* (= because this is important for all of us). **for the sake of sth/of doing sth** in order to get or keep sth: *The translation sacrifices naturalness for the sake of accuracy.* ◇ *She gave up smoking for the sake of her health.* ◇ *Don't get married* ***just for the sake of it.*** ◇ *Let's suppose,* ***for the sake of argument*** (= in order to have a discussion), *that interest rates went up by 2%.* ➲ more at OLD

sake² (also **saki**) /ˈsɑːki/ *noun* [U] a Japanese alcoholic drink made from rice ➲ see also SAKE¹

sa·laam /səˈlɑːm/ *verb* [I, T] **~ (sb)** (in some Eastern countries) to say hello to sb in a formal way by bending forward from the waist and putting your right hand on your FOREHEAD ▶ **sa·laam** *noun*

sal·acious /səˈleɪʃəs/ *adj.* (*formal*) (of stories, pictures, etc.) encouraging sexual desire or containing too much sexual detail ▶ **sal·acious·ness** *noun* [U]

salad 🔑 /ˈsæləd/ *noun*
1 🔑 [U, C] a mixture of raw vegetables such as LETTUCE, tomato and CUCUMBER, usually served with other food as part of a meal: *All main courses come with salad or vegetables.* ◇ *Is cold meat and salad OK for lunch?* ◇ *a* ***side salad*** (= a small bowl of salad served with the main course of a meal) ◇ *a* ***salad bowl*** (= a large bowl for serving salad in) ➲ COLLOCATIONS at COOKING ➲ see also CAESAR SALAD, GREEN SALAD **2** 🔑 [C, U] (in compounds) meat, fish, cheese, etc. served with salad: *a chicken salad* **3** 🔑 [U, C] (in compounds) raw or cooked vegetables, etc. that are cut into small pieces, often mixed with MAYONNAISE and served cold with other food: *potato salad* ◇ *a pasta salad* ➲ see also FRUIT SALAD **4** [U] any green vegetable, especially LETTUCE, that is eaten raw in a salad: *salad plants*
IDM **your ˈsalad days** (*old-fashioned*) the time when you are young and do not have much experience of life

ˈsalad cream *noun* [U] (*BrE*) a pale yellow sauce, similar to MAYONNAISE, sold in bottles and eaten on salads, in SANDWICHES, etc.

ˈsalad dressing *noun* [U, C] = DRESSING

sala·man·der /ˈsæləmændə(r)/ *noun* an animal like a LIZARD, with short legs and a long tail, that lives both on land and in water (= is an AMPHIBIAN) ➲ VISUAL VOCAB page V11

sa·lami /səˈlɑːmi/ *noun* [U, C] (*pl.* **sa·lamis**) a type of large spicy SAUSAGE served cold in thin slices

saˈlami slicing *noun* [U] (*informal*) the act of removing sth gradually by small amounts at a time

sal·ar·ied /ˈsælərid/ *adj.* **1** (of a person) receiving a salary: *a salaried employee* **2** (of a job) for which a salary is paid: *a salaried position*

sal·ary 🔑 /ˈsæləri/ *noun* (*pl.* **-ies**)
money that employees receive for doing their job, especially professional employees or people working in an office, usually paid every month: *an annual salary of $40 000* ◇ *a 9% salary increase* ◇ *She's* ***on a salary of*** *£24 000.* ◇ (*BrE*) *He gets a* ***basic salary*** *plus commission.* ◇ (*NAmE*) ***base salary*** ➲ compare WAGE ➲ SYNONYMS at INCOME

sal·ary·man /ˈsælərimæn/ *noun* (*pl.* **-men** /-men/) (especially in Japan) a WHITE-COLLAR worker (= one who works in an office)

sal·but·am·ol /sælˈbjuːtəmɒl; *NAmE* -mɔːl; -mɑːl/ *noun* [U] a drug that is used in the treatment of medical conditions such as ASTHMA

sale 🔑 /seɪl/ *noun*
1 🔑 [U, C] an act or the process of selling sth: *regulations governing the sale of alcoholic beverages* ◇ *I haven't* ***made a sale*** *all week.* ◇ *She gets 10% commission on each sale.* **2** 🔑 **sales** [pl.] the number of items sold: *Retail sales fell in November by 10%.* ◇ *Export sales were up by 32% last year.* ◇ *the* ***sales figures*** *for May* ◇ *a* ***sales drive/campaign*** (= a special effort to sell more) ➲ COLLOCATIONS at BUSINESS **3** 🔑 **sales** [U] (also **ˈsales department** [C]) the part of a company that deals with selling its products: *a sales and marketing director* ◇ *She works in sales/in the sales department.* ◇ *The Weldon Group has a 6 000 strong* ***sales force.*** **4** 🔑 [C] an occasion when a shop/store sells its goods at a lower price than usual: *The sale starts next week.* ◇ *the January sales* ◇ *I bought a coat* ***in the sales.*** ◇ *sale prices* **5** [C] an occasion when goods are sold, especially an AUCTION: *a contemporary art sale* ➲ see also CAR BOOT SALE, GARAGE SALE, JUMBLE SALE
IDM **for ˈsale** 🔑 available to be bought, especially from the owner: *I'm sorry, it's not for sale.* ◇ *They've* ***put their house up for sale.*** ◇ *an increase in the number of stolen vehicles being* ***offered for sale*** ◇ *a 'for sale' sign* **on ˈsale** **1** 🔑 available to be bought, especially in a shop/store: *Tickets are on sale from the booking office.* ◇ *The new model* ***goes on sale*** *next month.* **2** (*especially NAmE, SAfrE*) being offered at a reduced price: *All video equipment is on sale today and tomorrow.* **(on) ˌsale or reˈturn** (*BrE*) (of goods) supplied with the agreement that any item that is not sold can be sent back without having to be paid for

sale·able /ˈseɪləbl/ *adj.* good enough to be sold; that sb will want to buy: *a saleable product* ◇ *not in saleable condition* OPP **unsaleable**

ˌsale of ˈwork *noun* (*pl.* **ˌsales of ˈwork**) (*BrE*) a sale of things made by members of an organization, such as a church, often to make money for charity

sale·room /ˈseɪlruːm; -rʊm/ (*BrE*) (*NAmE* **sales·room**) *noun* a room where goods are sold at an AUCTION

ˈsales clerk (also **clerk**) (both *NAmE*) (*BrE* **ˈshop assistant, as·sist·ant**) *noun* a person whose job is to serve customers in a shop/store

sales·girl /ˈseɪlzɡɜːl; *NAmE* -ɡɜːrl/ *noun* a girl or woman who works in a shop/store

sales·man /ˈseɪlzmən/, **sales·woman** /ˈseɪlzwʊmən/ *noun* (*pl.* **-men** /-mən/, **-women** /-wɪmɪn/) a man or woman whose job is to sell goods, for example, in a shop/store: *a car salesman* ➲ note at GENDER

sales·man·ship /ˈseɪlzmənʃɪp/ *noun* [U] skill in persuading people to buy things

sales·per·son /ˈseɪlzpɜːsn; *NAmE* -pɜːrsn/ *noun* (*pl.* **-people**) a person whose job is to sell goods, for example, in a shop/store

ˈsales representative (also *informal* **ˈsales rep, rep**) *noun* an employee of a company who travels around a particular area selling the company's goods to shops/stores, etc.

sales·room /ˈseɪlzruːm; -rʊm/ (*NAmE*) (*BrE* **sale·room**) *noun* a room where goods are sold at an AUCTION

ˈsales slip *noun* (*NAmE*) = RECEIPT

ˈsales talk *noun* [U] talk that tries to persuade sb to buy sth

ˈsales tax *noun* [U, C] (in some countries) the part of the price you pay when you buy sth that goes to the government as tax

sales·woman *noun* ➲ SALESMAN

sali·cyl·ic acid /ˌsælɪˌsɪlɪk ˈæsɪd/ *noun* [U] a bitter chemical found in some plants, used in ASPIRIN (= a drug used for reducing pain and making your blood thinner)

sa·li·ent /ˈseɪliənt/ *adj.* [only before noun] most important or noticeable: *She pointed out the* ***salient features*** *of the new design.* ◇ *He summarized the* ***salient points.***

sa·line /ˈseɪlaɪn; *NAmE* -liːn/ *adj., noun*
■ **adj.** [usually before noun] (*technical*) containing salt: *Wash the lenses in saline solution.* ▶ **sal·in·ity** /səˈlɪnəti/ *noun* [U]: *to measure the salinity of the water*
■ **noun** [U] (*technical*) a mixture of salt in water

Salis·bury steak /ˌsɔːlzbri ˈsteɪk/ *noun* (*NAmE*) finely chopped beef mixed with egg and onions made into a flat, round shape and cooked under or over a strong heat

sal·iva /səˈlaɪvə/ *noun* [U] the liquid that is produced in your mouth that helps you to swallow food

S

sal·iv·ary /sə'laɪvəri; 'sælɪvəri; *NAmE* 'sæləveri/ *adj.* (*technical*) of or producing saliva

sali·vate /'sælɪveɪt/ *verb* [I] (*formal*) to produce more SALIVA in your mouth than usual, especially when you see or smell food: (*figurative*) *He was salivating over the thought of the million dollars.* ▶ **sali·va·tion** /ˌsælɪ'veɪʃn/ *noun* [U]

sal·low /'sæləʊ; *NAmE* -loʊ/ *adj., noun*
■ ***adj.*** (of a person's skin or face) having a slightly yellow colour that does not look healthy **SYN pasty**
■ ***noun*** a type of WILLOW tree that does not grow very tall

sally /'sæli/ *noun, verb*
■ ***noun*** (*pl.* **sal·lies**) **1** a remark that is intended to entertain or amuse sb **SYN witticism 2** a sudden attack by an enemy
■ ***verb*** (**sal·lies, sally·ing, sal·lied, sal·lied**)
PHR V ˌsally 'forth/'out (*old-fashioned* or *literary*) to leave a place in a determined or enthusiastic way.

sal·mon /'sæmən/ *noun* [C, U] (*pl.* **sal·mon**) a large fish with silver skin and pink flesh that is used for food. Salmon live in the sea but swim up rivers to lay their eggs: *a whole salmon* ◇ *smoked salmon* ◇ *wild and farmed salmon*

sal·mon·ella /ˌsælmə'nelə/ *noun* [U] a type of bacteria that makes people sick if they eat infected food; an illness caused by this bacteria: *cases of salmonella poisoning* ◇ *an outbreak of salmonella*

ˌsalmon 'pink *adj.* orange-pink in colour, like the flesh of a salmon ▶ **ˌsalmon 'pink** *noun* [U]

salon /'sælɒn; *NAmE* sə'lɑːn; sə'lɔːn/ *noun* **1** a shop/store that gives customers hair or beauty treatment or that sells expensive clothes: *a beauty salon* ◇ *a hairdressing salon* **2** (*old-fashioned*) a room in a large house used for entertaining guests **3** (in the past) a regular meeting of writers, artists and other guests at the house of a famous or important person: *a literary salon*

sal·oon /sə'luːn/ *noun* **1** (also **sa'loon car**) (both *BrE*) (*NAmE* **sedan**) a car with four doors and a BOOT/TRUNK (= space at the back for carrying things) which is separated from the part where the driver and passengers sit: *a five-seater family saloon* ➲ VISUAL VOCAB page V42 **2** (also **sa'loon bar**) (both *BrE*) = LOUNGE BAR **3** a bar where alcoholic drinks were sold in the western US and Canada in the past **4** a large comfortable room on a ship, used by the passengers to sit and relax in

sal·op·ettes /ˌsælə'pets/ *noun* [pl.] a piece of clothing worn for SKIING or sailing, consisting of trousers/pants with a part that comes up over your shoulders

salsa /'sælsə; *NAmE* 'sɑːlsə/ *noun* **1** [U] a type of Latin American dance music **2** [C, U] a dance performed to this music **3** [U] a sauce eaten with Mexican food

sal·sify /'sælsəfi/ *noun* [U] (*BrE*) a plant with a long root that is cooked and eaten as a vegetable

salt 🔑 /sɔːlt; *BrE* also sɒlt; *NAmE* sɔːlt/ *noun, verb, adj.*
■ ***noun* 1** 🔑 [U] a white substance that is added to food to give it a better flavour or to preserve it. Salt is obtained from mines and is also found in sea water. It is sometimes called **common salt** to distinguish it from other chemical salts. **SYN sodium chloride**: *Pass the salt, please.* ◇ *a pinch of salt* (= a small amount of it) ◇ *Season with salt and pepper.* ◇ *sea salt* ➲ see also ROCK SALT **2** [C] (*chemistry*) a chemical formed from a metal and an acid: *mineral salts* ➲ see also ACID SALT, EPSOM SALTS **3 salts** [pl.] a substance that looks or tastes like salt: *bath salts* (= used to give a pleasant smell to bath water) ➲ see also SMELLING SALTS
IDM the salt of the 'earth a very good and honest person that you can always depend on ➲ more at DOSE *n.*, PINCH *n.*, RUB *v.*, WORTH *adj.*
■ ***verb* 1** [usually passive] **~ sth** to put salt on or in food: *salted peanuts* ◇ *a pan of boiling salted water* **2 ~ sth** (**down**) to preserve food with salt: *salted fish* **3 ~ sth** to put salt on roads to melt ice or snow
PHR V ˌsalt sth↔a'way to save sth for the future, secretly and usually dishonestly: *She salted away the profits in foreign bank accounts.*
■ ***adj.*** [only before noun] containing, tasting of or preserved with salt: *salt water* ◇ *salt beef*

ˌsalt-and-'pepper *adj.* = PEPPER-AND-SALT

salt·box /'sɔːltbɒks; *NAmE* -bɑːks; *BrE* also 'sɒlt-/ *noun* (*NAmE*) a house that has two floors at the front and one floor at the back, with a roof that slopes down between the two floors

'salt cellar *noun* **1** (*BrE*) (*NAmE* **'salt shaker**) a small container for salt, usually with one hole in the top, that is used at the table ➲ VISUAL VOCAB page V19 **2** (*NAmE*) a small open dish containing salt

'salt flats *noun* [pl.] a flat area of land, covered with a layer of salt

salt·ine /sɔːl'tiːn; sɒl-; *NAmE* sɔːl-/ (also **ˌsaltine 'cracker**) *noun* (*NAmE*) a thin dry biscuit with salt on top of it

sal·tire /'sæltaɪə(r); 'sɔːl-/ (also **ˌsaltire 'cross**) *noun* **1** a cross in the shape of an X, especially on a COAT OF ARMS or a flag **2 the Saltire** the flag of Scotland, which is a white saltire on a blue background

'salt marsh (also **'salt meadow**) *noun* an area of open land near a coast that is regularly flooded by the sea

'salt pan *noun* an area of low land where sea water has EVAPORATED to leave salt

salt·petre (*US* **salt·peter**) /ˌsɔːlt'piːtə(r); *BrE* also ˌsɒlt-; *NAmE* ˌsɔːlt-/ *noun* [U] a white powder used for preserving food and making matches and GUNPOWDER

'salt truck (*US*) (*BrE* **grit·ter**) *noun* a large vehicle used for putting salt, sand or GRIT on the roads in winter when there is ice on them

'salt water *noun* [U] sea water; water containing salt ▶ **'salt·water** *adj.* [only before noun]: *saltwater fish* ➲ compare FRESHWATER

salty 🔑 /'sɔːlti; *BrE* also 'sɒlti; *NAmE* 'sɔːlti/ *adj.* (**saltier, salti·est**)
1 🔑 containing or tasting of salt: *salty food* ◇ *salty sea air* ➲ compare SWEET **2** (*old-fashioned*) (of language or humour) amusing and sometimes slightly rude ▶ **salti·ness** *noun* [U]: *She could taste the saltiness of her tears.*

sa·lu·bri·ous /sə'luːbriəs/ *adj.* (*formal*) (of a place) pleasant to live in; clean and healthy **OPP insalubrious**

salu·tary /'sæljətri; *NAmE* -teri/ *adj.* having a good effect on sb/sth, though often seeming unpleasant: *a* ***salutary lesson/experience/warning*** ◇ *The accident was a* ***salutary reminder*** *of the dangers of climbing.*

sa·lu·ta·tion /ˌsælju'teɪʃn/ *noun* **1** [C, U] (*formal*) something that you say to welcome or say hello to sb; the action of welcoming or saying hello to sb **2** [C] (*technical*) the words that are used in a letter to address the person you are writing to, for example 'Dear Sir'

sa·lute /sə'luːt/ *verb, noun*
■ ***verb* 1** [I, T] to touch the side of your head with the fingers of your right hand to show respect, especially in the armed forces: *The sergeant stood to attention and saluted.* ◇ **~ sb/sth** *to salute the flag/an officer* **2** [T] **~ sb/sth** (*formal*) to express respect and admiration for sb/sth **SYN acknowledge**: *The players saluted the fans before leaving the field.* ◇ *The president saluted the courage of those who had fought for their country.*
■ ***noun* 1** [C] the action of raising your right hand to the side of your head as a sign of respect, especially between soldiers and officers **2** [C, U] a thing that you say or do to show your admiration or respect for sb/sth or to welcome sb: *He raised his hat as a friendly salute.* ◇ *His first words were a salute to the people of South Africa.* ◇ *They all raised their glasses* ***in salute***. **3** [C] an official occasion when guns are fired into the air to show respect for an important person: *a 21-gun salute*

sal·vage /'sælvɪdʒ/ *noun, verb*
■ ***noun*** [U] **1** the act of saving things that have been, or are likely to be, damaged or lost, especially in a disaster or an accident: *the salvage of the wrecked tanker* ◇ *a* ***salvage company/operation/team*** **2** the things that are saved from a

disaster or an accident: *an exhibition of the salvage from the wreck*

■ ***verb*** **1** to save a badly damaged ship, etc. from being lost completely; to save parts or property from a damaged ship or from a fire, etc: **~ sth** *The wreck was salvaged by a team from the RAF.* ◇ *The house was built using salvaged materials.* ◇ **~ sth from sth** *We only managed to salvage two paintings from the fire.* **2 ~ sth** to manage to rescue sth from a difficult situation; to stop a bad situation from being a complete failure: *What can I do to salvage my reputation?* (= get a good reputation again) ◇ *He wondered what he could do to salvage the situation.* ◇ *United lost 5–2, salvaging a little pride with two late goals.*

'salvage yard *noun* (*NAmE*) a place where old machines, cars, etc. are broken up so that the metal can be sold or used again

sal·va·tion /sæl'veɪʃn/ *noun* [U] **1** (in Christianity) the state of being saved from the power of evil: *to pray for the salvation of the world* **2** a way of protecting sb from danger, disaster, loss, etc: *Group therapy classes have been his salvation.*

the Sal,vation 'Army *noun* [sing.] a Christian organization whose members wear military uniforms and work to help poor people

salve *noun, verb*

■ ***noun*** /sælv; *NAmE* also sæv/ [U, C] a substance that you put on a wound or sore skin to help it heal or to protect it ➲ see also LIPSALVE

■ ***verb*** /sælv/ **~ your conscience** (*formal*) to do sth that makes you feel less guilty

sal·ver /'sælvə(r)/ *noun* a large plate, usually made of metal, on which drinks or food are served at a formal event

salvo /'sælvəʊ; *NAmE* -voʊ/ *noun* (*pl.* **-os** or **-oes**) the act of firing several guns or dropping several bombs, etc. at the same time; a sudden attack: *The first salvo exploded a short distance away.* ◇ (*figurative*) *The newspaper article was* ***the opening salvo*** *in what proved to be a long battle.*

sal vola·tile /,sæl və'lætəli/ *noun* [U] a type of SMELLING SALTS

sal·war (also **shal·war**) /sʌl'wɑ:(r)/ *noun* light loose trousers/pants that are tight around the ankles, sometimes worn by S Asian women: *a salwar kameez* (= a salwar worn with a KAMEEZ)

Sa·mar·itan /sə'mærɪtən/ *noun*

IDM **a ,good Sa'maritan** a person who gives help and sympathy to people who need it ORIGIN From the Bible story of a person from Samaria who helps an injured man that nobody else will help

the Sa·mar·itans *noun* [pl.] a British charity that offers help to people who are very depressed and in danger of killing themselves, by providing a phone number that they can ring in order to talk to sb

sa·mar·ium /sə'meəriəm; *NAmE* -'mer-/ *noun* [U] (*symb.* Sm) a chemical element. Samarium is a hard silver-white metal used in making strong MAGNETS.

samba /'sæmbə/ *noun* a fast dance originally from Brazil; a piece of music for this dance

same 🔑 /seɪm/ *adj., pron., adv.*

■ ***adj.*** **1** 🔑 exactly the one or ones referred to or mentioned; not different: *We have lived in the same house for twenty years.* ◇ *Our children go to the* ***same*** *school* ***as*** *theirs.* ◇ *She's still the* ***same*** *fun-loving person* ***that*** *I knew at college.* ◇ *This one works in* ***exactly the same*** *way as the other.* ◇ *They both said* ***much the same*** *thing.* ◇ *He used* ***the very same*** (= exactly the same) *words.* ◇ *I resigned last Friday and left that same day.* **2** 🔑 exactly like the one or ones referred to or mentioned: *I bought the* ***same*** *car* ***as*** *yours* (= another car of that type). ◇ *She was wearing the* ***same*** *dress* ***that*** *I had on.* ◇ *The same thing happened to me last week.*

IDM Most idioms containing **same** are at the entries for the nouns and verbs in the idioms, for example **be in the same boat** is at **boat**. **'same old, 'same old** (*informal, especially NAmE*) used to say that a situation has not changed at all: *'How's it going?' 'Oh, same old, same old.'*

■ ***pron.*** **1** 🔑 **the ~** (**as...**) the same thing or things: *I would do the same again.* ◇ *I think the same as you do about this.* ◇ *Just do the same as me* (= as I do). ◇ *His latest movie is just* ***more of the same****—exotic locations, car chases and a final shoot-out.* ◇ (*informal*) *'I'll have coffee.' 'Same for me, please* (= I will have one too).*'* **2** 🔑 **the ~** (**as...**) having the same number, colour, size, quality, etc: *There are several brands and they're not all the same.* ◇ *I'd like one the same as yours.* **3 the same** (*BrE*) the same person: *'Was that George on the phone?' 'The same* (= yes, it was George).*'*

IDM **,all/,just the 'same** 🔑 despite this SYN **nevertheless**: *He's not very reliable, but I like him just the same.* ◇ *'Will you stay for lunch?' 'No, but thanks all the same.'* ◇ *All the same, there's some truth in what she says.* **be all the 'same to sb** to not be important to sb: *It's all the same to me whether we eat now or later.* **,one and the 'same** the same person or thing: *It turns out that her aunt and my cousin are one and the same.* **(the) ,same a'gain** 🔑 (*informal*) used to ask sb to serve you the same drink as before: *Same again, please!* **,same 'here** (*informal*) used to say that sth is also true of you: *'I can't wait to see it.' 'Same here.'* **(the) ,same to 'you** 🔑 (*informal*) used to answer a GREETING, an insult, etc.: *'Happy Christmas!' 'And the same to you!'* ◇ *'Get lost!' 'Same to you!'*

■ ***adv.*** 🔑 (usually **the same**) in the same way: *We treat boys exactly* ***the same as*** *girls.* ◇ (*informal*) *He gave me five dollars,* ***same as usual****.*

same·ness /'seɪmnəs/ *noun* [U] the quality of being the same; a lack of variety: *She grew tired of the sameness of the food.*

'same-sex *adj.* [only before noun] **1** of the same sex: *The child's same-sex parent acts as a role model.* **2** involving people of the same sex: *a same-sex relationship*

samey /'seɪmi/ *adj.* (*BrE, informal, disapproving*) not changing or different and therefore boring

sa·mosa /sə'məʊsə; *NAmE* -'moʊ-/ *noun* a type of hot spicy S Asian food consisting of a triangle of thin crisp PASTRY filled with meat or vegetables and fried

samo·var /'sæməvɑ:(r)/ *noun* a large container for heating water, used especially in Russia for making tea

samp /sæmp/ *noun* [U] (*SAfrE*) the inner parts of MAIZE seeds that are crushed roughly; a type of PORRIDGE that is made from this

sam·pan /'sæmpæn/ *noun* a small boat with a flat bottom used along the coast and rivers of China

sam·ple 🔑 /'sɑ:mpl; *NAmE* 'sæmpl/ *noun, verb*

■ ***noun*** **1** 🔑 a number of people or things taken from a larger group and used in tests to provide information about the group: *The interviews were given to a* ***random sample*** *of students.* ◇ *The survey covers a* ***representative sample*** *of schools.* ◇ *a sample survey* **2** 🔑 a small amount of a substance taken from a larger amount and tested in order to obtain information about the substance: *a blood sample* ◇ *Samples of the water contained pesticide.* ➲ COLLOCATIONS at SCIENTIFIC **3** 🔑 a small amount or example of sth that can be looked at or tried to see what it is like: *'I'd like to see a sample of your work,' said the manager.* ◇ *a* ***free sample*** *of shampoo* **4** (*technical*) a piece of recorded music or sound that is used in a new piece of music

■ ***verb*** **1 ~ sth** to try a small amount of a particular food to see what it is like; to experience sth for a short time to see what it is like: *I sampled the delights of Greek cooking for the first time.* **2 ~ sb/sth** (*technical*) to test, question, etc, part of sth or of a group of people in order to find out what the rest is like: *12% of the children sampled said they prefer cats to dogs.* **3 ~ sth** (*technical*) to record part of a piece of music, or a sound, in order to use it in a new piece of music

sam·pler /'sɑ:mplə(r); *NAmE* 'sæm-/ *noun* **1** a piece of cloth decorated with different STITCHES that people made in the past to show a person's skill at sewing **2** a collection that shows typical examples of sth, especially pieces of music

sam·pling /'sɑ:mplɪŋ; *NAmE* 'sæm-/ *noun* [U] **1** the process of taking a sample: *statistical sampling* **2** (*technical*)

S

the process of copying and recording parts of a piece of music in an electronic form so that they can be used in a different piece of music

ˈsampling error *noun* (*statistics*) a situation in which a set of results or figures does not show a true situation, because the group of people or things it was based on was not typical of a wider group

sam·urai /ˈsæmuraɪ/ *noun* (*pl.* **sam·urai**) (from *Japanese*) (in the past) a member of a powerful military class in Japan

sana·tor·ium /ˌsænəˈtɔːriəm/ (*NAmE* also **sani·tar·ium** /ˌsænəˈteəriəm; *NAmE* -ˈter-/) *noun* (*pl.* -riums or -ria /-riə/) a place like a hospital where patients who have a lasting illness or who are getting better after an illness are treated

sanc·tify /ˈsæŋktɪfaɪ/ *verb* (**sanc·ti·fies**, **sanc·ti·fied**, **sanc·ti·fy·ing**, **sanc·ti·fied**) [usually passive] (*formal*) **1 ~ sth** to make sth holy **2 ~ sth** to make sth seem right or legal; to give official approval to sth: *This was a practice sanctified by tradition.* ▸ **sanc·ti·fi·ca·tion** /ˌsæŋktɪfɪˈkeɪʃn/ *noun* [U]

sanc·ti·mo·ni·ous /ˌsæŋktɪˈməʊniəs; *NAmE* -ˈmoʊ-/ *adj.* (*disapproving*) giving the impression that you feel you are better and more moral than other people SYN **self-righteous** ▸ **sanc·ti·mo·ni·ous·ly** *adv.* **sanc·ti·mo·ni·ous·ness** *noun* [U]

sanc·tion /ˈsæŋkʃn/ *noun, verb*

■ ***noun* 1** [C, usually pl.] **~ (against sb)** an official order that limits trade, contact, etc. with a particular country, in order to make it do sth, such as obeying international law: *Trade sanctions were imposed against any country that refused to sign the agreement.* ◇ *The economic sanctions have been lifted.* ➲ COLLOCATIONS at INTERNATIONAL **2** [U] (*formal*) official permission or approval for an action or a change SYN **authorization**: *These changes will require the sanction of the court.* **3** [C] **~ (against sth)** a course of action that can be used, if necessary, to make people obey a law or behave in a particular way SYN **penalty**: *The ultimate sanction will be the closure of the restaurant.*

■ ***verb* 1 ~ sth** (*formal*) to give permission for sth to take place: *The government refused to sanction a further cut in interest rates.* **2 ~ sb/sth** (*technical*) to punish sb/sth; to impose a sanction (1) on sth

sanc·tity /ˈsæŋktəti/ *noun* [U] **1 ~ (of sth)** the state of being very important and worth protecting: *the* ***sanctity of marriage*** **2** the state of being holy: *a life of sanctity, like that of St Francis*

S

sanc·tu·ary /ˈsæŋktʃuəri; *NAmE* -ueri/ *noun* (*pl.* -ies) **1** [C] an area where wild birds or animals are protected and encouraged to breed SYN **reserve**: *a* ***bird/wildlife sanctuary*** **2** [U] safety and protection, especially for people who are being chased or attacked: *to take sanctuary in a place* ◇ *The government offered sanctuary to 4 000 refugees.* ◇ *She longed for the sanctuary of her own home.* **3** [C, usually sing.] a safe place, especially one where people who are being chased or attacked can stay and be protected: *The church became a sanctuary for the refugees.* **4** [C] a holy building or the part of it that is considered the most holy

sanc·tum /ˈsæŋktəm/ *noun* [usually sing.] (*formal*) **1** a private room where sb can go and not be disturbed: *She once allowed me into her* ***inner sanctum***. **2** a holy place

sand 🔑 /sænd/ *noun, verb*

■ ***noun* 1** 🔑 [U] a substance that consists of very small fine grains of rock. Sand is found on beaches, in deserts, etc: *a* ***grain of sand*** ◇ *Concrete is a mixture of sand and cement.* ◇ *His hair was the colour of sand.* ◇ *The children were playing in the sand* (= for example, in a SANDPIT). ➲ VISUAL VOCAB page V4 **2** 🔑 [U, C, usually pl.] a large area of sand on a beach: *We went for a walk along the sand.* ◇ *children playing on the sand* ◇ *miles of golden sands* ➲ SYNONYMS at COAST ➲ see also SANDY IDM see HEAD *n.*, SHIFT *v.*

■ ***verb* ~ sth (down)** to make sth smooth by rubbing it with sandpaper or using a sander

san·dal /ˈsændl/ *noun* a type of light open shoe that is worn in warm weather. The top part consists of leather bands that attach the SOLE to your foot. ➲ VISUAL VOCAB page V52

san·dalled (*BrE*) (*US* **san·daled**) /ˈsændld/ *adj.* [only before noun] wearing sandals: *sandalled feet*

san·dal·wood /ˈsændlwʊd/ *noun* [U] a type of oil with a sweet smell that is obtained from a hard tropical wood (also called sandalwood) and is used to make PERFUME

sand·bag /ˈsændbæg/ *noun, verb*

■ ***noun*** a bag filled with sand used to build a wall as a protection against floods or explosions

■ ***verb*** (-gg-) **1 ~ sth** to put sandbags in or around sth as protection against floods or explosions **2 ~ sb** (*informal, especially NAmE*) to attack sb by criticizing them strongly; to treat sb badly

sand·bank /ˈsændbæŋk/ *noun* a raised area of sand in a river or the sea ➲ VISUAL VOCAB page V4

sand·bar /ˈsændbɑː(r)/ *noun* a long mass of sand at the point where a river meets the sea that is formed by the movement of the water

sand·blast /ˈsændblɑːst; *NAmE* -blæst/ *verb* [often passive] **~ sth** to clean, polish, decorate, etc. a surface by firing sand at it from a special machine

sand·box /ˈsændbɒks; *NAmE* -bɑːks/ (*NAmE*) (*BrE* **sand·pit**) *noun* an area in the ground or a shallow container, filled with sand for children to play in ➲ VISUAL VOCAB page V32

sand·cas·tle /ˈsændkɑːsl; *NAmE* -kæsl/ *noun* a pile of sand made to look like a castle, usually by a child on a beach

ˈsand dune *noun* = DUNE

sand·er /ˈsændə(r)/ *noun* an electric tool with a rough surface used for making wood smooth

s and h (also **s & h**) *abbr.* (*NAmE*) shipping and handling ➲ compare P. AND P.

ˈsand iron *noun* (*BrE*) = SAND WEDGE

S & L /ˌes ənd ˈel/ *abbr.* SAVINGS AND LOAN ASSOCIATION

sand·lot /ˈsændlɒt; *NAmE* -lɑːt/ *adj.* [only before noun] (*NAmE*) (of a sport) played for enjoyment rather than as a job for money

the sand·man /ˈsændmæn/ *noun* [sing.] an imaginary man who is said to help children get to sleep

ˈsand martin *noun* a bird like a small SWALLOW, that makes its nest in banks of sand

sand·paper /ˈsændpeɪpə(r)/ *noun, verb*

■ ***noun*** [U] strong paper with a rough surface covered with sand or a similar substance, used for rubbing surfaces in order to make them smooth

■ ***verb*** (also **sand**) **~ sth (down)** to make sth smooth by rubbing it with sandpaper

sand·piper /ˈsændpaɪpə(r)/ *noun* a small bird with long legs and a long beak that lives near rivers and lakes

sand·pit /ˈsændpɪt/ (*BrE*) (*NAmE* **sand·box**) *noun* an area in the ground or a shallow container, filled with sand for children to play in ➲ VISUAL VOCAB page V32

sand·shoe /ˈsændʃuː/ *noun* (*ScotE, AustralE, NZE*) a PLIMSOLL (= a type of light cloth sports shoe with a rubber SOLE)

sand·stone /ˈsændstəʊn; *NAmE* -stoʊn/ *noun* [U] a type of stone that is formed of grains of sand tightly pressed together, used in building

sand·storm /ˈsændstɔːm; *NAmE* -stɔːrm/ *noun* a storm in a desert in which sand is blown into the air by strong winds

ˈsand trap (also **trap**) *noun* (both *NAmE*) = BUNKER

ˈsand wedge (*BrE* also **ˈsand iron**) *noun* a GOLF CLUB used for hitting the ball out of sand

sand·wich /ˈsænwɪtʃ; -wɪdʒ/ *noun, verb*

■ ***noun* 1** (also *BrE informal* **sar·nie**) two slices of bread, often spread with butter, with a layer of meat, cheese, etc. between them: *a cheese sandwich* ◇ *a* ***sandwich bar*** (= a place that sells sandwiches) ➲ see also CLUB SAND-

WICH, OPEN SANDWICH **2** (*BrE*) (in compounds) a SPONGE CAKE consisting of two layers with jam and/or cream between them
■ ***verb***
PHR V **'sandwich sb/sth between sb/sth** [usually passive] to fit sth/sb into a very small space between two other things or people, or between two times: *I was sandwiched between two fat men on the bus.* **ˌsandwich A and B to'gether** (**with sth**) to put sth between two things to join them: *Sandwich the cakes together with cream.*

'sandwich board *noun* a pair of boards with advertisements on them that sb wears at the front and back of their body as they walk around in public

'sandwich course *noun* (*BrE*) a course of study which includes periods of study and periods of working in business or industry

sandy /'sændi/ *adj.* (**sand·ier, sand·iest**) **1** covered with or containing sand: *a sandy beach* ◇ *sandy soil* **2** (of hair) having a light colour, between yellow and red

sane /seɪn/ *adj.* (**saner, san·est**) **1** having a normal healthy mind; not mentally ill **SYN** **of sound mind**: *No sane person would do that.* ◇ *Being able to get out of the city at the weekend* ***keeps me sane.*** **2** sensible and reasonable: *the sane way to solve the problem* **OPP** **insane** ⊃ see also SANITY ▶ **sane·ly** *adv.*

sang *past tense* of SING

sang·froid /sɒŋ'frwɑː; *NAmE* sɑːŋ-/ *noun* [U] (from *French*) the ability to remain calm in a difficult or dangerous situation

san·goma /sʌŋ'gəʊmə; sʌŋ'gɔːmə; *NAmE* -'goʊ-/ *noun* (*SAfrE*) a person who is believed to have magic powers that can be used, for example, to find out why sb is ill/sick or protect sb from being harmed

san·gria /'sæŋgriə; sæŋ'griːə/ *noun* [U] (from *Spanish*) an alcoholic drink made of red wine mixed with fruit, and sometimes with LEMONADE or BRANDY added

san·guin·ary /'sæŋgwɪnəri; *NAmE* -neri/ *adj.* (*formal*) involving or liking killing and blood

san·guine /'sæŋgwɪn/ *adj.* **~** (**about sth**) (*formal*) cheerful and confident about the future **SYN** **optimistic**: *They are less sanguine about the company's long-term prospects.* ◇ *He tends to* ***take a sanguine view*** *of the problems involved.* ▶ **san·guine·ly** *adv.*

sani·tar·ium (*NAmE*) = SANATORIUM

sani·tary /'sænətri; *NAmE* -teri/ *adj.* **1** [only before noun] connected with keeping places clean and healthy to live in, especially by removing human waste: *Overcrowding and* ***poor sanitary conditions*** *led to disease in the refugee camps.* ◇ *The hut had no cooking or sanitary facilities.* **2** clean; not likely to cause health problems **SYN** **hygienic**: *The new houses were more sanitary than the old ones had been.* **OPP** **insanitary**

'sanitary towel (*BrE*) (*NAmE* **'sanitary napkin**) *noun* a thick piece of soft material that women wear outside their body to absorb the blood during their PERIOD ⊃ compare TAMPON

sani·ta·tion /ˌsænɪ'teɪʃn/ *noun* [U] the equipment and systems that keep places clean, especially by removing human waste: *disease resulting from poor sanitation*

sani·tize (*BrE* also **-ise**) /'sænɪtaɪz/ *verb* (*formal*) **1 ~ sth** (*disapproving*) to remove the parts of sth that could be considered unpleasant: *This sanitized account of his life does not mention his time in prison.* **2 ~ sth** to clean sth thoroughly using chemicals to remove bacteria **SYN** **disinfect**

san·ity /'sænəti/ *noun* [U] **1** the state of having a normal healthy mind: *His behaviour was so strange that I began to doubt his sanity.* ◇ *to* ***keep/preserve your sanity*** **2** the state of being sensible and reasonable: *After a series of road accidents the police pleaded for sanity among drivers.* **OPP** **insanity** ⊃ see also SANE

sank *past tense* of SINK

sans /sænz/ *prep.* (*literary* or *humorous*) without: *There were no potatoes so we had fish and chips sans the chips.*

San·skrit /'sænskrɪt/ *noun* [U] an ancient language of India belonging to the Indo-European family, in which the Hindu holy texts are written and on which many modern languages are based

sans serif (also **san·serif**) /ˌsæn 'serɪf/ *noun* [U] (*technical*) (in printing) a TYPEFACE in which the letters have no SERIF

Santa Claus /'sæntə klɔːz/ (also **Santa**) (*BrE* also **ˌFather 'Christmas**) *noun* an imaginary old man with red clothes and a long white beard. Parents tell small children that he brings them presents at Christmas.

sap /sæp/ *noun, verb*
■ ***noun* 1** [U] the liquid in a plant or tree that carries food to all its parts: *Maple syrup is made from sap extracted from the sugar maple tree.* **2** [C] (*informal, especially NAmE*) a stupid person that you can easily trick, or treat unfairly
■ ***verb*** (**-pp-**) to make sth/sb weaker; to destroy sth gradually: **~ sth** *The hot sun sapped our energy.* ◇ **~ sb** (**of sth**) *Years of failure have sapped him of his confidence.*

sapi·ent /'seɪpiənt/ *adj.* (*literary*) having great intelligence or knowledge ▶ **sapi·ence** /-əns/ *noun* [U] **sapi·ent·ly** *adv.*

sap·ling /'sæplɪŋ/ *noun* a young tree

sapo·dilla /ˌsæpə'dɪlə/ *noun* a large tropical American tree that produces a fruit that can be eaten and CHICLE (= a substance used in chewing gum)

sap·per /'sæpə(r)/ *noun* (*BrE*) a soldier whose job is to build or repair roads, bridges, etc.

sap·phic /'sæfɪk/ *noun* (*formal*) relating to LESBIANS ▶ **sap·phism** /'sæfɪzəm/ *noun* [U]

sap·phire /'sæfaɪə(r)/ *noun* **1** [C, U] a clear, bright blue PRECIOUS STONE **2** [U] a bright blue colour ▶ **sap·phire** *adj.*: *sapphire eyes*

sappy /'sæpi/ *adj.* (**sap·pier, sap·piest**) **1** (*NAmE, informal*) = SOPPY **2** (of plants) full of SAP (= liquid)

sap·wood /'sæpwʊd/ *noun* [U] the soft younger outer layers of the wood of a tree, inside the BARK ⊃ compare HEARTWOOD

Saran Wrap™ /sə'ræn ræp/ *noun* [U] (*NAmE*) = PLASTIC WRAP

sar·casm /'sɑːkæzəm; *NAmE* 'sɑːrk-/ *noun* [U] a way of using words that are the opposite of what you mean in order to be unpleasant to sb or to make fun of them: *'That will be useful,' she snapped with heavy sarcasm* (= she really thought it would not be useful at all). ◇ *a* ***hint/touch/trace of sarcasm*** *in his voice*

sar·cas·tic /sɑː'kæstɪk; *NAmE* sɑːr'k-/ (also *BrE informal* **sarky**) *adj.* showing or expressing sarcasm: *sarcastic comments* ◇ *a sarcastic manner* ◇ *'There's no need to be sarcastic,' she said.* ▶ **sar·cas·tic·al·ly** /-kli/ *adv.*

sar·coma /sɑː'kəʊmə; *NAmE* sɑːr'koʊmə/ *noun* (*medical*) a harmful (= MALIGNANT) lump (= a TUMOUR) that grows in certain parts of the body such as muscle or bone

sar·copha·gus /sɑː'kɒfəgəs; *NAmE* sɑːr'kɑːf-/ *noun* (*pl.* **sar·coph·agi** /sɑː'kɒfəgaɪ; *NAmE* sɑːr'kɑːf-/) a stone COFFIN (= box that a dead person is buried in), especially one that is decorated, used in ancient times

sar·dine /ˌsɑː'diːn; *NAmE* ˌsɑːr'd-/ *noun* a small young sea fish (for example, a young PILCHARD) that is either eaten fresh or preserved in tins/cans
IDM (**packed, crammed, etc.**) **like sar'dines** (*informal*) pressed tightly together in a way that is uncomfortable or unpleasant

sar·don·ic /sɑː'dɒnɪk; *NAmE* sɑːr'dɑːnɪk/ *adj.* (*disapproving*) showing that you think that you are better than other people and do not take them seriously **SYN** **mocking**: *a sardonic smile* ▶ **sar·don·ic·al·ly** /-kli/ *adv.*

sarge /sɑːdʒ; *NAmE* sɑːrdʒ/ *noun* (*informal*) used to talk to or about a SERGEANT

sari /'sɑːri/ *noun* a long piece of cloth that is wrapped around the body and worn as the main piece of clothing by women in S Asia

S

sarin /ˈsɑːrɪn/ *noun* [U] a type of poisonous gas used in chemical weapons

sarky /ˈsɑːki; *NAmE* ˈsɑːrki/ *adj.* (**sark·ier**, **sarki·est**) (*BrE, informal*) = SARCASTIC

sar·nie /ˈsɑːni; *NAmE* ˈsɑːrni/ *noun* (*BrE, informal*) = SANDWICH

sar·ong /səˈrɒŋ; *NAmE* -ˈrɔːŋ; -ˈrɑːŋ/ *noun* a long piece of cloth wrapped around the body from the waist or the chest, worn by Malaysian and Indonesian men and women

sar·panch /ˈsɑːpʌntʃ; *NAmE* ˈsɑːrp-/ *noun* (in some S Asian countries) the head of a village or of a PANCHAYAT

SARS /sɑːz; *NAmE* sɑːrz/ *noun* [U] the abbreviation for 'severe acute respiratory syndrome' (an illness that is easily spread from person to person, which affects the lungs and can sometimes cause death): *No new SARS cases have been reported in the region.*

sar·sa·par·illa /ˌsɑːspəˈrɪlə; ˌsɑːsəpə-; *NAmE* ˌsɑːrs-/ *noun* **1** [U] a dried substance that is used to flavour drinks and medicines, obtained from a plant also called sarsaparilla **2** [U, C] a a drink made with sarsaparilla

sar·tor·ial /sɑːˈtɔːriəl; *NAmE* sɑːrˈt-/ *adj.* [only before noun] (*formal*) relating to clothes, especially men's clothes, and the way they are made or worn ▶ **sar·tor·ial·ly** /-riəli/ *adv.*

SAS /ˌes eɪ ˈes/ *abbr.* Special Air Service (a group of highly trained soldiers in Britain who are used on very secret or difficult military operations)

SASE *noun* (*NAmE*) the abbreviation used in writing for 'self-addressed stamped envelope' (an envelope on which you have written your name and address and put a stamp so that sb else can use it to send sth to you) ➲ compare SAE

sash /sæʃ/ *noun* **1** a long strip of cloth worn around the waist or over one shoulder, especially as part of a uniform **2** either of a pair of windows, one above the other, that are opened and closed by sliding them up and down inside the frame

sashay /ˈsæʃeɪ; *NAmE* sæˈʃeɪ/ *verb* [I] **+ adv./prep.** to walk in a very confident but relaxed way, especially in order to be noticed

ˈ**sash cord** *noun* a string or rope with a weight at one end attached to a sash window allowing it to stay open in any position

sash·imi /ˈsæʃɪmi; *NAmE* sɑːˈʃiːmi/ *noun* [U, C] (from *Japanese*) a Japanese dish consisting of slices of raw fish, served with sauce

ˌ**sash ˈwindow** *noun* a window that consists of two separate parts, one above the other that you open by sliding one of the parts up or down ➲ VISUAL VOCAB page V15

Sas·quatch /ˈsæskwætʃ; -wɒtʃ; *NAmE* -wɑːtʃ/ *noun* = BIGFOOT

sass /sæs/ *noun, verb*

■ ***noun*** [U] (*informal, especially NAmE*) behaviour or talk that is rude and lacking respect

■ ***verb*** **~ sb** (*NAmE, informal*) to speak to sb in a rude way, without respect: *Don't sass your mother!*

sas·sa·fras /ˈsæsəfræs/ *noun* a N American tree with pleasant-smelling leaves and BARK. Its leaves are sometimes used to make a type of tea.

Sas·sen·ach /ˈsæsənæk; -næx/ *noun* (*ScotE, disapproving* or *humorous*) an English person ▶ **Sas·sen·ach** *adj.*

sassy /ˈsæsi/ *adj.* (**sas·sier**, **sas·si·est**) (*informal, especially NAmE*) **1** (*disapproving*) rude; showing a lack of respect **2** (*approving*) fashionable and confident: *his sassy, streetwise daughter*

SAT *noun* **1 SAT™** /ˌes eɪ ˈtiː/ (in the US) the abbreviation for 'Scholastic Aptitude Test' (a test taken by HIGH SCHOOL students who want to go to a college or university): *to take the SAT* ◇ *I scored 1050 on the SAT.* ◇ *a SAT score* **2** /sæt/ (in Britain) the abbreviation for 'Standard Assessment Task' (now officially called NCT)

sat *past tense, past part.* of SIT

Satan /ˈseɪtn/ *noun* the DEVIL

sa·tan·ic /səˈtænɪk; *NAmE* also seɪˈt-/ *adj.* **1** (often **Sa·tan·ic**) connected with the worship of the DEVIL: *satanic cults* **2** (*formal*) morally bad and evil SYN **demonic** ▶ **sa·tan·ic·al·ly** /-kli/ *adv.*

sa·tan·ism /ˈseɪtənɪzəm/ *noun* [U] the worship of Satan ▶ **sa·tan·ist** /ˈseɪtənɪst/ *noun*

satay /ˈsæteɪ; *NAmE* ˈsɑː-/ *noun* [U, C] a SE Asian dish consisting of meat or fish cooked on sticks and served with a sauce made with PEANUTS

satchel /ˈsætʃəl/ *noun* a bag with a long strap, that you hang over your shoulder or wear on your back, used especially for carrying school books ➲ VISUAL VOCAB page V57

sat·com (also **SATCOM**) /ˈsætkɒm; *NAmE* -kɑːm/ *noun* [U] satellite communications

sate /seɪt/ *verb* **~ sth** (*formal*) to satisfy a desire

sated /ˈseɪtɪd/ *adj.* [not usually before noun] **~ (with sth)** (*formal*) having had so much of sth that you do not need any more: *sated with pleasure*

sat·el·lite /ˈsætəlaɪt/ *noun* **1** an electronic device that is sent into space and moves around the earth or another planet. It is used for communicating by radio, television, etc. and for providing information: *a **weather/communications satellite*** ◇ *The interview came live **by satellite** from Hollywood.* ◇ ***satellite television/TV*** (= broadcast using a satellite) ◇ *a **satellite broadcast/channel/picture*** ➲ COLLOCATIONS at TELEVISION **2** a natural object that moves around a larger natural object in space: *The moon is a satellite of earth.* **3** a town, a country or an organization that is controlled by and depends on another larger or more powerful one: *satellite states*

ˈ**satellite dish** *noun* a piece of equipment that receives signals from a satellite, used to enable people to watch satellite television

ˈ**satellite station** *noun* **1** a company that broadcasts television programmes using a satellite **2** a place where special equipment is used to follow the movements of satellites and receive information from them

sati (also **sut·tee**) /ˈsʌtiː; sʌˈtiː/ *noun* **1** [U] the former practice in Hinduism of a wife burning herself with the body of her dead husband **2** [C] a wife who did this

sa·ti·ate /ˈseɪʃieɪt/ *verb* [usually passive] **~ sb/sth** (*formal*) to give sb so much of sth that they do not feel they want any more ▶ **sa·ti·ation** /ˌseɪʃiˈeɪʃn/ *noun* [U]

sa·ti·ety /səˈtaɪəti/ *noun* [U] (*formal* or *technical*) the state or feeling of being completely full of food, or of having had enough of sth

satin /ˈsætɪn; *NAmE* ˈsætn/ *noun, adj.*

■ ***noun*** [U] a type of cloth with a smooth shiny surface: *a white satin ribbon*

■ ***adj.*** [only before noun] having the smooth shiny appearance of satin: *The paint has a satin finish.*

sat·iny /ˈsætɪni; *NAmE* ˈsætni/ *adj.* looking or feeling like satin: *her satiny skin*

sat·ire /ˈsætaɪə(r)/ *noun* [U, C] a way of criticizing a person, an idea or an institution in which you use humour to show their faults or weaknesses; a piece of writing that uses this type of criticism: ***political/social satire*** ◇ *a work full of **savage/biting satire*** ◇ *The novel is a stinging satire on American politics.*

sa·tir·ic·al /səˈtɪrɪkl/ (also *less frequent* **sa·tir·ic** /səˈtɪrɪk/) *adj.* using satire to criticize sb/sth: *a satirical magazine* ▶ **sa·tir·ic·al·ly** /-kli/ *adv.*

sat·ir·ist /ˈsætərɪst/ *noun* a person who writes or uses SATIRE

sat·ir·ize (*BrE* also **-ise**) /ˈsætəraɪz/ *verb* **~ sb/sth** to use SATIRE to show the faults in a person, an organization, a system, etc.

sat·is·fac·tion 🔑 /ˌsætɪsˈfækʃn/ *noun* **1** 🔑 [U, C] the good feeling that you have when you have achieved sth or when sth that you wanted to happen does happen; sth that gives you this feeling: *to **gain/get/derive satisfaction** from sth* ◇ *a **look/smile of satisfaction*** ◇ *She looked back on her career **with** great **satisfaction**.* ◇ *He **had***

*the **satisfaction of** seeing his book become a best-seller.* ◇ *She didn't want to **give him the satisfaction of** seeing her cry.* ◇ *The company is trying to improve **customer satisfaction**.* ◇ *He was enjoying all the satisfactions of being a parent.* ➲ see also DISSATISFACTION **2** [U] the act of FULFILLING a need or desire: *the satisfaction of sexual desires* ◇ *the satisfaction of your ambitions* **3** [U] (*formal*) an acceptable way of dealing with a complaint, a debt, an injury, etc: *I complained to the manager but I didn't get any satisfaction.*

WORD FAMILY
satisfaction *noun* (≠ dissatisfaction)
satisfactory *adj.* (≠ unsatisfactory)
satisfy *verb*
satisfying *adj.* (≠ unsatisfying)
satisfied *adj.* (≠ dissatisfied) (≠ unsatisfied)

IDM **to sb's satis'faction** **1** if you do sth **to sb's satisfaction**, they are pleased with it: *The affair was settled to the complete satisfaction of the client.* **2** if you prove sth **to sb's satisfaction**, they believe or accept it: *Can you demonstrate to our satisfaction that your story is true?*

Synonyms

satisfaction

happiness • pride • contentment • fulfilment

These are all words for the good feeling that you have when you are happy or when you have achieved sth.

satisfaction the good feeling that you have when you have achieved sth or when sth that you wanted to happen does happen: *He derived great satisfaction from knowing that his son was happy.*

happiness the good feeling that you have when you are happy: *Money can't buy you happiness.*

pride a feeling of pleasure or satisfaction that you get when you or people who are connected with you have done sth well or own sth that other people admire: *The sight of her son graduating filled her with pride.*

contentment (*rather formal*) a feeling of happiness or satisfaction with what you have: *They found contentment in living a simple life.*

fulfilment a feeling of happiness or satisfaction with what you do or have done: *her search for personal fulfilment*

SATISFACTION, HAPPINESS, CONTENTMENT OR FULFILMENT?

You can feel **satisfaction** at achieving almost anything, small or large; you feel **fulfilment** when you do sth useful and enjoyable with your life. **Happiness** is the feeling you have when things give you pleasure and can be quite a lively feeling; **contentment** is a quieter feeling that you get when you have learned to find pleasure in things.

PATTERNS
- satisfaction/happiness/pride/contentment/fulfilment **in** sth
- **real** satisfaction/happiness/pride/contentment/fulfilment
- **true** satisfaction/happiness/contentment/fulfilment
- **great** satisfaction/happiness/pride
- **quiet** satisfaction/pride/contentment
- to **feel** satisfaction/happiness/pride/contentment
- to **bring sb** satisfaction/happiness/pride/contentment/fulfilment
- to **find** satisfaction/happiness/contentment/fulfilment

sat·is·fac·tory /ˌsætɪsˈfæktəri/ *adj.* good enough for a particular purpose SYN **acceptable**: *a **satisfactory explanation/answer/solution/conclusion*** ◇ *The work is satisfactory but not outstanding.* ◇ *The existing law is not **entirely/wholly satisfactory**.* OPP **unsatisfactory** ▸ **sat·is·fac·tor·ily** /-tərəli/ *adv.*: *Her disappearance has never been satisfactorily explained.* ◇ *Our complaint was dealt with satisfactorily.*

sat·is·fied 🔑 /ˈsætɪsfaɪd/ *adj.*
1 🔑 pleased because you have achieved sth or because sth that you wanted to happen has happened: *a satisfied smile* ◇ *a satisfied customer* ◇ **~ with sb/sth** *She's never satisfied with what she's got.* OPP **dissatisfied** ➲ SYNONYMS at HAPPY **2** 🔑 **~ (that...)** | **~ (with sth)** believing or accepting that sth is true SYN **convinced**: *I'm satisfied that they are telling the truth.* ➲ compare UNSATISFIED

sat·isfy 🔑 /ˈsætɪsfaɪ/ *verb* (**sat·is·fies**, **sat·is·fy·ing**, **sat·is·fied**, **sat·is·fied**)
1 🔑 **~ sb** (not used in the progressive tenses) to make sb pleased by doing or giving them what they want: *Nothing satisfies him—he's always complaining.* ◇ *The proposed plan will not satisfy everyone.* **2** 🔑 **~ sth** to provide what is wanted, needed or asked for: *The food wasn't enough to **satisfy his hunger**.* ◇ *to **satisfy sb's curiosity*** ◇ *The education system must **satisfy the needs** of all children.* ◇ *We cannot **satisfy demand** for the product.* ◇ *She failed to satisfy all the requirements for entry to the college.* **3** 🔑 (not used in the progressive tenses) (*formal*) to make sb certain sth is true or has been done: **~ sb** *Her explanation did not satisfy the teacher.* ◇ **~ sb of sth** *People need to be satisfied of the need for a new system.* ◇ **~ sb/yourself (that)...** *Once I had satisfied myself (that) it was the right decision, we went ahead.*

sat·is·fy·ing 🔑 /ˈsætɪsfaɪɪŋ/ *adj.*
giving pleasure because it provides sth you need or want: *a satisfying meal* ◇ *a satisfying experience* ◇ ***It's satisfying to** play a game really well.* ▸ **sat·is·fy·ing·ly** *adv.*

Synonyms

satisfying

rewarding • pleasing • gratifying • fulfilling

These words all describe an experience, activity or fact that gives you pleasure because it provides sth you need or want.

satisfying that gives you pleasure because it provides sth you need or want: *It's satisfying to play a game really well.*

rewarding (of an experience or activity) that makes you happy because you think it is useful or important; worth doing: *Nursing can be a very rewarding career.*

pleasing (*rather formal*) that gives you pleasure, especially to look at, hear or think about: *It was a simple but pleasing design.*

gratifying (*formal*) that gives you pleasure, especially because it makes you feel that you have done well: *It is gratifying to see such good results.*

fulfilling (of an experience or activity) that makes you happy, because it makes you feel your skills and talents are being used: *I'm finding the work much more fulfilling now.*

SATISFYING, REWARDING OR FULFILLING?

Almost any experience, important or very brief, can be **satisfying**. **Rewarding** and **fulfilling** are used more for longer, more serious activities, such as jobs or careers. **Satisfying** and **fulfilling** are more about your personal satisfaction or happiness; **rewarding** is more about your sense of doing sth important and being useful to others.

PATTERNS
- a satisfying/rewarding/gratifying/fulfilling **experience/feeling**
- (a) satisfying/rewarding/fulfilling **job/career/work**
- **to find sth** satisfying/rewarding/pleasing/gratifying

sat·nav (also **sat nav**) /ˈsætnæv/ *noun* [U, C] (*BrE*) the abbreviation for 'satellite navigation' (a computer system that uses information obtained from SATELLITES to guide the driver of a vehicle): *The drivers all have satnav in the van.* ➲ VISUAL VOCAB page V42 ➲ compare GPS

sat·suma /sætˈsuːmə/ *noun* a type of small orange without seeds and with loose skin that comes off easily

S

sat·ur·ate /ˈsætʃəreɪt/ *verb* **1 ~ sth** to make sth completely wet SYN **soak**: *The continuous rain had saturated the soil.* **2** [often passive] **~ sth/sb (with/in sth)** to fill sth/sb completely with sth so that it is impossible or useless to add any more: *The company had saturated the market for personal organizers* (= so that no new buyers could be found).

sat·ur·ated /ˈsætʃəreɪtɪd/ *adj.* **1** [not usually before noun] completely wet SYN **soaked** ➲ SYNONYMS at WET **2** [usually before noun] (*chemistry*) if a chemical SOLUTION (= a liquid with sth dissolved in it) is **saturated**, it contains the greatest possible amount of the substance that has been dissolved in it: *a saturated solution of sodium chloride* **3** [usually before noun] (of colours) very strong: *saturated reds*

ˌsaturated ˈfat *noun* [C, U] a type of fat found, for example, in butter, fried food and many types of meat, which encourages the harmful development of CHOLESTEROL ➲ see also MONOUNSATURATED FAT, POLYUNSATURATED FAT, TRANS-FATTY ACID, UNSATURATED FAT

sat·ur·ation /ˌsætʃəˈreɪʃn/ *noun* [U] **1** (often *figurative*) the state or process that happens when no more of sth can be accepted or added because there is already too much of it or too many of them: *a business beset by price wars and* ***market saturation*** (= the fact that no new customers can be found) ◇ ***saturation bombing*** *of the city* (= covering the whole city) ◇ *There was* ***saturation coverage*** (= so much that it was impossible to avoid it or add to it) *of the event by the media.* **2** (*chemistry*) the degree to which sth is absorbed in sth else, expressed as a PERCENTAGE of the greatest possible

ˌsatuˈration point *noun* [U, sing.] **1** the stage at which no more of sth can be accepted or added because there is already too much of it or too many of them: *The market for computer games has reached saturation point.* **2** (*chemistry*) the stage at which no more of a substance can be absorbed into a liquid or VAPOUR

Sat·ur·day 0-w /ˈsætədeɪ; -di; *NAmE* -tərd-/ *noun* [C, U] (*abbr.* Sat.)
the day of the week after Friday and before Sunday HELP To see how **Saturday** is used, look at the examples at **Monday**. ORIGIN From the Old English for 'day of Saturn', translated from Latin *Saturni dies*.

Sat·urn /ˈsætɜːn; -tən; *NAmE* -tɜːrn/ *noun* a large planet in the SOLAR SYSTEM that has rings around it and is 6th in order of distance from the sun

Sat·ur·na·lia /ˌsætəˈneɪliə; *NAmE* -tərˈn-/ *noun* [U] an ancient Roman festival that took place in December, around the time that Christmas now takes place

sat·ur·na·lian /ˌsætəˈneɪliən; *NAmE* -tərˈn-/ *adj.* **1** relating to Saturnalia **2** involving wild celebrations

sat·ur·nine /ˈsætənaɪn; *NAmE* -tərn-/ *adj.* (*literary*) (of a person or their face) looking serious and threatening

satyr /ˈsætə(r); *NAmE* also ˈseɪtər/ *noun* (in ancient Greek stories) a god of the woods, with a man's face and body and a GOAT's legs and horns

sauce 0-w /sɔːs/ *noun*
1 0-w [C, U] a thick liquid that is eaten with food to add flavour to it: ***tomato/cranberry/chilli, etc. sauce*** ◇ *chicken in a white sauce* ◇ *ice cream with a hot fudge sauce* ➲ see also SOY SAUCE, TARTARE SAUCE, WHITE SAUCE **2** [U] (*old-fashioned, BrE, informal*) talk or behaviour that is annoying or lacking in respect SYN **cheek**
IDM **what's ˌsauce for the ˈgoose is ˌsauce for the ˈgander** (*old-fashioned, saying*) what one person is allowed to do, another person must be allowed to do in a similar situation

ˈsauce boat *noun* a long low JUG used for serving or pouring sauce at a meal

sauce·pan /ˈsɔːspən; *NAmE* -pæn/ (*especially BrE*) (*NAmE* usually **pot**) *noun* a deep round metal pot with a lid and one long handle or two short handles, used for cooking things over heat ➲ VISUAL VOCAB page V24

sau·cer /ˈsɔːsə(r)/ *noun* a small shallow round dish that a cup stands on; an object that is shaped like this: *cups and saucers* ➲ VISUAL VOCAB page V19 ➲ see also FLYING SAUCER

saucy /ˈsɔːsi/ *adj.* (sau·cier, sau·ci·est) rude or referring to sex in a way that is amusing but not offensive SYN **cheeky**: *saucy jokes* ◇ *a saucy smile* ▶ **sau·cily** /-ɪli/ *adv.*

sauer·kraut /ˈsaʊəkraʊt; *NAmE* ˈsaʊərk-/ *noun* [U] (from *German*) CABBAGE (= a type of green vegetable) that is preserved in salt water and then cooked

sauna /ˈsɔːnə; ˈsaʊnə/ *noun* a period of time in which you sit or lie in a room (also called a sauna) which has been heated to a very high temperature. Some saunas involve the use of steam: *a hotel with a swimming pool and sauna* ◇ *to* ***have/take a sauna***

saun·ter /ˈsɔːntə(r)/ *verb* [I] **+ adv./prep.** to walk in a slow relaxed way SYN **stroll**: *He sauntered by, looking as if he had all the time in the world.* ▶ **saun·ter** *noun* [sing.]: *This part of the route should be an easy saunter.*

saur·ian /ˈsɔːriən/ *adj., noun* (*biology*)
■ ***adj.*** relating to LIZARDS
■ ***noun*** a large REPTILE, especially a DINOSAUR

saus·age /ˈsɒsɪdʒ; *NAmE* ˈsɔːs-/ *noun* [C, U] a mixture of finely chopped meat, fat, bread, etc. in a long tube of skin, cooked and eaten whole or served cold in thin slices: ***beef/pork sausages*** ◇ *200g of garlic sausage* ➲ see also LIVER SAUSAGE
IDM **not a ˈsausage** (*old-fashioned, BrE, informal*) nothing at all

ˈsausage dog *noun* (*BrE, informal*) = DACHSHUND

ˈsausage meat *noun* [U] the mixture of finely chopped meat, fat, bread, etc. used for making sausages

ˌsausage ˈroll *noun* (*BrE*) a small tube of PASTRY filled with sausage meat and cooked

ˈsausage tree *noun* a large African tree that produces large grey fruit that hang downwards and have a similar shape to a sausage

sauté /ˈsəʊteɪ; *NAmE* soʊˈteɪ/ *verb* (**sauté·ing, sautéed, sautéed** or **sauté·ing, sautéd, sautéd**) **~ sth** to fry food quickly in a little hot fat ▶ **sauté** *adj.* [only before noun]: *sauté potatoes*

sav·age /ˈsævɪdʒ/ *adj., noun, verb*
■ ***adj.*** **1** aggressive and violent; causing great harm SYN **brutal**: *savage dogs* ◇ *She had been badly hurt in what police described as 'a savage attack'.* ◇ *savage public spending cuts* **2** involving very strong criticism: *The article was a savage attack on the government's record.* **3** [only before noun] (*old-fashioned, taboo*) an offensive way of referring to groups of people or customs that are considered to be simple and not highly developed SYN **primitive**: *a savage tribe* ▶ **sav·age·ly** *adv.*: *savagely attacked/criticized* ◇ *'No!' he snarled savagely.*
■ ***noun*** **1** (*old-fashioned, taboo*) an offensive word for sb who belongs to a people that is simple and not developed: *the development of the human race from primitive savages* **2** a cruel and violent person: *He described the attack as the work of savages.*
■ ***verb*** [usually passive] **1 ~ sb** (of an animal) to attack sb violently, causing serious injury: *She was* ***savaged to death*** *by a bear.* **2 ~ sb/sth** (*formal*) to criticize sb/sth severely: *Her latest novel has been savaged by the critics.*

sav·agery /ˈsævɪdʒri/ *noun* [U] behaviour that is very cruel and violent SYN **violence**: *The police were shocked by the savagery of the attacks.*

sa·van·nah (also **sa·vanna**) /səˈvænə/ *noun* [C, U] a wide flat open area of land, especially in Africa, that is covered with grass but has few trees ➲ compare VELD

sav·ant /ˈsævənt; *NAmE* sæˈvɑːnt/ *noun* (*formal*) **1** a person with great knowledge and ability **2** a person who is less intelligent than others but who has particular unusual abilities that other people do not have

save 0-w /seɪv/ *verb, noun, prep., conj.*
■ ***verb***
▸ KEEP SAFE **1** 0-w [T] to keep sb/sth safe from death, harm, loss, etc: **~ sb/sth** *to* ***save sb's life*** ◇ *Doctors were unable to*

save her. ◇ *He's trying to save their marriage.* ◇ *She needs to win the next two games to save the match.* ◇ (*figurative*) *Thanks for doing that. You* **saved my life** (= helped me a lot). ◇ **~ sb/sth** (**from sth**) *to save a rare species (from extinction)* ◇ **~ sb/sth from doing sth** *She saved a little girl from falling into the water.*

▸ MONEY **2** [I, T] to keep money instead of spending it, especially in order to buy a particular thing: *I'm not very good at saving.* ◇ **~** (**up**) (**for sth**) *I'm saving for a new bike.* ◇ *We've been saving up to go to Australia.* ◇ **~ sth** (**up**) (**for sth**) *You should save a little each week.* ◇ *I've saved almost £100 so far.*

▸ COLLECT STH **3** [T] **~ sth** to collect sth because you like it or for a special purpose: *I've been saving theatre programmes for years.* ◇ *If you save ten tokens you can get a T-shirt.*

▸ KEEP FOR FUTURE **4** [T] to keep sth to use or enjoy in the future: **~ sth** (**for sth/sb**) *He's saving his strength for the last part of the race.* ◇ *We'll eat some now and save some for tomorrow.* ◇ *Save some food for me.* ◇ **~ sb sth** *Save me some food.*

▸ NOT WASTE **5** [T, I] to avoid wasting sth or using more than necessary: **~ sth** *We'll take a cab to save time.* ◇ *Book early and save £50!* ◇ *We should try to save water.* ◇ **~ sth on sth** *The government is trying to save £1 million on defence.* ◇ **~ sb sth** (**on sth**) *If we go this way it will save us two hours on the trip.* ◇ **~ on sth** *I save on fares by walking to work.*

▸ AVOID STH BAD **6** [T] to avoid doing sth difficult or unpleasant; to make sb able to avoid doing sth difficult or unpleasant: **~ sb from doing sth** *The prize money saved her from having to find a job.* ◇ **~ sth** *She did it herself to save argument.* ◇ **~ sb sth** *Thanks for sending that letter for me—it saved me a trip.* ◇ **~ doing sth** *He's grown a beard to save shaving.* ◇ **~ sb doing sth** *If you phone for an appointment, it'll save you waiting.*

▸ IN SPORT **7** [T, I] **~** (**sth**) (in football (SOCCER), etc.) to prevent an opponent's shot from going in the goal: *to save a penalty* ◇ *The goalie saved Johnson's long-range shot.* ◇ (*BrE*) *The goalie saved brilliantly from Johnson's long-range shot.*

▸ COMPUTING **8** [T, I] **~** (**sth**) to make a computer keep work, for example by putting it on a disk: *Save data frequently.*

Synonyms

save

budget • economize • tighten your belt

These words all mean to spend less money.

save to keep money instead of spending it, often in order to buy a particular thing: *I'm saving for a new car.*

budget to be careful about the amount of money you spend; to plan to spend an amount of money for a particular purpose: *If we budget carefully we'll be able to afford the trip.*

economize to use less money, time, etc. than you normally use

tighten your belt (*rather informal*) to spend less money because there is less available: *With the price increases, we are all having to tighten our belts.*

PATTERNS

- to save up/budget **for** sth
- to **have to** save/budget/economize/tighten our belts
- to **try to/manage to** save/budget/economize

IDM **not be able to do sth to ˌsave your ˈlife** (*informal*) to be completely unable to do sth: *He can't interview people to save his life.* **save sb's ˈbacon/ˈneck** (*informal*) to rescue sb from a very difficult situation **save the ˈday/situˈation** to prevent failure or defeat, when this seems certain to happen: *Gerrard's late goal saved the day for Liverpool.* **save** (**sb's**) **ˈface** to avoid or help sb avoid embarrassment: *She was fired, but she saved face by telling everyone she'd resigned.* **save your ˈbreath** (*informal*) used to tell sb that it is not worth wasting time and effort saying sth because it will not change anything: *Save your breath—you'll never persuade her.* **save your** (**own**) **ˈskin/ˈhide/ˈneck** to try to avoid death, punishment, etc, especially by leaving others in an extremely difficult situation: *To save his own skin, he lied and blamed the accident on his friend.*

■ ***noun*** (in football, etc.) an action by the GOALKEEPER that stops a goal being scored: *He made a spectacular save.*

■ ***prep.*** (also **save for**) (*old use* or *formal*) except sth: *They knew nothing about her save her name.*

■ ***conj.*** (*old use* or *formal*) except: *They found out nothing more save that she had borne a child.*

Synonyms

save

rescue • bail out • redeem

These words all mean to prevent sb/sth from dying, losing sth, being harmed or embarrassed.

save to prevent sb/sth from dying, being harmed or destroyed or losing sth: *Doctors were unable to save him.* ◇ *a campaign to save the panda from extinction*

rescue to save sb/sth from a dangerous or harmful situation: *They were rescued by a passing cruise ship.*

bail sb out to rescue sb/sth from a difficult situation, especially by providing money: *Don't expect me to bail you out if it all goes wrong.*

redeem (*formal, religion*) to save sb from the power of evil: *He was a sinner, redeemed by the grace of God.*
NOTE **Redeem** is also used in non-religious language in the phrase *redeem a situation*, which means to prevent a situation from being as bad as it might be.

PATTERNS

- to save/rescue/redeem sb/sth **from** sth
- to save/rescue/redeem a **situation**
- to save/redeem **sinners/mankind**
- to rescue sb/bail sb out **financially**

saver /ˈseɪvə(r)/ *noun* **1** a person who saves money and puts it in a bank, etc. for future use **2** (often in compounds) something that helps you spend less money or use less of the thing mentioned: *a* ***money/time saver*** ➲ see also LIFESAVER

Savile Row /ˌsævl ˈrəʊ; *NAmE* ˈroʊ/ *noun* a street in London, England with many shops/stores that sell expensive clothes for men that are often specially made for each person: *He was wearing a Savile Row suit.*

sav·ing /ˈseɪvɪŋ/ *noun*
1 [C] an amount of sth such as time or money that you do not need to use or spend: *Buy three and make a saving of 55p.* ◇ *With the new boiler you can make big savings on fuel bills.* **2** **savings** [pl.] money that you have saved, especially in a bank, etc: *He put all his savings into buying a boat.* ◇ *I opened a* ***savings account*** *at my local bank.* ➲ COLLOCATIONS at FINANCE **3** **-saving** (in adjectives) that prevents the waste of the thing mentioned or stops it from being necessary: *energy-saving modifications* ◇ *labour-saving devices* ◇ *space-saving fitted furniture* ➲ see also FACE-SAVING

ˌsaving ˈgrace *noun* [usually sing.] the one good quality that a person or thing has that prevents them or it from being completely bad

ˌsavings and ˈloan association (*US*) (*BrE* **ˈbuilding society**) *noun* (*abbr.* S&L) an organization like a bank that lends money to people who want to buy a house. People also save money with a building society.

sa·viour (*especially US* **sa·vior**) /ˈseɪvjə(r)/ *noun* **1** [usually sing.] a person who rescues sb/sth from a dangerous or difficult situation: *The new manager has been hailed as the saviour of the club.* **2** **the Saviour** [sing.] used in the Christian religion as another name for Jesus Christ

S

savoir faire /ˌsævwɑː ˈfeə(r); *NAmE* ˌsævwɑːr ˈfer/ *noun* [U] (from *French, approving*) the ability to behave in the appropriate way in social situations

sa·vory (*NAmE*) = SAVOURY

sa·vour (*especially US* **savor**) /ˈseɪvə(r)/ *verb, noun*

■ ***verb* 1 ~ sth** to enjoy the full taste or flavour of sth, especially by eating or drinking it slowly SYN **relish**: *He ate his meal slowly, savouring every mouthful.* **2 ~ sth** to enjoy a feeling or an experience thoroughly SYN **relish**: *I wanted to savour every moment.*

PHR V **ˈsavour of sth** [no passive] (*formal*) to seem to have an amount of sth, especially sth bad: *His recent comments savour of hypocrisy.*

■ ***noun*** [usually sing.] (*formal* or *literary*) a taste or smell, especially a pleasant one: (*figurative*) *For Emma, life had lost its savour.*

sa·voury (*especially US* **sa·vory**) /ˈseɪvəri/ *adj., noun*

■ ***adj.* 1** having a taste that is salty not sweet: *savoury snacks* **2** having a pleasant taste or smell: *a savoury smell from the kitchen* ➲ see also UNSAVOURY

■ ***noun*** [usually pl.] (*pl.* -ies) a small amount of a food with a salty taste, not a sweet one, often served at a party, etc.

savoy /səˈvɔɪ/ (also **saˌvoy ˈcabbage**) *noun* [U, C] a type of CABBAGE with leaves that are not smooth

savvy /ˈsævi/ *noun, adj.*

■ ***noun*** [U] (*informal*) practical knowledge or understanding of sth: *political savvy*

■ ***adj.*** (**sav·vier, sav·vi·est**) (*informal, especially NAmE*) having practical knowledge and understanding of sth; having COMMON SENSE: *savvy shoppers*

saw /sɔː/ *noun, verb* ➲ see also SEE *v.*

■ ***noun* 1** (often in compounds) a tool that has a long blade with sharp points (called TEETH) along one of its edges. A saw is moved backwards and forwards by hand or driven by electricity and is used for cutting wood or metal. ➲ see also CHAINSAW, CIRCULAR SAW, FRETSAW, HACKSAW, HANDSAW, JIGSAW **2** (*old-fashioned*) a short phrase or sentence that states a general truth about life or gives advice

■ ***verb*** (**sawed, sawn** /sɔːn/) (*NAmE* also **sawed, sawed**) **1** [I, T] to use a saw to cut sth: *The workmen sawed and hammered all day.* ◇ **+ adv./prep.** *He accidentally sawed through a cable.* ◇ **~ sth (+ adv./prep.)** *She sawed the plank in half.* **2** [I, T] **~ (away) (at sth)** | **~ sth** to move sth backwards and forwards on sth as if using a saw: *She sawed away at her violin.* ◇ *He was sawing energetically at a loaf of bread.*

PHR V **ˌsaw sth↔ˈdown** to cut sth and bring it to the ground using a saw: *The tree had to be sawn down.* **ˌsaw sth↔ˈoff** | **ˌsaw sth ˈoff sth** to remove sth by cutting it with a saw: *We sawed the dead branches off the tree.* **ˌsaw sth↔ˈup (into sth)** to cut sth into pieces with a saw: *We sawed the wood up into logs.*

saw·dust /ˈsɔːdʌst/ *noun* [U] very small pieces of wood that fall as powder when wood is cut with a SAW

saw·horse /ˈsɔːhɔːs; *NAmE* -hɔːrs/ *noun* a wooden frame that supports wood that is being cut with a SAW

sawm /saʊm; *NAmE* soʊm/ *noun* [U] the Muslim practice of not eating or drinking in the day during the ninth month of the Muslim year, called RAMADAN

saw·mill /ˈsɔːmɪl/ *noun* a factory in which wood is cut into boards using machinery

ˌsawn-off ˈshotgun (*BrE*) (*NAmE* **ˌsawed-off ˈshotgun**) *noun* a SHOTGUN with part of its BARREL cut off

sax /sæks/ *noun* (*informal*) = SAXOPHONE

Saxon /ˈsæksn/ *noun* a member of a race of people once living in NW Germany, some of whom settled in Britain in the 5th and 6th centuries ➲ see also ANGLO-SAXON ▶ **Saxon** *adj.*: *Saxon churches/kings*

saxo·phone /ˈsæksəfəʊn; *NAmE* -foʊn/ (also *informal* **sax**) *noun* a metal musical instrument that you blow into, used especially in JAZZ ➲ VISUAL VOCAB page V30

sax·opho·nist /sækˈsɒfənɪst; *NAmE* ˈsæksəfoʊnɪst/ *noun* a person who plays the saxophone

say 🔑 /seɪ/ *verb, noun, exclamation*

■ ***verb*** (**says** /sez/, **said, said** /sed/)

▸ SPEAK **1** 🔑 [I, T] to speak or tell sb sth, using words: **+ speech** *'Hello!' she said.* ◇ *'That was marvellous,' said Daniel.* HELP In stories the subject often comes after **said, says** or **say** when it follows the actual words spoken, unless it is a pronoun.: **~ sth** *Be quiet, I have something to say.* ◇ *I didn't believe a word she said.* ◇ *That's a terrible* ***thing to say.*** ◇ *He knew that if he wasn't back by midnight, his parents would* ***have something to say about it*** (= be angry). ◇ **~ sth to sb** *She said nothing to me about it.* ◇ **~ to sb/yourself + speech** *I* ***said to myself*** (= thought), *'That can't be right!'* ◇ **~ (that)** *... He said (that) his name was Sam.* ◇ **it is said that...** *It is said that she lived to be over 100.* ◇ **~ (what, how, etc...)** *She finds it hard to say what she feels.* ◇ *'That's impossible!'* ***'So you say*** (= but I think you may be wrong).*'* ◇ *'Why can't I go out now?' 'Because I* ***say so.'*** ◇ *'What do you want it for?'* ***'I'd rather not say.'*** ◇ **~ to do sth** *He said to meet him here.* ◇ **sb/sth is said to be/have sth** *He is said to have been a brilliant scholar.*

▸ REPEAT WORDS **2** 🔑 [T] **~ sth** to repeat words, phrases, etc: *to say a prayer* ◇ *Try to say that line with more conviction.*

▸ EXPRESS OPINION **3** 🔑 [T, I] to express an opinion on sth: **~ sth** ***Say what you like*** (= although you disagree) *about her, she's a fine singer.* ◇ ***I'll say this for them,*** *they're a very efficient company.* ◇ *Anna thinks I'm lazy—* ***what do you say*** (= what is your opinion)? ◇ **~ (that)...** ***I can't say I blame*** *her for resigning* (= I think she was right). ◇ ***I say*** (= suggest) *we go without them.* ◇ ***I wouldn't say*** *they were rich* (= in my opinion they are not rich). ◇ ***That's not to say*** *it's a bad movie* (= it is good but it is not without faults). ◇ **~ (what, how, etc...)** ***It's hard to say*** *what caused the accident.* ◇ *'When will it be finished?'* ***'I couldn't say*** (= I don't know).*'*

▸ GIVE EXAMPLE **4** 🔑 [T, no passive] to suggest or give sth as an example or a possibility: **~ sth/sb** *You could learn the basics in,* ***let's say,*** *three months.* ◇ *Let's take any writer, say* (= for example) *Dickens...* ◇ **~ (that)...** *Say you lose your job: what would you do then?*

▸ SHOW THOUGHTS/FEELINGS **5** 🔑 [T] **~ sth (to sb)** to make thoughts, feelings, etc. clear to sb by using words, looks, movements, etc: *His angry glance* ***said it all.*** ◇ *That* ***says it all*** *really, doesn't it?* (= it shows clearly what is true) ◇ *Just what is the artist trying to say in her work?*

▸ GIVE WRITTEN INFORMATION **6** 🔑 [T, no passive] (of sth that is written or can be seen) to give particular information or instructions: **+ speech** *The notice said 'Keep Out'.* ◇ **~ sth** *The clock said three o'clock.* ◇ **~ (that)...** *The instructions say (that) we should leave it to set for four hours.* ◇ **~ where, why, etc...** *The book doesn't say where he was born.* ◇ **~ to do sth** *The guidebook says to turn left.*

IDM **before you can say Jack ˈRobinson** (*old-fashioned*) very quickly; in a very short time **ˌgo without ˈsaying** to be very obvious or easy to predict: *Of course I'll help you.* ***That goes without saying.*** **have something, nothing, etc. to ˈsay for yourself** to be ready, unwilling, etc. to talk or give your views on sth: *She doesn't have much to say for herself* (= doesn't take part in conversation). ◇ *He had plenty to say for himself* (= he had a lot of opinions and was willing to talk). ◇ *Late again—what have you got to say for yourself* (= what is your excuse)? **ˌhaving ˈsaid that** (*informal*) used to introduce an opinion that makes what you have just said seem less strong: *I sometimes get worried in this job. Having said that, I enjoy doing it, it's a challenge.* **ˈI'll say!** (*old-fashioned, informal*) used for emphasis to say 'yes': *'Does she see him often?' 'I'll say! Nearly every day.'* **I ˈmust say** (*informal*) used to emphasize an opinion: *Well, I must say, that's the funniest thing I've heard all week.* **ˌI ˈsay** (*old-fashioned, BrE, informal*) **1** used to express surprise, shock, etc.: *I say! What a huge cake!* **2** used to attract sb's attention or introduce a new subject of conversation: *I say, can you lend me five pounds?* **it says a ˈlot, very ˈlittle, etc. for sb/sth** (*informal*) it shows a good/bad quality that sb/sth has: *It says a lot for her that she never lost her temper.* ◇ *It didn't say much for their efficiency that the order arrived a week late.* **I ˌwouldn't say ˈno (to sth)** (*informal*) used to say that you would like sth or to accept sth that is offered: *I wouldn't say no to a pizza.* ◇ *'Tea, Brian?' 'I wouldn't say no.'* **ˌleast ˈsaid ˌsoonest ˈmended** (*BrE, saying*) a bad situation will pass or be forgotten most quickly if nothing more is said about it **the less/least said the ˈbetter** the best thing to do is say as little as possible about sth **ˌnever say ˈdie** (*saying*) do not stop hoping **not say boo to a ˈgoose** (*BrE*) (*NAmE* **not say boo to ˈanyone**) to be very shy or gentle: *He's so nervous he wouldn't say boo to a goose.* **ˈnot to say** used to introduce a stronger way of describing sth: *a difficult, not to say impossible, task* **say ˈcheese** used to ask sb to smile before you take their photograph **say ˈno (to sth)** 0‑w to refuse an offer, a suggestion, etc: *If you don't invest in this, you're saying no to a potential fortune.* **ˌsay no ˈmore** (*informal*) used to say that you understand exactly what sb means or is trying to say, so it is unnecessary to say anything more: *'They went to Paris together.' 'Say no more!'* **ˌsay your ˈpiece** to say exactly what you feel or think **say ˈwhat?** (*NAmE, informal*) used to express surprise at what sb has just said: *'He's getting married.' 'Say what?'* **say ˈwhen** used to ask sb to tell you when you should stop pouring a drink or serving food for them because they have enough **ˈthat is to say** in other words: *three days from now, that is to say on Friday* **that's not ˈsaying much** used to say that sth is not very unusual or special: *She's a better player than me, but that's not saying much* (= because I am a very bad player). **that ˈsaid** used to introduce an opinion that makes what you have just said seem less strong **there's no ˈsaying** used to say that it is impossible to predict what might happen: *There's no saying how he'll react.* **there's something, not much, etc. to be said for sth/doing sth** there are/are not good reasons for doing sth, believing sth or agreeing with sth **to ˌsay the ˈleast** without exaggerating at all: *I was surprised, to say the least.* **to say ˈnothing of sth** used to introduce a further fact or thing in addition to those already mentioned SYN **not to mention**: *It was too expensive, to say nothing of the time it wasted.* **well ˈsaid!** (*informal*) I agree completely: *'We must stand up for ourselves.' 'Well said, John.'* **ˌwhat do/would you ˈsay (to sth/doing sth)** (*informal*) would you like sth/to do sth?: *What do you say to eating out tonight?* ◇ *Let's go away for a weekend. What do you say?* **what/whatever sb says, ˈgoes** (*informal*, often *humorous*) a particular person must be obeyed: *Sarah wanted the kitchen painted green, and what she says, goes.* **whatever you ˈsay** (*informal*) used to agree to sb's suggestion because you do not want to argue **when ˌall is said and ˈdone** when everything is considered: *I know you're upset, but when all's said and done it isn't exactly a disaster.* **who can ˈsay (...)?** used to say that nobody knows the answer to a question: *Who can say what will happen next year?* **who ˈsays (...)?** (*informal*) used to disagree with a statement or an opinion: *Who says I can't do it?* **who's to say (...)?** used to say that sth might happen or might have happened in a particular way, because nobody really knows: *Who's to say we would not have succeeded if we'd had more time?* **you can say ˈthat again** (*informal*) I agree with you completely: *'He's in a bad mood today.' 'You can say that again!'* **you can't say ˈfairer (than ˈthat)** (*BrE, informal*) used to say that you think the offer you are making is reasonable or generous: *Look, I'll give you £100 for it. I can't say fairer than that.* **you don't ˈsay!** (*informal*, often *ironic*) used to express surprise: *'They left without us.' 'You don't say!'* (= I'm not surprised) **you ˈsaid it!** (*informal*) **1** (*BrE*) used to agree with sb when they say sth about themselves that you would not have been rude enough to say yourself: *'I know I'm not the world's greatest cook.' 'You said it!'* **2** (*NAmE*) used to agree with sb's suggestion ⊃ more at DARE *v.*, EASY *adj.*, ENOUGH *pron.*, GLAD, LET *v.*, MEAN *v.*, MIND *v.*, NEEDLESS, RECORD *n.*, SOON, SORRY *adj.*, SUFFICE, WORD *n.*

■ ***noun*** [sing., U] **~ (in sth)** the right to influence sth by giving your opinion before a decision is made: *We had no say in the decision to sell the company.* ◇ *People want a greater say in local government.* ◇ *The judge has the final say on the sentence.*

IDM **have your ˈsay** (*informal*) to have the opportunity to express yourself fully about sth: *She won't be happy until she's had her say.* ⊃ see also SAY YOUR PIECE

■ ***exclamation*** (*NAmE, informal*) **1** used for showing surprise or pleasure: *Say, that's a nice haircut!* **2** used for attracting sb's attention or for making a suggestion or comment: *Say, how about going to a movie tonight?*

Which Word?

say / tell

- **Say** never has a person as the object. You **say something** or **say something to somebody**. **Say** is often used when you are giving somebody's exact words: *'Sit down', she said.* ◇ *Anne said, 'I'm tired.'* ◇ *Anne said (that) she was tired.* ◇ *What did he say to you?* You cannot use 'say about', but **say something about** is correct: *I want to say something /a few words /a little about my family.* **Say** can also be used with a clause when the person you are talking to is not mentioned: *She didn't say what she intended to do.*
- **Tell** usually has a person as the object and often has two objects: *Have you told him the news yet?* It is often used with 'that' clauses: *Anne told me (that) she was tired.* **Tell** is usually used when somebody is giving facts or information, often with *what, where*, etc: *Can you tell me when the movie starts?* (BUT: *Can you give me some information about the school?*) **Tell** is also used when you are giving somebody instructions: *The doctor told me to stay in bed.* ◇ *The doctor told me (that) I had to stay in bed.* OR *The doctor said (that) I had to stay in bed.* NOT ~~*The doctor said me to stay in bed.*~~

say·ing /ˈseɪɪŋ/ *noun* a well-known phrase or statement that expresses sth about life that most people believe is wise and true: *'Accidents will happen', **as the saying goes**.*

ˈsay-so *noun* [sing.] (*informal*) permission that sb gives to do sth: *Nothing could be done without her say-so.*
IDM **on sb's ˈsay-so** based on a statement that sb makes without giving any proof: *He hired and fired people on his partner's say-so.*

ˈS-bend *noun* a bend in a road or pipe that is shaped like an S

scab /skæb/ *noun* **1** [C] a hard dry covering that forms over a wound as it heals **2** [U] a skin disease of animals **3** [U] a disease of plants, especially apples and potatoes, that causes a rough surface **4** [C] (*informal, disapproving*) a worker who refuses to join a strike or takes the place of sb on strike SYN **blackleg**

scab·bard /ˈskæbəd; *NAmE* -bərd/ *noun* a cover for a SWORD that is made of leather or metal SYN **sheath**

scab·by /ˈskæbi/ *adj.* covered in scabs

sca·bies /ˈskeɪbiːz/ *noun* [U] a skin disease that causes ITCHING and small red raised spots

scab·rous /ˈskeɪbrəs; ˈskæb-/ *adj.* **1** (*formal*) offensive or shocking in a sexual way SYN **indecent** **2** (*technical*) having a rough surface SYN **scaly**: *scabrous skin*

scads /skædz/ *noun* [pl.] **~ (of sth)** (*informal, especially NAmE*) large numbers or amounts of sth: *scads of $20 bills*

scaf·fold /ˈskæfəʊld; *NAmE* -foʊld/ *noun* **1** a platform used when EXECUTING criminals by cutting off their heads or hanging them from a rope **2** a structure made of scaffolding, for workers to stand on when they are working on a building

scaf·fold·ing /ˈskæfəldɪŋ/ *noun* [U] poles and boards that are joined together to make a structure for workers to stand on when they are working high up on the outside wall of a building

sca·lar /ˈskeɪlə(r)/ *adj.* (*mathematics*) (of a quantity) having size but no direction ⊃ compare VECTOR ▶ **sca·lar** *noun*

scala·wag /ˈskæləwæg/ (*NAmE*) (*BrE* **scally·wag**) *noun* (*informal*) a person, especially a child, who behaves badly, but not in a serious way SYN **scamp**

scald /skɔːld/ *verb, noun*

■ ***verb*** **~ sth/yourself** to burn yourself or part of your body

S

with very hot liquid or steam: *Be careful not to scald yourself with the steam.* ◇ (*figurative*) *Tears scalded her eyes.* ➲ SYNONYMS at BURN ➲ COLLOCATIONS at INJURY

■ ***noun*** an injury to the skin from very hot liquid or steam

scald·ing /ˈskɔːldɪŋ/ *adj.* hot enough to SCALD: *scalding water* ◇ (*figurative*) *Scalding tears poured down her face.* ▸ **scald·ing** *adv.*: *scalding hot*

scales

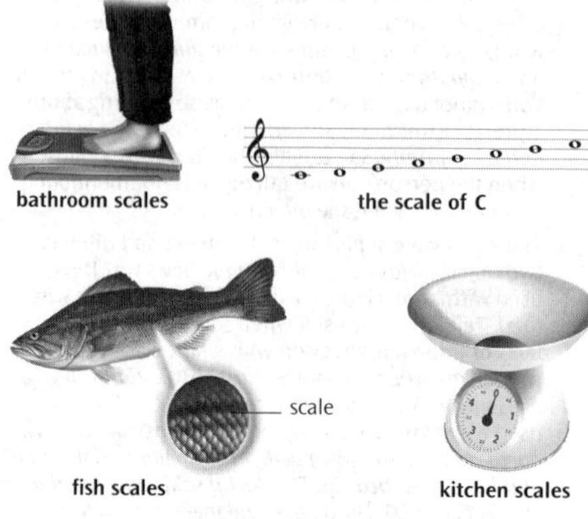

bathroom scales

the scale of C

fish scales

kitchen scales

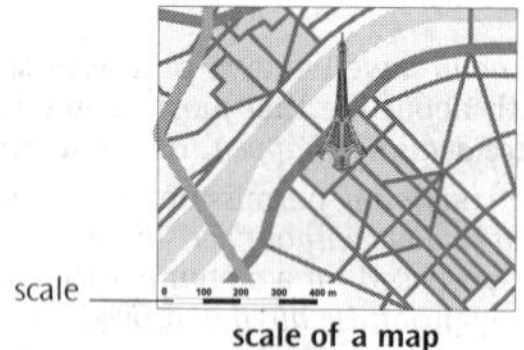

scale of a map

scale 🔑 /skeɪl/ *noun, verb*

■ ***noun***

▸ SIZE **1** 🔑 [sing., U] the size or extent of sth, especially when compared with sth else: *They entertain* ***on a large scale*** (= they hold expensive parties with a lot of guests). ◇ *Here was corruption* ***on a grand scale.*** ◇ *On a global scale, 77% of energy is created from fossil fuels.* ◇ *to achieve* ***economies of scale*** *in production* (= to produce many items so the cost of producing each one is reduced) ◇ **~ of sth** *It was impossible to comprehend* ***the full scale*** *of the disaster.* ◇ *It was not until morning that* ***the sheer scale*** *of the damage could be seen* (= how great it was). ➲ see also FULL-SCALE, LARGE-SCALE, SMALL-SCALE

▸ RANGE OF LEVELS **2** 🔑 [C] a range of levels or numbers used for measuring sth: *a five-point pay scale* ◇ *to evaluate performance on a scale from 1 to 10* ➲ see also RICHTER SCALE, SLIDING SCALE, TIMESCALE **3** 🔑 [C, usually sing.] the set of all the different levels of sth, from the lowest to the highest: ***At the other end of the scale,*** *life is a constant struggle to get enough to eat.* ◇ *the social scale*

▸ MARKS FOR MEASURING **4** 🔑 [C] a series of marks at regular intervals on an instrument that is used for measuring: *How much does it read on the scale?*

▸ WEIGHING INSTRUMENT **5** 🔑 **scales** [pl.] (*NAmE* also **scale**) an instrument for weighing people or things: ***bathroom/kitchen/weighing scales*** ◇ (*figurative*) *the* ***scales of justice*** (= represented as the two pans on a BALANCE (5)) ➲ VISUAL VOCAB page V21

▸ OF MAP/DIAGRAM/MODEL **6** 🔑 [C] the relation between the actual size of sth and its size on a map, diagram or model that represents it: *a scale of 1:25 000* ◇ *a* ***scale model/drawing*** ◇ *Both plans are drawn to the same scale.* ◇ *Is this diagram* ***to scale*** (= are all its parts the same size and shape in relation to each other as they are in the thing represented)?

▸ IN MUSIC **7** [C] a series of musical notes moving upwards or downwards, with fixed intervals between each note, especially a series of eight starting on a particular note: *the scale of C major* ◇ *to practise scales on the piano* ➲ compare KEY *n.* (5), OCTAVE

▸ OF FISH/REPTILE **8** [C] any of the thin plates of hard material that cover the skin of many fish and REPTILES

▸ IN WATER PIPES, ETC. **9** (*BrE* also **fur**) [U] a hard greyish-white substance that is sometimes left inside water pipes and containers for heating water ➲ see also LIMESCALE

▸ ON TEETH **10** [U] a hard substance that forms on teeth, especially when they are not cleaned regularly ➲ compare PLAQUE IDM see TIP *v.*

■ ***verb***

▸ CLIMB **1 ~ sth** (*formal*) to climb to the top of sth very high and steep: *the first woman to scale Mount Everest* ◇ (*figurative*) *He has* ***scaled the heights*** *of his profession.*

▸ FISH **2 ~ sth** to remove the small flat hard pieces of skin from a fish

▸ TEETH **3 ~ sth** to remove TARTAR from the teeth by SCRAPING: *The dentist scaled and polished my teeth.*

▸ CHANGE SIZE **4 ~ sth (from sth) (to sth)** (*technical*) to change the size of sth: *Text can be scaled from 4 points to 108 points without any loss of quality.*

PHR V **ˌscale sth↔ˈdown** (*NAmE* also **ˌscale sth↔ˈback**) to reduce the number, size or extent of sth: *We are thinking of scaling down our training programmes next year.* ◇ *The IMF has scaled back its growth forecasts for the next decade.* ➲ SYNONYMS at CUT **ˌscale sth↔ˈup** to increase the size or number of sth

sca·lene tri·angle /ˌskeɪliːn ˈtraɪæŋɡl/ *noun* (*geometry*) a triangle whose sides are all of different lengths ➲ VISUAL VOCAB page V58

scal·lion /ˈskæliən/ *noun* (*NAmE, IrishE*) = GREEN ONION, SPRING ONION

scal·lop /ˈskɒləp; *NAmE* ˈskæləp/ *noun, verb*

■ ***noun*** **1** a SHELLFISH that can be eaten, with two flat round shells that fit together: *a scallop shell* **2** any one of a series of small curves cut on the edge of a piece of cloth, PASTRY, etc. for decoration

■ ***verb*** [usually passive] **~ sth** to decorate the edge of sth with small curves: *a scalloped edge*

scally /ˈskæli/ *noun* (*pl.* **-ies**) (*BrE, informal*) (used especially in Liverpool in NW England) a boy or young man who behaves badly or causes trouble

scally·wag /ˈskæliwæɡ/ (*BrE*) (*NAmE* **scala·wag**) *noun* (*informal*) a person, especially a child, who behaves badly, but not in a serious way SYN **scamp**

scalp /skælp/ *noun, verb*

■ ***noun*** **1** the skin that covers the part of the head where the hair grows **2** (in the past) the skin and hair that was removed from the head of a dead enemy by some Native American peoples as a sign of victory **3** (*informal*) a symbol of the fact that sb has been defeated or punished: *They have claimed some impressive scalps in their bid for the championship.*

■ ***verb*** **1 ~ sb** to remove the skin and hair from the top of an enemy's head as a sign of victory **2** (*NAmE*) (*BrE* **tout**) **~ sth** to sell tickets for a popular event illegally, at a price that is higher than the official price, especially outside a theatre, STADIUM, etc.

scal·pel /ˈskælpəl/ *noun* a small sharp knife used by doctors in medical operations

scalp·er /ˈskælpə(r)/ (*NAmE*) (*BrE* **tout**, **ˈticket tout**) *noun* a person who buys tickets for concerts, sports events, etc. and then sells them to other people at a higher price: *ticket scalpers*

scaly /ˈskeɪli/ *adj.* (**scali·er**, **scali·est**) (of skin) covered with SCALES (8), or hard and dry, with small pieces that come off

ˌscaly ˈanteater *noun* = PANGOLIN

scam /skæm/ *noun* (*informal*) a clever and dishonest plan for making money ➲ COLLOCATIONS at CRIME

scamp /skæmp/ *noun* (*old-fashioned*) a child who enjoys playing tricks and causing trouble SYN **scallywag**

scam·per /ˈskæmpə(r)/ *verb* [I] **+ adv./prep.** (especially of children or small animals) to move quickly with short light steps

S

scampi /ˈskæmpi/ *noun* [U+sing./pl. v.] (*BrE*) large PRAWNS (= a type of sea creature) covered with BREADCRUMBS or BATTER and fried: *scampi and chips*

scan /skæn/ *verb, noun*
■ ***verb*** (-nn-) **1** [T] to look at every part of sth carefully, especially because you are looking for a particular thing or person SYN **scrutinize**: **~ sth for sth** *He scanned the horizon for any sign of land.* ◇ **~ sth** *She scanned his face anxiously.* **2** [T, I] to look quickly but not very carefully at a document, etc: **~ sth** (**for sth**) *I scanned the list quickly for my name.* ◇ **~ through sth** (**for sth**) *She scanned through the newspaper over breakfast.* **3** [T] **~ sth** to get an image of an object, a part of sb's body, etc. on a computer by passing X-RAYS, ULTRASOUND waves or ELECTROMAGNETIC waves over it in a special machine: *Their brains are scanned so that researchers can monitor the progress of the disease.* **4** [T] **~ sth** (of a light, RADAR, etc.) to pass across an area: *Concealed video cameras scan every part of the compound.* **5** [I, T] **~** (**sth**) (*computing*) (of a program) to examine a computer program or document in order to look for a virus: *This software is designed to scan all new files for viruses.* **6** [T] **~ sth** (*computing*) to pass light over a picture or document using a SCANNER in order to copy it and put it in the memory of a computer: *How do I scan a photo and attach it to an email?* **7** [I] (of poetry) to have a regular rhythm according to fixed rules: *This line doesn't scan.*
PHR V ˌ**scan sth ˈinto sth** | ˌ**scan sth ˈin** (*computing*) to pass light over a picture or document using a SCANNER in order to copy it and put it in the memory of a computer: *Text and pictures can be scanned into the computer.*
■ ***noun*** **1** [C] a medical test in which a machine produces a picture of the inside of a person's body on a computer screen after taking X-RAYS: *to have a brain scan* **2** [C] a medical test for pregnant women in which a machine uses ULTRASOUND to produce a picture of a baby inside its mother's body: *to have a scan* **3** [sing.] the act of looking quickly through sth written or printed, usually in order to find sth

scan·dal /ˈskændl/ *noun* **1** [C, U] behaviour or an event that people think is morally or legally wrong and causes public feelings of shock or anger: *a series of sex scandals* ◇ *to* ***cause/create a scandal*** ◇ *The* ***scandal broke*** (= became known to the public) *in May.* ◇ *There has been* ***no hint of scandal*** *during his time in office.* **2** [U] talk or reports about the shocking or immoral things that people have done or are thought to have done: *to spread scandal* ◇ *newspapers full of scandal* **3** [sing.] **~** (**that...**) an action, attitude, etc. that you think is shocking and not at all acceptable SYN **disgrace**: ***It is a scandal that*** *such a large town has no orchestra.*

scan·dal·ize (*BrE* also **-ise**) /ˈskændəlaɪz/ *verb* **~ sb** to do sth that people find very shocking SYN **outrage**: *She scandalized her family with her extravagant lifestyle.*

scan·dal·mon·ger /ˈskændlmʌŋɡə(r)/ *noun* (*disapproving*) a person who spreads stories about the shocking or immoral things that other people have done

scan·dal·ous /ˈskændələs/ *adj.* **1** shocking and unacceptable SYN **disgraceful**: *a scandalous waste of money* ◇ **it is scandalous that...** *It is scandalous that he has not been punished.* **2** [only before noun] containing talk about the shocking or immoral things that people have done or are thought to have done: *scandalous stories* ▶ **scan·dal·ous·ly** *adv.*: *scandalously low pay*

ˈ**scandal sheet** *noun* (*disapproving*) a newspaper or magazine that is mainly concerned with shocking stories about the immoral behaviour and private lives of famous or important people

Scan·di·navia /ˌskændɪˈneɪviə/ *noun* [U] a cultural region in NW Europe consisting of Norway, Sweden and Denmark and sometimes also Iceland, Finland and the Faroe Islands ▶ **Scan·di·navian** /ˌskændɪˈneɪviən/ *adj., noun*

scan·dium /ˈskændiəm/ *noun* [U] (*symb.* Sc) a chemical element. Scandium is a silver-white metal found in various minerals.

scan·ner /ˈskænə(r)/ *noun* **1** a device for examining sth or recording sth using light, sound or X-RAYS: *The identity cards are examined by an electronic scanner.* **2** (*computing*) a device which copies pictures and documents so that they can be stored on a computer: *a document scanner* ➲ VISUAL VOCAB pages V54, V56 ➲ see also FLATBED SCANNER **3** a machine used by doctors to produce a picture of the inside of a person's body on a computer screen: *a body scanner* **4** a piece of equipment for receiving and sending RADAR signals

scan·sion /ˈskænʃn/ *noun* [U] (*technical*) the rhythm of a line of poetry

scant /skænt/ *adj.* [only before noun] hardly any; not very much and not as much as there should be: *I* ***paid scant attention to*** *what she was saying.* ◇ *The firefighters went back into the house with* ***scant regard for*** *their own safety.*

scanty /ˈskænti/ *adj.* (**scant·ier, scanti·est**) **1** too little in amount for what is needed: *Details of his life are scanty.* **2** (of clothes) very small and not covering much of your body: *a scanty bikini* ▶ **scant·ily** *adv.*: *scantily dressed models*

-scape *combining form* (in nouns) a view or scene of: *landscape* ◇ *seascape* ◇ *moonscape*

scape·goat /ˈskeɪpɡəʊt; *NAmE* -ɡoʊt/ *noun* a person who is blamed for sth bad that sb else has done or for some failure SYN **fall guy**: *She felt she had been made a scapegoat for her boss's incompetence.* ▶ **scape·goat** *verb* **~ sb/sth**

scap·ula /ˈskæpjʊlə/ *noun* (*pl.* **scapu·lae** /-liː/ or **scapu·las**) (*anatomy*) the SHOULDER BLADE ➲ VISUAL VOCAB page V48

scar /skɑː(r)/ *noun, verb*
■ ***noun*** **1** a mark that is left on the skin after a wound has healed: *a scar on his cheek* ◇ *Will the operation leave a scar?* ◇ *scar tissue* **2** a permanent feeling of great sadness or mental pain that a person is left with after an unpleasant experience: *His years in prison have* ***left*** *deep* ***scars***. **3** something unpleasant or ugly that spoils the appearance or public image of sth: *The town still bears the scars of war.* ◇ *Racism has been a scar on the game.* **4** an area of a hill or CLIFF where there is exposed rock and no grass
■ ***verb*** (-rr-) [often passive] **1 ~ sb/sth** (of a wound, etc.) to leave a mark on the skin after it has healed: *His face was badly scarred.* **2 ~ sb** (of an unpleasant experience) to leave sb with a feeling of sadness or mental pain: *The experience left her* ***scarred for life***. **3 ~ sth** to spoil the appearance of sth: *The hills are scarred by quarries.* ◇ *battle-scarred buildings*

scarab /ˈskærəb/ (also ˈ**scarab beetle**) *noun* a large black BEETLE (= an insect with a hard shell); a design showing a scarab beetle

scarce /skeəs; *NAmE* skers/ *adj., adv.*
■ ***adj.*** (**scar·cer, scar·cest**) if sth is **scarce**, there is not enough of it and it is only available in small quantities: ***scarce resources*** ◇ *Details of the accident are scarce.* ◇ *Food was becoming scarce.*
IDM ˌ**make yourself ˈscarce** (*informal*) to leave somewhere and stay away for a time in order to avoid an unpleasant situation
■ ***adv.*** (*literary*) only just; almost not: *I can scarce remember him.*

scarce·ly /ˈskeəsli; *NAmE* ˈskers-/ *adv.* **1** only just; almost not: *I can scarcely believe it.* ◇ *We scarcely ever meet.* ◇ *Scarcely a week goes by without some new scandal in the papers.* **2** used to say that sth happens immediately after sth else happens: *He had scarcely put the phone down when the doorbell rang.* ◇ *Scarcely had the game started when it began to rain.* **3** used to suggest that sth is not at all reasonable or likely: *It was scarcely an occasion for laughter.* ◇ *She could scarcely complain, could she?* ➲ note at HARDLY

scar·city /ˈskeəsəti; *NAmE* ˈskers-/ *noun* [U, C] (*pl.* **-ies**) if there is a **scarcity of** sth, there is not enough of it and it is difficult to obtain it SYN **shortage**: *a time of scarcity* ◇ *a scarcity of resources*

scare 0-w /skeə(r); *NAmE* sker/ *verb, noun*
■ ***verb*** **1** 0-w [T] to frighten sb: **~ sb** *You scared me.* ◇ **it scares sb to do sth** *It scared me to think I was alone in the building.*

S

➲ SYNONYMS at FRIGHTEN **2** [I] to become frightened: *He doesn't scare easily.* ➲ see also SCARY

IDM **scare the 'shit out of sb | scare sb 'shitless** (*taboo, slang*) to frighten sb very much ➲ more at DAYLIGHTS, DEATH, LIFE

PHR V ˌ**scare sb↔a'way/'off** 🔑 to make sb go away by frightening them: *They managed to scare the bears away.* '**scare sb into doing sth** to frighten sb in order to make them do sth: *Local businesses were scared into paying protection money.* ˌ**scare sb↔'off** to make sb afraid of or nervous about doing sth, especially without intending to: *Rising prices are scaring customers off.* ˌ**scare 'up sth** (*NAmE, informal*) to find or make sth by using whatever is available: *I'll see if I can scare up enough chairs for us all.*

■ ***noun* 1** 🔑 [C] (used especially in newspapers) a situation in which a lot of people are anxious or frightened about sth: *a* ***bomb/health scare*** ◇ *recent scares about pesticides in food* ◇ *a* ***scare story*** (= a news report that spreads more anxiety or fear about sth than is necessary) ◇ *to cause a major scare* ◇ ***scare tactics*** (= ways of persuading people to do sth by frightening them) **2** 🔑 [sing.] a sudden feeling of fear: *You* ***gave me a scare!*** ◇ *We've had quite a scare.* ➲ see also SCARY

scare·crow /'skeəkrəʊ; *NAmE* 'skerkroʊ/ *noun* a figure made to look like a person, that is dressed in old clothes and put in a field to frighten birds away

scared 🔑 /skeəd; *NAmE* skerd/ *adj.* frightened of sth or afraid that sth bad might happen: **~ (of doing sth)** *She is scared of going out alone.* ◇ **~ (of sb/sth)** *He's scared of heights.* ◇ **~ (to do sth)** *People are scared to use the buses late at night.* ◇ **~ (that...)** *I'm scared (that) I'm going to fall.* ◇ *The thieves got scared and ran away.* ◇ *a scared look* ◇ *I was* ***scared to death*** (= very frightened). ◇ *We were* ***scared stiff*** (= very frightened). ➲ SYNONYMS at AFRAID IDM see SHADOW *n.*, WIT, WITLESS

scaredy-cat /'skeədi kæt; *NAmE* 'skerdi/ (*US* also '**fraidy cat**) *noun* (*informal, disapproving*) a children's word for a person who is easily frightened

scare·mon·ger /'skeəmʌŋgə(r); *NAmE* 'skerm-/ *noun* (*disapproving*) a person who spreads stories deliberately to make people frightened or nervous ▸ **scare·monger·ing** *noun* [U]

'**scare quotes** *noun* [pl.] QUOTATION MARKS that a writer puts around a word or phrase to show that it is used in an unusual way, usually one that the writer does not agree with: *This pronouncement came from the organization's 'scientific' committee (the scare quotes are mine).*

scarf /skɑːf; *NAmE* skɑːrf/ *noun, verb*

■ ***noun*** (*pl.* scarves /skɑːvz; *NAmE* skɑːrvz/ or *less frequent* scarfs) a piece of cloth that is worn around the neck, for example for warmth or decoration. Women also wear scarves over their shoulders or hair: *a woollen/silk scarf* ➲ VISUAL VOCAB page V53

■ ***verb*** (*NAmE*) (*BrE* **scoff**) [I, T] **~ (sth)** (*informal*) to eat a lot of sth quickly

scar·ify /'skærɪfaɪ; 'skeə-; *NAmE* 'sker-/ *verb* (scari·fies, scari·fy·ing, scari·fied, scari·fied) (*technical*) **1 ~ sth** to break up an area of grass, etc. and remove pieces of material from it that are not wanted **2 ~ sth** to make cuts in the surface of sth, especially skin

scar·let /'skɑːlət; *NAmE* 'skɑːrlət/ *adj.* bright red in colour: *scarlet berries* ◇ *She* ***went scarlet*** *with embarrassment.* ▸ **scar·let** *noun* [U]

ˌ**scarlet 'fever** *noun* [U] a serious infectious disease that causes fever and red marks on the skin

ˌ**scarlet 'woman** *noun* (*old-fashioned*) a woman who has sexual relationships with many different people

scarp /skɑːp; *NAmE* skɑːrp/ *noun* (*technical*) a very steep slope

scar·per /'skɑːpə(r); *NAmE* 'skɑːrp-/ *verb* [I] (*BrE, informal*) to run away; to leave: *The police arrived, so we scarpered.*

Scart /skɑːt; *NAmE* skɑːrt/ (also **SCART**) *noun* a device with 21 pins, used to connect video equipment to, for example, a television: *a Scart socket*

scarves *pl.* of SCARF

scary /'skeəri; *NAmE* 'skeri/ *adj.* (scari·er, scari·est) (*informal*) frightening: *It was a really scary moment.* ◇ *a scary movie* ➲ see also SCARE *v.*

scat /skæt/ *noun* [U] a style of JAZZ singing in which the voice is made to sound like a musical instrument

scath·ing /'skeɪðɪŋ/ *adj.* criticizing sb or sth very severely SYN **withering**: *a* ***scathing attack*** *on the new management* ◇ **~ about sb/sth** *He was scathing about the government's performance.* ▸ **scath·ing·ly** *adv.*: *'Oh, she's just a kid,' he said scathingly.*

scato·logic·al /ˌskætə'lɒdʒɪkl; *NAmE* -'lɑːdʒ-/ *adj.* (*formal*) connected with human waste from the body in an unpleasant way: *scatological humour*

scat·ter /'skætə(r)/ *verb, noun*

■ ***verb* 1** [T] to throw or drop things in different directions so that they cover an area of ground: **~ sth** *They scattered his ashes at sea.* ◇ **~ sth on/over/around sth** *Scatter the grass seed over the lawn.* ◇ **~ sth with sth** *Scatter the lawn with grass seed.* **2** [I, T] to move or to make people or animals move very quickly in different directions SYN **disperse**: *At the first gunshot, the crowd scattered.* ◇ **~ sb/sth** *The explosion scattered a flock of birds roosting in the trees.*

■ ***noun*** [usually sing.] (also **scat·ter·ing** /'skætərɪŋ/ [sing.]) a small amount or number of things spread over an area: *a scattering of houses*

scat·ter·brain /'skætəbreɪn; *NAmE* -tərb-/ *noun* (*informal*) a person who is always losing or forgetting things and cannot think in an organized way ▸ **scat·ter·brained** *adj.*

'**scatter cushion** (*BrE*) (*NAmE* '**throw pillow**) *noun* a small CUSHION that can be placed on furniture, on the floor, etc. for decoration ➲ VISUAL VOCAB page V18

'**scatter diagram** (also **scat·ter·gram** /'skætəgræm; *NAmE* -tərg-/) *noun* (*statistics*) a diagram that shows the relationship between two VARIABLES by creating a pattern of dots

scat·tered /'skætəd; *NAmE* -tərd/ *adj.* spread far apart over a wide area or over a long period of time: *a few scattered settlements* ◇ *sunshine with scattered showers* ◇ *Her family are scattered around the world.*

scatter·gun /'skætəgʌn; *NAmE* -tərg-/ (*BrE*) (*NAmE* **scatter·shot** /'skætəʃɒt; *NAmE* -tərʃɑːt/) *adj.* [only before noun] referring to a way of doing or dealing with sth by considering many different possibilities, people, etc. in a way that is not well organized: *The scattergun approach to marketing means that the campaign is not targeted at particular individuals.*

scatty /'skæti/ *adj.* (scat·tier, scat·ti·est) (*BrE, informal*) tending to forget things and behave in a slightly silly way

scav·enge /'skævɪndʒ/ *verb* **1** [T, I] (of a person, an animal or a bird) to search through waste for things that can be used or eaten: **~ sth (from sth)** *Much of their furniture was scavenged from other people's garbage.* ◇ **~ (through sth) (for sth)** *Dogs and foxes scavenged through the trash cans for something to eat.* **2** [T, I] (of animals or birds) to eat dead animals that have been killed by another animal, by a car, etc: **~ sth** *Crows scavenge carrion left on the roads.* ◇ **~ (on sth)** *Some fish scavenge on dead fish in the wild.*

scav·en·ger /'skævɪndʒə(r)/ *noun* an animal, a bird or a person that scavenges

'**scavenger hunt** *noun* a game in which players have to find various objects

SCE /ˌes siː 'iː/ *abbr.* Scottish Certificate of Education (exams taken by Scottish school students at two different levels at the ages of 16 and 17-18) ➲ see also HIGHER, STANDARD GRADE

scen·ario AW /sə'nɑːriəʊ; *NAmE* sə'næriοʊ/ *noun* (*pl.* -os) **1** a description of how things might happen in the future: *Let me suggest a* ***possible scenario***. ◇ *The* ***worst-case scenario*** (= the worst possible thing that could happen) *would be for the factory to be closed down.* ◇ *a* ***nightmare***

S

scenario **2** a written outline of what happens in a film/movie or play SYN **synopsis**

scene 0-π /siːn/ *noun*
▸ PLACE **1** 0-π [C, usually sing.] ~ (**of sth**) the place where sth happens, especially sth unpleasant: *the* ***scene of the accident/attack/crime*** ◇ *Firefighters* ***were on the scene*** *immediately.* ➲ SYNONYMS at PLACE
▸ EVENT **2** 0-π [C] ~ (**of sth**) an event or a situation that you see, especially one of a particular type: *The team's victory produced scenes of joy all over the country.* ◇ *She witnessed some very distressing scenes.*
▸ IN MOVIE/PLAY, ETC. **3** 0-π [C] a part of a film/movie, play or book in which the action happens in one place or is of one particular type: *The movie opens with a scene in a New York apartment.* ◇ ***love/sex scenes*** ◇ *I got very nervous before my big scene* (= the one where I have a very important part). **4** 0-π [C] one of the small sections that a play or an OPERA is divided into: *Act I, Scene 2 of 'Macbeth'*
▸ AREA OF ACTIVITY **5** **the scene, the... scene** [sing.] (*informal*) a particular area of activity or way of life and the people who are part of it: *After years at the top, she just vanished from the scene.* ◇ *the* ***club/dance/music, etc. scene*** ◇ *A newcomer has appeared on the* ***fashion scene****.*
▸ VIEW **6** 0-π [C] a view that you see: *a delightful rural scene* ◇ *They went abroad for* ***a change of scene*** (= to see and experience new surroundings). ➲ SYNONYMS at VIEW
▸ PAINTING/PHOTOGRAPH **7** 0-π [C] a painting, drawing, or photograph of a place and the things that are happening there: *an exhibition of Parisian street scenes*
▸ ARGUMENT **8** [C, usually sing.] a loud, angry argument, especially one that happens in public and is embarrassing: *She had* ***made a scene*** *in the middle of the party.* ◇ *'Please leave,' he said. 'I don't want a scene.'*
IDM **behind the 'scenes** **1** in the part of a theatre, etc. that the public does not usually see: *The students were able to go behind the scenes to see how programmes are made.* **2** in a way that people in general are not aware of: *A lot of negotiating has been going on behind the scenes.* ◇ *behind-the-scenes work* **not sb's 'scene** (*informal*) not the type of thing that sb likes or enjoys doing **set the 'scene (for sth)** **1** to create a situation in which sth can easily happen or develop: *His arrival set the scene for another argument.* **2** to give sb the information and details they need in order to understand what comes next: *The first part of the programme was just setting the scene.*

ˌscene-of-ˈcrime *adj.* [only before noun] (*BrE*) relating to the part of the police service that examines the physical evidence of a crime that is present in the place where the crime was committed: *a scene-of-crime officer*

scen·ery /ˈsiːnəri/ *noun* [U] **1** the natural features of an area, such as mountains, valleys, rivers and forests, when you are thinking about them being attractive to look at: *The scenery is magnificent.* ◇ *to enjoy the scenery* ➲ SYNONYMS at COUNTRY **2** the painted background that is used to represent natural features or buildings on a theatre stage

scenic /ˈsiːnɪk/ *adj.* **1** [usually before noun] having beautiful natural scenery: *an area of scenic beauty* ◇ *They took the* ***scenic route*** *back to the hotel.* ◇ *a scenic drive* **2** [only before noun] connected with scenery in a theatre: *scenic designs* ▸ **scen·ic·al·ly** /-kli/ *adv.*: *scenically attractive areas*

scent /sent/ *noun, verb*
■ ***noun*** **1** [U, C] the pleasant smell that sth has: *The air was filled with the scent of wild flowers.* ◇ *These flowers have no scent.* **2** [U, C, usually sing.] the smell that a person or an animal leaves behind and that other animals such as dogs can follow SYN **trail**: *The dogs must have lost her scent.* **3** [U] (*especially BrE*) a liquid with a pleasant smell that you wear on your skin to make it smell nice: *a bottle of scent* **4** ~ **of sth** [sing.] the feeling that sth is present or is going to happen very soon: *The scent of victory was in the air.*
IDM **put/throw sb off the 'scent** to do sth to stop sb from finding you or discovering sth **on the 'scent (of sth)** close to discovering sth
■ ***verb*** **1** ~ **sth** to find sth by using the sense of smell: *The dog scented a rabbit.* **2** ~ **sth** to begin to feel that sth exists or is about to happen SYN **sense**: *The press could scent a scandal.* ◇ *By then, the team was scenting victory.* **3** [often passive] ~ **sth** (**with sth**) to give sth a particular, pleasant smell: *Roses scented the night air.*

scent·ed /ˈsentɪd/ *adj.* having a strong pleasant smell

scent·less /ˈsentləs/ *adj.* without a smell

scep·ter (*NAmE*) = SCEPTRE

scep·tic (*BrE*) (*NAmE* **skep·tic**) /ˈskeptɪk/ *noun* a person who usually doubts that claims or statements are true, especially those that other people believe in ➲ see also EURO-SCEPTIC

scep·tical (*BrE*) (*NAmE* **skep·tical**) /ˈskeptɪkl/ *adj.* ~ (**about/of sth**) having doubts that a claim or statement is true or that sth will happen: *I am sceptical about his chances of winning.* ◇ *The public remain sceptical of these claims.* ◇ *She looked highly sceptical.* ▸ **scep·tic·al·ly** (*BrE*) (*NAmE* **skep·tic·al·ly**) /-kli/ *adv.*

scep·ti·cism (*BrE*) (*NAmE* **skep·ti·cism**) /ˈskeptɪsɪzəm/ *noun* [U, sing.] an attitude of doubting that claims or statements are true or that sth will happen: *Such claims should be regarded with a certain amount of scepticism.*

sceptre (*US* **scep·ter**) /ˈseptə(r)/ *noun* a decorated ROD carried by a king or queen at ceremonies as a symbol of their power ➲ compare MACE, ORB

Schad·en·freude /ˈʃɑːdnfrɔɪdə/ *noun* [U] (from *German*) a feeling of pleasure at the bad things that happen to other people

sched·ule 0-π AW /ˈʃedjuːl; *NAmE* ˈskedʒuːl/ *noun, verb*
■ ***noun*** **1** 0-π [C, U] a plan that lists all the work that you have to do and when you must do each thing: *I have a hectic schedule for the next few days.* ◇ *We're working to a* ***tight schedule*** (= we have a lot of things to do in a short time). ◇ *Filming began* ***on schedule*** (= at the planned time). ◇ *The new bridge has been finished two years* ***ahead of schedule****.* ◇ *The tunnel project has already fallen* ***behind schedule****.* **2** 0-π [C] (*NAmE*) = TIMETABLE: *a train schedule* ◇ *Chinese will be on the school schedule from next year.* **3** [C] a list of the television and radio programmes that are on a particular channel and the times that they start: *The channel's schedules are filled with old films and repeats.* **4** [C] a written list of things, for example prices, rates or conditions: *tax schedules* ➲ note at AGENDA
■ ***verb*** **1** 0-π [usually passive] to arrange for sth to happen at a particular time: ~ **sth** (**for sth**) *The meeting is scheduled for Friday afternoon.* ◇ *One of the scheduled events is a talk on alternative medicine.* ◇ *We'll be stopping here for longer than scheduled.* ◇ ~ **sb/sth to do sth** *I'm scheduled to arrive in LA at 5 o'clock.* **2** ~ **sth** (**as sth**) (*formal*) to include sth in an official list of things: *The substance has been scheduled as a poison.* ▸ **sched·uler** *noun*: *The President's schedulers allowed 90 minutes for TV interviews.*

ˌscheduled ˈcaste *noun* (in India) a CASTE (= division of society) that is listed in the Eighth Schedule of the Indian Constitution and recommended for special help in education and employment

ˈscheduled flight *noun* a plane service that leaves at a regular time each day or week ➲ compare CHARTER FLIGHT

ˌscheduled ˈtribe *noun* (in India) a TRIBE that is listed in the Eighth Schedule of the Indian Constitution and recommended for special help in education and employment

schema /ˈskiːmə/ *noun* (*pl.* **sche·mas** or **sche·mata** /-mətə; skiːˈmɑːtə/) (*technical*) an outline of a plan or theory

sche·mat·ic AW /skiːˈmætɪk/ *adj.* **1** in the form of a diagram that shows the main features or relationships but not the details: *a schematic diagram* **2** according to a fixed plan or pattern: *The play has a very schematic plot.* ▸ **sche·mat·ic·al·ly** AW /-kli/ *adv.*: *The process is shown schematically in figure 3.*

S

sche·ma·tize (*BrE* also **-ise**) /ˈskiːmətaɪz/ *verb* **~ sth** (*technical*) to organize sth in a system: *schematized data*

scheme 🔑 AW /skiːm/ *noun, verb*

■ ***noun* 1** 🔑 (*BrE*) a plan or system for doing or organizing sth: *a training scheme* ◇ **~ (for doing sth)** *a local scheme for recycling newspapers* ◇ **~ (to do sth)** *to **introduce/operate a scheme** to improve links between schools and industry* ◇ *Under the new scheme only successful schools will be given extra funding.* ➲ see also COLOUR SCHEME, PENSION SCHEME **2** 🔑 a plan for getting money or some other advantage for yourself, especially one that involves cheating other people: *an elaborate scheme to avoid taxes*

IDM **the/sb's ˈscheme of things** the way things seem to be organized; the way sb wants everything to be organized: *My personal problems are not really important in the **overall scheme of things**.* ◇ *I don't think marriage figures in his scheme of things.*

■ ***verb* 1** [I, T] (*disapproving*) to make secret plans to do sth that will help yourself and possibly harm others SYN **plot**: **~ (against sb)** *She seemed to feel that we were all scheming against her.* ◇ **~ to do sth** *His colleagues, meanwhile, were busily scheming to get rid of him.* ◇ **~ sth** *Her enemies were scheming her downfall.* **2** [T] **~ sth** (*SAfrE, informal*) to think or form an opinion about sth: *What do you scheme?* ◇ *'Do you think he'll come?' 'I scheme so.'*

schemer /ˈskiːmə(r)/ *noun* (*disapproving*) a person who plans secretly to do sth for their own advantage

schem·ing /ˈskiːmɪŋ/ *adj.* (*formal*) often planning secretly to do sth for your own advantage, especially by cheating other people

the Schengen agreement /ˈʃeŋən əgriːmənt/ *noun* an agreement between the countries of the European Union to remove controls at their borders so that, for example, people can move freely from one country to another without needing to show their passports

scherzo /ˈskeətsəʊ; *NAmE* ˈskertsoʊ/ *noun* (*pl.* **-os**) (from *Italian*) a short, lively piece of music, that is often part of a longer piece

schil·ling /ˈʃɪlɪŋ/ *noun* the former unit of money in Austria (replaced in 2002 by the euro)

schism /ˈskɪzəm; ˈsɪzəm/ *noun* [C, U] (*formal*) strong disagreement within an organization, especially a religious one, that makes its members divide into separate groups ▶ **schis·mat·ic** /skɪzˈmætɪk; sɪzˈmætɪk/ *adj.*

schist /ʃɪst/ *noun* [U] a type of rock formed of layers of different minerals, that breaks naturally into thin flat pieces

schiz·oid /ˈskɪtsɔɪd/ *adj.* (*technical*) similar to or suffering from schizophrenia: *schizoid tendencies*

schizo·phre·nia /ˌskɪtsəˈfriːniə/ *noun* [U] a mental illness in which a person becomes unable to link thought, emotion and behaviour, leading to WITHDRAWAL from reality and personal relationships

schizo·phren·ic /ˌskɪtsəˈfrenɪk/ *noun, adj.*

■ ***noun*** a person who suffers from schizophrenia

■ ***adj.* 1** suffering from schizophrenia **2** (*informal*) frequently changing your mind about sth or holding opinions about sth that seem to oppose each other

schlep (also **schlepp**) /ʃlep/ *verb* (**-pp-**) (*informal, especially NAmE*) **1** [I] **+ adv./prep.** to go somewhere, especially if it is a slow, difficult journey, or you do not want to go **2** [T] **~ sth (+ adv./prep.)** to carry or pull sth heavy: *I'm not schlepping these suitcases all over town.* ORIGIN From Yiddish *shlepn*, 'to drag'. ▶ **schlep** (also **schlepp**) *noun* [sing.]

schlock /ʃlɒk; *NAmE* ʃlɑːk/ *noun* [U] (*NAmE, informal*) things that are cheap and of poor quality

schmaltz /ʃmɔːlts/ *noun* [U] (*informal, disapproving*) the quality of being too SENTIMENTAL ▶ **schmaltzy** *adj.* (**schmaltz·ier, schmaltzi·est**)

schmo (also **shmo**) /ʃməʊ; *NAmE* ʃmoʊ/ *noun* (*pl.* **-oes**) (*NAmE, informal, disapproving*) a person who is stupid or foolish in an annoying way

schmooze /ʃmuːz/ *verb* [I, T] **~ (with) sb** (*informal, especially NAmE*) to talk in an informal and friendly way with sb, especially in order to gain an advantage by persuading people to like you and do what you want SYN **chat** ▶ **schmooz·er** *noun*

schmuck /ʃmʌk/ *noun* (*informal, disapproving, especially NAmE*) a stupid person: *He's such a schmuck!*

schnapps /ʃnæps/ *noun* [U] (from *German*) a strong alcoholic drink made from grain

schnau·zer /ˈʃnaʊzə(r)/ *noun* a dog with short rough hair which forms curls

schnook /ʃnʊk/ *noun* (*NAmE, informal, disapproving*) a stupid or unimportant person

scholar /ˈskɒlə(r); *NAmE* ˈskɑːl-/ *noun* **1** a person who knows a lot about a particular subject because they have studied it in detail: *a classical scholar* ◇ *He was the most distinguished scholar in his field.* **2** a student who has been given a scholarship to study at a school, college or university: *a Rhodes scholar* **3** (*BrE, informal*) a clever person who works hard at school: *I was never much of a scholar.*

schol·ar·ly /ˈskɒləli; *NAmE* ˈskɑːlərli/ *adj.* **1** (of a person) spending a lot of time studying and having a lot of knowledge about an academic subject SYN **academic 2** connected with academic study SYN **academic**: *a scholarly journal*

schol·ar·ship /ˈskɒləʃɪp; *NAmE* ˈskɑːlərʃɪp/ *noun* **1** [C] an amount of money given to sb by an organization to help pay for their education: *She **won a scholarship** to study at Stanford.* ◇ *He went to drama school **on a scholarship**.* **2** [U] the serious study of an academic subject and the knowledge and methods involved SYN **learning**: *a magnificent work of scholarship*

scho·las·tic /skəˈlæstɪk/ *adj.* [only before noun] (*formal*) **1** connected with schools and education: *scholastic achievements* **2** connected with scholasticism

scho·las·ti·cism /skəˈlæstɪsɪzəm/ *noun* [U] a system of philosophy, based on religious principles and writing, that was taught in universities in the Middle Ages

school 🔑 /skuːl/ *noun, verb*

■ ***noun***

▸ WHERE CHILDREN LEARN **1** 🔑 [C] a place where children go to be educated: *My brother and I went to the same school.* ◇ (*formal*) *Which school do they attend?* ◇ *I'm going to the school today to talk to Kim's teacher.* ◇ *We need more money for roads, hospitals and schools.* ◇ *school buildings* **2** 🔑 [U] (used without *the* or *a*) the process of learning in a school; the time during your life when you go to a school: (*BrE*) *to **start/leave school*** ◇ (*NAmE*) *to **start/quit school*** ◇ *Where did you go to school?* ◇ (*BrE*) *All my kids are still **at school**.* ◇ (*NAmE*) *All my kids are still **in school**.* ◇ (*NAmE*) *to **teach school*** (= teach in a school) ◇ *The transition from school to work can be difficult.* ➲ COLLOCATIONS at EDUCATION **3** 🔑 [U] (used without *the* or *a*) the time during the day when children are working in a school: *Shall I meet you after school today?* ◇ *School begins at 9.* ◇ *The kids are **at/in school** until 3.30.* ◇ ***after-school** activities*

▸ STUDENTS AND TEACHERS **4** 🔑 **the school** [sing.] all the children or students and the teachers in a school: *I had to stand up in front of the whole school.*

▸ FOR PARTICULAR SKILL **5** 🔑 [C] (often in compounds) a place where people go to learn a particular subject or skill: *a **drama/language/riding, etc. school***

▸ COLLEGE/UNIVERSITY **6** 🔑 [C, U] (*NAmE, informal*) a college or university; the time that you spend there: *famous schools like Yale and Harvard* ◇ *Where did you go to school?* ➲ see also GRADUATE SCHOOL **7** 🔑 [C] a department of a college or university that teaches a particular subject: *the **business/medical/law school*** ◇ *the School of Dentistry*

▸ OF WRITERS/ARTISTS **8** [C] a group of writers, artists, etc. whose style of work or opinions have been influenced by the same person or ideas: *the Dutch school of painting*

▸ OF FISH **9** [C] a large number of fish or other sea animals, swimming together: *a school of dolphins* ➲ compare SHOAL HELP There are many compounds ending in **school**. You will find them at their place in the alphabet.

IDM **school(s) of ˈthought** a way of thinking that a number of people share: *There are two schools of thought about how this illness should be treated.* ➲ more at OLD

■ ***verb***

▸ YOURSELF/ANIMAL **1** (*formal*) to train sb/yourself/an animal to do sth: **~ sb/sth/yourself** (**in sth**) *to school a horse* ◇ *She had schooled herself in patience.* ◇ **~ sb/sth/yourself to do sth** *I have schooled myself to remain calm under pressure.* ▸ CHILD **2 ~ sb** (*formal*) to educate a child: *She should be schooled with her peers.*

British / American

at / in school

- In *BrE* somebody who is attending school is **at school**: *I was at school with her sister.* In *NAmE* **in school** is used: *I have a ten-year-old in school.* **In school** in *NAmE* can also mean 'attending a university'.

Grammar Point

school

- When a **school** is being referred to as an institution, you do not need to use *the*: *When do the children finish school?* When you are talking about a particular building, *the* is used: *I'll meet you outside the school.* **Prison**, **jail**, **court**, and **church** work in the same way: *Her husband spent three years in prison.*

➲ note at COLLEGE, HOSPITAL

ˈschool age *noun* [U] the age or period when a child normally attends school: *children of school age* ◇ *school-age children*

school·boy /ˈsku:lbɔɪ/ *noun* a boy who attends school ➲ SYNONYMS at STUDENT

school·child /ˈsku:ltʃaɪld/ *noun* (*pl.* **school·chil·dren** /-tʃɪldrən/) (also *informal* **school·kid**) a child who attends school ➲ SYNONYMS at STUDENT

school·days /ˈsku:ldeɪz/ *noun* [pl.] the period in your life when you go to school: *She hadn't seen Laura since her schooldays.*

ˈschool district *noun* (in the US) an area that contains several schools that are governed together

ˈschool friend (also *less frequent* **school·mate**) *noun* (*especially BrE*) a friend who attends or attended the same school as you: *She met up with some of her old* (= former) *school friends.*

school·girl /ˈsku:lgɜ:l; *NAmE* -gɜ:rl/ *noun* a girl who attends school ➲ SYNONYMS at STUDENT

school·house /ˈsku:lhaʊs/ *noun* **1** a school building, especially a small one in a village in the past **2** a house for a teacher next to a small school

schoolie /ˈsku:li/ *noun* (*AustralE*) a school student at the end of his or her time at school

ˈSchoolies Week (also **Schoolies**) *noun* [U] (in Australia) a time in November or December each year when Year 12 (final-year) school students celebrate leaving school by having a holiday/vacation in a town with a beach

school·ing /ˈsku:lɪŋ/ *noun* [U] (*formal*) the education you receive at school: *secondary schooling* ◇ *He had very little schooling.*

school·kid /ˈsku:lkɪd/ *noun* (*informal*) = SCHOOLCHILD

ˌschool-ˈleaver *noun* (*BrE*) a person who has just left school, especially when they are looking for a job: *the problem of rising unemployment among school-leavers*

school·marm /ˈsku:lmɑ:m; *NAmE* -mɑ:rm/ *noun* (*disapproving, especially NAmE*) a woman who teaches in a school, especially one who is old-fashioned and strict ▸ **school·marm·ish** *adj.*

school·mas·ter /ˈsku:lmɑ:stə(r); *NAmE* -mæs-/, **school·mis·tress** /ˈsku:lmɪstrəs/ *noun* (*old-fashioned, especially BrE*) a teacher in a school, especially a private school ➲ compare MASTER

school·mate /ˈsku:lmeɪt/ *noun* (*especially BrE*) = SCHOOL FRIEND

school·room /ˈsku:lru:m; -rʊm/ *noun* (*old-fashioned*) a classroom

the ˈschool run *noun* [sing.] (*BrE*) the journey that parents make to take their children to school or to bring them home again

school·teach·er /ˈsku:lti:tʃə(r)/ *noun* a person whose job is teaching in a school

school·work /ˈsku:lwɜ:k; *NAmE* -wɜ:rk/ *noun* [U] work that students do at school or for school: *She is struggling to keep up with her schoolwork.*

school·yard /ˈsku:ljɑ:d; *NAmE* -jɑ:rd/ *noun* (*NAmE*) an outdoor area of a school for children to play in ➲ compare PLAYGROUND

schooner /ˈsku:nə(r)/ *noun* **1** a sailing ship with two or more MASTS (= posts that support the sails) **2** a tall glass for SHERRY or beer

schtick, schtuck, schtum, schtup = SHTICK, SHTOOK, SHTUM, SHTUP

schwa (also **shwa**) /ʃwɑ:/ *noun* (*phonetics*) a vowel sound in parts of words that are not stressed, for example the 'a' in *about* or the 'e' in *moment*; the PHONETIC symbol for this, /ə/

sci·at·ic /saɪˈætɪk/ *adj.* [only before noun] (*anatomy*) of the hip or of the nerve which goes from the PELVIS to the THIGH (= the **sciatic nerve**)

sci·at·ica /saɪˈætɪkə/ *noun* [U] pain in the back, hip and outer side of the leg, caused by pressure on the sciatic nerve

sci·ence 🔑 /ˈsaɪəns/ *noun*
1 🔑 [U] knowledge about the structure and behaviour of the natural and physical world, based on facts that you can prove, for example by experiments: *new developments in science and technology* ◇ *the advance of modern science* ◇ *the laws of science* **2** 🔑 [U] the study of science: ***science students/teachers/courses*** **3** 🔑 [U, C] a particular branch of science: *to study one of the sciences* ➲ compare ART (6), HUMANITIES **4** [sing.] a system for organizing the knowledge about a particular subject, especially one concerned with aspects of human behaviour or society: *a science of international politics* ➲ see also DOMESTIC SCIENCE, EARTH SCIENCE, LIFE SCIENCES, NATURAL SCIENCE, POLITICAL SCIENCE, ROCKET SCIENCE, SOCIAL SCIENCE
IDM see BLIND *v.*

ˈscience fair *noun* (*NAmE*) a competition in which students at a school compete to present the best science project

ˌscience ˈfiction (also *informal* **ˈsci-fi**) (*abbr.* **SF**) *noun* [U] a type of book, film/movie, etc. that is based on imagined scientific discoveries of the future, and often deals with space travel and life on other planets

ˈscience park *noun* an area where there are a lot of companies or organizations involved in scientific research and development

S

sci·en·tif·ic 🔑 /ˌsaɪənˈtɪfɪk/ *adj.* [usually before noun]
1 🔑 involving science; connected with science: *a scientific discovery* ◇ *scientific knowledge* ◇ *sites of scientific interest* **2** (of a way of doing sth or thinking) careful and logical: *He took a very **scientific approach** to management.* ◇ *We need to be more scientific about this problem.* OPP **unscientific** ➲ compare NON-SCIENTIFIC ▸ **sci·en·tif·ic·al·ly** /-kli/ *adv.*

sci·en·tism /ˈsaɪəntɪzəm/ *noun* [U] **1** a way of thinking or expressing ideas that is considered to be typical of scientists **2** complete belief in scientific methods, or in the truth of scientific knowledge

sci·en·tist 🔑 /ˈsaɪəntɪst/ *noun*
a person who studies one or more of the NATURAL SCIENCES (= for example, physics, chemistry and biology): *a research scientist* ◇ *nuclear scientists* ◇ *scientists and engineers* ◇ *the cartoon figure of the mad scientist working in his*

Collocations

Scientific research

Theory

- **formulate/advance** a theory/hypothesis
- **build/construct/create/develop** a simple/theoretical/mathematical model
- **develop/establish/provide/use** a theoretical/conceptual framework
- **advance/argue/develop** the thesis that...
- **explore** an idea/a concept/a hypothesis
- **make** a prediction/an inference
- **base** a prediction/your calculations on sth
- **investigate/evaluate/accept/challenge/reject** a theory/hypothesis/model

Experiment

- **design** an experiment/a questionnaire/a study/a test
- **do** research/an experiment/an analysis
- **make** observations/measurements/calculations
- **carry out/conduct/perform** an experiment/a test/a longitudinal study/observations/clinical trials
- **run** an experiment/a simulation/clinical trials
- **repeat** an experiment/a test/an analysis
- **replicate** a study/the results/the findings
- **observe/study/examine/investigate/assess** a pattern/a process/a behaviour/(*especially US*) a behavior
- **fund/support** the research/project/study
- **seek/provide/get/secure** funding for research

Results

- **collect/gather/extract** data/information
- **yield** data/evidence/similar findings/the same results
- **analyse/examine** the data/soil samples/a specimen
- **consider/compare/interpret** the results/findings
- **fit** the data/model
- **confirm/support/verify** a prediction/a hypothesis/the results/the findings
- **prove** a conjecture/hypothesis/theorem
- **draw/make/reach** the same conclusions
- **read/review** the records/literature
- **describe/report** an experiment/a study
- **present/publish/summarize** the results/findings
- **present/publish/read/review/cite** a paper in a scientific journal

S

laboratory ➲ see also COMPUTER SCIENTIST, POLITICAL SCIENTIST, SOCIAL SCIENTIST

Sci·en·tol·ogy™ /ˌsaɪənˈtɒlədʒi; *NAmE* -ˈtɑːl-/ *noun* [U] a religious system based on getting knowledge of yourself and spiritual FULFILMENT through courses of study and training ▸ **sci·en·tolo·gist** *noun*

sci-fi /ˈsaɪ faɪ/ *noun* [U] (*informal*) = SCIENCE FICTION

scimi·tar /ˈsɪmɪtə(r)/ *noun* a short curved SWORD with one sharp edge, used especially in Eastern countries

scin·tilla /sɪnˈtɪlə/ *noun* [sing.] ~ (**of sth**) (*formal*) (usually in negative sentences) a very small amount of sth: *There is not a scintilla of truth in what she says.*

scin·til·lat·ing /ˈsɪntɪleɪtɪŋ/ *adj.* very clever, amusing and interesting: *a scintillating performance* ◇ *Statistics on unemployment levels hardly make for scintillating reading.*

scion /ˈsaɪən/ *noun* **1** (*formal* or *literary*) a young member of a family, especially a famous or important one **2** (*technical*) a piece of a plant, especially one cut to make a new plant

sci·rocco ➲ SIROCCO

ˈscissor kick (also **ˈscissors kick**) *noun* **1** (in swimming) a strong kick with the legs moving in opposite directions **2** (in football (SOCCER)) an action of kicking the ball while jumping sideways in the air

scis·sors 🔑 /ˈsɪzəz; *NAmE* ˈsɪzərz/ *noun* [pl.] a tool for cutting paper or cloth, that has two sharp blades with handles, joined together in the middle: *a pair of scissors* ➲ VISUAL VOCAB pages V17, V23 ➲ see also NAIL SCISSORS ▸ **scis·sor** *adj.* [only before noun]: *The legs move in a scissor action.*

sclera /ˈsklɪərə; *NAmE* ˈsklɪrə/ (-**rae** /-riː/ or -**ras** /-rəz; *NAmE* -lɪr-/) *noun* (*anatomy*) the white part of the eye ➲ VISUAL VOCAB page V48

scler·osis /skləˈrəʊsɪs; *NAmE* -ˈroʊ-/ *noun* [U] (*medical*) a condition in which soft TISSUE in the body becomes hard, in a way that is not normal ➲ see also MULTIPLE SCLEROSIS ▸ **scler·otic** /skləˈrɒtɪk; *NAmE* -ˈrɑːt-/ *adj.*

scoff /skɒf; *NAmE* skɔːf; skɑːf/ *verb* **1** [I, T] ~ (**at sb/sth**) | + **speech** to talk about sb/sth in a way that makes it clear that you think they are stupid or ridiculous SYN **mock**: *He scoffed at our amateurish attempts.* ◇ *Don't scoff—she's absolutely right.* **2** (*BrE*) (*NAmE* **scarf**) [T] ~ (**sth**) (*informal*) to eat a lot of sth quickly: *Who scoffed all the grapes?*

scoff·law /ˈskɒflɔː; *NAmE* ˈskɔːf-; ˈskɑːf-/ *noun* (*NAmE*, *informal*) a person who often breaks the law but in a way that is not very serious

scold /skəʊld; *NAmE* skoʊld/ *verb* [T, I] ~ **sb** (**for sth/for doing sth**) | (+ **speech**) (*formal*) to speak angrily to sb, especially a child, because they have done sth wrong SYN **rebuke**: *He scolded them for arriving late.* ▸ **scolding** *noun* [usually sing.]: *I **got a scolding** from my mother.*

scoli·osis /ˌskəʊliˈəʊsɪs; ˌskɒl-; *NAmE* ˌskoʊliˈoʊsɪs/ *noun* [U] (*medical*) a condition in which the SPINE is curved in a way that is not normal

scone /skɒn; skəʊn; *NAmE* skɑːn; skoʊn/ *noun* a small round cake, sometimes with dried fruit in it and often eaten with butter, jam and cream spread on it

scoop /skuːp/ *noun*, *verb*

■ ***noun* 1** [C] a tool like a large spoon with a deep bowl, used for picking up substances in powder form like flour, or for serving food like ice cream: *Use an ice-cream scoop.* ➲ VISUAL VOCAB page V23 **2** [C] the amount picked up by a scoop: *two scoops of mashed potato* **3** [C] a piece of important or exciting news that is printed in one newspaper before other newspapers know about it **4 the scoop** [U] (*NAmE*, *informal*) the latest information about sb/sth, especially details that are not generally known: *I got the inside scoop on his new girlfriend.*

■ ***verb* 1** to move or lift sth with a scoop or sth like a scoop: ~ **sth** (+ **adv./prep.**) *She scooped ice cream into their bowls.* ◇ *First, scoop a hole in the soil.* ◇ *Scoop out the melon flesh.* ◇ ~ **sth up** (+ **adv./prep.**) *He quickly scooped the money up from the desk.* **2** ~ **sb/sth** (**up**) (+ **adv./prep.**) to move or lift sb/sth with a quick continuous movement: *She scooped the child up in her arms.* **3** ~ **sb/sth** to publish a story before all the other newspapers, television companies, etc: *The paper had inside information and scooped all its rivals.* **4** ~ **sth** (*informal*) to win sth, especially a large sum of money or a prize: *He scooped £10 000 on the lottery.*

scooped /skuːpt/ (also **scoop**) *adj.* [only before noun] (of the neck of a woman's dress, etc.) cut low and round: *a **scooped neck/neckline***

scoot /skuːt/ *verb* [I] (+ **adv./prep.**) (*informal*) to go or leave somewhere in a hurry: *I'd better scoot or I'll be late.*

scoot·er /ˈskuːtə(r)/ *noun* **1** (*BrE*) (also ˈ**motor scooter** *NAmE*, *BrE*) a light motorcycle, usually with small wheels and a curved metal cover at the front to protect the rider's legs ➲ VISUAL VOCAB page V41 **2** a child's vehicle with two small wheels attached to a narrow board with a vertical handle. The rider holds the handle, puts one foot on the board and pushes against the ground with the other.

scope AW /skəʊp; *NAmE* skoʊp/ *noun*, *verb*

■ ***noun*** [U] **1** the opportunity or ability to do or achieve sth SYN **potential**: ~ (**for sth**) *There's still plenty of scope for improvement.* ◇ *Her job offers very **little scope** for promotion.* ◇ ~ (**for sb**) (**to do sth**) *The extra money will give us the scope to improve our facilities.* ◇ *First try to do something that is **within your scope**.* **2** the range of things that a subject, an organization, an activity, etc. deals with: *Our powers are limited **in scope**. ◇ This subject lies **beyond the scope of** our investigation. ◇ These issues were **outside the scope** of the article.* **3 -scope** (in nouns) an instrument for looking through or watching sth with: *microscope ◇ telescope*

■ ***verb*** **1 ~ sth** (*informal*) to look at or examine sth thoroughly: *His eyes scoped the room, trying to spot her in the crowd.* **2 ~ sth (out)** (*especially NAmE*) to examine sth carefully before you start work on it so that you know the size of the task: *The information helped us scope the project.*

PHR V **,scope sth↔'out** to look at sth carefully in order to see what it is like

scorch /skɔːtʃ; *NAmE* skɔːrtʃ/ *verb* **1** [T, I] **~ (sth) | ~ sth + adj.** to burn and slightly damage a surface by making it too hot; to be slightly burned by heat: *I scorched my dress when I was ironing it. ◇ Don't stand so near the fire—your coat is scorching!* ➲ SYNONYMS at BURN **2** [T, I] **~ (sth)** to become or to make sth become dry and brown, especially from the heat of the sun or from chemicals: *scorched grass ◇ The leaves will scorch if you water them in the sun.* **3** [I] **+ adv./prep.** (*BrE, informal*) to move very fast: *The car scorched off down the road.*

scorched 'earth policy *noun* (in a war) a policy of destroying anything in a particular area that may be useful to the enemy

scorch·er /'skɔːtʃə(r); *NAmE* 'skɔːrtʃ-/ *noun* (*informal*) **1** a very hot day **2** (*BrE*) (used mainly in newspapers) a very good stroke, shot, etc. in a sport: *a scorcher of a free kick*

scorch·ing /'skɔːtʃɪŋ; *NAmE* 'skɔːrtʃ-/ *adj.* (*informal*) **1** very hot SYN **baking** **2** (*especially BrE*) used to emphasize how strong, powerful, etc. sth is: *a scorching critique of the government's economic policy*

'scorch mark *noun* a mark made on a surface by burning

score 🔑 /skɔː(r)/ *noun, verb*

■ ***noun***

▸ POINTS/GOALS, ETC. **1** 🔑 [C] the number of points, goals, etc. scored by each player or team in a game or competition: *a **high/low score** ◇ What's the score now? ◇ **The final score** was 4–3. ◇ I'll **keep (the) score**.* **2** 🔑 [C] (*especially NAmE*) the number of points sb gets for correct answers in a test: *test scores ◇ an IQ score of 120 ◇ a perfect score*

▸ MUSIC **3** [C] a written or printed version of a piece of music showing what each instrument is to play or what each voice is to sing: *an orchestral score ◇ the score of Verdi's 'Requiem'* **4** [C] the music written for a film/movie or play: *an award for best original score*

▸ TWENTY **5** [C] (*pl.* **score**) a set or group of 20 or approximately 20: *Several cabs and a score of cars were parked outside. ◇ Doyle's success brought imitators **by the score*** (= very many). ◇ *the biblical age of three score years and ten* (= 70)

▸ MANY **6 scores** [pl.] very many: *There were scores of boxes and crates, all waiting to be checked and loaded.*

▸ CUT **7** [C] a cut in a surface, made with a sharp tool

▸ FACTS ABOUT SITUATION **8 the score** [sing.] (*informal*) the real facts about the present situation: ***What's the score?** ◇ You don't have to lie to me. I **know the score**.*

IDM **on 'that/'this score** as far as that/this is concerned: *You don't have to worry on that score.* ➲ more at EVEN *v.*, SETTLE *v.*

■ ***verb***

▸ GIVE/GET POINTS/GOALS **1** 🔑 [I, T] to win points, goals, etc. in a game or competition: *Fraser scored again in the second half. ◇* **~ sth** *to **score a goal/try/touchdown/victory*** **2** [I] to keep a record of the points, goals, etc. won in a game or competition: *Who's going to score?* **3** 🔑 [T, I] to gain marks in a test or an exam: **~ sth** *She scored 98% in the French test. ◇* **+ adv./prep.** *Girls usually score highly in language exams.* **4** [T] **~ sth** to give sth/sb a particular number of points: *The tests are scored by psychologists. ◇ Score each criterion on a scale of 1 to 5. ◇ a scoring system* **5** [T] **~ sth** to be worth a particular number of points: *Each correct answer will score two points.*

▸ SUCCEED **6** [T, I] to succeed; to have an advantage: **~ (sth)** *The army continued to score successes in the south. ◇ She's scored again with her latest blockbuster. ◇* **~ over sth** *Bicycles score over other forms of transport in towns.*

▸ ARRANGE/WRITE MUSIC **7** [T, usually passive] to arrange a piece of music for one or more musical instruments or for voices: **~ sth for sth** *The piece is scored for violin, viola and cello. ◇* **~ sth** *The director invited him to score the movie* (= write the music for it).

▸ CUT **8** [T] **~ sth** to make a cut or mark on a surface: *Score the card first with a knife.*

▸ HAVE SEX **9** [I] **~ (with sb)** (*slang*) (especially of a man) to have sex with a new partner: *Did you score last night?*

▸ BUY DRUGS **10** [T, I] **~ (sth)** (*slang*) to buy or get illegal drugs

IDM **,score a 'point/'points (off/against/over sb)** = SCORE OFF SB

PHR V **'score off sb** [no passive] (*especially BrE*) to show that you are better than sb, especially by making clever remarks, for example in an argument: *He was always trying to score off his teachers.* **,score sth↔'out/'through** to draw a line or lines through sth: *Her name had been scored out on the list.*

score·board /'skɔːbɔːd; *NAmE* 'skɔːrbɔːrd/ *noun* a large board on which the score in a game or competition is shown

score·card /'skɔːkɑːd; *NAmE* 'skɔːrkɑːrd/ *noun* a card or piece of paper that people watching or playing a game can use to write the score on, or on which the score can be officially recorded

'score draw *noun* (*BrE*) the result of a football (SOCCER) match in which both teams score the same number of goals

score·less /'skɔːləs; *NAmE* 'skɔːrləs/ *adj.* (of a game) without either team getting any points, goals, etc: *a scoreless draw*

score·line /'skɔːlaɪn; *NAmE* 'skɔːrl-/ *noun* (*BrE*) (used mainly in newspapers) the final score or result in a game, competition, etc: *a 2–1 scoreline ◇ The team did not play as badly as the scoreline suggests.*

scorer /'skɔːrə(r)/ *noun* **1** (in sports) a player who scores points, goals, etc: *United's **top scorer*** **2** a person who keeps a record of the points, goals, etc. scored in a game or competition **3 a high/low ~** a person who gets a high/low number of points in a test or exam

'score sheet *noun* (*BrE*) a piece of paper on which the score of a game can be officially recorded

IDM **get your name on the 'score sheet** (*informal*) (used in newspapers) to score a goal, etc.

scorn /skɔːn; *NAmE* skɔːrn/ *noun, verb*

■ ***noun*** [U] a strong feeling that sb/sth is stupid or not good enough, usually shown by the way you speak SYN **contempt**: *Her fellow teachers **greeted** her proposal **with scorn**. ◇* **~ for sb/sth** *They had nothing but scorn for his political views.*

IDM **pour/heap 'scorn on sb/sth** to speak about sb/sth in a way that shows that you do not respect them or have a good opinion of them

■ ***verb*** **1 ~ sb/sth** to feel or show that you think sb/sth is stupid and you do not respect them or it SYN **dismiss**: *She scorned their views as old-fashioned.* **2** (*formal*) to refuse to have or do sth because you are too proud: **~ sth** *to scorn an invitation ◇* **~ to do sth** *She would have scorned to stoop to such tactics.* IDM see HELL

scorn·ful /'skɔːnfl; *NAmE* 'skɔːrnfl/ *adj.* showing or feeling scorn SYN **contemptuous**: *a scornful laugh ◇* **~ of sth** *He was scornful of such 'female' activities as cooking.* ▸ **scorn·ful·ly** /-fəli/ *adv.*: *She laughed scornfully.*

Scor·pio /'skɔːpiəʊ; *NAmE* 'skɔːrpioʊ/ *noun* **1** [U] the 8th sign of the ZODIAC, the SCORPION **2** [C] (*pl.* **-os**) a person born when the sun is in this sign, that is between 23 October and 21 November, approximately

scor·pion /'skɔːpiən; *NAmE* 'skɔːrp-/ *noun* a small creature like an insect with six legs, two front CLAWS (= curved and pointed arms) and a long tail that curves over

S

its back and can give a poisonous sting. Scorpions live in hot countries. ➲ VISUAL VOCAB page V11

Scot /skɒt; *NAmE* skɑːt/ *noun* **1** a person from Scotland **2 the Scots** [pl.] the people of Scotland ➲ note at SCOTTISH

Scotch /skɒtʃ; *NAmE* skɑːtʃ/ *noun, adj.*
▪ ***noun* 1** [U] the type of WHISKY made in Scotland: *a bottle of Scotch* **2** [C] a glass of Scotch: *Do you want a Scotch?*
▪ ***adj.*** of or connected with Scotland ➲ note at SCOTTISH

scotch /skɒtʃ; *NAmE* skɑːtʃ/ *verb* **~ sth** to stop sth from happening; to take action to end sth: *Plans for a merger have been scotched.* ◇ *Rumours that he had fled the country were promptly scotched by his wife.*

ˌScotch ˈbonnet *noun* a type of very hot CHILLI

ˌScotch ˈbroth *noun* [U] (*BrE*) a thick soup containing vegetables and BARLEY (= a type of grain)

ˌScotch ˈegg *noun* (*BrE*) a boiled egg covered with SAUSAGE MEAT and BREADCRUMBS, fried and eaten cold

ˈScotch tape™ (*NAmE*) (*BrE* **Sel·lo·tape™**, **ˈsticky tape**) *noun* [U] clear plastic tape that is sticky on one side, used for sticking things together ➲ VISUAL VOCAB page V56

ˌscot-ˈfree *adv.* (*informal*) without receiving the punishment you deserve: *They **got off scot-free** because of lack of evidence.* ORIGIN This idiom comes from the old English word 'scot' meaning 'tax'. People were scot-free if they didn't have to pay the tax.

Scot·land Yard /ˌskɒtlənd ˈjɑːd; *NAmE* ˌskɑːtlənd ˈjɑːrd/ *noun* [U+sing./pl. v.] (in Britain) the main office of the London police, especially the department that deals with serious crimes in London: *Scotland Yard's anti-terrorist squad* ◇ *Scotland Yard has/have been called in.*

Scots /skɒts; *NAmE* skɑːts/ *adj., noun*
▪ ***adj.*** of or connected with Scotland, and especially with the English language as spoken in Scotland or the Scots language: *He spoke with a Scots accent.* ◇ *She comes from an old Scots family.*
▪ ***noun*** [U] a language spoken in Scotland, closely related to English but with many differences

Scot·tie /ˈskɒti; *NAmE* ˈskɑːti/ *noun* (*informal*) = SCOTTISH TERRIER

Scot·tish /ˈskɒtɪʃ; *NAmE* ˈskɑːtɪʃ/ *adj.* of or connected with Scotland or its people: *the Scottish Highlands* ◇ *Scottish dancing*

S

More About

describing things from Scotland

- The adjective **Scottish** is the most general word used to describe the people and things of Scotland, while **Scots** is only used to describe its people, its law and especially its language: *Scottish dancing* ◇ *the Scottish parliament* ◇ *a well-known Scots poet* ◇ *a slight Scots accent.*
- The adjective **Scotch** is now mainly used in fixed expressions such as *Scotch whisky* and *Scotch broth* and sounds old-fashioned or insulting if it is used in any other way.
- The noun **Scotch** means whisky, and the noun **Scots** refers to a language spoken in Scotland, closely related to English. A person who comes from Scotland is a **Scot**: *The Scots won their match against England.*

➲ note at BRITISH

the ˌScottish ˈNational Party *noun* [sing.+ sing./pl. v.] (*abbr.* **SNP**) a Scottish political party which wants Scotland to be an independent nation

the ˌScottish ˈParliament *noun* [sing.+ sing./pl. v.] the parliament elected by the people of Scotland which has powers to make its own laws in areas such as education and health

ˌScottish ˈterrier (also **Scot·tie**, *informal*) *noun* a small TERRIER (= type of dog) with rough hair and short legs

scoun·drel /ˈskaʊndrəl/ *noun* (*old-fashioned*) a man who treats other people badly, especially by being dishonest or immoral SYN **rogue**

scour /ˈskaʊə(r)/ *verb* **1 ~ sth** (**for sb/sth**) to search a place or thing thoroughly in order to find sb/sth SYN **comb**: *We scoured the area for somewhere to pitch our tent.* **2 ~ sth** (**out**) to clean sth by rubbing its surface hard with rough material: *I had to scour out the pans.* **3 ~ sth** (**away/out**) | **~ sth** (**from/out of sth**) to make a passage, hole, or mark in the ground, rocks, etc. as the result of movement, especially over a long period: *The water had raced down the slope and scoured out the bed of a stream.*

scour·er /ˈskaʊərə(r)/ (also **ˈscouring pad**) *noun* a small ball of wire or stiff plastic used for cleaning pans

scourge /skɜːdʒ; *NAmE* skɜːrdʒ/ *noun, verb*
▪ ***noun* 1** [usually sing.] **~** (**of sb/sth**) (*formal*) a person or thing that causes trouble or suffering: ***the scourge of war/disease/poverty*** ◇ *Inflation was the scourge of the 1970s.* **2** a WHIP used to punish people in the past
▪ ***verb* 1** [usually passive] **~ sb** (*literary*) to cause trouble or suffering to sb: *He lay awake, scourged by his conscience.* **2 ~ sb** (*old use*) to hit sb with a scourge SYN **whip**

Scouse /skaʊs/ *noun* (*BrE, informal*) **1** (also **Scouser** /ˈskaʊsə(r)/) [C] a person from Liverpool in NW England **2** [U] a way of speaking, used by people from Liverpool ▸ **Scouse** *adj.*: *a Scouse accent*

scout /skaʊt/ *noun, verb*
▪ ***noun* 1 the Scouts** [pl.] an organization (officially called the **Scout Association**) originally for boys, which trains young people in practical skills and does a lot of activities with them, for example camping: *to join the Scouts* **2** (*BrE*) a boy or girl who is a member of the Scouts: *Both my brothers were scouts.* ◇ *a scout troop* ➲ see also BOY SCOUT, GUIDE ➲ compare BROWNIE **3** a person, an aircraft, etc. sent ahead to get information about the enemy's position, strength, etc. **4** = TALENT SCOUT
▪ ***verb* 1** [T, I] to search an area or various areas in order to find or discover sth: **~ sth** (**for sb/sth**) *They scouted the area for somewhere to stay the night.* ◇ **~** (**around**) (**for sb/sth**) *The kids were scouting around for wood for the fire.* ◇ *a military scouting party* **2** [I, T] **~** (**sb**) to look for sports players, actors, musicians, etc. who have special ability, so you can offer them work: *He scouts for Manchester United.*
PHR V **ˌscout sth↔ˈout** to find out what an area is like or where sth is, by searching: *We went ahead to scout out the lie of the land.*

Scout·er /ˈskaʊtə(r)/ *noun* a person who is the leader of a group of scouts

scout·ing /ˈskaʊtɪŋ/ *noun* [U] the activities that boy and girl SCOUTS take part in; the Scout organization

scout·mas·ter /ˈskaʊtmɑːstə(r); *NAmE* -mæstər/ (also **ˈscout leader**) *noun* the adult in charge of a group of BOY SCOUTS

scowl /skaʊl/ *verb, noun*
▪ ***verb*** [I] **~** (**at sb/sth**) to look at sb/sth in an angry or annoyed way SYN **glower**
▪ ***noun*** an angry look or expression: *He looked up at me with a scowl.*

Scrab·ble™ /ˈskræbl/ *noun* [U] a board game in which players try to make words from letters printed on small plastic blocks and connect them to words that have already been placed on the board

scrab·ble /ˈskræbl/ *verb* [I] **~** (**around/about**) (**for sth**) | **+ adv./prep.** (*especially BrE*) to try to find or to do sth in a hurry or with difficulty, often by moving your hands or feet about quickly, without much control: *She scrabbled around in her bag for her glasses.* ◇ *He was scrabbling for a foothold on the steep slope.* ◇ *a sound like rats scrabbling on the other side of the wall*

scrag·gly /ˈskrægli/ *adj.* (*NAmE, informal*) thin and growing in a way that is not even: *a scraggly beard*

scraggy /ˈskrægi/ *adj.* (**scrag·gier**, **scrag·gi·est**) (*disapproving*) (of people or animals) very thin and not looking healthy SYN **scrawny**: *a scraggy old cat*

scram /skræm/ *verb* (-mm-) [I] (*old-fashioned, informal*) (usually used in orders) to go away quickly: *Scram! I don't want you here.*

scram·ble /ˈskræmbl/ *verb, noun*

■ ***verb***

▸ WALK/CLIMB **1** [I] **+ adv./prep.** to move quickly, especially with difficulty, using your hands to help you SYN **clamber**: *She managed to scramble over the wall.* ◇ *He* ***scrambled to his feet*** *as we came in.*

▸ PUSH/FIGHT **2** [I] to push, fight or compete with others in order to get or to reach sth: **~ for sth** *The audience scrambled for the exits.* ◇ **~ to do sth** *Shoppers were scrambling to get the best bargains.*

▸ ACHIEVE STH WITH DIFFICULTY **3** [T] to manage to achieve sth with difficulty, or in a hurry, without much control: **~ sth** *Cork scrambled a 1–0 win over Monaghan.* ◇ **~ sth + adv./prep.** *Rooney managed to scramble the ball into the net.*

▸ EGGS **4** [T, usually passive] **~ sth** to cook an egg by mixing the white and yellow parts together and heating them, sometimes with milk and butter: *scrambled eggs*

▸ TELEPHONE/RADIO **5** [T, often passive] **~ sth** to change the way that a telephone or radio message sounds so that only people with special equipment can understand it: *scrambled satellite signals*

▸ CONFUSE THOUGHTS **6** [T] **~ sth** to confuse sb's thoughts, ideas, etc. so that they have no order: *Alcohol seemed to have scrambled his brain.*

▸ AIRCRAFT **7** [T, I, usually passive] **~ (sth)** to order that planes, etc. should take off immediately in an emergency; to take off immediately in an emergency: *A helicopter was scrambled to help rescue three young climbers.* ◇ *They scrambled as soon as the call came through.*

■ ***noun***

▸ DIFFICULT WALK/CLIMB **1** [sing.] a difficult walk or climb over rough ground, especially one in which you have to use your hands

▸ PUSH/FIGHT **2** [sing.] **~ (for sth)** a situation in which people push, fight or compete with each other in order to get or do sth SYN **free for all**: *There was a mad scramble for the best seats.*

▸ MOTORCYCLE RACE **3** [C] a race for motorcycles over rough ground

scram·bler /ˈskræmblə(r)/ *noun* a device that changes radio or telephone signals or messages so that they cannot be understood by other people

scram·bling /ˈskræmblɪŋ/ *noun* [U] (*BrE*) = MOTOCROSS

scrap /skræp/ *noun, verb*

■ ***noun*** **1** [C] a small piece of sth, especially paper, cloth, etc: *She scribbled his phone number on a scrap of paper.* ◇ (*figurative*) *scraps of information* ◇ (*figurative*) *She was just a scrap of a thing* (= small and thin). **2** [sing.] (usually with a negative) a small amount of sth SYN **bit**: *It won't make a* ***scrap of difference.*** ◇ *There's not a scrap of evidence to support his claim.* ◇ *a barren landscape without a scrap of vegetation* **3 scraps** [pl.] food left after a meal: *Give the scraps to the dog.* **4** [U] things that are not wanted or cannot be used for their original purpose, but which have some value for the material they are made of: *We sold the car* ***for scrap*** (= so that any good parts can be used again). ◇ ***scrap metal*** ◇ *a* ***scrap dealer*** (= a person who buys and sells scrap) **5** [C] (*informal*) a short fight or disagreement SYN **squabble, scuffle**: *He was always getting into scraps at school.* ➲ see also SCRAPPY

■ ***verb*** (-pp-) **1** [T, often passive] **~ sth** to cancel or get rid of sth that is no longer practical or useful: *They had been forced to scrap plans for a new school building.* ◇ *The oldest of the aircraft were scrapped.* **2** [I] (*informal*) to fight with sb: *The bigger boys started scrapping.*

scrap·book /ˈskræpbʊk/ *noun* a book with empty pages where you can stick pictures, newspaper articles, etc.

scrape /skreɪp/ *verb, noun*

■ ***verb***

▸ REMOVE **1** [T] to remove sth from a surface by moving sth sharp and hard like a knife across it: **~ sth (+ adv./prep.)** *She scraped the mud off her boots.* ◇ **~ sth + adj.** *The kids had scraped their plates clean.*

▸ DAMAGE **2** [T] to rub sth by accident so that it gets damaged or hurt: **~ sth** *She fell and scraped her knee.* ◇ **~ sth + adv./prep.** *I scraped the side of my car on the wall.* ◇ *Sorry, I've scraped some paint off the car.* ◇ *The wire had scraped the skin from her fingers.*

▸ MAKE SOUND **3** [I, T] to make an unpleasant noise by rubbing against a hard surface; to make sth do this: (**+ adv./prep.**) *I could hear his pen scraping across the paper.* ◇ *We could hear her scraping away at the violin.* ◇ **~ sth (+ adv./prep.)** *Don't scrape your chairs on the floor.*

▸ WIN WITH DIFFICULTY **4** [T, I] **~ (sth)** to manage to win or to get sth with difficulty: *The team scraped a narrow victory last year.* ◇ (*BrE*) *I just scraped a pass in the exam.* ◇ *They* ***scraped a living*** *by playing music on the streets.* ◇ *The government* ***scraped home*** (= just won) *by three votes.*

▸ MAKE HOLE IN GROUND **5** [T] **~ sth (out)** to make a hole or hollow place in the ground: *He found a suitable place, scraped a hole and buried the bag in it.*

▸ PULL HAIR BACK **6** [T] **~ your hair back** to pull your hair tightly back, away from your face: *Her hair was scraped back from her face in a ponytail.*

IDM **scrape (the bottom of) the ˈbarrel** (*disapproving*) to have to use whatever things or people you can get, because there is not much choice available ➲ more at BOW[1] *v.*

PHR V ˌ**scrape ˈby (on sth)** to manage to live on the money you have, but with difficulty: *I can just scrape by on what my parents give me.* ˌ**scrape ˈin** | ˌ**scrape ˈinto sth** to manage to get a job, a position, a place at college, etc, but with difficulty: *He scraped in with 180 votes.* ◇ *Our team just scraped into the semi-finals.* ˌ**scrape sth↔ˈout** to remove sth from inside sth else, using sth sharp or hard like a knife: *Scrape out the flesh of the melon with a spoon.* ˌ**scrape ˈthrough** | ˌ**scrape ˈthrough sth** to succeed in doing sth with difficulty, especially in passing an exam: *I might scrape through the exam if I'm lucky.* ˌ**scrape sth↔toˈgether/ˈup** to obtain or collect together sth, but with difficulty: *We managed to scrape together eight volunteers.*

■ ***noun***

▸ ACTION/SOUND **1** [sing.] the action or unpleasant sound of one thing rubbing roughly against another: *the scrape of iron on stone*

▸ DAMAGE **2** [C] an injury or a mark caused by rubbing against sth rough: *She emerged from the overturned car with only a few scrapes and bruises.*

▸ DIFFICULT SITUATION **3** [C] (*old-fashioned*) a difficult situation that you have caused yourself: *He was always getting into scrapes as a boy.*

scraper /ˈskreɪpə(r)/ *noun* a tool used for scraping, for example for scraping mud from shoes or ice from a car

scrap·heap /ˈskræphiːp/ *noun* a pile of things, especially of metal, that are no longer wanted or useful

IDM **on the ˈscrapheap** (*informal*) no longer wanted or considered useful

scra·pie /ˈskreɪpi/ *noun* [U] a serious disease that affects the NERVOUS SYSTEM of sheep

scrap·ing /ˈskreɪpɪŋ/ *noun* [usually pl.] a small amount of sth produced by scratching a surface

ˈscrap paper *noun* [U] loose pieces of paper used for writing notes on

scrappy /ˈskræpi/ *adj.* (**scrap·pier, scrap·pi·est**) **1** consisting of individual sections, events, etc. that are not organized into a whole SYN **bitty**: *a scrappy essay* **2** (*especially BrE*) not tidy and often of poor quality: *The note was written on a scrappy bit of paper.* ➲ see also SCRAP *n.*

scrap·yard /ˈskræpjɑːd; *NAmE* -jɑːrd/ (*BrE*) (also **junk·yard** *NAmE, BrE*) *noun* a place where old cars, machines, etc. are collected, so that parts of them, or the metal they are made of, can be sold to be used again

scratch 0‒ᴡ /skrætʃ/ *verb, noun, adj.*

■ ***verb***

▸ RUB WITH YOUR NAILS **1** 0‒ᴡ [T, I] to rub your skin with your nails, usually because it is ITCHING: **~ sth/yourself** *John yawned and scratched his chin.* ◇ *The dog scratched itself be-*

S

hind the ear. ◇ **~** (**at sth**) *Try not to scratch.* ◇ *She scratched at the insect bites on her arm.*

▸ CUT SKIN **2** [T, I] to cut or damage your skin slightly with sth sharp: **~** (**sb/sth/yourself**) *I'd scratched my leg and it was bleeding.* ◇ *Does the cat scratch?* ◇ **~ sb/sth/yourself on sth** *She scratched herself on a nail.*

▸ DAMAGE SURFACE **3** [T] **~ sth** to damage the surface of sth, especially by accident, by making thin shallow marks on it: *Be careful not to scratch the furniture.* ◇ *The car's paintwork is badly scratched.*

▸ MAKE/REMOVE MARK **4** [T] **~ sth + adv./prep.** to make or remove a mark, etc. on sth deliberately, by rubbing it with sth hard or sharp: *They scratched lines in the dirt to mark out a pitch.* ◇ *We scratched some of the dirt away.* ◇ (*figurative*) *You can scratch my name off the list.*

▸ MAKE SOUND **5** [I] (**+ adv./prep.**) to make an irritating noise by rubbing sth with sth sharp: *His pen scratched away on the paper.*

▸ A LIVING **6** [T] **~ a living** to make enough money to live on, but with difficulty

▸ CANCEL **7** [T, I] to decide that sth cannot happen or sb/sth cannot take part in sth, before it starts: **~ sb/sth** *to scratch a rocket launch* ◇ **~ sb/sth** (**from sth**) *The horse was scratched from the race because of injury.* ◇ **~** (**from sth**) *She had scratched because of a knee injury.*

IDM **scratch your 'head** (**over sth**) to think hard in order to find an answer to sth **scratch the 'surface** (**of sth**) to deal with, understand, or find out about only a small part of a subject or problem **,you scratch 'my back and ,I'll scratch 'yours** (*saying*) used to say that if sb helps you, you will help them, even if this is unfair to others

PHR V **,scratch a'bout/a'round** (**for sth**) to search for sth, especially with difficulty **,scratch sth↔'out** to remove a word, especially a name, from sth written, usually by putting a line through it

■ ***noun***

▸ MARK/CUT **1** [C] a mark, a cut or an injury made by scratching sb's skin or the surface of sth: *Her hands were covered in scratches from the brambles.* ◇ *a scratch on the paintwork* ◇ *It's **only a scratch*** (= a very slight injury). ◇ *He escaped **without a scratch*** (= was not hurt at all).

▸ SOUND **2** [sing.] the unpleasant sound of sth sharp or rough being rubbed against a surface

▸ WITH YOUR NAILS **3** [sing.] the act of scratching a part of your body when it ITCHES: *Go on, have a good scratch!*

IDM **from 'scratch 1** without any previous preparation or knowledge: *I learned German from scratch in six months.* **2** from the very beginning, not using any of the work done earlier: *They decided to dismantle the machine and start again from scratch.* **up to 'scratch** as good as sth/sb should be SYN **satisfactory**: *His work simply isn't up to scratch.* ◇ *It'll take months to bring the band up to scratch.*

■ ***adj.*** (*BrE*) **1** put together in a hurry using whatever people or materials are available: *a scratch team* **2** (especially in GOLF) with no HANDICAP: *a scratch player*

'scratch card *noun* a card that you buy that has an area that you scratch off to find out if you have won some money or a prize

'scratch pad *noun* (*NAmE*) a small book of cheap paper for writing notes on

'scratch paper *noun* [U] (*NAmE*) cheap paper, or loose sheets of paper, for writing notes on

scratchy /'skrætʃi/ *adj.* (**scratch·ier, scratchi·est**) **1** (of clothes or cloth) rough and unpleasant to the touch SYN **itchy 2** (of a record, voice, etc.) making a rough, unpleasant sound like sth being scratched across a surface: *a scratchy recording of Mario Lanza* ◇ *a scratchy pen* **3** (of writing or drawings) done without care

scrawl /skrɔːl/ *verb, noun*

■ ***verb*** [T, I] to write sth in a careless untidy way, making it difficult to read SYN **scribble**: **~ sth** (**across/in/on/over sth**) *I tried to read his directions, scrawled on a piece of paper.* ◇ **~ across/in/on/over sth** *Someone had scrawled all over my notes.*

■ ***noun*** a careless untidy way of writing; sth written in this way SYN **scribble**: *Her signature was an illegible scrawl.* ◇ *I can't be expected to read this scrawl!* ◇ *The paper was covered in scrawls.*

scrawny /'skrɔːni/ *adj.* (**scrawn·ier, scrawni·est**) (*disapproving*) (of people or animals) very thin in a way that is not attractive SYN **scraggy**

scream /skriːm/ *verb, noun*

■ ***verb*** **1** [I, T] to give a loud, high cry, because you are hurt, frightened, excited, etc. SYN **shriek**: *He covered her mouth to stop her from screaming.* ◇ **~ in/with sth** *The kids were screaming with excitement.* ◇ **~ out** (**in/with sth**) *People ran for the exits, screaming out in terror.* ◇ **~ yourself + adj.** *The baby was screaming itself hoarse.* **2** [T, I] to shout sth in a loud, high voice because of fear, anger, etc. SYN **yell**: **+ speech** *'Help!' she screamed.* ◇ **~** (**out**) (**for sth/sb**) *Someone was screaming for help.* ◇ **~ at sb** (**to do sth**) *He screamed at me to stop.* ◇ **~ sth** (**out**) (**at sb**) *She screamed abuse at him.* ◇ **~** (**out**) **that...** *His sister screamed out that he was crazy.* ➲ SYNONYMS at SHOUT **3** [I] to make a loud, high noise; to move fast, making this noise SYN **screech**: *Lights flashed and sirens screamed.* ◇ **+ adv./prep.** *The powerboat screamed out to sea.*

IDM **scream blue 'murder** (*BrE*) (*NAmE* **scream bloody 'murder**) to scream loudly and for a long time, especially in order to protest about sth

PHR V **,scream 'out** (**for sth**) to be in need of attention in a very noticeable way SYN **call out**: *These books scream out to be included in a list of favourites.*

■ ***noun*** **1** [C] a loud high cry made by sb who is hurt, frightened, excited, etc; a loud high noise: *She let out a scream of pain.* ◇ *They ignored the baby's screams.* ◇ *He drove off with a scream of tyres.* **2** [sing.] (*old-fashioned, informal*) a person or thing that causes you to laugh: *He's a scream.*

scream·ing·ly /'skriːmɪŋli/ *adv.* extremely: *It was screamingly obvious what we should do next.*

scree /skriː/ *noun* [U, C] an area of small loose stones, especially on a mountain, which may slide when you walk on them ➲ VISUAL VOCAB page V4

screech /skriːtʃ/ *verb, noun*

■ ***verb*** **1** [I, T] to make a loud high unpleasant sound; to say sth using this sound: *Monkeys were screeching in the trees.* ◇ *The wind screeched in his ears.* ◇ *screeching brakes* ◇ *He screeched with pain.* ◇ **+ speech** *'No, don't!' she screeched.* ◇ **~** (**sth**) (**at sb**) *He screeched something at me.* **2** [I] (**+ adv./prep.**) (of a vehicle) to make a loud high unpleasant noise as it moves: *The car **screeched to a halt** outside the hospital.* ◇ *A police car screeched out of a side street.*

■ ***noun*** a loud high unpleasant cry or noise: *a **screech of brakes/tyres*** ◇ *She suddenly let out a screech.*

screed /skriːd/ *noun* a long piece of writing, especially one that is not very interesting

screen /skriːn/ *noun, verb*

■ ***noun***

▸ OF TV/COMPUTER **1** [C] the flat surface at the front of a television, computer, or other electronic device, on which you see pictures or information: *a computer screen* ◇ *a monitor with a 21 inch screen* ◇ *They were staring at the television screen.* ◇ *Move your cursor to the top of the screen.* ◇ *the screen display* ◇ *Can you do a printout of this screen for me* (= of all the information on it)? ➲ VISUAL VOCAB page V54 ➲ see also ON-SCREEN

▸ FILMS/MOVIES/TV **2** [C] the large flat surface that films/movies or pictures are shown on: *a **cinema/movie screen*** ◇ *an eight-screen cinema* ◇ *The movie will be coming to your screens shortly.* **3** (often **the screen**) [sing., U] films/movies or television in general: *He has adapted the play for the screen.* ◇ *Some actors never watch themselves **on screen**.* ◇ *She was a star of **stage and screen*** (= plays and films/movies). ◇ *a screen actor* ➲ see also OFF-SCREEN, SILVER SCREEN, SMALL SCREEN **4** [C] the data or images shown on a computer screen: *Press the F1 key to display a help screen.*

▸ PIECE OF FURNITURE **5** [C] a vertical piece of furniture or equipment that is fixed or that can be moved to divide a room or to keep one area hidden or separate: *The nurse put a screen around the bed.* ➲ see also FIRE SCREEN

▸ FOR HIDING/PROTECTING STH/SB **6** [C] **~** (**of sth**) something that prevents sb from seeing or being aware of sth, or that protects sb/sth: *We planted a screen of tall trees.* ◇ (*figurative*) *All the research was conducted behind a screen of secrecy.* ➲ see also SMOKESCREEN, SUNSCREEN, WINDSCREEN

▸ ON WINDOW/DOOR **7** [C] (*especially NAmE*) a wire or plastic net that is held in a frame and fastened on a window, or a door, to let in air but keep out insects: *screen doors*

▸ IN CHURCH **8** [C] a wood or stone structure in a church, that partly separates the main area from the ALTAR or CHOIR

IDM see RADAR

■ *verb*

▸ HIDE STH/SB **1** **~ sth/sb** (**from sth/sb**) to hide or protect sth/sb by placing sth in front of or around them SYN **shield**: *Dark glasses screened his eyes from the sun.*

▸ PROTECT SB **2** **~ sb from sb/sth** to protect sb from sth dangerous or unpleasant, especially to protect sb who has done sth illegal or dishonest SYN **shield**

▸ FOR DISEASE **3** [often passive] **~ sb** (**for sth**) to examine people in order to find out if they have a particular disease or illness: *Men over 55 should be regularly screened for prostate cancer.*

▸ CHECK **4** **~ sb** (of a company, an organization, etc.) to find out information about people who work or who want to work for you in order to make sure that they can be trusted: *Government employees may be screened by the security services.* **5** **~ sth** to check sth to see if it is suitable or if you want it: *I use my voicemail to screen my phone calls.*

▸ SHOW FILM/MOVIE/PROGRAMME **6** [usually passive] **~ sth** to show a film/movie, etc. in a cinema/movie theater or on television: *a list of films to be screened as part of the festival* ➲ COLLOCATIONS at TELEVISION

PHR V ˌ**screen sth↔ˈoff** [often passive] to separate part of a room, etc. from the rest of it by putting a screen around it: *Beds can be screened off to give patients more privacy.* ˌ**screen sb↔ˈout** to decide not to allow sb to join an organization, enter a country, etc. because you think they may cause trouble ˌ**screen sth↔ˈout** to prevent sth harmful from entering or going through sth: *The ozone layer screens out dangerous rays from the sun.*

ˈ**Screen Actors Guild** *noun* (*abbr.* SAG) (in the US) an organization that protects the interests of actors in films and television

ˈ**screen dump** *noun* a copy of what is on a computer screen at a particular time; the act of printing this out

screener /ˈskriːnə(r)/ *noun* a person who checks people and their luggage at an airport

screen·ing /ˈskriːnɪŋ/ *noun* **1** [C] the act of showing a film/movie or television programme: *This will be the movie's first screening in this country.* **2** [U, C] the testing or examining of a large number of people or things for disease, faults, etc: *breast cancer screening*

screen·play /ˈskriːnpleɪ/ *noun* the words that are written for a film/movie (= the SCRIPT), together with instructions for how it is to be acted and filmed ➲ COLLOCATIONS at CINEMA

ˈ**screen-print** *verb* [T, I] **~** (**sth**) to force ink or metal onto a surface through a screen of silk or artificial material to produce a picture ▸ ˈ**screen print** *noun*

ˈ**screen saver** *noun* a computer program that replaces a screen display on a computer with another, moving, display after a particular length of time, to stop the screen from being damaged

screen·shot /ˈskriːnʃɒt; *NAmE* -ʃɑːt/ *noun* (*computing*) an image of the display on a screen, used when showing how a program works

ˈ**screen test** *noun* a test to see if sb is suitable to appear in a film/movie

screen·writer /ˈskriːnraɪtə(r)/ *noun* a person who writes SCREENPLAYS ➲ compare PLAYWRIGHT, SCRIPTWRITER

screw 0-w /skruː/ *noun, verb*

■ *noun* **1** 0-w [C] a thin pointed piece of metal like a nail with a raised SPIRAL line (called a THREAD) along it and a line or cross cut into its head. Screws are turned and pressed into wood, metal, etc. with a SCREWDRIVER in order to fasten two things together: *One of the screws is loose.* ◇ *Now tighten all the screws.* ➲ COLLOCATIONS at DECORATE ➲ VISUAL VOCAB page V17 ➲ see also CORKSCREW **2** [C] an act of turning a screw **3** [sing.] (*taboo, slang*) an act of having sex **4** [sing.] (*taboo, slang*) a partner in sex: *a good screw* **5** [C] a PROPELLER on a ship, a boat or an aircraft **6** [C] (*BrE, slang*) a prison officer

IDM **have a ˈscrew loose** to be slightly strange in your behaviour **put the ˈscrews on** (**sb**) to force sb to do sth by frightening and threatening them ➲ more at TURN *n.*

■ *verb* **1** 0-w [T] **~ sth + adv./prep.** to fasten one thing to another or make sth tight with a screw or screws: *The bookcase is screwed to the wall.* ◇ *You need to screw all the parts together.* ◇ *Now screw down the lid.* ➲ compare UNSCREW **2** 0-w [T] to twist sth around in order to fasten it in place: **~ sth + adv./prep.** *She screwed the cap back on the jar.* ◇ **~ sth + adj.** *Screw the bolt tight.* ➲ compare UNSCREW **3** 0-w [I] (**+ adv./prep.**) to be attached by screwing: *The bulb should just screw into the socket.* ◇ *The lid simply screws on.* **4** [T] to squeeze sth, especially a piece of paper, into a tight ball: **~ sth up** (**into sth**) *I screwed up the letter and threw it into the fire.* ◇ **~ sth** (**up**) **into sth** *Screw the foil into a little ball.* ➲ see also SCREWED-UP **5** [T] (*slang*) to cheat sb, especially by making them pay too much money for sth: **~ sb** *We've been screwed.* ◇ **~ sb for sth** *How much did they screw you for* (= how much did you have to pay)? **6** [I, T] **~** (**sb**) (*taboo, slang*) to have sex with sb

IDM **screw ˈhim, ˈyou, ˈthat, etc.** (*taboo, slang*) an offensive way of showing that you are annoyed or do not care about sb/sth **screw up your ˈcourage** to force yourself to be brave enough to do sth: *I finally screwed up my courage and went to the dentist.* ➲ more at HEAD *n.*

PHR V ˌ**screw aˈround** (*taboo, slang*) to have sex with a lot of different people ˌ**screw sth ˈfrom/ˈout of sb** to force sb to give you sth: *They screwed the money out of her by threats.* ˌ**screw ˈup** (*slang, especially NAmE*) to do sth badly or spoil sth SYN **mess up**: *You really screwed up there!* ➲ related noun SCREW-UP ˌ**screw sb↔ˈup** (*slang*) to upset or confuse sb so much that they are not able to deal with problems in their life: *Her father's death really screwed her up.* ➲ see also SCREWED-UP ˌ**screw sth↔ˈup** **1** to fasten sth with screws: *to screw up a crate* **2** (*BrE*) to fasten sth by turning it: *I screwed up the jar and put it back on the shelf.* **3** (*slang*) to do sth badly or spoil sth: *Don't screw it up this time.* ➲ related noun SCREW-UP ˌ**screw your ˈeyes/ˈface↔up** to contract the muscles of your eyes or face because the light is too strong, you are in pain, etc: *He took a sip of the medicine and screwed up his face.*

screw·ball /ˈskruːbɔːl/ *noun* (*informal, especially NAmE*) a strange or crazy person

screw·cap /ˈskruːkæp/ *noun* a top for a container, especially a wine bottle, that screws onto it ▸ **screw·cap** *adj.* [only before noun]: *screwcap bottles/wine*

screw·driver /ˈskruːdraɪvə(r)/ *noun* **1** a tool with a narrow blade that is specially shaped at the end, used for turning screws ➲ VISUAL VOCAB page V17 **2** a COCKTAIL (= an alcoholic drink) made from VODKA and orange juice

ˌ**screwed-ˈup** *adj.* **1** (*informal*) upset and anxious, especially because of sth bad that has happened to you in the past: *an extremely screwed-up kid* **2** (*especially BrE*) twisted into a ball: *a screwed-up tissue* **3** if your face or eyes are **screwed-up**, the muscles are tight, because you are worried, in pain, etc, or because the light is too bright

ˈ**screw-top** (also ˈ**screw-topped**) *adj.* [only before noun] (of a container) having a top or lid that screws onto it ➲ VISUAL VOCAB page V29

ˈ**screw-up** *noun* (*pl.* **screw-ups**) (*slang*) an occasion when you do sth badly or spoil sth

screwy /ˈskruːi/ *adj.* (*informal*) strange or crazy

scrib·ble /ˈskrɪbl/ *verb, noun*

■ *verb* **1** [T, I] to write sth quickly and carelessly, especially because you do not have much time SYN **scrawl**: **~ sth** *He scribbled a note to his sister before leaving.* ◇ **~ sth down** *She scribbled down her phone number and pushed it into his*

S

hand. ◇ **~ (away)** *Throughout the interview the journalists scribbled away furiously.* **2** [I] (**+ adv./prep.**) to draw marks that do not mean anything: *Someone had scribbled all over the table in crayon.*

■ ***noun*** **1** [U, sing.] careless and untidy writing SYN **scrawl**: *How do you expect me to read this scribble?* **2** [C, usually pl.] marks or pictures that seem to have no meaning SYN **scrawl**: *The page was covered with a mass of scribbles.*

scrib·bler /ˈskrɪblə(r)/ *noun* **1** (*disapproving* or *humorous*) a journalist, author or other writer **2** (*CanE*) a book with plain paper for writing in, especially for children at school

scribe /skraɪb/ *noun* a person who made copies of written documents before printing was invented

scrim·mage /ˈskrɪmɪdʒ/ *noun* **1** a confused struggle or fight SYN **scrum** **2** (in AMERICAN FOOTBALL) a period of play that begins with the ball being placed on the ground **3** (*NAmE*) a practice game of AMERICAN FOOTBALL, BASKETBALL, etc.

scrimp /skrɪmp/ *verb* [I] to spend very little money on the things that you need to live, especially so that you can save it to spend on sth else: *They* ***scrimped and saved*** *to give the children a good education.*

scrip /skrɪp/ *noun* (*business*) an extra share in a business, given out instead of a DIVIDEND

script /skrɪpt/ *noun, verb*

■ ***noun*** **1** [C] a written text of a play, film/movie, broadcast, talk, etc: *That line isn't in the original script.* **2** [U] writing done by hand: *She admired his neat script.* ➲ see also MANUSCRIPT **3** [U, C] a set of letters in which a language is written SYN **alphabet**: *a document in Cyrillic script* **4** [C] (*BrE*) a candidate's written answer or answers in an exam **5** [U, C] (*computing*) a series of instructions for a computer, carried out in a particular order, for example when a link in a website is clicked: *The bug was caused by an error in the script.*

■ ***verb*** [often passive] **~ sth** to write the script for a film/movie, play, etc.

script·ed /ˈskrɪptɪd/ *adj.* read from a script: *a scripted talk* OPP **unscripted**

scrip·tor·ium /skrɪpˈtɔːriəm/ *noun* (*pl.* **scrip·tor·iums** or **scrip·toria** /-ˈtɔːriə/) (*old use*) a room for writing in, especially in a MONASTERY

scrip·ture /ˈskrɪptʃə(r)/ *noun* **1 Scripture** [U] (also **the Scriptures** [pl.]) the Bible **2 scriptures** [pl.] the holy books of a particular religion: *Hindu scriptures* ▶ **scrip·tural** /ˈskrɪptʃərəl/ *adj.*: *scriptural references*

S

script·writer /ˈskrɪptraɪtə(r)/ *noun* a person who writes the words for films/movies, television and radio plays ➲ compare PLAYWRIGHT, SCREENWRITER

scrof·ula /ˈskrɒfjʊlə; *NAmE* ˈskrɔːf-/ *noun* [U] (especially in the past) a disease in which the GLANDS swelled, probably a form of TUBERCULOSIS

scroll /skrəʊl; *NAmE* skroʊl/ *noun, verb*

■ ***noun*** **1** a long roll of paper for writing on **2** a decoration cut in stone or wood with a curved shape like a roll of paper

■ ***verb*** [I, T] (*computing*) to move text on a computer screen up or down so that you can read different parts of it: **+ adv./prep.** *Use the arrow keys to scroll through the list of files.* ◇ *Scroll down to the bottom of the document.* ◇ **~ sth** *Use the arrow keys to scroll the list of files.*

ˈ**scroll bar** *noun* (*computing*) a strip at the edge of a computer screen that you use to scroll through a file with, using a mouse ➲ VISUAL VOCAB page V55

Scrooge /skruːdʒ/ *noun* [usually sing.] (*informal, disapproving*) a person who is very unwilling to spend money ORIGIN From **Ebenezer Scrooge**, a character in Charles Dickens' *A Christmas Carol* who is extremely mean.

scrote /skrəʊt; *NAmE* skroʊt/ *noun* (*BrE, informal*) an insulting word for a man that you do not like or are angry with

scro·tum /ˈskrəʊtəm; *NAmE* ˈskroʊ-/ *noun* (*pl.* **scro·tums** or **scrota** /ˈskrəʊtə; *NAmE* ˈskroʊ-/) the bag of skin that contains the TESTICLES in men and most male animals

scrounge /skraʊndʒ/ *verb, noun*

■ ***verb*** [T, I] (*informal, disapproving*) to get sth from sb by asking them for it rather than by paying for it SYN **cadge**: **~ (sth) (off/from sb)** *He's always scrounging free meals off us.* ◇ **~ (for sth)** *What is she scrounging for this time?* ▶ **scroun·ger** *noun*: *a campaign against welfare scroungers*

■ ***noun***

IDM **on the ˈscrounge** (*BrE, informal, disapproving*) trying to get sth by persuading sb to give it to you

scrub /skrʌb/ *verb, noun*

■ ***verb*** (**-bb-**) **1** [T, I] to clean sth by rubbing it hard, perhaps with a brush and usually with soap and water: **~ sth/yourself** *I found him in the kitchen, scrubbing the floor.* ◇ **~ sth/yourself down** *She scrubbed the counters down with bleach.* ◇ **~ (at sth)** *The woman scrubbed at her face with a tissue.* ◇ **~ sth/yourself + adj.** *Scrub the vegetables clean.* **2** [T] **~ sth** (*informal*) to cancel sth that you have arranged to do

PHR V ˌ**scrub sth↔ˈoff** | **scrub sth off sth** to remove sth from the surface of an object by rubbing it hard with a brush, etc: *This treatment involves scrubbing off the top layer of dead skin.* ˌ**scrub sth↔ˈout** to clean the inside of sth by rubbing it hard with a brush and usually with soap and water ˌ**scrub ˈup** (of a doctor, nurse, etc.) to wash your hands and arms before performing a medical operation

■ ***noun*** **1** [sing.] an act of scrubbing sth: *I've given the floor a good scrub.* **2** [U] small bushes and trees: *The bird disappeared into the scrub.* **3** (also **scrub·land**) [U] an area of dry land covered with small bushes and trees **4 scrubs** [pl.] (*technical*) the special clothes worn by SURGEONS when they are doing medical operations

scrub·ber /ˈskrʌbə(r)/ *noun* **1** (*BrE, informal*) an offensive word for a PROSTITUTE or for a woman who has sex with a lot of men **2** a brush or other object that you use for cleaning things, for example pans

ˈ**scrubbing brush** (*BrE*) (*NAmE* ˈ**scrub brush**) *noun* a stiff brush for cleaning floors and other surfaces

scrubby /ˈskrʌbi/ *adj.* **1** covered with small bushes and trees: *a scrubby hillside* **2** (of trees) small and not fully developed: *scrubby vegetation*

scrub·land /ˈskrʌblənd/ *noun* [U] = SCRUB (3)

ˈ**scrub nurse** (*NAmE*) (*BrE* ˈ**theatre nurse**) *noun* a nurse with special training, who helps during operations

ˈ**scrub room** *noun* a place in a hospital next to an operating room/theatre, where doctors and nurses get ready for operations

scruff /skrʌf/ *noun* (*BrE, informal*) a dirty or untidy person

IDM **by the scruff of the/sb's ˈneck** roughly holding the back of an animal's or person's neck: *She grabbed him by the scruff of the neck and threw him out.*

scruffy /ˈskrʌfi/ *adj.* (**scruff·ier**, **scruffi·est**) (*informal*) dirty or untidy SYN **shabby**: *He looked a little scruffy.* ◇ *scruffy pair of jeans* ▶ **scruff·ily** *adv.* **scruffi·ness** *noun* [U]

scrum /skrʌm/ *noun* **1** (also *formal* **scrum·mage**) a part of a RUGBY game when players from both sides link themselves together in a group, with their heads down, and push against the other side. The ball is then thrown between them and each side tries to get it. **2** the group of players who link themselves together in a scrum **3** (*especially BrE*) a crowd of people who are pushing each other: *There was a real scrum when the bus arrived.*

ˌ**scrum ˈhalf** *noun* (in RUGBY) a player who puts the ball into the scrum

scrum·mage /ˈskrʌmɪdʒ/ *noun, verb*

■ ***noun*** (*formal*) = SCRUM

■ ***verb*** (also ˌ**scrum ˈdown**) [I] (*sport*) to form a SCRUM during a game of RUGBY

scrummy /ˈskrʌmi/ *adj.* (**scrum·mier**, **scrum·mi·est**) (*BrE, informal*) tasting very good SYN **delicious**: *a scrummy cake*

scrump·tious /ˈskrʌmpʃəs/ *adj.* (*informal*) tasting very good **SYN delicious**

scrumpy /ˈskrʌmpi/ *noun* [U] (*BrE*) a type of strong CIDER (= an alcoholic drink made from apples), made especially in the west of England

scrunch /skrʌntʃ/ *verb* **1** [I] to make a loud sound like the one that is made when you walk on GRAVEL (= small stones) **SYN crunch**: *The snow scrunched underfoot.* **2** [T] **~ sth (up)** to squeeze sth into a small round shape in your hands: *He scrunched up the note and threw it on the fire.* **3** [T] **~ sth (up)** to make sth become smaller: *The hedgehog scrunched itself up into a ball.* **4** [T] **~ sth** to create a HAIRSTYLE with loose curls by squeezing the hair with the hands ▶ **scrunch** *noun* [sing.]: *the scrunch of tyres on the gravel*

ˌscrunch-ˈdry *verb* **~ sth** to create a HAIRSTYLE with loose curls by drying the hair while squeezing it with your hand

scrunchy (also **scrunchie**) /ˈskrʌntʃi/ *noun* (*pl.* -ies) a RUBBER BAND covered in cloth used to fasten hair away from the face

scru·ple /ˈskruːpl/ *noun, verb*

■ ***noun*** [C, usually pl., U] a feeling that prevents you from doing sth that you think may be morally wrong: *I overcame my moral scruples.* ◇ *He* ***had no scruples about*** *spying on her.* ◇ *She is totally* ***without scruple***.

■ ***verb*** [I] **not scruple to do sth** (*formal*) to be willing to do sth even if it might be wrong or immoral

scru·pu·lous /ˈskruːpjələs/ *adj.* **1** careful about paying attention to every detail **SYN meticulous**: *You must be scrupulous about hygiene when you're preparing a baby's feed.* ◇ *scrupulous attention to detail* **2 ~ (in sth/in doing sth)** careful to be honest and do what is right: *He was scrupulous in all his business dealings.* **OPP unscrupulous** ▶ **scru·pu·lous·ly** *adv.*: *Her house is scrupulously clean.* ◇ *to be scrupulously honest* **scru·pu·lous·ness** *noun* [U]

scru·tin·eer /ˌskruːtəˈnɪə(r); *NAmE* -ˈnɪr/ *noun* (*BrE*) a person who checks that an election or other vote is organized correctly and fairly

scru·tin·ize (*BrE* also **-ise**) /ˈskruːtənaɪz/ *verb* **~ sb/sth** to look at or examine sb/sth carefully: *She leaned forward to scrutinize their faces.* ◇ *The statement was carefully scrutinized before publication.*

scru·tiny /ˈskruːtəni/ *noun* [U] (*formal*) careful and thorough examination **SYN inspection**: *Her argument doesn't really stand up to scrutiny.* ◇ *Foreign policy has* ***come under*** *close* ***scrutiny*** *recently.* ◇ *The documents should be available for* ***public scrutiny***.

scuba-diving /ˈskuːbə daɪvɪŋ/ (also **scuba**) *noun* [U] the sport or activity of swimming underwater using special breathing equipment consisting of a container of air which you carry on your back and a tube through which you breathe the air: *to go* ***scuba-diving*** ➲ VISUAL VOCAB page V34

scud /skʌd/ *verb* (-dd-) [I] **+ adv./prep.** (*literary*) (of clouds) to move quickly across the sky

scuff /skʌf/ *verb* **1 ~ sth (on sth)** to make a mark on the smooth surface of sth when you rub it against sth rough: *I scuffed the heel of my shoe on the stonework.* **2 ~ your feet, heels, etc.** to drag your feet along the ground as you walk ▶ **scuffed** *adj.*: *After only one day, his shoes were already scuffed and dirty.* **scuff** (also ˈ**scuff mark**) *noun*

scuf·fle /ˈskʌfl/ *noun, verb*

■ ***noun*** **~ (with sb)** | **~ (between A and B)** a short and not very violent fight or struggle: ***Scuffles broke out*** *between police and demonstrators.* ➲ SYNONYMS at FIGHT

■ ***verb*** **1** [I] **~ (with sb)** (of two or more people) to fight or struggle with each other for a short time, in a way that is not very serious: *She scuffled with photographers as she left her hotel.* **2** [I] **+ adv./prep.** to move quickly making a quiet rubbing noise: *Some animal was scuffling in the bushes.*

scuf·fling /ˈskʌflɪŋ/ *noun* [U] a low noise made by sth moving around: *He could hear whispering and scuffling on the other side of the door.*

scull /skʌl/ *noun, verb*

■ ***noun*** **1** [C, usually pl.] one of a pair of small OARS used by a single person ROWING a boat, one in each hand **2 sculls** [pl.] a race between small light boats with pairs of sculls: ***single/double sculls*** (= with one/two people in each boat) **3** [C] a small light boat used in sculls races

■ ***verb*** [I] to ROW a boat using sculls

scull·er /ˈskʌlə(r)/ *noun* a person who ROWS with sculls

scull·ery /ˈskʌləri/ *noun* (*pl.* -ies) a small room next to the kitchen in an old house, originally used for washing dishes, etc.

scull·ing /ˈskʌlɪŋ/ *noun* [U] the sport of racing with SCULLS

sculpt /skʌlpt/ *verb* [usually passive] **1** to make figures or objects by CARVING or shaping wood, stone, CLAY, metal, etc: **~ sth (in sth)** *a display of animals sculpted in ice* ◇ **~ sth (from/out of sth)** *The figures were sculpted from single blocks of marble.* ➲ COLLOCATIONS at ART **2 ~ sth** to give sth a particular shape: *a coastline sculpted by the wind and sea*

sculp·tor /ˈskʌlptə(r)/ *noun* a person who makes SCULPTURES

sculp·tress /ˈskʌlptrəs/ *noun* a woman who makes SCULPTURES ➲ note at GENDER

sculp·ture /ˈskʌlptʃə(r)/ *noun* **1** [C, U] a work of art that is a solid figure or object made by CARVING or shaping wood, stone, CLAY, metal, etc: *a marble sculpture of Venus* ◇ *He collects modern sculpture.* ➲ COLLOCATIONS at ART **2** [U] the art of making sculptures: *the techniques of sculpture in stone* ▶ **sculp·tural** /ˈskʌlptʃərəl/ *adj.*: *sculptural decoration*

sculp·tured /ˈskʌlptʃəd; *NAmE* -tʃərd/ *adj.* [usually before noun] **1** (of figures or objects) CARVED or shaped from wood, stone, CLAY, metal, etc. **2** (*approving*) (of part of the body) having a clear and pleasing shape: *sculptured cheekbones*

scum /skʌm/ *noun* **1** [U, sing.] a layer of bubbles or an unpleasant substance that forms on the surface of a liquid: *Skim off any scum.* ◇ *stinking water covered by a thick green scum* **2** [U, pl.] (*informal*) an insulting word for people that you strongly disapprove of: *Don't waste your sympathy on scum like that.* ◇ *Drug dealers are* ***the scum of the earth*** (= the worst people there are). ▶ **scummy** /ˈskʌmi/ *adj.*: *scummy water* ◇ *scummy people dropping litter*

scum·bag /ˈskʌmbæg/ *noun* (*slang, offensive*) an unpleasant person

scunge /skʌndʒ/ *noun* (*AustralE, NZE, informal*) **1** [U] dirt **2** [C] an unpleasant person **3** [C] a person who does not like to spend money

scungy /ˈskʌndʒi/ *adj.* (**scun·gier**, **scun·gi·est**) (*AustralE, NZE, informal*) **1** dirty and unpleasant **2** not liking to spend money

scup·per /ˈskʌpə(r)/ *verb* **~ sth** (*BrE, informal*) to cause sb/sth to fail **SYN foil**: *The residents' protests scuppered his plans for developing the land.*

scur·ril·ous /ˈskʌrələs; *NAmE* ˈskɜːr-/ *adj.* (*formal*) very rude and insulting, and intended to damage sb's reputation: *scurrilous rumours* ▶ **scur·ril·ous·ly** *adv.*

scurry /ˈskʌri; *NAmE* ˈskɜːri/ *verb* (**scur·ries**, **scurry·ing**, **scur·ried**, **scur·ried**) [I] **+ adv./prep.** to run with quick short steps **SYN scuttle**: *She said goodbye and scurried back to work.* ◇ *Ants scurried around the pile of rotting food.* ▶ **scurry** *noun* [sing.]

scurvy /ˈskɜːvi; *NAmE* ˈskɜːrvi/ *noun* [U] a disease caused by a lack of VITAMIN C from not eating enough fruit and vegetables

scut·tle /ˈskʌtl/ *verb, noun*

■ ***verb*** **1** [I] **+ adv./prep.** to run with quick short steps **SYN scurry**: *She scuttled off when she heard the sound of his voice.* ◇ *He held his breath as a rat scuttled past.* **2** [T] **~ sth** to deliberately cause sth to fail **SYN foil**: *Shareholders successfully scuttled the deal.* **3** [T] **~ sth** to sink a

S

ship deliberately by making holes in the side or bottom of it
■ ***noun*** = COAL SCUTTLE

scuttle·butt /ˈskʌtlbʌt/ *noun* [U] (*NAmE, slang*) stories about other people's private lives, that may be unkind or not true **SYN** **gossip**

scuzzy /ˈskʌzi/ *adj.* (**scuzz·ier, scuz·zi·est**) (*informal, especially NAmE*) dirty and unpleasant

Scylla and Cha·ryb·dis /ˌsɪlə ənd kəˈrɪbdɪs; *NAmE* also tʃəˈr-/ *noun* used to refer to a situation in which an attempt to avoid one danger increases the risk from another danger **ORIGIN** From ancient Greek stories in which a female sea creature (called Scylla) tried to catch and eat sailors who passed between her cave and a whirlpool (called Charybdis).

scythe /saɪð/ *noun, verb*
■ ***noun*** a tool with a long handle and a slightly curved blade, used for cutting long grass, etc.
■ ***verb*** [T, I] **~ (sth)** to cut grass, etc. with a scythe: *the scent of newly scythed grass*

SD card /ˌes ˈdiː kɑːd; *NAmE* kɑːrd/ *noun* the abbreviation for 'secure digital card' (= a type of MEMORY CARD, used with DIGITAL cameras, mobile/cell phones, music players, etc.)

SDHC card /ˌes diː eɪtʃ ˈsiː kɑːd; *NAmE* kɑːrd/ *noun* the abbreviation for 'secure digital high capacity card' (= a type of MEMORY CARD, that can store more data than an SD card)

the SDLP /ˌes diː el ˈpiː/ *abbr.* (in Northern Ireland) Social Democratic and Labour Party (a political party of the left that is supported mainly by Catholics)

SE *abbr.* south-east; south-eastern: *SE Asia*

sea 🔑 /siː/ *noun*
1 🔑 (often **the sea**) [U] (also *literary* **seas** [pl.]) (*especially BrE*) the salt water that covers most of the earth's surface and surrounds its continents and islands: *to travel **by sea*** ◇ *a cottage **by the sea*** ◇ *The waste was dumped **in the sea**.* ◇ *The wreck is lying at the bottom of the sea.* ◇ *We left port and headed for **the open sea*** (= far away from land). ◇ *the cold seas of the Arctic* ◇ *a sea voyage* ◇ *a hotel room with sea view* ➲ see also THE HIGH SEAS, OCEAN **2** 🔑 [C] (often **Sea**, especially as part of a name) a large area of salt water that is part of an ocean or surrounded by land: *the North Sea* ◇ *the Caspian Sea* ➲ **VISUAL VOCAB** page V4 **3** 🔑 [C] (also **seas** [pl.]) the movement of the waves of the sea: *It was a calm sea.* ◇ *The sea was very rough.* **4** [sing.] **~ of sth** a large amount of sth that stretches over a wide area: *He looked down at the sea of smiling faces before him.*
IDM **at ˈsea 1** 🔑 on the sea, especially in a ship, or in the sea: *It happened on the second night at sea.* ◇ *They were **lost at sea**.* **2** confused and not knowing what to do: *I'm **all at sea** with these new regulations.* **go to ˈsea** to become a sailor **out to ˈsea** far away from land where the sea is deepest: *She fell overboard and was swept out to sea.* **put (out) to ˈsea** to leave a port or HARBOUR by ship or boat ➲ more at DEVIL, FISH *n.*

British/American

sea / ocean

- In *BrE*, the usual word for the mass of salt water that covers most of the earth's surface is the **sea**. In *NAmE*, the usual word is the **ocean**: *A swimmer drowned in the sea/ocean this morning.*
- The names of particular areas of seas, however, are fixed: *the Mediterranean Sea* ◇ *the Atlantic Ocean*.
- **Sea/ocean** are also used if you go to the coast on holiday/vacation: *We're spending a week by the sea/at the ocean in June.* In *NAmE* it is also common to say: *We're going to the beach for vacation.*

➲ note at COAST

ˌsea ˈair *noun* [U] air near the sea/ocean, thought to be good for the health: *a breath of sea air*

ˈsea anemone *noun* a simple, brightly coloured sea creature that sticks onto rocks and looks like a flower

the sea·bed /ˈsiːbed/ *noun* [sing.] the floor of the sea/ocean

sea·bird /ˈsiːbɜːd; *NAmE* -bɜːrd/ *noun* a bird that lives close to the sea, for example on CLIFFS or islands, and gets its food from it ➲ **VISUAL VOCAB** page V10

sea·board /ˈsiːbɔːd; *NAmE* -bɔːrd/ *noun* the part of a country that is along its coast: *Australia's eastern seaboard*

sea·borg·ium /siːˈbɔːgiəm; *NAmE* -ˈbɔːrg-/ *noun* [U] (*symb.* Sg) a RADIOACTIVE chemical element. Seaborgium is produced when atoms COLLIDE (= crash into each other).

sea·borne /ˈsiːbɔːn; *NAmE* -bɔːrn/ *adj.* [only before noun] carried in ships: *a seaborne invasion*

ˌsea ˈbreeze *noun* a wind blowing from the sea/ocean towards the land

ˈsea change *noun* [usually sing.] a strong and noticeable change in a situation

ˌsea ˈcucumber *noun* an INVERTEBRATE animal that lives in the sea, with a thick body that is covered with lumps

ˈsea dog *noun* (*informal*) a sailor who is old or who has a lot of experience

sea·farer /ˈsiːfeərə(r); *NAmE* -fer-/ *noun* (*old-fashioned* or *formal*) a sailor

sea·far·ing /ˈsiːfeərɪŋ; *NAmE* -fer-/ *adj.* [only before noun] connected with work or travel on the sea/ocean: *a seafaring nation* ▸ **sea·far·ing** *noun* [U]

ˈsea fish *noun* (*pl.* **sea fish**) a fish that lives in the sea, rather than in rivers or lakes

sea·food /ˈsiːfuːd/ *noun* [U] fish and sea creatures that can be eaten, especially SHELLFISH: *a seafood restaurant* ◇ *a seafood cocktail*

ˈsea fret *noun* = FRET

sea·front /ˈsiːfrʌnt/ (often **the seafront**) *noun* [sing.] the part of a town facing the sea/ocean: *the grand houses along the seafront* ➲ **VISUAL VOCAB** page V4

sea·going /ˈsiːgəʊɪŋ; *NAmE* -goʊ-/ *adj.* [only before noun] (of ships) built for crossing the sea/ocean

sea·grass /ˈsiːgrɑːs; *NAmE* -græs/ *noun* [U] a plant like grass that grows in or close to the sea

ˌsea-ˈgreen *adj.* bluish-green in colour, like the sea ▸ **ˌsea ˈgreen** *noun* [U]

sea·gull /ˈsiːgʌl/ *noun* = GULL: *a flock of seagulls*

ˈsea horse *noun* a small sea fish that swims in a vertical position and has a head that looks like the head of a horse

seal 🔑 /siːl/ *verb, noun*
■ ***verb***
▸ CLOSE ENVELOPE **1** 🔑 **~ sth (up/down)** to close an envelope, etc. by sticking the edges of the opening together: *Make sure you've signed the cheque before sealing the envelope.* ◇ *a **sealed bid*** (= one that is kept in a sealed envelope and therefore remains secret until all other bids have been received)
▸ CLOSE CONTAINER **2** 🔑 [often passive] **~ sth (up) (with sth)** to close a container tightly or fill a crack, etc, especially so that air, liquid, etc. cannot get in or out: *The organs are kept in sealed plastic bags.*
▸ COVER SURFACE **3** [often passive] **~ sth (with sth)** to cover the surface of sth with a substance in order to protect it: *The floors had been stripped and sealed with varnish.*
▸ MAKE STH DEFINITE **4 ~ sth** to make sth definite, so that it cannot be changed or argued about: *to seal a contract* ◇ *They drank a glass of wine to seal their new friendship.* ◇ *The discovery of new evidence **sealed his fate*** (= nothing could prevent what was going to happen to him).
▸ CLOSE BORDERS/EXITS **5 ~ sth** (of the police, army, etc.) to prevent people from passing through a place: *Troops have*

sealed the borders between the countries. IDM see LIP, SIGN *v.*

PHR V **,seal sth↔'in** to prevent sth that is contained in sth else from escaping **'seal sth in sth** to put sth in an envelope, container, etc. and seal it: *The body was sealed in a lead coffin.* **,seal sth↔'off** 🔑 (of the police, army) to prevent people from entering a particular area

■ ***noun***

▸ OFFICIAL MARK **1** 🔑 [C] an official design or mark, stamped on a document to show that it is genuine and carries the authority of a particular person or organization: *The letter bore the president's seal.*

▸ MAKING STH DEFINITE **2** [sing.] a thing that makes sth definite: *The project has been given the government's* ***seal of approval*** (= official approval). ◇ *I looked upon the gift as a seal on our friendship.*

▸ ON CONTAINERS **3** 🔑 [C] a substance, strip of material, etc. used to fill a crack so that air, liquid, etc. cannot get in or out: *a jar with a rubber seal in the lid* ◇ *Only drink bottled water and check the seal isn't broken.*

▸ ON LETTERS/BOXES **4** [C] a piece of WAX (= a soft substance produced by BEES), soft metal or paper that is placed across the opening of sth such as a letter or box and which has to be broken before the letter or box can be opened: *He broke the wax seal and unrolled the paper.* **5** [C] a piece of metal, a ring, etc. with a design on it, used for stamping a WAX or metal seal

▸ SEA ANIMAL **6** [C] a sea animal that eats fish and lives around coasts. There are many types of seal, some of which are hunted for their fur: *a colony of seals* ◇ *grey seals basking on the rocks*

IDM **set the 'seal on sth** (*formal*) to make sth definite or complete: *Her election to the premiership set the seal on a remarkable political career.* **under 'seal** (*formal*) (of a document) in a sealed envelope that cannot be opened before a particular time

'sea lane *noun* an official route at sea that is regularly used by ships

seal·ant /'siːlənt/ (also **seal·er**) *noun* [U, C] a substance that is put onto a surface to stop air, water, etc. from entering or escaping from it

'sea legs *noun* [pl.] the ability to walk easily on a moving ship and not to feel sick at sea: *It won't take you long to find your sea legs.*

seal·er /'siːlə(r)/ *noun* **1** = SEALANT **2** a person who hunts SEALS

'sea level *noun* [U] the average height of the sea/ocean, used as the basis for measuring the height of all places on land: *50 metres above sea level*

sea·lift /'siːlɪft/ *noun* an operation to take people, soldiers, food, etc. to or from an area by ship, especially in an emergency ▸ **sea·lift** *verb* ➲ compare AIRLIFT

seal·ing /'siːlɪŋ/ *noun* [U] the activity of hunting SEALS

'sealing wax *noun* [U] a type of WAX that melts quickly when it is heated and becomes hard quickly when it cools, used in the past for SEALING letters, etc.

'sea lion *noun* a large SEAL (= a sea animal with thick fur, that eats fish and lives around the coast) that lives by the Pacific Ocean

seal·skin /'siːlskɪn/ *noun* [U] the skin and fur of some types of SEAL, used for making clothes

seam /siːm/ *noun* **1** a line along which two edges of cloth, etc. are joined or sewn together: *a shoulder seam* **2** a thin layer of coal or other material, between layers of rock under the ground: *They struck a* ***rich seam*** *of iron ore.* ◇ (*figurative*) *The book is a* ***rich seam of*** *information.* **3** a line where two edges meet, for example the edges of wooden boards

IDM **be bursting/bulging at the 'seams** (*informal*) to be very full, especially of people **be falling/coming apart at the 'seams** (*informal*) to be going very badly wrong and likely to stop functioning completely: *She was falling apart at the seams, spending most of her time in tears.* ➲ more at FRAY *v.*

sea·man /'siːmən/ *noun* (*pl.* **-men** /-mən/) a member of the navy or a sailor on a ship below the rank of an officer: *Seaman Bates* ◇ *a merchant seaman* ➲ see also ABLE SEAMAN, ORDINARY SEAMAN

sea·man·ship /'siːmənʃɪp/ *noun* [U] skill in sailing a boat or ship

seamed /siːmd/ *adj.* **1** having a seam or seams: *seamed stockings* **2** (*literary*) covered with deep lines: *an old man with a brown seamed face*

'sea mile *noun* = NAUTICAL MILE

seam·less /'siːmləs/ *adj.* **1** without a SEAM: *a seamless garment* **2** with no spaces or pauses between one part and the next: *a seamless flow of talk* ▸ **seam·less·ly** *adv.*

seam·stress /'siːmstrəs; 'sem-/ *noun* (*old-fashioned*) a woman who can sew and make clothes or whose job is sewing and making clothes

seamy /'siːmi/ *adj.* (**seam·ier**, **seami·est**) unpleasant and immoral SYN **sordid**: *a seamy sex scandal* ◇ *the* ***seamier side of*** *life*

se·ance /'seɪɒ̃s; *NAmE* 'seɪɑːns/ *noun* a meeting at which people try to make contact with and talk to the spirits of dead people

sea·plane /'siːpleɪn/ (*NAmE* also **hydro·plane**) *noun* a plane that can take off from and land on water ➲ VISUAL VOCAB page V43

sea·port /'siːpɔːt; *NAmE* -pɔːrt/ *noun* a town with a HARBOUR used by large ships: *the Baltic seaports*

'sea power *noun* **1** [U] the ability to control the seas with a strong navy **2** [C] a country with a strong navy

sear /sɪə(r); *NAmE* sɪr/ *verb* **1** [T] **~ sth** to burn the surface of sth in a way that is sudden and powerful: *The heat of the sun seared their faces.* ◇ *Sear the meat first* (= cook the outside of it quickly at a high temperature) *to retain its juices.* **2** [I, T] (*formal*) to cause sb to feel sudden and great pain: **+ adv./prep.** *The pain seared along her arm.* ◇ **~ sb** *Feelings of guilt seared him.* ➲ see also SEARING

search 🔑 /sɜːtʃ; *NAmE* sɜːrtʃ/ *noun, verb*

■ ***noun*** **1** 🔑 **~** (**for sb/sth**) an attempt to find sb/sth, especially by looking carefully for them/it: *a long search for the murder weapon* ◇ *Detectives carried out a thorough search of the building.* ◇ *She went into the kitchen* ***in search of*** (= looking for) *a drink.* ◇ *The search for a cure goes on.* ◇ ***The search is on*** (= has begun) *for someone to fill the post.* ◇ *Eventually the search was called off.* ◇ *a* ***search and rescue*** *team* **2** 🔑 (*computing*) an act of looking for information in a computer DATABASE or network: *to do a search on the Internet*

■ ***verb*** **1** 🔑 [I, T] to look carefully for sth/sb; to examine a particular place when looking for sb/sth: **~** (**for sth/sb**) *She searched in vain for her passport.* ◇ *Police searched for clues in the area.* ◇ **+ adv./prep.** *The customs officers searched through our bags.* ◇ *I've* ***searched high and low*** *for those files.* ◇ **~ sth** *His house had clearly been searched and the book was missing.* ◇ **~ sth for sth/sb** *Police searched the area for clues.* ◇ *Firefighters searched the buildings for survivors.* ◇ *searching the Web for interesting sites* **2** 🔑 [T] (especially of the police) to examine sb's clothes, their pockets, etc. in order to find sth that they may be hiding: **~ sb** *Visitors are regularly searched as they enter the building.* ◇ **~ sb for sth** *The youths were arrested and searched for anything that would incriminate them.* ➲ see also STRIP-SEARCH **3** 🔑 [I] **~** (**for sth**) to think carefully about sth, especially in order to find the answer to a problem: *He searched desperately for something to say.* ➲ see also SOUL-SEARCHING

IDM **,search 'me** (*informal*) used to emphasize that you do not know the answer to sb's question: *'Why didn't she say anything?' 'Search me!'*

PHR V **,search sth/sb↔'out** to look for sth/sb until you find them SYN **track down**: *Fighter pilots searched out and attacked enemy aircraft.*

search·able /'sɜːtʃəbl; *NAmE* 'sɜːrtʃ-/ *adj.* (of a computer DATABASE or network) having information organized in such way that it can be searched for using a computer: *a searchable database*

S

ˈ**search engine** *noun* a computer program that searches the Internet for information, especially by looking for documents containing a particular word or group of words

search·er /ˈsɜːtʃə(r); *NAmE* ˈsɜːrtʃ-/ *noun* **1** a person who is trying to find sth/sb **2** (*computing*) a program that helps you find information in a computer DATABASE or network; a search engine

search·ing /ˈsɜːtʃɪŋ; *NAmE* ˈsɜːrtʃ-/ *adj.* [usually before noun] (of a look, a question, etc.) trying to find out the truth about sth; thorough and serious: *a **searching investigation/analysis/examination*** ◇ *He gave her a long **searching look**.* ◇ *The police asked him some **searching questions**.* ▶ **search·ing·ly** *adv.*

search·light /ˈsɜːtʃlaɪt; *NAmE* ˈsɜːrtʃ-/ *noun* a powerful lamp that can be turned in any direction, used, for example, for finding people or vehicles at night

ˈ**search party** *noun* [C+sing./pl. v.] an organized group of people who are looking for a person or thing that is missing or lost

ˈ**search warrant** *noun* an official document that allows the police to search a building, for example to look for stolen property

sear·ing /ˈsɪərɪŋ; *NAmE* ˈsɪrɪŋ/ *adj.* [usually before noun] (*formal*) **1** so strong that it seems to burn you: *the searing heat of a tropical summer* ◇ *searing pain* **2** (of words or speech) powerful and critical: *a searing attack on the government* ▶ **sear·ing·ly** *adv.* ➲ see also SEAR

sea·scape /ˈsiːskeɪp/ *noun* a picture or view of the sea ➲ compare TOWNSCAPE

ˈ**sea shanty** *noun* (*BrE*) = SHANTY

sea·shell /ˈsiːʃel/ *noun* the shell of a small creature that lives in the sea, often found empty when the creature has died

sea·shore /ˈsiːʃɔː(r)/ (usually **the seashore**) *noun* [usually sing.] the land along the edge of the sea or ocean, usually where there is sand and rocks ➲ SYNONYMS at COAST ➲ VISUAL VOCAB page V4

sea·sick /ˈsiːsɪk/ *adj.* [not usually before noun] feeling ill/sick or wanting to VOMIT when you are travelling on a boat or ship: *to **be/feel/get seasick*** ▶ ˈ**sea·sick·ness** *noun* [U]

sea·side /ˈsiːsaɪd/ (often **the seaside**) *noun* [sing.] (*especially BrE*) an area that is by the sea, especially one where people go for a day or a holiday/vacation: *a trip to the seaside* ◇ *a day **at/by the seaside*** ➲ SYNONYMS at COAST ▶ **sea·side** *adj.* [only before noun]: *a seaside resort* ◇ *a seaside vacation home*

S

sea·son 🔑 /ˈsiːzn/ *noun, verb*

■ *noun* **1** 🔑 any of the four main periods of the year: spring, summer, autumn/fall and winter: *the changing seasons* **2 the dry/rainy/wet ~** a period of the year in tropical countries when it is either very dry or it rains a lot **3** 🔑 a period of time during a year when a particular activity happens or is done: *the **cricket/hunting/shooting, etc. season*** ◇ *He scored his first goal of the season on Saturday.* ◇ *The female changes colour during the **breeding season**.* ◇ *The hotels are always full during **the peak season*** (= when most people are on holiday/vacation). ◇ (*BrE*) *the **holiday season*** ◇ (*NAmE*) *the **tourist season*** ◇ (*NAmE*) *the **holiday season*** (= the time of Thanksgiving, Hanukkah, Christmas and New Year) ◇ (*BrE*) *the **festive season*** (= Christmas and New Year) ➲ see also CLOSE SEASON, HIGH SEASON, LOW SEASON, OFF SEASON, THE SILLY SEASON **4** a period of time in which a play is shown in one place; a series of plays, films/movies or television programmes: *The play opens for a second season in London next week.* ◇ *a season of films by Alfred Hitchcock* **5** a period of time during one year when a particular style of clothes, hair, etc. is popular and fashionable: *This season's look is soft and romantic.*

IDM **in** ˈ**season** **1** (of fruit or vegetables) easily available and ready to eat because it is the right time of year for them **2** (of a female animal) ready to reproduce SYN **on heat** **out of** ˈ**season** **1** (of fruit or vegetables) not easily available because it is not the right time of year for them **2** at the times of year when few people go on holiday/vacation: *Hotels are cheaper out of season.* **season's** ˈ**greetings** used at Christmas to wish sb an enjoyable holiday

■ *verb* [T, I] **~ (sth) (with sth)** to add salt, pepper, etc. to food in order to give it more flavour: *Season the lamb with garlic.* ◇ *Add the mushrooms, and season to taste* (= add as much salt, pepper, etc. as you think is necessary).

sea·son·able /ˈsiːznəbl/ *adj.* usual or suitable for the time of year: *seasonable temperatures* OPP **unseasonable**

sea·son·al /ˈsiːzənl/ *adj.* **1** happening or needed during a particular season; varying with the seasons: *seasonal workers brought in to cope with the Christmas period* ◇ *seasonal variations in unemployment figures* **2** typical of or suitable for the time of year, especially Christmas: *seasonal decorations* OPP **unseasonal** ▶ **sea·son·al·ly** /-nəli/ *adv.*: *seasonally adjusted unemployment figures* (= not including the changes that always happen in different seasons)

ˌ**seasonal afˈfective disorder** *noun* [U] (*abbr.* SAD) a medical condition in which a person feels sad and tired during late autumn/fall and winter when there is not much light from the sun

sea·son·al·ity /ˌsiːzəˈnæləti/ *noun* [U, sing.] (*technical*) the fact of varying with the seasons: *a high degree of climatic seasonality*

sea·soned /ˈsiːznd/ *adj.* **1** [usually before noun] (of a person) having a lot of experience of a particular activity: *a **seasoned campaigner/performer/traveller, etc.*** **2** (of food) with salt, pepper, etc. added to it: *The sausage was very **highly seasoned**.* **3** (of wood) made suitable for use by being left outside

sea·son·ing /ˈsiːzənɪŋ/ *noun* [U, C] a substance used to add flavour to food, especially salt and pepper

ˈ**season ticket** *noun* a ticket that you can use many times within a particular period, for example on a regular train or bus journey, or for a series of games, and that costs less than paying separately each time: ***an annual/a monthly/a weekly season ticket*** ◇ *a **season ticket holder***

seat 🔑 /siːt/ *noun, verb*

■ *noun*

▸ PLACE TO SIT **1** 🔑 a place where you can sit, for example a chair: *She sat back in her seat.* ◇ *He put his shopping on the seat behind him.* ◇ *Please **take a seat*** (= sit down). ◇ *Ladies and gentlemen, please **take your seats*** (= sit down). ◇ *a **window/corner seat*** (= one near a window/in a corner) ◇ *a **child seat*** (= for a child in a car) ◇ *Would you prefer a **window seat** or an **aisle seat**?* (= on a plane) ◇ *We used the branch of an old tree as a seat.* ◇ *We all filed back to our seats in silence.* ➲ SYNONYMS at SIT ➲ VISUAL VOCAB page V42 ➲ see also BACK SEAT, BUCKET SEAT, HOT SEAT, LOVE SEAT, PASSENGER SEAT

▸ -SEATER **2** (in nouns and adjectives) with the number of seats mentioned: (*BrE*) *a ten-seater minibus* ◇ *an all-seater stadium* (= in which nobody is allowed to stand)

▸ PART OF CHAIR **3** the part of a chair, etc. on which you actually sit: *a steel chair with a plastic seat*

▸ IN PLANE/TRAIN/THEATRE **4** 🔑 a place where you pay to sit in a plane, train, theatre, etc: *to **book/reserve a seat*** (= for a concert, etc.) ◇ *There are no seats left on that flight.*

▸ OFFICIAL POSITION **5** 🔑 an official position as a member of a parliament, council, committee, etc: *a seat on the city council/in Parliament/in Congress* ◇ *to **win/lose a seat*** (= in an election) ◇ (*BrE*) *to **take your seat*** (= to begin your duties, especially in Parliament) ◇ *The majority of seats on the board will be held by business representatives.* ➲ see also SAFE SEAT

▸ TOWN/CITY **6 ~ of sth** (*formal*) a place where people are involved in a particular activity, especially a city that has a university or the offices of a government: *Washington is the **seat of government** of the US.* ◇ *a university town renowned as a **seat of learning***

▸ COUNTRY HOUSE **7** (also ˌ**country** ˈ**seat**) (both *BrE*) a large house in the country, that belongs to a member of the upper class: *the family seat in Norfolk*

▸ PART OF BODY **8** (especially *formal*) the part of the body on which a person sits SYN **buttocks**
▸ PART OF TROUSERS/PANTS **9** the part of a pair of trousers/pants that covers a person's seat
IDM (**fly**) **by the seat of your 'pants** (*informal*) to act without careful thought and without a plan that you have made in advance, hoping that you will be lucky and be successful SYN **wing it be in the 'driving seat** (*BrE*) (*NAmE* **be in the 'driver's seat**) to be the person in control of a situation ➲ more at BACK SEAT, BUM *n.*, EDGE *n.*
■ *verb*
▸ SIT DOWN **1 ~ sb/yourself** (*formal*) to give sb a place to sit; to sit down in a place: *Please wait to be seated* (= in a restaurant, etc.). ◇ *Please* ***be seated*** (= sit down). ◇ *He seated himself behind the desk.* ➲ SYNONYMS at SIT
▸ OF BUILDING/VEHICLE **2 ~ sb** to have enough seats for a particular number of people: *The aircraft seats 200 passengers.*

'seat belt (also **'safety belt**) *noun* a belt that is attached to the seat in a car or a plane and that you fasten around yourself so that you are not thrown out of the seat if there is an accident: *Fasten your seat belts.* ➲ COLLOCATIONS at DRIVING ➲ VISUAL VOCAB page V42

seat·ing /'siːtɪŋ/ *noun* [U] places to sit; seats: *The theatre has seating for about 500 people.* ◇ *The room had a* ***seating capacity*** *of over 200.* ◇ *the* ***seating arrangements*** *for the conference*

seat·mate /'siːtmeɪt/ *noun* a person that you sit next to when you are travelling, especially on a plane

'sea turtle *noun* (*NAmE*) = TURTLE

'sea urchin (also **ur·chin**) *noun* a small sea creature with a round shell which is covered with SPIKES

,sea 'wall *noun* a large strong wall built to stop the sea from flowing onto the land

sea·ward /'siːwəd; *NAmE* -wərd/ *adj.* towards the sea; in the direction of the sea: *the seaward side of the coastal road* ▸ **sea·ward** (also **sea·wards** /-wədz; *NAmE* -wərdz/) *adv.*: *Her gaze was fixed seawards.*

'sea water *noun* [U] water from the sea or ocean, that is salty

sea·way /'siːweɪ/ *noun* a passage from the sea through the land along which large ships can travel

sea·weed /'siːwiːd/ *noun* [U, C] a plant that grows in the sea or ocean, or on rocks at the edge of the sea or ocean. There are many different types of seaweed, some of which are eaten as food. ➲ VISUAL VOCAB page V4

sea·worthy /'siːwɜːði; *NAmE* -wɜːrði/ *adj.* (of a ship) in a suitable condition to sail ▸ **sea·worthi·ness** *noun* [U]

se·ba·ceous /sɪ'beɪʃəs/ *adj.* [usually before noun] (*biology*) producing a substance like oil in the body: *the sebaceous glands in the skin*

seb·or·rhoea (*NAmE* **seb·or·rhea**) /ˌsebə'rɪə; *NAmE* -'riːə/ *noun* [U] a medical condition of the skin in which an unusually large amount of SEBUM is produced by the SEBACEOUS GLANDS ▸ **seb·or·rhoe·ic** (*NAmE* **seb·or·rhe·ic**) /ˌsebə'riːɪk/ *adj.*

sebum /'siːbəm/ *noun* [U] an oil-like substance produced by the SEBACEOUS GLANDS

Sec. (*US* also **Secy.**) *abbr.* SECRETARY

sec /sek/ *noun* **a sec** [sing.] (*informal*) a very short time; a second: *Stay there. I'll be back* ***in a sec.*** ◇ *Hang on* (= wait) *a sec.*

sec. *abbr.* second(s)

SECAM /'siːkæm/ *noun* [U] a television broadcasting system that is used in France and some other countries ➲ compare NTSC, PAL

seca·teurs /ˌsekə'tɜːz; *NAmE* -'tɜːrz/ *noun* [pl.] (*BrE*) a garden tool like a pair of strong scissors, used for cutting plant STEMS and small branches: *a pair of secateurs* ➲ VISUAL VOCAB page V16

se·cede /sɪ'siːd/ *verb* [I] **~** (**from sth**) (*formal*) (of a state, country, etc.) to officially leave an organization of states, countries, etc. and become independent: *The Republic of Panama seceded from Colombia in 1903.*

se·ces·sion /sɪ'seʃn/ *noun* [U, C] **~** (**from sth**) the fact of an area or group becoming independent from the country or larger group that it belongs to

se·ces·sion·ist /sɪ'seʃənɪst/ *adj.* [only before noun] supporting or connected with secession ▸ **se·ces·sion·ist** *noun*: *a military campaign against the secessionists*

se·clude /sɪ'kluːd/ *verb* **~ yourself/sb** (**from sb/sth**) (*formal*) to keep yourself/sb away from contact with other people

se·cluded /sɪ'kluːdɪd/ *adj.* **1** (of a place) quiet and private; not used or disturbed by other people: ***a secluded garden/beach/spot, etc.*** **2** without much contact with other people SYN **solitary**: *to lead a secluded life*

se·clu·sion /sɪ'kluːʒn/ *noun* [U] the state of being private or of having little contact with other people: *the seclusion and peace of the island*

sec·ond[1] 🔑 /'sekənd/ *det., ordinal number, adv., noun, verb* ➲ see also SECOND[2]
■ ***det., ordinal number*** **1** 🔑 happening or coming next after the first in a series of similar things or people; 2nd: *This is the second time it's happened.* ◇ *Italy scored a second goal just after half-time.* ◇ *the second of June/June 2nd* ◇ *He was the second to arrive.* ◇ *We have one child and are expecting our second in July.* **2** 🔑 next in order of importance, size, quality, etc. to one other person or thing: *Osaka is Japan's* ***second-largest*** *city.* ◇ *Birmingham, the UK's second city* ◇ *The spreadsheet application is* ***second only to*** *word processing in terms of popularity.* ◇ *As a dancer, he is* ***second to none*** (= nobody is a better dancer than he is). **3** 🔑 [only before noun] another; in addition to one that you already own or use: *They have a second home in Tuscany.*
■ ***adv.*** **1** 🔑 after one other person or thing in order or importance: *She* ***came second*** *in the marathon.* ◇ *One of the smaller parties* ***came a close second*** (= *nearly won*). ◇ *I agreed to speak second.* ◇ *He is a writer first and a scientist second.* ◇ *I came* ***second*** (***to***) ***last*** (= the one before the last one) *in the race.* **2** 🔑 used to introduce the second of a list of points you want to make in a speech or piece of writing SYN **secondly**: *She did it first because she wanted to, and second because I asked her to.* ➲ LANGUAGE BANK at FIRST, PROCESS
■ ***noun*** **1** 🔑 [C] (*symb.* ″) (*abbr.* **sec.**) a unit for measuring time. There are 60 seconds in one minute: *She can run 100 metres in just over 11 seconds.* ◇ ***For several seconds*** *he did not reply.* ◇ *The light flashes* ***every 5 seconds.*** ◇ *The water flows at about 1.5 metres* ***per second.*** **2** 🔑 [C] (also *informal* **sec**) a very short time SYN **moment**: *I'll be with you* ***in a second.*** ◇ *They had finished* ***in/within seconds.*** ➲ see also SPLIT SECOND **3** [C] (*symb.* ″) a unit for measuring angles. There are 60 seconds in one minute: *1° 6′ 10″* (= one degree, six minutes and ten seconds) **4 seconds** [pl.] (*informal*) a second amount of the same food that you have just eaten: *Seconds, anybody?* **5** [C, usually pl.] an item that is sold at a lower price than usual because it is not perfect **6** (also **,second 'gear**) [U] one of four or five positions of the gears in a vehicle: *When it's icy, move off* ***in second.*** **7** [C] a level of university degree at British universities. An **upper second** is a good degree and a **lower second** is average. ➲ compare FIRST *n.* (4), THIRD *n.* (2) **8** [C] a person whose role is to help and support sb else, for example in a BOXING match or in a formal DUEL in the past
IDM see JUST *adv.*, WAIT *v.*
■ ***verb*** **~ sth** to state officially at a meeting that you support another person's idea, suggestion, etc. so that it can be discussed and/or voted on: *Any proposal must be seconded by two other members of the committee.* ◇ (*informal*) *'Thank God that's finished.' 'I'll second that!* (= I agree)' ➲ compare PROPOSE

se·cond[2] /sɪ'kɒnd; *NAmE* -'kɑːnd/ *verb* [usually passive] **~ sb** (**from sth**) (**to sth**) (*especially BrE*) to send an employee to another department, office, etc. in order to do a different job for a short period of time: *Each year two teachers are seconded to industry for six months.* ➲ see also SECOND[1] ▸ **se·cond·ment** (*BrE*) *noun* [U, C]: *They met while she was* ***on secondment*** *from the Foreign Office.*

S

sec·ond·ary 0-w /'sekəndri; *NAmE* -deri/ *adj.* **1** 0-w less important than sth else: *That is just a* **secondary consideration**. ◇ *Experience is what matters—age is of* **secondary importance**. ◇ **~ to sth** *Raising animals was only secondary to other forms of farming.* **2** 0-w happening as a result of sth else: *a secondary infection* ◇ *a secondary effect* ◇ *a secondary colour* (= made from mixing two primary colours) **3** 0-w [only before noun] connected with teaching children of 11-18 years: *secondary teachers* ◇ *the secondary curriculum* ➲ compare ELEMENTARY, PRIMARY, TERTIARY ▸ **sec·ond·ar·ily** /'sekəndrəli; *NAmE* ˌsekən'derəli/ *adv.*: *Their clothing is primarily functional and only secondarily decorative.*

ˌsecondary eduˈcation *noun* [U] (*especially BrE*) education for children between the ages of 11 and 18: *primary and secondary education*

ˈsecondary industry *noun* [U, C] (*economics*) the section of industry that uses RAW MATERIALS to make goods ➲ compare PRIMARY INDUSTRY, TERTIARY INDUSTRY

ˌsecondary ˈmodern *noun* (in Britain until the 1970s) a school for young people between the ages of 11 and 16 who did not go to a GRAMMAR SCHOOL

ˌsecondary ˈpicketing *noun* [U] (*BrE*) the act of preventing workers who are not involved in a strike from supplying goods to the company where the strike is held

ˈsecondary school *noun* a school for young people between the ages of 11 and 16 or 18 ➲ compare PRIMARY SCHOOL, HIGH SCHOOL

ˈsecondary source *noun* a book or other source of information where the writer has taken the information from some other source and not collected it himself or herself ➲ compare PRIMARY SOURCE

ˌsecondary ˈstress *noun* [U, C] (*phonetics*) the second strongest stress that is put on a syllable in a word or a phrase when it is spoken ➲ compare PRIMARY STRESS

ˌsecond ˈbest *adj.* **1** not as good as the best: *The two teams seemed evenly matched but Arsenal* **came off second best** (= did not win). ◇ *my second-best suit* **2** not exactly what you want; not perfect: *a second-best solution* ▸ **ˌsecond ˈbest** *noun* [U]: *Sometimes you have to* **settle for** (= be content with) **second best**.

ˌsecond ˈchamber *noun* (*especially BrE*) = UPPER HOUSE

ˌsecond ˈclass *noun* [U] **1** a way of travelling on a train or ship that costs less and is less comfortable than FIRST CLASS. In Britain this is now usually called **standard class**. **2** (in Britain) the class of mail that costs less and takes longer to arrive than FIRST CLASS **3** (in the US) the system of sending newspapers and magazines by mail **4** [U, sing.] the second highest standard of degree given by a British university, often divided into upper second class and lower second class

ˌsecond-ˈclass *adj.* **1** (*disapproving*) (of a person) less important than other people: *Older people should not be treated as* **second-class citizens**. **2** of a lower standard or quality than the best: *a second-class education* **3** [only before noun] connected with the less expensive way of travelling on a train, ship, etc: **second-class carriages/compartments/passengers** **4** [only before noun] (in Britain) connected with letters, packages, etc. that you pay less to send and that are delivered less quickly: **second-class letters/stamps** **5** (in the US) connected with the system of sending newspapers and magazines by mail **6** [only before noun] used to describe a British university degree which is good but not of the highest class: *Applicants should have at least a second-class honours degree.* ▸ **ˌsecond ˈclass** *adv.*: *to send a letter second class* ◇ *to travel second class*

the ˌSecond ˈComing *noun* [sing.] a day in the future when Christians believe Jesus Christ will come back to earth

ˌsecond ˈcousin *noun* a child of a cousin of your mother or father

ˌsecond-deˈgree *adj.* [only before noun] **1 ~ murder, assault, burglary, etc.** (*especially NAmE*) murder, etc. that is less serious than FIRST-DEGREE crimes **2 ~ burns** burns of the second most serious of three kinds, causing BLISTERS but no permanent marks ➲ compare FIRST-DEGREE, THIRD-DEGREE

sec·ond·er /'sekəndə(r)/ *noun* a person who SECONDS a proposal, etc. (= supports it so that it can be discussed) ➲ compare PROPOSER

ˌsecond-geneˈration *adj.* **1** used to describe people who were born in the country they live in but whose parents came to live there from another country: *She was a second-generation Japanese-American.* **2** (of a product, technology, etc.) at a more advanced stage of development than an earlier form: *second-generation hand-held computers*

ˌsecond-ˈguess *verb* **1** [T] **~ sb/sth** to guess what sb will do before they do it: *It was impossible to second-guess the decision of the jury.* **2** [T, I] **~ (sb/sth)** (*especially NAmE*) to criticize sb after a decision has been made; to criticize sth after it has happened

ˈsecond hand *noun* the hand on some watches and clocks that shows seconds ➲ picture at CLOCK

ˌsecond-ˈhand *adj.* **1** not new; owned by sb else before: *a second-hand bookshop* (= for selling second-hand books) ◇ (*especially BrE*) *second-hand cars* **2** (often *disapproving*) (of news, information, etc.) learned from other people, not from your own experience: *second-hand opinions* ▸ **ˌsecond-ˈhand** *adv.*: *I bought the camera second-hand.* ◇ *I only heard about it second-hand.* ➲ compare FIRST-HAND

ˌsecond ˈhome *noun* **1** [C] a house or flat/apartment that sb owns as well as their main home and uses, for example, for holidays/vacations **2** [sing.] a place where sb lives and which they know as well as, and like as much as, their home

ˌsecond in comˈmand *noun* a person who has the second highest rank in a group and takes charge when the leader is not there

ˌsecond ˈlanguage *noun* a language that sb learns to speak well and that they use for work or at school, but that is not the language they learned first: *ESL or English as a Second Language*

ˌsecond ˈlanguage acquisition *noun* [U] (*abbr.* SLA) (*linguistics*) the learning of a second language

ˌsecond lieuˈtenant *noun* an officer of lower rank in the army or the US AIR FORCE just below the rank of a LIEUTENANT

ˌSecond ˈLife™ *noun* [U] (*abbr.* SL) a VIRTUAL WORLD on the Internet where people can communicate with each other, play games and pretend to live another life

sec·ond·ly /'sekəndli/ *adv.* used to introduce the second of a list of points you want to make in a speech or piece of writing: *Firstly, it's expensive, and secondly, it's too slow.*

ˈsecond name *noun* (*especially BrE*) **1** a family name or surname **2** a second personal name: *His second name is Willem, after his grandfather.*

ˌsecond ˈnature *noun* [U] **~ (to sb) (to do sth)** something that you do very easily and naturally, because it is part of your character or you have done it so many times

the ˌsecond ˈperson *noun* [sing.] (*grammar*) the form of a pronoun or verb used when addressing sb: *In the phrase 'you are', the verb 'are' is in the second person and the word 'you' is a second-person pronoun.* ➲ compare THE FIRST PERSON, THE THIRD PERSON

ˌsecond-ˈrate *adj.* not very good or impressive SYN **mediocre**: *a second-rate player*

ˌsecond ˈsight *noun* [U] the ability that some people seem to have to know or see what will happen in the future or what is happening in a different place

ˌsecond-ˈstring *adj.* [only before noun] (*especially NAmE*) (usually of a player in a sports team) only used occasionally where sb/sth else is not available: *a second-string quarterback* ▸ **ˌsecond ˈstring** *noun*: *Wilson was a second string for New Zealand in last week's match.*

S

ˌsecond ˈwind *noun* [sing.] (*informal*) new energy that makes you able to continue with sth that had made you tired

the ˌSecond ˌWorld ˈWar (also **ˌWorld ˌWar ˈTwo**) *noun* [sing.] the second large international war, that was fought between 1939 and 1945

se·crecy /ˈsiːkrəsi/ *noun* [U] the fact of making sure that nothing is known about sth; the state of being secret: *the need for absolute secrecy in this matter* ◇ *Everyone involved was* ***sworn to secrecy.*** ◇ *The whole affair is still* ***shrouded in secrecy.***

se·cret 🔑 /ˈsiːkrət/ *adj., noun*

■ ***adj.*** **1** 🔑 known about by only a few people; kept hidden from others: ***secret information/meetings/talks*** ◇ **~ (from sb)** *He tried to* ***keep it secret*** *from his family.* ◇ *Details of the proposals remain secret.* ◇ *a secret passage leading to the beach* ➲ see also TOP SECRET **2** 🔑 [only before noun] used to describe actions and behaviour that you do not tell other people about: *He's a secret drinker.* ◇ *her secret fears* ◇ *a secret room* **3** [not usually before noun] **~ (about sth)** (of a person or their behaviour) liking to have secrets that other people do not know about; showing this SYN **secretive**: *They were so secret about everything.* ◇ *Jessica caught a secret smile flitting between the two of them.* ▶ **se·cret·ly** 🔑 *adv.*: *The police had secretly filmed the conversations.* ◇ *She was secretly pleased to see him.*

■ ***noun*** **1** 🔑 [C] something that is known about by only a few people and not told to others: *Can you* ***keep a secret?*** ◇ *The location of the ship is* ***a closely guarded secret.*** ◇ *Shall we* ***let him in on*** (= tell him) ***the secret?*** ◇ *He* ***made no secret of*** *his ambition* (= he didn't try to hide it). ◇ *She was dismissed for revealing trade secrets.* ◇ ***official/State secrets*** **2** 🔑 (usually **the secret**) [sing.] the best or only way to achieve sth; the way a particular person achieves sth: *Careful planning is the secret of success.* ◇ *She still looks so young. What's her secret?* **3** [C, usually pl.] a thing that is not yet fully understood or that is difficult to understand: *the secrets of the universe*

IDM **in ˈsecret** 🔑 without other people knowing about it: *The meeting was held in secret.* ➲ more at GUILTY *adj.*, OPEN *adj.*

ˌsecret ˈagent (also **agent**) *noun* a person who is used by a government to find out secret information about other countries or governments SYN **spy**

sec·re·tar·ial /ˌsekrəˈteəriəl; *NAmE* -ˈter-/ *adj.* involving or connected with the work of a secretary: *secretarial work*

sec·re·tar·iat /ˌsekrəˈteəriət; -iæt; *NAmE* -ˈter-/ *noun* the department of a large international or political organization which is responsible for running it, especially the office of a SECRETARY GENERAL

sec·re·tary 🔑 /ˈsekrətri; *NAmE* -teri/ *noun* (*pl.* **-ies**) (*abbr.* **Sec.**)

1 🔑 a person who works in an office, working for another person, dealing with letters and telephone calls, typing, keeping records, arranging meetings with people, etc: *a* ***legal/medical secretary*** ◇ *Please contact my secretary to make an appointment.* ➲ see also PRIVATE SECRETARY **2** 🔑 an official of a club, society, etc. who deals with writing letters, keeping records, and making business arrangements: *the membership secretary* **3 Secretary** = SECRETARY OF STATE ➲ see also HOME SECRETARY, PERMANENT UNDERSECRETARY **4** 🔑 (*US*) the head of a government department, chosen by the President: *Secretary of the Treasury* **5** 🔑 (in Britain) an assistant of a government minister, an AMBASSADOR, etc. ➲ see also UNDERSECRETARY

ˌSecretary ˈGeneral *noun* the person who is in charge of the department that deals with the running of a large international or political organization: *the former Secretary General of NATO*

ˌSecretary of ˈState *noun* **1** (also **Sec·re·tary**) (in Britain) the head of an important government department: *the Secretary of State for Education* ◇ *the Education Secretary* ◇ *the Foreign Secretary* **2** (in the US) the head of the government department that deals with foreign affairs

se·crete /sɪˈkriːt/ *verb* **1 ~ sth** (of part of the body or a plant) to produce a liquid substance: *Insulin is secreted by the pancreas.* **2 ~ sth (in sth)** (*formal*) to hide sth, especially sth small: *The drugs were secreted in the lining of his case.*

se·cre·tion /sɪˈkriːʃn/ *noun* (*technical*) **1** [U] the process by which liquid substances are produced by parts of the body or plants: *the secretion of bile by the liver* **2** [C, usually pl.] a liquid substance produced by parts of the body or plants: *bodily secretions*

se·cret·ive /ˈsiːkrətɪv/ *adj.* **~ (about sth)** tending or liking to hide your thoughts, feelings, ideas, etc. from other people: *He's very secretive about his work.* ▶ **se·cret·ive·ly** *adv.* **se·cret·ive·ness** *noun* [U]

ˌsecret poˈlice *noun* [sing.+ sing./pl. v.] a police force that works secretly to make sure that citizens behave as their government wants

ˌsecret ˈservice *noun* [usually sing.] a government department that is responsible for protecting its government's military and political secrets and for finding out the secrets of other governments

sect /sekt/ *noun* (sometimes *disapproving*) a small group of people who belong to a particular religion but who have some beliefs or practices which separate them from the rest of the group

sect·ar·ian /sekˈteəriən; *NAmE* -ˈter-/ *adj.* [usually before noun] (often *disapproving*) connected with the differences that exist between groups of people who have different religious views: ***sectarian attacks/violence*** ◇ *attempts to break down the* ***sectarian divide*** *in Northern Ireland*

sect·ar·ian·ism /sekˈteəriənɪzəm; *NAmE* -ˈter-/ *noun* [U] (often *disapproving*) strong support for one particular religious or political group, especially when this leads to violence between different groups

sec·tion 🔑 AW /ˈsekʃn/ *noun, verb*

■ ***noun***

▸ PART/PIECE **1** 🔑 [C] any of the parts into which sth is divided: *That section of the road is still closed.* ◇ *The library has a large biology section.* ◇ *the tail section of the plane* **2** 🔑 [C] a separate part of a structure from which the whole can be put together: *The shed comes in sections that you assemble yourself.*

▸ OF DOCUMENT/BOOK **3** 🔑 [C] a separate part of a document, book, etc: *These issues will be discussed more fully in the next section.* ◇ *the sports section of the newspaper*

▸ GROUP OF PEOPLE **4** 🔑 [C] a separate group within a larger group of people: *an issue that will affect large sections of the population* ◇ *the brass section of an orchestra* ➲ see also RHYTHM SECTION

▸ OF ORGANIZATION **5** [C] a department in an organization, institution, etc. SYN **division**: *He's the director of the finance section.*

▸ DISTRICT **6** [C] (*NAmE*) a district of a town, city or county: *the Dorchester section of Boston*

▸ MEASUREMENT **7** [C] (*NAmE*) a measure of land, equal to one square mile

▸ DIAGRAM **8** [C] a drawing or diagram of sth as it would look if it were cut from top to bottom or from one side to the other: *The illustration shows a section through a leaf.* ◇ *The architect drew the house* ***in section.*** ➲ see also CROSS SECTION

▸ MEDICAL **9** [C, U] (*medical*) the act of cutting or separating sth in an operation: *The surgeon performed a section* (= made a cut) *on the vein.* ➲ see also CAESAREAN **10** [C] (*medical, biology*) a very thin flat piece cut from body TISSUE to be looked at under a MICROSCOPE: *to examine a section from the kidney*

■ ***verb***

▸ MEDICAL/BIOLOGY **1 ~ sth** (*medical*) to divide body TISSUE by cutting **2 ~ sth** (*biology*) to cut animal or plant TISSUE into thin slices in order to look at it under a MICROSCOPE

▸ MENTAL PATIENT **3** [often passive] **~ sb** (*BrE*) to officially order a mentally ill person to go and receive treatment in a PSYCHIATRIC hospital, using a law that can force them to stay there until they are successfully treated

S

PHR V ˌ**section sth**↔ˈ**off** to separate an area from a larger one: *Parts of the town had been sectioned off.*

sec·tion·al /ˈsekʃənl/ *adj.* [usually before noun] **1** connected with one particular group within a community or an organization: *the sectional interests of managers and workers* **2** made of separate sections: *a sectional building* **3** connected with a CROSS SECTION of sth (= a surface or an image formed by cutting through sth from top to bottom): *a sectional drawing*

ˌ**Section ˈEight** *noun* (*NAmE*) **1** [U] (in the past) a part of US army law that dealt with dismissing a soldier who was considered not suitable **2** [C] (*informal*) a soldier who has been dismissed from the US army because he is not mentally fit

sec·tor 0‑w AW /ˈsektə(r)/ *noun*
1 0‑w a part of an area of activity, especially of a country's economy: *the manufacturing sector* ◇ *service-sector jobs* (= in hotels, restaurants, etc.) ➲ **COLLOCATIONS** at ECONOMY ➲ see also THE PRIVATE SECTOR, THE PUBLIC SECTOR **2** 0‑w a part of a particular area, especially an area under military control: *each sector of the war zone* **3** (*geometry*) a part of a circle lying between two straight lines drawn from the centre to the edge ➲ **VISUAL VOCAB** page V58

secu·lar /ˈsekjələ(r)/ *adj.* **1** not connected with spiritual or religious matters: *secular music* ◇ *Ours is a secular society.* **2** (of priests) living among ordinary people rather than in a religious community

secu·lar·ism /ˈsekjələrɪzəm/ *noun* [U] (*technical*) the belief that religion should not be involved in the organization of society, education, etc. ▶ **secu·lar·ist** /-lərɪst/ *adj.* [usually before noun]

secu·lar·iza·tion (*BrE* also **-isa·tion**) /ˌsekjələraɪˈzeɪʃn; *NAmE* -rəˈz-/ *noun* [U] the process of removing the influence or power that religion has over sth

secu·lar·ize (*BrE* also **-ise**) /ˈsekjələraɪz/ *verb* [often passive] **~ sth** to make sth SECULAR; to remove sth from the control or influence of religion: *a secularized society*

se·cure 0‑w AW /sɪˈkjʊə(r); *NAmE* səˈkjʊr/ *adj., verb*
■ ***adj.***
▸ HAPPY/CONFIDENT **1** 0‑w feeling happy and confident about yourself or a particular situation: *At last they were able to* ***feel secure*** *about the future.* ◇ *She finished the match,* ***secure in the knowledge that*** *she was through to the next round.* **OPP** **insecure**
▸ CERTAIN/SAFE **2** 0‑w likely to continue or be successful for a long time **SYN** **safe**: *a* ***secure job/income*** ◇ *It's not a very secure way to make a living.* ◇ *The future of the company looks secure.* **OPP** **insecure** **3** 0‑w **~** (**against/from sth**) that cannot be affected or harmed by sth: *Information must be stored so that it is secure from accidental deletion.*
▸ BUILDING/DOOR/ROOM **4** 0‑w guarded and/or made stronger so that it is difficult for people to enter or leave: *Check that all windows and doors have been made as secure as possible.* ◇ *a secure unit for child offenders* **OPP** **insecure**
▸ FIRM **5** 0‑w not likely to move, fall down, etc. **SYN** **stable**: *The aerial doesn't look very secure to me.* ◇ *It was difficult to maintain a secure foothold on the ice.* ◇ (*figurative*) *Our relationship was now on a more secure footing.* **OPP** **insecure**
▶ **se·cure·ly** AW *adv.*: *She locked the door securely behind her.* ◇ *Make sure the ropes are securely fastened.*
■ ***verb*** (*formal*)
▸ GET STH **1** to obtain or achieve sth, especially when this means using a lot of effort: **~ sth** *to* ***secure a contract/deal*** ◇ *The team managed to secure a place in the finals.* ◇ *She secured 2 000 votes.* ◇ **~ sth for sb/sth/yourself** *He secured a place for himself at law school.* ◇ **~ sb/sth/yourself sth** *He secured himself a place at law school.*
▸ FASTEN FIRMLY **2** **~ sth** (**to sth**) to attach or fasten sth firmly: *She secured the rope firmly to the back of the car.*
▸ PROTECT FROM HARM **3** to protect sth so that it is safe and difficult to attack or damage: **~ sth against sth** *to secure a property against intruders* ◇ **~ sth** *The windows were secured with locks and bars.* ◇ (*figurative*) *a savings plan that will secure your child's future*
▸ A LOAN **4** **~ sth** to legally agree to give sb property or goods that are worth the same amount as the money that you have borrowed from them, if you are unable to pay the money back: *a loan secured on the house*

se·cur·ity 0‑w AW /sɪˈkjʊərəti; *NAmE* səˈkjʊr-/ *noun* (*pl.* -ies)
▸ PROTECTION **1** 0‑w [U] the activities involved in protecting a country, building or person against attack, danger, etc: ***national security*** (= the defence of a country) ◇ *airport security* ◇ *They carried out* ***security checks*** *at the airport.* ◇ *The visit took place amidst* ***tight security*** (= the use of many police officers). ◇ *the* ***security forces/services*** (= the police, army, etc.) ◇ *a* ***high/maximum security prison*** (= for dangerous criminals) ➲ **COLLOCATIONS** at INTERNATIONAL ➲ see also HIGH-SECURITY **2** 0‑w [U+sing./pl. v.] the department of a large company or organization that deals with the protection of its buildings, equipment and staff: *Security was/were called to the incident.* **3** 0‑w [U] protection against sth bad that might happen in the future: *financial security* ◇ ***Job security*** (= the guarantee that you will keep your job) *is a thing of the past.*
▸ FEELING HAPPY/SAFE **4** 0‑w [U] the state of feeling happy and safe from danger or worry: *the security of a loving family life* ◇ *She'd allowed herself to be lulled into* ***a false sense of security*** (= a feeling that she was safe when in fact she was in danger).
▸ FOR A LOAN **5** [U, C] a valuable item, such as a house, that you agree to give to sb if you are unable to pay back the money that you have borrowed from them: *His home and business are being held* ***as security for*** *the loan.*
▸ SHARES IN COMPANY **6** **securities** [pl.] (*finance*) documents proving that sb is the owner of shares, etc. in a particular company ➲ see also SOCIAL SECURITY

seˈcurity blanket *noun* **1** a BLANKET or other object that a child holds in order to feel safe **2** something that provides protection against attack, danger, etc: *A firewall provides an essential security blanket for your computer network.* **3** (*BrE*) official orders or measures that prevent people from knowing about, seeing, etc. sth: *The government has thrown a security blanket around the talks.*

the Seˈcurity Council (also **the ˌUN Seˈcurity Council**, **the ˌUnited Nations Seˈcurity Council**) *noun* [sing.] the part of the United Nations that tries to keep peace and order in the world, consisting of representatives of fifteen countries

seˈcurity guard *noun* a person whose job is to guard money, valuables, a building, etc.

seˈcurity risk *noun* a person who cannot be given secret information because they are a danger to a particular country, organization, etc, especially because of their political beliefs

Seˈcurity Service *noun* a government organization that protects a country and its secrets from enemies

Secy. *abbr.* (*US*) = SEC.

sedan /sɪˈdæn/ (*NAmE*) (*BrE* **sal·oon**, **saˈloon car**) *noun* a car with four doors and a BOOT/TRUNK (= space at the back for carrying things) which is separated from the part where the driver and passengers sit ➲ **VISUAL VOCAB** page V42

seˌdan ˈchair *noun* a box containing a seat for one person, carried on poles by two people, used in the 17th and 18th centuries

sed·ate /sɪˈdeɪt/ *adj., verb*
■ ***adj.*** [usually before noun] **1** slow, calm and relaxed **SYN** **unhurried**: *We followed the youngsters at a more sedate pace.* **2** quiet, especially in a way that lacks excitement: *a sedate country town* **3** (of a person) quiet and serious in a way that seems formal: *a sedate, sober man*
▶ **sed·ate·ly** *adv.*
■ ***verb*** [often passive] **~ sb/sth** to give sb drugs in order to make them calm and or to make them sleep **SYN** **tranquillize**: *Most of the patients are heavily sedated.*

sed·ation /sɪˈdeɪʃn/ *noun* [U] the act of giving sb drugs in order to make them calm or to make them sleep; the state that results from this: *The victim's wife was last night being kept* ***under sedation*** *in the local hospital.*

seda·tive /ˈsedətɪv/ *noun* a drug that makes sb go to sleep or makes them feel calm and relaxed **SYN** **tranquillizer** ▸ **seda·tive** *adj.* [usually before noun]: *the sedative effect of the drug*

sed·en·tary /ˈsedntri; *NAmE* -teri/ *adj.* **1** (of work, activities, etc.) in which you spend a lot of time sitting down: *a* ***sedentary job/occupation/lifestyle*** **2** (of people) spending a lot of time sitting down and not moving: *He became increasingly sedentary in later life.* **3** (*technical*) (of people or animals) that stay and live in the same place or area: *Rhinos are largely sedentary animals.* ◇ *a sedentary population*

Seder /ˈseɪdə(r)/ *noun* a Jewish CEREMONIAL service and dinner on the first night or first two nights of Passover

sedge /sedʒ/ *noun* [U] a plant like grass that grows in wet ground or near water

sedi·ment /ˈsedɪmənt/ *noun* [U] **1** the solid material that settles at the bottom of a liquid **2** (*geology*) sand, stones, mud, etc. carried by water or wind and left, for example, on the bottom of a lake, river, etc.

sedi·ment·ary /ˌsedɪˈmentri/ *adj.* (*geology*) connected with or formed from the sand, stones, mud, etc. that settle at the bottom of lakes, etc: *sedimentary rocks*

sedi·men·ta·tion /ˌsedɪmenˈteɪʃn/ *noun* [U] (*geology*) the process of depositing sediment

se·di·tion /sɪˈdɪʃn/ *noun* [U] (*formal*) the use of words or actions that are intended to encourage people to oppose a government **SYN** **insurrection** ▸ **se·di·tious** /sɪˈdɪʃəs/ *adj.*: *seditious activity*

se·duce /sɪˈdjuːs; *NAmE* -ˈduːs/ *verb* **1** **~ sb** to persuade sb to have sex with you, especially sb who is younger or who has less experience than you **2** **~ sb (into sth/into doing sth)** to persuade sb to do sth that they would not usually agree to do by making it seem very attractive **SYN** **entice**: *The promise of huge profits seduced him into parting with his money.*

se·du·cer /sɪˈdjuːsə(r); *NAmE* sɪˈduːsər/ *noun* a person who persuades sb to have sex with them

se·duc·tion /sɪˈdʌkʃn/ *noun* **1** [U, C] the act of persuading sb to have sex with you: *Cleopatra's seduction of Caesar* **2** [C, usually pl., U] **~ (of sth)** the qualities or features of sth that make it seem attractive **SYN** **enticement**: *Who could resist the seductions of the tropical island?*

se·duc·tive /sɪˈdʌktɪv/ *adj.* **1** sexually attractive: *a seductive woman* ◇ *She used her most seductive voice.* **2** attractive in a way that makes you want to have or do sth **SYN** **tempting**: *The idea of retiring to the south of France is highly seductive.* ▸ **se·duc·tive·ly** *adv.* **se·duc·tive·ness** *noun* [U]

se·duc·tress /sɪˈdʌktrəs/ *noun* a woman who persuades sb to have sex with her

sedu·lous /ˈsedjʊləs; *NAmE* ˈsedʒələs/ *adj.* (*formal*) showing great care and effort in your work **SYN** **diligent** ▸ **sedu·lous·ly** *adv.*

see 🔑 /siː/ *verb, noun*

■ ***verb*** (**saw** /sɔː/, **seen** /siːn/)

▸ USE EYES **1** 🔑 [T, I] (not used in the progressive tenses) to become aware of sb/sth by using your eyes: **~ (sb/sth)** *She looked for him but couldn't see him in the crowd.* ◇ *The opera was the place to* ***see and be seen*** (= by other important or fashionable people). ◇ **~ (that)...** *He could see (that) she had been crying.* ◇ **~ what, how, etc...** *Did you see what happened?* ◇ **~ sb/sth + adj.** *I hate to see you unhappy.* ◇ **~ sb/sth doing sth** *She was seen running away from the scene of the crime.* ◇ **~ sb/sth do sth** *I saw you put the key in your pocket.* ◇ **sb/sth is seen to do sth** *He was seen to enter the building about the time the crime was committed.* **2** 🔑 [I] (not usually used in the progressive tenses) to have or use the power of sight: *She will never see again* (= she has become blind). ◇ *On a clear day you* ***can see*** *for miles from here.* ◇ **~ to do sth** *It was getting dark and I* ***couldn't see*** *to read.*

▸ WATCH **3** 🔑 [T] (not usually used in the progressive tenses) **~ sth** to watch a game, television programme, performance, etc: *Did you see that programme on Brazil last night?* ◇ *In the evening we went to see a movie.* ◇ *Fifty thousand people saw the match.* ➲ SYNONYMS at LOOK

▸ LOOK UP INFORMATION **4** 🔑 [T] (used in orders) **~ sth** to look at sth in order to find information: *See page 158.*

▸ MEET BY CHANCE **5** 🔑 [T] **~ sb** (not usually used in the progressive tenses) to be near and recognize sb; to meet sb by chance: *Guess who I saw at the party last night!*

▸ VISIT **6** 🔑 [T] **~ sb** to visit sb: *Come and see us again soon.*

▸ HAVE MEETING **7** 🔑 [T] **~ sb (about sth)** to have a meeting with sb: *You ought to see a doctor about that cough.* ◇ *What is it you want to see me about?*

▸ SPEND TIME **8** 🔑 [T] (often used in the progressive tenses) **~ sb** to spend time with sb: ***Are you seeing anyone*** (= having a romantic relationship with anyone)? ◇ *They've been* ***seeing a lot of each other*** (= spending a lot of time together) *recently.*

▸ UNDERSTAND **9** 🔑 [I, T] (not usually used in the progressive tenses) to understand sth: *'It opens like this.' 'Oh, I see.'* ◇ **~ sth** *He didn't see the joke.* ◇ *I don't think she* ***saw the point*** *of the story.* ◇ *I can see both sides of the argument.* ◇ *Make Lydia* ***see reason*** (= be sensible), *will you?* ◇ **~ (that)...** ***Can't you see*** *(that) he's taking advantage of you?* ◇ ***I don't see that it matters*** *what Josh thinks.* ◇ **~ what, why, etc...** *'It's broken.' 'Oh yes,* ***I see what you mean.****'* ◇ *'Can we go swimming?'* ***'I don't see why not*** (= yes, you can).*'* ◇ **be seen to do sth** *The government not only has to do something, it must* ***be seen to be doing something*** (= people must be aware that it is doing sth). ➲ SYNONYMS at UNDERSTAND

▸ HAVE OPINION **10** 🔑 [T] **~ sth + adv./prep.** (not usually used in the progressive tenses) to have an opinion of sth: *I* ***see things*** *differently now.* ◇ *Try to see things from her point of view.* ◇ *Lack of money is the main problem,* ***as I see it*** (= in my opinion). ◇ ***The way I see it,*** *you have three main problems.* ➲ SYNONYMS at REGARD

▸ IMAGINE **11** 🔑 [T] (not used in the progressive tenses) to consider sth as a future possibility; to imagine sb/sth as sth: **~ sb/sth doing sth** *I can't see her changing her mind.* ◇ **~ sb/sth as sth** *His colleagues see him as a future director.* ➲ SYNONYMS at IMAGINE

▸ FIND OUT **12** 🔑 [I, T] (not usually used in the progressive tenses) to find out sth by looking, asking or waiting: *'Has the mail come yet?' 'I'll just go and see.'* ◇ *'Is he going to get better?' 'I don't know, we'll just have to* ***wait and see.****'* ◇ *We'll have a great time,* ***you'll see.*** ◇ **~ what, how, etc...** *Go and see what the kids are doing, will you?* ◇ *We'll have to* ***see how it goes.*** ◇ **~ (that)...** *I see (that) interest rates are going up again.* ◇ **it is seen that...** ***It can be seen that*** *certain groups are more at risk than others.* **13** 🔑 [I, T] (not usually used in the progressive tenses) to find out or decide sth by thinking or considering: *'Will you be able to help us?' 'I don't know, I'll have to see.'* ◇ *'Can I go to the party?'* ***'We'll see*** (= I'll decide later). ◇ **~ what, whether, etc...** ***I'll see what I can do*** *to help.*

▸ MAKE SURE **14** [T] (not usually used in the progressive tenses) **~ that...** to make sure that you do sth or that sth is done: *See that all the doors are locked before you leave.*

▸ EXPERIENCE **15** [T] (not used in the progressive tenses) **~ sth** to experience or suffer sth: *He has seen a great deal in his long life.* ◇ *I hope I never live to* ***see the day*** *when computers finally replace books.* ◇ *It didn't surprise her—she* ***had seen it all before.***

▸ WITNESS EVENT **16** [T] (not used in the progressive tenses) **~ sth** to be the time when an event happens: *Next year sees the centenary of Mahler's death.* **17** [T] (not used in the progressive tenses) **~ sth** to be the place where an event happens **SYN** **witness**: *This stadium has seen many thrilling football games.*

▸ HELP **18** [T] **~ sb + adv./prep.** to go with sb to help or protect them: *I saw the old lady across* (= helped her cross) *the road.* ◇ *May I* ***see you home*** (= go with you as far as your house)? ◇ *My secretary will* ***see you out*** (= show you the way out of the building).

IDM Most idioms containing **see** are at the entries for the nouns and adjectives in the idioms, for example **not see the wood for the trees** is at **wood**. **for all (the world)**

S

to ˈsee clearly visible; in a way that is clearly visible ˌ**let me ˈsee/let's see** 🗝 (*informal*) used when you are thinking or trying to remember sth: *Now let me see—how old is she now?* **see sth ˈcoming** to realize that there is going to be a problem before it happens: *We should have seen it coming. There was no way he could keep going under all that pressure.* ˌ**see for yourˈself** to find out or look at sth yourself in order to be sure that what sb is saying is true: *If you don't believe me, go and see for yourself!* **see sb/sth for what they ˈare/it ˈis** to realize that sb/sth is not as good, pleasant, etc. as they/it seem **seeing that...** (also *informal* **seeing as (how)...**) because of the fact that...: *Seeing that he's been off sick all week he's unlikely to come.* **ˈsee you (aˈround)** | **(I'll) be ˈseeing you** | ˌ**see you ˈlater** (*informal*) goodbye: *I'd better be going now. See you!* **you ˈsee** 🗝 (*informal*) used when you are explaining sth: *You see, the thing is, we won't be finished before Friday.*

Synonyms

see

spot • catch • glimpse

These words all mean to become aware of sb/sth by using your eyes, especially suddenly or when it is not easy to see them/it.

- **see** to become aware of sb/sth by using your eyes: *She looked for him but couldn't see him in the crowd.* ◇ *He could see (that) she had been crying.*
- **spot** to see or notice sb/sth, especially suddenly or when they are not easy to see or notice: *I've just spotted a mistake on the front cover.*
- **catch** to see or notice sth for a moment, but not clearly or completely: *She* ***caught sight*** *of a car in the distance.* ◇ *He* ***caught a glimpse*** *of himself in the mirror.*
- **glimpse** (*literary*) to see sb/sth for a moment, but not clearly or completely: *He'd glimpsed her through the window as he passed.*

PATTERNS

- to see/spot **that/how/what/where/who...**
- to **suddenly** see/spot/catch/glimpse sb/sth

PHR V ˈ**see about sth** 🗝 to deal with sth: *I must see about* (= prepare) *lunch.* ◇ *He says he won't help, does he? Well,* ***we'll soon see about that*** (= I will demand that he does help). ◇ **~ doing sth** *I'll have to see about getting that roof repaired.* ˈ**see sth in sb/sth** to find sb/sth attractive or interesting: ***I don't know what she sees in him.*** ˌ**see sb↔ˈoff 1** to go to a station, an airport, etc. to say goodbye to sb who is starting a journey **2** (*BrE*) to force sb to leave a place, for example by chasing them: *The dogs saw them off in no time.* **3** (*BrE*) to defeat sb in a game, fight, etc: *The home team saw off the challengers by 68 points to 47.* ˌ**see sb↔ˈout** (not used in the progressive tenses) (*BrE*) to last longer than the rest of sb's life: *I've had this coat for years, and I'm sure it will see me out.* ˌ**see sth↔ˈout** (not used in the progressive tenses) (*BrE*) to reach the end or last until the end of sth: *They had enough fuel to see the winter out.* ◇ *He saw out his career in Italy.* ˌ**see ˈover sth** (*BrE*) to visit and look at a place carefully: *We need to see over the house before we can make you an offer.* ˌ**see ˈthrough sb/sth** (not used in the progressive tenses) to realize the truth about sb/sth: *We saw through him from the start.* ◇ *I can see through your little game* (= I am aware of the trick you are trying to play on me). ˌ**see sth ˈthrough** (not usually used in the progressive tenses) to not give up doing a task, project, etc. until it is finished: *She's determined to see the job through.* ˌ**see sb ˈthrough** | ˌ**see sb ˈthrough sth** (not used in the progressive tenses) to give help or support to sb for a particular period of time: *Her courage and good humour saw her through.* ◇ *I only have $20 to see me through the week.* ˈ**see to sth** 🗝 to deal with sth: *Will you see to the arrangements for the next meeting?* ◇ *Don't worry—****I'll see to it.*** ◇ *We'll have to get that door seen to* (= repaired). ˈ**see to it that...** to make sure that...: *Can you see to it that the fax goes this afternoon?*
■ ***noun*** (*formal*) the district or office of a BISHOP or an ARCHBISHOP: *the Holy See* (= the office of the POPE)

seed 🗝 /siːd/ *noun, verb*
■ ***noun***
▸ **OF PLANTS/FRUIT 1** 🗝 [C, U] the small hard part produced by a plant, from which a new plant can grow: *a packet of wild flower seeds* ◇ *sesame seeds* ◇ ***Sow the seeds*** *outdoors in spring.* ◇ *These vegetables can be* ***grown from seed.*** ◇ ***seed potatoes*** (= used for planting) ➲ COLLOCATIONS at LIFE ➲ VISUAL VOCAB pages V8, V28 ➲ see also BIRDSEED **2** [C] (*NAmE*) = PIP (2) ➲ VISUAL VOCAB page V26
▸ **BEGINNING 3** [C, usually pl.] **~ (of sth)** the beginning of a feeling or a development which continues to grow: *the seeds of rebellion* ◇ *This* ***planted the seeds of*** *doubt in my mind.*
▸ **IN TENNIS 4** [C] (especially in TENNIS) one of the best players in a competition. The seeds are given a position in a list to try and make sure that they do not play each other in the early parts of the competition: *The top seed won comfortably.* ◇ *the number one seed*
▸ **OF A MAN 5** [U] (*old-fashioned* or *humorous*) SEMEN **6** [U] (*literary*) all the people who are the children, grandchildren, etc. of one man
IDM **go/run to ˈseed 1** (especially of a vegetable plant) to produce flowers and seeds as well as leaves **2** to become much less attractive or good because of lack of attention: *After his divorce, he let himself go to seed.* ➲ more at SOW *v.*
■ ***verb***
▸ **OF A PLANT 1** [I] to produce seeds **2** [T] **~ itself** to produce other plants using its own seeds
▸ **AREA OF GROUND 3** [T, usually passive] **~ sth (with sth)** to plant seeds in an area of ground: *a newly seeded lawn*
▸ **IN TENNIS 4** [T, usually passive] **~ sb** to make sb a seed in a competition: *He has been seeded 14th at Wimbledon next week.*

seed·bed /ˈsiːdbed/ *noun* **1** an area of soil which has been specially prepared for planting seeds in **2** [usually sing.] **~ (of/for sth)** a place or situation in which sth can develop

ˈ**seed cake** *noun* [C, U] a cake containing CARAWAY seeds

seed·corn /ˈsiːdkɔːn; *NAmE* -kɔːrn/ *noun* [U] **1** the grain that is kept for planting the next year's crops **2** people or things that will be successful or useful in the future

seed·ed /ˈsiːdɪd/ *adj.* [usually before noun] **1** (especially of a TENNIS player) given a number showing that they are one of the best players in a particular competition: *a seeded player* **2** (of fruit) with the seeds removed: *seeded tomatoes*

seed·less /ˈsiːdləs/ *adj.* [usually before noun] (of fruit) having no seeds: *seedless grapes*

seed·ling /ˈsiːdlɪŋ/ *noun* a young plant that has grown from a seed ➲ VISUAL VOCAB page V16

ˈ**seed money** (also ˈ**seed capital**) *noun* [U] money to start a new business, project, etc.

ˈ**seed pearl** *noun* a small PEARL

seeds·man /ˈsiːdzmən/ *noun* (*pl.* **-men** /-mən/) a person who grows and sells seeds

seedy /ˈsiːdi/ *adj.* (**seed·ier, seedi·est**) (*disapproving*) dirty and unpleasant, possibly connected with immoral or illegal activities: *a seedy bar* ◇ *the seedy world of prostitution* ◇ *a seedy-looking man* ▸ **seedi·ness** *noun* [U]

ˌ**Seeing ˈEye dog™** *noun* (*NAmE*) = GUIDE DOG

seek 🗝 AW /siːk/ *verb* (**sought, sought** /sɔːt/) (*formal*) **1** 🗝 [T, I] to look for sth/sb: **~ sth/sb** *Drivers are advised to seek alternative routes.* ◇ **~ for sth/sb** (*BrE*) *They sought in vain for somewhere to shelter.* **2** 🗝 [T, I] **~ (sth)** to try to obtain or achieve sth: *to seek funding for a project* ◇ *Highly qualified secretary seeks employment.* (= in an advertisement) ◇ *We are currently seeking new ways of expanding our membership.* **3** 🗝 [T] to ask sb for sth: **~ sth** *I think it's time we sought legal advice.* ◇ **~ sth from sb** *She managed to calm him down and seek help from a neighbour.* **4** [I] **~ to do sth** to try to do sth SYN **attempt**: *They quickly sought to* *distance themselves from the protesters.* **5 -seeking** (in adjectives and nouns) looking for or trying to get the thing mentioned; the activity of doing this: *attention-seeking behaviour* ◇ *Voluntary work can provide a framework for job-seeking.* ➲ see also HEAT-SEEKING, SELF-SEEKING ➲ see also HIDE-AND-SEEK

IDM **seek your 'fortune** (*literary*) to try to find a way to become rich, especially by going to another place

PHR V **,seek sb/sth 'out** to look for and find sb/sth, especially when this means using a lot of effort

seek·er /'si:kə(r)/ *noun* (often in compounds) a person who is trying to find or get the thing mentioned: ***an attention/a publicity seeker*** ◇ *seekers after the truth* ➲ see also ASYLUM SEEKER, JOB SEEKER

seem 0-w /si:m/ *linking verb*
1 0-w **~ (to sb) (to be) sth** (not used in the progressive tenses) to give the impression of being or doing sth SYN **appear**: **+ adj.** *You seem happy.* ◇ *Do whatever seems best to you.* ◇ **+ noun** *He seems a nice man.* ◇ **~ like sth** *It seemed like a good idea at the time.* ◇ **~ (as though...)** *It always seemed as though they would get married.* ◇ *'He'll be there, then?' '**So it seems** (= people say so).'* ◇ **it seems that ...** *It seems that they know what they're doing.* ◇ **~ to do/be/have sth** *They seem to know what they're doing.* **2** 0-w **~ to do/be/have sth** used to make what you say about your thoughts, feelings or actions less strong: *I seem to have left my book at home.* ◇ *I can't seem to* (= I've tried, but I can't) *get started today.* **3** 0-w **it seems** | **it would seem** used to suggest that sth is true when you are not certain or when you want to be polite: **~ (that)...** *It would seem that we all agree.* ◇ **+ adj.** *It seems only reasonable to ask students to buy a dictionary.* ➲ LANGUAGE BANK at IMPERSONAL, OPINION, PERHAPS

seem·ing /'si:mɪŋ/ *adj.* [only before noun] (*formal*) appearing to be sth that may not be true SYN **apparent**: *a seeming impossibility* ◇ *She handled the matter with seeming indifference.*

seem·ing·ly /'si:mɪŋli/ *adv.* **1** in a way that appears to be true but may in fact not be: *a seemingly stupid question* ◇ *a **seemingly endless** journey* **2** (*formal*) according to what you have read or heard SYN **apparently**: *Seemingly, he borrowed the money from the bank.*

seem·ly /'si:mli/ *adj.* (*old-fashioned* or *formal*) appropriate for a particular social situation OPP **unseemly**

seen *past part.* of SEE

seep /si:p/ *verb* [I] **+ adv./prep.** (especially of liquids) to flow slowly and in small quantities through sth or into sth SYN **trickle**: *Blood was beginning to seep through the bandages.* ◇ *Water seeped from a crack in the pipe.* ◇ (*figurative*) *Gradually the pain seeped away.*

seep·age /'si:pɪdʒ/ *noun* [U, C, usually pl.] the process by which a liquid flows slowly and in small quantities through sth; the result of this process: *Water gradually escapes by seepage through the ground.* ◇ *oil seepages*

seer /sɪə(r); *NAmE* sɪr/ *noun* (*literary*) (especially in the past) a person who claims that they can see what is going to happen in the future SYN **prophet**

seer·sucker /'sɪəsʌkə(r); *NAmE* 'sɪrs-/ *noun* [U] a type of light cotton cloth with a pattern of raised lines and squares on its surface

'see-saw *noun, verb*
■ *noun* **1** (*NAmE* also **'teeter-totter**) [C] a piece of equipment for children to play on consisting of a long flat piece of wood that is supported in the middle. A child sits at each end and makes the see-saw move up and down. **2** [sing.] a situation in which things keep changing from one state to another and back again
■ *verb* [I] **~ (from A to B)** to keep changing from one situation, opinion, emotion, etc. to another and back again: *Her emotions see-sawed from anger to fear.* ◇ *Share prices see-sawed all day.*

seethe /si:ð/ *verb* [I] **1** to be extremely angry about sth but try not to show other people how angry you are SYN **fume**: *She seethed silently in the corner.* ◇ **~ with sth** *He marched off, seething with frustration.* ◇ **~ at sth** *Inwardly he was seething at this challenge to his authority.* **2 ~ (with sth)** (*formal*) (of a place) to be full of a lot of people or animals, especially when they are all moving around: *The resort is seething with tourists all year round.* ◇ *He became caught up in a **seething mass** of arms and legs.* **3** (*formal*) (of liquids) to move around quickly and violently: *The grey ocean seethed beneath them.*

'see-through *adj.* (of cloth) very thin so that you can see through it: *a see-through blouse*

seg·ment *noun, verb*
■ *noun* /'segmənt/ **1** a part of sth that is separate from the other parts or can be considered separately: *She cleaned a small segment of the painting.* ◇ *Lines divided the area into segments.* **2** one of the sections of an orange, a lemon, etc. ➲ VISUAL VOCAB page V26 **3** (*geometry*) a part of a circle separated from the rest by a single line ➲ VISUAL VOCAB page V58 **4** (*phonetics*) the smallest speech sound that a word can be divided into
■ *verb* /seg'ment/ [often passive] **~ sth** (*technical*) to divide sth into different parts: *Market researchers often segment the population on the basis of age and social class.* ◇ *The worm has a segmented body* (= with different sections joined together).

seg·men·tal /seg'mentl/ *adj.* (*phonetics*) relating to the individual sounds that make up speech, as opposed to PROSODIC features such as stress and INTONATION

seg·men·ta·tion /,segmen'teɪʃn/ *noun* [U, C, usually pl.] (*technical*) the act of dividing sth into different parts; one of these parts

seg·re·gate /'segrɪgeɪt/ *verb* (*formal*) **1 ~ sb (from sb)** to separate people of different races, religions or sexes and treat them in a different way: *a culture in which women are segregated from men* ◇ *a racially segregated community* ◇ *a segregated school* (= one for students of one race or religion only) OPP **integrate** **2 ~ sth (from sth)** to keep one thing separate from another: *In all our restaurants, smoking and non-smoking areas are segregated from each other.*

seg·re·ga·tion /,segrɪ'geɪʃn/ *noun* [U] (*formal*) **1** the act or policy of separating people of different races, religions or sexes and treating them in a different way: ***racial/religious segregation*** ◇ *segregation by age and sex* ➲ COLLOCATIONS at RACE **2** (*formal*) the act of separating people or things from a larger group: *the segregation of smokers and non-smokers in restaurants*

seg·re·ga·tion·ist /,segrɪ'geɪʃənɪst/ *adj.* supporting the separation of people according to their sex, race or religion: *segregationist policies* ▸ **seg·re·ga·tion·ist** *noun*

segue /'segweɪ/ *verb* [I] **+ adv./prep.** to move smoothly from one song, subject, place, etc. to another: *a spiritual that segued into a singalong chorus* ◇ *He then segued into a discussion of atheism.* ▸ **segue** *noun*

seine /seɪn/ (also **'seine net**) *noun* a type of fishing net which hangs down in the water and is pulled together at the ends to catch fish

seis·mic /'saɪzmɪk/ *adj.* [only before noun] **1** connected with or caused by EARTHQUAKES: *seismic waves* **2** having a very great effect; of very great size: *a **seismic shift** in the political process*

seis·mo·graph /'saɪzməgrɑ:f; *NAmE* -græf/ *noun* an instrument that measures and records information about EARTHQUAKES

seis·mol·ogy /saɪz'mɒlədʒi; *NAmE* -'mɑ:l-/ *noun* [U] the scientific study of EARTHQUAKES ▸ **seis·mo·logic·al** /,saɪzmə'lɒdʒɪkl; *NAmE* -'lɑ:dʒ-/ *adj.*: *the National Seismological Institute* **seis·molo·gist** /-dʒɪst/ *noun*

seize /si:z/ *verb* **1** to take sb/sth in your hand suddenly and using force SYN **grab**: **~ sth from sb** *She tried to seize the gun from him.* ◇ **~ sb/sth** *He seized her by the arm.* ◇ *She **seized hold of** my hand.* **2 ~ sth (from sb)** to take control of a place or situation, often suddenly and violently: *They seized the airport in a surprise attack.* ◇ *The army has **seized control of** the country.* ◇ *He **seized power** in a military coup.* **3 ~ sb** to arrest or capture sb: *The men were seized as they left the building.* **4 ~ sth** to take illegal or stolen

S

goods away from sb: *A large quantity of drugs was seized during the raid.* **5 ~ a chance, an opportunity, the initiative, etc.** to be quick to make use of a chance, an opportunity, etc. SYN **grab**: *The party* ***seized*** *the initiative* ***with both hands*** (= quickly and with enthusiasm). **6 ~ sb** (of an emotion) to affect sb suddenly and deeply: *Panic seized her.* ◇ *He* ***was seized by*** *curiosity.* **7** = SEIZE UP
PHR V ˈ**seize on/upon sth** to suddenly show a lot of interest in sth, especially because you can use it to your advantage SYN **pounce on/upon**: *The rumours were eagerly seized upon by the local press.* ˌ**seize** ˈ**up** (*NAmE* also **seize**) **1** (of the parts of a machine) to stop moving or working correctly **2** if a part of your body **seizes up**, you are unable to move it easily and it is often painful

seiz·ure /ˈsiːʒə(r)/ *noun* **1** [U, C] **~ (of sth)** the use of legal authority to take sth from sb; an amount of sth that is taken in this way: *The court ordered the seizure of his assets.* ◇ *the largest ever seizure of cocaine at a British port* **2** [U] **~ (of sth)** the act of using force to take control of a country, town, etc: *the army's seizure of power* ◇ *the seizure of Burma by Japan in 1942* **3** (*old-fashioned*) [C] a sudden attack of an illness, especially one that affects the brain

sel·dom /ˈseldəm/ *adv.* not often SYN **rarely**: *He had seldom seen a child with so much talent.* ◇ *She* ***seldom, if ever,*** *goes to the theatre.* ◇ *They seldom watch television these days.* ◇ (*literary*) *Seldom had he seen such beauty.*

se·lect 🔑 AW /sɪˈlekt/ *verb, adj.*
■ *verb* **1** 🔑 to choose sb/sth from a group of people or things, usually according to a system: **~ sb/sth for sth** *He hasn't been selected for the team.* ◇ *All our hotels have been* ***carefully selected*** *for the excellent value they provide.* ◇ **~ sb/sth as sth** *She was selected as the parliamentary candidate for Bath.* ◇ **~ sb/sth** *a* ***randomly selected*** *sample of 23 schools* ◇ *selected poems of T.S. Eliot* ◇ *This model is available at selected stores only.* ◇ **~ sb/sth to do sth** *Six theatre companies have been selected to take part in this year's festival.* ◇ **~ what, which, etc...** *Select what you want from the options available.* ➲ SYNONYMS at CHOOSE **2 ~ sth** (*computing*) to mark sth on a computer screen; to choose sth, especially from a menu: *Select the text you want to format by holding down the left button on your mouse.* ◇ *Select 'New Mail' from the 'Send' menu.*
■ *adj.* **1** [only before noun] carefully chosen as the best out of a larger group of people or things: *a select wine list* ◇ *Only a* ***select few*** (= a small number of people) *have been invited to the wedding.* **2** (of a society, club, place, etc.) used by people who have a lot of money or a high social position SYN **exclusive**: *They live in a very select area.* ◇ *a select club*

seˌlect comˈmittee *noun* (*BrE*) a small group of politicians or experts that have been chosen to examine a particular subject or problem

se·lect·ee /sɪˌlekˈtiː/ *noun* **1** a person who is chosen for sth **2** (*NAmE*) a person who is chosen to do MILITARY SERVICE

se·lec·tion 🔑 AW /sɪˈlekʃn/ *noun*
1 🔑 [U] the process of choosing sb/sth from a group of people or things, usually according to a system: *The final team selection will be made tomorrow.* ◇ *the* ***random selection*** *of numbers* ◇ *selection criteria* ◇ *the selection process* **2** 🔑 [C] a number of people or things that have been chosen from a larger group: *A selection of readers' comments are published below.* ➲ SYNONYMS at CHOICE **3** 🔑 [C] a collection of things from which sth can be chosen SYN **choice, range**: *The showroom has a* ***wide selection*** *of kitchens.* ➲ see also NATURAL SELECTION

se·lec·tion·al /sɪˈlekʃənl/ *adj.* (*linguistics*) used to describe the process by which each word limits what kind of words can be used with it in normal language: *'Eat' has the selectional restriction that it must be followed by a kind of food, so 'I eat sky' is not possible.*

seˈlection committee *noun* a group of people who choose, for example, the members of a sports team

se·lect·ive AW /sɪˈlektɪv/ *adj.* **1** [usually before noun] affecting or concerned with only a small number of people or things from a larger group: *the selective breeding of cattle* ◇ *selective strike action* **2 ~ (about/in sth)** tending to be careful about what or who you choose: *You will have to be selective about which information to include in the report.* ◇ *Their admissions policy is very selective.* ◇ *a selective school* (= one that chooses which children to admit, especially according to ability) ▸ **se·lect·ive·ly** AW *adv.*: *The product will be selectively marketed in the US* (= only in some areas). **se·lect·iv·ity** /səˌlekˈtɪvəti/ *noun* [U]: *Schools are tending towards greater selectivity.*

seˌlective ˈservice *noun* [U] (*NAmE*) a system in which people have to spend a period of time in the armed forces by law

se·lect·or AW /sɪˈlektə(r)/ *noun* **1** (*BrE*) a person who chooses the members of a particular sports team **2** a device in an engine, a piece of machinery, etc. that allows you to choose a particular function

sel·en·ium /səˈliːniəm/ *noun* [U] (*symb.* Se) a chemical element. Selenium is a grey substance that is used in making electrical equipment and coloured glass. A lack of selenium in the human body can lead to illnesses such as DEPRESSION.

self 🔑 /self/ *noun* (*pl.* **selves** /selvz/)
1 🔑 [C, usually sing.] the type of person you are, especially the way you normally behave, look or feel: *You'll soon be feeling* ***your old self*** *again* (= feeling well or happy again). ◇ *He's not* ***his usual happy self*** *this morning.* ◇ *Only with a few people could she be* ***her real self*** (= show what she was really like rather than what she pretended to be). ◇ *his* ***private/professional self*** (= how he behaves at home/work) **2** [U] (also **the self** [sing.]) (*formal*) a person's personality or character that makes them different from other people: *Many people living in institutions have lost their sense of self* (= the feeling that they are individual people). ◇ *the inner self* (= a person's emotional and spiritual character) ◇ *a lack of confidence in the self* **3** [U] (*formal*) your own advantage or pleasure rather than that of other people: *She didn't do it for any reason of self.* **4** [C] used to refer to a person: *You didn't hurt your little self, did you?* ◇ *We look forward to seeing Mrs Brown and* ***your good self*** *this evening.* IDM see FORMER

self- 🔑 /self/ *combining form*
(in nouns and adjectives) of, to or by yourself or itself: *self-control* ◇ *self-addressed* ◇ *self-taught*

ˌ**self-abˈsorbed** *adj.* only concerned about or interested in yourself ▸ ˌ**self-abˈsorp·tion** *noun* [U]

ˌ**self-aˈbuse** *noun* [U] **1** behaviour by which a person does harm to himself or herself **2** (*old-fashioned*) = MASTURBATION

ˌ**self-ˈaccess** *noun* [U] a method of learning in which students choose their materials and use them to study on their own: *a* ***self-access centre/library***

ˌ**self-actual·iˈza·tion** *noun* [U] the fact of using your skills and abilities and achieving as much as you can possibly achieve SYN **self-realization**

ˌ**self-adˈdressed** *adj.* if an envelope is **self-addressed**, sb has written their own address on it

ˌ**self-adˈhesive** *adj.* [usually before noun] covered on one side with a sticky substance so that it can be stuck to sth without the use of glue, etc: *self-adhesive tape*

ˌ**self-anˈalysis** *noun* [U] the study of your own character and behaviour, especially your reasons for doing things

ˌ**self-apˈpoint·ed** *adj.* [usually before noun] (usually *disapproving*) giving yourself a particular title, job, etc, especially without the agreement of other people

ˌ**self-apˈprais·al** *noun* [U, C] an act or the process of judging your own work or achievements

ˌ**self-asˈsembly** *adj.* (*BrE*) (of furniture) bought in several parts that you have to put together yourself: *cheap self-assembly kitchen units* ▸ ˌ**self-asˈsembly** *noun* [U]: *kitchen units for self-assembly*

ˌ**self-asˈsert·ive** *adj.* very confident and not afraid to express your opinions ▸ ˌ**self-asˈsertion**, ˌ**self-asˈsert·ive·ness** *noun* [U]

ˌself-asˈsess·ment *noun* [U] **1** the process of judging your own progress, achievements, etc. **2** (*BrE*) a system of paying tax in which you calculate yourself how much you should pay

ˌself-asˈsured *adj.* having a lot of confidence in yourself and your abilities SYN **confident** ▸ **ˌself-asˈsurance** *noun* [U]

ˌself-aˈwareness *noun* [U] knowledge and understanding of your own character ▸ **ˌself-aˈware** *adj.*

ˈself-build *noun* [U, C] (*BrE*) the building of homes by their owners; a home that is built in this way: *self-build houses*

ˌself-ˈcatering *adj.* [usually before noun] (*BrE*) a **self-catering** holiday is one which provides you with accommodation and the equipment that is necessary to cook your own meals: *self-catering accommodation* ▸ **ˌself-ˈcatering** *noun* [U]: (*BrE*) *All prices are based on a week's self-catering in shared accommodation.*

ˌself-ˈcentred (*especially US* **ˌself-ˈcentered**) *adj.* (*disapproving*) tending to think only about yourself and not thinking about the needs or feelings of other people ▸ **ˌself-ˈcentred·ness** (*especially US* **ˌself-ˈcentered·ness**) *noun* [U]

ˌself-conˈfessed *adj.* [only before noun] admitting that you are a particular type of person or have a particular problem, especially a bad one: *a self-confessed thief*

ˌself-ˈconfident *adj.* having confidence in yourself and your abilities SYN **self-assured**, **confident**: *a self-confident child* ◇ *a self-confident manner* ▸ **ˌself-ˈconfidence** *noun* [U]: *He has no self-confidence.*

ˌself-congratu·ˈla·tion *noun* [U] (usually *disapproving*) a way of behaving that shows that you think you have done sth very well and are pleased with yourself ▸ **ˌself-conˈgratu·la·tory** *adj.*: *The winners gave themselves a self-congratulatory round of applause.*

ˌself-ˈconscious *adj.* **1** ~ (**about sth**) nervous or embarrassed about your appearance or what other people think of you: *He's always been self-conscious about being so short.* **2** (often *disapproving*) done in a way that shows you are aware of the effect that is being produced: *The humour of the play is self-conscious and contrived.* OPP **unself-conscious** ▸ **ˌself-ˈconscious·ly** *adv.*: *She was self-consciously aware of his stare.* **ˌself-ˈconscious·ness** *noun* [U]

ˌself-conˈtained *adj.* **1** not needing or depending on other people: *Her father was a quiet self-contained man.* **2** able to operate or exist without outside help or influence SYN **independent**: *a self-contained community* ◇ *Each chapter is self-contained and can be studied in isolation.* **3** [usually before noun] (*BrE*) (of a flat/apartment) having its own kitchen, bathroom and entrance: *self-contained accommodation*

ˌself-contraˈdict·ory *adj.* containing two ideas or statements that cannot both be true ▸ **ˌself-contraˈdic·tion** *noun* [U]

ˌself-conˈtrol *noun* [U] the ability to remain calm and not show your emotions even though you are feeling angry, excited, etc: *to* ***lose/regain*** *your* ***self-control*** ◇ *It took all his self-control not to shout at them.* ▸ **ˌself-conˈtrolled** *adj.*

ˌself-corˈrect·ing *adj.* [usually before noun] that corrects or adjusts itself without outside help: *The economic market is a self-correcting mechanism, that does not need regulation by government.*

ˌself-ˈcriticism *noun* [U] the process of looking at and judging your own faults or weaknesses ▸ **ˌself-ˈcritical** *adj.*: *Don't be too self-critical.*

ˌself-deˈception *noun* [U] the act of making yourself believe sth that you know is not true

ˌself-deˈfeat·ing *adj.* causing more problems and difficulties instead of solving them; not achieving what you wanted to achieve but having an opposite effect: *Paying children too much attention when they misbehave can be self-defeating.*

ˌself-deˈfence (*BrE*) (*NAmE* **ˌself-deˈfense**) *noun* [U] **1** something you say or do in order to protect yourself when you are being attacked, criticized, etc: *The man later told police that he was acting* ***in self-defence.*** **2** the skill of being able to protect yourself from physical attack without using weapons: *I'm taking classes in self-defence.*

ˌself-deˈlusion *noun* [U] the act of making yourself believe sth that you know is not true

ˌself-deˈnial *noun* [U] the act of not having or doing the things you like, either because you do not have enough money, or for moral or religious reasons SYN **abstinence**

ˌself-ˈdeprecat·ing *adj.* done in a way that makes your own achievements or abilities seem unimportant: *He gave a self-deprecating shrug.* ▸ **ˌself-depreˈca·tion** *noun* [U]

ˌself-deˈstruct *verb* [I] (especially of a machine, etc.) to destroy itself, usually by exploding: *This tape will self-destruct in 30 seconds.* ◇ (*figurative*) *In the last half-hour of the movie the plot rapidly self-destructs.*

ˌself-deˈstruc·tion *noun* [U] the act of doing things to deliberately harm yourself ▸ **ˌself-deˈstruc·tive** *adj.*

ˌself-deˌtermiˈn·ation *noun* [U] (*formal*) **1** the right of a country or a region and its people to be independent and to choose their own government and political system SYN **independence** **2** the right or ability of a person to control their own FATE

ˌself-deˈvelop·ment *noun* [U] the process by which a person's character and abilities are developed: *Staff are encouraged to use the library for professional self-development.*

ˌself-ˈdiscip·line *noun* [U] the ability to make yourself do sth, especially sth difficult or unpleasant: *It takes a lot of self-discipline to go jogging in winter.*

ˌself-disˈcov·ery *noun* [U] the process of understanding more about yourself in order to make yourself happier: *David left his boring job to go on a* ***journey of self-discovery.***

ˌself-ˈdoubt *noun* [U, C] the feeling that you are not good enough

ˌself-ˈdrive *adj.* [only before noun] (*BrE*) **1** a **self-drive** car is one that you hire and drive yourself **2** a **self-drive** holiday is one on which you use your own car or a car you hire to travel to the holiday area

ˌself-ˈeducated *adj.* having learned things by reading books, etc. rather than at school or college

ˌself-efˈfacing *adj.* not wanting to attract attention to yourself or your abilities SYN **modest**: *He was a shy, self-effacing man.* ▸ **ˌself-efˈface·ment** *noun* [U]

ˌself-emˈployed *adj.* working for yourself and not employed by a company, etc: *a self-employed musician* ◇ *retirement plans for the self-employed* (= people who are self-employed) ▸ **ˌself-emˈploy·ment** *noun* [U]

ˌself-eˈsteem *noun* [U] a feeling of being happy with your own character and abilities SYN **self-worth**: *to have* ***high/low self-esteem*** ◇ *You need to build your self-esteem.*

ˌself-ˈevident *adj.* obvious and needing no further proof or explanation: *The dangers of such action are self-evident.* ◇ *a self-evident truth* ▸ **ˌself-ˈevident·ly** *adv.*

ˌself-exˌamiˈn·ation *noun* [U] **1** the study of your own behaviour and beliefs to find out if they are right or wrong **2** the act of checking your body for any signs of illness

ˌself-exˈplana·tory *adj.* easy to understand and not needing any more explanation

ˌself-exˈpres·sion *noun* [U] the expression of your thoughts or feelings, especially through activities such as writing, painting, dancing, etc: *You should encourage your child's attempts at self-expression.*

ˌself-fulˈfil·ling *adj.* [usually before noun] a **self-fulfilling** PROPHECY is one that becomes true because people expect it to be true and behave in a way that will make it happen: *If you expect to fail, you will fail. It's a* ***self-fulfilling prophecy.***

S

ˌ**self-fulˈfil·ment** (*BrE*) (also ˌ**self-fulˈfill·ment** *NAmE*) *noun* [U] the feeling of being happy and satisfied that you have everything you want or need

ˌ**self-ˈgovern·ment** *noun* [U] the government or control of a country or an organization by its own people or members, not by others ▸ ˌ**self-ˈgovern·ing** *adj.*

ˌ**self-ˈharm** *noun* [U] the practice of deliberately injuring yourself, for example by cutting yourself, as a result of having serious emotional or mental problems ▸ ˌ**self-ˈharm** *verb* [I]: *As a teenager I was self-harming regularly.*

ˌ**self-ˈhelp** *noun* [U] the act of relying on your own efforts and abilities in order to solve your problems, rather than depending on other people for help ▸ ˌ**self-ˈhelp** *adj.* [only before noun]: *a self-help discussion group for people suffering from depression* (= whose members help each other)

ˌ**self-ˈimage** *noun* the opinion or idea you have of yourself, especially of your appearance or abilities: *to have a* ***positive/negative self-image***

ˌ**self-imˈport·ant** *adj.* (*disapproving*) thinking that you are more important than other people **SYN arrogant** ▸ ˌ**self-imˈport·ance** *noun* [U] ˌ**self-imˈport·ant·ly** *adv.*

ˌ**self-imˈposed** *adj.* [usually before noun] a **self-imposed** task, duty, etc. is one that you force yourself to do rather than one that sb else forces you to do

ˌ**self-imˈprove·ment** *noun* [U] the process by which a person improves their knowledge, status, character, etc. by their own efforts

ˌ**self-inˈduced** *adj.* (of illness, problems, etc.) caused by yourself: *self-induced vomiting*

ˌ**self-inˈdulgent** *adj.* (*disapproving*) allowing yourself to have or do things that you like, especially when you do this too much or too often ▸ ˌ**self-inˈdulgence** *noun* [U]

ˌ**self-inˈflict·ed** *adj.* a **self-inflicted** injury, problem, etc. is one that you cause for yourself: *a self-inflicted wound*

ˌ**self-ˈinterest** *noun* [U] (*disapproving*) the fact of sb only considering their own interests and of not caring about things that would help other people: *Not all of them were acting out of self-interest.* ▸ ˌ**self-ˈinterest·ed** *adj.*

self·ish /ˈselfɪʃ/ *adj.* caring only about yourself rather than about other people: *selfish behaviour* ◇ *Do you think I'm being selfish by not letting her go?* ◇ *What a selfish thing to do!* ◇ *It was selfish of him to leave all the work to you.* **OPP unselfish, selfless** ▸ **self·ish·ly** *adv.*: *She looked forward, a little selfishly, to a weekend away from her family.* **self·ish·ness** *noun* [U]

ˌ**self-ˈknowledge** *noun* [U] an understanding of yourself

self·less /ˈselfləs/ *adj.* thinking more about the needs, happiness, etc. of other people than about your own: *a life of selfless service to the community* **OPP selfish** ▸ **self·less·ly** *adv.* **self·less·ness** *noun* [U]

ˌ**self-ˈlove** *noun* [U] (*approving*) the feeling that your own happiness and wishes are important

ˌ**self-ˈmade** *adj.* [usually before noun] having become rich and successful through your own hard work rather than having had money given to you: *He was proud of the fact that he was a* ***self-made man.***

ˌ**self-ˈmotivated** *adj.* if a person is **self-motivated**, they are capable of hard work and effort without the need for encouragement ▸ ˌ**self-motiˈva·tion** *noun* [U]

ˌ**self-mutiˈla·tion** *noun* [U] the act of wounding yourself, especially when this is a sign of mental illness

ˌ**self-oˈpinion·ated** *adj.* (*disapproving*) believing that your own opinions are always right and refusing to listen to those of other people **SYN opinionated**

ˌ**self-perˈpetu·at·ing** *adj.* continuing without any outside influence: *Revenge leads to a self-perpetuating cycle of violence.*

ˌ**self-ˈpity** *noun* [U] (often *disapproving*) a feeling of pity for yourself, especially because of sth unpleasant or unfair that has happened to you: *She's not someone who likes to* ***wallow in self-pity.*** ▸ ˌ**self-ˈpitying** *adj.*

ˌ**self-ˈportrait** *noun* a painting, etc. that you do of yourself

ˌ**self-posˈsessed** *adj.* able to remain calm and confident in a difficult situation ▸ ˌ**self-posˈses·sion** *noun* [U]: *He soon recovered his usual self-possession.*

ˌ**self-preser·ˈva·tion** *noun* [U] the fact of protecting yourself in a dangerous or difficult situation: *She was held back by some sense of self-preservation.*

ˌ**self-proˈclaimed** *adj.* (often *disapproving*) giving yourself a particular title, job, etc. without the agreement or permission of other people

ˌ**self-proˈmotion** *noun* [U] (*disapproving*) the activity of making people notice you and your abilities, especially in a way that annoys other people: *The article was a piece of blatant self-promotion.*

ˌ**self-raising ˈflour** (*US* ˈ**baking flour**, ˌ**self-rising ˈflour**) *noun* [U] flour that contains BAKING POWDER ➲ compare PLAIN FLOUR

ˌ**self-realiˈza·tion** *noun* [U] the fact of using your skills and abilities and achieving as much as you can possibly achieve **SYN self-actualization**

self-referen·tial /ˌself refəˈrenʃl/ *adj.* (*technical*) (of a work of literature) referring to the fact of actually being a work of literature, or to the author, or to other works that the author has written

ˌ**self-reˈgard** *noun* [U] a good opinion of yourself, which is considered bad if you have too little or too much: *He suffers from a lack of self-regard.* ▸ ˌ**self-reˈgard·ing** *adj.*: *His biography is nothing but self-regarding nonsense.*

ˌ**self-ˈregulat·ing** *adj.* something that is **self-regulating** controls itself: *a self-regulating economy* ▸ ˌ**self-reguˈla·tion** *noun* [U]

ˌ**self-reˈliant** *adj.* able to do or decide things by yourself, rather than depending on other people for help **SYN independent** ▸ ˌ**self-reˈliance** *noun* [U]

ˌ**self-reˈspect** *noun* [U] a feeling of pride in yourself that what you do, say, etc. is right and good

ˌ**self-reˈspect·ing** *adj.* [only before noun] (especially in negative sentences) having pride in yourself because you believe that what you do is right and good: *No self-respecting journalist would ever work for that newspaper.*

ˌ**self-reˈstraint** *noun* [U] the ability to stop yourself doing or saying sth that you want to because you know it is better not to: *She* ***exercised*** *all her* ***self-restraint*** *and kept quiet.*

ˌ**self-ˈrighteous** *adj.* (*disapproving*) feeling or behaving as if what you say or do is always morally right, and other people are wrong **SYN sanctimonious** ▸ ˌ**self-ˈright·eous·ly** *adv.* ˌ**self-ˈrighteous·ness** *noun* [U]

ˌ**self-rising ˈflour** (also ˈ**baking flour**) (both *US*) (*BrE* ˌ**self-raising ˈflour**) *noun* [U] flour that contains BAKING POWDER ➲ compare ALL-PURPOSE FLOUR

ˌ**self-ˈrule** *noun* [U] the governing of a country or an area by its own people

ˌ**self-ˈsacrifice** *noun* [U] (*approving*) the act of not allowing yourself to have or do sth in order to help other people: *the courage and self-sacrifice of those who fought in the war* ▸ ˌ**self-ˈsacrifi·cing** *adj.*

self·same /ˈselfseɪm/ *adj.* [only before noun] **the, this, etc. selfsame...** used to emphasize that two people or things are the same **SYN identical**: *Jane had been wondering that selfsame thing.*

ˌ**self-ˈsatisfied** *adj.* (*disapproving*) too pleased with yourself or your own achievements **SYN smug**: *He had a self-satisfied smirk on his face.* ▸ ˌ**self-satisˈfac·tion** *noun* [U]: *a look of self-satisfaction*

ˌ**self-ˈseeking** *adj.* (*disapproving*) interested only in your own needs and interests rather than thinking about the needs of other people ▸ ˌ**self-ˈseeking** *noun* [U]

ˌ**self-seˈlection** *noun* [U] a situation in which people decide for themselves to do sth rather than being chosen to do it ▸ ˌ**self-seˈlect·ing** *adj.*: *a self-selecting group* ˌ**self-seˈlected** *adj.*

ˌ**self-ˈservice** *adj.* [usually before noun] a **self-service** shop/store, restaurant, etc. is one in which customers serve themselves and then pay for the goods ▶ ˌ**self-ˈservice** *noun* [U]: *The cafe provides quick self-service at low prices.*

ˌ**self-ˈserving** *adj.* (*disapproving*) interested only in gaining an advantage for yourself

ˌ**self-ˈstarter** *noun* (*approving*) a person who is able to work on their own and make their own decisions without needing anyone to tell them what to do

ˌ**self-ˈstorage** *noun* [U] a service that provides a place where you can store things and a key so that you can get them when you need them: *self-storage facilities/units*

ˌ**self-ˈstudy** *noun* [U] the activity of learning about sth without a teacher to help you ▶ ˌ**self-ˈstudy** *adj.*: *self-study materials*

ˌ**self-ˈstyled** *adj.* [only before noun] (*disapproving*) using a name or title that you have given yourself, especially when you do not have the right to do it

ˌ**self-sufˈficient** *adj.* ~ (**in sth**) able to do or produce everything that you need without the help of other people: *The country is totally self-sufficient in food production.* ▶ ˌ**self-sufˈficiency** *noun* [U]

ˌ**self-supˈport·ing** *adj.* having enough money to be able to operate without financial help from other people

ˌ**self-ˈtaught** *adj.* having learned sth by reading books, etc, rather than by sb teaching you: *a self-taught artist*

ˌ**self-ˈwilled** *adj.* (*disapproving*) determined to do what you want without caring about other people SYN **headstrong**

ˌ**self-ˈworth** *noun* [U] a feeling of confidence in yourself that you are a good and useful person SYN **self-esteem**

selkie /ˈselki/ (also **silkie**) *noun* (in Scottish stories) an imaginary creature which sometimes looks like a human and sometimes looks like a SEAL

sell 🔑 /sel/ *verb, noun*

■ *verb* (**sold, sold** /səʊld; *NAmE* soʊld/)

▸ EXCHANGE FOR MONEY **1** 🔑 [T, I] to give sth to sb in exchange for money: ~ **sth** (**to sb**) (**for sth**) *I sold my car to James for £800.* ◇ ~ **sb sth** (**for sth**) *I sold James my car for £800.* ◇ ~ (**sth**) (**at sth**) *They* **sold** *the business* **at a profit/loss** (= they gained/lost money when they sold it). ◇ *We offered them a good price but they wouldn't sell.*

▸ OFFER FOR SALE **2** 🔑 [T] ~ **sth** to offer sth for people to buy: *Most supermarkets sell a range of organic products.* ◇ *Do you sell stamps?* ◇ *to sell insurance* ➲ compare CROSS-SELLING

▸ BE BOUGHT **3** 🔑 [T, I] to be bought by people in the way or in the numbers mentioned; to be offered at the price mentioned: ~ (**sth**) *The magazine sells 300 000 copies a week.* ◇ *The book sold well and was reprinted many times.* ◇ *The new design just didn't sell* (= nobody bought it). ◇ ~ **for/at sth** *The pens sell for just 50p each.*

▸ PERSUADE **4** [I, T] to make people want to buy sth: *You may not like it but advertising sells.* ◇ ~ **sth** *It is quality not price that sells our products.* **5** 🔑 [T] ~ **sth/yourself** (**to sb**) to persuade sb that sth is a good idea, service, product, etc; to persuade sb that you are the right person for a job, position, etc: *Now we have to try and sell the idea to management.* ◇ *You really have to sell yourself at a job interview.*

▸ TAKE MONEY/REWARD **6** [T] ~ **yourself** (**to sb**) (*disapproving*) to accept money or a reward from sb for doing sth that is against your principles SYN **prostitute** ➲ see also SALE

IDM **be ˈsold on sth** (*informal*) to be very enthusiastic about sth **sell your ˈbody** to have sex with sb in exchange for money **sell sb down the ˈriver** (*informal*) to give poor or unfair treatment to sb you have promised to help ORIGIN From the custom of buying and selling slaves on the plantations on the Mississippi river in America. Slaves who caused trouble for their masters could be sold to plantation owners lower down the river, where conditions would be worse. **sell sb/yourself ˈshort** to not value sb/yourself highly enough and show this by the way you treat or present them/yourself **sell your ˈsoul** (**to the devil**) to do anything, even sth bad or dishonest, in return for money, success or power ➲ more at HOT *adj.*, PUP

PHR V ˌ**sell sth↔ˈoff 1** 🔑 to sell things cheaply because you want to get rid of them or because you need the money **2** 🔑 to sell all or part of an industry, a company or land: *The Church sold off the land for housing.* ➲ related noun SELL-OFF ˌ**sell sth↔ˈon** to sell to sb else sth that you have bought not long before: *She managed the business for a year and then sold it on.* ˌ**sell ˈout** | **be ˌsold ˈout** 🔑 (of tickets for a concert, sports game, etc.) to be all sold: *The tickets sold out within hours.* ◇ *This week's performances are completely sold out.* ˌ**sell ˈout** (**of sth**) | **be ˌsold ˈout** (**of sth**) to have sold all the available items, tickets, etc: *I'm sorry, we've sold out of bread.* ◇ *We are already sold out for what should be a fantastic game.* ˌ**sell ˈout** (**to sb/sth**) **1** (*disapproving*) to change or give up your beliefs or principles: *He's a talented screenwriter who has sold out to TV soap operas.* **2** to sell your business or a part of your business: *The company eventually sold out to a multinational media group.* ➲ related noun SELL-OUT ˌ**sell ˈup** | ˌ**sell sth↔ˈup** (*especially BrE*) to sell your home, possessions, business, etc, usually because you are leaving the country or retiring

■ *noun* [sing.] (*informal*) something that is not as good as it seemed to be: *The band only played for about half an hour —it was a real sell.* ➲ see also HARD SELL

ˈ**sell-by date** (*BrE*) (*US* ˈ**pull date**) *noun* the date printed on food packages, etc. after which the food must not be sold: *This milk is past its sell-by date.* ◇ (*figurative*) *These policies are way past their sell-by date.*

sell·er /ˈselə(r)/ *noun* **1** a person who sells sth: *a flower seller* ◇ *The law is intended to protect both the buyer and the seller.* ➲ see also BOOKSELLER ➲ compare VENDOR **2 a good, poor, etc.** ~ a product that has been sold in the amounts or way mentioned: *This particular model is one of our biggest sellers.* ➲ see also BEST-SELLER

IDM **a ˌseller's ˈmarket** a situation in which people selling sth have an advantage, because there is not a lot of a particular item for sale, and prices can be kept high

ˈ**selling point** *noun* a feature of sth that makes people want to buy or use it: *The price is obviously one of the main selling points.* ◇ *Sales departments try to identify a product's USP or 'unique selling point'.*

ˈ**selling price** *noun* the price at which sth is sold ➲ compare ASKING PRICE, COST PRICE

ˈ**sell-off** *noun* **1** (*BrE*) the sale by the government of an industry or a service to individual people or private companies **2** (*NAmE, business*) the sale of a large number of STOCKS and SHARES, after which their value usually falls

Sel·lo·tape™ /ˈseləteɪp/ *noun* (also ˈ**sticky tape**) (both *BrE*) (*NAmE* ˈ**Scotch tape™**) [U] clear plastic tape that is sticky on one side, used for sticking things together: *a roll of Sellotape* ◇ *The envelope was stuck down with Sellotape.* ➲ VISUAL VOCAB page V56

sel·lo·tape /ˈseləteɪp/ *verb* ~ **sth** (**to sth**) (*BrE*) to join or stick things together with Sellotape: *We found a note sellotaped to the front door.*

ˈ**sell-out** *noun* [usually sing.] **1** a play, concert, etc. for which all the tickets have been sold: *Next week's final looks like being a sell-out.* ◇ *a sell-out tour* **2** a situation in which sb is not loyal to a person or group who trusted them, by not doing sth that they promised to do, or by doing sth that they promised not to do: *The workers see the deal as a union sell-out to management.*

selt·zer /ˈseltsə(r)/ *noun* [U, C] FIZZY water (= with bubbles), usually containing minerals, used as a drink

selv·edge (also **selv·age** especially in *NAmE*) /ˈselvɪdʒ/ *noun* an edge that is made on a piece of cloth, which stops the threads from coming apart (= stops it FRAYING)

selves *pl.* of SELF

se·man·tic /sɪˈmæntɪk/ *adj.* [usually before noun] (*linguistics*) connected with the meaning of words and sentences ▶ **se·man·tic·al·ly** /-kli/ *adv.*: *semantically related words*

seˌmantic ˈfield *noun* (*linguistics*) a set of words with related meanings

S

se·man·tics /sɪˈmæntɪks/ *noun* [U] (*linguistics*) **1** the study of the meanings of words and phrases **2** the meaning of words, phrases or systems

sema·phore /ˈseməfɔː(r)/ *noun, verb*
- ***noun*** [U] a system for sending signals in which you hold your arms or two flags in particular positions to represent different letters of the alphabet
- ***verb*** [I, T] **~ (sth)** | **~ that...** to send a message to sb by semaphore or a similar system of signals

semb·lance /ˈsembləns/ *noun* [sing., U] **~ of sth** (*formal*) a situation in which sth seems to exist although this may not, in fact, be the case: *The ceasefire brought about a semblance of peace.* ◇ *Life at last returned to some semblance of normality.*

semen /ˈsiːmən/ *noun* [U] the whitish liquid containing SPERM that is produced by the sex organs of men and male animals

se·mes·ter /sɪˈmestə(r)/ *noun* one of the two periods that the school or college year is divided into: *the **spring/fall semester*** ➲ see also TERM ➲ compare TRIMESTER

semi /ˈsemi/ *noun* (*pl.* semis) **1** (*BrE, informal*) a SEMI-DETACHED house (= one that is joined to another house by one shared wall): *suburban semis* **2** (*NAmE*) = SEMI-TRAILER **3** = SEMI-FINAL

semi- /ˈsemi/ *prefix* (in adjectives and nouns) half; partly: *semicircular* ◇ *semi-final*

ˌsemi-ˈarid *adj.* (*technical*) (of land or climate) dry; with little rain

ˌsemi-autoˈmat·ic *adj.* (of a gun) able to load bullets automatically, and therefore very quickly, but not firing automatically ▶ **ˌsemi-autoˈmat·ic** *noun*

semi·breve /ˈsemibriːv/ (*BrE*) (*NAmE* **ˈwhole note**) *noun* (*music*) a note that lasts as long as four CROTCHETS/QUARTER NOTES ➲ picture at MUSIC

semi·circle /ˈsemisɜːkl; *NAmE* -sɜːrkl/ *noun* **1** (*geometry*) one half of a circle ➲ VISUAL VOCAB page V58 **2** the line that forms the edge of a semicircle **3** a thing, or a group of people or things, shaped like a semicircle: *a semicircle of chairs* ◇ *We sat in a semicircle round the fire.* ▶ **semi·cir·cu·lar** /ˌsemiˈsɜːkjələ(r); *NAmE* -ˈsɜːrk-/ *adj.*: *a semicircular driveway*

semi·colon /ˌsemiˈkəʊlən; *NAmE* ˈsemikoʊ-/ *noun* the mark (;) used to separate the parts of a complicated sentence or items in a detailed list, showing a pause that is longer than a comma but shorter than a full stop/period ➲ compare COLON

semi·con·duct·or /ˌsemikənˈdʌktə(r)/ *noun* (*technical*) **1** a solid substance that CONDUCTS electricity in particular conditions, better than INSULATORS but not as well as CONDUCTORS **2** a device containing a semiconductor used in ELECTRONICS

ˌsemi-deˈtached *adj.* (of a house) joined to another house by a wall on one side that is shared ▶ **ˌsemi-deˈtached** *noun* (*BrE*) ➲ VISUAL VOCAB page V14 ➲ compare DETACHED ➲ see also SEMI, TERRACED

ˌsemi-ˈfinal (also **semi**) *noun* one of the two games or parts of a sports competition that are held to decide who will compete in the last part (the FINAL): *He's through to the semi-final of the men's singles.* ▶ **ˌsemi-ˈfinalist** *noun*: *They are semi-finalists for the fourth year in succession.*

semi·metal /ˈsemimetl/ *noun* (*BrE*) = METALLOID

sem·inal /ˈsemɪnl/ *adj.* **1** (*formal*) very important and having a strong influence on later developments: *a **seminal work/article/study*** **2** [usually before noun] (*technical*) of or containing SEMEN: *seminal fluid*

sem·inar /ˈsemɪnɑː(r)/ *noun* **1** a class at a university or college when a small group of students and a teacher discuss or study a particular topic: *Teaching is by lectures and seminars.* ◇ *a graduate seminar* ◇ *a seminar room* ➲ COLLOCATIONS at EDUCATION **2** a meeting for discussion or training: *a one-day management seminar*

sem·in·ar·ian /ˌsemɪˈneəriən; *NAmE* -ˈner-/ *noun* a student in a seminary

sem·in·ary /ˈsemɪnəri; *NAmE* -neri/ *noun* (*pl.* -ies) a college where priests, ministers or RABBIS are trained

Sem·in·ole /ˈsemɪnəʊl; *NAmE* -oʊl/ *noun* (*pl.* **Sem·in·ole** or **Sem·in·oles**) a member of a Native American people, many of whom live in the US states of Oklahoma and Florida

semi·ot·ics /ˌsemiˈɒtɪks; *NAmE* -ˈɑːtɪks/ *noun* [U] the study of signs and symbols and of their meaning and use ▶ **semi·ot·ic** *adj.*: *semiotic analysis*

ˌsemi-ˈprecious *adj.* [usually before noun] (of a JEWEL) less valuable than the most valuable types of JEWELS

ˌsemi-proˈfes·sion·al *adj.* **semi-professional** musicians or sports players are paid for what they do, but do not do it as their main job ▶ **ˌsemi-proˈfes·sion·al** *noun*

semi·quaver /ˈsemikweɪvə(r)/ (*BrE*) (*NAmE* **ˌsixˈteenth note**) *noun* (*music*) a note that lasts half as long as a QUAVER/EIGHTH NOTE ➲ picture at MUSIC

ˌsemi-ˈskilled *adj.* [usually before noun] (of workers) having some special training or qualifications, but less than skilled people: *a semi-skilled machine operator* ◇ *semi-skilled jobs* (= for people who have some special training)

ˌsemi-ˈskimmed *adj.* (*BrE*) (of milk) that has had a lot of the fat removed

Sem·ite /ˈsemaɪt/ *noun* a member of the peoples who speak Semitic languages, including Arabs and Jews

Sem·it·ic /səˈmɪtɪk/ *adj.* **1** of or connected with the language group that includes Hebrew and Arabic **2** of or connected with the people who speak Semitic languages, especially Hebrew and Arabic

semi·tone /ˈsemitəʊn; *NAmE* -toʊn/ (*BrE*) (*NAmE* **ˈhalf step**, **ˈhalf-tone**) *noun* (*music*) half a TONE on a musical SCALE, for example the INTERVAL between C and C♯ or between E and F ➲ compare STEP *n.* (10)

ˈsemi-trailer *noun* (*NAmE*) a TRAILER that has wheels at the back and is supported at the front by the vehicle that is pulling it

ˌsemi-ˈtropic·al *adj.* = SUBTROPICAL

semi·vowel /ˈsemivaʊəl/ *noun* (*phonetics*) a speech sound that sounds like a vowel but functions as a consonant, for example /w/ and /j/ in the English words *wet* and *yet*

semo·lina /ˌseməˈliːnə/ *noun* [U] **1** large hard grains of WHEAT used when crushed for making PASTA and sweet dishes **2** a sweet dish made from semolina and milk, eaten for DESSERT in Britain and for breakfast in the US

sem·tex /ˈsemteks/ *noun* [U] a powerful EXPLOSIVE that is used for making bombs, often illegally

Sen. *abbr.* SENATOR: *Sen. John K Nordqvist*

sen·ate 0-π /ˈsenət/ *noun* (usually **the Senate**) **1** 0-π [sing.] one of the two groups of elected politicians who make laws in some countries, for example in the US, Australia, Canada and France. The Senate is smaller than the other group but higher in rank. Many state parliaments in the US also have a Senate: *a member of the Senate* ◇ *a Senate committee* ➲ COLLOCATIONS at POLITICS ➲ compare CONGRESS, THE HOUSE OF REPRESENTATIVES **2** [C, usually sing., U] (in some countries) the group of people who control a university: *the senate of Loughborough University* **3** [sing.] (in ancient Rome) the most important council of the government; the building where the council met

sen·ator 0-π /ˈsenətə(r)/ *noun* (often **Senator**) (*abbr.* **Sen.**) a member of a senate: *Senator McCarthy* ◇ *She has served as a Democratic senator for North Carolina since 2009.* ▶ **sen·at·or·ial** /ˌsenəˈtɔːriəl/ *adj.* [only before noun]: *a senatorial candidate*

send 0-π /send/ *verb* (**sent**, **sent** /sent/)
▸ **BY MAIL/RADIO** **1** 0-π to make sth go or be taken to a place, especially by post/mail, email, radio, etc: **~ sth** *to send a letter/package/cheque/fax/email* ◇ *She sent the letter by airmail.* ◇ (*BrE*) *to send sth by post* ◇ (*NAmE*) *to send sth by mail*

S

◇ **~ sth to sb** *A radio signal was sent to the spacecraft.* ◇ *The CD player was faulty so we sent it back to the manufacturers.* ◇ *Have you sent a postcard to your mother yet?* ◇ **~ sb sth** *Have you sent your mother a postcard yet?* ◇ *I'll send you a text message.*
▸ MESSAGE **2** to tell sb sth by sending them a message: **~ sth** *My parents **send their love**.* ◇ **~ sth to sb** *What sort of message is that sending to young people?* ◇ **~ sb sth** *He **sent** me **word** to come.* ◇ **~ sth (that)...** *She **sent word** (that) she could not come.* ◇ **~ to do sth** (*formal*) *She sent to say that she was coming home.*
▸ SB SOMEWHERE **3** to tell sb to go somewhere or to do sth; to arrange for sb to go somewhere: **~ sb** *Ed couldn't make it so they sent me instead.* ◇ **~ sb + adv./prep.** *She sent the kids to bed early.* ◇ *to send sb to prison/boarding school* ◇ **~ sb to do sth** *I've sent Tom to buy some milk.*
▸ MAKE STH MOVE QUICKLY **4** to make sth/sb move quickly or suddenly: **~ sth/sb doing sth** *Every step he took sent the pain shooting up his leg.* ◇ *The punch **sent him flying**.* ◇ **~ sth/sb + adv./prep.** *The report sent share prices down a further 8p.*
▸ MAKE SB REACT **5** to make sb behave or react in a particular way: **~ sb to sth** *Her music always sends me to sleep.* ◇ **~ sb into sth** *Her account of the visit sent us into fits of laughter.* ◇ **~ sb + adj.** *All the publicity nearly sent him crazy.*
IDM **send sb 'packing** (*informal*) to tell sb firmly or rudely to go away ➲ more at COVENTRY, LOVE *n.*, THING
PHR V **,send a'way (to sb) (for sth)** = SEND OFF (FOR STH) **,send sb↔'down** (*BrE*) **1** (*informal*) to send sb to prison **2** (*old-fashioned*) to order a student to leave a university because of bad behaviour **'send for sb** to ask or tell sb to come to you, especially in order to help you: *Send for a doctor, quickly!* **'send for sth** to ask sb to bring or deliver sth to you: *His son found him and sent for help.* ◇ *She sent for the latest sales figures.* **,send sb 'forth** (*old-fashioned* or *literary*) to send sb away from you to another place **,send 'forth sth** (*formal*) to produce a sound, signal, etc. so that other people can hear it, receive it, etc: *He opened his mouth and sent forth a stream of noise.* **,send sb↔'in** to order sb to go to a place to deal with a difficult situation: *Troops were sent in to restore order.* **,send sth↔'in** to send sth by post/mail to a place where it will be dealt with: *Have you sent in your application yet?* **,send 'off (for sth)** | **,send a'way (to sb) (for sth)** to write to sb and ask them to send you sth by post/mail: *I've sent off for some books for my course.* **,send sb↔'off** (*BrE*) (in a sports game) to order sb to leave the field because they have broken the rules of the game: *Beckham was sent off for a foul in the second half.* ➲ related noun SENDING-OFF **,send sth↔'off** to send sth to a place by post/mail: *I'm sending the files off to my boss tomorrow.* **,send sth↔'on 1** to send sth to a place so that it arrives before you get there: *We sent our furniture on by ship.* **2** to send a letter that has been sent to sb's old address to their new address SYN **forward 3** to send sth from one place/person to another: *They arranged for the information to be sent on to us.* **,send 'out for sth** to ask a restaurant or shop/store to deliver food to you at home or at work: *Let's send out for a pizza.* **,send sth↔'out 1** to send sth to a lot of different people or places: *Have the invitations been sent out yet?* **2** to produce sth, such as light, a signal, sound, etc. SYN **emit** **,send sb/sth↔'up** (*informal*) to make people laugh at sb/sth by copying them/it in a funny way: *a TV programme that sends up politicians* ➲ related noun SEND-UP **,send sb↔'up** (*US, informal*) to send sb to prison

send·er /'sendə(r)/ *noun* a person who sends sth: *If undelivered, please return to sender.*

,sending-'off *noun* (*pl.* sendings-off) (*BrE*) (in football (SOCCER)) a situation when a REFEREE tells a player to leave the field because they have broken the rules in a serious way

'send-off *noun* (*informal*) an occasion when people come together to say goodbye to sb who is leaving

'send-up *noun* (*informal*) an act of making sb/sth look silly by copying them in a funny way

Sen·eca /'senəkə/ *noun* (*pl.* Sen·eca or Sen·ecas) a member of a Native American people, many of whom now live in the US states of New York and Ohio

sen·es·cence /sɪ'nesns/ *noun* [U] (*formal* or *technical*) the process of becoming old and showing the effects of being old ▸ **sen·es·cent** *adj.*

se·nile /'siːnaɪl/ *adj.* behaving in a confused or strange way, and unable to remember things, because you are old: *I think she's **going senile**.* ➲ COLLOCATIONS at AGE ▸ **sen·il·ity** /sə'nɪləti/ *noun* [U]: *an old man on the verge of senility*

,senile de'mentia *noun* [U] a serious mental DISORDER in old people that causes loss of memory, loss of control of the body, etc.

se·nior /'siːniə(r)/ *adj., noun*
■ ***adj.***
▸ OF HIGH RANK **1** **~ (to sb)** high in rank or status; higher in rank or status than others: *a **senior officer/manager/lecturer*** ◇ *a **senior partner** in a law firm* ◇ *a **senior post/position*** ◇ *I have ten years' experience at senior management level.* ◇ (*BrE*) *Junior nurses usually work alongside more senior nurses.* ◇ *He is senior to me.* ◇ *The meeting should be chaired by the most senior person present.* OPP **junior**
▸ IN SPORT **2** [only before noun] for adults or people at a more advanced level: *to take part in senior competitions* ◇ *He won the senior men's 400 metres.*
▸ FOR OLDER PEOPLE **3** [only before noun] for SENIOR CITIZENS (= older people, especially those who have retired from work): *Get one third off rail fares with a senior railcard.* ◇ *senior discounts/concessions*
▸ FATHER **4 Senior** (*abbr.* Snr., Sr) used after the name of a man who has the same name as his son, to avoid confusion ➲ compare JUNIOR
▸ SCHOOL/COLLEGE **5** [only before noun] (*BrE*) (of a school or part of a school) for children over the age of 11 or 13 **6** [only before noun] (*NAmE*) connected with the last year in HIGH SCHOOL or college: *the senior prom*
■ ***noun***
▸ OLDER PERSON **1** a person who is older than sb else: *She was ten years his senior.* ◇ *My brother is my senior by two years.* ➲ compare JUNIOR **2** (*especially NAmE*) = SENIOR CITIZEN
▸ HIGHER RANK **3** a person who is higher in rank or status: *She felt unappreciated both by her colleagues and her seniors.*
▸ IN SPORT **4** adults or people who have reached an advanced level: *tennis coaching for juniors and seniors*
▸ IN SCHOOL/COLLEGE **5** (*BrE*) a child at a senior school; an older child in a school **6** (in the US and some other countries) a student in the last year at a HIGH SCHOOL or college: *high school seniors* ➲ compare SOPHOMORE

,senior 'citizen (also **se·nior** especially in *NAmE*) *noun* an older person, especially sb who has retired from work. People often call sb a 'senior citizen' to avoid saying that they are old or using the word 'old-age pensioner'.

,senior 'common room *noun* (*abbr.* SCR) (*BrE*) a room used for social activities by teaching staff in a college or university

,senior 'high school (also **,senior 'high**) *noun* (in the US) a school for young people between the ages of 14 and 18 ➲ compare JUNIOR HIGH SCHOOL

se·ni·or·ity /,siːni'ɒrəti; *NAmE* -'ɔːr-; -'ɑːr-/ *noun* [U] **1** the fact of being older or of a higher rank than others: *a position of seniority* **2** the rank that you have in a company because of the length of time you have worked there: *a lawyer with five years' seniority* ◇ *Should promotion be based on merit or seniority?*

,senior 'moment *noun* (*humorous*) an occasion when sb forgets sth, or does not think clearly (thought to be typical of what happens when people get older): *It was an important meeting and a bad time to **have a senior moment**.*

sen·sa·tion /sen'seɪʃn/ *noun* **1** [C] a feeling that you get when sth affects your body: *a **tingling/burning, etc. sensation*** ◇ *I had a sensation of falling, as if in a dream.* **2** [U] the ability to feel through your sense of touch SYN **feeling**: *She seemed to have lost all sensation in her*

S

arms. **3** [C, usually sing.] a general feeling or impression that is difficult to explain; an experience or a memory: *He had the eerie sensation of being watched.* ◇ *When I arrived, I had the sensation that she had been expecting me.* **4** [C, usually sing., U] very great surprise, excitement, or interest among a lot of people; the person or the thing that causes this surprise: *News of his arrest* ***caused a sensation.*** ◇ *The band became a sensation overnight.*

sen·sa·tion·al /sen'seɪʃənl/ *adj.* **1** causing great surprise, excitement, or interest SYN **thrilling**: *The result was a sensational 4–1 victory.* **2** (*disapproving*) (of a newspaper, etc.) trying to get your interest by presenting facts or events as worse or more shocking than they really are **3** (*informal*) extremely good; wonderful SYN **fantastic**: *You look sensational in that dress!* ▸ **sen·sa·tion·al·ly** /-ʃənəli/ *adv.*: *They won sensationally against the top team.* ◇ *The incident was sensationally reported in the press.* ◇ *He's sensationally good-looking!*

sen·sa·tion·al·ism /sen'seɪʃənəlɪzəm/ *noun* [U] (*disapproving*) a way of getting people's interest by using shocking words or by presenting facts and events as worse or more shocking than they really are ▸ **sen·sa·tion·al·ist** /-ʃənəlɪst/ *adj.*: *sensationalist headlines*

sen·sa·tion·al·ize (*BrE* also **-ise**) /sen'seɪʃənəlaɪz/ *verb* **~ sth** (*disapproving*) to exaggerate a story so that it seems more exciting or shocking than it really is

sense 🔑 /sens/ *noun, verb*

■ ***noun***

▸ SIGHT/HEARING, ETC. **1** 🔑 [C] one of the five powers (sight, hearing, smell, taste and touch) that your body uses to get information about the world around you: *the five senses* ◇ *Dogs have a keen* (= strong) ***sense of smell.*** ◇ ***the sense organs*** (= eyes, ears, nose, etc.) ◇ *I could hardly believe the evidence of my own senses* (= what I could see, hear, etc.). ◇ *The mixture of sights, smells and sounds around her made her senses reel.* ➲ see also SIXTH SENSE

▸ FEELING **2** 🔑 [C] a feeling about sth important: *He felt an overwhelming sense of loss.* ◇ *a* ***strong sense of purpose/identity/duty, etc.*** ◇ *Helmets can give cyclists a* ***false sense of security.*** ◇ *I* ***had the sense that*** *he was worried about something.*

▸ UNDERSTANDING/JUDGEMENT **3** 🔑 [sing.] an understanding about sth; an ability to judge sth: *One of the most important things in a partner is a* ***sense of humour*** (= the ability to find things funny or make people laugh). ◇ *He has a very good* ***sense of direction*** (= finds the way to a place easily). ◇ *She has lost all sense of direction in her life.* ◇ *Always try to keep a* ***sense of proportion*** (= of the relative importance of different things). ◇ *a* ***sense of rhythm/timing*** ◇ *Alex doesn't have any* ***dress sense*** (= does not know which clothes look attractive). ➲ see also ROAD SENSE **4** 🔑 [U] good understanding and judgement; knowledge of what is sensible or practical behaviour: *You should* ***have the sense to*** *take advice when it is offered.* ◇ ***There's no sense in*** (= it is not sensible) *worrying about it now.* ◇ *Can't you* ***talk sense*** (= say sth sensible)? ◇ *There's a lot of sense in what Mary says.* ➲ see also COMMON SENSE, GOOD SENSE

▸ NORMAL STATE OF MIND **5 senses** [pl.] a normal state of mind; the ability to think clearly: *If she threatens to leave, it should* ***bring him to his senses.*** ◇ *He waited for Dora to* ***come to her senses*** *and return.* ◇ (*old-fashioned*) *Are you* ***out of your senses?*** *You'll be killed!* ◇ (*old-fashioned*) *Why does she want to marry him? She must have* ***taken leave of her senses.***

▸ MEANING **6** 🔑 [C] the meaning that a word or phrase has; a way of understanding sth: *The word 'love' is used in different senses by different people.* ◇ *education in its broadest sense* ◇ *He was a true friend,* ***in every sense of the word*** (= in every possible way). ◇ ***In a sense*** (= in one way) *it doesn't matter any more.* ◇ ***In some senses*** (= in one or more ways) *the criticisms were justified.* ◇ (*formal*) ***In no sense*** *can the issue be said to be resolved.* ◇ *There is a sense in which we are all to blame for the tragedy.* ➲ note at SENSIBLE

IDM **knock/talk some 'sense into sb** to try and persuade sb to stop behaving in a stupid way, sometimes using rough or violent methods **make 'sense 1** 🔑 to have a meaning that you can easily understand: *This sentence doesn't make sense.* **2** 🔑 to be a sensible thing to do: *It makes sense to buy the most up-to-date version.* **3** 🔑 to be easy to understand or explain: *John wasn't making much sense on the phone.* ◇ *Who would send me all these flowers? It makes no sense.* **make 'sense of sth** to understand sth that is difficult or has no clear meaning **see 'sense** to start to be sensible or reasonable **a sense of oc'casion** a feeling or understanding that an event is important or special: *Candles on the table gave the evening a sense of occasion.* ➲ more at LEAVE *n.*

■ ***verb*** (not used in the progressive tenses)

▸ BECOME AWARE **1** to become aware of sth even though you cannot see it, hear it, etc: **~ sth** *Sensing danger, they started to run.* ◇ **~ (that)...** *Lisa sensed that he did not believe her.* ◇ *Thomas, she sensed, could convince anyone of anything.* ◇ **~ sb/sth doing sth** *He sensed someone moving around behind him.* ◇ **~ sb/sth do sth** *He sensed something move in the bushes.* ◇ **~ how, what, etc...** *She could sense how nervous he was.*

▸ OF MACHINE **2 ~ sth** to discover and record sth: *equipment that senses the presence of toxic gases*

sense·less /'sensləs/ *adj.* **1** (*disapproving*) having no meaning or purpose SYN **pointless**: *senseless violence* ◇ *His death was a senseless waste of life.* ◇ *It's senseless to continue any further.* **2** [not before noun] unconscious: *He was beaten senseless.* ◇ *She drank herself senseless.* **3** not using good judgement: *The police blamed senseless drivers who went too fast.* ▸ **sense·less·ly** *adv.*

sens·ibil·ity /ˌsensə'bɪləti/ *noun* (*pl.* -ies) **1** [U, C] the ability to experience and understand deep feelings, especially in art and literature: *a man of impeccable manners, charm and sensibility* ◇ *artistic sensibility* **2 sensibilities** [pl.] a person's feelings, especially when the person is easily offended or influenced by sth: *The article offended her religious sensibilities.*

sens·ible 🔑 /'sensəbl/ *adj.*

1 🔑 (of people and their behaviour) able to make good judgements based on reason and experience rather than emotion; practical: *She's a sensible sort of person.* ◇ *I think that's a very sensible idea.* ◇ *Say something sensible.* ◇ *I think* ***the sensible thing*** *would be to take a taxi home.* **2** (of clothes, etc.) useful rather than fashionable: *sensible shoes* **3** (*formal* or *literary*) aware of sth: *I am sensible of the fact that mathematics is not a popular subject.* OPP for sense 3 INSENSIBLE HELP Use **silly** (sense 1) or **impractical** (senses 1 and 2) as the opposite for the other senses. ▸ **sens·ibly** /-əbli/ *adv.*: *to behave sensibly* ◇ *He decided, very sensibly, not to drive when he was so tired.* ◇ *She's always very sensibly dressed.*

Which Word?

sensible / sensitive

Sensible and **sensitive** are connected with two different meanings of sense.

- **Sensible** refers to your ability to make good judgements: *She gave me some very sensible advice.* ◇ *It wasn't very sensible to go out on your own so late at night.*
- **Sensitive** refers to how easily you react to things and how much you are aware of things or other people: *a soap for sensitive skin* ◇ *This movie may upset a sensitive child.*

sen·si·tive 🔑 /'sensətɪv/ *adj.*

▸ TO PEOPLE'S FEELINGS **1** 🔑 aware of and able to understand other people and their feelings: *a sensitive and caring man* ◇ **~ to sth** *She is very sensitive to other people's feelings.* OPP **insensitive**

▸ TO ART/MUSIC/LITERATURE **2** 🔑 able to understand art, music and literature and to express yourself through them: *an actor's sensitive reading of the poem* ◇ *a sensitive portrait*

▸ EASILY UPSET **3** 🔑 easily offended or upset: *You're far too*

S

sensitive. ◇ **~ about sth** *He's very sensitive about his weight.* ◇ **~ to sth** *She's very sensitive to criticism.* OPP **insensitive**
▸ INFORMATION/SUBJECT **4** that you have to treat with great care because it may offend people or make them angry or embarrassed: *Health care is a politically sensitive issue.*
▸ TO COLD/LIGHT/FOOD, ETC. **5** reacting quickly or more than usual to sth: *sensitive areas of the body* ◇ **~ to sth** *My teeth are very sensitive to cold food.* OPP **insensitive**
▸ TO SMALL CHANGES **6 ~ (to sth)** able to measure very small changes: *a sensitive instrument* ◇ (*figurative*) *The Stock Exchange is very sensitive to political change.* OPP **insensitive**
▸ **sen·si·tive·ly** *adv.*: *She handled the matter sensitively.* ◇ *He writes sensitively.* IDM see NERVE *n.*

sen·si·tiv·ity /ˌsensəˈtɪvəti/ *noun* (*pl.* -ies)
▸ TO PEOPLE'S FEELINGS **1** [U] **~ (to sth)** the ability to understand other people's feelings: *sensitivity to the needs of children* ◇ *She pointed out with tact and sensitivity exactly where he had gone wrong.*
▸ TO ART/MUSIC/LITERATURE **2** [U] the ability to understand art, music and literature and to express yourself through them: *She played with great sensitivity.*
▸ BEING EASILY UPSET **3** [U, C, usually pl.] a tendency to be easily offended or upset by sth: *He's a mixture of anger and sensitivity.* ◇ *She was blind to the feelings and sensitivities of other people.* OPP **insensitivity**
▸ OF INFORMATION/SUBJECT **4** [U] the fact of needing to be treated very carefully because it may offend or upset people: *Confidentiality is important because of the sensitivity of the information.*
▸ TO FOOD/COLD/LIGHT, ETC. **5** [U, C, usually pl.] (*technical*) the quality of reacting quickly or more than usual to sth: *food sensitivity* ◇ *allergies and sensitivities* ◇ *Some children develop a sensitivity to cow's milk.* ◇ *The eyes of some fish have a greater sensitivity to light than ours do.*
▸ TO SMALL CHANGES **6** [U] the ability to measure very small changes: *the sensitivity of the test*

sen·si·tize (*BrE* also **-ise**) /ˈsensətaɪz/ *verb* [usually passive] **1 ~ sb/sth (to sth)** to make sb/sth more aware of sth, especially a problem or sth bad: *People are becoming more sensitized to the dangers threatening the environment.* **2 ~ sb/sth (to sth)** (*technical*) to make sb/sth sensitive to physical or chemical changes, or to a particular substance ▸ **sen·si·tiza·tion, -isa·tion** /ˌsensətaɪˈzeɪʃn; *NAmE* -təˈz-/ *noun* [U]

sen·sor /ˈsensə(r)/ *noun* a device that can react to light, heat, pressure, etc. in order to make a machine, etc. do sth or show sth: *security lights with an infrared sensor* (= that come on when a person is near them)

sens·ory /ˈsensəri/ *adj.* [usually before noun] (*technical*) connected with your physical senses: *sensory organs* ◇ *sensory deprivation*

sens·ual /ˈsenʃuəl/ *adj.* **1** connected with your physical feelings; giving pleasure to your physical senses, especially sexual pleasure: *sensual pleasure* **2** suggesting an interest in physical pleasure, especially sexual pleasure: *sensual lips* ◇ *He was darkly sensual and mysterious.* ▸ **sen·su·al·ity** /ˌsenʃuˈæləti/ *noun* [U]: *the sensuality of his poetry* **sen·su·al·ly** /-ʃuəli/ *adv.*

sen·su·ous /ˈsenʃuəs/ *adj.* **1** giving pleasure to your senses: *sensuous music* ◇ *I'm drawn to the poetic, sensuous qualities of her paintings.* **2** suggesting an interest in sexual pleasure: *his full sensuous lips* ▸ **sen·su·ous·ly** *adv.* **sen·su·ous·ness** *noun* [U]

sent *past tense, past part.* of SEND

sen·tence /ˈsentəns/ *noun, verb*
■ ***noun* 1** [C] (*grammar*) a set of words expressing a statement, a question or an order, usually containing a subject and a verb. In written English sentences begin with a capital letter and end with a full stop/period (.), a question mark (?) or an exclamation mark/exclamation point (!). **2** [C, U] the punishment given by a court: ***a jail/prison sentence*** ◇ *a* ***light/heavy sentence*** ◇ *to be* ***under sentence of death*** ◇ *The judge* ***passed sentence*** (= said what the punishment would be). ◇ *The prisoner has* ***served*** (= completed) ***his sentence*** *and will be released tomorrow.* ⊃ COLLOCATIONS at JUSTICE ⊃ see also DEATH SENTENCE, LIFE SENTENCE
■ ***verb*** [often passive] **~ sb (to sth)** | **~ sb to do sth** to say officially in court that sb is to receive a particular punishment: *to be sentenced to death/life imprisonment/three years in prison*

ˈsentence adverb *noun* (*grammar*) an adverb that expresses the speaker's attitude towards, or gives the subject of, the whole of the rest of the sentence: *In 'Luckily, I didn't tell anyone' and 'Financially, we have a serious problem', 'luckily' and 'financially' are sentence adverbs.*

sen·ten·cer /ˈsentənsə(r)/ *noun* (*formal*) a person who decides on the punishment for sb who is guilty of a crime: *The judge was considered a tough sentencer.*

sen·ten·tious /senˈtenʃəs/ *adj.* (*formal, disapproving*) trying to sound important or intelligent, especially by expressing moral judgements ▸ **sen·ten·tious·ly** *adv.*

sen·tient /ˈsentiənt; ˈsenʃnt/ *adj.* [usually before noun] (*formal*) able to see or feel things through the senses: *Man is a sentient being.*

sen·ti·ment /ˈsentɪmənt/ *noun* **1** [C, U] (*formal*) a feeling or an opinion, especially one based on emotions: *the spread of nationalist sentiments* ◇ *This is a sentiment I wholeheartedly agree with.* ◇ *Public sentiment is against any change to the law.* **2** [U] (sometimes *disapproving*) feelings of pity, romantic love, sadness, etc. which may be too strong or not appropriate: *There was no fatherly affection, no display of sentiment.* ◇ *There is no room for sentiment in business.*

sen·ti·men·tal /ˌsentɪˈmentl/ *adj.* **1** connected with your emotions, rather than reason: *She kept the letters for sentimental reasons.* ◇ *The ring wasn't worth very much but it had great* ***sentimental value***. **2** (often *disapproving*) producing emotions such as pity, romantic love or sadness, which may be too strong or not appropriate; feeling these emotions too much: *a slushy, sentimental love story* ◇ *He's not the sort of man who gets* ***sentimental about*** *old friendships.* OPP **unsentimental** ▸ **sen·ti·men·tal·ly** /-təli/ *adv.*

sen·ti·men·tal·ist /ˌsentɪˈmentəlɪst/ *noun* (sometimes *disapproving*) a person who is sentimental about things

sen·ti·men·tal·ity /ˌsentɪmenˈtæləti/ *noun* [U] (*disapproving*) the quality of being too sentimental

sen·ti·men·tal·ize (*BrE* also **-ise**) /ˌsentɪˈmentəlaɪz/ *verb* [T, I] **~ (sth)** (*disapproving*) to present sth in an emotional way, emphasizing its good aspects and not mentioning its bad aspects: *Jackie was careful not to sentimentalize country life.*

sen·ti·nel /ˈsentɪnl/ *noun* (*literary*) a soldier whose job is to guard sth SYN **sentry**: (*figurative*) *a tall round tower* ***standing sentinel*** *over the river*

sen·try /ˈsentri/ *noun* (*pl.* -ies) a soldier whose job is to guard sth: *to be on sentry duty*

ˈsentry box *noun* a small shelter for a sentry to stand in

sepal /ˈsepl/ *noun* (*technical*) a part of a flower, like a leaf, that lies under and supports the PETALS (= the delicate coloured parts that make up the head of the flower). Each flower has a ring of sepals called a CALYX. ⊃ VISUAL VOCAB page V9

sep·ar·able /ˈsepərəbl/ *adj.* **1 ~ (from sth)** that can be separated from sth, or considered separately: *The moral question is not entirely separable from the financial one.* **2** (*grammar*) (of a phrasal verb) that can be used with the object going either between the verb and the PARTICLE or after the particle: *The phrasal verb 'tear up' is separable because you can say 'She tore the letter up' or 'She tore up the letter'.* OPP **inseparable** ▸ **sep·ar·abil·ity** /ˌseprəˈbɪləti/ *noun* [U]

sep·ar·ate *adj., verb*
■ ***adj.*** /ˈseprət/ **1 ~ (from sth/sb)** forming a unit by itself; not joined to sth else: *separate bedrooms* ◇ *Raw meat must be* ***kept separate*** *from cooked meat.* ◇ *The school is housed in two separate buildings.* **2** [usually before noun] differ-

S

ent; not connected: *It happened on three separate occasions.* ◇ *For the past three years they have been leading totally separate lives.* ▸ **sep·ar·ate·ness** *noun* [U, sing.]: *Japan's long-standing sense of separateness and uniqueness*

WORD FAMILY
separate *adj.*
separately *adv.*
separable *adj.* (≠ inseparable)
separate *verb*
separated *adj.*
separation *noun*

IDM **go your separate 'ways** **1** to end a relationship with sb **2** to go in a different direction from sb you have been travelling with ➲ more at COVER *n.*

■ ***verb*** /'sepəreɪt/ **1** [I, T] to divide into different parts or groups; to divide things into different parts or groups: *Stir the sauce constantly so that it does not separate.* ◇ **~ sth** *Separate the eggs* (= separate the YOLK from the white). ◇ **~ sth from/and sth** *It is impossible to separate belief from emotion.* ◇ **~ sth into sth** *Make a list of points and separate them into 'desirable' and 'essential'.* **2** [I, T] to move apart; to make people or things move apart: *South America and Africa separated 200 million years ago.* ◇ **~ from sth** *South America separated from Africa 200 million years ago.* ◇ **~ into sth** *We separated into several different search parties.* ◇ **~ sb/sth** *Police tried to separate the two men who were fighting.* ◇ *The war separated many families.* ◇ **~ sb/sth from/and sb/sth** *Those suffering from infectious diseases were separated from the other patients.* **3** [T] to be between two people, areas, countries, etc. so that they are not touching or connected: **~ sb/sth** *A thousand kilometres separates the two cities.* ◇ **~ sb/sth from/and sb** *A high wall separated our back yard from the playing field.* **4** [I] to stop living together as a couple with your husband, wife or partner: *They separated last year.* ◇ **~ from sb** *He separated from his wife after 20 years of marriage.* ➲ COLLOCATIONS at MARRIAGE **5** [T] **~ sb/sth** (**from sb/sth**) to make sb/sth different in some way from sb/sth else SYN **divide**: *Politics is the only thing that separates us* (= that we disagree about). ◇ *The judges found it impossible to separate the two contestants* (= they gave them equal scores). ◇ *Only four points separate the top three teams.* IDM see MAN *n.*, SHEEP, WHEAT

PHR V **,separate 'out** | **,separate sth↔'out** to divide into different parts; to divide sth into different parts: *to separate out different meanings*

sep·ar·ated /'sepəreɪtɪd/ *adj.* no longer living with your husband, wife or partner: *Her parents are separated but not divorced.* ◇ **~ from sb** *He's been separated from his wife for a year.* ➲ COLLOCATIONS at MARRIAGE

sep·ar·ate·ly /'seprətli/ *adv.* **~ (from sb/sth)** as a separate person or thing; not together: *They were photographed separately and then as a group.* ◇ *Last year's figures are shown separately.*

sep·ar·ates /'seprəts/ *noun* [pl.] individual pieces of clothing, for example skirts, jackets, and trousers/pants, that are designed to be worn together in different combinations

'separate school *noun* (*CanE*) a public school for Catholic children in some parts of Canada

sep·ar·ation /,sepə'reɪʃn/ *noun* **1** [U, sing.] the act of separating people or things; the state of being separate: **~ (from sb/sth)** *the state's eventual separation from the federation* ◇ **~ (between A and B)** *the need for a clear separation between Church and State* **2** [C] a period of time that people spend apart from each other: *They were reunited after a separation of more than 20 years.* **3** [C] a decision that a husband and wife make to live apart while they are still legally married: *a legal separation* ➲ compare DIVORCE

the ,separation of 'powers *noun* [sing.] the principle of the US Constitution that the political power of the government is divided between the President, Congress and the Supreme Court ➲ compare CHECKS AND BALANCES

sep·ar·at·ist /'seprətɪst/ *noun* a member of a group of people within a country who want to separate from the rest of the country and form their own government: *Basque separatists* ▸ **sep·ar·at·ism** /'seprətɪzəm/ *noun* [U] **sep·ar·at·ist** *adj.*: *a separatist movement*

sep·ar·ator /'sepəreɪtə(r)/ *noun* a machine for separating things

Seph·ardi /se'fɑːdi; *NAmE* -'fɑːrdi/ *noun* (*pl.* **Seph·ar·dim**) a Jew whose ANCESTORS came from Spain or N Africa ➲ compare ASHKENAZI ▸ **Seph·ar·dic** /-ɪk/ *adj.*

sepia /'siːpiə/ *noun* [U] **1** a brown substance used in inks and paints and used in the past for printing photographs **2** a reddish-brown colour ▸ **sepia** *adj.* [usually before noun]: ***sepia ink/prints/photographs***

sepoy /'siːpɔɪ/ *noun* **1** in the past, an Indian soldier serving under a British or European officer **2** (*IndE*) a soldier or police officer of the lowest rank

sep·sis /'sepsɪs/ *noun* [U] (*medical*) an infection of part of the body in which PUS is produced

Sep·tem·ber /sep'tembə(r)/ *noun* [U, C] (*abbr.* Sept.) the 9th month of the year, between August and October HELP To see how **September** is used, look at the examples at **April**.

sep·tet /sep'tet/ *noun* **1** [C+sing./pl. v.] a group of seven musicians or singers **2** [C] a piece of music for seven musicians or singers

sep·tic /'septɪk/ *adj.* (of a wound or part of the body) infected with harmful bacteria: *a septic finger* ◇ *A dirty cut may go septic.*

septi·cae·mia (*BrE*) (*NAmE* **septi·ce·mia**) /,septɪ'siːmiə/ *noun* [U] (*medical*) infection of the blood by harmful bacteria SYN **blood poisoning**

,septic 'tank *noun* a large container, usually underground, that holds human waste from toilets until the action of bacteria makes it liquid enough to be absorbed by the ground

sep·tua·gen·ar·ian /,septjuədʒə'neəriən; *NAmE* -tʃuədʒə'ner-/ *noun* (*formal*) a person between 70 and 79 years old

sep·tum /'septəm/ *noun* (*pl.* **septa** /'septə/) (*anatomy*) a thin part that separates two hollow areas, for example the part of the nose between the NOSTRILS

se·pul·chral /sə'pʌlkrəl/ *adj.* (*literary*) making you think of death SYN **funereal**: *He spoke in sepulchral tones.* — sounding sad and serious; making you think of death SYN **funereal**: *He spoke in sepulchral tones.*

sep·ul·chre (*US* **sep·ul·cher**) /'seplkə(r)/ *noun* (*old use*) a place for a dead body, either cut in rock or built of stone

se·quel /'siːkwəl/ *noun* **~ (to sth)** **1** a book, film/movie, play, etc. that continues the story of an earlier one: *a sequel to the hit movie 'Madagascar'* ➲ compare PREQUEL **2** [usually sing.] something that happens after an earlier event or as a result of an earlier event: *There was an interesting sequel to these events later in the year.*

se·quence AW /'siːkwəns/ *noun, verb*

■ ***noun*** **1** [C] a set of events, actions, numbers, etc. which have a particular order and which lead to a particular result: *He described **the sequence of events** leading up to the robbery.* **2** [C, U] the order that events, actions, etc. happen in or should happen in: *The tasks had to be performed in a particular sequence.* ◇ *Number the pages **in sequence**.* ◇ *These pages are **out of sequence**.* **3** [C] a part of a film/movie that deals with one subject or topic or consists of one scene

■ ***verb*** **1 ~ sth** (*technical*) to arrange things into a sequence **2 ~ sth** (*biology*) to identify the order in which a set of GENES or parts of MOLECULES are arranged: *The human genome has now been sequenced.* ▸ **se·quen·cing** *noun* [U]: *a gene sequencing project*

the ,sequence of 'tenses *noun* [sing.] (*grammar*) the rules according to which the tense of a SUBORDINATE CLAUSE depends on the tense of a main clause, so that,

S

for example, 'I think *that you* are *wrong*' becomes 'I thought *that you* were *wrong*' in the past tense

se·quen·cer /ˈsiːkwənsə(r)/ *noun* an electronic instrument for recording and storing sounds so that they can be played later as part of a piece of music

se·quen·tial AW /sɪˈkwenʃl/ *adj.* (*formal*) following in order of time or place: *sequential data processing* ▶ **se·quen·tial·ly** AW /-ʃəli/ *adv.*: *data stored sequentially on a computer*

se·ques·ter /sɪˈkwestə(r)/ *verb* (*law*) **1** = SEQUESTRATE **2** ~ **sb** to keep a JURY together in a place, in order to prevent them from talking to other people about a court case, or learning about it in the newspapers, on television, etc.

se·ques·tered /sɪˈkwestəd; *NAmE* -tərd/ *adj.* [usually before noun] (*literary*) (of a place) quiet and far away from people

se·ques·trate /ˈsiːkwəstreɪt; sɪˈkwes-/ (also **se·ques·ter**) *verb* ~ **sth** (*law*) to take control of sb's property or ASSETS until a debt has been paid ▶ **se·ques·tra·tion** /ˌsiːkwəˈstreɪʃn/ *noun* [U, C]

se·quin /ˈsiːkwɪn/ *noun* a small round shiny disc sewn onto clothing as decoration ▶ **se·quinned** (*NAmE* **se·quined**) /ˈsiːkwɪnd/ *adj.* [usually before noun]

se·quoia /sɪˈkwɔɪə/ *noun* a very tall N American tree, a type of redwood

sera *pl.* of SERUM

ser·aph /ˈserəf/ *noun* (*pl.* **ser·aph·im** /-fɪm/ or **ser·aphs**) an ANGEL of the highest rank ➲ compare CHERUB

ser·aph·ic /səˈræfɪk/ *adj.* (*literary*) **1** as beautiful, pure, etc. as an angel: *a* ***seraphic child/nature*** **2** extremely happy: *a seraphic smile*

ser·en·ade /ˌserəˈneɪd/ *noun, verb*

■ ***noun*** **1** a song or tune played or sung at night by a lover outside the window of the woman he loves **2** a gentle piece of music in several parts, usually for a small group of instruments

■ ***verb*** ~ **sb** to sing or play music to sb (as done in the past by a man singing under her window to the woman he loved)

ser·en·dip·ity /ˌserənˈdɪpəti/ *noun* [U] the fact of sth interesting or pleasant happening by chance ▶ **ser·en·dip·it·ous** /-ˈdɪpətəs/ *adj.*: *serendipitous discoveries*

se·rene /səˈriːn/ *adj.* calm and peaceful: *a lake, still and serene in the sunlight* ▶ **se·rene·ly** *adv.*: *serenely beautiful* ◇ *She smiled serenely.* **se·ren·ity** /səˈrenəti/ *noun* [U, sing.]: *The hotel offers a haven of peace and serenity away from the bustle of the city.*

serf /sɜːf; *NAmE* sɜːrf/ *noun* (in the past) a person who was forced to live and work on land that belonged to a LANDOWNER whom they had to obey

serf·dom /ˈsɜːfdəm; *NAmE* ˈsɜːrf-/ *noun* [U] the system under which crops were grown by serfs; the state of being a serf: *the abolition of serfdom in Russia in 1861*

serge /sɜːdʒ; *NAmE* sɜːrdʒ/ *noun* [U] a type of strong cloth made of wool, used for making clothes: *a blue serge suit*

ser·geant /ˈsɑːdʒənt; *NAmE* ˈsɑːrdʒ-/ *noun* (*abbr.* Sergt, Sgt) **1** a member of one of the middle ranks in the army and the AIR FORCE, below an officer: *Sergeant Salter* ➲ see also FLIGHT SERGEANT, STAFF SERGEANT **2** (in Britain) a police officer just below the rank of an INSPECTOR **3** (in the US) a police officer just below the rank of a LIEUTENANT or CAPTAIN ➲ see also SARGE

ˌsergeant ˈmajor *noun* (often used as a title) **1** a soldier of middle rank in the British army who is responsible for helping the officer who organizes the affairs of a particular REGIMENT (= a large group of soldiers) **2** a soldier in the US army of the highest rank of NON-COMMISSIONED OFFICERS

ser·ial /ˈsɪəriəl; *NAmE* ˈsɪr-/ *noun, adj.*

■ ***noun*** a story on television or the radio, or in a magazine, that is broadcast or published in several separate parts

■ ***adj.*** **1** [usually before noun] (*technical*) arranged in a series: *tasks carried out in the same serial order* **2** [only before noun] doing the same thing in the same way several times: *a serial rapist* **3** [only before noun] (of a story, etc.) broadcast or published in several separate parts: *a novel in serial form* ▶ **seri·al·ly** /-iəli/ *adv.*

seri·al·ize (*BrE* also **-ise**) /ˈsɪəriəlaɪz; *NAmE* ˈsɪr-/ *verb* ~ **sth** to publish or broadcast sth in parts as a serial: *The novel was serialized on TV in six parts.* ▶ **seri·al·iza·tion, -isa·tion** /ˌsɪəriəlaɪˈzeɪʃn; *NAmE* ˌsɪriələˈz-/ *noun* [C, U]: *a newspaper serialization of the book*

ˌserial ˈkiller *noun* a person who murders several people one after the other in a similar way

ˌserial moˈnogamy *noun* [U] the fact or custom of having more than one husband, wife or sexual partner in your life, but only one at a time

ˈserial number *noun* a number put on a product, such as a camera, television, etc. in order to identify it

ˈserial port *noun* (*computing*) a point on a computer where you connect a device such as a mouse that sends or receives data one BIT at a time

ser·ies 🗝 AW /ˈsɪəriːz; *NAmE* ˈsɪr-/ *noun* (*pl.* **ser·ies**) **1** 🗝 [C, usually sing.] ~ **of sth** several events or things of a similar kind that happen one after the other: *The incident sparked off a whole* ***series of events*** *that nobody had foreseen.* ◇ *the latest in a series of articles on the nature of modern society* **2** 🗝 [C] a set of radio or television programmes that deal with the same subject or that have the same characters ➲ COLLOCATIONS at TELEVISION **3** [C] (*sport*) a set of sports games played between the same two teams: *the* ***World Series*** (= in BASEBALL) ◇ *England have lost the* ***Test series*** (= of CRICKET matches) *against India.* **4** [U, C] (*technical*) an electrical CIRCUIT in which the current passes through all the parts in the correct order

serif /ˈserɪf/ *noun* a short line at the top or bottom of some styles of printed letters: *a serif typeface* ➲ compare SANS SERIF

Synonyms

serious

grave • earnest • solemn

These words all describe sb who thinks and behaves carefully and sensibly, but often without much joy or laughter.

serious thinking about things in a careful and sensible way; not laughing about sth: *He's not really a very serious person.* ◇ ***Be serious*** *for a moment; this is important.*

grave (*rather formal*) (of a person) serious in manner, as if sth sad, important, or worrying has just happened: *He looked very grave as he entered the room.*

earnest serious and sincere: *The earnest young doctor answered all our questions.*

solemn looking or sounding very serious, without smiling; done or said in a very serious and sincere way: *Her expression grew solemn.* ◇ *I made a* ***solemn promise*** *that I would return.*

PATTERNS

- a(n) serious/grave/earnest/solemn **expression/face**
- a serious/solemn **mood/atmosphere**

ser·ious 🗝 /ˈsɪəriəs; *NAmE* ˈsɪr-/ *adj.*

▸ BAD **1** 🗝 bad or dangerous: *a* ***serious illness/problem/offence*** ◇ *to cause* ***serious injury/damage*** ◇ *They pose a serious threat to security.* ◇ *The consequences could be serious.*

▸ NEEDING THOUGHT **2** 🗝 needing to be thought about carefully; not only for pleasure: *a serious article* ◇ *a serious newspaper* ◇ *It's time to give serious consideration to this matter.*

▸ IMPORTANT **3** 🗝 that must be treated as important: *We need to get down to the serious business of working out costs.* ◇ *The team is a serious contender for the title this year.*

S

▸ NOT SILLY **4** ⊶ thinking about things in a careful and sensible way; not silly: ***Be serious** for a moment; this is important.* ◇ *I'm afraid I'm not a very serious person.*

▸ NOT JOKING **5** ⊶ sincere about sth; not joking or meant as a joke: *Believe me, I'm **deadly*** (= extremely) ***serious**.* ◇ *Don't laugh, it's a serious suggestion.* ◇ **~ (about doing sth)** *Is she serious about wanting to sell the house?* ◇ **~ (about sb/sth)** *He's really serious about Penny and wants to get engaged.* ◇ (*informal*) ***You can't be serious!*** (= you must be joking) ◇ *You think I did it? **Be serious!*** (= what you suggest is ridiculous)

▸ LARGE AMOUNT **6** (*informal*) used to emphasize that there is a large amount of sth: *You can earn serious money doing that.* ◇ *I'm ready to do some serious eating* (= I am very hungry).

ser·ious·ly ⊶ /ˈsɪəriəsli; *NAmE* ˈsɪr-/ *adv.* **1** ⊶ in a serious way: *to be **seriously ill/injured*** ◇ *You're not seriously expecting me to believe that?* ◇ *They are seriously concerned about security.* ◇ *Smoking can seriously damage your health.* **2** ⊶ used at the beginning of a sentence to show a change from joking to being more serious: *Seriously though, it could be really dangerous.* **3** (*informal*) very; extremely: *They're seriously rich.*
IDM **take sb/sth ˈseriously** ⊶ to think that sb/sth is important and deserves your attention and respect: *We take threats of this kind very seriously.* ◇ *Why can't you ever take anything seriously?*

ser·ious·ness /ˈsɪəriəsnəs; *NAmE* ˈsɪr-/ *noun* [U, sing.] the state of being serious: *He spoke with a seriousness that was unusual in him.*
IDM **in all ˈseriousness** very seriously; not as a joke

ser·mon /ˈsɜːmən; *NAmE* ˈsɜːrmən/ *noun* **1** a talk on a moral or religious subject, usually given by a religious leader during a service ➲ SYNONYMS at SPEECH ➲ COLLOCATIONS at RELIGION **2** (*informal, usually disapproving*) moral advice that a person tries to give you in a long talk

ser·mon·ize (*BrE* also **-ise**) /ˈsɜːmənaɪz; *NAmE* ˈsɜːrm-/ *verb* [I] (*disapproving*) to give moral advice, especially when it is boring or not wanted SYN **moralize**

sero·tonin /ˌserəˈtəʊnɪn; *NAmE* -ˈtoʊn-/ *noun* [U] a chemical in the brain that affects how messages are sent from the brain to the body, and also affects how a person feels

ser·pent /ˈsɜːpənt; *NAmE* ˈsɜːrp-/ *noun* (*literary*) a snake, especially a large one

ser·pen·tine /ˈsɜːpəntaɪn; *NAmE* ˈsɜːrpəntiːn/ *adj.* (*literary*) bending and twisting like a snake SYN **winding**: *the serpentine course of the river*

ser·rated /səˈreɪtɪd/ *adj.* having a series of sharp points on the edge like a SAW: *a knife with a **serrated edge*** ➲ VISUAL VOCAB page V23

ser·ra·tion /seˈreɪʃn/ *noun* a part on an edge or the blade of a knife that is sharp and pointed like a SAW

ser·ried /ˈserid/ *adj.* [usually before noun] (*literary*) standing or arranged closely together in rows or lines: *serried ranks of soldiers*

serum /ˈsɪərəm; *NAmE* ˈsɪrəm/ *noun* (*pl.* **sera** /-rə/ or **ser·ums**) **1** [U] (*biology*) the thin liquid that remains from blood when the rest has CLOTTED **2** [U, C] (*medical*) serum taken from the blood of an animal and given to people to protect them from disease, poison, etc: *snakebite serum* **3** [U] any liquid like water in body TISSUE

ser·vant ⊶ /ˈsɜːvənt; *NAmE* ˈsɜːrv-/ *noun* **1** ⊶ a person who works in another person's house, and cooks, cleans, etc. for them: *a domestic servant* ◇ *They treat their mother like a servant.* **2** a person who works for a company or an organization: *a public servant* ➲ see also CIVIL SERVANT **3** a person or thing that is controlled by sth: *He was willing to make himself a servant of his art.*
IDM see OBEDIENT

serve ⊶ /sɜːv; *NAmE* sɜːrv/ *verb, noun*

■ *verb*

▸ FOOD/DRINK **1** ⊶ [T, I] to give sb food or drink, for example at a restaurant or during a meal: **~ (sth)** *Breakfast is served between 7 and 10 a.m.* ◇ *Pour the sauce over the pasta and serve immediately.* ◇ *Shall I serve?* ◇ **~ sth with sth** *Serve the lamb with new potatoes and green beans.* ◇ **~ sth to sb** *They served a wonderful meal to more than fifty delegates.* ◇ **~ sb with sth** *The delegates were served with a wonderful meal.* ◇ **~ sb sth** *She served us a delicious lunch.* ◇ **~ sth + adj.** *The quiche can be served hot or cold.* **2** [T] **~ sb/sth** (of an amount of food) to be enough for sb/sth: *This dish will serve four hungry people.*

▸ CUSTOMERS **3** ⊶ [T, I] **~ (sb)** (*especially BrE*) to help a customer or sell them sth in a shop/store: *Are you being served?* ◇ *She was serving behind the counter.*

▸ BE USEFUL **4** ⊶ [T] **~ sth/sb** to be useful to sb in achieving or satisfying sth: *These experiments **serve** no useful **purpose**.* ◇ *Most of their economic policies **serve the interests** of big business.* ◇ *How can we best **serve the needs** of future generations?* ◇ *His linguistic ability **served him well** in his chosen profession.*

▸ PROVIDE STH **5** ⊶ [T] to provide an area or a group of people with a product or service: **~ sb/sth** *The centre will serve the whole community.* ◇ **~ sb/sth with sth** *The town is well served with buses and major road links.*

▸ BE SUITABLE **6** [I] **~ (as sth)** to be suitable for a particular use, especially when nothing else is available: *The sofa will serve as a bed for a night or two.*

▸ HAVE PARTICULAR RESULT **7** [I, T] to have a particular effect or result: **~ as sth** *The judge said the punishment would serve as a warning to others.* ◇ **~ to do sth** *The attack was unsuccessful and **served only to** alert the enemy.*

▸ WORK **8** ⊶ [I, T] to work or perform duties for a person, an organization, a country, etc: **~ (as sth)** *He served as a captain in the army.* ◇ **~ in/on/with sth** *She served in the medical corps.* ◇ **~ under/with sb** *He served under Edward Heath in the 1970s.* ◇ **~ sth** *I wanted to work somewhere where I could serve the community.* ◇ **~ sb (as sth)** *He served the family faithfully for many years* (= as a servant). **9** [T, I] to spend a period of time in a particular job or training for a job: **~ sth** *He served a one-year apprenticeship.* ◇ **~ as sth** *She was elected to serve as secretary of the local party.*

▸ TIME IN PRISON **10** [T] **~ sth** to spend a period of time in prison: *prisoners serving life sentences* ◇ *She is serving two years for theft.* ◇ *He has **served time*** (= been to prison) *before.*

▸ OFFICIAL DOCUMENT **11** [T] (*law*) to give or send sb an official document, especially one that orders them to appear in court: **~ sth (on sb)** *to **serve a writ/summons** on sb* ◇ **~ sb with sth** *to serve sb with a writ/summons*

▸ IN SPORT **12** [I, T] (in TENNIS, etc.) to start playing by throwing the ball into the air and hitting it: *Who's serving?* ◇ **~ sth** *She served an ace.*

IDM **it serves sb ˈright (for doing sth)** ⊶ used to say that sth that has happened to sb is their own fault and they deserve it: *Left you, did she? It serves you right for being so selfish.* **serve your/its ˈturn** (*BrE*) to be useful for a particular purpose or period of time **serve two ˈmasters** (usually used in negative sentences) to support two opposing parties, principles, etc. at the same time ➲ more at FIRST *adv.*, MEMORY

PHR V **ˌserve sth↔ˈout 1** to continue doing sth, especially working or staying in prison, for a fixed period of time that has been set: *He has three more years in prison before he's served out his sentence.* ◇ (*BrE*) *They didn't want me to serve out my notice.* **2** (*BrE*) to share food or drink between a number of people: *I went around the guests serving out drinks.* **ˌserve sth↔ˈup 1** to put food onto plates and give it to people: *He served up a delicious meal.* **2** to give, offer or provide sth: *She served up the usual excuse.* ◇ *The teams served up some fantastic entertainment.*

■ ***noun*** (in TENNIS, etc.) the action of serving the ball to your opponent

ser·ver /ˈsɜːvə(r); *NAmE* ˈsɜːrv-/ *noun* **1** (*computing*) a computer program that controls or supplies information to several computers connected in a network; the main computer on which this program is run ➲ COLLOCATIONS at EMAIL **2** (*sport*) a player who is serving, for example in

TENNIS **3** [usually pl.] a kitchen UTENSIL (= tool) used for putting food onto sb's plate: *salad servers* ➲ VISUAL VOCAB page V19 **4** (*NAmE*) a person who serves food in a restaurant; a waiter or waitress **5** a person who helps a priest during a church service

serv·ery /'sɜːvəri; *NAmE* 'sɜːrv-/ *noun* (*pl.* -ies) (*BrE*) part of a restaurant where you collect your food to take back to your table

ser·vice 🔑 /'sɜːvɪs; *NAmE* 'sɜːrv-/ *noun, verb*

■ ***noun***

▸ PROVIDING STH **1** 🔑 [C] a system that provides sth that the public needs, organized by the government or a private company: *the **ambulance/bus/telephone, etc. service*** ◇ *The government aims to improve **public services**, especially education.* ◇ ***Essential services*** (= the supply of water, gas, electricity) *will be maintained.* ➲ see also EMERGENCY SERVICES, POSTAL SERVICE **2** 🔑 (also **Service**) [C] an organization or a company that provides sth for the public or does sth for the government: *the prison service* ◇ *the BBC World Service* ➲ see also CIVIL SERVICE, DIPLOMATIC SERVICE, FIRE SERVICE, HEALTH SERVICE, INTERNAL REVENUE SERVICE, NATIONAL HEALTH SERVICE, SECRET SERVICE, SECURITY SERVICE, SOCIAL SERVICES **3** 🔑 [C, U] a business whose work involves doing sth for customers but not producing goods; the work that such a business does: *financial services* ◇ *the development of new **goods and services*** ◇ *Smith's Catering Services* (= a company) *offers the best value.* ◇ *We guarantee (an) excellent service.* ◇ *the **service sector*** (= the part of the economy involved in this type of business) ◇ *a service industry*

▸ IN HOTEL/SHOP/RESTAURANT **4** 🔑 [U] the serving of customers in hotels, restaurants, and shops/stores: *The food was good but the service was very slow.* ◇ *10% will be added to your bill for service.* ◇ *Our main concern is to provide quality **customer service**.* ➲ COLLOCATIONS at RESTAURANT ➲ see also ROOM SERVICE, SELF-SERVICE

▸ WORK FOR ORGANIZATION **5** 🔑 [U] **~ (to sth)** the work that sb does for an organization, etc, especially when it continues for a long time or is admired very much: *She has just celebrated 25 years' service with the company.* ◇ *The employees have good **conditions of service**.* ◇ *After retiring, she became involved in **voluntary service** in the local community.* ➲ see also JURY SERVICE

▸ OF VEHICLE/MACHINE **6** [U] the use that you can get from a vehicle or machine; the state of being used: *That computer gave us very good service.* ◇ *The ship will be taken out of service within two years.* **7** [C, U] an examination of a vehicle or machine followed by any work that is necessary to keep it operating well: *a service engineer* ◇ (*BrE*) *I had taken the car in for a service.* ◇ (*NAmE*) *for service* ➲ see also AFTER-SALES SERVICE

▸ SKILLS/HELP **8** [usually pl.] (*formal*) the particular skills or help that a person is able to offer: **~ (of sb)** *You need the services of a good lawyer.* ◇ **~ (as sb/sth)** *He offered his services as a driver.*

▸ ARMY/NAVY/AIR FORCE **9** [C, usually pl., U] the army, the navy and the AIR FORCE; the work done by people in them: *Most of the boys went straight into **the services**.* ◇ *He **saw service** in North Africa.* ◇ *a service family* ➲ see also ACTIVE SERVICE, MILITARY SERVICE, NATIONAL SERVICE

▸ RELIGIOUS CEREMONY **10** 🔑 [C] a religious ceremony: ***morning/evening service*** ◇ *to **hold/attend a service*** ◇ *a **funeral/marriage/memorial, etc. service*** ➲ COLLOCATIONS at RELIGION

▸ BUS/TRAIN **11** [C, usually sing.] a bus, train, etc. that goes regularly to a particular place at a particular time: *the cancellation of the 10.15 service to Glasgow*

▸ ON MOTORWAY **12** **services** [sing.+ sing./pl. v.] (*BrE*) a place beside a MOTORWAY where you can stop for petrol, a meal, the toilets, etc: *motorway services* ◇ *It's five miles to the next services.* ➲ see also SERVICE AREA, SERVICE STATION

▸ IN TENNIS **13** [C] an act of hitting the ball in order to start playing; the way that you hit it SYN **serve**: *It's your service* (= your turn to start playing). ◇ *Her service has improved.*

▸ SET OF PLATES, ETC. **14** [C] a complete set of plates, dishes, etc. that match each other: *a tea service* (= cups, SAUCERS, a TEAPOT and plates, for serving tea) ➲ see also DINNER SERVICE

▸ BEING SERVANT **15** [U] (*old-fashioned*) the state or position of being a servant: *to **be in/go into service*** (= to be/become a servant)

▸ OF OFFICIAL DOCUMENT **16** [U] (*law*) the formal giving of an official document, etc. to sb: *the service of a demand for payment*

IDM **at the 'service of sb/sth | at sb's 'service** completely available for sb to use or to help sb: *Health care must be at the service of all who need it.* ◇ (*formal* or *humorous*) *If you need anything, I am **at your service**.* **be of 'service (to sb)** (*formal*) to be useful or helpful: *Can I be of service to anyone?* **do sb a/no 'service** (*formal*) to do sth that is helpful/not helpful to sb: *She was doing herself no service by remaining silent.* ➲ more at PRESS *v.*

■ ***verb***

▸ VEHICLE/MACHINE **1** [usually passive] **~ sth** to examine a vehicle or machine and repair it if necessary so that it continues to work correctly: *We need to have the car serviced.*

▸ PROVIDE STH **2** **~ sth/sb** to provide people with sth they need, such as shops/stores, or a transport system SYN **serve**: *Botley is well serviced by a regular bus route into Oxford.* ◇ *This department services the international sales force* (= provides services for it).

▸ PAY INTEREST **3** **~ sth** (*technical*) to pay interest on money that has been borrowed: *The company can no longer **service its debts**.*

ser·vice·able /'sɜːvɪsəbl; *NAmE* 'sɜːrv-/ *adj.* suitable to be used: *The carpet is worn but still serviceable.*

'service area *noun* (*BrE*) a place on a MOTORWAY where you can stop and buy food, petrol, have a meal, go to the toilet, etc.

'service charge *noun* **1** an amount of money that is added to a bill, as an extra charge for a service: *That will be $50, plus a service charge of $2.50.* **2** (*BrE*) an amount of money that is added to a bill in a restaurant, for example 10% of the total, that goes to pay for the work of the staff **3** an amount of money that is paid to the owner of an apartment building for services such as putting out rubbish/garbage, cleaning the stairs, etc.

'service club *noun* (*NAmE*) an organization whose members do things to help their local community

'service industry *noun* [U, C] (*economics*) = TERTIARY INDUSTRY

ser·vice·man /'sɜːvɪsmən; *NAmE* 'sɜːrv-/, **ser·vice·woman** /'sɜːvɪswʊmən; *NAmE* 'sɜːrv-/ *noun* (*pl.* **-men** /-mən/, **-women** /-wɪmɪn/) a man or woman who is a member of the armed forces ➲ note at GENDER

'service provider *noun* a business company that provides a service to customers, especially one that connects customers to the Internet: *an Internet service provider*

'service road (*NAmE* also **'frontage road**) *noun* a side road that runs parallel to a main road, that you use to reach houses, shops/stores, etc.

'service station *noun* **1** = GAS STATION, PETROL STATION **2** (*BrE*) an area and building beside a MOTORWAY where you can buy food and petrol, go to the toilet, etc: *a motorway service station*

ser·vicing /'sɜːvɪsɪŋ; *NAmE* 'sɜːrv-/ *noun* [U] **1** the act of checking and repairing a vehicle, machine, etc. to keep it in good condition: *Like any other type of equipment it requires regular servicing.* **2** (*finance*) the act of paying interest on money that has been borrowed: *debt servicing*

ser·vi·ette /ˌsɜːvi'et; *NAmE* ˌsɜːrv-/ *noun* (*BrE*) a piece of cloth or paper used at meals for protecting your clothes and cleaning your lips and fingers SYN **napkin**

ser·vile /'sɜːvaɪl; *NAmE* 'sɜːrvl; -vaɪl/ *adj.* (*disapproving*) wanting too much to please sb and obey them SYN **fawning** ▸ **ser·vil·ity** /sɜː'vɪləti; *NAmE* sɜːr'v-/ *noun* [U]

serv·ing /'sɜːvɪŋ; *NAmE* 'sɜːrvɪŋ/ *noun* an amount of food for one person: *This recipe will be enough for four servings.*

ser·vi·tor /'sɜːvɪtə(r); *NAmE* 'sɜːrv-/ *noun* (*old use*) a male servant

S

ser·vi·tude /ˈsɜːvɪtjuːd; *NAmE* ˈsɜːrvətuːd/ *noun* [U] (*formal*) the condition of being a SLAVE or being forced to obey another person SYN **slavery**

servo /ˈsɜːvəʊ; *NAmE* ˈsɜːrvoʊ/ *noun* (*pl.* -os) (*technical*) a part of a machine that controls a larger piece of machinery

ses·ame /ˈsesəmi/ *noun* [U] a tropical plant grown for its seeds and their oil, which are used in cooking: *sesame seeds* ➲ see also OPEN SESAME

ses·sion 0- /ˈseʃn/ *noun*
1 0- [C] a period of time that is spent doing a particular activity: *a* ***photo/recording/training, etc. session*** ◇ *The course is made up of 12 two-hour sessions.* ➲ see also JAM SESSION **2** 0- [C, U] a formal meeting or series of meetings of a court, a parliament, etc; a period of time when such meetings are held: *a session of the UN General Assembly* ◇ *The court is now* ***in session***. ◇ *The committee met* ***in closed session*** (= with nobody else present). ➲ see also QUARTER SESSIONS **3** [C] a school or university year **4** [C] an occasion when people meet to play music, especially Irish music, in a pub/bar

ˈ**session musician** *noun* a musician who is hired to play on recordings but is not a permanent member of a band

set 0- /set/ *verb, noun, adj.*
■ ***verb*** (set·ting, set, set)
▸ PUT/START **1** 0- [T] **~ sth/sb + adv./prep.** to put sth/sb in a particular place or position: *She set a tray down on the table.* ◇ *They ate everything that was set in front of them.* ◇ *The house is set* (= located) *in fifty acres of parkland.* **2** 0- [T] to cause sb/sth to be in a particular state; to start sth happening: **~ sb/sth + adv./prep.** *Her manner immediately* ***set*** *everyone* ***at*** *their* ***ease***. ◇ *He pulled the lever and* ***set*** *the machine* ***in motion***. ◇ **~ sb/sth + adj.** *The hijackers* ***set*** *the hostages* ***free***. ◇ **~ sb/sth doing sth** *Her remarks set me thinking.*
▸ PLAY/BOOK/MOVIE **3** 0- [T, usually passive] **~ sth + adv./prep.** to place the action of a play, novel or film/movie in a particular place, time, etc: *The novel is set in London in the 1960s.*
▸ CLOCK/MACHINE **4** 0- [T] **~ sth** (**+ adv./prep.**) to prepare or arrange sth so that it is ready for use or in position: *She set the camera on automatic.* ◇ *I set my watch by* (= make it show the same time as) *the TV.* ◇ *Set the alarm for 7 o'clock.*
▸ TABLE **5** 0- [T] **~ a/the table** (**for sb/sth**) to arrange knives, forks, etc. on a table for a meal: *Could you set the table for dinner?* ◇ *The table was set for six guests.*
▸ JEWELLERY **6** [T, usually passive] to put a PRECIOUS STONE into a piece of jewellery: **~ A in B** *She had the sapphire set in a gold ring.* ◇ **~ B with A** *Her bracelet was set with emeralds.*
▸ ARRANGE **7** 0- [T] **~ sth** to arrange or fix sth; to decide on sth: *They haven't* ***set a date*** *for their wedding yet.* ◇ *The government has set strict limits on public spending this year.*
▸ EXAMPLE/STANDARD, ETC. **8** 0- [T] **~ sth** to fix sth so that others copy it or try to achieve it: *This could* ***set a new fashion***. ◇ *They* ***set high standards*** *of customer service.* ◇ *I am unwilling to* ***set a precedent***. ◇ *She* ***set a*** *new world* ***record*** *for the high jump.* ◇ *I rely on you to* ***set a good example***.
▸ WORK/TASK **9** 0- [T] **~ sth** (**for sb**) | **~ sb** (**to do sth**) to give sb a piece of work, a task, etc: **~ sth** *Who will be setting* (= writing the questions for) *the French exam?* ◇ **~ sth for sth** *What books have been set* (= are to be studied) *for the English course?* ◇ **~ sth for sb/yourself** *She's set a difficult task for herself.* ◇ **~ sb/yourself sth** *She's set herself a difficult task.* ◇ **~ sb/yourself to do sth** *I've set myself to finish the job by the end of the month.*
▸ BECOME FIRM **10** 0- [I] to become firm or hard: *Leave the concrete to set for a few hours.* ◇ **+ adj.** *The glue had set hard.*
▸ FACE **11** [T, usually passive] **~ sth** to fix your face into a firm expression: *Her jaw was set in a determined manner.*
▸ HAIR **12** [T] **~ sth** to arrange sb's hair while it is wet so that it dries in a particular style: *She had her hair washed and set.*
▸ BONE **13** [T, I] **~** (**sth**) to put a broken bone into a fixed position and hold it there, so that it will heal; to heal in this way: *The surgeon set her broken arm.*
▸ FOR PRINTING **14** [T] **~ sth** (*technical*) to use a machine or computer to arrange writing and images on pages in order to prepare a book, newspaper, etc. for printing ➲ see also TYPESETTER
▸ WORDS TO MUSIC **15** [T] **~ sth** (**to sth**) to write music to go with words: *Schubert set many poems to music.*
▸ OF SUN/MOON **16** 0- [I] to go down below the HORIZON: *We sat and watched the sun setting.* ➲ see also SUNSET OPP **rise**

IDM Idioms containing **set** are at the entries for the nouns and adjectives in the idioms, for example **set the pace** is at **pace** *n.*

PHR V ˈ**set about sb** (*BrE, old-fashioned, informal*) to attack sb ˈ**set about sth** | ˌ**set about** ˈ**doing sth** [no passive] to start doing sth: *She set about the business of cleaning the house.* ◇ *We need to set about finding a solution.*
set sb aˈgainst sb to make sb oppose a friend, relative, etc: *She accused her husband of setting the children against her.* **set sth** (**off**) **against sth 1** to judge sth by comparing good or positive qualities with bad or negative ones: *Set against the benefits of the new technology, there is also a strong possibility that jobs will be lost.* **2** (*finance*) to record sth as a business cost as a way of reducing the amount of tax you must pay: *to set capital costs off against tax*
ˌ**set sb/sth aˈpart (from sb/sth)** to make sb/sth different from or better than others: *Her elegant style sets her apart from other journalists.* ˌ**set sth↔aˈpart** (**for sth**) [usually passive] to keep sth for a special use or purpose: *Two rooms were set apart for use as libraries.*
ˌ**set sth↔aˈside 1** to move sth to one side until you need it **2** to save or keep money or time for a particular purpose: *She tries to set aside some money every month.* **3** to not consider sth, because other things are more important SYN **disregard**: *Let's set aside my personal feelings for now.* **4** (*law*) to state that a decision made by a court is not legally valid: *The verdict was set aside by the Appeal Court.*
ˌ**set sth/sb↔ˈback** to delay the progress of sth/sb by a particular time: *The bad weather set back the building programme by several weeks.* ➲ related noun SETBACK ˌ**set sb ˈback sth** [no passive] (*informal*) to cost sb a particular amount of money: *The repairs could set you back over £200.* ˌ**set sth ˈback** (**from sth**) [usually passive] to place sth, especially a building, at a distance from sth: *The house is set well back from the road.*
ˌ**set sb↔ˈdown** (*BrE*) (of a bus or train, or its driver) to stop and allow sb to get off: *Passengers may be set down and picked up only at the official stops.* ˌ**set sth↔ˈdown 1** to write sth down on paper in order to record it **2** to give sth as a rule, principle, etc: *The standards were set down by the governing body.*
ˌ**set ˈforth** (*literary*) to start a journey ˌ**set sth↔ˈforth** (*formal*) to present sth or make it known SYN **expound**: *The President set forth his views in a television broadcast.*
ˌ**set ˈin** (of rain, bad weather, infection, etc.) to begin and seem likely to continue: *The rain seemed to have set in for the day.* ˌ**set sth ˈin/ˈinto sth** [usually passive] to fasten sth into a flat surface so that it does not stick out from it: *a plaque set into the wall*
ˌ**set ˈoff** 0- to begin a journey: *We set off for London just after ten.* ˌ**set sth↔ˈoff 1** 0- to make a bomb, etc. explode: *A gang of boys were setting off fireworks in the street.* **2** 0- to make an alarm start ringing: *Opening this door will set off the alarm.* **3** to start a process or series of events: *Panic on the stock market set off a wave of selling.* **4** to make sth more noticeable or attractive by being placed near it: *That blouse sets off the blue of her eyes.* ˌ**set sb ˈoff** (**doing sth**) to make sb start doing sth such as laughing, crying or talking
ˈ**set on/upon sb** [usually passive] to attack sb suddenly: *I opened the gate, and was immediately set on by a large dog.* ˈ**set sb/sth on sb** to make a person or an animal attack sb suddenly: *The farmer threatened to set his dogs on us.*
ˌ**set ˈout 1** 0- to leave a place and begin a journey: *They set out on the last stage of their journey.* **2** to begin a job, task, etc. with a particular aim or goal: *She set out to break the world record.* ◇ *They succeeded in what they set out to do.* ˌ**set sth↔ˈout 1** to arrange or display things: *Her work is always very well set out.* **2** to present ideas, facts, etc. in an organized way, in speech or writing: *He set out his objec-*

S

tions to the plan. ◇ *She set out the reasons for her resignation in a long letter.*
ˌ**set ˈto** (*old-fashioned, informal*) to begin doing sth in a busy or determined way
ˌ**set sb↔ˈup** **1** to provide sb with the money that they need in order to do sth: *A bank loan helped to set him up in business.* **2** (*informal*) to make sb healthier, stronger, more lively, etc: *The break from work really set me up for the new year.* **3** (*informal*) to trick sb, especially by making them appear guilty of sth: *He denied the charges, saying the police had set him up.* ➲ related noun SET-UP ˌ**set sth↔ˈup** **1** 🔑 to build sth or put sth somewhere: *The police set up roadblocks on routes out of the city.* **2** 🔑 to make a piece of equipment or a machine ready for use: *She set up her stereo in her bedroom.* **3** 🔑 to arrange for sth to happen: *I've set up a meeting for Friday.* **4** 🔑 to create sth or start it: *to set up a business* ◇ *A fund will be set up for the dead men's families.* **5** to start a process or a series of events: *The slump on Wall Street set up a chain reaction in stock markets around the world.* ➲ related noun SET-UP ˌ**set (yourself) ˈup (as sb)** to start running a business: *She took out a bank loan and set up on her own.* ◇ *After leaving college, he set himself up as a freelance photographer.*

■ ***noun***

▸ GROUP **1** 🔑 [C] **~ (of sth)** a group of similar things that belong together in some way: *a set of six chairs* ◇ *a complete set of her novels* ◇ *a set of false teeth* ◇ *a new set of rules to learn* ◇ *You can borrow my keys—I have a spare set.* ➲ see also TEA SET **2** 🔑 [C] a group of objects used together, for example for playing a game: *a chess set* **3** [C+sing./pl. v.] (sometimes *disapproving*) a group of people who have similar interests and spend a lot of time together socially: *the smart set* (= rich, fashionable people) ◇ *Dublin's literary set* ➲ see also THE JET SET
▸ TV/RADIO **4** [C] a piece of equipment for receiving television or radio signals
▸ FOR PLAY/MOVIE **5** [C] the SCENERY used for a play, film/movie, etc: *We need volunteers to help build and paint the set.* **6** [C, U] a place where a play is performed or part of a film/movie is filmed: *The cast must all be on (the) set by 7 in the morning.*
▸ IN SPORT **7** [C] one section of a match in games such as TENNIS or VOLLEYBALL: *She won **in straight sets*** (= without losing a set).
▸ MATHEMATICS **8** [C] a group of things that have a shared quality: *set theory*
▸ POP MUSIC **9** [C] a series of songs or pieces of music that a musician or group performs at a concert
▸ CLASS **10** [C] (*BrE*) a group of school students with a similar ability in a particular subject: *She's in the top set for French.*
▸ OF FACE/BODY **11** [sing.] **~ of sth** the way in which sb's face or body is fixed in a particular expression, especially one showing determination: *She admired the firm set of his jaw.*
▸ HAIR **12** [sing.] an act of arranging hair in a particular style while it is wet: *A **shampoo and set** costs £15.*
▸ BECOMING FIRM **13** [sing.] the state of becoming firm or solid
▸ ANIMAL'S HOME **14** [C] = SETT
▸ PLANT **15** [C] a young plant, SHOOT etc. for planting: *onion sets*

■ ***adj.***

▸ IN POSITION **1** in a particular position: *a house set in 40 acres of parkland* ◇ *He had close-set eyes.*
▸ PLANNED **2** [usually before noun] planned or fixed: *Each person was given set jobs to do.* ◇ *The school funds a set number of free places.* ◇ *Mornings in our house always follow a set pattern.* ➲ see also SET BOOK
▸ OPINIONS/IDEAS **3** not likely to change: ***set ideas/opinions/views** on how to teach* ◇ *As people get older, they get **set in their ways**.*
▸ MEAL **4** [only before noun] (of a meal in a restaurant) having a fixed price and a limited choice of dishes: *a **set dinner/lunch/meal*** ◇ *Shall we have the **set menu**?*
▸ LIKELY/READY **5** likely to do sth; ready for sth or to do sth: **~ for sth** *The team looks set for victory.* ◇ **~ to do sth** *Interest rates look set to rise again.* ◇ *Be set to leave by 10 o'clock.* ➲ LANGUAGE BANK at EXPECT
▸ FACE **6** [usually before noun] (of a person's expression) fixed; not natural: *a set smile* ◇ *His face took on a set expression.*

IDM **be (dead) set against sth/against doing sth** to be strongly opposed to sth: *Why are you so dead set against the idea?* **be ˈset on sth/on doing sth** to want to do or have sth very much; to be determined to do sth ➲ more at MARK *n.*

ˈ**set-aside** *noun* [U] a system in which the government pays farmers not to use some of their land for growing crops; the land that the farmers are paid not to use

set·back /ˈsetbæk/ *noun* a difficulty or problem that delays or prevents sth, or makes a situation worse: *The team **suffered a** major **setback** when their best player was injured.* ◇ *The breakdown in talks represents a temporary setback in the peace process.*

ˌ**set ˈbook** (also ˌ**set ˈtext**) *noun* (both *BrE*) a book that students must study for a particular exam

seth /seɪt/ *noun* (*IndE*) **1** a MERCHANT (= a person who sells goods in large quantities) or BANKER (= a person with an important job in a bank) **2** a rich man **3** a title added to a name to indicate high social status

ˌ**set ˈphrase** *noun* a phrase that is always used in the same form: *Don't worry about the grammar, just learn this as a set phrase.*

ˌ**set ˈpiece** *noun* **1** a part of a play, film/movie, piece of music, etc. that has a well-known pattern or style, and is used to create a particular effect **2** a move in a sports game that is well planned and practised

ˌ**set ˈpoint** *noun* (especially in TENNIS) a point that, if won by a player, will win them the SET (7)

ˈ**set square** (*BrE*) (*NAmE* **tri·angle**) *noun* an instrument for drawing straight lines and angles, made from a flat piece of plastic or metal in the shape of a triangle with one angle of 90° ➲ VISUAL VOCAB page V57

sett (also **set**) /set/ *noun* a hole in the ground where a BADGER lives

set·tee /seˈtiː/ *noun* (*BrE*) a long comfortable seat with a back and arms, for two or more people to sit on SYN **sofa, couch**

set·ter /ˈsetə(r)/ *noun* **1** a large dog with long hair, sometimes used in hunting. There are several types of setter. **2** (often in compounds) a person who sets sth: *a quiz setter* ➲ see also JET-SETTER, PACESETTER, TRENDSETTER

set·ting /ˈsetɪŋ/ *noun* **1** a set of surroundings; the place at which sth happens: *a **rural/an ideal/a beautiful/an idyllic, etc. setting*** ◇ *It was **the perfect setting** for a wonderful Christmas.* ➲ SYNONYMS at ENVIRONMENT **2** the place and time at which the action of a play, novel, etc. takes place: *short stories with a contemporary setting* **3** a position at which the controls on a machine can be set, to set the speed, height, temperature, etc: *The performance of the engine was tested at different settings.* **4** (*music*) music written to go with a poem, etc: *Schubert's setting of a poem by Goethe* **5** a piece of metal in which a PRECIOUS STONE is fixed to form a piece of jewellery **6** a complete set of equipment for eating with (knife, fork, spoon, glass, etc.) for one person, arranged on a table: *a place setting*

set·tle 🔑 /ˈsetl/ *verb, noun*

■ ***verb***

▸ END ARGUMENT **1** 🔑 [T, I] **~ (sth)** to put an end to an argument or a disagreement: *to **settle a dispute/an argument/a matter*** ◇ *It's time you **settled your differences** with your father.* ◇ *There is pressure on the unions to settle.* ◇ *The company has agreed to **settle out of court*** (= come to an agreement without going to court).
▸ DECIDE/ARRANGE **2** 🔑 [T, often passive] to decide or arrange sth finally: **~ sth** *It's all **settled**—we're leaving on the nine o'clock plane.* ◇ *Bob will be there? **That settles it**. I'm not coming.* ◇ *He had to **settle his affairs*** (= arrange all his personal business) *in Paris before he could return home.* ◇ **it is settled that…** *It's been settled that we leave on the nine o'clock plane.*
▸ CHOOSE PERMANENT HOME **3** 🔑 [I] **+ adv./prep.** to make a place your permanent home: *She settled in Vienna after her father's death.* **4** 🔑 [T, usually passive, I] **~ sth** | **+ adv./prep.**

S

(of a group of people) to make your permanent home in a country or an area as COLONISTS: *This region was settled by the Dutch in the nineteenth century.*
▸ INTO COMFORTABLE POSITION/STATE **5** [I, T] to make yourself or sb else comfortable in a new position: **~ (back) (+ adv./prep.)** *Ellie settled back in her seat.* ◇ **~ sb/yourself (+ adv./prep.)** *He settled himself comfortably in his usual chair.* ◇ *I settled her on the sofa and put a blanket over her.* **6** [T] **~ sth + adv./prep.** to put sth carefully in a position so that it does not move: *She settled the blanket around her knees.* **7** [I, T] to become or make sb/sth become calm or relaxed: *The baby wouldn't settle.* ◇ **~ sb/sth** *I took a pill to help settle my nerves.* ◇ *This should settle your stomach.*
▸ COME TO REST **8** [I] **~ (on/over sth)** to fall from above and come to rest on sth; to stay for some time on sth: *Dust had settled on everything.* ◇ *Two birds settled on the fence.* ◇ *I don't think the snow will settle* (= remain on the ground without melting). ◇ *His gaze settled on her face.*
▸ SINK DOWN **9** [I, T] **~ (sth)** to sink slowly down; to make sth do this: *The contents of the package may have settled in transit.*
▸ PAY MONEY **10** [T, I] to pay the money that you owe: **~ sth** *Please settle your bill before leaving the hotel.* ◇ *The insurance company is refusing to settle her claim.* ◇ **~ (up) (with sb)** *Let me settle with you for the meal.* ◇ *I'll pay now—we can settle up later.*
IDM **settle a 'score/an ac'count (with sb)** | **settle an old 'score** to hurt or punish sb who has harmed or cheated you in the past: *'Who would do such a thing?' 'Maybe someone with an old score to settle.'* ⊃ more at DUST *n.*
PHR V **,settle 'down 1** 0‑ to get into a comfortable position, either sitting or lying: *I settled down with a book.* **2** 0‑ to start to have a quieter way of life, living in one place: *When are you going to get married and settle down?* ⊃ COLLOCATIONS at AGE **,settle 'down** | **,settle sb↔'down** 0‑ to become or make sb become calm, less excited, etc: *It always takes the class a while to settle down at the start of the lesson.* **settle (down) to sth** to begin to give your attention to sth: *They finally settled down to a discussion of the main issues.* ◇ *He found it hard to settle to his work.* **'settle for sth** to accept sth that is not exactly what you want but is the best that is available: *In the end they had to settle for a draw.* ◇ *I couldn't afford the house I really wanted, so I had to* **settle for second best**. **,settle 'in** | **,settle 'into sth** to move into a new home, job, etc. and start to feel comfortable there: *How are the kids settling into their new school?* **'settle on sth** to choose or make a decision about sth after thinking about it: *Have you settled on a name for the baby yet?* **'settle sth on sb** (*law*) to formally arrange to give money or property to sb, especially in a WILL
■ ***noun*** an old-fashioned piece of furniture with a long wooden seat and a high back and arms, often also with a box for storing things under the seat

set·tled /'setld/ *adj.* **1** not likely to change or move: *settled weather* ◇ *a settled way of life* **2** comfortable and happy with your home, job, way of life, etc. OPP **unsettled**

settle·ment /'setlmənt/ *noun* **1** [C] an official agreement that ends an argument between two people or groups: *to* ***negotiate a*** *peace* ***settlement*** ◇ *The management and unions have* ***reached a settlement*** *over new working conditions.* ◇ *an* ***out-of-court settlement*** (= money that is paid to sb or an agreement that is made to stop sb going to court) **2** [U] the action of reaching an agreement: *the settlement of a dispute* **3** [C] (*law*) the conditions, or a document stating the conditions, on which money or property is given to sb: *a* ***divorce/marriage/property, etc. settlement*** **4** [U] the action of paying back money that you owe: *the settlement of a debt* ◇ *a cheque* ***in settlement*** *of a bill* **5** [C] a place where people have come to live and make their homes, especially where few or no people lived before: *signs of an Iron Age settlement* **6** [U] the process of people making their homes in a place: *the settlement of the American West*

'settlement house *noun* (*especially NAmE*) a public building in an area of a large city that has social problems, that provides social services such as advice and training to the people who live there

set·tler /'setlə(r)/ *noun* a person who goes to live in a new country or region: *white settlers in Africa*

,set-'to *noun* [sing.] (*informal, especially BrE*) a small fight or an argument

,set-,top 'box *noun* a device that changes a DIGITAL television signal into a form which can be seen on an ordinary television

'set-up *noun* [usually sing.] (*informal*) **1** a way of organizing sth; a system: *I've only been here a couple of weeks and I don't really know the set-up.* **2** a situation in which sb tricks you or makes it seem as if you have done sth wrong: *He didn't steal the goods. It was a set-up.*

sevak /'seɪvæk/ *noun* (*IndE*) **1** a male servant **2** a male SOCIAL WORKER

seven 0‑ /'sevn/ *number*
7 HELP There are examples of how to use numbers at the entry for **five**.
IDM **the seven-year 'itch** (*informal, humorous*) the desire for new sexual experience that is thought to be felt after seven years of marriage ⊃ more at SIX

the ,seven 'seas *noun* [pl.] all of the earth's oceans

the ,Seven 'Sisters *noun* [pl.] **1** the Pleiades, a group of seven stars **2** a group of seven traditional women's (or formerly women's) universities in the eastern US with high academic standards and a high social status

seven·teen 0‑ /,sevn'tiːn/ *number*
17 ▸ **seven·teenth** /,sevn'tiːnθ/ *ordinal number, noun* HELP There are examples of how to use ordinal numbers at the entry for **fifth**.

sev·enth 0‑ /'sevnθ/ *ordinal number, noun*
■ ***ordinal number*** 7th HELP There are examples of how to use ordinal numbers at the entry for **fifth**.
IDM **in seventh 'heaven** extremely happy: *Now that he's been promoted he's in seventh heaven.*
■ ***noun*** each of seven equal parts of sth

Seventh-Day Adventist /,sevnθ deɪ 'ædvəntɪst/ *noun* a member of a Christian religious group that believes that Christ will soon return to Earth

sev·enty 0‑ /'sevnti/
1 *number* 70 **2** *noun* **the seventies** [pl.] numbers, years or temperatures from 70 to 79 ▸ **seven·ti·eth** /'sevntiəθ/ *ordinal number, noun* HELP There are examples of how to use ordinal numbers at the entry for **fifth**.
IDM **in your 'seventies** between the ages of 70 and 79

sever /'sevə(r)/ *verb* (*formal*) **1** to cut sth into two pieces; to cut sth off sth: **~ sth** *to sever a rope* ◇ *a severed artery* ◇ **~ sth from sth** *His hand was severed from his arm.* **2 ~ sth** to completely end a relationship or all communication with sb SYN **break off**: *The two countries have* ***severed*** *all diplomatic* ***links***.

sev·eral 0‑ /'sevrəl/ *det., pron., adj.*
■ ***det., pron.*** 0‑ more than two but not very many: *Several letters arrived this morning.* ◇ *He's written several books about India.* ◇ *Several more people than usual came to the meeting.* ◇ *If you're looking for a photo of Alice you'll find several in here.* ◇ *Several of the paintings were destroyed in the fire.*
■ ***adj.*** (*formal*) separate: *They said goodbye and went their* ***several ways***.

sev·er·al·ly /'sevrəli/ *adv.* (*formal* or *law*) separately: *Tenants are* ***jointly and severally*** *liable for payment of the rent.*

sev·er·ance /'sevərəns/ *noun* [sing., U] (*formal*) **1** the act of ending a connection or relationship: *the severance of diplomatic relations* **2** the act of ending sb's work contract: *employees given notice of severance* ◇ ***severance pay/terms***

se·vere 0‑ /sɪ'vɪə(r); *NAmE* -'vɪr/ *adj.* (**se·verer**, **se·ver·est**)
▸ VERY BAD **1** 0‑ extremely bad or serious: *a severe handicap* ◇ *His injuries are severe.* ◇ *severe weather conditions* ◇ *a se-*

S

vere winter (= one during which the weather conditions are extremely bad) ◇ *The party suffered severe losses during the last election.* ◇ *a severe shortage of qualified staff*
▸ PUNISHMENT **2** ~ **(on/with sb)** punishing sb in an extreme way when they break a particular set of rules SYN **harsh**: *The courts are becoming more severe on young offenders.* ◇ *a **severe punishment/sentence***
▸ NOT KIND **3** not kind or sympathetic and showing disapproval of sb/sth SYN **stern**: *a severe expression* ◇ *She was a severe woman who seldom smiled.*
▸ VERY DIFFICULT **4** extremely difficult and requiring a lot of skill or ability SYN **stiff**: *The marathon is a severe test of stamina.*
▸ STYLE/APPEARANCE/CLOTHING **5** (*disapproving*) extremely plain and lacking any decoration: *Modern furniture is a little too severe for my taste.* ◇ *Her hair was short and severe.*
▸ **se·vere·ly** *adv.*: *severely disabled* ◇ *areas severely affected by unemployment* ◇ *Anyone breaking the law will be severely punished.* ◇ *a severely critical report* ◇ *Her hair was tied severely in a bun.* **se·ver·ity** /sɪˈverəti/ *noun* [U]: *A prison sentence should match the severity of the crime.* ◇ *The chances of a full recovery will depend on the severity of her injuries.* ◇ *the severity of the problem* ◇ *He frowned with mock severity.* ◇ *The elaborate facade contrasts strongly with the severity of the interior.*

sev·ika /ˈseɪvɪkə/ *noun* (*IndE*) **1** a female servant **2** a female SOCIAL WORKER

Sev·ille orange /ˌsevɪl ˈɒrɪndʒ; *NAmE* ˈɔːr-; ˈɑːr-/ *noun* a type of bitter orange, used in making MARMALADE

sew /səʊ; *NAmE* soʊ/ *verb* (**sewed**, **sewn** /səʊn; *NAmE* soʊn/ or **sewed**)
1 [I, T] to use a needle and thread to make STITCHES in cloth: *My mother taught me how to sew.* ◇ *to sew by hand/machine* ◇ **~ sth** *to sew a seam* **2** [T] to make, repair or attach sth using a needle and thread: **~ sth** *She sews all her own clothes.* ◇ **~ sth on** *Can you sew a button on for me?* ◇ *Surgeons were able to sew the finger back on.*
PHR V ˌ**sew sth**↔ˈ**up** **1** to join or repair sth by sewing: *to sew up a seam* **2** [often passive] (*informal*) to arrange sth in an acceptable way: *It didn't take me long to sew up the deal.* ◇ *They think they **have** the election **sewn up*** (= they think they are definitely going to win).

sew·age /ˈsuːɪdʒ; *BrE* also ˈsjuː-/ *noun* [U] used water and waste substances that are produced by human bodies, that are carried away from houses and factories through special pipes (=SEWERS): *a ban on the dumping of raw sewage* (= that has not been treated with chemicals) *at sea* ◇ *sewage disposal* ➲ compare WASTEWATER

ˈ**sewage farm** *noun* (*BrE*) = SEWAGE WORKS

ˈ**sewage plant** (also **sewage** ˈ**treatment plant**) *noun* (*especially NAmE*) = SEWAGE WORKS

ˈ**sewage works** (also **sewage** ˈ**treatment works**, **sewage dis**ˈ**posal works**) *noun* [C+sing./pl. v.] (*BrE*) a place where chemicals are used to clean sewage so that it can then be allowed to go into rivers, etc. or used to make MANURE

sewer /ˈsuːə(r); *BrE* also ˈsjuː-/ *noun* an underground pipe that is used to carry sewage away from houses, factories, etc.

sew·er·age /ˈsuːərɪdʒ; *BrE* also ˈsjuː-/ *noun* [U] the system by which sewage is carried away from houses, factories, etc. and is cleaned and made safe by adding chemicals to it

ˈ**sewer grate** *noun* (*US*) = GRATE (2)

sew·ing /ˈsəʊɪŋ; *NAmE* ˈsoʊ-/ *noun* [U]
1 the activity of making, repairing or decorating things made of cloth using a needle and thread: *knitting and sewing* ➲ VISUAL VOCAB page V35 **2** something that is being sewn: *a pile of sewing*

ˈ**sewing machine** *noun* a machine that is used for sewing things that are made of cloth ➲ VISUAL VOCAB page V35

sewn *past part.* of SEW

sex AW /seks/ *noun, verb*
■ ***noun*** **1** [U, C] the state of being male or female SYN **gender**: *How can you tell what sex a fish is?* ◇ *a process that allows couples to choose the sex of their baby* ◇ *Please indicate your sex and date of birth below.* ◇ ***sex discrimination*** (= the act of treating men and women differently in an unfair way) **2** [C] either of the two groups that people, animals and plants are divided into according to their function of producing young: *a member of **the opposite sex*** ◇ ***single-sex** schools* ➲ see also FAIR SEX **3** [U] physical activity between two people in which they touch each other's sexual organs, and which may include SEXUAL INTERCOURSE: *It is illegal to **have sex** with a person under the age of 16.* ◇ *gay sex* ◇ *the **sex act*** ◇ *a **sex attack*** ◇ *a **sex shop*** (= one selling magazines, objects, etc. that are connected with sex) ◇ ***sex education** in schools* ◇ *These drugs may affect your **sex drive*** (= your interest in sex and the ability to have it). ➲ see also SAFE SEX, SEXUAL INTERCOURSE **4** **-sexed** (in adjectives) having the amount of sexual activity or desire mentioned: *a highly-sexed woman*
■ ***verb*** **~ sth** (*technical*) to examine an animal in order to find out whether it is male or female
PHR V ˌ**sex sb**↔ˈ**up** (*informal*) to make sb feel sexually excited ˌ**sex sth**↔ˈ**up** (*informal*) to make sth seem more exciting and interesting: *The profession is trying to sex up its image.*

sexa·gen·ar·ian /ˌseksədʒəˈneəriən; *NAmE* -ˈner-/ *noun* a person between 60 and 69 years old

ˈ**sex appeal** *noun* [U] the quality of being attractive in a sexual way: *He exudes sex appeal.*

ˈ**sex change** *noun* [usually sing.] a medical operation in which parts of a person's body are changed so that they become like a person of the opposite sex

ˈ**sex chromosome** *noun* (*biology*) a CHROMOSOME that decides the sex of an animal or a plant ➲ see also X CHROMOSOME, Y CHROMOSOME

sex·ism AW /ˈseksɪzəm/ *noun* [U] the unfair treatment of people, especially women, because of their sex; the attitude that causes this: *legislation designed to combat sexism in the work place* ◇ *a study of sexism in language*

sex·ist /ˈseksɪst/ *noun* (*disapproving*) a person who treats other people, especially women, unfairly because of their sex or who makes offensive remarks about them ▸ **sex·ist** *adj.*: *a sexist attitude* ◇ *sexist language*

sex·less /ˈseksləs/ *adj.* **1** that is neither male nor female, or does not seem to be either male or female: *a sexless figure* **2** in which there is no sexual desire or activity

ˈ**sex life** *noun* a person's sexual activities: *ways to improve your sex life*

ˈ**sex maniac** *noun* a person who wants to have sex more often than is normal and who thinks about it all the time

ˈ**sex object** *noun* a person considered only for their sexual attraction and not for their character or their intelligence

ˈ**sex offender** *noun* a person who has been found guilty of illegal sexual acts

sex·ology /sekˈsɒlədʒi; *NAmE* -ˈsɑːl-/ *noun* [U] the scientific study of human sexual behaviour ▸ **sex·olo·gist** /-dʒɪst/ *noun*

sex·pot /ˈsekspɒt; *NAmE* -pɑːt/ *noun* (*informal*) a person who is thought to be sexually attractive

ˈ**sex symbol** *noun* a famous person who is thought by many people to be sexually attractive

sex·tant /ˈsekstənt/ *noun* an instrument for measuring angles and distances, used to calculate the exact position of a ship or an aircraft

sex·tet /seksˈtet/ *noun* **1** [C+sing./pl. v.] a group of six musicians or singers who play or sing together **2** [C] a piece of music for six musicians or singers

sex·ton /ˈsekstən/ *noun* a person whose job is to take care of a church and its surroundings, ring the church bell, etc.

sex·tu·plet /ˈsekstʊplət; sekˈstjuːplət; -ˈstʌp-/ *noun* one of six children born at the same time to the same mother

S

ˈ**sex typing** *noun* [U] **1** (*psychology*) the process of putting people into categories according to what people consider to be typical of each sex **2** (*biology*) the process of finding out whether a person or other living thing is male or female, especially in difficult cases when special tests are necessary

sex·ual 🔑 AW /ˈsekʃuəl/ *adj.*
1 🔑 [usually before noun] connected with the physical activity of sex: *sexual behaviour* ◇ *They were not having a sexual relationship at the time.* ◇ *Her interest in him is purely sexual.* ◇ ***sexual orientation*** (= whether you are HETEROSEXUAL or HOMOSEXUAL) **2** [only before noun] connected with the process of producing young: *the* ***sexual organs*** (= the PENIS, VAGINA, etc.) ◇ *sexual reproduction* **3** [usually before noun] connected with the state of being male or female: *sexual characteristics* ▶ **sex·ual·ly** 🔑 AW /ˈsekʃəli/ *adv.*: *sexually abused children* ◇ *She finds him sexually attractive.* ◇ *sexually explicit* ◇ *Girls become sexually mature earlier than boys.*

ˌ**sexual ˈharassment** *noun* [U] comments about sex, physical contact, etc. usually happening at work, that a person finds annoying and offensive

ˌ**sexual ˈintercourse** (also **inter·course**) (also *formal* **co·itus**) *noun* [U] (*formal*) the physical activity of sex, usually describing the act of a man putting his PENIS inside a woman's VAGINA

sexu·al·ity AW /ˌsekʃuˈæləti/ *noun* [U] the feelings and activities connected with a person's sexual desires: ***male/female sexuality*** ◇ *He was confused about his sexuality.*

sex·ual·ize (*BrE* also **-ise**) /ˈsekʃuəlaɪz/ *verb* **~ sb/sth** to make sb/sth seem sexually attractive ▶ **sex·ual·iza·tion, -isa·tion** /ˌsekʃuəlaɪˈzeɪʃn/ *noun* [U]

ˌ**sexually transˌmitted diˈsease** *noun* [C, U] (*abbr.* **STD**) any disease that is spread through sexual intercourse, such as SYPHILIS

ˈ**sex worker** *noun* a polite way of referring to a PROSTITUTE

sexy /ˈseksi/ *adj.* (**sex·ier, sexi·est**) **1** (of a person) sexually attractive: *the sexy lead singer* ◇ *She looked incredibly sexy in a black evening gown.* **2** sexually exciting: *sexy underwear* ◇ *a sexy look* **3** (of a person) sexually excited: *The music and wine began to make him feel sexy.* **4** exciting and interesting: *a sexy new range of software* ◇ *Accountancy just isn't sexy.* ▶ **sex·ily** *adv.* **sexi·ness** *noun* [U]

SF /ˌes ˈef/ *abbr.* SCIENCE FICTION

SFX /ˌes ef ˈeks/ *abbr.* SPECIAL EFFECTS

SGML /ˌes dʒiː em ˈel/ *abbr.* (*computing*) Standard Generalized Mark-up Language (a system used for marking text on a computer so that the text can be read on a different computer system or displayed in different forms)

Sgt (*especially BrE*) (also **Sgt.** *NAmE, BrE*) *abbr.* SERGEANT: *Sgt Williams*

sh (also **shh**) /ʃ/ *exclamation* the way of writing the sound people make when they are telling sb to be quiet: *Sh! Keep your voice down!*

shabby /ˈʃæbi/ *adj.* (**shab·bier, shab·bi·est**) **1** (of buildings, clothes, objects, etc.) in poor condition because they have been used a lot SYN **scruffy**: *She wore shabby old jeans and a T-shirt.* **2** (of a person) badly dressed in clothes that have been worn a lot SYN **scruffy**: *The old man was shabby and unkempt.* **3** (of behaviour) unfair or unreasonable SYN **shoddy**: *She tried to make up for her shabby treatment of him.* ▶ **shab·bily** /ˈʃæbɪli/ *adv.*: *shabbily dressed* ◇ *I think you were very shabbily treated.* **shab·bi·ness** *noun* [U]

shack /ʃæk/ *noun, verb*
■ ***noun*** a small building, usually made of wood or metal, that has not been built well
■ ***verb***
PHR V ˌ**shack ˈup with sb** | **be ˌshacked ˈup with sb** (*slang*) to start/be living with sb that you have a sexual relationship with, but that you are not married to: *I hear he's shacked up with some woman.*

shackle /ˈʃækl/ *verb* **1 ~ sb** to put shackles on sb: *The hostage had been shackled to a radiator.* ◇ *The prisoners were kept shackled during the trial.* **2** [usually passive] **~ sb/sth** to prevent sb from behaving or speaking as they want

shackles /ˈʃæklz/ *noun* [pl.] **1** two metal rings joined together by a chain and placed around a prisoner's wrists or ankles to prevent them from escaping or moving easily **2 ~ (of sth)** (*formal*) a particular state, set of conditions or circumstances, etc. that prevent you from saying or doing what you want: *a country struggling to free itself from the shackles of colonialism*

shade 🔑 /ʃeɪd/ *noun, verb*
■ ***noun***

▸ OUT OF SUN **1** 🔑 [U] **~ (of sth)** an area that is dark and cool under or behind sth, for example a tree or building, because the sun's light does not get to it: *We sat down* ***in the shade of*** *the wall.* ◇ *The temperature can reach 40°C* ***in the shade.*** ◇ *The trees provide shade for the animals in the summer.* ➲ see also SHADY
▸ ON LAMP, ETC. **2** 🔑 [C] a thing that you use to prevent light from coming through or to make it less bright: *I bought a new shade for the lamp.* ◇ *an eyeshade* ➲ see also LAMPSHADE, SUNSHADE
▸ ON WINDOW **3** [C] (also ˈ**window shade**) (both *NAmE*) = BLIND ➲ VISUAL VOCAB page V18
▸ OF COLOUR **4** 🔑 [C] **~ (of sth)** a particular form of a colour, that is, how dark or light it is: *a* ***delicate/pale/rich/soft shade*** *of blue* ➲ SYNONYMS at COLOUR
▸ IN PICTURE **5** [U] the dark areas in a picture, especially the use of these to produce variety: *The painting needs more* ***light and shade.***
▸ OF OPINION/FEELING **6** [C, usually pl.] **~ of sth** a different kind or level of opinion, feeling, etc: *politicians of all shades of opinion* ◇ *The word has many shades of meaning.*
▸ SLIGHTLY **7 a shade** [sing.] a little; slightly SYN **touch**: *He was feeling a shade disappointed.*
▸ FOR EYES **8 shades** [pl.] (*informal*) = SUNGLASSES
▸ GHOST **9** [C] (*literary*) the spirit of a dead person; a GHOST

Which Word?

shade / shadow

- **Shade** [U] is an area or a part of a place that is protected from the heat of the sun and so is darker and cooler: *Let's sit in the shade for a while.*
- A **shadow** [C] is the dark shape made when a light shines on a person or an object: *As the sun went down we cast long shadows on the lawn.*
- **Shadow** [U] is an area of darkness in which it is difficult to distinguish things easily: *Her face was in deep shadow.*

IDM **put sb/sth in the ˈshade** to be much better or more impressive than sb/sth: *I tried hard but her work put mine in the shade.* **shades of sb/sth** (*informal*) used when you are referring to things that remind you of a particular person, thing or time: *short skirts and long boots—shades of the 1960s*
■ ***verb***
▸ FROM DIRECT LIGHT **1** to prevent direct light from reaching sth: **~ sb/sth** *The courtyard was shaded by high trees.* ◇ **~ sb/sth from/against sth** *She shaded her eyes against the sun.*
▸ LAMP **2** [usually passive] **~ sth** to provide a screen for a lamp, light, etc. to make it less bright: *a shaded lamp*
▸ PART OF PICTURE **3** to make a part of a drawing, etc. darker, for example with an area of colour or with pencil lines:

~ sth *What do the shaded areas on the map represent?* ◇ **~ sth in** *I'm going to shade this part in.*
▸ JUST WIN **4 ~ sth** (*BrE, informal*) to just win a contest
PHR V **ˌshade ˈinto sth** to change gradually into sth else, so that you cannot tell where one thing ends and the other thing begins: *The scarlet of the wings shades into pink at the tips.* ◇ *Distrust of foreigners can shade into racism.*

shad·ing /ˈʃeɪdɪŋ/ *noun* **1** [U] the use of colour, pencil lines, etc. to give an impression of light and shade in a picture or to emphasize areas of a map, diagram, etc. **2 shadings** [pl.] slight differences that exist between different aspects of the same thing

shadow 🔑 /ˈʃædəʊ; *NAmE* -doʊ/ *noun, verb, adj.*
■ ***noun***
▸ DARK SHAPE **1** 🔑 [C] the dark shape that sb/sth's form makes on a surface, for example on the ground, when they are between the light and the surface: *The children were having fun, chasing each other's shadows.* ◇ *The ship's sail* ***cast a shadow*** *on the water.* ◇ *The shadows lengthened as the sun went down.* ◇ (*figurative*) *He didn't want to* ***cast a shadow on*** (= spoil) *their happiness.* ➲ picture at SHADE ➲ note at SHADE
▸ DARKNESS **2** 🔑 [U] (also **shadows** [pl.]) DARKNESS in a place or on sth, especially so that you cannot easily see who or what is there: *His face was deep* ***in shadow***, *turned away from her.* ◇ *I thought I saw a figure standing in the shadows.* ➲ note at SHADE
▸ SMALL AMOUNT **3** [sing.] **~ of sth** a very small amount of sth SYN **hint**: *A shadow of a smile touched his mouth.* ◇ *She knew* ***beyond a shadow of a doubt*** (= with no doubt at all) *that he was lying.*
▸ INFLUENCE **4** [sing.] **~ of sb/sth** the strong (usually bad) influence of sb/sth: *The new leader wants to escape from the shadow of his predecessor.* ◇ *These people have been living for years* ***under the shadow*** *of fear.*
▸ UNDER EYES **5 shadows** [pl.] dark areas under sb's eyes, because they are tired, etc.
▸ SB THAT FOLLOWS SB **6** [C] a person or an animal that follows sb else all the time
▸ STH NOT REAL **7** [C] a thing that is not real or possible to obtain: *You can't spend all your life* ***chasing shadows***. ➲ see also EYESHADOW, FIVE O'CLOCK SHADOW
IDM **be frightened/nervous/scared of your own ˈshadow** to be very easily frightened; to be very nervous **in/under the ˈshadow of 1** very close to: *The new market is in the shadow of the City Hall.* **2** when you say that sb is **in/under the shadow of** another person, you mean that they do not receive as much attention as that person ➲ more at FORMER
■ ***verb***
▸ FOLLOW AND WATCH **1 ~ sb** to follow and watch sb closely and often secretly: *He was shadowed for a week by the secret police.* **2 ~ sb** to be with sb who is doing a particular job, so that you can learn about it: *It is often helpful for teachers to shadow managers in industry.*
▸ COVER WITH SHADOW **3 ~ sth** to cover sth with a shadow: *A wide-brimmed hat shadowed her face.* ◇ *The bay was shadowed by magnificent cliffs.* ➲ see also OVERSHADOW
■ ***adj.*** [only before noun] (*BrE, politics*) used to refer to senior politicians of the main opposition party who would become government ministers if their party won the next election: *the shadow Chancellor* ◇ *the shadow Cabinet*

ˈshadow-box *verb* [I] to BOX with an imaginary opponent, especially for physical exercise or in order to train ▸ **ˈshadow-boxing** *noun* [U]

shad·owy /ˈʃædəʊi; *NAmE* -doʊi/ *adj.* **1** dark and full of shadows: *Someone was waiting in the shadowy doorway.* **2** [usually before noun] difficult to see because there is not much light: ***Shadowy figures*** *approached them out of the fog.* **3** [usually before noun] that not much is known about: *the shadowy world of terrorism*

shady /ˈʃeɪdi/ *adj.* (**shadi·er**, **shadi·est**) **1** protected from direct light from the sun by trees, buildings, etc: *a shady garden* ◇ *We went to find somewhere cool and shady to have a drink.* **2** (of a tree, etc.) providing shade from the sun **3** [usually before noun] (*informal*) seeming to be dishonest or illegal: *a shady businessman/deal*

shaft /ʃɑːft; *NAmE* ʃæft/ *noun, verb*
■ ***noun* 1** (often in compounds) a long, narrow, usually vertical passage in a building or underground, used especially for a lift/elevator or as a way of allowing air in or out: *a* ***lift/elevator shaft*** ◇ *a mineshaft* ◇ *a ventilation shaft* **2** the long narrow part of an arrow, HAMMER, GOLF CLUB, etc. **3** (often in compounds) a metal bar that joins parts of a machine or an engine together, enabling power and movement to be passed from one part to another ➲ see also CAMSHAFT, CRANKSHAFT **4** [usually pl.] either of the two poles at the front of a CARRIAGE or CART between which a horse is fastened in order to pull it **5 ~ of light, sunlight, etc.** (*literary*) a narrow strip of light: *A shaft of moonlight fell on the lake.* ◇ (*figurative*) *a shaft of inspiration* **6 ~ of pain, fear, etc.** (*literary*) a sudden strong feeling of pain, etc. that travels through your body: *Shafts of fear ran through her as she heard footsteps behind her.* **7 ~ of sth** (*formal*) a clever remark that is intended to upset or annoy sb: *a shaft of wit*
IDM **give sb the ˈshaft** (*NAmE, informal*) to treat sb unfairly
■ ***verb* ~ sb** (*informal*) to treat sb unfairly or cheat them

shag /ʃæɡ/ *noun, verb, adj.*
■ ***noun* 1** [U] a strong type of TOBACCO cut into long thin pieces **2** [C] a large black bird with a long neck that lives near the sea **3** [C, usually sing.] (*BrE, taboo, slang*) an act of sex with sb
■ ***verb*** (-gg-) [I, T] **~ (sb)** (*BrE, taboo, slang*) to have sex with sb
■ ***adj.*** [only before noun] used to describe a carpet, etc, usually made of wool, that has long threads

shagged /ʃæɡd/ (also **ˌshagged ˈout**) *adj.* [not before noun] (*BrE, taboo, slang*) very tired

shaggy /ˈʃæɡi/ *adj.* (**shag·gier**, **shag·gi·est**) **1** (of hair, fur, etc.) long and untidy: *a shaggy mane of hair* **2** having long untidy hair, fur, etc: *a huge shaggy white dog*

ˌshaggy-ˈdog story *noun* a very long joke with a silly or disappointing ending

shah /ʃɑː/ *noun* the title of the kings of Iran in the past

shaikh = SHEIKH

shake 🔑 /ʃeɪk/ *verb, noun*
■ ***verb*** (**shook** /ʃʊk/, **shaken** /ˈʃeɪkən/)
▸ OBJECT/BUILDING/PERSON **1** 🔑 [I, T] to move or make sb/sth move with short quick movements from side to side or up and down: *The whole house shakes when a train goes past.* ◇ **~ sb/sth** *Shake the bottle well before use.* ◇ *He shook her violently by the shoulders.* ◇ **~ sb/sth + adj.** *She* ***shook*** *her hair* ***loose***. **2** 🔑 [T] **~ sth + adv./prep.** to move sth in a particular direction by shaking: *She bent down to shake a pebble out of her shoe.*
▸ YOUR HEAD **3** 🔑 [T] **~ your head** to turn your head from side to side as a way of saying 'no' or to show sadness, disapproval, doubt, etc: *She shook her head in disbelief.*
▸ HANDS **4** 🔑 [T] to take sb's hand and move it up and down as a way of saying hello or to show that you agree about sth **~ hands (with sb) (on sth)**: *Do people in Italy shake hands when they meet?* ◇ *They shook hands on the deal* (= to show that they had reached an agreement). ◇ **~ sb's hand** *He shook my hand warmly.* ◇ **~ sb by the hand** *Our host shook each of us warmly by the hand.*
▸ YOUR FIST **5** [T] **~ your fist (at sb)** to show that you are angry with sb; to threaten sb by shaking your FIST (= closed hand)
▸ OF BODY **6** 🔑 [I] **~ (with sth)** to make short quick movements that you cannot control, for example because you are cold or afraid SYN **tremble**: *He was shaking with fear.* ◇ *I was* ***shaking like a leaf***. ◇ *Her hands had started to shake.*
▸ OF VOICE **7** 🔑 [I] **~ (with sth)** (of sb's voice) to sound unsteady, usually because you are nervous, upset or angry
▸ SHOCK SB **8** 🔑 [T] (not used in the progressive tenses) to shock or upset sb very much: **~ sb** *He was badly shaken by the news of her death.* ◇ **~ sb up** *The accident really shook her up.*
▸ BELIEF/IDEA **9** [T] **~ sth** to make a belief or an idea less certain: *The incident had* ***shaken her faith*** *in him.* ◇ *This an-*

S

nouncement is bound to ***shake the confidence*** *of the industry.*

▸ GET RID OF **10** [T] to get rid of sth: **~ sth off** *I can't seem to shake off this cold.* ◇ **~ sth** *He couldn't shake the feeling that there was something wrong.*

IDM **shake in your 'shoes** (*informal*) to be very frightened or nervous **shake a 'leg** (*old-fashioned, informal*) used to tell sb to start to do sth or to hurry ➲ more at FOUNDATION

PHR V **,shake 'down** (*informal*) to become familiar with a new situation and begin to work well in it **,shake sb/sth↔'down** (*NAmE, informal*) **1** to search a person or place in a very thorough way ➲ related noun SHAKEDOWN **2** to threaten sb in order to get money from them **,shake sb↔'off** to get away from sb who is chasing or following you **'shake on sth** to shake hands in order to show that sth has been agreed: *They shook on the deal.* ◇ *Let's* ***shake on it.*** **,shake sth↔'out** to open or spread sth by shaking, especially so that bits of dirt, dust, etc. come off it: *to shake out a duster* **,shake sb↔'up** to surprise sb and make them think about sth in a different way, become more active, etc. **,shake sth↔'up** to make important changes in an organization, a profession, etc. in order to make it more efficient ➲ related noun SHAKE-UP

■ ***noun***

▸ MOVEMENT **1** 0‑w [C, usually sing.] an act of shaking sth/sb: *Give the bottle a good shake before opening.* ◇ *He dismissed the idea with a firm shake of his head* (= turning it from side to side to mean 'no'). ◇ *She gave him a shake to wake him.* ➲ see also HANDSHAKE

▸ OF BODY **2** **the shakes** [pl.] (*informal*) a physical condition in which you cannot stop your body from shaking because of fear, illness, or because you have drunk too much alcohol: *I always* ***get the shakes*** *before exams.*

▸ DRINK **3** [C] = MILKSHAKE: *a strawberry shake*

IDM **in two 'shakes | in a couple of 'shakes** (*informal*) very soon ➲ more at FAIR *adj.*, GREAT *adj.*

shake·down /ˈʃeɪkdaʊn/ *noun* (*NAmE, informal*) **1** a situation in which sb tries to force sb else to give them money using violence, threats, etc. **2** a thorough search of sb/sth: *a police shakedown of the area* **3** a test of a vehicle to see if there are any problems before it is used generally

shaken /ˈʃeɪkən/ (also **shaken 'up**) *adj.* [not usually before noun] shocked, upset or frightened by sth

'shake-out *noun* [usually sing.] **1** a situation in which people lose their jobs and less successful companies are forced to close because of competition and difficult economic conditions **2** = SHAKE-UP

S

shaker /ˈʃeɪkə(r)/ *noun* **1** (often in compounds) a container that is used for shaking things: *a salt shaker* ◇ *a cocktail shaker* ➲ VISUAL VOCAB page V19 **2** **Shaker** a member of a religious group in the US who live in a community in a very simple way and do not marry or have partners **IDM** see MOVER

'shake-up (also **'shake-out**) *noun* **~ (in/of sth)** a situation in which a lot of changes are made to a company, an organization, etc. in order to improve the way in which it works: *a management shake-up*

shak·ing /ˈʃeɪkɪŋ/ *noun* [sing., U] the act of shaking sth/sb or the fact of being shaken

shaky /ˈʃeɪki/ *adj.* (**shaki·er, shaki·est**) **1** shaking and feeling weak because you are ill/sick, emotional or old **SYN** **unsteady**: *Her voice sounded shaky on the phone.* ◇ *The old man was very shaky on his feet.* **2** not firm or safe; not certain: *That ladder looks a little shaky.* ◇ (*figurative*) *Her memories of the accident are a little shaky.* ◇ (*figurative*) *The protesters are* ***on shaky ground*** (= it is not certain that their claims are valid). **3** not seeming very successful; likely to fail **SYN** **uncertain**: *Business is looking shaky at the moment.* ◇ *After a shaky start, they fought back to win 3–2.* ▸ **shaki·ly** /-ɪli/ *adv.*: *'Get the doctor,' he whispered shakily.*

shale /ʃeɪl/ *noun* [U] a type of soft stone that splits easily into thin flat layers ▸ **shaly** *adj.*

shall 0‑w /ʃəl; *strong form* ʃæl/ *modal verb* (*negative* **shall not** *short form* **shan't** /ʃɑːnt/; *NAmE* ʃænt/, *pt* **should** /ʃʊd/, *negative* **should not** *short form* **shouldn't** /ˈʃʊdnt/) (*especially BrE*)

1 0‑w (becoming *old-fashioned*) used with *I* and *we* for talking about or predicting the future: *This time next week I shall be in Scotland.* ◇ *We shan't be gone long.* ◇ *I said that I should be pleased to help.* **2** 0‑w used in questions with *I* and *we* for making offers or suggestions or asking advice: *Shall I send you the book?* ◇ *What shall we do this weekend?* ◇ *Let's look at it again, shall we?* **3** (*old-fashioned* or *formal*) used to show that you are determined, or to give an order or instruction: *He is determined that you shall succeed.* ◇ *Candidates shall remain in their seats until all the papers have been collected.* ➲ note at MODAL

Grammar Point

shall / will

- In modern English the traditional difference between **shall** and **will** has almost disappeared, and **shall** is not used very much at all, especially in *NAmE*. **Shall** is now only used with *I* and *we*, and often sounds formal and old-fashioned. People are more likely to say: *I'll* (= I will) *be late* and *'You'll* (= you will) *apologize immediately.' 'No I won't!'*
- In *BrE* **shall** is still used with *I* and *we* in questions or when you want to make a suggestion or an offer: *What shall I wear to the party?* ◇ *Shall we order some coffee?* ◇ *I'll drive, shall I?*

➲ note at SHOULD

shal·lot /ʃəˈlɒt; *NAmE* -ˈlɑːt/ *noun* a vegetable like a small onion with a very strong taste ➲ VISUAL VOCAB page V27

shal·low 0‑w /ˈʃæləʊ; *NAmE* -loʊ/ *adj.* (**shal·low·er, shal·low·est**)

1 0‑w not having much distance between the top or surface and the bottom: *a shallow dish* ◇ *They were playing in* ***the shallow end*** (= of the swimming pool). ◇ *These fish are found in shallow waters around the coast.* **OPP** **deep** **2** (*disapproving*) (of a person, an idea, a comment, etc.) not showing serious thought, feelings, etc. about sth **SYN** **superficial** **3** **shallow breathing** involves taking in only a small amount of air each time ▸ **shal·low·ly** *adv.*: *He was breathing shallowly.* **shal·low·ness** *noun* [U]

shal·lows /ˈʃæləʊz; *NAmE* -loʊz/ **the shallows** *noun* [pl.] a shallow place in a river or the sea

sha·lom /ʃəˈlɒm; *NAmE* -ˈloʊm/ *exclamation* a Hebrew word for 'hello' or 'goodbye' that means 'peace'

shalt /ʃælt/ *verb* **thou shalt** (*old use*) used to mean 'you shall', when talking to one person

shal·war = SALWAR

sham /ʃæm/ *noun, adj., verb*

■ ***noun*** (*disapproving*) **1** [sing.] a situation, feeling, system, etc. that is not as good or true as it seems to be: *The latest crime figures are a complete sham.* **2** [C, usually sing.] a person who pretends to be sth that they are not **3** [U] behaviour, feelings, words, etc. that are intended to make sb/sth seem to be better than they really are: *Their promises turned out to be full of sham and hypocrisy.*

■ ***adj.*** [only before noun] (usually *disapproving*) not genuine but intended to seem real **SYN** **false**: *a sham marriage*

■ ***verb*** (**-mm-**) [I, T] **~ (sth) | + adj.** to pretend sth: *Is he really sick or is he just shamming?*

shaman /ˈʃeɪmən; ˈʃɑːmən; ˈʃæmən/ *noun* a person in some religions and societies who is believed to be able to contact good and evil spirits and cure people of illnesses ▸ **sha·man·ic** /ʃəˈmænɪk/ *adj.*

shama·teur /ˈʃæmətə(r); -tʃə(r)/ *noun* (*disapproving*) a person who makes money playing a sport but is officially an AMATEUR ▸ **shama·teur·ism** /ˈʃæmətərɪzəm; -tʃər-/ *noun* [U]

shamba /ˈʃæmbə/ *noun* (*EAfrE*) a small farm or a field that is used for growing crops

sham·ble /ˈʃæmbl/ *verb* [I] (+ **adv./prep.**) to walk in an awkward or lazy way, dragging your feet along the ground

sham·bles /ˈʃæmblz/ *noun* [sing.] (*informal*) **1** a situation in which there is a lot of confusion **SYN mess**: *The press conference was a complete shambles.* ◇ *What a shambles!* ◇ *The government is* ***in a shambles*** *over Europe.* **2** a place which is dirty or untidy **SYN mess**: *The house was a shambles.*

sham·bol·ic /ʃæmˈbɒlɪk; *NAmE* -ˈbɑːl-/ *adj.* (*BrE, informal*) lacking order or organization **SYN chaotic, disorganized**

shame 0‑ /ʃeɪm/ *noun, verb, exclamation*

■ ***noun*** **1** 0‑ [U] the feelings of sadness, embarrassment and GUILT that you have when you know that sth you have done is wrong or stupid: *His face burned with shame.* ◇ *She hung her head in shame.* ◇ *He could not live with the shame of other people knowing the truth.* ◇ ***To my shame*** (= I feel shame that) *I refused to listen to her side of the story.* **2** [U] (*formal*) (only used in questions and negative sentences) the ability to feel shame at sth you have done: *Have you no shame?* **3** 0‑ **a shame** [sing.] used to say that sth is a cause for feeling sad or disappointed **SYN pity**: ***What a shame*** *they couldn't come.* ◇ ***It's a shame about*** *Tim, isn't it?* ◇ ***It's a shame that*** *she wasn't here to see it.* ◇ *It would be* ***a crying shame*** (= a great shame) *not to take them up on the offer.* **4** 0‑ [U] the loss of respect that is caused when you do sth wrong or stupid: *There is* ***no shame in*** *wanting to be successful.* ◇ (*formal*) *She felt that her failure would* ***bring shame on*** *her family.*

IDM **put sb/sth to ˈshame** to be much better than sb/sth: *Their presentation put ours to shame.* **ˈshame on you, him, etc.** (*informal*) used to say that sb should feel ashamed for sth they have said or done ➲ more at NAME *v.*

■ ***verb*** **1 ~ sb** to make sb feel ashamed: *His generosity shamed them all.* **2 ~ sb** (*formal*) to make sb feel that they have lost honour or respect: *You have shamed your family.*

PHR V **ˈshame sb into doing sth** to persuade sb to do sth by making them feel ashamed not to do it: *She shamed her father into promising more help.*

■ ***exclamation*** (*SAfrE*) used to express sympathy, or to show that you like sb/sth: *Shame, she's so cute!*

shame·faced /ˌʃeɪmˈfeɪst/ *adj.* feeling or looking ashamed because you have done sth bad or stupid **SYN sheepish**: *a shamefaced smile* ▸ **shame·faced·ly** /ˌʃeɪmˈfeɪstli; -ˈfeɪsɪdli/ *adv.*

shame·ful /ˈʃeɪmfl/ *adj.* that should make you feel ashamed **SYN disgraceful**: *shameful behaviour* ◇ *It was shameful the way she was treated.* ▸ **shame·ful·ly** /-fəli/ *adv.*

shame·less /ˈʃeɪmləs/ *adj.* (*disapproving*) not feeling ashamed of sth you have done, although other people think you should **SYN unashamed** ▸ **shame·less·ly** *adv.* (usually *disapproving* but sometimes *approving*): *The whole film is shamelessly romantic and glamorous.* **shame·less·ness** *noun* [U]

sham·ing /ˈʃeɪmɪŋ/ *adj.* causing sb to feel ashamed: *a shaming defeat by a less experienced team*

sham·my /ˈʃæmi/ *noun* (*pl.* -ies) (also ˌ**shammy ˈleather**) [U, C] (*informal*) = CHAMOIS (2)

sham·poo /ʃæmˈpuː/ *noun, verb*

■ ***noun*** (*pl.* -os) **1** [C, U] a liquid soap that is used for washing your hair; a similar liquid used for cleaning carpets, furniture covers or a car: *a shampoo for greasy hair* ◇ *carpet shampoo* **2** [C, usually sing.] an act of washing your hair using shampoo: *Rinse the hair thoroughly after each shampoo.* ◇ *a shampoo and set* (= an act of washing and styling sb's hair)

■ ***verb*** (**sham·pooed, sham·pooed**) **~ sth** to wash or clean hair, carpets, etc. with shampoo

sham·rock /ˈʃæmrɒk; *NAmE* -rɑːk/ *noun* a small plant with three leaves on each STEM. The shamrock is the national symbol of Ireland.

shandy /ˈʃændi/ *noun* (*pl.* -ies) (*especially BrE*) **1** [U] a drink made by mixing beer with LEMONADE **2** [C] a glass or can of shandy: *Two shandies, please.*

shang·hai /ˌʃæŋˈhaɪ/ *verb* (**shang·hai·ing** /-ˈhaɪɪŋ/, **shang·haied, shang·haied** /-ˈhaɪd/) **~ sb (into doing sth)** (*old-fashioned, informal*) to trick or force sb into doing sth that they do not really want to do

Shangri-La /ˌʃæŋgri ˈlɑː/ *noun* [sing.] a place that is extremely beautiful and where everything seems perfect, especially a place far away from modern life **ORIGIN** From the name of an imaginary valley in Tibet in James Hilton's novel *Lost Horizon*, where people do not grow old.

shank /ʃæŋk/ *noun* **1** the straight narrow part between the two ends of a tool or an object **2** the part of an animal's or a person's leg between the knee and ankle **3** the top part of the leg of an animal, cooked and eaten: *braised lamb shanks*

IDM **(on) Shanks's ˈpony** (*BrE, informal*) walking, rather than travelling by car, bus, etc. **SYN on foot**

shan't /ʃɑːnt; *NAmE* ʃænt/ *short form* shall not

shanty /ˈʃænti/ *noun* (*pl.* -ies) **1** a small house, built of pieces of wood, metal and cardboard, where very poor people live, especially on the edge of a big city **2** (also ˈ**sea shanty**) (*US* **chanty, chantey**) a song that sailors traditionally used to sing while pulling ropes, etc.

ˈshanty town *noun* an area in or near a town where poor people live in shanties

shape 0‑ /ʃeɪp/ *noun, verb*

■ ***noun*** **1** 0‑ [C, U] the form of the outer edges or surfaces of sth; an example of sth that has a particular form: *a rectangular shape* ◇ *The pool was* ***in the shape of*** *a heart.* ◇ *The island was originally circular* ***in shape.*** ◇ *Squares, circles and triangles are types of shape.* ◇ *Candles come in* ***all shapes and sizes.*** ◇ *You can recognize the fish by the shape of their fins.* ◇ *This old T-shirt has completely lost its shape.* ◇ (*figurative*) *The government provides money* ***in the shape of*** (= consisting of) *grants and student loans.* ➲ VISUAL VOCAB page V58 **2** 0‑ [C] a person or thing that is difficult to see clearly **SYN figure**: *Ghostly shapes moved around in the dark.* **3** 0‑ [U] the physical condition of sb/sth: *What sort of shape was the car in after the accident?* ◇ *He's* ***in good shape*** *for a man of his age.* ◇ *I like to* ***keep in shape*** (= keep fit). **4** [U] the particular qualities or characteristics of sth: *Will new technology change the shape of broadcasting?*

IDM **get (yourself) into ˈshape** to take exercise, eat healthy food, etc. in order to become physically fit **get/knock/lick sb into ˈshape** to train sb so that they do a particular job, task, etc. well **get/knock/lick sth into ˈshape** to make sth more acceptable, organized or successful: *I've got all the information together but it still needs knocking into shape.* **give ˈshape to sth** (*formal*) to express or explain a particular idea, plan, etc. **in ˈany (way,) shape or form** (*informal*) of any type: *I don't approve of violence in any shape or form.* **out of ˈshape** **1** not having the normal shape: *The wheel had been twisted out of shape.* **2** (of a person) not in good physical condition **the ˌshape of ˌthings to ˈcome** the way things are likely to develop in the future **take ˈshape** to develop and become more complete or organized ➲ more at BENT *adj.*

■ ***verb*** **1** 0‑ [T] to make sth into a particular shape: **~ A into B** *Shape the dough into a ball.* ◇ **~ sth** *This tool is used for shaping wood.* **2** 0‑ [T] **~ sb/sth** to have an important influence on the way that sb/sth develops: *His ideas had been shaped by his experiences during the war.* ◇ *She had a leading role in shaping party policy.* **3** [I] **~ to do sth** to prepare to do sth, especially hit or kick sth: *She was shaping to hit her second shot.*

IDM **ˈshape up or ship ˈout** (*NAmE, informal*) used to tell sb that if they do not improve, work harder, etc. they will have to leave their job, position, etc.: *He finally faced up to his drug problem when his band told him to shape up or ship out.*

PHR V ˌ**shape ˈup** **1** to develop in a particular way, especially in a good way: *Our plans are shaping up nicely* (= showing signs that they will be successful). **2** (*informal*) to improve your behaviour, work harder, etc: *If he doesn't shape up, he'll soon be out of a job.*

S

shaped ⚷ /ʃeɪpt/ *adj.* having the type of shape mentioned: *a huge balloon* ***shaped like*** *a giant cow* ◇ *almond-shaped eyes* ◇ *an L-shaped room* ➲ see also PEAR-SHAPED

shape·less /ˈʃeɪpləs/ *adj.* [usually before noun] (often *disapproving*) **1** not having any definite shape: *a shapeless sweater* **2** lacking clear organization SYN **unstructured**: *a shapeless and incoherent story* ▶ **shape·less·ly** *adv.* **shape·less·ness** *noun* [U]

shape·ly /ˈʃeɪpli/ *adj.* (especially of a woman's body) having an attractive curved shape

shard /ʃɑːd; *NAmE* ʃɑːrd/ (also **sherd**) *noun* a piece of broken glass, metal, etc: *shards of glass*

share ⚷ /ʃeə(r); *NAmE* ʃer/ *verb, noun*

■ ***verb***

▸ USE AT SAME TIME **1** ⚷ [T, I] **~ (sth) (with sb)** to have or use sth at the same time as sb else: *Sue shares a house with three other students.* ◇ *There isn't an empty table. Would you mind sharing?*

▸ DIVIDE BETWEEN PEOPLE **2** ⚷ [T] **~ sth (out) (among/between sb)** to divide sth between two or more people: *We shared the pizza between the four of us.* ➲ see also JOB-SHARING, POWER-SHARING

▸ GIVE SOME OF YOURS **3** ⚷ [T, I] **~ (sth) (with sb)** to give some of what you have to sb else; to let sb use sth that is yours: *Eli shared his chocolate with the other kids.* ◇ *The conference is a good place to share information and exchange ideas.* ◇ *John had no brothers or sisters and wasn't used to sharing.*

▸ FEELINGS/IDEAS/PROBLEMS **4** ⚷ [T, I] to have the same feelings, ideas, experiences, etc. as sb else: **~ sth** *They shared a common interest in botany.* ◇ *a view that is widely shared* ◇ *shared values* ◇ **~ sth with sb** *People often share their political views with their parents.* ◇ **~ in sth** *I didn't really share in her love of animals.* **5** ⚷ [T, I] to tell other people about your ideas, experiences and feelings: **~ sth** *Men often don't like to share their problems.* ◇ *The two friends shared everything—they had no secrets.* ◇ **~ (sth with sb)** *Would you like to share your experience with the rest of the group?* ◇ *The group listens while one person shares* (= tells other people about their experiences, feelings, etc.).

▸ BLAME/RESPONSIBILITY **6** ⚷ [I, T] to be equally involved in sth or responsible for sth: **~ in sth** *I try to get the kids to share in the housework.* ◇ **~ sth (with sb)** *Both drivers shared the blame for the accident.*

IDM **share and share aˈlike** (*saying*) used to say that everyone should share things equally and in a fair way ➲ more at TROUBLE *n.*

■ ***noun***

▸ PART/AMOUNT OF STH **1** ⚷ [C, usually sing.] **~ (of/in sth)** one part of sth that is divided between two or more people: *How much was your share of the winnings?* ◇ *Next year we hope to have a bigger share of the market.* ◇ (*BrE*) *I'm looking for a* ***flat share*** (= a flat that is shared by two or more people who are not related). ➲ see also MARKET SHARE, TIMESHARE **2** ⚷ [sing.] the part that sb has in a particular activity that involves several people: *We all did our share.* ◇ **~ of sth** *Everyone must accept their share of the blame.* **3** ⚷ [sing.] **~ (of sth)** an amount of sth that is thought to be normal or acceptable for one person: *I've had my share of luck in the past.* ◇ *I've done my share of worrying for one day!*

▸ IN BUSINESS **4** ⚷ [C] **~ (in sth)** any of the units of equal value into which a company is divided and sold to raise money. People who own shares receive part of the company's profits: *shares in British Telecom* ◇ *a fall in* ***share prices*** ➲ compare STOCK *n.* (4) ➲ see also ORDINARY SHARE

▸ FARM EQUIPMENT **5** [C] (*NAmE*) = PLOUGHSHARE IDM see CAKE *n.*, FAIR *adj.*, LION, PIE

-share *combining form* **1** (in nouns) an arrangement to divide sth between two or more people, groups, etc: *a job-share* (= a job that is done by two people who each work for part of the week) ◇ (*BrE*) *a nanny share* (= an arrangement for sb to work for two families) ➲ see also TIMESHARE **2** (in verbs) using an arrangement to divide sth between two or more people, groups, etc: (*especially BrE*) *We encourage people to carshare to reduce congestion on the roads.* ◇ (*NAmE*) *to rideshare*

share·crop·per /ˈʃeəkrɒpə(r); *NAmE* ˈʃerkrɑːpər/ *noun* (*especially NAmE*) a farmer who gives part of his or her crop as rent to the owner of the land

share·hold·er /ˈʃeəhəʊldə(r); *NAmE* ˈʃerhoʊ-/ *noun* an owner of shares in a company or business

share·hold·ing /ˈʃeəhəʊldɪŋ; *NAmE* ˈʃerhoʊ-/ *noun* the amount of a company or business that sb owns in the form of shares

ˈ**share index** *noun* [usually sing.] a list that shows the current value of shares on the STOCK MARKET, based on the prices of shares of particular companies

ˈ**share option** (*BrE*) (*NAmE* ˈ**stock option**) *noun* a right given to employees to buy shares in their company at a fixed price

ˈ**share-out** *noun* [usually sing.] (*BrE*) an act of dividing sth between two or more people; the amount of sth that one person receives when it is divided

share·ware /ˈʃeəweə(r); *NAmE* ˈʃerwer/ *noun* [U] (*computing*) computer software (= programs, etc.) that is available free for a user to test, after which they must pay if they wish to continue using it ➲ compare FREEWARE

sha·ria (also **sha·riah**) /ʃəˈriːə/ *noun* [U] the system of religious laws that Muslims follow

shark /ʃɑːk; *NAmE* ʃɑːrk/ *noun* **1** a large sea fish with very sharp teeth and a pointed FIN on its back. There are several types of shark, some of which can attack people swimming. **2** (*informal, disapproving*) a person who is dishonest in business, especially sb who gives bad advice and gets people to pay too much for sth ➲ see also LOAN SHARK

sharp ⚷ /ʃɑːp; *NAmE* ʃɑːrp/ *adj., adv., noun*

■ ***adj.*** (**sharp·er, sharp·est**)

▸ EDGE/POINT **1** ⚷ having a fine edge or point, especially of sth that can cut or make a hole in sth: *a sharp knife* ◇ *sharp teeth* OPP **blunt**

▸ RISE/DROP/CHANGE **2** ⚷ [usually before noun] sudden and rapid, especially of a change in sth: *a sharp drop in prices* ◇ *a sharp rise in crime* ◇ *a sharp increase in unemployment* ◇ *He heard a* ***sharp intake of breath***. ◇ *We need to give young criminals a* ***short, sharp shock*** (= a punishment that is very unpleasant for a short time).

▸ CLEAR/DEFINITE **3** ⚷ [usually before noun] clear and definite: *a sharp outline* ◇ *The photograph is not very sharp* (= there are no clear contrasts between areas of light and shade). ◇ *She drew a* ***sharp distinction*** *between domestic and international politics.* ◇ *In* ***sharp contrast*** *to her mood, the clouds were breaking up to reveal a blue sky.* ◇ *The issue must be brought into sharper focus.*

▸ MIND/EYES **4** ⚷ (of people or their minds, eyes, etc.) quick to notice or understand things or to react: *to have sharp eyes* ◇ *a girl of sharp intelligence* ◇ *a sharp sense of humour* ◇ *He kept a sharp lookout for any strangers.* ◇ *It was very sharp of you to see that!*

▸ CRITICAL **5** ⚷ (of a person or what they say) critical or severe: *sharp criticism* ◇ *Emma has a* ***sharp tongue*** (= she often speaks in an unpleasant or unkind way). ◇ **~ with sb** *He was very sharp with me when I was late.*

▸ SOUNDS **6** ⚷ [usually before noun] loud, sudden and often high in tone: *She read out the list in sharp, clipped tones.* ◇ *There was a sharp knock on the door.*

▸ FEELING **7** ⚷ (of a physical feeling or an emotion) very strong and sudden, often like being cut or wounded SYN **intense**: *He winced as a sharp pain shot through his leg.* ◇ *Polly felt a sharp pang of jealousy.*

▸ CURVES **8** ⚷ changing direction suddenly: *a sharp bend in the road* ◇ *a sharp turn to the left*

▸ FLAVOUR/SMELL **9** ⚷ strong and slightly bitter: *The cheese has a distinctively sharp taste.* ➲ SYNONYMS at BITTER

▸ FROST/WIND **10** ⚷ used to describe a very cold or very severe FROST or wind ➲ see also RAZOR-SHARP

▸ CLEVER AND DISHONEST **11** (*disapproving*) (of a person or their way of doing business) clever but possibly dishonest: *His lawyer's a* ***sharp operator***. ◇ *The firm had to face some* ***sharp practice*** *from competing companies.*

▸ CLOTHES **12** [usually before noun] (of clothes or the way sb

S

dresses) fashionable and new: *The consultants were a group of men in **sharp suits**.* ◇ *Todd is a **sharp dresser**.*
▸ FACE/FEATURES **13** not full or round in shape: *a man with a thin face and sharp features* (= a pointed nose and chin)
▸ IN MUSIC **14** used after the name of a note to mean a note a SEMITONE/HALF TONE higher: *the Piano Sonata in C sharp minor* ➲ picture at MUSIC **OPP flat** ➲ compare NATURAL **15** above the correct PITCH (= how high or low a note sounds): *That note sounded sharp.* **OPP flat**
▶ **sharp·ness** *noun* [C, U]: *There was a sudden sharpness in her voice.*
IDM **look 'sharp** (*BrE, informal*) used in orders to tell sb to be quick or to hurry: *You'd better look sharp or you'll be late.* **not the sharpest knife in the 'drawer | not the sharpest tool in the 'box** (*informal, humorous*) not intelligent: *He's not exactly the sharpest knife in the drawer, is he?* **the 'sharp end (of sth)** (*BrE, informal*) the place or position of greatest difficulty or responsibility: *He started work at the sharp end of the business, as a salesman.*
■ ***adv.***
▸ EXACTLY **1** used after an expression for a time of day to mean 'exactly': *Please be here at seven o'clock sharp.*
▸ LEFT/RIGHT **2** (*BrE*) **~ left/right** turning suddenly to the left or right
▸ MUSIC **3** (*comparative* **sharp·er**, no *superlative*) above the correct PITCH (= how high or low a note sounds) **OPP flat**
■ ***noun*** **1** (*music*) a note played a SEMITONE/HALF TONE higher than the note that is named. The written symbol is (♯): *It's a difficult piece to play, full of sharps and flats.* **OPP flat** ➲ compare NATURAL **2 sharps** [pl.] (*medical*) things with a sharp edge or point, such as needles and SYRINGES: *the safe disposal of sharps*

sharp·en /ˈʃɑːpən; *NAmE* ˈʃɑːrpən/ *verb* **1** [T, I] **~ (sth)** to make sth sharper; to become sharper: *This knife needs sharpening.* ◇ *The outline of the trees sharpened as it grew lighter.* **2** [I, T] **~ (sth)** if a sense or feeling **sharpens** or sth **sharpens** it, it becomes stronger and/or clearer: *The sea air sharpened our appetites.* **3** [T] **~ sth** to make a disagreement between people, or an issue on which people disagree, clearer and more likely to produce a result: *There is a need to sharpen the focus of the discussion.* **4** [I, T] to become or make sth better, more skilful, more effective, etc. than before **SYN improve**: **~ (up)** *He needs to sharpen up before the Olympic trials.* ◇ **~ sth (up)** *She's doing a course to sharpen her business skills.* **5** [I, T] **~ (sth)** if your voice **sharpens** or sth **sharpens** it, it becomes high and loud in an unpleasant way

sharp·en·er /ˈʃɑːpnə(r); *NAmE* ˈʃɑːrp-/ *noun* (usually in compounds) a tool or machine that makes things sharp: *a pencil sharpener* ◇ *a knife sharpener* ➲ VISUAL VOCAB page V56

ˌsharp-ˈeyed *adj.* able to see very well and quick to notice things **SYN observant**: *A sharp-eyed reader spotted the mistake in yesterday's paper.*

sharp·ish /ˈʃɑːpɪʃ; *NAmE* ˈʃɑːrpɪʃ/ *adv.* (*BrE, informal*) quickly; in a short time

sharp·ly 🗝 /ˈʃɑːpli; *NAmE* ˈʃɑːrpli/ *adv.*
1 🗝 in a critical, rough or severe way: *The report was sharply critical of the police.* ◇ *'Is there a problem?' he asked sharply.* **2** 🗝 suddenly and by a large amount: *Profits fell sharply following the takeover.* ◇ *The road fell sharply to the sea.* **3** 🗝 in a way that clearly shows the differences between two things: *Their experiences contrast sharply with those of other children.* **4** 🗝 quickly and suddenly or loudly: *She moved sharply across the room to block his exit.* ◇ *He rapped sharply on the window.* **5** 🗝 used to emphasize that sth has a sharp point or edge: *sharply pointed*

sharp·shoot·er /ˈʃɑːpʃuːtə(r); *NAmE* ˈʃɑːrp-/ *noun* a person who is skilled at shooting a gun

shat *past tense, past part.* of SHIT

shat·ter /ˈʃætə(r)/ *verb* **1** [I, T] to suddenly break into small pieces; to make sth suddenly break into small pieces: **~ (into sth)** *He dropped the vase and it shattered into pieces on the floor.* ◇ *the sound of shattering glass* ◇ **~ sth (into sth)** *The explosion shattered all the windows in the building.* **2** [T, I] to destroy sth completely, especially sb's feelings, hopes or beliefs; to be destroyed in this way: **~ sth (into sth)** *Anna's self-confidence had been completely shattered.* ◇ *Her experience of divorce shattered her illusions about love.* ◇ **~ (into sth)** *My whole world shattered into a million pieces.* **3** [T] **~ sb** to make sb feel extremely shocked and upset: *The unexpected death of their son shattered them.*

shat·tered /ˈʃætəd; *NAmE* -tərd/ *adj.* **1** very shocked and upset: *The experience left her feeling absolutely shattered.* **2** (*BrE, informal*) very tired **SYN exhausted**

shat·ter·ing /ˈʃætərɪŋ/ *adj.* **1** very shocking and upsetting: *a shattering experience* ◇ *The news of his death came as a shattering blow.* **2** very loud **SYN deafening** ▶ **shat·ter·ing·ly** *adv.*

ˈshatter-proof *adj.* designed not to SHATTER: *shatter-proof glass*

shauri /ˈʃaʊriː/ *noun* (*EAfrE*) something that needs to be discussed or decided; something that causes a problem

shave 🗝 /ʃeɪv/ *verb, noun*
■ ***verb*** **1** 🗝 [I, T] to cut hair from the skin, especially the face, using a RAZOR: *Mike cut himself shaving.* ◇ **~ sb/sth/yourself** *The nurse washed and shaved him.* ◇ *a shaved head* ➲ VISUAL VOCAB page V49 ➲ see also SHAVEN **2** [T] **~ sth** to cut a small amount off a price, etc: *The firm had shaved profit margins.*
PHR V **ˌshave sth↔ˌoff | ˌshave sth ˈoff sth 1** to remove a beard or MOUSTACHE by shaving: *Charles decided to shave off his beard.* **2** to cut very thin pieces from the surface of wood, etc: *I had to shave a few millimetres off the door to make it shut.* **3** to reduce a number by a very small amount: *He shaved a tenth of a second off the world record.*
■ ***noun*** an act of shaving: *I need a shave.* ◇ *to have a shave*
IDM see CLOSE² *adj.*

shaven /ˈʃeɪvn/ *adj.* with all the hair shaved off: *a shaven head* ➲ see also CLEAN-SHAVEN ➲ compare UNSHAVEN ➲ VISUAL VOCAB page V49

shaver /ˈʃeɪvə(r)/ (also **eˌlectric ˈrazor**) *noun* an electric tool for shaving ➲ VISUAL VOCAB page V21 ➲ compare RAZOR

ˈshaving cream, **ˈshaving foam** *noun* [U] special cream or FOAM for spreading over the face with a **shaving brush** before shaving

shav·ings /ˈʃeɪvɪŋz/ *noun* [pl.] thin pieces cut from a piece of wood, etc. using a sharp tool, especially a PLANE

Sha·vu·oth /ʃəˈvuːəs; ˌʃɑːvʊˈɒt; *NAmE* ʃəˈvuːoʊt; -oʊθ/ (also **ˌFeast of ˈWeeks**, **Pente·cost**) *noun* [U] a Jewish festival that takes place 50 days after the second day of Passover

shawl /ʃɔːl/ *noun* a large piece of cloth worn by a woman around the shoulders or head, or wrapped around a baby

Shaw·nee /ʃɔːˈniː/ *noun* (*pl.* **Shaw·nee** or **Shaw·nees**) a member of a Native American people, many of whom now live in the US state of Oklahoma

she 🗝 /ʃi; *strong form* ʃiː/ *pron., noun*
■ ***pron.*** 🗝 (used as the subject of a verb) a female person or animal that has already been mentioned or is easily identified: *'What does your sister do?' 'She's a dentist.'* ◇ *Doesn't she* (= the woman we are looking at) *look like Sue?* ➲ compare HER ➲ note at GENDER
■ ***noun*** **1** [sing.] (*informal*) a female: *What a sweet little dog. Is it a he or a she?* **2 she-** (in compound nouns) a female animal: *a she-wolf*

s/he *pron.* used in writing by some people when the subject of the verb could be either female (she) or male (he): *If a student does not attend all the classes, s/he will not be allowed to take the exam.*

shea butter /ˈʃiː bʌtə(r); *BrE* also ˈʃiːə; *NAmE* also ˈʃeɪ/ *noun* [U] a type of fat obtained from the nuts of the **shea tree**, used in foods and COSMETICS

sheaf /ʃiːf/ *noun* (*pl.* **sheaves** /ʃiːvz/) **1** a number of pieces of paper tied or held together **2** a bunch of WHEAT tied together after being cut

S

shear /ʃɪə(r); *NAmE* ʃɪr/ *verb* (**sheared**, **shorn** /ʃɔːn; *NAmE* ʃɔːrn/ or **sheared**) **1** [T] **~ sth** to cut the wool off a sheep: *It was time for the sheep to be shorn.* ◇ *sheep shearing* **2** [T] **~ sth** (*formal*) to cut off sb's hair: *shorn hair* **3** [I, T] **~ (sth)** (**off**) (*technical*) (especially of metal) to break under pressure; to cut through sth and make it break: *The bolts holding the wheel in place sheared off.*
PHR V **be 'shorn of sth** (*literary*) to have sth important taken away from you: *Shorn of his power, the deposed king went into exile.*

shears /ʃɪəz; *NAmE* ʃɪrz/ *noun* [pl.] a garden tool like a very large pair of scissors, used for cutting bushes and HEDGES: *a pair of garden shears* ➲ VISUAL VOCAB page V16 ➲ see also PINKING SHEARS

shear·water /ˈʃɪəwɔːtə(r); *NAmE* ˈʃɪr-/ *noun* a bird with long wings that often flies low over the sea

sheath /ʃiːθ/ *noun* (*pl.* **sheaths** /ʃiːðz/) **1** a cover that fits closely over the blade of a knife or other sharp weapon or tool ➲ picture at SWORD **2** any covering that fits closely over sth for protection: *the sheath around an electric cable* **3** (*BrE*) = CONDOM **4** a woman's dress that fits the body closely

sheathe /ʃiːð/ *verb* **1 ~ sth** (*literary*) to put a knife or SWORD into a sheath **2** [usually passive] **~ sth** (**in/with sth**) to cover sth in a material, especially in order to protect it

'sheath knife *noun* a short knife with a SHEATH (= cover)

sheaves *pl.* of SHEAF

she·bang /ʃɪˈbæŋ/ *noun*
IDM **the whole she'bang** (*informal*) the whole thing; everything

she·been /ʃɪˈbiːn/ *noun* (*informal*) (especially in Ireland, Scotland and South Africa) a place where alcoholic drinks are sold, usually illegally

shed /ʃed/ *noun, verb*
■ ***noun*** (often in compounds) **1** a small simple building, usually built of wood or metal, used for keeping things in: *a bicycle shed* ◇ (*BrE*) *a garden shed* ➲ VISUAL VOCAB page V16 **2** (*BrE*) a large industrial building, used for working in or keeping equipment: *an engine shed* **3** (*AustralE, NZE*) a building with open sides where the wool is cut off sheep (= they are SHEARED) or where cows are MILKED ➲ see also COWSHED, POTTING SHED, WOODSHED
■ ***verb*** (**shed·ding, shed, shed**)
▸ GET RID OF **1 ~ sth** (often used in newspapers) to get rid of sth that is no longer wanted: *The factory is shedding a large number of jobs.* ◇ *a quick way to shed unwanted pounds* (= extra weight or fat on your body) ◇ *Museums have been trying hard to shed their stuffy image.*
▸ DROP **2 ~ sth** (*formal*) to let sth fall; to drop sth: *Luke shed his clothes onto the floor.* ◇ *A duck's feathers shed water immediately.* **3 ~ sth** (*BrE*) (of a vehicle) to lose or drop what it is carrying: *The traffic jam was caused by a lorry* ***shedding its load.***
▸ SKIN/LEAVES **4 ~ sth** if an animal **sheds** its skin, or a plant **sheds** leaves, it loses them naturally
▸ LIGHT **5 ~ sth** (**on/over sb/sth**) to send light over sth; to let light fall somewhere: *The candles shed a soft glow on her face.*
▸ TEARS **6 ~ tears** (*formal* or *literary*) to cry: *She shed no tears when she heard he was dead.*
▸ BLOOD **7 ~ blood** (*formal*) to kill or injure people, especially in a war ➲ see also BLOODSHED IDM see LIGHT *n.*

she'd /ʃiːd/ *short form* **1** she had **2** she would

'she-devil *noun* a very cruel woman

shed·load /ˈʃedləʊd; *NAmE* -loʊd/ *noun* **~ (of sth)** (*BrE, informal*) a large amount of sth, especially money: *The project cost a shedload of money.* ◇ *This should save you shedloads.*

sheen /ʃiːn/ *noun* [sing., U] a soft smooth shiny quality SYN **shine**: *hair with a healthy sheen*

sheep 0‑w /ʃiːp/ *noun* (*pl.* **sheep**) an animal with a thick coat, kept on farms for its meat (called MUTTON or LAMB) or its wool: *a flock of sheep* ◇ *Sheep were grazing in the fields.* ➲ compare EWE, LAMB, RAM ➲ see also BLACK SHEEP
IDM **like 'sheep** (*disapproving*) if people behave **like sheep**, they all do what the others are doing, without thinking for themselves **sort out/separate the ˌsheep from the ˈgoats** to distinguish people who are good at sth, intelligent, etc. from those who are not ➲ more at COUNT *v.*, WELL *adv.*, WOLF *n.*

'sheep dip *noun* [U, C] a liquid which is used to kill insects, etc. in a sheep's coat; the container in which sheep are put to treat them with this

sheep·dog /ˈʃiːpdɒg; *NAmE* -dɔːg; -dɑːg/ *noun* **1** a dog that is trained to help control sheep on a farm **2** (*BrE*) a dog of a breed that is often used for controlling sheep, especially a COLLIE ➲ see also OLD ENGLISH SHEEPDOG

sheep·fold /ˈʃiːpfəʊld; *NAmE* -foʊld/ *noun* an area in a field surrounded by a fence or wall where sheep are kept for safety

sheep·herd·er /ˈʃiːphɜːdə(r); *NAmE* -hɜːrd-/ *noun* (*NAmE*) = SHEPHERD

sheep·ish /ˈʃiːpɪʃ/ *adj.* looking or feeling embarrassed because you have done sth silly or wrong SYN **shamefaced**: *Mary gave her a sheepish grin.* ▸ **sheep·ish·ly** *adv.*

sheep·skin /ˈʃiːpskɪn/ *noun* [U, C] the skin of a sheep with the wool still on it: *a* ***sheepskin coat/rug***

sheer /ʃɪə(r); *NAmE* ʃɪr/ *adj., adv., verb*
■ ***adj.*** **1** [only before noun] used to emphasize the size, degree or amount of sth: *The area is under threat from the sheer number of tourists using it.* ◇ *We were impressed by the sheer size of the cathedral.* **2** [only before noun] complete and not mixed with anything else SYN **utter**: *The concert was sheer delight.* ◇ *I only agreed out of sheer desperation.* **3** very steep: ***sheer cliffs/slopes*** ◇ *Outside there was a sheer drop down to the sea below.* **4** (of cloth, etc.) thin, light and almost transparent: *sheer nylon*
■ ***adv.*** straight up or down: *The cliffs rise sheer from the beach.* ◇ *The ground dropped sheer away at our feet.*
■ ***verb***
PHR V **ˌsheer aˈway/ˈoff (from sth)** to change direction suddenly, especially in order to avoid hitting sth: (*figurative*) *Her mind sheered away from images she did not wish to dwell on.*

sheet 0‑w /ʃiːt/ *noun*
▸ ON BED **1** 0‑w a large piece of thin cloth used on a bed to lie on or lie under: *Have you* ***changed the sheets*** (= put clean sheets on the bed)? ◇ *He slid between the sheets and closed his eyes.* ➲ VISUAL VOCAB page V20 ➲ see also DUST SHEET
▸ OF PAPER **2** 0‑w a piece of paper for writing or printing on, etc. usually in a standard size: *a* ***clean/blank sheet of paper*** (= with no writing on it) ◇ *Pick up one of our free information sheets at reception.*
▸ FLAT THIN PIECE **3** 0‑w a flat thin piece of any material, normally square or RECTANGULAR: *a* ***sheet of glass/steel*** ◇ ***sheet metal*** (= metal that has been made into thin sheets) ◇ *Place the dough on a* ***baking sheet*** (= for cooking sth in an oven).
▸ WIDE FLAT AREA **4** 0‑w a wide flat area of sth, covering the surface of sth else: *The road was covered with a sheet of ice.*
▸ OF FIRE/WATER **5** a large moving mass of fire or water: *a sheet of flame* ◇ *The rain was coming down* ***in sheets*** (= very heavily).
▸ ON SAIL **6** (*technical*) a rope or chain fastened to the lower corner of a sail to hold it and to control the angle of the sail
HELP There are other compounds ending **sheet**. You will find them at their place in the alphabet. IDM see CLEAN *adj.*

'sheet anchor *noun* a person or thing that you can depend on in a difficult situation

sheet·ing /ˈʃiːtɪŋ/ *noun* [U] **1** metal, plastic, etc. made into flat thin pieces: ***metal/plastic/polythene sheeting*** **2** cloth used for making sheets for beds

S

ˌ**sheet ˈlightning** *noun* [U] LIGHTNING that appears as a broad area of light in the sky ➲ compare FORKED LIGHTNING

ˈ**sheet music** *noun* [U] printed music as opposed to recorded music; printed music published on separate sheets of paper that are not fastened together to form a book

sheikh /ʃeɪk; ʃiːk/ (also **shaikh** /ʃeɪk/) *noun* **1** an Arab prince or leader; the head of an Arab family, village, etc. **2** a leader in a Muslim community or organization

sheikh·dom /ˈʃeɪkdəm; ˈʃiːk-/ *noun* an area of land ruled by a sheikh

sheila /ˈʃiːlə/ *noun* (*AustralE, NZE, slang*) a girl or young woman

shekel /ˈʃekl/ *noun* **1** the unit of money in Israel **2** an ancient silver coin used by the Jews

shel·duck /ˈʃeldʌk/ *noun* (*pl.* **shel·duck** or **shelducks**) a type of wild DUCK that lives on or near the coast

shelf 🔑 /ʃelf/ *noun* (*pl.* **shelves** /ʃelvz/)
1 🔑 a flat board, made of wood, metal, glass, etc, fixed to the wall or forming part of a cupboard/closet, BOOKCASE, etc, for things to be placed on: *I helped him put up some shelves in his bedroom.* ◇ *The book I wanted was on the top shelf.* ◇ ***supermarket/library shelves*** ◇ *empty shelves* ➲ COLLOCATIONS at DECORATE, SHOPPING ➲ VISUAL VOCAB page V22 **2** (*geology*) a thing shaped like a shelf, especially a piece of rock sticking out from a CLIFF or from the edge of a mass of land under the sea: *the continental shelf* ➲ see also SHELVE
IDM **on the ˈshelf** (*informal*) **1** not wanted by anyone; not used **2** (*old-fashioned*) (especially of women) considered to be too old to get married **off the ˈshelf** that can be bought immediately and does not have to be specially designed or ordered: *I bought this package off the shelf.* ◇ *off-the-shelf software packages* ➲ compare OFF THE PEG at PEG *n.*

ˈ**shelf life** *noun* [usually sing.] the length of time that food, etc. can be kept before it is too old to be sold

ˈ**shelf-stacker** *noun* a person whose job is to fill shelves with goods to be sold, especially in a supermarket

shell 🔑 /ʃel/ *noun, verb*
▪ ***noun*** **1** 🔑 [C, U] the hard outer part of eggs, nuts, some seeds and some animals: *We collected shells on the beach.* ◇ *snail shells* ◇ *walnut shells* ◇ *earrings made out of coconut shell* ➲ picture at SHELLFISH ➲ VISUAL VOCAB pages V11, V26, V28 ➲ see also EGGSHELL, NUTSHELL, SEASHELL, TORTOISESHELL **2** [C] any object that looks like the shell of a SNAIL or sea creature: *pasta shells* **3** [C] a metal case filled with EXPLOSIVE, to be fired from a large gun **4** (*NAmE*) = CARTRIDGE **5** [C] the walls or outer structure of sth, for example, an empty building or ship after a fire or a bomb attack: *The house was now a shell gutted by flames.* ◇ (*figurative*) *My life has been an empty shell since he died.* **6** [C] any structure that forms a hard outer frame: *the body shell of a car* **7** [sing.] the outer layer of sb's personality; how they seem to be or feel: *She had developed a shell of indifference.*
IDM **come out of your ˈshell** to become less shy and more confident when talking to other people **to go, retreat, etc. into your ˈshell** to become shyer and avoid talking to other people
▪ ***verb*** **1** [T, I] **~ (sth)** to fire shells at sth: *They shelled the city all night.* ◇ *Just as they were leaving, the rebels started shelling.* **2** [T] **~ sth** to remove the shell or covering from nuts, PEAS, etc.
PHR V ˌ**shell ˈout (for sth)** | ˌ**shell sth↔ˈout (for sth)** (*informal*) to pay a lot of money for sth SYN **fork out**: *The band shelled out $100 000 for a mobile recording studio.*

she'll /ʃiːl/ *short form* she will

shel·lac /ʃəˈlæk; ˈʃelæk/ *noun, verb*
▪ ***noun*** [U] a natural substance used in making varnish to protect surfaces and make them hard
▪ ***verb*** (-ck-) **1 ~ sth** to cover sth with shellac **2** [usually passive] **~ sb** (*NAmE, informal*) to defeat sb very easily: *The Republicans got shellacked in the elections.*

shell·fire /ˈʃelfaɪə(r)/ *noun* [U] attacks or explosions caused by SHELLS being fired from large guns

shellfish

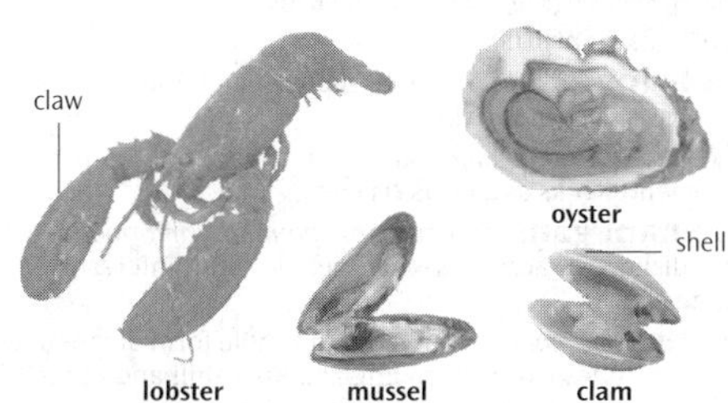

shell·fish /ˈʃelfɪʃ/ *noun* (*pl.* **shell·fish**) a creature with a shell, that lives in water, especially one of the types that can be eaten. OYSTERS and CRABS are both shellfish. ➲ compare CRUSTACEAN, MOLLUSC

ˈ**shell game** *noun* (*NAmE*) **1 the ˈshell game** a game in which three cups are moved around, and players must guess which is the one with a small object underneath **2** an act by an organization or a politician that tricks people in a clever way

shell·ing /ˈʃelɪŋ/ *noun* [U] the firing of SHELLS from large guns: *We suffered weeks of heavy shelling.*

ˈ**shell shock** *noun* [U] a mental illness that can affect soldiers who have been in battle for a long time

ˈ**shell-shocked** *adj.* **1** shocked, confused or anxious because of a difficult situation, and unable to think or act normally **2** suffering from shell shock

ˈ**shell suit** *noun* (*BrE*) a loose pair of trousers/pants and matching jacket worn as informal clothes. Shell suits are made of a light, slightly shiny, material and are often brightly coloured. ➲ compare TRACKSUIT

shel·ter 🔑 /ˈʃeltə(r)/ *noun, verb*
▪ ***noun*** **1** 🔑 [U] the fact of having a place to live or stay, considered as a basic human need: *Human beings need food, clothing and shelter.* **2** 🔑 [U] **~ (from sth)** protection from rain, danger or attack: *to* ***take shelter*** *from the storm* ◇ *The fox was running for the shelter of the trees.* ◇ *People were desperately seeking shelter from the gunfire.* **3** 🔑 [C] (often in compounds) a structure built to give protection, especially from the weather or from attack: *They built a rough shelter from old pieces of wood.* ◇ *an air-raid shelter* ➲ see also BUS SHELTER **4** [C] a building, usually owned by a charity, that provides a place to stay for people without a home, or protection for people or animals who have been badly treated: *a night shelter for the homeless* ◇ *an animal shelter* ➲ see also HOSTEL
▪ ***verb*** **1** 🔑 [T] to give sb/sth a place where they are protected from the weather or from danger; to protect sb/sth: **~ sb/sth from sb/sth** *Trees shelter the house from the wind.* ◇ **~ sb/sth** *helping the poor and sheltering the homeless* ◇ *Perhaps I sheltered my daughter too much* (= protected her too much from unpleasant or difficult experiences). **2** 🔑 [I] **~ (from sth)** to stay in a place that protects you from the weather or from danger: *We sheltered from the rain in a doorway.*

shel·tered /ˈʃeltəd; *NAmE* -tərd/ *adj.* **1** (of a place) protected from bad weather: *a sheltered beach* **2** (sometimes *disapproving*) protected from the more unpleasant aspects or difficulties of life: *She had a very sheltered childhood.* ◇ *They both lead very sheltered lives.* **3** [only before noun] (*BrE*) (of houses, flats/apartments, etc.) designed for people, especially old people, who can still live fairly independent lives, but with staff available to help them if necessary: ***sheltered accommodation/housing*** ◇ *a* ***sheltered workshop*** *for the blind*

shelve /ʃelv/ *verb* **1** [T] **~ sth** to decide not to continue with a plan, either for a short time or permanently SYN **put on ice**: *The government has shelved the idea until at least next year.* **2** [T] **~ sth** to put books, etc. on a shelf

S

3 [I] (+ **adv./prep.**) (of land) to slope downwards: *The beach shelved gently down to the water.*

shelves *pl.* of SHELF

shelv·ing /'ʃelvɪŋ/ *noun* [U] shelves; material for making shelves: *wooden shelving*

'she-male *noun* (*informal*) a TRANSSEXUAL, especially one who works as a PROSTITUTE

she·nani·gans /ʃɪ'nænɪgənz/ *noun* [pl.] (*informal*) secret or dishonest activities that people find interesting or amusing

Sheng /ʃeŋ/ *noun* [U] (in Kenya) a simple form of language that includes words from English, Kiswahili and other African languages, used especially between young people in cities

shep·herd /'ʃepəd; *NAmE* -ərd/ *noun, verb*

■ ***noun*** (*NAmE* also **sheep·herd·er**) a person whose job is to take care of sheep

■ ***verb* ~ sb + adv./prep.** to guide sb or a group of people somewhere, making sure they go where you want them to go

shep·herd·ess /ˌʃepə'des; 'ʃepədəs; *NAmE* ˌʃepər'des; 'ʃepərdəs/ *noun* (*old-fashioned*) a woman who takes care of sheep

ˌshepherd's 'pie (also **ˌcottage 'pie**) *noun* [C, U] (*especially BrE*) a dish of MINCED (= finely chopped) meat covered with a layer of MASHED potato

sher·bet /'ʃɜːbət; *NAmE* 'ʃɜːrbət/ *noun* **1** [U] (*BrE*) a powder that tastes of fruit and FIZZES when you put it in your mouth, eaten as a sweet/candy **2** [C, U] (*NAmE*, becoming *old-fashioned*) = SORBET

sherd /ʃɜːd; *NAmE* ʃɜːrd/ *noun* = SHARD

sher·iff /'ʃerɪf/ *noun* **1** (in the US) an elected officer responsible for keeping law and order in a county or town **2** (often **High Sheriff**) (in England and Wales) an officer representing the king or queen in counties, and some cities, who performs some legal duties and attends ceremonies **3** (in Scotland) a judge **4** (in Canada) an official who works in a court preparing court cases

'sheriff court *noun* a lower court in Scotland

Sher·lock /'ʃɜːlɒk; *NAmE* 'ʃɜːrlɑːk/ (also **Sherlock Holmes** /həʊmz; *NAmE* hoʊmz/) *noun* (*informal*, sometimes *ironic*) a person who tries to find an explanation for a crime or sth mysterious or who shows that they understand sth quickly, especially sth that is not obvious: *Oh, well done, Sherlock. Did you figure that out all by yourself?* ORIGIN From Sherlock Holmes, a very clever detective in stories by Arthur Conan Doyle, published in the late 19th and early 20th centuries.

S

Sherpa /'ʃɜːpə; *NAmE* 'ʃɜːrpə/ *noun* a member of a Himalayan people, who often guide people in the mountains, sometimes carrying their bags, etc.

sherry /'ʃeri/ *noun* (*pl.* **-ies**) **1** [U, C] a strong yellow or brown wine, originally from southern Spain. It is often drunk before meals: ***sweet/dry sherry*** ◇ ***cream sherry*** (= a type of very sweet sherry) ◇ *fine quality sherries* ◇ *a **sherry glass*** (= a type of small narrow wine glass) **2** [C] a glass of sherry: *I'll have a sherry.*

sher·wani /ʃɜː'wɑːni; *NAmE* ʃɜːr'w-/ *noun* a knee-length coat with buttons up to the neck, sometimes worn by men from S Asia

she's *short form* **1** /ʃiːz; ʃiz/ she is **2** /ʃiːz/ she has

Shetland pony /ˌʃetlənd 'pəʊni; *NAmE* 'poʊni/ *noun* a very small, strong horse with a rough coat

shh = SH

Shia (also **Shi'a**) /'ʃɪə/ *noun* (*pl.* **Shia** or **Shias**) **1** [U] one of the two main branches of the Islamic religion ➲ compare SUNNI **2** [C] (also **Shi·ite, Shi'ite**) a member of the Shia branch of Islam

shi·atsu /ʃi'ætsuː/ *noun* [U] (from *Japanese*) = ACUPRESSURE

shib·bo·leth /'ʃɪbəleθ/ *noun* (*formal*) **1** an old idea, principle or phrase that is no longer accepted by many people as important or appropriate to modern life **2** a custom, word, etc. that distinguishes one group of people from another ORIGIN From a Hebrew word meaning 'ear of corn'. In the Bible story, Jephthah, the leader of the Gileadites, was able to use it as a test to tell which were his own men, because others found the 'sh' sound difficult to pronounce.

shied *past tense, past part.* of SHY

shield /ʃiːld/ *noun, verb*

■ ***noun* 1** a large piece of metal or leather carried by soldiers in the past to protect the body when fighting **2** = RIOT SHIELD **3** a person or thing used to protect sb/sth, especially by forming a barrier: *The gunman used the hostages as a **human shield**.* ◇ *Water is not an effective shield against the sun's more harmful rays.* ◇ *She hid her true feelings behind a shield of cold indifference.* **4** a plate or screen that protects a machine or the person using it from damage or injury **5** an object in the shape of a shield, given as a prize in a sports competition, etc. ➲ picture at MEDAL **6** a drawing or model of a shield showing a COAT OF ARMS **7** (*NAmE*) a police officer's BADGE

■ ***verb* 1** to protect sb/sth from danger, harm or sth unpleasant: **~ sth against sth** *I shielded my eyes against the glare.* ◇ **~ sb/sth from sb/sth** *The ozone layer shields the earth from the sun's ultraviolet rays.* ◇ *You can't shield her from the truth forever.* ◇ **~ sb/sth** *Police believe that somebody is shielding the killer.* **2 ~ sth** to put a shield around a piece of machinery, etc. in order to protect the person using it

shift 🔑 AW /ʃɪft/ *verb, noun*

■ ***verb***

▸ MOVE **1** 🔑 [I, T] to move, or move sth, from one position or place to another: *Lydia shifted uncomfortably in her chair.* ◇ **~ (from...) (to...)** *The action of the novel shifts from Paris to London.* ◇ **~ sth** *Could you help me shift some furniture?* ◇ **~ sth (from...) (to...)** *He shifted his gaze from the child to her.* ◇ *She shifted her weight from one foot to the other.* **2** [I, T] **~ (yourself)** (*BrE, informal*) to move quickly SYN **hurry**

▸ SITUATION/OPINION/POLICY **3** 🔑 [I] (of a situation, an opinion, a policy etc.) to change from one state, position, etc. to another: *Public attitudes towards marriage have shifted over the past 50 years.* ◇ **~ (from...) (to/towards/toward...)** *The balance of power shifted away from workers towards employers.* **4** [T] to change your opinion of or attitude towards sth, or change the way that you do sth: **~ sth** *We need to shift the focus of this debate.* ◇ **~ sth (from...) (to/towards/toward...)** *The new policy shifted the emphasis away from fighting inflation.*

▸ RESPONSIBILITY **5** [T] **~ responsibility/blame (for sth) (onto sb)** to make sb else responsible for sth you should do or sth bad that you have done: *He tried to shift the blame for his mistakes onto his colleagues.*

▸ REMOVE MARK **6** [T] **~ sth** to remove sth such as a dirty mark SYN **get rid of**: *a detergent that shifts even the most stubborn stains*

▸ SELL GOODS **7** [T] **~ sth** to sell goods, especially goods that are difficult to sell: *They cut prices drastically to try and shift stock.*

▸ IN VEHICLE **8** [I] (*NAmE*) to change the gears when you are driving a vehicle: *to shift into second gear*

IDM **shift your 'ground** (usually *disapproving*) to change your opinion about a subject, especially during a discussion **(the) ˌshifting 'sands (of sth)** used to describe a situation that changes so often that it is difficult to understand or deal with it

PHR V **ˌshift for your'self** (*BrE*) to do things without help from other people: *You're going to have to shift for yourself from now on.*

■ ***noun***

▸ CHANGE **1** 🔑 [C] **~ (in sth)** a change in position or direction: *a dramatic shift in public opinion* ◇ *a shift of emphasis* ➲ see also PARADIGM SHIFT

▸ PERIOD OF WORK **2** 🔑 [C] a period of time worked by a group of workers who start work as another group finishes: *to be on the **day/night shift** at the factory* ◇ *to work an eight-hour shift* ◇ *working in shifts* ◇ ***shift workers/work***

➲ COLLOCATIONS at JOB ➲ see also SWING SHIFT **3** 🔑 [C+sing./pl. v.] the workers who work a particular shift: *The night shift has/have just come off duty.*
▸ ON COMPUTER **4** [U] the system on a computer keyboard or TYPEWRITER that allows capital letters or a different set of characters to be typed; the key that operates this system: *a shift key* ◇ *Press shift + F11 to insert a new worksheet.*
▸ CLOTHING **5** [C] a woman's simple straight dress **6** [C] a simple straight piece of clothing worn by women in the past as underwear

shift·er /ˈʃɪftə(r)/ *noun* (*especially NAmE*) the GEARBOX of a vehicle or the set of gears on a bicycle

ˌshifting ˌculti'vation *noun* [U] (*technical*) a way of farming in some tropical countries in which farmers use an area of land until it cannot be used for growing plants any more, then move to a new area of land

shift·less /ˈʃɪftləs/ *adj.* (*disapproving*) lazy and having no ambition to succeed in life

shifty /ˈʃɪfti/ *adj.* (**shift·ier**, **shifti·est**) (*informal*) seeming to be dishonest; looking guilty about sth SYN **furtive**: *shifty eyes* ◇ *to look shifty* ▸ **shift·ily** /-ɪli/ *adv.*

shii·take (also **shi·take**) /ʃɪˈtɑːki; ʃiː-/ (also ˌ**shiitake** ˈ**mushroom**) *noun* (from *Japanese*) a type of Japanese or Chinese MUSHROOM

Shi·ite (also **Shi'ite**) /ˈʃiːaɪt/ *noun* a member of the Shia branch of Islam ➲ compare SUNNI ▸ **Shi·ite** (also **Shi'ite**) *adj.* [usually before noun]

shil·ling /ˈʃɪlɪŋ/ *noun* **1** a British coin in use until 1971, worth 12 old pence. There were 20 shillings in one pound. **2** the unit of money in Kenya, Uganda, Tanzania and Somalia

shilly-shally /ˈʃɪli ʃæli/ *verb* (**shilly-shallies**, **shilly-shally·ing**, **shilly-shallied**, **shilly-shallied**) [I] (*informal, disapproving*) to take a long time to do sth, especially to make a decision SYN **dither**: *Stop shilly-shallying and make up your mind.*

shim /ʃɪm/ *noun* (*NAmE*) a thin piece of wood, rubber, metal, etc. which is thicker at one end than the other, that you use to fill a space between two things that do not fit well together

shim·mer /ˈʃɪmə(r)/ *verb, noun*
■ ***verb*** [I] to shine with a soft light that seems to move slightly: *The sea was shimmering in the sunlight.* ➲ SYNONYMS at SHINE
■ ***noun*** [U, sing.] a shining light that seems to move slightly: *a shimmer of moonlight in the dark sky*

shimmy /ˈʃɪmi/ *verb* (**shim·mies**, **shimmy·ing**, **shim·mied**, **shim·mied**) [I] **+ adv./prep.** to dance or move in a way that involves shaking your hips and shoulders

shin /ʃɪn/ *noun, verb*
■ ***noun*** the front part of the leg below the knee ➲ VISUAL VOCAB page V48
■ ***verb*** (-nn-) (*BrE*) (*NAmE* **shinny**)
PHR V ˈ**shin/ˈshinny up/down sth** (*informal*) to climb up or down sth quickly, using your hands and legs: *He shinned down the drainpipe and ran off.*

ˈ**shin bone** *noun* the front and larger bone of the two bones in the lower part of the leg between the knee and the ankle SYN **tibia** ➲ VISUAL VOCAB page V48

shin·dig /ˈʃɪndɪɡ/ *noun* (*informal*) a big noisy party

shine 🔑 /ʃaɪn/ *verb, noun*
■ ***verb*** (**shone**, **shone** /ʃɒn; *US* ʃoʊn/) HELP In sense 2 in *NAmE* **shined** can also be used for the past tense and past participle . In sense 3 **shined** is used for the past tense and past participle. **1** 🔑 [I] to produce or reflect light; to be bright: *The sun shone brightly in a cloudless sky.* ◇ *The dark polished wood shone like glass.* ◇ (*figurative*) *Her eyes were shining with excitement.* ◇ *Excitement was shining in her eyes.* **2** 🔑 (*NAmE* also **shined**, **shined**) [T] **~ sth** (**+ adv./prep.**) to aim or point the light of a lamp, etc. in a particular direction: *He shone the flashlight around the cellar.* ◇ (*figurative*) *Campaigners are shining a spotlight on the world's diminishing natural resources.* **3** (**shined**, **shined**) [T] **~ sth** to polish sth; to make sth smooth and bright: *He shined shoes and sold newspapers to make money.* **4** [I] to be very good at sth: *He failed to shine academically but he was very good at sports.* ◇ *She has set a **shining example** of loyal service over four decades.* ➲ see also SHINY IDM see HAY, KNIGHT *n.*, RISE *v.*
PHR V ˌ**shine** ˈ**through** (**sth**) (of a quality) to be easy to see or notice: *Her old professional skills shone through.*
■ ***noun*** [sing.] the bright quality that sth has when light is reflected on it: *a shampoo that gives your hair body and shine*
IDM **take a** ˈ**shine to sb/sth** (*informal*) to begin to like sb very much as soon as you see or meet them **take the** ˈ**shine off sth** (*informal*) to make sth seem much less good than it did at first ➲ more at RAIN *n.*

Synonyms

shine

gleam • glow • sparkle • glisten • shimmer • glitter • twinkle • glint

These words all mean to produce or reflect light.

shine to produce or reflect light, especially brightly: *The sun was shining and the sky was blue.*

gleam to shine with a clear bright or pale light, especially a reflected light: *Moonlight gleamed on the water.*

glow (often of sth hot or warm) to produce a dull steady light: *The end of his cigarette glowed red.*

sparkle to shine brightly with small flashes of light: *The diamonds sparkled in the light.*

glisten (of sth wet) to shine: *The road glistened wet after the rain.*

shimmer to shine with a soft light that seems to shake slightly: *Everything seemed to shimmer in the heat.*

glitter to shine brightly with small flashes of reflected light: *The ceiling of the cathedral glittered with gold.*

SPARKLE OR GLITTER?

There is very little difference in meaning between these two words. **Glitter** can sometimes suggest a lack of depth, but this is more frequent in the figurative use of **glitter** as a noun: *the superficial glitter of show business.* **Sparkle** is also often used to talk about light reflected off a surface, but things that produce light can also sparkle: *Stars sparkled in the sky.*

twinkle to shine with a light that changes rapidly from bright to faint to bright again: *Stars twinkled in the sky.*

glint to give small bright flashes of reflected light: *The blade of the knife glinted in the darkness.*

PATTERNS

- to shine/gleam/sparkle/glisten/shimmer/glitter/glint **on** sth
- to shine/gleam/glow/sparkle/glisten/shimmer/glitter/twinkle/glint **with** sth
- to shine/gleam/sparkle/glisten/shimmer/glitter/glint **in the sunlight**
- to shine/gleam/glisten/shimmer/glitter/glint **in the moonlight**
- the **stars** shine/sparkle/glitter/twinkle
- sb's **eyes** shine/gleam/glow/sparkle/glisten/glitter/twinkle/glint
- to shine/gleam/glow/glitter **brightly**
- to shine/gleam/glow/shimmer **softly**

shiner /ˈʃaɪnə(r)/ *noun* (*informal*) an area of dark skin that can form around sb's eye when they receive a blow to it SYN **black eye**

shin·gle /ˈʃɪŋɡl/ *noun* **1** [U] a mass of small smooth stones on a beach or at the side of a river: *a shingle beach* ➲ VISUAL VOCAB page V4 **2** [C, U] a small flat piece of wood that is used to cover a wall or roof of a building **3** [C] (*NAmE*) a board with a sign on it, in front of a doctor's or lawyer's

S

office: *He* ***hung out his own shingle*** (= started a business as a doctor or lawyer).

shin·gled /ˈʃɪŋɡld/ *adj.* (of a roof, building, etc.) covered with shingles (2)

shin·gles /ˈʃɪŋɡlz/ *noun* [U] (*medical*) a disease that affects the nerves and produces a band of painful spots on the skin

shin·gly /ˈʃɪŋɡli/ *adj.* (of a beach) covered in shingle

ˈ**shin guard** (*BrE* also ˈ**shin pad**) *noun* a piece of thick material that is used to protect the lower front part of the leg when playing sports

shinny /ˈʃɪni/ *verb, noun*

■ ***verb*** (**shin·nies, shinny·ing, shin·nied, shin·nied**) (*NAmE*) (*BrE* **shin**)

PHR V ˈ**shin/ˈshinny up/down sth** (*informal*) to climb up or down sth quickly, using your hands and legs

■ ***noun*** (also ˈ**shinny hockey**) [U] an informal form of ICE HOCKEY, played especially by children

ˈ**shin splints** *noun* [pl.] sharp pain in the front parts of the lower legs caused by too much exercise, especially on a hard surface

Shinto /ˈʃɪntəʊ; *NAmE* -toʊ/ (also **Shin·to·ism** /ˈʃɪntəʊɪzəm; *NAmE* -toʊ-/) *noun* [U] a Japanese religion whose practices include the worship of ANCESTORS and a belief in nature spirits

shinty /ˈʃɪnti/ *noun* [U] a Scottish game similar to HOCKEY, played with curved sticks by teams of twelve players

shiny 0-w /ˈʃaɪni/ *adj.* (**shini·er, shini·est**) smooth and bright; reflecting the light: *shiny black hair*

IDM **shiny new** (*approving*) very new and attractive: *shiny new stuff/software*

ship 0-w /ʃɪp/ *noun, verb*

■ ***noun*** 0-w a large boat that carries people or goods by sea: *There are two restaurants* ***on board ship.*** ◇ *a* ***sailing/cargo/cruise ship*** ◇ *a* ***ship's captain/crew/company/cook*** ◇ *Raw materials and labour come* ***by ship****, rail or road.* ➲ COLLOCATIONS at TRAVEL ➲ VISUAL VOCAB page V44 ➲ see also AIRSHIP, FLAGSHIP, LIGHTSHIP IDM see JUMP *v.*, SINK *v.*, SPOIL *v.*, TIGHT

■ ***verb*** (-pp-) **1** [T] **~ sb/sth + adv./prep.** to send or transport sb/sth by ship or by another means of transport: *The company ships its goods all over the world.* ◇ *He was arrested and shipped back to the UK for trial.* **2** [I, T] to be available to be bought; to make sth available to be bought: *The software is due to ship next month.* ◇ **~ sth** *The company continues to ship more computer systems than its rivals.* **3** [T] **~ water** (of a boat, etc.) to have water coming in over the sides IDM see SHAPE *v.*

PHR V ˌ**ship sb↔ˈoff** (*disapproving*) to send sb to a place where they will stay: *The children were shipped off to a boarding school at an early age.*

-ship *suffix* (in nouns) **1** the state or quality of: *ownership* ◇ *friendship* **2** the status or office of: *citizenship* ◇ *professorship* **3** skill or ability as: *musicianship* **4** the group of: *membership*

ship·board /ˈʃɪpbɔːd; *NAmE* -bɔːrd/ *adj.* [only before noun] happening on a ship: *shipboard romances*

ship·build·er /ˈʃɪpbɪldə(r)/ *noun* a person or company that builds ships ▶ **ship·build·ing** *noun* [U]: *the shipbuilding industry*

ship·load /ˈʃɪpləʊd; *NAmE* -loʊd/ *noun* as many goods or passengers as a ship can carry

ship·mate /ˈʃɪpmeɪt/ *noun* sailors who are **shipmates** are sailing on the same ship as each other

ship·ment /ˈʃɪpmənt/ *noun* **1** [U] the process of sending goods from one place to another: *The goods are ready for shipment.* ◇ *the illegal shipment of arms* ◇ *shipment costs* **2** [C] a load of goods that are sent from one place to another: *arms shipments* ◇ *a shipment of arms*

ship·owner /ˈʃɪpəʊnə(r); *NAmE* -oʊn-/ *noun* a person or company that owns a ship or ships

ship·per /ˈʃɪpə(r)/ *noun* a person or company that arranges for goods to be sent from one place to another, especially by ship

ship·ping /ˈʃɪpɪŋ/ *noun* [U] **1** ships in general or considered as a group: *The canal is open to shipping.* ◇ *international* ***shipping lanes*** (= routes for ships) **2** the activity of carrying people or goods from one place to another by ship: *a shipping company* ◇ *She arranged for the shipping of her furniture to England.*

ˈ**shipping forecast** (*BrE*) (*US* **the** ˈ**shipping news** [U]) *noun* a radio broadcast giving a report for ships on the weather conditions at sea

ˈ**ship's chandler** *noun* = CHANDLER

ship·shape /ˈʃɪpʃeɪp/ *adj.* [not usually before noun] clean and neat; in good condition and ready to use

ˌ**ship-to-ˈshore** *adj.* [only before noun] providing communication between people on a ship and people on land: *a ship-to-shore radio*

ship·wreck /ˈʃɪprek/ *noun, verb*

■ ***noun*** **1** [U, C] the loss or destruction of a ship at sea because of a storm or because it hits rocks, etc: *They narrowly escaped shipwreck in a storm in the North Sea.* **2** [C] a ship that has been lost or destroyed at sea: *The contents of shipwrecks belong to the state.*

■ ***verb*** **be shipwrecked** to be left somewhere after the ship that you have been sailing in has been lost or destroyed at sea ▶ **ship·wrecked** *adj.*: *a shipwrecked sailor*

ship·yard /ˈʃɪpjɑːd; *NAmE* -jɑːrd/ *noun* a place where ships are built or repaired: *shipyard workers*

shire /ˈʃaɪə(r); *or, in compounds,* -ʃə(r)/ *noun* (*BrE*) **1** [C] (*old use*) a county (now used in the names of some counties in Britain, for example *Hampshire, Yorkshire*) **2 the Shires**, (also **the Shire Counties**) [pl.] counties in central England that are in country areas

ˈ**shire horse** *noun* a large powerful horse, used for pulling loads

shirk /ʃɜːk; *NAmE* ʃɜːrk/ *verb* [I, T] to avoid doing sth you should do, especially because you are too lazy: *Discipline in the company was strict and no one shirked.* ◇ **~ from sth/doing sth** *A determined burglar will not shirk from breaking a window to gain entry.* ◇ **~ sth/doing sth** *She never shirked her responsibilities.* ▶ **shirk·er** *noun*

shirt 0-w /ʃɜːt; *NAmE* ʃɜːrt/ *noun* a piece of clothing (usually for men), worn on the upper part of the body, made of light cloth, with sleeves and usually with a COLLAR and buttons down the front: *to wear a shirt and tie* ◇ *a short-sleeved shirt* ◇ *a football shirt* ➲ VISUAL VOCAB page V51 ➲ see also NIGHTSHIRT, POLO SHIRT, STUFFED SHIRT, SWEATSHIRT, T-SHIRT

IDM **keep your** ˈ**shirt on** (*informal*) used to tell sb not to get angry: *Keep your shirt on! It was only a joke.* **put your** ˈ**shirt on sb/sth** (*BrE, informal*) to bet all your money on sb/sth **the** ˌ**shirt off sb's** ˈ**back** anything that sb has, including the things they really need themselves, that sb else takes from them or they are willing to give

ˈ**shirt front** *noun* the front part of a shirt, especially the stiff front part of a formal white shirt

shirt·sleeve /ˈʃɜːtsliːv; *NAmE* ˈʃɜːrt-/ *noun* [usually pl.] a sleeve of a shirt

IDM **in (your)** ˈ**shirtsleeves** wearing a shirt without a jacket, etc. on top of it

ˈ**shirt tail** *noun* the part of a shirt that is below the waist and is usually inside your trousers/pants

shirty /ˈʃɜːti; *NAmE* ˈʃɜːrti/ *adj.* **~ (with sb)** (*BrE, informal*) angry or annoyed with sb about sth, and acting in a rude way

shish kebab /ˈʃɪʃ kɪbæb/ *noun* (*especially NAmE*) = KEBAB

shit /ʃɪt/ *exclamation, noun, verb, adj.*

■ ***exclamation*** (*taboo, slang*) a swear word that many people find offensive, used to show that you are angry or annoyed: *Shit! I've lost my keys!* HELP Less offensive exclam-

S

ations to use are **blast, darn it** (especially *NAmE*), **damn** or (*BrE*) **bother**.

■ ***noun*** (*taboo, slang*) **1** [U] solid waste matter from the BOWELS SYN **excrement**: *a pile of dog shit on the path* HELP A more polite way to express this example would be 'a pile of dog poo/poop'. **2** [sing.] an act of emptying solid waste matter from the BOWELS: *to have/take a shit* **3** [U] stupid remarks or writing; nonsense: *You're talking shit!* ◇ *She's so full of shit.* ➲ see also BULLSHIT **4** [C] (*disapproving*) an unpleasant person who treats other people badly: *He's an arrogant little shit.* **5** [U] criticism or unfair treatment: *I'm not going to take any shit from them.*

IDM **beat, kick, etc. the 'shit out of sb** to attack sb violently so that you injure them **in the 'shit | in ˌdeep 'shit** in trouble: *I'll be in the shit if I don't get this work finished today.* **like 'shit** really bad, ill/sick etc; really badly: *I woke up feeling like shit.* ◇ *We get treated like shit in this job.* **no 'shit!** (often *ironic*) used to show that you are surprised, impressed, etc. or that you are pretending to be **not give a 'shit (about sb/sth)** to not care at all about sb/sth: *He doesn't give a shit about anybody else.* **shit 'happens** used to express the idea that we must accept that bad things often happen without reason **when the ˌshit hits the 'fan** when sb in authority finds out about sth bad or wrong that sb has done: *When the shit hits the fan, I don't want to be here.* ➲ more at BUG *v.*, CROCK, SCARE *v.*

■ ***verb*** (**shit·ting, shit, shit**) (*taboo, slang*) HELP **shat** /ʃæt/ and, in *BrE*, **shit·ted** are also used for the past tense and past participle. **1** [I, T] **~ (sth)** to empty solid waste matter from the BOWELS HELP A more polite way of expressing this is 'to go to the toilet/lavatory' (*BrE*), 'to go to the bathroom' (*NAmE*) or 'to go'. A more formal expression is 'to empty the bowels'. **2** [T] **~ yourself** to empty solid waste matter from the BOWELS by accident **3** [T] **~ yourself** to be very frightened

■ ***adj.*** (*taboo, slang, especially BrE*) very bad: *You're shit and you know you are!* ◇ *They're a shit team.*

shi·take *noun* = SHIITAKE

shite /ʃaɪt/ *exclamation, noun* [U] (*BrE, taboo, slang*) another word for SHIT

'shit-faced *adj.* (*taboo, slang*) very drunk

shit·hole /'ʃɪthəʊl; *NAmE* -hoʊl/ *noun* (*taboo, slang*) a very dirty or unpleasant place

'shit-hot *adj.* (*taboo, slang*) extremely good at sth: *a shit-hot lawyer*

shit·house /'ʃɪthaʊs/ *noun* (*taboo, slang*) a toilet/bathroom

shit·less /'ʃɪtləs/ *adj.* (*taboo, slang*) IDM see SCARE *v.*

ˌshit-'scared *adj.* [not before noun] (*taboo, slang*) very frightened

'shit stirrer *noun* (*BrE, taboo, slang*) a person who tries to make situations in which people disagree even worse ▶ **'shit stirring** *noun* [U]

shitty /'ʃɪti/ *adj.* (*taboo, slang*) **1** unpleasant; very bad **2** unfair or unkind: *What a shitty way to treat a friend!*

shiver /'ʃɪvə(r)/ *verb, noun*

■ ***verb*** [I] (of a person) to shake slightly because you are cold, frightened, excited, etc: *Don't stand outside shivering—come inside and get warm!* ◇ *He shivered at the thought of the cold, dark sea.* ◇ **~ with sth** *to **shiver with cold/excitement/pleasure, etc.***

■ ***noun*** **1** [C] a sudden shaking movement of your body because you are cold, frightened, excited, etc: *The sound of his voice **sent shivers down her spine**.* ◇ *He felt a cold shiver of fear run through him.* **2 the shivers** [pl.] shaking movements of your body because of fear or a high temperature: *I don't like him. He **gives me the shivers**.* ◇ *Symptoms include headaches, vomiting and the shivers.*

shiv·ery /'ʃɪvəri/ *adj.* shaking with cold, fear, illness, etc.

shmo = SCHMO

shoal /ʃəʊl; *NAmE* ʃoʊl/ *noun* **1** a large number of fish swimming together as a group ➲ compare SCHOOL (9) **2** a small hill of sand just below the surface of the sea

shock 0⊷ /ʃɒk; *NAmE* ʃɑːk/ *noun, verb*

■ ***noun***

▸ SURPRISE **1** 0⊷ [C, usually sing., U] a strong feeling of surprise as a result of sth happening, especially sth unpleasant; the event that causes this feeling: *The news of my promotion **came as a shock**.* ◇ *He's still in **a state of shock**.* ◇ *I got a terrible shock the other day.* ◇ *She still hadn't got over the shock of seeing him again.* ◇ (*informal*) *If you think the job will be easy, **you're in for a shock**.* ◇ *Losing in the first round was **a shock to the system*** (= it was a more of a shock because it was not expected). ◇ *The team suffered a shock defeat in the first round.* ➲ see also CULTURE SHOCK

▸ MEDICAL **2** 0⊷ [U] a serious medical condition, usually the result of injury in which a person has lost a lot of blood and they are extremely weak: *She was taken to hospital **suffering from shock**.* ◇ *He isn't seriously injured but he is **in (a state of) shock**.* ➲ see also SHELL SHOCK, TOXIC SHOCK SYNDROME

▸ VIOLENT SHAKING **3** 0⊷ [C, U] a violent shaking movement that is caused by an explosion, EARTHQUAKE, etc: *The shock of the explosion could be felt up to six miles away.* ◇ *The bumper absorbs shock on impact.*

▸ FROM ELECTRICITY **4** 0⊷ [C] = ELECTRIC SHOCK: *Don't touch that wire or you'll **get a shock**.*

▸ OF HAIR **5** a thick mass of hair on a person's head

IDM **ˌshock 'horror** (*BrE, informal*, often *humorous*) used when you pretend to be shocked by sth that is not really very serious or surprising ➲ see also SHOCK-HORROR *adj.*

■ ***verb***

▸ SURPRISE AND UPSET **1** 0⊷ [T] to surprise and upset sb: **~ sb** *It shocks you when something like that happens.* ◇ *We were all shocked at the news of his death.* ◇ **~ sb that...** *Neighbours were shocked that such an attack could happen in their area.* ◇ **~ sb to do sth** ***I was shocked to** hear that he had resigned.*

▸ OFFEND/DISGUST **2** 0⊷ [I, T] (of bad language, immoral behaviour, etc.) to make sb feel offended or disgusted: *These movies deliberately set out to shock.* ◇ **~ sb (to do sth)** *She enjoys shocking people by saying outrageous things.*

▶ **shocked** 0⊷ *adj.*: *For a few minutes we stood in **shocked silence**.*

Synonyms

shock

appal • horrify • disgust • sicken • repel

These words all mean to surprise and upset sb very much.

shock [often passive] to surprise sb, usually in a way that upsets them: *We were all shocked at the news of his death.*

appal/appall to shock and upset sb very much: *The brutality of the crime has appalled the public.*

horrify to make sb feel extremely shocked, upset or frightened: *The whole country was horrified by the killings.*

disgust to make sb feel shocked and almost ill because sth is so unpleasant: *The level of violence in the movie really disgusted me.*

sicken (*BrE*) to make sb feel very shocked, angry and almost ill because sth is so unpleasant: *The public is becoming sickened by these images of violence and death.*

repel [often passive] (*rather formal*) to make sb feel rather disgusted: *I was repelled by the smell of drink on his breath.*

PATTERNS

- shocked/appalled/horrified/disgusted **at** sb/sth
- to shock/appal/horrify/disgust sb **that...**
- to shock/appal/horrify/disgust/sicken sb **to think/see/hear...**
- **sb's behaviour** shocks/appals sb
- **violence/an idea** shocks/appals/horrifies/disgusts sb

S

ˈshock absorber *noun* a device that is fitted to each wheel of a vehicle in order to reduce the effects of travelling over rough ground, so that passengers can be more comfortable

shock·er /ˈʃɒkə(r); *NAmE* ˈʃɑːk-/ *noun* (*informal*) **1** a film/movie, piece of news or person that shocks you **2** something that is of very low quality

ˈshock-headed (also **ˈshock-haired**) *adj.* (of people) having a lot of thick untidy hair

ˈshock-horror *adj.* intending to make people very shocked or very angry: *a shock-horror advertising campaign* ➲ see also SHOCK *n.*

shock·ing 🔑 /ˈʃɒkɪŋ; *NAmE* ˈʃɑːk-/ *adj.*
1 🔑 that offends or upsets people; that is morally wrong: *shocking behaviour* ◇ *shocking news* ◇ *It is shocking that they involved children in the crime.* ◇ *a shocking waste of money* **2** (*informal, especially BrE*) very bad: *The house was left in a shocking state.* ▸ **shock·ing·ly** *adv.*: *a shockingly high mortality rate*

ˌshocking ˈpink *adj.* very bright pink in colour ▸ **ˌshocking ˈpink** *noun* [U]

ˈshock jock *noun* (*informal, especially NAmE*) a DISC JOCKEY on a radio show who deliberately expresses opinions or uses language that many people find offensive

shock·proof /ˈʃɒkpruːf; *NAmE* ˈʃɑːk-/ *adj.* made so that it cannot be damaged if it is dropped or hit: *My watch is shockproof and waterproof.*

ˈshock tactics *noun* [pl.] actions that are done to deliberately shock people in order to persuade them to do sth or to react in a particular way

ˈshock therapy (also **ˈshock treatment**) *noun* [U] a way of treating mental illness by giving ELECTRIC SHOCKS or a drug that has a similar effect

ˈshock troops *noun* [pl.] soldiers who are specially trained to make sudden attacks on the enemy

ˈshock wave *noun* **1** a movement of very high air pressure that is caused by an explosion, EARTHQUAKE, etc. **2 shock waves** [pl.] feelings of shock that people experience when sth bad happens suddenly: *The murder sent shock waves through the whole community.*

shod /ʃɒd; *NAmE* ʃɑːd/ *adj.* (*literary*) wearing shoes of the type mentioned: *She turned on her elegantly shod heel.* ➲ see also SHOE, SHOEING, SHOD, SHOD *V.*

shoddy /ˈʃɒdi; *NAmE* ˈʃɑːdi/ *adj.* (**shod·dier, shod·di·est**) **1** (of goods, work, etc.) made or done badly and with not enough care SYN **second-rate**: *shoddy goods* ◇ *shoddy workmanship* **2** dishonest or unfair: *shoddy treatment* ▸ **shod·dily** *adv.* **shod·di·ness** *noun* [U]

shoe 🔑 /ʃuː/ *noun, verb*
■ ***noun* 1** 🔑 one of a pair of outer coverings for your feet, usually made of leather or plastic: *a pair of shoes* ◇ *He took his shoes and socks off.* ◇ *What's your shoe size?* ◇ *a shoe brush* ◇ *shoe polish* ➲ VISUAL VOCAB page V52 ➲ see also SNOWSHOE **2** = HORSESHOE
IDM **be in sb's shoes | put yourself in sb's shoes** to be in, or imagine that you are in, another person's situation, especially when it is an unpleasant or difficult one: *I wouldn't like to be in your shoes when they find out about it.* **if ˌI were in ˈyour shoes** used to introduce a piece of advice you are giving to sb: *If I were in your shoes, I'd resign immediately.* **if the shoe fits** (**, wear it**) (*NAmE*) (*BrE* **if the cap fits** (**, wear it**)) if you feel that a remark applies to you, you should accept it and take it as a warning or criticism **the shoe is on the other ˈfoot** (*NAmE*) (*BrE* **the boot is on the other ˈfoot**) used to say that a situation has changed so that sb now has power or authority over the person who used to have power or authority over them ➲ more at FILL *V.*, SHAKE *V.*, STEP *V.*
■ ***verb*** (**shoe·ing, shod, shod** /ʃɒd; *NAmE* ʃɑːd/) **~ sth** to put one or more HORSESHOES on a horse: *The horses were sent to the blacksmith to be shod.*

shoe·box /ˈʃuːbɒks; *NAmE* -bɑːks/ *noun* **1** a box in which you take a pair of new shoes home from a shop **2** (*disapproving*) a very small house with a square shape and no interesting features, especially one that is very similar to all the ones around it

shoe·horn /ˈʃuːhɔːn; *NAmE* -hɔːrn/ *noun, verb*
■ ***noun*** a curved piece of plastic or metal, used to help your heel slide into a shoe
■ ***verb* ~ sth + adv./prep.** to succeed in putting sth into a small space or a place where it does not fit very easily: *They managed to shoehorn the material onto just one CD.*

shoe·lace /ˈʃuːleɪs/ (also **lace**) (*NAmE* also **shoe·string**) *noun* a long thin piece of material like string that goes through the holes on a shoe and is used to fasten it: *a pair of shoelaces* ◇ *to* ***tie/untie*** *your* ***shoelaces*** ◇ *Your shoelace is undone.* ➲ VISUAL VOCAB page V52

shoe·maker /ˈʃuːmeɪkə(r)/ *noun* a person whose job is making shoes and boots ➲ compare COBBLER ▸ **shoe·mak·ing** *noun* [U]

shoe·shine /ˈʃuːʃaɪn/ *noun* [U] (*especially NAmE*) the activity of cleaning people's shoes for money: *a shoeshine stand on West 32nd Street*

shoe·string /ˈʃuːstrɪŋ/ *noun, adj.*
■ ***noun*** (*NAmE*) = SHOELACE
IDM **on a ˈshoestring** (*informal*) using very little money: *In the early years, the business was run on a shoestring.*
■ ***adj.*** [only before noun] (*informal*) that uses very little money: *The club exists on a shoestring budget.*

ˌshoestring poˈtatoes *noun* [pl.] (*NAmE*) potatoes cut into long thin strips and fried in oil

ˈshoe tree *noun* an object shaped like a shoe that you put inside a shoe when you are not wearing it to help the shoe keep its shape

sho·gun /ˈʃəʊgən; *NAmE* ˈʃoʊ-/ *noun* (in the past) a Japanese military leader

Shona /ˈʃəʊnə; *NAmE* ˈʃoʊ-/ *noun* [U] a language spoken by the Shona peoples of southern Africa, used in Zimbabwe and other parts of southern Africa

shone *past tense, past part.* of SHINE

shonky /ˈʃɒŋki; *NAmE* ˈʃɔːŋ-; ˈʃɑːŋ-/ *adj.* (**shonk·ier, shonki·est**) (*AustralE, NZE, informal*) not honest or legal

shoo /ʃuː/ *verb, exclamation*
■ ***verb*** (**shoo·ing, shooed, shooed**) **~ sb/sth** (**+ adv./prep.**) to make sb/sth go away or to another place, especially by saying 'shoo' and waving your arms and hands: *He shooed the dog out of the kitchen.*
■ ***exclamation*** used to tell a child or an animal to go away

shoo·fly pie /ˌʃuːflaɪ ˈpaɪ/ *noun* [C, U] (*NAmE*) an open PIE filled with brown sugar and TREACLE/MOLASSES ORIGIN From the need to say *shoo!* to the flies that the sugar attracts.

ˈshoo-in *noun* **~ (for sth) | ~ (to do sth)** (*NAmE, informal*) a person or team that will win easily

shook *past tense, past part.* of SHAKE

shoot 🔑 /ʃuːt/ *verb, noun, exclamation*
■ ***verb*** (**shot, shot** /ʃɒt; *NAmE* ʃɑːt/)
▸ WEAPON **1** 🔑 [I, T] to fire a gun or other weapon; to fire sth from a weapon: *Don't shoot—I surrender.* ◇ **~ (sth) (at sb/sth)** *troops shooting at the enemy* ◇ *The police rarely* ***shoot to kill*** (= try to kill the people they shoot at). ◇ **~ sth (from sth)** *He shot an arrow from his bow.* ◇ *They shot the lock off* (= removed it by shooting). ➲ COLLOCATIONS at WAR **2** 🔑 [T] to kill or wound a person or an animal with a bullet, etc: **~ sb/sth/yourself** *A man was shot in the leg.* ◇ *He shot himself during a fit of depression.* ◇ *The guards were ordered to* ***shoot on sight*** *anyone trying to escape.* ◇ **~ sb/sth + adj.** *Three people were* ***shot dead*** *during the robbery.* **3** [T, I] **~ (sth)** (of a gun or other weapon) to fire bullets, etc: *This is just a toy gun—it doesn't shoot real bullets.*
▸ FOR SPORT **4** 🔑 [T, I] **~ (sth)** to hunt and kill birds and animals with a gun as a sport: *to shoot pheasants* ◇ *They* ***go shooting*** *in Scotland.*
▸ MOVE QUICKLY **5** 🔑 [I, T] to move suddenly or quickly in one direction; to make sb/sth move in this way: **+ adv./prep.** *A plane shot across the sky.* ◇ *His hand shot out to grab*

S

her. ◇ *Flames were shooting up through the roof.* ◇ (*figurative*) *The band's last single shot straight to number one in the charts.* ◇ **~ sth + adv./prep.** *He shot out his hand to grab her.*

▸ OF PAIN **6** [I] to move suddenly and quickly and be very sharp: *a shooting pain in the back* ◇ **+ adv./prep.** *The pain shot up her arm.*

▸ DIRECT AT SB **7** [T, no passive] to direct sth at sb suddenly or quickly: **~ sth at sb** *Journalists were shooting questions at the candidates.* ◇ *She shot an angry glance at him.* ◇ **~ sb sth** *She shot him an angry glance.*

▸ FILM/PHOTOGRAPH **8** 🔑 [I, T] to make a film/movie or photograph of sth: *Cameras ready? OK, shoot!* ◇ **~ sth (+ adv./prep.)** *Where was the movie shot?* ◇ *The movie was shot in black and white.*

▸ IN SPORTS **9** [I, T] (in football (SOCCER), HOCKEY, etc.) to try to kick, hit or throw the ball into a goal or to score a point: **~ (at sth)** *He should have shot instead of passing.* ◇ (*especially NAmE*) **~ sth** *After school we'd be on the driveway* ***shooting baskets*** (= playing BASKETBALL). **10** [T] **~ sth** (*informal*) (in GOLF) to make a particular score in a complete ROUND or competition: *She shot a 75 in the first round.*

▸ PLAY GAME **11** [T] **~ sth** (*especially NAmE*) to play particular games: *to shoot pool*

IDM **be/get 'shot of sb/sth** (*BrE, informal*) to get rid of sb/sth so you no longer have the problems they cause: *I'll be glad to get shot of this car.* **have shot your 'bolt** (*informal*) to have used all your power, money or supplies **be like shooting ˌfish in a 'barrel** (*informal*) used to emphasize how easy it is to do sth: *What do you mean you can't do it? It'll be like shooting fish in a barrel!* **shoot the 'breeze/'bull** (*NAmE, informal*) to have a conversation in an informal way SYN **chat**: *We sat around in the bar, shooting the breeze.* **ˌshoot from the 'hip** to react quickly without thinking carefully first **ˌshoot yourself in the 'foot** (*informal*) to do or say sth that will cause you a lot of trouble or harm, especially when you are trying to get an advantage for yourself **ˌshoot it 'out (with sb)** (*informal*) to fight against sb with guns, especially until one side is killed or defeated: *The gang decided to shoot it out with the police.* ➲ related noun SHOOT-OUT **shoot the 'messenger** to blame the person who gives the news that sth bad has happened, instead of the person who is really responsible: *Don't shoot the messenger!* **ˌshoot your 'mouth off (about sth)** (*informal*) **1** to talk with too much pride about sth **2** to talk about sth that is private or secret **shoot the 'rapids** to go in a boat over part of a river where the water flows very fast

PHR V **ˌshoot sb/sth↔'down 1** 🔑 to make sb/sth fall to the ground by shooting them/it: *Several planes were shot down by enemy fire.* **2** to be very critical of sb's ideas, opinions, etc: *His latest theory has been* ***shot down in flames.*** **'shoot for sth** (*NAmE, informal*) to try to achieve or get sth, especially sth difficult: *We've been shooting for a pay raise for months.* **ˌshoot 'off** (*informal*) to leave very quickly SYN **dash off**: *I had to shoot off at the end of the meeting.* **ˌshoot sth 'off** (*NAmE*) to light FIREWORKS and make them go off SYN **let off, set off** **ˌshoot 'through** (*AustralE, NZE, informal*) to leave, especially in order to avoid sb/sth: *I was only five when my Dad shot through.* **ˌshoot 'up 1** to grow very quickly: *Their kids have shot up since I last saw them.* **2** to rise suddenly by a large amount: *Ticket prices shot up last year.* ➲ LANGUAGE BANK at INCREASE **3** (*slang*) to INJECT an illegal drug directly into your blood **ˌshoot sth↔'up 1** to cause great damage to sth by shooting **2** [no passive] (*slang*) to INJECT an illegal drug directly into your blood

■ ***noun***

▸ PLANT **1** the part that grows up from the ground when a plant starts to grow; a new part that grows on plants or trees: *new green shoots* ◇ *bamboo shoots* ➲ VISUAL VOCAB page V9

▸ FILM/PHOTOGRAPHS **2** an occasion when sb takes professional photographs for a particular purpose or makes a film/movie: *a fashion shoot* ➲ see also PHOTO SHOOT

▸ FOR SPORT **3** (*especially BrE*) an occasion when a group of people hunt and shoot animals or birds for sport; the land where this happens

■ ***exclamation*** **1** (*NAmE*) used to show that you are annoyed when you do sth stupid or when sth goes wrong (to avoid saying 'shit'): *Shoot! I've forgotten my book!* **2** (*especially NAmE*) used to tell sb to say what they want to say: *You want to tell me something? OK, shoot!*

'shoot-'em-up *adj.* (*informal*) a **shoot-'em-up** computer game, etc. is one involving a lot of violence with guns

shoot·er /'ʃuːtə(r)/ *noun* **1** (especially in compounds) a person or weapon that shoots ➲ see also PEA-SHOOTER, SHARPSHOOTER, SIX-SHOOTER, TROUBLESHOOTER **2** (*informal*) a gun **3** (*NAmE*) (used especially in news reports) a person who uses a gun to kill people

shoot·ing 🔑 /'ʃuːtɪŋ/ *noun*
1 🔑 [C] a situation in which a person is shot with a gun: *Terrorist groups claimed responsibility for the shootings and bomb attacks.* ◇ *a serious shooting incident* **2** [U] the sport of shooting animals and birds with guns: *grouse shooting* **3** 🔑 [U] the process of filming a film/movie: *Shooting began early this year.*

'shooting gallery *noun* **1** a place where people shoot guns at objects for practice or to win prizes **2** (*especially NAmE*) a place where people go to take drugs

'shooting match *noun* an occasion when people or groups fight or attack each other
IDM **the whole 'shooting match** (*BrE, informal*) everything, or a situation which includes everything

ˌshooting 'star (also **ˌfalling 'star**) *noun* a small METEOR (= a piece of rock in outer space) that travels very fast and burns with a bright light as it enters the earth's atmosphere

'shooting stick *noun* a pointed stick that has a handle at the top which opens out to make a simple seat

'shoot-out *noun* a fight that is fought with guns until one side is killed or defeated ➲ see also PENALTY SHOOT-OUT

shop 🔑 /ʃɒp; *NAmE* ʃɑːp/ *noun, verb*

■ ***noun***

▸ WHERE YOU BUY STH **1** 🔑 [C] (*especially BrE*) a building or part of a building where you can buy goods or services: *a shoe shop* ◇ *There's a little gift shop around the corner.* ◇ (*BrE*) *a butcher's shop* ◇ (*NAmE*) *a butcher shop* ◇ (*BrE*) *I'm just going down* ***to the shops.*** *Can I get you anything?* ➲ COLLOCATIONS at SHOPPING ➲ VISUAL VOCAB page V2 ➲ see also BAKESHOP, BUCKET SHOP, COFFEE SHOP, CORNER SHOP, FACTORY SHOP

▸ FOR MAKING/REPAIRING THINGS **2** (also **work·shop**) [C] (especially in compounds) a place where things are made or repaired, especially part of a factory where a particular type of work is done: *a repair shop* ◇ *a paint shop* (= where cars are painted) ➲ see also BODY SHOP

▸ SHOPPING **3** [sing.] (*BrE, informal*) an act of going shopping, especially for food and other items needed in the house: *I* ***do a*** *weekly* ***shop*** *at the supermarket.*

▸ SCHOOL SUBJECT **4** (also **'shop class**) [U] (both *NAmE*) = INDUSTRIAL ARTS

▸ ROOM FOR TOOLS **5** (also **work·shop**) [C] (*NAmE*) a room in a house where tools are kept for making repairs to the house, building things out of wood, etc.

IDM **all 'over the shop** (*BrE, informal*) = ALL OVER THE PLACE at PLACE *n.* **ˌset up 'shop** to start a business ➲ more at BULL, HIT *v.*, MIND *v.*, SHUT *v.*, TALK *v.*

■ ***verb*** (-pp-)

▸ BUY **1** 🔑 [I] **~ (for sth)** to buy things in shops/stores: *to shop for food* ◇ *He likes to shop at the local market.* ◇ *She was determined to go out and* ***shop till she dropped.*** **2** 🔑 **go shopping** [I] to spend time going to shops/stores and looking for things to buy: *There should be plenty of time to go shopping before we leave New York.* ◇ *'Where's Mum?' 'She went shopping.'*

▸ TELL POLICE ABOUT SB **3** [T] **~ sb (to sb)** (*BrE, informal*) to give information to sb, especially to the police, about sb who has committed a crime: *He didn't expect his own mother to shop him to the police.*

PHR V **ˌshop a'round (for sth)** to compare the quality or prices of goods or services that are offered by different

S

shops/stores, companies, etc. so that you can choose the best: *Shop around for the best deal.*

shop·ahol·ic /ˌʃɒpəˈhɒlɪk; *NAmE* ˌʃɑːpəˈhɔːlɪk; -ˈhɑːl-/ *noun* (*informal*) a person who enjoys shopping very much and spends too much time or money doing it ▸ **shop·ahol·ic** *adj.*

ˈ**shop assistant** (also **as·sist·ant**) (both *BrE*) (*NAmE* ˈ**sales clerk, clerk**) *noun* a person whose job is to serve customers in a shop/store

ˈ**shop-bought** (*BrE*) (*NAmE* **store-bought**) *adj.* [only before noun] bought from a shop/store and not made at home: *shop-bought cakes*

shop·fit·ting /ˈʃɒpfɪtɪŋ; *NAmE* ˈʃɑːp-/ *noun* [U] the business of putting equipment and furniture into shops/stores ▸ **shop·fit·ter** *noun*

ˌ**shop** ˈ**floor** *noun* [sing.] **1** the area in a factory where the goods are made by the workers: *to work* ***on the shop floor*** **2** the workers in a factory, not the managers

shop·front /ˈʃɒpfrʌnt; *NAmE* ˈʃɑːp-/ (*BrE*) (*NAmE* **storefront**) *noun* the outside of a shop/store that faces the street

shop·house /ˈʃɒphaʊs; *NAmE* ˈʃɑːp-/ *noun* (in SE Asia) a shop that opens onto the street and is used as the owner's home

shop·keep·er /ˈʃɒpkiːpə(r); *NAmE* ˈʃɑːp-/ (also **store·keep·er** especially in *NAmE*) *noun* a person who owns or manages a shop/store, usually a small one

shop·lift·ing /ˈʃɒplɪftɪŋ; *NAmE* ˈʃɑːp-/ *noun* [U] the crime of stealing goods from a shop/store by deliberately leaving without paying for them ➲ COLLOCATIONS at SHOPPING ▸ **shop·lift** *verb* [I] **shop·lift·er** *noun*: *Shoplifters will be prosecuted.*

shop·lot /ˈʃɒplɒt; *NAmE* ˈʃɑːplɑːt/ *noun* (*SEAsianE*) the amount of space that a shop/store fills

shop·per /ˈʃɒpə(r); *NAmE* ˈʃɑːp-/ *noun* a person who buys goods from shops/stores: *The streets were full of Christmas shoppers.* ➲ see also MYSTERY SHOPPER, PERSONAL SHOPPER

shop·ping 0‑w /ˈʃɒpɪŋ; *NAmE* ˈʃɑːp-/ *noun* [U] **1** 0‑w the activity of going to shops/stores and buying things: *to* ***go shopping*** ◇ (*BrE*) *When shall I* ***do the shopping****?* ◇ (*BrE*) *We* ***do our shopping*** *on Saturdays.* ◇ *a shopping basket* ◇ *a shopping trolley* ◇ (*NAmE*) *a shopping cart* ➲ see also WINDOW-SHOPPING **2** 0‑w (*especially BrE*) the things that you have bought from shops/stores: *to put the shopping in the car*

S

ˈ**shopping arcade** *noun* = ARCADE (3)

ˈ**shopping bag** *noun* **1** a large, strong bag made of cloth, plastic, etc. used for carrying your shopping ➲ VISUAL VOCAB page V29 **2** (*NAmE*) (*BrE* ˈ**carrier bag, car·rier**) a paper or plastic bag for carrying shopping

ˈ**shopping centre** (*BrE*) (*NAmE* ˈ**shopping center**) *noun* a group of shops/stores built together, sometimes under one roof ➲ VISUAL VOCAB page V2

ˈ**shopping list** *noun* a list that you make of all the things that you need to buy when you go shopping: (*figurative*) *The union presented a shopping list of demands to the management.*

ˈ**shopping mall** *noun* (*especially NAmE*) = MALL

ˈ**shop-soiled** (*BrE*) (*NAmE* **shop·worn**) *adj.* (of goods) dirty or not in perfect condition because they have been in a shop/store for a long time: *a sale of shop-soiled goods at half price*

ˌ**shop** ˈ**steward** *noun* (*especially BrE*) a person who is elected by members of a TRADE/LABOR UNION in a factory or company to represent them in meetings with managers

ˈ**shop talk** *noun* [U] talk about your work or your business

ˌ**shop** ˈ**window** (*BrE*) (*NAmE* ˌ**store** ˈ**window**) (also **window**) *noun* the glass at the front of a shop/store and the area behind it where goods are shown to the public

Collocations

Shopping

Shopping

- **go/go out/be out** shopping
- **go to** (*especially BrE*) the shops/(*especially NAmE*) a store/(*especially NAmE*) the mall
- **do** (*BrE*) the shopping/(*especially NAmE*) the grocery shopping/a bit of window-shopping
- (*NAmE, informal*) **hit/hang out at** the mall
- **try on** clothes/shoes
- **indulge in** some retail therapy
- **go on** a spending spree
- **cut/cut back on/reduce** your spending
- **be/get caught** shoplifting
- **donate sth to/take sth to/find sth in** (*BrE*) a charity shop/(*NAmE*) a thrift store
- **buy/sell/find sth at** (*BrE*) a car boot sale/(*BrE*) a jumble sale/a garage sale/(*NAmE*) a yard sale
- **find/get/pick up** a bargain

At the shop/store

- **load/push/wheel** (*BrE*) a trolley/(*NAmE*) a cart
- **stand in/wait in** (*BrE*) the checkout queue/(*NAmE*) the checkout line
- (*NAmE*) **stand in line**/(*BrE*) **queue** at the checkout
- **bag** (*especially NAmE*) (your) groceries
- **pack (away)** (*especially BrE*) your shopping
- **stack/stock/restock** the shelves at a store (with sth)
- **be (found) on/appear on** supermarket/shop/store shelves
- **be in/have in/be out of/run out of** stock
- **deal with/help/serve** customers
- **run** a special promotion
- **be on** special offer

Buying goods

- **make/complete** a purchase
- **buy/purchase sth** online/by mail order
- **make/place/take** an order for sth
- **buy/order sth** in bulk/in advance
- **accept/take** credit cards
- **pay** (in) cash/by (credit/debit) card/(*BrE*) with a gift voucher/(*NAmE*) with a gift certificate
- **enter** your PIN number
- **ask for/get/obtain** a receipt
- **return/exchange** an item/a product
- **be entitled to/ask for/demand** a refund
- **compare** prices
- **offer (sb)/give (sb)/get/receive** a 30% discount

shop·worn /ˈʃɒpwɔːn; *NAmE* ˈʃɑːpwɔːrn/ (*NAmE*) (*BrE* ˈ**shop-soiled**) *adj.* (of goods) dirty or not in perfect condition because they have been in a shop/store for a long time: (*figurative*) *a shopworn argument* (= that is no longer new or useful)

shore /ʃɔː(r)/ *noun, verb*

▪ ***noun*** **1** [C, U] the land along the edge of the sea or ocean, a lake or another large area of water: *a* ***rocky/sandy shore*** ◇ *to swim from the boat* ***to the shore*** ◇ *a house* ***on the shores of*** *the lake* ◇ *The ship was anchored* ***off shore***. **2 shores** [pl.] (especially *literary*) a country, especially one with a coast: *foreign shores* ◇ *What brings you to these shores?*

▪ ***verb***

PHR V ˌ**shore sth**↔ˈ**up 1** to support part of a building or other large structure by placing large pieces of wood or metal against or under it so that it does not fall down **2** to help to support sth that is weak or going to fail

shore·line /ˈʃɔːlaɪn; *NAmE* ˈʃɔːrl-/ *noun* [usually sing.] the edge of the sea, the ocean or a lake: *a rocky shoreline* ◇ *The road follows the shoreline for a few miles.*

shorn *past part.* of SHEAR

short 0‑w /ʃɔːt; *NAmE* ʃɔːrt/ *adj., adv., noun, verb*

■ ***adj.*** (short·er, short·est)

▸ LENGTH/DISTANCE **1** 0‑w measuring or covering a small length or distance, or a smaller length or distance than usual: *He had short curly hair.* ➲ VISUAL VOCAB page V49: *a short walk* ◇ *a short skirt* OPP **long**

▸ HEIGHT **2** 0‑w (of a person) small in height: *She was short and dumpy.* OPP **tall**

▸ TIME **3** 0‑w lasting or taking a small amount of time or less time than usual: *I'm going to France for a short break.* ◇ *Which is the shortest day of the year?* ◇ *a short book* (= taking a short time to read, because it does not have many pages) ◇ *She has a very **short memory*** (= remembers only things that have happened recently). ◇ (*informal*) ***Life's too short*** *to sit around moping.* ◇ *It was all over in a relatively **short space of time**.* OPP **long** **4** [only before noun] (of a period of time) seeming to have passed very quickly: *Just two short years ago he was the best player in the country.* OPP **long**

▸ NOT ENOUGH **5** 0‑w [not before noun] **~** (**of sth**) not having enough of sth; lacking sth: *I'm afraid I'm a little short* (= of money) *this month.* ◇ *She is not short of excuses when things go wrong.* **6 ~ on sth** (*informal*) lacking or not having enough of a particular quality: *He was a big strapping guy but short on brains.* **7** 0‑w [not before noun] not easily available; not supplying as much as you need: *Money was short at that time.* **8** [not before noun] **~** (**of sth**) less than the number, amount or distance mentioned or needed: *Her last throw was only three centimetres short of the world record.* ◇ *The team was five players short.* ◇ *She was just short of her 90th birthday when she died.*

▸ OF BREATH **9 ~ of breath** having difficulty breathing, for example because of illness

▸ NAME/WORD **10 ~ for sth** being a shorter form of a name or word: *Call me Jo—it's short for Joanna.* ◇ *file transfer protocol or FTP **for short***

▸ RUDE **11** [not before noun] **~** (**with sb**) (of a person) speaking to sb using few words in a way that seems rude: *I'm sorry I was short with you earlier—I had other things on my mind.*

▸ VOWEL **12** (*phonetics*) a **short** vowel is pronounced for a shorter time than other vowels: *Compare the short vowel in 'full' and the long vowel in 'fool'.* OPP **long** ➲ see also SHORTLY ▸ **short·ness** *noun* [U]: *She suffered from shortness of breath.*

IDM **a ˌbrick short of a ˈload, two ˌsandwiches short of a ˈpicnic, etc.** (*informal*) (of a person) stupid; not very intelligent **get the short end of the ˈstick** (*NAmE*) (*BrE* **ˌdraw the short ˈstraw**) to be the person in a group who is chosen or forced to perform an unpleasant duty or task **give sb/sth/get short ˈshrift** to give sb/get little attention or sympathy **have/be on a short ˈfuse** to have a tendency to get angry quickly and easily: *You may find your temper on a short fuse when confronting your teenager.* **in ˌshort ˈorder** quickly and without trouble **in the ˈshort run** concerning the immediate future: *In the short run, unemployment may fall.* **in ˌshort supˈply** not existing in large enough quantities to satisfy demand: *Basic foodstuffs were in short supply.* ◇ *Sunshine will be in short supply for the west coast.* **little/nothing short of ˈsth** used when you are saying that sth is almost true, or is equal to sth: *Last year's figures were little short of disastrous.* ◇ *The transformation has been nothing short of a miracle.* **make short ˈwork of sth/sb** to defeat, deal with sth/sb quickly: *Liverpool made short work of the opposition* (= in a football/SOCCER game). ◇ *He made short work of his lunch* (= ate it quickly). **ˌshort and ˈsweet** (*informal*) pleasant but not lasting a long time: *We haven't much time so I'll keep it short and sweet.* ➲ more at DRAW *v.*, LIFE *n.*, LONG *adj.*, MEASURE *n.*, NOTICE *n.*, TERM *n.*, THICK *adj.*

■ ***adv.*** (short·er, short·est) **1** if you **go short of** or **run short of** sth, you do not have enough of it: *I'd never let you go short of anything.* ◇ *Mothers regularly go short of food to ensure their children have enough.* ◇ *They had **run short of*** (= used most of their supply of) *fuel.* **2** not as far as you need or expect: *All too often you pitch the ball short.* **3** before the time expected or arranged; before the natural time: *a career tragically **cut short** by illness* ◇ *I'm afraid I'm going to have to **stop** you **short** there, as time is running out.*

IDM **be caught ˈshort** (*BrE* also **be taken ˈshort**) **1** (*BrE, informal*) to suddenly feel an urgent need to go to the toilet/bathroom **2** to be put at a disadvantage **come ˈshort** (*SAfrE, informal*) to have an accident; to get into trouble **fall ˈshort of sth** to fail to reach the standard that you expected or need: *The hotel fell far short of their expectations.* **short of** (**doing**) **sth** without sth; without doing sth; unless sth happens: *Short of a miracle, we're certain to lose.* ◇ *Short of asking her to leave* (= and we don't want to do that) *there's not a lot we can do about the situation.* **pull, bring, etc. sb up ˈshort** to make sb suddenly stop what they are doing: *I was brought up short by a terrible thought.* ➲ more at SELL *v.*, STOP *v.*

■ ***noun*** (*informal*) ➲ see also SHORTS **1** (*BrE*) a small strong alcoholic drink, for example of WHISKY **2** a short film/movie, especially one that is shown before the main film **3** (*informal*) = SHORT CIRCUIT

IDM **in ˈshort** in a few words: *His novels belong to a great but vanished age. They are, in short, old-fashioned.* ➲ more at LONG *adj.*

■ ***verb*** [I, T] **~** (**sth**) (**out**) (*informal*) = SHORT-CIRCUIT

short·age /ˈʃɔːtɪdʒ; *NAmE* ˈʃɔːrt-/ *noun* [C, U] a situation when there is not enough of the people or things that are needed: ***food/housing/water shortages*** ◇ *a shortage of funds* ◇ ***There is no shortage of*** (= there are plenty of) *things to do in the town.*

ˈshort-arse (*BrE*) (*US* **ˈshort-ass**) *noun* (*slang, disapproving*) a person who is not very tall

ˌshort ˌback and ˈsides *noun* [sing.] (*BrE, old-fashioned*) a way of cutting a man's hair so that the hair is very short at the sides and the back of the head

short·bread /ˈʃɔːtbred; *NAmE* ˈʃɔːrt-/ (*BrE* also **short·cake**) *noun* [U] a rich crisp biscuit/cookie made with flour, sugar and a lot of butter

short·cake /ˈʃɔːtkeɪk; *NAmE* ˈʃɔːrt-/ *noun* [U] **1** (*BrE*) = SHORTBREAD **2** a cake with a PASTRY base and cream and fruit on top: *strawberry shortcake*

ˌshort-ˈchange *verb* [often passive] **1 ~ sb** to give back less than the correct amount of money to sb who has paid for sth with more than the exact price: *I think I've been short-changed at the bar.* **2 ~ sb** to treat sb unfairly by not giving them what they have earned or deserve

ˌshort ˈcircuit (also *informal* **short**) *noun* a failure in an electrical CIRCUIT, when electricity travels along the wrong route because of damaged wires or a fault in the connections between the wires

ˌshort-ˈcircuit (also *informal* **short**) *verb* **1** [I, T] **~** (**sth**) to have a short circuit; to make sth have a short circuit: *The wires had short-circuited and burnt out.* **2** [T] **~ sth** to succeed in doing sth more quickly than usual, without going through all the usual processes

short·com·ing /ˈʃɔːtkʌmɪŋ; *NAmE* ˈʃɔːrt-/ *noun* [usually pl.] a fault in sb's character, a plan, a system, etc. SYN **defect**

short·crust pastry /ˌʃɔːtkrʌst ˈpeɪstri; *NAmE* ˌʃɔːrt-/ *noun* [U] a type of PASTRY that CRUMBLES easily, used for making PIES, etc.

ˌshort ˈcut (also **ˈshort cut**) *noun* **1** a quicker or shorter way of getting to a place: *You can **take a short cut** across the field.* **2** a way of doing sth that is quicker than the usual way: *There are no short cuts to economic recovery.*

short·en /ˈʃɔːtn; *NAmE* ˈʃɔːrtn/ *verb* [T, I] to make sth shorter; to become shorter: **~** (**sth**) *Injury problems could shorten his career.* ◇ *a shortened version of the game* ◇ *In November the temperatures drop and the days shorten.* ◇ **~ sth to sth** *Her name's Katherine, generally shortened to Kay.* OPP **lengthen**

short·en·ing /ˈʃɔːtnɪŋ; *NAmE* ˈʃɔːrt-/ *noun* [U] fat that is used for making PASTRY

S

short·fall /ˈʃɔːtfɔːl; *NAmE* ˈʃɔːrt-/ *noun* **~ (in sth)** if there is **a shortfall in** sth, there is less of it than you need or expect SYN **deficit**

short·hair /ˈʃɔːtheə(r); *NAmE* ˈʃɔːrther/ *noun* a breed of cat with short hair ➲ compare LONGHAIR

short·hand /ˈʃɔːthænd; *NAmE* ˈʃɔːrt-/ *noun* **1** (*NAmE* also **sten·og·raphy**) [U] a quick way of writing using special signs or abbreviations, used especially to record what sb is saying: *typing and shorthand* ◇ *to take sth down* ***in shorthand*** ◇ *a shorthand typist* **2** [U, C, usually sing.] **~ (for sth)** a shorter way of saying or referring to sth, which may not be as accurate as the more complicated way of saying it

ˌshort-ˈhanded *adj.* [not usually before noun] not having as many workers or people who can help as you need SYN **short-staffed**

ˈshort-haul *adj.* [only before noun] that involves transporting people or goods over short distances, especially by plane OPP **long-haul**

short·horn /ˈʃɔːthɔːn; *NAmE* ˈʃɔːrthɔːrn/ *noun* a breed of cow with short horns

shortie = SHORTY

short·list /ˈʃɔːtlɪst; *NAmE* ˈʃɔːrt-/ *noun, verb*

■ ***noun*** [usually sing.] a small number of candidates for a job, etc, who have been chosen from all the people who applied: *to draw up a shortlist* ◇ *a shortlist for a literary prize* ◇ *She is* ***on my shortlist*** *of great singers.*

■ ***verb*** [usually passive] **~ sb/sth (for sth)** (*BrE*) to put sb/sth on a shortlist for a job, prize, etc: *Candidates who are shortlisted for interview will be contacted by the end of the week.*

ˌshort-ˈlived *adj.* lasting only for a short time

short·ly 0-w /ˈʃɔːtli; *NAmE* ˈʃɔːrt-/ *adv.*
1 0-w a short time; not long: *She arrived shortly after us.* ◇ *I saw him shortly before he died.* **2** 0-w soon: *I'll be ready shortly.* **3** in an angry and impatient way SYN **sharply**

ˌshort-order ˈcook *noun* a person who works in a restaurant cooking food that can be prepared quickly

ˌshort-ˈrange *adj.* [usually before noun] **1** (of weapons) designed to travel only over short distances: *short-range missiles* **2** (of plans, etc.) connected with a short period of time in the future: *a short-range weather forecast* ➲ compare LONG-RANGE

shorts /ʃɔːts; *NAmE* ʃɔːrts/ *noun* [pl.] **1** short trousers/ pants that end above or at the knee: *a pair of tennis shorts* ◇ *He was wearing a T-shirt and shorts.* ➲ VISUAL VOCAB page V51 **2** (*NAmE*) = BOXER SHORTS

S

ˌshort-ˈsighted *adj.* **1** (*especially BrE*) (*NAmE* usually **near·sighted**) able to see things clearly only if they are very close to you OPP **long-sighted** **2** not thinking carefully about the possible effects of sth or what might happen in the future: *a short-sighted policy* ▶ **ˌshort ˈsight** (also **ˌshort-ˈsighted·ness**) *noun* [U]: *She suffered from short sight.* ◇ *Many people accused the government of short-sightedness.* **ˌshort-ˈsighted·ly** *adv.*

ˌshort-ˈstaffed *adj.* [not usually before noun] having fewer members of staff than you need or usually have SYN **short-handed** ➲ see also UNDERSTAFFED

ˌshort-ˈstay *adj.* [only before noun] (*BrE*) (of a place) where you only stay for a short time: *a short-stay car park*

ˌshort ˈstory *noun* a story, usually about imaginary characters and events, that is short enough to be read from beginning to end without stopping

ˌshort ˈtemper *noun* [sing.] a tendency to become angry very quickly and easily ▶ **ˌshort-ˈtempered** *adj.*

ˌshort-ˈterm *adj.* [usually before noun] lasting a short time; designed only for a short period of time in the future: *a short-term loan* ◇ *to find work on a short-term contract* ◇ *short-term plans* ◇ *a short-term solution to the problem* ◇ *His* ***short-term memory*** (= the ability to remember things that happened a short time ago) *is failing.* ➲ compare LONG-TERM

ˌshort-ˈtermism *noun* [U] a way of thinking or planning that is concerned with the advantages or profits you could have now, rather than the effects in the future

ˌshort ˈtime *noun* [U] (*BrE*) if workers are put on **short time**, they work for fewer hours than usual, because there is not enough work to do or not enough money to pay them

ˌshort ˈwave *noun* [C, U] (*abbr.* **SW**) a radio wave that has a FREQUENCY between 3 and 30 MEGAHERTZ ➲ compare LONG WAVE, MEDIUM WAVE

shorty (also **shortie**) /ˈʃɔːti; *NAmE* ˈʃɔːrti/ *noun* (*pl.* **-ies**) (*informal*) a person who is shorter than average

Sho·shone /ʃəʊˈʃəʊni; *NAmE* ʃoʊˈʃoʊni/ *noun* (*pl.* **Sho·shone** or **Sho·shones**) a member of a Native American people many of whom now live in the US state of Wyoming

shot 0-w /ʃɒt; *NAmE* ʃɑːt/ *noun, adj.* ➲ see also SHOOT, SHOT, SHOT *v.*

■ ***noun***

▸ WITH GUN **1** 0-w [C] **~ (at sb/sth)** the act of firing a gun; the sound this makes: *The man fired several shots from his pistol.* ◇ *Someone* ***took a shot at*** *the car.* ◇ *We heard some shots in the distance.* ➲ see also GUNSHOT, POTSHOT **2** [C] **a good, bad, etc. ~** a person who shoots a gun in a particular way (well, badly, etc.)

▸ BULLETS **3** (also **ˌlead ˈshot**) [U] a large number of small metal balls that you fire together from a SHOTGUN ➲ see also BUCKSHOT **4** [C] (*pl.* **shot**) a large stone or metal ball that was shot from a CANNON or large gun in the past

▸ REMARK/ACTION **5** [C] a remark or an action that is usually one of a series, and is aimed against sb/sth that you are arguing or competing with: *This statement was* ***the opening shot*** *in the argument.* ◇ *The supermarket* ***fired the first shot*** *in a price war today.*

▸ ATTEMPT **6** [C, usually sing.] **~ (at sth/at doing sth)** (*informal*) the act of trying to do or achieve sth: *The team are looking good for a shot at the title.* ◇ *I've never produced a play before but I'll* ***have a shot at*** *it.* ◇ *I'm willing to* ***give it a shot.*** ◇ *Just* ***give it your best shot*** (= try as hard as you can) *and you'll be fine.*

▸ IN SPORT **7** 0-w [C] the action of hitting, kicking or throwing the ball in order to score a point or goal in a game: *Taylor scored with a low shot into the corner of the net.* ◇ *Good shot!* **8** (often **the shot**) [sing.] the heavy ball that is used in the sports competition called THE SHOT-PUT

▸ PHOTOGRAPH **9** [C] a photograph: *I got some good shots of people at the party.* ➲ see also MUGSHOT, SNAPSHOT ➲ SYNONYMS at PHOTOGRAPH

▸ SCENE IN FILM/MOVIE **10** [C] a scene in a film/movie that is filmed continuously by one camera: *the opening shot of a character walking across a desert*

▸ DRUG **11** [C] (*informal, especially NAmE*) a small amount of a drug that is put into your body using a SYRINGE SYN **injection**: *a flu shot* (= to protect you against flu) ◇ *a shot of morphine*

▸ DRINK **12** [C] (*informal*) a small amount of a drink, especially a strong alcoholic one: *a shot of whisky*

▸ OF SPACECRAFT **13** [C] an occasion when a SPACECRAFT is sent into space: *The space shot was shown live on television.*

▸ HORSE/DOG IN RACE **14** [sing.] (used with numbers) a horse, dog, etc. that has the particular chance of winning a race that is mentioned: *The horse is a 10–1 shot.* HELP You will find other compounds ending in **shot** at their place in the alphabet.

IDM **like a ˈshot** (*informal*) very quickly and without hesitating: *If I had the chance to go there, I'd go like a shot.* **a shot across the/sb's ˈbows** something that you say or do as a warning to sb about what might happen if they do not change, etc. **a shot in the ˈarm** something that gives sb/ sth the help or encouragement they need ➲ more at BIG *adj.*, CALL *v.*, DARK *n.*, LONG *adj.*, PARTING *adj.*

■ ***adj.*** **1 ~ (with sth)** (of cloth, hair, etc.) having another colour showing through or mixed with the main colour: *shot silk* **2** [not before noun] (*informal*) in a very bad condition; destroyed: *The brakes on this car are shot.* ◇ *I'm shot—I'm too old for this job.* ◇ *After the accident his nerves were* ***shot to pieces.***

IDM **be/get ˈshot of sb/sth** (*BrE, informal*) to get rid of sb/ sth so you no longer have the problems they cause **shot**

through with sth containing a lot of a particular colour, quality or feature: *a voice shot through with emotion*

shot·gun /ˈʃɒtɡʌn; *NAmE* ˈʃɑːt-/ *noun* a long gun that fires a lot of small metal bullets (called SHOT) and is used especially for shooting birds or animals ➲ see also SAWN-OFF SHOTGUN IDM see RIDE *v.*

ˌshotgun ˈwedding (also **ˌshotgun ˈmarriage**) *noun* (*old-fashioned, informal*) a wedding that has to take place quickly because the woman is pregnant

shot·making /ˈʃɒtmeɪkɪŋ; *NAmE* ˈʃɑːt-/ *noun* [U] (in GOLF, TENNIS, etc.) a way of playing in which a player takes risks in order to win more points

Shoto·kan /ʃəʊˈtəʊkæn; *NAmE* ʃoʊˈtoʊ-/ *noun* [U] (from *Japanese*) a popular form of KARATE

the ˈshot-put *noun* [sing.] (also **ˈshot-putting**, **ˌputting the ˈshot**) the event or sport of throwing a heavy metal ball (called a SHOT) as far as possible

Grammar Point

should / ought / had better

- **Should** and **ought to** are both used to say that something is the best thing or the right thing to do, but **should** is much more common: *You should take the baby to the doctor's.* ◇ *I ought to give up smoking.* In questions, **should** is usually used instead of **ought to**: *Should we call the doctor?*
- **Had better** can also be used to say what is the best thing to do in a situation that is happening now: *We'd better hurry or we'll miss the train.*
- You form the past by using **should have** or **ought to have**: *She should have asked for some help.* ◇ *You ought to have been more careful.*
- The forms **should not** or **shouldn't** (and **ought not to** or **oughtn't to**, which are rare in *NAmE* and formal in *BrE*) are used to say that something is a bad idea or the wrong thing to do: *You shouldn't drive so fast.*
- The forms **should not have** or **shouldn't have** and, much less frequently, **ought not to have** or **oughtn't to have** are used to talk about the past: *I'm sorry, I shouldn't have lost my temper.*

should 0▬ /ʃəd; *strong form* ʃʊd/ *modal verb* (*negative* **should not**, *short form* **shouldn't** /ˈʃʊdnt/)
1 0▬ used to show what is right, appropriate, etc, especially when criticizing sb's actions: *You shouldn't drink and drive.* ◇ *He should have been more careful.* ◇ *A present for me? You* ***shouldn't have!*** (= used to thank sb politely) **2** 0▬ used for giving or asking for advice: *You should stop worrying about it* ◇ *Should I call him and apologize?* ◇ *I should wait a little longer,* ***if I were you.*** ◇ (*ironic*) *'She doesn't think she'll get a job.' 'She should worry, with all her qualifications* (= she does not need to worry).*'* **3** 0▬ used to say that you expect sth is true or will happen: *We should arrive before dark.* ◇ *I should have finished the book by Friday.* ◇ *The roads should be less crowded today.* **4** 0▬ used to say that sth that was expected has not happened: *It should be snowing now, according to the weather forecast.* ◇ *The bus should have arrived ten minutes ago.* **5** (*BrE, formal*) used after *I* or *we* instead of *would* for describing what you would do if sth else happened first: *If I were asked to work on Sundays, I should resign.* **6** (*formal*) used to refer to a possible event or situation: *If you should change your mind, do let me know.* ◇ *In case you should need any help, here's my number.* ◇ *Should anyone call* (= if anyone calls), *please tell them I'm busy.* **7** 0▬ used as the past form of *shall* when reporting what sb has said: *He asked me what time he should come.* (= His words were: 'What time shall I come?') ◇ (*BrE, formal*) *I said (that) I should be glad to help.* **8** 0▬ (*BrE*) used after *that* when sth is suggested or arranged: *She recommended that I should take some time off.* ◇ *In order that training should be effective it must be planned systematically.* HELP In both *NAmE* and *BrE* this idea can be expressed without 'should': *She recommended that I take some time off.* ◇ *In order that training be effective...* **9** used after *that* after many adjectives that describe feelings: *I'm anxious that we should allow plenty of time.* ◇ *I find it astonishing that he should be so rude to you.* **10** (*BrE, formal*) used with *I* and *we* in polite requests: *I should like to call my lawyer.* ◇ *We should be grateful for your help.* **11** 0▬ used with *I* and *we* to give opinions that you are not certain about: *I should imagine it will take about three hours.* ◇ *'Is this enough food for everyone?' '****I should think so.****'* ◇ *'Will it matter?' '****I shouldn't think so.****'* **12** used for expressing strong agreement: *'I know it's expensive but it will last for years.' '****I should hope so too!****'* ◇ *'Nobody will oppose it.' '****I should think not!****'* **13 why, how, who, what ~ sb/sth do** used to refuse sth or to show that you are annoyed at a request; used to express surprise about an event or a situation: *Why should I help him? He's never done anything for me.* ◇ *How should I know where you've left your bag?* ◇ *I got on the bus and who should be sitting in front of me but Tony!* **14** used to tell sb that sth would amuse or surprise them if they saw or experienced it: *You should have seen her face when she found out!* ➲ note at MODAL

Grammar Point

should / would

- In modern English, the traditional difference between **should** and **would** in reported sentences, conditions, requests, etc. has disappeared and **should** is not used very much at all. In spoken English the short form **'d** is usually used: *I said I'd (I would) be late.* ◇ *He'd (he would) have liked to have been an actor.* ◇ *I'd (I would) really prefer tea.*
- The main use of **should** now is to tell somebody what they ought to do, to give advice, or to add emphasis: *We should really go and visit them soon.* ◇ *You should have seen it!*

shoul·der 0▬ /ˈʃəʊldə(r); *NAmE* ˈʃoʊ-/ *noun, verb*
■ ***noun***
▸ PART OF BODY **1** 0▬ [C] either of the two parts of the body between the top of each arm and the neck: *He slung the bag over his shoulder.* ◇ *She tapped him on the shoulder.* ◇ *He looked back over his shoulder.* ◇ *She* ***shrugged her shoulders*** (= showing that she didn't know or care). ◇ *an* ***off-the-shoulder*** *dress* ◇ *He carried the child on his shoulders.* ➲ COLLOCATIONS at PHYSICAL ➲ VISUAL VOCAB page V48
▸ -SHOULDERED **2** (in adjectives) having the type of shoulders mentioned: *broad-shouldered* ➲ see also ROUND-SHOULDERED
▸ CLOTHING **3** 0▬ [C] the part of a piece of clothing that covers the shoulder: *a jacket with padded shoulders*
▸ MEAT **4** [U, C] **~ (of sth)** meat from the top part of one of the front legs of an animal that has four legs
▸ OF MOUNTAIN/BOTTLE, ETC. **5** [C] **~ (of sth)** a part of sth, such as a bottle or mountain, that is shaped like a shoulder: *The village lay just around the shoulder of the hill.*
▸ SIDE OF ROAD **6** [C] (*NAmE*) an area of ground at the side of a road where vehicles can stop in an emergency: *No shoulder for next 5 miles.* ➲ see also HARD SHOULDER, SOFT SHOULDER
IDM **be looking over your ˈshoulder** to be anxious and have the feeling that sb is going to do sth unpleasant or harmful to you **on sb's shoulders** if blame, GUILT, etc. is **on sb's shoulders**, they must take responsibility for it **put your shoulder to the ˈwheel** to start working very hard at a particular task **a shoulder to ˈcry on** used to describe a person who listens to your problems and gives you sympathy **ˌshoulder to ˈshoulder (with sb) 1** physically close to sb **2** as one group that has the same aims, opinions, etc. ➲ more at CHIP *n.*, COLD *adj.*, HEAD *n.*, OLD, RUB *v.*, STRAIGHT *adv.*
■ ***verb***
▸ ACCEPT RESPONSIBILITY **1** [T] **~ sth** to accept the responsibility for sth: *to* ***shoulder the responsibility/blame*** *for sth*

S

◇ *women who shoulder the double burden of childcare and full-time work*

▸ PUSH WITH SHOULDER **2** [T, I] to push forward with your shoulder in order to get somewhere **~ your way + adv./prep.**: *He shouldered his way through the crowd and went after her.* ◇ **+ adv./prep.** *She shouldered past a woman with a screaming baby.* **3** [T] **~ sb/sth + adv./prep.** to push sb/sth out of your way with your shoulder: *He shouldered the man aside.*

▸ CARRY ON SHOULDER **4** [T] **~ sth** to carry sth on your shoulder: *She shouldered her bag and set off home.*

'shoulder bag *noun* a bag, especially a HANDBAG, that is carried over the shoulder with a long narrow piece of leather, etc. ➲ VISUAL VOCAB page V52

'shoulder blade *noun* either of the two large flat bones at the top of the back SYN **scapula** ➲ VISUAL VOCAB page V48

ˌshoulder-'high *adj.* as high as a person's shoulders: *a shoulder-high wall* ▸ **ˌshoulder-'high** *adv.*: *They carried him shoulder-high through the crowd.*

'shoulder-length *adj.* (especially of hair) long enough to reach your shoulders ➲ VISUAL VOCAB page V49

'shoulder pad *noun* [usually pl.] **1** a small piece of thick cloth that is sewn into the shoulder of a dress, jacket, etc. to make a person's shoulders look bigger **2** a piece of hard plastic that people wear under their shirts to protect their shoulders when playing AMERICAN FOOTBALL, ICE HOCKEY, etc. ➲ VISUAL VOCAB page V36

'shoulder strap *noun* **1** a strip of cloth on a dress or other piece of clothing that goes over your shoulder from the front to the back **2** a long strip of cloth, leather, etc. that is attached to a bag so that you can carry it over your shoulder

'shoulder surfing *noun* [U] (*informal*) the practice of watching a person who is getting money from a machine, filling out a form, etc, in order to find out their personal information

shout 0‑ /ʃaʊt/ *verb, noun*

■ *verb* **1** 0‑ [I, T] to say sth in a loud voice; to speak loudly/angrily to sb: *Stop shouting and listen!* ◇ **~ for sth** *I shouted for help but nobody came.* ◇ **~ at sb** *Then he started shouting and swearing at her.* ◇ **~ at sb to do sth** *She shouted at him to shut the gate.* ◇ **~ sth (at/to sb)** *to shout abuse/encouragement/orders* ◇ **~ that...** *He shouted that he couldn't swim.* ◇ **~ yourself + adj.** *She shouted herself hoarse, cheering on the team.* ◇ **+ speech** *'Run!' he shouted.* **2** 0‑ [I] **~ (out)** to make a loud noise: *She shouted out in pain when she tried to move her leg.* **3** [I, T] (*AustralE, NZE*) to buy drinks or food for sb in a bar, restaurant, etc: *I'll shout—what are you drinking?* ◇ **~ (sb) sth** *Who's going to shout me a drink?*

PHR V **ˌshout sb↔'down** to shout so that sb who is speaking cannot be heard: *The speaker was shouted down by a group of protesters.* **ˌshout sth↔'out** to say sth in a loud voice so that it can be clearly heard: *Don't shout out all the answers.* ◇ **+ speech** *'I'm over here!' I shouted out.*

■ *noun* **1** 0‑ a loud cry of anger, fear, excitement, etc: *angry shouts* ◇ *a shout of anger* ◇ *I heard her warning shout too late.* **2** (*BrE, informal*) a person's turn to buy drinks: *What are you drinking? It's my shout.*

IDM **be ˌin with a 'shout (of sth/of doing sth)** (*informal*) to have a good chance of winning sth or of achieving sth **give sb a 'shout** (*informal*) to tell sb sth: *Give me a shout when you're ready.*

shout·ing /'ʃaʊtɪŋ/ *noun* [U] loud cries from a number of people: *Didn't you hear all the shouting?*

IDM **be all over bar the 'shouting** (*BrE*) (of an activity or a competition) to be almost finished or decided, so that there is no doubt about the final result **within 'shouting distance** (*especially NAmE*) (*BrE* also **within 'spitting distance (of sth)**) (*informal*) very close

'shouting match *noun* an argument or a disagreement when people shout loudly at each other

Synonyms

shout

yell • cry • scream • cheer • bellow • raise your voice

These words all mean to say sth in a very loud voice.

shout to say sth in a loud voice; to speak loudly and often angrily to sb: *Stop shouting and listen!* ◇ *'Run!' he shouted.*

yell to shout loudly, for example because you are angry, excited, frightened or in pain: *She yelled at the boy to get down from the wall.*

cry (*rather formal* or *literary*) to shout loudly: *She ran over to the window and cried for help.*

scream to shout sth in a loud high voice because you are afraid, angry or excited: *He screamed at me to stop.*

cheer (especially of a crowd of people) to shout loudly to show support or praise for sb, or to give them encouragement: *We all cheered as the team came onto the field.*

bellow to shout in a loud deep voice, especially because you are angry: *'Quiet!' the teacher bellowed.*

raise your voice to speak loudly to sb, especially because you are angry: *She never once raised her voice to us.*

PATTERNS

- to shout/yell/cry/raise your voice **to** sb
- to shout/yell/scream/bellow **at** sb
- to shout/yell/cry out/scream/bellow **in** pain/anguish/rage, etc.
- to shout/cry out/scream **for** joy/excitement/delight, etc.
- to shout/yell/cry out/scream **with** excitement/triumph, etc.
- to shout/yell/scream/bellow at sb **to do sth**
- to shout/yell/scream **abuse**
- to shout/yell/cry/scream **for help**

'shout-out *noun* (*informal, especially NAmE*) a public expression of thanks or welcome: *This is a shout-out to all our sponsors and advertisers.*

shouty /'ʃaʊti/ *adj.* (*informal*) doing or involving a lot of shouting: *a shouty conversation on the stairs*

shove /ʃʌv/ *verb, noun*

■ *verb* **1** [I, T] to push sb/sth in a rough way: *The crowd was* ***pushing and shoving*** *to get a better view.* ◇ **+ adv./prep.** *The door wouldn't open no matter how hard she shoved.* ◇ **~ sb/sth (+ adv./prep.)** *He shoved her down the stairs.* **2** [T] **~ sth (+ adv./prep.)** (*informal*) to put sth somewhere roughly or carelessly: *She shoved the book into her bag and hurried off.* ◇ *He came over and shoved a piece of paper into my hand.* ◇ *Shove your suitcase under the bed.*

IDM **'shove it** (*informal, especially NAmE*) used to say rudely that you will not accept or do sth: *'The boss wants that report now.' 'Yeah? Tell him he can shove it.'*

PHR V **ˌshove 'off** (*BrE, informal*) used to tell sb rudely to go away **ˌshove 'up** (*BrE, informal*) to move in order to make a space for sb to sit down beside you: *Shove up! Jan wants to sit down.*

■ *noun* [usually sing.] a strong push: *You have to* ***give*** *the door* ***a shove*** *or it won't close.* IDM see PUSH *n.*

shovel /'ʃʌvl/ *noun, verb*

■ *noun* **1** a tool with a long handle and a broad blade with curved edges, used for moving earth, snow, sand, etc: *workmen with picks and shovels* ◇ (*NAmE*) *The children took their* ***pails and shovels*** *to the beach.* ➲ VISUAL VOCAB page V16 ➲ compare SPADE **2** the part of a large machine or vehicle that digs or moves earth

■ *verb* (-ll-, *US* -l-) **~ sth (+ adv./prep.)** to lift and move earth, stones, coal, etc. with a shovel: *A gang of workmen were shovelling rubble onto a truck.* ◇ *They went out in freezing conditions to shovel snow.* ◇ (*NAmE*) *to* ***shovel the sidewalk/driveway*** (= to remove snow) ◇ (*figurative*) *He sat at the table, shovelling food into his mouth.*

S

shovel·ful /ˈʃʌvlfʊl/ *noun* the amount that a shovel can hold

show 🔑 /ʃəʊ; *NAmE* ʃoʊ/ *verb, noun*

■ ***verb*** (**showed**, **shown** /ʃəʊn; *NAmE* ʃoʊn/ or, rarely, **showed**)

▸ MAKE CLEAR **1** 🔑 [T] to make sth clear; to prove sth: **~ (that)...** *The figures clearly show that her claims are false.* ◇ **~ sb that...** *Market research has shown us that people want quality, not just low prices.* ◇ **~ sth** *a report showing the company's current situation* ◇ **~ sb/sth to be/have sth** *His new book shows him to be a first-rate storyteller.* ◇ **~ (sb) how, what, etc...** *This shows how people are influenced by TV advertisements.* ➲ LANGUAGE BANK at ILLUSTRATE

▸ LET SB SEE STH **2** 🔑 [T] to let sb see sth: **~ sth** *You have to show your ticket as you go in.* ◇ **~ sth to sb** *If there's a letter from France please show it to me.* ◇ *Have you shown your work to anyone?* ◇ **~ sb sth** *Have you shown anyone your work?*

▸ TEACH **3** 🔑 [T] to help sb to do sth by letting them watch you do it or by explaining it: **~ sth to sb** *She showed the technique to her students.* ◇ **~ sb sth** *She showed her students the technique.* ◇ *Can you show me how to do it?*

▸ POINT **4** 🔑 [T] **~ sb sth** to point to sth so that sb can see where or what it is: *He showed me our location on the map.* ◇ **~ sb which, what, etc...** *Show me which picture you drew.*

▸ GUIDE **5** 🔑 [T] to lead or guide sb to a place: **~ sb + adv./prep.** *The attendant showed us to our seats.* ◇ *We were shown into the waiting room.* ◇ **~ sb sth** *I'll go first and **show** you **the way**.* ➲ SYNONYMS at TAKE

▸ QUALITY/BEHAVIOUR/FEELING **6** 🔑 [T] to make it clear that you have a particular quality: **~ sth** *to show great courage* ◇ **~ yourself + adj.** *She had shown herself unable to deal with money.* ◇ **~ yourself to be/have sth** *He has shown himself to be ready to make compromises.* ◇ **~ that...** *He has shown that he is ready to make compromises.* **7** 🔑 [T] to behave in a particular way towards sb: **~ sth (for/to sb)** *They showed no respect for their parents.* ◇ **~ sb sth** *They showed their parents no respect.* **8** 🔑 [I, T] if a feeling or quality **shows**, or if you **show** it, people can see it: *Fear showed in his eyes.* ◇ *She tried not to let her disappointment show.* ◇ *She's nearly forty now. **And it shows*** (= it's obvious). ◇ **~ sth** *Her expression showed her disappointment.* ◇ *James began to **show signs of** impatience.* ◇ **~ how, what, etc...** *She tried not to show how disappointed she was.*

▸ BE VISIBLE **9** 🔑 [I, T] if sth **shows**, people can see it. If sth **shows** a mark, dirt, etc, the mark can be seen: *She had a warm woollen hat and scarf on that left only her eyes and nose showing.* ◇ **~ sth** *Their new white carpet showed every mark.*

▸ INFORMATION **10** 🔑 [T] (not usually used in the progressive tenses) **~ sth** to give particular information, or a time or measurement: *The map shows the principal towns and rivers.* ◇ *The clock showed midnight.* ◇ *The end-of-year accounts show a loss.*

▸ OF PICTURE/PHOTOGRAPH **11** 🔑 [T] **~ sth** | **~ sb/sth (as sth)** | **~ sb/sth doing sth** to be of sb/sth; to represent sb/sth: *She had objected to a photo showing her in a bikini.*

▸ FOR PUBLIC TO SEE **12** 🔑 [I, T] to be or make sth available for the public to see: *The movie is now showing at all major movie theaters.* ◇ **~ sth** *The movie is being shown now.* ◇ *She plans to show her paintings early next year.*

▸ PROVE **13** [T, no passive] (*informal*) to prove that you can do sth or are sth: **~ sb (sth)** *They think I can't do it, but I'll show them!* ◇ **~ yourself to be/have sth** *He has shown himself to be a caring father.*

▸ ARRIVE **14** [I] (*informal, especially NAmE*) to arrive where you have arranged to meet sb or do sth: *I waited an hour but he didn't show.* ➲ see also SHOW UP

▸ ANIMAL **15** [T] **~ sth** to enter an animal in a competition

IDM **it goes to ˈshow** used to say that sth proves sth: *It just goes to show what you can do when you really try.* **show sb the ˈdoor** to ask sb to leave, because they are no longer welcome **show your ˈface** to appear among your friends or in public: *She stayed at home, afraid to show her face.* **show your ˈhand/ˈcards** (*BrE*) (*NAmE* **tip your ˈhand**) to make your plans or intentions known **show sb who's ˈboss** to make it clear to sb that you have more power and authority than they have **show the ˈway** to do sth first so that other people can follow **show ˈwilling** (*BrE*) to show that you are ready to help, work hard, etc. if necessary **(have) something, nothing, etc. to ˈshow for sth** (to have) something, nothing, etc. as a result of sth: *All those years of hard work, and nothing to show for it!* ➲ more at FLAG *n.*, PACE *n.*, ROPE *n.*

PHR V **ˌshow sb aˈround/ˈround (sth)** 🔑 to be a guide for sb when they visit a place for the first time to show them what is interesting: *We were shown around the school by one of the students.* ◇ *Has anyone shown you round yet?* **ˌshow ˈoff** 🔑 (*informal, disapproving*) to try to impress others by talking about your abilities, possessions, etc: *He's just showing off because that girl he likes is here.* ➲ related noun SHOW-OFF **ˌshow sb/sth↔ˈoff** 🔑 to show people sb/sth that you are proud of: *She wanted to show off her new husband at the party.* ◇ **~ how, what, etc...** *He likes to show off how well he speaks French.* **ˌshow sth↔ˈoff** 🔑 (of clothing) to make sb look attractive, by showing their best features: *a dress that shows off her figure* **ˌshow ˈthrough** | **ˌshow ˈthrough sth** to be able to be seen behind or under sth else: *The writing on the other side of the page shows through.* ◇ (*figurative*) *When he spoke, his bitterness showed through.* ◇ *Veins showed through her pale skin.* **ˌshow ˈup** 🔑 (*informal*) to arrive where you have arranged to meet sb or do sth: *It was getting late when she finally showed up.* **ˌshow ˈup** | **ˌshow sth↔ˈup** to become visible; to make sth become visible: *a broken bone showed up on the X-ray* ◇ *The harsh light showed up the lines on her face.* **ˌshow sb↔ˈup 1** (*BrE, informal*) to make sb feel embarrassed by behaving badly: *He showed me up by snoring during the concert.* **2** to make sb feel embarrassed by doing sth better than them

■ ***noun***

▸ ENTERTAINMENT **1** 🔑 [C] a theatre performance, especially one that includes singing and dancing: *to go to a show* ◇ *a one-woman/-man show* ◇ *to put on/stage a show* ◇ *She's the **star of the show**!* ➲ see also FLOOR SHOW, ROADSHOW **2** 🔑 [C] a programme on television or the radio: *to **host a show*** ◇ *a **TV/radio show*** ◇ *a **quiz show*** ➲ COLLOCATIONS at TELEVISION ➲ see also CHAT SHOW, GAME SHOW, ROADSHOW, TALK SHOW **3** [C] (*NAmE, informal*) a concert, especially of rock music

▸ OF COLLECTION OF THINGS **4** 🔑 [C, U] an occasion when a collection of things are brought together for people to look at: *an agricultural show* ◇ *The latest computers will be **on show** at the exhibition.* ➲ see also FASHION SHOW, PEEP SHOW

▸ OF FEELING **5** [C] an action or a way of behaving that shows how you feel SYN **display**: *a show of emotion* ◇ *a show of support* ◇ ***a show of force/strength** by the army*

▸ INSINCERE ACT **6** [U, sing.] something that is done only to give a good impression, but is not sincere: *He may seem charming, but it's all show!* ◇ *She pretends to be interested in opera, but it's only **for show**.* ◇ *He **made a great show of** affection, but I knew he didn't mean it.*

▸ COLOURFUL SIGHT **7** [C, U] a brightly coloured or pleasing sight SYN **display**: *a lovely show of spring flowers*

▸ EVENT/SITUATION **8** [sing.] (*informal*) an event, a business or a situation where sth is being done or organized: *She runs the whole show.* ◇ *I won't interfere—it's your show.*

▸ GOOD/POOR SHOW **9** [C, usually sing.] (*informal, especially BrE*) something that is done in a particular way: *The team **put on a good show** in the competition.* ◇ *It's a poor show if he forgets your birthday.*

IDM **for ˈshow** intended to be seen but not used: *These items are just for show—they're not for sale.* **get the ˌshow on the ˈroad** (*informal*) to start an activity or a journey: *Let's get this show on the road!* **(jolly) good ˈshow!** (*old-fashioned, BrE, informal*) used to show you like sth or to say that sb has done sth well **a show of ˈhands** a group of people each raising a hand to vote for or against sth ➲ more at DOG *n.*, STEAL

ˌshow-and-ˈtell *noun* [U] an activity in which children have to bring sth to show their class and talk about it to them

show·boat /ˈʃəʊbəʊt; *NAmE* ˈʃoʊboʊt/ *verb, noun*

■ ***verb*** [I] (*informal, often disapproving*) to behave in a way

S

that tries to show people how clever, skilful, etc. you are ▶ **show·boat·ing** *noun* [U]

■ ***noun*** (*NAmE*) a boat on which musical shows are performed

ˈ**show business** (also *informal* **show·biz** /ˈʃəʊbɪz; *NAmE* ˈʃoʊ-/) *noun* [U] the business of providing public entertainment, for example in the theatre, in films/movies or in television: *to* ***be in show business*** ◇ *show-business* ***people/stars*** ◇ *That's showbiz!*

show·case /ˈʃəʊkeɪs; *NAmE* ˈʃoʊ-/ *noun* **1** [usually sing.] **~ (for sb/sth)** an event that presents sb's abilities or the good qualities of sth in an attractive way: *The festival was a showcase for young musicians.* **2** a box with a glass top or sides that is used for showing objects in a shop/store, museum, etc. ▶ **show·case** *verb*: **~ sth** *Jack found a film role that showcased all his talents.*

show·down /ˈʃəʊdaʊn; *NAmE* ˈʃoʊ-/ *noun* [usually sing.] an argument, a fight or a test that will settle a disagreement that has lasted for a long time: *Management are facing a showdown with union members today.* ◇ *Fans gathered outside the stadium for the final showdown* (= the game that will decide the winner of the competition).

shower 0‑ᵗ /ˈʃaʊə(r)/ *noun, verb*

■ ***noun*** **1** 0‑ᵗ a piece of equipment producing a spray of water that you stand under to wash yourself; the small room or part of a room that contains a shower: *a hotel room with bath and shower* ◇ *He's* ***in the shower.*** ◇ *a shower cubicle* ➲ VISUAL VOCAB page V21 **2** 0‑ᵗ the act of washing yourself with a shower: (*especially BrE*) *to* ***have a shower*** ◇ (*especially NAmE*) *to* ***take a shower*** ◇ *shower gel* **3** 0‑ᵗ a short period of rain or snow: *scattered showers* ◇ *April showers* ◇ *We were caught in a heavy shower.* ◇ *snow showers* ◇ *wintry showers* (= of snow) **4** a large number of things that arrive or fall together: *a shower of leaves* ◇ *a shower of sparks from the fire* ◇ *a shower of kisses* **5** (*NAmE*) a party at which you give presents to a woman who is getting married or having a baby: *a* ***bridal/baby shower***

■ ***verb*** **1** [I] to wash yourself under a shower: *She showered and dressed and went downstairs.* **2** [I] **~ (down) on sb/sth** | **~ down** to fall onto sb/sth, especially in a lot of small pieces: *Volcanic ash showered down on the town after the eruption.* **3** [T] **~ sb with sth** to drop a lot of small things onto sb: *The bride and groom were showered with rice as they left the church.* ◇ *The roof collapsed, showering us with dust and debris.* **4** [T] to give sb a lot of sth: **~ sb with sth** *He showered her with gifts.* ◇ **~ sth on sb** *He showered gifts on her.*

S

show·ery /ˈʃaʊəri/ *adj.* (of the weather) with frequent showers of rain: *a showery day*

show·girl /ˈʃəʊɡɜːl; *NAmE* ˈʃoʊɡɜːrl/ *noun* a female performer who sings and dances in a musical show

show·ground /ˈʃəʊɡraʊnd; *NAmE* ˈʃoʊ-/ *noun* a large outdoor area where FAIRS, farm shows, etc. take place

ˈ**show house** (also ˈ**show home**) (both *BrE*) (*NAmE* ˈ**model home**) *noun* a house in a group of new houses that has been painted and filled with furniture, so that people who might want to buy one of the houses can see what they will be like

show·ing /ˈʃəʊɪŋ; *NAmE* ˈʃoʊ-/ *noun* **1** an act of showing a film/movie: *There are three showings a day.* **2** [usually sing.] evidence of how well or how badly sb/sth is performing: *the* ***strong/poor showing*** *of the Green Party in the election* ◇ *On* (= judging by) *last week's showing, the team is unlikely to win today.*

show·jump·ing /ˈʃəʊdʒʌmpɪŋ; *NAmE* ˈʃoʊ-/ *noun* [U] the sport of riding a horse and jumping over a set of fences as quickly as possible ➲ VISUAL VOCAB page V38

show·man /ˈʃəʊmən; *NAmE* ˈʃoʊ-/ *noun* (*pl.* **-men** /-mən/) **1** a person who does things in an entertaining way and is good at getting people's attention **2** a person who organizes public entertainments, especially at FAIRGROUNDS

show·man·ship /ˈʃəʊmənʃɪp; *NAmE* ˈʃoʊ-/ *noun* [U] skill in doing things in an entertaining way and getting a lot of attention

shown *past part.* of SHOW

ˈ**show-off** *noun* (*informal, disapproving*) a person who tries to impress other people by showing how good he or she is at doing sth

show·piece /ˈʃəʊpiːs; *NAmE* ˈʃoʊ-/ *noun* an excellent example of sth that people are meant to see and admire

show·place /ˈʃəʊpleɪs; *NAmE* ˈʃoʊ-/ *noun* a place of great beauty, historical interest, etc. that is open to the public

show·room /ˈʃəʊruːm; -rʊm; *NAmE* ˈʃoʊ-/ *noun* a large shop/store in which goods for sale, especially cars and electrical goods, are displayed: *a car showroom*

ˈ**show-stopper** *noun* (*informal*) a performance that is very impressive and receives a lot of APPLAUSE from the audience ▶ ˈ**show-stopping** *adj.* [only before noun]: *a show-stopping performance*

show·time /ˈʃəʊtaɪm; *NAmE* ˈʃoʊ-/ *noun* [U] the time that a theatre performance will begin: *It's five minutes to showtime and the theatre is packed.* ◇ (*figurative, NAmE*) *Everybody ready? It's showtime!*

ˈ**show trial** *noun* an unfair trial of sb in court, organized by a government for political reasons, not in order to find out the truth

showy /ˈʃəʊi; *NAmE* ˈʃoʊi/ *adj.* (often *disapproving*) so brightly coloured, large or exaggerated that it attracts a lot of attention SYN **ostentatious**: *showy flowers* ▶ **show·ily** /-ɪli/ *adv.* **showi·ness** *noun* [U]

shrank *past tense* of SHRINK

shrap·nel /ˈʃræpnəl/ *noun* [U] small pieces of metal that are thrown up and away from an exploding bomb

shred /ʃred/ *verb, noun*

■ ***verb*** (-dd-) **~ sth** to cut or tear sth into small pieces: *Serve the fish on a bed of shredded lettuce.* ◇ *He was accused of shredding documents relating to the case* (= putting them in a SHREDDER).

■ ***noun*** **1** [usually pl.] a small thin piece that has been torn or cut from sth SYN **scrap**: *shreds of paper* ◇ *His jacket had been* ***torn to shreds*** *by the barbed wire.* **2** [usually sing.] **~ of sth** (used especially in negative sentences) a very small amount of sth: *There is* ***not a shred of evidence*** *to support his claim.*

IDM **in ˈshreds 1** very badly damaged SYN **in tatters**: *Her nerves were in shreds.* ◇ *The country's economy is in shreds.* **2** torn in many places: *The document was in shreds on the floor.* **pick/pull/tear sb/sth to ˈpieces/ˈshreds** (*informal*) to criticize sb, or their work or ideas, very severely

shred·der /ˈʃredə(r)/ *noun* a machine that tears sth into small pieces, especially paper, so that nobody can read what was printed on it

shrew /ʃruː/ *noun* **1** a small animal like a mouse with a long nose **2** (*old-fashioned*) a bad-tempered unpleasant woman

shrewd /ʃruːd/ *adj.* (**shrewd·er**, **shrewd·est**) **1** clever at understanding and making judgements about a situation SYN **astute**: *a shrewd businessman* ◇ *She is a shrewd judge of character.* **2** showing good judgement and likely to be right: *a shrewd move* ◇ *I* ***have a shrewd idea*** *who the mystery caller was.* ▶ **shrewd·ly** *adv.* **shrewd·ness** *noun* [U]

shrew·ish /ˈʃruːɪʃ/ *adj.* (*old-fashioned*) (of women) bad-tempered and always arguing

Shri (also **Sri**) /ʃriː; sriː/ *noun* (*IndE*) **1** a title used before the names of gods or holy books, showing respect **2** a title of respect for a man

shriek /ʃriːk/ *verb, noun*

■ ***verb*** **1** [I] to give a loud high shout, for example when you are excited, frightened or in pain SYN **scream**: **~ (in sth)** *She shrieked in fright.* ◇ **~ with sth** *The audience was shrieking with laughter.* ◇ **~ at sb** (*figurative*) *The answer shrieked at her* (= was very obvious). **2** [T] to say sth in a loud, high voice SYN **scream**: **~ sth (at sb)** *She was shrieking abuse at them as they carried her off.* ◇ **+ speech** *'Look out!' he shrieked.*

■ ***noun*** a loud high shout, for example one that you make when you are excited, frightened or in pain: *She let out a piercing shriek.* ◇ *a shriek of delight*

shrift /ʃrɪft/ *noun* IDM see SHORT *adj.*

shrike /ʃraɪk/ *noun* a bird with a strong beak, that catches small birds and insects and sticks them on THORNS

shrill /ʃrɪl/ *adj., verb*

■ ***adj.*** (shrill·er, shrill·est) **1** (of sounds or voices) very high and loud, in an unpleasant way SYN **piercing**: *a shrill voice* **2** loud and determined but often unreasonable: *shrill demands/protests* ▸ **shrilly** /ˈʃrɪlli/ *adv.* **shrill·ness** *noun* [U]

■ ***verb*** **1** [I] to make an unpleasant high loud sound: *Behind him, the telephone shrilled.* **2** [T] **+ speech** to say sth in a loud, high voice SYN **shriek**: *'Wait for me!' she shrilled.*

Shri·mati (also **Sri·mati**) /ˈʃriːmʌti; ˈsriː-/ *noun* (*IndE*) a title of respect or affection for a woman

shrimp /ʃrɪmp/ *noun* (*pl.* **shrimps** or **shrimp**) **1** a small SHELLFISH that can be eaten, like a PRAWN but smaller. Shrimps turn pink when cooked. **2** (*NAmE*) = PRAWN: *grilled shrimp*

shrimp·ing /ˈʃrɪmpɪŋ/ *noun* [U] the activity of catching shrimps: *a shrimping net* ▸ **shrimp·er** *noun*: (*especially NAmE*) *shrimpers and fishermen in the Gulf of Mexico*

shrine /ʃraɪn/ *noun* **1** a place where people come to worship because it is connected with a holy person or event: **~ (to sb/sth)** *a shrine to the Virgin Mary* ◇ **~ (of sb/sth)** *to visit the shrine of Mecca* **2 ~ (for sb)** | **~ (to sb/sth)** a place that people visit because it is connected with sb/sth that is important to them: *Wimbledon is a shrine for all lovers of tennis.*

shrink /ʃrɪŋk/ *verb, noun*

■ ***verb*** (shrank /ʃræŋk/, shrunk /ʃrʌŋk/) or (shrunk, shrunk) **1** [I, T] **~ (sth)** to become smaller, especially when washed in water that is too hot; to make clothes, cloth, etc. smaller in this way: *My sweater shrank in the wash.* **2** [I, T] to become or to make sth smaller in size or amount: *The tumour had shrunk to the size of a pea.* ◇ *The market for their products is shrinking.* ◇ **~ sth** *There was a movie called 'Honey, I Shrunk the Kids'.* ◇ *Television in a sense has shrunk the world.* ➲ see also SHRUNKEN **3** [I] **+ adv./prep.** to move back or away from sth because you are frightened or shocked SYN **cower**: *He shrank back against the wall as he heard them approaching.*

IDM **a ˌshrinking ˈviolet** (*humorous*) a way of describing a very shy person

PHR V **ˈshrink from sth** to be unwilling to do sth that is difficult or unpleasant: *We made it clear to them that we would not shrink from confrontation.* ◇ **~ doing sth** *They did not shrink from doing what was right.*

■ ***noun*** (*slang, humorous*) a PSYCHIATRIST or PSYCHOLOGIST

shrink·age /ˈʃrɪŋkɪdʒ/ *noun* [U] the process of becoming smaller in size; the amount by which sth becomes smaller: *the shrinkage of heavy industry* ◇ *She bought a slightly larger size to allow for shrinkage.*

ˈshrink-wrapped *adj.* wrapped tightly in a thin plastic covering

shrivel /ˈʃrɪvl/ *verb* (-ll-, *US* -l-) [I, T] to become or make sth dry and WRINKLED as a result of heat, cold or being old: **~ (up)** *The leaves on the plant had shrivelled up from lack of water.* ◇ **~ sth (up)** *The hot weather had shrivelled the grapes in every vineyard.* ▸ **shriv·elled** *adj.*: *a shrivelled old man*

shroom /ʃruːm; ʃrʊm/ (*informal, especially NAmE*) (also **magic mushroom** *BrE* or becoming *old-fashioned, NAmE*) *noun* a type of MUSHROOM that has an effect like some drugs and that may make people who eat it HALLUCINATE (= see things that are not there) ▸ **shroom** *verb* [I]: *Joe was shrooming last night and has a killer headache today.*

shroud /ʃraʊd/ *noun, verb*

■ ***noun*** **1** a piece of cloth that a dead person's body is wrapped in before it is buried **2 ~ of sth** (*literary*) a thing that covers, surrounds or hides sth: *The organization is cloaked in a shroud of secrecy.* ◇ *a shroud of smoke*

■ ***verb*** [usually passive] **1 ~ sth in sth** (of DARKNESS, clouds, cloth, etc.) to cover or hide sth: *The city was shrouded in mist.* **2 ~ sth in sth** to hide information or keep it secret and mysterious: *His family background **is shrouded in mystery**.*

ˈshroud-waving *noun* [U] (*BrE*) the practice of warning about the bad effect on medical care if more money is not provided by the government to pay for more doctors, hospitals, etc.

Shrove Tuesday /ˌʃrəʊv ˈtjuːzdeɪ; -di; *NAmE* ˌʃroʊv ˈtuːz-/ *noun* [U, C] (in the Christian Church) the day before the beginning of Lent ➲ compare MARDI GRAS, PANCAKE DAY ➲ see also ASH WEDNESDAY

shrub /ʃrʌb/ *noun* a large plant that is smaller than a tree and that has several STEMS of wood coming from the ground SYN **bush**

shrub·bery /ˈʃrʌbəri/ *noun* [C, U] (*pl.* **-ies**) an area planted with shrubs

shrubby /ˈʃrʌbi/ *adj.* (of plants) like a SHRUB

shrug /ʃrʌg/ *verb, noun*

■ ***verb*** (-gg-) [I, T, no passive] to raise your shoulders and then drop them to show that you do not know or care about sth: *Sam shrugged and said nothing.* ◇ **~ sth** *'I don't know,' Anna replied, shrugging her shoulders.*

■ ***noun*** **1** [usually sing.] an act of raising your shoulders and then dropping them to show that you do not know or care about sth: *Andy gave a shrug. 'It doesn't matter.'* **2** [C] a very short knitted piece of clothing that is open at the front and usually has sleeves made from the same piece as the back and front

PHR V **ˌshrug sth ˈoff/aˈside** to treat sth as if it is not important SYN **dismiss**: *Shrugging off her injury, she played on.* ◇ *He shrugged aside suggestions that he resign.* **ˌshrug sb/sth ˈoff/aˈway** to push sb/sth back or away with your shoulders: *Kevin shrugged off his jacket.* ◇ *She shrugged him away angrily.*

shrunk *past tense, past part.* of SHRINK

shrunk·en /ˈʃrʌŋkən/ *adj.* [usually before noun] that has become smaller (and less attractive) SYN **wizened**: *a shrunken old woman*

shtetl /ˈʃtetl/ *noun* a small Jewish town or village in eastern Europe in the past

shtick (also **schtick**) /ʃtɪk/ *noun* [U, sing.] (*especially NAmE*) **1** a style of humour that is typical of a particular performer **2** a particular ability that sb has

shtook (also **schtuck**) /ʃtʊk/ *noun* [U]

IDM **be in ˈshtook** (*BrE, informal*) to be in serious trouble

shtum (also **schtum**) /ʃtʊm/ *noun* [U]

IDM **keep/stay ˈshtum** (*BrE, informal*) to not speak: *Police have appealed for witnesses, but it seems the locals are keeping shtum.*

shtup (also **schtup**) /ʃtʊp/ *verb* (-pp-) **~ sb** (*NAmE, slang*) to have sex with sb

shuck /ʃʌk/ *noun, verb*

■ ***noun*** (*NAmE*) the outer covering of a nut, plant, etc. or an OYSTER or a CLAM

■ ***verb*** **~ sth** (*NAmE*) to remove the shell or covering of nuts, SHELLFISH, etc.

shucks /ʃʌks/ *exclamation* (*old-fashioned, NAmE, informal*) used to express embarrassment or disappointment

shud·der /ˈʃʌdə(r)/ *verb, noun*

■ ***verb*** **1** [I] to shake because you are cold or frightened, or because of a strong feeling: *Just thinking about the accident makes me shudder.* ◇ **~ with sth** *Alone in the car, she shuddered with fear.* ◇ **~ at sth** ***I shuddered at the thought** of all the trouble I'd caused.* ◇ **~ to do sth** ***I shudder to think** how much this is all going to cost* (= I don't want to think about it because it is too unpleasant). **2** [I] (of a vehicle, machine, etc.) to shake very hard: *The bus shuddered to a halt.*

■ ***noun*** [usually sing.] **1** a shaking movement you make because you are cold, frightened or disgusted: *a shudder of fear* ◇ *She gave an involuntary shudder.* **2** a strong shaking movement: *The elevator rose with a shudder.*

S

shuf·fle /ˈʃʌfl/ *verb, noun*
■ ***verb* 1** [I] **+ adv./prep.** to walk slowly without lifting your feet completely off the ground: *He shuffled across the room to the window.* ◇ *The line shuffled forward a little.* **2** [T, I] **~ (sth)** to move from one foot to another; to move your feet in an awkward or embarrassed way: *Jenny shuffled her feet and blushed with shame.* **3** [T, I] **~ (sth)** to mix cards up in a PACK/DECK of PLAYING CARDS before playing a game: *Shuffle the cards and deal out seven to each player.* **4** [T] **~ sth** to move paper or things into different positions or a different order: *I shuffled the documents on my desk.*
■ ***noun*** [usually sing.] **1** a slow walk in which you take small steps and do not lift your feet completely off the ground **2** the act of mixing cards before a card game: *Give the cards a good shuffle.* **3** a type of dancing in which you take small steps and do not lift your feet completely off the ground **4** = RESHUFFLE
IDM **lose sb/sth in the ˈshuffle** [usually passive] (*NAmE*) to not notice sb/sth or pay attention to sb/sth because of a confusing situation: *Middle children tend to get lost in the shuffle.* **on ˈshuffle** (of pieces of music stored on a music player, such as an MP3 player) not in any special order: *I put the iPod on shuffle and hit play.*

shuf·fle·board /ˈʃʌflbɔːd; *NAmE* -bɔːrd/ *noun* [U] a game in which players use long sticks to push discs towards spaces with numbers on a board

shufti /ˈʃʊfti/ *noun* [sing.]
IDM **have a shufti (at sth)** (*BrE, informal*) to have a quick look at sth

shun /ʃʌn/ *verb* (-nn-) **~ sb/sth** to avoid sb/sth: *She was shunned by her family when she remarried.* ◇ *an actor who shuns publicity*

shunt /ʃʌnt/ *verb, noun*
■ ***verb* 1 ~ sth** to move a train or a coach/car of a train from one track to another **2 ~ sb/sth + adv./prep.** (usually *disapproving*) to move sb/sth to a different place, especially a less important one: *John was shunted sideways to a job in sales.*
■ ***noun* 1** (*BrE, informal*) a road accident in which one vehicle crashes into the back of another **2** (*medical*) a small tube put in your body in a medical operation to allow the blood or other FLUID to flow from one place to another

shush /ʃʊʃ/ *exclamation, verb*
■ ***exclamation*** used to tell sb to be quiet
■ ***verb* ~ sb** to tell sb to be quiet, especially by saying 'shush', or by putting your finger against your lips: *Lyn shushed the children.*

shut 🔑 /ʃʌt/ *verb, adj.*
■ ***verb*** (**shut·ting, shut, shut**) **1** 🔑 [T, I] **~ (sth)** to make sth close; to become closed: *Philip went into his room and shut the door behind him.* ◇ *I can't shut my suitcase—it's too full.* ◇ *She shut her eyes and fell asleep immediately.* ◇ *He shut his book and looked up.* ◇ *The window won't shut.* ◇ *The doors open and shut automatically.* **2** 🔑 [I, T] **~ (sth)** (*BrE*) when a shop/store, restaurant, etc. **shuts** or when sb **shuts** it, it stops being open for business and you cannot go into it: *The bank shuts at 4.* ➲ note at CLOSE[1]
IDM **shut your ˈmouth/ˈface!** (*slang*) a rude way of telling sb to be quiet or stop talking **shut up ˈshop** (*BrE, informal*) to close a business permanently or to stop working for the day ➲ more at DOOR, EAR, EYE *n.*, MOUTH *n.*
PHR V **ˌshut sb/sth↔aˈway** to put sb/sth in a place where other people cannot see or find them **ˌshut yourself aˈway** to go somewhere where you will be completely alone **ˌshut ˈdown** 🔑 (of a factory, shop/store, etc. or a machine) to stop opening for business; to stop working ➲ related noun SHUTDOWN **ˌshut sth↔ˈdown** 🔑 to stop a factory, shop/store, etc. from opening for business; to stop a machine from working: *The computer system will be shut down over the weekend.* ➲ related noun SHUTDOWN **ˌshut sb/yourself ˈin (sth)** 🔑 to put sb in a room and keep them there; to go to a room and stay there: *She shut the dog in the shed while she prepared the barbecue.* **ˈshut sth in sth** to trap sth by closing a door, lid, etc. on it: *Sam shut his finger in the car door.* **ˌshut ˈoff** (of a machine, tool, etc.) to stop working: *The engines shut off automatically in an emergency.* **ˌshut sth↔ˈoff 1** to stop a machine, tool, etc. from working **2** to stop a supply of gas, water, etc. from flowing or reaching a place: *A valve immediately shuts off the gas when the lid is closed.* **ˌshut yourself ˈoff (from sth)** to avoid seeing people or having contact with anyone: *Martin shut himself off from the world to write his book.* **ˌshut sb/sth ˈoff from sth** to separate sb/sth from sth: *Bosnia is shut off from the Adriatic by the mountains.* **ˌshut sb/sth↔ˈout (of sth) 1** 🔑 to prevent sb/sth from entering a place: *Mum, Ben keeps shutting me out of the bedroom!* ◇ *sunglasses that shut out 99% of the sun's harmful rays* **2** to not allow a person to share or be part of your thoughts; to stop yourself from having particular feelings: *I wanted to shut John out of my life for ever.* ◇ *She learned to shut out her angry feelings.* ◇ *If you shut me out, how can I help you?* **ˌshut ˈup** 🔑 (*informal*) to stop talking (often used as an order as a rude way of telling sb to stop talking): *Just shut up and listen!* ◇ *Will you tell Mike to shut up?* ◇ *When they'd finally shut up, I started again.* **ˌshut sb ˈup** to make sb stop talking SYN **silence**: *She kicked Anne under the table to shut her up.* **ˌshut sth↔ˈup** to close a room, house, etc. **ˌshut sb/sth ˈup (in sth)** 🔑 to keep sb/sth in a place and prevent them from going anywhere
■ ***adj.*** [not before noun] **1** 🔑 not open SYN **closed**: *The door was shut.* ◇ *She slammed the door shut.* ◇ *Keep your eyes shut.* **2** 🔑 (*BrE*) not open for business SYN **closed**: *Unfortunately the bank is shut now.*

shut·down /ˈʃʌtdaʊn/ *noun* the act of closing a factory or business or stopping a large machine from working, either temporarily or permanently: *factory shutdowns* ◇ *the nuclear reactor's emergency shutdown procedures*

ˈshut-eye *noun* [U] (*informal*) sleep

ˈshut-in *noun* (*NAmE*) a person who cannot leave their home very easily because they are ill/sick or disabled

shut·out /ˈʃʌtaʊt/ *noun* (*NAmE*) a game in which one team prevents the other from scoring

shut·ter /ˈʃʌtə(r)/ *noun* **1** [usually pl.] one of a pair of wooden or metal covers that can be closed over the outside of a window to keep out light or protect the windows from damage: *to* ***open/close the shutters*** ◇ (*BrE, figurative*) *More than 70 000 shopkeepers have been forced to* ***put up the shutters*** (= close down their businesses) *in the past year.* ➲ VISUAL VOCAB pages V15, V18 **2** the part of a camera that opens to allow light to pass through the LENS when you take a photograph
IDM **ˌbring/ˌput down the ˈshutters** to stop letting sb know what your thoughts or feelings are; to stop letting yourself think about sth

shut·ter·bug /ˈʃʌtəbʌg; *NAmE* ˈʃʌtər-/ *noun* (*NAmE, informal*) a person who likes to take a lot of photographs

shut·tered /ˈʃʌtəd; *NAmE* -tərd/ *adj.* with the shutters closed; with shutters fitted

ˈshutter speed *noun* the length of time that a camera's SHUTTER remains open

shut·tle /ˈʃʌtl/ *noun, verb*
■ ***noun* 1** a plane, bus or train that travels regularly between two places: *a shuttle service between London and Edinburgh* **2** = SPACE SHUTTLE **3** a pointed tool used in making cloth to pull a thread backwards and forwards over the other threads that pass along the length of the cloth **4 the Shuttle** [sing.] a train service that takes cars and their passengers through the Channel Tunnel between England and France
■ ***verb* 1** [I] **~ (between A and B)** to travel between two places frequently: *Her childhood was spent shuttling between her mother and father.* **2** [T] **~ sb (+ adv./prep.)** to carry people between two places that are close, making regular journeys between the two places: *A bus shuttles passengers back and forth from the station to the terminal.*

shuttle·cock /ˈʃʌtlkɒk; *NAmE* -kɑːk/ (*NAmE* also **birdie**) *noun* the object that players hit backwards and forwards in the game of BADMINTON ➲ VISUAL VOCAB page V37

ˌshuttle diˈplomacy *noun* [U] international talks in which people travel between two or more countries in order to talk to the different governments involved

shwa *noun* = SCHWA

shy 🔑 /ʃaɪ/ *adj., verb*

■ **adj.** (shyer, shy·est) **1** 🔑 (of people) nervous or embarrassed about meeting and speaking to other people SYN **timid**: *a quiet, shy man* ◇ *Don't be shy—come and say hello.* ◇ *She was too shy to ask anyone for help.* ◇ *As a teenager I was* ***painfully shy.*** ◇ *She's very shy with adults.* **2** 🔑 showing that sb is nervous or embarrassed about meeting and speaking to other people: *a shy smile* **3** (of animals) easily frightened and not willing to come near people: *The panda is a shy creature.* **4** [not before noun] **~ of/about (doing) sth** afraid of doing sth or being involved in sth: *The band has never been shy of publicity.* ◇ *He disliked her and had never been shy of saying so.* **5** [not before noun] **~ (of sth)** (*informal, especially NAmE*) lacking the amount that is needed: *He died before Christmas, only a month shy of his 90th birthday.* ◇ *We are still two players shy (of a full team).* **6 -shy** (in compounds) avoiding or not liking the thing mentioned: *camera-shy* (= not liking to be photographed) ◇ *He's always been work-shy.* ▶ **shyly** *adv.* **shy·ness** *noun* [U] IDM see FIGHT *v.*, ONCE *adv.*

■ **verb** (shies, shy·ing, shied, shied /ʃaɪd/) [I] **~ (at sth)** (especially of a horse) to turn away with a sudden movement because it is afraid or surprised: *My horse shied at the unfamiliar noise.* ➲ see also COCONUT SHY

PHR V **,shy a'way (from sth)** to avoid doing sth because you are nervous or frightened: *Hugh never shied away from his responsibilities.* ◇ *The newspapers have shied away from investigating the story.*

shy·ster /'ʃaɪstə(r)/ *noun* (*informal, especially NAmE*) a dishonest person, especially a lawyer

SI /,es 'aɪ/ *abbr.* International System (used to describe units of measurement; from French 'Système International'): *SI units*

Siamese cat /,saɪəmi:z 'kæt/ (also **Siam·ese**) *noun* a cat with short pale fur and a brown face, ears, tail and feet

,Siamese 'twin *noun* = CONJOINED TWIN

sib /sɪb/ *noun* (*biology*) a brother or sister

sibi·lant /'sɪbɪlənt/ *adj., noun*

■ **adj.** (*formal* or *literary*) making an 's' or 'sh' sound: *the sibilant sound of whispering*

■ **noun** (*phonetics*) a sibilant sound made in speech, such as /s/ and /z/ in the English words *sip* and *zip*

sib·ling /'sɪblɪŋ/ *noun* (*formal* or *technical*) a brother or sister: *squabbles between siblings* ◇ ***sibling rivalry*** (= competition between brothers and sisters)

sibyl /'sɪbl/ *noun* **1** in ancient times, a woman who was thought to be able to communicate messages from a god **2** (*literary*) a woman who can predict the future

sic /sɪk; si:k/ *adv., verb*

■ **adv.** (from *Latin*) written after a word that you have copied from somewhere, to show that you know that the word is wrongly spelled or wrong in some other way: *In the letter to parents it said: 'The school is proud of it's [sic] record of excellence'.*

■ **verb** (-cc-) **~ sb** (*NAmE, informal*) to attack sb: *Sic him, Duke!* (= said to a dog)

PHR V **'sic sth on sb** (*NAmE, informal*) to tell a dog to attack sb

sick 🔑 /sɪk/ *adj., noun, verb*

■ **adj.**

▸ ILL **1** 🔑 physically or mentally ill: *a sick child* ◇ *Her mother's very sick.* ◇ *Peter has* ***been off sick*** (= away from work because he is ill) *for two weeks.* ◇ *Emma has just* ***called in sick*** (= telephoned to say she will not be coming to work because she is ill). ◇ *Britain's workers* ***went sick*** (= did not go to work because they were ill) *for a record number of days last year.* ◇ (*NAmE*) *I can't afford to* ***get sick*** (= become ill). ➲ COLLOCATIONS at ILL

▸ WANTING TO VOMIT **2** 🔑 [not usually before noun] (*especially BrE*) feeling that you want to VOMIT: *Mum, I* ***feel sick!*** ◇ *If you eat any more cake you'll* ***make yourself sick.*** ◇ *a sick feeling in your stomach*

▸ -SICK **3** (in compounds) feeling sick as a result of travelling on a ship, plane, etc: *seasick* ◇ *airsick* ◇ *carsick* ◇ *travel-sick*

▸ BORED **4** 🔑 (*informal*) bored with or annoyed about sth that has been happening for a long time, and wanting it to stop: **~ of sb/sth** *I'm sick of the way you've treated me.* ◇ *I'm* ***sick and tired of*** *your moaning.* ◇ *I'm* ***sick to death*** *of all of you!* ◇ **~ of doing sth** *We're sick of waiting around like this.*

▸ CRUEL/STRANGE **5** (*informal*) (especially of humour) dealing with suffering, disease or death in a cruel way that some people think is offensive: *a sick joke* ◇ *That's really sick.* **6** (*informal*) getting enjoyment from doing strange or cruel things: *a sick mind* ◇ *People think I'm sick for having a rat as a pet.* ◇ *We live in a sick society.* ➲ see also HOMESICK, LOVESICK

IDM **be 'sick** 🔑 (*BrE*) to bring food from your stomach back out through your mouth SYN **vomit**: *I was sick three times in the night.* ◇ *She had been* ***violently sick.*** **be worried 'sick; be 'sick with worry** to be extremely worried: *Where have you been? I've been worried sick about you.* **fall 'sick** (also *old-fashioned* **take 'sick**) (*formal*) to become ill/sick **make sb 'sick** to make sb angry or disgusted: *His hypocrisy makes me sick.* **(as) sick as a 'dog** (*informal*) feeling very ill/sick; VOMITING a lot **(as) sick as a 'parrot** (*BrE, humorous*) very disappointed **sick at 'heart** (*formal*) very unhappy or disappointed **sick to your 'stomach 1** feeling very angry or worried: *Nora turned sick to her stomach on hearing this news.* **2** (*NAmE*) feeling that you want to VOMIT

■ **noun**

▸ VOMIT **1** [U] (*BrE, informal*) food that you bring back up from your stomach through your mouth SYN **vomit**

▸ ILL PEOPLE **2 the sick** [pl.] people who are ill/sick: *All the sick and wounded were evacuated.*

■ **verb**

PHR V **,sick sth↔'up** (*BrE, informal*) to bring sth up from the stomach back out through your mouth SYN **vomit**

'sick bag *noun* a paper bag on a boat or plane into which you can VOMIT

sick·bay /'sɪkbeɪ/ *noun* a room or rooms, for example on a ship or in a school, with beds for people who are ill/sick

sick·bed /'sɪkbed/ *noun* [sing.] the bed on which a person who is ill/sick is lying: *The President left his sickbed to attend the ceremony.*

,sick 'building syndrome *noun* [U] a condition that affects people who work in large offices, making them feel tired and causing headaches, sore eyes and breathing problems, thought to be caused by, for example, the lack of fresh air or by chemicals in the air

sick·en /'sɪkən/ *verb* (*BrE*) **1** [T] **~ sb** to make sb feel very shocked and angry SYN **disgust** **2** [I] to become ill/sick: (*old-fashioned*) *The baby sickened and died before his first birthday.* ◇ (*BrE*) *Faye hasn't eaten all day—she must* ***be sickening for something.***

sick·en·ing /'sɪkənɪŋ/ *adj.* **1** making you feel disgusted or shocked SYN **repulsive**: *the sickening stench of burnt flesh* **2** making you afraid that sb has been badly hurt or that sth has been broken: *Her head hit the ground with a sickening thud.* **3** (*informal*) making you feel jealous or annoyed: *'She's off to the Bahamas for a month.' 'How sickening!'* ▶ **sick·en·ing·ly** *adv.*

sickie /'sɪki/ *noun* (*BrE, informal*) a day when you say that you are ill/sick and cannot go to work when it is not really true: *to pull/throw/chuck a sickie*

sickle /'sɪkl/ *noun* a tool with a curved blade and a short handle, used for cutting grass, etc. ➲ see also HAMMER AND SICKLE

'sick leave *noun* [U] permission to be away from work because of illness; the period of time spent away from work: *to be on sick leave*

,sickle-cell a'naemia (also **'sickle-cell disease**) *noun* [U] a serious form of ANAEMIA (= a disease of the blood) that is found mostly in people of African family origins, and which is passed down from parents to children

sick·ly /'sɪkli/ *adj.* (sick·lier, sick·li·est) **1** often ill/sick: *He was a sickly child.* **2** not looking healthy and strong

S

SYN **frail**: *She looked pale and sickly.* ◇ *sickly plants* **3** that makes you feel sick, especially because it is too sweet or full of false emotion: *a sickly sweet smell* ◇ *She gave me a sickly smile.* **4** (of colours) unpleasant to look at: *a sickly green colour*

sick·ness /ˈsɪknəs/ *noun* **1** [U] illness; bad health: *She's been off work because of sickness.* ◇ *insurance against sickness and unemployment* ⊃ SYNONYMS at ILLNESS **2** [U, C, usually sing.] a particular type of illness or disease: ***altitude/travel/radiation, etc. sickness*** ⊃ see also SLEEPING SICKNESS **3** [U] (*especially BrE*) the feeling that you are likely to VOMIT (= bring food back up from the stomach to the mouth); the fact of VOMITING SYN **nausea**: *symptoms include sickness and diarrhoea* ◇ *The sickness passed off after a while.* ⊃ see also MORNING SICKNESS **4** [sing.] a feeling of great sadness, disappointment or disgust

ˈsickness benefit *noun* [U] (*BrE*) money paid by the government to people who are away from work because of illness ⊃ compare SICK PAY

sicko /ˈsɪkəʊ; *NAmE* -koʊ/ *noun* (*pl.* -os) (*informal, especially NAmE*) a person who gets enjoyment from doing strange and cruel things: *child molesters and other sickos*

sick·out /ˈsɪkaʊt/ *noun* (*NAmE*) a strike in which all the workers at a company say they are sick and stay at home

ˈsick pay *noun* [U] pay given to an employee who is away from work because of illness ⊃ compare SICKNESS BENEFIT

sick·room /ˈsɪkruːm; -rʊm/ *noun* a room in which a person who is ill/sick is lying in bed

side 🔑 /saɪd/ *noun, verb*

■ ***noun***

▸ LEFT/RIGHT **1** 🔑 [C, usually sing.] either of the two halves of a surface, an object or an area that is divided by an imaginary central line: *They drive on the left-hand side of the road in Japan.* ◇ *the right side of the brain* ◇ *satellite links to the other side of the world* ◇ *She was on the far side of the room.* ◇ *They crossed from one side of London to the other.* ◇ *Keep on your side of the bed!* **2** 🔑 [C, usually sing.] a position or an area to the left or right of sth: *There is a large window **on either side of** the front door.* ◇ *He crossed the bridge to **the other side** of the river.* ◇ *people on both sides of the Atlantic* ◇ *She tilted her head **to one side**.*

▸ NOT TOP OR BOTTOM **3** 🔑 [C] one of the flat surfaces of sth that is not the top or bottom, front or back: *Write your name on the side of the box.* ◇ *There's a scratch on the side of my car.* ◇ *The kitchen door is at the side of the house.* ◇ *a **side door/entrance/window*** ◇ *Now lay the jar on its side.* **4** 🔑 [C] the vertical or sloping surface around sth, but not the top or bottom of it: *A path went up the side of the hill.* ◇ *Brush the sides of the tin with butter.* ⊃ see also HILLSIDE, MOUNTAINSIDE

▸ EDGE **5** 🔑 [C] a part or an area of sth near the edge and away from the middle: *She sat on the side of the bed.* ◇ *A van was parked at the side of the road.* ◇ *the south side of the lake* ⊃ see also BEDSIDE, FIRESIDE, RINGSIDE, RIVERSIDE, ROADSIDE, SEASIDE

▸ OF BODY **6** 🔑 [C, usually sing.] either the right or left part of a person's body, from the ARMPIT (= where the arm joins the body) to the hip: *She has a pain down her right side.* ◇ *He was lying on his side.*

▸ NEAR TO SB/STH **7** 🔑 [sing.] a place or position very near to sb/sth: *Keep close to my side.* ◇ *Her husband stood at her side.*

▸ OF STH FLAT AND THIN **8** 🔑 [C] either of two surfaces of sth flat and thin, such as paper or cloth: *Write on one side of the paper only.* ◇ *Fry the steaks for two minutes on each side.*

▸ PAGE **9** [C] the amount of writing needed to fill one side of a sheet of paper: *He told us not to write more than three sides.*

▸ MATHEMATICS **10** 🔑 [C] any of the flat surfaces of a solid object: *A cube has six sides.* **11** 🔑 [C] any of the lines that form a flat shape such as a square or triangle: *a shape with five sides* ◇ *The farm buildings form three sides of a square.* ⊃ VISUAL VOCAB page V58

▸ -SIDED **12** used in adjectives to state the number or type of sides: *a six-sided object* ◇ *a glass-sided container*

▸ IN WAR/ARGUMENT **13** 🔑 [C] one of the two or more people or groups taking part in an argument, war, etc: *We have finally reached an agreement acceptable to all sides.* ◇ *At some point during the war he seems to have **changed sides**.* ◇ *to be **on the winning/losing side*** **14** 🔑 [C] one of the opinions, attitudes or positions held by sb in an argument, a business arrangement, etc: *We heard both **sides of the argument**.* ◇ *I just want you to hear my **side of the story** first.* ◇ *Will you keep your **side of the bargain**?*

▸ ASPECT **15** 🔑 [C] a particular aspect of sth, especially a situation or a person's character: *These poems reveal her gentle side.* ◇ *This is a side of Alan that I never knew existed.* ◇ *It's good you can see **the funny side** of the situation.* ◇ *I'll take care of that side of things.*

▸ FEELING THAT YOU ARE BETTER **16** [U] (*BrE, informal*) a feeling that you are better than other people: *There was **no side** to him at all.*

▸ SPORTS TEAM **17** [C] (*BrE*) a sports team: *The French have a very strong side.* ◇ *We were **on the winning/losing side**.*

▸ OF FAMILY **18** [C] the part of your family that people belong to who are related either to your mother or to your father: *a cousin on my father's side* (= a child of my father's brother or sister)

▸ FOOD **19** (*NAmE, informal*) = SIDE DISH: *Your dinner comes with a choice of two sides.*

▸ MEAT **20** [C] **a ~ of beef/bacon, etc.** one of the two halves of an animal that has been killed for meat

▸ TV CHANNEL **21** [C] (*old-fashioned, BrE, informal*) a television channel: *What's on the other side?*

IDM **come down on ˈone side of the fence or the ˈother** to choose between two possible choices **from ˌside to ˈside** 🔑 moving to the left and then to the right and then back again: *He shook his head slowly from side to side.* ◇ *The ship rolled from side to side.* **get on the right/wrong ˈside of sb** to make sb pleased with you/annoyed with you **have sth on your ˈside** to have sth as an advantage that will make it more likely that you will achieve sth **let the ˈside down** (*especially BrE*) to fail to give your friends, family, etc. the help and support they expect, or to behave in a way that makes them disappointed **not leave sb's ˈside** to stay with sb, especially in order to take care of them **on/from all ˈsides | on/from every ˈside** in or from all directions; everywhere: *We realized we were surrounded on all sides.* ◇ *Disaster threatens on every side.* **on the ˈbig, ˈsmall, ˈhigh, etc. side** (*informal*) slightly too big, small, high, etc: *These shoes are a little on the tight side.* **on the other side of the ˈfence** in a situation that is different from the one that you are in **on the ˌright/ˌwrong side of ˈ40, ˈ50, etc.** (*informal*) younger or older than 40, 50, etc. years of age **on the ˈside** (*informal*) **1** in addition to your main job: *a mechanic who buys and sells cars on the side* **2** secretly or illegally: *He's married but he has a girlfriend on the side.* **3** (*especially NAmE*) (of food in a restaurant) served at the same time as the main part of the meal, but on a separate plate **on/to one ˈside 1** out of your way: *I left my bags on one side.* **2** to be dealt with later: *I put his complaint to one side until I had more time.* ◇ *Leaving that to one side for a moment, are there any other questions?* **be on sb's side** to support and agree with sb: *I'm definitely on your side in this.* ◇ *Whose side are you on anyway?* **the other side of the ˈcoin** the aspect of a situation that is the opposite of or contrasts with the one you have been talking about **ˌside by ˈside 1** 🔑 close together and facing in the same direction: *There were two children ahead, walking side by side.* **2** together, without any difficulties: *We have been using both systems, side by side, for two years.* ◇ *The two communities exist happily side by side.* **take ˈsides** to express support for sb in a disagreement: *She didn't think it was wise to take sides in their argument.* **take/draw sb to one ˈside** to speak to sb in private, especially in order to warn or tell them about sth **this side of...** before a particular time, event, age, etc: *They aren't likely to arrive this side of midnight.* ⊃ more at BED *n.*, BIT, BRIGHT *adj.*, CREDIT *n.*, DISTAFF, ERR, GRASS *n.*, KNOW *v.*, LAUGH *v.*, RIGHT *adj.*, SAFE *adj.*, SPLIT *v.*, THORN, TIME *n.*, TWO, WRONG *adj.*

S

■ *verb*

PHR V **'side with sb (against sb/sth)** to support one person or group in an argument against sb else: *The kids always sided with their mother against me.*

side·bar /ˈsaɪdbɑː(r)/ *noun* **1** a short article in a newspaper or magazine that is printed next to a main article, and gives extra information **2** a narrow area on the side of a computer screen or a WEB PAGE that is separate from the main part of the page

side·board /ˈsaɪdbɔːd; *NAmE* -bɔːrd/ (*NAmE* also **buf·fet**) *noun* **1** a piece of furniture in a DINING ROOM for putting food on before it is served, with drawers for storing knives, forks, etc. ➲ **VISUAL VOCAB** page V19 **2** = SIDEBURN

side·burn /ˈsaɪdbɜːn; *NAmE* -bɜːrn/ (*BrE* also **side·board**) *noun* [usually pl.] hair that grows down the sides of a man's face in front of his ears ➲ **VISUAL VOCAB** page V49

side·car /ˈsaɪdkɑː(r)/ *noun* a small vehicle attached to the side of a motorcycle in which a passenger can ride

'side dish (*NAmE informal* **side**) *noun* a small amount of food, for example a salad, served with the main course of a meal **SYN** **side order**

'side effect *noun* [usually pl.] **1** an extra and usually bad effect that a drug has on you, as well as curing illness or pain **2** an unexpected result of a situation or course of action that happens as well as the result you were aiming for

'side-foot *verb* **~ sth** to kick a ball with the inside part of your foot

'side issue *noun* an issue that is less important than the main issue, and may take attention away from it

side·kick /ˈsaɪdkɪk/ *noun* (*informal*) a person who helps another more important or more intelligent person: *Batman and his young sidekick Robin*

side·light /ˈsaɪdlaɪt/ *noun* **1 ~ (on sb/sth)** a piece of information, usually given by accident or in connection with another subject, that helps you to understand sb/sth **2** (*BrE*) either of a pair of small lights at the front of a vehicle

side·line /ˈsaɪdlaɪn/ *noun, verb*

■ *noun* **1** [C] an activity that you do as well as your main job in order to earn extra money **2 sidelines** [pl.] the lines along the two long sides of a sports field, TENNIS COURT, etc. that mark the outer edges; the area just outside these: *The coach stood on the sidelines yelling instructions to the players.*

IDM **on/from the 'sidelines** watching sth but not actually involved in it: *He was content to watch from the sidelines as his wife built up a successful business empire.*

■ *verb* [usually passive] **1 ~ sb** to prevent sb from playing in a team, especially because of an injury: *The player has been sidelined by a knee injury.* **2 ~ sb** to prevent sb from having an important part in sth that other people are doing: *The vice-president is increasingly being sidelined.*

side·long /ˈsaɪdlɒŋ; *NAmE* -lɔːŋ/ *adj.* [only before noun] (of a look) out of the corner of your eye, especially in a way that is secret or disapproving: *She cast* ***a sidelong glance*** *at Eric to see if he had noticed her blunder.* ▸ **side·long** *adv.*: *She looked sidelong at him.*

ˌside-'on *adv.* (*BrE*) coming from the side rather than from the front or back: *The car hit us side-on.*

'side order *noun* a small amount of food ordered in a restaurant to go with the main dish, but served separately **SYN** **side dish**: *a side order of fries*

'side plate *noun* a small plate used for bread or other food that goes with a meal ➲ **VISUAL VOCAB** page V19

sid·er·eal /saɪˈdɪəriəl; *NAmE* -ˈdɪr-/ *adj.* (*astronomy*) related to the stars that are far away, not the sun or planets

'side road *noun* a smaller and less important road leading off a main road

'side-saddle *adv.* if you ride a horse **side-saddle**, you ride with both your legs on the same side of the horse

'side salad *noun* a salad served with the main course of a meal

side·show /ˈsaɪdʃəʊ; *NAmE* -ʃoʊ/ *noun* **1** a separate small show or attraction at a FAIR or CIRCUS where you pay to see a performance or take part in a game **2** an activity or event that is much less important than the main activity or event

'side-splitting *adj.* (*informal*) extremely funny; making people laugh a lot: *side-splitting anecdotes* ▸ **'side-splittingly** *adv.*: *side-splittingly funny*

side·step /ˈsaɪdstep/ *verb* (**-pp-**) **1** [T] **~ sth** to avoid answering a question or dealing with a problem: *Did you notice how she neatly sidestepped the question?* **2** [T, I] **~ (sth)** to avoid sth, for example being hit, by stepping to one side: *He cleverly sidestepped the tackle.*

'side street *noun* a less important street leading off a road in a town

side·swipe /ˈsaɪdswaɪp/ *noun* **1** (*NAmE*) a hit from the side: *a sideswipe by a truck* **2 ~ (at sb/sth)** (*informal*) a critical comment made about sb/sth while you are talking about sb/sth completely different: *It was a good speech, but he couldn't resist taking a sideswipe at his opponent.* ▸ **side·swipe** *verb*: **~ sb/sth** (*NAmE*) *The bus sideswiped two parked cars.*

side·track /ˈsaɪdtræk/ *verb* [usually passive] **~ sb (into doing sth)** to make sb start to talk about or do sth that is different from the main thing that they are supposed to be talking about or doing **SYN** **distract**: *I was supposed to be writing a letter but I'm afraid I* ***got sidetracked.***

'side view *noun* a view of sth from the side: *The picture shows a side view of the house.*

side·walk /ˈsaɪdwɔːk/ (*NAmE*) (*BrE* **pave·ment**) *noun* a flat part at the side of a road for people to walk on ➲ **VISUAL VOCAB** page V3

'sidewalk artist (*NAmE*) (*BrE* **'pavement artist**) *noun* an artist who draws pictures in CHALK on the PAVEMENT/SIDEWALK, hoping to get money from people who pass

side·ward /ˈsaɪdwəd; *NAmE* -wərd/ *adj.* to, towards or from the side: *a sideward glance* ▸ **side·ward** (also **side·wards**) *adv.*: *He was blown sidewards by the wind.*

side·ways 🔑 /ˈsaɪdweɪz/ *adv.*

1 🔑 to, towards or from the side: *He looked sideways at her.* ◇ *The truck skidded sideways across the road.* ◇ *He has been moved sideways* (= moved to another job at the same level as before, not higher or lower). **2** 🔑 with one side facing forwards: *She sat sideways on the chair.* ▸ **side·ways** 🔑 *adj.*: *She slid him a sideways glance.* ◇ *a sideways move* **IDM** see KNOCK *v.*

'side whiskers *noun* [pl.] hair growing on the sides of a man's face down to, but not on, the chin

side·wind·er /ˈsaɪdwaɪndə(r)/ *noun* a poisonous N American snake that moves sideways across the desert by throwing its body in an S shape

sid·ing /ˈsaɪdɪŋ/ *noun* **1** a short track beside a main railway/railroad line, where trains can stand when they are not being used **2** (*NAmE*) material used to cover and protect the outside walls of buildings

sidle /ˈsaɪdl/ *verb* [I] **+ adv./prep.** to walk somewhere in a shy or uncertain way as if you do not want to be noticed: *She sidled up to me and whispered something in my ear.*

SIDS /ˌes aɪ diː ˈes; sɪdz/ *noun* [U] the abbreviation for 'sudden infant death syndrome' (the sudden death while sleeping of a baby which appears to be healthy) **SYN** **cot death**

siege /siːdʒ/ *noun* **1** a military operation in which an army tries to capture a town by surrounding it and stopping the supply of food, etc. to the people inside: *the siege of Troy* ◇ *The siege was finally lifted* (= ended) *after six months.* ◇ *The police placed the city centre under a virtual* ***state of siege*** (= it was hard to get in or out). **2** a situation in which the police surround a building where people are living or hiding, in order to make them come out ➲ see also BESIEGE

IDM **under 'siege 1** surrounded by an army or the police in a siege **2** being criticized all the time or put under pressure by problems, questions, etc. **lay 'siege to sth 1** to begin a siege of a town, building, etc. **2** to surround a

S

building, especially in order to speak to or question the person or people living or working there

'siege mentality *noun* [sing., U] a feeling that you are surrounded by enemies and must protect yourself

sie·mens /'si:mənz/ *noun* (*abbr.* S) (*physics*) the standard unit for measuring how well an object CONDUCTS electricity

si·enna /si'enə/ *noun* [U] a type of dark yellow or red CLAY used for giving colour to paints, etc.

si·erra /si'erə/ *noun* (especially in place names) a long range of steep mountains with sharp points, especially in Spain and America: *the Sierra Nevada*

si·esta /si'estə/ *noun* a rest or sleep taken in the early afternoon, especially in hot countries: *to **have/take a siesta*** ➲ compare NAP

sieve /sɪv/ *noun, verb*

■ ***noun*** a tool for separating solids from liquids or larger solids from smaller solids, made of a wire or plastic net attached to a ring. The liquid or small pieces pass through the net but the larger pieces do not. ➲ VISUAL VOCAB page V23

IDM **have a memory/mind like a 'sieve** (*informal*) to have a very bad memory; to forget things easily

■ ***verb*** **~ sth** to put sth through a sieve

sie·vert /'si:vət; *NAmE* -vərt/ *noun* (*abbr.* Sv) (*physics*) a unit for measuring the effect of RADIATION

sift /sɪft/ *verb* **1** [T] **~ sth** to put flour or some other fine substance through a SIEVE/SIFTER: *Sift the flour into a bowl.* **2** [T, I] to examine sth very carefully in order to decide what is important or useful or to find sth important: **~ sth** *We will sift every scrap of evidence.* ◇ **~ through sth** *Crash investigators have been sifting through the wreckage of the aircraft.* **3** [T] **~ sth (out) from sth** to separate sth from a group of things: *She looked quickly through the papers, sifting out from the pile anything that looked interesting.*

PHR V **,sift sth↔'out 1** to remove sth that you do not want from a substance by putting it through a SIEVE: *Put the flour through a sieve to sift out the lumps.* **2** to separate sth, usually sth you do not want, from a group of things: *We need to sift out the applications that have no chance of succeeding.*

sift·er /'sɪftə(r)/ *noun* **1** (*NAmE*) a small SIEVE used for sifting flour ➲ VISUAL VOCAB page V23 **2** a container with a lot of small holes in the top, used for shaking flour or sugar onto things: *a sugar sifter*

S

sigh /saɪ/ *verb, noun*

■ ***verb*** **1** [I] to take and then let out a long deep breath that can be heard, to show that you are disappointed, sad, tired, etc: *He **sighed deeply** at the thought.* ◇ **~ with sth** *She **sighed with relief** that it was all over.* **2** [T] **+ speech** to say sth with a sigh: *'Oh well, better luck next time,' she sighed.* **3** [I] (*literary*) (especially of the wind) to make a long sound like a sigh

■ ***noun*** an act or the sound of sighing: *to **give/heave/let out a sigh*** ◇ *a deep sigh* ◇ *'I'll wait,' he said with a sigh.* ◇ *We all **breathed a sigh of relief** when it was over.*

sight 🔑 /saɪt/ *noun, verb*

■ ***noun***

▸ ABILITY TO SEE **1** 🔑 [U] the ability to see SYN **eyesight**: *to lose your sight* (= to become blind) ◇ *She has very good sight.* ◇ *The disease has affected her sight.* ◇ *He has very little sight in his right eye.*

▸ ACT OF SEEING **2** 🔑 [U] **~ of sb/sth** the act of seeing sb/sth: *After ten days at sea, we had our first sight of land.* ◇ *I have been known to faint **at the sight of** blood.* ◇ *The soldiers were given orders to shoot **on sight*** (= as soon as they saw sb). ◇ *She **caught sight** of a car in the distance.*

▸ HOW FAR YOU CAN SEE **3** 🔑 [U] the area or distance within which sb can see or sth can be seen: *There was no one **in sight**.* ◇ *At last we **came in sight of** a few houses.* ◇ *A bicycle came into sight on the main road.* ◇ *The end is **in sight*** (= will happen soon). ◇ *Leave any valuables in your car **out of sight**.* ◇ *Keep **out of sight*** (= stay where you cannot be seen). ◇ *She never lets her daughter **out of her sight*** (= always keeps her where she can see her). ◇ *Get out of my sight!* (= Go away!) ◇ *The boat disappeared **from sight**.* ◇ *The house was **hidden from sight** behind some trees.* ◇ *He had placed himself directly in my **line of sight**.*

Synonyms

sight

view • vision

These are all words for the area or distance that you can see from a particular position.

sight the area or distance that you can see from a particular position: *He looked up the street, but there was no one in sight.* ◇ *Leave any valuables in your car out of sight.*

view (*rather formal*) the area or distance that you can see from a particular position: *The lake soon came into view.*

vision the area that you can see from a particular position: *The couple moved outside her field of vision* (= total area you can see from a particular position).

SIGHT, VIEW OR VISION?

View is more literary than **sight** or **vision**. It is the only word for talking about how well you can see: ~~*I didn't have a good sight/vision of the stage.*~~ **Vision** must always be used with a possessive pronoun: *my/his/her etc. (field of) vision*. It is not used with the prepositions *in, into* and *out of* that are very frequent with **sight** and **view**: ~~*There was nobody in vision.*~~ ◇ ~~*A tall figure came into vision.*~~

PATTERNS

- **in/out of** sight/view
- **in/within** sight/view **of** sth
- to **come into/disappear from** sight/view/sb's vision
- to **come in** sight/view **of** sb/sth
- to **block** sb's view/vision
- sb's **line of** sight/vision
- sb's **field of** view/vision

▸ WHAT YOU CAN SEE **4** 🔑 [C] a thing that you see or can see: *It's a spectacular sight as the flamingos lift into the air.* ◇ *The museum attempts to recreate **the sights and sounds of** wartime Britain.* ◇ *He was a **sorry sight**, soaked to the skin and shivering.* ◇ *The bird is now a rare sight in this country.* ➲ SYNONYMS at VIEW

▸ INTERESTING PLACES **5** 🔑 **sights** [pl.] the interesting places, especially in a town or city, that are often visited by tourists: *We're going to Paris for the weekend to **see the sights**.*

▸ RIDICULOUS/UNTIDY PERSON **6 a sight** [sing.] (*informal, especially BrE*) a person or thing that looks ridiculous, untidy, unpleasant, etc: *She looks a sight in that hat!*

▸ ON GUN/TELESCOPE **7** [C, usually pl.] a device that you look through to aim a gun, etc. or to look at sth through a TELESCOPE, etc: *He had the deer **in his sights** now.* ◇ (*figurative*) *Even as a young actress, she always had Hollywood firmly in her sights* (= as her final goal).

IDM **at first 'sight 1** 🔑 when you first begin to consider sth: *At first sight, it may look like a generous offer, but always read the small print.* **2** 🔑 when you see sb/sth for the first time: *It was **love at first sight*** (= we fell in love the first time we saw each other). **hate, be sick of, etc. the 'sight of sb/sth** (*informal*) to hate, etc. sb/sth very much: *I can't stand the sight of him!* **in the sight of sb/in sb's sight** (*formal*) in sb's opinion: *We are all equal in the sight of God.* **lose 'sight of sb/sth 1** to become no longer able to see sb/sth: *They finally lost sight of land.* **2** to stop considering sth; to forget sth: *We must not lose sight of our original aim.* **,out of 'sight, ,out of 'mind** (*saying*) used to say sb will quickly be forgotten when they are no longer with you **raise/lower your 'sights** to expect more/less from a situation **set your sights on sth/on doing sth** to decide that you want sth and to try very hard to get it: *She's set her sights on getting into Harvard.* **a (damn, etc.) sight better, etc. | a (damn, etc.) sight too good, etc.**

(*informal*) very much better; much too good, etc: *She's done a darn sight better than I have.* ◇ *It's worth a damn sight more than I thought.* **a ˌsight for sore ˈeyes** (*informal*) a person or thing that you are pleased to see; something that is very pleasant to look at **sight unˈseen** if you buy sth **sight unseen**, you do not have an opportunity to see it before you buy it ⊃ more at HEAVE *v.*, KNOW *v.*, NOWHERE, PRETTY *adj.*

■ *verb* **~ sth** (*formal*) to suddenly see sth, especially sth you have been looking for: *After twelve days at sea, they sighted land.*

sight·ed /ˈsaɪtɪd/ *adj.* **1** able to see; not blind: *the blind parents of sighted children* **2 -sighted** (in compounds) able to see in the way mentioned: *partially sighted* ◇ *short-sighted* ◇ *long-sighted*

sight·ing /ˈsaɪtɪŋ/ *noun* an occasion when sb sees sb/sth, especially sth unusual or sth that lasts for only a short time: *a reported sighting of the Loch Ness monster*

sight·less /ˈsaɪtləs/ *adj.* (*literary*) unable to see SYN **blind**: *The statue stared down at them with sightless eyes.*

ˈsight-line *noun* = LINE OF SIGHT

ˈsight-read *verb* [I, T] **~ (sth)** to play or sing written music when you see it for the first time, without practising it first ▸ **ˈsight-reader** *noun* **ˈsight-reading** *noun* [U]

sight·see·ing /ˈsaɪtsiːɪŋ/ *noun* [U] the activity of visiting interesting buildings and places as a tourist: *to go sightseeing* ◇ *Did you have a chance to* **do any sightseeing?** ◇ *a sightseeing tour of the city* ⊃ COLLOCATIONS at TRAVEL ▸ **sight·see** *verb* [I] (only used in the progressive tenses) **sight·seer** *noun* SYN **tourist**: *Oxford attracts large numbers of sightseers.*

sigma /ˈsɪɡmə/ *noun* the 18th letter of the Greek alphabet (Σ, σ)

sign 0-w /saɪn/ *noun, verb*

■ *noun*

▸ SHOWING STH **1** 0-w [C, U] an event, an action, a fact, etc. that shows that sth exists, is happening or may happen in the future SYN **indication**: **~ (of sth/sb)** *Headaches may be a sign of stress.* ◇ *There is no sign of John anywhere.* ◇ *Call the police at the first sign of trouble.* ◇ *There was no* **sign of life** *in the house* (= there seemed to be nobody there). ◇ *Her work is* **showing some signs of** *improvement.* ◇ **~ (of doing sth)** *The gloomy weather* **shows no sign of** *improving.* ◇ *The fact that he didn't say 'no' immediately is a* **good sign**. ◇ **~ (that…)** *If an interview is too easy, it's* **a sure sign that** *you haven't got the job.* ◇ *If I had noticed the* **warning signs**, *none of this would have happened.*

▸ FOR INFORMATION/WARNING **2** 0-w [C] a piece of paper, wood or metal that has writing or a picture on it that gives you information, instructions, a warning, etc: *a* **road/traffic sign** ◇ *a* **shop/pub sign** ◇ *The sign on the wall said 'Now wash your hands'.* ◇ **Follow the signs** *for the city centre.*

▸ MOVEMENT/SOUND **3** 0-w [C] a movement or sound that you make to tell sb sth: *He* **gave a** *thumbs-up* **sign**. ◇ *She nodded as a sign for us to sit down.* ⊃ see also V-SIGN

▸ SYMBOL **4** 0-w [C] a mark used to represent sth, especially in mathematics: *a plus/minus sign* (+/−) ◇ *a dollar/pound sign* ($/£)

▸ STAR SIGN **5** [C] (*informal*) = STAR SIGN: *What sign are you?*

IDM **a ˌsign of the ˈtimes** something that you feel shows what things are like now, especially how bad they are

■ *verb*

▸ YOUR NAME **1** 0-w [I, T] to write your name on a document, letter, etc. to show that you have written it, that you agree with what it says, or that it is genuine: *Sign here, please.* ◇ **~ sth** *Sign your name here, please.* ◇ *You haven't signed the letter.* ◇ *to sign a cheque* ◇ *The treaty was signed on 24 March.* ◇ *The player was signing autographs for a group of fans.* ◇ **~ yourself + noun** *He signed himself 'Jimmy'.*

▸ CONTRACT **2** [T, I] to arrange for sb, for example a sports player or musician, to sign a contract agreeing to work for your company; to sign a contract agreeing to work for a company: **~ sb** *United have just signed a new goalie.* ◇ **~ for sth** *He signed for United yesterday.* ◇ **~ with sth** *The band signed with Virgin Records.*

▸ MAKE MOVEMENT/SOUND **3** [I, T] **~ (to/for sb) (to do sth)** | **~ that…** to make a request or tell sb to do sth by using a sign, especially a hand movement SYN **signal**: *The hotel manager signed to the porter to pick up my case.*

▸ FOR DEAF PERSON **4** [I, T] to use sign language to communicate with sb: *She learnt to sign to help her deaf child.* ◇ **~ sth** *An increasing number of plays are now being signed.* ▸ **sign·er** *noun*: *the signers of the petition* ◇ *signers communicating information to deaf people*

IDM **ˌsigned and ˈsealed** | **ˌsigned, ˌsealed and deˈliver·ed** definite, because all the legal documents have been signed **sign on the dotted ˈline** (*informal*) to sign a document to show that you have agreed to buy sth or do sth: *Just sign on the dotted line and the car is yours.* ⊃ more at PLEDGE *n.*

PHR V **ˌsign sth↔aˈway** to lose your rights or property by signing a document **ˈsign for sth** to sign a document to show that you have received sth **ˌsign ˈin/ˈout** | **ˌsign sb↔ˈin/ˈout** to write your/sb's name when you arrive at or leave an office, a club, etc: *All visitors must sign in on arrival.* ◇ *You must sign guests out when they leave the club.* **ˌsign ˈoff 1** (*BrE*) to end a letter SYN **finish**: *She signed off with 'Yours, Janet'.* **2** to end a broadcast by saying goodbye

Synonyms

sign

indication • symptom • symbol • indicator • signal

These are all words for an event, action or fact that shows that sth exists, is happening or may happen in the future.

sign an event, action or fact that shows that sth exists, is happening or may happen in the future: *Headaches may be a sign of stress.*

indication (*rather formal*) a remark or sign that shows that sth is happening or what sb is thinking or feeling: *They gave no* **indication as to** *how the work should be done.*

SIGN OR INDICATION?

An **indication** often comes in the form of sth that sb says; a **sign** is usually sth that happens or sth that sb does.

symptom a change in your body or mind that shows that you are not healthy; a sign that sth exists, especially sth bad: *Symptoms include a sore throat.* ◇ *The rise in inflation was just one symptom of the poor state of the economy.*

symbol a person, object or event that represents a more general quality or situation: *The dove is a universal symbol of peace.*

indicator (*rather formal*) a sign that shows you what sth is like or how a situation is changing: *the economic indicators*

signal an event, action or fact that shows that sth exists, is happening or may happen in the future: *Chest pains can be a warning signal of heart problems.*

SIGN OR SIGNAL?

Signal is often used to talk about an event, action or fact that suggests to sb that they should do sth. **Sign** is not usually used in this way: ~~*Reducing prison sentences would send the wrong signs to criminals.*~~

PATTERNS

- a(n) sign/indication/symptom/symbol/indicator/signal **of** sth
- a(n) sign/indication/symptom/indicator/signal **that…**
- a **clear** sign/indication/symptom/symbol/indicator/signal
- an **obvious** sign/indication/symptom/symbol/indicator
- an **early** sign/indication/symptom/indicator/signal
- an **outward** sign/indication/symbol
- **to give** a(n) sign/indication/signal

S

or playing a piece of music ˌ**sign sth↔ˈoff** to give your formal approval to sth, by signing your name ˌ**sign ˈoff on sth** (*NAmE, informal*) to express your approval of sth formally and definitely: *The President hasn't signed off on this report.* ˌ**sign ˈon** (*BrE, informal*) to sign a form stating that you are an unemployed person so that you can receive payment from the government ˌ**sign ˈon/ˈup** | ˌ**sign sb↔ˈon/ˈup** to sign a form or contract which says that you agree to do a job or become a soldier; to persuade sb to sign a form or contract like this SYN **enlist**: *He signed on for five years in the army.* ◇ *The company has signed up three top models for the fashion show.* ˌ**sign sth↔ˈover (to sb)** to give your rights or property to sb else by signing a document: *She has signed the house over to her daughter.* ˌ**sign ˈup (for sth)** to arrange to do a course of study by adding your name to the list of people doing it ˌ**sign ˈup to sth** **1** (*BrE*) to commit yourself to a project or course of action, especially one that you have agreed with a group of other people, countries or organizations: *How many countries have signed up to the Kyoto protocol on climate change?* **2 ~ to do sth** to agree to take part in sth: *We have about 100 people signed up to help so far.*

sign·age /ˈsaɪnɪdʒ/ *noun* [U] (*technical*) signs, especially ones that give instructions or directions to the public

sig·nal 🔑 /ˈsɪɡnəl/ *noun, verb, adj.*

■ ***noun*** **1** 🔑 a movement or sound that you make to give sb information, instructions, a warning, etc. SYN **sign**: ***a danger/warning/distress, etc. signal*** ◇ *At an agreed signal they left the room.* ◇ *The siren was a signal for everyone to leave the building.* ◇ *When I **give the signal**, run!* ◇ (*NAmE*) *All I get is a **busy signal** when I dial his number* (= his phone is being used). ◇ ***hand signals*** (= movements that CYCLISTS and drivers make with their hands to tell other people that they are going to stop, turn, etc.) ➲ see also TURN SIGNAL **2** 🔑 an event, an action, a fact, etc. that shows that sth exists or is likely to happen SYN **indication**: *The rise in inflation is a **clear signal** that the government's policies are not working.* ◇ *Chest pains can be a **warning signal** of heart problems.* ◇ *Reducing prison sentences would **send the wrong signals** to criminals.* ➲ SYNONYMS at SIGN **3** 🔑 a piece of equipment that uses different coloured lights to tell drivers to go slower, stop, etc, used especially on railways/railroads and roads: *traffic signals* ◇ *a stop signal* **4** 🔑 a series of electrical waves that carry sounds, pictures or messages, for example to a radio, television or mobile/cell phone: *TV signals* ◇ *a high-frequency signal* ◇ *a radar signal* ◇ *to **detect/pick up signals*** ◇ *to **emit a signal*** ◇ *I couldn't **get a signal** on my cell phone.*

■ ***verb*** (-ll-, *US* -l-) **1** 🔑 [I, T] to make a movement or sound to give sb a message, an order, etc: *Don't fire until I signal.* ◇ *Did you signal before you turned right?* ◇ **~ (to sb) (for sth)** *He signalled to the waiter for the bill.* ◇ **~ to/for sb to do sth** *He signalled to us to join him.* ◇ **~ sb to do sth** *She signalled him to follow.* ◇ **~ sth** *The referee signalled a foul.* ◇ **~ (that)** ... *She signalled (that) it was time to leave.* ◇ **~ which, what, etc...** *You must signal which way you are going to turn.* **2** [T] **~ sth** to be a sign that sth exists or is likely to happen SYN **indicate**: *This announcement signalled a clear change of policy.* ◇ *The scandal surely signals the end of his political career.* **3** [T] to do sth to make your feelings or opinions known: **~ sth** *He signalled his discontent by refusing to vote.* ◇ **~ (that)...** *She has signalled (that) she is willing to stand as a candidate.*

■ ***adj.*** [only before noun] (*formal*) important and noticeable: *a signal honour* ▶ **sig·nal·ly** /-nəli/ *adv.*: *They have signally failed to keep their election promises.*

ˈ**signal box** *noun* (*BrE*) a building beside a railway/railroad from which rail signals are operated

sig·nal·ler (*US* also **sig·nal·er**) /ˈsɪɡnələ(r)/ *noun* = SIGNALMAN

sig·nal·man /ˈsɪɡnəlmən/ *noun* (*pl.* **-men** /-mən/) (also **sig·nal·ler**) (*BrE*) **1** a person whose job is operating signals on a railway **2** a person trained to give and receive signals in the army or navy

ˌ**signal-to-ˈnoise ratio** *noun* **1** (*technical*) the strength of an electronic signal that you want to receive, compared to the strength of the signals that you do not want **2** a measure of how much useful information you receive, compared to information which is not useful

sig·na·tory /ˈsɪɡnətri; *NAmE* -tɔːri/ *noun* (*pl.* **-ies**) **~ (to/of sth)** (*formal*) a person, a country or an organization that has signed an official agreement: *a signatory of the Declaration of Independence* ◇ *Many countries are signatories to/of the Berne Convention.*

sig·na·ture 🔑 /ˈsɪɡnətʃə(r)/ *noun*

1 🔑 [C] your name as you usually write it, for example at the end of a letter: *Someone had forged her signature on the cheque.* ◇ *They collected 10 000 signatures for their petition.* ◇ *He was attacked for having **put his signature to** the deal.* **2** [U] (*formal*) the act of signing sth: *Two copies of the contract will be sent to you for signature.* **3** [C, usually sing.] a particular quality that makes sth different from other similar things and makes it easy to recognize: *Bright colours are his signature.* ➲ see also DIGITAL SIGNATURE, KEY SIGNATURE, TIME SIGNATURE

ˈ**signature tune** *noun* (*BrE*) a short tune played at the beginning and end of a particular television or radio programme, or one that is connected with a particular performer ➲ compare THEME MUSIC

sign·board /ˈsaɪnbɔːd; *NAmE* -bɔːrd/ *noun* a piece of wood that has some information on it, such as a name, and is displayed outside a shop/store, hotel, etc.

sig·net ring /ˈsɪɡnət rɪŋ/ *noun* a ring with a design cut into it, that you wear on your finger ➲ VISUAL VOCAB page V53

sig·nifi·cance AW /sɪɡˈnɪfɪkəns/ *noun* [U, C] **1** the importance of sth, especially when this has an effect on what happens in the future: *a decision of major political significance* ◇ *The new drug has great significance for the treatment of the disease.* ◇ *They discussed the **statistical significance** of the results.* **2** the meaning of sth: *She couldn't grasp the full significance of what he had said.* ◇ *Do these symbols have any particular significance?* ➲ compare INSIGNIFICANCE

sig·nifi·cant 🔑 AW /sɪɡˈnɪfɪkənt/ *adj.*

1 🔑 large or important enough to have an effect or to be noticed: *a highly significant discovery* ◇ *The results of the experiment are not **statistically significant**.* ◇ *There are no significant differences between the two groups of students.* ◇ *Your work has shown a significant improvement.* ◇ ***It is significant that** girls generally do better in examinations than boys.* ➲ compare INSIGNIFICANT **2** 🔑 having a particular meaning: *It is significant that he changed his will only days before his death.* **3** [usually before noun] having a special or secret meaning that is not understood by everyone SYN **meaningful**: *a **significant look/smile***

sig·nifi·cant·ly 🔑 AW /sɪɡˈnɪfɪkəntli/ *adv.*

1 🔑 in a way that is large or important enough to have an effect on sth or to be noticed: *The two sets of figures are not significantly different.* ◇ *Profits have increased significantly over the past few years.* **2** 🔑 in a way that has a particular meaning: *Significantly, he did not deny that there might be an election.* **3** in a way that has a special or secret meaning: *She paused significantly before she answered.*

sigˌnificant ˈother *noun* (often *humorous*) your husband, wife, partner or sb that you have a special relationship with

sig·ni·fi·ca·tion /ˌsɪɡnɪfɪˈkeɪʃn/ *noun* (*formal* or *linguistics*) [U, C] the exact meaning of sth, especially a word or phrase

sig·ni·fied /ˈsɪɡnɪfaɪd/ *noun* (*linguistics*) the meaning expressed by a LINGUISTIC sign, rather than its form ➲ compare SIGNIFIER

sig·ni·fier /ˈsɪɡnɪfaɪə(r)/ *noun* (*linguistics*) the form of a LINGUISTIC sign, for example its sound or its printed form, rather than the meaning it expresses ➲ compare SIGNIFIED

sig·nify AW /ˈsɪɡnɪfaɪ/ *verb* (**sig·ni·fies**, **sig·ni·fy·ing**, **sig·ni·fied**, **sig·ni·fied**) (*formal*) **1** [T] to be a sign of sth SYN **mean**: **~ sth** *This decision signified a radical change*

S

in their policies. ◇ **~ that...** *This mark signifies that the products conform to an approved standard.* ◇ *The white belt signifies that he's an absolute beginner.* **2** [T] to do sth to make your feelings, intentions, etc. known: **~ sth** *She signified her approval with a smile.* ◇ **~ that...** *He nodded to signify that he agreed.* **3** [I] (usually used in questions or negative sentences) to be important or to matter: *His presence no longer signified.*

sign·ing /ˈsaɪnɪŋ/ *noun* **1** [U] the act of writing your name at the end of an official document to show that you accept it: *the signing of the Treaty of Rome* **2** [C] (*BrE*) a person who has just signed a contract to join a particular sports team or record or film company **3** [U] the act of making an official contract that arranges for sb to join a sports team or a record or film company **4** [U] the act of using sign language: *the use of signing in classrooms*

ˈsign language *noun* [U, C] a system of communicating with people who cannot hear, by using hand movements rather than spoken words

sign·post /ˈsaɪnpəʊst; *NAmE* -poʊst/ *noun, verb*

■ ***noun*** a sign at the side of a road giving information about the direction and distance of places: *Follow the signposts to the superstore.* ◇ (*figurative*) *The chapter headings are useful signposts to the content of the book.* ➲ VISUAL VOCAB page V3

■ ***verb*** (*BrE*) **1** [usually passive] **~ sth** to mark a road, place, etc. with signposts: *The route is well signposted.* **2 ~ sth** to show clearly the way that an argument, a speech, etc. will develop: *You need to signpost for the reader the various points you are going to make.* ▸ **sign·post·ing** *noun* [U]

sign·writer /ˈsaɪnraɪtə(r)/ (also **ˈsign painter**) *noun* a person who paints signs and advertisements for shops/stores and businesses ▸ **ˈsign·writing** *noun* [U]

Sikh /siːk/ *noun* a member of a religion (called **Sikhism**) that developed in Punjab in the late 15th century and is based on a belief that there is only one God ▸ **Sikh** *adj.*

sil·age /ˈsaɪlɪdʒ/ *noun* [U] grass or other green crops that are stored without being dried and are used to feed farm animals in winter

si·lence 🔑 /ˈsaɪləns/ *noun, verb, exclamation*

■ ***noun*** **1** 🔑 [U] a complete lack of noise or sound SYN **quiet**: *Their footsteps echoed in the silence.* ◇ *A scream broke the silence of the night.* ◇ *I need **absolute silence** when I'm working.* **2** 🔑 [C, U] a situation when nobody is speaking: *an **embarrassed/awkward silence*** ◇ *a moment's stunned silence* ◇ *I got used to his long silences.* ◇ *They finished their meal **in total silence**.* ◇ *She lapsed into silence again.* ◇ *There was a **deafening silence*** (= one that is very noticeable). ◇ *a two-minute silence in honour of those who had died* **3** [U, sing.] a situation in which sb refuses to talk about sth or to answer questions: *She **broke her** public **silence** in a TV interview.* ◇ **~ (on sth)** *The company's silence on the subject has been taken as an admission of guilt.* ◇ *the **right to silence*** (= the legal right not to say anything when you are arrested) ◇ *There is **a conspiracy of silence** about what is happening* (= everyone has agreed not to discuss it). **4** [U] a situation in which people do not communicate with each other by letter or telephone: *The phone call came after months of silence.*

IDM **ˌsilence is ˈgolden** (*saying*) it is often best not to say anything ➲ more at HEAVY *adj.*, PREGNANT

■ ***verb*** **1 ~ sb/sth** to make sb/sth stop speaking or making a noise: *She silenced him with a glare.* ◇ *Our bombs silenced the enemy's guns* (= they destroyed them). **2 ~ sb/sth** to make sb stop expressing opinions that are opposed to yours: *All protest had been silenced.* ◇ *Her recent achievements have silenced her critics.*

■ ***exclamation*** (*formal*) used to tell people to be quiet: *Silence in court!*

si·len·cer /ˈsaɪlənsə(r)/ *noun* **1** (*BrE*) (*NAmE* **muf·fler**) a device that is fixed to the EXHAUST of a vehicle in order to reduce the amount of noise that the engine makes ➲ VISUAL VOCAB page V41 **2** a device that is fixed to the end of a gun in order to reduce the amount of noise that it makes when it is fired

si·lent 🔑 /ˈsaɪlənt/ *adj.*

1 🔑 (of a person) not speaking: *to **remain/stay/keep silent*** ◇ *They huddled together in silent groups.* ◇ *As the curtain rose, the audience **fell silent**.* ◇ *He gave me **the silent treatment*** (= did not speak to me because he was angry). **2** 🔑 [only before noun] (especially of a man) not talking very much SYN **quiet**: *He's the **strong silent** type.* **3** 🔑 where there is little or no sound; making little or no sound SYN **quiet**: *At last the traffic **fell silent**.* ◇ *The streets were silent and deserted.* **4** 🔑 [only before noun] not expressed with words or sound: *a **silent prayer/protest*** ◇ *They nodded in **silent agreement**.* **5 ~ (on/about sth)** not giving information about sth; refusing to speak about sth: *The report is strangely silent on this issue.* ◇ *the right to **remain silent*** (= the legal right not to say anything when you are arrested) **6** [only before noun] (of old films/movies) with pictures but no sound: *a **silent film/movie*** ◇ *stars of the **silent screen*** **7** (of a letter in a word) written but not pronounced: *The 'b' in 'lamb' is silent.*

si·lent·ly /ˈsaɪləntli/ *adv.* **1** without speaking: *They marched silently through the streets.* **2** without making any or much sound SYN **quietly**: *She crept silently out of the room.* **3** without using words or sounds to express sth: *She prayed silently.* ◇ *He silently agreed with much of what she had said.*

IDM **sit/stand ˌsilently ˈby** to do or say nothing to help sb or deal with a difficult situation

the ˌsilent maˈjority *noun* [usually sing.] the large number of people in a country who think the same as each other, but do not express their views publicly

ˌsilent ˈpartner (*NAmE*) (*BrE* **ˌsleeping ˈpartner**) *noun* a person who has put money into a business company but who is not actually involved in running it

sil·hou·ette /ˌsɪluˈet/ *noun, verb*

■ ***noun*** **1** [C, U] the dark outline or shape of a person or an object that you see against a light background: *the silhouette of chimneys and towers* ◇ *The mountains stood out **in silhouette**.* **2** [C] the shape of a person's body or of an object: *The dress is fitted to give you a flattering silhouette.* **3** [C] a picture that shows sb/sth as a black shape against a light background, especially one that shows the side view of a person's face

■ ***verb*** [usually passive] **~ sb/sth (against sth)** to make sth appear as a silhouette: *A figure stood in the doorway, silhouetted against the light.*

sil·ica /ˈsɪlɪkə/ *noun* [U] (*symb.* SiO_2) a chemical containing silicon found in sand and in rocks such as QUARTZ, used in making glass and CEMENT

ˈsilica gel *noun* [U] a substance made from silica in the form of grains, which keeps things dry by absorbing water

sili·cate /ˈsɪlɪkeɪt/ *noun* [C, U] **1** (*chemistry*) any COMPOUND containing SILICON and OXYGEN: *aluminium silicate* **2** a mineral that contains silica. There are many different silicates and they form a large part of the earth's CRUST.

sil·icon /ˈsɪlɪkən/ *noun* [U] (*symb.* **Si**) a chemical element. Silicon exists as a grey solid or as a brown powder and is found in rocks and sand. It is used in making glass and TRANSISTORS.

ˌsilicon ˈchip *noun* a very small piece of silicon used to carry a complicated electronic CIRCUIT

sili·cone /ˈsɪlɪkəʊn; *NAmE* -koʊn/ *noun* [U] a chemical containing silicon. There are several different types of silicone, used to make paint, artificial rubber, VARNISH, etc: *a silicone breast implant*

ˌSilicon ˈValley *noun* [U] the area in California where there are many companies connected with the computer and ELECTRONICS industries, sometimes used to refer to any area where there are a lot of computer companies

sili·cosis /ˌsɪlɪˈkəʊsɪs; *NAmE* -ˈkoʊ-/ *noun* [U] (*medical*) a serious lung disease caused by breathing in dust containing SILICA

silk 🔑 /sɪlk/ *noun*

1 🔑 [U] fine soft thread produced by SILKWORMS **2** 🔑 [U] a type of fine smooth cloth made from silk thread: *a silk*

S

blouse ◊ silk stockings ◊ made of pure silk ◊ Her skin was **as smooth as silk.** ➲ see also WATERED SILK **3** [U] silk thread used for sewing **4 silks** [pl.] clothes made of silk, especially the coloured shirts worn by people riding horses in a race (=JOCKEYS) **5** [C] (*BrE, law*) a type of lawyer who represents the government (= a KING'S/QUEEN'S COUNSEL): *to take silk* (= to become this type of lawyer)

IDM **make a silk ˌpurse out of a sow's ˈear** to succeed in making sth good out of material that does not seem very good at all

silk·en /ˈsɪlkən/ *adj.* (*literary*) **1** [usually before noun] soft, smooth and shiny like silk: *silken hair* **2** [usually before noun] smooth and gentle: *her silken voice* **3** [only before noun] made of silk: *silken ribbons*

silkie /ˈsɪlki/ *noun* = SELKIE

ˈsilk screen *noun* **1** [U] a method of printing in which ink is forced through a design cut in a piece of fine cloth: *silk-screen prints* **2** [C] a picture, etc. produced by this method: *Warhol's silk screen of Marilyn Monroe* ▶ **ˈsilk-screen** *verb* **~ sth**

silk·worm /ˈsɪlkwɜːm; *NAmE* -wɜːrm/ *noun* a CATERPILLAR (= a small creature like a WORM with legs) that produces silk thread

silky /ˈsɪlki/ *adj.* (**silk·ier**, **silki·est**) **1** soft, smooth and shiny like silk: *silky fur* **2** [usually before noun] smooth and gentle: *He spoke in a silky tone.* **3** made of silk or cloth that looks like silk: *a silky dress* ▶ **silk·ily** *adv.*: *'How have I changed?' he asked silkily.* **silki·ness** *noun* [U] **silky** *adv.*: *The leaves are grey and silky smooth.*

sill /sɪl/ *noun* **1** = WINDOWSILL **2** a piece of metal that forms part of the frame of a vehicle below the doors

silly 0-ᴡ /ˈsɪli/ *adj., noun*

■ ***adj.*** (**sil·lier**, **sil·li·est**) **1** 0-ᴡ showing a lack of thought, understanding or judgement SYN **foolish**: *a silly idea* ◊ *That was* ***a silly thing to do!*** ◊ *Her work is full of silly mistakes.* ◊ *'I can walk home.' 'Don't be silly—it's much too far!'* ◊ *You silly boy!* **2** 0-ᴡ stupid or embarrassing, especially in a way that is more typical of a child than an adult SYN **ridiculous**: *a silly sense of humour* ◊ *a silly game* ◊ *I* ***feel silly*** *in these clothes.* ◊ *She had a silly grin on her face.* ◊ (*especially BrE*) *I got it for a silly price* (= very cheap). **3** 0-ᴡ not practical or serious: *We had to wear these silly little hats.* ◊ *Why worry about a silly thing like that?* ▶ **sil·li·ness** *noun* [U]

IDM **ˌdrink, ˌlaugh, ˌshout, etc. yourself ˈsilly** (*informal*) to drink, laugh, shout, etc. so much that you cannot behave in a sensible way **play ˈsilly buggers** (*BrE, informal*) to behave in a stupid and annoying way ➲ more at GAME *n.*

■ ***noun*** (*BrE* also **ˌsilly ˈbilly**) [sing.] (*informal*) often used when speaking to children to say that they are not behaving in a sensible way: *No, silly, those aren't your shoes!*

the ˈsilly season *noun* [sing.] (*BrE*) the time, usually in the summer, when newspapers are full of unimportant stories because there is little serious news

silo /ˈsaɪləʊ; *NAmE* -loʊ/ *noun* (*pl.* **-os**) **1** a tall tower on a farm used for storing grain, etc. ➲ VISUAL VOCAB page V2 **2** an underground place where nuclear weapons or dangerous substances are kept **3** an underground place where SILAGE is made and stored

silt /sɪlt/ *noun, verb*

■ ***noun*** [U] sand, mud, etc. that is carried by flowing water and is left at the mouth of a river or in a HARBOUR ▶ **silty** *adj.*: *silty soils*

■ ***verb***

PHR V **ˌsilt sth↔ˈup** | **ˌsilt ˈup** to block sth with silt; to become blocked with silt: *Sand has silted up the river delta.* ◊ *The harbour has now silted up.*

sil·ver 0-ᴡ /ˈsɪlvə(r)/ *noun, adj., verb*

■ ***noun*** **1** 0-ᴡ [U] (*symb.* **Ag**) a chemical element. Silver is a greyish-white PRECIOUS METAL used for making coins, jewellery, decorative objects, etc: *a silver chain* ◊ *made of* ***solid silver*** ◊ *a silver mine* **2** [U] coins that are made of silver or a metal that looks like silver: *I need £2 in silver for the parking meter.* **3** 0-ᴡ [U] dishes, decorative objects, etc. that are made of silver: *They've had to sell the family silver to pay the bills.* **4** 0-ᴡ [U] a shiny greyish-white colour ➲ see also SILVERY **5** [U, C] = SILVER MEDAL: *She won silver in last year's championships.* ◊ *The team won two silvers and a bronze.*

IDM **on a silver ˈplatter** if you are given sth **on a silver platter**, you do not have to do much to get it: *These rich kids expect to have it all handed to them on a silver platter.* ➲ more at BORN, CLOUD *n.*, CROSS *v.*

■ ***adj.*** 0-ᴡ shiny greyish-white in colour: *a silver car* ◊ *silver hair* ➲ see also SILVERY

■ ***verb*** **1** [usually passive] **~ sth** to cover the surface of sth with a thin layer of silver or sth that looks like silver **2 ~ sth** (especially *literary*) to make sth become bright like silver: *Moonlight was silvering the countryside.*

ˌsilver anniˈversary *noun* (*especially US*) **1** (also **ˌsilver ˈwedding anniversary** *BrE, NAmE*) (*BrE* **ˌsilver ˈwedding**) the 25th anniversary of a wedding **2** (*BrE* **ˌsilver ˈjubilee**) the 25th anniversary of an important event; a celebration of sth that began 25 years ago

silver·back /ˈsɪlvəbæk; *NAmE* -vərb-/ *noun* a male adult GORILLA with white or silver hair across its back

ˌsilver ˈband *noun* (*BrE*) a BRASS BAND which uses silver-coloured instruments

ˌsilver ˈbirch *noun* [C, U] a tree with smooth, very pale grey or white BARK and thin branches, that grows in northern countries

sil·ver·fish /ˈsɪlvəfɪʃ; *NAmE* -vərf-/ *noun* (*pl.* **sil·ver·fish**) a small silver insect without wings that lives in houses and that can cause damage to materials such as cloth and paper

ˌsilver ˈfoil *noun* [U] (*BrE*) = FOIL

ˌsilver ˈjubilee (*BrE*) (*US* **ˌsilver anniˈversary**) *noun* [usually sing.] the 25th anniversary of an important event; a celebration of sth that began 25 years ago: *the silver jubilee of the Queen's accession* ◊ *The college celebrated its silver jubilee last year.* ➲ compare DIAMOND JUBILEE, GOLDEN JUBILEE

ˌsilver ˈmedal *noun* [C] (also **sil·ver** [U, C]) a MEDAL that is given to the person or the team that wins the second prize in a race or competition: *an Olympic silver medal winner* ➲ compare BRONZE MEDAL, GOLD MEDAL ▶ **ˌsilver ˈmedallist** (*BrE*) (*NAmE* **ˌsilver ˈmedalist**) *noun*: *He's an Olympic silver medallist.*

ˌsilver ˈpaper *noun* [U] (*BrE*) very thin, shiny sheets of ALUMINIUM/ALUMINUM that are used for wrapping chocolate, etc.

ˌsilver ˈplate *noun* [U] metal that is covered with a thin layer of silver; objects that are made of this metal ▶ **ˌsilver-ˈplated** *adj.*

the ˌsilver ˈscreen *noun* [sing.] (*old-fashioned*) the film/movie industry

ˌsilver ˈservice *noun* [U] a style of serving food at formal meals in which the person serving uses a silver fork and spoon

sil·ver·smith /ˈsɪlvəsmɪθ; *NAmE* -vərs-/ *noun* a person who makes, repairs or sells articles made of silver

ˌsilver ˈsurfer *noun* (*informal*) an old person who spends a lot of time using the Internet

sil·ver·tail /ˈsɪlvəteɪl; *NAmE* ˈsɪlvər-/ *noun* (*AustralE, informal*) a famous or socially important person

ˌsilver ˈtongue *noun* (*formal*) great skill at persuading people to do or to believe what you say ▶ **ˌsilver-ˈtongued** *adj.*

sil·ver·ware /ˈsɪlvəweə(r); *NAmE* -vərwer/ *noun* [U] **1** objects that are made of or covered with silver, especially knives, forks, dishes, etc. that are used for eating and serving food: *a piece of silverware* **2** (also **flat·ware**) (both *NAmE*) (also **cut·lery** especially in *BrE*) knives, forks and spoons, used for eating and serving food **3** (*BrE, informal*) a silver cup that you win in a sports competition SYN **trophy**

S

ˌsilver ˈwedding (*BrE*) (*US* **ˌsilver anniˈversary**) (also **ˌsilver ˈwedding anniversary** *US, BrE*) *noun* the 25th anniversary of a wedding: *They celebrated their silver wedding in May.* ➲ compare DIAMOND WEDDING, GOLDEN WEDDING, RUBY WEDDING

sil·very /ˈsɪlvəri/ *adj.* [usually before noun] **1** shiny like silver; having the colour of silver: *silvery light* ◇ *a silvery grey colour* **2** (*literary*) (especially of a voice) having a pleasant musical sound

sim /sɪm/ *noun* (*informal*) a computer or video game that SIMULATES (= artificially creates the feeling of experiencing) an activity such as flying an aircraft or playing a sport

ˈSIM card *noun* the abbreviation for 'subscriber identification module' (a plastic card inside a mobile/cell phone that stores information to identify the phone and the person using it) ➲ COLLOCATIONS at PHONE

sim·ian /ˈsɪmiən/ *adj.* (*technical*) like a MONKEY or an ape; connected with monkeys or apes

simi·lar 🔑 AW /ˈsɪmələ(r)/ *adj.*
like sb/sth but not exactly the same: *We have very similar interests.* ◇ **~ (to sb/sth)** *My teaching style is similar to that of most other teachers.* ◇ **~ (in sth)** *The two houses are similar in size.* ◇ *The brothers look very similar.* ◇ *All our patients have broadly similar problems.* OPP **different, dissimilar**

simi·lar·ity AW /ˌsɪməˈlærəti/ *noun* (*pl.* -ies) **1** [U, sing.] the state of being like sb/sth but not exactly the same SYN **resemblance**: **~ (between A and B)** *The report highlights the similarity between the two groups.* ◇ **~ (to sb/sth)** *She bears a* ***striking similarity*** *to her mother.* ◇ **~ (in sth)** *There is some similarity in the way they sing.* ◇ *They are both doctors but that is where the similarity ends.* **2** [C] a feature that things or people have that makes them like each other SYN **resemblance**: *a study of the similarities and differences between the two countries* ◇ **~ in/of sth** *similarities in/of style* ◇ **~ to/with sb/sth** *The karate bout has many similarities to a boxing match.* OPP **difference, dissimilarity**

simi·lar·ly 🔑 AW /ˈsɪmələli; *NAmE* -lərli/ *adv.*
1 🔑 in almost the same way: *Husband and wife were similarly successful in their chosen careers.* **2** 🔑 used to say that two facts, actions, statements, etc. are like each other: *The United States won most of the track and field events. Similarly, in swimming, the top three places went to Americans.*

Language Bank

similarly

Making comparisons

- This chart **provides a comparison of** the ways that teenage boys and girls in the UK spend their free time.
- In many cases, the results for boys and girls are virtually **the same/identical**.
- In many cases, the results for boys are virtually **the same as/identical to** the results for girls.
- **Both** boys **and** girls spend the bulk of their free time with friends.
- Most of the boys do more than two hours of sport a week, **as do** many of the girls.
- **Like** many of the girls, most of the boys spend a large part of their free time using the Internet.
- The girls particularly enjoy using social networking websites. **Similarly**, nearly all the boys said they spent at least two to three hours a week on these sites.

➲ Language Banks at CONTRAST, ILLUSTRATE, PROPORTION, SURPRISING

sim·ile /ˈsɪməli/ *noun* [C, U] (*technical*) a word or phrase that compares sth to sth else, using the words *like* or *as*, for example *a face like a mask* or *as white as snow*; the use of such words and phrases ➲ compare METAPHOR

si·mili·tude /sɪˈmɪlɪtjuːd; *NAmE* -tuːd/ *noun* [U] (*formal*) **~ (between A and B)** | **~ (to sb/sth)** the state of being similar to sth: *the similitude between humans and gorillas*

sim·mer /ˈsɪmə(r)/ *verb, noun*
■ *verb* **1** [T, I] **~ (sth)** to cook sth by keeping it almost at boiling point; to be cooked in this way: *Simmer the sauce gently for 10 minutes.* ◇ *Leave the soup to simmer.* ➲ COLLOCATIONS at COOKING **2** [I] **~ (with sth)** to be filled with a strong feeling, especially anger, which you have difficulty controlling SYN **seethe**: *She was still simmering with resentment.* ◇ *Anger simmered inside him.* **3** [I] (of an argument, a disagreement, etc.) to develop for a period of time without any real anger or violence being shown: *This argument has been simmering for months.*
PHR V **ˌsimmer ˈdown** (*informal*) to become calm after a period of anger or excitement: *I left him alone until he simmered down.*
■ *noun* [sing.] the state when sth is almost boiling: *Bring the sauce to a simmer and cook for 5 minutes.*

sim·nel cake /ˈsɪmnəl keɪk/ *noun* [C, U] a type of cake made with dried fruit, traditionally eaten in Britain at Easter

Simon says /ˌsaɪmən ˈsez/ *noun* [U] a children's game in which players should only do what a person says if he/she says 'Simon says...' at the beginning of the instruction

sim·pat·ico /sɪmˈpætɪkəʊ; *NAmE* -koʊ/ *adj.* (*informal*, from *Spanish*) **1** (of a person) pleasant; easy to like **2** (of a person) with similar interests and ideas to yours SYN **compatible**

sim·per /ˈsɪmpə(r)/ *verb* [I, T] to smile in a silly and annoying way: *a silly simpering girl* ◇ **+ speech** *'You're such a darling,' she simpered.* ▸ **sim·per** *noun* [sing.] **sim·per·ing·ly** /ˈsɪmpərɪŋli/ *adv.*

sim·ple 🔑 /ˈsɪmpl/ *adj.* (**sim·pler, sim·plest**)
HELP You can also use **more simple** and **most simple**.
▸ EASY **1** 🔑 not complicated; easy to understand or do SYN **easy**: *a simple solution* ◇ *The answer is really quite simple.* ◇ *This machine is very simple to use.* ◇ *We lost because we played badly. It's* ***as simple as that***. ◇ *Give the necessary information but* ***keep it simple***.
▸ BASIC/PLAIN **2** 🔑 basic or plain without anything extra or unnecessary: *simple but elegant clothes* ◇ *We had a simple meal of soup and bread.* ◇ *The accommodation is simple but spacious.* OPP **fancy**
▸ FOR EMPHASIS **3** used before a noun to emphasize that it is exactly that and nothing else: *Nobody wanted to believe the simple truth.* ◇ *It was a matter of simple survival.* ◇ *It's nothing to worry about—just a simple headache.* ◇ *I had to do it* ***for the simple reason that*** (= because) *I couldn't trust anyone else.* ➲ SYNONYMS at PLAIN
▸ WITH FEW PARTS **4** 🔑 [usually before noun] consisting of only a few parts; not complicated in structure: *simple forms of life, for example amoebas* ◇ *a simple machine* ◇ (*grammar*) *a* ***simple sentence*** (= one with only one verb)
▸ ORDINARY **5** 🔑 [only before noun] (of a person) ordinary; not special: *I'm a simple country girl.*
▸ NOT INTELLIGENT **6** [not usually before noun] (of a person) not very intelligent; not mentally normal: *He's not mad—just a little simple.*
▸ GRAMMAR **7** used to describe the present or past tense of a verb that is formed without using an auxiliary verb, as in *She loves him* (= the simple present tense) or *He arrived late* (= the simple past tense) ➲ see also SIMPLY IDM see PURE

ˌsimple ˈfracture *noun* an injury when a bone in your body is broken but does not come through the skin ➲ compare COMPOUND FRACTURE

ˌsimple ˈinterest *noun* [U] (*finance*) interest that is paid only on the original amount of money that you invested, and not on any interest that it has earned ➲ compare COMPOUND INTEREST

ˌsimple-ˈminded *adj.* (*disapproving*) not intelligent; not able to understand how complicated things are: *a simple-minded person* ◇ *a simple-minded approach*

simple·ton /ˈsɪmpltən/ *noun* (*old-fashioned*) a person who is not very intelligent and can be tricked easily

S

sim·plex /ˈsɪmpleks/ *noun* (*linguistics*) a simple word that is not made of other words ➲ compare COMPOUND

sim·pli·city /sɪmˈplɪsəti/ *noun* (*pl.* -ies) **1** [U] the quality of being easy to understand or use: *the relative simplicity of the new PC* ◊ ***For the sake of simplicity****, let's divide the discussion into two parts.* **2** [U] (*approving*) the quality of being natural and plain: *the simplicity of the architecture* ◊ *the simplicity of country living* **3** [C, usually pl.] an aspect of sth that is easy, natural or plain: *the simplicities of our old way of life*

IDM **be simˌplicity itˈself** to be very easy or plain

sim·pli·fi·ca·tion /ˌsɪmplɪfɪˈkeɪʃn/ *noun* **1** [U, sing.] the process of making sth easier to do or understand: *Complaints have led to (a) simplification of the rules.* **2** [C] the thing that results when you make a problem, statement, system, etc. easier to understand or do: *A number of simplifications have been made to the taxation system.* ➲ compare OVERSIMPLIFICATION at OVERSIMPLIFY

sim·plify /ˈsɪmplɪfaɪ/ *verb* (**sim·pli·fies, sim·pli·fy·ing, sim·pli·fied, sim·pli·fied**) **~ sth** to make sth easier to do or understand: *The application forms have now been simplified.* ◊ *I hope his appointment will* ***simplify matters****.* ◊ *a simplified version of the story for young children*

sim·plis·tic /sɪmˈplɪstɪk/ *adj.* (*disapproving*) making a problem, situation, etc. seem less difficult or complicated than it really is ▶ **sim·plis·tic·al·ly** /-kli/ *adv.*

simp·ly 0‑w /ˈsɪmpli/ *adv.*
1 0‑w used to emphasize how easy or basic sth is SYN **just**: *Simply add hot water and stir.* ◊ *The runway is simply a strip of grass.* ◊ *Fame is often* ***simply a matter of*** *being in the right place at the right time.* ◊ *You can enjoy all the water sports, or simply lie on the beach.* **2** used to emphasize a statement SYN **absolutely**: *You simply must see the play.* ◊ *The view is simply wonderful!* ◊ *That is simply not true!* ◊ *I haven't seen her for simply ages.* **3** 0‑w in a way that is easy to understand: *The book explains grammar simply and clearly.* ◊ *Anyway,* ***to put it simply****, we still owe them £2 000.* **4** 0‑w in a way that is natural and plain: *The rooms are simply furnished.* ◊ *They live simply* (= they do not spend much money). **5** used to introduce a summary or an explanation of sth that you have just said or done: *I don't want to be rude,* ***it's simply that*** *we have to be careful who we give this information to.*

sim·sim /ˈsɪmsɪm/ *noun* [U] an E African word for SESAME (= a type of plant whose seeds and their oil are used in cooking)

S

simu·lac·rum /ˌsɪmjuˈleɪkrəm/ *noun* (*pl.* **simu·lacra** /-krə/) (*formal*) something that looks like sb/sth else or that is made to look like sb/sth else SYN **copy**

simu·late AW /ˈsɪmjuleɪt/ *verb* **1 ~ sth** to pretend that you have a particular feeling SYN **feign**: *I tried to simulate surprise at the news.* **2 ~ sth** to create particular conditions that exist in real life using computers, models, etc, usually for study or training purposes: *Computer software can be used to simulate conditions on the seabed.* **3 ~ sth** to be made to look like sth else: *a gas heater that simulates a coal fire*

simu·lated AW /ˈsɪmjuleɪtɪd/ *adj.* [only before noun] not real, but made to look, feel, etc. like the real thing: *simulated leather* ◊ *'How wonderful!' she said with simulated enthusiasm.* ◊ *The experiments were carried out under simulated examination conditions.*

simu·la·tion AW /ˌsɪmjuˈleɪʃn/ *noun* **1** [C, U] a situation in which a particular set of conditions is created artificially in order to study or experience sth that could exist in reality: *a computer simulation of how the planet functions* ◊ *a simulation model* **2** [U] the act of pretending that sth is real when it is not: *the simulation of genuine concern*

simu·la·tor /ˈsɪmjuleɪtə(r)/ *noun* a piece of equipment that artificially creates a particular set of conditions in order to train sb to deal with a situation that they may experience in reality: *a flight simulator*

sim·ul·cast /ˈsɪmlkɑːst; *NAmE* also ˈsaɪm-/ *verb* (**sim·ul·cast, sim·ul·cast**) **~ sth** to broadcast sth on radio and television at the same time or on both AM and FM radio ▶ **sim·ul·cast** *noun*

sim·ul·tan·eous /ˌsɪmlˈteɪniəs; *NAmE* ˌsaɪml-/ *adj.* happening or done at the same time as sth else: *There were several simultaneous attacks by the rebels.* ◊ ***simultaneous translation/interpreting*** ▶ **sim·ul·tan·eity** /ˌsɪmltəˈneɪəti; *NAmE* ˌsaɪmltəˈniːəti/ *noun* [U] **sim·ul·tan·eous·ly** *adv.*: *The game will be broadcast simultaneously on TV and radio.* ➲ LANGUAGE BANK at PROCESS

ˌsimulˌtaneous eˈquations *noun* [pl.] (*mathematics*) EQUATIONS involving two or more unknown quantities that have the same values in each equation

SIN /ˌes aɪ ˈen/ *abbr.* (*CanE*) SOCIAL INSURANCE NUMBER

sin /sɪn/ *noun, verb, abbr.*
■ ***noun*** **1** [C] an offence against God or against a religious or moral law: *to commit a sin* ◊ *Confess your sins to God and he will forgive you.* ◊ *The Bible says that stealing is a sin.* ➲ COLLOCATIONS at RELIGION ➲ see also MORTAL SIN, ORIGINAL SIN **2** [U] the act of breaking a religious or moral law: *a life of sin* **3** [C, usually sing.] (*informal*) an action that people strongly disapprove of: *It's a sin to waste taxpayers' money like that.* ➲ see also SINFUL, SINNER
IDM **be/do sth for your sins** (*informal, humorous, especially BrE*) used to say that sth that sb does is like a punishment: *She works with us in Accounts, for her sins!* **(as) miserable/ugly as ˈsin** (*informal*) used to emphasize that sb is very unhappy or ugly ➲ more at MULTITUDE, LIVE[1]
■ ***verb*** (-nn-) [I] to break a religious or moral law: *Forgive me, Lord, for I have sinned.* ◊ **~ against sb/sth** *He was* ***more sinned against than sinning*** (= although he did wrong, other people treated him even worse).
■ ***abbr.*** (*mathematics*) SINE

ˈsin bin *noun* (*informal*) (in some sports, for example ICE HOCKEY) a place away from the playing area where the REFEREE sends a player who has broken the rules

since 0‑w /sɪns/ *prep., conj., adv.*
■ ***prep.*** **1** 0‑w (used with the present perfect or past perfect tense) from a time in the past until a later past time, or until now: *She's been off work since Tuesday.* ◊ *We've lived here since 2006.* ◊ *I haven't eaten since breakfast.* ◊ *He's been working in a bank since leaving school.* ◊ *Since the party she had only spoken to him once.* ◊ *'They've split up.'* ***'Since when?'*** ◊ *That was years ago. I've changed jobs* ***since then****.*
HELP Use **for**, not **since**, with a period of time: *I've been learning English for five years.* ◊ ~~*I've been learning English since five years.*~~ **2 ~ when?** used when you are showing that you are angry about sth: *Since when did he ever listen to me?*
■ ***conj.*** **1** 0‑w (used with the present perfect, past perfect or simple present tense in the main clause) from an event in the past until a later past event, or until now: *Cath hasn't phoned since she went to Berlin.* ◊ *It was the first time I'd had visitors since I'd moved to London.* ◊ *It's twenty years since I've seen her.* ◊ *How long is it since we last went to the theatre?* ◊ *She had been worrying* ***ever since*** *the letter arrived.* **2** 0‑w because; as: *We thought that, since we were in the area, we'd stop by and see them.*
■ ***adv.*** (used with the present perfect or past perfect tense) **1** 0‑w from a time in the past until a later past time, or until now: *He left home two weeks ago and we haven't heard from him since.* ◊ *The original building has* ***long since*** (= long before now) *been demolished.* **2** 0‑w at a time after a particular time in the past: *We were divorced two years ago and she has since remarried.*

sin·cere 0‑w /sɪnˈsɪə(r); *NAmE* -ˈsɪr/ *adj.* (*superlative* **sin·cerest**, no *comparative*)
1 0‑w (of feelings, beliefs or behaviour) showing what you really think or feel SYN **genuine**: *a sincere attempt to resolve the problem* ◊ *sincere regret* ◊ *Please accept our sincere thanks.* ◊ *a sincere apology* **2** 0‑w (of a person) saying only what you really think or feel SYN **honest**: *He seemed sincere enough when he said he wanted to help.* ◊ **~ in sth** *She is never completely sincere in what she says about people.* OPP **insincere** ▶ **sin·cer·ity** /sɪnˈserəti/ *noun* [U]: *She*

spoke with total sincerity. ◇ *I can say* **in all sincerity** *that I knew nothing of these plans.*

sin·cere·ly ⚿ /sɪnˈsɪəli; *NAmE* -ˈsɪrli/ *adv.* in a way that shows what you really feel or think about sb/sth: *I sincerely believe that this is the right decision.* ◇ *'I won't let you down.' 'I sincerely hope not.'*
IDM **Yours sincerely** ⚿ (*BrE*) (*NAmE* **Sincerely** (**yours**)) (*formal*) used at the end of a formal letter before you sign your name, when you have addressed sb by their name ➲ WRITING TUTOR page WT24

Sindhi /ˈsɪndi/ *noun* [U] a language spoken in Sind in Pakistan and in western India

sine /saɪn/ *noun* (*abbr.* sin) (*mathematics*) the RATIO of the length of the side opposite one of the angles in a RIGHT-ANGLED triangle that are less than 90° to the length of the longest side ➲ compare COSINE, TANGENT

sine·cure /ˈsɪnɪkjʊə(r); ˈsaɪn-; *NAmE* -kjʊr/ *noun* (*formal*) a job that you are paid for even though it involves little or no work

sine die /ˌsaɪni ˈdaɪiː; ˌsɪneɪ ˈdiːeɪ/ *adv.* (from *Latin*, *formal, law*) without a future date being arranged: *The case was adjourned sine die.*

sine qua non /ˌsɪneɪ kwɑː ˈnəʊn; *NAmE* ˈnoʊn/ *noun* [sing.] **~ (of/for sth)** (from *Latin*, *formal*) something that is essential before you can achieve sth else

sinew /ˈsɪnjuː/ *noun* **1** [C, U] a strong band of TISSUE in the body that joins a muscle to a bone **2** [usually pl.] (*literary*) a source of strength or power IDM see STRAIN *v.*

sinewy /ˈsɪnjuːi/ *adj.* (of a person or an animal) having a thin body and strong muscles SYN **wiry**

sin·ful /ˈsɪnfl/ *adj.* (*formal*) morally wrong or evil SYN **immoral**: *sinful thoughts* ◇ *It is sinful to lie.* ◇ (*informal*) *It's sinful to waste good food!* ▶ **sin·ful·ly** /-fəli/ *adv.* **sin·ful·ness** *noun* [U]

sing ⚿ /sɪŋ/ *verb* (**sang** /sæŋ/, **sung** /sʌŋ/)
1 ⚿ [I, T] to make musical sounds with your voice in the form of a song or tune: *She usually sings in the shower.* ◇ *I just can't sing in tune!* ◇ **~ to sb** *He was singing softly to the baby.* ◇ **~ sth to sb** *Will you sing a song to us?* ◇ **~ sb sth** *Will you sing us a song?* ◇ **~ sth** *Now I'd like to sing a song by the Beatles.* ◇ **~ sb to sleep** *She* **sang the baby to sleep** (= sang until the baby went to sleep). ➲ COLLOCATIONS at MUSIC **2** ⚿ [I] (of birds) to make high musical sounds: *The birds were singing outside my window.* **3** [I] (**+ adv./prep.**) to make a high ringing sound like a whistle: *Bullets sang past my ears.* ▶ **sing** *noun* [sing.]: *Let's have a sing.*
IDM **sing a different 'tune** to change your opinion about sb/sth or your attitude towards sb/sth **sing from the same 'hymn/'song sheet** (*BrE*, *informal*) to show that you are in agreement with each other by saying the same things in public ➲ more at FAT *adj.*
PHR V **ˌsing aˈlong (with sb/sth)** | **ˌsing aˈlong (to sth)** to sing together with sb who is already singing or while a record, radio, or musical instrument is playing: *Do sing along if you know the words.* ➲ related noun SINGALONG **ˈsing of sth** (*old-fashioned* or *formal*) to mention sth in a song or a poem, especially to praise it **ˌsing ˈout** to sing or say sth clearly and loudly: *A voice suddenly sang out above the rest.* **ˌsing ˈup** (*BrE*) (*NAmE* **ˌsing ˈout**) to sing more loudly: *Sing up, let's hear you.*

sing·along /ˈsɪŋəlɒŋ; *NAmE* -lɔːŋ; -lɑːŋ/ (*BrE* also **ˈsing-song**) *noun* an informal occasion at which people sing songs together

singe /sɪndʒ/ *verb* (**singe·ing, singed, singed**) [T, I] **~ (sth)** to burn the surface of sth slightly, usually by mistake; to be burnt in this way: *He singed his hair as he tried to light his cigarette.* ◇ *the smell of singeing fur* ➲ SYNONYMS at BURN

sing·er ⚿ /ˈsɪŋə(r)/ *noun* a person who sings, or whose job is singing, especially in public: *She's a wonderful singer.* ◇ *an opera singer*

sing·ing ⚿ /ˈsɪŋɪŋ/ *noun* [U] the activity of making musical sounds with your voice: *the beautiful singing of birds* ◇ *choral singing* ◇ *There was singing and dancing all night.* ◇ *a singing teacher* ◇ *She has a beautiful singing voice.*

sin·gle ⚿ /ˈsɪŋgl/ *adj., noun, verb*
■ ***adj.***
▸ ONE **1** ⚿ [only before noun] only one: *He sent her a single red rose.* ◇ *a* **single-sex school** (= for boys only or for girls only) ◇ *All these jobs can now be done by one single machine.* ◇ *I couldn't understand a single word she said!* ◇ *the European* **single currency**, *the euro* ◇ (*BrE*) *a* **single honours** *degree* (= for which you study only one subject)
▸ FOR EMPHASIS **2** ⚿ [only before noun] used to emphasize that you are referring to one particular person or thing on its own: *Unemployment is the single most important factor in the growing crime rates.* ◇ *We eat rice* **every single day**.
▸ NOT MARRIED **3** ⚿ (of a person) not married or having a romantic relationship with sb: *The apartments are ideal for single people living alone.* ◇ *Are you still single?* ➲ see also SINGLE PARENT
▸ FOR ONE PERSON **4** ⚿ [only before noun] intended to be used by only one person: *a* **single bed/room** ➲ VISUAL VOCAB page V20 ➲ compare DOUBLE *adj.* (3)
▸ TICKET **5** [only before noun] (*BrE*) (also **one-way** *NAmE, BrE*) a **single** ticket, etc. can be used for travelling to a place but not back again: *a single ticket* ◇ *How much is the single fare to Glasgow?* ➲ compare RETURN *n.* (7) IDM see FILE *n.*, GLANCE *n.*
■ ***noun***
▸ TICKET **1** [C] (*BrE*) a ticket that allows you to travel to a place but not back again: *How much is a single to York?* ➲ compare RETURN *n.* (7)
▸ MUSIC **2** [C] a piece of recorded music, usually popular music, that consists of one song; a CD that a single is recorded on: *The band releases its new single next week.* ➲ compare ALBUM
▸ ROOM **3** ⚿ [C] a room in a hotel, etc. for one person ➲ compare DOUBLE *n.* (5)
▸ MONEY **4** [C] (*NAmE*) a bill/note that is worth one dollar ➲ compare DOUBLE *n.* (5)
▸ UNMARRIED PEOPLE **5 singles** [pl.] people who are not married and do not have a romantic relationship with sb else: *They organize parties for singles.* ◇ *a* **singles bar/club**
▸ IN SPORT **6 singles** [U+sing./pl. v.] (especially in TENNIS) a game when only one player plays against one other; a series of two or more of these games: *the women's singles champion* ◇ *the first round of the men's singles* ◇ *a singles match* ◇ *She's won three singles titles this year.* ➲ compare DOUBLES *n.* (6) **7** [C] (in CRICKET) a hit from which a player scores one RUN (= point) **8** [C] (in BASEBALL) a hit that only allows the player to run to FIRST BASE
■ ***verb***
PHR V **ˌsingle sb/sth↔ˈout (for sth/as sb/sth)** to choose sb/sth from a group for special attention: *She was singled out for criticism.* ◇ *He was singled out as the outstanding performer of the games.*

ˌsingle ˈbed (*NAmE* also **ˌtwin ˈbed**) *noun* a bed big enough for one person ➲ VISUAL VOCAB page V20

ˌsingle-ˈbreast·ed *adj.* (of a jacket or coat) having only one row of buttons that fasten in the middle ➲ compare DOUBLE-BREASTED

ˌsingle ˈcombat *noun* [U] fighting between two people, usually with weapons

ˌsingle ˈcream *noun* [U] (*BrE*) thin cream which is used in cooking and for pouring over food ➲ compare DOUBLE CREAM

ˌsingle-ˈdecker *noun* a bus with only one level ➲ VISUAL VOCAB page V46 ➲ compare DOUBLE-DECKER

ˌsingle ˈfigures *noun* [pl.] a number that is less than ten: *Inflation is down to single figures.* ◇ *The number of people who fail each year is now* **in single figures**.

ˌsingle-ˈhanded *adv.* on your own with nobody helping you SYN **alone**: *to sail around the world single-handed* ▶ **ˌsingle-ˈhanded** *adj.*: *a single-handed voyage* **ˌsingle-ˈhanded·ly** *adv.*

ˌsingle ˈmarket *noun* [usually sing.] (*economics*) a group of countries that have few or no restrictions on the move-

S

ment of goods, money and people between the members of the group

ˌsingle-ˈminded *adj.* only thinking about one particular aim or goal because you are determined to achieve sth: *the single-minded pursuit of power* ◇ *She is very single-minded about her career.* ▶ **ˌsingle-ˈminded·ly** *adv.* **ˌsingle-ˈminded·ness** *noun* [U]

single·ness /ˈsɪŋɡlnəs/ *noun* [U] **1 ~ of purpose** the ability to think about one particular aim or goal because you are determined to succeed **2** the state of not being married or having a partner

ˌsingle ˈparent *noun* a person who takes care of their child or children without a husband, wife or partner: *a single-parent family*

sing·let /ˈsɪŋɡlət/ *noun* (*BrE*) a piece of clothing without sleeves, worn under or instead of a shirt; a similar piece of clothing worn by runners, etc. ➲ compare VEST

single·ton /ˈsɪŋɡltən/ *noun* **1** a single item of the kind that you are talking about **2** a person who is not married or in a romantic relationship **3** a person or an animal that is not a twin, etc.

ˌsingle transˌferable ˈvote *noun* [sing.] (*politics*) a system for electing representatives in which a person's vote can be given to their second or third choice if their first choice is defeated, or if their first choice wins with more votes than they need

ˌsingle-ˈuse *adj.* [only before noun] made to be used once only: *disposable single-use cameras*

sin·gly /ˈsɪŋɡli/ *adv.* alone; one at a time SYN **individually**: *The stamps are available singly or in books of ten.* ◇ *Guests arrived singly or in groups.*

ˈsing-song *noun, adj.*
- ***noun* 1** [C] (*BrE*) = SINGALONG **2** [sing.] a way of speaking in which a person's voice keeps rising and falling
- ***adj.*** [only before noun] a **sing-song** voice keeps rising and falling

sin·gu·lar /ˈsɪŋɡjələ(r)/ *noun, adj.*
- ***noun*** [sing.] (*grammar*) a form of a noun or verb that refers to one person or thing: *The singular of 'bacteria' is 'bacterium'.* ◇ *The verb should be* ***in the singular.*** ➲ compare PLURAL
- ***adj.* 1** (*grammar*) connected with or having the singular form: *a* ***singular noun/verb/ending*** **2** (*formal*) very great or obvious SYN **outstanding**: *landscape of singular beauty* **3** (*literary*) unusual; strange SYN **eccentric**: *a singular style of dress*

S

sin·gu·lar·ity /ˌsɪŋɡjuˈlærəti/ *noun* [U] (*formal*) the quality of sth that makes it unusual or strange

sin·gu·lar·ly /ˈsɪŋɡjələli; *NAmE* -lərli/ *adv.* (*formal*) very; in an unusual way: *singularly beautiful* ◇ *He chose a singularly inappropriate moment to make his request.*

Sin·hal·ese /ˌsɪnhəˈliːz; ˌsɪnə-/ *noun* (*pl.* **Sin·hal·ese**) **1** [C] a member of a race of people living in Sri Lanka **2** [U] the language of the Sinhalese ▶ **Sin·hal·ese** *adj.*

sin·is·ter /ˈsɪnɪstə(r)/ *adj.* seeming evil or dangerous; making you think sth bad will happen: *There was something cold and sinister about him.* ◇ *There is another, more sinister, possibility.*

sink 0⊸ /sɪŋk/ *verb, noun, adj.*
- ***verb*** (**sank** /sæŋk/, **sunk** /sʌŋk/) or (*less frequent* **sunk**, **sunk**)
- ▸ IN WATER/MUD, ETC. **1** 0⊸ [I] to go down below the surface or towards the bottom of a liquid or soft substance: *The ship sank to the bottom of the sea.* ◇ *We're sinking!* ◇ *The wheels started to sink into the mud.* ◇ *to* ***sink like a stone***
- ▸ BOAT **2** 0⊸ [T] **~ sth** to damage a boat or ship so that it goes below the surface of the sea, etc: *a battleship sunk by a torpedo*
- ▸ FALL/SIT DOWN **3** [I] **+ adv./prep.** (of a person) to move downwards, especially by falling or sitting down SYN **collapse**: *I sank into an armchair.* ◇ *She* ***sank back*** *into her seat, exhausted.* ◇ *The old man had* ***sunk to his knees.***
- ▸ MOVE DOWNWARDS **4** 0⊸ [I] (of an object) to move slowly downwards: *The sun was sinking in the west.* ◇ *The foundations of the building are starting to sink.*
- ▸ BECOME WEAKER **5** [I] to decrease in amount, volume, strength, etc: *The pound has sunk to its lowest recorded level against the dollar.* ◇ *He is clearly sinking fast* (= getting weaker quickly and will soon die).
- ▸ OF VOICE **6** [I] to become quieter SYN **fade**: *Her voice sank to a whisper.*
- ▸ DIG IN GROUND **7** [T] **~ sth** to make a deep hole in the ground SYN **drill**: *to* ***sink a well/shaft/mine*** **8** [T] **~ sth** (**+ adv./prep.**) to place sth in the ground by digging: *to sink a post into the ground* ➲ see also SUNKEN
- ▸ PREVENT SUCCESS **9** [T] **~ sth/sb** (*informal*) to prevent sb or sb's plans from succeeding: *I think I've just sunk my chances of getting the job.* ◇ *If the car breaks down, we'll* ***be sunk*** (= have serious problems).
- ▸ BALL **10** [T] **~ sth** to hit a ball into a hole in GOLF or SNOOKER: *He sank a 12-foot putt to win the match.*
- ▸ ALCOHOL **11** [T] **~ sth** (*BrE*, *informal*) to drink sth quickly, especially a large amount of alcohol

IDM **be ˈsunk in sth** to be in a state of unhappiness or deep thought: *She just sat there, sunk in thought.* (**like rats**) **deserting/leaving a sinking ˈship** (*humorous, disapproving*) used to talk about people who leave an organization, a company, etc. that is having difficulties, without caring about the people who are left **sink your ˈdifferences** to agree to forget about your disagreements **a/that ˈsinking feeling** (*informal*) an unpleasant feeling that you get when you realize that sth bad has happened or is going to happen **ˌsink or ˈswim** to be in a situation where you will either succeed by your own efforts or fail completely: *The new students were just left to sink or swim.* **ˌsink so ˈlow | sink to sth** to have such low moral standards that you do sth very bad: *Stealing from your friends? How could you sink so low?* ◇ *I can't believe that anyone would sink to such depths.* ➲ more at HEART

PHR V **ˌsink ˈin | ˌsink ˈinto sth 1** (of words, an event, etc.) to be fully understood or realized: *He paused to allow his words to sink in.* ◇ *The full scale of the disaster has yet to sink in.* **2** (of liquids) to go down into another substance through the surface: *The rain sank into the dry ground.* **ˈsink into sth** to go gradually into a less active, happy or pleasant state: *She sank into a deep sleep.* ◇ *He sank deeper into depression.* **ˌsink ˈinto sth | ˌsink sth ˈinto sth** to go, or to make sth sharp go, deep into sth solid: *The dog sank its teeth into my leg* (= bit it). ◇ *I felt her nails sink into my wrist.* **ˌsink sth ˈinto sth** to spend a lot of money on a business or an activity, for example in order to make money from it in the future: *We sank all our savings into the venture.*

- ***noun* 1** a large open container in a kitchen that has taps/faucets to supply water and that you use for washing dishes in: *Don't just leave your dirty plates in the sink!* ◇ *I felt chained to the kitchen sink* (= I had to spend all my time doing jobs in the house). ➲ picture at PLUG ➲ VISUAL VOCAB page V22 **2** (*especially NAmE*) = WASHBASIN IDM see KITCHEN
- ***adj.*** [only before noun] (*BrE*) located in a poor area where social conditions are bad: *the misery of life in* ***sink estates*** ◇ *a* ***sink school***

sink·er /ˈsɪŋkə(r)/ *noun* a weight that is attached to a FISHING LINE or net to keep it under the water IDM see HOOK *n.*

sink·hole /ˈsɪŋkhəʊl; *NAmE* -hoʊl/ (also **ˈswallow hole**) *noun* (*geology*) a large hole in the ground that a river flows into, created over a long period of time by water that has fallen as rain

sin·ner /ˈsɪnə(r)/ *noun* (*formal*) a person who has committed a SIN or SINS (= broken God's law)

Sinn Fein /ˌʃɪn ˈfeɪn/ *noun* [U+sing./pl. v.] an Irish political party that wants Northern Ireland and the Republic of Ireland to become one country

Sino- /ˈsaɪnəʊ; *NAmE* -noʊ/ *combining form* (in nouns and adjectives) Chinese: *Sino-Japanese relations*

sinu·ous /ˈsɪnjuəs/ *adj.* (*literary*) turning while moving, in an elegant way; having many curves: *a sinuous movement* ◊ *the sinuous grace of a cat* ◊ *the sinuous course of the river* ▸ **sinu·ous·ly** *adv.*

si·nus /ˈsaɪnəs/ *noun* any of the hollow spaces in the bones of the head that are connected to the inside of the nose: *blocked sinuses*

si·nus·itis /ˌsaɪnəˈsaɪtɪs/ *noun* [U] the painful swelling of the sinuses

-sion ➲ -ION

Sioux /suː/ *noun* (*pl.* **Sioux**) a member of a Native American people many of whom live in the US state of South Dakota

sip /sɪp/ *verb, noun*

■ ***verb*** (-pp-) [I, T] to drink sth, taking a very small amount each time: **~ (at sth)** *She sat there, sipping at her tea.* ◊ **~ sth** *He slowly sipped his wine.*

■ ***noun*** a very small amount of a drink that you take into your mouth: *to **have/take a sip** of water*

si·phon (also **sy·phon**) /ˈsaɪfn/ *noun, verb*

■ ***noun*** a tube that is used for moving liquid from one container to another, using pressure from the atmosphere

■ ***verb* 1 ~ sth (+ adv./prep.)** to move a liquid from one container to another, using a siphon: *I siphoned the gasoline out of the car into a can.* ◊ *The waste liquid needs to be siphoned off.* **2 ~ sth (+ adv./prep.)** (*informal*) to remove money from one place and move it to another, especially dishonestly or illegally SYN **divert**: *She has been accused of **siphoning off** thousands of pounds from the company into her own bank account.*

sippy cup /ˈsɪpi kʌp/ *noun* (*NAmE, informal*) a cup with a lid that has holes in it so that a baby can suck liquid from it

sir 🔑 /sɜː(r); sə(r)/ *noun*

1 🔑 used as a polite way of addressing a man whose name you do not know, for example in a shop/store or restaurant, or to show respect: *Good morning, sir. Can I help you?* ◊ *Are you ready to order, sir?* ◊ *'Report to me tomorrow, corporal!' 'Yes, sir!'* ◊ *'Thank you very much.' 'You're welcome, sir. Have a nice day.'* ➲ compare MA'AM ➲ see also MADAM **2** 🔑 **Dear Sir/Sirs** used at the beginning of a formal business letter when you do not know the name of the man or people that you are dealing with: *Dear Sir/Sirs* ◊ *Dear Sir or Madam* **3** 🔑 **Sir** a title that is used before the first name of a man who has received one of the highest British honours (= a KNIGHT), or before the first name of a BARONET: *Sir Paul McCartney* ◊ *Thank you, Sir Paul.* ➲ compare LADY **4** (*BrE*) used as a form of address by children in school to a male teacher: *Please, sir, can I open a window?* ➲ compare MISS

IDM ▸ **ˌno ˈsir!** | **ˌno siˈree!** (*informal, especially NAmE*) certainly not: *We will never allow that to happen! No sir!* **ˌyes ˈsir!** | **ˌyes siˈree!** (*informal, especially NAmE*) used to emphasize that sth is true: *That's a fine car you have. Yes sir!*

sire /ˈsaɪə(r)/ *noun, verb*

■ ***noun* 1** (*technical*) the male parent of an animal, especially a horse ➲ compare DAM **2** (*old use*) a word that people used when they addressed a king

■ ***verb* 1 ~ sth** to be the male parent of an animal, especially a horse **2 ~ sth** (*old-fashioned* or *humorous*) to become the father of a child

siree (also **sir·ree**) /səˈriː/ *exclamation* (*NAmE, informal*) used for emphasis, especially after 'yes' or 'no': *He's not going to do it, no siree.*

siren /ˈsaɪrən/ *noun* **1** a device that makes a long loud sound as a signal or warning: *an air-raid siren* ◊ *A police car raced past with its siren wailing.* **2** (in ancient Greek stories) any of a group of sea creatures that were part woman and part bird, or part woman and part fish, whose beautiful singing made sailors sail towards them into rocks or dangerous waters **3** a woman who is very attractive or beautiful but also dangerous **4 ~ voices/song/call** (*literary*) the TEMPTATION to do sth that seems very attractive but that will have bad results: *The government must resist the siren voices calling for tax cuts.*

sir·loin /ˈsɜːlɔɪn; *NAmE* ˈsɜːrl-/ (also **ˌsirloin ˈsteak**) *noun* [U, C] good quality beef that is cut from a cow's back

si·rocco (also **sci·rocco**) /sɪˈrɒkəʊ; *NAmE* sɪˈrɑːkoʊ/ *noun* (*pl.* -os) a hot wind that blows from Africa into southern Europe

sis /sɪs/ *noun* (*informal*) sister (used when you are speaking to her)

sisal /ˈsaɪsl/ *noun* [U] strong FIBRES made from the leaves of a tropical plant also called sisal, used for making rope, floor coverings, etc.

sissy (*BrE* also **cissy**) /ˈsɪsi/ *noun* (*pl.* -ies) (*informal, disapproving*) a boy that other men or boys laugh at because they think he is weak or frightened, or only interested in the sort of things girls like SYN **wimp** ▸ **sissy** *adj.*

sis·ter 🔑 /ˈsɪstə(r)/ *noun*

1 🔑 a girl or woman who has the same mother and father as another person: *She's my sister.* ◊ *an **older/younger sister*** ◊ (*informal*) *a **big/little/kid sister*** ◊ *We're sisters.* ◊ *Do you have any **brothers or sisters?*** ◊ *My best friend has been like a sister to me* (= very close). ➲ see also HALF-SISTER, STEPSISTER **2** used for talking to or about other members of a women's organization or other women who have the same ideas, purpose, etc. as yourself: *They supported their sisters in the dispute.* **3 Sister** (*BrE*) a senior female nurse who is in charge of a hospital WARD ➲ see also CHARGE NURSE **4 Sister** a female member of a religious group, especially a NUN: *Sister Mary* ◊ *the Sisters of Charity* **5** (in the US) a member of a SORORITY (= a club for a group of female students at a college or university) **6** (*NAmE, informal*) used by black people as a form of address for a black woman **7** (usually used as an adjective) a thing that belongs to the same type or group as sth else: *our sister company in Italy* ◊ *a sister ship*

sis·ter·hood /ˈsɪstəhʊd; *NAmE* -tərh-/ *noun* **1** [U] the close loyal relationship between women who share ideas and aims **2** [C+sing./pl. v.] a group of women who live in a community together, especially a religious one

ˈsister-in-law *noun* (*pl.* **sisters-in-law**) the sister of your husband or wife; your brother's wife; the wife of your husband or wife's brother ➲ compare BROTHER-IN-LAW

sis·ter·ly /ˈsɪstəli; *NAmE* -tərli/ *adj.* typical of or like a sister: *She gave him a sisterly kiss.*

Sisy·phean /ˌsɪsɪˈfiːən/ *adj.* (of a task) impossible to complete ORIGIN From the Greek myth in which **Sisyphus** was punished for the bad things he had done in his life with the never-ending task of rolling a large stone to the top of a hill, from which it always rolled down again.

sit 🔑 /sɪt/ *verb* (**sit·ting, sat, sat** /sæt/)

▸ **ON CHAIR, ETC. 1** 🔑 [I] to rest your weight on your bottom with your back vertical, for example on/in a chair: *She sat and stared at the letter in front of her.* ◊ **+ adv./prep.** *May I sit here?* ◊ *Just sit still!* ◊ *He went and sat beside her.* ◊ *She was sitting at her desk.* ◊ **~ doing sth** *We sat talking for hours.* ➲ see also SIT DOWN **2** [T] **~ sb + adv./prep.** to put sb in a sitting position: *He lifted the child and sat her on the wall.*

▸ **OF THINGS 3** [I] to be in a particular place: **+ adv./prep.** *A large bus was sitting outside.* ◊ *The pot was sitting in a pool of water.* ◊ *The jacket sat beautifully on her shoulders* (= fitted well). ◊ **+ adj.** *The box sat unopened on the shelf.*

▸ **HAVE OFFICIAL POSITION 4** [I] to have an official position as sth or as a member of sth: **~ as sth** *He was sitting as a temporary judge.* ◊ *They both sat as MPs in the House of Commons.* ◊ **~ in/on sth** *She sat on a number of committees.* ◊ **~ for sth** *For years he sat for Henley* (= was the MP for that CONSTITUENCY).

▸ **OF PARLIAMENT, ETC. 5** [I] (of a parliament, committee, court of law, etc.) to meet in order to do official business: *Parliament sits for less than six months of the year.*

▸ **EXAM 6** [T, I] (rather *formal*) to do an exam: (*BrE*) **~ sth** *Candidates will sit the examinations in June.* ◊ *Most of the students sit at least 5 GCSEs.* ◊ (*especially NAmE*) **~ for sth** *He was about to sit for his entrance exam.*

▸ **OF BIRD 7** [I] (**+ adv./prep.**) to rest on a branch, etc. or to stay on a nest to keep the eggs warm

S

▸ OF DOG **8** [I] to sit on its bottom with its front legs straight: *Rover! Sit!*

▸ TAKE CARE OF CHILDREN **9** [I] **~ (for sb)** = BABYSIT: *Who's sitting for you?* ➲ see also HOUSE-SIT

Synonyms

sit

sit down • be seated • take a seat • perch

These words all mean to rest your weight on your bottom with your back upright, for example on a chair.

sit to rest your weight on your bottom with your back upright, for example on a chair: *May I sit here?* ◇ *Sit still, will you!* NOTE **Sit** is usually used with an adverb or prepositional phrase to show where or how sb sits, but sometimes another phrase or clause is used to show what sb does while they are sitting: *We sat talking for hours.*

sit down/sit yourself down to move from a standing position to a sitting position: *Please sit down.* ◇ *Come in and sit yourselves down.*

be seated (*formal*) to be sitting: *She was seated at the head of the table.* NOTE **Be seated** is often used as a formal way of inviting sb to sit down: Please be seated.

take a seat to sit down NOTE **Take a seat** is used especially as a polite way of inviting sb to sit down: *Please take a seat.*

perch (*rather informal*) to sit on sth, especially on the edge of sth: *She perched herself on the edge of the bed.* NOTE **Perch** is always used with an adverb or prepositional phrase to show where sb is perching.

PATTERNS

- to sit/sit down/be seated/take a seat/perch **on** sth
- to sit/sit down/be seated/take a seat **in** sth

IDM **be ˌsitting ˈpretty** (*informal*) to be in a good situation, especially when others are not **sit at sb's ˈfeet** to admire sb very much, especially a teacher or sb from whom you try to learn **sit comfortably, easily, well, etc. (with sth)** to seem right, natural, suitable, etc. in a particular place or situation: *His views did not sit comfortably with the management line.* **sit in ˈjudgement (on/over/upon sb)** to decide whether sb's behaviour is right or wrong, especially when you have no right to do this: *How dare you sit in judgement on me?* **sit on the ˈfence** to avoid becoming involved in deciding or influencing sth: *He tends to sit on the fence at meetings.* **ˌsit ˈtight 1** to stay where you are rather than moving away or changing position: *We sat tight and waited to be rescued.* **2** to stay in the same situation, without changing your mind or taking any action: *Shareholders are being advised to sit tight until the crisis passes.* ➲ more at BOLT *adv.*, LAUREL, SILENTLY

PHR V **ˌsit aˈbout/aˈround** (often *disapproving*) to spend time doing nothing very useful: *I'm far too busy to sit around here.* ◇ **~ doing sth** *He just sits around watching TV.* **ˌsit ˈback 1** to sit on sth, usually a chair, in a relaxed position: *He sat back in his chair and started to read.* **2** to relax, especially by not getting too involved in or anxious about sth: *She's not the kind of person who can sit back and let others do all the work.* **ˌsit ˈby** to take no action to stop sth bad or wrong from happening: *We cannot just sit by and watch this tragedy happen.* **ˌsit ˈdown | ˌsit yourself ˈdown** 0‑ to move from a standing position to a sitting position: *Please sit down.* ◇ *He sat down on the bed.* ◇ *They sat down to consider the problem.* ◇ *Come in and sit yourselves down.* **ˌsit ˈdown and do sth** to give sth time and attention in order to try to solve a problem or achieve sth: *This is something that we should sit down and discuss as a team.* **ˈsit for sb/sth** [no passive] to be a model for an artist or a photographer: *to sit for your portrait* ◇ *She sat for Augustus John.* **ˌsit ˈin for sb** to do sb's job or perform their duties while they are away, sick, etc. SYN **stand in for** **ˌsit ˈin on sth** to attend a meeting, class, etc. in order to listen to or learn from it rather than to take an active part **ˈsit on sth** (*informal*) to have received a letter, report, etc. from sb and then not replied or taken any action concerning it: *They have been sitting on my application for a month now.* **ˌsit sth↔ˈout 1** to stay in a place and wait for sth unpleasant or boring to finish: *We sat out the storm in a cafe.* **2** to not take part in a dance, game or other activity **ˈsit through sth** to stay until the end of a performance, speech, meeting, etc. that you think is boring or too long: *We had to sit through nearly two hours of speeches.* **ˌsit ˈup 1** to be or move yourself into a sitting position, rather than lying down or leaning back: *Sit up straight—don't slouch.* **2** to not go to bed until later than usual: *We sat up half the night, talking.* **ˌsit ˈup (and do sth)** (*informal*) to start to pay careful attention to what is happening, being said, etc: *The proposal had made his clients* ***sit up and take notice.*** **ˌsit sb ˈup** to move sb into a sitting position after they have been lying down

Grammar Point

sit

- You can use *on*, *in* and *at* with **sit**. You **sit on** a chair, a step, the edge of the table, etc. You **sit in** an armchair. If you are **sitting at** a table, desk, etc. you are sitting in a chair close to it, usually so that you can eat a meal, do some work, etc.

sitar /sɪˈtɑː(r); ˈsɪtɑː(r)/ *noun* a musical instrument from S Asia like a GUITAR, with a long neck and two sets of metal strings ➲ VISUAL VOCAB page V31

sit·com /ˈsɪtkɒm; *NAmE* -kɑːm/ (also *formal* **ˌsituation ˈcomedy**) *noun* [C, U] a regular programme on television that shows the same characters in different amusing situations

ˈsit-down *noun* [sing.] (*BrE, informal*) a rest while sitting in a chair: *I need a cup of tea and a sit-down.* ▸ **ˈsit-down** *adj.* [only before noun]: *a sit-down protest* (= in which people sit down to block a road or the entrance to a building until people listen to their demands) ◇ *a sit-down meal for 50 wedding guests* (= served to people sitting at tables)

site 0‑ AW /saɪt/ *noun, verb*

■ ***noun* 1** 0‑ a place where a building, town, etc. was, is or will be located: *the site of a sixteenth century abbey* ◇ *to work on a* ***building/construction site*** ◇ *A site has been chosen for the new school.* ◇ *All the materials are* ***on site*** *so that work can start immediately.* ➲ SYNONYMS at PLACE **2** 0‑ a place where sth has happened or that is used for sth: *the site of the battle* ◇ *an archaeological site* ◇ *a* ***camping/caravan site*** **3** 0‑ (*computing*) a place on the Internet where a company, an organization, a university, etc. puts information ➲ COLLOCATIONS at EMAIL ➲ see also MIRROR SITE, WEBSITE

■ ***verb*** [often passive] **~ sth + adv./prep.** to build or place sth in a particular position: *There was a meeting to discuss the siting of the new school.* ◇ *The castle is magnificently sited high up on a cliff.*

ˈsit-in *noun* a protest in which a group of workers, students, etc. refuse to leave their factory, college, etc. until people listen to their demands: *to* ***hold/stage a sit-in***

sit·ter /ˈsɪtə(r)/ *noun* **1** a person who sits or stands somewhere so that sb can paint a picture of them or photograph them **2** (*especially NAmE*) = BABYSITTER **3** (*BrE, informal*) (in football (SOCCER)) an easy chance to score a goal

sit·ting /ˈsɪtɪŋ/ *noun* **1** a period of time during which a court or a parliament deals with its business **2** a time when a meal is served in a hotel, etc. to a number of people at the same time: *A hundred people can be served* ***at one sitting*** (= at the same time). **3** a period of time that a person spends sitting and doing an activity: *I read the book* ***in one sitting.*** **4** a period of time when sb sits or stands to have their picture painted or be photographed

ˌsitting ˈduck (also **ˌsitting ˈtarget**) *noun* a person or thing that is easy to attack

ˈ**sitting room** *noun* (*BrE*) = LIVING ROOM

ˌ**sitting ˈtenant** *noun* (*BrE*) a person who is living in a rented house or flat and who has the legal right to stay there

situ ➲ IN SITU

situ·ate /ˈsɪtʃueɪt/ *verb* (*formal*) **1** ~ **sth + adv./prep.** to build or place sth in a particular position **2** ~ **sth + adv./prep.** to consider how an idea, event, etc. is related to other things that influence your view of it: *Let me try and situate the events in their historical context.*

situ·ated /ˈsɪtʃueɪtɪd/ *adj.* [not before noun] (*formal*) **1** in a particular place or position: *My bedroom was situated on the top floor of the house.* ◇ *The hotel is* ***beautifully situated*** *in a quiet spot near the river.* ◇ *All the best theatres and restaurants are situated within a few minutes' walk of each other.* **2** (of a person, an organization, etc.) in a particular situation or in particular circumstances: *Small businesses are well situated to benefit from the single market.*

Synonyms

situation

circumstances • position • conditions • things • the case • state of affairs

These are all words for the conditions and facts that are connected with and affect the way things are.

situation all the things that are happening at a particular time and in a particular place: *the present economic situation*

circumstances the facts that are connected with and affect a situation, an event or an action; the conditions of a person's life, especially the money they have: *The ship sank in mysterious circumstances.*

position the situation that sb is in, especially when it affects what they can and cannot do: *She felt she was in a position of power.*

conditions the circumstances in which people live, work or do things; the physical situation that affects how sth happens: *We were forced to work outside in freezing conditions.*

CIRCUMSTANCES OR CONDITIONS?

Circumstances refers to sb's financial situation; **conditions** are things such as the quality and amount of food or shelter they have. The **circumstances** that affect an event are the facts surrounding it; the **conditions** that affect it are usually physical ones, such as the weather.

things (*rather informal*) the general situation, as it affects sb: *Hi, Jane!* ***How are things?*** ◇ *Think things over before you decide.*

the case the true situation: *If that is the case* (= if the situation described is true), *we need more staff.*

state of affairs a situation: *How did this unhappy state of affairs come about?*

SITUATION OR STATE OF AFFAIRS?

State of affairs is mostly used with *this*. It is also used with adjectives describing how good or bad a situation is, such as *happy, sorry, shocking, sad* and *unhappy*, as well as those relating to time, such as *present* and *current*. **Situation** is much more frequent and is used in a wider variety of contexts.

PATTERNS

- **in** (a) particular situation/circumstances/position/state of affairs
- the/sb's **economic/financial/social** situation/circumstances/position/conditions
- (a/an) **happy/unhappy** situation/circumstances/position/state of affairs
- to **look at/review** the situation/circumstances/conditions/things

situ·ation 0➔ /ˌsɪtʃuˈeɪʃn/ *noun* **1** 0➔ all the circumstances and things that are happening at a particular time and in a particular place: *to be* ***in a*** *difficult* ***situation*** ◇ *You could get into* ***a situation where*** *you have to decide immediately.* ◇ *We have all been in similar embarrassing situations.* ◇ *the present* ***economic/financial/political, etc. situation*** ◇ *He could see no way out of the situation.* ◇ *In your situation, I would look for another job.* ◇ *What we have here is a crisis situation.* ◇ *I'm in a* ***no-win situation*** (= whatever I do will be bad for me). **2** (*formal*) the kind of area or surroundings that a building or town has: *The town is in a delightful situation in a wide green valley.* **3** (*old-fashioned* or *formal*) a job: ***Situations Vacant*** (= the title of the section in a newspaper where jobs are advertised) IDM see SAVE *v.* ▶ **situ·ation·al** /ˌsɪtʃuˈeɪʃənl/ *adj.*

ˌ**situation ˈcomedy** *noun* [C, U] (*formal*) = SITCOM

ˈ**sit-up** (also **crunch**) *noun* an exercise for making your stomach muscles strong, in which you lie on your back on the floor and raise the top part of your body to a sitting position ➲ VISUAL VOCAB page V35

six 0➔ /sɪks/ *number* 6 HELP There are examples of how to use numbers at the entry for **five**.

IDM **at ˌsixes and ˈsevens** (*informal*) in confusion; not well organized **be ˌsix feet ˈunder** (*informal*) to be dead and in a grave **hit/knock sb for ˈsix** (*BrE*) to affect sb very deeply **it's six of ˌone and half a dozen of the ˈother** (*saying*) used to say that there is not much real difference between two possible choices

the ˌSix ˈCounties *noun* [pl.] a way of referring to Northern Ireland, used especially by people who want the whole of Ireland to be one country

ˌ**six-ˈfigure** *adj.* [only before noun] used to describe a number that is 100 000 or more: *a six-figure salary*

six·fold /ˈsɪksfəʊld; *NAmE* -foʊld/ *adj., adv.* ➲ -FOLD

ˈ**six-gun** *noun* = SIX-SHOOTER

the ˌSix ˈNations *noun* [sing.] a RUGBY competition between England, France, Ireland, Italy, Scotland and Wales

ˈ**six-pack** *noun* **1** a set of six bottles or cans sold together, especially of beer **2** (*informal*) stomach muscles that are very strong and that you can see clearly across sb's stomach

six·pence /ˈsɪkspəns/ *noun* a British coin in use until 1971, worth six old pence

ˈ**six-shooter** (also ˈ**six-gun**) *noun* (*especially NAmE*) a small gun that holds six bullets

six·teen 0➔ /ˌsɪksˈtiːn/ *number* 16 ▶ **six·teenth** /ˌsɪksˈtiːnθ/ *ordinal number, noun* HELP There are examples of how to use ordinal numbers at the entry for **fifth**.

ˌ**sixˈteenth note** (*NAmE*) (*BrE* **semi·quaver**) *noun* (*music*) a note that lasts half as long as a QUAVER/EIGHTH NOTE ➲ picture at MUSIC

sixth 0➔ /sɪksθ/ *ordinal number, noun*
■ ***ordinal number*** 6th HELP There are examples of how to use ordinal numbers at the entry for **fifth**.
■ ***noun*** each of six equal parts of sth

ˈ**sixth form** *noun* [usually sing.] (*BrE*) the two final years at school for students between the ages of 16 and 18 who are preparing to take A LEVELS (= advanced level exams): *Sue is in the sixth form now.*

ˌ**sixth-form ˈcollege** *noun* (in Britain) a school for students over the age of 16

ˈ**sixth-former** *noun* (*BrE*) a student who is in the sixth form at school

ˌ**sixth ˈsense** *noun* [sing.] a special ability to know sth without using any of the five senses that include sight, touch, etc: *My sixth sense told me to stay here and wait.*

sixty 0➔ /ˈsɪksti/ **1** *number* 60 **2** *noun* **the sixties** [pl.] numbers, years or temperatures from 60 to 69 ▶ **six·ti·eth** /ˈsɪkstiəθ/ *ordinal*

S

number, noun HELP There are examples of how to use ordinal numbers at the entry for **fifth**.

IDM **in your 'sixties** between the ages of 60 and 69

the ˌsixty-four ˌthousand ˌdollar 'question *noun* (*informal*) the thing that people most want to know, or that is most important ORIGIN From the name of a US television show which gave prizes of money to people who answered questions correctly. The correct answer to the last question was worth $64 000.

size /saɪz/ *noun, verb*

■ *noun*

▸ HOW LARGE/SMALL **1** [U, C] how large or small a person or thing is: *an area **the size of*** (= the same size as) *Wales* ◇ *They complained about the size of their gas bill.* ◇ *Dogs come **in all shapes and sizes**.* ◇ *The facilities are excellent for a town that size.* ◇ *The kitchen is **a good size*** (= not small). ◇ *It's similar **in size** to a tomato.* **2** [U] the large amount or extent of sth: *You should have seen the size of their house!* ◇ *We were shocked at the size of his debts.*

▸ OF CLOTHES/SHOES/GOODS **3** [C, U] one of a number of standard measurements in which clothes, shoes and other goods are made and sold: *The jacket was the wrong size.* ◇ *It's not my size.* ◇ *They didn't have the jacket **in my size**.* ◇ *She's a size 12 in clothes.* ◇ *The hats are made in three sizes: small, medium and large.* ◇ *I need a bigger/smaller size.* ◇ *What size do you take?* ◇ *She takes (a) size 5 in shoes.* ◇ *Do you have these shoes in (a) size 5?* ◇ *Try this one **for size*** (= to see if it is the correct size). ◇ *The glass can be **cut to size*** (= cut to the exact measurements) *for you.* HELP To ask about the size of something, you usually say: *How big?* You use: *What size?* to ask about something that is produced in fixed measurements.

▸ -SIZED/-SIZE **4** (in adjectives) having the size mentioned: *a medium-sized house* ◇ *Cut it into bite-size pieces.* ➲ see also KING-SIZE, MAN-SIZED, PINT-SIZED, QUEEN-SIZE

▸ STICKY SUBSTANCE **5** [U] a sticky substance that is used for making material stiff or for preparing walls for WALLPAPER

IDM **cut sb down to 'size** to show sb that they are not as important as they think they are **that's about the 'size of it** (*informal*) that's how the situation seems to be: *'So they won't pay up?' 'That's about the size of it.'*

■ *verb*

▸ GIVE SIZE **1** [usually passive] **~ sth** to mark the size of sth; to give a size to sth: *The screws are sized in millimetres.*

▸ CHANGE SIZE **2** [usually passive] **~ sth** to change the size of sth: *The fonts can be sized according to what effect you want.*

▸ MAKE STICKY **3 ~ sth** to cover sth with a sticky substance called SIZE

PHR V **ˌsize sb/sth↔'up** (*informal*) to form a judgement or an opinion about sb/sth SYN **sum up**: *She knew that he was looking at her, sizing her up.* ◇ *He sized up the situation very quickly.*

size·able (also **siz·able**) /'saɪzəbl/ *adj.* fairly large SYN **considerable**: *The town has a sizeable Sikh population.*

ˌsize 'zero *noun* [U, C] (in the US) the smallest size for women's clothes, used to describe women who are extremely thin: *size zero models and celebrities* ◇ *She is a size zero.*

siz·zle /'sɪzl/ *verb* [I] to make the sound of food frying in hot oil: *sizzling sausages* ▸ **siz·zle** *noun* [sing.]

siz·zling /'sɪzlɪŋ/ *adj.* **1** very hot: *sizzling summer temperatures* **2** very exciting: *a sizzling love affair*

sjam·bok /'ʃæmbɒk; *NAmE* -bɑːk/ *noun* (*SAfrE*) a long, stiff WHIP made of leather

ska /skɑː/ *noun* [U] a type of fast popular music with strong rhythms, developed in Jamaica in the 1960s and that developed into REGGAE

skank /skæŋk/ *noun* (*informal, especially NAmE*) an unpleasant person

skanky /'skæŋki/ *adj.* (*informal, especially NAmE*) very unpleasant

skate /skeɪt/ *verb, noun*

■ *verb* **1** [I, T] to move on skates (usually referring to ICE SKATING, if no other information is given): *Can you skate?* ◇ *It was so cold that we were able to **go skating** on the lake.* ◇ **~ sth** *He skated an exciting programme at the American Championships.* **2** [I] to ride on a SKATEBOARD IDM see THIN *adj.*

PHR V **ˌskate 'over sth** to avoid talking about or considering a difficult subject: *He politely skated over the issue.*

■ *noun* **1** = ICE SKATE, ROLLER SKATE: *a pair of skates* ➲ VISUAL VOCAB page V36 **2** (*pl.* skate or skates) a large flat sea fish that can be eaten

IDM **get/put your 'skates on** (*BrE, informal*) used to tell sb to hurry: *Get your skates on or you'll miss the bus.*

skate·board /'skeɪtbɔːd; *NAmE* -bɔːrd/ *noun* a short narrow board with small wheels at each end, which you stand on and ride as a sport: *a **skateboard park/ramp*** ▸ **skate·board** *verb* [I] **skate·board·er** *noun* **skate·board·ing** *noun* [U]: *a skateboarding magazine* ➲ VISUAL VOCAB page V34

skate·park /'skeɪtpɑːk; *NAmE* -'pɑːrk/ *noun* an area built for people to use SKATEBOARDS, with slopes, curves, etc.

skater /'skeɪtə(r)/ *noun* **1** a person who skates for pleasure or as a sport: *a **figure/speed skater*** ➲ see also ICE SKATER **2** = SKATEBOARDER: *Extreme skaters perform jumps, spins, flips, etc.*

'skate shoe (*especially NAmE*) (also **Heely™** especially in *BrE*) *noun* a sports shoe that has one or more wheels underneath it

skat·ing /'skeɪtɪŋ/ *noun* [U] **1** (also **'ice skating**) the sport or activity of moving on ice on SKATES: *to go skating* ➲ see also FIGURE-SKATING, SPEED SKATING **2** = ROLLER SKATING IDM see THIN *adj.*

'skating rink (also **rink**) *noun* **1** = ICE RINK ➲ VISUAL VOCAB page V34 **2** an area or a building where you can ROLLER SKATE

ske·dad·dle /skɪ'dædl/ *verb* [I] (*informal, humorous*) to move away or leave a place quickly, especially in order to avoid sb

skeet·er /'skiːtə(r)/ *noun* (*NAmE, informal, humorous*) = MOSQUITO

skeet shooting /'skiːt ʃuːtɪŋ/ (*NAmE*) (*BrE* **ˌclay 'pigeon shooting**) *noun* a sport in which a disc of baked clay (called a **clay pigeon**) is thrown into the air for people to shoot at

skein /skeɪn/ *noun* a long piece of wool, thread, or YARN that is loosely tied together

skel·etal /'skelətl/ *adj.* **1** (*technical*) connected with the skeleton of a person or an animal **2** looking like a skeleton: *skeletal figures dressed in rags* **3** that exists only in a basic form, as an outline: *He has written only a skeletal plot for the book so far.*

skel·eton /'skelɪtn/ *noun* **1** [C] the structure of bones that supports the body of a person or an animal; a model of this structure: *The human skeleton consists of 206 bones.* ◇ *a dinosaur skeleton* ➲ VISUAL VOCAB page V48 **2** [C] (*informal*) a very thin person or animal **3** [C, usually sing.] the main structure that supports a building, etc. SYN **framework**: *Only the concrete skeleton of the factory remained.* **4** [C, usually sing.] the basic outline of a plan, piece of writing, etc. to which more details can be added later: *Examples were used to flesh out the skeleton of the argument.* **5** [C] **~ staff, crew, etc.** the smallest number of people, etc. that you need to do sth: *There will only be a skeleton staff on duty over the holiday.* ◇ *We managed to operate a skeleton bus service during the strike.* **6** [C] (*sport*) a type of SLEDGE/SLED (= a vehicle for sliding over ice) for racing, used by one person lying on their front with their feet pointing backwards **7** [U] the sport or event of racing down a special track of ice on a skeleton: *Canada won gold and silver in the skeleton.*

IDM **a skeleton in the 'cupboard** (*BrE*) (also **a skeleton in the 'closet** *NAmE, BrE*) (*informal*) something shocking, embarrassing, etc. that has happened to you or your family in the past that you want to keep secret

ˈ**skeleton key** *noun* a key that will open several different locks

skelm /skelm/ *noun* (*SAfrE*) a person that you believe is a criminal or that you do not trust

skep·tic (*NAmE*) (*BrE* **scep·tic**) /ˈskeptɪk/ *noun* a person who usually doubts that claims or statements are true, especially those that other people believe in

skep·tical (*NAmE*) (*BrE* **scep·tical**) /ˈskeptɪkl/ *adj.* **~ (about/of sth)** having doubts that a claim or statement is true or that sth will happen: *I am skeptical about his chances of winning.* ◇ *The public remain skeptical of these claims.* ◇ *She looked highly skeptical.* ▶ **skep·tic·al·ly** (*NAmE*) (*BrE* **scep·tic·al·ly**) /-kli/ *adv.*

skep·ti·cism (*NAmE*) (*BrE* **scep·ti·cism**) /ˈskeptɪsɪzəm/ *noun* [U, sing.] an attitude of doubting that claims or statements are true or that sth will happen: *Such claims should be regarded with a certain amount of skepticism.*

sketch /sketʃ/ *noun, verb*
■ ***noun*** **1** a simple picture that is drawn quickly and does not have many details: *The artist is making sketches for his next painting.* ◇ *She drew a* ***sketch map*** *of the area to show us the way.* ➲ SYNONYMS at PICTURE ➲ COLLOCATIONS at ART **2** a short funny scene on television, in the theatre, etc: *The drama group did a sketch about a couple buying a new car.* **3** a short report or story that gives only basic details about sth: *a biographical sketch of the Prime Minister*
■ ***verb*** **1** [T, I] **~ (sb/sth)** to make a quick drawing of sb/sth: *He quickly sketched the view from the window.* **2** [T] **~ sth (out)** to give a general description of sth, giving only the basic facts SYN **outline**: *She sketched out her plan for tackling the problem.*
PHR V ˌ**sketch sth↔ˈin** to give more information or details about sth

sketch·book /ˈsketʃbʊk/ (also ˈ**sketch pad**) *noun* a book of sheets of paper for drawing on

sketchy /ˈsketʃi/ *adj.* (**sketch·ier**, **sketch·iest**) not complete or detailed and therefore not very useful SYN **rough**: *He gave us a very sketchy account of his visit.* ◇ *sketchy notes* ▶ **sketch·ily** *adv.* **sketchi·ness** *noun* [U]

skew /skjuː/ *verb* **1** [T] **~ sth** to change or influence sth with the result that it is not accurate, fair, normal, etc: *to skew the statistics* **2** [I] **+ adv./prep.** (*BrE*) to move or lie at an angle, especially in a position that is not normal: *The ball skewed off at a right angle.*

skew·bald /ˈskjuːbɔːld/ *adj.* (of a horse) with areas on it of white and another colour, usually not black ➲ compare PIEBALD ▶ **skew·bald** *noun*: *He was riding a skewbald.*

skewed /skjuːd/ *adj.* **1** (of information) not accurate or correct SYN **distorted**: *skewed statistics* **2 ~ (towards sb/sth)** directed towards a particular group, place, etc. in a way that may not be accurate or fair: *The book is heavily skewed towards American readers.* **3** not straight or level: *The car had ended up skewed across the road.* ➲ see also ASKEW

skew·er /ˈskjuːə(r)/ *noun, verb*
■ ***noun*** a long thin pointed piece of metal or wood that is pushed through pieces of meat, vegetables, etc. to hold them together while they are cooking, or used to test whether sth is completely cooked
■ ***verb*** **~ sth** to push a skewer or other thin pointed object through sth

ˌ**skew-ˈwhiff** *adj.* (*BrE, informal*) not straight

ski /skiː/ *noun, adj., verb*
■ ***noun*** (*pl.* **skis**) **1** one of a pair of long narrow pieces of wood, metal or plastic that you attach to boots so that you can move smoothly over snow: *a pair of skis* ➲ VISUAL VOCAB pages V39, V43 **2** = WATERSKI
■ ***adj.*** [only before noun] connected with the sport of skiing: *ski boots* ◇ *the ski slopes*
■ ***verb*** (**ski·ing, skied, skied**) **1** [I] (**+ adv./prep.**) to move over snow on skis, especially as a sport **2 go skiing** [I] to spend time skiing for pleasure: *We went skiing in France in March.* ➲ see also SKIING, WATERSKI

skid /skɪd/ *verb, noun*
■ ***verb*** (**-dd-**) [I] (usually of a vehicle) to slide sideways or forwards in an uncontrolled way: *The car skidded on the ice and went straight into the wall.* ◇ *The taxi* ***skidded to a halt*** *just in time.* ◇ *Her foot skidded on the wet floor and she fell heavily.*
■ ***noun*** **1** the movement of a vehicle when it suddenly slides sideways in an uncontrolled way: *The motorbike* ***went into a skid.*** ◇ *The* ***skid marks*** *on the road showed how fast the car had been travelling.* **2** a part that is underneath some aircraft, beside the wheels, and is used for landing: *the skids of a helicopter* ➲ VISUAL VOCAB page V43
IDM **put the ˈskids under sb/sth** (*informal*) to stop sb/sth from being successful or making progress **be on the ˈskids** (*informal*) to be in a bad situation that will get worse

skid·pan /ˈskɪdpæn/ *noun* an area with a surface that is especially prepared so that drivers can practise controlling skids

ˌ**skid ˈrow** *noun* [U] (*informal, especially NAmE*) used to describe the poorest part of a town, the sort of place where people who have no home or job and who drink too much alcohol live: *to be on skid row*

skier /ˈskiːə(r)/ *noun* a person who skis

skies *pl.* of SKY

skiff /skɪf/ *noun* a small light boat for ROWING or sailing, usually for one person

skif·fle /ˈskɪfl/ *noun* a type of music popular in the 1950s, that was a mixture of JAZZ and FOLK MUSIC

ski·ing /ˈskiːɪŋ/ *noun* [U] the sport or activity of moving over snow on skis: *to* ***go skiing*** ◇ ***downhill/cross-country skiing*** ◇ *a* ***skiing holiday/instructor/lesson/vacation***

ski·joring /ˈskiːdʒɔːrɪŋ; ˌskiːˈdʒɔːr-/ *noun* [U] the activity of being pulled over snow or ice on skis, by a horse or dog

ˈ**ski jump** *noun* a very steep artificial slope that ends suddenly and that is covered with snow. People ski down the slope, jump off the end and see how far they can travel through the air before landing. ▶ ˈ**ski jumper** *noun* ˈ**ski jumping** *noun* [U]: *Is ski jumping an Olympic sport?* ◇ *the Swiss ski-jumping team*

skil·ful 🔑 (*especially US* **skill·ful**) /ˈskɪlfl/ *adj.*
1 🔑 (of a person) good at doing sth, especially sth that needs a particular ability or special training SYN **accomplished**: *a skilful player/performer/teacher* **2** 🔑 made or done very well SYN **professional**: *Thanks to her skilful handling of the affair, the problem was averted.* ▶ **skil·ful·ly** 🔑 /-fəli/ *adv.*

ˈ**ski lift** *noun* a machine for taking SKIERS up a slope so that they can then ski down

skill 🔑 /skɪl/ *noun*
1 🔑 [U] the ability to do sth well: *The job requires skill and an eye for detail.* ◇ **~ in/at sth/doing sth** *What made him remarkable as a photographer was his skill in capturing the moment.* **2** 🔑 [C] a particular ability or type of ability: *We need people with practical skills like carpentry.* ◇ *management skills*

S

skilled 🔑 /skɪld/ *adj.*
1 🔑 having enough ability, experience and knowledge to be able to do sth well: *a skilled engineer/negotiator/craftsman* ◇ *a shortage of* ***skilled labour*** (= people who have had training in a skill) ◇ **~ in/at sth/doing sth** *She is* ***highly skilled*** *at dealing with difficult customers.* **2** 🔑 (of a job) needing special abilities or training SYN **expert**: *Furniture-making is very skilled work.* OPP **unskilled**

skil·let /ˈskɪlɪt/ *noun* (*NAmE*) = FRYING PAN ➲ VISUAL VOCAB page V24

skill·ful (*NAmE*) = SKILFUL

ˈ**skill set** *noun* a person's range of skills or abilities

skim /skɪm/ *verb* (**-mm-**) **1** [T] to remove fat, cream, etc. from the surface of a liquid: **~ sth off/from sth** *Skim the scum off the jam and let it cool.* ◇ **~ sth** *Skim the jam and let it cool.* **2** [I, T, no passive] to move quickly and lightly over a surface, not touching it or only touching it occasionally; to make sth do this: **~ along/over, etc. sth** *We watched the birds skimming over the lake.* ◇ **~ sth** *The speedboat took* off, skimming the waves. ◇ (*figurative*) *This report has barely* ***skimmed the surface*** *of the subject.* ◇ **~ sth across, over, etc. sth** (*BrE*) *Small boys were skimming stones across the water.* ➲ see also SKIP **3** [I, T] to read sth quickly in order to find a particular point or the main points: **~ through/over sth** *He skimmed through the article trying to find his name.* ◇ **~ sth** *I always skim the financial section of the newspaper.* **4** [T] **~ sth (from sth)** (*informal*) to steal small amounts of money frequently over a period of time **5** [I, T] **~ (sth)** to illegally copy electronic information from a credit card in order to use it without the owner's permission

PHR V ˌ**skim sth/sb↔ˈoff** to take for yourself the best part of sth, often in an unfair way

ˌ**skimmed ˈmilk** (*BrE*) (also ˌ**skim ˈmilk** *NAmE, BrE*) *noun* [U] milk that contains less fat than normal because the cream has been removed from it

skimp /skɪmp/ *verb* [I] **~ (on sth)** to try to spend less time, money, etc. on sth than is really needed: *Older people should not skimp on food or heating.*

skimpy /ˈskɪmpi/ *adj.* (**skimp·ier, skimpi·est**) **1** (of clothes) very small and not covering much of your body: *a skimpy dress* **2** (*disapproving*) not large enough in amount or size: *a skimpy meal* ◇ *They provided only skimpy details.*

skin 🔑 /skɪn/ *noun, verb*

■ ***noun***

▸ ON BODY **1** 🔑 [U, C] the layer of TISSUE that covers the body: *to have* ***dark/fair/olive, etc. skin*** ◇ *The snake sheds its skin once a year.* ◇ *cosmetics for sensitive skins* ◇ *skin cancer* ➲ COLLOCATIONS at PHYSICAL ➲ see also FORESKIN, REDSKIN

▸ -SKINNED **2** (in adjectives) having the type of skin mentioned: *dark-skinned* ◇ *fair-skinned* ➲ see also THICK-SKINNED, THIN-SKINNED

▸ OF DEAD ANIMAL **3** 🔑 [C, U] (often in compounds) the skin of a dead animal with or without its fur, used for making leather, etc: *The skins are removed and laid out to dry.* ◇ *a tiger skin rug*

▸ OF FRUIT/VEGETABLES **4** 🔑 [C, U] the outer layer of some fruit and vegetables: *Remove the skins by soaking the tomatoes in hot water.* ➲ VISUAL VOCAB page V26 ➲ see also BANANA SKIN ➲ compare PEEL, RIND, ZEST

▸ OF SAUSAGE **5** [C, U] the thin outer layer of a SAUSAGE: *Prick the skins before grilling.*

▸ ON LIQUIDS **6** [C, U] the thin layer that forms on the surface of some liquids, especially when they become cold: *A skin had formed on the top of the milk.*

▸ OUTSIDE LAYER **7** [C] a layer that covers the outside of sth: *the outer skin of the earth* ◇ *the metal skin of the aircraft* **8** [C] a special cover for any small electronic device that you can carry with you so that you can listen to music: *You can create your own custom skin for your iPod.*

▸ IN A COMPUTER PROGRAM **9** [C] (*computing*) the INTERFACE of a computer program (= the way a computer program presents information on screen), that the user can change to suit their particular preferences

IDM **by the ˌskin of your ˈteeth** (*informal*) if you do sth **by the skin of your teeth**, you only just manage to do it **get under sb's ˈskin** (*informal*) to annoy sb: *Don't let him get under your skin.* **have got sb under your ˈskin** (*informal*) to be extremely attracted to sb **it's no skin off ˈmy, ˈyour, ˈhis, etc. nose** (*informal*) used to say that sb is not upset or annoyed about sth because it does not affect them in a bad way **make your ˈskin crawl** to make you feel afraid or full of disgust (**nothing but/all/only**) **skin and ˈbone** (*informal*) extremely thin in a way that is not attractive or healthy ➲ more at JUMP *v.*, SAVE *v.*, THICK *adj.*, THIN *adj.*

■ ***verb*** (-nn-)

▸ ANIMAL/FRUIT/VEGETABLE **1 ~ sth** to take the skin off an animal, a fruit or a vegetable: *You'll need four ripe tomatoes, skinned and chopped.*

▸ PART OF BODY **2 ~ sth** to rub the skin off part of your body by accident: *He skinned his knees climbing down the tree.*

IDM see EYE *n.*, WAY *n.*

PHR V ˌ**skin ˈup** (*BrE, informal*) to make a cigarette containing MARIJUANA

skin·care /ˈskɪnkeə(r); *NAmE* -ker/ *noun* [U] the use of creams and special products to look after your skin

ˌ**skin-ˈdeep** *adj.* [not usually before noun] (of a feeling or an attitude) not as important or strongly felt as it appears to be SYN **superficial** IDM see BEAUTY

ˈ**skin-diving** *noun* [U] the sport or activity of swimming underwater with simple breathing equipment but without a special suit for protection: *to go skin-diving* ▸ ˈ**skin-diver** *noun*

skin·flint /ˈskɪnflɪnt/ *noun* (*informal, disapproving*) a person who does not like spending money SYN **miser**

skin·ful /ˈskɪnfʊl/ *noun* [usually sing.] (*BrE, slang*) a large quantity of alcohol to drink, enough to make you very drunk

ˈ**skin graft** *noun* a medical operation in which healthy skin is taken from one part of sb's body and placed over another part to replace skin that has been burned or damaged; a piece of skin that is moved in this way

skin·head /ˈskɪnhed/ *noun* a young person with very short hair, especially one who is violent, aggressive and RACIST

skink /skɪŋk/ *noun* a LIZARD with short legs or with no legs

skinny /ˈskɪni/ *adj., noun*

■ ***adj.*** (**skin·nier, skin·ni·est**) **1** (*informal*, usually *disapproving*) very thin, especially in a way that you find unpleasant or ugly: *skinny legs* **2** (of clothes) designed to fit closely to the body: *a skinny sweater* **3** (*NAmE, informal*) low in fat: *a skinny latte*

■ ***noun*** [U] **the ~ (on sb/sth)** (*NAmE, informal*) information about sb/sth, especially details that are not generally known: *This book gives you the skinny on Hollywood.*

ˈ**skinny-dipping** *noun* [U] (*informal*) swimming without any clothes on

skint /skɪnt/ *adj.* [not usually before noun] (*BrE, informal*) having no money

skin·tight /ˌskɪnˈtaɪt/ *adj.* (of clothes) fitting very closely to the body

skip /skɪp/ *verb, noun*

■ ***verb*** (-pp-)

▸ MOVE WITH JUMPS **1** [I] (**+ adv./prep.**) to move forwards lightly and quickly making a little jump with each step: *She skipped happily along beside me.*

▸ JUMP OVER ROPE **2** [I] (*BrE*) (*NAmE* **jump ˈrope**, ˌ**skip ˈrope**) [T] to jump over a rope which is held at both ends by yourself or by two other people and is passed again and again over your head and under your feet: *The girls were skipping in the playground.* ◇ *She likes to skip rope as a warm-up.*

▸ NOT DO STH **3** [T] **~ sth** to not do sth that you usually do or should do: *I often skip breakfast altogether.* ◇ (*especially NAmE*) *She decided to* ***skip class*** *that afternoon.* **4** [T, I] to leave out sth that would normally be the next thing that you would do, read, etc: **~ sth** *You can skip the next chapter if you have covered the topic in class.* ◇ **~ over sth** *I skipped over the last part of the book.* ◇ **~ to sth** *I suggest we skip to the last item on the agenda.*

▸ CHANGE QUICKLY **5** [I] **+ adv./prep.** to move from one place to another or from one subject to another very quickly: *She kept skipping from one topic of conversation to another.*

▸ LEAVE SECRETLY **6** [T] **~ sth** to leave a place secretly or suddenly: *The bombers skipped the country shortly after the blast.*

▸ STONES **7** (*BrE* also **skim**) [T] **~ sth (across, over, etc. sth)** to make a flat stone jump across the surface of water: *The boys were skipping stones across the pond.*

IDM ˈ**skip it** (*informal*) used to tell sb rudely that you do not want to talk about sth or repeat what you have said: *'What were you saying?' 'Oh, skip it!'*

PHR V ˌ**skip ˈoff/ˈout** to leave secretly or suddenly ˌ**skip ˈout on sb** (*NAmE*) to leave sb, especially when they need you

S

■ ***noun***
▸ MOVEMENT **1** a skipping movement: *She gave a skip and a jump and was off down the street.*
▸ CONTAINER FOR WASTE **2** (*BrE*) (*NAmE* **Dumpster™**) a large open container for putting old bricks, rubbish/garbage, etc. in. The skip is then loaded on a lorry/truck and taken away.

ˌski pants *noun* [pl.] **1** trousers/pants worn for skiing **2** narrow trousers/pants made from a type of cloth that stretches and with a part that goes under the foot

ˈski-plane *noun* a plane with two parts like skis fixed to the bottom so that it can land on snow or ice ➲ VISUAL VOCAB page V43

ˈski pole (*BrE* also **ˈski stick**) *noun* a stick used to push yourself forward while skiing

skip·per /ˈskɪpə(r)/ *noun, verb*
■ ***noun*** **1** the captain of a small ship or fishing boat **2** (*informal, especially BrE*) the captain of a sports team
■ ***verb*** **~ sth** to be the captain of a boat, sports team, etc: *to skipper a yacht* ◇ (*especially BrE*) *He skippered the team to victory.*

ˈskipping rope (*BrE*) (*NAmE* **ˈjump rope**) *noun* a piece of rope, usually with a handle at each end, that you hold, turn over your head and then jump over, for fun or to keep fit ➲ VISUAL VOCAB page V32

skir·mish /ˈskɜːmɪʃ; *NAmE* ˈskɜːrmɪʃ/ *noun, verb*
■ ***noun*** **1** a short fight between small groups of soldiers, etc, especially one that is not planned **2** a short argument, especially between political opponents
■ ***verb*** [I] to take part in a short fight or argument ▸ **skir·mish·er** *noun* **skir·mish·ing** *noun* [U]: *There are reports of skirmishing along the border.*

skirt 🔑 /skɜːt; *NAmE* skɜːrt/ *noun, verb*
■ ***noun*** **1** 🔑 [C] a piece of clothing for a woman or girl that hangs from the waist: *a **long/short/straight/pleated, etc. skirt*** ➲ VISUAL VOCAB page V50 **2** [C] (also **skirts** [pl.]) the part of a dress, coat, etc. that hangs below the waist **3** [C] an outer covering or part used to protect the base of a vehicle or machine: *the rubber skirt around the bottom of a hovercraft* ➲ VISUAL VOCAB page V44
■ ***verb*** **1** [T, I] to be or go around the edge of sth: **~ sth** *They followed the road that skirted the lake.* ◇ **~ around/round sth** *I skirted around the field and crossed the bridge.* **2** [T, I] to avoid talking about a subject, especially because it is difficult or embarrassing: **~ sth** *He carefully skirted the issue of where they would live.* ◇ **~ around/round sth** *She tactfully skirted around the subject of money.*

ˈskirting board (also **skirt·ing**) (both *BrE*) (*NAmE* **base·board**) *noun* [C, U] a narrow piece of wood that is fixed along the bottom of the walls in a house

ˈski run (also **run**) *noun* a track that is marked on a slope that you ski down

skit /skɪt/ *noun* **~ (on sth)** a short piece of humorous writing or a performance that makes fun of sb/sth by copying them: *a skit on daytime TV programmes*

ˈski tow *noun* **1** a machine which pulls you up the mountain on your skis **2** a rope which pulls you when you are WATERSKIING

skit·ter /ˈskɪtə(r)/ *verb* [I] **+ adv./prep.** to run or move very quickly and lightly

skit·tish /ˈskɪtɪʃ/ *adj.* **1** (of horses) easily excited or frightened and therefore difficult to control **2** (of people) not very serious and with ideas and feelings that keep changing **3** (*especially NAmE, business*) likely to change suddenly: *skittish financial markets* ▸ **skit·tish·ly** *adv.* **skit·tish·ness** *noun* [U]

skit·tle /ˈskɪtl/ *noun* **1** [C] (in Britain) a wooden or plastic object used in the game of skittles **2** **skittles** [U] (in Britain) a game in which players roll a ball at nine skittles and try to knock over as many of them as possible ➲ compare TENPIN BOWLING

skive /skaɪv/ *verb* [I, T] (*BrE, informal*) to avoid work or school by staying away or leaving early SYN **bunk off**: *'Where's Tom?' 'Skiving as usual.'* ◇ **~ off** *She always skives off early on Fridays.* ◇ **~ sth** *I skived the last lecture.* ▸ **skiver** *noun*

skivvy /ˈskɪvi/ *noun, verb*
■ ***noun*** (*pl.* **-ies**) **1** [C] (*BrE, informal*) a servant, usually female, who does all the dirty or boring jobs in a house: *He treats his wife like a skivvy.* **2** **skiv·vies** [pl.] (*NAmE, informal*) underwear, especially men's underwear
■ ***verb*** (**skiv·vies**, **skivvy·ing**, **skiv·vied**, **skiv·vied**) [I] (*BrE, informal*) to do dirty or boring jobs

skolly /ˈskɒli; *NAmE* ˈskɑːli/ *noun* (*pl.* **-ies**) (*SAfrE, informal*) a young person who commits crimes or behaves badly

skua /ˈskjuːə/ *noun* a large brownish bird that lives near the sea. It eats fish, which it sometimes takes from other birds.

skul·dug·gery (also **skull·dug·gery**) /skʌlˈdʌɡəri/ *noun* [U] (*old-fashioned* or *humorous*) dishonest behaviour or activities

skulk /skʌlk/ *verb* [I] **+ adv./prep.** (*disapproving*) to hide or move around secretly, especially when you are planning sth bad: *There was someone skulking behind the bushes.*

skull /skʌl/ *noun* **1** the bone structure that forms the head and surrounds and protects the brain SYN **cranium**: *a fractured skull* ➲ VISUAL VOCAB page V48 **2** (*informal*) the head or the brain: *Her skull was crammed with too many thoughts.* ◇ (*informal*) *When will he **get it into his thick skull** that I never want to see him again!*

ˌskull and ˈcrossbones *noun* [sing.] a picture of a human skull above two crossed bones, used in the past on the flags of PIRATE ships, and now used as a warning on containers with dangerous substances inside

skull·cap /ˈskʌlkæp/ *noun* a small round cap worn on top of the head, especially by male Jews and Catholic BISHOPS, CARDINALS, etc. ➲ see also YARMULKE

skull·dug·gery = SKULDUGGERY

skunk /skʌŋk/ (*NAmE* also **pole·cat**) *noun* **1** [C] a small black and white N American animal that can produce a strong unpleasant smell to defend itself when it is attacked **2** [U] (*slang*) = SKUNKWEED IDM see DRUNK *adj.*

skunk·weed /ˈskʌŋkwiːd/ (also *slang* **skunk**) *noun* [U] a strong type of CANNABIS

skunk·works /ˈskʌŋkwɜːkz; *NAmE* -wɜːrkz/ *noun* (*pl.* **skunk·works**) (*NAmE, informal*) a small laboratory or department of a large company used for doing new scientific research or developing new products

sky 🔑 /skaɪ/ *noun, verb*
■ ***noun*** 🔑 [C, U] (*pl.* **skies**) the space above the earth that you can see when you look up, where clouds and the sun, moon and stars appear HELP You usually say **the sky**. When **sky** is used with an adjective, use **a... sky**. You can also use the plural form **skies**, especially when you are thinking about the great extent of the sky: *What's that in the sky?* ◇ *The sky suddenly went dark and it started to rain.* ◇ *the night sky* ◇ *a cloudless sky* ◇ *cloudless skies* ◇ *a land of blue skies and sunshine* ◇ *The skies above London were ablaze with a spectacular firework display.* ➲ COLLOCATIONS at WEATHER
IDM **the sky's the ˈlimit** (*informal*) there is no limit to what sb can achieve, earn, do, etc: *With a talent like his, the sky's the limit.* ➲ more at GREAT *adj.*, PIE, PRAISE *v.*
■ ***verb*** (**skies**, **sky·ing**, **skied**, **skied**) **~ sth** to hit a ball very high into the air: *She skied her tee shot.*

ˌsky-ˈblue *adj.* bright blue in colour, like the sky on a clear day ▸ **ˌsky ˈblue** *noun* [U]

sky·box /ˈskaɪbɒks; *NAmE* -bɑːks/ *noun* (*NAmE*) an area of expensive seats, separated from other areas, high up in a sports ground

sky·cap /ˈskaɪkæp/ *noun* (*NAmE*) a person whose job is to carry people's bags at an airport

sky·div·ing /ˈskaɪdaɪvɪŋ/ *noun* [U] a sport in which you jump from a plane and fall for as long as you safely can before opening your PARACHUTE: *to go skydiving* ➲ VISUAL VOCAB page V40 ▸ **sky·diver** *noun*

S

ˌsky-ˈhigh *adj.* very high; too high: *His confidence is still sky-high.* ◇ *sky-high interest rates* ▶ **ˌsky-ˈhigh** *adv.*: *After the election, prices went sky-high.*

sky·lark /ˈskaɪlɑːk; *NAmE* -lɑːrk/ *noun* a small bird that sings while it flies high up in the sky

sky·light /ˈskaɪlaɪt/ *noun* a small window in a roof ➲ VISUAL VOCAB page V15

sky·line /ˈskaɪlaɪn/ *noun* the outline of buildings, trees, hills, etc. seen against the sky: *the New York skyline*

ˈsky marshal *noun* = AIR MARSHAL

Skype™ /skaɪp/ *noun* [U] a telephone system that works by direct communication between users' computers on the Internet, without the need for a central SERVER ➲ compare VOIP

Skype·cast /ˈskaɪpkɑːst; *NAmE* -kæst/ *noun* a public telephone call on Skype in which many people take part in a discussion, that may be recorded and made available on the Internet ▶ **Skype·cast·ing** /ˈskaɪpkɑːstɪŋ; *NAmE* -kæst-/ *noun* [U]: *A Skypecasting session can include up to 100 people.*

sky·rocket /ˈskaɪrɒkɪt; *NAmE* -rɑːk-/ *verb* [I] (of prices, etc.) to rise quickly to a very high level

sky·scraper /ˈskaɪskreɪpə(r)/ *noun* a very tall building in a city ➲ VISUAL VOCAB pages V2, V13

ˈsky surfing *noun* [U] the sport of jumping from a plane and travelling through the air on a board before landing with a PARACHUTE

sky·wards /ˈskaɪwədz; *NAmE* -wərdz/ (also **sky·ward**) *adv.* towards the sky; up into the sky: *She pointed skywards.* ◇ *The rocket soared skywards.*

SLA /ˌes el ˈeɪ/ *abbr.* (*linguistics*) SECOND LANGUAGE ACQUISITION

slab /slæb/ *noun* **1** a thick flat piece of stone, wood or other hard material: *a **slab of marble/concrete*** ◇ *The road was paved with smooth **stone slabs**.* ◇ ***paving slabs*** ◇ *a dead body **on the slab*** (= on a table in a MORTUARY) **2** a thick, flat slice or piece of sth: *a slab of chocolate* ◇ *slabs of meat*

slack /slæk/ *adj., noun, verb*

■ ***adj.*** (**slack·er**, **slack·est**) **1** not stretched tight **SYN** **loose**: *She was staring into space, her mouth slack.* ◇ *The rope suddenly went slack.* ◇ *slack muscles* **2** (of business) not having many customers or sales; not busy: *a slack period* **3** (*disapproving*) not putting enough care, attention or energy into sth and so not doing it well enough: *He's been very slack in his work lately.* ◇ *Discipline in the classroom is very slack.* ▶ **slack·ly** *adv.*: *Her arms hung slackly by her sides.* **slack·ness** *noun* [U]

■ ***noun*** [U] ➲ see also SLACKS **1** the part of a rope, etc. that is hanging loosely: *There's too much slack in the tow rope.* **2** people, money or space that should be used more fully in an organization: *There's very little slack in the budget.* **3** very small pieces of coal

IDM **cut sb some ˈslack** (*informal*) to be less critical of sb or less strict with them: *Hey, cut him some slack! He's doing his best!* **take up the ˈslack** **1** to improve the way money or people are used in an organization **2** to pull on a rope, etc. until it is tight

■ ***verb*** [I] to work less hard than you usually do or should do

PHR V **ˌslack ˈoff (on sth)** to do sth more slowly or with less energy than before

slack·en /ˈslækən/ *verb* **1** [I, T] to gradually become, or to make sth become, slower, less active, etc. **SYN** **relax**: **~ (off)** *We've been really busy, but things are starting to slacken off now.* ◇ **~ sth** *She slackened her pace a little* (= walked a little more slowly). **2** [I, T] to become, or to make sth become, less tight **SYN** **loosen**: *His grip slackened and she pulled away from him.* ◇ **~ sth** *He slackened the ropes slightly.*

slack·er /ˈslækə(r)/ *noun* (*informal, disapproving*) a person who is lazy and avoids work

slacks /slæks/ *noun* [pl.] (*old-fashioned* or *NAmE, formal*) trousers/pants for men or women, that are not part of a suit: *a pair of slacks*

slag /slæg/ *noun, verb*

■ ***noun*** **1** [U] the waste material that remains after metal has been removed from rock **2** [C] (*BrE, slang*) an offensive word for a woman, used to suggest that she has a lot of sexual partners

■ ***verb*** (-gg-)

PHR V **ˌslag sb↔ˈoff** (*BrE, slang*) to say cruel or critical things about sb: *I hate the way he's always slagging off his colleagues.*

ˈslag heap *noun* (*BrE*) a large pile of slag from a mine

slain *past part.* of SLAY

slake /sleɪk/ *verb* (*literary*) **1** **~ your thirst** to drink so that you no longer feel thirsty **SYN** **quench** **2** **~ sth** to satisfy a desire

sla·lom /ˈslɑːləm/ *noun* a race for people on SKIS or in CANOES along a winding course marked by poles

slam /slæm/ *verb, noun*

■ ***verb*** (-mm-) **1** [I, T] to shut, or to make sth shut, with a lot of force, making a loud noise **SYN** **bang**: *I heard the door slam behind him.* ◇ **+ adj.** *A window slammed shut in the wind.* ◇ **~ sth** *He stormed out of the house, slamming the door as he left.* ◇ **~ sth + adj.** *She slammed the lid shut.* ◇ **+ adv./prep.** *She slammed out of the room* (= went out and slammed the door behind her). **2** [T] **~ sth + adv./prep.** to put, push or throw sth into a particular place or position with a lot of force: *She slammed down the phone angrily.* ◇ *He slammed on the brakes* (= stopped the car very suddenly). **3** [T] **~ sb/sth** (used especially in newspapers) to criticize sb/sth very strongly **IDM** see DOOR

PHR V **ˌslam ˈinto/aˈgainst sb/sth** | **ˌslam sth ˈinto/aˈgainst sb/sth** to crash into sth with a lot of force; to make sth crash into sth with a lot of force ➲ SYNONYMS at CRASH

■ ***noun*** [usually sing.] an act of slamming sth; the noise of sth being slammed: *She gave the door a good hard slam.* ➲ see also GRAND SLAM

ˈslam dunk *noun* **1** (in BASKETBALL) the act of jumping up and putting the ball through the net with a lot of force **2** (*NAmE, informal*) something that is certain to be successful: *Politically, this issue is a slam dunk for the party.*

ˈslam-dunk *verb* **~ sth** (in BASKETBALL) to jump up and put the ball through the net with a lot of force

slam·mer /ˈslæmə(r)/ *noun* **1** **the slammer** [sing.] (*slang*) prison **2** [C] (also **teˌquila ˈslammer**) an alcoholic drink made by mixing TEQUILA and LEMONADE, which is drunk quickly after covering the glass and hitting it on the table to make the drink fill with bubbles

slan·der /ˈslɑːndə(r); *NAmE* ˈslæn-/ *noun, verb*

■ ***noun*** [C, U] a false spoken statement intended to damage the good opinion people have of sb; the legal offence of making this kind of statement: *a vicious slander on the company's good name* ◇ *He's suing them for slander.* ➲ compare LIBEL ▶ **slan·der·ous** /-dərəs/ *adj.*: *a slanderous remark*

■ ***verb*** **~ sb/sth** to make a false spoken statement about sb that is intended to damage the good opinion that people have of them: *He angrily accused the investigators of slandering both him and his family.* ➲ compare LIBEL

slang /slæŋ/ *noun* [U] very informal words and expressions that are more common in spoken language, especially used by a particular group of people, for example, children, criminals, soldiers, etc: *teenage slang* ◇ *a **slang word/expression/term*** ➲ see also RHYMING SLANG

ˈslanging match *noun* (*BrE, informal*) an angry argument in which people insult each other

slangy /ˈslæŋi/ *adj.* (**slang·ier**, **slangi·est**) containing a lot of slang: *a slangy style*

slant /slɑːnt; *NAmE* slænt/ *verb, noun*

■ ***verb*** **1** [I, T] to slope or to make sth slope in a particular direction or at a particular angle **+ adv./prep.** (*literary*): *The sun slanted through the window.* ◇ **~ sth + adv./prep.** *Slant your skis a little more to the left.* **2** [T] **~ sth** (**+ adv./prep.**) (sometimes *disapproving*) to present information

based on a particular way of thinking, especially in an unfair way: *The findings of the report had been slanted in favour of the manufacturers.*
■ ***noun* 1** a sloping position: *The sofa faced the fire* **at a slant**. ◇ *Cut the flower stems* **on the slant**. **2 ~ (on sth/sb)** a way of thinking about sth, especially one that shows support for a particular opinion or side in a disagreement: *She put a* **new slant** *on the play.*

slant·ed /ˈslɑːntɪd; *NAmE* ˈslæntɪd/ *adj.* **1** sloping in one direction: *She had slanted brown eyes.* **2 ~ (towards sb/sth)** tending to be in favour of one person or thing in a way that may be unfair to others: *a biased and slanted view of events*

slant·ing /ˈslɑːntɪŋ; *NAmE* ˈslæntɪŋ/ *adj.* not straight or level; sloping: *slanting eyes/handwriting/rain*

slap /slæp/ *verb, noun, adv.*
■ ***verb*** (-pp-) **1** [T] **~ sb/sth (+ adv./prep.)** to hit sb/sth with the flat part of your hand SYN **smack**: *She slapped his face hard.* ◇ *She slapped him hard across the face.* ◇ *'Congratulations!' he said, slapping me on the back.* **2** [T] **~ sth + adv./prep.** to put sth on a surface in a quick, careless and often noisy way, especially because you are angry: *He slapped the newspaper down on the desk.* ◇ *She slapped a $10 bill into my hand.* **3** [I] **+ adv./prep.** to hit against sth with the noise of sb being slapped: *The water slapped against the side of the boat.* ➲ see also HAPPY SLAPPING
PHR V **ˌslap sb aˈbout/aˈround** (*informal*) to hit sb regularly or often: *Her ex-husband used to slap her around.* **ˌslap sb/sth↔ˈdown** (*informal*) to criticize sb in an unfair way, often in public, so that they feel embarrassed or less confident **ˈslap sth on sb/sth** (*informal*) to order, especially in a sudden or an unfair way, that sth must happen or sb must do sth: *The company slapped a ban on using email on the staff.* **ˌslap sth ˈon sth** (*informal*) to increase the price of sth suddenly: *They've slapped 50p on the price of a pack of cigarettes.* **ˌslap sth ˈon sth | ˌslap sth↔ˈon** to spread sth on a surface in a quick, careless way: *Just slap some paint on the walls and it'll look fine.* ◇ *I'd better slap some make-up on before I go out.*
■ ***noun* 1** [C] the action of hitting sb/sth with the flat part of your hand: *She gave him a slap across the face.* ◇ *He gave me a hearty slap on the back.* **2** [sing.] the noise made by hitting sb/sth with the flat part of your hand; a similar noise made by sth else: *the gentle slap of water against the shore* **3** [U] (*BrE, informal*) = MAKE-UP (1)
IDM **slap and ˈtickle** (*old-fashioned, BrE, informal*) enthusiastic kissing and CUDDLING between lovers **a slap in the ˈface** an action that seems to be intended as a deliberate insult to sb **a slap on the ˈwrist** (*informal*) a warning or mild punishment
■ ***adv.*** (also **ˌslap ˈbang**) (*informal*) **1** straight, and with great force: *Storming out of her room, she went slap into Luke.* **2** exactly: *Their apartment is slap bang in the middle of town.*

slap·dash /ˈslæpdæʃ/ *adj.* done, or doing sth, too quickly and carelessly: *She has a very slapdash approach to keeping accounts.* ◇ *a slapdash piece of writing*

ˌslap-ˈhappy *adj.* (*informal*) **1** cheerful, but careless about things that should be taken seriously: *a slap-happy approach to life* **2** (*especially NAmE*) = PUNCH-DRUNK

slap·head /ˈslæphed/ *noun* (*BrE, informal*) an unkind way of referring to a man with little or no hair on his head

slap·per /ˈslæpə(r)/ *noun* (*BrE, slang*) an offensive word for a woman, used to suggest that she has a lot of sexual partners

slap·stick /ˈslæpstɪk/ *noun* [U] the type of humour that is based on simple actions, for example people hitting each other, falling down, etc.

ˈslap-up *adj.* [only before noun] (*BrE, informal*) (of a meal) large and very good

slash /slæʃ/ *verb, noun*
■ ***verb* 1 ~ sth** to make a long cut with a sharp object, especially in a violent way SYN **slit**: *Someone had slashed the tyres on my car.* ◇ *She tried to kill herself by slashing her wrists.* ◇ *We had to* **slash our way** *through the undergrowth with sticks.* **2** [often passive] **~ sth** (*informal*) (often used in newspapers) to reduce sth by a large amount: *to* **slash costs/prices/fares, etc.** ◇ *The workforce has been slashed by half.* ➲ SYNONYMS at CUT
PHR V **ˈslash at sb/sth (with sth)** to attack sb violently with a knife, etc.
■ ***noun* 1** [C] a sharp movement made with a knife, etc. in order to cut sb/sth **2** [C] a long narrow wound or cut: *a slash across his right cheek* ◇ (*figurative*) *Her mouth was a slash of red lipstick.* **3** [C] (*BrE* also **ob·lique**) the symbol (/) used to show alternatives, as in *lunch and/or dinner* and *4/5 people* and to write FRACTIONS, as in ¾ ➲ see also BACKSLASH, FORWARD SLASH **4 a slash** [sing.] (*BrE, slang*) an act of URINATING: *He's just nipped out to have a slash.*

ˌslash-and-ˈburn *adj.* **1** relating to a method of farming in which existing plants, crops, etc. are cut down and burned before new seeds are planted: *slash-and-burn agriculture* **2** aggressive and causing a lot of harm or damage

slash·er /ˈslæʃə(r)/ (also **ˈslasher film**, **ˈslasher movie**) *noun* a frightening film/movie, in which an unknown person kills a lot of people

slat /slæt/ *noun* **1** one of a series of thin flat pieces of wood, metal or plastic, used in furniture, fences, etc. ➲ VISUAL VOCAB page V18 **2** (*technical*) a part of the wing of an aircraft, on the front of the wing, that can be moved up or down to control upward or downward movement ➲ VISUAL VOCAB page V43

slate /sleɪt/ *noun, verb*
■ ***noun* 1** [U] a type of dark grey stone that splits easily into thin flat layers: *a slate quarry* ◇ *The sea was the colour of slate.* **2** [C] a small thin piece of slate, used for covering roofs: *A loose slate had fallen from the roof.* **3** [C] (*NAmE*) a list of the candidates in an election: *a slate of candidates* ◇ *the Democratic slate* **4** [C] a small sheet of slate in a wooden frame, used in the past in schools for children to write on
IDM see CLEAN *adj.*, WIPE *v.*
■ ***verb* 1 ~ sb/sth (for sth)** (*BrE*) to criticize sb/sth, especially in a newspaper: *to slate a book/play/writer* **2** [usually passive] to plan that sth will happen at a particular time in the future: **~ sth for sth** *The houses were first slated for demolition five years ago.* ◇ **~ sth to do sth** *The new store is slated to open in spring.* **3** [usually passive] (*informal, especially NAmE*) to suggest or choose sb for a job, position, etc: **~ sb for sth** *I was told that I was being slated for promotion.* ◇ **~ sb to do sth** *He is slated to play the lead in the new musical.*

slated /ˈsleɪtɪd/ *adj.* covered with pieces of SLATE: *a slated roof*

ˌslate-ˈgrey *adj.* bluish-grey in colour, like slate

slather /ˈslæðə(r)/ *verb*
PHR V **ˈslather sth on sth | ˈslather with/in sth | ˌslather sth↔ˈon** to cover sth with a thick layer of a substance: *hot dogs slathered with mustard*

slat·ted /ˈslætɪd/ *adj.* [usually before noun] made of slats (= thin pieces of wood): *slatted blinds*

slat·tern /ˈslætən; *NAmE* -tərn/ *noun* (*old-fashioned*) a dirty untidy woman ▸ **slat·tern·ly** *adj.*: *a slatternly girl*

slaty (also **slatey**) /ˈsleɪti/ *adj.* **1** having a dark grey colour: *a slaty sky* **2** containing SLATE; like SLATE: *slaty rock*

slaugh·ter /ˈslɔːtə(r)/ *noun, verb*
■ ***noun*** [U] **1** the killing of animals for their meat: *cows taken for slaughter* **2** the cruel killing of large numbers of people at one time, especially in a war SYN **massacre**: *the wholesale slaughter of innocent people* IDM see LAMB *n.*
■ ***verb* 1 ~ sth** to kill an animal, usually for its meat SYN **butcher 2 ~ sb/sth** to kill a large number of people or animals violently SYN **massacre**: *Men, women and children were slaughtered and villages destroyed.* **3 ~ sb/sth** (*informal*) to defeat sb/sth by a large number of points in a sports game, competition, etc: *We were slaughtered 10–1 by the home team.*

slaugh·ter·house /ˈslɔːtəhaʊs; *NAmE* -tərh-/ *noun* (*BrE* also **ab·at·toir**) a building where animals are killed for food

S

Slav /slɑːv/ *noun* a member of any of the races of people of central and eastern Europe who speak Slavic languages

slave /sleɪv/ *noun, verb*

■ ***noun*** **1** a person who is owned by another person and is forced to work for them: *She treated her daughter like a slave.* **2** a person who is so strongly influenced by sth that they cannot live without it, or cannot make their own decisions: **~ of sth** *We are slaves of the motor car.* ◇ **~ to sth** *Sue's a slave to fashion.* **3** (*technical*) a device that is directly controlled by another one

■ ***verb*** [I] **~** (**away**) (**at sth**) to work very hard: *I've been slaving away all day trying to get this work finished.* ◇ *I haven't got time to spend hours* ***slaving over a hot stove*** (= doing a lot of cooking).

'slave-driver *noun* (*disapproving*) a person who makes people work extremely hard SYN **tyrant**

ˌslave 'labour (*especially US* **ˌslave 'labor**) *noun* [U] **1** work that is done by slaves; the slaves who do the work: *Huge palaces were built by slave labour.* **2** (*informal*) work that is very hard and very badly paid: *I left because the job was just slave labour.*

slaver[1] /'slævə(r)/ *verb* [I] (usually of an animal) to let SALIVA (= the liquid produced in the mouth) run out of the mouth, especially when hungry or excited: *slavering dogs*

slaver[2] /'sleɪvə(r)/ *noun* **1** (in the past) a person who bought and sold SLAVES **2** a ship that was used in the past for carrying SLAVES

slav·ery /'sleɪvəri/ *noun* [U] **1** the state of being a SLAVE: *to* ***be sold into slavery*** **2** the practice of having SLAVES: *the abolition of slavery* OPP **freedom**

'slave trade *noun* [sing.] the buying and selling of people as SLAVES, especially in the 17th–19th centuries

Slav·ic /'slɑːvɪk/ (also **Slav·on·ic**) *adj.* of or connected with Slavs or their languages, which include Russian, Polish, Czech and a number of other languages

slav·ish /'sleɪvɪʃ/ *adj.* (*disapproving*) following or copying sb/sth exactly without having any original thought at all: *a slavish adherence to the rules* ▸ **slav·ish·ly** *adv.*

Sla·von·ic /slə'vɒnɪk; *NAmE* -'vɑːn-/ *adj.* = SLAVIC

slay /sleɪ/ *verb* (**slew** /sluː/, **slain** /sleɪn/) **1 ~ sb/sth** (*old-fashioned* or *literary*) to kill sb/sth in a war or a fight: *St George slew the dragon.* **2 ~ sb** (*especially NAmE*) (used especially in newspapers) to murder sb: *Two passengers were slain by the hijackers.* **3 ~ sb** (*old-fashioned, informal, especially NAmE*) to have a strong effect on sb, especially to make them laugh: *Those old movies still slay me!* ▸ **slay·ing** *noun*: (*especially NAmE*) *the drug-related slayings of five people*

S

sleaze /sliːz/ *noun* **1** [U] dishonest or illegal behaviour, especially by politicians or business people: *allegations of sleaze* ◇ *The candidate was seriously damaged by the sleaze factor.* **2** [U] behaviour or conditions that are unpleasant and not socially acceptable, especially because sex is involved: *the sleaze of a town that was once a naval base* **3** [C] (also **sleaze·bag** /'sliːzbæg/, **sleaze·ball** /'sliːzbɔːl/ especially in *NAmE*) a dishonest or immoral person

sleazy /'sliːzi/ *adj.* (**sleaz·ier**, **sleazi·est**) (*informal*) **1** (of a place) dirty, unpleasant and not socially acceptable, especially because sex is involved SYN **disreputable**: *a sleazy bar* **2** (of people) immoral and unpleasant: *a sleazy reporter* ▸ **sleazi·ness** *noun* [U]

sled /sled/ *noun, verb* (**-dd-**) (*especially NAmE*) = SLEDGE ▸ **sled·ding** /'sledɪŋ/ *noun* [U]

sledge /sledʒ/ (*BrE*) (also **sled** *NAmE, BrE*) *noun, verb*

■ ***noun*** a vehicle for travelling over snow and ice, with long narrow strips of wood or metal instead of wheels. Larger sledges are pulled by horses or dogs and smaller ones are used for going down hills as a sport or for pleasure. ➲ compare SLEIGH, TOBOGGAN

■ ***verb*** [I] to ride on a sledge/sled: *We were hoping we could* ***go sledging***.

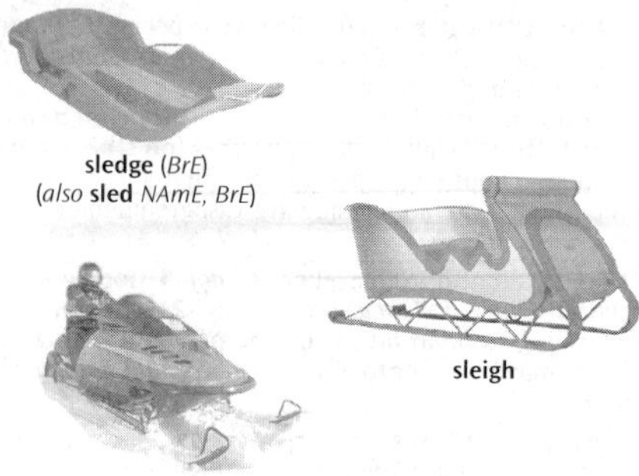

sledge·ham·mer /'sledʒhæmə(r)/ *noun* a large heavy hammer with a long handle

IDM **use a ˌsledgehammer to crack a 'nut** to use more force than is necessary

sledg·ing /'sledʒɪŋ/ *noun* [U] **1** (*BrE*) (*NAmE* **sledding**) the activity of riding on a sledge: *to* ***go sledging*** **2** (in CRICKET) insults to players in the opposing team in order to destroy their concentration ➲ compare TRASH TALK

sleek /sliːk/ *adj., verb*

■ ***adj.*** (**sleek·er**, **sleek·est**) **1** (*approving*) smooth and shiny SYN **glossy**: *sleek black hair* ◇ *the sleek dark head of a seal* **2** (*approving*) having an elegant smooth shape: *a sleek yacht* ◇ *the* ***sleek lines*** *of the new car* **3** (often *disapproving*) (of a person) looking rich, and dressed in elegant and expensive clothes: *a sleek and ambitious politician* ▸ **sleek·ly** *adv.* **sleek·ness** *noun* [U]

■ ***verb*** **~ sth** (**back/down**) to make sth, especially hair, smooth and shiny: *His glossy hair was sleeked back over his ears.*

sleep 0-w /sliːp/ *verb, noun*

■ ***verb*** (**slept**, **slept** /slept/) **1** 0-w [I] (**+ adv./prep.**) to rest with your eyes closed and your mind and body not active: *to* ***sleep well/deeply/soundly/badly*** ◇ *I* ***couldn't sleep*** *because of the noise.* ◇ *I had to sleep on the sofa.* ◇ *He slept solidly for ten hours.* ◇ *I slept at my sister's house last night* (= stayed the night there). ◇ *We both slept right through* (= were not woken up by) *the storm.* ◇ *She only sleeps for four hours a night.* ◇ *We sometimes* ***sleep late*** *at the weekends* (= until late in the morning). ◇ *I put the sleeping baby down gently.* ◇ *What are our* ***sleeping arrangements*** *here* (= where shall we sleep)? HELP It is more common to say that somebody **is asleep** than to say that somebody **is sleeping**. **Sleep** can only be used in the passive with a preposition such as **in** or **on**: *It was clear her bed hadn't been slept in.* **2** [T, no passive] **~ sb** to have enough beds for a particular number of people: *The apartment sleeps six.* ◇ *The hotel sleeps 120 guests.*

IDM **let sleeping dogs 'lie** (*saying*) to avoid mentioning a subject or sth that happened in the past, in order to avoid any problems or arguments **sleep like a 'log/'baby** (*informal*) to sleep very well **sleep 'tight** (*informal*) used especially to children before they go to bed to say that you hope they sleep well: *Goodnight, sleep tight!* ➲ more at ROUGH *adv.*, WINK *n.*

PHR V **ˌsleep a'round** (*informal, disapproving*) to have sex with a lot of different people **ˌsleep 'in** to sleep until after the time you usually get up in the morning **ˌsleep sth↔'off** to get better after sth, especially drinking too much alcohol, by sleeping: *Let's leave him to* ***sleep it off***. **'sleep on sth** (*informal*) to delay making a decision about sth until the next day, so that you have time to think about it: *Could I sleep on it and let you know tomorrow?* **ˌsleep 'over** to stay the night at sb else's home: *It's very late now—why don't you sleep over?* ◇ *Can I sleep over at my friend's house?* ➲ related noun SLEEPOVER **'sleep together** | **'sleep with sb** (*informal*) to have sex with sb, especially sb you are not married to: *I know he's going out with her, but I don't think they're sleeping together.* ◇ *Everyone knows she sleeps with the boss.*

■ ***noun*** **1** 0-w [U] the natural state of rest in which your eyes are closed, your body is not active, and your mind is not conscious: *I need to* ***get some sleep****.* ◇ *I didn't* ***get much sleep*** *last night.* ◇ *Can you give me something to help me* ***get to sleep*** (= start sleeping)*?* ◇ ***Go to sleep****—it's late.* ◇ *He cried out* ***in his sleep****.* ◇ *Anxiety can be caused by* ***lack of sleep****.* ◇ *His talk nearly* ***sent me to sleep*** (= it was boring). ◇ *Try to go* ***back to sleep****.* **2** 🗝 [sing.] a period of sleep: *Did you have a good sleep?* ◇ *Ros fell into a deep sleep.* ◇ *I'll feel better after a* ***good night's sleep*** (= a night when I sleep well). **3** [U] (*informal*) the substance that sometimes forms in the corners of your eyes after you have been sleeping

IDM **be able to do sth in your 'sleep** (*informal*) to be able to do sth very easily because you have done it many times before **ˌgo to 'sleep** (*informal*) if part of your body **goes to sleep**, you lose the sense of feeling in it, usually because it has been in the same position for too long **not lose 'sleep/lose no 'sleep over sth** to not worry much about sth: *It's not worth losing sleep over.* **put sb to 'sleep** (*informal*) to make sb unconscious before an operation by using drugs (called an ANAESTHETIC) **put sth to 'sleep** to kill a sick or injured animal by giving it drugs so that it dies without pain. People say 'put to sleep' to avoid saying 'kill'. ➲ more at WINK *n.*

Synonyms

sleep

doze • nap • snooze

These words all mean to rest with your eyes closed and your mind and body not active.

sleep to rest with your eyes shut and your mind and body not active: *Did you sleep well?* ◇ *I couldn't sleep last night.* **NOTE** It is more usual to say that sb is **asleep** than that they are **sleeping**; but if you use an adverb to say how they are sleeping, use **sleeping**: *'What's Ashley doing?' 'Sh! She's asleep.'* ◇ *The baby was sleeping peacefully.* ◇ ~~*The baby was asleep peacefully.*~~

doze to sleep lightly, waking up easily, often when you are not in bed: *He was dozing in front of the TV.*

nap to sleep for a short time, especially during the day.

snooze (*informal*) to sleep lightly for a short time, especially during the day and usually not in bed: *My brother was snoozing on the sofa.*

PATTERNS

- to sleep/doze **lightly/fitfully**
- to doze/snooze **gently**

sleep·er /ˈsliːpə(r)/ *noun* **1** (used with an adjective) a person who sleeps in a particular way: *a* ***heavy/light/sound sleeper*** **2** a person who is asleep: *Only the snores of the sleepers broke the silence of the house.* **3** a night train with beds for passengers on it: *the London–Edinburgh sleeper* **4** = SLEEPING CAR **5** (*BrE*) (*NAmE* **tie**) one of the heavy pieces of wood or concrete on which the rails on a railway/railroad track are laid ➲ VISUAL VOCAB page V47 **6** (*informal, especially NAmE*) a film/movie, play or book that for a long time is not very successful and then is suddenly a success **7** (also **ˌsleeper 'agent**) a SPY who is sent to live in a country as a normal citizen and is not used until much later **8** (*BrE*) a ring or piece of metal that you wear in an ear that has been PIERCED (= had a hole made in it) to keep the hole from closing

'sleeping bag *noun* a thick warm bag that you use for sleeping in, for example when you are camping ➲ VISUAL VOCAB page V20

ˌSleeping 'Beauty *noun* used to refer to sb who has been asleep for a long time: *OK, Sleeping Beauty, time to get up.* **ORIGIN** From the European fairy tale about a beautiful girl who sleeps for a hundred years and is woken up when a prince kisses her.

'sleeping car (also **sleep·er**) *noun* a coach/car on a train with beds for people to sleep in

ˌsleeping 'partner (*BrE*) (*NAmE* **ˌsilent 'partner**) *noun* a person who has put money into a business company but who is not actually involved in running it

'sleeping pill (*BrE* also **'sleeping tablet**) *noun* a pill containing a drug that helps you to sleep

ˌsleeping po'liceman *noun* (*BrE, informal*) = SPEED HUMP

'sleeping sickness *noun* [U] a tropical disease carried by the TSETSE FLY that causes a feeling of wanting to go to sleep and usually causes death

sleep·less /ˈsliːpləs/ *adj.* **1** [only before noun] without sleep: *I've had a few* ***sleepless nights*** *recently.* **2** [not before noun] not able to sleep: *She lay sleepless until dawn.* ▶ **sleep·less·ly** *adv.* **sleep·less·ness** *noun* [U] **SYN** **insomnia**: *to suffer from sleeplessness*

sleep·over /ˈsliːpəʊvə(r); *NAmE* -oʊ-/ (*NAmE* also **'slumber party**) *noun* a party for children or young people when a group of them spend the night at one house

sleep·walk /ˈsliːpwɔːk/ *verb* [I] to walk around while you are asleep ▶ **sleep·walk·er** (also *formal* **som·nam·bu·list**) *noun*

sleepy /ˈsliːpi/ *adj.* (**sleep·ier, sleepi·est**) **1** needing sleep; ready to go to sleep **SYN** **drowsy**: *a sleepy child* ◇ *He had begun to feel sleepy.* ◇ *The heat and the wine made her sleepy.* **2** (of places) quiet and where nothing much happens: *a sleepy little town* ▶ **sleep·ily** /-ɪli/ *adv.*: *She yawned sleepily.* **sleepi·ness** *noun* [U]

sleepy·head /ˈsliːpihed/ *noun* (*informal*) a way of addressing sb who is not completely awake: *Come on sleepyhead — time to get up.*

sleet /sliːt/ *noun, verb*

■ ***noun*** [U] a mixture of rain and snow

■ ***verb*** [I] when **it is sleeting**, a mixture of rain and snow is falling from the sky

sleeve 🗝 /sliːv/ *noun*

1 🗝 a part of a piece of clothing that covers all or part of your arm: *a dress with* ***short/long sleeves*** ◇ *Dan* ***rolled up his sleeves*** *and washed his hands.* ➲ VISUAL VOCAB pages V50, V51 ➲ see also SHIRTSLEEVE **2** **-sleeved** (in adjectives) having sleeves of the type mentioned: *a short-sleeved shirt* ➲ VISUAL VOCAB page V51 **3** (also **jacket** especially in *NAmE*) a stiff paper or cardboard envelope for a record: *a colourful sleeve design* **4** a tube that covers a part of a machine to protect it ▶ **sleeve·less** *adj.*: *a sleeveless dress* ➲ VISUAL VOCAB page V50

IDM **have/keep sth up your 'sleeve** to keep a plan or an idea secret until you need to use it ➲ more at ACE *n.*, CARD *n.*, LAUGH *v.*, ROLL *v.*, TRICK *n.*, WEAR *v.*

'sleeve note *noun* (*BrE*) = LINER NOTE

sleigh /sleɪ/ *noun* a SLEDGE (= a vehicle that slides over snow), especially one pulled by horses: *a sleigh ride* ➲ picture at SLEDGE

sleight of hand /ˌslaɪt əv ˈhænd/ *noun* [U] **1** (also *formal* **le·ger·de·main**) skilful movements of your hand that other people cannot see: *The trick is done simply by sleight of hand.* **2** the fact of tricking people in a clever way: *Last year's profits were more the result of financial sleight of hand than genuine growth.*

slen·der /ˈslendə(r)/ *adj.* (**slen·derer, slen·derest**) **HELP** You can also use **more slender** and **most slender**. **1** (*approving*) (of people or their bodies) thin in an attractive or elegant way **SYN** **slim**: *her slender figure* ◇ *long, slender fingers* **2** thin or narrow: *a glass with a slender stem* **3** small in amount or size and hardly enough: *to win by a* ***slender margin/majority*** ◇ *people of* ***slender means*** (= with little money) ◇ *Australia held a slender 1–0 lead at half-time.* ▶ **slen·der·ness** *noun* [U]

slept *past tense, past part.* of SLEEP

sleuth /sluːθ/ *noun* (*old-fashioned* or *humorous*) a person who investigates crimes **SYN** **detective**: *an amateur sleuth*

sleuth·ing /ˈsluːθɪŋ/ *noun* [U] the act of investigating a crime or mysterious event: *to do some private sleuthing*

slew /sluː/ *verb, noun* ➲ see also SLAY *v.*

■ ***verb*** [I, T] (especially of a vehicle) to turn or slide suddenly in another direction; to make a vehicle do this: **+ adv./**

S

prep. *The car skidded and slewed sideways.* ◇ **~ sth + adv./prep.** *He slewed the motorbike over as they hit the freeway.*
■ ***noun*** [sing.] **~ of sth** (*informal, especially NAmE*) a large number or amount of sth

slice 0-w /slaɪs/ *noun, verb*
■ ***noun* 1** 0-w a thin flat piece of food that has been cut off a larger piece: *a slice of bread* ◇ *Cut the meat into thin slices.* **2** (*informal*) a part or share of sth: *Our firm is well placed to grab a large slice of the market.* **3** a kitchen UTENSIL (= tool) that you use to lift and serve pieces of food: *a fish slice* ➲ VISUAL VOCAB page V23 **4** (*sport*) (in GOLF, TENNIS, etc.) a stroke that makes the ball spin to one side rather than going straight ahead
IDM **a ˌslice of ˈlife** a film/movie, play or book that gives a very realistic view of ordinary life ➲ more at ACTION, CAKE *n.*, PIE
■ ***verb* 1** 0-w [T] **~ sth (up)** to cut sth into slices: *to slice (up) onions* ◇ *Slice the cucumber thinly.* ◇ *a sliced loaf* ➲ COLLOCATIONS at COOKING ➲ VISUAL VOCAB page V25 ➲ see also SALAMI SLICING **2** 0-w [I] to cut sth easily with or as if with a sharp blade: **+ adv./prep.** *He accidentally* ***sliced through*** *his finger.* ◇ *A piece of glass sliced into his shoulder.* ◇ (*figurative*) *Her speech sliced through all the confusion surrounding the situation.* ◇ **~ sth (+ adj.)** *The knife sliced his jacket.* ◇ *He sliced the fruit open.* ◇ (*figurative*) *The ship sliced the water.* **3** [T] **~ sth** (*sport*) to hit a ball so that it spins and does not move in the expected direction: *He managed to slice a shot over the net.* **4** [T] **~ sth** (in GOLF) to hit the ball so that it flies away in a curve, when you do not mean to **5** [T] **~ sth** (*NAmE, informal*) to reduce sth by a large amount: *The new tax has sliced annual bonuses by 30 percent.*
IDM **ˌslice and ˈdice (sth)** (*computing*) to divide information into small parts in order to study it more closely or to see it in different ways: *The software lets you slice and dice the data and display it in different formats.* ➲ more at WAY *n.*
PHR V **ˌslice sth↔ˈoff/aˈway** | **ˌslice sth ˈoff sth** to cut sth from a larger piece: *Slice a piece off.* ◇ (*figurative*) *He sliced two seconds off the world record.*

ˌsliced ˈbread *noun* [U] bread that is sold already cut into slices: *a loaf of sliced bread*
IDM **the best thing since sliced ˈbread** (*informal*) if you say that sth is **the best thing since sliced bread**, you think it is extremely good, interesting, etc.

slick /slɪk/ *adj., noun, verb*
■ ***adj.*** (**slick·er, slick·est**) **1** (sometimes *disapproving*) done or made in a way that is clever and efficient but often does not seem to be sincere or lacks important ideas: *a slick advertising campaign* ◇ *a slick performance* **2** (sometimes *disapproving*) speaking very easily and smoothly but in a way that does not seem sincere SYN **glib**: *slick TV presenters* ◇ *a slick salesman* **3** done quickly and smoothly SYN **skilful**: *The crowd enjoyed the team's slick passing.* ◇ *a slick gear change* **4** smooth and difficult to hold or move on SYN **slippery**: *The roads were slick with rain.* ▶ **slick·ly** *adv.*: *The magazine is slickly produced.* **slick·ness** *noun* [U]
■ ***noun* 1** (also **ˈoil slick**) an area of oil that is floating on the surface of the sea **2** a small area of sth wet and shiny: *a slick of sweat*
■ ***verb*** [usually passive] **~ sth + adv./prep.** to make hair very flat and smooth by putting oil, water, etc. on it: *His hair was* ***slicked back/down*** *with gel.*

slick·er /ˈslɪkə(r)/ *noun* (*NAmE*) a long loose coat that keeps you dry in the rain ➲ see also CITY SLICKER

slide 0-w /slaɪd/ *verb, noun*
■ ***verb*** (**slid, slid** /slɪd/)
▸ MOVE SMOOTHLY/QUIETLY **1** 0-w [I, T] to move easily over a smooth or wet surface; to make sth move in this way: (**+ adv./prep.**) *We slid down the grassy slope.* ◇ *The drawers slide in and out easily.* ◇ **~ sth + adv./prep.** *She slid her hand along the rail.* ◇ **~ (sth) + adj.** *The automatic doors slid open.* **2** 0-w [I, T] to move quickly and quietly, for example in order not to be noticed; to make sth move in this way SYN **slip**: **+ adv./prep.** *He slid into bed.* ◇ *She slid out while no one was looking.* ◇ **~ sth + adv./prep.** *The man slid the money quickly into his pocket.*
▸ BECOME LOWER/WORSE **3** [I] **~ (from...) (to...)** to become gradually lower or of less value: *Shares slid to a 10-year low.* **4** [I] **~ (down/into/towards sth)** to move gradually into a worse situation: *The industry has slid into decline.* ◇ *They were sliding towards bankruptcy.* ◇ *He got depressed and began to* ***let things slide*** (= failed to give things the attention they needed).
■ ***noun***
▸ BECOMING LOWER/WORSE **1** [C, usually sing.] a change to a lower or worse condition: *a downward slide in the price of oil* ◇ *the team's slide down the table* ◇ *talks to prevent* ***a slide into*** *civil war* ◇ *The economy is* ***on the slide*** (= getting worse).
▸ ON ICE **2** [sing.] a long, smooth movement on ice or a smooth surface SYN **skid**: *Her car went into a slide.*
▸ FOR CHILDREN **3** [C] a structure with a steep slope that children use for sliding down: *to go down the slide* ➲ VISUAL VOCAB page V32
▸ FALL OF ROCK **4** [C] a sudden fall of a large amount of rock or earth down a hill SYN **landslide**: *I was afraid of starting a slide of loose stones.*
▸ PHOTOGRAPH **5** [C] a small piece of film held in a frame that can be shown on a screen when you shine a light through it SYN **transparency**: *a talk with colour slides*
▸ COMPUTERS **6** [C] one page of an electronic presentation, that may contain text and images, that is usually viewed on a computer screen or projected onto a larger screen: *I'm still working on the slides for my presentation.*
▸ FOR MICROSCOPE **7** [C] a small piece of glass that sth is placed on so that it can be looked at under a MICROSCOPE ➲ VISUAL VOCAB page V57
▸ PART OF MUSICAL INSTRUMENT **8** [C] a part of a musical instrument or other device that slides backwards and forwards ➲ VISUAL VOCAB page V30
▸ FOR HAIR **9** [C] (*BrE*) = HAIRSLIDE

ˈslide projector *noun* a piece of equipment for displaying SLIDES (= small pieces of film held in frames) on a screen ➲ compare DATA PROJECTOR, OVERHEAD PROJECTOR

sli·der /ˈslaɪdə(r)/ *noun* **1** a device for controlling sth such as the volume of a radio, which you slide up and down or from side to side **2** (*computing*) an ICON that you can slide up and down or from side to side with the mouse **3** a FRESHWATER TURTLE from N America

ˈslide rule *noun* a long narrow instrument like a ruler, with a middle part that slides backwards and forwards, used for calculating numbers

ˈslide show (also **slide·show**) *noun* **1** a number of slides (= small pieces of film held in frames) shown to an audience using a SLIDE PROJECTOR, often during a lecture **2** (*computing*) a piece of software that shows a number of images on a computer screen in a particular order: *a slideshow presentation*

ˌsliding ˈdoor *noun* a door that slides across an opening rather than swinging away from it

ˌsliding ˈscale *noun* a system in which the rate at which sth is paid varies according to particular conditions: *Fees are calculated* ***on a sliding scale*** *according to income* (= richer people pay more).

slight 0-w /slaɪt/ *adj., noun, verb*
■ ***adj.*** (**slight·er, slight·est**) **1** 0-w very small in degree: *a slight increase/change/delay/difference* ◇ *I woke up with a slight headache.* ◇ *The damage was slight.* ◇ *She takes offence at the slightest thing* (= is very easily offended). ◇ *There was* ***not the slightest*** *hint of trouble.* **2** small and thin in size: *a slight woman* **3** (*formal*) not deserving serious attention: *This is a very slight novel.*
IDM **not in the ˈslightest** not at all: *He didn't seem to mind in the slightest.*
■ ***noun*** **~ (on sb/sth)** an act or a remark that criticizes sth or offends sb SYN **insult**: *Nick took her comment as a slight on his abilities as a manager.*
■ ***verb*** [usually passive] **~ sb** to treat sb rudely or without respect SYN **insult**: *She* ***felt slighted*** *because she hadn't been*

S

invited. ▸ **slight·ing** *adj.* [only before noun]: *slighting remarks*

slight·ly 🔑 /ˈslaɪtli/ *adv.*
1 🔑 a little: *a slightly different version* ◇ *We took a slightly more direct route.* ◇ *I knew her slightly.* ◇ *'Are you worried?' 'Only slightly.'* **2** a **slightly built** person is small and thin

slim /slɪm/ *adj., verb, noun*
■ ***adj.*** (**slim·mer, slim·mest**) **1** (*approving*) (of a person) thin, in a way that is attractive: *a slim figure/body/waist* ◇ *She was tall and slim.* ◇ *How do you manage to stay so slim?* ◇ (*figurative*) *Many companies are a lot slimmer than they used to be* (= have fewer workers). **2** thinner than usual: *a* ***slim volume*** *of poetry* **3** not as big as you would like or expect SYN **small**: *a* ***slim chance*** *of success* ◇ *The party was returned to power with a* ***slim majority.*** ➲ see also SLIMMER, SLIMMING ▸ **slim·ness** *noun* [U]
■ ***verb*** (**-mm-**) [I] (*BrE*) (usually used in the progressive tenses) to try to become thinner, for example by eating less SYN **diet**: *You can still eat breakfast when you are slimming.* ➲ COLLOCATIONS at DIET
PHR V ˌ**slim** ˈ**down** to become thinner, for example as a result of eating less ˌ**slim** ˈ**down** | ˌ**slim sth**↔ˈ**down** to make a company or an organization smaller, by reducing the number of jobs in it; to be made smaller in this way: *They're restructuring and slimming down the workforce.* ◇ *The industry may have to slim down even further.* ◇ *the new, slimmed-down company* ➲ see also SLIMMING
■ ***noun*** [U] an African word for AIDS

slime /slaɪm/ *noun* [U] any unpleasant thick liquid substance: *The pond was full of mud and green slime.* ➲ see also SLIMY

slime·ball /ˈslaɪmbɔːl/ (also **slime·bag** /ˈslaɪmbæɡ/) *noun* (*informal*) an unpleasant or disgusting person

slim·line /ˈslɪmlaɪn/ *adj.* [only before noun] **1** smaller or thinner in design than usual: *a slimline phone* **2** (*BrE*) (of a drink) containing very little sugar: *slimline tonic water*

slim·mer /ˈslɪmə(r)/ *noun* (*BrE*) a person who is trying to lose weight: *a calorie-controlled diet for slimmers* ➲ see also SLIM

slim·ming /ˈslɪmɪŋ/ *noun* [U] (*BrE*) the practice of trying to lose weight: *a slimming club* ➲ see also SLIM

slimy /ˈslaɪmi/ *adj.* (**slimi·er, slimi·est**) **1** like or covered with SLIME: *thick slimy mud* ◇ *The walls were black, cold and slimy.* **2** (*informal, disapproving*) (of a person or their manner) polite and extremely friendly in a way that is not sincere or honest

sling /slɪŋ/ *verb, noun*
■ ***verb*** (**slung, slung** /slʌŋ/) **1** (*informal, especially BrE*) to throw sth somewhere in a careless way SYN **chuck**: **~ sth + adv./prep.** *Don't just sling your clothes on the floor.* ◇ **~ sb sth** *Sling me an apple, will you?* ➲ see also MUD-SLINGING **2** [often passive] **~ sth + adv./prep.** to put sth somewhere where it hangs loosely: *Her bag was slung over her shoulder.* ◇ *We slung a hammock between two trees.* **3** [often passive] **~ sb + adv./prep.** (*informal*) to put sb somewhere by force; to make sb leave somewhere: *They were slung out of the club for fighting.*
IDM **sling your** ˈ**hook** (*BrE, informal*) (used especially in orders) to go away
PHR V ˌ**sling** ˈ**off at sb** (*AustralE, NZE, informal*) to laugh at sb in an unkind way
■ ***noun*** **1** a band of cloth that is tied around a person's neck and used to support a broken or injured arm: *He had his arm* ***in a sling.*** **2** a device consisting of a band, ropes, etc. for holding and lifting heavy objects: *The engine was lifted in a sling of steel rope.* **3** a device like a bag for carrying a baby on your back or in front of you **4** (in the past) a simple weapon made from a band of leather, etc, used for throwing stones SYN **catapult**

sling·back /ˈslɪŋbæk/ *noun* a woman's shoe that is open at the back with a narrow piece of leather, etc. around the heel ➲ VISUAL VOCAB page V52

sling·shot /ˈslɪŋʃɒt; *NAmE* -ʃɑːt/ (*NAmE*) (*BrE* **cata·pult**) *noun* a stick shaped like a Y with a rubber band attached to it, used by children for shooting stones ➲ picture at CATAPULT

slink /slɪŋk/ *verb* (**slunk, slunk** /slʌŋk/) [I] **+ adv./prep.** to move somewhere very quietly and slowly, especially because you are ashamed or do not want to be seen SYN **creep**: *John was trying to slink into the house by the back door.* ◇ *The dog howled and slunk away.*

slinky /ˈslɪŋki/ *adj.* (**slink·ier, slinki·est**) **1** (of a woman's clothes) fitting closely to the body in a sexually attractive way **2** (of movement or sound) smooth and slow, often in a way that is sexually attractive

slip 🔑 /slɪp/ *verb, noun*
■ ***verb*** (**-pp-**)
▸ SLIDE/FALL **1** 🔑 [I] **~ (over)** to slide a short distance by accident so that you fall or nearly fall: *She slipped over on the ice and broke her leg.* ◇ *As I ran up the stairs, my foot slipped and I fell.*
▸ OUT OF POSITION **2** 🔑 [I] (**+ adv./prep.**) to slide out of position or out of your hand: *His hat had slipped over one eye.* ◇ *The fish slipped out of my hand.* ◇ *The child* ***slipped from his grasp*** *and ran off.* ◇ (*figurative*) *She was careful not to let her control slip.*
▸ GO/PUT QUICKLY **3** 🔑 [I] **+ adv./prep.** to go somewhere quickly and quietly, especially without being noticed SYN **creep**: *She slipped out of the house before the others were awake.* ◇ *The ship slipped into the harbour at night.* ◇ (*figurative*) *She knew that time was slipping away.* **4** 🔑 [T] to put sth somewhere quickly, quietly or secretly: **~ sth + adv./prep.** *Anna slipped her hand into his.* ◇ *I managed to slip a few jokes into my speech.* ◇ *I managed to* ***slip in*** *a few jokes.* ◇ **~ sth to sb** *They'd slipped some money to the guards.* ◇ **~ sb sth** *They'd slipped the guards some money.*
▸ BECOME WORSE **5** 🔑 [I] to fall to a lower level; to become worse: *His popularity has slipped recently.* ◇ *That's three times she's beaten me—I* ***must be slipping!***
▸ INTO DIFFICULT SITUATION **6** [I] **+ adv./prep.** to pass into a particular state or situation, especially a difficult or unpleasant one: *He began to* ***slip into*** *debt.* ◇ *The patient had* ***slipped into*** *a coma.* ◇ *We seem to have slipped behind schedule.*
▸ CLOTHES ON/OFF **7** [I, T] to put clothes on or to take them off quickly and easily: **+ adv./prep.** *to* ***slip into/out of a dress*** ◇ **~ sth + adv./prep.** *to* ***slip your shoes on/off*** ◇ *He slipped a coat over his sweatshirt.*
▸ GET FREE **8** [T] to get free; to make sth/sb/yourself free from sth: **~ sth** *The ship had slipped its moorings in the night.* ◇ **~ (sth) + adj.** *The animal had* ***slipped free*** *and escaped.*
IDM **let** ˈ**slip sth** to give sb information that is supposed to be secret: *I happened to* ***let it slip*** *that he had given me £1 000 for the car.* ◇ *She tried not to let slip what she knew.* **let sth** ˈ**slip (through your fingers)** to miss or fail to use an opportunity: *Don't let the chance to work abroad slip through your fingers.* **slip your** ˈ**mind** if sth **slips your mind**, you forget it or forget to do it ˌ**slip one** ˈ**over on sb** (*informal*) to trick sb **slip through the** ˈ**net** when sb/sth **slips through the net**, an organization or a system fails to find them and deal with them: *We tried to contact all former students, but one or two slipped through the net.* ➲ more at GEAR *n.*, TONGUE *n.*
PHR V ˌ**slip a**ˈ**way** to stop existing; to disappear or die: *Their support gradually slipped away.* ˌ**slip** ˈ**out** when sth **slips out**, you say it without really intending to: *I'm sorry I said that. It just slipped out.* ˌ**slip** ˈ**up** (*informal*) to make a careless mistake: *We can't afford to slip up.* ➲ related noun SLIP-UP
■ ***noun***
▸ SMALL MISTAKE **1** a small mistake, usually made by being careless or not paying attention: *He recited the whole poem without making a single slip.* ➲ see also FREUDIAN SLIP ➲ SYNONYMS at MISTAKE
▸ PIECE OF PAPER **2** a small piece of paper, especially one for writing on or with sth printed on it: *I wrote it down on a slip of paper.* ◇ *a betting slip* ➲ see also PAYSLIP
▸ ACT OF SLIPPING **3** an act of slipping: *One slip and you could fall to your death.*
▸ CLOTHING **4** a piece of women's underwear like a thin dress or skirt, worn under a dress

S

▸ IN CRICKET **5** a player who stands behind and to one side of the BATSMAN and tries to catch the ball; the position on the field where this player stands
IDM **give sb the 'slip** (*informal*) to escape or get away from sb who is following or chasing you **a 'slip of a boy, girl, etc.** (*old-fashioned*) a small or thin, usually young, person **a slip of the 'pen/'tongue** a small mistake in sth that you write or say: *Did I call you Richard? Sorry, Robert, just a slip of the tongue.* **there's ˌmany a 'slip 'twixt ˌcup and 'lip** (*saying*) nothing is completely certain until it really happens because things can easily go wrong

'slip case *noun* a stiff cover that a book or other object fits into

'slip cover (*NAmE*) (*BrE* **ˌloose 'cover**) *noun* a cover for a chair, etc. that you can take off, for example to wash it

'slip knot *noun* a knot that can slide easily along the rope, etc. on which it is tied, in order to make the LOOP or rope tighter or looser

'slip-on *noun* a shoe that you can slide your feet into without having to tie LACES: *a* ***pair of slip-ons*** ◇ *slip-on shoes*

slip·page /'slɪpɪdʒ/ *noun* [U, C, usually sing.] **1** failure to achieve an aim or complete a task by a particular date **2** a slight or gradual fall in the amount, value, etc. of sth

ˌslipped 'disc *noun* a painful condition caused when one of the discs between the bones of the SPINE in a person's back moves out of place

slip·per /'slɪpə(r)/ *noun* a loose soft shoe that you wear in the house: *a pair of slippers* ➲ **VISUAL VOCAB** page V52 ➲ see also CARPET SLIPPER

slip·pered /'slɪpəd; *NAmE* -pərd/ *adj.* wearing slippers: *slippered feet*

slip·pery /'slɪpəri/ *adj.* **1** (also *informal* **slippy**) difficult to hold or to stand or move on, because it is smooth, wet or polished: *slippery like a fish* ◇ *In places the path can be wet and slippery.* ◇ *His hand was slippery with sweat.* **2** (*informal*) (of a person) that you cannot trust: *Don't believe what he says—he's a slippery customer.* **3** (*informal*) (of a situation, subject, problem, etc.) difficult to deal with and that you have to think about carefully: *Freedom is a slippery concept* (= because its meaning changes according to your point of view).
IDM **the/a slippery 'slope** a course of action that is difficult to stop once it has begun, and can lead to serious problems or disaster

slippy /'slɪpi/ *adj.* (**slip·pier**, **slip·piest**) (*informal*) = SLIPPERY

S

'slip road (*BrE*) (*NAmE* **ramp**) *noun* a road used for driving onto or off a major road such as a MOTORWAY or INTERSTATE ➲ compare ACCESS ROAD

slip·shod /'slɪpʃɒd; *NAmE* -ʃɑːd/ *adj.* done without care; doing things without care **SYN** **careless**

slip·stream /'slɪpstriːm/ *noun* [sing.] the stream of air behind a vehicle that is moving very fast

'slip-up *noun* (*informal*) a careless mistake

slip·way /'slɪpweɪ/ *noun* a sloping track leading down to water, on which ships are built or pulled up out of the water for repairs, or from which they are launched

slit /slɪt/ *noun, verb*
■ ***noun*** a long narrow cut or opening: *a long skirt with a slit up the side* ◇ *His eyes narrowed into slits.*
■ ***verb*** (**slit·ting**, **slit**, **slit**) to make a long narrow cut or opening in sth: **~ sth** *Slit the roll with a sharp knife.* ◇ *The child's throat had been slit.* ◇ *Her skirt was slit at both sides* (= designed with an opening at the bottom on each side). ◇ **~ sth + adj.** *He slit open the envelope and took out the letter.*

'slit-eyed *adj.* having narrow eyes (often used in an offensive way to refer to people from E Asia)

slither /'slɪðə(r)/ *verb* **1** [I] **+ adv./prep.** to move somewhere in a smooth, controlled way, often close to the ground **SYN** **glide**: *The snake slithered away as we approached.* **2 + adv./prep.** to move somewhere without much control, for example because the ground is steep or wet **SYN** **slide**: *We slithered down the slope to the road.* ◇ *They were slithering around on the ice.*

slith·ery /'slɪðəri/ *adj.* difficult to hold or stand on because it is wet or smooth; moving in a slithering way

slitty-eyed /ˌslɪti 'aɪd/ *adj.* (*offensive*) having narrow eyes (often used in an offensive way to refer to people from E Asia)

sliver /'slɪvə(r)/ *noun* a small or thin piece of sth that is cut or broken off from a larger piece: *slivers of glass* ◇ (*figurative*) *A sliver of light showed under the door.*

Sloane /sləʊn; *NAmE* sloʊn/ *noun* (*BrE, informal*, often *disapproving*) a young person, especially a woman, from a rich upper-class background, especially one who lives in a fashionable area of London

slob /slɒb; *NAmE* slɑːb/ *noun, verb*
■ ***noun*** (*informal, disapproving*) a person who is lazy and dirty or untidy: *Get out of bed, you fat slob!*
■ ***verb*** (**-bb-**)
PHR V **ˌslob a'round/'out** (*BrE, informal*) to spend time being lazy and doing nothing

slob·ber /'slɒbə(r); *NAmE* 'slɑːb-/ *verb* [I] to let SALIVA come out of your mouth **SYN** **dribble**
PHR V **'slobber over sb/sth** (*informal, disapproving*) to show how much you like or want sb/sth without any pride or control

sloe /sləʊ; *NAmE* sloʊ/ *noun* a bitter wild fruit like a small PLUM that grows on a bush called a BLACKTHORN

ˌsloe 'eyes *noun* [pl.] attractive, dark eyes, usually ones that are long and thin ▸ **ˌsloe-'eyed** *adj.*

ˌsloe 'gin *noun* [U] a strong alcoholic drink made by leaving sloes in GIN so that the gin has the flavour and the colour of the sloes

slog /slɒg; *NAmE* slɑːg/ *verb, noun*
■ ***verb*** (**-gg-**) (*informal*) **1** [I, T] to work hard and steadily at sth, especially sth that takes a long time and is boring or difficult: **~ (away) (at sth)** *He's been slogging away at that piece of music for weeks.* ◇ **~ (through sth)** *The teacher made us slog through long lists of vocabulary.* ◇ **~ your way through sth** *She slogged her way through four piles of ironing.* **2** [I, T] to walk or travel somewhere steadily, with great effort or difficulty: **+ adv./prep.** *I've been slogging around the streets of London all day.* ◇ **~ your way through sth** *He started to slog his way through the undergrowth.* **3** [T, I] **~ (sth) (+ adv./prep.)** to hit a ball very hard but often without skill
IDM **ˌslog it 'out** (*BrE, informal*) to fight or compete in order to prove who is the strongest, the best, etc. ➲ more at GUT *n.*
■ ***noun*** [U, C, usually sing.] a period of hard work or effort: *Writing the book took ten months of hard slog.* ◇ *It was a long slog to the top of the mountain.*

slo·gan /'sləʊgən; *NAmE* 'sloʊ-/ (also *NAmE informal* **'tag line**) *noun* a word or phrase that is easy to remember, used for example by a political party or in advertising to attract people's attention or to suggest an idea quickly: *an* ***advertising slogan*** ◇ *a* ***campaign slogan*** ◇ *The crowd began chanting anti-government* ***slogans***.

slo·gan·eer·ing /ˌsləʊgə'nɪərɪŋ; *NAmE* ˌsloʊgə'nɪrɪŋ/ *noun* [U] (*disapproving*) the use of slogans in advertisements, by politicians, etc.

slo-mo /'sləʊ məʊ; *NAmE* 'sloʊ moʊ/ *noun* [U] (*informal*) = SLOW MOTION

sloop /sluːp/ *noun* a small sailing ship with one MAST (= a post to support the sails)

slop /slɒp; *NAmE* slɑːp/ *verb, noun*
■ ***verb*** (**-pp-**) **1** [I] **+ adv./prep.** (of a liquid) to move around in a container, often so that some liquid comes out over the edge: *Water was slopping around in the bottom of the boat.* ◇ *As he put the glass down the beer slopped over onto the table.* **2** [T] **~ sth (+ adv./prep.)** to make liquid or food come out of a container in an untidy way **SYN** **spill**: *He got out of the bath, slopping water over the sides.* ◇ *She slopped some beans onto a plate.*
PHR V **ˌslop a'bout/a'round** (*BrE, informal*) **1** to spend

time relaxing or being lazy: *He used to slop around all day in his pyjamas.* **2** to move around in water, mud. etc. ˌ**slop ˈout** (*BrE*) when prisoners **slop out**, they empty the containers that they use as toilets

■ ***noun*** [U] (also **slops** [pl.]) **1** waste food, sometimes fed to animals **2** liquid or partly liquid waste, for example URINE or dirty water from baths: *a slop bucket*

slope 0➡ /sləʊp; *NAmE* sloʊp/ *noun, verb*

■ ***noun*** **1** 0➡ [C] a surface or piece of land that slopes (= is higher at one end than the other) SYN **incline**: *a grassy slope* ◇ *The town is built **on a slope**.* **2** 0➡ [C, usually pl.] an area of land that is part of a mountain or hill: *the eastern slopes of the Andes* ◇ *ski slopes* ◇ *He spends all winter **on the slopes*** (=SKIING). ➲ VISUAL VOCAB page V4 **3** 0➡ [sing., U] the amount by which sth slopes: *a **gentle/steep slope*** ◇ *a slope of 45 degrees* ◇ *the angle of slope* IDM see SLIPPERY

■ ***verb*** **1** 0➡ [I] (+ **adv./prep.**) (of a horizontal surface) to be at an angle so that it is higher at one end than the other: *The garden slopes away towards the river.* ◇ *sloping shoulders* **2** 0➡ [I] (+ **adv./prep.**) (of sth vertical) to be at an angle rather than being straight or vertical: *His handwriting slopes backwards.* ◇ *It was a very old house with sloping walls.* **3** [I] + **adv./prep.** (*BrE, informal*) to go somewhere quietly, especially in order to avoid sth/sb SYN **slink**: *They got bored waiting for him and **sloped off**.*

sloppy /ˈslɒpi; *NAmE* ˈslɑːpi/ *adj.* (**slop·pier, slop·pi·est**) **1** that shows a lack of care, thought or effort: *sloppy thinking* ◇ *Your work is sloppy.* ◇ *a sloppy worker* **2** (of clothes) loose and without much shape SYN **baggy**: *a sloppy T-shirt* **3** (*informal, especially BrE*) romantic in a silly or embarrassing way: *a sloppy love story* **4** containing too much liquid: *Don't make the mixture too sloppy.* ◇ (*informal*) *She gave him a big sloppy kiss.* ► **slop·pily** /-ɪli/ *adv.*: *a sloppily run department* **slop·pi·ness** *noun* [U]: *There is no excuse for sloppiness in your work.*

sloppy joe /ˌslɒpi ˈdʒəʊ; *NAmE* ˌslɑːpi ˈdʒoʊ/ *noun* (*NAmE*) finely chopped meat served in a spicy tomato sauce inside a BUN (= bread roll)

slosh /slɒʃ; *NAmE* slɑːʃ/ *verb* (*informal*) **1** [I] + **adv./prep.** (of liquid) to move around making a lot of noise or coming out over the edge of sth: *The water was sloshing around under our feet.* ◇ *Some of the paint sloshed out of the can.* **2** [T] ~ **sth + adv./prep.** to make liquid move in a noisy way; to use liquid carelessly: *The children were sloshing water everywhere.* ◇ *She sloshed coffee into the mugs.* **3** [I] + **adv./prep.** to walk noisily in water or mud: *We all sloshed around in the puddles.*

PHR V ˌ**slosh aˈbout/aˈround** (*BrE, informal*) (especially of money) to be available or present in large quantities

sloshed /slɒʃt; *NAmE* slɑːʃt/ *adj.* (*informal*) drunk

slot /slɒt; *NAmE* slɑːt/ *noun, verb*

■ ***noun*** **1** a long narrow opening, into which you put or fit sth: *to put some coins in the slot* **2** a position, a time or an opportunity for sb/sth, for example in a list, a programme of events or a series of broadcasts: *He has a regular slot on the late-night programme.* ◇ *Their album has occupied the Number One slot for the past six weeks.* ◇ *the airport's take-off and landing slots*

■ ***verb*** (-tt-) [T, I] to put sth into a space that is available or designed for it; to fit into such a space: ~ **sth + adv./prep.** *He slotted a cassette into the VCR.* ◇ *The bed comes in sections which can be quickly **slotted together**.* ◇ + **adv./prep.** *The dishwasher slots neatly between the cupboards.* IDM see PLACE *n.*

PHR V ˌ**slot sb/sth↔ˈin** to manage to find a position, a time or an opportunity for sb/sth: *I can slot you in between 3 and 4.* ◇ *We slotted in some extra lessons before the exam.*

sloth /sləʊθ; *NAmE* sloʊθ/ *noun* **1** [C] a S American animal that lives in trees and moves very slowly **2** [U] (*formal*) the bad habit of being lazy and unwilling to work

sloth·ful /ˈsləʊθfl; *NAmE* ˈsloʊθfl/ *adj.* (*formal*) lazy

ˈ**slot machine** *noun* **1** (*BrE*) a machine with an opening for coins, used for selling things such as cigarettes and bars of chocolate **2** (*especially NAmE*) (also ˌ**one-armed ˈbandit** *NAmE, BrE*) (*BrE* also ˈ**fruit machine**) a gambling machine that you put coins into and that gives money back if particular pictures appear together on the screen

slot·ted /ˈslɒtɪd; *NAmE* ˈslɑːt-/ *adj.* [usually before noun] (*technical*) **1** having a SLOT or SLOTS in it **2** (of a screw) having a SLOT in it rather than a cross shape ➲ compare PHILLIPS

ˌ**slotted ˈspoon** *noun* a large spoon with holes in it

slouch /slaʊtʃ/ *verb, noun*

■ ***verb*** [I] (+ **adv./prep.**) to stand, sit or move in a lazy way, often with your shoulders and head bent forward: *Sit up straight. Don't slouch.*

■ ***noun*** [usually sing.] a way of standing or sitting in which your shoulders are not straight, so that you look tired or lazy

IDM **be no ˈslouch** (*informal*) to be very good at sth or quick to do sth: *She's no slouch on the guitar.*

slouchy /ˈslaʊtʃi/ *adj.* (**slouch·ier, slouchi·est**) **1** (*disapproving*) holding your body in a lazy way, often with your shoulders and head bent forward: *his slouchy posture* **2** (*approving*) (of clothes) without a firm outline; not stiff: *The slouchy suede boots look great with slim pants.*

slough[1] /slʌf/ *verb* to lose a layer of dead skin, etc: ~ **sth** *a snake sloughing its skin* ◇ ~ **sth off** *Slough off dead skin cells by using a facial scrub.*

PHR V ˌ**slough sth↔ˈoff** (*formal*) to get rid of sth that you no longer want: *Responsibilities are not sloughed off so easily.*

slough[2] /slaʊ; *NAmE* sluː/ *noun* (*literary*) **1** [sing.] ~ **of misery, despair, etc.** a state of sadness with no hope **2** [C] a very soft wet area of land

the Slough of Des·pond /ˌslaʊ əv dɪˈspɒnd; *NAmE* dɪˈspɑːnd/ *noun* [sing.] a mental state in which a person feels no hope and is very afraid: *He was sinking into the Slough of Despond.* ORIGIN From the name of a place that Christian, the main character, must travel through in John Bunyan's *The Pilgrim's Progress*.

slov·en·ly /ˈslʌvnli/ *adj.* careless, untidy or dirty in appearance or habits: *He grew lazy and slovenly in his habits.* ► **slov·en·li·ness** *noun* [U]

slow 0➡ /sləʊ; *NAmE* sloʊ/ *adj., adv., verb*

■ ***adj.*** (**slow·er, slow·est**)

► NOT FAST **1** 0➡ not moving, acting or done quickly; taking a long time; not fast: *a slow driver* ◇ *Progress was slower than expected.* ◇ *The country is experiencing slow but steady economic growth.* ◇ *Collecting data is a **painfully slow** process.* ◇ *a slow, lingering death* ◇ *Oh you're so slow; come on, hurry up!* ◇ *The slow movement opens with a cello solo.* ◇ *She gave a slow smile.* **2** 0➡ not going or allowing you to go at a fast speed: *I missed the fast train and had to get the slow one* (= the one that stops at all the stations).

► WITH DELAY **3** 0➡ hesitating to do sth or not doing sth immediately: ~ **to do sth** *She wasn't slow to realize what was going on.* ◇ ~ **in doing sth** *His poetry was slow in achieving recognition.* ◇ ~ **doing sth** *They were very slow paying me.*

► NOT CLEVER **4** 0➡ not quick to learn; finding things hard to understand: *He's the slowest in the class.*

► NOT BUSY **5** not very busy; containing little action SYN **sluggish**: *Sales are slow* (= not many goods are being sold).

► WATCH/CLOCK **6** [not before noun] showing a time earlier than the correct time: *My watch is five minutes slow* (= it shows 1.45 when it is 1.50).

► IN PHOTOGRAPHY **7 slow** film is not very sensitive to light ► **slow·ness** *noun* [U]: *There was impatience over the slowness of reform.*

IDM **do a slow ˈburn** (*NAmE, informal*) to slowly get angry ➲ more at MARK *n.*, UPTAKE

■ ***adv.*** (**slow·er, slow·est**) (used especially in the comparative and superlative forms, or in compounds) at a slow speed SYN **slowly**: *Could you go a little slower?* ◇ *slow-drying paint* ◇ *slow-moving traffic* ◇ (*NAmE*) *Drive slow!*

IDM **go ˈslow** (**on sth**) to show less enthusiasm for achieving sth: *The government is going slow on tax reforms.* ➲ see also GO-SLOW

■ ***verb*** [I, T] to go or to make sth/sb go at a slower speed or be

S

less active: *Economic growth has slowed a little.* ◇ *The bus* ***slowed to a halt.*** ◇ **~ down/up** *The car slowed down as it approached the junction.* ◇ *The game slowed up little in the second half.* ◇ *You must slow down* (= work less hard) *or you'll make yourself ill.* ◇ **~ sth/sb down/up** *The ice on the roads was slowing us down.* ◇ **~ sth/sb** *We hope to slow the spread of the disease.* ➲ see also SLOWDOWN

Which Word?

slow / slowly

- **Slowly** is the usual adverb from the adjective **slow**. **Slow** is sometimes used as an adverb in informal language, on road signs, etc. It can also be used to form compounds: *Slow. Major road ahead.* ◇ *a slow-acting drug* ◇ ~~*They walk very slow.*~~ In the comparative both **slower** and **more slowly** are used: *Can you speak slower/more slowly?*

slow·coach /ˈsləʊkəʊtʃ; *NAmE* ˈsloʊkoʊtʃ/ (*BrE*) (*NAmE* ˈ**slow·poke**) *noun* (*informal*) a person who moves, acts or works too slowly

ˈ**slow cooker** *noun* an electric pot used for cooking meat and vegetables slowly in liquid

slow·down /ˈsləʊdaʊn; *NAmE* ˈsloʊ-/ *noun* **1** a reduction in speed or activity: *a slowdown in economic growth* **2** (*NAmE*) (*BrE* ˌ**go-ˈslow**) a protest that workers make by doing their work more slowly than usual ➲ compare WORK-TO-RULE

ˌ**slow ˈfood** *noun* [U] traditional food and ways of producing, cooking and eating it ➲ compare FAST FOOD

ˈ**slow lane** *noun* [sing.] the part of a major road such as a MOTORWAY or INTERSTATE where vehicles drive slowest
IDM **in the ˈslow lane** not making progress as fast as other people, countries, companies, etc.

slow·ly 🔑 /ˈsləʊli; *NAmE* ˈsloʊli/ *adv.* at a slow speed; not quickly: *to move slowly* ◇ *Please could you speak more slowly?* ◇ *The boat chugged slowly along.* ◇ *He found that life moved slowly in the countryside.* ◇ *Don't rush into a decision.* ***Take it slowly.*** ◇ *Slowly things began to improve.* ➲ note at SLOW
IDM ˌ**slowly but ˈsurely** making slow but definite progress: *We'll get there slowly but surely.*

ˌ**slow ˈmotion** *noun* [U] (in a film/movie or on television) the method of showing action at a much slower speed than it happened in real life: *Some scenes were filmed* ***in slow motion.*** ◇ *a slow-motion replay*

slow·poke /ˈsləʊpəʊk; *NAmE* ˈsloʊpoʊk/ (*NAmE*) (*BrE* **slow·coach**) *noun* (*informal*) a person who moves, acts or works too slowly

ˈ**slow-witted** *adj.* not able to think quickly; slow to learn or understand things OPP **quick-witted**

ˈ**slow-worm** (also **blind·worm**) *noun* a small European REPTILE with no legs, like a snake

SLR /ˌes el ˈɑː(r)/ *abbr.* single-lens reflex (used to describe a camera in which there is only one LENS which both forms the image on the film and provides the image in the VIEW-FINDER)

slub /slʌb/ *noun* a lump or thick place in wool or thread ▸ **slubbed** /slʌbd/ *adj.*

sludge /slʌdʒ/ *noun* [U] **1** thick, soft, wet mud or a substance that looks like it SYN **slime**: *There was some sludge at the bottom of the tank.* **2** industrial or human waste that has been treated: *industrial sludge* ◇ *the use of sewage sludge as a fertilizer on farm land*

slug /slʌg/ *noun, verb*
■ ***noun*** **1** a small soft creature, like a SNAIL without a shell, that moves very slowly and often eats garden plants ➲ VISUAL VOCAB page V11 **2** (*informal*) a small amount of a strong alcoholic drink: *He took another slug of whisky.* **3** (*informal, especially NAmE*) a bullet **4** (*NAmE, informal*) a piece of metal shaped like a coin used to get things from machines, etc, sometimes illegally
■ ***verb*** (-gg-) **1 ~ sb** (*informal*) to hit sb hard, especially with your closed hand **2 ~ sth** (in BASEBALL) to hit the ball hard
IDM ˌ**slug it ˈout** to fight or compete until it is clear who has won

slug·fest /ˈslʌgfest/ *noun* (*informal, especially NAmE*) an angry argument in which people insult each other: *The battle between the two Democrats is turning into a nasty little slugfest.*

slug·gard /ˈslʌgəd; *NAmE* -gərd/ *noun* (*formal*) a slow, lazy person ▸ **slug·gard·ly** *adj.*

slug·ger /ˈslʌgə(r)/ *noun* (*NAmE, informal*) **1** (in BASEBALL) a player who hits the ball, especially one who hits it very hard and for long distances **2** (*approving*) used when speaking to or about sb, especially a young boy, who tries really hard at sth, and that you feel affection for: *Hang in there, slugger. You can do it!*

slug·gish /ˈslʌgɪʃ/ *adj.* moving, reacting or working more slowly than normal and in a way that seems lazy: *sluggish traffic* ◇ *a sluggish economy* ◇ *the sluggish black waters of the canal* ◇ *He felt very heavy and sluggish after the meal.* ▸ **slug·gish·ly** *adv.* **slug·gish·ness** *noun* [U]

sluice /sluːs/ *noun, verb*
■ ***noun*** (also ˈ**sluice gate**) a sliding gate or other device for controlling the flow of water out of or into a CANAL, etc.
■ ***verb*** **1** [T] **~ sth (down/out)** | **~ sth (with sth)** to wash sth with a stream of water: *The ship's crew was sluicing down the deck.* **2** [I] **+ adv./prep.** (of water) to flow somewhere in large quantities

slum /slʌm/ *noun, verb*
■ ***noun*** an area of a city that is very poor and where the houses are dirty and in bad condition: *a slum area* ◇ ***city/urban slums*** ◇ *She was brought up in the slums of Leeds.*
■ ***verb*** (-mm-) [I] (usually **be slumming**) (*informal*) to spend time in places or conditions that are much worse than those you are used to: *There are plenty of ways you can cut costs on your trip without slumming.*
IDM ˈ**slum it** (often *humorous*) to accept conditions that are worse than those you are used to: *Several businessmen had to slum it in economy class.*

slum·ber /ˈslʌmbə(r)/ *noun, verb*
■ ***noun*** [U, C, usually pl.] (*literary*) sleep; a time when sb is asleep: *She fell into a deep and peaceful slumber.*
■ ***verb*** [I] (*literary*) to sleep

ˈ**slumber party** *noun* (*NAmE*) = SLEEPOVER

slum·lord /ˈslʌmlɔːd; *NAmE* -lɔːrd/ *noun* (*NAmE, informal*) a person who owns houses or flats/apartments in a poor area and who charges very high rent for them even though they are in bad condition

slump /slʌmp/ *verb, noun*
■ ***verb*** **1** [I] to fall in price, value, number, etc, suddenly and by a large amount SYN **drop**: *Sales have slumped this year.* ◇ **~ by sth** *Profits slumped by over 50%.* ◇ **~ (from sth) (to sth)** *The paper's circulation has slumped to 90 000.* **2** [I] **+ adv./prep.** to sit or fall down heavily: *The old man slumped down in his chair.* ◇ *She slumped to her knees.*
■ ***noun*** **1 ~ (in sth)** a sudden fall in sales, prices, the value of sth, etc. SYN **decline**: *a slump in profits* **2** a period when a country's economy or a business is doing very badly: *the slump of the 1930s* ◇ *The toy industry is in a slump.* ➲ compare BOOM *n.* (1)

slumped /slʌmpt/ *adj.* [not usually before noun] **~ (against/over sth)** sitting with your body leaning forward, for example because you are asleep or unconscious: *The driver was slumped exhausted over the wheel.*

slung *past tense, past part.* of SLING

slunk *past tense, past part.* of SLINK

slur /slɜː(r)/ *verb, noun*
■ ***verb*** (-rr-) **1 ~ sth** | **+ speech** to pronounce words in a way that is not clear so that they run into each other, usually because you are drunk or tired: *She had drunk too much and her speech was slurred.* **2 ~ sth** (*music*) to play or sing a group of two or more musical notes so that each one runs

S

smoothly into the next **3 ~ sb/sth** to harm sb's reputation by making unfair or false statements about them

■ ***noun*** **1 ~** (**on sb/sth**) an unfair remark about sb/sth that may damage other people's opinion of them SYN **insult**: *She had dared to **cast a slur** on his character.* ◇ (*especially NAmE*) *The crowd started throwing bottles and shouting **racial slurs**.* **2** (*music*) a curved sign used to show that two or more notes are to be played smoothly and without a break

slurp /slɜːp; *NAmE* slɜːrp/ *verb* (*informal*) **1** [T, I] to make a loud noise while you are drinking sth: **~ sth** *He was slurping his tea.* ◇ **~** (**from sth**) *She slurped noisily from her cup.* **2** [I] to make a noise like this: *The water slurped in the tank.* ▶ **slurp** *noun* [usually sing.]: *She took a slurp from her mug.*

slurry /ˈslʌri; *NAmE* ˈslɜːri/ *noun* [U] a thick liquid consisting of water mixed with animal waste, CLAY, coal dust or CEMENT

slush /slʌʃ/ *noun* [U] **1** partly melted snow that is usually dirty: *In the city the clean white snow had turned to grey slush.* **2** (*informal, disapproving*) stories, films/movies or feelings that are considered to be silly and without value because they are too emotional and romantic ▶ **slushy** *adj.*: *slushy pavements* ◇ *slushy romantic fiction*

ˈ**slush fund** *noun* (*disapproving*) a sum of money kept for illegal purposes, especially in politics

slut /slʌt/ *noun* (*disapproving, offensive*) **1** a woman who has many sexual partners **2** a woman who is very untidy or lazy ▶ **slut·tish** *adj.*

sly /slaɪ/ *adj.* **1** (*disapproving*) acting or done in a secret or dishonest way, often intending to trick people SYN **cunning**: *a sly political move* ◇ (*humorous*) *You sly old devil! How long have you known?* **2** [usually before noun] suggesting that you know sth secret that other people do not know SYN **knowing**: *a **sly smile/grin/look/glance, etc.*** ▶ **slyly** *adv.*: *He glanced at her slyly.* **sly·ness** *noun* [U]

IDM **on the** ˈ**sly** secretly; not wanting other people to discover what you are doing: *He has to visit them on the sly.*

smack /smæk/ *verb, noun, adv.*

■ ***verb*** **1** [T] **~ sb/sth** (*especially BrE*) to hit sb with your open hand, especially as a punishment: *I think it's wrong to smack children.* ➲ compare SPANK **2** [T] **~ sth + adv./prep.** to put sth somewhere with a lot of force so that it makes a loud noise SYN **bang**: *She smacked her hand down on to the table.* ◇ *He smacked a fist into the palm of his hand.* **3** [I] **+ adv./prep.** to hit against sth with a lot of force SYN **crash**: *Two players accidentally smacked into each other.* IDM see LIP

PHR V ˈ**smack of sth** to seem to contain or involve a particular unpleasant quality: *Her behaviour smacks of hypocrisy.* ◇ *Today's announcement smacks of a government cover-up.* ˌ**smack sb**↔ˈ**up** (*BrE, informal*) to hit sb hard with your hand, many times

■ ***noun*** **1** [C] (*especially BrE*) a sharp hit given with your open hand, especially to a child as a punishment: *You'll get a smack on your backside if you're not careful.* **2** [C] (*informal*) a hard hit given with a closed hand SYN **punch**: *a smack on the jaw* **3** [C, usually sing.] a short loud sound: *She closed the ledger with a smack.* **4** [C] (*informal*) a loud kiss: *a **smack on the lips/cheek*** **5** [U] (*slang*) the drug HEROIN: *smack addicts* **6** [C] (*BrE*) a small fishing boat

■ ***adv.*** (*informal*) **1** (*NAmE* also ˈ**smack-dab**) exactly or directly in a place: *It landed **smack in the middle** of the carpet.* **2** with sudden, violent force, often making a loud noise: *The car drove smack into a brick wall.*

smack·er /ˈsmækə(r)/ *noun* **1** (*informal*) a loud kiss **2** (*slang*) a British pound or US dollar

smack·ing /ˈsmækɪŋ/ *noun* [sing., U] (*especially BrE*) an act of hitting sb, especially a child, several times with your open hand, as a punishment: *He gave both of the children a good smacking.* ◇ *We don't approve of smacking.*

small 🔑 /smɔːl/ *adj., adv., noun*

■ ***adj.*** (**small·er**, **small·est**)

▸ NOT LARGE **1** 🔑 not large in size, number, degree, amount, etc: *a small house/town/car/man* ◇ *A much smaller number of students passed than I had expected.* ◇ *They're having a relatively small wedding.* ◇ *That dress is too small for you.* ◇ *'I don't agree,' he said in a small* (= quiet) *voice.* **2** 🔑 (*abbr.* S) used to describe one size in a range of sizes of clothes, food, products used in the house, etc.: *small, medium, large* ◇ *This is too big—have you got a small one?* **3** 🔑 not as big as sth else of the same kind: *the small intestine*

▸ YOUNG **4** 🔑 young: *They have three small children.* ◇ *We travelled around a lot when I was small.* ◇ *As a small boy he had spent most of his time with his grandparents.*

▸ NOT IMPORTANT **5** 🔑 slight; not important: *I made only a few small changes to the report.* ◇ *She noticed several small errors in his work.* ◇ *Everything had been planned down to the smallest detail.* ◇ *It was **no small** achievement getting her to agree to the deal.*

▸ BUSINESS **6** 🔑 [usually before noun] not doing business on a very large scale: *a small farmer* ◇ *The government is planning to give more help to small businesses.*

▸ LETTERS **7** [usually before noun] not written or printed as capitals: *Should I write 'god' **with a small** 'g' or a capital?* ◇ *She's a socialist **with a small** 's'* (= she has socialist ideas but is not a member of a socialist party).

▸ NOT MUCH **8** [only before noun] (used with uncountable nouns) little; not much: *The government has small cause for optimism.* ◇ *They have small hope of succeeding.*

▶ **small·ness** *noun* [U]

IDM **be grateful/thankful for small** ˈ**mercies** to be happy that a situation that is bad is not as bad as it could have been: *Well, at least you weren't hurt. I suppose we should be grateful for small mercies.* **it's a** ˌ**small** ˈ**world** (*saying*) used to express your surprise when you meet sb you know in an unexpected place, or when you are talking to sb and find out that you both know the same person **look/feel** ˈ**small** to look or feel stupid, weak, ashamed, etc. ➲ more at BIG *adj.*, GREAT *adj.*, HOUR, STILL *adj.*, SWEAT *v.*, WAY *n.*, WONDER *n.*

■ ***adv.*** (**small·er**, **small·est**) **1** into small pieces: *Chop the cabbage up small.* **2** in a small size: *You can fit it all in if you write very small.*

■ ***noun*** **1 the ~ of the/sb's back** [sing.] the lower part of the back where it curves in ➲ VISUAL VOCAB page V48 **2 smalls** [pl.] (*old-fashioned, BrE, informal*) small items of clothing, especially underwear

ˈ**small ads** *noun* [pl.] (*BrE, informal*) = CLASSIFIED ADVERTISEMENTS

ˈ**small arms** *noun* [pl.] small light weapons that you can carry in your hands

ˌ**small** ˈ**beer** (*BrE*) (*NAmE* ˌ**small po**ˈ**tatoes**) *noun* [U] (*informal*) a person or thing that has no great importance or value, especially when compared with sb/sth else

ˈ**small-bore** *adj.* **1** a **small-bore** gun is narrow inside **2** (*informal, especially NAmE*) not important: *small-bore issues*

ˌ**small** ˈ**capitals** (also ˌ**small** ˈ**caps**) *noun* [pl.] (*technical*) capital letters which are the same height as LOWER-CASE letters

ˌ**small** ˈ**change** *noun* [U] **1** coins of low value: *Have you got any small change for the phone?* **2** something that is of little value when compared with sth else

ˌ**small** ˈ**claims court** *noun* a local court which deals with cases involving small amounts of money

ˌ**small** ˈ**fortune** *noun* [usually sing.] (*informal*) a lot of money: *That holiday cost me a small fortune.*

ˈ**small fry** *noun* [U+sing./pl. v.] (*informal*) people or things that are considered unimportant compared to sb/sth else: *That's small fry to her.* ◇ *People like us are small fry to such a large business.*

small·hold·er /ˈsmɔːlhəʊldə(r); *NAmE* -hoʊ-/ *noun* (*BrE*) a person who owns or rents a small piece of land for farming

small·hold·ing /ˈsmɔːlhəʊldɪŋ; *NAmE* -hoʊ-/ *noun* a small piece of land used for farming

small·ish /ˈsmɔːlɪʃ/ *adj.* fairly small: *a smallish town*

ˌ**small-**ˈ**minded** *adj.* (*disapproving*) having fixed opinions and ways of doing things and not willing to change them or consider other people's opinions or feelings; interested in small problems and details and not in things which are

S

really important **SYN intolerant, petty** ▶ **ˌsmall-ˈminded·ness** *noun* [U]

ˌsmall poˈtatoes (*NAmE*) (*BrE* **ˌsmall ˈbeer**) *noun* [U] (*informal*) a person or thing that has no great importance or value, especially when compared with sb/sth else

small·pox /ˈsmɔːlpɒks; *NAmE* -pɑːks/ *noun* [U] a serious infectious disease (now extremely rare) that causes fever, leaves permanent marks on the skin and often causes death

the ˌsmall ˈprint (*BrE*) (*NAmE* **the ˌfine ˈprint**) *noun* [U] the important details of an agreement or a legal document that are usually printed in small type and are therefore easy to miss: *Read all the small print before signing.*

ˌsmall-ˈscale *adj.* **1** (of an organization, activity, etc.) not large in size or extent; limited in what it does: *small-scale farming* ◇ *a small-scale study of couples in second marriages* **2** (of maps, drawings, etc.) drawn to a small scale so that not many details are shown **OPP large-scale**

the ˌsmall ˈscreen *noun* [sing.] television (when contrasted with cinema): *This will be the film's first showing on the small screen.* ◇ *his first small-screen role*

ˈsmall talk *noun* [U] polite conversation about ordinary or unimportant subjects, especially at social occasions

ˈsmall-time *adj.* [only before noun] (*informal, disapproving*) (often of criminals) not very important or successful **SYN petty**: *a small-time crook* ➲ compare BIG TIME

ˈsmall-town *adj.* [only before noun] **1** (*disapproving*) not showing much interest in new ideas or what is happening outside your own environment **SYN narrow-minded**: *small-town values* **2** connected with a small town: *small-town America* (= people who live in small towns in America)

smarmy /ˈsmɑːmi; *NAmE* ˈsmɑːrmi/ *adj.* (**smarm·ier, smarmi·est**) (*informal, disapproving*) too polite in a way that is not sincere **SYN smooth**: *a smarmy salesman*

smart 🔑 /smɑːt; *NAmE* smɑːrt/ *adj., verb*

■ ***adj.*** (**smart·er, smart·est**)

▸ CLEAN/NEAT **1** 🔑 (*especially BrE*) (of people) looking clean and neat; well dressed in fashionable and/or formal clothes: *You look very smart in that suit.* **2** 🔑 (*especially BrE*) (of clothes, etc.) clean, neat and looking new and attractive: *They were wearing their smartest clothes.*

▸ INTELLIGENT **3** 🔑 (*especially NAmE*) intelligent: *She's smarter than her brother.* ◇ *That was a* ***smart*** *career* ***move***. ◇ *OK, I admit it was not the smartest thing I ever did* (= it was a stupid thing to do). ➲ SYNONYMS at INTELLIGENT

▸ FASHIONABLE **4** (*especially BrE*) connected with fashionable rich people: *smart restaurants* ◇ *She mixes with* ***the smart set***.

▸ QUICK **5** (of a movement, etc.) quick and usually done with force **SYN brisk**: *He was struck with a smart crack on the head.* ◇ *We set off at a smart pace.*

▸ COMPUTER-CONTROLLED **6** (of a device, especially of a weapon/bomb) controlled by a computer, so that it appears to act in an intelligent way: *smart bombs* ◇ *This smart washing machine will dispense an optimal amount of water for the load.*

▶ **smart·ly** *adv.*: (*especially BrE*) *smartly dressed* ◇ *He ran off pretty smartly* (= quickly and suddenly). **smart·ness** *noun* [U]

■ ***verb*** **1** [I] **~ (from sth)** to feel a sharp stinging pain in a part of your body: *His eyes were smarting from the smoke.* **2** [I] **~ (from/over sth)** to feel upset about a criticism, failure, etc: *They are still smarting from the 4–0 defeat last week.* ➲ see also SMARTS

smart alec (*BrE*) (*NAmE* **smart aleck**) /ˈsmɑːt ælɪk; *NAmE* ˈsmɑːrt/ (also **ˈsmarty-pants**) (*BrE* also **ˈsmart-arse**) (*NAmE* also **ˈsmart-ass**) *noun* (*informal, disapproving*) a person who thinks they are very clever and likes to show people this in an annoying way

ˈsmart bomb *noun* a weapon controlled by an electronic device that is intended to cause damage to the target while avoiding damage to other people, buildings, etc. that are in the area

ˈsmart card *noun* a small plastic card on which information is stored in electronic form ➲ see also CHIP CARD

smart·en /ˈsmɑːtn; *NAmE* ˈsmɑːrtn/ *verb*

PHR V **ˌsmarten sb/sth↔ˈup | ˌsmarten (yourself) ˈup** (*especially BrE*) to make yourself, another person or a place look neater or more attractive: *The hotel has been smartened up by the new owners.*

smart·ish /ˈsmɑːtɪʃ; *NAmE* ˈsmɑːrt-/ *adj., adv.* (*informal, especially BrE*) quick; quickly: *We set off at a smartish pace.* ◇ *You'd better move smartish.*

the ˈsmart money *noun* [U] **1** money that is invested or bet by people who have expert knowledge: *It seems the smart money is no longer in insurance* (= is no longer being invested in insurance companies). ◇ *The smart money is on him for the best actor award.* **2** people who have expert knowledge of sth: *The smart money says that he's likely to withdraw from the leadership campaign.*

smart·phone /ˈsmɑːtfəʊn; *NAmE* ˈsmɑːrtfoʊn/ *noun* a mobile phone/cell phone that also has some of the functions of a computer

smarts /smɑːts; *NAmE* smɑːrts/ *noun* [U] (*NAmE, informal*) intelligence: *She made it to the top on her smarts.*

ˈsmarty-pants *noun* = SMART ALEC

smash 🔑 /smæʃ/ *verb, noun*

■ ***verb***

▸ BREAK **1** 🔑 [T, I] **~ (sth)** to break sth, or to be broken, violently and noisily into many pieces: *Several windows had been smashed.* ◇ *He smashed the radio to pieces.* ◇ *The glass bowl smashed into a thousand pieces.*

▸ HIT VERY HARD **2** 🔑 [I, T] to move with a lot of force against sth solid; to make sth do this: **+ adv./prep.** *the sound of waves smashing against the rocks* ◇ *The car smashed into a tree.* ◇ **~ sth + adv./prep.** *Mark smashed his fist down on the desk.* ➲ SYNONYMS at CRASH **3** 🔑 [T, I] to hit sth very hard and break it, in order to get through it: **~ sth + adv./prep.** *They had to smash holes in the ice.* ◇ *The elephant smashed its way through the trees.* ◇ **~ sth + adj.** *We had to smash the door open.* ◇ **+ adv./prep.** *They had smashed through a glass door to get in.* **4** [T] **~ sth/sb (+ adv./prep.)** to hit sth/sb very hard **SYN slam**: *He smashed the ball into the goal.*

▸ DESTROY/DEFEAT **5** [T] **~ sth/sb** to destroy, defeat or put an end to sth/sb: *Police say they have smashed a major drugs ring.* ◇ *She has smashed the world record* (= broken it by a large amount).

▸ CRASH VEHICLE **6** [T] **~ sth (up)** to crash a vehicle: *He's smashed (up) his new car.* ➲ SYNONYMS at CRASH

▸ IN TENNIS, ETC. **7** [T] **~ sth** to hit a high ball downwards and very hard over the net

PHR V **ˌsmash sth↔ˈdown** to make sth fall down by hitting it hard and breaking it: *The police had to smash the door down.* **ˌsmash sth↔ˈin** to make a hole in sth by hitting it with a lot of force: *Vandals had smashed the door in.* ◇ (*informal*) *I wanted to* ***smash his face in*** (= hit him hard in the face). **ˌsmash sth↔ˈup** to destroy sth deliberately: *Youths had broken into the bar and smashed the place up.*

■ ***noun***

▸ ACT OF BREAKING **1** 🔑 [sing.] an act of breaking sth noisily into pieces; the sound this makes: *The cup hit the floor with a smash.*

▸ VEHICLE CRASH **2** [C] (*BrE*) an accident in which a vehicle hits another vehicle: *a car smash*

▸ IN TENNIS, ETC. **3** [C] a way of hitting the ball downwards and very hard

▸ SONG/MOVIE/PLAY **4** (also **ˌsmash ˈhit**) [C] a song, film/movie or play that is very popular: *her latest chart smash*

ˌsmash-and-ˈgrab *adj.* [only before noun] (*BrE*) relating to the act of stealing from a shop/store by breaking a window and taking the goods you can see or reach easily: *a smash-and-grab raid*

smashed /smæʃt/ *adj.* [not before noun] (*slang*) very drunk

smash·er /ˈsmæʃə(r)/ *noun* (*old-fashioned, BrE, informal*) a very good or attractive person or thing

smash·ing /ˈsmæʃɪŋ/ *adj.* (*old-fashioned, BrE, informal*) very good or enjoyable SYN **great**: *We had a smashing time.*

ˈ**smash-up** *noun* (*informal*) a crash in which vehicles are very badly damaged

smat·ter·ing /ˈsmætərɪŋ/ *noun* [sing.] **~ (of sth)** a small amount of sth, especially knowledge of a language: *He only has a smattering of French.*

smear /smɪə(r); *NAmE* smɪr/ *verb, noun*
■ ***verb*** **1** [T] to spread an OILY or soft substance over a surface in a rough or careless way SYN **daub**: **~ sth on/over sth** *The children had smeared mud on the walls.* ◇ **~ sth with sth** *The children had smeared the walls with mud.* **2** [T] **~ sth** to make sth dirty or GREASY: *His glasses were smeared.* ◇ *smeared windows* **3** [T] **~ sb/sth** to damage sb's reputation by saying unpleasant things about them that are not true SYN **slander**: *The story was an attempt to smear the party leader.* **4** [T, I] **~ (sth)** to rub writing, a drawing, etc. so that it is no longer clear; to become not clear in this way SYN **smudge**: *The last few words of the letter were smeared.*
■ ***noun*** **1** an OILY or dirty mark: *a smear of jam* ➲ SYNONYMS at MARK **2** a story that is not true about sb that is intended to damage their reputation, especially in politics: *He was a victim of a **smear campaign**.* **3** (*BrE*) = SMEAR TEST

ˈ**smear test** (also **smear**, ˌ**cervical** ˈ**smear**) (all *BrE*) (*NAmE* ˈ**Pap smear**) *noun* a medical test in which a very small amount of TISSUE from a woman's CERVIX is removed and examined for cancer cells

Vocabulary Building

Smells

Describing smells

These adjectives describe pleasant smells:
- **scented** candles
- **aromatic** oils
- **fragrant** perfume
- **sweet-smelling** flowers

To describe unpleasant smells you can use:
- **smelly** cheese
- **stinking** fish
- **musty** old books
- **acrid** smoke

Types of smell

Pleasant smells:
- the rich **aroma** of fresh coffee
- a herb with a delicate **fragrance**
- a rose's sweet **perfume**
- the **scent** of wild flowers

Unpleasant smells:
- nasty household **odours**
- the **stench** of rotting meat
- the **stink** of stale sweat
- the **reek** of beer and tobacco

smell 🔑 /smel/ *verb, noun*
■ ***verb*** (**smelled, smelled**) (*BrE* also **smelt, smelt** /smelt/) **1** 🔑 [I] to have a particular smell: **+ adj.** *The room smelt damp.* ◇ *Dinner smells good.* ◇ *a bunch of sweet-smelling flowers* ◇ **~ of sth** *His breath smelt of garlic.* ◇ **~ like sth** *What does the perfume smell like?* **2** 🔑 [T, no passive] (not used in the progressive tenses; often with *can* or *could*) to notice or recognize a particular smell: **~ sth** *He said he could smell gas when he entered the room.* ◇ *The dog had smelt a rabbit.* ◇ *I could smell alcohol on his breath.* ◇ **~ sth doing sth** *Can you smell something burning?* ◇ **~ (that)…** *I could smell that something was burning.* **3** [I] (not used in the progressive tenses; often with *can* or *could*) to be able to notice and recognize smells: *I can't smell because I've got a bad cold.* **4** 🔑 [T] **~ sth** (not usually used in the passive) to put your nose near sth and breathe in so that you can discover or identify its smell SYN **sniff**: *Smell this and tell me what you think it is.* ◇ *I bent down to smell the flowers.* **5** 🔑 [I] (not used in the progressive tenses) to have an unpleasant smell: *The drains smell.* ◇ ***It smells** in here.* ◇ *He hadn't washed for days and was beginning to smell.* **6** [T, no passive] **~ sth** to feel that sth exists or is going to happen: *He smelt danger.* ◇ *I can smell trouble.*
IDM **come up/out of sth smelling of** ˈ**roses** (*informal*) to still have a good reputation, even though you have been involved in sth that might have given people a bad opinion of you ˌ**smell a** ˈ**rat** (*informal*) to suspect that sth is wrong about a situation ➲ more at ROSE *n.*, WAKE *v.*
PHR V ˌ**smell sb/sth**↔ˈ**out** **1** to be aware of fear, danger, trouble, etc. in a situation: *He could always smell out fear.* **2** to find sth by smelling: *dogs trained to smell out drugs*
■ ***noun*** **1** 🔑 [C, U] the quality of sth that people and animals sense through their noses: *a **faint/strong smell** of garlic* ◇ *a **sweet/fresh/musty smell*** ◇ *There was a smell of burning in the air.* ◇ *The smells from the kitchen filled the room.* **2** 🔑 [sing.] an unpleasant smell: *What's that smell?* ◇ *Yuk! What a smell!* **3** 🔑 [U] the ability to sense things with the nose: *Dogs have a very good **sense of smell**.* ◇ *Taste and smell are closely connected.* **4** [C] the act of smelling sth SYN **sniff**: *He took one smell of the liquid and his eyes began to water.*
IDM see SWEET *adj.*

ˈ**smelling salts** *noun* [pl.] a chemical with a very strong smell, kept in a small bottle, used especially in the past for putting under the nose of a person who has become unconscious

smelly /ˈsmeli/ *adj.* (**smell·ier, smelli·est**) (*informal*) having an unpleasant smell: *smelly feet*

smelt /smelt/ *verb* **~ sth** to heat and melt ORE (= rock that contains metal) in order to obtain the metal it contains: *a method of smelting iron* ➲ see also SMELL *v.*

smelt·er /ˈsmeltə(r)/ *noun* a piece of equipment for smelting metal

smidgen (also **smidg·eon, smid·gin**) /ˈsmɪdʒən/ *noun* [sing.] **~ (of sth)** (*informal*) a small piece or amount of sth: *'Sugar?' 'Just a smidgen.'*

smile 🔑 /smaɪl/ *verb, noun*
■ ***verb*** **1** 🔑 [I] to make a smile appear on your face: *to **smile sweetly/faintly/broadly, etc.*** ◇ *He smiled with relief.* ◇ *He never seems to smile.* ◇ **~ at sb/sth** *She smiled at him and he **smiled back**.* ◇ *I had to smile at* (= was amused by) *his optimism.* **2** [T] to say or express sth with a smile: **~ sth** *She smiled her thanks.* ◇ **+ speech** *'Perfect,' he smiled.* **3** [T, no passive] **~ sth** to give a smile of a particular type: *to smile a small smile* ◇ *She smiled a smile of dry amusement.* IDM see EAR
PHR V ˈ**smile on sb/sth** (*formal*) if luck, etc. **smiles on** you, you are lucky or successful
■ ***noun*** 🔑 the expression that you have on your face when you are happy, amused, etc. in which the corners of your mouth turn upwards: *'Oh, hello,' he said, **with a smile**.* ◇ *She **gave a** wry **smile**.* ◇ *He had a big smile on his face.* ◇ *I'm going to **wipe that smile off your face*** (= make you stop thinking this is funny).
IDM **all** ˈ**smiles** looking very happy, especially soon after you have been looking worried or sad: *Twelve hours later she was all smiles again.*

smiley /ˈsmaɪli/ *noun* **1** a simple picture of a smiling face that is drawn as a circle with two eyes and a curved mouth **2** a simple picture or series of keyboard symbols :-) that represents a smiling face. The symbols are used, for example, in email or text messages to show that the person sending the message is pleased or joking.

smil·ing·ly /ˈsmaɪlɪŋli/ *adv.* with a smile or smiles

smirk /smɜːk; *NAmE* smɜːrk/ *verb* [I] to smile in a silly or unpleasant way that shows that you are pleased with yourself, know sth that other people do not know, etc: *It was hard not to smirk.* ◇ *He smirked unpleasantly when we told him the bad news.* ▶ **smirk** *noun*: *She had a self-satisfied smirk on her face.*

smite /smaɪt/ *verb* (**smote** /sməʊt; *NAmE* smoʊt/, **smit·ten** /ˈsmɪtn/) (*old use* or *literary*) **1 ~ sb/sth** to hit sb/sth hard; to attack or punish sb **2 ~ sb** to have a great effect on sb, especially an unpleasant or serious one ➲ see also SMITTEN

smith /smɪθ/ *noun* = BLACKSMITH ➲ see also GOLDSMITH, GUNSMITH, LOCKSMITH, SILVERSMITH

smith·er·eens /ˌsmɪðəˈriːnz/ *noun* [pl.]
IDM **smash, blow, etc. sth to smitheˈreens** (*informal*) to destroy sth completely by breaking it into small pieces

smithy /ˈsmɪði; *NAmE* -θi/ *noun* (*pl.* -ies) a place where a BLACKSMITH works

smit·ten /ˈsmɪtn/ *adj.* [only before noun] **1 ~ (with/by sb/sth)** (especially *humorous*) suddenly feeling that you are in love with sb: *From the moment they met, he was completely smitten by her.* **2 ~ with/by sth** severely affected by a feeling, disease, etc. ➲ see also SMITE

smock /smɒk; *NAmE* smɑːk/ *noun* **1** a loose comfortable piece of clothing like a long shirt, worn especially by women **2** a long loose piece of clothing worn over other clothes to protect them from dirt, etc: *an artist's smock*

smock·ing /ˈsmɒkɪŋ; *NAmE* ˈsmɑːk-/ *noun* [U] decoration on clothing consisting of very small tight folds which are sewn together

smog /smɒg; *NAmE* smɑːg/ *noun* [U, C] a form of air pollution that is or looks like a mixture of smoke and FOG, especially in cities: *attempts to reduce smog caused by traffic fumes* ➲ VISUAL VOCAB page V6 ▸ **smoggy** *adj.*

smoke 0‑w /sməʊk; *NAmE* smoʊk/ *noun, verb*

■ ***noun*** **1** 0‑w [U] the grey, white or black gas that is produced by sth burning: *cigarette smoke* ◇ *Clouds of thick black smoke billowed from the car's exhaust.* **2** 0‑w [C, usually sing.] (*informal*) an act of smoking a cigarette: *Are you coming outside for a smoke?*

IDM **go up in ˈsmoke 1** to be completely burnt: *The whole house went up in smoke.* **2** if your plans, hopes, etc. **go up in smoke**, they fail completely (**there is**) **no smoke without ˈfire** (*BrE*) (*NAmE* **where there's smoke, there's ˈfire**) (*saying*) if sth bad is being said about sb/sth, it usually has some truth in it **a smoke-filled ˈroom** (*disapproving*) a decision that people describe as being made in a **smoke-filled room** is made by a small group of people at a private meeting, rather than in an open and DEMOCRATIC way ➲ more at BLOW *v.*

■ ***verb*** **1** 0‑w [T, I] **~ (sth)** to suck smoke from a cigarette, pipe, etc. into your mouth and let it out again: *He was smoking a large cigar.* ◇ *How many cigarettes do you smoke a day?* ◇ *Do you mind if I smoke?* **2** 0‑w [I] to use cigarettes, etc. in this way as a habit: *Do you smoke?* ◇ *She smokes heavily.* ➲ see also CHAIN-SMOKE **3** 0‑w [I] to produce smoke: *smoking factory chimneys* ◇ *the smoking remains of burnt-out cars* **4** 0‑w [T, usually passive] **~ sth** to preserve meat or fish by hanging it in smoke from wood fires to give it a special taste: *smoked salmon*

PHR V **ˌsmoke sb/sth↔ˈout 1** to force sb/sth to come out of a place by filling it with smoke: *to smoke out wasps from a nest* **2** to take action to discover where sb is hiding or to make a secret publicly known: *The police are determined to smoke out the leaders of the gang.*

ˈsmoke alarm (also **ˈsmoke detector**) *noun* a device that makes a loud noise if smoke is in the air to warn you of a fire

ˈsmoke bomb *noun* a bomb that produces clouds of smoke when it explodes

ˌsmoked ˈglass *noun* [U] glass that has been deliberately made dark by smoke

ˈsmoke-free *adj.* free from cigarette smoke; where smoking is not allowed: *a smoke-free working environment*

smoke·less /ˈsməʊkləs; *NAmE* ˈsmoʊk-/ *adj.* [usually before noun] **1** able to burn without producing smoke: *smokeless fuels* **2** free from smoke: *a smokeless zone* (= where smoke from factories or houses is not allowed)

smoker /ˈsməʊkə(r); *NAmE* ˈsmoʊk-/ *noun* a person who smokes TOBACCO regularly: *a **heavy smoker*** (= sb who smokes a lot) ◇ *a **smoker's cough*** ◇ *a **cigarette/cigar/pipe smoker*** OPP **non-smoker**

smoke·screen /ˈsməʊkskriːn; *NAmE* ˈsmoʊk-/ *noun* **1** something that you do or say in order to hide what you are really doing or intending **2** a cloud of smoke used to hide soldiers, ships, etc. during a battle

ˈsmoke shop *noun* (*NAmE*) a shop/store selling cigarettes, TOBACCO, etc.

ˈsmoke signal *noun* [usually pl.] **1** a signal that is sent to sb who is far away, using smoke **2** a sign of what sb is thinking or doing

smoke·stack /ˈsməʊkstæk; *NAmE* ˈsmoʊk-/ *noun* (*especially NAmE*) **1** a tall CHIMNEY that takes away smoke from factories **2** (*BrE* also **fun·nel**) a metal CHIMNEY, for example on a ship or an engine, through which smoke comes out

Smokey the Bear /ˌsməʊki ðə ˈbeə(r); *NAmE* ˌsmoʊki ðə ˈber/ *noun* **1** the symbol used by the US Forest Service on signs and advertising about preventing forest fires **2** (also **ˌSmokey ˈBear**, **ˈSmokey**) (*informal*) (in the US) a member of the police force that is responsible for the highway

smok·ing 0‑w /ˈsməʊkɪŋ; *NAmE* ˈsmoʊk-/ *noun* [U] the activity or habit of smoking cigarettes, etc: *No Smoking* (= for example, on a notice) ◇ *Would you like smoking or non-smoking?* (= for example, in a restaurant) ◇ *He's trying **to give up smoking**.* ➲ compare NON-SMOKING

ˌsmoking ˈgun *noun* [sing.] (*informal*) something that seems to prove that sb has done sth wrong or illegal: *This memo could be the smoking gun that investigators have been looking for.*

ˈsmoking jacket *noun* a man's comfortable jacket worn in the past, often made of VELVET

smoko /ˈsməʊkəʊ; *NAmE* ˈsmoʊkoʊ/ *noun* (*pl.* -os) (*AustralE, NZE, informal*) a rest from work, for example to smoke a cigarette

smoky /ˈsməʊki; *NAmE* ˈsmoʊki/ *adj.* (**smoki·er, smoki·est**) **1** full of smoke: *a smoky atmosphere* ◇ *a smoky pub* **2** producing a lot of smoke: *a smoky fire* **3** tasting or smelling like smoke: *a smoky flavour* **4** having the colour or appearance of smoke: *smoky blue glass* OPP **clear**

smol·der (*NAmE*) = SMOULDER

smooch /smuːtʃ/ *verb* [I] (*informal*) to kiss and hold sb closely, especially when you are dancing slowly

smoodge /smuːdʒ/ *verb* [I] **~ (to sb)** (*AustralE, NZE, informal*) to behave in a friendly way towards sb because you want them to give you sth or do sth for you ▸ **smoodge** *noun* [U]: *What's wrong with a bit of smoodge between friends?*

smooth 0‑w /smuːð/ *adj., verb*

■ ***adj.*** (**smooth·er, smooth·est**)

▸ FLAT/EVEN **1** 0‑w completely flat and even, without any lumps, holes or rough areas: *a lotion to make your skin feel soft and smooth* ◇ *The water was as smooth as glass.* ◇ *a paint that gives a smooth, silky finish* ◇ *Over the years, the stone steps had worn smooth.* OPP **rough**

▸ WITHOUT LUMPS **2** 0‑w (of a liquid mixture) without any lumps: *Mix the flour with the milk to form a smooth paste.*

▸ WITHOUT PROBLEMS **3** 0‑w happening or continuing without any problems: *They are introducing new measures to ensure the smooth running of the business.* ◇ *They could not ensure a smooth transfer of political power.*

▸ MOVEMENT **4** 0‑w even and regular, without sudden stops and starts: *The car's improved suspension gives you a smoother ride.* ◇ *The plane made a smooth landing.* ◇ *She swung herself over the gate in one smooth movement.*

▸ MAN **5** (often *disapproving*) (of people, especially men, and their behaviour) very polite and pleasant, but in a way that is often not very sincere SYN **smarmy**: *I don't like him. He's far too smooth for me.* ◇ *He's something of a **smooth operator**.*

▸ DRINK/TASTE **6** pleasant and not bitter: *This coffee has a smooth, rich taste.*

▸ VOICE/MUSIC **7** nice to hear, and without any rough or unpleasant sounds
▶ **smooth·ness** *noun* [U]: *the smoothness of her skin* ◇ *They admired the smoothness and efficiency with which the business was run.* IDM see ROUGH *n.*
■ *verb* **1** to make sth smooth: **~ sth (back/down/out)** *He smoothed his hair back.* ◇ *She was smoothing out the creases in her skirt.* ◇ **~ sth + adj.** *He took the letter and smoothed it flat on the table.* **2 ~ sth on/into/over sth** to put a layer of a soft substance over a surface: *Smooth the icing over the top of the cake.*
IDM **smooth the 'path/'way** to make it easier for sb/sth to develop or make progress: *These negotiations are intended to smooth the path to a peace treaty.* **smooth (sb's) ruffled 'feathers** to make sb feel less angry or offended
PHR V **,smooth sth↔a'way/'out** to make problems or difficulties disappear **,smooth sth↔'over** to make problems or difficulties seem less important or serious, especially by talking to people: *She spoke to both sides in the dispute in an attempt to smooth things over.*

smoothie /'smu:ði/ *noun* **1** (*informal*) a man who dresses well and talks very politely and confidently but who is often not honest or sincere **2** a drink made of fruit or fruit juice mixed with milk or ice cream

smooth·ly 🔑 /'smu:ðli/ *adv.*
1 🔑 in an even way, without suddenly stopping and starting again: *Traffic is now flowing smoothly again.* ◇ *The engine was running smoothly.* **2** 🔑 without problems or difficulties: *The interview **went smoothly**.* **3** in a calm or confident way: *'Would you like to come this way?' he said smoothly.* **4** 🔑 in a way that produces a smooth surface or mixture: *The colours blend smoothly together.*

,smooth 'muscle *noun* [U] (*anatomy*) the type of muscle found in the organs inside the body, that is not under conscious control

,smooth-'talking *adj.* (usually *disapproving*) talking very politely and confidently, especially to persuade sb to do sth, but in a way that may not be honest or sincere

s'more /smɔ:(r)/ *noun* (*NAmE*) a cooked MARSHMALLOW eaten with chocolate between two GRAHAM CRACKERS (= a type of cookie) that is traditionally cooked over a fire when camping

smor·gas·bord /'smɔ:gəsbɔ:d; *NAmE* 'smɔ:rgəsbɔ:rd/ *noun* [U, sing.] (from *Swedish*) a meal at which you serve yourself from a large range of hot and cold dishes

smote *past tense of* SMITE

smother /'smʌðə(r)/ *verb* **1 ~ sb (with sth)** to kill sb by covering their face so that they cannot breathe SYN **suffocate**: *He smothered the baby with a pillow.* **2 ~ sth/sb with/in sth** to cover sth/sb thickly or with too much of sth: *a rich dessert smothered in cream* ◇ *She smothered him with kisses.* **3 ~ sth** to prevent sth from developing or being expressed SYN **stifle**: *to **smother a yawn/giggle/grin*** ◇ *The voices of the opposition were effectively smothered.* **4 ~ sb** to give sb too much love or protection so that they feel restricted: *Her husband was very loving, but she felt smothered.* **5 ~ sth** to make a fire stop burning by covering it with sth: *He tried to smother the flames with a blanket.*

smoul·der (*especially US* **smol·der**) /'sməʊldə(r); *NAmE* 'smoʊ-/ *verb* **1** [I] to burn slowly without a flame: *The bonfire was still smouldering the next day.* ◇ *a smouldering cigarette* ◇ (*figurative*) *The feud smouldered on for years.* **2** [I] (*formal*) to be filled with a strong emotion that you do not fully express SYN **burn**: **~ (with sth)** *His eyes smouldered with anger.* ◇ **~ (in sth)** *Anger smouldered in his eyes.*

SMS /,es em 'es/ *noun, verb*
■ *noun* **1** [U] the abbreviation for 'short message service' (a system for sending short written messages from one mobile/cell phone to another) **2** [C] a message sent by SMS SYN **text, text message**: *I'm trying to send an SMS.* ➲ COLLOCATIONS at PHONE ➲ compare EMS
■ *verb* [T, I] **~ (sb)** to send a message to sb by SMS SYN **text, text message**: *He SMSed me every day.* ◇ *If you have any comments, just email or SMS.* ◇ *She spends her time chatting and SMSing.*

smudge /smʌdʒ/ *noun, verb*
■ *noun* a dirty mark with no clear shape SYN **smear**: *a smudge of lipstick on a cup*
■ *verb* **1** [T, I] **~ (sth)** to touch or rub sth, especially wet ink or paint, so that it is no longer clear; to become not clear in this way: *He had smudged his signature with his sleeve.* ◇ *Tears had smudged her mascara.* ◇ *Her lipstick had smudged.* **2** [T] **~ sth** to make a dirty mark on a surface SYN **smear**: *The mirror was smudged with fingerprints.*

smudgy /'smʌdʒi/ *adj.* **1** with dirty marks on **2** (of a picture, writing, etc.) with edges that are not clear SYN **blurred**

smug /smʌg/ *adj.* (*disapproving*) looking or feeling too pleased about sth you have done or achieved SYN **complacent**: *a **smug expression/smile/face, etc.*** ◇ *What are you looking so smug about?* ▶ **smug·ly** *adv.* **smug·ness** *noun* [U]

smug·gle /'smʌgl/ *verb* **~ sth/sb (+ adv./prep.)** to take, send or bring goods or people secretly and illegally into or out of a country, etc: *They were caught smuggling diamonds into the country.* ◇ *He managed to smuggle a gun into the prison.* ◇ *smuggled drugs* ➲ COLLOCATIONS at CRIME

smug·gler /'smʌglə(r)/ *noun* a person who takes goods into or out of a country illegally

smug·gling /'smʌglɪŋ/ *noun* [U] the crime of taking, sending or bringing goods secretly and illegally into or out of a country: *drug smuggling*

smut /smʌt/ *noun* **1** [U] (*informal*) stories, pictures or comments about sex that deal with it in a way that some people find offensive **2** [U, C] dirt, ASH, etc. that causes a black mark on sth; a black mark made by this

smutty /'smʌti/ *adj.* [usually before noun] (*informal*) (of stories, pictures and comments) dealing with sex in a way that some people find offensive: *smutty jokes*

snack /snæk/ *noun, verb*
■ *noun* **1** (*informal*) a small meal or amount of food, usually eaten in a hurry: *a mid-morning snack* ◇ *I only have time for a snack at lunchtime.* ◇ *Do you serve bar snacks?* ◇ *a snack lunch* **2** (*AustralE, informal*) a thing that is easy to do: *It'll be a snack.*
■ *verb* [I] **~ on sth** to eat snacks between or instead of main meals: *It's healthier to snack on fruit rather than chocolate.*

'snack bar *noun* a place where you can buy a small quick meal, such as a SANDWICH

snaf·fle /'snæfl/ *verb* **~ sth** (*BrE, informal*) to take sth quickly for yourself, especially before anyone else has had the time or opportunity

snafu /snæ'fu:/ *noun* [sing.] (*NAmE, informal*) a situation in which nothing happens as planned: *It was another bureaucratic snafu.*

snag /snæg/ *noun, verb*
■ *noun* **1** (*informal*) a problem or difficulty, especially one that is small, hidden or unexpected SYN **difficulty**: *There is just one small snag—where is the money coming from?* ◇ *Let me know if you run into any snags.* **2** an object or a part of an object that is rough or sharp and may cut sth **3** (*AustralE, NZE, informal*) a SAUSAGE
■ *verb* (-gg-) **1** [T, I] to catch or tear sth on sth rough or sharp; to become caught or torn in this way: **~ sth on/in sth** *I snagged my sweater on the wire fence.* ◇ **~ sth** *The fence snagged my sweater.* ◇ **~ (on/in sth)** *The nets snagged on some rocks.* **2** [T] **~ sth (from sb)** (*NAmE, informal*) to succeed in getting sth quickly, often before other people: *I snagged a ride from Joe.*

snag·gle /'snægl/ *noun, verb*
■ *noun* an untidy or confused collection of things: *a snaggle of restrictions*
■ *verb* [I] to become twisted, untidy or confused: *My hair snaggles when I wash it.*

'snaggle-tooth *noun* (*informal*) a tooth which sticks out or is a strange shape ▶ **'snaggle-toothed** *adj.*

S

snail /sneɪl/ *noun* a small soft creature with a hard round shell on its back, that moves very slowly and often eats garden plants. Some types of snail can be eaten. ➲ VISUAL VOCAB page V11

IDM **at a 'snail's pace** very slowly

'snail mail *noun* [U] (*informal, humorous*) used especially by people who use email to describe the system of sending letters by ordinary mail

snake 0‑‑ /sneɪk/ *noun, verb*

■ ***noun*** 0‑‑ a REPTILE with a very long thin body and no legs. There are many types of snake, some of which are poisonous: *a snake coiled up in the grass* ◇ *Venomous snakes spit and hiss when they are cornered.*

IDM **a ˌsnake (in the 'grass)** (*disapproving*) a person who pretends to be your friend but who cannot be trusted

■ ***verb*** [I, T] to move like a snake, in long twisting curves; to go in a particular direction in long twisting curves SYN **meander**: **+ adv./prep.** *The road snaked away into the distance.* ◇ **~ its way + adv./prep.** *The procession snaked its way through narrow streets.*

snake·bite /'sneɪkbaɪt/ *noun* [C, U] **1** a wound that you get when a poisonous snake bites you **2** an alcoholic drink made of equal parts of beer and CIDER

Snake·board™ /'sneɪkbɔːd; *NAmE* -bɔːrd/ *noun* ➲ STREETBOARD

'snake charmer *noun* an entertainer who seems to be able to control snakes and make them move by playing music to them

'snake eyes *noun* [pl.] (*informal*) a result in a game when you throw two dice and both show one dot

'snake oil *noun* [U] (*informal, especially NAmE*) something, for example medicine, that sb tries to sell you, but that is not effective or useful: *a snake-oil salesman*

snake·pit /'sneɪkpɪt/ *noun* **1** a hole in the ground in which snakes are kept **2** a place which is extremely unpleasant or dangerous

ˌsnakes and 'ladders (*BrE*) *noun* [U] a children's game played on a special board with pictures of snakes and LADDERS on it. Players move their pieces up the ladders to go forward and down the snakes to go back. ➲ see also CHUTES AND LADDERS ➲ VISUAL VOCAB page V33

snake·skin /'sneɪkskɪn/ *noun* [U] the skin of a snake, used for making expensive shoes, bags, etc.

snaky /'sneɪki/ *adj.* (*AustralE, NZE, informal*) angry: *What are you snaky about?*

snap /snæp/ *verb, noun, adj., exclamation*

■ ***verb*** (-pp-)

▸ BREAK **1** [T, I] to break sth suddenly with a sharp noise; to be broken in this way: **~ sth** *The wind had snapped the tree in two.* ◇ **~ sth off (sth)** *He snapped a twig off a bush.* ◇ **~ (off)** *Suddenly, the rope snapped.* ◇ *The branch she was standing on must have snapped off.*

▸ OPEN/CLOSE/MOVE INTO POSITION **2** [I, T] to move, or to move sth, into a particular position quickly, especially with a sudden sharp noise: **+ adj.** *The lid snapped shut.* ◇ *His eyes snapped open.* ◇ **+ adv./prep.** *He snapped to attention and saluted.* ◇ **~ sth + adj.** *She snapped the bag shut.*

▸ SPEAK IMPATIENTLY **3** [T, I] to speak or say sth in an impatient, usually angry, voice: **+ speech** *'Don't just stand there,' she snapped.* ◇ **~ (at sb)** *I was tempted to snap back angrily at him.* ◇ **~ sth** *He snapped a reply.*

▸ OF ANIMAL **4** [I] **~ (at sb/sth)** to try to bite sb/sth SYN **nip**: *The dogs snarled and snapped at our heels.*

▸ TAKE PHOTOGRAPH **5** [T, I] (*informal*) to take a photograph: **~ sth** *A passing tourist snapped the incident.* ◇ **~ (away)** *She seemed oblivious to the crowds of photographers snapping away.*

▸ LOSE CONTROL **6** [I] to suddenly be unable to control your feelings any longer because the situation has become too difficult: *My patience finally snapped.* ◇ *When he said that, something snapped inside her.* ◇ *And that did it. I snapped.*

▸ FASTEN CLOTHING **7** [I, T] **~ (sth)** (*NAmE*) to fasten a piece of clothing with a snap

IDM **snap your 'fingers** to make a sharp noise by moving your second or third finger quickly against your thumb, to attract sb's attention, or to mark the beat of music, for example **ˌsnap 'out of it/sth** | **ˌsnap sb 'out of it/sth** [no passive] (*informal*) to make an effort to stop feeling unhappy or depressed; to help sb to stop feeling unhappy: *You've been depressed for weeks. It's time you snapped out of it.* **ˌsnap 'to it** (*informal*) used, especially in orders, to tell sb to start working harder or more quickly ➲ more at HEAD *n.*

PHR V **ˌsnap sth↔'out** to say sth in a sharp unpleasant way: *The sergeant snapped out an order.* **ˌsnap sth↔'up** (*informal*) to buy or obtain sth quickly because it is cheap or you want it very much: *All the best bargains were snapped up within hours.* ◇ (*figurative*) *She's been snapped up by Hollywood to star in two major movies.*

■ ***noun***

▸ SHARP NOISE **1** [C] a sudden sharp noise, especially one made by sth closing or breaking: *She closed her purse with a snap.* ◇ *the snap of a twig*

▸ PHOTOGRAPH **2** (also **snap·shot**) [C] a photograph, especially one taken quickly: *holiday snaps*

▸ CARD GAME **3 Snap** [U] a card game in which players take turns to put cards down and try to be the first to call out 'snap' when two similar cards are put down together

▸ FASTENER **4** (*NAmE*) (*BrE* **'press stud**, **pop·per**) a type of button used for fastening clothes, consisting of two metal or plastic sections that can be pressed together ➲ VISUAL VOCAB page V51 ➲ see also BRANDY SNAP, COLD SNAP

IDM **be a 'snap** (*NAmE, informal*) to be very easy to do: *This job's a snap.*

■ ***adj.*** [only before noun] made or done quickly and without careful thought or preparation: *It was a* ***snap decision.*** ◇ *They held a* ***snap election.***

■ ***exclamation*** **1** you say **snap!** in the card game called 'Snap' when two cards that are the same are put down **2** (*BrE, informal*) people say **snap!** to show that they are surprised when two things are the same: *Snap! I've just bought that CD too!*

snap·dragon /'snæpdrægən/ *noun* a small garden plant with red, white, yellow or pink flowers that open and shut like a mouth when squeezed

snap·per /'snæpə(r)/ *noun* **1** [C, U] a fish that lives in warm seas and is used for food **2** [C] (*informal, BrE*) a photographer, especially one who takes pictures of famous people for newspapers and magazines

snappy /'snæpi/ *adj.* (**snap·pier**, **snap·pi·est**) **1** (of a remark, title, etc.) clever or amusing and short: *a snappy slogan* ◇ *a snappy answer* **2** [usually before noun] (*informal*) attractive and fashionable: *a snappy outfit* ◇ *She's a* ***snappy dresser.*** **3** (of people or their behaviour) tending to speak to people in a bad-tempered, impatient way **4** lively; quick: *a snappy tune* ▸ **snap·pily** *adv.*: *He summarized the speech snappily.* ◇ *snappily dressed* ◇ *'What?' she asked snappily.* **snap·pi·ness** *noun* [U]

IDM **ˌmake it 'snappy** (*informal*) used to tell sb to do sth quickly or to hurry

snap·shot /'snæpʃɒt; *NAmE* -ʃɑːt/ *noun* **1** = SNAP: *snapshots of the children* ➲ SYNONYMS at PHOTOGRAPH **2** [usually sing.] a short description or a small amount of information that gives you an idea of what sth is like

snare /sneə(r); *NAmE* sner/ *noun, verb*

■ ***noun*** **1** a device used for catching small animals and birds, especially one that holds their leg so that they cannot escape SYN **trap** **2** (*formal*) a situation which seems attractive but is unpleasant and difficult to escape from **3** the metal strings that are stretched across the bottom of a snare drum

■ ***verb*** **~ sth/sb** to catch sth, especially an animal, in a snare SYN **trap**: *to snare a rabbit* ◇ (*figurative*) *Her one thought was to snare a rich husband.* ◇ (*figurative*) *He found himself snared in a web of intrigue.*

'snare drum *noun* a small drum with metal strings across one side that make a continuous sound when the drum is hit ➲ VISUAL VOCAB page V30

snarf /snɑːf; *NAmE* snɑːrf/ *verb* **~ sth** (*informal, especially NAmE*) to eat or drink sth very quickly or in a way that people think is GREEDY: *The kids snarfed up all the cookies.*

snarky /ˈsnɑːki; *NAmE* ˈsnɑːrki/ *adj.* (*NAmE, informal*) criticizing sb in an unkind way: *a snarky remark*

snarl /snɑːl; *NAmE* snɑːrl/ *verb, noun*

■ ***verb* 1** [I] **~ (at sb/sth)** (of dogs, etc.) to show the teeth and make a deep angry noise in the throat: *The dog snarled at us.* **2** [T] to speak in an angry or bad-tempered way: **+ speech (at sb)** *'Get out of here!' he snarled.* ◇ **~ sth (at sb)** *She snarled abuse at anyone who happened to walk past.*

PHR V **ˌsnarl ˈup** | **ˌsnarl sth↔ˈup 1** to involve sb/sth in a situation that stops their movement or progress; to become involved in a situation like this: *The accident snarled up the traffic all day.* **2** to become caught or twisted; to make sth do this: *The sheets kept getting snarled up.* ➲ related noun SNARL-UP

■ ***noun* 1** [usually sing.] a deep sound that an animal makes when it is angry and shows its teeth: *The dog bared its teeth in a snarl.* **2** [usually sing.] an act of speaking in an angry or bad-tempered way; the sound you make when you are angry, in pain, etc: *a snarl of hate* **3** = SNARL-UP: *rush-hour traffic snarls* **4** (*informal*) something that has become twisted in an untidy way: *She used conditioner to remove the snarls from her hair.*

ˈsnarl-up (also **snarl**) *noun* (*BrE, informal*) a situation in which traffic is unable to move **SYN** **jam**

snatch /snætʃ/ *verb, noun*

■ ***verb* 1** [T, I] to take sth quickly and often rudely or roughly **SYN** **grab**: **~ sth (+ adv./prep.)** *She managed to snatch the gun from his hand.* ◇ *Gordon snatched up his jacket and left the room.* ◇ **(+ adv./prep.)** *Hey, you kids! Don't all snatch!* **2** [T] **~ sb/sth (from sb/sth)** to take sb/sth away from a person or place, especially by force; to steal sth **SYN** **steal**: *The raiders snatched $100 from the cash register.* ◇ *The baby was snatched from its parents' car.* **3** [T] **~ sth** to take or get sth quickly, especially because you do not have much time: *I managed to snatch an hour's sleep.* ◇ *The team snatched a dramatic victory in the last minute of the game.*

PHR V **ˈsnatch at sth 1** to try to take hold of sth with your hands: *He snatched at the steering wheel but I pushed him away.* **2** to take an opportunity to do sth: *We snatched at every moment we could be together.*

■ ***noun* 1** a very small part of a conversation or some music that you hear **SYN** **snippet**: *a snatch of music* ◇ *I only caught snatches of the conversation.* **2** an act of moving your hand very quickly to take or steal sth: *a bag snatch* ◇ *to **make a snatch** at sth* **3** (*taboo, slang*) an offensive word for a woman's outer sex organs

IDM **in ˈsnatches** for short periods rather than continuously: *Sleep came to him in brief snatches.*

snatch·er /ˈsnætʃə(r)/ *noun* (often in compounds) a person who takes sth quickly with their hand and steals it: *a purse snatcher*

ˈsnatch squad *noun* [C+sing./pl. v.] a group of police officers or soldiers whose job is to remove people from a crowd who are considered to be causing trouble

snazzy /ˈsnæzi/ *adj.* (**snaz·zier, snaz·zi·est**) (*informal*) (of clothes, cars, etc.) fashionable, bright and modern, and attracting your attention **SYN** **jazzy, smart**: *a snazzy tie*

sneak /sniːk/ *verb, noun, adj.*

■ ***verb*** **HELP** The usual past form is **sneaked**, but **snuck** is now very common in informal speech in *NAmE* and some people use it in *BrE* too. However, many people think that it is not correct and it should not be used in formal writing. **1** [I] **+ adv./prep.** to go somewhere secretly, trying to avoid being seen **SYN** **creep**: *I sneaked up the stairs.* **2** [T] to do sth or take sb/sth somewhere secretly, often without permission: **~ sth** *We sneaked a look at her diary.* ◇ **~ sth to sb** *I managed to sneak a note to him.* ◇ **~ sb sth** *I managed to sneak him a note.* **3** [T] **~ sth** (*informal*) to secretly take sth small or unimportant **SYN** **pinch**: *I sneaked a cake when they were out of the room.* **4** [I] **~ (on sb) (to sb)** (*old-fashioned, BrE, disapproving*) to tell an adult that another child has done sth wrong, especially in order to cause trouble **SYN** **snitch**: *Did you sneak on me to the teacher?*

PHR V **ˌsneak ˈup (on sb/sth)** to move towards sb very quietly so that they do not see or hear you until you reach them: *He sneaked up on his sister and shouted 'Boo!'.*

■ ***noun*** (*old-fashioned, BrE, disapproving*) a person, especially a child, who tells sb about sth wrong that another person has done **SYN** **snitch**

■ ***adj.*** [only before noun] done without any warning: *a sneak attack*

sneak·er /ˈsniːkə(r)/ (*NAmE*) (*BrE* **train·er, ˈtraining shoe**) *noun* [usually pl.] a shoe that you wear for sports or as informal clothing: *He wore old jeans and a pair of sneakers.* ➲ VISUAL VOCAB page V52

sneak·ing /ˈsniːkɪŋ/ *adj.* [only before noun] if you have a **sneaking** feeling for sb or about sth, you do not want to admit it to other people, because you feel embarrassed, or you are not sure that this feeling is right: *She had always had a sneaking affection for him.* ◇ *I have a sneaking suspicion that she knows more than she's telling us.*

ˌsneak ˈpreview *noun* an opportunity to see sth before it is officially shown to the public

ˈsneak thief *noun* a person who steals things without using force or breaking doors or windows

sneaky /ˈsniːki/ *adj.* (**sneak·ier, sneaki·est**) (*informal*) behaving in a secret and sometimes dishonest or unpleasant way **SYN** **crafty**: *That was a sneaky trick!* ▶ **sneak·ily** /-ɪli/ *adv.*

sneer /snɪə(r); *NAmE* snɪr/ *verb, noun*

■ ***verb*** [I, T] to show that you have no respect for sb by the expression on your face or by the way you speak **SYN** **mock**: **~ (at sb/sth)** *He sneered at people who liked pop music.* ◇ *a sneering comment* ◇ **+ speech** *'You? A writer?' she sneered.* ▶ **sneer·ing·ly** /ˈsnɪərɪŋli; *NAmE* ˈsnɪr-/ *adv.*

■ ***noun*** [usually sing.] an unpleasant look, smile or comment that shows you do not respect sb/sth: *A faint sneer of satisfaction crossed her face.*

sneeze /sniːz/ *verb, noun*

■ ***verb*** [I] to have air come suddenly and noisily out through your nose and mouth in a way that you cannot control, for example because you have a cold: *I've been sneezing all morning.*

IDM **not to be ˈsneezed at** (*informal*) good enough to be accepted or considered seriously: *In those days, $20 was not a sum to be sneezed at.*

■ ***noun*** the act of sneezing or the noise you make when you sneeze: *coughs and sneezes* ◇ *She gave a violent sneeze.*

snicker /ˈsnɪkə(r)/ *verb* (*especially NAmE*) (*BrE* also **snig·ger**) [I] **~ (at sb/sth)** to laugh in a quiet unpleasant way, especially at sth rude or at sb's problems or mistakes **SYN** **titter** ▶ **snicker** *noun*

snide /snaɪd/ *adj.* (*informal*) criticizing sb/sth in an unkind and indirect way: ***snide comments/remarks*** ▶ **snide·ly** *adv.*

sniff /snɪf/ *verb, noun*

■ ***verb* 1** [I] to breathe air in through your nose in a way that makes a sound, especially when you are crying, have a cold, etc: *We all had colds and couldn't stop sniffing and sneezing.* **2** [T, I] to breathe air in through the nose in order to discover or enjoy the smell of sth **SYN** **smell**: **~ sth** *sniffing the fresh morning air* ◇ *to sniff glue* ◇ **~ (at sth)** *The dog sniffed at my shoes.* ➲ see also GLUE-SNIFFING **3** [T, I] **+ speech** | **~ (sth)** to say sth in a complaining or disapproving way: *'It's hardly what I'd call elegant,' she sniffed.*

IDM **not to be ˈsniffed at** (*informal*) good enough to be accepted or considered seriously: *In those days, $20 was not a sum to be sniffed at.*

PHR V **ˌsniff aˈround/ˈround** (*informal*) to try to find out information about sb/sth, especially secret information: *We don't want journalists sniffing around.* **ˈsniff around/round sb** [no passive] (*especially BrE*) to try to get sb as a lover, employee, etc: *Hollywood agents have been sniffing around him.* **ˈsniff at sth** to show no interest in or respect for sth **ˌsniff sb/sth↔ˈout 1** to discover or find sb/sth by using your sense of smell: *The dogs are trained to sniff out drugs.* **2** (*informal*) to discover or find sb/sth by looking: *Journalists are good at sniffing out a scandal.*

■ ***noun* 1** [C] an act or the sound of sniffing: *She took a deep sniff of the perfume.* ◇ *My mother gave a sniff of disapproval.*

◇ *His sobs soon turned to sniffs.* **2** [sing.] **~ of sth** an idea of what sth is like or that sth is going to happen: *The sniff of power went to his head.* ◇ *They make threats but back down at the first sniff of trouble.* **3** [sing.] **~ of sth** a small chance of sth: *She didn't get even a sniff at a medal.*
IDM **have a (good) ˌsniff aˈround** to examine a place carefully

ˈ**sniffer dog** *noun* (*informal, especially BrE*) a dog that is trained to find drugs or EXPLOSIVES by smell

snif·fle /ˈsnɪfl/ *verb, noun*
■ *verb* [I, T] (+ **speech**) to sniff or keep sniffing, especially because you are crying or have a cold
■ *noun* an act or the sound of sniffling: *After a while, her sniffles died away.*
IDM **get, have, etc. the ˈsniffles** (*informal*) to get, have, etc. a slight cold

sniffy /ˈsnɪfi/ *adj.* **~ (about sth)** (*informal*) not approving of sth/sb because you think they are not good enough for you

snif·ter /ˈsnɪftə(r)/ *noun* **1** (*especially NAmE*) a large glass used for drinking BRANDY **2** (*old-fashioned, BrE, informal*) a small amount of a strong alcoholic drink

snig·ger /ˈsnɪɡə(r)/ *verb, noun*
■ *verb* (*BrE*) (also **snicker** *NAmE, BrE*) [I, T] **~ (at sb/sth)** | **+ speech** to laugh in a quiet unpleasant way, especially at sth rude or at sb's problems or mistakes SYN **titter**: *What are you sniggering at?*
■ *noun* (*BrE*) (also **snicker** *NAmE, BrE*) a quiet unpleasant laugh, especially at sth rude or at sb's problems or mistakes SYN **titter**

snip /snɪp/ *verb, noun*
■ *verb* (**-pp-**) [T, I] to cut sth with scissors using short quick strokes: **~ sth** *Snip a tiny hole in the paper.* ◇ **~ (at/through sth)** *She snipped at the loose threads hanging down.*
PHR V **ˌsnip sth↔ˈoff** to remove sth by cutting it with scissors in short quick strokes
■ *noun* **1** [C] an act of cutting sth with scissors; the sound that this makes: *Make a series of small snips along the edge of the fabric.* ◇ *Snip, snip, went the scissors.* **2 snips** [pl.] a tool like large scissors, used for cutting metal **3 a snip** [sing.] (*BrE, informal*) a thing that is cheap and good value SYN **bargain**: *It's a snip at only £25.*

snipe /snaɪp/ *verb, noun*
■ *verb* **1** [I] **~ (at sb/sth)** to shoot at sb from a hiding place, usually from a distance: *Gunmen continued to snipe at people leaving their homes to find food.* **2** [I] **~ (at sb/sth)** to criticize sb in an unpleasant way ▸ **snip·ing** *noun* [U]: *Aid workers remain in the area despite continuous sniping.*
■ *noun* (*pl.* **snipe**) a bird with a long straight beak that lives on wet ground

sniper /ˈsnaɪpə(r)/ *noun* a person who shoots at sb from a hidden position

snip·pet /ˈsnɪpɪt/ *noun* **1** a small piece of information or news: *Have you got any interesting snippets for me?* ◇ *a snippet of information* **2** a short piece of a conversation, piece of music, etc. SYN **snatch, extract**

snippy /ˈsnɪpi/ *adj.* (*NAmE, informal*) rude; not showing respect

snit /snɪt/ *noun*
IDM **be in a ˈsnit** (*NAmE*) to be bad-tempered and refuse to speak to anybody for a time because you are angry about sth

snitch /snɪtʃ/ *verb* [I] **~ (on sb) (to sb)** (*informal, disapproving*) to tell a parent, teacher, etc. about sth wrong that another child has done SYN **sneak**: *Johnnie snitched on me to his mom.* ▸ **snitch** *noun*: *You little snitch! I'll never tell you anything again!*

snivel /ˈsnɪvl/ *verb* (**-ll-**, *US* **-l-**) [I] to cry and complain in a way that people think is annoying SYN **whine**

sniv·el·ling (*especially US* **sniv·el·ing**) /ˈsnɪvlɪŋ/ *adj.* [only before noun] (*disapproving*) tending to cry or complain a lot in a way that annoys people: *a snivelling little brat*

snob /snɒb; *NAmE* snɑːb/ *noun* (*disapproving*) **1** a person who admires people in the higher social classes too much and has no respect for people in the lower social classes: *She's such a snob!* **2** a person who thinks they are much better than other people because they are intelligent or like things that many people do not like: *an* ***intellectual snob*** ◇ *a* ***food/wine, etc. snob*** ◇ *There is a* ***snob value*** *in driving the latest model.*

snob·bery /ˈsnɒbəri; *NAmE* ˈsnɑːb-/ *noun* [U] (*disapproving*) the attitudes and behaviour of people who are snobs: *intellectual snobbery* ➲ see also INVERTED SNOBBERY

snob·bish /ˈsnɒbɪʃ; *NAmE* ˈsnɑːb-/ (also *informal* **snobby** /ˈsnɒbi; *NAmE* ˈsnɑːbi/) *adj.* (*disapproving*) thinking that having a high social class is very important; feeling that you are better than other people because you are more intelligent or like things that many people do not like ▸ **snob·bish·ness** *noun* [U]

snog /snɒɡ; *NAmE* snɑːɡ/ *verb* (**-gg-**) [I, T] (*BrE, informal*) (of two people) to kiss each other, especially for a long time: *They were snogging on the sofa.* ◇ **~ sb** *I caught him snogging my friend.* ▸ **snog** *noun* [sing.]

snood /snuːd/ *noun* a net or bag worn over the hair at the back of a woman's head for decoration

snook /snuːk/ *noun* IDM see COCK *v.*

snook·er /ˈsnuːkə(r)/ *noun, verb*
■ *noun* **1** [U] a game for two people played on a long table covered with green cloth. Players use CUES (= long sticks) to hit a white ball against other balls (15 red and 6 of other colours) in order to get the coloured balls into pockets at the edge of the table, in a particular set order: *to* ***play snooker*** ◇ *a* ***game of snooker*** ◇ *a* ***snooker hall/player/table, etc.*** ➲ compare BILLIARDS, POOL **2** [C] a position in snooker in which one player has made it very difficult for the opponent to play a shot within the rules
■ *verb* [usually passive] **1 ~ sb** (in the game of snooker) to have your opponent in a snooker (2) **2 ~ sb/sth** (*BrE, informal*) to make it impossible for sb to do sth, especially sth they want to do: *Any plans I'd had for the weekend were by now well and truly snookered.* **3 ~ sb** (*NAmE, informal*) to cheat or trick sb

snoop /snuːp/ *verb, noun*
■ *verb* [I] (*informal, disapproving*) to find out private things about sb, especially by looking secretly around a place: **~ (around/round sth)** *Someone's been snooping around my apartment.* ◇ **~ (on sb)** *journalists snooping on politicians*
■ *noun* **1** (also **snoop·er**) a person who looks around a place secretly to find out private things about sb **2** [sing.] a secret look around a place: *He had a snoop around her office.*

snoot /snuːt/ *noun* (*NAmE, informal*) **1** a person's nose **2** (*disapproving*) a person who treats other people as if they are not as good or as important as them

snooty /ˈsnuːti/ (also *informal* **snotty**) *adj.* (**snoot·ier, snooti·est**) (*disapproving*) treating people as if they are not as good or as important as you SYN **snobbish** ▸ **snoot·ily** *adv.* **snooti·ness** *noun* [U]

snooze /snuːz/ *verb* [I] (*informal*) to have a short light sleep, especially during the day and usually not in bed: *My brother was snoozing on the sofa.* ➲ SYNONYMS at SLEEP ▸ **snooze** *noun* [sing.]: *I often have a snooze after lunch.*

ˈ**snooze button** *noun* a button on a CLOCK RADIO which you press when you wake up, so that you can sleep a little longer and be woken up again after a short time

snore /snɔː(r)/ *verb, noun*
■ *verb* [I] to breathe noisily through your nose and mouth while you are asleep: *I could hear Paul snoring in the next room.* ▸ **snorer** *noun* **snor·ing** *noun* [U]: *loud snoring*
■ *noun* noisy breathing while you are asleep: *She lay awake listening to his snores.*

snor·kel /ˈsnɔːkl; *NAmE* ˈsnɔːrkl/ *noun* a tube that you can breathe air through when you are swimming under the surface of the water ➲ VISUAL VOCAB page V34 ▸ **snor·kel** *verb* (**-ll-**, *especially US* **-l-**) [I]

S

snor·kel·ling (*especially US* **snor·kel·ing**) /ˈsnɔːkəlɪŋ; *NAmE* ˈsnɔːrk-/ *noun* [U] the sport or activity of swimming underwater with a snorkel: *to go snorkelling* ➲ VISUAL VOCAB page V34

snort /snɔːt; *NAmE* snɔːrt/ *verb, noun*
■ ***verb*** **1** [I, T] to make a loud sound by breathing air out noisily through your nose, especially to show that you are angry or amused: *The horse snorted and tossed its head.* ◇ **~ with sth** *to snort with laughter* ◇ **~ in sth** *She snorted in disgust.* ◇ **+ speech** *'You!' he snorted contemptuously.* **2** [T] **~ sth** to take drugs by breathing them in through the nose: *to snort cocaine*
■ ***noun*** **1** a loud sound that you make by breathing air out noisily through your nose, especially to show that you are angry or amused: *to **give a snort*** ◇ *a snort of disgust* ◇ *I could hear the snort and stamp of a horse.* **2** a small amount of a drug that is breathed in through the nose; an act of taking a drug in this way: *to take a snort of cocaine*

snot /snɒt; *NAmE* snɑːt/ *noun* [U] (*informal*) a word that some people find offensive, used to describe the liquid substance (=MUCUS) that is produced in the nose

snotty /ˈsnɒti; *NAmE* ˈsnɑːti/ *adj.* (**snot·tier, snot·ti·est**) (also ˌ**snotty-ˈnosed**) (*informal*) **1** = SNOOTY **2** full of or covered in snot: *a snotty nose* ◇ *snotty kids*

snout /snaʊt/ *noun* **1** the long nose and area around the mouth of some types of animal, such as a pig ➲ VISUAL VOCAB page V10 ➲ compare MUZZLE **2** (*informal, humorous*) a person's nose **3** a part of sth that sticks out at the front: *the snout of a pistol*

snow 🔑 /snəʊ; *NAmE* snoʊ/ *noun, verb*
■ ***noun*** **1** 🔑 [U] small soft white pieces (called FLAKES) of frozen water that fall from the sky in cold weather; this substance when it is lying on the ground: ***Snow was falling*** *heavily.* ◇ *We had snow in May this year.* ◇ *The snow was beginning to melt.* ◇ *Children were playing in the snow.* ◇ *20 cm of snow were expected today.* ◇ *The snow didn't settle* (= stay on the ground). ◇ *Her skin was **as white as snow**.* ➲ COLLOCATIONS at WEATHER ➲ VISUAL VOCAB page V4 **2 snows** [pl.] (*literary*) an amount of snow that falls in one particular place or at one particular time: *the first snows of winter* ◇ *the snows of Everest*
IDM **as clean, pure, etc. as the driven ˈsnow** extremely clean, pure, etc.
■ ***verb*** **1** 🔑 [I] when **it snows**, snow falls from the sky: *It's been snowing heavily all day.* **2** [T] **~ sb** (*NAmE, informal*) to impress sb a lot by the things you say, especially if these are not true or not sincere: *He really snowed me with all his talk of buying a Porsche.*
IDM **be snowed ˈin/ˈup** to be unable to leave a place because of heavy snow **be snowed ˈunder (with sth)** to have more things, especially work, than you feel able to deal with: *I'd love to come but I'm completely snowed under at the moment.* **be snowed ˈup** (especially of a road) to be blocked with snow

snow·ball /ˈsnəʊbɔːl; *NAmE* ˈsnoʊ-/ *noun, verb*
■ ***noun*** **1** [C] a ball that you make out of snow to throw at sb/sth in a game: *a snowball fight* **2** [sing.] (often used as an adjective) a situation that develops more and more quickly as it continues: *All this publicity has had a **snowball effect** on the sales of their latest album.* **3** [C] a COCKTAIL (= a type of alcoholic drink) that contains ADVOCAAT and LEMONADE
IDM **not have a ˌsnowball's chance in ˈhell** (*informal*) to have no chance at all
■ ***verb*** [I] if a problem, a plan, an activity, etc. **snowballs**, it quickly becomes much bigger, more serious, more important, etc.

the ˈSnow Belt *noun* [sing.] (*informal*) the northern and north-eastern states of the US where the winters are very cold

snow·bird /ˈsnəʊbɜːd; *NAmE* ˈsnoʊbɜːrd/ *noun* (*NAmE, informal*) a person who spends the winter in a warmer climate, especially an old person from the north of the US, or from Canada, who spends the winter in the south

ˈsnow-blind *adj.* unable to see because of the light reflected from a large area of snow ▶ **ˈsnow-blindness** *noun* [U]

snow·blow·er /ˈsnəʊbləʊə(r); *NAmE* ˈsnoʊbloʊər/ *noun* a machine that removes snow from roads or paths by blowing it to one side

snow·board /ˈsnəʊbɔːd; *NAmE* ˈsnoʊbɔːrd/ *noun* a long wide board that a person stands on to move over snow in the sport of snowboarding ➲ VISUAL VOCAB page V40

snow·board·ing /ˈsnəʊbɔːdɪŋ; *NAmE* ˈsnoʊbɔːrd-/ *noun* [U] the sport of moving over snow on a snowboard: *to go snowboarding* ◇ *Snowboarding is now an Olympic sport.* ▶ **snow·board·er** *noun* ➲ VISUAL VOCAB page V40

snow·bound /ˈsnəʊbaʊnd; *NAmE* ˈsnoʊ-/ *adj.* **1** (of a person or vehicle) trapped in a particular place and unable to move because a lot of snow has fallen **2** (of a road or building) that you cannot use or reach because a lot of snow has fallen

ˈsnow cannon (*BrE*) (also **ˈsnow gun** *US, BrE*) *noun* a machine which makes artificial snow and blows it onto SKI slopes

ˈsnow-capped *adj.* (*literary*) (of mountains and hills) covered with snow on top

ˈsnow chains *noun* [pl.] chains that are put on the wheels of a car so that it can drive over snow

ˈsnow-covered (also *literary* **ˈsnow-clad**) *adj.* [usually before noun] covered with snow: *snow-covered fields*

snow·drift /ˈsnəʊdrɪft; *NAmE* ˈsnoʊ-/ *noun* a deep pile of snow that has been blown together by the wind

snow·drop /ˈsnəʊdrɒp; *NAmE* ˈsnoʊdrɑːp/ *noun* a small white flower that appears in early spring

snow·fall /ˈsnəʊfɔːl; *NAmE* ˈsnoʊ-/ *noun* [C, U] an occasion when snow falls; the amount of snow that falls in a particular place in a period of time: *a **heavy/light snowfall*** ◇ *an area of low snowfall* ◇ *What is the average annual snowfall for this state?*

snow·field /ˈsnəʊfiːld; *NAmE* ˈsnoʊ-/ *noun* a large area that is always covered with snow, for example in the mountains

snow·flake /ˈsnəʊfleɪk; *NAmE* ˈsnoʊ-/ *noun* a small soft piece of frozen water that falls from the sky as snow

ˈsnow gun (*BrE* also **ˈsnow cannon**) *noun* a machine which makes artificial snow and blows it onto SKI slopes

ˈsnow job *noun* (*NAmE, informal*) an attempt to trick sb or to persuade them to support sth by telling them things that are not true, or by praising them too much

the snow·line /ˈsnəʊlaɪn; *NAmE* ˈsnoʊ-/ *noun* [sing.] the level on mountains above which snow never melts completely ➲ VISUAL VOCAB page V4

snow·man /ˈsnəʊmæn; *NAmE* ˈsnoʊ-/ *noun* (*pl.* **-men** /-men/) a figure like a man that people, especially children, make out of snow for fun

snow·mobile /ˈsnəʊməbiːl; *NAmE* ˈsnoʊmoʊ-/ (also **ski-mobile**) *noun* a vehicle that can move over snow and ice easily ➲ picture at SLEDGE

ˈsnow pea (*NAmE*) (*BrE* **mange·tout**) *noun* [usually pl.] a type of very small PEA that grows in long, flat green PODS that are cooked and eaten whole

snow·plough (*NAmE* **snow·plow**) /ˈsnəʊplaʊ; *NAmE* ˈsnoʊ-/ *noun, verb*
■ ***noun*** a vehicle or machine for cleaning snow from roads or railways
■ ***verb*** [I] to bring the two points of your SKIS together, in order to go slower or stop

snow·shoe /ˈsnəʊʃuː; *NAmE* ˈsnoʊ-/ *noun* one of a pair of flat frames that you attach to the bottom of your shoes so that you can walk on deep snow without sinking in

snow·slide /ˈsnəʊslaɪd; *NAmE* ˈsnoʊ-/ *noun* (*NAmE*) = AVALANCHE

snow·storm /ˈsnəʊstɔːm; *NAmE* ˈsnoʊstɔːrm/ *noun* a very heavy fall of snow, usually with a strong wind

ˌ**snow-ˈwhite** *adj.* pure white in colour: *snow-white sheets*

S

snowy /ˈsnəʊi; *NAmE* ˈsnoʊi/ *adj.* (**snow·ier**, **snowi·est**) **1** [usually before noun] covered with snow: *snowy fields* **2** (of a period of time) when a lot of snow falls: *a snowy weekend* **3** (*literary*) very white, like new snow: *snowy hair*

SNP /ˌes en ˈpiː/ *abbr.* SCOTTISH NATIONAL PARTY

Snr *abbr.* = SR

snub /snʌb/ *verb, noun*

■ *verb* (-bb-) **1** **~ sb** to insult sb, especially by ignoring them when you meet SYN **cold-shoulder**: *I tried to be friendly, but she snubbed me completely.* **2** **~ sth** to refuse to attend or accept sth, for example as a protest SYN **boycott**: *All the country's leading players snubbed the tournament.*

■ *noun* **~ (to sb)** an action or a comment that is deliberately rude in order to show sb that you do not like or respect them SYN **insult**: *Her refusal to attend the dinner is being seen as a deliberate snub to the President.*

■ *adj.* [only before noun] (of a nose) short, flat and turned up at the end ▸ **ˌsnub-ˈnosed** *adj.*: *a snub-nosed child* ◇ *a snub-nosed revolver* (= with a short BARREL)

snuck *past tense, past part.* of SNEAK

snuff /snʌf/ *verb, noun*

■ *verb* **1** [T] **~ sth (out)** to stop a small flame from burning, especially by pressing it between your fingers or covering it with sth SYN **extinguish** **2** [I, T] **~ (sth)** (of an animal) to smell sth by breathing in noisily through the nose: *The dogs were snuffing gently at my feet.*

IDM **ˈsnuff it** (*BrE, slang, humorous*) to die

PHR V **ˌsnuff sth↔ˈout** to stop or destroy sth completely: *An innocent child's life has been snuffed out by this senseless shooting.*

■ *noun* [U] TOBACCO in the form of a powder that people take by breathing it into their noses

IDM **ˌup to ˈsnuff** (*NAmE*) (*BrE* **ˌup to the ˈmark**) as good as it/they should be SYN **up to scratch**

snuff·box /ˈsnʌfbɒks; *NAmE* -bɑːks/ *noun* a small, usually decorated, box for holding snuff

snuf·fle /ˈsnʌfl/ *verb, noun*

■ *verb* **1** [I, T] (**+ speech**) to breathe noisily because you have a cold or you are crying SYN **sniff**: *I could hear the child snuffling in her sleep.* **2** [I] **~ (about/around)** if an animal **snuffles**, it breathes noisily through its nose, especially while it is smelling sth

■ *noun* (also *less frequent* **snuf·fling**) an act or the sound of snuffling: *The silence was broken only by the snuffles of the dogs.* ◇ *His breath came in snuffles.*

IDM **get, have, etc. the ˈsnuffles** (*informal*) to get/have a cold

S

ˈsnuff movie *noun* a film/movie that shows a real murder, intended as entertainment

snug /snʌg/ *adj., noun*

■ *adj.* **1** warm, comfortable and protected, especially from the cold SYN **cosy**: *a snug little house* ◇ *I spent the afternoon snug and warm in bed.* **2** fitting sb/sth closely: *The elastic at the waist gives a nice snug fit.* ▸ **snug·ly** *adv.*: *I left the children tucked up snugly in bed.* ◇ *The lid should fit snugly.* **snug·ness** *noun* [U]

■ *noun* (*BrE*) a small comfortable room in a pub, with seats for only a few people

snug·gle /ˈsnʌgl/ *verb* [I, T] to get into, or to put sb/sth into, a warm comfortable position, especially close to sb: **+ adv./prep.** *The child* ***snuggled up to*** *her mother.* ◇ *He* ***snuggled down*** *under the bedclothes.* ◇ *She snuggled closer.* ◇ **~ sth + adv./prep.** *He snuggled his head onto her shoulder.*

So. *abbr.* (*NAmE*) south; southern

so 🔑 /səʊ; *NAmE* soʊ/ *adv., conj., noun*

■ *adv.* **1** 🔑 to such a great degree: *Don't look so angry.* ◇ *There's no need to worry so.* ◇ **~ ... (that)...** *She spoke so quietly (that) I could hardly hear her.* ◇ **~ ... as to do sth** *I'm not so stupid as to believe that.* ◇ (*formal, especially BrE*) ***Would you be so kind as to*** *lock the door when you leave?* **2** 🔑 very; extremely: *I'm so glad to see you.* ◇ *We have so much to do.* ◇ *Their attitude is* ***so very*** *English.* ◇ *The article was* ***just so much*** (= nothing but) *nonsense.* ◇ (*BrE*) *He sat there* ***ever so*** *quietly.* ◇ (*BrE*) *I do love it so.* **3** 🔑 **not ~ ... (as ...)** (used in comparisons) not to the same degree: *I haven't enjoyed myself so much for a long time.* ◇ *It wasn't so good as last time.* ◇ *It's not so easy as you'd think.* ◇ *He was not so quick a learner as his brother.* ◇ *It's* ***not so much*** *a hobby* ***as*** *a career* (= more like a career than a hobby). ◇ (*disapproving*) *Off she went* ***without so much as*** (= without even) *a 'goodbye'.* **4** used to show the size, amount or number of sth: *The fish was about so big* (= said when using your hands to show the size). ◇ *There are* ***only so many*** (= only a limited number of) *hours in a day.* **5** 🔑 used to refer back to sth that has already been mentioned: *'Is he coming?' 'I hope so.'* ◇ *'Did they mind?' 'I* ***don't think so****.'* ◇ *If she notices, she never* ***says so****.* ◇ *I might be away next week.* ***If so****, I won't be able to see you.* ◇ *We are very busy—****so much so that*** *we won't be able to take time off this year.* ◇ *Programs are expensive, and* ***even more so*** *if you have to keep altering them.* ◇ *I hear that you're a writer—****is that so*** (= is that true)? ◇ *He thinks I dislike him but that just isn't so.* ◇ *George is going to help me, or* ***so he says*** (= that is what he says). ◇ *They asked me to call them and I* ***did so*** (= I called). **6** 🔑 also: *Times have changed and* ***so have I****.* ◇ *'I prefer the first version.' '****So do we****.'* HELP You cannot use **so** with negative verbs. Use **neither** or **either**: *'I'm not hungry.' '****Neither am I/I'm not*** *very hungry* ***either****.'* **7** used to agree that sth is true, especially when you are surprised: *'You were there, too.' 'So I was—I'd forgotten.'* ◇ *'There's another one.' 'So there is.'* **8** (*informal*) used, often with a negative, before adjectives and noun phrases to emphasize sth that you are saying: *He is* ***so not*** *the right person for you.* ◇ *That is* ***so not*** *cool.* **9** (*informal*) used, especially by children, to say that what sb says is not the case and the opposite is true: *'You're not telling the truth, are you?' 'I am, so!'* **10** used when you are showing sb how to do sth or telling them how sth happened: *Stand with your arms out, so.* ◇ (*literary*) ***So it was that*** *he finally returned home.*

IDM **and ˈso forth | and ˈso on (and ˈso forth)** 🔑 used at the end of a list to show that it continues in the same way: *We discussed everything—when to go, what to see and so on.* **... or so** 🔑 used after a number, an amount, etc. to show that it is not exact: *There were twenty or so* (= about twenty) *people there.* ◇ *We stayed for an hour or so.* **so as to do sth** with the intention of doing sth: *We went early so as to get good seats.* **so ˈbe it** (*formal*) used to show that you accept sth and will not try to change it or cannot change it: *If he doesn't want to be involved, then so be it.* **ˌso much for ˈsth** **1** used to show that you have finished talking about sth: *So much for the situation in Germany. Now we turn our attention to France.* **2** (*informal*) used to suggest that sth has not been successful or useful: *So much for that idea!* **so... that** (*formal*) in such a way that: *The programme has been so organized that none of the talks overlap.* **(all) the ˈmore so because...** used to give an important extra reason why sth is true: *His achievement is remarkable; all the more so because he had no help at all.*

■ *conj.* **1** 🔑 used to show the reason for sth: *It was still painful so I went to see a doctor.* **2** 🔑 **~ (that...)** used to show the result of sth: *Nothing more was heard from him so that we began to wonder if he was dead.* **3** 🔑 **~ (that...)** used to show the purpose of sth: *But I gave you a map so you wouldn't get lost!* ◇ *She worked hard so that everything would be ready in time.* **4** 🔑 used to introduce the next part of a story: *So after shouting and screaming for an hour she walked out in tears.* **5** 🔑 (*informal*) used to show that you think sth is not important, especially after sb has criticized you for it: *So I had a couple of drinks on the way home. What's wrong with that?* ◇ *'You've been smoking again.' 'So?'* **6** 🔑 (*informal*) used to introduce a comment or a question: *So, let's see. What do we need to take?* ◇ *So, what have you been doing today?* **7** (*informal*) used when you are making a final statement: *So, that's it for today.* **8** (*informal*) used in questions to refer to sth that has just been said: *So there's nothing we can do about it?* ◇ *'I've just got back from a trip to Rome.' 'So, how was it?'* **9** used when stating that two events, situations, etc. are similar: ***Just as*** *large companies are having to cut back,* ***so*** *small businesses are being forced to close.*

IDM **so ˈwhat?** (*informal*) used to show that you think sth is not important, especially after sb has criticized you for it:

'He's fifteen years younger than you!' 'So what?' ◇ *So what if nobody else agrees with me?*
■ ***noun*** = SOH

soak /səʊk; *NAmE* soʊk/ *verb, noun*
■ ***verb*** **1** [T, I] to put sth in liquid for a time so that it becomes completely wet; to become completely wet in this way: **~ sth** (**in sth**) *I usually soak the beans overnight.* ◇ *If you soak the tablecloth before you wash it, the stains should come out.* ◇ **~** (**in sth**) *Leave the apricots* ***to soak*** *for 20 minutes.* ◇ *I'm going to go and soak in the bath.* **2** [T] **~ sb/sth** to make sb/sth completely wet SYN **drench**: *A sudden shower of rain soaked the spectators.* **3** [T] **~ sb** (*informal*) to obtain a lot of money from sb by making them pay very high taxes or prices: *He was accused of soaking his clients.*
PHR V **'soak into/through sth** | **soak 'in** (of a liquid) to enter or pass through sth: *Blood had soaked through the bandage.* **,soak sth↔'off/'out** to remove sth by leaving it in water **,soak sth↔'up 1** to take in or absorb liquid: *Use a cloth to soak up some of the excess water.* **2** to absorb sth into your senses, your body or your mind: *We were just sitting soaking up the atmosphere.*
■ ***noun*** (also **soak·ing**) [sing.] **1** an act of leaving sth in a liquid for a period of time; an act of making sb/sth wet: *Give the shirt a good soak before you wash it.* **2** (*informal*) a period of time spent in a bath

soaked /səʊkt; *NAmE* soʊkt/ *adj.* **1** [not usually before noun] **~** (**with sth**) very wet SYN **drenched**: *He woke up soaked with sweat.* ◇ *You're* ***soaked through!*** (= completely wet) ◇ *They were* ***soaked to the skin.*** ◇ *You'll* ***get soaked*** *if you go out in this rain.* ◇ *Your clothes are soaked!* ➲ SYNONYMS at WET **2 -soaked** used with nouns to form adjectives describing sth that is made completely wet with the thing mentioned: *a blood-soaked cloth* ◇ *rain-soaked clothing*

soak·ing /'səʊkɪŋ; *NAmE* 'soʊ-/ (also **,soaking 'wet**) *adj.* completely wet SYN **sopping**: *That coat is soaking—take it off.* ◇ *We arrived home soaking wet.*

so-and-so /'səʊ ən səʊ; *NAmE* 'soʊ ən soʊ/ *noun* (*pl.* **so-and-sos**) (*informal*) **1** [usually sing.] used to refer to a person, thing, etc. when you do not know their name or when you are talking in a general way: *What would you say to Mrs So-and-so who has called to complain about a noisy neighbour?* **2** an annoying or unpleasant person. People sometimes say **so-and-so** to avoid using an offensive word: *He's an ungrateful so-and-so.*

soap 🗝 /səʊp; *NAmE* soʊp/ *noun, verb*
■ ***noun*** **1** 🗝 [U, C] a substance that you use with water for washing your body: *soap and water* ◇ *a* ***bar/piece of soap*** ◇ *soap bubbles* **2** [C] (*informal*) = SOAP OPERA: *soaps on TV* ◇ *She's a US soap star.*
■ ***verb*** **~ yourself/sb/sth** to rub yourself/sb/sth with soap ➲ see also SOFT-SOAP

soap·box /'səʊpbɒks; *NAmE* 'soʊpbɑːks/ *noun* a small temporary platform that sb stands on to make a speech in a public place, usually outdoors
IDM **get/be on your 'soapbox** (*informal*) to express the strong opinions that you have about a particular subject

'soap flakes *noun* [pl.] very small thin pieces of soap that are sold in boxes, used for washing clothes by hand

'soap opera (also *informal* **soap**) *noun* [C, U] a story about the lives and problems of a group of people which is broadcast every day or several times a week on television or radio ➲ COLLOCATIONS at TELEVISION

'soap powder *noun* [U, C] (*BrE*) a powder made from soap and other substances that you use for washing your clothes, especially in a machine

soap·stone /'səʊpstəʊn; *NAmE* 'soʊpstoʊn/ *noun* [U] a type of soft stone that feels like soap, used in making decorative objects

soap·suds /'səʊpsʌdz; *NAmE* 'soʊp-/ *noun* [pl.] = SUDS

soapy /'səʊpi; *NAmE* 'soʊpi/ *adj.* [usually before noun] **1** full of soap; covered with soap **2** tasting or feeling like soap

soar /sɔː(r)/ *verb* **1** [I] if the value, amount or level of sth **soars**, it rises very quickly SYN **rocket**: ***soaring costs/prices/temperatures*** ◇ *Unemployment has soared to 18%.* **2** [I] **~** (**up**) (**into sth**) to rise quickly and smoothly up into the air: *The rocket soared* (*up*) *into the air.* ◇ (*figurative*) *Her spirits soared* (= she became very happy and excited). **3** [I] to fly very high in the air or remain high in the air: *an eagle soaring high above the cliffs* **4** [I] to be very high or tall: *soaring mountains* ◇ *The building soared above us.* **5** [I] when music **soars**, it becomes higher or louder: *soaring strings*

soar·away /'sɔːrəweɪ/ *adj.* [only before noun] (*BrE*) (especially of success) very great; growing very quickly

SOB /,es əʊ 'biː; *NAmE* ,es oʊ 'biː/ *noun* (*slang, especially NAmE*) = SON OF A BITCH

sob /sɒb; *NAmE* sɑːb/ *verb, noun*
■ ***verb*** (**-bb-**) **1** [I] to cry noisily, taking sudden, sharp breaths: *I heard a child sobbing loudly.* ◇ *He started to sob uncontrollably.* **2** [T] to say sth while you are crying: **+ speech** *'I hate him,' she sobbed.* ◇ **~ sth** (**out**) *He sobbed out his troubles.*
IDM **sob your 'heart out** to cry noisily for a long time because you are very sad
■ ***noun*** an act or the sound of sobbing: *He gave a deep sob.* ◇ *Her body was racked* (= shaken) *with sobs.*

sober /'səʊbə(r); *NAmE* 'soʊ-/ *adj., verb*
■ ***adj.*** **1** [not usually before noun] not drunk (= not affected by alcohol): *I promised him that I'd stay sober tonight.* ◇ *He was* ***as sober as a judge*** (= completely sober). **2** (of people and their behaviour) serious and sensible: *a sober assessment of the situation* ◇ *He is honest, sober and hard-working.* ◇ ***On sober reflection*** (= after some serious thought), *I don't think I really need a car after all.* **3** (of colours or clothes) plain and not bright: *a sober grey suit* ▶ **sober·ly** *adv.* IDM see STONE COLD
■ ***verb*** [T, I] **~** (**sb**) to make sb behave or think in a more serious and sensible way; to become more serious and sensible: *The bad news sobered us for a while.* ◇ *He suddenly sobered.*
PHR V **,sober 'up** | **,sober sb 'up** to become or to make sb no longer drunk: *Stay here with us until you've sobered up.*

sober·ing /'səʊbərɪŋ; *NAmE* 'soʊ-/ *adj.* making you feel serious and think carefully: *a* ***sobering effect/experience/thought, etc.*** ◇ ***It is sobering*** *to realize that this is not a new problem.*

so·bri·ety /sə'braɪəti/ *noun* [U] (*formal*) **1** the state of being sober (= not being drunk) OPP **insobriety** **2** the fact of being sensible and serious

so·bri·quet /'səʊbrɪkeɪ; *NAmE* 'soʊ-/ (also **sou·bri·quet**) *noun* (*formal*) an informal name or title that you give sb/sth SYN **nickname**

'sob story *noun* (*informal, disapproving*) a story that sb tells you just to make you feel sorry for them, especially one that does not have that effect or is not true

Soc. *abbr.* (in writing) SOCIETY: *Royal Geographical Soc.*

soca /'səʊkə; *NAmE* 'soʊ-/ *noun* [U] a type of dance music, originally from the Caribbean, which mixes SOUL and CALYPSO

,so-'called AW *adj.* **1** [only before noun] used to show that you do not think that the word or phrase that is being used to describe sb/sth is appropriate: *the opinion of a so-called 'expert'* ◇ *How have these so-called improvements helped the local community?* **2** [usually before noun] used to introduce the word that people usually use to describe sth: *artists from the so-called 'School of London'*

soc·cer /'sɒkə(r); *NAmE* 'sɑːk-/ (*BrE* also **foot·ball**) (also *BrE formal* **As,sociation 'football**) (also *BrE informal* **footy, footie**) *noun* [U] a game played by two teams of 11 players, using a round ball which players kick up and down the playing field. Teams try to kick the ball into the other team's goal: *soccer players* ◇ *a* ***soccer pitch/team/match*** ➲ VISUAL VOCAB page V36

'soccer mom *noun* (*NAmE, informal*) a mother who spends a lot of time taking her children to activities such as sports and music lessons, used as a way of referring to a typical mother from the MIDDLE CLASSES

S

so·ci·able /ˈsəʊʃəbl; *NAmE* ˈsoʊ-/ (also *less frequent* **so·cial**) *adj.* (of people) enjoying spending time with other people SYN **gregarious**: *She's a sociable child who'll talk to anyone.* ◇ *I'm not feeling very sociable this evening.* ◇ *We had a very sociable weekend* (= we did a lot of things with other people). ➲ compare ANTISOCIAL OPP **unsociable** ▶ **so·ci·abil·ity** /ˌsəʊʃəˈbɪləti; *NAmE* ˌsoʊ-/ *noun* [U]

so·cial 🗝 /ˈsəʊʃl; *NAmE* ˈsoʊʃl/ *adj., noun*

■ *adj.*

▸ CONNECTED WITH SOCIETY **1** 🗝 [only before noun] connected with society and the way it is organized: *social issues/problems/reforms* ◇ *a call for social and economic change* **2** 🗝 [only before noun] connected with your position in society: ***social class/background*** ◇ *social advancement* (= improving your position in society)

▸ ACTIVITIES WITH OTHERS **3** 🗝 [only before noun] connected with activities in which people meet each other for pleasure: *a busy **social life*** ◇ *Team sports help to develop a child's **social skills*** (= the ability to talk easily to other people and do things in a group). ◇ *Social events and training days are arranged for all the staff.* ◇ *Join a social club to make new friends.*

▸ ANIMALS **4** [only before noun] (*technical*) living naturally in groups, rather than alone

▸ FRIENDLY **5** = SOCIABLE

▶ **so·cial·ly** 🗝 /-ʃəli/ *adv.*: *The reforms will bring benefits, socially and politically.* ◇ *This type of behaviour is no longer socially acceptable.* ◇ *a socially disadvantaged family* (= one that is poor and from a low social class) ◇ *We meet at work, but never socially.* ◇ *Carnivores are usually socially complex mammals.*

■ *noun* **1** [C] (*old-fashioned*) a party that is organized by a group or club **2 the social** [U] (*BrE, informal*) = SOCIAL SECURITY: *We're living on the social now.*

ˌsocial ˈbookmarking *noun* [U] (*computing*) a way of BOOKMARKING (= storing and labelling) the addresses of pages on the Internet, using a special service that enables you to make them available to other Internet users

ˌsocial ˈclimber *noun* (*disapproving*) a person who tries to improve their position in society by becoming friendly with people who belong to a higher social class

ˌsocial ˈconscience *noun* [sing., U] the state of being aware of the problems that affect a lot of people in society, such as being poor or having no home, and wanting to do sth to help these people

ˌsocial ˈcontract (also **ˌsocial ˈcompact**) *noun* [sing.] an agreement among citizens to behave in a way that benefits everybody

ˌsocial deˈmocracy *noun* [U, C] a political system that combines the principles of SOCIALISM with the greater personal freedom of DEMOCRACY; a country that has this political system of government ▶ **ˌsocial ˈdemocrat** *noun* **ˌsocial demoˈcratic** *adj.* [only before noun]

ˌsocial engiˈneering *noun* [U] the attempt to change society and to deal with social problems according to particular political beliefs, for example by changing the law

ˈsocial fund *noun* [usually sing.] a sum of money that can be used to help people who have financial, family or other social problems

ˌsocial ˈhousing *noun* [U] (in Britain) houses or flats/apartments that are provided by a local council or another organization for people to buy or rent at a low price

ˌSocial Inˈsurance number *noun* (*abbr.* SIN) a number that the Canadian government uses to identify you, and that you use when you fill out official forms, apply for a job, etc.

so·cial·ism /ˈsəʊʃəlɪzəm; *NAmE* ˈsoʊ-/ *noun* [U] a set of political and economic theories based on the belief that everyone has an equal right to a share of a country's wealth and that the government should own and control the main industries ➲ compare CAPITALISM, COMMUNISM, SOCIAL DEMOCRACY

so·cial·ist /ˈsəʊʃəlɪst; *NAmE* ˈsoʊ-/ *noun* a person who believes in or supports socialism; a member of a political party that believes in socialism ▶ **so·cial·ist** *adj.* [usually before noun]: *a socialist country* ◇ *socialist beliefs* ◇ *the ruling Socialist Party*

so·cial·is·tic /ˌsəʊʃəˈlɪstɪk; *NAmE* ˌsoʊ-/ *adj.* [usually before noun] (often *disapproving*) having some of the features of socialism

ˌsocialist ˈrealism *noun* [U] a theory that was put into practice in some COMMUNIST countries, especially in the Soviet Union under Stalin, that art, music and literature should be used to show people the principles of a SOCIALIST society and encourage them to support it

so·cial·ite /ˈsəʊʃəlaɪt; *NAmE* ˈsoʊ-/ *noun* (sometimes *disapproving*) a person who goes to a lot of fashionable parties and is often written about in the newspapers, etc.

so·cial·iza·tion (*BrE* also **-isa·tion**) /ˌsəʊʃəlaɪˈzeɪʃn; *NAmE* ˌsoʊʃələˈz-/ *noun* [U] (*formal*) the process by which sb, especially a child, learns to behave in a way that is acceptable in their society

so·cial·ize (*BrE* also **-ise**) /ˈsəʊʃəlaɪz; *NAmE* ˈsoʊ-/ *verb* **1** [I] ~ (**with sb**) to meet and spend time with people in a friendly way, in order to enjoy yourself SYN **mix**: *I enjoy socializing with the other students.* ◇ *Maybe you should socialize more.* **2** [T, often passive] **~ sb** (**to do sth**) (*formal*) to teach people to behave in ways that are acceptable to their society: *The family has the important function of socializing children.* **3** [T, usually passive] **~ sth** to organize sth according to the principles of SOCIALISM

ˌsocialized ˈmedicine *noun* [U] (*US*) medical and hospital care provided by the government for everyone by paying for it with public money

ˌsocial ˈnetworking *noun* [U] communication with people who share your interests using a website or other service on the Internet: *a social networking site* ➲ COLLOCATIONS at EMAIL

ˌsocial psyˈchology *noun* [U] the study of people's behaviour, attitudes, etc. in society ▶ **ˌsocial psyˈchologist** *noun*

ˌsocial ˈscience *noun* **1** [U] (also **ˌsocial ˈstudies**) the study of people in society **2** [C] a particular subject connected with the study of people in society, for example geography, ECONOMICS or SOCIOLOGY

ˌsocial ˈscientist *noun* a person who studies social science

ˌsocial ˈsecretary *noun* the person who organizes social activities for an organization or for another person

ˌsocial seˈcurity *noun* [U] **1** (*BrE*) (also **wel·fare** *NAmE, BrE*) money that the government pays regularly to people who are poor, unemployed, sick, etc: *to live on social security* ◇ *social security payments* **2 Social Security** (in the US) a system in which people pay money regularly to the government when they are working and receive payments from the government when they are unable to work, especially when they are sick or too old to work ➲ compare NATIONAL INSURANCE

ˌSocial Seˈcurity number *noun* (*abbr.* SSN) (in the US) an official identity number that everyone is given when they are born

ˌsocial ˈservices *noun* [pl.] a system that is organized by the local government to help people who have financial or family problems; the department or the people who provide this help: *a leaflet on the range of social services available* ◇ *the local social services department*

ˌsocial ˈstudies *noun* [pl.] = SOCIAL SCIENCE (1)

ˈsocial work *noun* [U] paid work that involves giving help and advice to people living in the community who have financial or family problems

ˈsocial worker *noun* a person whose job is social work

so·ci·etal /səˈsaɪətl/ *adj.* [only before noun] (*technical*) connected with society and the way it is organized

so·ci·ety 🗝 /səˈsaɪəti/ *noun* (*pl.* -ies)

1 🗝 [U] people in general, living together in communities: *policies that will benefit society as a whole* ◇ *Racism exists at*

S

all levels of society. ◇ They carried out research into the roles of men and women in today's society **2** [C, U] a particular community of people who share the same customs, laws, etc: *modern industrial societies ◇ demand created by a consumer society ◇ Can Britain ever be a classless society? ◇ They were discussing the problems of Western society.* **3** [C] (*abbr.* Soc.) (especially in names) a group of people who join together for a particular purpose: *a member of the drama society ◇ the American Society of Newspaper Editors* ➲ see also BUILDING SOCIETY, FRIENDLY SOCIETY **4** [U] the group of people in a country who are fashionable, rich and powerful: *Their daughter married into* ***high society***. ◇ *a society wedding* **5** [U] (*formal*) the state of being with other people SYN **company**: *He was a solitary man who avoided the society of others.*

socio- /ˈsəʊsiəʊ; *NAmE* ˈsoʊsioʊ/ *combining form* (in nouns, adjectives and adverbs) connected with society or the study of society: *socio-economic ◇ sociolinguistics*

so·cio·cul·tural /ˌsəʊsiəʊˈkʌltʃərəl; *NAmE* ˌsoʊsioʊ-/ *adj.* relating to society and culture

ˌsocio-ˌecoˈnomic *adj.* relating to society and economics: *people from different socio-economic backgrounds*

socio·lect /ˈsəʊsiəʊlekt; *NAmE* ˈsoʊsioʊ-/ *noun* (*linguistics*) a variety of a language that the members of a particular social class or social group speak

socio·lin·guis·tics /ˌsəʊsiəʊlɪŋˈɡwɪstɪks; *NAmE* ˌsoʊsioʊ-/ *noun* [U] the study of the way language is affected by differences in social class, region, sex, etc. ▶ **socio·lin·guis·tic** /ˌsəʊsiəʊlɪŋˈɡwɪstɪk; *NAmE* ˌsoʊsioʊ-/ *adj.*

soci·olo·gist /ˌsəʊsiˈɒlədʒɪst; *NAmE* ˌsoʊsiˈɑːl-/ *noun* a person who studies sociology

soci·ology /ˌsəʊsiˈɒlədʒi; *NAmE* ˌsoʊsiˈɑːl-/ *noun* [U] the scientific study of the nature and development of society and social behaviour ▶ **socio·logic·al** /ˌsəʊsiəˈlɒdʒɪkl; *NAmE* ˌsoʊsiəˈlɑːdʒ-/ *adj.*: *sociological theories* **socio·logic·al·ly** /-kli/ *adv.*

socio·path /ˈsəʊsiəʊpæθ; *NAmE* ˈsoʊsioʊ-/ *noun* a person who has a mental illness and who behaves in an aggressive or dangerous way towards other people

socio·politic·al /ˌsəʊsiəʊpəˈlɪtɪkl; *NAmE* ˌsoʊsioʊ-/ *adj.* relating to society and politics

sock /sɒk; *NAmE* sɑːk/ *noun, verb*

■ ***noun*** **1** a piece of clothing that is worn over the foot, ankle and lower part of the leg, especially inside a shoe: *a pair of socks* **2** (*informal*) a strong blow, especially with the FIST: *He gave him a sock on the jaw.*

IDM **blow/knock sb's ˈsocks off** (*informal*) to surprise or impress sb very much **put a ˈsock in it** (*old-fashioned, BrE, informal*) used to tell sb to stop talking or making a noise ➲ more at PULL *v.*

■ ***verb*** **~ sb** (*informal*) to hit sb hard: *She got angry and socked him in the mouth.* ◇ (*figurative*) *The banks are socking customers with higher charges.*

IDM **ˈsock it to sb** (*informal* or *humorous*) to do sth or tell sb sth in a strong and effective way: *Go in there and sock it to 'em!*

PHR V **ˌsock sth↔aˈway** (*NAmE*) to save money

socket /ˈsɒkɪt; *NAmE* ˈsɑːkɪt/ *noun* **1** (also **ˈpower point**) (both *BrE*) (*NAmE* **out·let, re·cep·tacle**) a device in a wall that you put a plug into in order to connect electrical equipment to the power supply of a building: *a wall socket* ➲ picture at PLUG **2** a device on a piece of electrical equipment that you can fix a plug, a light BULB, etc. into: *an aerial socket on the television* **3** a curved hollow space in the surface of sth that another part fits into or moves around in: *His eyes bulged in their sockets.*

sod /sɒd; *NAmE* sɑːd/ *noun, verb*

■ ***noun*** **1** (*BrE, taboo, slang*) used to refer to a person, especially a man, that you are annoyed with or think is unpleasant: *You stupid sod!* **2** (*BrE, taboo, slang*) used with an adjective to refer to a person, especially a man: *The poor old sod got the sack yesterday.* ◇ *You lucky sod!* HELP You can use words like **man**, **boy**, **devil** or **thing** instead. **3** (*BrE, taboo, slang*) a thing that is difficult or causes problems: *It was a real sod of a job.* **4** [usually sing.] (*formal* or *literary*) a layer of earth with grass growing on it; a piece of this that has been removed: *under the sod* (= in your grave)

■ ***verb*** (-dd-) **~ sth** (*BrE, taboo, slang*) (only used in orders) a swear word that many people find offensive, used when sb is annoyed about sth or to show that they do not care about sth: *Sod this car! It's always breaking down.* ◇ *Oh, sod it! I'm not doing any more.* IDM see LARK *n.*

PHR V **ˌsod ˈoff** (*BrE, taboo, slang*) (usually used in orders) to go away: *Sod off, the pair of you!*

soda /ˈsəʊdə; *NAmE* ˈsoʊdə/ *noun* **1** [U, C] = SODA WATER: *a Scotch and soda* **2** (also *old-fashioned* **ˈsoda pop**) (both *NAmE*) [U, C] a sweet FIZZY drink (= a drink with bubbles) made with soda water, fruit flavour and sometimes ice cream: *He had an ice-cream soda.* **3** [U] a chemical substance in common use that is a COMPOUND of SODIUM: ***baking/washing soda*** ➲ see also CAUSTIC SODA, SODIUM BICARBONATE, SODIUM CARBONATE

ˈsoda bread *noun* [U] bread that rises because of SODIUM BICARBONATE that is added instead of YEAST (popular in Ireland)

ˈsoda fountain *noun* (*NAmE*) **1** (*BrE* **ˈsoda siphon**) a bottle containing soda water or another drink, with a device that you press to pour the drink and put bubbles into it **2** (*old-fashioned*) a type of bar where you can buy sodas to drink, ICE CREAMS, etc.

ˌsod ˈall *noun* [U] (*BrE, taboo, slang*) a phrase that some people find offensive, used to mean 'none at all' or 'nothing at all'

ˈsoda pop *noun* (*old-fashioned*) = SODA (2)

ˈsoda siphon (*BrE*) (*NAmE* **ˈsoda fountain**) *noun* a bottle containing soda water or another drink, with a device that you press to pour the drink and put bubbles into it

ˈsoda water (also **soda**) *noun* **1** [U] FIZZY water (= water with bubbles) used as a drink on its own or to mix with alcoholic drinks or fruit juice (originally made with SODIUM BICARBONATE) **2** [C] a glass of soda water

sod·den /ˈsɒdn; *NAmE* ˈsɑːdn/ *adj.* **1** extremely wet SYN **soaked**: *sodden grass* **2 -sodden** extremely wet with the thing mentioned: *a rain-sodden jacket*

sod·ding /ˈsɒdɪŋ; *NAmE* ˈsɑːd-/ *adj.* [only before noun] (*BrE, taboo, slang*) a swear word that many people find offensive, used to emphasize a comment or an angry statement: *I couldn't understand a sodding thing!*

so·dium /ˈsəʊdiəm; *NAmE* ˈsoʊ-/ *noun* [U] (*symb.* Na) a chemical element. Sodium is a soft silver-white metal that is found naturally only in COMPOUNDS, such as salt.

S

ˌsodium biˈcarbonate (also **biˌcarbonate of ˈsoda**, **ˈbaking soda**) (also *informal* **bi·carb**) *noun* [U] (*symb.* $NaHCO_3$) a chemical in the form of a white powder that dissolves and is used in baking to make cakes, etc. rise and become light, and in making FIZZY drinks and some medicines

sodium carbonate /ˌsəʊdiəm ˈkɑːbənət; *NAmE* ˌsoʊdiəm ˈkɑːrbənət/ (also **ˈwashing soda**) *noun* [U] (*symb.* Na_2CO_3) a chemical in the form of white CRYSTALS or powder that dissolves and is used in making glass, soap and paper, and for making water soft

ˌsodium ˈchloride *noun* [U] (*symb.* NaCl) common salt (a chemical made up of SODIUM and CHLORINE)

Sodom and Gom·or·rah /ˌsɒdəm ən ɡəˈmɒrə; *NAmE* ˌsɑːdəm ən ɡəˈmɔːrə/ *noun* a place that is full of people behaving in a sexually immoral way: *The village had a reputation as a latter-day Sodom and Gomorrah.* ORIGIN From the names of two cities in the Bible which were destroyed by God to punish the people for their sexually immoral behaviour.

sod·om·ite /ˈsɒdəmaɪt; *NAmE* ˈsɑːd-/ *noun* (*old-fashioned, formal*) a person who practises sodomy

sod·om·ize (*BrE* also **-ise**) /ˈsɒdəmaɪz; *NAmE* ˈsɑːd-/ *verb* **~ sb** (*disapproving*) to have ANAL sex with sb

sod·omy /ˈsɒdəmi; *NAmE* ˈsɑːd-/ *noun* [U] a sexual act in which a man puts his PENIS in sb's, especially another man's, ANUS

ˌ**Sod's ˈLaw** *noun* [U] (*BrE, humorous*) the tendency for things to happen in just the way that you do not want, and in a way that is not useful: *We always play better when we are not being recorded—but that's Sod's Law, isn't it?* ◇ *It was Sod's Law—the only day he could manage was the day I couldn't miss work.*

sofa /ˈsəʊfə; *NAmE* ˈsoʊfə/ *noun* a long comfortable seat with a back and arms, for two or more people to sit on SYN **settee, couch** ➲ VISUAL VOCAB page V18

ˈ**sofa bed** *noun* a sofa that can be folded out to form a bed ➲ VISUAL VOCAB page V20

soft 🔑 /sɒft; *NAmE* sɔːft/ *adj.* (**soft·er, soft·est**)
▸ NOT HARD **1** 🔑 changing shape easily when pressed; not stiff or firm: *soft margarine* ◇ *soft feather pillows* ◇ *The grass was soft and springy.* **2** 🔑 less hard than average: *soft rocks such as limestone* ◇ *soft cheeses* OPP **hard**
▸ NOT ROUGH **3** 🔑 smooth and pleasant to touch: *soft skin* OPP **rough**
▸ WITHOUT ANGLES/EDGES **4** not having sharp angles or hard edges: *This season's fashions focus on warm tones and soft lines.* ◇ *The moon's pale light cast soft shadows.*
▸ LIGHT/COLOURS **5** [usually before noun] not too bright, in a way that is pleasant and relaxing to the eyes: *a soft pink* ◇ *the soft glow of candlelight* OPP **harsh**
▸ RAIN/WIND **6** not strong or violent SYN **light**: *A soft breeze rustled the trees.*
▸ SOUNDS **7** not loud, and usually pleasant and gentle SYN **quiet**: *soft background music* ◇ *a soft voice*
▸ SYMPATHETIC **8** kind and sympathetic; easily affected by other people's suffering: *Julia's soft heart was touched by his grief.* OPP **hard**
▸ NOT STRICT **9** (usually *disapproving*) not strict or severe; not strict or severe enough SYN **lenient**: **~ (on sb/sth)** *The government is not becoming soft on crime.* ◇ **~ (with sb)** *If you're too soft with these kids they'll never respect you.* OPP **tough**
▸ CRAZY **10** (*informal, disapproving*) stupid or crazy: *He must be going* ***soft in the head***.
▸ NOT BRAVE/TOUGH ENOUGH **11** (*informal, disapproving*) not brave enough; wanting to be safe and comfortable: *Stay in a hotel? Don't be so soft. I want to camp out under the stars.*
▸ TOO EASY **12** (*disapproving*) not involving much work; too easy and comfortable: *They had got too used to the soft life at home.* OPP **hard**
▸ WATER **13** not containing mineral salts and therefore good for washing: *You won't need much soap—the water here is very soft.* OPP **hard**
▸ CONSONANTS **14** (*phonetics*) not sounding hard, for example 'c' in 'city' and 'g' in 'general' OPP **hard**
▶ **soft·ness** *noun* [U, sing.]: *the softness of her skin* ◇ *the softness of the water* ➲ see also SOFTLY
IDM **have a soft ˈspot for sb/sth** (*informal*) to like sb/sth: *She's always had a soft spot for you.* ➲ more at OPTION, TOUCH *n.*

soft·ball /ˈsɒftbɔːl; *NAmE* ˈsɔːft-/ *noun* **1** [U] a game similar to BASEBALL but played on a smaller field with a larger, softer ball **2** [C] the ball used in softball

ˌ**soft-ˈboiled** *adj.* (of eggs) boiled for a short time so that the YOLK is still soft or liquid ➲ compare HARD-BOILED

ˌ**soft ˈcentre** *noun* (*BrE*) **1** [usually pl.] a chocolate with a soft mixture inside **2** if sb has a **soft centre**, they are not really as severe as they seem ▶ ˌ**soft-ˈcentered** *adj.*

ˈ**soft-core** *adj.* [usually before noun] showing or describing sexual activity without being too detailed or shocking ➲ compare HARD-CORE

ˌ**soft ˈdrink** *noun* a cold drink that does not contain alcohol ➲ compare HARD *adj.* (11)

ˌ**soft ˈdrug** *noun* an illegal drug, such as CANNABIS, that some people take for pleasure, that is not considered very harmful or likely to cause ADDICTION ➲ compare HARD DRUG

soft·en /ˈsɒfn; *NAmE* ˈsɔːfn/ *verb* **1** [I, T] to become, or to make sth softer: *Fry the onions until they soften.* ◇ **~ sth** *a lotion to soften the skin* ◇ *Linseed oil will soften stiff leather.* **2** [I, T] **~ (sth)** to become or to make sth less bright, rough or strong: *Trees soften the outline of the house.* **3** [I, T] to become or to make sb/sth more sympathetic and less severe or critical: *She felt herself softening towards him.* ◇ *His face softened as he looked at his son.* ◇ **~ sb/sth** *She softened her tone a little.* **4** [T] **~ sth** to reduce the force or the unpleasant effects of sth SYN **cushion**: *Airbags are designed to soften the impact of a car crash.* IDM see BLOW *n.*
PHR V ˌ**soften sb↔ˈup** (*informal*) **1** to try to persuade sb to do sth for you by being very nice to them before you ask them: *Potential customers are softened up with free gifts before the sales talk.* **2** to make an enemy weaker and easier to attack

soft·en·er /ˈsɒfnə(r); *NAmE* ˈsɔːf-/ *noun* **1** [C] a device that is used with chemicals to make hard water soft: *a water softener* **2** [U, C] a substance that you add when washing clothes to make them feel soft

ˌ**soft ˈerror** *noun* (*computing*) an error or fault that makes a program or OPERATING SYSTEM stop working, but that can often be corrected by switching the computer off then on again

ˌ**soft ˈfocus** *noun* [U] a method of producing a photograph so that the edges of the image are not clear, in order to make it look more romantic and attractive

ˌ**soft ˈfruit** *noun* [C, U] small fruits without large seeds or hard skin, such as STRAWBERRIES or CURRANTS ➲ VISUAL VOCAB page V26

ˌ**soft ˈfurnishings** *noun* [pl.] (*BrE*) CUSHIONS, curtains and other things made from cloth that are found in a house

ˈ**soft goods** *noun* [pl.] **1** things that are made of cloth, such as clothes and curtains **2** (*business*) any type of cloth SYN **textiles**

ˌ**soft-ˈhearted** *adj.* kind, sympathetic and emotional SYN **kind-hearted** OPP **hard-hearted**

softie (also **softy**) /ˈsɒfti; *NAmE* ˈsɔːfti/ *noun* (*pl.* **-ies**) (*informal*) a kind, sympathetic or emotional person: *There's no need to be afraid of him—he's a big softie.*

soft·ly 🔑 /ˈsɒftli; *NAmE* ˈsɔːftli/ *adv.* in a soft way: *She closed the door softly behind her.* ◇ *'I missed you,' he said softly.* ◇ *The room was softly lit by a lamp.* ◇ *a softly tailored suit*

ˌ**softly-ˈsoftly** *adj.* (*BrE, informal*) (of a way of doing sth) careful and patient, with no sudden actions: *The police used a* ***softly-softly approach*** *with him.*

ˌ**softly-ˈspoken** *adj.* = SOFT-SPOKEN

ˈ**soft pedal** *noun* (*music*) a PEDAL on a piano that is pressed to make the sound quieter

ˌ**soft-ˈpedal** *verb* (-ll-, *US* also -l-) [T, I] **~ (on) sth** (*informal*) to treat sth as less serious or important than it really is: *Television has been accused of soft-pedalling bad news.*

ˌ**soft ˈporn** *noun* [U] films/movies, books, pictures, etc. that show or describe sexual activity in a way that is sexually exciting but not in a very detailed or violent way ➲ compare HARD PORN

ˌ**soft ˈsell** *noun* [sing.] a method of selling that involves persuading sb to buy sth rather than using pressure or aggressive methods ➲ compare HARD SELL

ˈ**soft-shoe** *noun, verb*
■ **noun** [U] a type of dance like TAP, performed with soft shoes which do not make a noise: *a soft-shoe shuffle*
■ **verb** **1** [I] to perform a soft-shoe dance **2** [I] **+ adv./prep.** to move somewhere very quietly, without attracting attention

ˌ**soft ˈshoulder** *noun* (*NAmE*) a strip of ground with a soft surface at the edge of a road ➲ compare VERGE

ˌ**soft-ˈsoap** *verb* **~ sb** (*informal*) to say nice things to sb in order to persuade them to do sth ▶ ˌ**soft ˈsoap** *noun* [U]

ˌ**soft-ˈspoken** (also *less frequent* ˌ**softly-ˈspoken**) *adj.* having a gentle and quiet voice

S

ˌ**soft** ˈ**target** *noun* a person or thing that it is very easy to attack

ˌ**soft** ˈ**tissue** *noun* [U, C] (*anatomy*) the parts of the body that are not bone, for example the skin and muscles

ˈ**soft top** *noun* a type of car that has a soft roof that can be folded down or removed; the roof of such a car ➲ see also CONVERTIBLE

ˌ**soft** ˈ**toy** (*BrE*) (also ˌ**stuffed** ˈ**animal** *NAmE, BrE*) *noun* a toy in the shape of an animal, made of cloth and filled with a soft substance ➲ **VISUAL VOCAB** page V32

soft·ware O‑ /ˈsɒftweə(r); *NAmE* ˈsɔːftwer/ *noun* [U] the programs, etc. used to operate a computer: ***application/system software*** ◇ ***design/educational/music-sharing, etc. software*** ◇ *to* ***install/run*** *a piece of* ***software*** ◇ *Will the* ***software run*** *on my machine?* ➲ compare HARDWARE

ˈ**software engineer** *noun* a person who writes computer programs

ˈ**software package** *noun* (*computing*) = PACKAGE (4)

soft·wood /ˈsɒftwʊd; *NAmE* ˈsɔːft-/ *noun* [U, C] wood from trees such as PINE, that is cheap to produce and can be cut easily ➲ compare HARDWOOD

softy = SOFTIE

soggy /ˈsɒgi; *NAmE* ˈsɑːgi/ *adj.* (**sog·gier**, **sog·gi·est**) wet and soft, usually in a way that is unpleasant: *We squelched over the soggy ground.* ◇ *soggy bread*

soh (also **so**) /səʊ; *NAmE* soʊ/ (also **sol**) *noun* (*music*) the fifth note of a MAJOR SCALE

soi-disant /ˌswɑː diːˈzɒ̃; *NAmE* -ˈzɑ̃ː/ *adj.* [only before noun] (from *French*) used to show sb's description of himself/herself, usually when you do not agree with it: *a soi-disant novelist*

soi·gnée /ˈswɑːnjeɪ; *NAmE* swɑːnˈjeɪ/ *adj.* (from *French*, *formal*) (of a woman) elegant; carefully and neatly dressed

Synonyms

soil

mud • dust • clay • land • earth • dirt • ground

These are all words for the top layer of the earth in which plants grow.

soil the top layer of the earth in which plants grow: *Plant the seedlings in damp soil.*

mud wet soil that is soft and sticky: *The car wheels got stuck in the mud.*

dust a fine powder that consists of very small pieces of rock, earth, etc: *A cloud of dust rose as the truck set off.*

clay a type of heavy sticky soil that becomes hard when it is baked and is used to make things such as pots and bricks: *The tiles are made of clay.*

land an area of ground, especially of a particular type: *an area of rich, fertile land*

earth the substance that plants grow in. **NOTE** **Earth** is often used about the soil found in gardens or used for gardening: *She put some earth into the pot.*

dirt (*especially NAmE*) soil, especially loose soil: *Pack the dirt firmly around the plants.*

ground an area of soil: *The car got stuck in the muddy ground.* ◇ *They drove across miles of rough, stony ground.* **NOTE** **Ground** is not used for loose soil: ~~*a handful of dry ground*~~

PATTERNS

- **good/rich** soil/land/earth
- **fertile/infertile** soil/land/ground
- to **dig** the soil/mud/clay/land/earth/ground
- to **cultivate** the soil/land/ground

soil O‑ /sɔɪl/ *noun, verb*

▪ **noun** [U, C] **1** O‑ the top layer of the earth in which plants, trees, etc. grow: ***poor/dry/acid/sandy/fertile, etc. soil*** ◇ *the study of rocks and soils* ◇ *soil erosion* **2** (*literary*) a country; an area of land: *It was the first time I had set foot on African soil.*

▪ **verb** [often passive] **~ sth** (*formal*) to make sth dirty: *soiled linen* ◇ (*figurative*) *I don't want you* ***soiling your hands*** *with this sort of work* (= doing sth unpleasant or wrong). ➲ see also SHOP-SOILED

ˈ**soil science** *noun* [U] the study of soil, for example the study of its structure or characteristics

soirée /ˈswɑːreɪ; *NAmE* swɑːˈreɪ/ *noun* (from *French*, *formal*) a formal party in the evening, especially at sb's home

so·journ /ˈsɒdʒən; *NAmE* ˈsoʊdʒɜːrn/ *noun* (*literary*) a temporary stay in a place away from your home ▶ **so·journ** *verb* [I] **+ adv./prep.**

sol /sɒl; *NAmE* soʊl/ *noun* = SOH

sol·ace /ˈsɒləs; *NAmE* ˈsɑːləs/ *noun* [U, sing.] (*formal*) a feeling of emotional comfort when you are sad or disappointed; a person or thing that makes you feel better or happier when you are sad or disappointed **SYN** **comfort**: *He sought solace in the whisky bottle.* ◇ *She turned to Rob for solace.* ◇ *His grandchildren were a solace in his old age.* ▶ **so·lace** *verb*: **~ sb** (*literary*) *She smiled, as though solaced by the memory.*

solar /ˈsəʊlə(r); *NAmE* ˈsoʊ-/ *adj.* [only before noun] **1** of or connected with the sun: *solar radiation* ◇ *the solar cycle* **2** using the sun's energy: ***solar power/heating*** ➲ **COLLOCATIONS** at ENVIRONMENT ➲ **VISUAL VOCAB** page V7

ˌ**solar** ˈ**cell** *noun* a device that converts light and heat energy from the sun into electricity

ˈ**solar cooker** *noun* (*IndE*) a container for cooking food that uses heat from the sun

sol·ar·ium /səˈleəriəm; *NAmE* -ˈler-/ *noun* a room whose walls are mainly made of glass, or which has special lamps, where people go to get a SUNTAN (= make their skin go brown) using light from the sun or artificial light

ˌ**solar** ˈ**panel** *noun* a piece of equipment on a roof that uses light and heat energy from the sun to produce hot water and electricity ➲ **VISUAL VOCAB** page V7

solar plexus /ˌsəʊlə ˈpleksəs; *NAmE* ˌsoʊlər/ *noun* [sing.] **1** (*anatomy*) a system of nerves at the base of the stomach **2** (*informal*) the part of the body at the top of the stomach, below the RIBS: *a painful punch in the solar plexus*

ˈ**solar system** *noun* **1 the solar system** [sing.] the sun and all the planets that move around it **2** [C] any group of planets that all move around the same star

ˌ**solar** ˈ**year** *noun* the time it takes the earth to go around the sun once, approximately 365¼ days

S

sold *past tense, past part.* of SELL

sol·der /ˈsəʊldə(r); ˈsɒldə(r); *NAmE* ˈsɑːdər/ *noun, verb*

▪ **noun** [U] a mixture of metals that is heated and melted and then used to join metals, wires, etc. together

▪ **verb** **~ sth (to/onto sth)** | **~ (A and B together)** to join pieces of metal or wire with solder

ˈ**soldering iron** *noun* a tool that is heated and used for joining metals and wires by soldering them

sol·dier O‑ /ˈsəʊldʒə(r); *NAmE* ˈsoʊl-/ *noun, verb*

▪ **noun** O‑ a member of an army, especially one who is not an officer: *soldiers in uniform* ◇ *soldiers on duty* ➲ see also FOOT SOLDIER

▪ **verb**

PHR V ˌ**soldier** ˈ**on** to continue with what you are doing or trying to achieve, especially when this is difficult or unpleasant

sol·dier·ing /ˈsəʊldʒərɪŋ; *NAmE* ˈsoʊl-/ *noun* [U] the life or activity of being a soldier

sol·dier·ly /ˈsəʊldʒəli; *NAmE* ˈsoʊldʒərli/ *adj.* typical of a good soldier

ˌ**soldier of** ˈ**fortune** *noun* a person who fights for any country or person who will pay them **SYN** **mercenary**

sol·diery /ˈsəʊldʒəri; NAmE ˈsoʊl-/ *noun* [U+sing./pl. v.] (*old-fashioned*) a group of soldiers, especially of a particular kind

ˌsold ˈout *adj.* **1** if a concert, match, etc. is **sold out**, there are no more tickets available for it **2** if a shop/store is **sold out** of a product, it has no more of it left to sell

sole AW /səʊl; NAmE soʊl/ *adj., noun, verb*
■ ***adj.*** [only before noun] **1** only; single: *the **sole surviving** member of the family* ◇ *My **sole reason** for coming here was to see you.* ◇ *This is the sole means of access to the building.* **2** belonging to one person or group; not shared: *She has **sole responsibility** for the project.* ◇ *the **sole owner***
■ ***noun*** **1** [C] the bottom surface of the foot: *The hot sand burned the **soles of their feet**.* ➲ VISUAL VOCAB page V48 **2** [C] the bottom part of a shoe or sock, not including the heel: *leather soles* ➲ VISUAL VOCAB page V52 ➲ compare HEEL *n.* (3) **3 -soled** (in adjectives) having the type of soles mentioned: *rubber-soled shoes* **4** [U, C] (*pl.* sole) a flat sea fish that is used for food
■ ***verb*** [usually passive] **~ sth** to repair a shoe by replacing the sole

sol·ecism /ˈsɒlɪsɪzəm; NAmE ˈsɑːl-/ *noun* (*formal*) **1** a mistake in the use of language in speech or writing **2** an example of bad manners or unacceptable behaviour

sole·ly AW /ˈsəʊlli; NAmE ˈsoʊlli/ *adv.* only; not involving sb/sth else: *She was motivated solely by self-interest.* ◇ *Selection is based solely on merit.* ◇ *He became solely responsible for the firm.*

sol·emn /ˈsɒləm; NAmE ˈsɑːləm/ *adj.* **1** (of a person) not happy or smiling SYN **serious**: *Her face grew solemn.* ◇ *a solemn expression* OPP **cheerful** **2** done, said, etc. in a very serious and sincere way: *a **solemn oath/undertaking/vow, etc.*** **3** (of a religious ceremony or formal occasion) performed in a serious way: *a solemn ritual* ▶ **sol·emn·ly** *adv.*: *He nodded solemnly.* ◇ *She solemnly promised not to say a word to anyone about it.* ◇ *The choir walked solemnly past.*

so·lem·nity /səˈlemnəti/ *noun* **1** [U] the quality of being solemn: *He was smiling, but his eyes retained a look of solemnity.* ◇ *He was buried with great pomp and solemnity.* **2 solemnities** [pl.] (*formal*) formal things that people do at a serious event or occasion: *to observe the solemnities of the occasion*

sol·em·nize (*BrE* also **-ise**) /ˈsɒləmnaɪz; NAmE ˈsɑːl-/ *verb* **~ sth** (*formal*) to perform a religious ceremony, especially a marriage

so·len·oid /ˈsɒlənɔɪd; ˈsəʊl-; NAmE ˈsoʊl-; ˈsɑːl-/ *noun* (*physics*) a piece of wire, wound into circles, which acts as a MAGNET when carrying an electric current

ˌsol-ˈfa *noun* (also **ˌtonic ˌsol-ˈfa**) (*music*) a system of naming the notes of the SCALE, used in teaching singing

so·licit /səˈlɪsɪt/ *verb* **1** [T, I] (*formal*) to ask sb for sth, such as support, money or information; to try to get sth or persuade sb to do sth: **~ sth (from sb)** *They were planning to solicit funds from a number of organizations.* ◇ **~ sb (for sth)** *Historians and critics are solicited for their opinions.* ◇ **~ (for sth)** *to solicit for money* ◇ **~ sb to do sth** *Volunteers are being solicited to assist with the project.* **2** [I, T] **~ (sb)** (of a PROSTITUTE) to offer to have sex with people in return for money: *Prostitutes solicited openly in the streets.* ◇ *the crime of soliciting* ▶ **so·lici·ta·tion** /səˌlɪsɪˈteɪʃn/ *noun* [U, C] (*especially NAmE*): *the solicitation of money for election funds*

so·lici·tor /səˈlɪsɪtə(r)/ *noun* **1** (*BrE*) a lawyer who prepares legal documents, for example for the sale of land or buildings, advises people on legal matters, and can speak for them in some courts of law ➲ note at LAWYER **2** (*NAmE*) a person whose job is to visit or telephone people and try to sell them sth **3** (*NAmE*) the most senior legal officer of a city, town or government department

Soˌlicitor ˈGeneral *noun* (*pl.* **Solicitors General**) a senior legal officer in Britain or the US, next in rank below the ATTORNEY GENERAL

so·lici·tous /səˈlɪsɪtəs/ *adj.* (*formal*) being very concerned for sb and wanting to make sure that they are comfortable, well or happy SYN **attentive** ▶ **so·lici·tous·ly** *adv.* (*formal*)

so·lici·tude /səˈlɪsɪtjuːd; NAmE -tuːd/ *noun* [U] **~ (for sb/sth)** (*formal*) anxious care for sb's comfort, health or happiness: *I was touched by his solicitude for the boy.*

solid O-w /ˈsɒlɪd; NAmE ˈsɑːl-/ *adj., noun*
■ ***adj.***
▸ NOT LIQUID/GAS **1** O-w hard or firm; not in the form of a liquid or gas: *The planet Jupiter may have no solid surface at all.* ◇ *The boat bumped against a solid object.* ◇ *She had refused all solid food.* ◇ *It was so cold that the stream had **frozen solid**.* ◇ *The boiler uses **solid fuel**.*
▸ WITHOUT HOLES OR SPACES **2** O-w having no holes or spaces inside; not hollow: *They were drilling through solid rock.* ◇ *The stores are **packed solid*** (= very full and crowded) *at this time of year.*
▸ STRONG **3** O-w strong and made well: *These chains seem fairly solid.*
▸ RELIABLE **4** O-w that you can rely on; having a strong basis: *As yet, they have no solid evidence.* ◇ *This provided a solid foundation for their marriage.* ◇ *The Irish team were **solid as a rock** in defence.*
▸ GOOD BUT NOT SPECIAL **5** definitely good and steady but perhaps not excellent or special: *2008 was a year of solid achievement.* ◇ *He's a solid player.*
▸ MATERIAL **6** O-w [only before noun] made completely of the material mentioned (that is, the material is not only on the surface): *a solid gold bracelet*
▸ PERIOD OF TIME **7** (*informal*) without a pause; continuous: *The essay represents a solid week's work.* ◇ *It rained for two hours solid this afternoon.*
▸ COLOUR **8** of the colour mentioned and no other colour: *One cat is black and white, the other solid black.*
▸ SHAPE **9** (*geometry*) a shape that is **solid** has length, width and height and is not flat: *A cube is a solid figure.* ➲ VISUAL VOCAB page V58
▸ IN AGREEMENT **10** in complete agreement; agreed on by everyone: *The strike was solid, supported by all the members.* ➲ see also ROCK SOLID
■ ***noun***
▸ NOT LIQUID/GAS **1** O-w a substance or an object that is solid, not a liquid or a gas: *liquids and solids* ◇ *The baby is not yet on solids* (= eating solid food).
▸ SHAPE **2** (*geometry*) a shape which has length, width and height, such as a CUBE

soli·dar·ity /ˌsɒlɪˈdærəti; NAmE ˌsɑːl-/ *noun* [U] support by one person or group of people for another because they share feelings, opinions, aims, etc: *community solidarity* ◇ **~ with sb** *to **express/show solidarity** with sb* ◇ *Demonstrations were held as **a gesture of solidarity** with the hunger strikers.*

so·lid·ify /səˈlɪdɪfaɪ/ *verb* (**so·lidi·fies, so·lidi·fy·ing, so·lidi·fied, so·lidi·fied**) **1** [I, T] **~ (into sth)** | **~ (sth)** to become solid; to make sth solid: *The mixture will solidify into toffee.* ◇ *solidified lava* **2** [I, T] (*formal*) (of ideas, etc.) to become or to make sth become more definite and less likely to change: **~ (into sth)** *Vague objections to the system solidified into firm opposition.* ◇ **~ sth** *They solidified their position as Britain's top band.* ▶ **so·lidi·fi·ca·tion** /səˌlɪdɪfɪˈkeɪʃn/ *noun* [U]

so·lid·ity /səˈlɪdəti/ *noun* [U] the quality or state of being solid: *the strength and solidity of Romanesque architecture* ◇ *Her writings have extraordinary depth and solidity.* ◇ *the solidity of his support for his staff*

sol·id·ly /ˈsɒlɪdli; NAmE ˈsɑːl-/ *adv.* **1** in a firm and strong way: *a large, solidly-built house* ◇ *He stood solidly in my path.* **2** continuously; without stopping: *It rained solidly for three hours.* **3** agreeing with or supporting sb/sth completely: *The state is solidly Republican.*

ˌsolid-ˈstate *adj.* (*technical*) using or containing solid SEMICONDUCTORS: *a solid-state radio*

so·lilo·quy /səˈlɪləkwi/ *noun* [C, U] (*pl.* -ies) a speech in a play in which a character, who is alone on the stage, speaks his or her thoughts; the act of speaking thoughts in this way SYN **monologue**: *Hamlet's famous soliloquy,*

'To be or not to be…' ◇ the playwright's use of soliloquy ▶ **so·lilo·quize, -ise** /sə'lɪləkwaɪz/ *verb* [I]

sol·ip·sism /'sɒlɪpsɪzəm; *NAmE* 'sɑːl-/ *noun* [U] (*philosophy*) the theory that only the SELF exists or can be known ▶ **sol·ip·sis·tic** /ˌsɒlɪp'sɪstɪk; *NAmE* ˌsɑːl-/ *adj.*

soli·taire /ˌsɒlɪ'teə(r); *NAmE* 'sɑːləter/ *noun* **1** [U] (*BrE*) a game for one person in which you remove pieces from their places on a special board after moving other pieces over them. The aim is to finish with only one piece left on the board. **2** (*NAmE*) (*BrE* **pa·tience**) [U] a card game for only one player **3** [C] a single PRECIOUS STONE; a piece of jewellery with a single precious stone in it

soli·tary /'sɒlətri; *NAmE* 'sɑːləteri/ *adj., noun*
■ ***adj.*** **1** [usually before noun] done alone; without other people: *She enjoys long solitary walks.* ◇ *He led a solitary life.* **2** (of a person or an animal) enjoying being alone; frequently spending time alone: *He was a solitary child.* ◇ *Tigers are solitary animals.* **3** (of a person, thing or place) alone, with no other people or things around SYN **single**: *a solitary farm* ◇ *A solitary light burned dimly in the hall.* **4** [usually before noun] (especially in negative sentences and questions) only one SYN **single**: *There was not a solitary shred of evidence* (= none at all). ▶ **soli·tari·ness** *noun* [U]
■ ***noun*** (*pl.* -ies) **1** [U] (*informal*) = SOLITARY CONFINEMENT **2** [C] (*formal*) a person who chooses to live alone

ˌsolitary conˈfinement (also *informal* **soli·tary**) *noun* [U] a punishment in which a prisoner is kept alone in a separate cell: *to be in solitary confinement*

soli·tude /'sɒlɪtjuːd; *NAmE* 'sɑːlətuːd/ *noun* [U] the state of being alone, especially when you find this pleasant SYN **privacy**: *She longed for peace and solitude.*

solo /'səʊləʊ; *NAmE* 'soʊloʊ/ *adj., noun*
■ ***adj.*** [only before noun] **1** done by one person alone, without anyone helping them: *his first solo flight* ◇ *a solo effort* **2** connected with or played as a musical solo: *a solo artist* (= for example a singer who sings on their own, not as part of a group) ◇ *a piece for solo violin* ▶ **solo** *adv.*: *She wanted to fly solo across the Atlantic.* ◇ *After three years with the band he decided to* ***go solo****.*
■ ***noun*** (*pl.* -os) **1** a piece of music, dance or entertainment performed by only one person: *a guitar solo* ⊃ compare DUET **2** a flight in which the pilot flies alone without an INSTRUCTOR (= teacher)

solo·ist /'səʊləʊɪst; *NAmE* 'soʊloʊ-/ *noun* a person who plays an instrument or performs alone

Solo·mon /'sɒləmən; *NAmE* 'sɑːl-/ *noun* used to talk about a very wise person: *In this job you need to exhibit the wisdom of Solomon.* ORIGIN From Solomon in the Bible, a king of Israel who was famous for being wise.

sol·stice /'sɒlstɪs; *NAmE* 'sɑːlstəs/ *noun* either of the two times of the year at which the sun reaches its highest or lowest point in the sky at midday, marked by the longest and shortest days: *the* ***summer/winter solstice*** ⊃ VISUAL VOCAB page V59

sol·uble /'sɒljəbl; *NAmE* 'sɑːl-/ *adj.* **1** ~ **(in sth)** that can be dissolved in a liquid: *soluble aspirin* ◇ *Glucose is soluble in water.* **2** (*formal*) (of a problem) that can be solved OPP **insoluble** ▶ **solu·bil·ity** /ˌsɒlju'bɪləti; *NAmE* ˌsɑːl-/ *noun* [U]

so·lu·tion 0-w /sə'luːʃn/ *noun*
1 0-w [C] ~ **(to sth)** a way of solving a problem or dealing with a difficult situation SYN **answer**: *Attempts to* ***find a solution*** *have failed.* ◇ *There's no simple solution to this problem.* ◇ *Do you have a better solution?* **2** 0-w [C] ~ **(to sth)** an answer to a PUZZLE or to a problem in mathematics: *The solution to last week's quiz is on page 81.* **3** 0-w [C, U] a liquid in which sth is dissolved: *an alkaline solution* ◇ *saline solution* **4** [U] the process of dissolving a solid or gas in a liquid: *the solution of glucose in water*

solve 0-w /sɒlv; *NAmE* sɑːlv; sɔːlv/ *verb*
1 0-w ~ **sth** to find a way of dealing with a problem or difficult situation: *Attempts are being made to solve the problem of waste disposal.* **2** 0-w ~ **sth** to find the correct answer or explanation for sth: *to* ***solve an equation/a puzzle/a riddle*** ◇ *to* ***solve a crime/mystery***

solv·ency /'sɒlvənsi; *NAmE* 'sɑːl-/ *noun* [U] the state of not being in debt (= not owing money)

solv·ent /'sɒlvənt; *NAmE* 'sɑːl-/ *noun, adj.*
■ ***noun*** [U, C] a substance, especially a liquid, that can dissolve another substance
■ ***adj.*** **1** [not usually before noun] having enough money to pay your debts; not in debt OPP **insolvent** **2** (*technical*) able to dissolve another substance, or be dissolved in another substance: *Lead is more solvent in acidic water.*

ˈsolvent abuse *noun* [U] the practice of breathing in gases from glue or similar substances in order to produce a state of excitement ⊃ see also GLUE-SNIFFING

solv·er /'sɒlvə(r); *NAmE* 'sɑːl-; 'sɔːl-/ *noun* a person who finds an answer to a problem or a difficult situation: *She's a good* ***problem solver****.*

sombre (*BrE*) (*US* **som·ber**) /'sɒmbə(r); *NAmE* 'sɑːm-/ *adj.* **1** dark in colour; dull SYN **drab**: *dressed in sombre shades of grey and black* **2** sad and serious SYN **melancholy**: *Paul was in a* ***sombre mood****.* ◇ *The year ended on a sombre note.* ▶ **sombre·ly** (*BrE*) (*US* **som·berly**) *adv.* **sombre·ness** (*BrE*) (*US* **som·berness**) *noun* [U]

som·brero /sɒm'breərəʊ; *NAmE* sɑːm'breroʊ/ *noun* (*pl.* -os) a Mexican hat for men that is tall with a very wide BRIM, turned up at the edges ⊃ VISUAL VOCAB page V53

some 0-w *det., pron., adv.*
■ ***det.*** /səm; *strong form* sʌm/ **1** 0-w used with uncountable nouns or plural countable nouns to mean 'an amount of' or 'a number of', when the amount or number is not given: *There's still some wine in the bottle.* ◇ *Have some more vegetables.* HELP In negative sentences and questions **any** is usually used instead of 'some': *I don't want any more vegetables.* ◇ *Is there any wine left?* However, **some** is used in questions that expect a positive reply: *Would you like some milk in your coffee?* ◇ *Didn't you borrow some books of mine?* **2** 0-w /sʌm/ used to refer to certain members of a group or certain types of a thing, but not all of them: *Some people find this more difficult than others.* ◇ *I like some modern music* (= but not all of it). **3** 0-w /sʌm/ a large number or amount of sth: *It was with some surprise that I heard the news.* ◇ *We've known each other for some years now.* ◇ *We're going to be working together for* ***some time*** (= a long time). **4** 0-w /sʌm/ a small amount or number of sth: *There is some hope that things will improve.* **5** 0-w used with singular nouns to refer to a person, place, thing or time that is not known or not identified: *There must be some mistake.* ◇ *He's in* ***some kind of*** *trouble.* ◇ *She won a competition in* ***some*** *newspaper* ***or other****.* ◇ *I'll see you again some time, I'm sure.* **6** /sʌm/ (*informal*, sometimes *ironic*) used to express a positive or negative opinion about sb/sth: *That was some party!* ◇ *Some expert you are! You know even less than me.*
■ ***pron.*** /sʌm/ ~ **(of sb/sth)** **1** 0-w used to refer to an amount of sth or a number of people or things when the amount or number is not given: *Some disapprove of the idea.* ◇ *You'll find some in the drawer.* ◇ *Here are some of our suggestions.* HELP In negative sentences and questions **any** is usually used instead of 'some': *I don't want any.* ◇ *Do you have any of the larger ones?* However, **some** is used in questions that expect a positive reply: *Would you like some?* ◇ *Weren't you looking for some of those?* **2** 0-w a part of the whole number or amount being considered: *All these students are good, but some work harder than others.* ◇ *Some of the music was weird.*
IDM **… and ˈthen some** (*informal*) and a lot more than that: *We got our money's worth and then some.*
■ ***adv.*** /sʌm/ **1** used before numbers to mean 'approximately': *Some thirty people attended the funeral.* **2** (*NAmE, informal*) to some degree: *He needs feeding up some.* ◇ *'Are you finding the work any easier?' 'Some.'*

-some *suffix* **1** (in adjectives) producing; likely to: *fearsome* ◇ *quarrelsome* **2** (in nouns) a group of the number mentioned: *a foursome*

some·body 0-w /'sʌmbədi/ *pron.* = SOMEONE: *Somebody should have told me.* ◇ *She thinks she's really somebody in that car.* OPP **nobody**

S

'some day (also **someday**) *adv.* at some time in the future: *Some day he'll be famous.*

some·how 0-■ /ˈsʌmhaʊ/ *adv.*
1 0-■ (also *NAmE informal* **some·way, some·ways**) in a way that is not known or certain: *We must stop him from seeing her somehow.* ◇ ***Somehow or other*** *I must get a new job.* **2** 0-■ for a reason that you do not know or understand: *Somehow, I don't feel I can trust him.* ◇ *She looked different somehow.*

some·one 0-■ /ˈsʌmwʌn/ (also **some·body**) *pron.*
1 0-■ a person who is not known or mentioned by name: *There's someone at the door.* ◇ *Someone's left their bag behind.* ◇ *It's time for someone new* (= a new person) *to take over.* ◇ *It couldn't have been me—it must have been* ***someone else*** (= a different person). ◇ *Should we call a doctor* ***or someone?*** HELP The difference between **someone** and **anyone** is the same as the difference between **some** and **any**. Look at the notes there. **2** an important person: *He was a small-time lawyer keen to* ***be someone.*** ➲ compare NOBODY

some·place /ˈsʌmpleɪs/ *adv., pron.* (*NAmE*) = SOMEWHERE: *It has to go someplace.* ◇ *Can't you do that* ***someplace else?*** ◇ *We need to find* ***someplace to*** *live.*

som·er·sault /ˈsʌməsɔːlt; *NAmE* -mərs-/ *noun, verb*
■ ***noun*** a movement in which sb turns over completely, with their feet over their head, on the ground or in the air: *to* ***do/turn a somersault*** ◇ *He turned back somersaults.* ◇ (*figurative*) *Her heart did a complete somersault when she saw him.*
■ ***verb*** [I] (+ **adv./prep.**) to turn over completely in the air: *The car hit the kerb and somersaulted into the air.*

some·thing 0-■ /ˈsʌmθɪŋ/ *pron., adv.*
■ ***pron.*** **1** 0-■ a thing that is not known or mentioned by name: *We stopped for something to eat.* ◇ *Give me* ***something to do.*** ◇ *There's something wrong with the TV.* ◇ ***There's something about*** *this place that frightens me.* ◇ *Don't just stand there.* ***Do something!*** ◇ *His name is Alan something* (= I don't know his other name). ◇ *She's a professor of* ***something or other*** (= I'm not sure what) *at Leeds.* ◇ *He's* ***something in*** (= has a job connected with) *television.* ◇ *The car hit a tree* ***or something.*** ◇ *I could just eat* ***a little something.*** HELP The difference between **something** and **anything** is the same as the difference between **some** and **any**. Look at the notes there. **2** 0-■ (*informal*) a thing that is thought to be important or worth taking notice of: *There's* ***something in*** (= some truth or some fact or opinion worth considering in) *what he says.* ◇ *It's* ***quite something*** (= a thing that you should feel happy about) *to have a job at all these days.* ◇ *'We should finish by tomorrow.'* ***'That's something*** (= a good thing), *anyway.'* **3** 0-■ (*informal*) used to show that a description or an amount, etc. is not exact: *She called at* ***something after*** *ten o'clock.* ◇ *a new comedy aimed at* ***thirty-somethings*** (= people between thirty and forty years old) ◇ *It tastes* ***something like*** *melon.* ◇ *They pay six pounds an hour.* ***Something like that.*** ◇ *She found herself* ***something of a*** (= to some degree a) *celebrity.* ◇ *The programme's* ***something to do with*** (= in some way about) *the environment.* ◇ *He gave her a wry look,* ***something between*** *amusement and regret.*
IDM **'make something of yourself** to be successful in life **something 'else 1** 0-■ a different thing; another thing: *He said something else that I thought was interesting.* **2** (*informal*) a person, a thing or an event that is much better than others of a similar type: *I've seen some fine players, but she's something else.*
■ ***adv.*** (*non-standard*) used with an adjective to emphasize a statement: *She was swearing something terrible.*

some·time /ˈsʌmtaɪm/ *adv., adj.*
■ ***adv.*** (also **'some time**) at a time that you do not know exactly or has not yet been decided: *I saw him sometime last summer.* ◇ *We must get together sometime.*
■ ***adj.*** [only before noun] (*formal*) **1** used to refer to what sb used to be: *Thomas Atkins, sometime vicar of this parish* **2** (*NAmE*) used to refer to what sb does occasionally: *a sometime contributor to this magazine*

some·times 0-■ /ˈsʌmtaɪmz/ *adv.*
occasionally rather than all of the time: *Sometimes I go by car.* ◇ *He sometimes writes to me.* ◇ *I like to be on my own sometimes.*

some·way /ˈsʌmweɪ/ (also **someways**) *adv.* (*NAmE, informal*) = SOMEHOW

some·what 0-■ AW /ˈsʌmwɒt; *NAmE* -wʌt/ *adv.*
to some degree SYN **rather**: *I was somewhat surprised to see him.* ◇ *The situation has changed somewhat since we last met.* ◇ *What happened to them remains* ***somewhat of*** *a mystery.*

some·where 0-■ /ˈsʌmweə(r); *NAmE* -wer/ (*NAmE* also **some·place**) *adv.*
in, at or to a place that you do not know or do not mention by name: *I've seen him somewhere before.* ◇ *Can we go somewhere warm?* ◇ *I've already looked there—it must be* ***somewhere else.*** ◇ *He went to school in York* ***or somewhere*** (= I'm not sure where). ◇ *They live* ***somewhere or other*** *in France.* HELP The difference between **somewhere** and **anywhere** is the same as the difference between **some** and **any**. Look at the notes there. ▶ **some·where** (*NAmE* also **some·place**) *pron.*: *We need to find* ***somewhere to*** (= a place to) *live.* ◇ *I know somewhere we can go.*
IDM **'get somewhere** (*informal*) to make progress in what you are doing **somewhere around, between, etc. sth** approximately the number or amount mentioned: *It cost somewhere around two thousand dollars.*

som·mer /ˈsɒmə; *NAmE* ˈsɑːmə/ *adv.* (*SAfrE, informal*) just; simply: *He sommer hit me without saying anything.*

som·nam·bu·list /sɒmˈnæmbjəlɪst; *NAmE* sɑːm-/ *noun* (*formal*) = SLEEPWALKER ▶ **som·nam·bu·lism** /-lɪzəm/ *noun* [U]

som·no·lent /ˈsɒmnələnt; *NAmE* ˈsɑːm-/ *adj.* (*formal*) **1** almost asleep: *a somnolent cat* ◇ (*figurative*) *a somnolent town* **2** making you feel tired: *a somnolent Sunday afternoon* ▶ **som·no·lence** *noun* [U]

son 0-■ /sʌn/ *noun*
1 0-■ [C] a person's male child: *We have two sons and a daughter.* ◇ *They have three grown-up sons.* ◇ *He's the son of an Oxford professor.* ◇ *Maine & Sons, Grocers* (= the name of a company on a sign) ➲ COLLOCATIONS at CHILD **2** [sing.] (*informal*) a friendly form of address that is used by an older man to a young man or boy: *Well, son, how can I help you?* **3** [C] (*literary*) a man who belongs to a particular place or country, etc: *one of France's most famous sons* **4 my son** (*formal*) used by a priest to address a boy or man **5 the Son** [sing.] Jesus Christ as the second member of the TRINITY: *the Father, the Son and the Holy Spirit* IDM see FATHER *n.*, FAVOURITE *adj.*, PRODIGAL

sonar /ˈsəʊnɑː(r); *NAmE* ˈsoʊ-/ *noun* [U] equipment or a system for finding objects underwater using sound waves ➲ compare RADAR

son·ata /səˈnɑːtə/ *noun* a piece of music for one instrument or for one instrument and a piano, usually divided into three or four parts

son et lu·mi·ère /ˌsɒn eɪ ˈluːmjeə(r); *NAmE* ˌsɔːn eɪ luːmˈjer/ *noun* [U] (from *French*) a performance held at night at a famous place that tells its history with special lights and sound

song 0-■ /sɒŋ; *NAmE* sɔːŋ/ *noun*
1 0-■ [C] a short piece of music with words that you sing: *a* ***folk/love/pop, etc. song*** ◇ *We* ***sang a song*** *together.* ➲ COLLOCATIONS at MUSIC ➲ see also SWANSONG **2** 0-■ [U] songs in general; music for singing: *The story is told through song and dance.* ◇ *Suddenly he* ***burst into song*** (= started to sing). ➲ see also PLAINSONG **3** [U, C] the musical sounds that birds make: *the song of the blackbird*
IDM **for a 'song** (*informal*) very cheaply; at a low price **a song and 'dance (about sth) 1** (*BrE, informal, disapproving*) if you make a **song and dance** about sth, you complain or talk about it too much when this is not necessary **2** [C] (*NAmE, informal*) a long explanation about sth, or excuse for sth **on 'song** (*informal*) working or performing well ➲ more at SING *v.*

S

song·bird /ˈsɒŋbɜːd; *NAmE* ˈsɔːŋbɜːrd/ *noun* a bird that has a musical call, for example a BLACKBIRD or THRUSH

song·book /ˈsɒŋbʊk; *NAmE* ˈsɔːŋ-/ *noun* a book containing the music and words of different songs

song·smith /ˈsɒŋsmɪθ; *NAmE* ˈsɔːŋ-/ *noun* (*informal*) a person who writes popular songs

song·ster /ˈsɒŋstə(r); *NAmE* ˈsɔːŋ-/ *noun* (*old-fashioned*) **1** a word sometimes used in newspapers to mean 'singer' **2** a SONGBIRD

song·stress /ˈsɒŋstrəs; *NAmE* ˈsɔːŋ-/ *noun* a word sometimes used in newspapers to mean 'a woman singer'

song·writer /ˈsɒŋraɪtə(r); *NAmE* ˈsɔːŋ-/ *noun* a person who writes the words and usually also the music for songs: ***singer-songwriter** Paul Simon*

song·writ·ing /ˈsɒŋraɪtɪŋ; *NAmE* ˈsɔːŋ-/ *noun* [U] the process of writing songs

sonic /ˈsɒnɪk; *NAmE* ˈsɑːnɪk/ *adj.* (*technical*) connected with sound or the speed of sound: *sonic waves*

ˌsonic ˈboom *noun* the EXPLOSIVE sound that is made when an aircraft travels faster than the speed of sound

ˈson-in-law *noun* (*pl.* ˈsons-in-law) the husband of your daughter ➲ compare DAUGHTER-IN-LAW

son·net /ˈsɒnɪt; *NAmE* ˈsɑːnɪt/ *noun* a poem that has 14 lines, each containing 10 syllables, and a fixed pattern of RHYME: *Shakespeare's sonnets*

sonny /ˈsʌni/ *noun* [sing.] (*old-fashioned*) a word used by an older person to address a young man or boy

ˌson of a ˈbitch *noun* (*pl.* **sons of bitches**) (also **SOB** especially in *NAmE*) (*taboo, slang*) an offensive word for a person that you think is bad or very unpleasant: *I'll kill that son of a bitch when I get my hands on him!*

ˌson of a ˈgun *noun* (*NAmE, informal*) **1** a person or thing that you are annoyed with: *My car's at the shop—the son of a gun broke down again.* **2** used to express the fact that you are surprised or annoyed: *Well, son of a gun—and I thought the old guy couldn't dance!* **3** (*old-fashioned*) used by a man to address or talk about a male friend that he admires and likes: *Frank, you old son of a gun—I haven't seen you for months.*

son·or·ous /ˈsɒnərəs; *NAmE* ˈsɑːn-/ *adj.* (*formal*) having a pleasant full deep sound: *a sonorous voice* ▶ **son·or·ity** /səˈnɒrəti; *NAmE* -ˈnɔːr-/ *noun* [U, C]: *the rich sonority of the bass* **son·or·ous·ly** *adv.*

sook /suːk; sʊk/ *noun* (*informal, AustralE, NZE, CanE*) **1** a person who is not brave SYN **coward**, **crybaby** **2** a young cow that has been fed from a bottle, not by its mother

soon 0‑w /suːn/ *adv.* (soon·er, soon·est)
1 0‑w in a short time from now; a short time after sth else has happened: *We'll be home soon./We'll soon be home.* ◇ *She sold the house* ***soon after*** *her husband died.* ◇ *I soon realized the mistake.* ◇ *It soon became clear that the programme was a failure.* ◇ (*informal*) ***See you soon!*** **2** 0‑w early; quickly: ***How soon*** *can you get here?* ◇ *We'll deliver the goods* ***as soon as*** *we can.* ◇ *Please send it* ***as soon as possible.*** ◇ *Next Monday is* ***the soonest*** *we can deliver.* ◇ *They arrived home sooner than expected.* ◇ ***The sooner*** *we set off,* ***the sooner*** *we will arrive.* ◇ *The note said, 'Call Bill soonest'* (= as soon as possible). ◇ ***All too soon*** *the party was over.* ➲ see also ASAP

IDM **no sooner said than ˈdone** used to say that sth was, or will be, done immediately **no sooner... than...** 0‑w used to say that sth happens immediately after sth else: *No sooner had she said it than she burst into tears.* ➲ note at HARDLY **the ˌsooner the ˈbetter** very soon; as soon as possible: *'When shall I tell him?' 'The sooner the better.'* **ˌsooner or ˈlater** 0‑w at some time in the future, even if you are not sure exactly when: *Sooner or later you will have to make a decision.* **ˌsooner rather than ˈlater** after a short time rather than after a long time: *We urged them to sort out the problem sooner rather than later.* **I, etc. would sooner do sth (than sth else)** to prefer to do sth (than do sth else): *She'd sooner share a house with other students than live at home with her parents.* ➲ more at ANY TIME, JUST *adv.*, SAY *v.*

soot /sʊt/ *noun* [U] black powder that is produced when wood, coal, etc. is burnt ➲ see also SOOTY

soothe /suːð/ *verb* **1 ~ sb** to make sb who is anxious, upset, etc. feel calmer SYN **calm**: *The music soothed her for a while.* **2 ~ sth** to make a TENSE or painful part of your body feel more comfortable SYN **relieve**: *This should soothe the pain.* ◇ *Take a warm bath to soothe tense, tired muscles.* ▶ **sooth·ing** *adj.*: *a soothing voice/lotion* **sooth·ing·ly** *adv.*: *'There's no need to worry,' he said soothingly.*

PHR V **ˈsoothe sth↔away** to remove a pain or an unpleasant feeling

sooth·er /ˈsuːðə(r)/ *noun* (*CanE*) a specially shaped rubber or plastic object for a baby to suck SYN **dummy**

sooth·say·er /ˈsuːθseɪə(r)/ *noun* (*old use*) a person who is believed to be able to tell what will happen in the future

sooty /ˈsʊti/ *adj.* **1** covered with SOOT **2** of the colour of SOOT

sop /sɒp; *NAmE* sɑːp/ *noun* [usually sing.] **~ (to sb/sth)** a small, not very important, thing that is offered to sb who is angry or disappointed in order to make them feel better

soph·ist /ˈsɒfɪst; *NAmE* ˈsɑːf-/ *noun* **1** a teacher of philosophy in ancient Greece, especially one with an attitude of doubting that statements are true **2** a person who uses clever but wrong arguments

so·phis·ti·cate /səˈfɪstɪkeɪt/ *noun* (*formal*) a sophisticated person

so·phis·ti·cated /səˈfɪstɪkeɪtɪd/ *adj.* **1** having a lot of experience of the world and knowing about fashion, culture and other things that people think are socially important: *the sophisticated pleasures of city life* ◇ *Mark is a smart and sophisticated young man.* ➲ compare NAIVE **2** (of a machine, system, etc.) clever and complicated in the way that it works or is presented: *highly sophisticated computer systems* ◇ *Medical techniques are becoming more sophisticated all the time.* **3** (of a person) able to understand difficult or complicated ideas: *a sophisticated audience* OPP **unsophisticated**

so·phis·ti·ca·tion /səˌfɪstɪˈkeɪʃn/ *noun* [U] the quality of being sophisticated

soph·is·try /ˈsɒfɪstri; *NAmE* ˈsɑːf-/ *noun* (*pl.* **-ies**) (*formal*) **1** [U] the use of clever arguments to persuade people that sth is true when it is really false **2** [C] a reason or an explanation that tries to show that sth is true when it is really false

sopho·more /ˈsɒfəmɔː(r); *NAmE* ˈsɑːf-/ *noun* (*US*) **1** a student in the second year of a course of study at a college or university **2** a HIGH SCHOOL student in the 10th grade ➲ compare FRESHMAN, JUNIOR, SENIOR

sop·or·if·ic /ˌsɒpəˈrɪfɪk; *NAmE* ˌsɑːp-/ *adj.* (*formal*) making you want to go to sleep: *the soporific effect of the sun*

sop·ping /ˈsɒpɪŋ; *NAmE* ˈsɑːp-/ (also **ˌsopping ˈwet**) *adj.* (*informal*) very wet SYN **soaking**

soppy /ˈsɒpi; *NAmE* ˈsɑːpi/ (*especially BrE*) (**sop·pier**, **sop·pi·est**) (*NAmE* usually **sappy**) *adj.* (*informal*) silly and SENTIMENTAL; full of unnecessary emotion: *soppy love songs*

sop·rano /səˈprɑːnəʊ; *NAmE* səˈprɑːnoʊ; -ˈpræn-/ *noun*, *adj.*
■ ***noun*** (*pl.* -os /-nəʊz; *NAmE* -noʊz/) a singing voice with the highest range for a woman or boy; a singer with a soprano voice ➲ compare ALTO, MEZZO-SOPRANO, TREBLE
■ ***adj.*** [only before noun] (of a musical instrument) with the highest range of notes in its group: *a soprano saxophone* ➲ compare ALTO, BASS, TENOR

soˌprano reˈcorder (*NAmE*) (*BrE* **ˌdescant reˈcorder**) *noun* (*music*) the most common size of RECORDER (= a musical instrument in the shape of a pipe that you blow into), with a high range of notes

sor·bet /ˈsɔːbeɪ; *NAmE* ˈsɔːrbət/ (*BrE* also ˈ**water ice**) *noun* [C, U] a sweet frozen food made from sugar, water and fruit juice, often eaten as a DESSERT

S

sor·cer·er /ˈsɔːsərə(r); *NAmE* ˈsɔːrs-/ *noun* (in stories) a man with magic powers, who is helped by evil spirits

sor·cer·ess /ˈsɔːsərəs; *NAmE* ˈsɔːrs-/ *noun* (in stories) a woman with magic powers, who is helped by evil spirits

sor·cery /ˈsɔːsəri; *NAmE* ˈsɔːrs-/ *noun* [U] magic that uses evil spirits SYN **black magic**

sor·did /ˈsɔːdɪd; *NAmE* ˈsɔːrdɪd/ *adj.* **1** immoral or dishonest: *It was a shock to discover the truth about his sordid past.* ◇ *I didn't want to hear* **the sordid details** *of their relationship.* **2** very dirty and unpleasant SYN **squalid**: *people living in sordid conditions*

sore 0-ᵣ /sɔː(r)/ *adj., noun*

■ ***adj.*** **1** 0-ᵣ if a part of your body is **sore**, it is painful, and often red, especially because of infection or because a muscle has been used too much: *to have a sore throat* ◇ *His feet were sore after the walk.* ◇ *My stomach is still sore* (= painful) *after the operation.* ➲ SYNONYMS at PAINFUL **2** [not before noun] **~ (at sb/about sth)** (*informal, especially NAmE*) upset and angry, especially because you have been treated unfairly SYN **annoyed** ▶ **sore·ness** *noun* [U]: *an ointment to reduce soreness and swelling*

IDM **a ˌsore ˈpoint** a subject that makes you feel angry or upset when it is mentioned: *It's a sore point with Sue's parents that the children have not been baptized yet.* **stand/stick out like a sore ˈthumb** to be very noticeable in an unpleasant way ➲ more at BEAR *n.*, SIGHT *n.*

■ ***noun*** a painful, often red, place on your body where there is a wound or an infection SYN **wound**: *open sores* ➲ see also BEDSORE, CANKER SORE, COLD SORE

sore·ly /ˈsɔːli; *NAmE* ˈsɔːrli/ *adv.* seriously; very much: *I was* **sorely tempted** *to complain, but I didn't.* ◇ *If you don't come to the reunion you'll be* **sorely missed**.

sor·ghum /ˈsɔːgəm; *NAmE* ˈsɔːrgəm/ *noun* [U] very small grain grown as food in tropical countries; the plant that produces this grain

sor·or·ity /səˈrɒrəti; *NAmE* -ˈrɔːr-; -ˈrɑːr-/ *noun* (*pl.* -ies) (*NAmE*) a club for a group of women students at an American college or university ➲ compare FRATERNITY

sor·rel /ˈsɒrəl; *NAmE* ˈsɔːr-/ *noun* [U] a plant with leaves that taste bitter and are used in cooking as a HERB

sor·row /ˈsɒrəʊ; *NAmE* ˈsɑːroʊ/ *noun, verb*

■ ***noun*** **1** [U] **~ (at/for/over sth)** (*rather formal*) a feeling of great sadness because sth very bad has happened SYN **grief**: *He expressed his sorrow at the news of her death.* ◇ *They said that the decision was made* **more in sorrow than in anger**. **2** [C] a very sad event or situation: *the joys and sorrows of childhood*

■ ***verb*** [I] (*literary*) to feel or express great sadness: *the sorrowing relatives*

S

sor·row·ful /ˈsɒrəʊfl; *NAmE* ˈsɑːroʊ-/ *adj.* (*literary*) very sad: *her sorrowful eyes* ▶ **sor·row·ful·ly** /-fəli/ *adv.*

sorry 0-ᵣ /ˈsɒri; *NAmE* ˈsɑːri; ˈsɔːri/ *adj., exclamation*

■ ***adj.*** (**sor·rier, sor·ri·est**) HELP You can also use **more sorry** and **most sorry**. **1** 0-ᵣ [not before noun] feeling sad and sympathetic: **~ (that)...** *I'm sorry that your husband lost his job.* ◇ **~ (to see, hear, etc.)** *We're sorry to hear that your father's in hospital again.* ◇ **~ (about sth)** *No one is sorrier than I am about what happened.* **2** 0-ᵣ [not before noun] feeling sad and ashamed about sth that has been done: **~ (about sth)** *We're very sorry about the damage to your car.* ◇ **~ (for sth/doing sth)** *He says he's really sorry for taking the car without asking.* ◇ **~ (that)...** *She was sorry that she'd lost her temper.* ◇ *If you* **say you're sorry** *we'll forgive you.* **3** 0-ᵣ [not before noun] feeling disappointed about sth and wishing you had done sth different or had not done sth: **~ (that)...** *She was sorry that she'd lost contact with Mary.* ◇ *You'll be sorry if I catch you!* ◇ **~ to do sth** *I was genuinely sorry to be leaving college.* **4** [only before noun] very sad or bad, especially making you feel pity or disapproval: *The business is in a* **sorry state**. ◇ *They were a* **sorry sight** *when they eventually got off the boat.*

IDM **be/feel sorry for sb** 0-ᵣ to feel pity or sympathy for sb: *He decided to help Jan as he felt sorry for her.* **feel sorry for yourself** (*informal, disapproving*) to feel unhappy; to pity yourself: *Stop feeling sorry for yourself and think about other people for a change.* **I'm sorry 1** 0-ᵣ used when you are apologizing for sth: *I'm sorry, I forgot.* ◇ *Oh, I'm sorry. Have I taken the one you wanted?* ◇ *I'm sorry. I can't make it tomorrow.* **2** 0-ᵣ used for disagreeing with sb or politely saying 'no': *I'm sorry, I don't agree.* ◇ *I'm sorry, I'd rather you didn't go.* **3** 0-ᵣ used for introducing bad news: *I'm sorry to have to tell you you've failed.* **I'm ˈsorry to say** used for saying that sth is disappointing: *He didn't accept the job, I'm sorry to say.* ➲ more at SAFE *adj.*

■ ***exclamation*** **1** 0-ᵣ used when you are APOLOGIZING for sth: *Sorry I'm late!* ◇ *Did I stand on your foot? Sorry!* ◇ *Sorry to bother you, but could I speak to you for a moment?* ◇ *Sorry, we don't allow dogs in the house.* ◇ *He didn't even* **say sorry**. **2** 0-ᵣ (*especially BrE*) used for asking sb to repeat sth that you have not heard clearly: *Sorry? Could you repeat the question?* **3** 0-ᵣ used for correcting yourself when you have said sth wrong: *Take the first turning, sorry, the third turning on the right.*

sort 0-ᵣ /sɔːt; *NAmE* sɔːrt/ *noun, verb*

■ ***noun*** **1** 0-ᵣ [C] a group or type of people or things that are similar in a particular way SYN **kind**: *'***What sort of** *music do you like?' 'Oh,* **all sorts**.*'* ◇ **This sort of** *problem is quite common./***These sorts of** *problems are quite common.* ◇ *He's the sort of person who only cares about money.* ◇ *For dessert there's a fruit pie* **of some sort** (= you are not sure what kind). ◇ *Most people went on training courses* **of one sort or another** (= of various types) *last year.* ◇ (*informal*) *There were snacks—peanuts, olives,* **that sort of thing**. ◇ (*informal*) *There are* **all sorts of** *activities* (= many different ones) *for kids at the campsite.* ◇ (*informal*) **What sort of** *price did you want to pay?* (= approximately how much) ◇ (*informal*) **What sort of** *time do you call this?* (= I'm very angry that you have come so late.) ➲ note at KIND **2** [C, usually sing.] (*informal, especially BrE*) a particular type of person: *My brother would never cheat on his wife; he's not that sort.* **3** (*computing*) [sing.] the process of putting data in a particular order: *to do a sort*

IDM **it takes all sorts** (**to make a world**) (*saying*) used to say that you think sb's behaviour is very strange or unusual but that everyone is different and likes different things **of ˈsorts** (*informal*) used when you are saying that sth is not a good example of a particular type of thing: *He offered us an apology of sorts.* **out of ˈsorts** (*especially BrE*) ill/sick or upset: *She was tired and out of sorts by the time she arrived home.* **sort of** (*informal*) **1** 0-ᵣ to some extent but in a way that you cannot easily describe: *She sort of pretends that she doesn't really care.* ◇ *'Do you understand?' 'Sort of.'* **2** 0-ᵣ (also **sort of like**) (*BrE, informal*) used when you cannot think of a good word to use to describe sth, or what to say next: *We're sort of doing it the wrong way.* **a sort of sth** 0-ᵣ (*informal*) used for describing sth in a not very exact way: *I had a sort of feeling that he wouldn't come.* ◇ *They're a sort of greenish-blue colour.* ➲ more at KIND *n.*

■ ***verb*** **1** 0-ᵣ to arrange things in groups or in a particular order according to their type, etc; to separate things of one type from others: **~ sth** *sorting the mail* ◇ **~ sth into sth** *The computer sorts the words into alphabetical order.* ◇ *Rubbish can easily be separated and sorted into plastics, glass and paper.* ◇ **~ sth from sth** *Women and children sorted the ore from the rock.* ➲ see also SORT OUT **2** 0-ᵣ [often passive] **~ sth** (*informal, especially BrE*) to deal with a problem successfully or organize sth/sb properly: *I'm really busy—can you sort it?* ➲ compare SORTED *adj.* IDM see MAN *n.*, SHEEP, WHEAT

PHR V **ˌsort itself ˈout** (of a problem) to stop being a problem without anyone having to take action: *It will all sort itself out in the end.* **ˌsort sth↔ˈout 1** 0-ᵣ (*informal*) to organize the contents of sth; to tidy sth: *The cupboards need sorting out.* **2** to organize sth successfully: *If you're going to the bus station, can you sort out the tickets for tomorrow?* **ˌsort sth↔ˈout (from sth)** to separate sth from a larger group: *Could you sort out the toys that can be thrown away?* ➲ related noun SORT-OUT **ˌsort sth/sb/yourself ˈout** 0-ᵣ (*especially BrE*) to deal with sb's/your own problems successfully: *If you can wait a moment, I'll sort it all out for you.* ◇ *You load up the car and I'll sort the kids out.* **ˌsort sb↔ˈout** (*informal*) to deal with sb who is causing trouble, etc. especially by punishing or attacking them: *Wait till I get my hands on him—I'll soon sort him out!* **ˈsort through sth (for sth)** to look through a number of things, either in order to find sth or to put them in order: *I sorted through my paperwork.* ◇ *She sorted through her suitcase for something to wear.*

ˈsort code (*BrE*) (*US* **ˈrouting number**) *noun* a number that is used to identify a particular bank

sorted /ˈsɔːtɪd; *NAmE* ˈsɔːrt-/ *adj.* [not before noun] (*BrE, informal*) completed, solved or organized: *Don't worry. We'll soon have this sorted.* ◇ *It's our problem. We'll* ***get it sorted.*** ◇ *It's all sorted.* ◇ *It's time you* ***got yourself sorted.*** ➲ compare SORT *v.* (2)

sor·tie /ˈsɔːti; *NAmE* ˈsɔːrti/ *noun* **1** a flight that is made by an aircraft during military operations; an attack made by soldiers SYN **raid** **2** a short trip away from your home or the place where you are SYN **foray** **3 ~ into sth** an effort that you make to do or join sth new SYN **foray**: *His first sortie into politics was unsuccessful.*

ˈsorting office *noun* (*BrE*) a place where mail is sorted before being delivered

ˈsort-out *noun* (*BrE, informal*) an act of arranging or organizing the contents of sth in a tidy or neat way and removing things you do not want

SOS /ˌes əʊ ˈes; *NAmE* oʊ/ *noun* [sing.] **1** a signal or message that a ship or plane sends when it needs urgent help: *to send an SOS* ◇ *an SOS message* **2** an urgent request for help: *We've received an SOS from the area asking for food parcels.* ➲ see also MAYDAY

sosa·tie /səˈsɑːti/ *noun* (*SAfrE*) small pieces of meat or vegetables that are cooked on a stick, usually over an open fire SYN **kebab**

ˌso-ˈso *adj.* (*informal*) not particularly good or bad; average: *'How are you feeling today?' 'So-so.'* ▶ **ˌso-ˈso** *adv.*: *I only did so-so in the exam.*

sotto voce /ˌsɒtəʊ ˈvəʊtʃi; *NAmE* ˌsɑːtoʊ ˈvoʊ-/ *adv.* (from *Italian, formal*) in a quiet voice so that not everyone can hear ▶ **sotto voce** *adj.*

sou /suː/ *noun* [sing.] (*old-fashioned, BrE, informal*) if you do not have a **sou**, you have no money at all

sou·bri·quet /ˈsuːbrɪkeɪ/ *noun* = SOBRIQUET

souf·flé /ˈsuːfleɪ; *NAmE* suːˈfleɪ/ *noun* [C, U] a dish made from egg whites, milk and flour mixed together to make it light, flavoured with cheese, fruit, etc. and baked until it rises: *a cheese soufflé*

sough /saʊ; sʌf/ *verb* [I] (*literary*) (especially of the wind) to make a soft whistling sound

sought AW *past tense, past part.* of SEEK

ˈsought after *adj.* wanted by many people, because it is of very good quality or difficult to get or to find: *This design is the most sought after.* ◇ *a much sought-after actress*

souk /suːk/ *noun* a market in an Arab country

soul 0-w /səʊl; *NAmE* soʊl/ *noun*

▸ SPIRIT OF PERSON **1** 0-w [C] the spiritual part of a person, believed to exist after death: *He believed his immortal soul was in peril.* ◇ *The howling wind sounded like the wailing of lost souls* (= the spirits of dead people who are not in heaven). ➲ COLLOCATIONS at RELIGION

▸ INNER CHARACTER **2** 0-w [C] a person's inner character, containing their true thoughts and feelings: *There was a feeling of restlessness deep in her soul.*

▸ SPIRITUAL/MORAL/ARTISTIC QUALITIES **3** 0-w [sing.] the spiritual and moral qualities of humans in general SYN **psyche**: *the dark side of the human soul* **4** [U, C] strong and good human feeling, especially that gives a work of art its quality or enables sb to recognize and enjoy that quality: *It was a very polished performance, but it lacked soul.* **5** [sing.] **the ~ of sth** a perfect example of a good quality: *He is the soul of discretion.*

▸ PERSON **6** [C] (becoming *old-fashioned*) a person of a particular type: *She's lost all her money, poor soul.* ◇ *You're a brave soul.* **7** [C] (especially in negative sentences) a person: *There wasn't a soul in sight* (= nobody was in sight). ◇ *Don't tell a soul* (= do not tell anyone). ◇ (*literary*) *a village of 300 souls* (= with 300 people living there)

▸ MUSIC **8** (also ˈ**soul music**) [U] a type of music that expresses strong emotions, made popular by African American musicians: *a soul singer*

IDM **good for the ˈsoul** (*humorous*) good for you, even if it seems unpleasant: *'Want a ride?' 'No thanks. Walking is good for the soul.'* ➲ more at BARE *v.*, BODY, GOD, HEART, LIFE, SELL *v.*

ˈsoul-destroy·ing *adj.* (of a job or task) very dull and boring, because it has to be repeated many times or because there will never be any improvement

ˈsoul food *noun* [U] the type of food that was traditionally eaten by black people in the southern US

soul·ful /ˈsəʊlfl; *NAmE* ˈsoʊlfl/ *adj.* expressing deep feelings, especially feelings of sadness or love: *soulful eyes* ◇ *a soulful song* ▶ **soul·ful·ly** /-fəli/ *adv.* **soul·ful·ness** *noun* [U]

soul·less /ˈsəʊlləs; *NAmE* ˈsoʊl-/ *adj.* **1** (of things and places) lacking any attractive or interesting qualities that make people feel happy SYN **depressing**: *They live in soulless concrete blocks.* **2** (of a person) lacking the ability to feel emotions

soul·mate /ˈsəʊlmeɪt; *NAmE* ˈsoʊlmeɪt/ *noun* a person that you have a special friendship with because you understand each other's feelings and interests

ˈsoul music *noun* [U] = SOUL (8)

ˈsoul-searching *noun* [U] the careful examination of your thoughts and feelings, for example in order to reach the correct decision or solution to sth

sound 0-w /saʊnd/ *noun, verb, adj., adv.*

■ ***noun***

▸ STH YOU HEAR **1** 0-w [C] something that you can hear SYN **noise**: *a* ***high/low sound*** ◇ *a* ***clicking/buzzing/scratching, etc. sound*** ◇ *the different sounds and smells of the forest* ◇ *She heard the sound of footsteps outside.* ◇ *He crept into the house trying not to* ***make a sound.*** **2** 0-w [U] continuous rapid movements (called VIBRATIONS) that travel through air or water and can be heard when they reach a person's or an animal's ear: *Sound travels more slowly than light.* ➲ note at NOISE

▸ FROM TELEVISION/RADIO **3** 0-w [U] what you can hear coming from a television, radio, etc, or as part of a film/movie: *Could you* ***turn the sound up/down?*** ◇ *The* ***sound quality*** *of the tapes was excellent.*

▸ OF MUSICIANS **4** [C, U] the effect that is produced by the music of a particular singer or group of musicians: *I like their sound.*

▸ IMPRESSION **5** [sing.] **the ~ of sth** the idea or impression that you get of sb/sth from what sb says or what you read: *They had a wonderful time* ***by the sound of it.*** ◇ ***From the sound of things*** *you were lucky to find him.* ◇ *They're consulting a lawyer?* ***I don't like the sound of that.***

▸ WATER **6** [C] (often in place names) a narrow passage of water that joins two larger areas of water SYN **strait**

IDM **like, etc. the sound of your own ˈvoice** (*disapproving*) to like talking a lot or too much, usually without wanting to listen to other people **within (the) sound of sth** (*BrE*) near enough to be able to hear sth: *a house within sound of the sea*

■ ***verb*** (not usually used in the progressive tenses)

▸ GIVE IMPRESSION **1** 0-w *linking verb* to give a particular impression when heard or read about: **+ adj.** *His voice sounded strange on the phone.* ◇ *She didn't sound surprised when I told her the news.* ◇ *His explanation sounds reasonable to me.* ◇ *Leo* ***made it sound*** *so easy. But it wasn't.* ◇ **+ noun** *She sounds just the person we need for the job.* ◇ **~ like sb/sth** *You sounded just like your father when you said that.* ◇ **~ as if/as though...** *I hope I don't sound as if/as though I'm criticizing you.* HELP In spoken English people often use **like** instead of **as if** or **as though**, especially in *NAmE*, but this is not considered correct in written *BrE*.

▸ -SOUNDING **2** (in adjectives) giving the impression of having a particular sound: *an Italian-sounding name* ◇ *fine-sounding words*

▸ PRODUCE SOUND **3** [I, T] to produce a sound; to make sth

S

such as a musical instrument produce a sound: *The bell sounded for the end of the class.* ◇ (*BrE*) **~ sth** *Passing motorists sounded their horns in support.*
▸ GIVE WARNING/SIGNAL **4** 🔑 [T] **~ sth** to give a signal such as a warning by making a sound: *When I saw the smoke, I tried to* ***sound the alarm.*** ◇ (*figurative*) *Scientists have* ***sounded a note of caution*** *on the technique.* ◇ *Leaving him out of the team may* ***sound the death knell*** *for our chances of winning* (= signal the end of our chances).
▸ PRONOUNCE **5** [T] **~ sth** (*technical*) to pronounce sth: *You don't sound the 'b' in the word 'comb'.*
▸ MEASURE DEPTH **6** [T, I] **~ (sth)** (*technical*) to measure the depth of the sea or a lake by using a line with a weight attached, or an electronic instrument
IDM **(it) ˌsounds like a plan to ˈme** (*especially NAmE*) used to agree to a suggestion that you think is good ➲ more at NOTE *n.*, SUSPICIOUSLY
PHR V **ˌsound ˈoff (about sth)** (*informal, disapproving*) to express your opinions loudly or in an aggressive way **ˌsound sb↔ˈout (about/on sth)** | **ˌsound sth↔ˈout** to try to find out from sb what they think about sth, often in an indirect way: *I wanted to sound him out about a job.* ◇ *They decided to sound out her interest in the project.*
■ ***adj.*** (sound·er, sound·est)
▸ RELIABLE **1** sensible; that you can rely on and that will probably give good results: *a person of sound judgement* ◇ *He gave me some very sound advice.* ◇ *This gives the design team a sound basis for their work.* ◇ *The proposal makes sound commercial sense.* ◇ *Their policies are environmentally sound.* OPP **unsound**
▸ THOROUGH **2** [only before noun] good and thorough: *a sound knowledge/understanding of sth* ◇ *He has* ***a sound grasp of*** *the issues.*
▸ NOT DAMAGED/HURT **3** in good condition; not damaged, hurt, etc: *We arrived home* ***safe and sound.*** ◇ *to be* ***of sound mind*** (= not mentally ill) ◇ *The house needs attention but the roof is sound.* OPP **unsound**
▸ SLEEP **4** [usually before noun] deep and peaceful: *to have a sound night's sleep* ◇ *to be a* ***sound sleeper***
▸ GOOD, BUT NOT EXCELLENT **5** good and accurate, but not excellent: *a sound piece of writing* ◇ *a sound tennis player*
▸ PHYSICAL PUNISHMENT **6** severe: *to give sb a sound beating*
▸ **sound·ness** *noun* [U]: *soundness of judgement* ◇ *financial soundness* ◇ *the soundness of the building's foundations* ➲ see also SOUNDLY
IDM **(as) sound as a ˈbell** (*informal*) in perfect condition
■ ***adv.*** **~ asleep** very deeply asleep

sound·alike /ˈsaʊndəlaɪk/ *noun* a person who sounds very similar to sb who is famous

S

the ˈsound barrier *noun* [sing.] the point at which an aircraft's speed is the same as the speed of sound, causing reduced control, a very loud noise (called a SONIC BOOM) and various other effects: *to break the sound barrier* (= to travel faster than the speed of sound)

ˈsound bite *noun* a short phrase or sentence taken from a longer speech, especially a speech made by a politician, that is considered to be particularly effective or appropriate

ˈsound card *noun* (*computing*) a device that can be put into a computer to allow the use of sound with MULTIMEDIA software

sound·check /ˈsaʊndtʃek/ *noun* a process of checking that the equipment used for recording music, or for playing music at a concert, is working correctly and producing sound of a good quality

ˈsound effect *noun* [usually pl.] a sound that is made artificially, for example the sound of the wind or a battle, and used in a film/movie, play, computer game, etc. to make it more realistic

ˈsound engineer *noun* a person who works in a recording or broadcasting studio and whose job is to control the levels and balance of sound

sound·ing /ˈsaʊndɪŋ/ *noun* **1 soundings** [pl.] careful questions that are asked in order to find out people's opinions about sth: *They will* ***take soundings*** *among party members.* ◇ *What do your soundings show?* **2** [C] a measurement that is made to find out how deep water is: *They* ***took soundings*** *along the canal.*

ˈsounding board *noun* a person or group of people that you discuss your ideas with before you make them known or reach a decision

sound·less /ˈsaʊndləs/ *adj.* without making any sound; silent: *Her lips parted in a soundless scream.* ▸ **sound·less·ly** *adv.*

sound·ly /ˈsaʊndli/ *adv.* **1** if you sleep **soundly**, you sleep very well and very deeply **2** in a way that is sensible or can be relied on: *a soundly based conclusion* **3** completely and thoroughly: *The team was soundly defeated.* **4** strongly; firmly: *These houses are soundly built.* **5** very well, but not in an excellent way: *He played soundly.* **6** (of physical punishment) severely: *He was soundly beaten by his mother.*

sound·proof /ˈsaʊndpruːf/ (also **sound·proofed**) *adj.* made so that sound cannot pass through it or into it: *a soundproof room* ▸ **sound·proof** *verb* **~ sth**

ˈsound stage *noun* a platform or a special area where sound can be recorded, for example for a film/movie

ˈsound system *noun* equipment for playing recorded or live music and for making it louder

sound·track /ˈsaʊndtræk/ *noun* **1** all the music, speech and sounds that are recorded for a film/movie: *The soundtrack of 'Casablanca' took weeks to edit.* **2** some of the music, and sometimes some speech, from a film/movie or musical that is released on CD, the Internet, etc. for people to buy: *I've just bought the soundtrack of the latest Miyazaki movie.* ➲ COLLOCATIONS at CINEMA

ˈsound wave *noun* a VIBRATION in the air, in water, etc. that we hear as sound

soup 🔑 /suːp/ *noun, verb*
■ ***noun*** 🔑 [U, C] a liquid food made by boiling meat, vegetables, etc. in water, often eaten as the first course of a meal: *a bowl of soup* ◇ *chicken soup* ◇ (*BrE*) ***tinned/packet soups*** ◇ (*NAmE*) ***canned/packaged soups*** ◇ ***a soup spoon/plate*** ➲ VISUAL VOCAB page V19
IDM **from ˌsoup to ˈnuts** (*NAmE, informal*) from beginning to end: *She told me the whole story from soup to nuts.* **in the ˈsoup** (*informal*) in trouble: *We're all in the soup now.*
■ ***verb***
PHR V **ˌsoup sth↔ˈup** (*informal*) to make changes to sth such as a car or computer, so that it is more powerful or exciting than before

soup·çon /ˈsuːpsɒn; *NAmE* ˈ-sɑːn/ *noun* [sing.] (from *French*, sometimes *humorous*) a very small amount

ˈsoup kitchen *noun* a place where people who have no money can get soup and other food free

soupy /ˈsuːpi/ *adj.* **1** similar to soup: *a soupy stew* **2** (of the air) very damp and unpleasant **3** (*informal*) emotional in a way that is exaggerated and embarrassing

sour 🔑 /ˈsaʊə(r)/ *adj., verb*
■ ***adj.*** **1** 🔑 having a taste like that of a lemon or of fruit that is not ready to eat: *sour apples* ◇ *a sour flavour* OPP **sweet** ➲ see also SWEET-AND-SOUR ➲ SYNONYMS at BITTER **2** 🔑 (especially of milk) having an unpleasant taste or smell because it is not fresh: *to* ***turn/go sour*** ➲ SYNONYMS at BITTER **3** (of people) not cheerful; bad-tempered and unpleasant: *a sour and disillusioned woman* ◇ *a sour face* ◇ *The meeting ended on a* ***sour note*** *with several people walking out.* ▸ **sour·ly** *adv.*: *'Who asked you?' he said sourly.* **sour·ness** *noun* [U]
IDM **go/turn ˈsour** to stop being pleasant or working properly: *Their relationship soon went sour.* **sour ˈgrapes** (*saying*) used to show that you think sb is jealous and is pretending that sth is not important: *He said he didn't want the job anyway, but that's just sour grapes.*
■ ***verb*** **1** [I, T] (of relationships, attitudes, people, etc.) to change so that they become less pleasant or friendly than before; to make sth do this: *The atmosphere at the house soured.* ◇ **~ sth** *The disagreement over trade tariffs has soured relations between the two countries.* **2** [I, T] **~ (sth)** if milk **sours** or if sth **sours** it, it becomes sour and has an unpleasant taste or smell

source 0-ᴛ AW /sɔːs; *NAmE* sɔːrs/ *noun, verb*
■ ***noun* 1** 0-ᴛ a place, person or thing that you get sth from: *renewable **energy sources** ◇ Your local library will be a useful **source of** information. ◇ What is their main source of income?* **2** 0-ᴛ [usually pl.] a person, book or document that provides information, especially for study, a piece of written work or news: *He refused to name his sources. ◇ Government sources indicated yesterday that cuts may have to be made. ◇ source material ◇ Historians use a wide range of **primary and secondary sources** for their research.* **3** 0-ᴛ a person or thing that causes sth, especially a problem: *a source of violence ◇ a source of confusion* **4** the place where a river or stream starts: *the source of the Nile* ➲ VISUAL VOCAB page V4
IDM **at 'source** at the place or the point that sth comes from or begins: *Is your salary taxed at source* (= by your employer)*?*
■ ***verb*** [often passive] **~ sth (from...)** (*business*) to get sth from a particular place: *We source all the meat sold in our stores from British farms.* ➲ see also OUTSOURCE

source·book /'sɔːsbʊk; *NAmE* 'sɔːrs-/ *noun* a collection of texts on a particular subject, used especially as an introduction to the subject

'source code *noun* [U] (*computing*) a computer program written in text form that must be translated into MACHINE CODE before it can run on a computer

,sour 'cream (*BrE* also **,soured 'cream**) *noun* [U] cream that has been made sour by adding bacteria to it, used in cooking

sour·dough /'saʊədəʊ; *NAmE* 'saʊərdoʊ/ *noun* [U] DOUGH (= a mixture of flour, fat and water) that is left to FERMENT so that it has a sour taste, used for making bread; bread made with this DOUGH

'sour-faced *adj.* [usually before noun] (of a person) having a bad-tempered or unpleasant expression

sour·puss /'saʊəpʊs; *NAmE* 'saʊərpʊs/ *noun* (*informal*) a person who is not cheerful or pleasant

sousa·phone /'suːzəfəʊn; *NAmE* -foʊn/ *noun* a BRASS instrument like a TUBA, used in marching bands in the US

souse /saʊs/ *verb* **~ sth/sb** [usually passive] to SOAK sth/sb completely in a liquid

soused /saʊst/ *adj.* **1** [only before noun] (of fish) preserved in salt water and VINEGAR: *soused herring* **2** (*old-fashioned, informal*) drunk

south 0-ᴛ /saʊθ/ *noun, adj., adv.*
■ ***noun*** [U, sing.] (*abbr.* S, So.) **1** 0-ᴛ (usually **the south**) the direction that is on your right when you watch the sun rise; one of the four main points of the COMPASS: *Which way is south? ◇ warmer weather coming from the south ◇ He lives **to the south of*** (= further south than) *the city.* ➲ picture at COMPASS ➲ compare EAST, NORTH, WEST **2** 0-ᴛ **the south, the South** the southern part of a country, a region or the world: *birds flying to the south for the winter ◇ They bought a villa in the South of France. ◇ Houses are less expensive in the North than in the South* (= of England). **3 the South** the southern states of the US ➲ see also THE DEEP SOUTH **4 the South** the poorer countries in the southern half of the world
■ ***adj.*** (*abbr.* S, So.) [only before noun] **1** 0-ᴛ in or towards the south: *South Wales ◇ They live on the south coast.* **2** 0-ᴛ a **south wind** blows from the south ➲ compare SOUTHERLY
■ ***adv.* 1** 0-ᴛ towards the south: *This room faces south.* **2 ~ of sth** nearer to the south than sth: *They live ten miles south of Bristol.* **3 ~ of sth** (*informal, NAmE* or *finance*) less or lower than sth: *The drug is achieving revenues just south of $1 billion per quarter.* OPP **north**
IDM **down 'south** (*informal*) to or in the south, especially of England: *They've gone to live down south.*

,South A'merica *noun* [U] the continent which is to the south of Central America and N America ➲ compare LATIN AMERICA

south·bound /'saʊθbaʊnd/ *adj.* travelling or leading towards the south: *southbound traffic ◇ the southbound carriageway of the motorway*

the ,South-'East *noun* (*BrE*) the south-eastern part of England which is the richest part of the country and has the highest population

,south-'east *noun* (usually **the south-east**) [sing.] (*abbr.* SE) the direction or region at an equal distance between south and east ➲ picture at COMPASS ▶ **,south-'east** *adv., adj.*

,south-'easter·ly *adj.* **1** [only before noun] in or towards the south-east **2** [usually before noun] (of winds) blowing from the south-east

,south-'eastern *adj.* [only before noun] (*abbr.* SE) connected with the south-east

,south-'eastwards (also **,south-'eastward**) *adv.* towards the south-east ▶ **,south-'eastward** *adj.*

south·er·ly /'sʌðəli; *NAmE* -ərli/ *adj., noun*
■ ***adj.* 1** [only before noun] in or towards the south: *travelling in a southerly direction* **2** [usually before noun] (of winds) blowing from the south: *a warm southerly breeze* ➲ compare SOUTH
■ ***noun*** (*pl.* -ies) a wind that blows from the south

south·ern 0-ᴛ /'sʌðən; *NAmE* -ərn/ (also **Southern**) *adj.* (*abbr.* S) [usually before noun]
located in the south or facing south; connected with or typical of the south part of the world or a region: *the southern slopes of the mountains ◇ southern Spain ◇ a southern accent*

,southern 'belle *noun* (*old-fashioned, NAmE*) a young attractive woman from the southern US

the ,Southern 'Cone *noun* [sing.] the region of S America which consists of Brazil, Paraguay, Uruguay, Argentina and Chile

the ,Southern 'Cross *noun* [sing.] a group of stars in the shape of a cross that can be seen from the southern HEMISPHERE

south·ern·er /'sʌðənə(r); *NAmE* -ərn-/ *noun* a person who comes from or lives in the southern part of a country

the ,Southern 'Lights *noun* [pl.] (also **aur·ora aus·tra·lis**) bands of coloured light that are sometimes seen in the sky at night in the most southern countries of the world

south·ern·most /'sʌðənməʊst; *NAmE* -ərnmoʊst/ *adj.* [usually before noun] furthest south: *the southernmost part of the island*

south·paw /'saʊθpɔː/ *noun* (*informal, especially NAmE*) a person who prefers to use their left hand rather than their right, especially in a sport such as BOXING

the ,South 'Pole *noun* [sing.] the point of the earth that is furthest south ➲ VISUAL VOCAB page V59

,south-south-'east *noun* [sing.] (*abbr.* SSE) the direction at an equal distance between south and south-east ▶ **,south-south-'east** *adv.*

,south-south-'west *noun* [sing.] (*abbr.* SSW) the direction at an equal distance between south and south-west ▶ **,south-south-'west** *adv.*

south·wards /'saʊθwədz; *NAmE* -wərdz/ (also **south·ward**) *adv.* towards the south: *to turn southwards* ▶ **south·ward** *adj.*: *in a southward direction*

,south-'west *noun* (usually **the south-west**) [sing.] (*abbr.* SW) the direction or region at an equal distance between south and west ➲ picture at COMPASS ▶ **,south-'west** *adv., adj.*

,south-'wester·ly *adj.* **1** [only before noun] in or towards the south-west **2** [usually before noun] (of winds) blowing from the south-west

,south-'western *adj.* [only before noun] (*abbr.* SW) connected with the south-west

,south-'westwards (also **,south-'westward**) *adv.* towards the south-west ▶ **,south-'westward** *adj.*

sou·venir /,suːvə'nɪə(r); *NAmE* -'nɪr; 'suːvənɪr/ *noun* a thing that you buy and/or keep to remind yourself of a

S

place, an occasion or a holiday/vacation; something that you bring back for other people when you have been on holiday/vacation SYN **memento**: *I bought the ring **as a souvenir of** Greece.* ◇ *a **souvenir shop*** ➲ COLLOCATIONS at TRAVEL

souv·la·ki /suː'vlæki/ *noun* [U, C] a Greek dish consisting of pieces of meat cooked on sticks

sou'·wester /ˌsaʊ'westə(r)/ *noun* **1** a hat made of shiny material that keeps out the rain, with a long wide piece at the back to protect the neck ➲ VISUAL VOCAB page V53 **2** a strong wind or storm coming from the south-west

sov·er·eign /'sɒvrɪn; *NAmE* 'sɑːvrən/ *noun, adj.*
▪ ***noun* 1** (*formal*) a king or queen **2** an old British gold coin worth one pound
▪ ***adj.*** (*formal*) **1** [only before noun] (of a country or state) free to govern itself; completely independent SYN **autonomous 2** having complete power or the greatest power in the country: *a sovereign ruler*

sov·er·eign·ty /'sɒvrənti; *NAmE* 'sɑːv-/ *noun* [U] (*formal*) **1 ~ (over sth)** complete power to govern a country: *The country claimed sovereignty over the island.* ◇ *the sovereignty of Parliament* ◇ (*figurative*) *the idea of consumer sovereignty* **2** the state of being a country with freedom to govern itself: *The declaration proclaimed the **full sovereignty** of the republic.* ➲ COLLOCATIONS at INTERNATIONAL

So·viet /'səʊviət; 'sɒv-; *NAmE* 'soʊviet; 'sɑːv-/ *adj.* [usually before noun] connected with the former USSR

so·viet /'səʊviət; 'sɒv-; *NAmE* 'soʊviet; 'sɑːv-/ *noun* **1** [C] an elected local, district or national council in the former USSR **2 the Soviets** [pl.] (*especially NAmE*) the people of the former USSR

sow[1] /səʊ; *NAmE* soʊ/ *verb* ➲ see also SOW[2] (**sowed, sown** /səʊn; *NAmE* soʊn/ or **sowed, sowed**) **1** [T, I] to plant or spread seeds in or on the ground: **~ (sth)** *Sow the seeds in rows.* ◇ *Water well after sowing.* ◇ **~ sth with sth** *The fields around had been sown with wheat.* ➲ COLLOCATIONS at FARMING **2** [T] **~ sth (in sth)** to introduce or spread feelings or ideas, especially ones that cause trouble: *to sow doubt in sb's mind* ◇ *to sow confusion*

IDM **sow the seeds of sth** to start the process that leads to a particular situation or result **sow (your) wild 'oats** (of young men) to go through a period of wild behaviour while young, especially having a lot of romantic or sexual relationships ➲ more at REAP

sow[2] /saʊ/ *noun* a female pig ➲ compare BOAR, HOG ➲ see also SOW[1] IDM see SILK

sower /'səʊə(r); *NAmE* 'soʊ-/ *noun* a person or machine that puts seeds in the ground

soya /'sɔɪə/ (*BrE*) (*NAmE* **soy**) *noun* [U] the plant on which soya beans grow; the food obtained from soya beans: *a soya crop* ◇ *soya flour*

'soya bean (*BrE*) (*NAmE* **soy·bean** /'sɔɪ biːn/) *noun* a type of BEAN, originally from SE Asia, that is used instead of meat or animal PROTEIN in some types of food

'soya milk *noun* [U] a liquid made from soya beans, used instead of milk

soy sauce /ˌsɔɪ 'sɔːs/ (also ˌ**soya 'sauce**) *noun* [U] a thin dark brown sauce that is made from soya beans and has a salty taste, used in Chinese and Japanese cooking

soz·zled /'sɒzld; *NAmE* 'sɑːzld/ *adj.* (*BrE, slang*) very drunk

spa /spɑː/ *noun* **1** a place where water with minerals in it, which is considered to be good for your health, comes up naturally out of the ground; the name given to a town that has such a place and where there are, or were, places where people could drink the water: *Leamington Spa* ◇ *a spa town* ◇ *spa waters* **2** a place where people can relax and improve their health, with, for example, a swimming pool: *a superb **health spa** which includes sauna, Turkish bath and fitness rooms* **3** (*especially NAmE*) = JACUZZI

space 0-ᴛ /speɪs/ *noun, verb*
▪ ***noun***
▸ EMPTY AREA **1** 0-ᴛ [U] an amount of an area or of a place that is empty or that is available for use SYN **room**: ***floor/office/shelf, etc. space*** ◇ *We must make good use of the available space.* ◇ *That desk **takes up** too much **space**.* ◇ *There is very little **storage space** in the department.* ◇ *Can we **make space** for an extra chair?* ◇ *How much **disk space** will it take up?* (= on a computer) **2** 0-ᴛ [C] an area or a place that is empty: *a large/small/narrow/wide space* ◇ *a space two metres by three metres* ◇ *a **parking space*** ◇ *crowded together in a confined space* ◇ *I'll clear a space for your books.* ◇ *Put it in the space between the table and the wall.* **3** 0-ᴛ [U] the quality of being large and empty, allowing you to move freely SYN **spaciousness**: *The room has been furnished and decorated to give a feeling of space.* **4** 0-ᴛ [C, U] a large area of land that has no buildings on it: *the **wide open spaces** of the Canadian prairies* ◇ *It's a city with fine buildings and plenty of **open space**.* ➲ SYNONYMS at LAND
▸ OUTSIDE EARTH'S ATMOSPHERE **5** 0-ᴛ (also ˌ**outer 'space**) [U] the area outside the earth's atmosphere where all the other planets and stars are: *the first woman in space* ◇ *the possibility of visitors from **outer space*** ◇ *a space flight/mission*
▸ PERIOD OF TIME **6** [C, usually sing.] a period of time: *Forty-four people died **in the space of** five days.* ◇ *They had achieved a lot **in a short space of time**.* ◇ *Leave a space of two weeks between appointments.*
▸ IN WRITING/PRINTING **7** [U, C] the part of a line, page or document that is empty: *Don't waste space by leaving a wide margin.* ◇ *There was not enough space to print all the letters we received.* ◇ *Leave a space after the comma.*
▸ FREEDOM **8** [U] the freedom and the time to think or do what you want to: *She was upset and **needed space**.* ◇ *You have to **give** teenagers plenty of **space**.* ➲ see also BREATHING SPACE
▸ WHERE THINGS EXIST/MOVE **9** [U] the whole area in which all things exist and move: *It is quite possible that space and time are finite.*

IDM **look/stare/gaze into 'space** to look straight in front of you without looking at a particular thing, usually because you are thinking about sth ➲ more at WASTE *n.*, WATCH *v.*

▪ ***verb*** [often passive] **~ sth (+ adv./prep.)** to arrange things so that they have regular spaces between them: ***evenly spaced** plants* ◇ *a row of **closely spaced** dots* ◇ *Space the posts about a metre apart.*

PHR V ˌ**space 'out** (*informal, especially NAmE*) to take no notice of what is happening around you, especially as a result of taking drugs ➲ see also SPACED OUT ˌ**space sth↔'out** to arrange things with a wide space between them: *The houses are spaced out in this area of town.*

'space-age *adj.* [usually before noun] (*informal*) (especially of design or technology) very modern and advanced: *a space-age kitchen*

'space bar *noun* a bar on the keyboard of a computer or TYPEWRITER that you press to make spaces between words ➲ VISUAL VOCAB page V54

'space cadet *noun* (*slang*) a person who behaves strangely and often forgets things, as though he or she is using drugs

space·craft /'speɪskrɑːft; *NAmE* -kræft/ *noun* (*pl.* **spacecraft**) a vehicle that travels in space

ˌ**spaced 'out** (also **spacey**) *adj.* (*informal*) not completely conscious of what is happening around you, often because of taking drugs

'space heater *noun* (*NAmE*) an electric device for heating a room

space·man /'speɪsmæn/ *noun* (*pl.* **-men** /-men/) **1** (*informal*) a man who travels into space; an ASTRONAUT **2** (in stories) a creature that visits the earth from another planet SYN **alien** ➲ see also SPACEWOMAN

'space probe *noun* = PROBE

the 'space race *noun* competition between the US and the Soviet Union in the 1950s and 60s to be the first to explore space

space·ship /'speɪsʃɪp/ *noun* a vehicle that travels in space, carrying people

S

ˈspace shuttle (also **shuttle**) *noun* a SPACECRAFT designed to be used, for example, for travelling between the earth and a space station

ˈspace station *noun* a large structure that is sent into space and remains above the earth as a base for people working and travelling in space

space·suit /ˈspeɪssuːt; *BrE* also -sjuːt/ *noun* a special suit that covers the whole body and has a supply of air, allowing sb to survive and move around in space

ˈspace-time *noun* [U] (*physics*) the universe considered as a CONTINUUM with four measurements—length, width, depth and time—inside which any event or physical object is located

space·walk /ˈspeɪswɔːk/ *noun* a period of time that an ASTRONAUT spends in space outside a SPACECRAFT

space·woman /ˈspeɪswʊmən/ *noun* (*pl.* -women /-wɪmɪn/) a woman who travels into space

spacey /ˈspeɪsi/ *adj.* = SPACED OUT

spa·cial = SPATIAL

spa·cing /ˈspeɪsɪŋ/ *noun* [U] **1** the amount of space that is left between things, especially between the words or lines printed on a page: ***single/double spacing*** (= with one or two lines left between lines of type) **2** the amount of time that is left between things happening

spa·cious /ˈspeɪʃəs/ *adj.* (*approving*) (of a room or building) large and with plenty of space for people to move around in SYN **roomy** ▸ **spa·cious·ly** *adv.* **spa·cious·ness** *noun* [U]: *White walls can give a feeling of spaciousness.*

spade /speɪd/ *noun* **1** [C] a garden tool with a broad metal blade and a long handle, used for digging: *Turn the soil over with a spade.* ◇ (*BrE*) *The children took their **buckets and spades** to the beach.* ➲ VISUAL VOCAB page V16 ➲ compare SHOVEL **2 spades** [pl., U] one of the four sets of cards (called SUITS) in a PACK/DECK of cards. The cards have a black design shaped like pointed leaves with short STEMS: *the five/queen/ace of spades* ➲ VISUAL VOCAB page V32 **3** [C] a card from the set of spades: *You must play a spade if you have one.* **4** [C] (*taboo, slang*) an offensive word for a black person

IDM **in ˈspades** (*informal*) in large amounts or to a great degree: *He'd got his revenge now, and in spades.* ➲ more at CALL *v.*

spade·work /ˈspeɪdwɜːk; *NAmE* -wɜːrk/ *noun* [U] the hard work that has to be done in order to prepare for sth

spa·ghetti /spəˈɡeti/ *noun* [U] PASTA in the shape of long thin pieces that look like string when they are cooked

spa·ghetti bol·ognese (also **spa·ghetti bol·ognaise**) /spəˌɡeti ˌbɒləˈneɪz; *NAmE* ˌboʊlənˈjeɪz/ *noun* [U, C] a dish of spaghetti with a sauce of meat, tomatoes, etc.

spaˌghetti ˈwestern *noun* a film/movie about COWBOYS, made in Europe by Italian companies

spake /speɪk/ (*old use*) *past tense* of SPEAK

spam /spæm/ *noun* [U] **1 Spam™** finely chopped cooked meat that has been pressed together in a container, usually sold in cans and served cold in slices **2** (*informal*) advertising material sent by email to people who have not asked for it ➲ COLLOCATIONS at EMAIL ➲ compare JUNK MAIL, SPIM

spam·ming /ˈspæmɪŋ/ *noun* [U] (*informal*) the practice of sending mail, especially advertising material, through the Internet to a large number of people who have not asked for it ▸ **spam·mer** /ˈspæmə(r)/ *noun*

span /spæn/ *noun, verb, adj.*

■ ***noun*** **1** the length of time that sth lasts or is able to continue: *I worked with him over a span of six years.* ◇ *The project must be completed within a specific **time span**.* ◇ *Small children have a short **attention span**.* ➲ see also LIFESPAN **2 ~ (of sth)** a range or variety of sth: *Managers have a **wide span of** control.* ◇ *These forests cover a broad span of latitudes.* **3** the part of a bridge or an ARCH between one vertical support and another: *The bridge crosses the river in a single span.* **4** the width of sth from one side to the other: *The kite has a span of 1.5 metres.* ➲ see also WINGSPAN

■ ***verb*** (-nn-) **1 ~ sth** to last all through a period of time or to cover the whole of it: *His acting career spanned 55 years.* ◇ *Family photos spanning five generations were stolen.* **2 ~ sth** to include a large area or a lot of things: *The operation, which spanned nine countries, resulted in 200 arrests.* **3 ~ sth** to stretch right across sth, from one side to the other SYN **cross**: *a series of bridges spanning the river*

■ ***adj.*** IDM see SPICK

span·dex /ˈspændeks/ *noun* = LYCRA

span·gle /ˈspæŋɡl/ *verb, noun*

■ ***verb*** [usually passive] **~ sth (with sth)** to cover or to decorate sth with small pieces of sth shiny ➲ see also STAR-SPANGLED BANNER

■ ***noun*** a small piece of shiny metal or plastic used to decorate clothes SYN **sequin**

Spang·lish /ˈspæŋɡlɪʃ/ *noun* [U] (*informal*) language which is a mixture of Spanish and English, especially a type of Spanish that includes many English words

span·iel /ˈspænjəl/ *noun* a dog with large soft ears that hang down. There are several types of spaniel.

Span·ish /ˈspænɪʃ/ *adj., noun*

■ ***adj.*** from or connected with Spain

■ ***noun*** [U] the language of Spain and of most countries in Central and S America

ˌSpanish ˈfly *noun* (*pl.* ˌSpanish ˈflies) **1** [C] a bright green insect that has a strong smell and produces a harmful substance **2** [U] a poisonous mixture made from the crushed bodies of these insects, that is said to give people a strong desire to have sex

the ˌSpanish Inquiˈsition *noun* [sing.] **1** the organization set up by the Roman Catholic Church in Spain in the 15th century to punish people who opposed its beliefs, known for its cruel and severe methods **2** (often *humorous*) used to say that you do not like the fact that sb is questioning you a lot about sth: *What is this? The Spanish Inquisition?*

ˌSpanish ˈmoss *noun* [U] a tropical American plant that has long thin grey leaves and that grows over trees

spank /spæŋk/ *verb* **~ sb/sth** to hit sb, especially a child, several times on their bottom as a punishment ➲ compare SMACK ▸ **spank** *noun*

spank·ing /ˈspæŋkɪŋ/ *noun, adv., adj.*

■ ***noun*** [C, U] a series of hits on the bottom, given to sb, especially a child, as a punishment: *to give sb a spanking* ◇ *I don't agree with spanking.*

■ ***adv.*** (*informal*) when you say that sth is **spanking** new, etc. you are emphasizing that it is very new, etc.

■ ***adj.*** [only before noun] (*informal*) very fast, good or impressive: *The horse set off **at a spanking pace**.*

span·ner /ˈspænə(r)/ (*BrE*) (also **wrench** *NAmE, BrE*) *noun* a metal tool with a specially shaped end for holding and turning NUTS and BOLTS (= small metal rings and pins that hold things together) ➲ VISUAL VOCAB page V17 ➲ compare ADJUSTABLE SPANNER

IDM **(throw) a ˈspanner in the works** (*BrE*) (*NAmE* **(throw) a (ˈmonkey) ˈwrench in the works**) (to cause) a delay or problem with sth that sb is planning or doing

spar /spɑː(r)/ *verb, noun*

■ ***verb*** (-rr-) **1** [I] **~ (with sb)** to make the movements used in BOXING, either in training or to test the speed of your opponent's reaction **2** [I] **~ (with sb)** to argue with sb, usually in a friendly way

■ ***noun*** **1** a strong pole used to support the sails, etc. on a ship **2** a structure that supports the wing of an aircraft

spare 0→ /speə(r); *NAmE* sper/ *adj., verb, noun*

■ ***adj.***

▸ NOT USED/NEEDED **1** 0→ [usually before noun] that is not being used or is not needed at the present time: *We've got a spare bedroom, if you'd like to stay.* ◇ *I'm afraid I haven't got any **spare cash**.* ◇ *Are there any tickets **going spare** (= are there any available, not being used by sb else)?*

▸ EXTRA **2** 0→ [only before noun] kept in case you need to replace the one you usually use; extra: *a spare key/tyre* ◇ *Take some spare clothes in case you get wet.*

S

▸ TIME **3** 🔑 available to do what you want with rather than work: *He's studying music in his* ***spare time.*** ◇ *I haven't had a spare moment this morning.*
▸ PERSON **4** thin, and usually quite tall
IDM **go 'spare** (*BrE, informal*) to become very angry or upset
■ ***verb***
▸ TIME/MONEY/ROOM/THOUGHT, ETC. **1** to make sth such as time or money available to sb or for sth, especially when it requires an effort for you to do this: **~ sth/sb** *I'd love to have a break, but I can't spare the time just now.* ◇ *Could you spare one of your staff to help us out?* ◇ **~ sth/sb for sb/sth** *We can only spare one room for you.* ◇ *You should* ***spare a thought for*** (= think about) *the person who cleans up after you.* ◇ **~ sb sth** *Surely you can spare me a few minutes?*
▸ SAVE SB PAIN/TROUBLE **2** to save sb/yourself from having to go through an unpleasant experience: **~ sb/yourself sth** *He wanted to spare his mother any anxiety.* ◇ *Please* ***spare me*** (= do not tell me) ***the*** *gruesome* ***details.*** ◇ *You could have spared yourself an unnecessary trip by phoning in advance.* ◇ **~ sb/yourself from sth** *She was spared from the ordeal of appearing in court.*
▸ NOT HARM/DAMAGE **3** [usually passive] **~ sb/sth (from sth)** (*formal*) to allow sb/sth to escape harm, damage or death, especially when others do not escape it: **~ sb/sth (from sth)** *They killed the men but spared the children.* ◇ *During the bombing only one house was spared* (= was not hit by a bomb). ◇ **~ sb/sth sth** *Hong Kong was spared a direct hit, but the storm still brought heavy rains and powerful winds.*
▸ NO EFFORT/ EXPENSE, ETC. **4 ~ no effort, expense, etc.** to do everything possible to achieve sth or to do sth well without trying to limit the time or money involved: *He spared no effort to make her happy again.* ◇ ***No expense was spared*** *in furnishing the new office.*
▸ WORK HARD **5 not ~ yourself** to work as hard as possible
IDM **spare sb's 'blushes** (*BrE*) to save sb from an embarrassing situation **spare sb's 'feelings** to be careful not to do or say anything that might upset sb **to 'spare** if you have time, money, etc. **to spare**, you have more than you need: *I've got absolutely no money to spare this month.* ◇ *We arrived at the airport with five minutes to spare.*
■ ***noun* 1** 🔑 an extra thing that you keep in case you need to replace the one you usually use (used especially about a tyre of a car): *to get the spare out of the boot/trunk* ◇ *I've lost my key and I haven't got a spare.* **2 spares** [pl.] (*especially BrE*) = SPARE PARTS: *It can be difficult to get spares for some older makes of car.*

,spare 'part *noun* [usually pl.] a new part that you buy to replace an old or broken part of a car, machine, etc.

,spare 'rib *noun* a RIB of PORK (= meat from a pig) with most of the meat cut off: *barbecued spare ribs*

,spare 'tyre (*BrE*) (*NAmE* **,spare 'tire**) *noun* **1** an extra wheel for a car **2** (*humorous*) a large roll of fat around sb's waist

spar·ing /'speərɪŋ; *NAmE* 'sper-/ *adj.* careful to use or give only a little of sth: *Doctors now advise only* ***sparing use of*** *such creams.* ◇ **~ with sth** *He was always sparing with his praise.* ▸ **spar·ing·ly** *adv.*: *Use the cream very sparingly.*

spark /spɑːk; *NAmE* spɑːrk/ *noun, verb*
■ ***noun* 1** [C] a very small burning piece of material that is produced by sth that is burning or by hitting two hard substances together: *A shower of sparks flew up the chimney.* **2** [C] a small flash of light produced by an electric current: *sparks from a faulty light switch* ◇ *A spark ignites the fuel in a car engine.* **3** [C, usually sing.] **~ of sth** a small amount of a particular quality or feeling SYN **glimmer**: *a spark of hope* **4** [U, sing.] a special quality of energy, intelligence or enthusiasm that makes sb very clever, amusing, etc: *As a writer he seemed to lack creative spark.* **5** [C] an action or event that causes sth important to develop, especially trouble or violence: *the sparks of revolution* **6** [C, usually pl.] feelings of anger or excitement between people: ***Sparks flew*** *at the meeting* (= there was a lot of argument).
IDM see BRIGHT *adj.*
■ ***verb* 1** [T] to cause sth to start or develop, especially suddenly: **~ sth** *The proposal would spark a storm of protest around the country.* ◇ *Winds brought down power lines, sparking a fire.* ◇ **~ sth off** *The riots were sparked off by the arrest of a local leader.* **2** [I] to produce small flashes of fire or electricity: *a sparking, crackling fire* ◇ (*figurative*) *The game suddenly sparked to life.*
PHR V **,spark 'up sth** (*BrE*) to begin a conversation, an argument, a friendship, etc, often suddenly: *I tried to spark up a conversation with her.*

spar·kle /'spɑːkl; *NAmE* 'spɑːrkl/ *verb, noun*
■ ***verb* 1** [I] **~ (with sth)** to shine brightly with small flashes of light: *sparkling eyes* ◇ *Her jewellery sparkled in the candlelight.* ➲ note at SHINE **2** [I] **~ (with sth)** to be full of life, enthusiasm or humour: *He always sparkles at parties.*
■ ***noun*** [C, U] **1** a series of flashes of light produced by light hitting a shiny surface: *the sparkle of glass* ◇ (*figurative*) *There was a sparkle of excitement in her eyes.* **2** the quality of being lively and original: *The performance lacked sparkle.*

spark·ler /'spɑːklə(r); *NAmE* 'spɑːrk-/ *noun* a type of small FIREWORK that you hold in your hand and light. It burns with many bright SPARKS.

spark·ling /'spɑːklɪŋ; *NAmE* 'spɑːrk-/ *adj.* **1** (also *less frequent, informal* **sparkly** /'spɑːkli; *NAmE* 'spɑːrkli/) shining and flashing with light: *the calm and sparkling waters of the lake* ◇ *sparkling blue eyes* **2** (of drinks) containing bubbles of gas SYN **fizzy**: *a sparkling wine* ◇ *sparkling mineral water* **3** interesting and amusing: *a sparkling conversation/personality* **4** excellent; of very good quality SYN **brilliant**: *The champion was* ***in sparkling form.***

'spark plug (also **plug**) (*BrE* also **'sparking plug**) *noun* a part in a car engine that produces a SPARK (= a flash of electricity) which makes the fuel burn and starts the engine

sparky /'spɑːki; *NAmE* 'spɑːrki/ *adj.* (*BrE, informal*) full of life; interesting and amusing: *a sparky personality*

'sparring partner *noun* **1** a person that you regularly have friendly arguments or discussions with **2** (in BOXING) a person that a BOXER regularly practises with

spar·row /'spærəʊ; *NAmE* -roʊ/ *noun* a small brown and grey bird, common in many parts of the world

spar·row·hawk /'spærəʊhɔːk; *NAmE* -roʊ-/ *noun* a small BIRD OF PREY (= a bird that kills other creatures for food) of the HAWK family

sparse /spɑːs; *NAmE* spɑːrs/ *adj.* (*comparative* **sparser**, no *superlative*) only present in small amounts or numbers and often spread over a large area: *the sparse population of the islands* ◇ *Vegetation becomes sparse higher up the mountains.* ◇ *The information available on the subject is sparse.* ▸ **sparse·ly** *adv.*: *a* ***sparsely populated*** *area* **sparse·ness** *noun* [U]

spar·tan /'spɑːtn; *NAmE* 'spɑːrtn/ *adj.* (of conditions) simple or severe; lacking anything that makes life easier or more pleasant ORIGIN From **Sparta**, a powerful city in ancient Greece, where the people were not interested in comfort or luxury. OPP **luxurious**

spasm /'spæzəm/ *noun* **1** [C, U] a sudden and often painful contracting of a muscle, which you cannot control: *a muscle spasm* ◇ *The injection sent his leg* ***into spasm.*** **2** [C] **~ (of sth)** a sudden strong feeling or reaction that lasts for a short time: *a* ***spasm of anxiety/anger/coughing/pain, etc.***

spas·mod·ic /spæz'mɒdɪk; *NAmE* -'mɑːd-/ *adj.* **1** happening suddenly for short periods of time; not regular or continuous: *There was spasmodic fighting in the area yesterday.* **2** (*technical*) caused by your muscles becoming tight in a way that you cannot control: *spasmodic movements* ▸ **spas·mod·ic·al·ly** /-kli/ *adv.*

spas·tic /'spæstɪk/ *adj.* **1** (*medical* or *old-fashioned*) having or caused by CEREBRAL PALSY, an illness which makes it difficult for sb to control their muscles and movements. Using this word is now often considered offensive: *spastic children* ◇ *spastic reactions* **2** (*informal*) an offensive word, sometimes used by children to mean 'stupid' ▸ **spas·tic** *noun*

S

spat /spæt/ *noun* **1** (*informal*) a short argument or disagreement about sth unimportant **2** [usually pl.] a cloth covering for the ankle that was worn in the past by men over the shoe and fastened with buttons at the side ➲ see also SPIT, SPITTING, SPAT, SPAT *v.*

spate /speɪt/ *noun* [usually sing.] **~ of sth** a large number of things, which are usually unpleasant, that happen suddenly within a short period of time: *The bombing was the latest in a spate of terrorist attacks.*

IDM **in (full) 'spate** (*especially BrE*) (of a river) containing more water and flowing more strongly than usual: *After heavy rain, the river was in spate.* ◇ (*figurative*) *Celia was* ***in full spate*** (= completely involved in talking and not likely to stop or able to be interrupted).

spa·tial (also **spa·cial**) /ˈspeɪʃl/ *adj.* (*formal* or *technical*) relating to space and the position, size, shape, etc. of things in it: *changes taking place in the spatial distribution of the population* ◇ *the development of a child's spatial awareness* (= the ability to judge the positions and sizes of objects) ▸ **spa·tial·ly** /-ʃəli/ *adv.*

spat·ter /ˈspætə(r)/ *verb, noun*

■ ***verb*** **1** [T] to cover sb/sth with drops of liquid, dirt, etc, especially by accident SYN **splash**: **~ sb/sth** *blood-spattered walls* ◇ **~ sb/sth with sth** *As the bus passed, it spattered us with mud.* ◇ **~ sth on/over sb/sth** *Oil was spattered on the floor.* **2** [I] **+ adv./prep.** (of liquid) to fall on a surface in drops, often noisily: *We heard the rain spattering on the roof.*

■ ***noun*** (also **spat·ter·ing**) [sing.] **~ (of sth)** a number of drops of a liquid or small amounts of sth that hit a surface; the noise this makes: *a spatter of rain against the window* ◇ *a spattering of blood* ◇ (*figurative*) *a spatter of applause*

spat·ula /ˈspætʃələ/ *noun* **1** a tool with a broad flat blade used for mixing and spreading things, especially in cooking and painting ➲ VISUAL VOCAB pages V23, V24, V57 **2** (*especially NAmE*) (*BrE* usually **'fish slice**) a kitchen UTENSIL that has a broad flat blade with narrow holes in it, attached to a long handle, used for turning and lifting food when cooking ➲ VISUAL VOCAB page V23 **3** (*BrE*) (*NAmE* **'tongue depressor**) a thin flat instrument that doctors use for pressing the tongue down when they are examining sb's throat

spawn /spɔːn/ *verb, noun*

■ ***verb*** **1** [I, T] **~ (sth)** (of fish, FROGS, etc.) to lay eggs **2** [T] **~ sth** (often *disapproving*) to cause sth to develop or be produced: *The band's album spawned a string of hit singles.*

■ ***noun*** [U] a soft substance containing the eggs of fish, FROGS etc. ➲ see also FROGSPAWN

spay /speɪ/ *verb* **~ sth** (*technical*) to remove the OVARIES of a female animal, to prevent it from breeding: *Have you had your cat spayed?*

spaza /ˈspɑːzə/ *noun* (*SAfrE*) a small shop/store that sb operates from their home, selling food, drinks, cigarettes, etc. to local people, especially in a TOWNSHIP

speak 0‑m /spiːk/ *verb* (**spoke** /spəʊk; *NAmE* spoʊk/, **spoken** /ˈspəʊkən; *NAmE* ˈspoʊ-/)

WORD FAMILY
speak *verb*
speaker *noun*
speech *noun*
spoken *adj.* (≠ unspoken)

▸ HAVE CONVERSATION **1** 0‑m [I] to talk to sb about sth; to have a conversation with sb: **~ (to sb) (about sth/sb)** *I've spoken to the manager about it.* ◇ *The President refused to speak to the waiting journalists.* ◇ *'Can I speak to Susan?' 'Speaking.'* (= at the beginning of a telephone conversation) ◇ *'Do you know him?' 'Not to speak to.'* (= only by sight) ◇ *I saw her in the street but we didn't speak.* ◇ (*especially NAmE*) **~ (with sb) (about sth/sb)** *Can I speak with you for a minute?* ➲ SYNONYMS at TALK

▸ USE VOICE **2** 0‑m [I] to use your voice to say sth: *He can't speak because of a throat infection.* ◇ *Please speak more slowly.* ◇ *Without speaking, she stood up and went out.* ◇ *He speaks with a strange accent.* ◇ *She has a beautiful speaking voice.*

▸ MENTION/DESCRIBE **3** 0‑m [I] **~ of/about sth/sb** to mention or describe sth/sb: *She still speaks about him with great affection.* ◇ *Witnesses spoke of a great ball of flame.* ◇ *Speaking of travelling,* (= referring back to a subject just mentioned) *are you going anywhere exciting this year?* ➲ note at MENTION

▸ A LANGUAGE **4** 0‑m [T] (not used in the progressive tenses) **~ sth** to be able to use a particular language: *to speak several languages* ◇ *to speak a little Urdu* ◇ *Do you speak English?* **5** 0‑m [T, I] to use a particular language to express yourself: **~ sth** *What language is it they're speaking?* ◇ **~ in sth** *Would you prefer it if we spoke in German?*

▸ -SPEAKING **6** (in adjectives) speaking the language mentioned: *French-speaking Canada* ◇ *non-English-speaking students*

▸ MAKE SPEECH **7** 0‑m [I] (**+ adv./prep.**) to make a speech to an audience: *to speak in public* ◇ *to speak on the radio* ◇ *to speak at a conference* ◇ *Professor Wilson was invited to speak about the results of his research.* ◇ *She* ***spoke in favour of*** *the new tax.* ◇ *He has a number of* ***speaking engagements*** *this week.*

▸ SAY/STATE **8** [T] **~ sth** to say or state sth: *She was clearly* ***speaking the truth.*** ◇ *He spoke the final words of the play.*

IDM **be on 'speaking terms (with sb)** | **be 'speaking (to sb)** to be willing to be polite or friendly towards sb, especially after an argument: *She's not been on speaking terms with her uncle for years.* ◇ *Are they speaking to each other again yet?* **'generally, 'broadly, 'roughly, 'relatively, etc. speaking** used to show that what you are saying is true in a general, etc. way: *Generally speaking, the more you pay, the more you get.* ◇ *There are, broadly speaking, two ways of doing this.* ◇ *Personally speaking, I've always preferred Italian food.* ➲ LANGUAGE BANK at GENERALLY **no .../nothing to 'speak of** such a small amount that it is not worth mentioning: *They've got no friends to speak of.* ◇ *She's saved a little money but nothing to speak of.* **,so to 'speak** used to emphasize that you are expressing sth in an unusual or amusing way: *They were all very similar. All cut from the same cloth, so to speak.* **speak for it'self/them'selves** to be so easy to see and understand that you do not need to say anything else about it/them: *Her success speaks for itself.* **speak for my'self/her'self/him'self, etc.** to express what you think or want yourself, rather than sb else doing it for you: *I'm quite capable of speaking for myself, thank you!* **speak for your'self** (*informal*) used to tell sb that a general statement they have just made is not true of you: *'We didn't play very well.' 'Speak for yourself!'* (= I think that I played well.) **speaking as sth** used to say that you are the type of person mentioned and are expressing your opinion from that point of view: *Speaking as a parent, I'm very concerned about standards in education.* **speak your 'mind** to say exactly what you think, in a very direct way **,speak out of 'turn** to say sth when you should not, for example because it is not the right time or you are not the right person to say it **speak 'volumes (about/for sth/sb)** to tell you a lot about sth/sb, without the need for words **speak 'well/'ill of sb** (*formal*) to say good or bad things about sb ➲ more at ACTION *n.*, DEVIL, FACT, ILL *n.*, LANGUAGE, MANNER, STRICTLY, TURN *n.*

PHR V **'speak for sb** to state the views or wishes of a person or a group; to act as a representative for sb **'speak of sth** (*formal*) to be evidence that sth exists or is present: *Everything here speaks of perfect good taste.* **,speak 'out (against sth)** 0‑m to state your opinions publicly, especially in opposition to sth and in a way that takes courage ➲ see also OUTSPOKEN **'speak to sb (about sth)** (*informal*) to talk to sb in a serious way about sth wrong they have done, to try to stop them doing it again **,speak 'up** 0‑m usually used in orders to tell sb to speak more loudly: *Please speak up—we can't hear you at the back.* **,speak 'up (for sb/sth)** 0‑m to say what you think clearly and freely, especially in order to support or defend sb/sth

-speak /spiːk/ *combining form* (in nouns) (*informal*, often *disapproving*) the language used by a particular group of people, especially when it is difficult for other people to understand or they find it annoying: *management-speak* ◇ *Visitors to websites don't want to read marketing-speak.*

speak·easy /ˈspiːkiːzi/ *noun* (*pl.* **-ies**) a place in the US where people could buy alcohol illegally, at the time in

S

the 1920s and 1930s when it was illegal to make or sell alcohol

speak·er 0-w /ˈspiːkə(r)/ *noun*
1 0-w a person who gives a talk or makes a speech: *He was a* ***guest speaker*** *at the conference.* ◇ *She was a brilliant* ***public speaker.*** **2** 0-w a person who is or was speaking: *I looked around to see who the speaker was.* **3** 0-w a person who speaks a particular language: *Chinese speakers* ◇ *a* ***native speaker*** *of English* **4** (**the**) **Speaker** the title of the person whose job is to control the discussions in a parliament: *the Speaker of the House of Commons/Representatives* **5** 0-w the part of a radio, computer or piece of musical equipment that the sound comes out of ➲ VISUAL VOCAB page V18 ➲ see also LOUDSPEAKER

Synonyms

speaker

communicator • gossip • talker

These are all words for a person who talks or who is talking, especially in a particular way.

speaker a person who is or was speaking; a person who speaks a particular language: *I looked around to see who the speaker was.* ◇ *a fluent Arabic speaker*

communicator (*rather formal*) a person who is able to describe their ideas and feelings clearly to others: *The ideal candidate will be an effective communicator.*

gossip (*disapproving*) a person who enjoys talking about other people's private lives: *Myra is a dear, but she's also a terrible gossip.*

talker a person who talks in a particular way or who talks a lot: *He's a very persuasive talker.* ◇ *She's a (great) talker* (= she talks a lot).

SPEAKER OR TALKER?

Talker is used when you are talking about how much sb talks or how well they talk. It is not used for the person who is or was talking: ~~*I looked round to see who the talker was.*~~ You can say that sb is *a good/persuasive speaker* but that means that they are good at making speeches. If you mean that they speak well in conversation, use **talker**.

PATTERNS

- a **good/great** speaker/communicator/talker
- an **effective/excellent** speaker/communicator

S

speak·er·phone /ˈspiːkəfəʊn; *NAmE* -ərfoʊn/ *noun* a telephone that can be used without being held, because it contains a MICROPHONE and a LOUDSPEAKER

spear /spɪə(r); *NAmE* spɪr/ *noun, verb*
■ ***noun*** **1** a weapon with a long wooden handle and a sharp metal point used for fighting, hunting and fishing in the past ➲ picture at SWORD **2** the long pointed STEM of some plants ➲ VISUAL VOCAB page V27
■ ***verb*** **~ sth/sb** to throw or push a spear or other pointed object through sth/sb: *They were standing in the river spearing fish.* ◇ *She speared an olive with her fork.*

spear·head /ˈspɪəhed; *NAmE* ˈspɪrhed/ *noun, verb*
■ ***noun*** [usually sing.] a person or group that begins an activity or leads an attack against sb/sth
■ ***verb*** **~ sth** to begin an activity or lead an attack against sb/sth: *He is* ***spearheading a campaign*** *for a new stadium in the town.*

spear·mint /ˈspɪəmɪnt; *NAmE* ˈspɪrm-/ *noun* [U] a type of MINT used especially in making sweets/candy and TOOTHPASTE: *spearmint chewing gum* ➲ compare PEPPERMINT

spec /spek/ *noun, verb*
■ ***noun*** (*BrE*) a detailed description of sth, especially the design and materials needed to produce sth: *We want the machine manufactured to our own spec.* ➲ see also SPECIFICATION, SPECS

IDM **on ˈspec** (*BrE, informal*) when you do sth **on spec**, you are trying to achieve sth without organizing it in advance, but hoping you will be lucky
■ ***verb*** (-cc-) **~ sth** (*BrE*) to design and make sth to a particular standard: *The camera is well specced at the price.*

speccy = SPECKY

spe·cial 0-w /ˈspeʃl/ *adj., noun*
■ ***adj.*** **1** 0-w [usually before noun] not ordinary or usual; different from what is normal SYN **exceptional**: *The school will only allow this in special circumstances.* ◇ *Some of the officials have special privileges.* ◇ *There is* ***something special*** *about this place.* **2** 0-w more important than others; deserving or getting more attention than usual: *What are your special interests?* ◇ *She's a very special friend.* ◇ *Our special guest on next week's show will be...* ◇ *Don't lose it — it's special.* **3** 0-w organized or intended for a particular purpose: *a special event* ◇ *These teachers need special training.* **4** 0-w used by or intended for one particular person or group of people: *She has a special way of smiling.* ◇ *He sent a special message to the men.* **5** 0-w [only before noun] better or more than usual: *As an only child she got special attention.* ◇ *Please take special care of it.* ➲ compare ESPECIAL
■ ***noun*** **1** something that is not usually available but is provided for a particular purpose or on one occasion: *an election-night special on television* ◇ *The menu changes regularly and there are daily specials to choose from.* **2** (*informal, especially NAmE*) a price for a particular product in a shop/store or restaurant that is lower than usual: *There's a special on coffee this week.*

IDM **on ˈspecial** (*especially NAmE*) on sale at a lower price for a short period of time: *The chocolates were on special at my local store.*

ˈspecial agent *noun* a DETECTIVE who works for the FEDERAL government in the US, for example for the FBI

ˈSpecial Branch *noun* [U+sing./pl. v.] (also **the Special Branch** [sing.+ sing./pl. v.]) the department of the British police force that deals with the defence of the country against political crimes and TERRORISM

ˌspecial ˈconstable *noun* (in Britain) a person who is not a professional police officer but who is trained to help the police force, especially during an emergency

ˌspecial deˈlivery *noun* [U] a service that delivers a letter, etc. faster than normal

ˌspecial deˈvelopment area (also **ˌspecial ˈarea**) *noun* an area of the UK for which special laws exist in order to help the economy to develop

ˌspecial eduˈcation *noun* [U] the education of children who have physical or learning problems

ˌspecial efˈfects (also **SFX**) *noun* [pl.] unusual or exciting pieces of action in films/movies or television programmes, that are created by computers or clever photography to show things that do not normally exist or happen

ˌspecial ˈinterest group (also **ˌspecial ˈinterest**) *noun* (*especially NAmE*) a group of people who work together to achieve sth that they are particularly interested in, especially by putting pressure on the government, etc.

spe·cial·ism /ˈspeʃəlɪzəm/ *noun* **1** [C] an area of study or work that sb SPECIALIZES in: *a business degree with a specialism in computing* ◇ *Dr Crane's specialism is tropical diseases.* **2** [U] the fact of SPECIALIZING in a particular subject

spe·cial·ist 0-w /ˈspeʃəlɪst/ *noun*
1 0-w a person who is an expert in a particular area of work or study: *a specialist in Japanese history* **2** 0-w a doctor who has SPECIALIZED in a particular area of medicine: *a cancer specialist* ➲ compare GENERALIST ▶ **spe·cial·ist** *adj.* [only before noun]: *specialist magazines* ◇ *You need some specialist advice.*

spe·ci·al·ity /ˌspeʃiˈæləti/ (*BrE*) (also **spe·cial·ty** *NAmE, BrE*) *noun* (*pl.* -ies) **1** a type of food or product that a restaurant or place is famous for because it is so good: *Seafood is a speciality on the island.* ◇ *local specialities* **2** an area of work or study that sb gives most of their attention to and knows a lot about; sth that sb is good at: *My speciality is international tax law.*

spe·cial·ize (*BrE* also **-ise**) /ˈspeʃəlaɪz/ *verb* [I] **~ (in sth)** to become an expert in a particular area of work, study or business; to spend more time on one area of work, etc. than on others: *Many students prefer not to specialize too soon.* ◇ *He specialized in criminal law.* ◇ *The shop specializes in hand-made chocolates.* ▶ **spe·cial·iza·tion, -isa·tion** /ˌspeʃəlaɪˈzeɪʃn; *NAmE* -ləˈz-/ *noun* [U, C]

spe·cial·ized (*BrE* also **-ised**) /ˈspeʃəlaɪzd/ *adj.* designed or developed for a particular purpose or area of knowledge: *specialized equipment* ◇ *specialized skills*

ˌspecial ˈlicence *noun* (*BrE*) a licence allowing two people to get married at a time or place that is not usually allowed

spe·cial·ly 🔑 /ˈspeʃəli/ *adv.*
1 🔑 for a particular purpose, person, etc: *The ring was specially made for her.* ◇ *a specially designed diet plan* ◇ *We came specially to see you.* **2** (*informal*) more than usual or more than other things: *It will be hard to work today—specially when it's so warm and sunny outside.* ◇ *I hate homework. Specially history.* ➲ note at ESPECIALLY

ˌspecial ˈneeds *noun* [pl.] (*especially BrE*) needs that a person has because of mental or physical problems: *She teaches children with special needs.*

ˌspecial ˈoffer *noun* [C, U] a product that is sold at less than its usual price, especially in order to persuade people to buy it; the act of offering goods in this way: *Shop around for special offers.* ◇ *a special offer on perfume* ◇ *French wine is* ***on special offer*** *this week.*

ˌspecial ˈpleading *noun* [U] trying to persuade sb about sth by mentioning only the arguments that support your opinion and ignoring the arguments that do not support it

ˌspecial ˈschool *noun* a school for children who have physical or learning problems

spe·cialty /ˈspeʃəlti/ *noun* (*pl.* **-ies**) (*especially NAmE* or *medical*) = SPECIALITY: *regional specialties* ◇ *specialty stores* ◇ *Her specialty is taxation law.* ◇ *Doctors training for General Practice must complete programmes in a number of specialties, including Paediatrics.*

spe·cies /ˈspiːʃiːz/ *noun* (*pl.* **spe·cies**) a group into which animals, plants, etc. that are able to breed with each other and produce healthy young are divided, smaller than a GENUS and identified by a Latin name: *a rare species of beetle* ◇ *There are many species of dog(s).* ◇ *a conservation area for* ***endangered species***

the ˈspecies barrier *noun* [sing.] the natural system which is thought to prevent diseases spreading from one type of animal or plant to another

spe·cies·ism /ˈspiːʃiːzɪzəm/ *noun* [U] (*disapproving*) the belief that humans are more important than animals, which causes people to treat animals badly ▶ **spe·cies·ist** *adj., noun*

spe·cif·ic 🔑 AW /spəˈsɪfɪk/ *adj.*
1 🔑 detailed and exact SYN **precise**: *I gave you specific instructions.* ◇ *'I'd like your help tomorrow.' 'Can you* ***be more specific*** *(= tell me exactly what you want)?'* **2** 🔑 [usually before noun] connected with one particular thing only SYN **particular**: *children's television programmes aimed at a specific age group* ◇ *The money was collected for a specific purpose.* ◇ *children with specific learning difficulties* (= in one area only) **3 ~ to sth** (*formal*) existing only in one place or limited to one thing SYN **peculiar**: *a belief that is specific to this part of Africa*

spe·cif·ic·al·ly 🔑 AW /spəˈsɪfɪkli/ *adv.*
1 🔑 in a detailed and exact way: *I specifically told you not to go near the water!* **2** 🔑 connected with or intended for one particular thing only: *liquid vitamins specifically designed for children* ◇ *a magazine aimed specifically at working women* **3** 🔑 used when you want to add more detailed and exact information: *The newspaper, or more specifically, the editor, was taken to court for publishing the photographs.*

speci·fi·ca·tion AW /ˌspesɪfɪˈkeɪʃn/ *noun* [C, U] a detailed description of how sth is, or should be, designed or made: *the technical specifications of the new model* (= of car) ◇ *The house has been built exactly* ***to our specifications.*** ◇ *The office was furnished* ***to a high specification.***

speˌcific ˈgravity *noun* [U] = RELATIVE DENSITY

speci·fi·city AW /ˌspesɪˈfɪsəti/ *noun* [U] (*formal*) the quality of being specific

spe·cif·ics AW /spəˈsɪfɪks/ *noun* [pl.] the details of a subject that you need to think about or discuss: *Okay, that's the broad plan—let's get down to the specifics.*

spe·cify AW /ˈspesɪfaɪ/ *verb* (**speci·fies, speci·fy·ing, speci·fied, speci·fied**) to state sth, especially by giving an exact measurement, time, exact instructions, etc: **~ sth** *Remember to specify your size when ordering clothes.* ◇ **~ who, what, etc...** *The contract clearly specifies who can operate the machinery.* ◇ **~ that...** *The regulations specify that calculators may not be used in the examination.* ▶ **spe·ci·fi·able** AW /ˈspesɪfaɪəbl/ *adj.*

speci·men /ˈspesɪmən/ *noun* **1** a small amount of sth that shows what the rest of it is like SYN **sample**: *Astronauts have brought back specimens of rock from the moon.* ➲ COLLOCATIONS at SCIENTIFIC **2** a single example of sth, especially an animal or a plant: *The aquarium has some interesting specimens of unusual tropical fish.* ◇ (*humorous*) *They were fine specimens of British youth!* ➲ SYNONYMS at EXAMPLE **3** a small quantity of blood, URINE, etc. that is taken from sb and tested by a doctor: *to* ***provide/take a specimen***

spe·cious /ˈspiːʃəs/ *adj.* (*formal*) seeming right or true but actually wrong or false SYN **misleading**: *a specious argument*

speck /spek/ *noun* a very small spot; a small piece of dirt, etc: *The ship was now just a speck in the distance.* ◇ *specks of dust* ➲ SYNONYMS at MARK

speckle /ˈspekl/ *noun* [usually pl.] a small coloured mark or spot on a background of a different colour

speck·led /ˈspekld/ *adj.* covered with small marks or spots SYN **flecked**

specky (also **speccy**) /ˈspeki/ *adj.* (*BrE, offensive*) wearing glasses

specs /speks/ *noun* [pl.] **1** (*informal, especially BrE*) = GLASSES: *I need a new pair of specs.* **2** (*NAmE*) ➲ SPEC

spec·tacle /ˈspektəkl/ *noun* **1 spectacles** [pl.] (*formal*) = GLASSES: *a pair of spectacles* ◇ *a spectacle case* (= to put your glasses in) **2** [C, U] a performance or an event that is very impressive and exciting to look at: *The carnival parade was a magnificent spectacle.* **3** [C] a sight or view that is very impressive to look at: *The sunset was a stunning spectacle.* **4** [sing.] an unusual or surprising sight or situation that attracts a lot of attention: *I remember the sad spectacle of her standing in her wedding dress, covered in mud.*
IDM **make a ˈspectacle of yourself** to draw attention to yourself by behaving or dressing in a ridiculous way in public

spec·tacu·lar /spekˈtækjələ(r)/ *adj., noun*
■ ***adj.*** very impressive SYN **breathtaking**: *spectacular scenery* ◇ *Messi scored a spectacular goal.* ◇ *It was a spectacular achievement on their part.* ▶ **spec·tacu·lar·ly** *adv.*: *It has been a spectacularly successful year.*
■ ***noun*** an impressive show or performance: *a Christmas TV spectacular*

spec·tate /spekˈteɪt/ *verb* [I] to watch sth, especially a sports event

spec·ta·tor /spekˈteɪtə(r); *NAmE* ˈspekteɪtər/ *noun* a person who is watching an event, especially a sports event

specˈtator sport *noun* a sport that many people watch; a sport that is interesting to watch

spec·tra *pl.* of SPECTRUM

spec·tral /ˈspektrəl/ *adj.* **1** (*literary*) like a GHOST; connected with a ghost **2** (*technical*) connected with a SPECTRUM: *spectral bands*

spectre (*US* **spec·ter**) /ˈspektə(r)/ *noun* **1 ~ (of sth)** something unpleasant that people are afraid might hap-

S

pen in the future: *The country is haunted by the spectre of civil war.* ◇ *These weeks of drought have once again* ***raised the spectre*** *of widespread famine.* **2** (*literary*) a GHOST: *Was he a spectre returning to haunt her?*

spec·trom·eter /spek'trɒmɪtə(r); *NAmE* -'trɑːm-/ *noun* (*technical*) a piece of equipment for measuring the WAVELENGTHS of SPECTRA

spec·tro·scope /'spektrəskəʊp; *NAmE* -skoʊp/ *noun* (*technical*) a piece of equipment for forming and looking at SPECTRA ▸ **spec·tro·scop·ic** /ˌspektrə'skɒpɪk; *NAmE* -'skɑːp-/ *adj.*: *spectroscopic analysis*

spec·tros·copy /spek'trɒskəpi; *NAmE* -'trɑːs-/ *noun* [U] (*chemistry, physics*) the study of forming and looking at SPECTRA using spectrometers, spectroscopes, etc.

spec·trum /'spektrəm/ *noun* (*pl.* **spec·tra** /'spektrə/) **1** a band of coloured lights in order of their WAVELENGTHS, as seen in a RAINBOW and into which light may be separated: *A spectrum is formed by a ray of light passing through a prism.* ◇ *Red and violet are at opposite ends of the spectrum.* **2** a range of sound waves or several other types of wave: *the* ***electromagnetic/radio/sound spectrum*** **3** [usually sing.] a complete or wide range of related qualities, ideas, etc: *a broad spectrum of interests* ◇ *We shall hear views from across the political spectrum.*

specu·late /'spekjuleɪt/ *verb* **1** [I, T] to form an opinion about sth without knowing all the details or facts: **~ (about/on/as to sth)** *We all speculated about the reasons for her resignation.* ◇ **~ why, how, etc...** *It is useless to speculate why he did it.* ◇ **~ that...** *We can speculate that the stone circles were used in some sort of pagan ceremony.* **2** [I] **~ (in/on sth)** to buy goods, property, shares, etc, hoping to make a profit when you sell them, but with the risk of losing money: *He likes to speculate on the stock market.*

specu·la·tion /ˌspekju'leɪʃn/ *noun* **1** [U, C] the act of forming opinions about what has happened or what might happen without knowing all the facts: **~ (that...)** *There was widespread speculation that she was going to resign.* ◇ *His private life is the subject of much speculation.* ◇ **~ (about/over sth)** *Today's announcement ends months of speculation about the company's future.* ◇ *She dismissed the newspaper reports as* ***pure speculation.*** ◇ *Our speculations proved right.* **2** [U, C] **~ (in sth)** the activity of buying and selling goods or shares in a company in the hope of making a profit, but with the risk of losing money

specu·la·tive /'spekjələtɪv; *NAmE* also 'spekjəleɪtɪv/ *adj.* **1** based on guessing or on opinions that have been formed without knowing all the facts **2** showing that you are trying to guess sth: *She cast a speculative look at Kate.* **3** (of business activity) done in the hope of making a profit but involving the risk of losing money ▸ **specu·la·tive·ly** *adv.*

specu·la·tor /'spekjuleɪtə(r)/ *noun* a person who buys and sells goods or shares in a company in the hope of making a profit: *property speculators*

specu·lum /'spekjələm/ *noun* (*medical*) a metal instrument that is used to make a hole or tube in the body wider so it can be examined

sped *past tense, past part.* of SPEED

speech 0‑ᵂ /spiːtʃ/ *noun*
1 0‑ᵂ [C] **~ (on/about sth)** a formal talk that a person gives to an audience: *to* ***give/make/deliver a speech*** *on human rights* ◇ *He made the announcement* ***in a speech*** *on television.* ◇ *Several people made speeches at the wedding.* **2** 0‑ᵂ [U] the ability to speak: *I seemed to have lost the* ***power of speech.*** ◇ *a speech defect* ◇ ***freedom of speech*** (= the right to say openly what you think) **3** 0‑ᵂ [U] the way in which a particular person speaks: *Her speech was slurred—she was clearly drunk.* **4** 0‑ᵂ [U] the language used when speaking: *This expression is used mainly in speech, not in writing.* ◇ *speech sounds* **5** [C] a group of lines that an actor speaks in a play in the theatre: *She has the longest speech in the play.* ➲ see also FIGURE OF SPEECH

Synonyms

speech

lecture • **address** • **talk** • **sermon**

These are all words for a talk given to an audience.

speech a formal talk given to an audience: *Several people made speeches at the wedding.*

lecture a talk given to a group of people to tell them about a particular subject, often as part of a university or college course: *a lecture on the Roman army* ◇ *a course/series of lectures*

address a formal speech given to an audience: *a televised presidential address*

SPEECH OR ADDRESS?

A **speech** can be given on a public or private occasion; an **address** is always public: ~~*He gave an address at the wedding.*~~

talk a fairly informal session in which sb tells a group of people about a subject: *She gave an interesting talk on her visit to China.*

sermon a talk on a moral or religious subject, usually given by a religious leader during a service: *to preach a sermon*

PATTERNS

- a **long/short** speech/lecture/address/talk/sermon
- a **keynote** speech/lecture/address
- to **write/prepare/give/deliver/hear** a(n) speech/lecture/address/talk/sermon
- to **attend/go to** a lecture/talk

'speech act *noun* (*linguistics*) something that sb says, considered as an action, for example 'I forgive you'

'speech bubble *noun* a circle around the words that sb says in a CARTOON

'speech community *noun* all the people who speak a particular language or variety of a language: *the Kodava speech community in India* ◇ *speech communities such as high school students or hip hop fans*

'speech day *noun* an event held once a year in some British schools at which there are speeches and prizes

speechi·fy·ing /'spiːtʃɪfaɪɪŋ/ *noun* [U] (*informal, disapproving*) the act of making speeches in a very formal way, trying to sound important

speech·less /'spiːtʃləs/ *adj.* not able to speak, especially because you are extremely angry or surprised: *Laura was speechless with rage.* ▸ **speech·less·ly** *adv.* **speech·less·ness** *noun* [U]

'speech marks *noun* [pl.] = QUOTATION MARKS

'speech recognition (also **'voice recognition**) *noun* [U] technology that allows a computer to understand spoken words

'speech synthesis *noun* [U] the production of speech from written language by a computer

ˌspeech 'therapy *noun* [U] special treatment to help people who have problems in speaking clearly, for example in pronouncing particular sounds ▸ **ˌspeech 'therapist** *noun*

'speech-writer *noun* a person whose job is to write speeches for a politician or public figure

speed 0‑ᵂ /spiːd/ *noun, verb*
■ ***noun***
▸ RATE OF MOVEMENT/ACTION **1** 0‑ᵂ [C, U] the rate at which sb/sth moves or travels: *He reduced speed and turned sharp left.* ◇ *The train began to* ***pick up speed*** (= go faster). ◇ *The car was* ***gathering speed.*** ◇ *a* ***speed*** *of 50 mph/80 kph* ◇ *at* ***high/low/full/top speed*** ◇ ***at breakneck speed*** (= fast in a way that is dangerous) ◇ *travelling at* ***the speed of light/sound*** ➲ see also AIRSPEED, GROUND SPEED **2** 0‑ᵂ [C, U] the rate at which sth happens or is done: *the processing speed of the computer* ◇ *This course is designed so that stu-*

dents can progress at their own speed. ◇ *We aim to increase the speed of delivery* (= how quickly goods are sent). **3** [U] the quality of being quick or rapid: *The accident was due to excessive speed.* ◇ *She was overtaken by the* ***speed of events*** (= things happened more quickly than she expected). ◇ (*formal*) *A car flashed past them* ***at speed*** (= fast).
▸ IN PHOTOGRAPHY **4** [C] a measurement of how sensitive film for cameras, etc. is to light **5** [C] the time taken by a camera SHUTTER to open and close: *shutter speeds*
▸ ON BICYCLE/CAR **6** [C] (especially in compounds) a gear on a bicycle, in a car, etc: *a four-speed gearbox* ◇ *a ten-speed mountain bike*
▸ DRUG **7** [U] (*informal*) an illegal AMPHETAMINE drug that is taken to give feelings of excitement and energy
IDM **full speed/steam a'head** with as much speed or energy as possible **up to 'speed (on sth) 1** (of a person, company, etc.) performing at an expected rate or level: *the cost of* ***bringing*** *the chosen schools* ***up to speed*** **2** (of a person) having the most recent and accurate information or knowledge: *Are you up to speed yet on the latest developments?* ➲ more at HASTE, TURN *n.*
■ ***verb*** (**speed·ed, speed·ed** HELP In senses 1 and 2 **sped** is also used for the past tense and past participle.)
▸ MOVE/HAPPEN QUICKLY **1** [I] **+ adv./prep.** (*formal*) to move along quickly: *He sped away on his bike.* **2** [T] **~ sb/sth + adv./prep.** (*formal*) to take sb/sth somewhere very quickly, especially in a vehicle: *The cab speeded them into the centre of the city.* **3** [T] **~ sth** (*formal*) to make sth happen more quickly: *The drugs will speed her recovery.*
▸ DRIVE TOO FAST **4** [I] (usually used in the progressive tenses) to drive faster than the speed that is legally allowed: *The police caught him speeding.*
PHR V **,speed 'up | ,speed sth↔'up** to move or happen faster; to make sth move or happen faster: *The train soon speeded up.* ◇ *Can you try and* ***speed things up*** *a bit?*

speed·boat /'spi:dbəʊt; *NAmE* -boʊt/ *noun* a boat with a motor that can travel very fast ➲ VISUAL VOCAB page V44

'speed breaker *noun* (*IndE*) a SPEED HUMP

'speed camera *noun* (*BrE*) a machine which takes pictures of vehicles that are being driven too fast. The pictures are then used as evidence so that the drivers can be punished. ➲ COLLOCATIONS at DRIVING

'speed dating *noun* [U] meeting people at an event organized for single people who want to begin a romantic relationship, where you are allowed to spend only a few minutes talking to one person before you have to move on to meet the next person

'speed hump (*especially BrE*) (*NAmE* usually **'speed bump**) (also *BrE informal* **,sleeping po'liceman**) *noun* a raised area across a road that is put there to make traffic go slower

speed·ing /'spi:dɪŋ/ *noun* [U] the traffic offence of driving faster than the legal limit ➲ COLLOCATIONS at DRIVING

'speed limit *noun* the highest speed at which you can legally drive on a particular road: *You should always keep to the speed limit.* ◇ *to* ***break/exceed the speed limit*** ◇ *The road has a 30 mph speed limit.* ➲ COLLOCATIONS at DRIVING

speedo /'spi:dəʊ; *NAmE* -doʊ/ *noun* (*pl.* **-os**) **1** (*BrE, informal*) = SPEEDOMETER **2 Speedo™** [usually pl.] a SWIMMING COSTUME, especially a style of tight TRUNKS for men and boys: *a pair of Speedos*

speed·om·eter /spi:'dɒmɪtə(r); *NAmE* -'dɑ:m-/ (also *informal* **speedo**) *noun* an instrument in a vehicle which shows how fast the vehicle is going ➲ VISUAL VOCAB page V42

'speed-read *verb* [I, T] **~ (sth)** to read sth very quickly, paying attention to the general meaning of sentences and phrases rather than to every word ▸ **'speed-reading** *noun* [U]

'speed skating *noun* [U] the sport of SKATING on ice as fast as possible ➲ compare FIGURE-SKATING

speed·ster /'spi:dstə(r)/ *noun* (*informal*) **1** a person who drives a vehicle very fast **2** a machine or vehicle that works well at high speeds

'speed trap (*BrE* also **'radar trap**) *noun* a place on a road where police use special equipment to catch drivers who are going too fast

speed·way /'spi:dweɪ/ *noun* **1** [U] (*BrE*) the sport of racing motorcycles on a special track **2** [C] (*NAmE*) a special track for racing cars or motorcycles on

speed·well /'spi:dwel/ *noun* [U, C] a small wild plant with bright blue or pinkish-white flowers

speedy /'spi:di/ *adj.* (**speed·ier, speedi·est**) **1** happening or done quickly or without delay SYN **rapid**: *We wish you* ***a speedy recovery*** (= from an illness or injury). ◇ *a speedy reply* **2** moving or working very quickly: *speedy computers* ➲ SYNONYMS at FAST ▸ **speed·ily** *adv.*: *All enquiries will be dealt with as speedily as possible.*

spele·olo·gist /,spi:li'ɒlədʒɪst; *NAmE* -'ɑ:lə-/ *noun* a scientist who studies CAVES or a person who goes into caves as a sport ➲ compare CAVER, POTHOLER, SPELUNKER ▸ **spele·ology** /,spi:li'ɒlədʒi; *NAmE* -'ɑ:lə-/ *noun* [U]

spell /spel/ *verb, noun*
■ ***verb*** (**spelt, spelt** /spelt/ or **spelled, spelled**) **1** [T] **~ sth** to say or write the letters of a word in the correct order: *How do you spell your surname?* ◇ *I thought her name was Catherine, but it's Kathryn spelt with a 'K'.* **2** [I, T] to form words correctly from individual letters: *I've never been able to spell.* ◇ **~ sth + adj.** *You've spelt my name wrong.* ➲ see also MISSPELL **3** [T] **~ sth** (of letters of a word) to form words when they are put together in a particular order: *C—A—T spells 'cat'.* **4** [T] **~ sth (for sb/sth)** to have sth, usually sth bad, as a result; to mean sth, usually sth bad: *The crop failure spelt disaster for many farmers.* **5** [T] **~ sb** (*NAmE, informal*) to replace for a short time sb who is doing a particular activity so that they can rest: *Carter will be here in an hour to spell you.*
PHR V **,spell sth↔'out 1** to explain sth in a simple, clear way: *You know what I mean—I'm sure I don't need to spell it out.* ◇ **~ why, what, etc...** *Let me spell out why we need more money.* **2** to say or write the letters of a word in the right order: *Could you spell that name out again?*
■ ***noun*** **1** [C] a short period of time during which sth lasts: *a spell of warm weather* ◇ *a* ***cold/hot/wet/bright, etc. spell*** ◇ *There will be rain at first, with* ***sunny spells*** *later.* ◇ *She went to the doctor complaining of* ***dizzy spells.*** **2** [C] a period of time doing sth or working somewhere: *She had a spell as a singer before becoming an actress.* ◇ *I spent a* ***brief spell*** *on the Washington Post.* **3** [C] words that are thought to have magic power or to make a piece of magic work; a piece of magic that happens when sb says these magic words: *a* ***magic spell*** ◇ *a book of spells* ◇ *The wizard recited a spell.* ◇ *to* ***cast/put a spell on sb*** ◇ *to be* ***under a spell*** (= affected by magic) **4** [sing.] a quality that a person or thing has that makes them so attractive or interesting that they have a strong influence on you SYN **charm**: *I completely* ***fell under her spell.*** IDM see WEAVE *v.*

spell·bind·ing /'spelbaɪndɪŋ/ *adj.* holding your attention completely SYN **enthralling**: *a spellbinding performance*

spell·bound /'spelbaʊnd/ *adj.* [not usually before noun] with your attention completely held by what you are listening to or watching: *a storyteller who can hold audiences spellbound*

spell·check /'speltʃek/ *verb* **~ sth** to use a computer program to check your writing to see if your spelling is correct ▸ **spell·check** *noun* = SPELLCHECKER

spell·checker /'speltʃekə(r)/ *noun* a computer program that checks your writing to see if your spelling is correct

spell·er /'spelə(r)/ *noun* if sb is a **good/bad speller**, they find it easy/difficult to spell words correctly

spell·ing /'spelɪŋ/ *noun*
1 [U] the act of forming words correctly from individual letters; the ability to do this: *a* ***spelling mistake*** ◇ *the differences between British and American spelling* ◇ *My spelling is terrible.* **2** [C] the way that a particular word is written: *a list of difficult spellings*

S

'spelling bee *noun* a competition in which people have to spell words

spelt *past tense, past part.* of SPELL

spe·lunk·ing /spɪ'lʌŋkɪŋ/ (*NAmE*) (*BrE* **cav·ing, pot·hol·ing**) *noun* [U] the sport or activity of going into CAVES under the ground ➲ VISUAL VOCAB page V34 ▶ **spe·lunk·er** /spɪ'lʌŋkə(r)/ *noun* (*NAmE*) (*BrE* **caver, pot·holer**)

spend 0‒ /spend/ *verb, noun*

▪ ***verb*** (**spent, spent** /spent/) **1** 0‒ [T, I] to give money to pay for goods, services, etc: **~ sth** *I've spent all my money already.* ◇ **~ sth on sth/on doing sth** *She spent £100 on a new dress.* ◇ **~ (sth doing sth)** *The company has spent thousands of pounds updating their computer systems.* ◇ *I just can't seem to stop spending.* **2** 0‒ [T] to use time for a particular purpose; to pass time: **~ sth + adv./prep.** *We spent the weekend in Paris.* ◇ *How do you spend your spare time?* ◇ **~ sth on sth** *How long did you spend on your homework?* ◇ **~ sth doing sth** *I spend too much time watching television.* ◇ **~ sth in doing sth** *Most of her life was spent in caring for others.* **3** 0‒ [T, often passive] to use energy, effort, etc, especially until it has all been used: **~ sth on sth** *She spends too much effort on things that don't matter.* ◇ **~ itself** *The storm had finally spent itself.* ➲ see also SPENT

IDM **spend the 'night with sb** **1** to stay with sb for a night: *My daughter's spending the night with a friend.* **2** (also **spend the 'night together**) to stay with sb for a night and have sex with them **spend a 'penny** (*old-fashioned, BrE*) people say 'spend a penny' to avoid saying 'use the toilet'

▪ ***noun*** [sing.] (*informal*) the amount of money spent for a particular purpose or over a particular length of time:

spend·er /'spendə(r)/ *noun* a person who spends money in the particular way mentioned: *a big spender* (= who spends a lot of money)

spend·ing /'spendɪŋ/ *noun* [U] the amount of money that is spent by a government or an organization: *to increase **public spending*** ➲ SYNONYMS at COSTS

'spending money *noun* [U] money that you can spend on personal things for pleasure or entertainment

spend·thrift /'spendθrɪft/ *noun* (*disapproving*) a person who spends too much money or who wastes money ▶ **spend·thrift** *adj.* [usually before noun]

spent /spent/ *adj.* **1** [usually before noun] that has been used, so that it cannot be used again: *spent matches* **2** (*formal*) very tired SYN **exhausted**: *After the gruelling test, he felt totally spent.*

IDM **a ,spent 'force** a person or group that no longer has any power or influence ➲ see also SPEND *v.*

S

sperm /spɜːm; *NAmE* spɜːrm/ *noun* (*pl.* **sperm** or **sperms**) **1** [C] a cell that is produced by the sex organs of a male and that can combine with a female egg to produce young: *He has a low **sperm count*** (= very few live male cells). **2** [U] the liquid that is produced by the male sex organs that contains these cells SYN **semen** ➲ COLLOCATIONS at LIFE

sperm·ato·zoon /,spɜːmətə'zəʊən; *NAmE* ,spɜːrmətə'zoʊən/ *noun* (*pl.* **sperm·ato·zoa** /-'zəʊə; *NAmE* -'zoʊə/) (*biology*) a sperm

'sperm bank *noun* a place where sperm is kept and then used to help women become pregnant artificially

spermi·cide /'spɜːmɪsaɪd; *NAmE* 'spɜːrm-/ *noun* [U, C] a substance that kills sperm, used during sex to prevent the woman from becoming pregnant ▶ **spermi·cidal** /,spɜːmɪ'saɪdl; *NAmE* ,spɜːrm-/ *adj.* [only before noun]

'sperm whale *noun* a large WHALE that is hunted for its oil and fat ➲ VISUAL VOCAB page V10

spew /spjuː/ *verb* **1** [I, T] to flow out quickly, or to make sth flow out quickly, in large amounts: **+ adv./prep.** *Flames spewed from the aircraft's engine.* ◇ **~ sth + adv./prep.** *Massive chimneys were spewing out smoke.* **2** [I, T] (*BrE, informal*) to VOMIT (= bring food from the stomach back out through the mouth): **~ (up)** *He spewed up on the pavement.* ◇ **~ sth (up)** *She spewed up the entire meal.*

SPF /,es piː 'ef/ *abbr.* sun protection factor (a number that tells you how much protection a particular cream or liquid gives you from the harmful effects of the sun)

sphag·num /'sfægnəm/ (also **'Sphagnum moss**) *noun* [U] a type of MOSS that grows in wet areas, used especially for planting plants in pots, making FERTILIZER, etc.

sphere AW /sfɪə(r); *NAmE* sfɪr/ *noun* **1** (*geometry*) a solid figure that is completely round, with every point on its surface at an equal distance from the centre ➲ VISUAL VOCAB page V58 **2** any object that is completely round, for example a ball **3** an area of activity, influence or interest; a particular section of society SYN **domain**: *the political sphere* ◇ *This area was formerly within the **sphere of influence** of the US.* ◇ *He and I moved in totally different social spheres.* **4 -sphere** (in nouns) a region that surrounds a planet, especially the earth: *ionosphere* ◇ *atmosphere*

spher·ic·al AW /'sferɪkl; *NAmE* also 'sfɪr-/ *adj.* shaped like a sphere SYN **round** ▶ **spher·ic·al·ly** AW /-kli/ *adv.*

spher·oid /'sfɪərɔɪd; *NAmE* 'sfɪr-/ *noun* (*technical*) a solid object that is approximately the same shape as a sphere

sphinc·ter /'sfɪŋktə(r)/ *noun* (*anatomy*) a ring of muscle that surrounds an opening in the body and can contract to close it: *the anal sphincter*

sphinx /sfɪŋks/ *noun* (often **the Sphinx**) an ancient Egyptian stone statue of a creature with a human head and the body of a LION lying down. In ancient Greek stories the Sphinx spoke in RIDDLES.

spic /spɪk/ *noun* (*taboo, slang, especially NAmE*) a very offensive word for a person from a country where Spanish is spoken, for example a Mexican or Puerto Rican

IDM **,spic and 'span** = SPICK AND SPAN at SPICK

spice 0‒ /spaɪs/ *noun, verb*

▪ ***noun*** **1** 0‒ [C, U] one of the various types of powder or seed that come from plants and are used in cooking. Spices have a strong taste and smell: *common spices such as ginger and cinnamon* ◇ *a spice jar* ➲ VISUAL VOCAB page V28 **2** [U] extra interest or excitement: *We need an exciting trip to add some spice to our lives.* IDM see VARIETY

▪ ***verb*** **1 ~ sth (up) (with sth)** to add spice to food in order to give it more flavour **2 ~ sth (up) (with sth)** to add interest or excitement to sth: *He exaggerated the details to spice up the story.*

spick /spɪk/ *adj.*

IDM **,spick and 'span** (also **,spic and 'span**) [not usually before noun] neat and clean: *Their house is always spick and span.*

spicy 0‒ /'spaɪsi/ *adj.* (**spici·er, spici·est**) **1** 0‒ (of food) having a strong taste because spices have been used to flavour it SYN **hot** **2** (*informal*) (of a story, piece of news, etc.) exciting and slightly shocking ▶ **spici·ness** *noun* [U]

spider 0‒ /'spaɪdə(r)/ *noun* a small creature with eight thin legs. Many spiders spin webs (= nets of thin threads) to catch insects for food. ➲ VISUAL VOCAB page V11

'spider monkey *noun* a S American MONKEY with very long arms and legs and a long PREHENSILE tail ➲ VISUAL VOCAB page V10

'spider's web (*especially BrE*) (also **'spider web** especially in *NAmE*) (also **web**) *noun* a fine net of threads made by a spider to catch insects: (*figurative*) *to be caught in a spider's web of confusion* ➲ see also COBWEB

spi·dery /'spaɪdəri/ *adj.* long and thin, like the legs of a spider: *spidery fingers* ◇ *spidery writing* (= consisting of thin lines that are not very clear)

spied *past tense, past part.* of SPY

spiel /ʃpiːl; spiːl/ *noun* (*informal*, usually *disapproving*) a long speech that sb has used many times, that is intended to persuade you to believe sth or buy sth

spies /spaɪz/ *noun pl.* of SPY

spiff /spɪf/ *verb*

PHR V **,spiff 'up** | **,spiff sb/sth↔'up** (*NAmE, informal*) to make yourself/sb/sth look neat and attractive

spif·fing /ˈspɪfɪŋ/ *adj.* (*BrE, old-fashioned, informal*) extremely good or pleasant SYN **excellent**

spiffy /ˈspɪfi/ *adj.* (*NAmE, informal*) attractive and fashionable

spigot /ˈspɪɡət/ *noun* **1** (*technical*) a device in a tap/faucet that controls the flow of liquid from a container **2** (*US*) any tap/faucet, especially one outdoors

spike /spaɪk/ *noun, verb*

■ ***noun*** **1** [C] a thin object with a sharp point, especially a pointed piece of metal, wood, etc: *a row of iron spikes on a wall* ◇ *Her hair stood up in spikes.* ➲ see also SPIKE HEEL **2** [C, usually pl.] a metal point attached to the SOLE of a sports shoe to prevent you from slipping while running ➲ compare CLEAT **3 spikes** [pl.] shoes fitted with these metal spikes, used for running: *a pair of spikes* **4** [C] a long pointed group of flowers that grow together on a single STEM **5** [C, usually sing.] (*informal, especially NAmE*) a sudden large increase in sth: *a spike in oil prices*

■ ***verb*** **1** [T] **~ sb/sth (on sth)** to push a sharp piece of metal, wood, etc. into sb/sth; to injure sth on a sharp point SYN **stab 2** [T] **~ sth (with sth)** to add alcohol, poison or a drug to sb's drink or food without them knowing: *He gave her a drink spiked with tranquillizers.* ◇ (*figurative*) *Her words were spiked with malice.* **3** [T] **~ sth** to reject sth that a person has written or said; to prevent sth from happening or being made public: *The article was spiked for fear of legal action against the newspaper.* **4** [I] **~ (to sth)** (*especially NAmE*) to rise quickly and reach a high value: *The US dollar spiked to a three-month high.*

IDM **spike sb's ˈguns** (*BrE*) to spoil the plans of an opponent

spiked /ˈspaɪkt/ *adj.* with one or more spikes: *spiked running shoes* ◇ *short spiked hair*

ˌspike ˈheel *noun* a very thin high heel on a woman's shoe; a shoe with such a heel SYN **stiletto**

spiky /ˈspaɪki/ *adj.* **1** having sharp points: *spiky plants, such as cacti* **2** (of hair) sticking straight up from the head ➲ VISUAL VOCAB page V49 **3** (*BrE*) (of people) easily annoyed or offended ► **spiki·ness** *noun* [U]

spill /spɪl/ *verb, noun*

■ ***verb*** (**spilled, spilled**) (*BrE* also **spilt, spilt** /spɪlt/) **1** [I, T] (especially of liquid) to flow over the edge of a container by accident; to make liquid do this: *Water had spilled out of the bucket onto the floor.* ◇ **~ sth** *He startled her and made her spill her drink.* ◇ *Thousands of gallons of crude oil were spilled into the ocean.* **2** [I] **+ adv./prep.** (of people) to come out of a place in large numbers and spread out: *The doors opened and people spilled into the street.* ◇ (*figurative*) *Light spilled from the windows.*

IDM **spill the ˈbeans** (*informal*) to tell sb sth that should be kept secret or private **spill (sb's) ˈblood** (*formal* or *literary*) to kill or wound people **spill your ˈguts (to sb)** (*NAmE, informal*) to tell sb everything you know or feel about sth, because you are upset ➲ more at CRY *v.*

PHR V **ˌspill sth↔ˈout** | **ˌspill ˈout** to tell sb all about a problem etc. very quickly; to come out quickly: *Has she been spilling out her troubles to you again?* ◇ *When he started to speak, the words just spilled out.* **ˌspill ˈover (into sth)** **1** to fill a container and go over the edge: *She filled the glass so full that the water spilled over.* ◇ (*figurative*) *Her emotions suddenly spilled over.* **2** to start in one area and then affect other areas: *Unrest has spilt over into areas outside the city.* ➲ related noun OVERSPILL, SPILLOVER

■ ***noun*** **1** (also *formal* **spill·age**) [C, U] an act of letting a liquid come or fall out of a container; the amount of liquid that comes or falls out: *Many seabirds died as a result of the oil spill.* ◇ *I wiped up the coffee spills on the table.* **2** [C] a long match, or a thin piece of twisted paper, used for lighting fires, oil lamps, etc. **3** [C, usually sing.] a fall, especially from a bicycle or a boat: *to take a spill* IDM see THRILL *n.*

spill·age /ˈspɪlɪdʒ/ *noun* [U, C] (*formal*) = SPILL: *Put the bottle in a plastic bag in case of spillage.*

spilli·kins /ˈspɪlɪkɪnz/ (*BrE*) (*NAmE* **jack·straw**) *noun* [U] a game in which you remove a small stick from a pile, without moving any of the other sticks

spill·over /ˈspɪləʊvə(r); *NAmE* -oʊ-/ *noun* [C, U] **1** something that is too large or too much for the place where it starts, and spreads to other places: *A second room was needed for the spillover of staff and reporters.* **2** the results or the effects of sth that have spread to other situations or places

spill·way /ˈspɪlweɪ/ *noun* (*technical*) a passage for the extra water from a DAM (= a wall across a river that holds water back)

spim /spɪm/ *noun* [U] (*informal*) advertising sent as messages on the Internet to people who have not asked for it ➲ compare SPAM ORIGIN From the letters for *SPam via Instant Messaging.*

spin 🔑 /spɪn/ *verb, noun*

■ ***verb*** (**spin·ning, spun, spun** /spʌn/)

▸ TURN ROUND QUICKLY **1** 🔑 [I, T] to turn round and round quickly; to make sth do this: (**+ adv./prep.**) *The plane was spinning out of control.* ◇ *a spinning ice skater* ◇ *My head is spinning* (= I feel as if my head is going around and I can't balance). ◇ **~ (round/around)** *The dancers spun round and round.* ◇ **~ sth (round/around)** *to spin a ball/coin/wheel* **2** 🔑 [I, T] **~ (sb) round/around** | **+ adv./prep.** to turn round quickly once; to make sb do this: *He spun around to face her.*

▸ MAKE THREAD **3** [I, T] to make thread from wool, cotton, silk, etc. by twisting it: *She sat by the window spinning.* ◇ **~ sth** *to spin and knit wool* ◇ **~ A into B** *spinning silk into thread* ◇ **~ B from A** *spinning thread from silk*

▸ OF SPIDER/SILKWORM **4** [T] **~ sth** to produce thread from its body to make a web or COCOON: *a spider spinning a web*

▸ DRIVE/TRAVEL QUICKLY **5** [I] **+ adv./prep.** to drive or travel quickly: *They went spinning along the roads on their bikes.*

▸ DRY CLOTHES **6** [T] **~ sth** to remove the water from clothes that have just been washed, in a SPIN DRYER

▸ PRESENT INFORMATION **7** [T] **~ sth (as sth)** to present information or a situation in a particular way, especially one that makes you or your ideas seem good: *An aide was already spinning the senator's defeat as 'almost as good as an outright win'.*

IDM **spin (sb) a ˈyarn, ˈtale, etc.** to try to make sb believe a long story that is not true ➲ more at HEEL *n.*

PHR V **ˌspin ˈoff (from sth)** | **ˌspin sth↔ˈoff (from sth)** to happen or to produce sth as a new or unexpected result of sth that already exists: *products spinning off from favourite books* ➲ related noun SPIN-OFF **ˌspin sth↔ˈoff** (*business*) (*especially NAmE*) to form a new company from parts of an existing one: *The transportation operation will be spun off into a separate company.* **ˌspin sth↔ˈout** to make sth last as long as possible

■ ***noun***

▸ FAST TURNING MOVEMENT **1** [C, U] a very fast turning movement: *the earth's spin* ◇ *the spin of a wheel* ◇ *Give the washing a short spin.* **2** [C, usually sing.] if an aircraft goes into a **spin**, it falls and turns round rapidly

▸ IN CAR **3** [C] (*informal, becoming old-fashioned*) a short ride in a car for pleasure: *Let's **go for a spin**.*

▸ IN TENNIS/CRICKET **4** [U] the way you make a ball turn very fast when you throw it or hit it: *She puts a lot of spin on the ball.* ◇ *a **spin bowler*** (= in CRICKET, a BOWLER who uses spin) ➲ see also TOPSPIN

▸ ON INFORMATION **5** [sing., U] (*informal*) a way of presenting information or a situation in a particular way, especially one that makes you or your ideas seem good: *Politicians put their own spin on the economic situation.*

IDM **in a (flat) ˈspin** very confused, worried or excited: *Her resignation put her colleagues in a spin.*

spina bif·ida /ˌspaɪnə ˈbɪfɪdə/ *noun* [U] a medical condition in which some bones in the SPINE have not developed normally at birth, often causing PARALYSIS (= loss of control or feeling) in the legs

spin·ach /ˈspɪnɪtʃ; -ɪdʒ/ *noun* [U] a vegetable with large dark green leaves that are cooked or eaten in salads

spinal /ˈspaɪnl/ *adj.* [usually before noun] (*technical*) connected with the SPINE (= the long bone in the back): *spinal injuries*

ˌspinal ˈcolumn *noun* the SPINE

S

ˌ**spinal ˈcord** *noun* the mass of nerves inside the SPINE that connects all parts of the body to the brain ➲ VISUAL VOCAB page V48

ˈ**spinal tap** (*NAmE*) (*BrE* ˌ**lumbar ˈpuncture**) *noun* the removal of liquid from the lower part of the SPINE with a hollow needle

spin·dle /ˈspɪndl/ *noun* **1** a long straight part that turns in a machine, or that another part of the machine turns around **2** a thin pointed piece of wood used for spinning wool into thread by hand

spindly /ˈspɪndli/ *adj.* (*informal*, often *disapproving*) very long and thin and not strong: *spindly legs*

ˈ**spin doctor** *noun* (*informal*) a person whose job is to present information to the public about a politician, an organization, etc. in the way that seems most positive

ˌ**spin ˈdryer** (also ˌ**spin ˈdrier**) *noun* (*BrE*) a machine that partly dries clothes that you have washed by turning them round and round very fast to remove the water ➲ compare TUMBLE DRYER ▶ ˌ**spin-ˈdry** *verb* **~ sth**

spine /spaɪn/ *noun* **1** the row of small bones that are connected together down the middle of the back SYN **backbone** ➲ VISUAL VOCAB page V48 **2** any of the sharp pointed parts like needles on some plants and animals: *Porcupines use their spines to protect themselves.* ➲ see also SPINY **3** the narrow part of the cover of a book that the pages are joined to

ˈ**spine-chilling** *adj.* (of a book, film/movie, etc.) frightening in an exciting way ▶ ˈ**spine-chiller** *noun*

spine·less /ˈspaɪnləs/ *adj.* **1** (*disapproving*) (of people) weak and easily frightened **2** (of animals) having no SPINE (= the long bone in the back) **3** (of animals or plants) having no SPINES (= sharp parts like needles)

spi·net /spɪˈnet; *NAmE* ˈspɪnət/ *noun* **1** a kind of HARPSICHORD (= an early type of musical instrument), played like a piano **2 ~ piano/organ** (*US*) a small piano/electronic organ

ˈ**spine-tingling** *adj.* (of an event, a piece of music, etc.) enjoyable because it is very exciting or frightening

spin·naker /ˈspɪnəkə(r)/ *noun* a large extra sail on a racing YACHT that you use when the wind is coming from behind ➲ VISUAL VOCAB page V45

spin·ner /ˈspɪnə(r)/ *noun* **1** (in CRICKET) a BOWLER who uses SPIN (4) when throwing the ball **2** a person who spins thread **3** a device that spins around, used on a fishing line to attract fish

S

spin·ney /ˈspɪni/ *noun* (*BrE*) a small area of trees SYN **copse**

spin·ning /ˈspɪnɪŋ/ *noun* [U] **1** the art or the process of twisting wool, etc. to make thread **2 Spinning™** a type of exercise performed on an EXERCISE BIKE, usually in a class

ˈ**spinning wheel** *noun* a simple machine that people used in their homes in the past for twisting wool, etc. It has a large wheel operated with the foot.

ˈ**spin-off** *noun* **~ (from/of sth) 1** an unexpected but useful result of an activity that is designed to produce sth else: *commercial spin-offs from medical research* **2** a book, a film/movie, a television programme, or an object that is based on a book, film/movie or television series that has been very successful: *The TV comedy series is a spin-off of the original movie.* ◇ *spin-off merchandise from the latest Disney movie*

spin·ster /ˈspɪnstə(r)/ *noun* (*old-fashioned*, often *disapproving*) a woman who is not married, especially an older woman who is not likely to marry HELP This word should not now be used to mean simply a woman who is not married. ➲ compare BACHELOR ▶ **spin·ster·hood** /-hʊd/ *noun* [U]: *For most women, marriage used to bring a higher status than spinsterhood.*

spiny /ˈspaɪni/ *adj.* (of animals or plants) having sharp points like needles ➲ see also SPINE

ˌ**spiny ˈanteater** *noun* = ECHIDNA

spiral /ˈspaɪrəl/ *noun, adj., verb*

■ ***noun* 1** a shape or design, consisting of a continuous curved line that winds around a central point, with each curve further away from the centre: *The birds circled in a slow spiral above the house.* **2** a continuous harmful increase or decrease in sth, that gradually gets faster and faster: *the destructive spiral of violence in the inner cities* ◇ *measures to control the inflationary spiral* ◇ *the* ***upward/downward spiral*** *of sales*

■ ***adj.*** moving in a continuous curve that winds around a central point: *A snail's shell is spiral in form.* ▶ **spir·al·ly** *adv.*

■ ***verb*** (-ll-, *NAmE* usually -l-) **1** [I] (**+ adv./prep.**) to move in continuous circles, going upwards or downwards: *The plane spiralled down to the ground.* **2** [I] to increase rapidly: *the spiralling cost of health care* ◇ **+ adv./prep.** *Prices are spiralling out of control.*

PHR V ˌ**spiral ˈdown/ˈdownward** to decrease rapidly

ˌ**spiral-ˈbound** *adj.* (of a book) held together by wire which is wound through holes along one edge

ˌ**spiral ˈstaircase** *noun* a set of stairs that curve upwards around a central post

spir·ant /ˈspaɪərənt/ (*NAmE*) (*BrE* **frica·tive**) *noun, adj.* (*phonetics*) a speech sound made by forcing breath out through a narrow space in the mouth with the lips, teeth or tongue in a particular position, for example /f/ and /ʃ/ in *fee* and *she* ▶ **spir·ant** (*NAmE*) (*BrE* **frica·tive**) *adj.* ➲ compare PLOSIVE

spire /ˈspaɪə(r)/ *noun* a tall pointed structure on the top of a building, especially a church

spirit 🔑 /ˈspɪrɪt/ *noun, verb*

■ ***noun***

▸ MIND/FEELINGS/CHARACTER **1** 🔑 [U, C] the part of a person that includes their mind, feelings and character rather than their body: *the power of the human spirit to overcome difficulties* **2** 🔑 **spirits** [pl.] a person's feelings or state of mind: *to be in* ***high/low spirits*** ◇ *You must try and* ***keep your spirits up*** (= stay cheerful). ◇ *My* ***spirits sank*** *at the prospect of starting all over again.* **3** [C] (always with an adjective) a person of the type mentioned: *a brave spirit* ◇ ***kindred spirits*** (= people who like the same things as you) ➲ see also FREE SPIRIT

▸ COURAGE/DETERMINATION **4** 🔑 [U] courage, determination or energy: *Show a little* ***fighting spirit***. ◇ *Although the team lost, they played with tremendous spirit.* ◇ *They took away his freedom and broke his spirit.*

▸ LOYAL FEELINGS **5** 🔑 [U, sing.] loyal feelings towards a group, team or society: *There's not much* ***community spirit*** *around here.* ➲ see also TEAM SPIRIT

▸ ATTITUDE **6** [sing.] a state of mind or mood; an attitude: *We approached the situation in the wrong spirit.* ◇ *'OK, I'll try'.* ***'That's the spirit*** (= the right attitude).' ◇ *The party went well because everyone* ***entered into the spirit of things***. ➲ see also PARTY SPIRIT

▸ TYPICAL QUALITY **7** [sing.] the typical or most important quality or mood of sth: *The exhibition captures the* ***spirit of the age/times***.

▸ REAL MEANING **8** [U] the real or intended meaning or purpose of sth: *Obey the spirit, not the letter* (= the narrow meaning of the words) *of the law.*

▸ SOUL **9** 🔑 [C] the soul thought of as separate from the body and believed to live on after death; a GHOST: *He is dead, but his spirit lives on.* ◇ *It was believed that people could be possessed by evil spirits.* ➲ see also THE HOLY SPIRIT

▸ IMAGINARY CREATURE **10** [C] (*old-fashioned*) an imaginary creature with magic powers, for example, a FAIRY or an ELF

▸ ALCOHOL **11** 🔑 [C, usually pl.] (*especially BrE*) a strong alcoholic drink: *I don't drink whisky or brandy or any other spirits.* **12** [U] a special type of alcohol used in industry or medicine ➲ see also METHYLATED SPIRIT, SURGICAL SPIRIT, WHITE SPIRIT

IDM **in ˈspirit** in your thoughts: *I shall be with you in spirit* (= thinking about you though not with you physically). **the ˌspirit is ˈwilling (but the ˌflesh is ˈweak)** (*humorous*, *saying*) you intend to do good things but you are too lazy, weak or busy to actually do them **as/when/if the ˌspirit**

ˈ**moves you** as/when/if you feel like it: *I'll go for a run this evening, if the spirit moves me.* ➲ more at FIGHT *v.*, RAISE *v.*
■ ***verb*** **~ sth + adv./prep.** to take sb/sth away in a quick, secret or mysterious way: *After the concert, the band was* ***spirited away*** *before their fans could get near them.*

spir·it·ed /ˈspɪrɪtɪd/ *adj.* [usually before noun] full of energy, determination or courage: *a spirited young woman* ◇ *a spirited discussion* ◇ *She put up a spirited defence in the final game.* ➲ compare DISPIRITED ➲ see also HIGH-SPIRITED, PUBLIC-SPIRITED ▸ **spir·it·ed·ly** *adv.*

spir·it·less /ˈspɪrɪtləs/ *adj.* (*formal*) without energy, enthusiasm or determination

ˈ**spirit level** (also **level**) *noun* a glass tube partly filled with liquid, with a bubble of air inside. Spirit levels are used to test whether a surface is level, by the position of the bubble. ➲ VISUAL VOCAB page V17

spir·it·ual 0‑ /ˈspɪrɪtʃuəl/ *adj.*, *noun*
■ ***adj.*** [usually before noun] **1** 0‑ connected with the human spirit, rather than the body or physical things: *a spiritual experience* ◇ *spiritual development* ◇ *a lack of spiritual values in the modern world* ◇ *We're concerned about your* ***spiritual welfare.*** OPP **material** **2** 0‑ connected with religion: *a spiritual leader* ➲ compare TEMPORAL ▸ **spir·itu·al·ly** /-tʃuəli/ *adv.*: *a spiritually uplifting book*
IDM **your ˌspiritual ˈhome** the place where you are happiest, especially a country where you feel you belong more than in your own country because you share the ideas and attitudes of the people who live there
■ ***noun*** (also ˌ**Negro ˈspiritual**) a religious song of the type originally sung by black SLAVES in America

spir·itu·al·ism /ˈspɪrɪtʃuəlɪzəm/ *noun* [U] the belief that people who have died can send messages to living people, usually through a MEDIUM (= a person who has special powers)

spir·itu·al·ist /ˈspɪrɪtʃuəlɪst/ *noun* a person who believes that people who have died can send messages to living people

spir·itu·al·ity /ˌspɪrɪtʃuˈæləti/ *noun* [U] the quality of being concerned with religion or the human spirit

spir·it·ual·ized (*BrE* also **-ised**) /ˈspɪrɪtʃuəlaɪzd/ *adj.* (*formal*) raised to a spiritual level: *She tends to have intense, spiritualized friendships.*

spit /spɪt/ *verb*, *noun*
■ ***verb*** (**spit·ting, spat, spat** /spæt/ HELP **spit** is also sometimes used for the past tense and past participle, especially in *NAmE*)
▸ FROM MOUTH **1** [T] to force liquid, food, etc. out of your mouth: **~ sth (out)** *She took a mouthful of food and then suddenly spat it out.* ◇ **~ sth (from sth)** *He was spitting blood from a badly cut lip.* **2** [I] to force SALIVA (= the liquid that is produced in the mouth) out of your mouth, often as a sign of anger or lack of respect: *He coughed and spat.* ◇ **~ at/on/in sb/sth** *The prisoners were spat on by their guards.* ◇ *She spat in his face and went out.*
▸ SAY STH ANGRILY **3** [T] to say sth in an angry or aggressive way: **+ speech** *'You liar!' she spat.* ◇ **~ sth (at sb)** *He was dragged out of the court, spitting abuse at the judge and jury.*
▸ OF AN ANIMAL **4** [I] to make a short angry sound: *Snakes spit and hiss when they are cornered.*
▸ OF STH COOKING/BURNING **5** [I] to make a noise and throw out fat, SPARKS, etc: *sausages spitting in the frying pan* ◇ *The logs on the fire crackled and spat.*
▸ RAIN **6** [I] (*informal*) (only used in the progressive tenses) when **it is spitting**, it is raining lightly
IDM ˌ**spit it ˈout** (*informal*) usually used in orders to tell sb to say sth when they seem frightened or unwilling to speak: *If you've got something to say, spit it out!* **spit ˈvenom/ˈblood** to show that you are very angry; to speak in an angry way **within ˈspitting distance (of sth)** (*BrE*) (also **within ˈshouting distance** *NAmE*, *BrE*) (*informal*) very close
PHR V ˌ**spit ˈup** (*NAmE*, *informal*) (especially of a baby) to VOMIT (= bring food from the stomach back out through the mouth)
■ ***noun***
▸ IN/FROM MOUTH **1** [U] the liquid that is produced in your mouth SYN **saliva** **2** [C, usually sing.] the act of spitting liquid or food out of your mouth
▸ PIECE OF LAND **3** [C] a long thin piece of land that sticks out into the sea/ocean, a lake, etc. ➲ VISUAL VOCAB page V4
▸ FOR COOKING MEAT **4** [C] a long thin straight piece of metal that you put through meat to hold and turn it while you cook it over a fire
IDM ˌ**spit and ˈpolish** (*informal*) thorough cleaning and polishing of sth

spite 0‑ /spaɪt/ *noun*, *verb*
■ ***noun*** [U] a feeling of wanting to hurt or upset sb SYN **malice**: *I'm sure he only said it* ***out of spite.***
IDM **in ˈspite of sth** 0‑ if you say that sb did sth **in spite of** a fact, you mean it is surprising that that fact did not prevent them from doing it SYN **despite**: *In spite of his age, he still leads an active life.* ◇ *They went swimming in spite of all the danger signs.* ◇ *English became the official language for business* ***in spite of the fact that*** *the population was largely Chinese.* ➲ LANGUAGE BANK at HOWEVER **in ˈspite of yourself** if you do sth **in spite of yourself**, you do it although you did not intend or expect to: *He fell asleep, in spite of himself.*
■ ***verb*** (only used in the infinitive with *to*) **~ sb** to deliberately annoy or upset sb: *They're playing the music so loud just to spite us.* IDM see NOSE *n.*

spite·ful /ˈspaɪtfl/ *adj.* behaving in an unkind way in order to hurt or upset sb SYN **malicious** ▸ **spite·ful·ly** /-fəli/ *adv.*: *'I don't need you,' she said spitefully.* **spite·ful·ness** *noun* [U]

spit-roast /ˈspɪt rəʊst; *NAmE* roʊst/ *verb* **~ sth** to cook meat on a SPIT *n.* (4)

ˌ**spitting ˈimage** *noun*
IDM **be the spitting image of sb** to look exactly like sb else: *She's the spitting image of her mother.*

spit·tle /ˈspɪtl/ *noun* [U] (*old-fashioned*) the liquid that forms in the mouth SYN **saliva, spit**

spit·toon /spɪˈtuːn/ *noun* a container, used especially in the past, for people to SPIT into

spiv /spɪv/ *noun* (*old-fashioned*, *BrE*, *slang*, *disapproving*) a man who makes his money by being dishonest in business, especially one who dresses in a way that makes people believe he is rich and successful

splash /splæʃ/ *verb*, *noun*
■ ***verb*** **1** [I] **+ adv./prep.** (of liquid) to fall noisily onto a surface: *Water splashed onto the floor.* ◇ *Rain splashed against the windows.* **2** [T] to make sb/sth wet by making water, mud, etc. fall on them/it: **~ sth on/onto/over sb/sth** *He splashed cold water on his face.* ◇ **~ sb/sth with sth** *He splashed his face with cold water.* ◇ *My clothes were splashed with mud.* ◇ **~ sb/sth** *Stop splashing me!* **3** [I] (**+ adv./prep.**) to move through water making drops fly everywhere: *The kids were splashing through the puddles.* ◇ *People were having fun in the pool, swimming or just splashing around.* **4** [T] **~ sth with sth** [usually passive] to decorate sth with areas of bright colour, not in a regular pattern: *The walls were splashed with patches of blue and purple.*
PHR V ˈ**splash sth across/over sth** to put a photograph, news story, etc. in a place where it will be easily noticed ˌ**splash ˈdown** (of a SPACECRAFT) to land in the sea or ocean ➲ related noun SPLASHDOWN ˌ**splash ˈout (on sth)** | ˌ**splash sth↔ˈout (on/for sth)** (*BrE*, *informal*) to spend a lot of money on sth: *We're going to splash out and buy a new car.* ◇ *He splashed out hundreds of pounds on designer clothes.*
■ ***noun*** **1** [C] the sound of sth hitting liquid or of liquid hitting sth: *We heard the splash when she fell into the pool.* **2** [C] a small amount of liquid that falls onto sth; the mark that this makes: *splashes of water on the floor* ◇ *dark splashes of mud on her skirt* **3** [C] a small area of bright colour or light that contrasts with the colours around it: *These flowers will give a splash of colour throughout the summer.* **4** [sing.] (*BrE*, *informal*) a small amount of liquid that you add to a drink: *coffee with just a splash of milk* ➲ compare

S

DASH **5** [sing.] an article in a newspaper, etc. that is intended to attract a lot of attention

IDM **make, cause, etc. a 'splash** (*informal*) to do sth in a way that attracts a lot of attention or causes a lot of excitement

splash·back /'splæʃbæk/ *noun* (*BrE*) a surface behind a sink or cooker/stove which protects the wall from liquids ➲ VISUAL VOCAB page V22

splash·down /'splæʃdaʊn/ *noun* [C, U] a landing of a SPACECRAFT in the sea/ocean

splashy /'splæʃi/ *adj.* (**splash·ier, splashi·est**) (*especially NAmE*) bright and very easy to notice

splat /splæt/ *noun* [sing.] (*informal*) the sound made by sth wet hitting a surface with force: *The tomato hit the wall with a splat.* ▸ **splat** *adv.*: *The omelette fell splat onto the floor.*

splat·ter /'splætə(r)/ *verb* **1** [I] (+ **adv./prep.**) (of large drops of liquid) to fall or hit sth noisily: *Heavy rain splattered on the roof.* **2** [T, I] to drop or throw water, paint, mud, etc. on sb/sth; to make sb/sth wet or dirty by landing on them in large drops: **~ sb/sth** (+ **adv./prep.**) *The walls were splattered with blood.* ◊ **+ adv./prep.** *Coffee had splattered across the front of his shirt.*

splay /spleɪ/ *verb* [T, I] **~ (sth) (out)** to make fingers, legs, etc. become further apart from each other or spread out; to be spread out wide apart: *She lay on the bed, her arms and legs splayed out.* ◊ *His long fingers splayed across her back.*

ˌsplay-'foot *noun* a broad flat foot which turns away from the other foot ▸ **ˌsplay-'footed** *adj.*

spleen /spliːn/ *noun* **1** [C] a small organ near the stomach that controls the quality of the blood cells: *a ruptured spleen* ➲ VISUAL VOCAB page V48 **2** [U] (*literary*) anger: *He* ***vented his spleen*** (= shouted in an angry way) *on the assembled crowd.* ➲ see also SPLENETIC

splen·did /'splendɪd/ *adj., exclamation*

■ ***adj.*** (*especially BrE*) **1** (*old-fashioned*) excellent; very good SYN **great**: *What a splendid idea!* ◊ *We've all had a splendid time.* **2** very impressive; very beautiful: *splendid scenery* ◊ *The hotel stands* ***in splendid isolation****, surrounded by moorland.* ▸ **splen·did·ly** *adv.*: *You all played splendidly.*

■ ***exclamation*** (*old-fashioned, especially BrE*) used to show that you approve of sth, or are pleased: *You're both coming? Splendid!*

splen·dif·er·ous /splen'dɪfərəs/ *adj.* (*informal, humorous*) extremely good or pleasant

S

splen·dour (*especially US* **splen·dor**) /'splendə(r)/ *noun* **1** [U] grand and impressive beauty SYN **grandeur**: *a view of Rheims Cathedral, in all its splendour* ◊ *The palace has been restored to its former splendour.* **2 splendours** [pl.] the beautiful and impressive features or qualities of sth, especially a place: *the splendours of Rome* (= its fine buildings, etc.)

splen·et·ic /splə'netɪk/ *adj.* (*formal*) often bad-tempered and angry

splice /splaɪs/ *verb, noun*

■ ***verb*** **1 ~ sth (together)** to join the ends of two pieces of rope by twisting them together **2 ~ sth (together)** to join the ends of two pieces of film, tape, etc. by sticking them together

IDM **get 'spliced** (*old-fashioned, BrE, informal*) to get married

■ ***noun*** the place where two pieces of film, tape, rope, etc. have been joined

spli·cer /'splaɪsə(r)/ *noun* a person or machine that joins pieces of tape, cable, etc. together

spliff /splɪf/ *noun* (*BrE, slang*) a cigarette containing CANNABIS

splint /splɪnt/ *noun* a long piece of wood or metal that is tied to a broken arm or leg to keep it still and in the right position

splin·ter /'splɪntə(r)/ *noun, verb*

■ ***noun*** a small thin sharp piece of wood, metal, glass, etc. that has broken off a larger piece SYN **shard**

■ ***verb*** **1** [I, T] (of wood, glass, stone, etc.) to break, or to make sth break, into small, thin sharp pieces SYN **shatter**: *The mirror cracked but did not splinter.* ◊ **~ sth** *The impact splintered the wood.* **2** [I] (of a group of people) to divide into smaller groups that are no longer connected; to separate from a larger group: *The party began to splinter.* ◊ **~ (off) (from sth)** *Several firms have splintered off from the original company.*

'splinter group *noun* a small group of people that has separated from a larger one, especially in politics

split 🔑 /splɪt/ *verb, noun*

■ ***verb*** (**split·ting, split, split**)

▸ DIVIDE **1** 🔑 [T, I] **~ (sth)** to divide, or to make a group of people divide, into smaller groups that have very different opinions: *a debate that has* ***split*** *the country* ***down the middle*** ◊ *The committee split over government subsidies.* **2** 🔑 [T, I] to divide, or to make sth divide, into two or more parts: **~ sth (into sth)** *She split the class into groups of four.* ◊ **~ (into sth)** *The results split neatly into two groups.* ➲ see also SPLIT UP **3** 🔑 [T] to divide sth into two or more parts and share it between different people, activities, etc: **~ sth (with sb)** *She split the money she won with her brother.* ◊ **~ sth between sb/sth** *His time is split between the London and Paris offices.* ➲ see also SPLIT UP

▸ TEAR **4** 🔑 [I, T] to tear, or to make sth tear, along a straight line: *Her dress had split along the seam.* ◊ **~ (sth) open** *The cushion split open and sent feathers everywhere.* ◊ **~ sth** *Don't tell me you've split another pair of pants!*

▸ CUT **5** [T] to cut sb's skin and make it BLEED: **~ sth open** *She split her head open on the cupboard door.* ◊ **~ sth** *How did you split your lip?*

▸ END RELATIONSHIP **6** [I] (*informal*) to leave sb and stop having a relationship with them: **~ (with sb)** *The singer split with his wife last June.* ◊ **~ (from sb)** *She intends to split from the band at the end of the tour.* ➲ see also SPLIT UP

▸ LEAVE **7** [I] (*old-fashioned, informal*) to leave a place quickly: *Let's split!*

IDM **split the 'difference** (when discussing a price, etc.) to agree on an amount that is at an equal distance between the two amounts that have been suggested **split 'hairs** to pay too much attention in an argument to differences that are very small and not important **split an in'finitive** to place an adverb between 'to' and the infinitive of a verb, for example to say 'to strongly deny a rumour'. Some people consider this to be bad English style. **split your 'sides (laughing/with laughter)** to laugh a lot at sb/sth **split the 'ticket** (*US, politics*) to vote for candidates from more than one party ➲ more at MIDDLE *n.*

PHR V **ˌsplit a'way/'off (from sth)** | **ˌsplit sth↔a'way/'off (from sth)** to separate from, or to separate sth from, a larger object or group: *A rebel faction has split away from the main group.* ◊ *The storm split a branch off from the main trunk.* **'split on sb (to sb)** (*BrE, informal*) to tell sb in authority about sth wrong, dishonest, etc. that sb else has done: *Don't worry—he won't split on us.* **ˌsplit 'up (with sb)** 🔑 to stop having a relationship with sb: *My parents split up last year.* ◊ *She's split up with her boyfriend.* **ˌsplit sb 'up** to make two people stop having a relationship with each other: *My friend is doing her best to split us up.* **ˌsplit sb 'up** | **ˌsplit 'up** 🔑 to divide a group of people into smaller parts; to become divided up in this way: *We were split up into groups to discuss the question.* ◊ *Let's split up now and meet again at lunchtime.* **ˌsplit sth↔'up** 🔑 to divide sth into smaller parts: *The day was split up into 6 one-hour sessions.*

■ ***noun***

▸ DISAGREEMENT **1** 🔑 [C] (*informal*) a disagreement that divides a group of people or makes sb separate from sb else: **~ (within sth)** *a damaging split within the party leadership* ◊ **~ (with sb/sth)** *the years following his bitter split with his wife* ◊ **~ (between A and B)** *There have been reports of a split between the Prime Minister and the Cabinet.*

▸ DIVISION **2** 🔑 [sing.] a division between two or more things; one of the parts that sth is divided into: *He demanded a 50–50 split in the profits.*

▸ TEAR/HOLE **3** 🗝 [C] a long crack or hole made when sth tears: *There's a big split in the tent.*
▸ BANANA DISH **4** [C] a sweet dish made from fruit, especially a BANANA cut in two along its length, with cream, ice cream, etc. on top: *a banana split*
▸ BODY POSITION **5 the splits** [pl.] (*US* also **split** [sing.]) a position in which you stretch your legs flat across the floor in opposite directions with the rest of your body vertical: *a gymnast **doing the splits***

ˌsplit ˈend *noun* a hair on your head that has divided into parts at the end because it is dry or in poor condition

ˌsplit inˈfinitive *noun* (*grammar*) the form of the verb with 'to', with an adverb placed between 'to' and the verb, as in *She seems to really like it*. Some people consider this to be bad English style.

ˌsplit-ˈlevel *adj.* (of a room, floor, etc.) having parts at different levels

ˌsplit ˈpea *noun* [usually pl.] a type of dried PEA, split into halves

ˌsplit-persoˈnality disorder *noun* = MULTIPLE-PERSONALITY DISORDER

ˌsplit ˈscreen *noun* a way of displaying two or more pictures or pieces of information at the same time on a television, cinema or computer screen ▸ **ˌsplit-ˈscreen** *adj.* [only before noun]: *a movie with several split-screen sequences*

ˌsplit ˈsecond *noun* a very short moment of time: *Their eyes met **for a split second**.*

ˌsplit-ˈsecond *adj.* [only before noun] done very quickly or very accurately: *She had to make a split-second decision.* ◇ *The success of the raid depended on **split-second timing**.*

ˌsplit ˈshift *noun* two separate periods of time that you spend working in a single day, with several hours between them: *I work split shifts in a busy restaurant.*

splits·ville /ˈsplɪtsvɪl/ *noun* [sing.] (*NAmE, slang*) the end of a relationship: *Within three months of the honeymoon, it was splitsville for Ron and Mimi.*

ˌsplit ˈticket *noun* (in elections in the US) a vote in which sb votes for candidates from two different parties ▸ **ˌsplit-ˈticket** *adj.*: *a split-ticket vote*

split·ting /ˈsplɪtɪŋ/ *adj.* [only before noun] if you have a **splitting headache**, you have a very bad pain in your head

splodge /splɒdʒ; *NAmE* splɑːdʒ/ (*BrE*) (also **splotch** /splɒtʃ; *NAmE* splɑːtʃ/ *NAmE, BrE*) *noun* a large mark or spot of ink, paint, mud, etc; a small area of colour or light

splosh /splɒʃ; *NAmE* splɑːʃ/ *verb, noun* (*BrE, informal*)
■ ***verb*** [I] **+ adv./prep.** to move through water, making soft sounds: *Children were sploshing about in the pool.*
■ ***noun* 1** the soft sound of sth moving through or falling into water **2** a small amount of liquid that moves through the air

splurge /splɜːdʒ; *NAmE* splɜːrdʒ/ *noun, verb*
■ ***noun*** [usually sing.] (*informal*) an act of spending a lot of money on sth that you do not really need
■ ***verb*** [T, I] **~ (sth) (on sth)** (*informal*) to spend a lot of money on sth that you do not really need

splut·ter /ˈsplʌtə(r)/ *verb, noun*
■ ***verb* 1** [T, I] to speak quickly and with difficulty, making soft SPITTING sounds, because you are angry or embarrassed SYN **sputter**: **+ speech (out)** *'But, but...you can't!' she spluttered.* ◇ **~ (with sth)** *Her father spluttered with indignation.* **2** [I] to make a series of short EXPLOSIVE sounds SYN **sputter**: *The firework spluttered and went out.* ◇ *She fled from the blaze, **coughing and spluttering**.*
■ ***noun*** a short EXPLOSIVE sound: *The car started with a loud splutter.*

spoil 🗝 /spɔɪl/ *verb, noun*
■ ***verb*** (**spoiled, spoiled** /spɔɪld/) (*BrE* also **spoilt, spoilt** /spɔɪlt/) **1** 🗝 [T] **~ sth** to change sth good into sth bad, unpleasant, useless, etc. SYN **ruin**: *Our camping trip was spoilt by bad weather.* ◇ *Don't let him spoil your evening.* ◇ *The tall buildings have spoiled the view.* ◇ *Don't eat too many nuts—you'll **spoil your appetite** (= will no longer be hungry at the proper time to eat).* ◇ (*BrE*) *spoiled ballot papers* (= not valid because not correctly marked) **2** 🗝 [T] **~ sb** to give a child everything that they ask for and not enough discipline in a way that has a bad effect on their character and behaviour SYN **overindulge**: *She spoils those kids of hers.* **3** [T] **~ sb/yourself** to make sb/yourself happy by doing sth special: *Why not spoil yourself with a weekend in a top hotel?* ◇ *He really spoiled me on my birthday.* **4** [I] (of food) to become bad so that it can no longer be eaten SYN **go off**
IDM **be ˈspoiling for a fight** to want to fight with sb very much **spoil the ˌship for a haˈp'orth/haˈpennyworth of ˈtar** (*saying*) to spoil sth good because you did not spend enough money or time on a small but essential part of it ⊃ more at COOK *n.*
■ ***noun* 1 the spoils** [pl.] (*formal* or *literary*) goods taken from a place by thieves or by an army that has won a battle or war **2 spoils** [pl.] the profits or advantages that sb gets from being successful: *the spoils of high office* **3** [U] (*technical*) waste material that is brought up when a hole is dug, etc.

spoil·age /ˈspɔɪlɪdʒ/ *noun* [U] (*technical*) the decay of food which means that it can no longer be used

spoil·er /ˈspɔɪlə(r)/ *noun* **1** a part of an aircraft's wing that can be raised in order to interrupt the flow of air over it and so slow the aircraft's speed **2** a raised part on a fast car that prevents it from being lifted off the road when travelling very fast **3** (*especially NAmE*) a candidate for a political office who is unlikely to win but who may get enough votes to prevent one of the main candidates from winning **4** a person or thing that intends or is intended to stop sb/sth being successful **5** information that you are given about what is going to happen in a film/movie, television series etc. before it is shown to the public **6** a newspaper story, book, etc. that is produced very quickly in order to take attention away from one produced by a COMPETITOR that appears at the same time

spoil·sport /ˈspɔɪlspɔːt; *NAmE* -spɔːrt/ *noun* (*informal*) a person who spoils other people's enjoyment, for example by not taking part in an activity or by trying to stop other people from doing it: *Don't be such a spoilsport!*

the ˈspoils system *noun* [sing.] the arrangement in US politics which allows the President to give government jobs to supporters after winning an election

spoilt /spɔɪlt/ (*BrE*) (also **spoiled** /spɔɪld/ *NAmE, BrE*) *adj.* (of a child) rude and badly behaved because they are given everything they ask for and not enough discipline: *a spoiled brat* ◇ *He's **spoilt rotten*** (= a lot).
IDM **be spoilt for ˈchoice** (*BrE*) to have such a lot of things to choose from that it is very difficult to make a decision

spoke /spəʊk; *NAmE* spoʊk/ *noun* one of the thin bars or long straight pieces of metal that connect the centre of a wheel to its outer edge, for example on a bicycle ⊃ VISUAL VOCAB page V41
IDM **put a ˈspoke in sb's wheel** (*BrE*) to prevent sb from putting their plans into operation ⊃ see also SPEAK, SPOKE, SPOKEN *v.*

spoken 🗝 /ˈspəʊkən; *NAmE* ˈspoʊ-/ *adj.*
1 🗝 involving speaking rather than writing; expressed in speech rather than in writing: *spoken English* ◇ *spoken commands* **2** (following an adverb) speaking in the way mentioned: *a quietly spoken man* ⊃ see also OUTSPOKEN

ˈspoken for *adj.* [not before noun] already claimed or being kept for sb: *I'm afraid you can't sit there—those seats are spoken for.* ◇ (*old-fashioned*) *Liza is already spoken for* (= she is already married or has a partner).

the ˌspoken ˈword *noun* [sing.] language expressed in speech, rather than being written or sung

spokes·man /ˈspəʊksmən; *NAmE* ˈspoʊ-/, **spokes·woman** /ˈspəʊkswʊmən; *NAmE* ˈspoʊ-/ *noun* (*pl.* **-men** /-mən/, **-women** /-wɪmɪn/) a person who speaks on behalf of a group or an organization: *a police spokesman* ◇ **~ for sb/sth** *A spokeswoman for the government denied the rumours.* ⊃ note at GENDER

S

Synonyms

spoken

oral • vocal

These words all describe producing language using the voice, rather than writing.

spoken (of language) produced using the voice; said rather than written: *an exam in spoken English*

oral [usually before noun] spoken rather than written: *There will be a test of both oral and written French.*

SPOKEN OR ORAL?

Both of these words can be used to refer to language skills and the communication of information: *spoken/oral French* ◇ *a spoken/oral presentation*. In these cases **oral** is slightly more technical than **spoken**. **Oral** but not **spoken** can also be used with words such as *tradition*, *culture* and *legends* to talk about the way in which people pass stories down from one generation to the next, and in legal contexts followed by words such as *evidence* and *hearing*.

vocal [usually before noun] connected with the voice: *vocal music* ◇ *the vocal organs* (= the tongue, lips, etc.) NOTE **Vocal** is used to talk about the ability to produce sounds using the voice, and is often used in musical contexts when referring to singing.

PATTERNS

- spoken/oral **French/English/Japanese, etc.**
- spoken/oral **language skills**

spokes·per·son /ˈspəʊkspɜːsn; *NAmE* ˈspoʊkspɜːrsn/ *noun* (*pl.* **-persons** or **-people**) ~ (**for sb/sth**) a person who speaks on behalf of a group or an organization

spon·dee /ˈspɒndiː; *NAmE* ˈspɑːn-/ *noun* (*technical*) a unit of sound in poetry consisting of two strong or long syllables

sponge /spʌndʒ/ *noun, verb*

■ ***noun*** **1** [C] a piece of artificial or natural material that is soft and light and full of holes and can hold water easily, used for washing or cleaning: (*figurative*) *His mind was like a sponge, ready to absorb anything.* ➲ VISUAL VOCAB pages V21, V49 **2** [U] artificial sponge used for filling furniture, CUSHIONS, etc. **3** [C] a simple sea creature with a light body full of holes, from which natural sponge is obtained **4** [C, U] (*BrE*) = SPONGE CAKE: *a chocolate sponge*

■ ***verb*** **1** [T] ~ **sb/yourself/sth** (**down**) to wash sb/yourself/sth with a wet cloth or SPONGE SYN **wipe**: *She sponged his hot face.* ◇ *Take your jacket off and I'll sponge it down with water.* **2** [T] ~ **sth + adv./prep.** to remove sth using a wet cloth or SPONGE SYN **wash**: *We tried to sponge the blood off my shirt.* **3** [I] ~ (**off/on sb**) (*informal, disapproving*) to get money, food, etc. regularly from other people without doing anything for them or offering to pay SYN **scrounge**: *He spent his life sponging off his relatives.*

ˈ**sponge bag** (also ˈ**toilet bag**, ˈ**wash·bag**) (all *BrE*) (*NAmE* ˈ**toiletry bag**) *noun* a small bag for holding your soap, TOOTHBRUSH, etc. when you are travelling ➲ VISUAL VOCAB page V21

ˈ**sponge bath** *noun* (*NAmE*) an act of washing the whole of sb's body when they cannot get out of bed because they are sick, injured or old

ˈ**sponge cake** (also **sponge**) *noun* [C, U] (*BrE*) a light cake made from eggs, sugar and flour, with or without fat

ˌ**sponge ˈpudding** *noun* [U, C] (*BrE*) a hot DESSERT (= a sweet dish) like a sponge cake that usually has jam or fruit on top

spon·ger /ˈspʌndʒə(r)/ *noun* (*informal*) a person who gets money, food, etc. from other people without doing anything for them or offering to pay

spongi·form /ˈspʌndʒɪfɔːm; *NAmE* -fɔːrm/ *adj.* (*technical*) having or relating to a structure with holes in it like a SPONGE ➲ see also BSE

spongy /ˈspʌndʒi/ *adj.* soft and able to absorb water easily like a SPONGE SYN **springy**: *spongy moss* ◇ *The ground was soft and spongy.* ◇ *The bread had a spongy texture.* ▸ **spon·gi·ness** *noun* [U]

spon·sor /ˈspɒnsə(r); *NAmE* ˈspɑːn-/ *noun, verb*

■ ***noun*** **1** a person or company that pays for a radio or television programme, or for a concert or sporting event, usually in return for advertising: *The race organizers are trying to attract sponsors.* **2** a person who agrees to give sb money for a charity if that person succeeds in completing a particular activity: *I'm collecting sponsors for next week's charity run.* **3** a person or company that supports sb by paying for their training or education **4** a person who introduces and supports a proposal for a new law, etc: *the sponsor of the new immigration bill* **5** a person who agrees to be officially responsible for another person **6** a person who presents a child for Christian BAPTISM or CONFIRMATION SYN **godparent**

■ ***verb*** **1** ~ **sth** (of a company, etc.) to pay the costs of a particular event, programme, etc. as a way of advertising: *sports events sponsored by the tobacco industry* **2** ~ **sth** to arrange for sth official to take place: *The US is sponsoring negotiations between the two sides.* **3** ~ **sb** (**for sth/to do sth**) to agree to give sb money for a charity if they complete a particular task: *Will you sponsor me for a charity walk I'm doing?* ◇ *a sponsored swim* **4** ~ **sb** (**through sth**) to support sb by paying for their training or education: *She found a company to sponsor her through college.* **5** ~ **sth** to introduce a proposal for a new law, etc: *The bill was sponsored by a Labour MP.*

spon·sor·ship /ˈspɒnsəʃɪp; *NAmE* ˈspɑːnsərʃɪp/ *noun* **1** [U, C] financial support from a sponsor: *a $50 million sponsorship deal* ◇ *The project needs to raise £8 million in sponsorship.* ◇ *We need to find sponsorships for the expedition.* **2** [U] the act of sponsoring sb/sth or being sponsored: *the senator's sponsorship of the job training legislation*

spon·tan·eity /ˌspɒntəˈneɪəti; *NAmE* ˌspɑːn-/ *noun* [U] the quality of being spontaneous

spon·tan·eous /spɒnˈteɪniəs; *NAmE* spɑːn-/ *adj.* **1** not planned but done because you suddenly want to do it: *a spontaneous offer of help* ◇ *The audience burst into spontaneous applause.* **2** often doing things without planning to, because you suddenly want to do them **3** (*technical*) happening naturally, without being made to happen: *spontaneous remission of the disease* **4** done naturally, without being forced or practised: *a tape recording of spontaneous speech* ◇ *a wonderfully spontaneous performance of the piece* ▸ **spon·tan·eous·ly** *adv.*: *We spontaneously started to dance.* ◇ *The bleeding often stops spontaneously.*

sponˌtaneous comˈbustion *noun* [U] the burning of a mineral or vegetable substance caused by chemical changes inside it and not by fire or heat from outside

spoof /spuːf/ *noun, verb*

■ ***noun*** (*informal*) a humorous copy of a film/movie, television programme, etc. that exaggerates its main features: *It's a spoof on horror movies.*

■ ***verb*** **1** ~ **sth** to copy a film/movie, television programme, etc. in an amusing way by exaggerating its main features: *It is a movie that spoofs other movies.* **2** ~ **sth** to send an email that appears to come from sb else's email address: *Someone has been spoofing my address.* ▸ **spoof·ing** *noun* [U]

spook /spuːk/ *noun, verb*

■ ***noun*** (*informal*) **1** a GHOST: *a castle haunted by spooks* **2** (*especially NAmE*) a SPY: *a CIA spook*

■ ***verb*** [T, usually passive, I] ~ (**sb/sth**) (*informal, especially NAmE*) to frighten a person or an animal; to become frightened: *We were spooked by the strange noises and lights.* ◇ *The horse spooked at the siren.*

spooky /ˈspuːki/ *adj.* (**spook·ier**, **spooki·est**) HELP You can also use **more spooky** and **most spooky**. (*informal*) strange and frightening SYN **creepy**: *a spooky old house* ◇ *I was just thinking about her when she phoned. Spooky!*

spool /spuːl/ *noun, verb*
■ ***noun*** (*especially NAmE*) = REEL (1): *a spool of thread* ➲ VISUAL VOCAB page V35
■ ***verb*** **1** [T] **~ sth + adv./prep.** to wind sth onto or off a spool **2** [T, I] **~ (sth)** (*computing*) to move data and store it for a short time, for example on a disk, especially before it is printed

spoon 🔑 /spuːn/ *noun, verb*
■ ***noun*** **1** 🔑 a tool that has a handle with a shallow bowl at the end, used for stirring, serving and eating food: *a soup spoon* ◇ *a wooden spoon* ➲ VISUAL VOCAB page V19 ➲ see also DESSERTSPOON, GREASY SPOON, TABLESPOON, TEASPOON **2** = SPOONFUL IDM see BORN
■ ***verb*** **~ sth + adv./prep.** to lift and move food with a spoon: *She spooned the sauce over the chicken pieces.*

spoon·bill /ˈspuːnbɪl/ *noun* a large bird with long legs, a long neck and a beak that is wide and flat at the end

spoon·er·ism /ˈspuːnərɪzəm/ *noun* a mistake in which you change around the first sounds of two words by mistake when saying them, often with a humorous result, for example *well-boiled icicle* for *well-oiled bicycle* ORIGIN Named after **W.A. Spooner** (1844–1930), the head of New College, Oxford, who was said to have made many mistakes like this when he spoke.

ˈ**spoon-feed** *verb* **1** (*disapproving*) to teach people sth in a way that gives them too much help and does not make them think for themselves: **~ sb (with sth)** *The students here do not expect to be spoon-fed.* ◇ **~ sth to sb** *They had information spoon-fed to them.* **2 ~ sb** to feed sb, especially a baby, with a spoon

spoon·ful /ˈspuːnfʊl/ (also **spoon**) *noun* the amount that a spoon can hold: *two spoonfuls of sugar*

spoor /spʊə(r); *NAmE* spʊr/ *noun* [sing.] a track or smell that a wild animal leaves as it travels

spor·ad·ic /spəˈrædɪk/ *adj.* happening only occasionally or at intervals that are not regular SYN **intermittent**: ***sporadic fighting/gunfire/violence, etc.*** ◇ *sporadic outbreaks of the disease* ▶ **spor·ad·ic·al·ly** /-kli/ *adv.*: *She attended lectures only sporadically.* ◇ *Fighting continued sporadically for two months.*

spore /spɔː(r)/ *noun* (*biology*) one of the very small cells that are produced by some plants and that develop into new plants: *Ferns, mosses and fungi spread by means of spores.* ➲ COLLOCATIONS at LIFE

spor·ran /ˈspɒrən; *NAmE* ˈspɑː-/ *noun* a flat bag, usually made of leather or fur, that is worn by men in front of the KILT as part of the Scottish national dress

sport 🔑 /spɔːt; *NAmE* spɔːrt/ *noun, verb*
■ ***noun*** **1** 🔑 [U] (*BrE*) (*NAmE* **sports** [pl.]) activity that you do for pleasure and that needs physical effort or skill, usually done in a special area and according to fixed rules: *There are excellent facilities for sport and recreation.* ◇ *I'm not interested in sport.* ◇ *the use of drugs in sport* **2** 🔑 [C] a particular form of sport: *What's your favourite sport?* ◇ ***team/water sports*** ◇ *a sports club* ➲ VISUAL VOCAB pages V36–V39 ➲ see also BLOOD SPORT, FIELD SPORTS, SPECTATOR SPORT, WINTER SPORTS **3** [C] (*AustralE, NZE, informal*) used as a friendly way of addressing sb, especially a man: *Good on you, sport!* **4** [U] (*formal*) enjoyment or fun: *The comments were only made **in sport**.* ◇ *to **make sport of*** (= to joke about) ***sb/sth*** **5** [C] (*biology*) a plant or an animal that is different in a noticeable way from its usual type
IDM **be a (good) ˈsport** (*informal*) to be generous, cheerful and pleasant, especially in a difficult situation: *She's a good sport.* ◇ *Go on, be a sport* (= used when asking sb to help you).
■ ***verb*** **1** [T] **~ sth** to have or wear sth in a proud way SYN **wear**: *to sport a beard* ◇ *She was sporting a T-shirt with the company's logo on it.* **2** [I] **+ adv./prep.** (*literary*) to play in a happy and lively way

sport·ing /ˈspɔːtɪŋ; *NAmE* ˈspɔːrtɪŋ/ *adj.* **1** [only before noun] connected with sports: *a major sporting event* ◇ *a range of sporting activities* ◇ *His main sporting interests are golf and tennis.* ◇ (*NAmE*) *a store selling sporting goods* **2** (*especially BrE*) fair and generous in your treatment of other people, especially in a game or sport OPP for sense 2 UNSPORTING ▶ **sport·ing·ly** *adv.*: *He sportingly agreed to play the point again.*
IDM **a ˌsporting ˈchance** a reasonable chance of success

ˈ**sports car** (*US* also ˈ**sport car**) *noun* a low fast car, often with a roof that can be folded back ➲ VISUAL VOCAB page V42

sports·cast /ˈspɔːtskɑːst; *NAmE* ˈspɔːrtskæst/ *noun* (*NAmE*) a television or radio broadcast of sports news or a sports event

sports·cast·er /ˈspɔːtskɑːstə(r); *NAmE* ˈspɔːrtskæstər/ *noun* (*NAmE*) a person who introduces and presents a sportscast

ˈ**sports centre** *noun* (*BrE*) a building where the public can go to play many different kinds of sports, swim, etc.

ˈ**sports day** (*BrE*) (*NAmE* ˈ**field day**) *noun* a special day at school when there are no classes and children compete in sports events

ˈ**sports jacket** (*NAmE* also ˈ**sport jacket**) *noun* a man's jacket for informal occasions, sometimes made of TWEED

sports·man /ˈspɔːtsmən; *NAmE* ˈspɔːrts-/, **sports·woman** /ˈspɔːtswʊmən; *NAmE* ˈspɔːrts-/ *noun* (*pl.* **-men** /-mən/, **-women** /-wɪmɪn/) (*especially BrE*) a person who takes part in sport, especially sb who is very good at it SYN **athlete**: *a keen sportswoman* ◇ *He is one of this country's top professional sportsmen.* ➲ note at GENDER

sports·man·like /ˈspɔːtsmənlaɪk; *NAmE* ˈspɔːrts-/ *adj.* behaving in a fair, generous and polite way, especially when playing a sport or game: *a sportsmanlike attitude*

sports·man·ship /ˈspɔːtsmənʃɪp; *NAmE* ˈspɔːrts-/ *noun* [U] fair, generous and polite behaviour, especially when playing a sport or game

sports·per·son /ˈspɔːtspɜːsn; *NAmE* ˈspɔːrtspɜːrsn/ *noun* (*pl.* **-per·sons** or **-people**) (*especially BrE*) a person who takes part in sport, especially sb who is very good at it SYN **athlete**

ˈ**sports shirt** (*NAmE* also ˈ**sport shirt**) *noun* a man's shirt for informal occasions

sports·wear /ˈspɔːtsweə(r); *NAmE* ˈspɔːrtswer/ *noun* [U] **1** (*especially BrE*) clothes that are worn for playing sports, or in informal situations **2** (*especially NAmE*) clothes that are worn in informal situations

ˌ**sport uˈtility vehicle** *noun* (*abbr.* SUV) (*especially NAmE*) a type of large car, often with FOUR-WHEEL DRIVE and made originally for travelling over rough ground ➲ VISUAL VOCAB page V42

sporty /ˈspɔːti; *NAmE* ˈspɔːrti/ *adj.* (**sport·ier**, **sporti·est**) (*informal*) **1** (*especially BrE*) liking or good at sport: *I'm not very sporty.* **2** (of clothes) bright, attractive and informal; looking suitable for wearing for sports: *a sporty cotton top* **3** (of cars) fast and elegant: *a sporty Mercedes*

spot 🔑 /spɒt; *NAmE* spɑːt/ *noun, verb, adj.*
■ ***noun***
▸ SMALL MARK **1** 🔑 a small round area that has a different colour or feels different from the surface it is on: *Which has spots, the leopard or the tiger?* ◇ *The male bird has a red spot on its beak.* ◇ (*BrE*) *She was wearing a black skirt with white spots.* ➲ see also BEAUTY SPOT, SUNSPOT ➲ SYNONYMS at PATCH **2** 🔑 a small dirty mark on sth: *His jacket was covered with spots of mud.* ◇ *rust spots* ➲ SYNONYMS at MARK **3** 🔑 [usually pl.] a small mark or lump on a person's skin, sometimes with a yellow head to it: *The baby's whole body was covered in small red spots.* ◇ (*BrE*) *teenagers worried about their spots* ➲ compare PIMPLE, RASH, ZIT
▸ PLACE **4** 🔑 a particular area or place: *a **quiet/secluded/lonely, etc. spot*** ◇ *He showed me **the exact spot** where he had asked her to marry him.* ◇ *She stood **rooted to the spot** with fear* (= unable to move). ◇ *a tourist spot* ➲ see also BLACK SPOT, BLIND SPOT, HOT SPOT, NIGHTSPOT, TROUBLE SPOT ➲ SYNONYMS at PLACE
▸ SMALL AMOUNT **5** [usually sing.] **~ of sth** (*BrE, informal*) a small amount of sth SYN **bit**: *He's in a spot of trouble.*

S

6 [usually pl.] **~ (of sth)** a small amount of a liquid: *I felt a few spots of rain.*
▸ PART OF SHOW **7** a part of a television, radio, club or theatre show that is given to a particular entertainer or type of entertainment: *a **guest/solo spot***
▸ IN COMPETITION **8** a position in a competition or an event: *two teams battling for top spot*
▸ LIGHT **9** (*informal*) = SPOTLIGHT
IDM **in a (tight) 'spot** (*informal*) in a difficult situation **on the 'spot 1** immediately: *He answered the question on the spot.* ◇ *an on-the-spot parking fine* **2** at the actual place where sth is happening: *An ambulance was on the spot within minutes.* ◇ *an on-the-spot report* **3** (*NAmE* also **in 'place**) in one exact place, without moving in any direction: *Running on the spot is good exercise.* **put sb on the 'spot** to make sb feel awkward or embarrassed by asking them a difficult question: *The interviewer's questions really put him on the spot.* ➲ more at BRIGHT *adj.*, GLUE *v.*, HIT *v.*, KNOCK *v.*, LEOPARD, RIVET *v.*, SOFT, TIGHT
■ ***verb*** (-tt-) **1** (not used in the progressive tenses) to see or notice a person or thing, especially suddenly or when it is not easy to do so: **~ sb/sth** *I finally spotted my friend in the crowd.* ◇ *I've just spotted a mistake on the front cover.* ◇ *Can you spot the difference between these two pictures?* ◇ **~ sb/sth doing sth** *Neighbours spotted smoke coming out of the house.* ◇ **~ that...** *No one spotted that the gun was a fake.* ◇ **~ what, where, etc...** *I soon spotted what the mistake was.* ➲ see also SPOTTER ➲ SYNONYMS at SEE **2 ~ sb/sth sth** (*NAmE, sport*) to give your opponent or the other team an advantage: *We spotted the opposing team two goals.*
IDM **be spotted with sth** to be covered with small round marks of sth: *His shirt was spotted with oil.*
■ ***adj.*** [only before noun] (*business*) connected with a system of trading where goods are delivered and paid for immediately after sale: *spot prices*

,spot 'check *noun* a check that is made suddenly and without warning on a few things or people chosen from a group to see that everything is as it should be: *to carry out random spot checks on vehicles*

'spot kick *noun* (*BrE*) = PENALTY KICK

spot·less /'spɒtləs; *NAmE* 'spɑːt-/ *adj.* perfectly clean SYN **immaculate**: *a spotless white shirt* ◇ *She keeps the house spotless.* ◇ *(figurative) He has a spotless record so far.* ▸ **spot·less·ly** *adv.*: *spotlessly clean*

spot·light /'spɒtlaɪt; *NAmE* 'spɑːt-/ *noun, verb*
■ ***noun*** **1** (also *informal* **spot**) [C] a light with a single, very bright BEAM that can be directed at a particular place or person: *The room was lit by spotlights.* ➲ VISUAL VOCAB page V18 **2 the spotlight** [U] the area of light that is made by a spotlight: *She stood alone on stage in the spotlight.* **3 the spotlight** [U] attention from newspapers, television and the public: *Unemployment is once again **in the spotlight**.* ◇ *The issue will come **under the spotlight** when parliament reassembles.* ◇ *The report has **turned the spotlight on** the startling rise in street crime.*
■ ***verb*** (**spot·lit, spot·lit** /-lɪt/ HELP Especially in sense 2, **spot·light·ed** is also used for the past tense and past participle.) **1 ~ sth** to shine a spotlight on sb/sth: *a spotlit stage* **2 ~ sth** to give special attention to a problem, situation, etc. so that people notice it SYN **highlight**: *The programme spotlights financial problems in the health service.*

,spot 'on *adj.* [not before noun] (*BrE, informal*) exactly right: *His assessment of the situation was spot on.*

spot·ted /'spɒtɪd; *NAmE* 'spɑːt-/ (also **spotty**) *adj.* **1** (of cloth, etc.) having a regular pattern of round dots on it: *a black and white spotted dress* **2** having marks on it, sometimes in a pattern: *a leopard's spotted coat*

,spotted 'dick *noun* [U] (*BrE*) a hot DESSERT (= a sweet dish) like a SPONGE CAKE with dried fruit in it

spot·ter /'spɒtə(r); *NAmE* 'spɑːt-/ *noun* **1** (especially in compounds) a person who looks for a particular type of thing or person, as a hobby or job: *a talent spotter* (= sb who visits clubs and theatres looking for new performers) ➲ see also TRAINSPOTTER **2** (also **'spotter plane**) a plane used for finding out what an enemy is doing

spotty /'spɒti; *NAmE* 'spɑːti/ *adj.* **1** (*BrE*, usually *disapproving*) (of a person) having a lot of spots on the skin SYN **pimply**: *a spotty adolescent* ◇ *a spotty face* **2** (*NAmE*) = PATCHY (2) **3** = SPOTTED: *a spotty dress*

spouse /spaʊs; spaʊz/ *noun* (*formal* or *law*) a husband or wife ▸ **spou·sal** /'spaʊzl; 'spaʊsl/ *adj.* [only before noun]: (*formal*) *spousal consent* ◇ *spousal abuse*

spout /spaʊt/ *noun, verb*
■ ***noun*** **1** a pipe or tube on a container, that you can pour liquid out through: *the spout of a teapot* ➲ VISUAL VOCAB page V22 **2** a stream of liquid coming out of somewhere with great force SYN **fountain**
IDM **be/go up the 'spout** (*BrE, slang*) to be/go wrong; to be spoilt or not working: *Well, that's my holiday plans gone up the spout!*
■ ***verb*** **1** [T, I] to send out sth, especially a liquid, in a stream with great force; to come out of sth in this way SYN **pour**: **~ sth (from sth)** *The wound was still spouting blood.* ◇ **~ from/out of sth** *Clear water spouted from the fountains.* **2** [I] (of a WHALE) to send out a stream of water from a hole in its head **3** [I, T] (*informal, disapproving*) to speak a lot about sth; to repeat sth in a boring or annoying way: **~ (off/on) (about sth)** *He's always spouting off about being a vegetarian.* ◇ *What are you spouting on about now?* ◇ **~ sth** *He could spout poetry for hours.* ◇ *She could do nothing but spout insults.*

sprain /spreɪn/ *verb* **~ sth** to injure a joint in your body, especially your wrist or ankle, by suddenly twisting it: *I stumbled and sprained my ankle.* ➲ COLLOCATIONS at INJURY ➲ SYNONYMS at INJURE ▸ **sprain** *noun*: *a bad ankle sprain*

sprang *past tense of* SPRING

sprat /spræt/ *noun* a very small European sea fish that is used for food

sprawl /sprɔːl/ *verb, noun*
■ ***verb*** **1** [I] (+ **adv./prep.**) to sit or lie with your arms and legs spread out in a relaxed or awkward way: *He was sprawling in an armchair in front of the TV.* ◇ *Something hit her and **sent her sprawling** to the ground.* ◇ *I tripped and **went sprawling**.* **2** [I] + **adv./prep.** to spread in an untidy way; to cover a large area: *The town sprawled along the side of the lake.*
■ ***noun*** **1** [C, usually sing., U] a large area covered with buildings that spreads from the city into the countryside in an ugly way: *attempts to control the fast-growing **urban sprawl*** **2** [C, usually sing.] an act of spreading to cover a large area in an untidy way; sth that spreads like this

sprawled /sprɔːld/ *adj.* sitting or lying with your arms and legs spread out in a lazy or awkward way: *He was lying sprawled in an armchair, watching TV.*

sprawl·ing /'sprɔːlɪŋ/ *adj.* [only before noun] spreading in an untidy way: *a modern sprawling town*

spray 🔑 /spreɪ/ *noun, verb*
■ ***noun*** **1** 🔑 [U, C] very small drops of a liquid that are sent through the air, for example by the wind: *sea spray* ◇ *A cloud of fine spray came up from the waterfall.* ◇ (*figurative*) *a spray of machine-gun bullets* **2** 🔑 [U, C] (especially in compounds) a substance that is forced out of a container such as an AEROSOL, in very small drops: *a can of insect spray* (= used to kill insects) ◇ *body spray* ➲ VISUAL VOCAB page V29 ➲ see also HAIRSPRAY **3** 🔑 [C] a device or container, for example an AEROSOL, that you use to apply liquid in fine drops: *a throat spray* **4** [C] an act of applying liquid to sth in very small drops: *I gave the plants a quick spray.* **5** [C] a small branch of a tree or plant, with its leaves and flowers or BERRIES, that you use for decoration SYN **sprig** **6** [C] an attractive arrangement of flowers or jewellery, that you wear: *a spray of orchids*
■ ***verb*** **1** 🔑 [T, I] to cover sb/sth with very small drops of a liquid that are forced out of a container or sent through the air: **~ (sth) (on/onto/over sb/sth)** *Spray the conditioner onto your wet hair.* ◇ *Champagne sprayed everywhere.* ◇ **~ sb/sth (with sth)** *The crops are regularly sprayed with pesticide.* ◇ **~ sth + adj.** *She's had the car sprayed blue.* **2** [T, I] to cover sb/sth with a lot of small things with a lot

of force: **~ sb/sth with sth** *The gunman sprayed the building with bullets.* ◇ **+ adv./prep.** *Pieces of glass sprayed all over the room.* **3** [I] (especially of a male cat) to leave small amounts of URINE to mark its own area

ˈspray can *noun* a small metal container that has paint in it under pressure and that you use to spray paint onto sth

spray·er /ˈspreɪə(r)/ *noun* a piece of equipment used for spraying liquid, especially paint or a substance used to kill insects that damage crops: *a **paint/crop sprayer***

ˈspray gun *noun* a device for spraying paint onto a surface, that works by air pressure

ˈspray-on *adj.* [only before noun] (*especially BrE*) that you can spray onto sth/sb from a special container: *a spray-on water repellent for shoes*

ˈspray paint *noun* [U] paint that is kept in a container under pressure and that you can spray onto sth ▸ **ˈspray-paint** *verb* **~ A (with B) | ~ B (on A)**

spread ⊶ /spred/ *verb, noun*

■ ***verb*** **(spread, spread)**

▸ OPEN/ARRANGE **1** ⊶ [T] **~ sth (out) (on/over sth)** to open sth that has been folded so that it covers a larger area than before: *to spread a cloth on a table* ◇ *Sue spread the map out on the floor.* ◇ *The bird spread its wings.* **2** ⊶ [T] **~ sth (out) (on/over sth)** to arrange objects so that they cover a large area and can be seen easily: *Papers had been spread out on the desk.*

▸ ARMS/LEGS **3** ⊶ [T] **~ sth (out)** to move your arms, legs, fingers, etc. far apart from each other: *She spread her arms and the child ran towards her.*

▸ AMONG PEOPLE **4** ⊶ [I, T] to affect or make sth affect, be known by, or used by more and more people: (**+ adv./prep.**) *The disease spreads easily.* ◇ *Within weeks, his confidence had spread throughout the team.* ◇ *Use of computers **spread rapidly** during that period.* ◇ **~ sth** *to **spread rumours/lies** about sb* ◇ *The disease is spread by mosquitoes.*

▸ COVER LARGE AREA **5** ⊶ [I, T] to cover, or to make sth cover, a larger and larger area: (**+ adv./prep.**) *The fire rapidly spread to adjoining buildings.* ◇ *Water began to spread across the floor.* ◇ *A smile spread slowly across her face.* ◇ **~ sth** *Using too much water could spread the stain.* **6** ⊶ [T] **~ sb/sth** to cause sb/sth to be in a number of different places: *Seeds and pollen are spread by the wind.* ◇ *We have 10 000 members spread all over the country.* **7** [I] **~ (out) + adv./prep.** to cover a large area: *The valley spread out beneath us.*

▸ SOFT LAYER **8** ⊶ [T, I] to put a layer of a substance onto the surface of sth; to be able to be put onto a surface: **~ (A on/over B)** *to spread butter on pieces of toast* ◇ **~ (B with A)** *pieces of toast spread with butter* ◇ *If the paint is too thick, it will not spread evenly.*

▸ DIVIDE/SHARE **9** ⊶ [T] to separate sth into parts and divide them between different times or different people: **~ sth** *Why not pay monthly and spread the cost of your car insurance?* ◇ **~ sth (out) (over sth)** *A series of five interviews will be spread over two days.* ◇ **~ sth between sb/sth** *We attempted to spread the workload between the departments.*

IDM **spread like ˈwildfire** (of news, etc.) to become known by more and more people very quickly **spread your ˈnet** to consider a wide range of possibilities or cover a large area, especially to try to find sb/sth: *They have spread their net far and wide in the search for a new team coach.* **spread your ˈwings** to become more independent and confident and try new activities, etc. **spread the ˈword** to tell people about sth **spread yourself too ˈthin** to try to do so many different things at the same time that you do not do any of them well

PHR V **ˌspread ˈout | ˌspread yourself ˈout 1** ⊶ to stretch your body or arrange your things over a large area: *There's more room to spread out in first class.* ◇ *Do you have to spread yourself out all over the sofa?* **2** ⊶ to separate from other people in a group, to cover a larger area: *The searchers spread out to cover the area faster.*

■ ***noun***

▸ INCREASE **1** ⊶ [U] an increase in the amount or number of sth that there is, or in the area that is affected by sth: *to prevent the spread of disease* ◇ *to encourage the spread of information* ◇ *the spread of a city into the surrounding areas* ➲ see also MIDDLE-AGE SPREAD

▸ RANGE/VARIETY **2** [C, usually sing.] a range or variety of people or things: *a **broad spread** of opinions*

▸ ON BREAD **3** [C, U] a soft food that you put on bread: *Use a low-fat spread instead of butter.* ◇ *cheese spread*

▸ AREA COVERED **4** [C, usually sing.] **~ (of sth)** the area that sth exists in or happens in: *The company has a good geographical spread of hotels in this country.* **5** [C, usually sing.] **~ (of sth)** how wide sth is or the area that sth covers: *The bird's wings have a spread of nearly a metre.*

▸ IN NEWSPAPER/MAGAZINE **6** [C] an article or advertisement in a newspaper or magazine, especially one that covers two opposite pages: *The story continued with **a double-page spread** on the inside pages.* ➲ see also CENTRE SPREAD

▸ MEAL **7** [C] (*informal*) a large meal, especially one that is prepared for a special occasion: *They had laid on a huge spread for the party.*

▸ OF LAND/WATER **8** [C, usually sing.] **~ (of sth)** (*NAmE*) an area of land or water: *a vast spread of water* ◇ *They have a huge spread in California* (= a large farm or RANCH).

▸ FINANCE **9** [U] the difference between two rates or prices

▸ ON BED **10** [C] (*NAmE*) = BEDSPREAD

ˌspread ˈbetting *noun* [U] a type of betting on a sports event in which you bet money on whether you think the predicted number of goals, points, etc. is too high or too low. The amount of money you win or lose depends on the extent to which you are right or wrong. ▸ **ˌspread ˈbet** *noun*

spread·eagled /ˌspredˈiːɡld/ (*BrE*) (*NAmE* **spread-eagle**) *adj.* [not usually before noun] in a position with your arms and legs spread out ▸ **spread·eagle** /ˌspredˈiːɡl/ *verb* **~ sb**

spread·er /ˈspredə(r)/ *noun* a device or machine that spreads things: *a muck spreader*

spread·sheet /ˈspredʃiːt/ *noun* a computer program that is used, for example, when doing financial or project planning. You enter data in rows and columns and the program calculates costs, etc. from it.

Sprech·ge·sang /ˈʃprexɡəzæŋ/ *noun* [U] (from *German, music*) a style of singing which is between speaking and singing

spree /spriː/ *noun* **1** a short period of time that you spend doing one particular activity that you enjoy, but often too much of it: *a **shopping/spending spree*** ◇ *He's out **on a spree**.* **2** (used especially in newspapers) a period of activity, especially criminal activity: *to go on a killing spree*

sprig /sprɪɡ/ *noun* a small STEM with leaves on it from a plant or bush, used in cooking or as a decoration: *a sprig of parsley/holly/heather*

spright·ly /ˈspraɪtli/ (also *less frequent* **spry**) *adj.* (especially of older people) full of life and energy SYN **lively**: *a sprightly 80-year-old* ▸ **spright·li·ness** *noun* [U]

spring

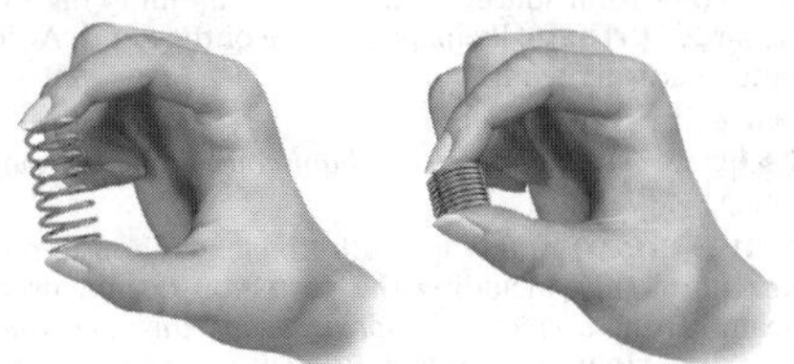

spring ⊶ /sprɪŋ/ *noun, verb*

■ ***noun***

▸ SEASON **1** ⊶ [U, C] the season between winter and summer when plants begin to grow: *flowers that bloom **in spring/in the spring*** ◇ *He was born in the spring of 1944.* ◇ *There's a feeling of spring in the air today.* ◇ *spring flowers*

▸ TWISTED WIRE **2** ⊶ [C] a twisted piece of metal that can be pushed, pressed or pulled but which always returns to its original shape or position afterwards: *bed springs* **3** [U] the

S

ability of a spring to return to its original position: *The mattress has lost its spring.*

▸ WATER **4** [C] a place where water comes naturally to the surface from under the ground: *a mountain spring* ◇ *spring water*

▸ CHEERFUL QUALITY **5** [U, sing.] a cheerful, lively quality: *She walked along **with a spring in her step**.*

▸ SUDDEN JUMP **6** [C] a quick sudden jump upwards or forwards: *With a spring, the cat leapt on to the table.* IDM see JOY

■ ***verb*** (sprang /spræŋ/, sprung /sprʌŋ/) (*NAmE* also sprung, sprung)

▸ JUMP/MOVE SUDDENLY **1** [I] (+ **adv./prep.**) (of a person or an animal) to move suddenly and with one quick movement in a particular direction SYN **leap**: *He turned off the alarm and sprang out of bed.* ◇ *Everyone **sprang to their feet*** (= stood up suddenly) *when the principal walked in.* ◇ *The cat crouched ready to spring.* ◇ (*figurative*) *to **spring to sb's defence/assistance*** (= to quickly defend or help sb) **2** [I] (of an object) to move suddenly and violently: **+ adv./prep.** *The branch sprang back and hit him in the face.* ◇ **+ adj.** *She turned the key and the lid sprang open.*

▸ SURPRISE **3** [T] to do sth, ask sth or say sth that sb is not expecting: **~ sth** *She sprang a surprise by winning the tournament.* ◇ **~ sth on sb** *I'm sorry to **spring it on you**, but I've been offered another job.*

▸ APPEAR SUDDENLY **4** [I] **+ adv./prep.** to appear or come somewhere suddenly: *Tears sprang to her eyes.*

▸ FREE PRISONER **5** [T] **~ sb** (*informal*) to help a prisoner to escape: *Plans to spring the hostages have failed.*

IDM **ˌspring into ˈaction** | **ˌspring into/to ˈlife** (of a person, machine, etc.) to suddenly start working or doing sth: *'Let's go!' he said, springing into action.* ◇ *The town springs into life* (= becomes busy) *during the carnival.* **spring a ˈleak** (of a boat or container) to develop a hole through which water or another liquid can pass **spring a ˈtrap 1** to make a trap for catching animals close suddenly **2** to try to trick sb into doing or saying sth; to succeed in this ➲ more at HOPE *n.*, MIND *n.*

PHR V **ˈspring for sth** (*NAmE, informal*) to pay for sth for sb else: *I'll spring for the drinks tonight.* **ˈspring from sth** (*formal*) to be caused by sth; to start from sth: *The idea for the novel sprang from a trip to India.* **ˈspring from...** (*informal*) to appear suddenly and unexpectedly from a particular place: *Where on earth did you spring from?* **ˌspring ˈup** to appear or develop quickly and/or suddenly

spring·board /ˈsprɪŋbɔːd; *NAmE* -bɔːrd/ *noun* **1** a strong board that you jump on and use to help you jump high in DIVING and GYMNASTICS **2 ~ (for/to sth)** something that helps you start an activity, especially by giving you ideas: *The document provided a springboard for a lot of useful discussion.* ▸ **spring·board** *verb* [I, T]: **~ (sth) (into sth)** *The company expects that this strategic move would allow it to springboard into the US market.*

spring·bok /ˈsprɪŋbɒk; *NAmE* -bɑːk/ *noun* **1** [C] a small ANTELOPE from southern Africa that can jump high into the air **2 Springboks** [pl.] the name of the South African national RUGBY team

ˌspring ˈchicken *noun*

IDM **be no ˌspring ˈchicken** (*humorous*) to be no longer young

ˌspring-ˈclean *verb* [T, I] **~ (sth)** to clean a house, room, etc. thoroughly, including the parts you do not usually clean: *Fran decided to spring-clean the apartment.* ▸ **ˌspring ˈclean** *noun* [sing.]: (*BrE*) *The place needed a good spring clean before we could move in.*

ˌspring ˈgreens *noun* [pl.] leaves of young CABBAGE plants of certain types

ˌspring-ˈloaded *adj.* containing a metal spring that presses one part against another

ˌspring ˈonion (*BrE*) (*NAmE* **ˌgreen ˈonion, scal·lion**) *noun* a type of small onion with a long green STEM and leaves. Spring onions are often eaten raw in salads. ➲ VISUAL VOCAB page V27

ˌspring ˈroll (*especially BrE*) *noun* a type of Chinese food consisting of a tube of thin PASTRY, filled with vegetables and/or meat and fried until it is crisp ➲ see also EGG ROLL

ˌspring ˈtide *noun* a TIDE in which there is a very great rise and fall of the sea, and which happens near the new moon and the full moon each month

spring·time /ˈsprɪŋtaɪm/ *noun* [U] the season of spring: *a visit to Holland **in springtime/in the springtime***

springy /ˈsprɪŋi/ (**spring·ier, springi·est**) *adj.* **1** returning quickly to the original shape after being pushed, pulled, stretched, etc: *We walked across the springy grass.* **2** full of energy and confidence: *She's 73, but hasn't lost that youthful, springy step.*

sprin·kle /ˈsprɪŋkl/ *verb, noun*

■ ***verb*** **1** [T] to shake small pieces of sth or drops of a liquid on sth: **~ A on/onto/over B** *Sprinkle chocolate on top of the cake.* ◇ *She sprinkled sugar over the strawberries.* ◇ **~ B with A** *She sprinkled the strawberries with sugar.* **2** [T, usually passive] **~ sth with sth** to include a few of sth in sth else SYN **strew**: *His poems are sprinkled with quotations from ancient Greek.* **3** [I] (*NAmE*) if **it sprinkles**, it rains lightly SYN **drizzle**: *It's only sprinkling. We can still go out.*

■ ***noun*** [sing.] **1** = SPRINKLING: *Add a sprinkle of cheese and serve.* **2** (*especially NAmE*) light rain: *We've only had a few sprinkles (of rain) recently.*

sprink·ler /ˈsprɪŋklə(r)/ *noun* **1** a device with holes in that is used to spray water in drops on plants, soil or grass ➲ VISUAL VOCAB page V16 **2** a device inside a building which automatically sprays out water if there is a rise in temperature because of a fire

sprin·kles /ˈsprɪŋklz/ (*NAmE*) (*BrE* **ˌhundreds and ˈthousands**) *noun* [pl.] extremely small pieces of coloured sugar, used to decorate cakes, etc.

sprink·ling /ˈsprɪŋklɪŋ/ (also **sprin·kle**) *noun* a small amount of a substance that is dropped somewhere, or a number of things or people that are spread or included somewhere: *Add a sprinkling of pepper.* ◇ *Most were men, but there was also a sprinkling of young women.*

sprint /sprɪnt/ *verb, noun*

■ ***verb*** [I, T] to run or swim a short distance very fast: **+ adv./prep.** *He sprinted for the line.* ◇ *Three runners sprinted past.* ◇ *She jumped out of the car and sprinted for the front door.* ◇ **~ sth** *I sprinted the last few metres.*

■ ***noun*** **1** a race in which the people taking part run, swim, etc. very fast over a short distance: *a 100-metre sprint* ◇ *the world sprint champion* ➲ VISUAL VOCAB page V38 **2** [usually sing.] a short period of running, swimming, etc. very fast: *a sprint for the line* ◇ *a sprint for the bus* ◇ *She won in a sprint finish.* ▸ **sprint·er** *noun*

sprite /spraɪt/ *noun* (in stories) a small creature with magic powers, especially one that likes playing tricks

spritz /sprɪts/ *verb* **~ sth** (*especially NAmE*) to spray very small drops of liquid on sth quickly: *Lightly spritz your hair with water.* ▸ **spritz** *noun*

spritz·er /ˈsprɪtsə(r)/ *noun* a drink made with wine (usually white) mixed with either SODA WATER or SPARKLING mineral water (= with bubbles in it): *a white wine spritzer*

sprocket /ˈsprɒkɪt; *NAmE* ˈsprɑːkɪt/ *noun* **1** (also **sprocket wheel**) a wheel with a row of teeth around the edge that connect with the holes of a bicycle chain or with holes in a film, etc. in order to turn it **2** one of the teeth on such a wheel

sprocket wheel

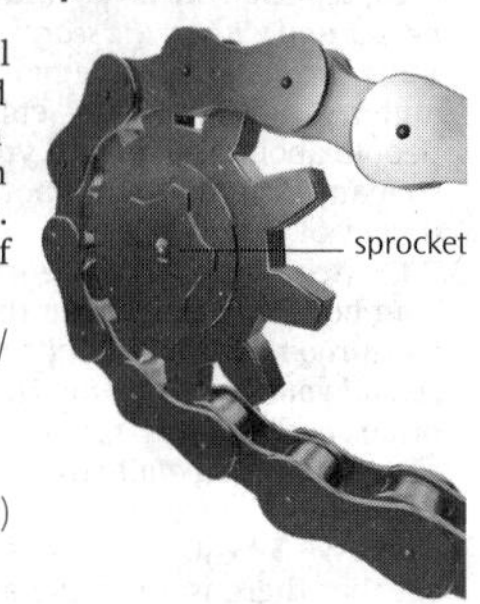

sprog /sprɒg; *NAmE* sprɑːg/ *noun* (*BrE, informal, humorous*) a child or baby

sprout /spraʊt/ *verb, noun*

■ ***verb*** **1** [I] (of plants or seeds) to produce new leaves or BUDS; to start to grow: *new leaves sprouting from the trees* ◇ *The seeds will sprout in a few days.* **2** [I, T] to appear; to develop sth, especially in large numbers: *Hundreds of*

mushrooms had sprouted up overnight. ◇ **~ sth** *The town has sprouted shopping malls, discos and nightclubs in recent years.* **4** [T, I] to start to grow sth; to start to grow on sb/sth: **~ sth** *Tim has sprouted a beard since we last saw him.* ◇ **~ from sth** *Hair sprouted from his chest.*
■ ***noun* 1** = BRUSSELS SPROUT **2** a new part growing on a plant

spruce /spruːs/ *noun, verb, adj.*
■ ***noun* 1** [C, U] an EVERGREEN forest tree with leaves like needles **2** [U] the soft wood of the spruce, used, for example, in making paper
■ ***verb***
PHR V **ˌspruce ˈup | ˌspruce sb/sth/yourself↔ˈup** to make sb/sth/yourself clean and neat: *She spruced up for the interview.* ◇ *The city is sprucing up its museums and galleries.*
■ ***adj.*** (of people or places) neat and clean in appearance

spruit /spreɪt/ *noun* (*SAfrE*) a stream, sometimes one that only flows when there has been a lot of rain

sprung /sprʌŋ/ *adj.* fitted with metal springs: *a sprung mattress* ➲ see also SPRING, SPRANG, SPRUNG *v.*

spry /spraɪ/ *adj.* = SPRIGHTLY

spud /spʌd/ *noun* (*especially BrE, informal*) a potato

spume /spjuːm/ *noun* [U] (*literary*) the mass of white bubbles that forms in waves when the sea is rough SYN **foam**

spun *past part.* of SPIN

spunk /spʌŋk/ *noun* **1** [U] (*informal*) courage; determination **2** [U] (*BrE, taboo, slang*) = SEMEN **3** [C] (*informal, AustralE, informal*) a sexually attractive person

spunky /ˈspʌŋki/ *adj.* (*informal*) **1** brave and determined; full of enthusiasm: *She is bright, tough and spunky.* **2** (*AustralE, informal*) sexually attractive: *a top babe with a spunky boyfriend*

spur /spɜː(r)/ *noun, verb*
■ ***noun* 1** a sharp pointed object that riders sometimes wear on the heels of their boots and use to encourage their horse to go faster **2** [usually sing.] **~ (to sth)** a fact or an event that makes you want to do sth better or more quickly SYN **motivation**: *His speech was a powerful spur to action.* **3** an area of high ground that sticks out from a mountain or hill **4** a road or a railway/railroad track that leads from the main road or line
IDM **on the ˌspur of the ˈmoment** suddenly, without planning in advance: *I phoned him up on the spur of the moment.* ◇ *a spur-of-the-moment decision* **win/earn your ˈspurs** (*formal*) to achieve fame or success
■ ***verb*** (-rr-) **1** to encourage sb to do sth or to encourage them to try harder to achieve sth: **~ sb/sth (on) to sth/to do sth** *Her difficult childhood spurred her on to succeed.* ◇ **~ sb/sth into sth** *I was* ***spurred into action*** *by the letter.* ◇ **~ sb/sth (on)** *The band has been spurred on by the success of their last single.* **2 ~ sth** to make sth happen faster or sooner: *The agreement is essential to spurring economic growth around the world.* **3 ~ sth** to encourage a horse to go faster, especially by pushing the spurs on your boots into its side

spuri·ous /ˈspjʊəriəs; *NAmE* ˈspjʊr-/ *adj.* **1** false, although seeming to be genuine: *He had managed to create the entirely spurious impression that the company was thriving.* **2** based on false ideas or ways of thinking: *a spurious argument* ► **spuri·ous·ly** *adv.*

spurn /spɜːn; *NAmE* spɜːrn/ *verb* **~ sb/sth** to reject or refuse sb/sth, especially in a proud way SYN **shun**: *Eve spurned Mark's invitation.* ◇ *a spurned lover*

spurt /spɜːt; *NAmE* spɜːrt/ *verb, noun*
■ ***verb* 1** [I, T] (of liquid or flames) to burst or pour out suddenly; to produce sudden, powerful streams of liquid or flames: **~ (from sth)** *Blood was spurting from her nose.* ◇ **~ out (of/from sth)** *Red and yellow flames spurted out of the fire.* ◇ **~ sth** *Her nose was spurting blood.* ◇ **~ sth + adv./prep.** *The volcano spurted clouds of steam and ash high into the air.* **2** [I] **+ adv./prep.** to increase your speed for a short time to get somewhere faster: *She spurted past me to get to the line first.*
■ ***noun* 1** an amount of liquid or flames that comes out of somewhere with great force: *a great spurt of blood* **2** a sudden increase in speed, effort, activity or emotion for a short period of time: *You'd better* ***put on a spurt*** (= hurry up) *if you want to finish that work today.* ◇ *Babies get very hungry during growth spurts.* ◇ *a sudden spurt of anger*
IDM **in ˈspurts** in short periods of great activity, powerful movement, etc, rather than in a steady, continuous way: *The water came out of the tap in spurts.*

sput·nik /ˈspʌtnɪk; ˈspʊt-/ *noun* (from *Russian*) a SATELLITE of the type that was put into space by the Soviet Union

sput·ter /ˈspʌtə(r)/ *verb* **1** [I] if an engine, a lamp or a fire **sputters**, it makes a series of short EXPLOSIVE sounds SYN **splutter**: *sputtering fireworks* **2** [T] **+ speech | ~ sth** to speak quickly and with difficulty, making soft SPITTING sounds, because you are angry or shocked SYN **splutter**: *'W-What?' sputtered Anna.*

spu·tum /ˈspjuːtəm/ *noun* [U] (*medical*) liquid from the throat or lungs, especially when it is coughed up because of disease: *blood in the sputum*

spy /spaɪ/ *noun, verb*
■ ***noun*** (*pl.* **spies**) a person who tries to get secret information about another country, organization or person, especially sb who is employed by a government or the police: *He was denounced as a foreign spy.* ◇ *a police spy* ◇ *a* ***spy plane/satellite*** (= used to watch the activities of the enemy) ◇ *Video spy cameras are being used in public places.*
■ ***verb*** (**spies, spy·ing, spied, spied**) **1** [I] to collect secret information about another country, organization or person: *He spied for his government for more than ten years.* **2** [T] **~ sb/sth** (*literary* or *formal*) to suddenly see or notice sb/sth: *In the distance we spied the Pacific for the first time.*
IDM **ˌspy out the ˈland** to collect information before deciding what to do
PHR V **ˈspy on sb/sth** to watch sb/sth secretly: *Have you been spying on me?* **ˌspy sth↔ˈout** to get information about sth

spy·glass /ˈspaɪɡlɑːs; *NAmE* -ɡlæs/ *noun* a small TELESCOPE

spy·hole /ˈspaɪhəʊl; *NAmE* -hoʊl/ *noun* a small hole in a door that you can look through to see who is on the other side before opening the door

spy·mas·ter /ˈspaɪmɑːstə(r); *NAmE* -mæs-/ *noun* a person who controls a group of spies

Sq. *abbr.* (used in written addresses) SQUARE: *6 Hanover Sq.*

sq (also **sq.** especially in *NAmE*) *abbr.* (in measurements) square: *10 sq cm*

squab·ble /ˈskwɒbl; *NAmE* ˈskwɑːbl/ *verb* [I] **~ (with sb) (about/over sth)** to argue noisily about sth that is not very important SYN **bicker**: *My sisters were squabbling over what to watch on TV.* ► **squab·ble** *noun*: *family squabbles* ◇ *There were endless squabbles over who should sit where.*

squad /skwɒd; *NAmE* skwɑːd/ *noun* [C+sing./pl. v.] **1** a section of a police force that deals with a particular type of crime: *the* ***drugs/fraud, etc. squad*** ➲ see also FLYING SQUAD **2** (in sport) a group of players, runners, etc. from which a team is chosen for a particular game or match: *the* ***Olympic/national squad*** ◇ *They still have not named their squad for the World Cup qualifier.* **3** a small group of soldiers working or being trained together ➲ see also FIRING SQUAD **4** a group of people who have a particular task ➲ see also DEATH SQUAD, HIT SQUAD

ˈsquad car *noun* a police car

squad·die /ˈskwɒdi; *NAmE* ˈskwɑːdi/ *noun* (*BrE, slang*) a new soldier; a soldier of low rank

squad·ron /ˈskwɒdrən; *NAmE* ˈskwɑːd-/ *noun* [C+sing./pl. v.] a group of military aircraft or ships forming a section of a military force: *a* ***bomber/fighter squadron***

ˈsquadron leader *noun* an officer of high rank in the British AIR FORCE

squalid /ˈskwɒlɪd; *NAmE* ˈskwɑːlɪd/ *adj.* (*disapproving*) **1** (of places and living conditions) very dirty and unpleas-

S

ant **SYN filthy**: *squalid housing* ◇ *squalid, overcrowded refugee camps* **2** (of situations or activities) involving low moral standards or dishonest behaviour **SYN sordid**: *It was a squalid affair involving prostitutes and drugs.*

squall /skwɔːl/ *noun, verb*
■ ***noun*** a sudden strong and violent wind, often during rain or snow storms
■ ***verb*** [I] (usually used in the progressive tenses) (*disapproving*) to cry very loudly and noisily: *squalling kids*

squally /ˈskwɔːli/ *adj.* (of weather) involving sudden, violent and strong winds: *squally showers*

squalor /ˈskwɒlə(r); *NAmE* ˈskwɑːl-/ *noun* [U] dirty and unpleasant conditions: *the poverty and squalor of the slums* ◇ *He had lost his job and was living* ***in squalor***.

squan·der /ˈskwɒndə(r); *NAmE* ˈskwɑːn-/ *verb* **~ sth (on sb/sth)** to waste money, time, etc. in a stupid or careless way: *He squandered all his money on gambling.*

square 0━ /skweə(r); *NAmE* skwer/ *adj., noun, verb, adv.*
■ ***adj.***
▸ SHAPE **1** 0━ (*geometry*) having four straight equal sides and four angles of 90°: *a square room* ➲ VISUAL VOCAB page V58 **2** 0━ forming an angle of 90° exactly or approximately: *The book had rounded, not square, corners.* ◇ *square shoulders* ◇ *He had a firm, square jaw.*
▸ MEASUREMENT **3** 0━ used after a unit of measurement to say that sth measures the same amount on each of four sides: *a carpet four metres square* **4** 0━ (*abbr.* **sq**) used after a number to give a measurement of area: *an area of 36 square metres*
▸ BROAD/SOLID **5** used to describe sth that is broad or that looks solid in shape: *a man of* ***square build*** ➲ see also FOUR-SQUARE
▸ LEVEL/PARALLEL **6** [not before noun] **~ (with sth)** level with or parallel to sth: *tables arranged square with the wall*
▸ WITH MONEY **7** (*informal*) if two people are **square**, neither of them owes money to the other: *Here's the £10 I owe you —now we're square.*
▸ IN SPORT **8 ~ (with sb)** if two teams are **square**, they have the same number of points: *The teams were* ***all square*** *at half-time.*
▸ FAIR/HONEST **9** fair or honest, especially in business matters: *a* ***square deal*** ◇ *Are you being square with me?*
▸ IN AGREEMENT **10 ~ with sth** in agreement with sth: *That isn't quite square with what you said yesterday.*
▸ BORING **11** (*informal, disapproving*) (of a person) considered to be boring, for example because they are old-fashioned or work too hard at school

S

IDM **a square ˈmeal** a good, satisfying meal: *He looks as though he hasn't had a square meal for weeks.* **a square ˈpeg (in a round ˈhole)** (*BrE, informal*) a person who does not feel happy or comfortable in a particular situation, or who is not suitable for it
■ ***noun***
▸ SHAPE **1** 0━ [C] a shape with four straight sides of equal length and four angles of 90°; a piece of sth that has this shape: *First break the chocolate into squares.* ◇ *The floor was tiled in squares of grey and white marble.* ➲ see also SET SQUARE, T-SQUARE
▸ IN TOWN **2** 0━ [C] an open area in a town, usually with four sides, surrounded by buildings: *The hotel is just off the* ***main square***. ◇ *the* ***market/town/village square*** **3 Square** [sing.] (*abbr.* **Sq.**) (used in addresses): *They live at 95 Russell Square.*
▸ MATHEMATICS **4** [C] the number obtained when you multiply a number by itself: *The square of 7 is 49.*
▸ BORING PERSON **5** [C] (*informal, disapproving*) a person who is considered to be boring, for example because they are old-fashioned or because they work too hard at school

IDM **back to square ˈone** a return to the situation you were in at the beginning of a project, task, etc, because you have made no real progress: *If this suggestion isn't accepted, we'll be back to square one.*
■ ***verb***
▸ SHAPE **1** to make sth have straight edges and corners: **~ sth** *It was like trying to* ***square a circle***. *That is, it was impossible.* ◇ **~ sth off** *The boat is rounded at the front but squared off at the back.*
▸ MATHEMATICS **2** [usually passive] **~ sth** to multiply a number by itself: *Three squared is written* 3^2. ◇ *Four squared equals 16.*
▸ SHOULDERS **3 ~ yourself/your shoulders** to make your back and shoulders straight to show you are ready or determined to do sth: *Bruno squared himself to face the waiting journalists.*
▸ IN SPORT **4 ~ sth** (*especially BrE*) to make the number of points you have scored in a game or competition equal to those of your opponents: *His goal squared the game 1–1.*
▸ PAY MONEY **5 ~ sb** (*informal*) to pay money to sb in order to get their help: *They must have squared the mayor before they got their plan underway.*

PHR V ˌ**square sth**↔**aˈway** [usually passive] (*NAmE*) to put sth in order; to finish sth completely ˌ**square ˈoff (against sb)** (*NAmE*) to fight or prepare to fight sb ˌ**square ˈup (to sb/sth) 1** to face a difficult situation and deal with it in a determined way **2** to face sb as if you are going to fight them ˌ**square ˈup (with sb)** to pay money that you owe: *Can I leave you to square up with the waiter?* ˈ**square sth with sth** | ˈ**square with sth** to make two ideas, facts or situations agree or combine well with each other; to agree or be CONSISTENT with another idea, fact or situation: *The interests of farmers need to be squared with those of consumers.* ◇ *How can you* ***square this with your conscience?*** ◇ *Your theory does not square with the facts.* ˈ**square sth with sb** to ask permission or check with sb that they approve of what you want to do: *I think I'll be able to come, but I'll square it with my parents first.*
■ ***adv.*** (only used *after* the verb) directly; not at an angle **SYN squarely**: *I looked her square in the face.* IDM see FAIR *adv.*

ˈ**square-bashing** *noun* [U] (*BrE, informal*) training for soldiers, which involves marching and holding weapons in different positions

ˌ**square ˈbracket** (*BrE*) (*NAmE* **bracket**) *noun* [usually pl.] either of a pair of marks, [ ], placed at the beginning and end of extra information in a text, especially comments made by an editor

squared /skweəd; *NAmE* skwerd/ *adj.* marked with squares; divided into squares: *squared paper*

ˈ**square dance** *noun* **1** a traditional dance from the US in which groups of four couples dance together, starting the dance by facing each other in a square **2** a social event at which people dance square dances

square·head /ˈskweəhed; *NAmE* ˈskwer-/ *noun* (*informal, especially NAmE*) **1** a person who is stupid or not able to do sth **2** an offensive word for a person from Germany, Holland or Scandinavia; a person whose family originally came from there

ˈ**square knot** *noun* (*NAmE*) = REEF KNOT

square·ly /ˈskweəli; *NAmE* ˈskwerli/ *adv.* (usually used *after* the verb) **1** directly; not at an angle or to one side: *She looked at me squarely in the eye.* ◇ *He stood squarely in front of them, blocking the entrance.* ◇ (*figurative*) *We must meet the challenge squarely* (= not try to avoid it). **2** directly or exactly; without confusion: *The responsibility for the crisis rests squarely on the government.* IDM see FAIRLY

the ˌ**Square ˈMile** *noun* [sing.] (*BrE, informal*) a name used for the City of London, where there are many banks and financial businesses

ˌ**square ˈroot** *noun* (*mathematics*) a number which when multiplied by itself produces a particular number: *The square root of 64* ($\sqrt{64}$) *is 8* ($8 \times 8 = 64$). ➲ compare CUBE ROOT

squar·ish /ˈskweərɪʃ; *NAmE* ˈskwer-/ *adj.* almost square in shape

squash /skwɒʃ; *NAmE* skwɑːʃ; skwɔːʃ/ *verb, noun*
■ ***verb*** **1** [T] to press sth so that it becomes soft, damaged or flat, or changes shape: **~ sth/sb** *The tomatoes at the bottom of the bag had been squashed.* ◇ **~ sth against sth** *He squashed his nose against the window.* ◇ **~ sth + adj.** *Squash your cans flat before recycling.* ➲ picture at SQUEEZE **2** [I, T]

to push sb/sth or yourself into a space that is too small: **+ adv./prep.** *We all squashed into the back of the car.* ◇ **~ sb/sth + adv./prep.** *How many people are they going to try and squash into this bus?* ◇ *She was squashed between the door and the table.* **3** [T] **~ sth** to stop sth from continuing; to destroy sth because it is a problem for you **SYN** **quash**: *to squash a plan/an idea/a revolt* ◇ *If parents don't answer children's questions, their natural curiosity will be squashed.* ◇ *The statement was an attempt to squash the rumours.*

PHR V ˌ**squash** ˈ**up** (**against sb/sth**) | ˌ**squash sb/sth**↔ˈ**up** (**against sb/sth**) to move so close to sb/sth else that it is uncomfortable: *We squashed up to make room for Sue.* ◇ *I was squashed up against the wall.*

■ ***noun*** **1** (also *formal* ˈ**squash rackets**) [U] a game for two players, played in a COURT surrounded by four walls, using RACKETS and a small rubber ball: *a **squash court*** ◇ *to **play squash*** ➲ VISUAL VOCAB page V37 **2** [U, C] (*BrE*) a drink made with fruit juice, sugar and water: *a glass of **orange/lemon squash*** ◇ *Two orange squashes, please.* **3** [C, U] (*pl.* **squash**, *BrE* also **squashes**) a type of vegetable that grows on the ground. **Winter squash** have hard skin and orange flesh. **Summer squash** have soft yellow or green skin and white flesh. ➲ VISUAL VOCAB page V27 **4** [sing.] (*informal*) if sth is a **squash**, there is hardly enough room for everything or everyone to fit into a small space: *It's a real squash with six of us in the car.*

squashy /ˈskwɒʃi; *NAmE* ˈskwɑːʃi; ˈskwɔːʃi/ *adj.* soft and easy to crush or squeeze

squat /skwɒt; *NAmE* skwɑːt/ *verb, noun, adj.*

■ ***verb*** (-tt-) **1** [I] **~** (**down**) to sit on your heels with your knees bent up close to your body **2** [I, T] **~** (**sth**) to live in a building or on land which is not yours, without the owner's permission: *They ended up squatting in the empty houses on Oxford Road.*

■ ***noun*** **1** (*especially BrE*) a building that people are living in without permission and without paying rent: *to live in a squat* **2** a squatting position of the body **3** = SQUAT THRUST

■ ***adj.*** short and wide or fat, in a way that is not attractive: *a squat tower* ◇ *a squat muscular man with a shaven head*

squat·ter /ˈskwɒtə(r); *NAmE* ˈskwɑːt-/ *noun* a person who is living in a building or on land without permission and without paying rent

ˈ**squat thrust** (also **squat**) *noun* an exercise in which you start with your hands on the floor and your knees bent, and then quickly move both legs backwards and forwards together

squaw /skwɔː/ *noun* (*old use*) a word for a Native American woman that is now often considered offensive

squawk /skwɔːk/ *verb* **1** [I] (of birds) to make a loud sharp sound: *The parrot squawked and flew away.* **2** [T, I] (**+ speech**) to speak or make a noise in a loud, sharp voice because you are angry, surprised, etc: *'You did what?!' she squawked.* ▸ **squawk** *noun*: *The bird gave a startled squawk.* ◇ *a squawk of protest*

squeak /skwiːk/ *verb, noun*

■ ***verb*** **1** [I] to make a short high sound that is not very loud: *My new shoes squeak.* ◇ *The mouse ran away, squeaking with fear.* ◇ *One wheel makes a horrible squeaking noise.* **2** [T, I] (**+ speech**) to speak in a very high voice, especially when you are nervous or excited: *'Let go of me!' he squeaked nervously.* **3** [I] **+ adv./prep.** to only just manage to win sth, pass a test, etc: *We squeaked into the final with a goal in the last minute.*

■ ***noun*** a short, high cry or sound, that is not usually very loud ➲ see also BUBBLE AND SQUEAK

squeak·er /ˈskwiːkə(r)/ *noun* (*informal, especially NAmE*) a competition or election won by only a small amount or likely to be won by only a small amount

squeaky /ˈskwiːki/ *adj.* making a short, high sound; squeaking: *squeaky floorboards* ◇ *a high squeaky voice*

ˌ**squeaky** ˈ**clean** *adj.* (*informal*) **1** completely clean, and therefore attractive: *squeaky clean hair* **2** morally correct in every way; that cannot be criticized

squeal /skwiːl/ *verb, noun*

■ ***verb*** **1** [I] to make a long, high sound: *The pigs were squealing.* ◇ *The car squealed to a halt.* ◇ *Children were running around squealing with excitement.* **2** [T, I] (**+ speech**) to speak in a very high voice, especially when you are excited or nervous: *'Don't!' she squealed.* **3** [I] **~** (**on sb**) (*informal, disapproving*) to give information, especially to the police, about sth illegal that sb has done

■ ***noun*** a long high cry or sound: *a squeal of pain* ◇ *a squeal of delight* ◇ *He stopped with a squeal of brakes.*

squeam·ish /ˈskwiːmɪʃ/ *adj.* **1** easily upset, or made to feel sick by unpleasant sights or situations, especially when the sight of blood is involved **2** not wanting to do sth that might be considered dishonest or immoral **3 the squeamish** *noun* [pl.] people who are squeamish: *This movie is not for the squeamish.* ▸ **squeam·ish·ness** *noun* [U]

squee·gee /ˈskwiːdʒiː/ *noun* **1** a tool with a rubber edge and a handle, used for removing water from smooth surfaces such as windows ➲ VISUAL VOCAB page V17 **2** (also ˈ**squeegee mop**) a tool for washing floors, that has a long handle with two thick pieces of soft material at the end, which may be squeezed together using a piece of machinery attached to the handle ➲ VISUAL VOCAB page V17

ˈ**squeegee merchant** *noun* (*BrE, informal*) a person who cleans the front windows of cars that have stopped in traffic and then asks the driver to pay them money, even if the driver did not want them to do it

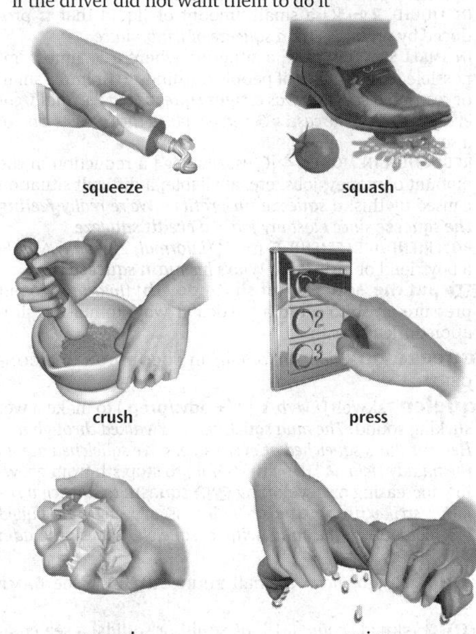

squeeze squash crush press crumple wring

squeeze 🔑 /skwiːz/ *verb, noun*

■ ***verb***

▸ PRESS WITH FINGERS **1** 🔑 [T, I] **~** (**sth**) to press sth firmly, especially with your fingers: *to squeeze a tube of toothpaste* ◇ *to squeeze the trigger of a gun* (= to fire it) ◇ *He squeezed her hand and smiled at her.* ◇ *Just take hold of the tube and squeeze.*

▸ GET LIQUID OUT **2** 🔑 [T] to get liquid out of sth by pressing or twisting it hard: **~ sth out of/from sth** *to squeeze the juice from a lemon* ◇ (*figurative*) *She felt as if every drop of emotion had been squeezed from her.* ◇ **~ sth** (**out**) *He took off his wet clothes and squeezed the water out.* ◇ *freshly squeezed orange juice* ◇ **~ sth + adj.** *Soak the cloth in warm water and then squeeze it dry.*

▸ INTO/THROUGH SMALL SPACE **3** [T, I] to force sb/sth/yourself into or through a small space: **~ sb/sth into, through, etc. sth** *We managed to squeeze six people into the car.* ◇ (*figurative*) *We managed to squeeze a lot into a week* (= we did a lot

S

of different things). ◊ **~ into, through, etc. sth** *to squeeze into a tight dress/a parking space* ◊ *to squeeze through a gap in the hedge* ◊ **~ through, in, past, etc.** *If you move forward a little, I can squeeze past.*

▸ THREATEN **4** [T] **~ sb (for sth)** (*informal*) to get sth by putting pressure on sb, threatening them, etc: *He's squeezing me for £500.*

▸ LIMIT MONEY **5** [T] **~ sb/sth** to strictly limit or reduce the amount of money that sb/sth has or can use: *High interest rates have squeezed the industry hard.*

IDM ˌ**squeeze sb** ˈ**dry** to get as much money, information, etc. out of sb as you can

PHR V ˌ**squeeze sb/sth↔**ˈ**in** to give time to sb/sth, although you are very busy: *If you come this afternoon the doctor will try to squeeze you in.* ˌ**squeeze sb/sth↔**ˈ**out (of sth)** to prevent sb/sth from continuing to do sth or be in business: *Supermarkets are squeezing out small shops.* ˌ**squeeze sth** ˈ**out of/**ˈ**from sb** to get sth by putting pressure on sb, threatening them, etc: *to squeeze a confession from a suspect* ˌ**squeeze** ˈ**up (against sb/sth)** | ˌ**squeeze sb↔**ˈ**up (against sb/sth)** to move close to sb/sth so that you are pressed against them/it: *There'll be enough room if we all squeeze up a little.* ◊ *I sat squeezed up against the wall.*

■ ***noun***

▸ PRESSING WITH FINGERS **1** 0‑w [C, usually sing.] an act of pressing sth, usually with your hands: *He gave my hand a little squeeze.* ◊ *Give the tube another squeeze.*

▸ OF LIQUID **2** 0‑w [C] a small amount of liquid that is produced by pressing sth: *a squeeze of lemon juice*

▸ IN SMALL SPACE **3** [sing.] a situation where it is almost impossible for a number of people or things to fit into a small or restricted space: *It was **a tight squeeze** but we finally got everything into the case.* ◊ *Seven people in the car was a bit of a squeeze.*

▸ REDUCTION IN MONEY **4** [C, usually sing.] a reduction in the amount of money, jobs, etc. available; a difficult situation caused by this: ***a squeeze on** profits* ◊ *We're really **feeling the squeeze** since I lost my job.* ◊ *a **credit squeeze***

▸ BOYFRIEND/GIRLFRIEND **5** [sing.] (*informal, especially NAmE*) a boyfriend or girlfriend: *Who's his **main squeeze**?*

IDM **put the** ˈ**squeeze on sb (to do sth)** (*informal*) to put pressure on sb to act in a particular way; to make a situation difficult for sb

ˈ**squeeze box** *noun* (*informal*) an ACCORDION or a CONCERTINA

squelch /skweltʃ/ *verb* **1** [I] (**+ adv./prep.**) to make a wet sucking sound: *The mud squelched as I walked through it.* ◊ *Her wet shoes squelched at every step.* ◊ *We squelched across the muddy field.* **2** [T] **~ sth** (*NAmE*) to stop sth from growing, increasing or developing SYN **squash**: *to squelch a rumour/strike/fire* ▸ **squelch** *noun* [usually sing.]: *He pulled his foot out of the mud with a squelch.* **squelchy** *adj.*: *squelchy ground*

squib /skwɪb/ *noun* a small FIREWORK IDM see DAMP *adj.*

squid /skwɪd/ *noun* [C, U] (*pl.* **squid** or **squids**) a sea creature that has a long soft body, eight arms and two TENTACLES (= long thin parts like arms) around its mouth, and that is sometimes used for food

squidgy /ˈskwɪdʒi/ *adj.* (*informal, especially BrE*) soft and wet, and easily SQUASHED

squiffy /ˈskwɪfi/ *adj.* (*BrE, informal*) slightly drunk

squig·gle /ˈskwɪgl/ *noun* a line, for example in sb's HANDWRITING, that is drawn or written in a careless way with twists and curls in it: *Are these dots and squiggles supposed to be your signature?* ▸ **squig·gly** /ˈskwɪgli/ *adj.*

squil·lion /ˈskwɪljən/ *noun* (*informal*, often *humorous*) a very large number: *a squillion-dollar budget*

squint /skwɪnt/ *verb, noun*

■ ***verb*** **1** [I, T] to look at sth with your eyes partly shut in order to keep out bright light or to see better: *to squint into the sun* ◊ *She was squinting through the keyhole.* ◊ *He squinted at the letter in his hand.* ◊ **~ sth** *When he squinted his eyes, he could just make out a house in the distance.* **2** [I] (*BrE*) (of an eye) to look in a different direction from the other eye: *His left eye squints a little.* **3** [I] to have eyes that look in different directions

■ ***noun*** **1** [C, usually sing.] a condition of the eye muscles which causes each eye to look in a different direction: *He was born with a squint.* **2** [sing.] (*BrE, informal*) a short look: ***Have a squint** at this.*

squire /ˈskwaɪə(r)/ *noun* **1** (also **Squire**) (in the past in England) a man of high social status who owned most of the land in a particular country area **2 Squire** (*BrE, informal* or *humorous*) used by a man as a friendly way of addressing another man: *What can I get you, Squire?* **3** (in the past) a young man who was an assistant to a KNIGHT before becoming a knight himself

squire·archy /ˈskwaɪərɑːki; *NAmE* ‑ɑːrki/ *noun* [C+sing./pl. v.] (in the past in England) the people of high social status who owned large areas of land, considered as a social or political group

squirm /skwɜːm; *NAmE* skwɜːrm/ *verb* **1** [I] to move around a lot making small twisting movements, because you are nervous, uncomfortable, etc. SYN **wriggle**: (**+ adv./prep.**) *The children were squirming restlessly in their seats.* ◊ **+ adj.** *Someone grabbed him but he managed to squirm free.* **2** [I] to feel great embarrassment or shame: *It made him squirm to think how badly he'd messed up the interview.*

squir·rel /ˈskwɪrəl; *NAmE* ˈskwɜːrəl/ *noun, verb*

■ ***noun*** a small animal with a long thick tail and red, grey or black fur. Squirrels eat nuts and live in trees. ➲ VISUAL VOCAB page V10 ➲ see also GROUND SQUIRREL

■ ***verb*** (‑ll‑, *especially US* ‑l‑)

PHR V ˌ**squirrel sth↔a**ˈ**way** to hide or store sth so that it can be used later: *She had money squirrelled away in various bank accounts.*

squir·rel·ly /ˈskwɪrəli; *NAmE* ˈskwɜːrəli/ *adj.* (*NAmE, informal*) **1** unable to keep still or be quiet: *squirrelly kids* **2** crazy

squirt /skwɜːt; *NAmE* skwɜːrt/ *verb, noun*

■ ***verb*** **1** [T, I] to force liquid, gas, etc. in a thin fast stream through a narrow opening; to be forced out of a narrow opening in this way SYN **spurt**: **~ sth (+ adv./prep.)** *The snake can squirt poison from a distance of a metre.* ◊ *I desperately squirted water on the flames.* ◊ (**+ adv./prep.**) *When I cut the lemon, juice squirted in my eye.* **2** [T] to hit sb/sth with a stream of water, gas, etc. SYN **spray**: **~ sb/sth (with sth)** *The children were squirting each other with water from the hose.* ◊ **~ sth (at sb)** *He squirted a water pistol at me* (= made the water come out of it).

■ ***noun*** **1** a thin, fast stream of liquid that comes out of a small opening SYN **spray**: *a squirt of perfume* **2** (*informal, disapproving*) a word used to refer to a short, young or unimportant person that you do not like or that you find annoying

ˈ**squirt gun** *noun* (*NAmE*) = WATER PISTOL

squish /skwɪʃ/ *verb* (*informal*) **1** [I, T] **~ (sth)** if sth soft **squishes** or **is squished**, it is crushed out of shape when it is pressed **2** [I] to make a soft wet sucking sound

squishy /ˈskwɪʃi/ *adj.* (*informal*) soft and wet

squit /skwɪt/ *noun* (*BrE*) **1** (*offensive*) a small or unimportant person **2 the squits** (also **the squit·ters** /ˈskwɪtəz; *NAmE* ‑tərz/) [pl.] (*informal*) = DIARRHOEA

Sr (also **Snr**) (both *BrE*) (also **Sr.** *NAmE, BrE*) *abbr.* SENIOR ➲ compare JR

Sri, Srimati = SHRI, SHRIMATI

SS *abbr.* **1** SAINTS: *SS Philip and James* **2** /ˌes ˈes/ STEAMSHIP: *the SS Titanic*

SSN /ˌes es ˈen/ *abbr.* SOCIAL SECURITY NUMBER

St *abbr.* **1** (also **st**) (both *BrE*) (also **St., st.** *NAmE, BrE*) (used in written addresses) Street: *Fleet St* **2 St.** (*NAmE*) State **3** (also **St.** especially in *NAmE*) SAINT

st (*BrE*) (also **st.** *NAmE, BrE*) *abbr.* STONE (a British measurement of weight): *9st 2lb*

stab /stæb/ *verb, noun*

■ ***verb*** (‑bb‑) **1** [T] **~ sb** to push a sharp, pointed object, especially a knife, into sb, killing or injuring them: *He was* *stabbed to death in a racist attack.* ◇ *She stabbed him in the arm with a screwdriver.* **2** [T, I] to make a short, aggressive or violent movement with a finger or pointed object **SYN** **jab, prod**: **~ sth** (**at/into/through sth**) *He stabbed his finger angrily at my chest.* ◇ **~ sb/sth** (**with sth**) *She stabbed the air with her fork.* ◇ **~ at/into/through sth** (*figurative*) *The pain stabbed at his chest.*

IDM **stab sb in the ˈback** to do or say sth that harms sb who trusts you **SYN** **betray**

■ ***noun*** **1** an act of stabbing or trying to stab sb/sth; a wound caused by stabbing: *He received several stabs in the chest.* ◇ *She died of a single* ***stab wound*** *to the heart.* **2** a sudden sharp pain or unpleasant feeling: *She felt a sudden* ***stab of pain*** *in the chest.* ◇ *a* ***stab of guilt/fear/pity/jealousy, etc.*** **3** [usually sing.] (*informal*) an attempt to do sth: **~** (**at sth**) *He found the test difficult but nevertheless* ***made a*** *good* ***stab at*** *it.* ◇ **~** (**at doing sth**) *Countless people* ***have had a stab at*** *solving the riddle.*

IDM **a ˌstab in the ˈback** (*informal*) an act that harms sb, done by a person they thought was a friend ➲ more at DARK *n.*

stab·bing /ˈstæbɪŋ/ *noun, adj.*

■ ***noun*** an occasion when a person is stabbed with a knife or other pointed object: *a fatal stabbing*

■ ***adj.*** [usually before noun] (of pain) very sharp, sudden and strong

sta·bil·ity **AW** /stəˈbɪləti/ *noun* [U] the quality or state of being steady and not changing or being disturbed in any way (= the quality of being stable): ***political/economic/social stability*** ◇ *the stability of the dollar on the world's money markets* ◇ *Being back with their family should provide emotional stability for the children.* **OPP** **instability**

sta·bil·ize (*BrE* also **-ise**) **AW** /ˈsteɪbəlaɪz/ *verb* [I, T] to become or to make sth become firm, steady and unlikely to change; to make sth stable: *The patient's condition stabilized.* ◇ **~ sth** *government measures to stabilize prices* ◇ *Doctors stabilized the patient's condition.* ➲ compare DESTABILIZE ▸ **sta·bil·iza·tion, -isa·tion** **AW** /ˌsteɪbəlaɪˈzeɪʃn; *NAmE* -ləˈz-/ *noun* [U]: *economic stabilization*

sta·bil·izer (*BrE* also **-iser**) /ˈsteɪbəlaɪzə(r)/ *noun* **1** a device that keeps sth steady, especially one that stops an aircraft or a ship from rolling to one side **2** **stabilizers** [pl.] (*BrE*) (*NAmE* ˈ**training wheels**) small wheels that are fitted at each side of the back wheel on a child's bicycle to stop it from falling over ➲ VISUAL VOCAB page V41 **3** (*technical*) a chemical that is sometimes added to food or paint to stop the various substances in it from becoming separate

stable 🔑 **AW** /ˈsteɪbl/ *adj., noun, verb*

> **WORD FAMILY**
> **stable** *adj.* (≠ unstable)
> **stability** *noun* (≠ instability)
> **stabilize** *verb*

■ ***adj.*** **1** 🔑 firmly fixed; not likely to move, change or fail **SYN** **steady**: *stable prices* ◇ *a stable relationship* ◇ *This ladder doesn't seem very stable.* ◇ *The patient's condition is stable* (= it is not getting worse). **2** 🔑 (of a person) calm and reasonable; not easily upset **SYN** **balanced**: *Mentally, she is not very stable.* **3** (*technical*) (of a substance) staying in the same chemical or ATOMIC state: *chemically stable* **OPP** **unstable** ▸ **sta·bly** /ˈsteɪbli/ *adv.*

■ ***noun*** **1** 🔑 [C] a building in which horses are kept ➲ VISUAL VOCAB page V2 **2** 🔑 (*BrE* also **stables**) [C+sing./pl. v.] an organization that keeps horses for a particular purpose: (*BrE*) *a* ***riding/racing stables*** ◇ *His stables are near Oxford.* **3** [C] a group of RACEHORSES owned or trained by the same person: *There have been just three winners from his stable this season.* **4** [sing.] a group of people who work or trained in the same place; a group of products made by the same company: *actors from the same stable* ◇ *the latest printer from the Epson stable*

■ ***verb*** **~ sth** to put or keep a horse in a stable: *Where do you stable your pony?*

ˈ**stable boy**, ˈ**stable girl** (*BrE* also ˈ**stable lad**) *noun* a person who works in a stable

ˈ**stable companion** *noun* = STABLEMATE

ˌ**stable ˈdoor** (*BrE*) (*NAmE* ˌ**Dutch ˈdoor**) *noun* a door which is divided into two parts so that the top part can be left open while the bottom part is kept shut

IDM **close, lock, etc. the stable door after the horse has ˈbolted** (*BrE*) (*US* **close, etc. the barn door after the horse has eˈscaped**) to try to prevent or avoid loss or damage when it is already too late to do so

stable·man /ˈsteɪblmæn/ *noun* (*pl.* **-men** /-men/) a person who works in a stable

stable·mate /ˈsteɪblmeɪt/ *noun* **1** a horse, especially a racing horse, from the same stable as another horse **2** (also ˈ**stable companion**) a person or product from the same organization as another person or product: *the 'Daily Mirror' newspaper and its Scottish stablemate the 'Daily Record'*

stab·ling /ˈsteɪblɪŋ/ *noun* [U] buildings or space where horses can be kept

stac·cato /stəˈkɑːtəʊ; *NAmE* -toʊ/ *adj.* **1** (*music*) with each note played separately in order to produce short, sharp sounds: *staccato sounds* **OPP** **legato** **2** with short, sharp sounds: *a peculiar staccato voice* ◇ *staccato bursts of gunfire* ▸ **stac·cato** *adv.*

stack /stæk/ *noun, verb*

■ ***noun*** **1** [C] a pile of sth, usually neatly arranged: *a stack of books* ◇ *a stack hi-fi system* (= where a radio, CD player, etc. are arranged on top of each other) ➲ see also HAYSTACK **2** [C] **~** (**of sth**) (*informal, especially BrE*) a large number or amount of sth; a lot of sth: *stacks of money* ◇ *There's a stack of unopened mail waiting for you at the house.* ◇ *I've got stacks of work to do.* **3** [C] a tall CHIMNEY, especially on a factory ➲ see also CHIMNEY STACK, SMOKESTACK **4** **the stacks** [pl.] the part of a library, sometimes not open to the public, where books that are not often needed are stored **5** [C] (*computing*) a way of storing information in a computer in which the most recently stored item is the first to be RETRIEVED (= found or got back) **6** [C] (*geology*) a tall thin part of a CLIFF that has been separated from the land and stands on its own in the sea **IDM** see BLOW *v.*

■ ***verb*** **1** [T, I] **~** (**sth**) (**up**) to arrange objects neatly in a pile; to be arranged in this way: *to stack boxes* ◇ *logs stacked up against a wall* ◇ *Do these chairs stack?* ◇ *stacking chairs* **2** [T] **~ sth** (**with sth**) to fill sth with piles of things: *They were busy stacking the shelves with goods.* **3** [I, T] **~** (**sth**) (**up**) if aircraft **stack** (**up**) or **are stacked** (**up**) over an airport, there are several flying around waiting for their turn to land

IDM ˈ**stack it** (*informal*) to fall over or off sth, especially in a way that makes you look silly and makes other people laugh: *I tried a spin on the ice and stacked it.*

PHR V ˌ**stack ˈup** **1** to keep increasing in quantity until there is a large pile, a long line, etc: *Cars quickly stacked up behind the bus.* **2** (used especially in questions or in negatives) to compare with sb/sth else; to be as good as sb/sth else **SYN** **measure up**: *Let's try him in the job and see how he stacks up.* ◇ **~ against sb/sth** *A mobile home simply doesn't stack up against a traditional house.* **3** (used especially in negatives) to seem reasonable; to make sense: *That can't be right. It just doesn't stack up.*

stacked /stækt/ *adj.* [not usually before noun] if a surface is **stacked with** objects, there are large numbers or piles of them on it: *a table stacked with glasses*

IDM **the cards/odds are stacked aˈgainst you** you are unlikely to succeed because the conditions are not good for you **the cards/odds are stacked in your ˈfavour** you are likely to succeed because the conditions are good and you have an advantage

sta·dium /ˈsteɪdiəm/ *noun* (*pl.* **sta·diums** or **sta·dia** /ˈsteɪdiə/) a large sports ground surrounded by rows of seats and usually other buildings: *a* ***football/sports stadium*** ◇ *an* ***all-seater stadium***

staff 🔑 /stɑːf; *NAmE* stæf/ *noun, verb*

■ ***noun*** **1** 🔑 [C, usually sing., U] all the workers employed in an organization considered as a group: *medical staff* ◇ (*BrE*) *teaching staff* ◇ (*BrE*) *We have 20 part-time* ***members***

S

of staff. ◇ (*NAmE*) ***staff members*** ◇ ***staff development/training*** ◇ *a* ***staff restaurant/meeting*** ◇ (*especially BrE*) *a lawyer* ***on the staff*** *of the Worldwide Fund for Nature* ➲ COLLOCATIONS at JOB ➲ see also GROUND STAFF **2** [sing.] (*NAmE*) the people who work at a school, college or university, but who do not teach students: *students, faculty and staff* **3** [C+sing./pl. v.] a group of senior army officers who help a commanding officer: *a staff officer* ➲ see also CHIEF OF STAFF, GENERAL STAFF **4** [C] (*old-fashioned* or *formal*) a long stick used as a support when walking or climbing, as a weapon, or as a symbol of authority **5** (*especially NAmE*) (*BrE* also **stave**) [C] (*music*) a set of five lines on which music is written ➲ picture at MUSIC

IDM **the ˌstaff of ˈlife** (*literary*) a basic food, especially bread

■ ***verb*** [T, usually passive] **~ sth** to work in an institution, a company, etc; to provide people to work there: *The advice centre is staffed entirely by volunteers.* ◇ *The charity provided money to staff and equip two hospitals.* ◇ *a fully staffed department* ➲ see also OVERSTAFFED, SHORT-STAFFED, UNDERSTAFFED ▶ **staf·fing** *noun* [U]: *staffing levels*

Grammar Point

staff

- In *BrE* **staff** (sense 1) can be singular: *a staff of ten* (= a group of ten people) or plural: *I have ten staff working for me*. If it is the subject of a verb, this verb is plural: *The staff in this shop are very helpful.*
- In *NAmE* **staff** (senses 1 and 2) can only be singular: *a staff of ten* (but not ~~ten staff~~). ◇ *The staff in this store is very helpful.*
- The plural form **staffs** is less frequent but is used in both *BrE* and *NAmE* to refer to more than one group of people: *the senator and his staff (singular)* ◇ *senators and their staffs (plural).*

staff·er /ˈstɑːfə(r); *NAmE* ˈstæf-/ *noun* (*NAmE*) a member of staff in a big organization

ˈstaff nurse *noun* (in Britain) a qualified hospital nurse

ˈstaff officer *noun* a military officer who helps an officer of very high rank or who works at a military HEADQUARTERS or a government department

staff·room /ˈstɑːfruːm; -rʊm; *NAmE* ˈstæf-/ *noun* (*BrE*) a room in a school where teachers can go when they are not teaching

S

ˈstaff sergeant *noun* a member of the army or the US AIR FORCE just above the rank of a SERGEANT: *Staff Sergeant Bob Woods*

stag /stæɡ/ *noun* a male DEER ➲ compare BUCK, DOE, HART

IDM **go ˈstag** (*NAmE, old-fashioned, informal*) (of a man) to go to a party without a partner

ˈstag beetle *noun* a large insect with a mouth that has parts like the horns of an animal

stage 0-w /steɪdʒ/ *noun, verb*

■ ***noun***

▸ PERIOD/STATE **1** 0-w [C] a period or state that sth/sb passes through while developing or making progress: *This technology is still in its* ***early stages****.* ◇ *The children are at different stages of development.* ◇ *The product is at the design stage.* ◇ *People tend to work hard* ***at this stage*** *of life.* ◇ ***At one stage*** *it looked as though they would win.* ◇ *Don't worry about the baby not wanting to leave you—it's* ***a stage they go through.***

▸ PART OF PROCESS **2** 0-w [C] a separate part that a process, etc. is divided into SYN **phase**: *We did the first stage of the trip by train.* ◇ *The police are building up a picture of the incident* ***stage by stage.*** ◇ *The pay increase will be introduced* ***in stages*** (= not all at once). ◇ *We can take the argument one stage further.* ➲ LANGUAGE BANK at PROCESS

▸ THEATRE **3** 0-w [C] a raised area, usually in a theatre, etc. where actors, dancers, etc. perform: *The audience threw flowers onto the stage.* ◇ *There were more than 50 people* ***on stage*** *in one scene.* ◇ *They marched* ***off stage*** *to the sound of trumpets.* ➲ see also BACKSTAGE, OFFSTAGE, ONSTAGE **4** 0-w (often **the stage**) [sing.] the theatre and the world of acting as a form of entertainment: *His parents didn't want him to* ***go on the stage*** (= to be an actor). ◇ *She was a popular star of* ***stage and screen*** (= theatre and cinema/movies).

▸ IN POLITICS **5** [sing.] an area of activity where important things happen, especially in politics: *She was forced to the centre of* ***the political stage.*** ◇ *Germany is playing a leading role on* ***the international stage.*** ➲ see also CENTRE STAGE

▸ CARRIAGE **6** [C] (*old-fashioned, informal*) = STAGECOACH ➲ see also LANDING STAGE

IDM **set the ˈstage for sth** to make it possible for sth to happen; to make sth likely to happen

■ ***verb*** **1 ~ sth** to organize and present a play or an event for people to see: *to stage a ceremony/an event/an exhibition* ◇ *The local theatre group is staging a production of 'Hamlet'.* ◇ *Birmingham has bid to stage the next national athletics championships.* **2 ~ sth** to organize and take part in action that needs careful planning, especially as a public protest: *to* ***stage a strike/demonstration/march/protest*** **3 ~ sth** to make sth happen: *The dollar* ***staged a recovery*** *earlier today.* ◇ *After five years in retirement, he* ***staged a comeback*** *to international tennis.*

stage·coach /ˈsteɪdʒkəʊtʃ; *NAmE* -koʊtʃ/ *noun* a large CARRIAGE pulled by horses, that was used in the past to carry passengers, and often mail, along a regular route

stage·craft /ˈsteɪdʒkrɑːft; *NAmE* -kræft/ *noun* [U] skill in presenting plays in a theatre

ˈstage direction *noun* a note in the text of a play telling actors when to come on to or leave the stage, what actions to perform, etc.

ˌstage ˈdoor *noun* the entrance at the back of a theatre used by actors, staff, etc.

ˈstage fright *noun* [U] nervous feelings felt by performers before they appear in front of an audience

stage·hand /ˈsteɪdʒhænd/ *noun* a person whose job is to help move SCENERY, etc. in a theatre, to prepare the stage for the next play or the next part of a play

ˌstage ˈleft *adv.* on the left side of a stage in a theatre, as seen by an actor facing the audience

ˌstage-ˈmanage *verb* **1 ~ sth** to act as stage manager for a performance in a theatre **2 ~ sth** to arrange and carefully plan an event that the public will see, especially in order to give a particular impression

ˌstage ˈmanager *noun* the person who is responsible for the stage, lights, SCENERY, etc. during the performance of a play in a theatre

ˈstage name *noun* a name that an actor uses instead of his or her real name

ˌstage ˈright *adv.* on the right side of a stage in a theatre, as seen by an actor facing the audience

ˈstage-struck *adj.* enjoying the theatre a lot and wishing very much to become an actor

ˌstage ˈwhisper *noun* **1** words that are spoken quietly by an actor to the audience and that the other people on stage are not supposed to hear **2** words that are spoken quietly by sb but that they in fact want everyone to hear: *'I knew this would happen,' she said in a stage whisper.*

stagey = STAGY

stag·fla·tion /stæɡˈfleɪʃn/ *noun* [U] an economic situation where there is high INFLATION (= prices rising continuously) but no increase in the jobs that are available or in business activity

stag·ger /ˈstæɡə(r)/ *verb* **1** [I, T] to walk with weak unsteady steps, as if you are about to fall SYN **totter**: (**+ adv./prep.**) *The injured woman staggered to her feet.* ◇ *He staggered home, drunk.* ◇ *We seem to stagger from one crisis to the next.* ◇ (*figurative*) *The company is* ***staggering under the weight*** *of a £10m debt.* ◇ **~ sth** *I managed to stagger the last few steps.* **2** [T] to shock or surprise sb very much SYN amaze: ~ sb *Her remarks staggered me.* ◇ **it staggers sb that...** *It staggers me that the government is doing nothing about it.* **3** [T] ~ **sth** to arrange for events that would normally happen at the same time to start or happen at different times: *There were so many runners that they had to stagger the start.* ▶ **stag·ger** *noun*: *to walk with a stagger*

stag·gered /ˈstæɡəd; *NAmE* -ɡərd/ *adj.* **1** [not before noun] ~ **(at/by sth)** | ~ **(to hear, learn, see, etc.)** very surprised and shocked at sth you are told or at sth that happens SYN **amazed**: *I was staggered at the amount of money the ring cost.* **2** arranged in such a way that not everything happens at the same time: *staggered working hours* (= people start and finish at different times)

stag·ger·ing /ˈstæɡərɪŋ/ *adj.* (rather *informal*) so great, shocking or surprising that it is difficult to believe SYN **astounding** ▶ **stag·ger·ing·ly** *adv.*: *staggeringly beautiful/expensive*

sta·ging /ˈsteɪdʒɪŋ/ *noun* **1** [C, U] the way in which a play is produced and presented on stage: *a modern staging of 'King Lear'* **2** [U] a temporary platform used for standing or working on

ˈ**staging post** *noun* a place where people, planes, ships, etc. regularly stop during a long journey

stag·nant /ˈstæɡnənt/ *adj.* **1** **stagnant** water or air is not moving and therefore smells unpleasant **2** not developing, growing or changing SYN **static**: *a stagnant economy*

stag·nate /stæɡˈneɪt; *NAmE* ˈstæɡneɪt/ *verb* **1** [I] to stop developing or making progress: *Profits have stagnated.* ◇ *I feel I'm stagnating in this job.* **2** [I] to be or become stagnant: *The water in the pond was stagnating.* ▶ **stag·na·tion** /stæɡˈneɪʃn/ *noun* [U]: *a period of economic stagnation*

ˈ**stag night** *noun* [usually sing.] **1** (*BrE*) the night before a man's wedding, often spent with his male friends **2** (also ˈ**stag party**) (both *BrE*) (*NAmE* ˈ**bachelor party**) a party that a man has with his male friends just before he gets married, often the night before ➲ compare HEN PARTY

stagy (also **stagey**) /ˈsteɪdʒi/ *adj.* not natural, as if it is being acted by sb in a play

staid /steɪd/ *adj.* (**staid·er**, **staid·est**) not amusing or interesting; boring and old-fashioned

stain /steɪn/ *verb, noun*

■ ***verb*** **1** [T, I] to leave a mark that is difficult to remove on sth; to be marked in this way: ~ **(sth) (with sth)** *I hope it doesn't stain the carpet.* ◇ *This carpet stains easily.* ◇ ~ **sth + adj.** *The juice from the berries stained their fingers red.* **2** [T] to change the colour of sth using a coloured liquid: ~ **sth** *to stain wood* ◇ *Stain the specimen before looking at it under the microscope.* ◇ ~ **sth + adj.** *They stained the floors dark brown.* **3** [T] ~ **sth** (*formal*) to damage the opinion that people have of sth: *The events had stained the city's reputation unfairly.*

■ ***noun*** **1** [C] a dirty mark on sth, that is difficult to remove: ***a blood/a coffee/an ink, etc. stain*** ◇ ***stubborn stains*** (= that are very difficult to remove) ◇ *How can I get this stain out?* ◇ *The carpet has been treated so that it is* ***stain-resistant*** (= it does not stain easily). ➲ SYNONYMS at MARK **2** [U, C] a liquid used for changing the colour of wood or cloth **3** [sing.] **a ~ on sth** (*formal*) something that damages a person's reputation, so that people think badly of them

stained /steɪnd/ *adj.* (often in compounds) covered with stains or marked with a stain: *My dress was stained.* ◇ *paint-stained jeans* ➲ SYNONYMS at DIRTY

ˌ**stained** ˈ**glass** *noun* [U] pieces of coloured glass that are put together to make windows, especially in churches

stain·less steel /ˌsteɪnləs ˈstiːl/ *noun* [U] a type of steel that does not RUST (= change colour)

stair 0‑ᴡ /steə(r); *NAmE* ster/ *noun*

1 0‑ᴡ **stairs** [pl.] a set of steps built between two floors inside a building: *We had to carry the piano up three* ***flights of stairs.*** ◇ *The children ran* ***up/down the stairs.*** ◇ ***at the bottom/top of the stairs*** ◇ *He remembered passing her* ***on the stairs.*** ➲ see also DOWNSTAIRS, UPSTAIRS **2** 0‑ᴡ [C] one of the steps in a set of stairs: *How many stairs are there up to the second floor?* ➲ picture at STAIRCASE **3** [sing.] (*literary*) = STAIRCASE: *The house had a panelled hall and a fine oak stair.* ▶ **stair** *adj.* [only before noun]: *the stair carpet*

IDM **below** ˈ**stairs** (*old-fashioned*, *BrE*) in the part of a house where the servants lived in the past

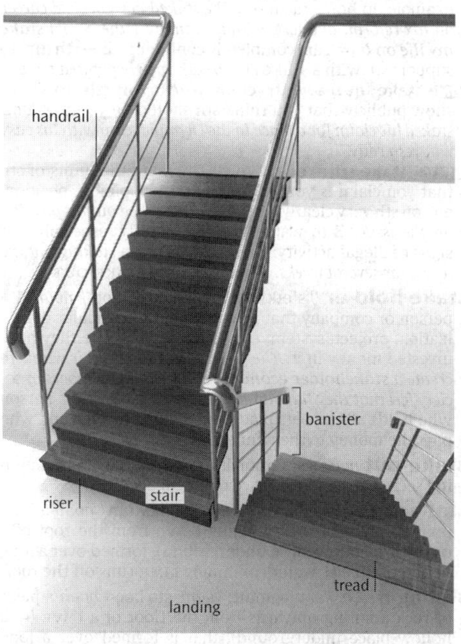

stair·case /ˈsteəkeɪs; *NAmE* ˈsterk-/ *noun* a set of stairs inside a building including the posts and rails (= BANISTERS) that are fixed at the side: *a marble/stone/wooden staircase* ➲ see also SPIRAL STAIRCASE

stair·lift /ˈsteəlɪft; *NAmE* ˈsterl-/ *noun* a piece of equipment in the form of a seat that sb can sit on to be moved up and down stairs, used by people who find it difficult to walk up and down stairs without help

stair·way /ˈsteəweɪ; *NAmE* ˈsterweɪ/ *noun* a set of stairs inside or outside a building

stair·well /ˈsteəwel; *NAmE* ˈsterwel/ *noun* [usually sing.] the space in a building in which the stairs are built

stake /steɪk/ *noun, verb*

■ ***noun*** **1** [C] a wooden or metal post that is pointed at one end and pushed into the ground in order to support sth, mark a particular place, etc. ➲ VISUAL VOCAB page V16 **2 the stake** [sing.] a wooden post that sb could be tied to in former times before being burnt to death (= killed by fire) as a punishment: *Joan of Arc was* ***burnt at the stake.*** **3** [C] money that sb invests in a company: *a 20% stake in the business* **4** [sing.] ~ **in sth** an important part or share in a business, plan, etc. that is important to you and that you want to be successful: *She has a personal stake in the success of the play.* ◇ *Many young people no longer feel they have a stake in society.* **5** [C] something that you risk losing, especially money, when you try to predict the result of a race, game, etc, or when you are involved in an activity that can succeed or fail: *How much was the stake* (= how much did you bet)? ◇ *They were playing cards for* ***high stakes*** (= a lot of money). **6 stakes** [pl.] the money that is paid to the winners in horse racing **7 stakes** [U] used in the names of some horse races

IDM **at** ˈ**stake** that can be won or lost, depending on the success of a particular action: *We cannot afford to take risks when people's lives are at stake.* ◇ *The prize at stake is a place in the final.* **go to the** ˈ**stake over/for sth** to be prepared to do anything in order to defend your opinions or beliefs **in the... stakes** used to say how much of a particular quality a person has, as if they were in a competition in which some people are more successful than others: *John doesn't do too well in the personality stakes.* ➲ more at UP *v.*

■ ***verb*** **1 ~ sth (on sth)** to risk money or sth important on the result of sth SYN **bet**: *He staked £25 on the favourite* (= for example, in horse racing). ◇ *She staked her political career on tax reform, and lost.* ◇ *That's him over there—I'd* ***stake my life on it*** (= I am completely confident). **2 ~ sth (up)** to support sth with a stake (1): *to stake newly planted trees*

IDM **stake (out) a/your 'claim (to/for/on sth)** to say or show publicly that you think sth should be yours: *Adams staked his claim for a place in the Olympic team with his easy win yesterday.*

PHR V **,stake sth↔'out 1** to clearly mark the limits of sth that you claim is yours **2** to state your opinion, position, etc. on sth very clearly: *The President staked out his position on the issue.* **3** to watch a place secretly, especially for signs of illegal activity: *Detectives had been staking out the house for several weeks.* ➲ related noun STAKE-OUT

stake·hold·er /'steɪkhəʊldə(r); *NAmE* -hoʊ-/ *noun* **1** a person or company that is involved in a particular organization, project, system, etc, especially because they have invested money in it: *The government has said it wants to create a* ***stakeholder economy*** *in which all members of society feel that they have an interest in its success.* **2** a person who holds all the bets placed on a game or race and who pays the money to the winner

'stake-out *noun* a situation in which police watch a building secretly to find evidence of illegal activities

stal·ac·tite /'stæləktaɪt; *NAmE* stə'læktaɪt/ *noun* a long pointed piece of rock hanging down from the roof of a CAVE (= a hollow place underground), formed over a long period of time as water containing LIME runs off the roof

stal·ag·mite /'stæləgmaɪt; *NAmE* stə'læg-/ *noun* a piece of rock pointing upwards from the floor of a CAVE (= a hollow place underground), that is formed over a long period of time from drops of water containing LIME that fall from the roof

stale /steɪl/ *adj.* **1** (of food, especially bread and cake) no longer fresh and therefore unpleasant to eat **2** (of air, smoke, etc.) no longer fresh; smelling unpleasant: *stale cigarette smoke* ◇ *stale sweat* **3** something that is **stale** has been said or done too many times before and is no longer interesting or exciting: *stale jokes* ◇ *Their marriage had* ***gone stale.*** **4** a person who is **stale** has done the same thing for too long and so is unable to do it well or produce any new ideas: *After ten years in the job, she felt stale and needed a change.* ▶ **stale·ness** *noun* [U]

S

stale·mate /'steɪlmeɪt/ *noun* **1** [U, C, usually sing.] a disagreement or a situation in a competition in which neither side is able to win or make any progress SYN **impasse**: *The talks ended in (a) stalemate.* **2** [U, sing.] (in CHESS) a situation in which a player cannot successfully move any of their pieces and the game ends without a winner ➲ compare CHECKMATE

Sta·lin·ism /'stɑːlɪnɪzəm/ *noun* [U] the policies and beliefs of Stalin, especially that the Communist party should be the only party and that the central government should control the whole political and economic system ▶ **Sta·lin·ist** *adj., noun*

stalk /stɔːk/ *noun, verb*

■ ***noun*** **1** a thin STEM that supports a leaf, flower or fruit and joins it to another part of the plant or tree; the main STEM of a plant: *flowers on long stalks* ◇ *celery stalks* ◇ *He ate the apple, stalk and all.* ➲ VISUAL VOCAB pages V9, V26 **2** a long thin structure that supports sth, especially an organ in some animals, and joins it on to another part: *Crabs have eyes on stalks.*

■ ***verb*** **1** [T, I] **~ (sth/sb)** to move slowly and quietly towards an animal or a person, in order to kill, catch or harm it or them: *The lion was stalking a zebra.* ◇ *He stalked his victim as she walked home, before attacking and robbing her.* **2** [T] **~ sb** to illegally follow and watch sb over a long period of time, in a way that is annoying or frightening: *She claimed that he had been stalking her over a period of three years.* **3** [I] **+ adv./prep.** to walk in an angry or proud way: *He stalked off without a word.* **4** [T, I] **~ (sth)** to move through a place in an unpleasant or threatening way: *The gunmen stalked the building, looking for victims.* ◇ (*figurative*) *Fear stalks the streets of the city at night.*

stalk·er /'stɔːkə(r)/ *noun* **1** a person who follows and watches another person over a long period of time in a way that is annoying or frightening **2** a person who follows an animal quietly and slowly, especially in order to kill or capture it

stalk·ing /'stɔːkɪŋ/ *noun* [U] the crime of following and watching sb over a long period of time in a way that is annoying or frightening

'stalking horse *noun* [sing.] **1** a person or thing that is used to hide the real purpose of a particular course of action **2** a politician who competes against the leader of their party in order to see how much support the leader has; a stronger candidate can then compete against the leader more seriously

stall /stɔːl/ *noun, verb*

■ ***noun*** **1** [C] a table or small shop with an open front that people sell things from, especially at a market SYN **stand**: *a market stall* ➲ VISUAL VOCAB page V3 ➲ see also BOOKSTALL **2** [C] a section inside a farm building that is large enough for one animal to be kept in **3** [C] (*especially NAmE*) a small area in a room, surrounded by glass, walls, etc, that contains a shower or toilet **4 the stalls** (also **the 'orchestra stalls**) (both *BrE*) [pl.] (*NAmE* **the orchestra** [sing.]) the seats that are nearest to the stage in a theatre: *the front row of the stalls* **5** [C, usually pl.] the seats at the front of a church where the CHOIR (= singers) and priests sit **6** [C, usually sing.] a situation in which a vehicle's engine suddenly stops because it is not getting enough power **7** [C, usually sing.] a situation in which an aircraft loses speed and goes steeply downwards

■ ***verb*** **1** [I, T] (of a vehicle or an engine) to stop suddenly because of a lack of power or speed; to make a vehicle or engine do this: *The car stalled and refused to start again.* ◇ **~ sth** *I stalled the car three times during my driving test.* **2** [I] **~ (on/over sth)** to try to avoid doing sth or answering a question so that you have more time: *They are still stalling on the deal.* ◇ *'What do you mean?' she asked,* ***stalling for time.*** **3** [T] **~ sb** to make sb wait so that you have more time to do sth: *See if you can stall her while I finish searching her office.* **4** [T, I] **~ (sth)** to stop sth from happening until a later date; to stop making progress: *attempts to revive the stalled peace plan* ◇ *Discussions have once again stalled.*

stall·hold·er /'stɔːlhəʊldə(r); *NAmE* -hoʊ-/ *noun* (*BrE*) a person who sells things from a stall in a market, etc.

stal·lion /'stæliən/ *noun* a fully grown male horse, especially one that is used for breeding ➲ compare COLT, GELDING, MARE

stal·wart /'stɔːlwət; *NAmE* -wərt/ *noun, adj.*

■ ***noun*** **~ (of sth)** a loyal supporter who does a lot of work for an organization, especially a political party

■ ***adj.*** [usually before noun] **1** loyal and able to be relied on, even in a difficult situation SYN **faithful**: *stalwart supporters* **2** (*formal*) physically strong

sta·men /'steɪmən/ *noun* (*technical*) a small thin male part in the middle of a flower that produces POLLEN and is made up of a STALK supporting an ANTHER. The centre of each flower usually has several stamens. ➲ VISUAL VOCAB page V9

stam·ina /'stæmɪnə/ *noun* [U] the physical or mental strength that enables you to do sth difficult for long periods of time: *It takes a lot of stamina to run a marathon.* ➲ COLLOCATIONS at DIET

stam·mer /'stæmə(r)/ *verb, noun*

■ ***verb*** [I, T] to speak with difficulty, repeating sounds or words and often stopping, before saying things correctly SYN **stutter**: *Many children stammer but grow out of it.* ◇ **+ speech** *'W-w-what?' he stammered.* ◇ **~ sth (out)** *She was barely able to stammer out a description of her attacker.* ▶ **stam·mer·er** *noun*

■ ***noun*** [sing.] a problem that sb has in speaking in which they repeat sounds or words or often pause before saying things correctly

stamp 0-ᴛ /stæmp/ *noun, verb*

■ ***noun***

▸ ON LETTER/PACKAGE **1** 0-ᴛ (also *formal* ˈ**postage stamp**) [C] a small piece of paper with a design on it that you buy and stick on an envelope or a package before you post it: *a 28p stamp* ◇ *Could I have three first-class stamps, please?* ◇ *He has been collecting stamps since he was eight.* ◇ *a* ***stamp album*** ➲ VISUAL VOCAB page V35

▸ PRINTING TOOL **2** 0-ᴛ [C] a tool for printing the date or a design or mark onto a surface: *a date stamp* ➲ see also RUBBER STAMP

▸ PRINTED DESIGN/WORDS **3** 0-ᴛ [C] a design or words made by stamping sth onto a surface: *The passports, with the visa stamps, were waiting at the embassy.* ◇ (*figurative*) *The project has the government's* ***stamp of approval.***

▸ PROOF OF PAYMENT **4** [C] a small piece of paper with a design on it, stuck on a document to show that a particular amount of money has been paid: *a TV licence stamp*

▸ CHARACTER/QUALITY **5** [sing.] **~** (**of sth**) (*formal*) the mark or sign of a particular quality or person: *All his work* ***bears the stamp*** *of authority.* **6** [sing.] (*formal*) a kind or class, especially of people: *men of a different stamp*

▸ OF FOOT **7** [sing.] an act or sound of stamping the foot: *The stamp of hoofs alerted Isabel.*

■ ***verb***

▸ FOOT **1** 0-ᴛ [T, I] **~** (**sth**) to put your foot down heavily and noisily on the ground: *I tried* ***stamping my feet*** *to keep warm.* ◇ *Sam* ***stamped his foot*** *in anger.* ◇ *The audience were stamping and cheering.*

▸ WALK **2** [I] **+ adv./prep.** to walk with loud heavy steps SYN **stomp**: *She turned and stamped out of the room.*

▸ PRINT DESIGN/WORDS **3** 0-ᴛ [T, often passive] to print letters, words, a design, etc. onto sth using a special tool: **~ A** (**with B**) *The box was stamped with the maker's name.* ◇ *Wait here to have your passport stamped.* ◇ **~ B on A** *I'll stamp the company name on your cheque.* ◇ *The maker's name was stamped in gold on the box.* ➲ see also RUBBER-STAMP, STAMP STH ON STH

▸ SHOW FEELING/QUALITY **4** [T, usually passive] to make a feeling show clearly on sb's face, in their actions, etc: **~ A with B** *Their faces were stamped with hostility.* ◇ **~ B over, across, etc. A** *The crime had revenge stamped all over it.* **5** [T] **~ sb as sth** to show that sb has a particular quality: *Her success has stamped her as one of the country's top riders.*

▸ ON LETTER/PACKAGE **6** [T, usually passive] **~ sth** to stick a stamp on a letter or package

▸ CUT OUT OBJECT **7** [T] **~ sth** (**out**) (**of/from sth**) to cut and shape an object from a piece of metal or plastic using a special machine or tool

PHR V ˈ**stamp on sth 1** to put your foot down with force on sth: *The child stamped on the spider.* **2** to stop sth from happening or stop sb from doing sth, especially by using force or authority: *All attempts at modernization were stamped on by senior officials.* ˈ**stamp sth on sth** to make sth have an important effect or influence on sth: *She stamped her own interpretation on the role.* ˌ**stamp sth**↔ˈ**out 1** to get rid of sth that is bad, unpleasant or dangerous, especially by using force or a lot of effort SYN **eliminate**: *to stamp out racism* **2** to put out a fire by bringing your foot down heavily on it

ˈ**stamp collecting** *noun* [U] the hobby of collecting stamps from different countries ➲ VISUAL VOCAB page V35 ▸ ˈ**stamp collector** *noun*

ˈ**stamp duty** *noun* [U] a tax in Britain on some legal documents

ˌ**stamped addressed** ˈ**envelope** *noun* (*abbr.* SAE) (*BrE*) an envelope on which you have written your name and address and put a stamp so that sb else can use it to send sth to you: *Please enclose a stamped addressed envelope to get your test results.*

stam·pede /stæmˈpiːd/ *noun, verb*

■ ***noun*** [C, usually sing.] **1** a situation in which a group of people or large animals such as horses suddenly start running in the same direction, especially because they are frightened or excited: *A stampede broke out when the doors opened.* **2** a situation in which a lot of people are trying to do or achieve the same thing at the same time: *Falling interest rates has led to a stampede to buy property.*

■ ***verb*** **1** [I, T] **~** (**sth**) (of large animals or people) to run in a stampede; to make animals do this: *a herd of stampeding elephants* ◇ *A huge bunch of kids came stampeding down the corridor.* **2** [T, usually passive] **~ sb** (**into sth/into doing sth**) to make sb rush into doing sth without giving them time to think about it: *I refuse to be stampeded into making any hasty decisions.*

ˈ**stamping ground** (*NAmE* also ˈ**stomping ground**) *noun* (*informal*) a place that sb likes and where they often go SYN **haunt**

stance /stæns; *BrE* also stɑːns/ *noun* **1** **~** (**on sth**) the opinions that sb has about sth and expresses publicly SYN **position**: *What is the newspaper's stance on the war?* **2** the way in which sb stands, especially when playing a sport

stanch /stɔːntʃ; stæntʃ/ *verb* (*especially NAmE*) = STAUNCH

stan·chion /ˈstæntʃən; ˈstɑːn-/ *noun* (*formal*) a vertical pole used to support sth

stand 0-ᴛ /stænd/ *verb, noun*

■ ***verb*** (**stood, stood** /stʊd/)

▸ ON FEET/BE VERTICAL **1** 0-ᴛ [I] to be on your feet; to be in a vertical position: *She was too weak to stand.* ◇ *a bird standing on one leg* ◇ ***Don't just stand there****—do something!* ◇ *I was standing only a few feet away.* ◇ *We all* ***stood around*** *in the corridor waiting.* ◇ *to* ***stand on your head/hands*** (= to be upside down, balancing on your head/hands) ◇ *After the earthquake, only a few houses were* ***left standing.*** ◇ **+ adj.** ***Stand still*** *while I take your photo.* **2** 0-ᴛ [I] to get up onto your feet from another position: *Everyone stood when the President came in.* ◇ **~ up** *We stood up in order to get a better view.*

▸ PUT UPRIGHT **3** [T] **~ sth/sb + adv./prep.** to put sth/sb in a vertical position somewhere: *Stand the ladder up against the wall.* ◇ *I stood the little girl on a chair so that she could see.*

▸ BE IN PLACE/CONDITION **4** 0-ᴛ [I] **+ adv./prep.** to be in a particular place: *The castle stands on the site of an ancient battlefield.* ◇ *An old oak tree once stood here.* **5** [I] (**+ adj.**) to be in a particular condition or situation: *The house* ***stood empty*** *for a long time.* ◇ *'You're wrong about the date—it was 1988.' '****I stand corrected*** (= accept that I was wrong).' ◇ *You never* ***know where you stand with*** *her—one minute she's friendly, the next she'll hardly speak to you.* ◇ ***As things stand,*** *there is little chance of a quick settlement of the dispute.*

▸ BE AT HEIGHT/LEVEL **6** [I] **+ noun** (not used in the progressive tenses) to be a particular height: *The tower stands 30 metres high.* **7** [I] **~ at sth** to be at a particular level, amount, height, etc: *Interest rates stand at 3%.* ◇ *The world record then stood at 6.59 metres.*

▸ OF CAR/TRAIN, ETC. **8** [I] **+ adv./prep.** to be in a particular place, especially while waiting to go somewhere: *The train standing at platform 3 is for London, Victoria.*

▸ OF LIQUID/MIXTURE **9** [I] to remain still, without moving or being moved: *Mix the batter and let it stand for twenty minutes.* ◇ *standing pools of rainwater*

▸ OFFER/DECISION **10** [I] if an offer, a decision, etc. made earlier **stands**, it is still valid: *My offer still stands.* ◇ *The world record stood for 20 years.*

▸ BE LIKELY TO DO STH **11** [I] **~ to do sth** to be in a situation where you are likely to do sth: *You stand to make a lot from this deal.*

▸ HAVE OPINION **12** [I] **~** (**on sth**) to have a particular attitude or opinion about sth or towards sb: ***Where do you stand*** *on private education?*

▸ DISLIKE **13** 0-ᴛ [T, no passive] (not used in the progressive tenses) used especially in negative sentences and questions to emphasize that you do not like sb/sth SYN **bear**: **~ sb/sth** *I* ***can't stand*** *his brother.* ◇ *I can't stand the sight of blood.* ◇ *I* ***can't stand it*** *when you do that.* ◇ **~ doing sth** *She couldn't stand being kept waiting.* ◇ **~ sb/sth doing sth** *I*

S

can't stand people interrupting all the time. ◇ How do you stand him being here all the time? ➲ SYNONYMS at HATE

▸ SURVIVE TREATMENT **14** [T] **~ sth** used especially with *can/could* to say that sb/sth can survive sth or can TOLERATE sth without being hurt or damaged: *His heart won't stand the strain much longer.* ◇ *Modern plastics can stand very high and very low temperatures.*

▸ BUY DRINK/MEAL **15** [T, no passive] to buy a drink or meal for sb: **~ sth** *He stood drinks all round.* ◇ **~ sb sth** *She was kind enough to stand us a meal.*

▸ IN ELECTION **16** (*especially BrE*) (*NAmE* usually **run**) [I] **~ (for/as sth)** to be a candidate in an election: *He* ***stood for parliament*** (= tried to get elected as an MP). ◇ *She stood unsuccessfully as a candidate in the local elections.*

IDM Idioms containing **stand** are at the entries for the nouns and adjectives in the idioms, for example **stand on ceremony** is at **ceremony**.

PHR V **ˌstand aˈside 1** to move to one side: *She stood aside to let us pass.* **2** to not get involved in sth: *Don't stand aside and let others do all the work.* **3** to stop doing a job so sb else can do it

ˌstand ˈback (from sth) 1 to move back from a place: *The police ordered the crowd to stand back.* **2** to be located away from sth: *The house stands back from the road.* **3** to think about a situation as if you are not involved in it: *It's time to stand back and look at your career so far.*

ˌstand beˈtween sb/sth and sth to prevent sb from getting or achieving sth: *Only one game stood between him and victory.*

ˌstand ˈby 1 to be present while sth bad is happening but not do anything to stop it: *How can you stand by and see him accused of something he didn't do?* ➲ related noun BYSTANDER **2** to be ready for action: *The troops are standing by.* ➲ related noun STANDBY **ˈstand by sb** to help sb or be friends with them, even in difficult situations: *her famous song, 'Stand by your man'* **ˈstand by sth** to still believe or agree with sth you said, decided or agreed earlier: *She still stands by every word she said.*

ˌstand ˈdown 1 ~ (as sth) to leave a job or position: *He stood down to make way for someone younger.* **2** (of a witness) to leave the WITNESS BOX/STAND in court after giving evidence

ˈstand for sth [no passive] **1** (not used in the progressive tenses) to be an abbreviation or symbol of sth: *'The book's by T.C. Smith.' 'What does the 'T.C.' stand for?'* **2** to support sth: *I hated the organization and all it stood for* (= the ideas that it supported). **3 not stand for sth** to not let sb do sth or sth happen: *I'm not standing for it any longer.*

ˌstand ˈin (for sb) to take sb's place SYN **deputize**: *My assistant will stand in for me while I'm away.* ➲ related noun STAND-IN

ˌstand ˈout (as sth) to be much better or more important than sb/sth: *Four points stand out as being more important than the rest.* ➲ see also OUTSTANDING **ˌstand ˈout (from/against sth)** to be easily seen; to be noticeable: *The lettering stood out well against the dark background.* ◇ *She's the sort of person who* ***stands out in a crowd.***

ˌstand ˈover sb be near sb and watch them: *I don't like you standing over me while I'm cooking.*

ˌstand ˈup to be on your feet: *There were no seats left so I had to stand up.* ◇ *You'll look taller if you* ***stand up straight.***

ˌstand sb ˈup (*informal*) to deliberately not meet sb you have arranged to meet, especially sb you are having a romantic relationship with: *I've been stood up!* **ˌstand ˈup for sb/sth** to support or defend sb/sth: *Always stand up for your friends.* ◇ *You must stand up for your rights.* ◇ *She had learnt to stand up for herself.* **ˌstand ˈup (to sth)** to remain valid even when tested, examined closely, etc: *His argument simply doesn't stand up to close scrutiny.* ◇ *I'm afraid this document will never stand up in a court of law.* **ˌstand ˈup to sb** to resist sb; to not accept bad treatment from sb without complaining: *It was brave of her to stand up to those bullies.* **ˌstand ˈup to sth** (of materials, products, etc.) to remain in good condition despite rough treatment SYN **withstand**: *The carpet is designed to stand up to a lot of wear and tear.*

Synonyms

stand

get up • stand up • rise • get to your feet • be on your feet

These words all mean to be in an upright position with your weight on your feet, or to put yourself in this position.

stand to be in an upright position with your weight on your feet : *She was too weak to stand.* ◇ ***Stand still*** *when I'm talking to you!* NOTE **Stand** is usually used with an adverb or prepositional phrase to show where or how sb stands, but sometimes another phrase or clause is used to show what sb does while they are standing: *We stood talking for a few minutes.* ◇ *He stood and looked out to sea.*

get up to get into a standing position from a sitting, kneeling or lying position: *Please don't get up!*

stand up to be in a standing position; to stand after sitting: *Stand up straight!* ◇ *Everyone would stand up when the teacher entered the classroom.*

STAND, GET UP OR STAND UP?

Stand usually means 'to be in a standing position' but can also mean 'to get into a standing position'. **Stand up** can be used with either of these meanings, but its use is more restricted: it is used especially when sb tells sb or a group of people to stand. **Get up** is the most frequent way of saying 'get into a standing position', and this can be from a sitting, kneeling or lying position; if you **stand up**, this is nearly always after sitting, especially on a chair. If you want to tell sb politely that they do not need to move from their chair, use **get up**: ~~*Please don't stand up!*~~

rise (*formal*) to get into a standing position from a sitting, kneeling or lying position: *Would you all rise, please, to welcome our visiting speaker.*

get to your feet to stand up after sitting, kneeling or lying: *I helped her to get to her feet.*

be on your feet to be standing up: *I've been on my feet all day.*

■ ***noun***

▸ OPINION **1** [usually sing.] **~ (on sth)** an attitude towards sth or an opinion that you make clear to people: *to take a firm stand on sth* ◇ *He was criticized for his tough stand on immigration.*

▸ DEFENCE **2** [usually sing.] a strong effort to defend yourself or your opinion about sth: *We must* ***make a stand against*** *further job losses.* ◇ *the rebels' desperate last stand*

▸ FOR SHOWING/HOLDING STH **3** a table or a vertical structure that goods are sold from, especially in the street or at a market SYN **stall**: *a hamburger/newspaper stand* ➲ see also NEWS-STAND **4** (*especially BrE*) a table or a vertical structure where things are displayed or advertised, for example at an exhibition: *a* ***display/an exhibition/a trade stand*** **5** (often in compounds) a piece of equipment or furniture that you use for holding a particular type of thing: *a* ***bicycle/microphone/cake, etc. stand*** ➲ VISUAL VOCAB pages V41, V57 ➲ see also HATSTAND, MUSIC STAND, NIGHTSTAND, WASHSTAND

▸ AT SPORTS GROUND **6** a large sloping structure at a STADIUM with rows where people sit or stand to watch the game ➲ see also GRANDSTAND

▸ IN COURT **7** [usually sing.] = WITNESS BOX: *He* ***took the stand*** *as the first witness.*

▸ IN CRICKET **8** [usually sing.] the period of time in which two people who are BATTING (= hitting the ball) play together and score points: *Clinch and Harris shared an* ***opening stand*** *of 69.*

▸ FOR BAND/ORCHESTRA, ETC. **9** a raised platform for a band, an ORCHESTRA, a speaker, etc. ➲ see also BANDSTAND

▸ FOR TAXIS/BUSES, ETC. **10** a place where taxis, buses, etc.

park while they are waiting for passengers ➲ compare TAXI RANK

▸ OF PLANTS/TREES **11 ~** (**of sth**) (*technical*) a group of plants or trees of one kind: *a stand of pines*

▸ OF LAND **12** (*SAfrE*) a piece of land that you can buy and use for building a house, etc. on: *A developer bought the land and divided it into stands.* ➲ see also HANDSTAND, ONE-NIGHT STAND IDM see FIRM *adj.*

'stand-alone *adj.* [usually before noun] (especially of a computer) able to be operated on its own without being connected to a larger system

stand·ard 0-π /'stændəd; *NAmE* -dərd/ *noun, adj.*

■ ***noun***

▸ LEVEL OF QUALITY **1** 0-π [C, U] **~** (**of sth**) a level of quality, especially one that people think is acceptable: *a fall in academic standards* ◇ *We aim to maintain* ***high standards*** *of customer care.* ◇ *The standard of this year's applications is very low.* ◇ *He failed to* ***reach the required standard,*** *and did not qualify for the race.* ◇ *Her work is not* ***up to standard*** (= of a good enough standard). ◇ *Who* ***sets the standard*** *for water quality?* ◇ *A number of Britain's beaches fail to* ***meet*** *European* ***standards*** *on cleanliness.* ◇ *In the shanty towns there are very poor* ***living standards.*** ➲ see also STANDARD OF LIVING, SUBSTANDARD **2** 0-π [C, usually pl.] a level of quality that is normal or acceptable for a particular person or in a particular situation: *You'd better* ***lower your standards*** *if you want to find somewhere cheap to live.* ◇ *It was a simple meal by Eddie's standards.* ◇ *The equipment is slow and heavy* ***by modern standards.***

▸ LEVEL OF BEHAVIOUR **3** 0-π **standards** [pl.] a level of behaviour that sb considers to be morally acceptable: *a man of high moral standards* ◇ *Standards aren't what they used to be.* ➲ see also DOUBLE STANDARD

▸ UNIT OF MEASUREMENT **4** [C] a unit of measurement that is officially used; an official rule used when producing sth: *a reduction in the weight standard of silver coins* ◇ *industry standards* ➲ see also GOLD STANDARD

▸ FLAG **5** [C] a flag that is used during official ceremonies, especially one connected with a particular military group

▸ SONG **6** [C] a song that has been recorded by many different singers

■ ***adj.***

▸ AVERAGE/NORMAL **1** 0-π average or normal rather than having special or unusual features: *A standard letter was sent to all candidates.* ◇ *Televisions are a standard feature in most hotel rooms.* ◇ *the standard rate of tax* (= paid by everyone) ◇ *It is* ***standard practice*** *to search visitors as they enter the building.* ◇ *All vehicles come with a CD player* ***as standard.***

▸ SIZE/MEASUREMENT **2** 0-π [usually before noun] following a particular standard set, for example, by an industry: *standard sizes of clothes*

▸ BOOK/WRITER **3** [only before noun] read by most people who are studying a particular subject

▸ LANGUAGE **4** [usually before noun] (of spelling, pronunciation, grammar, etc.) believed to be correct and used by most people: *Standard English* ➲ compare NON-STANDARD, SUBSTANDARD

'standard-bearer *noun* a leader in a political group or campaign

,standard de'duction *noun* [usually sing.] (*US*) a fixed amount of money that you can earn free of tax

,standard devi'ation *noun* (*mathematics*) the amount by which measurements in a set vary from the average for the set

,standard 'error *noun* (*statistics*) a method of measuring how accurate an estimate is

'Standard Grade *noun* (in Scotland) an exam in a particular subject at a lower level than HIGHERS. Standard Grades are usually taken in a number of different subjects at the age of 16.

stand·ard·ize (*BrE* also **-ise**) /'stændədaɪz; *NAmE* -dərd-/ *verb* **~ sth** to make objects or activities of the same type have the same features or qualities; to make sth standard: *a standardized contract/design/test* ▸ **stand·ard·iza·tion, -isa·tion** /stændədaɪ'zeɪʃn; *NAmE* -dərdə'z-/ *noun* [U]: *the standardization of components*

'standard lamp (*BrE*) (also **'floor lamp** *NAmE, BrE*) *noun* a tall lamp that stands on the floor ➲ VISUAL VOCAB page V18

,standard of 'living *noun* (*pl.* **,standards of 'living**) the amount of money and level of comfort that a particular person or group has

'standard time *noun* [U] the official time of a country or an area

stand·by /'stændbaɪ/ *noun, adj.*

■ ***noun*** (*pl.* **stand·bys**) a person or thing that can always be used if needed, for example if sb/sth else is not available or if there is an emergency: *I always keep a pizza in the freezer as a standby.* ◇ *a standby electricity generator*

IDM **on 'standby 1** ready to do sth immediately if needed or asked: *The emergency services were* ***put on standby*** *after a bomb warning.* **2** ready to travel or go somewhere if a ticket or sth that is needed suddenly becomes available: *He was* ***put on standby*** *for the flight to New York.*

■ ***adj.*** [only before noun] a **standby** ticket for a flight, concert, etc. cannot be bought in advance and is only available a very short time before the plane leaves or the performance starts

'stand-down *noun* [U, C] a period when people, especially soldiers, relax after a period of duty or danger

stand·ee /stæn'diː/ *noun* (*NAmE, ScotE*) a person who is standing, for example in a bus or at a concert

'stand-in *noun* **1** a person who does sb's job for a short time when they are not available **2** a person who replaces an actor in some scenes in a film/movie, especially dangerous ones

stand·ing /'stændɪŋ/ *adj., noun*

■ ***adj.*** [only before noun] **1** existing or arranged permanently, not formed or made for a particular situation: *a standing army* ◇ (*BrE*) *a* ***standing charge*** (= an amount of money that you pay in order to use a service, such as gas or water) ◇ *a* ***standing committee*** ◇ *It's a* ***standing joke*** (= something that a group of people regularly laugh at). ◇ *We have a* ***standing invitation*** *to visit them anytime.* **2** done from a position in which you are standing rather than sitting or running: *a* ***standing jump/start*** ◇ *The speaker got a* ***standing ovation*** (= people stood up to clap after the speech). ➲ see also FREE-STANDING

■ ***noun*** **1** [U] the position or reputation of sb/sth within a group of people or in an organization SYN **status**: *the* ***high/low standing*** *of politicians with the public* ◇ *The contract has no legal standing.* **2** [U] the period of time that sth has existed: *a friendship of many years' standing* ➲ see also LONG-STANDING **3 standings** [pl.] a list of people, teams, etc. showing their positions in a sports competition

,standing 'order *noun* [C, U] an instruction that you give to your bank to pay sb a fixed amount of money from your account on the same day each week/month, etc. ➲ compare BANKER'S ORDER, DIRECT DEBIT

'standing room *noun* [U] space for people to stand in, especially in a theatre, sports ground, etc: *standing room for 12 000 supporters* ◇ *It was* ***standing room only*** *at the concert* (= all the seats were sold).

'standing stone *noun* a tall vertical stone that was shaped and put up by PREHISTORIC people in western Europe SYN **menhir**

'stand-off *noun* **~** (**between A and B**) a situation in which no agreement can be reached SYN **deadlock**

,stand-off 'half (also **,fly 'half**) *noun* (in RUGBY) a player who plays behind the SCRUM HALF

stand-offish /,stænd 'ɒfɪʃ; *NAmE* -'ɔːf-; -'ɑːf-/ *adj.* (*informal*) not friendly towards other people SYN **aloof**

stand·out /'stændaʊt/ *noun* (*NAmE, informal*) a person or thing that is very noticeable because they are or it is better, more impressive, etc. than others in a group ▸ **stand·out** *adj.* [only before noun]: *the standout track on this album*

S

stand·pipe /ˈstændpaɪp/ *noun* a pipe that is connected to a public water supply and used to provide water outside a building

stand·point /ˈstændpɔɪnt/ *noun* [usually sing.] an opinion or a way of thinking about ideas or situations SYN **perspective**: *a* ***political/theoretical, etc. standpoint*** ◇ *He is writing* ***from the standpoint*** *of someone who knows what life is like in prison.*

St Andrew's Day /ˌsnt ˈændruːz deɪ; *NAmE* ˌseɪnt/ *noun* 30 November, a Christian festival of the national SAINT of Scotland

stand·still /ˈstændstɪl/ *noun* [sing.] a situation in which all activity or movement has stopped SYN **halt**: *The security alert* ***brought*** *the airport* ***to a standstill.*** ◇ *Traffic in the northbound lane is* ***at a*** *complete* ***standstill.***

ˌstand-ˈto *noun* [U] the state of being ready to fight or attack

ˈstand-up *adj., noun*

■ ***adj.*** [only before noun] **1 stand-up** comedy consists of one person standing in front of an audience and telling jokes **2** (*especially BrE*) a **stand-up** argument, fight, etc. is one in which people shout loudly at each other or are violent towards each other **3** worn, used, etc. in a vertical position: *a stand-up collar*

■ ***noun*** **1** [U] stand-up comedy: *When did you start doing stand-up?* **2** [C] a person who performs stand-up comedy: *She started out as a stand-up.*

stank *past tense of* STINK

Stan·ley knife™ /ˈstænli naɪf/ *noun* (*BrE*) a very sharp knife with a blade in the shape of a triangle that can be replaced

stanza /ˈstænzə/ *noun* (*technical*) a group of lines in a repeated pattern that form a unit in some types of poem SYN **verse**

staphylo·coc·cus /ˌstæfɪləˈkɒkəs; *NAmE* -ˈkɑːk-/ *noun* (*medical*) a type of bacteria that can cause infections in some parts of the body such as the skin and eyes

staple /ˈsteɪpl/ *adj., noun, verb*

■ ***adj.*** [only before noun] forming a basic, large or important part of sth: *The staple crop is rice.* ◇ *Jeans are a staple part of everyone's wardrobe.*

■ ***noun*** **1** a small piece of wire that is used in a device called a STAPLER and is pushed through pieces of paper and bent over at the ends in order to fasten the pieces of paper together ➲ VISUAL VOCAB page V56 **2** a small piece of metal in the shape of a U that is hit into wooden surfaces using a HAMMER, used especially for holding electrical wires in place **3** a basic type of food that is used a lot: *Aid workers helped distribute corn, milk and other staples.* **4** something that is produced by a country and is important for its economy: *Rubber became the staple of the Malayan economy.* **5 ~ (of sth)** a large or important part of sth: *Royal gossip is a staple of the tabloid press.*

■ ***verb*** **~ sth + adv./prep.** to attach one thing to another using a staple or staples: *Staple the invoice to the receipt.* ◇ *Staple the invoice and the receipt together.*

ˌstaple ˈdiet *noun* [U, C] **~ (of sth) 1** the food that a person or an animal normally eats: *a staple diet of meat and potatoes* ◇ *Bamboo is the panda's staple diet.* **2** something that is used a lot: *Sex and violence seem to be the staple diet of television drama.*

ˈstaple gun *noun* a device for fixing paper to walls, etc. using STAPLES

stapler /ˈsteɪplə(r)/ *noun* a small device used for putting staples into paper, etc. ➲ VISUAL VOCAB page V56

ˈstaple remover *noun* a small device used for removing staples from paper, etc. ➲ VISUAL VOCAB page V56

star 0⊸ /stɑː(r)/ *noun, verb*

■ ***noun***

▸ IN SKY **1** 0⊸ [C] a large ball of burning gas in space that we see as a point of light in the sky at night: *There was a big moon and hundreds of stars were shining overhead.* ◇ *Sirius is the brightest star in the sky.* ◇ *We camped out* ***under the stars.*** ➲ see also FALLING STAR, LODESTAR, POLE STAR, SHOOTING STAR, STARRY

▸ SHAPE **2** 0⊸ [C] an object, a decoration, a mark, etc, usually with five or six points, whose shape represents a star: *a horse with a white star on its forehead* ◇ *a sheriff's star* ◇ *I've put a star by the names of the girls in the class.* ◇ *a four-star general*

▸ MARK OF QUALITY **3** 0⊸ [C, usually sing.] a mark that represents a star and tells you how good sth is, especially a hotel or restaurant: ***three-/four-/five-star*** *hotels* ◇ *What star rating does this restaurant have?*

▸ PERFORMER **4** 0⊸ [C] a famous and excellent singer, performer, sports player, etc: ***pop/rock/Hollywood, etc. stars*** ◇ *a* ***football/tennis, etc. star*** ◇ *He's so good—I'm sure he'll be a big star.* ◇ *She acts well but she hasn't got* ***star quality.*** ◇ *The best models receive* ***star treatment.*** ➲ see also ALL-STAR, FILM STAR, MEGASTAR, MOVIE STAR, SUPERSTAR **5** 0⊸ [C] a person who has the main part, or one of the main parts, in a film/movie, play, etc: *She was the star of many popular television series.* ◇ *The* ***star of the show*** *was a young Italian singer.* ◇ *the* ***star role/part*** ➲ see also STAR TURN

▸ BEST OF GROUP **6** [C] (often used before another noun) a person or thing that is the best of a group: *a star student* ◇ *Paula is the star of the class.* ◇ *He was the* ***star performer*** *at the championships.* ◇ *The* ***star prize*** *is a weekend for two in Paris.* ◇ *The monkey was* ***the star attraction*** (= the best or most popular act) *at the show.*

▸ HELPFUL PERSON **7** [C, usually sing.] (*informal*) used to show that you feel very grateful for sth that sb has done or that you think they are wonderful: *Thanks! You're a star!*

▸ INFLUENCE ON SB'S FUTURE **8 stars** [pl.] a description of what sb thinks is going to happen to sb in the future, based on the position of the stars and planets when they were born SYN **horoscope**: *Do you read your stars in the paper?*

IDM **see ˈstars** (*informal*) to see flashes of light in front of your eyes, usually because you have been hit on the head **ˈstars in your eyes** if sb has **stars in their eyes**, they have dreams of becoming famous, especially as an entertainer ➲ more at REACH *v.*, THANK

■ ***verb*** (-rr-)

▸ PERFORM IN MOVIE/PLAY **1** 0⊸ [I] **~ (with/opposite sb) (in sth)** to have one of the main parts in a film/movie, play, etc: *She starred opposite Cary Grant in 'Bringing up Baby'.* ◇ *No one has yet been chosen for the* ***starring role*** (= the main part). ➲ COLLOCATIONS at CINEMA **2** 0⊸ [T, no passive] **~ sb** if a film/movie, play, etc. **stars** sb, that person has one of the main parts: *a movie starring Meryl Streep and Pierce Brosnan* ◇ *The studio wants to star her in a sequel to last year's hit.* ➲ see also CO-STAR

▸ MARK WITH SYMBOL **3** [T, usually passive] **~ sth** to put a symbol shaped like a star (= an ASTERISK) next to a word, etc. in order to make people notice it: *Treat all the sections that have been starred as priority.*

ˌstar ˈanise *noun* [U, C] a small fruit in the shape of a star, used in cooking as a spice ➲ VISUAL VOCAB page V28

star·board /ˈstɑːbəd; *NAmE* ˈstɑːrbərd/ *noun* [U] the side of a ship or an aircraft that is on the right when you are facing forward ➲ compare PORT

star·burst /ˈstɑːbɜːst; *NAmE* ˈstɑːrbɜːrst/ *noun* a bright light in the shape of a star, or a shape that looks like a star exploding

starch /stɑːtʃ; *NAmE* stɑːrtʃ/ *noun, verb*

■ ***noun*** **1** [U, C] a white CARBOHYDRATE food substance found in potatoes, flour, rice, etc; food containing this: *There's too much starch in your diet.* ◇ *You need to cut down on starches.* **2** [U] starch prepared in powder form or as a spray and used for making clothes, sheets, etc. stiff

■ ***verb*** [usually passive] **~ sth** to make clothes, sheets, etc. stiff using starch: *a starched white shirt*

starchy /ˈstɑːtʃi; *NAmE* ˈstɑːrtʃi/ *adj.* **1** (of food) containing a lot of starch **2** (*informal, disapproving*) (of a person or their behaviour) very formal; not friendly or relaxed

ˈstar-crossed *adj.* (*literary*) not able to be happy because of bad luck or FATE: *Shakespeare's star-crossed lovers, Romeo and Juliet*

S

star·dom /ˈstɑːdəm; *NAmE* ˈstɑːrdəm/ *noun* [U] the state of being famous as an actor, a singer, etc: *The group is being* ***tipped for stardom*** (= people say they will be famous). ◇ *She* ***shot to stardom*** *in a Broadway musical.*

star·dust /ˈstɑːdʌst; *NAmE* ˈstɑːrd-/ *noun* [U] **1** a magic quality that some famous people with a great natural ability seem to have **2** (*astronomy*) stars that are very far from the earth and appear like bright dust in the sky at night

stare 🔑 /steə(r); *NAmE* ster/ *verb, noun*

■ ***verb*** 🔑 [I] **~ (at sb/sth)** to look at sb/sth for a long time: *I screamed and everyone stared.* ◇ *I stared blankly at the paper in front of me.* ◇ *He sat* ***staring into space*** (= looking at nothing). ◇ *She looked at them with dark staring eyes.*

IDM **be staring sb in the ˈface 1** to be obvious or easy to see: *The answer was staring us in the face.* **2** to be certain to happen: *Defeat was staring them in the face.* **be staring sth in the ˈface** to be unable to avoid sth: *They were staring defeat in the face.*

PHR V **ˌstare sb ˈout** (*BrE*) (also **ˌstare sb ˈdown** *NAmE, BrE*) to look into sb's eyes for a long time until they feel embarrassed and are forced to look a way

■ ***noun*** 🔑 an act of looking at sb/sth for a long time, especially in a way that is unfriendly or that shows surprise: *She gave him a blank stare.* ➲ SYNONYMS at LOOK

Synonyms

stare

gaze • peer • glare

These words all mean to look at sb/sth for a long time.

stare to look at sb/sth for a long time, especially with surprise or fear, or because you are thinking: *I screamed and everyone stared.*

gaze (*rather formal*) to look steadily at sb/sth for a long time, especially with surprise or love, or because you are thinking: *We all gazed at Marco in amazement.*

peer to look closely or carefully at sth, especially when you cannot see it clearly

glare to look angrily at sb/sth for a long time: *I looked at her and she glared stonily back.*

PATTERNS

- to stare/gaze/peer/glare **at** sb/sth
- to stare/gaze/peer/glare **suspiciously**
- to stare/gaze/peer **anxiously/intently**
- to stare/gaze/glare **wildly/fiercely**

star·fish /ˈstɑːfɪʃ; *NAmE* ˈstɑːrfɪʃ/ *noun* (*pl.* **star·fish**) a flat sea creature in the shape of a star with five arms

star·fruit /ˈstɑːfruːt; *NAmE* ˈstɑːrf-/ *noun* (*pl.* **star·fruit**) a green or yellow tropical fruit with a shape like a star ➲ VISUAL VOCAB page V26

star·gazer /ˈstɑːɡeɪzə(r); *NAmE* ˈstɑːrɡ-/ *noun* (*informal*) a person who studies ASTROLOGY or ASTRONOMY ▶ **star·gaz·ing** *noun* [U]

stark /stɑːk; *NAmE* stɑːrk/ *adj., adv.*

■ ***adj.*** (**stark·er, stark·est**) **1** (often *disapproving*) looking severe and without any colour or decoration: *I think white would be too stark for the bedroom.* ◇ *The hills stood stark against the winter sky.* **2** unpleasant; real, and impossible to avoid SYN **bleak**: *The author paints a stark picture of life in a prison camp.* ◇ *a stark choice* ◇ *The remains of the building stand as a stark reminder of the fire.* ◇ *He now faces the* ***stark reality*** *of life in prison.* ➲ SYNONYMS at PLAIN **3** very different to sth in a way that is easy to see SYN **clear**: *stark differences* ◇ *Social divisions in the city are stark.* ◇ *The good weather was* ***in stark contrast to*** *the storms of previous weeks.* **4** [only before noun] complete and total SYN **utter**: *The children watched in stark terror.* ▶ **stark·ly** *adv.*: *The interior is starkly simple.* ◇ *The lighthouse stood out starkly against the dark sky.* ◇ *We are starkly aware of the risks.* **stark·ness** *noun* [U]

■ ***adv.*** **~ naked** completely naked IDM see RAVING

stark·ers /ˈstɑːkəz; *NAmE* ˈstɑːrkərz/ *adj.* [not before noun] (*BrE, informal*) not wearing any clothes SYN **naked**

star·less /ˈstɑːləs; *NAmE* ˈstɑːrləs/ *adj.* with no stars in the sky: *a starless night*

star·let /ˈstɑːlət; *NAmE* ˈstɑːrlət/ *noun* a young woman actor who plays small parts and hopes to become famous

star·light /ˈstɑːlaɪt; *NAmE* ˈstɑːrl-/ *noun* [U] light from the stars: *We walked home by starlight.*

star·ling /ˈstɑːlɪŋ; *NAmE* ˈstɑːrlɪŋ/ *noun* a common bird with dark shiny feathers and a noisy call

star·lit /ˈstɑːlɪt; *NAmE* ˈstɑːrlɪt/ *adj.* with light from the stars: *a starlit night*

ˈstar network *noun* (*computing*) a network in which computers are connected to a central unit, rather than to each other

ˌStar of ˈDavid *noun* (*pl.* **Stars of David**) a star with six points that is used as a symbol of Judaism and the state of Israel

starry /ˈstɑːri/ *noun* [usually before noun] **1** (of the sky) full of stars: *a beautiful starry night* **2** looking like a star: *starry flowers* **3** (of eyes) shining like stars

ˌstarry-ˈeyed *adj.* (*informal*) full of emotion, hopes or dreams about sb/sth in a way that is not realistic

the ˌStars and ˈStripes *noun* [sing.] the national flag of the US

star·ship /ˈstɑːʃɪp; *NAmE* ˈstɑːrʃ-/ *noun* (in SCIENCE FICTION) a large SPACECRAFT in which people or other creatures travel through space

ˈstar sign (also *informal* **sign**) *noun* one of the twelve signs of the ZODIAC: *'What's your star sign?' 'Aquarius.'*

the ˌStar-ˌSpangled ˈBanner *noun* [sing.] the national ANTHEM (= song) of the US

ˈstar-struck *adj.* very impressed by famous people such as actors, football players, etc.

ˈstar-studded *adj.* including many famous performers: *a star-studded cast*

start 🔑 /stɑːt; *NAmE* stɑːrt/ *verb, noun*

■ ***verb***

▸ DOING STH **1** 🔑 [T, I] to begin doing or using sth: **~ sth** *I start work at nine.* ◇ *He's just started a new job.* ◇ *I only started* (= began to read) *this book yesterday.* ◇ *We need to start* (= begin using) *a new jar of coffee.* ◇ *The kids start school next week.* ◇ **~ to do sth** *It started to rain.* ◇ *Mistakes were starting to creep in.* ◇ **~ doing sth** *She started laughing.* ◇ **~ (on sth)** *It's a long story. Where shall I start?* ◇ *It's time you started on your homework.* ◇ *Can you start* (= a new job) *on Monday?* ◇ **~ by doing sth** *Let's start by reviewing what we did last week.* ◇ **+ adj.** *The best professional musicians* ***start young.*** ➲ note at BEGIN

▸ HAPPENING **2** 🔑 [I, T] to start happening; to make sth start happening: *When does the class start?* ◇ *Have you any idea where the rumour started?* ◇ **~ sth** *Who started the fire?* ◇ *Do you start the day with a good breakfast?* ◇ *You're always trying to start an argument.* ◇ **~ sb/sth doing sth** *The news started me thinking.*

▸ MACHINE/VEHICLE **3** 🔑 [T, I] **~ (sth)** when you **start** a machine or a vehicle or it **starts**, it begins to operate: *Start the engines!* ◇ *I can't get the car started.* ◇ *The car won't start.*

▸ EXISTING **4** 🔑 [I, T] to begin to exist; to make sth begin to exist: **~ (up)** *There are a lot of small businesses starting up in that area.* ◇ **~ sth (up)** *They decided to start a catering business.*

▸ JOURNEY **5** 🔑 [I] **~ (out)** to begin a journey; to leave SYN **set off, set out**: *What time are we starting tomorrow?*

▸ GOING/WALKING **6** [I] **+ adv./prep.** to begin to move in a particular direction: *I started after her* (= began to follow her) *to tell her the news.* ◇ *He started for the door, but I blocked his way.*

▸ IN PARTICULAR WAY/FROM PLACE/LEVEL **7** 🔑 [I, T] to begin, or to begin sth such as a career, in a particular way that changed later: **~ as sth** *She started as a secretary but ended up running the department.* ◇ **~ out/off (as sth)** *The com-*

S

pany started out with 30 employees. ◇ **~ sth (as sth)** *He* **started life** *as a teacher before turning to journalism.* **8** [I] **+ adv./prep.** to begin from a particular place, amount or situation: *The trail starts just outside the town.* ◇ *Hotel prices start at €50 a night for a double room.* ◇ *The evening started badly when the speaker failed to turn up.*

▸ MOVE SUDDENLY **9** [I] to move suddenly and quickly because you are surprised or afraid SYN **jump**: *The sudden noise made her start.*

IDM ˌ**don't (you) 'start** (*informal*) used to tell sb not to complain or be critical: *Don't start! I told you I'd be late.* **get 'started** to begin doing sth: *It's nearly ten o'clock. Let's get started.* **you, he, she, etc. 'started it** (*informal*) you, he, she, etc. began a fight or an argument: *'Stop fighting, you two!' 'He started it!'* **'start something** (*informal*) to cause trouble **to 'start with 1** used when you are giving the first and most important reason for sth: *To start with it's much too expensive...* **2** at the beginning: *The club had only six members to start with.* ◇ *I'll have melon to start with.* ◇ *She wasn't keen on the idea to start with.* ➲ more at ALARM *n.*, BALL *n.*, FOOT *n.*

PHR V ˌ**start 'back** to begin to return somewhere ˌ**start 'off 1** to begin to move: *The horse started off at a steady trot.* **2** to begin happening; to begin doing sth: *The discussion started off mildly enough.* **3** to begin by doing or being sth: *Let's start off with some gentle exercises.* ◇ *We started off by introducing ourselves.* ◇ **+ adj.** *The leaves start off green but turn red later.* ◇ **~ doing sth** *I started off working quite hard, but it didn't last.* ˌ**start sb 'off (on sth) 1** [no passive] to make sb begin doing sth: *What started her off on that crazy idea?* ◇ *Don't say anything to her—you'll start her off again* (= make her get angry). ◇ **~ doing sth** *Kevin started us all off laughing.* **2** to help sb begin doing sth: *My mother started me off on the piano when I was three.* ◇ **~ doing sth** *His father started him off farming.* **'start on sb** [no passive] to attack sb physically or with words ˌ**start 'on at sb (about sth)** | ˌ**start 'on (at sb) about sth** (*informal*) to begin to complain about sth or criticize sb: *She started on at me again about getting some new clothes.* ◇ *Don't start on about him not having a job.* ˌ**start 'out 1** to begin to do sth, especially in business or work: *to start out in business* ◇ *She started out on her legal career in 2001.* **2** to have a particular intention when you begin sth: **~ to do sth** *I started out to write a short story, but it soon developed into a novel.* ˌ**start 'over** (*especially NAmE*) to begin again: *She wasn't happy with our work and made us start over.* ˌ**start 'up** | ˌ**start sth↔'up** to begin working, happening, etc; to make sth do this: *I heard his car start up.* ◇ *Start up the engines!* ➲ see also START-UP

■ *noun*

▸ BEGINNING **1** [C, usually sing.] the point at which sth begins: *a perfect start to the day* ◇ *Things didn't look too hopeful at the start of the year.* ◇ *The meeting* **got off to a good/bad start** (= started well/badly). ◇ *The trip was a disaster* **from start to finish**. ◇ *We've had problems* **(right) from the start**. ◇ (*informal*) *This could be the start of something big.* **2** [sing.] the act or process of beginning sth: *I'll paint the ceiling if you* **make a start on** *the walls.* ◇ *I want to make an early start in the morning.* ◇ *She's moving abroad to make a* **fresh start** (= to begin a new life). ➲ see also FALSE START, KICK-START

▸ OPPORTUNITY **3** [C, usually sing.] the opportunity that you are given to begin sth in a successful way: *They worked hard to give their children a good* **start in life**. ◇ *The job gave him his start in journalism.*

▸ IN RACE **4 the start** [sing.] the place where a race begins: *The runners lined up at the start.* **5** [C, usually sing.] an amount of time or distance that sb has as an advantage over other people at the beginning of a race: *She went into the second round with a five-minute start on the rest of the cyclists.* ◇ *I gave the younger children a start.* ➲ see also HEAD START **6** [C, usually pl.] (*sport*) a race or competition that sb has taken part in: *She has been beaten only once in six starts.*

▸ SUDDEN MOVEMENT **7** [C, usually sing.] an act of moving your body quickly and suddenly because you are surprised, afraid, etc: *She woke from the dream* **with a start**. ◇ *You gave me quite a start!*

IDM **for a 'start** (*informal*) used to emphasize the first of a list of reasons, opinions, etc.: *I'm not working there—for a start, it's too far to travel.* ➲ more at FIT *n.*, FLYING START

Synonyms

start

begin • start off • kick off • commence • open

These words are all used to talk about things happening from the beginning, or people doing the first part of sth.

start to begin to happen or exist; to begin in a particular way or from a particular point: *When does the class start?*

begin to start to happen or exist; to start in a particular way or from a particular point; to start speaking: *When does the concert begin?*

START OR BEGIN?

There is not much difference in meaning between these words. **Start** is more frequent in spoken English and in business contexts; **begin** is more frequent in written English and is often used when you are describing a series of events: *The story begins on the island of Corfu.* **Start** is not used to mean 'begin speaking': ~~*'Ladies and gentlemen,' he started.*~~

start off (*rather informal*) to start happening or doing sth; to start by doing or being sth: *The discussion started off mildly enough.*

kick off (*informal*) to start an event or activity, especially in a particular way; (of an event, activity, etc.) to start, especially in a particular way: *Tom will kick off with a few comments.* ◇ *The festival kicks off on Monday, September 13.*

commence (*formal*) to start happening: *The meeting is scheduled to commence at noon.*

open to start an event or activity in a particular way; (of an event, film/movie or book) to start, especially in a particular way: *The story opens with a murder.*

PATTERNS

- to start/begin/start off/kick off/commence/open **with** sth
- to start/begin/start off/kick off/commence/open **by** doing sth
- to start/begin/start off/commence **as** sth
- a **campaign/season/meeting** starts/begins/starts off/kicks off/commences/opens
- a **film/movie/book** starts/begins/starts off/opens

start·er /'stɑːtə(r); *NAmE* 'stɑːrt-/ *noun* **1** (*especially BrE*) (*NAmE* usually **ap·pe·tiz·er**) a small amount of food that is served before the main course of a meal ➲ COLLOCATIONS at RESTAURANT ➲ compare HORS D'OEUVRE **2** a person, horse, car, etc. that is in a race at the beginning: *Only 8 of the 28 starters completed the course.* ➲ compare NON-STARTER **3** a person who gives the signal for a race to start **4** a device used for starting the engine of a vehicle **5** a person who begins doing a particular activity in the way mentioned: *He was a* **late starter** *in the theatre* (= older than most people when they start). ◇ *a* **slow starter** ➲ see also SELF-STARTER **6** (often used as an adjective) something that is intended to be used by sb who is starting to do sth: *a* **starter home** (= a small home for sb who is buying property for the first time) ◇ *a* **starter kit/pack**

IDM **for 'starters** (*informal*) used to emphasize the first of a list of reasons, opinions, etc, or to say what happens first **under ˌstarter's 'orders** (of a runner, rider, etc.) waiting for a signal to start a race

'starting blocks (also **the blocks**) *noun* [pl.] the two blocks on the ground that runners push their feet against at the beginning of a race ➲ VISUAL VOCAB page V38

'starting gate *noun* a barrier that is raised to let horses or dogs start running in a race

ˈ**starting pistol** *noun* a gun used for signalling the start of a race

ˈ**starting point** *noun* **1 ~ (for sth)** a thing, an idea or a set of facts that can be used to begin a discussion or process: *The article served as a useful starting point for our discussion.* **2** the place where you begin a journey

ˈ**starting price** *noun* the final ODDS that are given for a horse or dog just before a race begins

star·tle /ˈstɑːtl; *NAmE* ˈstɑːrtl/ *verb* to surprise sb suddenly in a way that slightly shocks or frightens them: **~ sb/sth** *I didn't mean to startle you.* ◇ *The explosion startled the horse.* ◇ *I was startled by her question.* ◇ **it startles sb to do sth** *It startled me to find her sitting in my office.* ➲ SYNONYMS at SURPRISE ▶ **star·tled** /ˈstɑːtld; *NAmE* ˈstɑːrtld/ *adj.*: *She looked at him with startled eyes.* ◇ *He looked startled.* ◇ *She jumped back like a startled rabbit.*

start·ling /ˈstɑːtlɪŋ; *NAmE* ˈstɑːrt-/ *adj.* **1** extremely unusual and surprising: *a startling discovery* **2** (of a colour) extremely bright: *startling blue eyes* ▶ **start·ling·ly** *adv.*

ˈ**start-up** *adj., noun*
■ ***adj.*** [only before noun] connected with starting a new business or project: *start-up costs*
■ ***noun*** a company that is just beginning to operate, especially an Internet company

ˌ**star ˈturn** *noun* [usually sing.] the main performer or entertainer in a show

star·va·tion /stɑːˈveɪʃn; *NAmE* stɑːrˈv-/ *noun* [U] the state of suffering and death caused by having no food: *to* ***die of/from starvation*** ◇ *Millions will* ***face starvation*** *next year as a result of the drought.* ◇ *a* ***starvation diet*** (= one in which you do not have much to eat) ◇ *They were on* ***starvation wages*** (= extremely low wages).

starve /stɑːv; *NAmE* stɑːrv/ *verb* **1** [I, T] to suffer or die because you do not have enough food to eat; to make sb suffer or die in this way: *The animals were left to starve to death.* ◇ *pictures of starving children* ◇ *The new job doesn't pay as much but we won't starve!* ◇ **~ sb/yourself** *She's starving herself to try to lose weight.* **2 -starved** (in adjectives) not having sth that you need: *supply-starved rebels* ➲ see also CASH-STARVED

IDM **be ˈstarving (for sth)** (also **be ˈstarved** especially in *NAmE*) (*informal*) to feel very hungry: *When's the food coming? I'm starving!*

PHR V ˌ**starve sb into ˈsth/into ˈdoing sth** to force sb to do sth by not allowing them to get any food or money ˌ**starve sb/sth of ˈsth** (*NAmE* also ˌ**starve sb/sth for ˈsth**) [usually passive] to not give sth that is needed: *I felt starved of intelligent conversation.* ◇ *The department has been starved of resources.* ˌ**starve sb↔ˈout (of sth)** to force sb to leave a particular building or area by not allowing them to get any food

stash /stæʃ/ *verb, noun*
■ ***verb*** **~ sth + adv./prep.** (*informal*) to store sth in a safe or secret place: *She has a fortune* ***stashed away*** *in various bank accounts.*
■ ***noun*** [usually sing.] (*informal*) an amount of sth that is kept secretly: *a stash of money*

sta·sis /ˈsteɪsɪs/ *noun* [U, C] (*pl.* **sta·ses** /-siːz/) (*formal*) a situation in which there is no change or development

stat /stæt/ *noun* (*NAmE, informal*) = STATISTIC

state 🔑 /steɪt/ *noun, adj., verb*
■ ***noun***
▸ CONDITION OF SB/STH **1** 🔑 [C] the mental, emotional or physical condition that a person or thing is in: *a confused* ***state of mind*** ◇ *He was in a state of permanent depression.* ◇ *anxieties about the state of the country's economy* ◇ *The building is in a bad* ***state of repair*** (= needs to be repaired). ◇ *She was in a* ***state of shock.*** ◇ (*BrE, informal*) *Look at the state of you! You can't go out looking like that.* ◇ *You're* ***not in a fit state*** *to drive.* ➲ SYNONYMS at CONDITION
▸ COUNTRY **2** 🔑 (also **State**) [C] a country considered as an organized political community controlled by one government: *the Baltic States* ◇ *European Union member states* ➲ see also CITY STATE, NATION STATE, POLICE STATE, WELFARE STATE ➲ note at COUNTRY
▸ PART OF COUNTRY **3** 🔑 (also **State**) [C] (*abbr.* **St.**) an organized political community forming part of a country: *the states of Victoria and Western Australia* ◇ *the southern states of the US*
▸ GOVERNMENT **4** 🔑 (also **the State**) [U, sing.] the government of a country: ***matters/affairs of state*** ◇ *people who are financially dependent on the state* ◇ *a state-owned company* ◇ *They wish to limit the power of the State.*
▸ OFFICIAL CEREMONY **5** [U] the formal ceremonies connected with high levels of government or with kings and queens: *The president was driven* ***in state*** *through the streets.*
▸ THE US **6 the States** [pl.] (*informal*) the United States of America: *I've never been to the States.*

IDM **be in/get into a ˈstate** (*informal, especially BrE*) **1** to be/become excited or anxious: *She was in a real state about her exams.* **2** to be dirty or untidy: *What a state this place is in!* **in a state of ˈgrace** (in the Roman Catholic Church) having been forgiven by God for the wrong or evil things you have done **a state of afˈfairs** a situation: *This state of affairs can no longer be ignored.* ➲ SYNONYMS at SITUATION **the state of ˈplay 1** the stage that has been reached in a process, etc. which has not yet been completed: *What is the current state of play in the peace talks?* **2** (*especially BrE*) the score in a sports match, especially in CRICKET

■ ***adj.*** (also **State**) [only before noun]
▸ GOVERNMENT **1** 🔑 provided or controlled by the government of a country: *state education* ◇ *families dependent on state benefits* (= in Britain, money given by the government to people who are poor) ◇ *state secrets* (= information that could be harmful to a country if it were discovered by an enemy)
▸ OFFICIAL **2** connected with the leader of a country attending an official ceremony: *The Queen is on a state visit to Moscow.* ◇ *the state opening of Parliament* ◇ *the state apartments* (= used for official ceremonies)
▸ PART OF COUNTRY **3** 🔑 connected with a particular state of a country, especially in the US: *a* ***state prison/hospital/university, etc.*** ◇ ***state police/troopers*** ◇ *a state tax*

■ ***verb*** **1** 🔑 to formally write or say sth, especially in a careful and clear way: **~ sth** *He has already stated his intention to run for election.* ◇ *The facts are clearly stated in the report.* ◇ *There is no need to* ***state the obvious*** (= to say sth that everyone already knows). ◇ **~ how, what, etc...** *State clearly how many tickets you require.* ◇ **~ that...** *He stated categorically that he knew nothing about the deal.* ◇ **it is stated that...** *It was stated that standards at the hospital were dropping.* ◇ **sth is stated to be/have sth** *The contract was stated to be invalid.* ➲ SYNONYMS at DECLARE **2** [usually passive] **~ sth** to fix or announce the details of sth, especially on a written document: *This is not one of their stated aims.* ◇ *You must arrive at the time stated.* ◇ *Do not exceed the stated dose* (= of medicine).

state·craft /ˈsteɪtkrɑːft; *NAmE* -kræft/ *noun* [U] skill in managing state and political affairs

the ˈState Department *noun* the US government department of foreign affairs

state·hood /ˈsteɪthʊd/ *noun* [U] **1** the fact of being an independent country and of having the rights and powers of a country **2** the condition of being one of the states within a country such as the US or Australia: *West Virginia was granted statehood in 1863.*

ˈ**state house** *noun* [usually sing.] (in the US) a building in which a state LEGISLATURE (= parliament) meets

state·less /ˈsteɪtləs/ *adj.* not officially a citizen of any country ▶ **state·less·ness** *noun* [U]

state·let /ˈsteɪtlət/ *noun* a small state, especially one that is formed when a larger state breaks up

ˌ**state ˈline** *noun* the line between two states in the US: *the Nevada-California state line*

state·ly /ˈsteɪtli/ *adj.* **1** impressive in size, appearance or manner SYN **majestic**: *an avenue of stately chestnut trees* ◇ *a tall, stately woman* **2** slow, formal and elegant: *a stately dance* ◇ *The procession made its stately progress through the streets of the city.* ▶ **state·li·ness** *noun* [U]

S

ˌstately ˈhome *noun* (*BrE*) a large, impressive house of historical interest, especially one that the public may visit ➲ VISUAL VOCAB page V13

Synonyms

statement

comment • announcement • remark • declaration • observation

These are all words for sth that you say or write, especially sth that gives information or an opinion.

statement something that you say or write that gives information or an opinion, often in a formal way: *A government spokesperson made a statement to the press.*

comment something that you say or write that gives an opinion on sth or is a response to a question about a particular situation: *She made helpful comments on my work.*

announcement a spoken or written statement that informs people about sth: *the announcement of a peace agreement*

remark something that you say or write that gives an opinion or thought about sb/sth: *He made a number of rude remarks about the food.*

declaration (*rather formal*) an official or formal statement, especially one that states an intention, belief or feeling, or that gives information: *the declaration of war*

observation (*rather formal*) a comment, especially one based on sth you have seen, heard or read: *He began by making a few general observations about the report.*

COMMENT, REMARK OR OBSERVATION?

A **comment** can be official or private. A **remark** can be made in public or private but is always unofficial and the speaker may not have considered it carefully. An **observation** is unofficial but is usually more considered than a remark.

PATTERNS

- a(n) statement/comment/announcement/remark/declaration/observation **about** sth
- a(n) statement/comment/observation **on** sth
- a(n) **public/official** statement/comment/announcement/declaration
- to **make** a(n) statement/comment/announcement/remark/declaration/observation
- to **issue** a(n) statement/announcement/declaration

S

state·ment 🔑 /ˈsteɪtmənt/ *noun, verb*
■ ***noun*** **1** 🔑 [C] something that you say or write that gives information or an opinion: *Are the following statements true or false?* ◇ *Your statement is misleading.* ◇ *Is that a statement or a question?* ◇ *The play makes a strong political statement.* ➲ see also FASHION STATEMENT **2** 🔑 [C] **~ (on/about sth)** a formal or official account of facts or opinions SYN **declaration**: ***a formal/ a public/a written/an official statement*** ◇ *A government spokesperson **made a statement** to the press.* ◇ *The prime minister is expected to **issue a statement** on the policy change this afternoon.* ◇ *The police asked me to **make a statement*** (= a written account of facts concerning a crime, used in court if legal action follows). **3** 🔑 [C] a printed record of money paid, received, etc: *The directors are responsible for preparing the company's financial statements.* ◇ *My bank sends me monthly statements.* ➲ see also BANK STATEMENT **4** [C] (in England and Wales) an official report on a child's special needs made by a local education authority: *a statement of special educational needs* **5** [U] (*formal*) the act of stating or expressing sth in words SYN **expression**: *When writing instructions, clarity of statement is the most important thing.*
IDM **ˌmake a ˈstatement** to express or reveal an opinion or characteristic in a very clear way, although often without words: *The cleaning staff extended their strike mainly to make a statement about how determined they were.* ◇ *The way you dress makes a statement about you.*
■ ***verb*** [often passive] **~ sb** (in England and Wales) to officially decide and report that a child has special needs for his or her education: *statemented children*

ˌstate of ˈsiege *noun* a situation in which the government limits people's freedom to enter or leave a city, town or building

ˌstate of the ˈart *adj.* using the most modern or advanced techniques or methods; as good as it can be at the present time: *The system was state of the art.* ◇ *a state-of-the-art system*

the ˌState of the ˈUnion Address *noun* [sing.] (in the US) a speech about the achievements and plans of the government that the President gives to Congress once a year

state·room /ˈsteɪtruːm; -rʊm/ *noun* **1** a private room on a large ship **2** a room used by important government members, members of a royal family, etc. on formal occasions

ˌstate's atˈtorney *noun* (*US*) a lawyer who represents a state in a court

ˈstate school *noun* **1** (*BrE*) (*NAmE* **ˈpublic school**) a school that is paid for by the government and provides free education ➲ compare PRIVATE SCHOOL, PUBLIC SCHOOL **2** (*NAmE*) = STATE UNIVERSITY

ˌstate's ˈevidence *noun* [U] (*US, law*) if a criminal **turns state's evidence**, he or she gives evidence against the people who committed a crime with him or her

state·side /ˈsteɪtsaɪd/ *adj., adv.* (*US, informal*) connected with the US; in or towards the US (used when the person speaking is not in the US): *When are you next planning a trip stateside?*

states·man /ˈsteɪtsmən/ *noun* (*pl.* **-men** /-mən/) a wise, experienced and respected political leader: *the party's **elder statesman***

states·man·like /ˈsteɪtsmənlaɪk/ *adj.* having or showing the qualities and abilities of a statesman: *He was commended for his statesmanlike handling of the crisis.*

states·man·ship /ˈsteɪtsmənʃɪp/ *noun* [U] skill in managing state affairs

states·per·son /ˈsteɪtspɜːsn; *NAmE* -pɜːrsn/ *noun* (*pl.* **-people**) a wise, experienced and respected political leader

ˌstates' ˈrights *noun* [pl.] (in the US) the rights of each state in relation to the national government, such as the right to make some laws and to have its own police force

ˌstate ˈtrooper (also **troop·er**) *noun* (*NAmE*) (in the US) a member of a State police force

ˈstate university (also **ˈstate school**) *noun* (both *NAmE*) a university that is managed by a state of the US

state·wide /ˈsteɪtwaɪd/ *adj., adv.* happening or existing in all parts of a state of the US: *a statewide election* ◇ *She won 10% of the vote statewide.*

static /ˈstætɪk/ *adj., noun*
■ ***adj.*** **1** not moving, changing or developing: *Prices on the stock market, which have been static, are now rising again.* ◇ *a static population level* **2** (*physics*) (of a force) acting as a weight but not producing movement: *static pressure* OPP **dynamic**
■ ***noun*** [U] **1** noise or other effects that disturb radio or television signals and are caused by particular conditions in the atmosphere **2** (also **ˌstatic elecˈtricity**) electricity that gathers on or in an object which is not a CONDUCTOR of electricity: *My hair gets full of static when I brush it.* **3 statics** the science that deals with the forces that balance each other to keep objects in a state of rest ➲ compare DYNAMICS **4** (*NAmE, informal*) angry or critical comments or behaviour

sta·tin /ˈstætɪn/ *noun* a drug that people take to lower the level of CHOLESTEROL (= a substance in the body that can cause heart disease) in their blood. There are several types of statin.

sta·tion 0-w /ˈsteɪʃn/ *noun, verb*

■ ***noun***

▸ FOR TRAINS/BUSES **1** 0-w a place where trains stop so that passengers can get on and off; the buildings connected with this: *I get off at the next station.* ◇ *the main station* ◇ *Penn Station* ◇ *a* ***train station*** ◇ (*BrE* also) *a* ***railway station*** ◇ (*BrE*) ***a tube/an underground station*** ◇ (*NAmE*) *a* ***subway station*** **2** 0-w (usually in compounds) a place where buses stop; the buildings connected with this: *a* ***bus/coach station*** HELP In Britain, the word **station** on its own usually refers to the train station: *Can you tell me the way to the station?* In the US it is usual to say which station you are talking about: *the train station* ◇ *the Greyhound Bus station*

▸ FOR WORK/SERVICE **3** 0-w (usually in compounds) a place or building where a service is organized and provided or a special type of work is done: *a police station* ◇ (*BrE*) *a* ***petrol station*** ◇ (*NAmE*) *a* ***gas station*** ◇ *an agricultural research station* ◇ *a pollution monitoring station* ➲ compare SPACE STATION

▸ RADIO/TV COMPANY **4** 0-w (often in compounds) a radio or television company and the programmes it broadcasts: *a local* ***radio/TV station*** ◇ *He tuned to another station.*

▸ SOCIAL POSITION **5** (*old-fashioned* or *formal*) your social position: *She was definitely getting ideas* ***above her station.***

▸ POSITION **6** a place where sb has to wait and watch or be ready to do work if needed: *You are not to leave your station without permission.* ➲ see also DOCKING STATION

▸ LARGE FARM **7** (usually in compounds) a large sheep or CATTLE farm in Australia or New Zealand

▸ FOR ARMY/NAVY **8** a small base for the army or navy; the people living in it: *a naval station* ➲ see also ACTION STATIONS IDM see PANIC *n.*

■ ***verb***

▸ ARMED FORCES **1** [often passive] **~ sb + adv./prep.** to send sb, especially from one of the armed forces, to work in a place for a period of time: *troops stationed abroad*

▸ GO TO POSITION **2 ~ sb/yourself + adv./prep.** (*formal*) to go somewhere and stand or sit there, especially to wait for sth; to send sb somewhere to do this: *She stationed herself at the window to await his return.*

ˈstation agent (*US*) (*BrE* **sta·tion·mas·ter**) *noun* a person in charge of a train station

sta·tion·ary /ˈsteɪʃənri; *NAmE* -neri/ *adj.* **1** not moving; not intended to be moved: *I remained stationary.* ◇ *The car collided with a stationary vehicle.* ◇ *a stationary exercise bike* OPP **mobile 2** not changing in condition or quantity SYN **static**: *a stationary population*

sta·tion·er /ˈsteɪʃənə(r)/ *noun* (*especially BrE*) **1** a person who owns or manages a shop selling stationery **2 stationer's** (*pl.* **stationers**) a shop that sells stationery: *Is there a stationer's near here?*

sta·tion·ery /ˈsteɪʃənri; *NAmE* -neri/ *noun* [U] **1** materials for writing and for using in an office, for example paper, pens and envelopes ➲ VISUAL VOCAB page V56 **2** special paper for writing letters on

ˈstation house *noun* (*NAmE*) = POLICE STATION

sta·tion·mas·ter /ˈsteɪʃnmɑːstə(r); *NAmE* -mæs-/ (*BrE*) (*US* **ˈstation agent**) *noun* a person in charge of a train station

ˈstation wagon (*NAmE*) (*BrE* **eˈstate car, estate**) *noun* a car with a lot of space behind the back seats and a door at the back for loading large items ➲ VISUAL VOCAB page V42

stat·ism /ˈsteɪtɪzəm/ *noun* [U] a political system in which the central government controls social and economic affairs ▸ **stat·ist** *adj., noun*

stat·is·tic AW /stəˈtɪstɪk/ *noun* **1 statistics** (also *informal* **stats**) [pl.] a collection of information shown in numbers: ***crime/unemployment, etc. statistics*** ◇ *According to official statistics the disease killed over 500 people.* ◇ ***Statistics show*** *that far more people are able to ride a bicycle than can drive a car.* ◇ *These statistics are misleading.* ➲ see also VITAL STATISTICS **2 statistics** (also *informal* **stats**) [U] the science of collecting and analysing statistics: *There is a compulsory course in statistics.* **3** (*NAmE informal* **stat**) [C] a piece of information shown in numbers: *An important statistic is that 94 per cent of crime relates to property.* ◇ *I felt I was no longer being treated as a person but as a statistic.* ▸ **stat·is·tic·al** AW /stəˈtɪstɪkl/ *adj.*: *statistical analysis* **stat·is·tic·al·ly** AW /-kli/ *adv.*: *The difference between the two samples was not* ***statistically significant.***

stat·is·ti·cian AW /ˌstætɪˈstɪʃn/ *noun* a person who studies or works with statistics

sta·tive /ˈsteɪtɪv/ *adj.* (*linguistics*) (of verbs) describing a state rather than an action. **Stative** verbs (for example *be, seem, understand, like, own*) are not usually used in the progressive tenses. ➲ compare DYNAMIC

stats /stæts/ *noun* (*informal*) = STATISTICS

ˈstat sheet *noun* (*NAmE*) a piece of paper or a document which gives details of sth in the form of numbers, especially of a team's or a player's performance

statu·ary /ˈstætʃuəri; *NAmE* -eri/ *noun* [U] (*formal*) statues: *a collection of marble statuary*

statue 0-w /ˈstætʃuː/ *noun*
a figure of a person or an animal in stone, metal, etc, usually the same size as in real life or larger ➲ COLLOCATIONS at ART ➲ VISUAL VOCAB page V2

the ˌStatue of ˈLiberty *noun* a statue at the entrance of New York HARBOUR, which represents a female figure carrying a book of laws in one hand and a TORCH in the other and is a symbol of welcome to people coming to live in the US

statu·esque /ˌstætʃuˈesk/ *adj.* (*formal*) (usually of a woman) tall and beautiful in an impressive way; like a statue SYN **imposing**

statu·ette /ˌstætʃuˈet/ *noun* a small statue

stat·ure /ˈstætʃə(r)/ *noun* [U] (*formal*) **1** the importance and respect that a person has because of their ability and achievements: *an actress of considerable stature* ◇ *The orchestra has* ***grown in stature.*** **2** a person's height: *a woman of short stature* ◇ *He is small in stature.*

sta·tus 0-w AW /ˈsteɪtəs; *NAmE* also ˈstætəs/ *noun* [usually sing.]
1 0-w [U, C] the legal position of a person, group or country: *They were granted refugee status.* ◇ *The party was denied legal status.* **2** 0-w [U, C, usually sing.] the social or professional position of sb/sth in relation to others: *low status jobs* ◇ *to have a high social status* ◇ *Women are only asking to be given equal status with men.* ◇ *She achieved celebrity status overnight.* **3** 0-w [U] high rank or social position: *The job brings with it status and a high income.* **4** 0-w [U, C, usually sing.] the level of importance that is given to sth: *the high status accorded to science in our culture* **5** [U] the situation at a particular time during a process: *What is the current status of our application for funds?*

ˈstatus bar *noun* (*computing*) an area that you see along the bottom of your computer screen that gives you information about the program that you are using or the document that you are working on

status quo /ˌsteɪtəs ˈkwəʊ; *NAmE* ˈkwoʊ/ *noun* [sing.] (from *Latin*) the situation as it is now, or as it was before a recent change: *to* ***defend/restore the status quo*** ◇ *conservatives who want to* ***maintain the status quo***

ˈstatus symbol *noun* a possession that people think shows their high social status and wealth: *Exotic pets are the latest status symbol.*

stat·ute /ˈstætʃuːt/ *noun* **1** a law that is passed by a parliament, council, etc. and formally written down: *Penalties are laid down* ***in the statute.*** ◇ *Corporal punishment was banned* ***by statute*** *in 1987.* **2** a formal rule of an organization or institution: ***Under the statutes*** *of the university they had no power to dismiss him.*

ˈstatute book *noun* a collection of all the laws made by a government: *It's not yet* ***on the statute book*** (= it has not yet become law).

ˈstatute law *noun* [U] all the written laws of a parliament, etc. as a group ➲ compare CASE LAW, COMMON LAW

S

ˌstatute of limiˈtations *noun* (*law*) the legal limit on the period of time within which action can be taken on a crime or other legal question

statu·tory /ˈstætʃətri; *NAmE* -tɔːri/ *adj.* [usually before noun] fixed by law; that must be done by law: *The authority failed to carry out its statutory duties.* ◇ *When you buy foods you have certain statutory rights.* ▶ **statu·tor·ily** *adv.*

ˌstatutory ˈholiday *noun* (*CanE*) a public holiday that is fixed by law

ˌstatutory ˈinstrument *noun* (*law*) a law or other rule which has legal status

ˌstatutory ofˈfence (*BrE*) (*NAmE* **ˌstatutory ofˈfense**) *noun* (*law*) a crime that is described by law and can be punished by a court

ˌstatutory ˈrape *noun* [U] (*NAmE*, *law*) the crime of having sex with sb who is not legally old enough

staunch /stɔːntʃ/ *adj.*, *verb*
▪ ***adj.*** (*superlative* **staunch·est**, no *comparative*) strong and loyal in your opinions and attitude SYN **faithful**: *a staunch supporter of the monarchy* ◇ *one of the president's staunchest allies* ◇ *a staunch Catholic* ▶ **staunch·ly** *adv.*: *She staunchly defended the new policy.* ◇ *The family was staunchly Protestant.* **staunch·ness** *noun* [U]
▪ ***verb*** (also **stanch** especially in *NAmE*) **~ sth** (*formal*) to stop the flow of sth, especially blood

stave /steɪv/ *noun*, *verb*
▪ ***noun*** **1** a strong stick or pole: *fence staves* **2** (*BrE*) (also **staff** *NAmE*, *BrE*) (*music*) a set of five lines on which music is written ➲ picture at MUSIC
▪ ***verb*** (**staved**, **staved** or **stove**, **stove** /stəʊv; *NAmE* stoʊv/)
PHR V **ˌstave sth↔ˈin** to break or damage sth by pushing it or hitting it from the outside: *The side of the boat was staved in when it hit the rocks.* **ˌstave sth↔ˈoff** (**staved**, **staved**) to prevent sth bad from affecting you for a period of time; to delay sth: *to stave off hunger*

stay 🔑 /steɪ/ *verb*, *noun*
▪ ***verb*** **1** 🔑 [I] to continue to be in a particular place for a period of time without moving away: *to stay in bed* ◇ *'Do you want a drink?' 'No, thanks, I can't stay.'* ◇ *Stay there and don't move!* ◇ *We ended up staying for lunch.* ◇ *She **stayed at home*** (= did not go out to work) *while the children were young.* ◇ *I'm **staying late** at the office tonight.* ◇ *My hat won't stay on!* ◇ *Can you **stay behind** after the others have gone and help me clear up?* ◇ *We stayed to see what would happen.* ◇ **~ doing sth** *They stayed talking until well into the night.* HELP In spoken English **stay** can be used with **and** plus another verb, instead of with **to** and the infinitive, to show purpose or to tell somebody what to do: *I'll stay and help you.* ◇ *Can you stay and keep an eye on the baby?* **2** 🔑 [I] to continue to be in a particular state or situation SYN **remain**: **+ adj.** *He never stays angry for long.* ◇ *I can't stay awake any longer.* ◇ *The store stays open until late on Thursdays.* ◇ **+ adv./prep.** *I don't know why they stay together* (= remain married or in a relationship). ◇ *Inflation stayed below 4% last month.* ◇ **+ noun** *We promised to stay friends for ever.* **3** 🔑 [I] to live in a place temporarily as a guest or visitor: *We found out we were staying in the same hotel.* ◇ *My sister's coming to stay next week.* ◇ *He's staying with friends this weekend.* ◇ *I stayed three nights at my cousin's house.* HELP In Indian, Scottish and South African English **stay** can mean 'to live in a place permanently': *Where do you stay* (= where do you live)?
IDM **be here to ˈstay** | **have come to ˈstay** to be accepted or used by most people and therefore a permanent part of our lives: *It looks like televised trials are here to stay.* **stay!** used to tell a dog not to move **stay the ˈcourse** to continue doing sth until it has finished or been completed, even though it is difficult: *Very few of the trainees have stayed the course.* **stay your ˈhand** (*old-fashioned* or *literary*) to stop yourself from doing sth; to prevent you from doing sth **stay the ˈnight** (*especially BrE*) to sleep at sb's house for one night: *You can always stay the night at our house.* **stay ˈput** (*informal*) if sb/sth **stays put**, they continue to be in the place where they are or where they have been put ➲ more at CLEAR *adv.*, LOOSE *adj.*
PHR V **ˌstay aˈround** (*informal*) to not leave somewhere: *I'll stay around in case you need me.* **ˌstay aˈway (from sb/sth)** 🔑 to not go near a particular person or place: *I want you to stay away from my daughter.* **ˌstay ˈin** to not go out or to remain indoors: *I feel like staying in tonight.* **ˌstay ˈon** to continue studying, working, etc. somewhere for longer than expected or after other people have left **ˌstay ˈout** **1** to continue to be outdoors or away from your house at night **2** (of workers) to continue to be on strike **ˌstay ˈout of sth** **1** 🔑 to not become involved in sth that does not concern you **2** 🔑 to avoid sth: *to stay out of trouble* **ˌstay ˈover** to sleep at sb's house for one night **ˌstay ˈup** to go to bed later than usual: *You've got school tomorrow. I don't want you **staying up late**.*
▪ ***noun*** **1** 🔑 a period of staying; a visit: *I enjoyed my stay in Prague.* ◇ *an overnight stay* **2** a rope or wire that supports a ship's MAST, a pole, etc. ➲ see also MAINSTAY
IDM **a ˌstay of exeˈcution** (*law*) a delay in following the order of a court: *to grant a stay of execution*

ˈstay-at-home *noun*, *adj.*
▪ ***noun*** (*informal*, often *disapproving*) a person who rarely goes out or does anything exciting
▪ ***adj.*** a **stay-at-home** mother or father is one who stays at home to take care of their children instead of going out to work

stay·cation /ˌsteɪˈkeɪʃn/ *noun* a holiday/vacation that you spend at or near your home

stay·er /ˈsteɪə(r)/ *noun* (*BrE*) a person or an animal, especially a horse, with the ability to keep going in a tiring race or competition

ˈstaying power *noun* [U] the ability to continue doing sth difficult or tiring until it is finished SYN **stamina**

St Bernard /ˌsnt ˈbɜːnəd; *NAmE* ˌseɪnt bɜːrˈnɑːrd/ *noun* a large strong dog, originally from Switzerland, where it was trained to help find people who were lost in the snow

St Chris·to·pher /ˌsnt ˈkrɪstəfə; *NAmE* ˌseɪnt ˈkrɪstəfər/ *noun* a small MEDAL with a picture of St Christopher (the PATRON SAINT of travellers) on it, that some people wear or carry with them when they go on a journey because they believe it will protect them from danger

STD /ˌes tiː ˈdiː/ *noun* **1** the abbreviation for 'sexually transmitted disease' (a disease that is passed from one person to another during sexual activity) **2** (*BrE*) the abbreviation for 'subscriber trunk dialling' (a system of making direct telephone calls over long distances)

St David's Day /ˌsnt ˈdeɪvɪdz deɪ; *NAmE* ˌseɪnt/ *noun* 1 March, a Christian festival of the national SAINT of Wales, when many Welsh people wear a DAFFODIL

stead /sted/ *noun*
IDM **in sb's/sth's ˈstead** (*formal*) instead of sb/sth: *Foxton was dismissed and John Smith was appointed in his stead.* **stand sb in good ˈstead** to be useful or helpful to sb when needed: *Your languages will stand you in good stead when it comes to finding a job.*

stead·fast /ˈstedfɑːst; *NAmE* -fæst/ *adj.* (*literary*, *approving*) not changing in your attitudes or aims SYN **firm**: *steadfast loyalty* ◇ **~ in sth** *He remained steadfast in his determination to bring the killers to justice.* ▶ **stead·fast·ly** *adv.* **stead·fast·ness** *noun* [U]

steady 🔑 /ˈstedi/ *adj.*, *verb*, *adv.*, *exclamation*
▪ ***adj.*** (**stead·ier**, **steadi·est**) **1** 🔑 developing, growing, etc. gradually and in an even and regular way SYN **constant**: *five years of steady economic growth* ◇ *a steady decline in numbers* ◇ *We are making slow but steady progress.* ◇ *The castle receives a **steady stream** of visitors.* **2** 🔑 not changing and not interrupted SYN **regular**: *His breathing was steady.* ◇ *a **steady job/income*** ◇ *She drove at a steady 50 mph.* ◇ *They set off at a steady pace.* ◇ *a **steady boyfriend/girlfriend*** (= with whom you have a serious relationship or one that has lasted a long time) ◇ *to have a steady relationship* **3** 🔑 firmly fixed, supported or balanced; not shaking or likely to fall down: *He held the boat steady as she got in.* ◇ *I met his steady gaze.* ◇ *Such fine work requires a good eye and a **steady hand**.* OPP **unsteady** **4** (of a per-

S

son) sensible; who can be relied on ▶ **stead·ily** 0-ᴛ *adv.*: *The company's exports have been increasing steadily.* ◇ *The situation got steadily worse.* ◇ *He looked at her steadily.* ◇ *The rain fell steadily.* **steadi·ness** *noun* [U]

IDM **(as) steady as a 'rock** extremely steady and calm; that you can rely on ➲ more at READY *adj.*

■ ***verb*** (**stead·ies, steady·ing, stead·ied, stead·ied**) **1** [T, I] **~ (yourself/sb/sth)** to stop yourself/sb/sth from moving, shaking or falling; to stop moving, shaking or falling: *She steadied herself against the wall.* ◇ *The lift rocked slightly, steadied, and the doors opened.* **2** [I] to stop changing and become regular again: *Her heartbeat steadied.* ◇ **~ against sth** *The pound steadied against the dollar.* **3** [T] **~ sb/sth** to make sb/sth calm: *He took a few deep breaths to* ***steady his nerves.***

■ ***adv.*** in a way that is steady and does not change or shake: *In trading today the dollar* ***held steady*** *against the yen.*

IDM **go 'steady (with sb)** (*old-fashioned, informal*) to have a romantic or sexual relationship with sb, in which you see the other person regularly

■ ***exclamation*** (*informal*) **1 ~ on** (becoming *old-fashioned*) used to tell sb to be careful about what they are saying or doing, for example because it is extreme or not appropriate: *Steady on! You can't say things like that about somebody you've never met.* **2** used to tell sb to be careful: *Steady! Don't fall off.*

steak /steɪk/ *noun* **1** (also *less frequent* **beef·steak**) [U, C] a thick slice of good quality beef: ***fillet/rump/sirloin steak*** ◇ *How would you like your steak done?* ◇ *a* ***steak knife*** (= one with a special blade for eating steak with) ➲ VISUAL VOCAB page V19 **2** [U, C] a thick slice of any type of meat: *pork steak* ◇ *a gammon steak* **3** [U] (often in compounds) beef that is not of the best quality, often sold in small pieces and used in PIES, STEWS, etc: ***braising/stewing steak*** ◇ *a steak and kidney pie* **4** [C] a large thick piece of fish: *a cod steak*

steak·house /'steɪkhaʊs/ *noun* a restaurant that serves mainly steak

steak tar·tare /ˌsteɪk tɑː'tɑː(r); *NAmE* tɑːr'tɑːr; 'tɑːrtər/ *noun* [U, C] (from *French*) a dish made with raw chopped beef and raw eggs

steal 0-ᴛ /stiːl/ *verb, noun*

■ ***verb*** (**stole** /stəʊl; *NAmE* stoʊl/, **stolen** /'stəʊlən; *NAmE* 'stoʊ-/) **1** 0-ᴛ [I, T] to take sth from a person, shop/store, etc. without permission and without intending to return it or pay for it: **~ (from sb/sth)** *We found out he'd been stealing from us for years.* ◇ **~ sth (from sb/sth)** *My wallet was stolen.* ◇ *I* ***had*** *my wallet* ***stolen.*** ◇ *Thieves stole jewellery worth over £10 000.* ◇ *It's a crime to handle stolen goods.* ◇ (*figurative*) *to steal sb's ideas* ➲ COLLOCATIONS at CRIME **2** [I] + **adv./prep.** to move secretly and quietly so that other people do not notice you **SYN** **creep**: *She stole out of the room so as not to wake the baby.* ◇ (*figurative*) *A chill stole over her body.* **3** [T] **~ sth** (in BASEBALL) to run to the next BASE before another player from your team hits the ball, so that you are closer to scoring: *He tried to steal second base but was out.*

IDM **steal a 'glance/'look (at sb/sth)** to look at sb/sth quickly so that nobody sees you doing it **steal sb's 'heart** (*literary*) to make sb fall in love with you **steal a 'kiss (from sb)** (*literary*) to kiss sb suddenly or secretly **steal a 'march (on sb)** [no passive] to gain an advantage over sb by doing sth before them **steal the 'show** [no passive] to attract more attention and praise than other people in a particular situation: *As always, the children stole the show.* **steal sb's 'thunder** to get the attention, success, etc. that sb else was expecting, usually by saying or doing what they had intended to say or do

■ ***noun*** (*NAmE*) (in BASEBALL) the act of running to another BASE while the PITCHER is throwing the ball

IDM **be a 'steal** (*informal, especially NAmE*) to be for sale at an unexpectedly low price: *This suit is a steal at $80.*

stealth /stelθ/ *noun, adj.*

■ ***noun*** [U] the fact of doing sth in a quiet or secret way: *The government was accused of trying to introduce the tax* ***by stealth.*** ◇ *Lions rely on stealth when hunting.*

■ ***adj.*** [only before noun] (of an aircraft) designed in a way that makes it difficult to be discovered by RADAR: *a stealth bomber*

'stealth tax *noun* (*BrE, disapproving*) a new tax that is collected in way that is not very obvious, so people are less aware that they are paying it

stealthy /'stelθi/ *adj.* doing things quietly or secretly; done quietly or secretly: *a stealthy animal* ◇ *a stealthy movement* ▶ **stealth·ily** /-ɪli/ *adv.*

steam 0-ᴛ /stiːm/ *noun, verb*

■ ***noun*** [U] **1** 0-ᴛ the hot gas that water changes into when it boils: *Steam rose from the boiling kettle.* **2** 0-ᴛ the power that is produced from steam under pressure, used to operate engines, machines, etc: *the introduction of steam in the 18th century* ◇ *steam power* ◇ *the steam age* ◇ *a* ***steam train/engine*** **3** very small drops of water that form in the air or on cold surfaces when warm air suddenly cools **SYN** **condensation**: *She wiped the steam from her glasses.*

IDM **full speed/steam a'head** with as much speed or energy as possible **ˌget up/ˌpick up 'steam 1** (*informal*) to become gradually more powerful, active, etc: *His election campaign is beginning to get up steam.* **2** (of a vehicle) to increase speed gradually **ˌlet off 'steam** (*informal*) to get rid of your energy, anger or strong emotions by doing sth active or noisy **ˌrun out of 'steam** (*informal*) to lose energy and enthusiasm and stop doing sth, or do it less well **get, etc. somewhere under your own 'steam** (*informal*) to go somewhere without help from other people

■ ***verb*** **1** [I] to send out steam: *a mug of steaming hot coffee* **2** [T, I] **~ (sth)** to place food over boiling water so that it cooks in the steam; to be cooked in this way: *steamed fish* ➲ COLLOCATIONS at COOKING ➲ VISUAL VOCAB page V24 **3** [I] + **adv./prep.** (of a boat, ship, etc.) to move using the power produced by steam: *The boat steamed across the lake.* **4** [I] + **adv./prep.** (especially of a person) to go somewhere very quickly: *He spotted her steaming down the corridor towards him.* ◇ (*figurative*) *The company is steaming ahead with its investment programme.*

IDM **be/get (all) steamed 'up (about/over sth)** (*BrE*) (*NAmE* **be 'steamed (about sth)**) (*informal*) to be/become very angry or excited about sth

PHR V **ˌsteam sth↔'off** | **ˌsteam sth 'off sth** to remove one piece of paper from another using steam to make the glue that is holding them together softer **ˌsteam sth↔'open** to open an envelope using steam to make the glue softer **ˌsteam 'up** | **ˌsteam sth↔'up** to become, or to make sth become, covered with steam: *As he walked in, his glasses steamed up.*

steam·boat /'stiːmbəʊt; *NAmE* -boʊt/ *noun* a boat driven by steam, used especially in the past on rivers and along coasts

steam·er /'stiːmə(r)/ *noun* **1** a boat or ship driven by steam ➲ see also PADDLE STEAMER **2** a metal container with small holes in it, that is placed over a pan of boiling water in order to cook food in the steam ➲ VISUAL VOCAB page V24

steam·ing /'stiːmɪŋ/ *adj., noun*

■ ***adj.*** **1** (*BrE, informal*) very angry **2** (also **ˌsteaming 'hot**) very hot

■ ***noun*** [U] (*informal*) a crime in which a group of thieves move quickly through a crowded public place, stealing things as they go

steam·roll·er /'stiːmrəʊlə(r); *NAmE* -roʊ-/ *noun, verb*

■ ***noun*** a large slow vehicle with a ROLLER, used for making roads flat

■ ***verb*** (*NAmE* usually **'steam roll**) [T, I] **~ (sb/sth) (+ adv./prep.)** to defeat sb or force them to do sth, using your power or authority: *The team steamrollered their way to victory.* ◇ *She knew that she'd let herself be steamrollered.*

steam·ship /'stiːmʃɪp/ *noun* (*abbr.* SS) a ship driven by steam

'steam shovel *noun* (*especially NAmE*) a large machine for digging, that originally worked by steam

S

steamy /'stiːmi/ *adj.* (steam·ier, steami·est) **1** full of steam; covered with steam: *a steamy bathroom* ◇ *steamy windows* ◇ *the steamy heat of Tokyo* **2** (*informal*) sexually exciting SYN **erotic**

steed /stiːd/ *noun* (*literary* or *humorous*) a horse to ride on

steel 0‑w /stiːl/ *noun, verb*

■ ***noun*** **1** 0‑w [U] a strong hard metal that is made of a mixture of iron and CARBON: *the iron and steel industry* ◇ *The frame is made of steel.* ◇ *The bridge is reinforced with huge steel girders.* ➲ see also STAINLESS STEEL **2** 0‑w [U] the industry that produces steel: *Steel used to be important in South Wales.* ◇ *steel workers* ◇ *a steel town* **3** [C] a long thin straight piece of steel with a rough surface, used for rubbing knives on to make them sharp ➲ VISUAL VOCAB page V23 **4** [U] (*old use* or *literary*) weapons that are used for fighting: *the clash of steel*

IDM **of 'steel** having a quality like steel, especially a strong, cold or hard quality: *She felt a hand of steel* (= a strong, firm hand) *on her arm.* ◇ *You need a cool head and **nerves of steel*** (= great courage). ◇ *There was a hint of steel in his voice* (= he sounded cold and firm).

■ ***verb*** to prepare yourself to deal with sth unpleasant: **~ yourself** (**for/against sth**) *As she waited, she steeled herself for disappointment.* ◇ **~ yourself to do sth** *He steeled himself to tell them the truth.*

ˌsteel 'band *noun* a group of musicians who play music on drums that are made from empty metal oil containers. Steel bands originally came from the West Indies.

ˌsteel 'drum (also **ˌsteel 'pan**) *noun* a musical instrument used in West Indian music, made from a metal oil container which is hit in different places with two sticks to produce different notes ➲ VISUAL VOCAB page V30

ˌsteel 'wool (*BrE* also **ˌwire 'wool**) *noun* [U] a mass of fine steel threads that you use for cleaning pots and pans, making surfaces smooth, etc.

steel·work·er /'stiːlwɜːkə(r); *NAmE* -wɜːrk-/ *noun* a person who works in a place where steel is made

steel·works /'stiːlwɜːks; *NAmE* -wɜːrks/ *noun* (*pl.* steel·works) [C+sing./pl. v.] a factory where steel is made

steely /'stiːli/ *adj.* **1** (of a person's character or behaviour) strong, hard and unfriendly: *a cold, steely voice* ◇ *a look of steely determination* **2** like steel in colour: *steely blue eyes* ▸ **steeli·ness** *noun* [U]

steep 0‑w /stiːp/ *adj., verb*

■ ***adj.*** (steep·er, steep·est) **1** 0‑w (of a slope, hill, etc.) rising or falling quickly, not gradually: *a **steep hill/slope/bank*** ◇ *a **steep climb/descent/drop*** ◇ *a steep flight of stairs* ◇ *The path grew steeper as we climbed higher.* **2** 0‑w [usually before noun] (of a rise or fall in an amount) sudden and very big SYN **sharp**: *a steep decline in the birth rate* ◇ *a steep rise in unemployment* **3** (*informal*) (of a price or demand) too much; unreasonable SYN **expensive**: *£2 for a cup of coffee seems a little steep to me.* ▸ **steep·ly** 0‑w *adv.*: *a steeply sloping roof* ◇ *The path climbed steeply upwards.* ◇ *Prices rose steeply.* **steep·ness** *noun* [U]

■ ***verb***

IDM **be 'steeped in sth** (*formal*) to have a lot of a particular quality: *a city steeped in history*

PHR V **'steep sth in sth** to put food in a liquid and leave it for some time so that it becomes soft and flavoured by the liquid **'steep yourself in sth** (*formal*) to spend a lot of time thinking or learning about sth: *They spent a month steeping themselves in Chinese culture.*

steep·en /'stiːpən/ *verb* [I, T] **~** (**sth**) to become or to make sth become steeper: *After a mile, the slope steepened.*

steeple /'stiːpl/ *noun* a tall pointed tower on the roof of a church, often with a SPIRE on it

steeple·chase /'stiːpltʃeɪs/ (also **chase**) *noun* **1** a long race in which horses have to jump over fences, water, etc. ➲ compare FLAT RACING **2** a long race in which people run and jump over gates and water, etc. around a track

steeple·chaser /'stiːpltʃeɪsə(r)/ *noun* a horse or a person that takes part in steeplechases

steeple·jack /'stiːpldʒæk/ *noun* a person whose job is painting or repairing towers, tall CHIMNEYS, etc.

steer 0‑w /stɪə(r); *NAmE* stɪr/ *verb, noun*

■ ***verb*** **1** 0‑w [T, I] **~** (**sth /sb**) (**+ adv./prep.**) to control the direction in which a boat, car, etc. moves: *He steered the boat into the harbour.* ◇ (*figurative*) *He took her arm and steered her towards the door.* ◇ *You row and I'll steer.* **2** 0‑w [T, I] **~** (**sth**) (**+ adv./prep.**) (of a boat, car, etc.) to move in a particular direction: *The ship steered a course between the islands.* ◇ *The ship steered into port.* **3** [T] **~ sth + adv./prep.** to take control of a situation and influence the way in which it develops: *He managed to steer the conversation away from his divorce.* ◇ *She steered the team to victory.* ◇ *The skill is in steering a middle course between the two extremes.* IDM see CLEAR *adv.*

■ ***noun*** **1** [sing.] (*BrE*) a piece of advice or information that helps you do sth or avoid a problem: *Can anyone give me a steer on this?* **2** [C] a BULL (= a male cow) that has been CASTRATED (= had part of its sex organs removed), kept for its meat ➲ compare BULLOCK, OX

steer·age /'stɪərɪdʒ; *NAmE* 'stɪr-/ *noun* [U] (in the past) the part of a ship where passengers with the cheapest tickets used to travel

steer·ing /'stɪərɪŋ; *NAmE* 'stɪr-/ *noun* [U] the machinery in a vehicle that you use to control the direction it goes in ➲ see also POWER STEERING

'steering column *noun* the part of a car or other vehicle that the STEERING WHEEL is fitted on

'steering committee (also **'steering group**) *noun* a group of people that a government or an organization chooses to direct an activity and to decide how it will be done

'steering wheel *noun* the wheel that the driver turns to control the direction that a vehicle goes in ➲ VISUAL VOCAB page V42

stego·saur /'stegəsɔː(r)/ (also **stego·saurus** /ˌstegə'sɔːrəs/) *noun* a DINOSAUR with a small head, four legs and two rows of SPIKES along its back

stein /staɪn/ *noun* (from *German*) a large decorated cup for drinking beer, usually made of EARTHENWARE and often with a lid

stel·lar /'stelə(r)/ *adj.* [usually before noun] **1** (*technical*) connected with the stars ➲ compare INTERSTELLAR **2** (*informal*) excellent: *a stellar performance*

stem /stem/ *noun, verb*

■ ***noun*** **1** the main long thin part of a plant above the ground from which the leaves or flowers grow; a smaller part that grows from this and supports flowers or leaves ➲ VISUAL VOCAB page V9 **2** the long thin part of a wine glass between the bowl and the base ➲ VISUAL VOCAB page V19 **3** the thin tube of a TOBACCO pipe **4 -stemmed** (in adjectives) having one or more stems of the type mentioned: *a long-stemmed rose* **5** (*grammar*) the main part of a word that stays the same when endings are added to it: *'Writ' is the stem of the forms 'writes', 'writing' and 'written'.*

IDM **from ˌstem to 'stern** all the way from the front of a ship to the back

■ ***verb*** (-mm-) **~ sth** to stop sth that is flowing from spreading or increasing: *The cut was bandaged to stem the bleeding.* ◇ *They discussed ways of **stemming the flow** of smuggled drugs.* ◇ *The government had failed to **stem the tide** of factory closures.*

PHR V **'stem from sth** (not used in the progressive tenses) to be the result of sth ➲ LANGUAGE BANK at BECAUSE OF

'stem cell *noun* a basic type of cell which can divide and develop into cells with particular functions. All the different kinds of cells in the human body develop from stem cells.

stem·ware /'stemweə(r); *NAmE* -wer/ *noun* [U] (*technical*) glasses and glass bowls that have a STEM

stench /stentʃ/ *noun* [sing.] a strong, very unpleasant smell SYN **reek**: *an overpowering stench of rotting fish* ◇ (*figurative*) *The stench of treachery hung in the air.*

sten·cil /'stensl/ *noun, verb*

■ ***noun*** a thin piece of metal, plastic or card with a design cut out of it, that you put onto a surface and paint over so that

S

the design is left on the surface; the pattern or design that is produced in this way

■ ***verb*** (-ll-, *NAmE* also -l-) [T, I] **~ (sth)** to make letters or a design on sth using a stencil

steno /ˈstenəʊ; *NAmE* -noʊ/ *noun* (*pl.* **-os**) (*NAmE, informal*) **1** [C] = STENOGRAPHER **2** [U] = STENOGRAPHY

sten·og·raph·er /stəˈnɒɡrəfə(r); *NAmE* -ˈnɑːɡ-/ (also *informal* **steno**) *noun* (*especially NAmE*) a person whose job is to write down what sb else says, using a quick system of signs or abbreviations

sten·og·raphy /stəˈnɒɡrəfi; *NAmE* -ˈnɑːɡ-/ (also *informal* **steno**) *noun* [U] (*NAmE*) = SHORTHAND

stent /stent/ *noun* (*medical*) a small support that is put inside a BLOOD VESSEL tube in the body, for example in order to stop sth blocking it

sten·tor·ian /stenˈtɔːriən/ *adj.* (*formal*) (of a voice) loud and powerful

step 0-π /step/ *noun, verb*

■ ***noun***

▸ MOVEMENT/SOUND **1** 0-π [C] the act of lifting your foot and putting it down in order to walk or move somewhere; the sound this makes: *a baby's first steps* ◇ *He* **took a step** *towards the door.* ◇ *We heard steps outside.* ⊃ see also FOOTSTEP, GOOSE-STEP

▸ WAY OF WALKING **2** [C, usually sing.] the way that sb walks: *He walked with a quick light step.*

▸ DISTANCE **3** 0-π [C] the distance that you cover when you take a step: *It's only a few steps further.* ◇ *He turned around and* **retraced his steps** (= went back the way he had come). ◇ *She moved a step closer to me.* ◇ *The hotel is only a short step from the beach.*

▸ IN SERIES/PROCESS **4** 0-π [C] one of a series of things that you do in order to achieve sth: *This was a first step towards a united Europe.* ◇ *It's a* **big step** *giving up your job and moving halfway across the world.* ◇ *We are* **taking steps** *to prevent pollution.* ◇ *This won't solve the problem but it's* **a step in the right direction**. ◇ *The new drug is a major* **step forward** *in the treatment of the disease.* ⊃ SYNONYMS at ACTION **5** 0-π [C] one of a series of things that sb does or that happen, which forms part of a process SYN **stage**: *Having completed the first stage, you can move on to step 2.* ◇ *I'd like to take this idea* **a step further**. ◇ *This was a big* **step up** (= to a better position) *in his career.* ◇ *I'll explain it to you* **step by step**. ◇ *a* **step-by-step** *guide to building your own home*

▸ STAIR **6** 0-π [C] a surface that you put your foot on in order to walk to a higher or lower level, especially one of a series: *She was sitting on the bottom step of the staircase.* ◇ *We walked down some stone steps to the beach.* ◇ *A short* **flight of steps** *led up to the door.* ⊃ VISUAL VOCAB pages V15, V17 ⊃ see also DOORSTEP

▸ IN DANCE **7** [C, usually pl.] a series of movements that you make with your feet and which form a dance ⊃ see also QUICKSTEP

▸ EXERCISE **8** [U] (often in compounds) a type of exercise that you do by stepping on and off a raised piece of equipment: *step aerobics* ◇ *a step class*

▸ LADDER **9 steps** [pl.] (*BrE*) a STEPLADDER: *a pair of steps* ◇ *We need the steps to get into the attic.*

▸ IN MUSIC **10** [C] (*NAmE*) the interval between two notes that are next to each other in a SCALE ⊃ compare TONE (7), SEMITONE

IDM **break ˈstep** to change the way you are walking so that you do not walk in the same rhythm as the people you are walking or marching with **fall into ˈstep (beside/with sb)** to change the way you are walking so that you start walking in the same rhythm as the person you are walking with: *He caught her up and fell into step beside her.* **in/out of ˈstep (with sb/sth) 1** putting your feet on the ground in the right/wrong way, according to the rhythm of the music or the people you are moving with **2** having ideas that are the same as or different from other people's: *She was out of step with her colleagues.* **mind/watch your ˈstep 1** to walk carefully **2** to behave in a careful and sensible way **one step ˌforward, two steps ˈback** (*saying*) used to say that every time you make progress, sth bad happens that means that the situation is worse than before **a/one step aˈhead (of sb/sth)** when you are **one step ahead** of sb/sth, you manage to avoid them or to achieve sth more quickly than they do **a/one step at a ˈtime** when you do sth **one step at a time** you do it slowly and gradually

■ ***verb*** (-pp-) [I] **+ adv./prep.** to lift your foot and move it in a particular direction or put it on or in sth; to move a short distance: *to step onto/off a bus* ◇ *I stepped forward when my name was called out.* ◇ *She stepped aside to let them pass.* ◇ *We stepped carefully over the broken glass.* ◇ *I turned around quickly and stepped on his toes.* ◇ (*figurative*) *Going into the hotel is like stepping back in time.*

IDM **step into the ˈbreach** to do sb's job or work when they are suddenly or unexpectedly unable to do it **step into sb's ˈshoes** to continue a job or the work that sb else has started **ˈstep on it** (*informal*) used especially in orders to tell sb to drive faster **step on sb's ˈtoes** (*NAmE, informal*) = TREAD ON SB'S TOES at TREAD **step out of ˈline | be/get out of ˈline** to behave badly or break the rules **step up to the ˈplate** (*especially NAmE*) to do what is necessary in order to benefit from an opportunity or deal with a crisis: *It's important for world leaders to step up to the plate and honor their commitments on global warming.*

PHR V **ˌstep aˈside/ˈdown** to leave an important job or position and let sb else take your place **ˌstep ˈback (from sth)** to think about a situation calmly, as if you are not involved in it yourself: *We are learning to step back from ourselves and identify our strengths and weaknesses.* **ˌstep ˈforward** to offer to help sb or give information **ˌstep ˈin** to help sb in a disagreement or difficult situation: *A local businessman stepped in with a large donation for the school.* ◇ *The team coach was forced to step in to stop the two athletes from coming to blows.* **ˌstep ˈout** (*especially NAmE*) to go out: *I'm just going to step out for a few minutes.* **ˌstep ˈup** to come forward: *She stepped up to receive her prize.* **ˌstep sth↔ˈup** to increase the amount, speed, etc. of sth: *He has stepped up his training to prepare for the race.*

step- /step-/ *combining form* (in nouns) related as a result of one parent marrying again: *stepmother*

step·brother /ˈstepbrʌðə(r)/ *noun* the son from an earlier marriage of your STEPMOTHER or STEPFATHER ⊃ compare HALF-BROTHER

ˈstep change *noun* [usually sing.] (*BrE*) a big change or improvement in sth: *His speech called for a step change in attitudes to the environment in the 21st century.*

step·child /ˈsteptʃaɪld/ *noun* (*pl.* **step·chil·dren** /-tʃɪldrən/) a child of your husband or wife by an earlier marriage

step·daugh·ter /ˈstepdɔːtə(r)/ *noun* a daughter that your husband or wife has from an earlier marriage to another person

S

step·fam·ily /ˈstepfæməli/ *noun* (*pl.* **-ies**) the family that is formed when sb marries a person who already has children

step·father /ˈstepfɑːðə(r)/ *noun* the man who is married to your mother but who is not your real father

Step·ford wife /ˌstepfəd ˈwaɪf; *NAmE* -fərd/ *noun* a woman who does not behave or think in an independent way, always following the accepted rules of society and obeying her husband without thinking: *She's gradually turning into a Stepford wife.* ORIGIN From the title of the book and film/movie *The Stepford Wives*, in which a group of women who behave in this way are in fact robots.

step·lad·der /ˈsteplædə(r)/ *noun* a short LADDER that is made of two parts, one with steps, that are joined together at the top, so that it can stand on its own or be folded flat for carrying or storing ⊃ VISUAL VOCAB page V17

step·mother /ˈstepmʌðə(r)/ *noun* the woman who is married to your father but who is not your real mother

step·ney /ˈstepni/ *noun* (*IndE*) a spare wheel for a car

ˈstep-parent *noun* a stepmother or stepfather

steppe /step/ *noun* [C, usually pl., U] a large area of land with grass but few trees, especially in SE Europe and Siberia: *the vast Russian steppes*

ˈ**stepping stone** *noun* **1** one of a line of flat stones that you step on in order to cross a stream or river **2** something that allows you to make progress or begin to achieve sth: *a stepping stone to a more lucrative career*

step·sis·ter /ˈstepsɪstə(r)/ *noun* the daughter from an earlier marriage of your STEPMOTHER or STEPFATHER ➲ compare HALF-SISTER

step·son /ˈstepsʌn/ *noun* a son that your husband or wife has from an earlier marriage to another person

step·wise /ˈstepwaɪz/ *adj.* **1** in a series of steps, rather than continuously **2** (*music*) (of a MELODY) moving in a way that uses only the notes that are next to each other in a SCALE

-ster *suffix* (in nouns) a person who is connected with or has the quality of: *gangster* ◇ *youngster*

stereo /ˈsteriəʊ; *NAmE* -oʊ/ *noun* (*pl.* -os) **1** (also ˈ**stereo system**) [C] a machine that plays CDs, etc, sometimes with a radio, that has two separate SPEAKERS so that you hear different sounds from each: *a **car/personal stereo*** ◇ *Let's put some music on the stereo.* **2** [U] the system for playing recorded music, speech, etc. in which the sound is directed through two channels: *to broadcast **in stereo*** ➲ compare MONO ▸ **stereo** (also *formal* **stereo·phon·ic** /ˌsteriəˈfɒnɪk; *NAmE* -ˈfɑːnɪk/) *adj.* [only before noun]: *stereo sound* ➲ compare QUADRAPHONIC

stereo·scop·ic /ˌsteriəˈskɒpɪk; *NAmE* -ˈskɑːpɪk/ *adj.* **1** (*technical*) able to see objects with length, width and depth, as humans do: *stereoscopic vision* **2** (of a picture, photograph, etc.) that is made so that you see the objects in it with length, width, and depth when you use a special machine SYN **three-D**

stereo·type /ˈsteriətaɪp/ *noun, verb*

■ ***noun*** a fixed idea or image that many people have of a particular type of person or thing, but which is often not true in reality: ***cultural/gender/racial stereotypes*** ◇ *He doesn't conform to the usual stereotype of the businessman with a dark suit and briefcase.* ➲ COLLOCATIONS at RACE ▸ **stereo·typ·ical** /ˌsteriəˈtɪpɪkl/ *adj.*: *the stereotypical image of feminine behaviour* **stereo·typ·ical·ly** /-kli/ *adv.*

■ ***verb*** [often passive] to form a fixed idea about a person or thing which may not really be true: **~ sb** *Children from certain backgrounds tend to be stereotyped by their teachers.* ◇ **~ sb as sth** *Why are professors stereotyped as absent-minded?* ▸ **stereo·typed** *adj.*: *a play full of stereotyped characters* **stereo·typ·ing** *noun* [U]: *sexual stereotyping*

ster·ile /ˈsteraɪl; *NAmE* ˈsterəl/ *adj.* **1** (of humans or animals) not able to produce children or young animals SYN **infertile** ➲ compare FERTILE **2** completely clean and free from bacteria: *sterile bandages* ◇ *sterile water* **3** (of a discussion, an argument, etc.) not producing any useful result SYN **fruitless**: *a sterile debate* **4** lacking individual personality, imagination or new ideas: *The room felt cold and sterile.* ◇ *He felt creatively and emotionally sterile.* **5** (of land) not good enough to produce crops ▸ **ster·il·ity** /stəˈrɪləti/ *noun* [U]: *The disease can cause sterility in men and women.* ◇ *the meaningless sterility of statistics* ◇ *She contemplated the sterility of her existence.*

ster·il·ize (*BrE* also **-ise**) /ˈsterəlaɪz/ *verb* **1** [often passive] **~ sth** to kill the bacteria in or on sth: *to sterilize surgical instruments* ◇ *sterilized milk/water* **2** [usually passive] **~ sb/sth** to make a person or an animal unable to have babies, especially by removing or blocking their sex organs ▸ **ster·il·iza·tion, -isa·tion** /ˌsterəlaɪˈzeɪʃn; *NAmE* -ləˈz-/ *noun* [U, C]

ster·il·izer (*BrE* also **-iser**) /ˈsterəlaɪzə(r)/ *noun* a machine or piece of equipment that you use to make objects or substances completely clean and free from bacteria

ster·ling /ˈstɜːlɪŋ; *NAmE* ˈstɜːrlɪŋ/ *noun, adj.*

■ ***noun*** [U] the money system of Britain, based on the pound: *the value of sterling* ◇ *You can be paid in pounds sterling or American dollars.*

■ ***adj.*** [usually before noun] (*formal*) of excellent quality: *He has done **sterling work** on the finance committee.*

ˌ**sterling** ˈ**silver** *noun* [U] silver of a particular standard of PURITY

stern /stɜːn; *NAmE* stɜːrn/ *adj., noun*

■ ***adj.*** (**stern·er, stern·est**) **1** serious and often disapproving; expecting sb to obey you SYN **strict**: *a **stern face/expression/look*** ◇ *a **stern warning*** ◇ *Her voice was stern.* ◇ *The police are planning sterner measures to combat crime.* **2** serious and difficult: *We face stern opposition.* ▸ **stern·ly** *adv.* **stern·ness** *noun* [U]

IDM **be made of sterner** ˈ**stuff** to have a stronger character and to be more determined in dealing with problems than other people

■ ***noun*** the back end of a ship or boat ➲ VISUAL VOCAB page V44 ➲ compare BOW[1] *n.*, POOP IDM see STEM *n.*

ster·num /ˈstɜːnəm; *NAmE* ˈstɜːrnəm/ *noun* (*pl.* **ster·nums** or **sterna** /-nə/) (*anatomy*) the BREASTBONE ➲ VISUAL VOCAB page V48

ster·oid /ˈsterɔɪd; *BrE* also ˈstɪər-; *NAmE* also ˈstɪr-/ *noun* a chemical substance produced naturally in the body. There are several different steroids and they can be used to treat various diseases and are also sometimes used illegally by people playing sports to improve their performance.

stetho·scope /ˈsteθəskəʊp; *NAmE* -skoʊp/ *noun* an instrument that a doctor uses to listen to sb's heart and breathing

stet·son (*BrE*) (*NAmE* **Stetson™**) /ˈstetsn/ *noun* a tall hat with a wide BRIM, worn especially by American COWBOYS

steve·dore /ˈstiːvədɔː(r)/ *noun* a person whose job is moving goods on and off ships ➲ see also DOCKER

stew /stjuː; *NAmE* stuː/ *noun, verb*

■ ***noun*** [U, C] a dish of meat and vegetables cooked slowly in liquid in a container that has a lid: *beef stew and dumplings* ◇ *I'm making a stew for lunch.*

IDM **get (yourself)/be in a** ˈ**stew (about/over sth)** (*informal*) to become/feel very anxious or upset about sth

■ ***verb*** **1** [T, I] **~ (sth)** to cook sth slowly, or allow sth to cook slowly, in liquid in a closed dish: *stewed apples* ◇ *The meat needs to stew for two hours.* ➲ see also STEWED **2** [I] (**+ adv./prep.**) to think or worry about sth: *I've been stewing over the problem for a while.* ◇ *Leave him to stew.*

IDM **let sb stew in their own** ˈ**juice** (*informal*) to leave sb to worry and suffer the unpleasant effects of their own actions

stew·ard /ˈstjuːəd; *NAmE* ˈstuːərd/ *noun* **1** a man whose job is to take care of passengers on a ship, an aircraft or a train and who brings them meals, etc. **2** a person who helps to organize a large public event, for example a race, public meeting, etc. SYN **marshal** **3** a person whose job is to arrange for the supply of food to a college, club, etc. ➲ see also SHOP STEWARD **4** a person employed to manage another person's property, especially a large house or land

stew·ard·ess /ˌstjuːəˈdes; ˈstjuːə-; *NAmE* ˈstuːərdəs/ *noun* **1** (*old-fashioned*) a female FLIGHT ATTENDANT **2** a woman whose job is to take care of the passengers on a ship or train ➲ note at GENDER

stew·ard·ship /ˈstjuːədʃɪp; *NAmE* ˈstuːərdʃɪp/ *noun* [U] (*formal*) the act of taking care of or managing sth, for example property, an organization, money or valuable objects: *The organization certainly prospered under his stewardship.*

stewed /stjuːd; *NAmE* stuːd/ *adj.* (of tea) tasting too strong and bitter because it has been left in the pot too long

St George's Day /ˌsnt ˈdʒɔːdʒɪz deɪ; *NAmE* ˌseɪnt ˈdʒɔːrdʒɪz/ *noun* 23 April, the day of the national SAINT of England

STI /ˌes tiː ˈaɪ/ *noun* the abbreviation for 'sexually transmitted infection' (an infection that is passed from one person to another during sexual activity)

stick 🔑 /stɪk/ *verb, noun*

■ ***verb*** (**stuck, stuck** /stʌk/)

▸ PUSH STH IN **1** 🔑 [T, I] to push sth, usually a sharp object, into sth; to be pushed into sth: **~ sth + adv./prep.** *The nurse stuck the needle into my arm.* ◇ *Don't stick your fingers*

S

through the bars of the cage. ◇ **+ adv./prep.** *I found a nail sticking in the tyre.*
▸ ATTACH **2** [T, I] to fix sth to sth else, usually with a sticky substance; to become fixed to sth in this way: **~ sth + adv./prep.** *He stuck a stamp on the envelope.* ◇ *We used glue to stick the broken pieces together.* ◇ *I stuck the photos into an album.* ◇ **+ adv./prep.** *Her wet clothes were sticking to her body.* ◇ *The glue's useless—the pieces just won't stick.*
▸ PUT **3** [T] **~ sth + adv./prep.** (*informal*) to put sth in a place, especially quickly or carelessly: *Stick your bags down there.* ◇ *He stuck his hands in his pockets and strolled off.* ◇ *Can you stick this on the noticeboard?* ◇ *Peter stuck his head around the door and said, 'Coffee, anyone?'* ◇ (*informal*) *Stick 'em up!* (= put your hands above your head — I have a gun!) **4** [T] **sb can stick sth** (*informal*) used to say in a rude and angry way that you are not interested in what sb has, offers, does, etc.: *I got sick of my boss's moaning and told him he could stick the job.*
▸ BECOME FIXED **5** [I] **~ (in sth)** to become fixed in one position and impossible to move SYN **jam**: *The key has stuck in the lock.* ◇ *This drawer keeps sticking.*
▸ DIFFICULT SITUATION **6** [T] (*BrE, informal*) (usually used in negative sentences and questions) to accept a difficult or unpleasant situation or person SYN **stand**: **~ sth/sb** *I don't know how you stick that job.* ◇ *The problem is, my mother can't stick my boyfriend.* ◇ **~ doing sth** *John can't stick living with his parents.*
▸ BECOME ACCEPTED **7** [I] to become accepted: *The police couldn't* ***make the charges stick*** (= show them to be true). ◇ *His friends called him Bart and* ***the name has stuck*** (= has become the name that everyone calls him).
▸ IN CARD GAMES **8** [I] to not take any more cards ➲ see also STUCK

IDM **stick in your 'mind** (of a memory, an image, etc.) to be remembered for a long time: *One of his paintings in particular sticks in my mind.* **stick in your 'throat/'craw** (*informal*) **1** (of words) to be difficult or impossible to say **2** (of a situation) to be difficult or impossible to accept; to make you angry **stick your 'neck out** (*informal*) to do or say sth when there is a risk that you may be wrong **stick to your 'guns** (*informal*) to refuse to change your mind about sth even when other people are trying to persuade you that you are wrong ➲ more at BOOT *n.*, FINGER *n.*, KNIFE *n.*, MILE, MUD, NOSE *n.*, OAR, SORE *adj.*, TELL

PHR V **,stick a'round** (*informal*) to stay in a place, waiting for sth to happen or for sb to arrive: *Stick around; we'll need you to help us later.* **'stick at sth** to continue to work in a serious and determined way to achieve sth: *If you want to play an instrument well, you've got to* ***stick at it***. **'stick by sb** [no passive] to be loyal to a person and support them, especially in a difficult situation **'stick by sth** [no passive] to do what you promised or planned to do: *They stuck by their decision.* **,stick sth↔'down** (*informal*) to write sth somewhere: *I think I'll stick my name down on the list.* **,stick 'out** to be noticeable or easily seen SYN **stand out**: *They wrote the notice in big red letters so that it would stick out.* **,stick 'out (of sth) | ,stick sth↔'out (of sth)** to be further out than sth else or come through a hole; to push sth further out than sth else or through a hole: *His ears stick out.* ◇ *She stuck her tongue out at me.* ◇ *Don't stick your arm out of the car window.* **,stick it/sth 'out** (*informal*) to continue doing sth to the end, even when it is difficult or boring: *She didn't like the course but she* ***stuck it out*** *to get the certificate.* **,stick 'out for sth** (*informal*) to refuse to give up until you get what you need or want: *They are sticking out for a higher pay rise.* **'stick to sth 1** to continue doing sth despite difficulties: *She finds it impossible to stick to a diet.* **2** to continue doing or using sth and not want to change it: *He promised to help us and he* ***stuck to his word*** (= he did as he had promised). ◇ *'Shall we meet on Friday this week?' 'No, let's stick to Saturday.'* ◇ *She stuck to her story.* **,stick to'gether** (*informal*) (of people) to stay together and support each other **,stick 'up** to point upwards or be above a surface: *The branch was sticking up out of the water.* **,stick 'up for sb/yourself/sth** [no passive] (*informal*) to support or defend sb/yourself/sth: *Stick up for what you believe.* ◇ *She taught her children to stick up for themselves at school.* ◇ *Don't worry—I'll stick up for you.* **'stick with sb/sth** [no passive] (*informal*) **1** to stay close to sb so that they can help you **2** to continue with sth or continue doing sth: *They decided to stick with their original plan.*

sticks

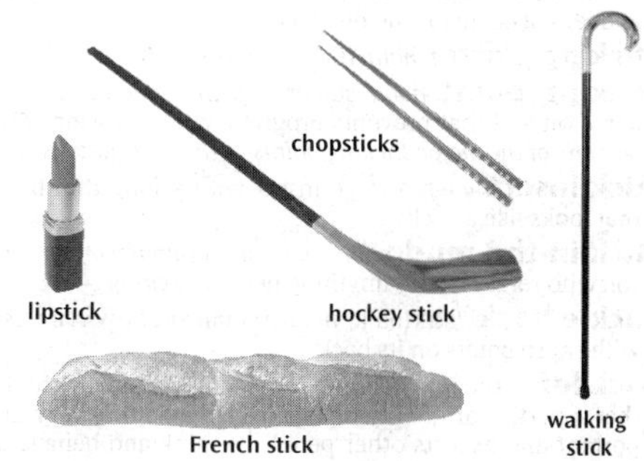

■ ***noun***
▸ FROM TREE **1** [C] a thin piece of wood that has fallen or been broken from a tree: *We collected dry sticks to start a fire.* ◇ *The boys were throwing sticks and stones at the dog.* ◇ *Her arms and legs were like sticks* (= very thin).
▸ FOR WALKING **2** [C] (*especially BrE*) = WALKING STICK: *The old lady leant on her stick as she talked.* ➲ see also SHOOTING STICK, WHITE STICK
▸ IN SPORT **3** [C] a long thin object that is used in some sports to hit or control the ball: *a hockey stick* ➲ VISUAL VOCAB page V36
▸ LONG THIN PIECE **4** [C] (often in compounds) a long thin piece of sth: *a stick of dynamite* ◇ *carrot sticks* ◇ (*NAmE*) *a stick of butter* ➲ VISUAL VOCAB page V29 ➲ see also FRENCH STICK **5** [C] (often in compounds) a thin piece of wood or plastic that you use for a particular purpose: *pieces of pineapple on sticks* ➲ see also CHOPSTICK, COCKTAIL STICK, DRUMSTICK, MATCHSTICK, YARDSTICK
▸ OF GLUE, ETC. **6** [C] a quantity of a substance, such as solid glue, that is sold in a small container with round ends and straight sides, and can be pushed further out of the container as it is used ➲ see also LIPSTICK
▸ IN PLANE/VEHICLE **7** [C] (*informal, especially NAmE*) the control stick of a plane ➲ see also JOYSTICK **8** [C] (*informal, especially NAmE*) a handle used to change the gears of a vehicle ➲ see also GEAR LEVER, STICK SHIFT
▸ FOR ORCHESTRA **9** [C] a BATON, used by the person who CONDUCTS an ORCHESTRA
▸ CRITICISM **10** [U] (*BrE, informal*) criticism or severe words: *The referee* ***got a lot of stick*** *from the home fans.*
▸ COUNTRY AREAS **11 the sticks** [pl.] (*informal*, usually *disapproving*) country areas, a long way from cities: *We live* ***out in the sticks***.
▸ PERSON **12** [C] (*old-fashioned, BrE, informal*) a person: *He's not such a bad* ***old stick***. HELP There are many other compounds ending in **stick**. You will find them at their place in the alphabet. IDM see BEAT *v.*, BIG *adj.*, CARROT, CLEFT *adj.*, SHORT *adj.*, UP *v.*, WRONG *adj.*

sticka·bil·ity /ˌstɪkəˈbɪləti/ *noun* [U] (*informal*) **1** (*NAmE* also **stick-to-itiveness**) the ability to keep doing sth, even if it is sometimes boring SYN **persistence, tenacity**: *The long list of jobs on her CV suggests a lack of stickability.* **2** (of a website) the ability to keep visitors interested for more than a short time

stick·ball /ˈstɪkbɔːl/ *noun* an informal game similar to BASEBALL, played with a stick and a rubber ball

stick·er /ˈstɪkə(r)/ *noun* a sticky label with a picture or message on it, that you stick onto sth: *bumper stickers* (= on cars) ◇ *a sticker album* (= to collect stickers in) ➲ SYNONYMS at LABEL

'sticker price *noun* (*NAmE*) the price that is marked on sth, especially a car

S

'sticker shock *noun* [U] (*NAmE*) the unpleasant feeling that people experience when they find that sth is much more expensive than they expected

'stick figure (*NAmE*) (*BrE* **'matchstick figure**) *noun* a picture of a person drawn only with thin lines for the arms and legs, a circle for the head, etc.

'sticking plaster *noun* (*BrE*) = PLASTER (3)

'sticking point *noun* something that people do not agree on and that prevents progress in a discussion: *This was one of the major sticking points in the negotiations.*

'stick insect *noun* a large insect with a long thin body that looks like a stick

'stick-in-the-mud *noun* (*informal, disapproving*) a person who refuses to try anything new or exciting

stickle·back /'stɪklbæk/ *noun* a small FRESHWATER fish with sharp points on its back

stick·ler /'stɪklə(r)/ *noun* **~ (for sth)** a person who thinks that a particular quality or type of behaviour is very important and expects other people to think and behave in the same way: *a stickler for punctuality*

'stick-on *adj.* [only before noun] (of an object) with glue on one side so that it sticks to sth: *stick-on labels*

stick·pin /'stɪkpɪn/ *noun* (*NAmE*) a decorative pin that is worn on a tie to keep it in place, or as a piece of jewellery

'stick shift *noun* (*NAmE, informal*) **1** (*NAmE* also **'gear shift**) (*BrE* **'gear lever**, **'gear·stick**) a handle used to change the gears of a vehicle **2** a vehicle that has a stick shift ➲ compare AUTOMATIC *n.*

stick-to-itiveness /ˌstɪk 'tuː ɪtəvnəs/ *noun* [U] (*NAmE, informal*) = STICKABILITY

'stick-up *noun* (*informal, especially NAmE*) = HOLD-UP: *This is a stick-up!*

sticky 🗝 /'stɪki/ *adj., noun*

■ ***adj.*** (stick·ier, sticki·est) **1** 🗝 made of or covered in a substance that sticks to things that touch it: *sticky fingers covered in jam* ◇ *Stir in the milk to make a soft but not sticky dough.* **2** 🗝 (of paper, labels, etc.) with glue on one side so that you can stick it to a surface **3** (*informal*) (of the weather) hot and damp **4** (*informal*) (of a person) feeling hot and uncomfortable SYN **sweaty** **5** (*informal*) difficult or unpleasant: *a sticky situation* **6** (*computing*) (of a website) so interesting and well organized that the people who visit it stay there for a long time ▶ **stick·ily** /-ɪli/ *adv.* **sticki·ness** *noun* [U]

IDM **have sticky 'fingers** (*informal*) to be likely to steal sth **a ˌsticky 'wicket** (*BrE, informal*) a difficult situation ➲ more at END *n.*

■ ***noun*** (*pl.* -ies) (also **'sticky note**) a small piece of sticky paper that you use for writing a note on, and that can be easily removed ➲ compare POST-IT

sticky·beak /'stɪkibiːk/ *noun* (*AustralE, NZE, informal*) a person who tries to find out information about other people's private lives in a way that is annoying or rude ▶ **sticky·beak** *verb* [I]: *I don't mean to stickybeak, but when is he going to leave?*

'sticky tape *noun* [U] (*BrE*) = SELLOTAPE

stiff 🗝 /stɪf/ *adj., adv., noun, verb*

■ ***adj.*** (stiff·er, stiff·est)

▸ DIFFICULT TO BEND/MOVE **1** 🗝 firm and difficult to bend or move: *stiff cardboard* ◇ *a stiff brush* ◇ *The windows were stiff and she couldn't get them open.*

▸ MUSCLES **2** 🗝 when a person is **stiff**, their muscles hurt when they move them: *I'm really stiff after that bike ride yesterday.* ◇ *I've got a* ***stiff neck***.

▸ MIXTURE **3** 🗝 thick and almost solid; difficult to stir: *Whisk the egg whites until stiff.*

▸ DIFFICULT/SEVERE **4** more difficult or severe than usual: *It was a* ***stiff climb*** *to the top of the hill.* ◇ *The company faces* ***stiff competition*** *from its rivals.* ◇ *The new proposals have met with* ***stiff opposition***. ◇ *There are* ***stiff fines*** *for breaking the rules.* ◇ *a* ***stiff breeze/wind*** (= one that blows strongly)

▸ NOT FRIENDLY **5** (of a person or their behaviour) not friendly or relaxed: *The speech he made to welcome them was stiff and formal.*

▸ PRICE **6** (*informal*) costing a lot or too much: *There's a stiff $30 entrance fee to the exhibition.*

▸ ALCOHOLIC DRINK **7** [only before noun] strong; containing a lot of alcohol: *a stiff whisky*

▶ **stiff·ly** 🗝 *adv.* **stiff·ness** *noun* [U]: *pain and stiffness in her legs*

IDM **(keep) a stiff upper 'lip** to keep calm and hide your feelings when you are in pain or in a difficult situation

■ ***adv.*** **1** (*informal*) very much; to an extreme degree: *be* ***bored/scared/worried stiff*** **2** **frozen ~** (of wet material) very cold and hard because the water has become ice: *The clothes on the washing line were frozen stiff.* ◇ *I came home from the game frozen stiff* (= very cold).

■ ***noun*** (*slang*) the body of a dead person

■ ***verb*** **~ sb** (*NAmE, informal*) to cheat sb or not pay them what you owe them, especially by not leaving any money as a tip

ˌstiff-'arm *verb* (*NAmE*) = STRAIGHT-ARM

stiff·en /'stɪfn/ *verb* **1** [I, T] to make yourself or part of your body firm, straight and still, especially because you are angry or frightened: **~ (with sth)** *She stiffened with fear.* ◇ **~ sth (with sth)** *I stiffened my back and faced him.* **2** [I, T] (of part of the body) to become, or to make sth become, difficult to bend or move: **~ (up)** *My muscles had stiffened up after the climb.* ◇ **~ sth** *stiffened muscles* **3** [T, I] **~ (sth)** to make an attitude or idea stronger or more powerful; to become stronger SYN **strengthen**: *The threat of punishment has only* ***stiffened their resolve*** (= made them even more determined to do sth). **4** [T] **~ sth (with sth)** to make sth, such as cloth, firm and unable to bend

ˌstiff-'necked *adj.* proud and refusing to change

stiffy /'stɪfi/ *noun* (*pl.* -ies) (*taboo, slang*) an ERECTION (1) of a man's PENIS

stifle /'staɪfl/ *verb* **1** [T] **~ sth** to prevent sth from happening; to prevent a feeling from being expressed SYN **suppress**: *She managed to stifle a yawn.* ◇ *They hope the new rules will not stifle creativity.* ◇ *The government failed to stifle the unrest.* **2** [I, T] to feel unable to breathe, or to make sb unable to breathe, because it is too hot and/or there is no fresh air SYN **suffocate**: *I felt I was stifling in the airless room.* ◇ **~ sb** *Most of the victims were stifled by the fumes.* ▶ **stif·ling** /'staɪflɪŋ/ *adj.*: *a stifling room* ◇ *'It's stifling in here—can we open a window?'* ◇ *At 25, she found family life stifling.* **stif·ling·ly** *adv.*: *The room was stiflingly hot.*

stigma /'stɪgmə/ *noun* **1** [U, C, usually sing.] feelings of disapproval that people have about particular illnesses or ways of behaving: *the social stigma of alcoholism* ◇ *There is no longer any stigma attached to being divorced.* **2** [C] (*biology*) the part in the middle of a flower where POLLEN is received ➲ VISUAL VOCAB page V9

stig·mata /'stɪgmətə; stɪg'mɑːtə/ *noun* [pl.] marks that look like the wounds made by nails on the body of Jesus Christ, believed by some Christians to have appeared as holy marks on the bodies of some SAINTS

stig·ma·tize (*BrE* also **-ise**) /'stɪgmətaɪz/ *verb* [usually passive] **~ sb/sth** (*formal*) to treat sb in a way that makes them feel that they are very bad or unimportant ▶ **stig·ma·tiza·tion**, **-isa·tion** /ˌstɪgmətaɪ'zeɪʃn; *NAmE* -tə'z-/ *noun* [U]

stile

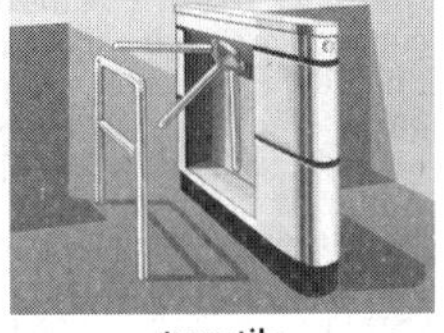
turnstile

stile /staɪl/ *noun* a set of steps that help people climb over a fence or gate in a field, etc. ➲ VISUAL VOCAB page V3

stil·etto /stɪˈletəʊ; *NAmE* -toʊ/ *noun* (*pl.* -os or -oes) **1** (also ˌ**stiletto ˈheel**) (*especially BrE*) a woman's shoe with a very high narrow heel; the heel on such a shoe SYN **spike heel** ➲ VISUAL VOCAB page V52 **2** a small knife with a narrow pointed blade

still /stɪl/ *adv., adj., noun, verb*

■ ***adv.*** **1** continuing until a particular point in time and not finishing: *I wrote to them last month and I'm still waiting for a reply.* ◇ *Mum, I'm still hungry!* ◇ *Do you still live at the same address?* ◇ *There's still time to change your mind.* ◇ *It was, and still is, my favourite movie.* **2** despite what has just been said: *We searched everywhere but we still couldn't find it.* ◇ *The weather was cold and wet. Still, we had a great time.* **3** used for making a comparison stronger: *The next day was warmer still.* ◇ *If you can manage to get two tickets that's better still.* **4 ~ more/another** even more: *There was still more bad news to come.* IDM see LESS *adv.*

■ ***adj.*** **1** not moving; calm and quiet: *still water* ◇ ***Keep still*** *while I brush your hair.* ◇ *The kids found it hard to* ***stay still.*** ◇ *Can't you* ***sit still?*** ◇ *We stayed in a village where* ***time has stood still*** (= life has not changed for many years). **2** with no wind: *a still summer's day* ◇ *the still night air* **3** (*BrE*) (of a drink) not containing bubbles of gas; not FIZZY: *still mineral water*

IDM **the still of the ˈnight** (*literary*) the time during the night when it is quiet and calm **a/the still small ˈvoice** (*literary*) the voice of God or your CONSCIENCE, that tells you to do what is morally right **still waters run ˈdeep** (*saying*) a person who seems to be quiet or shy may surprise you by knowing a lot or having deep feelings

■ ***noun*** **1** a photograph of a scene from a film/movie or video: *a publicity still from his new movie* **2** a piece of equipment that is used for making strong alcoholic drinks: *a whisky still* ➲ see also DISTIL

■ ***verb*** [I, T] (*literary*) to become calm and quiet; to make sth calm and quiet: *The wind stilled.* ◇ **~ sb/sth** *She spoke quietly to still the frightened child.* ◇ (*figurative*) *to still sb's doubts/fears*

still·birth /ˈstɪlbɜːθ; *NAmE* -bɜːrθ/ *noun* [C, U] a birth in which the baby is born dead

still·born /ˈstɪlbɔːn; *NAmE* -bɔːrn/ *adj.* **1** born dead: *a stillborn baby* **2** not successful; not developing

ˌ**still ˈlife** *noun* [U, C] (*pl.* **still lifes**) the art of painting or drawing arrangements of objects such as flowers, fruit, etc; a painting, etc. like this

still·ness /ˈstɪlnəs/ *noun* [U] the quality of being quiet and not moving: *The sound of footsteps on the path broke the stillness.*

stilt /stɪlt/ *noun* [usually pl.] **1** one of a set of posts that support a building so that it is high above the ground or water **2** one of two long pieces of wood that have a step on the side that you can stand on, so that you can walk above the ground: *a circus performer* ***on stilts***

stilt·ed /ˈstɪltɪd/ *adj.* (*disapproving*) (of a way of speaking or writing) not natural or relaxed; too formal: *We made stilted conversation for a few moments.* ▸ **stilt·ed·ly** *adv.*

Stil·ton™ /ˈstɪltən/ *noun* [U, C] a type of English cheese with blue lines of MOULD running through it and a strong flavour

stimu·lant /ˈstɪmjələnt/ *noun* (*formal*) **1** a drug or substance that makes you feel more awake and gives you more energy: *Coffee and tea are mild stimulants.* **2 ~ (to sth)** an event or activity that encourages more activity

stimu·late /ˈstɪmjuleɪt/ *verb* **1 ~ sth** to make sth develop or become more active; to encourage sth: *The exhibition has stimulated interest in her work.* ◇ *The article can be used to stimulate discussion among students.* **2** to make sb interested and excited about sth: **~ sb** *Parents should give children books that stimulate them.* ◇ *Both men and women are stimulated by erotic photos* (= sexually). ◇ **~ sb to do sth** *The conference stimulated him to study the subject in more depth.* **3 ~ sth** (*technical*) to make a part of the body function: *The women were given fertility drugs to stimulate the ovaries.* ▸ **stimu·la·tion** /ˌstɪmjuˈleɪʃn/ *noun* [U]: *sensory/intellectual/sexual/visual/physical stimulation*

stimu·lat·ing /ˈstɪmjuleɪtɪŋ/ *adj.* **1** full of interesting or exciting ideas; making people feel enthusiastic SYN **inspiring**: *a stimulating discussion* ◇ *a stimulating teacher* ➲ SYNONYMS at INTERESTING **2** making you feel more active and healthy: *shower gel containing plant extracts that have a stimulating effect on the skin*

stimu·lus /ˈstɪmjələs/ *noun* (*pl.* **stim·uli** /-laɪ/) **~ (to/for sth)** | **~ (to do sth)** **1** [usually sing.] something that helps sb/sth to develop better or more quickly: *Books provide children with ideas and a stimulus for play.* ◇ *The new tax laws should act as a stimulus to exports.* **2** something that produces a reaction in a human, an animal or a plant: ***sensory/verbal/visual*** *stimuli* ◇ *The animals were conditioned to respond to* ***auditory stimuli*** (= sounds).

sting /stɪŋ/ *verb, noun*

■ ***verb*** (**stung, stung** /stʌŋ/) **1** [T, I] **~ (sb/sth)** (of an insect or plant) to touch your skin or make a very small hole in it so that you feel a sharp pain: *I was stung on the arm by a wasp.* ◇ *Be careful of the nettles—they sting!* **2** [I, T] to feel, or to make sb feel, a sharp pain in a part of their body: *I put some antiseptic on the cut and it stung for a moment.* ◇ *My eyes were stinging from the smoke.* ◇ **~ sth** *Tears stung her eyes.* ➲ SYNONYMS at HURT **3** [T] to make sb feel angry or upset: **~ sb** *He was stung by their criticism.* ◇ *They launched a stinging attack on the government.* ◇ **~ sb to/into sth** *Their cruel remarks stung her into action.* ◇ **~ sb into doing sth** *He was stung into answering in his defence.* **4** [T, often passive] **~ sb (for sth)** (*informal*) to charge sb more money than they expected; to charge sb who did not expect to pay: *I got stung for a £100 meal.*

PHR V ˈ**sting sb for sth** (*BrE, informal*) to borrow money from sb

■ ***noun*** **1** (*NAmE* also **sting·er**) [C] the sharp pointed part of an insect or creature that can go into the skin leaving a small, painful and sometimes poisonous wound: *the sting of a bee* ◇ *The scorpion has a sting in its tail.* ➲ VISUAL VOCAB page V11 **2** [C] a wound that is made when an insect, a creature or a plant stings you: *A wasp or bee sting is painful but not necessarily serious.* **3** [C, U] any sharp pain in your body or mind: *the sting of salt in a wound* ◇ *He smiled at her, trying to* ***take the sting out of*** *his words* (= trying to make the situation less painful or difficult). **4** [C] a clever secret plan by the police to catch criminals: *a sting operation to catch heroin dealers in Detroit* **5** [C] (*especially NAmE*) a clever plan by criminals to cheat people out of a lot of money

IDM **a ˌsting in the ˈtail** (*informal*) an unpleasant feature that comes at the end of a story, an event, etc. and spoils it

ˈ**stinging nettle** *noun* = NETTLE

sting·ray /ˈstɪŋreɪ/ *noun* a large wide flat sea fish that has a long tail with a sharp sting in it that can cause serious wounds

stingy /ˈstɪndʒi/ *adj.* (**stin·gier, stin·gi·est**) (*informal*) not given or giving willingly; not generous, especially with money SYN **mean**: *You're stingy!* (= not willing to spend money) ◇ *Don't be so stingy with the cream!* ▸ **stingi·ness** *noun* [U]

stink /stɪŋk/ *verb, noun*

■ ***verb*** (**stank** /stæŋk/, **stunk** /stʌŋk/) or (**stunk, stunk**) (*informal*) **1** [I] **~ (of sth)** to have a strong, unpleasant smell SYN **reek**: *Her breath stank of garlic.* ◇ ***It stinks*** *of smoke in here.* **2** [I] **~ (of sth)** to seem very bad, unpleasant or dishonest: *The whole business stank of corruption.* ◇ *'What do you think of the idea?' 'I think* ***it stinks.****'*

PHR V ˌ**stink sth↔ˈout** to fill a place with a strong, unpleasant smell

■ ***noun*** (*informal*) **1** [C, usually sing.] a very unpleasant smell SYN **reek**: *the stink of sweat and urine* **2** [sing.] a lot of trouble and anger about sth: *The whole business caused quite a stink.* ◇ *We'll* ***kick up a stink*** (= complain a lot and cause trouble) *if they try to close the school down.*

ˈ**stink bomb** *noun* a container that produces a very bad smell when it is broken. Stink bombs are used for playing tricks on people.

stink·er /ˈstɪŋkə(r)/ *noun* (*informal*) a person or thing that is very unpleasant or difficult

stink·ing /ˈstɪŋkɪŋ/ *adj., adv.*

■ ***adj.*** **1** having a very strong, unpleasant smell: *I was pushed into a filthy, stinking room.* **2** [only before noun] (*informal, especially BrE*) very bad or unpleasant: *I've got a stinking cold.* **3** [only before noun] (*BrE, informal*) showing a lot of anger: *I wrote them a stinking letter to complain.*

■ ***adv.*** (*informal*, usually *disapproving*) extremely: *They must be* ***stinking rich****.*

stinky /ˈstɪŋki/ *adj.* (stink·ier, stink·iest) (*informal*) **1** having an extremely bad smell **2** extremely unpleasant or bad

stint /stɪnt/ *noun, verb*

■ ***noun*** **~ (as sth)** a period of time that you spend working somewhere or doing a particular activity: *He* ***did a stint*** *abroad early in his career.* ◇ *a two-year stint in the Navy*

■ ***verb*** [I, T] (usually used in negative sentences) to provide or use only a small amount of sth: **~ (on sth)** *She never stints on the food at her parties.* ◇ **~ yourself** *We don't need to stint ourselves—have some more!* ➲ see also UNSTINTING

sti·pend /ˈstaɪpend/ *noun* (*formal*) an amount of money that is paid regularly to sb, especially a priest, as wages or money to live on: *a monthly stipend* ◇ (*especially NAmE*) *a summer internship with a small stipend*

sti·pen·diary /staɪˈpendiəri; *NAmE* -dieri/ *noun* (*pl.* -ies) (also **sti,pendiary ˈmagistrate**) (in Britain) a MAGISTRATE who is paid for his or her work

stip·ple /ˈstɪpl/ *verb* [often passive] **~ sth** (*technical*) to paint or draw sth using small dots or marks ▸ **stip·pling** /ˈstɪplɪŋ/ *noun* [U]

stipu·late /ˈstɪpjuleɪt/ *verb* (*formal*) to state clearly and firmly that sth must be done, or how it must be done **SYN** **specify**: **~ sth** *A delivery date is stipulated in the contract.* ◇ **~ that…** *The job advertisement stipulates that the applicant must have three years' experience.* ◇ **~ what, how, etc…** *The policy stipulates what form of consent is required.* ▸ **stipu·la·tion** /ˌstɪpjuˈleɪʃn/ *noun* [C, U]: *The only stipulation is that the topic you choose must be related to your studies.*

stir 🔑 /stɜː(r)/ *verb, noun*

■ ***verb*** (-rr-)

▸ MIX **1** 🔑 [T] to move a liquid or substance around, using a spoon or sth similar, in order to mix it thoroughly: **~ sth** *She stirred her tea.* ◇ **~ sth into sth** *The vegetables are stirred into the rice while it is hot.* ◇ **~ sth in** *Stir in the milk until the sauce thickens.* ➲ SYNONYMS at MIX ➲ COLLOCATIONS at COOKING

▸ MOVE **2** [I, T] to move, or to make sth move, slightly: *She heard the baby stir in the next room.* ◇ **~ sth/sb** *A slight breeze was stirring the branches.* ◇ *A noise stirred me from sleep.* **3** [I, T] to move, or to make sb move, in order to do sth: *You haven't stirred from that chair all evening!* ◇ **~ yourself/sb** *Come on, stir yourself. You're late!* ◇ *Their complaints have finally stirred him into action.*

▸ FEELINGS **4** [T] **~ sb (to sth)** to make sb excited or make them feel sth strongly: *a book that really stirs the imagination* ◇ *She was stirred by his sad story.* **5** [I] (of a feeling or a mood) to begin to be felt: *A feeling of guilt began to stir in her.*

▸ CAUSE TROUBLE **6** [T, I] **~ (it)** (*BrE, informal, disapproving*) to try to cause trouble: *You're just stirring it!* ➲ see also STIRRER

IDM **stir the ˈblood** to make sb excited **stir your ˈstumps** (*old-fashioned, BrE, informal*) to begin to move; to hurry

PHR V **ˌstir sb↔ˈup** to encourage sb to do sth; to make sb feel they must do sth **ˌstir sth↔ˈup 1** to make people feel strong emotions: *to stir up hatred* **2** to try to cause arguments or problems: *to stir up a debate* ◇ *Whenever he's around, he always manages to* ***stir up trouble****.* ◇ *We've got enough problems without you trying to* ***stir things up****.* **3** to make sth move around in water or air: *The wind stirred up a lot of dust.*

■ ***noun*** **1** [sing.] excitement, anger or shock that is felt by a number of people **SYN** **commotion**: *Her resignation* ***caused quite a stir****.* **2** [C, usually sing.] the action of stirring sth: *Could you give the rice a stir?*

ˈstir-crazy *adj.* (*informal, especially NAmE*) showing signs of mental illness because of being kept in prison

ˈstir-fry *verb, noun* (*pl.* -ies)

■ ***verb*** **~ sth** to cook thin strips of vegetables or meat quickly by stirring them in very hot oil: *stir-fried chicken* ➲ COLLOCATIONS at COOKING ➲ VISUAL VOCAB page V24

■ ***noun*** a hot dish made by stir-frying small pieces of meat, fish and/or vegetables

stir·rer /ˈstɜːrə(r)/ *noun* (*BrE, informal, disapproving*) a person who likes causing trouble, especially between other people, by spreading secrets

stir·ring /ˈstɜːrɪŋ/ *noun, adj.*

■ ***noun*** **~ (of sth)** the beginning of a feeling, an idea or a development: *She felt a stirring of anger.*

■ ***adj.*** [usually before noun] causing strong feelings; exciting: *a stirring performance* ◇ *stirring memories*

stir·rup /ˈstɪrəp/ *noun* one of the metal rings that hang down on each side of a horse's SADDLE, used to support the rider's foot

ˈstirrup pants *noun* [pl.] women's tight trousers/pants with a narrow strip of cloth at the bottom of each leg that fits under the foot

stitch /stɪtʃ/ *noun, verb*

■ ***noun*** **1** [C] one of the small lines of thread that you can see on a piece of cloth after it has been sewn; the action that produces this: *Try to keep the stitches small and straight.* ➲ VISUAL VOCAB page V35 **2** [C] one of the small circles of wool that you make around the needle when you are knitting: *to* ***drop a stitch*** (= to lose one that you have made) **3** [C, U] (especially in compounds) a particular style of sewing or knitting that you use to make the pattern you want: *chain stitch* **4** [C] a short piece of thread, etc. that doctors use to sew the edges of a wound together: *The cut needed eight stitches.* ➲ COLLOCATIONS at INJURY **5** [C, usually sing.] a sudden pain in the side of your body, usually caused by running or laughing: *Can we slow down? I've got a stitch.*

IDM **in ˈstitches** (*informal*) laughing a lot: *The play* ***had us in stitches****.* **not have a stitch ˈon | not be wearing a ˈstitch** (*informal*) to be naked **a stitch in ˈtime (saves ˈnine)** (*saying*) it is better to deal with sth immediately because if you wait it may become worse or more difficult and cause extra work

■ ***verb*** **1 ~ sth (+ adv./prep.)** to use a needle and thread to repair, join, or decorate pieces of cloth **SYN** **sew**: *Her wedding dress was stitched by hand.* ◇ (*figurative*) *An agreement was hastily stitched together* (= made very quickly). **2 ~ sth (up)** to sew the edges of a wound together: *The cut will need to be stitched.*

PHR V **ˌstitch sb↔ˈup** (*BrE, informal*) to cheat sb or put them in a position where they seem guilty of sth they have not done **ˌstitch sth↔ˈup 1** to use a needle and thread to join things together **2** (*BrE, informal*) to arrange or complete sth: *to stitch up a deal* ◇ *They think they have the US market stitched up.*

stitch·ing /ˈstɪtʃɪŋ/ *noun* [U] a row of stitches

ˈstitch-up *noun* (*BrE, informal*) a situation in which sb deliberately cheats you or causes you to be wrongly blamed for sth

St John's Wort /snt ˌdʒɒnz ˈwɜːt; *NAmE* seɪnt ˌdʒɑːnz ˈwɜːrt/ *noun* [U, C] a HERB with yellow flowers, used in medicines

stoat /stəʊt; *NAmE* stoʊt/ *noun* a small wild animal with a long body and brown fur that, in northern areas, turns white in winter. The white fur is called ERMINE.

stock 🔑 /stɒk; *NAmE* stɑːk/ *noun, verb, adj.*

■ ***noun***

▸ SUPPLY **1** 🔑 [U, C] a supply of goods that is available for sale in a shop/store: *We have a fast turnover of stock.* ◇ *That particular model is not currently* ***in stock****.* ◇ *I'm afraid we're temporarily* ***out of stock****.* ◇ *We don't carry a large stock of pine furniture.* ➲ COLLOCATIONS at SHOPPING **2** 🔑 [C, U] **~ (of sth)** a supply of sth that is available for use: *She's built up a good stock of teaching materials over the years.* ◇ *Food*

S

stocks are running low. ◇ *a country's* ***housing stock*** (= all the houses available for living in)

▸ FINANCE **3** [U] the value of the shares in a company that have been sold **4** [C, usually pl.] a share that sb has bought in a company or business: *stock prices* ◇ *(NAmE) to invest in* ***stocks and bonds*** ➲ compare SHARE *n.* (4) **5** [U, C] (*BrE*) money that is lent to a government at a fixed rate of interest; an official document that gives details of this: *government stock* ◇ *to invest in* ***stocks and shares***

▸ FARM ANIMALS **6** [U] farm animals, such as cows and sheep, that are kept for their meat, wool, etc: *breeding stock* ➲ see also LIVESTOCK

▸ FAMILY/ANCESTORS **7** [U] **of farming, noble, French, etc. ~** having the type of family or ANCESTORS mentioned SYN **descent**

▸ FOOD **8** [U, C] a liquid made by cooking bones, meat, etc. in water, used for making soups and sauces: *vegetable stock*

▸ FOR PUNISHMENT **9 stocks** [pl.] a wooden structure with holes for the feet, used in the past to lock criminals in as a form of punishment, especially in a public place ➲ compare PILLORY

▸ RESPECT **10** [U] (*formal*) the degree to which sb is respected or liked by other people: *Their* ***stock is high/low.***

▸ OF GUN **11** [C] the part of a gun that you hold against your shoulder when firing it

▸ PLANT **12** [U, C] a garden plant with brightly coloured flowers with a sweet smell

▸ THEATRE **13** [C] (*NAmE*) = STOCK COMPANY ➲ see also LAUGHING STOCK, ROLLING STOCK

IDM **on the 'stocks** in the process of being made, built or prepared: *Our new model is already on the stocks and will be available in the spring.* **put 'stock in sth** (*especially NAmE*) to have a particular amount of belief in sth: *She no longer puts much stock in their claims.* **take 'stock (of sth)** to stop and think carefully about the way in which a particular situation is developing in order to decide what to do next ➲ more at LOCK *n.* ➲ see also STOCKTAKING

■ ***verb*** **1 ~ sth** (of a shop/store) to keep a supply of a particular type of goods to sell: *Do you stock green tea?* **2** [often passive] **~ sth (with sth)** to fill sth with food, books, etc: *The pond was well stocked with fish.* ◇ *a well-stocked library*

PHR V **,stock sth↔'up** to fill sth with goods, food, etc: *We need to stock up the freezer.* **,stock 'up (on/with sth)** to buy a lot of sth so that you can use it later: *We ought to stock up on film before our trip.*

■ ***adj.*** [only before noun] **1** (*disapproving*) a **stock** excuse, answer, etc. is one that is often used because it is easy and convenient, but that is not very original: *'No comment,' was the actor's stock response.* **2** usually available for sale in a shop/store SYN **standard**: *stock sizes*

stock·ade /stɒ'keɪd; *NAmE* stɑː'k-/ *noun* a line or wall of strong wooden posts built to defend a place

stock·broker /'stɒkbrəʊkə(r); *NAmE* 'stɑːkbroʊ-/ (also **broker**) *noun* a person or an organization that buys and sells shares for other people

'stockbroker belt *noun* [sing.] (*BrE*) an area outside a large city, where many rich people live

stock·brok·ing /'stɒkbrəʊkɪŋ; *NAmE* 'stɑːkbroʊ-/ *noun* [U] the work of a stockbroker

'stock car *noun* an ordinary car that has been made stronger for use in stock-car racing

'stock-car racing *noun* [U] (*BrE*) (*NAmE* **,demolition 'derby**) a type of race in which the competing cars are allowed to hit each other

'stock company *noun* (*NAmE*) **1** a company owned by people who have shares in it **2** (also **stock**) a theatre company that does several different plays in a season; a REPERTORY company

'stock cube *noun* a solid CUBE made from the dried juices of meat or vegetables, sold in packs and used for making soups, sauces, etc.

'stock exchange *noun* [usually sing.] a place where shares in companies are bought and sold; all of the business activity involved in doing this: *the London Stock Exchange* ◇ *to lose money on the stock exchange*

stock·fish /'stɒkfɪʃ; *NAmE* 'stɑːk-/ *noun* **1** [U] COD or similar fish that is dried without salt **2** [C] (*pl.* **stock·fish** or **stock·fishes**) (*SAfrE*) a large sea fish that is used for food

stock·hold·er /'stɒkhəʊldə(r); *NAmE* 'stɑːkhoʊ-/ *noun* (*especially NAmE*) a person who owns STOCKS and shares in a business

stock·inet (also **stock·in·ette**) /,stɒkɪ'net; *NAmE* ,stɑːk-/ *noun* [U] a type of soft cloth that stretches easily and is used for making bandages

stock·ing /'stɒkɪŋ; *NAmE* 'stɑːk-/ *noun* **1** either of a pair of thin pieces of clothing that fit closely over a woman's legs and feet: *a pair of silk stockings* ➲ compare TIGHTS ➲ see also BODY STOCKING **2** = CHRISTMAS STOCKING

IDM **in your ,stocking(ed) 'feet** wearing socks or stockings but not shoes

'stocking filler (*BrE*) (*NAmE* **'stocking stuffer**) *noun* a small present that is put in a CHRISTMAS STOCKING

,stock-in-'trade *noun* [U] a person's **stock-in-trade** is sth that they do, say or use very often or too often: *Famous people and their private lives are the stock-in-trade of the popular newspapers.*

stock·ist /'stɒkɪst; *NAmE* 'stɑːk-/ *noun* (*BrE*) a shop/store or company that sells a particular product or type of goods SYN **retailer**

stock·job·ber /'stɒkdʒɒbə(r); *NAmE* 'stɑːkdʒɑːb-/ *noun* = JOBBER

stock·man /'stɒkmən; *NAmE* 'stɑːk-/ *noun* (*pl.* **-men** /-mən/) **1** a man whose job is to take care of farm animals **2** (*NAmE*) a man who owns farm animals **3** (*NAmE*) a man who is in charge of the goods in a WAREHOUSE, etc.

'stock market (also **market**) *noun* the business of buying and selling shares in companies and the place where this happens; a STOCK EXCHANGE: *to make money on the stock market* ◇ *a stock market crash* (= when prices of shares fall suddenly and people lose money) ➲ COLLOCATIONS at ECONOMY

'stock option (*NAmE*) (*BrE* **'share option**) *noun* a right given to employees to buy shares in their company at a fixed price

stock·pile /'stɒkpaɪl; *NAmE* 'stɑːk-/ *noun, verb*

■ ***noun*** a large supply of sth that is kept to be used in the future if necessary: *the world's stockpile of nuclear weapons*

■ ***verb*** **~ sth** to collect and keep a large supply of sth

stock·pot /'stɒkpɒt; *NAmE* 'stɑːkpɑːt/ *noun* a pot in which meat, fish, vegetables, or bones are cooked to make STOCK

stock·room /'stɒkruːm; -rʊm; *NAmE* 'stɑːk-/ *noun* a room for storing things in a shop/store, an office, etc.

,stock-'still *adv.* without moving at all: *We stood stock-still watching the animals.*

stock·tak·ing /'stɒkteɪkɪŋ; *NAmE* 'stɑːk-/ *noun* [U] **1** (*especially BrE*) the process of making a list of all the goods in a shop/store or business ➲ compare INVENTORY **2** the process of thinking carefully about your own situation or position

stocky /'stɒki; *NAmE* 'stɑːki/ *adj.* (**stock·ier**, **stocki·est**) (of a person) short, with a strong, solid body SYN **thickset** ▸ **stock·ily** *adv.*

stock·yard /'stɒkjɑːd; *NAmE* 'stɑːkjɑːrd/ *noun* a place where farm animals are kept for a short time before they are sold at a market

stodge /stɒdʒ; *NAmE* stɑːdʒ/ *noun* [U] (*BrE, informal*, usually *disapproving*) heavy food that makes you feel very full

stodgy /'stɒdʒi; *NAmE* 'stɑːdʒi/ *adj.* (*informal, especially BrE*) **1** (of food) heavy and making you feel very full **2** serious and boring; not exciting

stoep /stuːp; stʊp/ *noun* (*SAfrE*) a raised area outside the door of a house, with a roof over it, where you can sit and relax, eat meals, etc.

stogy (also **stogie**) /'stəʊgi; *NAmE* 'stoʊgi/ *noun* (*pl.* **-ies**) (*NAmE*) a cheap cigar

S

stoic /ˈstəʊɪk; *NAmE* ˈstoʊɪk/ *noun* (*formal*) a person who is able to suffer pain or trouble without complaining or showing what they are feeling ▸ **stoic** (also **sto·ic·al** /-kl/) *adj.*: *her stoic endurance* ◇ *his stoical acceptance of death* **sto·ic·al·ly** /-kli/ *adv.* ORIGIN From the **Stoics**, a group of ancient Greek philosophers, who believed that wise people should not allow themselves to be affected by painful or pleasant experiences.

sto·icism /ˈstəʊɪsɪzəm; *NAmE* ˈstoʊ-/ *noun* [U] (*formal*) the fact of not complaining or showing what you are feeling when you are suffering: *She endured her long illness with stoicism.*

stoke /stəʊk; *NAmE* stoʊk/ *verb* **1** ~ **sth** (**up**) (**with sth**) to add fuel to a fire, etc: *to stoke up a fire with more coal* ◇ *to stoke a furnace* **2** ~ **sth** (**up**) to make people feel sth more strongly: *to stoke up envy* **3** ~ **sth** (**up**) to make sth increase or develop more quickly: *They were accused of stoking the crisis.*

PHR V ˌ**stoke** ˈ**up** (**on/with sth**) (*informal*) to eat or drink a lot of sth, especially so that you do not feel hungry later: *Stoke up for the day on a good breakfast.*

stoked /stəʊkt; *NAmE* stoʊkt/ *adj.* (*NAmE*, *informal*) excited and pleased about sth: *I'm really stoked that they chose me for the team.*

stoker /ˈstəʊkə(r); *NAmE* ˈstoʊ-/ *noun* a person whose job is to add coal or other fuel to a fire, etc, especially on a ship or a steam train

stok·vel /ˈstɒkfel; *NAmE* ˈstɑːk-/ *noun* (*SAfrE*) a group of people who agree to pay regular amounts of money and take turns to receive all or part of what is collected

stole /stəʊl; *NAmE* stoʊl/ *noun* a piece of clothing consisting of a wide band of cloth or fur, worn by a woman around the shoulders; a similar piece of clothing worn by a priest ➲ see also STEAL, STOLE, STOLEN *v.*

stolid /ˈstɒlɪd; *NAmE* ˈstɑːl-/ *adj.* (usually *disapproving*) not showing much emotion or interest; remaining always the same and not reacting or changing ▸ **stol·id·ly** *adv.* **stol·id·ity** /stəˈlɪdəti/ *noun* [U]

stoma /ˈstəʊmə; *NAmE* ˈstoʊ-/ *noun* **1** (*biology*) a tiny PORE (= hole) in the outer layer of a plant's leaf or STEM **2** (*biology*) a small opening like a mouth, in some animals **3** (*medical*) an artificial opening made in an organ of the body, especially in the COLON or TRACHEA

stom·ach 0‑ᴡ /ˈstʌmək/ *noun, verb*

■ ***noun*** 0‑ᴡ the organ inside the body where food goes when you swallow it; the front part of the body below the chest: *stomach pains* ◇ *an upset stomach* ◇ (*BrE* also) *a stomach upset* ◇ *It's not a good idea to drink* (= alcohol) *on **an empty stomach*** (= without having eaten anything). ◇ *You shouldn't exercise **on a full stomach**.* ◇ *The attacker kicked him in the stomach.* ◇ *Lie on your stomach with your arms by your side.* ➲ COLLOCATIONS at PHYSICAL ➲ VISUAL VOCAB page V48 ➲ see also TUMMY

IDM **have no** ˈ**stomach for sth 1** to not want to eat sth: *She had no stomach for the leftover stew.* **2** to not have the desire or courage to do sth: *They had no stomach for a fight.* **turn your** ˈ**stomach** to make you feel upset, sick or disgusted: *Pictures of the burnt corpses turned my stomach.* ➲ more at BUTTERFLY, EYE *n.*, FEEL *v.*, PIT *n.*, PUMP *v.*, STRONG

■ ***verb*** (especially in negative sentences or questions) **1** ~ **sth** to approve of sth and be able to enjoy it; to enjoy being with a person: *I **can't stomach** violent films.* ◇ *I find him very **hard to stomach**.* **2** ~ **sth** to be able to eat sth without feeling ill/sick: *She **couldn't stomach** any breakfast.*

ˈ**stomach ache** *noun* [C, U] pain in or near your stomach

ˈ**stomach pump** *noun* a machine with a tube that doctors use to remove poisonous substances from sb's stomach through their mouth

stomp /stɒmp; *NAmE* stɑːmp; stɔːmp/ *verb* [I] + **adv./prep.** (*informal*) to walk, dance, or move with heavy steps: *She stomped angrily out of the office.*

stompie /ˈstɒmpi; *NAmE* ˈstɑːm-/ *noun* (*SAfrE, informal*) a cigarette that has been partly smoked; the end of a cigarette that is thrown away after it has been smoked

ˈ**stomping ground** *noun* (*NAmE, informal*) = STAMPING GROUND

stone 0‑ᴡ /stəʊn; *NAmE* stoʊn/ *noun, verb*

■ ***noun***

▸ HARD SUBSTANCE **1** 0‑ᴡ [U] (often used before nouns or in compounds) a hard solid mineral substance that is found in the ground, often used for building: *Most of the houses are built of stone.* ◇ *stone walls* ◇ *a stone floor* ◇ *a flight of stone steps* ➲ see also DRYSTONE WALL, LIMESTONE, SANDSTONE, SOAPSTONE **2** 0‑ᴡ [C] (*especially BrE*) a small piece of rock of any shape: *a pile of stones* ◇ *Some children were throwing stones into the lake.* ➲ see also HAILSTONE, PHILOSOPHER'S STONE **3** 0‑ᴡ [C] (usually in compounds) a piece of stone shaped for a particular purpose: *These words are carved on the stone beside his grave.* ➲ see also CORNERSTONE, FOUNDATION STONE, GRAVESTONE, HEADSTONE, LODESTONE, MILLSTONE, PAVING STONE, STEPPING STONE, TOMBSTONE

▸ JEWEL **4** [C] = PRECIOUS STONE

▸ IN FRUIT **5** [C] (*especially BrE*) (*NAmE* usually **pit**) a hard shell containing the nut or seed in the middle of some types of fruit: ***cherry/peach stones*** ➲ VISUAL VOCAB page V26

▸ IN BODY **6** [C] (often in compounds) a small piece of hard material that can form in the BLADDER or KIDNEY and cause pain: *kidney stones* ➲ see also GALLSTONE

▸ MEASUREMENT OF WEIGHT **7** [C] (*pl.* stone) (*abbr.* st) (in Britain) a unit for measuring weight, equal to 6.35 kg or 14 pounds: *He weighs over 15 stone.* ◇ *She's trying to lose a stone.*

IDM **carved/set in** ˈ**stone** (of a decision, plan, etc.) unable to be changed: *People should remember that our proposals aren't set in stone.* **leave no stone un**ˈ**turned** to try every possible course of action in order to find or achieve sth **a** ˈ**stone's throw** a very short distance away: *We live just a stone's throw from here.* ◇ *The hotel is within a stone's throw of the beach.* ➲ more at BLOOD *n.*, HEART, KILL *v.*, PEOPLE *n.*, ROLL *v.*

■ ***verb***

▸ THROW STONES **1** [usually passive] ~ **sb/sth** to throw stones at sb/sth: *Shops were looted and vehicles stoned.* ◇ *to be **stoned to death*** (= as a punishment)

▸ FRUIT **2** (*BrE*) (also **pit** *NAmE, BrE*) ~ **sth** to remove the stone from the inside of a fruit: *stoned black olives*

IDM ˌ**stone the** ˈ**crows** | ˌ**stone** ˈ**me** (*old-fashioned, BrE*) used to express surprise, shock, anger, etc.

the ˈ**Stone Age** *noun* [sing.] the very early period of human history when tools and weapons were made of stone: (*figurative*) *My dad's taste in music is from the Stone Age* (= very old-fashioned). ▸ ˈ**stone-age** *adj.* [only before noun]: (*figurative*) *stone-age* (= very out-of-date) *computers*

ˌ**stone** ˈ**circle** *noun* a circle of large tall vertical stones from PREHISTORIC times, thought to have been used for religious or other ceremonies

ˌ**stone** ˈ**cold** *adj.* completely cold, when it should be warm or hot: *The soup was stone cold.*

IDM ˌ**stone-cold** ˈ**sober** having drunk no alcohol at all

stoned /stəʊnd; *NAmE* stoʊnd/ *adj.* [not usually before noun] (*informal*) not behaving or thinking normally because of the effects of a drug such as MARIJUANA or alcohol

ˌ**stone** ˈ**dead** *adj.* (*BrE*) completely dead or completely destroyed

ˌ**stone** ˈ**deaf** *adj.* completely unable to hear

stone·ground /ˈstəʊngraʊnd; *NAmE* ˈstoʊn-/ *adj.* (of flour for bread, etc.) made by being crushed between heavy stones

stone·mason /ˈstəʊnmeɪsn; *NAmE* ˈstoʊn-/ *noun* a person whose job is cutting and preparing stone for buildings

stone·wall /ˌstəʊnˈwɔːl; *NAmE* ˈstoʊn-/ *verb* [T, I] ~ (**sb/sth**) (especially in politics) to delay a discussion or decision by refusing to answer questions or by talking a lot

stone·ware /ˈstəʊnweə(r); *NAmE* ˈstoʊnwer/ *noun* [U] pots, dishes, etc. made from CLAY that contains a small amount of the hard stone called FLINT

stone·washed /ˈstəʊnwɒʃt; *NAmE* ˈstoʊnwɔːʃt; -wɑːʃt/ *adj.* (of jeans, etc.) washed in a special way so that the cloth loses some colour and looks older

stone·work /ˈstəʊnwɜːk; *NAmE* ˈstoʊnwɜːrk/ *noun* [U] the parts of a building that are made of stone

stoni·ly /ˈstəʊnɪli; *NAmE* ˈstoʊn-/ *adv.* in a way that shows a lack of feeling or sympathy: *She stared stonily at him for a minute.*

stonk·er /ˈstɒŋkə(r); *NAmE* ˈstɑːŋk-; ˈstɔːŋk-/ *noun* (*BrE, informal*) an extremely large or impressive thing

stonk·ing /ˈstɒŋkɪŋ; *NAmE* ˈstɑːŋk-; ˈstɔːŋk-/ *adj.* [usually before noun] (*BrE, informal*) extremely large or impressive

stony /ˈstəʊni; *NAmE* ˈstoʊni/ *adj.* (**stoni·er**, **stoni·est**) **1** having a lot of stones on it or in it: *stony soil* **2** showing a lack of feeling or sympathy SYN **cold**: *They listened to him in stony silence.*
IDM **fall on stony ˈground** to fail to produce the result or the effect that you hope for; to have little success **stony ˈbroke** = FLAT BROKE at FLAT *adv.*

ˌstony-ˈfaced *adj.* not showing any friendly feelings

stood *past tense, past part.* of STAND

stooge /stuːdʒ/ *noun* **1** (*informal*, usually *disapproving*) a person who is used by sb to do things that are unpleasant or dishonest **2** a performer in a show whose role is to appear silly so that the other performers can make jokes about him or her

stool /stuːl/ *noun* **1** (often in compounds) a seat with legs but with nothing to support your back or arms: *a bar stool* ◇ *a piano stool* ➲ VISUAL VOCAB pages V20, V22, V31 **2** (*medical*) a piece of solid waste from your body IDM see TWO

ˈstool pigeon *noun* (*informal*) a person, especially a criminal, who helps the police to catch another criminal, for example by spending time with them and getting secret information SYN **informer**

stoop /stuːp/ *verb, noun*
■ ***verb*** **1** [I] **~ (down)** to bend your body forwards and downwards: *She stooped down to pick up the child.* ◇ *The doorway was so low that he had to stoop.* **2** [I] to stand or walk with your head and shoulders bent forwards: *He tends to stoop because he's so tall.*
IDM **stoop so ˈlow (as to do sth)** (*formal*) to drop your moral standards far enough to do sth bad or unpleasant: *She was unwilling to believe anyone would stoop so low as to steal a ring from a dead woman's finger.*
PHR V **ˈstoop to sth** to drop your moral standards to do sth bad or unpleasant: *You surely don't think I'd stoop to that!* ◇ **~ doing sth** *I didn't think he'd stoop to cheating.*
■ ***noun*** **1** [sing.] if sb has a **stoop**, their shoulders are always bent forward **2** [C] (*NAmE*) a raised area outside the door of a house with steps leading up to it

stooped /stuːpt/ *adj.* **1** standing or walking with your head and shoulders bent forwards **2** **stooped shoulders** are bent forwards

stop 0‑w /stɒp; *NAmE* stɑːp/ *verb, noun*
■ ***verb*** (-pp-)
▸ NOT MOVE **1** 0‑w [I, T] to no longer move; to make sb/sth no longer move: *The car stopped at the traffic lights.* ◇ *We stopped for the night in Port Augusta.* ◇ **~ sb/sth** *He was stopped by the police for speeding.*
▸ NOT CONTINUE **2** 0‑w [I, T] to no longer continue to do sth; to make sb/sth no longer do sth: **~ (doing sth)** *That phone never stops ringing!* ◇ *Please stop crying and tell me what's wrong.* ◇ *She criticizes everyone and the trouble is, she* ***doesn't know when to stop.*** ◇ *Can't you just stop?* ◇ **~ sb/sth** *Stop me* (= make me stop talking) *if I'm boring you.* ◇ ***Stop it!*** *You're hurting me.* ◇ **~ what…** *Mike immediately stopped what he was doing.* HELP Notice the difference between **stop doing sth** and **stop to do sth**: *We stopped taking pictures* means 'We were no longer taking pictures.'; *We stopped to take pictures* means 'We stopped what we were doing so that we could start taking pictures.'
▸ END **3** 0‑w [I, T] to end or finish; to make sth end or finish: *When is this fighting going to stop?* ◇ *The bus service stops at midnight.* ◇ **~ doing sth** *Has it stopped raining yet?* ◇ **~ sth** *Doctors couldn't stop the bleeding.* ◇ *The referee was forced to stop the game because of heavy snow.*
▸ PREVENT **4** 0‑w [T] to prevent sb from doing sth; to prevent sth from happening: **~ sb/sth** *I want to go and you can't stop me.* ◇ *We need more laws to stop pollution.* ◇ ***There's no stopping us now*** (= nothing can prevent us from achieving what we want to achieve). ◇ **~ sb/sth from doing sth** ***There's nothing to stop you*** *from accepting the offer.* ◇ *You can't stop people from saying what they think.* ◇ (*BrE* also) **~ sb/sth doing sth** *You can't stop people saying what they think.*
▸ FOR SHORT TIME [I] **5** 0‑w to end an activity for a short time in order to do sth: **~ for sth** *I'm hungry. Let's stop for lunch.* ◇ **~ to do sth** *We stopped to admire the scenery.* ◇ *People just don't* ***stop to think*** *about the consequences.* HELP In spoken English, **stop** can be used with **and** plus another verb, instead of with **to** and the infinitive, to show purpose: *He stopped and bought some flowers.* ◇ *Let's stop and look at the map.*
▸ NOT FUNCTION **6** 0‑w [I, T] to no longer work or function; to make sth no longer work or function: *Why has the engine stopped?* ◇ *I felt as if my heart had stopped.* ◇ **~ sth** *I stopped the tape and pressed rewind.*
▸ STAY **7** [I] (*BrE, informal*) to stay somewhere for a short time, especially at sb's house: *I'm not stopping. I just came to give you this message.* ◇ **~ for sth** *Can you stop for tea?*
▸ MONEY **8** [T] to prevent money from being paid: **~ sth** *to* ***stop a cheque*** (= tell the bank not to pay it) ◇ **~ sth from sth** (*BrE*) *Dad threatened to stop £1 a week from our pocket money if we didn't clean our rooms.*
▸ CLOSE HOLE **9** [T] **~ sth (up) (with sth)** to block, fill or close a hole, an opening, etc: *Stop up the other end of the tube, will you?* ◇ *I stopped my ears but still heard her cry out.*
IDM **stop at ˈnothing** to be willing to do anything to get what you want, even if it is dishonest or wrong **ˌstop the ˈclock** to stop measuring time in a game or an activity that has a time limit **ˌstop ˈshort | ˌstop sb ˈshort** to suddenly stop, or make sb suddenly stop, doing sth: *He stopped short when he heard his name.* **stop short of sth/of doing sth** to be unwilling to do sth because it may involve a risk, but to nearly do it: *She stopped short of calling the president a liar.* ➲ more at BUCK *n.*, TRACK *n.*
PHR V **ˌstop ˈby (sth)** to make a short visit somewhere: *I'll stop by this evening for a chat.* ◇ *Could you stop by the store on the way home for some bread?* **ˌstop ˈin** (*BrE, informal*) to stay at home rather than go out **ˌstop ˈoff (at/in…)** to make a short visit somewhere during a trip in order to do sth: *We stopped off at a hotel for the night.* **ˌstop ˈout** (*BrE, informal*) to stay out late at night **ˌstop ˈover (at/in…)** to stay somewhere for a short time during a long journey: *I wanted to stop over in India on the way to Australia.* ➲ related noun STOPOVER **ˌstop ˈup** (*BrE, informal*) to stay up late
■ ***noun***
▸ ACT OF STOPPING **1** 0‑w an act of stopping or stopping sth; the state of being stopped: *The trip included an overnight stop in Brussels.* ◇ *She* ***brought*** *the car* ***to a stop.*** ◇ *Work has temporarily* ***come to a stop*** *while the funding is reviewed.* ◇ *It is time to* ***put a stop to*** *the violence.* ◇ *Babies do not grow at a steady rate but* ***in stops and starts.*** ➲ see also NON-STOP, WHISTLE-STOP
▸ OF BUS/TRAIN **2** 0‑w a place where a bus or train stops regularly for passengers to get on or off: *I get off at the next stop.* ◇ *Is this your stop?* ➲ see also BUS STOP, PIT STOP, REQUEST STOP
▸ PUNCTUATION **3** (*BrE*) = FULL STOP
▸ MUSIC **4** a row of pipes on an organ that produce the different sounds **5** a handle on an organ that the player pushes in or pulls out to control the sound produced by the pipes
▸ PHONETICS **6** a speech sound made by stopping the flow of air coming out of the mouth and then suddenly releasing it, for example /p, k, t/ SYN **plosive** ➲ see also GLOTTAL STOP IDM see FULL STOP, PULL *v.*

S

stop·cock /ˈstɒpkɒk; *NAmE* ˈstɑːpkɑːk/ (also **cock**) *noun* a tap that controls the flow of liquid or gas through a pipe

stop·gap /ˈstɒpɡæp; *NAmE* ˈstɑːp-/ *noun* something that you use or do for a short time while you are looking for sth better: *The arrangement was only intended as a stopgap.* ◇ *a stopgap measure*

ˌstop-ˈgo (*especially BrE*) (*especially NAmE* **ˌstop-and-ˈgo**) *adj.* [usually before noun] (*disapproving*) **1** starting and then stopping: *stop-go driving in heavy traffic* **2** used to describe the policy of first restricting and then encouraging economic activity and growth: *the damaging stop-go economic cycle*

ˈstop light *noun* [C] **1** (*BrE*) a red TRAFFIC LIGHT **2** (also **stop·lights** [pl.]) (*NAmE*) = TRAFFIC LIGHT **3** (*NAmE*) = BRAKE LIGHT

stop·over /ˈstɒpəʊvə(r); *NAmE* ˈstɑːpoʊ-/ (*NAmE* also **lay·over**) *noun* a short stay somewhere between two parts of a journey: *We had a two-day stopover in Fiji on the way to Australia.* ➲ **COLLOCATIONS** at TRAVEL

stop·page /ˈstɒpɪdʒ; *NAmE* ˈstɑːp-/ *noun* **1** [C] a situation in which people stop working as part of a protest or strike **2** [C] (*sport*) an interruption in the game for a particular reason: *Play resumed quickly after the stoppage.* ◇ ***stoppage time*** (= added on at the end of the game if there have been stoppages) **3** [C] a situation in which sth does not move forward or is blocked: *a stoppage of blood to the heart* **4 stoppages** [pl.] (*old-fashioned, BrE, formal*) an amount of money that an employer takes from people's wages for tax and other payments

stop·per /ˈstɒpə(r); *NAmE* ˈstɑːp-/ (*NAmE* also **plug**) *noun* an object that fits into the top of a bottle to close it ➲ **VISUAL VOCAB** page V57 ▶ **stop·per** *verb* **~ sth**

ˈstopping train *noun* (*BrE*) a train that stops at a lot of stations between main stations

ˌstop ˈpress *noun* [U] late news that is added to a newspaper after printing has begun

ˈstop street *noun* (*SAfrE*) a place where one road joins or crosses another at which there is a sign indicating that vehicles must stop before continuing

stop·watch /ˈstɒpwɒtʃ; *NAmE* ˈstɑːpwɑːtʃ/ *noun* a watch that you can stop and start by pressing buttons, in order to time a race, etc. accurately

stor·age /ˈstɔːrɪdʒ/ *noun* [U] **1** the process of keeping sth in a particular place until it is needed; the space where things can be kept: *tables that fold flat for storage* ◇ *There's a lot of storage space in the loft.* ◇ *food storage facilities* ◇ *We need more storage now.* ➲ see also COLD STORAGE **2** (*computing*) the process of keeping information, etc. on a computer; the way it is kept: *the storage and retrieval of information* ◇ *data storage* **3** the process of paying to keep furniture, etc. in a special building until you want it: *When we moved we had to put our furniture **in storage** for a while.*

S

ˈstorage battery (*NAmE*) (*BrE* **ac·cu·mu·la·tor**) *noun* a large battery that you can fill with electrical power (= that you can RECHARGE)

ˈstorage heater *noun* (*BrE*) an electric HEATER that stores heat when electricity is cheaper, for example at night

store 🔑 /stɔː(r)/ *noun, verb*

■ ***noun*** **1** 🔑 [C] a large shop that sells many different types of goods: *a big department store* ➲ see also CHAIN STORE, VARIETY STORE **2** 🔑 [C] (*NAmE*) a shop, large or small: *a health food store* ◇ *a liquor store* ➲ **COLLOCATIONS** at SHOPPING ➲ see also CONSIGNMENT STORE, CONVENIENCE STORE, GENERAL STORE, PACKAGE STORE **3** [C] a quantity or supply of sth that you have and use: *her secret store of chocolate* ◇ *a vast store of knowledge* **4** [pl.] **stores** goods of a particular kind or for a particular purpose: *medical stores* **5** [C] (often **stores**) a place where goods of a particular kind are kept: *a grain store* ◇ *weapons stores*

IDM **in store (for sb)** waiting to happen to sb: *We don't know what life **holds in store** for us.* ◇ *If she had known what **lay in store** for her, she would never have agreed to go.* ◇ *They think it'll be easy but they have a **surprise in store**.* **set/put (great, etc.) ˈstore by sth** to consider sth to be important: *She sets great store by her appearance.* ◇ *It is unwise to put too much store by these statistics.* ➲ more at HIT *v.*, MIND *v.*

■ ***verb*** **1** 🔑 **~ sth (away/up)** to put sth somewhere and keep it there to use later: *animals storing up food for the winter* ◇ *He hoped the electronic equipment was safely stored away.* **2** 🔑 **~ sth** to keep information or facts in a computer or in your brain: *Thousands of pieces of data are stored in a computer's memory.*

PHR V **ˌstore sth↔ˈup** to not express strong feelings or deal with problems when you have them, especially when this causes problems later: *She had stored up all her anger and eventually snapped.* ◇ *By ignoring your feelings you are only **storing up trouble** for yourself.*

ˈstore-bought (*NAmE*) (*BrE* **ˈshop-bought**) *adj.* [only before noun] bought from a shop/store and not made at home: *store-bought cookies*

ˈstore-brand (*US*) (*BrE* **ˌown-ˈbrand, ˌown-ˈlabel**) *adj.* used to describe goods that are marked with the name of the shop/store in which they are sold rather than with the name of the company that produced them

ˈstore card *noun* a card that a particular shop/store provides for regular customers so that they can use it to buy goods that they will pay for later ➲ compare CREDIT CARD

ˈstore detective *noun* a person employed by a large shop/store to watch customers and make sure they do not steal goods

store·front /ˈstɔːfrʌnt; *NAmE* ˈstɔːrf-/ *noun* (*NAmE*) **1** (*BrE* **shop·front**) the outside of a shop/store that faces the street **2** a room at the front of a shop/store: *They run their business from a small storefront.* ◇ *a storefront office* **3** a place on the Internet where you can buy goods and services: *Welcome to our **online storefront**.*

store·house /ˈstɔːhaʊs; *NAmE* ˈstɔːrh-/ *noun* **1** a building where things are stored SYN **warehouse 2 ~ of information, knowledge, etc.** a place or thing that has or contains a lot of information

store·keep·er /ˈstɔːkiːpə(r); *NAmE* ˈstɔːrk-/ *noun* (*especially NAmE*) = SHOPKEEPER

store·room /ˈstɔːruːm; -rʊm/ *noun* a room used for storing things

ˈstore window (*NAmE*) (*BrE* **ˌshop ˈwindow**) (also **window**) *noun* the glass at the front of a shop/store and the area behind it where goods are shown to the public

storey (*especially BrE*) (*especially US* **story**) /ˈstɔːri/ *noun* (*pl.* **stor·eys**, *NAmE* **stor·ies**) **1** a level of a building; a floor: *the **upper/lower storey** of the house* ◇ *a **single-storey/two-storey** building* ➲ see also MULTI-STOREY ➲ **VISUAL VOCAB** page V14 **2 -storeyed** (*BrE*) (*NAmE* **-storied**) (in adjectives) (of a building) having the number of levels mentioned: *a four-storeyed building*

Which Word?

storey / floor

- You use **storey** (*BrE*)/**story** (*NAmE*) mainly when you are talking about the number of levels a building has: *a five-storey house* ◇ *The office building is five storeys high.*
- **Floor** is used mainly to talk about which particular level in the building someone lives on, goes to, etc: *His office is on the fifth floor.*

➲ note at FLOOR

stor·ied /ˈstɔːrid/ *adj.* (*NAmE*) **1** [only before noun] mentioned in stories; famous; well known: *the rock star's storied career* **2 -storied** = -STOREYED at STOREY

stork /stɔːk; *NAmE* stɔːrk/ *noun* a large black and white bird with a long beak and neck and long legs, that lives near water but often builds its nest on the top of a high building. There is a tradition that says that it is storks that bring people their new babies.

storm 0-w /stɔːm; *NAmE* stɔːrm/ *noun*, *verb*
■ ***noun*** **1** 0-w very bad weather with strong winds and rain, and often THUNDER and LIGHTNING: ***fierce/heavy/violent storms*** ◇ *A few minutes later* ***the storm broke*** (= began). ◇ *I think we're* ***in for a storm*** (= going to have one). ◇ *storm damage* ➲ SYNONYMS at RAIN ➲ COLLOCATIONS at WEATHER **2** (in compounds) very bad weather of the type mentioned: *a* ***thunderstorm/snowstorm/sandstorm*** ➲ see also ELECTRICAL STORM, RAINSTORM **3** 0-w **~ (of sth)** a situation in which a lot of people suddenly express very strong feelings about sth: *a storm of protest* ◇ *A political* ***storm is brewing*** *over the Prime Minister's comments.* **4 ~ of sth** a sudden loud noise that is caused by emotion or excitement SYN **roar**: *a storm of applause* ➲ see also BRAINSTORM
IDM **a storm in a 'teacup** (*BrE*) (*NAmE* **a tempest in a 'teapot**) a lot of anger or worry about sth that is not important **take sth/sb by 'storm 1** to be extremely successful very quickly in a particular place or among particular people: *The play took London by storm.* **2** to attack a place suddenly and capture it ➲ more at CALM *n.*, PORT
■ ***verb*** **1** [T, I] to suddenly attack a place: **~ sth** *Police stormed the building and captured the gunman.* ◇ **~ into sth** *Soldiers stormed into the city at dawn.* **2** [I] **+ adv./prep.** to go somewhere quickly and in an angry, noisy way: *She stormed into my office waving a newspaper.* ◇ *He burst into tears and stormed off.* **3** [T] **+ speech** to say sth in a loud angry way: *'Don't you know who I am?' she stormed.*

'storm cloud *noun* [usually pl.] a dark cloud that you see when bad weather is coming: (*figurative*) *The storm clouds of revolution were gathering.*

'storm door *noun* an extra door that is fitted to the outside door of a house, etc. to give protection from bad weather

storm·ing /'stɔːmɪŋ; *NAmE* 'stɔːrm-/ *adj.* [only before noun] (*BrE*) (of a performance) very impressive; done with a lot of energy: *Arsenal scored three late goals in a storming finish.*

'storm-tossed *adj.* [only before noun] (*literary*) affected or damaged by storms

'storm trooper *noun* a soldier who is specially trained for violent attacks, especially one in Nazi Germany in the 1930s and 1940s

'storm water *noun* [U] water covering the ground in large quantities because of heavy rain

'storm window *noun* an extra window that is fitted to a window of a house to give protection from bad weather

stormy /'stɔːmi; *NAmE* 'stɔːrmi/ *adj.* (**storm·ier**, **stormi·est**) **1** with strong winds and heavy rain or snow: *a dark and stormy night* ◇ *stormy weather* ◇ *stormy seas* (= with big waves) **2** full of strong feelings and angry arguments: *a stormy debate* ◇ *a stormy relationship*

story 0-w /'stɔːri/ *noun* (*pl.* **-ies**)
1 0-w **~ (about/of sth/sb)** a description of events and people that the writer or speaker has invented in order to entertain people: ***adventure/detective/love, etc. stories*** ◇ *a story about time travel* ◇ *Shall I* ***tell you a story?*** ◇ *He* ***read*** *the children* ***a story.*** ◇ *a* ***bedtime story*** ➲ COLLOCATIONS at LITERATURE ➲ see also FAIRY STORY, GHOST STORY, SHORT STORY **2** 0-w **~ (about/of sth/sb)** an account, often spoken, of what happened to sb or of how sth happened: *It was many years before* ***the full story*** *was made public.* ◇ *The police didn't believe her story.* ◇ *We must stick to our story about the accident.* ◇ *I can't decide until I've heard* ***both sides of the story.*** ◇ *It's a story of courage.* ◇ *Many years later I returned to Africa but* ***that's another story*** (= I am not going to talk about it now). ➲ see also COCK AND BULL STORY, HARD-LUCK STORY, LIFE STORY, SHAGGY-DOG STORY, SOB STORY, SUCCESS STORY, TALL STORY ➲ SYNONYMS at REPORT **3** 0-w an account of past events or of how sth has developed: *He told us the story of his life.* ◇ *the story of the Beatles* ◇ *the story of the building of the bridge* **4** 0-w a report in a newspaper, magazine or news broadcast: *a front-page story* ◇ *Now for a summary of tonight's main news stories.* ➲ see also COVER STORY, LEAD STORY **5** 0-w (also **story·line**) the series of events in a book, film/movie, play, etc. SYN **plot**: *Her novels always have the same basic story.* **6** (*informal*) something that sb says which is not true: *She knew the child had been* ***telling stories*** *again.* **7** (*NAmE*) = STOREY
IDM **the story goes (that)...** | **so the story goes** used to describe sth that people are saying although it may not be correct: *She never saw him again—or so the story goes.* **that's the ˌstory of my 'life** (*informal*) when you say **that's the story of my life** about an unfortunate experience you have had, you mean you have had many similar experiences ➲ more at LIKELY *adj.*, LONG *adj.*, OLD, PITCH *v.*, TELL

story·board /'stɔːribɔːd; *NAmE* -bɔːrd/ *noun* a series of drawings or pictures that show the outline of the story of a film/movie, etc. ▶ **story·board** *verb* **~ sth** **storyboarding** *noun* [U]: *the storyboarding process*

story·book /'stɔːribʊk/ *noun* a book of stories for children: *a picture in a storybook* ◇ *storybook characters* ◇ *storybook adventures* (= like the ones in stories for children)

story·line /'stɔːrilaɪn/ *noun* the basic story in a novel, play, film/movie, etc. SYN **plot**

story·tell·er /'stɔːritelə(r)/ *noun* a person who tells or writes stories ▶ **story·tell·ing** *noun* [U]

stoup /stuːp/ *noun* (*technical*) a stone container for holy water in a church

stout /staʊt/ *adj.*, *noun*
■ ***adj.*** (**stout·er**, **stout·est**) **1** (of a person) rather fat SYN **plump** **2** [usually before noun] strong and thick: *a stout pair of shoes* **3** [usually before noun] (*formal*) brave and determined: *He put up a stout defence in court.* ▶ **stout·ly** *adv.*: *He was tall and stoutly built.* ◇ *'I disagree,' said Polly stoutly.* **stout·ness** *noun* [U]
■ ***noun*** [U, C] strong dark beer made with MALT or BARLEY

ˌstout-'hearted *adj.* (*old-fashioned, literary*) brave and determined

stove 0-w /stəʊv; *NAmE* stoʊv/ *noun*
1 0-w a piece of equipment that can burn various fuels and is used for heating rooms: *a* ***gas/wood-burning stove*** **2** 0-w (*especially NAmE*) (*BrE* also **cook·er**) (*NAmE* also **range**) a large piece of equipment for cooking food, containing an oven and gas or electric rings on top: *She put a pan of water on the stove.* ◇ (*NAmE, BrE*) *Most people don't want to spend hours* ***slaving over a hot stove*** (= cooking). ➲ see also STAVE, STOVE, STOVE *V.*

stove·top /'stəʊvtɒp; *NAmE* 'stoʊvtɑːp/ *noun* (*NAmE*) (*BrE* **hob**) the top part of a cooker where food is cooked in pans; a similar surface that is built into a kitchen unit and is separate from the oven: *stovetop cooking* ➲ VISUAL VOCAB page V22

stow /stəʊ; *NAmE* stoʊ/ *verb* **~ sth (away) (in sth)** to put sth in a safe place: *She found a seat, stowed her backpack and sat down.*
PHR V **ˌstow a'way** to hide in a ship, plane, etc. in order to travel secretly ➲ related noun STOWAWAY

stow·age /'stəʊɪdʒ; *NAmE* 'stoʊ-/ *noun* [U] space provided for stowing things away, in a boat or a plane

stow·away /'stəʊəweɪ; *NAmE* 'stoʊ-/ *noun* a person who hides in a ship or plane before it leaves, in order to travel without paying or being seen

St Pat·rick's Day /ˌsnt 'pætrɪks deɪ; *NAmE* ˌseɪnt/ *noun* 17 March, a Christian festival of the national SAINT of Ireland, when many Irish people wear a SHAMROCK

strad·dle /'strædl/ *verb* **1 ~ sth/sb** to sit or stand with one of your legs on either side of sb/sth: *He swung his leg over the motorcycle, straddling it easily.* **2 ~ sth** to cross, or exist on both sides of, a river, a road or an area of land: *The mountains straddle the French-Swiss border.* **3 ~ sth** to exist within, or include, different periods of time, activities or groups of people: *a writer who straddles two cultures*

strafe /strɑːf; *NAmE* streɪf/ *verb* **~ sth** to attack a place with bullets or bombs from an aircraft flying low

S

strag·gle /ˈstræɡl/ *verb* **1** [I] (+ **adv./prep.**) to grow, spread or move in an untidy way in different directions: *The town straggled to an end and the fields began.* **2** [I] (+ **adv./prep.**) to move slowly behind a group of people that you are with so that you become separated from them: *On the way the kids straggled behind us.*

strag·gler /ˈstræɡlə(r)/ *noun* [usually pl.] a person or an animal that is among the last or the slowest in a group to do sth, for example, to finish a race or leave a place

strag·gly /ˈstræɡli/ *adj.* growing or hanging in a way that does not look tidy or attractive: *a thin woman with grey, straggly hair*

straight O‑ /streɪt/ *adv., adj., noun*

■ ***adv.*** (straight·er, straight·est)

▸ NOT IN CURVE **1** O‑ not in a curve or at an angle; in a straight line: *Keep* ***straight on*** *for two miles.* ◇ *Can you stretch your arms out straighter?* ◇ *He was too tired to walk straight.* ◇ *I can't shoot straight* (= accurately). ◇ *She looked me straight in the eye.*

▸ IMMEDIATELY **2** O‑ by a direct route; immediately: *Come straight home after school.* ◇ *I was so tired I went straight to bed.* ◇ *She went straight from college to a top job.* ◇ *I'm going to the library* ***straight after*** *the class.* ◇ *I'll come* ***straight to the point****—your work isn't good enough.*

▸ IN LEVEL/CORRECT POSITION **3** O‑ in or into a level or vertical position; in or into the correct position: *Sit up straight!* ◇ *She pulled her hat straight.*

▸ HONESTLY **4** honestly and directly: *I told him straight that I didn't like him.* ◇ *Are you* ***playing straight*** *with me?*

▸ WITHOUT INTERRUPTION **5** continuously without interruption: *They had been working for 16 hours straight.*

IDM **go ˈstraight** (*informal*) to stop being a criminal and live an honest life **play it ˈstraight** to be honest and not try to trick sb **ˌstraight aˈway** O‑ immediately; without delay SYN **at once**: *I'll do it straight away.* **ˌstraight from the ˈshoulder** if you say sth **straight from the shoulder**, you are being very honest and direct, even if what you are saying is critical **ˌstraight ˈoff/ˈout** (*informal*) without hesitating: *She asked him straight off what he thought about it all.* **ˌstraight ˈup** (*BrE, informal*) used to ask if what sb has said is true or to emphasize that what you have said is true: *I saw it—straight up!* ➲ more at HIT *v.*, HORSE *n.*, THINK *v.*

■ ***adj.*** (straight·er, straight·est)

▸ WITHOUT CURVES **1** O‑ without a bend or curve; going in one direction only: *a straight line* ◇ *a straight road* ◇ *long straight hair* (= without curls) ◇ *a boat sailing* ***in a straight line*** ◇ *straight-backed chairs*

▸ CLOTHING **2** O‑ not fitting close to the body and not curving away from the body: *a straight skirt*

▸ AIM/BLOW **3** going directly to the correct place: *a straight punch to the face*

▸ IN LEVEL/CORRECT POSITION **4** O‑ positioned in the correct way; level, vertical or parallel to sth: *Is my tie straight?*

▸ CLEAN/NEAT **5** [not usually before noun] clean and neat, with everything in the correct place: *It took hours to get the house straight.*

▸ HONEST **6** honest and direct: *a straight answer to a straight question* ◇ *I don't think you're being straight with me.* ◇ *It's time for some* ***straight talking***. ➲ SYNONYMS at HONEST

▸ CHOICE **7** [only before noun] simple; involving only two clear choices: *It was a* ***straight choice*** *between taking the job and staying out of work.* ◇ (*BrE*) *The election was a* ***straight fight*** *between the two main parties.*

▸ ACTOR/PLAY **8** [only before noun] (of an actor or a play) not connected with comedy or musical theatre, but with serious theatre

▸ WITHOUT INTERRUPTION **9** [only before noun] one after another in a series, without interruption SYN **consecutive**: *The team has had five straight wins.*

▸ ALCOHOLIC DRINK **10** (*NAmE*) (*BrE* **neat**) not mixed with water or anything else

▸ NORMAL/BORING **11** (*informal*) you can use **straight** to describe a person who is normal and ordinary, but who you consider dull and boring

▸ SEX **12** (*informal*) HETEROSEXUAL OPP **gay**

▸ **straight·ness** *noun* [U]

IDM **get sth ˈstraight** to make a situation clear; to make sure that you or sb else understands the situation: *Let's get this straight—you really had no idea where he was?* **put/set sb ˈstraight (about/on sth)** to correct sb's mistake; to make sure that sb knows the correct facts when they have had the wrong idea or impression **(earn/get) straight ˈA's** (*especially NAmE*) (to get) the best marks/grades in all your classes: *a straight A student* **the ˌstraight and ˈnarrow** (*informal*) the honest and morally acceptable way of living: *His wife is trying to keep him on the straight and narrow.* **a straight ˈface** if you keep a **straight face**, you do not laugh or smile, although you find sth funny ➲ see also STRAIGHT-FACED ➲ more at RAMROD, RECORD *n.*

■ ***noun***

▸ SEX **1** (*informal*) a person who has sexual relationships with people of the opposite sex, rather than the same sex: *gays and straights*

▸ OF ROAD/TRACK **2** (*NAmE* also **straight·away**) a straight part of a RACETRACK or road ➲ see also THE HOME STRAIGHT

ˌstraight-ˈarm (also **ˌstiff-ˈarm**) (both *NAmE*) (*BrE* **ˌhand sb↔ˈoff**) *verb* **~ sb** (in sport) to push away a player who is trying to stop you, with your arm straight

ˌstraight ˈarrow *noun* (*NAmE, informal*) a person who is very honest or who never does anything exciting or different

straight·away /ˌstreɪtəˈweɪ/ *adv., noun*

■ ***adv.*** ➲ STRAIGHT *adv.*

■ ***noun*** (*NAmE*) = STRAIGHT *n.* (2)

ˈstraight edge *noun* a strip of wood, metal or plastic with a straight edge used for drawing accurate straight lines, or checking them

straight·en /ˈstreɪtn/ *verb* **1** [T, I] to become straight; to make sth straight: **~ sth (out)** *I straightened my tie and walked in.* ◇ **~ (out)** *The road bends here then straightens out.* **2** [T, I] to make your body straight and vertical: **~ sth** *He stood up and straightened his shoulders.* ◇ **~ sth/yourself up** *I straightened myself up to answer the question.* ◇ **~ (up)** *Straighten up slowly, then repeat the exercise ten times.*

PHR V **ˌstraighten sb↔ˈout** to help sb to deal with problems or understand a confused situation **ˌstraighten sth↔ˈout** to deal with a confused situation by organizing things that are causing problems: *I need time to straighten out my finances.* **ˌstraighten sth↔ˈup** to make sth neat and tidy

ˌstraight-ˈfaced *adj.* without laughing or smiling, even though you may be amused

straight·for·ward AW /ˌstreɪtˈfɔːwəd; *NAmE* -ˈfɔːrwərd/ *adj.* **1** easy to do or to understand; not complicated SYN **easy**: *a straightforward process* ◇ *It's quite straightforward to get here.* **2** (of a person or their behaviour) honest and open; not trying to trick sb or hide sth ▸ **straight·for·ward·ly** *adv.*: *Let me put it more straightforwardly.* **straight·for·ward·ness** *noun* [U]

straight·jacket *noun* = STRAITJACKET

ˌstraight-ˈlaced *adj.* = STRAIT-LACED

ˈstraight man *noun* a person in a show whose role is to provide the main entertainer with opportunities to make jokes

ˌstraight ˈticket *noun* (in elections in the US) a vote in which sb chooses all the candidates from the same party ➲ compare SPLIT TICKET ▸ **ˌstraight-ˈticket** *adj.*: *straight-ticket voting*

strain O‑ /streɪn/ *noun, verb*

■ ***noun***

▸ WORRY/ANXIETY **1** O‑ [U, C] pressure on sb/sth because they have too much to do or manage, or sth very difficult to deal with; the problems, worry or anxiety that this produces: *Their marriage is* ***under great strain*** *at the moment.* ◇ *These repayments are* ***putting a strain on*** *our finances.* ◇ *Relax, and let us* ***take the strain*** (= do things for you). ◇ *The transport service cannot cope with the strain of so many additional passengers.* ◇ *You will learn to cope* *with the* ***stresses and strains*** *of public life.* ◇ *I found it a strain having to concentrate for so long.* ➲ SYNONYMS at PRESSURE

▸ PHYSICAL PRESSURE **2** 🔑 [U, C] the pressure that is put on sth when a physical force stretches, pushes, or pulls it: *The rope broke* ***under the strain.*** ◇ *You should try not to place too much strain on muscles and joints.* ◇ *The ground here cannot* ***take the strain*** *of a large building.* ◇ *The cable has a 140kg* ***breaking strain*** (= it will break when it is stretched or pulled by a force greater than this).

▸ INJURY **3** [C, U] an injury to a part of your body, such as a muscle, that is caused by using it too much or by twisting it: *a* ***calf/groin/leg strain*** ◇ *muscle strain*

▸ TYPE OF PLANT/ANIMAL/DISEASE **4** [C] a particular type of plant or animal, or of a disease caused by bacteria, etc: *a new strain of mosquitoes resistant to the poison* ◇ *This is only one of the many strains of the disease.*

▸ IN SB'S CHARACTER **5** [C, usually sing.] a particular tendency in the character of a person or group, or a quality in their manner SYN **streak**: *He had a definite strain of snobbery in him.*

▸ OF MUSIC **6** [C, usually pl.] (*formal*) the sound of music being played or sung: *She could hear the strains of Mozart through the window.*

■ ***verb***

▸ INJURE **1** [T] **~ sth/yourself** to injure yourself or part of your body by making it work too hard: *to strain a muscle* ➲ SYNONYMS at INJURE ➲ COLLOCATIONS at INJURY

▸ MAKE EFFORT **2** [T, I] to make an effort to do sth, using all your mental or physical strength: **~ sth to do sth** *I* ***strained my ears*** (= listened very hard) *to catch what they were saying.* ◇ **~ sth** *Necks were strained for a glimpse of the stranger.* ◇ **~ to do sth** *People were straining to see what was going on.* ◇ **~ (sth) (for sth)** *He burst to the surface, straining for air.* ◇ *Bend gently to the left without straining.*

▸ STRETCH TO LIMIT **3** [T] **~ sth** to try to make sth do more than it is able to do: *The sudden influx of visitors is straining hotels in the town to the limit.* ◇ *His constant complaints were straining our patience.* ◇ *The dispute has strained relations between the two countries* (= made them difficult).

▸ PUSH/PULL HARD **4** [I] **+ adv./prep.** to push hard against sth; to pull hard on sth: *She strained against the ropes that held her.* ◇ *The dogs were* ***straining at the leash,*** *eager to get to the park.*

▸ SEPARATE SOLID FROM LIQUID **5** [T] to pour food, etc. through sth with very small holes in it, for example a SIEVE, in order to separate the solid part from the liquid part: **~ sth** *Use a colander to strain the vegetables.* ◇ **~ sth off** *Strain off any excess liquid.*

IDM **strain at the 'leash** (*informal*) to want to do sth very much: *Like all youngsters, he's straining at the leash to leave home.* **strain every 'nerve/'sinew (to do sth)** (*formal*) to try as hard as you can to do sth ➲ more at CREAK *v.*

strained /streɪnd/ *adj.* **1** showing the effects of worry or pressure SYN **tense**: *Her face looked strained and weary.* ◇ *He spoke in a low, strained voice.* **2** (of a situation) not relaxed or friendly SYN **tense**: *There was a strained atmosphere throughout the meeting.* ◇ *Relations between the two families are strained.* **3** not natural; produced by a deliberate effort SYN **forced**: *She gave a strained laugh.*

strain·er /ˈstreɪnə(r)/ *noun* a kitchen UTENSIL (= a tool) with a lot of small holes in it, used for separating solids from liquids: *a tea-strainer*

strait /streɪt/ *noun* **1** (also **straits**) [pl.] (especially in the names of places) a narrow passage of water that connects two seas or large areas of water: *the Strait(s) of Gibraltar* **2 straits** [pl.] a very difficult situation especially because of lack of money: *The factory is* ***in dire straits.*** ◇ *She found herself in desperate financial straits.*

strait·ened /ˈstreɪtnd/ *adj.* [only before noun] (*formal*) without enough money or as much money as there was before: *The family of eight was living* ***in straitened circumstances.***

strait·jacket (also **straight·jacket**) /ˈstreɪtdʒækɪt/ *noun* **1** a piece of clothing like a jacket with long arms which are tied to prevent the person wearing it from behaving violently. Straitjackets are sometimes used to control people who are mentally ill. **2** (*disapproving*) a thing that stops sth from growing or developing: *the straitjacket of taxation*

strait-laced (also **straight-laced**) /ˌstreɪt ˈleɪst/ *adj.* (*disapproving*) having strict or old-fashioned ideas about people's moral behaviour

strand /strænd/ *noun, verb*

■ ***noun*** **1** a single thin piece of thread, wire, hair, etc: *a strand of wool* ◇ *a few strands of dark hair* ◇ *She wore a single strand of pearls around her neck.* **2** one of the different parts of an idea, a plan, a story, etc: *We heard every strand of political opinion.* ◇ *The author draws the different strands of the plot together in the final chapter.* **3** (*literary* or *IrishE*) the land along the edge of the sea or ocean, or of a lake or river

■ ***verb*** [usually passive] **1 ~ sb** to leave sb in a place from which they have no way of leaving: *The strike left hundreds of tourists stranded at the airport.* **2 ~ sth** to make a boat, fish, WHALE, etc. be left on land and unable to return to the water: *The ship was stranded on a sandbank.*

strange 🔑 /streɪndʒ/ *adj.* (**stran·ger, stran·gest**)

1 🔑 unusual or surprising, especially in a way that is difficult to understand: *A strange thing happened this morning.* ◇ *She was looking at me in a very strange way.* ◇ **~ (that)** *... It's strange (that) we haven't heard from him.* ◇ **~ (how...)** *It's strange how childhood impressions linger.* ◇ ***That's strange****—the front door's open.* ◇ *I'm looking forward to the exam,* ***strange as it may seem.*** ◇ *There was* ***something strange*** *about her eyes.* ◇ ***Strange to say,*** *I don't really enjoy television.* **2** 🔑 not familiar because you have not been there before or met the person before: *a strange city* ◇ *to wake up in a strange bed* ◇ *Never accept lifts from strange men.* ◇ **~ to sb** *At first the place was strange to me.* ▸ **strange·ness** *noun* [U]

IDM **feel 'strange** 🔑 to not feel comfortable in a situation; to have an unpleasant physical feeling: *She felt strange sitting at her father's desk.* ◇ *It was terribly hot and I started to feel strange.* ➲ more at TRUTH

strange·ly 🔑 /ˈstreɪndʒli/ *adv.* in an unusual or surprising way: *She's been acting very strangely lately.* ◇ *The house was strangely quiet.* ◇ *strangely shaped rocks* ◇ ***Strangely enough,*** *I don't feel at all nervous.*

strang·er 🔑 /ˈstreɪndʒə(r)/ *noun*

1 🔑 a person that you do not know: *There was a* ***complete stranger*** *sitting at my desk.* ◇ *They got on well together although they were* ***total strangers.*** ◇ *We've told our daughter not to speak to strangers.* ◇ **~ to sb** *She remained a stranger to me.* **2** 🔑 a person who is in a place that they have not been in before: *Sorry, I don't know where the bank is. I'm a stranger here myself.* ◇ **~ to...** *He must have been a stranger to the town.*

IDM **be no/a 'stranger to sth** (*formal*) to be familiar/not familiar with sth because you have/have not experienced it many times before: *He is no stranger to controversy.*

stran·gle /ˈstræŋgl/ *verb* **1 ~ sb** to kill sb by squeezing or pressing on their throat and neck: *to strangle sb to death* ◇ *He strangled her with her own scarf.* **2 ~ sth** to prevent sth from growing or developing: *The current monetary policy is strangling the economy.*

stran·gled /ˈstræŋgld/ *adj.* (of a cry, sb's voice, etc.) not clear because it stops before it has completely finished: *There was a strangled cry from the other room.*

strangle·hold /ˈstræŋglhəʊld; *NAmE* -hoʊld/ *noun* [sing.] **1** a strong hold around sb's neck that makes it difficult for them to breathe **2 ~ (on sth)** complete control over sth that makes it impossible for it to grow or develop well: *The company now had a stranglehold on the market.*

stran·gler /ˈstræŋglə(r)/ *noun* a person who kills sb by squeezing their throat tightly

stran·gu·lated /ˈstræŋgjuleɪtɪd/ *adj.* **1** (*medical*) (of a part of the body) squeezed so tightly that blood etc. cannot pass through it **2** (*formal*) (of a voice) sounding as though the throat is tightly squeezed, usually because of fear or worry: *He gave a strangulated squawk.*

S

stran·gu·la·tion /ˌstræŋɡjuˈleɪʃn/ *noun* [U] **1** the act of killing sb by squeezing their throat tightly; the state of being killed in this way: *to die of slow strangulation* **2** (*disapproving*) the act of preventing sth from growing or developing: *the strangulation of the human spirit*

strap /stræp/ *noun, verb*

■ ***noun*** a strip of leather, cloth or other material that is used to fasten sth, keep sth in place, carry sth or hold onto sth: *the shoulder straps of her dress* ◇ *a watch with a leather strap* ➲ VISUAL VOCAB pages V41, V52

■ ***verb*** (-pp-) **1 ~ sth + adv./prep.** to fasten sb/sth in place using a strap or straps: *He strapped the knife to his leg.* ◇ *Everything had to be strapped down to stop it from sliding around.* ◇ *Are you strapped in* (= wearing a seat belt in a car, plane, etc.)? **2 ~ sth (up)** to wrap strips of material around a wound or an injured part of the body SYN **bandage**: *I have to keep my leg strapped up for six weeks.*

strap·less /ˈstræpləs/ *adj.* (especially of a dress or BRA) without straps

strapped /stræpt/ *adj.* **~ (for cash, funds, etc.)** (*informal*) having little or not enough money

strap·ping /ˈstræpɪŋ/ *adj.* [only before noun] (*informal*) (of people) big, tall and strong: *a strapping lad*

strappy /ˈstræpi/ *adj.* (**strap·pier, strap·pi·est**) (*informal*) (of shoes or clothes) having straps: *white strappy sandals*

strata *pl.* of STRATUM

strata·gem /ˈstrætədʒəm/ *noun* (*formal*) a trick or plan that you use to gain an advantage or to trick an opponent

stra·tegic AW /strəˈtiːdʒɪk/ (also *less frequent* **stra·tegic·al** /-dʒɪkl/) *adj.* [usually before noun] **1** done as part of a plan that is meant to achieve a particular purpose or to gain an advantage: *strategic planning* ◇ *a strategic decision to sell off part of the business* ◇ *Cameras were set up at strategic points* (= in places where they would be most effective) *along the route.* **2** connected with getting an advantage in a war or other military situation: *Malta was of vital strategic importance during the war.* **3** (of weapons, especially nuclear weapons) intended to be fired at an enemy's country rather than used in a battle ➲ compare TACTICAL (3) ▸ **stra·tegic·al·ly** AW /-kli/ *adv.*: *a strategically placed microphone* ◇ *a strategically important target*

strat·egist AW /ˈstrætədʒɪst/ *noun* a person who is skilled at planning things, especially military activities

strat·egy 0‑ AW /ˈstrætədʒi/ *noun* (*pl.* -ies) **1** 0‑ [C] a plan that is intended to achieve a particular purpose: *the government's economic strategy* ◇ **~ for doing sth** *to develop a strategy for dealing with unemployment* ◇ **~ to do sth** *It's all part of an overall strategy to gain promotion.* **2** 0‑ [U] the process of planning sth or putting a plan into operation in a skilful way: *marketing strategy* **3** 0‑ [U, C] the skill of planning the movements of armies in a battle or war; an example of doing this: *military strategy* ◇ *defence strategies* ➲ COLLOCATIONS at WAR ➲ compare TACTIC

strati·fi·ca·tion /ˌstrætɪfɪˈkeɪʃn/ *noun* [U] (*technical*) the division of sth into different layers or groups: *social stratification*

strat·ify /ˈstrætɪfaɪ/ *verb* (**strati·fies, strati·fy·ing, strati·fied, strati·fied**) [usually passive] **~ sth** (*formal* or *technical*) to arrange sth in layers or STRATA: *a highly stratified society* ◇ *stratified rock*

strato·sphere /ˈstrætəsfɪə(r); *NAmE* -sfɪr/ *noun* **the stratosphere** [sing.] the layer of the earth's atmosphere between about 10 and 50 kilometres above the surface of the earth ➲ compare IONOSPHERE ▸ **strato·spher·ic** /ˌstrætəˈsferɪk; *NAmE* also -ˈsfɪr-/ *adj.*: *stratospheric clouds*

IDM **in/into the ˈstratosphere** at or to an extremely high level: *The technology boom sent share prices into the stratosphere.*

stra·tum /ˈstrɑːtəm; *NAmE* ˈstreɪtəm/ *noun* (*pl.* **strata** /-tə/) **1** (*geology*) a layer or set of layers of rock, earth, etc. **2** (*formal*) a class in a society: *people from all social strata*

stra·tus /ˈstreɪtəs; ˈstrɑːtəs/ *noun* [U] (*technical*) a type of cloud that forms a continuous grey sheet covering the sky

stra·vaig (also **stra·vage**) /strəˈveɪɡ/ *verb* [I] (+ **adv./prep.**) (*IrishE, ScotE*) to walk around without an aim

straw /strɔː/ *noun* **1** [U] STEMS of WHEAT or other grain plants that have been cut and dried. Straw is used for making MATS, hats, etc, for packing things to protect them, and as food for animals or for them to sleep on: *a mattress filled with straw* ◇ *a straw hat* ➲ compare HAY **2** [C] a single STEM or piece of straw: *He was leaning over the gate chewing on a straw.* **3** (also **ˈdrinking straw**) a thin tube of plastic or paper that you suck a drink through ➲ VISUAL VOCAB page V29

IDM **clutch/grasp at ˈstraws** to try all possible means to find a solution or some hope in a difficult or unpleasant situation, even though this seems very unlikely **the last/final ˈstraw | the ˌstraw that breaks the camel's ˈback** the last in a series of bad events, etc. that makes it impossible for you to accept a situation any longer **a straw in the ˈwind** (*BrE*) a small sign of what might happen in the future ➲ more at BRICK *n.*, DRAW *v.*

straw·berry /ˈstrɔːbəri; *NAmE* -beri/ *noun* (*pl.* -ies) a soft red fruit with very small yellow seeds on the surface, that grows on a low plant: *strawberries and cream* ◇ *strawberry plants* ➲ VISUAL VOCAB page V26

ˌstrawberry ˈblonde (also **ˌstrawberry ˈblond**) *adj.* (of hair) a light reddish-yellow colour

ˌstraw ˈpoll (*NAmE* also **ˌstraw ˈvote**) *noun* an occasion when a number of people are asked in an informal way to give their opinion about sth or to say how they are likely to vote in an election

stray /streɪ/ *verb, adj., noun*

■ ***verb*** **1** [I] (+ **adv./prep.**) to move away from the place where you should be, without intending to: *He strayed into the path of an oncoming car.* ◇ *Her eyes kept straying over to the clock on the wall.* **2** [I] (+ **adv./prep.**) to begin to think about or discuss a different subject from the one you should be thinking about or discussing: *My mind kept straying back to our last talk together.* ◇ *We seem to be straying from the main theme of the debate.* **3** [I] (of a person who is married or in a relationship) to have a sexual relationship with sb who is not your usual partner

■ ***adj.*** [only before noun] **1** (of animals normally kept as pets) away from home and lost; having no home: *stray dogs* **2** separated from other things or people of the same kind: *A civilian was killed by a* ***stray bullet***. ◇ *a few stray hairs*

■ ***noun*** **1** an animal that has got lost or separated from its owner or that has no owner ➲ see also WAIF **2** a person or thing that is not in the right place or is separated from others of the same kind

streak /striːk/ *noun, verb*

■ ***noun*** **1** a long thin mark or line that is a different colour from the surface it is on: *streaks of grey in her hair* ◇ *dirty streaks on the window* ➲ SYNONYMS at MARK **2** a part of a person's character, especially an unpleasant part: *a ruthless/vicious/mean streak* ◇ *a streak of cruelty* **3** a series of successes or failures, especially in a sport or in gambling: *a streak of good luck* ◇ *to hit* (= have) *a* ***winning streak*** ◇ *to be on a* ***winning/losing streak*** ◇ *a* ***lucky/unlucky streak***

■ ***verb*** **1** [T] to mark or cover sth with streaks: **~ sth** *Tears streaked her face.* ◇ *She's had her hair streaked* (= had special chemicals put on her hair so that it has attractive coloured lines in it). ◇ **~ sth with sth** *His face was streaked with mud.* **2** [I] **+ adv./prep.** to move very fast in a particular direction SYN **speed**: *A car pulled out and streaked off down the road.* **3** [I] (+ **adv./prep.**) (*informal*) to run through a public place with no clothes on as a way of getting attention

streak·er /ˈstriːkə(r)/ *noun* a person who runs through a public place with no clothes on as a way of getting attention

streaky /ˈstriːki/ *adj.* marked with lines of a different colour: *streaky blonde hair* ◇ *The wallpaper was streaky with grease.* ◇ (*BrE*) *streaky bacon* (= with layers of fat in it)

stream 0‑ /striːm/ *noun, verb*

■ ***noun*** **1** 0‑ a small narrow river: *mountain streams* ➲ VISUAL VOCAB page V2 ➲ see also DOWNSTREAM, UP-

STREAM, THE GULF STREAM **2** ~ (**of sth**) a continuous flow of liquid or gas: *A stream of blood flowed from the wound.* ➲ see also BLOODSTREAM **3** ~ (**of sth/sb**) a continuous flow of people or vehicles: *I've had a **steady stream** of visitors.* ◇ *Cars filed past in an endless stream.* **4** ~ **of sth** a large number of things that happen one after the other: *a **constant stream of** enquiries* ◇ *The agency provided me with a **steady stream** of work.* **5** (*especially BrE*) a group of students of the same age and level of ability in some schools: *She was put into the fast stream.*

IDM **be/come on 'stream** to be in operation or available: *The new computer system comes on stream next month.*

■ ***verb*** **1** [I, T] (of liquid or gas) to move or pour out in a continuous flow; to produce a continuous flow of liquid or gas: (+ **adv./prep.**) *Tears streamed down his face.* ◇ *a streaming cold* (= with a lot of liquid coming from the nose) ◇ ~ **with sth** *Her head was streaming with blood.* ◇ ~ **from sth** *Blood was streaming from her head.* ◇ *Black smoke streamed from the exhaust.* ◇ ~ **sth** *The exhaust streamed black smoke.* **2** (of people or things) [I] + **adv./prep.** to move somewhere in large numbers, one after the other: *People streamed across the bridge.* **3** [I] to move freely, especially in the wind or water: *Her scarf streamed behind her.* **4** (*especially BrE*) (*NAmE* usually **track**) [T, usually passive] ~ **sb** (in schools) to put school students into groups according to their ability: *Pupils are streamed for French and Maths.* **5** [T] ~ **sth** (*computing*) to play video or sound on a computer by receiving it as a continuous stream, from the Internet for example, rather than needing to wait until the whole of the material has been DOWNLOADED

stream·er /'stri:mə(r)/ *noun* **1** a long narrow piece of coloured paper, used to decorate a place for a party or other celebration **2** a long narrow piece of cloth or other material

stream·ing /'stri:mɪŋ/ *noun* [U] (*especially BrE*) = BANDING: *Streaming within comprehensive schools is common practice.*

stream·line /'stri:mlaɪn/ *verb* [usually passive] **1** ~ **sth** to give sth a smooth even shape so that it can move quickly and easily through air or water: *The cars all have a new streamlined design.* **2** ~ **sth** to make a system, an organization, etc. work better, especially in a way that saves money: *The production process is to be streamlined.*

ˌstream of 'consciousness *noun* [U] a continuous flow of ideas, thoughts, and feelings, as they are experienced by a person; a style of writing that expresses this without using the usual methods of description and conversation

street /stri:t/ *noun, adj.*

■ ***noun*** **1** [C] (*abbr.* St, st) a public road in a city or town that has houses and buildings on one side or both sides: *The bank is just across the street.* ◇ *to walk **along/down/up the street*** ◇ *the town's narrow cobbled streets* ◇ *92nd Street* ◇ *10 Downing Street* ◇ *He is used to being recognized **in the street**.* ◇ *a **street map/plan** of York* ◇ ***street theatre/musicians*** ◇ *My office is **at street level*** (= on the ground floor). ◇ *It's not safe to **walk the streets** at night.* ➲ note at ROAD ➲ see also BACKSTREET, HIGH STREET, SIDE STREET **2** [sing.] the ideas and opinions of ordinary people, especially people who live in cities, which are considered important: *The feeling I get from the street is that we have a good chance of winning this election.* ◇ *The **word on the street** is that it's not going to happen.*

IDM (**out**) **on the 'streets/'street** (*informal*) without a home; outside, not in a house or other building: *the problems of young people living on the streets* ◇ *If it had been left to me I would have put him out on the street long ago.* **on/walking the 'streets** working as a PROSTITUTE **'streets ahead** (**of sb/sth**) (*BrE, informal*) much better or more advanced than sb/sth else: *a country that is streets ahead in the control of environmental pollution* **the streets are ˌpaved with 'gold** (*saying*) used to say that it seems easy to make money in a place (**right**) **up your 'street** (*especially BrE*) (*NAmE* usually (**right**) **up your 'alley**) (*informal*) very suitable for you because it is sth that you know a lot about or are very interested in: *This job seems right up your street.* ➲ more at EASY *adj.*, HIT *v.*, MAN *n.*

■ ***adj.*** [only before noun] informal and based on the daily life of ordinary people in cities: *street sports such as skateboarding and skating* ◇ *street newspapers sold by the homeless* ◇ *street culture/dance/law*

street·board /'stri:tbɔ:d; *NAmE* -bɔ:rd/ (also **Snakeboard™**) *noun* two small boards joined with a short pole and with wheels on, which you stand on and ride as a sport ▸ **street·board·ing** (also **snake·board·ing**) *noun* [U]

street·car /'stri:tkɑ:(r)/ (also **trol·ley**) (both *US*) (*BrE* **tram, tram·car**) *noun* a vehicle driven by electricity, that runs on rails along the streets of a town and carries passengers ➲ VISUAL VOCAB page V47

'street cred (also **cred**) (*informal*) (also *less frequent* **'street credibility**) *noun* [U] a way of behaving and dressing that is acceptable to young people, especially those who live in cities and have experienced the problems of real life: *Those clothes do nothing for your street cred.*

ˌstreet 'furniture *noun* [U] (*technical*) equipment such as road signs, street lights, etc. placed at the side of a road

'street light (*BrE* also **'street lamp**) *noun* a light at the top of a tall post in the street ➲ compare LAMP POST ➲ VISUAL VOCAB page V2

'street people *noun* (*especially NAmE*) people who have no home and who live outside in a town SYN **the homeless**

'street-smart *adj.* (*NAmE*) = STREETWISE ➲ compare BOOK-SMART

'street smarts *noun* [pl.] (*NAmE, informal*) the knowledge and experience that is needed to deal with the difficulties and dangers of life in a big city

ˌstreet 'theatre (*BrE*) (*NAmE* **ˌstreet 'theater**) *noun* [U] plays or other performances that are done in the street

'street value *noun* [usually sing.] a price for which sth that is illegal or has been obtained illegally can be sold: *drugs with a street value of over £1 million*

street·walk·er /'stri:twɔ:kə(r)/ *noun* (*old-fashioned*) a PROSTITUTE who looks for customers on the streets

street·wise /'stri:twaɪz/ (*NAmE* also **'street-smart**) *adj.* (*informal*) having the knowledge and experience that is needed to deal with the difficulties and dangers of life in a big city

strength /streŋθ/ *noun*

▸ BEING PHYSICALLY STRONG **1** [U, sing.] the quality of being physically strong: *He pushed against the rock with all his strength.* ◇ *It may take a few weeks for you to build up your strength again.* ◇ *He had a physical strength that matched his outward appearance.* ◇ ~ **to do sth** *She didn't have the strength to walk any further.* **2** [U] the ability that sth has to resist force or hold heavy weights without breaking or being damaged: *the strength of a rope* ➲ see also INDUSTRIAL-STRENGTH

▸ BEING BRAVE **3** [U, sing.] the quality of being brave and determined in a difficult situation: *During this ordeal he was able to draw strength from his faith.* ◇ *She has a remarkable **inner strength**.* ◇ *You have shown great **strength of character**.*

▸ POWER/INFLUENCE **4** [U] the power and influence that sb/sth has: *Political power depends upon economic strength.* ◇ *Their superior military strength gives them a huge advantage.* ◇ *to negotiate from **a position of strength*** ◇ *The rally was intended to be **a show of strength** by the socialists.*

▸ OF OPINION/FEELING **5** [U] how strong or deeply felt an opinion or a feeling is: *the strength of public opinion* ◇ *This view has recently gathered strength* (= become stronger or more widely held). ◇ *I was surprised by the strength of her feelings.*

▸ ADVANTAGE **6** [C] a quality or an ability that a person or thing has that gives them an advantage: *The ability to keep*

S

calm is one of her many strengths. ◇ the **strengths and weaknesses** of an argument
▸ OF NATURAL FORCE **7** [U] how strong a natural force is: *the strength of the sun* ◇ *wind strength* ◇ *the strength and direction of the tide*
▸ OF FLAVOUR **8** [U, C] how strong a particular flavour or substance is: *Add more curry powder depending on the strength required.* ◇ *a range of beers with different strengths* (= with different amounts of alcohol in them)
▸ OF CURRENCY **9** [U] how strong a country's CURRENCY (= unit of money) is in relation to other countries' CURRENCIES: *the strength of the dollar*
▸ NUMBER IN GROUP **10** [U] the number of people in a group, a team or an organization: *The strength of the workforce is about to be doubled from 3 000 to 6 000.* ◇ *The team will be back* ***at full strength*** (= with all the best players) *for the next match.* ◇ *The protesters turned out* ***in strength*** (= in large numbers). ◇ *These cuts have left the local police force* ***under strength*** (= with fewer members than it needs).
IDM **go from ˌstrength to ˈstrength** to become more and more successful: *Since her appointment the department has gone from strength to strength.* **on the strength of sth** because sb has been influenced or persuaded by sth: *I got the job on the strength of your recommendation.* ➲ more at TOWER *n.*

strength·en /ˈstreŋθn/ *verb* [I, T] to become stronger; to make sb/sth stronger: *Her position in the party has strengthened in recent weeks.* ◇ *Yesterday the pound strengthened against the dollar.* ◇ *The wind had strengthened overnight.* ◇ **~ sb/sth** *Repairs are necessary to strengthen the bridge.* ◇ *The exercises are designed to strengthen your stomach muscles.* ◇ *The move is clearly intended to strengthen the President's position as head of state.* ◇ *The new manager has strengthened the side by bringing in several younger players.* ◇ *Their attitude only strengthened his resolve to fight on.* ◇ *The new evidence will strengthen their case.* OPP **weaken**

strenu·ous /ˈstrenjuəs/ *adj.* **1** needing great effort and energy SYN **arduous**: *a strenuous climb* ◇ *Avoid* ***strenuous exercise*** *immediately after a meal.* ◇ *How about a stroll in the park?* ***Nothing too strenuous.*** **2** showing great energy and determination: *The ship went down although* ***strenuous efforts*** *were made to save it.* ▸ **strenu·ous·ly** *adv.*: *He still works out strenuously every morning.* ◇ *The government* ***strenuously denies*** *the allegations.*

strep throat /ˌstrep ˈθrəʊt; *NAmE* ˈθroʊt/ *noun* (*NAmE, informal*) an infection of the throat

strepto·coc·cus /ˌstreptəˈkɒkəs; *NAmE* -ˈkɑːkəs/ *noun* (*pl.* **streptococci** /ˌstreptəˈkɒkaɪ; *NAmE* -ˈkɑːkaɪ/) (*medical*) a type of bacteria, some types of which can cause serious infections and illnesses

S

stress AW /stres/ *noun, verb*
■ *noun*
▸ MENTAL PRESSURE **1** [U, C] pressure or worry caused by the problems in sb's life: *Things can easily go wrong when people are* ***under stress.*** ◇ *to suffer from stress* ◇ *coping with stress* ◇ *She failed to withstand the* ***stresses and strains*** *of public life.* ◇ ***stress-related*** *illnesses* ◇ ***emotional/mental stress*** ◇ *Stress is often a factor in the development of long-term sickness.* ◇ ***stress management*** (= dealing with stress) ➲ SYNONYMS at PRESSURE ➲ COLLOCATIONS at DIET
▸ PHYSICAL PRESSURE **2** [U, C] **~ (on sth)** pressure put on sth that can damage it or make it lose its shape: *When you have an injury you start putting stress on other parts of your body.* ◇ *a* ***stress fracture*** *of the foot* (= one caused by such pressure)
▸ EMPHASIS **3** [U] **~ (on sth)** special importance given to sth: *She* ***lays*** *great* ***stress on*** *punctuality.* ◇ *I think the company places too much stress on cost and not enough on quality.*
▸ ON WORD/SYLLABLE **4** [U, C] (*phonetics*) an extra force used when pronouncing a particular word or syllable: *We worked on pronunciation, stress and intonation.* ◇ ***primary/secondary stress*** ◇ *In 'strategic' the stress falls on the second syllable* ➲ compare INTONATION
▸ IN MUSIC **5** [U, C] extra force used when making a particular sound in music
▸ ILLNESS **6** [U] illness caused by difficult physical conditions: *Those most vulnerable to heat stress are the elderly.*
■ *verb*
▸ EMPHASIZE **1** [T] to emphasize a fact, an idea, etc: **~ sth** *He stressed the importance of a good education.* ◇ **~ that...** *I must stress that everything I've told you is strictly confidential.* ◇ **+ speech** *'There is,' Johnson stressed, 'no real alternative.'* ◇ **it is stressed that...** *It must be stressed that this disease is very rare.* ◇ **~ how, what, etc...** *I cannot stress too much how important this is.*
▸ WORD/SYLLABLE **2** [T] **~ sth** to give extra force to a word or syllable when saying it: *You stress the first syllable in 'happiness'.* **3** [I, T] to become or make sb become too anxious or tired to be able to relax: **~ out** *I try not to stress out when things go wrong.* ◇ **~ sb (out)** *Driving in cities really stresses me (out).*

Synonyms

stress
emphasize

These words both mean to give extra force to a syllable, word or phrase when you are saying it.

stress to give extra force to a word or syllable when saying it: *You stress the first syllable in 'happiness'.*

emphasize to give extra force to a word or phrase when saying it, especially to show that it is important: *'Let nothing ... nothing,' he emphasized the word, 'tempt you.'*

stressed AW /strest/ *adj.*
1 (also *informal* **ˌstressed ˈout**) [not before noun] too anxious and tired to be able to relax **2** (of a syllable) pronounced with emphasis OPP **unstressed** **3** [only before noun] (*technical*) that has had a lot of physical pressure put on it: *stressed metal*

stress·ful AW /ˈstresfl/ *adj.* causing a lot of anxiety and worry: *a stressful job* ◇ *It was a stressful time for all of us.*

ˈstress mark *noun* a mark used to show where the stress is placed on a particular word or syllable ➲ see also PRIMARY STRESS, SECONDARY STRESS

ˈstress-timed *adj.* (*phonetics*) (of a language) having a regular rhythm of PRIMARY STRESSES. English is considered to be a stress-timed language. ➲ compare SYLLABLE-TIMED

stretch /stretʃ/ *verb, noun*
■ *verb*
▸ MAKE BIGGER/LOOSER **1** [T, I] **~ (sth)** to make sth longer, wider or looser, for example by pulling it; to become longer, etc. in this way: *Is there any way of stretching shoes?* ◇ *This sweater has stretched.* **2** [I] (of cloth) to become bigger or longer when you pull it and return to its original shape when you stop: *The jeans stretch to provide a perfect fit.*
▸ PULL TIGHT **3** [T] to pull sth so that it is smooth and tight: **~ sth** *Stretch the fabric tightly over the frame.* ◇ **~ sth + adj.** *Make sure that the rope is stretched tight.*
▸ YOUR BODY **4** [I, T] to put your arms or legs out straight and contract your muscles: *He stretched and yawned lazily.* ◇ **~ sth** *The exercises are designed to stretch and tone your leg muscles.*
▸ REACH WITH ARM **5** [I, T] to put out an arm or a leg in order to reach sth: **+ adv./prep.** *She stretched across the table for the butter.* ◇ **~ sth + adv./prep.** *I stretched out a hand and picked up the book.*
▸ OVER AREA **6** [I] **+ adv./prep.** to spread over an area of land SYN **extend**: *Fields and hills stretched out as far as we could see.*
▸ OVER TIME **7** [I] **+ adv./prep.** to continue over a period of time: *The town's history stretches back to before 1500.* ◇ *The talks look set to stretch into a second week.*
▸ MONEY/SUPPLIES/TIME **8** [I] **~ (to sth)** (used in negative sentences and questions about an amount of money) to be enough to buy or pay for sth: *I need a new car, but my savings won't stretch to it.* **9** [T] **~ sb/sth** to make use of a lot of

your money, supplies, time, etc: *The influx of refugees has* ***stretched*** *the country's resources* ***to the limit.*** ◇ *We can't take on any more work—we're fully stretched as it is.*

▸ SB'S SKILL/INTELLIGENCE **10** [T] **~ sb/sth** to make use of all sb's skill, intelligence, etc: *I need a job that will stretch me.*

▸ TRUTH/BELIEF **11** [T] **~ sth** to use sth in a way that would not normally be considered fair, acceptable, etc: *He admitted that he had maybe* ***stretched the truth*** *a little* (= not been completely honest). ◇ *The play's plot* ***stretches*** *credulity* ***to the limit.***

IDM **stretch your 'legs** (*informal*) to go for a short walk after sitting for some time: *It was good to get out of the car and stretch our legs.* **stretch a 'point** to allow or do sth that is not usually acceptable, especially because of a particular situation ➲ more at RULE *n.*

PHR V **ˌstretch 'out | ˌstretch yourself 'out** to lie down, usually in order to relax or sleep: *He stretched himself out on the sofa and fell asleep.*

■ ***noun***

▸ AREA OF LAND/WATER **1** [C] **~ (of sth)** an area of land or water, especially a long one: *an unspoilt stretch of coastline* ◇ *a particularly dangerous stretch of road* ◇ *You rarely see boats on this stretch of the river.*

▸ PERIOD OF TIME **2** [C] a continuous period of time SYN **spell**: *They worked in four-hour stretches.* ◇ *She used to read for hours* ***at a stretch*** (= without stopping). **3** [C, usually sing.] (*informal*) a period of time that sb spends in prison: *He did a ten-year stretch for fraud.*

▸ OF BODY **4** [C, U] an act of stretching out your arms or legs or your body and contracting the muscles; the state of being stretched: *We got out of the car and* ***had a*** *good* ***stretch.*** ◇ *Only do these more difficult stretches when you are warmed up.* ◇ *Stay in this position and feel the stretch in your legs.*

▸ OF FABRIC **5** [U] the ability to be made longer or wider without breaking or tearing: *You need a material with plenty of stretch in it.* ◇ *stretch jeans*

▸ ON RACETRACK **6** [C, usually sing.] a straight part at the end of a racing track SYN **straight**: *the* ***finishing/home stretch*** ◇ (*figurative*) *The campaign has entered its final stretch.*

IDM **at full 'stretch** using as much energy as possible, or the greatest possible amount of supplies: *Fire crews have been operating at full stretch.* **not by any stretch of the imagination | by no stretch of the imagination** used to say strongly that sth is not true, even if you try to imagine or believe it: *She could not, by any stretch of the imagination, be called beautiful.*

stretch·er /ˈstretʃə(r)/ *noun, verb*

■ ***noun*** a long piece of strong cloth with a pole on each side, used for carrying sb who is sick or injured and who cannot walk: *He was carried off on a stretcher.* ◇ *stretcher cases* (= people too badly injured to be able to walk)

■ ***verb*** **~ sb + adv./prep.** [usually passive] to carry sb somewhere on a stretcher: *He was stretchered off the pitch with a broken leg.*

ˈstretcher-bearer *noun* a person who helps to carry a stretcher, especially in a war or when there is a very serious accident

ˌstretch ˈlimo *noun* (also *formal* **ˌstretch limouˈsine**) a very large car that has been made longer so that it can have extra seats

ˈstretch marks *noun* [pl.] the marks that are left on a person's skin after it has been stretched, particularly after a woman has been pregnant

stretchy /ˈstretʃi/ *adj.* (**stretch·ier, stretchi·est**) that can easily be made longer or wider without tearing or breaking: *stretchy fabric*

strew /struː/ *verb* (**strewed, strewed** or **strewed, strewn** /struːn/) **1** [usually passive] to cover a surface with things SYN **scatter**: **~ A on, over, across, etc. B** *Clothes were strewn across the floor.* ◇ **~ B with A** *The floor was strewn with clothes.* ◇ (*figurative*) *The way ahead is strewn with difficulties.* **2 ~ sth** to be spread or lying over a surface: *Leaves strewed the path.*

strewth /struːθ/ *exclamation* (*old-fashioned, BrE, slang*) used to express surprise, anger, etc.

stri·ation /straɪˈeɪʃn/ *noun* [usually pl.] (*technical*) a striped pattern on sth, especially on a muscle

stricken /ˈstrɪkən/ *adj.* (*formal*) **1** seriously affected by an unpleasant feeling or disease or by a difficult situation: *She raised her stricken face and begged for help.* ◇ *We went to the aid of the stricken boat.* ◇ **~ with/by sth** *Whole villages were stricken with the disease.* ◇ *He was stricken by a heart attack on his fiftieth birthday.* **2** (in compounds) seriously affected by the thing mentioned: *poverty-stricken families* ➲ see also GRIEF-STRICKEN, HORROR-STRICKEN, PANIC-STRICKEN

strict 🔑 /strɪkt/ *adj.* (**strict·er, strict·est**)

1 🔑 that must be obeyed exactly: ***strict rules/regulations/discipline*** ◇ *She left* ***strict instructions*** *that she was not to be disturbed.* ◇ *He told me* ***in the strictest confidence*** (= on the understanding that I would tell nobody else). ◇ *She's on a very strict diet.* **2** 🔑 demanding that rules, especially rules about behaviour, should be obeyed: *a* ***strict teacher/parent/disciplinarian*** ◇ *She's very strict about things like homework.* ◇ *They were always very strict with their children.* **3** 🔑 obeying the rules of a particular religion, belief, etc. exactly: *a strict Muslim* ◇ *a strict vegetarian* **4** [usually before noun] very exact and clearly defined: *It wasn't illegal* ***in the strict sense*** *(****of the word****).* ▸ **strict·ness** *noun* [U]

strict·ly 🔑 /ˈstrɪktli/ *adv.*

1 🔑 with a lot of control and rules that must be obeyed: *She was brought up very strictly.* ◇ *The industry is strictly regulated.* **2** 🔑 used to emphasize that sth happens or must happen in all circumstances SYN **absolutely**: *Smoking is strictly forbidden.* ◇ *My letter is, of course, strictly private and confidential.* **3** in all details; exactly: *This is not strictly true.* **4** used to emphasize that sth only applies to one particular person, thing or situation SYN **purely**: *We'll look at the problem from a strictly legal point of view.* ◇ *I know we're friends, but this is strictly business.*

IDM **ˈstrictly speaking** if you are using words or rules in their exact or correct sense: *Strictly speaking, the book is not a novel, but a short story.*

stric·ture /ˈstrɪktʃə(r)/ *noun* (*formal*) **1** [usually pl.] **~ (on sb/sth)** a severe criticism, especially of sb's behaviour **2 ~ (against/on sth)** a rule or situation that restricts your behaviour SYN **restriction**: *strictures against civil servants expressing political opinions*

stride /straɪd/ *verb, noun*

■ ***verb*** (*pt* **strode** /strəʊd; *NAmE* stroʊd/) [I] (not used in the perfect tenses) **+ adv./prep.** to walk with long steps in a particular direction: *We strode across the snowy fields.* ◇ *She came striding along to meet me.*

■ ***noun*** **1** one long step; the distance covered by a step SYN **pace**: *He crossed the room in two strides.* ◇ *I was gaining on the other runners* ***with every stride.*** **2** your way of walking or running: *his familiar purposeful stride* ◇ *She did not slow her stride until she was face to face with us.* **3** an improvement in the way sth is developing: *We're* ***making great strides*** *in the search for a cure.* **4 strides** [pl.] (*AustralE, informal*) trousers/pants

IDM **get into your 'stride** (*BrE*) (*NAmE* **hit (your) 'stride**) to begin to do sth with confidence and at a good speed after a slow, uncertain start **put sb off their 'stride** to make sb take their attention off what they are doing and stop doing it so well **(match sb) ˌstride for 'stride** to keep doing sth as well as sb else, even though they keep making it harder for you **take sth in your 'stride** (*BrE*) (*NAmE* **take sth in 'stride**) to accept and deal with sth difficult without letting it worry you too much **without breaking 'stride** (*especially NAmE*) without stopping what you are doing

stri·dent /ˈstraɪdnt/ *adj.* **1** having a loud, rough and unpleasant sound: *a strident voice* ◇ *strident music* **2** aggressive and determined: *He is a strident advocate of nuclear power.* ◇ *strident criticism* ▸ **stri·dency** /ˈstraɪdənsi/ *noun* [U] **stri·dent·ly** *adv.*

S

strife /straɪf/ *noun* **1** [U] (*formal* or *literary*) angry or violent disagreement between two people or groups of people SYN **conflict**: *civil strife* ◇ *The country was torn apart by strife.* **2** (*AustralE, NZE*) trouble or difficulty of any kind

strike /straɪk/ *verb, noun*

■ ***verb*** (**struck, struck** /strʌk/)
▸ HIT SB/STH **1** [T] **~ sb/sth** (*formal*) to hit sb/sth hard or with force: *The ship struck a rock.* ◇ *The child ran into the road and was struck by a car.* ◇ *The tree was* ***struck by lightning.*** ◇ *He fell, striking his head on the edge of the table.* ◇ *The stone struck her on the forehead.* ➲ SYNONYMS at HIT **2** [T] **~ sb/sth (sth)** (*formal*) to hit sb/sth with your hand or a weapon: *She struck him in the face.* ◇ *He struck the table with his fist.* ◇ *Who struck the first blow* (= started the fight)*?*
▸ KICK/HIT BALL **3** [T] **~ sth** (*formal*) to hit or kick a ball, etc: *He walked up to the penalty spot and struck the ball firmly into the back of the net.*
▸ ATTACK **4** [I] to attack sb/sth, especially suddenly: *The lion crouched ready to strike.* ◇ *Police fear that the killer may strike again.*
▸ OF DISASTER/DISEASE **5** [I, T] to happen suddenly and have a harmful or damaging effect on sb/sth: *Two days later tragedy struck.* ◇ **~ sb/sth** *The area was struck by an outbreak of cholera.*
▸ THOUGHT/IDEA/IMPRESSION **6** [T] (not used in the progressive tenses) (of a thought or an idea) to come into sb's mind suddenly: **~ sb** *An awful thought has just struck me.* ◇ *I was struck by her resemblance to my aunt.* ◇ **it strikes sb how, what, etc...** *It suddenly struck me how we could improve the situation.* **7** [T] to give sb a particular impression: **~ sb (as sth)** *His reaction struck me as odd.* ◇ *How does the idea strike you?* ◇ *She strikes me as a very efficient person.* ◇ **it strikes sb that...** *It strikes me that nobody is really in favour of the changes.*
▸ OF LIGHT **8** [T] **~ sth** to fall on a surface: *The windows sparkled as the sun struck the glass.*
▸ DUMB/DEAF/BLIND **9** [T] **~ sb + adj.** [usually passive] to put sb suddenly into a particular state: ***to be struck dumb/deaf/blind***
▸ OF WORKERS **10** [I] **~ (for sth)** to refuse to work, because of a disagreement over pay or conditions: *The union has voted to strike for a pay increase of 6%.* ◇ *Striking workers picketed the factory.*
▸ MATCH **11** [T, I] **~ (sth)** to rub sth such as a match against a surface so that it produces a flame; to produce a flame when rubbed against a rough surface: *to strike a match on a wall* ◇ *The sword struck sparks off the stone floor.* ◇ *The matches were damp and he couldn't make them strike.*
▸ OF CLOCK **12** [I, T] to show the time by making a ringing noise, etc. SYN **chime**: *Did you hear the clock strike?* ◇ **~ sth** *The clock has just struck three.*
▸ MAKE SOUND **13** [T] **~ sth** to produce a musical note, sound, etc. by pressing a key or hitting sth: *to strike a chord on the piano*
▸ GOLD/OIL, ETC. **14** [T] **~ sth** to discover gold, oil, etc. by digging or DRILLING: *They had struck oil!*
▸ GO WITH PURPOSE **15** [I] **~ (off/out)** to go somewhere with great energy or purpose: *We left the road and struck off across the fields.*

IDM **be 'struck by/on/with sb/sth** (*informal*) to be impressed or interested by sb/sth; to like sb/sth very much: *I was struck by her youth and enthusiasm.* ◇ *We're not very struck on that new restaurant.* **strike a 'balance (between A and B)** to manage to find a way of being fair to two opposing things; to find an acceptable position which is between two things **strike a 'bargain/'deal** to make an agreement with sb in which both sides have an advantage **strike a blow for/against/at sth** to do sth in support of/against a belief, principle, etc: *He felt that they had struck a blow for democracy.* **strike fear, etc. into sb/sb's heart** (*formal*) to make sb be afraid, etc. **strike 'gold** to find or do sth that brings you a lot of success or money: *He has struck gold with his latest novel.* **strike it 'rich** (*informal*) to get a lot of money, especially suddenly or unexpectedly **strike (it) 'lucky** (*informal*) to have good luck **strike a 'pose/an 'attitude** to hold your body in a particular way to create a particular impression **strike while the iron is 'hot** (*saying*) to make use of an opportunity immediately ORIGIN This expression refers to a blacksmith making a shoe for a horse. He has to strike/hammer the iron while it is hot enough to bend into the shape of the shoe. **within 'striking distance (of sth)** near enough to be reached or attacked easily; near enough to reach or attack sth easily: *The beach is within striking distance.* ◇ *The cat was now within striking distance of the duck.* ➲ more at CHORD, HARD *adj.*, HOME *adv.*, LIGHTNING *n.*, NOTE *n.*, PAY DIRT

PHR V **'strike at sb/sth 1** to try to hit sb/sth, especially with a weapon: *He struck at me repeatedly with a stick.* **2** to cause damage or have a serious effect on sb/sth: *to strike at the root of the problem* ◇ *criticisms that* ***strike at the heart of*** *the party's policies* **,strike 'back (at/against sb)** to try to harm sb in return for an attack or injury you have received **,strike sb 'down** [usually passive] **1** (of a disease, etc.) to make sb unable to lead an active life; to make sb seriously ill; to kill sb: *He was struck down by cancer at the age of thirty.* **2** to hit sb very hard, so that they fall to the ground **,strike sth ↔'down** (*especially NAmE*) to decide that a law is illegal and should not apply: *The Supreme Court struck down a Texas state law.* **,strike sth↔'off** to remove sth with a sharp blow; to cut sth off: *He struck off the rotten branches with an axe.* **,strike sb/sth 'off (sth)** (also **,strike sb/sth 'from sth**) to remove sb/sth's name from sth, such as the list of members of a professional group: *Strike her name off the list.* ◇ *The doctor was struck off* (= not allowed to continue to work as a doctor) *for incompetence.* **,strike 'out 1** to start being independent: *I knew it was time I struck out on my own.* **2** (*NAmE, informal*) to fail or be unsuccessful: *The movie struck out and didn't win a single Oscar.* **,strike 'out (at sb/sth) 1** to aim a sudden violent blow at sb/sth: *He lost his temper and struck out wildly.* **2** to criticize sb/sth, especially in a public speech or in a book or newspaper: *In a recent article she strikes out at her critics.* **,strike 'out | ,strike sb↔'out** (in BASEBALL) to fail to hit the ball three times and therefore not be allowed to continue hitting; to make sb do this ➲ related noun STRIKEOUT **,strike sth↔'out/'through** to remove sth by drawing a line through it SYN **cross out**: *The editor struck out the whole paragraph.* **,strike 'out (for/towards sth)** to move in a determined way (towards sth): *He struck out* (= started swimming) *towards the shore.* **,strike 'up (with sth) | ,strike 'up sth** (of a band, an ORCHESTRA, etc.) to begin to play a piece of music: *The orchestra struck up and the curtain rose.* ◇ *The band struck up a waltz.* **,strike 'up sth (with sb)** to begin a friendship, a relationship, a conversation, etc: *He would often strike up conversations with complete strangers.*

■ ***noun***
▸ OF WORKERS **1** a period of time when an organized group of employees of a company stops working because of a disagreement over pay or conditions: *the train drivers' strike* ◇ *a strike by teachers* ◇ *an* ***unofficial/a one-day strike*** ◇ *Air traffic controllers are threatening to* ***come out on/go on strike.*** ◇ *Half the workforce are now* ***(out) on strike.*** ◇ *The train drivers have voted to* ***take strike action.*** ◇ *The student union has called for a* ***rent strike*** (= a refusal to pay rent as a protest). ➲ see also GENERAL STRIKE, HUNGER STRIKE
▸ ATTACK **2** a military attack, especially by aircraft dropping bombs: *an* ***air strike*** ◇ *They decided to launch a* ***pre-emptive strike.***
▸ HITTING/KICKING **3** [usually sing.] an act of hitting or kicking sth/sb: *His spectacular strike in the second half made the score 2–0.* ➲ see also BIRD STRIKE, LIGHTNING
▸ IN BASEBALL **4** an unsuccessful attempt to hit the ball
▸ IN BOWLING **5** a situation in TENPIN BOWLING when a player knocks down all the pins with the first ball
▸ DISCOVERY OF OIL **6** [usually sing.] a sudden discovery of sth valuable, especially oil
▸ BAD THING/ACTION **7** (*NAmE*) **~ (against sb/sth)** a bad thing or action that damages sb/sth's reputation: *The amount of fuel that this car uses is a big strike against it.*

IDM **,three strikes and you're 'out | the ,three 'strikes rule** used to describe a law which says that people who commit three crimes will automatically go to prison ORIGIN From baseball, in which a batter who misses the ball three times is out.

'strike-bound *adj.* unable to operate because employees have stopped working as a protest: *a strike-bound airport*

'strike-breaker *noun* a person who continues to work while other employees are on strike; a person who is employed to replace people who are on strike ➲ compare BLACKLEG ▸ **'strike-breaking** *noun* [U]

'strike force *noun* [C+sing./pl. v.] a military or police force that is ready to act quickly when necessary

strike·out /'straɪkaʊt/ *noun* (in BASEBALL) a situation in which the player who is supposed to be hitting the ball has to stop because he or she has tried to hit the ball three times and failed

striker /'straɪkə(r)/ *noun* **1** a worker who has stopped working because of a disagreement over pay or conditions **2** (in football (SOCCER)) a player whose main job is to attack and try to score goals

'strike rate *noun* [usually sing.] (*sport*) the number of times a player is successful in relation to the number of times they try to score or win

'strike zone *noun* (in BASEBALL) the area between a BATTER's upper arms and their knees, to which the ball must be PITCHED

strik·ing 0-ᵾ /'straɪkɪŋ/ *adj.*
1 0-ᵾ interesting and unusual enough to attract attention SYN **marked**: *a striking feature* ◇ *She bears* ***a striking resemblance*** *to her older sister.* ◇ ***In striking contrast to*** *their brothers, the girls were both intelligent and charming.* ➲ LANGUAGE BANK at SURPRISING **2** 0-ᵾ very attractive, often in an unusual way SYN **stunning**: *striking good looks* ▸ **strik·ing·ly** *adv.*: *The two polls produced strikingly different results.* ◇ *She is strikingly beautiful.*

Strim·mer™ /'strɪmə(r)/ *noun* (*BrE*) an electric garden tool held in the hands and used for cutting grass that is difficult to cut with a larger machine ➲ VISUAL VOCAB page V16

Strine /'straɪn/ (also **strine**) *noun* (*informal*) **1** [U] Australian English, especially when spoken in an informal way and with a strong accent **2** [C] an Australian ▸ **Strine** *adj.*: *a Strine accent*

string 0-ᵾ /strɪŋ/ *noun, verb, adj.*
■ *noun*
▸ FOR TYING/FASTENING **1** 0-ᵾ [U, C] material made of several threads twisted together, used for tying things together; a piece of string used to fasten or pull sth or keep sth in place: *a* ***piece/length of string*** ◇ *He wrapped the package in brown paper and tied it with string.* ◇ *The key is hanging on a string by the door.* ➲ picture at ROPE ➲ see also DRAWSTRING, G-STRING, THE PURSE STRINGS
▸ THINGS JOINED **2** 0-ᵾ [C] a set or series of things that are joined together, for example on a string: *a string of pearls* ◇ *The molecules join together to form long strings.* ➲ VISUAL VOCAB page V53
▸ SERIES **3** [C] a series of things or people that come closely one after another: *a string of hits* ◇ *He owns a string of racing stables.*
▸ COMPUTING **4** [C] a series of characters (= letters, numbers, etc.)
▸ MUSICAL INSTRUMENTS **5** [C] a tightly stretched piece of wire, NYLON, or CATGUT on a musical instrument, that produces a musical note when the instrument is played ➲ VISUAL VOCAB pages V30, V31 **6 the strings** [pl.] the group of musical instruments in an ORCHESTRA that have strings, for example VIOLINS; the people who play them: *The opening theme is taken up by the strings.* ➲ VISUAL VOCAB page V30 ➲ compare BRASS, PERCUSSION, WOODWIND
▸ ON TENNIS RACKET **7** [C] any of the tightly stretched pieces of NYLON, etc. in a RACKET, used for hitting balls in TENNIS and some other games
▸ CONDITIONS **8 strings** [pl.] special conditions or restrictions: *Major loans like these always come with strings.* ◇ *It's a business proposition, pure and simple.* ***No strings attached.***
IDM **have another string/more strings to your bow** (*BrE*) to have more than one skill or plan that you can use if you need to ➲ more at APRON, LONG *adj.*, PULL *v.*
■ *verb* (strung, strung /strʌŋ/)
▸ HANG DECORATION **1** to hang or tie sth in place, especially as decoration: **~ sth + adv./prep.** *We strung paper lanterns up in the trees.* ◇ **~ A on, along, in, etc. B** *Flags were strung out along the route.* ◇ **~ B with A** *The route was strung with flags.*
▸ JOIN THINGS **2 ~ sth + adv./prep.** to put a series of small objects on string, etc; to join things together with string, etc. SYN **thread**: *She had strung the shells on a silver chain.* ◇ (*figurative*) *carbon atoms strung together to form giant molecules*
▸ RACKET/MUSICAL INSTRUMENT **3 ~ sth** to put a string or strings on a RACKET or musical instrument ➲ see also HIGHLY STRUNG
PHR V **,string sb a'long** (*informal*) to allow sb to believe sth that is not true, for example that you love them, intend to help them, etc: *She has no intention of giving you a divorce; she's just stringing you along.* **,string a'long** (**with sb**) (*BrE, informal*) to go somewhere with sb, especially because you have nothing else to do **,string sth↔'out** to make sth last longer than expected or necessary: *They seem determined to string the talks out for an indefinite period.* ➲ see also STRUNG OUT **,string sth↔to'gether** to combine words or phrases to form sentences: *I can barely string two words together in Japanese.* **,string sb↔'up** (*informal*) to kill sb by hanging them, especially illegally
■ *adj.* [only before noun]
▸ MUSICAL INSTRUMENT **1** consisting of musical instruments that have strings; connected with these musical instruments: *a string quartet* ◇ *a string player*
▸ MADE OF STRING **2** made of string or sth like string: *a string bag/vest*

,string 'bass *noun* a word for a DOUBLE BASS, used especially by JAZZ musicians

,string 'bean *noun* **1** (*BrE*) = RUNNER BEAN **2** (*NAmE*) = GREEN BEAN

,stringed 'instrument *noun* any musical instrument with strings that you play with your fingers or with a BOW ➲ VISUAL VOCAB page V30

strin·gent /'strɪndʒənt/ *adj.* (*formal*) **1** (of a law, rule, regulation, etc.) very strict and that must be obeyed: *stringent air quality regulations* **2** (of financial conditions) difficult and very strictly controlled because there is not much money: *the government's stringent economic policies* ▸ **strin·gency** /-nsi/ *noun* [U]: *a period of financial stringency* **strin·gent·ly** *adv.*: *The rules are stringently enforced.*

string·er /'strɪŋə(r)/ *noun* a journalist who is not on the regular staff of a newspaper, but who often supplies stories for it

,string 'vest *noun* (*especially BrE*) a man's VEST made from a type of cloth with a regular pattern of large holes

stringy /'strɪŋi/ *adj.* (*disapproving*) **1** (of hair) long and thin and looking as if it has not been washed **2** (of food) containing long thin pieces like string and difficult to chew: *tough, stringy meat* **3** (of a person or part of their body) thin so that you can see the muscles: *a stringy neck*

strip 0-ᵾ /strɪp/ *verb, noun*
■ *verb* (-pp-)
▸ TAKE OFF CLOTHES **1** 0-ᵾ [I, T] to take off all or most of your clothes or another person's clothes SYN **undress**: *I stripped and washed myself all over.* ◇ **~ down to sth** *She stripped down to her underwear.* ◇ **~ (sth) off** *We stripped off and ran down to the water.* ◇ **~ sb (to sth)** *He stood there* ***stripped to the waist*** (= he had no clothes on the upper part of his body). ◇ **~ sb + adj.** *He was* ***stripped naked*** *and left in a cell.* **2** [I] to take off your clothes as a form of entertainment; to perform a STRIPTEASE
▸ REMOVE LAYER **3** 0-ᵾ [T] to remove a layer from sth, especially so that it is completely exposed: **~ sth (off)** *Strip off all the existing paint.* ◇ *After the guests had gone, I stripped all*

S

the beds (= removed all the sheets in order to wash them). ◇ **~ A off/from B** *Deer had stripped all the bark off the tree.* ◇ **~ B of A** *Deer had stripped the tree of its bark.*
▸ REMOVE EVERYTHING **4** [T] to remove all the things from a place and leave it empty: **~ sth (out)** *We had to strip out all the old wiring and start again.* ◇ **~ sth + adj.** *Thieves had stripped the house bare.*
▸ MACHINE **5** [T] **~ sth (down)** to separate a machine, etc. into parts so that they can be cleaned or repaired SYN **dismantle**: *They taught us how to strip down a car engine and put it back together again.*
▸ PUNISHMENT **6** [T] **~ sb of sth** to take away property or honours from sb, as a punishment: *He was disgraced and stripped of his title.*
PHR V **ˌstrip sth↔aˈway 1** to remove a layer from sth: *First, you need to strip away all the old plaster.* **2** to remove anything that is not true or necessary: *The movie aims to strip away the lies surrounding Kennedy's life.*
■ ***noun***
▸ LONG, NARROW PIECE **1** a long narrow piece of paper, metal, cloth, etc: *a strip of material* ◇ *Cut the meat into strips.* ➲ see also RUMBLE STRIP **2** a long narrow area of land, sea, etc: *the Gaza Strip* ◇ *The islands are separated by a narrow strip of water.* ➲ see also AIRSTRIP, LANDING STRIP
▸ OF SPORTS TEAM **3** [usually sing.] (*BrE*) (*NAmE* **uniform**) the uniform that is worn by the members of a sports team when they are playing: *Juventus in their famous black and white strip* ◇ *the team's* ***away strip*** (= that they use when playing games away from home) ➲ VISUAL VOCAB page V36
▸ TAKING CLOTHES OFF **4** [usually sing.] an act of taking your clothes off, especially in a sexually exciting way and in front of an audience: *to do a strip* ◇ *a strip show* ➲ see also STRIPTEASE
▸ STREET **5** (*NAmE*) a street that has many shops, stores, restaurants, etc. along it: *Sunset Strip*
▸ PICTURE STORY **6** (*NAmE*) = COMIC STRIP IDM see TEAR[1] *v.*

ˌstrip carˈtoon (also **cartoon**) *noun* (*BrE*) = COMIC STRIP

ˈstrip club (also **ˈstrip joint** especially in *NAmE*) *noun* a club where people go to watch performers take their clothes off in a sexually exciting way

stripe /straɪp/ *noun*
1 a long narrow line of colour, that is a different colour from the areas next to it: *a zebra's black and white stripes* ◇ *a white tablecloth with red stripes* ➲ see also PINSTRIPE, THE STARS AND STRIPES **2** a narrow piece of cloth, often in the shape of a V, that is worn on the uniform of a soldier or police officer to show their rank **3** (*especially NAmE*) a type, category or opinion: *politicians* ***of every stripe*** ◇ *commentators* ***of all*** *political* ***stripes*** ◇ *She's an educator* ***of a*** *very* ***different*** *stripe.*

striped /straɪpt/ (also *BrE informal* **stripy**) *adj.* marked with a pattern of stripes: *a striped shirt* ◇ *a blue and white striped jacket* ➲ VISUAL VOCAB page V50

ˈstrip light *noun* a light consisting of a long glass tube that is used especially in offices, kitchens, etc. ▸ **ˈstrip lighting** *noun* [U]

strip·ling /ˈstrɪplɪŋ/ *noun* (*old-fashioned* or *humorous*) a young man who is older than a boy but who does not seem to be a real man yet

ˈstrip mall *noun* (*NAmE*) a line of shops/stores and restaurants beside a main road

ˈstrip mining *noun* [U] (*NAmE*) a type of mining in which coal is taken out of the ground near the surface ➲ see also OPENCAST

ˌstripped-ˈdown *adj.* [usually before noun] **1** keeping only the most basic or essential features, with everything else removed: *a stripped-down version of the song* **2** (of a machine or vehicle) taken to pieces, with all the parts removed

strip·per /ˈstrɪpə(r)/ *noun* **1** [C] a performer who takes his or her clothes off in a sexually exciting way in front of an audience: *a male stripper* **2** [U, C] (especially in compounds) a substance or tool that is used for removing paint, etc. from sth: *paint stripper*

ˈstrip search *noun* an act of searching a person for illegal drugs, weapons, etc, for example at an airport or in a prison, after they have been made to take off all their clothes ▸ **ˈstrip-search** *verb* **~ sb**

strip·tease /ˈstrɪptiːz/ *noun* [C, U] a form of entertainment, for example in a bar or club, when a performer removes his or her clothes in a sexually exciting way, usually to music, in front of an audience

stripy (also **stripey**) /ˈstraɪpi/ *adj.* (*BrE, informal*) = STRIPED: *a stripy jumper*

strive /straɪv/ *verb* (**strove** /strəʊv; *NAmE* stroʊv/, **striven** /ˈstrɪvn/) or (*less frequent* **strived, strived**) [I] (*formal*) to try very hard to achieve sth: **~ (for th)** *We encourage all members to strive for the highest standards.* ◇ **~ (against sth)** *striving against corruption* ◇ **~ to do sth** *Newspaper editors all strive to be first with a story.* ▸ **striv·ing** *noun* [U, sing.]: *our striving for perfection*

strobe /strəʊb; *NAmE* stroʊb/ (also **ˈstrobe light**) *noun* a bright light that flashes rapidly on and off, used especially at DISCOS

strob·ing /ˈstrəʊbɪŋ; *NAmE* ˈstroʊb-/ *noun* [U] (*technical*) the effect, sometimes seen in the lines and stripes in a television picture, of sudden movements or flashing

strode *past tense* of STRIDE

stroke /strəʊk; *NAmE* stroʊk/ *noun, verb*
■ ***noun***
▸ HITTING MOVEMENT **1** an act of hitting a ball, for example with a BAT or RACKET: *What a beautiful stroke!* ◇ *He won by two strokes* (= in GOLF, by taking two fewer strokes than his opponent). **2** a single movement of the arm when hitting sb/sth: *His punishment was six strokes of the cane.*
▸ IN SWIMMING/ROWING **3** any of a series of repeated movements in swimming or ROWING: *She took a few more strokes to reach the bank.* ➲ VISUAL VOCAB page V37 **4** (often in compounds) a style of swimming: *Butterfly is the only stroke I can't do.* ➲ see also BACKSTROKE, BREASTSTROKE **5** the person who sets the speed at which everyone in a boat ROWS
▸ GENTLE TOUCH **6** [usually sing.] (*especially BrE*) an act of moving your hand gently over a surface, usually several times: *He gave the cat a stroke.*
▸ OF PEN/BRUSH **7** a mark made by moving a pen, brush, etc. once across a surface: *to paint with fine brush strokes* ◇ ***At the stroke of a pen*** (= by signing sth) *they removed thousands of people from the welfare system.*
▸ ACTION **8 ~ (of sth)** a single successful action or event: *Your idea was a* ***stroke of genius.*** ◇ *It was a* ***stroke of luck*** *that I found you here.* ◇ *It was a* ***bold stroke*** *to reveal the identity of the murderer on the first page.* ◇ *She* ***never does a stroke*** (***of work***) (= never does any work). ➲ see also MASTERSTROKE
▸ OF CLOCK **9** each of the sounds made by a clock or bell giving the hours: *At the first stroke it will be 9 o'clock exactly.* ◇ ***on the stroke of*** *three* (= at 3 o'clock exactly)
▸ ILLNESS **10** a sudden serious illness when a blood VESSEL (= tube) in the brain bursts or is blocked, which can cause death or the loss of the ability to move or to speak clearly: *to* ***have/suffer a stroke*** ◇ *The stroke left him partly paralysed.*
IDM **at a (single) ˈstroke | at one ˈstroke** with a single immediate action: *They threatened to cancel the whole project at a stroke.* **put sb off their ˈstroke** (*BrE*) to make sb make a mistake or hesitate in what they are doing
■ ***verb***
▸ TOUCH GENTLY **1 ~ sth** (*especially BrE*) to move your hand gently and slowly over an animal's fur or hair: *He's a beautiful dog. Can I stroke him?* ➲ see also PET **2 ~ sth/sb** to move your hand gently over a surface, sb's hair, etc: *He stroked her hair affectionately.*
▸ MOVE STH GENTLY **3 ~ sth + adv./prep.** to move sth some-

where with a gentle movement: *She stroked away his tears.* ◇ *He stroked the ball between the posts.*
▸ BE NICE TO SB **4 ~ sb** (*informal, especially NAmE*) to be very nice to sb, especially to get them to do what you want

'stroke play (also **'medal play**) *noun* [U] a way of playing GOLF in which your score depends on the number of times you hit the ball in the whole game, rather than on the number of holes that you win ➲ compare MATCH PLAY

stroll /strəʊl; *NAmE* stroʊl/ *verb, noun*
■ ***verb*** [I] (**+ adv./prep.**) to walk somewhere in a slow relaxed way: *People were strolling along the beach.*
■ ***noun*** a slow relaxed walk: *We went for a stroll in the park.*

stroll·er /'strəʊlə(r); *NAmE* 'stroʊ-/ *noun* **1** a person who is enjoying a slow relaxed walk **2** (*NAmE*) (*BrE* **buggy, push·chair**) a small folding seat on wheels in which a small child sits and is pushed along ➲ picture at PUSHCHAIR

strong 🔑 /strɒŋ; *NAmE* strɔːŋ/ *adj.* (**strong·er** /-ɡə(r)/, **strong·est** /-ɡɪst/)

> **WORD FAMILY**
> strong *adj.*
> strongly *adv.*
> strength *noun*
> strengthen *verb*

▸ HAVING PHYSICAL POWER **1** 🔑 (of people, animals, etc.) having a lot of physical power so that you can lift heavy weights, do hard physical work, etc: *strong muscles* ◇ *She wasn't a strong swimmer* (= she could not swim well). ◇ *He's strong enough to lift a car!* **2** 🔑 (of a natural or physical force) having great power: *Stay indoors in the middle of the day, when the sun is strongest.* ◇ *a **strong wind/current*** ◇ *a strong magnet* **3** 🔑 having a powerful effect on the body or mind: *a strong drug*
▸ HAVING POWER OVER PEOPLE **4** 🔑 having a lot of power or influence: *a **strong leader/government*** **5 the strong** [pl.] people who are rich or powerful
▸ HARD TO RESIST/DEFEAT/ATTACK **6** 🔑 very powerful and difficult for people to fight against or defeat: *a strong team* ◇ (*figurative*) *The temptation to tell her everything was very strong.* **7** 🔑 (of an argument, evidence, etc.) difficult to attack or criticize: *There is strong evidence of a link between exercise and a healthy heart.* ◇ *You have a strong case for getting your job back.*
▸ OPINION/BELIEF/FEELING **8** [only before noun] (of a person) holding an opinion or a belief very firmly and seriously **SYN** **firm**: *a **strong supporter/opponent** of the government* **9** 🔑 (of an opinion, a belief or a feeling) very powerful: *strong support for the government* ◇ *People have strong feelings about this issue.*
▸ NOT EASILY BROKEN **10** 🔑 (of objects) not easily broken or damaged; made well: *a strong chair*
▸ NOT EASILY UPSET **11** 🔑 not easily upset or frightened; not easily influenced by other people: *You need strong nerves to ride a bike in London.* ◇ *It's difficult, I know. But be strong!* ◇ *a strong personality* ➲ see also HEADSTRONG, STRONG-MINDED, STRONG-WILLED
▸ LIKELY TO SUCCEED **12** 🔑 likely to succeed or happen: *a strong candidate for the job* ◇ *You're **in a strong position** to negotiate a deal.* ◇ *There's **a strong possibility** that we'll lose the game.*
▸ GOOD AT STH **13** good at sth: *The play has a very strong cast.* ◇ *Mathematics was never my **strong point*** (= I was never very good at it).
▸ NUMBER **14** 🔑 great in number: *There was a strong police presence at the demonstration.* **15** used after numbers to show the size of a group: *a 5 000-strong crowd* ◇ *The crowd was 5 000 strong.*
▸ HEALTHY **16** 🔑 (of a person) not easily affected by disease; healthy: *Are you feeling stronger now after your rest?* ➲ SYNONYMS at WELL
▸ FIRMLY ESTABLISHED **17** 🔑 firmly established; difficult to destroy: *a strong marriage* ◇ *The college has strong links with local industry.*
▸ BUSINESS **18** 🔑 (of prices, an economy, etc.) having a value that is high or increasing: *strong share prices* ◇ *The euro is getting stronger against the dollar.* **19** (of a business or an industry) in a safe financial position: *Their catering business remained strong despite the recession.*
▸ EASY TO SEE/HEAR/FEEL/SMELL **20** 🔑 easy to see, hear, feel or smell; very great or INTENSE: *a strong smell* ◇ *a strong feeling of nausea* ◇ *a strong voice* (= loud) ◇ *strong colours* ◇ *a face with strong features* (= large and noticeable) ◇ *She spoke with a strong Australian accent.* ◇ *He was under strong pressure to resign.*
▸ FOOD **21** 🔑 having a lot of flavour: *strong cheese*
▸ DRINKS **22** 🔑 containing a lot of a substance: *strong black coffee*
▸ WORDS **23** (of words or language) having a lot of force, often causing offence to people: *The movie has been criticized for **strong language*** (= swearing).
▸ GRAMMAR **24** [usually before noun] (of a verb) forming the past tense and past participle by changing a vowel, not by adding a regular ending, for example *sing, sang*
▸ PHONETICS **25** [usually before noun] used to describe the way some words are pronounced when they have stress. For example, the strong form of *and* is /ænd/ . **OPP** **weak**
▸ **strong·ly** 🔑 *adv.*: *a strongly built boat* ◇ *a light shining strongly* ◇ *a strongly worded protest* ◇ *He was strongly opposed to the idea.* ◇ *This is an issue I feel strongly about* (= I have firm opinions about). ◇ *The room smelt strongly of polish.*
IDM **be a bit 'strong** (*BrE, informal*) used to say that you think what sb has said is unfair or too critical **be 'strong on sth 1** to be good at sth: *I'm not very strong on dates* (= I can't remember the dates of important events). **2** to have a lot of sth: *The report was strong on criticism, but short on practical suggestions.* **be sb's 'strong suit** to be a subject that sb knows a lot about: *I'm afraid geography is not my strong suit.* **come on 'strong** (*informal*) to make your feelings clear in an aggressive way, especially your sexual feelings towards sb **going 'strong** (*informal*) to continue to be healthy, active or successful: *My grandmother is 90 and still going strong.* **,have a ,strong 'stomach** to be able to see or do unpleasant things without feeling sick or upset ➲ more at CARD *n.*

'strong-arm *adj.* [only before noun] (*disapproving*) using threats or violence in order to make people do what you want: *to use **strong-arm tactics** against your political opponents*

strong·box /'strɒŋbɒks; *NAmE* 'strɔːŋbɑːks/ *noun* a strong, usually metal, box for keeping valuable things in

,strong 'force *noun* (*physics*) one of the four FUNDAMENTAL FORCES in the universe, which holds the parts of the NUCLEUS of an atom together ➲ see also ELECTROMAGNETISM, GRAVITY, WEAK FORCE

strong·hold /'strɒŋhəʊld; *NAmE* 'strɔːŋhoʊld/ *noun* **1** an area in which there is a lot of support for a particular belief or group of people, especially a political party: *a Republican stronghold/a stronghold of Republicanism* **2** a castle or a place that is strongly built and difficult to attack **3** an area where there are a large number of a particular type of animal: *This valley is one of the last strongholds of the Siberian tiger.*

strong·man /'strɒŋmæn; *NAmE* 'strɔːŋ-/ *noun* (*pl.* **-men** /-men/) **1** a leader who uses threats or violence to rule a country **2** a physically very strong man, especially sb who performs in a CIRCUS

,strong-'minded *adj.* having strong opinions that are not easily influenced by what other people think or say **SYN** **determined**

strong·room /'strɒŋruːm; -rʊm; *NAmE* 'strɔːŋ-/ *noun* a room, for example in a bank, with thick walls and a strong solid door, where valuable items are kept

,strong 'safety *noun* (in AMERICAN FOOTBALL) a defending player who plays opposite the attacking team's strongest side

,strong-'willed *adj.* determined to do what you want to do, even if other people advise you not to

stron·tium /'strɒntiəm; 'strɒnʃ-; *NAmE* 'strɑːnʃ-; 'strɑːnt-/ *noun* [U] (*symb.* **Sr**) a chemical element. Strontium is a soft silver-white metal.

strop /strɒp; *NAmE* strɑːp/ *noun* [sing.] (*BrE, informal*) a very bad mood when you are annoyed about sth: ***Don't get in a strop**—I'm only a few minutes late.*

S

strophe /ˈstrəʊfi; *NAmE* ˈstroʊfi/ *noun* (*technical*) a group of lines forming a section of a poem ➲ compare STANZA ▸ **stroph·ic** /ˈstrəʊfɪk; *NAmE* ˈstroʊf-/ *adj.*

stroppy /ˈstrɒpi; *NAmE* ˈstrɑːpi/ *adj.* (*BrE, informal*) (**strop·pier, strop·pi·est**) (of a person) easily annoyed and difficult to deal with: *Don't* **get stroppy** *with me—it isn't my fault!*

strove *past tense* of STRIVE

struck *past tense, past part.* of STRIKE

struc·tural AW /ˈstrʌktʃərəl/ *adj.* [usually before noun] connected with the way in which sth is built or organized: *Storms have caused structural damage to hundreds of homes.* ◇ *structural changes in society* ▸ **struc·tur·al·ly** AW /-ərəli/ *adv.*: *The building is structurally sound.* ◇ *The languages are structurally different.*

ˌstructural enginˈeer *noun* a person whose job is to plan large buildings, bridges, etc.

struc·tur·al·ism /ˈstrʌktʃərəlɪzəm/ *noun* [U] (in literature, language and social science) a theory that considers any text as a structure whose various parts only have meaning when they are considered in relation to each other ➲ compare DECONSTRUCTION ▸ **struc·tur·al·ist** /-rəlɪst/ *noun, adj.*: *a structuralist approach*

ˌstructural linˈguistics *noun* [U] the part of LINGUISTICS that deals with language as a system of related structures

Synonyms

structure

framework • form • composition • construction • fabric

These are all words for the way the different parts of sth combine together or the way that sth has been made.

structure the way in which the parts of sth are connected together or arranged; a particular arrangement of parts: *the structure of the building/human body* ◇ *the social structure of society* ◇ *the grammatical structures of a language* ◇ *a salary structure*

framework a set of beliefs, ideas or rules that forms the basis of a system or society: *The report provides a framework for further research.*

form [U] the arrangement of parts in a whole, especially in a work of art of piece of writing: *As a photographer, shape and form were more important to him than colour.*

composition [U] (*rather formal*) the different parts or people that combine to form sth; the way in which they combine: *recent changes in the composition of the workforce*

construction [U] the way that sth has been built or made: *ships of steel construction*

fabric (*rather formal*) the basic structure of a society or an organization that enables it to function successfully: *This is a trend which threatens* **the very fabric of society**.

PATTERNS

- the **basic** structure/framework/form/composition/construction/fabric of sth
- a **simple/complex** structure/framework/form
- the **economic/political/social** structure/framework/composition/fabric of sth
- the **chemical/genetic** structure/composition of sth

struc·ture 0-w AW /ˈstrʌktʃə(r)/ *noun, verb*
■ *noun* **1** 0-w [U, C] the way in which the parts of sth are connected together, arranged or organized; a particular arrangement of parts: *the structure of the building* ◇ *changes in the social and economic structure of society* ◇ *the grammatical structures of a language* ◇ *a salary structure* **2** 0-w [C] a thing that is made of several parts, especially a building: *a stone/brick/wooden structure* ➲ SYNONYMS at BUILDING **3** 0-w [U, C] the state of being well organized or planned with all the parts linked together; a careful plan: *Your essay needs (a) structure.*
■ *verb* [usually passive] to arrange or organize sth into a system or pattern: **~ sth** *How well does the teacher structure the lessons?* ◇ *Make use of the toys in structured group activities.* ◇ **~ sth around sth** *The exhibition is structured around the themes of work and leisure.*

stru·del /ˈstruːdl/ *noun* [U, C] (from *German*) a cake made from pieces of fruit, especially apple, rolled in thin PASTRY and baked

strug·gle 0-w /ˈstrʌgl/ *verb, noun*
■ *verb* **1** 0-w [I] to try very hard to do sth when it is difficult or when there are a lot of problems: **~ (for sth)** *a country struggling for independence* ◇ *Shona* **struggled for breath.** ◇ *life as a struggling artist* (= one who is very poor) ◇ **~ to do sth** *They struggled just to pay their bills.* **2** 0-w [I] **+ adv./prep.** to move somewhere or do sth with difficulty: *I struggled up the hill with the heavy bags.* ◇ *Paul struggled out of his wheelchair.* **3** 0-w [I] to fight against sb/sth in order to prevent a bad situation or result: **~ (against sb/sth)** *He struggled against cancer for two years.* ◇ **~ (with sb/sth)** *Lisa struggled with her conscience before talking to the police.* **4** 0-w [I] to fight sb or try to get away from them: *I struggled and screamed for help.* ◇ **~ together** *Ben and Jack struggled together on the grass.* ◇ **~ with sb** *James was hit in the mouth as he struggled with the raiders.* ◇ **+ adj.** *How did she manage to* **struggle free**? **5** [I] **~ (with sb) (for sth)** to compete or argue with sb, especially in order to get sth: *rival leaders struggling for power*
PHR V **ˌstruggle aˈlong/ˈon** to continue despite problems
■ *noun* **1** 0-w [C] a hard fight in which people try to obtain or achieve sth, especially sth that sb else does not want them to have: *a* **power/leadership struggle** ◇ **~ (with sb) (for/against sth)** *a struggle for independence* ◇ **~ (with sb) (to do sth)** *He is engaged in a bitter struggle with his rival to get control of the company.* ◇ **~ (between A and B)** *the struggle between good and evil* ◇ *She will not give up her children without a struggle.* ➲ SYNONYMS at CAMPAIGN **2** 0-w [C] a physical fight between two people or groups of people, especially when one of them is trying to escape, or to get sth from the other: *There were no signs of a struggle at the murder scene.* ➲ SYNONYMS at FIGHT **3** 0-w [sing.] **~ (to do sth)** something that is difficult for you to do or achieve SYN **effort**: *It was a real struggle to be ready on time.*

strum /strʌm/ *verb* (**-mm-**) [I, T] **~ (on) sth** to play a GUITAR or similar instrument by moving your fingers up and down across the strings: *As she sang she strummed on a guitar.*

strum·pet /ˈstrʌmpɪt/ *noun* (*old use, disapproving*) a PROSTITUTE, or a woman who looks and behaves like one

strung *past tense, past part.* of STRING

ˌstrung ˈout *adj.* [not before noun] **1** spread out in a line: *a group of riders strung out along the beach* **2 ~ (on sth)** (*slang*) strongly affected by an illegal drug such as HEROIN

ˌstrung ˈup *adj.* [not before noun] (*BrE, informal*) very nervous, worried or excited

strut /strʌt/ *verb, noun*
■ *verb* (**-tt-**) [I] to walk proudly with your head up and chest out to show that you think you are important: *The players strutted and posed for the cameras.*
IDM **ˌstrut your ˈstuff** (*informal*) to proudly show your ability, especially at dancing or performing
■ *noun* **1** a long thin piece of wood or metal used to support or make part of a vehicle or building stronger **2** [sing.] (*disapproving*) an act of walking in a proud and confident way

strych·nine /ˈstrɪkniːn/ *noun* [U] a poisonous substance used in very small amounts as a medicine

St Swithin's Day /ˌsnt ˈswɪðɪnz deɪ; *NAmE* ˌseɪnt/ *noun* 15 July, a Christian festival. In Britain it is said that if it rains on this day it will rain for the next forty days.

stub /stʌb/ *noun, verb*
■ *noun* **1** a short piece of a cigarette, pencil, etc. that is left

S

when the rest of it has been used **2** the small part of a ticket, cheque, etc. that you keep as a record when you have given the main part to sb ➲ picture at MONEY

■ *verb* (-bb-) **~ your toe** (**against/on sth**) to hurt your toe by accident by hitting it against sth hard

PHR V ˌ**stub sth**↔ˈ**out** to stop a cigarette, etc. from burning by pressing the end against sth hard

stub·ble /ˈstʌbl/ *noun* [U] **1** the lower short stiff part of the STEMS of crops such as WHEAT that are left in the ground after the top part has been cut and collected **2** the short stiff hairs that grow on a man's face when he has not shaved recently ➲ VISUAL VOCAB page V49 ▶ **stub·bly** /ˈstʌbli/ *adj.*

stub·born /ˈstʌbən; *NAmE* -bərn/ *adj.* **1** (often *disapproving*) determined not to change your opinion or attitude SYN **obstinate**: *He was too stubborn to admit that he was wrong.* ◇ *She can be* ***as stubborn as a mule.*** ◇ *stubborn pride* ◇ *a stubborn resistance to change* ◇ *a stubborn refusal to listen* **2** difficult to get rid of or deal with SYN **persistent**: *a* ***stubborn cough/stain*** ◇ *a stubborn problem* ▶ **stub·born·ly** *adv.*: *She stubbornly refused to pay.* ◇ *Unemployment remains stubbornly high.* **stub·born·ness** *noun* [U]

stubby /ˈstʌbi/ *adj.*, *noun*

■ *adj.* [usually before noun] short and thick: *stubby fingers*

■ *noun* (*pl.* -ies) (*AustralE, NZE*) **1** [C] (*informal*) a small fat bottle of beer usually holding 0.375 litres **2 Stubbies™** [pl.] a pair of short trousers/pants for men

stucco /ˈstʌkəʊ; *NAmE* -koʊ/ *noun* [U] a type of PLASTER that is used for covering ceilings and the outside walls of buildings ▶ **stuc·coed** *adj.*: *a stuccoed wall*

stuck /stʌk/ *adj.* [not before noun] ➲ see also STICK *v.* **1** unable to move or to be moved: *The wheels were stuck in the mud.* ◇ *This drawer keeps* ***getting stuck.*** ◇ *She got the key stuck in the lock.* ◇ *I can't get out—I'm stuck.* **2** in an unpleasant situation or place that you cannot escape from: *We were stuck in traffic for over an hour.* ◇ *I hate being stuck at home all day.* **3 ~** (**on sth**) unable to answer or understand sth: *I got stuck on the first question.* ◇ *I'll help you if you're stuck.* **4 ~** (**for sth**) not knowing what to do in a particular situation: *If you're stuck for something to do tonight, come out with us.* ◇ *I've never known him to be stuck for words before.* **5 ~ with sb/sth** (*informal*) unable to get rid of sb/sth that you do not want: *I was stuck with him for the whole journey.*

IDM ˌ**get stuck ˈin** | ˌ**get stuck ˈinto sth** (*BrE, informal*) to start doing sth in an enthusiastic way, especially to start eating ➲ more at GROOVE, ROCK *n.*, TIME WARP

ˌ**stuck-ˈup** *adj.* (*informal, disapproving*) thinking that you are more important than other people and behaving in an unfriendly way towards them SYN **snobbish**

stud /stʌd/ *noun* **1** [C] a small piece of jewellery with a part that is pushed through a hole in your ear, nose, etc: *diamond studs* ➲ VISUAL VOCAB page V53 **2** [C] a small round piece of metal that is attached to the surface of sth, especially for decoration: *a leather jacket with studs on the back* **3** [C, usually pl.] (*BrE*) one of several small metal or plastic objects that are fixed to the bottom part of a FOOTBALL BOOT or running shoe ➲ VISUAL VOCAB page V53 ➲ compare CLEAT **4** [C] a small metal object used in the past for fastening a COLLAR onto a shirt ➲ see also PRESS STUD **5** [C, U] an animal, especially a horse, that is kept for breeding; a place where animals, especially horses, are kept for breeding: *a stud farm* ◇ *The horse was retired from racing and* ***put out to stud*** (= kept for breeding). **6** [C] (*informal*) a man who has many sexual partners and who is thought to be sexually attractive

stud·ded /ˈstʌdɪd/ *adj.* **1** decorated with small raised pieces of metal: *a studded leather belt* **2 ~ with sth** having a lot of sth on or in it: *The sky was clear and studded with stars.* ◇ *an essay studded with quotations* ➲ see also STAR-STUDDED ▶ **stud** *verb* (-dd-): **~ sth** *Stars studded the sky.*

stu·dent 🔑 /ˈstjuːdnt; *NAmE* ˈstuː-/ *noun* **1** 🔑 a person who is studying at a university or college: *a* ***medical/science, etc. student*** ◇ *a* ***graduate/postgraduate/research student*** ◇ *an* ***overseas student*** ◇ *a* ***student teacher/nurse*** ◇ *a* ***student grant/loan*** (= money that is given/lent to students to pay for their studies) ◇ ***student fees*** (= to pay for the cost of teaching) ◇ *She's a student at Sussex University.* ➲ see also MATURE STUDENT **2** 🔑 a person who is studying at a school, especially a SECONDARY SCHOOL: *a 15-year-old high school student* ➲ compare PUPIL ➲ see also A STUDENT **3 ~ of sth** (*formal*) a person who is very interested in a particular subject: *a keen student of human nature*

Synonyms

student

pupil • schoolboy/schoolchild/schoolgirl

These are all words for a child that attends school.

student a person who is studying in a school, especially an older child: *Students are required to be in school by 8.30.* ◇ *Any high school student could tell you the answer.*

pupil (*BrE*) a person who is being taught, especially a child in a school: *The school has over 850 pupils.* NOTE **Pupil** is used only in British English and is starting to become old-fashioned. **Student** is often preferred, especially by teachers and other people involved in education, and especially when talking about older children.

schoolboy/schoolgirl/schoolchild a boy, girl or child who attends school: *Since she was a schoolgirl she had dreamed of going on the stage.* NOTE These words emphasize the age of the children or this period in their lives; they are less often used to talk about teaching and learning: ~~*an able schoolboy/schoolgirl/schoolchild*~~

PATTERNS

- a(n) **good/bright/able/brilliant/star/outstanding** student/pupil
- a **naughty** schoolboy/schoolgirl/schoolchild
- a **disruptive** student/pupil
- a(n) **ex-/former** student/pupil
- a **school** student/pupil
- to **teach** students/pupils/schoolboys/schoolgirls/schoolchildren

More About

students

- A **student** is a person who is studying at a school, college, university, etc.
- An **undergraduate** is a student who is studying for their first degree at a university or college.
- In *BrE*, a **graduate** is a person who has completed a first degree at a university or college. In *NAmE* **graduate** is usually used with another noun and can also apply to a person who has finished high school: *a high school graduate* ◇ *a graduate student.*
- A **postgraduate** is a person who has finished a first degree and is doing advanced study or research. This is the usual term in *BrE*, but it is formal in *NAmE* and **graduate student** is usually used instead.

stu·dent·ship /ˈstjuːdəntʃɪp; *NAmE* ˈstuː-/ *noun* (*BrE*) one of a small number of places that a university gives to students who wish to continue studying or to do research after they have finished their degree; an amount of money that is given to a student who wins one of these places

ˌ**students' ˈunion** (also ˌ**student ˈunion**) *noun* **1** a building where students at a university or college can go to meet socially **2** (*BrE*) an association of students at a particular university or college, concerned with students' rights, living conditions, etc.

S

ˌ**student ˈteaching** (*US*) (*BrE* ˈ**teaching practice**) *noun* [U] the part of a course for people who are training to become teachers which involves teaching classes of students

stud·ied /ˈstʌdid/ *adj.* [only before noun] (*formal*) deliberate and carefully planned: *She introduced herself with studied casualness.*

stu·dio 0ᵂ /ˈstjuːdiəʊ; *NAmE* ˈstuːdioʊ/ *noun* (*pl.* -os) **1** 0ᵂ a room where radio or television programmes are recorded and broadcast from, or where music is recorded: *a **television studio** ◇ a **studio audience*** (= one in a studio, that can be seen or heard as a programme is broadcast) ◇ *a **recording studio*** **2** 0ᵂ a place where films/movies are made or produced **3** 0ᵂ a company that makes films/movies: *She works for a major Hollywood studio. ◇ a studio executive* **4** 0ᵂ a room where an artist works: *a sculptor's studio* **5** a place where dancing is taught or where dancers practise: *a dance studio* **6** (*BrE* also ˈ**studio flat**) (*NAmE* also ˈ**studio apartment**) a small flat/apartment with one main room for living and sleeping in and usually a kitchen and bathroom

stu·di·ous /ˈstjuːdiəs; *NAmE* ˈstuː-/ *adj.* spending a lot of time studying or reading SYN **scholarly**: *a studious young man*

stu·di·ous·ly /ˈstjuːdiəsli; *NAmE* ˈstuː-/ *adv.* in a way that is carefully planned and deliberate: *He studiously avoided answering the question.*

stud·muf·fin /ˈstʌdmʌfɪn/ *noun* (*informal, especially NAmE*) a man who is considered sexually attractive

study 0ᵂ /ˈstʌdi/ *noun, verb*

▪ ***noun*** (*pl.* -ies)

▸ ACTIVITY OF LEARNING **1** 0ᵂ [U] the activity of learning or gaining knowledge, either from books or by examining things in the world: *a room set aside for **private study** ◇ **academic/literary/scientific, etc. study** ◇ It is important to develop good **study skills**. ◇ Physiology is the study of how living things work.* **2** 0ᵂ **studies** [pl.] (*formal*) a particular person's learning activities, for example at a college or university: *to continue your studies*

▸ ACADEMIC SUBJECT **3** 0ᵂ **studies** [U+sing./pl. v.] used in the names of some academic subjects: *business/media/American studies*

▸ DETAILED EXAMINATION **4** 0ᵂ [U] the act of considering or examining sth in detail: *These proposals deserve careful study.* **5** 0ᵂ [C] a piece of research that examines a subject or question in detail: *to **make/carry out/conduct a study** ◇ **This study shows/confirms/suggests** that... ◇ a detailed study of how animals adapt to their environment* ⇨ COLLOCATIONS at SCIENTIFIC ⇨ see also CASE STUDY

▸ ROOM **6** 0ᵂ [C] a room, especially in sb's home, used for reading and writing

▸ ART **7** [C] a drawing or painting of sth, especially one done for practice or before doing a larger picture: *a study of Chartres Cathedral ◇ a nude study*

▸ MUSIC **8** (*BrE*) (also **étude** *NAmE, BrE*) [C] a piece of music designed to give a player practice in technical skills

▸ PERFECT EXAMPLE **9** [sing.] **~ (in sth)** (*formal*) a perfect example of sth: *His face was a study in concentration.*

IDM see BROWN *adj.*

▪ ***verb*** (stud·ies, study·ing, stud·ied, stud·ied)

▸ LEARN **1** 0ᵂ [T, I] **~ (for sth)** to spend time learning about a subject by reading, going to college, etc: **~ (sth)** *How long have you been studying English? ◇ Don't disturb Jane, she's studying for her exams.* ◇ **~ (sth) at...** *My brother studied at the Royal College of Art.* ◇ **~ (sth) under...** *a composer who studied under Nadia Boulanger* (= was taught by Nadia Boulanger) ◇ **~ to do/be sth** *Nina is studying to be an architect.* ⇨ COLLOCATIONS at EDUCATION

▸ EXAMINE CAREFULLY **2** 0ᵂ [T] **~ sth** to watch, or look at sb/sth carefully in order to find out sth: *Scientists are studying photographs of the planet for signs of life. ◇ He studied her face thoughtfully. ◇ Fran was studying the menu.* **3** 0ᵂ [T] to examine sth carefully in order to understand it: **~ sth** *We will study the report carefully before making a decision.* ◇ **~ how, what, etc...** *The group will study how the region coped with the loss of thousands of jobs.* ⇨ SYNONYMS at EXAMINE

ˈ**study bedroom** *noun* (*BrE*) a student's room containing a bed and a desk

ˈ**study hall** *noun* [U] (*NAmE*) a period of time during the school day when students study quietly on their own, usually with a teacher present

stuff 0ᵂ /stʌf/ *noun, verb*

▪ ***noun*** [U] **1** 0ᵂ (*informal*, sometimes *disapproving*) used to refer to a substance, material, group of objects, etc. when you do not know the name, when the name is not important or when it is obvious what you are talking about: *What's all that sticky stuff on the carpet? ◇ The chairs were covered in some sort of plastic stuff. ◇ This wine is good stuff.* ◇ (*disapproving*) *I don't know how you can eat that stuff! ◇ They sell stationery **and stuff*** (**like that**). ◇ *Where's all my stuff* (= my possessions)? ◇ (*disapproving*) *Could you move all that stuff off the table?* ⇨ see also FOODSTUFF ⇨ SYNONYMS at THING **2** 0ᵂ (*informal*) used to refer in a general way to things that people do, say, think, etc: *I've got loads of stuff to do today. ◇ I like reading **and stuff**. ◇ The band did some **great stuff** on their first album. ◇ This is all **good stuff**. Well done! ◇ What's all this 'Mrs Smith' stuff? Call me Anna. ◇ I don't believe in **all that stuff** about ghosts.* **3 ~** (**of sth**) (*formal* or *literary*) the most important feature of sth; something that sth else is based on or is made from: *The trip was magical; the stuff of which dreams are made. ◇ Parades and marches were **the very stuff of** politics in the region. ◇ Let's see what stuff you're made of* (= what sort of person you are). ⇨ see also HOT STUFF

IDM **do your ˈstuff** (*informal*) to do what you are good at or what you have been trained to do: *Some members of the team are just not doing their stuff* (= doing as well as they should). ◇ (*figurative*) *The medicine has clearly done its stuff.* **not give a ˈstuff** (*BrE, slang*) to not care at all about sth ˌ**stuff and ˈnonsense** *exclamation* (*old-fashioned, informal*) used to describe sth that is stupid or not true ⇨ more at KID *n.*, KNOW *v.*, STERN *adj.*, STRUT *v.*, SWEAT *v.*

▪ ***verb*** **1** to fill a space or container tightly with sth: **~ A with B** *She had 500 envelopes to stuff with leaflets.* ◇ **~ B in, into, under, etc. A** *She had 500 leaflets to stuff into envelopes.* ◇ **~ sth** *The fridge is stuffed to bursting.* ◇ **~ sth + adj.** *All the drawers **were stuffed full of** letters and papers.* **2 ~ sth + adv./prep.** to push sth quickly and carelessly into a small space SYN **shove**: *She stuffed the money under a cushion. ◇ His hands were stuffed in his pockets.* **3 ~ sth** to fill a vegetable, chicken, etc. with another type of food: *Are you going to stuff the turkey? ◇ stuffed peppers* **4** (*informal*) to eat a lot of food or too much food; to give sb a lot or too much to eat: **~ sb/yourself** *He sat at the table stuffing himself.* ◇ **~ sb/yourself with sth** *Don't stuff the kids with chocolate before their dinner.* ◇ **~ your face** *We stuffed our faces at the party.* **5** [usually passive] **~ sth** to fill the dead body of an animal with material and preserve it, so that it keeps its original shape and appearance: *They had had their pet dog stuffed.*

IDM **get ˈstuffed** (*BrE, informal*) used to tell sb in a rude and angry way to go away, or that you do not want sth ˈ**stuff it** (*informal*) used to show that you have changed your mind about sth or do not care about sth: *I didn't want a part in the play, then I thought—stuff it—why not?* **you, etc. can stuff sth** (*informal*) used to tell sb in a rude and angry way that you do not want sth: *I told them they could stuff their job.*

stuffed /stʌft/ *adj.* [not before noun] (*informal*) having eaten so much that you cannot eat anything else SYN **full**

ˌ**stuffed ˈanimal** *noun* **1** (*especially NAmE*) (*BrE* also ˌ**soft ˈtoy**) a toy in the shape of an animal, made of cloth and filled with a soft substance ⇨ VISUAL VOCAB page V32 **2** a dead animal that has been STUFFED: *stuffed animals in glass cases*

ˌ**stuffed ˈshirt** *noun* (*informal, disapproving*) a person who is very serious, formal or old-fashioned

ˌ**stuffed ˈup** *adj.* if you are **stuffed up**, your nose is blocked and you are not able to breathe easily

S

stuff·ing /ˈstʌfɪŋ/ *noun* [U] **1** (*NAmE* also **dress·ing**) a mixture of finely chopped food, such as bread, onions and HERBS, placed inside a chicken, etc. before it is cooked to give it flavour **2** soft material used to fill CUSHIONS, toys, etc. SYN **filling** IDM see KNOCK *v.*

stuffy /ˈstʌfi/ *adj.* (**stuff·ier**, **stuffi·est**) **1** (of a building, room, etc.) warm in an unpleasant way and without enough fresh air: *a stuffy room* ◇ *It gets very hot and stuffy in here in summer.* **2** (*informal, disapproving*) very serious, formal, boring or old-fashioned: *a stuffy, formal family* ◇ *plain, stuffy clothes* **3** (*especially NAmE*) if you have a **stuffy** nose, your nose is blocked because you have a cold ▶ **stuffi·ness** *noun* [U]

stul·ti·fy·ing /ˈstʌltɪfaɪɪŋ/ *adj.* (*formal*) making you feel very bored and unable to think of new ideas: *the stultifying effects of work that never varies* ▶ **stul·tify** *verb* (**stul·ti·fies**, **stul·ti·fy·ing**, **stul·ti·fied**, **stul·ti·fied**) **~ sb** **stul·ti·fy·ing·ly** *adv.*

stum·ble /ˈstʌmbl/ *verb* **1** [I] to hit your foot against sth while you are walking or running and almost fall SYN **trip**: *The child stumbled and fell.* ◇ **~ over/on sth** *I stumbled over a rock.* **2** [I] **+ adv./prep.** to walk or move in an unsteady way: *We were stumbling around in the dark looking for a candle.* **3** [I] **~ (over/through sth)** to make a mistake or mistakes and stop while you are speaking, reading to sb or playing music: *In her nervousness she stumbled over her words.* ◇ *I stumbled through the piano piece with difficulty.* ▶ **stum·ble** *noun*

PHR V ˈ**stumble across/on/upon sth/sb** to discover sth/sb unexpectedly: *Police have stumbled across a huge drugs ring.* ˈ**stumble into sth** to become involved in sth by chance: *I stumbled into acting when I left college.*

ˈ**stumbling block** *noun* **~ (to sth)** | **~ (to doing sth)** something that causes problems and prevents you from achieving your aim SYN **obstacle**

stump /stʌmp/ *noun, verb*

■ ***noun* 1** [C] the bottom part of a tree left in the ground after the rest has fallen or been cut down **2** [C] the end of sth or the part that is left after the main part has been cut, broken off or worn away: *the stump of a pencil* **3** [C] the short part of sb's leg or arm that is left after the rest has been cut off **4** [C, usually pl.] (in CRICKET) one of the set of three vertical wooden sticks (called **the stumps**) that form the WICKET **5 the stump** [sing.] (*informal, especially NAmE*) the fact of a politician before an election going to different places and trying to get people's support by making speeches: *The senator gave his standard stump speech.* ◇ *politicians* ***on the stump*** IDM see STIR *v.*

■ ***verb* 1** [T, usually passive] **~ sb** (*informal*) to ask sb a question that is too difficult for them to answer or give them a problem that they cannot solve SYN **baffle**: *I'm stumped. I don't know how they got here before us.* ◇ *Kate was* ***stumped for words*** (= unable to answer). **2** [I] **+ adv./prep.** to walk in a noisy, heavy way, especially because you are angry or upset SYN **stomp**: *He stumped off, muttering under his breath.* **3** [I, T] **+ adv./prep.** | **~ sth** (*NAmE*) to travel around making political speeches, especially before an election: *He stumped around the country trying to build up support.* **4** [T] **~ sb** (in CRICKET) to put a BATSMAN out of the game by touching the stumps with the ball when he or she is out of the area in which the ball can be hit

PHR V ˌ**stump ˈup (for sth)** | ˌ**stump ˈup sth (for sth)** (*BrE, informal*) to pay money for sth SYN **cough up**: *We were asked to stump up for the repairs.* ◇ *Who is going to stump up the extra money?*

stumpy /ˈstʌmpi/ *adj.* (*disapproving*) short and thick SYN **stubby**: *stumpy fingers* ◇ *a stumpy tail*

stun /stʌn/ *verb* (**-nn-**) **1 ~ sb/sth** to make a person or an animal unconscious for a short time, especially by hitting them on the head SYN **knock out**: *The fall stunned me for a moment.* ◇ *The animals are stunned before slaughter.* **2 ~ sb** to surprise or shock sb so much that they cannot think clearly or speak SYN **astound** ➲ SYNONYMS at SURPRISE **3 ~ sb** to impress sb very much SYN **amaze**: *They were stunned by the view from the summit.* ▶ **stunned** *adj.*: *She was too stunned to speak.* ◇ *There was a* ***stunned silence*** *when I told them the news.*

stung *past tense, past part.* of STING

ˈ**stun grenade** *noun* a small bomb that shocks people so that they cannot do anything, without seriously injuring them

ˈ**stun gun** *noun* a weapon that makes a person or an animal unconscious or unable to move for a short time, usually by giving them a small electric shock

stunk *past part.* of STINK

stun·ner /ˈstʌnə(r)/ *noun* (*informal*) **1** a person (especially a woman) or a thing that is very attractive or exciting to look at **2** something, such as a piece of news, that is very surprising or shocking

stun·ning /ˈstʌnɪŋ/ *adj.* (rather *informal*) **1** extremely attractive or impressive SYN **beautiful**: *You look absolutely stunning!* ◇ *a stunning view of the lake* **2** extremely surprising or shocking: *He suffered a stunning defeat in the election.* ▶ **stun·ning·ly** *adv.*: *stunningly beautiful* ◇ *a stunningly simple idea*

stunt /stʌnt/ *noun, verb*

■ ***noun* 1** a dangerous and difficult action that sb does to entertain people, especially as part of a film/movie: *He did all his own stunts.* ◇ *a stunt pilot* ➲ COLLOCATIONS at CINEMA **2** (sometimes *disapproving*) something that is done in order to attract people's attention: *a publicity stunt* **3** (*informal*) a stupid or dangerous act: *I've had enough of her childish stunts.* ◇ *Don't you ever* ***pull a stunt*** *like that again!*

■ ***verb* ~ sb/sth** to prevent sb/sth from growing or developing as much as they/it should: *The constant winds had stunted the growth of plants and bushes.* ◇ *His illness had not stunted his creativity.*

stunt·ed /ˈstʌntɪd/ *adj.* that has not been able to grow or develop as much as it should: *stunted trees* ◇ *the stunted lives of children deprived of education*

stunt·man /ˈstʌntmæn/, **stunt·woman** /ˈstʌntwʊmən/ *noun* (*pl.* **-men** /-men/, **-women** /-wɪmɪn/) a person whose job is to do dangerous things in place of an actor in a film/movie, etc; a person who does dangerous things in order to entertain people

stu·pefy /ˈstjuːpɪfaɪ; *NAmE* ˈstuː-/ *verb* (**stu·pe·fies**, **stu·pe·fy·ing**, **stu·pe·fied**, **stu·pe·fied**) [often passive] **~ sb** to surprise or shock sb; to make sb unable to think clearly: *He was stupefied by the amount they had spent.* ◇ *She was stupefied with cold.* ▶ **stu·pe·fac·tion** /ˌstjuːpɪˈfækʃn; *NAmE* ˌstuː-/ *noun* [U]

stu·pe·fy·ing /ˈstjuːpɪfaɪɪŋ; *NAmE* ˈstuː-/ *adj.* **1** making you unable to think clearly: *stupefying boredom* **2** very surprising or shocking ▶ **stu·pe·fy·ing·ly** *adv.*: *The party was stupefyingly dull.*

stu·pen·dous /stjuːˈpendəs; *NAmE* stuː-/ *adj.* extremely large or impressive, especially greater or better than you expect SYN **staggering**: *stupendous achievements* ◇ *stupendous costs* ▶ **stu·pen·dous·ly** *adv.*

stu·pid 0‑w /ˈstjuːpɪd; *NAmE* ˈstuː-/ *adj., noun*

■ ***adj.*** (**stu·pider**, **stu·pidest**) HELP **more stupid** and **most stupid** are also common **1** 0‑w showing a lack of thought or good judgement SYN **foolish**, **silly**: *a stupid mistake* ◇ *It was a pretty stupid thing to do.* ◇ *I was* ***stupid enough*** *to believe him.* ◇ ***It was stupid of you*** *to get involved.* **2** 0‑w (*disapproving*) (of a person) slow to learn or understand things; not clever or intelligent: *He'll manage—he isn't stupid.* ◇ *Forgetting my notes made me* ***look stupid.*** **3** [only before noun] (*informal*) used to emphasize that you are annoyed with sb/sth: *I can't get the stupid thing open!* ◇ *Get your stupid feet off the chair!* ▶ **stu·pid·ly** *adv.*: *I stupidly agreed to lend him the money.* ◇ *Todd stared stupidly at the screen.*

■ ***noun*** [sing.] (*informal*) if you call sb **stupid**, you are telling them, usually in a joking way, that you think they are not being very intelligent: *Yes, stupid, it's you I'm talking to!*

stu·pid·ity /stjuːˈpɪdəti; *NAmE* stuː-/ *noun* (*pl.* **-ies**) **1** [U, C, usually pl.] behaviour that shows a lack of thought or good judgement: *I couldn't believe my own stupidity.* ◇ *the*

S

errors and stupidities of youth **2** [U] the state or quality of being slow to learn and not clever or intelligent

stu·por /ˈstjuːpə(r); *NAmE* ˈstuː-/ *noun* [sing., U] a state in which you are unable to think, hear, etc. clearly, especially because you have drunk too much alcohol, taken drugs or had a shock: *He drank himself into a stupor.* ◇ *a drunken stupor*

sturdy /ˈstɜːdi; *NAmE* ˈstɜːrdi/ *adj.* (**stur·dier, stur·di·est**) **1** (of an object) strong and not easily damaged SYN **robust**: *a sturdy pair of boots* ◇ *a sturdy table* **2** (of people and animals, or their bodies) physically strong and healthy: *a man of sturdy build* ◇ *sturdy legs* ◇ *a sturdy breed of cattle* **3** not easily influenced or changed by other people SYN **firm, determined**: *The village has always maintained a sturdy independence.* ▸ **stur·dily** /-ɪli/ *adv.*: *The boat was sturdily made.* ◇ *a sturdily built young man* ◇ *a sturdily independent community* **stur·di·ness** *noun* [U]

stur·geon /ˈstɜːdʒən; *NAmE* ˈstɜːrdʒən/ *noun* [C, U] (*pl.* **stur·geon** or **stur·geons**) a large sea and FRESHWATER fish that lives in northern regions. Sturgeon are used for food and the eggs (called CAVIAR) are also eaten.

stut·ter /ˈstʌtə(r)/ *verb, noun*

■ ***verb*** **1** [T, I] to have difficulty speaking because you cannot stop yourself from repeating the first sound of some words several times SYN **stammer**: **+ speech** *'W-w-what?' he stuttered.* ◇ **~ (sth)** *I managed to stutter a reply.* **2** [I] (of a vehicle or an engine) to move or start with difficulty, making short sharp noises or movements: *The car stuttered along in first gear.*

■ ***noun*** [sing.] a speech problem in which a person finds it difficult to say the first sound of a word and repeats it several times: *He had a terrible stutter.*

St ˈValentine's Day /ˌsnt ˈvæləntaɪnz deɪ; *NAmE* ˌseɪnt/ *noun* the day (14 February), when people send a card to the person that they love, often without signing their name on it

sty /staɪ/ *noun* **1** (*pl.* **sties**) = PIGSTY **2** (also **stye**) (*pl.* **sties** or **styes**) an infection of the EYELID (= the skin above or below the eye) which makes it red and sore

Sty·gian /ˈstɪdʒiən/ *adj.* [usually before noun] (*literary*) very dark, and therefore frightening: *Stygian gloom* ORIGIN From the **Styx**, the river in the underworld which the souls of the dead had to cross in Greek myth.

style 0-w AW /staɪl/ *noun, verb*

■ ***noun***

▸ WAY STH IS DONE **1** 0-w [C, U] **~ (of sth)** the particular way in which sth is done: *a style of management* ◇ *a management style* ◇ *furniture to suit your style of living* ◇ *a study of different teaching styles* ◇ *I* **like your style** (= I like the way you do things). ◇ *Caution was* **not her style** (= not the way she usually behaved). ◇ *I'm surprised he rides a motorbike—I'd have thought big cars were* **more his style** (= what suited him). ➲ see also LIFESTYLE

▸ DESIGN OF CLOTHES/HAIR **2** 0-w [C] a particular design of sth, especially clothes: *We stock a wide variety of styles and sizes.* ◇ *Have you thought about having your hair in a shorter style?* ➲ COLLOCATIONS at FASHION ➲ see also HAIRSTYLE **3** 0-w [U] the quality of being fashionable in the clothes that you wear: *style-conscious teenagers* ◇ *Short skirts are back* **in style** (= fashionable).

▸ BEING ELEGANT **4** 0-w [U] the quality of being elegant and made to a high standard: *The hotel has been redecorated but it's lost a lot of its style.* ◇ *She does everything with style and grace.*

▸ OF BOOK/PAINTING/BUILDING **5** 0-w [C, U] the features of a book, painting, building, etc. that make it typical of a particular author, artist, historical period, etc: *a style of architecture* ◇ *a fine example of Gothic style* ◇ *a parody written* **in the style of** *Molière*

▸ USE OF LANGUAGE **6** [U, C] the correct use of language: *It's not considered good style to start a sentence with 'but'.* ◇ *Please follow* **house style** (= the rules of spelling, etc. used by a particular publishing company).

▸ -STYLE **7** (in adjectives) having the type of style mentioned: *Italian-style gardens* ◇ *a buffet-style breakfast* ➲ see also OLD-STYLE

▸ IN A PLANT **8** (*biology*) the long thin part of a flower that carries the STIGMA ➲ VISUAL VOCAB page V9

IDM **in (great, grand, etc.) style** in an impressive way: *She always celebrates her birthday in style.* ◇ *He won the championship in great style.* ➲ more at CRAMP *v.*

■ ***verb***

▸ CLOTHES/HAIR, ETC. **1 ~ sth** to design, make or shape sth in a particular way: *an elegantly styled jacket* ◇ *He'd had his hair styled at an expensive salon.*

▸ GIVE NAME/TITLE **2 ~ sb/sth/yourself + noun** (*formal*) to give sb/sth/yourself a particular name or title: *He styled himself Major Carter.*

PHR V **ˈstyle sth/yourself on sth/sb** to copy the style, manner or appearance of sb/sth SYN **model**: *a coffee bar styled on a Parisian cafe* ◇ *He styled himself on Elvis Presley.*

ˈstyle sheet *noun* (*computing*) a file which is used for creating documents in a particular style

sty·li *pl.* of STYLUS

styl·ing AW /ˈstaɪlɪŋ/ *noun* [U] **1** the act of cutting and/or shaping hair in a particular style: *styling gel* **2** the way in which sth is designed: *The car has been criticized for its outdated body styling.*

styl·ish AW /ˈstaɪlɪʃ/ *adj.* (*approving*) fashionable; elegant and attractive SYN **classy**: *his stylish wife* ◇ *a stylish restaurant* ◇ *It was a stylish performance by both artists.* ▸ **styl·ish·ly** *adv.* **styl·ish·ness** *noun* [U]

styl·ist /ˈstaɪlɪst/ *noun* **1** a person whose job is cutting and shaping people's hair **2** a writer who takes great care to write or say sth in an elegant or unusual way **3** a person whose job is to create or design a particular style or image for a product, a person, an advertisement, etc. **4** a person who designs fashionable clothes **5** (in sport or music) a person who performs with style

styl·is·tic /staɪˈlɪstɪk/ *adj.* [only before noun] connected with the style an artist uses in a particular piece of art, writing or music: *stylistic analysis* ◇ *stylistic features* ▸ **styl·is·tic·al·ly** /-kli/ *adv.*

styl·is·tics /staɪˈlɪstɪks/ *noun* [U] the study of style and the methods used in written language

styl·ized (*BrE* also **-ised**) AW /ˈstaɪlaɪzd/ *adj.* drawn, written, etc. in a way that is not natural or realistic: *a stylized drawing of a house* ◇ *the highly stylized form of acting in Japanese theatre* ▸ **styl·iza·tion, -isa·tion** /ˌstaɪlaɪˈzeɪʃn; *NAmE* -ləˈz-/ *noun* [U]

Stylo·phone™ /ˈstaɪləfəʊn; *NAmE* -foʊn/ *noun* a small electronic musical instrument played by touching its keyboard with a STYLUS

sty·lus /ˈstaɪləs/ *noun* (*pl.* **sty·luses** or **sty·li** /ˈstaɪlaɪ/) **1** a device on a RECORD PLAYER that looks like a small needle and is placed on the record in order to play it **2** (*computing*) a special pen used to write text or draw an image on a special computer screen ➲ VISUAL VOCAB page V54

sty·mie /ˈstaɪmi/ *verb* (**sty·mie·ing** or **sty·mying, sty·mied, sty·mied**) **~ sb/sth** (*informal*) to prevent sb from doing sth that they have planned or want to do; to prevent sth from happening SYN **foil**

styp·tic /ˈstɪptɪk/ *adj.* (*medical*) able to stop the loss of blood from a wound: *I use a styptic pencil on shaving cuts.*

Styro·foam™ /ˈstaɪrəfəʊm; *NAmE* -foʊm/ *noun* [U] (*especially NAmE*) = POLYSTYRENE: *Styrofoam cups*

sua·sive /ˈsweɪsɪv/ *adj.* (*linguistics*) (of verbs) having a meaning that includes the idea of persuading ▸ **sua·sion** /ˈsweɪʒn/ *noun* [U]

suave /swɑːv/ *adj.* (especially of a man) confident, elegant and polite, sometimes in a way that does not seem sincere ▸ **suave·ly** *adv.*

sub /sʌb/ *noun, verb*

■ ***noun*** (*informal*) **1** = SUBMARINE **2** a substitute who replaces another player in a team: *He came on as sub.* **3** (*BrE*) a SUBSCRIPTION (= money that you pay regularly when you are a member of a club, etc.) **4** (*BrE*) a SUBEDITOR **5** (*NAmE, informal*) a SUBSTITUTE TEACHER

■ ***verb*** **1** [T] **~ sb** to replace a sports player with another player during a game SYN **substitute**: *He was subbed after just five minutes because of a knee injury.* **2** [I] **~ (for sb)** to do sb else's job for them for a short time SYN **substitute** **3** [T] **~ sth for sth** to use sth instead of sth else, especially instead of the thing you would normally use SYN **substitute**: *For a lower-calorie version of the recipe, try subbing milk for cream.* **4** [T] **~ sb sth** (*BrE, informal*) to lend sb money for a short time: *Could you sub me £50 till next week?*

sub- /sʌb/ *prefix* **1** (in nouns and adjectives) below; less than: *sub-zero temperatures* ◇ *a subtropical* (= almost tropical) *climate* ◇ *substandard* **2** (in nouns and adjectives) under: *subway* ◇ *submarine* **3** (in verbs and nouns) a smaller part of sth: *subdivide* ◇ *subset*

sub·al·tern /ˈsʌbltən; *NAmE* səˈbɔːltərn/ *noun* any officer in the British army who is lower in rank than a captain

ˌsub-ˈaqua *adj.* [only before noun] (*BrE*) connected with sports that are done underwater: *sub-aqua diving* ◇ *sub-aqua equipment*

sub·atom·ic /ˌsʌbəˈtɒmɪk; *NAmE* -ˈtɑːm-/ *adj.* [usually before noun] (*physics*) smaller than, or found in, an atom: *subatomic particles*

sub·clause /ˈsʌbklɔːz/ *noun* (*law*) one of the parts of a clause (= section) in a legal document

sub·com·mit·tee /ˈsʌbkəmɪti/ *noun* [C+sing./pl. v.] a smaller committee formed from a main committee in order to study a particular subject in more detail

sub·com·pact /ˈsʌbkəmpækt/ *noun* (*NAmE*) a small car, smaller than a COMPACT

sub·con·scious /ˌsʌbˈkɒnʃəs; *NAmE* -ˈkɑːn-/ *adj., noun*
■ ***adj.*** [usually before noun] connected with feelings that influence your behaviour even though you are not aware of them: *subconscious desires* ◇ *the subconscious mind* ➲ compare CONSCIOUS, UNCONSCIOUS ▸ **sub·con·scious·ly** *adv.*: *Subconsciously, she was looking for the father she had never known.*
■ ***noun*** **the/your subconscious** [sing.] the part of your mind that contains feelings that you are not aware of ➲ compare THE UNCONSCIOUS

sub·con·tin·ent /ˌsʌbˈkɒntɪnənt; *NAmE* -ˈkɑːn-/ *noun* [usually sing.] a large land mass that forms part of a continent, especially the part of Asia that includes India, Pakistan and Bangladesh: *the Indian subcontinent*

sub·con·tract *verb, noun*
■ ***verb*** /ˌsʌbkənˈtrækt; *NAmE* ˌsʌbˈkɑːntrækt/ to pay a person or company to do some of the work that you have been given a contract to do: **~ sth (to sb/sth)** *We subcontracted the work to a small engineering firm.* ◇ **~ sb/sth (to do sth)** *We subcontracted a small engineering firm to do the work.* ▸ **sub·con·tract·ing** *noun* [U]
■ ***noun*** /ˌsʌbˈkɒntrækt; *NAmE* -kɑːn-/ a contract to do part of the work that has been given to another person or company

sub·con·tract·or /ˌsʌbkənˈtræktə(r); *NAmE* sʌbˈkɑːntræk-/ *noun* a person or company that does part of the work given to another person or company

sub·cul·ture /ˈsʌbkʌltʃə(r)/ *noun* (sometimes *disapproving*) the behaviour and beliefs of a particular group of people in society that are different from those of most people: *the **criminal/drug/youth, etc. subculture***

sub·cuta·ne·ous /ˌsʌbkjuˈteɪniəs/ *adj.* [usually before noun] (*technical*) under the skin: *a subcutaneous injection* ▸ **sub·cuta·ne·ous·ly** *adv.*

sub·dir·ec·tory /ˈsʌbdərektəri; -dɪ-; -daɪ-/ *noun* (*pl.* **-ies**) (*computing*) a DIRECTORY (= list of files or programs) which is inside another directory

sub·div·ide /ˈsʌbdɪvaɪd; ˌsʌbdɪˈvaɪd/ *verb* [T, often passive, I] **~ (sth) (into sth)** to divide sth into smaller parts; to be divided into smaller parts

sub·div·ision *noun* **1** /ˌsʌbdɪˈvɪʒn/ [U] the act of dividing a part of sth into smaller parts **2** /ˈsʌbdɪvɪʒn/ [C] one of the smaller parts into which a part of sth has been divided: *a police subdivision* (= the area covered by one particular police force) ◇ *subdivisions within the Hindu caste system* **3** /ˈsʌbdɪvɪʒn/ [C] (*NAmE*) an area of land that has been divided up for building houses on

sub·due /səbˈdjuː; *NAmE* -ˈduː/ *verb* (rather *formal*) **1 ~ sb/sth** to bring sb/sth under control, especially by using force SYN **defeat**: *Troops were called in to subdue the rebels.* **2 ~ sth** to calm or control your feelings SYN **suppress**: *Julia had to subdue an urge to stroke his hair.*

sub·dued /səbˈdjuːd; *NAmE* -ˈduːd/ *adj.* **1** (of a person) unusually quiet, and possibly unhappy: *He seemed a bit subdued to me.* ◇ *She was in a subdued mood.* ◇ *The reception was a subdued affair.* **2** (of light or colours) not very bright: *subdued lighting* **3** (of sounds) not very loud: *a subdued conversation* **4** (of business activity) not very busy; with not much activity: *a period of subdued trading*

sub·edi·tor /ˌsʌbˈedɪtə(r)/ (also *informal* **sub**) *noun* (*BrE*) a person whose job is to check and make changes to the text of a newspaper or magazine before it is printed ▸ **sub·edit** *verb* [I, T] **~ (sth)**

sub·group /ˈsʌbgruːp/ *noun* a smaller group made up of members of a larger group

sub·head·ing /ˌsʌbˈhedɪŋ/ *noun* a title given to any of the sections into which a longer piece of writing has been divided

sub·human /ˌsʌbˈhjuːmən/ *adj.* (*disapproving*) not working or behaving like a normal human; not fit for humans: *subhuman behaviour* ◇ *They were living in subhuman conditions.* ➲ compare INHUMAN, SUPERHUMAN

sub·ject 🔑 *noun, adj., verb*
■ ***noun*** /ˈsʌbdʒɪkt; -dʒekt/
▸ OF CONVERSATION/BOOK **1** 🔑 a thing or person that is being discussed, described or dealt with: *an unpleasant **subject of conversation*** ◇ *books on many different subjects* ◇ *a magazine article **on the subject of** space travel* ◇ *I have nothing more to say on the subject.* ◇ *I wish you'd **change the subject*** (= talk about sth else). ◇ *How did we **get onto the subject of** marriage?* ◇ *We seem to have **got off the subject** we're meant to be discussing.* ◇ *Nelson Mandela is the subject of a new biography.* ◇ *Climate change is still very much a **subject for debate**.*
▸ AT SCHOOL/COLLEGE **2** 🔑 an area of knowledge studied in a school, college, etc: *Biology is my favourite subject.*
▸ OF PICTURE/PHOTOGRAPH **3** a person or thing that is the main feature of a picture or photograph, or that a work of art is based on: *Focus the camera on the subject.* ◇ *Classical landscapes were a popular subject with many 18th century painters.*
▸ OF EXPERIMENT **4** a person or thing being used to study sth, especially in an experiment: *We need male subjects between the ages of 18 and 25 for the experiment.*
▸ GRAMMAR **5** a noun, noun phrase or pronoun representing the person or thing that performs the action of the verb (*I* in *I sat down.*), about which sth is stated (*the house* in *the house is very old*) or, in a passive sentence, that is affected by the action of the verb (*the tree* in *the tree was blown down in the storm*) ➲ compare OBJECT *n.* (4), PREDICATE
▸ OF COUNTRY **6** a person who has the right to belong to a particular country, especially one with a king or queen: *a British subject*
■ ***adj.*** /ˈsʌbdʒekt; -dʒɪkt/ (*formal*) **1 ~ to sth** likely to be affected by sth, especially sth bad: *Flights are subject to delay because of the fog.* **2 ~ to sth** depending on sth in order to be completed or agreed: *The article is ready to publish, subject to your approval.* ◇ *All the holidays on offer are subject to availability.* **3 ~ to sth/sb** under the authority of sth/sb: *All nuclear installations are subject to international safeguards.* **4** [only before noun] controlled by the government of another country: *subject peoples*
■ ***verb*** /səbˈdʒekt/ **~ sth (to sth)** (*formal*) to bring a country or group of people under your control, especially by using force: *The Roman Empire subjected most of Europe to its rule.* ▸ **sub·jec·tion** /səbˈdʒekʃn/ *noun* [U]

PHR V **subˈject sb/sth to sth** [often passive] to make sb/sth experience, suffer or be affected by sth, usually sth unpleasant: *to be subjected to ridicule* ◇ *The city was subjected to heavy bombing.* ◇ *The defence lawyers claimed that the prisoners had been subjected to cruel and degrading treatment.*

sub·ject·ive /səbˈdʒektɪv/ *adj.* **1** based on your own ideas or opinions rather than facts and therefore sometimes unfair: *a highly subjective point of view* ◇ *Everyone's opinion is bound to be subjective.* **2** (of ideas, feelings or experiences) existing in sb's mind rather than in the real world **3** [only before noun] (*grammar*) the **subjective** case is the one which is used for the subject of a sentence OPP **objective** ▶ **sub·ject·ive·ly** *adv.*: *People who are less subjectively involved are better judges.* ◇ *subjectively perceived changes* **sub·ject·iv·ity** /ˌsʌbdʒekˈtɪvəti/ *noun* [U]: *There is an element of subjectivity in her criticism.*

sub·ject·iv·ism /səbˈdʒektɪvɪzəm/ *noun* [U] (*philosophy*) the theory that all knowledge and moral values are subjective rather than based on truth that actually exists in the real world

ˈsubject matter *noun* [U] the ideas or information contained in a book, speech, painting, etc: *The artist was revolutionary in both subject matter and technique.* ◇ *She's searching for subject matter for her new book.*

sub ju·dice /ˌsʌb ˈdʒuːdəsi; -seɪ; -keɪ/ *adj.* [not usually before noun] (from *Latin, law*) if a legal case is **sub judice**, it is still being discussed in court and it is therefore illegal for anyone to talk about it in newspapers, etc.

sub·ju·gate /ˈsʌbdʒugeɪt/ *verb* [usually passive] **~ sb/sth** (*formal*) to defeat sb/sth; to gain control over sb/sth: *a subjugated race* ◇ *Her personal ambitions had been subjugated to* (= considered less important than) *the needs of her family.* ▶ **sub·ju·ga·tion** /ˌsʌbdʒuˈgeɪʃn/ *noun* [U]: (*formal*) *the subjugation of Ireland by England*

sub·junct·ive /səbˈdʒʌŋktɪv/ *noun* (*grammar*) the form (or MOOD) of a verb that expresses wishes, possibility or UNCERTAINTY; a verb in this form: *The verb is in the subjunctive.* ◇ *In 'I wish I were taller', 'were' is a subjunctive.* ▶ **sub·junct·ive** *adj.*: *the subjunctive mood*

sub·let /ˌsʌbˈlet/ *verb* (**sub·let·ting, sub·let, sub·let**) [T, I] **~ (sth) (to sb)** to rent to sb else all or part of a property that you rent from the owner ➲ COLLOCATIONS at HOUSE

ˌsub lieuˈtenant *noun* an officer in the British navy just below the rank of LIEUTENANT

sub·lim·ate /ˈsʌblɪmeɪt/ *verb* **~ sth** (*psychology*) to direct your energy, especially sexual energy, to socially acceptable activities such as work, exercise, art, etc. SYN **channel** ▶ **sub·lim·ation** /ˌsʌblɪˈmeɪʃn/ *noun* [U]

S

sub·lime /səˈblaɪm/ *adj., noun*

▪ ***adj.*** **1** of very high quality and causing great admiration: *sublime beauty* ◇ *a sublime combination of flavours* **2** (*formal*, often *disapproving*) (of a person's behaviour or attitudes) extreme, especially in a way that shows they are not aware of what they are doing or are not concerned about what happens because of it: *the sublime confidence of youth* ▶ **sub·lime·ly** *adv.*: *sublimely beautiful* ◇ *She was sublimely unaware of the trouble she had caused.* **sub·lim·ity** /səˈblɪməti/ *noun* [U]

▪ ***noun*** **the sublime** [sing.] something that is sublime: *He transforms the most ordinary subject into the sublime.*

IDM **from the sublime to the riˈdiculous** used to describe a situation in which sth serious, important or of high quality is followed by sth silly, unimportant or of poor quality

sub·lim·inal /ˌsʌbˈlɪmɪnl/ *adj.* affecting your mind even though you are not aware of it: *subliminal advertising* ▶ **sub·lim·in·al·ly** *adv.*

ˌsub-maˈchine gun *noun* a light MACHINE GUN that you can hold in your hands to fire

sub·mar·ine /ˌsʌbməˈriːn; ˈsʌbməriːn/ *noun, adj.*

▪ ***noun*** (also *informal* **sub**) **1** a ship that can travel underwater: *a nuclear submarine* ◇ *a submarine base* **2** (also **ˌsubmarine ˈsandwich, hero**) (all *NAmE*) a long bread roll split open along its length and filled with various types of food

▪ ***adj.*** [only before noun] (*technical*) existing or located under the sea: *submarine plant life* ◇ *submarine cables*

sub·mar·iner /sʌbˈmærɪnə(r); *NAmE* also ˌsʌbməˈriːnər/ *noun* a sailor who works on a submarine

sub·merge /səbˈmɜːdʒ; *NAmE* -ˈmɜːrdʒ/ *verb* **1** [I, T] to go under the surface of water or liquid; to put sth or make sth go under the surface of water or liquid: *The submarine had had time to submerge before the warship could approach.* ◇ **~ sth** *The fields had been submerged by floodwater.* **2** [T] **~ sth** to hide ideas, feelings, opinions, etc. completely: *Doubts that had been submerged in her mind suddenly resurfaced.* ▶ **sub·merged** *adj.*: *Her submerged car was discovered in the river by police divers.* **sub·mer·sion** /səbˈmɜːʃn; *NAmE* -ˈmɜːrʒn/ *noun* [U]

sub·mers·ible /səbˈmɜːsəbl; *NAmE* -ˈmɜːrs-/ *adj., noun*

▪ ***adj.*** (*NAmE* also **sub·merg·ible** /səbˈmɜːdʒəbl; *NAmE* -ˈmɜːrdʒ-/) that can be used underwater: *a submersible camera*

▪ ***noun*** a SUBMARINE (= a ship that can travel underwater) that goes underwater for short periods

sub·mis·sion AW /səbˈmɪʃn/ *noun* **1** [U] the act of accepting that sb has defeated you and that you must obey them SYN **surrender**: *a gesture of submission* ◇ *to **beat/force/starve sb into submission*** **2** [U, C] the act of giving a document, proposal, etc. to sb in authority so that they can study or consider it; the document, etc. that you give: *When is the final date for the submission of proposals?* ◇ *They prepared a report for submission to the council.* ◇ *All parties will have the opportunity to **make submissions** relating to this case.* **3** [C] (*law*) a statement that is made to a judge in court

sub·mis·sive /səbˈmɪsɪv/ *adj.* too willing to accept sb else's authority and willing to obey them without questioning anything they want you to do: *He expected his daughters to be meek and submissive.* ◇ *She followed him like a submissive child.* OPP **assertive** ▶ **sub·mis·sive·ly** *adv.*: *'You're right and I was wrong,' he said submissively.* **sub·mis·sive·ness** *noun* [U]

sub·mit AW /səbˈmɪt/ *verb* (**-tt-**) **1** [T] **~ sth (to sb/sth)** to give a document, proposal, etc. to sb in authority so that they can study or consider it: *to **submit an application/a claim/a complaint*** ◇ *Completed projects must be submitted by 10 March.* **2** [I, T] (*formal*) to accept the authority, control or greater strength of sb/sth; to agree to sth because of this SYN **give in to sb/sth, yield**: **~ (to sb/sth)** *She refused to submit to threats.* ◇ **~ yourself (to sb/sth)** *He submitted himself to a search by the guards.* **3** [T] **~ that...** (*law* or *formal*) to say or suggest sth: *Counsel for the defence submitted that the evidence was inadmissible.*

sub·nor·mal /ˌsʌbˈnɔːml; *NAmE* -ˈnɔːrml/ *adj.* **1** (*technical*) lower than normal: *subnormal temperatures* **2** (sometimes *offensive*) having less than the normal level of intelligence: *educationally subnormal children*

sub·note·book /ˌsʌbˈnəʊtbʊk; *NAmE* -ˈnoʊt-/ (also **subnote** /ˈsʌbnəʊt; *NAmE* -noʊt/, **ˈmini-note**) *noun* a small LAPTOP computer ➲ compare NETBOOK, NOTEBOOK

sub·or·din·ate AW *adj., noun, verb*

▪ ***adj.*** /səˈbɔːdɪnət; *NAmE* -ˈbɔːrd-/ **1 ~ (to sb)** having less power or authority than sb else in a group or an organization: *In many societies women are subordinate to men.* **2 ~ (to sth)** less important than sth else SYN **secondary**: *All other issues are subordinate to this one.*

▪ ***noun*** /səˈbɔːdɪnət; *NAmE* -ˈbɔːrd-/ a person who has a position with less authority and power than sb else in an organization SYN **inferior**: *the relationship between subordinates and superiors*

▪ ***verb*** /səˈbɔːdɪneɪt; *NAmE* -ˈbɔːrd-/ **~ sb/sth (to sb/sth)** to treat sb/sth as less important than sb/sth else: *Safety considerations were subordinated to commercial interests.* ▶ **sub·or·din·ation** AW /səˌbɔːdɪˈneɪʃn; *NAmE* -ˌbɔːrd-/ *noun* [U]

suˌbordinate ˈclause (also **deˌpendent ˈclause**) *noun* (*grammar*) a group of words that is not a sentence but adds information to the main part of a sentence, for example *when it rang* in *She answered the phone when it rang.* ➲ compare COORDINATE CLAUSE, MAIN CLAUSE

su,bordinating con'junction *noun* (*grammar*) a word that begins a subordinate clause, for example 'although' or 'because' ➲ compare COORDINATING CONJUNCTION

sub·orn /sə'bɔːn; *NAmE* sə'bɔːrn/ *verb* **~ sb** (*law*) to pay or persuade sb to do sth illegal, especially to tell lies in court: *to suborn a witness*

sub·par /,sʌb'pɑː(r)/ *adj.* (*especially NAmE*) below a level of quality that is usual or expected: *a subpar performance*

sub·plot /'sʌbplɒt; *NAmE* -plɑːt/ *noun* a series of events in a play, novel, etc. that is separate from but linked to the main story

sub·poena /sə'piːnə/ *noun, verb*

■ ***noun*** (*law*) a written order to attend court as a witness to give evidence

■ ***verb*** **~ sb (to do sth)** (*law*) to order sb to attend court and give evidence as a witness: *The court subpoenaed her to appear as a witness.* ➲ COLLOCATIONS at JUSTICE

,sub-'post office *noun* (*BrE*) a small local post office

sub·prime /,sʌb'praɪm/ *adj.* (*finance*) connected with the practice of lending money to people who may not be able to pay the money back, because they have a bad CREDIT RATING: *subprime mortgages/loans/lending* ◇ *subprime lenders/borrowers*

sub·rou·tine /'sʌbruːtiːn/ (also **sub·pro·gram** /'sʌbprəʊgræm; *NAmE* -proʊ-/) *noun* (*computing*) a set of instructions which repeatedly perform a task within a program

sub-Saharan /,sʌb sə'hɑːrən/ *adj.* [only before noun] from or relating to areas in Africa that are south of the Sahara Desert: *sub-Saharan Africa*

sub·scribe /səb'skraɪb/ *verb* **1** [I] **~ (to sth)** to pay an amount of money regularly in order to receive or use sth: *Which journals does the library subscribe to?* ◇ *We subscribe to several sports channels* (= on TV). ◇ *He subscribed to a newsgroup* (= on the Internet). **2** [I] **~ (to sth)** to pay money regularly to be a member of an organization or to support a charity: *He subscribes regularly to Amnesty International.* **3** [I] **~ (for sth)** (*finance*) to apply to buy shares in a company ➲ see also OVERSUBSCRIBED **4** [T, usually passive] **~ sth** to apply to take part in an activity, use a service, etc: *The tour of Edinburgh is fully subscribed.*

PHR V **sub'scribe to sth** (*formal*) to agree with or support an opinion, a theory, etc. SYN **believe in sth**: *The authorities no longer subscribe to the view that disabled people are unsuitable as teachers.*

sub·scriber /səb'skraɪbə(r)/ *noun* **1** a person who pays money, usually once a year, to receive regular copies of a magazine or newspaper **2** (*BrE*) a person who gives money regularly to help the work of an organization such as a charity **3** a person who pays to receive a service: *subscribers to cable television*

sub·scrip·tion /səb'skrɪpʃn/ *noun* [C, U] **1** an amount of money you pay, usually once a year, to receive regular copies of a newspaper or magazine, etc; the act of paying this money: *an annual subscription* ◇ **~ (to/for sth)** *to* ***take out a subscription*** *to 'Newsweek'* ◇ *to* ***cancel/renew a subscription*** ◇ *Copies are available by subscription.* **2** (*BrE*) a sum of money that you pay regularly to a charity, or to be a member of a club or to receive a service; the act of paying this money SYN **donation**: *a monthly subscription to Oxfam* **3** the act of people paying money for sth to be done: *A statue in his memory was erected by* ***public subscription.*** ➲ SYNONYMS at PAYMENT

sub'scription concert *noun* (*BrE*) any of the concerts in a series for which the tickets are sold in advance

sub·sec·tion /'sʌbsekʃn/ *noun* a part of a section, especially of a legal document

sub·se·quent AW /'sʌbsɪkwənt/ *adj.* (*formal*) happening or coming after sth else OPP **previous**: *subsequent generations* ◇ *Subsequent events confirmed our doubts.* ◇ *Developments on this issue will be dealt with in a subsequent report.*

sub·se·quent·ly AW /'sʌbsɪkwəntli/ *adv.* (*formal*) afterwards; later; after sth else has happened: *The original interview notes were subsequently lost.* ◇ *Subsequently, new guidelines were issued to all employees.*

'subsequent to *prep.* (*formal*) after; following: *There have been further developments subsequent to our meeting.*

sub·ser·vi·ent /səb'sɜːviənt; *NAmE* -'sɜːrv-/ *adj.* **1 ~ (to sb/sth)** (*disapproving*) too willing to obey other people: *The press was accused of being subservient to the government.* **2 ~ (to sth)** (*formal*) less important than sth else: *The needs of individuals were subservient to those of the group as a whole.* ▸ **sub·ser·vi·ence** /-əns/ *noun* [U]

sub·set /'sʌbset/ *noun* (*technical*) a smaller group of people or things formed from the members of a larger group

sub·side /səb'saɪd/ *verb* **1** [I] to become calmer or quieter: *She waited nervously for his anger to subside.* ◇ *I took an aspirin and the pain gradually subsided.* **2** [I] (of water) to go back to a normal level: *The flood waters gradually subsided.* **3** [I] (of land or a building) to sink to a lower level; to sink lower into the ground: *Weak foundations caused the house to subside.*

sub·sid·ence /səb'saɪdns; 'sʌbsɪdns/ *noun* [U] the process by which an area of land sinks to a lower level than normal, or by which a building sinks into the ground

sub·sidi·ar·ity /səb,sɪdi'ærəti; ,sʌbsɪdi-; *NAmE* -'erəti/ *noun* [U] the principle that a central authority should not be very powerful, and should only control things which cannot be controlled by local organizations

sub·sid·iary AW /səb'sɪdiəri; *NAmE* -dieri/ *adj., noun*

■ ***adj.*** **1 ~ (to sth)** connected with sth but less important than it SYN **additional**: *subsidiary information* ◇ *a subsidiary matter* ◇ (*BrE*) *I'm taking History as a* ***subsidiary subject*** (= one that is not studied in as great depth as a main subject). **2** (of a business company) owned or controlled by another company

■ ***noun*** (*pl.* **-ies**) a business company that is owned or controlled by another larger company

sub·sid·ize (*BrE* also **-ise**) AW /'sʌbsɪdaɪz/ *verb* **~ sb/sth** to give money to sb or an organization to help pay for sth; to give a subsidy SYN **fund**: *The housing projects are subsidized by the government.* ◇ *She's not prepared to subsidize his gambling any longer.* ▸ **sub·sid·iza·tion, -isa·tion** /,sʌbsɪdaɪ'zeɪʃn; *NAmE* -də'z-/ *noun* [U]

sub·sidy AW /'sʌbsədi/ *noun* (*pl.* **-ies**) [C, U] money that is paid by a government or an organization to reduce the costs of services or of producing goods so that their prices can be kept low: *agricultural subsidies* ◇ *to reduce the level of subsidy* ➲ COLLOCATIONS at FARMING

sub·sist /səb'sɪst/ *verb* **1** [I] **~ (on sth)** to manage to stay alive, especially with limited food or money: *Old people often subsist on very small incomes.* **2** [I] (*formal*) to exist; to be valid: *The terms of the contract subsist.*

sub·sist·ence /səb'sɪstəns/ *noun* [U] the state of having just enough money or food to stay alive: *Many families are living below the level of subsistence.* ◇ *to live below (the)* ***subsistence level*** ◇ *They had no visible means of subsistence.* ◇ ***subsistence agriculture/farming*** (= growing enough only to live on, not to sell) ◇ ***subsistence crops*** ◇ *He worked a 16-hour day for a* ***subsistence wage*** (= enough money to buy only basic items).

sub·soil /'sʌbsɔɪl/ *noun* [U] the layer of soil between the surface of the ground and the hard rock underneath it ➲ compare TOPSOIL

sub·son·ic /,sʌb'sɒnɪk; *NAmE* -'sɑːn-/ *adj.* less than the speed of sound; flying at less than the speed of sound ➲ compare SUPERSONIC

sub·stance 🔑 /'sʌbstəns/ *noun*

1 🔑 [C] a type of solid, liquid or gas that has particular qualities: *a* ***chemical/radioactive, etc. substance*** ◇ ***banned/illegal substances*** (= drugs) ◇ *a sticky substance* **2** [U] the quality of being based on facts or the truth: *It was* malicious gossip, completely **without substance**. ◇ The commission's report **gives substance to** these allegations. ◇ There is some substance in what he says. **3** [U] the most important or main part of sth: *Love and guilt form* **the substance of** *his new book.* ◇ *I agreed with what she said* **in substance**, *though not with every detail.* **4** [U] (*formal*) importance SYN **significance**: *matters* **of substance** ◇ *Nothing of any substance was achieved in the meeting.*

IDM **a man/woman of 'substance** (*formal*) a rich and powerful man or woman

sub·standard /ˌsʌbˈstændəd; *NAmE* -ərd/ *adj.* not as good as normal; not acceptable SYN **inferior**: *substandard goods*

sub·stan·tial 0-π /səbˈstænʃl/ *adj.*
1 0-π large in amount, value or importance SYN **considerable**: *substantial sums of money* ◇ *a substantial change* ◇ *Substantial numbers of people support the reforms.* ◇ *He ate a substantial breakfast.* **2** 0-π [usually before noun] (*formal*) large and solid; strongly built: *a substantial house*

sub·stan·tial·ly 0-π /səbˈstænʃəli/ *adv.*
1 0-π very much; a lot SYN **considerably**: *The costs have increased substantially.* ◇ *The plane was substantially damaged in the crash.* **2** (*formal*) mainly; in most details, even if not completely: *What she says is substantially true.*

sub·stan·ti·ate /səbˈstænʃieɪt/ *verb* **~ sth** (*formal*) to provide information or evidence to prove that sth is true: *The results of the tests substantiated his claims.* ▸ **sub·stan·ti·ation** /səbˌstænʃiˈeɪʃn/ *noun* [U]

sub·stan·tive /səbˈstæntɪv; ˈsʌbstəntɪv/ *adj., noun*
▪ ***adj.*** (*formal*) dealing with real, important or serious matters: *substantive issues* ◇ *The report concluded that no substantive changes were necessary.*
▪ ***noun*** (*old-fashioned, grammar*) a noun

sub·sta·tion /ˈsʌbsteɪʃn/ *noun* a place where the strength of electric power from a POWER STATION is reduced before it is passed on to homes and businesses

sub·sti·tute 0-π AW /ˈsʌbstɪtjuːt; *NAmE* -tuːt/ *noun, verb*
▪ ***noun*** **1** 0-π a person or thing that you use or have instead of the one you normally use or have: *a meat substitute* ◇ *a substitute family* ◇ **~ for sb/sth** *Paul's father only saw him as a substitute for his dead brother.* ◇ *The course teaches you the theory but* **there's no substitute for** *practical experience.* ◇ *The local bus service was a* **poor substitute for** *their car.* **2** 0-π (also *informal* **sub**) a player who replaces another player in a sports game: *He was brought on as (a) substitute after half-time.*
▪ ***verb*** 0-π [I, T] to take the place of sb/sth else; to use sb/sth instead of sb/sth else: **~ for sb/sth** *Nothing can substitute for the advice your doctor is able to give you.* ◇ **~ A for B** *Margarine can be substituted for butter in this recipe.* ◇ **~ B with/by A** *Butter can be substituted with margarine in this recipe.* ◇ **~ sb/sth** *Beckham was substituted in the second half after a knee injury* (= somebody else played instead of Beckham in the second half). HELP When **for**, **with** or **by** are not used, as in the last example, it can be difficult to tell whether the person or thing mentioned is being used, or has been replaced by somebody or something else. The context will usually make this clear. ▸ **sub·sti·tu·tion** AW /ˌsʌbstɪˈtjuːʃn; *NAmE* -ˈtuː-/ *noun* [U, C]: *the substitution of low-fat spreads for butter* ◇ *Two substitutions were made during the game.*

ˌsubstitute ˈteacher (also *informal* **sub**) (both *NAmE*) (*BrE* **supˈply teacher**) *noun* a teacher employed to do the work of another teacher who is away because of illness, etc.

sub·strate /ˈsʌbstreɪt/ *noun* (*technical*) a substance or layer which is under sth or on which sth happens, for example the surface on which a living thing grows and feeds

sub·stra·tum /ˈsʌbstrɑːtəm; *NAmE* ˈsʌbstreɪtəm/ *noun* (*pl.* **sub·strata** /ˈsʌbstrɑːtə; *NAmE* ˈsʌbstreɪtə/) (*technical*) a layer of sth, especially rock or soil, that is below another layer

sub·struc·ture /ˈsʌbstrʌktʃə(r)/ *noun* a base or structure that is below another structure and that supports it: *a substructure of timber piles* ◇ (*figurative*) *the substructure of national culture* ➲ compare SUPERSTRUCTURE

sub·sume /səbˈsjuːm; *NAmE* -ˈsuːm/ *verb* [usually passive] **~ sth + adv./prep.** (*formal*) to include sth in a particular group and not consider it separately: *All these different ideas can be subsumed under just two broad categories.*

sub·tend /səbˈtend/ *verb* **~ sth** (*geometry*) (of a line or CHORD) to be opposite to an ARC or angle

sub·ter·fuge /ˈsʌbtəfjuːdʒ; *NAmE* -tərf-/ *noun* [U, C] (*formal*) a secret, usually dishonest, way of behaving

sub·ter·ra·nean /ˌsʌbtəˈreɪniən/ *adj.* [usually before noun] (*formal*) under the ground: *a subterranean cave*

sub·text /ˈsʌbtekst/ *noun* a hidden meaning or reason for doing sth

sub·title /ˈsʌbtaɪtl/ *noun, verb*
▪ ***noun*** **1** [usually pl.] words that translate what is said in a film/movie into a different language and appear on the screen at the bottom. Subtitles are also used, especially on television, to help deaf people (= people who cannot hear well): *a Polish film with English subtitles* ◇ *Is the movie dubbed or are there subtitles?* **2** a second title of a book that appears after the main title and gives more information
▪ ***verb*** [usually passive] to give a subtitle or subtitles to a book, film/movie, etc: **~ sth** *a Spanish film subtitled in English* ◇ **~ sth + noun** *The book is subtitled 'New language for new times'.* ➲ compare DUB

sub·tle /ˈsʌtl/ *adj.* (**sub·tler**, **sub·tlest**) HELP **more subtle** is also common **1** (often *approving*) not very noticeable or obvious: ***subtle colours/flavours/smells, etc.*** ◇ *There are* ***subtle differences*** *between the two versions.* ◇ *She's been dropping subtle hints about what she'd like as a present.* **2** (of a person or their behaviour) behaving in a clever way, and using indirect methods, in order to achieve sth: *I decided to try a more subtle approach.* **3** organized in a clever way: *a subtle plan* ◇ *a subtle use of lighting in the play* **4** good at noticing and understanding things: *The job required a subtle mind.* ▸ **subtly** /ˈsʌtli/ *adv.*: *Her version of events is subtly different from what actually happened.* ◇ *Not very subtly, he raised the subject of money.*

subtle·ty /ˈsʌtlti/ *noun* (*pl.* **-ies**) **1** [U] the quality of being subtle: *It's a thrilling movie even though it lacks subtlety.* **2** [C, usually pl.] the small but important details or aspects of sth: *the subtleties of language*

sub·total /ˈsʌbtəʊtl; *NAmE* -toʊtl/ *noun* the total of a set of numbers which is then added to other totals to give a final number

sub·tract /səbˈtrækt/ *verb* [T, I] **~ (sth) (from sth)** to take a number or an amount away from another number or amount SYN **take away**: *6 subtracted from 9 is 3* OPP **add** ▸ **sub·trac·tion** /səbˈtrækʃn/ *noun* [U, C] ➲ compare ADDITION

sub·trop·ic·al /ˌsʌbˈtrɒpɪkl; *NAmE* -ˈtrɑːp-/ (also **ˌsemiˈtropical**) *adj.* in or connected with regions that are near tropical parts of the world

the sub·trop·ics /ˌsʌbˈtrɒpɪks; *NAmE* -ˈtrɑːp-/ *noun* [pl.] the regions of the earth which are near the TROPICS

sub·urb /ˈsʌbɜːb; *NAmE* -ɜːrb/ *noun* (also *NAmE informal* **the burbs**) an area where people live that is outside the centre of a city: *a suburb of London* ◇ *a London suburb* ◇ *They live* ***in the suburbs.*** ➲ COLLOCATIONS at TOWN

sub·ur·ban /səˈbɜːbən; *NAmE* -ˈbɜːrb-/ *adj.* **1** in or connected with a suburb: *suburban areas* ◇ *a suburban street* ◇ *life in suburban London* **2** (*disapproving*) boring and ordinary: *a suburban lifestyle*

sub·ur·ban·ite /səˈbɜːbənaɪt; *NAmE* -ˈbɜːrb-/ *noun* (often *disapproving*) a person who lives in the SUBURBS of a city

sub·ur·bia /səˈbɜːbiə; *NAmE* -ˈbɜːrb-/ *noun* [U] (often *disapproving*) the SUBURBS and the way of life, attitudes, etc. of the people who live there

S

sub·ven·tion /səbˈvenʃn/ *noun* (*formal*) an amount of money that is given by a government, etc. to help an organization

sub·ver·sive /səbˈvɜːsɪv; *NAmE* -ˈvɜːrs-/ *adj.* trying or likely to destroy or damage a government or political system by attacking it secretly or indirectly SYN **seditious** ▶ **sub·ver·sive** *noun*: *He was a known political subversive.* **sub·ver·sive·ly** *adv.* **sub·ver·sive·ness** *noun* [U]

sub·vert /səbˈvɜːt; *NAmE* -ˈvɜːrt/ *verb* (*formal*) **1** [T, I] **~ (sth)** to try to destroy the authority of a political, religious, etc. system by attacking it secretly or indirectly SYN **undermine 2** [T] **~ sth** to try to destroy a person's belief in sth or sb SYN **undermine** ▶ **sub·ver·sion** /səbˈvɜːʃn; *NAmE* -ˈvɜːrʒn/ *noun* [U]

sub·way /ˈsʌbweɪ/ *noun* **1** (*NAmE*) an underground railway/railroad system in a city: *the New York subway* ◇ *a **subway station/train*** ◇ *a downtown subway stop* ◇ *to **ride/take the subway*** ➲ note at UNDERGROUND ➲ VISUAL VOCAB page V47 **2** (*BrE*) a path that goes under a road, etc. which people can use to cross to the other side SYN **underpass**

sub·woof·er /ˈsʌbwʊfə(r)/ *noun* (*technical*) a part of a LOUDSPEAKER that produces very low sounds

ˌ**sub-ˈzero** *adj.* [usually before noun] (of temperatures) below zero

suc·ceed 0‑ᵂ /səkˈsiːd/ *verb*
1 0‑ᵂ [I] to achieve sth that you have been trying to do or get; to have the result or effect that was intended: *Our plan succeeded.* ◇ **~ in doing sth** *He succeeded in getting a place at art school.* ◇ *I tried to discuss it with her but **only succeeded** in making her angry* (= I failed and did the opposite of what I intended). ➲ see also SUCCESS **2** 0‑ᵂ [I] to be successful in your job, earning money, power, respect, etc: *You will have to work hard if you are to succeed.* ◇ **~ in sth** *She doesn't have the ruthlessness required to succeed in business.* ◇ **~ as sth** *He had hoped to succeed as a violinist.* ➲ see also SUCCESS **3** [T] **~ sb/sth** to come next after sb/sth and take their/its place or position SYN **follow**: *Who succeeded Kennedy as President?* ◇ *Their early success was succeeded by a period of miserable failure.* ◇ *Strands of DNA are reproduced through **succeeding generations**.* ➲ see also SUCCESSION **4** [I] **~ (to sth)** to gain the right to a title, property, etc. when sb dies: *She succeeded to the throne* (= became queen) *in 1558.* ➲ see also SUCCESSION
IDM **nothing succeeds like sucˈcess** (*saying*) when you are successful in one area of your life, it often leads to success in other areas

Synonyms

successful

profitable • commercial • lucrative • economic

These words all describe sb/sth that is making or is likely to make money.

successful making a lot of money, especially by being popular: *The play was very successful on Broadway.* ◇ *The company has had another successful year.*

profitable making a profit: *a highly profitable business*

commercial [only before noun] making or intended to make a profit: *The movie was not a commercial success* (= made no profit).

lucrative (of business or work) producing or paying a large amount of money; making a large profit: *They do a lot of business in lucrative overseas markets.*

economic (often used in negative sentences) (of a process, business or activity) producing enough profit to continue: *Small local shops stop being economic when a supermarket opens up nearby.*

PATTERNS
- a successful/profitable/lucrative **business**
- a successful/profitable/lucrative **year**
- a(n) commercial/economic **success**

suc·cess 0‑ᵂ /səkˈses/ *noun*
1 0‑ᵂ [U] the fact that you have achieved sth that you want and have been trying to do or get; the fact of becoming rich or famous or of getting a high social position: *What's the secret of your success?* ◇ **~ (in doing sth)** *I didn't **have much success in** finding a job.* ◇ **~ (in sth)** *They didn't have much success in life.* ◇ *Confidence is **the key to success**.* ◇ *economic success* ◇ *Their plan will probably **meet with little success**.* ◇ *She was surprised by the book's success* (= that it had sold a lot of copies). **2** 0‑ᵂ [C] a person or thing that has achieved a good result and been successful: *The party was a big success.* ◇ *He's proud of his daughter's successes.* ◇ *She wasn't a success as a teacher.* ◇ *He was determined to **make a success** of the business.* OPP **failure** IDM see ROARING, SUCCEED, SWEET *adj.*

suc·cess·ful 0‑ᵂ /səkˈsesfl/ *adj.*
1 0‑ᵂ achieving your aims or what was intended: **~ (in sth/in doing sth)** *They were successful in winning the contract.* ◇ **~ (at sth/at doing sth)** *I wasn't very successful at keeping the news secret.* ◇ *We congratulated them on the successful completion of the project.* **2** 0‑ᵂ having become popular and/or made a lot of money: *The play was very successful on Broadway.* ◇ *a successful actor* ◇ *The company has had another successful year.* OPP **unsuccessful** ▶ **suc·cess·ful·ly** 0‑ᵂ /-fəli/ *adv.*

suc·ces·sion AW /səkˈseʃn/ *noun* **1** [C, usually sing.] a number of people or things that follow each other in time or order SYN **series**: *a succession of visitors* ◇ *He's been hit by a succession of injuries since he joined the team.* ◇ *She has won the award for the third year **in succession**.* ◇ *They had three children **in quick succession**.* ◇ *The gunman fired three times **in rapid succession**.* **2** [U] the regular pattern of one thing following another thing: *the succession of the seasons* **3** [U] the act of taking over an official position or title; the right to take over an official position or title, especially to become the king or queen of a country: *He became chairman **in succession to** Bernard Allen.* ◇ *She's third **in order of succession** to the throne.* ➲ see also SUCCEED

sucˈcession planning *noun* [U] (*business*) the process of training and preparing employees in a company or an organization so that there will always be sb to replace a senior manager who leaves

suc·ces·sive AW /səkˈsesɪv/ *adj.* [only before noun] following immediately one after the other SYN **consecutive**: *This was their fourth successive win.* ◇ *Successive governments have tried to tackle the problem.* ▶ **suc·ces·sive·ly** AW *adv.*: *This concept has been applied successively to painting, architecture and sculpture.*

suc·ces·sor AW /səkˈsesə(r)/ *noun* **~ (to sb/sth)** a person or thing that comes after sb/sth else and takes their/its place: *Who's the likely successor to him as party leader?* ◇ *Their latest release is a **worthy successor** to their popular debut album.* ➲ compare PREDECESSOR

sucˈcess story *noun* a person or thing that is very successful

suc·cinct /səkˈsɪŋkt/ *adj.* (*approving*) expressed clearly and in a few words SYN **concise**: *Keep your answers as succinct as possible.* ◇ *a succinct explanation* ▶ **suc·cinct·ly** *adv.*: *You put that very succinctly.* **suc·cinct·ness** *noun* [U]

suc·co·tash /ˈsʌkətæʃ/ *noun* [U] (*US*) a dish of CORN (MAIZE) and BEANS cooked together

Suc·coth /sʊˈkəʊt; ˈsʌkəθ; *NAmE* ˈsuːkoʊt; suːˈkoʊt/ (also ˌ**Feast of ˈTabernacles**) *noun* [U] a Jewish festival that takes place in the autumn/fall, during which shelters are made using natural materials

suc·cour (*US* **suc·cor**) /ˈsʌkə(r)/ *noun, verb*
- ***noun*** [U] (*literary*) help that you give to sb who is suffering or having problems
- ***verb*** **~ sb** (*literary*) to help sb who is suffering or having problems

suc·cu·bus /ˈsʌkjʊbəs/ *noun* (*pl.* **suc·cu·bi** /-baɪ/) (*literary*) a female evil spirit, supposed to have sex with a sleeping man ➲ compare INCUBUS

S

suc·cu·lent /ˈsʌkjələnt/ *adj., noun*
■ ***adj.*** **1** (*approving*) (of fruit, vegetables and meat) containing a lot of juice and tasting good SYN **juicy**: *a succulent pear/steak* **2** (*technical*) (of plants) having leaves and STEMS that are thick and contain a lot of water ▸ **suc·cu·lence** /-əns/ *noun* [U]
■ ***noun*** (*technical*) any plant with leaves and STEMS that are thick and contain a lot of water, for example a CACTUS

suc·cumb /səˈkʌm/ *verb* [I] to not be able to fight an attack, an illness, a TEMPTATION, etc: *The town succumbed after a short siege.* ◇ **~ to sth** *His career was cut short when he succumbed to cancer.* ◇ *He finally succumbed to Lucy's charms and agreed to her request.*

such 0┳ /sʌtʃ/ *det., pron.*
1 0┳ of the type already mentioned: *They had been invited to a Hindu wedding and were not sure what happened on such occasions.* ◇ *He said he didn't have time or made* ***some such*** *excuse.* ◇ *She longed to find somebody who understood her problems, and in him she thought she had found such a person.* ◇ *We were second-class citizens and they treated us* ***as such****.* ◇ *Accountants were boring. Such* (= that) *was her opinion before meeting Ian!* **2** 0┳ of the type that you are just going to mention: ***There is no such thing*** *as a free lunch.* ◇ *Such advice as he was given* (= it was not very much) *has proved almost worthless.* ◇ *The knot was fastened* ***in such a way*** *that it was impossible to undo.* ◇ *The damage was such that it would cost thousands to repair.* **3** 0┳ **~ (is, was, etc.) sth that...** used to emphasize the great degree of sth: *This issue was of such importance that we could not afford to ignore it.* ◇ *Why are you in such a hurry?* ◇ (*informal*) *It's such a beautiful day!* ◇ (*formal*) *Such is the elegance of this typeface that it is still a favourite of designers.*
IDM **... and such** and similar things or people: *The centre offers activities like canoeing and sailing and such.* **as ˈsuch** 0┳ as the word is usually understood; in the exact sense of the word: *The new job is not a promotion as such, but it has good prospects.* ◇ *'Well, did they offer it to you?' 'No, not as such, but they said I had a good chance.'* **such as 1** 0┳ for example: *Wild flowers such as primroses are becoming rare.* ◇ *'There are loads of things to do.' 'Such as?'* (= give me an example) **2** 0┳ of a kind that; like: *Opportunities such as this did not come every day.* ➲ LANGUAGE BANK at E.G. **ˌsuch as it ˈis/they ˈare** used to say that there is not much of sth or that it is of poor quality: *The food, such as it was, was served at nine o'clock.*

ˈsuch-and-such *pron., det.* (*informal*) used for referring to sth without saying exactly what it is: *Always say at the start of an application that you're applying for such-and-such a job because...*

S

such·like /ˈsʌtʃlaɪk/ *pron.* things of the type mentioned: *You can buy brushes, paint, varnish and suchlike there.* ▸ **such·like** *det.*: *food, drink, clothing and suchlike provisions*

suck 0┳ /sʌk/ *verb, noun*
■ ***verb*** **1** 0┳ [T] **~ sth (+ adv./prep.)** to take liquid, air, etc. into your mouth by using the muscles of your lips: *to suck the juice from an orange* ◇ *She was noisily sucking up milk through a straw.* **2** 0┳ [I, T] to keep sth in your mouth and pull on it with your lips and tongue: **~ at/on sth** *The baby sucked at its mother's breast.* ◇ *She sucked on a mint.* ◇ **~ sth** *She sucked a mint.* ◇ *Stop sucking your thumb!* **3** 0┳ [T] to take liquid, air, etc. out of sth: **~ sth + adv./prep.** *The pump sucks air out through the valve.* ◇ **~ sth + adj.** *Greenfly can literally suck a plant dry.* **4** [T] **~ sb/sth + adv./prep.** to pull sb/sth with great force in a particular direction: *The canoe was sucked down into the whirlpool.* **5 sth sucks** [I] (*slang*) used to say that sth is very bad: *Their new CD sucks.* ➲ compare ROCK *v.* (4)
IDM **ˌsuck it and ˈsee** (*BrE, informal*) used to say that the only way to know if sth is suitable is to try it **ˌsuck it ˈup** (*NAmE, informal*) to accept sth bad and deal with it well, controlling your emotions ➲ more at DRY *adj.*, TEACH
PHR V **ˌsuck sb ˈin** | **ˌsuck sb ˈinto sth** [usually passive] to involve sb in an activity or a situation, especially one they do not want to be involved in **ˌsuck ˈup (to sb)** (*informal, disapproving*) to try to please sb in authority by praising them too much, helping them, etc, in order to gain some advantage for yourself
■ ***noun*** [usually sing.] an act of sucking

suck·er /ˈsʌkə(r)/ *noun, verb*
■ ***noun*** **1** (*informal*) a person who is easily tricked or persuaded to do sth **2 ~ for sb/sth** (*informal*) a person who cannot resist sb/sth or likes sb/sth very much: *I've always been a sucker for men with green eyes.* **3** a special organ on the body of some animals that enables them to stick to a surface ➲ VISUAL VOCAB page V11 **4** a disc shaped like a cup, usually made of rubber or plastic, that sticks to a surface when you press it against it **5** a part of a tree or bush that grows from the roots rather than from the main STEM or the branches and can form a new tree or bush **6** (*NAmE, slang*) used to refer in a general way to a person or thing, especially for emphasis: *The pilot said, 'I don't know how I got the sucker down safely.'* **7** (*NAmE, informal*) = LOLLIPOP
■ ***verb***
PHR V **ˌsucker sb ˈinto sth/into doing sth** (*NAmE, informal*) to persuade sb to do sth that they do not really want to do, especially by using their lack of knowledge or experience: *I was suckered into helping.*

ˈsucker punch *noun* a blow that the person who receives it is not expecting ▸ **ˈsucker punch** *verb* **~ sb**

suckle /ˈsʌkl/ *verb* **1** [T] **~ sb/sth** (of a woman or female animal) to feed a baby or young animal with milk from the breast or UDDER: *a cow suckling her calves* ◇ (*old-fashioned*) *a mother suckling a baby* **2** [I] (of a baby or young animal) to drink milk from its mother's breast or UDDER

suck·ling /ˈsʌklɪŋ/ *noun* (*old-fashioned*) a baby or young animal that is still drinking milk from its mother IDM see MOUTH *n.*

ˈsuck·ling pig *noun* [U, C] a young pig still taking milk from its mother, that is cooked and eaten

su·crose /ˈsuːkrəʊz; -krəʊs; *NAmE* -kroʊs; -kroʊz/ *noun* [U] (*chemistry*) the form of sugar that is obtained from SUGAR CANE and SUGAR BEET

suc·tion /ˈsʌkʃn/ *noun* [U] the process of removing air or liquid from a space or container so that sth else can be sucked into it or so that two surfaces can stick together: *Vacuum cleaners work by suction.* ◇ *a* ***suction pump/pad*** ▸ **suc·tion** *verb* **~ sth** (*technical*)

sud·den 0┳ /ˈsʌdn/ *adj.*
happening or done quickly and unexpectedly: *a sudden change* ◇ *Don't make any sudden movements.* ◇ *His death was very sudden.* ◇ *It was only decided yesterday. It's all been very sudden.* ▸ **sud·den·ness** *noun* [U]
IDM **ˌall of a ˈsudden** quickly and unexpectedly: *All of a sudden someone grabbed me around the neck.*

ˌsudden ˈdeath *noun* [U] a way of deciding the winner of a game when the scores are equal at the end. The players or teams continue playing and the game ends as soon as one of them gains the lead: *a sudden-death play-off in golf*

sud·den·ly 0┳ /ˈsʌdənli/ *adv.*
quickly and unexpectedly: *'Listen!' said Doyle suddenly.* ◇ *I suddenly realized what I had to do.* ◇ *It all happened so suddenly.*

su·doku /ˌsuˈdəʊkuː; -ˈdɒk-; *NAmE* -ˈdoʊk-; -ˈdɑːk-/ *noun* [C, U] a number puzzle with nine squares, each containing nine smaller squares, in which you have to put the numbers one to nine so that a number appears only once in each of the nine squares and in each row of nine across and down the puzzle: *He passes the time doing sudokus.* ➲ VISUAL VOCAB page V33

suds /sʌdz/ (also **soap·suds**) *noun* **1** [pl.] a mass of very small bubbles that forms on top of water that has soap in it SYN **lather**: *She was up to her elbows in suds.* **2** [U] (*old-fashioned, NAmE, informal*) beer

sue /suː; *BrE* also sjuː/ *verb* **1** [T, I] **~ (sb) (for sth)** to make a claim against sb in court about sth that they have said or done to harm you: *to sue sb for breach of contract* ◇ *to sue sb for $10 million* (= in order to get money from sb) ◇ *to sue sb for damages* ◇ *They threatened to sue if the work was not completed.* **2** [I] **~ for sth** (*formal*) to formally ask for sth, especially in court: *to sue for divorce* ◇ *The rebels were forced to sue for peace.*

suede /sweɪd/ *noun* [U] soft leather with a surface like VELVET on one side, used especially for making clothes and shoes: *a suede jacket*

suet /'su:ɪt; *BrE* also 'sju:ɪt/ *noun* [U] hard fat from around the KIDNEYS of cows, sheep, etc, used in cooking: *suet pudding* (= one made using suet)

suf·fer 0-w /'sʌfə(r)/ *verb*
1 0-w [I] to be badly affected by a disease, pain, sadness, a lack of sth, etc: *I hate to see animals suffering.* ◇ **~ from sth** *He suffers from asthma.* ◇ *road accident victims suffering from shock* ◇ *Many companies are suffering from a shortage of skilled staff.* ◇ **~ for sth** *He made a rash decision and now he is suffering for it.* **2** 0-w [T] **~ sth** to experience sth unpleasant, such as injury, defeat or loss: *He suffered a massive heart attack.* ◇ *The party suffered a humiliating defeat in the general election.* ◇ *The company suffered huge losses in the last financial year.* **3** 0-w [I] to become worse: *His school work is suffering because of family problems.*
IDM **not suffer fools 'gladly** to have very little patience with people that you think are stupid

suf·fer·ance /'sʌfərəns/ *noun* [U]
IDM **on 'sufferance** if you do sth **on sufferance**, sb allows you to do it although they do not really want you to: *He's only staying here on sufferance.*

suf·fer·er /'sʌfərə(r)/ *noun* a person who suffers, especially sb who is suffering from a disease: *cancer sufferers* ◇ *She received many letters of support from fellow sufferers.*

suf·fer·ing 0-w /'sʌfərɪŋ/ *noun*
1 0-w [U] physical or mental pain: *Death finally brought an end to her suffering.* ◇ *This war has caused widespread human suffering.* **2 sufferings** [pl.] feelings of pain and unhappiness: *The hospice aims to ease the sufferings of the dying.*

suf·fice /sə'faɪs/ *verb* [I] (*formal*) (not used in the progressive tenses) to be enough for sb/sth: *Generally a brief note or a phone call will suffice.* ◇ **~ to do sth** *One example will suffice to illustrate the point.*
IDM **suffice (it) to say (that)...** used to suggest that although you could say more, what you do say will be enough to explain what you mean

suf·fi·ciency AW /sə'fɪʃnsi/ *noun* [sing.] **~ (of sth)** (*formal*) an amount of sth that is enough for a particular purpose

suf·fi·cient 0-w AW /sə'fɪʃnt/ *adj.*
enough for a particular purpose; as much as you need: *Allow sufficient time to get there.* ◇ **~ to do sth** *These reasons are not sufficient to justify the ban.* ◇ **~ for sth/sb** *Is £100 sufficient for your expenses?* OPP **insufficient** ➲ see also SELF-SUFFICIENT ▶ **suf·fi·cient·ly** 0-w AW *adv.*: *The following day she felt sufficiently well to go to work.*

suf·fix /'sʌfɪks/ *noun* (*grammar*) a letter or group of letters added to the end of a word to make another word, such as *-ly* in *quickly* or *-ness* in *sadness* ➲ compare AFFIX, PREFIX

suf·fo·cate /'sʌfəkeɪt/ *verb* **1** [I, T] to die because there is no air to breathe; to kill sb by not letting them breathe air: *Many dogs have suffocated in hot cars.* ◇ **~ sb/sth** *The couple were suffocated by fumes from a faulty gas fire.* ◇ *He put the pillow over her face and suffocated her.* ◇ (*figurative*) *She felt suffocated by all the rules and regulations.* **2** [I] **be suffocating** if **it is suffocating**, it is very hot and there is little fresh air: *Can I open a window? It's suffocating in here!* ▶ **suf·fo·ca·tion** /ˌsʌfə'keɪʃn/ *noun* [U]: *to die of suffocation*

suf·fo·cat·ing /'sʌfəkeɪtɪŋ/ *adj.* **1** making it difficult to breathe normally SYN **stifling**: *The afternoon heat was suffocating.* **2** restricting what sb/sth can do: *Some marriages can sometimes feel suffocating.*

suf·fra·gan /'sʌfrəgən/ (also **suffragan 'bishop**) *noun* a BISHOP who is an assistant to a bishop of a particular DIOCESE

suf·frage /'sʌfrɪdʒ/ *noun* [U] the right to vote in political elections: *universal suffrage* (= the right of all adults to vote) ◇ *women's suffrage*

suf·fra·gette /ˌsʌfrə'dʒet/ *noun* a member of a group of women who, in Britain and the US in the early part of the 20th century, worked to get the right for women to vote in political elections

suf·fuse /sə'fju:z/ *verb* [often passive] **~ sb/sth (with sth)** (*literary*) (especially of a colour, light or feeling) to spread all over or through sb/sth: *Her face was suffused with colour.* ◇ *Colour suffused her face.*

Sufi /'su:fi/ *noun* a member of a Muslim group who try to become united with God through prayer and MEDITATION and by living a very simple, strict life ▶ **Suf·ism** *noun* [U]

su·fur·ia /su:'fu:riə/ *noun* (*EAfrE*) a metal pot used for cooking

sugar 0-w /'ʃʊgə(r)/ *noun, verb, exclamation*
■ ***noun*** **1** 0-w [U] a sweet substance, often in the form of white or brown CRYSTALS, made from the juices of various plants, used in cooking or to make tea, coffee, etc. sweeter: *a **sugar plantation/refinery/bowl*** ◇ *This juice contains **no added sugar**.* ◇ *Do you **take sugar*** (= have it in your tea, coffee, etc.)? ➲ see also BROWN SUGAR, CANE SUGAR, CASTER SUGAR, GRANULATED SUGAR, ICING SUGAR **2** 0-w [C] the amount of sugar that a small spoon can hold or that is contained in a small CUBE, added to tea, coffee, etc: *How many sugars do you take in coffee?* **3** [C, usually pl.] (*technical*) any of various sweet substances that are found naturally in plants, fruit, etc: *fruit sugars* ◇ *a person's **blood sugar** level* (= the amount of GLUCOSE in their blood) **4** [U] (*informal, especially NAmE*) a way of addressing sb that you like or love: *See you later, sugar.*
■ ***verb*** **~ sth** to add sugar to sth; to cover sth in sugar
IDM see PILL
■ ***exclamation*** used to show that you are annoyed when you do sth stupid or when sth goes wrong (to avoid saying 'shit'): *Oh sugar! I've forgotten my book!*

'sugar beet *noun* [U] a plant with a large round root, from which sugar is made

'sugar cane *noun* [U] a tall tropical plant with thick STEMS from which sugar is made

'sugar-coat *verb* **~ sth** to do sth that makes an unpleasant situation seem less unpleasant

ˌsugar-'coated *adj.* **1** covered with sugar **2** (*disapproving*) made to seem attractive, in a way that tricks people: *a sugar-coated promise*

'sugar cube (*especially NAmE*) (*BrE* also **'sugar lump**) *noun* a small CUBE of sugar, used in cups of tea or coffee

'sugar daddy *noun* (*informal*) a rich older man who gives presents and money to a much younger woman, usually in return for sex

sug·ar·ing /'ʃʊgərɪŋ/ *noun* [U] **1** a way of removing hair from your skin using a mixture of sugar and water **2** the process of boiling juice from a MAPLE tree until it becomes sugar

'sugar lump (also *informal* **lump**) (both *BrE*) (also **'sugar cube** *NAmE, BrE*) *noun* a small CUBE of sugar, used in cups of tea or coffee

sugar·plum /'ʃʊgəplʌm; *NAmE* -gərp-/ *noun* (*especially NAmE*) a small round sweet/candy

'sugar snap (also **ˌsugar snap 'pea**, **'sugar pea**) *noun* a type of PEA which is eaten while still in its POD

sug·ary /'ʃʊgəri/ *adj.* **1** containing sugar; tasting of sugar: *sugary snacks* **2** (*disapproving*) seeming too full of emotion in a way that is not sincere SYN **sentimental**: *a sugary smile* ◇ *sugary pop songs*

sug·gest 0-w /sə'dʒest; *NAmE* also səg'dʒ-/ *verb*
1 0-w to put forward an idea or a plan for other people to think about SYN **propose**: **~ sth (to sb)** *May I suggest a white wine with this dish, Sir?* ◇ **~ itself (to sb)** *A solution immediately suggested itself to me* (= I immediately thought of a solution). ◇ **~ (that)...** *I suggest (that) we go out to eat.* ◇ **~ doing sth** *I suggested going in my car.* ◇ **it is suggested that...** *It has been suggested that bright children take their exams early.* ◇ (*BrE* also) *It has been suggested that*

S

bright children should take their exams early. ➲ LANGUAGE BANK at ARGUE **2** 🔑 to tell sb about a suitable person, thing, method, etc. for a particular job or purpose SYN **recommend**: **~ sb/sth for sth** *Who would you suggest for the job?* ◇ **~ sb/sth as sth** *She suggested Paris as a good place for the conference.* ◇ **~ sb/sth** *Can you suggest a good dictionary?* HELP You cannot 'suggest somebody something': ~~Can you suggest me a good dictionary?~~: **~ how, what, etc...** *Can you suggest how I might contact him?* **3** 🔑 to put an idea into sb's mind; to make sb think that sth is true SYN **indicate**: **~ (that)...** *All the evidence suggests (that) he stole the money.* ◇ **~ sth** *The symptoms suggest a minor heart attack.* ◇ **~ sth to sb** *What do these results suggest to you?* **4** to state sth indirectly SYN **imply**: **~ (that)...** *Are you suggesting (that) I'm lazy?* ◇ **~ sth** *I would never suggest such a thing.*

sug·gest·ible /sə'dʒestəbl; *NAmE* also səg'dʒ-/ *adj.* easily influenced by other people: *He was young and highly suggestible.*

sug·ges·tion 🔑 /sə'dʒestʃən; *NAmE* also səg'dʒ-/ *noun*

1 🔑 [C] an idea or a plan that you mention for sb else to think about: *Can I **make a suggestion**?* ◇ *Do you **have any suggestions**?* ◇ **~ (for/about/on sth)** *I'd like to hear your suggestions for ways of raising money.* ◇ *Are there any suggestions about how best to tackle the problem?* ◇ *We welcome any comments and suggestions on these proposals.* ◇ **~ (that ...)** *He agreed with my suggestion that we should change the date.* ◇ *We are **open to suggestions*** (= willing to listen to ideas from other people). ◇ *We need to get it there by four. **Any suggestions?*** **2** 🔑 [U, C, usually sing.] a reason to think that sth, especially sth bad, is true SYN **hint**: **~ of sth** *A spokesman dismissed any suggestion of a boardroom rift.* ◇ **~ that...** *There was no suggestion that he was doing anything illegal.* **3** [C, usually sing.] a slight amount or sign of sth SYN **trace**: *She looked at me with just a suggestion of a smile.* **4** [U] putting an idea into people's minds by connecting it with other ideas: *Most advertisements work through suggestion.* ◇ *the power of suggestion*

IDM **at/on sb's sug'gestion** because sb suggested it: *At his suggestion, I bought the more expensive printer.*

sug·gest·ive /sə'dʒestɪv; *NAmE* also səg'dʒ-/ *adj.* **1 ~ (of sth)** reminding you of sth or making you think about sth: *music that is suggestive of warm summer days* **2** making people think about sex: *suggestive jokes* ▸ **sug·gest·ive·ly** *adv.*: *He leered suggestively.*

sui·cidal /ˌsuːɪ'saɪdl; *BrE* also ˌsjuːɪ-/ *adj.* **1** people who are **suicidal** feel that they want to kill themselves: *On bad days I even felt suicidal.* ◇ *suicidal tendencies* **2** very dangerous and likely to lead to death; likely to cause very serious problems or disaster: *a suicidal leap into the swollen river* ◇ ***It would be suicidal** to risk going out in this weather.* ◇ *The new economic policies could prove suicidal for the party.* ▸ **sui·cid·al·ly** /-dəli/ *adv.*: *suicidally depressed*

sui·cide /'suːɪsaɪd; *BrE* also 'sjuːɪ-/ *noun* **1** [U, C] the act of killing yourself deliberately: *to **commit suicide*** ◇ *an **attempted suicide*** (= one in which the person survives) ◇ *a **suicide letter/note*** (= written before sb tries to commit suicide) ◇ *a **suicide bomber*** (= who expects to die while trying to kill other people with a bomb) ➲ see also ASSISTED SUICIDE **2** [U] a course of action that is likely to ruin your career, position in society, etc: *It would have been political suicide for him to challenge the allegations in court.* **3** [C] (*formal*) a person who commits suicide

'suicide pact *noun* an agreement between two or more people to kill themselves at the same time

sui generis /ˌsuːi 'dʒenərɪs; ˌsuːaɪ; 'genərɪs/ *adj.* (from *Latin, formal*) different from all other people or things SYN **unique**

suit 🔑 /suːt; *BrE* also sjuːt/ *noun, verb*

■ ***noun* 1** 🔑 a set of clothes made of the same cloth, including a jacket and trousers/pants or a skirt: *a business suit* ◇ *a pinstripe suit* ◇ *a **two-/three-piece suit*** (= of two/three pieces of clothing) ➲ VISUAL VOCAB page V50 ➲ see also DINNER SUIT, JUMPSUIT, LEISURE SUIT, LOUNGE SUIT, SAILOR SUIT, SHELL SUIT, SWEATSUIT, TRACKSUIT, TROUSER SUIT **2** 🔑 a set of clothing worn for a particular activity: *a diving suit* ◇ *a suit of armour* ➲ see also BOILER SUIT, SPACESUIT, SWIMSUIT, WETSUIT **3** any of the four sets that form a PACK/DECK of cards: *The suits are called hearts, clubs, diamonds and spades.* ➲ VISUAL VOCAB page V32 **4** = LAWSUIT: *to **file/bring a suit** against sb* ◇ *a divorce suit* ➲ see also PATERNITY SUIT **5** [usually pl.] (*informal*) a person with an important job as a manager in a company or organization, especially one thought of as being mainly concerned with financial matters or as having a lot of influence IDM see BIRTHDAY, FOLLOW, STRONG

■ ***verb*** [no passive] (not used in the progressive tenses) **1** 🔑 to be convenient or useful for sb: **~ sb/sth** *Choose a computer to suit your particular needs.* ◇ *If we met at 2, would that suit you?* ◇ *If you want to go by bus, that **suits me fine**.* ◇ *He can be very helpful, but only when it suits him.* ◇ **it suits sb to do sth** *It suits me to start work at a later time.* **2** 🔑 **~ sb** (especially of clothes, colours, etc.) to make you look attractive: *Blue suits you. You should wear it more often.* ◇ *I don't think this coat really suits me.* **3 ~ sb/sth** (*especially BrE*) (usually used in negative sentences) to be right or good for sb/sth: *This hot weather doesn't suit me.*

IDM **suit your/sb's book** (*BrE, informal*) to be convenient or useful for you/sb **suit sb ˌdown to the 'ground** (*BrE, informal*) to be very convenient or acceptable for sb: *This job suits me down to the ground.* **ˌsuit your'self** (*informal*) **1** to do exactly what you would like: *I choose my assignments to suit myself.* **2** usually used in orders to tell sb to do what they want, even though it annoys you: *'I think I'll stay in this evening.' 'Suit yourself!'*

PHR V **'suit sth to sth/sb** to make sth appropriate for sth/sb: *He can suit his conversation to whoever he's with.*

suit·able 🔑 /'suːtəbl; *BrE* also 'sjuː-/ *adj.*

right or appropriate for a particular purpose or occasion: *a suitable candidate* ◇ **~ for sth/sb** *This programme is not suitable for children.* ◇ *a suitable place for a picnic* ◇ **~ to do sth** *I don't have anything suitable to wear for the party.* ◇ *Would now be a suitable moment to discuss my report?* OPP **unsuitable** ▸ **suit·abil·ity** /ˌsuːtə'bɪləti; *BrE* also ˌsjuː-/ *noun* [U]: *There is no doubt about her suitability for the job.*

suit·ably /'suːtəbli; *BrE* also 'sjuː-/ *adv.* **1** in a way that is right or appropriate for a particular purpose or occasion: *I am not really suitably dressed for a party.* ◇ *suitably qualified candidates* **2** showing the feelings, etc. that you would expect in a particular situation: *He was suitably impressed when I told him I'd won.*

suit·case 🔑 /'suːtkeɪs; *BrE* also 'sjuː-/ (also **case**) *noun*

a case with flat sides and a handle, used for carrying clothes, etc. when you are travelling: *to **pack/unpack a suitcase*** ➲ VISUAL VOCAB page V52

suite /swiːt/ *noun* **1** a set of rooms, especially in a hotel: *a **hotel/private/honeymoon suite*** ◇ *a **suite of rooms/offices*** ➲ see also EN SUITE **2** a set of matching pieces of furniture: *a **bathroom/bedroom suite*** ◇ (*BrE*) *a **three-piece suite** with two armchairs and a sofa* **3** a piece of music made up of three or more related parts, for example pieces from an OPERA: *Stravinsky's Firebird Suite* **4** (*computing*) a set of related computer programs: *a suite of software development tools*

suit·ed 🔑 /'suːtɪd; *BrE* also 'sjuː-/ *adj.* [not before noun] **1** 🔑 right or appropriate for sb/sth: **~ (to sb/sth)** *She was **ideally suited** to the part of Eva Peron.* ◇ *This diet is suited to anyone who wants to lose weight fast.* ◇ **~ (for sb/sth)** *He is not really suited for a teaching career.* OPP **unsuited** **2** 🔑 if two people are **suited** or **well suited**, they are likely to make a good couple: *Jo and I are very well suited.* ◇ *They were not suited to one another.* OPP **unsuited** **3** wearing a suit, or a suit of the type mentioned: *sober-suited city businessmen*

suit·ing /'suːtɪŋ; *BrE* also 'sjuːtɪŋ/ *noun* [U] cloth made especially of wool, used for making suits: *men's suiting*

S

suitor /ˈsuːtə(r); *BrE* also ˈsjuː-/ *noun* **1** (*old-fashioned*) a man who wants to marry a particular woman **2** (*business*) a company that wants to buy another company

su·kuma wiki /sʊˌkuːmə ˈwiːkiː/ *noun* [U] (*EAfrE*) a vegetable with dark green leaves that are cooked; KALE: *a meal of ugali and sukuma wiki*

sul·fate, sul·fide, sul·fur, sul·fur·ic acid (*US*) = SULPHATE, SULPHIDE, SULPHUR, SULPHURIC ACID

sulk /sʌlk/ *verb, noun*

■ ***verb*** [I] (*disapproving*) to look angry and refuse to speak or smile because you want people to know that you are upset about sth: *He went off to sulk in his room.*

■ ***noun*** (*BrE* also **the sulks** [pl.]) a period of not speaking and being bad-tempered because you are angry about sth: *Jo was **in a sulk** upstairs.* ◇ *to have the sulks*

sulky /ˈsʌlki/ *adj.* (*disapproving*) bad-tempered or not speaking because you are angry about sth: *Sarah had looked sulky all morning.* ◇ *a sulky child* ▸ **sulk·ily** /-ɪli/ *adv.* **sulki·ness** *noun* [U]

sul·len /ˈsʌlən/ *adj.* (*disapproving*) **1** bad-tempered and not speaking, either on a particular occasion or because it is part of your character: *Bob looked pale and sullen.* ◇ *She gave him a sullen glare.* ◇ *sullen teenagers* **2** (*literary*) (of the sky or weather) dark and unpleasant ▸ **sul·len·ly** *adv.* **sul·len·ness** *noun* [U]

sully /ˈsʌli/ *verb* (**sul·lies, sully·ing, sul·lied, sul·lied**) (*formal* or *literary*) **1 ~ sth** to spoil or reduce the value of sth **2 ~ sth** to make sth dirty

sul·phate (*BrE*) (*US* **sul·fate**) /ˈsʌlfeɪt/ *noun* [C, U] (*chemistry*) a COMPOUND of SULPHURIC ACID and a chemical element: *copper sulphate*

sul·phide (*BrE*) (*US* **sul·fide**) /ˈsʌlfaɪd/ *noun* [C, U] (*chemistry*) a COMPOUND of sulphur and another chemical element

sul·phur (*BrE*) (*US* **sul·fur**) /ˈsʌlfə(r)/ *noun* [U] (*symb.* S) a chemical element. Sulphur is a pale yellow substance that produces a strong unpleasant smell when it burns and is used in medicine and industry. HELP The spelling **sulfur** has been adopted by the International Union of Pure and Applied Chemistry and by the Royal Society of Chemistry in the UK. However, **sulphur** still remains the usual spelling in British, Irish, South African and Indian English. Both spellings are used in Canadian, Australian and New Zealand English. ▸ **sul·phur·ous** (*BrE*) (*US* **sul·fur·ous**) /ˈsʌlfərəs/ *adj.*: *sulphurous fumes*

ˌsulphur diˈoxide (*BrE*) (*US* **ˌsulfur diˈoxide**) *noun* [U] (*symb.* SO_2) a poisonous gas with a strong smell, that is used in industry and causes air pollution

sul·phur·ic acid (*BrE*) (*US* **sul·fur·ic acid**) /sʌlˌfjʊərɪk ˈæsɪd; *NAmE* -ˌfjʊr-/ *noun* [U] (*symb.* H_2SO_4) a strong clear acid

sul·tan /ˈsʌltən/ *noun* the title given to Muslim rulers in some countries: *the Sultan of Brunei*

sul·tana /sʌlˈtɑːnə; *NAmE* -ˈtænə/ *noun* **1** (*BrE*) (*NAmE* **ˌgolden ˈraisin**) a small dried GRAPE without seeds, used in cakes, etc. **2** the wife, mother, sister or daughter of a sultan

sul·tan·ate /ˈsʌltəneɪt/ *noun* **1** the rank or position of a SULTAN **2** an area of land that is ruled over by a SULTAN: *the Sultanate of Oman* **3** the period of time during which sb is a SULTAN

sul·try /ˈsʌltri/ *adj.* (**sul·trier, sul·tri·est**) **1** (of the weather or air) very hot and uncomfortable SYN **muggy**: *a sultry summer afternoon* **2** (*formal*) (of a woman or her appearance) sexually attractive; seeming to have strong sexual feelings SYN **sexy**: *a sultry smile* ◇ *a sultry singer* ▸ **sul·tri·ness** *noun* [U]

sum 0-w AW /sʌm/ *noun, verb*

■ ***noun*** **1** 0-w [C] **~ (of sth)** an amount of money: *You will be fined the sum of £200.* ◇ *a large sum of money* ◇ *a six-figure sum* ➲ see also LUMP SUM **2** 0-w [C, usually sing.] **~ (of sth)** the number you get when you add two or more numbers together: *The sum of 7 and 12 is 19.* **3** (also **ˌsum ˈtotal**) [sing.] **the ~ of sth** all of sth, especially when you think that it is not very much: *This is the sum of my achievements so far.* **4** [C] a simple problem that involves calculating numbers: *to **do a sum** in your head* ◇ *I was good at sums at school.* ◇ *If I've got my sums right, I should be able to afford the rent.*

IDM **be greater/more than the ˌsum of its ˈparts** to be better or more effective as a group than you would think just by looking at the individual members of the group **in ˈsum** (*formal*) used to introduce a short statement of the main points of a discussion, speech, etc.

■ ***verb*** (-mm-)

PHR V **ˌsum ˈup** | **ˌsum sth↔ˈup 1** 0-w to state the main points of sth in a short and clear form SYN **summarize**: ***To sum up**, there are three main ways of tackling the problem...* ◇ **~ what...** *Can I just sum up what we've agreed so far?* ➲ LANGUAGE BANK at CONCLUSION **2** (of a judge) to give a summary of the main facts and arguments in a legal case, near the end of a trial ➲ related noun SUMMING-UP **ˌsum sb/sth↔ˈup 1** to describe or show the most typical characteristics of sb/sth, especially in a few words: *Totally lazy—that just about sums him up.* **2** to form or express an opinion of sb/sth SYN **size up**: *She quickly summed up the situation and took control.* ➲ related noun SUMMING-UP

summa cum laude /ˌsʊmə ˌkʊm ˈlɔːdi; ˈlaʊdeɪ/ *adv., adj.* (from *Latin*) (in the US) at the highest level of achievement that students can reach when they finish their studies at college: *He graduated summa cum laude from Harvard.* ➲ compare CUM LAUDE, MAGNA CUM LAUDE

sum·mar·ize (*BrE* also **-ise**) AW /ˈsʌməraɪz/ *verb* [T, I] **~ (sth)** to give a summary of sth (= a statement of the main points): *The results of the research are summarized at the end of the chapter.* ➲ LANGUAGE BANK at CONCLUSION

sum·mary 0-w AW /ˈsʌməri/ *noun, adj.*

■ ***noun*** 0-w (*pl.* -ies) a short statement that gives only the main points of sth, not the details: *The following is a summary of our conclusions.* ◇ *a news summary* ◇ *a two-page summary of a government report* ◇ ***In summary**, this was a disappointing performance.* ➲ WRITING TUTOR page WT14

■ ***adj.*** [only before noun] **1** (*formal*) giving only the main points of sth, not the details: *a summary financial statement* ◇ *I made a summary report for the records.* **2** (sometimes *disapproving*) done immediately, without paying attention to the normal process that should be followed: ***summary justice/execution*** ◇ *a summary judgement* ▸ **sum·mar·ily** /ˈsʌmərəli; *NAmE* səˈmerəli/ *adv.*: *to be summarily dismissed/executed*

sum·mat /ˈsʌmət; ˈsəmət/ *noun* (*NEngE, non-standard*) a way of writing a spoken form of 'something'

sum·ma·tion AW /sʌˈmeɪʃn/ *noun* **1** [usually sing.] (*formal*) a summary of what has been done or said: *What he said was a fair summation of the discussion.* **2** (*formal*) a collection of different parts that forms a complete account or impression of sb/sth: *The exhibition presents a summation of the artist's career.* **3** (*NAmE, law*) a final speech that a lawyer makes near the end of a trial in court, after all the evidence has been given

sum·mer 0-w /ˈsʌmə(r)/ *noun* [U, C] the warmest season of the year, coming between spring and autumn/fall: *We're going away **in the summer**.* ◇ *It's very hot here **in summer**.* ◇ *in the summer of 2009* ◇ *late/early summer* ◇ *this/next/last summer* ◇ *a cool/hot/wet summer* ◇ *It is now **high summer*** (= the hottest part of summer). ◇ *a summer's day* ◇ *a summer dress* ◇ *the **summer holidays/vacation*** ◇ *two summers ago* ➲ see also INDIAN SUMMER IDM see SWALLOW *n.*

ˈsummer camp *noun* [C, U] (in the US) a place where children go during the summer and take part in sports and other activities

ˈsummer house *noun* **1** a small building in a garden/yard for sitting in in good weather **2** (also **ˈsummer home**) (*NAmE*) a house that sb lives in only during the summer

S

ˌsummer ˈpudding *noun* [C, U] (*BrE*) a cold DESSERT (= a sweet dish) made from BERRIES surrounded by slices of bread that have absorbed their juice

ˈsummer school *noun* [C, U] courses that are held in the summer at a university or college or, in the US, at a school

ˌsummer ˈstock *noun* [U] (*NAmE*) the production of special plays and other entertainment in areas where people are on holiday/vacation

ˈsummer student *noun* (*CanE*) a student, especially a university student, who is working at a job for the summer

ˈsummer time (*BrE*) (*NAmE* **ˈdaylight saving time**) *noun* [U] the period during which in some countries the clocks are put forward one hour, so that it is light for an extra hour in the evening

sum·mer·time /ˈsʌmətaɪm; *NAmE* -mərt-/ *noun* [U] the season of summer: *It's beautiful here in (the) summertime.*

sum·mery /ˈsʌməri/ *adj.* typical of or suitable for the summer: *summery weather* ◇ *a light summery dress* **OPP** **wintry**

ˌsumming-ˈup *noun* (*pl.* **summings-up**) **1** a speech that the judge makes near the end of a trial in court, in which he or she reminds the JURY about the evidence and the most important points in the case before the JURY makes its decision **2** an occasion when sb states the main points of an argument, etc.

sum·mit /ˈsʌmɪt/ *noun* **1** the highest point of sth, especially the top of a mountain: *We reached the summit at noon.* ◇ *This path leads to the summit.* ◇ (*figurative*) *the summit of his career* ➲ VISUAL VOCAB page V4 **2** an official meeting or series of meetings between the leaders of two or more governments at which they discuss important matters: *a summit in Moscow* ◇ *a summit conference* ➲ COLLOCATIONS at INTERNATIONAL

sum·mon /ˈsʌmən/ *verb* **1 ~ sb (to do sth)** (*formal*) to order sb to appear in court **SYN** **summons**: *He was summoned to appear before the magistrates.* **2 ~ sb (to sth)** | **~ sb to do sth** (*formal*) to order sb to come to you: *In May 1688 he was urgently summoned to London.* ◇ *She summoned the waiter.* **3 ~ sth** (*formal*) to arrange an official meeting **SYN** **convene**: *to summon a meeting* **4 ~ sth** (*formal*) to call for or try to obtain sth: *to* ***summon assistance/help/reinforcements*** **5 ~ sth (up)** to make an effort to produce a particular quality in yourself, especially when you find it difficult **SYN** **muster**: *She was trying to summon up the courage to leave him.* ◇ *I couldn't even summon the energy to get out of bed.*
PHR V **ˌsummon sth↔ˈup** to make a feeling, an idea, a memory, etc. come into your mind **SYN** **evoke**: *The book summoned up memories of my childhood.*

S

sum·mons /ˈsʌmənz/ *noun, verb*
■ ***noun*** (*pl.* **sum·monses** /-zɪz/) **1** (*NAmE* also **cit·ation**) an order to appear in court: *to issue a summons against sb* ◇ *The police have been unable to* ***serve a summons on*** *him.* ◇ *She received a summons to appear in court the following week.* **2** an order to come and see sb: *to obey a royal summons*
■ ***verb*** to order sb to appear in court **SYN** **summon**: **~ sb (for sth)** *She was summonsed for speeding.* ◇ **~ sb to do sth** *He was summonsed to appear in court.*

sumo /ˈsuːməʊ; *NAmE* -moʊ/ (also **ˌsumo ˈwrestling**) *noun* [U] a Japanese style of WRESTLING, in which the people taking part are extremely large: *a sumo wrestler*

sump /sʌmp/ *noun* **1** a hole or hollow area in which liquid waste collects **2** (*NAmE* also **ˈoil pan**) the place under an engine that holds the engine oil

sump·tu·ous /ˈsʌmptʃuəs/ *adj.* (*formal*) very expensive and looking very impressive: *a sumptuous meal* ◇ *We dined in sumptuous surroundings.* ▸ **sump·tu·ous·ly** *adv.* **sump·tu·ous·ness** *noun* [U]

ˌsum ˈtotal *noun* [sing.] (sometimes *disapproving*) the whole of sth; everything: *A photo, a book of poems and a gold ring—this was the sum total of his possessions.*

sun 🔑 /sʌn/ *noun, verb*
■ ***noun*** **1** 🔑 **the sun, the Sun** [sing.] the star that shines in the sky during the day and gives the earth heat and light: *the sun's rays* ◇ *the* ***rising/setting sun*** ◇ ***The sun was shining*** *and birds were singing.* ◇ *The sun was just setting.* ➲ COLLOCATIONS at WEATHER **2** 🔑 (usually **the sun**) [sing., U] the light and heat from the sun **SYN** **sunshine**: *the warmth of the afternoon sun* ◇ *This room gets the sun in the mornings.* ◇ *We sat* ***in the sun.*** ◇ *The sun was blazing hot.* ◇ *Too much sun ages the skin.* ◇ *We did our best to keep* ***out of the sun.*** ◇ *They've booked a holiday* ***in the sun*** (= in a place where it is warm and the sun shines a lot). ◇ *Her face had obviously* ***caught the sun*** (= become red or brown) *on holiday.* ◇ *I was driving westwards and I* ***had the sun in my eyes*** (= the sun was shining in my eyes). ➲ see also SUNNY **3** [C] (*technical*) any star around which planets move
IDM **under the ˈsun** used to emphasize that you are talking about a very large number of things: *We talked about everything under the sun.* **with the ˈsun** when the sun rises or sets: *I get up with the sun.* ➲ more at HAY, PLACE *n.*
■ ***verb*** (**-nn-**) **~ yourself** to sit or lie in a place where the sun is shining on you: *We lay sunning ourselves on the deck.*

ˈsun-baked *adj.* **1** made hard and dry by the heat of the sun: *sun-baked earth* **2** receiving a lot of light and heat from the sun: *sun-baked beaches*

sun·bathe /ˈsʌnbeɪð/ *verb* [I] to sit or lie in the sun, especially in order to go brown (get a SUNTAN) ➲ note at BATH

sun·beam /ˈsʌnbiːm/ *noun* a stream of light from the sun

sun·bed /ˈsʌnbed/ *noun* a bed for lying on under a SUNLAMP ➲ compare SUNLOUNGER

the Sun·belt /ˈsʌnbelt/ *noun* [sing.] the southern and south-western parts of the US that are warm for most of the year

sun·block /ˈsʌnblɒk; *NAmE* -blɑːk/ *noun* [U, C] a cream that you put on your skin to protect it completely from the harmful effects of the sun

sun·burn /ˈsʌnbɜːn; *NAmE* -bɜːrn/ *noun* [U] the condition of having painful red skin because you have spent too much time in the sun ➲ compare SUNTAN

sun·burned /ˈsʌnbɜːnd; *NAmE* -bɜːrnd/ (also **sun·burnt** /ˈsʌnbɜːnt; *NAmE* -bɜːrnt/) *adj.* **1** suffering from sunburn: *Her shoulders were badly sunburned.* **2** (*BrE*) (of a person or of skin) having an attractive brown colour from being in the sun **SYN** **tanned**: *She looked fit and sunburned.*

sun·burst /ˈsʌnbɜːst; *NAmE* -bɜːrst/ *noun* an occasion when the sun appears from behind the clouds and sends out bright streams of light

sun·cream /ˈsʌnkriːm/ *noun* [U, C] (*especially BrE*) cream that you put on your skin to protect it from the harmful effects of the sun

sun·dae /ˈsʌndeɪ; -di/ *noun* a cold DESSERT (= a sweet dish) of ice cream covered with a sweet sauce, nuts, pieces of fruit, etc, usually served in a tall glass

Sun·day 🔑 /ˈsʌndeɪ; -di/ *noun* (*abbr.* **Sun.**)
1 🔑 [C, U] the day of the week after Saturday and before Monday, thought of as either the first or the last day of the week **HELP** To see how **Sunday** is used, look at the examples at **Monday.** **ORIGIN** From the Old English for 'day of the sun', translated from Latin *dies solis*. **2** [C, usually pl.] (*BrE, informal*) a newspaper published on a Sunday
IDM **your ˌSunday ˈbest** (*informal, humorous*) your best clothes ➲ more at MONTH

ˈSunday school *noun* [C, U] a class that is organized by a church or SYNAGOGUE where children can go for a short time on Sundays to learn about the Christian or Jewish religion

ˈsun deck *noun* the part of a ship where passengers can sit to enjoy the sun, or a similar area beside a restaurant or swimming pool

sun·der /ˈsʌndə(r)/ *verb* **~ sth/sb (from sth/sb)** (*formal* or *literary*) to split or break sth/sb apart, especially by force ➲ see also ASUNDER

sun·dial /ˈsʌndaɪəl/ *noun* a device used outdoors, especially in the past, for telling the time when the sun is shining. A pointed piece of metal throws a shadow on a flat surface that is marked with the hours like a clock, and the shadow moves around as the sun moves across the sky.

sundial

sun·down /ˈsʌndaʊn/ *noun* [U] (*especially NAmE*) the time when the sun goes down and night begins SYN **sunset**

sun·down·er /ˈsʌndaʊnə(r)/ *noun* (*BrE, informal*) an alcoholic drink, drunk around the time when the sun goes down

ˈ**sun-drenched** *adj.* [only before noun] (*approving*) having a lot of hot sun: *sun-drenched Mediterranean beaches*

sun·dress /ˈsʌndres/ *noun* a dress that does not cover the arms, neck or shoulders, worn in hot weather

ˈ**sun-dried** *adj.* [only before noun] (especially of food) dried naturally by the heat of the sun: *sun-dried tomatoes*

sun·dries /ˈsʌndriz/ *noun* [pl.] various items, especially small ones, that are not important enough to be named separately

sun·dry /ˈsʌndri/ *adj.* [only before noun] (*formal*) various; not important enough to be named separately: *a watch, a diary and sundry other items*

IDM ˌ**all and ˈsundry** (*informal*) everyone, not just a few special people: *She was known to all and sundry as Bella.* ◇ *The club is open to all and sundry.*

sun·flower /ˈsʌnflaʊə(r)/ *noun* a very tall plant with large yellow flowers, grown in gardens or for its seeds and their oil that are used in cooking: *sunflower oil* ➲ VISUAL VOCAB page V9

sung *past part.* of SING

sun·glasses /ˈsʌnglɑːsɪz; *NAmE* -glæs-/ (also *informal* **shades**) *noun* [pl.] a pair of glasses with dark glass in them that you wear to protect your eyes from bright light from the sun: *a pair of sunglasses* ➲ see also DARK GLASSES

ˈ**sun hat** *noun* a hat worn to protect the head and neck from the sun ➲ VISUAL VOCAB page V53

sunk *past part.* of SINK

sunk·en /ˈsʌŋkən/ *adj.* **1** [only before noun] that has fallen to the bottom of the sea or the ocean, or of a lake or river SYN **submerged**: *a sunken ship* ◇ *sunken treasure* **2** (of eyes or cheeks) hollow and deep as a result of disease, getting old, or not having enough food **3** [only before noun] at a lower level than the area around: *a sunken garden*

ˈ**sun-kissed** *adj.* [usually before noun] made warm or brown by the sun: *sun-kissed bodies on the beach*

sun·lamp /ˈsʌnlæmp/ *noun* a lamp that produces ULTRAVIOLET light that has the same effect as the sun and can turn the skin brown

sun·less /ˈsʌnləs/ *adj.* without any sun; receiving no light from the sun SYN **gloomy**: *a sunless day* OPP **sunny**

sun·light /ˈsʌnlaɪt/ *noun* [U] the light from the sun: *a **ray/pool of sunlight*** ◇ ***shafts of** bright **sunlight*** ◇ *The morning sunlight flooded into the room.*

sun·lit /ˈsʌnlɪt/ *adj.* [usually before noun] receiving light from the sun: *sunlit streets*

ˈ**sun lounge** (*BrE*) (also **sun·room** *NAmE, BrE*) *noun* a room with large windows, and often a glass roof, that lets in a lot of light

sun·loun·ger /ˈsʌnlaʊndʒə(r)/ *noun* (*BrE*) a chair with a long seat that supports your legs, used for sitting or lying on in the sun ➲ compare LOUNGER, SUNBED ➲ VISUAL VOCAB page V16

Sunni /ˈsʊni; ˈsʌni/ *noun* (*pl.* **Sunni** or **Sun·nis**) **1** [U] one of the two main branches of the Islamic religion ➲ compare SHIA **2** [C] a member of the Sunni branch of Islam ➲ compare SHIITE ▶ **Sun·nite** /ˈsʊnaɪt; ˈsʌn-/ *adj.* [usually before noun]

sun·nies /ˈsʌniz/ [pl.], *noun* (*AustralE, NZE, informal*) SUNGLASSES

sunny /ˈsʌni/ *adj.* (**sun·nier, sun·ni·est**) **1** with a lot of bright light from the sun: *a sunny day* ◇ *sunny weather* ◇ *The outlook for the weekend is hot and sunny.* ◇ *a sunny garden* ◇ *Italy was at its sunniest.* **2** cheerful and happy: *a sunny disposition*

ˈ**sunny side** *noun* the side of sth that receives most light from the sun: (*figurative*) *the sunny side of life* (= the more cheerful aspects of life)

IDM ˌ**sunny side ˈup** (*NAmE*) (of an egg) fried on one side only

sun·rise /ˈsʌnraɪz/ *noun* **1** [U] the time when the sun first appears in the sky in the morning SYN **dawn**: *We got up **at sunrise**.* **2** [C, usually sing.] the colours in the part of the sky where the sun first appears in the morning: *the pinks and yellows of the sunrise*

ˈ**sunrise industry** *noun* a new industry, especially one connected with ELECTRONICS or computers, that is successful and growing ➲ compare SUNSET INDUSTRY

sun·roof /ˈsʌnruːf/ *noun* (*pl.* **-roofs**) a part of the roof of a car that you can open to let air and light in

sun·room /ˈsʌnruːm; -rʊm/ (*especially NAmE*) (*BrE* also ˈ**sun lounge**) *noun* a room with large windows, and often a glass roof, that lets in a lot of light

sun·screen /ˈsʌnskriːn/ *noun* [C, U] a cream or liquid that you put on your skin to protect it from the harmful effects of the sun: *a high factor* (= strong) *sunscreen*

sun·set /ˈsʌnset/ *noun, adj., verb*

■ ***noun*** **1** [U] the time when the sun goes down and night begins: *Every evening **at sunset** the flag was lowered.* **2** [C] the colours in the part of the sky where the sun slowly goes down in the evening: *a spectacular sunset* **3** [C] a fixed period of time after which a law or the effect of a law will end: *There is a five-year sunset on the new tax.*

■ ***adj.*** [only before noun] **1** used to describe a colour that is like one of the colours in a sunset: *sunset yellow* **2** used to describe sth that is near its end, or that happens at the end of sth: *This is his sunset tour after fifty years as a singer.* **3** (of a law or the effect of a law) designed to end or to end sth after a fixed period of time: *a two-year sunset clause in the new law*

■ ***verb*** (-tt-) [I, T] **~ (sth)** (of a law or the effect of a law) to end or to end sth after a fixed period of time: *The tax relief will sunset after a year.*

ˈ**sunset industry** *noun* an old industry that has started to become less successful ➲ compare SUNRISE INDUSTRY

ˈ**sunset provision** (also ˈ**sunset clause**) *noun* (*law*) part of a law, rule or agreement that states that it will no longer apply from a particular date

sun·shade /ˈsʌnʃeɪd/ *noun* **1** a light umbrella or other object such as an AWNING, that is used to protect people from hot sun: *a child's buggy fitted with a sunshade* ➲ VISUAL VOCAB page V16 ➲ compare PARASOL **2 sun·shades** [pl.] a pair of dark glasses that you wear to protect your eyes from bright light from the sun, especially ones that fix on to your ordinary glasses

sun·shine /ˈsʌnʃaɪn/ *noun* [U] **1** the light and heat of the sun: *the warm spring sunshine* ➲ COLLOCATIONS at WEATHER **2** (*informal*) happiness: *She brought sunshine into our dull lives.* **3** (*BrE, informal*) used for addressing sb in a friendly, or sometimes a rude way: *Hello, sunshine!* ◇ *Look, sunshine, who do you think you're talking to?* IDM see RAY

ˈ**sunshine law** *noun* (*US*) a law that forces government organizations to make certain types of information available to the public

sun·spot /ˈsʌnspɒt; *NAmE* -spɑːt/ *noun* a dark area that sometimes appears on the sun's surface

sun·stroke /ˈsʌnstrəʊk; *NAmE* -stroʊk/ *noun* [U] an illness with fever, weakness, headache, etc. caused by too much direct sun, especially on the head

sun·tan /ˈsʌntæn/ *noun* [usually sing.] = TAN: *Where have you been to get that suntan?* ➲ compare SUNBURN

S

▶ **sun·tan** *adj.* [only before noun]: *suntan oil* **sun·tanned** *adj.* = TANNED: *a suntanned face*

sun·trap /ˈsʌntræp/ *noun* a place that is sheltered from the wind and gets a lot of sun

sun·up /ˈsʌnʌp/ *noun* [U] (*especially NAmE*) the time when the sun rises and day begins

ˈ**sun-worship·per** *noun* (*informal*) a person who enjoys lying in the sun very much

sup /sʌp/ *verb* (-pp-) [I, T] **~ (sth)** (*NEngE* or *old-fashioned*) to drink sth, especially in small amounts ▶ **sup** *noun*

super /ˈsuːpə(r); *BrE* also ˈsjuː-/ *adj., adv., noun*
- ■ ***adj.*** (*informal*, becoming *old-fashioned*) extremely good: *a super meal* ◇ *We had a super time in Italy.* ◇ *She was super* (= very kind) *when I was having problems.*
- ■ ***adv.*** (*informal*) especially; particularly: *He's been super understanding.*
- ■ ***noun*** **1** (*BrE, informal*) a SUPERINTENDENT in the police **2** (*NAmE*) a SUPERINTENDENT of a building

super- /ˈsuːpə(r); *BrE* also ˈsjuː-/ *combining form* **1** (in adjectives, adverbs and nouns) extremely; more or better than normal: *super-rich* ◇ *superhuman* ◇ *superglue* **2** (in nouns and verbs) above; over: *superstructure* ◇ *superimpose*

super·abun·dance /ˌsuːpərəˈbʌndəns; *BrE* also ˌsjuː-/ *noun* [sing., U] (*formal*) much more than enough of sth ▶ **super·abun·dant** *adj.*

super·annu·ated /ˌsuːpərˈænjueɪtɪd; *BrE* also ˌsjuː-/ *adj.* [usually before noun] (*formal* or *humorous*) (of people or things) too old for work or to be used for their original purpose: *superannuated rock stars*

super·annu·ation /ˌsuːpərˌænjuˈeɪʃn; *BrE* also ˌsjuː-/ *noun* [U] (*especially BrE*) a pension that you get, usually from your employer, when you stop working when you are old and that you pay for while you are working; the money that you pay for this

su·perb /suːˈpɜːb; sjuː-; *NAmE* suːˈpɜːrb/ *adj.* excellent; of very good quality: *a superb player* ◇ *The car's in superb condition.* ◇ *His performance was absolutely superb.* ◇ *You look superb.* ➲ SYNONYMS at EXCELLENT ▶ **su·perb·ly** *adv.*: *a superbly illustrated book* ◇ *She plays superbly.*

the ˈSuper Bowl™ *noun* an AMERICAN FOOTBALL game played every year to decide the winner of the National Football League

super·bug /ˈsuːpəbʌɡ; ˈsjuː-; *NAmE* ˈsuːpərb-/ *noun* a type of bacteria that cannot easily be killed by ANTIBIOTICS ➲ see also MRSA

super·cen·ter (*US*) (*BrE* **super·centre**) /ˈsuːpəsentə(r); ˈsjuː-; *NAmE* ˈsuːpər-/ *noun* (*especially US*) a very large shop/store, especially a grocery store that also sells lots of other goods

super·charged /ˈsuːpətʃɑːdʒd; ˈsjuː-; *NAmE* ˈsuːpərtʃɑːrdʒd/ *adj.* **1** (of an engine) powerful because it is supplied with air or fuel at a pressure that is higher than normal **2** (*informal*) stronger, more powerful or more effective than usual: *supercharged words, like 'terrorism' or 'fascism'* ▶ **super·charg·er** *noun*: *VW's supercharger for its 16-valve engine*

super·cili·ous /ˌsuːpəˈsɪliəs; ˌsjuː-; *NAmE* ˌsuːpərˈs-/ *adj.* (*disapproving*) behaving towards other people as if you think you are better than they are **SYN** **superior** ▶ **super·cili·ous·ly** *adv.* **super·cili·ous·ness** *noun* [U]

super·com·puter /ˈsuːpəkəmpjuːtə(r); ˈsjuː-; *NAmE* ˈsuːpərk-/ *noun* a powerful computer with a large amount of memory and a very fast CENTRAL PROCESSING UNIT

super·con·duct·iv·ity /ˌsuːpəˌkɒndʌkˈtɪvəti; ˌsjuː-; *NAmE* ˌsuːpərˌkɑːn-/ *noun* [U] (*physics*) the property (= characteristic) of some substances at very low temperatures to let electricity flow with no RESISTANCE

super·con·duct·or /ˈsuːpəkəndʌktə(r); ˈsjuː-; *NAmE* ˈsuːpərk-/ *noun* (*physics*) a substance that has SUPERCONDUCTIVITY

super·con·tin·ent /ˈsuːpəkɒntɪnənt; ˈsjuː-; *NAmE* ˈsuːpərkɑːn-/ *noun* (*geology*) any of the very large areas of land, for example Gondwana or Laurasia, that existed millions of years ago

super-duper /ˌsuːpə ˈduːpə(r); ˌsjuː-; *NAmE* ˌsuːpər/ *adj.* (*old-fashioned, informal*) excellent

super·ego /ˌsuːpərˈiːɡəʊ; ˌsjuː-; *NAmE* ˌsuːpərˈiːɡoʊ/ *noun* [usually sing.] (*pl.* -os) (*psychology*) the part of the mind that makes you aware of right and wrong and makes you feel guilty if you do wrong ➲ compare EGO, ID

super·fi·cial /ˌsuːpəˈfɪʃl; ˌsjuː-; *NAmE* ˌsuːpərˈf-/ *adj.* **1** (often *disapproving*) not studying or looking at sth thoroughly; seeing only what is obvious: *a superficial analysis* ◇ *The book shows only a superficial understanding of the historical context.* **2** appearing to be true, real or important until you look at it more carefully: *superficial differences/similarities* ◇ *When you first meet her, she gives a superficial impression of warmth and friendliness.* **3** (of a wound or damage) only affecting the surface and therefore not serious: *a superficial injury* ◇ *superficial burns* **4** (*disapproving*) not concerned with anything serious or important and lacking any depth of understanding or feeling **SYN** **shallow**: *a superficial friendship* ◇ *The guests engaged in superficial chatter.* ◇ *She's so superficial!* **5** (*technical*) of or on the surface of sth: *superficial veins* ◇ *a superficial deposit of acidic soils* ▶ **super·fi·ci·al·ity** /ˌsuːpəˌfɪʃiˈæləti; ˌsjuː-; *NAmE* ˌsuːpərˌf-/ *noun* [U] **super·fi·cial·ly** /-ʃəli/ *adv.*

super·fine /ˈsuːpəfaɪn; ˈsjuː-; *NAmE* ˈsuːpərf-/ *adj.* (*technical*) **1** extremely light or thin; made of extremely small pieces: *superfine fibres* ◇ *superfine powder* **2** of extremely good quality: *superfine cloth*

su·per·flu·ous /suːˈpɜːfluəs; sjuː-; *NAmE* suːˈpɜːrf-/ *adj.* (*formal*) more than you need or want **SYN** **unnecessary**: *She gave him a look that made words superfluous.* ▶ **su·per·flu·ity** /ˌsuːpəˈfluːəti; ˌsjuː-; *NAmE* ˌsuːpərˈf-/ *noun* [U, sing.] (*formal*) **su·per·flu·ous·ly** *adv.*

super·food *noun* /ˈsuːpəfuːd; ˈsjuː-; *NAmE* ˈsuːpər-/ a type of food that some people think is very good for you and helps to prevent disease: *the health benefits of so-called superfoods*

super·glue /ˈsuːpəɡluː; ˈsjuː-; *NAmE* ˈsuːpərɡ-/ *noun* [U] a very strong glue that sticks very quickly and is used in small quantities for repairing things

super·grass /ˈsuːpəɡrɑːs; ˈsjuː-; *NAmE* ˈsuːpərɡræs/ *noun* (*BrE, informal*) a criminal who informs the police about the activities of a large number of other criminals, usually in order to get a less severe punishment ➲ compare GRASS *n.* (5)

super·group /ˈsuːpəɡruːp; ˈsjuː-; *NAmE* ˈsuːpərɡ-/ *noun* a very successful and very famous band that plays rock music, especially one whose members have already become famous in other bands

super·heated /ˌsuːpəˈhiːtɪd; ˌsjuː-; *NAmE* ˌsuːpərˈh-/ *adj.* (*physics*) **1** (of a liquid) that has been heated under pressure above its boiling point without becoming a gas **2** (of a gas) that has been heated above its temperature of SATURATION (= below which it becomes a liquid)

super·heavy·weight /ˌsuːpəˈheviweɪt; ˌsjuː-; *NAmE* ˌsuːpərˈh-/ *noun* a BOXER of the heaviest class, weighing 91 kilograms or more

super·hero /ˈsuːpəhɪərəʊ; ˈsjuː-; *NAmE* ˈsuːpərhɪroʊ; -hiːroʊ/ *noun* (*pl.* -oes) a character in a story, film/movie, etc. who has unusual strength or power and uses it to help people; a real person who has done sth unusually brave to help sb **OPP** **supervillain**

super·high·way /ˌsuːpəˈhaɪweɪ; ˌsjuː-; *NAmE* ˌsuːpərˈh-/ *noun* **1** (*NAmE, old-fashioned*) = INTERSTATE **2** = INFORMATION SUPERHIGHWAY

super·human /ˌsuːpəˈhjuːmən; ˌsjuː-; *NAmE* ˌsuːpərˈh-/ *adj.* having much greater power, knowledge, etc. than is normal **SYN** **heroic**: *superhuman strength* ◇ *It took an almost* ***superhuman effort*** *to contain his anger.* ➲ compare SUBHUMAN

super·im·pose /ˌsuːpərɪm'pəʊz; ˌsjuː-; *NAmE* ˌsuːpərɪm'poʊz/ *verb* **1 ~ sth (on/onto sth)** to put one image on top of another so that the two can be seen combined: *A diagram of the new road layout was superimposed on a map of the city.* **2 ~ sth (on/onto sth)** to add some of the qualities of one system or pattern to another one in order to produce sth that combines the qualities of both: *She has tried to superimpose her own attitudes onto this ancient story.* ▶ **super·im·pos·it·ion** /ˌsuːpərˌɪmpə'zɪʃn; *BrE* also ˌsjuː-/ *noun* [U]

super·in·tend /ˌsuːpərɪn'tend; *BrE* also ˌsjuː-/ *verb* **~ sth** (*formal*) to be in charge of sth and make sure that everything is working, being done, etc. as it should be **SYN supervise** ▶ **super·in·tend·ence** /-əns/ *noun* [U]

super·in·tend·ent /ˌsuːpərɪn'tendənt; *BrE* also ˌsjuː-/ *noun* **1** a person who has a lot of authority and manages and controls an activity, a place, a group of workers, etc: *a park superintendent* ◇ *the superintendent of schools in Dallas* **2** (*abbr.* **Supt**) (in Britain) a police officer just above the rank of CHIEF INSPECTOR: *Superintendent Livesey* **3** (*abbr.* **Supt.**) (in the US) the head of a police department **4** (*NAmE*) a person whose job is to be in charge of a building and make small repairs, etc. to it

su·per·ior 0‑ᵕ /suː'pɪəriə(r); sjuː-; *NAmE* suː'pɪr-/ *adj., noun*

■ ***adj.*** **1** 0‑ᵕ **~ (to sb/sth)** better in quality than sb/sth else; greater than sb/sth else: ***vastly superior*** ◇ *superior intelligence* ◇ *This model is technically superior to its competitors.* ◇ *Liverpool were clearly the superior team.* ◇ *The enemy won because of their superior numbers* (= there were more of them). **OPP inferior** **2** 0‑ᵕ **~ (to sb)** higher in rank, importance or position: *my superior officer* ◇ *superior status* ◇ *a superior court of law* **OPP inferior** **3** (*disapproving*) showing by your behaviour that you think you are better than others **SYN arrogant**: *a superior manner* ◇ *He always looks so superior.* **4** (used especially in advertisements) of very good quality; better than other similar things: *superior apartments*

■ ***noun*** **1** a person of higher rank, status or position: *your social superiors* ◇ *He's my **immediate superior*** (= the person directly above me). ◇ *I'm going to complain to your superiors.* **OPP inferior** **2** used in titles for the head of a religious community: *Mother Superior*

su·per·ior·ity /suːˌpɪəri'ɒrəti; sjuː-; *NAmE* suːˌpɪri'ɔːr-; -'ɑːr-/ *noun* [U] **1 ~ (in sth)** | **~ (to/over sth/sb)** the state or quality of being better, more skilful, more powerful, greater, etc. than others: *the superiority of this operating system* ◇ *to have **naval/air superiority*** (= more ships/planes than the enemy) **2** behaviour that shows that you think you are better than other people: *an air of superiority* **OPP inferiority**

suˌperi'ority complex *noun* a feeling that you are better or more important than other people, often as a way of hiding your feelings of failure

su·per·la·tive /su'pɜːlətɪv; sjuː-; *NAmE* suː'pɜːrl-/ *adj., noun*

■ ***adj.*** **1** excellent **SYN first-rate**: *a superlative performance* **2** (*grammar*) relating to adjectives or adverbs that express the highest degree of sth, for example *best, worst, slowest* and *most difficult* ➲ compare COMPARATIVE ▶ **su·per·la·tive·ly** *adv.*

■ ***noun*** (*grammar*) the form of an adjective or adverb that expresses the highest degree of sth: *It's hard to find enough superlatives to describe this book.* ➲ compare COMPARATIVE

super·man /'suːpəmæn; 'sjuː-; *NAmE* 'suːpərm-/ *noun* (*pl.* **-men** /-men/) a man who is unusually strong or intelligent or who can do sth extremely well ➲ compare SUPERWOMAN

super·mar·ket 0‑ᵕ /'suːpəmɑːkɪt; 'sjuː-; *NAmE* 'suːpərmɑːrkət/ (*NAmE* also **'grocery store**) *noun* a large shop/store that sells food, drinks and goods used in the home. People choose what they want from the shelves and pay for it as they leave.

super·max /'suːpəmæks; 'sjuː-; *NAmE* 'suːpər-/ *noun* (*especially NAmE*) a maximum security prison, intended for very dangerous prisoners

super·model /'suːpəmɒdl; 'sjuː-; *NAmE* 'suːpərmɑːdl/ *noun* a very famous and highly paid fashion model

super·nat·ural /ˌsuːpə'nætʃrəl; ˌsjuː-; *NAmE* ˌsuːpər'n-/ *adj.* **1** that cannot be explained by the laws of science and that seems to involve gods or magic **SYN paranormal**: *supernatural powers* ◇ *supernatural strength* ➲ compare NATURAL **2 the supernatural** *noun* [sing.] events, forces or powers that cannot be explained by the laws of science and that seem to involve gods or magic **SYN the paranormal**: *a belief in the supernatural* ▶ **super·nat·ur·al·ly** /-'nætʃrəli/ *adv.*

super·nova /ˌsuːpə'nəʊvə; ˌsjuː-; *NAmE* ˌsuːpər'noʊvə/ *noun* (*pl.* **super·novae** /-viː/ or **super·novas**) (*astronomy*) a star that suddenly becomes much brighter because it is exploding ➲ compare NOVA

super·numer·ary /ˌsuːpə'njuːmərəri; ˌsjuː-; *NAmE* ˌsuːpər'nuːməreri/ *adj.* (*formal*) more than you normally need; extra

super·ordin·ate /ˌsuːpər'ɔːdɪnət; ˌsjuː-; *NAmE* -'ɔːrd-/ (also **hyper·nym**) *noun* (*linguistics*) a word with a general meaning that includes the meanings of other particular words, for example 'fruit' is the superordinate of 'apple', 'orange', etc. ➲ compare HYPONYM ▶ **super·ordin·ate** *adj.* ➲ compare SUBORDINATE

super·pose /ˌsuːpə'pəʊz; ˌsjuː-; *NAmE* ˌsuːpər'poʊz/ *verb* **~ sth** to put sth on or above sth else: *They had superposed a picture of his head onto someone else's body.* ▶ **super·pos·ition** *noun* /-pə'zɪʃn/

super·power /'suːpəpaʊə(r); 'sjuː-; *NAmE* 'suːpərp-/ *noun* one of the countries in the world that has very great military or economic power and a lot of influence, for example the US

super·script /'suːpəskrɪpt; 'sjuː-; *NAmE* 'suːpərs-/ *adj.* (*technical*) written or printed above the normal line of writing or printing ▶ **super·script** *noun* [U]

super·sede /ˌsuːpə'siːd; ˌsjuː-; *NAmE* ˌsuːpər's-/ *verb* **~ sth/sb** [often passive] to take the place of sth/sb that is considered to be old-fashioned or no longer the best available: *The theory has been superseded by more recent research.*

super·size /'suːpəsaɪz; 'sjuː-; *NAmE* 'suːpər-/ *adj., verb*

■ ***adj.*** (also **super·sized**) bigger than normal: *supersize portions of fries* ◇ *supersized clothing*

■ ***verb*** [T, I] **~ (sb/sth)** to make sb/sth bigger; to become bigger: *We are being supersized into obesity* (= made very fat) *by the fast food industry.* ◇ *TV ads encourage kids to supersize.*

super·sonic /ˌsuːpə'sɒnɪk; ˌsjuː-; *NAmE* ˌsuːpər'sɑːnɪk/ *adj.* faster than the speed of sound: *a supersonic aircraft* ◇ *supersonic flight* ➲ compare SUBSONIC

super·star /'suːpəstɑː(r); 'sjuː-; *NAmE* 'suːpərs-/ *noun* a very famous performer, for example an actor, a singer or a sports player

super·state /'suːpəsteɪt; 'sjuː-; *NAmE* 'suːpərs-/ *noun* a very powerful state, especially one that is formed by several nations joining or working together: *the European superstate*

super·sti·tion /ˌsuːpə'stɪʃn; ˌsjuː-; *NAmE* ˌsuːpər's-/ *noun* [U, C] (often *disapproving*) the belief that particular events happen in a way that cannot be explained by reason or science; the belief that particular events bring good or bad luck: *According to superstition, breaking a mirror brings bad luck.*

super·sti·tious /ˌsuːpə'stɪʃəs; ˌsjuː-; *NAmE* ˌsuːpər's-/ *adj.* believing in superstitions: *superstitious beliefs* ◇ *I'm superstitious about the number 13.* ▶ **super·sti·tious·ly** *adv.*

super·store /'suːpəstɔː(r); 'sjuː-; *NAmE* 'suːpərs-/ *noun* a very large supermarket or a large shop/store that sells a wide variety of one type of goods: *a computer superstore*

super·struc·ture /'suːpəstrʌktʃə(r); 'sjuː-; *NAmE* 'suːpərs-/ *noun* **1** a structure that is built on top of sth, for

S

example the upper parts of a ship or the part of a building above the ground ➲ compare SUBSTRUCTURE **2** (*formal*) the systems and beliefs in a society that have developed from more simple ones

super·tank·er /ˈsuːpətæŋkə(r); ˈsjuː-; *NAmE* ˈsuːpərt-/ *noun* a very large ship for carrying oil, etc.

ˌSuper ˈTuesday *noun* [sing.] (*informal*) a day on which several US states hold PRIMARY elections

super·vene /ˌsuːpəˈviːn; ˌsjuː-; *NAmE* ˌsuːpərˈv-/ *verb* [I] (*formal*) to happen, especially unexpectedly, and have a powerful effect on the existing situation

super·vil·lain /ˈsuːpəvɪlən; ˈsjuː; *NAmE* ˈsuːpər-/ *noun* a very bad character in a story, especially one with magical powers OPP **superhero**

super·vise /ˈsuːpəvaɪz; ˈsjuː-; *NAmE* ˈsuːpərv-/ *verb* [T, I] to be in charge of sb/sth and make sure that everything is done correctly, safely, etc: **~ (sb/sth)** *to supervise building work* ◇ **~ sb doing sth** *She supervised the children playing near the pool.* ▶ **super·vi·sion** /ˌsuːpəˈvɪʒn; ˌsjuː-; *NAmE* ˌsuːpərˈv-/ *noun* [U, C]: *Very young children should not be left to play without supervision.* ◇ *The drug should only be used* ***under*** *medical* ***supervision****.* ◇ *I have weekly supervisions* (= meetings with a TUTOR or SUPERVISOR).

ˌsuperˈvision order *noun* (*law*) in the UK, an order made by a court which says that the local government or a PROBATION OFFICER must be responsible for a child, help them and check that they behave well

super·visor /ˈsuːpəvaɪzə(r); ˈsjuː-; *NAmE* ˈsuːpərv-/ *noun* a person who supervises sb/sth: *I have a meeting with my supervisor about my research topic.* ▶ **super·vis·ory** /ˌsuːpəˈvaɪzəri; ˌsjuː-; *NAmE* ˌsuːpərˈv-/ *adj.*: *She has a supervisory role on the project.*

super·woman /ˈsuːpəwʊmən; ˈsjuː-; *NAmE* ˈsuːpərw-/ *noun* (*pl.* **-women** /-wɪmɪn/) a woman who is unusually strong or intelligent or who can do sth extremely well, especially a woman who has a successful career and also takes care of her home and family ➲ compare SUPERMAN

su·pine /ˈsuːpaɪn; *BrE* also ˈsjuː-/ *adj.* (*formal*) **1** lying flat on your back: *a supine position* ➲ compare PRONE **2** (*disapproving*) not willing to act or disagree with sb because you are lazy or morally weak ▶ **su·pine·ly** *adv.*

sup·per /ˈsʌpə(r)/ *noun* [U, C] the last meal of the day, either a main meal, usually smaller and less formal than dinner, or a SNACK eaten before you go to bed: *I'll do my homework after supper.* ◇ *What's for supper?* ◇ *We'll have an early supper tonight.* ➲ note at MEAL ➲ compare TEA (6)

S

sup·plant /səˈplɑːnt; *NAmE* -ˈplænt/ *verb* **~ sb/sth** (*formal*) to take the place of sb/sth (especially sb/sth older or less modern) SYN **replace**

sup·ple /ˈsʌpl/ *adj.* **1** able to bend and move parts of your body easily into different positions: *her slim, supple body* ◇ *These exercises will help to keep you supple.* **2** soft and able to bend easily without cracking: *Moisturizing cream helps to keep your skin soft and supple.* ▶ **supple·ness** *noun* [U]

sup·ple·ment AW *noun, verb*

■ ***noun*** /ˈsʌplɪmənt/ **1** a thing that is added to sth else to improve or complete it: ***vitamin/dietary supplements*** (=VITAMINS and other foods eaten in addition to what you usually eat) ◇ **~ to sth** *Industrial sponsorship is a supplement to government funding.* **2** an extra separate section, often in the form of a magazine, that is sold with a newspaper: *the Sunday* ***colour supplements*** **3 ~ (to sth)** a book or a section at the end of a book that gives extra information or deals with a special subject: *the supplement to the Oxford English Dictionary* **4** (*BrE*) an amount of money that you pay for an extra service or item, especially in addition to the basic cost of a holiday/vacation SYN **surcharge**: *There is a £10 supplement for a single room.* ◇ *Safety deposit boxes are available* ***at a supplement****.*

■ ***verb*** /ˈsʌplɪment/ to add sth to sth in order to improve it or make it more complete: **~ sth with sth** *a diet supplemented with vitamin pills* ◇ **~ sth** *He supplements his income by giving private lessons.* ▶ **sup·ple·men·ta·tion** /ˌsʌplɪmenˈteɪʃn/ *noun* [U]

sup·ple·men·tary AW /ˌsʌplɪˈmentri/ (*especially BrE*) (*NAmE* usually **sup·ple·men·tal** /ˌsʌplɪˈmentl/) *adj.* provided in addition to sth else in order to improve or complete it SYN **additional**: *supplementary information*

suppleˌmentary ˈangle *noun* (*mathematics*) either of two angles which together make 180° ➲ compare COMPLEMENTARY ANGLE

sup·ple·tion /səˈpliːʃn/ *noun* [U] (*linguistics*) the use of a word as a particular form of a verb when the word is not related to the main form of the verb, for example 'went' as the past tense of 'go' ▶ **sup·ple·tive** /səˈpliːtɪv/ *adj.*

sup·pli·cant /ˈsʌplɪkənt/ (also **sup·pli·ant** /ˈsʌpliənt/) *noun* (*formal*) a person who asks for sth in a HUMBLE way, especially from God or a powerful person

sup·pli·ca·tion /ˌsʌplɪˈkeɪʃn/ *noun* [U, C] (*formal*) the act of asking for sth with a very HUMBLE request or prayer: *She knelt in supplication.*

sup·plier /səˈplaɪə(r)/ *noun* a person or company that supplies goods: *a leading supplier of computers in the UK*

sup·ply 🔑 /səˈplaɪ/ *noun, verb*

■ ***noun*** **1** 🔑 [C] an amount of sth that is provided or available to be used: *The water supply is unsafe.* ◇ *Supplies of food are almost exhausted.* ◇ *We cannot guarantee adequate supplies of raw materials.* ◇ *Books were in* ***short supply*** (= there were not enough of them). **2** 🔑 **supplies** [pl.] the things such as food, medicines, fuel, etc. that are needed by a group of people, for example an army or EXPEDITION: *Our supplies were running out.* ◇ *a transport plane carrying food and* ***medical supplies*** *for refugees* **3** 🔑 [U] the act of supplying sth: *The UN has agreed to allow the supply of emergency aid.* ◇ *A stroke can disrupt the supply of oxygen to the brain.* ◇ *The electricity supply* (= the system supplying electricity) *had been cut off.*

■ ***verb*** 🔑 (**sup·plies**, **sup·ply·ing**, **sup·plied**, **sup·plied**) to provide sb/sth with sth that they need or want, especially in large quantities: **~ sth to sb/sth** *Foreign governments supplied arms to the rebels.* ◇ **~ sb/sth with sth** *Foreign governments supplied the rebels with arms.* ◇ **~ sb/sth** *Local schools supply many of the volunteers.* ◇ *foods supplying our daily vitamin needs*

supˌply and deˈmand *noun* [U] (*economics*) the relationship between the amount of goods or services that are available and the amount that people want to buy, especially when this controls prices

supˈply chain *noun* [usually sing.] (*business*) the series of processes involved in the production and supply of goods, from when they are first made, grown, etc. until they are bought or used

supˈply line *noun* a route along which food, equipment, etc. is transported to an army during a war

supˈply-side *adj.* [only before noun] (*economics*) connected with the policy of reducing taxes in order to encourage economic growth

supˈply teacher (*BrE*) (*NAmE* **ˈsubstitute teacher**) *noun* a teacher employed to do the work of another teacher who is away because of illness, etc.

sup·port 🔑 /səˈpɔːt; *NAmE* səˈpɔːrt/ *verb, noun*

■ ***verb***

▸ ENCOURAGE/GIVE HELP **1** 🔑 to help or encourage sb/sth by saying or showing that you agree with them/it SYN **back**: **~ sb/sth** *to support a proposal* ◇ *These measures are* ***strongly supported*** *by environmental groups.* ◇ *If you raise it at the meeting, I'll support you.* ◇ **~ sb/sth in sth** *The government supported the unions in their demand for a minimum wage.* **2** 🔑 **~ sb** to give or be ready to give help to sb if they need it: *an organization that supports people with AIDS* ◇ *The company will support customers in Europe* (= solve their problems with a product).

▸ PROVIDE MONEY, ETC. **3** 🔑 **~ sth** to help or encourage sth to be successful by giving it money SYN **sponsor**: *Several major companies are supporting the project.* **4** 🔑 **~ sb/sth/yourself** to provide everything necessary, especially money, so that sb/sth can live or exist: *Mark has two children to support from his first marriage.* ◇ *He turned to crime* *to support his drug habit.* ◇ *The atmosphere of Mars could not support life.*

▸ HOLD IN POSITION **5** ⚷ **~ sb/sth** to hold sb/sth in position; to prevent sb/sth from falling: *a platform supported by concrete pillars* ◇ *Support the baby's head when you hold it.*

▸ HELP PROVE STH **6** ⚷ **~ sth** to help to show that sth is true SYN **corroborate**: *The witness's story was not supported by the evidence.* ⮌ LANGUAGE BANK at EVIDENCE

▸ SPORTS TEAM **7** ⚷ **~ sb/sth** (*BrE*) to like a particular sports team, watch their games, etc: *Which team do you support?*

▸ POP/ROCK CONCERT **8 ~ sb/sth** (of a band or singer) to perform in a pop or rock concert before the main performer: *They were supported by a local Liverpool band.*

▸ COMPUTER **9 ~ sth** (of a computer or computer system) to allow a particular program, language or device to be used with it: *This digital audio player supports multiple formats.*

■ ***noun***

▸ ENCOURAGEMENT/MONEY **1** ⚷ [U] **~** (**for sth**) encouragement and help that you give to sb/sth because you approve of them and want them to be successful: *There is strong public support for the change.* ◇ *Can I rely on your support* (= will you vote for me) *in the election?* ◇ *Only a few people spoke* ***in support of*** *the proposal.* ◇ *Local businesses have provided* ***financial support.*** ◇ *She has no visible means of support* (= no work, income etc.).

▸ HELP **2** ⚷ [U] sympathy and help that you give to sb who is in a difficult or unhappy situation: *Her family and friends have given her lots of support.* ⮌ see also MORAL SUPPORT

▸ HOLDING IN POSITION **3** ⚷ [C] a thing that holds sth and prevents it from falling: *The supports under the bridge were starting to bend.* ◇ (*figurative*) *When my father died, Jim was a real support.* **4** ⚷ [U] the act of holding sth firmly in position or preventing it from falling: *I wrapped a bandage around my ankle to give it some support.* ◇ *She held on to his arm for support.* **5** ⚷ [C] something you wear to hold an injured or weak part of your body firmly in position: *a* ***knee/back support***

▸ PROOF **6** ⚷ [U] evidence that helps to show that sth is true or correct: *The statistics offer further support for our theory.*

▸ POP/ROCK CONCERT **7** [U] a band or singer who performs in a pop or rock concert before the main performer: *The support (act) has yet to be confirmed.*

▸ TECHNICAL HELP **8** [U] technical help that a company gives to customers using their computers or other products: *We offer free* ***technical support.***

sup·port·er ⚷ /sə'pɔːtə(r); *NAmE* -'pɔːrt-/ *noun* **1** ⚷ a person who supports a political party, an idea, etc: *a* ***strong/loyal/staunch supporter*** ◇ *Labour supporters* **2** ⚷ (*BrE*) a person who supports a particular sports team SYN **fan**: *I'm an Arsenal supporter.* ⮌ see also ATHLETIC SUPPORTER

sup'port group *noun* a group of people who meet to help each other with a particular problem: *a support group for single parents*

sup·port·ing /sə'pɔːtɪŋ; *NAmE* -'pɔːrt-/ *adj.* [only before noun] **1** a **supporting** actor in a play or film/movie has an important part but not the leading one: *The movie featured Robert Lindsay in a* ***supporting role.*** **2** (*formal*) helping to show that sth is true: *There was a wealth of supporting evidence.* **3** carrying the weight of sth: *a supporting wall*

sup·port·ive /sə'pɔːtɪv; *NAmE* -'pɔːrt-/ *adj.* giving help, encouragement or sympathy to sb: *a supportive family* ◇ *She was very supportive during my father's illness.*

sup·pose ⚷ /sə'pəʊz; *NAmE* sə'poʊz/ *verb* **1** ⚷ [I, T] to think or believe that sth is true or possible (based on the knowledge that you have): *Getting a visa isn't as simple as you might suppose.* ◇ *Prices will go up,* ***I suppose.*** ◇ **~ sb/sth to be/have sth** (*formal*) *This combination of qualities is* ***generally supposed*** *to be extremely rare.* ◇ **~ sb/sth** (**to be/have**) **sth** | **~ sb/sth + adj.** (*formal*) *She had supposed him (to be) very rich.* ◇ **~ sb/sth + noun** (*formal*) *I had supposed his wife a younger woman.* ◇ **~** (**that**)... *I don't suppose for a minute that he'll agree* (= I'm sure that he won't). ◇ ***Why do you suppose*** *he resigned?* ◇ ***There is no reason to suppose*** *she's lying.* ◇ *I suppose you think it's funny, do you?* (= showing anger). HELP 'That' is nearly always left out, especially in speech. **2** ⚷ [T] to pretend that sth is true; to imagine what would happen if sth were true: **~** (**that**)... *Suppose flights are fully booked on that day —which other day could we go?* ◇ *Let us suppose, for example, that you are married with two children.* ◇ **~ sth** (*formal*) *The theory supposes the existence of life on other planets.* ◇ **~ sb/sth** (**to be/have**) **sth** | **~ sb/sth + adj./noun** (*formal*) *Suppose him (to be) dead—what then?* **3** ⚷ [I, T] used to make a statement, request or suggestion less direct or less strong: *I could take you in the car,* ***I suppose*** (= but I don't really want to). ◇ *'Can I borrow the car?'* ***'I suppose so'*** (= Yes, but I'm not happy about it). ◇ **~** (**that**)... ***I don't suppose*** (***that***) *I could have a look at your newspaper, could I?* ◇ *Suppose we take a later train?*

IDM **be supposed to do/be sth 1** ⚷ to be expected or required to do/be sth according to a rule, a custom, an arrangement, etc: *You're supposed to buy a ticket, but not many people do.* ◇ *I thought we were supposed to be paid today.* ◇ *The engine doesn't sound like it's supposed to.* ◇ *You were supposed to be here an hour ago!* ◇ *How was I supposed to know you were waiting for me?* ◇ *'Yes and no.'* ***'What is that supposed to mean?'*** (= showing that you are annoyed) **2** ⚷ to be generally believed or expected to be/do sth: *I haven't seen it myself, but it's supposed to be a great movie.* **not be supposed to do sth** ⚷ to not be allowed to do sth: *You're not supposed to walk on the grass.*

sup·posed /sə'pəʊzd; *NAmE* sə'poʊzd/ *adj.* [only before noun] used to show that you think that a claim, statement or way of describing sb/sth is not true or correct, although it is generally believed to be SYN **alleged**: *This is the opinion of the supposed experts.* ◇ *When did this supposed accident happen?*

sup·posed·ly /sə'pəʊzɪdli; *NAmE* -'poʊ-/ *adv.* according to what is generally thought or believed but not known for certain SYN **allegedly**: *The novel is supposedly based on a true story.*

sup·pos·ing /sə'pəʊzɪŋ; *NAmE* -'poʊ-/ *conj.* **~** (**that**) used to ask sb to pretend that sth is true or to imagine that sth will happen: *Supposing (that) you are wrong, what will you do then?* ◇ *But supposing he sees us?*

sup·pos·ition /ˌsʌpə'zɪʃn/ *noun* (*formal*) **1** [C] **~** (**that...**) an idea that you think is true although you may not be able to prove it SYN **assumption**: *The police are working on the supposition that he was murdered.* **2** [U] the act of believing or claiming that sth is true even though it cannot be proved: *The report is based entirely on supposition.*

sup·posi·tory /sə'pɒzətri; *NAmE* sə'pɑːzətɔːri/ *noun* (*pl.* -ies) a small piece of solid medicine that is placed in the RECTUM or VAGINA and left to dissolve gradually

S

sup·press /sə'pres/ *verb* **1 ~ sth** (usually *disapproving*) (of a government, ruler, etc.) to put an end, often by force, to a group or an activity that is believed to threaten authority SYN **quash**: *The rebellion was brutally suppressed.* **2 ~ sth** (usually *disapproving*) to prevent sth from being published or made known: *The police were accused of suppressing vital evidence.* **3 ~ sth** to prevent yourself from having or expressing a feeling or an emotion: *to suppress a smile* ◇ *She was unable to suppress her anger.* **4 ~ sth** to prevent sth from growing, developing or continuing: *drugs that suppress the appetite*

sup·pres·sant /sə'presnt/ *noun* a drug that is used to prevent one of the body's functions from working normally: *an appetite suppressant*

sup·pres·sion /sə'preʃn/ *noun* [U] the act of SUPPRESSING sth: *the suppression of a rebellion* ◇ *the suppression of emotion*

sup·pres·sor /sə'presə(r)/ *noun* a thing or person that SUPPRESSES sb/sth: *the body's pain suppressors*

sup·pur·ate /'sʌpjureɪt/ *verb* [I] (*formal*) (of a cut, wound, etc.) to produce a thick yellow liquid (called PUS) because of infection ▸ **sup·pur·ation** /ˌsʌpju'reɪʃn/ *noun* [U]

supra·nation·al /ˌsuːprə'næʃnəl; *BrE* also ˌsjuː-/ *adj.* (*formal*) involving more than one country

supra·seg·men·tal /ˌsuːprəseg'mentl; *BrE* also ˌsjuː-/ *adj.* (*phonetics*) relating to features of speech such as stress and INTONATION as opposed to individual speech sounds

su·prema·cist /suː'preməsɪst; *BrE* also sjuː-/ *noun* a person who believes that their own race is better than others and should be in power: *a white supremacist*

su·prem·acy /suː'preməsi; *BrE* also sjuː-/ *noun* [U] a position in which you have more power, authority or status than anyone else: *the battle for supremacy in the region* ◇ *the dangerous notion of white supremacy* (= that white races are better than others and should control them) ◇ **~ over sb/sth** *The company has established total supremacy over its rivals.*

su·preme /suː'priːm; *BrE* also sjuː-/ *adj.* [usually before noun] **1** highest in rank or position: *the Supreme Commander of the armed forces* ◇ *the supreme champion* ◇ *It is an event in which she* ***reigns supreme.*** **2** very great or the greatest in degree: *to make the* ***supreme sacrifice*** (= die for what you believe in) ◇ *a supreme effort* ◇ *She smiled with supreme confidence.*

the Suˌpreme 'Being *noun* [sing.] (*formal*) God

the Suˌpreme 'Court (also **ˌHigh 'Court**) *noun* [sing.] the highest court in a country or state

su·preme·ly /suː'priːmli; *BrE* also sjuː-/ *adv.* extremely: *supremely confident* ◇ *They managed it all supremely well.*

su·premo /suː'priːməʊ; sjuː-; *NAmE* suː'priːmoʊ/ *noun* (*pl.* **-os**) (*BrE, informal*) a person who has the most power or authority in a particular business or activity: *the Microsoft supremo, Bill Gates*

Supt (also **Supt.** especially in *NAmE*) *abbr.* (in the police force) SUPERINTENDENT: *Chief Supt Pauline Clark*

sura (also **surah**) /'sʊərə; *NAmE* 'sʊrə/ *noun* a chapter or section of the Koran

sur·charge /'sɜːtʃɑːdʒ; *NAmE* 'sɜːrtʃɑːrdʒ/ *noun, verb*
■ ***noun*** **~ (on sth)** an extra amount of money that you must pay in addition to the usual price SYN **supplement**
■ ***verb*** **~ sb (sth)** to make sb pay a surcharge: *We were surcharged £50 for travelling on a Friday.*

sur·coat /'sɜːkəʊt; *NAmE* 'sɜːrkoʊt/ *noun* a piece of clothing without sleeves, worn in the past over a suit of ARMOUR

sure 🗝 /ʃʊə(r); ʃɔː(r); *NAmE* ʃʊr/ *adj., adv.*
■ ***adj.*** (**surer, sur·est**) HELP You can also use **more sure** and **most sure**, especially in sense 1. **1** 🗝 [not before noun] confident that you know sth or that you are right SYN **certain**: *'Is that John over there?'* ***'I'm not sure'.*** ◇ *You don't sound very sure.* ◇ **~ (that)...** *I'm pretty sure (that) he'll agree.* ◇ *Are you sure you don't mind?* ◇ **~ of sth** *I hope you are sure of your facts.* ◇ **~ about sth** *Are you sure about that?* ◇ **~ how, whether, etc...** *Ask me if you're* ***not sure how*** *to do it.* ◇ *I'm* ***not sure whether*** *I should tell you this.* OPP **unsure** **2** 🗝 [not before noun] certain that you will receive sth or that sth will happen: **~ of sth** *You're always sure of a warm welcome there.* ◇ **~ of doing sth** *England must win this game to be sure of qualifying for the World Cup.* **3** 🗝 **~ to do sth** certain to do sth or to happen: *The exhibition is sure to be popular.* ◇ *It's sure to rain.* ➲ SYNONYMS at CERTAIN **4** [usually before noun] that can be trusted or relied on: *It's a* ***sure sign*** *of economic recovery.* ◇ *There's only one sure way to do it.* ◇ *He is a* ***sure bet*** *for the presidential nominations* (= certain to succeed). ➲ SYNONYMS at CERTAIN **5** [usually before noun] steady and confident: *We admired her sure touch at the keyboard.*
IDM **be sure to do sth** used to tell sb to do sth: *Be sure to give your family my regards.* HELP In spoken English **and** plus another verb can be used instead of **to** and the infinitive: *Be sure and call me tomorrow.* **for 'sure** 🗝 (*informal*) without doubt: *No one knows for sure what happened.* ◇ *I think he'll be back on Monday, but I can't say for sure.* ◇ ***One thing is for sure****—it's not going to be easy.* ◇ (*NAmE*) *'Will you be there?' 'For sure.'* **make 'sure (of sth/that...) 1** 🗝 to do sth in order to be certain that sth else happens: *Make sure (that) no one finds out about this.* ◇ *They scored another goal and made sure of victory.* ◇ *Our staff will do their best to make sure you enjoy your visit.* **2** 🗝 to check that sth is true or has been done: *She looked around to make sure that she was alone.* ◇ *I think the door's locked, but I'll just go and make sure.* **'sure of yourself** (sometimes *disapproving*) very confident: *She seems very sure of herself.* **ˌsure 'thing** (*informal, especially NAmE*) used to say 'yes' to a suggestion or request: *'Are you coming?' 'Sure thing.'* **to be 'sure** (*formal*) used to admit that sth is true: *He is intelligent, to be sure, but he's also very lazy.*
■ ***adv.*** (*informal, especially NAmE*) **1** 🗝 used to say 'yes' to sb: *'Will you open the wine?' 'Sure, where is it?'* ◇ *Did it hurt? Sure it hurt.* **2** used to emphasize sth that you are saying: *Boy, it sure is hot.* ◇ *'Amazing view'. 'Sure is.'* ◇ *That song* ***sure as hell*** *sounds familiar.* ◇ *He sure looked unhappy.* **3** used to reply to sb who has just thanked you for sth: *'Thanks for the ride.' 'Sure—anytime.'*
IDM **(as) sure as eggs is 'eggs** (*old-fashioned, BrE, informal*) used to say that sth is definitely true **ˌsure e'nough** used to say that sth happened as expected: *I said he'd forget, and sure enough he did.*

Synonyms

sure

confident • convinced • certain • positive • clear

These words all describe sb who knows without doubt that sth is true or will happen.

sure [not before noun] without any doubt that you are right, that sth is true, that you will get sth or that sth will happen: *'Is that John over there?' 'I'm not sure.'* ◇ *Are you sure about that?* ◇ *England must win this game to be sure of qualifying.* NOTE **Sure** is often used in negative statements and questions, because there is some doubt or anxiety over the matter. If there is no doubt, people often say *quite sure*: *I'm quite sure (that) I left my bag here* (= I have no doubt about it).

confident completely sure that sth will happen in the way that you want or expect: *I'm quite confident that you'll get the job.* ◇ *The team feels confident of winning.* NOTE **Confident** is a stronger and more definite word than **sure** and is more often used in positive statements, when you feel no anxiety.

convinced [not before noun] completely sure that sth is true or right, especially because the evidence seems to prove it or sb else has persuaded you to believe it: *I'm convinced that she's innocent.*

certain [not usually before noun] sure that you are right or that sth is true: *Are you absolutely certain about this?*

SURE OR CERTAIN?

Like **sure**, **certain** is often used in negative statements and questions. It is slightly more formal than **sure**; **sure** is more frequent, especially in spoken English.

positive [not before noun] (*rather informal*) completely sure that sth is true: *She was positive that he'd been there.* ◇ *'Are you sure?' 'Positive.'*

clear (often used in negative statements and questions) having no doubt or confusion about sth: *My memory isn't really clear on that point.*

PATTERNS

- sure/confident/convinced/certain/positive/clear **about** sth
- sure/confident/convinced/certain **of** sth
- sure/confident/convinced/certain/positive/clear **that...**
- sure/certain/clear **who/what/how**, etc.
- **to feel** sure/confident/convinced/certain/positive
- **quite/absolutely/completely/fairly/pretty** sure/confident/convinced/certain/positive/clear
- **not altogether** sure/confident/convinced/certain/clear

'sure-fire *adj.* [only before noun] (*informal*) certain to be successful or to happen as you expect: *a sure-fire success*

S

ˌ**sure-ˈfooted** (also **foot·sure**) *adj.* **1** not likely to fall when walking or climbing on rough ground **2** confident and unlikely to make mistakes, especially in difficult situations

sure·ly 0‑ /ˈʃʊəli; ˈʃɔːli; *NAmE* ˈʃʊrli/ *adv.*
1 0‑ used to show that you are almost certain of what you are saying and want other people to agree with you: *Surely we should do something about it?* ◇ *It's surely only a matter of time before he is found, isn't it?* **2** 0‑ used with a negative to show that sth surprises you and you do not want to believe it: *Surely you don't think I was responsible for this?* ◇ *'They're getting married.' '**Surely not!**'* ◇ *They won't go, surely?* **3** (*formal*) without doubt; certainly: *He knew that if help did not arrive soon they would surely die.* **4** (*old-fashioned, NAmE, informal*) used to say 'yes' to sb or to agree to sth **IDM** see SLOWLY

Which Word?

surely / certainly

- You use **surely**, especially in *BrE*, to show that you are almost certain about what you are saying and you want other people to agree with you: *Surely this can't be right?* **Surely** in negative sentences shows that something surprises you and you do not want to believe it: *You're surely not thinking of going, are you?*
- **Certainly** usually means 'without doubt' or 'definitely', and is used to show that you strongly believe something or to emphasize that something is really true: *I'll certainly remember this trip!* In informal *NAmE* this would be: *I'll sure remember this trip!*
- Compare: *The meal was certainly too expensive* (= there is no doubt about it) and *The meal was surely too expensive?* (= that is my opinion. Don't you agree?).
- In formal language only, **surely** can be used to mean 'without doubt': *This will surely end in disaster.*

➲ note at COURSE, SURE

sure·ness /ˈʃʊənəs; ˈʃɔːn-; *NAmE* ˈʃʊrn-/ *noun* [U] the quality of being confident and steady; not hesitating or doubting: *an artist's sureness of touch* ◇ *her sureness that she had done the right thing*

surety /ˈʃʊərəti; ˈʃɔːr-; *NAmE* ˈʃʊr-/ *noun* [C, U] (*pl.* -ies) (*law*) **1** money given as a promise that you will pay a debt, appear in court, etc: *She was granted bail with a surety of $500.* **2** a person who accepts responsibility if sb else does not pay a debt, appear in court, etc: *to act as surety for sb*

surf /sɜːf; *NAmE* sɜːrf/ *noun, verb*
■ ***noun*** [U] large waves in the sea or ocean, and the white FOAM that they produce as they fall on the beach, on rocks, etc: *the sound of surf breaking on the beach* ◇ *Sydney, surf capital of the world* (= where the sport of surfing is very popular)
■ ***verb*** **1** (often **go surfing**) [I, T] **~ (sth)** to take part in the sport of riding on waves on a SURFBOARD **2** [T] **~ the Net/Internet** to use the Internet: *I was surfing the Net looking for information on Indian music.*

sur·face 0‑ /ˈsɜːfɪs; *NAmE* ˈsɜːrfɪs/ *noun, verb*
■ ***noun*** **1** 0‑ [C] the outside or top layer of sth: *an uneven road surface* ◇ *We'll need a flat surface to play the game on.* ◇ *Teeth have a hard surface layer called enamel.* ◇ *a broad leaf with a large **surface area*** **2** 0‑ [C, usually sing.] the top layer of an area of water or land: *the earth's surface* ◇ *These plants float on the surface of the water.* **3** 0‑ [C] the flat upper part of a piece of furniture, that is used for working on: *a work surface* ◇ *She's cleaned all the kitchen surfaces.* **4** [sing.] the outer appearance of a person, thing or situation; the qualities that you see or notice, that are not hidden: *Rage bubbled just below the surface of his mind.*
IDM **on the ˈsurface** when not thought about deeply or thoroughly; when not looked at carefully: *It seems like a good idea on the surface but there are sure to be problems.* ◇ *On the surface, he appeared unchanged.* ➲ more at SCRATCH *v.*
■ ***verb*** **1** [I] to come up to the surface of water **SYN** **emerge**: *The ducks dived and surfaced again several metres away.* **2** [I] to suddenly appear or become obvious after having been hidden for a while **SYN** **emerge**: *Doubts began to surface.* ◇ *She surfaced again years later in London.* **3** [I] (*informal*) to wake up or get up after being asleep: *He finally surfaced around noon.* **4** [T] **~ sth** to put a surface on a road, path, etc.

ˈ**surface mail** *noun* [U] letters, etc. carried by road, rail or sea, not by air

ˈ**surface structure** *noun* (*grammar*) the structure of a well-formed sentence in a language, rather than its UNDERLYING form ➲ compare DEEP STRUCTURE

ˌ**surface ˈtension** *noun* [U] (*technical*) the property (= characteristic) of liquids by which they form a layer at their surface, and which makes sure that this surface covers as small an area as possible

ˌ**surface-to-ˈair** *adj.* [only before noun] (especially of MISSILES) fired from the ground or from ships and aimed at aircraft

ˌ**surface-to-ˈsurface** *adj.* [only before noun] (especially of MISSILES) fired from the ground or from ships and aimed at another point on the ground or a ship

sur·fac·tant /sɜːˈfæktənt; *NAmE* sɜːrˈf-/ *noun* [C, U] **1** (*technical*) a substance that reduces the SURFACE TENSION of a liquid, often forming bubbles in the liquid **2** (*medical*) a substance that keeps the lungs working well to prevent breathing problems

surf·board /ˈsɜːfbɔːd; *NAmE* ˈsɜːrfbɔːrd/ (also **board**) *noun* a long narrow board used for SURFING

sur·feit /ˈsɜːfɪt; *NAmE* ˈsɜːrfɪt/ *noun* [usually sing.] **~ (of sth)** (*formal*) an amount that is too large **SYN** **excess**

surf·er /ˈsɜːfə(r); *NAmE* ˈsɜːrfər/ *noun* **1** a person who goes SURFING **2** (also ˈ**Net surfer**) (*informal*) a person who spends a lot of time using the Internet ➲ see also SILVER SURFER

surfie /ˈsɜːfi; *NAmE* ˈsɜːrfi/ *noun* (*AustralE, NZE, informal*) a person who is enthusiastic about SURFING, especially a young man

surf·ing /ˈsɜːfɪŋ; *NAmE* ˈsɜːrf-/ *noun* [U] **1** the sport of riding on waves while standing on a narrow board called a SURFBOARD: *to go surfing* ➲ **VISUAL VOCAB** page V40 **2** the activity of looking at different things on the Internet in order to find sth interesting, or of changing between TV channels in order to find an interesting programme

ˈ**surf lifesaver** *noun* (*AustralE, NZE*) = LIFEGUARD

ˌ**surf 'n' ˈturf** *noun* [U] (*NAmE*) SEAFOOD and STEAK served together as a meal

surge /sɜːdʒ; *NAmE* sɜːrdʒ/ *verb, noun*
■ ***verb*** **1** [I] **+ adv./prep.** to move quickly and with force in a particular direction: *The gates opened and the crowd surged forward.* ◇ *Flood waters surged into their homes.* **2** [I] (**+ adv./prep.**) to fill sb with a strong feeling **SYN** **sweep**: *Relief surged through her.* **3** [I] (of prices, profits, etc.) to suddenly increase in value: *Share prices surged.* ➲ related noun UPSURGE **4** [I] (of the flow of electrical power) to increase suddenly
■ ***noun*** **1 ~ (of sth)** a sudden increase of a strong feeling **SYN** **rush**: *She felt a sudden surge of anger.* ◇ *a surge of excitement* ➲ see also UPSURGE **2** a sudden increase in the amount or number of sth; a large amount of sth: **~ (in sth)** *a surge in consumer spending* ◇ *We are having trouble keeping up with the recent surge in demand.* ◇ **~ (of sth)** *After an initial surge of interest, there has been little call for our services.* ➲ see also UPSURGE **3 ~ (of sth)** a sudden, strong forward or upward movement: *a tidal surge* **4** a sudden increase in the flow of electrical power through a system: *An electrical surge damaged the computer's disk drive.*

sur·geon /ˈsɜːdʒən; *NAmE* ˈsɜːrdʒən/ *noun* a doctor who is trained to perform surgery (= medical operations that involve cutting open a person's body): *a **brain/heart, etc. surgeon*** ➲ compare PHYSICIAN

ˌ**Surgeon ˈGeneral** *noun* (*pl.* **Surgeons General**) (in the US) the head of a public health service or of a medical ser-

S

vice in the armed forces: *Surgeon General's warning: cigarette smoking causes cancer*

sur·gery /ˈsɜːdʒəri; *NAmE* ˈsɜːrdʒ-/ *noun* (*pl.* -ies) **1** [U] medical treatment of injuries or diseases that involves cutting open a person's body and often removing or replacing some parts; the branch of medicine connected with this treatment: ***major/minor surgery*** ◇ *to* ***undergo*** *heart surgery* ◇ *He will require surgery on his left knee.* HELP In American English the countable form can be used: *She had three surgeries over ten days.* ➲ COLLOCATIONS at ILL ➲ see also OPEN-HEART SURGERY, PLASTIC SURGERY **2** [U, C] (*BrE*) the time during which a doctor, dentist or VET is available to see patients: ***morning/afternoon/evening surgery*** ◇ *surgery hours* ◇ *Is there a surgery this evening?* **3** [C] (*BrE*) (*NAmE* **office**) a place where a doctor, dentist or VET sees patients: *a* ***doctor's/dentist's surgery*** **4** [C] (*BrE*) a time when people can meet their Member of Parliament to ask questions and get help: *a constituency surgery*

sur·gi·cal /ˈsɜːdʒɪkl; *NAmE* ˈsɜːrdʒ-/ *adj.* [only before noun] used in or connected with surgery: *surgical procedures* ◇ *a surgical ward* (= for patients having operations) ▸ **sur·gi·cal·ly** /-kli/ *adv.*: *The lumps will need to be surgically removed.*

ˌsurgical ˈspirit (*BrE*) (*NAmE* ˈ**rubbing alcohol**) *noun* [U] a clear liquid, consisting mainly of alcohol, used for cleaning wounds, etc.

surly /ˈsɜːli; *NAmE* ˈsɜːrli/ *adj.* (**sur·lier, sur·li·est**) bad-tempered and rude: *a surly youth* ▸ **sur·li·ness** *noun* [U]

sur·mise *verb, noun*

■ ***verb*** /səˈmaɪz; *NAmE* sərˈm-/ [T, I] **~ (sth)** | **~ (that)...** | **~ what, where, etc...** | **+ speech** (*formal*) to guess or suppose sth using the evidence you have, without definitely knowing SYN **conjecture**: *From the looks on their faces, I surmised that they had had an argument.*

■ ***noun*** /ˈsɜːmaɪz; *NAmE* ˈsɜːrm-/ [U, C, usually sing.] (*formal*) a guess based on some facts that you know already: *This is pure surmise on my part.*

sur·mount /səˈmaʊnt; *NAmE* sərˈm-/ *verb* (*formal*) **1 ~ sth** to deal successfully with a difficulty SYN **overcome**: *She was well aware of the difficulties that had to be surmounted.* **2** [usually passive] **~ sth** to be placed on top of sth: *a high column surmounted by a statue*

sur·name 0→ /ˈsɜːneɪm; *NAmE* ˈsɜːrn-/ *noun* (*especially BrE*) a name shared by all the members of a family (written last in English names) ➲ compare FAMILY NAME, LAST NAME

S

sur·pass /səˈpɑːs; *NAmE* sərˈpæs/ *verb* [T, I] **~ (sb/sth/yourself)** (*formal*) to do or be better than sb/sth: *He hopes one day to surpass the world record.* ◇ *Its success has* ***surpassed all expectations.*** ◇ *Her cooking was always good, but this time she had* ***surpassed herself*** (= done better than her own high standards). ◇ *scenery of surpassing beauty*

sur·plice /ˈsɜːpləs; *NAmE* ˈsɜːrp-/ *noun* a loose white piece of clothing with wide sleeves worn by priests and singers in the CHOIR during church services

sur·plus /ˈsɜːpləs; *NAmE* ˈsɜːrp-/ *noun, adj.*

■ ***noun*** [C, U] **1** an amount that is extra or more than you need: *food surpluses* ◇ *Wheat was* ***in surplus*** *that year.* **2** the amount by which the amount of money received is greater than the amount of money spent: *a trade surplus of £400 million* ◇ *The balance of payments was* ***in surplus*** *last year* (= the value of exports was greater than the value of imports). ➲ COLLOCATIONS at INTERNATIONAL ➲ compare DEFICIT

■ ***adj.*** more than is needed or used: *surplus cash* ◇ *Surplus grain is being sold for export.* ◇ **~ to sth** *These items are* ***surplus to requirements*** (= not needed).

sur·prise 0→ /səˈpraɪz; *NAmE* sərˈp-/ *noun, verb*

■ ***noun*** **1** 0→ [C] an event, a piece of news, etc. that is unexpected or that happens suddenly: *What a nice surprise!* ◇ *a surprise attack* ◇ *There are few surprises in this year's budget.* ◇ *I have a surprise for you!* ◇ *It* ***comes as no surprise to*** *learn that they broke their promises.* ◇ *Her letter* ***came as a*** *complete* ***surprise.*** ◇ *There are lots of* ***surprises in store for*** *visitors to the gallery.* ◇ *Visitors to the gallery are* ***in for a few surprises.*** **2** 0→ [U, C] a feeling caused by sth happening suddenly or unexpectedly: *a look of surprise* ◇ *She looked up* ***in surprise.*** ◇ **~ (at sth)** *He gasped* ***with surprise*** *at her strength.* ◇ **~ (at seeing, hearing, etc.)** *They couldn't conceal their surprise at seeing us together.* ◇ *I* ***got a surprise*** *when I saw the bill.* ◇ ***Much to my surprise,*** *I passed.* ◇ ***To everyone's surprise,*** *the plan succeeded.* ◇ *Imagine our surprise when he walked into the room!* **3** [U] the use of methods that cause feelings of surprise: *A successful campaign should have* ***an element of surprise.***

IDM **surˌprise, surˈprise** (*informal*) **1** (*ironic*, often *disapproving*) used to show that sth is not a surprise to you, as you could easily have predicted that it would happen or be true: *One of the candidates was the manager's niece, and surprise, surprise, she got the job.* **2** used when giving sb a surprise: *Surprise, surprise! Look who's here!* **take sb/sth by surˈprise** to attack or capture sb/sth unexpectedly or without warning: *The police took the burglars by surprise.* **take sb by surˈprise** to happen unexpectedly so that sb is slightly shocked; to surprise sb: *His frankness took her by surprise.*

■ ***verb*** **1** 0→ to make sb feel surprised: **~ sb** *It wouldn't surprise me if they got married soon.* ◇ **~ sb how, what, etc...** *It's always surprised me how popular he is.* ◇ **it surprises sb that...** *It surprises me that you've never sung professionally.* ◇ **it surprises sb to do sth** *Would it surprise you to know that I'm thinking of leaving?* **2 ~ sb** to attack, discover, etc. sb suddenly and unexpectedly: *The army attacked at night to surprise the rebels.* ◇ *We arrived home early and surprised a burglar trying to break in.*

Synonyms

surprise

startle • amaze • stun • astonish • take sb aback • astound

These words all mean to make sb feel surprised.

surprise to give sb the feeling that you get when sth happens that you do not expect or do not understand, or sth that you do expect does not happen; to make sb feel surprised: *The outcome didn't surprise me at all.*

startle to surprise sb suddenly in a way that slightly shocks or frightens them: *Sorry, I didn't mean to startle you.* ◇ *The explosion startled the horse.*

amaze to surprise sb very much: *Just the huge size of the place amazed her.*

stun (*rather informal*) (often in newspapers) to surprise or shock sb so much that they cannot think clearly or speak

astonish to surprise sb very much: *The news astonished everyone.*

AMAZE OR ASTONISH?

These two words have the same meaning and in most cases you can use either. If you are talking about sth that both surprises you and makes you feel ashamed, use **astonish**: *He was astonished by his own stupidity.*

take sb aback [usually passive] (especially of sth negative) to surprise or shock sb: *We were rather taken aback by her hostile reaction.*

astound to surprise or shock sb very much: *His arrogance astounded her.*

PATTERNS

- **It** surprises sb/startles sb/amazes sb/stuns sb/astonishes sb/takes sb aback/astounds sb
- to surprise/startle/amaze/stun/astonish/astound sb **that...**
- to surprise/amaze sb **what/how...**
- to surprise/startle/amaze/stun/astonish/astound sb **to know/find/learn/see/hear...**
- to be surprised/startled/stunned **into** (doing) sth

sur·prised 0-w /sə'praɪzd; *NAmE* sər'p-/ *adj.* feeling or showing surprise: *a surprised look* ◇ *She looked surprised when I told her.* ◇ ~ (**at/by sb/sth**) *I was surprised at how quickly she agreed.* ◇ *I'm surprised at you, behaving like that in front of the kids.* ◇ ~ (**to see, hear, etc.**) *They were surprised to find that he'd already left.* ◇ ~ (**that...**) *You shouldn't be surprised (that) he didn't come.* ◇ ***Don't be surprised if*** *I pretend not to recognise you.* ◇ *'Will she cancel the party?' '**I wouldn't be surprised.**'* ➲ compare UNSURPRISED

sur·pris·ing 0-w /sə'praɪzɪŋ; *NAmE* sər'p-/ *adj.* causing surprise: *It's not surprising (that) they lost.* ◇ *We had a surprising amount in common.* ◇ *It's surprising what people will do for money.* ▶ **sur·pris·ing·ly** 0-w *adv.*: *She looked surprisingly well.* ◇ *Surprisingly, he agreed straight away.* ◇ ***Not surprisingly*** *on such a hot day, the beach was crowded.*

Language Bank

surprising

Highlighting interesting data

- **What is surprising** about these results **is** that boys are more likely to be left-handed than girls.
- **Surprisingly**, boys are more likely to be left-handed than girls.
- **Interestingly**, even when both parents are left-handed, there is still only a 26% chance of their children being left-handed.
- **One of the most interesting** findings is that only 2% of the left-handers surveyed have two left-handed parents.
- **It is interesting to note that** people are more likely to be left-handed if their mother is left-handed than if their father is.
- **The most striking** feature of these results **is** that left-handed mothers are more likely to have left-handed children.

➲ Language Banks at CONTRAST, EMPHASIS, ILLUSTRATE, SIMILARLY

sur·real /sə'riːəl/ (also *less frequent* **sur·real·is·tic**) *adj.* very strange; more like a dream than reality, with ideas and images mixed together in a strange way

sur·real·ism /sə'riːəlɪzəm/ *noun* [U] a 20th century style and movement in art and literature in which images and events that are not connected are put together in a strange or impossible way, like a dream, to try to express what is happening deep in the mind ▶ **sur·real·ist** *adj.* [usually before noun]: *a surrealist painter/painting* **sur·real·ist** *noun*: *the surrealist Salvador Dali*

sur·real·is·tic /sə,riːə'lɪstɪk/ *adj.* **1** = SURREAL **2** connected with surrealism: *a surrealistic painting*

sur·ren·der /sə'rendə(r)/ *verb, noun*

■ ***verb*** **1** [I, T] to admit that you have been defeated and want to stop fighting; to allow yourself to be caught, taken prisoner, etc. SYN **give in:** ~ (**to sb**) *The rebel soldiers were forced to surrender.* ◇ ~ **yourself** (**to sb**) *The hijackers eventually surrendered themselves to the police.* **2** (*formal*) to give up sth/sb when you are forced to SYN **relinquish:** ~ **sth/sb to sb** *He agreed to surrender all claims to the property.* ◇ *They surrendered their guns to the police.* ◇ ~ **sth/sb** *The defendant was released to await trial but had to surrender her passport.*

PHR V **sur'render to sth** | **sur'render yourself to sth** (*formal*) to stop trying to prevent yourself from having a feeling, habit, etc. and allow it to control what you do: *He finally surrendered to his craving for drugs.*

■ ***noun*** [U, sing.] **1** ~ (**to sb/sth**) an act of admitting that you have been defeated and want to stop fighting: *They demanded (an)* ***unconditional surrender.*** ➲ COLLOCATIONS at WAR **2** the fact of allowing yourself to be controlled by sth: *They accused the government of a surrender to business interests.* **3** ~ **of sth** (**to sb**) an act of giving sth to sb else even though you do not want to, especially after a battle, etc: *They insisted on the immediate surrender of all weapons.*

sur'render value *noun* the amount of money that you get if you end a life insurance policy before its official end date

sur·rep·ti·tious /ˌsʌrəp'tɪʃəs; *NAmE* ˌsɜːr-/ *adj.* done secretly or quickly, in the hope that other people will not notice SYN **furtive:** *She sneaked a surreptitious glance at her watch.* ▶ **sur·rep·ti·tious·ly** *adv.*

sur·ro·gacy /'sʌrəgəsi; *NAmE* 'sɜːr-/ *noun* [U] the practice of giving birth to a baby for another woman who is unable to have babies herself

sur·ro·gate /'sʌrəgət; *NAmE* 'sɜːr-/ *adj.* (*formal*) used to describe a person or thing that takes the place of, or is used instead of, sb/sth else: *She saw him as a sort of surrogate father.* ▶ **sur·ro·gate** *noun*

ˌsurrogate 'mother *noun* a woman who gives birth to a baby for another woman who is unable to have babies herself

sur·round 0-w /sə'raʊnd/ *verb, noun*

■ ***verb*** **1** 0-w to be all around sth/sb: ~ **sth/sb** *Tall trees surround the lake.* ◇ *the membranes surrounding the brain* ◇ *As a child I was surrounded by love and kindness.* ◇ ~ **sth/sb with sth** *The lake is surrounded with/by trees.* **2** 0-w to move into position all around sb/sth, especially so as to prevent them from escaping; to move sb/sth into position in this way: ~ **sb/sth** *Police surrounded the building.* ◇ ~ **sb/sth with sb/sth** *They've surrounded the building with police.* **3** ~ **sth/sb** to be closely connected with sth/sb: *publicity surrounding the divorce* **4** ~ **yourself with sb/sth** to choose to have particular people or things near you all the time: *I like to surround myself with beautiful things.*

■ ***noun*** a border or an area around the edge of sth, especially one that is decorated ➲ VISUAL VOCAB page V18

sur·round·ing 0-w /sə'raʊndɪŋ/ *adj.* [only before noun] that is near or around sth: *Oxford and the surrounding area*

sur·round·ings 0-w /sə'raʊndɪŋz/ *noun* [pl.] everything that is around or near sb/sth SYN **environment:** *to work in pleasant surroundings* ◇ *The buildings have been designed to blend in with their surroundings.* ➲ SYNONYMS at ENVIRONMENT

sur'round sound *noun* [U] a system for reproducing sound using several SPEAKERS (= the pieces of equipment that the sound comes out of) placed around the person listening in order to produce a more realistic sound

sur·tax /'sɜːtæks; *NAmE* 'sɜːrt-/ *noun* [U] a tax charged at a higher rate than the normal rate, on income above a particular level

Sur·titles™ /'sɜːtaɪtlz; *NAmE* 'sɜːrt-/ *noun* [pl.] words that translate what is being sung in an OPERA, or spoken in a play in the theatre, into a different language and appear on a screen above or beside the stage

sur·veil·lance /sɜː'veɪləns; *NAmE* sɜːr'v-/ *noun* [U] the act of carefully watching a person suspected of a crime or a place where a crime may be committed SYN **observation:** *The police are keeping the suspects* ***under*** *constant* ***surveillance.*** ◇ ***surveillance cameras/equipment***

sur·vey 0-w AW *noun, verb*

■ ***noun*** /'sɜːveɪ; *NAmE* 'sɜːrveɪ/ **1** 0-w an investigation of the opinions, behaviour, etc. of a particular group of people, which is usually done by asking them questions: *A recent survey showed 75% of those questioned were in favour of the plan.* ◇ *The* ***survey revealed*** *that...* ◇ *to* ***conduct/carry out a survey*** **2** 0-w the act of examining and recording the measurements, features, etc. of an area of land in order to make a map or plan of it: *an aerial survey* (= made by taking photographs from an aircraft) ◇ *a geological survey* **3** (*BrE*) an examination of the condition of a house, etc, usually done for sb who is thinking of buying it **4** a general

S

study, view or description of sth: *a comprehensive survey of modern music*

■ ***verb*** /sə'veɪ; *NAmE* sər'veɪ/ **1** 0‑ **~ sth** to look carefully at the whole of sth, especially in order to get a general impression of it SYN **inspect**: *The next morning we surveyed the damage caused by the fire.* ◇ *He surveyed himself in the mirror before going out.* **2 ~ sth** to study and give a general description of sth: *This chapter briefly surveys the current state of European politics.* **3 ~ sth** to measure and record the features of an area of land, for example in order to make a map or in preparation for building **4 ~ sth** (*BrE*) to examine a building to make sure it is in good condition **5** 0‑ **~ sb/sth** to investigate the opinions or behaviour of a group of people by asking them a series of questions SYN **interview**: *We surveyed 500 smokers and found that over three quarters would like to give up.*

'survey course *noun* (*NAmE*) a college course that gives an introduction to a subject for people who are thinking about studying it further

sur·vey·or /sə'veɪə(r); *NAmE* sər'v-/ *noun* **1** a person whose job is to examine and record the details of a piece of land **2** (*BrE*) (*NAmE* **in·spect·or**) a person whose job is to examine a building to make sure it is in good condition, usually done for sb who is thinking of buying it **3** (*BrE*) an official whose job is to check that sth is accurate, of good quality, etc: *the surveyor of public works* ➲ see also QUANTITY SURVEYOR

sur·viv·able /sə'vaɪvəbl; *NAmE* sər'v-/ *adj.* (of an accident or experience) able to be survived: *a survivable air crash*

sur·vival AW /sə'vaɪvl; *NAmE* sər'v-/ *noun* **1** [U] the state of continuing to live or exist, often despite difficulty or danger: *the* ***struggle/battle/fight for survival*** ◇ *His only* ***chance of survival*** *was a heart transplant.* ◇ *Exporting is necessary for our economic survival.* **2** [C] **~ (from sth)** something that has continued to exist from an earlier time SYN **relic**: *The ceremony is a survival from pre-Christian times.*

IDM **the sur,vival of the 'fittest** the principle that only the people or things that are best adapted to their surroundings will continue to exist

sur·vival·ist /sə'vaɪvəlɪst; *NAmE* sər'v-/ *noun* a person who prepares for a dangerous or unpleasant situation such as a war by learning how to survive outdoors, practising how to use weapons, storing food, etc. ▶ **sur·vival·ism** /sə'vaɪvəlɪzəm; *NAmE* sər'v-/ *noun* [U]

sur'vival kit *noun* a set of emergency equipment, including food, medical supplies and tools

sur·vive 0‑ AW /sə'vaɪv; *NAmE* sər'v-/ *verb* **1** 0‑ [I] to continue to live or exist: *She was the last surviving member of the family.* ◇ *Of the six people injured in the crash, only two survived.* ◇ (*humorous*) *'How are you these days?' 'Oh, surviving.'* ◇ *Don't worry, it's only a scratch—you'll survive.* ◇ **~ from sth** *Some strange customs have survived from earlier times.* ◇ **~ on sth** *I can't survive on £40 a week* (= it is not enough for my basic needs). ◇ **~ as sth** *He survived as party leader until his second election defeat.* **2** 0‑ [T] to continue to live or exist despite a dangerous event or time: **~ sth** *The company managed to survive the crisis.* ◇ *Many birds didn't survive the severe winter.* ◇ **~ sth + adj.** *Few buildings survived the war intact.* **3** [T] **~ sb/sth** to live or exist longer than sb/sth SYN **outlive**: *She survived her husband by ten years.*

sur·vivor AW /sə'vaɪvə(r); *NAmE* sər'v-/ *noun* a person who continues to live, especially despite being nearly killed or experiencing great danger or difficulty: *the* ***sole/only survivor*** *of the massacre* ◇ *The plane crashed in an area of dense jungle. There were no survivors.* ◇ *There are only a few survivors from the original team* (= members who remain in it while others have been replaced). ◇ *She'll cope. She's one of life's great survivors* (= sb who deals very well with difficult situations).

sus = SUSS

sus·cep·ti·bil·ity /sə,septə'bɪləti/ *noun* (*pl.* -ies) **1** [U, sing.] **~ (to sth)** the state of being very likely to be influenced, harmed or affected by sth: *susceptibility to disease* **2 susceptibilities** [pl.] a person's feelings which are likely to be easily hurt SYN **sensibilities**: *It was all carried out without any consideration for the susceptibilities of the bereaved family.*

sus·cep·tible /sə'septəbl/ *adj.* **1** [not usually before noun] **~ (to sb/sth)** very likely to be influenced, harmed or affected by sb/sth: *He's highly susceptible to flattery.* ◇ *Some of these plants are more susceptible to frost damage than others.* ◇ *Salt intake may lead to raised blood pressure in susceptible adults.* **2** easily influenced by feelings and emotions SYN **impressionable**: *She was both charming and susceptible.* **3 ~ (of sth)** (*formal*) allowing sth; capable of sth: *Is this situation not susceptible of improvement by legislation?*

sushi /'su:ʃi/ *noun* [U] a Japanese dish of small cakes of cold cooked rice, flavoured with VINEGAR and served with raw fish, etc. on top: *a sushi bar*

sus·pect 0‑ *verb, noun, adj.*

> **WORD FAMILY**
> **suspect** *verb*
> **suspected** *adj.*
> **suspicion** *noun*
> **suspicious** *adj.*
> **suspiciously** *adv.*
> **suspect** *noun, adj.*

■ ***verb*** /sə'spekt/ (not used in the progressive tenses) **1** 0‑ [T, I] to have an idea that sth is probably true or likely to happen, especially sth bad, but without having definite proof: **~ (sth)** *If you suspect a gas leak, do not strike a match or even turn on an electric light.* ◇ *Suspecting nothing, he walked right into the trap.* ◇ *As I had suspected all along, he was not a real policeman.* ◇ **~ (that)...** *I began to suspect (that) they were trying to get rid of me.* ◇ **it is suspected that...** *It was suspected that the drugs had been brought into the country by boat.* ◇ **~ sb/sth to be/have sth** *She suspected him to be an impostor.* **2** 0‑ [T] to have an idea that sb is guilty of sth, without having definite proof: **~ sb/sth of sth** *He resigned after being suspected of theft.* ◇ **~ sb/sth of doing sth** *The drug is suspected of causing over 200 deaths.* ◇ **~ sb/sth** *Whom do the police suspect?* **3** [T] **~ sth** to be suspicious about sth; to not trust sth: *I suspected her motives in offering to help.* ▶ **sus·pected** *adj.*: *a suspected broken arm* ◇ *suspected tax evasion* ◇ *suspected terrorists*

■ ***noun*** 0‑ /'sʌspekt/ a person who is suspected of a crime or of having done sth wrong: *a murder suspect* ◇ *He is the* ***prime suspect*** *in the case.*

■ ***adj.*** /'sʌspekt/ **1** that may be false and that cannot be relied on SYN **questionable**: *Some of the evidence they produced was highly suspect.* **2** that you suspect to be dangerous or illegal SYN **suspicious**: *a suspect package* (= one that may contain drugs, a bomb, etc.)

sus·pend AW /sə'spend/ *verb* **1 ~ sth/sb (from sth) (by/on sth)** (*formal*) to hang sth from sth else: *A lamp was suspended from the ceiling.* ◇ *Her body was found suspended by a rope.* **2 ~ sth** to officially stop sth for a time; to prevent sth from being active, used, etc. for a time: *Production has been suspended while safety checks are carried out.* ◇ *The constitution was suspended as the fighting grew worse.* ◇ *In the theatre we willingly* ***suspend disbelief*** (= temporarily believe that the characters, etc. are real). **3 ~ sth** to officially delay sth; to arrange for sth to happen later than planned: *The introduction of the new system has been suspended until next year.* ◇ *to suspend judgement* (= delay forming or expressing an opinion) **4** [usually passive] **~ sb (from sth)** to officially prevent sb from doing their job, going to school, etc. for a time: *The police officer was suspended while the complaint was investigated.* **5 be suspended in sth** (*technical*) to float in liquid or air without moving ➲ see also SUSPENSION

su,spended ani'mation *noun* [U] **1** the state of being alive but not conscious or active **2** a feeling that you cannot do anything because you are waiting for sth to happen

su,spended 'sentence *noun* a punishment given to a criminal in court which means that they will only go to prison if they commit another crime within a particular period of time

sus·pend·er /sə'spendə(r)/ *noun* **1** [C, usually pl.] (*BrE*) (*NAmE* **gar·ter**) a short circle of ELASTIC for holding up a sock or STOCKING **2 suspenders** (*NAmE*) (*BrE* **braces**) [pl.] long narrow pieces of cloth, leather, etc. for holding trousers/pants up. They are fastened to the top of the trousers/pants at the front and back and passed over the shoulders. ➲ VISUAL VOCAB page V50

su'spender belt *noun* (*BrE*) (*NAmE* '**garter belt**) a piece of women's underwear like a belt, worn around the waist, used for holding STOCKINGS up

sus·pense /sə'spens/ *noun* [U] a feeling of worry or excitement that you have when you feel that sth is going to happen, sb is going to tell you some news, etc: *a tale of mystery and suspense* ◇ *Don't* ***keep us in suspense****. Tell us what happened!* ◇ *I couldn't bear the suspense a moment longer.*

sus·pen·sion AW /sə'spenʃn/ *noun* **1** [U, C] the act of officially removing sb from their job, school, team, etc. for a period of time, usually as a punishment: *suspension from school* ◇ *The two players are appealing against their suspensions.* **2** [U, sing.] the act of delaying sth for a period of time, until a decision has been taken: *These events have led to the suspension of talks.* **3** [U, C] the system by which a vehicle is supported on its wheels and which makes it more comfortable to ride in when the road surface is not even **4** [C, U] (*technical*) a liquid with very small pieces of solid matter floating in it; the state of such a liquid ➲ see also SUSPEND

su'spension bridge *noun* a bridge that hangs from steel cables that are supported by towers at each end ➲ VISUAL VOCAB page V12

sus·pi·cion 0→ /sə'spɪʃn/ *noun*
1 0→ [U, C] a feeling that sb has done sth wrong, illegal or dishonest, even though you have no proof: *They drove away slowly to avoid arousing suspicion.* ◇ *He was arrested* ***on suspicion of*** *murder.* ◇ **~ (that...)** *I have* ***a sneaking suspicion*** *that she's not telling the truth.* ➲ see also SUSPECT **2** 0→ [C] **~ (that...)** a feeling or belief that sth is true, even though you have no proof: *I have a horrible suspicion that we've come to the wrong station.* **3** 0→ [U, C] the feeling that you cannot trust sb/sth: *Their offer was greeted with some suspicion.* **4** [sing.] **~ of sth** (*formal*) a small amount of sth SYN **hint**: *His mouth quivered in the suspicion of a smile.*
IDM **above/beyond su'spicion** too good, honest, etc. to have done sth wrong, illegal or dishonest: *Nobody who was near the scene of the crime is above suspicion.* **under su'spicion (of sth)** suspected of doing sth wrong, illegal or dishonest: *The whole family is currently under suspicion of her murder.* ◇ *A number of doctors* ***came under suspicion*** *of unethical behaviour.* ➲ more at FINGER *n.*

sus·pi·cious 0→ /sə'spɪʃəs/ *adj.*
1 0→ **~ (of/about sb/sth)** feeling that sb has done sth wrong, illegal or dishonest, without having any proof: *They became suspicious of his behaviour and contacted the police.* ◇ *a suspicious look* ◇ *You have a very* ***suspicious mind*** (= you always think that people are behaving in an illegal or dishonest way). **2** 0→ making you feel that sth is wrong, illegal or dishonest: *Didn't you notice anything suspicious in his behaviour?* ◇ *She died in* ***suspicious circumstances****.* ◇ *Police are not treating the fire as suspicious.* ◇ *It was all very suspicious.* **3** 0→ **~ (of sb/sth)** not willing or able to trust sb/sth SYN **sceptical**: *I was suspicious of his motives.* ◇ *Many were suspicious of reform.* ➲ see also SUSPECT

sus·pi·cious·ly /sə'spɪʃəsli/ *adv.* **1** in a way that shows you think sb has done sth wrong, illegal or dishonest: *The man looked at her suspiciously.* **2** in a way that makes people think sth wrong, illegal or dishonest is happening: *Let me know if you see anyone acting suspiciously.* **3** in a way that shows you think there may be sth wrong with sth: *She eyed the fish on her plate suspiciously.*
IDM **look/sound suspiciously like sth** (often *humorous*) to be very similar to sth: *Their latest single sounds suspiciously like the last one.*

suss (also **sus**) /sʌs/ *verb* [T, I] **~ (sb/sth) (out)** | **~ that...** | **~ how, what, etc...** (*BrE, informal*) to realize sth; to understand the important things about sb/sth: *I think I've got him sussed* (= now I understand him). ◇ *If you want to succeed in business you have to suss out the competition.* ◇ *He cheated on her for years, but she never sussed.*

sussed /sʌst/ *adj.* (*BrE, informal*) knowing what you need to know about the situations and people around you, so that you are not easily tricked and are able to take care of yourself

sus·tain AW /sə'steɪn/ *verb* **1 ~ sb/sth** to provide enough of what sb/sth needs in order to live or exist: *Which planets can sustain life?* ◇ *The love and support of his family sustained him during his time in prison.* **2 ~ sth** to make sth continue for some time without becoming less SYN **maintain**: *a period of sustained economic growth* ◇ *a sustained attack* ◇ *She managed to sustain everyone's interest until the end of her speech.* **3 ~ sth** (*formal*) to experience sth bad SYN **suffer**: *to* ***sustain damage/an injury/a defeat*** ◇ *The company* ***sustained losses*** *of millions of dollars.* **4 ~ sth** to provide evidence to support an opinion, a theory, etc. SYN **uphold**: *The evidence is not detailed enough to sustain his argument.* **5 ~ sth** (*formal*) to support a weight without breaking or falling SYN **bear**: *The ice will not sustain your weight.* **6 ~ sth** (*law*) to decide that a claim, etc. is valid SYN **uphold**: *The court sustained his claim that the contract was illegal.* ◇ ***Objection sustained!*** (= said by a judge when a lawyer makes an OBJECTION in court)

sus·tain·able AW /sə'steɪnəbl/ *adj.* **1** involving the use of natural products and energy in a way that does not harm the environment: *sustainable forest management* ◇ *an environmentally sustainable society* **2** that can continue or be continued for a long time: *sustainable economic growth* OPP **unsustainable** ▶ **sus·tain·abil·ity** AW /sə,steɪnə'bɪləti/ *noun* [U] **sus·tain·ably** /-bli/ *adv.*

sus·ten·ance AW /'sʌstənəns/ *noun* [U] (*formal*) **1** the food and drink that people, animals and plants need to live and stay healthy: *There's not much sustenance in a bowl of soup.* ◇ *(figurative) Arguing would only give further sustenance to his allegations.* **2 ~ (of sth)** the process of making sth continue to exist: *Elections are essential for the sustenance of parliamentary democracy.*

sutra /'su:trə/ *noun* **1** a rule or statement in Sanskrit literature, or a set of rules **2** a Buddhist or Jainist holy text

sut·tee = SATI

su·ture /'su:tʃə(r)/ *noun, verb*
■ ***noun*** (*medical*) a STITCH or stitches made when sewing up a wound, especially after an operation
■ ***verb*** **~ sth** (*medical*) to sew up a wound

SUV /,es ju: 'vi:/ *abbr.* SPORT UTILITY VEHICLE

su·zer·ainty /'su:zəreɪnti; -rənti/ *noun* [U] (*formal*) the right of a country to rule over another country

Sv *abbr.* SIEVERT

svelte /svelt; sfelt/ *adj.* (*approving*) (of a person, especially a woman) thin and attractive

Sven·gali /sven'gɑ:li/ *noun* a person who has the power to control another person's mind, make them do bad things, etc. ORIGIN From the name of a character in George du Maurier's novel *Trilby*.

SW *abbr.* **1** (*especially BrE*) SHORT WAVE: *SW and LW radio* **2** south-west; south-western: *SW Australia*

swab /swɒb; *NAmE* swɑ:b/ *noun, verb*
■ ***noun*** **1** a piece of soft material used by a doctor, nurse, etc. for cleaning wounds or taking a sample from sb's body for testing **2** an act of taking a sample from sb's body, with a swab: *to take a throat swab*
■ ***verb*** (-bb-) **1 ~ sth** to clean or remove liquid from a wound, etc, using a swab **2 ~ sth (down)** to clean or wash a floor, surface, etc. using water and a cloth, etc.

swad·dle /'swɒdl; *NAmE* 'swɑ:dl/ *verb* **~ sb/sth** (*old-fashioned*) to wrap sb/sth, especially a baby, tightly in clothes or a piece of cloth

'swaddling clothes *noun* [pl.] strips of cloth used in the past for wrapping a baby tightly

S

swag /swæg/ *noun* **1** [U] (*old-fashioned, informal*) goods that have been stolen SYN **loot** **2** [C, usually pl.] cloth that is hung in large curved folds as decoration, especially above a window **3** (*AustralE, NZE*) a pack of things tied or wrapped together and carried by a traveller **4** [C, usually pl.] a bunch of flowers or fruit that is CARVED onto walls, etc. as decoration

swag·ger /ˈswæɡə(r)/ *verb, noun*
■ ***verb*** [I] (+ **adv./prep.**) (usually *disapproving*) to walk in an extremely proud and confident way SYN **strut**
■ ***noun*** [sing.] (*disapproving*) a way of walking or behaving that seems too confident

swag·man /ˈswæɡmæn/ *noun* (*pl.* **-men** /-men/) (*AustralE, NZE, old use*) a man who travels around looking for work, carrying his possessions wrapped in a cloth

Swa·hili /swəˈhiːli; swɑːˈh-/ (also **Ki·swa·hili**) *noun* [U] a language widely used in E Africa, especially between people who speak different first languages

swain /sweɪn/ *noun* (*old use* or *humorous*) a young man who is in love

swal·low 0-w /ˈswɒləʊ; *NAmE* ˈswɑːloʊ/ *verb, noun*
■ ***verb***
▸ FOOD/DRINK **1** 0-w [T, I] to make food, drink, etc. go down your throat into your stomach: **~ (sth)** *Always chew food well before swallowing it.* ◇ *I had a sore throat and it hurt to swallow.* ◇ **~ sth + adj.** *The pills should be swallowed whole.*
▸ MOVE THROAT MUSCLES **2** 0-w [I] to move the muscles of your throat as if you were swallowing sth, especially because you are nervous: *She* ***swallowed hard*** *and told him the bad news.*
▸ COMPLETELY COVER **3** [T, often passive] to take sb/sth in or completely cover it so that they cannot be seen or no longer exist separately: **~ sb/sth** *I watched her walk down the road until she was swallowed by the darkness.* ◇ **~ sb/sth up** *Large areas of countryside have been swallowed up by towns.*
▸ USE UP MONEY **4** [T] **~ sb/sth (up)** to use up sth completely, especially an amount of money: *Most of my salary gets swallowed (up) by the rent and bills.*
▸ BELIEVE **5** [T] to accept that sth is true; to believe sth: **~ sth** *I found her excuse very* ***hard to swallow.*** ◇ **~ sth + adj.** *He told her a pack of lies, but she* ***swallowed it whole.***
▸ FEELINGS **6** [T] **~ sth** to hide your feelings: *to swallow your doubts* ◇ *You're going to have to* ***swallow your pride*** *and ask for your job back.*
▸ ACCEPT INSULTS **7** [T] **~ sth** to accept insults, criticisms, etc. without complaining or protesting: *I was surprised that he just sat there and swallowed all their remarks.* IDM see BITTER *adj.*
■ ***noun***
▸ BIRD **1** a small bird with long pointed wings and a tail with two points, that spends the winter in Africa but flies to northern countries for the summer
▸ OF FOOD/DRINK **2** an act of swallowing; an amount of food or drink that is swallowed at one time
IDM **one ˌswallow doesn't make a ˈsummer** (*saying*) you must not take too seriously a small sign that sth is happening or will happen in the future, because the situation could change

ˈswallow dive (*BrE*) (*NAmE* **ˈswan dive**) *noun* a DIVE performed with your arms stretched out sideways until you are close to the water

ˈswallow hole *noun* = SINKHOLE

swam *past tense* of SWIM

swami /ˈswɑːmi/ *noun* (also used as a title) a Hindu religious teacher: *Swami Vivekanand*

swamp /swɒmp; *NAmE* swɑːmp/ *noun, verb*
■ ***noun*** [C, U] an area of ground that is very wet or covered with water and in which plants, trees, etc. are growing SYN **marsh**: *tropical swamps* ▸ **swampy** *adj.*: *swampy ground*
■ ***verb*** [often passive] **1** to make sb have more of sth than they can deal with SYN **inundate**: **~ sb/sth with sth** *The department was swamped with job applications.* ◇ **~ sb/sth** *In summer visitors swamp the island.* **2 ~ sth** to fill or cover sth with a lot of water SYN **engulf**: *The little boat was swamped by the waves.*

ˈswamp fever *noun* [U] **1** a serious disease that affects horses **2** (*old-fashioned*) = MALARIA

swamp·land /ˈswɒmplænd; *NAmE* ˈswɑːmp-/ *noun* [U, pl.] a large area of SWAMP

swan /swɒn; *NAmE* swɑːn/ *noun, verb*
■ ***noun*** a large bird that is usually white and has a long thin neck. Swans live on or near water.
■ ***verb*** (-nn-) [I] + **adv./prep.** (*BrE, informal, disapproving*) to go around enjoying yourself in a way that annoys other people or makes them jealous: *They've gone swanning off to Paris for the weekend.*

ˈswan dive (*NAmE*) (*BrE* **ˈswallow dive**) *noun* a DIVE performed with your arms stretched out sideways until you are close to the water

swank /swæŋk/ *verb* [I] (*old-fashioned, BrE, informal, disapproving*) to behave in way that is too proud or confident

swanky /ˈswæŋki/ (**swank·ier, swanki·est**) (*especially BrE*) (also **swank** especially in *NAmE*) *adj.* (*informal, approving*) fashionable and expensive in a way that is intended to impress people: *a swanky new hotel*

swan·song /ˈswɒnsɒŋ; *NAmE* ˈswɑːnsɔːŋ/ *noun* [sing.] the last piece of work produced by an artist, a musician, etc. or the last performance by an actor, ATHLETE, etc.

swap (also **swop**) /swɒp; *NAmE* swɑːp/ *verb, noun*
■ ***verb*** (-pp-) **1** [I, T] to give sth to sb and receive sth in exchange: **~ (sth) (with sb)** *I've finished this magazine. Can I swap with you?* ◇ **~ sth for sth** *I swapped my red scarf for her blue one.* ◇ **~ sth** *Can we* ***swap places****? I can't see the screen.* ◇ *We spent the evening in the pub* ***swapping stories*** (= telling each other stories) *about our travels.* ◇ **~ sb sth for sth** *I swapped him my CD for his posters.* **2** [I] **~ (over)** to start doing sb else's job, etc. while they do yours: *I'll drive there and then we'll swap over on the way back.* **3** [T] (*especially BrE*) to replace one person or thing with another: **~ sb/sth (for sb/sth)** *I think I'll swap this sweater for one in another colour.* ◇ **~ sb/sth (over)** *I'm going to swap you over. Mike will go first and Jon will go second.* IDM see PLACE *n.*
■ ***noun*** **1** [usually sing.] an act of exchanging one thing or person for another: *Let's* ***do a swap****. You work Friday night and I'll do Saturday.* **2** a thing or person that has been exchanged for another: *Most of my football stickers are swaps.*

ˈswap meet *noun* (*especially NAmE*) an occasion at which people buy and sell or exchange items that interest them: *a swap meet for collectors of Star Trek memorabilia*

sward /swɔːd; *NAmE* swɔːrd/ *noun* [C, U] (*literary*) an area of grass

swarm /swɔːm; *NAmE* swɔːrm/ *noun, verb*
■ ***noun*** **~ (of sth) 1** a large group of insects, especially BEES, moving together in the same direction: *a* ***swarm of bees/locusts/flies*** **2** a large group of people, especially when they are all moving quickly in the same direction SYN **horde**
■ ***verb*** **1** [I] + **adv./prep.** (often *disapproving*) (of people, animals, etc.) to move around in a large group: *Tourists were swarming all over the island.* **2** (of BEES and other flying insects) to move around together in a large group, looking for a place to live
PHR V **ˈswarm with sb/sth** to be full of people or things: *The capital city is swarming with police.*

swar·thy /ˈswɔːði; *NAmE* ˈswɔːrði/ *adj.* (especially of a person or their face) having dark skin

swash /swɒʃ; *NAmE* swɔːʃ; swɑːʃ/ *noun* [sing.] (*technical*) the flow of water up the beach after a wave has BROKEN

swash·buck·ling /ˈswɒʃbʌklɪŋ; *NAmE* ˈswɔːʃ-; ˈswɑːʃ-/ *adj.* [only before noun] (especially of films/movies) set in the past and full of action, adventure, fighting with SWORDS, etc: *a swashbuckling tale of adventure on the high seas* ◇ *the swashbuckling hero of Hollywood epics*

swas·tika /ˈswɒstɪkə; *NAmE* ˈswɑːs-/ *noun* an ancient symbol in the form of a cross with its ends bent at an angle

S

of 90°, used in the 20th century as the symbol of the German Nazi party

swat /swɒt; *NAmE* swɑːt/ *verb* (-tt-) **~ sth** to hit sth, especially an insect, using your hand or a flat object ▸ **swat** *noun*

swatch /swɒtʃ; *NAmE* swɑːtʃ/ *noun* a small piece of cloth used to show people what a larger piece would look or feel like

swathe /sweɪð/ *noun, verb*

■ ***noun*** (also **swath** /swɒθ; *NAmE* swɑːθ/) (*formal*) **1** a long strip of land, especially one on which the plants or crops have been cut: *The combine had cut a swathe around the edge of the field.* ◇ *Development has affected vast swathes of our countryside.* **2** a large strip or area of sth: *The mountains rose above a swathe of thick cloud.*

IDM **cut a 'swathe through sth** (of a person, fire, etc.) to pass through a particular area destroying a large part of it

■ ***verb*** [usually passive] **~ sb/sth** (**in sth**) (*formal*) to wrap or cover sb/sth in sth: *He was lying on the hospital bed, swathed in bandages.*

'SWAT team *noun* (*especially US*) a group of police officers who are especially trained to deal with violent situations. SWAT stands for 'Special Weapons and Tactics'.

sway /sweɪ/ *verb, noun*

■ ***verb*** **1** [I, T] to move slowly from side to side; to move sth in this way: (**+ adv./prep.**) *The branches were swaying in the wind.* ◇ *Vicky swayed and fell.* ◇ **~ sth** (**+ adv./prep.**) *They danced rhythmically, swaying their hips to the music.* **2** [T, often passive] **~ sb** to persuade sb to believe sth or do sth SYN **influence**: *He's easily swayed.* ◇ *She wasn't swayed by his good looks or his clever talk.*

■ ***noun*** [U] **1** a movement from side to side **2** (*literary*) power or influence over sb: *Rebel forces* ***hold sway*** *over much of the island.* ◇ *He was quick to exploit those who fell* ***under his sway.***

swear 0-w /sweə(r); *NAmE* swer/ *verb* (**swore** /swɔː(r)/, **sworn** /swɔːn; *NAmE* swɔːrn/)

1 0-w [I] to use rude or offensive language, usually because you are angry: *She fell over and swore loudly.* ◇ **~ at sb/sth** *Why did you let him swear at you like that?* **2** 0-w [T, no passive] to make a serious promise to do sth SYN **vow**: **~ sth** *He swore revenge on the man who had killed his father.* ◇ **~ (that)...** *I swear (that) I'll never leave you.* HELP 'That' is usually left out, especially in speech.: **~ to do sth** *She made him swear not to tell anyone.* **3** 0-w [T] to promise that you are telling the truth: **~ (that)...** *She swore (that) she'd never seen him before.* ◇ ***I could have sworn*** (= I am sure) *I heard the phone ring.* ◇ **~ to sb/on sth (that)...** ***I swear to God*** *I had nothing to do with it.* **4** 0-w [I, T] to make a public or official promise, especially in court: **~** (**on sth**) *Witnesses were required to swear on the Bible.* ◇ **~ that...** *Are you willing to stand up in court and swear that you don't recognize him?* ◇ **~ to do sth** *Remember, you have sworn to tell the truth.* ◇ **~ sth** *Barons had to swear an oath of allegiance to the king.* **5** [T] **~ sb to secrecy/silence** to make sb promise not to tell sth to anyone: *Everyone was sworn to secrecy about what had happened.* ➲ see also SWORN

IDM **swear 'blind** (*informal*) to say that sth is definitely true **swear like a 'trooper** (*old-fashioned, BrE*) to often use very rude or offensive language

PHR V **'swear by sb/sth 1** to name sb/sth to show that you are making a serious promise: *I swear by almighty God that I will tell the truth.* **2** (not used in the progressive tenses) to be certain that sth is good or useful: *She swears by meditation as a way of relieving stress.* **ˌswear sb↔'in** | **ˌswear sb 'into sth** [often passive] to make sb promise to do a job correctly, to be loyal to an organization, a country, etc: *He was sworn in as president.* ◇ *The new prime minister was sworn into office.* ➲ related noun SWEARING-IN **ˌswear 'off sth** (*informal*) to promise that you will not do or use sth again: *I decided to swear off burgers forever.* **'swear to sth** (*informal*) to say that sth is definitely true: *I think I put the keys back in the drawer, but I couldn't swear to it* (= I'm not completely sure).

swear·ing 0-w /'sweərɪŋ; *NAmE* 'swerɪŋ/ *noun* [U] rude or offensive language: *I was shocked at the swearing.*

ˌswearing-'in *noun* [U, sing.] the act of publicly asking sb to promise to be loyal and perform their duties well when they start a new job, etc: *the swearing-in of the new President*

'swear word *noun* a rude or offensive word, used, for example, to express anger SYN **expletive**

sweat 0-w /swet/ *noun, verb*

■ ***noun***

▸ LIQUID ON SKIN **1** 0-w [U] drops of liquid that appear on the surface of your skin when you are hot, ill/sick or afraid SYN **perspiration**: *beads of sweat* ◇ *She wiped the sweat from her face.* ◇ *By the end of the match, the sweat was pouring off him.* ➲ see also SWEATY **2** 0-w [usually sing.] the state of being covered with sweat: *I woke up in a sweat.* ◇ *She completed the routine without even* ***working up a sweat.*** ◇ *He* ***breaks out in a sweat*** *just at the thought of flying.* ◇ *He started having night sweats.* ➲ see also COLD SWEAT

▸ HARD WORK **3** [U] hard work or effort: (*informal*) *Growing your own vegetables sounds like a lot of sweat.* ◇ (*literary*) *She achieved success by* ***the sweat of her brow*** (= by working very hard).

▸ CLOTHES **4 sweats** [pl.] (*informal, especially NAmE*) a SWEATSUIT or SWEATPANTS: *I hung around the house all day in my sweats.*

IDM **be/get in a 'sweat** (**about sth**) to be/become anxious or frightened about sth **break 'sweat** (*BrE*) (*NAmE* **break a 'sweat**) (*informal*) to use a lot of physical effort: *He hardly needed to break sweat to reach the final.* **no 'sweat** (*informal*) used to tell sb that sth is not difficult or a problem when they thank you or ask you to do sth: *'Thanks for everything.' 'Hey, no sweat!'* ➲ more at BLOOD *n.*

■ ***verb***

▸ PRODUCE LIQUID ON SKIN/SURFACE **1** 0-w [I, T] when you **sweat**, drops of liquid appear on the surface of your skin, for example when you are hot, ill/sick or afraid SYN **perspire**: *to sweat heavily* ◇ **~ sth** *He was* ***sweating buckets*** (= a lot). **2** [I] if sth **sweats**, the liquid that is contained in it appears on its surface: *The cheese was beginning to sweat.*

▸ WORK HARD **3** [I] **~** (**over sth**) to work hard at sth: *Are you still sweating over that report?*

▸ WORRY **4** [I] (*informal*) to worry or feel anxious about sth: *They really made me sweat during the interview.*

▸ HEAT FOOD **5** [T, I] **~** (**sth**) (*BrE*) if you **sweat** meat or vegetables or let them **sweat**, you heat them slowly with a little fat in a pan that is covered with a lid

IDM **don't 'sweat it** (*NAmE, informal*) used to tell sb to stop worrying about sth **don't sweat the 'small stuff** (*NAmE, informal*) used to tell sb not to worry about small details or unimportant things **sweat 'blood** (*informal*) to work very hard ➲ more at GUT *n.*

PHR V **ˌsweat sth↔'off** to lose weight by doing a lot of hard exercise to make yourself sweat **ˌsweat it 'out** (*informal*) to be waiting for sth difficult or unpleasant to end, and be feeling anxious about it

sweat·band /'swetbænd/ *noun* a band of cloth worn around the head or wrist, for absorbing sweat

ˌsweated 'labour *noun* [U] (*BrE*) hard work that is done for low wages in poor conditions; the people who do this work

sweat·er 0-w /'swetə(r)/ *noun*

a knitted piece of clothing made of wool or cotton for the upper part of the body, with long sleeves. In British English the word is used to describe a piece of clothing with no buttons. In American English a sweater can have buttons and be like a jacket. ➲ VISUAL VOCAB page V51

sweat·pants /'swetpænts/ (also *informal* **sweats**) *noun* [pl.] (*especially NAmE*) loose warm trousers/pants, usually made of thick cotton and worn for relaxing or playing sports in

sweat·shirt /'swetʃɜːt; *NAmE* -ʃɜːrt/ *noun* a piece of clothing for the upper part of the body, with long sleeves, usually made of thick cotton and often worn for sports

S

sweat·shop /ˈswetʃɒp; *NAmE* -ʃɑːp/ *noun* (*disapproving*) a place where people work for low wages in poor conditions

sweat·suit /ˈswetsuːt; *BrE* also -sjuːt/ *noun* (also *informal* **sweats** [pl.]) (both *NAmE*) a sweatshirt and SWEATPANTS worn together, for relaxing or playing sports in

sweaty /ˈsweti/ *adj.* (sweat·ier, sweati·est) **1** covered or damp with sweat: *sweaty feet* ◇ *He felt all hot and sweaty.* **2** [only before noun] making you become hot and covered with sweat: *It was sweaty work, under the hot sun.*

swede /swiːd/ (*BrE*) (*NAmE* **ru·ta·baga**) (*ScotE* **tur·nip**) *noun* [C, U] a large round yellow root vegetable ➲ VISUAL VOCAB page V27

sweep 🔑 /swiːp/ *verb, noun*

■ ***verb*** (swept, swept /swept/)

▸ WITH BRUSH OR HAND **1** 🔑 [T, I] to clean a room, surface, etc. using a BROOM (= a type of brush on a long handle): **~ (sth)** *to sweep the floor* ◇ **~ sth + adj.** *The showroom had been emptied and swept clean.* **2** 🔑 [T] **~ sth + adv./prep.** to remove sth from a surface using a brush, your hand, etc: *She swept the crumbs into the wastebasket.* ◇ *He swept the leaves up into a pile.*

▸ MOVE QUICKLY/WITH FORCE **3** [T] **~ sb/sth + adv./prep.** to move or push sb/sth suddenly and with a lot of force: *The little boat was swept out to sea.* ◇ *She let herself be swept along by the crowd.* **4** [I, T] (of weather, fire, etc.) to move suddenly and/or with force over an area or in a particular direction: **+ adv./prep.** *Rain swept in through the broken windows.* ◇ **~ sth** *Strong winds regularly sweep the islands.*

▸ OF A PERSON **5** [I] **+ adv./prep.** to move quickly and/or smoothly, especially in a way that impresses or is intended to impress other people: *Without another word she swept out of the room.* ◇ (*figurative*) *He swept into the lead with an almost perfect performance.* **6** [T] **~ sth + adv./prep.** to move sth, especially your hand or arm, quickly and smoothly in a particular direction: *He rushed to greet her, sweeping his arms wide.*

▸ OF FEELINGS **7** [I] **+ adv./prep.** to suddenly affect sb strongly: *A wave of tiredness swept over her.* ◇ *Memories came sweeping back.*

▸ OF IDEAS/FASHIONS **8** [I, T] to spread quickly: **+ adv./prep.** *Rumours of his resignation swept through the company.* ◇ **~ sth** *the latest craze sweeping America*

▸ LOOK/MOVE OVER AREA **9** [I, T] to move over an area, especially in order to look for sth: **+ adv./prep.** *His eyes swept around the room.* ◇ **~ sth** *Searchlights swept the sky.*

▸ TOUCH SURFACE **10** [T] **~ sth** to move, or move sth, over a surface, touching it lightly: *Her dress swept the ground as she walked.*

▸ HAIR **11** [T] **~ sth + adv./prep.** to brush, COMB, etc. your hair in a particular direction: *Her hair was swept back from her face.*

▸ OF LANDSCAPE **12** [I] **+ adv./prep.** to form a long smooth curve: *The hotel gardens sweep down to the beach.*

▸ IN SPORT **13** [T] **~ sth** (*NAmE*) to win all the games in a series of games against another team or all the parts of a contest: *The Blue Jays have a chance to sweep the series.* ◇ *New Jersey swept Detroit last season.*

IDM **sweep the ˈboard** to win all the prizes, etc. in a competition ˌ**sweep sb off their ˈfeet** to make sb fall suddenly and deeply in love with you **sweep (sb) to ˈpower** to win an election by a large number of votes; to make sb win an election with a large number of votes **sweep to ˈvictory** to win a contest easily: *Obama swept to victory in 2008.* **sweep sth under the ˈcarpet** (*US* also **sweep sth under the ˈrug**) to try to stop people from finding out about sth wrong, illegal, embarrassing, etc. that has happened or that you have done IDM see VICTORY *n.*

PHR V ˌ**sweep sb aˈlong/aˈway** [usually passive] to make sb very interested or involved in sth, especially in a way that makes them forget everything else: *They were swept along by the force of their emotions.* ˌ**sweep sth↔aˈside** to ignore sth completely: *All their advice was swept aside.* ˌ**sweep sth↔aˈway** to get rid of sth completely: *Any doubts had long since been swept away.* ˌ**sweep sth↔ˈout** to remove all the dust, dirt, etc. from a room or building using a brush ˌ**sweep sb↔ˈup** to lift sb up with a sudden smooth movement: *He swept her up into his arms.*

■ ***noun***

▸ WITH BRUSH **1** [C, usually sing.] an act of cleaning a room, surface, etc. using a BROOM: *Give the room a good sweep.*

▸ CURVING MOVEMENT **2** [C] a smooth curving movement: *He indicated the door with a sweep of his arm.*

▸ LANDSCAPE **3** [C, usually sing.] a long, often curved, piece of road, river, coast, etc: *the broad sweep of white cliffs around the bay*

▸ RANGE **4** [U] the range of an idea, a piece of writing, etc. that considers many different things: *Her book covers the long sweep of the country's history.*

▸ MOVEMENT/SEARCH OVER AREA **5** [C] a movement over an area, for example in order to search for sth or attack sth: *The rescue helicopter made another sweep over the bay.*

▸ CHIMNEY **6** [C] = CHIMNEY SWEEP

▸ GAMBLING **7** [C] (*NAmE* also **sweeps**) (*informal*) = SWEEPSTAKE

▸ IN SPORT **8** [C] (*NAmE*) a series of games that a team wins against another team; the fact of winning all the parts of a contest: *a World Series sweep*

▸ TELEVISION **9 the sweeps** [pl.] (*NAmE*) a time when television companies examine their programmes to find out which ones are the most popular, especially in order to calculate advertising rates IDM see CLEAN *adj.*

sweep·er /ˈswiːpə(r)/ *noun* **1** a person whose job is to sweep sth: *a road sweeper* **2** a thing that sweeps sth: *a carpet sweeper* ➲ see also MINESWEEPER **3** (*BrE*) (in football (SOCCER)) a player who plays behind the other defending players in order to try and stop anyone who passes them

sweep·ing /ˈswiːpɪŋ/ *adj.* **1** [usually before noun] having an important effect on a large part of sth: ***sweeping reforms/changes*** ◇ *Security forces were given sweeping powers to search homes.* **2** [usually before noun] (*disapproving*) too general and failing to think about or understand particular examples: *a* ***sweeping generalization/statement*** **3 ~ victory** a victory by a large number of votes, etc. **4** [only before noun] forming a curved shape: *a sweeping gesture* (= with your hand or arm) ◇ *a sweeping staircase*

sweep·stake /ˈswiːpsteɪk/ (*NAmE* also **sweep·stakes**) *noun* a type of betting in which the winner gets all the money bet by everyone else

sweet 🔑 /swiːt/ *adj., noun*

■ ***adj.*** (sweet·er, sweet·est)

▸ FOOD/DRINK **1** 🔑 containing, or tasting as if it contains, a lot of sugar: *a cup of hot sweet tea* ◇ *sweet food* ◇ *I had a craving for something sweet.* ◇ *This wine is too sweet for me.* ➲ compare BITTER, SALTY OPP **sour**

▸ SMELL **2** 🔑 having a pleasant smell SYN **fragrant**: *a sweet-smelling rose* ◇ *The air was sweet with incense.*

▸ SOUND **3** having a pleasant sound: *a sweet voice*

▸ PURE **4** pleasant and not containing any harmful substances: *the sweet air of a mountain village*

▸ SATISFYING **5** making you feel happy and/or satisfied: *Goodnight.* ***Sweet dreams.*** ◇ *I can't tell you how sweet this victory is.*

▸ ATTRACTIVE **6** (*especially BrE*) (especially of children or small things) attractive SYN **cute**: *His sister's a sweet young thing.* ◇ *You look sweet in this photograph.* ◇ *We stayed in a sweet little hotel on the seafront.*

▸ KIND **7** having or showing a kind character: *She gave him her sweetest smile.* ◇ *It was* ***sweet of them to*** *offer to help.*

▸ GOOD **8 Sweet!** (*NAmE, informal*) used to show that you approve of sth: *Free tickets? Sweet!*

IDM **be ˈsweet on sb** (*old-fashioned, informal*) to like sb very much in a romantic way **have a sweet ˈtooth** (*informal*) to like food that contains a lot of sugar **in your ˌown sweet ˈtime/ˈway** how and when you want to, even though this might annoy other people: *He always does the work, but in his own sweet time.* **keep sb ˈsweet** (*informal*) to say or do pleasant things in order to keep sb in a good mood so that they will agree to do sth for you **she's ˈsweet** (*AustralE, NZE, informal*) everything is all right **sweet FˈA** | **sweet Fanny ˈAdams** (*BrE, informal*) nothing at all. People say 'sweet FA' to avoid saying 'fuck all'. **sweet ˈnothings** romantic words: *to whisper sweet nothings in sb's ear* **the**

S

sweet smell of suc'cess (*informal*) the pleasant feeling of being successful ➲ more at HOME *n.*, ROSE *n.*, SHORT *adj.*

■ ***noun***

▸ FOOD **1** [C] (*BrE*) a small piece of sweet food, usually made with sugar and/or chocolate and eaten between meals SYN **candy**: *a packet of boiled sweets* ◇ *a sweet shop* **2** [C, U] (*BrE*) a sweet dish eaten at the end of a meal SYN **afters, dessert, pudding**: *I haven't made a sweet today.* ◇ *Would you like some more sweet?*

▸ PERSON **3** [U] (*old-fashioned*) a way of addressing sb that you like or love: *Don't you worry, my sweet.*

,sweet-and-'sour *adj.* [only before noun] (of food) cooked in a sauce that contains sugar and VINEGAR or lemon: *Chinese sweet-and-sour pork*

sweet·bread /'swi:tbred/ *noun* [usually pl.] the THYMUS (= an organ in the neck) or the PANCREAS (= an organ near the stomach) of a young cow or sheep, eaten as food

sweet·corn /'swi:tkɔ:n; *NAmE* -kɔ:rn/ (*BrE*) (*NAmE* **corn**) *noun* [U] the yellow seeds of a type of MAIZE (CORN) plant, also called sweetcorn, which grow on thick STEMS and are cooked and eaten as a vegetable: *tinned sweetcorn* ➲ VISUAL VOCAB page V27 ➲ see also CORN ON THE COB

sweet·en /'swi:tn/ *verb* **1 ~ sth** to make food or drinks taste sweeter by adding sugar, etc. **2 ~ sb (up)** (*informal*) to try to make sb more willing to help you, agree to sth, etc. by giving them money, praising them, etc. **3 ~ sth** to make sth more pleasant or acceptable IDM see PILL

sweet·en·er /'swi:tnə(r)/ *noun* **1** [U, C] a substance used to make food or drink taste sweeter, used instead of sugar: *artificial sweetener(s)* ➲ COLLOCATIONS at DIET **2** [C] (*informal*) something that is given to sb in order to persuade them to do sth, especially when this is done in a secret or dishonest way

sweet·heart /'swi:thɑ:t; *NAmE* -hɑ:rt/ *noun* **1** [sing.] (*informal*) used to address sb in a way that shows affection: *Do you want a drink, sweetheart?* **2** [C] (becoming *old-fashioned*) a person with whom sb is having a romantic relationship: *They were childhood sweethearts.*

sweetie /'swi:ti/ *noun* (*informal*) **1** [C] (*BrE*) a child's word for a sweet/a piece of candy **2** [C] a person who is kind and easy to like: *He's a real sweetie.* **3** [sing.] used to address sb in a way that shows affection

sweet·ish /'swi:tɪʃ/ *adj.* fairly sweet

sweet·ly /'swi:tli/ *adv.* **1** in a pleasant way: *She smiled sweetly at him.* **2** in a way that smells sweet: *a sweetly scented flower* **3** in a way that is without difficulties or problems: *Everything went sweetly and according to plan.* ◇ *He headed the ball sweetly into the back of the net.*

sweet·meat /'swi:tmi:t/ *noun* (*old use*) a sweet/candy; any food preserved in sugar

sweet·ness /'swi:tnəs/ *noun* [U] **1** the quality of being pleasant: *a smile of great sweetness* **2** the quality of tasting or smelling sweet: *The air was filled with the sweetness of mimosa.*

IDM **be (all) ,sweetness and 'light 1** (of a person) to be pleasant, friendly and polite **2** (of a situation) to be enjoyable and easy to deal with

,sweet 'pea *noun* a climbing garden plant with pale flowers that have a sweet smell ➲ VISUAL VOCAB page V9

,sweet 'pepper (*BrE* also **pep·per**) (*NAmE* also **'bell pepper**) *noun* a hollow fruit, usually red, green or yellow, eaten as a vegetable either raw or cooked ➲ VISUAL VOCAB page V27

'sweet po'tato *noun* [C, U] a root vegetable that looks like a red potato, but that is yellow inside and tastes sweet ➲ VISUAL VOCAB page V27

'sweet spot *noun* **1** the area on a BAT which hits the ball in the most effective way **2** a location or combination of characteristics that produces the best results: *This series aims to hit a sweet spot between romantic comedy and thriller.*

'sweet-talk *verb* **~ sb (into sth/into doing sth)** (*disapproving*) to try to persuade sb to do sth by praising them and telling them things they like to hear: *I can't believe you let him sweet-talk you into working for him!* ▸ **'sweet talk** *noun* [U]

sweet Wil·liam /,swi:t 'wɪljəm/ *noun* a garden plant with groups of red, pink, or white flowers that smell sweet

swell 0-π /swel/ *verb, noun, adj.*

■ ***verb*** (**swelled** /sweld/, **swol·len** /'swəʊlən; *NAmE* 'swoʊ-/ or **swelled, swelled**) **1** 0-π [I] **~ (up)** to become bigger or rounder: *Her arm was beginning to swell up where the bee had stung her.* **2** [I, T] to curve out or make sth curve out: **~ (out)** *The sails swelled (out) in the wind.* ◇ **~ sth (out)** *The wind swelled (out) the sails.* **3** [T, I] to increase or make sth increase in number or size: **~ sth (to sth)** *Last year's profits were swelled by a fall in production costs.* ◇ *We are looking for more volunteers to* ***swell the ranks*** (= increase the number) *of those already helping.* ◇ **~ (to sth)** *Membership has swelled to over 20 000.* OPP **shrink 4** [I] (of a sound) to become louder: *The cheering swelled through the hall.* **5** [I] **~ (with sth)** to be filled with a strong emotion: *to swell with pride* ➲ see also SWOLLEN

■ ***noun*** **1** [C, usually sing.] the movement of the sea when it rises and falls without the waves breaking: *The boat was caught in a heavy* (= strong) *swell.* **2** [sing.] (*formal*) the curved shape of sth, especially a part of the body: *the firm swell of her breasts* **3** [sing.] a situation in which sth increases in size, number, strength, etc: *a growing swell of support* ◇ *a swell of pride* ➲ see also GROUNDSWELL **4** [sing.] (of music or noise) a gradual increase in the volume of sth SYN **crescendo 5** (*old-fashioned, informal*) an important or fashionable person

■ ***adj.*** (*old-fashioned, NAmE, informal*) very good, enjoyable, etc: *We had a swell time.*

swell·ing 0-π /'swelɪŋ/ *noun*

1 0-π [U] the condition of being larger or rounder than normal (= of being SWOLLEN): *Use ice to reduce the swelling.* **2** 0-π [C] a place on your body that has become larger or rounder than normal as the result of an illness or injury: *The fall left her with a painful swelling above her eye.*

swel·ter /'sweltə(r)/ *verb* [I] to be very hot in a way that makes you feel uncomfortable: *Passengers sweltered in temperatures of over 90°F.* ▸ **swel·ter·ing** *adj.* SYN **stifling**: *sweltering heat* **swel·ter·ing·ly** *adv.*: *swelteringly hot*

swept *past tense, past part.* of SWEEP

,swept-'back *adj.* [only before noun] **1** (of hair) pulled back from your face **2** (of an aircraft wing) pointing backwards

'swept-up *adj.* = UPSWEPT

swerve /swɜ:v; *NAmE* swɜ:rv/ *verb* [I] (especially of a vehicle) to change direction suddenly, especially in order to avoid hitting sb/sth: *She swerved sharply to avoid a cyclist.* ◇ *The bus suddenly swerved into his path.* ◇ *The ball swerved into the net.* ▸ **swerve** *noun*

swift /swɪft/ *adj., noun*

■ ***adj.*** (**swift·er, swift·est**) **1** happening or done quickly and immediately; doing sth quickly: *swift action* ◇ *a swift decision* ◇ **~ to do sth** *The White House was swift to deny the rumours.* **2** moving very quickly; able to move very quickly: *a swift current* ◇ *a swift runner* ➲ SYNONYMS at FAST ▸ **swift·ly** *adv.*: *She moved swiftly to the rescue.* **swift·ness** *noun* [U, sing.]

■ ***noun*** a small bird with long narrow wings, similar to a SWALLOW

swig /swɪg/ *verb* (-gg-) **~ sth** (*informal*) to take a quick drink of sth, especially alcohol: *They sat around swigging beer from bottles.* ▸ **swig** *noun*: *She took a swig of wine.*

swill /swɪl/ *verb, noun*

■ ***verb*** **1** [T] **~ sth (out/down)** (*especially BrE*) to clean sth by pouring large amounts of water in, on or through it SYN **rinse**: *She swilled the glasses with clean water.* **2** [T] **~ sth (down)** (*informal*) to drink sth quickly and/or in large quantities **3** [T, I] to move, or to make a liquid move, in a particular direction or around a particular place: **~ sth + adv./prep.** *He swilled the juice around in his glass.* ◇ **+ adv./prep.** *Water swilled around in the bottom of the boat.*

S

■ *noun* **1** (also **pig·swill**) [U] a mixture of waste food and water that is given to pigs to eat **2** [U] (*informal*) drink or food that is unpleasant or of a poor quality **3** [C, usually sing.] (*informal*) a large amount of a drink that you take into your mouth: *He had a quick swill of wine.*

swim 0-w /swɪm/ *verb, noun*

■ *verb* (swim·ming, swam /swæm/, swum /swʌm/) **1** 0-w [I, T] (of a person) to move through water in a horizontal position using the arms and legs: *I can't swim.* ◇ *The boys swam across the lake.* ◇ *They spent the day swimming and sunbathing.* ◇ **~ sth** *Can you swim backstroke yet?* ◇ *How long will it take her to swim the Channel?* ⊃ note at BATH **2** 0-w [I] **go swimming** to spend time swimming for pleasure: *I go swimming twice a week.* **3** 0-w [I] (**+ adv./prep.**) (of a fish, etc.) to move through or across water: *A shoal of fish swam past.* ◇ *Ducks were swimming around on the river.* **4** [I] (usually **be swimming**) to be covered with a lot of liquid: **~ (in sth)** *The main course was swimming in oil.* ◇ **~ (with sth)** *Her eyes were swimming with tears.* **5** [I] (of objects, etc.) to seem to be moving around, especially when you are ill/sick or drunk: *The pages swam before her eyes.* **6** [I] to feel confused and/or as if everything is spinning around: *His head swam and he swayed dizzily.* IDM see SINK *v.*

■ *noun* **1** [sing.] a period of time during which you swim: *Let's **go for a swim.*** **2** (*especially NAmE*) (in compounds) related to or used for swimming: *a swim meet* (= a swimming competition between teams) ◇ *swim trunks*

IDM **in the 'swim (of things)** (*informal*) involved in things that are happening in society or in a particular situation

swim·mer /'swɪmə(r)/ *noun* a person who can swim; a person who is swimming: *a **good/strong swimmer*** ◇ *They watched the swimmers splashing through the water.* ◇ *a shallow pool for **non-swimmers***

swim·ming 0-w /'swɪmɪŋ/ *noun* [U] the sport or activity of swimming: *Swimming is a good form of exercise.* ⊃ VISUAL VOCAB page V37

'swimming bath *noun* [usually pl.] (*old-fashioned, BrE*) a public swimming pool inside a building

'swimming cap (also **'swimming hat**) (both *BrE*) (also **'bathing cap** *NAmE, BrE*) *noun* a soft rubber or plastic cap that fits closely over your head to keep your hair dry while you are swimming

'swimming costume *noun* (*BrE*) = SWIMSUIT

swim·ming·ly /'swɪmɪŋli/ *adv.* (*informal*) without any problems or difficulties: *We hope everything will **go swimmingly**.*

S

'swimming pool 0-w (also **pool**) *noun* **1** 0-w an area of water that has been created for people to swim in: *an **indoor/outdoor swimming pool*** ◇ *a **heated swimming pool*** ◇ *an **open-air swimming pool*** **2** 0-w the building that contains a public swimming pool: *She trained five times a week at her local swimming pool.*

'swimming trunks (also **trunks**) (*NAmE* also **'swim trunks**) *noun* [pl.] a piece of clothing covering the lower part of the body and sometimes the top part of the legs, worn by men and boys for swimming: *a pair of swimming trunks* ⊃ picture at TRUNK

swim·suit /'swɪmsu:t; *BrE* also -sju:t/ *noun* (*BrE* also **'swimming costume**) (also **'bathing suit** *NAmE* or *old-fashioned*) a piece of clothing worn for swimming, especially the type worn by women and girls

swim·wear /'swɪmweə(r); *NAmE* -wer/ *noun* [U] clothing that you wear for swimming

swin·dle /'swɪndl/ *verb, noun*

■ *verb* to cheat sb in order to get sth, especially money, from them: **~ sb (out of sth)** *They swindled him out of hundreds of dollars.* ◇ **~ sth (out of sb)** *They swindled hundreds of dollars out of him.* ▶ **swind·ler** /'swɪndlə(r)/ *noun* SYN **conman**

■ *noun* [usually sing.] a situation in which sb uses dishonest or illegal methods in order to get money from a company, another person, etc. SYN **con**: *an insurance swindle*

swine /swaɪn/ *noun* (*pl.* swines or swine) **1** [C] (*informal*) an unpleasant person: *He's an arrogant little swine!* **2** [C] (*BrE, informal*) a difficult or unpleasant thing or task: *The car can be a swine to start.* **3 swine** [pl.] (*old use* or *technical*) pigs: *a herd of swine* ◇ ***swine fever*** (= a disease of pigs) IDM see PEARL

'swine flu *noun* [U] **1** a serious illness that affects pigs **2** a serious illness spread between humans, that is GENETICALLY similar to swine flu in pigs, that in some cases causes death

swine·herd /'swaɪnhɜ:d; *NAmE* -hɜ:rd/ *noun* (*old use*) a person whose job is to take care of pigs

swing 0-w /swɪŋ/ *verb, noun*

■ *verb* (swung, swung /swʌŋ/)

▸ HANG AND MOVE **1** 0-w [I, T] to move backwards or forwards or from side to side while hanging from a fixed point; to make sth do this: *His arms swung as he walked.* ◇ *As he pushed her, she swung higher and higher* (= while sitting on a swing). ◇ **~ from sth** *A set of keys swung from her belt.* ◇ **~ sth** *He sat on the stool, swinging his legs.* **2** 0-w [I, T] to move from one place to another by holding sth that is fixed and pulling yourself along, up, etc: **+ adv./prep.** *The gunshot sent monkeys swinging away through the trees.* ◇ **~ yourself + adv./prep.** *He swung himself out of the car.*

▸ MOVE IN CURVE **3** 0-w [I, T] to move or make sth move with a wide curved movement: **+ adv./prep.** *A line of cars swung out of the palace gates.* ◇ **~ sth + adv./prep.** *He swung his legs over the side of the bed.* ◇ **+ adj.** *The door swung open.* ◇ **~ sth + adj.** *She swung the door open.*

▸ TURN QUICKLY **4** [I, T] to turn or change direction suddenly; to make sth do this: **+ adv./prep.** *The bus swung sharply to the left.* ◇ **~ sth + adv./prep.** *He swung the camera around to face the opposite direction.*

▸ TRY TO HIT **5** [I, T] to try to hit sb/sth: **~ at sb/sth** *She swung at me with the iron bar.* ◇ **~ sth (at sb/sth)** *He swung another punch in my direction.*

▸ CHANGE OPINION/MOOD **6** [I, T] to change or make sb/sth change from one opinion, mood, etc. to another: **~ (from A) (to B)** *The state has swung from Republican to Democrat.* ◇ **~ (between A and B)** *His emotions swung between fear and curiosity.* ◇ *The game could swing either way* (= either side could win it). ◇ **~ sb/sth (to sth)** *I managed to swing them round to my point of view.*

▸ DO/GET STH **7** [T] (*informal*) to succeed in getting or achieving sth, sometimes in a slightly dishonest way: **~ sth** *We're trying to **swing it** so that we can travel on the same flight.* ◇ **~ sb sth** *Is there any chance of you swinging us a couple of tickets?*

▸ OF MUSIC **8** [I] to have a strong rhythm

▸ OF PARTY **9** [I] (*informal*) if a party, etc. **is swinging**, there are a lot of people there having a good time

IDM **swing the 'balance** = TIP THE BALANCE/SCALE at TIP *v.* **swing both 'ways** (*informal*) to be BISEXUAL (= sexually attracted to both men and women) **,swing for the 'fences** (*NAmE*) to really try to achieve sth great, even when it is not reasonable to expect to be so successful: *entrepreneurs who think big and swing for the fences* **,swing into 'action** to start doing sth quickly and with a lot of energy **,swing the 'lead** (*old-fashioned, BrE, informal*) (usually used in the progressive tenses) to pretend to be ill/sick when in fact you are not, especially to avoid work: *I don't think there's anything wrong with her—she's just swinging the lead.* ORIGIN The lead was a weight at the bottom of a line that sailors used to measure how deep water was when the ship was near land. 'Swinging the lead' was thought to be an easy task, and came to mean avoiding hard work. ⊃ more at ROOM *n.*

PHR V **,swing 'by | 'swing by sth** (*NAmE, informal*) to visit a place or person for a short time SYN **drop by**: *I'll swing by your house on the way home from work.*

■ *noun*

▸ MOVEMENT **1** 0-w [C] a swinging movement or rhythm: *He took a wild swing at the ball.* ◇ *the swing of her hips*

▸ OF OPINION/MOOD **2** 0-w [C] a change from one opinion or situation to another; the amount by which sth changes: *He is liable to abrupt **mood swings*** (= for example from being very happy to being very sad). ◇ *Voting showed a 10% swing to Labour.*

▸ HANGING SEAT **3** 🔑 [C] a seat for swinging on, hung from above on ropes or chains: *The kids were playing on the swings.* ➲ VISUAL VOCAB page V32
▸ IN GOLF **4** [sing.] the swinging movement you make with your arms and body when you hit the ball in the game of GOLF: *I need to work on my swing.*
▸ MUSIC **5** [U] a type of JAZZ with a smooth rhythm, played especially by big dance bands in the 1930s
▸ JOURNEY **6** [sing.] (*NAmE*) a quick journey, especially one made by a politician, in which sb visits several different places in a short time: *a three-day campaign swing through California*

IDM **get in/into the ˈswing (of sth)** (*informal*) to get used to an activity or a situation and become fully involved in it **go with a ˈswing** (*BrE*) **1** (of a party or an activity) to be lively and enjoyable **2** (of music) to have a strong rhythm **in full ˈswing** having reached a very lively level: *When we arrived the party was already in full swing.* **ˌswings and ˈroundabouts** (*BrE, informal*) used to say that there are advantages and disadvantages whatever decision you make: *If you earn more, you pay more in tax, so it's all swings and roundabouts.*

ˌswing ˈbridge *noun* (*BrE*) a bridge that can be moved to one side to allow tall ships to pass

ˌswing ˈdoor (*BrE*) (*NAmE* **ˌswinging ˈdoor**) *noun* a door that you can open in either direction and that closes itself when you stop holding it open

swinge·ing /ˈswɪndʒɪŋ/ *adj.* [usually before noun] (*BrE*) **1** large and likely to cause people problems, especially financial problems: *swingeing cuts in benefits* ◇ *swingeing tax increases* **2** extremely critical of sb/sth: *a swingeing attack on government policy*

swing·er /ˈswɪŋə(r)/ *noun* (*old-fashioned, informal*) **1** a person who is fashionable and has an active social life **2** a person who has sex with many different people

swing·ing /ˈswɪŋɪŋ/ *adj.* [usually before noun] (*old-fashioned, informal*) lively and fashionable

ˌswinging ˈdoor (*NAmE*) (*BrE* **ˌswing ˈdoor**) *noun* a door that you can open in either direction and that closes itself when you stop holding it open

ˈswing set *noun* a frame for children to play on including one or more SWINGS and often a SLIDE

ˈswing shift *noun* (*NAmE, informal*) the SHIFT (= period of time worked each day) from 3 or 4 o'clock in the afternoon until 11 or 12 at night; the workers who work this SHIFT

ˌswing ˈstate *noun* (*politics*) (in an election for president in the US) a state where none of the candidates can be certain of getting the most support

ˌswing ˈvote *noun* [C, sing.] (*NAmE*) the votes of people who do not always vote for the same political party and have not decided which party to vote for in an election

ˌswing ˈvoter (*NAmE*) (*BrE* **ˌfloating ˈvoter**) *noun* a person who does not always vote for the same political party and who has not decided which party to vote for in an election

ˌswing-ˈwing *adj.* [only before noun] used to describe an aircraft wing that can be moved forward for landing, etc. and backward for rapid flight

swipe /swaɪp/ *verb, noun*
■ ***verb*** **1** [I, T] **~ (at) sb/sth** to hit or try to hit sb/sth with your hand or an object by swinging your arm: *He swiped at the ball and missed.* **2** [T] **~ sth** (*informal*) to steal sth SYN **pinch** **3** [T] **~ sth** to pass a plastic card, such as a credit card, through a special machine that is able to read the information that is stored on it
■ ***noun*** **~ (at sb/sth)** (*informal*) **1** an act of hitting or trying to hit sb/sth by swinging your arm or sth that you are holding: *She **took a swipe at** him with her umbrella.* **2** an act of criticizing sb/sth: *He used the interview to **take a swipe at** his critics.*

ˈswipe card (also **ˈkey card** especially in *NAmE*) *noun* a special plastic card with information recorded on it which can be read by an electronic device: *Access to the building is by swipe card only.*

swirl /swɜːl; *NAmE* swɜːrl/ *verb, noun*
■ ***verb*** [I, T] to move around quickly in a circle; to make sth do this: (**+ adv./prep.**) *The water swirled down the drain.* ◇ *A long skirt swirled around her ankles.* ◇ *swirling mists* ◇ **~ sth** (**+ adv./prep.**) *He took a mouthful of water and swirled it around his mouth.*
■ ***noun*** **1** the movement of sth that twists and turns in different directions and at different speeds **2** a pattern or an object that twists in circles

swish /swɪʃ/ *verb, noun, adj.*
■ ***verb*** [I, T] to move quickly through the air in a way that makes a soft sound; to make sth do this: (**+ adv./prep.**) *A large car swished past them and turned into the embassy gates.* ◇ *The pony's tail swished.* ◇ **~ sth** (**+ adv./prep.**) *The pony swished its tail.* ◇ *She swished her racket aggressively through the air.*
■ ***noun*** [sing.] the movement or soft sound made by sth moving quickly, especially through the air
■ ***adj.*** (*BrE, informal*) looking expensive and fashionable SYN **smart**: *a swish restaurant*

Swiss /swɪs/ *adj., noun* (*pl.* **Swiss**)
■ ***adj.*** from or connected with Switzerland
■ ***noun*** a person from Switzerland

ˌSwiss ˈArmy knife™ *noun* a small knife with several different blades and tools such as scissors, that fold into the handle

ˈSwiss ball™ *noun* = EXERCISE BALL

ˌSwiss ˈchard *noun* [U] = CHARD

ˌSwiss ˈcheese *noun* [U, C] any hard cheese with holes in it

ˌSwiss ˈroll (*BrE*) (*NAmE* **ˈjelly roll**) *noun* a thin flat cake that is spread with jam, etc. and rolled up

switch 🔑 /swɪtʃ/ *noun, verb*
■ ***noun*** **1** 🔑 a small device that you press or move up and down in order to turn a light or piece of electrical equipment on and off: *a light switch* ◇ *an on-off switch* ◇ *That was in the days before electricity was available **at the flick of a switch**.* ◇ *Which switch do I press to turn it off?* ◇ *to throw a switch* (= to move a large switch) **2** a change from one thing to another, especially when this is sudden and complete: **~ (in/of sth)** *a switch of priorities* ◇ **~ (from A to B)** *She made the switch from full-time to part-time work when her first child was born.* ◇ *a policy switch* **3** (*NAmE*) the POINTS on a railway/railroad line **4** a thin stick that bends easily: *a riding switch*
■ ***verb*** **1** 🔑 [I, T] to change or make sth change from one thing to another: **~ (over) (from sth) (to sth)** *We're in the process of switching over to a new system of invoicing.* ◇ **~ between A and B** *Press these two keys to switch between documents on screen.* ◇ **~ sth (over) (from sth) (to sth)** *When did you switch jobs?* **2** [T] to exchange one thing for another SYN **swap**: **~ sth** *The dates of the last two exams have been switched.* ◇ **~ sth over/around/round** *I see you've switched the furniture around* (= changed its position). ◇ **~ sth with sth** *Do you think she'll notice if I switch my glass with hers?* **3** [I, T] to do sb else's job for a short time or work during different hours so that they can do your job or work during your usual hours SYN **swap**: **~ (with sb)** *I can't work next weekend—will you switch with me?* ◇ **~ sth (with sb)** *Have you been able to switch your shift with anyone?* ◇ **~ (sth) (over/around/round)** *Can we switch our shifts around?*

PHR V **ˌswitch ˈoff** (*informal*) to stop thinking about sth or paying attention to sth: *When I hear the word 'football' I switch off* (= because I am not interested in it). ◇ *The only time he really switches off* (= stops thinking about work, etc.) *is when we're on vacation.* **ˌswitch ˈoff/ˈon | ˌswitch sth↔ˈoff/ˈon** 🔑 to turn a light, machine, etc. off/on by pressing a button or switch: *Please switch the lights off as you leave.* ◇ *How do you switch this thing on?* **ˌswitch ˈover | ˌswitch sth↔ˈover** (*BrE*) to change stations on a radio or television

switch·back /ˈswɪtʃbæk/ *noun* **1** a road or railway/railroad track that has many sharp bends as it goes up a steep

S

hill, or one that rises and falls steeply many times **2** (*NAmE*) a 180 degree bend in a road that is going up a steep hill **3** (*old-fashioned, BrE*) = ROLLER COASTER

switch·blade /ˈswɪtʃbleɪd/ (*especially NAmE*) (*BrE* also **ˈflick knife**) *noun* a knife with a blade inside the handle that jumps out quickly when a button is pressed

switch·board /ˈswɪtʃbɔːd; *NAmE* -bɔːrd/ *noun* the central part of a telephone system used by a company, etc, where telephone calls are answered and PUT THROUGH (= connected) to the appropriate person or department; the people who work this equipment: *a switchboard operator* ◇ *Call the switchboard and ask for extension 410.* ◇ *Hundreds of fans jammed the switchboard for over an hour.*

ˌswitched ˈon *adj.* **1 ~ (to sth)** aware of new things that are happening: *We're trying to get people switched on to the benefits of healthy eating.* ◇ *an organization for switched-on young people* **2** made to feel interested and excited: *People get really switched on by this music.*

ˈswitch-hitter *noun* (in BASEBALL) a player who can hit with the BAT on either side of their body

switch·over /ˈswɪtʃəʊvə(r); *NAmE* -oʊ-/ *noun* a change from one system, method, policy, etc. to another: *the switchover from analogue to digital TV*

swivel /ˈswɪvl/ *noun, verb*

■ ***noun*** (often used as an adjective) a device used to connect two parts of an object together, allowing one part to turn around without moving the other: *a swivel chair* (= one on which the seat turns around without moving the base) ➲ VISUAL VOCAB page V56

■ ***verb*** (-ll-, *US* -l-) **1** [T, I] **~ (sth) (+ adv./prep.)** to turn or make sth turn around a fixed central point SYN **spin**: *She swivelled the chair around to face them.* **2** [I, T] **~ (sth) (+ adv./prep.)** to turn or move your body, eyes or head around quickly to face another direction SYN **swing**: *He swivelled around to look at her.*

swizz (also **swiz**) /swɪz/ *noun* [usually sing.] (*BrE, informal*) something unfair or disappointing: *What a swizz!*

swiz·zle stick /ˈswɪzl stɪk/ *noun* a stick used to remove the bubbles from SPARKLING drinks such as CHAMPAGNE

swol·len 0→ /ˈswəʊlən; *NAmE* ˈswoʊlən/ *adj.* **1** 0→ (of a part of the body) larger than normal, especially as a result of a disease or an injury: *swollen glands* ◇ *Her eyes were red and swollen from crying.* **2** (of a river) containing more water than normal ➲ see also SWELL *v.*

swoon /swuːn/ *verb* **1** [I] **~ (over sb)** to feel very excited, emotional, etc. about sb that you think is sexually attractive, so that you almost become unconscious: *He's used to having women swooning over him.* **2** [I] (*old-fashioned*) to become unconscious SYN **faint** ▶ **swoon** *noun* [sing.]: (*old-fashioned*) *to go into a swoon*

S

swoop /swuːp/ *verb, noun*

■ ***verb*** **1** [I] (+ **adv./prep.**) (of a bird or plane) to fly quickly and suddenly downwards, especially in order to attack sb/sth SYN **dive**: *The aircraft swooped down over the buildings.* **2** [I] **~ (on sb/sth)** (especially of police or soldiers) to visit or attack sb/sth suddenly and without warning

■ ***noun*** **1** an act of moving suddenly and quickly through the air in a downward direction, as a bird does SYN **dive** **2 ~ (on sth/sb)** an act of arriving somewhere or attacking sth/sb in a way that is sudden and unexpected SYN **raid**: *Large quantities of drugs were found during a police swoop on the star's New York home.* IDM see FELL *adj.*

swoosh /swuːʃ/ *verb* [I] + **adv./prep.** to move quickly through the air in a way that makes a sound: *Cars and trucks swooshed past.* ▶ **swoosh** *noun* [sing.]

swop = SWAP

sword /sɔːd; *NAmE* sɔːrd/ *noun* a weapon with a long metal blade and a handle: *to* ***draw/sheathe a sword*** (= to take it out/put it into its cover)

IDM **put sb to the ˈsword** (*old-fashioned* or *literary*) to kill sb with a sword **a/the sword of ˈDamocles** (*literary*) a bad or unpleasant thing that might happen to you at any time and that makes you feel worried or frightened ORIGIN From the legend in which **Damocles** had to sit at a meal at the court of Dionysius with a sword hanging by a single hair above his head. He had praised Dionysius' happiness, and Dionysius wanted him to understand how quickly happiness can be lost. **turn swords into ˈploughshares** (*literary*) to stop fighting and return to peaceful activities ➲ more at CROSS *v.*, DOUBLE-EDGED, PEN *n.*

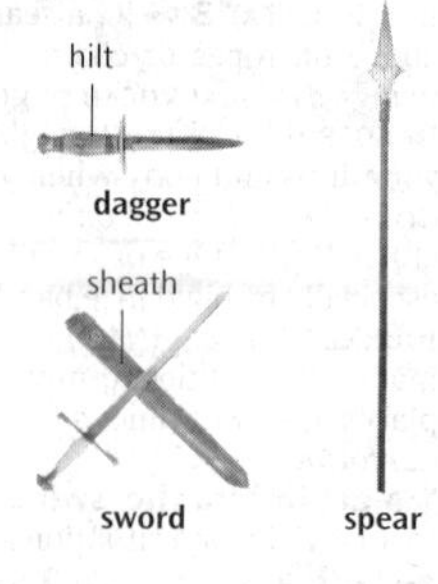

ˈsword dance *noun* a Scottish dance in which people dance between and over SWORDS that are placed on the ground

sword·fish /ˈsɔːdfɪʃ; *NAmE* ˈsɔːrd-/ *noun* [C, U] (*pl.* **swordfish**) a large sea fish with a very long thin pointed upper JAW

sword·play /ˈsɔːdpleɪ; *NAmE* ˈsɔːrd-/ *noun* [U] **1** the sport or skill of FENCING **2** clever and amusing comments and replies that are made quickly SYN **repartee**

swords·man /ˈsɔːdzmən; *NAmE* ˈsɔːrdz-/ *noun* (*pl.* **-men** /-mən/) (usually used with an adjective) a person who fights with a SWORD: *a fine swordsman*

swords·man·ship /ˈsɔːdzmənʃɪp; *NAmE* ˈsɔːrdz-/ *noun* [U] skill in fighting with a SWORD

swore *past tense* of SWEAR

sworn /swɔːn; *NAmE* swɔːrn/ *adj.* [only before noun] **1** made after you have promised to tell the truth, especially in court: *a sworn statement* **2 ~ enemies** people, countries, etc. that have a strong hatred for each other ➲ see also SWEAR *v.*

swot /swɒt; *NAmE* swɑːt/ *noun, verb*

■ ***noun*** (*BrE*) (*US* **grind**) (*informal, disapproving*) a person who spends too much time studying

■ ***verb*** (-tt-) [I] **~ (for sth)** (*BrE, informal*) to study very hard, especially in order to prepare for an exam

PHR V **ˌswot sth↔ˈup** | **ˌswot ˈup on sth** (*BrE, informal*) to study a particular subject very hard, especially in order to prepare for an exam: *Make sure you swot up on the company before the interview.*

ˈSWOT analysis *noun* a study done by an organization in order to find its strengths and weaknesses, and what problems or opportunities it should deal with. **SWOT** is formed from the initial letters of 'strengths', 'weaknesses', 'opportunities' and 'threats'.

swum *past part.* of SWIM

swung *past tense, past part.* of SWING

syb·ar·it·ic /ˌsɪbəˈrɪtɪk/ *adj.* [usually before noun] (*formal*) connected with a desire for pleasure: *his sybaritic lifestyle*

syca·more /ˈsɪkəmɔː(r)/ *noun* **1** [C, U] (*especially BrE*) a European tree of the MAPLE family, with leaves that have five points and seeds shaped like a pair of wings ➲ VISUAL VOCAB page V8 **2** [C] (*especially NAmE*) an American PLANE TREE **3** [U] the valuable hard wood of the European sycamore

syco·phant /ˈsɪkəfænt/ *noun* (*formal, disapproving*) a person who praises important or powerful people too much and in a way that is not sincere, especially in order to get sth from them ▶ **syco·phancy** /ˈsɪkəfənsi/ *noun* [U] **syco·phan·tic** /ˌsɪkəˈfæntɪk/ *adj.*: *a sycophantic review*

syl·lab·ary /ˈsɪləbəri; *NAmE* -beri/ *noun* (*pl.* **-ies**) (*technical*) a set of written characters representing syllables and used as an alphabet in some languages

syl·lab·ic /sɪˈlæbɪk/ *adj.* (*phonetics*) **1** based on syllables: *syllabic stress* **2** (of a consonant) forming a whole syllable, for example /l/ in *settle*

syl·lable /ˈsɪləbl/ *noun* any of the units into which a word is divided, containing a vowel sound and usually one or more consonants: *a word with two syllables* ◇ *a two-syllable* *word* ◇ *'Potato' is stressed on the second syllable.* IDM see WORD *n.*

'syllable-timed *adj.* (*phonetics*) (of a language) having a regular rhythm of syllables ➲ compare STRESS-TIMED

syl·la·bub /'sɪləbʌb/ *noun* [C, U] (*BrE*) a cold DESSERT (= a sweet dish) made from cream that has been mixed very quickly with sugar, wine, fruit juice, etc. to make it thick

syl·la·bus /'sɪləbəs/ *noun* (*pl.* **syl·la·buses** or *less frequent* **syl·labi** /'sɪləbaɪ/) a list of the topics, books, etc. that students should study in a particular subject at school or college ➲ COLLOCATIONS at EDUCATION ➲ compare CURRICULUM

syl·lo·gism /'sɪlədʒɪzəm/ *noun* (*technical*) a way of arguing in which two statements are used to prove that a third statement is true, for example: 'All humans must die; I am a human; therefore I must die.' ▸ **syl·lo·gist·ic** /ˌsɪlə'dʒɪstɪk/ *adj.* [only before noun]

sylph /sɪlf/ *noun* **1** an imaginary spirit **2** a girl or woman who is thin and attractive

sylph·like /'sɪlflaɪk/ *adj.* (of a woman or girl) thin in an attractive way

syl·van /'sɪlvən/ *adj.* (*literary*) connected with forests and trees

sym·bi·osis /ˌsɪmbaɪ'əʊsɪs; *NAmE* -'oʊsɪs/ *noun* [U, C] (*pl.* **sym·bi·oses** /-'əʊsiːz; *NAmE* -'oʊsiːz/) **1** (*biology*) the relationship between two different living creatures that live close together and depend on each other in particular ways, each getting particular benefits from the other **2** a relationship between people, companies, etc. that is to the advantage of both ▸ **sym·bi·ot·ic** /-'ɒtɪk; *NAmE* -'ɑːtɪk/ *adj.*: *a symbiotic relationship* **sym·bi·ot·ic·al·ly** /ˌsɪmbaɪ'ɒtɪkli; *NAmE* -'ɑːtɪk-/ *adv.*

sym·bol 0⊸ AW /'sɪmbl/ *noun*
1 0⊸ **~ (of sth)** a person, an object, an event, etc. that represents a more general quality or situation: *White has always been a symbol of purity in Western cultures.* ◇ *Mandela became a symbol of the anti-apartheid struggle.* ➲ SYNONYMS at SIGN **2** 0⊸ **~ (for sth)** a sign, number, letter, etc. that has a fixed meaning, especially in science, mathematics and music: *What is the chemical symbol for copper?* ◇ *A list of symbols used on the map is given in the index.* ➲ see also SEX SYMBOL, STATUS SYMBOL

sym·bol·ic AW /sɪm'bɒlɪk; *NAmE* -'bɑːlɪk/ *adj.* **~ (of sth)** containing symbols, or being used as a symbol: *The dove is symbolic of peace.* ◇ *The Channel Tunnel has enormous symbolic significance for a united Europe.* ◇ *The new regulations are largely symbolic* (= they will not have any real effect). ▸ **sym·bol·ic·al·ly** AW /sɪm'bɒlɪkli; *NAmE* -'bɑːlɪk-/ *adv.*: *a symbolically significant gesture*

sym·bol·ism AW /'sɪmbəlɪzəm/ *noun* [U] the use of symbols to represent ideas, especially in art and literature ➲ COLLOCATIONS at LITERATURE ▸ **sym·bol·ist** /'sɪmbəlɪst/ *adj.*, *noun*: *the symbolist poet Rimbaud*

sym·bol·ize (*BrE* also **-ise**) AW /'sɪmbəlaɪz/ *verb* **~ sth** to be a symbol of sth SYN **represent**: *The use of light and dark symbolizes good and evil.* ◇ *He came to symbolize his country's struggle for independence.*

sym·met·rical /sɪ'metrɪkl/ (also **sym·met·ric** /sɪ'metrɪk/) *adj.* (of a body, a design, an object, etc.) having two halves, parts or sides that are the same in size and shape: *a symmetrical pattern* OPP **asymmetric** ▸ **sym·met·ric·al·ly** /-kli/ *adv.*

sym·metry /'sɪmətri/ *noun* [U] **1** the exact match in size and shape between two halves, parts or sides of sth: *the perfect symmetry of the garden design* ➲ picture at AXIS **2** the quality of being very similar or equal: *the increasing symmetry between men's and women's jobs*

sym·pa·thet·ic 0⊸ /ˌsɪmpə'θetɪk/ *adj.*
1 0⊸ **~ (to/towards sb)** kind to sb who is hurt or sad; showing that you understand and care about their problems: *a sympathetic listener* ◇ *I did not feel at all sympathetic towards Kate.* ◇ *I'm here if you need a* **sympathetic ear** (= sb to talk to about your problems). **2** 0⊸ **~ (to/towards sb/sth)** showing that you approve of sb/sth or that you share their views and are willing to support them: *to be sympathetic to the party's aims* ◇ *Russian newspapers are largely sympathetic to the president.* **3** (of a person) easy to like: *a* **sympathetic character** *in a novel* ◇ *I don't find her a very sympathetic person.* HELP This meaning is not very common and you should use **likeable** or **pleasant** instead. OPP **unsympathetic** ▸ **sym·pa·thet·ic·al·ly** *adv.*: *to smile at sb sympathetically* ◇ *We hope this application will be treated sympathetically* (= it will be approved).

sym·pa·thize (*BrE* also **-ise**) /'sɪmpəθaɪz/ *verb* **1** [I, T] **~ (with sb/sth)** | **+ speech** to feel sorry for sb; to show that you understand and feel sorry about sb's problems: *I find it very hard to sympathize with him.* **2** [I] **~ with sb/sth** to support sb/sth: *He has never really sympathized with the aims of Animal Rights activists.*

sym·pa·thizer (*BrE* also **-iser**) /'sɪmpəθaɪzə(r)/ *noun* a person who supports or approves of sb/sth, especially a political cause or party: *communist sympathizers*

sym·pathy 0⊸ /'sɪmpəθi/ *noun* (*pl.* -ies)
1 0⊸ [U, C, usually pl.] the feeling of being sorry for sb; showing that you understand and care about sb's problems: *to* **express/feel sympathy** *for sb* ◇ *I* **have no sympathy for** *Jan, it's all her own fault.* ◇ *I wish he'd show me a little more sympathy.* ◇ **Our** *heartfelt* **sympathy goes out** *to the victims of the war.* ◇ (*formal*) *May we* **offer our** *deepest* **sympathies** *on the death of your wife.* **2** 0⊸ [U, C, usually pl.] the act of showing support for or approval of an idea, a cause, an organization, etc: *The seamen went on strike* **in sympathy with** (= to show their support for) *the dockers.* ◇ *Her sympathies lie with the anti-abortion lobby.* **3** [U] friendship and understanding between people who have similar opinions or interests: *There was no personal sympathy between them.*
IDM **in 'sympathy with sth** happening because sth else has happened: *Share prices slipped in sympathy with the German market.* **out of 'sympathy with sb/sth** not agreeing with or not wanting to support sb/sth

sym·phony /'sɪmfəni/ *noun* (*pl.* -ies) a long complicated piece of music for a large ORCHESTRA, in three or four main parts (called MOVEMENTS): *Beethoven's Fifth Symphony* ➲ COLLOCATIONS at MUSIC ▸ **sym·phon·ic** /sɪm'fɒnɪk; *NAmE* -'fɑːn-/ *adj.*: *Mozart's symphonic works*

'symphony orchestra *noun* a large ORCHESTRA that plays CLASSICAL music: *the Boston Symphony Orchestra*

sym·po·sium /sɪm'pəʊziəm; *NAmE* -'poʊ-/ *noun* (*pl.* **sym·po·sia** /-ziə/ or **sym·po·siums**) **~ (on sth)** a meeting at which experts have discussions about a particular subject; a small conference

symp·tom /'sɪmptəm/ *noun* **1** a change in your body or mind that shows that you are not healthy: *flu symptoms* ◇ *Look out for symptoms of depression.* ◇ *Symptoms include a headache and sore throat.* **2** a sign that sth exists, especially sth bad SYN **indication**: *The rise in inflation was just one symptom of the poor state of the economy.* ➲ SYNONYMS at SIGN

symp·tom·at·ic /ˌsɪmptə'mætɪk/ *adj.* being a sign of an illness or a problem: *a symptomatic infection* ◇ **~ of sth** *These disagreements are symptomatic of the tensions within the party.*

symp·tom·ize /'sɪmptəmaɪz/ *verb* **~ sth** (*US*) to be a sign or SYMPTOM of sth

syn·aes·the·sia (also **syn·es·the·sia**) /ˌsɪnəs'θiːziə; *NAmE* -'θiːʒə/ *noun* [U] (*biology*) the fact of experiencing some things in a different way from most other people, for example experiencing colours as sounds or shapes as tastes, or feeling sth in one part of the body when a different part is STIMULATED

syna·gogue /'sɪnəgɒg; *NAmE* -gɑːg/ *noun* a building where Jews meet for religious worship and teaching

syn·apse /'saɪnæps; 'sɪn-/ *noun* (*biology*) a connection between two nerve cells ▸ **syn·ap·tic** /saɪ'næptɪk; sɪ'n-/ *adj.*: *the synaptic membranes*

sync (also **synch**) /sɪŋk/ *noun* [U] (*informal*)
IDM **in 'sync 1** moving or working at exactly the same

S

time and speed as sb/sth else: *The soundtrack is **not in sync** with the picture.* **2** in agreement with sb/sth; working well with sb/sth: *His opinions were in sync with those of his colleagues.* **out of 'sync 1** not moving or working at exactly the same time and speed as sb/sth else **2** not in agreement with sb/sth; not working well with sb/sth ➲ see also LIP-SYNC, SYNCHRONIZATION

syn·chron·ic /sɪŋˈkrɒnɪk; *NAmE* -ˈkrɑːn-/ *adj.* (*linguistics*) relating to a language as it is at a particular point in time ➲ compare DIACHRONIC

syn·chron·icity /ˌsɪŋkrəˈnɪsəti/ *noun* [U] (*technical*) the fact of two or more things happening at exactly the same time

syn·chron·ize (*BrE* also **-ise**) /ˈsɪŋkrənaɪz/ *verb* [I, T] to happen at the same time or to move at the same speed as sth; to make sth do this: **~ (with sth)** *The sound track did not synchronize with the action.* ◇ **~ sth (with sth)** *Let's synchronize our watches* (= make them show exactly the same time). ▸ **syn·chron·iza·tion, -isa·tion** /ˌsɪŋkrənaɪˈzeɪʃn; *NAmE* -nəˈz-/ (also *informal* **sync**) *noun* [U]

ˌsynchronized 'swimming (*BrE* also **-ised**) *noun* [U] a sport in which groups of SWIMMERS move in patterns in the water to music

syn·chron·ous /ˈsɪŋkrənəs/ *adj.* (*technical*) happening or existing at the same time

syn·cline /ˈsɪŋklaɪn/ *noun* (*geology*) an area of ground where layers of rock in the earth's surface have been folded into a curve that is lower in the middle than at the ends ➲ compare ANTICLINE

syn·co·pated /ˈsɪŋkəpeɪtɪd/ *adj.* (*music*) in **syncopated** rhythm the strong beats are made weak and the weak beats are made strong ▸ **syn·co·pa·tion** /ˌsɪŋkəˈpeɪʃn/ *noun* [U]

syn·cope /ˈsɪŋkəpi/ *noun* [U] (*phonetics*) the dropping of a sound or sounds in the middle of a word when it is spoken, for example the pronunciation of *library* as /ˈlaɪbri/ ➲ compare APOCOPE

syn·cre·tism /ˈsɪŋkrətɪzəm/ *noun* [U] **1** (*technical*) the mixing of different religions, philosophies or ideas **2** (*linguistics*) the mixing of different forms of the same word during the development of a language

syn·dic·al·ism /ˈsɪndɪkəlɪzəm/ *noun* [U] the belief that factories, businesses, etc. should be owned and managed by all the people who work in them

syn·dic·al·ist /ˈsɪndɪkəlɪst/ *noun* a person who believes in syndicalism ▸ **syn·dic·al·ist** *adj.*

S

syn·di·cate *noun, verb*
- ***noun*** /ˈsɪndɪkət/ a group of people or companies who work together and help each other in order to achieve a particular aim
- ***verb*** /ˈsɪndɪkeɪt/ [usually passive] **~ sth** to sell an article, a photograph, a television programme, etc. to several different newspapers, etc: *His column is syndicated throughout the world.* ▸ **syn·di·ca·tion** /ˌsɪndɪˈkeɪʃn/ *noun* [U]

syn·drome /ˈsɪndrəʊm; *NAmE* -droʊm/ *noun* **1** a set of physical conditions that show you have a particular disease or medical problem: *PMS or premenstrual syndrome* ◇ *This syndrome is associated with frequent coughing.* ➲ see also AIDS, DOWN'S SYNDROME, ECONOMY CLASS SYNDROME, SICK BUILDING SYNDROME, TOURETTE'S SYNDROME **2** a set of opinions or a way of behaving that is typical of a particular type of person, attitude or social problem: *With teenagers, be prepared for the 'Me, me, me!' syndrome* (= they think of themselves first).

syn·ec·doche /sɪˈnekdəki/ *noun* [U, C] (*technical*) a word or phrase in which a part of sth is used to represent a whole, or a whole is used to represent a part of sth. For example, in 'Australia lost by two goals', *Australia* is used to represent the Australian team.

syn·ergy /ˈsɪnədʒi; *NAmE* -ərdʒi/ *noun* [U, C] (*pl.* **-ies**) (*technical*) the extra energy, power, success, etc. that is achieved by two or more people or companies working together, instead of on their own ▸ **syn·er·gis·tic** /ˌsɪnəˈdʒɪstɪk; *NAmE* ˌsɪnər-/ *adj.* **syn·er·gis·tic·al·ly** /-kli/ *adv.*

synod /ˈsɪnəd; *BrE* also -nɒd/ *noun* an official meeting of Church members to discuss religious matters and make important decisions

syno·nym /ˈsɪnənɪm/ *noun* a word or expression that has the same or nearly the same meaning as another in the same language: *'Big' and 'large' are synonyms.* ➲ compare ANTONYM

syn·onym·ous /sɪˈnɒnɪməs; *NAmE* -ˈnɑːn-/ *adj.* **1** (of words or expressions) having the same, or nearly the same, meaning **2 ~ (with sth)** so closely connected with sth that the two things appear to be the same: *Wealth is not necessarily synonymous with happiness.* ▸ **syn·onym·ous·ly** *adv.*

syn·onymy /sɪˈnɒnɪmi; *NAmE* -ˈnɑːn-/ *noun* [U] the fact of two or more words or expressions having the same meaning

syn·op·sis /sɪˈnɒpsɪs; *NAmE* -ˈnɑːp-/ *noun* (*pl.* **syn·op·ses** /-siːz/) a summary of a piece of writing, a play, etc. ▸ **syn·op·tic** /sɪˈnɒptɪk; *NAmE* -ˈnɑːp-/ *adj.* (*formal*)

syn·ovial /saɪˈnəʊviəl; sɪˈn-; *NAmE* sɪˈnoʊ-/ *adj.* (*biology*) (of a joint) having a MEMBRANE (= a piece of very thin skin) containing liquid between the bones, which allows the joint to move freely

syn·tac·tic /sɪnˈtæktɪk/ *adj.* (*linguistics*) connected with SYNTAX ▸ **syn·tac·tic·al·ly** /-kli/ *adv.*: *to be syntactically correct*

syn·tagm /ˈsɪntæm/ *noun* (also **syn·tagma** /ˌsɪnˈtægmə/) (*linguistics*) a unit of language consisting of sets of PHONEMES, words, or phrases that are arranged in order ▸ **syn·tag·mat·ic** /ˌsɪntægˈmætɪk/ *adj.*

syn·tax /ˈsɪntæks/ *noun* [U] **1** (*linguistics*) the way that words and phrases are put together to form sentences in a language; the rules of grammar for this ➲ compare MORPHOLOGY **2** (*computing*) the rules that state how words and phrases must be used in a computer language

synth /sɪnθ/ *noun* (*informal*) = SYNTHESIZER

syn·the·sis /ˈsɪnθəsɪs/ *noun* (*pl.* **syn·the·ses** /-siːz/) **1** [U, C] **~ (of sth)** the act of combining separate ideas, beliefs, styles, etc; a mixture or combination of ideas, beliefs, styles, etc: *the synthesis of art with everyday life* ◇ *a synthesis of traditional and modern values* **2** [U] (*technical*) the natural chemical production of a substance in animals and plants: *protein synthesis* **3** [U] (*technical*) the artificial production of a substance that is present naturally in animals and plants: *the synthesis of penicillin* **4** [U] (*technical*) the production of sounds, music or speech by electronic means: *speech synthesis*

syn·the·size (*BrE* also **-ise**) /ˈsɪnθəsaɪz/ *verb* **1 ~ sth** (*technical*) to produce a substance by means of chemical or BIOLOGICAL processes **2 ~ sth** to produce sounds, music or speech using electronic equipment **3 ~ sth** to combine separate ideas, beliefs, styles, etc.

syn·the·sizer (*BrE* also **-iser**) /ˈsɪnθəsaɪzə(r)/ (also *informal* **synth**) *noun* an electronic machine for producing different sounds. Synthesizers are used as musical instruments, especially for copying the sounds of other instruments, and for copying speech sounds: *a speech synthesizer* ➲ compare KEYBOARD (3)

syn·thet·ic /sɪnˈθetɪk/ *adj., noun*
- ***adj.*** **1** artificial; made by combining chemical substances rather than being produced naturally by plants or animals SYN **man-made**: *synthetic drugs/fabrics* ➲ SYNONYMS at ARTIFICIAL **2** (also **ag·glu·tin·ative**) (*linguistics*) (of languages) using changes to the ends of words rather than separate words to show the functions of words in a sentence ➲ compare ANALYTIC ▸ **syn·thet·ic·al·ly** /-kli/ *adv.*
- ***noun*** an artificial substance or material: *cotton fabrics and synthetics*

syph·ilis /ˈsɪfɪlɪs/ *noun* [U] a disease that gets worse over a period of time, spreading from the sexual organs to the skin, bones, muscles and brain. It is caught by having sex with an infected person. ▸ **syph·il·it·ic** /ˌsɪfɪˈlɪtɪk/ *adj.*

sy·phon = SIPHON

syr·inge /sɪˈrɪndʒ/ *noun, verb*
■ *noun* **1** (also **hypo·der·mic**, ˌ**hypodermic syˈringe**) a plastic or glass tube with a long hollow needle that is used for putting drugs, etc. into a person's body or for taking a small amount of blood from a person **2** a plastic or glass tube with a rubber part at the end, used for sucking up liquid and then pushing it out ➲ VISUAL VOCAB page V57
■ *verb* **~ sth** to clean sb's ear by spraying liquid into it with a SYRINGE: *I had my ears syringed.*

syrup /ˈsɪrəp/ *noun* [U] **1** a sweet liquid made from sugar and water, often used in cans of fruit: *pears in syrup* **2** any thick sweet liquid made with sugar, used especially as a sauce ➲ see also CORN SYRUP, GOLDEN SYRUP, MAPLE SYRUP

syr·upy /ˈsɪrəpi/ *adj.* **1** thick and sticky like syrup; containing syrup **2** (*disapproving*) extremely emotional and romantic and therefore unpleasant; too SENTIMENTAL: *a syrupy romantic novel*

sys·tem 🔑 /ˈsɪstəm/ *noun*
1 🔑 [C] an organized set of ideas or theories or a particular way of doing sth: *the British educational system* ◇ **~ for doing sth** *a new system for assessing personal tax bills* ◇ **~ of sth** *a system of government* ➲ see also BINARY, METRIC SYSTEM **2** 🔑 [C] a group of things, pieces of equipment, etc. that are connected or work together: *a transport system* ◇ *heating systems* ◇ *a stereo system* ◇ *a security system* ➲ see also ECOSYSTEM, EXPERT SYSTEM, OPERATING SYSTEM, PUBLIC ADDRESS SYSTEM, SOLAR SYSTEM **3** 🔑 [C] a human or an animal body, or a part of it, when it is being thought of as the organs and processes that make it function: *You have to wait until the drugs have passed out of your system.* ◇ *the male reproductive system* ➲ see also CENTRAL NERVOUS SYSTEM, DIGESTIVE SYSTEM, IMMUNE SYSTEM **4 the system** [sing.] (*informal*, usually *disapproving*) the rules or people that control a country or an organization, especially when they seem to be unfair because you cannot change them: *You can't* ***beat the system*** (= you must accept it). ◇ *young people rebelling against the system*
IDM **get sth out of your ˈsystem** (*informal*) to do sth so that you no longer feel a very strong emotion or have a strong desire: *I was very angry with him, but now I feel I've got it out of my system.*

sys·tem·at·ic /ˌsɪstəˈmætɪk/ *adj.* done according to a system or plan, in a thorough, efficient or determined way: *a* ***systematic approach to*** *solving the problem* ◇ *a systematic attempt to destroy the organization* ◇ *The prisoner was subjected to systematic torture.* OPP **unsystematic** ▸ **sys·tem·at·ic·al·ly** /-kli/ *adv.*: *The search was carried out systematically.*

sys·tem·atize (*BrE* also **-ise**) /ˈsɪstəmətaɪz/ *verb* **~ sth** (*formal*) to arrange sth according to a system SYN **organize** ▸ **sys·tem·atiza·tion**, **-isa·tion** /ˌsɪstəmətaɪˈzeɪʃn; *NAmE* -təˈz-/ *noun* [U]

sys·tem·ic /sɪˈstemɪk; sɪˈstiːmɪk/ *adj.* (*technical*) **1** affecting or connected with the whole of sth, especially the human body **2** **systemic** chemicals or drugs that are used to treat diseases in plants or animals enter the body of the plant or animal and spread to all parts of it: *systemic weed-killers* ▸ **sys·tem·ic·al·ly** *adv.*

ˈ**system operator** (also ˈ**systems operator**) *noun* (*computing*) a person who manages a computer system or electronic communication service

ˈ**systems analyst** *noun* a person whose job is to analyse the needs of a business company or an organization and then design processes for working efficiently using computer programs ▸ ˈ**systems analysis** *noun* [U]

ˈ**system unit** *noun* (*computing*) the main part of a computer, separate from the keyboard and monitor, that contains the unit that controls all the other parts of the system

sys·tole /ˈsɪstəli/ *noun* (*medical*) the part of the heart's rhythm when the heart PUMPS blood ➲ compare DIASTOLE ▸ **sys·tol·ic** /ˌsɪsˈtɒlɪk; *NAmE* -ˈtɑːl-/ *adj.*

S

Tt

T (also **t**) /tiː/ *noun* [C, U] (*pl.* **Ts, T's, t's** /tiːz/) the 20th letter of the English alphabet: *'Tin' begins with (a) T/'T'.* ➲ see also T-BONE STEAK, T-JUNCTION, T-SHIRT, T-SQUARE
IDM **to a 'T/'tee** (*informal*) used to say that sth is exactly right for sb, succeeds in doing sth in exactly the right way, etc.: *Her new job suits her to a T.* ◇ *The novel captures the feeling of the pre-war period to a T.* ➲ more at DOT *v.*

TA /ˌtiː ˈeɪ/ *abbr.* **1** (*BrE*) TERRITORIAL ARMY **2** (*NAmE*) TEACHING ASSISTANT

ta /tɑː/ *exclamation* (*BrE, slang*) thank you

taa·rab /ˈtɑːrʌb/ *noun* [U] a type of music that is popular in E Africa, especially along the coast, and that is influenced by Arabian and Indian music

tab /tæb/ *noun, verb*
■ ***noun*** **1** a small piece of paper, cloth, metal, etc. that sticks out from the edge of sth, and that is used to give information about it, or to hold it, fasten it, etc: *Insert tab A into slot 1* (= for example to make a model, box, etc.). **2** = TAB STOP **3** (*NAmE*) = PULL TAB **4** a bill for goods you receive but pay for later, especially for food or drinks in a restaurant or bar; the price or cost of sth: *a bar tab* ◇ *Can I put it on my tab?* ◇ *The tab for the meeting could be $3 000.* **5** (*informal*) a small solid piece of an illegal drug: *a tab of Ecstasy* **6** = TABLATURE: *guitar tabs*
IDM **keep (close) tabs on sb/sth** (*informal*) to watch sb/sth carefully in order to know what is happening so that you can control a particular situation: *It's not always possible to keep tabs on everyone's movements.* ➲ more at PICK *v.*
■ ***verb*** (**-bb-**) **1 ~ sb (as) sth** (*especially NAmE*) to say that sb is suitable for a particular job or role or describe them in a particular way: *He has been tabbed by many people as a future champion.* **2 ~ sth** to use the TAB KEY when you are using a keyboard

tab·ard /ˈtæbəd; -bɑːd; *NAmE* -bərd; -bɑːrd/ *noun* a simple piece of clothing consisting of back and front sections without sleeves, and a hole for the head

Tab·asco™ /təˈbæskəʊ; *NAmE* -koʊ/ *noun* [U] a red spicy sauce made from PEPPERS

tab·bou·leh /təˈbuːleɪ; *BrE* also ˈtæbuːleɪ/ *noun* [U] an Arab dish consisting of crushed WHEAT with chopped tomatoes, onions and HERBS

tabby /ˈtæbi/ *noun* (*pl.* **-ies**) (also **ˈtabby cat**) a cat with brown or grey fur marked with dark lines or spots

tab·er·nacle /ˈtæbənækl; *NAmE* -bərn-/ *noun* **1** [C] a place of worship for some groups of Christians: *a Mormon tabernacle* **2 the tabernacle** [sing.] a small place of worship that could be moved, used by the Jews in ancient times when they were travelling in the desert

ˈtab key (also **tab**, *formal* **tabu·la·tor**) *noun* a button on a keyboard that you use to move to a certain fixed position in a line of a document that you are typing

tabla /ˈtæblə; ˈtʌb-/ *noun* a pair of small drums played with the hands and used in S Asian music, usually to accompany other instruments

tab·lat·ure /ˈtæblətʃə(r)/ (also **tab**) *noun* [U, C] a way of representing musical notes on paper by showing the position of the fingers on a musical instrument rather than the actual notes; an example of this: *The book contains lyrics and guitar tablatures for over 100 songs.*

table 0-ᵣ /ˈteɪbl/ *noun, verb*
■ ***noun***
▸ FURNITURE **1** 0-ᵣ a piece of furniture that consists of a flat top supported by legs: *a kitchen table* ◇ *A table for two, please* (= in a restaurant). ◇ *I'd like to* ***book a table*** *for tonight* (= in a restaurant). ◇ *to* ***set the table*** (= to put the plates, knives, etc. on it for a meal) ◇ (*BrE* also) *to* ***lay the table*** ◇ *to* ***clear the table*** (= take away the dirty plates, etc. at the end of a meal) ◇ *He questioned her next morning over the breakfast table* (= during breakfast). ◇ (*BrE, formal*) *Children must learn to behave* ***at table***. ◇ *a* ***billiard/snooker/pool table*** ➲ VISUAL VOCAB page V34 HELP There are many compounds ending in **table**. You will find them at their place in the alphabet.
▸ PEOPLE **2** the people sitting at a table for a meal or to play cards, etc: *He kept the whole table entertained with his jokes.* ➲ see also ROUND-TABLE
▸ LIST OF FACTS/NUMBERS **3** 0-ᵣ a list of facts or numbers arranged in a special order, usually in rows and columns: *a* ***table of contents*** (= a list of the main points or information in a book, usually at the front of the book) ◇ *Table 2 shows how prices and earnings have increased over the past 20 years.* ➲ see also THE PERIODIC TABLE
▸ IN SPORT **4** a list of sports teams, countries, schools, etc. that shows their position in a competition, etc: *If Arsenal win this game they'll go to the top of the table.* ◇ *school performance league tables*
▸ MATHEMATICS **5** = MULTIPLICATION TABLE: *Do you know your six times table?* ➲ see also TURNTABLE, WATER TABLE
IDM ˌ**bring sth to the ˈparty/ˈtable** to contribute sth useful to a discussion, project, etc: *What Hislop brought to the table was real commitment and energy.* **on the ˈtable 1** (*BrE*) (of a plan, suggestion, etc.) offered to people so that they can consider or discuss it: *Management have put several new proposals on the table.* **2** (*especially NAmE*) (of a plan, suggestion, etc.) not going to be discussed or considered until a future date **turn the ˈtables (on sb)** to change a situation so that you are now in a stronger position than the person who used to be in a stronger position than you ➲ more at CARD *n.*, DRINK *v.*, WAIT *v.*
■ ***verb*** **1 ~ sth** (*BrE*) to present sth formally for discussion: *They have tabled a motion for debate at the next Party Conference.* **2 ~ sth** (*NAmE*) to leave an idea, a proposal, etc. to be discussed at a later date: *They voted to table the proposal until the following meeting.*

tab·leau /ˈtæbləʊ; *NAmE* -loʊ/ *noun* (*pl.* **tab·leaux** /-ləʊ; -ləʊz; *NAmE* -loʊ; -loʊz/) **1** a scene showing, for example, events and people from history, that is presented by a group of actors who do not move or speak: *The procession included a tableau of the Battle of Hastings.* ◇ (*figurative*) *She stood at the door observing the peaceful domestic tableau around the fire.* **2** a work of art, especially a set of statues, showing a group of people, animals, etc.

table·cloth /ˈteɪblklɒθ; *NAmE* -klɔːθ; -klɑːθ/ *noun* a cloth that you use for covering a table, especially when you have a meal ➲ VISUAL VOCAB page V19

ˈtable dancing *noun* [U] sexually exciting dancing which is performed close to a customer's table in a bar or club

table d'hôte /ˌtɑːbl ˈdəʊt; *NAmE* ˈdoʊt/ *adj.* a **table d'hôte** meal in a restaurant costs a fixed price and there are only a limited number of dishes to choose from: *the table d'hôte menu* ▸ **table d'hôte** *noun* [U]: *The restaurant offers both table d'hôte and à la carte.*

ˈtable football (*BrE*) (*NAmE* **foosball**) *noun* [U] an indoor game for two people or teams, played by moving rows of small models of football (SOCCER) players in order to move a ball on a board that has marks like a football (SOCCER) field

ˈtable lamp *noun* a small lamp that you can put on a table, etc. ➲ VISUAL VOCAB page V18

table·land /ˈteɪbllænd/ *noun* a large area of high flat land SYN **plateau**

ˈtable linen *noun* [U] the cloths that you use during a meal, for example TABLECLOTHS and NAPKINS

ˈtable manners *noun* [pl.] the behaviour that is considered correct while you are having a meal at a table with other people

ˈtable mat *noun* (*BrE*) a small piece of wood or cloth that you put under a hot dish or plate to protect the surface of the table ➲ VISUAL VOCAB page V19

ˈtable napkin *noun* = NAPKIN

table·spoon /ˈteɪblspuːn/ *noun* **1** a large spoon, used especially for serving food ➲ VISUAL VOCAB page V19

2 (also **table·spoon·ful** /-fʊl/) (*abbr.* **tbsp**) the amount a tablespoon can hold: *Add two tablespoons of water.*

tab·let 🔑 /ˈtæblət/ *noun*
1 🔑 (*especially BrE*) a small round solid piece of medicine that you swallow SYN **pill**: *vitamin tablets* ◇ *Take two tablets with water before meals.* **2** an amount of another substance in a small round solid piece: *water purification tablets* **3** a flat piece of stone that has words written on it, especially one that has been fixed to a wall in memory of an important person or event SYN **plaque**: (*figurative*) *We can be very flexible—our entry requirements are not set in* ***tablets of stone*** (= they can be changed). **4 ~ of soap** (*old-fashioned, formal*) a piece of soap **5** (*NAmE*) a number of pieces of paper for writing or drawing on, that are fastened together at one edge ➲ see also GRAPHICS TABLET

ˈ**table tennis** (also *informal* ˈ**ping-pong** both *BrE*) (*NAmE* ˈ**Ping-Pong™**) *noun* [U] a game played like TENNIS with BATS and a small plastic ball on a table with a net across it ➲ VISUAL VOCAB page V37

table·top /ˈteɪbltɒp; *NAmE* -tɑːp/ *noun* the top or the surface of a table ▸ **table·top** *adj.* [only before noun]: *a tabletop machine* (= that can be used on a table) ◇ (*BrE*) *a tabletop sale* (= where goods for sale are displayed on tables)

ˌ**Tablet PˈC™** *noun* a small computer that is easy to carry, with a large touch screen and sometimes without a physical keyboard

table·ware /ˈteɪblweə(r); *NAmE* -wer/ *noun* [U] the word used in shops/stores, etc. for items that you use for meals, such as plates, glasses, knives and forks

ˈ**table wine** *noun* [U, C] a fairly cheap wine, suitable for drinking with meals

tab·loid /ˈtæblɔɪd/ *noun* **1** a newspaper with small pages (usually half the size of those in larger papers) ➲ compare BERLINER, BROADSHEET **2** (sometimes *disapproving*) a newspaper of this size with short articles and a lot of pictures and stories about famous people, often thought of as less serious than other newspapers: *The story made the front page in all the tabloids.* ➲ compare QUALITY NEWSPAPER ➲ see also RED-TOP ▸ **tab·loid** *adj.* [only before noun]: *a serious paper in a new tabloid format* ◇ *tabloid journalists* ◇ *a tabloid newspaper* ◇ *the tabloid press*

taboo /təˈbuː/ *noun* (*pl.* **ta·boos**) **~ (against/on sth) 1** a cultural or religious custom that does not allow people to do, use or talk about a particular thing as people find it offensive or embarrassing: *an incest taboo* ◇ *a taboo on working on a Sunday* ◇ *to* ***break/violate a taboo*** ◇ *Death is one of the great taboos in our culture.* **2** a general agreement not to do sth or talk about sth: *The subject is still a taboo in our family.* ▸ **taboo** *adj.*: *in the days when sex was a* ***taboo subject***

taˈboo word *noun* a word that many people consider offensive or shocking, for example because it refers to sex, the body or people's race

tabor /ˈteɪbə(r)/ *noun* a musical instrument like a small drum, used in the past

ˈ**tab stop** (also **tab**) *noun* a fixed position in a line of a document that you are typing that shows where a piece of text or a column of figures, etc. will begin

tabu·lar /ˈtæbjələ(r)/ *adj.* [usually before noun] presented or arranged in a TABLE (= in rows and columns): *tabular data* ◇ *The results are presented* ***in tabular form***.

tab·ula rasa /ˌtæbjʊlə ˈrɑːzə/ *noun* (*pl.* **tab·ulae rasae** /ˌtæbjʊliː ˈrɑːziː/) (from *Latin, formal*) **1** a situation in which there are no fixed ideas about how sth should develop **2** the human mind as it is at birth, with no ideas or thoughts in it

tabu·late /ˈtæbjuleɪt/ *verb* **~ sth** to arrange facts or figures in columns or lists so that they can be read easily ▸ **tabu·la·tion** /ˌtæbjuˈleɪʃn/ *noun* [U, C]

tabu·la·tor /ˈtæbjuleɪtə(r)/ *noun* = TAB KEY

tacho·graph /ˈtækəgrɑːf; *NAmE* -græf/ *noun* a device that is used in vehicles such as large lorries/trucks and some types of buses to measure their speed, how far they have travelled and when the driver has stopped to rest

tach·om·eter /tæˈkɒmɪtə(r); *NAmE* -ˈkɑːm-/ *noun* a device that measures the rate that sth turns and is used to measure the speed of an engine in a vehicle

tacit /ˈtæsɪt/ *adj.* [usually before noun] that is suggested indirectly or understood, rather than said in words: ***tacit approval/support/knowledge*** ◇ *By* ***tacit agreement****, the subject was never mentioned again.* ▸ **tacit·ly** *adv.*

taci·turn /ˈtæsɪtɜːn; *NAmE* -tɜːrn/ *adj.* (*formal*) tending not to say very much, in a way that seems unfriendly ▸ **taci·turn·ity** /ˌtæsɪˈtɜːnəti; *NAmE* -ˈtɜːrn-/ *noun* [U]

tack /tæk/ *noun, verb*
■ ***noun* 1** [U, sing.] the way in which you deal with a particular situation; the direction of your words or thoughts: *a complete* ***change of tack*** ◇ *It was a brave decision to* ***change tack*** *in the middle of the project.* ◇ *When threats failed, she decided to* ***try/take a different tack****.* ◇ *His thoughts wandered off* ***on another tack****.* **2** [C, U] (*technical*) the direction that a boat with sails takes as it sails at an angle to the wind in order to fill its sails: *They were sailing on (a)* ***port/starboard tack*** (= with the wind coming from the left/right side). **3** [C] a small nail with a sharp point and a flat head, used especially for fixing a carpet to the floor: *a carpet tack* ➲ compare NAIL *n.* (2) **4** [C] (*NAmE*) = THUMBTACK ➲ VISUAL VOCAB page V56 ➲ see also BLU-TACK **5** [C] a long loose STITCH used for holding pieces of cloth together temporarily, before you sew them finally **6** [U] (*technical*) the equipment that you need for riding a horse, such as a SADDLE and BRIDLE IDM see BRASS
■ ***verb* 1** [T] **~ sth + adv./prep.** to fasten sth in place with a tack or tacks SYN **nail**: *The carpet was tacked to the floor.* **2** [T] **~ sth (+ adv./prep.)** to fasten pieces of cloth together temporarily with long loose STITCHES before sewing them finally **3** [I] (*technical*) to change the direction of a sailing boat so that the wind blows onto the sails from the opposite side; to do this several times in order to travel in the direction that the wind is coming from
PHR V ˌ**tack sth↔ˈon** | ˌ**tack sth ˈonto sth** (*informal*) to add sth to sth that already exists, especially in a careless way: *The poems were tacked on at the end of the book.*

tackie (also **tak·kie**) /ˈtæki/ *noun* (*SAfrE*) **1** a shoe with a rubber SOLE (= the part underneath), worn when dressing informally or for taking part in sports ➲ compare TRAINER **2** (*informal*) a tyre on a car, etc.

tackle 🔑 /ˈtækl/ *verb, noun*
■ ***verb* 1** 🔑 [T] **~ sth** to make a determined effort to deal with a difficult problem or situation: *The government is determined to tackle inflation.* **2** 🔑 [T] **~ sb (about sth)** to speak to sb about a problem or difficult situation SYN **confront**: *I tackled him about the money he owed me.* **3** [T, I] **~ (sb)** (in football (SOCCER), HOCKEY, etc.) to try and take the ball from an opponent: *He was tackled just outside the penalty area.* **4** [I, T] **~ (sb)** (in RUGBY or AMERICAN FOOTBALL) to make an opponent fall to the ground in order to stop them running **5** [T] **~ sb** to deal with sb who is violent or threatening you: *He tackled a masked intruder at his home.*
■ ***noun* 1** [C] an act of trying to take the ball from an opponent in football (SOCCER), etc; an act of knocking an opponent to the ground in RUGBY or AMERICAN FOOTBALL ➲ VISUAL VOCAB page V36 **2** [C] (*NAmE*) (in AMERICAN FOOTBALL) a player whose job is to stop opponents by knocking them to the ground **3** [U] the equipment used to do a particular sport or activity, especially fishing ➲ see also BLOCK AND TACKLE **4** [U] (*BrE, slang*) a man's sexual organs

tack·ler /ˈtæklə(r)/ *noun* (*BrE*) a player who tries to TACKLE an opponent in some sports

tacky /ˈtæki/ *adj.* (**tack·ier, tacki·est**) **1** (*informal*) cheap, badly made and/or lacking in taste: *tacky souvenirs* ◇ *The movie had a really tacky ending.* **2** (of paint, glue, etc.) not dry and therefore slightly sticky ▸ **tacki·ness** *noun* [U]

taco /ˈtækəʊ; *NAmE* ˈtɑːkoʊ/ *noun* (*pl.* **-os**) (from *Spanish*) a type of Mexican food consisting of a crisp fried PANCAKE that is folded over and filled with meat, BEANS, etc.

T

tact /tækt/ *noun* [U] the ability to deal with difficult or embarrassing situations carefully and without doing or saying anything that will annoy or upset other people SYN **sensitivity**: *Settling the dispute required great tact and diplomacy.* ◇ *She is not exactly known for her tact.*

tact·ful /ˈtæktfl/ *adj.* careful not to say or do anything that will annoy or upset other people SYN **diplomatic**: *That wasn't a very tactful thing to say!* ◇ *I tried to find a tactful way of telling her the truth.* OPP **tactless** ▸ **tact·ful·ly** /-fəli/ *adv.*: *a tactfully worded reply* ◇ *I tactfully suggested he should see a doctor.*

tac·tic /ˈtæktɪk/ *noun* **1** [C, usually pl.] the particular method you use to achieve sth: *They tried all kinds of tactics to get us to go.* ◇ *This was just the latest in a series of* ***delaying tactics.*** ◇ *The manager discussed tactics with his team.* ◇ *Confrontation is not always the best tactic.* ◇ *It's time to try a change of tactic.* **2 tactics** [pl.] the art of moving soldiers and military equipment around during a battle or war in order to use them in the most effective way ➲ compare STRATEGY

tac·tic·al /ˈtæktɪkl/ *adj.* **1** [usually before noun] connected with the particular method you use to achieve sth SYN **strategic**: *tactical planning* ◇ *to have a tactical advantage* ◇ *Telling your boss you were looking for a new job was a* ***tactical error*** (= it was the wrong thing to do at that time). **2** [usually before noun] carefully planned in order to achieve a particular aim SYN **strategic**: *a tactical decision* ➲ see also TACTICAL VOTING **3** [only before noun] (especially of weapons) used or having an effect over short distances or for a short time: ***tactical weapons/missiles*** ➲ compare STRATEGIC (3) **4** [only before noun] connected with military tactics: *He was given tactical command of the operation.* ▸ **tac·tic·al·ly** /-kli/ *adv.*: *At the time, it was tactically the right thing to do.* ◇ *The enemy was tactically superior.*

ˌtactical ˈvoting *noun* [U] (*BrE*) the act of voting for a particular person or political party, not because you support them, but in order to prevent sb else from being elected

tac·ti·cian /tækˈtɪʃn/ *noun* a person who is very clever at planning the best way to achieve sth

tact·ile /ˈtæktaɪl; *NAmE* -tl/ *adj.* [usually before noun] connected with the sense of touch; using your sense of touch: *tactile stimuli* ◇ *visual and tactile communication* ◇ *tactile fabric* (= pleasant to touch) ◇ *tactile maps* (= that you can touch and feel) ◇ *He's a very tactile man* (= he enjoys touching people).

tact·less /ˈtæktləs/ *adj.* saying or doing things that are likely to annoy or to upset other people SYN **insensitive**: *a tactless remark* ◇ *It was tactless of you to comment on his hair!* OPP **tactful** ▸ **tact·less·ly** *adv.* **tact·less·ness** *noun* [U]

tad /tæd/ *noun* **a tad** [sing.] (*informal*) a very small amount: *Could you turn the sound down just a tad?* ▸ **a tad** *adv.*: *It's a tad too expensive for me.*

tad·pole /ˈtædpəʊl; *NAmE* -poʊl/ (*NAmE* also **polli·wog**) *noun* a small creature with a large head and a small tail, that lives in water and is the young form of a FROG or TOAD ➲ VISUAL VOCAB page V11

tae kwon do /ˌtaɪ ˌkwɒn ˈdəʊ; *NAmE* ˌkwɑːn ˈdoʊ/ *noun* [U] a Korean system of fighting without weapons, similar to KARATE

taf·feta /ˈtæfɪtə/ *noun* [U] a type of stiff shiny cloth made from silk or a similar material, used especially for making dresses

Taffy /ˈtæfi/ *noun* (*pl.* **-ies**) (also **Taff** /tæf/) (*BrE, informal,* often *offensive*) a person from Wales

taffy /ˈtæfi/ *noun* (*pl.* **-ies**) [U, C] (*NAmE*) a type of soft sweet/candy made of brown sugar boiled until it is very thick and given different shapes and colours

tag /tæg/ *noun, verb*

■ ***noun*** **1** [C] (often in compounds) a small piece of paper, cloth, plastic, etc. attached to sth to identify it or give information about it: *He put name tags on all his shirts.* ◇ *a gift tag* (= tied to a present) ◇ *The police use electronic tags to monitor the whereabouts of young offenders on probation.* ➲ SYNONYMS at LABEL ➲ see also PRICE TAG **2** [C, usually sing.] a name or phrase that is used to describe a person or thing in some way: *They are finally ready to drop the tag 'the new Beatles'.* ◇ *The 'lucky' tag stuck for years.* **3** [C] (*linguistics*) a word or phrase that is added to a sentence for emphasis, for example *I do* in *Yes, I do* ➲ see also QUESTION TAG **4** [C] (*computing*) a set of letters or symbols that are put before and after a piece of text or data in order to identify it or show that it is to be treated in a particular way **5** [C] a short QUOTATION or saying in a foreign language: *the Latin tag 'Si vis pacem, para bellum.'* (= if you want peace, prepare for war) **6** (*BrE* also **tig**) [U] a children's game in which one child chases the others and tries to touch one of them **7** [C] a symbol or name used by a GRAFFITI writer and painted in a public place

■ ***verb*** (**-gg-**) **1 ~ sth/sb** to fasten a tag onto sth/sb: *Each animal was tagged with a number for identification.* ➲ see also ELECTRONIC TAGGING **2 ~ sb/sth as sth** to give sb/sth a name that describes what they are or do SYN **label**: *The country no longer wanted to be tagged as a Third World nation.* **3 ~ sth** (*computing*) to add a set of letters or symbols to a piece of text or data in order to identify it or show that it is to be treated in a particular way

PHR V **ˌtag aˈlong** (**behind/with sb**) to go somewhere with sb, especially when you have not been asked or invited **ˌtag sth↔ˈon** | **ˌtag sth ˈonto sth** to add sth to the end of sth that already exists, especially in a careless way: *An apology was tagged onto the end of the letter.*

Taga·log /təˈgɑːlɒg; *NAmE* -lɔːg/ *noun* [U] the national language spoken in the Philippine islands

ta·gine (also **ta·jine**) /təˈʒiːn; təˈdʒiːn/ *noun* **1** [C, U] a hot dish made with meat and vegetables, cooked with liquid and spices in a closed container **2** [C] a container made of CLAY, with a pointed lid, for cooking and serving tagine, originally used in North Africa

taglia·telle /ˌtæljəˈteli; *NAmE* ˌtɑːl-/ *noun* [U] (from *Italian*) PASTA in the shape of long flat strips

ˈtag line *noun* (*NAmE, informal*) **1** = PUNCHLINE **2** = SLOGAN

ˈtag question *noun* (*grammar*) = QUESTION TAG

ˈtag team *noun* **1** a team of two WRESTLERS who take turns to fight in the same match **2** (*informal, especially NAmE*) two people working or performing together: *The show used a tag team of interviewers.*

ta·hini /tɑːˈhiːni; təˈh-/ (also **ta·hina** /tɑːˈhiːnə; təˈh-/) *noun* [U] a thick mixture made with crushed SESAME SEEDS, eaten in the Middle East

t'ai chi ch'uan /ˌtaɪ tʃiː ˈtʃwɑːn/ (also **ˌt'ai ˈchi**) *noun* [U] (from *Chinese*) a Chinese system of exercises consisting of sets of very slow controlled movements

taiga /ˈtaɪgə/ *noun* [sing., U] forest that grows in wet ground in far northern regions of the earth: *the Siberian taiga*

tail 🔑 /teɪl/ *noun, verb*

■ ***noun***

▸ OF BIRD/ANIMAL/FISH **1** 🔑 [C] the part that sticks out and can be moved at the back of the body of a bird, an animal or a fish: *The dog ran up, wagging its tail.* ◇ *The male has beautiful tail feathers.* ➲ VISUAL VOCAB page V10 ➲ see also PONYTAIL

▸ -TAILED **2** (in adjectives) having the type of tail mentioned: *a white-tailed eagle*

▸ OF PLANE/SPACECRAFT **3** 🔑 [C] the back part of a plane, SPACECRAFT, etc: *the tail wing* ➲ VISUAL VOCAB page V43

▸ BACK/END OF STH **4** [C] **~** (**of sth**) a part of sth that sticks out at the back like a tail: *the tail of a kite* **5** [C] **~** (**of sth**) the last part of sth that is moving away from you: *the tail of the procession* ➲ see also TAIL END

▸ JACKET **6 tails** [pl.] (also **tail·coat** [C]) a long jacket divided at the back below the waist into two pieces that become narrower at the bottom, worn by men at very formal events: *The men all wore top hat and tails.* ➲ see also COAT-TAILS, SHIRT TAIL ➲ compare DINNER JACKET, MORNING COAT

T

▸ SIDE OF COIN **7 tails** [U] the side of a coin that does not have a picture of the head of a person on it, used as one choice when a coin is TOSSED to decide sth ➲ compare HEADS *n.* (5)
▸ PERSON WHO FOLLOWS SB **8** [C] (*informal*) a person who is sent to follow sb secretly and find out information about where that person goes, what they do, etc: *The police have **put a tail on him**.*
▸ **tail·less** *adj.*: *Manx cats are tailless.*
IDM **on sb's 'tail** (*informal*) following behind sb very closely, especially in a car **the tail (is) wagging the 'dog** used to describe a situation in which the most important aspect is being influenced and controlled by sb/sth that is not as important **turn 'tail** to run away from a fight or dangerous situation **with your tail between your 'legs** (*informal*) feeling ashamed or unhappy because you have been defeated or punished ➲ more at BRIGHT-EYED, CHASE *v.*, HEAD *n.*, NOSE *n.*, STING *n.*
■ *verb* **~ sb** to follow sb closely, especially in order to watch where they go and what they do SYN **shadow**: *A private detective had been tailing them for several weeks.* IDM see TOP *v.*
PHR V **,tail a'way/'off** (*especially BrE*) to become smaller or weaker: *The number of tourists tails off in October.* ◊ *'But why...?' Her voice tailed away.* **,tail 'back** (of traffic) to form a tailback

tail·back /'teɪlbæk/ *noun* **1** [C] (*BrE*) a long line of traffic that is moving slowly or not moving at all, because sth is blocking the road **2** [C, U] = HALFBACK

tail·board /'teɪlbɔːd; *NAmE* -bɔːrd/ *noun* = TAILGATE

tail·bone /'teɪlbəʊn; *NAmE* -boʊn/ *noun* the small bone at the bottom of the SPINE SYN **coccyx** ➲ VISUAL VOCAB page V48

tail·coat /'teɪlkəʊt; *NAmE* -koʊt/ *noun* a long jacket divided at the back below the waist into two pieces that become narrower at the bottom, worn by men at formal events SYN **tails**

,tail 'end *noun* [sing.] the very last part of sth: *the tail end of the queue*

tail·gate /'teɪlgeɪt/ *noun, verb*
■ *noun* **1** (also **tail·board**) a door at the back of a lorry/truck that opens downwards and that you can open or remove when you are loading or unloading the vehicle **2** the door that opens upwards at the back of a car that has three or five doors (called a HATCHBACK)
■ *verb* **1** [I, T] **~ (sb/sth)** (*informal, especially NAmE*) to drive too closely behind another vehicle **2** [I] (*NAmE*) to eat food and drinks outdoors, served from the tailgate of a car

'tail light *noun* a red light at the back of a car, bicycle or train ➲ VISUAL VOCAB page V42

tailor /'teɪlə(r)/ *noun, verb*
■ *noun* a person whose job is to make men's clothes, especially sb who makes suits, etc. for individual customers
■ *verb* to make or adapt sth for a particular purpose, a particular person, etc: **~ sth to/for sb/sth** *Special programmes of study are tailored to the needs of specific groups.* ◊ **~ sth to do sth** *Most travel agents are prepared to tailor travel arrangements to meet individual requirements.*

tailored /'teɪləd; *NAmE* -lərd/ *adj.* **1** (of clothes) made to fit well or closely: *a tailored jacket* **2** made for a particular person or purpose SYN **tailor-made**

tailor·ing /'teɪlərɪŋ/ *noun* [U] **1** the style or the way in which a suit, jacket, etc. is made: *Clever tailoring can flatter your figure.* **2** the job of making men's clothes

,tailor-'made *adj.* **1 ~ (for sb/sth)** | **~ (to sth/to do sth)** made for a particular person or purpose, and therefore very suitable: *a tailor-made course of study* ◊ *a trip tailor-made just for you* ◊ *She seems tailor-made for the job* (= perfectly suited for it). **2** (of clothes) made by a TAILOR for a particular person SYN **bespoke**: *a tailor-made suit*

tail·piece /'teɪlpiːs/ *noun* **1 ~ (to sth)** a part that you add to the end of a piece of writing to make it longer or complete **2** (*music*) a piece of wood that the lower ends of the strings of some musical instruments are attached to

tail·pipe /'teɪlpaɪp/ *noun* (*especially NAmE*) = EXHAUST (2)

tail·plane /'teɪlpleɪn/ *noun* a small horizontal wing at the back of an aircraft ➲ VISUAL VOCAB page V43

tail·spin /'teɪlspɪn/ *noun* [sing.] **1** a situation in which a pilot loses control of an aircraft and it spins as it falls quickly towards the ground, with the back making larger circles than the front **2** a situation that suddenly becomes much worse and is not under control: *Following the announcement, share prices went into a tailspin.*

tail·wind /'teɪlwɪnd/ *noun* a wind that blows from behind a moving vehicle, a runner, etc. ➲ compare HEADWIND

taint /teɪnt/ *verb, noun*
■ *verb* [often passive] **~ sth (with sth)** (*formal*) to damage or spoil the quality of sth or the opinion that people have of sb/sth: *The administration was tainted with scandal.*
▸ **taint·ed** *adj.*: *tainted drinking water*
■ *noun* [usually sing.] the effect of sth bad or unpleasant that spoils the quality of sb/sth: *to be free from the taint of corruption*

tai·pan /'taɪpæn/ *noun* (from *Chinese*) **1** a foreign person who is in charge of a business in China **2** an extremely poisonous Australian snake

ta·jine = TAGINE

take 🔑 /teɪk/ *verb, noun*
■ *verb* (**took** /tʊk/, **taken** /'teɪkən/)
▸ CARRY/LEAD **1** 🔑 [T] to carry or move sth from one place to another: **~ sth (with you)** *I forgot to take my bag with me when I got off the bus.* ◊ **~ sth to sb/sth** *Take this to the bank for me, would you?* ◊ *Shall I take a gift to my host family?* ◊ **~ sb sth** *Shall I take my host family a gift?* **2** 🔑 [T] to go with sb from one place to another, especially to guide or lead them: **~ sb** *It's too far to walk—I'll take you by car.* ◊ **~ sb to sth** *A boy took us to our room.* ◊ **~ sb doing sth** *I'm taking the kids swimming later.* ◊ **~ sb to do sth** *The boys were taken to see their grandparents most weekends.* **3** 🔑 [T] **~ sb/sth + adv./prep.** to make sb/sth go from one level, situation, etc. to another: *Her energy and talent took her to the top of her profession.* ◊ *The new loan takes the total debt to $100 000.* ◊ *I'd like to take my argument a stage further.* ◊ *He believes he has the skills to take the club forward.* ◊ *We'll take the matter forward at our next meeting* (= discuss it further).
▸ REACH AND HOLD **4** 🔑 [T] **~ sb/sth** to put your hands or arms around sb/sth and hold them/it; to reach for sb/sth and hold them/it: *I passed him the rope and he took it.* ◊ *Free newspapers: please take one.* ◊ *Can you take* (= hold) *the baby for a moment?* ◊ *He took her hand/took her by the hand* (= held her hand, for example to lead her somewhere). ◊ *She took the child in her arms and kissed him.*
▸ REMOVE **5** 🔑 [T] **~ sth/sb + adv./prep.** to remove sth/sb from a place or a person: *Will you take your books off the table?* ◊ *The sign must be taken down.* ◊ *He took some keys out of his pocket.* ◊ *My name had been taken off the list.* ◊ *She was playing with a knife, so I took it away from her.* ◊ (*informal*) *She was playing with a knife, so I took it off her.* ◊ (*figurative*) *The new sports centre will **take the pressure off** the old one.* **6** 🔑 [T] **~ sth** to remove sth without permission or by mistake: *Someone has taken my scarf.* ◊ *Did the burglars take anything valuable?* ◊ (*figurative*) *The storms **took the lives** of 50 people.* **7** 🔑 [T] to get sth from a particular source: **~ sth from sth** *The scientists are taking water samples from the river.* ◊ *The machine takes its name from its inventor.* ◊ **~ sth out of sth** *Part of her article is taken straight* (= copied) *out of my book.*
▸ CAPTURE **8** 🔑 [T] to capture a place or person; to get control of sth: **~ sth (from sb)** *The rebels succeeded in taking the town.* ◊ *The state has **taken control of** the company.* ◊ **~ sb + noun** *The rebels took him prisoner.* ◊ *He was **taken prisoner** by the rebels.*
▸ CHOOSE/BUY **9** 🔑 [T] **~ sth** to choose, buy or rent sth: *I'll take the grey jacket.* ◊ *We took a room at the hotel for two nights.* **10** [T] **~ sth** (*formal*) to buy a newspaper or magazine regularly: *We take the 'Express'.*
▸ EAT/DRINK **11** 🔑 [T] **~ sth** to eat, drink, etc. sth: *Do you take sugar in your coffee?* ◊ *The doctor has given me some*

T

medicine to take for my cough. ◇ *He started taking drugs* (= illegal drugs) *at college.*

▸ MATHEMATICS **12** [T] **~ A (away) from B | B ~ away A | ~ A away** (not used in the progressive tenses) to reduce one number by the value of another SYN **subtract**: *Take 5 from 12 and you're left with 7.* ◇ (*informal*) *80 take away 5 is 75.*

▸ WRITE DOWN **13** 0‑w [T] **~ sth** to find out and record sth; to write sth down: *The police officer took my name and address.* ◇ *Did you* ***take notes*** *in the class?*

▸ PHOTOGRAPH **14** 0‑w [T] **~ sth** to photograph sb/sth: *to* ***take a photograph/picture/snapshot*** *of sb/sth* ◇ *to* ***have your picture/photo taken***

▸ MEASUREMENT **15** 0‑w [T] **~ sth** to test or measure sth: *to take sb's temperature* ◇ *I need to have my blood pressure taken.*

▸ SEAT **16** 0‑w [T] **~ sth** to sit down in or use a chair, etc: *Are these seats taken?* ◇ *Come in;* ***take a seat.*** ➲ SYNONYMS at SIT

▸ GIVE EXAMPLE **17** [T] **~ sb/sth** used to introduce sb/sth as an example: *Lots of couples have problems in the first year of marriage. Take Ann and Paul.*

▸ ACCEPT/RECEIVE **18** 0‑w [T] (not usually used in the progressive tenses or in the passive) **~ sth** to accept or receive sth: *If they offer me the job, I'll take it.* ◇ *She was accused of taking bribes.* ◇ *Does the hotel take credit cards?* ◇ *I'll take the call in my office.* ◇ *Why should I* ***take the blame*** *for somebody else's mistakes?* ◇ *If you* ***take my advice*** *you'll have nothing more to do with him.* ◇ *Will you take $10 for the book* (= will you sell it for $10)? ◇ *The store took* (= sold goods worth) *$100 000 last week.* **19** 0‑w [T] (not usually used in the progressive tenses) **~ sb** to accept sb as a customer, patient, etc: *The school doesn't take boys* (= only has girls). ◇ *The dentist can't take any new patients.* **20** [T] (not usually used in the progressive tenses) **~ sth** to experience or be affected by sth: *The school took the full force of the explosion.* ◇ *Can the ropes* ***take the strain*** (= not break)? ◇ *The team took a terrible beating.* **21** 0‑w [T, no passive] **~ sth** (not usually used in the progressive tenses) to be able to bear sth: *She can't* ***take criticism.*** ◇ *I don't think I can take much more of this heat.* ◇ *I find his attitude a little* ***hard to take.*** **22** 0‑w [T] **~ sth/sb + adv./prep.** to react to sth/sb in a particular way: *He took the criticism surprisingly well.* ◇ *These threats are not to be taken lightly.* ◇ *I wish you'd take me seriously.* ◇ *She took it in the spirit in which it was intended.*

▸ CONSIDER **23** 0‑w [T] (not used in the progressive tenses) to understand or consider sth in a particular way: **~ sth (as sth)** *She took what he said as a compliment.* ◇ *How am I supposed to take that remark?* ◇ *Taken overall, the project was a success.* ◇ **~ sth to do sth** *What did you take his comments to mean?* **24** [T] (not used in the progressive tenses) to consider sb/sth to be sb/sth, especially when you are wrong: **~ sb/sth for sb/sth** *Even the experts took the painting for a genuine Van Gogh.* ◇ *Of course I didn't do it!* ***What do you take me for*** (= what sort of person do you think I am)? ◇ **~ sb/sth to be sb/sth** *I took the man with him to be his father.*

▸ HAVE FEELING/OPINION **25** 0‑w [T] (not usually used in the progressive tenses) **~ sth** to have a particular feeling, opinion or attitude: *My parents always* ***took an interest*** *in my hobbies.* ◇ *Don't* ***take offence*** (= be offended) *at what I said.* ◇ *I* ***took a dislike*** *to him.* ◇ *He takes the view that children are responsible for their own actions.*

▸ ACTION **26** 0‑w [T] **~ sth** to use a particular course of action in order to deal with or achieve sth: *The government is* ***taking action*** *to combat drug abuse.* ◇ *We need to take a different approach to the problem.* **27** 0‑w [T] **~ sth** used with nouns to say that sb is doing sth, performing an action, etc.: *to take a step/walk/stroll* ◇ *to take a bath/shower/wash* ◇ *to take a look/glance* ◇ *to take a bite/drink/sip* ◇ *to take a deep breath* ◇ *to take a break/rest* ◇ (*BrE*) *No decision will be taken on the matter until next week.*

▸ FORM/POSITION **28** [T] **~ sth** to have a particular form, position or state: *Our next class will take the form of a debate.* ◇ *The new President takes office in January.*

▸ TIME **29** 0‑w [T, no passive, I] to need or require a particular amount of time: **~ sth** *The journey to the airport takes about half an hour.* ◇ **~ sth to do sth** ***It takes*** *about half an hour to get to the airport.* ◇ *That cut is taking a long time to heal.* ◇ **~ sb sth (to do sth)** *It took her three hours to repair her bike.* ◇ *It'll take her time to recover from the illness.* ◇ **~ sth for sb to do sth** *It'll* ***take time*** (= take a long time) *for her to recover from the illness.* ◇ **+ adv.** *I need a shower—I won't take long.* ➲ note at LAST[1]

▸ NEED **30** [T, no passive] to need or require sth in order to happen or be done: **~ sb/sth to do sth** *It only takes one careless driver to cause an accident.* ◇ *It doesn't take much to make her angry.* ◇ **~ sth** (*informal*) *He didn't take much persuading* (= he was easily persuaded). **31** [T, no passive] (not used in the progressive tenses) **~ sth** (of machines, etc.) to use sth in order to work: *All new cars take unleaded petrol.*

▸ SIZE OF SHOES/CLOTHES **32** [T, no passive] (not used in the progressive tenses) **~ sth** to wear a particular size in shoes or clothes: *What size shoes do you take?*

▸ HOLD/CONTAIN **33** [T, no passive] (not used in the progressive tenses) **~ sth/sb** to have enough space for sth/sb; to be able to hold or contain a particular quantity: *The bus can take 60 passengers.* ◇ *The tank takes 50 litres.*

▸ TEACH/LEAD **34** [T] **~ sb (for sth) | ~ sth** to be the teacher or leader in a class or a religious service: *The head teacher usually takes us for French.*

▸ STUDY **35** [T] **~ sth** to study a subject at school, college, etc: *She is planning to take a computer course.* ◇ *How many subjects are you taking this year?*

▸ EXAM **36** [T] **~ sth** to do an exam or a test: *When did you take your driving test?*

▸ TRANSPORT/ROAD **37** [T] **~ sth** to use a form of transport, a road, a path, etc. to go to a place: *to* ***take the bus/plane/train*** ◇ *to take a cab* ◇ *Take the second road on the right.* ◇ *It's more interesting to take the coast road.*

▸ GO OVER/AROUND **38** [T] **~ sth (+ adv./prep.)** to go over or around sth: *The horse took the first fence well.* ◇ *He takes bends much too fast.*

▸ IN SPORTS **39** [T] **~ sth** (of a player in a sports game) to kick or throw the ball from a fixed or agreed position: *to* ***take a penalty/free kick/corner***

▸ VOTE/SURVEY **40** [T] **~ sth** to use a particular method to find out people's opinions: *to* ***take a vote/poll/survey***

▸ BE SUCCESSFUL **41** [I] to be successful; to work: *The skin graft failed to take.*

▸ GRAMMAR **42** [T] (not used in the progressive tenses) **~ sth** (of verbs, nouns, etc.) to have or require sth when used in a sentence or other structure: *The verb 'rely' takes the preposition 'on'.*

IDM Most idioms containing **take** are at the entries for the nouns and adjectives in the idioms, for example **take the biscuit** is at **biscuit**. **I, you, etc. can't take sb 'anywhere** (*informal*, often *humorous*) used to say that you cannot trust sb to behave well in public **have (got) what it 'takes** (*informal*) to have the qualities, ability, etc. needed to be successful **take sth as it 'comes | take sb as they 'come** to accept sth/sb without wishing it/them to be different or without thinking about it/them very much in advance: *She takes life as it comes.* **'take it (that...)** to suppose; to assume: *I take it you won't be coming to the party?* **take it from 'me (that...)** (*informal*) used to emphasize that what you are going to say is the truth: *Take it from me—he'll be a millionaire before he's 30.* **take it on/upon yourself to do sth** to decide to do sth without asking permission or advice **sb can take it or 'leave it 1** used to say that you do not care if sb accepts or rejects your offer **2** used to say that sb does not have a strong opinion about sth: *Dancing? I can take it or leave it.* **take it/a lot 'out of sb** (*informal*) to make sb physically or mentally tired: *Taking care of small children really takes it out of you.* **take some/a lot of 'doing** (*informal*) to need a lot of effort or time; to be very difficult to do **,take 'that!** (*informal*) used as an exclamation when you are hitting sb or attacking them in some other way

PHR V **,take sb a'back** [usually passive] to shock or surprise sb very much

,take 'after sb [no passive] **1** (not used in the progressive tenses) to look or behave like an older member of your family, especially your mother or father: *Your daughter*

doesn't take after you at all. **2** (*NAmE, informal*) to follow sb quickly: *I was afraid that if I started running the man would take after me.*

ˌtake aˈgainst sb/sth [no passive] (*old-fashioned, BrE*) to start not liking sb/sth for no clear reason

ˌtake sb/sth↔aˈpart (*informal*) **1** to defeat sb easily in a game or competition **2** to criticize sb/sth severely **ˌtake sth↔aˈpart** to separate a machine or piece of equipment into the different parts that it is made of SYN **dismantle**

ˌtake sth↔aˈway 1 🔑 to make a feeling, pain, etc. disappear: *I was given some pills to take away the pain.* **2** 🔑 (*BrE*) (*NAmE* **ˌtake sth↔ˈout**) to buy cooked food at a restaurant and carry it away to eat, for example at home: *Two burgers to take away, please.* ➔ related noun TAKEAWAY, TAKEOUT

ˌtake aˈway from sth [no passive] to make the effort or value of sth seem less SYN **detract from**: *I don't want to take away from his achievements, but he couldn't have done it without my help.*

ˌtake sb↔ˈback to allow sb, such as your husband, wife or partner, to come home after they have left because of a problem **ˌtake sb ˈback (to...)** to make sb remember sth: *The smell of the sea took him back to his childhood.* **ˌtake sth↔ˈback 1** 🔑 if you **take** sth **back** to a shop/store, or a shop/store **takes** sth **back**, you return sth that you have bought there, for example because it is the wrong size or does not work **2** to admit that sth you said was wrong or that you should not have said it: *OK, I take it all back!*

ˌtake sth↔ˈdown 1 🔑 to remove a structure, especially by separating it into pieces: *to take down a tent* **2** to pull down a piece of clothing worn below the waist without completely removing it: *to take down your trousers/pants* **3** 🔑 to write sth down: *Reporters took down every word of his speech.*

ˌtake sb↔ˈin 1 🔑 to allow sb to stay in your home: *to take in lodgers* ◇ *He was homeless, so we took him in.* **2** 🔑 [often passive] to make sb believe sth that is not true SYN **deceive**: *Don't be taken in by his charm—he's ruthless.* ➔ SYNONYMS at CHEAT **ˌtake sth↔ˈin 1** 🔑 to absorb sth into the body, for example by breathing or swallowing: *Fish take in oxygen through their gills.* ➔ related noun INTAKE **2** to make a piece of clothing narrower or tighter OPP **let out 3** [no passive] to include or cover sth: *The tour takes in six European capitals.* **4** [no passive] to go to see or visit sth such as a film/movie: *I generally take in a show when I'm in New York.* **5** 🔑 to take notice of sth with your eyes: *He took in every detail of her appearance.* **6** 🔑 to understand or remember sth that you hear or read: *Halfway through the chapter I realized I hadn't taken anything in.*

ˌtake ˈoff 🔑 **1** 🔑 (of an aircraft, etc.) to leave the ground and begin to fly: *The plane took off an hour late.* ➔ related noun TAKE-OFF OPP **land 2** (*informal*) to leave a place, especially in a hurry: *When he saw me coming he took off in the opposite direction.* **3** (of an idea, a product, etc.) to become successful or popular very quickly or suddenly: *The new magazine has really taken off.* **ˌtake sb↔ˈoff 1** to copy sb's voice, actions or manner in an amusing way SYN **impersonate 2** (in sports, entertainment, etc.) to make sb stop playing, acting, etc. and leave the field or the stage: *He was taken off after twenty minutes.* **ˌtake sth↔ˈoff 1** 🔑 to remove sth, especially a piece of clothing from your/sb's body: *to take off your coat* ◇ *He took off my wet boots and made me sit by the fire.* OPP **put on 2** 🔑 to have a period of time as a break from work: *I've decided to take a few days off next week.* **3** [often passive] to stop a public service, television programme, performances of a show, etc: *The show was taken off because of poor audience figures.* **4** to remove some of sb's hair, part of sb's body, etc: *The hairdresser asked me how much she should take off.* ◇ *The explosion nearly took his arm off.* **ˌtake yourself/sb ˈoff (to...)** (*informal*) to leave a place; to make sb leave a place **ˌtake sb ˈoff sth** [often passive] to remove sb from sth such as a job, position, piece of equipment, etc: *The officer leading the investigation has been taken off the case.* ◇ *After three days she was taken off the ventilator.* **ˌtake sth ˈoff sth 1** to remove an amount of money or a number of marks, points, etc. in order to reduce the total: *The manager took $10 off the bill.* ◇ *That experience took ten years off my life* (= made me feel ten years older). **2** [often passive] to stop sth from being sold: *The slimming pills were taken off the market.*

ˌtake sb↔ˈon 1 🔑 (*especially BrE*) to employ sb: *to take on new staff* ◇ *She was taken on as a trainee.* **2** [no passive] to play against sb in a game or contest; to fight against sb: *to take somebody on at tennis* ◇ *The rebels took on the entire Roman army.* **ˌtake sth↔ˈon** [no passive] to begin to have a particular quality, appearance, etc: *The chameleon can take on the colours of its background.* ◇ *His voice took on a more serious tone.* **ˌtake sth/sb↔ˈon 1** to decide to do sth; to agree to be responsible for sth/sb: *I can't take on any extra work.* ◇ *We're not taking on any new clients at present.* **2** (of a bus, plane or ship) to allow sb/sth to enter: *The bus stopped to take on more passengers.* ◇ *The ship took on more fuel at Freetown.*

ˌtake sb↔ˈout to go to a restaurant, theatre, club, etc. with sb you have invited **ˌtake sb/sth↔ˈout** (*informal*) to kill sb or destroy sth: *They took out two enemy bombers.* **ˌtake sth↔ˈout 1** to remove sth from inside sb's body, especially a part of it: *How many teeth did the dentist take out?* **2** to obtain an official document or service: *to* ***take out an insurance policy/a mortgage/a loan*** ◇ *to take out an ad in a newspaper* **3** (*NAmE*) (*BrE* **ˌtake sth↔aˈway**) to buy cooked food at a restaurant and carry it away to eat, for example at home ➔ related noun TAKEAWAY, TAKEOUT **ˌtake sth↔ˈout (against sb)** to start legal action against sb by means of an official document: *The police have taken out a summons against the driver of the car.* **ˌtake sth↔ˈout (of sth)** to obtain money by removing it from your bank account **ˌtake sth ˈout of sth** to remove an amount of money from a larger amount, especially as a payment: *The fine will be taken out of your wages.* **ˌtake it/sth ˈout on sb** to behave in an unpleasant way towards sb because you feel angry, disappointed, etc, although it is not their fault: *OK, so you had a bad day. Don't take it out on me.* ◇ *She tended to take her frustrations out on her family.* **ˌtake sb ˈout of himself/ herself** to make sb forget their worries and become less concerned with their own thoughts and situation

ˌtake ˈover (from sth) to become bigger or more important than sth else; to replace sth: *Try not to let negative thoughts take over.* ◇ *It has been suggested that mammals took over from dinosaurs 65 million years ago.* **ˌtake ˈover (from sb)** | **ˌtake sth↔ˈover (from sb) 1** 🔑 to begin to have control of or responsibility for sth, especially in place of sb else **2** 🔑 to gain control of a political party, a country, etc: *The army is threatening to take over if civil unrest continues.* **ˌtake sth↔ˈover** 🔑 to gain control of a business, a company, etc, especially by buying shares: *CBS Records was taken over by Sony.* ➔ related noun TAKEOVER

ˌtake sb ˈthrough sth to help sb learn or become familiar with sth, for example by talking about each part in turn: *The director took us through the play scene by scene.*

ˈtake to sth [no passive] **1** to go away to a place, especially to escape from danger: *The rebels took to the hills.* **2** to begin to do sth as a habit: **~ doing sth** *I've taken to waking up very early.* **3** to develop an ability for sth: *She took to tennis as if she'd been playing all her life.* **ˈtake to sb/sth** [no passive] to start liking sb/sth: *I took to my new boss immediately.* ◇ *He hasn't taken to his new school.*

ˌtake ˈup to continue, especially starting after sb/sth else has finished: *The band's new album takes up where their last one left off.* **ˌtake ˈup sth** 🔑 to fill or use an amount of space or time: *The table takes up too much room.* ◇ *I won't take up any more of your time.* **ˌtake sth↔ˈup 1** to make sth such as a piece of clothing shorter: *This skirt needs taking up.* OPP **let down 2** 🔑 to learn or start to do sth, especially for pleasure: *They've taken up golf.* ◇ *She has taken up* (= started to learn to play) *the oboe.* **3** to start or begin sth such as a job: *He takes up his duties next week.* **4** to join in singing or saying sth: *to take up the chorus* ◇ *Their protests were later taken up by other groups.* **5** to continue sth that sb else has not finished, or that has not been mentioned for some time: *She took up the story where Tim had left off.* ◇ *I'd like to take up the point you raised earlier.* **6** to move into a particular position: *I took up my position by the door.* **7** to accept sth that is offered or available: *to take up a challenge* ◇ *She took up his offer of a drink.* **ˌtake ˈup with sb** (*informal*) to begin to be friendly with sb, especially sb with a bad reputation **ˌtake sb ˈup on sth 1** to question sb about sth, because you do not agree with them: *I must take*

T

you up on that point. **2** (*informal*) to accept an offer, a bet, etc. from sb: *Thanks for the invitation—we'll take you up on it some time.* ˌ**take sth ˈup with sb** to speak or write to sb about sth that they may be able to deal with or help you with: *They decided to take the matter up with their MP.* **be ˌtaken ˈup with sth/sb** to be giving all your time and energy to sth/sb
be ˈtaken with sb/sth to find sb/sth attractive or interesting: *We were all very taken with his girlfriend.* ◇ *I think he's quite taken with the idea.*
■ ***noun*** **1** a scene or part of a film/movie that is filmed at one time without stopping the camera: *We managed to get it right in just two takes.* **2** [usually sing.] (*informal*) an amount of money that sb receives, especially the money that is earned by a business during a particular period of time SYN **takings**: *How much is my share of the take?* **3 ~ on sth** (*informal*) the particular opinion or idea that sb has about sth: *What's his take on the plan?* ◇ *a new take on the Romeo and Juliet story* (= a way of presenting it) ➲ see also DOUBLE TAKE
IDM **be on the ˈtake** (*informal*) to accept money from sb for helping them in a dishonest or illegal way

Synonyms

take

lead • escort • drive • show • walk • guide • usher • direct

These words all mean to go with sb from one place to another.

take to go with sb from one place to another, for example in order to show them sth or to show them the way to a place: *It's too far to walk—I'll take you by car.*

lead to go with or go in front of sb in order to show them the way or to make them go in the right direction: *Firefighters led the survivors to safety.*

escort to go with sb in order to protect or guard them or to show them the way: *The president arrived, escorted by twelve bodyguards.*

drive to take sb somewhere in a car, taxi, etc: *My mother drove us to the airport.*

show to take sb to a particular place, in the right direction, or along the correct route: *The attendant showed us to our seats.*

walk to go somewhere with sb on foot, especially in order to make sure that they get there safely; to take an animal, especially a dog, for a walk or make an animal walk somewhere: *He always walked her home.* ◇ *Have you walked the dog yet today?*

guide to show sb the way to a place, often by going with them; to show sb a place that you know well: *She guided us through the busy streets.* ◇ *We were guided around the museums.*

usher (*rather formal*) to politely take or show sb where they should go, especially within a building: *She ushered her guests to their seats.*

direct (*rather formal*) to tell or show sb how to get somewhere or where to go: *A young woman directed them to the station.*

PATTERNS
- to take/lead/escort/drive/show/walk/guide/usher/direct sb **to/out of/into** sth
- to take/lead/escort/drive/show/walk/guide sb **around/round**
- to take/lead/escort/drive/walk sb **home**
- to take/lead/escort/guide sb **to safety**
- to lead/show **the way**

take·away /ˈteɪkəweɪ/ (*BrE*) (*NAmE* ˈ**take·out**) (also ˈ**carry-out** *US, ScotE*) *noun* **1** a restaurant that cooks and sells food that you take away and eat somewhere else **2** a meal that you buy at this type of restaurant: *Let's have a takeaway tonight.*

take·down /ˈteɪkdaʊn/ *noun* **1** a move in which a WRESTLER quickly gets his/her opponent down to the floor from a standing position **2** (*informal*) an arrest or unexpected visit by the police

ˈ**take-home pay** *noun* [U] the amount of money that you earn after you have paid tax, etc.

ˈ**take-off** *noun* **1** [U, C] the moment at which an aircraft leaves the ground and starts to fly: *The plane is ready for take-off.* ◇ *take-off speed* ◇ (*figurative*) *The local economy is poised for take-off.* OPP **landing 2** [C, U] the moment when your feet leave the ground when you jump **3** [C] if you do a **take-off** of sb, you copy the way they speak or behave, in a humorous way to entertain people

take·over /ˈteɪkəʊvə(r); *NAmE* -oʊ-/ *noun* [C, U] **1** an act of taking control of a company by buying most of its shares: *a **takeover bid** for the company* ➲ COLLOCATIONS at BUSINESS **2** an act of taking control of a country, an area or a political organization by force

taker /ˈteɪkə(r)/ *noun* **1** [usually pl.] a person who is willing to accept sth that is being offered: *They won't find many takers for the house at that price.* **2** (often in compounds) a person who takes sth: *drug takers* ◇ *It is better to be a giver than a taker.*

ˈ**take-up** *noun* [U, sing.] the rate at which people accept sth that is offered or made available to them: *a low take-up of government benefits*

tak·ings /ˈteɪkɪŋz/ *noun* [pl.] (*BrE*) the amount of money that a shop/store, theatre, etc. receives from selling goods or tickets over a particular period of time: *The box office takings are up on last week.*

tak·kie = TACKIE

tala /ˈtɑːlə/ *noun* a traditional pattern of rhythm in CLASSICAL Indian music

tal·cum pow·der /ˈtælkəm paʊdə(r)/ (also *informal* **talc** /tælk/) *noun* [U] a fine soft powder, usually with a pleasant smell, that you put on your skin to make it feel smooth and dry

tale /teɪl/ *noun* **1** a story created using the imagination, especially one that is full of action and adventure: *Dickens' 'A Tale of Two Cities'* ◇ *a **fairy/moral/romantic, etc. tale*** ➲ see also FOLK TALE **2** an exciting spoken description of an event, which may not be completely true: *I love listening to his tales of life at sea.* ◇ *I've heard tales of people seeing ghosts in that house.* ◇ *The team's **tale of woe** continued on Saturday* (= they lost another match). ◇ *Her experiences provide a **cautionary tale*** (= a warning) *for us all.* ➲ see also TELLTALE IDM see OLD, TELL

tal·ent /ˈtælənt/ *noun* **1** [C, U] a natural ability to do sth well: *to **have** great artistic **talent*** ◇ *a man **of many talents*** ◇ **~ (for sth/for doing sth)** *She showed considerable talent for getting what she wanted.* ◇ *a **talent competition/contest/show*** (= in which people perform, to show how well they can sing, dance, etc.) **2** [U, C] people or a person with a natural ability to do sth well: *There is **a wealth of** young **talent** in British theatre.* ◇ *He is a great talent.* **3** [U] (*BrE, slang*) people who are sexually attractive: *He likes to spend his time chatting up the local talent.*

tal·ent·ed /ˈtæləntɪd/ *adj.* having a natural ability to do sth well: *a talented player*

ˈ**talent scout** (also **scout**, ˈ**talent spotter**) *noun* a person whose job is to find people who are good at singing, acting, sport, etc. in order to give them work

tal·is·man /ˈtælɪzmən/ *noun* an object that is thought to have magic powers and to bring good luck

talk 0-w /tɔːk/ *verb, noun*
■ ***verb***
▸ SPEAK TO SB **1** 0-w [I, T] to say things; to speak in order to give information or to express feelings, ideas, etc: *Stop talking and listen!* ◇ *We talked on the phone for over an hour.* ◇ **~ (to/with sb) (about sb/sth)** *Who were you talking to just now?* ◇ *We looked around the school and talked with the principal.* ◇ *Ann and Joe **aren't talking** to each other right*

T

now (= they refuse to speak to each other because they have argued). ◇ *When they get together, all they talk about is football.* ◇ ***What are you talking about?*** (= used when you are surprised, annoyed and/or worried by sth that sb has just said) ◇ ***I don't know what you're talking about*** (= used to say that you did not do sth that sb has accused you of). ◇ **~ of sth** *Mary is talking of looking for another job.* ◇ **~ yourself + adj.** *We* ***talked ourselves hoarse****, catching up on all the news.*

▸ DISCUSS **2** 🔑 [I, T] to discuss sth, usually sth serious or important: *This situation can't go on. We need to talk.* ◇ *The two sides in the dispute say they are ready to talk.* ◇ **~ (to/with sb) (about sth)** *Talk to your doctor if you're still worried.* ◇ **~ sth** *to talk business*

▸ SAY WORDS **3** 🔑 [I, T] to say words in a language: *The baby is just starting to talk.* ◇ **~ in sth** *We couldn't understand them because they were talking in Chinese.* ◇ **~ sth** *Are they talking Swedish or Danish?*

▸ SENSE/NONSENSE **4** [T] **~ sth** to say things that are/are not sensible: *She talks a lot of sense.* ◇ (*BrE*) *You're talking rubbish!* ◇ *See if you can* ***talk some sense into him*** (= persuade him to be sensible).

▸ FOR EMPHASIS **5** [T] **be talking sth** (*informal*) used to emphasize an amount of money, how serious sth is, etc.: *We're talking £500 for three hours' work.*

▸ ABOUT PRIVATE LIFE **6** [I] to talk about a person's private life SYN **gossip**: *Don't phone me at work—****people will talk****.*

▸ GIVE INFORMATION **7** [I] to give information to sb, especially unwillingly: *The police questioned him but he refused to talk.*

IDM **look who's ˈtalking | ˈyou can/can't talk | you're a ˈfine one to talk** (*informal*) used to tell sb that they should not criticize sb else for sth because they do the same things too: *'George is so careless with money.' 'Look who's talking!'* **now you're ˈtalking** (*informal*) used when you like what sb has suggested very much **ˈtalk about...** (*informal*) used to emphasize sth: *Talk about mean! She didn't even buy me a card.* **talk ˈdirty** (*informal*) to talk to sb about sex in order to make them sexually excited **talk a good ˈgame** (*NAmE*) to talk in a way that sounds convincing, but may not be sincere **talk the hind leg off a ˈdonkey** (*informal*) to talk too much, especially about boring or unimportant things **talking of sb/sth** (*informal, especially BrE*) used when you are going to say more about a subject that has already been mentioned: *Talking of Sue, I met her new boyfriend last week.* **talk ˈshop** (usually *disapproving*) to talk about your work with the people you work with, especially when you are also with other people who are not connected with or interested in it **ˌtalk the ˈtalk** (*informal*, sometimes *disapproving*) to be able to talk in a confident way that makes people think you are good at what you do: *You can talk the talk, but can you walk the walk?* (= can you act in a way that matches your words?) **talk through your ˈhat** (*old-fashioned, informal*) to say silly things while you are talking about a subject you do not understand **talk ˈtough (on sth)** (*informal, especially NAmE*) to tell people very strongly what you want **talk ˈturkey** (*informal, especially NAmE*) to talk about sth seriously **talk your way out of sth/of doing sth** to make excuses and give reasons for not doing sth; to manage to get yourself out of a difficult situation: *I managed to talk my way out of having to give a speech.* **ˈyou can/can't talk** (*informal*) = LOOK WHO'S TALKING **you're a ˈfine one to talk** (*informal*) = LOOK WHO'S TALKING ➲ more at DEVIL, KNOW *v.*, LANGUAGE, MONEY, SENSE *n.*, TURN *n.*

PHR V **ˌtalk aˈround/ˈround sth** to talk about sth in a general way without dealing with the most important parts of it **ˈtalk at sb** to speak to sb without listening to what they say in reply **ˌtalk ˈback (to sb)** to answer sb rudely, especially sb in authority ➲ related noun BACK TALK **ˌtalk sb/sth↔ˈdown** to help a pilot of a plane to land by giving instructions from the ground **ˌtalk sth↔ˈdown** to make sth seem less important or successful than it really is: *You shouldn't talk down your own achievements.* **ˌtalk ˈdown to sb** to speak to sb as if they were less important or intelligent than you **ˌtalk sb ˈinto/ˈout of sth** to persuade sb to do/not to do sth: *I didn't want to move abroad but Bill talked me into it.* ◇ **~ doing sth** *She tried to talk him out of leaving.* **ˌtalk sth↔ˈout** to discuss sth thoroughly in order to make a decision, solve a problem, etc. **ˌtalk sth↔ˈover (with sb)** to discuss sth thoroughly, especially in order to reach an agreement or make a decision: *You'll find it helpful to talk things over with a friend.* **ˌtalk sb ˈround (to sth)** (*BrE*) to persuade sb to accept sth or agree to sth: *We finally managed to talk them round to our way of thinking.* **ˌtalk sb ˈthrough sth** to explain to sb how sth works so that they can do it or understand it: *Can you talk me through the various investment options?* **ˌtalk sth ↔ˈthrough** to discuss sth thoroughly until you are sure you understand it **ˌtalk sb/sth ˈup** to describe sb/sth in a way that makes them sound better than they really are

■ ***noun***

▸ CONVERSATION **1** 🔑 [C] **~ (with sb) (about sth)** a conversation or discussion: *I* ***had a*** *long* ***talk*** *with my boss about my career prospects.* ◇ *I had to have a heart-to-heart talk with her.* ➲ SYNONYMS at DISCUSSION

▸ FORMAL DISCUSSIONS **2** 🔑 **talks** [pl.] formal discussions between governments or organizations: ***arms/pay/peace, etc. talks*** ◇ *to* ***hold talks*** ◇ **~ (between A and B) (on/over sth)** ***Talks*** *between management and workers* ***broke down*** *over the issue of holiday pay.* ◇ *A further* ***round of talks*** *will be needed if the dispute is to be resolved.*

▸ SPEECH **3** 🔑 [C] **~ (on sth)** a speech or lecture on a particu-

Synonyms

talk

discuss • speak • communicate • debate • consult

These words all mean to share news, information, ideas or feelings with another person or other people, especially by talking with them.

talk to speak in order to give information, express feelings or share ideas: *We talked on the phone for over an hour.*

discuss (*rather formal*) to talk and share ideas on a subject or problem with other people, especially in order to decide sth: *Have you discussed the problem with anyone?* NOTE You cannot say 'discuss about sth': ~~*I'm not prepared to discuss about this on the phone.*~~

speak to talk to sb about sth; to have a conversation with sb: *I've spoken to the manager about it.* ◇ *'Can I speak to Susan?' 'Speaking.'* (= at the beginning of a telephone conversation)

TALK OR SPEAK?

Speak can suggest a more formal level of communication than **talk**. You **speak** to sb about sth to try to achieve a particular goal or to tell them to do sth. You **talk** to sb in order to be friendly or to ask their advice: *Have you talked to your parents about the problems you're having?* ◇ *I've spoken to Ed about it and he's promised not to let it happen again.*

communicate (*rather formal*) to exchange information or ideas with sb: *We only communicate by email.* ◇ *Dolphins use sound to communicate with each other.* NOTE **Communicate** is often used when the speaker wants to draw attention to the means of communication used.

debate to discuss sth, especially formally, before making a decisionor finding a solution: *Politicians will be debating the bill later this week.*

consult (*rather formal*) to discuss sth with sb in order to get their permission for sth, or to help you make a decision: *You shouldn't have done it without consulting me.*

PATTERNS

- to talk/discuss sth/speak/communicate/debate/consult **with** sb
- to talk/speak **to** sb
- to talk/speak to sb/consult sb **about** sth
- to talk/speak **of** sth

T

lar subject: *She **gave a talk** on her visit to China.* ➲ SYNONYMS at SPEECH
▸ WORDS WITHOUT ACTIONS **4** [U] (*informal*) words that are spoken, but without the necessary facts or actions to support them: *It's just talk. He'd never carry out his threats.* ◇ *Don't pay any attention to her—she's **all talk**.*
▸ STORIES/RUMOURS **5** [U] **~ (of sth/of doing sth) | ~ (that...)** stories that suggest a particular thing might happen in the future: *There was talk in Washington of sending in troops.* ◇ *She dismissed the stories of her resignation as newspaper talk.*
▸ TOPIC/WAY OF SPEAKING **6** [U] (often in compounds) a topic of conversation or a way of speaking: *business talk* ◇ *She said it was just **girl talk** that a man wouldn't understand.* ◇ *The book teaches you how to understand Spanish **street talk*** (= slang). ◇ *It was tough talk, coming from a man who had begun the year in a hospital bed.* ➲ see also SMALL TALK, SWEET TALK, TRASH TALK
IDM **the talk of sth** the person or thing that everyone is talking about in a particular place: *Overnight, she became **the talk of the town*** (= very famous). ➲ more at FIGHT *v.*

talka·tive /ˈtɔːkətɪv/ *adj.* liking to talk a lot: *He's not very talkative, is he?* ◇ *She was in a talkative mood.*

talk·back /ˈtɔːkbæk/ *noun* [U] (*technical*) a system that allows people working in a recording or broadcasting studio to talk to each other without their voices being recorded or heard on the radio

talk·er /ˈtɔːkə(r)/ *noun* a person who talks in a particular way or who talks a lot: *a brilliant talker* ◇ *She's a (great) talker* (= she talks a lot). ◇ *He's more a talker than a doer* (= he talks instead of doing things). ➲ SYNONYMS at SPEAKER IDM see FAST *adj.*

talkie /ˈtɔːki/ *noun* [usually pl.] (*old-fashioned, especially NAmE*) a film/movie that has sounds and not just pictures ➲ see also WALKIE-TALKIE

ˌtalking ˈdrum *noun* a type of drum from W Africa whose sound can be changed in order to communicate different messages

ˌtalking ˈhead *noun* (*informal*) a person on television who talks straight to the camera: *The election broadcast consisted largely of talking heads.*

ˈtalking point *noun* **1** (*BrE*) a subject that is talked about or discussed by many people: *The judge's decision became a legal talking point.* **2** (*NAmE*) an item that sb will speak about at a meeting, often one that supports a particular argument

ˈtalking shop *noun* (*BrE, disapproving*) a place where there is a lot of discussion and argument but no action is taken

ˈtalking-to *noun* [sing.] (*informal*) a serious talk with sb who has done sth wrong: *to give sb a good talking-to*

ˈtalk radio *noun* [U] radio programmes in which sb discusses a particular subject with people who telephone the radio station to give their opinions

ˈtalk show *noun* **1** (*especially NAmE*) (*BrE* also **ˈchat show**) a television or radio programme in which famous people are asked questions and talk in an informal way about their work and opinions on various topics: *a talk-show host* **2** a television or radio programme in which a PRESENTER introduces a particular topic which is then discussed by the audience

talk·time /ˈtɔːktaɪm/ *noun* [U] the amount of time that a mobile/cell phone can be used for calls without needing more power or more payments

tall 0‐π /tɔːl/ *adj.* (tall·er, tall·est)
1 0‐π (of a person, building, tree, etc.) having a greater than average height: *She's tall and thin.* ◇ *tall chimneys* ◇ *the tallest building in the world* ◇ *a tall glass of iced tea* OPP **short 2** 0‐π used to describe or ask about the height of sb/sth: *How tall are you?* ◇ *He's six feet tall and weighs 200 pounds.* ➲ note at HIGH ▸ **tall·ness** *noun* [U]
IDM **stand ˈtall** (*especially NAmE*) to show that you are proud and able to deal with anything **be a ˌtall ˈorder** (*informal*) to be very difficult to do ➲ more at OAK, WALK *v.*

tall·boy /ˈtɔːlbɔɪ/ (*BrE*) (*NAmE* **high·boy**) *noun* a tall piece of furniture with drawers, used for storing clothes in

tal·low /ˈtæləʊ; *NAmE* -loʊ/ *noun* [U] animal fat used for making CANDLES, soap, etc.

ˌtall ˈpoppy syndrome *noun* [U] (*informal, especially AustralE*) the fact of criticizing people who are richer or more successful than others

ˌtall ˈstory (*especially BrE*) (*NAmE* usually **ˌtall ˈtale**) *noun* a story that is difficult to believe because what it describes seems exaggerated and not likely to be true

tally /ˈtæli/ *noun, verb*
■ ***noun*** (*pl.* -ies) a record of the number or amount of sth, especially one that you can keep adding to: *He hopes to improve on his tally of three goals in the past nine games.* ◇ ***Keep a tally** of how much you spend while you're away.*
■ ***verb*** (tal·lies, tally·ing, tal·lied, tal·lied) **1** [I] **~ (with sth)** to be the same as or to match another person's account of sth, another set of figures, etc. SYN **match up**: *Her report of what happened tallied exactly with the story of another witness.* **2** [T] **~ sth (up)** to calculate the total number, cost, etc. of sth

ˌtally-ˈho *exclamation* used in hunting for telling the dogs that a FOX has been seen

the Tal·mud /ˈtælmʊd; *NAmE* also ˈtɑːl-/ *noun* [sing.] a collection of ancient writings on Jewish law and traditions ▸ **Tal·mud·ic** /ˌtælˈmʊdɪk; -ˈmjuːd-; *NAmE* also ˌtɑːl-/ *adj.*

talon /ˈtælən/ *noun* a long sharp curved nail on the feet of some birds, especially BIRDS OF PREY (= birds that kill other creatures for food) ➲ VISUAL VOCAB page V10

taluk /ˈtɑːlʊk/ (also **taluka** /ˈtɑːlʊkɑː/) *noun* (in some countries in S Asia) a smaller division of a district that governs itself

tam·ar·ind /ˈtæmərɪnd/ *noun* a tropical tree that produces fruit, also called tamarinds, that are often preserved and used in Asian cooking

tam·bour /ˈtæmbʊə(r); *NAmE* -bʊr/ *noun* a type of drum

tam·bour·ine /ˌtæmbəˈriːn/ *noun* a musical instrument that has a round wooden frame, sometimes covered with plastic or skin, with metal discs around the edge. To play it you shake it or hit it with your hand. ➲ VISUAL VOCAB page V30

tame /teɪm/ *adj., verb*
■ ***adj.*** (tamer, tam·est) **1** (of animals, birds, etc.) not afraid of people, and used to living with them OPP **wild 2** (*informal*) not interesting or exciting: *You'll find life here pretty tame after New York.* **3** (*informal*) (of a person) willing to do what other people ask: *I have a tame doctor who'll always give me a sick note when I want a day off.* ▸ **tame·ly** *adv.* **tame·ness** *noun* [U]
■ ***verb*** **~ sth** to make sth tame or easy to control: *Lions can never be completely tamed.* ◇ *She made strenuous efforts to tame her anger.*

tamer /ˈteɪmə(r)/ *noun* (usually in compounds) a person who trains wild animals: *a lion-tamer*

Tamil /ˈtæmɪl/ *noun* **1** [C] a member of a race of people living in Tamil Nadu in southern India and in Sri Lanka **2** [U] the language of the Tamils ▸ **Tamil** *adj.*

Tam·many Hall /ˌtæməni ˈhɔːl/ *noun* a dishonest political organization that had a lot of influence in New York City in the 19th and early 20th centuries (sometimes used to refer to any dishonest political organization)

tam-o'shanter /ˌtæməˈʃæntə(r)/ *noun* a round hat made of wool with a small ball made of wool in the centre, originally worn in Scotland

tam·oxi·fen /təˈmɒksɪfen; *NAmE* -ˈmɑːks-/ *noun* [U] (*medical*) a drug that is used especially to treat breast cancer

tamp /tæmp/ *verb* **~ sth (down)** to press sth down firmly, especially into a closed space

Tam·pax™ /ˈtæmpæks/ *noun* [C, U] (*pl.* **Tam·pax**) a type of TAMPON

tam·per /ˈtæmpə(r)/ *verb*
PHR V ˈ**tamper with sth** to make changes to sth without permission, especially in order to damage it **SYN** **interfere with**: *Someone had obviously tampered with the brakes of my car.*

ˈ**tamper-proof** *adj.* something that is **tamper-proof** is specially designed so that it cannot be easily changed or damaged: *a tamper-proof identity card*

tamp·ing /ˈtæmpɪŋ/ *adj.* (*WelshE, informal*) very angry

tam·pon /ˈtæmpɒn; *NAmE* -pɑːn/ *noun* a specially shaped piece of cotton material that a woman puts inside her VAGINA to absorb blood during her PERIOD ➲ compare SANITARY TOWEL

tan /tæn/ *verb, noun, adj., abbr.*
■ ***verb*** (-nn-) **1** [I, T] **~ (sb/sth)** if a person or their skin **tans** or is **tanned**, they become brown as a result of spending time in the sun **2** [T] **~ sth** to make animal skin into leather by treating it with chemicals **IDM** see HIDE *n.*
■ ***noun*** **1** [U] a yellowish-brown colour **2** (also **sun·tan**) [C] the brown colour that sb with pale skin goes when they have been in the sun: *to get a tan*
■ ***adj.*** yellowish brown in colour
■ ***abbr.*** (*mathematics*) TANGENT

tan·dem /ˈtændəm/ *noun* a bicycle for two riders, one behind the other ➲ VISUAL VOCAB page V41
IDM **in** ˈ**tandem** (**with sb/sth**) a thing that works or happens **in tandem** with sth else works together with it or happens at the same time as it

tan·doori /tænˈdʊəri; *NAmE* -ˈdʊri/ *noun* [U] (often used as an adjective) a method of cooking meat on a long straight piece of metal (called a SPIT) in a CLAY oven, originally used in S Asia: *tandoori chicken* ◇ *a tandoori restaurant*

tang /tæŋ/ *noun* [usually sing.] a strong sharp taste or smell: *the tang of lemons* ▶ **tangy** /ˈtæŋi/ *adj.*: *a refreshing tangy lemon flavour*

tan·gent /ˈtændʒənt/ *noun* **1** (*geometry*) a straight line that touches the outside of a curve but does not cross it ➲ VISUAL VOCAB page V58 **2** (*abbr.* tan) (*mathematics*) the RATIO of the length of the side opposite an angle in a RIGHT-ANGLED triangle to the length of the side next to it ➲ compare COSINE, SINE
IDM **fly/go off at a** ˈ**tangent** (*BrE*) (*NAmE* **go off on a** ˈ**tangent**) (*informal*) to suddenly start saying or doing sth that does not seem to be connected to what has gone before

tan·gen·tial /tænˈdʒenʃl/ *adj.* **1** (*formal*) having only a slight or indirect connection with sth: *a tangential argument* **2** (*geometry*) of or along a tangent ▶ **tan·gen·tial·ly** *adj.*

tan·ger·ine /ˌtændʒəˈriːn; *NAmE* ˈtændʒəriːn/ *noun* **1** [C] a type of small sweet orange with loose skin that comes off easily **2** [U] a deep orange-yellow colour ▶ **tan·ger·ine** *adj.*: *a tangerine evening gown*

tangi /ˈtæŋi/ *noun* (*NZE*) a Maori funeral, or meal that is held after the ceremony

tan·gible /ˈtændʒəbl/ *adj.* **1** [usually before noun] that can be clearly seen to exist: ***tangible benefits/improvements/results, etc.*** ◇ ***tangible assets*** (= a company's buildings, machinery, etc.) **2** that you can touch and feel: *The tension between them was* ***almost tangible.*** **OPP** **intangible** ▶ **tan·gibly** /ˈtændʒəbli/ *adv.*

tan·gle /ˈtæŋgl/ *noun, verb*
■ ***noun*** **1** a twisted mass of threads, hair, etc. that cannot be easily separated: *a tangle of branches* ◇ *Her hair was a mass of tangles.* **2** a state of confusion or lack of order: *His financial affairs are in a tangle.* **3** (*informal*) a disagreement or fight
■ ***verb*** [T, I] **~ (sth) up** to twist sth into an untidy mass; to become twisted in this way: *She had tangled up the sheets on the bed as she lay tossing and turning.*
PHR V ˈ**tangle with sb/sth** to become involved in an argument or a fight with sb/sth

tan·gled /ˈtæŋgld/ *adj.* **1** twisted together in an untidy way: *tangled hair/bed clothes* **2** complicated, and not easy to understand: *tangled financial affairs*

tango /ˈtæŋgəʊ; *NAmE* -goʊ/ *noun, verb*
■ ***noun*** (*pl.* -os /-gəʊz; *NAmE* -goʊz/) a fast S American dance with a strong beat, in which two people hold each other closely; a piece of music for this dance
■ ***verb*** (**tango·ing, tan·goed, tan·goed**) [I] to dance the tango
IDM **it takes** ˈ**two to tango** (*informal*) used to say that two people or groups, and not just one, are responsible for sth that has happened (usually sth bad)

tank 🔑 /tæŋk/ *noun, verb*
■ ***noun*** **1** 🔑 a large container for holding liquid or gas: *a hot water tank* ◇ *a fuel tank* ◇ *a fish tank* (= for keeping fish in) ➲ VISUAL VOCAB pages V34, V41 ➲ see also SEPTIC TANK, THINK TANK **2** 🔑 (also **tank·ful** /-fʊl/) the contents of a tank or the amount it will hold: *We drove there and back on one tank of petrol.* **3** 🔑 a military vehicle covered with strong metal and armed with guns. It can travel over very rough ground using wheels that move inside metal belts. **4** (*IndE*) an artificial pool, lake or RESERVOIR
■ ***verb*** **1** [I] (*NAmE*) (of a company or a product) to fail completely: *The company's shares tanked on Wall Street.* **2** [T, I] **~ (sth)** (*NAmE, sport*) to lose a game, especially deliberately: *She was accused of tanking the match.*
PHR V ˌ**tank (sth)** ˈ**up** (*NAmE*) to fill a car with petrol/gas: *He tanked up and drove off.* ◇ *We stopped to tank the car up.*

tank·ard /ˈtæŋkəd; *NAmE* -ərd/ *noun* a large, usually metal, cup with a handle, that is used for drinking beer from

ˌ**tanked** ˈ**up** (*BrE*) (*NAmE* **tanked**) *adj.* (*informal*) very drunk

ˈ**tank engine** *noun* a steam engine that carries its own fuel and water inside, rather than using another small truck

tank·er /ˈtæŋkə(r)/ *noun* a ship or lorry/truck that carries oil, gas or petrol/gas in large quantities: *an oil tanker* ➲ VISUAL VOCAB page V46 ➲ see also SUPERTANKER

tank·ini /ˌtæŋˈkiːni/ *noun* a SWIMSUIT in two pieces, consisting of a short top without sleeves and the bottom half of a BIKINI

ˈ**tank top** *noun* **1** (*BrE*) a sweater without sleeves **2** (*NAmE*) a piece of clothing like a T-SHIRT without sleeves

ˈ**tank tread** *noun* (*especially NAmE*) (also ˈ**Caterpillar track™** especially in *BrE*) *noun* a metal belt fastened around the wheels of a heavy vehicle, used for travelling over rough or soft ground ➲ VISUAL VOCAB page V47

tanned /tænd/ (also **sun·tanned**) *adj.* having a brown skin colour as a result of being in the sun

tan·ner /ˈtænə(r)/ *noun* a person whose job is to TAN animal skins to make leather

tan·nery /ˈtænəri/ *noun* (*pl.* -ies) a place where animal skins are TANNED and made into leather

tan·nie /ˈtʌni/ *noun* (*SAfrE, informal*) **1** an aunt; a friendly form of address for a woman who is older than you **2** (sometimes *disapproving*) a woman, especially one with old-fashioned views or tastes

tan·nin /ˈtænɪn/ (also ˌ**tannic** ˈ**acid**) *noun* [U] a yellowish or brownish substance found in the BARK of some trees and the fruit of many plants, used especially in making leather, ink and wine ▶ **tan·nic** /ˈtænɪk/ *adj.*

Tan·noy™ /ˈtænɔɪ/ *noun* (*BrE*) a system with LOUDSPEAKERS used for giving information in a public place: *to make an announcement over the Tannoy*

tan·tal·ize (*BrE* also **-ise**) /ˈtæntəlaɪz/ *verb* **~ sb/sth** to make a person or an animal want sth that they cannot have or do ▶ **tan·tal·iz·ing, -is·ing** *adj.*: *The tantalizing aroma of fresh coffee wafted towards them.* ◇ *a* ***tantalizing glimpse*** *of the future* **tan·tal·iz·ing·ly, -is·ing·ly** *adv.*: *The branch was tantalizingly out of reach.*

tan·ta·lum /ˈtæntələm/ *noun* [U] (*symb.* Ta) a chemical element. Tantalum is a hard silver-grey metal used in the production of electronic parts and of metal plates and pins for connecting broken bones.

T

tan·ta·mount /ˈtæntəmaʊnt/ *adj.* **~ to sth** (*formal*) having the same bad effect as sth else: *If he resigned it would be tantamount to admitting that he was guilty.*

tan·tra /ˈtæntrə/ *noun* **1** [C] an ancient Hindu or Buddhist text **2** [U] behaviour based on these texts, including prayer and MEDITATION ▶ **tan·tric** /ˈtæntrɪk/ *adj.*

tan·trum /ˈtæntrəm/ *noun* a sudden short period of angry, unreasonable behaviour, especially in a child: *to* ***have/throw a tantrum*** ◇ *Children often have* ***temper tantrums*** *at the age of two or thereabouts.*

Taoi·seach /ˈtiːʃəx/ *noun* the Prime Minister of the Irish Republic

Tao·ism /ˈdaʊɪzəm; ˈtaʊ-/ *noun* [U] a Chinese philosophy based on the writings of Lao-tzu ▶ **Tao·ist** /ˈdaʊɪst; ˈtaʊ-/ *noun, adj.*

tap 0━ /tæp/ *verb, noun*

■ ***verb*** (**-pp-**) **1** 0━ [I, T] to hit sb/sth quickly and lightly: **~ (away) (at sth)** *Someone tapped at the door.* ◇ *He was busy tapping away at his computer.* ◇ **~ sb/sth** *Ralph tapped me on the shoulder.* **2** 0━ [T, I] **~ (sth)** if you **tap** your fingers, feet, etc. or they **tap**, you hit them gently against a table, the floor, etc, for example to the rhythm of music: *He kept tapping his fingers on the table.* ◇ *The music set everyone's feet tapping.* **3** [T, I] to make use of a source of energy, knowledge, etc. that already exists: **~ sth** *We need to tap the expertise of the people we already have.* ◇ **~ into sth** *The movie seems to tap into a general sentimentality about animals.* **4** [T] **~ sth** (*especially BrE*) to fit a device to a telephone so that sb's calls can be listened to secretly: *He was convinced his phone was being tapped.* ➲ see also WIRETAPPING **5** [T] **~ sth** to cut into a tree in order to get liquid from it **6** [T, usually passive] **~ sb** (*NAmE*) to choose sb to do a particular job: *Richards has been tapped to replace the retiring chairperson.* **7** [T] **~ sth** (*phonetics*) to produce a TAP (6) SYN **flap**

PHR V **ˈtap sb for sth** (*BrE, informal*) to persuade sb to give you sth, especially money **ˌtap sth↔ˈin/ˈout** to put information, numbers, letters, etc. into a machine by pressing buttons: *Tap in your PIN number.* **ˌtap sth↔ˈout 1** to hit a surface gently to the rhythm of music: *She tapped out the beat on the table.* **2** to write sth using a computer or a mobile/cell phone: *I tapped out a text message to Mandy.*

■ ***noun*** **1** 0━ (*especially BrE*) (*NAmE* usually **fau·cet**) [C] a device for controlling the flow of water from a pipe into a bath/BATHTUB or SINK: *bath taps* ◇ *the* ***hot/cold tap*** (= the tap that hot/cold water comes out of) ◇ ***Turn the tap on/off.*** ◇ *Don't leave the tap running.* ◇ *the sound of a* ***dripping tap*** ➲ picture at PLUG ➲ **VISUAL VOCAB** pages V21, V22 ➲ see also TAP WATER **2** [C] a device for controlling the flow of liquid or gas from a pipe or container: *a gas tap* ◇ *beer taps* **3** 0━ [C] a light hit with your hand or fingers: *a* ***tap at/on*** *the door* ◇ *He felt a tap on his shoulder and turned round.* **4** [C] an act of fitting a device to a telephone so that sb's telephone calls can be listened to secretly: *a phone tap* **5** [U] = TAP-DANCING **6** [C] (*phonetics*) a speech sound which is produced by striking the tongue quickly and lightly against the part of the mouth behind the upper front teeth. The /t/ in *later* in American English and the /r/ in *very* in some British accents are examples of taps. SYN **flap**

IDM **on ˈtap 1** available to be used at any time: *We have this sort of information on tap.* **2** beer that is **on tap** is in a BARREL with a tap on it **3** (*NAmE*) something that is **on tap** is being discussed or prepared and will happen soon

tapas /ˈtæpəs; -pæs/ *noun* [pl.] (from *Spanish*) small amounts of a variety of Spanish dishes, served with drinks in a bar

ˈtap dance *noun* [U, C] a style of dancing in which you tap the rhythm of the music with your feet, wearing special shoes with pieces of metal on the heels and toes ▶ **ˈtap dancer** *noun* **ˈtap-dancing** (also **tap**) *noun* [U]

tape 0━ AW /teɪp/ *noun, verb*

■ ***noun*** **1** 0━ [U] a long narrow strip of MAGNETIC material that is used for recording sounds, pictures or information ➲ see also MAGNETIC TAPE, VIDEOTAPE **2** 0━ [C] a CASSETTE that contains sounds, or sounds and pictures, that have been recorded: *a* ***blank tape*** (= a tape that has nothing recorded on it) ◇ *I lent her my Bob Marley tapes.* ◇ *Police seized various books and tapes.* **3** 0━ [U] a long narrow strip of material with a sticky substance on one side that is used for sticking things together: ***adhesive/sticky tape*** ➲ see also INSULATING TAPE, MASKING TAPE, SCOTCH TAPE, SELLOTAPE **4** [C, U] a narrow strip of material that is used for tying things together or as a label: *The papers were in a pile, tied together with a tape.* ➲ see also RED TAPE, TICKER TAPE **5** [C] a long narrow strip of material that is stretched across the place where a race will finish: *the finishing tape* **6** [C] = TAPE MEASURE

■ ***verb*** **1** **~ sb/sth** to record sb/sth on MAGNETIC tape using a special machine: *Private conversations between the two had been taped and sent to a newspaper.* **2** **~ sth (up)** to fasten sth by sticking or tying it with tape: *Put it in a box and tape it up securely.* **3** **~ sth + adv./prep.** to stick sth onto sth else using sticky tape: *Someone had taped a message on the door.* **4** **~ sth (up)** (*NAmE*) to tie a bandage firmly around an injury or a wound: *That's a nasty cut—come on, we'll get it all taped up.*

IDM **have (got) sb/sth ˈtaped** (*BrE, informal*) to understand sb/sth completely and to have learned how to deal with them/it successfully: *He can't fool me—I've got him taped.*

ˈtape measure (also **tape**, **ˈmeasuring tape**) *noun* a long narrow strip of plastic, cloth or FLEXIBLE metal that has measurements marked on it and is used for measuring the length of sth

taper /ˈteɪpə(r)/ *verb, noun*

■ ***verb*** [I, T] to become gradually narrower; to make sth become gradually narrower: *The tail tapered to a rounded tip.* ◇ **~ sth** *The pots are wide at the base and tapered at the top.*

PHR V **ˌtaper ˈoff** to become gradually less in number, amount, degree, etc: *The number of applicants for teaching posts has tapered off.* **ˌtaper sth↔ˈoff** to make sth become gradually less in number, amount, degree, etc: *They are gradually tapering off production of the older models.*

■ ***noun*** **1** a long thin piece of wood, paper, etc. that is used for lighting fires or lamps **2** a long thin CANDLE **3** [usually sing.] the way that sth gradually decreases in size, becoming thinner

ˈtape-record *verb* **~ sth** to record sth on tape: *a tape-recorded interview*

ˈtape recorder *noun* a machine that is used for recording and playing sounds on tape

ˈtape recording *noun* something that has been recorded on tape: *a tape recording of the interview*

tape·script /ˈteɪpskrɪpt/ *noun* the printed text of a recording of speech

tap·es·try /ˈtæpəstri/ *noun* [C, U] (*pl.* **-ies**) a picture or pattern that is made by WEAVING coloured wool onto heavy cloth; the art of doing this: *medieval tapestries* ◇ *tapestry cushions* ◇ *crafts such as embroidery and tapestry* ▶ **tap·es·tried** *adj.*: *tapestried walls*

tape·worm /ˈteɪpwɜːm; *NAmE* -wɜːrm/ *noun* a long flat WORM that lives in the INTESTINES of humans and animals

ˈtap-in *noun* (in sport) an easy light hit of the ball into the goal or hole from a close position: *The pass left Tevez with a simple tap-in.*

tapi·oca /ˌtæpiˈəʊkə; *NAmE* -ˈoʊkə/ *noun* [U] hard white grains obtained from the CASSAVA plant, often cooked with milk to make a DESSERT (= a sweet dish)

tapir /ˈteɪpə(r)/ *noun* an animal like a pig with a long nose, that lives in Central and S America and SE Asia

ˌtap-ˈpenalty *noun* (in RUGBY) a situation where a player is allowed a free kick of the ball because the other team has broken a rule, and chooses to touch it lightly with the foot then immediately pick it up

tap·root /ˈtæpruːt/ *noun* the main root of a plant that grows straight downwards and produces smaller side roots

'tap water *noun* [U] water supplied through pipes to taps/faucets in a building: *Is the tap water safe to drink?*

tar /tɑː(r)/ *noun, verb*

■ ***noun*** [U] **1** a thick black sticky liquid that becomes hard when cold. Tar is obtained from coal and is used especially in making roads. **2** a substance similar to tar that is formed by burning TOBACCO: *low-tar cigarettes* IDM see SPOIL *v.*

■ ***verb*** (-rr-) **~ sth** to cover sth with tar: *a tarred road*

IDM **tar and 'feather sb** to put tar on sb then cover them with feathers, as a punishment **be tarred with the same 'brush (as sb)** to be thought to have the same faults, etc. as sb else

tara·ma·sa·lata /ˌtærəməsəˈlɑːtə/ *noun* [U] (*BrE*) a type of Greek food made from fish eggs

ta·ran·tula /təˈræntʃələ/ *noun* a large spider covered with hair that lives in hot countries. Some types of tarantula have a poisonous bite.

tardy /ˈtɑːdi; *NAmE* ˈtɑːrdi/ *adj.* **~ (in doing sth)** (*formal*) slow to act, move or happen; late in happening or arriving: *The law is often tardy in reacting to changing attitudes.* ◇ *people who are tardy in paying their bills* ◇ (*NAmE*) *to be tardy for school* ▸ **tar·dily** /ˈtɑːdɪli; *NAmE* ˈtɑːrd-/ *adv.* **tar·di·ness** *noun* [U]

tare /teə(r); *NAmE* ter/ *noun* (*literary* or *technical*) a plant growing where you do not want it SYN **weed**

Synonyms

target

objective • goal • object • end

These are all words for sth that you are trying to achieve.

target a result that you try to achieve: *Set yourself targets that you can reasonably hope to achieve.* ◇ *attainment targets in schools*

objective (*rather formal*) something that you are trying to achieve: *What is the main objective of this project?*

goal something that you hope to achieve: *He continued to pursue his goal of becoming an actor.*

TARGET, OBJECTIVE OR GOAL?

A **target** is usually officially recorded in some way, for example by an employer or by a government committee. It is often specific, and in the form of figures, such as number of sales or exam passes, or a date. People often set their own **objectives**: these are things that they wish to achieve, often as part of a project or a talk they are giving. **Goals** are often long-term, and relate to people's life and career plans or the long-term plans of a company or organization.

object the purpose of sth; sth that you plan to achieve: *The object is to educate people about road safety.*

end something that you plan to achieve: *He joined the society for political ends.* ◇ *That's only OK if you believe that **the end justifies the means*** (= bad methods of doing sth are acceptable if the final result is good). NOTE **End** is usually used in the plural or in particular fixed expressions.

PATTERNS

- to work **towards** a(n) target/objective/goal
- an **ambitious/major/long-term/short-term/future** target/objective/goal
- **economic/financial/business** targets/objectives/goals
- to **set/agree on/identify/reach/meet/exceed** a(n) target/objective/goal
- to **achieve** a(n) target/objective/goal/end

tar·get 0‑w AW /ˈtɑːɡɪt; *NAmE* ˈtɑːrɡɪt/ *noun, verb*

■ ***noun*** **1** 0‑w a result that you try to achieve: *business goals and targets* ◇ *attainment targets* ◇ ***Set yourself targets*** *that you can reasonably hope to achieve.* ◇ *to **meet/achieve a target*** ◇ *a **target date** of April 2012* ◇ *The university will **reach its target** of 5 000 students next September.* ◇ *The new sports complex is **on target** to open in June.* ◇ *a **target area/audience/group*** (= the particular area, audience, etc. that a product, programme, etc. is aimed at) ➲ COLLOCATIONS at BUSINESS **2** 0‑w an object, a person or a place that people aim at when attacking: *They bombed military and civilian targets.* ◇ **~ for sb/sth** *Doors and windows are an **easy target** for burglars.* ◇ *It's a **prime target*** (= an obvious target) *for terrorist attacks.* ◇ **~ of sth** (*figurative*) *He's become the target of a lot of criticism recently.* **3** an object that people practise shooting at, especially a round board with circles on it: *to aim at a target* ◇ *to **hit/miss the target*** ◇ ***target practice*** ➲ VISUAL VOCAB page V34

■ ***verb*** (**tar·get·ing, tar·get·ed, tar·get·ed**) [usually passive] **1 ~ sb/sth** to aim an attack or a criticism at sb/sth: *The missiles were mainly targeted at the United States.* ◇ *The company has been targeted by animal rights groups for its use of dogs in drugs trials.* **2 ~ sb** to try to have an effect on a particular group of people: *The campaign is clearly targeted at the young.* ◇ *a new magazine that targets single men*

'target language *noun* (*linguistics*) **1** (also **'object language**) a language into which a text is being translated **2** a foreign language that sb is learning

tar·iff /ˈtærɪf/ *noun* **1** a tax that is paid on goods coming into or going out of a country ➲ SYNONYMS at TAX ➲ COLLOCATIONS at INTERNATIONAL **2** a list of fixed prices that are charged by a hotel or restaurant for rooms, meals, etc, or by a company for a particular service **3** (*BrE, law*) a level of punishment for sb who has been found guilty of a crime

Tar·mac™ /ˈtɑːmæk; *NAmE* ˈtɑːrmæk/ *noun* [U] **1** (also *less frequent* **tar·mac·adam** /ˌtɑːməˈkædəm; *NAmE* ˌtɑːrm-/) (*NAmE* also **black·top**) a black material used for making road surfaces, that consists of small stones mixed with TAR **2 the tarmac** an area with a Tarmac surface, especially at an airport: *Three planes were standing on the tarmac, waiting to take off.*

tar·mac /ˈtɑːmæk; *NAmE* ˈtɑːrmæk/ *verb* (-ck-) (*NAmE* also **blacktop**) **~ sth** to cover a surface with Tarmac: *tarmacked roads*

tarn /tɑːn; *NAmE* tɑːrn/ *noun* a small lake in the mountains

tar·na·tion /tɑːˈneɪʃn; *NAmE* tɑːrˈn-/ *exclamation* (*old-fashioned, especially NAmE*) a word that people use to show that they are annoyed with sb/sth

tar·nish /ˈtɑːnɪʃ; *NAmE* ˈtɑːrnɪʃ/ *verb, noun*

■ ***verb*** **1** [I, T] if metal **tarnishes** or sth **tarnishes** it, it no longer looks bright and shiny: *The mirrors had tarnished with age.* ◇ **~ sth** *The silver candlesticks were tarnished and dusty.* **2** [T] **~ sth** to spoil the good opinion people have of sb/sth SYN **taint**: *He hopes to improve the newspaper's somewhat tarnished public image.*

■ ***noun*** [sing., U] a thin layer on the surface of a metal that makes it look dull and not bright

tarot /ˈtærəʊ; *NAmE* -roʊ/ *noun* [sing., U] a set of special cards with pictures on them, used for telling sb what will happen to them in the future

tar·paulin /tɑːˈpɔːlɪn; *NAmE* tɑːrˈp-/ (also *NAmE informal* **tarp**) *noun* [C, U] a large sheet made of heavy WATERPROOF material, used to cover things with and to keep rain off

tar·ra·gon /ˈtærəɡən/ *noun* [U] a plant with leaves that have a strong taste and are used in cooking as a HERB ➲ VISUAL VOCAB page V28

tarry /ˈtæri/ *verb* (**tar·ries, tarry·ing, tar·ried, tar·ried**) [I] (*old use* or *literary*) to stay in a place, especially when you ought to leave; to delay coming to or going from a place SYN **linger**

tar·sal /ˈtɑːsl; *NAmE* ˈtɑːrsl/ *noun* (*anatomy*) one of the small bones in the ankle and upper foot

tart /tɑːt; *NAmE* tɑːrt/ *noun, adj., verb*

■ ***noun*** **1** [C, U] an open PIE filled with sweet food such as fruit: *a strawberry tart* ➲ compare FLAN, QUICHE **2** [C] (*BrE, informal, disapproving*) a woman who you think behaves or dresses in a way that is immoral and is intended

T

to make men sexually excited ➲ see also TARTY **3** [C] (*slang*) a PROSTITUTE
■ ***adj.*** **1** having an unpleasant sour taste: *tart apples* **2** [usually before noun] (of remarks, etc.) quick and unkind: *a tart reply* SYN **sharp** ▸ **tart·ly** *adv.*: *'Too late!' said my mother tartly.* **tart·ness** *noun* [U]
■ ***verb***
PHR V **ˌtart yourself ˈup** (*informal*) (especially of a woman) to make yourself more attractive by putting on nice clothes, jewellery, make-up, etc. **ˌtart sth↔ˈup** (*informal*) to decorate or improve the appearance of sth, often in a way that other people do not think is attractive

tar·tan /ˈtɑːtn; *NAmE* ˈtɑːrtn/ *noun* **1** [U, C] a pattern of squares and lines of different colours and widths that cross each other at an angle of 90°, used especially on cloth, and originally from Scotland: *a tartan rug* ➲ VISUAL VOCAB page V50 **2** [C] a tartan pattern connected with a particular group of families (= a CLAN) in Scotland: *the MacLeod tartan* **3** [U] cloth, especially made of wool, that has a tartan pattern ➲ compare PLAID

tar·tar /ˈtɑːtə(r); *NAmE* ˈtɑːrt-/ *noun* **1** [U] a hard substance that forms on teeth **2** [C] (*old-fashioned*) a person in a position of authority who is very bad-tempered

tar·tare sauce (*NAmE* **tar·tar sauce**) /ˌtɑːtə ˈsɔːs; *NAmE* ˌtɑːrtər/ *noun* [U] a thick cold white sauce made from MAYONNAISE, chopped onions and CAPERS, usually eaten with fish

tar·tar·ic acid /tɑːˌtærɪk ˈæsɪd; *NAmE* tɑːrˌt-/ *noun* [U] (*chemistry*) a type of acid that is found in GRAPES that are not ready to eat

tarty /ˈtɑːti; *NAmE* ˈtɑːrti/ *adj.* (*disapproving*) (of a woman) dressing or behaving in a way that is intended to attract sexual attention

Tar·zan /ˈtɑːzæn; *NAmE* ˈtɑːrz-/ *noun* a man with a very strong body ORIGIN From the novel *Tarzan of the Apes* by Edgar Rice Burroughs about a man who lived with wild animals.

taser /ˈteɪzə(r)/ *noun* a gun that fires DARTS that give a person a small electric shock and makes them unable to move for a short time

task 0➸ AW /tɑːsk; *NAmE* tæsk/ *noun, verb*
■ ***noun*** **1** 0➸ a piece of work that sb has to do, especially a hard or unpleasant one: *to* ***perform/carry out/complete/undertake a task*** ◇ ***a daunting/an impossible/a formidable/an unenviable, etc. task*** ◇ *a* ***thankless task*** (= an unpleasant one that nobody wants to do and nobody thanks you for doing) ◇ *Our first task is to set up a communications system.* ◇ *Detectives are now faced with* ***the task of*** *identifying the body.* ◇ *Getting hold of this information was* ***no easy task*** (= was difficult). **2** an activity which is designed to help achieve a particular learning goal, especially in language teaching: *task-based learning*
IDM **take sb to ˈtask (for/over sth)** to criticize sb strongly for sth they have done
■ ***verb*** [usually passive] **~ sb (with sth)** (*formal*) to give sb a task to do

ˈtask force *noun* **1** a military force that is brought together and sent to a particular place **2** a group of people who are brought together to deal with a particular problem

task·mas·ter /ˈtɑːskmɑːstə(r); *NAmE* ˈtæskmæstər/ *noun* a person who gives other people work to do, often work that is difficult: *She was* ***a hard taskmaster.***

tas·sel /ˈtæsl/ *noun* a bunch of threads that are tied together at one end and hang from CUSHIONS, curtains, clothes, etc. as a decoration ➲ VISUAL VOCAB page V52

tassel

tas·selled (*BrE*) (*US* **tas·seled**) /ˈtæsld/ *adj.* decorated with tassels

taste 0➸ /teɪst/ *noun, verb*
■ ***noun***
▸ FLAVOUR **1** 0➸ [C, U] the particular quality that different foods and drinks have that allows you to recognize them when you put them in your mouth: *a* ***salty/bitter/sweet, etc. taste*** ◇ *I don't like the taste of olives.* ◇ *This dish has an unusual combination of tastes and textures.* ◇ *The soup has very little taste.*
▸ SENSE **2** 0➸ [U] the sense you have that allows you to recognize different foods and drinks when you put them in your mouth: *I've lost my sense of taste.*
▸ SMALL QUANTITY **3** 0➸ [C, usually sing.] a small quantity of food or drink that you try in order to see what it is like: *Just have a taste of this cheese.*
▸ SHORT EXPERIENCE **4** [sing.] a short experience of sth: *This was my* ***first taste*** *of live theatre.* ◇ *Although we didn't know it, this incident was* ***a taste of things to come.***
▸ ABILITY TO CHOOSE WELL **5** 0➸ [U] a person's ability to choose things that people recognize as being of good quality or appropriate: *He has very* ***good taste*** *in music.* ◇ *They've got more money than taste.* ◇ *The room was furnished with taste.*
▸ WHAT YOU LIKE **6** 0➸ [C, U] what a person likes or prefers: **~ (for sth)** *That trip gave me a taste for foreign travel.* ◇ **~ (in sth)** *She has very expensive tastes in clothes.* ◇ *The colour and style is* ***a matter*** *of personal* ***taste.*** ◇ *Modern art is not* ***to everyone's taste.*** ◇ *There are trips to suit all tastes.*
IDM **be in bad, poor, the worst possible, etc. ˈtaste** to be offensive and not at all appropriate: *Most of his jokes were in very poor taste.* **be in good, the best possible, etc. ˈtaste** to be appropriate and not at all offensive **leave a bad/nasty ˈtaste in the mouth** (of events or experiences) to make you feel disgusted or ashamed afterwards **to ˈtaste** in the quantity that is needed to make sth taste the way you prefer: *Add salt and pepper to taste.* ➲ more at ACCOUNT *V.*, ACQUIRE, MEDICINE
■ ***verb*** (not used in the progressive tenses)
▸ HAVE FLAVOUR **1** 0➸ *linking verb* to have a particular flavour: **+ adj.** *It tastes sweet.* ◇ **~ of sth** *The ice tasted of mint.* ◇ **~ like sth** *This drink tastes like sherry.* **2 -tasting** (in adjectives) having a particular flavour: *foul-tasting medicine*
▸ RECOGNIZE FLAVOUR **3** 0➸ [T] **~ sth** (often used with *can* or *could*) to be able to recognize flavours in food and drink: *You can taste the garlic in this stew.*
▸ TEST FLAVOUR **4** 0➸ [T] **~ sth** to test the flavour of sth by eating or drinking a small amount of it SYN **try**: *Taste it and see if you think there's enough salt in it.*
▸ EAT/DRINK **5** 0➸ [T] **~ sth** to eat or drink food or liquid: *I've never tasted anything like it.*
▸ HAVE SHORT EXPERIENCE **6** [T] **~ sth** to have a short experience of sth, especially sth that you want more of: *He had tasted freedom only to lose it again.*

ˈtaste bud *noun* [usually pl.] one of the small structures on the tongue that allow you to recognize the flavours of food and drink

taste·ful /ˈteɪstfl/ *adj.* (especially of clothes, furniture, decorations, etc.) attractive and of good quality and showing that the person who chose them can recognize good things ▸ **taste·ful·ly** /-fəli/ *adv.*: *The bedroom was tastefully furnished.*

taste·less /ˈteɪstləs/ *adj.* **1** having little or no flavour: *tasteless soup* **2** offensive and not appropriate: *tasteless jokes* **3** showing a lack of the ability to choose things that people recognize as attractive and of good quality ▸ **taste·less·ly** *adv.* **taste·less·ness** *noun* [U]

taster /ˈteɪstə(r)/ *noun* **1** a person whose job is to judge the quality of wine, tea, etc. by tasting it **2** (*informal, especially BrE*) a small example of sth for you to try in order to see if you would like more of it

-tastic /ˈtæstɪk/ *suffix* (in adjectives) (*BrE, informal*) used to emphasize that sb/sth of a particular type is extremely good: *We have a toptastic line-up of stars for you tonight.* ◇ *Try this new choctastic recipe!* ➲ see also POPTASTIC

tast·ing /ˈteɪstɪŋ/ *noun* an event at which people can try different kinds of food and drink, especially wine, in small quantities: *a wine tasting*

tasty /ˈteɪsti/ *adj.* (**tasti·er, tasti·est**) **1** (*approving*) having a strong and pleasant flavour: *a tasty meal* ◇ *something tasty* to eat **2** (*BrE, informal*, sometimes *offensive*) a word that some men use about women that they think are sexually attractive ▶ **tasti·ness** *noun* [U]

tat /tæt/ *noun* [U] (*BrE, informal*) goods that are cheap and of low quality ➲ see also TIT FOR TAT

ta-ta /ˌtæ 'tɑː/ *exclamation* (*BrE, informal*) goodbye: *Ta-ta for now!*

tat·ami /tə'tɑːmi; 'tætəmi/ *noun* (from *Japanese*) a traditional Japanese floor covering made from dried RUSHES

tater /'teɪtə(r)/ *noun* [usually pl.] (*slang*) a potato

tat·tered /'tætəd; *NAmE* -tərd/ *adj.* old and torn; in bad condition: *tattered clothes* ◇ (*figurative*) *tattered relationships* ◇ (*figurative*) *the hotel's tattered reputation*

tat·ters /'tætəz; *NAmE* -tərz/ *noun* [pl.] clothes or pieces of cloth that are badly torn

IDM **in tatters 1** torn in many places: *His clothes were in tatters.* **2** ruined or badly damaged SYN **in shreds**: *Her reputation was in tatters.* ◇ *The government's education policy lies in tatters.*

tat·tie /'tæti/ *noun* (*ScotE, informal*) a potato

tat·tle /'tætl/ *verb* [I] **~ (on sb) (to sb)** (*informal, disapproving, especially NAmE*) to tell sb, especially sb in authority, about sth bad that sb else has done SYN **tell on sb**

tat·tle·tale /'tætlteɪl/ (*NAmE*) (*BrE* **tell·tale**) *noun* (*informal, disapproving*) a child who tells an adult what another child has done wrong

tat·too /tə'tuː; *NAmE* tæ'tuː/ *noun, verb*

▪ ***noun*** (*pl.* **-oos**) **1** a picture or design that is marked permanently on a person's skin by making small holes in the skin with a needle and filling them with coloured ink: *His arms were covered in tattoos.* ➲ COLLOCATIONS at FASHION **2** (*especially BrE*) an outdoor show by members of the armed forces that includes marching, music and military exercises **3** [usually sing.] a rapid and continuous series of taps or hits, especially on a drum as a military signal

▪ ***verb*** to mark sb's skin with a tattoo: **~ A on B** *He had a heart tattooed on his shoulder.* ◇ **~ B (with A)** *His shoulder was tattooed with a heart.*

tat·too·ist /tə'tuːɪst; *NAmE* tæ't-/ *noun* a person who draws tattoos on people's skin, as a job

tatty /'tæti/ *adj.* (*informal, especially BrE*) (**tat·tier, tat·ti·est**) in a bad condition because it has been used a lot or has not been cared for well SYN **shabby**: *a tatty carpet*

tau /tɔː; taʊ/ *noun* the 19th letter of the Greek alphabet (Τ, τ)

taught *past tense, past part.* of TEACH

taunt /tɔːnt/ *verb, noun*

▪ ***verb* ~ sb** to try to make sb angry or upset by saying unkind things about them, laughing at their failures, etc: *The other kids continually taunted him about his size.*

▪ ***noun*** an insulting or unkind remark that is intended to make sb angry or upset: *Black players often had to endure racist taunts.*

taupe /təʊp; *NAmE* toʊp/ *noun* [U] a brownish-grey colour ▶ **taupe** *adj.*

taur·ine /'tɔːriːn/ *noun* [U] an acid substance which is sometimes used in drinks that are designed to make you feel more active

Taurus /'tɔːrəs/ *noun* **1** [U] the second sign of the ZODIAC, the BULL **2** [sing.] a person born when the sun is in this sign, that is between 21 April and 21 May ▶ **Taur·ean** /'tɔːriən/ *noun, adj.*

taut /tɔːt/ *adj.* **1** stretched tightly: *Keep the rope taut.* **2** showing that you are anxious or TENSE: *Her face was taut and pale.* **3** (of a person or their body) with firm muscles; not fat: *His body was solid and taut.* **4** (of a piece of writing, etc.) tightly controlled, with no unnecessary parts in it ▶ **taut·ly** *adv.* **taut·ness** *noun* [U]

taut·en /'tɔːtn/ *verb* [I, T] **~ (sth)** to become taut; to make sth taut

tau·tol·ogy /tɔː'tɒlədʒi; *NAmE* -'tɑːl-/ *noun* [U, C] a statement in which you say the same thing twice in different words, when this is unnecessary, for example 'They spoke in turn, one after the other.' ▶ **tauto·logic·al** /ˌtɔːtə'lɒdʒɪkl; *NAmE* -'lɑːdʒ-/ *adj.* **tau·tolo·gous** /tɔː'tɒləgəs; *NAmE* -'tɑːl-/ *adj.*

tav·ern /'tævən; *NAmE* -vərn/ *noun* (*old use* or *literary*) a pub or an INN

taw·dry /'tɔːdri/ *adj.* (*disapproving*) **1** intended to be bright and attractive but cheap and of low quality: *tawdry jewellery* **2** involving low moral standards; extremely unpleasant or offensive: *a tawdry affair* ▶ **taw·dri·ness** *noun* [U]

tawny /'tɔːni/ *adj.* brownish-yellow in colour: *the lion's tawny mane*

ˌtawny 'owl *noun* a reddish-brown or grey European BIRD OF PREY (= a bird that kills other creatures for food) of the OWL family

tax 0‑ᴡ /tæks/ *noun, verb*

▪ ***noun*** 0‑ᴡ [C, U] money that you have to pay to the government so that it can pay for public services. People pay tax according to their income and businesses pay tax according to their profits. Tax is also often paid on goods and services: *to* ***raise/cut taxes*** ◇ ***tax increases/cuts*** ◇ *changes in* ***tax rates*** ◇ *to pay over £1 000* ***in tax*** ◇ *profits* ***before/after tax*** ◇ **~ on sth** *a tax on cigarettes* ➲ COLLOCATIONS at ECONOMY ➲ see also CORPORATION TAX, COUNCIL TAX, DIRECT TAX, INDIRECT TAX, INHERITANCE TAX, POLL TAX, ROAD TAX, SALES TAX, STEALTH TAX, VALUE ADDED TAX, WITHHOLDING TAX

▪ ***verb* 1** 0‑ᴡ **~ sb/sth** to put a tax on sb/sth; to make sb pay tax: *Any interest payments are taxed as part of your income.* ◇ *His declared aim was to tax the rich.* **2 ~ sth** (*BrE*) to pay tax on a vehicle so that you may use it on the roads: *The car is taxed until July.* **3 ~ sb/sth** to need a great amount of physical or mental effort: *The questions did not tax me.* ◇ *The problem is currently* ***taxing the brains*** *of the nation's experts* (= making them think very hard).

PHR V **'tax sb with sth** (*formal*) to accuse sb of doing sth wrong: *I taxed him with avoiding his responsibility as a parent.*

Synonyms

tax

duty • customs • tariff • rates

These are all words for money that you have to pay to the government.

tax money that you have to pay to the government so that it can pay for public services: *income tax* ◇ *tax cuts*

duty a tax that you pay on things that you buy, especially those that you bring into a country: *The company has to pay customs duties on all imports.*

customs tax that is paid when goods are brought in from other countries

tariff a tax that is paid on goods coming into or going out of a country, often in order to protect industry from cheap imports: *A general tariff was imposed on foreign imports.*

rates (in Britain) a tax paid by businesses to a local authority for land and buildings that they use, and in the past also paid by anyone who owned a house: *Business rates are very high in the city centre.*

PATTERNS

- (a) tax/duty/tariff/rates **on** sth
- to pay an amount of money **in** tax/duty/customs/rates
- to **pay** (a) tax/duty/customs/tariff/rates
- to **collect** taxes/duties/rates
- to **increase/raise/reduce** taxes/duty/tariffs/rates
- to **cut** taxes/duties/rates
- to **impose** a tax/duty/tariff
- to **put** a tax/duty **on** sth

T

tax·able /ˈtæksəbl/ *adj.* (of money) that you have to pay tax on: *taxable income*

tax·ation /tækˈseɪʃn/ *noun* [U] **1** money that has to be paid as taxes: *to reduce taxation* **2** the system of collecting money by taxes: *changes in the taxation structure*

ˈtax avoidance *noun* [U] ways of paying only the smallest amount of tax that you legally have to ➲ compare TAX EVASION

ˈtax bracket (*BrE* also **ˈtax band**) *noun* a range of different incomes on which the same rate of tax must be paid: *There are now only two tax brackets—22% and 40%.*

ˈtax break *noun* a special advantage or reduction in taxes that the government gives to particular people or organizations

ˈtax collector *noun* a person whose job is collecting the tax that people must pay on the money they earn

ˈtax credit *noun* **1** money that is taken off your total tax bill **2** money provided by the government to people who need financial help, especially if they have children or are on a low income

ˌtax-deˈduct·ible *adj.* (of costs) that can be taken off your income before the amount of tax that you have to pay is calculated

ˌtax-deˈferred *adj.* (*NAmE*) that you only pay tax on later: *a tax-deferred savings plan*

ˈtax disc *noun* = ROAD FUND LICENCE

ˈtax dodge *noun* (*informal*) a way of paying less tax, legally or illegally ▸ **ˈtax dodger** *noun*

ˈtax evasion *noun* [U] the crime of deliberately not paying all the taxes that you should pay ➲ compare TAX AVOIDANCE

ˌtax-eˈxempt *adj.* that is not taxed: *tax-exempt savings*

ˈtax exile *noun* a rich person who has left their own country and gone to live in a place where the taxes are lower

ˌtax-ˈfree *adj.* (of money, goods, etc.) that you do not have to pay tax on: *a tax-free allowance* ▸ **ˌtax-ˈfree** *adv.*

ˈtax haven *noun* a place where taxes are low and where people choose to live or officially register their companies because taxes are higher in their own countries

taxi 🔑 /ˈtæksi/ *noun, verb*
■ ***noun*** **1** 🔑 (also **cab, taxi·cab**) a car with a driver that you pay to take you somewhere. Taxis usually have METERS which show how much money you have to pay: *a* ***taxi driver/ride*** ◇ *We'd better* ***take a taxi.*** ◇ *I came home* ***by taxi.*** ◇ *to* ***order/hail/call a taxi*** ➲ VISUAL VOCAB page V47 **2** in some places in Africa, a small bus with a driver that you pay to take you somewhere. Taxis usually have fixed routes and stop wherever passengers need to get on or off. ➲ see also DALA-DALA, MATATU
■ ***verb*** (**taxi·ing, tax·ied, tax·ied**) [I] (of a plane) to move slowly along the ground before taking off or after landing

taxi·der·mist /ˈtæksɪdɜːmɪst; *NAmE* -dɜːrm-/ *noun* a person whose job is taxidermy

taxi·dermy /ˈtæksɪdɜːmi; *NAmE* -dɜːrmi/ *noun* [U] the art of STUFFING dead animals, birds and fish with a special material so that they look like living ones and can be displayed

tax·ing /ˈtæksɪŋ/ *adj.* needing a great amount of physical or mental effort SYN **demanding**: *a taxing job* ◇ *This shouldn't be too taxing for you.* ➲ SYNONYMS at DIFFICULT

ˈtax inspector *noun* (*BrE*) = INSPECTOR OF TAXES

ˈtaxi rank (*BrE*) (also **ˈtaxi stand** *NAmE, BrE*) *noun* a place where taxis park while they are waiting for passengers ➲ VISUAL VOCAB page V2

ˈtaxi squad *noun* (in AMERICAN FOOTBALL) **1** a group of players who practise with the first team but who do not play in games **2** four extra players on a team who play when other players are injured

taxi·way /ˈtæksiweɪ/ *noun* the hard path that a plane uses as it moves to and from the RUNWAY (= the hard surface where planes take off and land)

tax·man /ˈtæksmæn/ *noun* (*pl.* **-men** /-men/) **1 the taxman** [sing.] (*informal*) a way of referring to the government department that is responsible for collecting taxes: *He had been cheating the taxman for years.* **2** [C] a person whose job is to collect taxes

tax·ono·mist /tækˈsɒnəmɪst; *NAmE* -ˈsɑːnə-/ *noun* a person who studies or is skilled in taxonomy

tax·onomy /tækˈsɒnəmi; *NAmE* -ˈsɑːnə-/ *noun* (*pl.* **-ies**) **1** [U] the scientific process of CLASSIFYING things (= arranging them into groups): *plant taxonomy* **2** [C] a particular system of CLASSIFYING things ▸ **taxo·nom·ic** /ˌtæksəˈnɒmɪk; *NAmE* -ˈnɑːmɪk/ *adj.*

tax·pay·er /ˈtækspeɪə(r)/ *noun* a person who pays tax to the government, especially on the money that they earn

ˈtax relief (also **relief**) *noun* [U] a reduction in the amount of tax you have to pay

ˈtax return *noun* an official document in which you give details of the amount of money that you have earned so that the government can calculate how much tax you have to pay

ˈtax shelter *noun* a way of using or investing money so that you can legally avoid paying tax on it

ˈtax year *noun* (*BrE*) = FINANCIAL YEAR

tay·berry /ˈteɪbəri; *NAmE* -beri/ *noun* (*pl.* **-ies**) a dark red soft fruit that is a combination of a BLACKBERRY and a RASPBERRY

TB *abbr.* **1** /ˌtiː ˈbiː/ TUBERCULOSIS **2** (in writing) TERABYTE

Tb (also **Tbit**) *abbr.* (in writing) TERABIT

TBA /ˌtiː biː ˈeɪ/ *abbr.* (used in notices about events) to be announced: *party with live band (TBA)*

ˈT-bar *noun* **1** (also **ˈT-bar lift**) a machine which pulls two people up a mountain on SKIS together **2** a T-shaped strip of leather, etc. on a shoe

TBC /ˌtiː biː ˈsiː/ *abbr.* (used in notices about events) to be confirmed: *The four-day course will run from March 8–11 (TBC).*

ˈT-bill *abbr.* (*NAmE, informal*) = TREASURY BILL

ˈT-bone steak *noun* a thick slice of beef containing a bone in the shape of a T

tbsp (also **tbs**) *abbr.* (*pl.* **tbsp** or **tbsps**) TABLESPOONFUL: *Add 3 tbsp sugar.*

TCP/IP /ˌtiː siː ˌpiː aɪ ˈpiː/ *abbr.* (*computing*) transmission control protocol/Internet protocol (a system that controls the connection of computers to the Internet)

TD /ˌtiː ˈdiː/ *noun* the abbreviation for 'Teachta Dála', 'Member of the Dáil' (a member of the LOWER HOUSE of the parliament of the Republic of Ireland)

te (*BrE*) (*NAmE* **ti**) /tiː/ *noun* (*music*) the 7th note of a MAJOR SCALE

tea 🔑 /tiː/ *noun*
1 🔑 [U] the dried leaves (called TEA LEAVES) of the tea bush ➲ see also GREEN TEA **2** 🔑 [U] a hot drink made by pouring boiling water onto tea leaves. It may be drunk with milk or lemon and/or sugar added: *a* ***cup/mug/pot of tea*** ◇ ***lemon/iced tea*** ◇ *Would you like tea or coffee?* ◇ *Do you take sugar in your tea?* **3** 🔑 [C] a cup of tea: *Two teas, please.* **4** [U, C] a hot drink made by pouring boiling water onto the leaves of other plants: ***camomile/mint/herb, etc. tea*** ➲ see also BEEF TEA **5** [U, C] the name used by some people in Britain for the cooked meal eaten in the evening, especially when it is eaten early in the evening: *You can have your tea as soon as you come home from school.* ➲ compare DINNER, SUPPER **6** [U, C] (*BrE*) a light meal eaten in the afternoon or early evening, usually with SANDWICHES and/or biscuits and cakes and with tea to drink ➲ note at MEAL ➲ see also CREAM TEA, HIGH TEA
IDM **not for all the tea in ˈChina** (*old-fashioned*) not even for a great reward: *I wouldn't do your job. Not for all the tea in China!* ➲ more at CUP *n.*

ˈ**tea bag** *noun* a small thin paper bag containing tea leaves, which you pour boiling water onto in order to make tea

ˈ**tea break** *noun* (*BrE*) a short period of time when people stop working and drink tea, coffee, etc.

ˈ**tea caddy** (also **caddy**) *noun* (*especially BrE*) a small box with a lid that you keep tea in

tea·cake /ˈtiːkeɪk/ *noun* (*BrE*) a small flat round cake made of a bread-like mixture, usually containing dried fruit: *toasted teacakes*

tea·cart /ˈtiːkɑːt; *NAmE* -kɑːrt/ (also ˈ**tea wagon**) (both *US*) (*BrE* ˈ**tea trolley**) *noun* a small table on wheels that is used for serving drinks and food

ˈ**tea ceremony** *noun* a Japanese ceremony in which tea is served and drunk according to complicated rules

teach 0-ᴛ /tiːtʃ/ *verb* (**taught, taught** /tɔːt/)
1 0-ᴛ [I, T] to give lessons to students in a school, college, university, etc; to help sb learn sth by giving information about it: *She teaches at our local school.* ◇ *He taught for several years before becoming a writer.* ◇ **~ sth** *I'll be teaching history and sociology next term.* ◇ (*NAmE*) *to* ***teach school*** (= teach in a school) ◇ **~ sth to sb** *He teaches English to advanced students.* ◇ **~ sb sth** *He teaches them English.* **2** 0-ᴛ [T] to show sb how to do sth so that they will be able to do it themselves: **~ (sb to do) sth** *Could you teach me to do that?* ◇ **~ sb how, what, etc...** *My father taught me how to ride a bike.* **3** 0-ᴛ [T] to make sb feel or think in a different way: **~ sb to do sth** *She taught me to be less critical of other people.* ◇ **~ (sb) that...** *My parents taught me that honesty was always the best policy.* ◇ **~ sb sth** *Our experience as refugees taught us many valuable lessons.* **4** [T, no passive] (*informal*) to persuade sb not to do sth again by making them suffer so much that they are afraid to do it: **~ sb to do sth** *Lost all your money?* ***That'll teach you*** *to gamble.* ◇ *I'll teach you to call* (= punish you for calling) *me a liar!* ◇ **~ sb sth** *The accident* ***taught me a lesson*** *I'll never forget.*
IDM **teach your grandmother to suck ˈeggs** (*BrE, informal*) to tell or show sb how to do sth that they can already do well, and probably better than you can (**you can't**) **teach an old dog new ˈtricks** (*saying*) (you cannot) successfully make people change their ideas, methods of work, etc, when they have had them for a long time **teach to the ˈtest** to teach students only what is necessary in order to pass a particular test, rather than help them develop a range of skills

Vocabulary Building

Teach and teachers

Verbs

- **teach** *John teaches French at the local school.* ◇ *She taught me how to change a tyre.*
- **educate** *Our priority is to educate people about the dangers of drugs.*
- **instruct** *Members of staff should be instructed in the use of fire equipment.*
- **train** *She's a trained midwife.* ◇ *He's training the British Olympic swimming team.*
- **coach** *He's the best football player I've ever coached.* ◇ *She coaches some of the local children in maths.* (*BrE*)
- **tutor** *She tutors some of the local children in math.* (*NAmE*)

Nouns

- **teacher** *school/college teachers*
- **instructor** *a swimming/science instructor*
- **trainer** *a horse trainer* ◇ *Do you have a personal trainer?*
- **coach** *a football coach*
- **tutor** *tutors working with migrant children*

teach·able /ˈtiːtʃəbl/ *adj.* **1** (of a subject) that can be taught **2** (of a person) able to learn by being taught

teach·er 0-ᴛ /ˈtiːtʃə(r)/ *noun*
a person whose job is teaching, especially in a school: *a history/science, etc. teacher* ◇ *primary school teachers* ◇ *There is a growing need for qualified teachers of Business English.* ➲ note at TEACH

ˌ**teacher** ˈ**training** *noun* [U] the process of teaching or learning the skills you need to be a teacher in a school ▶ ˌ**teacher** ˈ**trainer** *noun*: *experienced teachers and teacher trainers*

ˈ**tea chest** *noun* (*BrE*) a large light wooden box lined with metal in which tea is transported. Tea chests are sometimes used for transporting personal possessions, for example, when moving to another home.

ˈ**teach-in** *noun* an informal lecture and discussion on a subject of public interest

teach·ing 0-ᴛ /ˈtiːtʃɪŋ/ *noun*
1 0-ᴛ [U] the work of a teacher: *She wants to go into teaching* (= make it a career). ◇ *the teaching profession* **2** 0-ᴛ [C, usually pl., U] the ideas of a particular person or group, especially about politics, religion or society, that are taught to other people: *the teachings of Lenin* ◇ *views that go against traditional Christian teaching*

ˈ**teaching assistant** *noun* **1** a person who is not a qualified teacher who helps a teacher in a school **2** (*abbr.* TA) (both *NAmE*) (also ˈ**teaching fellow** *US, BrE*) a GRADUATE student who teaches UNDERGRADUATE classes at a university or college, takes discussion or practical classes, marks written work, etc.

ˈ**teaching practice** (*BrE*) (*NAmE* ˌ**student** ˈ**teaching**) *noun* [U] the part of a course for people who are training to become teachers which involves teaching classes of students

ˈ**tea cloth** *noun* (*BrE*) = TEA TOWEL

ˈ**tea cosy** (*BrE*) (*NAmE* ˈ**tea cozy**) *noun* a cover placed over a TEAPOT in order to keep the tea warm

tea·cup /ˈtiːkʌp/ *noun* a cup in which tea is served
IDM see STORM *n.*

ˈ**tea dance** *noun* a social event held in the afternoon, especially in the past, at which people dance, drink tea, and eat a small meal

teak /tiːk/ *noun* [U] the strong hard wood of a tall Asian tree, used especially for making furniture

tea·ket·tle /ˈtiːketl/ *noun* a metal container with a lid, handle and a SPOUT, used for boiling water

teal /tiːl/ *noun* **1** [C] (*pl.* **teal**) a small wild DUCK **2** [U] (*especially NAmE*) a bluish-green colour

ˈ**tea leaf** *noun* a small piece of a dried leaf of the tea bush; used especially in the plural to describe what is left at the bottom of a cup or pot after the tea has been made

tea·light /ˈtiːlaɪt/ *noun* a small CANDLE that is used for decoration and which often gives off a pleasant smell

team 0-ᴛ **AW** /tiːm/ *noun, verb*
■ ***noun*** [C+sing./pl. v.] **1** 0-ᴛ a group of people who play a particular game or sport against another group of people: *a* ***football/baseball, etc. team*** ◇ *a* ***team event*** (= one played by groups of people rather than individual players) ◇ (*BrE*) *Whose team are you in?* ◇ (*NAmE*) *Whose team are you on?* ◇ *The team is/are not playing very well this season.* **2** 0-ᴛ a group of people who work together at a particular job: *the sales team* ◇ *a* ***team leader/member*** ◇ *A team of experts has/have been called in to investigate.* **3** two or more animals that are used together to pull a CART, etc.
■ ***verb*** [usually passive] **~ sb/sth** (**with sb/sth**) to put two or more things or people together in order to do sth or to achieve a particular effect: *He was teamed with his brother in the doubles.*
PHR V ˌ**team** ˈ**up** (**with sb**) to join with another person or group in order to do sth together ˌ**team sb/sth** ˈ**up** (**with sb**) to put two or more people or things together in order to do sth or to achieve a particular effect

ˈ**team handball** *noun* [U] (*US*) = HANDBALL

team·mate /ˈtiːmmeɪt/ *noun* a member of the same team or group as yourself

T

ˈteam player *noun* a person who is good at working as a member of a team, usually in their job

ˌteam ˈspirit *noun* [U] (*approving*) the desire and willingness of people to work together and help each other as part of a team

team·ster /ˈtiːmstə(r)/ *noun* (*NAmE*) a person whose job is driving a truck SYN **truck driver**

team·work /ˈtiːmwɜːk; *NAmE* -wɜːrk/ *noun* [U] the activity of working well together as a team: *She stressed the importance of good teamwork.*

ˈtea party *noun* a social event at which people eat cake, drink tea, etc. in the afternoon

tea·pot /ˈtiːpɒt; *NAmE* -pɑːt/ *noun* a container with a SPOUT, a handle and a lid, used for making and serving tea ➲ VISUAL VOCAB page V22 IDM see TEMPEST

tear¹ 🔑 /teə(r); *NAmE* ter/ *verb, noun* ➲ see also TEAR²

■ ***verb*** (**tore** /tɔː(r)/, **torn** /tɔːn; *NAmE* tɔːrn/)

▸ DAMAGE **1** 🔑 [T, I] to damage sth by pulling it apart or into pieces or by cutting it on sth sharp; to become damaged in this way SYN **rip**: **~ (sth) (+ adv./prep.)** *I tore my jeans on the fence.* ◇ *I tore a hole in my jeans.* ◇ *He tore the letter in two.* ◇ *a torn handkerchief* ◇ *Careful—the fabric tears very easily.* ◇ **~ sth + adj.** *I tore the package open.* **2** [T] **~ sth in sth** to make a hole in sth by force SYN **rip**: *The blast tore a hole in the wall.*

▸ REMOVE FROM STH/SB **3** 🔑 [T] **~ sth + adv./prep.** to remove sth from sth else by pulling it roughly or violently SYN **rip**: *The storm nearly tore the roof off.* ◇ *I tore another sheet from the pad.* ◇ *He tore his clothes off* (= took them off quickly and carelessly) *and dived into the lake.* **4** [T] to pull yourself/sb away by force from sb/sth that is holding you or them: **~ yourself/sb from sb/sth** *She tore herself from his grasp.* ◇ **~ yourself/sb + adj.** *He tore himself free.*

▸ INJURE MUSCLE **5** [T] **~ sth** to injure a muscle, etc. by stretching it too much: *a torn ligament*

▸ MOVE QUICKLY **6** [I] **+ adv./prep.** to move somewhere very quickly or in an excited way: *He tore off down the street.* ◇ *A truck tore past the gates.*

▸ -TORN **7** (in adjectives) very badly affected or damaged by sth: *to bring peace to a strife-torn country* ◇ *a strike-torn industry* ➲ see also WAR-TORN

IDM **tear sb/sth aˈpart, to ˈshreds, to ˈbits, etc.** to destroy or defeat sb/sth completely or criticize them or it severely: *We tore the other team apart in the second half.* ◇ *The critics tore his last movie to shreds.* **ˌtear at your ˈheart** | **ˌtear your ˈheart out** (*formal*) to strongly affect you in an emotional way **tear your ˈhair (out)** (*informal*) to show that you are very angry or anxious about sth: *She's keeping very calm—anyone else would be tearing their hair out.* **(be in) a tearing ˈhurry/ˈrush** (*especially BrE*) (to be) in a very great hurry **be torn (between A and B)** to be unable to decide or choose between two people, things or feelings: *I was torn between my parents and my friend.* **tear sb ˈoff a strip** | **tear a ˈstrip off sb** (*BrE, informal*) to speak angrily to sb who has done sth wrong **ˌthat's ˈtorn it** (*BrE, informal*) used to say that sth has happened to spoil your plans ➲ more at HEART, LIMB, LOOSE *adj.*, PIECE *n.*, SHRED *n.*

PHR V **ˌtear sb↔aˈpart/ˈup** to make sb feel very unhappy or worried SYN **rip sb apart**: *It tears me apart to think I might have hurt her feelings.* **ˌtear sth↔aˈpart 1** to destroy sth violently, especially by pulling it to pieces: *The dogs tore the fox apart.* **2** to make people in a country, an organization or other place fight or argue with each other: *Racial strife is tearing our country apart.* **3** to search a place, making it look untidy and causing damage: *They tore the room apart, looking for money.* SYN **rip sth apart** **ˈtear at sth** to pull or cut sth violently so that it tears: *He tore at the meat with his bare hands.* **ˌtear yourself aˈway (from sth)** | **ˌtear sth aˈway (from sth)** to leave somewhere even though you would prefer to stay there; to take sth away from somewhere: *Dinner's ready, if you can tear yourself away from the TV.* ◇ *She was unable to tear her eyes away from him* (= could not stop looking at him). **ˌtear sth↔ˈdown** to pull or knock down a building, wall, etc. SYN **demolish** **ˌtear ˈinto sb/sth 1** to attack sb/sth physically or with words **2** to start doing sth with a lot of energy: *They tore into their food as if they were starving.* **ˌtear sb↔ˈup** = TEAR SB APART **ˌtear sth↔ˈup** 🔑 to destroy a document, etc. by tearing it into pieces SYN **rip sth up**: *She tore up all the letters he had sent her.* ◇ (*figurative*) *He accused the leader of tearing up the party's manifesto* (= of ignoring it).

■ ***noun*** a hole that has been made in sth by tearing: *This sheet has a tear in it.* IDM see WEAR *n.*

tear² 🔑 /tɪə(r); *NAmE* tɪr/ *noun* [usually pl.] ➲ see also TEAR¹

a drop of liquid that comes out of your eye when you cry: *A tear rolled down his face.* ◇ *She left the room* ***in tears*** (= crying). ◇ *He suddenly* ***burst into tears*** (= began to cry). ◇ *As he listened to the music, his* ***eyes filled with tears***. ◇ *Their story will* ***move you to tears*** (= make you cry). ◇ *They* ***reduced her to tears*** (= made her cry, especially by being cruel or unkind). ◇ *Ann* ***wiped a tear*** *from her eye.* ◇ *The memory* ***brought a tear to her eye*** (= made her cry). ◇ *Most of the audience was* ***on the verge of tears***. ◇ *I was* ***close to tears*** *as I told them the news.* ◇ *Desperately she* ***fought back the tears*** (= tried not to cry). ◇ *to* ***shed tears*** *of happiness* ◇ *tears of pain, joy, etc.* ◇ *The* ***tears welled up*** *in his eyes.* ▸ **teary** /ˈtɪəri; *NAmE* ˈtɪri/ *adj.*: *teary eyes* ◇ *a teary smile/goodbye* IDM see BLOOD *n.*, BORED, CROCODILE, END *v.*

tear·away /ˈteərəweɪ; *NAmE* ˈter-/ *noun* (*BrE, informal*) a young person who is difficult to control and often does stupid, dangerous and/or illegal things

tear·drop /ˈtɪədrɒp; *NAmE* ˈtɪrdrɑːp/ *noun* a single tear that comes from your eye

tear duct /ˈtɪə dʌkt; *NAmE* ˈtɪr/ *noun* a tube through which tears pass from the tear GLANDS to the eye, or from the eye to the nose ➲ VISUAL VOCAB page V48

tear·ful /ˈtɪəfl; *NAmE* ˈtɪrfl/ *adj.* **1** (of a person) crying, or about to cry: *She suddenly became very tearful.* **2** (of an event, etc.) at which people feel emotional and cry: *a tearful farewell* ▸ **tear·ful·ly** /-fəli/ *adv.* **tear·ful·ness** *noun* [U]

tear gas /ˈtɪə gæs; *NAmE* ˈtɪr/ *noun* [U] a gas that makes your eyes sting and fill with tears, used by the police or army to control crowds

tear-jerker /ˈtɪə dʒɜːkə(r); *NAmE* ˈtɪr dʒɜːrkər/ *noun* (*informal*) a film/movie, story, etc. that is designed to make people feel sad SYN **weepy**

tear-off /ˈteər ɒf; *NAmE* ˈter ɔːf; ɑːf/ *adj.* [only before noun] relating to sth that can be removed by being torn off, especially part of a sheet of paper: *a tear-off slip*

ˈtea room (also **ˈtea shop**) *noun* (*BrE*) a restaurant in which tea, coffee, cakes and SANDWICHES are served

tear-stained /ˈtɪə steɪnd; *NAmE* ˈtɪr/ *adj.* (especially of sb's face or cheeks) wet with tears

tease /tiːz/ *verb, noun*

■ ***verb*** **1** [I, T] **~ (sb)** | **~ (sb) + speech** to laugh at sb and make jokes about them, either in a friendly way or in order to annoy or embarrass them: *Don't get upset—I was only teasing.* ◇ *I used to get teased about my name.* **2** [T] **~ sth** to annoy an animal, especially by touching it, pulling its tail, etc. **3** [I, T] **~ (sb)** (*disapproving*) to make sb sexually excited, especially when you do not intend to have sex with them **4** [T] **~ sth (+ adv./prep.)** to pull sth gently apart into separate pieces: *to tease wool into strands* **5** (*NAmE*) (*BrE* **back·comb**) [T] **~ sth** to COMB your hair in the opposite direction to the way it grows so that it looks thicker

PHR V **ˌtease sth↔ˈout 1** to remove knots from hair, wool, etc. by gently pulling or brushing it **2** to spend time trying to find out information or the meaning of sth, especially when this is complicated or difficult: *The teacher helped them tease out the meaning of the poem.*

■ ***noun*** [usually sing.] **1** a person who likes to play tricks and jokes on other people, especially by telling them sth that is not true or by not telling them sth that they want to know **2** an act that is intended as a trick or joke **3** (*disapproving*) a person who pretends to be attracted to sb, makes them sexually excited and then refuses to have sex with them

T

tea·sel (also **tea·zle**) /ˈtiːzl/ *noun* a plant which has large flowers with SPIKES, used in the past for brushing cloth to give it a smooth surface

teaser /ˈtiːzə(r)/ *noun* **1** (*informal*) a difficult problem or question ➲ see also BRAIN-TEASER **2** (also ˈ**teaser ad**) an advertisement for a product that does not mention the name of the product or say much about it but is intended to make people interested and likely to pay attention to later advertisements

ˈ**tea set** (*BrE*) (also ˈ**tea service** *NAmE, BrE*) *noun* a set consisting of a TEAPOT, sugar bowl, cups, plates, etc, used for serving tea

ˈ**tea shop** *noun* (*BrE*) = TEA ROOM

teas·ing·ly /ˈtiːzɪŋli/ *adv.* **1** in a way that is intended to make sb feel embarrassed, annoyed, etc. **2** in a way that suggests sth and makes sb want to know more **3** in a way that is intended to make sb sexually excited

tea·spoon /ˈtiːspuːn/ *noun* **1** a small spoon for putting sugar into tea and other drinks ➲ VISUAL VOCAB page V19 **2** (also **tea·spoon·ful** /-fʊl/) (*abbr.* **tsp**) the amount a teaspoon can hold: *Add two teaspoons of salt.*

teat /tiːt/ *noun* **1** (*BrE*) (*NAmE* **nip·ple**) the rubber part at the end of a baby's bottle that the baby sucks in order to get milk, etc. from the bottle **2** one of the parts of a female animal's body that the young animals suck in order to get milk

tea·time /ˈtiːtaɪm/ *noun* [U] (*BrE*) the time during the afternoon or early evening when people have the meal called tea

ˈ**tea towel** (also ˈ**tea cloth**) (both *BrE*) (*NAmE* **dish·towel**) *noun* a small towel used for drying cups, plates, knives, etc. after they have been washed ➲ VISUAL VOCAB page V22

ˈ**tea tree** *noun* a small Australian and New Zealand tree. The oil from its leaves can be used to treat wounds and skin problems.

ˈ**tea trolley** (*BrE*) (*US* ˈ**tea·cart**, ˈ**tea wagon**) *noun* a small table on wheels that is used for serving drinks and food

tea·zle *noun* = TEASEL

tebi·bit /ˈtebibɪt/ *noun* (*abbr.* **Tib**, **Tibit**) (*computing*) = TERABIT (2)

tebi·byte /ˈtebibaɪt/ *noun* (*abbr.* **TiB**) (*computing*) = TERABYTE (2)

tech /tek/ *noun* (*BrE, informal*) = TECHNICAL COLLEGE ➲ see also HIGH-TECH, LOW-TECH

techie (also **techy**) /ˈteki/ *noun* (*pl.* **-ies**) (*informal*) a person who is expert in or enthusiastic about technology, especially computers

tech·ne·tium /tekˈniːʃiəm/ *noun* [U] (*symb.* **Tc**) a chemical element. Technetium is found naturally as a product of URANIUM or made artificially from MOLYBDENUM.

tech·nical 0‑w AW /ˈteknɪkl/ *adj.*
1 0‑w [usually before noun] connected with the practical use of machinery, methods, etc. in science and industry: *We offer free technical support for those buying our software.* ◇ *a technical education* ◇ *technical drawing* (= especially taught as a school subject) **2** 0‑w [usually before noun] connected with the skills needed for a particular job, sport, art, etc: *Skaters score extra points for technical complexity.* **3** 0‑w connected with a particular subject and therefore difficult to understand if you do not know about that subject: *The article is full of* ***technical terms****.* ◇ *The guide is too technical for a non-specialist.* **4** 0‑w [only before noun] connected with the details of a law or set of rules: *Their lawyers spent days arguing over technical details.*

ˈ**technical college** (also *BrE informal* **tech**) *noun* a college where students can study mainly practical subjects

ˌ**technical ˈfoul** *noun* (in BASKETBALL) an act of breaking certain rules of the game, especially ones relating to fair play

ˌ**technical ˈhitch** *noun* a temporary problem or difficulty, especially one caused by a piece of machinery or equipment

tech·ni·cal·ity /ˌteknɪˈkæləti/ *noun* (*pl.* **-ies**) **1 technicalities** [pl.] the small details of how to do sth or how sth works **2** a small detail in a law or set of rules, especially one that does not seem fair: *She was released* ***on a technicality*** (= because of a small detail in the law).

ˌ**technical ˈknockout** *noun* (in BOXING) a victory when the opponent is still standing but is unable to continue fighting

tech·nic·al·ly AW /ˈteknɪkli/ *adv.* **1** according to the exact meaning, facts etc: ***Technically*** *(****speaking****), the two countries are still at war.* ◇ *It is still* ***technically possible*** *for them to win* (= but it seems unlikely). **2** in a way that is connected with the skills needed for a particular job, sport, art, etc: *As a musician, she is technically accomplished.* **3** in a way that is connected with the practical use of machinery, methods, etc. in science and industry: *a technically advanced society* ◇ *In those days recording sound was not* ***technically possible****.*

ˌ**technical supˈport** (also *informal* ˌ**tech supˈport**) *noun* **1** [U] technical help that a company gives to customers using their computers or other products: *All our software licences include technical support.* **2** [U+sing./pl. v.] a department in a company that provides technical help to its workers or customers: *I called tech support and they fixed it.*

tech·ni·cian /tekˈnɪʃn/ *noun* **1** a person whose job is keeping a particular type of equipment or machinery in good condition: *laboratory technicians* **2** a person who is very skilled at the technical aspects of an art, a sport, etc.

Tech·ni·color™ /ˈteknɪkʌlə(r)/ *noun* [U] a process of producing colour film, as used in cinema films/movies

tech·ni·col·our (*especially US* **tech·ni·color**) /ˈteknɪkʌlə(r)/ *noun* [U] (*informal*) the state of having many bright colours: *The rooms were painted in* ***glorious technicolour****.*

tech·ni·kon /ˈteknɪkɒn; *NAmE* -kɑːn/ (also *informal* **tech**) *noun* (*SAfrE*) a type of college or university that teaches mainly practical subjects

tech·nique 0‑w AW /tekˈniːk/ *noun*
1 0‑w [C] a particular way of doing sth, especially one in which you have to learn special skills: *The artist combines different techniques in the same painting.* ◇ *marketing techniques* **2** 0‑w [U, sing.] the skill with which sb is able to do sth practical: *Her technique has improved a lot over the past season.*

techno /ˈteknəʊ; *NAmE* -noʊ/ *noun* [U] a type of fast, electronic dance music, typically with little or no singing

techno- /ˈteknəʊ; *NAmE* -noʊ/ *combining form* (in nouns, adjectives and adverbs) connected with technology: *technophobe* (= a person who is afraid of technology)

tech·no·bab·ble /ˈteknəʊbæbl; *NAmE* -noʊ-/ *noun* [U] (*informal, disapproving*) words or expressions connected with computers and technology that are difficult for ordinary people to understand

tech·no·cracy /tekˈnɒkrəsi; *NAmE* -ˈnɑːk-/ *noun* [U, C] (*pl.* **-ies**) a social or political system in which people with scientific knowledge have a lot of power

tech·no·crat /ˈteknəkræt/ *noun* an expert in science, engineering, etc. who has a lot of power in politics and/or industry ▸ **tech·no·crat·ic** /ˌteknəˈkrætɪk/ *adj.* [usually before noun]

tech·nolo·gist /tekˈnɒlədʒɪst; *NAmE* -ˈnɑːl-/ *noun* an expert in technology

tech·nol·ogy 0‑w AW /tekˈnɒlədʒi; *NAmE* -ˈnɑːl-/ *noun* (*pl.* **-ies**)
1 0‑w [U, C] scientific knowledge used in practical ways in industry, for example in designing new machines: *science and technology* ◇ *recent advances in medical technology* ◇ *to make use of the most modern technologies* ➲ see also HIGH TECHNOLOGY, INFORMATION TECHNOLOGY **2** 0‑w [U] machinery or equipment designed using technology: *The company has invested in the latest technology.* ▸ **tech·no·logic·al** AW /ˌteknəˈlɒdʒɪkl; *NAmE* -ˈlɑːdʒ-/

T

adj.: *technological advances* ◇ *technological change* ◇ *a major technological breakthrough* **tech·no·logic·al·ly** AW /-kli/ *adv.*: *technologically advanced*

tech·no·phile /ˈteknəʊfaɪl; *NAmE* -noʊ-/ *noun* a person who is enthusiastic about new technology

tech·no·phobe /ˈteknəʊfəʊb; *NAmE* -noʊfoʊb/ *noun* a person who is afraid of, dislikes or avoids new technology

ˈ**tech support** *noun* (*informal*) = TECHNICAL SUPPORT

techy = TECHIE

tec·ton·ic /tekˈtɒnɪk; *NAmE* -ˈtɑːnɪk/ *adj.* [only before noun] (*geology*) connected with the structure of the earth's surface ➲ see also PLATE TECTONICS

teddy bear /ˈtedi beə(r); *NAmE* ber/ (*BrE* also **teddy** *pl.* -ies) *noun* a soft toy BEAR ➲ VISUAL VOCAB page V32

ˈ**Teddy boy** (also *informal* **ted** /ted/) *noun* (in Britain in the 1950s) a member of a group of young men who liked ROCK AND ROLL music and who had their own style of dressing (usually wearing narrow trousers/pants, long jackets and pointed shoes)

te·di·ous /ˈtiːdiəs/ *adj.* lasting or taking too long and not interesting SYN **boring**: *The journey soon became tedious.* ◇ *We had to listen to the tedious details of his operation.* ➲ SYNONYMS at BORING ▶ **te·di·ous·ly** *adv.* **te·di·ous·ness** *noun* [U]

te·dium /ˈtiːdiəm/ *noun* [U] the quality of being boring SYN **boredom**: *She longed for something to relieve the tedium of everyday life.*

tee /tiː/ *noun, verb*

■ ***noun*** **1** a flat area on a GOLF COURSE from which players hit the ball: *to drive off from the first tee* ◇ *a tee shot* **2** a small piece of plastic or wood that you stick in the ground to support a GOLF ball before you hit it IDM see T

■ ***verb*** (teed, teed)

PHR V ˌ**tee** ˈ**off** to hit a GOLF ball from a tee, especially at the start of a match ˌ**tee sb**↔ˈ**off** (*NAmE, informal*) to make sb angry or annoyed ˌ**tee sth**↔ˈ**up** | ˌ**tee** ˈ**up** to prepare to hit a GOLF ball by placing it on a tee

teed off /ˌtiːd ˈɒf; *NAmE* ˈɔːf; ˈɑːf/ *adj.* (*NAmE, informal*) annoyed or angry

tee-hee /ˌtiː ˈhiː/ *noun* used to represent the sound of a quiet laugh

teem /tiːm/ *verb* [I] (usually **be teeming**) (of rain) to fall heavily SYN **pour**: *The rain was teeming down.* ◇ ***It was teeming with*** *rain.*

PHR V ˈ**teem with sth** (usually **be** ˈ**teeming with sth**) to be full of people, animals, etc. moving around: *The streets were teeming with tourists.* ◇ *a river teeming with fish*

teem·ing /ˈtiːmɪŋ/ *adj.* present in large numbers; full of people, animals, etc. that are moving around: *teeming insects* ◇ *the teeming streets of the city*

T

teen·age /ˈtiːneɪdʒ/ (also *informal* **teen** especially in *NAmE*) *adj.* [usually before noun] between 13 and 19 years old; connected with people of this age: *teenage girls/boys* ◇ *teenage rebellion* ◇ *teen magazines*

teen·aged /ˈtiːneɪdʒd/ *adj.* between 13 and 19 years old: *They have two teenaged daughters.*

teen·ager /ˈtiːneɪdʒə(r)/ (also *informal* **teen** especially in *NAmE*) *noun* a person who is between 13 and 19 years old: *a magazine aimed at teenagers*

teens /tiːnz/ *noun* [pl.] the years of a person's life when they are between 13 and 19 years old: *She began writing poetry* ***in her teens.*** ◇ *to be in your* ***early/late teens***

teeny /ˈtiːni/ *adj.* (*informal*) (teen·ier, teeni·est) **1** (also **teeny-weeny** /ˌtiːni ˈwiːni/, **teensy** /ˈtiːnzi/, **teensy-weensy** /ˌtiːnzi ˈwiːnzi/) very small SYN **tiny** **2** connected with people between 13 and 19 years old: *teeny magazines*

teeny-bopper /ˈtiːni bɒpə(r); *NAmE* bɑːp-/ *noun* (*old-fashioned, informal*) a young girl between the ages of about 10 and 13, who is very interested in pop music, fashionable clothes, etc.

tee·pee = TEPEE

ˈ**tee shirt** = T-SHIRT

tee·ter /ˈtiːtə(r)/ *verb* [I] to stand or move in an unsteady way so that you look as if you are going to fall: *She teetered after him in her high-heeled shoes.*

IDM **teeter on the** ˈ**brink/**ˈ**edge of sth** to be very close to a very unpleasant or dangerous situation: *The country is teetering on the brink of civil war.*

ˈ**teeter-totter** *noun* (*NAmE*) = SEE-SAW

teeth *pl.* of TOOTH

teethe /tiːð/ *verb* [I] when a baby **is teething**, its first teeth are starting to grow

ˈ**teething troubles** (also ˈ**teething problems**) *noun* [pl.] small problems that a company, product, system, etc. has at the beginning

tee·total /ˌtiːˈtəʊtl; *NAmE* -ˈtoʊtl/ *adj.* never drinking alcohol: *He's strictly teetotal.* ▶ **tee·total·ism** *noun* [U]

tee·total·ler (*BrE*) (*US* **tee·total·er**) /ˌtiːˈtəʊtlə(r); *NAmE* -ˈtoʊ-/ *noun* a person who does not drink alcohol

TEFL /ˈtefl/ *abbr.* (*BrE*) teaching English as a foreign language

Tef·lon™ /ˈteflɒn; *NAmE* ˈteflɑːn/ *noun, adj.*

■ ***noun*** [U] a substance used especially to cover the inside of cooking pans, that stops food from sticking to them

■ ***adj.*** (especially of a politician) still having a good reputation after making a mistake or doing sth that is not legal: *The Teflon Prime Minister has survived another crisis.*

tel. (also **Tel.**) *abbr.* (in writing) telephone number

telco /ˈtelkəʊ; *NAmE* -koʊ/ *noun* (*pl.* -os) (used especially in newspapers) a TELECOMMUNICATIONS company: *Telcos were struggling to make money from broadband services.*

tele- /ˈteli/ *combining form* (in nouns, verbs, adjectives and adverbs) **1** over a long distance; far: *telepathy* ◇ *telescopic* **2** connected with television: *teletext* **3** done using a telephone: *telesales*

tele·bank·ing /ˈtelibæŋkɪŋ/ *noun* [U] = TELEPHONE BANKING

tele·cam·era /ˈtelikæmərə/ *noun* a video camera used in VIDEOCONFERENCING

tele·cast /ˈtelikɑːst; *NAmE* -kæst/ *noun* (*especially NAmE*) a broadcast on television ▶ **tele·cast** *verb* (**tele·cast, tele·cast**) [usually passive]: **~ sth** *The event will be telecast simultaneously to nearly 150 cities.* **tele·cast·er** *noun*

tele·com·mu·ni·ca·tions /ˌtelikəˌmjuːnɪˈkeɪʃnz/ (also *informal* **tele·coms** /ˈtelikɒmz; *NAmE* -kɑːmz/) *noun* [pl.] the technology of sending signals, images and messages over long distances by radio, telephone, television, SATELLITE, etc: *technological developments in telecommunications* ◇ *the telecommunications industry* ▶ **tele·com·mu·ni·ca·tion** (also *informal* **tele·com** /ˈtelikɒm; *NAmE* -kɑːm/) *adj.* [only before noun]: *a telecommunication company*

tele·com·mute /ˌtelikəˈmjuːt/ *verb* [I] to work from home, communicating with your office, customers and others by telephone, email, etc. ▶ **tele·com·muter** *noun* SYN **teleworker** **tele·com·mut·ing** *noun* [U] SYN **teleworking**

tele·con·fer·ence /ˈtelikɒnfərəns; *NAmE* -kɑːn-/ *noun* a conference or discussion at which members are in different places and speak to each other using telephone and video connections ▶ **tele·con·fer·ence** *verb* [I] **tele·con·fer·enc·ing** /ˈtelikɒnfərənsɪŋ; *NAmE* -kɑːn-/ *noun* [U]

tele·cot·tage /ˈtelikɒtɪdʒ; *NAmE* -kɑːt-/ *noun* a room or small building in a countryside area that is filled with computer equipment for the use of people living in the area

tele·film /ˈtelifɪlm/ *noun* a film/movie that is made specially to be shown on television

tele·gen·ic /ˌtelɪˈdʒenɪk/ *adj.* a **telegenic** person looks good on television

tele·gram /ˈtelɪɡræm/ *noun* a message sent by TELEGRAPH and then printed and given to sb

tele·graph /ˈtelɪɡrɑːf; *NAmE* -ɡræf/ *noun, verb*
- ***noun*** [U] a method of sending messages over long distances, using wires that carry electrical signals
- ***verb* 1** [I, T] **~ (sth)** to send a message by telegraph **2** [T] **~ sth** to make it clear to people what you are going to do, often without intending to

tele·graph·ic /ˌtelɪˈɡræfɪk/ *adj.* connected with sending messages by telegraph: *You will need to arrange a telegraphic transfer from your bank to ours.*

ˈtelegraph pole (*BrE*) (*NAmE* **ˈtelephone pole**) *noun* a tall wooden pole used for carrying telephone or telegraph wires high above the ground

tel·eg·raphy /təˈleɡrəfi/ *noun* [U] the process of sending messages by telegraph

tele·kin·esis /ˌtelɪkɪˈniːsɪs; *BrE* also -kaɪˈn-/ *noun* [U] the ability to move objects without touching them, using mental powers

tele·mark /ˈtelɪmɑːk; *NAmE* -mɑːrk/ *noun* [U] (in SKIING or SKI JUMPING) a style of turning or landing with one SKI forward and bent knees

tele·mar·ket·ing /ˈtelimɑːkɪtɪŋ; *NAmE* -mɑːrk-/ (*BrE* also **tele·sales**) *noun* [U] a method of selling things and taking orders for sales by telephone

tele·mat·ics /ˌtelɪˈmætɪks/ *noun* [U] the use or study of technology which allows information to be sent over long distances using computers

tele·meter /ˈtelimiːtə(r)/ *noun* (*technical*) a device for sending, receiving and measuring scientific data over a long distance ▸ **tele·meter** *verb*: **~ sth (to sth)** *Data from these instruments is telemetered to the laboratory.*

tel·em·etry /təˈlemətri/ *noun* [U] (*technical*) the process of using special equipment to send, receive and measure scientific data over long distances

tele·ology /ˌtiːliˈɒlədʒi; *NAmE* -ˈɑːlə-/ *noun* [U, sing.] (*philosophy*) the theory that events and developments are meant to achieve a purpose and happen because of that ▸ **teleo·logic·al** /ˌtiːliəˈlɒdʒɪkl; *NAmE* -ˈlɑːdʒ-/ *adj.*

tele·op·er·ate /ˌteliˈɒpəreɪt; *NAmE* -ˈɑːpə-/ *verb* **~ sth (from sth)** to operate a machine which is not in the same place as you: *Equipment on the space station is teleoperated from earth.*

tele·path·ic /ˌtelɪˈpæθɪk/ *adj.* **1** using telepathy: *telepathic communication* **2** (of a person) able to communicate by telepathy: *How do I know what he's thinking? I'm not telepathic!* ▸ **tele·path·ic·al·ly** /-kli/ *adv.*

tel·ep·athy /təˈlepəθi/ *noun* [U] the direct communication of thoughts or feelings from one person to another without using speech, writing, or any other normal method

tele·phone 🔑 /ˈtelɪfəʊn; *NAmE* -foʊn/ *noun, verb*
- ***noun* 1** 🔑 [C, U] a system for talking to sb else over long distances, using wires or radio; a machine used for this: *The* ***telephone rang*** *and Pat answered it.* ◇ *You can reserve seats* ***over the telephone.*** ◇ *I need to* ***make a telephone call.*** ◇ ***telephone lines/networks/services*** ➲ COLLOCATIONS at PHONE **2** 🔑 [C] the part of the telephone that you hold in your hand and speak into SYN **handset, receiver** ➲ see also PHONE

IDM **be on the ˈtelephone 1** to be using the telephone: *He's on the telephone at the moment.* ◇ *You're wanted* (= sb wants to speak to you) *on the telephone.* **2** (*BrE*) to have a telephone in your home or place of work: *We're not on the telephone at the cottage.*
- ***verb*** 🔑 [I, T] (*formal, especially BrE*) to speak to sb by telephone SYN **call, phone**: *Please write or telephone for details.* ◇ *He telephoned to say he'd be late.* ◇ **~ sth** *You can telephone your order 24 hours a day.* ◇ *I was about to telephone the police.* ➲ note at PHONE

ˌtelephone ˈbanking (also **ˈtele·bank·ing**) *noun* [U] activities relating to your bank account, which you do using the telephone

ˈtelephone booth *noun* = PHONE BOOTH

ˈtelephone box *noun* (*BrE*) = PHONE BOX

ˈtelephone directory (also **ˈphone book, ˈtelephone book**) *noun* a book that lists the names, addresses and telephone numbers of people in a particular area: *to look up a number in the telephone directory*

ˈtelephone exchange (also **exchange**) *noun* a place where telephone calls are connected so that people can speak to each other

ˈtelephone kiosk *noun* (*BrE*) = PHONE BOX

ˈtelephone number (also **ˈphone number**) *noun* the number of a particular telephone, that you use when you make a call to it

ˈtelephone pole (*NAmE*) (*BrE* **ˈtelegraph pole**) *noun* a tall wooden pole used for carrying telephone or telegraph wires high above the ground

ˈtelephone tapping (also **ˈphone tapping**) *noun* [U] the practice of connecting a piece of equipment to a telephone in order to listen secretly to other people's telephone conversations

tel·eph·on·ist /təˈlefənɪst/ *noun* (*BrE*) = OPERATOR

tel·eph·ony /təˈlefəni/ *noun* [U] the process of sending messages and signals by telephone

tele·photo lens /ˌtelifəʊtəʊ ˈlenz; *NAmE* -foʊtoʊ/ *noun* a camera LENS that produces a large image of an object that is far away and allows you to take photographs of it

tele·port /ˈtelipɔːt; *NAmE* -pɔːrt/ *verb* [I, T] **~ (sb/sth)** (usually in SCIENCE FICTION) to move sb/sth immediately from one place to another a distance away, using special equipment; to be moved in this way: *The search party was teleported down to the planet's surface.* ▸ **tele·por·ta·tion** /ˌtelipɔːˈteɪʃn; *NAmE* -pɔːrˈt-/ *noun* [U]

tele·print·er /ˈteliprɪntə(r)/ (*NAmE* also **tele·type·writer**) *noun* a machine that prints out TELEX messages that have been typed in another place and sent by telephone lines

tele·prompt·er /ˈteliprɒmptə(r); *NAmE* -prɑːm-/ (*especially NAmE*) (*BrE* also **Auto·cue™**) *noun* a device used by people who are speaking in public, especially on television, which displays the words that they have to say

tele·sales /ˈteliseɪlz/ (*BrE*) (also **tele·mar·ket·ing** *NAmE, BrE*) *noun* [U] a method of selling things and taking orders for sales by telephone

tele·scope /ˈtelɪskəʊp; *NAmE* -skoʊp/ *noun, verb*
- ***noun*** a piece of equipment shaped like a tube, containing LENSES, that you look through to make objects that are far away appear larger and nearer: *to look at the stars through a telescope* ➲ picture at BINOCULARS ➲ see also RADIO TELESCOPE
- ***verb* 1** [I, T] **~ (sth)** to become shorter, or make sth shorter, by sliding sections inside one another **2** [T] **~ sth (into sth)** to reduce sth so that it happens in less time: *Three episodes have been telescoped into a single programme.*

tele·scop·ic /ˌtelɪˈskɒpɪk; *NAmE* -ˈskɑːpɪk/ *adj.* **1** connected with or using a telescope; making things look larger as a telescope does: *a rifle with a telescopic sight* **2** made of sections that can slide into each other to make the object longer or shorter: *a telescopic aerial* ▸ **tele·scop·ic·al·ly** /-kli/ *adv.*

tele·shop·ping /ˈteliʃɒpɪŋ; *NAmE* -ʃɑːp-/ *noun* [U] shopping that is done using the telephone or television

tele·text /ˈtelitekst/ *noun* [U] a service providing written news and information using television: *See if the results are* ***on teletext.***

tele·thon /ˈteləθɒn; *NAmE* -θɑːn/ *noun* a very long television show, broadcast to raise money for charity

tele·type·writer /ˌteliˈtaɪpraɪtə(r)/ *noun* (*NAmE*) = TELEPRINTER

tele·van·gel·ist /ˌtelɪˈvændʒəlɪst/ *noun* (especially in the US) a person who appears regularly on television to try to persuade people to become Christians and to give money ▸ **tele·van·gel·ism** *noun* [U]

T

tele·vise /ˈtelɪvaɪz/ *verb* [usually passive] **~ sth** to broadcast sth on television: *a televised debate* ◇ *to televise a novel* ◇ *The speech will be televised live.*

Collocations

Television

Watching

- **watch** television/TV/a show/(*BrE*) a programme/(*NAmE*) a program/a documentary/a pilot/a rerun/a repeat
- **see** (*especially BrE*) an ad/(*especially NAmE*) a commercial/the news/the weather
- **catch/miss** a show/a programme/a program/an episode/the news
- **pick up/reach for/grab** the remote (control)
- **change/switch** channel
- **surf (through)**/(*especially NAmE*) **flip through**/(*especially BrE*) **flick through** the channels
- **sit in front of/switch on/switch off/turn on/turn off** the television/the TV/the TV set
- **have/install** satellite (TV)/cable (TV)/a satellite dish

Showing

- **show** a programme/a documentary/an ad/a commercial
- **screen** a programme/a documentary
- **run** an ad/a commercial
- **broadcast**/(*especially NAmE*) **air/repeat** a show/a programme/a documentary/an episode/a series
- **go out/air/be recorded** live
- **attract/draw (in)/pull (in)** viewers
- **be a hit with** viewers/audiences/critics
- **get** (low/high) ratings

Appearing

- **be on/appear on** television/TV/a TV show
- **take part in** a phone-in/a game show/a quiz show/a reality TV show
- **host** a show/a programme/series/a game show/a quiz show/a talk show/(*BrE*) a chat show
- **be/become/work as a** (*BrE*) TV presenter/talk-show host/sports commentator/anchorman/(*BrE*) newsreader
- **read/present** the news
- **appear/perform** live (on TV)

Programme-making

- **do/film/make** a show/a programme/a documentary/an episode/a pilot/a series/an ad/a commercial
- **work on** a soap (opera)/a pilot (episode)/a sitcom
- **write/produce** a drama/sitcom/spin-off/comedy series

tele·vi·sion O-w /ˈtelɪvɪʒn/ *noun* (*abbr.* TV)
1 O-w (also **ˈtelevision set**) (also *BrE informal* **telly**) [C] a piece of electrical equipment with a screen on which you can watch programmes with moving pictures and sounds: *a **colour television*** ◇ *a **widescreen television*** ◇ *a **plasma screen television*** ◇ *to **turn the television on/off*** **2** O-w (also *BrE informal* **telly**) [U] the programmes broadcast on television: *We don't do much in the evenings except **watch television**.* **3** O-w [U] the system, process or business of broadcasting television programmes: ***satellite/terrestrial/cable/digital television*** ◇ *the television news* ◇ *a television documentary* ◇ *a **television company/presenter*** ◇ *I'd like to work **in television*** (= for a television company). ➲ see also CABLE TELEVISION, CLOSED-CIRCUIT TELEVISION
IDM **on (the) ˈtelevision** O-w (also *informal* **on TV**) (also *BrE informal* **on the ˈtelly**) being broadcast by television; appearing in a television programme: *What's on television tonight?* ◇ *Is there anything good on the telly tonight?* ◇ *It was on TV yesterday.* ◇ *I recognize you. Aren't you on television?*

tele·vis·ual /ˌteliˈvɪʒuəl/ *adj.* relating to or suitable for television: *a major televisual event*

tele·work·ing /ˈteliwɜːkɪŋ; *NAmE* -wɜːrk-/ *noun* [U] (*BrE*) the practice of working from home, communicating with your office, customers and others by telephone, email, etc. SYN **telecommuting** ▸ **tele·worker** *noun* SYN **telecommuter**

telex /ˈteleks/ *noun, verb*
■ ***noun*** **1** [U] an international system of communication in which messages are typed on a special machine and sent by the telephone system **2** [C] a message sent or received by telex **3** [C] (*informal*) a machine for sending and receiving messages by telex
■ ***verb*** [I, T] **~ (sth)** to send a message by telex

tell O-w /tel/ *verb* (**told**, **told** /təʊld; *NAmE* toʊld/)
▸ GIVE INFORMATION **1** O-w [T] (of a person) to give information to sb by speaking or writing: **~ sth to sb** *He told the news to everybody he saw.* ◇ **~ sb sth** *He told everybody he saw the news.* ◇ *Did she tell you her name?* ◇ ***What did I tell you?*** (= you should have listened to my advice) ◇ **~ sb (about sth)** *Why wasn't I told about the accident?* ◇ **~ sb/yourself (that)...** *They've told us (that) they're not coming.* ◇ ***I kept telling myself** (that) everything was OK.* ◇ *Are you telling me you didn't have any help with this?* (= I don't believe what you have said) ◇ **~ sb where, what, etc...** *Tell me where you live.* ◇ **~ sb + speech** *'I'm ready to go now,' he told her.* ➲ note at SAY **2** O-w [T] (of some writing, an instrument, a sign, etc.) to give information about sth: **~ sb sth** *The advertisement told us very little about the product.* ◇ **~ sb how, where, etc...** *This gauge tells you how much fuel you have left.* ◇ **~ sb (that)...** *The sound of his breathing told her (that) he was asleep.*
▸ EXPRESS IN WORDS **3** O-w [T] to express sth in words: **~ sth** *to **tell stories/jokes/lies*** ◇ *Are you sure you're **telling the truth**?* ◇ **~ sb how, what, etc...** ***I can't tell you** how happy I am.*
▸ SECRET **4** [I] (*informal*) to let sb know a secret: *Promise you won't tell.* ◇ *'Who are you going out with tonight?' '**That would be telling!**'* (= it's a secret)
▸ ORDER **5** O-w [T] to order or advise sb to do sth: **~ sb/yourself to do sth** *He was told to sit down and wait.* ◇ *There was a sign telling motorists to slow down.* ◇ *I kept telling myself to keep calm.* ◇ **~ sb sth** *Do what I tell you.* ◇ **~ sb** *Children must **do as they're told**.* ◇ **~ sb what, when, etc...** *Don't tell me what to do!* ◇ **~ sb (that)...** *The doctor told me (that) I should eat less fat.* ➲ SYNONYMS at ORDER ➲ note at SAY
▸ KNOW/JUDGE **6** O-w [I, T] (not used in the progressive tenses) to know, see or judge sth correctly: *I think he's happy. **It's hard to tell.*** ◇ ***As far as I can tell**, she's enjoying the course.* ◇ **~ (that)...** *I could tell (that) he was angry from his expression.* ◇ **~ how, if, etc...** *'That's not an original.' 'How can you tell?'* ◇ *The only way to tell if you like something is by trying it.*
▸ DISTINGUISH **7** O-w [T] (not used in the progressive tenses or in the passive) to distinguish one thing or person from another: **~ sth** *It was hard to **tell the difference between** the two versions.* ◇ **~ A from B** *Can you tell Tom from his twin brother?* ◇ **~ A and B apart** *It's difficult to **tell them apart**.* ◇ **~ which, what, etc...** *The kittens look exactly alike—how can you **tell which is which**?*
▸ HAVE EFFECT **8** [I] **~ (on sb)** to have an effect on sb/sth, especially a bad one: *The strain was beginning to tell on the rescue team.*
IDM **all ˈtold** with all people, etc. counted and included: *There are 52 people coming, all told.* **don't ˈtell me** (*informal*) used to say that you know or can guess what sb is going to say, especially because it is typical of them: *Don't tell me you were late again!* **I/I'll ˌtell you ˈwhat** (*informal*) used to introduce a suggestion: *I'll tell you what—let's stay in instead.* **I ˈtell you** | **I can ˈtell you** | **I'm ˈtelling you** (*informal*) used to emphasize what you are saying, especially when it is surprising or difficult to believe: *It isn't cheap, I can tell you!* ◇ *I'm telling you, that's exactly what she said.* **I ˈtold you (so)** (*informal*) used when sth bad has

T

happened, to remind sb that you warned them about it and they did not listen to you **ˌlive, etc. to ˌtell the ˈtale** to survive a difficult or dangerous experience so that you can tell others what really happened **tell a ˈdifferent story/tale** to give some information that is different from what you expect or have been told **tell its own tale/story** to explain itself, without needing any further explanation or comment: *Her face told its own story.* **ˈtell me** (*informal*) used to introduce a question: *Tell me, have you had lunch yet?* **ˈtell me about it** (*informal*) used to say that you understand what sb is talking about and have had the same experience: *'I get so annoyed with Steve!' 'Tell me about it. He drives me crazy.'* **tell me aˈnother!** (*informal*) used to tell sb that you do not believe what they have said **tell ˈtales (about sth/on sb)** (*BrE*) to tell sb about sth that another person has done wrong ➲ related noun TELLTALE **tell the ˈtime** (*BrE*) (*NAmE* **tell ˈtime**) to read the time from a clock, etc: *She's only five—she hasn't learnt to tell the time yet.* **tell sb where to get ˈoff/where they can get ˈoff** (*BrE, informal*) to make it clear to sb that you will no longer accept their bad behaviour **tell sb where to ˈput/ˈstick sth | tell sb what they can ˈdo with sth** (*informal*) to make it clear to sb that you are angry and are rejecting what they are offering you **there's no ˈtelling** used to say that it is impossible to know what happened or will happen: *There's no telling how they'll react.* **to tell (you) the ˈtruth** (*informal*) used when admitting sth: *To tell the truth, I fell asleep in the middle of her talk.* **you can never ˈtell | you never can ˈtell** (*saying*) you can never be sure, for example because things are not always what they appear to be **you're telling ˈme!** (*informal*) I completely agree with you ➲ more at HEAR, KISS *v.*, LITTLE *adj.*, THING, TIME *n.*, TRUTH

PHR V **ˌtell aˈgainst sb** (*BrE, formal*) to be a disadvantage to sb: *Her lack of experience told against her.* **ˈtell of sth** (*formal* or *literary*) to make sth known; to give an account of sth: *notices telling of the proposed job cuts* **ˌtell sb↔ˈoff (for sth/for doing sth)** (*informal*) to speak angrily to sb for doing sth wrong SYN **scold**: *I told the boys off for making so much noise.* ◇ *Did you get told off?* ➲ related noun TELLING-OFF **ˈtell on sb** (*informal*) to tell a person in authority about sth bad that sb has done: *Promise not to tell on me!*

ˌtell-ˈall *adj.* [only before noun] (of a book, an interview in a newspaper or magazine, etc.) in which sb, usually sb famous, admits sth that may shock people: *a tell-all book/memoir/autobiography*

tell·er /ˈtelə(r)/ *noun* **1** a person whose job is to receive and pay out money in a bank **2** a machine that pays out money automatically: *automatic teller machines* **3** a person whose job is to count votes, especially in a parliament **4** (usually in compounds) a person who tells stories, etc: *a foul-mouthed teller of lies* ➲ see also FORTUNE-TELLER, STORYTELLER

tell·ing /ˈtelɪŋ/ *adj.* **1** having a strong or important effect; effective: *a telling argument* **2** showing effectively what sb/sth is really like, but often without intending to: *The number of homeless people is a telling comment on the state of society.* ▶ **tell·ing·ly** *adv.*

ˌtelling-ˈoff *noun* [usually sing.] (*pl.* **ˌtellings-ˈoff**) (*BrE, informal*) the act of speaking angrily to sb, especially a child, because they have done sth bad

tell·tale /ˈtelteɪl/ *adj., noun*
- *adj.* [only before noun] showing that sth exists or has happened: ***telltale clues/marks/signs/sounds*** ◇ *The telltale smell of cigarettes told her that he had been in the room.*
- *noun* (*BrE*) (*NAmE* **tat·tle·tale**) (*informal, disapproving*) a child who tells an adult what another child has done wrong

tel·lur·ium /teˈljʊəriəm; *NAmE* teˈlʊr-/ *noun* [U] (*symb.* Te) a chemical element. Tellurium is a shiny silver-white substance that breaks easily, found in SULPHIDE ORES.

telly /ˈteli/ *noun* (*pl.* -ies) (*BrE, informal*) **1** [C] a television set SYN **TV**: *He spends most evenings just sitting in front of the telly.* **2** [U] the programmes broadcast on television SYN **TV**: *daytime telly* ◇ *Is there anything good **on telly**?* ◇ *I don't want to **watch telly**.*

tel·net /ˈtelnet/ *noun* [U] (*computing*) a computer system which allows you to use data and programs on another computer; a connection made using this system ▶ **tel·net** *verb* (-tt-) [I, T] **~ (to) sth | ~ in**

Tel·ugu /ˈteləguː/ *noun* [U] a language spoken in Andhra Pradesh in SE India

tem·blor /ˈtemblə(r)/ *noun* (*NAmE*) an EARTHQUAKE (= a sudden, violent shaking of the earth's surface)

tem·er·ity /təˈmerəti/ *noun* [U] (*formal*) extremely confident behaviour that people are likely to consider rude: *He **had the temerity to** call me a liar!*

temp /temp/ *noun, verb, abbr.*
- ***noun*** a temporary employee in an office
- ***verb*** [I] (*informal*) to do a temporary job or a series of temporary jobs: *I've been temping for an employment agency.* ➲ COLLOCATIONS at JOB
- ***abbr.*** (also **temp.** especially in *NAmE*) temperature: *Max temp 17 °C*

tem·per /ˈtempə(r)/ *noun, verb*
- ***noun*** **1** [C, usually sing., U] if sb has a **temper**, they become angry very easily: *a **violent/short/quick, etc. temper*** ◇ *He must learn to **control his temper**.* ◇ *She broke the plates in a **fit of temper**.* ◇ *After an hour of waiting, **tempers began to fray*** (= people began to get angry). **2** [C, usually sing.] a short period of feeling very angry: *to **fly into a temper*** ◇ *She says awful things when she's **in a temper**.* **3** [C] the way that you are feeling at a particular time SYN **mood**: *Come back when you're in a better temper.* ◇ *to be **in a bad/foul, etc. temper*** **4 -tempered** (in adjectives) having a particular type of temper: ***good-/bad-tempered*** ◇ *a sweet-tempered child* HELP You will find other compounds ending in **-tempered** at their place in the alphabet.

IDM **lose/keep your ˈtemper (with sb)** to fail/manage to control your anger: *She lost her temper with a customer and shouted at him.* ◇ *I struggle to keep my temper with the kids when they misbehave.* ➲ more at QUICK *adj.*
- ***verb*** **1 ~ sth (with sth)** (*formal*) to make sth less severe by adding sth that has the opposite effect: *Justice must be tempered with mercy.* **2 ~ sth** (*technical*) to make metal as hard as it needs to be by heating and then cooling it

tem·pera /ˈtempərə/ *noun* [U] a kind of paint in which the colour is mixed with egg and water; a method of painting that uses this kind of paint

tem·pera·ment /ˈtemprəmənt/ *noun* **1** [C, U] a person's or an animal's nature as shown in the way they behave or react to situations or people: *to have an artistic temperament* ◇ *a horse with an excellent temperament* ◇ *She's a dreamer and a romantic **by temperament**.* **2** [U] the tendency to get emotional and excited very easily and behave in an unreasonable way: *an actor given to displays of temperament*

tem·pera·men·tal /ˌtemprəˈmentl/ *adj.* **1** (usually *disapproving*) having a tendency to become angry, excited or upset easily, and to behave in an unreasonable way: *You never know what to expect with her. She's so temperamental.* ◇ (*figurative*) *The printer's being temperamental this morning.* **2** connected with sb's nature and personality: *They are firm friends in spite of temperamental differences.* ▶ **tem·pera·men·tal·ly** /-təli/ *adv.*: *I'm temperamentally unsuited to this job.*

tem·per·ance /ˈtempərəns/ *noun* [U] **1** (*old-fashioned*) the practice of not drinking alcohol because of your moral or religious beliefs **2** (*formal*) the practice of controlling your behaviour, the amount you eat, etc, so that it is always reasonable SYN **moderation**

tem·per·ate /ˈtempərət/ *adj.* **1** [usually before noun] (*technical*) (of a climate or region) having a mild temperature without extremes of heat or cold **2** (*formal*) behaving in a calm and controlled way OPP of sense 2 INTEMPERATE ▶ **tem·per·ate·ly** *adv.*

ˈtemperate zone *noun* [C, usually sing.] (*technical*) an area of the Earth that is not near the EQUATOR or the South or North Pole

T

tem·pera·ture 0‑w /ˈtemprətʃə(r); *NAmE* also -tʃʊr/ *noun* [C, U] (*abbr.* temp)
1 0‑w the measurement in degrees of how hot or cold a thing or place is: ***high/low temperatures*** ◇ *a* ***fall/drop in temperature*** ◇ *a* ***rise in temperature*** ◇ *The temperature has risen (by) five degrees.* ◇ *Heat the oven to a temperature of 200°C* (= degrees CENTIGRADE). ◇ *Some places have had temperatures in the 40s* (= over 40° CENTIGRADE). ➲ see also ABSOLUTE TEMPERATURE, ROOM TEMPERATURE **2** 0‑w the measurement of how hot sb's body is: *to* ***take sb's temperature*** (= measure the temperature of sb's body using a special instrument) ◇ (*BrE*) *Does he* ***have a temperature*** (= is it higher than normal, because of illness)? ◇ *She's* ***running a temperature*** (= it is higher than normal). ◇ *He's in bed with a temperature of 40°.* HELP In *NAmE* you can *take sb's temperature* but in the other examples the word **fever** is used. ➲ compare FEVER
IDM **raise/lower the ˈtemperature** to increase/decrease the amount of excitement, emotion, etc. in a situation: *His angry refusal to agree raised the temperature of the meeting.*

tem·pest /ˈtempɪst/ *noun* (*formal* or *literary*) a violent storm
IDM **a tempest in a ˈteapot** (*NAmE*) (*BrE* **a storm in a ˈteacup**) a lot of anger or worry about sth that is not important

tem·pes·tu·ous /temˈpestʃuəs/ *adj.* **1** (*formal*) full of extreme emotions SYN **stormy**: *a tempestuous relationship* **2** (*formal* or *literary*) caused by or affected by a violent storm SYN **stormy**: *tempestuous seas*

tem·plate /ˈtempleɪt/ *noun* **1** a shape cut out of a hard material, used as a model for producing exactly the same shape many times in another material **2** a thing that is used as a model for producing other similar examples: *If you need to write a lot of similar letters, set up a template on your computer.*

tem·ple /ˈtempl/ *noun* **1** a building used for the worship of a god or gods, especially in religions other than Christianity: *the Temple of Diana at Ephesus* ◇ *a* ***Buddhist/Hindu/Sikh temple*** ◇ (*NAmE*) *to go to temple* (= to a service in a SYNAGOGUE, where Jews worship) ➲ COLLOCATIONS at RELIGION **2** each of the flat parts at the sides of the head, at the same level as the eyes and higher: *He had black hair, greying at the temples.* ➲ VISUAL VOCAB page V48

tempo /ˈtempəʊ; *NAmE* -poʊ/ *noun* [C, U] (*pl.* -os or, in sense 1, *technical* **tempi** /ˈtempiː/) **1** the speed or rhythm of a piece of music: *a* ***slow/fast tempo*** ◇ *It's a difficult piece, with numerous changes of tempo.* **2** the speed of any movement or activity SYN **pace**: *the increasing tempo of life in Western society*

tem·poral /ˈtempərəl/ *adj.* **1** (*formal*) connected with the real physical world, not spiritual matters: *Although spiritual leader of millions of people, the Pope has no temporal power.* **2** (*formal*) connected with or limited by time: *a universe which has spatial and temporal dimensions* **3** (*anatomy*) near the TEMPLE(s) at the side of the head: *the right temporal lobe of the brain*

tem·por·ary 0‑w AW /ˈtemprəri; *NAmE* -pəreri/ *adj.* lasting or intended to last or be used only for a short time; not permanent: *temporary relief from pain* ◇ *I'm looking for some* ***temporary work.*** ◇ *They had to move into* ***temporary accommodation.*** ◇ *a* ***temporary measure/solution/arrangement*** ◇ *More than half the staff are temporary.* OPP **permanent** ▸ **tem·por·ar·ily** 0‑w AW /ˈtemprərəli; *NAmE* ˌtempəˈrerəli/ *adv.*: *We regret this service is temporarily unavailable.* **tem·por·ari·ness** *noun* [U]

tem·por·ize (*BrE* also **-ise**) /ˈtempəraɪz/ *verb* [I] (*formal*) to delay making a decision or giving a definite answer, in order to gain time

tempt /tempt/ *verb* **1** to attract sb or make sb want to do or have sth, even if they know it is wrong: **~ sb (into sth/into doing sth)** *I was tempted by the dessert menu.* ◇ *Don't tempt thieves by leaving valuables clearly visible.* ◇ **~ sb to do sth** *I was tempted to take the day off.* **2** to persuade or try to persuade sb to do sth that you want them to do, for example by offering them sth: **~ sb (into sth/into doing sth)** *How can we tempt young people into engineering?* ◇ **~ sb to do sth** *Nothing would tempt me to live here.*
IDM **tempt ˈfate/ˈprovidence** to do sth too confidently in a way that might mean that your good luck will come to an end

temp·ta·tion /tempˈteɪʃn/ *noun* **1** [C, U] the desire to do or have sth that you know is bad or wrong: *the temptation of easy profits* ◇ *to* ***give way to/yield to temptation*** ◇ *I couldn't* ***resist the temptation*** *to open the letter.* ◇ *Don't* ***put temptation in her way*** *by offering her a cigarette.* **2** [C] a thing that makes sb want to do or have sth that they know is bad or wrong: *An expensive bicycle is a temptation to thieves.*

tempt·er /ˈtemptə(r)/ *noun* a person who tries to persuade sb to do sth, especially sth bad or wrong

tempt·ing /ˈtemptɪŋ/ *adj.* something that is **tempting** is attractive, and makes people want to have it, do it, etc: *It was a tempting offer.* ◇ *That cake looks very tempting.* ◇ *It's tempting to speculate about what might have happened.* ▸ **tempt·ing·ly** *adv.*

temp·tress /ˈtemptrəs/ *noun* (*old-fashioned* or *humorous*) a woman who TEMPTS sb, especially one who deliberately makes a man want to have sex with her

tem·pura /ˈtempʊrə; temˈpuːrə/ *noun* [U, C] a Japanese dish consisting of pieces of vegetables or fish that have been fried in BATTER (= a mixture of flour, egg and water)

ten 0‑w /ten/ *number*
10 HELP There are examples of how to use numbers at the entry for **five**.
IDM ˌ**ten out of ˈten (for sth)** (*BrE*, often *ironic*) used to say that sb has guessed sth correctly or done sth very well: *Not brilliant, Robyn, but I'll give you ten out of ten for effort.* ˌ**ten to ˈone** very probably: *Ten to one he'll be late.*

ten·able /ˈtenəbl/ *adj.* **1** (of a theory, an opinion, etc.) easy to defend against attack or criticism: *a tenable position* ◇ *The old idea that this work was not suitable for women was no longer tenable.* OPP **untenable 2** [not before noun] (of a job, position, etc, especially in a university) that can be held for a particular period of time: *The lectureship is tenable for a period of three years.*

ten·acious /təˈneɪʃəs/ *adj.* (*formal*) **1** that does not stop holding sth or give up sth easily; determined: *a tenacious grip* ◇ *She's a tenacious woman. She never gives up.* ◇ *The party has kept its tenacious hold on power for more than twenty years.* **2** continuing to exist, have influence, etc. for longer than you might expect SYN **persistent**: *a tenacious illness* ▸ **ten·acious·ly** *adv.*: *Though seriously ill, he still clings tenaciously to life.* **ten·acity** /təˈnæsəti/ *noun* [U]: *They competed with skill and tenacity.*

ten·ancy /ˈtenənsi/ *noun* (*pl.* -ies) **1** [C] (*BrE*) a period of time that you rent a house, land, etc. for: *a three-month tenancy* ◇ *a tenancy agreement* ➲ COLLOCATIONS at HOUSE **2** [C, U] the right to live or work in a building or on land that you rent: *They had taken over the tenancy of the farm.*

ten·ant /ˈtenənt/ *noun, verb*
■ ***noun*** a person who pays rent for the use of a room, building, land, etc. to the person who owns it: *They had evicted their tenants for non-payment of rent.* ◇ *The decorating was done by a previous tenant.* ◇ *tenant farmers* (= ones who do not own their own farms) ➲ COLLOCATIONS at HOUSE
■ ***verb*** [usually passive] **~ sth** to live or work in a place as a tenant: *a tenanted farm*

tench /tentʃ/ *noun* (*pl.* **tench**) a European FRESHWATER fish

tend 0‑w /tend/ *verb*
1 0‑w [I] **~ to do sth** to be likely to do sth or to happen in a particular way because this is what often or usually happens: *Women tend to live longer than men.* ◇ *When I'm tired, I tend to make mistakes.* ◇ *It tends to get very cold here in the winter.* ◇ *People* ***tend to think*** *that the problem will never affect them.* ➲ LANGUAGE BANK at GENERALLY **2** [I] **~ (to/towards sth)** to take a particular direction or often have a particular quality: *His views tend towards the extreme.* ◇ *Prices have tended downwards over recent years.* **3** [T, I] to care for sb/sth: **~ sb/sth** *a shepherd tending his sheep* ◇ *Doc-*

T

tors and nurses tended the injured. ◇ *well-tended gardens* ◇ **~ to sb/sth** *Ambulance crews were tending to the injured.* **4** [T] **~ sth** (*NAmE*) to serve customers in a store, bar, etc: *He had a job* ***tending bar*** *in San Francisco.*

ten·dency 🔑 /ˈtendənsi/ *noun* (*pl.* -ies) **1** 🔑 [C] if sb/sth has a particular **tendency**, they are likely to behave or act in a particular way: *to* ***display*** *artistic, etc.* ***tendencies*** ◇ **~** (**for sb/sth**) (**to do sth**) *I* ***have a tendency*** *to talk too much when I'm nervous.* ◇ *There is a tendency for this disease to run in families.* ◇ **~** (**to/towards sth**) *She has a strong natural tendency towards caution.* **2** 🔑 [C] **~** (**for sb/sth**) (**to do sth**) | **~** (**to/towards sth**) a new custom that is starting to develop **SYN** **trend**: *There is a growing tendency among employers to hire casual staff.* **3** [C+sing./pl. v.] (*BrE*) a group within a larger political group, whose views are more extreme than those of the rest of the group

ten·den·tious /tenˈdenʃəs/ *adj.* (*formal*, usually *disapproving*) (of a speech, piece of writing, theory, etc.) expressing a strong opinion that people are likely to disagree with **SYN** **controversial** ▶ **ten·den·tious·ly** *adv.* **SYN** **controversially** **ten·den·tious·ness** *noun* [U]

ten·der /ˈtendə(r)/ *adj., noun, verb*

■ ***adj.*** (**ten·derer, ten·derest**) **HELP** **more tender** and **most tender** are also common **1** kind, gentle and loving: *tender words* ◇ *What he needs now is a lot of* ***tender loving care*** (= sympathetic treatment). **2** (of food) easy to bite through and cut: *This meat is extremely tender.* **OPP** **tough** **3** (of part of the body) painful when you touch it **SYN** **sore** **4** easily hurt or damaged **SYN** **delicate**: *tender young plants* ▶ **ten·der·ly** *adv.* **ten·der·ness** *noun* [U]

IDM **at a ˌtender ˈage** | **at the tender age of...** used in connection with sb who is still young and does not have much experience: *He left home at the tender age of 15.* ◇ *She shouldn't be having to deal with problems like this* ***at such a tender age.***

■ ***noun*** **1** a formal offer to supply goods or do work at a stated price **SYN** **bid**: *Cleaning services have been* ***put out to tender*** (= companies have been asked to make offers to supply these services). ◇ *a competitive tender* **2** a truck attached to a steam engine, carrying fuel and water **3** a small boat, used for carrying people or goods between a larger boat and land

■ ***verb*** **1** [I] **~** (**for sth**) to make a formal offer to supply goods or do work at a stated price: *Local firms were invited to tender for the building contract.* **2** [T] **~ sth** (**to sb**) (*formal*) to offer or give sth to sb: *He has* ***tendered his resignation*** *to the Prime Minister.*

tend·er·foot /ˈtendəfʊt; *NAmE* -dərf-/ *noun* (*pl.* **tend·er·feet** or **tend·er·foots**) (*NAmE*, *informal*) a person who is new to sth and not experienced **SYN** **greenhorn**

ˌtender-ˈhearted *adj.* having a kind and gentle nature

ten·der·ize (*BrE* also **-ise**) /ˈtendəraɪz/ *verb* **~ sth** to make meat softer and easier to cut and eat by preparing it in a particular way

ten·der·loin /ˈtendəlɔɪn; *NAmE* -dərl-/ *noun* [U] good quality meat from the back or side of a cow or pig

ten·don /ˈtendən/ *noun* a strong band of TISSUE in the body that joins a muscle to a bone ➲ **COLLOCATIONS** at INJURY

ten·dril /ˈtendrəl/ *noun* **1** a thin curling STEM that grows from a climbing plant. A plant uses tendrils to attach itself to a wall or other support. ➲ **VISUAL VOCAB** page V9 **2** (*literary*) a thin curling piece of sth such as hair

tene·ment /ˈtenəmənt/ *noun* a large building divided into flats/apartments, especially in a poor area of a city: *a tenement block*

tenet /ˈtenɪt/ *noun* (*formal*) one of the principles or beliefs that a theory or larger set of beliefs is based on: *one of the* ***basic/central tenets*** *of Christianity*

ten·fold /ˈtenfəʊld; *NAmE* -foʊld/ *adj., adv.* ➲ -FOLD

ˌten-gallon ˈhat *noun* a large hat with a broad BRIM, traditionally worn by COWBOYS

ten·ner /ˈtenə(r)/ *noun* (*BrE*, *informal*) £10 or a ten-pound note: *You can have it for a tenner.*

ten·nis /ˈtenɪs/ (also *formal* **ˌlawn ˈtennis**) *noun* [U] a game in which two or four players use RACKETS to hit a ball backwards and forwards across a net on a specially marked COURT ➲ **VISUAL VOCAB** page V37: *to* ***play tennis*** ◇ ***a tennis player/tournament/club/court***

ˌtennis ˈelbow *noun* [U] painful swelling of the elbow caused by too much repeated twisting of the arm

ˈtennis racket (also **ˈtennis rac·quet**) *noun* the RACKET that you use when you play tennis

ˈtennis shoe (*NAmE* also **athˈletic shoe**) *noun* a sports shoe that is made of strong cotton cloth or leather

tenon /ˈtenən/ *noun* (*technical*) an end of a piece of wood that has been cut to fit into a MORTISE so that the two are held together

tenor /ˈtenə(r)/ *noun, adj.*

■ ***noun*** **1** [C] a man's singing voice with a range just below the lowest woman's voice; a man with a tenor voice ➲ compare ALTO, BARITONE, BASS, COUNTERTENOR **2** [sing.] a musical part written for a tenor voice **3** [sing.] **the ~ of sth** (*formal*) the general character or meaning of sth: *I was encouraged by the general tenor of his remarks.*

■ ***adj.*** [only before noun] (of a musical instrument) with a range of notes similar to that of a tenor voice: *a tenor saxophone* ➲ compare ALTO, BASS, SOPRANO

ˌten ˈpence (also **ˌten pence ˈpiece, 10p** /ˌten ˈpiː/) *noun* a British coin worth ten pence: *Have you got a ten pence piece?*

ten·pin /ˈtenpɪn/ *noun* **1** [C] any of the ten bottle-shaped objects that players try to knock over in the game of TENPIN BOWLING **2** **ten·pins** [U] (*NAmE*) = TENPIN BOWLING

ˌtenpin ˈbowling (*NAmE* also **ten·pins**) *noun* [U] a game in which players try to knock over tenpins by rolling a heavy ball at them, played indoors, especially in a BOWLING ALLEY ➲ **VISUAL VOCAB** page V34 ➲ compare SKITTLE

tense **AW** /tens/ *adj., noun, verb*

■ ***adj.*** **1** (of a person) nervous or worried, and unable to relax: *He's a very tense person.* ◇ *She sounded tense and angry.* **2** (of a situation, an event, a period of time, etc.) in which people have strong feelings such as worry, anger, etc. that often cannot be expressed openly: *I spent a tense few weeks waiting for the results of the tests.* ◇ *The atmosphere in the meeting was getting more and more tense.* **3** (of a muscle or other part of the body) tight rather than relaxed: *A massage will relax those tense muscles.* **4** (of wire, etc.) stretched tightly **SYN** **taut** **5** (*phonetics*) (of a speech sound) produced with the muscles of the speech organs stretched tight **OPP** **lax** ▶ **tense·ly** **AW** *adv.* **tense·ness** *noun* [U]

■ ***noun*** (*grammar*) any of the forms of a verb that may be used to show the time of the action or state expressed by the verb: *the* ***past/present/future tense***

■ ***verb*** [T, I] if you **tense** your muscles, or you or your muscles **tense**, they become tight and stiff, especially because you are not relaxed: **~ sth/yourself** (**up**) *She tensed her muscles in anticipation of the blow.* ◇ *He tensed himself, listening to see if anyone had followed him.* ◇ **~** (**up**) *His muscles tensed as he got ready to run.* ◇ *She tensed, hearing the strange noise again.*

IDM **be/get tensed ˈup** to become or feel nervous or worried so that you cannot relax

ten·sile /ˈtensaɪl; *NAmE* ˈtensl/ *adj.* (*technical*) **1** [only before noun] used to describe the extent to which sth can stretch without breaking: *the* ***tensile strength*** *of rope* **2** that can be drawn out or stretched: *tensile cable*

ten·sion 🔑 **AW** /ˈtenʃn/ *noun, verb*

■ ***noun*** **1** 🔑 [U, C, usually pl.] **~** (**between A and B**) a situation in which people do not trust each other, or feel unfriendly towards each other, and which may cause them to attack each other: *There is mounting tension along the border.* ◇ ***international/racial/political tensions*** **2** [C, U] **~** (**between A and B**) a situation in which the fact that there are different needs or interests causes difficulties: *There is often a tension between the aims of the company and the*

T

wishes of the employees. **3** [U] a feeling of anxiety and stress that makes it impossible to relax: ***nervous tension*** ◇ *We laughed and that helped* ***ease the tension.*** ➲ SYNONYMS at PRESSURE **4** [U] the feeling of fear and excitement that is created by a writer or a film/movie director: *dramatic tension* ◇ *As the movie progresses the tension builds.* **5** [U] the state of being stretched tight; the extent to which sth is stretched tight: *muscular tension* ◇ *Adjust the string tension of your tennis racket to suit your style of playing.* ➲ see also SURFACE TENSION
■ ***verb*** **~ sth** (*technical*) to make a wire, sail, etc. tight and stretched

ten·sor /ˈtensə(r); -sɔː(r)/ *noun* (*anatomy*) a muscle that TIGHTENS or stretches part of the body

tent 0⊸ /tent/ *noun*
a shelter made of a large sheet of CANVAS, NYLON, etc. that is supported by poles and ropes fixed to the ground, and is used especially for camping: *to* ***put up/take down a tent*** ◇ *to* ***pitch*** (= put up) ***a tent*** ◇ *Food will be served in the* ***hospitality tent*** (= for example at an outdoor show). ➲ see also A-FRAME TENT, DOME TENT, FRAME TENT, OXYGEN TENT, PUP TENT, RIDGE TENT, WALL TENT

ten·tacle /ˈtentəkl/ *noun* **1** [C] a long thin part of the body of some creatures, such as SQUID, used for feeling or holding things, for moving or for getting food: (*figurative*) *Tentacles of fear closed around her body.* ➲ VISUAL VOCAB page V11 **2 tentacles** [pl.] (usually *disapproving*) the influence that a large place, organization or system has and that is hard to avoid: *The tentacles of satellite television are spreading even wider.*

ten·ta·tive /ˈtentətɪv/ *adj.* **1** (of an arrangement, agreement, etc.) not definite or certain because you may want to change it later: *We made a* ***tentative arrangement*** *to meet on Friday.* ◇ *tentative conclusions* **2** not behaving or done with confidence SYN **hesitant**: *a tentative greeting* ◇ *I'm taking the first* ***tentative steps*** *towards fitness.*
▸ **ten·ta·tive·ly** *adv.* **ten·ta·tive·ness** *noun* [U]

tent·ed /ˈtentɪd/ *adj.* consisting of tents; like a tent: *a tented village*

ten·ter·hooks /ˈtentəhʊks; *NAmE* -tərh-/ *noun* [pl.]
IDM **(be) on ˈtenterhooks** (*NAmE* also **be on ˌpins and ˈneedles**) (to be) very anxious or excited while you are waiting to find out sth or see what will happen: *I've been on tenterhooks all week waiting for the results.* ORIGIN From **tenterhook**, a hook which in the past was used to keep material stretched on a drying frame during manufacture.

tenth 0⊸ /tenθ/ *ordinal number, noun*
■ ***ordinal number*** 0⊸ 10th HELP There are examples of how to use ordinal numbers at the entry for **fifth**.
■ ***noun*** 0⊸ each of ten equal parts of sth IDM see POSSESSION

ˈtent peg *noun* = PEG ➲ picture at PEG

tenu·ous /ˈtenjuəs/ *adj.* **1** so weak or uncertain that it hardly exists: *a tenuous hold on life* ◇ *His links with the organization turned out to be, at best, tenuous.* **2** extremely thin and easily broken ▸ **tenu·ous·ly** *adv.*

ten·ure /ˈtenjə(r)/ *noun* [U] **1** the period of time when sb holds an important job, especially a political one; the act of holding an important job: *his four-year tenure as President* ◇ *She knew that tenure of high political office was beyond her.* **2** the right to stay permanently in your job, especially as a teacher at a university: *It's still extremely difficult to get tenure.* **3** the legal right to live in a house or use a piece of land

ten·ured /ˈtenjəd; *NAmE* -jərd/ *adj.* [usually before noun] **1** (of an official job) that you can keep permanently: *a tenured post* **2** (of a person, especially a teacher at a university) having the right to keep their job permanently: *a tenured professor*

tepee (also **tee·pee**) /ˈtiːpiː/ *noun* a type of tall tent shaped like a CONE, used by Native Americans in the past ➲ see also WIGWAM

tepid /ˈtepɪd/ *adj.* **1** slightly warm, sometimes in a way that is not pleasant SYN **lukewarm**: *tepid tea* ◇ *a tepid bath* ➲ SYNONYMS at COLD **2** not enthusiastic SYN **lukewarm**: *The play was greeted with tepid applause.*

te·quila /təˈkiːlə/ *noun* **1** [U] a strong alcoholic drink made in Mexico from a tropical plant **2** [C] a glass of tequila

tera- /ˈterə/ *combining form* (in nouns; used in units of measurement) **1** 10^{12}, or 1 000 000 000 000 **2** 2^{40}, or 1 099 511 627 776

tera·bit /ˈterəbɪt/ *noun* (*abbr.* **Tb**, **Tbit**) (*computing*) **1** a unit of computer memory or data, equal to one million million, or 10^{12} (= 1 000 000 000 000) BITS **2** (also **tebi·bit**) a unit of computer memory or data, equal to 2^{40} (= 1 099 511 627 776) BITS

tera·byte /ˈterəbaɪt/ *noun* (*abbr.* **TB**) (*computing*) **1** a unit of computer memory or data, equal to one million million, or 10^{12} (= 1 000 000 000 000) BYTES **2** (also **tebi·byte**) a unit of computer memory or data, equal to 2^{40} (= 1 099 511 627 776) BYTES

ter·bium /ˈtɜːbiəm; *NAmE* ˈtɜːrb-/ *noun* [U] (*symb.* **Tb**) a chemical element. Terbium is a silver-white metal used in LASERS, X-RAYS and television TUBES.

ter·cen·ten·ary /ˌtɜːsenˈtiːnəri; *NAmE* ˌtɜːrsenˈtenəri/ *noun* (*pl.* **-ies**) the 300th anniversary of sth: *the tercentenary of the school's foundation* ◇ *tercentenary celebrations*

ter·gi·ver·sate /ˈtɜːdʒɪvəseɪt; ˌtɜːdʒɪˈvɜːseɪt; *NAmE* tərˈdʒɪvərseɪt; ˈtɜːrdʒɪvərseɪt/ *verb* (*formal*) **1** [I] to make statements that deliberately hide the truth or that avoid answering a question directly **2** [I] to stop being loyal to one person, group, or religion and begin to support another ▸ **ter·gi·ver·sa·tion** /ˌtɜːdʒɪvəˈseɪʃn; *NAmE* ˌtɜːrdʒɪvərˈseɪʃn/ *noun* [U]

teri·yaki /ˌteriˈjɑːki; *BrE* also -ˈjæki/ *noun* [U, C] a Japanese dish consisting of meat or fish that has been left in a sweet sauce and then cooked

term 0⊸ /tɜːm; *NAmE* tɜːrm/ *noun, verb*
■ ***noun*** ➲ see also TERMS **1** 0⊸ [C] a word or phrase used as the name of sth, especially one connected with a particular type of language: *a* ***technical/legal/scientific, etc. term*** ◇ *a term of abuse* ◇ *'Register' is the term commonly used to describe different levels of formality in language.* ➲ SYNONYMS at WORD ➲ LANGUAGE BANK at DEFINE **2** 0⊸ (*NAmE* also **tri·mes·ter**) [C, U] (especially in Britain) one of the three periods in the year during which classes are held in schools, universities, etc: *the* ***spring/summer/autumn/fall term*** ◇ *Many students now have paid employment* ***during term.*** ◇ (*BrE*) *It's nearly the* ***end of term.*** ◇ (*NAmE*) *the* ***end of the term*** ➲ see also SEMESTER, TERMLY, TERM-TIME **3** 0⊸ [C] a period of time for which sth lasts; a fixed or limited time: *during the president's first* ***term of/in office*** ◇ *He faces a maximum* ***prison/jail term*** *of 25 years.* ◇ *a long term of imprisonment* **4** [sing.] (*formal*) the end of a particular period of time, especially one for which an agreement, etc. lasts: *the term of the loan* ◇ *His life had reached its natural term.* ◇ (*medical*) *The pregnancy went to* ***full term*** (= lasted the normal length of time). **5** [C] (*mathematics*) each of the various parts in a series, an EQUATION, etc.
IDM **in terms of | in ... terms** ➲ IN TERMS OF at TERMS **in the ˈlong/ˈshort/ˈmedium term** used to describe what will happen a long, short, etc. time in the future: *Such a development seems unlikely, at least in the short term* (= it will not happen for quite a long time). ➲ see also LONG-TERM, MEDIUM-TERM, SHORT-TERM
■ ***verb*** [often passive] **~ sb/sth + noun/adj.** (*formal*) to use a particular name or word to describe sb/sth: *At his age, he can hardly be termed a young man.* ◇ *REM sleep is termed 'active' sleep.*

ter·ma·gant /ˈtɜːməgənt; *NAmE* ˈtɜːrm-/ *noun* (*formal*) a woman who is very strict or who tries to tell people what to do, in an unpleasant way

ter·min·al AW /ˈtɜːmɪnl; *NAmE* ˈtɜːrm-/ *noun, adj.*
■ ***noun*** **1** a building or set of buildings at an airport where air passengers arrive and leave: *A second terminal was opened in 2008.* **2** a place, building or set of buildings

where journeys by train, bus or boat begin or end: *a railway/bus/ferry terminal* **3** (*computing*) a piece of equipment, usually consisting of a keyboard and a screen that joins the user to a central computer system **4** (*technical*) a point at which connections can be made in an electric CIRCUIT: *a* ***positive/negative terminal***

■ ***adj.*** **1** (of an illness or a disease) that cannot be cured and will lead to death, often slowly: *He has terminal lung cancer.* ◇ *The illness is usually terminal.* ◇ (*figurative*) *She's suffering from terminal* (= very great) *boredom.* **2** (of a person) suffering from an illness that cannot be cured and will lead to death: *a terminal patient* **3** certain to get worse and come to an end: *The industry is* ***in terminal decline.*** **4** [only before noun] (*formal* or *technical*) at the end of sth: *a terminal branch of a tree* ◇ *terminal examinations* (= at the end of a course, etc.) ▶ **ter·min·al·ly** /-nəli/ *adv.*: *a hospice for the terminally ill* ◇ *a terminally dull film*

ter·min·ate AW /ˈtɜːmɪneɪt; *NAmE* ˈtɜːrm-/ *verb* (*formal*) **1** [I, T] to end; to make sth end: *Your contract of employment terminates in December.* ◇ **~ sth** *The agreement was terminated immediately.* ◇ *to terminate a pregnancy* (= to perform or have an ABORTION) **2** [I] (of a bus or train) to end a journey/trip: *This train terminates at London Victoria.*

ter·min·ation AW /ˌtɜːmɪˈneɪʃn; *NAmE* ˌtɜːrm-/ *noun* **1** [U, C] (*formal*) the act of ending sth; the end of sth: *Failure to comply with these conditions will result in termination of the contract.* **2** [C] (*medical*) a medical operation to end a PREGNANCY at an early stage SYN **abortion**

ter·min·ology /ˌtɜːmɪˈnɒlədʒi; *NAmE* ˌtɜːrməˈnɑːl-/ *noun* (*pl.* **-ies**) **1** [U, C] the set of technical words or expressions used in a particular subject: *medical terminology* ➲ **SYNONYMS** at LANGUAGE **2** [U] words used with particular meanings: *The disagreement arose over a different use of terminology.* ➲ **SYNONYMS** at LANGUAGE ▶ **ter·mino·logic·al** /ˌtɜːmɪnəˈlɒdʒɪkl; *NAmE* ˌtɜːrmənəˈlɑːdʒ-/ *adj.*

ter·minus /ˈtɜːmɪnəs; *NAmE* ˈtɜːrm-/ *noun* (*pl.* **ter·mini** /ˈtɜːmɪnaɪ; *NAmE* ˈtɜːrm-/) the last station at the end of a railway/railroad line or the last stop on a bus route

ter·mite /ˈtɜːmaɪt; *NAmE* ˈtɜːrm-/ *noun* an insect that lives in organized groups, mainly in hot countries. Termites do a lot of damage by eating the wood of trees and buildings: *a termite colony*

term·ly /ˈtɜːmli; *NAmE* ˈtɜːrm-/ *adj.* (*BrE*) happening in each of the periods that the school or college year is divided into: *termly reports*

ˈterm paper *noun* (in an American school or college) a long piece of written work that a student does on a subject that is part of a course of study

terms /tɜːmz; *NAmE* tɜːrmz/ *noun* [pl.] **1** the conditions that people offer, demand or accept when they make an agreement, an arrangement or a contract: *peace terms* ◇ ***Under the terms of the agreement,*** *their funding of the project will continue until 2015.* ◇ *They failed to agree on the terms of a settlement.* ◇ *These are the* ***terms and conditions*** *of your employment.* **2** conditions that you agree to when you buy, sell, or pay for sth; a price or cost: *to buy sth* ***on easy terms*** (= paying for it over a long period) ◇ *My terms are £20 a lesson.* **3** a way of expressing yourself or of saying sth: *We wish to protest in the* ***strongest possible terms*** (= to say we are very angry). ◇ *I'll try to explain in simple terms.* ◇ *The letter was brief, and* ***couched in*** *very polite* ***terms.*** ➲ **SYNONYMS** at LANGUAGE

IDM **be on good, friendly, bad, etc. ˈterms (with sb)** to have a good, friendly, etc. relationship with sb: *I had no idea that you and he were on such intimate terms* (= were such close friends). ◇ *He is still on excellent terms with his ex-wife.* ◇ *I'm on* ***first-name terms*** *with my boss now* (= we call each other by our first names). **come to ˈterms (with sb)** to reach an agreement with sb; to find a way of living or working together **come to ˈterms with sth** to accept sth unpleasant by learning to deal with it: *She is still coming to terms with her son's death.* **in terms of ˈsth | in... terms** used to show what aspect of a subject you are talking about or how you are thinking about it: *The job is great in terms of salary, but it has its disadvantages.* ◇ *What does this mean in terms of cost?* ◇ *In practical terms this law may be difficult to enforce.* ◇ *The decision was disastrous in political terms.* ◇ *He's talking in terms of starting a completely new career.* **on your own ˈterms | on sb's ˈterms** according to the conditions that you or sb else decides: *I'll only take the job on my own terms.* ◇ *I'm not doing it on your terms.* ➲ more at CONTRADICTION, EQUAL, SPEAK, UNCERTAIN

ˌterms of ˈreference *noun* [pl.] the limits that are set on what an official committee or report has been asked to do: *The matter, they decided, lay outside the commission's terms of reference.*

ˈterm-time *noun* [U] (*BrE*) the period of time when classes are held at a school, college, or university, as opposed to the holidays/vacations ▶ **ˈterm-time** *adj.* [only before noun]: *Please give your term-time address.*

tern /tɜːn; *NAmE* tɜːrn/ *noun* a bird with long pointed wings and a tail with two points that lives near the sea

ter·race /ˈterəs/ *noun* **1** [C] (*BrE*) (often in the names of streets) a continuous row of similar houses that are joined together in one block: *12 Albert Terrace* **2** [C] a flat, hard area, especially outside a house or restaurant, where you can sit, eat and enjoy the sun: *a sun terrace* ◇ *a roof terrace* ◇ *All rooms have a balcony or terrace.* ➲ see also PATIO **3 terraces** [pl.] (*BrE*) the wide steps at a football (SOCCER) ground where people can stand to watch the game **4** [C] one of a series of flat areas of ground that are cut into the side of a hill like steps so that crops can be grown there

ter·raced /ˈterəst/ *adj.* **1** (*BrE*) used to describe houses that form part of a terrace, or streets with houses in terraces: *a terraced cottage* ◇ *terraced housing* ◇ *terraced streets* **2** (of a slope or the side of a hill) having a series of flat areas of ground like steps cut into it

ˌterraced ˈhouse (also *less frequent* **ˌterrace ˈhouse**) (both *BrE*) (*NAmE* **ˈrow house, town·house**) *noun* a house that is one of a row of houses that are joined together on each side ➲ **VISUAL VOCAB** page V14

ter·ra·cing /ˈterəsɪŋ/ *noun* [U] **1** (*BrE*) an area with wide steps at a football (SOCCER) ground where people can stand to watch the game **2** a slope or the side of a hill that has had flat areas like steps cut into it

terra·cotta /ˌterəˈkɒtə; *NAmE* -ˈkɑːtə/ *noun* [U] **1** reddish-brown CLAY that has been baked but not GLAZED, used for making pots, etc. **2** a reddish-brown colour

terra firma /ˌterə ˈfɜːmə; *NAmE* ˈfɜːrmə/ *noun* [U] (from *Latin*, usually *humorous*) safe dry land, as contrasted with water or air SYN **dry land**: *After two days at sea, it was good to be back on terra firma again.*

terra·form /ˈterəfɔːm; *NAmE* -fɔːrm/ *verb* **~ sth** to make a planet more like Earth, so that people can live on it

ter·rain /təˈreɪn/ *noun* [C, U] used to refer to an area of land when you are mentioning its natural features, for example, if it is rough, flat, etc.: ***difficult/rough/mountainous, etc. terrain*** ➲ **SYNONYMS** at COUNTRY

terˈrain park *noun* an outdoor area with special features designed for winter sports, especially SNOWBOARDING (= moving over snow on a special board)

terra·pin /ˈterəpɪn/ *noun* a small TURTLE (= a REPTILE with a hard round shell), that lives in warm rivers and lakes in N America ➲ compare TORTOISE

ter·rar·ium /teˈreəriəm; *NAmE* -ˈrer-/ *noun* a glass container for growing plants in or for keeping small animals such as TURTLES or snakes in

ter·res·trial /təˈrestriəl/ *adj.* **1** (*technical*) (of animals and plants) living on the land or on the ground, rather than in water, in trees or in the air **2** connected with the planet Earth: *terrestrial life* ➲ compare CELESTIAL, EXTRATERRESTRIAL **3** (of television and broadcasting systems) operating on earth rather than from a SATELLITE

ter·rible 0‑w /ˈterəbl/ *adj.* **1** 0‑w very unpleasant; making you feel very unhappy, upset or frightened: *a terrible experience* ◇ *What terrible* *news!* ◇ *I've just had a terrible thought.* **2** 🔑 causing great harm or injury; very serious: *a terrible accident* ◇ *He had suffered terrible injuries.* **3** 🔑 [not before noun] unhappy or ill/sick: *I feel terrible—I think I'll go to bed.* **4** 🔑 (*informal*) of very bad quality; very bad: *a terrible meal* ◇ *Your driving is terrible!* **5** 🔑 [only before noun] used to show the great extent or degree of sth bad: *a terrible mistake* ◇ *to be in terrible pain* ◇ *The room was in a terrible mess.* ◇ (*informal*) *I had a terrible job* (= it was very difficult) *to persuade her to come.*

Synonyms

terrible

awful • horrible • dreadful • vile • horrendous

These words all describe sth that is very unpleasant.

terrible very bad or unpleasant; making you feel unhappy, frightened, upset, ill, guilty or disapproving: *What terrible news!* ◇ *That's a terrible thing to say!*

awful (*rather informal*) very bad or unpleasant; used to describe sth that you do not like or that makes you feel depressed, ill, guilty or disapproving: *That's an awful colour.* ◇ *The weather last summer was awful.*

horrible (*rather informal*) very unpleasant; used to describe sth that you do not like: *The coffee tasted horrible.*

dreadful (*rather informal, especially BrE*) very bad or unpleasant; used to describe sth that you do not like or that you disapprove of: *What dreadful weather!*

vile (*informal*) extremely bad or unpleasant: *There was a vile smell coming from the room.* ◇ *He was in a vile mood.*

horrendous (*rather informal*) extremely unpleasant and unacceptable: *The traffic around the city was horrendous.*

PATTERNS

- terrible/awful/horrible/dreadful **for** sb
- a(n) terrible/awful/horrible/dreadful/vile **thing**
- a(n) terrible/awful/horrible/vile **smell**
- terrible/awful/horrible/dreadful/vile/horrendous **conditions**
- terrible/awful/horrible/dreadful/vile **weather**
- terrible/awful/dreadful **news**

ter·ribly 🔑 /ˈterəbli/ *adv.* **1** 🔑 (*especially BrE*) very: *I'm terribly sorry—did I hurt you?* ◇ *It's terribly important for parents to be consistent.* **2** 🔑 very much; very badly: *I miss him terribly.* ◇ *They suffered terribly when their son was killed.* ◇ *The experiment went terribly wrong.*

ter·rier /ˈteriə(r)/ *noun* a small active dog. There are many types of terrier. ➲ see also BULL TERRIER, PIT BULL TERRIER, YORKSHIRE TERRIER

ter·rif·ic /təˈrɪfɪk/ *adj.* **1** (*informal*) excellent; wonderful: *I feel absolutely terrific today!* ◇ *She's doing a terrific job.* ➲ SYNONYMS at GREAT **2** (*informal*) very large; very great: *I've got a terrific amount of work to do.* ◇ *We drove along at a terrific speed.*

ter·rif·ic·al·ly /təˈrɪfɪkli/ *adv.* (*informal*) extremely (usually used about positive qualities): *terrifically exciting*

ter·ri·fied /ˈterɪfaɪd/ *adj.* very frightened: **~ (of sb/sth)** *to be terrified of spiders* ◇ **~ (of doing sth)** *I'm terrified of losing you.* ◇ **~ (that...)** *He was terrified (that) he would fall.* ◇ **~ (at sth)** *She was terrified at the thought of being alone.* ➲ SYNONYMS at AFRAID IDM see WIT

ter·rify /ˈterɪfaɪ/ *verb* (**ter·ri·fies**, **ter·ri·fy·ing**, **ter·ri·fied**, **ter·ri·fied**) **~ sb** to make sb feel extremely frightened: *Flying terrifies her.* ➲ SYNONYMS at FRIGHTEN ▸ **ter·ri·fy·ing** *adj.*: *It was a terrifying experience.* **ter·ri·fy·ing·ly** *adv.*

ter·rine /teˈriːn/ *noun* [U, C] a soft mixture of finely chopped meat, fish, etc. pressed into a container and served cold, especially in slices as the first course of a meal

Ter·ri·tor·ial /ˌterəˈtɔːriəl/ *noun* (in Britain) a member of the Territorial Army

ter·ri·tor·ial /ˌterəˈtɔːriəl/ *adj.* **1** connected with the land or sea that is owned by a particular country: *territorial disputes* ◇ *Both countries feel they have territorial claims to* (= have a right to own) *the islands.* **2** (of animals, birds, etc.) guarding and defending an area of land that they believe to be their own: *territorial instincts* ◇ *Cats are very territorial.* ▸ **ter·ri·tori·al·ity** /ˌterəˌtɔːriˈæləti/ *noun* [U]: *the instinctive territoriality of some animals* **ter·ri·tori·al·ly** *adv.*: *The country was trying to expand territorially.*

the ˌTerritorial ˈArmy *noun* [sing.+ sing./pl. v.] (*abbr.* TA) (in Britain) a military force of people who are not professional soldiers but who train as soldiers in their free time

ˌterritorial ˈwaters *noun* [pl.] the parts of a sea or an ocean which are near a country's coast and are legally under its control

ter·ri·tory /ˈterətri; *NAmE* -tɔːri/ *noun* (*pl.* **-ies**) **1** [C, U] land that is under the control of a particular country or ruler: ***enemy/disputed/foreign territory*** ◇ *occupied territories* ◇ *They have refused to allow UN troops to be stationed in their territory.* ➲ COLLOCATIONS at WAR **2** [C, U] an area that one person, group, animal, etc. considers as their own and defends against others who try to enter it: *Mating blackbirds will defend their territory against intruders.* ◇ (*figurative*) *This type of work is **uncharted territory** for us.* ◇ (*figurative*) *Legal problems are Andy's territory* (= he deals with them). **3** [C, U] an area of a town, country, etc. that sb has responsibility for in their work or another activity: *Our representatives cover a very large territory.* **4** [U] a particular type of land: *unexplored territory* **5** (also **Territory**) [C] a country or an area that is part of the US, Australia or Canada but is not a state or PROVINCE: *Guam and American Samoa are US territories.*
IDM **ˌcome/ˌgo with the ˈterritory** to be a normal and accepted part of a particular job, situation, etc: *She has to work late most days, but in her kind of job that goes with the territory.* ➲ more at NEUTRAL *adj.*

ter·ror /ˈterə(r)/ *noun* **1** [U, sing.] a feeling of extreme fear: *a feeling of **sheer/pure terror*** ◇ *Her eyes were wild with terror.* ◇ *People fled from the explosion **in terror**.* ◇ *She **lives in terror of*** (= is constantly afraid of) *losing her job.* ◇ *Some women have a terror of losing control in the birth process.* ◇ (*literary*) *The very name of the enemy **struck terror into** their hearts.* ➲ SYNONYMS at FEAR **2** [C] a person, situation or thing that makes you very afraid: *These street gangs have become the terror of the neighbourhood.* ◇ *Death **holds no terrors for*** (= does not frighten or worry) *me.* ◇ *The terrors of the night were past.* **3** [U] violent action or the threat of violent action that is intended to cause fear, usually for political purposes SYN **terrorism**: *a campaign of terror* ◇ *terror tactics* ➲ see also REIGN OF TERROR **4** [C] (*informal*) a person (usually a child) or an animal that causes you trouble or is difficult to control: *Their kids are real little terrors.*

ter·ror·ism /ˈterərɪzəm/ *noun* [U] the use of violent action in order to achieve political aims or to force a government to act: *an act of terrorism* ➲ COLLOCATIONS at CRIME

ter·ror·ist /ˈterərɪst/ *noun* a person who takes part in terrorism: *The terrorists are threatening to blow up the plane.* ◇ *a **terrorist attack/bomb/group***

ter·ror·ize (*BrE* also **-ise**) /ˈterəraɪz/ *verb* to frighten and threaten people so that they will not oppose sth or will do as they are told: **~ sb** *drug dealers terrorizing the neighbourhood* ◇ **~ sb into doing sth** *People were terrorized into leaving their homes.*

ˈterror-stricken *adj.* extremely frightened

terry /ˈteri/ *noun* [U] a type of soft cotton cloth that absorbs liquids and has a surface covered with raised LOOPS of thread, used especially for making towels

terse /tɜːs; *NAmE* tɜːrs/ *adj.* using few words and often not seeming polite or friendly: *a terse style* ◇ *The President issued a terse statement denying the charges.* ▸ **terse·ly** *adv.* **terse·ness** *noun* [U]

ter·tiary /ˈtɜːʃəri; *NAmE* ˈtɜːrʃieri; -ʃəri/ *adj.* third in order, rank or importance: *the tertiary sector* (= the area of industry that deals with services rather than materials or goods) ◇ (*BrE*) *tertiary education* (= at university or college level) ➲ compare PRIMARY, SECONDARY

ˈ**tertiary college** *noun* (in Britain) a college that provides education for people aged 16 and older, but that is not a university

ˈ**tertiary industry** (also ˈ**service industry**) *noun* [U, C] (*economics*) the part of a country's economy that provides services ➲ compare PRIMARY INDUSTRY, SECONDARY INDUSTRY

tery·lene™ /ˈterəliːn/ *noun* [U] (*BrE*) a light strong artificial material, used for making clothes, etc.

TESL /ˈtesl/ *abbr.* teaching English as a second language

TESOL /ˈtiːsɒl; ˈtesɒl; *NAmE* -sɑːl; -sɔːl/ *abbr.* **1** teaching English to speakers of other languages **2** (*NAmE*) teachers of English to speakers of other languages (an organization of teachers)

tes·sel·lated /ˈtesəleɪtɪd/ *adj.* (*technical*) made from small flat pieces arranged in a pattern: *a tessellated pavement*

test 0‑ᴡ /test/ *noun, verb*

■ ***noun***

▸ OF KNOWLEDGE/ABILITY **1** 0‑ᴡ an examination of sb's knowledge or ability, consisting of questions for them to answer or activities for them to perform: *an **IQ/intelligence/aptitude test*** ◇ *to **take a test*** ◇ (*BrE*) *to **do a test*** ◇ **~ (on sth)** *a test on irregular verbs* ◇ *to **pass/fail a test*** ◇ (*BrE*) *a good mark **in the test*** ◇ (*NAmE*) *a good grade **on the test*** ➲ COLLOCATIONS at EDUCATION ➲ note at EXAM ➲ see also DRIVING TEST

▸ OF HEALTH **2** 0‑ᴡ a medical examination to discover what is wrong with you or to check the condition of your health: *a test for AIDS* ◇ *an eye test* ◇ *a pregnancy test* ◇ *When can I get my **test results**?* ➲ see also BLOOD TEST, BREATH TEST

▸ OF MACHINE/PRODUCT, ETC. **3** 0‑ᴡ an experiment to discover whether or how well sth works, or to find out more information about it: *laboratory tests* ◇ *a nuclear test* ◇ *Tests have shown high levels of pollutants in the water.* ◇ *I'll run a diagnostic test to see why the server keeps crashing.* ➲ see also ACID TEST, BLIND TEST, FIELD TEST, MEANS TEST, ROAD TEST

▸ OF STRENGTH, ETC. **4** a situation or an event that shows how good, strong, etc. sb/sth is: *The local elections will be a good test of the government's popularity.*

▸ IN CRICKET, ETC. **5 Test** = TEST MATCH

IDM **put sb/sth to the ˈtest** to put sb/sth in a situation which will show what their or its true qualities are: *His theories have never really been put to the test.* **stand the test of ˈtime** to prove to be good, popular, etc. over a long period of time ➲ more at TEACH *v.*

■ ***verb***

▸ KNOWLEDGE/ABILITY **1** 0‑ᴡ [T, I] to find out how much sb knows, or what they can do by asking them questions or giving them activities to perform: **~ sb (on sth)** *Children are tested on core subjects at ages 7, 11 and 14.* ◇ **~ (sth)** *We test your English before deciding which class to put you in.* ◇ *Schools use various methods of testing.* **2** [I] **~ well/badly** to perform well/badly in a test of knowledge or ability: *students who tested well in reading*

▸ HEALTH **3** 0‑ᴡ [T, I] to examine the blood, a part of the body, etc. to find out what is wrong with a person, or to check the condition of their health: **~ sb/sth** *to test sb's eyesight/hearing* ◇ **~ sb/sth for sth** *The doctor tested him for hepatitis.* ◇ **+ adj. (for sth)** *to **test positive/negative*** ◇ *Two athletes tested positive for steroids.*

▸ MACHINE/PRODUCT, ETC. **4** 0‑ᴡ [T] to use or try a machine, substance, etc. to find out how well it works or to find out more information about it: **~ sth** *Test your brakes regularly.* ◇ **~ sth on sb/sth** *Our beauty products are not tested on animals.* ◇ **~ sth for sth** *The water is regularly tested for purity.* ◇ **~ sth out** *They opened a single store in Europe to test out the market.* ➲ see also FIELD-TEST **5** [I] **~ well/badly** (of a machine or product) to perform well/badly in a test of how well it works: *The ad had tested badly with consumers.*

▸ STRENGTH, ETC. **6** [T] **~ sb/sth** to be difficult and therefore need all your strength, ability, etc: *The long climb tested our fitness and stamina.* ➲ see also TESTING

IDM **test the ˈwaters** to find out what the situation is before doing sth or making a decision ➲ more at TRIED

PHR V ˈ**test for sth** | ˈ**test sth for sth** to examine sth to see if a particular substance, etc. is present: *testing for oil* ◇ *The software has been tested for viruses.*

test·able /ˈtestəbl/ *adj.* that can be tested: *testable hypotheses*

tes·ta·ment /ˈtestəmənt/ *noun* (*formal*) **1** [C, usually sing., U] **~ (to sth)** a thing that shows that sth else exists or is true SYN **testimony**: *The new model is a testament to the skill and dedication of the workforce.* **2** [C] = WILL: *This is the last will and testament of...* ➲ see also NEW TESTAMENT, OLD TESTAMENT

ˈ**test ban** *noun* an agreement between countries to stop testing nuclear weapons: *a test ban treaty*

ˈ**test bed** *noun* a piece of equipment used for testing new machinery, especially aircraft engines: (*figurative*) *The country is an ideal test bed for emerging technologies.*

ˈ**test case** *noun* a legal case or other situation whose result will be used as an example when decisions are being made on similar cases in the future

ˈ**test drive** *noun* an occasion when you drive a vehicle that you are thinking of buying so that you can see how well it works and if you like it ▸ ˈ**test-drive** *verb* **~ sth**

test·er /ˈtestə(r)/ *noun* **1** a person or thing that tests sth: *testers of new software* **2** a small container of a product, such as PERFUME, that you can try in a shop/store to see if you like it

tes·tes *pl.* of TESTIS

ˈ**test flight** *noun* a flight during which an aircraft or part of its equipment is tested

tes·ticle /ˈtestɪkl/ *noun* either of the two organs that produce SPERM, located in a bag of skin below the PENIS ▸ **tes·ticu·lar** /tesˈtɪkjələ(r)/ *adj.* [only before noun]: *testicular cancer*

test·ify /ˈtestɪfaɪ/ *verb* (**testi·fies**, **testi·fy·ing**, **testi·fied**, **testi·fied**) **1** [I, T] to make a statement that sth happened or that sth is true, especially as a witness in court: **~ (against/for sb)** *She refused to testify against her husband.* ◇ *There are several witnesses who will testify for the defence.* ◇ **~ about sth** *He was summoned to testify before a grand jury about his role in the affair.* ◇ **~ to sth/to doing sth** *Evans testified to receiving $200 000 in bribes.* ◇ **~ (that)...** *He testified (that) he was at the theatre at the time of the murder.* ◇ **+ speech** *'I was approached by a man I did not recognize,' she testified.* **2** [T] **~ (that)...** (*formal*) to say that you believe sth is true because you have evidence of it: *Too many young people are unable to write or spell well, as employers will testify.* **3** [I] (*especially NAmE*) to express your belief in God publicly

PHR V ˈ**testify to sth** (*formal*) to show or be evidence that sth is true SYN **evidence**: *The film testifies to the courage of ordinary people during the war.*

tes·ti·mo·nial /ˌtestɪˈməʊniəl; *NAmE* -ˈmoʊ-/ *noun* **1** a formal written statement, often by a former employer, about sb's abilities, qualities and character; a formal written statement about the quality of sth: *a glowing testimonial* ◇ *The catalogue is full of testimonials from satisfied customers.* **2** a thing that is given or done to show admiration for sb or to thank sb: *a testimonial game* (= to raise money for a particular player)

tes·ti·mony /ˈtestɪməni; *NAmE* -moʊni/ *noun* (*pl.* -ies) **1** [U, sing.] **~ (to sth)** (*formal*) a thing that shows that sth else exists or is true SYN **testament**: *This increase in exports **bears testimony to** the successes of industry.* ◇ *The pyramids are an eloquent testimony to the ancient Egyptians' engineering skills.* **2** [C, U] a formal written or spoken

T

statement saying what you know to be true, usually in court: *a sworn testimony* ◇ *Can I refuse to give testimony?*

test·ing /ˈtestɪŋ/ *noun, adj.*
- **noun** [U] the activity of testing sb/sth in order to find sth out, see if it works, etc: *nuclear testing* ◇ *testing and assessment in education*
- **adj.** (of a problem or situation) difficult to deal with and needing particular strength or abilities

ˈtesting ground *noun* **1** a place or situation used for testing new ideas and methods to see if they work **2** a place used for testing machines, etc. to see if they work correctly: *a piece of land in use as a tank testing ground*

tes·tis /ˈtestɪs/ *noun* (*pl.* **tes·tes** /-tiːz/) (*anatomy*) a TESTICLE

ˈTest match (also **Test**) *noun* a CRICKET or RUGBY match played between the teams of two different countries, usually as part of a series of matches on a tour

tes·tos·ter·one /teˈstɒstərəʊn; *NAmE* teˈstɑːstəroʊn/ *noun* a HORMONE (= chemical substance produced in the body) that causes men to develop the physical and sexual features that are characteristic of the male body ➲ compare OESTROGEN, PROGESTERONE

ˈtest pilot *noun* a pilot whose job is to fly aircraft in order to test their performance

ˌtest ˈrun *noun* = TRIAL RUN

ˈtest tube *noun* a small glass tube, closed at one end, that is used in scientific experiments ➲ VISUAL VOCAB page V57

ˈtest-tube baby *noun* a baby that grows from an egg that is FERTILIZED outside the mother's body and then put back inside to continue developing normally ➲ see also IN VITRO

testy /ˈtesti/ *adj.* easily annoyed or irritated SYN **irritable** ▶ **test·ily** /-ɪli/ *adv.*: *'Leave me alone,' she said testily.*

tet·anus /ˈtetənəs/ *noun* [U] a disease in which the muscles, especially the JAW muscles, become stiff, caused by bacteria entering the body through cuts or wounds

tetchy /ˈtetʃi/ *adj.* bad-tempered; likely to get angry easily or without good reason SYN **irritable** ▶ **tetch·ily** /-ɪli/ *adv.*

tête-à-tête /ˌteɪt ɑː ˈteɪt/ *noun* (from *French*) a private conversation between two people

tether /ˈteðə(r)/ *verb, noun*
- **verb ~ sth (to sth)** to tie an animal to a post so that it cannot move very far
- **noun** a rope or chain used to tie an animal to sth, allowing it to move around in a small area IDM see END *n.*

tetra·he·dron /ˌtetrəˈhiːdrən; -ˈhed-/ *noun* (*geometry*) a solid shape with four flat sides that are triangles ➲ VISUAL VOCAB page V58

T

tet·ral·ogy /teˈtrælədʒi/ *noun* (*pl.* -ies) a group of four books, films/movies, etc. that have the same subject or characters

Tetra Pak™ /ˈtetrə pæk/ *noun* a type of cardboard container in which milk or other drinks are sold

Teut·on·ic /tjuːˈtɒnɪk; *NAmE* tuːˈtɑːnɪk/ *adj.* [usually before noun] (*informal*, often *disapproving*) showing qualities considered typical of German people: *The preparations were made with Teutonic thoroughness.*

Tex-Mex /ˌteks ˈmeks/ *adj.* [only before noun] connected with the variety of Mexican cooking, music, etc. that is found in Texas and the SW part of the US

text 0- AW /tekst/ *noun, verb*
- **noun 1** 0- [U] the main printed part of a book or magazine, not the notes, pictures, etc: *My job is to lay out the text and graphics on the page.* **2** 0- [U] any form of written material: *a computer that can process text* ◇ *printed text* **3** [C] = TEXT MESSAGE **4** 0- [C] the written form of a speech, a play, an article, etc: *The newspaper had printed the full text of the president's speech.* **5** 0- [C] a book, play, etc, especially one studied for an exam: *a literary text* ◇ (*BrE*) *'Macbeth' is a set text this year.* ➲ COLLOCATIONS at LITERATURE **6** 0- [C] a piece of writing that you have to answer questions about in an exam or a lesson SYN **passage**: *Read the text carefully and then answer the questions.* **7** [C] (*NAmE*) = TEXTBOOK: *medical texts* **8** [C] a sentence or short passage from the Bible that is read out and discussed by sb, especially during a religious service
- **verb** [T, I] to send sb a written message using a mobile/cell phone: **~ (sb)** *Text me when you're on your way.* ◇ *Kids seem to be texting non-stop these days.* ◇ **~ sb sth** *I'll text you the final score.* ➲ see also SMS, TEXT-MESSAGE

text·book /ˈtekstbʊk/ *noun, adj.*
- **noun** (*NAmE* also **text**) a book that teaches a particular subject and that is used especially in schools and colleges: *a* ***school/medical/history, etc. textbook*** ➲ VISUAL VOCAB page V57
- **adj.** [only before noun] used to describe sth that is done exactly as it should be done, in the best possible way: *a* ***textbook example*** *of how the game should be played*

ˈtext editor *noun* (*computing*) a system or program that allows you to make changes to text

texter /ˈtekstə(r)/ *noun* (*especially BrE*) a person who sends TEXT MESSAGES

tex·tile /ˈtekstaɪl/ *noun* **1** [C] any type of cloth made by WEAVING or knitting: *a factory producing a range of textiles* ◇ *the textile industry* ◇ *a textile designer* ➲ note at FABRIC **2 textiles** [pl.] the industry that makes cloth

ˈtext message (also **text**) *noun* a written message that you send using a mobile/cell phone: *Send a text message to this number to vote.* ➲ COLLOCATIONS at PHONE ▶ **ˈtext-message** (also **text**) *verb* [T, I]: **~ (sb) (sth)** *I text-messaged him to say we were waiting in the pub.* **ˈtext-messaging** (also **text·ing**) *noun* [U]

ˌtext-to-ˈspeech *noun* (*abbr.* TTS) [U] (*computing*) a computer program that converts text into spoken language: *text-to-speech software* ◇ *a TTS package*

text·ual AW /ˈtekstʃuəl/ *adj.* [usually before noun] connected with or contained in a text: *textual analysis* ◇ *textual errors*

tex·tural /ˈtekstʃərəl/ *adj.* (*technical*) relating to texture: *the textural characteristics of the rocks*

tex·ture /ˈtekstʃə(r)/ *noun* [C, U] **1** the way a surface, substance or piece of cloth feels when you touch it, for example how rough, smooth, hard or soft it is: *the soft texture of velvet* ◇ *She uses a variety of different colours and textures in her wall hangings.* **2** the way food or drink tastes or feels in your mouth, for example whether it is rough, smooth, light, heavy, etc: *The two cheeses were very different in both taste and texture.* **3** the way that different parts of a piece of music or literature are combined to create a final impression: *the rich texture of the symphony*

tex·tured /ˈtekstʃəd; *NAmE* -tʃərd/ *adj.* with a surface that is not smooth, but has a particular texture: *textured wallpaper*

ˌtextured ˈvegetable protein *noun* (*abbr.* TVP) a substance that looks like meat, but which is made from SOYA BEANS

TFT /ˌtiː ef ˈtiː/ *noun* a piece of technology used to make flat screens for computers, mobile phones/cell phones, etc. (the abbreviation for thin film transistor): *a 17 in TFT screen*

TG /ˌtiː ˈdʒiː/ *abbr.* TRANSFORMATIONAL GRAMMAR

-th *suffix* **1** (in ordinal numbers): *sixth* ◇ *fifteenth* ◇ *hundredth* **2** (in nouns) the action or process of: *growth*

thali /ˈtɑːli/ *noun* (*IndE*) **1** a metal plate on which food is served **2** a set meal at a restaurant

thal·ido·mide /θəˈlɪdəmaɪd/ *noun* [U] a SEDATIVE drug which was used until the 1960s, when it was discovered that if given to pregnant women, it prevented some babies from developing normal arms and legs

thal·lium /ˈθæliəm/ *noun* [U] (*symb.* Tl) a chemical element. Thallium is a soft silver-white metal whose COMPOUNDS are very poisonous.

than 0- /ðən; *rare strong form* ðæn/ *prep., conj.*
1 0- used to introduce the second part of a comparison: *I'm older than her.* ◇ *There was more whisky in it than soda.*

◇ *He loves me more than you do.* ◇ *It was much better than I'd expected.* ◇ *You should know better than to behave like that.* ◇ *I'd rather email than phone, if that's OK by you.* **2** ⊶ **more/less/fewer, etc. ~** used for comparing amounts, numbers, distances, etc.: *It never takes more than an hour.* ◇ *It's less than a mile to the beach.* ◇ *There were fewer than twenty people there.* **3** used in expressions showing that one thing happens straight after another: ***No sooner*** *had I sat down* ***than*** *there was a loud knock on the door.* ◇ ***Hardly*** *had we arrived* ***than*** *the problems started.* IDM see OTHER *adj.*

thang /θæŋ/ *noun* (*NAmE, informal*) a way of saying or writing the word 'thing', that represents the pronunciation of the southern US

thank ⊶ /θæŋk/ *verb* to tell sb that you are grateful for sth: **~ sb for sth** *I must write and thank Mary for the present.* ◇ *In his speech, he thanked everyone for all their hard work.* ◇ **~ sb for doing sth** *She said goodbye and thanked us for coming.* ◇ **~ sb** *There's no need to thank me—I enjoyed doing it.*
IDM **have sb to thank (for sth)** used when you are saying who is responsible for sth: *I have my parents to thank for my success.* **I'll thank you for sth/to do sth** (*formal*) used to tell sb that you are annoyed and do not want them to do sth: *I'll thank you to mind your own business.* **thank 'God/'goodness/'heaven(s) (for sth)** ⊶ used to say that you are pleased about sth: *Thank God you're safe!* ◇ *'Thank goodness for that!' she said with a sigh of relief.* HELP Some people find the phrase **thank God** offensive. **thank your lucky 'stars** to feel very grateful and lucky about sth **sb won't 'thank you for sth** used to say that sb will not be pleased or will be annoyed about sth: *John won't thank you for interfering.*

thank·ful /ˈθæŋkfl/ *adj.* [not usually before noun] pleased about sth good that has happened, or sth bad that has not happened: **~ (to do sth)** *I was thankful to see they'd all arrived safely.* ◇ **~ (for sth)** *He wasn't badly hurt—that's something to be thankful for.* ◇ **~ (that...)** *I was thankful that he hadn't been hurt.* IDM see SMALL *adj.*

thank·ful·ly /ˈθæŋkfəli/ *adv.* **1** used to show that you are pleased that sth good has happened or that sth bad has been avoided SYN **fortunately**: *There was a fire in the building, but thankfully no one was hurt.* **2** in a pleased or grateful way: *I accepted the invitation thankfully.*

thank·less /ˈθæŋkləs/ *adj.* unpleasant or difficult to do and unlikely to bring you any rewards or thanks from anyone: *Sometimes being a mother and a housewife felt like* ***a thankless task.***

thanks ⊶ /θæŋks/ *exclamation, noun*
■ ***exclamation*** ➲ see also THANK YOU **1** ⊶ used to show that you are grateful to sb for sth they have done: **~ (for doing sth)** *Thanks for lending me the money.* ◇ **~ (for sth)** ***Many thanks*** *for your support.* ◇ *'How are you?' 'Fine, thanks* (= thanks for asking).' **2** ⊶ a polite way of accepting sth that sb has offered you: *'Would you like a coffee?' 'Oh, thanks.'* ◇ *'Here's the change.'* ***'Thanks very much.'*** **3** ⊶ **no thanks** a polite way of refusing sth that sb has offered you: *'Would you like some more?' 'No thanks.'*
■ ***noun*** ⊶ [pl.] **~ (to sb) (for sth)** words or actions that show that you are grateful to sb for sth SYN **gratitude**: *How can I ever express my thanks to you for all you've done?* ◇ *Thanks are due to all those who worked so hard for so many months.* ◇ *She murmured her thanks.* ➲ see also VOTE OF THANKS
IDM **no thanks to sb/sth** despite sb/sth; with no help from sb/sth: *We managed to get it finished in the end—no thanks to him* (= he didn't help). **thanks a lot** **1** ⊶ used to show that you are very grateful to sb for sth they have done: *Thanks a lot for all you've done.* **2** (*ironic*) used to show that you are annoyed that sb has done sth because it causes trouble or difficulty for you: *'I'm afraid I've finished all the milk.' 'Well, thanks a lot!'* **thanks to sb/sth** ⊶ (sometimes *ironic*) used to say that sth has happened because of sb/sth: *It was all a great success—thanks to a lot of hard work.* ◇ *Everyone knows about it now, thanks to you!*

thanks·giv·ing /ˌθæŋksˈɡɪvɪŋ/ *noun* **1 Thanksgiving (Day)** [U, C] a public holiday in the US (on the fourth Thursday in November) and in Canada (on the second Monday in October), originally to give thanks to God for the HARVEST and for health: *We always eat turkey on Thanksgiving.* ◇ *Are you going home for Thanksgiving?* ➲ compare HARVEST FESTIVAL **2** [U] (*formal*) the expression of thanks to God

ˈthank you ⊶ *exclamation, noun*
■ ***exclamation*** ➲ see also THANKS **1** ⊶ used to show that you are grateful to sb for sth they have done: **~ (for sth)** *Thank you for your letter.* ◇ **~ (for doing sth)** ***Thank you very much*** *for sending the photos.* **2** ⊶ a polite way of accepting sth that sb has offered you: *'Would you like some help with that?' 'Oh, thank you.'* **3** ⊶ **no thank you** a polite way of refusing sth that sb has offered you: *'Would you like some more cake?' 'No thank you.'* **4** used at the end of a sentence to tell sb firmly that you do not need their help or advice: *'Shall I do that?' 'I can do it myself, thank you.'*
■ ***noun*** ⊶ [usually sing.] **~ (to sb) (for sth)** an act, a gift, a comment, etc. intended to thank sb for sth they have done: *The actor sent a big thank you to all his fans for their letters of support.* ◇ *She took the money without so much as a thank you.* ◇ *a thank-you letter*

that ⊶ *det., pron., conj., adv.*
■ ***det.*** /ðæt/ (*pl.* **those** /ðəʊz; *NAmE* ðoʊz/) **1** ⊶ used for referring to a person or thing that is not near the speaker or as near to the speaker as another: *Look at that man over there.* ◇ *How much are those apples at the back?* **2** ⊶ used for referring to sb/sth that has already been mentioned or is already known about: *I was living with my parents at that time.* ◇ *That incident changed their lives.* ◇ *Have you forgotten about that money I lent you last week?* ◇ *That dress of hers is too short.*
■ ***pron.*** /ðæt/ (*pl.* **those** /ðəʊz; *NAmE* ðoʊz/) **1** ⊶ used for referring to a person or thing that is not near the speaker, or not as near to the speaker as another: *Who's that?* ◇ *That's Peter over there.* ◇ *Hello. Is that Jo?* ◇ *That's a nice dress.* ◇ *Those look riper than these.* **2** ⊶ used for referring to sb/sth that has already been mentioned, or is already known about: *What can I do about that?* ◇ *Do you remember when we went to Norway? That was a good trip.* ◇ *That's exactly what I think.* **3** (*formal*) used for referring to people or things of a particular type: *Those present were in favour of change.* ◇ *There are those who say* (= some people say) *she should not have got the job.* ◇ *Salaries are higher here than those in my country.* **4** ⊶ /ðət; *rare strong form* ðæt/ (*pl.* **that**) used as a relative pronoun to introduce a part of a sentence which refers to the person, thing or time you have been talking about: *Where's the letter that came yesterday?* ◇ *Who was it that won the US Open?* ◇ *The watch (that) you gave me keeps perfect time.* ◇ *The people (that) I spoke to were very helpful.* ◇ *It's the best novel (that) I've ever read.* ◇ *We moved here the year (that) my mother died.* HELP In spoken and informal written English **that** is nearly always left out when it is the object of the verb or is used with a preposition.
IDM **and (all) 'that** (*BrE, informal*) and everything else connected with an activity, a situation, etc. SYN **and so on**: *Did you bring the contract and (all) that?* **that is (to say)** used to say what sth means or to give more information: *He's a local government administrator, that is to say a civil servant.* ◇ *You'll find her very helpful—if she's not too busy, that is.* ➲ LANGUAGE BANK at I.E. **ˌthat's ˈit** (*informal*) **1** ⊶ used to say that sb is right, or is doing sth right: *No, the other one... that's it.* ◇ *That's it, carry on!* **2** ⊶ used to say that sth is finished, or that no more can be done: *That's it, the fire's out now.* ◇ *That's it for now, but if I get any news I'll let you know.* ◇ *A week to go, and that's it!* **3** used to say that you will not accept sth any longer: *That's it, I've had enough!* **4** ⊶ used to talk about the reason for sth: *So that's it—the fuse had gone.* ◇ *You don't love me any more, is that it?* **ˌthat's ˈthat** (*informal*) used to say that your decision cannot be changed: *Well I'm not going, and that's that.*
■ ***conj.*** /ðət; *rare strong form* ðæt/ **1** ⊶ used after some verbs, adjectives and nouns to introduce a new part of the sentence: *She said (that) the story was true.* ◇ *It's pos-*

T

sible (that) he has not received the letter. ◇ The fact (that) he's older than me is not relevant. HELP In spoken and informal written English **that** is usually left out after reporting verbs and adjectives. It is less often left out after nouns. **2** **so... that...** used to express a result: *She was so tired (that) she couldn't think straight.* HELP In informal English **that** is often left out. **3** (*literary*) used for expressing a hope or a wish: *Oh that I could see him again!*

■ ***adv.*** /ðæt/ **1** used when saying how much or showing how long, big, etc. sth is with your hands: *I can't walk that far* (= as far as that). ◇ *It's about that long.* **2** **not (all) ~** not very, or not as much as has been said: *It isn't all that cold.* ◇ *There aren't that many people here.* **3** (*BrE, informal*) used to emphasize how much: *I was that scared I didn't know what to do.*

tha·ta·way /ˈðætəweɪ/ *adv.* (*informal*) in that direction: *They went thataway!*

thatch /θætʃ/ *noun, verb*

■ ***noun*** **1** [U, C] dried STRAW, REEDS, etc. used for making a roof; a roof made of this material: *a roof made of thatch* ◇ *The thatch was badly damaged in the storm.* **2** [sing.] **~ of hair** (*informal*) thick hair on sb's head

■ ***verb*** **~ sth** to cover the roof of a building with thatch ▸ **thatched** *adj.*: *They live in a thatched cottage.* ➲ VISUAL VOCAB page V14

thatch·er /ˈθætʃə(r)/ *noun* a person whose job is thatching roofs

Thatch·er·ite /ˈθætʃəraɪt/ *adj.* connected with or supporting the policies of the former British Prime Minister, Margaret Thatcher (= thought of as being right-wing) ▸ **Thatch·er·ite** *noun*

thaw /θɔː/ *verb, noun*

■ ***verb*** **1** [I] **~ (out)** (of ice and snow) to turn back into water after being frozen SYN **melt** OPP **freeze** **2** [I] when **it thaws** or **is thawing**, the weather becomes warm enough to melt snow and ice: *It's starting to thaw.* **3** [I, T] **~ (sth) (out)** to become, or to let frozen food become, soft or liquid ready for cooking ➲ compare DEFROST, DE-ICE, UNFREEZE: *Leave the meat to thaw completely before cooking.* **4** [I, T] **~ (sth) (out)** to become, or make sth become, a normal temperature after being very cold: *I could feel my ears and toes start to thaw out.* **5** [I] **~ (out)** to become more friendly and less formal: *Relations between the two countries thawed a little after the talks.*

■ ***noun*** **1** [C, usually sing.] a period of warmer weather following one of cold weather, causing snow and ice to melt **2** [sing.] **~ (in sth)** a situation in which the relations between two enemy countries become more friendly

the /ðə; ði; *strong form* ðiː/ *definite article*

1 used to refer to sb/sth that has already been mentioned or is easily understood: *There were three questions. The first two were relatively easy but the third one was hard.* ◇ *There was an accident here yesterday. A car hit a tree and the driver was killed.* ◇ *The heat was getting to be too much for me.* ◇ *The nights are getting longer.* **2** used to refer to sb/sth that is the only, normal or obvious one of their kind: *the Mona Lisa* ◇ *the Nile* ◇ *the Queen* ◇ *What's the matter?* ◇ *The phone rang.* ◇ *I patted her on the back.* ◇ *How's the* (= your) *baby?* **3** used when explaining which person or thing you mean: *the house at the end of the street* ◇ *The people I met there were very friendly.* ◇ *It was the best day of my life.* ◇ *You're the third person to ask me that.* ◇ *Friday the thirteenth* ◇ *Alexander the Great* **4** used to refer to a thing in general rather than a particular example: *He taught himself to play the violin.* ◇ *The dolphin is an intelligent animal.* ◇ *They placed the African elephant on their endangered list.* ◇ *I heard it on the radio.* ◇ *I'm usually out during the day.* **5** used with adjectives to refer to a thing or a group of people described by the adjective: *With him, you should always expect the unexpected.* ◇ *the unemployed* ◇ *the French* **6** used before the plural of sb's last name to refer to a whole family or a married couple: *Don't forget to invite the Jordans.* **7** enough of sth for a particular purpose: *I wanted it but I didn't have the money.* **8** used with a unit of measurement to mean 'every': *My car does forty miles to the gallon.* ◇ *You get paid by the hour.* **9** used with a unit of time to mean 'the present': *Why not have the dish of the day?* ◇ *She's flavour of the month with him.* **10** /ðiː/ used, stressing *the*, to show that the person or thing referred to is famous or important: *Sheryl Crow? Not 'the Sheryl Crow?* ◇ *At that time London was 'the place to be.*

IDM **the more, less, etc..., the more, less, etc...** used to show that two things change to the same degree: *The more she thought about it, the more depressed she became.* ◇ *The less said about the whole thing, the happier I'll be.*

the·atre (*especially US* **theater**) /ˈθɪətə(r); *NAmE* ˈθiːətər/ *noun*

1 [C] a building or an outdoor area where plays and similar types of entertainment are performed: *Broadway theatres* ◇ *an open-air theatre* ◇ *How often do you* ***go to the theatre?*** ➲ VISUAL VOCAB page V2 ➲ see also LECTURE THEATRE **2** (also ˈ**movie theater**) (both *NAmE*) (*BrE* **cin·ema**) [C] a building in which films/movies are shown **3** [U] plays considered as entertainment: *an evening of live music and theatre* ◇ (*BrE*) *I like music, theatre and cinema.* ◇ *current ideas about what makes good theatre* (= what makes good entertainment when performed) **4** [U] (also **the theatre** [sing.]) the work of writing, producing and acting in plays: *I want to work in theatre.* ◇ *He was essentially a man of the theatre.* **5** [C, U] (*BrE*) = OPERATING THEATRE: *a theatre sister* (= a nurse who helps during operations) ◇ *He's still* ***in theatre.*** **6** [C, usually sing.] **~ (of war, etc.)** (*formal*) the place in which a war or fighting takes place

theatre·goer (*especially US* **theater·goer**) /ˈθɪətəgəʊə(r); *NAmE* ˈθiːətərgoʊər/ (also **play·goer**) *noun* a person who goes regularly to the theatre ▸ **theatre·going** (*especially US* **theater·going**) *adj.*: *the theatregoing public*

ˌ**theatre-in-the-ˈround** (*especially US* ˌ**theater-in-the-ˈround**) *noun* [U] a way of performing plays on a stage which is surrounded by the audience

ˈ**theatre nurse** (*BrE*) (*NAmE* ˈ**scrub nurse**) *noun* a nurse with special training, who helps during operations

the·at·ri·cal /θiˈætrɪkl/ *adj.* **1** [only before noun] connected with the theatre: *a theatrical agent* **2** (often *disapproving*) (of behaviour) exaggerated in order to attract attention or create a particular effect: *a theatrical gesture* ▸ **the·at·ri·cal·ly** /-kli/ *adv.*

the·at·ri·cal·ity /θiˌætrɪˈkæləti/ *noun* [U] the exaggerated quality of sth that is intended to attract attention or create a particular effect

the·at·ri·cals /θiˈætrɪklz/ *noun* [pl.] **1** performances of plays: *amateur theatricals* **2** (also **the·at·rics** especially in *NAmE*) behaviour that is exaggerated and emotional in order to attract attention

thee /ðiː/ *pron.* (*old use* or *dialect*) a word meaning 'you', used when talking to only one person who is the object of the verb: *We beseech thee, O Lord.* ➲ compare THOU

theft /θeft/ *noun* [U, C] **~ (of sth)** the crime of stealing sth from a person or place: *car theft* ◇ *Police are investigating the theft of computers from the company's offices.* ➲ compare BURGLARY, ROBBERY ➲ see also IDENTITY THEFT, THIEF

their /ðeə(r); *NAmE* ðer/ *det.*

(the possessive form of *they*) **1** of or belonging to them: *Their parties are always fun.* ◇ *Which is their house?* **2** used instead of *his* or *her* to refer to a person whose sex is not mentioned or not known: *If anyone calls, ask for their number so I can call them back.* ➲ note at GENDER

theirs /ðeəz; *NAmE* ðerz/ *pron.*

(the possessive form of *they*) of or belonging to them: *Theirs are the children with very fair hair.* ◇ *It's a favourite game of theirs.*

the·ism /ˈθiːɪzəm/ *noun* [U] belief in the existence of God or gods OPP **atheism**

them /ðəm; *strong form* ðem/ *pron.*

(the object form of *they*) **1** used when referring to people, animals or things as the object of a verb or preposition, or after the verb *be*: *Tell them the news.* ◇ *What are*

T

you doing with those matches? Give them to me. ◇ *Did you eat all of them?* ◇ *It's them.* **2** 🔑 used instead of *him* or *her* to refer to a person whose sex is not mentioned or not known: *If anyone comes in before I get back, ask them to wait.*

the·mat·ic AW /θɪˈmætɪk; θiː-/ *adj.* [usually before noun] connected with the theme or themes of sth: *the thematic structure of a text* ▸ **the·mat·ic·al·ly** AW /-kli/ *adv.*: *The books have been grouped thematically.*

the,matic ˈrole (also **ˈtheta role**) *noun* (*linguistics*) the function that a noun phrase has in relation to a verb, for example AGENT or PATIENT

theme 🔑 AW /θiːm/ *noun, adj.*
■ ***noun*** **1** 🔑 the subject or main idea in a talk, piece of writing or work of art: *North American literature is the main theme of this year's festival.* ◇ *The President stressed a favourite campaign theme—greater emphasis on education.* ◇ *The naked male figure was always the central theme of Greek art.* ◇ *The stories are all* ***variations on the theme*** *of unhappy marriage.* ➲ COLLOCATIONS at LITERATURE **2** (*music*) a short tune that is repeated or developed in a piece of music **3** = THEME MUSIC: *the theme from 'The Godfather'* **4** (*old-fashioned, NAmE*) a short piece of writing on a particular subject, done for school **5** (*linguistics*) the part of a sentence or clause that contains information that is not new to the reader or audience ➲ compare RHEME
■ ***adj.*** (*BrE*) **~ pub/bar/restaurant, etc.** a pub, bar, etc. that is designed to reflect a particular subject or period of history: *an Irish theme pub*

themed /θiːmd/ *adj.* [usually before noun] (*BrE*) (of an event or a place of entertainment) designed to reflect a particular subject or period of history: *a themed restaurant*

ˈtheme music *noun* [U] (also **theme**, **ˈtheme song**, **ˈtheme tune** [C]) music that is played at the beginning and end and/or is often repeated in a film/movie, television programme, etc. ➲ compare SIGNATURE TUNE

ˈtheme park *noun* a large park where people go to enjoy themselves, for example by riding on large machines such as ROLLER COASTERS, and where much of the entertainment is connected with one subject or idea: *a western-style theme park*

them·self /ðəmˈself/ *pron.* (the reflexive form of *they*) used instead of *himself* or *herself* to refer to a person whose sex is not mentioned or not known: *Does anyone here consider themself a good cook?* HELP Although **themself** is fairly common, especially in spoken English, many people think it is not correct.

them·selves 🔑 /ðəmˈselvz/ *pron.*
1 🔑 (the reflexive form of *they*) used when people or animals performing an action are also affected by it: *They seemed to be enjoying themselves.* ◇ *The children were arguing amongst themselves.* ◇ *They've bought themselves a new car.* **2** 🔑 used to emphasize *they* or a plural subject: *They themselves had had a similar experience.* ◇ *Don and Julie paid for it themselves.* **3** 🔑 used instead of *himself* or *herself* to refer to a person whose sex is not mentioned or not known: *There wasn't anyone who hadn't enjoyed themselves.* HELP Although this use of **themselves** is fairly common, especially in spoken English, many people think it is not correct.
IDM **(all) by themˈselves** **1** alone; without anyone else: *They wanted to spend the evening by themselves.* **2** without help: *They did the cooking by themselves.* **(all) to themˈselves** for them alone; not shared with anyone

then 🔑 /ðen/ *adv., adj.*
■ ***adv.*** **1** 🔑 used to refer to a particular time in the past or future: *Life was harder then because neither of us had a job.* ◇ *Things were very different* ***back then.*** ◇ *She grew up in Zimbabwe, or Rhodesia as it then was.* ◇ *I saw them at Christmas but haven't heard a thing* ***since then.*** ◇ *I've been invited too, so I'll see you then.* ◇ *There's a room free in Bob's house next week but you can stay with us* ***until then.*** ◇ *Call again next week. They should have reached a decision* ***by then.*** ◇ ***Just then*** (= at that moment) *there was a knock at the door.* ◇ *She left in 1984 and* ***from then on*** *he lived alone.* ◇ *I took one look at the car and offered to buy it* ***there and then/then and there*** (= immediately). **2** 🔑 used to introduce the next item in a series of actions, events, instructions, etc.: *He drank a glass of whisky, then another and then another.* ◇ *First cook the onions, then add the mushrooms.* ◇ *We lived in France and then Italy before coming back to England.* ➲ LANGUAGE BANK at PROCESS **3** 🔑 used to show the logical result of a particular statement or situation: *If you miss that train then you'll have to get a taxi.* ◇ *'My wife's got a job in Glasgow.' 'I take it you'll be moving, then.'* ◇ *'You haven't done anything to upset me.' 'So what's wrong, then?'* ◇ *Why don't you hire a car? Then you'll be able to visit more of the area.* **4** used to introduce additional information: *She's been very busy at work* ***and then*** *there was all that trouble with her son.* **5** (*formal*) used to introduce a summary of sth that has just been said: *These, then, are the main areas of concern.* **6** used to show the beginning or end of a conversation, statement, etc.: *Right then, where do you want the table to go?* ◇ *'I really have to go.' 'OK. Bye, then.'* ◇ *OK then, I think we've just about covered everything on the agenda.*
IDM **...and ˈthen some** (*informal*) used to emphasize the large amount or number of sth, and to say that you have not mentioned everything: *There are Indian, Chinese, Mexican, Thai restaurants... and then some!* **but ˈthen | then aˈgain | but then aˈgain** (*informal*) used to introduce additional information or information that contrasts with sth that has just been said: *She was early, but then again, she always is.* ◇ *'So you might accept their offer?' 'Yes, then again I might not.'* ➲ more at NOW *adv.*
■ ***adj.*** [only before noun] used to describe sb who had a particular title, job, etc. at the time in the past that is being discussed: *That decision was taken by the then president.*

thence /ðens/ *adv.* (*old use* or *formal*) from that place; following that: *They made their way from Spain to France and thence to England.* ◇ *He was promoted to manager, thence to a partnership in the firm.*

thence·forth /ˌðensˈfɔːθ; *NAmE* -ˈfɔːrθ/ (also **thence·for·ward** /ˌðensˈfɔːwəd; *NAmE* -ˈfɔːrwərd/) *adv.* (*old use* or *formal*) starting from that time

theo- /ˈθiːəʊ; *NAmE* ˈθiːoʊ/ *combining form* (in nouns, adjectives and adverbs) connected with God or a god

the·oc·racy /θiˈɒkrəsi; *NAmE* θiˈɑːk-/ *noun* (*pl.* -ies) **1** [U] government of a country by religious leaders **2** [C] a country that is governed by religious leaders ▸ **theo·crat·ic** /ˌθiːəˈkrætɪk/ *adj.*: *theocratic rule*

the·odo·lite /θiˈɒdəlaɪt; *NAmE* θiˈɑːd-/ *noun* a piece of equipment used by SURVEYORS for measuring angles

theo·lo·gian /ˌθiːəˈləʊdʒən; *NAmE* -ˈloʊ-/ *noun* a person who studies theology

the·ology /θiˈɒlədʒi; *NAmE* -ˈɑːlə-/ *noun* (*pl.* -ies) **1** [U] the study of religion and beliefs: *a degree in Theology* ◇ *a theology student* **2** [C] a set of religious beliefs: *the theologies of the East* ▸ **theo·logic·al** /ˌθiːəˈlɒdʒɪkl; *NAmE* -ˈlɑːdʒ-/ *adj.*: (*BrE*) *a theological college* ◇ (*NAmE*) *a theological seminary* **theo·logic·al·ly** /-kli/ *adv.*

the·orem /ˈθɪərəm; *NAmE* ˈθiːə-; ˈθɪr-/ *noun* (*technical*) a rule or principle, especially in mathematics, that can be proved to be true ➲ COLLOCATIONS at SCIENTIFIC

the·or·etic·al AW /ˌθɪəˈretɪkl; *NAmE* ˌθiːə-/ *adj.* [usually before noun] **1** concerned with the ideas and principles on which a particular subject is based, rather than with practice and experiment: *a theoretical approach* ◇ *theoretical physics* ◇ *The first year provides students with a sound theoretical basis for later study.* OPP **experimental, practical** **2** that could possibly exist, happen or be true, although this is unlikely: *It's a theoretical possibility.* ▸ **the·or·etic·al·ly** AW /-kli/ *adv.*: *theoretically sound conclusions* ◇ *It is theoretically possible for him to overrule their decision, but highly unlikely.*

the·or·ist AW /ˈθɪərɪst; *NAmE* ˈθiːə-; ˈθɪr-/ (also **the·or·et·ician** /ˌθɪərəˈtɪʃn; *NAmE* ˌθiːə-; ˌθɪr-/) *noun* a person who develops ideas and principles about a particular subject in order to explain why things happen or exist

T

the·or·ize (*BrE* also **-ise**) /'θɪəraɪz; *NAmE* 'θiːə-/ *verb* [I, T] **~ (about/on sth)** | **~ sth** | **~ that...** to suggest facts and ideas to explain sth; to form a theory or theories about sth: *The study theorizes about the role of dreams in peoples' lives.* ▶ **the·or·iz·ing, -is·ing** *noun* [U]

the·ory 🔑 AW /'θɪəri; *NAmE* 'θɪri; 'θiːəri/ *noun* (*pl.* -ies)
1 🔑 [C, U] a formal set of ideas that is intended to explain why sth happens or exists: *According to the theory of relativity, nothing can travel faster than light.* ➲ COLLOCATIONS at SCIENTIFIC **2** 🔑 [U] the principles on which a particular subject is based: *the theory and practice of language teaching* **3** 🔑 [C] **~ (that...)** an opinion or idea that sb believes is true but that is not proved: *I have this theory that most people prefer being at work to being at home.*
IDM **in 'theory** 🔑 used to say that a particular statement is supposed to be true but may in fact be wrong: *In theory, these machines should last for ten years or more.* ◇ *That sounds fine in theory, but have you really thought it through?*

the·oso·phy /θi'ɒsəfi; *NAmE* θi'ɑːs-/ *noun* **1** [U, C] a religious system of thought that tries to know God by means of MEDITATION, prayer, etc. **2 Theosophy** [U] the belief of a religious group, the Theosophical Society, started in New York in 1875

thera·peut·ic /ˌθerə'pjuːtɪk/ *adj.* **1** [usually before noun] designed to help treat an illness: *the therapeutic properties of herbs* **2** helping you to relax: *Painting can be very therapeutic.* ▶ **thera·peut·ic·al·ly** /-kli/ *adv.*

thera·peut·ics /ˌθerə'pjuːtɪks/ *noun* [U] the branch of medicine concerned with the treatment of diseases

ther·ap·ist /'θerəpɪst/ *noun* **1** (especially in compounds) a specialist who treats a particular type of illness or problem, or who uses a particular type of treatment: *a speech therapist* ◇ *a beauty therapist* ➲ see also OCCUPATIONAL THERAPIST, PHYSIOTHERAPIST **2** = PSYCHOTHERAPIST

ther·apy /'θerəpi/ *noun* (*pl.* -ies) **1** [U, C] the treatment of a physical problem or an illness: *Most leukaemia patients undergo some sort of* ***drug therapy*** (= treatment using drugs). ◇ ***alternative/complementary/natural therapies*** (= treatments that do not use traditional drugs) ➲ COLLOCATIONS at ILL **2** [U] = PSYCHOTHERAPY: *a therapy group* ◇ *She's* ***in therapy.*** ➲ see also CHEMOTHERAPY, GROUP THERAPY, HORMONE REPLACEMENT THERAPY, OCCUPATIONAL THERAPY, PHYSIOTHERAPY, RADIOTHERAPY, RETAIL THERAPY, SPEECH THERAPY

Thera·vada /ˌθerə'vɑːdə/ (also **ˌTheraˌvada 'Buddhism**) *noun* [U] one of the two major forms of Buddhism ➲ compare MAHAYANA

T

there 🔑 /ðeə(r); *NAmE* ðer/ *adv., exclamation*
■ ***adv.*** **1** 🔑 **there is, are, was, were, etc.** used to show that sth exists or happens: *There's a restaurant around the corner.* ◇ *There are two people waiting outside.* ◇ *Has there been an accident?* ◇ *I don't want there to be any misunderstanding.* ◇ *There seemed to be no doubt about it.* ◇ *There comes a point where you give up.* ◇ *There remains the problem of finance.* ◇ *Suddenly there was a loud bang.* ◇ (*informal*) *There's only four days left.* ◇ (*literary*) ***There once was*** *a poor farmer who had four sons.* **2** 🔑 in, at or to that place or position: *We went on to Paris and stayed there eleven days.* ◇ *I hope we get there in time.* ◇ *It's there, right in front of you!* ◇ ***There it is****—just behind the chair.* ◇ *'Have you seen my pen?' 'Yes, it's* ***over there.****'* ◇ *There are a lot of people* ***back there*** (= behind) *waiting to get in.* ◇ *I'm not going* ***in there****—it's freezing!* ◇ *We're* ***almost there*** (= we have almost arrived). ◇ *Can I get* ***there and back*** *in a day?* ◇ *I left in 2008 and I haven't been* ***back there*** *since.* ◇ *Hello, is Bob there please?* (= used when calling sb on the phone) ◇ *I took one look at the car and offered to buy it* ***there and then/then and there*** (= immediately). **3** 🔑 existing or available: *I went to see if my old school was still there.* ◇ *The money's there if you need it.* **4** at that point (in a story, an argument, etc.): *'I feel...' There she stopped.* ◇ *I don't agree with you there.* **5** used to attract sb's attention: *Hello, there!* ◇ *You there! Come back!* ◇ ***There you are!*** *I've been looking for you everywhere.* **6** used to attract sb's attention to a particular person, thing or fact: *There's the statue I was telling you about.* ◇ *That woman there is the boss's wife.* ◇ ***There goes*** *the last bus* (= we've just missed it). ◇ ***There goes*** *the phone* (= it's ringing). ◇ (*humorous*) ***There goes*** *my career!* (= my career is ruined) ◇ *So,* ***there you have it****: that's how it all started.* **7 ~ to do sth** used to show the role of a person or thing in a situation: *The fact is, they're there to make money.*
IDM **ˌbeen 'there, ˌdone 'that** (*informal*) used to show that you think a place or an activity is not very interesting or impressive because you have already experienced it: *Not Spain again! Been there, done that, got the T-shirt.* **be 'there for sb** to be available if sb wants to talk to you or if they need help: *You know I'll always be there for you.* **by 'there** (*WelshE*) there; to there: *He's over by there.* **have been there be'fore** (*informal*) to know all about a situation because you have experienced it **not all 'there** (*informal*) not very intelligent, especially because of mental illness **ˌso 'there!** (*informal*) used to show that you are determined not to change your attitude or opinion: *Well, you can't have it, so there!* **ˌthere it 'is** (*informal*) that is the situation: *It's crazy, I know, but there it is.* **'there's a good boy, girl, dog, etc.** (*informal*) used to praise or encourage small children or animals: *Finish your lunch, there's a good boy.* **there's lovely, nice, etc.** (*WelshE*) used to say that sth has a particular quality **ˌthere's 'sth for you** (*informal*) used to say that sth is a very good example of sth: *She visited him every day he was in the hospital. There's devotion for you.* ◇ (*ironic*) *He didn't even say thank you. There's gratitude for you!* **ˌthere or therea'bouts** (*BrE, informal*) used to say that sth is very good, even if it is not perfect: *At the end of the tournament, he'll be there or thereabouts* (= he may not win, but he will be one of the best players). **ˌthere, 'there!** (*informal*) used to persuade a small child to stop crying or being upset: *There, there! Never mind, you'll soon feel better.* **ˌthere you 'are** (also **ˌthere you 'go**) (*informal*) **1** 🔑 used when giving sb a thing they want or have asked for: *There you are—that'll be £3.80, please.* ◇ *OK, there you go.* **2** used when explaining or showing sth to sb: *You switch on, push in the DVD and there you are!* ◇ *There you are! I told you it was easy!* **3** used when you are talking about sth that happens in a typical way or about a situation that cannot be changed: *There you go—that's what they're like.* ◇ *I know it's not ideal but there you go...* **ˌthere you go a'gain** (*informal*) used to criticize sb when they behave in a way that is typical of them: *There you go again—jumping to conclusions.* ➲ more at HERE *adv.*
■ ***exclamation*** used to express satisfaction that you were right about sth or to show that sth annoys you: *There now! What did I tell you?* (= you can see that I was right) ◇ *There! That didn't hurt too much, did it?* ◇ *There! You've gone and woken the baby!*

there·abouts /ˌðeərə'baʊts; *NAmE* ˌðerə-/ *adv.* (usually used after *or*) **1** near the place mentioned: *He comes from Leeds or thereabouts.* **2** used to say that a particular number, quantity, time, etc. is not exact: *They paid $100 000 or thereabouts for the house.* IDM see THERE *adv.*

there·after /ˌðeər'ɑːftə(r); *NAmE* ˌðer'æf-/ *adv.* (*formal*) after the time or event mentioned: *She married at 17 and gave birth to her first child shortly thereafter.* ➲ compare HEREAFTER

there·by AW /ˌðeə'baɪ; *NAmE* ˌðer'baɪ/ *adv.* (*formal*) used to introduce the result of the action or situation mentioned: *Regular exercise strengthens the heart, thereby reducing the risk of heart attack.*

there·fore 🔑 /'ðeəfɔː(r); *NAmE* 'ðerf-/ *adv.* used to introduce the logical result of sth that has just been mentioned: *He's only 17 and therefore not eligible to vote.* ◇ *There is still much to discuss. We shall, therefore, return to this item at our next meeting.*

there·from /ˌðeə'frɒm; *NAmE* ˌðer'frʌm/ *adv.* (*formal* or *law*) from the thing mentioned: *The committee will examine the agreement and any problems arising therefrom.*

there·in /ˌðeər'ɪn; *NAmE* ˌðer-/ *adv.* (*law* or *formal*) in the place, object, document, etc. mentioned: *The insurance policy covers the building and any fixtures contained therein.*

Language Bank

therefore

Ways of saying 'For this reason...'

- Today's children eat more junk food and get less exercise than previous generations of children. It is not surprising, **therefore**, that rates of childhood obesity are on the increase.
- Children who grow up on a diet of junk food find it difficult to change this habit later in life. It is essential, **therefore**, that parents encourage healthy eating from an early age.
- Children who grow up on a diet of junk food find it difficult to change this habit later in life. **For this reason**, **/This is why** it is essential that children eat healthily from an early age.
- Eating habits formed in childhood tend to continue into adult life. **Thus**, the best way to prevent heart disease among adults is to encourage healthy eating from an early age.
- Eating habits formed in childhood tend to continue into adult life, **hence** the importance of encouraging healthy eating from an early age.

➲ Language Banks at BECAUSE OF, CAUSE, CONSEQUENTLY, EMPHASIS, VITAL

IDM ▸ **therein lies...** used to emphasize the result or consequence of a particular situation: *He works extremely hard and therein lies the key to his success.*

there·of /ˌðeər'ɒv; *NAmE* ˌðer'ʌv/ *adv.* (*law* or *formal*) of the thing mentioned: *Is the property or any part thereof used for commercial activity?*

there·on /ˌðeər'ɒn; *NAmE* ˌðer'ɑːn; -'ɔːn/ *adv.* (*law* or *formal*) on the thing mentioned: *a meeting to discuss the annual accounts and the auditors' report thereon*

there's /ðeəz; *NAmE* ðerz/ *short form* **1** there is **2** there has

there·to /ˌðeə'tuː; *NAmE* ˌðer'tuː/ *adv.* (*law* or *formal*) to the thing mentioned: *The lease entitles the holder to use the buildings and any land attached thereto.*

there·under /ˌðeər'ʌndə(r); *NAmE* ˌðer-/ *adv.* (*law* or *formal*) under the thing mentioned: *This savings plan is only available under the Finance Act 1990 and any regulations made thereunder.*

there·upon /ˌðeərə'pɒn; *NAmE* ˌðerə'pɑːn/ *adv.* (*formal*) **1** immediately after the situation mentioned; as a direct result of the situation mentioned: *The audience thereupon rose cheering to their feet.* **2** on the thing mentioned: *a large notice with black letters printed thereupon*

there·with /ˌðeə'wɪð; -'wɪθ; *NAmE* ˌðer'w-/ *adv.* (*old use* or *formal*) **1** with or in the thing mentioned **2** soon or immediately after that

therm /θɜːm; *NAmE* θɜːrm/ *noun* a unit of heat, used in Britain for measuring a gas supply

ther·mal /'θɜːml; *NAmE* 'θɜːrml/ *adj., noun*

■ ***adj.*** [only before noun] **1** (*technical*) connected with heat: *thermal energy* **2** (of clothing) designed to keep you warm by preventing heat from escaping from the body: *thermal underwear* **3** (of streams, lakes, etc.) in which the water has been naturally heated by the earth: *thermal springs* ▸ **ther·mal·ly** /-əli/ *adv.*

■ ***noun*** **1** [C] a rising current of warm air used, for example, by a GLIDER to gain height **2 thermals** [pl.] (*especially BrE*) warm underwear that prevents heat from escaping from the body

ˌthermal 'imaging *noun* [U] (*technical*) the process of producing an image of sth or finding out where sth is, using the heat that comes from it: *Rescue teams are using thermal imaging to locate survivors of the earthquake.*

thermo- /'θɜːməʊ; *NAmE* -moʊ/ *combining form* (in nouns, adjectives and adverbs) connected with heat: *thermonuclear* ◇ *thermometer*

thermo·dynam·ics /ˌθɜːməʊdaɪ'næmɪks; *NAmE* ˌθɜːrmoʊ-/ *noun* [U] the science that deals with the relations between heat and other forms of energy: *the laws of thermodynamics* ▸ **thermo·dynam·ic** *adj.*

therm·om·eter /θə'mɒmɪtə(r); *NAmE* θər'mɑːm-/ *noun* an instrument used for measuring the temperature of the air, a person's body, etc: *a thermometer reading*

thermo·nuclear /ˌθɜːməʊ'njuːkliə(r); *NAmE* ˌθɜːrmoʊ'nuːk-/ *adj.* connected with nuclear reactions that only happen at very high temperatures

thermo·plas·tic /ˌθɜːməʊ'plæstɪk; *NAmE* ˌθɜːrmoʊ-/ *noun* [U] (*technical*) a plastic material that can be easily shaped and bent when it is heated, and that becomes hard when it is cooled

Ther·mos™ /'θɜːməs; *NAmE* 'θɜːrməs/ (*BrE* also **'Thermos flask**) (*NAmE* also **'Thermos bottle**) *noun* a particular kind of VACUUM FLASK (= a container like a bottle with double walls with a VACUUM between them, used for keeping liquids hot or cold) ➲ compare FLASK

the thermo·sphere /'θɜːməsfɪə(r); *NAmE* 'θɜːrməsfɪr/ *noun* [sing.] (*technical*) the region of the atmosphere above the MESOSPHERE

thermo·stat /'θɜːməstæt; *NAmE* 'θɜːrm-/ *noun* a device that measures and controls the temperature of a machine or room, by switching the heating or cooling system on and off as necessary ▸ **thermo·stat·ic** /ˌθɜːmə'stætɪk; *NAmE* ˌθɜːrm-/ *adj.* [only before noun] **thermo·stat·ic·al·ly** /-kli/ *adv.*

the·saurus /θɪ'sɔːrəs/ *noun* (*pl.* **the·sauri** /θɪ'sɔːraɪ/ or **the·saur·uses** /-rəsɪz/) a book that lists words in groups that have similar meanings

these ➲ THIS

thesis AW /'θiːsɪs/ *noun* (*pl.* **theses** /'θiːsiːz/) **1** ~ (**on sth**) a long piece of writing completed by a student as part of a university degree, based on their own research **2** a statement or an opinion that is discussed in a logical way and presented with evidence in order to prove that it is true: *These latest findings support the thesis that sexuality is determined by nature rather than choice.* ➲ COLLOCATIONS at SCIENTIFIC

thes·pian /'θespiən/ *noun* (often *humorous*) an actor ▸ **thes·pian** *adj.*

theta /'θiːtə/ *noun* the 8th letter of the Greek alphabet (Θ, *θ*)

'theta role *noun* = THEMATIC ROLE

they 🔑 /ðeɪ/ *pron.* (used as the subject of a verb) **1** 🔑 people, animals or things that have already been mentioned or are easily identified: *'Where are John and Liz?' 'They went for a walk.'* ◇ *They* (= the things you are carrying) *go on the bottom shelf.* **2** 🔑 used instead of *he* or *she* to refer to a person whose sex is not mentioned or not known: *If anyone arrives late they'll have to wait outside.* ➲ note at GENDER **3** 🔑 people in general: *The rest, as they say, is history.* **4** 🔑 people in authority or experts: *They cut my water off.* ◇ *They now say that red wine is good for you.*

they'd /ðeɪd/ *short form* **1** they had **2** they would

they'll /ðeɪl/ *short form* they will

they're /ðeə(r); *NAmE* ðer; *NAmE weak form* ðər/ *short form* they are

they've /ðeɪv/ *short form* they have

thia·mine (also **thia·min**) /'θaɪəmɪn; -miːn/ *noun* [U] a VITAMIN of the B group, found in grains, BEANS and LIVER

thick 🔑 /θɪk/ *adj., noun, adv.*

■ ***adj.*** (**thick·er**, **thick·est**)

▸ DISTANCE BETWEEN SIDES **1** 🔑 having a larger distance between opposite sides or surfaces than other similar objects or than normal: *a thick slice of bread* ◇ *a thick book* (= one that has a lot of pages) ◇ *a thick coat* (= one made of heavy cloth) ◇ *thick fingers* ◇ *Everything was covered with a thick layer of dust.* **2** 🔑 used to ask about or state the distance between opposite sides or surfaces: *How thick are the walls?* ◇ *They're two feet thick.*

T

▸ HAIR/FUR/TREES **3** 🗝 growing closely together in large numbers: *thick dark hair* ◇ *a thick forest*
▸ LIQUID **4** 🗝 not flowing very easily: *thick soup* ◇ *The effect will be ruined if the paint is too thick.*
▸ FOG/SMOKE/AIR **5** 🗝 difficult to see through; difficult to breathe in: *The plane crashed in thick fog.* ◇ *thick smoke* ◇ **~ with sth** *The air was thick with dust.* ◇ *(figurative) The atmosphere was thick with tension.*
▸ WITH LARGE NUMBER/AMOUNT **6 ~ with sb/sth** having a large number of people or a large amount of sth in one place: *The beach was thick with sunbathers.*
▸ STUPID **7** (*BrE, informal*) (of a person) slow to learn or understand things: *Are you thick, or what?*
▸ ACCENT **8** (sometimes *disapproving*) easily recognized as being from a particular country or area SYN **strong**: *a thick Brooklyn accent*
▸ VOICE **9 ~** (**with sth**) deep and not as clear as normal, especially because of illness or emotion: *His voice was thick with emotion.*
▸ FRIENDLY WITH SB **10 ~** (**with sb**) (*informal*) very friendly with sb, especially in a way that makes other people suspicious: *You seem to be very thick with the boss!* ➲ see also THICKLY, THICKNESS

IDM **give sb/get a thick 'ear** (*BrE, informal*) to hit sb/be hit on the head as a punishment (**as**) **thick as 'thieves** (*informal*) (of two or more people) very friendly, especially in a way that makes other people suspicious (**as**) **thick as two short 'planks** (*BrE, informal*) (of a person) very stupid **a thick 'head** (*informal*) a physical condition in which your head is painful or you cannot think clearly as a result of an illness or of drinking too much alcohol **your thick 'head** (*informal*) used to show that you are annoyed that sb does not understand sth: *When will you get it into your thick head that I don't want to see you again!* **a ˌthick 'skin** the ability to accept criticism, insults, etc. without becoming upset OPP **a thin skin** ➲ see also THICK-SKINNED ➲ more at BLOOD *n.*, GROUND *n.*

■ ***noun*** [U]

IDM **in the 'thick of sth** involved in the busiest or most active part of sth **through ˌthick and 'thin** even when there are problems or difficulties: *He's supported the team for over ten years through thick and thin.*

■ ***adv.*** (**thick·er, thick·est**) in a way that produces a wide piece or deep layer of sth: *Make sure you cut the bread nice and thick.*

IDM **lay it on 'thick** (*informal*) to talk about sb/sth in a way that makes them or it seem much better or much worse than they really are; to exaggerate sth: *Praise them when necessary, but don't lay it on too thick.* **thick and 'fast** quickly and in large quantities: *Questions were coming at them thick and fast.*

T

thick·en /ˈθɪkən/ *verb* [I, T] to become thicker; to make sth thicker: *Stir until the sauce has thickened.* ◇ *It was a dangerous journey through thickening fog.* ◇ **~ sth** *Thicken the stew with flour.* IDM see PLOT *n.*

thick·en·er /ˈθɪkənə(r)/ *noun* a substance used to make a liquid thicker: *paint thickeners*

thicket /ˈθɪkɪt/ *noun* **1** a group of bushes or small trees growing closely together **2** a large number of things that are not easy to understand or separate

thick·head /ˈθɪkhed/ (also **thicko**) *noun* (*BrE, informal*) a stupid person

thick·head·ed /ˌθɪkˈhedɪd/ *adj.* stupid

thick·ly 🗝 /ˈθɪkli/ *adv.*
1 🗝 in a way that produces a wide piece or deep layer of sth: *thickly sliced bread* ◇ *Apply the paint thickly in even strokes.* **2 ~ wooded, populated, etc.** having a lot of trees, people, etc. close together **3** in a deep voice that is not as clear as normal, especially because of illness or emotion

thick·ness 🗝 /ˈθɪknəs/ *noun*
1 🗝 [U, C] the size of sth between opposite surfaces or sides SYN **width**: *Use wood of at least 12 mm thickness.* ◇ *The board is available in four thicknesses.* **2** [C] **~** (**of sth**) a layer of sth: *The jacket was lined with a double thickness (= two layers) of fabric.*

thicko /ˈθɪkəʊ; *NAmE* -oʊ/ *noun* (*pl.* **-os**) (*BrE, informal*) = THICKHEAD

thick·set /θɪkˈset/ *adj.* (especially of a man) having a strong heavy body

ˌthick-'skinned *adj.* **1** (of a person) not easily upset by criticism or unkind comments **2** (of fruit) having a thick skin OPP **thin-skinned**

thief 🗝 /θiːf/ *noun* (*pl.* **thieves** /θiːvz/)
a person who steals sth from another person or place: *a **car/jewel, etc. thief*** ➲ COLLOCATIONS at CRIME ➲ see also THEFT IDM see HONOUR *n.*, THICK *adj.*

thiev·ing /ˈθiːvɪŋ/ *noun* [U] (*informal*) the act of stealing things ▶ **thiev·ing** *adj.*: (*informal*) *You've no right to take that, you thieving swine!*

thigh /θaɪ/ *noun* **1** the top part of the leg between the knee and the hip ➲ COLLOCATIONS at PHYSICAL ➲ VISUAL VOCAB page V48 **2** the top part of the leg of a chicken, etc, cooked and eaten

'thigh bone *noun* the large thick bone in the top part of the leg between the hip and the knee SYN **femur** ➲ VISUAL VOCAB page V48

thim·ble /ˈθɪmbl/ *noun* a small metal or plastic object that you wear on the end of your finger to protect it when sewing

thimble·ful /ˈθɪmblfʊl/ *noun* a very small amount of a liquid, especially alcohol

thin 🗝 /θɪn/ *adj., adv., verb*
■ ***adj.*** (**thin·ner, thin·nest**)
▸ NOT THICK **1** 🗝 having a smaller distance between opposite sides or surfaces than other similar objects or than normal: *Cut the vegetables into thin strips.* ◇ *A number of thin cracks appeared in the wall.* ◇ *The body was hidden beneath a thin layer of soil.* ◇ *a thin blouse* (= of light cloth) ➲ see also PAPER-THIN ➲ SYNONYMS at NARROW
▸ NOT FAT **2** 🗝 (of a person or part of the body) (sometimes *disapproving*) not covered with much flesh: *He was tall and thin, with dark hair.* ◇ *She was looking pale and thin.* ◇ *He is as **thin as a rake*** (= very thin). ◇ *thin legs*
▸ HAIR **3** 🗝 not growing closely together or in large amounts: *thin grey hair*
▸ LIQUID **4** 🗝 containing more liquid than is normal or expected SYN **runny**: *The sauce was thin and tasteless.*
▸ SMOKE **5** fairly easy to see through: *They fought their way through where the smoke was thinner.*
▸ AIR **6** containing less OXYGEN than normal
▸ SOUND **7** (*disapproving*) high and weak: *Her thin voice trailed off into silence.*
▸ SMILE **8** not sincere or enthusiastic: *He gave a thin smile.*
▸ LIGHT **9** not very bright: *the thin grey light of dawn*
▸ POOR QUALITY **10** of poor quality; lacking an important quality: *a thin excuse* (= one that people are not likely to believe) ◇ *Their arguments all sound a little thin to me.*
▶ **thin·ness** /ˈθɪnnəs/ *noun* [U] ➲ see also THINLY

IDM **be skating/walking on thin 'ice** to be taking a risk **disappear, vanish, etc. into thin 'air** to disappear suddenly in a mysterious way **have a thin 'time (of it)** (*BrE, informal*) to have many problems or difficulties to deal with; to not be successful **out of thin 'air** from nowhere or nothing, as if by magic **the thin end of the 'wedge** (*especially BrE*) an event or action that is the beginning of sth more serious and/or unpleasant **thin on 'top** (*informal*) without much hair on the head: *He's starting to get a little thin on top* (= he's losing his hair). **a ˌthin 'skin** the lack of ability to accept criticism, insults, etc. without becoming upset SYN **sensitive** OPP **a thick skin** ➲ see also THIN-SKINNED ➲ more at GROUND *n.*, LINE *n.*, SPREAD *v.*, THICK *adj.*, WEAR *v.*

■ ***adv.*** (**thin·ner, thin·nest**) in a way that produces a thin piece or layer of sth: *Don't spread it too thin.* ◇ *I like my bread sliced thin.*

■ ***verb*** (**-nn-**)
▸ LIQUID **1** [T] **~ sth** (**down**) (**with sth**) to make a liquid less thick or strong by adding water or another substance: *Thin the paint with water.*

▸ OF HAIR **2** [I] to become less thick: *a middle-aged man with thinning hair*
▸ BECOME LESS THICK **3** [I, T] to become less thick or fewer in number; to make sth less thick or fewer, for example by removing some things or people: *The clouds thinned and the moon shone through.* ◇ **~ out** *The crowd had thinned out and only a few people were left.* ◇ **~ sth (out)** *Thin out the seedlings to about 10cm apart.*

Vocabulary Building

Saying that somebody is thin

Thin is the most usual word: *Steve is tall and thin and has brown hair.* It is sometimes used with a negative meaning: *Mother looked thin and tired after her long illness.*

The following words all express praise or admiration:

- **Slim** means pleasantly thin. It is often used to describe women who have controlled their weight by diet or exercise: *She has a beautifully slim figure.*
- A **slender** girl or woman is thin and graceful.
- A **lean** man is thin and fit.
- **Willowy** describes a woman who is attractively tall and thin.

The following words are more negative in their meaning:

- **Skinny** means very thin, often in a way that is not attractive: *a skinny little kid.*
- **Bony** describes parts of the body when they are so thin that the bones can be seen: *the old man's bony hands.*
- **Scrawny** suggests that a person is thin, weak and not attractive: *a scrawny old woman.*
- **Gaunt** describes a person who is a little too thin and looks sad or ill.
- **Underweight** is used in medical contexts to describe people who are too thin because they are ill or have not had enough food: *Women who smoke risk giving birth to underweight babies.*
- **Emaciated** describes a serious condition resulting from illness or lack of food.
- **Anorexic** is a medical term, but is now also used informally to describe a girl or woman who is so thin that you are worried about them.

It is more acceptable to talk to somebody about how thin or slim they are than about how fat they are.

➲ note at FAT

thine /ðaɪn/ *pron., det.* (*old use*)
■ ***pron.*** a word meaning 'yours', used when talking to only one person
■ ***det.*** the form of *thy* that is used before a vowel or 'h', meaning 'your'

thing 🔑 /θɪŋ/ *noun*
▸ OBJECT **1** 🔑 [C] an object whose name you do not use because you do not need to or want to, or because you do not know it: *Can you pass me that thing over there?* ◇ *She's very fond of sweet things* (= sweet foods). ◇ *He's just bought one of those exercise things.* ◇ *Turn that thing off while I'm talking to you!* **2** 🔑 [C] an object that is not alive in the way that people and plants are: *Don't treat her like that—she's a person, not a thing!* ◇ *He's good at making things with his hands.* ◇ *She took no interest in the people and things around her.*
▸ POSSESSIONS/EQUIPMENT **3** 🔑 **things** [pl.] (rather *informal*) objects, clothing or tools that belong to sb or are used for a particular purpose: *Shall I help you pack your things?* ◇ *Bring your swimming things with you.* ◇ *I'll just clear away the breakfast things.* ◇ *Put your things* (= coat, etc.) *on and let's go.*
▸ ANYTHING **4 a thing** [sing.] used with negatives to mean 'anything' in order to emphasize what you are saying: *I haven't got a thing to wear!* ◇ *There wasn't a thing we could do to help.* ◇ *Ignore what he said—it* ***doesn't mean a thing.***
▸ FACT/EVENT/SITUATION/ACTION **5** 🔑 [C] a fact, an event, a situation or an action; what sb says or thinks: *There are a lot of things she doesn't know about me.* ◇ *There's another thing I'd like to ask you.* ◇ *A terrible thing happened last night.* ◇ *He found* ***the whole thing*** (= the situation) *very boring.* ◇ *I've got loads of things to do today.* ◇ ***The main thing*** *to remember is to switch off the burglar alarm.* ◇ *I like camping, climbing and* ***that sort of thing.*** ◇ *She said* ***the first thing*** *that came into her head.* ◇ *'Why did you tell her our secret?' 'I did* ***no such thing!'*** ◇ *Let's forget* ***the whole thing*** (= everything). **6** 🔑 **things** [pl.] (rather *informal*) the general situation, as it affects sb: *Things haven't gone entirely to plan.* ◇ (*informal*) *Hi, Jane!* ***How are things?*** ◇ ***Think things over*** *before you decide.* ◇ ***As things stand*** *at present, he seems certain to win.* ◇ ***All things considered*** (= considering all the difficulties or problems), *she's done very well.* ◇ *Why do you make things so difficult for yourself?*
➲ SYNONYMS at SITUATION
▸ WHAT IS NEEDED/RIGHT **7** 🔑 [C, usually sing.] what is needed or socially acceptable: *You need something to cheer you up—I know just the thing!* ◇ *to say* ***the right/wrong thing*** ◇ *The best thing to do is to apologize.*
▸ THINGS OF PARTICULAR TYPE **8 things** [pl.] (*formal*) (followed by an adjective) all that can be described in a particular way: *She loves all things Japanese.*
▸ CREATURE **9** [C] (used with an adjective) a living creature: *All living things are composed of cells.*
▸ PERSON/ANIMAL **10** [C] (with an adjective) (*informal*) used to talk to or about a person or an animal, to show how you feel about them: *You silly thing!* ◇ *You must be starving, you poor things.* ◇ *The cat's very ill, poor old thing.*

Synonyms

things

stuff • property • possessions • junk • belongings • goods • valuables

These are all words for objects or items, especially ones that you own or have with you at a particular time.

things (*rather informal*) objects, clothing or tools that you own or that are used for a particular purpose: *Shall I help you pack your things?* ◇ *Bring your swimming things.*

stuff [U] (*informal*) used to refer to a group of objects when you do not know their names, when the names are not important or when it is obvious what you are talking about: *Where's all my stuff?*

property [U] (*rather formal*) a thing or things that are owned by sb: *This building is government property.* ◇ *Be careful not to damage other people's property.*

possessions things that you own, especially sth that can be moved: *Prisoners were allowed no personal possessions except letters and photographs.*

junk [U] things that are considered useless or of little value: *I've cleared out all that old junk from the attic.*

belongings possessions that can be moved, especially ones that you have with you at a particular time: *Please make sure you have all your belongings with you when leaving the plane.*

goods (*technical* or *rather formal*) possessions that can be moved: *He was found guilty of* ***handling stolen goods.***

valuables things that are worth a lot of money, especially small personal things such as jewellery or cameras: *Never leave cash or other valuables lying around.*

PATTERNS

- **personal** things/stuff/property/possessions/belongings
- to **collect/gather/pack** (up) your things/stuff/possessions/belongings
- to **search** sb's/your/the things/stuff/property/belongings
- to **go through** sb's/your/the things/stuff/belongings

T

IDM **A is ˈone thing, B is aˈnother | it's ˈone thing to do A, it's aˈnother thing to do B** B is very different from A, for example it is more difficult, serious or important: *Romance is one thing, marriage is quite another.* ◇ *It's one thing to tease your sister, but it's another to hit her.* **ˌall/ˌother things being ˈequal** if the conditions stay the same; if other conditions are the same: *All things being equal, we should finish the job tomorrow.* **and ˈthings (like ˈthat)** (*informal*) used when you do not want to complete a list: *She likes nice clothes and things like that.* ◇ *I've been busy shopping and things.* **be all things to all ˈmen/ˈpeople 1** (of people) to please everyone by changing your attitudes or opinions to suit different people **2** (of things) to be understood or used in different ways by different people **come to/be the same ˈthing** to have the same result or meaning **be a ˈgood thing (that)...** to be lucky that...: *It's a good thing we got here early.* **be no bad ˈthing (that)...** used to say that although sth seems to be bad, it could have good results: *We didn't want the press to get hold of the story, but it might be no bad thing.* **be onto a good ˈthing** to have found a job, situation or style of life that is pleasant or easy **ˈdo things to sb** (*informal*) to have a powerful emotional effect on sb: *That song just does things to me.* **do your own ˈthing** (*informal*) to do what you want to do or what interests you, without thinking about other people; to be independent **ˌfirst/ˌlast ˈthing** early in the morning/late in the evening: *I need the report on my desk first thing Monday morning.* **ˌfirst things ˈfirst** (often *humorous*) the most important matters must be dealt with first: *We have a lot to discuss, but, first things first, let's have a cup of coffee!* **for ˈone thing** used to introduce one of two or more reasons for doing sth: *'Why don't you get a car?' 'Well, for one thing, I can't drive!'* **have a ˈthing about sb/sth** (*informal*) to have a strong like or dislike of sb/sth in a way that seems strange or unreasonable: *She has a thing about men with beards.* **it isn't my, his, etc. ˈthing** it isn't sth that you really enjoy or are interested in **it's a... thing** (*informal*) it is sth that only a particular group understands: *You wouldn't know what it means—it's a girl thing.* **know/tell sb a ˈthing or two (about sb/sth)** (*informal*) to know/tell sb some useful, interesting or surprising information about sb/sth: *She's been married five times, so she knows a thing or two about men!* **make a (big) ˈthing of/about sth** (*informal*) to make sth seem more important than it really is **not know, etc. the first thing aˈbout sth/sb** to know nothing at all about sth/sb **not ˌquite the ˈthing 1** not considered socially acceptable: *It wouldn't be quite the thing to turn up in running gear.* **2** (*old-fashioned*) not healthy or normal **(just) ˌone of those ˈthings** used to say that you do not want to discuss or think about sth bad or unpleasant that has happened, but just accept it: *It wasn't your fault. It was just one of those things.* **ˌone (damned/damn) thing after aˈnother** (*informal*) used to complain that a lot of unpleasant things keep happening to you **ˌone thing leads to aˈnother** used to suggest that the way one event or action leads to others is so obvious that it does not need to be stated: *He offered me a ride home one night, and, well, one thing led to another and now we're married!* **be ˈseeing/ˈhearing things** (*informal, humorous*) to imagine that you can see or hear sth that is in fact not there **there's only ˌone thing ˈfor it** there is only one possible course of action **these ˌthings are sent to ˈtry us** (*saying*) used to say that you should accept an unpleasant situation or event because you cannot change it **the ˌthing ˈis** (*informal*) used to introduce an important fact, reason or explanation: *I'm sorry my assignment isn't finished. The thing is, I've had a lot of other work this week.* **the ˌthing (about/with sth/sb) ˈis** used to introduce a problem about sth/sb: *The thing with Karl is, he's always late.* **the (whole)... thing** (*informal*) a situation or an activity of the type mentioned: *She really didn't want to be involved in the whole family thing.* **ˌthings that go ˌbump in the ˈnight** (*informal, humorous*) used to refer to GHOSTS and other SUPERNATURAL things that cannot be explained **too ˈmuch of a good thing** used to say that, although sth is pleasant, you do not want to have too much of it **(what) with ˌone thing and aˈnother** (*informal*) because you have been busy with various problems, events or things you had to do: *I completely forgot her birthday, what with one thing and another.* ➲ more at CHANCE *n.*, CLOSE² *adj.*, CLOSE² *adv.*, DAY, DECENT, DONE, EASY *adv.*, NATURE, NEAR *adj.*, ONLY *adj.*, OVERDO, PUSH *v.*, REAL, SCHEME *n.*, SHAPE *n.*, SURE *adj.*, TURN *v.*, WAY *n.*, WORK *v.*

Vocabulary Building

Other words for thing

Instead of using the word **thing**, try to use more precise and interesting words, especially in formal written English.

- **aspect** *That was the most puzzling aspect of the situation.* (*...the most puzzling thing about...*)
- **attribute** *Curiosity is an essential attribute for a journalist.* (*...an essential thing for a journalist to have.*)
- **characteristic** *This bird has several interesting characteristics.* (*There are several interesting things about this bird.*)
- **detail** *I want to know every detail of what happened.* (*... everything about...*)
- **feature** *Noise is a familiar feature of city life.* (*...a familiar thing in city life.*)
- **issue** *She has campaigned on many controversial issues.* (*...many controversial things.*)
- **matter** *We have several important matters to deal with at this meeting.* (*...several important things...*)
- **point** *That's a very interesting point you made.* (*...a very interesting thing you said.*)
- **subject** *The book covers a number of subjects.* (*...a number of things.*)
- **topic** *We discussed a wide range of topics.* (*...a wide range of things.*)
- **trait** *Her generosity is one of her most attractive traits.* (*...one of the most attractive things about her.*)
- Don't use **thing** after an adjective when the adjective can be used on its own: *Having your own computer is very useful.* ◇ ~~*Having your own computer is a very useful thing.*~~
- It is often more natural to use words like **something**, **anything**, etc. instead of **thing**: *I have something important to tell you.* ◇ ~~*I have an important thing to tell you.*~~ ◇ *Do you want anything else?* ◇ ~~*Do you want any other thing?*~~
- It is more natural to say **a lot, a great deal, much**, etc. rather than **many things**: *I have so much to tell you.* ◇ ~~*I have so many things to tell you.*~~ ◇ *She knows a lot about basketball.* ◇ ~~*She knows many things about basketball.*~~

thing·ummy /ˈθɪŋəmi/ *noun* (*pl.* -ies) (also **thing·ama·bob** /ˈθɪŋəməbɒb; *NAmE* -bɑːb/, **thing·uma·jig** /ˈθɪŋəmədʒɪɡ/, **thingy**) (*informal*) used to refer to a person or thing whose name you do not know or have forgotten, or which you do not want to mention: *It's one of those thingummies for keeping papers together.* ◇ *Is thingummy going to be there? You know, that woman from the Sales Department?*

thingy /ˈθɪŋi/ *noun* (*pl.* -ies) = THINGUMMY

think 🔑 /θɪŋk/ *verb, noun*

■ ***verb*** (**thought, thought** /θɔːt/)

▸ HAVE OPINION/BELIEF **1** 🔑 [T, I] (not used in the progressive tenses) to have a particular idea or opinion about sth/sb; to believe sth: **~ (that)...** *Do you think (that) they'll come?* ◇ *I thought I heard a scream.* ◇ *I didn't think you liked sports.* ◇ ***Am I right in thinking*** *that you used to live here?* ◇ *I think this is their house, but I'm not sure.* ◇ *He ought to resign, I think.* ◇ *We'll need about 20 chairs,* ***I should think.*** ◇ **it is thought that...** ***It was*** *once* ***thought that*** *the sun travelled around the earth.* ◇ **~ sth (about sth)** *What did you think about the idea?* ◇ *Well, I like it.* ***What do you think?*** ◇ **~ so** *'Will we make it in time?' 'I* ***think so.****'* ◇ *'Is he any good?' 'I*

T

don't think so.' ◇ **~ sb/sth + adj.** *I think it highly unlikely that I'll get the job.* ◇ *She thought him kind and generous.* ◇ **sb/sth is thought to be sb/sth** *He's thought to be one of the richest men in Europe.* ➲ LANGUAGE BANK at ACCORDING TO, OPINION

▸ USE MIND **2** [I, T] to use your mind to consider sth, to form connected ideas, to try to solve problems, etc: *Are animals able to think?* ◇ *Let me think* (= give me time before I answer). ◇ **~ (about sth)** *I can't tell you now—I'll have to* ***think about it.*** ◇ *She* ***had thought*** *very* ***deeply*** *about this problem.* ◇ *All he ever thinks about is money.* ◇ *I'm sorry, I* ***wasn't thinking*** (= said when you have upset or offended sb accidentally). ◇ **~ what, how, etc...** *He was trying to think what to do.* **3** [T] (usually used in the progressive tenses) to have ideas, words or images in your mind: **~ sth** *You're very quiet. What are you thinking?* ◇ **~ what, how, etc...** *I was just thinking what a long way it is.* ◇ **+ speech** *'I must be crazy,' she thought.*

▸ IMAGINE **4** [T, no passive, I] to form an idea of sth; to imagine sth: **~ where, how, etc...** *We couldn't think where you'd gone.* ◇ *Just think how nice it would be to see them again.* ◇ **~ (that)...** *I can't think (that) he would be so stupid.* ◇ **~ (sth)** *Just think—we'll be lying on the beach this time tomorrow.* ◇ *If I'm late home, my mother always* ***thinks the worst.*** ◇ *Try to* ***think yourself into*** *the role.* ➲ SYNONYMS at IMAGINE

▸ EXPECT **5** [T] to expect sth: **~ (that)...** *I never thought (that) I'd see her again.* ◇ *The job took longer than we thought.* ◇ *You'd think she'd have been grateful for my help* (= but she wasn't). ◇ **~ to do sth** (*formal*) *Who would have thought to find you here?*

▸ IN A PARTICULAR WAY **6** [I, T] (*informal*) [no passive] to think in a particular way or on a particular subject: **+ adj.** *Let's think positive.* ◇ *You need to* ***think big*** (= aim to achieve a lot). ◇ **~ sth** *If you want to make money, you've got to think money.*

▸ SHOWING ANGER/SURPRISE **7** [T] **~ (that)...** used in questions to show that you are angry or surprised: *What do you think you're doing?*

▸ BEING LESS DEFINITE/MORE POLITE **8** [T, I] used to make sth you say sound less definite or more polite: **~ (that)...** *I thought we could go out tonight.* ◇ *Twenty guests are enough, I would have thought.* ◇ ***Do you think*** *you could open the window?* ◇ **~ so** *'You've made a mistake.' 'I don't think so.'*

▸ INTEND **9** [T, I] **~ (that...)** to intend sth; to have a plan about sth: *I think I'll go for a swim.* ◇ *I'm thinking in terms of about 70 guests at the wedding.*

▸ REMEMBER **10** [T] to remember sth; to have sth come into your mind: **~ to do sth** *I didn't think* (= it did not occur to me) *to tell her.* ◇ **~ where, what, etc...** *I can't think where I put the keys.*

IDM **come to ˈthink of it** used when you suddenly remember sth or realize that it might be important: *Come to think of it, he did mention seeing you.* **I ˌdon't ˈthink so** (*informal*) used to say very strongly that you do not agree with sth, or that sth is not possible: *Me? Fail? I don't think so.* **if/when you ˈthink about it** used to draw attention to a fact that is not obvious or has not previously been mentioned: *It was a difficult situation, when you think about it.* **I ˈthought as much** that is what I expected or suspected: *'He said he'd forgotten.' 'I thought as much.'* **ˌthink aˈgain** to consider a situation again and perhaps change your idea or intention **think aˈloud/out ˈloud** to say what your thoughts are as you have them **think ˈbetter of it/of doing sth** to decide not to do sth after thinking further about it **SYN** **reconsider**: *Rosie was about to protest but thought better of it.* **think (the) ˈbetter of sb** to have a higher opinion of sb: *She has behaved appallingly—I must say I thought better of her.* **think nothing ˈof it** (*formal*) used as a polite response when sb has said sorry to you or thanked you **think ˈnothing of sth/of doing sth** to consider an activity to be normal and not particularly unusual or difficult: *She thinks nothing of walking thirty miles a day.* **think on your ˈfeet** to be able to think and react to things very quickly and effectively without any preparation **ˌthink out of the ˈbox** to think about sth, or how to do sth, in a way that is new, different or shows imagination **ˈthink straight** to think in a clear or logical way **think ˈtwice about sth/about doing sth** to think carefully before deciding to do sth: *You should think twice about employing someone you've never met.* **think the world, highly, a lot, not much, poorly, little, etc. of sb/sth** to have a very good, poor, etc. opinion of sb/sth: *He thinks the world of his daughter.* ◇ *I don't think much of her idea.* **to think (that...)** used to show that you are surprised or shocked by sth: *To think that my mother wrote all those books and I never knew!* ➲ more at FIT *adj.*, GREAT *adj.*, ILL *adv.*, LET *v.*, LIKE *v.*, OWN *v.*

PHR V **ˈthink about/of sb/sth** **1** to consider sb/sth when you are doing or planning sth: *Don't you ever think about other people?* **2** to consider doing sth **SYN** **contemplate**: **~ doing sth** *She's thinking of changing her job.* **ˌthink aˈhead (to sth)** to think about a future event or situation and plan for it **ˌthink ˈback (to sth)** to think about sth that happened in the past: *I keep thinking back to the day I arrived here.* **ˌthink for yourˈself** to form your own opinions and make decisions without depending on others **ˈthink of sth/sb** **1** to have an image or idea of sth/sb in your mind: *When I said that I wasn't thinking of anyone in particular.* **2** to create an idea in your imagination: *Can anybody think of a way to raise money?* ◇ *Have you thought of a name for the baby yet?* **3** [no passive] (used especially with *can*) to remember sth/sb: *I can think of at least three occasions when he arrived late.* ◇ *I can't think of her name at the moment.* **ˈthink of sb/sth as sb/sth** to consider sb/sth in a particular way: *I think of this place as my home.* ◇ *She is thought of as a possible director.* ➲ see also WELL THOUGHT OF **ˈthink of sth** to imagine an

Synonyms

think

believe • feel • reckon • be under the impression

These words all mean to have an idea that sth is true or possible or to have a particular opinion about sb/sth.

think to have an idea that sth is true or possible, although you are not completely certain; to have a particular opinion about sb/sth: *Do you think (that) they'll come?* ◇ *Well, I like it. What do you think?*

believe to have an idea that sth is true or possible, although you are not completely certain; to have a particular opinion about sb/sth: *Police believe (that) the man may be armed.*

THINK OR BELIEVE?

When you are expressing an idea that you have or that sb has of what is true or possible, **believe** is more formal than **think**. It is used especially for talking about ideas that other people have; **think** is used more often for talking about your own ideas: *Police believe...* ◇ *I think...* When you are expressing an opinion, **believe** is stronger than **think** and is used especially for matters of principle; **think** is used more for practical matters or matters of personal taste.

feel to have a particular opinion about sth that has happened or about what you/sb ought to do: *We all felt (that) we were unlucky to lose.*

reckon (*informal*) to think that sth is true or possible: *I reckon (that) I'm going to get that job.*

be under the impression that... to have an idea that sth is true: *I was under the impression that the work had already been completed.*

PATTERNS

- to think/believe/feel/reckon/be under the impression **that...**
- **It is** thought/believed/reckoned **that...**
- to **be** thought/believed/felt/reckoned **to be** sth
- to think/believe/feel sth **about** sb/sth
- to **sincerely/honestly/seriously/mistakenly** think/believe/feel

T

actual or a possible situation: *Just think of the expense!* ◇ **~ doing sth** *I couldn't think of letting you take the blame* (= I would not allow that to happen). ˌ**think sth↔ˈout** to consider or plan sth carefully: *It's a very well thought out plan.* ˌ**think sth↔ˈover** 0‑ to consider sth carefully, especially before reaching a decision: *He'd like more time to think things over.* ˌ**think sth↔ˈthrough** to consider a problem or a possible course of action fully ˌ**think sth↔ˈup** 0‑ (*informal*) to create sth in your mind SYN **devise, invent**: *Can't you think up a better excuse than that?*

■ ***noun*** [sing.]

IDM **have a ˈthink (about sth)** (*informal*) to think carefully about sth in order to make a decision about it: *I'll have a think and let you know tomorrow.* **you've got another think ˈcoming** (*informal*) used to tell sb that they are wrong about sth and must change their plans or opinions

think·able /ˈθɪŋkəbl/ *adj.* [not before noun] that you can imagine as a possibility: *Such an idea was scarcely thinkable ten years ago.* OPP **unthinkable**

think·er /ˈθɪŋkə(r)/ *noun* **1** a person who thinks seriously, and often writes about important things, such as philosophy or science: *Einstein was one of the greatest thinkers of the 20th century.* **2** a person who thinks in a particular way: *a clear thinker*

think·ing 0‑ /ˈθɪŋkɪŋ/ *noun, adj.*

■ ***noun*** [U] **1** 0‑ the process of thinking about sth: *I had to do some quick thinking.* ➲ see also LATERAL THINKING, WISHFUL THINKING **2** 0‑ ideas or opinions about sth: *What is the current thinking on this question?* ◇ *She explained the thinking behind the campaign.* IDM see WAY *n.*

■ ***adj.*** [only before noun] intelligent and able to think seriously about things: *the thinking woman's magazine*

ˈthinking cap *noun*

IDM **put your ˈthinking cap on** (*informal*) to try to solve a problem by thinking about it

ˈthink tank *noun* a group of experts who provide advice and ideas on political, social or economic issues

thin·ly /ˈθɪnli/ *adv.* **1** in a way that produces a thin piece or layer of sth: *Slice the potatoes thinly.* **2** with only a few things or people spread over a place so that there is a lot of space between them: *a thinly populated area* **3** in a way that is not sincere or enthusiastic: *She smiled thinly.* **4** in a way that does not hide the truth very well SYN **barely**: *The novel is a thinly disguised autobiography.*

thin·ner /ˈθɪnə(r)/ *noun* [U, C] a substance that is added to paint, VARNISH, etc. to make it less thick

ˌ**thin-ˈskinned** *adj.* **1** easily upset by criticism or insults **2** (of fruit) having a thin skin OPP **thick-skinned**

T

third 0‑ /θɜːd; *NAmE* θɜːrd/ *ordinal number, noun*

■ ***ordinal number*** 0‑ 3rd HELP There are examples of how to use ordinal numbers at the entry for **fifth**.

IDM **third time ˈlucky** (*US* also **third time is the ˈcharm**) used when you have failed to do sth twice and hope that you will succeed the third time

■ ***noun*** **1** 0‑ each of three equal parts of sth ➲ LANGUAGE BANK at PROPORTION **2 ~ (in sth)** a level of university degree at British universities, that is lower than average ➲ compare FIRST *n.* (4), SECOND *n.* (7)

the ˌthird ˈage *noun* [sing.] (*BrE*) the period of your life between MIDDLE AGE and OLD AGE, when you are still active

ˌ**third ˈclass** *noun* **1** [U, sing.] (especially in the past) the cheapest and least comfortable part of a train, ship, etc. **2** [U] (in the US) the class of mail used for sending advertisements, etc. **3** [U, sing.] the lowest standard of degree given by a British university

ˈthird-class *adj.* **1** (especially in the past) connected with the cheapest and least comfortable way of travelling on a train, ship, etc. **2** (in the US) connected with the class of mail used to send advertisements, etc. **3** [only before noun] used to describe the lowest standard of degree given by a British university **4** (*disapproving*) (of people) less important than other people: *They are treated as third-class citizens.* ▸ ˌ**third ˈclass** *adv.*: *to travel third class*

ˌ**third deˈgree** *noun* [sing.]

IDM **give sb the ˌthird deˈgree** (*informal*) to question sb for a long time and in a thorough way; to use threats or violence to get information from sb

ˌ**third-deˈgree** *adj.* **1 ~ burns** burns of the most serious kind, affecting TISSUE below the skin **2** (*NAmE*) **~ murder, assault, robbery, etc.** murder, etc. of the least serious of three kinds ➲ compare FIRST-DEGREE, SECOND-DEGREE

ˈthird-generation *adj.* (*abbr.* 3G) **1** used to describe technology that has been developed to send data to mobile phones/cell phones, etc. at much higher speeds than were possible before **2** used to describe any technology that is being developed that is more advanced than the earlier two stages

third·ly /ˈθɜːdli; *NAmE* ˈθɜːrd-/ *adv.* used to introduce the third of a list of points you want to make in a speech or piece of writing: *Thirdly, I would like to say that...*

ˌ**third ˈparty** *noun* (*law* or *formal*) a person who is involved in a situation in addition to the two main people involved

ˌ**third-party inˈsurance** *noun* [U] insurance that COVERS (= protects) you if you injure sb or damage sb's property

the ˌthird ˈperson *noun* [sing.] **1** (*grammar*) a set of pronouns and verb forms used by a speaker to refer to other people and things: *'They are' is the third person plural of the verb 'to be'.* **2** a way of writing a novel, etc. as the experience of sb else, using third person forms: *a book written **in the third person*** ➲ compare THE FIRST PERSON, THE SECOND PERSON

ˌ**third-ˈrate** *adj.* of very poor quality SYN **inferior**: *a third-rate actor*

the Third Reich /ˌθɜːd ˈraɪk; ˈraɪx; *NAmE* ˌθɜːrd/ *noun* [sing.] the Nazi rule of Germany between 1933 and 1945

ˌ**third ˈway** *noun* [sing.] a course of action or political policy that is between two extreme positions

the ˌThird ˈWorld *noun* [sing.] a way of referring to the poor or developing countries of Africa, Asia and Latin America, which is sometimes considered offensive: *the causes of poverty and injustice in the Third World* ◇ *Third-World debt* ➲ compare FIRST WORLD

thirst /θɜːst; *NAmE* θɜːrst/ *noun, verb*

■ ***noun*** **1** [U, sing.] the feeling of needing or wanting a drink: *He quenched his thirst with a long drink of cold water.* ◇ *She woke up with a raging thirst and a headache.* **2** [U] the state of not having enough water to drink: *Thousands are dying of thirst.* **3** [sing.] **~ (for sth)** a strong desire for sth SYN **craving**: *a thirst for knowledge*

■ ***verb*** [I] (*old use*) to be thirsty

PHR V **ˈthirst for sth** (*literary*) to feel a strong desire for sth SYN **crave**: *She thirsted for power.*

thirsty 0‑ /ˈθɜːsti; *NAmE* ˈθɜːrsti/ *adj.* (**thirst·ier, thirsti·est**)

1 0‑ needing or wanting to drink: *We were hungry and thirsty.* ◇ *Digging is **thirsty work*** (= makes you thirsty). **2 ~ for sth** having a strong desire for sth SYN **hungry** (5): *He is thirsty for power.* **3** (of plants, fields, etc.) dry; in need of water ▸ **thirst·ily** /-ɪli/ *adv.*: *Paul drank thirstily.*

thir·teen 0‑ /ˌθɜːˈtiːn; *NAmE* ˌθɜːrˈt-/ *number*

13 ▸ **thir·teenth** 0‑ /ˌθɜːˈtiːnθ; *NAmE* ˌθɜːrˈt-/ *ordinal number, noun* HELP There are examples of how to use ordinal numbers at the entry for **fifth**.

thirty 0‑ /ˈθɜːti; *NAmE* ˈθɜːrti/

1 0‑ *number* 30 **2** *noun* **the thirties** [pl.] numbers, years or temperatures from 30 to 39 ▸ **thir·ti·eth** 0‑ /ˈθɜːtiəθ; *NAmE* ˈθɜːrt-/ *ordinal number, noun* HELP There are examples of how to use ordinal numbers at the entry for **fifth**.

IDM **in your ˈthirties** between the ages of 30 and 39

this 0‑ /ðɪs/ *det., pron., adv.*

■ ***det., pron.*** (*pl.* **these** /ðiːz/) **1** 0‑ used to refer to a particular person, thing or event that is close to you, especially compared with another: *How long have you been living in* *this country?* ◇ *Well, make up your mind. Which do you want? This one or that one?* ◇ *I think you'll find these more comfortable than those.* ◇ *Is this your bag?* **2** used to refer to sth/sb that has already been mentioned: *There was a court case resulting from this incident.* ◇ *The boy was afraid and the dog had sensed this.* ◇ *What's this I hear about you getting married?* **3** used for introducing sb or showing sth to sb: *Hello, this is Maria Diaz* (= on the telephone). ◇ *Jo, this is Kate* (= when you are introducing them). ◇ *This is the captain speaking.* ◇ *Listen to this.* ◇ *Do it like this* (= in the way I am showing you). **4** used with periods of time related to the present: *this week/month/year* ◇ *I saw her this morning* (= today in the morning). ◇ *Do you want me to come this Tuesday* (= Tuesday of this week) *or next Tuesday?* ◇ *Do it* ***this minute*** (= now). ◇ *He never comes to see me* ***these days*** (= now, as compared with the past). **5 ~ sth of sb's** (*informal*) used to refer to sb/sth that is connected with a person, especially when you have a particular attitude towards it or them: *These new friends of hers are supposed to be very rich.* **6** (*informal*) used when you are telling a story or telling sb about sth: *There was this strange man sitting next to me on the plane.* ◇ *I've been getting these pains in my chest.*

IDM **ˌthis and ˈthat** | **ˌthis, ˌthat and the ˈother** (*informal*) various things or activities: *'What did you talk about?' 'Oh, this and that.'*

■ ***adv.*** to this degree; so: *It's about this high* (= as high as I am showing you with my hands). ◇ *I didn't think we'd get this far.*

this·tle /ˈθɪsl/ *noun* a wild plant with leaves with sharp points and purple, yellow or white flowers made up of a mass of narrow PETALS pointing upwards. The thistle is the national symbol of Scotland. ➲ VISUAL VOCAB page V9

thistle·down /ˈθɪsldaʊn/ *noun* [U] a very light soft substance that contains THISTLE seeds and is blown from THISTLES by the wind

thither /ˈðɪðə(r)/ *adv.* (*old use*) to or towards that place IDM see HITHER

tho' *adv.* an informal spelling of 'though'

thong /θɒŋ; *NAmE* θɔːŋ; θɑːŋ/ *noun* **1** a narrow strip of leather that is used to fasten sth or as a WHIP **2** a pair of women's KNICKERS or men's UNDERPANTS that has only a very narrow strip of cloth, like a string, at the back **3** (*NAmE, AustralE, NZE*) = FLIP-FLOP

thorax /ˈθɔːræks/ *noun* (*pl.* **thor·axes** or **thor·aces** /ˈθɔːrəsiːz/) **1** (*anatomy*) the part of the body that is surrounded by the RIBS, between the neck and the waist **2** the middle section of an insect's body, to which the legs and wings are attached ➲ VISUAL VOCAB page V11 ▶ **thor·acic** /θɔːˈræsɪk/ *adj.* [only before noun]

thor·ium /ˈθɔːriəm/ *noun* [U] (*symb.* Th) a chemical element. Thorium is a white RADIOACTIVE metal used as a source of nuclear energy.

thorn /θɔːn; *NAmE* θɔːrn/ *noun* **1** a small sharp pointed part on the STEM of some plants, such as ROSES ➲ VISUAL VOCAB page V9 **2** a tree or bush that has thorns ➲ see also BLACKTHORN, HAWTHORN **3** (*phonetics*) the letter that was used in Old English and Icelandic to represent the sounds /θ/ and /ð/ and later written as *th*

IDM **a thorn in sb's ˈflesh/ˈside** a person or thing that repeatedly annoys sb or stops them from doing sth

thorny /ˈθɔːni; *NAmE* ˈθɔːrni/ *adj.* (**thorn·ier**, **thorni·est**) **1** [usually before noun] causing difficulty or disagreement SYN **knotty**: *a* ***thorny question/issue/problem*** **2** having thorns: *a thorny bush*

thor·ough /ˈθʌrə; *NAmE* ˈθɜːroʊ/ *adj.* **1** done completely; with great attention to detail: *a thorough knowledge of the subject* ◇ *The police carried out a thorough investigation.* **2** [not usually before noun] (of a person) doing things very carefully and with great attention to detail: *She's very thorough and conscientious.* **3** (*BrE, informal*) used to emphasize how bad or annoying sb/sth is SYN **complete**: *Everything was in a thorough mess.* ▶ **thor·ough·ness** *noun* [U]: *I was impressed by the thoroughness of the report.* ◇ *I admire his thoroughness.*

thor·ough·bred /ˈθʌrəbred; *NAmE* ˈθɜːroʊb-/ *noun* an animal, especially a horse, of high quality, that has parents that are both of the same breed ▶ **thor·ough·bred** *adj.*: *a thoroughbred mare*

thor·ough·fare /ˈθʌrəfeə(r); *NAmE* ˈθɜːroʊfer/ *noun* a public road or street used by traffic, especially a main road in a city or town

thor·ough·going /ˌθʌrəˈgəʊɪŋ; *NAmE* ˌθɜːroʊˈgoʊɪŋ/ *adj.* [only before noun] **1** very thorough; looking at every detail: *a thoroughgoing revision of the text* **2** complete: *a thoroughgoing commitment to change*

thor·ough·ly /ˈθʌrəli; *NAmE* ˈθɜːr-/ *adv.* **1** very much; completely: *We thoroughly enjoyed ourselves.* ◇ *I'm thoroughly confused.* ◇ *a thoroughly professional performance* **2** completely and with great attention to detail: *Wash the fruit thoroughly before use.* ◇ *The work had not been done very thoroughly.*

those ➲ THAT

thou /ðaʊ/ *pron.* (*old use* or *dialect*) a word meaning 'you', used when talking to only one person who is the subject of the verb ➲ compare THEE

though /ðəʊ; *NAmE* ðoʊ/ *conj., adv.*

■ ***conj.*** **1** despite the fact that SYN **although**: *Anne was fond of Tim, though he often annoyed her.* ◇ *Though she gave no sign, I was sure she had seen me.* ◇ *His clothes, though old and worn, looked clean and of good quality.* ◇ *Strange though it may sound, I was pleased it was over.* **2** used to add a fact or an opinion that makes the previous statement less strong or less important: *They're very different, though they did seem to get on well when they met.* ◇ *He'll probably say no, though it's worth asking.* ➲ note at ALTHOUGH IDM see AS *conj.*, EVEN *adv.*

■ ***adv.*** used especially at the end of a sentence to add a fact or an opinion that makes the previous statement less strong or less important: *Our team lost. It was a good game though.* ◇ *'Have you ever been to Australia?' 'No. I'd like to, though.'* ➲ note at ALTHOUGH

thought /θɔːt/ *noun*

▸ STH YOU THINK **1** [C] something that you think of or remember: **~ of (sb/sth) doing sth** *I don't like the thought of you walking home alone.* ◇ **~ of sth** *The very thought of it makes me feel sick.* ◇ **~ (that...)** *She was struck by the sudden thought that he might already have left.* ◇ *I've just* ***had a thought*** (= an idea). ◇ *Would Mark be able to help?* ***It's just a thought.*** ◇ *'Why don't you try the other key?'* ***'That's a thought!'*** ◇ *I'd like to hear your thoughts on the subject.*

▸ MIND/IDEAS **2** **thoughts** [pl.] a person's mind and all the ideas that they have in it when they are thinking: *My thoughts turned to home.*

▸ PROCESS/ACT OF THINKING **3** [U] the power or process of thinking: *A good teacher encourages independence of thought.* ◇ *She was* ***lost in thought*** (= concentrating so much on her thoughts that she was not aware of her surroundings). **4** [U] the act of thinking seriously and carefully about sth SYN **consideration**: *I've given the matter careful thought.* ◇ *Not enough thought has gone into this essay.*

▸ CARE/WORRY **5** [C] **~ (for sb/sth)** a feeling of care or worry: ***Spare a thought*** *for those without enough to eat this winter.* ◇ ***Don't give it another thought*** (= to tell sb not to worry after they have said they are sorry). ◇ ***It's the thought that counts*** (= used to say that sb has been very kind even if they have only done sth small or unimportant).

▸ INTENTION **6** [U, C] an intention or a hope of doing sth: **~ (of doing sth)** *She had given up all thought of changing her job.* ◇ **~ (of sth)** *He acted with no thoughts of personal gain.*

▸ IN POLITICS/SCIENCE, ETC. **7** [U] ideas in politics, science, etc. connected with a particular person, group or period of history: *feminist thought* ➲ see also THINK *v.*

IDM **have ˌsecond ˈthoughts** to change your opinion after thinking about sth again **on ˈsecond thoughts** (*BrE*) (*NAmE* **on ˈsecond thought**) used to say that you have changed your opinion: *I'll wait here. No, on second*

T

thoughts, I'll come with you. **without a second 'thought** immediately; without stopping to think about sth further: *He dived in after her without a second thought.* ➲ more at COLLECT *v.*, FOOD, PAUSE *n.*, PENNY, PERISH, SCHOOL *n.*, TRAIN *n.*, WISH *n.*

thought·crime /ˈθɔːtkraɪm/ *noun* [U, C] an idea or opinion that is considered socially unacceptable or criminal ORIGIN From George Orwell's novel *Nineteen Eighty-Four.*

thought·ful /ˈθɔːtfl/ *adj.* **1** quiet, because you are thinking: *He looked thoughtful.* ◇ *They sat in thoughtful silence.* **2** (*approving*) showing that you think about and care for other people SYN **considerate, kind**: *It was very thoughtful of you to send the flowers.* **3** showing signs of careful thought: *a player who has a thoughtful approach to the game* ▸ **thought·ful·ly** /-fəli/ *adv.*: *Martin looked at her thoughtfully.* ◇ *She used the towel thoughtfully provided by her host.* **thought·ful·ness** *noun* [U]

thought·less /ˈθɔːtləs/ *adj.* (*disapproving*) not caring about the possible effects of your words or actions on other people SYN **inconsiderate**: *a thoughtless remark* ▸ **thought·less·ly** *adv.* **thought·less·ness** *noun* [U]

'thought police *noun* [pl.] a group of people who are seen as trying to control people's ideas and stop them from having their own opinions

'thought-provok·ing *adj.* making people think seriously about a particular subject or issue

thou·sand O-w /ˈθaʊznd/ *number* (*abbr.* K)
1 O-w 1000 HELP You say **a, one, two, etc. thousand** without a final 's' on 'thousand'. **Thousands (of...)** can be used if there is no number or quantity before it. Always use a plural verb with **thousand** or **thousands**, except when an amount of money is mentioned: *Four thousand (people) are expected to attend.* ◇ *Two thousand (pounds) was withdrawn from the account.* **2** O-w **a thousand** or **thousands (of...)** (usually *informal*) a large number: *There were thousands of people there.* **3 the thousands** the numbers from 1000 to 9 999: *The cost ran into the thousands.* HELP There are more examples of how to use numbers at the entry for **hundred**. IDM see BAT *v.*

thou·sandth O-w /ˈθaʊznθ/ *ordinal number, noun*
■ ***ordinal number*** O-w 1000th: *the city's thousandth anniversary*
■ ***noun*** O-w each of one thousand parts of sth: *a/one thousandth of a second*

thrall /θrɔːl/ *noun*
IDM **in (sb's/sth's) 'thrall | in 'thrall to sb/sth** (*literary*) controlled or strongly influenced by sb/sth

thrash /θræʃ/ *verb, noun*
■ ***verb* 1** [T] **~ sb/sth** to hit a person or an animal many times with a stick, etc. as a punishment SYN **beat 2** [I, T] to move or make sth move in a violent or uncontrolled way: **~ (about/around)** *Someone was thrashing around in the water, obviously in trouble.* ◇ **~ sth (about/around)** *A whale was thrashing the water with its tail.* ◇ *She thrashed her head from side to side.* **3** [T] **~ sb/sth** (*informal, especially BrE*) to defeat sb very easily in a game: *Scotland thrashed England 5–1.* ➲ compare WHIP *v.* (5)
PHR V **,thrash sth↔'out** (*informal*) to discuss a situation or problem thoroughly in order to decide sth
■ ***noun* 1** [U] a type of loud rock music **2** [C] (*old-fashioned, informal*) a party with music and dancing

thrash·ing /ˈθræʃɪŋ/ *noun* **1** an act of hitting sb very hard, especially with a stick: *to* ***give sb/get a thrashing*** **2** (*informal*) a severe defeat in a game

thread O-w /θred/ *noun, verb*
■ ***noun* 1** O-w [U, C] a thin string of cotton, wool, silk, etc. used for sewing or making cloth: *a needle and thread* ◇ *a robe embroidered with gold thread* ◇ *the delicate threads of a spider's web* ➲ picture at ROPE ➲ VISUAL VOCAB page V35 **2** [C] an idea or a feature that is part of sth greater; an idea that connects the different parts of sth: *A common thread runs through these discussions.* ◇ *The author skilfully draws together the different threads of the plot.* ◇ ***I lost the thread*** *of the argument* (= I could no longer follow it). **3** [C] **~ (of sth)** a long thin line of sth: *A thread of light emerged from the keyhole.* **4** [C] (*computing*) a series of connected messages on a MESSAGE BOARD on the Internet which have been sent by different people **5** [C] the raised line that runs around the length of a screw and that allows it to be fixed in place by twisting ➲ VISUAL VOCAB page V17 **6 threads** [pl.] (*old-fashioned, NAmE, slang*) clothes IDM see HANG *v.*, PICK *v.*
■ ***verb* 1** [T] **~ sth (+ adv./prep.)** to pass sth long and thin, especially thread, through a narrow opening or hole: *to thread a needle (with cotton)* ◇ *to thread cotton through a needle* ◇ *A tiny wire is threaded through a vein to the heart.* **2** [I, T] to move or make sth move through a narrow space, avoiding things that are in the way SYN **pick your way**: **+ adv./prep.** *The waiters threaded between the crowded tables.* ◇ **~ your way + adv./prep.** *It took me a long time to thread my way through the crowd.* **3** [T] **~ sth (onto sth)** to join two or more objects together by passing sth long and thin through them: *to thread beads (onto a string)* **4** [T] **~ sth** to pass film, tape, string, etc. through parts of a piece of equipment so that it is ready to use **5** [T, usually passive] **~ sth (with sth)** to sew or twist a particular type of thread into sth: *a robe threaded with gold and silver*

thread·bare /ˈθredbeə(r); *NAmE* -ber/ *adj.* **1** (of cloth, clothing, etc.) old and thin because it has been used a lot: *a threadbare carpet* **2** (of an argument, excuse, etc.) that does not have much effect, especially because it has been used too much

thread·ed /ˈθredɪd/ *adj.* (*technical*) (of a screw, etc.) having a THREAD (5)

'thread vein *noun* a very thin VEIN, especially one that can be seen through the skin

thread·worm /ˈθredwɜːm; *NAmE* -wɜːrm/ *noun* a small thin WORM that lives in the INTESTINES of humans and animals

threat O-w /θret/ *noun*
1 O-w [C, U] **~ (to do sth)** a statement in which you tell sb that you will punish or harm them, especially if they do not do what you want: *to make threats against sb* ◇ *She is prepared to* ***carry out her threat*** *to resign.* ◇ *He received* ***death threats*** *from right-wing groups.* ◇ *crimes involving violence or the threat of violence* **2** O-w [U, C, usually sing.] the possibility of trouble, danger or disaster: *These ancient woodlands are* ***under threat*** *from new road developments.* ◇ *There is a real threat of war.* **3** O-w [C, usually sing.] **~ (to sth)** a person or thing that is likely to cause trouble, danger, etc: *He is unlikely to be a threat to the Spanish player in the final.* ◇ *Drugs* ***pose a major threat to*** *our society.*

threat·en O-w /ˈθretn/ *verb*
1 O-w [T] to say that you will cause trouble, hurt sb, etc. if you do not get what you want: **~ sb** *They broke my windows and threatened me.* ◇ **~ sb with sth** *The attacker threatened them with a gun.* ◇ *He was threatened with dismissal if he continued to turn up late for work.* ◇ **~ sth** *The threatened strike has been called off.* ◇ **~ to do sth** *The hijackers threatened to kill one passenger every hour if their demands were not met.* ◇ **~ that...** *They threatened that passengers would be killed.* **2** O-w [I, T] to seem likely to happen or cause sth unpleasant: *A storm was threatening.* ◇ **~ to do sth** *This dispute threatens to split the party.* ◇ **~ sth** *The clouds threatened rain.* **3** O-w [T] **~ sth** to be a danger to sth SYN **endanger, put at risk**: *Pollution is threatening marine life.*

threat·en·ing O-w /ˈθretnɪŋ/ *adj.*
1 O-w expressing a threat of harm or violence SYN **menacing**: *threatening letters* ◇ *threatening behaviour* **2** O-w (of the sky, clouds, etc.) showing that bad weather is likely: *The sky was dark and threatening.* ▸ **threat·en·ing·ly** *adv.*: *He glared at her threateningly.*

three O-w /θriː/ *number*
3 HELP There are examples of how to use numbers at the entry for **five**.
IDM **the three 'Rs** (*old-fashioned*) reading, writing and ARITHMETIC, thought to be the most important parts of a child's education ➲ more at TWO

ˌthree-card ˈtrick *noun* a game in which players bet money on which is the queen out of three cards lying face down

ˌthree-ˈcornered *adj.* [usually before noun] **1** having three corners: *a three-cornered hat* **2** involving three people or groups: *a three-cornered contest*

ˌthree-ˈD (also **3-D**) *noun* [U] the quality of having, or appearing to have, length, width and depth (= three DIMENSIONS): *These glasses allow you to see the film in three-D.* ◇ *a three-D image*

ˌthree-day eˈventing *noun* = EVENTING

ˌthree-diˈmension·al *adj.* having, or appearing to have, length, width and depth: *three-dimensional objects*

three·fold /ˈθriːfəʊld; *NAmE* -foʊld/ *adj., adv.* ➲ -FOLD

ˌthree ˈfourths *noun* [pl.] (*US*) = THREE QUARTERS

three-legged race /ˌθriː ˈlegɪd reɪs/ *noun* a race in which people taking part run in pairs, the right leg of one runner being tied to the left leg of the other

ˌthree-line ˈwhip *noun* (in Britain) a written notice to Members of Parliament from their party leaders telling them that they must be present at a particular vote and must vote in a particular way

ˌthree-ˈpeat *noun* (*NAmE*) (used especially in newspapers) an occasion when a person or team wins a competition for the third time, especially in sport ▸ **ˌthree-ˈpeat** *verb* [I]

three·pence /ˌθriːˈpens; *formerly* ˈθrepəns/ *noun* [U] (*BrE*) the sum of three old pence

three·penny bit /ˌθrepəni ˈbɪt/ (also **ˌthree·penny ˈpiece**) *noun* a British coin in use until 1971, worth three old pence

ˌthree-ˈpiece *adj.* [only before noun] consisting of three separate parts or pieces: *a **three-piece suit*** (= a set of clothes consisting of trousers/pants, a jacket and a WAISTCOAT/VEST) ◇ (*BrE*) *a **three-piece suite*** (= a set of three pieces of furniture, usually a SOFA and two ARMCHAIRS)

ˌthree-point ˈturn *noun* a method of turning a car in a small space so that it faces in the opposite direction, by driving forwards, then backwards, then forwards again, in a series of curves

ˌthree-ˈquarter *adj.* [only before noun] used to describe sth which is three quarters of the usual size: *a three-quarter length coat*

ˌthree ˈquarters (*US* also **ˌthree ˈfourths**) *noun* **~ (of sth)** three of the four equal parts into which sth may be divided: *three quarters of an hour*

ˌthree-ring ˈcircus *noun* [sing.] (*NAmE, informal*) a place or situation with a lot of confusing or amusing activity

three·some /ˈθriːsəm/ *noun* **1** [C+sing./pl. v.] a group of three people **2** [C] an occasion when three people have sex together

ˈthree-star *adj.* [usually before noun] **1** having three stars in a system that measures quality. The highest standard is usually represented by four or five stars: *a three-star hotel* **2** (*NAmE*) having the third-highest military rank, and wearing uniform which has three stars on it: *a three-star general*

ˌthree-ˈway *adj.* [only before noun] happening or working in three ways or directions, or between three people: *a three-way switch* ◇ *a three-way discussion*

thren·ody /ˈθrenədi/ *noun* (*pl.* -ies) (*technical*) a song, poem or other expression of great sadness for sb who has died or for sth that has ended

thresh /θreʃ/ *verb* **1** [T] **~ sth** to separate grains of rice, WHEAT, etc. from the rest of the plant using a machine or, especially in the past, by hitting it with a special tool ➲ COLLOCATIONS at FARMING **2** [I, T] **~ (sth)** to make, or cause sth to make, uncontrolled movements SYN **thrash** ▸ **thresh·ing** *noun* [U]: *a threshing machine*

thresh·old /ˈθreʃhəʊld; *NAmE* -hoʊld/ *noun* **1** the floor or ground at the bottom of a DOORWAY, considered as the entrance to a building or room: *She stood hesitating on the threshold.* ◇ *He stepped across the threshold.* **2** the level at which sth starts to happen or have an effect: *He has a low **boredom threshold*** (= he gets bored easily). ◇ *I have a high **pain threshold*** (= I can suffer a lot of pain before I start to react). ◇ *My earnings are just above the **tax threshold*** (= more than the amount at which you start paying tax). **3** [usually sing.] the point just before a new situation, period of life, etc. begins: *She felt as though she was **on the threshold of** a new life.*

threw *past tense* of THROW

thrice /θraɪs/ *adv.* (*old use* or *formal*) three times

thrift /θrɪft/ *noun* [U] **1** (*approving*) the habit of saving money and spending it carefully so that none is wasted ➲ see also SPENDTHRIFT **2** a wild plant with bright pink flowers that grows by the sea/ocean

ˈthrift shop (also **ˈthrift store**) (both *NAmE*) (*BrE* **ˈcharity shop**) *noun* a shop/store that sells clothes and other goods given by people to raise money for a charity

thrifty /ˈθrɪfti/ *adj.* (*approving*) careful about spending money and not wasting things SYN **frugal**

thrill /θrɪl/ *noun, verb*

■ ***noun*** **1** a strong feeling of excitement or pleasure; an experience that gives you this feeling: **~ (to do sth)** *It **gave me a** big **thrill** to meet my favourite author in person.* ◇ **~ (of doing sth)** *the thrill of catching a really big fish* ◇ *She gets an obvious thrill out of performing.* **2** a sudden strong feeling that produces a physical effect: *A thrill of alarm ran through him.*

IDM **(the) thrills and ˈspills** (*informal*) the excitement that is involved in dangerous activities, especially sports

■ ***verb*** **~ sb** to excite or please sb very much: *This band has thrilled audiences all over the world.* ◇ *I was thrilled by your news.*

PHR V **ˈthrill to sth** (*formal*) to feel very excited at sth

thrilled /θrɪld/ *adj.* very excited and pleased: **~ (about/at/with sth)** *He was thrilled at the prospect of seeing them again.* ◇ **~ (to do sth)** *I was thrilled to be invited.* ◇ **~ (that…)** (*BrE*) *She was **thrilled to bits*** (= extremely pleased) *that he'd been offered the job.* ◇ *'Are you pleased?' 'I'm thrilled.'* ➲ SYNONYMS at GLAD

thrill·er /ˈθrɪlə(r)/ *noun* a book, play or film/movie with an exciting story, especially one about crime or SPYING

thrill·ing /ˈθrɪlɪŋ/ *adj.* exciting and enjoyable: *a thrilling experience/finish* ➲ SYNONYMS at EXCITING ▸ **thrill·ing·ly** *adv.*

ˈthrill ride *noun* a ride at an AMUSEMENT PARK that makes you feel very excited and frightened at the same time

thrive /θraɪv/ *verb* [I] to become, and continue to be, successful, strong, healthy, etc. SYN **flourish**: *New businesses thrive in this area.* ◇ *These animals rarely thrive in captivity.* ▸ **thriv·ing** *adj.*: *a thriving industry*

PHR V **ˈthrive on sth** to enjoy sth or be successful at sth, especially sth that other people would not like: *He thrives on hard work.*

throat 0→ /θrəʊt; *NAmE* θroʊt/ *noun*

1 0→ a passage in the neck through which food and air pass on their way into the body; the front part of the neck: *a sore throat* ◇ *A sob caught in his throat.* ◇ *He held the knife to her throat.* ◇ *Their throats had been cut.* ➲ VISUAL VOCAB page V48 **2 -throated** (in adjectives) having the type of throat mentioned: *a deep-throated roar* ◇ *a red-throated diver* ➲ see also CUT-THROAT

IDM **be at each other's ˈthroats** (of two or more people, groups, etc.) to be fighting or arguing with each other **cut your own ˈthroat** to do sth that is likely to harm you, especially when you are angry and trying to harm sb else **force/thrust/ram sth down sb's ˈthroat** (*informal*) to try to force sb to listen to and accept your opinions in a way that they find annoying ➲ more at CLEAR *v.*, FROG, JUMP *v.*, LUMP *n.*, STICK *v.*

throaty /ˈθrəʊti; *NAmE* ˈθroʊti/ *adj.* sounding low and rough: *a throaty laugh* ◇ *the throaty roar of the engines* ▸ **throat·ily** /-ɪli/ *adv.*

T

throb /θrɒb; *NAmE* θrɑːb/ *verb, noun*
■ ***verb*** (-bb-) **1** [I] **~ (with sth)** (of a part of the body) to feel a series of regular painful movements: *His head throbbed painfully.* ◇ *My feet were throbbing after the long walk home.* ➲ SYNONYMS at HURT **2** [I] to beat or sound with a strong, regular rhythm SYN **pulsate**: *The ship's engines throbbed quietly.* ◇ *a throbbing drumbeat* ◇ *The blood was throbbing in my veins.* ◇ **~ with sth** (*figurative*) *His voice was throbbing with emotion.*
■ ***noun*** (also **throb·bing**) [sing.] a strong regular beat; a feeling of pain that you experience as a series of strong beats: *the throb of the machines* ◇ *My headache faded to a dull throbbing.* ➲ see also HEART-THROB

throes /θrəʊz; *NAmE* θroʊz/ *noun* [pl.] violent pains, especially at the moment of death: *The creature went into its death throes.*
IDM **in the throes of sth/of doing sth** in the middle of an activity, especially a difficult or complicated one: *The country was in the throes of revolutionary change.*

throm·bosis /θrɒmˈbəʊsɪs; *NAmE* θrɑːmˈboʊ-/ *noun* [C, U] (*pl.* **throm·boses** /-siːz/) (*medical*) a serious condition caused by a blood CLOT (= a thick mass of blood) forming in a blood VESSEL (= tube) or in the heart ➲ see also CORONARY THROMBOSIS, DEEP VEIN THROMBOSIS

throne /θrəʊn; *NAmE* θroʊn/ *noun* **1** [C] a special chair used by a king or queen to sit on at ceremonies **2 the throne** [sing.] the position of being a king or queen: *Queen Elizabeth* ***came/succeeded to the throne*** *in 1952.* ◇ *when Henry VIII was* ***on the throne*** (= was king) IDM see POWER *n.*

throng /θrɒŋ; *NAmE* θrɔːŋ; θrɑːŋ/ *noun, verb*
■ ***noun*** (*literary*) a crowd of people: *We pushed our way through the throng.*
■ ***verb*** [I, T] (*literary*) to go somewhere or be present somewhere in large numbers: **+ adv./prep.** *The children thronged into the hall.* ◇ **~ to do sth** *People are thronging to see his new play.* ◇ **~ sth** *Crowds thronged the stores.*
PHR V ˈ**throng with sb/sth** | **be ˈthronged with sb/sth** to be full of people, cars, etc: *The cafes were thronging with students.* ◇ *The streets were thronged with people.*

throt·tle /ˈθrɒtl; *NAmE* ˈθrɑːtl/ *verb, noun*
■ ***verb*** **~ sb** to attack or kill sb by squeezing their throat in order to stop them from breathing SYN **strangle**: *He throttled the guard with his bare hands.* ◇ (*humorous*) *I like her, although I could cheerfully throttle her at times* (= because she is annoying). ◇ (*figurative*) *The city is being throttled by traffic.*
PHR V ˌ**throttle** (**sth**) ˈ**back**/ˈ**down**/ˈ**up** to control the supply of fuel or power to an engine in order to reduce/increase the speed of a vehicle: *I throttled back as we approached the runway.*
■ ***noun*** a device that controls the amount of fuel that goes into the engine of a vehicle, for example the ACCELERATOR in a car: *He drove along* ***at full throttle*** (= as fast as possible).

through 0-w /θruː/ *prep., adv., adj.*
■ ***prep.*** HELP For the special uses of **through** in phrasal verbs, look at the entries for the verbs. For example **get through sth** is in the phrasal verb section at **get. 1** 0-w from one end or side of sth/sb to the other: *The burglar got in through the window.* ◇ *The bullet went straight through him.* ◇ *Her knees had gone through* (= made holes in) *her jeans.* ◇ *The sand ran through* (= between) *my fingers.* ◇ *The path led through the trees to the river.* ◇ *The doctor pushed his way through the crowd.* ◇ *The Charles River flows through Boston.* **2 see, hear, etc. ~ sth** to see, hear, etc. sth from the other side of an object or a substance: *I couldn't hear their conversation through the wall.* ◇ *He could just make out three people through the mist.* **3** 0-w from the beginning to the end of an activity, a situation or a period of time: *The children are too young to sit through a concert.* ◇ *He will not live through the night.* ◇ *I'm halfway through* (= reading) *her second novel.* **4** 0-w past a barrier, stage or test: *Go through this gate, and you'll see the house on your left.* ◇ *He drove through a red light* (= passed it when he should have stopped). ◇ *First I have to get through the exams.* ◇ *The bill had a difficult passage through Parliament.* ◇ *I'd never have got through it all* (= a difficult situation) *without you.* **5** 0-w (also *informal* **thru**) (both *NAmE*) until, and including: *We'll be in New York Tuesday through Friday.* ➲ note at INCLUSIVE **6** 0-w by means of; because of: *You can only achieve success through hard work.* ◇ *It was through him* (= as a result of his help) *that I got the job.* ◇ *The accident happened through no fault of mine.*
■ ***adv.*** HELP For the special uses of **through** in phrasal verbs, look at the entries for the verbs. For example **carry sth through** is in the phrasal verb section at **carry. 1** 0-w from one end or side of sth to the other: *Put the coffee in the filter and let the water run through.* ◇ *The tyre's flat—the nail has gone right through.* ◇ *The onlookers stood aside to let the paramedics through.* ◇ *The flood was too deep to drive through.* **2** 0-w from the beginning to the end of a thing or period of time: *Don't tell me how it ends—I haven't read it all the way through yet.* ◇ *I expect I'll struggle through until payday.* **3** 0-w past a barrier, stage or test: *The lights were red but he drove straight through.* ◇ *Our team is through to* (= has reached) *the semi-finals.* **4** 0-w travelling through a place without stopping or without people having to get off one train and onto another: *'Did you stop in Oxford on the way?' 'No, we drove straight through.'* ◇ *This train goes straight through to York.* **5** 0-w connected by telephone: *Ask to be* ***put through*** *to me personally.* ◇ *I tried to call you but I couldn't* ***get through.*** **6** used after an adjective to mean 'completely': *We got wet through.*
IDM ˌ**through and ˈthrough** completely; in every way: *He's British through and through.*
■ ***adj.*** **1** [only before noun] **through** traffic travels from one side of a place to the other without stopping **2** [only before noun] a **through** train takes you to the final place you want to get to and you do not have to get off and get on another train **3** [only before noun] a **through** road or route is open at both ends and allows traffic to travel from one end to the other: *The village lies on a busy through road.* ◇ ***No through road*** (= the road is closed at one end). **4** [not before noun] **~ (with sth/sb)** (*especially NAmE*) used to show that you have finished using sth or have ended a relationship with sb: *Are you through with that newspaper?* ◇ *Todd and I are through.*

through·out 0-w /θruːˈaʊt/ *prep.*
1 0-w in or into every part of sth: *They export their products to markets throughout the world.* **2** 0-w during the whole period of time of sth: *The museum is open daily throughout the year.* ▸ **through·out** 0-w *adv.*: *The house was painted white throughout.* ◇ *The ceremony lasted two hours and we had to stand throughout.*

through·put /ˈθruːpʊt/ *noun* [U, C, usually sing.] (*technical*) the amount of work that is done, or the number of people that are dealt with, in a particular period of time

through·way = THRUWAY

throw 0-w /θrəʊ; *NAmE* θroʊ/ *verb, noun*
■ ***verb*** (**threw** /θruː/, **thrown** /θrəʊn; *NAmE* θroʊn/)
▸ WITH HAND **1** 0-w [T, I] to send sth from your hand through the air by moving your hand or arm quickly: **~ (sth)** *Stop throwing stones at the window!* ◇ *She threw the ball up and caught it again.* ◇ *They had a competition to see who could throw the furthest.* ◇ **~ sth to sb** *Don't throw it to him, give it to him!* ◇ **~ sb sth** *Can you throw me that towel?*
▸ PUT CARELESSLY **2** 0-w [T] **~ sth + adv./prep.** to put sth in a particular place quickly and carelessly: *Just throw your bag down over there.*
▸ MOVE WITH FORCE **3** 0-w [T] to move sth suddenly and with force: **~ sth + adv./prep.** *The boat was thrown onto the rocks.* ◇ *The sea throws up all sorts of debris on the beach.* ◇ **~ sth + adj.** *I threw open the windows to let the smoke out.*
▸ PART OF BODY **4** 0-w [T] **~ sth/yourself + adv./prep.** to move your body or part of it quickly or suddenly: *He threw back his head and roared with laughter.* ◇ *I ran up and threw my arms around him.* ◇ *Jenny threw herself onto the bed.*
▸ MAKE SB FALL **5** [T] **~ sb** to make sb fall quickly or violently to the ground: *Two riders were thrown* (= off their horses) *in the second race.*
▸ INTO PARTICULAR STATE **6** [T, usually passive] **~ sb/sth + adv./prep.** to make sb/sth be in a particular state: *Hun-*

dreds were thrown out of work. ◇ *We were thrown into confusion by the news.* ◇ *The problem was suddenly thrown into sharp focus.*

▸ DIRECT STH AT SB/STH **7** [T] **~ sth on/at sb/sth** to direct sth at sb/sth: *to throw doubt on the verdict* ◇ *to throw the blame on someone* ◇ *to throw accusations at someone* ◇ *He threw the question back at me* (= expected me to answer it myself).

▸ UPSET **8** [T] **~ sb** (*informal*) to make sb feel upset, confused, or surprised: *The news of her death really threw me.*

▸ DICE **9** [T] **~ sth** to roll a DICE or let it fall after shaking it; to obtain a particular number in this way: *Throw the dice!* ◇ *He threw three sixes in a row.*

▸ CLAY POT **10** [T] **~ sth** (*technical*) to make a CLAY pot, dish, etc. on a POTTER'S WHEEL: *a hand-thrown vase*

▸ LIGHT/SHADE **11** [T] **~ sth** (+ **adv./prep.**) to send light or shade onto sth: *The trees threw long shadows across the lawn.*

▸ YOUR VOICE **12** [T] **~ your voice** to make your voice sound as if it is coming from another person or place SYN **project**

▸ A PUNCH **13** [T] **~ a punch** to hit sb with your FIST

▸ SWITCH/HANDLE **14** [T] **~ sth** to move a switch, handle, etc. to operate sth

▸ BAD-TEMPERED BEHAVIOUR **15** [T] **~ sth** to have a sudden period of bad-tempered behaviour, violent emotion, etc: *She'll throw a fit if she finds out.* ◇ *Children often throw tantrums at this age.*

▸ A PARTY **16** [T] **~ a party** (*informal*) to give a party

▸ IN SPORTS/COMPETITIONS **17** [T] **~ sth** (*informal*) to deliberately lose a game or contest that you should have won: *He was accused of having thrown the game.*

IDM Idioms containing **throw** are at the entries for the nouns and adjectives in the idioms, for example **throw your hat into the ring** is at **hat**.

PHR V ˌ**throw sth↔aˈside** to reject sth such as an attitude, a way of life, etc. ˈ**throw yourself at sth/sb 1** to rush violently at sth/sb **2** (*informal, disapproving*) (usually of a woman) to be too enthusiastic in trying to attract a sexual partner ˌ**throw sth↔aˈway 1** 🔑 (also ˌ**throw sth↔ˈout**) to get rid of sth that you no longer want: *I don't need that—you can throw it away.* ◇ *That old chair should be thrown away.* **2** 🔑 to fail to make use of sth; to waste sth: *to throw away an opportunity* ➲ see also THROWAWAY ˌ**throw sth ˈback at sb** to remind sb of sth they have said or done in the past, especially to upset or annoy them ˌ**throw sb ˈback on sth** [usually passive] to force sb to rely on sth because nothing else is available: *There was no TV so we were thrown back on our own resources* (= had to entertain ourselves). ˌ**throw sth↔ˈin 1** to include sth with what you are selling or offering, without increasing the price: *You can have the piano for $200, and I'll throw in the stool as well.* **2** to add a remark to a conversation: *Jack threw in the odd encouraging comment.* ˌ**throw yourself/sth ˈinto sth** to begin to do sth with energy and enthusiasm ˌ**throw sth/sb↔ˈoff 1** to manage to get rid of sth/sb that is making you suffer, annoying you, etc: *to throw off a cold/your worries/your pursuers* **2** to take off a piece of clothing quickly and carelessly: *She entered the room and threw off her wet coat.* ˌ**throw sth↔ˈon** to put on a piece of clothing quickly and carelessly: *She just threw on the first skirt she found.* ˌ**throw sth↔ˈopen** (**to sb**) **1** to allow people to enter or visit a place where they could not go before **2** to allow people to discuss sth, take part in a competition, etc: *The debate will be thrown open to the audience.* ˌ**throw sb↔ˈout** (**of...**) 🔑 to force sb to leave a place: *You'll be thrown out if you don't pay the rent.* ˌ**throw sth↔ˈout 1** to say sth in a way that suggests you have not given it a lot of thought: *to throw out a suggestion* **2** to decide not to accept a proposal, an idea, etc. **3** = THROW STH AWAY **4** to produce smoke, light, heat, etc: *a small fire that threw out a lot of heat* **5** to confuse sth or make it wrong: *Our calculations of the cost of our trip were thrown out by changes in the exchange rate.* ˌ**throw sb ˈover** (*old-fashioned*) to stop being friends with sb or having a romantic relationship with them ˌ**throw sb↔toˈgether** [often passive] to bring people into contact with each other, often unexpectedly: *Fate had thrown them together.* ˌ**throw sth↔toˈgether** to make or produce sth in a hurry: *I threw together a quick meal.* ˌ**throw ˈup** to VOMIT SYN **be sick**: *The smell made me want to throw up.* ˌ**throw sth↔ˈup 1** to VOMIT food SYN **sick up**: *The baby's thrown up her dinner.* **2** to make people notice sth: *Her research has thrown up some interesting facts.* **3** to build sth suddenly or in a hurry: *They're throwing up new housing estates all over the place.* **4** to leave your job: *to throw up your career*

■ ***noun*** **1** the act of throwing sth, especially a ball or DICE: *a well-aimed throw* ◇ *It's your throw* (= it's your turn to throw the dice). ◇ *He threw me to the ground with a judo throw.* **2** the distance which sth is thrown: *a javelin throw of 57 metres* **3** a loose cloth cover that can be thrown over a SOFA, etc. ➲ **VISUAL VOCAB** page V18

IDM **$100, £50, etc. a ˈthrow** (*informal*) used to say how much items cost each: *The tickets for the dinner were £50 a throw.* ➲ more at STONE *n.*

Synonyms

throw

toss • hurl • fling • chuck • lob • bowl • pitch

These words all mean to send sth from your hand through the air.

throw to send sth from your hand or hands through the air: *Some kids were throwing stones at the window.* ◇ *She threw the ball and he caught it.*

toss to throw sth lightly or carelessly: *She tossed her jacket onto the bed.*

hurl to throw sth violently in a particular direction: *Rioters hurled a brick through the car's windscreen.*

fling to throw sb/sth somewhere with a lot of force, especially because you are angry or in a hurry: *She flung the letter down onto the table.*

chuck (*especially BrE, informal*) to throw sth carelessly: *I chucked him the keys.*

lob (*informal*) to throw sth so that it goes high through the air: *They were lobbing stones over the wall.*

bowl (in cricket) to throw the ball to the batsman

pitch (in baseball) to throw the ball to the batter

PATTERNS

- to throw/toss/hurl/fling/chuck/lob/bowl/pitch sth **at/to** sb/sth
- to throw/toss/fling/chuck sth **aside/away**
- to throw/toss/hurl/fling/chuck/lob/bowl/pitch a **ball**
- to throw/toss/hurl/fling/chuck **stones/rocks/a brick**
- to throw/toss/hurl/fling sth **angrily**
- to throw/toss sth **casually/carelessly**

throw·away /ˈθrəʊəweɪ; *NAmE* ˈθroʊ-/ *adj.* [only before noun] **1 ~ line/remark/comment** something you say quickly without careful thought, sometimes in order to be funny: *She was very upset at what to him was just a throwaway remark.* **2** (of goods, etc.) produced cheaply and intended to be thrown away after use SYN **disposable**: *throwaway products* ◇ *We live in a throwaway society* (= a society in which things are not made to last a long time).

throw·back /ˈθrəʊbæk; *NAmE* ˈθroʊ-/ *noun* [usually sing.] **~** (**to sth**) a person or thing that is similar to sb/sth that existed in the past: *The car's design is a throwback to the 1960s.*

throw·er /ˈθrəʊə(r); *NAmE* ˈθroʊ-/ *noun* a person who throws sth: *a discus thrower* ➲ see also FLAME-THROWER

ˈ**throw-in** *noun* (in football (SOCCER) and RUGBY) the act of throwing the ball back onto the playing field after it has gone outside the area

thrown *past part.* of THROW

ˈ**throw pillow** (*NAmE*) (*BrE* ˈ**scatter cushion**) *noun* a small CUSHION that can be placed on furniture, on the floor, etc. for decoration ➲ **VISUAL VOCAB** page V18

thru (*NAmE, informal*) = THROUGH *prep.* (5)

thrush /θrʌʃ/ *noun* **1** [C] a bird with a brown back and brown spots on its chest: *a song thrush* **2** [U] an infectious disease that affects the mouth and throat **3** [U] (*BrE*) (*NAmE* **'yeast infection**) an infectious disease that affects the VAGINA

thrust /θrʌst/ *verb, noun*

■ ***verb*** (**thrust, thrust**) **1** [T, I] to push sth/sb suddenly or violently in a particular direction; to move quickly and suddenly in a particular direction: **~ sth/sb/yourself + adv/prep.** *He thrust the baby into my arms and ran off.* ◇ *She thrust her hands deep into her pockets.* ◇ (*figurative*) *He tends to thrust himself forward too much.* ◇ **+ adv./prep.** *She thrust past him angrily and left.* **2** [I, T] **~ (at sb) (with sth)** | **~ (sth at sb)** to make a sudden strong forward movement at sb with a weapon, etc: *He thrust at me with a knife.* ◇ *a thrusting movement* IDM see THROAT

PHR V **,thrust sth↔a'side** to refuse to listen to sb's complaints, comments, etc: *All our objections were thrust aside.* **'thrust sth/sb on/upon sb** to force sb to accept or deal with sth/sb that they do not want: *She was annoyed at having three extra guests suddenly thrust on her.*

■ ***noun*** **1 the thrust** [sing.] the main point of an argument, a policy, etc: *The thrust of his argument was that change was needed.* **2** [C] a sudden strong movement that pushes sth/sb forward: *He killed her with a thrust of the knife.* **3** [U] (*technical*) the force that is produced by an engine to push a plane, ROCKET, etc. forward IDM see CUT *n.*

thrust·er /'θrʌstə(r)/ *noun* a small engine used to provide extra force, especially on a SPACECRAFT

thru·way (also **through·way**) /'θru:weɪ/ *noun* (*NAmE*) used in the names of some FREEWAYS (= important roads across or between states): *the New York State Thruway*

thud /θʌd/ *noun, verb*

■ ***noun*** a sound like the one which is made when a heavy object hits sth else: *His head hit the floor with a dull thud.*

■ ***verb*** (**-dd-**) **1** [I, T] **~ (sth) + adv./prep.** to fall or hit sth with a low dull sound: *His arrow thudded into the target.* **2** [I] (*literary*) (especially of the heart) to beat strongly

thug /θʌg/ *noun* a violent person, especially a criminal: *a gang of thugs* ▸ **thug·gish** /'θʌgɪʃ/ *adj.*: *thuggish brutality*

thug·gery /'θʌgəri/ *noun* [U] (*formal*) violent, usually criminal, behaviour

thu·lium /'θu:liəm; *BrE* also 'θju:-/ *noun* [U] (*symb.* **Tm**) a chemical element. Thulium is a soft silver-white metal.

thumb 🔑 /θʌm/ *noun, verb*

■ ***noun*** **1** 🔑 the short thick finger at the side of the hand, slightly apart from the other four: *She still* ***sucks her thumb*** *when she's worried.* ➲ VISUAL VOCAB page V48 ➲ see also GREEN THUMB **2** 🔑 the part of a glove that covers the thumb: *There's a hole in the thumb.*

IDM **be all (,fingers and) 'thumbs** to be awkward with your hands so that you drop things or are unable to do sth **hold 'thumbs** (*SAfrE*) to hope that your plans will be successful or that sth will take place in the way that you want it to: *Let's hold thumbs that you get the job.* **thumbs 'up/'down** (*informal*) used to show that sth has been accepted/rejected or that it is/is not a success: *Their proposals* ***were given the thumbs down.*** ◇ *It looks like it's thumbs up for their latest album.* ORIGIN In contests in ancient Rome the public put their thumbs up if they wanted a gladiator to live, and down if they wanted him to be killed. **under sb's 'thumb** (of a person) completely controlled by sb ➲ more at RULE *n.*, SORE *adj.*, TWIDDLE *v.*

■ ***verb*** **1** [I, T] to make a signal with your thumb to passing drivers to ask them to stop and take you somewhere: **+ adv./prep.** *He had thumbed all across Europe.* ◇ (*BrE*) **~ a lift** *We managed to thumb a lift with a lorry driver.* ◇ (*NAmE*) **~ a ride** *We managed to thumb a ride with a truck driver.* **2** [T] **~ sth (+ adv./prep.)** to touch or move sth with your thumb: *She thumbed off the safety catch of her pistol.* ➲ see also WELL THUMBED

IDM **thumb your 'nose at sb/sth** to make a rude sign with your thumb on your nose; to show that you have no respect for sb/sth: *The company just thumbs its nose at the legislation on pollution.*

PHR V **'thumb through sth** to turn the pages of a book quickly in order to get a general idea of what is in it

'thumb drive *noun* (*NAmE*) = FLASH DRIVE

'thumb index *noun* a series of cuts in the edge of a book, with letters of the alphabet on them, to help you to find the section that you want more easily

thumb·nail /'θʌmneɪl/ *noun* **1** the nail on the thumb **2** (also **,thumbnail 'image**) (*computing*) a very small picture on a computer screen which shows you what a larger picture looks like, or what a page of a document will look like when you print it

,thumbnail 'sketch *noun* a short description of sth, giving only the main details

'thumb piano (also **sansa**) *noun* an African musical instrument consisting of a row of metal strips, that you play with your fingers and thumbs

thumb·print /'θʌmprɪnt/ *noun* the mark made by the pattern of lines on the top of a person's thumb

thumb·screw /'θʌmskru:/ *noun* an instrument that was used in the past for TORTURING people by crushing their thumbs

thumb·suck /'θʌmsʌk/ *noun* [C, usually sing., U] (*SAfrE, informal*, often *disapproving*) a guess or estimate: *Their sales projections are a total thumbsuck.*

thumb·tack /'θʌmtæk/ (also **tack**) (both *NAmE*) (*BrE* **'drawing pin**) *noun* a short pin with a large round flat head, used especially for fastening paper to a board or wall ➲ VISUAL VOCAB page V56

thump /θʌmp/ *verb, noun*

■ ***verb*** **1** [T, I] **~ (sb/sth) (+ adv./prep.)** to hit sb/sth hard, especially with your closed hand: *He thumped the table angrily.* ◇ *She couldn't get her breath and had to be thumped on the back.* ◇ (*informal*) *I'll thump you if you say that again.* ◇ (*figurative*) *He thumped out a tune* (= played it very loudly) *on the piano.* **2** [I, T] to fall on or hit a surface hard, with a loud dull sound; to make sth do this: **+ adv./prep.** *A bird thumped against the window.* ◇ **~ sth + adv./prep.** *He thumped the report down on my desk.* **3** [I] to beat strongly: *My heart was thumping with excitement.* ➲ see also TUB-THUMPING

■ ***noun*** **1** the sound of sth heavy hitting the ground or another object: *There was a thump as the truck hit the bank.* **2** (*BrE, informal*) an act of hitting sb/sth hard: *She gave him a thump on the back.*

thump·ing /'θʌmpɪŋ/ *adj.* [only before noun] (*informal*) very big SYN **huge**: *a thumping majority* ▸ **thump·ing** *adv.*: (*BrE*) *He told us a thumping great lie.*

thun·der /'θʌndə(r)/ *noun, verb*

■ ***noun*** [U] **1** the loud noise that you hear after a flash of LIGHTNING, during a storm: *the rumble of distant thunder* ◇ *a* ***clap/crash/roll of thunder*** ◇ *Thunder crashed in the sky.* ➲ COLLOCATIONS at WEATHER **2** a loud noise like thunder: *the thunder of hooves* IDM see FACE *n.*, STEAL *v.*

■ ***verb*** **1** [I] when **it thunders**, there is a loud noise in the sky during a storm **2** [I] to make a very loud deep noise SYN **roar**: *A voice thundered in my ear.* ◇ *thundering traffic* **3** [I] **+ adv./prep.** to move very fast and with a loud deep noise SYN **roar**: *Heavy trucks kept thundering past.* **4** [T] **~ sth + adv./prep.** (*informal*) to make sth move somewhere very fast: *Essien thundered the ball past the goalie.* **5** [I, T] (*literary*) to shout, complain, etc. very loudly and angrily: **~ (sth)** *He thundered against the evils of television.* ◇ **+ speech** *'Sit still!' she thundered.*

thun·der·bolt /'θʌndəbəʊlt; *NAmE* 'θʌndərboʊlt/ *noun* a flash of LIGHTNING that comes at the same time as the noise of THUNDER and that hits sth: *The news hit them like a thunderbolt* (= was very shocking).

thun·der·box /'θʌndəbɒks; *NAmE* 'θʌndərbɑ:ks/ *noun* (*old-fashioned, BrE, informal*) a toilet, especially a simple one

thun·der·clap /'θʌndəklæp; *NAmE* -dərk-/ *noun* a loud crash made by THUNDER

thun·der·cloud /ˈθʌndəklaʊd; *NAmE* -dərk-/ *noun* a large dark cloud that produces THUNDER and LIGHTNING during a storm

thun·der·ous /ˈθʌndərəs/ *adj.* (*formal*) **1** very loud SYN **deafening**: *thunderous applause* **2** looking very angry: *his thunderous expression* ▶ **thun·der·ous·ly** *adv.*

thun·der·storm /ˈθʌndəstɔːm; *NAmE* ˈθʌndərstɔːrm/ *noun* a storm with THUNDER and LIGHTNING and usually very heavy rain

thun·der·struck /ˈθʌndəstrʌk; *NAmE* -dərs-/ *adj.* [not usually before noun] (*formal*) extremely surprised and shocked SYN **amazed**

thun·dery /ˈθʌndəri/ *adj.* (of weather) with THUNDER; suggesting that THUNDER is likely

Thurs·day 0‑ /ˈθɜːzdeɪ; -di; *NAmE* ˈθɜːrz-/ *noun* [C, U] (*abbr.* **Thur.**, **Thurs.**)
the day of the week after Wednesday and before Friday HELP To see how **Thursday** is used, look at the examples at **Monday**. ORIGIN From the Old English for 'day of thunder', translated from Latin *Jovis dies* 'Jupiter's day'. Jupiter was the god associated with thunder.

thus 0‑ /ðʌs/ *adv.* (*formal*)
1 0‑ in this way; like this: *Many scholars have argued thus.* ◇ *The universities have expanded, thus allowing many more people the chance of higher education.* **2** 0‑ as a result of sth just mentioned SYN **hence**, **therefore**: *He is the eldest son and thus heir to the title.* ◇ *We do not own the building. Thus, it would be impossible for us to make any major changes to it.* ➲ LANGUAGE BANK at THEREFORE IDM see FAR *adv.*

thwack /θwæk/ *verb* **~ sb/sth** to hit sb/sth hard, making a short loud sound ▶ **thwack** *noun*: *the thwack of bat on ball*

thwart /θwɔːt; *NAmE* θwɔːrt/ *verb* [often passive] to prevent sb from doing what they want to do SYN **frustrate**: **~ sth** *to thwart sb's plans* ◇ **~ sb (in sth)** *She* ***was thwarted in her attempt*** *to take control of the party.*

thy /ðaɪ/ (also **thine** before a vowel) *det.* (*old use*) a word meaning 'your', used when talking to only one person: *Honour thy father and thy mother.*

thyme /taɪm/ *noun* [U] a plant with small leaves that have a sweet smell and are used in cooking as a HERB ➲ VISUAL VOCAB page V28

thy·mus /ˈθaɪməs/ (also ˈ**thymus gland**) *noun* (*anatomy*) an organ in the neck that produces LYMPHOCYTES (= cells to fight infection)

thy·roid /ˈθaɪrɔɪd/ (also ˈ**thyroid gland**) *noun* (*anatomy*) a small organ at the front of the neck that produces HORMONES that control the way in which the body grows and functions

thy·self /ðaɪˈself/ *pron.* (*old use* or *dialect*) a word meaning 'yourself', used when talking to only one person

ti (*NAmE*) (*BrE* **te**) /tiː/ *noun* (*music*) the 7th note of a MAJOR SCALE

tiara /tiˈɑːrə/ *noun* a piece of jewellery like a small crown decorated with PRECIOUS STONES, worn by a woman, for example a princess, on formal occasions

TiB *abbr.* (in writing) TEBIBYTE

Tib *abbr.* (also **Tibit**) (in writing) TEBIBIT

tibia /ˈtɪbiə/ *noun* (*pl.* **tib·iae** /-bii:/) (*anatomy*) the SHIN BONE ➲ VISUAL VOCAB page V48 ➲ see also FIBULA

tic /tɪk/ *noun* a sudden quick movement of a muscle, especially in your face or head, that you cannot control

tick /tɪk/ *verb, noun*
■ *verb* **1** [I] (of a clock, etc.) to make short, light, regular repeated sounds to mark time passing: *In the silence we could hear the clock ticking.* ◇ *a ticking bomb* ◇ **~ away** *While we waited the taxi's meter kept ticking away.* **2** [T] (*BrE*) (*NAmE* **check**) **~ sth** to put a mark (✓) next to an item on a list, an answer, etc: *Please tick the appropriate box.* ◇ *Tick 'yes' or 'no' to each question.* ◇ *I've ticked the names of the people who have paid.*
IDM ˌ**tick all the/sb's** ˈ**boxes** (*BrE, informal*) to do exactly the right things to please sb: *This is a movie that ticks all the boxes.* **what makes sb** ˈ**tick** what makes sb behave in the way that they do: *I've never really understood what makes her tick.*
PHR V ˌ**tick aˈway/ˈby/ˈpast** (of time) to pass: *I had to get to the airport by two, and the minutes were ticking away.* ˌ**tick sth↔aˈway** (of a clock, etc.) to mark the time as it passes: *The clock ticked away the minutes.* ˌ**tick sb↔ˈoff 1** (*BrE, informal*) to speak angrily to sb, especially a child, because they have done sth wrong SYN **tell off** ➲ related noun TICKING OFF **2** (*NAmE, informal*) to make sb angry or annoyed ˌ**tick sb/sth** ˈ**off** (*BrE*) (*NAmE* ˌ**check sb/sth** ˈ**off**) to put a mark (✓) beside a name or an item on a list to show that sth has been dealt with ˌ**tick** ˈ**over** (*BrE*) (usually used in the progressive tenses) **1** (of an engine) to run slowly while the vehicle is not moving SYN **idle 2** (of a business, a system, an activity, etc.) to keep working slowly without producing or achieving much: *Just* ***keep things ticking over*** *while I'm away.*
■ *noun* **1** [C] (*BrE*) (*NAmE* ˈ**check mark**, **check**) a mark (✓) put beside a sum or an item on a list, usually to show that it has been checked or done or is correct: ***Put a tick*** *in the appropriate box if you would like further information about any of our products.* ➲ compare CROSS, X (4) **2** [C] a small insect that bites humans and animals and sucks their blood. There are several types of tick, some of which can carry diseases: *a tick bite* ➲ VISUAL VOCAB page V11 **3** (also **tick·ing**) [U] a short, light, regularly repeated sound, especially that of a clock or watch: *The only sound was the soft tick of the clock.* **4** [C] (*BrE, informal*) a moment: *Hang on a tick!* ◇ *I'll be with you in two ticks.* **5** [U] (*old-fashioned, BrE, informal*) permission to delay paying for sth that you have bought SYN **credit**: *Can I have these* ***on tick***?

tick·box /ˈtɪkbɒks; *NAmE* -bɑːks/ *noun* (*BrE*) = CHECKBOX

tick·er /ˈtɪkə(r)/ *noun* **1** = NEWS TICKER **2** (*old-fashioned, informal*) a person's heart

ˈ**ticker tape** *noun* [U] (*especially NAmE*) (in the past) long narrow strips of paper with information, for example STOCK MARKET prices, printed on them by a special TELEGRAPH machine: *a* ***ticker-tape parade*** *in the streets of New York* (= an occasion when people throw pieces of paper as part of a celebration, for example in honour of a famous person)

ticket 0‑ /ˈtɪkɪt/ *noun, verb*
■ *noun* **1** 0‑ **~ (for/to sth)** a printed piece of paper that gives you the right to travel on a particular bus, train, etc. or to go into a theatre, etc: *a* ***bus/theatre/plane, etc. ticket*** ◇ *free tickets to the show* ◇ *Tickets are available from the Arts Centre at £5.00.* ◇ *a* ***ticket office/machine/collector*** ◇ (*figurative*) *She hoped that getting this job would finally be her* ***ticket to success***. ➲ picture at LABEL ➲ see also MEAL TICKET, RETURN TICKET, SEASON TICKET **2** 0‑ a printed piece of paper with a number or numbers on it, that you buy in order to have the chance of winning a prize if the number or numbers are later chosen: *a* ***lottery/raffle ticket*** ◇ *There are three winning tickets.* **3** 0‑ a label that is attached to sth in a shop/store giving details of its price, size, etc. **4** an official notice that orders you to pay a FINE because you have done sth illegal while driving or parking your car SYN **fine**: *a* ***parking/speeding ticket*** **5** [usually sing.] (*especially NAmE*) a list of candidates that are supported by a particular political party in an election: *She ran for office on the Democratic ticket.* ➲ see also DREAM TICKET
IDM **be** ˈ**tickets** (*SAfrE, informal*) be the end: *It's tickets for the team that loses.* **just the** ˈ**ticket** (*BrE* also **just the** ˈ**job**) (*informal, approving*) exactly what is needed in a particular situation ˈ**that's the ticket** (*old-fashioned, BrE, informal*) used to say that sth is just what is needed or that everything is just right ➲ more at SPLIT *v.*
■ *verb* **1 ~ sth/sb** (*technical*) to produce and sell tickets for an event, a trip, etc; to give sb a ticket: *Passengers can now be ticketed electronically.* **2** [usually passive] **~ sb** (*especially NAmE*) to give sb an official notice that orders them to pay a FINE because they have done sth illegal while driving or parking a car: *Park illegally, and you're likely to be ticketed.*

T

ticket·ed /ˈtɪkɪtɪd/ *adj.* [usually before noun] a **ticketed** event is one for which you need a ticket to get in: *The museum holds both free and ticketed events.*
IDM **be ˈticketed for sth** (*especially NAmE*) to be intended for a particular purpose

ticket·ing /ˈtɪkɪtɪŋ/ *noun* [U] the process of producing and selling tickets: *ticketing systems*

ˈticket tout *noun* (*BrE*) = TOUT

tickety-boo /ˌtɪkəti ˈbuː/ *adj.* [not before noun] (*old-fashioned, BrE, informal*) very good or successful, with no problems

tick·ing /ˈtɪkɪŋ/ *noun* [U] a type of strong cotton cloth that is often striped, used especially for making MATTRESS and PILLOW covers

ˌticking ˈoff *noun* [sing.] (*old-fashioned, BrE, informal*) the act of telling sb that they have done sth to make you angry SYN **telling off**

tickle /ˈtɪkl/ *verb, noun*
■ ***verb*** **1** [T, I] **~ (sb/sth)** to move your fingers on a sensitive part of sb's body in a way that makes them laugh: *The bigger girls used to chase me and tickle me.* ◇ *Stop tickling!* **2** [T, I] **~ (sth)** to produce a slightly uncomfortable feeling in a sensitive part of the body; to have a feeling like this: *His beard was tickling her cheek.* ◇ *My throat tickles.* ◇ *a tickling cough* **3** [T] to amuse and interest sb: **~ sb/sth** *to tickle sb's imagination* ◇ **~ sb to do sth** *I was tickled to discover that we'd both done the same thing.*
IDM **be tickled ˈpink** (*informal*) to be very pleased or amused **tickle sb's ˈfancy** (*informal*) to please or amuse sb: *See if any of these tickle your fancy.*
■ ***noun*** [usually sing.] **1** an act of tickling sb: *She gave the child a little tickle.* **2** a slightly uncomfortable feeling in a part of your body: *to have a tickle in your throat* (= that makes you want to cough) IDM see SLAP *n.*

tick·lish /ˈtɪklɪʃ/ *adj.* **1** (of a person) sensitive to being tickled: *Are you ticklish?* **2** (*informal*) (of a situation or problem) difficult to deal with, and possibly embarrassing SYN **awkward** **3** (of a cough) that irritates your throat: *a dry ticklish cough*

tick-tock /ˌtɪk ˈtɒk; *NAmE* ˌtɪk ˈtɑːk/ *noun* [usually sing.] used to describe the sound of a large clock TICKING

ticky-tacky /ˌtɪki ˈtæki/ *noun* [U] (*NAmE, informal*) building material that is cheap and of low quality ▶ **ticky-tacky** *adj.*

tic-tac-toe (also **tick-tack-toe**) /ˌtɪk tæk ˈtəʊ; *NAmE* ˈtoʊ/ (*NAmE*) (*BrE* **ˌnoughts and ˈcrosses**) *noun* [U] a simple game in which two players take turns to write Os or Xs in a set of nine squares. The first player to complete a row of three Os or three Xs is the winner. ➲ VISUAL VOCAB page V33

tidal /ˈtaɪdl/ *adj.* connected with TIDES (= the regular rise and fall of the sea): *tidal forces* ◇ *a tidal river*

ˌtidal ˈwave *noun* **1** a very large ocean wave that is caused by a storm or an EARTHQUAKE, and that destroys things when it reaches the land **2 ~ (of sth)** a sudden increase in a particular feeling, activity or type of behaviour: *a tidal wave of crime*

tid·bit /ˈtɪdbɪt/ (*NAmE*) (*BrE* **tit·bit**) *noun* a small special piece of food SYN **morsel**

tid·dler /ˈtɪdlə(r)/ *noun* (*BrE, informal*) a very small fish

tid·dly /ˈtɪdli/ *adj.* (*BrE, informal*) **1** slightly drunk **2** very small SYN **tiny**

tiddly·winks /ˈtɪdliwɪŋks/ *noun* [U] a game in which players try to make small plastic discs jump into a cup by pressing them on the edge with a larger disc

tide /taɪd/ *noun, verb*
■ ***noun*** **1** [C, U] a regular rise and fall in the level of the sea, caused by the pull of the moon and sun; the flow of water that happens as the sea rises and falls: *the ebb and flow of the tide* ◇ *The* **tide is in/out**. ◇ *Is the tide coming in or going out?* ◇ *The body was washed up on the beach by the tide.* ➲ see also HIGH TIDE, LOW TIDE, NEAP TIDE, SPRING TIDE **2** [C, usually sing.] the direction in which the opinion of a large number of people seems to be moving: *It takes courage to speak out against the tide of opinion.* **3** [C, usually sing.] a large amount of sth unpleasant that is increasing and is difficult to control: *There is anxiety about the* **rising tide** *of crime.* **4** [sing.] **~ of sth** a feeling that you suddenly have that gets stronger and stronger: *A tide of rage surged through her.* **5 -tide** [sing.] (*old use*) (in compounds) a time or season of the year: *Christmastide*
IDM **go, swim, etc. with/against the ˈtide** to agree with/oppose the attitudes or opinions that most other people have **the ˈtide turned | turn the ˈtide** used to say that there is a change in sb's luck or in how successful they are being
■ ***verb***
PHR V **ˌtide sb ˈover (sth)** [no passive] to help sb during a difficult period by providing what they need: *Can you lend me some money to tide me over until I get paid?*

tide·line /ˈtaɪdlaɪn/ *noun* a line left or reached by the sea when the tide is at its highest point

tide·mark /ˈtaɪdmɑːk; *NAmE* -mɑːrk/ *noun* **1** a line that is made by the sea on a beach at the highest point that the sea reaches **2** (*BrE, informal*) a line that is left around the inside of a bath/BATHTUB by dirty water

ˈtide pool (*NAmE*) (*BrE* **ˈrock pool**) *noun* a small amount of water that collects between the rocks by the sea/ocean ➲ VISUAL VOCAB page V5

tide·water /ˈtaɪdwɔːtə(r)/ *noun* **1** [C] (*NAmE*) an area of land at or near the coast **2** [U, C] water that is brought by the TIDE

tid·ings /ˈtaɪdɪŋz/ *noun* [pl.] (*old-fashioned* or *humorous*) news: *I am the bearer of* **good tidings**. ◇ *He brought* **glad tidings**.

tidy 🔑 /ˈtaɪdi/ *adj., verb, noun*
■ ***adj.*** (**tidi·er**, **tidi·est**) **1** 🔑 (*especially BrE*) arranged neatly and with everything in order: *a tidy desk* ◇ *She* **keeps** *her flat very* **tidy**. ◇ *I like everything to be* **neat and tidy**. OPP **untidy** **2** 🔑 (*especially BrE*) keeping things neat and in order: *I'm a tidy person.* ◇ *tidy habits* OPP **untidy** **3** [only before noun] (*informal*) a **tidy** amount of money is fairly large SYN **considerable**: *It must have cost a tidy sum.* ◇ *a tidy profit* ▶ **tidi·ly** *adv.*: *The room was very tidily arranged.* **tidi·ness** *noun* [U]
■ ***verb*** 🔑 (**tidies**, **tidy·ing**, **tidied**, **tidied**) [I, T] (*especially BrE*) to make sth look neat by putting things in the place where they belong: *I spent all morning cleaning and tidying.* ◇ **~ up** *When you cook, could you please tidy up after yourself.* ◇ **~ sth (up)** *to tidy (up) a room*
PHR V **ˌtidy sth↔aˈway** (*BrE*) to put things in the place where they belong, especially where they cannot be seen, so that a room appears tidy **ˌtidy sth↔ˈup** to arrange or deal with sth so that it is well or correctly finished: *I tidied up the report before handing it in.*
■ ***noun*** (*pl.* **-ies**) (*BrE*) (especially in compounds) a container for putting small objects in, in order to keep a place tidy: *a desk tidy*

tie 🔑 /taɪ/ *verb, noun*
■ ***verb*** (**ties**, **tying**, **tied**, **tied**)
▸ FASTEN WITH STRING/ROPE **1** 🔑 [T] **~ sth (+ adv./prep.)** to attach or hold two or more things together using string, rope, etc; to fasten sb/sth with string, rope, etc: *She tied the newspapers in a bundle.* ◇ *He had to tie her hands together.* ◇ *They tied him to a chair with cable.* ◇ *Shall I tie the package or tape it?* ◇ *I tie back my hair when I'm cooking.* **2** 🔑 [T] **~ sth + adv./prep.** to fasten sth to or around sth else: *She tied a label on to the suitcase.* **3** 🔑 [T] **~ sth** to make a knot in a piece of string, rope, etc: *to tie a ribbon* ◇ *Can you help me tie my tie?* ◇ *Tie up your shoelaces!* ◇ *I tied a knot in the rope.* **4** [I] (**+ adv./prep.**) to be closed or fastened with a knot, etc: *The skirt ties at the waist.*
▸ CONNECT/LINK **5** [T, usually passive] **~ sb/sth (to sth/sb)** to connect or link sb/sth closely with sb/sth else: *Pay increases are tied to inflation.* ◇ *The house is tied to the job, so we'll have to move when I retire.*
▸ RESTRICT **6** [T, usually passive] to restrict sb and make them unable to do everything they want to: **~ sb** *to be tied by a contract* ◇ **~ sb to sth** *I want to work but I'm tied to the house*

T

with the baby. ◇ **~ sb to doing sth** *I don't want to be tied to coming home at a particular time.*

▸ IN GAME/COMPETITION **7** [I, T] (of two teams, etc.) to have the same number of points SYN **draw**: **~ (with sb)** *England tied 2–2 with Germany in the first round.* ◇ **~ for sth** *They tied for second place.* ◇ **~ sth** *The scores are tied at 3–3.* ◇ *Last night's vote was tied.*

▸ MUSIC **8** [T] **~ sth** to join notes with a tie ➲ see also TONGUE-TIED

IDM **tie sb/yourself (up) in 'knots** to become or make sb very confused ˌ**tie one 'on** (*old-fashioned, NAmE, slang*) to get very drunk ˌ**tie the 'knot** (*informal*) to get married ➲ more at APRON, HAND *n.*

PHR V ˌ**tie sb 'down (to sth/to doing sth)** to restrict sb's freedom, for example by making them accept particular conditions or by keeping them busy: *Kids tie you down, don't they?* ◇ *I don't want to tie myself down to coming back on a particular date.* ˌ**tie 'in (with sth)** to match or agree with sth: *This evidence ties in closely with what we already know.* ˌ**tie 'in (with sth)** | ˌ**tie sth↔'in (with sth)** to link sth or be linked to sth; to happen, or arrange for sth to happen, at the same time as sth else: *The concert will tie in with the festival of dance taking place the same weekend.* ➲ related noun TIE-IN ˌ**tie sth↔'off** to put a knot in the end of sth; to close sth with string, thread, etc: *to tie off a rope* ◇ *to tie off an artery* ˌ**tie 'up** | ˌ**tie sth↔'up 1** 🔑 to attach a boat to a fixed object with a rope: *We tied up alongside the quay.* ◇ *We tied the boat up.* **2** 🔑 to close sth with a knot; to be closed or fastened with a knot: *to tie up a garbage bag* ˌ**tie sb↔'up 1** 🔑 to tie sb's arms and legs tightly so that they cannot move or escape: *The gang tied up a security guard.* **2** [usually passive] to keep sb busy so that they have no time for other things: *I'm tied up in a meeting until 3.* ˌ**tie sth↔'up 1** 🔑 to attach an animal to sth with a rope, chain, etc: *He left his dog tied up to a tree.* **2** [usually passive] to connect or link sth to sth else: *Her behaviour is tied up with her feelings of guilt.* ➲ related noun TIE-UP **3** [often passive] to invest money so that it is not easily available for use: *Most of the capital is tied up in property.* **4** to deal with all the remaining details of sth: *We are hoping to tie up the deal by tomorrow.* ◇ *I went into the office for an hour to* **tie up any loose ends** (= finish remaining small jobs).

■ ***noun***

▸ CLOTHES **1** 🔑 (*NAmE* also **neck·tie**) a long narrow piece of cloth worn around the neck, especially by men, with a knot in front: *a* ***collar and tie*** ◇ *a striped silk tie* ➲ VISUAL VOCAB page V50 ➲ see also BLACK TIE, BOW TIE, OLD SCHOOL TIE, WHITE TIE

▸ FOR FASTENING **2** a piece of string or wire used for fastening or tying sth: *ties for closing plastic bags*

▸ CONNECTION **3** 🔑 [usually pl.] a strong connection between people or organizations: *family ties* ◇ *the ties of friendship* ◇ *economic ties* ◇ *The firm has close ties with an American corporation.*

▸ RESTRICTION **4** a thing that limits sb's freedom of action: *He was still a young man and he did not want any ties.*

▸ IN GAME/COMPETITION **5** a situation in a game or competition when two or more players have the same score: *The match ended in a tie.* ➲ compare DRAW *n.* (2) **6** (*BrE*) a sports match, especially a football (SOCCER) match, that is part of a larger competition: *the first leg of the Cup tie between Leeds and Roma*

▸ MUSIC **7** a curved line written over two notes of the same PITCH (= how high or low a note is) to show that they are to be played or sung as one note ➲ picture at MUSIC

▸ ON RAILWAY **8** (*NAmE*) (*BrE* **sleep·er**) one of the heavy pieces of wood or concrete on which the rails on a railway/railroad track are laid ➲ VISUAL VOCAB page V47

tie·break /ˈtaɪbreɪk/ (*BrE*) (*NAmE* **tie·break·er**) *noun* (in TENNIS) a period of extra play to decide who is the winner of a SET when both players have won six games

tie·breaker /ˈtaɪbreɪkə(r)/ *noun* **1** (*NAmE*) (*BrE* **tie-break**) (in TENNIS) a period of extra play to decide who is the winner of a SET when both players have won six games **2** an extra question in a competition to decide who is the winner when two or more of those taking part have equal scores

tied /taɪd/ *adj.* [only before noun] (*BrE*) (of a house) rented to sb on the condition that they work for the owner: *a tied cottage on a farm*

ˌ**tied 'house** *noun* (*BrE*) a pub that is owned by a particular BREWERY (= a company that produces beer) and that mainly sells the beer which that brewery produces ➲ compare FREE HOUSE

'tie-dye *verb* **~ sth** to make patterns on cloth by tying knots in it or tying string around it before you put it in a DYE, so that some parts receive more colour than others

'tie-in *noun* a product such as a book or toy that is connected with a new film/movie, television programme, etc.

tie·pin /ˈtaɪpɪn/ (*NAmE* also **'tie tack**) *noun* a small decorative pin that is worn on a tie to keep it in place

tier /tɪə(r); *NAmE* tɪr/ *noun* **1** a row or layer of sth that has several rows or layers placed one above the other: *a wedding cake with three tiers* ◇ *The seating is arranged* ***in tiers.*** **2** one of several levels in an organization or a system: *We have introduced an extra tier of administration.* ◇ *a two-tier system of management*

tiered /tɪəd; *NAmE* tɪrd/ *adj.* **1** arranged in tiers: *tiered seating* **2 -tiered** (in compounds) having the number of tiers mentioned: *a two-tiered system*

'tie-up *noun* **1 ~ (with sb/sth)** (*BrE*) an agreement between two companies to join together: *They're negotiating a tie-up with Ford.* **2 ~ (between A and B)** (*BrE*) a connection between two or more things: *a tie-up between politics and economics* **3** (*especially NAmE*) a situation in which sth stops working or moving forward: *a traffic tie-up*

TIFF /tɪf/ *noun* [U, C] (*computing*) the abbreviation for 'tagged image file format' (a form in which images can be stored and shown on a computer; an image created in this form)

tiff /tɪf/ *noun* (*informal*) a slight argument between close friends or lovers: *to have a tiff with sb*

tif·fin /ˈtɪfɪn/ *noun* [U] (*old-fashioned* or *IndE*) a small meal, especially lunch

tig /tɪg/ *noun* [U] (*BrE*) = TAG (6)

tiger /ˈtaɪgə(r)/ *noun* a large wild animal of the cat family, that has yellowish fur with black lines (=STRIPES) and lives in parts of Asia: *She* ***fought like a tiger*** *to be able to keep her children.* ➲ compare TIGRESS ➲ see also PAPER TIGER

ˌ**tiger e'conomy** *noun* the economy of a country that is growing very quickly

tiger·ish /ˈtaɪgərɪʃ/ *adj.* like a tiger, especially in being aggressive or showing great energy

tight 🔑 /taɪt/ *adj., adv.*

■ ***adj.*** (**tight·er**, **tight·est**)

▸ FIRM **1** 🔑 held or fixed in position firmly; difficult to move or undo: *He kept* ***a tight grip*** *on her arm.* ◇ *She twisted her hair into a tight knot.* ◇ *The screw was so tight that it wouldn't move.*

▸ CLOTHES **2** 🔑 fitting closely to your body and sometimes uncomfortable: *She was wearing a tight pair of jeans.* ◇ *These shoes are much too tight.* ◇ *The new sweater was a* ***tight fit.*** OPP **loose** ➲ see also SKINTIGHT

▸ CONTROL **3** 🔑 very strict and firm: *to* ***keep tight control*** *over sth* ◇ *We need tighter security at the airport.*

▸ STRETCHED **4** 🔑 stretched or pulled so that it cannot stretch much further: *The rope was stretched tight.*

▸ CLOSE TOGETHER **5** [usually before noun] with things or people packed closely together, leaving little space between them: *There was a tight group of people around the speaker.* ◇ *With six of us in the car it was* ***a tight squeeze.***

▸ MONEY/TIME **6** difficult to manage with because there is not enough: *We have a very tight budget.* ◇ *The president has a tight schedule today.*

▸ EXPRESSION/VOICE **7** looking or sounding anxious, upset, angry, etc: *'I'm sorry,' she said, with a tight smile.* ➲ see also UPTIGHT

▸ PART OF BODY **8** feeling painful or uncomfortable because

T

of illness or emotion SYN **constricted**: *He complained of having a tight chest.* ◇ *Her throat felt tight, just looking at her baby.*
▸ RELATIONSHIP **9** having a close relationship with sb else or with other people: *It was a tight community and newcomers were not welcome.* ➲ see also TIGHT-KNIT
▸ BEND/CURVE **10** curving suddenly rather than gradually: *The driver slowed down at a tight bend in the road.* ◇ *The plane flew around in a tight circle.*
▸ CONTEST/RACE **11** with runners, teams, etc. that seem to be equally good SYN **close**: *a tight race*
▸ NOT GENEROUS **12** (*informal, disapproving*) not wanting to spend much money; not generous SYN **mean**: *He's very tight with his money.*
▸ DRUNK **13** [not usually before noun] (*old-fashioned, informal*) drunk SYN **tipsy**
▸ -TIGHT **14** (in compounds) not allowing the substance mentioned to enter: *measures to make your home weather-tight* ➲ see also AIRTIGHT, WATERTIGHT
▸ **tight·ness** *noun* [U]
IDM **to keep a tight 'rein on sb/sth** to control sb/sth carefully or strictly **run a tight 'ship** to organize sth in a very efficient way, controlling other people very closely **a tight 'spot/'corner** a very difficult or dangerous situation
■ *adv.* (**tight·er**, **tight·est**) closely and firmly; tightly: ***Hold tight!*** ◇ *My suitcase was packed tight.* ◇ *His fists were clenched tight.* IDM see SIT, SLEEP *v.*

Which Word?

tight / tightly

■ **Tight** and **tightly** are both adverbs that come from the adjective **tight**. They have the same meaning, but **tight** is often used instead of **tightly** after a verb, especially in informal language, and in compounds: *packed tight* ◇ *a tight-fitting lid.* Before a past participle **tightly** is used: *clusters of tightly packed flowers.*

'tight-arse *noun* (*informal, disapproving*) **1** (*BrE*) a person who does not like spending money **2** (*BrE*) (*NAmE* **'tight-ass**) a person who controls their emotions and actions very carefully and does not like to break the rules ▸ **'tight-arsed** (*BrE*) (*NAmE* **'tight-assed**) *adj.*

tight·en /ˈtaɪtn/ *verb* **1** [I, T] to become or make sth become tight or tighter: **~ (up)** *The rope holding the boat suddenly tightened and broke.* ◇ *His mouth tightened into a thin line.* ◇ **~ sth (up)** *to tighten a lid/screw/rope/knot* ◇ *The nuts weren't properly tightened and the wheel came off.* ◇ *She tightened her grip on his arm.* **2** [T] **~ sth** to make sth become stricter: *to tighten security* OPP **loosen**
IDM **tighten your 'belt** to spend less money because there is less available ➲ SYNONYMS at SAVE
PHR V **,tighten 'up (on sth)** to become stricter or more careful: *Laws on gambling have tightened up recently.* ◇ *The police are tightening up on under-age drinking.*

,tight 'end *noun* (in AMERICAN FOOTBALL) an attacking player who plays close to the TACKLE

,tight-'fisted *adj.* not willing to spend or give much money SYN **mean, stingy**

,tight-'fitting *adj.* that fits very tightly or closely SYN **close-fitting**: *a tight-fitting skirt*

'tight head *noun* (in RUGBY) the player in the front row of a team in the SCRUM who is furthest from where the ball is put in

,tight-'knit (also **,tightly-'knit**) *adj.* (of a family or community) with all the members having strong friendly relationships with one another: *a tight-knit mining community*

,tight-'lipped *adj.* **1** not willing to talk about sth **2** keeping your lips pressed firmly together, especially because you are angry about sth

tight·ly 🔑 /ˈtaɪtli/ *adv.*
closely and firmly; in a tight manner: *Her eyes were tightly closed.* ◇ *He held on tightly to her arm.* ◇ *a tightly packed crowd of tourists* ➲ note at TIGHT

tight·rope /ˈtaɪtrəʊp; *NAmE* -roʊp/ *noun* a rope or wire that is stretched tightly high above the ground and that performers walk along, especially in a CIRCUS: *a tightrope walker*
IDM **tread/walk a 'tightrope** to be in a difficult situation in which you do not have much freedom of action and need to be extremely careful about what you do

tights /taɪts/ *noun* [pl.] **1** (*BrE*) (*NAmE* **panty·hose**) a piece of clothing made of very thin cloth that fits closely over a woman's hips, legs and feet: *a pair of tights* ➲ compare STOCKING **2** a piece of clothing similar to tights but made of thicker cloth, worn especially by dancers

tight·wad /ˈtaɪtwɒd; *NAmE* -wɑːd/ *noun* (*NAmE, informal*) a person who hates to spend or give money SYN **miser**

tig·ress /ˈtaɪgrəs/ *noun* a female TIGER

tike *noun* = TYKE

tikka /ˈtɪkə; *BrE* also ˈtiːkə/ *noun* [U, C] a spicy S Asian dish consisting of pieces of meat or vegetables which have been left in a sauce and then cooked: *chicken tikka*

til, 'til ➲ UNTIL

tilak /ˈtɪlæk/ *noun* a mark on the FOREHEAD of a Hindu, worn as a religious symbol or for decoration

til·apia /tɪˈlæpiə; -ˈleɪp-; *NAmE* -ˈlɑːp-/ *noun* (*pl.* **tilapia** or **tilapias**) [C, U] a FRESHWATER fish found in hot countries that is used for food

tilde /ˈtɪldə/ *noun* **1** the mark (~) placed over letters in some languages and some vowels in the International Phonetic Alphabet to show how they should be pronounced, as in *España*, *São Paulo* and *penchant* /ˈpɒ̃ʃɒ̃/ **2** (also **,swung 'dash**) the mark (~), used in this dictionary in some parts of an entry to represent the word in blue type at the top of the entry

tile /taɪl/ *noun, verb*
■ *noun* **1** a flat, usually square, piece of baked CLAY, carpet or other material that is used in rows for covering walls and floors: *ceramic floor tiles* ◇ *carpet tiles* **2** a piece of baked CLAY that is used in rows for covering roofs ➲ VISUAL VOCAB page V15 **3** any of the small flat pieces that are used in particular board games IDM see NIGHT
■ *verb* **1 ~ sth** to cover a surface with tiles: *a tiled bathroom* **2 ~ sth** (*computing*) to arrange several windows on a computer screen so that they fill the screen but do not cover each other

tiler /ˈtaɪlə(r)/ *noun* a person whose job is to lay tiles

til·ing /ˈtaɪlɪŋ/ *noun* [U] **1** an area covered with tiles ➲ VISUAL VOCAB page V21 **2** the work of covering a floor, wall, etc. with tiles

till 🔑 /tɪl/ *conj., prep., noun, verb*
■ *conj., prep.* = UNTIL: *We're open till 6 o'clock.* ◇ *Can't you wait till we get home?* ◇ *Just wait till you see it. It's great.*
HELP **Till** is generally felt to be more informal than **until** and is used much less often in writing. At the beginning of a sentence, **until** is usually used.
■ *noun* **1** (*BrE*) = CASH REGISTER **2** (*BrE, informal*) the place where you pay for goods in a large shop/store: *Please pay at the till.* ◇ *a long queue at the till* **3** (*especially NAmE*) the drawer where the money is put in a CASH REGISTER
IDM see FINGER *n.*
■ *verb* **~ sth** (*old use*) to prepare and use land for growing crops

till·age /ˈtɪlɪdʒ/ *noun* [U] (*old-fashioned*) **1** the process of preparing and using land for growing crops **2** land that is used for growing crops

till·er /ˈtɪlə(r)/ *noun* a bar that is used to turn the RUDDER of a small boat in order to steer it ➲ compare HELM

tilt /tɪlt/ *verb, noun*
■ *verb* **1** [I, T] to move, or make sth move, into a position with one side or end higher than the other SYN **tip**: (+ **adv./prep.**) *Suddenly the boat tilted to one side* ◇ *The seat tilts forward, when you press this lever.* ◇ **~ sth** (+ **adv./prep.**) *His hat was tilted slightly at an angle.* ◇ *She tilted her head back and looked up at me with a smile.* **2** [T, I] **~ (sth/**

sb) (**in favour of/away from sth/sb**) to make sth/sb change slightly so that one particular opinion, person, etc. is preferred or more likely to succeed than another; to change in this way: *The conditions may* ***tilt the balance*** *in favour of the Kenyan runners.* ◇ *Popular opinion has* ***tilted in favour*** *of the socialists.*

IDM **tilt at 'windmills** to waste your energy attacking imaginary enemies ORIGIN From Cervantes' novel *Don Quixote*, in which the hero thought that the windmills he saw were giants and tried to fight them.

PHR V **'tilt at sb/sth** (*BrE*) to attack sb/sth in speech or writing **'tilt at sth** (*BrE*) to try to win sth: *He was tilting at the top prize.*

■ ***noun*** **1** a position in which one end or side of sth is higher than the other; an act of tilting sth to one side: *The table is at a slight tilt.* ◇ *He answered with a tilt of his head.* **2** an attempt to win sth or defeat sb: *She aims to* ***have a tilt at*** *the world championship next year.*

IDM **(at) full 'tilt/'pelt** as fast as possible

tim·ber /ˈtɪmbə(r)/ *noun* **1** [U] trees that are grown to be used in building or for making things: *the timber industry* **2** [U] (*especially BrE*) (*NAmE* usually **lum·ber**) wood that is prepared for use in building, etc: *houses built of timber* **3** [C, usually pl.] a long heavy piece of wood used in building a house or ship: *roof timbers* **4 timber!** used to warn people that a tree that has been cut is about to fall

tim·bered /ˈtɪmbəd; *NAmE* -bərd/ *adj.* built of timbers; with a FRAMEWORK of timbers ➲ see also HALF-TIMBERED

'tim·ber yard (*BrE*) (*NAmE* **lum·ber·yard**) *noun* a place where wood for building, etc. is stored and sold

timbre /ˈtæmbə(r)/ *noun* (*formal*) the quality of sound that is produced by a particular voice or musical instrument

Tim·buktu (also **Tim·buctoo**) /ˌtɪmbʌkˈtuː/ *noun* a place that is very far away ORIGIN From the name of a town in northern Mali.

time 🔑 /taɪm/ *noun, verb*

■ ***noun*** ➲ see also TIMES

▸ MINUTES/HOURS/YEARS, ETC. **1** 🔑 [U] what is measured in minutes, hours, days, etc: *The changing seasons mark the* ***passing of time****.* ◇ *A visit to the museum will take you* ***back in time*** *to the 1930s.* ◇ *time and space* ◇ ***As time went by*** *we saw less and less of each other.* ◇ *Perceptions change* ***over time*** (= as time passes). ➲ see also FATHER TIME **2** 🔑 [U] the time shown on a clock in minutes and hours: ***What time is it/What's the time?*** ◇ *Do you have the time?* ◇ (*BrE*) ***What time do you make it?*** ◇ (*NAmE*) ***What time do you have?*** ◇ *The time is now half past ten.* ◇ (*BrE*) *Can she* ***tell the time*** *yet* (= say what time it is by looking at a clock)? ◇ (*NAmE*) *Can she* ***tell time*** *yet?* ◇ *My watch* ***keeps perfect time*** (= always shows the correct time). ◇ *Look at the time! We'll be late.* ◇ ***This time tomorrow*** *I'll be in Canada.* **3** 🔑 [U] the time measured in a particular part of the world: *Greenwich Mean Time* ◇ *6 o'clock* ***local time*** ➲ see also STANDARD TIME, SUMMER TIME **4** 🔑 [U, C] the time when sth happens or when sth should happen: *What time do you finish work?* ◇ *The baby loves bath time.* ◇ **~ (to do sth)** *I think it's time to go to bed.* ◇ **~ (for sth)** *It's time for lunch.* ◇ **~ (that)...** *It's time the kids were in bed.* ◇ ***By the time*** *you get there the meeting will be over.* ◇ *A computer screen shows arrival and departure times.* ◇ *The train arrived right* ***on time*** (= at exactly the correct time). ◇ *You'll feel differently about it* ***when the time comes*** (= when it happens). ➲ see also ANY TIME, CLOSING TIME, DRIVE TIME, NIGHT-TIME, OPENING TIME

▸ PERIOD **5** 🔑 [U] **~ (to do sth)** an amount of time; the amount of time available to work, rest, etc: *Allow plenty of time to get to the airport.* ◇ *I can probably* ***make the time*** *to see them.* ◇ *It* ***takes time*** *to make changes in the law.* ◇ *We have* ***no time to lose*** (= we must hurry). ◇ *He spends most of his time working.* ◇ *She doesn't have much* ***free/spare time****.* ◇ *What a* ***waste of time****!* ◇ *I didn't finish the test—****I ran out of time****.* ◇ ***Time's up****—have you worked out the answer yet?* ◇ *He never takes any* ***time off*** (= time spent not working). ◇ *Jane's worked here* ***for some time*** (= for a fairly long period of time). ◇ *Do it now please—not in three hours' time* (= three hours from now). ◇ *The journey time is two hours.* ➲ see also RESPONSE TIME **6** 🔑 **a time** [sing.] a period of time, either long or short, during which you do sth or sth happens: *His injuries will* ***take a long time*** *to heal.* ◇ *I lived in Egypt* ***for a time****.* ◇ *The early morning is the best* ***time of day****.* ◇ *Her parents died* ***a long time ago****.* ◇ ***At one time*** (= at a period of time in the past) *Emily was my best friend.* ◇ *Mr Curtis was the manager* ***in my time*** (= when I was working there). **7** 🔑 [U, pl.] a period of history connected with particular events or experiences in people's lives: *The movie is set* ***at the time of*** *the Russian Revolution.* ◇ *in ancient times* ◇ *the violent times we live in* (= the present period of history) ◇ *Times are hard for the unemployed.* ◇ ***Times have changed*** *since Grandma was young.* ➲ see also OLD-TIME

▸ OCCASION/EVENT **8** 🔑 [C] an occasion when you do sth or when sth happens: ***Every time*** *I hear that song I feel happy.* ◇ ***Next time*** *you're here let's have lunch together.* ◇ *He failed his driving test three times.* ◇ *He's determined to pass* ***this time****.* ◇ *When was the* ***last time*** *you saw her?* ◇ ***How many times*** (= how often) *do I have to tell you not to do that?* ◇ (*especially NAmE*) *I remember* ***one time*** (= once) *we had to abandon our car in the snow.* ◇ (*formal*) ***At no time did*** *I give my consent to the plan.* HELP To talk about the first or the last time you do sth, use **the first/last time (that) I...**: *This is the first time (that) I've been to London.* ◇ ~~*This is the first time for me to go to London.*~~ ◇ *That was the last time (that) I saw her.* **9** 🔑 [C] an event or occasion that you experience in a particular way: *Did you* ***have a good time*** *in Spain?* ◇ *I had an awful time in the hospital.*

▸ FOR RACE **10** [C, U] how long sb takes to run a race or complete an event: *The winner's time was 11.6 seconds.* ◇ *She completed the 500 metres* ***in record time*** (= faster than any previous runner). ◇ *one of the fastest times ever*

▸ IN MUSIC **11** [U] the number of beats in a BAR/MEASURE of music: *This piece is in four-four time.* ◇ *a slow waltz time* ◇ *The conductor* ***beat time*** *with a baton.* **12** [U] the correct speed and rhythm of a piece of music: *Try and dance* ***in time to*** *the music* (= with the same speed and rhythm). ◇ *Clap your hands to* ***keep time*** (= sing or move with the correct speed and rhythm). ◇ *to play* ***in/out of time*** (= follow/not follow the correct speed and rhythm) ◇ *He always plays in perfect time.* ➲ see also BIG TIME, SMALL-TIME

IDM **(and) about 'time ('too)** | **(and) not before 'time** used to say that sth should have happened before now **against 'time** if you do sth **against time**, you do it as fast as you can because you do not have much time: *They're working against time to try and get people out of the rubble alive.* **ahead of/behind 'time** earlier/later than was expected: *We finished 15 minutes ahead of time.* **ahead of your 'time** having advanced or new ideas that other people use or copy later **all the 'time** | **the whole 'time** **1** 🔑 during the whole of a particular period of time: *The letter was in my pocket all the time* (= while I was looking for it). **2** 🔑 very often; repeatedly: *She leaves the lights on all the time.* **at all 'times** 🔑 always: *Our representatives are ready to help you at all times.* **at the 'best of times** even when the circumstances are very good: *He's never very happy at the best of times—he'll be much worse now!* **at the same 'time 1** 🔑 at one time; together: *She was laughing and crying at the same time.* **2** 🔑 used to introduce a contrasting fact, etc. that must be considered: *You have to be firm, but at the same time you should try and be sympathetic.* **at a 'time** 🔑 separately or in groups of two, three, etc. on each occasion: *We had to go and see the principal one at a time.* ◇ *She ran up the stairs two at a time.* **at 'my, 'your, 'his, etc. time of life** at the age you are (especially when you are not young): *Eyesight doesn't get any better at my time of life.* **at 'times** 🔑 sometimes: *He can be really bad-tempered at times.* **before my, your, his, etc. 'time** **1** happening before you were born or can remember or before you lived, worked, etc. somewhere: *'Were you taught by Professor Pascal?' 'No, he was before my time.'* **2** before the usual time in sb's life when sth happens SYN **prematurely**: *She got old before her time.* **behind the 'times** old-fashioned in your ideas, methods, etc. **do 'time** (*informal*) to spend time in prison **every 'time** whenever there is a choice: *I don't really like cities—give*

T

me the countryside every time. **for the time 'being** for a short period of time but not permanently: *You can leave your suitcase here for the time being.* **from ˌtime to 'time** - occasionally but not regularly: *She has to work at weekends from time to time.* **have a lot of time for sb/sth** (*informal, especially BrE*) to like and be interested in sb/sth **have no time for sb/sth | not have much time for sb/sth** (*informal*) to dislike sb/sth: *I have no time for lazy people like Steve.* **have the ˌtime of your 'life** (*informal*) to enjoy yourself very much **have time on your 'hands | have time to 'kill** (*informal*) to have nothing to do or not be busy **in good 'time** early; with enough time so that you are not in a hurry **(all) in good 'time** (*informal*) used to say that sth will be done or will happen at the appropriate time and not before: *Be patient, Emily! All in good time.* **in (less than/next to) 'no time** so soon or so quickly that it is surprising: *The kids will be leaving home in no time.* **in 'time** after a period of time when a situation has changed SYN **eventually**: *They learned to accept their stepmother in time.* **in time (for sth/to do sth)** not late; with enough time to be able to do sth: *Will we be in time for the six o'clock train?* ◇ *The ambulance got there just in time* (= to save sb's life). **in your own (good) 'time** (*informal*) when you are ready and not sooner: *Don't hassle him! He'll do it in his own good time.* **in your own time** in your free time and not when you usually work or study **it's aˌbout/ˌhigh 'time** (*informal*) used to say that you think sb should do sth soon: *It's about time you cleaned your room!* **keep up/move with the 'times** to change and develop your ideas, way of working, etc. so that you do what is modern and what is expected **make good, etc. 'time** to complete a journey quickly: *We made excellent time and arrived in Spain in two days.* **'many a time | 'many's the time (that)...** (*old-fashioned*) many times; frequently **ˌnine times out of 'ten | ˌninety-ˌnine times out of a 'hundred** used to say that sth is usually true or almost always happens: *Nine times out of ten she gives the right answer.* **(and) not before 'time** = (AND) ABOUT TIME (TOO) **not give sb the ˌtime of 'day** to refuse to speak to sb because you do not like or respect them: *Since the success of her novel, people shake her hand who once wouldn't have given her the time of day.* **(there is) no time like the 'present** (*saying*) now is the best time to do sth, not in the future **of all 'time** that has ever existed: *Many rated him the best singer of all time.* ➲ see also ALL-TIME **take your 'time (over sth) | take your 'time to do sth/doing sth** **1** to use as much time as you need without hurrying: *There's no rush—take your time.* **2** used to say you think sb is late or is too slow in doing sth: *You certainly took your time getting here!* **take time 'out** to spend some time away from your usual work or activity in order to rest or do sth else instead: *She is taking time out from her music career for a year.* ➲ SYNONYMS at REST **ˌtime after 'time | ˌtime and (ˌtime) a'gain** often; on many or all occasions: *You will get a perfect result time after time if you follow these instructions.* **time and a 'half** one and a half times the usual rate of pay ➲ see also DOUBLE TIME **time 'flies** (*saying*) time seems to pass very quickly: *How time flies! I've got to go now.* ◇ *Time has flown since the holiday began.* ORIGIN This phrase is a translation of the Latin 'tempus fugit'. **time is 'money** (*saying*) time is valuable, and should not be wasted **time is on your 'side** used to say that sb can wait for sth to happen or can wait before doing sth **(the) next, first, second, etc. time 'round** on the next, first, etc. occasion that the same thing happens: *He repeated none of the errors he'd made first time round.* ◇ *This time round it was not so easy.* **time 'was (when)...** (*old-fashioned*) used to say that sth used to happen in the past **time (alone) will 'tell | only time will 'tell** (*saying*) used to say that you will have to wait for some time to find out the result of a situation: *Only time will tell if the treatment has been successful.* **the whole 'time** = ALL THE TIME ➲ more at BEAT *v.*, BIDE, BORROW, BUY *v.*, CALL *v.*, COURSE *n.*, DAY, DEVIL, EASY *adj.*, FIRST *det.*, FORTH, FULLNESS, GAIN *v.*, GIVE *v.*, HARD *adj.*, HIGH *adj.*, KILL *v.*, LONG *adj.*, LOST *adj.*, LUCK *n.*, MARK *v.*, MATTER *n.*, MOVE *v.*, NICK *n.*, NINETY, OLD, ONCE *adv.*, PASS *v.*, RACE *n.*, SIGN *n.*, STITCH *n.*, SWEET *adj.*, THIN *adj.*, THIRD, WHALE

■ ***verb***

▸ ARRANGE TIME **1** [often passive] to arrange to do sth or arrange for sth to happen at a particular time: **~ sth (for sth)** *She timed her arrival for shortly after 3.* ◇ *Their request was* ***badly timed*** (= it was made at the wrong time). ◇ *'I hope we're not too early.' 'You couldn't have timed it better!'* ◇ **~ sth to do sth** *Publication of his biography was* ***timed to coincide with*** *his 70th birthday celebrations.*

▸ MEASURE TIME **2** to measure how long it takes for sth to happen or for sb to do sth: **~ sth (at sth)** *The winner was timed at 20.4 seconds.* ◇ **~ how long...** *Time how long it takes you to answer the questions.*

▸ IN SPORT **3 ~ sth** to hit or kick a ball at a particular moment in a sports game: *She timed the pass perfectly.* ◇ *a beautifully timed shot* ➲ see also ILL-TIMED, MISTIME, TIMING, WELL TIMED

PHR V **ˌtime 'out | ˌtime sth'out** (of a computer program or task) to turn off, or turn sth off, automatically after a particular length of time even if the user has not finished: *My satellite connection timed out—it was so frustrating.*

ˌtime-and-'motion study *noun* a study to find out how efficient a company's working methods are

'time bomb *noun* **1** a bomb that can be set to explode at a particular time **2** a situation that is likely to cause serious problems in the future: *Rising unemployment is a political time bomb for the government.*

'time capsule *noun* a container that is filled with objects that people think are typical of the time they are living in. It is buried so that it can be discovered by people in the future.

'time card *noun* (*especially NAmE*) a piece of card on which the number of hours that sb has worked are recorded, usually by a machine

'time clock *noun* a special clock that records the exact time that sb starts and finishes work

'time-consum·ing *adj.* taking or needing a lot of time: *a difficult and time-consuming process*

'time frame *noun* the length of time that is used or available for sth

'time-honoured (*especially US* **-honored**) *adj.* respected because it has been used or done for a long time: *They showed their approval in the time-honoured way* (= by clapping, for example).

time·keep·er /'taɪmkiːpə(r)/ *noun* a person who records the time that is spent doing sth, for example at work or at a sports event
IDM **be a good/bad 'timekeeper** to be regularly on time/late for work

time·keep·ing /'taɪmkiːpɪŋ/ *noun* [U] **1** a person's ability to arrive in time for things, especially work **2** the activity of recording the time sth takes

'time lag (*also* **lag**, **'time lapse**) *noun* the period of time between two connected events: *There is a long time lag between when I do the work and when I get paid.*

'time-lapse *adj.* [only before noun] (of photography) using a method in which a series of individual pictures of a process are shown together so that sth that really happens very slowly is shown as happening very quickly: *a time-lapse sequence of a flower opening*

time·less /'taɪmləs/ *adj.* (*formal*) **1** not appearing to be affected by the passing of time or by changes in fashion: *her timeless beauty* **2** existing or continuing for ever SYN **unending**: *timeless eternity* ▸ **time·less·ly** *adv.* **time·less·ness** *noun* [U]

'time limit *noun* the length of time within which you must do or complete sth: *We have to set a time limit for the work.* ◇ *The work must be completed within a certain time limit.*

time·line /'taɪmlaɪn/ *noun* a horizontal line that is used to represent time, with the past towards the left and the future towards the right

'time lock *noun* **1** a lock with a device which prevents it from being opened until a particular time **2** (*computing*) part of a program which stops the program operating after a particular time

time·ly /ˈtaɪmli/ *adj.* happening at exactly the right time **SYN** **opportune**: *A nasty incident was prevented by the timely arrival of the police.* ◇ *This has been **a timely reminder** to us all.* **OPP** **untimely** ▶ **time·li·ness** *noun* [U]

ˈ**time machine** *noun* (in SCIENCE FICTION stories) a machine that enables you to travel in time to the past or the future

time·out /ˈtaɪmaʊt/ *noun* **1** (*NAmE*) a short period of rest during a sports game **2** (*computing*) an occasion when a process or program is automatically stopped after a certain amount of time because it has not worked successfully

time·piece /ˈtaɪmpiːs/ *noun* (*formal*) a clock or watch

ˌ**time-ˈpoor** *adj.* having very little or no free time because you work all the time: *products for customers who are time-poor but cash-rich*

timer /ˈtaɪmə(r)/ *noun* (often in compounds) a device that is used to measure the time that sth takes; a device that starts or stops a machine working at a particular time: *an oven timer* ➲ VISUAL VOCAB page V23 ➲ see also EGG TIMER, OLD-TIMER

ˈ**time-release** *adj.* [usually before noun] releasing an active substance, for example a drug, a little at a time

times /taɪmz/ **1** *prep.* (*informal*) multiplied by: *Five times two is/equals ten* (5 × 2 = 10). **2** *noun* [pl.] used in comparisons to show how much more, better, etc. sth is than sth else: *three times as long as sth* ◇ *three times longer than sth* ◇ *three times the length of sth* ➲ LANGUAGE BANK at PROPORTION

ˈ**time-saving** *adj.* [usually before noun] that reduces the amount of time it takes to do sth: *time-saving devices*

time·scale /ˈtaɪmskeɪl/ *noun* the period of time that it takes for sth to happen or be completed: *What's the timescale for the project?*

ˈ**time-server** *noun* (*disapproving*) a person who does as little work as possible in their job because they are just waiting until they leave for another job or retire ▶ ˈ**time-serving** *adj.*, *noun* [U]

time·share /ˈtaɪmʃeə(r); *NAmE* -ʃer/ *noun* **1** (also ˈ**time-sharing**) [U] an arrangement in which several people own a holiday/vacation home together and each uses it at a different time of the year: *timeshare apartments* **2** [C] a holiday/vacation home that you own in this way: *They have a timeshare in Florida.*

ˈ**time sheet** *noun* a piece of paper on which the number of hours that sb has worked are recorded

ˈ**time signal** *noun* a sound or sounds that show the exact time of day, especially a series of short high sounds that are broadcast on the radio

ˈ**time signature** *noun* (*music*) a sign at the start of a piece of music, usually in the form of numbers, showing the number of beats in each BAR/MEASURE ➲ picture at MUSIC

ˈ**time span** *noun* a period of time: *These changes have occurred over a long time span.*

ˈ**time switch** *noun* a switch that can be set to start and stop a machine working automatically at a particular time: *The heating is on a time switch.*

time·table 🗝 /ˈtaɪmteɪbl/ *noun, verb*

■ ***noun* 1** 🗝 (*especially BrE*) (*NAmE* usually **sched·ule**) a list showing the times at which particular events will happen: *a **bus/train timetable*** (= when they arrive and leave) ◇ *We have a new timetable each term* (= showing the times of each class in school). ◇ *Sport is no longer so important in the school timetable* (= all the subjects that are taught at schools). **2** 🗝 a plan of when you expect or hope particular events to happen **SYN** **schedule**: *I have a busy timetable this week* (= I have planned to do many things). ◇ *The government has set out its timetable for the peace talks.* ➲ note at AGENDA

■ ***verb*** [usually passive] **~ sth** (**for sth**) (*especially BrE*) to arrange for sth to take place at a particular time **SYN** **schedule**: *A series of discussion groups have been timetabled for the afternoons.* ▶ **time·tab·ling** *noun* [U]

ˈ**time trial** *noun* (in cycle racing and some other sports) a race in which the people who are taking part race on their own in as fast a time as possible, instead of racing against each other at the same time

ˈ**time warp** *noun* an imaginary situation, described for example in SCIENCE FICTION, in which it is possible for people or things from the past or the future to move to the present

IDM **be** (**stuck**) **in a ˈtime warp** not having changed at all from a time in the past although everything else has

ˈ**time-wasting** *noun* [U] **1** the act of wasting time **2** (*BrE*) (in sport) the act of playing more slowly towards the end of a game to prevent the opposing team from scoring ➲ compare RUN DOWN/OUT THE CLOCK ▶ ˈ**time-waster** *noun*

ˈ**time-worn** *adj.* old and used a lot, and therefore damaged, or no longer useful or interesting

ˈ**time zone** *noun* one of the 24 areas that the world is divided into, each with its own time that is one hour earlier than that of the time zone immediately to the east

timid /ˈtɪmɪd/ *adj.* shy and nervous; not brave: *He stopped in the doorway, too timid to go in.* ◇ *They've been rather timid in the changes they've made* (= they've been afraid to make any big changes). ◇ *a timid voice* ▶ **tim·id·ity** /tɪˈmɪdəti/ *noun* [U] **tim·id·ly** *adv.*

tim·ing /ˈtaɪmɪŋ/ *noun* **1** [U, C] the act of choosing when sth happens; a particular point or period of time when sth happens or is planned: *The timing of the decision was a complete surprise.* ◇ *Please check your flight timings carefully.* **2** [U] the skill of doing sth at exactly the right time: *an actor with a great sense of comic timing* ◇ *Your timing is perfect. I was just about to call you.* **3** [U] the repeated rhythm of sth; the skill of producing this: *She played the piano confidently but her timing was not good.* **4** [U] (*technical*) the rate at which an electric SPARK is produced in a vehicle's engine in order to make it work

tim·or·ous /ˈtɪmərəs/ *adj.* (*literary* or *formal*) nervous and easily frightened **SYN** **timid** ▶ **tim·or·ous·ly** *adv.*

tim·pani /ˈtɪmpəni/ (also *informal* **timps** /tɪmps/) *noun* [pl.] a set of large metal drums (also called KETTLEDRUMS) in an ORCHESTRA ▶ **tim·pan·ist** *noun*

tin 🗝 /tɪn/ *noun*

1 🗝 [U] (*symb.* Sn) a chemical element. Tin is a soft silver-white metal that is often mixed with other metals or used to cover them to prevent them from RUSTING: *a tin mine* ◇ *a tin box* **2** 🗝 [C] (also ˌ**tin ˈcan**) (both *BrE*) (also **can** *NAmE*, *BrE*) **~** (**of sth**) a metal container in which food and drink is sold; the contents of one of these containers: *a tin of beans* ◇ *Next, add two tins of tomatoes.* ➲ VISUAL VOCAB page V29 **3** 🗝 [C] (*BrE*) (also **can** *NAmE*, *BrE*) **~** (**of sth**) a metal container with a lid, in the shape of a CYLINDER, in which paint, glue, etc. is sold and stored; the contents of one of these containers: *a tin of varnish* ◇ *The bedroom needed three tins of paint* (= in order to paint it). **4** [C] a metal container with a lid used for keeping food in: *a biscuit/cake/cookie tin* ➲ VISUAL VOCAB page V29 **5** [C] (*BrE*) (*NAmE* **pan**) a metal container used for cooking food in: *a cake tin* ➲ VISUAL VOCAB page V24

IDM (**it**) **does** (**eˌxactly**) **what it says on the ˈtin** (*informal, saying*) used to say that sth is as good or effective as it claims to be, or that it really does what it claims to do. This expression is especially used when you are comparing publicity and advertisements with actual products: *I paid £150 for this camera and am more than happy with it. It does exactly what it says on the tin!*

ˌ**tin ˈcan** *noun* = TIN

tinc·ture /ˈtɪŋktʃə(r)/ *noun* [C, U] (*technical*) a substance dissolved in alcohol for use as a medicine

tin·der /ˈtɪndə(r)/ *noun* [U] dry material, especially wood or grass, that burns easily and can be used to light a fire:

T

The fire started late Saturday in tinder-dry grass near the Snake River.

tin·der·box /ˈtɪndəbɒks; *NAmE* ˈtɪndərbɑːks/ *noun* **1** a box containing dry material, used in the past for lighting a fire **2** (*formal*) a situation that is likely to become dangerous

tine /taɪn/ *noun* (*technical*) any of the points or sharp parts of, for example, a fork or the ANTLERS of a DEER ➲ VISUAL VOCAB page V19

tin·foil /ˈtɪnfɔɪl/ *noun* [U] metal made into very thin sheets, that is used for wrapping food, etc.

tinge /tɪndʒ/ *verb, noun*

■ ***verb*** [usually passive] **1 ~ sth (with sth)** to add a small amount of colour to sth: *white petals tinged with blue* **2 ~ sth (with sth)** to add a small amount of a particular emotion or quality to sth: *a look of surprise tinged with disapproval*

■ ***noun*** [usually sing.] a small amount of a colour, feeling or quality: *to feel a tinge of envy* ◇ *There was a faint pink tinge to the sky.* ➲ SYNONYMS at COLOUR

tin·gle /ˈtɪŋɡl/ *verb, noun*

■ ***verb*** **1** [I] (of a part of your body) to feel as if a lot of small sharp points are pushing into it: *The cold air made her face tingle.* ◇ *a tingling sensation* ➲ SYNONYMS at HURT **2** [I] **~ with sth** to feel an emotion strongly: *She was still tingling with excitement.*

■ ***noun*** [usually sing.] (also **ting·ling** [sing., U]) **1** a slight stinging or uncomfortable feeling in a part of your body **2** an exciting or uncomfortable feeling of emotion: *to feel a tingle of excitement*

tin·gly /ˈtɪŋɡli/ *adj.* causing or experiencing a slight feeling of tingling: *a tingly sensation*

tin·ker /ˈtɪŋkə(r)/ *noun, verb*

■ ***noun*** (in the past) a person who travelled from place to place, selling or repairing things

■ ***verb*** [I] **~ (with sth)** to make small changes to sth in order to repair or improve it, especially in a way that may not be helpful

tin·kle /ˈtɪŋkl/ *noun, verb*

■ ***noun*** [usually sing.] **1** (also **tink·ling** [sing., U]) a light high ringing sound: *the tinkle of glass breaking* **2** (*old-fashioned, BrE, informal*) a telephone call **3** (*BrE, informal*) an act of URINATING: *to have a tinkle*

■ ***verb*** [I, T] **~ (sth)** to make a series of light high ringing sounds; to make sth produce this sound: *A bell tinkled as the door opened.* ◇ *tinkling laughter*

tinned /tɪnd/ (*BrE*) (also **canned** *NAmE, BrE*) *adj.* (of food) preserved in a can: *tinned fruit*

T

tin·nitus /ˈtɪnɪtəs/ *noun* [U] (*medical*) an unpleasant condition in which sb hears ringing in their ears

tinny /ˈtɪni/ *adj., noun*

■ ***adj.*** (*especially BrE, disapproving*) **1** having a high thin sound like small pieces of metal hitting each other **2** having a taste like metal: *The beer tasted tinny.*

■ ***noun*** (also **tin·nie**) (*pl.* **-ies**) (*AustralE, NZE, informal*) a can of beer

ˈtin opener (*BrE*) (also **ˈcan opener** *NAmE, BrE*) *noun* a kitchen UTENSIL (= a tool) for opening tins of food ➲ VISUAL VOCAB page V23

ˌTin Pan ˈAlley *noun* [U] (*old-fashioned, informal*) people who write and publish popular songs ORIGIN From the name of the part of New York where many such people worked in the past.

tin·plate /ˈtɪnpleɪt/ *noun* [U] a metal material made from iron and steel and covered with a layer of tin

tin·pot /ˈtɪnpɒt; *NAmE* -pɑːt/ *adj.* [only before noun] (*BrE, disapproving*) (especially of a leader or government) not important and of little worth or use: *a tinpot dictator*

tin·sel /ˈtɪnsl/ *noun* [U] strips of shiny material like metal, used as decorations, especially at Christmas

Tin·sel·town /ˈtɪnsltaʊn/ *noun* [U] (*informal*) a way of referring to Hollywood in California, the centre of the US movie industry

tint /tɪnt/ *noun, verb*

■ ***noun*** **1** a shade or small amount of a particular colour; a faint colour covering a surface: *leaves with red and gold autumn tints* ◇ *the brownish tint of an old photo* ➲ SYNONYMS at COLOUR **2** an artificial colour used to change the colour of your hair; the act of colouring the hair with a tint: *a blond tint* ◇ *to have a tint*

■ ***verb*** **1** [usually passive] **~ sth (with sth)** to add a small amount of colour to sth **2 ~ sth** to change the colour of sb's hair with a tint ▸ **tint·ed** *adj.*: *tinted glasses*

ˌT-interˈsec·tion (*NAmE*) (*BrE* **ˈT-junction**) *noun* a place where one road joins another but does not cross it, so that the roads form the shape of the letter T

tin·tin·nabu·la·tion /ˌtɪntɪnæbjuˈleɪʃn/ *noun* [U, C] (*formal*) a ringing sound

ˌtin ˈwhistle (also **ˌpenny ˈwhistle**) *noun* a simple musical instrument like a short pipe with six holes, that you play by blowing

tiny 0-w /ˈtaɪni/ *adj.* (**tini·er**, **tini·est**) very small in size or amount: *a tiny baby* ◇ *Only a tiny minority hold such extreme views.* IDM see PATTER *n.*

-tion ➲ -ION

tip 0-w /tɪp/ *noun, verb*

■ ***noun***

▸ END OF STH **1** 0-w the thin pointed end of sth: *the tips of your fingers* ◇ *the tip of your nose* ◇ *the northern tip of the island* ➲ see also FINGERTIP **2** 0-w a small part that fits on or over the end of sth: *a walking stick with a rubber tip* ➲ see also FELT-TIP PEN, FILTER TIP

▸ ADVICE **3** 0-w a small piece of advice about sth practical SYN **hint**: **~ (on/for doing sth)** ***handy tips*** *for buying a computer* ◇ **~ (on/for sth)** *useful tips on how to save money* **4** (*informal*) a secret or expert piece of advice about what the result of a competition, etc. is likely to be, especially about which horse is likely to win a race: *a* ***hot tip*** *for the big race* **5** (*NAmE*) (also **ˈtip-off** especially in *BrE*) (*informal*) secret information that sb gives, for example to the police, to warn them about an illegal activity that is going to happen: *The man was arrested after an anonymous tip.*

▸ EXTRA MONEY **6** 0-w a small amount of extra money that you give to sb, for example sb who serves you in a restaurant: *to* ***leave a tip*** ◇ *He* ***gave*** *the waiter* ***a*** *generous* ***tip***.

▸ FOR RUBBISH **7** (*BrE*) a place where you can take rubbish/garbage and leave it

▸ UNTIDY PLACE **8** (*BrE, informal, disapproving*) an untidy place SYN **dump**: *Their flat is a tip!*

IDM **on the tip of your ˈtongue** if a word or name is **on the tip of your tongue**, you are sure that you know it but you cannot remember it **the tip of the ˈiceberg** only a small part of a much larger problem

■ ***verb*** (**-pp-**)

▸ LEAN/POUR/PUSH AT AN ANGLE **1** 0-w [I, T] to move so that one end or side is higher than the other; to move sth into this position SYN **tilt**: **(+ adv./prep.)** *The boat tipped to one side.* ◇ *The seat tips forward to allow passengers into the back.* ◇ **~ sth (+ adv./prep.)** *She tipped her head back and laughed loudly.* **2** 0-w [T] **~ sth/sb + adv./prep.** to make sth/sb come out of a container or its/their position by holding or lifting it/them at an angle: *She tipped the dirty water down the drain.* ◇ *The bus stopped abruptly, nearly tipping me out of my seat.* **3** [T] **~ sth + adv./prep.** to touch sth lightly so that it moves in a particular direction: *The goalkeeper just managed to tip the ball over the crossbar.*

▸ LEAVE RUBBISH **4** [I, T] **~ (sth)** (*BrE*) to leave rubbish/garbage somewhere outdoors in order to get rid of it: *'No tipping.'* (= for example, on a notice)

▸ GIVE EXTRA MONEY **5** 0-w [I, T] to give sb an extra amount of money to thank them for sth they have done for you as part of their job: *Americans were always welcome because they tended to tip heavily.* ◇ **~ sb** *Did you remember to tip the waiter?* ◇ **~ sb sth** *She tipped the porter a dollar.*

▸ PREDICT SUCCESS **6** [T] (*especially BrE*) to say in advance that sb/sth will be successful: **~ sb/sth (for sth)** *The band is being tipped for the top.* ◇ **~ sb/sth as sth** *The senator has*

been tipped by many as a future president. ◇ **~ sb/sth to do sth** *The actor is tipped to win an Oscar for his performance.*
▸ COVER END **7** [T, usually passive] **~ sth** (**with sth**) to cover the end or edge of sth with a colour, a substance, etc: *The wings are tipped with yellow.*

IDM **it is/was 'tipping** (**it**) **down** (*BrE, informal*) it is/was raining heavily **tip the 'balance/'scales** (also **swing the 'balance**) to affect the result of sth in one way rather than another: *In an interview, smart presentation can tip the scales in your favour.* **tip your 'hand** (*NAmE*) (*BrE* **show your 'hand/'cards**) to make your plans or intentions known **tip the scales at sth** to weigh a particular amount: *He tipped the scales at just over 80 kilos.* **tip sb the 'wink** | **tip the 'wink to sb** (*BrE, informal*) to give sb secret information that they can use to gain an advantage for themselves ➲ more at HAT *n.*

PHR V ˌ**tip sb↔'off** (**about sth**) (*informal*) to warn sb about sth that is going to happen, especially sth illegal: *Three men were arrested after police were tipped off about the raid.* ◇ **~ that...** *They were tipped off that he might be living in Wales.* ➲ related noun TIP-OFF ˌ**tip 'up/'over** | ˌ**tip sth↔'up/'over** 🔑 to fall or turn over; to make sth do this: *The mug tipped over, spilling hot coffee everywhere.* ◇ *We'll have to tip the sofa up to get it through the door.*

'tip-off *noun* (*especially BrE*) (*NAmE* usually **tip**) (*informal*) secret information that sb gives, for example to the police, to warn them about an illegal activity that is going to happen: *The man was arrested after an anonymous tip-off.*

tip·per /ˈtɪpə(r)/ *noun* **1** (used with an adjective) a person who gives sb a TIP (= a small amount of extra money to thank them for doing sth as part of their job) of the size mentioned: *She says that Americans are usually big tippers.* **2** (also **'tipper lorry/truck**) a lorry/truck with a container part that can be moved into a sloping position so that its load can slide off at the back

tip·pet /ˈtɪpɪt/ *noun* a long piece of fur worn in the past by a woman around the neck and shoulders, with the ends hanging down in front; a similar piece of clothing worn by judges, priests, etc.

Tipp-Ex™ /ˈtɪpeks/ *noun* [U] (*BrE*) a liquid, usually white, that you use to cover mistakes that you make when you are writing or typing, and that you can write on top of; a type of CORRECTION FLUID ▸ **tip·pex** *verb*: **~ sth** (**out**) *I tippexed out the mistakes.*

'tipping point *noun* the point at which the number of small changes over a period of time reaches a level where a further small change has a sudden and very great effect on a system or leads to an idea suddenly spreading quickly among a large number of people

tip·ple /ˈtɪpl/ *noun, verb*
■ ***noun*** [usually sing.] (*informal, especially BrE*) an alcoholic drink: *His favourite tipple was rum and lemon.*
■ ***verb*** [I, T] **~** (**sth**) (*informal, especially BrE*) to drink alcohol ▸ **tip·pler** /ˈtɪplə(r)/ *noun*

tip·ster /ˈtɪpstə(r)/ *noun* **1** a person who tells you, often in exchange for money, which horse is likely to win a race, so that you can bet on it and win money **2** (*especially NAmE*) a person who gives information to the police about a crime or criminal

tipsy /ˈtɪpsi/ *adj.* (*informal*) slightly drunk SYN **tight**

tip·toe /ˈtɪptəʊ; *NAmE* -toʊ/ *noun, verb*
■ ***noun***
IDM **on 'tiptoe/'tiptoes** standing or walking on the front part of your foot, with your heels off the ground, in order to make yourself taller or to move very quietly: *She had to stand on tiptoe to reach the top shelf.* ◇ *We crept around on tiptoes so as not to disturb him.*
■ ***verb*** [I] (+ **adv./prep.**) to walk using the front parts of your feet only, so that other people cannot hear you: *I tiptoed over to the window.*

ˌ**tip-'top** *adj.* [usually before noun] (*informal*) excellent: *The house is* ***in tip-top condition.***

'tip-up *adj.* (of a seat) moving up into a vertical position when nobody is sitting in it

tir·ade /taɪˈreɪd; *NAmE* ˈtaɪreɪd/ *noun* **~** (**against sb/sth**) a long angry speech criticizing sb/sth or accusing sb of sth: *She launched into a tirade of abuse against politicians.*

tire 🔑 /ˈtaɪə(r)/ *verb, noun*
■ ***verb*** [I, T] **~** (**sb**) to become tired and feel as if you want to sleep or rest; to make sb feel this way: *Her legs were beginning to tire.* ◇ *He has made a good recovery but still tires easily.*

IDM **never tire of doing sth** to do sth a lot, especially in a way that annoys people: *He went to Harvard—as he never tires of reminding us.*

PHR V **'tire of sth/sb** to become bored with sth/sb or begin to enjoy it/them less: *They soon tired of the beach and went for a walk.* ˌ**tire sb/yourself 'out** 🔑 to make sb/yourself feel very tired ➲ see also TIRED
■ ***noun*** 🔑 (*NAmE*) (*BrE* **tyre**) a thick rubber ring that fits around the edge of a wheel of a car, bicycle, etc: *a* ***front tire*** ◇ *a* ***back/rear tire*** ◇ *to pump up a tire* ◇ *a* ***flat/burst/punctured tire*** ◇ ***bald/worn tires*** ◇ *to check your tire pressure* ➲ VISUAL VOCAB pages V41, V42 ➲ see also SPARE TYRE

tired 🔑 /ˈtaɪəd; *NAmE* ˈtaɪərd/ *adj.*
1 🔑 feeling that you would like to sleep or rest; needing rest SYN **weary**: *to* ***be/look/feel tired*** ◇ *I'm too tired even to think.* ◇ *They were cold, hungry and* ***tired out*** (= very tired). ◇ *tired feet* **2** 🔑 feeling that you have had enough of sb/sth because you no longer find them/it interesting or because they make you angry or unhappy: **~ of sb/sth** *I'm* ***sick and tired*** *of all the arguments.* ◇ **~ of doing sth** *She was tired of hearing about their trip to India.* **3** boring because it is too familiar or has been used too much: *He always comes out with the same tired old jokes.* ▸ **tired·ly** *adv.*: *He shook his head tiredly.* **tired·ness** *noun* [U] ➲ see also DOG-TIRED

'tire iron *noun* (*NAmE*) a metal tool for taking tyres off wheels

tire·less /ˈtaɪələs; *NAmE* ˈtaɪərləs/ *adj.* (*approving*) putting a lot of hard work and energy into sth over a long period of time SYN **indefatigable**: *a tireless campaigner for human rights* ▸ **tire·less·ly** *adv.*

tire·some /ˈtaɪəsəm; *NAmE* ˈtaɪərsəm/ *adj.* making you feel annoyed SYN **annoying**: *Buying a house can be a very tiresome business.* ◇ *The children were being very tiresome.* ▸ **tire·some·ly** *adv.*

tir·ing 🔑 /ˈtaɪərɪŋ/ *adj.*
making you feel the need to sleep or rest SYN **exhausting**: *It had been a long tiring day.*

'tis /tɪz/ *short form* (*old use*) it is

tis·sue /ˈtɪʃuː; *BrE* also ˈtɪsjuː/ *noun* **1** [U] (also **tissues** [pl.]) a collection of cells that form the different parts of humans, animals and plants: ***muscle/brain/nerve, etc. tissue*** ◇ *scar tissue* **2** [C] a piece of soft paper that absorbs liquids, used especially as a HANDKERCHIEF: *a box of tissues* **3** (also **'tissue paper**) [U] very thin paper used for wrapping and packing things that break easily

IDM **a ˌtissue of 'lies** (*literary*) a story, an excuse, etc. that is full of lies

tit /tɪt/ *noun* **1** [usually pl.] (also **titty**) (*taboo, slang*) a woman's breast or NIPPLE **2** (*BrE, slang*) a stupid person **3** a small European bird. There are several types of tit: *a great tit* ➲ see also BLUE TIT

Titan /ˈtaɪtn/ (also **titan**) *noun* (*formal*) a person who is very large, strong, intelligent or important ORIGIN From the **Titans**, who in Greek mythology were the older gods who were defeated in a battle with Zeus.

ti·tan·ic /taɪˈtænɪk/ *adj.* (*formal*) very large, important, strong or difficult: *a titanic struggle between good and evil*

ti·tan·ium /tɪˈteɪniəm/ *noun* [U] (*symb.* Ti) a chemical element. Titanium is a silver-white metal used in making various strong light materials.

tit·bit /ˈtɪtbɪt/ (*BrE*) (*NAmE* **tid·bit**) *noun* **1** a small special piece of food SYN **morsel**: *She had saved a few titbits for*

T

her cat. **2** a small but interesting piece of news SYN **snippet**: *titbits of gossip*

titch /tɪtʃ/ *noun* (*BrE*, *informal* often *humorous*) used as a way of talking about or addressing a very small person

titchy /ˈtɪtʃi/ *adj.* (*BrE*, *informal*) very small

ˌtit for ˈtat *noun* [U] a situation in which you do sth bad to sb because they have done the same to you: *the routine tit for tat when countries expel each other's envoys* ◇ *tit-for-tat assassinations by rival gangs*

tithe /taɪð/ *noun* **1** (in the past) a tenth of the goods that sb produced or the money that they earned, that was paid as a tax to support the Church **2** (in some Christian Churches today) a tenth of a person's income, that they give to the Church

tit·il·late /ˈtɪtɪleɪt/ *verb* [I, T] (often *disapproving*) to interest or excite sb, especially in a sexual way: *titillating pictures* ◇ **~ sth** *a story intended to titillate the imagination of the public* ▶ **tit·il·la·tion** /ˌtɪtɪˈleɪʃn/ *noun* [U]

titi·vate /ˈtɪtɪveɪt/ *verb* **~ sth** to improve the appearance of sb/sth by making small changes: *She titivated her hair in the mirror.*

title 🔑 /ˈtaɪtl/ *noun, verb*

■ ***noun*** **1** 🔑 [C] the name of a book, poem, painting, piece of music, etc: *His poems were published under the title of 'Love and Reason'.* ◇ *the* **title track** *from their latest CD* (= the song with the same title as the disc) ◇ *She has sung the title role in 'Carmen'* (= the role of Carmen in that OPERA). **2** [C] a particular book or magazine: *The company publishes twenty new titles a year.* **3** 🔑 [C] a word in front of a person's name to show their rank or profession, whether or not they are married, etc: *The present duke inherited the title from his father.* ◇ *Give your name and title* (= Mr, Miss, Ms, Dr, etc.). ➲ note at NAME **4** 🔑 [C] a name that describes a job: *The official title of the job is 'Administrative Assistant'.* **5** [C] the position of being the winner of a competition, especially a sports competition: *the world heavyweight title* ◇ *She has three world titles.* **6** [U, C] **~ (to sth/to do sth)** (*law*) the legal right to own sth, especially land or property; the document that shows you have this right

■ ***verb*** [usually passive] **~ sth + noun** to give a book, piece of music, etc. a particular name: *Their first album was titled 'Made in Valmez'.*

ˈtitle bar *noun* (*computing*) a bar at the top of a computer screen, which shows the name of the program and file that is on the screen

titled /ˈtaɪtld/ *adj.* having a title such as Lord, LADY, etc.

ˈtitle deed *noun* [usually pl.] a legal document proving that sb is the owner of a particular house, etc.

ˈtitle-holder *noun* **1** a person or team that has defeated all the other people or teams taking part in an important competition: *the current Olympic title-holder* **2** (*technical*) (*NAmE*) the legal owner of sth

ˈtitle page *noun* a page at the front of a book that has the title and the author's name on it

ti·trate /taɪˈtreɪt; tɪ-/ *verb* **~ sth** (*chemistry*) to find out how much of a particular substance is in a liquid by measuring how much of another substance is needed to react with it ▶ **ti·tra·tion** /-ˈtreɪʃn/ *noun* [U]

tit·ter /ˈtɪtə(r)/ *verb* [I] to laugh quietly, especially in a nervous or embarrassed way SYN **giggle** ▶ **tit·ter** *noun*

tittle-tattle /ˈtɪtl tætl/ *noun* [U] (*informal*, *disapproving*) unimportant talk, usually not true, about other people and their lives SYN **gossip**

titty /ˈtɪti/ *noun* (*pl.* -ies) (*slang*) = TIT (1)

titu·lar /ˈtɪtjulə(r); *NAmE* -tʃə-/ *adj.* [only before noun] **1** (*formal*) having a particular title or status but no real power or authority SYN **nominal**: *the titular head of state* **2** the **titular** character of a book, play, film/movie, etc. is the one mentioned in the title SYN **eponymous**

tizzy /ˈtɪzi/ (also **tizz** /tɪz/) *noun* [sing.] (*informal*) a state of nervous excitement or confusion: *She was in a real tizzy before the meeting.*

ˈT-junction (*BrE*) (*NAmE* **ˌT-interˈsection**) *noun* a place where one road joins another but does not cross it, so that the roads form the shape of the letter T

TLC /ˌtiː el ˈsiː/ *noun* [U] (*informal*) the abbreviation for 'tender loving care' (care that you give sb to make them feel better): *What he needs now is just rest and a lot of TLC.*

Tlin·git /ˈtlɪŋgɪt/ *noun* (*pl.* **Tlin·git** or **Tlin·gits**) a member of a Native American people, many of whom live in the US state of Alaska

TM /ˌtiː ˈem/ *abbr.* **1** TRADEMARK **2** (*US* **T.M.**) TRANSCENDENTAL MEDITATION

tme·sis /ˈtmiːsɪs/ *noun* [U, C] (*pl.* **tme·ses** /-siːz/) (*linguistics*) the use of a word or words in the middle of another word, for example 'abso-bloody-lutely'

TNT /ˌtiː en ˈtiː/ *noun* [U] a powerful EXPLOSIVE

to 🔑 /*before consonants* tə; *before vowels* tu; *strong form* tuː/ *prep., infinitive marker, adv.*

■ ***prep.*** HELP For the special uses of **to** in phrasal verbs, look at the entries for the verbs. For example **see to sth** is in the phrasal verb section at **see**. **1** 🔑 in the direction of sth; towards sth: *I walked to the office.* ◇ *It fell to the ground.* ◇ *It was on the way to the station.* ◇ *He's going to Paris.* ◇ *my first visit to Africa* ◇ *He pointed to something on the opposite bank.* ◇ *Her childhood was spent travelling from place to place.* **2** 🔑 **~ the sth (of sth)** located in the direction mentioned from sth: *Place the cursor to the left of the first word.* ◇ *There are mountains to the north.* **3** 🔑 as far as sth: *The meadows lead down to the river.* ◇ *Her hair fell to her waist.* **4** 🔑 reaching a particular state: *The vegetables were cooked to perfection.* ◇ *He tore the letter to pieces.* ◇ *She sang the baby to sleep.* ◇ *The letter reduced her to tears* (= made her cry). ◇ *His expression changed from amazement to joy.* **5** 🔑 used to show the end or limit of a range or period of time: *a drop in profits from $105 million to around $75 million* ◇ *I'd say he was 25 to 30 years old* (= approximately 25 or 30 years old). ◇ *I like all kinds of music from opera to reggae.* ◇ *We only work from Monday to Friday.* ◇ *I watched the programme from beginning to end.* **6** 🔑 before the start of sth: *How long is it to lunch?* ◇ (*especially BrE*) *It's five to ten* (= five minutes before ten o'clock). **7** 🔑 used to show the person or thing that receives sth: *He gave it to his sister.* ◇ *I'll explain to you where everything goes.* ◇ *I am deeply grateful to my parents.* ◇ *Who did she address the letter to?* ◇ (*formal*) *To whom did she address the letter?* **8** 🔑 used to show the person or thing that is affected by an action: *She is devoted to her family.* ◇ *What have you done to your hair?* **9** 🔑 used to show that two things are attached or connected: *Attach this rope to the front of the car.* **10** 🔑 used to show a relationship between one person or thing and another: *She's married to an Italian.* ◇ *the Japanese ambassador to France* ◇ *the key to the door* ◇ *the solution to this problem* **11** 🔑 directed towards; concerning: *It was a threat to world peace.* ◇ *She made a reference to her recent book.* **12** 🔑 used to introduce the second part of a comparison or RATIO: *I prefer walking to climbing.* ◇ *The industry today is nothing to what it once was.* ◇ *We won by six goals to three.* **13** 🔑 used to show a quantity or rate: *There are 2.54 centimetres to an inch.* ◇ *This car does 30 miles to the gallon.* ➲ compare PER **14** 🔑 in honour of sb/sth: *a monument to the soldiers who died in the war* ◇ *Let's drink to Julia and her new job.* **15** while sth else is happening or being done: *He left the stage to prolonged applause.* **16** used after verbs of movement to mean 'with the intention of giving sth': *People rushed to her rescue and picked her up.* **17** 🔑 used to show sb's attitude or reaction to sth: *His music isn't really to my taste.* ◇ *To her astonishment, he smiled.* **18** 🔑 used to show what sb's opinion or feeling about sth is: *It sounded like crying to me.*

■ ***infinitive marker*** HELP **To** is often used before the base form of a verb to show that the verb is in the infinitive. The infinitive is used after many verbs and also after many nouns and adjectives. **1** 🔑 used to show purpose or intention: *I set out to buy food.* ◇ *I am going to tell you a story.* ◇ *She was determined to do well.* ◇ *His aim was to become* president. ◇ *To be honest with you, I don't remember what he said.* **2** 🔑 used to show the result of sth: *She managed to escape.* ◇ *It was too hot to go out.* ◇ *He couldn't get close enough to see.* **3** 🔑 used to show the cause of sth: *I'm sorry to hear that.* **4** 🔑 used to show an action that you want or are advised to do: *I'd love to go to France this summer.* ◇ *The leaflet explains how to apply for a place.* ◇ *I don't know what to say.* HELP **To** can also be used without a following verb when the missing verb is easy to understand: *He asked her to come but she said she didn't want to.* **5** 🔑 used to show sth that is known or reported about a particular person or thing: *The house was said to be haunted.* **6** 🔑 used to show that one action immediately follows another: *I reached the station only to find that my train had already left.* **7 am, is, are, was, were ~** used to show that you must or should do sth: *You are not to talk during the exam.* ◇ *She was to be here at 8.30 but she didn't arrive.*

▪ ***adv.*** (usually of a door) in or into a closed position: *Push the door to.* ➲ see also TOING

IDM ˌ**to and ˈfro** backwards and forwards: *She rocked the baby to and fro.* HELP For the special uses of **to** in phrasal verbs, look at the entries for the verbs. For example **set to** is in the phrasal verb section at **set**.

toad /təʊd; *NAmE* toʊd/ *noun* **1** a small animal like a FROG but with a drier and less smooth skin, that lives on land but breeds in water (= is an AMPHIBIAN) ➲ VISUAL VOCAB page V11 **2** (*informal, disapproving*) an unpleasant person

ˌ**toad-in-the-ˈhole** *noun* [U] a British dish of SAUSAGES cooked in BATTER

toad·stool /ˈtəʊdstuːl; *NAmE* ˈtoʊd-/ *noun* a FUNGUS with a round flat or curved head and a short STEM. Many types of toadstool are poisonous. ➲ compare MUSHROOM

toady /ˈtəʊdi; *NAmE* ˈtoʊdi/ *noun, verb*

▪ ***noun*** (*pl.* -ies) (*informal, disapproving*) a person who treats sb more important with special kindness or respect in order to gain their favour or help SYN **sycophant**

▪ ***verb*** (**toad·ies, toady·ing, toad·ied, toad·ied**) [I] **~ (to sb)** (*disapproving*) to treat sb more important with special kindness or respect in order to gain their favour or help

toast /təʊst; *NAmE* toʊst/ *noun, verb*

▪ ***noun*** **1** [U] slices of bread that have been made brown and crisp by heating them on both sides in a toaster or under a GRILL: *cheese on toast* ◇ *a piece of toast* ◇ *two **slices/rounds of toast*** ➲ see also FRENCH TOAST **2** [C] **~ (to sb/sth)** the act of a group of people wishing sb happiness, success, etc. by drinking a glass of sth, especially alcohol, at the same time: *I'd like to **propose a toast** to the bride and groom.* ◇ *The committee **drank a toast** to the new project.* **3** [sing.] **the ~ of...** a person who is praised by a lot of people in a particular place because of sth that they have done well: *The performance made her the toast of the festival.*

IDM **be ˈtoast** (*informal, especially NAmE*) to be likely to die or be destroyed: *One mistake and you're toast.*

▪ ***verb*** **1** [T] **~ sb/sth** to lift a glass of wine, etc. in the air and drink it at the same time as other people in order to wish sb/sth success, happiness, etc: *The happy couple were toasted in champagne.* ◇ *We toasted the success of the new company.* **2** [T, I] **~ (sth)** to make sth, especially bread, turn brown by heating it in a toaster or close to heat; to turn brown in this way: *a toasted sandwich* ◇ *Place under a hot grill until the nuts have toasted.* ➲ COLLOCATIONS at COOKING **3** [T] **~ sth** to warm a part of your body by placing it near a fire

toast·er /ˈtəʊstə(r); *NAmE* ˈtoʊ-/ *noun* an electrical machine that you put slices of bread in to make toast ➲ VISUAL VOCAB page V22

toastie /ˈtəʊsti; *NAmE* ˈtoʊsti/ *noun* (*BrE*) a SANDWICH that has been TOASTED

ˈ**toasting fork** *noun* a fork with a long handle used for TOASTING bread in front of a fire

toast·mas·ter /ˈtəʊstmɑːstə(r); *NAmE* ˈtoʊstmæstər/ *noun* a person who introduces the speakers at a formal dinner and calls for people to drink sth together in honour of particular people (= proposes TOASTS)

toasty /ˈtəʊsti; *NAmE* ˈtoʊ-/ *adj.* (*especially NAmE*) warm and comfortable

to·bacco /təˈbækəʊ; *NAmE* -koʊ/ *noun* [U, C] (*pl.* -os) the dried leaves of the tobacco plant that are used for making cigarettes, smoking in a pipe or chewing: *The government imposed a ban on tobacco advertising* (= the advertising of cigarettes and all other forms of tobacco).

to·bac·con·ist /təˈbækənɪst/ *noun* **1** a person who owns, manages or works in a shop/store selling cigarettes, tobacco for pipes, etc. **2 to·bac·con·ist's** (*pl.* **to·bac·con·ists**) a shop/store that sells cigarettes, tobacco, etc: *There's a tobacconist's on the corner.*

to·bog·gan /təˈbɒɡən; *NAmE* -ˈbɑːɡ-/ *noun, verb*

▪ ***noun*** a long light narrow SLEDGE (= a vehicle that slides over snow) sometimes curved up in front, used for sliding down slopes

▪ ***verb*** [I] to travel down a slope on snow or ice using a toboggan ▸ **to·bog·gan·ing** *noun* [U]

toc·cata /təˈkɑːtə/ *noun* a piece of music for a keyboard instrument which includes difficult passages designed to show the player's skill

toc·sin /ˈtɒksɪn; *NAmE* ˈtɑːk-/ *noun* (*old use*) a warning bell or signal

tod /tɒd; *NAmE* tɑːd/ *noun*

IDM **on your ˈtod** (*old-fashioned, BrE, informal*) on your own; alone

today 🔑 /təˈdeɪ/ *adv., noun*

▪ ***adv.*** **1** 🔑 on this day: *I've got a piano lesson later today.* ◇ *The exams start **a week today/today week*** (= one week from now). **2** 🔑 at the present period SYN **nowadays**: *Young people today face a very difficult future at work.*

▪ ***noun*** [U] **1** 🔑 this day: *Today is her tenth birthday.* ◇ *The review is in today's paper.* ◇ *I'm leaving a week from today.* **2** 🔑 the present period of time: *today's young people*

tod·dle /ˈtɒdl; *NAmE* ˈtɑːdl/ *verb* **1** [I] when a young child who has just learnt to walk **toddles**, he/she walks with short, unsteady steps **2** [I] **+ adv./prep.** (*informal*) to walk or go somewhere: *She toddles down to the park most afternoons.* ◇ *I locked the door and then toddled off to bed.*

tod·dler /ˈtɒdlə(r); *NAmE* ˈtɑːd-/ *noun* a child who has only recently learnt to walk

toddy /ˈtɒdi; *NAmE* ˈtɑːdi/ *noun* [C, U] (*pl.* -ies) a drink made with strong alcohol, sugar, hot water and sometimes spices

tod·ger /ˈtɒdʒə(r); *NAmE* ˈtɑːdʒər/ *noun* (*BrE, informal*) a man's PENIS

to-do /təˈduː/ *noun* [sing.] (*informal, becoming old-fashioned*) unnecessary excitement or anger about sth SYN **fuss**: *What a to-do!*

toe 🔑 /təʊ; *NAmE* toʊ/ *noun, verb*

▪ ***noun*** **1** 🔑 one of the five small parts that stick out from the foot: *the **big/little toe*** (= the largest/smallest toe) ◇ *I stubbed my toe on the step.* ◇ *Can you **touch your toes**?* (= by bending over while keeping your legs straight) ➲ VISUAL VOCAB page V48 **2** 🔑 the part of a sock, shoe, etc. that covers the toes ➲ VISUAL VOCAB page V52 **3 -toed** (in adjectives) having the type or number of toes mentioned: *open-toed sandals* ◇ *a three-toed sloth* ➲ see also PIGEON-TOED

IDM **keep sb on their ˈtoes** to make sure that sb is ready to deal with anything that might happen by doing things that they are not expecting: *Surprise visits help to keep the staff on their toes.* **make sb's ˈtoes curl** to make sb feel embarrassed or uncomfortable ➲ see also TOE-CURLING ➲ more at DIG *v.*, DIP *v.*, HEAD *n.*, STEP *v.*, TOP *n.*, TREAD *v.*

▪ ***verb***

IDM **toe the ˈline** (*NAmE* also **toe the ˈmark**) to say or do what sb in authority tells you to say or do, even if you do not share the same opinions, etc: *to toe the party line*

toe·cap /ˈtəʊkæp; *NAmE* ˈtoʊ-/ *noun* a piece of metal or leather that covers the front part of a shoe or boot to make it stronger

T

ˈ**toe-curling** *adj.* (*informal*) extremely embarrassing because of being very bad or silly ▶ ˈ**toe-curling·ly** *adv.*: *a toe-curlingly awful movie*

TOEFL™ /ˈtəʊfl; *NAmE* ˈtoʊfl/ *abbr.* Test of English as a Foreign Language (a test of a person's level of English that is taken in order to go to a university in the US)

toe·hold /ˈtəʊhəʊld; *NAmE* ˈtoʊhoʊld/ *noun* **1** a position in a place or an activity which you hope will lead to more power or success: *The firm is anxious to gain a toehold in Europe.* **2** a very small hole or space on a CLIFF, just big enough to put your foot in when you are climbing

TOEIC™ /ˈtəʊɪk; *NAmE* ˈtoʊɪk/ *noun* [U] the abbreviation for 'Test of English for International Communication' (a test that measures your ability to read and understand English if it is not your first language)

toe·nail /ˈtəʊneɪl; *NAmE* ˈtoʊ-/ *noun* the nail on a toe ➲ VISUAL VOCAB page V48

toe·rag /ˈtəʊræg; *NAmE* ˈtoʊ-/ *noun* (*BrE, slang*) used as a rude and offensive way of addressing sb you do not like or that you are angry with

ˈ**toe-tapping** *adj.* (*informal*) (of music) lively and making you want to move your feet

toey /ˈtəʊi; *NAmE* ˈtoʊi/ *adj.* (*AustralE, NZE, informal*) (of a person or an animal) nervous or not able to keep still

toff /tɒf; *NAmE* tɑːf/ *noun* (*BrE, informal*) a disapproving way of referring to sb from a high social class

tof·fee /ˈtɒfi; *NAmE* ˈtɔːfi; ˈtɑːfi/ *noun* [U, C] a hard sticky sweet/candy made by heating sugar, butter and water together and allowing it to cool

IDM **can't do sth for ˈtoffee** (*old-fashioned, BrE, informal*) if sb **can't do sth for toffee**, they are very bad at doing it: *He can't dance for toffee!*

ˈ**toffee apple** (*BrE*) (*NAmE* ˈ**candy apple**) *noun* an apple covered with a thin layer of hard toffee and fixed on a stick

ˈ**toffee-nosed** *adj.* (*old-fashioned, BrE, informal*) behaving as if you are better than other people, especially those of a lower social class SYN **snobbish**

tofu /ˈtəʊfuː; *NAmE* ˈtoʊfuː/ (also ˈ**bean curd**) *noun* [U] a soft white substance that is made from SOYA and used in cooking, often instead of meat

tog /tɒg; *NAmE* tɑːg/ *noun, verb*

■ *noun* (*BrE*) **1 togs** [pl.] (*informal*, becoming *old-fashioned*) clothes, especially ones that you wear for a particular purpose: *running togs* **2** a unit for measuring the warmth of DUVETS, etc.

■ *verb* (-gg-)

IDM **be ˌtogged ˈout/ˈup** (**in sth**) (*informal*) to be wearing clothes for a particular activity or occasion: *They were all togged up in their skiing gear.*

toga /ˈtəʊgə; *NAmE* ˈtoʊgə/ *noun* a loose outer piece of clothing worn by the citizens of ancient Rome

to·gether 🔑 /təˈgeðə(r)/ *adv., adj.*

■ *adv.* HELP For the special uses of **together** in phrasal verbs, look at the entries for the verbs. For example **pull yourself together** is in the phrasal verb section at **pull**. **1** 🔑 with or near to sb/sth else; with each other: *We grew up together.* ◇ *Together they climbed the dark stairs.* ◇ *Get all the ingredients together before you start cooking.* ◇ *Stay **close together**—I don't want anyone to get lost.* **2** 🔑 so that two or more things touch or are joined to or combined with each other: *He rubbed his hands together in satisfaction.* ◇ *She nailed the two boards together.* ◇ *Mix the sand and cement together.* ◇ ***Taken together**, these factors are highly significant.* ◇ *He has **more** money **than the rest of** us **put together**.* **3** 🔑 (of two people) in a close relationship, for example a marriage: *They split up after ten years together.* **4** 🔑 in or into agreement: *After the meeting the two sides in the dispute were no closer together.* **5** 🔑 at the same time: *They both spoke together.* ◇ (*informal*) ***All together now**: 'Happy birthday to you…'* **6 for hours, days, etc.** ~ (*formal*) for hours, days, etc. without stopping: *She sat for hours together just staring into space.*

IDM **together with 1** 🔑 including: *Together with the Johnsons, there were 12 of us in the villa.* **2** 🔑 in addition to; as well as: *I sent my order, together with a cheque for £40.*

■ *adj.* (*informal, approving*) (of a person) well organized and confident: *He's incredibly together for someone so young.*

to·gether·ness /təˈgeðənəs; *NAmE* -ðərn-/ *noun* [U] the happy feeling you have when you are with people you like, especially family and friends

tog·gle /ˈtɒgl; *NAmE* ˈtɑːgl/ *noun, verb*

■ *noun* **1** a short piece of wood, plastic, etc. that is put through a LOOP of thread to fasten sth, such as a coat or bag, instead of a button ➲ VISUAL VOCAB page V51 **2** (also ˈ**toggle switch**) (*computing*) a key on a computer that you press to change from one style or operation to another, and back again

■ *verb* [I, T] (*computing*) to press a key or set of keys on a computer keyboard in order to turn a feature on or off, or to move from one program, etc. to another: ~ (**between A and B**) *He toggled between the two windows.* ◇ ~ **sth** *This key toggles various views of the data.*

ˈ**toggle switch** *noun* **1** an electrical switch which you move up and down or backwards and forwards **2** (*computing*) = TOGGLE (2)

toil /tɔɪl/ *verb, noun*

■ *verb* (*formal*) **1** [I] to work very hard and/or for a long time, usually doing hard physical work SYN **slave away** **2** [I] + **adv./prep.** to move slowly and with difficulty SYN **slog**: *They toiled up the hill in the blazing sun.* ▶ **toil·er** *noun*

■ *noun* [U] (*formal* or *literary*) hard unpleasant work that makes you very tired: *a life of hardship and toil* ➲ see also TOILS

toi·let 🔑 /ˈtɔɪlət/ *noun*

1 🔑 [C] a large bowl attached to a pipe that you sit on or stand over when you get rid of waste matter from your body: *Have you flushed the toilet?* ◇ (*BrE*) *I need to **go to the toilet*** (= use the toilet). ◇ *a toilet seat* ◇ *toilet facilities* ◇ *Do you **need the toilet**?* ➲ VISUAL VOCAB page V21 **2** 🔑 (*BrE*) (*NAmE* **bath·room**) [C] a room containing a toilet: *Every flat has its own bathroom and toilet.* ◇ *Who's in the toilet?* **3** 🔑 (*BrE*) [C] (also **toi·lets** [pl.]) a room or small building containing several toilets, each in a separate smaller room: *public toilets* ◇ *Could you tell me where the ladies' toilet is, please?* **4** [U] (*old-fashioned*) the process of washing and dressing yourself, arranging your hair, etc.

British / American

toilet / bathroom

- In *BrE*, but not in *NAmE*, the room that has a toilet in it is usually referred to as a **toilet**. This room in people's houses can also be called the **lavatory**, or informally, the **loo**. An extra downstairs toilet in a house can be called the **cloakroom**. In public places, especially on signs, the words **toilets**, **Gents** (for men's toilets) or **Ladies** (for women's toilets) are used for a room or small building containing several toilets. You might also see **WC** or **Public Conveniences** on some signs.
- In *NAmE* the room that contains a toilet is usually called the **bathroom**, never the **toilet**. A room with a toilet in a public place can also be called a **restroom**, **ladies' room**, **women's room** or **men's room**. **Washroom** is also used, especially in Canada.

ˈ**toilet bag** *noun* (*BrE*) = SPONGE BAG

ˈ**toilet paper** (also ˈ**toilet tissue**) *noun* [U] thin soft paper used for cleaning yourself after you have used the toilet: *a roll of toilet paper* ➲ VISUAL VOCAB page V21

toi·let·ries /ˈtɔɪlətriz/ *noun* [pl.] things such as soap or TOOTHPASTE that you use for washing, cleaning your teeth, etc. ➲ VISUAL VOCAB page V21

ˈ**toilet roll** *noun* (*BrE*) a roll of toilet paper ➲ picture at ROLL

ˈ**toiletry bag** (*NAmE*) (*BrE* ˈ**sponge bag**, ˈ**toilet bag**, **wash·bag**) *noun* a small bag for holding your soap, TOOTHBRUSH, etc. when you are travelling ➲ VISUAL VOCAB page V21

ˈ**toilet soap** *noun* [U, C] soap that you use for washing yourself

ˈ**toilet-train** *verb* [usually passive] **~ sb** to teach a small child to use the toilet ▸ ˈ**toilet-trained** *adj.* ˈ**toilet-training** *noun* [U]

ˈ**toilet water** *noun* [U, C] a kind of PERFUME (= a pleasant smelling liquid for the skin) that has water added to it and is not very expensive

toils /tɔɪlz/ *noun* [pl.] (*formal* or *literary*) if you are caught in **the toils** of an unpleasant feeling or situation, you cannot escape from it SYN **snare**

toing /ˈtuːɪŋ/ *noun*

IDM ˌ**toing and ˈfroing 1** movement or travel backwards and forwards between two or more places: *All this toing and froing between London and New York takes it out of him.* **2** a lot of unnecessary or repeated activity or discussion: *After a great deal of toing and froing, I decided not to change jobs after all.*

toke /təʊk; *NAmE* toʊk/ *noun* (*informal*) an act of breathing in smoke from a cigarette containing MARIJUANA ▸ **toke** *verb* [I]

token /ˈtəʊkən; *NAmE* ˈtoʊ-/ *noun, adj.*

▪ ***noun* 1** a round piece of metal or plastic used instead of money to operate some machines or as a form of payment: *a parking token* **2** (*BrE*) a piece of paper that you pay for and that sb can exchange for sth in a shop/store: *a £20* ***book/record/gift token*** **3** a piece of paper that you can collect when you buy a particular product and then exchange for sth: *Collect six tokens for a free T-shirt.* **4** something that is a symbol of a feeling, a fact, an event, etc. SYN **expression**, **mark**: *Please accept this small gift* ***as a token of*** *our gratitude.*

IDM **by the same ˈtoken** for the same reasons: *The penalty for failure will be high. But, by the same token, the rewards for success will be great.*

▪ ***adj.*** [only before noun] **1** involving very little effort or feeling and intended only as a way of showing other people that you think sb/sth is important, when really you are not sincere: *The government has only made a token gesture towards helping the unemployed.* ◇ *There was one token woman on the committee* (= a woman who is included in the group to make it look as if women are always included, although that is not true). **2** done as a symbol to show that you are serious about sth and will keep a promise or an agreement or do more later: *The government agreed to send a small token force to the area.* ◇ *a one-day token strike* **3** (of a small amount of money) that you pay or charge sb only as a symbol, because a payment is expected SYN **nominal**: *We charge only a token fee for use of the facilities.*

token·ism /ˈtəʊkənɪzəm; *NAmE* ˈtoʊ-/ *noun* [U] (*disapproving*) the fact of doing sth only in order to do what the law requires or to satisfy a particular group of people, but not in a way that is really sincere: *Appointing one woman to the otherwise all-male staff could look like tokenism.*

to·kol·oshe /ˈtɒkɒlɒʃ; *NAmE* ˈtɑːkəlɑːʃ/ *noun* (*SAfrE*) an evil imaginary creature that some people believe can harm you while you are sleeping

Tok Pisin /ˌtɒk ˈpɪzən; -sən; *NAmE* ˌtɑːk/ (also **Pidgin**) *noun* [U] a CREOLE language based on English, used in Papua New Guinea

told *past tense, past part.* of TELL

tol·er·able /ˈtɒlərəbl; *NAmE* ˈtɑːl-/ *adj.* (*formal*) **1** fairly good, but not of the best quality SYN **reasonable**: *a tolerable degree of success* **2** that you can accept or bear, although unpleasant or painful SYN **bearable**: *At times, the heat was barely tolerable.* OPP **intolerable** ▸ **tol·er·ably** /ˈtɒlərəbli; *NAmE* ˈtɑːl-/ *adv.*: *He plays the piano tolerably (well).*

tol·er·ance /ˈtɒlərəns; *NAmE* ˈtɑːl-/ *noun* **1** [U] **~ (of/for sb/sth)** the willingness to accept or TOLERATE sb/sth, especially opinions or behaviour that you may not agree with, or people who are not like you: *She had no tolerance for jokes of any kind.* ◇ *religious tolerance* ◇ *a reputation for tolerance towards refugees* ➲ see also ZERO TOLERANCE OPP **intolerance 2** [C, U] **~ (to sth)** the ability to suffer sth, especially pain, difficult conditions, etc. without being harmed: *tolerance to cold* ◇ *Tolerance to alcohol decreases with age.* **3** [C, U] (*technical*) the amount by which the measurement of a value can vary without causing problems: *They were working to a tolerance of 0.0001 of a centimetre.*

tol·er·ant /ˈtɒlərənt; *NAmE* ˈtɑːl-/ *adj.* **1 ~ (of/towards sb/sth)** able to accept what other people say or do even if you do not agree with it: *He has a very tolerant attitude towards other religions.* **2 ~ (of sth)** (of plants, animals or machines) able to survive or operate in difficult conditions: *The plants are tolerant of frost.* OPP **intolerant** ▸ **tol·er·ant·ly** *adv.*

tol·er·ate /ˈtɒləreɪt; *NAmE* ˈtɑːl-/ *verb* **1** to allow sb to do sth that you do not agree with or like SYN **put up with**: **~ sth** *Their relationship was tolerated but not encouraged.* ◇ *This sort of behaviour will not be tolerated.* ◇ **~ (sb/sth) doing/being/having sth** *She refused to tolerate being called a liar.* **2 ~ sb/sth** to accept sb/sth that is annoying, unpleasant, etc. without complaining SYN **put up with**: *There is a limit to what one person can tolerate.* ◇ *I don't know how you tolerate that noise!* **3 ~ sth** to be able to be affected by a drug, difficult conditions, etc. without being harmed: *She tolerated the chemotherapy well.* ◇ *Few plants will tolerate sudden changes in temperature.*

tol·er·ation /ˌtɒləˈreɪʃn; *NAmE* ˌtɑːl-/ *noun* [U] a willingness to allow sth that you do not like or agree with to happen or continue SYN **tolerance**: *religious toleration*

toll /təʊl; *NAmE* toʊl/ *noun, verb*

▪ ***noun* 1** [C] money that you pay to use a particular road or bridge: *motorway tolls* ◇ *a* ***toll road/bridge*** ➲ SYNONYMS at RATE **2** [C, usually sing.] the amount of damage or the number of deaths and injuries that are caused in a particular war, disaster, etc: *The official* ***death toll*** *has now reached 7 000.* ◇ *the war's growing casualty toll* **3** [sing.] the sound of a bell ringing with slow regular strokes **4** [C] (*NAmE*) a charge for a telephone call that is calculated at a higher rate than a local call

IDM **take a heavy ˈtoll (on sb/sth)** | **take its ˈtoll (on sb/sth)** to have a bad effect on sb/sth; to cause a lot of damage, deaths, suffering, etc: *Illness had taken a heavy toll on her.* ◇ *The recession is taking its toll on the housing markets.*

▪ ***verb*** [I, T] when a bell **tolls** or sb **tolls** it, it is rung slowly many times, especially as a sign that sb has died: **~ (for sb)** *The Abbey bell tolled for those killed in the war.* ◇ **~ sth** *The bell tolled the hour.* ◇ (*figurative*) *The revolution* ***tolled the death knell*** (= signalled the end) *for the Russian monarchy.*

toll·booth /ˈtəʊlbuːð; *NAmE* ˈtoʊlbuːθ/ *noun* a small building by the side of a road where you pay to drive on a road, go over a bridge, etc.

ˌ**toll-ˈfree** *adj.* (*NAmE*) (of a telephone call to an organization or a service) that you do not have to pay for: *a toll-free number* ➲ see also FREEPHONE

toll·house cookie /ˌtəʊlhaʊs ˈkʊki; *NAmE* ˌtoʊl-/ *noun* (*US*) a crisp sweet biscuit/cookie that contains small pieces of chocolate

ˈ**toll plaza** *noun* (*US*) a row of TOLLBOOTHS across a road

Tom /tɒm; *NAmE* tɑːm/ *noun*

IDM **any/every ˌTom, ˌDick or ˈHarry** (usually *disapproving*) any ordinary person rather than the people you know or people who have special skills or qualities: *We don't want any Tom, Dick or Harry using the club bar.*

tom /tɒm; *NAmE* tɑːm/ *noun* = TOMCAT

toma·hawk /ˈtɒməhɔːk; *NAmE* ˈtɑːm-/ *noun* a light AXE used by Native Americans

to·mato 🔑 /təˈmɑːtəʊ; *NAmE* təˈmeɪtoʊ/ *noun* [C, U] (*pl.* -oes)

a soft fruit with a lot of juice and shiny red skin that is eaten as a vegetable either raw or cooked: *a bacon, lettuce*

T

and tomato sandwich ◇ *sliced tomatoes* ◇ *tomato plants* ➲ VISUAL VOCAB page V27

tomb /tuːm/ *noun* a large grave, especially one built of stone above or below the ground

tom·bola /tɒmˈbəʊlə; *NAmE* ˌtɑːmˈboʊlə/ *noun* [U, C] (*BrE*) a game in which you buy tickets with numbers on them. If the number on your ticket is the same as the number on one of the prizes, you win the prize.

tom·boy /ˈtɒmbɔɪ; *NAmE* ˈtɑːm-/ *noun* a young girl who enjoys activities and games that are traditionally considered to be for boys

tomb·stone /ˈtuːmstəʊn; *NAmE* -stoʊn/ *noun* a large, flat stone that lies over a grave or stands at one end, that shows the name, age, etc. of the person buried there ➲ compare GRAVESTONE, HEADSTONE

tom·cat /ˈtɒmkæt; *NAmE* ˈtɑːm-/ (also **tom**) *noun* a male cat

tome /təʊm; *NAmE* toʊm/ *noun* (*formal*) a large heavy book, especially one dealing with a serious topic

tom·fool /ˌtɒmˈfuːl; *NAmE* ˌtɑːm-/ *noun* (*old-fashioned*) a silly person ▸ **tom·fool** *adj.* [only before noun]

tom·fool·ery /tɒmˈfuːləri; *NAmE* tɑːm-/ *noun* [U] (*old-fashioned*) silly behaviour SYN **foolishness**

Tommy /ˈtɒmi; *NAmE* ˈtɑːmi/ *noun* (*old use, informal*) a British soldier

ˈ**tommy gun** *noun* a type of SUB-MACHINE GUN

tommy·rot /ˈtɒmirɒt; *NAmE* ˈtɑːmirɑːt/ *noun* [U] (*old-fashioned*) nonsense

tom·og·raphy /təˈmɒɡrəfi; *NAmE* -ˈmɑːɡ-/ *noun* [U] a way of producing an image of the inside of the human body or a solid object using X-RAYS or ULTRASOUND

to·mor·row 0‒ /təˈmɒrəʊ; *NAmE* təˈmɔːroʊ; -ˈmɑːr-/ *adv., noun*

■ ***adv.*** on or during the day after today: *I'm off now. See you tomorrow.* ◇ *She's leaving tomorrow.* ◇ *(especially BrE) They arrive* ***a week tomorrow/tomorrow week*** (= after a week, starting from tomorrow). IDM see JAM *n.*

■ ***noun*** [U] **1** 0‒ the day after today: *Today is Tuesday, so tomorrow is Wednesday.* ◇ ***tomorrow afternoon/morning/night/evening*** ◇ *I'll see you* ***the day after tomorrow****.* ◇ *The announcement will appear in tomorrow's newspapers.* ◇ *I want it done by tomorrow.* **2** 0‒ the future: *Who knows what changes tomorrow may bring?* ◇ *Tomorrow's workers will have to be more adaptable.*

IDM **do sth as if/like there's no toˈmorrow** to do sth a lot or as though you do not care what effects it will have: *I ate as if there was no tomorrow.* ◇ *She spends money like there's no tomorrow.*

T

ˈ**tom-tom** *noun* a tall narrow drum that you play with your hands ➲ VISUAL VOCAB page V30

ton 0‒ /tʌn/ *noun*

1 0‒ [C] (*pl.* **tons** or **ton**) a unit for measuring weight, in Britain 2 240 pounds (**long ton**) and in the US 2 000 pounds (**short ton**): (*informal*) *What have you got in this bag? It weighs a ton!* ➲ compare TONNE **2** [C] a unit for measuring the size of a ship. 1 ton is equal to 100 CUBIC feet. **3 tons** [pl.] (*informal*) a lot: *They've got tons of money.* ◇ *I've still got tons to do.* **4 a/the ton** (*BrE, informal*) 100, especially when connected with a speed of 100 miles per hour: *He was caught doing a ton.*

IDM **like a ton of ˈbricks** (*informal*) very heavily; very severely: *Disappointment hit her like a ton of bricks.* ◇ *They* ***came down on him like a ton of bricks*** (= criticized him very severely).

tonal /ˈtəʊnl; *NAmE* ˈtoʊnl/ *adj.* **1** (*technical*) relating to tones of sound or colour **2** (*music*) having a particular KEY OPP **atonal** ▸ **tonal·ly** *adv.*

ton·al·ity /təʊˈnæləti; *NAmE* toʊ-/ *noun* [U, C] (*pl.* -ies) (*music*) the quality of a piece of music that depends on the KEY in which it is written

tone 0‒ /təʊn; *NAmE* toʊn/ *noun, verb*

■ ***noun***

▸ OF VOICE **1** 0‒ [C] the quality of sb's voice, especially expressing a particular emotion: *speaking in* ***hushed/low/clipped/measured, etc. tones*** ◇ *a conversational tone* ◇ *a tone of surprise* ◇ *Don't speak to me in that* ***tone of voice*** (= in that unpleasant way). ◇ *There's no need to* ***take that tone*** *with me—it's not my fault we're late.*

▸ CHARACTER/ATMOSPHERE **2** 0‒ [sing.] the general character and attitude of sth such as a piece of writing, or the atmosphere of an event: *The overall tone of the book is gently nostalgic.* ◇ *She* ***set the tone for*** *the meeting with a firm statement of company policy.* ◇ *Trust you to* ***lower the tone*** *of the conversation* (= for example by telling a rude joke). ◇ *The article was moderate* ***in tone*** *and presented both sides of the case.*

▸ OF SOUND **3** 0‒ [C] the quality of a sound, especially the sound of a musical instrument or one produced by electronic equipment: *the full rich tone of the trumpet* ◇ *the volume and tone controls on a car stereo*

▸ COLOUR **4** [C] a shade of a colour: *a carpet in warm tones of brown and orange*

▸ OF MUSCLES/SKIN **5** [U] how strong and firm your muscles or skin are: *how to improve your* ***muscle/skin tone***

▸ ON TELEPHONE **6** [C] a sound heard on a telephone line: (*BrE*) *the* ***dialling tone*** ◇ (*NAmE*) *the* ***dial tone*** ◇ *Please speak after the tone* (= for example as an instruction on an answering machine).

▸ IN MUSIC **7** (*BrE*) (*US* ˈ**whole step**) [C] one of the five longer INTERVALS in a musical SCALE, for example the INTERVAL between C and D or between E and F♯ ➲ compare SEMITONE, STEP *n.* (10)

▸ PHONETICS **8** [C] the PITCH (= how high or low a sound is) of a syllable in speaking: *a* ***rising/falling tone*** **9** a particular PITCH pattern on a syllable in languages such as Chinese, that can be used to distinguish different meanings

▸ -TONED **10** (in adjectives) having the type of tone mentioned: *a bright-toned soprano* ◇ *olive-toned skin*

■ ***verb***

▸ MUSCLES/SKIN **1** [T] **~ sth (up)** to make your muscles, skin, etc. firmer and stronger: *Massage will help to tone up loose skin under the chin.* ◇ *a beautifully toned body*

▸ COLOUR **2** [I] **~ (in) (with sth)** (*BrE*) to match the colour of sth: *The beige of his jacket toned (in) with the cream shirt.*

PHR V ˌ**tone sth↔ˈdown 1** to make a speech, an opinion, etc. less extreme or offensive: *The language of the article will have to be toned down for the mass market.* **2** to make a colour less bright

ˌ**tone-ˈdeaf** *adj.* unable to hear the difference between musical notes

ˈ**tone language** *noun* a language in which differences in TONE *n.* (9) can change the meaning of words

tone·less /ˈtəʊnləs; *NAmE* ˈtoʊn-/ *adj.* (of a voice, etc.) dull or flat; not expressing any emotion or interest ▸ **tone·less·ly** *adv.*

ˈ**tone poem** *noun* a piece of music that is intended to describe a place or express an idea

toner /ˈtəʊnə(r); *NAmE* ˈtoʊ-/ *noun* [U, C] **1** a type of ink used in machines that print or photocopy **2** a liquid or cream used for making the skin on your face firm and smooth

ˈ**tone unit** (also ˈ**tone group**) *noun* (*phonetics*) the basic unit of INTONATION in a language which consists of one or more syllables with a complete PITCH movement

tongs /tɒŋz; *NAmE* tɔːŋz; tɑːŋz/ *noun* [pl.] **1** a tool with two long parts that are joined at one end, used for picking up and holding things: *a pair of tongs* ➲ VISUAL VOCAB pages V23, V24, V57 **2** (also ˈ**curling tongs**) (both *BrE*) (*NAmE* **curling iron**) a tool that is heated and used for curling hair IDM see HAMMER *n.*

tongue 0‒ /tʌŋ/ *noun, verb*

■ ***noun*** **1** 0‒ [C] the soft part in the mouth that moves around, used for tasting, swallowing, speaking, etc: *He clicked his tongue to attract their attention.* ◇ *She ran her tongue over her lips.* ◇ *It's very rude to* ***stick your tongue out*** *at people.* ➲ VISUAL VOCAB page V48 **2** [U, C] the tongue of some animals, cooked and eaten: *a slice of ox tongue*

3 [C] (*formal* or *literary*) a language: *None of the tribes speak the same tongue.* ◇ *I tried speaking to her in her native tongue.* ➲ see also MOTHER TONGUE **4** [sing.] a particular way of speaking: *He has a sharp tongue.* ◇ (*formal*) *I'll thank you to* ***keep a civil tongue in your head*** (= speak politely). ➲ see also SILVER TONGUE **5 -tongued** (in adjectives) speaking in the way mentioned: *sharp-tongued* **6** [C] a long narrow piece of leather under the LACES on a shoe ➲ VISUAL VOCAB page V52 **7** [C] **~ (of sth)** (*literary*) something that is long and narrow and shaped like a tongue: *a tongue of flame*

IDM **get your 'tongue around/round sth** to pronounce a difficult word correctly **,hold your 'tongue/'peace** (*old-fashioned*) to say nothing although you would like to give your opinion **roll/slip/trip off the 'tongue** to be easy to say or pronounce: *It's not a name that exactly trips off the tongue, is it?* **set 'tongues wagging** (*informal*) to cause people to start talking about sb's private affairs **with your tongue in your 'cheek | with tongue in 'cheek** if you say sth **with your tongue in your cheek**, you are not being serious and mean it as a joke ➲ more at BITE *v.*, FIND *v.*, LOOSE *adj.*, LOOSEN *v.*, SLIP *n.*, TIP *n.*, WATCH *v.*

■ ***verb*** **1 ~ sth** to stop the flow of air into a wind instrument with your tongue in order to make a note **2 ~ sth** to LICK sth with your tongue

,tongue and 'groove *noun* [U] wooden boards that have a long cut along one edge and a long RIDGE along the other, which are used to connect them together

'tongue depressor (*NAmE*) (*BrE* **spat·ula**) *noun* a thin flat instrument that doctors use for pressing the tongue down when they are examining sb's throat

,tongue-in-'cheek *adj.* not intended seriously; done or said as a joke: *a tongue-in-cheek remark* ▶ **,tongue-in-'cheek** *adv.*: *The offer was made almost tongue-in-cheek.*

'tongue-tied *adj.* not able to speak because you are shy or nervous

'tongue-twister *noun* a word or phrase that is difficult to say quickly or correctly, such as 'She sells sea shells on the seashore.'

tonic /'tɒnɪk; *NAmE* 'tɑːn-/ *noun* **1** (also **'tonic water**) [U, C] a clear FIZZY drink (= with bubbles in it) with a slightly bitter taste, that is often mixed with a strong alcoholic drink, especially GIN or VODKA: *a gin and tonic* **2** [C] a medicine that makes you feel stronger and healthier, taken especially when you feel tired: *herbal tonics* **3** [C, U] a liquid that you put on your hair or skin in order to make it healthier: *skin tonic* **4** [C, usually sing.] (*old-fashioned*) anything that makes people feel healthier or happier: *The weekend break was just the tonic I needed.* **5** [C] (*music*) the first note of a SCALE of eight notes **6** (also **,tonic 'sylla·ble**) [C] (*phonetics*) the syllable in a TONE UNIT on which a change in PITCH takes place

,tonic ,sol-'fa *noun* = SOL-FA

ton·ify /'təʊnɪfaɪ; *NAmE* 'toʊn-/ *verb* (**toni·fies, toni·fy·ing, toni·fied, toni·fied**) **~ sth** to make a part of the body firmer, smoother and stronger, by exercise or by applying special creams, etc.

to·night 0-w /tə'naɪt/ *adv.*, *noun*

■ ***adv.*** on or during the evening or night of today: *Will you have dinner with me tonight?* ◇ *It's cold tonight.*

■ ***noun*** [U] the evening or night of today: *Here are tonight's football results.* ◇ *Tonight will be cloudy.*

ton·nage /'tʌnɪdʒ/ *noun* [U, C] **1** the size of a ship or the amount it can carry, expressed in tons **2** the total amount that sth weighs

tonne 0-w /tʌn/ (*pl.* **tonnes** or **tonne**) (also **,metric 'ton**) *noun*
a unit for measuring weight, equal to 1 000 kilograms: *a record grain harvest of 236m tonnes* ◇ *a 17-tonne truck* ➲ compare TON

ton·sil /'tɒnsl; *NAmE* 'tɑːnsl/ *noun* either of the two small organs at the sides of the throat, near the base of the tongue: *I've had my tonsils out* (= removed). ➲ VISUAL VOCAB page V48

ton·sil·lec·tomy /,tɒnsə'lektəmi; *NAmE* ,tɑːn-/ *noun* (*pl.* **-ies**) (*medical*) a medical operation to remove the TONSILS

ton·sil·litis /,tɒnsə'laɪtɪs; *NAmE* ,tɑːn-/ *noun* [U] an infection of the tonsils in which they become swollen and sore

ton·sure /'tɒnʃə(r); *NAmE* 'tɑːn-/ *noun* the part of a MONK's or priest's head that has been shaved

Tony /'təʊni; *NAmE* 'toʊni/ *noun* (*pl.* **Tonys**) an award given in the US for achievement in the theatre

tony /'təʊni; *NAmE* 'toʊni/ *adj.* (*NAmE*, *informal*, becoming *old-fashioned*) fashionable and expensive

too 0-w /tuː/ *adv.*

1 0-w used before adjectives and adverbs to say that sth is more than is good, necessary, possible, etc.: *He's* ***far too*** *young to go on his own.* ◇ *This is too large a helping for me/ This helping is too large for me.* ◇ *Is it too much to ask for a little quiet?* ◇ *The dress was too tight for me.* ◇ *It's too late to do anything about it now.* ◇ *Accidents like this happen* ***all too*** (= much too) *often.* **2** 0-w (usually placed at the end of a clause) also; as well: *Can I come too?* ◇ *When I've finished painting the bathroom, I'm going to do the kitchen too.* ➲ note at ALSO ➲ see also ME-TOO **3** used to comment on sth that makes a situation worse: *She broke her leg last week—and on her birthday too!* **4** 0-w very: *I'm not too sure if this is right.* ◇ *I'm just going out—I won't be too long.* ◇ *She's* ***none too*** (= not very) *clever.* **5** used to emphasize sth, especially your anger, surprise or agreement with sth: *'He did apologize eventually.' 'I should think so too!'* ◇ *'She gave me the money.' 'About time too!'*

IDM **be too 'much (for sb)** 0-w to need more skill or strength than you have; to be more difficult, annoying, etc. than you can bear ➲ more at RIGHT *adj.*

took *past tense* of TAKE

tool 0-w /tuːl/ *noun*, *verb*

■ ***noun*** **1** 0-w an instrument such as a hammer, SCREWDRIVER, SAW, etc. that you hold in your hand and use for making things, repairing things, etc: *garden tools* ◇ *a cutting tool* ◇ *power tools* (= using electricity) ◇ *Always select the right tool for the job.* ➲ VISUAL VOCAB page V17 **2** 0-w a thing that helps you to do your job or to achieve sth: *research tools like questionnaires* ◇ *The computer is now an invaluable tool for the family doctor.* ◇ *Some of them carried the guns which were* ***the tools of their trade*** (= the things they needed to do their job). **3** a person who is used or controlled by another person or group: *The prime minister was an unwitting tool of the president.* **4** (*taboo, slang*) a PENIS IDM see DOWN *v.*

■ ***verb*** [I] **+ adv./prep.** (*NAmE*, *informal*) to drive around in a vehicle

PHR V **,tool 'up | ,tool sb/sth↔'up** (*technical*) to get or provide sb/sth with the equipment, etc. that is necessary to do or produce sth: *The factory is not tooled up to produce this type of engine.*

tool·bar /'tuːlbɑː(r)/ *noun* (*computing*) a row of symbols (=ICONS) on a computer screen that show the different things that you can do with a particular program

tool·box /'tuːlbɒks; *NAmE* -bɑːks/ *noun* a box with a lid for keeping tools in ➲ VISUAL VOCAB page V17

tooled /tuːld/ *adj.* (of leather) decorated with patterns made with a special heated tool

tool·kit /'tuːlkɪt/ *noun* **1** a set of tools in a box or bag **2** (*computing*) a set of software tools **3** the things that you need in order to achieve sth

tool·maker /'tuːlmeɪkə(r)/ *noun* a person or company that makes tools, especially ones used in industry ▶ **tool·mak·ing** /'tuːlmeɪkɪŋ/ *noun* [U]

toonie /'tuːni/ *noun* (*CanE*) the Canadian two-dollar coin

toot /tuːt/ *noun*, *verb*

■ ***noun*** a short high sound made by a car horn or a whistle: *She gave a sharp toot on her horn.*

■ ***verb*** [I, T] (*especially BrE*) when a car horn **toots** or you **toot** it, it makes a short high sound: *the sound of horns tooting* ◇ **~ sth** *Toot your horn to let them know we're here.* IDM see HORN

T

tooth 0→ /tuːθ/ *noun* (*pl.* teeth /tiːθ/)
1 0→ any of the hard white structures in the mouth used for biting and chewing food: *I've just* **had a tooth out** *at the dentist's.* ◇ *to* **brush/clean your teeth** ◇ **tooth decay** ◇ *She answered* **through clenched teeth** (= opening her mouth only a little because of anger). ◇ *The cat* **sank its teeth into** *his finger.* ➲ COLLOCATIONS at PHYSICAL ➲ VISUAL VOCAB page V48 ➲ see also BUCK TEETH, FALSE TEETH, MILK TOOTH, WISDOM TOOTH **2** a narrow pointed part that sticks out of an object: *the teeth on a saw* ➲ VISUAL VOCAB page V51 ➲ see also FINE-TOOTH COMB
IDM **cut your teeth on sth** to do sth that gives you your first experience of a particular type of work **cut a 'tooth** (of a baby) to grow a new tooth **get your 'teeth into sth** (*informal*) to put a lot of effort and enthusiasm into sth that is difficult enough to keep you interested: *Choose an essay topic that you can really get your teeth into.* **have 'teeth** (*BrE, informal*) (of an organization, a law, etc.) to be powerful and effective **in the teeth of sth** **1** despite problems, opposition, etc: *The new policy was adopted in the teeth of fierce criticism.* **2** in the direction that a strong wind is coming from: *They crossed the bay in the teeth of a howling gale.* **set sb's 'teeth on edge** (of a sound or taste) to make sb feel physically uncomfortable: *Just the sound of her voice sets my teeth on edge.* ➲ more at ARMED *v.*, BARE *v.*, BIT, EYE *n.*, EYE TEETH, FIGHT *v.*, GNASH, GRIT *v.*, HELL, KICK *v.*, KICK *n.*, LIE[2] *v.*, LONG *adj.*, RED *adj.*, SKIN *n.*, SWEET *adj.*

tooth·ache /'tuːθeɪk/ *noun* [U, C, usually sing.] a pain in your teeth or in one tooth: (*BrE*) *I've got toothache.* ◇ (*NAmE, BrE*) *I've got a toothache.*

tooth·brush /'tuːθbrʌʃ/ *noun* a small brush for cleaning your teeth ➲ VISUAL VOCAB page V21

ˌtoothbrush mous'tache *noun* a short MOUSTACHE cut with square corners

toothed /tuːθt; tuːðd/ *adj.* [only before noun] **1** (*technical*) having teeth: *a toothed whale* **2** **-toothed** (in compounds) having the type of teeth mentioned: *a gap-toothed smile*

the 'tooth fairy *noun* [sing.] an imaginary creature that is said to take away a tooth that a small child leaves near his or her bed at night and to leave a coin there in its place

tooth·less /'tuːθləs/ *adj.* **1** having no teeth: *a toothless old man* ◇ *She gave us a toothless grin.* **2** having no power or authority

tooth·paste /'tuːθpeɪst/ *noun* [U] a substance that you put on a brush and use to clean your teeth ➲ VISUAL VOCAB page V21

tooth·pick /'tuːθpɪk/ *noun* a short pointed piece of wood or plastic used for removing bits of food from between the teeth

tooth·some /'tuːθsəm/ *adj.* (*humorous*) (of food) tasting good SYN **tasty**

toothy /'tuːθi/ *adj.* a **toothy** smile shows a lot of teeth

too·tle /'tuːtl/ *verb* (*informal*) **1** [I] + **adv./prep.** to walk, drive, etc. somewhere without hurrying **2** [I, T] **~ (sth)** to produce a series of notes by blowing into a musical instrument

toot·sies /'tʊtsɪz/ *noun* [pl.] (*informal*) (used by or when speaking to young children) toes or feet

top 0→ /tɒp; *NAmE* tɑːp/ *noun, adj., verb*
■ ***noun***
▸ HIGHEST POINT **1** 0→ [C] the highest part or point of sth: *She was standing* **at the top** *of the stairs.* ◇ *Write your name at the top.* ◇ *The title is* **right at the top** *of the page.* ◇ *He filled my glass* **to the top**. ◇ *We climbed to the* **very top** *of the hill.* ◇ *Snow was falling on the mountain tops.* ◇ (*BrE*) *the top of the milk* (= the cream that rises to the top of a bottle of milk) ◇ *The wind was blowing in the tops of the trees.* ➲ see also ROOFTOP, TREETOP
▸ UPPER SURFACE **2** 0→ [C] the upper flat surface of sth: *Can you polish the top of the table?* ◇ *a desk top* ➲ see also HARDTOP, ROLL-TOP DESK, TABLETOP
▸ HIGHEST RANK **3** 0→ [sing.] **the ~ (of sth)** the highest or most important rank or position: *He's at the top of his profession.* ◇ *She is determined to make it to the top* (= achieve fame or success). ◇ *They finished the season at the top of the league.* ◇ *We have a lot of things to do, but packing is at the* **top of the list**. ◇ *This decision came from the top.*
▸ FARTHEST POINT **4** 0→ [sing.] **the ~ of sth** the end of a street, table, etc. that is farthest away from you or from where you usually come to it: *I'll meet you at the top of Thorpe Street.*
▸ OF PEN/BOTTLE **5** 0→ [C] a thing that you put on the end of sth to close it: *Where's the top of this pen?* ◇ *a bottle with a screw top* ➲ SYNONYMS at LID ➲ VISUAL VOCAB page V29
▸ CLOTHING **6** 0→ [C] a piece of clothing worn on the upper part of the body: *I need a top to go with this skirt.* ◇ *a* **track-suit/pyjama/bikini top** ➲ see also CROP TOP
▸ LEAVES OF PLANT **7** [C, usually pl.] the leaves of a plant that is grown mainly for its root: *Remove the green tops from the carrots.*
▸ AMOUNT OF MONEY **8** **tops** [pl.] (*BrE*) used after an amount of money to show that it is the highest possible: *It couldn't have cost more than £50, tops.*
▸ BEST **9** **tops** [pl.] (*old-fashioned, informal*) a person or thing of the best quality: *Among sports superstars she's (the) tops.* ◇ *In the survey the Brits come out tops for humour.*
▸ TOY **10** [C] a child's toy that spins on a point when it is turned round very quickly by hand or by a string: *She was so confused—her mind was* **spinning like a top**. ➲ see also BIG TOP
IDM **at the top of the 'tree** in the highest position or rank in a profession or career **at the top of your 'voice** as loudly as possible: *She was screaming at the top of her voice.* **come out on 'top** to win a contest or an argument: *In most boardroom disputes he tends to come out on top.* **from ˌtop to 'bottom** going to every part of a place in a very thorough way: *We cleaned the house from top to bottom.* **from ˌtop to 'toe** completely; all over: *She was dressed in green from top to toe.* **get on 'top of sb** to be too much for sb to manage or deal with: *All this extra work is getting on top of him.* **get on 'top of sth** to manage to control or deal with sth: *How will I ever get on top of all this work?* **off the ˌtop of your 'head** (*informal*) just guessing or using your memory, without taking time to think carefully or check the facts: *I can't remember the name off the top of my head, but I can look it up for you.* **on 'top** **1** 0→ on the highest point or surface: *a cake with cream on top* ◇ *Stand on top and look down.* ◇ *He's going bald on top* (= on the top of his head). **2** in a leading position or in control: *She remained on top for the rest of the match.* **3** in addition: *Look, here's 30 dollars, and I'll buy you lunch on top.* **on top of sth/sb** **1** 0→ on, over or covering sth/sb: *Books were piled on top of one another.* ◇ *Many people were crushed when the building collapsed on top of them.* **2** 0→ in addition to sth: *He gets commission on top of his salary.* ◇ *On top of everything else, my car's been stolen.* **3** very close to sth/sb: *We were all living on top of each other in that tiny apartment.* **4** in control of a situation: *Do you think he's really on top of his job?* **on ˌtop of the 'world** very happy or proud **ˌover the 'top** (*abbr.* OTT) (*informal, especially BrE*) done to an exaggerated degree and with too much effort: *His performance is completely over the top.* ◇ *an over-the-top reaction* **ˌtake sth from the 'top** (*informal*) to go back to the beginning of a song, piece of music, etc. and repeat it: *OK, everybody, let's take it from the top.* **up 'top** (*BrE, informal*) used to talk about a person's intelligence: *He hasn't got much up top* (= he isn't very intelligent). ➲ more at BLOW *v.*, HEAP *n.*, PILE *n.*, THIN *adj.*
■ ***adj.*** [usually before noun] **1** 0→ highest in position, rank or degree: *He lives on the top floor.* ◇ *She kept her passport in the top drawer.* ◇ *He's one of the top players in the country.* ◇ *She got the top job.* ◇ *He finished top in the exam.* ◇ *She got top marks for her essay.* ◇ *They're top of the league.* ◇ *The athletes are all on top form* (= performing their best). ◇ *Welfare reform is a top priority for the government.* ◇ *The car was travelling at top speed.* **2** (*BrE, informal*) very good: *He's a top bloke.*
■ ***verb*** (-pp-)
▸ BE MORE **1** **~ sth** to be higher than a particular amount: *Worldwide sales look set to top $1 billion.*
▸ BE THE BEST **2** **~ sth** to be in the highest position on a list

T

because you are the most successful, important, etc: *The band topped the charts for five weeks with their first single.*
▸ PUT ON TOP **3** [usually passive] **~ sth** (**with sth**) to put sth on the top of sth else: *fruit salad topped with cream*
▸ SAY/DO STH BETTER **4 ~ sth** to say or do sth that is better, funnier, more impressive, etc. than sth that sb else has said or done in the past: *I'm afraid the other company has topped your offer* (= offered more money).
▸ KILL YOURSELF **5 ~ yourself** (*BrE, informal*) to kill yourself deliberately
▸ CLIMB HILL **6 ~ sth** (*literary*) to reach the highest point of a hill, etc.
IDM **to top/cap it 'all** (*informal*) used to introduce the final piece of information that is worse than the other bad things that you have just mentioned **ˌtop and 'tail sth** (*BrE*) to cut the top and bottom parts off fruit and vegetables to prepare them to be cooked or eaten
PHR V **ˌtop sth↔'off** (**with sth**) to complete sth successfully by doing or adding one final thing **ˌtop 'out** (**at sth**) if sth **tops out** at a particular price, speed, etc. it does not rise any higher: *Inflation topped out at 12%.* **ˌtop sth↔'up** (*especially BrE*) **1** to fill a container that already has some liquid in it with more liquid: *Top the car up with oil before you set off.* ◇ *Top the oil up before you set off.* **2** to increase the amount of sth to the level you want or need: *She relies on tips to top up her wages.* ◇ (*BrE*) *I need to top up my mobile phone* (= pay more money so you can make more calls). ➲ related noun TOP-UP **ˌtop sb 'up** (*especially BrE*) to fill sb's glass or cup with sth more to drink: *Can I top you up?* ➲ related noun TOP-UP

topaz /ˈtəʊpæz; *NAmE* ˈtoʊ-/ *noun* [C, U] a clear yellow SEMI-PRECIOUS STONE: *a topaz ring*

ˌtop 'brass *noun* [sing.+ sing./pl. v.] (*BrE, informal*) = BRASS

ˌtop-'class *adj.* of the highest quality or standard: *a top-class performance*

top·coat /ˈtɒpkəʊt; *NAmE* ˈtɑːpkoʊt/ *noun* **1** the last layer of paint put on a surface ➲ compare UNDERCOAT **2** (*old-fashioned*) an OVERCOAT

ˌtop 'dog *noun* [usually sing.] (*informal*) a person, group or country that is better than all the others, especially in a situation that involves competition

ˌtop 'dollar *noun*
IDM **pay, earn, charge, etc. top 'dollar** (*informal*) pay, earn, charge, etc. a lot of money: *If you want the best, you have to pay top dollar.* ◇ *We can help you get top dollar when you sell your house.*

ˌtop-'down *adj.* **1** (of a plan, project, etc.) starting with a general idea to which details are added later ➲ compare BOTTOM-UP **2** starting from or involving the people who have higher positions in an organization: *a top-down management style*

ˌtop 'drawer *noun* [sing.] if sb/sth is out of **the top drawer**, they are of the highest social class or of the highest quality ▸ **ˌtop-'drawer** *adj.*

topee = TOPI

ˌtop-'end *adj.* [only before noun] among the best, most expensive, etc. examples of sth: *Many people are upgrading their mobiles to top-end models.*

ˌtop-'flight *adj.* of the highest quality; the best or most successful

ˌtop 'gear *noun* [U] (*BrE*) the highest gear in a vehicle: *They cruised along **in top gear**.* ◇ (*figurative*) *Her career is moving into top gear.*

ˌtop-'grossing *adj.* [only before noun] earning more money than other similar things or people: *the top-grossing movie of 2009*

ˌtop 'hat (also *informal* **top·per**) *noun* a man's tall black or grey hat, worn with formal clothes on very formal occasions ➲ VISUAL VOCAB page V53

ˌtop-'heavy *adj.* **1** too heavy at the top and therefore likely to fall **2** (of an organization) having too many senior staff compared to the number of workers

ˌtop-'hole *adj.* (*old-fashioned, BrE, informal*) excellent

topi (also **topee**) /ˈtəʊpi; *NAmE* ˈtoʊpi; toʊˈpiː/ *noun* a light hard hat worn to give protection from the sun in very hot countries

topi·ary /ˈtəʊpiəri; *NAmE* ˈtoʊpieri/ *noun* [U] the art of cutting bushes into shapes such as birds or animals

topic 0‑ AW /ˈtɒpɪk; *NAmE* ˈtɑːp-/ *noun*
a subject that you talk, write or learn about: *The main **topic of conversation** was Tom's new girlfriend.* ◇ *The article covered a wide range of topics.*
IDM **on topic** (*NAmE*) appropriate or relevant to the situation: *Keep the text short and on topic.* ◇ *Let's get back on topic.*

top·ic·al AW /ˈtɒpɪkl; *NAmE* ˈtɑːp-/ *adj.* **1** connected with sth that is happening or of interest at the present time: *a topical joke/reference* ◇ *topical events* **2** (*medical*) connected with, or put directly on, a part of the body ▸ **top·ic·al·ity** /ˌtɒpɪˈkæləti; *NAmE* ˌtɑːp-/ *noun* [U, sing.]

top·knot /ˈtɒpnɒt; *NAmE* ˈtɑːpnɑːt/ *noun* a way of arranging your hair in which it is tied up on the top of your head

top·less /ˈtɒpləs; *NAmE* ˈtɑːp-/ *adj.* (of a woman) not wearing any clothes on the upper part of the body so that her breasts are not covered: *a topless model* ◇ *a topless bar* (= where the female staff are topless) ▸ **top·less** *adv.*: *to sunbathe topless*

ˌtop-'level *adj.* [only before noun] involving the most important or best people in a company, an organization or a sport: *a top-level meeting* ◇ *top-level tennis*

top·most /ˈtɒpməʊst; *NAmE* ˈtɑːpmoʊst/ *adj.* [only before noun] (*formal*) highest: *the topmost branches of the tree*

ˌtop-'notch *adj.* (*informal*) excellent; of the highest quality

ˌtop of the 'range (*BrE*) (*NAmE* **ˌtop of the 'line**) *adj.* [usually before noun] used to describe the most expensive of a group of similar products: *Our equipment is top of the range.* ◇ *our top-of-the-range model*

top·og·raphy /təˈpɒɡrəfi; *NAmE* təˈpɑːɡ-/ *noun* [U] (*technical*) the physical features of an area of land, especially the position of its rivers, mountains, etc; the study of these features: *a map showing the topography of the island* ▸ **topo·graph·ic·al** /ˌtɒpəˈɡræfɪkl; *NAmE* ˌtɑːpə-/ (also **topo·graph·ic** /ˌtɒpəˈɡræfɪk; *NAmE* ˌtɑːpə-/) *adj.*: *a topographical map/feature* **topo·graph·ic·al·ly** /-kli/ *adv.*

top·ology /təˈpɒlədʒi; *NAmE* -ˈpɑːl-/ *noun* [U, C] (*technical*) the way the parts of sth are arranged and related: *The Canadian banking topology is relatively flat, with a few large banks controlling the entire market.*

topo·nym /ˈtɒpənɪm; *NAmE* ˈtɑːp-/ *noun* (*technical*) a place name

topos /ˈtɒpɒs; *NAmE* ˈtoʊpɑːs; ˈtɑːp-/ *noun* (*pl.* **topoi** /ˈtɒpɔɪ; *NAmE* ˈtoʊ-; ˈtɑː-/) (*technical*) a traditional subject or idea in literature

top·per /ˈtɒpə(r); *NAmE* ˈtɑːp-/ *noun* (*informal*) = TOP HAT

top·ping /ˈtɒpɪŋ; *NAmE* ˈtɑːp-/ *noun* [C, U] a layer of food that you put on top of a dish, cake, etc. to add flavour or to make it look nice

top·ple /ˈtɒpl; *NAmE* ˈtɑːpl/ *verb* **1** [I, T] to become unsteady and fall down; to make sth do this: **+ adv./prep.** *The pile of books toppled over.* ◇ **~ sb/sth + adv./prep.** *He brushed past, toppling her from her stool.* **2** [T] **~ sb/sth** to make sb lose their position of power or authority SYN **overthrow**: *a plot to topple the President*

ˌtop-'ranking *adj.* [only before noun] of the highest rank, status or importance in an organization, a sport, etc.

ˌtop-'rated *adj.* [only before noun] most popular with the public: *a top-rated TV show*

top·sail /ˈtɒpseɪl; ˈtɒpsl; *NAmE* ˈtɑːpseɪl; ˈtɑːpsl/ *noun* [usually sing.] the sail attached to the upper part of the MAST of a ship

ˌtop 'secret *adj.* that must be kept completely secret, especially from other governments: *This information has been classified top secret.* ◇ *top-secret documents*

T

ˌ**top-ˈshelf** *adj.* [only before noun] **1** (*BrE*) including pictures of naked people and/or sexual acts: *top-shelf magazines/DVDs* **2** (*especially NAmE*) of the highest class: *It is a top-shelf law firm.*

top·side /ˈtɒpsaɪd; *NAmE* ˈtɑːp-/ *noun* [U] (*BrE*) a piece of beef that is cut from the upper part of the leg

top·soil /ˈtɒpsɔɪl; *NAmE* ˈtɑːp-/ *noun* [U] the layer of soil nearest the surface of the ground ➲ compare SUBSOIL

top·spin /ˈtɒpspɪn; *NAmE* tɑːp-/ *noun* [U] (*sport*) the fast forward spinning movement that a player can give to a ball by hitting or throwing it in a special way

topsy-turvy /ˌtɒpsi ˈtɜːvi; *NAmE* ˌtɑːpsi ˈtɜːrvi/ *adj.* (*informal*) in a state of great confusion: *Everything's topsy-turvy in my life at the moment.*

ˌ**top ˈtable** (*BrE*) (*NAmE* ˌ**head ˈtable**) *noun* the table at which the most important guests sit at a formal dinner

the ˌ**top ˈten** *noun* [pl.] the ten pop records that have sold the most copies in a particular week

ˈ**top-up** *noun* (*BrE*) **1** a payment that you make to increase the amount of money, etc. to the level that is needed: *a phone top-up* (= to buy more time for calls) ◇ *Students will have to pay top-up fees* (= fees that are above the basic level). **2** (*informal*) an amount of a drink that you add to a cup or glass in order to fill it again: *Can I give anyone a top-up?*

ˈ**top-up card** *noun* a card that you buy for a mobile/cell phone so that you can make more calls to the value of the card

toque /təʊk; *NAmE* toʊk/ *noun* **1** a woman's small hat **2** (*CanE*) a close-fitting hat made of wool, sometimes with a ball of wool on the top

tor /tɔː(r)/ *noun* a small hill with rocks at the top, especially in parts of SW England

Torah /ˈtɔːrɑː; tɔːˈrɑː/ *noun* (usually **the Torah**) (in Judaism) the law of God as given to Moses and recorded in the first five books of the Bible

torch /tɔːtʃ; *NAmE* tɔːrtʃ/ *noun, verb*

▪ ***noun*** **1** (*BrE*) (also **flash·light** *NAmE, BrE*) a small electric lamp that uses batteries and that you can hold in your hand: *Shine the torch on the lock while I try to get the key in.* **2** (*NAmE*) = BLOWTORCH **3** a long piece of wood that has material at one end that is set on fire and that people carry to give light: *a flaming torch* ◇ *the Olympic torch* ◇ (*figurative*) *They struggled to keep the torch of idealism and hope alive.*

IDM **put sth to the ˈtorch** (*literary*) to set fire to sth deliberately ➲ more at CARRY

▪ ***verb*** **~ sth** to set fire to a building or vehicle deliberately in order to destroy it

torch·light /ˈtɔːtʃlaɪt; *NAmE* ˈtɔːrtʃ-/ *noun* [U] the light that is produced by an electric torch or by burning torches

ˈ**torch song** *noun* a type of sad romantic song about feelings of love for a person who does not share those feelings ▶ ˈ**torch singer** *noun*

tore *past tense* of TEAR

torea·dor /ˈtɒriədɔː(r); *NAmE* ˈtɔːr-/ *noun* a man, especially one riding a horse, who fights BULLS to entertain people, for example in Spain

tor·ment *noun, verb*

▪ ***noun*** /ˈtɔːment; *NAmE* ˈtɔːrm-/ [U, C] (*formal*) extreme suffering, especially mental suffering; a person or thing that causes this SYN **anguish**: *the cries of a man* ***in torment*** ◇ *She suffered years of mental torment after her son's death.* ◇ *The flies were a terrible torment.*

▪ ***verb*** /tɔːˈment; *NAmE* tɔːrˈm-/ **1 ~ sb** (*formal*) to make sb suffer very much SYN **plague**: *He was tormented by feelings of insecurity.* **2 ~ sb/sth** to annoy a person or an animal in a cruel way because you think it is amusing SYN **torture**

tor·ment·or /tɔːˈmentə(r); *NAmE* tɔːrˈm-/ *noun* (*formal*) a person who causes sb to suffer

torn *past part.* of TEAR

tor·nado /tɔːˈneɪdəʊ; *NAmE* tɔːrˈneɪdoʊ/ *noun* (*pl.* **-oes** or **-os**) a violent storm with very strong winds which move in a circle. There is often also a long cloud which is narrower at the bottom than the top. ➲ COLLOCATIONS at WEATHER

tor·pedo /tɔːˈpiːdəʊ; *NAmE* tɔːrˈpiːdoʊ/ *noun, verb*

▪ ***noun*** (*pl.* **-oes**) a long narrow bomb that is fired under the water from a ship or SUBMARINE and that explodes when it hits a ship, etc.

▪ ***verb*** (**tor·pe·does**, **tor·pe·do·ing**, **tor·pe·doed**, **tor·pe·doed**) **1 ~ sth** to attack a ship or make it sink using a torpedo **2 ~ sth** to completely destroy the possibility that sth could succeed: *Her comments had torpedoed the deal.*

tor·pid /ˈtɔːpɪd; *NAmE* ˈtɔːrpɪd/ *adj.* (*formal*) not active; with no energy or enthusiasm SYN **lethargic**

tor·por /ˈtɔːpə(r); *NAmE* ˈtɔːrp-/ *noun* [U, sing.] (*formal*) the state of not being active and having no energy or enthusiasm SYN **lethargy**: *In the heat they sank into a state of torpor.*

torque /tɔːk; *NAmE* tɔːrk/ *noun* [U] (*technical*) a twisting force that causes machinery, etc. to ROTATE (= turn around)

tor·rent /ˈtɒrənt; *NAmE* ˈtɔːr-; ˈtɑːr-/ *noun* **1** a large amount of water moving very quickly: *After the winter rains, the stream becomes a* ***raging torrent.*** ◇ *The rain was coming down* ***in torrents.*** **2** a large amount of sth that comes suddenly and violently SYN **deluge**: *a* ***torrent of abuse/criticism*** ◇ *a torrent of words*

tor·ren·tial /təˈrenʃl/ *adj.* (of rain) falling in large amounts

tor·rid /ˈtɒrɪd; *NAmE* ˈtɔːr-; ˈtɑːr-/ *adj.* [usually before noun] **1** full of strong emotions, especially connected with sex and love SYN **passionate**: *a torrid love affair* **2** (*formal*) (of a climate or country) very hot or dry: *a torrid summer* **3** (*BrE*) very difficult: *They face a torrid time in tonight's game.*

ˈ**torrid zone** *noun* [sing.] (*technical*) an area of the earth near the EQUATOR SYN **the tropics**

tor·sion /ˈtɔːʃn; *NAmE* ˈtɔːrʃn/ *noun* [U] (*technical*) twisting, especially of one end of sth while the other end is held fixed

torso /ˈtɔːsəʊ; *NAmE* ˈtɔːrsoʊ/ *noun* (*pl.* **-os**) **1** the main part of the body, not including the head, arms or legs SYN **trunk** **2** a statue of a torso

tort /tɔːt; *NAmE* tɔːrt/ *noun* [C, U] (*law*) something wrong that sb does to sb else that is not criminal, but that can lead to action in a CIVIL court

torte /ˈtɔːtə; tɔːt; *NAmE* ˈtɔːrtə; tɔːrt/ *noun* [C, U] a large cake filled with a mixture of cream, chocolate, fruit, etc.

tor·tilla /tɔːˈtiːə; *NAmE* tɔːrˈt-/ *noun* (from *Spanish*) **1** a thin Mexican PANCAKE made with CORN (MAIZE) flour or WHEAT flour, usually eaten hot and filled with meat, cheese, etc. **2** a Spanish dish made with eggs and potatoes fried together

torˈtilla chip *noun* a small flat hard piece of food, often shaped like a triangle, made from CORN (MAIZE)

tor·toise /ˈtɔːtəs; *NAmE* ˈtɔːrtəs/ *noun* a REPTILE with a hard round shell, that lives on land and moves very slowly. It can pull its head and legs into its shell. ➲ VISUAL VOCAB page V11 ➲ compare TERRAPIN, TURTLE

tor·toise·shell /ˈtɔːtəsʃel; ˈtɔːtəʃel; *NAmE* ˈtɔːrt-/ *noun* **1** [U] the hard shell of a TURTLE, especially the type with orange and brown marks, used for making COMBS and small decorative objects **2** (*NAmE* also ˈ**calico cat**) [C] a cat with black, brown, orange and white fur **3** [C] a BUTTERFLY with orange and brown marks on its wings

tor·tu·ous /ˈtɔːtʃuəs; *NAmE* ˈtɔːrtʃ-/ *adj.* [usually before noun] (*formal*) **1** (usually *disapproving*) not simple and direct; long, complicated and difficult to understand SYN **convoluted**: *tortuous language* ◇ *the long, tortuous process of negotiating peace* **2** (of a road, path, etc.) full of bends SYN **winding** ▶ **tor·tu·ous·ly** *adv.*

tor·ture /ˈtɔːtʃə(r); *NAmE* ˈtɔːrtʃ-/ *noun, verb*
■ ***noun*** [U, C] **1** the act of causing sb severe pain in order to punish them or make them say or do sth: *Many of the refugees have suffered torture.* ◇ *the use of torture* ◇ *terrible instruments of torture* ◇ *His confessions were made* ***under torture.*** ◇ *I heard stories of gruesome tortures in prisons.* **2** (*informal*) mental or physical suffering; sth that causes this: *The interview was sheer torture from start to finish.*
■ ***verb*** [often passive] **1** to hurt sb physically or mentally in order to punish them or make them tell you sth: **~ sb** *Many of the rebels were captured and tortured by secret police.* ◇ **~ sb into doing sth** *He was tortured into giving them the information.* **2 ~ sb** to make sb feel extremely unhappy or anxious SYN **torment**: *He spent his life tortured by the memories of his childhood.* ▶ **tor·turer** /ˈtɔːtʃərə(r); *NAmE* ˈtɔːrtʃ-/ *noun*

tor·tured /ˈtɔːtʃəd; *NAmE* ˈtɔːrtʃərd/ *adj.* [only before noun] suffering severely; involving a lot of suffering and difficulty: *a tortured mind*

Tory /ˈtɔːri/ *noun* (*pl.* -ies) (*informal*) a member or supporter of the British Conservative party: *The Tories* (= the Tory party) *lost the election.* ▶ **Tory** *adj.* [usually before noun]: *the Tory party* ◇ *Tory policies* **Tory·ism** *noun* [U]

tosa /ˈtəʊsə; *NAmE* ˈtoʊ-/ *noun* a large strong dog originally kept for fighting

tosh /tɒʃ; *NAmE* tɑːʃ/ *noun* [U] (*old-fashioned, BrE, slang*) nonsense SYN **rubbish**

toss /tɒs; *NAmE* tɔːs; tɑːs/ *verb, noun*
■ ***verb***
▸ THROW **1** [T] to throw sth lightly or carelessly: **~ sth + adv./prep.** *I tossed the book aside and got up.* ◇ **~ sth to sb** *He tossed the ball to Anna.* ◇ **~ sb sth** *He tossed Anna the ball.* ➲ SYNONYMS at THROW
▸ YOUR HEAD **2** [T] **~ sth** to move your head suddenly upwards, especially to show that you are annoyed or impatient: *She just tossed her head and walked off.*
▸ SIDE TO SIDE/UP AND DOWN **3** [I, T] to move or make sb/sth move from side to side or up and down: *Branches were tossing in the wind.* ◇ *I couldn't sleep but kept* ***tossing and turning*** *in bed all night.* ◇ **~ sb/sth** *Our boat was being tossed by the huge waves.*
▸ IN COOKING **4** [T] **~ sth** to shake or turn food in order to cover it with oil, butter, etc: *Drain the pasta and toss it in melted butter.* **5** [T] **~ a pancake** (*BrE*) to throw A PANCAKE upwards so that it turns over in the air and you can fry the other side
▸ COIN **6** [T, I] to throw a coin in the air in order to decide sth, especially by guessing which side is facing upwards when it lands SYN **flip**: **~ sth** *Let's* ***toss a coin.*** ◇ (*especially BrE*) **~ (sb) for sth** *There's only one ticket left—I'll toss you for it.* ◇ (*BrE*) **~ up (for sth)** *We tossed up to see who went first.* ◇ (*BrE*) **~ up between A and B** (*figurative*) *He had to toss up between* (= decide between) *paying the rent or buying food.* ➲ related noun TOSS-UP
PHR V **ˌtoss ˈoff** | **ˌtoss sb/yourself ˈoff** (*BrE, taboo, slang*) to give yourself sexual pleasure by rubbing your sex organs; to give sb sexual pleasure by rubbing their sex organs SYN **masturbate** **ˌtoss sth↔ˈoff** (*BrE*) to produce sth quickly and without much thought or effort
■ ***noun*** [usually sing.]
▸ OF COIN **1** an act of throwing a coin in the air in order to decide sth: *The final result was decided* ***on/by the toss of a coin.*** ◇ ***to win/lose the toss*** (= to guess correctly/wrongly which side of a coin will face upwards when it lands on the ground after it has been thrown in the air)
▸ OF HEAD **2 ~ of your head** an act of moving your head suddenly upwards, especially to show that you are annoyed or impatient: *She dismissed the question with a toss of her head.*
▸ THROW **3** an act of throwing sth, especially in a competition or game: *a toss of 10 metres*
IDM **not give a ˈtoss (about sb/sth)** (*BrE, slang*) to not care at all about sb/sth ➲ more at ARGUE

toss·er /ˈtɒsə(r); *NAmE* ˈtɔːs-; ˈtɑːs-/ *noun* (*BrE, slang*) a stupid or unpleasant person

toss·pot /ˈtɒspɒt; *NAmE* ˈtɔːspɑːt; ˈtɑːspɑːt/ *noun* (*BrE, slang*) an offensive word for an unpleasant or stupid person

ˈtoss-up *noun* [sing.] (*informal*) a situation in which either of two choices, results, etc. is equally possible: *'Have you decided on the colour yet?'* ***'It's a toss-up*** *between the blue and the green.'*

tot /tɒt; *NAmE* tɑːt/ *noun, verb*
■ ***noun*** **1** (*informal*) a very young child **2** (*especially BrE*) a small amount of a strong alcoholic drink in a glass
■ ***verb*** (-tt-)
PHR V **ˌtot sth↔ˈup** (*informal, especially BrE*) to add together several numbers or amounts in order to calculate the total SYN **add up**

total 0‑w /ˈtəʊtl; *NAmE* ˈtoʊtl/ *adj., noun, verb*
■ ***adj.*** [usually before noun] **1** 0‑w being the amount or number after everyone or everything is counted or added together: *the total profit* ◇ *This brought the total number of accidents so far this year to 113.* ◇ *The club has a total membership of 300.* **2** 0‑w including everything SYN **complete**: *The room was in total darkness.* ◇ *They wanted a total ban on handguns.* ◇ *The evening was a total disaster.* ◇ *I can't believe you'd tell a total stranger about it!*
■ ***noun*** the amount you get when you add several numbers or amounts together; the final number of people or things when they have all been counted: *You got 47 points on the written examination and 18 on the oral, making a total of 65.* ◇ *His businesses are worth a combined total of $3 billion.* ◇ *Out of a total of 15 games, they only won 2.* ◇ *The repairs came to over £500* ***in total*** (= including everything). ➲ see also GRAND TOTAL, RUNNING TOTAL, SUM TOTAL
■ ***verb*** (-ll-, *US* also -l-) **1 ~ sth** to reach a particular total: *Imports totalled $1.5 billion last year.* **2 ~ sth/sb (up)** to add up the numbers of sth/sb and get a total: *Each student's points were totalled and entered in a list.* **3 ~ sth** (*informal, especially NAmE*) to damage a car very badly, so that it is not worth repairing it ➲ see also WRITE STH OFF

to·tali·tar·ian /təʊˌtæləˈteəriən; *NAmE* toʊˌtæləˈter-/ *adj.* (*disapproving*) (of a country or system of government) in which there is only one political party that has complete power and control over the people ▶ **to·tali·tar·ian·ism** /-ɪzəm/ *noun* [U]

to·tal·ity /təʊˈtæləti; *NAmE* toʊ-/ *noun* [C, U] (*formal*) the state of being complete or whole; the whole number or amount: *The seriousness of the situation is difficult to appreciate* ***in its totality.***

to·tal·iza·tor (*BrE* also **-isa·tor**) /ˈtəʊtəlaɪzeɪtə(r); *NAmE* ˈtoʊt-/ (also **to·tal·izer, -iser** /ˈtəʊtəlaɪzə(r); *NAmE* ˈtoʊt-/) *noun* a device for showing the number and amount of bets put on a race

tot·al·ly 0‑w /ˈtəʊtəli; *NAmE* ˈtoʊ-/ *adv.* completely: *They come from totally different cultures.* ◇ *I'm still not totally convinced that he knows what he's doing.* ◇ *This behaviour is totally unacceptable.* ◇ (*informal, especially NAmE*) *'She's so cute!' 'Totally!'* (= I agree) ◇ (*informal*) *It's a totally awesome experience.*

ˌtotal ˌquality ˈmanagement *noun* [U] (*abbr.* TQM) a system of management that considers that every employee in an organization is responsible for keeping the highest standards in every aspect of the company's work

tote /təʊt; *NAmE* toʊt/ *noun, verb*
■ ***noun*** **1** (also **the Tote**) [sing.] a system of betting on horses in which the total amount of money that is bet on each race is divided among the people who bet on the winners **2** (also **ˈtote bag**) [C] (*NAmE*) a large bag for carrying things with you
■ ***verb*** **1 ~ sth** (*informal, especially NAmE*) to carry sth, especially sth heavy: *We arrived, toting our bags and suitcases.* **2 -toting** (in adjectives) carrying the thing mentioned: *gun-toting soldiers*

totem /ˈtəʊtəm; *NAmE* ˈtoʊ-/ *noun* an animal or other natural object that is chosen and respected as a special symbol of a community or family, especially among Native Americans; an image of this animal, etc. ▶ **to·tem·ic** /təʊˈtemɪk; *NAmE* toʊ-/ *adj.*: *totemic animals*

T

ˈ**totem pole** *noun* **1** a tall wooden pole that has symbols and pictures (called TOTEMS) CARVED or painted on it, traditionally made by Native Americans **2** (*NAmE, informal*) a range of different levels in an organization, etc: *I didn't want to be* ***low man on the totem pole*** *for ever.*

t'other /ˈtʌðə(r)/ *adj., pron.* (*BrE, dialect*) the other: *I saw it t'other day.* ◇ *They were talking of this, that and t'other.*

toto ➲ IN TOTO

tot·ter /ˈtɒtə(r); *NAmE* ˈtɑːt-/ *verb* **1** [I] (+ **adv./prep.**) to walk or move with weak unsteady steps, especially because you are drunk or ill/sick SYN **stagger** **2** [I] to be weak and seem likely to fall: *the tottering walls of the castle* ◇ *(figurative) a tottering dictatorship*

totty /ˈtɒti; *NAmE* ˈtɑːti/ *noun* [U] (*BrE, slang*) sexually attractive women (an expression used by men, and usually offensive to women)

tou·can /ˈtuːkæn/ *noun* a tropical American bird that is black with some areas of very bright feathers, and that has a very large beak

touch 0‐ᵂ /tʌtʃ/ *verb, noun*

■ *verb*

▸ WITH HAND/PART OF BODY **1** 0‐ᵂ [T] **~ sb/sth** to put your hand or another part of your body onto sb/sth: *Don't touch that plate—it's hot!* ◇ *Can you touch your toes?* (= bend and reach them with your hands) ◇ *I touched him lightly on the arm.* ◇ *He has hardly touched the ball all game.* ◇ (*figurative*) *I must do some more work on that article—I haven't touched it all week.*

▸ NO SPACE BETWEEN **2** 0‐ᵂ [I, T] (of two or more things, surfaces, etc.) to be or come so close together that there is no space between: *Make sure the wires don't touch.* ◇ **~ sth** *Don't let your coat touch the wet paint.* ◇ *His coat was so long it was almost touching the floor.*

▸ MOVE STH/HIT SB **3** 0‐ᵂ [T] (often in negative sentences) **~ sth/sb** to move sth, especially in such a way that you damage it; to hit or harm sb: *I told you not to touch my things.* ◇ *He said I kicked him, but I never touched him!*

▸ AFFECT SB/STH **4** 0‐ᵂ [T] **~ sb/sth** (**to do sth**) to make sb feel upset or sympathetic: *Her story touched us all deeply.* **5** [T] **~ sb/sth** (*old-fashioned* or *formal*) to affect or concern sb/sth: *These are issues that touch us all.*

▸ EAT/DRINK/USE **6** [T] (usually in negative sentences) **~ sth** to eat, drink or use sth: *You've hardly touched your food.* ◇ *He hasn't touched the money his aunt left him.*

▸ EQUAL SB **7** [T] (usually in negative sentences) **~ sb** to be as good as sb in skill, quality, etc: *No one can touch him when it comes to interior design.*

▸ REACH LEVEL **8** [T] **~ sth** to reach a particular level, etc: *The speedometer was touching 90.*

▸ BE INVOLVED WITH **9** [T] **~ sth/sb** to become connected with or work with a situation or person: *Everything she touches turns to disaster.* ◇ *His last two movies have been complete flops and now no studio will touch him.*

▸ OF SMILE **10** [T] **~ sth** to be seen on sb's face for a short time: *A smile touched the corners of his mouth.*

IDM **be touched with sth** to have a small amount of a particular quality: *His hair was touched with grey.* **not touch sb/sth with a ˈbargepole** (*BrE*) (*NAmE* **not touch sb/sth with a ten-foot ˈpole**) (*informal*) to refuse to get involved with sb/sth or in a particular situation **touch ˈbase** (**with sb**) (*informal*) to make contact with sb again **touch ˈbottom 1** to reach the ground at the bottom of an area of water **2** (*BrE*) to reach the worst possible state or condition ˌ**touch ˈwood** (*BrE*) (*NAmE* ˌ**knock on ˈwood**) (*saying*) used when you have just mentioned some way in which you have been lucky in the past, to avoid bringing bad luck: *I've been driving for over 20 years and never had an accident—touch wood!* ➲ more at CHORD, FORELOCK, HAIR, NERVE *n.*, RAW *n.*

PHR V ˌ**touch ˈdown 1** (of a plane, SPACECRAFT, etc.) to make contact with the ground as it lands: (*figurative*) *Tornadoes touched down in Alabama and Louisiana.* ➲ related noun TOUCHDOWN **2** (in RUGBY) to score a TRY by putting the ball on the ground behind the other team's goal line ➲ related noun TOUCHDOWN ˈ**touch sb for sth** (*informal*) to persuade sb to give or lend you sth, especially money ˌ**touch sth↔ˈoff** to make sth begin, especially a difficult or violent situation ˈ**touch on/upon sth** to mention or deal with a subject in only a few words, without going into detail: *In his speech he was only able to touch on a few aspects of the problem.* ˌ**touch sb↔ˈup** (*BrE, informal*) to touch sb sexually, usually in a way that is not expected or welcome SYN **grope** ˌ**touch sth↔ˈup** to improve sth by changing or adding to it slightly: *She was busy touching up her make-up in the mirror.*

■ *noun*

▸ SENSE **1** 0‐ᵂ [U] the sense that enables you to be aware of things and what they are like when you put your hands and fingers on them: *the sense of touch*

▸ WITH HAND/PART OF BODY **2** 0‐ᵂ [C, usually sing.] an act of putting your hand or another part of your body onto sb/sth: *The gentle touch of his hand on her shoulder made her jump.* ◇ *All this information is readily available* ***at the touch of a button*** (= by simply pressing a button). ◇ *This type of engraving requires a delicate touch.*

▸ WAY STH FEELS **3** [sing.] the way that sth feels when you put your hand or fingers on it or when it comes into contact with your body: *The body was cold* ***to the touch.*** ◇ *material with a smooth silky touch* ◇ *He could not bear the touch of clothing on his sunburnt skin.*

▸ SMALL DETAIL **4** [C] a small detail that is added to sth in order to improve it or make it complete: *I spent the morning* ***putting the finishing touches to*** *the report.* ◇ *Meeting them at the airport was a nice touch.*

▸ WAY OF DOING STH **5** [sing.] a way or style of doing sth: *She prefers to answer any fan mail herself for a more personal touch.* ◇ *Computer graphics will give your presentation the professional touch.* ◇ *He couldn't find his magic touch with the ball today* (= he didn't play well). ◇ *This meal is awful. I think I'm* ***losing my touch*** (= my ability to do sth).

▸ SMALL AMOUNT **6** [C, usually sing.] **~ of sth** a very small amount SYN **trace**: *There was a touch of sarcasm in her voice.*

▸ SLIGHTLY **7 a touch** [sing.] slightly; a little: *The music was a touch too loud for my liking.*

▸ IN FOOTBALL/RUGBY **8** [U] the area outside the lines that mark the sides of the playing field: *He kicked the ball into touch.*

IDM **be, get, keep, etc. in ˈtouch** (**with sb**) 0‐ᵂ to communicate with sb, especially by writing to them or telephoning them: *Are you still in touch with your friends from college?* ◇ *Thanks for showing us your products—we'll be in touch.* ◇ *I'm trying to get in touch with Jane. Do you have her number?* ◇ *Let's keep in touch.* ◇ *I'll put you in touch with someone in your area.* **be, keep, etc. in ˈtouch** (**with sth**) to know what is happening in a particular subject or area: *It is important to keep in touch with the latest research.* **be out of ˈtouch** (**with sb**) to no longer communicate with sb, so that you no longer know what is happening to them **be, become, etc. out of ˈtouch** (**with sth**) to not know or understand what is happening in a particular subject or area: *Unfortunately, the people making the decisions are out of touch with the real world.* **an easy/a soft ˈtouch** (*informal*) a person that you can easily persuade to do sth, especially to give you money: *Unfortunately, my father is no soft touch.* **lose ˈtouch** (**with sb/sth**) **1** to no longer have any contact with sb/sth: *I've lost touch with all my old friends.* **2** to no longer understand sth, especially how ordinary people feel ➲ more at COMMON *adj.*, KICK *v.*, LIGHT *adj.*

ˌ**touch-and-ˈgo** *adj.* [not usually before noun] (*informal*) used to say that the result of a situation is uncertain and that there is a possibility that sth bad or unpleasant will happen: *She's fine now, but it was touch-and-go for a while* (= there was a possibility that she might die).

touch·down /ˈtʌtʃdaʊn/ *noun* **1** [C, U] the moment when a plane or SPACECRAFT lands SYN **landing** **2** [C] (in RUGBY) an act of scoring points by putting the ball down on the area of ground behind the other team's GOAL LINE **3** [C] (in AMERICAN FOOTBALL) an act of scoring points by crossing the other team's GOAL LINE while carrying the ball, or receiving the ball when you are over the other team's GOAL LINE

tou·ché /ˈtuːʃeɪ; *NAmE* tuːˈʃeɪ/ *exclamation* (from *French*) used during an argument or a discussion to show that you accept that sb has answered your comment in a clever way and has gained an advantage by making a good point

touched /tʌtʃt/ *adj.* [not before noun] **1** feeling happy and grateful because of sth kind that sb has done; feeling emotional about sth: **~ (by sth)** *She was touched by their warm welcome.* ◇ *She was touched by the plight of the refugees.* ◇ **~ (that…)** *I was touched that he still remembered me.* **2** (*old-fashioned, informal*) slightly crazy

ˌtouch ˈfootball *noun* [U] (*NAmE*) a type of AMERICAN FOOTBALL in which touching is used instead of TACKLING ➲ compare FLAG FOOTBALL

touch·ing /ˈtʌtʃɪŋ/ *adj.* causing feelings of pity or sympathy; making you feel emotional SYN **moving**: *It was a touching story that moved many of us to tears.* ▸ **touch·ing·ly** *adv.*

ˈtouch judge *noun* (in RUGBY) a LINESMAN

touch·line /ˈtʌtʃlaɪn/ *noun* a line that marks the side of the playing field in football (SOCCER), RUGBY, etc.

ˈtouch pad *noun* (*computing*) a device which you touch in different places in order to operate a program

touch·paper /ˈtʌtʃpeɪpə(r)/ *noun* a piece of paper that burns slowly, that you light in order to start a FIREWORK burning

ˈtouch screen *noun* (*computing*) a computer screen which allows you to give instructions to the computer by touching areas on it

touch·stone /ˈtʌtʃstəʊn; *NAmE* -stoʊn/ *noun* [usually sing.] **~ (of/for sth)** (*formal*) something that provides a standard against which other things are compared and/or judged: *the touchstone for quality*

ˈTouch-Tone™ *adj.* (of a telephone or telephone system) producing different sounds when different numbers are pushed

ˈtouch-type *verb* [I] to type without having to look at the keys of a TYPEWRITER or keyboard

ˈtouch-up *noun* a quick improvement made to the appearance or condition of sth: *My lipstick needed a touch-up.*

touchy /ˈtʌtʃi/ *adj.* (**touch·ier, touchi·est**) **1** [not usually before noun] **~ (about sth)** (of a person) easily upset or offended SYN **sensitive**: *He's a little touchy about his weight.* **2** [usually before noun] (of a subject) that may upset or offend people and should therefore be dealt with carefully SYN **delicate, sensitive** ▸ **touchi·ness** *noun* [U]

ˌtouchy-ˈfeely *adj.* (*informal*, usually *disapproving*) expressing emotions too openly

tough 🔑 /tʌf/ *adj., noun, verb*

■ *adj.* (**tough·er, tough·est**)

▸ DIFFICULT **1** 🔑 having or causing problems or difficulties: *a tough childhood* ◇ *It was a tough decision to make.* ◇ *She's been having **a tough time of it*** (= a lot of problems) *lately.* ◇ *He faces the toughest test of his leadership so far.* ◇ *It can be tough trying to juggle a career and a family.*

▸ STRICT/FIRM **2** 🔑 demanding that particular rules be obeyed and showing a lack of sympathy for any problems or suffering that this may cause: **~ (on sb/sth)** *Don't be too tough on him—he was only trying to help.* ◇ **~ (with sb/sth)** *It's about time teachers started to **get tough with** bullies.* ◇ *The school **takes a tough line on*** (= punishes severely) *cheating.* OPP **soft**

▸ STRONG **3** 🔑 strong enough to deal successfully with difficult conditions or situations: *a tough breed of cattle* ◇ *He's not tough enough for a career in sales.* ◇ *She's a **tough cookie/customer*** (= sb who knows what they want and is not easily influenced by other people). **4** 🔑 (of a person) physically strong and likely to be violent: *You think you're so tough, don't you?* ◇ *He plays the **tough guy** in the movie.*

▸ MEAT **5** 🔑 difficult to cut or chew OPP **tender**

▸ NOT EASILY DAMAGED **6** not easily cut, broken, torn, etc: *a tough pair of shoes* ◇ *The reptile's skin is tough and scaly.*

▸ UNFORTUNATE **7** **~ (on sb)** (*informal*) unfortunate for sb in a way that seems unfair: *It was tough on her being dropped from the team like that.* ◇ (*ironic*) *'I can't get it finished in time.' 'Tough!* (= I don't feel sorry about it.)*'* ▸ **tough·ly** *adv.* **tough·ness** *noun* [U]

IDM (as) **tough as old ˈboots** | (as) **tough as ˈnails** (*informal*) **1** very strong and able to deal successfully with difficult conditions or situations **2** not feeling or showing any emotion **tough ˈluck** (*informal*) **1** (*BrE*) used to show sympathy for sth unfortunate that has happened to sb: *'I failed by one point.' 'That's tough luck.'* **2** (*ironic*) used to show that you do not feel sorry for sb who has a problem: *'If you take the car, I won't be able to go out.' 'Tough luck!'* ➲ more at ACT *n.*, GOING *n.*, HANG *v.*, NUT *n.*, TALK *v.*

■ *noun* (*old-fashioned, informal*) a person who regularly uses violence against other people

■ *verb*

PHR V **ˌtough sth↔ˈout** to stay firm and determined in a difficult situation: *You're just going to have to **tough it out**.*

tough·en /ˈtʌfn/ *verb* **1** [T, I] **~ (sth) (up)** to become or make sth stronger, so that it is not easily cut, broken, etc: *toughened glass* **2** [T] **~ sth (up)** to make sth such as laws or rules stricter: *The government is considering toughening up the law on censorship.* **3** [T] **~ sb (up)** to make sb stronger and more able to deal with difficult situations

toughie /ˈtʌfi/ *noun* (*informal*) **1** a person who is determined and not easily frightened **2** a very difficult choice or question

ˌtough ˈlove *noun* [U] the fact of helping sb who has problems by dealing with them in a strict way because you believe it is good for them

ˌtough-ˈminded *adj.* dealing with problems and situations in a determined way without being influenced by emotions SYN **hard-headed**

tou·pee /ˈtuːpeɪ; *NAmE* tuːˈpeɪ/ (also *informal* **rug** especially in *NAmE*) *noun* a small section of artificial hair, worn by a man to cover an area of his head where hair no longer grows

tour 🔑 /tʊə(r); tɔː(r); *NAmE* tʊr/ *noun, verb*

■ *noun* **1** 🔑 **~ (of/round/around sth)** a journey made for pleasure during which several different towns, countries, etc. are visited: *a **walking/sightseeing, etc. tour*** ◇ *a **coach tour** of northern France* ◇ *a **tour operator*** (= a person or company that organizes tours) ➲ SYNONYMS at TRIP ➲ COLLOCATIONS at TRAVEL ➲ see also PACKAGE TOUR, WHISTLE-STOP **2** 🔑 an act of walking around a town, building, etc. in order to visit it: *We were given a **guided tour*** (= by sb who knows about the place) *of the palace.* ◇ *a **tour guide*** ◇ *a **tour of inspection*** (= an official visit of a factory, classroom, etc. made by sb whose job is to check that everything is working as expected) **3** 🔑 an official series of visits made to different places by a sports team, an ORCHESTRA, an important person, etc: *The band is currently on a nine-day tour of France.* ◇ *The band is **on tour** in France.* ◇ *a concert tour* ◇ *The Prince will visit Boston on the last leg* (= part) *of his American tour.* ◇ *The soldiers all used to do a six-month **tour of duty** in Northern Ireland.*

■ *verb* 🔑 [T, I] to travel around a place, for example on holiday/vacation, or to perform, to advertise sth, etc: **~ sth** *He toured America with his one-man show.* ◇ *She toured the country promoting her book.* ◇ **~ around sth** *We spent four weeks touring around Europe.*

tour de force /ˌtʊə də ˈfɔːs; *NAmE* ˌtʊr də ˈfɔːrs/ *noun* (*pl.* **tours de force** /ˌtʊə də ˈfɔːs; *NAmE* ˌtʊr də ˈfɔːrs/) (from *French*) an extremely skilful performance or achievement: *a cinematic tour de force*

Tour·ette's syn·drome /tʊˈrets sɪndrəʊm; *NAmE* -droʊm/ *noun* [U] (*medical*) a DISORDER of the nerves in which a person makes a lot of small movements and sounds that they cannot control, including using swear words

tour·ism /ˈtʊərɪzəm; ˈtɔːr-; *NAmE* ˈtʊr-/ *noun* [U] the business activity connected with providing accommodation, services and entertainment for people who are visiting a place for pleasure: *The area is heavily dependent on tourism.* ◇ *the tourism industry* ➲ COLLOCATIONS at TRAVEL ➲ see also AGRITOURISM

T

tour·ist 0→ /ˈtʊərɪst; ˈtɔːr-; *NAmE* ˈtʊr-/ *noun*
1 0→ a person who is travelling or visiting a place for pleasure: *busloads of foreign tourists* ◇ *a popular* ***tourist attraction/destination/resort*** ◇ *the* ***tourist industry/sector*** ◇ *Further information is available from the local* ***tourist office.*** ➲ COLLOCATIONS at TRAVEL **2** (*BrE*) a member of a sports team that is playing a series of official games in a foreign country

ˈ**tourist class** *noun* [U] the cheapest type of ticket or accommodation that is available on a plane or ship or in a hotel

ˈ**tourist trap** *noun* (*informal, disapproving*) a place that attracts a lot of tourists and where food, drink, entertainment, etc. is more expensive than normal

tour·isty /ˈtʊərɪsti; ˈtɔːr-; *NAmE* ˈtʊr-/ *adj.* (*informal, disapproving*) attracting or designed to attract a lot of tourists: *Jersey is the most touristy of the islands.* ◇ *a shop full of touristy souvenirs*

tour·na·ment /ˈtʊənəmənt; ˈtɔːn-; ˈtɜːn-; *NAmE* ˈtʊrn-; ˈtɜːrn-/ *noun* **1** (*NAmE less frequent* **tour·ney**) a sports competition involving a number of teams or players who take part in different games and must leave the competition if they lose. The competition continues until there is only the winner left: *a* ***golf/squash/tennis, etc. tournament*** **2** a competition in the Middle Ages between soldiers on HORSEBACK fighting to show courage and skill

tour·ney /ˈtʊəni; ˈtɜːni; *NAmE* ˈtʊrni; ˈtɜːrni/ *noun* (*NAmE*) = TOURNAMENT (1)

tour·ni·quet /ˈtʊənɪkeɪ; *NAmE* ˈtɜːrnəkət/ *noun* a piece of cloth, etc. that is tied tightly around an arm or a leg to stop the loss of blood from a wound

tou·sle /ˈtaʊzl/ *verb* [usually passive] **~ sth** to make sb's hair untidy ▶ **tou·sled** *adj.*: *a boy with blue eyes and tousled hair*

tout /taʊt/ *verb, noun*
■ ***verb*** **1** [T] **~ sb/sth** (**as sth**) to try to persuade people that sb/sth is important or valuable by praising them/it: *She's being touted as the next leader of the party.* **2** [I, T] (*especially BrE*) to try to persuade people to buy your goods or services, especially by going to them and asking them directly: **~** (**for sth**) *the problem of unlicensed taxi drivers touting for business at airports* ◇ **~ sth** *He's busy touting his client's latest book around London publishers.* **3** [I, T] (*BrE*) (*NAmE* **scalp**) **~** (**sth**) to sell tickets for a popular event illegally, at a price that is higher than the official price, especially outside a theatre, STADIUM, etc.
■ ***noun*** (also ˈ**ticket tout**) (both *BrE*) (*NAmE* **scalp·er**) a person who buys tickets for concerts, sports events, etc. and then sells them to other people at a higher price

tout court /ˌtuː ˈkʊə(r); ˈkɔː(r); *NAmE* ˈkuːr/ *adv.* (from *French*) simply, with nothing to add: *It was a lie, tout court.*

tow /təʊ; *NAmE* toʊ/ *verb, noun*
■ ***verb*** **~ sth** (**away**) to pull a car or boat behind another vehicle, using a rope or chain: *Our car was towed away by the police.* ➲ SYNONYMS at PULL ➲ see also TOW BAR, TOW ROPE
■ ***noun*** [sing.] an act of one vehicle pulling another vehicle using a rope or chain: *The car broke down and we had to get somebody to give us a tow.* ◇ *a tow truck*
IDM **in tow 1** (*informal*) if you have sb **in tow**, they are with you and following closely behind: *She turned up with her mother in tow.* **2** if a ship is taken **in tow**, it is pulled by another ship

to·wards 0→ /təˈwɔːdz; *NAmE* tɔːrdz/ (also **to·ward** /təˈwɔːd; *NAmE* tɔːrd/ especially in *NAmE*) *prep.*
1 0→ in the direction of sb/sth: *They were heading towards the German border.* ◇ *She had her back towards me.* **2** 0→ getting closer to achieving sth: *This is a first step towards political union.* **3** 0→ close or closer to a point in time: *towards the end of April* **4** 0→ in relation to sb/sth: *He was warm and tender towards her.* ◇ *our attitude towards death* **5** with the aim of obtaining sth, or helping sb to obtain sth: *The money will go towards a new school building* (= will help pay for it).

ˈ**tow bar** *noun* a bar fixed to the back of a vehicle for TOWING (= pulling) another vehicle

towel 0→ /ˈtaʊəl/ *noun, verb*
■ ***noun*** a piece of cloth or paper used for drying things, especially your body: *Help yourself to a clean towel.* ◇ *a* ***hand/bath towel*** (= a small/large towel) ◇ *a* ***beach towel*** (= a large towel used for lying on in the sun) ◇ *a* ***kitchen towel*** (= a piece of paper from a roll that you use to clean up liquid, etc. in the kitchen) ➲ VISUAL VOCAB page V21 ➲ see also PAPER TOWEL, SANITARY TOWEL, TEA TOWEL
IDM **throw in the ˈtowel** (*informal*) to admit that you have been defeated and stop trying
■ ***verb*** (-ll-, *NAmE* also -l-) **~ yourself/sb/sth** (**down**) to dry yourself/sb/sth with a towel

tow·el·ling (*BrE*) (*US* **tow·el·ing**) /ˈtaʊəlɪŋ/ *noun* [U] a type of soft cotton cloth that absorbs liquids, used especially for making towels: *a towelling bathrobe*

ˈ**towel rail** (*BrE*) (*NAmE* ˈ**towel rack**) *noun* a bar or frame for hanging towels on in a bathroom ➲ VISUAL VOCAB page V21

tower 0→ /ˈtaʊə(r)/ *noun, verb*
■ ***noun*** **1** 0→ a tall narrow building or part of a building, especially of a church or castle: *a* ***clock/bell tower*** ◇ *the Tower of London* ◇ *the Eiffel Tower* **2** (often in compounds) a tall structure used for sending television or radio signals: *a television tower* **3** (usually in compounds) a tall piece of furniture used for storing things: *a CD tower* ➲ see also CONTROL TOWER, COOLING TOWER, IVORY TOWER, WATCHTOWER, WATER TOWER
IDM **a ˌtower of ˈstrength** a person that you can rely on to help, protect and comfort you when you are in trouble
■ ***verb***
PHR V **ˌtower ˈover/aˈbove sb/sth 1** to be much higher or taller than the people or things that are near: *The cliffs towered above them.* ◇ *He towered over his classmates.* **2** to be much better than others in ability, quality, etc: *She towers over other dancers of her generation.*

ˈ**tower block** *noun* (*BrE*) a very tall block of flats/apartments or offices

tower·ing /ˈtaʊərɪŋ/ *adj.* [only before noun] **1** extremely tall or high and therefore impressive: *towering cliffs* **2** of extremely high quality: *a towering performance* **3** (of emotions) extremely strong: *a towering rage*

tow·line /ˈtəʊlaɪn; *NAmE* ˈtoʊ-/ *noun* = TOW ROPE

town 0→ /taʊn/ *noun*
1 0→ [C, U] a place with many houses, shops/stores, etc. where people live and work. It is larger than a village but smaller than a city: *a university town* ◇ *They live in a rough part of town.* ◇ *The nearest town is ten miles away.* ◇ *We spent a month in the French town of Le Puy.* ➲ see also SMALL-TOWN HELP You will find other compounds ending in **town** at their place in the alphabet. **2** 0→ **the town** [sing.] the people who live in a particular town: *The whole town is talking about it.* **3** 0→ [U] the area of a town where most of the shops/stores and businesses are: *Can you give me a lift into town?* ➲ see also DOWNTOWN, MIDTOWN, OUT-OF-TOWN, UPTOWN **4** [U] (*especially NAmE*) a particular town where sb lives and works or one that has just been referred to: *I'll be in town next week if you want to meet.* ◇ *He married a girl from out of town.* ➲ see also OUT-OF-TOWN **5** [sing., U] life in towns or cities as opposed to life in the country: *Pollution is just one of the disadvantages of living in the town.*
IDM **go to ˈtown** (**on sth**) (*informal*) to do sth with a lot of energy, enthusiasm, etc, especially by spending a lot of money (**out**) **on the ˈtown** (*informal*) visiting restaurants, clubs, theatres, etc. for entertainment, especially at night: *a night on the town* ◇ *How about going out on the town tonight?* ➲ more at GAME *n.*, MAN *n.*, PAINT *v.*

ˌ**town and ˈgown** *noun* [U] the relationship between the people who live permanently in a town where there is a university and the members of the university

ˌ**town ˈcentre** *noun* (*BrE*) the main part of a town, where the shops/stores are ➲ compare DOWNTOWN

Collocations

Town and country

Town

- **live in** a city/a town/an urban environment/(informal) a concrete jungle/the suburbs/shanty towns/slums
- **live** (*especially NAmE*) downtown/in the downtown area/(*BrE*) in the city centre
- **enjoy/like** the hectic pace of life/the hustle and bustle of city life
- **cope with** the stress/pressure of urban life
- **get caught up in** the rat race
- **prefer/seek** the anonymity of life in a big city
- **be drawn by/resist** the lure of the big city
- **head for** the bright lights (of the big city/New York)
- **enjoy/love** the vibrant/lively nightlife
- **have/be close to** all the amenities
- **be surrounded by** towering skyscrapers/a soulless urban sprawl
- **use/travel by/rely on** (*BrE*) public transport/(*NAmE*) public transportation
- **put up with/get stuck in/sit in** massive/huge/heavy/endless/constant traffic jams
- **tackle/ease/reduce/relieve/alleviate** the heavy/severe traffic congestion
- **be affected/choked/damaged by** pollution

Country

- **live** in a village/the countryside/an isolated area/a rural backwater/(*informal*) the sticks
- **enjoy/like** the relaxed/slower pace of life
- **enjoy/love/explore** the great outdoors
- **look for/find/get/enjoy** a little peace and quiet
- **need/want** to get back/closer to nature
- **be surrounded by** open/unspoilt/picturesque countryside
- **escape/quit/get out of/leave** the rat race
- **seek/achieve** a better/healthy work-life balance
- **downshift** to a less stressful life
- **seek/start** a new life in the country
- (*BrE, informal*) **up sticks/**(*NAmE, informal*) **pull up stakes** and move to/head for...
- **create/build/foster** a strong sense of community
- **depend on/be employed in/work in** agriculture
- **live off/farm/work** the land
- **tackle/address** the problem of rural unemployment

ˌtown ˈclerk *noun* **1** (*NAmE*) a public officer in charge of the records of a town **2** (*BrE*) in the past, the person who was the secretary of, and gave legal advice to, the local government of a town

ˌtown ˈcrier (also **crier**) *noun* (in the past) a person whose job was to walk through a town shouting news, official ANNOUNCEMENTS, etc.

townee = TOWNIE

ˌtown ˈhall *noun* a building containing local government offices and, in Britain, usually a hall for public meetings, concerts, etc.

ˈtown house *noun* **1** (*BrE*) a house in a town owned by sb who also has a house in the country **2** (*BrE*) a tall narrow house in a town that is part of a row of similar houses: *an elegant Georgian town house* ➲ VISUAL VOCAB page V14 **3** (usually **ˈtownhouse**) (*NAmE*) = ROW HOUSE

townie /ˈtaʊni/ *noun* (*disapproving*) **1** (also **townee**) a person who lives in or comes from a town or city, especially sb who does not know much about life in the countryside **2** (*NAmE*) a person who lives in a town with a college or university but does not attend or work at it **3** (*BrE, informal*) a member of a group of young people who live in a town, all wear similar clothes, such as TRACKSUITS and caps, and often behave badly

ˌtown ˈmeeting *noun* a meeting when people in a town come together to discuss problems that affect the town and to give their opinions on various issues

ˌtown ˈplanner *noun* = PLANNER

ˌtown ˈplanning (also **plan·ning**) *noun* [U] the control of the development of towns and their buildings, roads, etc. so that they can be pleasant and convenient places for people to live in; the subject that studies this

town·scape /ˈtaʊnskeɪp/ *noun* **1** what you see when you look at a town, for example from a distance: *an industrial townscape* **2** (*technical*) a picture of a town ➲ compare LANDSCAPE, SEASCAPE

town·ship /ˈtaʊnʃɪp/ *noun* **1** (in South Africa in the past) a town or part of a town that black people had to live in, and where only black people lived **2** (in the US or Canada) a division of a county that is a unit of local government

towns·people /ˈtaʊnzpiːpl/ (also **towns·folk** /ˈtaʊnsfəʊk; *NAmE* -foʊk/) *noun* [pl.] people who live in towns, not in the countryside; the people who live in a particular town

tow·path /ˈtəʊpɑːθ; *NAmE* ˈtoʊpæθ/ *noun* a path along the bank of a river or CANAL, that was used in the past by horses pulling boats (called BARGES)

ˈtow rope (also **tow·line**) *noun* a rope that is used for pulling sth along, especially a vehicle

ˈtow truck (*especially NAmE*) (*BrE* usually **ˈbreakdown truck**) *noun* a truck that is used for taking cars away to be repaired when they have had a breakdown ➲ VISUAL VOCAB page V46

tox·ae·mia (*BrE*) (*NAmE* **tox·emia**) /tɒkˈsiːmiə; *NAmE* tɑːk-/ *noun* [U] (*medical*) infection of the blood by harmful bacteria SYN **blood poisoning**

toxic /ˈtɒksɪk; *NAmE* ˈtɑːk-/ *adj.* **1** containing poison; poisonous: *toxic chemicals/fumes/gases/substances* ◇ *to dispose of toxic waste* ◇ *Many pesticides are* ***highly toxic***. **2 ~ debt/loan/asset/investment** a level of debt or high-risk investment that causes very serious problems for a bank or other financial institution **3** [usually before noun] (*informal*) (of a person) having a very unpleasant personality, especially in the way they like to control and influence other people in a dishonest way

tox·icity /tɒkˈsɪsəti; *NAmE* tɑːk-/ *noun* (*pl.* -ies) (*technical*) **1** [U] the quality of being poisonous; the extent to which sth is poisonous: *substances with high levels of toxicity* **2** [C] the effect that a poisonous substance has: *Minor toxicities of this drug include nausea and vomiting.*

toxi·col·ogy /ˌtɒksɪˈkɒlədʒi; *NAmE* ˌtɑːksɪˈkɑːl-/ *noun* [U] the scientific study of poisons ▸ **toxi·colo·gical** /ˌtɒksɪkəˈlɒdʒɪkl; *NAmE* ˌtɑːksɪkəˈlɑːdʒɪkl/ *adj.* **toxi·colo·gist** /-dʒɪst/ *noun*

ˌtoxic ˈshock syndrome *noun* [U] a serious illness in women caused by harmful bacteria in the VAGINA, connected with the use of TAMPONS

toxin /ˈtɒksɪn; *NAmE* ˈtɑːk-/ *noun* a poisonous substance, especially one that is produced by bacteria in plants and animals

toxo·plas·mo·sis /ˌtɒksəʊplæzˈməʊsɪs; *NAmE* ˌtɑːksoʊplæzˈmoʊsɪs/ *noun* [U] (*medical*) a disease that can be dangerous to a baby while it is still in its mother's body, caught from infected meat, soil, or animal FAECES

toy 🔑 /tɔɪ/ *noun, adj., verb*

▪ ***noun*** **1** 🔑 an object for children to play with: ***cuddly/soft toys*** ◇ *The children were playing happily with their toys.* ➲ VISUAL VOCAB page V32 **2** an object that you have for enjoyment or pleasure rather than for a serious purpose SYN **plaything**: *executive toys* ◇ *His latest toy is the electric drill he bought last week.*

▪ ***adj.*** [only before noun] **1** 🔑 made as a copy of a particular thing and used for playing with: *a toy car* ◇ *toy soldiers* **2** (of a dog) of a very small breed: *a toy poodle*

▪ ***verb***

PHR V **ˈtoy with sth 1** to consider an idea or a plan, but not very seriously and not for a long time SYN **flirt with**: *I did briefly* **toy with the idea of** *living in France.* **2** to play with sth and move it around carelessly or without thinking: *He kept toying nervously with his pen.* ◇ *She hardly ate a thing, just toyed with a piece of cheese on her plate.*

'toy boy *noun* (*BrE*) (*NAmE* **'boy toy**) (*informal, humorous*) a woman's male lover who is much younger than she is

toyi-toyi /'tɔɪ tɔɪ/ *noun* [U] (*SAfrE*) a type of dance or march, used as a form of protest, in which you repeatedly move one leg up and down followed by the other

TPR /ˌtiː piː 'ɑː(r)/ *abbr.* TOTAL PHYSICAL RESPONSE

TQM /ˌtiː kjuː 'em/ *abbr.* TOTAL QUALITY MANAGEMENT

trace 🗝 AW /treɪs/ *verb, noun*

■ *verb* **1** 🗝 **~ sb/sth** (**to sth**) to find or discover sb/sth by looking carefully for them/it SYN **track down**: *We finally traced him to an address in Chicago.* **2** 🗝 **~ sth** (**back**) (**to sth**) to find the origin or cause of sth: *She could trace her family tree back to the 16th century.* ◇ *The leak was eventually traced to a broken seal.* ◇ *The police traced the call* (= used special electronic equipment to find out who made the telephone call) *to her ex-husband's number.* **3 ~ sth** (**from sth**) (**to sth**) to describe a process or the development of sth: *Her book traces the town's history from Saxon times to the present day.* **4 ~ sth** (**out**) to draw a line or lines on a surface: *She traced a line in the sand.* **5 ~ sth** to follow the shape or outline of sth: *He traced the route on the map.* ◇ *A tear traced a path down her cheek.* **6 ~ sth** to copy a map, drawing, etc. by drawing on transparent paper (= TRACING PAPER) placed over it

■ *noun* **1** 🗝 [C, U] a mark, an object or a sign that shows that sb/sth existed or was present: *It's exciting to discover traces of earlier civilizations.* ◇ *Police searched the area but found* **no trace of** *the escaped prisoners.* ◇ *Years of living in England had eliminated* **all trace of** *her American accent.* ◇ *The ship had vanished* **without** (**a**) **trace**. **2** 🗝 [C] **~ of sth** a very small amount of sth: *The post-mortem revealed traces of poison in his stomach.* ◇ *She spoke without a trace of bitterness.* **3** [C] (*technical*) a line or pattern on paper or a screen that shows information that is found by a machine: *The trace showed a normal heart rhythm.* **4** [C] **~ on sb/sth** a search to find out information about the identity of sb/sth, especially what number a telephone call was made from: *The police ran a trace on the call.* **5** [C, usually pl.] one of the two long pieces of leather that fasten a CARRIAGE or CART to the horse that pulls it IDM see KICK *v.*

trace·able AW /'treɪsəbl/ *adj.* **~** (**to sb/sth**) if sth is **traceable**, you can find out where it came from, where it has gone, when it began or what its cause was: *Most telephone calls are traceable.*

'trace element *noun* **1** a chemical substance that is found in very small amounts **2** a chemical substance that living things, especially plants, need only in very small amounts to be able to grow well

tracer /'treɪsə(r)/ *noun* **1** a bullet or SHELL (= a kind of bomb) that leaves a line of smoke or flame behind it **2** (*technical*) a RADIOACTIVE substance that can be seen in the human body and is used to find out what is happening inside the body

tra·cery /'treɪsəri/ *noun* (*pl.* **-ies**) **1** [U] (*technical*) a pattern of lines and curves in stone on the top part of some church windows **2** [U, C, usually sing.] (*literary*) an attractive pattern of lines and curves

trachea /trə'kiːə; *NAmE* 'treɪkiə/ *noun* (*pl.* **trach·eas** or **trach·eae** /-kiːiː/) (*anatomy*) the tube in the throat that carries air to the lungs SYN **windpipe** ➲ VISUAL VOCAB page V48

trache·ot·omy /ˌtræki'ɒtəmi; *NAmE* ˌtreɪki'ɑːt-/ *noun* (*pl.* **-ies**) (*medical*) a medical operation to cut a hole in sb's trachea so that they can breathe

tra·cing /'treɪsɪŋ/ *noun* a copy of a map, drawing, etc. that you make by drawing on a piece of transparent paper placed on top of it

'tracing paper *noun* [U] strong transparent paper that is placed on top of a drawing, etc. so that you can follow the lines with a pen or pencil in order to make a copy of it

track 🗝 /træk/ *noun, verb*

■ *noun*

▸ ROUGH PATH **1** 🗝 [C] a rough path or road, usually one that has not been built but that has been made by people walking there: *a muddy track through the forest* ➲ VISUAL VOCAB page V4 ➲ see also CART TRACK

▸ MARKS ON GROUND **2** 🗝 [C, usually pl.] marks left by a person, an animal or a moving vehicle: *We followed the bear's tracks in the snow.* ◇ *tyre tracks*

▸ FOR TRAIN **3** 🗝 [C, U] rails that a train moves along: ***railway/railroad tracks*** ◇ *India has thousands of miles of track.* **4** 🗝 [C] (*NAmE*) a track with a number at a train station that a train arrives at or leaves from: *The train for Chicago is on track 9.* ➲ note at PLATFORM

▸ FOR RACES **5** 🗝 [C] a piece of ground with a special surface for people, cars, etc. to have races on: *a running track* ◇ *a Formula One Grand Prix track* (= for motor racing) ➲ see also DIRT TRACK (2), TRACK AND FIELD

▸ DIRECTION/COURSE **6** [C] the path or direction that sb/sth is moving in: *Police are* **on the track of** (= searching for) *the thieves.* ◇ *She is on the* ***fast track*** *to promotion* (= will get it quickly). ➲ see also ONE-TRACK MIND

▸ ON TAPE/CD **7** 🗝 [C] a piece of music or song on a record, tape or CD: *a track from their latest album* **8** [C] part of a tape, CD or computer disk that music or information can be recorded on: *a sixteen track recording studio* ◇ *She sang on the backing track.* ➲ see also SOUNDTRACK

▸ FOR CURTAIN **9** [C] a pole or rail that a curtain moves along

▸ ON LARGE VEHICLE **10** [C] a continuous belt of metal plates around the wheels of a large vehicle such as a BULLDOZER that allows it to move over the ground

IDM **ˌback on 'track** going in the right direction again after a mistake, failure, etc: *I tried to get my life back on track after my divorce.* **be ˌon 'track** to be doing the right thing in order to achieve a particular result: *Curtis is on track for the gold medal.* **keep/lose track of sb/sth** to have/not have information about what is happening or where sb/sth is: *Bank statements help you keep track of where your money is going.* ◇ *I lost all track of time* (= forgot what time it was). **make 'tracks** (*informal*) to leave a place, especially to go home **on the right/wrong 'track** thinking or behaving in the right/wrong way **stop/halt sb in their 'tracks | stop/halt/freeze in your 'tracks** to suddenly make sb stop by frightening or surprising them; to suddenly stop because sth has frightened or surprised you: *The question stopped Alice in her tracks.* ➲ more at BEAT *v.*, COVER *v.*, HOT *adj.*, WRONG *adj.*

■ *verb*

▸ FOLLOW **1** [T, I] **~** (**sb/sth**) to find sb/sth by following the marks, signs, information, etc, that they have left behind them: *hunters tracking and shooting bears* **2** [T] **~ sb/sth | ~ where, how, etc...** to follow the movements of sb/sth, especially by using special electronic equipment: *We continued tracking the plane on our radar.* **3** [T] **~ sb/sth | ~ where, how, etc...** to follow the progress or development of sb/sth: *The research project involves tracking the careers of 400 graduates.* ➲ see also FAST-TRACK

▸ OF CAMERA **4** [I] **+ adv./prep.** to move in relation to the thing that is being filmed: *The camera eventually tracked away.*

▸ SCHOOL STUDENTS **5** (*NAmE*) = STREAM (4)

▸ LEAVE MARKS **6** [T] **~ sth** (**+ adv./prep.**) (*especially NAmE*) to leave dirty marks behind you as you walk: *Don't track mud on my clean floor.*

PHR V **ˌtrack sb/sth↔'down** to find sb/sth after searching in several different places SYN **trace**: *The police have so far failed to track down the attacker.*

ˌtrack and 'field (*NAmE*) (*BrE* **ath·let·ics**) *noun* sports that people compete in, such as running and jumping ➲ VISUAL VOCAB page V37

track·ball /'trækbɔːl/ (also **'tracker ball**, **roller·ball**) *noun* (*computing*) a device containing a ball that is used instead of a mouse to move the CURSOR around the screen

track·er /ˈtrækə(r)/ *noun* a person who can find people or wild animals by following the marks that they leave on the ground

ˈ**tracker ball** *noun* (*computing*) = TRACKBALL

ˈ**tracker dog** *noun* a dog that has been trained to help the police find people or EXPLOSIVES

ˈ**track event** *noun* [usually pl.] a sports event that is a race run on a track, rather than jumping or throwing sth ➲ VISUAL VOCAB page V38 ➲ compare FIELD EVENT

ˈ**tracking station** *noun* a place where people follow the movements of aircraft, etc. in the sky by RADAR or radio

ˈ**track·less trol·ley** (*US*) (*BrE* **trol·ley·bus**) *noun* a bus driven by electricity from a cable above the street

ˈ**track record** *noun* all the past achievements, successes or failures of a person or an organization: *He has a proven track record in marketing.*

track·suit /ˈtræksuːt/ (also ˈ**jogging suit**) *noun* a warm loose pair of trousers/pants and matching jacket worn for sports practice or as informal clothes ➲ compare SHELL SUIT

tract /trækt/ *noun* **1** (*biology*) a system of connected organs or TISSUES along which materials or messages pass: *the digestive tract* ◇ *a nerve tract* **2** an area of land, especially a large one SYN **stretch**: *vast tracts of forest* **3** (sometimes *disapproving*) a short piece of writing, especially on a religious, moral or political subject, that is intended to influence people's ideas

tract·able /ˈtræktəbl/ *adj.* (*formal*) easy to deal with or control SYN **manageable** OPP **intractable** ▸ **tract·abil·ity** /ˌtræktəˈbɪləti/ *noun* [U]

ˈ**tract house** (also ˈ**tract home**) *noun* (*NAmE*) a modern house built on an area of land where a lot of other similar houses have also been built

trac·tion /ˈtrækʃn/ *noun* [U] **1** the action of pulling sth along a surface; the power that is used for doing this **2** a way of treating a broken bone in your body that involves using special equipment to pull the bone gradually back into its correct place: *He spent six weeks* **in traction** *after he broke his leg.* **3** the force that stops sth, for example the wheels of a vehicle, from sliding on the ground

ˈ**traction engine** *noun* a vehicle, driven by steam or DIESEL oil, used in the past for pulling heavy loads

trac·tor /ˈtræktə(r)/ *noun* **1** a powerful vehicle with two large and two smaller wheels, used especially for pulling farm machinery ➲ VISUAL VOCAB pages V2, V47 **2** (*NAmE*) the front part of a tractor-trailer, where the driver sits ➲ VISUAL VOCAB pages V2, V46

ˈ**tractor-trailer** (also ˈ**trailer truck**) *noun* (*NAmE*) a large lorry/truck with two sections, one in front where the driver sits and one behind for carrying goods. The sections are connected by a FLEXIBLE joint so that the tractor-trailer can turn corners more easily. ➲ VISUAL VOCAB page V46 ➲ see also ARTICULATED

trad /træd/ (also *less frequent* ˈ**trad jazz**) (both *BrE*) *noun* [U] traditional JAZZ in the style of the 1920s, with free playing (=IMPROVISATION) against a background of fixed rhythms and combinations of notes ➲ see also DIXIELAND

trad·able (also **trade·able**) /ˈtreɪdəbl/ *adj.* (*technical*) that you can easily buy and sell or exchange for money or goods SYN **marketable**

trade 🔑 /treɪd/ *noun, verb*

■ ***noun* 1** 🔑 [U] the activity of buying and selling or of exchanging goods or services between people or countries: ***international/foreign trade*** ◇ *Trade between the two countries has increased.* ◇ *the international trade in oil* ◇ *the* ***arms/drugs, etc. trade*** ➲ COLLOCATIONS at BUSINESS, INTERNATIONAL ➲ see also BALANCE OF TRADE, FAIR-TRADE, FREE TRADE **2** 🔑 [C] a particular type of business: *the* ***building/food/tourist, etc. trade*** ◇ *He works in the* ***retail trade*** (= selling goods in shops/stores). ➲ see also RAG TRADE **3** **the trade** [sing.+ sing./pl. v.] a particular area of business and the people or companies that are connected with it: *They offer discounts to the trade* (= to people who are working in the same business). ◇ *a* ***trade magazine/journal*** ➲ see also STOCK-IN-TRADE **4** 🔑 [U, C] the amount of goods or services that you sell SYN **business**: *Trade was very good last month.* **5** 🔑 [U, C] a job, especially one that involves working with your hands and that requires special training and skills: *He was a carpenter* ***by trade.*** ◇ *When she leaves school, she wants to learn a trade.* ◇ *She was surrounded by* ***the tools of her trade*** (= everything she needs to do her job). ➲ SYNONYMS at WORK IDM see JACK *n.*, PLY *v.*, ROARING, TRICK *n.*

■ ***verb* 1** 🔑 [I, T] to buy and sell things: **~ (in sth) (with sb)** *The firm openly traded in arms.* ◇ *Early explorers traded directly with the Indians.* ◇ *trading partners* (= countries that you trade with) ◇ **~ sth (with sb)** *Our products are now traded worldwide.* **2** [I] to exist and operate as a business or company: *The firm has now ceased trading.* ◇ **~ as sb/sth** *They traded as 'Walker and Son'.* **3** [I, T] **~ (sth)** to be bought and sold, or to buy and sell sth, on a STOCK EXCHANGE: *Shares were trading at under half their usual value.* **4** [T] to exchange sth that you have for sth that sb else has: **~ (sb) sth** *to* ***trade secrets/insults/jokes*** ◇ **~ sth for sth** *She traded her posters for his CD.* ◇ **~ sth with sb** *I wouldn't mind* ***trading places*** *with her for a day.*

PHR V ˈ**trade at sth** (*US*) to buy goods or shop at a particular store ˌ**trade ˈdown** to spend less money on things than you used to: *Shoppers are trading down and looking for bargains.* ˌ**trade sth↔ˈin** to give sth used as part of the payment for sth new: *He traded in his old car for a new Mercedes.* ➲ related noun TRADE-IN ˌ**trade sth↔ˈoff (against/for sth)** to balance two things or situations that are opposed to each other: *They were attempting to trade off inflation against unemployment.* ➲ related noun TRADE-OFF ˈ**trade on sth** (*disapproving*) to use sth to your own advantage, especially in an unfair way SYN **exploit**: *They trade on people's insecurity to sell them insurance.* ˌ**trade ˈup 1** to sell sth in order to buy sth more expensive: *We're going to trade up to a larger house.* **2** to give sth you have used as part of the payment for sth more expensive

ˈ**trade balance** *noun* = BALANCE OF TRADE

ˈ**trade deficit** (also ˈ**trade gap**) *noun* [usually sing.] a situation in which the value of a country's imports is greater than the value of its exports

the ˌTrade Deˈscriptions Act *noun* [sing.] (in Britain) a law that states that goods must be described honestly when they are advertised or sold: *You could get them under the Trade Descriptions Act for that!*

ˈ**trade fair** (also ˈ**trade show**) *noun* an event at which many different companies show and sell their products

ˈ**trade-in** *noun* a method of buying sth by giving a used item as part of the payment for a new one; the used item itself: *the trade-in value of a car* ◇ *Do you have a trade-in?* ➲ see also PART EXCHANGE

trade·mark /ˈtreɪdmɑːk; *NAmE* -mɑːrk/ *noun* **1** (*abbr.* TM) a name, symbol or design that a company uses for its products and that cannot be used by anyone else: *'Big Mac' is McDonald's best-known trademark.* **2** a special way of behaving or dressing that is typical of sb and that makes them easily recognized

ˈ**trade name** *noun* **1** = BRAND NAME **2** a name that is taken and used by a company for business purposes

ˈ**trade-off** *noun* **~ (between sth and sth)** the act of balancing two things that are opposed to each other: *a trade-off between increased production and a reduction in quality*

trader /ˈtreɪdə(r)/ *noun* a person who buys and sells things as a job: ***small/independent/local traders*** ◇ ***bond/currency traders***

ˈ**trade route** *noun* (in the past) the route that people buying and selling goods used to take across land or sea

ˈ**trade school** *noun* (*NAmE*) a school where students go to learn a trade

ˌ**trade ˈsecret** *noun* a secret piece of information that is known only by the people at a particular company: *The recipe for their drink is a closely guarded trade secret.*

ˈ**trade show** *noun* = TRADE FAIR

T

trades·man /ˈtreɪdzmən/ *noun* (*pl.* -men /-mən/) **1** a person whose job involves going to houses to sell or deliver goods **2** (*especially BrE*) a person who sells goods, especially in a shop/store SYN **shopkeeper** **3** (*especially NAmE*) a skilled person, especially one who makes things by hand

trades·people /ˈtreɪdzpiːpl/ *noun* [pl.] **1** people whose job involves selling goods or services, especially people who own a shop/store **2** people whose job involves training and special skills, for example CARPENTERS

the ˌTrades ˌUnion ˈCongress *noun* [sing.] = TUC

ˌtrade ˈsurplus *noun* a situation in which the value of a country's exports is greater than the value of its imports

ˌtrade ˈunion (*BrE* also **ˌtrades ˈunion**) *noun* = UNION ▸ **ˌtrade ˈunionism** *noun* [U]: *the history of trade unionism*

ˌtrade ˈunionist (also **ˌtrades ˈunionist, union·ist**) *noun* a member of a trade/labor union

ˈtrade-up *noun* a sale of an object in order to buy sth similar but better and more expensive

ˈtrade winds *noun* [pl.] strong winds that blow all the time towards the EQUATOR and then to the west

trad·ing 0-w /ˈtreɪdɪŋ/ *noun* [U] the activity of buying and selling things: *new laws on Sunday trading* (= shops being open on Sundays) ◇ *Supermarkets everywhere reported excellent trading in the run-up to Christmas.* ◇ *Shares worth $8 million changed hands during a day of hectic trading.*

ˈtrading card *noun* (*especially NAmE*) one of a set of cards, often showing sports players or other famous people on them, that children collect and exchange with one another

ˈtrading estate *noun* (*BrE*) an area of land, often on the edge of a city or town, where there are a number of businesses and small factories ⊃ compare INDUSTRIAL ESTATE

ˈtrading floor *noun* an area in a STOCK EXCHANGE or bank where shares and other SECURITIES are bought and sold

ˈtrading post *noun* a small place in an area that is a long way from any town, used as a centre for buying and selling goods (especially in N America in the past)

trad·ition 0-w AW /trəˈdɪʃn/ *noun* [C, U] a belief, custom or way of doing sth that has existed for a long time among a particular group of people; a set of these beliefs or customs: ***religious/cultural, etc. traditions*** ◇ *This region is* ***steeped in tradition.*** ◇ *The company has a* ***long tradition*** *of fine design.* ◇ *The British are said to love tradition* (= to want to do things in the way they have always been done). ◇ *They* ***broke with tradition*** (= did things differently) *and got married quietly.* ◇ ***By tradition,*** *children play tricks on 1 April.* ◇ *There's a tradition in our family that we have a party on New Year's Eve.* ◇ *He's a politician* ***in the tradition of*** (= similar in style to) *Kennedy.*

trad·ition·al 0-w AW /trəˈdɪʃənl/ *adj.* **1** 0-w being part of the beliefs, customs or way of life of a particular group of people, that have not changed for a long time: *traditional dress* ◇ ***It's traditional*** *in America to eat turkey on Thanksgiving Day.* **2** 0-w (sometimes *disapproving*) following older methods and ideas rather than modern or different ones SYN **conventional**: *traditional methods of teaching* ◇ *Their marriage is very traditional.* ▸ **trad·ition·al·ly** 0-w AW /-ʃənəli/ *adv.*: *The festival is traditionally held in May.* ◇ *Housework has traditionally been regarded as women's work.*

trad·ition·al·ism /trəˈdɪʃənəlɪzəm/ *noun* [U] the belief that customs and traditions are more important for a society than modern ideas

trad·ition·al·ist AW /trəˈdɪʃənəlɪst/ *noun* a person who prefers tradition to modern ideas or ways of doing things ▸ **trad·ition·al·ist** *adj.*

ˈtrad jazz *noun* [U] = TRAD

tra·duce /trəˈdjuːs; *NAmE* -ˈduːs/ *verb* **~ sb** (*formal*) to say things about sb that are unpleasant or not true SYN **slander**

traf·fic 0-w /ˈtræfɪk/ *noun, verb*

■ ***noun*** [U] **1** 0-w the vehicles that are on a road at a particular time: ***heavy/rush-hour traffic*** ◇ ***local/through traffic*** ◇ *There's always a lot of traffic at this time of day.* ◇ *They were stuck* ***in traffic*** *and missed their flight.* ◇ *a plan to reduce* ***traffic congestion*** ◇ ***traffic police*** (= who control traffic on a road or stop drivers who are breaking the law) ◇ *The delay is due simply to the* ***volume of traffic.*** ⊃ COLLOCATIONS at DRIVING **2** the movement of ships, trains, aircraft, etc. along a particular route: *transatlantic traffic* ◇ *air traffic control* **3** the movement of people or goods from one place to another: ***commuter/freight/passenger traffic*** ◇ *the traffic of goods between one country and another* **4** the movement of messages and signals through an electronic communication system: *the computer servers that manage global Internet traffic* **5 ~** (**in sth**) illegal trade in sth: *the traffic in firearms*

■ ***verb*** (-ck-)

PHR V **ˈtraffic in sth** to buy and sell sth illegally: *to traffic in drugs* ▸ **traf·fick·er** *noun*: *a drugs trafficker* **traf·fick·ing** *noun* [U]: *drug trafficking*

ˈtraffic calming *noun* [U] (*BrE*) ways of making roads safer, especially for people who are walking or riding bicycles, by building raised areas, etc. to make cars go more slowly

ˈtraffic circle (also **ro·tary**) (both *NAmE*) (*BrE* **roundabout**) *noun* a place where two or more roads meet, forming a circle that all traffic must go around in the same direction

ˈtraffic cone *noun* = CONE

ˈtraffic island (*BrE* also **island, ref·uge**) (*US* also **ˈsafety island**) *noun* an area in the middle of a road where you can stand and wait for cars to go past until it is safe for you to cross

ˈtraffic jam *noun* a long line of vehicles on a road that cannot move or that can only move very slowly: *We were* ***stuck in a traffic jam.*** ⊃ COLLOCATIONS at DRIVING

ˈtraffic light *noun* [C] (also **ˈtraffic lights** [pl.]) (*NAmE* also **stop·lights** [pl.]) a signal that controls the traffic on a road, by means of red, orange and green lights that show when you must stop and when you can go: *Turn left at the traffic lights.* ⊃ VISUAL VOCAB page V2

ˈtraffic warden *noun* (*BrE*) a person whose job is to check that people do not park their cars in the wrong place or for longer than is allowed, and to report on those who do or tell them that they have to pay a FINE

tra·gedian /trəˈdʒiːdiən/ *noun* (*formal*) **1** a person who writes tragedies for the theatre **2** an actor in tragedies

tra·gedy /ˈtrædʒədi/ *noun* [C, U] (*pl.* -ies) **1** a very sad event or situation, especially one that involves death: ***It's a tragedy*** *that she died so young.* ◇ ***Tragedy struck*** *the family when their son was hit by a car and killed.* ◇ *The whole affair* ***ended in tragedy.*** **2** a serious play with a sad ending, especially one in which the main character dies; plays of this type: *Shakespeare's tragedies* ◇ *Greek tragedy* ⊃ compare COMEDY

tra·gic /ˈtrædʒɪk/ *adj.* **1** making you feel very sad, usually because sb has died or suffered a lot: *He was killed in a tragic accident at the age of 24.* ◇ *Cuts in the health service could have tragic consequences for patients.* ◇ *It would be tragic if her talent remained unrecognized.* **2** [only before noun] connected with tragedy (= the style of literature): *a* ***tragic actor/hero*** ▸ **tra·gic·al·ly** /-kli/ *adv.*: *Tragically, his wife was killed in a car accident.* ◇ *He died tragically young.*

ˌtragic ˈirony *noun* [U] (*technical*) a technique in literature in which a character's actions or thoughts are known to the reader or audience but not to the other characters in the story

tragi·com·edy /ˌtrædʒiˈkɒmədi; *NAmE* -ˈkɑːm-/ *noun* [C, U] (*pl.* -ies) **1** a play that is both funny and sad; plays of this type **2** an event or a situation that is both funny and sad ▸ **tragi·com·ic** /-ˈkɒmɪk; *NAmE* -ˈkɑːm-/ *adj.*

T

trail /treɪl/ *noun, verb*
■ ***noun* 1** a long line or series of marks that is left by sb/sth: *a trail of blood* ◇ *tourists who* ***leave a trail*** *of litter everywhere they go* ◇ *The hurricane left a trail of destruction behind it.* **2** a track, sign or smell that is left behind and that can be followed, especially in hunting: *The hounds were following the fox's trail.* ◇ *The police are still* ***on the trail of*** *the escaped prisoner.* ◇ *Fortunately the* ***trail was still warm*** (= clear and easy to follow). ◇ *The* ***trail had gone cold.*** **3** a path through the countryside: *a trail through the forest* ➲ see also NATURE TRAIL **4** a route that is followed for a particular purpose: *a* ***tourist trail*** (= of famous buildings) ◇ *politicians on the* ***campaign trail*** (= travelling around to attract support) IDM see BLAZE *v.*, HIT *v.*, HOT *adj.*
■ ***verb* 1** [T, I] to pull sth behind sb/sth, usually along the ground; to be pulled along in this way: **~ sth** *A jeep trailing a cloud of dust was speeding in my direction.* ◇ *I trailed my hand in the water as the boat moved along.* ◇ (**+ adv./prep.**) *The bride's dress trailed behind her.* **2** [I] **+ adv./prep.** to walk slowly because you are tired or bored, especially behind sb else: *The kids trailed around after us while we shopped for clothes.* **3** [I, T] (used especially in the progressive tenses) to be losing a game or other contest: *United were trailing 2–0 at half-time.* ◇ **~ by sth** *We were trailing by five points.* ◇ **~ in sth** *This country is still trailing badly in scientific research.* ◇ **~ sb/sth** *The Conservatives are trailing Labour in the opinion polls.* **4** [T] **~ sb/sth** to follow sb/sth by looking for signs that show you where they have been: *The police trailed Dale for days.* **5** [I] to grow or hang downwards over sth or along the ground; to move downwards over sth: *trailing plants* ◇ *He had tears trailing down his cheeks.*
PHR V **ˌtrail aˈway/ˈoff** (of sb's speech) to become gradually quieter and then stop: *His voice trailed away to nothing.* ◇ **+ speech** *'I only hope...', she trailed off.*

ˈtrail bike *noun* a light motorcycle that can be used on rough ground

trail·blazer /ˈtreɪlbleɪzə(r)/ *noun* a person who is the first to do or discover sth and so makes it possible for others to follow ➲ compare BLAZE A TRAIL at BLAZE ▸ **trail·blaz·ing** *adj.* [usually before noun]: *trailblazing scientific research*

trail·er /ˈtreɪlə(r)/ *noun* **1** a truck, or a container with wheels, that is pulled by another vehicle: *a car towing a trailer with a boat on it* ➲ VISUAL VOCAB page V47 ➲ see also TRACTOR-TRAILER **2** (*NAmE*) (*BrE* **mobile home**) a vehicle without an engine, that can be pulled by a car or truck or used as a home or an office when it is parked: *a* ***trailer park*** (= an area where trailers are parked and used as homes) ➲ VISUAL VOCAB page V14 **3** (*NAmE*) = MOBILE HOME (1) **4** (*especially BrE*) (*NAmE* usually **preview**) a series of short scenes from a film/movie or television programme, shown in advance to advertise it ➲ SYNONYMS at ADVERTISEMENT

ˈtrailer trash *noun* [U] (*NAmE, informal, offensive*) a way of referring to poor white people from a low social class

ˈtrailer truck *noun* (*NAmE*) = TRACTOR-TRAILER

ˌtrailing ˈedge *noun* (*technical*) the rear edge of sth moving, especially an aircraft wing ➲ VISUAL VOCAB page V43

train 🔑 /treɪn/ *noun, verb*
■ ***noun* 1** 🔑 a railway/railroad engine pulling a number of coaches/cars or trucks, taking people and goods from one place to another: *to* ***get on/off a train*** ◇ *I like travelling* ***by train.*** ◇ *a* ***passenger/commuter/goods/freight train*** ◇ *to* ***catch/take/get the train*** *to London* ◇ *a* ***train journey/driver*** ◇ *You have to* ***change trains*** *at Reading.* ➲ VISUAL VOCAB page V47 ➲ see also GRAVY TRAIN, ROAD TRAIN, WAGON TRAIN **2** a number of people or animals moving in a line: *a camel train* **3** [usually sing.] a series of events or actions that are connected: *His death set in motion a* ***train of events*** *that led to the outbreak of war.* **4** the part of a long formal dress that spreads out on the floor behind the person wearing it
IDM **bring sth in its ˈtrain** (*formal*) to have sth as a result: *Unemployment brings great difficulties in its train.* **in sb's ˈtrain** (*formal*) following behind sb: *In the train of the rich and famous came the journalists.* **set sth in ˈtrain** (*formal*) to prepare or start sth: *That telephone call set in train a whole series of events.* **a train of ˈthought** the connected series of thoughts that are in your head at a particular time: *The phone ringing interrupted my train of thought.*
■ ***verb* 1** 🔑 [T, I] to teach a person or an animal the skills for a particular job or activity; to be taught in this way: **~ sb/sth** *badly trained staff* ◇ **~ sb/sth to do sth** *They train dogs to sniff out drugs.* ◇ **~ (sb) (as/in/for sth)** *He trained as a teacher before becoming an actor.* ◇ *All members of the team have trained in first aid.* ◇ **~ to do/be sth** *Sue is training to be a doctor.* **2** 🔑 [I, T] to prepare yourself/sb for a particular activity, especially a sport, by doing a lot of exercise; to prepare a person or an animal in this way: **~ (for/in sth)** *athletes training for the Olympics* ◇ **~ sb/sth (for/in sth)** *She trains horses.* ◇ *He trains the Olympic team.* **3** [T] to develop a natural ability or quality so that it improves: **~ sth** *An expert with a trained eye will spot the difference immediately.* ◇ **~ sth to do sth** *You can train your mind to think positively.* **4** [T] **~ sth (around/along/up, etc.)** to make a plant grow in a particular direction: *Roses had been trained around the door.*
PHR V **ˈtrain sth at/on sb/sth** to aim a gun, camera, light, etc. at sb/sth

train·ee /ˌtreɪˈniː/ *noun* a person who is being taught how to do a particular job: *a management trainee* ◇ *a trainee teacher* ➲ COLLOCATIONS at JOB

train·er /ˈtreɪnə(r)/ *noun* **1** (also **ˈtraining shoe**) (both *BrE*) (*NAmE* **sneak·er**) [usually pl.] a shoe that you wear for sports or as informal clothing: *a pair of trainers* ➲ VISUAL VOCAB page V52 ➲ see also CROSS-TRAINER **2** a person who teaches people or animals to perform a particular job or skill well, or to do a particular sport: *teacher trainers* ◇ *a racehorse trainer* ◇ *Her trainer had decided she shouldn't run in the race.* ➲ see also PERSONAL TRAINER

train·ing 🔑 /ˈtreɪnɪŋ/ *noun* [U]
1 🔑 **~ (in sth/in doing sth)** the process of learning the skills that you need to do a job: *staff training* ◇ *Few candidates had received any training in management.* ◇ *a training course* ➲ COLLOCATIONS at EDUCATION, JOB **2** 🔑 the process of preparing to take part in a sports competition by doing physical exercises: *to be* ***in training*** *for a race*

ˈtraining college *noun* (*BrE*) a college that trains people for a job or profession: *a police training college*

ˈtraining shoe *noun* (*BrE*) = TRAINER

ˈtraining wheels (*NAmE*) (*BrE* **sta·bil·izers**) *noun* [pl.] small wheels that are fitted at each side of the back wheel on a child's bicycle to stop it from falling over ➲ VISUAL VOCAB page V41

train·man /ˈtreɪnmən/ *noun* (*pl.* -men /-mən/) (*NAmE*) a member of the team of people operating a train

ˈtrain set *noun* a toy train, together with the track that it runs on, a toy station, etc.

train·spot·ter /ˈtreɪnspɒtə(r); *NAmE* -spɑːt-/ *noun* (*BrE*) **1** a person who collects the numbers of railway engines as a hobby **2** (*disapproving*) a person who is interested in the details of a subject that other people think are boring ▸ **ˈtrain·spot·ting** *noun* [U]

traipse /treɪps/ *verb* [I] **+ adv./prep.** (*informal*) to walk somewhere slowly when you are tired and unwilling

trait /treɪt/ *noun* a particular quality in your personality: *personality traits*

trai·tor /ˈtreɪtə(r)/ *noun* **~ (to sb/sth)** a person who gives away secrets about their friends, their country, etc: *He was seen as a traitor to the socialist cause.* ◇ *She denied that she had* ***turned traitor*** (= become a traitor).

trai·tor·ous /ˈtreɪtərəs/ *adj.* (*formal*) giving away secrets about your friends, your country, etc. ▸ **trai·tor·ous·ly** *adv.*

tra·jec·tory /trəˈdʒektəri/ (*pl.* -ies) *noun* (*technical*) the curved path of sth that has been fired, hit or thrown into the air: *a missile's trajectory* ◇ (*figurative*) *My career seemed to be on a downward trajectory.*

T

tram /træm/ (also **tram·car**) (both *BrE*) (*US* **street·car**, **trol·ley**) *noun* a vehicle driven by electricity, that runs on rails along the streets of a town and carries passengers: *a tram route* ➲ VISUAL VOCAB page V47

tram·lines /ˈtræmlaɪnz/ *noun* [pl.] **1** the rails in the street that trams run on **2** (*BrE*) (*NAmE* **alley**) (*informal*) the pair of parallel lines on a TENNIS or BADMINTON COURT that mark the extra area that is used when four people are playing

tram·mel /ˈtræml/ *verb* (-ll-, *especially US* -l-) [often passive] **~ sb/sth** (*formal*) to limit sb's freedom of movement or activity SYN **restrict** ➲ compare UNTRAMMELLED

tramp /træmp/ *noun, verb*

■ ***noun*** **1** (also **hobo**) [C] a person with no home or job who travels from place to place, usually asking people in the street for food or money **2** [sing.] **the ~ of sb/sth** the sound of sb's heavy steps: *the tramp of marching feet* **3** [C, usually sing.] a long walk SYN **trek**: *We had a long tramp home.* **4** (*old-fashioned, NAmE, disapproving*) a woman who has many sexual partners

■ ***verb*** (also *NAmE informal* **tromp**) [I, T] to walk with heavy or noisy steps, especially for a long time: (**+ adv./prep.**) *We tramped across the wet grass to look at the statue.* ◇ *the sound of tramping feet* ◇ **~ sth** *She's been tramping the streets looking for a job.*

tram·ple /ˈtræmpl/ *verb* **1** [T, I] to step heavily on sb/sth so that you crush or harm them/it with your feet: **~ sb/sth** *People were* ***trampled underfoot*** *in the rush for the exit.* ◇ *He was* ***trampled to death*** *by a runaway horse.* ◇ **~ sb/sth down** *The campers had trampled the corn down.* ◇ **~ on/over sth** *Don't trample on the flowers!* **2** [I] **~ (on/over) sb/sth** to ignore sb's feelings or rights and treat them as if they are not important: *The government is trampling on the views of ordinary people.*

tram·po·line /ˈtræmpəliːn/ *noun, verb*

■ ***noun*** a piece of equipment that is used in GYMNASTICS for doing jumps in the air. It consists of a sheet of strong material that is attached by springs to a frame. ➲ VISUAL VOCAB page V32

■ ***verb*** [I] to jump on a trampoline ▸ **tram·po·lin·ing** *noun* [U]

tram·way /ˈtræmweɪ/ *noun* the rails that form the route for a TRAM

trance /trɑːns; *NAmE* træns/ *noun* **1** [C] a state in which sb seems to be asleep but is aware of what is said to them, for example if they are HYPNOTIZED: *to* ***go/fall into a trance*** **2** [C] a state in which you are thinking so much about sth that you do not notice what is happening around you SYN **daze** **3** (also **ˈtrance music**) [U] a type of electronic dance music with HYPNOTIC rhythms and sounds

tranche /trɑːnʃ/ *noun* (*finance*) (*BrE*) one of the parts into which an amount of money or a number of shares in a company is divided

tranny (also **tran·nie**) /ˈtræni/ *noun* (*pl.* -ies) (*informal*) **1** a TRANSSEXUAL or TRANSVESTITE **2** (*especially BrE*) a TRANSISTOR radio **3** a TRANSPARENCY (1)

tran·quil /ˈtræŋkwɪl/ *adj.* (*formal*) quiet and peaceful SYN **serene**: *a tranquil scene* ◇ *the tranquil waters of the lake* ◇ *She led a tranquil life in the country.* ▸ **tran·quil·lity** (*BrE*) (*NAmE* also **tran·quil·ity**) /træŋˈkwɪləti/ *noun* [U] **tran·quil·ly** *adv.*

tran·quil·lize (also **-ise**) (both *BrE*) (*NAmE* **tran·quil·ize**) /ˈtræŋkwəlaɪz/ *verb* **~ sb/sth** to make a person or an animal calm or unconscious, especially by giving them a drug (= a TRANQUILLIZER)

tran·quil·lizer (also **-iser**) (both *BrE*) (*NAmE* **tran·quil·izer**) /ˈtræŋkwəlaɪzə(r)/ *noun* a drug used to reduce anxiety: *She's on* (= is taking) *tranquillizers.*

trans- /trænz-; træns-/ *prefix* **1** (in adjectives) across; beyond: *transatlantic* ◇ *transcontinental* **2** (in verbs) into another place or state: *transplant* ◇ *transform*

trans·act /trænˈzækt/ *verb* [T, I] **~ (sth) (with sb)** (*formal*) to do business with a person or an organization: *buyers and sellers transacting business*

trans·ac·tion /trænˈzækʃn/ *noun* **1** [C] **~ (between A and B)** a piece of business that is done between people, especially an act of buying or selling SYN **deal**: *financial transactions between companies* ◇ *commercial transactions* **2** [U] **~ of sth** (*formal*) the process of doing sth: *the transaction of government business*

trans·at·lan·tic /ˌtrænzətˈlæntɪk/ *adj.* [only before noun] **1** crossing the Atlantic Ocean: *a transatlantic flight* **2** connected with countries on both sides of the Atlantic Ocean: *a transatlantic alliance* **3** on or from the other side of the Atlantic Ocean: *to speak with a transatlantic accent*

trans·ceiver /trænˈsiːvə(r)/ *noun* a radio that can both send and receive messages

tran·scend /trænˈsend/ *verb* **~ sth** (*formal*) to be or go beyond the usual limits of sth SYN **exceed**

tran·scend·ent /trænˈsendənt/ *adj.* (*formal*) going beyond the usual limits; extremely great ▸ **tran·scend·ence** /-dəns/ *noun* [U]: *the transcendence of God*

tran·scen·den·tal /ˌtrænsenˈdentl/ *adj.* [usually before noun] going beyond the limits of human knowledge, experience or reason, especially in a religious or spiritual way: *a transcendental experience*

ˌtranscenˌdental mediˈtation (*BrE*) (*NAmE* **Transcendental Meditation™**) *noun* [U] (*abbr.* TM) a method of making yourself calm by thinking deeply in silence and repeating a special phrase to yourself many times

trans·con·tin·en·tal /ˌtrænzˌkɒntɪˈnentl; ˌtræns-; *NAmE* -ˌkɑːn-/ *adj.* crossing a continent: *a transcontinental railway/railroad*

tran·scribe /trænˈskraɪb/ *verb* **1** to record thoughts, speech or data in a written form, or in a different written form from the original: **~ sth** *Clerks transcribe everything that is said in court.* ◇ *The interview was recorded and then transcribed.* ◇ **~ sth into sth** *How many official documents have been transcribed into Braille for blind people?* **2 ~ sth** (*technical*) to show the sounds of speech using a special PHONETIC alphabet **3 ~ sth (for sth)** to write a piece of music in a different form so that it can be played by another musical instrument or sung by another voice: *a piano piece transcribed for the guitar*

tran·script /ˈtrænskrɪpt/ *noun* **1** (also **tran·scrip·tion**) a written or printed copy of words that have been spoken: *a transcript of the interview* **2** (*especially NAmE*) an official record of a student's work that shows the courses they have taken and the marks/grades they have achieved

tran·scrip·tion /trænˈskrɪpʃn/ *noun* **1** [U] the act or process of representing sth in a written or printed form: *errors made in transcription* ◇ *phonetic transcription* **2** [C] = TRANSCRIPT: *The full transcription of the interview is attached.* **3** [C] something that is represented in writing: *This dictionary gives phonetic transcriptions of all headwords.* **4** [C] a change in the written form of a piece of music so that it can be played on a different instrument or sung by a different voice

trans·ducer /trænzˈdjuːsə(r); træns-; *NAmE* -ˈduːsər/ *noun* (*technical*) a device for producing an electrical signal from another form of energy such as pressure

tran·sept /ˈtrænsept/ *noun* (*architecture*) either of the two wide parts of a church shaped like a cross, that are built at RIGHT ANGLES to the main central part ➲ compare NAVE

tran·sex·ual = TRANSSEXUAL

ˌtrans-fatty ˈacid (also **ˌtrans-ˈfat**) *noun* [C, U] a type of fat produced when oils are changed by a chemical process into solids, for example to make MARGARINE. Trans-fatty acids are believed to encourage the harmful development of CHOLESTEROL: *foods that are low in trans-fatty acids* ➲ see also MONOUNSATURATED FAT, POLYUNSATURATED FAT, SATURATED FAT, UNSATURATED FAT

trans·fer 🔑 AW *verb, noun*

■ ***verb*** /trænsˈfɜː(r)/ (-rr-)

T

▸ TO NEW PLACE **1** ⊶ [I, T] to move from one place to another; to move sth/sb from one place to another: **~ (from...) (to ...)** *The film studio is transferring to Hollywood.* ◇ (*especially NAmE*) *If I spend a semester in Madrid, will my credits transfer?* ◇ **~ sth/sb (from...) (to...)** *How can I transfer money from my bank account to his?* ◇ *The patient was transferred to another hospital.* ◇ (*especially NAmE*) *I couldn't transfer all my credits from junior college.*

▸ TO NEW JOB/SCHOOL/SITUATION **2** ⊶ [I, T] to move from one job, school, situation, etc. to another; to arrange for sb to move: **~ (from...) (to...)** *Children usually transfer to secondary school at 11 or 12.* ◇ *He transferred to UCLA after his freshman year.* ◇ **~ sb (from...) (to...)** *Ten employees are being transferred from the sales department.*

▸ FEELING/DISEASE/POWER **3** [T, I] **~ (sth) (from...) (to...)** if you **transfer** a feeling, a disease, or power, etc, or if it **transfers** from one person to another, the second person has it, often instead of the first: *Joe had already transferred his affections from Lisa to Cleo.* ◇ *This disease is rarely transferred from mother to baby* (= so that the baby has it as well as the mother).

▸ PROPERTY **4** [T] **~ sth (to sb)** to officially arrange for sth to belong to sb else or for sb else to control sth SYN **sign over**: *He transferred the property to his son.*

▸ IN SPORT **5** [I, T] (*especially BrE*) to move, or to move sb, to a different sports team, especially a professional football (SOCCER) team: **~ (from...) (to...)** *He transferred to Everton for £6 million.* ◇ **~ sb (from...) (to...)** *He was transferred from Spurs to Arsenal for a huge fee.*

▸ TO NEW VEHICLE **6** [I, T] to change to a different vehicle during a journey; to arrange for sb to change to a different vehicle during a journey: **~ (from...) (to...)** *I transferred at Bahrain for a flight to Singapore.* ◇ **~ sb (from...) (to...)** *Passengers are transferred from the airport to the hotel by taxi.*

▸ INFORMATION/MUSIC, ETC. **7** ⊶ [T, I] to copy information, music, an idea, etc. from one method of recording or presenting it to another; to be recorded or presented in a different way: **~ sth (from sth) (to sth)** *You can transfer data to a memory stick in a few seconds.* ◇ **~ (from sth) (to sth)** *The novel does not transfer well to the movies.*

■ ***noun*** /ˈtrænsfɜː(r)/

▸ CHANGE OF PLACE/JOB/SITUATION **1** ⊶ [U, C] the act of moving sb/sth from one place, group or job to another; an occasion when this happens: *electronic* ***data transfer*** ◇ *the transfer of currency from one country to another* ◇ *He has asked for a transfer to the company's Paris branch.* ◇ *After the election there was a swift* ***transfer of power.***

▸ IN SPORT **2** [U, C] the act of moving a sports player from one club or team to another: *It was the first goal he had scored since his transfer from Chelsea.* ◇ *a transfer fee* ◇ *to be* ***on the transfer list*** (= available to join another club)

▸ CHANGE OF VEHICLE **3** [U, C] an act of changing to a different place, vehicle or route when you are travelling: *The transfer from the airport to the hotel is included in the price.*

▸ TRAIN/BUS TICKET **4** [C] (*NAmE*) a ticket that allows a passenger to continue their journey on another bus or train

▸ PICTURE **5** [C] (*especially BrE*) (*NAmE* usually **decal**) a picture or design that can be removed from a piece of paper and stuck onto a surface, for example by being pressed or heated

▸ PSYCHOLOGY **6** [U] (*psychology*) the process of using behaviour which has already been learned in one situation in a new situation ➲ see also LANGUAGE TRANSFER

trans·fer·able AW /trænsˈfɜːrəbl/ *adj.* that can be moved from one place, person or use to another: *This ticket is not transferable* (= it may only be used by the person who has bought it). ◇ *We aim to provide our students with* ***transferable skills*** (= that can be used in different jobs). ▸ **trans·fer·abil·ity** /ˌtrænsˌfɜːrəˈbɪləti/ *noun* [U]

trans·fer·ence AW /ˈtrænsfərəns; *NAmE* trænsˈfɜːrəns/ *noun* [U] (*technical* or *formal*) the process of moving sth from one place, person or use to another: *the transference of heat from the liquid to the container*

trans·fer·ral /trænsˈfɜːrəl/ *noun* [U] the action of transferring sth or sb

ˈtransfer student *noun* (*NAmE*) a student at a college or university who has completed classes at another college or university after leaving high school

trans·fig·ure /trænsˈfɪɡə(r); *NAmE* -ɡjər/ *verb* [often passive] **~ sb/sth** (*literary*) to change the appearance of a person or thing so that they look more beautiful ▸ **trans·fig·ur·ation** /ˌtrænsˌfɪɡəˈreɪʃn; *NAmE* -ɡjəˈr-/ *noun* [U]

trans·fix /trænsˈfɪks/ *verb* [usually passive] **~ sb** to make sb unable to move because they are afraid, surprised, etc. SYN **paralyse**: *Luisa stood transfixed with shock.*

trans·form ⊶ AW /trænsˈfɔːm; *NAmE* -ˈfɔːrm/ *verb* **1** ⊶ **~ sth/sb (from sth) (into sth)** to change the form of sth SYN **convert**: *The photochemical reactions transform the light into electrical impulses.* **2** ⊶ **~ sth/sb (from sth) (into sth)** to completely change the appearance or character of sth, especially so that it is better: *A new colour scheme will transform your bedroom.* ◇ *It was an event that would transform my life.*

trans·form·ation AW /ˌtrænsfəˈmeɪʃn; *NAmE* -fərˈm-/ *noun* **1** [C, U] a complete change in sb/sth: *The way in which we work has* ***undergone a*** *complete* ***transformation*** *in the past decade.* ◇ *What a transformation! You look great.* ◇ **~ (from sth) (to/into sth)** *the country's transformation from dictatorship to democracy* **2** [U] used in South Africa to describe the process of making institutions and organizations more DEMOCRATIC: *a lack of transformation in the private sector* ▸ **trans·form·ation·al** /-ʃənl/ *adj.*

ˌtransforˌmational ˈgrammar *noun* [U] (*abbr.* TG) (*linguistics*) a type of grammar that describes a language as a system that has a deep structure which changes in particular ways when real sentences are produced

trans·form·er /trænsˈfɔːmə(r); *NAmE* -ˈfɔːrm-/ *noun* a device for reducing or increasing the VOLTAGE of an electric power supply, usually to allow a particular piece of electrical equipment to be used

trans·fu·sion /trænsˈfjuːʒn/ *noun* [C, U] **1** = BLOOD TRANSFUSION **2 ~ of sth** the act of investing extra money in a place or an activity that needs it: *The project badly needs a transfusion of cash.* ▸ **trans·fuse** *verb*: **~ sth (into sb/sth)** *to transfuse blood into a patient*

trans·gen·der /trænzˈdʒendə(r); træns-/ *adj.* relating to TRANSSEXUALS and TRANSVESTITES: *transgender issues* ▸ **trans·gen·dered** *adj.*

trans·gen·ic /ˌtrænzˈdʒenɪk; ˈtræns-/ *adj.*, *noun* (*biology*)
■ ***adj.*** (of a plant or an animal) having GENETIC material introduced from another type of plant or animal SYN **genetically modified**: *transgenic crops* ▸ **trans·gen·ic·ally** /-kli/ *adv.*
■ ***noun*** **1 trans·gen·ics** [pl.] the study or practice of creating transgenic plants or animals **2** [C] a transgenic plant or animal

trans·gress /trænzˈɡres; træns-/ *verb* **~ sth** (*formal*) to go beyond the limit of what is morally or legally acceptable ▸ **trans·gres·sion** /trænzˈɡreʃn; træns-/ *noun* [C, U] **trans·gres·sor** *noun*

trans·hu·mance /trænsˈhjuːməns; *NAmE* trænz-/ *noun* [U] (*technical*) the practice of moving animals to different fields in different seasons, for example to higher fields in summer and lower fields in winter

tran·si·ent /ˈtrænziənt; *NAmE* ˈtrænʃnt/ *adj.*, *noun*
■ ***adj.*** (*formal*) **1** continuing for only a short time SYN **fleeting, temporary**: *the transient nature of speech* **2** staying or working in a place for only a short time, before moving on: *a city with a large transient population* (= of students, temporary workers, etc.) ▸ **tran·si·ence** /-əns/ *noun* [U]: *the transience of human life*
■ ***noun*** (*especially NAmE*) a person who stays or works in a place for only a short time, before moving on

tran·sis·tor /trænˈzɪstə(r); -ˈsɪst-/ *noun* **1** a small electronic device used in computers, radios, televisions, etc. for controlling an electric current as it passes along a CIR-

T

CUIT **2** (also **tran,sistor 'radio**) (also *informal* **tranny** especially in *BrE*) a small radio with transistors

tran·sit AW /'trænzɪt; -sɪt/ *noun, verb*

▪ ***noun*** **1** [U] the process of being moved or carried from one place to another: *The cost includes transit.* ◇ *goods damaged* ***in transit*** ◇ *transit times* **2** [U, C, usually sing.] the act of going through a place on the way to somewhere else: *the transit lounge at Vienna airport* ◇ *a* ***transit visa*** (= one that allows a person to pass through a country but not to stay there) **3** [U] (*NAmE*) the system of buses, trains, etc. which people use to travel from one place to another: *the city's* ***mass/public transit*** *system*

▪ ***verb*** [T, I] **~ (sth)** to pass across or through an area: *The ship is currently transiting the Gulf of Mexico.*

'transit camp *noun* a camp that provides temporary accommodation for REFUGEES

tran·si·tion AW /træn'zɪʃn; -'sɪʃn/ *noun* [U, C] the process or a period of changing from one state or condition to another: **~ (from sth) (to sth)** *the transition from school to full-time work* ◇ *He will remain head of state during the* ***period of transition*** *to democracy.* ◇ **~ (between A and B)** *We need to ensure a smooth transition between the old system and the new one.* ◇ *This course is useful for students who are* ***in transition*** (= in the process of changing) *from one training programme to another.* ▸ **tran·si·tion·al** AW /-ʃənl/ *adj.*: *a transitional period* ◇ *a transitional government*

tran'sition metal (also **tran'sition element**) *noun* (*chemistry*) one of the group of metals in the centre of the PERIODIC TABLE (= a list of all the chemical elements) which form coloured COMPOUNDS and often act as CATALYSTS (= substances that make chemical reactions happen faster)

tran·si·tive /'trænsətɪv/ *adj.* (*grammar*) (of verbs) used with a DIRECT OBJECT: *In 'She wrote a letter', the verb 'wrote' is transitive and the word 'letter' is the direct object.* OPP **intransitive** ▸ **tran·si·tive·ly** *adv.*: *The verb is being used transitively.*

tran·si·tiv·ity /,trænsə'tɪvəti; ,trænz-/ *noun* [U] (*grammar*) the fact of whether a particular verb is TRANSITIVE or INTRANSITIVE

tran·si·tory AW /'trænsətri; *NAmE* -tɔːri/ *adj.* (*formal*) continuing for only a short time SYN **fleeting, temporary**: *the transitory nature of his happiness*

'Transit van™ *noun* (*BrE*) a type of large van that is used for delivering goods, carrying equipment, etc.

trans·late O-w /træns'leɪt; trænz-/ *verb*

1 O-w [T, I] to express the meaning of speech or writing in a different language: **~ sth (from sth) (into sth)** *He translated the letter into English.* ◇ *Her books have been translated into 24 languages.* ◇ *Can you help me translate this legal jargon into plain English?* ◇ **~ sth (as sth)** *'Suisse' had been wrongly translated as 'Sweden'.* ◇ **~ (from sth) (into sth)** *I don't speak Greek so Dina offered to translate for me.* ◇ *My work involves translating from German.* **2** O-w [I] to be changed from one language to another: *Most poetry does not translate well.* ◇ **~ as sth** *The Welsh name translates as 'Land's End'.* **3** [T, I] to change sth, or to be changed, into a different form: **~ sth (into sth)** *It's time to translate words into action.* ◇ **~ into sth** *I hope all the hard work will translate into profits.* **4** [T, I] **~ (sth) (as sth)** to understand sth in a particular way or give sth a particular meaning SYN **interpret**: *the various words and gestures that we translate as love*

trans·la·tion O-w /træns'leɪʃn; trænz-/ *noun*

1 O-w [U] **~ (from sth) (into sth)** | **~ (of sth) (into sth)** the process of changing sth that is written or spoken into another language: *an error in translation* ◇ *He specializes in translation from Danish into English.* ◇ *The book loses something* ***in translation.*** ◇ *The irony is* ***lost in translation.*** **2** O-w [C, U] a text or work that has been changed from one language into another: *The usual translation of 'glasnost' is 'openness'.* ◇ *a* ***rough translation*** (= not translating everything exactly) ◇ *a* ***literal translation*** (= following the original words exactly) ◇ *a* ***free translation*** (= not following the original words exactly) ◇ *a* ***word-for-word translation*** ◇ *I have only read Tolstoy* ***in translation.*** ◇ *a copy of Dryden's translation of the Aeneid* **3** [U] **~ (of sth) into sth** the process of changing sth into a different form: *the translation of theory into practice*

trans·la·tor /træns'leɪtə(r); trænz-/ *noun* a person who translates writing or speech into a different language, especially as a job: *She works as a translator of technical texts.* ➲ compare INTERPRETER

trans·lit·er·ate /træns'lɪtəreɪt; trænz-/ *verb* **~ sth (into/as sth)** (*formal*) to write words or letters using letters of a different alphabet or language ▸ **trans·lit·er·ation** /,træns,lɪtə'reɪʃn; ,trænz-/ *noun* [C, U]

trans·lu·cent /træns'luːsnt; trænz-/ *adj.* (*formal*) allowing light to pass through but not transparent ▸ **trans·lu·cence** /-sns/ (also **trans·lu·cency** /-snsi/) *noun* [U]

trans·mi·gra·tion /,trænzmaɪ'greɪʃn; ,træns-/ *noun* [U] the passing of a person's soul after their death into another body

trans·mis·sion AW /træns'mɪʃn; trænz-/ *noun* (*formal*) **1** [U] the act or process of passing sth from one person, place or thing to another SYN **transfer**: *the transmission of the disease* ◇ *the risk of transmission* **2** [U] the act or process of sending out an electronic signal or message or of broadcasting a radio or television programme: *the transmission of computer data along telephone lines* ◇ *a break in transmission* (= of a radio or television broadcast) *due to a technical fault* **3** [C] a radio or television message or broadcast: *a live transmission from Sydney* **4** [U, C] the system in a vehicle by which power is passed from the engine to the wheels

trans·mit AW /træns'mɪt; trænz-/ *verb* (-tt-) **1** [T, I] **~ (sth) (from...) (to...)** to send an electronic signal, radio or television broadcast, etc: *signals transmitted from a satellite* ◇ *The ceremony was transmitted live by satellite to over fifty countries.* ◇ *a short-wave radio that can transmit as well as receive* **2** [T] (*formal*) to pass sth from one person to another SYN **transfer**: **~ sth** *sexually transmitted diseases* ◇ **~ sth to sb** *Parents can unwittingly transmit their own fears to their children.* **3** [T] **~ sth** (*technical*) to allow heat, light, sound, etc. to pass through SYN **conduct**

trans·mit·ter /træns'mɪtə(r); trænz-/ *noun* **1** a piece of equipment used for sending electronic signals, especially radio or television signals ➲ compare RECEIVER **2 ~ of sth** (*formal*) a person or thing that transmits sth from one person or thing to another: *Emphasis was placed on the school as a transmitter of moral values.*

trans·mog·rify /,trænz'mɒgrɪfaɪ; ,træns-; *NAmE* -'mɑːg-/ *verb* (**trans·mog·ri·fies, trans·mog·ri·fy·ing, trans·mog·ri·fied, trans·mog·ri·fied**) **~ sb/sth** (often *humorous*) to change sb/sth completely, especially in a surprising way SYN **transform** ▸ **trans·mog·ri·fi·ca·tion** /,trænz,mɒgrɪfɪ'keɪʃn; ,træns-; *NAmE* -,mɑːg-/ *noun* [U]

trans·mute /trænz'mjuːt; træns-/ *verb* [T, I] **~ (sth) (into sth)** (*formal*) to change, or make sth change, into sth different SYN **transform**: *It was once thought that lead could be transmuted into gold.* ▸ **trans·mu·ta·tion** /,trænzmjuː'teɪʃn; ,træns-/ *noun* [C, U]

trans·nation·al /,trænz'næʃnəl; ,træns-/ *adj.* (*business*) existing in or involving many different countries: *transnational corporations*

tran·som /'trænsəm/ *noun* **1** a bar of wood or stone across the top of a door or window **2** (*NAmE*) = FANLIGHT

trans·par·ency /træns'pærənsi/ *noun* (*pl.* -ies) **1** (also *informal* **tranny**) [C] a picture printed on a piece of film, usually in a frame, that can be shown on a screen by shining light through the film SYN **slide**: *an overhead transparency* (= used with an OVERHEAD PROJECTOR) **2** [U] the quality of sth, such as glass, that allows you to see through it **3** [U] the quality of sth, such as an excuse or a lie, that allows sb to see the truth easily: *They were shocked by the transparency of his lies.* **4** [U] the quality of sth, such as a situation or an argument, that makes it easy to understand: *a need for greater transparency in legal documents* ◇

T

The police reforms will ensure greater transparency and accountability.

trans·par·ent 🔑 /træns'pærənt/ *adj.* **1** 🔑 (of glass, plastic, etc.) allowing you to see through it: *The insect's wings are almost transparent.* OPP **opaque** **2** (of an excuse, a lie, etc.) allowing you to see the truth easily SYN **obvious**: *a man of transparent honesty* ◇ *a transparent attempt to buy votes* ◇ *Am I that transparent?* (= are my intentions that obvious?) **3** (of language, information, etc.) easy to understand: *a campaign to make official documents more transparent* OPP **opaque** ▸ **trans·par·ent·ly** *adv.*: *transparently obvious*

tran·spir·ation /ˌtrænspɪ'reɪʃn/ *noun* [U] (*biology*) the process of water passing out from the surface of a plant or leaf ⊃ compare PERSPIRATION

tran·spire /træn'spaɪə(r)/ *verb* (*formal*) **1** [T] (not usually used in the progressive tenses) **~ that...** if **it transpires that** sth has happened or is true, it is known or has been shown to be true: *It transpired that the gang had had a contact inside the bank.* ◇ *This story, it later transpired, was untrue.* **2** [I] to happen: *You're meeting him tomorrow? Let me know what transpires.* **3** [I, T] **~ (sth)** (*biology*) when plants or leaves **transpire**, water passes out from their surface

trans·plant *verb, noun*

■ ***verb*** /træns'plɑːnt; trænz-; *NAmE* -'plænt/ **1 ~ sth (from sb/sth) (into sb/sth)** to take an organ, skin, etc. from one person, animal, part of the body, etc. and put it into or onto another: *Surgeons have successfully transplanted a liver into a four-year-old boy.* ◇ *Patients often reject transplanted organs.* ⊃ compare IMPLANT **2 ~ sth** to move a growing plant and plant it somewhere else **3 ~ sb/sth (from...) (to...)** (*formal*) to move sb/sth to a different place or environment: *Japanese production methods have been transplanted into some British factories.* ▸ **trans·plan·ta·tion** /ˌtrænsplɑːn'teɪʃn; ˌtrænz-; *NAmE* -plæn-/ *noun* [U]: *liver transplantation* ◇ *the transplantation of entire communities overseas*

■ ***noun*** /'trænsplɑːnt; 'trænz-; *NAmE* -plænt/ **1** [C, U] a medical operation in which a damaged organ, etc. is replaced with one from another person: *to have a heart transplant* ◇ *a transplant operation* ◇ *a shortage of suitable kidneys for transplant* ⊃ COLLOCATIONS at ILL **2** [C] an organ, etc. that is used in a transplant operation: *There is always a chance that the body will reject the transplant.* ⊃ compare IMPLANT

tran·spon·der /træns'pɒndə(r); *NAmE* -'pɑːn-/ *noun* (*technical*) a piece of equipment that receives radio signals and automatically sends out another signal in reply

trans·port 🔑 AW *noun, verb*

■ ***noun*** /'trænspɔːt; *NAmE* -spɔːrt/ **1** 🔑 (*especially BrE*) (*NAmE* usually **trans·por·ta·tion**) [U] a system for carrying people or goods from one place to another using vehicles, roads, etc: ***air/freight/road transport*** ◇ *the government's transport policy* ⊃ see also PUBLIC TRANSPORT **2** 🔑 (*BrE*) (*NAmE* **trans·por·ta·tion**) [U] a vehicle or method of travel: *Applicants must have their own transport.* ◇ *Transport to and from the airport is included in the price.* ◇ *His bike is his only **means of transport**.* **3** 🔑 [U] (*especially BrE*) (also **trans·por·ta·tion** *NAmE, BrE*) the activity or business of carrying goods from one place to another using lorries/trucks, trains, etc: *The goods were damaged during transport.* ◇ *controls on the transport of nuclear waste* **4** [C] a ship, plane or lorry/truck used for carrying soldiers, supplies, etc. from one place to another **5 transports** [pl.] **~ of sth** (*literary*) strong feelings and emotions: *to be in transports of delight*

■ ***verb*** /træn'spɔːt; *NAmE* -'spɔːrt/ **1** 🔑 **~ sth/sb (+ adv./prep.)** to take sth/sb from one place to another in a vehicle: *to transport goods/passengers* **2** 🔑 **~ sth (+ adv./prep.)** to move sth somewhere by means of a natural process SYN **carry**: *The seeds are transported by the wind.* ◇ *Blood transports oxygen around the body.* **3 ~ sb (+ adv./prep.)** to make sb feel that they are in a different place, time or situation: *The book transports you to another world.* **4 ~ sb (+ adv./prep.)** (in the past) to send sb to a far away place as a punishment: *British convicts were transported to Australia for life.*

trans·port·able /træn'spɔːtəbl; *NAmE* -'spɔːrt-/ *adj.* [not usually before noun] that can be carried or moved from one place to another, especially by a vehicle

trans·por·ta·tion 🔑 AW /ˌtrænspɔː'teɪʃn; *NAmE* -pɔːr't-/ *noun* [U] **1** (*especially NAmE*) = TRANSPORT: *the transportation industry* ◇ *public transportation* (= the system of buses, trains, etc. provided for people to travel from one place to another) ◇ *The city is providing free transportation to the stadium from downtown.* ◇ *the transportation of heavy loads* ◇ *transportation costs* **2** (in the past) the act of sending criminals to a place that is far away as a form of punishment

'transport cafe *noun* (*BrE*) a CAFE at the side of a main road that serves cheap food and is used mainly by lorry/truck drivers ⊃ compare TRUCK STOP

trans·port·er AW /træn'spɔːtə(r); *NAmE* -'spɔːrt-/ *noun* a large vehicle used for carrying heavy objects, for example other vehicles: *a car transporter* ⊃ VISUAL VOCAB page V46

trans·pose /træn'spəʊz; *NAmE* -'spoʊz/ *verb* [often passive] **1 ~ sth** (*formal*) to change the order of two or more things SYN **reverse** **2 ~ sth (from sth) (to sth)** (*formal*) to move or change sth to a different place or environment or into a different form SYN **transfer**: *The director transposes Shakespeare's play from 16th century Venice to present-day England.* **3 ~ sth** (*music*) to write or play a piece of music or a series of notes in a different key ▸ **trans·pos·ition** /ˌtrænspə'zɪʃn/ *noun* [C, U]

trans·sex·ual (also **tran·sex·ual**) /trænz'sekʃuəl; træns-/ (also *informal* **tranny**) *noun* a person who feels emotionally that they want to live, dress, etc. as a member of the opposite sex, especially one who has a medical operation to change their sexual organs

tran·sub·stan·ti·ation /ˌtrænsəbˌstænʃi'eɪʃn/ *noun* [U] the belief that the bread and wine of the COMMUNION service become the actual body and blood of Jesus Christ after they have been BLESSED, even though they still look like bread and wine

trans·verse /'trænzvɜːs; 'træns-; *NAmE* -vɜːrs/ *adj.* [usually before noun] (*technical*) placed across sth SYN **diagonal**: *A transverse bar joins the two posts.*

ˌtransverse 'wave *noun* (*technical*) a wave that VIBRATES at 90° to the direction in which it is moving ⊃ compare LONGITUDINAL WAVE

trans·vest·ite /trænz'vestaɪt; træns-/ (also *informal* **tranny**) *noun* a person, especially a man, who enjoys dressing as a member of the opposite sex ▸ **trans·vest·ism** /trænz'vestɪzəm; træns-/ *noun* [U]

trap 🔑 /træp/ *noun, verb*

■ ***noun***

▸ FOR ANIMALS **1** 🔑 a piece of equipment for catching animals: *a fox with its leg in a trap* ◇ *A trap was laid, with fresh bait.* ⊃ see also MOUSETRAP

▸ TRICK **2** 🔑 a clever plan designed to trick sb, either by capturing them or by making them do or say sth that they did not mean to do or say: *She had **set a trap** for him and he had walked straight into it.* ⊃ see also BOOBY TRAP, RADAR TRAP, SAND TRAP, TOURIST TRAP

▸ BAD SITUATION **3** [usually sing.] an unpleasant situation from which it is hard to escape: *the unemployment trap* ◇ *Some women see marriage as a trap.* ⊃ see also DEATH-TRAP, POVERTY TRAP

▸ CARRIAGE **4** a light CARRIAGE with two wheels, pulled by a horse: *a pony and trap*

▸ MOUTH **5** (*slang*) mouth SYN **gob**: *Shut your trap!* (= a rude way of telling sb to be quiet) ◇ *to keep your trap shut* (= to not tell a secret)

▸ FOR RACING DOG **6** a CAGE from which a GREYHOUND (= a type of dog) is let out at the start of a race

▸ IN GOLF **7** (*NAmE*) = BUNKER

IDM **to fall into/avoid the trap of doing sth** to do/avoid doing sth that is a mistake but which seems at first to be a

T

good idea: *Parents often fall into the trap of trying to do everything for their children.* ➲ more at SPRING *v.*

■ ***verb*** (-pp-)

▸ IN DANGEROUS/BAD SITUATION **1** ~ **sb** (**+ adv./prep.**) to keep sb in a dangerous place or bad situation that they want to get out of but cannot: *Help! I'm trapped!* ◇ *They were trapped in the burning building.* ◇ *We became trapped by the rising floodwater.* ◇ *He was trapped in an unhappy marriage.* ◇ *I feel trapped in my job.*

▸ PART OF BODY/CLOTHING **2** ~ **sth** (**+ adv./prep.**) to have part of your body, your clothing, etc. held in a place so tightly that you cannot remove it and it may be injured or damaged: *I trapped my coat in the car door.* ◇ *The pain was caused by a trapped nerve.*

▸ CATCH **3** ~ **sth** to catch or keep sth in a place and prevent it from escaping, especially so that you can use it: *Solar panels trap energy from the sun.* **4** ~ **sb/sth** (**+ adv./prep.**) to force sb/sth into a place or situation that they cannot escape from, especially in order to catch them: *The escaped prisoners were eventually trapped in an underground garage and recaptured.* **5** ~ **sth** to catch an animal in a trap: *Raccoons used to be trapped for their fur.*

▸ TRICK **6** ~ **sb** (**into sth/into doing sth**) to trick sb into sth: *He felt he had been trapped into accepting the terms of the contract.*

trap·door /ˈtræpdɔː(r)/ *noun* a small door in a floor or ceiling

trap·eze /trəˈpiːz; *NAmE* træ-/ *noun* a wooden or metal bar hanging from two pieces of rope high above the ground, used especially by CIRCUS performers: *a trapeze artist*

tra·pez·ium /trəˈpiːziəm/ *noun* (*pl.* **tra·pez·iums** or **tra·pezia** /trəˈpiːziə/) (*geometry*) **1** (*BrE*) (*NAmE* **trap·ez·oid**) a flat shape with four straight sides, one pair of opposite sides being parallel and the other pair not parallel ➲ VISUAL VOCAB page V58 **2** (*NAmE*) (*BrE* **trap·ez·oid**) a flat shape with four straight sides, none of which are parallel

trap·ez·oid /ˈtræpəzɔɪd/ *noun* (*geometry*) **1** (*BrE*) (*NAmE* **tra·pez·ium**) a flat shape with four straight sides, none of which are parallel ➲ VISUAL VOCAB page V58 **2** (*NAmE*) (*BrE* **tra·pez·ium**) a flat shape with four straight sides, one pair of opposite sides being parallel and the other pair not parallel

trap·per /ˈtræpə(r)/ *noun* a person who traps and kills animals, especially for their fur

trap·pings /ˈtræpɪŋz/ *noun* [pl.] ~ (**of sth**) (*formal*, especially *disapproving*) the possessions, clothes, etc. that are connected with a particular situation, job or social position: *They enjoyed all the trappings of wealth.*

Trap·pist /ˈtræpɪst/ *adj.* belonging to a group of MONKS who have very strict rules, including a rule that they must not speak ▸ **Trap·pist** *noun*

trash /træʃ/ *noun, verb*

■ ***noun*** [U] **1** (*NAmE*) things that you throw away because you no longer want or need them ➲ note at RUBBISH **2** (*informal, disapproving*) objects, writing, ideas, etc. that you think are of poor quality: *What's this trash you're watching?* ◇ (*especially BrE*) *He's talking trash* (= nonsense). **3** (*NAmE, informal*) an offensive word used to describe people that you do not respect: ***white trash*** (= poor white people, especially those living in the southern US) ➲ see also TRAILER TRASH

■ ***verb*** (*informal*) **1** ~ **sth** to damage or destroy sth: *The band was famous for trashing hotel rooms.* **2** ~ **sth/sb** to criticize sth/sb very strongly **3** ~ **sth** (*NAmE*) to throw away sth that you do not want: *I'm leaving my old toys here—if you don't want them, just trash them.*

ˈtrash can *noun* (*NAmE*) **1** (*BrE* **ˈlitter bin**) a container for people to put rubbish/garbage in, in the street or in a public building **2** = GARBAGE CAN

ˈtrash talk (also **ˈtrash talking**) *noun* [U] (*NAmE, informal*) a way of talking which is intended to make sb, especially an opponent, feel less confident ➲ compare SLEDGING

trashy /ˈtræʃi/ *adj.* (*informal*) (**trash·ier, trashi·est**) of poor quality; with no value SYN **rubbishy**: *trashy TV shows*

trat·toria /ˌtrætəˈriːə/ *noun* (from *Italian*) an Italian restaurant serving simple food

trauma /ˈtrɔːmə; *NAmE* ˈtraʊmə/ *noun* **1** [U] (*psychology*) a mental condition caused by severe shock, especially when the harmful effects last for a long time **2** [C, U] an unpleasant experience that makes you feel upset and/or anxious: *She felt exhausted after the traumas of recent weeks.* **3** [U, C] (*medical*) an injury: *The patient suffered severe brain trauma.*

trau·mat·ic /trɔːˈmætɪk; *NAmE* traʊˈm-/ *adj.* **1** extremely unpleasant and causing you to feel upset and/or anxious: *a traumatic experience* ◇ *Divorce can be traumatic for everyone involved.* **2** [only before noun] (*psychology* or *medical*) connected with or caused by trauma: *traumatic amnesia* ➲ see also POST-TRAUMATIC STRESS DISORDER ▸ **trau·mat·ic·al·ly** /-kli/ *adv.*

trau·ma·tize (*BrE* also **-ise**) /ˈtrɔːmətaɪz; *NAmE* ˈtraʊm-/ *verb* [usually passive] ~ **sb** to shock and upset sb very much, often making them unable to think or work normally

trav·ail /ˈtræveɪl; trəˈveɪl/ *noun* [U, pl.] (*old use* or *literary*) an unpleasant experience or situation that involves a lot of hard work, difficulties and/or suffering

travel /ˈtrævl/ *verb, noun*

■ ***verb*** (-ll-, *especially US* -l-) **1** [I, T] to go from one place to another, especially over a long distance: *to travel around the world* ◇ *I go to bed early if I'm travelling the next day.* ◇ *I love travelling by train.* ◇ *We always travel first class.* ◇ *We travelled to California for the wedding.* ◇ *When I finished college I **went travelling** for six months* (= spent time visiting different places). ◇ ~ **sth** *He travelled the length of the Nile in a canoe.* ◇ *I travel 40 miles to work every day.* **2** [I] (**+ adv./prep.**) to go or move at a particular speed, in a particular direction, or a particular distance: *to travel at 50 miles an hour* ◇ *Messages travel along the spine from the nerve endings to the brain.* ◇ *News travels fast these days.* **3** [I] (of food, wine, an object, etc.) to be still in good condition after a long journey: *Some wines do not travel well.* **4** [I] (**+ adv./prep.**) (of a book, an idea, etc.) to be equally successful in another place and not just where it began: *Some writing travels badly in translation.* **5** [I] to go fast: *Their car can really travel!* **6** [I] (in BASKETBALL) to move while you are holding the ball, in a way that is not allowed

IDM **travel ˈlight** to take very little with you when you go on a trip

■ ***noun*** **1** [U] the act or activity of travelling: ***air/rail/space, etc. travel*** ◇ *travel expenses* ◇ *The job involves a considerable amount of **foreign travel**.* ◇ *the travel industry* ◇ *travel sickness* ◇ *a **travel bag/clock*** (= for use when travelling) ◇ *The pass allows **unlimited travel** on all public transport in the city.* **2** **travels** [pl.] time spent travelling, especially in foreign countries and for pleasure: *The novel is based on his travels in India.* ◇ *When are you off **on your travels*** (= going travelling)?

ˈtravel agency *noun* a company that arranges travel and/or accommodation for people going on a holiday/vacation or journey

ˈtravel agent *noun* **1** a person or business whose job is to make arrangements for people wanting to travel, for example buying tickets or arranging hotel rooms ➲ COLLOCATIONS at TRAVEL **2** **travel agent's** (*pl.* **travel agents**) a shop/store where you can go to arrange a holiday/vacation, etc: *He works in a travel agent's.* ➲ see also TRAVEL AGENCY

trav·ela·tor (also **trav·ola·tor**) /ˈtrævəleɪtə(r)/ *noun* a moving path, especially at an airport

trav·elled (*especially US* **trav·eled**) /ˈtrævld/ *adj.* (usually in compounds) **1** (of a person) having travelled the amount mentioned: *a much-travelled man* **2** (of a road, etc.) used the amount mentioned: *The path was steeper and less travelled than the previous one.*

trav·el·ler (*especially US* **trav·el·er**) /ˈtrævələ(r)/ *noun*

1 a person who is travelling or who often travels: *She is*

Collocations

Travel and tourism

Holidays/vacations

- **have/take** (*BrE*) a holiday/(*NAmE*) a vacation/a break/a day off/(*BrE*) a gap year
- **go on/be on** holiday/vacation/leave/honeymoon/safari/a trip/a tour/a cruise/a pilgrimage
- **go** backpacking/camping/hitchhiking/sightseeing
- **plan** a trip/a holiday/a vacation/your itinerary
- **book** accommodation/a hotel room/a flight/tickets
- **have/make/cancel** a reservation/(*especially BrE*) booking
- **rent** a villa/(*both BrE*) a holiday home/a holiday cottage
- (*especially BrE*) **hire**/(*especially NAmE*) **rent** a car/bicycle/moped
- **stay in** a hotel/a bed and breakfast/a youth hostel/a villa/(*both BrE*) a holiday home/a caravan
- **cost/charge $100 a/per night for** a single/double/twin/standard/(*BrE*) en suite room
- **check into/out of** a hotel/a motel/your room
- **pack/unpack** your suitcase/bags
- **call/order** room service
- **cancel/cut short** a trip/holiday/vacation

Foreign travel

- **apply for/get/renew** a/your passport
- **take out/buy/get** travel insurance
- **catch/miss** your plane/train/ferry/connecting flight
- **fly (in)/travel in** business/economy class
- **make/have** a brief/two-day/twelve-hour stopover/(*NAmE also*) layover in Hong Kong
- **experience/cause/lead to** delays
- **check (in)/collect/get/lose** (your) (*especially BrE*) luggage/(*especially NAmE*) baggage
- **be charged for/pay** excess baggage
- **board/get on/leave/get off** the aircraft/plane/ship/ferry
- **taxi down/leave/approach/hit/overshoot** the runway
- **experience/hit/encounter** severe turbulence
- **suffer from/recover from/get over your** jet lag/travel sickness

The tourist industry

- **attract/draw/bring** tourists/visitors
- **encourage/promote/hurt** tourism
- **promote/develop** ecotourism
- **build/develop/visit** a tourist/holiday/(*especially BrE*) seaside/beach/ski resort
- **work for/be operated by** a major hotel chain
- **be served by/compete with** low-cost/(*especially NAmE*) low-fare/budget airlines
- **book sth through/make a booking through/use** a travel agent
- **contact/check with** your travel agent/tour operator
- **book/be on/go on** a package deal/holiday/tour
- **buy/bring back** (tacky/overpriced) souvenirs

a frequent traveller to Belgium. ◇ *He passed the time chatting with fellow travellers.* ➲ see also COMMERCIAL TRAVELLER **2** (*BrE*) a person who does not live in one place but travels around, especially as part of a group: *New Age travellers* HELP **Traveller** is used especially to talk about travelling people of Irish origin, but is also used as a word for all travelling people, including people from the ROMANI community. ➲ compare GYPSY

ˈtraveller's cheque (*US* **ˈtraveler's check**) *noun* a cheque for a fixed amount, sold by a bank or TRAVEL AGENT, that can be exchanged for cash in foreign countries

trav·el·ling (*especially US* **trav·el·ing**) /ˈtrævəlɪŋ/ *adj., noun*
▪ ***adj.*** [only before noun] **1** going from place to place: ***a travelling circus/exhibition/performer, etc.*** ◇ *the travelling public* ◇ (*BrE*) ***travelling people*** (= people who have no fixed home, especially those living in a community that moves from place to place, also known as 'travellers') **2** used when you travel: *a travelling clock*
▪ ***noun*** [U] the act of travelling: *The job requires a lot of travelling.* ◇ *a* ***travelling companion***

ˌtravelling ˈsalesman (*especially US* **ˌtraveling ˈsalesman**) *noun* (*old-fashioned*) = SALES REPRESENTATIVE

trav·el·ogue (*NAmE* also **trav·elog**) /ˈtrævəlɒg; *NAmE* -lɔːg; -lɑːg/ *noun* a film/movie, broadcast or piece of writing about travel

ˈtravel-sick *adj.* (*BrE*) feeling sick because you are travelling in a vehicle ▸ **ˈtravel-sickness** (*BrE*) (also **ˈmotion sickness** *NAmE, BrE*) *noun* [U]

tra·verse *verb, noun*
▪ ***verb*** /trəˈvɜːs; *NAmE* -ˈvɜːrs/ **~ sth** (*formal* or *technical*) to cross an area of land or water
▪ ***noun*** /ˈtrævɜːs; *NAmE* -vɜːrs/ (in mountain climbing) an act of moving sideways or walking across a steep slope, not climbing up or down it; a place where this is possible or necessary

trav·esty /ˈtrævəsti/ *noun* (*pl.* **-ies**) **~ (of sth)** something that does not have the qualities or values that it should have, and as a result is often shocking or offensive SYN **parody**: *The trial was a* ***travesty of justice***.

trav·ola·tor = TRAVELATOR

trawl /trɔːl/ *verb, noun*
▪ ***verb*** **1** [T, I] to search through a large amount of information or a large number of people, places, etc. looking for a particular thing or person: **~ sth (for sth/sb)** *She trawled the shops for bargains.* ◇ **~ (through sth) (for sth/sb)** *The police are trawling through their files for similar cases.* **2** [I] **~ (for sth)** to fish for sth by pulling a large net with a wide opening through the water
▪ ***noun*** **1** a search through a large amount of information, documents, etc: *A quick trawl through the newspapers yielded five suitable job adverts.* **2** (also **ˈtrawl net**) a large net with a wide opening, that is dragged along the bottom of the sea by a boat in order to catch fish

trawl·er /ˈtrɔːlə(r)/ *noun* a fishing boat that uses large nets that it drags through the sea behind it

tray /treɪ/ *noun* **1** a flat piece of wood, metal or plastic with raised edges, used for carrying or holding things, especially food: *He brought her breakfast in bed on a tray.* ◇ *She came in with a tray of drinks.* ◇ *a tea tray* **2** (often in compounds) a shallow plastic box, used for various purposes: *a seed tray* (= for planting seeds in) ◇ *a cat's litter tray* ➲ VISUAL VOCAB pages V29, V56 ➲ see also BAKING TRAY, IN TRAY, OUT TRAY

TRC /ˌtiː ɑː ˈsiː; *NAmE* ɑːr/ *abbr.* Truth and Reconciliation Commission (an organization that was established in South Africa to investigate how people had been treated unfairly in the past)

treach·er·ous /ˈtretʃərəs/ *adj.* **1** that cannot be trusted; intending to harm you SYN **deceitful**: *He was weak, cowardly and treacherous.* ◇ *lying, treacherous words* **2** dangerous, especially when seeming safe: *The ice on the roads made driving conditions treacherous.* ▸ **treach·er·ous·ly** *adv.*

treach·ery /ˈtretʃəri/ *noun* [U, C] (*pl.* **-ies**) behaviour that involves not being loyal to sb who trusts you; an example of this: *an act of treachery*

trea·cle /ˈtriːkl/ *noun* [U] (*BrE*) **1** (*NAmE* **mo·las·ses**) a thick black sweet sticky liquid produced when sugar is REFINED (= made pure), used in cooking **2** = GOLDEN SYRUP: *a treacle tart*

trea·cly /ˈtriːkli/ *adj.* **1** (*BrE*) like treacle: *a treacly brown liquid* **2** expressing feelings of love in a way that seems false or exaggerated: *treacly music*

T

tread /tred/ *verb, noun*

■ **verb** (**trod** /trɒd; *NAmE* trɑːd/, **trod·den** /ˈtrɒdn; *NAmE* ˈtrɑːdn/ or **trod**) **1** [I] **~ (on/in/over sth/sb)** (*especially BrE*) to put your foot down while you are stepping or walking: *Ouch! You trod on my toe!* ◇ *Careful you don't tread in that puddle.* **2** [T] **~ sth** (**+ adv./prep.**) to crush or press sth with your feet **SYN** **trample**: *Don't tread ash into the carpet!* ◇ *The wine is still made by treading grapes in the traditional way.* **3** [T, I] **~ (sth)** (*formal* or *literary*) to walk somewhere: *Few people had trod this path before.* ◇ *He was treading quietly and cautiously.*

IDM **tread ˈcarefully, ˈwarily, etc.** to be very careful about what you do or say: *The government will have to tread very carefully in handling this issue.* **ˌtread a difficult, dangerous, solitary, etc. ˈpath** to choose and follow a particular way of life, way of doing sth, etc: *A restaurant has to tread the tricky path between maintaining quality and keeping prices down.* **ˌtread on sb's ˈheels** to follow sb closely **ˌtread on sb's ˈtoes** (*especially BrE*) (*NAmE* usually **ˌstep on sb's ˈtoes**) (*informal*) to offend or annoy sb, especially by getting involved in sth that is their responsibility **ˌtread ˈwater** **1** to keep yourself vertical in deep water by moving your arms and legs **2** to make no progress while you are waiting for sth to happen ➲ more at FOOL *n.*, LINE *n.*, TIGHTROPE

■ **noun** **1** [sing.] the way that sb walks; the sound that sb makes when they walk: *I heard his heavy tread on the stairs.* **2** [C, U] the raised pattern on the surface of a tyre on a vehicle: *The tyres were worn below the legal limit of 1.6 mm of tread.* **3** [C] the upper surface of a step or stair ➲ picture at STAIRCASE ➲ compare RISER

treadle /ˈtredl/ *noun* (especially in the past) a device worked by the foot to operate a machine

tread·mill /ˈtredmɪl/ *noun* **1** [sing.] work or a way of life that is boring or tiring because it involves always doing the same things: *I'd like to escape the office treadmill.* **2** [C] (especially in the past) a large wheel turned by the weight of people or animals walking on steps around its inside edge, and used to operate machinery **3** [C] an exercise machine that has a moving surface that you can walk or run on while remaining in the same place ➲ VISUAL VOCAB page V35

trea·son /ˈtriːzn/ (also **ˌhigh ˈtreason**) *noun* [U] the crime of doing sth that could cause danger to your country, such as helping its enemies during a war ▸ **treas·on·able** /ˈtriːzənəbl/ *adj.*: *a treasonable act*

treas·ure /ˈtreʒə(r)/ *noun, verb*

■ **noun** **1** [U] a collection of valuable things such as gold, silver and jewellery: *buried treasure* ◇ *a pirate's treasure chest* **2** [C, usually pl.] a highly valued object: *the priceless art treasures of the Uffizi Gallery* **3** [sing.] a person who is much loved or valued

■ **verb** **~ sth** to have or keep sth that you love and that is extremely valuable to you **SYN** **cherish**: *I treasure his friendship.* ◇ *This ring is my most treasured possession.*

ˈtreasure house *noun* a place that contains many valuable or interesting things: *The area is a treasure house of archaeological relics.*

ˈtreasure hunt *noun* a game in which players try to find a hidden prize by answering a series of questions that have been left in different places

treas·urer /ˈtreʒərə(r)/ *noun* a person who is responsible for the money and accounts of a club or an organization

ˈtreasure trove *noun* **1** [U, C, usually sing.] valuable things that are found hidden and whose owner is unknown **2** [C, usually sing.] a place, book, etc. containing many useful or beautiful things

treas·ury /ˈtreʒəri/ *noun* (*pl.* **-ies**) **1 the Treasury** [sing. + sing./pl. v.] (in Britain, the US and some other countries) the government department that controls public money **2** [C] a place in a castle, etc. where valuable things are stored

ˈtreasury bill (also *informal* **ˈT-bill**) *noun* a type of investment sold by the US government in which a fixed amount of money is paid back on a certain date

treat 0‑ᵂ /triːt/ *verb, noun*

■ **verb**

▸ BEHAVE TOWARDS SB/STH **1** 0‑ᵂ to behave in a particular way towards sb/sth: **~ sb/sth** (**with sth**) *to treat people with* ***respect/consideration/suspicion, etc.*** ◇ *Treat your keyboard with care and it should last for years.* ◇ **~ sb/sth like sth** *My parents still treat me like a child.* ◇ **~ sb/sth as sth**) *He was treated as a hero on his release from prison.*

▸ CONSIDER **2** 0‑ᵂ **~ sth as sth** to consider sth in a particular way: *I decided to treat his remark as a joke.* **3** 0‑ᵂ **~ sth + adv./prep.** to deal with or discuss sth in a particular way: *The question is treated in more detail in the next chapter.*

▸ ILLNESS/INJURY **4** 0‑ᵂ **~ sb** (**for sth**) (**with sth**) to give medical care or attention to a person, an illness, an injury, etc: *She was treated for sunstroke.* ◇ *The condition is usually treated with drugs and a strict diet.* ➲ COLLOCATIONS at INJURY

▸ USE CHEMICAL **5** 0‑ᵂ **~ sth** (**with sth**) to use a chemical substance or process to clean, protect, preserve, etc. sth: *to treat crops with insecticide* ◇ *wood treated with preservative*

▸ PAY FOR STH ENJOYABLE **6** **~ sb/yourself** (**to sth**) to pay for sth that sb/you will enjoy and that you do not usually have or do: *She treated him to lunch.* ◇ *Don't worry about the cost —I'll treat you.* ◇ *I'm going to treat myself to a new pair of shoes.*

▸ **treat·able** *adj.*: *a treatable infection*

IDM **treat sb like ˈdirt** (*informal*) to treat sb with no respect at all

PHR V **ˈtreat sb to sth** to entertain sb with sth special: *The crowd were treated to a superb display of tennis.*

■ **noun** something very pleasant and enjoyable, especially sth that you give sb or do for them: *We took the kids to the zoo* ***as a special treat.*** ◇ *You've never been to this area before? Then you're in for a real treat.* ◇ *When I was young chocolate was a treat.* ◇ *Let's go out for lunch—****my treat*** (= I will pay). ➲ SYNONYMS at PLEASURE

IDM **a ˈtreat** (*BrE, informal*) extremely well or good: *His idea worked a treat* (= was successful). ➲ more at TRICK *n.*

trea·tise /ˈtriːtɪs; -tɪz/ *noun* **~ (on sth)** (*formal*) a long and serious piece of writing on a particular subject

treat·ment 0‑ᵂ /ˈtriːtmənt/ *noun*

1 0‑ᵂ [U, C] **~ (for sth)** something that is done to cure an illness or injury, or to make sb look and feel good: *He is receiving treatment for shock.* ◇ *She is* ***responding*** *well* ***to treatment.*** ◇ *to require* ***hospital/medical treatment*** ◇ *There are various treatments available for this condition.* ◇ *Guests at the health spa receive a range of beauty treatments.* ➲ COLLOCATIONS at ILL **2** 0‑ᵂ [U] a way of behaving towards or dealing with a person or thing: *the brutal treatment of political prisoners* ◇ *Certain city areas have been singled out for special treatment.* **3** [U, C] a way of dealing with or discussing a subject, work of art, etc: *Shakespeare's treatment of madness in 'King Lear'* **4** [U, C] a process by which sth is cleaned, or protected against sth: *a sewage* ***treatment plant*** ◇ **~ for sth** *an effective treatment for dry rot*

treaty /ˈtriːti/ *noun* (*pl.* **-ies**) a formal agreement between two or more countries: *the Treaty of Rome* ◇ *a peace treaty* ◇ *to* ***draw up/sign/ratify a treaty*** ◇ *Under* ***the terms of the treaty,*** *La Rochelle was ceded to the English.* ➲ COLLOCATIONS at WAR

treble /ˈtrebl/ *noun, verb, det., adj.*

■ **noun** **1** [U] the high tones or part in music or a sound system: *to turn up the treble on the stereo* ➲ compare BASS **2** [C] a child's high voice; a boy who sings with a treble voice ➲ compare SOPRANO **3** [sing.] a musical part written for a treble voice **4** [sing.] (*BrE*) three successes in a row: *The victory completed a treble for the horse's owner.*

■ **verb** [I, T] to become, or to make sth, three times as much or as many **SYN** **triple**: *Cases of food poisoning have trebled in the last two years.* ◇ **~ sth** *He trebled his earnings in two years.*

■ **det.** [usually before noun] three times as much or as many: *Capital expenditure was treble the 2007 level.*

■ **adj.** [only before noun] high in tone: *a treble voice* ◇ *the* ***treble clef*** (= the symbol in music showing that the notes following it are high) ➲ picture at MUSIC ➲ compare BASS

tree 0-π /tri:/ *noun*
a tall plant that can live a long time. Trees have a thick central wooden TRUNK from which branches grow, usually with leaves on them: *an oak tree* ◇ *to* ***plant a tree*** ◇ *to* ***chop/cut down a tree*** ◇ *They followed a path through the trees.* ➲ COLLOCATIONS at LIFE ➲ VISUAL VOCAB page V8 ➲ compare BUSH, SHRUB ➲ see also BAY TREE, CHRISTMAS TREE, FAMILY TREE, GUM TREE, PLANE TREE
IDM **be out of your 'tree** (*informal*) to be behaving in a crazy or stupid way, perhaps because of drugs or alcohol ➲ more at APPLE *n.*, BARK *v.*, FOREST, GROW, TOP *n.*, WOOD

'tree diagram *noun* a diagram with lines that divide more and more as you move to lower levels to show the relationships between processes, people etc.

'tree house *noun* a structure built in the branches of a tree, usually for children to play on

'tree-hugger *noun* (*informal*, usually *disapproving*) a person who cares very much about the environment and tries to protect it

tree·less /'tri:ləs/ *adj.* without trees: *a treeless plain*

tree·line /'tri:laɪn/ *noun* [sing.] a level of land, for example on a mountain, above which trees will not grow

'tree structure *noun* (*computing*) a diagram that uses lines that divide into more and more lines to show the various levels of a computer program, and how each part relates to a part in the level above

'tree surgeon (also *formal* **ar·bor·ist**) *noun* a person whose job is treating trees that are damaged or have a disease, especially by cutting off branches, to try to preserve them ▸ **'tree surgery** *noun* [U]

tree·top /'tri:tɒp; *NAmE* -tɑ:p/ *noun* [usually pl.] the branches at the top of a tree: *birds nesting in the treetops*

tre·foil /'trefɔɪl; 'tri:fɔɪl/ *noun* **1** (*technical*) a plant whose leaves are divided into three similar parts, for example CLOVER **2** a decoration or a design shaped like a trefoil leaf

trek /trek/ *noun, verb*
▪ ***noun*** **1** a long, hard walk lasting several days or weeks, especially in the mountains **2** (*informal*) a long walk SYN **tramp**: *It's a long trek into town.*
▪ ***verb*** (-kk-) **1** [I] (+ **adv./prep.**) (*informal*) to make a long or difficult journey, especially on foot: *I hate having to trek up that hill with all the groceries.* **2** (also **go trekking**) [I] (+ **adv./prep.**) to spend time walking, especially in mountains and for enjoyment and interest: *We went trekking in Nepal.* ◇ *During the expedition, they trekked ten to thirteen hours a day.* ➲ see also PONY-TREKKING

trel·lis /'trelɪs/ *noun* [C, U] a light frame made of long narrow pieces of wood that cross each other, used to support climbing plants ➲ VISUAL VOCAB page V16

trem·ble /'trembl/ *verb, noun*
▪ ***verb*** **1** [I] ~ (**with sth**) to shake in a way that you cannot control, especially because you are very nervous, excited, frightened, etc: *My legs were trembling with fear.* ◇ *Her voice trembled with excitement.* ◇ *He opened the letter with trembling hands.* **2** [I] to shake slightly SYN **quiver**: *leaves trembling in the breeze* **3** [I] to be very worried or frightened: *I trembled at the thought of having to make a speech.*
▪ ***noun*** [C, usually sing.] (also **trem·bling** [C, U]) a feeling, movement or sound of trembling: *a tremble of fear* ◇ *She tried to control the trembling in her legs.*

trem·bly /'trembli/ *adj.* (*informal*) shaking from fear, cold, excitement, etc.

tre·men·dous /trə'mendəs/ *adj.* **1** very great SYN **huge**: *a tremendous explosion* ◇ *A tremendous amount of work has gone into the project.* **2** extremely good SYN **remarkable**: *It was a tremendous experience.* ▸ **tre·men·dous·ly** *adv.*: *tremendously exciting*

trem·olo /'tremələʊ; *NAmE* -loʊ/ *noun* (*pl.* -os) (*music*) a special effect in singing or playing a musical instrument made by repeating the same note or two notes very quickly

tremor /'tremə(r)/ *noun* **1** a small EARTHQUAKE in which the ground shakes slightly: *an earth tremor* **2** a slight shaking movement in a part of your body caused, for example, by cold or fear SYN **quiver**: *There was a slight tremor in his voice.*

tremu·lous /'tremjələs/ *adj.* (*literary*) shaking slightly because you are nervous; causing you to shake slightly SYN **trembling**: *a tremulous voice* ◇ *He was in a state of tremulous excitement.* ▸ **tremu·lous·ly** *adv.*

trench /trentʃ/ *noun* **1** a long deep hole dug in the ground, for example for carrying away water **2** a long deep hole dug in the ground in which soldiers can be protected from enemy attacks (for example in northern France and Belgium in the First World War): *life in the* ***trenches*** ◇ *trench warfare* **3** (also ˌ**ocean 'trench**) a long deep narrow hole in the ocean floor

tren·chant /'trentʃənt/ *adj.* (*formal*) (of criticism, remarks, etc.) expressed strongly and effectively, in a clear way SYN **incisive** ▸ **tren·chant·ly** *adv.*

'trench coat *noun* a long loose coat, worn especially to keep off rain, with a belt and pockets in the style of a military coat

trench·er /'trentʃə(r)/ *noun* a wooden plate used in the past for serving food

ˌ**trench 'foot** *noun* [U] a painful condition of the feet, in which the flesh begins to decay and die, caused by being in mud or water for too long

trend 0-π AW /trend/ *noun*
a general direction in which a situation is changing or developing: ***economic/social/political trends*** ◇ ~ (**towards sth**) *There is a* ***growing trend*** *towards earlier retirement.* ◇ ~ (**in sth**) ***current trends*** *in language teaching* ◇ ***a downward/an upward trend*** *in sales* ◇ *You seem to have* ***set*** (= started) *a new* ***trend***. ◇ *This trend is being reversed* (= is going in the opposite direction). ◇ *One region is attempting to* ***buck*** (= oppose or resist) *the* ***trend*** *of economic decline.* ◇ *The* ***underlying trend*** *of inflation is still upwards.* ➲ LANGUAGE BANK at FALL

trend·set·ter /'trendsetə(r)/ *noun* (often *approving*) a person who starts a new fashion or makes it popular ▸ **trend·set·ting** *adj.* [only before noun]

trendy /'trendi/ *adj., noun*
▪ ***adj.*** (**trend·ier**, **trendi·est**) (*informal*) very fashionable: *trendy clothes* ▸ **trend·ily** *adv.* **trendi·ness** *noun* [U]
▪ ***noun*** (*pl.* -ies) (*BrE, informal*, usually *disapproving*) a trendy person: *young trendies from art college*

trepi·da·tion /ˌtrepɪ'deɪʃn/ *noun* [U] (*formal*) great worry or fear about sth unpleasant that may happen

tres·pass /'trespəs/ *verb, noun*
▪ ***verb*** **1** [I] ~ (**on sth**) to enter land or a building that you do not have permission or the right to enter: *He told me I was trespassing on private land.* **2** [I] (*old use*) to do sth wrong
PHR V **'trespass on sth** (*formal*) to make unfair use of sb's time, help, etc. SYN **encroach on**: *I mustn't trespass on your time any longer.*
▪ ***noun*** **1** [U, C] an act of trespassing on land **2** [C] (*old use*) something that you do that is morally wrong SYN **sin**

tres·pass·er /'trespəsə(r)/ *noun* a person who goes onto sb's land without their permission: *The notice read: 'Trespassers will be prosecuted.'*

tresses /'tresɪz/ *noun* [pl.] (*literary*) a woman's long hair SYN **locks**

tres·tle /'tresl/ *noun* a wooden or metal structure with two pairs of sloping legs. Trestles are used in pairs to support a flat surface, for example the top of a table.

'trestle table *noun* a table that consists of a wooden top supported by trestles

trews /tru:z/ *noun* [pl.] trousers/pants, especially when they are made of TARTAN

trey /treɪ/ *noun* (in BASKETBALL) a shot that scores three points

tri- /traɪ/ *combining form* (in nouns and adjectives) three; having three: *tricycle* ◇ *triangular*

T

triad /ˈtraɪæd/ *noun* **1** (*formal*) a group of three related people or things **2** (also **Triad**) a Chinese secret organization involved in criminal activity

tri·age /ˈtriːɑːʒ; *NAmE* triːˈɑːʒ/ *noun* [U] (in a hospital) the process of deciding how seriously ill/sick or injured a person is, so that the most serious cases can be treated first

trial 0‑ /ˈtraɪəl/ *noun, verb*

■ ***noun***

▸ LAW **1** 0‑ [U, C] a formal examination of evidence in court by a judge and often a JURY, to decide if sb accused of a crime is guilty or not: *a murder trial* ◇ *He's* ***on trial*** *for murder.* ◇ *She will* ***stand trial/go on trial*** *for fraud.* ◇ *The men were arrested but not* ***brought to trial.*** ◇ *The case never* ***came to trial.*** ◇ *She is awaiting trial on corruption charges.* ◇ *He did not receive a fair trial.* ◇ *She was detained without trial.* ➲ COLLOCATIONS at JUSTICE

▸ TEST **2** 0‑ [C, U] the process of testing the ability, quality or performance of sb/sth, especially before you make a final decision about them: *The new drug is undergoing clinical trials.* ◇ *She agreed to employ me for* ***a trial period.*** ◇ *The system was introduced* ***on a trial basis*** *for one month.* ◇ *a* ***trial separation*** (= of a couple whose marriage is in difficulties) ◇ *We had the machine* ***on trial*** *for a week.* ◇ *a* ***trial of strength*** (= a contest to see who is stronger) ➲ COLLOCATIONS at SCIENTIFIC

▸ IN SPORT **3** [C, usually pl.] (*BrE*) (*NAmE* **try·out**) a competition or series of tests to find the best players for a sports team or an important event: *Olympic trials*

▸ FOR ANIMALS **4** [C, usually pl.] an event at which animals compete or perform: *horse trials*

▸ DIFFICULT EXPERIENCE **5** [C] an experience or a person that causes difficulties for sb: *the* ***trials and tribulations*** *of married life* ◇ **~ to sb** *She was a sore trial to her family at times.*

IDM ˌ**trial and ˈerror** the process of solving a problem by trying various methods until you find a method that is successful: *Children learn to use computer programs* ***by trial and error.***

■ ***verb*** (-ll-, *NAmE* -l-) [T, I] **~ (sth)** (*BrE*) to test the ability, quality or performance of sth to see if it will be effective or successful

ˈ**trial balloon** *noun* (*especially NAmE*) something that you say or do to find out what people think about a course of action before you take it

ˌ**trial ˈrun** (also ˌ**test ˈrun**) *noun* a test of how well sth new works, so that you can see if any changes are necessary

tri·angle 0‑ /ˈtraɪæŋgl/ *noun*

1 0‑ a flat shape with three straight sides and three angles; a thing in the shape of a triangle: (*BrE*) *a right-angled triangle* ◇ (*NAmE*) *a right triangle* ◇ *Cut the sandwiches into triangles.* ➲ VISUAL VOCAB page V58 **2** a simple musical instrument that consists of a long piece of metal bent into the shape of a triangle, that you hit with another piece of metal ➲ VISUAL VOCAB page V30 **3** a situation involving three people in a complicated relationship: *a love triangle* ➲ see also ETERNAL TRIANGLE **4** (*NAmE*) (*BrE* ˈ**set square**) an instrument for drawing straight lines and angles, made from a flat piece of plastic or metal in the shape of a triangle with one angle of 90°

tri·angu·lar /traɪˈæŋgjələ(r)/ *adj.* **1** shaped like a triangle **2** involving three people or groups: *a triangular contest in an election*

tri·angu·la·tion /traɪˌæŋgjuˈleɪʃn/ *noun* [U] (*technical*) a method of finding out distance and position, usually on a map, by measuring the distance between two fixed points and then measuring the angle from each of these to the third point

triˌanguˈlation point *noun* = TRIG POINT

tri·ath·lon /traɪˈæθlən/ *noun* a sporting event in which people compete in three different sports, usually swimming, cycling and running ➲ compare BIATHLON, DECATHLON, HEPTATHLON, PENTATHLON, TETRATHLON

tri·bal /ˈtraɪbl/ *noun, adj.*

■ ***adj.*** [usually before noun] connected with a tribe or tribes: *tribal art* ◇ *tribal leaders*

■ ***noun*** a member of a tribe, especially in S Asia

tri·bal·ism /ˈtraɪbəlɪzəm/ *noun* [U] **1** behaviour, attitudes, etc. that are based on being loyal to a tribe or other social group **2** the state of being organized in a tribe or tribes

ˈ**tri-band** *adj.* (of a mobile phone/cell phone) able to use three different ranges of radio waves so that it can be used in different regions of the world

tribe /traɪb/ *noun* **1** (sometimes *offensive*) (in developing countries) a group of people of the same race, and with the same customs, language, religion, etc, living in a particular area and often led by a chief: *tribes living in remote areas of the Amazonian rainforest* **2** (usually *disapproving*) a group or class of people, especially of one profession: *He had a sudden outburst against the whole tribe of actors.* **3** (*biology*) a group of related animals or plants: *a tribe of cats* **4** (*informal* or *humorous*) a large number of people: *One or two of the grandchildren will be there, but not the whole tribe.*

tribes·man /ˈtraɪbzmən/, **tribes·woman** /ˈtraɪbzwʊmən/ *noun* (*pl.* **-men** /-mən/, **-women** /-wɪmɪn/) a member of a tribe

tribes·people /ˈtraɪbzpiːpl/ *noun* [pl.] the people who belong to a particular tribe

tribu·la·tion /ˌtrɪbjuˈleɪʃn/ *noun* [C, U] (*literary* or *humorous*) great trouble or suffering: *the tribulations of modern life*

tri·bu·nal /traɪˈbjuːnl/ *noun* [C+sing./pl. v.] a type of court with the authority to deal with a particular problem or disagreement: *an international war crimes tribunal* ◇ *a military tribunal* ➲ see also INDUSTRIAL TRIBUNAL

trib·une /ˈtrɪbjuːn/ *noun* **1** an official elected by the people in ancient Rome to defend their rights; a popular leader **2** a raised area that sb stands on to make a speech in public

tribu·tary /ˈtrɪbjətri; *NAmE* -teri/ *noun* (*pl.* **-ies**) a river or stream that flows into a larger river or a lake ➲ VISUAL VOCAB page V4 ▸ **tribu·tary** *adj.* [only before noun]: *a tributary stream*

trib·ute /ˈtrɪbjuːt/ *noun* **1** [U, C] **~ (to sb)** an act, a statement or a gift that is intended to show your respect or admiration, especially for a dead person: *At her funeral her oldest friend* ***paid tribute to*** *her life and work.* ◇ *This book is a fitting tribute to the bravery of the pioneers.* ◇ *floral tributes* (= gifts of flowers at a funeral) **2** [sing.] **~ to sth/sb** showing the good effects or influence of sth/sb: *His recovery is a tribute to the doctors' skill.* **3** [U, C] (especially in the past) money given by one country or ruler to another, especially in return for protection or for not being attacked

ˈ**tribute band** *noun* a group of musicians who play the music of a famous band and copy the way they look and sound

trice /traɪs/ *noun*

IDM **in a ˈtrice** very quickly or suddenly SYN **in an instant**: *He was gone in a trice.*

tri·ceps /ˈtraɪseps/ *noun* (*pl.* **tri·ceps**) the large muscle at the back of the top part of the arm ➲ compare BICEPS

tri·cera·tops /traɪˈserətɒps; *NAmE* -tɑːps/ *noun* (*pl.* **tri·cera·tops** or **tri·cera·topses**) a large DINOSAUR with two large horns and one small horn on its very large head

trich·ology /trɪˈkɒlədʒi; *NAmE* -ˈkɑːl-/ *noun* [U] the study of the hair and SCALP ▸ **trich·olo·gist** /trɪˈkɒlədʒɪst; *NAmE* -ˈkɑːl-/ *noun*

trick 0‑ /trɪk/ *noun, verb, adj.*

■ ***noun***

▸ STH TO CHEAT SB **1** 0‑ something that you do to make sb believe sth which is not true, or to annoy sb as a joke: *They had to think of a trick to get past the guards.* ◇ *The kids are always* ***playing tricks on*** *their teacher.* ➲ see also CONFIDENCE TRICK, DIRTY TRICK

▸ STH CONFUSING **2** 0‑ something that confuses you so that you see, understand, remember, etc. things in the wrong way: *One of the problems of old age is that your memory can* start to **play tricks** on you. ◊ *Was there somebody standing there or was it* ***a trick of the light****?*

▸ ENTERTAINMENT **3** a clever action that sb/sth performs as a way of entertaining people: *He amused the kids with conjuring tricks.* ◊ *a card trick* ➲ see also HAT-TRICK

▸ GOOD METHOD **4** [usually sing.] a way of doing sth that works well; a good method: ***The trick is*** *to pick the animal up by the back of its neck.* ◊ *He used the old trick of attacking in order to defend himself.*

▸ IN CARD GAMES **5** the cards that you play or win in a single part of a card game: *I won six tricks in a row.*

IDM **a bag/box of 'tricks** (*informal*) a set of methods or equipment that sb can use **be up to your (old) 'tricks** (*informal, disapproving*) to be behaving in the same bad way as before **do the 'trick** (*informal*) to succeed in solving a problem or achieving a particular result: *I don't know what it was that did the trick, but I am definitely feeling much better.* **every trick in the 'book** every available method, whether it is honest or not: *He'll try every trick in the book to stop you from winning.* **have a 'trick, some more 'tricks, etc. up your sleeve** to have an idea, some plans, etc. that you keep ready to use if it becomes necessary **ˌtrick or 'treat** said by children who visit people's houses at Halloween and threaten to play tricks on people who do not give them sweets/candy **the ˌtricks of the 'trade** the clever ways of doing things, known and used by people who do a particular job or activity **ˌturn a 'trick** (*NAmE, slang*) to have sex with sb for money ➲ more at MISS *v.*, TEACH

■ ***verb*** to make sb believe sth which is not true, especially in order to cheat them: **~ sb** *I'd been tricked and I felt stupid.* ◊ **~ your way + adv./prep.** *He managed to trick his way past the security guards.* ➲ SYNONYMS at CHEAT

PHR V **ˌtrick sb 'into sth/into doing sth** to make sb do sth by means of a trick: *He tricked me into lending him £100.* **ˌtrick sb 'out of sth** to get sth from sb by means of a trick: *She was tricked out of her life savings.* **ˌtrick sb/sth↔'out (in/with sth)** (*literary*) to dress or decorate sb/sth in a way that attracts attention

■ ***adj.*** [only before noun] **1** intended to trick sb: *It was a* ***trick question*** (= one to which the answer seems easy but actually is not). ◊ *It's all done using* ***trick photography*** (= photography that uses clever techniques to show things that do not actually exist or are impossible). **2** (*NAmE*) (of part of the body) weak and not working well: *a trick knee*

trick·ery /ˈtrɪkəri/ *noun* [U] the use of dishonest methods to trick people in order to achieve what you want SYN **deception**

trickle /ˈtrɪkl/ *verb, noun*

■ ***verb*** **1** [I, T] to flow, or to make sth flow, slowly in a thin stream: (**+ adv./prep.**) *Tears were trickling down her cheeks.* ◊ **~ sth (+ adv./prep.)** *Trickle some oil over the salad.* **2** [I, T] **~ (sth) + adv./prep.** to go, or to make sth go, somewhere slowly or gradually: *People began trickling into the hall.* ◊ *News is starting to trickle out.*

PHR V **ˌtrickle 'down** (especially of money) to spread from rich to poor people through the economic system of a country

■ ***noun*** **1** a small amount of liquid, flowing slowly **2** [usually sing.] **~ (of sth)** a small amount or number of sth, coming or going slowly: *a steady trickle of visitors*

'trickle-down *noun* [U] the theory that if the richest people in society become richer, this will have a good effect on poorer people as well, for example by creating more jobs

trick·ster /ˈtrɪkstə(r)/ *noun* a person who tricks or cheats people

tricksy /ˈtrɪksi/ *adj.* (*informal*, usually *disapproving*) using ideas and methods that are intended to be clever but are too complicated

tricky /ˈtrɪki/ *adj.* (**trick·ier, tricki·est**) **1** (rather *informal*) difficult to do or deal with: *a tricky situation* ◊ *Getting it to fit exactly is a* ***tricky business****.* ◊ *The equipment can be tricky to install.* **2** (of people) clever but likely to trick you SYN **crafty**

tri·col·our (*US* **tri·color**) /ˈtrɪkələ(r); *NAmE* ˈtraɪkʌlər/ *noun* [C] a flag which has three bands of different colours, especially the French and Irish national flags

tri·cycle /ˈtraɪsɪkl/ (also *informal* **trike**) *noun* a vehicle similar to a bicycle, but with one wheel at the front and two at the back ➲ VISUAL VOCAB page V41

tri·dent /ˈtraɪdnt/ *noun* a weapon used in the past that looks like a long fork with three points

tried /traɪd/ *adj.* ➲ see also TRY *v.*

IDM **ˌtried and 'tested/'trusted** (*BrE*) (*NAmE* **ˌtried and 'true**) that you have used or relied on in the past successfully: *a tried and tested method for solving the problem*

tri·en·nial /traɪˈeniəl/ *adj.* happening every three years

trier /ˈtraɪə(r)/ *noun* a person who tries very hard at what they are doing and does their best

trifle /ˈtraɪfl/ *noun, verb*

■ ***noun*** **1 a trifle** [sing.] (used as an adverb) (*formal* or *humorous*) slightly: *She seemed a trifle anxious.* **2** [C] something that is not valuable or important: *$1000 is a mere trifle to her.* **3** [C, U] (*BrE*) a cold DESSERT (= a sweet dish) made from cake and fruit with wine and/or jelly poured over it, covered with CUSTARD and cream

■ ***verb***

PHR V **'trifle with sb/sth** (*formal*) (used especially in negative sentences) to treat sb/sth without genuine respect: *He is not a person to be trifled with.*

trif·ling /ˈtraɪflɪŋ/ *adj.* (*formal*) small and not important SYN **trivial**: *trifling details*

trig·ger AW /ˈtrɪɡə(r)/ *noun, verb*

■ ***noun*** **1** the part of a gun that you press in order to fire it: *to* ***pull/squeeze the trigger*** ◊ *He kept his finger on the trigger.* **2 ~ (for sth)** | **~ (to sth/to do sth)** something that is the cause of a particular reaction or development, especially a bad one: *The trigger for the strike was the closure of yet another factory.* **3** the part of a bomb that causes it to explode: *nuclear triggers*

■ ***verb*** **1 ~ sth (off)** to make sth happen suddenly SYN **set off**: *Nuts can trigger off a violent allergic reaction.* **2 ~ sth** to cause a device to start functioning SYN **set off**: *to trigger an alarm*

'trigger-happy *adj.* (*informal, disapproving*) too willing and quick to use violence, especially with guns

trig·onom·etry /ˌtrɪɡəˈnɒmətri; *NAmE* -ˈnɑːm-/ *noun* [U] the type of mathematics that deals with the relationship between the sides and angles of triangles ▸ **trig·ono·met·ric** /ˌtrɪɡənəˈmetrɪk/ (also **trig·ono·met·ric·al** /-kl/) *adj.*

trig point /ˈtrɪɡ pɔɪnt/ (also **triˌangu'lation point**) *noun* (*technical*) a position on a high place used as a REFERENCE POINT, especially by people who make and use maps. It is usually marked on the ground by a short stone PILLAR.

tri·graph /ˈtraɪɡrɑːf; *NAmE* -ɡræf/ *noun* (*linguistics*) a combination of three letters representing one sound, for example 'sch' in German

trike /traɪk/ *noun* (*informal*) = TRICYCLE

tri·lat·eral /ˌtraɪˈlætərəl/ *adj.* involving three groups of people or three countries: *trilateral talks* ➲ compare BILATERAL, MULTILATERAL, UNILATERAL

trilby /ˈtrɪlbi/ *noun* (*pl.* -ies) (*especially BrE*) a man's soft hat with a narrow BRIM and the top part pushed in from front to back ➲ VISUAL VOCAB page V53

tri·lin·gual /ˌtraɪˈlɪŋɡwəl/ *adj.* **1** able to speak three languages equally well: *He is trilingual in English, Spanish and Danish.* **2** using three languages; written in three languages: *trilingual education* ◊ *a trilingual menu*

trill /trɪl/ *noun, verb*

■ ***noun*** **1** a repeated short high sound made, for example, by sb's voice or by a bird **2** (*music*) the sound made when two notes next to each other in the musical SCALE are played or sung quickly several times one after the other **3** (also **roll**) (*phonetics*) a sound, usually an /r/, produced by making the tongue VIBRATE against a part of the mouth

■ ***verb*** **1** [I] to make repeated short high sounds

T

SYN **warble**: *A phone trilled on the desk.* ◇ *The canary was trilling away happily.* **2** [T] + **speech** to say sth in a high cheerful voice SYN **warble**: *'How wonderful!' she trilled.* **3** [T] **~ sth** (*phonetics*) to pronounce an 'r' sound by making a trill (3) ➲ compare ROLL (10)

tril·lion /ˈtrɪljən/ *number* **1** 🗝 1 000 000 000 000; one million million HELP You say **a, one, two, several, etc. trillion** without a final 's' on 'trillion'. **Trillions (of...)** can be used if there is no number or quantity before it. Always use a plural verb with **trillion** or **trillions**. **2** 🗝 **a trillion** or **trillions (of...)** (*informal*) a very large amount HELP There are more examples of how to use numbers at the entry for **hundred**. **3** (*old-fashioned, BrE*) one million million million; 1 000 000 000 000 000 000

tri·lo·bite /ˈtraɪləʊbaɪt; *NAmE* ˈtraɪlə-/ *noun* a small sea creature that lived millions of years ago and is now a FOSSIL

tril·ogy /ˈtrɪlədʒi/ *noun* (*pl.* -ies) a group of three books, films/movies, etc. that have the same subject or characters

trim /trɪm/ *verb, noun, adj.*

■ *verb* (-mm-) **1 ~ sth** to make sth neater, smaller, better, etc, by cutting parts from it: *to trim your hair* ◇ *to trim a hedge (back)* ◇ (*figurative*) *The training budget had been trimmed by £10 000.* **2 ~ sth (off sth)** | **~ sth (off/away)** to cut away unnecessary parts from sth: *Trim any excess fat off the meat.* ◇ *I trimmed two centimetres off the hem of the skirt.* **3** [usually passive] **~ sth (with sth)** to decorate sth, especially around its edges: *gloves trimmed with fur*

IDM **ˌtrim your ˈsails 1** to arrange the sails of a boat to suit the wind so that the boat moves faster **2** to reduce your costs

PHR V **ˌtrim ˈdown** | **ˌtrim sth↔ˈdown** to become smaller in size; to make sth smaller: *Using the diet he's trimmed down from 90 kilos to 70.*

■ *noun* **1** [C, usually sing.] an act of cutting a small amount off sth, especially hair: *a wash and trim* ◇ *The hedge needs a trim.* **2** [U, sing.] material that is used to decorate clothes, furniture, cars, etc, especially along the edges, by being a different colour, etc: *The car is available with black or red trim* (= the colour of the seats). ◇ *a blue jacket with a white trim*

IDM **in (good, etc.) ˈtrim** (*informal*) in good condition or order: *He* ***keeps in trim*** *by running every day.* ◇ *The team need to* ***get in trim*** *for the coming season.*

■ *adj.* **1** (of a person) looking thin, healthy and attractive: *She has kept very trim.* ◇ *a trim figure* **2** neat and well cared for SYN **well kept**: *a trim garden*

tri·maran /ˈtraɪməræn/ *noun* a fast sailing boat like a CATAMARAN, but with three HULLS instead of two

tri·mes·ter /traɪˈmestə(r)/ *noun* **1** (*medical*) a period of three months during the time when a woman is pregnant: *the first trimester of pregnancy* **2** (*NAmE*) = TERM: *The school year is divided into three trimesters.* ➲ compare SEMESTER

trim·mer /ˈtrɪmə(r)/ *noun* a machine for cutting the edges of bushes, grass and HEDGES: *a hedge-trimmer*

trim·ming /ˈtrɪmɪŋ/ *noun* **1 trimmings** (*NAmE* also **fixings**) [pl.] the extra things that it is traditional to have for a special meal or occasion: *a splendid feast of turkey with* ***all the trimmings*** **2 trimmings** [pl.] the small pieces of sth that are left when you have cut sth: *hedge trimmings* **3** [U, C, usually pl.] material that is used to decorate sth, for example along its edges: *a white blouse with blue trimming*

trin·ity /ˈtrɪnəti/ *noun* [sing.] **1 the Trinity** (in Christianity) the union of Father, Son and HOLY SPIRIT as one God **2** (*formal*) a group of three people or things

trin·ket /ˈtrɪŋkɪt/ *noun* a piece of jewellery or small decorative object that is not worth much money

trio /ˈtriːəʊ; *NAmE* ˈtriːoʊ/ *noun* (*pl.* -os) **1** [C+sing./pl. v.] a group of three people or things ➲ compare DUO **2** [C+sing./pl. v.] a group of three musicians or singers who play or sing together **3** [C] a piece of music for three musicians or singers: *a trio for piano, oboe and bassoon* ➲ compare DUET

trip 🗝 /trɪp/ *noun, verb*

■ *noun* **1** 🗝 a journey to a place and back again, especially a short one for pleasure or a particular purpose: *Did you have a good trip?* ◇ *We* ***went on a trip*** *to the mountains.* ◇ *a* ***day trip*** (= lasting a day) ◇ *a* ***boat/coach trip*** ◇ *a* ***business/school/shopping trip*** ◇ *They* ***took a trip*** *down the river.* ◇ *We had to* ***make several trips*** *to bring all the equipment over.* ➲ COLLOCATIONS at TRAVEL ➲ see also EGO TRIP, FIELD TRIP, ROUND TRIP **2** (*slang*) the experience that sb has if they take a powerful drug that affects the mind and makes them imagine things: *an acid* (= LSD) *trip* **3** an act of falling or nearly falling down, because you hit your foot against sth IDM see GUILT

■ *verb* (-pp-) **1** 🗝 [I] to catch your foot on sth and fall or almost fall: *She tripped and fell.* ◇ **~ over/on sth** *Someone will trip over that cable.* ◇ **~ over/up** *Be careful you don't trip up on the step.* **2** 🗝 [T] **~ sb** (*BrE* also **trip sb up**) to catch sb's foot and make them fall or almost fall: *As I passed, he stuck out a leg and tried to trip me up.* **3** [I] + **adv./prep.** (*literary*) to walk, run or dance with quick light steps: *She said goodbye and tripped off along the road.* **4** [T] **~ sth** to release a switch, etc. or to operate sth by doing so: *to trip a switch* ◇ *Any intruders will trip the alarm.* **5** [I] (*informal*) to be under the influence of a drug that makes you HALLUCINATE

IDM see MEMORY LANE, TONGUE *n.*

PHR V **ˌtrip ˈup** | **ˌtrip sb↔ˈup** to make a mistake; to deliberately make sb do this: *Read the questions carefully, because the examiners sometimes try to trip you up.*

Synonyms

trip

journey • tour • expedition • excursion • outing • day out

These are all words for an act of travelling to a place.

trip an act of travelling from one place to another, and usually back again: *a business trip* ◇ *a five-minute trip by taxi*

journey an act of travelling from one place to another, especially when they are a long way apart: *a long and difficult journey across the mountains*

TRIP OR JOURNEY?

A **trip** usually involves you going to a place and back again; a **journey** is usually one-way. A **trip** is often shorter than a **journey**, although it does not have to be: *a trip to New York* ◇ *a round-the-world trip.* It is often short in time, even if it is long in distance. **Journey** is more often used when the travelling takes a long time and is difficult. In North American English **journey** is not used for short trips: (*BrE*) *What is your journey to work like?*

tour a journey made for pleasure during which several different places are visited: *a tour of Bavaria*

expedition an organized journey with a particular purpose, especially to find out about a place that is not well known: *the first expedition to the South Pole*

excursion a short trip made for pleasure, especially one that has been organized for a group of people: *We went on an all-day excursion to the island.*

outing a short trip made for pleasure or education, usually with a group of people and lasting no more than a day: *The children were on a day's outing from school.*

day out a trip to somewhere for a day, especially for pleasure: *We had a day out at the beach.*

PATTERNS

- a(n) **foreign/overseas** trip/journey/tour/expedition
- a **bus/coach/train/rail** trip/journey/tour
- to **go on** a(n) trip/journey/tour/expedition/excursion/outing/day out
- to **set out/off on** a(n) trip/journey/tour/expedition/excursion
- to **make** a(n) trip/journey/tour/expedition/excursion

tri·par·tite /traɪˈpɑːtaɪt; *NAmE* -ˈpɑːrt-/ *adj.* [usually before noun] (*formal*) having three parts or involving three people, groups, etc.

tripe /traɪp/ *noun* [U] **1** the LINING of a cow's or pig's stomach, eaten as food **2** (*informal*) something that sb says or writes that you think is nonsense or not of good quality SYN **garbage, rubbish**

ˈ**trip hop** *noun* [U] a type of dance music, which is a mixture of HIP HOP and REGGAE, has a slow beat, and is intended to create a relaxed atmosphere

triple /ˈtrɪpl/ *adj., verb*

■ ***adj.*** [only before noun] **1** having three parts or involving three people or groups: *a triple heart bypass operation* ◇ *a triple alliance* ◇ *They're showing a* ***triple bill*** *of horror movies* (= three horror movies one after the other). **2** three times as much or as many as sth: *The amount of alcohol in his blood was triple the legal maximum.* ◇ *Its population is about triple that of Venice.* ▶ **triply** /ˈtrɪpli/ *adv.*

■ ***verb*** [I, T] **~ (sth)** to become, or to make sth, three times as much or as many SYN **treble**: *Output should triple by next year.*

the ˈtriple jump *noun* [sing.] a sporting event in which people try to jump as far forward as possible with three jumps. The first jump lands on one foot, the second on the other, and the third on both feet.

trip·let /ˈtrɪplət/ *noun* **1** one of three children born at the same time to the same mother **2** (*music*) a group of three equal notes to be played or sung in the time usually taken to play or sing two of the same kind

trip·li·cate /ˈtrɪplɪkət/ *noun*

IDM **in ˈtriplicate 1** done three times: *Each sample was tested in triplicate.* **2** (of a document) copied twice, so that there are three copies in total ➲ compare DUPLICATE

tri·pod /ˈtraɪpɒd; *NAmE* -pɑːd/ *noun* a support with three legs for a camera, TELESCOPE, etc. ➲ **VISUAL VOCAB** page V57

trip·per /ˈtrɪpə(r)/ *noun* (*BrE*) a person who is visiting a place for a short time for pleasure: *a day tripper*

trip·tych /ˈtrɪptɪk/ *noun* (*technical*) a picture that is painted or CARVED on three pieces of wood placed side by side, especially one over an ALTAR in a church

trip·wire /ˈtrɪpwaɪə(r)/ *noun* a wire that is stretched close to the ground as part of a device for catching sb/sth if they touch it

tri·reme /ˈtraɪriːm/ *noun* a long flat ship with three rows of OARS on each side, used in war by the ancient Greeks and Romans

tri·shaw /ˈtraɪʃɔː/ *noun* a light vehicle with three wheels and PEDALS, used in SE Asia to carry passengers

trite /traɪt/ *adj.* (of a remark, an opinion, etc.) dull and boring because it has been expressed so many times before; not original SYN **banal** ▶ **trite·ly** *adv.* **trite·ness** *noun* [U]

tri·tium /ˈtrɪtiəm/ *noun* [U] (*symb.* T) an ISOTOPE (= a different form) of hydrogen with a mass that is three times that of the usual isotope

tri·umph /ˈtraɪʌmf/ *noun, verb*

■ ***noun* 1** [C, U] a great success, achievement or victory: *one of the greatest triumphs of modern science* ◇ **~ over sb/sth** *It was a personal triumph over her old rival.* **2** [U] the feeling of great satisfaction or joy that you get from a great success or victory: *a shout of triumph* ◇ *The winning team returned home* ***in triumph***. **3** [sing.] **a ~ (of sth)** an excellent example of how successful sth can be: *Her arrest was a triumph of international cooperation.*

■ ***verb*** [I] **~ (over sb/sth)** to defeat sb/sth; to be successful: *As is usual in this kind of movie, good triumphs over evil in the end.* ◇ *France triumphed 3–0 in the final.*

tri·umph·al /traɪˈʌmfl/ *adj.* [usually before noun] done or made in order to celebrate a great success or victory

tri·umph·al·ism /traɪˈʌmfəlɪzəm/ *noun* [U] (*disapproving*) behaviour that celebrates a victory or success in a way that is too proud and intended to upset the people you have defeated ▶ **tri·umph·al·ist** *adj.*

tri·umph·ant /traɪˈʌmfənt/ *adj.* **1** very successful in a way that causes great satisfaction: *They emerged triumphant in the September election.* **2** showing great satisfaction or joy about a victory or success: *a triumphant smile* ▶ **tri·umph·ant·ly** *adv.*

tri·um·vir·ate /traɪˈʌmvərət/ *noun* (*formal*) a group of three powerful people or groups who control sth together

trivet /ˈtrɪvɪt/ *noun* a metal stand that you can put a hot dish, etc. on

trivia /ˈtrɪviə/ *noun* [U] **1** unimportant matters, details or information: *We spent the whole evening discussing domestic trivia.* **2** (usually in compounds) facts about many subjects that are used in a game to test people's knowledge: *a trivia quiz*

triv·ial /ˈtrɪviəl/ *adj.* not important or serious; not worth considering: *a trivial detail* ◇ *I know it* ***sounds trivial***, *but I'm worried about it.* ◇ *I'll try to fix it — but it's not trivial* (= it may be difficult to fix). ▶ **trivi·al·ly** /-iəli/ *adv.*

trivi·al·ity /ˌtrɪviˈæləti/ *noun* (*pl.* -ies) (*disapproving*) **1** [C] a matter that is not important: *I don't want to waste time on trivialities.* **2** [U] the state of being unimportant or dealing with unimportant things: *His speech was one of great triviality.*

trivi·al·ize (*BrE* also **-ise**) /ˈtrɪviəlaɪz/ *verb* **~ sth** (usually *disapproving*) to make sth seem less important, serious, difficult, etc. than it really is ▶ **trivi·al·iza·tion, -isa·tion** /ˌtrɪviəlaɪˈzeɪʃn; *NAmE* -ləˈz-/ *noun* [U]

tro·chee /ˈtrəʊkiː; *NAmE* ˈtroʊkiː/ *noun* (*technical*) a unit of sound in poetry consisting of one strong or long syllable followed by one weak or short syllable ▶ **tro·cha·ic** /trəʊˈkeɪɪk; *NAmE* troʊ-/ *adj.*

trod *past tense* of TREAD

trod·den *past part.* of TREAD

trog /trɒg; *NAmE* trɑːg/ *noun* (*BrE, informal*) a person with bad social skills and low intelligence

trog·lo·dyte /ˈtrɒglədaɪt; *NAmE* ˈtrɑːg-/ *noun* a person living in a CAVE, especially in PREHISTORIC times SYN **cave dweller**

troika /ˈtrɔɪkə/ *noun* (*formal*) a group of three politicians or countries working together

troil·ism /ˈtrɔɪlɪzəm/ *noun* [U] sexual activity involving three people

Tro·jan /ˈtrəʊdʒən; *NAmE* ˈtroʊ-/ *noun, adj.* a person from the ancient city of Troy in Asia Minor

IDM **work like a ˈTrojan** (*old-fashioned*) to work very hard

ˌ**Trojan ˈhorse** *noun* **1** a person or thing that is used to trick an enemy in order to achieve a secret purpose **2** (*computing*) a computer program that seems to be helpful but that is, in fact, designed to destroy data, etc. ORIGIN From the story in which the ancient Greeks hid inside a hollow wooden statue of a horse in order to enter the city of their enemies, Troy.

troll /trɒl; trəʊl; *NAmE* troʊl/ *noun, verb*

■ ***noun* 1** (in Scandinavian stories) a creature that looks like an ugly person. Some trolls are very large and evil, others are small and friendly but like to trick people. **2** (*informal*) a message to a discussion group on the Internet that sb deliberately sends to make other people angry; a person who sends a message like this

■ ***verb* 1** [I] **~ (for sth)** (*especially NAmE*) to catch fish by pulling a line with BAIT on it through the water behind a boat **2** [T, I] (*informal*) to search for or try to get sth: **~ sth for sth** *He trolled the Internet for advice on the disease.* ◇ **~ for sth** *Both candidates have been trolling for votes.*

trol·ley /ˈtrɒli; *NAmE* ˈtrɑːli/ *noun* **1** (*BrE*) (*NAmE* **cart**) a small vehicle with wheels that can be pushed or pulled along and is used for carrying things: *a* ***shopping/supermarket/luggage trolley*** ➲ **VISUAL VOCAB** page V29 **2** (*BrE*) (*US* **cart, wagon**) a small table on very small wheels,

T

used for carrying or serving food or drink: *a drinks trolley* ◇ *a tea trolley* **3** (*US*) = STREETCAR
IDM **off your 'trolley** (*BrE, informal*) crazy; stupid

trol·ley·bus /ˈtrɒlibʌs; *NAmE* ˈtrɑːl-/ (*BrE*) (*US* **'track-less trolley**) *noun* a bus driven by electricity from a cable above the street

'trolley car *noun* (*old-fashioned, US*) = STREETCAR

trol·lop /ˈtrɒləp; *NAmE* ˈtrɑːləp/ *noun* (*old-fashioned, offensive*) **1** a woman who has many sexual partners **2** a woman who is very untidy

trom·bone /trɒmˈbəʊn; *NAmE* trɑːmˈboʊn/ *noun* a large BRASS musical instrument that you blow into, with a sliding tube used to change the note ➲ VISUAL VOCAB page V30

trom·bon·ist /trɒmˈbəʊnɪst; *NAmE* trɑːmˈboʊ-/ *noun* a person who plays the trombone

tromp /trɒmp; *NAmE* trɑːmp/ *verb* (*NAmE, informal*) = TRAMP

trompe l'œil /ˌtrɒmp ˈlɔɪ; *NAmE* ˌtrɔːmp/ *noun* (*pl.* **trompe l'œils** /ˌtrɒmp ˈlɔɪ; *NAmE* ˌtrɔːmp/) (from *French*) a painting or design intended to make the person looking at it think that it is a real object

troop /truːp/ *noun, verb*
■ ***noun*** **1 troops** [pl.] soldiers, especially in large groups: *They announced the withdrawal of 12 000 troops from the area.* ◇ *The president decided to* **send in the troops**. ◇ *Russian troops* ➲ COLLOCATIONS at WAR **2** [C] one group of soldiers, especially in tanks or on horses: (*figurative*) *A troop of guests was moving towards the house.* **3** [C] a local group of SCOUTS ▸ **troop** *adj.* [only before noun]: *troop movements* (= of soldiers)
■ ***verb*** [I] **+ adv./prep.** (used with a plural subject) to walk somewhere together as a group: *After lunch we all trooped down to the beach.*

troop·er /ˈtruːpə(r)/ *noun* **1** a soldier of low rank in the part of an army that uses tanks or horses **2** (*NAmE*) = STATE TROOPER IDM see SWEAR

troop·ship /ˈtruːpʃɪp/ *noun* a ship used for transporting soldiers

trop ➲ DE TROP

trope /trəʊp; *NAmE* troʊp/ *noun* (*technical*) a word or phrase that is used in a way that is different from its usual meaning in order to create a particular mental image or effect. METAPHORS and SIMILES are tropes.

troph·ic /ˈtrəʊfɪk; ˈtrɒf-; *NAmE* ˈtroʊfɪk/ *adj.* (*biology*) **1** relating to feeding, and to the food necessary for growth **2** (of a HORMONE or its effect) causing the release of another HORMONE or other substance into the blood

T

ˌtrophic ˈlevel *noun* (*technical*) each of several levels in an ECOSYSTEM (= all the plants and animals in a particular area and their relationship with their surroundings). Each level consists of living creatures that share the same function in the FOOD CHAIN and get their food from the same source.

trophy /ˈtrəʊfi; *NAmE* ˈtroʊfi/ *noun, adj.*
■ ***noun*** (*pl.* **-ies**) **1** an object such as a silver cup that is given as a prize for winning a competition ➲ picture at MEDAL **2 Trophy** used in the names of some competitions and races in which a trophy is given to the winner **3** an object that you keep to show that you were successful in sth, especially hunting or war
■ ***adj.*** [only before noun] **~ building/art/girlfriend, etc.** (*informal, disapproving*) an impressive or beautiful thing or person that you have in order to make other people admire you: *We don't need a trophy building for our business.*

'trophy wife *noun* (*informal, disapproving*) a young attractive woman who is married to an older man and thought of as a trophy (= sth that shows that you are successful and impresses other people)

trop·ic /ˈtrɒpɪk; *NAmE* ˈtrɑːpɪk/ *noun* **1** [C, usually sing.] one of the two imaginary lines drawn around the world 23° 26′ north (**the Tropic of Cancer**) or south (**the Tropic of Capricorn**) of the EQUATOR **2 the tropics** [pl.] the area between the two tropics, which is the hottest part of the world SYN **the torrid zone**

trop·ic·al 0→ /ˈtrɒpɪkl; *NAmE* ˈtrɑːp-/ *adj.* coming from, found in or typical of the tropics: *tropical fish* ◇ *tropical Africa* ◇ *a tropical island*

tro·pism /ˈtrəʊpɪzəm; ˈtrɒp-; *NAmE* ˈtroʊpɪzəm/ *noun* [U] (*biology*) the action of a living thing turning all or part of itself in a particular direction, towards or away from sth such as a source of light

the tropo·sphere /ˈtrɒpəsfɪə(r); *NAmE* ˈtroʊpəsfɪr; ˈtrɑːp-/ *noun* [sing.] (*technical*) the lowest layer of the earth's atmosphere, between the surface of the earth and about 6-10 kilometres above the surface

trot /trɒt; *NAmE* trɑːt/ *verb, noun*
■ ***verb*** (**-tt-**) **1** [I] (of a horse or its rider) to move forward at a speed that is faster than a walk and slower than a CANTER **2** [T] **~ sth** to ride a horse in this way: *She trotted her pony around the field.* **3** [I] **+ adv./prep.** (of a person or an animal) to run or walk fast, taking short quick steps: *The children trotted into the room.* **4** [I] **+ adv./prep.** (*informal*) to walk or go somewhere: *The guide led the way and we trotted along behind him.* IDM see HOT *adj.*
PHR V **ˌtrot sth↔ˈout** (*informal, disapproving*) to give the same excuses, facts, explanations, etc. for sth that have often been used before: *They trotted out the same old excuses for the lack of jobs in the area.*
■ ***noun*** **1** [sing.] a trotting speed, taking short quick steps: *The horse slowed to a trot.* ◇ *The girl* **broke into a trot** *and disappeared around the corner.* **2** [C] a period of trotting
IDM **on the 'trot** (*BrE, informal*) **1** one after the other SYN **in succession**: *They've now won three games on the trot.* **2** busy all the time: *I've been on the trot all day.*

troth /trəʊθ; *NAmE* trɑːθ/ *noun* IDM see PLIGHT *v.*

Trot·sky·ist /ˈtrɒtskiɪst; *NAmE* ˈtrɑːt-/ (also **Trot·sky·ite** /ˈtrɒtskiaɪt; *NAmE* ˈtrɑːt-/) *noun* a supporter of the political ideas of Leon Trotsky, especially that SOCIALISM should be introduced all over the world by means of revolution ▸ **Trot·sky·ist** (also **Trot·sky·ite**) *adj.*

trot·ter /ˈtrɒtə(r); *NAmE* ˈtrɑːt-/ *noun* **1** a pig's foot, especially when cooked and eaten as food **2** a horse that has been trained to TROT fast in races

trou·ba·dour /ˈtruːbədɔː(r)/ *noun* (*literary*) a writer and performer of songs or poetry (after the French travelling performers of the 11th-13th centuries)

trouble 0→ /ˈtrʌbl/ *noun, verb*
■ ***noun***
▸ PROBLEM/WORRY **1** 0→ [U, C] a problem, worry, difficulty, etc. or a situation causing this: *We* **have trouble** *getting staff.* ◇ *He could* **make trouble for me** *if he wanted to.* ◇ **~ (with sb/sth)** *The* **trouble with you is** *you don't really want to work.* ◇ *We've never* **had** *much* **trouble with** *vandals around here.* ◇ ***Her trouble is*** *she's incapable of making a decision.* ◇ ***The trouble is*** (= what is difficult is) *there aren't any trains at that time.* ◇ ***The only trouble is*** *we won't be here then.* ◇ *No, I don't know his number—I have quite enough trouble remembering my own.* ◇ *financial troubles* ◇ *She was on the phone for an hour telling me her troubles.* ◇ *Our troubles aren't over yet.* ➲ see also TEETHING TROUBLES
▸ ILLNESS/PAIN **2** 0→ [U] illness or pain: *back trouble* ◇ *I've been having trouble with my knee.* ➲ SYNONYMS at ILLNESS
▸ WITH MACHINE **3** 0→ [U] something that is wrong with a machine, vehicle, etc: *mechanical trouble*
▸ DIFFICULT/VIOLENT SITUATION **4** 0→ [U] a situation that is difficult or dangerous; a situation in which you can be criticized or punished: *The company* **ran into trouble** *early on, when a major order was cancelled.* ◇ *A yachtsman* **got into trouble** *off the coast and had to be rescued.* ◇ *If I don't get this finished in time, I'll be* **in trouble**. ◇ *He's* **in trouble with** *the police.* ◇ *My brother was always* **getting me into trouble** *with my parents.* **5** 0→ [U] an angry or violent situation: *The police were expecting trouble after the match.* ◇ *If you're not in by midnight, there'll be trouble* (= I'll be very angry). ◇ *He had to throw out a few drunks who were causing trouble in the bar.*
▸ EXTRA EFFORT **6** 0→ [U] **~ (to sb)** extra effort or work

SYN **bother**: *I don't want to* **put you to a lot of trouble.** ◇ *I'll get it if you like, that will* **save you the trouble of** *going out.* ◇ *Making your own yogurt* **is more trouble than it's worth.** ◇ *She* **went to a lot of trouble** *to find the book for me.* ◇ *He thanked me for my trouble and left.* ◇ *Nothing is ever* **too much trouble** *for her* (= she's always ready to help). ◇ *I can call back later—it's* **no trouble** (= I don't mind). ◇ *I hope the children weren't too much trouble.*
▸ IN NORTHERN IRELAND **7 the Troubles** [pl.] the time of political and social problems in Northern Ireland, especially after 1968, when there was violence between Catholics and Protestants about whether Northern Ireland should remain part of the UK
IDM **get sb into 'trouble** (*old-fashioned*) to make a woman who is not married pregnant **give (sb) (some, no, any, etc.) 'trouble** to cause problems or difficulties: *My back's been giving me a lot of trouble lately.* ◇ *The children didn't give me any trouble at all when we were out.* **look for 'trouble** to behave in a way that is likely to cause an argument, violence, etc: *Drunken youths hang around outside looking for trouble.* **take trouble over/with sth | take trouble doing/to do sth** to try hard to do sth well: *They take a lot of trouble to find the right person for the right job.* **take the trouble to do sth** to do sth even though it involves effort or difficulty SYN **make the effort**: *She didn't even take the trouble to find out how to spell my name.* **a trouble ˌshared is a trouble 'halved** (*saying*) if you talk to sb about your problems and worries, instead of keeping them to yourself, they seem less serious ➲ more at ASK
■ *verb*
▸ MAKE SB WORRIED **1** [T] **~ sb** to make sb worried or upset: *What is it that's troubling you?*
▸ DISTURB **2** [T] (often used in polite requests) to disturb sb because you want to ask them sth SYN **bother**: **~ sb** *Sorry to trouble you, but could you tell me the time?* ◇ **~ sb with sth** *I don't want to trouble the doctor with such a small problem.* ◇ (*formal*) **~ sb to do sth** *Could I trouble you to open the window, please?*
▸ MAKE EFFORT **3** [I] **~ to do sth** (*BrE, formal*) (usually used in negative sentences) to make an effort to do sth SYN **bother**: *He rushed into the room without troubling to knock.*
▸ CAUSE PAIN **4** [T] **~ sb** (of a medical problem) to cause pain: *My back's been troubling me again.* IDM see POUR

troubled /'trʌbld/ *adj.* **1** (of a person) worried and anxious: *She looked into his troubled face.* **2** (of a place, situation or time) having a lot of problems: *a troubled marriage* ◇ *We live in* **troubled times.**

trouble·maker /'trʌblmeɪkə(r)/ *noun* a person who often causes trouble, especially by involving others in arguments or encouraging them to complain about people in authority

trouble·shoot /'trʌblʃuːt/ *verb* **1** [I, T] **~ (sth)** to analyse and solve serious problems for a company or other organization **2** [I, T] **~ (sth)** (*computing*) to identify and correct faults in a computer system ▸ **trouble·shoot·ing** *noun* [U]

trouble·shoot·er /'trʌblʃuːtə(r)/ *noun* a person who helps to solve problems in a company or an organization

trouble·some /'trʌblsəm/ *adj.* causing trouble, pain, etc. over a long period of time SYN **annoying, irritating**: *a troublesome cough/child/problem*

'trouble spot *noun* a place or country where trouble often happens, especially violence or war

trough /trɒf; *NAmE* trɔːf/ *noun* **1** [C] a long narrow open container for animals to eat or drink from **2 the trough** [sing.] (*informal*) if you say that people have their noses **in the trough**, you mean that they are trying to get a lot of money for themselves **3** [C] (*technical*) a long narrow region of low air pressure between two regions of higher pressure ➲ compare RIDGE **4** [C] a period of time when the level of sth is low, especially a time when a business or the economy is not growing: *There have been* **peaks and troughs** *in the long-term trend of unemployment.* **5** [C] a low area between two waves in the sea, or two hills

trounce /traʊns/ *verb* **~ sb** (*formal*) to defeat sb completely: *Brazil trounced Italy 5–1 in the final.*

troupe /truːp/ *noun* [C+sing./pl. v.] a group of actors, singers, etc. who work together

trouper /'truːpə(r)/ *noun* (*informal*) an actor or other person who has a lot of experience and who you can depend on

trou·ser *verb* **~ sth** (*BrE, informal*) to take or earn an amount of money SYN **pocket**

trou·sers O-w /'traʊzəz; *NAmE* -zərz/ (*especially BrE*) (*NAmE* usually **pants**) *noun* [pl.]
a piece of clothing that covers the body from the waist down and is divided into two parts to cover each leg separately: *a pair of grey trousers* ◇ *I was still* **in short trousers** (= still only a boy) *at the time.* ◇ *He dropped his trousers.* ➲ VISUAL VOCAB page V50 ▸ **trou·ser** *adj.* [only before noun]: *trouser pockets* IDM see CATCH *v.*, WEAR *v.*

'trouser suit (*BrE*) (*NAmE* **pant·suit**) *noun* a woman's suit of jacket and trousers/pants

trous·seau /'truːsəʊ; *NAmE* -soʊ/ *noun* (*pl.* **trous·seaus** or **trous·seaux** /-səʊz; *NAmE* -soʊz/) (*old-fashioned*) the clothes and other possessions collected by a woman who is soon going to get married, to begin her married life with

trout /traʊt/ *noun* **1** [C, U] (*pl.* **trout**) a common FRESHWATER fish that is used for food. There are several types of trout: *rainbow trout* ◇ *trout fishing* ◇ *Shall we have trout for dinner?* ➲ VISUAL VOCAB page V10 **2** [C, usually sing.] (usually **old trout**) (*informal, disapproving*) a bad-tempered or annoying old woman

trove /trəʊv; *NAmE* troʊv/ *noun* ➲ TREASURE TROVE

trowel /'traʊəl/ *noun* **1** a small garden tool with a curved blade for lifting plants and digging holes ➲ VISUAL VOCAB page V16 **2** a small tool with a flat blade, used in building for spreading CEMENT or PLASTER
IDM **lay it on with a 'trowel** (*informal*) to talk about sb/sth in a way that makes them or it seem much better or much worse than they really are; to exaggerate sth: *He was laying the flattery on with a trowel.*

troy /trɔɪ/ *noun* [U] a system for measuring PRECIOUS METALS and PRECIOUS STONES

tru·ancy /'truːənsi/ *noun* [U] the practice of staying away from school without permission

tru·ant /'truːənt/ *noun* a child who stays away from school without permission ▸ **tru·ant** *verb* [I]: *A number of pupils have been truanting regularly.*
IDM **play 'truant** (*BrE*) (*NAmE old-fashioned, informal* **play 'hooky**) to stay away from school without permission ➲ COLLOCATIONS at EDUCATION ➲ see also BUNK OFF, SKIVE

truce /truːs/ *noun* an agreement between enemies or opponents to stop fighting for an agreed period of time; the period of time that this lasts: *to* **call/break** *a* **truce** ➲ COLLOCATIONS at WAR

T

truck O-w /trʌk/ *noun, verb*
■ *noun* O-w **1** (*especially NAmE*) (*BrE* also **lorry**) a large vehicle for carrying heavy loads by road: *a truck driver* ➲ COLLOCATIONS at DRIVING ➲ VISUAL VOCAB page V46 **2** (*BrE*) (*NAmE* **car**) an open railway vehicle for carrying goods or animals: *a cattle truck* **3** a vehicle that is open at the back, used for carrying goods, soldiers, animals, etc: *a delivery/garbage/farm truck* **4** a vehicle for carrying things, that is pulled or pushed by hand ➲ see also FORK-LIFT TRUCK, PICKUP TRUCK, SALT TRUCK
IDM **have/want no truck with sb/sth** (*BrE*) to refuse to deal with sb; to refuse to accept or consider sth: *We in this party will have no truck with illegal organizations.*
■ *verb* **~ sth** (+ **adv./prep.**) (*especially NAmE*) to take sth somewhere by truck ▸ **truck·ing** *noun* [U]: *trucking companies*

truck·er /'trʌkə(r)/ *noun* (*especially NAmE*) a person whose job is driving a truck

'truck farm (*US*) (*BrE* ˌ**market 'garden**) *noun* a type of farm where vegetables are grown for sale ▸ **'truck farmer** *noun* **'truck farming** *noun* [U]

truck·load /'trʌkləʊd; *NAmE* -loʊd/ *noun* **~ (of sb/sth)** the amount of sb/sth that fills a truck (often used to express the fact that an amount is large)

'truck stop *noun* (*NAmE*) a place at the side of a main road where lorry/truck drivers can stop for a time and can rest, get sth to eat, etc. ➲ compare TRANSPORT CAFE

trucu·lent /'trʌkjələnt/ *adj.* (*formal, disapproving*) tending to argue or be bad-tempered; slightly aggressive ▸ **trucu·lence** /-ləns/ *noun* [U] **trucu·lent·ly** *adv.*

trudge /trʌdʒ/ *verb, noun*

■ ***verb*** [I] to walk slowly or with heavy steps, because you are tired or carrying sth heavy: **+ noun** *He trudged the last two miles to the town.* ◇ **+ adv./prep.** *The men trudged up the hill, laden with supplies.*

■ ***noun*** [sing.] a long tiring walk

true 🗝 /tru:/ *adj., adv., noun*

> **WORD FAMILY**
> true *adj.* (≠ untrue)
> truth *noun*
> truthful *adj.* (≠ untruthful)
> truthfully *adv.*
> truly *adv.*

■ ***adj.*** (truer, tru·est)

▸ CORRECT **1** 🗝 connected with facts rather than things that have been invented or guessed: *Indicate whether the following statements are* **true** *or* **false**. ◇ *Is it true she's leaving?* ◇ *All the rumours turned out to be true.* ◇ *That's not strictly* (= completely) *true.* ◇ *The novel is based on* **a true story**. ◇ *His excuse just doesn't* **ring** (= sound) **true**. ◇ *Unfortunately, these findings do not* **hold true** (= are not valid) *for women and children.* ◇ *The music is dull and uninspiring, and* **the same is true of** *the acting.* ◇ *You never spoke a truer word* (= used to emphasize that you agree with what sb has just said). **OPP** **untrue**

▸ REAL **2** 🗝 real or exact, especially when this is different from how sth seems: *the true face of war* (= what it is really like rather than what people think it is like) ◇ *The true cost of these experiments to the environment will not be known for years to come.* ◇ *He reveals his true character to very few people.* **3** 🗝 [usually before noun] having the qualities or characteristics of the thing mentioned: *It was true love between them.* ◇ *He's a true gentleman.* ◇ *The painting is a masterpiece in the truest sense of the word.* ◇ *He is credited with inventing the first true helicopter.*

▸ ADMITTING FACT **4** 🗝 used to admit that a particular fact or statement is correct, although you think that sth else is more important: *It's true that he could do the job, but would he fit in with the rest of the team?* ◇ *'We could get it cheaper.' 'True, but would it be as good?'* ➲ LANGUAGE BANK at NEVERTHELESS

▸ LOYAL **5** showing respect and support for a particular person or belief in a way that does not change, even in different situations: *a true friend* ◇ **~ to sb/sth** *She has always been true to herself* (= done what she thought was good, right, etc.). ◇ *He was* **true to his word** (= did what he promised to do).

▸ ACCURATE **6 ~ (to sth)** being an accurate version or copy of sth: *The movie is not true to the book.* **7** [not usually before noun] (*old-fashioned* or *literary*) straight and accurate: *His aim was true* (= he hit the target).

IDM **come 'true** 🗝 (of a hope, wish, etc.) to become reality: *Winning the medal was like* **a dream come true**. **too ,good to be 'true** used to say that you cannot believe that sth is as good as it seems: *'I'm afraid you were quoted the wrong price.' 'I thought it was too good to be true.'* **your true 'colours** (often *disapproving*) your real character, rather than the one that you usually allow other people to see **true to 'form** used to say that sb is behaving in the way that you expect them to behave, especially when this is annoying **true to 'life** (of a book, film/movie, etc.) seeming real rather than invented ➲ more at RING² *v.*, TRIED

■ ***adv.*** (*old-fashioned* or *literary*)

▸ STRAIGHT **1** in a direct line: *The arrow flew straight and true to the target.*

▸ CORRECTLY **2** **speak ~** to tell the truth: *He had spoken truer than he knew.*

■ ***noun***

IDM **,out of 'true** if an object is **out of true**, it is not straight or in the correct position

> **Synonyms**
>
> **true**
>
> **right • correct**
>
> These words all describe sth that cannot be doubted as fact and includes no mistakes.
>
> **true** connected with facts rather than things that have been invented or guessed: *Are the following statements true or false?* ◇ *Is it* **true (that)** *she's leaving?*
>
> **right** that is true and cannot be doubted as a fact: *I got about half the answers right.* ◇ *What's the right time?*
>
> **correct** right according to the facts and without any mistakes: *Only one of the answers is correct.* ◇ *Check that all the details are correct.*
>
> **RIGHT OR CORRECT?**
>
> **Correct** is more formal than **right** and is more likely to be used in official or formal instructions or documents.
>
> **PATTERNS**
>
> ■ right/correct **about** sb/sth
> ■ the true/right/correct **answer**
> ■ the right/correct **time**

,true-'blue *adj.* **1** (*BrE*) strongly supporting the British Conservative Party: *true-blue Tory voters* **2** (*especially NAmE*) being a loyal supporter of a particular person, group, principle, etc; being a typical example of sth: *a true-blue Californian*

,true-'life *adj.* [only before noun] a **true-life** story is one that actually happened rather than one that has been invented

,true 'north *noun* [U] north according to the earth's AXIS (= the imaginary line through the earth's centre from north to south) ➲ compare MAGNETIC NORTH

truf·fle /'trʌfl/ *noun* **1** an expensive type of FUNGUS that grows underground, used in cooking **2** a soft round sweet/candy made of chocolate

trug /trʌg/ *noun* a shallow BASKET used for carrying garden tools, plants, etc.

tru·ism /'tru:ɪzəm/ *noun* a statement that is clearly true and does not therefore add anything interesting or important to a discussion

truly 🗝 /'tru:li/ *adv.*

1 🗝 used to emphasize that a particular statement, feeling, etc. is sincere or genuine: *I'm truly sorry that things had to end like this.* **2** 🗝 used to emphasize a particular quality: *a truly memorable occasion* **3** 🗝 used to emphasize that a particular description is accurate or correct: *a truly democratic system of government* ◇ (*informal*) *Well,* ***really and truly****, things were better than expected.*

IDM **yours truly 1** 🗝 **Yours Truly** (*NAmE, formal*) used at the end of a formal letter before you sign your name **2** (*informal*, often *humorous*) I/me: *Steve came first, Robin second, and yours truly came last.* ➲ more at WELL *adv.*

trump /trʌmp/ *noun, verb*

■ ***noun*** **1** (also **'trump card**) [C] (in some card games) a card that belongs to the SUIT (= one of the four sets in a PACK/DECK of cards) that has been chosen for a particular game to have a higher value than the other three suits: *I played a trump and won the trick.* **2** **trumps** [U+sing./pl. v.] (in some card games) the SUIT that has been chosen for a particular game to have a higher value than the other three suits: *What's trumps?* ◇ *Clubs are trumps.*

IDM **,come up/,turn up 'trumps** to do what is necessary to make a particular situation successful, especially when this is sudden or unexpected: *I didn't honestly think he'd pass the exam but he came up trumps on the day.*

■ ***verb*** **1 ~ sth (with sth)** (in some card games) to play a trump card that beats sb else's card **2 ~ sth/sb** to beat sth that sb says or does by saying or doing sth even better

PHR V ˌtrump sth↔ˈup to make up a false story about sb/sth, especially accusing them of doing sth wrong: *She was arrested on a trumped-up charge.*

ˈ**trump card** *noun* **1** = TRUMP (1) **2** something that gives you an advantage over other people, especially when they do not know what it is and you are able to use it to surprise them

trump·ery /ˈtrʌmpəri/ *noun* [U] (*old-fashioned*) objects of little value ▸ **trump·ery** *adj.*

trum·pet /ˈtrʌmpɪt/ *noun, verb*

▪ ***noun* 1** a BRASS musical instrument made of a curved metal tube that you blow into, with three VALVES for changing the note ➲ VISUAL VOCAB page V30 **2** a thing shaped like a trumpet, especially the open flower of a DAFFODIL ➲ VISUAL VOCAB page V9 IDM see BLOW *v.*

▪ ***verb* 1** [T] **~ sth (as sth)** | **+ speech** to talk about sth publicly in a proud or enthusiastic way: *to trumpet somebody's achievements* ◇ *Their marriage was trumpeted as the wedding of the year.* **2** [I] (especially of an ELEPHANT) to make a loud noise

trum·pet·er /ˈtrʌmpɪtə(r)/ *noun* a person who plays a trumpet

trun·cate /trʌŋˈkeɪt; *NAmE* ˈtrʌŋkeɪt/ *verb* [usually passive] **~ sth** (*formal*) to make sth shorter, especially by cutting off the top or end: *My article was published in truncated form.* ▸ **trun·ca·tion** *noun* [U, C]

trun·cheon /ˈtrʌntʃən/ (also **baton**) (both *especially BrE*) (*NAmE* usually **night·stick**) *noun* a short thick stick that police officers carry as a weapon

trun·dle /ˈtrʌndl/ *verb* **1** [I, T] **~ (sth) + adv./prep.** to move or roll somewhere slowly and noisily; to move sth slowly and noisily, especially sth heavy, with wheels: *A train trundled across the bridge.* **2** [I] **+ adv./prep.** (of a person) to walk slowly with heavy steps

PHR V ˌ**trundle sth↔ˈout** (*disapproving, especially BrE*) to mention or do sth that you have often mentioned or done before: *A long list of reasons was trundled out to justify their demands.*

trunk /trʌŋk/ *noun* **1** [C] the thick main STEM of a tree, that the branches grow from ➲ VISUAL VOCAB page V8 **2** (*NAmE*) (*BrE* **boot**) [C] the space at the back of a car that you put bags, cases, etc. in ➲ VISUAL VOCAB page V42 **3** [C] the long nose of an ELEPHANT ➲ VISUAL VOCAB page V10 **4 trunks** [pl.] = SWIMMING TRUNKS **5** [C] a large strong box with a lid used for storing or transporting clothes, books, etc. ➲ VISUAL VOCAB page V52 **6** [C, usually sing.] the main part of the human body apart from the head, arms and legs ➲ see also TORSO

trunks

ˈ**trunk call** *noun* (*old-fashioned, BrE*) a telephone call to a place that is a long distance away but in the same country

ˈ**trunk road** *noun* (*BrE*) an important main road

truss /trʌs/ *noun, verb*

▪ ***noun* 1** a special belt with a thick piece of material, worn by sb suffering from a HERNIA in order to support the muscles **2** a frame made of pieces of wood or metal used to support a roof, bridge, etc.

▪ ***verb* 1 ~ sb/sth (up)** to tie up sb's arms and legs so that they cannot move **2 ~ sth** to tie the legs and wings of a chicken, etc. before it is cooked

trust O━ /trʌst/ *noun, verb*

▪ ***noun* 1** O━ [U] **~ (in sb/sth)** the belief that sb/sth is good, sincere, honest, etc. and will not try to harm or trick you: *Her trust in him was unfounded.* ◇ *a partnership* ***based on trust*** ◇ *It has taken years to* ***earn their trust.*** ◇ *If you* ***put your trust in*** *me, I will not let you down.* ◇ *She will not* ***betray your trust*** (= do sth that you have asked her not to do). ◇ *He was appointed to a* ***position of trust*** (= a job involving a lot of responsibility, because people trust him). **2** [C, U] (*law*) an arrangement by which an organization or a group of people has legal control of money or property that has been given to sb, usually until that person reaches a particular age; an amount of money or property that is controlled in this way: *He* ***set up a trust*** *for his children.* ◇ *The money will be* ***held in trust*** *until she is 18.* ◇ *Our fees depend on the value of the trust.* ➲ see also UNIT TRUST **3** [C] (*law*) an organization or a group of people that invests money that is given or lent to it and uses the profits to help a charity: *a charitable trust* **4** [C] (*business*) (*especially NAmE*) a group of companies that work together illegally to reduce competition, control prices, etc: *anti-trust laws*

IDM **in sb's ˈtrust** | **in the trust of sb** being taken care of by sb: *The family pet was left in the trust of a neighbour.* **take sth on ˈtrust** to believe what sb says even though you do not have any proof or evidence to show that it is true

▪ ***verb* 1** to have confidence in sb; to believe that sb is good, sincere, honest, etc: **~ sb** *She trusts Alan implicitly.* ◇ **~ sb to do sth** *You can trust me not to tell anyone.* **2 ~ sth** to

Synonyms

trust

depend on sb/sth • rely on sb/sth • count on sb/sth • believe in sb

These words all mean to believe that sb/sth will do what you hope or expect of them or that what they tell you is correct or true.

trust to believe that sb is good, honest, sincere, etc. and that they will do what you expect of them or do the right thing; to believe that sth is true or correct: *You can trust me not to tell anyone.* ◇ *Don't trust what you read in the newspapers!*

depend on/upon sb/sth (often used with *can/cannot/could/could not*) to trust sb/sth to do what you expect or want, to do the right thing, or to be true or correct: *He was the sort of person you could depend on.* ◇ *Can you depend on her version of what happened?*

rely on/upon sb/sth (used especially with *can/cannot/could/could not* and *should/should not*) to trust sb/sth to do what you expect or want, or to be honest, correct or good enough: *Can I rely on you to keep this secret?* ◇ *You can't rely on any figures you get from them.*

TRUST, DEPEND OR RELY ON/UPON SB/STH?

You can **trust** a person but not a thing or system. You can **trust** sb's *judgement or advice*, but not their support. You can **depend on** sb's *support*, but not their judgement or advice. **Rely on/upon sb/sth** is used especially with *you can/could* or *you should* to give advice or a promise: ~~*I don't really rely on his judgement.*~~ ◇ *You can't really rely on his judgement.*

count on sb/sth (often used with *can/cannot/could/could not*) to be sure that sb will do what you need them to do, or that sth will happen as you want it to happen: *I'm counting on you to help me.* ◇ *We can't count on the good weather lasting.*

believe in sb to feel that you can trust sb and/or that they will be successful: *They need a leader they can believe in.*

PATTERNS

- to trust/depend on/rely on/count on sb/sth **to do sth**
- to trust/believe **in** sb/sth
- to trust/rely on **sb's advice/judgement**
- to depend on/rely on/count on **sb's support**
- to **completely** trust/depend on/rely on/believe in sb/sth

T

believe that sth is true or correct or that you can rely on it: *He trusted her judgement.* ◇ *Don't trust what the newspapers say!* **3 ~** (**that**)... (*formal*) to hope and expect that sth is true: *I trust (that) you have no objections to our proposals?*
IDM **not trust sb an 'inch** to not trust sb at all **trust 'you, 'him, 'her, etc. (to do sth)** (*informal*) used when sb does or says sth that you think is typical of them: *Trust John to forget Sue's birthday!* ➲ more at TRIED
PHR V **'trust in sb/sth** (*formal*) to have confidence in sb/sth; to believe that sb/sth is good and can be relied on: *She needs to trust more in her own abilities.* **'trust to sth** [no passive] to put your confidence in sth such as luck, chance, etc. because there is nothing else to help you: *I stumbled along in the dark, trusting to luck to find the right door.* **'trust sb with sth/sb** to give sth/sb to a person to take care of because you believe they would be very careful with it/them: *I'd trust her with my life.*

trust·ee /trʌ'sti:/ *noun* **1** a person or an organization that has control of money or property that has been put into a TRUST for sb **2** a member of a group of people that controls the financial affairs of a charity or other organization

trustee·ship /trʌ'sti:ʃɪp/ *noun* [U, C] **1** the job of being a trustee **2** the responsibility for governing a particular region, given to a country by the United Nations Organization; a region that is governed by another country in this way

'trust fund *noun* money that is controlled for sb by an organization or a group of people

trust·ing /'trʌstɪŋ/ *adj.* tending to believe that other people are good, honest, etc: *If you're too trusting, other people will take advantage of you.* ▸ **trust·ing·ly** *adv.*

'trust territory *noun* a region governed by the United Nations Organization or by another country that has been chosen by the United Nations Organization

trust·worthy /'trʌstwɜ:ði; *NAmE* -wɜ:rði/ *adj.* that you can rely on to be good, honest, sincere, etc. **SYN** **reliable** ▸ **trust·worthi·ness** *noun* [U]

trusty /'trʌsti/ *adj.*, *noun*
■ ***adj.*** [only before noun] (*old use* or *humorous*) that you have had a long time and have always been able to rely on **SYN** **reliable**: *a trusty friend* ◇ *She spent years touring Europe with her trusty old camera.*
■ ***noun*** (*pl.* -ies) (*informal*) a prisoner who is given special advantages because of good behaviour

truth 🔑 /tru:θ/ *noun* (*pl.* truths /tru:ðz/)
1 🔑 **the truth** [sing.] the true facts about sth, rather than the things that have been invented or guessed: *Do you think she's **telling the truth**?* ◇ *We are determined to get at* (= discover) *the truth.* ◇ ***The truth** (**of the matter**) **is** we can't afford to keep all the staff on.* ◇ *I don't think you are telling me **the whole truth** about what happened.* **2** 🔑 [U] the quality or state of being based on fact: *There is no truth in the rumours.* ◇ *There is not **a grain of truth** in what she says.* **OPP** **falsity** **3** [C] a fact that is believed by most people to be true: *universal truths* ◇ *She was forced to face up to a few unwelcome truths about her family.* ➲ compare UNTRUTH ➲ see also HALF-TRUTH, HOME TRUTH
IDM **if (the) ˌtruth be 'known/'told** used to tell sb the true facts about a situation, especially when these are not known by other people **in 'truth** (*formal*) used to emphasize the true facts about a situation: *She laughed and chatted but was, in truth, not having much fun.* **ˌnothing could be ˌfurther from the 'truth** used to say that a fact or comment is completely false **to tell (you) the 'truth** (*informal*) used when admitting sth: *To tell you the truth, I'll be glad to get home.* **ˌtruth is stranger than 'fiction** (*saying*) used to say that things that actually happen are often more surprising than stories that are invented **(the) ˌtruth will 'out** (*saying*) used to say that people will find out the true facts about a situation even if you try to keep them secret ➲ more at BEND *v.*, ECONOMICAL, MOMENT

'truth drug *noun* a drug that is believed to be able to put sb into a state where they will answer questions with the truth

truth·ful /'tru:θfl/ *adj.* **1 ~** (**about sth**) (of a person) saying only what is true **SYN** **honest**: *They were less than truthful about their part in the crime.* ◇ *Are you being completely truthful with me?* **2** (of a statement) giving the true facts about sth: *a truthful answer* **OPP** **untruthful** ▸ **truth·ful·ly** /-fəli/ *adv.*: *She answered all their questions truthfully.* **truth·ful·ness** *noun* [U]

try 🔑 /traɪ/ *verb*, *noun*
■ ***verb*** (**tries**, **try·ing**, **tried**, **tried**) **1** 🔑 [I, T] to make an attempt or effort to do or get sth: *I don't know if I can come but I'll try.* ◇ **~ to do sth** *What are you trying to do?* ◇ *I tried hard not to laugh.* ◇ **~ your best/hardest** (**to do sth**) *She tried her best to solve the problem.* ◇ *Just try your hardest.* **HELP** In spoken English **try** can be used with **and** plus another verb, instead of with **to** and the infinitive: *I'll try and get you a new one tomorrow.* ◇ *Try and finish quickly.* In this structure, only the form **try** can be used, not **tries**, **trying** or **tried**. **2** 🔑 [T] to use, do or test sth in order to see if it is good, suitable, etc: **~ sth** *Have you tried this new coffee? It's very good.* ◇ *'Would you like to try some raw fish?' 'Why not? **I'll try anything once!**'* ◇ *Have you ever tried windsurfing?* ◇ ***Try** these shoes **for size**—they should fit you.* ◇ *She tried the door, but it was locked.* ◇ **~ doing sth** *John isn't here. Try phoning his home number.* **HELP** Notice the difference between **try to do sth** and **try doing sth**: *You should try to eat more fruit.* means 'You should make an effort to eat more fruit.'; *You should try eating more fruit.* means 'You should see if eating more fruit will help you' (to feel better, for example). **3** [T] to examine evidence in court and decide whether sb is innocent or guilty: **~ sb** (**for sth**) *He was tried for murder.* ◇ **~ sth** *The case was tried before a jury.*
IDM **ˌnot for want/lack of 'trying** used to say that although sb has not succeeded in sth, they have tried very hard: *They haven't won a game yet, but it isn't for want of trying.* **try your 'hand** (**at sth**) to do sth such as an activity or a sport for the first time **ˌtry it 'on** (**with sb**) (*BrE*, *informal*, *disapproving*) **1** to behave badly towards sb or try to get sth from them, even though you know this will make them angry: *Children often try it on with new teachers.* **2** to try to start a sexual relationship with sb **try your 'luck** (**at sth**) to do sth that involves risk or luck, hoping to succeed: *My grandparents emigrated to Canada to try their luck there.* **try sb's 'patience** to make sb feel impatient ➲ more at DAMNEDEST, LEVEL *adj.*, THING
PHR V **'try for sth** to make an attempt to get or win sth **ˌtry sth↔'on** 🔑 to put on a piece of clothing to see if it fits and how it looks: *Try the shoes on before you buy them.* **ˌtry 'out for sth** (*especially NAmE*) to compete for a position or place in sth, or to be a member of a team: *She's trying out for the school play.* ➲ related noun TRYOUT **ˌtry sb/sth↔'out** (**on sb**) 🔑 to test or use sb/sth in order to see how good or effective they are: *They're trying out a new presenter for the show.* ➲ related noun TRYOUT
■ ***noun*** (*pl.* **tries**) **1** [usually sing.] an act of trying to do sth **SYN** **attempt**: *I doubt they'll be able to help but it's **worth a try*** (= worth asking them). ◇ **~** (**at sth/at doing sth**) *Why don't you **have a try** at convincing him?* ◇ (*NAmE*) *The US negotiators decided to **make another try at** reaching a settlement.* ◇ *I don't think I'll be any good at tennis, but I'll **give it a try**.* ◇ (*informal*) *'What's that behind you?' '**Nice try*** (= at making me turn round), *but you'll have to do better than that!'* **2** (in RUGBY) an act of scoring points by touching the ground behind your opponents' GOAL LINE with the ball: *to score a try*

ˌtry-and-'buy *adj.* [only before noun] (especially of computer programs and equipment) that can be used free for a limited period of time, during which you can decide whether you want to buy it or not

try·ing /'traɪɪŋ/ *adj.* annoying or difficult to deal with: *These are trying times for all of us.*

try·out /'traɪaʊt/ *noun* **1** an act of testing how good or effective sb/sth is before deciding whether to use them in the future **2** (*NAmE*) (*BrE* **trial**) a competition or series of tests to find the best players for a sports team or an important event

tryst /trɪst/ *noun* (*literary* or *humorous*) a secret meeting between lovers

tsar (also **tzar**, **czar**) /zɑ:(r)/ *noun* **1** the title of the EMPEROR of Russia in the past: *Tsar Nicholas II* **2** (in compounds) (*informal*) an official whose job is to advise the government on policy in a particular area: (*BrE*) *a drugs tsar* ◇ (*NAmE*) *a drug tsar*

tsar·ina (also **tzar·ina**, **czar·ina**) /zɑ:ˈri:nə/ *noun* the title of the EMPRESS of Russia in the past

tsar·ism (also **tzar·ism**, **czar·ism**) /ˈzɑ:rɪzəm/ *noun* [U] the Russian system of government by a tsar, which existed before 1917 ▶ **tsar·ist** (also **tzar·ist**, **czar·ist**) *noun, adj.*

tsetse fly /ˈtsetsi flaɪ/ *noun* an African fly that bites humans and animals and sucks their blood and can spread a disease called SLEEPING SICKNESS

ˈT-shirt (also **ˈtee shirt**) *noun* an informal shirt with short sleeves and no COLLAR or buttons, or just a few buttons at the top ➲ VISUAL VOCAB page V51

tsk tsk /ˌtəsk ˈtəsk/ *exclamation* used in writing to represent the sound you make with your tongue when you disapprove of something: *So you were out drinking again last night were you? Tsk tsk!*

tsotsi /ˈtsɒtsi; *NAmE* ˈtsɑ:t-/ *noun* (*SAfrE*) a young black criminal

Tsotsi·taal /ˈtsɒtsitɑ:l; *NAmE* ˈtsɑ:t-/ *noun* [U] (*SAfrE*) a simple form of language that includes words from Afrikaans and African languages, used especially between young black people in cities or TOWNSHIPS

tsp *abbr.* (*pl.* **tsp** or **tsps**) TEASPOONFUL: *1 tsp chilli powder*

ˈT-square *noun* a plastic or metal instrument in the shape of a T for drawing or measuring RIGHT ANGLES (= of 90°)

tsu·nami /tsu:ˈnɑ:mi/ *noun* (from *Japanese*) an extremely large wave in the sea caused, for example, by an EARTHQUAKE SYN **tidal wave**

tub /tʌb/ *noun* **1** a large round container without a lid, used for washing clothes in, growing plants in, etc: *There were tubs of flowers on the balcony.* **2** a small wide, usually round, plastic or paper container with a lid, used for food, etc: *a tub of margarine* ➲ VISUAL VOCAB page V29 **3** (*informal, especially NAmE*) = BATHTUB: *They found her lying in the tub.* ➲ see also HOT TUB

tuba /ˈtju:bə; *NAmE* ˈtu:bə/ *noun* a large BRASS musical instrument that you play by blowing, and that produces low notes ➲ VISUAL VOCAB page V30

tubal /ˈtju:bl; *NAmE* ˈtu:bl/ *adj.* (*medical*) connected with the FALLOPIAN TUBES: *a tubal pregnancy*

tubby /ˈtʌbi/ *adj.* (*informal*) (of a person) short and slightly fat SYN **stout**

tube 0ᴋ /tju:b; *NAmE* tu:b/ *noun*

▸ PIPE **1** 0ᴋ [C] a long hollow pipe made of metal, plastic, rubber, etc, through which liquids or gases move from one place to another ➲ see also CATHODE RAY TUBE, INNER TUBE, TEST TUBE **2** 0ᴋ [C] a hollow object in the shape of a pipe or tube: *a bike's inner tube* ◇ *the cardboard tube from the centre of a toilet roll*

▸ CONTAINER **3** 0ᴋ [C] ~ (**of sth**) a long narrow container made of soft metal or plastic, with a lid, used for holding thick liquids that can be squeezed out of it: *a tube of toothpaste* ➲ VISUAL VOCAB page V29 **4** (*AustralE, informal*) a can of beer: *a tube of lager*

▸ PART OF BODY **5** [C] a part inside the body that is shaped like a tube and through which air, liquid, etc. passes: *bronchial tubes* ➲ VISUAL VOCAB page V48 ➲ see also FALLOPIAN TUBES

▸ UNDERGROUND RAILWAY **6** (also **The Tube™**) [sing.] (*BrE*) the underground railway system in London: *a* ***tube station/train*** ◇ *We came* ***by tube***. ➲ note at UNDERGROUND

▸ TELEVISION **7 the tube** [sing.] (*NAmE, informal*) the television

▸ IN EAR **8** (*NAmE*) (*BrE* **grom·met**) [C] a small tube placed in a child's ear in order to DRAIN liquid from it

IDM **go down the ˈtube/ˈtubes** (*informal*) (of a plan, company, situation, etc.) to fail: *The education system is going down the tubes.*

tuber /ˈtju:bə(r); *NAmE* ˈtu:-/ *noun* the short thick round part of an underground STEM or root of some plants, such as potatoes, which stores food and from which new plants grow ▶ **tu·ber·ous** /ˈtju:bərəs; *NAmE* ˈtu:-/ *adj.*

tu·ber·cle /ˈtju:bəkl; *NAmE* ˈtu:b-/ *noun* **1** (*anatomy, biology*) a small round lump, especially on a bone or on the surface of an animal or plant **2** (*medical*) a small swollen area in the lung caused by TUBERCULOSIS

tu·ber·cu·losis /tju:ˌbɜ:kjuˈləʊsɪs; *NAmE* tu:ˌbɜ:rkjəˈloʊsɪs/ *noun* [U] (*abbr.* **TB**) a serious infectious disease in which swellings appear on the lungs and other parts of the body ▶ **tu·ber·cu·lar** /tju:ˈbɜ:kjələ(r); *NAmE* tu:ˈbɜ:rk-/ *adj.*: *a tubercular infection*

ˈtube top (*NAmE*) (*BrE* **ˈboob tube**) *noun* a piece of women's clothing that is made of cloth that stretches and covers the chest

ˈtube well *noun* a pipe with holes in the sides near the end, that is put into the ground and used with a PUMP operated by hand to bring water up from under the ground

tub·ing /ˈtju:bɪŋ; *NAmE* ˈtu:bɪŋ/ *noun* [U] metal, plastic, etc. in the shape of a tube: *a length of copper tubing* ➲ VISUAL VOCAB page V57

ˈtub-thumping *noun* [U] (*BrE, disapproving*) the act of giving your opinions about sth in a loud and aggressive way ▶ **ˈtub-thumping** *adj.*

tu·bu·lar /ˈtju:bjələ(r); *NAmE* ˈtu:-/ *adj.* **1** made of tubes or of parts that are shaped like tubes: *a tubular metal chair* **2** shaped like a tube

ˌtubular ˈbells *noun* [pl.] a musical instrument which sounds like a set of bells, consisting of a row of hanging metal tubes that are hit with a stick

TUC /ˌti: ju: ˈsi:/ *abbr.* Trades Union Congress (an organization to which many British TRADE/LABOR UNIONS belong)

tuck /tʌk/ *verb, noun*

■ ***verb*** **1 ~ sth + adv./prep.** to push, fold or turn the ends or edges of clothes, paper, etc. so that they are held in place or look neat: *She tucked up her skirt and waded into the river.* ◇ *The sheets should be tucked in neatly* (= around the bed). ◇ *Tuck the flap of the envelope in.* **2 ~ sth + adv./prep.** to put sth into a small space, especially to hide it or keep it safe or comfortable: *She tucked her hair (up) under her cap.* ◇ *He sat with his legs tucked up under him.* ◇ *The letter had been tucked under a pile of papers.* **3 ~ sth + adv./prep.** to cover sb with sth so that they are warm and comfortable: *She tucked a blanket around his legs.*

PHR V **ˌtuck sth↔aˈway 1 be tucked away** to be located in a quiet place, where not many people go: *The shop is tucked away down a backstreet.* **2** to hide sth somewhere or keep it in a safe place: *She kept his letters tucked away in a drawer.* ◇ *They have thousands of pounds tucked away in a savings account.* **3** (*BrE, informal*) to eat a lot of food **ˌtuck sb ˈin/ˈup** to make sb feel comfortable in bed by pulling the covers up around them: *I tucked the children in and said goodnight.* **ˌtuck ˈin | ˌtuck ˈinto sth** (*BrE, informal*) to eat a lot of food, especially when it is done quickly and with enthusiasm: *Come on, tuck in everyone!* ◇ *He was tucking into a huge plateful of pasta.*

■ ***noun*** **1** [C] a fold that is sewn into a piece of clothing or cloth, either for decoration or to change the shape of it **2** [C] (*informal*) a medical operation in which skin and/or fat is removed to make sb look younger or thinner **3** [U] (*old-fashioned, BrE, informal*) food, especially sweets, etc. eaten by children at school

tuck·er /ˈtʌkə(r)/ *noun* [U] (*AustralE, NZE, informal*) food IDM see BIB

Tudor /ˈtju:də(r); *NAmE* ˈtu:-/ *adj.* connected with the time when kings and queens from the Tudor family ruled England (1485-1603): *Tudor architecture*

Tues·day 0ᴋ /ˈtju:zdeɪ; -di; *NAmE* ˈtu:-/ *noun* [C, U] (*abbr.* **Tue.**, **Tues.**)
the day of the week after Monday and before Wednesday HELP To see how **Tuesday** is used, look at the examples at **Monday**. ORIGIN Originally translated from the Latin for

T

'day of Mars' *dies Marti* and named after the Germanic god *Tiw*.

tuft /tʌft/ *noun* **~ (of sth)** a number of pieces of hair, grass, etc. growing or held closely together at the base

tuft·ed /'tʌftɪd/ *adj.* [usually before noun] having a tuft or tufts; growing in tufts: *a tufted carpet* ◇ *a tufted duck*

tug /tʌg/ *verb, noun*

■ ***verb*** (-gg-) **1** [I, T] to pull sth hard, often several times: **~ (at/on sth)** *She tugged at his sleeve to get his attention.* ◇ (*figurative*) *a sad story that* ***tugs at your heartstrings*** (= makes you feel sad) ◇ **~ sth** *The baby was tugging her hair.* ◇ **~ sth + adj.** *He tugged the door open.* **2** [T] **~ sth + adv./prep.** to pull sth hard in a particular direction: *He tugged the hat down over his head.* ➲ SYNONYMS at PULL IDM see FORELOCK

■ ***noun*** **1** (also **tug·boat** /'tʌgbəʊt; *NAmE* -boʊt/) a small powerful boat for pulling ships, especially into a HARBOUR or up a river ➲ VISUAL VOCAB page V44 **2** a sudden hard pull: *I felt a tug at my sleeve.* ◇ *She gave her sister's hair a sharp tug.* **3** [usually sing.] a sudden strong emotional feeling: *a tug of attraction*

ˌtug of 'love *noun* [sing.] (*BrE, informal*) a situation in which a child's parents are divorced or no longer living together and are fighting over who the child should live with

ˌtug of 'war *noun* [sing., U] **1** a sporting event in which two teams pull at opposite ends of a rope until one team drags the other over a line on the ground **2** a situation in which two people or groups try very hard to get or keep the same thing

tu·ition /tju'ɪʃn; *NAmE* tu-/ *noun* [U] **1 ~ (in sth)** (*formal*) the act of teaching sth, especially to one person or to people in small groups: *She received private tuition in French.* ➲ COLLOCATIONS at EDUCATION **2** (also **tu'ition fees** [pl.]) the money that you pay to be taught, especially in a college or university

tulip /'tju:lɪp; *NAmE* 'tu:-/ *noun* a large, brightly coloured spring flower, shaped like a cup, on a tall STEM ➲ VISUAL VOCAB page V9

tulle /tju:l; *NAmE* tu:l/ *noun* [U] a type of soft fine cloth made of silk, NYLON, etc. and full of very small holes, used especially for making VEILS and dresses

tum /tʌm/ *noun* (*BrE, informal*) a person's stomach or the area around the stomach

tum·ble /'tʌmbl/ *verb, noun*

■ ***verb*** **1** [I, T] **~ (sb/sth) + adv./prep.** to fall downwards, often hitting the ground several times, but usually without serious injury; to make sb/sth fall in this way: *He slipped and tumbled down the stairs.* **2** [I] **~ (down)** to fall suddenly and in a dramatic way: *The scaffolding came tumbling down.* ◇ (*figurative*) *World records tumbled at the last Olympics.* ➲ see also TUMBLEDOWN **3** [I] to fall rapidly in value or amount: *The price of oil is still tumbling.* **4** [I] **+ adv./prep.** to move or fall somewhere in a relaxed, uncontrolled, or noisy way: *A group of noisy children tumbled out of the bus.* ◇ *Thick golden curls tumbled down over her shoulders.* **5** [I] to perform ACROBATICS on the floor, especially SOMERSAULTS (= a jump in which you turn over completely in the air)

PHR V **'tumble to sth/sb** (*BrE, informal*) to suddenly understand sth or be aware of sth

■ ***noun*** **1** [C, usually sing.] a sudden fall: *The jockey* ***took a nasty tumble*** *at the third fence.* ◇ *Share prices* ***took a sharp tumble*** *following news of the merger.* ➲ see also ROUGH AND TUMBLE **2** [sing.] **~ (of sth)** an untidy group of things: *a tumble of blond curls*

tumble·down /'tʌmbldaʊn/ *adj.* [usually before noun] (of a building) old and in a poor condition so that it looks as if it is falling down SYN **dilapidated**

ˌtumble 'dryer (also **ˌtumble-'drier**) (both *BrE*) *noun* a machine that uses hot air to dry clothes after they have been washed ➲ compare SPIN DRYER

tum·bler /'tʌmblə(r)/ *noun* **1** a glass for drinking out of, with a flat bottom, straight sides and no handle or STEM ➲ VISUAL VOCAB page V19 **2** (also **tum·bler·ful** /-fʊl/) the amount held by a tumbler **3** (*old-fashioned*) an ACROBAT who performs SOMERSAULTS (= a jump in which you turn over completely in the air)

tumble·weed /'tʌmblwi:d/ *noun* [U] a plant that grows like a bush in the desert areas of N America and Australia. In the autumn/fall, it breaks off just above the ground and is blown around like a ball by the wind.

tum·bril /'tʌmbrəl/ *noun* an open vehicle used for taking people to their deaths at the GUILLOTINE during the French Revolution

tu·mes·cent /tju:'mesnt; *NAmE* tu:-/ *adj.* (*formal*) (especially of parts of the body) larger than normal, especially as a result of sexual excitement SYN **swollen** ▶ **tu·mes·cence** /-sns/ *noun* [U]

tummy /'tʌmi/ *noun* (*pl.* -ies) (*informal*) (used especially by children or when speaking to children) the stomach or the area around the stomach: *Mum, my tummy hurts.* ◇ *to have (a) tummy ache* ◇ *a* ***tummy bug/upset*** (= an illness when you feel sick or VOMIT)

'tummy button *noun* (*BrE, informal*) = NAVEL

tu·mour (*especially US* **tu·mor**) /'tju:mə(r); *NAmE* 'tu:-/ *noun* a mass of cells growing in or on a part of the body where they should not, usually causing medical problems: *a brain tumour* ◇ *a* ***benign/malignant*** (= harmless/harmful) ***tumour***

tu·mult /'tju:mʌlt; *NAmE* 'tu:-/ *noun* [U, C, usually sing.] (*formal*) **1** a confused situation in which there is usually a lot of noise and excitement, often involving large numbers of people **2** a state in which your thoughts or feelings are confused

tu·mul·tu·ous /tju:'mʌltʃuəs; *NAmE* tu:-/ *adj.* [usually before noun] **1** very loud; involving strong feelings, especially feelings of approval: *tumultuous applause* ◇ *a* ***tumultuous reception/welcome*** **2** involving a lot of change and confusion and/or violence SYN **tempestuous**: *the tumultuous years of the English Civil War*

tu·mu·lus /'tju:mjələs; *NAmE* 'tu:-/ *noun* (*pl.* **tu·muli** /-laɪ/) (*technical*) a large pile of earth built over the grave of an important person in ancient times

tun /tʌn/ *noun* (*old-fashioned*) a large round wooden container for beer, wine, etc. SYN **barrel**

tuna /'tju:nə; *NAmE* 'tu:nə/ *noun* [C, U] (*pl.* **tuna** or **tunas**) (also **'tuna fish**) (*BrE* also *less frequent* **tunny**) a large sea fish that is used for food: *fishing for tuna* ◇ *tuna steaks* ◇ *a tin/can of tuna in vegetable oil*

tun·dra /'tʌndrə/ *noun* [U] the large flat Arctic regions of northern Europe, Asia and N America where no trees grow and where the soil below the surface of the ground is always frozen

tune 0-w /tju:n; *NAmE* tu:n/ *noun, verb*

■ ***noun*** 0-w [C] a series of musical notes that are sung or played in a particular order to form a piece of music: *He was humming a familiar tune.* ◇ *I don't know the title but I recognize the tune.* ◇ *It was a catchy tune* (= song). ◇ *a football song sung* ***to the tune of*** (= using the tune of) *'When the saints go marching in'* ➲ COLLOCATIONS at MUSIC ➲ see also SIGNATURE TUNE, THEME TUNE

IDM **be ˌin/ˌout of 'tune (with sb/sth)** to be/not be in agreement with sb/sth; to have/not have the same opinions, feelings, interests, etc. as sb/sth: *These proposals are perfectly in tune with our own thoughts on the subject.* ◇ *The President is out of tune with public opinion.* **ˌin/ˌout of 'tune** to be/not be singing or playing the correct musical notes to sound pleasant: *None of them could sing in tune.* ◇ *The piano is out of tune.* **to the tune of sth** (*informal*) used to emphasize how much money sth has cost: *The hotel has been refurbished to the tune of a million dollars.* ➲ more at CALL *v.*, CHANGE *v.*, DANCE *v.*, PAY *v.*, SING

■ ***verb*** **1 ~ sth** to adjust a musical instrument so that it plays at the correct PITCH: *to tune a guitar* **2 ~ sth** to adjust an engine so that it runs smoothly and as well as possible **3** [usually passive] **~ sth (in) (to sth)** to adjust the controls on a radio or television so that you can receive a particular programme or channel: *The radio was tuned (in) to the BBC World Service.* ◇ (*informal*) ***Stay tuned*** *for the news coming up next.* **4 ~ sth (to sth)** to prepare or adjust sth so that it is suitable for a particular situation: *His speech was tuned to what the audience wanted to hear.*

PHR V ˌ**tune** ˈ**in (to sth)** to listen to a radio programme or watch a television programme ˌ**tune** ˈ**in to sb/sth** to become aware of other people's thoughts and feelings, etc. ˌ**tune** ˈ**out** | ˌ**tune sb/sth**↔ˈ**out** to stop listening to sth: *When she started talking about her job, he just tuned out.* ˌ**tune** ˈ**up** | ˌ**tune sth**↔ˈ**up** to adjust musical instruments so that they can play together: *The orchestra was tuning up as we entered the hall.*

ˌ**tuned** ˈ**in** *adj.* [not before noun] **~ (to sth)** aware of what is happening in a particular situation: *The resort is tuned in to the tastes of young and old alike.*

tune·ful /ˈtjuːnfl; *NAmE* ˈtuːnfl/ *adj.* having a pleasant tune or sound **OPP** **tuneless** ▸ **tune·ful·ly** /-fəli/ *adv.* **tune·ful·ness** *noun* [U]

tune·less /ˈtjuːnləs; *NAmE* ˈtuːn-/ *adj.* not having a pleasant tune or sound **OPP** **tuneful** ▸ **tune·less·ly** *adv.*

tuner /ˈtjuːnə(r); *NAmE* ˈtuː-/ *noun* **1** (especially in compounds) a person who tunes musical instruments, especially pianos **2** the part of a radio, television, etc. that you move in order to change the signal and receive the radio or television station that you want **3** an electronic device that receives a radio signal and sends it to an AMPLIFIER so that it can be heard

tune·smith /ˈtjuːnsmɪθ; *NAmE* ˈtuːn-/ *noun* (*informal*) a person who writes popular music

tung·sten /ˈtʌŋstən/ *noun* [U] (*symb.* W) a chemical element. Tungsten is a very hard silver-grey metal, used especially in making steel and in FILAMENTS for LIGHT BULBS.

tunic /ˈtjuːnɪk; *NAmE* ˈtuː-/ *noun* **1** a loose piece of clothing covering the body down to the knees, usually without sleeves, as worn in ancient Greece and Rome **2** a piece of women's clothing like a tunic, that reaches to the hips and is worn over trousers/pants or a skirt **3** (*BrE*) a tightly fitting jacket worn as part of a uniform by police officers, soldiers, etc.

ˈ**tuning fork** *noun* a small metal instrument with two long parts joined together at one end, that produces a particular musical note when you hit it and is used in TUNING musical instruments

ˈ**tuning peg** *noun* = PEG (4) ➲ picture at PEG

tun·nel 🔑 /ˈtʌnl/ *noun, verb*

▪ ***noun*** **1** 🔑 a passage built underground, for example to allow a road or railway/railroad to go through a hill, under a river, etc: *a* ***railway/railroad tunnel*** ◇ *the Channel Tunnel* ➲ see also WIND TUNNEL **2** an underground passage made by an animal **IDM** see LIGHT *n.*

▪ ***verb*** (-ll-, *NAmE* also -l-) [I, T] to dig a tunnel under or through the ground: **+ adv./prep.** *The engineers had to tunnel through solid rock.* ◇ **~ your way + adv./prep.** *The rescuers tunnelled their way in to the trapped miners.*

ˌ**tunnel** ˈ**vision** *noun* [U] **1** (*medical*) a condition in which sb cannot see things that are not straight ahead of them **2** (*disapproving*) an inability to see or understand all the aspects of a situation, an argument, etc. instead of just one part of it

tunny /ˈtʌni/ *noun* (*pl.* **tunny**) (*BrE*) = TUNA

tup·pence (also **two·pence**) /ˈtʌpəns/ *noun* [U] (*BrE, informal*) the sum of two pence

IDM **not care/give** ˈ**tuppence for sb/sth** to think that sb/sth is not important or that they have no value

tup·penny /ˈtʌpəni/ *adj.* [only before noun] (*BrE, informal*) = TWOPENNY

Tup·per·ware™ /ˈtʌpəweə(r); *NAmE* ˈtʌpərwer/ *noun* [U] plastic containers used mainly for storing food

tur·ban /ˈtɜːbən; *NAmE* ˈtɜːrbən/ *noun* **1** a long piece of cloth wound tightly around the head, worn, for example, by Muslim or Sikh men **2** a woman's hat that looks like a turban ▸ **tur·baned** /ˈtɜːbənd; *NAmE* ˈtɜːrb-/ *adj.*: *turbaned Sikhs*

tur·bid /ˈtɜːbɪd; *NAmE* ˈtɜːrbɪd/ *adj.* (*formal*) (of liquid) full of mud, dirt, etc. so that you cannot see through it **SYN** **muddy** ▸ **tur·bid·ity** /tɜːˈbɪdəti; *NAmE* tɜːrˈb-/ *noun* [U]

tur·bine /ˈtɜːbaɪn; *NAmE* ˈtɜːrb-/ *noun* a machine or an engine that receives its power from a wheel that is turned by the pressure of water, air or gas ➲ see also WIND TURBINE

turbo·char·ger /ˈtɜːbəʊtʃɑːdʒə(r); *NAmE* ˈtɜːrboʊtʃɑːrdʒər/ (also **turbo** *pl.* -os) *noun* a system driven by a turbine that gets its power from an engine's EXHAUST gases. It sends the mixture of petrol/gas and air into the engine at high pressure, making it more powerful. ▸ **turbo·charge** *verb*: **~ sth** *turbocharged engines*

turbo·jet /ˈtɜːbəʊdʒet; *NAmE* ˈtɜːrboʊ-/ *noun* **1** a TURBINE engine that produces forward movement by forcing out a stream of hot air and gas behind it **2** a plane that gets its power from this type of engine

turbo·prop /ˈtɜːbəʊprɒp; *NAmE* ˈtɜːrboʊprɑːp/ *noun* **1** a TURBINE engine that produces forward movement by turning a PROPELLER (= a set of spinning blades) **2** a plane that gets its power from this type of engine

tur·bot /ˈtɜːbət; *NAmE* ˈtɜːrbət/ *noun* [C, U] (*pl.* **tur·bot** or **tur·bots**) a large flat European sea fish that is used for food

tur·bu·lence /ˈtɜːbjələns; *NAmE* ˈtɜːrb-/ *noun* [U] **1** a situation in which there is a lot of sudden change, confusion, disagreement and sometimes violence **SYN** **upheaval** **2** a series of sudden and violent changes in the direction that air or water is moving in: *We experienced severe turbulence during the flight.* ➲ COLLOCATIONS at TRAVEL

tur·bu·lent /ˈtɜːbjələnt; *NAmE* ˈtɜːrb-/ *adj.* [usually before noun] **1** in which there is a lot of sudden change, confusion, disagreement and sometimes violence: *a short and turbulent career in politics* ◇ *a turbulent part of the world* **2** (of air or water) changing direction suddenly and violently: *The aircraft is designed to withstand turbulent conditions.* ◇ *a* ***turbulent sea/storm*** (= caused by turbulent water/air) **3** (of people) noisy and/or difficult to control **SYN** **unruly**: *a turbulent crowd*

turd /tɜːd; *NAmE* tɜːrd/ *noun* (*taboo, slang*) **1** a lump of solid waste from the BOWELS: *dog turds* **2** an offensive word for an unpleasant person

tur·een /tjuˈriːn; təˈriːn/ *noun* a large deep dish with a lid, used for serving vegetables or soup

turf /tɜːf; *NAmE* tɜːrf/ *noun, verb*

▪ ***noun*** (*pl.* **turfs** or **turves** /tɜːvz; *NAmE* tɜːrvz/) **1** [U, C] short grass and the surface layer of soil that is held together by its roots; a piece of this that has been cut from the ground and is used especially for making LAWNS (= the area of grass in a garden/yard): *newly laid turf* ◇ (*especially BrE*) *the hallowed turf of Wimbledon, etc.* (= the grass used for playing a sport on) **2** [U, C] PEAT that is cut to be used as fuel; a piece of this **3 the turf** [sing.] the sport of horse racing **4** [U] **sb's ~** (*informal, especially NAmE*) the place where sb lives and/or works, especially when they think of it as their own: *He feels more confident on* ***home turf.***

▪ ***verb*** **~ sth** to cover an area of ground with turf

PHR V ˌ**turf sb** ˈ**out (of sth)** | ˌ**turf sb** ˈ**off (sth)** (*BrE, informal*) to make sb leave a place, an organization, etc. **SYN** **throw out**: *He was turfed out of the party.* ◇ *The boys were turfed off the bus.*

ˈ**turf accountant** *noun* (*BrE, formal*) = BOOKMAKER

ˈ**turf war** *noun* a violent disagreement between two groups of people about who should control a particular area, activity or business: *a vicious turf war between rival gangs of drug dealers*

tur·gid /ˈtɜːdʒɪd; *NAmE* ˈtɜːrdʒɪd/ *adj.* (*formal*) **1** (of language, writing, etc.) boring, complicated and difficult to understand **2** swollen; containing more water than usual: *the turgid waters of the Thames*

tur·ista /tuˈrɪstə/ *noun* [U] (*NAmE, informal*) DIARRHOEA that is suffered by sb who is visiting a foreign country

T

tur·key /ˈtɜːki; *NAmE* ˈtɜːrki/ *noun* (*pl.* -eys) **1** [C] a large bird that is often kept for its meat, eaten especially at Christmas in Britain and at Thanksgiving in the US ➲ VISUAL VOCAB page V10 **2** [U] meat from a turkey: *roast turkey* **3** [C] (*NAmE, informal*) a failure: *His latest movie is a real turkey.* **4** [C] (*NAmE, informal*) a stupid or useless person ➲ see also COLD TURKEY IDM see TALK *v.*

ˈ**turkey shoot** *noun* (*informal, especially NAmE*) a battle or contest in which one side is much stronger than the other and able to win very easily

Turk·ish /ˈtɜːkɪʃ; *NAmE* ˈtɜːrkɪʃ/ *adj., noun*
▪ *adj.* from or connected with Turkey
▪ *noun* [U] the language of Turkey

ˌ**Turkish ˈbath** *noun* a type of bath in which you sit in a room full of hot steam, have a MASSAGE and then a cold shower or bath; a building where this treatment takes place

ˌ**Turkish ˈcoffee** *noun* [U, C] very strong, usually very sweet, black coffee

ˌ**Turkish deˈlight** *noun* [U, C] a sweet/candy made from a substance like jelly that is flavoured with fruit and covered with fine white sugar

tur·meric /ˈtɜːmərɪk; *NAmE* ˈtɜːrm-/ *noun* [U] a yellow powder made from the root of an Asian plant, used in cooking as a spice, especially in CURRY ➲ VISUAL VOCAB page V28

tur·moil /ˈtɜːmɔɪl; *NAmE* ˈtɜːrm-/ *noun* [U, sing.] a state of great anxiety and confusion SYN **confusion**: ***emotional/mental/political turmoil*** ◇ *His statement* ***threw*** *the court* ***into turmoil****.* ◇ *Her mind was* ***in*** *(****a****)* ***turmoil****.*

turn 0-w /tɜːn; *NAmE* tɜːrn/ *verb, noun*
▪ *verb*
▸ MOVE ROUND **1** 0-w [I, T] to move or make sth move around a central point: *The wheels of the car began to turn.* ◇ *I can't get the screw to turn.* ◇ **~ sth** (**+ adv./prep.**) *He turned the key in the lock.* ◇ *She turned the wheel sharply to the left.*
▸ CHANGE POSITION/DIRECTION **2** 0-w [I, T] to move your body or part of your body so as to face or start moving in a different direction: *We turned and headed for home.* ◇ *She turned to look at me.* ◇ **+ adv./prep.** *He turned back to his work.* ◇ *I turned away and looked out of the window.* ◇ **~ sth** (**+ adv./prep.**) *He turned his back to the wall.* ◇ *She turned her head away.* ➲ see also TURN OVER **3** 0-w [T] **~ sth + adv./prep.** to move sth so that it is in a different position or facing a different direction: *She turned the chair on its side to repair it.* ◇ *Turn the sweater inside out before you wash it.* ➲ see also TURN OVER **4** 0-w [I, T] to change the direction you are moving or travelling in; to make sth change the direction it is moving in: **~ (into sth)** *He turned into a narrow street.* ◇ **~ sth** *The man* ***turned the corner*** *and disappeared.* ◇ **~ sth into sth** *I turned the car into the car park.* **5** 0-w [I] (**+ adv./prep.**) (of a road or river) to curve in a particular direction: *The road turns to the left after the church.*
▸ AIM/POINT **6** [T, I] to aim or point sth in a particular direction: **~ sth (on/to sb/sth/yourself)** *Police turned water cannon on the rioters.* ◇ *He turned the gun on himself.* ◇ *She looked at him then turned her attention back to me.* ◇ **~ to sb/sth/yourself** *His thoughts turned to his dead wife.*
▸ OF TIDE IN SEA **7** [I] to start to come in or go out: *The tide is turning—we'd better get back.*
▸ LET SB/STH GO **8** [T] to make or let sb/sth go into a particular place or state: **~ sth + adv./prep.** *They turned the horse into the field.* ◇ **~ sth + adj.** *to turn the dogs loose*
▸ FOLD **9** [T] **~ sth + adv./prep.** to fold sth in a particular way: *She turned down the blankets and climbed into bed.* ◇ *He turned up the collar of his coat and hurried out into the rain.*
▸ CARTWHEEL/SOMERSAULT **10** [T, no passive] **~ sth** to perform a movement by moving your body in a circle: *to turn cartwheels/somersaults*
▸ PAGE **11** 0-w [T, I] if you **turn** a page of a book or magazine, you move it so that you can read the next page: **~ sth** *He sat turning the pages idly.* ◇ **~ to sth** *Turn to p.23.*
▸ GAME **12** [I, T] **~ (sth) (around)** if a game **turns** or sb **turns** it, it changes the way it is developing so that a different person or team starts to win
▸ BECOME **13** 0-w *linking verb* to change into a particular state or condition; to make sth do this: **+ adj.** *The leaves were turning brown.* ◇ *The weather has turned cold.* ◇ *He turned nasty when we refused to give him the money.* ◇ *He decided to* ***turn professional****.* ◇ **~ sth + adj.** *The heat turned the milk sour.* ◇ **+ noun** *She turned a deathly shade of white when she heard the news.* ◇ *He's a lawyer turned politician* (= he used to be a lawyer but is now a politician). ➲ SYNONYMS at BECOME
▸ AGE/TIME **14** *linking verb* (not used in the progressive tenses) **+ noun** to reach or pass a particular age or time: *She turns 21 in June.* ◇ *It's turned midnight.*
▸ STOMACH **15** [I, T] **~ (your stomach)** when your stomach **turns** or sth **turns** your stomach, you feel as though you will VOMIT
▸ WOOD **16** [T] **~ sth** to shape sth on a LATHE: *to turn a chair leg* ◇ *turned boxes and bowls*

IDM Most idioms containing **turn** are at the entries for the nouns and adjectives in the idioms, for example **not turn a hair** is at **hair**. **as it/things turned ˈout** as was shown or proved by later events: *I didn't need my umbrella, as it turned out* (= because it didn't rain). **be well, badly, etc. turned ˈout** to be well, badly, etc. dressed **turn round/around and do sth** (*informal*) used to report what sb says or does, when this is surprising or annoying: *How could she turn round and say that, after all I've done for her?*

PHR V ˌ**turn aˈgainst sb** | ˌ**turn sb aˈgainst sb** to stop or make sb stop being friendly towards sb: *She turned against her old friend.* ◇ *After the divorce he tried to turn the children against their mother.*

ˌ**turn aˈround/ˈround** | ˌ**turn sb/sth aˈround/ˈround** 0-w to change position or direction so as to face the other way; to make sb/sth do this: *Turn around and let me look at your back.* ◇ *I turned my chair round to face the fire.* ˌ**turn aˈround/ˈround** | ˌ**turn sth↔aˈround/ˈround** if a business, economy, etc. **turns around** or sb **turns it around**, it starts being successful after it has been unsuccessful for a time ➲ related noun TURNAROUND

ˌ**turn sb↔aˈway (from sth)** to refuse to allow sb to enter a place: *Hundreds of people were turned away from the stadium* (= because it was full). ◇ *They had nowhere to stay so I couldn't turn them away.*

ˌ**turn ˈback** | ˌ**turn sb/sth↔ˈback** 0-w to return the way you have come; to make sb/sth do this: *The weather became so bad that they had to turn back.* ◇ (*figurative*) *We said we would do it—there can be no turning back.* ◇ *Our car was turned back at the border.* ➲ SYNONYMS at RETURN

ˌ**turn sb/sth↔ˈdown** 0-w to reject or refuse to consider an offer, a proposal, etc. or the person who makes it: *Why did she turn down your invitation?* ◇ *He has been turned down for ten jobs so far.* ◇ *He asked her to marry him but she turned him down.* ˌ**turn sth↔ˈdown** 0-w to reduce the noise, heat, etc. produced by a piece of equipment by moving its controls: *Please turn the volume down.* ◇ **+ adj.** *He turned the lights down low.*

ˌ**turn ˈin 1** to face or curve towards the centre: *Her feet turn in.* **2** (*old-fashioned*) to go to bed ˌ**turn sb↔ˈin** (*informal*) to take sb to the police or sb in authority because they have committed a crime: *She threatened to turn him in to the police.* ◇ *He decided to turn himself in.* ˌ**turn sth↔ˈin 1** to give back sth that you no longer need: *You must turn in your pass when you leave the building.* **2** (*especially NAmE*) to give sth to sb in authority: *They turned in a petition with 80 000 signatures.* ◇ *I haven't even turned in Monday's work yet.* **3** to achieve a score, performance, profit, etc: *The champion turned in a superb performance to retain her title.* ˌ**turn ˈin on yourself** to become too concerned with your own problems and stop communicating with others

ˌ**turn (from sth) ˈinto sth** 0-w to become sth: *Our dream holiday turned into a nightmare.* ◇ *In one year she turned from a problem child into a model student.* ˌ**turn sb/sth (from sth) ˈinto sth** 0-w to make sb/sth become sth: *Ten years of prison had turned him into an old man.* ◇ *The prince was turned into a frog by the witch.*

ˌ**turn ˈoff** | ˌ**turn ˈoff sth** [no passive] to leave a road in order to travel on another: *Is this where we turn off?* ◇ *The* *jet began to turn off the main runway.* **ˌturn ˈoff** (*informal*) to stop listening to or thinking about sb/sth: *I couldn't understand the lecture so I just turned off.* **ˌturn sb↔ˈoff 1** to make sb feel bored or not interested: *People had been turned off by both candidates in the election.* **2** to stop sb feeling sexually attracted; to make sb have a feeling of disgust ➲ related noun TURN-OFF **ˌturn sth↔ˈoff** 🔑 to stop the flow of electricity, gas, water, etc. by moving a switch, button, etc: *to turn off the light* ◇ *Please turn the television off before you go to bed.*

ˈturn on sb to attack sb suddenly and unexpectedly: *The dogs suddenly turned on each other.* ◇ *Why are you all turning on me* (= criticizing or blaming me)? **ˈturn on sth** [no passive] **1** (*BrE*) to depend on sth: *Much turns on the outcome of the current peace talks.* **2** [no passive] to have sth as it main topic: *The discussion turned on the need to raise standards.* **ˌturn sb↔ˈon** (*informal*) to make sb excited or interested, especially sexually: *Jazz has never really turned me on.* ◇ *She gets turned on by men in uniform.* ➲ related noun TURN-ON **ˌturn sb ˈon (to sth)** (*informal*) to make sb become interested in sth or to use sth for the first time: *He turned her on to jazz.* **ˌturn sth↔ˈon** 🔑 to start the flow of electricity, gas, water, etc. by moving a switch, button, etc: *to turn on the heating* ◇ *I'll turn the television on.* ◇ (*figurative*) *He really knows how to* ***turn on the charm*** (= suddenly become pleasant and attractive).

ˌturn ˈout 1 to be present at an event: *A vast crowd turned out to watch the procession.* ➲ related noun TURNOUT **2** (used with an adverb or adjective, or in questions with *how*) to happen in a particular way; to develop or end in a particular way: *Despite our worries everything turned out well.* ◇ *You never know how your children will turn out.* ◇ **+ adj.** *If the day turns out wet, we may have to change our plans.* **3** to point away from the centre: *Her toes turn out.* **4** 🔑 to be discovered to be; to prove to be: **~ that…** *It turned out that she was a friend of my sister.* ◇ **~ to be/have sth** *The job turned out to be harder than we thought.* ◇ *The house they had offered us turned out to be a tiny apartment.* **ˌturn sb/sth↔ˈout** to produce sb/sth: *The factory turns out 900 cars a week.* **ˌturn sb ˈout (of/from sth)** to force sb to leave a place **ˌturn sth↔ˈout 1** to switch a light or a source of heat off: *Remember to turn out the lights when you go to bed.* **2** (*BrE*) to clean sth thoroughly by removing the contents and organizing them again: *to turn out the attic* **3** to empty sth, especially your pockets **4** to make sth point away from the centre: *She turned her toes out.*

ˌturn ˈover 1 🔑 to change position so that the other side is facing towards the outside or the top: *If you turn over you might find it easier to get to sleep.* ◇ *The car skidded and turned over.* ◇ (*figurative*) *The smell made my stomach turn over* (= made me feel sick). **2** (of an engine) to start or to continue to run **3** to change to another channel when you are watching television **ˌturn ˈover sth** to do business worth a particular amount of money in a particular period of time: *The company turns over £3.5 million a year.* ➲ related noun TURNOVER **ˌturn sth↔ˈover 1** 🔑 to make sth change position so that the other side is facing towards the outside or the top: *Brown the meat on one side, then turn it over and brown the other side.* **2** to think about sth carefully: *She kept turning over the events of the day in her mind.* **3** (of a shop/store) to sell goods and replace them: *A supermarket will turn over its stock very rapidly.* ➲ related noun TURNOVER **4** (*informal*) to steal from a place: *Burglars had turned the house over.* **5** to make an engine start running **ˌturn sb↔ˈover to sb** to deliver sb to the control or care of sb else, especially sb in authority: *Customs officials turned the man over to the police.* **ˌturn sth↔ˈover to sb** to give the control of sth to sb: *He turned the business over to his daughter.* **ˌturn sth↔ˈover to sth** to change the use or function of sth: *The factory was turned over to the manufacture of aircraft parts.*

ˈturn to sb/sth 🔑 to go to sb/sth for help, advice, etc: *She has nobody she can turn to.*

ˌturn ˈup 1 🔑 to be found, especially by chance, after being lost: *Don't worry about the letter—I'm sure it'll turn up.* **2** 🔑 (of a person) to arrive: *We arranged to meet at 7.30, but she never turned up.* **3** (of an opportunity) to happen, especially by chance: *He's still hoping something* (= for example, a job or a piece of luck) *will turn up.* ➲ related noun TURN-UP **ˌturn sth↔ˈup 1** 🔑 to increase the sound, heat, etc. of a piece of equipment: *Could you turn the TV up?* ◇ **+ adj.** *The music was turned up loud.* **2** (*BrE*) to make a piece of clothing shorter by folding and sewing it up at the bottom OPP **let down** ➲ related noun TURN-UP **3** to find sth: *Our efforts to trace him turned up nothing.*

■ ***noun*** [C]

▸ MOVEMENT **1** 🔑 an act of turning sb/sth around: *Give the handle a few turns.*

▸ OF ROAD/VEHICLE **2** 🔑 a change in direction in a vehicle: ***Make a left/right turn*** *into West Street.* ➲ see also THREE-POINT TURN, U-TURN **3** (*especially NAmE*) (*BrE* also **turn·ing**) a place where a road leads away from the one you are travelling on **4** a bend or corner in a road: *a lane full of* ***twists and turns***

▸ TIME **5** 🔑 the time when sb in a group of people should or is allowed to do sth: *When it's your turn, take another card.* ◇ *Please* ***wait your turn.*** ◇ ***Whose turn is it*** *to cook?* ◇ *Steve* ***took a turn*** *driving while I slept.*

▸ CHANGE **6** an unusual or unexpected change in what is happening: *a surprising* ***turn of events*** ◇ *His health has* ***taken a turn for the*** *worse* (= suddenly got worse). ◇ *Events took a dramatic turn in the weeks that followed.* ◇ *The book is,* ***by turns,*** *funny and very sad.* ➲ see also ABOUT-TURN

▸ PERFORMANCE **7** a short performance or piece of entertainment such as a song, etc: *Everyone got up on stage to do a turn.* ➲ see also STAR TURN

▸ WALK **8** (*old-fashioned*) a short walk: *We took a turn around the park.*

▸ ILLNESS **9** (*old-fashioned*) a feeling of illness: *a funny turn* (= a feeling that you may faint)

IDM **at every ˈturn** everywhere or every time you try and do sth: *At every turn I met with disappointment.* **(do sb) a good ˈturn** (to do) sth that helps sb: *Well, that's my good turn for the day.* **done to a ˈturn** (*BrE*) cooked for exactly the right amount of time **give sb a ˈturn** (*old-fashioned*) to frighten or shock sb **in ˈturn 1** 🔑 one after the other in a particular order: *The children called out their names in turn.* **2** as a result of sth in a series of events: *Increased production will, in turn, lead to increased profits.* **ˌone good ˌturn deserves aˈnother** (*saying*) you should help sb who has helped you **on the ˈturn** (*especially BrE*) going to change soon: *His luck is on the turn.* **speak/talk ˌout of ˈturn** to say sth that you should not because it is the wrong situation or because it offends sb **take ˈturns (in sth/to do sth)** 🔑 (*BrE* also **take it in ˈturns**) if people **take turns** or **take it in turns** to do sth, they do it one after the other to make sure it is done fairly: *The male and female birds take turns in sitting on the eggs.* ◇ *We take it in turns to do the housework.* **the ˌturn of the ˈcentury/ˈyear** the time when a new century/year starts: *It was built at the turn of the century.* **a ˌturn of ˈmind** a particular way of thinking about things **a ˌturn of ˈphrase** a particular way of describing sth **a ˌturn of the ˈscrew** an extra amount of pressure, CRUELTY, etc. added to a situation that is already difficult to bear or understand **a ˌturn of ˈspeed** a sudden increase in your speed or rate of progress; the ability to suddenly increase your speed: *He put on an impressive turn of speed in the last lap.* ➲ more at HAND *n.*, SERVE *v.*

turn·about /ˈtɜːnəbaʊt; *NAmE* ˈtɜːrn-/ *noun* [sing.] **~ (in sth)** a sudden and complete change in sb/sth SYN **reversal**

turn·around /ˈtɜːnəraʊnd; *NAmE* ˈtɜːrn-/ (*BrE* also **turn·round**) *noun* [usually sing.] **1** the amount of time it takes to unload a ship or plane at the end of one journey and load it again for the next one **2** the amount of time it takes to do a piece of work that you have been given and return it **3** a situation in which sth changes from bad to good: *a turnaround in the economy* **4** a complete change in sb's opinion, behaviour, etc.

turn·coat /ˈtɜːnkəʊt; *NAmE* ˈtɜːrnkoʊt/ *noun* (*disapproving*) a person who leaves one political party, religious group, etc. to join one that has very different views

turn·ing /ˈtɜːnɪŋ; *NAmE* ˈtɜːrnɪŋ/ (*BrE*) (also **turn** *NAmE*, *BrE*) *noun* a place where a road leads away from the one

T

you are travelling on: *Take the first turning on the right.* ◇ *I think we must have taken a wrong turning somewhere.*

'turning circle *noun* the smallest circle that a vehicle can turn around in

'turning point *noun* **~ (in sth)** the time when an important change takes place, usually with the result that a situation improves: *The promotion* ***marked a turning point in*** *her career.*

tur·nip /'tɜːnɪp; *NAmE* 'tɜːrnɪp/ *noun* [C, U] **1** a round white, or white and purple, root vegetable ➲ VISUAL VOCAB page V27 **2** (*ScotE*) = SWEDE ➲ VISUAL VOCAB page V27

turn·key /'tɜːnkiː; *NAmE* 'tɜːrn-/ *adj.* (especially of computer systems) complete and ready to use immediately

'turn-off *noun* **1** a place where a road leads away from another larger or more important road: *We missed the turn-off for the airport.* **2** [usually sing.] (*informal*) a person or thing that people do not find interesting, attractive or sexually exciting: *The city's crime rate is a serious turn-off to potential investors.* ◇ *I find beards a real turn-off.*

'turn-on *noun* [usually sing.] (*informal*) a person or thing that people find sexually exciting

turn·out /'tɜːnaʊt; *NAmE* 'tɜːrn-/ *noun* [C, usually sing., U] **1** the number of people who attend a particular event: *This year's festival attracted a record turnout.* **2** the number of people who vote in a particular election: *a* ***high/low/poor turnout*** ◇ *a 60% turnout of voters*

turn·over /'tɜːnəʊvə(r); *NAmE* 'tɜːrnoʊ-/ *noun* **1** [C, usually sing., U] **~ (of sth)** the total amount of goods or services sold by a company during a particular period of time: *an annual turnover of $75 million* ◇ *a fall in turnover* ➲ COLLOCATIONS at BUSINESS **2** [sing.] **~ (of sb)** the rate at which employees leave a company and are replaced by other people: *a high turnover of staff* **3** [sing.] **~ (of sth)** the rate at which goods are sold in a shop/store and replaced by others: *a fast turnover of stock* **4** [C] a small PIE in the shape of a triangle or half a circle, filled with fruit or jam

turn·pike /'tɜːnpaɪk; *NAmE* 'tɜːrn-/ (also **pike**) (both *NAmE*) *noun* a wide road, where traffic can travel fast for long distances and that drivers must pay a TOLL to use

turn·round /'tɜːnraʊnd; *NAmE* 'tɜːrn-/ *noun* (*BrE*) = TURNAROUND

'turn signal (*NAmE*) (*BrE* **in·di·ca·tor**) (also *informal* **blink·er** *NAmE, BrE*) *noun* a light on a vehicle that flashes to show that the vehicle is going to turn left or right ➲ VISUAL VOCAB page V42

turn·stile /'tɜːnstaɪl; *NAmE* 'tɜːrn-/ *noun* a gate at the entrance to a public building, STADIUM, etc. that turns in a circle when pushed, allowing one person to go through at a time ➲ picture at STILE

turn·table /'tɜːnteɪbl; *NAmE* 'tɜːrn-/ *noun* **1** the round surface on a RECORD PLAYER that you place the record on to be played **2** a large round surface that is able to move in a circle and onto which a railway/railroad engine is driven in order to turn it to go in the opposite direction

'turn-up *noun* (*BrE*) **1** (*NAmE* **cuff**) [C] the bottom of the leg of a pair of trousers/pants that has been folded over on the outside **2** [sing.] (*informal*) something surprising or unexpected that happens: *He actually offered to help? That's* ***a turn-up for the books!***

tur·pen·tine /'tɜːpəntaɪn; *NAmE* 'tɜːrp-/ (also *informal* **turps** /tɜːps; *NAmE* tɜːrps/) *noun* [U] a clear liquid with a strong smell, used especially for making paint thinner and for cleaning paint from brushes and clothes

tur·pi·tude /'tɜːpɪtjuːd; *NAmE* 'tɜːrpətuːd/ *noun* [U] (*formal*) very immoral behaviour SYN **wickedness**

tur·quoise /'tɜːkwɔɪz; *NAmE* 'tɜːrk-/ *noun* **1** [C, U] a blue or greenish-blue SEMI-PRECIOUS STONE: *a turquoise brooch* **2** [U] a greenish-blue colour ▸ **tur·quoise** *adj.*: *a turquoise dress*

tur·ret /'tʌrət; *NAmE* 'tɜːrət/ *noun* **1** a small tower on top of a wall or building, especially a castle ➲ VISUAL VOCAB page V13 **2** a small metal tower on a ship, plane or TANK that can usually turn around and from which guns are fired

tur·ret·ed /'tʌrətɪd; *NAmE* 'tɜːr-/ *adj.* [usually before noun] having one or more turrets

tur·tle /'tɜːtl; *NAmE* 'tɜːrtl/ *noun* **1** (*NAmE* also ˌ**sea 'turtle**) a large REPTILE with a hard round shell, that lives in the sea ➲ VISUAL VOCAB page V11 **2** (*NAmE, informal*) any REPTILE with a large shell, for example a TORTOISE or TERRAPIN

IDM **turn 'turtle** (of a boat) to turn over completely while sailing

'turtle dove *noun* a wild DOVE (= a type of bird) with a pleasant soft call, thought to be a very loving bird

turtle·neck /'tɜːtlnek; *NAmE* 'tɜːrtl-/ *noun* **1** (also ˌ**turtleneck 'sweater**) a sweater with a high part fitting closely around the neck **2** (*NAmE*) (*BrE* ˌ**polo neck**) a high round COLLAR made when the neck of a piece of clothing is folded over; a piece of clothing with a polo neck ➲ VISUAL VOCAB page V51

turves *pl.* of TURF

tusk /tʌsk/ *noun* either of the long curved teeth that stick out of the mouth of ELEPHANTS and some other animals ➲ VISUAL VOCAB page V10 ➲ see also IVORY

tus·sle /'tʌsl/ *noun, verb*

■ ***noun*** **~ (for/over sth)** a short struggle, fight or argument especially in order to get sth: *He was injured during a tussle for the ball.*

■ ***verb*** [I] **~ (with sb/sth)** to fight or compete with sb/sth, especially in order to get sth: *The children were tussling with one another for the ball.*

tus·sock /'tʌsək/ *noun* a small area of grass that is longer and thicker than the grass around it ▸ **tus·socky** *adj.*: *tussocky grass*

tut /tʌt/ (also ˌ**tut-'tut**) *exclamation, noun* used as the written or spoken way of showing the sound that people make when they disapprove of sth: *Tut-tut, I expected better of you.* ◇ *tut-tuts of disapproval* ▸ **tut** (also ˌ**tut-'tut**) *verb* (-tt-) [I]: *He tut-tutted under his breath.*

tutee /tjuː'tiː; *NAmE* tuː-/ *noun* a person who is taught or given advice by a TUTOR

tu·tel·age /'tjuːtəlɪdʒ; *NAmE* 'tuː-/ *noun* [U] (*formal*) **1** the teaching and instruction that one person gives to another SYN **tuition** **2** the state of being protected or controlled by another person, organization or country: *parental tutelage*

tutor /'tjuːtə(r); *NAmE* 'tuː-/ *noun, verb*

■ ***noun*** **1** a private teacher, especially one who teaches an individual student or a very small group **2** (*especially BrE*) a teacher whose job is to pay special attention to the studies or health, etc. of a student or a group of students: *his history tutor* ◇ *He was my* ***personal tutor*** *at university.* ◇ *She's in my* ***tutor group*** *at school.* **3** (*BrE*) a teacher, especially one who teaches adults or who has a special role in a school or college: *a part-time adult education tutor* **4** (*NAmE*) an assistant LECTURER in a college **5** a book of instruction in a particular subject, especially music: *a violin tutor*

■ ***verb*** **1** [T] **~ sb (in sth)** to be a tutor to an individual student or a small group; to teach sb, especially privately: *He tutors students in mathematics.* **2** [I] to work as a tutor: *Her work was divided between tutoring and research.*

tu·tor·ial /tjuː'tɔːriəl; *NAmE* tuː-/ *noun, adj.*

■ ***noun*** **1** a period of teaching in a university that involves discussion between an individual student or a small group of students and a tutor **2** a short book or computer program that gives information on a particular subject or explains how sth is done: *An online tutorial is provided.*

■ ***adj.*** connected with the work of a tutor: *tutorial staff* ◇ (*BrE*) *a tutorial college* (= a private school that prepares students for exams)

tutti-frutti /ˌtuːti 'fruːti/ *noun* [U] a type of ice cream that contains pieces of fruit of various kinds

tutu /'tuːtuː/ *noun* a BALLET dancer's skirt made of many layers of material. Tutus may be either short and stiff, sticking out from the waist, or long and bell-shaped.

tu-whit, tu-whoo /təˌwɪt tə'wuː/ *noun* used to represent the sound that an OWL makes

tux·edo /tʌk'si:dəʊ; *NAmE* -doʊ/ *noun* (*pl.* -os) (also *informal* **tux** /tʌks/) (*especially NAmE*) **1** (*BrE* also ˈ**dinner suit**) a black or white jacket and trousers/pants, worn with a BOW TIE at formal occasions in the evening **2** (*BrE* also ˈ**dinner jacket**) a black or white jacket worn with a BOW TIE at formal occasions in the evening ORIGIN From Tuxedo Park in New York, where it was first worn.

TV /ˌti: 'vi:/ *noun* [C, U] television: *What's* **on TV** *tonight?* ◇ *We're buying a new TV with the money.* ◇ *Almost all homes have at least one* **TV set**. ◇ *All rooms have a bathroom and colour TV.* ◇ *a* **TV series/ show/programme** ◇ **satellite/cable/digital TV** ◇ *She's a highly paid TV presenter.* ➲ COLLOCATIONS at TELEVISION ➲ VISUAL VOCAB page V18 ➲ see also PAY TV

ˌ**TV** ˈ**dinner** *noun* a meal that you can buy already cooked and prepared, that you only have to heat up before you can eat it

TVP™ /ˌti: ˌvi: 'pi:/ *abbr.* TEXTURED VEGETABLE PROTEIN

TW *abbr.* (*pl.* TW) TERAWATT(S)

twad·dle /'twɒdl; *NAmE* 'twɑ:dl/ *noun* [U] (*old-fashioned, informal*) something that has been said or written that you think is stupid and not true SYN **nonsense**

twain /tweɪn/ *number* (*old use*) two

IDM **never the ˌtwain shall ˈmeet** (*saying*) used to say that two things are so different that they cannot exist together

twang /twæŋ/ *noun, verb*

■ ***noun*** [usually sing.] **1** used to describe a way of speaking, usually one that is typical of a particular area and especially one in which the sounds are produced through the nose as well as the mouth **2** a sound that is made when a tight string, especially on a musical instrument, is pulled and released

■ ***verb*** [I, T] to make a sound like a tight wire or string being pulled and released; to make sth do this: *The bed springs twanged.* ◇ **~ sth** *Someone was twanging a guitar in the next room.*

'twas /twɒz; *NAmE* twʌz/ *abbr.* (*literary*) it was

twat /twæt; twɒt; *NAmE* twɑ:t/ *noun* (*taboo, slang, especially BrE*) **1** an offensive word for an unpleasant or stupid person **2** an offensive word for the outer female sex organs

tweak /twi:k/ *verb, noun*

■ ***verb*** **1 ~ sth** to pull or twist sth suddenly: *She tweaked his ear playfully.* **2 ~ sth** to make slight changes to a machine, system, etc. to improve it: *I think you'll have to tweak these figures a little before you show them to the boss.*

■ ***noun*** **1** a sharp pull or twist: *She gave his ear a tweak.* **2** a slight change that you make to a machine, system, etc. to improve it

twee /twi:/ *adj.* (*BrE, informal, disapproving*) very pretty, in a way that you find unpleasant and silly; appearing SENTIMENTAL: *The room was decorated with twee little pictures of animals.*

tweed /twi:d/ *noun* **1** [U] a type of thick rough cloth made of wool that has small spots of different coloured thread in it: *a tweed jacket* **2 tweeds** [pl.] clothes made of tweed

Tweedle·dum and Tweedle·dee /ˌtwi:dl'dʌm ən twi:dl'di:/ *noun* [pl.] two people or things that are not different from each other ORIGIN From two characters in *Through the Looking Glass* by Lewis Carroll who look the same and say the same things.

tweedy /'twi:di/ *adj.* **1** made of or looking like tweed: *a tweedy jacket* **2** (*BrE, informal*, often *disapproving*) used to describe the sort of person who often wears tweeds and therefore shows that they belong to the social class of rich people who live in the country

tween /twi:n/ (also **tween·er** *especially BrE* **tween·ager** /'twi:neɪdʒə(r)/) *noun* a child between the ages of about 10 and 12 SYN **pre-teen**

tween·er /twi:nə(r)/ *noun* **1** = TWEEN **2** a person or thing that is between two categories, classes or age groups: *The film is a tweener, neither indie nor mainstream.*

tweet /twi:t/ *noun, verb*

■ ***noun*** **1** the short high sound made by a small bird **2** (also **twitter**) a message sent using the Twitter SOCIAL NETWORKING service

■ ***verb*** = TWITTER

tweet·er /'twi:tə(r)/ *noun* a LOUDSPEAKER for reproducing the high notes in a SOUND SYSTEM ➲ compare WOOFER

tweez·ers /'twi:zəz; *NAmE* -ərz/ *noun* [pl.] a small tool with two long thin parts joined together at one end, used for picking up very small things or for pulling out hairs: *a pair of tweezers* ➲ VISUAL VOCAB page V21

ˌ**Twelfth** ˈ**Night** *noun* [U] **1** January 6th, the day of the Christian festival of EPIPHANY **2** the evening of January 5th, the day before EPIPHANY, which traditionally marks the end of Christmas celebrations

twelve /twelv/ *number* 12 ▸ **twelfth** /twelfθ/ *ordinal number, noun* HELP There are examples of how to use ordinal numbers at the entry for **fifth**.

twelve·month /'twelvmʌnθ/ *noun* [sing.] (*old use*) a year

ˈ**twelve-note** (also **do·deca·phon·ic**, ˈ**twelve-tone**) *adj.* [only before noun] (*music*) used to describe a system of music which uses the twelve notes in the scale equally rather than using a particular KEY

twenty /'twenti/

1 *number* 20 **2** *noun* **the twenties** [pl.] numbers, years or temperatures from 20 to 29 ▸ **twen·ti·eth** /'twentiəθ/ *ordinal number, noun* HELP There are examples of how to use ordinal numbers at the entry for **fifth**.

IDM **in your** ˈ**twenties** between the ages of 20 and 29

ˌ**twenty-ˈfirst** *noun* [sing.] (*informal, especially BrE*) a person's 21st birthday and the celebrations for this occasion

ˌ**twenty-ˌfour** ˈ**seven** (also **24/7**) *adv.* (*informal*) twenty-four hours a day, seven days a week (used to mean 'all the time'): *He's on duty twenty-four seven.*

ˌ**twenty** ˈ**pence** (also ˌ**twenty pence** ˈ**piece**, **20p** /ˌtwenti 'pi:/) *noun* a British coin worth 20 pence: *You need two 20ps for the machine.*

ˌ**twenty-ˌtwenty** ˈ**vision** (also **20/20 vision**) *noun* [U] the ability to see perfectly

'twere /twɜ:(r)/ *abbr.* (*old use*) it were

twerp /twɜ:p; *NAmE* twɜ:rp/ *noun* (*old-fashioned, informal*) a stupid or annoying person

twice /twaɪs/ *adv.*

1 two times; on two occasions: *I don't know him well; I've only met him twice.* ◇ *They go there* **twice a week/ month/year**. ◇ *a* **twice-monthly/yearly** *newsletter* **2** double in quantity, rate, etc: *an area twice the size of Wales* ◇ *Cats sleep twice as much as people.* ◇ *At 56 he's twice her age.*

IDM **twice** ˈ**over** not just once but twice: *There was enough of the drug in her stomach to kill her twice over.* ➲ more at LIGHTNING *n.*, ONCE *adv.*, THINK *v.*

twid·dle /'twɪdl/ *verb, noun*

■ ***verb*** [I, T] (*BrE*) to twist or turn sth with your fingers often because you are nervous or bored: **~ with sth** *He twiddled with the radio knob until he found the right programme.* ◇ **~ sth** *She was twiddling the ring on her finger.*

IDM **twiddle your thumbs 1** to move your thumbs around each other with your fingers joined together **2** to do nothing while you are waiting for sth to happen

■ ***noun*** **1** (*BrE*) a twist or turn: *a twiddle of the knob* **2** a decorative twist in a pattern, piece of music, etc: *twiddles on the clarinet*

twid·dly /'twɪdli/ *adj.* (*BrE, informal*) detailed or complicated SYN **fiddly**

twig /twɪg/ *noun, verb*

■ ***noun*** a small very thin branch that grows out of a larger branch on a bush or tree ➲ VISUAL VOCAB page V8

■ ***verb*** (-gg-) [I, T] **~ (sth)** | **~ what...** | **~ (that)...** (*BrE, informal*) to suddenly understand or realize sth: *Haven't you twigged yet?* ◇ *I finally twigged what he meant.*

twi·light /'twaɪlaɪt/ *noun, adj.*

■ ***noun*** [U] **1** the faint light or the period of time at the end of the day after the sun has gone down: *It was hard to see him clearly* **in the twilight**. ◇ *We went for a walk along the beach* **at twilight**. **2 the ~ (of sth)** the final stage of sth when it

T

becomes weaker or less important than it was: *the twilight years* (= the last years of your life)
■ ***adj.*** [only before noun] **1** (*formal*) used to describe a state in which things are strange and mysterious, or where things are kept secret and do not seem to be part of the real world: *the **twilight world of** the occult* ◇ *They lived in the **twilight zone** on the fringes of society.* **2** used to describe a situation or area of thought that is not clearly defined

twi·lit /ˈtwaɪlɪt/ *adj.* (*literary*) lit by twilight

twill /twɪl/ *noun* [U] a type of strong cloth that is made in a particular way to produce a surface of raised DIAGONAL lines: *a cotton twill skirt*

'twill /twɪl/ *abbr.* (*old use*) it will

twin 🔑 /twɪn/ *noun, verb, adj.*
■ ***noun*** **1** 🔑 one of two children born at the same time to the same mother: *She's expecting twins.* ➲ **COLLOCATIONS** at CHILD ➲ see also CONJOINED TWIN, FRATERNAL TWIN, IDENTICAL TWIN, SIAMESE TWIN **2** one of two similar things that make a pair
■ ***verb*** (-nn-) **1** [usually passive] **~ sth** (**with sth**) to make a close relationship between two towns or areas: *Oxford is twinned with Bonn in Germany.* **2 ~ sth** (**with sth**) to join two people or things closely together: *The opera twins the themes of love and death.*
■ ***adj.*** [only before noun] **1** 🔑 used to describe one of a pair of children who are twins: ***twin boys/girls*** ◇ *a **twin brother/sister*** **2** used to describe two things that are used as a pair: *a ship with twin propellers* **3** used to describe two things that are connected, or present or happening at the same time: *The prison service has the twin goals of punishment and rehabilitation.*

ˌtwin ˈbed *noun* **1** [usually pl.] one of a pair of single beds in a room: *Would you prefer twin beds or a double?* **2** (*NAmE*) (*BrE* **ˌsingle ˈbed**) a bed big enough for one person: *sheets to fit a twin bed* ➲ **VISUAL VOCAB** page V20

ˌtwin-ˈbedded *adj.* (of a room) having two single beds in it

ˌtwin ˈbedroom *noun* a room in a hotel, etc. that has two single beds

twine /twaɪn/ *noun, verb*
■ ***noun*** [U] strong string that has two or more STRANDS (= single thin pieces of thread or string) twisted together
■ ***verb*** [I, T] **~ (sth) around/round/through/in sth** to wind or twist around sth; to make sth do this: *ivy twining around a tree trunk* ◇ *She twined her arms around my neck.*

ˌtwin-ˈengined *adj.* (of an aircraft) having two engines

twinge /twɪndʒ/ *noun* **1** a sudden short feeling of pain: *He **felt a twinge** in his knee.* **2 ~** (**of sth**) a sudden short feeling of an unpleasant emotion: *a twinge of disappointment*

T

twin·kle /ˈtwɪŋkl/ *verb, noun*
■ ***verb*** **1** [I] to shine with a light that keeps changing from bright to faint to bright again: *Stars twinkled in the sky.* ◇ *twinkling lights in the distance* ➲ **SYNONYMS** at SHINE **2** [I] **~ (with sth)** | **~ (at sb)** if your eyes **twinkle**, you have a bright expression because you are happy or excited: *twinkling blue eyes* ◇ *Her eyes twinkled with merriment.*
■ ***noun*** [sing.] **1** an expression in your eyes that shows you are happy or amused about sth: *He looked at me with a **twinkle in his eye.*** **2** a small light that keeps changing from bright to faint to bright again: *the twinkle of stars* ◇ *the twinkle of the harbour lights in the distance*

twink·ling /ˈtwɪŋklɪŋ/ *noun* [sing.] (*old-fashioned, informal*) a very short time
IDM **in the ˌtwinkling of an ˈeye** very quickly **SYN** **in an instant**

twin·set /ˈtwɪnset/ *noun* (*BrE*) a woman's matching sweater and CARDIGAN that are designed to be worn together

ˌtwin ˈtown *noun* one of two towns in different countries that have a special relationship with each other: *a visit to Lyon, Birmingham's twin town in France*

twirl /twɜːl; *NAmE* twɜːrl/ *verb, noun*
■ ***verb*** **1** [I, T] **~ (sb) (around/round)** to move or dance round and round; to make sb do this: *She twirled around in front of the mirror.* ◇ *He held her hand and twirled her around.* **2** [T] **~ sth** (**around/about**) to make sth turn quickly and lightly round and round **SYN** **spin**: *He twirled his hat in his hand.* ◇ *She sat twirling the stem of the glass in her fingers.* **3** [T] **~ sth** to twist or curl sth with your fingers: *He kept twirling his moustache.*
■ ***noun*** the action of a person spinning around once: *Kate **did a twirl** in her new dress.*

twist 🔑 /twɪst/ *verb, noun*
■ ***verb***
▸ BEND INTO SHAPE **1** 🔑 [T] **~ sth** (**into sth**) to bend or turn sth into a particular shape: *Twist the wire to form a circle.* **2** 🔑 [T, I] to bend or turn sth into a shape or position that is not normal or natural; to be bent or turned in this way: **~ sth (+ adv./prep.)** *He grabbed me and twisted my arm behind my back.* ◇ **(+ adv./prep.)** *Her face twisted in anger.*
▸ TURN BODY **3** [T, I] to turn part of your body around while the rest stays still: **~ sth (+ adv./prep.)** *He twisted his head around to look at her.* ◇ **(+ adv./prep.)** *She twisted in her chair when I called her name.* **4** 🔑 [I, T] to turn your body with quick sharp movements and change direction often: *I **twisted and turned** to avoid being caught.* ◇ **+ adv./prep.** *She tried unsuccessfully to twist free.* ◇ **~ sth/yourself + adv./prep.** *He managed to twist himself round in the restricted space.*
▸ TURN WITH HAND **5** 🔑 [T] **~ sth (+ adv./prep.)** to turn sth around in a circle with your hand: *Twist the knob to the left to open the door.* ◇ *Nervously I twisted the ring on my finger.*
▸ OF ROADS/RIVERS **6** 🔑 [I] to bend and change direction often: *The road **twists and turns** along the coast.* ◇ *narrow twisting streets* ◇ *a twisting staircase*
▸ ANKLE/WRIST/KNEE **7** 🔑 [T] **~ sth** to injure part of your body, especially your ankle, wrist or knee, bending it in an awkward way: *She fell and twisted her ankle.*
▸ WIND AROUND **8** 🔑 [T] **~ sth (+ adv./prep.)** to wind sth around or through an object: *She twisted a scarf around her head.* ◇ *The telephone cable has **got twisted*** (= wound around itself). **9** 🔑 [I] **~ (round/around sth)** to move or grow by winding around sth: *A snake was twisting around his arm.*
▸ FACTS **10** [T] **~ sth** to deliberately change the meaning of what sb has said, or to present facts in a particular way, in order to benefit yourself or harm sb else **SYN** **misrepresent**: *You always twist everything I say.* ◇ *The newspaper was accused of twisting the facts.*
▸ THREADS **11** [T] **~ sth (into sth)** to turn or wind threads, etc. together to make sth longer or thicker: *They had twisted the sheets into a rope and escaped by climbing down it.*
IDM **twist sb's ˈarm** (*informal*) to persuade or force sb to do sth ➲ more at KNIFE *n.*, LITTLE FINGER
PHR V **ˌtwist sth↔ˈoff** to turn and pull sth with your hand to remove it from sth: *I twisted off the lid and looked inside.* ◇ *a twist-off top*
■ ***noun***
▸ ACTION OF TURNING **1** 🔑 [C] the action of turning sth with your hand, or of turning a part of your body: *She gave the lid another twist and it came off.* ◇ *He gave a shy smile and a little twist of his head.*
▸ UNEXPECTED CHANGE **2** 🔑 [C] an unexpected change or development in a story or situation: *the twists and turns of his political career* ◇ *The story has taken another twist.* ◇ *The disappearance of a vital witness added a **new twist** to the case.* ◇ *By a curious **twist of fate** we met again only a week or so later.*
▸ IN ROAD/RIVER **3** 🔑 [C] a sharp bend in a road or river: *The car followed the **twists and turns** of the mountain road.*
▸ SHAPE **4** [C] a thing that has been twisted into a particular shape: *mineral water with a twist of lemon*
▸ DANCE **5 the twist** [sing.] a fast dance that was popular in the 1960s, in which you twist from side to side
IDM **round the bend/twist** (*informal, especially BrE*) crazy: *She's gone completely round the twist.* ➲ more at KNICKERS

twist·ed 🔑 /ˈtwɪstɪd/ *adj.*
1 🔑 bent or turned so that the original shape is lost: *After the crash the car was a mass of twisted metal.* ◇ *a twisted ankle* (= injured by being turned suddenly) ◇ *She gave a small twisted smile.* ➲ picture at CURVED **2** (of a person's

mind or behaviour) not normal; strange in an unpleasant way: *Her experiences had left her **bitter and twisted**.*

twist·er /'twɪstə(r)/ *noun* (*NAmE, informal*) a violent storm that is caused by a powerful spinning column of air SYN **tornado**

twisty /'twɪsti/ *adj.* (especially of a road) having many bends or turns SYN **winding, zigzag**

twit /twɪt/ *noun* (*informal, especially BrE*) a silly or annoying person

twitch /twɪtʃ/ *verb, noun*

■ ***verb* 1** [I, T] **~ (sth)** if a part of your body **twitches**, or if you **twitch** it, it makes a sudden quick movement, sometimes one that you cannot control: *Her lips twitched with amusement.* ◇ *The cats watched each other, their tails twitching.* **2** [T, I] **~ (sth)** to give sth a short sharp pull; to be pulled in this way: *He twitched the package out of my hands.* ◇ *The curtains twitched as she rang the bell.*

■ ***noun* 1** a sudden quick movement that you cannot control in one of your muscles: *She has a twitch in her left eye.* ◇ *a nervous twitch* **2** a sudden quick movement or feeling: *He greeted us with a mere twitch of his head.* ◇ *At that moment she felt the first twitch of anxiety.*

twitch·er /'twɪtʃə(r)/ *noun* (*BrE, informal*) a person who is very keen on finding and watching rare birds

twitchy /'twɪtʃi/ *adj.* (*informal*) **1** nervous or anxious about sth SYN **jittery 2** making sudden quick movements

Twit·ter™ /'twɪtə(r)/ *noun* [U] a SOCIAL NETWORKING service that allows you to send out short regular messages about what you are doing, that people can access on the Internet or on their mobile/cell phones ➲ compare MICROBLOGGING *n.*, TWEET *n.*

twit·ter /'twɪtə(r)/ *verb, noun*

■ ***verb* 1** (also **tweet**) [I] when birds **twitter**, they make a series of short high sounds **2** [I, T] **~ (on) (about sth)** | **+ speech** (*especially BrE*) to talk quickly in a high excited voice, especially about sth that is not very important **3** (also **tweet**) [I] to send a message using the Twitter SOCIAL NETWORKING service

■ ***noun*** [sing.] **1** (also **twit·tering**) a series of short high sounds that birds make **2** (*informal*) a state of nervous excitement **3** = TWEET

'twixt /twɪkst/ *prep.* (*old use*) between IDM see SLIP *n.*

two 🗝 /tu:/ *number*

2 HELP There are examples of how to use numbers at the entry for **five**.

IDM **a 'day, 'moment, 'pound, etc. or two** one or a few days, moments, pounds, etc: *May I borrow it for a day or two?* **fall between two 'stools** (*BrE*) to fail to be or to get either of two choices, both of which would have been acceptable **in 'two** in or into two pieces or halves: *He broke the bar of chocolate in two and gave me half.* **in ˌtwos and 'threes** two or three at a time; in small numbers: *People arrived in twos and threes.* **it takes two to do sth** (*saying*) one person cannot be completely responsible for sth: *You can't put all the blame on him. It takes two to make a marriage.* **not have two beans, brain cells, etc. to rub to'gether** (*informal*) to have no money; to be very stupid, etc. **put ˌtwo and ˌtwo to'gether** to guess the truth from what you see, hear, etc: *He's inclined to **put two and two together and make five*** (= reaches the wrong conclusion from what he sees, hears, etc.). **that makes 'two of us** (*informal*) I am in the same position or I agree with you: *'I'm tired!' 'That makes two of us!'* **two ˌsides of the same 'coin** used to talk about two ways of looking at the same situation ➲ more at MIND *n.*, SHAKE *n.*

'two-bit *adj.* [only before noun] (*informal, especially NAmE*) not good or important: *She wanted to be more than just a two-bit secretary.*

ˌtwo 'bits *noun* [pl.] (*old-fashioned, NAmE, informal*) 25 cents

ˌtwo-di'mension·al *adj.* flat; having no depth; appearing to have only two DIMENSIONS: *a two-dimensional drawing* ◇ (*figurative*) *The novel was criticized for its two-dimensional characters* (= that did not seem like real people).

ˌtwo-'edged *adj.* **1** (of a blade, knife, etc.) having two sharp edges for cutting **2** having two possible meanings or results, one good and one bad: *a two-edged remark* ◇ *Fame can be **a two-edged sword**.*

ˌtwo-'faced *adj.* (*informal, disapproving*) not sincere; not acting in a way that supports what you say that you believe; saying different things to different people about a particular subject SYN **hypocritical**

ˌtwo 'fingers *noun* [pl.] (*BrE, informal*) a sign that you make by holding up your hand with the inside part facing towards you and making a V-shape with your first and second fingers (used as a way of being rude to other people): *I gave him the two fingers.* ➲ compare V-SIGN

two·fold /'tu:fəʊld; *NAmE* -foʊld/ *adj.* (*formal*) **1** consisting of two parts: *The problem was twofold.* **2** twice as much or as many: *a twofold increase in demand* ▶ **two·fold** *adv.*: *Her original investment has increased twofold.*

ˌtwo-'handed *adj.* using or needing both hands: *a two-handed backhand* (= in TENNIS) ◇ *a two-handed catch*

ˌtwo-'hander *noun* (*especially BrE*) a play that is written for only two actors

twonk /twɒŋk; *NAmE* twɑ:ŋk/ *noun* (*BrE, slang*) a stupid person

ˌtwo 'pence (also **ˌtwo pence 'piece, 2p** /ˌtu: 'pi:/) *noun* a British coin worth two pence

two·pence /'tʌpəns/ *noun* (*BrE*) = TUPPENCE

two·penny (also *informal* **tup·penny**) /'tʌpəni; *NAmE* also 'tu:peni/ *adj.* (*BrE*) costing or worth two old pence: *a twopenny stamp*

ˌtwo-'piece *noun* a set of clothes consisting of two matching pieces of clothing, for example a skirt and jacket or trousers/pants and a jacket ▶ **ˌtwo-'piece** *adj.*: *a two-piece suit*

'two-ply *adj.* (of wool, wood or other material) with two threads or thicknesses

ˌtwo-'seater *noun* a vehicle, an aircraft or a piece of furniture with seats for two people ➲ VISUAL VOCAB page V18

two·some /'tu:səm/ *noun* a group of two people who do sth together SYN **pair**

'two-star *adj.* [usually before noun] **1** having two stars in a system that measures quality. The highest standard is usually represented by four or five stars: *a two-star hotel* **2** (*NAmE*) having the fourth-highest military rank, and wearing uniform which has two stars on it

'two-step *noun* a dance with long, sliding steps; the music for this dance

'two-stroke *adj.* (of an engine or vehicle) with a PISTON that makes two movements, one up and one down, in each power CYCLE ➲ compare FOUR-STROKE

'two-time *verb* **~ sb** (*informal*) to not be faithful to a person you have a relationship with, especially a sexual one, by having a secret relationship with sb else at the same time: *Are you sure he's not two-timing you?* ▶ **'two-timer** *noun*

'two-tone *adj.* [only before noun] having two different colours or sounds

'twould /twʊd/ *abbr.* (*old use*) it would

ˌtwo-ˌup ˌtwo-'down *noun* (*BrE, informal*) a house with two rooms on the bottom floor and two bedrooms upstairs

ˌtwo-'way *adj.* [usually before noun] **1** moving in two different directions; allowing sth to move in two different directions: *two-way traffic* ◇ *two-way trade* ◇ *a two-way switch* (= that allows electric current to be turned on or off from either of two points) **2** (of communication between people) needing equal effort from both people or groups involved: *Friendship is a two-way process.* **3** (of radio equipment, etc.) used both for sending and receiving signals

ˌtwo-way 'mirror *noun* a piece of glass that is a mirror on one side, but that you can see through from the other

ty·coon /taɪ'ku:n/ *noun* a person who is successful in business or industry and has become rich and powerful: *a **business/property/media tycoon***

T

tyke (also **tike**) /taɪk/ *noun* (*informal*) **1** a small child, especially one who behaves badly **2** (*BrE*) a person from Yorkshire

tym·pa·num /ˈtɪmpənəm/ *noun* (*pl.* **tym·pa·nums** or **tym·pana** /ˈtɪmpənə/) (*anatomy*) the EARDRUM

type 🗝 /taɪp/ *noun, verb*

▪ ***noun*** **1** 🗝 [C] **~ (of sth)** a class or group of people or things that share particular qualities or features and are part of a larger group; a kind or sort: *different racial types* ◇ *a rare blood type* ◇ *There are three main types of contract(s).* ◇ *Bungalows are a type of house.* ◇ *She mixes with all types of people.* ◇ *She mixes with people of all types.* ◇ *I love this type of book.* ◇ *I love these types of books.* ◇ (*informal*) *I love these type of books.* ◇ *What do you charge for this type of work?* ◇ *What do you charge for work of this type?* ◇ *It is the first car of its type to have this design feature.* **2** [sing.] (*informal*) a person of a particular character, with particular features, etc: *She's the artistic type.* ◇ *He's not the type to be unfaithful.* ◇ *She's* ***not my type*** (= not the kind of person I am usually attracted to). **3 -type** (in adjectives) having the qualities or features of the group, person or thing mentioned: *a police-type badge* ◇ *a continental-type cafe* **4** [U] letters that are printed or typed: *The type was too small for me to read.* ◇ *The important words are in bold type.*

▪ ***verb*** **1** 🗝 [I, T] to write sth using a computer or TYPEWRITER: *How fast can you type?* ◇ *typing errors* ◇ **~ sth (out/in/up)** *This letter will need to be typed (out) again.* ◇ *Type (in) the filename, then press 'Return'.* ◇ *Has that report been* ***typed up*** *yet?* **2** [T] **~ sb/sth** (*technical*) to find out the group or class that a person or thing belongs to: *Blood samples were taken from patients for typing.*

type·cast /ˈtaɪpkɑːst; *NAmE* -kæst/ *verb* (**type·cast, type·cast**) [usually passive] **~ sb (as sth)** if an actor is **typecast**, he or she is always given the same kind of character to play: *She didn't want to be typecast as a dumb blonde.*

type·face /ˈtaɪpfeɪs/ *noun* a set of letters, numbers, etc. of a particular design, used in printing: *I'd like the heading to be in a different typeface from the text.*

type·script /ˈtaɪpskrɪpt/ *noun* [C, U] a copy of a text or document that has been typed

type·set·ter /ˈtaɪpsetə(r)/ *noun* a person, machine or company that prepares a book, etc. for printing ▸ **type·set** *verb* (**type·set·ting, type·set, type·set**): **~ sth** *Pages can now be typeset on-screen.* **type·set·ting** *noun* [U]: *computerized typesetting*

type·writer /ˈtaɪpraɪtə(r)/ *noun* a machine that produces writing similar to print. It has keys that you press to make metal letters or signs hit a piece of paper through a strip of cloth covered with ink. ➲ see also TYPIST

type·writ·ing /ˈtaɪpraɪtɪŋ/ *noun* = TYPING

type·writ·ten /ˈtaɪprɪtn/ *adj.* written using a typewriter or computer

ty·phoid /ˈtaɪfɔɪd/ (also *less frequent* **ˌtyphoid ˈfever**) *noun* [U] a serious infectious disease that causes fever, red spots on the chest and severe pain in the BOWELS, and sometimes causes death: *a typhoid epidemic*

ty·phoon /taɪˈfuːn/ *noun* a violent tropical storm with very strong winds ➲ compare CYCLONE, HURRICANE

ty·phus /ˈtaɪfəs/ *noun* [U] a serious infectious disease that causes fever, headaches, purple marks on the body and often death

typ·ical 🗝 /ˈtɪpɪkl/ *adj.*

1 🗝 having the usual qualities or features of a particular type of person, thing or group **SYN representative**: *a typical Italian cafe* ◇ *This is a typical example of Roman pottery.* ◇ **~ of sb/sth** *This meal is typical of local cookery.* ◇ **~ for sb/sth** *The weather at the moment is not typical for July.* **OPP atypical** **2** 🗝 happening in the usual way; showing what sth is usually like **SYN normal**: *A typical working day for me begins at 7.30.* **OPP untypical** **3** 🗝 **~ (of sb/sth)** (often *disapproving*) behaving in the way that you expect: *It was typical of her to forget.* ◇ *He spoke with typical enthusiasm.* ◇ (*informal*) *She's late again—typical!*

typ·ic·al·ly 🗝 /ˈtɪpɪkli/ *adv.*

1 🗝 used to say that sth usually happens in the way that you are stating: *The factory typically produces 500 chairs a week.* ◇ *A typically priced meal will be around $10.* **2** 🗝 in a way that shows the usual qualities or features of a particular type of person, thing or group: *typically American hospitality* ◇ *Mothers typically worry about their children.* **3** 🗝 in the way that you expect sb/sth to behave: *Typically, she couldn't find her keys.* ◇ *He was typically modest about his achievements.*

typ·ify /ˈtɪpɪfaɪ/ *verb* (**typi·fies, typi·fy·ing, typi·fied, typi·fied**) (not usually used in the progressive tenses) **1 ~ sth** to be a typical example of sth: *clothes that typify the 1960s* ◇ *the new style of politician, typified by the Prime Minister* **2 ~ sth** to be a typical feature of sth: *the haunting guitar melodies that typify the band's music*

typ·ing /ˈtaɪpɪŋ/ (also *less frequent* **type·writ·ing**) *noun* [U] **1** the activity or job of using a TYPEWRITER or computer to write sth: *to do the typing* ◇ *typing errors* ◇ *a* ***typing pool*** (= a group of people who share a company's typing work) **2** writing that has been done on a TYPEWRITER or computer

typ·ist /ˈtaɪpɪst/ *noun* **1** a person who works in an office typing letters, etc. **2** a person who uses a TYPEWRITER or computer keyboard: *I'm quite a fast typist.*

typo /ˈtaɪpəʊ; *NAmE* -poʊ/ *noun* (*pl.* **-os**) (*informal*) a small mistake in a typed or printed text

typ·og·raph·er /taɪˈpɒɡrəfə(r); *NAmE* -ˈpɑːɡ-/ *noun* a person who is skilled in typography

typ·og·raphy /taɪˈpɒɡrəfi; *NAmE* -ˈpɑːɡ-/ *noun* [U] the art or work of preparing books, etc. for printing, especially of designing how text will appear when it is printed ▸ **typo·graph·ic·al** /ˌtaɪpəˈɡræfɪkl/ (also **typo·graph·ic** /ˌtaɪpəˈɡræfɪk/) *adj.*: *a typographical error* ◇ *typographic design* **typo·graph·ic·al·ly** /-kli/ *adv.*

typ·ology /taɪˈpɒlədʒi; *NAmE* -ˈpɑːl-/ *noun* (*pl.* **-ies**) (*technical*) a system of dividing things into different types

tyr·an·nical /tɪˈrænɪkl/ (also *formal* **tyr·an·nous** /ˈtɪrənəs/) *adj.* using power or authority over people in an unfair and cruel way **SYN autocratic, dictatorial**

tyr·an·nize (*BrE* also **-ise**) /ˈtɪrənaɪz/ *verb* [T, I] to use your power to treat sb in a cruel or unfair way: **~ sb/sth** *a father tyrannizing his children* ◇ **~ over sb/sth** *a political leader who tyrannizes over his people* ➲ see also TYRANT

tyr·an·no·saur /tɪˈrænəsɔː(r); taɪ-/ (also **tyr·an·no·saurus** /tɪˌrænəˈsɔːrəs/) *noun* a very large DINOSAUR that stood on two legs, had large powerful JAWS and two short front legs

tyr·anny /ˈtɪrəni/ *noun* [U, C] (*pl.* **-ies**) **1** unfair or cruel use of power or authority: *a victim of oppression and tyranny* ◇ *The children had no protection against the tyranny of their father.* ◇ *the tyrannies of Nazi rule* ◇ (*figurative*) *These days it seems we must all submit to the tyranny of the motor car.* **2** the rule of a tyrant; a country under this rule **SYN dictatorship**: *Any political system refusing to allow dissent becomes a tyranny.*

tyr·ant /ˈtaɪrənt/ *noun* a person who has complete power in a country and uses it in a cruel and unfair way **SYN dictator**: *The country was ruled by a succession of tyrants.* ◇ (*figurative*) *His boss is a complete tyrant.*

tyre 🗝 (*BrE*) (*NAmE* **tire**) /ˈtaɪə(r)/ *noun*

a thick rubber ring that fits around the edge of a wheel of a car, bicycle, etc: *a* ***front tyre*** ◇ *a* ***back/rear tyre*** ◇ *to pump up a tyre* ◇ *a* ***flat/burst/punctured tyre*** ◇ ***bald/worn tyres*** ➲ COLLOCATIONS at DRIVING ➲ VISUAL VOCAB pages V41, V42 ➲ see also SPARE TYRE

tyro /ˈtaɪrəʊ; *NAmE* -roʊ/ *noun* (*pl.* **-os**) a person who has little or no experience of sth or is beginning to learn sth **SYN novice**

tzar, tzar·ina, tzar·ism, tzar·ist = TSAR, TSARINA, TSARISM, TSARIST

T

Uu

U /juː/ *noun, abbr.*
■ ***noun*** (also **u**) [C, U] (*pl.* **Us**, **U's**, **u's** /juːz/) the 21st letter of the English alphabet: *'Under' begins with (a) U/'U'.* ➲ see also U-BOAT, U-TURN
■ ***abbr.*** (*BrE*) universal (the label of a film/movie that is suitable for anyone including children): *Aladdin, certificate U*

ˈU-bend *noun* a section of pipe shaped like a U, especially one that carries away used water

uber- (also **über-**) /ˈuːbə(r)/ *combining form* (from *German, informal*) (in nouns and adjectives) of the greatest or best kind; to a very large degree: *His girlfriend was a real uber-babe, with long blonde hair and a big smile.* ◇ *This stylish new restaurant is futuristic and uber-cool.*

ubi·qui·tous /juːˈbɪkwɪtəs/ *adj.* [usually before noun] (*formal* or *humorous*) seeming to be everywhere or in several places at the same time; very common: *the ubiquitous bicycles of university towns* ◇ *the ubiquitous movie star, Tom Hanks* ▸ **ubi·qui·tous·ly** *adv.* **ubi·quity** /juːˈbɪkwəti/ *noun* [U]: *the ubiquity of the mass media*

ˈU-boat *noun* a German SUBMARINE (= a ship that can travel underwater)

ubuntu /ʊˈbʊntʊ/ *noun* [U] (*SAfrE*) the idea that people are not only individuals but live in a community and must share things and care for each other

u.c. *abbr.* (in writing) UPPER CASE

UCAS /ˈjuːkæs/ *abbr.* (in Britain) Universities and Colleges Admissions Service (an official organization that deals with applications to study at universities and colleges)

UDA /ˌjuː diː ˈeɪ/ *abbr.* Ulster Defence Association (an illegal military organization in Northern Ireland that wants Northern Ireland to remain part of the UK)

udder /ˈʌdə(r)/ *noun* an organ shaped like a bag that produces milk and hangs underneath the body of a cow, GOAT, etc.

UDR /ˌjuː diː ˈɑː(r)/ *abbr.* Ulster Defence Regiment (a branch of the British army in Northern Ireland, now forming part of the Royal Irish Regiment)

UEFA /juˈeɪfə/ *abbr.* Union of European Football Associations

U-ey /ˈjuːi/ *noun* (*informal, especially AustralE*) a turn of 180° that a vehicle makes so that it can move forwards in the opposite direction SYN **U-turn**

UFO (also **ufo**) /ˌjuː ef ˈəʊ; ˈjuːfəʊ; *NAmE* ˌjuː ef ˈoʊ; ˈjuːfoʊ/ *noun* (*pl.* **UFOs** or **ufos**) the abbreviation for 'Unidentified Flying Object' (a strange object that some people claim to have seen in the sky and believe is a SPACECRAFT from another planet) ➲ compare FLYING SAUCER

ufol·ogy /juːˈfɒlədʒi; *NAmE* -ˈfɑːl-/ *noun* [U] the study of UFOs

ugali /uːˈɡɑːli/ *noun* [U] (*EAfrE*) a type of food made with flour from CORN (MAIZE) or MILLET, usually eaten with meat or vegetable STEW

ugh (also **urgh**) *exclamation* the way of writing the sound (/ɜː/ /ʊx/) that people make when they think that sth is disgusting or unpleasant: *Ugh! How can you eat that stuff?*

Ugli™ /ˈʌɡli/ (also **ˈUgli fruit**) *noun* a large CITRUS fruit with a rough, yellowish-orange skin and sweet flesh with a lot of juice

ugly 🔑 /ˈʌɡli/ *adj.* (**ug·lier**, **ugli·est**)
1 🔑 unpleasant to look at SYN **unattractive**: *an ugly face* ◇ *an ugly building* **2** 🔑 (of an event, a situation, etc.) unpleasant or dangerous; involving threats or violence: *an ugly incident* ◇ *There were ugly scenes in the streets last night as rioting continued.* ▸ **ugli·ness** *noun* [U] IDM see REAR *v.*, SIN *n.*

ˌugly ˈduckling *noun* a person or thing that at first does not seem attractive or likely to succeed but that later becomes successful or much admired ORIGIN From the title of a story by Hans Christian Andersen, in which a young swan thinks it is an ugly young duck until it grows up into a beautiful adult swan.

uh *exclamation* the way of writing the sound /ʌ/ or /ɜː/ that people make when they are not sure about sth, when they do not hear or understand sth you have said, or when they want you to agree with what they have said: *Uh, yeah, I guess so.* ◇ *'Are you ready yet?' 'Uh? Oh. Yes.'* ◇ *We can discuss this another time, uh?*

UHF /ˌjuː eɪtʃ ˈef/ *abbr.* ultra-high frequency (a range of radio waves used for high-quality radio and television broadcasting)

ˈuh-huh *exclamation* the way of writing the sound that people make when they understand or agree with what you have said, when they want you to continue or when they are answering 'Yes': *'Did you read my note?' 'Uh-huh.'*

ˈuh-oh (also **ˈoh-oh**) *exclamation* the way of writing the sound that people make when they want to say that they have done sth wrong or that they think there will be trouble: *Uh-oh. I forgot to write that letter.* ◇ *Uh-oh! Turn the TV off. Here comes Dad!*

UHT /ˌjuː eɪtʃ ˈtiː/ *abbr.* (*BrE*) ultra heat treated. UHT milk has been heated to a very high temperature in order to make it last for a long time.

uh-uh *exclamation* the way of writing the sound /ˈʌ ʌ/ that people make when they are answering 'No' to a question

uja·maa /ˌʊdʒæˈmɑː/ *noun* [U] (in Tanzania) SOCIALISM

UK (also **U.K.** especially in *US*) /ˌjuː ˈkeɪ/ *abbr.* UNITED KINGDOM

uku·lele /ˌjuːkəˈleɪli/ *noun* a musical instrument with four strings, like a small GUITAR

ulcer /ˈʌlsə(r)/ *noun* a sore area on the outside of the body or on the surface of an organ inside the body which is painful and may BLEED or produce a poisonous substance: *a stomach ulcer* ➲ see also MOUTH ULCER

ul·cer·ate /ˈʌlsəreɪt/ *verb* [I, T, usually passive] **~ (sth)** (*medical*) to become, or make sth become, covered with ulcers ▸ **ul·cer·ation** /ˌʌlsəˈreɪʃn/ *noun* [U, C]

ulna /ˈʌlnə/ *noun* (*pl.* **ulnae** /-niː/) (*anatomy*) the longer bone of the two bones in the lower part of the arm between the elbow and the wrist, on the side opposite the thumb ➲ see also RADIUS (3) ➲ VISUAL VOCAB page V48

ul·ter·ior /ʌlˈtɪəriə(r); *NAmE* -ˈtɪr-/ *adj.* [only before noun] (of a reason for doing sth) that sb keeps hidden and does not admit: *She must have some* ***ulterior motive*** *for being nice to me—what does she really want?*

ul·tim·ate 🔑 AW /ˈʌltɪmət/ *adj., noun*
■ ***adj.*** [only before noun] **1** 🔑 happening at the end of a long process SYN **final**: *our* ***ultimate goal/aim/objective/target*** ◇ *We will accept ultimate responsibility for whatever happens.* ◇ *The ultimate decision lies with the parents.* **2** 🔑 most extreme; best, worst, greatest, most important, etc: *This race will be the ultimate test of your skill.* ◇ *Silk sheets are the ultimate luxury.* **3** from which sth originally comes SYN **basic, fundamental**: *the ultimate truths of philosophy and science*
■ ***noun*** [sing.] **the ~ in sth** (*informal*) the best, most advanced, greatest, etc. of its kind: *the ultimate in modern design*

ˈultimate fighting (also **ˈextreme fighting**) *noun* [U] a sport that combines different styles of fighting such as BOXING, WRESTLING and MARTIAL ARTS and in which there are not many rules

ul·tim·ate·ly 🔑 AW /ˈʌltɪmətli/ *adv.*
1 🔑 in the end; finally: *Ultimately, you'll have to make the decision yourself.* ◇ *A poor diet will ultimately lead to illness.* **2** at the most basic and important level: *All life depends ultimately on oxygen.*

ul·ti·matum /ˌʌltɪˈmeɪtəm/ *noun* (*pl.* **ul·ti·matums** or **ul·ti·ma·ta**) a final warning to a person or country that if they do not do what you ask, you will use force or take action against them: *to issue an ultimatum*

ultra /ˈʌltrə/ *noun* a person who holds extreme views, especially in politics

ultra- /ˈʌltrə/ *prefix* (in adjectives and nouns) extremely; beyond a particular limit: *ultra-modern* ◇ *ultraviolet* ➲ compare INFRA-

ˌultra-high ˈfrequency *noun* [U] = UHF

ultra·light /ˈʌltrəlaɪt/ (*NAmE*) (*BrE* **micro·light**) *noun* a very small light aircraft for one or two people ➲ VISUAL VOCAB page V43

ultra·mar·ine /ˌʌltrəməˈriːn/ *noun* [U] a bright blue colour

ultra·short /ˌʌltrəˈʃɔːt; *NAmE* -ˈʃɔːrt/ *adj.* (of radio waves) having a very short WAVELENGTH (shorter than 10 metres), with a FREQUENCY greater than 30 MEGAHERTZ ➲ compare LONG WAVE, MEDIUM WAVE, SHORT WAVE

ultra·son·ic /ˌʌltrəˈsɒnɪk; *NAmE* -ˈsɑːn-/ *adj.* [usually before noun] (of sounds) higher than humans can hear: *ultrasonic waves*

ultra·sound /ˈʌltrəsaʊnd/ *noun* **1** [U] sound that is higher than humans can hear **2** [U, C] a medical process that produces an image of what is inside your body: *Ultrasound showed she was expecting twins.*

ultra·vio·let /ˌʌltrəˈvaɪələt/ (*abbr.* UV) *adj.* [usually before noun] (*physics*) of or using ELECTROMAGNETIC waves that are just shorter than those of VIOLET light in the SPECTRUM and that cannot be seen: *ultraviolet rays* (= that cause the skin to go darker) ◇ *an ultraviolet lamp* ➲ compare INFRARED

ulu·late /ˈjuːljʊleɪt; ˈʌljʊleɪt; *NAmE* ˈʌljəl-/ *verb* [I] (*literary*) to give a long cry SYN **wail** ▸ **ulu·la·tion** /-leɪʃn/ *noun* [U, C]

um *exclamation* the way of writing the sound /ʌm/ or /əm/ that people make when they hesitate, or do not know what to say next: *Um, I'm not sure how to ask you this....*

umami /uːˈmɑːmi/ *noun* [U] a taste found in some foods that is neither sweet, sour, bitter nor salty: *Tomatoes have lots of umami.*

umber /ˈʌmbə(r)/ *noun* [U] a dark brown or yellowish-brown colour used in paints

um·bil·ical cord /ʌmˌbɪlɪkl ˈkɔːd; *NAmE* ˈkɔːrd/ *noun* a long piece of TISSUE that connects a baby to its mother before it is born and is cut at the moment of birth

um·bil·icus /ʌmˈbɪlɪkəs; ˌʌmbɪˈlaɪkəs/ *noun* (*pl.* **um·bil·ici** /ʌmˈbɪlɪsaɪ; ˌʌmbɪˈlaɪsaɪ; -kaɪ/ or **um·bil·icuses**) (*technical*) the NAVEL

umbra /ˈʌmbrə/ *noun* (*pl.* **um·bras** or **um·brae** /ˈʌmbriː/) (*technical*) **1** the darkest part of a shadow **2** the area on the earth or the moon which is the darkest during an ECLIPSE ➲ compare PENUMBRA

um·brage /ˈʌmbrɪdʒ/ *noun*

IDM **take ˈumbrage (at sth)** (*formal* or *humorous*) to feel offended, insulted or upset by sth, often without a good reason SYN **take offence**

U

um·brella 0-w /ʌmˈbrelə/ *noun*

1 0-w (also *BrE informal* **brolly**) an object with a round folding frame of long straight pieces of metal covered with material, that you use to protect yourself from the rain or from hot sun: *I put up my umbrella.* ◇ *colourful beach umbrellas* ➲ compare PARASOL, SUNSHADE **2** a thing that contains or includes many different parts or elements: *Many previously separate groups are now operating under the umbrella of a single authority.* ◇ *an* **umbrella organization/group/fund** ◇ *'Contact sports' is an* **umbrella term** *for a variety of different sports.* **3** a country or system that protects people

um·faan /ʊmˈfɑːn/ *noun* (*pl.* **um·faans** or **ba·fana** /bɑːˈfɑːnə/) (*SAfrE*) **1** a young black man who is not married **2** a young black boy

um·laut /ˈʊmlaʊt/ *noun* the mark placed over a vowel in some languages to show how it should be pronounced, as over the *u* in the German word *für* ➲ compare ACUTE ACCENT, CIRCUMFLEX, GRAVE², TILDE

UMPC /ˌjuː em piː ˈsiː/ *noun* (*computing*) a very small computer that is easy to carry, often with a touch screen and sometimes without a physical keyboard (the abbreviation for 'ultra-mobile personal computer')

um·pire /ˈʌmpaɪə(r)/ *noun, verb*

■ ***noun*** (also *NAmE informal* **ump**) (in sports such as TENNIS and BASEBALL) a person whose job is to watch a game and make sure that rules are not broken ➲ VISUAL VOCAB page V36 ➲ compare REFEREE

■ ***verb*** [I, T] to act as an umpire: *We need someone to umpire.* ◇ **~ sth** *to umpire a game of baseball*

ump·teen /ˌʌmpˈtiːn/ *det.* (*informal*) very many: *I've told this story umpteen times.* ▸ **ump·teen** *pron.*: *Umpteen of them all arrived at once.* **ump·teenth** /ˌʌmpˈtiːnθ/ *det.*: *'This is crazy,' she told herself* ***for the umpteenth time*** (= she had done it many times before).

UN (also **U.N.** especially in *US*) /ˌjuː ˈen/ *abbr.* United Nations (an association of many countries that aims to help economic and social conditions improve and to solve political problems in the world in a peaceful way): *the UN Security Council* ◇ *a UN peacekeeping plan*

un- /ʌn/ *prefix* **1** (in adjectives, adverbs and nouns) not; the opposite of: *unable* ◇ *unconsciously* ◇ *untruth* **2** (in verbs that describe the opposite of a process): *unlock* ◇ *undo*

'un /ən/ *pron.* (*BrE, informal*) a way of saying or writing 'one': *That was a good 'un.* ◇ *The little 'uns* (= the small children) *couldn't keep up.*

un·abashed /ˌʌnəˈbæʃt/ *adj.* not ashamed, embarrassed or affected by people's disapproval, when other people would be OPP **abashed** ▸ **un·abashed·ly** /-ʃɪdli/ *adv.*

un·abated /ˌʌnəˈbeɪtɪd/ *adj.* [not usually before noun] (*formal*) without becoming any less strong: *The rain* ***continued unabated.***

un·able 0-w /ʌnˈeɪbl/ *adj.* [not before noun]

~ to do sth (rather *formal*) not having the skill, strength, time, knowledge, etc. to do sth: *He lay there, unable to move.* ◇ *I tried to contact him but was unable to.* OPP **able**

un·abridged /ˌʌnəˈbrɪdʒd/ *adj.* (of a novel, play, speech, etc.) complete, without being made shorter in any way OPP **abridged**

un·ac·cent·ed /ʌnˈæksentɪd/ *adj.* **1** (of sb's speech) having no regional or foreign accent **2** (*phonetics*) (of a syllable) having no stress

un·accept·able 0-w /ˌʌnəkˈseptəbl/ *adj.*

that you cannot accept, allow or approve of: *Such behaviour is totally unacceptable in a civilized society.* ◇ *Noise from the factory has reached an unacceptable level.* OPP **acceptable** ▸ **un·accept·ably** /-bli/ *adv.*: *unacceptably high levels of unemployment*

un·accom·pan·ied AW /ˌʌnəˈkʌmpənid/ *adj.*

1 (*formal*) without a person going together with sb/sth: *No unaccompanied children allowed.* ◇ ***unaccompanied luggage/baggage*** (= travelling separately from its owner) **2** (*music*) performed without anyone else playing or singing at the same time: *a sonata for unaccompanied violin* **3** (*formal*) **~ by sth** not together with a particular thing: *Mere words, unaccompanied by any violence, cannot amount to an assault.*

un·account·able /ˌʌnəˈkaʊntəbl/ *adj.* (*formal*) **1** impossible to understand or explain SYN **inexplicable**: *For some unaccountable reason, the letter never arrived.* **2 ~ (to sb/sth)** not having to explain or give reasons for your actions to anyone: *Too many government departments are unaccountable to the general public.* OPP **accountable**

un·account·ably /ˌʌnəˈkaʊntəbli/ *adv.* (*formal*) in a way that is very difficult to explain; without any obvious reason SYN **inexplicably**: *He has been unaccountably delayed.*

un·account·ed for /ˌʌnəˈkaʊntɪd fɔː(r)/ *adj.* [not before noun] **1** a person or thing that is **unaccounted for** cannot be found and people do not know what has happened to them or it: *At least 300 civilians are unaccounted for after* *the bombing raids.* **2** not explained: *In the story he gave the police, half an hour was left unaccounted for.*

un·accus·tomed /ˌʌnəˈkʌstəmd/ *adj.* (*formal*) **1 ~ to sth/to doing sth** not in the habit of doing sth; not used to sth: *He was unaccustomed to hard work.* ◇ *I am unaccustomed to being told what to do.* **2** [usually before noun] not usual, normal or familiar: *The unaccustomed heat made him weary.* OPP **accustomed**

un·achiev·able /ˌʌnəˈtʃiːvəbl/ *adj.* that you cannot manage to reach or obtain: *unachievable goals* OPP **achievable**

un·acknow·ledged /ˌʌnəkˈnɒlɪdʒd; *NAmE* -ˈnɑːl-/ *adj.* **1** not receiving the thanks or praise that is deserved: *Her contribution to the research went largely unacknowledged.* **2** that people do not admit as existing or true; that people are not aware of: *unacknowledged feelings* **3** not publicly or officially recognized: *the unacknowledged leader of the group*

un·ac·quaint·ed /ˌʌnəˈkweɪntɪd/ *adj.* **~ (with sth/sb)** (*formal*) not familiar with sth/sb; having no experience of sth: *visitors unacquainted with local customs* OPP **acquainted**

un·adjust·ed /ˌʌnəˈdʒʌstɪd/ *adj.* (*statistics*) (of figures) not adjusted according to particular facts or circumstances: *Unadjusted figures which do not take tourism into account showed that unemployment fell in July.*

un·adorned /ˌʌnəˈdɔːnd; *NAmE* -ˈdɔːrnd/ *adj.* (*formal*) without any decoration SYN **simple**: *The walls were plain and unadorned.*

un·adul·ter·ated /ˌʌnəˈdʌltəreɪtɪd/ *adj.* **1** [usually before noun] you use **unadulterated** to emphasize that sth is complete or total SYN **undiluted**: *For me, the holiday was sheer unadulterated pleasure.* **2** not mixed with other substances; not ADULTERATED SYN **pure**: *unadulterated foods*

un·ad·ven·tur·ous /ˌʌnədˈventʃərəs/ *adj.* not willing to take risks or try new and exciting things SYN **cautious** OPP **adventurous**

un·affect·ed AW /ˌʌnəˈfektɪd/ *adj.* **1 ~ (by sth)** not changed or influenced by sth; not affected by sth: *People's rights are unaffected by the new law.* ◇ *Some members of the family may remain unaffected by the disease.* **2** (*approving*) (of a person or their behaviour) natural and sincere OPP **affected**

un·affili·ated /ˌʌnəˈfɪlieɪtɪd/ *adj.* **~ (with sth)** not belonging to or connected with a political party or a large organization SYN **independent** OPP **affiliated**

un·afford·able /ˌʌnəˈfɔːdəbl; *NAmE* -əˈfɔːrd-/ *adj.* costing so much that people do not have enough money to pay for it: *Health insurance is now unaffordable for many people.* OPP **affordable**

un·afraid /ˌʌnəˈfreɪd/ *adj.* [not before noun] (*formal*) not afraid or nervous; not worried about what might happen: **~ (of sth)** *She was unafraid of conflict.* ◇ **~ (to do sth)** *He's unafraid to speak his mind.*

un·aid·ed AW /ʌnˈeɪdɪd/ *adj.* (*formal*) without help from anyone or anything: *He can now walk unaided.*

un·ali·en·able /ʌnˈeɪliənəbl/ *adj.* = INALIENABLE

un·alloyed /ˌʌnəˈlɔɪd/ *adj.* (*formal*) not mixed with anything else, such as negative feelings SYN **pure**: *unalloyed joy*

un·alter·able AW /ʌnˈɔːltərəbl/ *adj.* (*formal*) that cannot be changed SYN **immutable**: *the unalterable laws of the universe*

un·altered AW /ʌnˈɔːltəd; *NAmE* -tərd/ *adj.* that has not changed or been changed: *This practice has* ***remained unaltered*** *for centuries.*

un·am·bigu·ous AW /ˌʌnæmˈbɪɡjuəs/ *adj.* clear in meaning; that can only be understood in one way: *an unambiguous statement* ◇ *The message was clear and unambiguous—'Get out!'* OPP **ambiguous** ▸ **un·am·bigu·ous·ly** AW *adv.*

un·am·bi·tious /ˌʌnæmˈbɪʃəs/ *adj.* **1** (of a person) not interested in becoming successful, rich, powerful, etc. **2** not involving a lot of effort, time, money, etc. or anything new: *an unambitious plan* OPP **ambitious**

ˌun-Aˈmerican *adj.* against American values or interests

unan·im·ity /ˌjuːnəˈnɪməti/ *noun* [U] complete agreement about sth among a group of people

unani·mous /juˈnænɪməs/ *adj.* **1** if a decision or an opinion is **unanimous**, it is agreed or shared by everyone in a group: *a unanimous vote* ◇ *unanimous support* ◇ *The decision was not unanimous.* **2 ~ (in sth)** if a group of people are **unanimous**, they all agree about sth: *Local people are unanimous in their opposition to the proposed new road.* ▸ **unani·mous·ly** *adv.*: *The motion was passed unanimously.*

un·announced /ˌʌnəˈnaʊnst/ *adj.* happening without anyone being told or warned in advance: *She just turned up unannounced on my doorstep.* ◇ *an unannounced increase in bus fares*

un·answer·able /ʌnˈɑːnsərəbl; *NAmE* ʌnˈæn-/ *adj.* **1** an **unanswerable** argument, etc. is one that nobody can question or disagree with SYN **irrefutable**: *They presented an unanswerable case for more investment.* **2** an **unanswerable** question is one that has no answer or that you cannot answer

un·answered /ʌnˈɑːnsəd; *NAmE* -sərd/ *adj.* **1** (of a question, problem, etc.) that has not been answered: *Many questions about the crime* ***remain unanswered.*** **2** (of a letter, telephone call, etc.) that has not been replied to: *unanswered letters*

un·antici·pated AW /ˌʌnænˈtɪsɪpeɪtɪd/ *adj.* (*formal*) that you have not expected or predicted; that you have not anticipated: *unanticipated costs*

un·apolo·get·ic /ˌʌnəˌpɒləˈdʒetɪk; *NAmE* -ˌpɑːl-/ *adj.* not saying that you are sorry about sth, even in situations in which other people might expect you to OPP **apologetic** ▸ **un·apolo·get·ic·al·ly** /-kli/ *adv.*

un·appeal·ing /ˌʌnəˈpiːlɪŋ/ *adj.* not attractive or pleasant: *The room was painted in an unappealing shade of brown.* ◇ *The prospect of studying for another five years was distinctly unappealing.* OPP **appealing**

un·appe·tiz·ing (*BrE* also **-is·ing**) /ʌnˈæpɪtaɪzɪŋ/ *adj.* (of food) unpleasant to eat; looking as if it will be unpleasant to eat OPP **appetizing**

un·appre·ci·ated AW /ˌʌnəˈpriːʃieɪtɪd/ *adj.* [not usually before noun] not having your work or your qualities recognized and enjoyed by other people; not appreciated: *He was in a job where he felt unappreciated and undervalued.*

un·approach·able AW /ˌʌnəˈprəʊtʃəbl; *NAmE* -ˈproʊ-/ *adj.* (of a person) unfriendly and not easy to talk to OPP **approachable**

un·argu·able /ʌnˈɑːɡjuəbl; *NAmE* -ˈɑːrɡ-/ *adj.* (*formal*) that nobody can disagree with: *unarguable proof* ➲ compare ARGUABLE ▸ **un·argu·ably** *adv.*: *She is unarguably one of the country's finest athletes.*

un·armed /ˌʌnˈɑːmd; *NAmE* ˌʌnˈɑːrmd/ *adj.* **1** not carrying a weapon: *unarmed civilians* **2** not involving the use of weapons: *The soldiers were trained in* ***unarmed combat.*** OPP **armed**

un·ashamed /ˌʌnəˈʃeɪmd/ *adj.* feeling no shame or embarrassment about sth, especially when people might expect you to ➲ compare ASHAMED ▸ **un·ashamed·ly** /ˌʌnəˈʃeɪmɪdli/ *adv.*: *She wept unashamedly.* ◇ *an unashamedly sentimental song*

un·asked /ˌʌnˈɑːskt; *NAmE* ˌʌnˈæskt/ *adj.* **1** an **unasked** question is one that you have not asked even though you would like to know the answer **2** without being invited or asked: *He came to the party unasked.* ◇ *She brought him, unasked, the relevant file.*

unˈasked-for *adj.* that has not been asked for or requested: *unasked-for advice*

un·assail·able /ˌʌnəˈseɪləbl/ *adj.* (*formal*) that cannot be destroyed, defeated or questioned: *The party now has*

U

an unassailable lead. ◇ Their ten-point lead puts the team in an almost unassailable position.

un·assigned AW /ˌʌnəˈsaɪnd/ *adj.* not given to or reserved for any particular person or purpose

un·assist·ed AW /ˌʌnəˈsɪstɪd/ *adj.* not helped by anyone or anything SYN **unaided**: *She could not move unassisted.*

un·assum·ing /ˌʌnəˈsjuːmɪŋ; *NAmE* ˌʌnəˈsuː-/ *adj.* (*approving*) not wanting to draw attention to yourself or to your abilities or status SYN **modest**

un·attached AW /ˌʌnəˈtætʃt/ *adj.* **1** not married or involved in a romantic relationship SYN **single**: *He was still unattached at the age of 34.* **2** not connected with or belonging to a particular group or organization ➲ compare ATTACHED

un·attain·able AW /ˌʌnəˈteɪnəbl/ *adj.* impossible to achieve or reach: *an unattainable goal* OPP **attainable**

un·attend·ed /ˌʌnəˈtendɪd/ *adj.* (*formal*) without the owner present; not being watched or cared for: *unattended vehicles* ◇ *Never leave young children unattended.*

un·attract·ive /ˌʌnəˈtræktɪv/ *adj.* **1** not attractive or pleasant to look at: *an unattractive brown colour* **2** not good, interesting or pleasant: *one of the unattractive aspects of the free market economy* OPP **attractive** ▸ **un·attract·ive·ly** *adv.*

un·author·ized (*BrE* also **-ised**) /ʌnˈɔːθəraɪzd/ *adj.* without official permission: *No access for unauthorized personnel.* OPP **authorized**

un·avail·able AW /ˌʌnəˈveɪləbl/ *adj.* [not usually before noun] **~ (to sb/sth)** **1** that cannot be obtained: *Such luxuries are unavailable to ordinary people.* **2** not able or not willing to see, meet or talk to sb: *The minister was* ***unavailable for comment.*** OPP **available** ▸ **un·avail·abil·ity** *noun* [U]

un·avail·ing /ˌʌnəˈveɪlɪŋ/ *adj.* (*formal*) without success SYN **unsuccessful**: *Their efforts were unavailing.*

un·avoid·able /ˌʌnəˈvɔɪdəbl/ *adj.* impossible to avoid or prevent: *unavoidable delays* OPP **avoidable** ▸ **un·avoid·ably** /-əbli/ *adv.*: *I was unavoidably delayed.*

un·aware AW /ˌʌnəˈweə(r); *NAmE* -ˈwer/ *adj.* [not before noun] not knowing or realizing that sth is happening or that sth exists: **~ of sth** *He was completely unaware of the whole affair.* ◇ **~ that…** *She was unaware that I could see her.* OPP **aware** ▸ **un·aware·ness** *noun* [U]

un·awares /ˌʌnəˈweəz; *NAmE* -ˈwerz/ *adv.* **1** when not expected: *The camera had* ***caught her unawares.*** ◇ *The announcement* ***took me unawares.*** ◇ *She came upon him unawares when he was searching her room.* **2** (*formal*) without noticing or realizing: *He slipped unawares into sleep.*

un·bal·ance /ˌʌnˈbæləns/ *verb* **1 ~ sth** to make sth no longer balanced, for example by giving too much importance to one part of it **2 ~ sb/sth** to make sb/sth unsteady so that they are likely to fall down **3 ~ sb** to make sb slightly crazy or mentally ill

un·bal·anced /ˌʌnˈbælənst/ *adj.* **1** [not usually before noun] (of a person) slightly crazy; mentally ill **2** [usually before noun] giving too much or too little importance to one part or aspect of sth: *an unbalanced article* ◇ *an unbalanced diet*

unban /ˌʌnˈbæn/ *verb* (-nn-) **~ sth** to allow sth that was banned before OPP **ban**

un·bear·able /ʌnˈbeərəbl; *NAmE* -ˈber-/ *adj.* too painful, annoying or unpleasant to deal with or accept SYN **intolerable**: *The heat was becoming unbearable.* ◇ *unbearable pain* ◇ *He's been unbearable since he won that prize.* OPP **bearable** ▸ **un·bear·ably** /-əbli/ *adv.*: *unbearably hot*

un·beat·able /ʌnˈbiːtəbl/ *adj.* **1** (of a team, player, etc.) impossible to defeat SYN **invincible** **2** (of prices, value, etc.) impossible to improve: *unbeatable offers*

un·beat·en /ʌnˈbiːtn/ *adj.* (*sport*) not having been defeated: *The team are unbeaten in their last four games.* ◇ *They will be putting their* ***unbeaten record*** *to the test next Saturday.*

un·be·com·ing /ˌʌnbɪˈkʌmɪŋ/ *adj.* (*formal*) **1** not suiting a particular person SYN **unflattering**: *She was wearing an unbecoming shade of purple.* **2 ~ (to/of sb)** not appropriate or acceptable SYN **inappropriate**: *He was accused of conduct unbecoming to an officer.* OPP **becoming**

un·be·fit·ting /ˌʌnbɪˈfɪtɪŋ/ *adj.* **~ (of/for/to sb/sth)** (*formal*) not suitable or good enough for sb/sth: *His behaviour is unbefitting of a university professor.* ◇ *The amount of litter in the streets is unbefitting for a historic city.*

un·be·known /ˌʌnbɪˈnəʊn; *NAmE* -ˈnoʊn/ (also *less frequent* **un·be·knownst** /ˌʌnbɪˈnəʊnst; *NAmE* -ˈnoʊnst/) *adj.* **~ to sb** (*formal*) without the person mentioned knowing: *Unbeknown to her they had organized a surprise party.*

un·belief /ˌʌnbɪˈliːf/ *noun* [U] (*formal*) lack of belief, or the state of not believing, especially in God, a religion, etc. ➲ compare BELIEF, DISBELIEF

un·believ·able /ˌʌnbɪˈliːvəbl/ *adj.* **1** (*informal*) used to emphasize how good, bad or extreme sth is SYN **incredible**: *We had an unbelievable* (= very good) *time in Paris.* ◇ *Conditions in the prison camp were unbelievable* (= very bad). ◇ *The cold was unbelievable* (= it was extremely cold). ◇ ***It's unbelievable that*** (= very shocking) *they have permitted this trial to go ahead.* **2** very difficult to believe and unlikely to be true SYN **incredible**: *I found the whole story bizarre, not to say unbelievable.* ▸ **un·believ·ably** *adv.*: *unbelievably bad/good* ◇ *Unbelievably it actually works.*

un·believer /ˌʌnbɪˈliːvə(r)/ *noun* (*formal*) a person who does not believe, especially in God, a religion, etc. OPP **believer**

un·believ·ing /ˌʌnbɪˈliːvɪŋ/ *adj.* (*formal*) feeling or showing that you do not believe sb/sth: *She stared at us with unbelieving eyes.* ◇ *He gazed at the letter, unbelieving.*

un·bend /ˌʌnˈbend/ *verb* (**un·bent**, **un·bent** /ˌʌnˈbent/) **1** [I] to relax and become less strict or formal in your behaviour or attitude **2** [T, I] **~ (sth)** to make sth that was bent become straight; to become straight

un·bend·ing /ˌʌnˈbendɪŋ/ *adj.* (often *disapproving*) unwilling to change your opinions, decisions, etc. SYN **inflexible**

un·biased AW (also **un·biassed**) /ʌnˈbaɪəst/ *adj.* fair and not influenced by your own or sb else's opinions, desires, etc. SYN **impartial**: *unbiased advice* ◇ *an unbiased judge* OPP **biased**

un·bid·den /ʌnˈbɪdn/ *adj.* (*literary*) (usually used after the verb) without being asked, invited or expected SYN **unasked**: *He walked into the room unbidden.*

un·bleached /ʌnˈbliːtʃt/ *adj.* not made whiter by the use of chemicals; not bleached: *unbleached flour*

un·blem·ished /ʌnˈblemɪʃt/ *adj.* (*formal*) not spoiled, damaged or marked in any way: *He had an unblemished reputation.* ◇ *her pale unblemished skin*

un·blink·ing /ʌnˈblɪŋkɪŋ/ *adj.* (*formal*) if sb has an **unblinking stare** or looks with **unblinking eyes**, they look very steadily at sth and do not BLINK ▸ **un·blink·ing·ly** *adv.*

un·block /ˌʌnˈblɒk; *NAmE* -ˈblɑːk/ *verb* **~ sth** to clean sth, for example a pipe, by removing sth that is blocking it

un·born /ˌʌnˈbɔːn; *NAmE* -ˈbɔːrn/ *adj.* [usually before noun] not yet born: *her unborn baby*

un·bound·ed /ʌnˈbaʊndɪd/ *adj.* (*formal*) having, or seeming to have, no limits SYN **boundless**, **infinite**: *her unbounded energy*

un·bowed /ˌʌnˈbaʊd/ *adj.* (*literary*) not defeated or not ready to accept defeat: *The losing team left the field* ***bloody but unbowed.***

un·break·able /ʌnˈbreɪkəbl/ *adj.* impossible to break SYN **indestructible**: *This new material is virtually unbreakable.* OPP **breakable**

un·bridge·able /ʌnˈbrɪdʒəbl/ *adj.* an **unbridgeable** gap or difference between two people or groups or their opinions is one that cannot be closed or made less wide

un·bridled /ʌnˈbraɪdld/ *adj.* [usually before noun] (*formal*) not controlled and therefore extreme: *unbridled passion*

un·broken /ʌnˈbrəʊkən; *NAmE* -ˈbroʊ-/ *adj.* **1** not interrupted or disturbed in any way: *a single unbroken line* ◇ *30 years of virtually unbroken peace* ◇ *my first night of unbroken sleep since the baby was born* **2** (of a record in a sport, etc.) that has not been improved on

un·buckle /ˌʌnˈbʌkl/ *verb* **~ sth** to undo the BUCKLE of a belt, shoe, etc.

un·bur·den /ˌʌnˈbɜːdn; *NAmE* -ˈbɜːrdn/ *verb* **1 ~ your·self/sth** (**of sth**) (**to sb**) (*formal*) to talk to sb about your problems or sth you have been worrying about, so that you feel less anxious: *She needed to unburden herself to somebody.* **2 ~ sb/sth** (**of sth**) to take sth that causes a lot of work or worry away from sb/sth **OPP** **burden**

un·but·ton /ˌʌnˈbʌtn/ *verb* **~ sth** to undo the buttons on a piece of clothing: *He unbuttoned his shirt.* **OPP** **button (up)**

un·but·toned /ˌʌnˈbʌtnd/ *adj.* informal and relaxed: *Staff respond well to her unbuttoned style of management.*

unˈcalled for *adj.* (of behaviour or remarks) not fair or appropriate **SYN** **unnecessary**: *His comments were uncalled for.* ◇ *uncalled-for comments*

un·canny /ʌnˈkæni/ *adj.* strange and difficult to explain **SYN** **weird**: *I had an uncanny feeling I was being watched.* ◇ *It was uncanny really, almost as if she knew what I was thinking.* ▸ **un·can·nily** /-ɪli/ *adv.*: *He looked uncannily like someone I knew.*

unˈcared for *adj.* not taken care of **SYN** **neglected**: *The garden looked uncared for.* ◇ *an uncared-for garden*

un·car·ing /ʌnˈkeərɪŋ; *NAmE* -ˈker-/ *adj.* (*disapproving*) not sympathetic about the problems or suffering of other people **SYN** **callous** **OPP** **caring**

un·ceas·ing /ʌnˈsiːsɪŋ/ *adj.* (*formal*) continuing all the time **SYN** **incessant**: *unceasing efforts* ◇ *Planes passed overhead with unceasing regularity.* ▸ **un·ceas·ing·ly** *adv.*: *Snow fell unceasingly.*

un·cen·sored /ʌnˈsensəd; *NAmE* -sərd/ *adj.* (of a report, film/movie, etc.) not CENSORED (= having had parts removed that are not considered suitable for the public): *an uncensored newspaper article*

un·cere·mo·ni·ous /ˌʌnˌserəˈməʊniəs; *NAmE* -ˈmoʊ-/ *adj.* (*formal*) done roughly and rudely: *He was bundled out of the room with unceremonious haste.* ➲ compare CEREMONIOUS

un·cere·mo·ni·ous·ly /ˌʌnˌserəˈməʊniəsli; *NAmE* -ˈmoʊ-/ *adv.* (*formal*) in a rough or rude way, without caring about a person's feelings: *They dumped his belongings unceremoniously on the floor.*

un·cer·tain 🔑 /ʌnˈsɜːtn; *NAmE* ʌnˈsɜːrtn/ *adj.* **1** 🔑 [not before noun] **~ (about/of sth)** feeling doubt about sth; not sure: *They're both uncertain about what to do.* ◇ *I'm still uncertain of my feelings for him.* **OPP** **certain** **2** 🔑 likely to change, especially in a negative or unpleasant way: *Our future looks uncertain.* ◇ *a man of uncertain temper* **3** 🔑 not definite or decided **SYN** **unclear**: *It is uncertain what his role in the company will be.* **4** not confident **SYN** **hesitant**: *The baby took its first uncertain steps.*
IDM **in ˌno unˌcertain ˈterms** clearly and strongly: *I told him what I thought of him in no uncertain terms.*

un·cer·tain·ly /ʌnˈsɜːtnli; *NAmE* -ˈsɜːrtn-/ *adv.* without confidence **SYN** **hesitantly**: *They smiled uncertainly at one another.*

un·cer·tainty /ʌnˈsɜːtnti; *NAmE* -ˈsɜːrtn-/ *noun* (*pl.* -ies) **1** [U] the state of being uncertain: *There is considerable uncertainty about the company's future.* ◇ *He had an air of uncertainty about him.* **2** [C] something that you cannot be sure about; a situation that causes you to be or feel uncertain: *life's uncertainties* ◇ *the uncertainties of war*

un·chal·lenge·able /ʌnˈtʃælɪndʒəbl/ *adj.* that cannot be questioned or argued with; that cannot be challenged: *unchallengeable evidence*

un·chal·lenged /ʌnˈtʃælɪndʒd/ *adj.* **1** not doubted; accepted without question; not challenged: *She could not allow such a claim to* **go unchallenged**. **2** (of a ruler or leader, or their position) not opposed by anyone: *He is in a position of unchallenged authority.* **3** without being stopped and asked to explain who you are, what you are doing, etc: *I walked into the building unchallenged.*

un·change·able /ʌnˈtʃeɪndʒəbl/ *adj.* that cannot be changed: *unchangeable laws* ➲ compare CHANGEABLE

un·changed /ʌnˈtʃeɪndʒd/ *adj.* [not usually before noun] that has stayed the same and not changed: *My opinion remains unchanged.*

un·chan·ging /ʌnˈtʃeɪndʒɪŋ/ *adj.* that always stays the same and does not change: *unchanging truths*

un·char·ac·ter·is·tic /ˌʌnˌkærəktəˈrɪstɪk/ *adj.* **~ (of sb)** not typical of sb; not the way sb usually behaves: *The remark was quite uncharacteristic of her.* **OPP** **characteristic** ▸ **un·char·ac·ter·is·tic·al·ly** /-kli/ *adv.*: *The children had been uncharacteristically quiet.*

un·char·it·able /ʌnˈtʃærɪtəbl/ *adj.* unkind and unfair in the way that you judge people: *uncharitable thoughts* **OPP** **charitable** ▸ **un·char·it·ably** /-əbli/ *adv.*

un·chart·ed **AW** /ˌʌnˈtʃɑːtɪd; *NAmE* -ˈtʃɑːrt-/ *adj.* [usually before noun] **1** that has not been visited or investigated before; not familiar: *They set off into the country's uncharted interior.* ◇ (*figurative*) *The party is sailing in* **uncharted waters** (= a situation it has not been in before). ◇ (*figurative*) *I was moving into* **uncharted territory** (= a completely new experience) *with this relationship.* **2** not marked on a map: *The ship hit an uncharted rock.*

un·checked /ˌʌnˈtʃekt/ *adj.* if sth harmful is **unchecked**, it is not controlled or stopped from getting worse: *The fire was allowed to burn unchecked.* ◇ *The rise in violent crime must not* **go unchecked**. ◇ *The plant will soon choke ponds and waterways if* **left unchecked**.

un·chris·tian /ˌʌnˈkrɪstʃən/ *adj.* not showing the qualities you expect of a Christian; not kind or thinking about other people's feelings **OPP** **christian**

un·civil /ˌʌnˈsɪvl/ *adj.* (*formal*) not polite **OPP** **civil** ➲ see also INCIVILITY

un·civ·il·ized (*BrE* also **-ised**) /ʌnˈsɪvəlaɪzd/ *adj.* (*disapproving*) **1** (of people or their behaviour) not behaving in a way that is acceptable according to social or moral standards **2** (of people or places) not having developed a modern culture and way of life: *I have worked in the wildest and most uncivilized parts of the world.* **OPP** **civilized**

un·claimed /ˌʌnˈkleɪmd/ *adj.* that nobody has claimed as belonging to them or being owed to them

un·clas·si·fied /ʌnˈklæsɪfaɪd/ *adj.* **1** (of documents, information, etc.) not officially secret; available to everyone **OPP** **classified** **2** (*technical*) that has not been CLASSIFIED as being the member of a particular group: (*BrE*) *A high proportion of candidates get low or unclassified grades* (= their work is not good enough to receive a grade). **3** (*BrE*) (of a road) not large or important enough to be given a number

uncle 🔑 /ˈʌŋkl/ *noun* **1** 🔑 the brother of your mother or father; the husband of your aunt: *Uncle Ian* ◇ *I'm going to visit my uncle.* ◇ *I've just become an uncle* (= because your brother/sister has had a baby). **2** used by children, with a first name, to address a man who is a close friend of their parents **IDM** see BOB

un·clean /ˌʌnˈkliːn/ *adj.* **1** (*formal*) dirty and therefore likely to cause disease: *unclean water* **OPP** **clean** **2** considered to be bad, immoral or not pure in a religious way, and therefore not to be touched, eaten, etc. **SYN** **impure**: *unclean thoughts* ◇ *unclean food*

un·clear /ˌʌnˈklɪə(r); *NAmE* -ˈklɪr/ *adj.* **1** not clear or definite; difficult to understand or be sure about: *His motives*

U

are unclear. ◇ *It is unclear whether there is any damage.* ◇ *Your diagrams are unclear.* **2 ~ (about sth)** | **~ (as to sth)** not fully understanding sth SYN **uncertain**: *I'm unclear about what you want me to do.*

ˌUncle ˈSam *noun* (*informal*) a way of referring to the United States of America or the US government (sometimes shown as a tall man with a white beard and a tall hat): *He owed $20 000 in tax to Uncle Sam.*

ˌUncle ˈTom *noun* (*taboo, offensive*) sometimes used in the past to refer to a black man who wants to please or serve white people ORIGIN From a character in the novel *Uncle Tom's Cabin* by Harriet Beecher Stowe.

un·clothed /ˌʌnˈkləʊðd; *NAmE* -ˈkloʊðd/ *adj.* (*formal*) not wearing any clothes SYN **naked** OPP **clothed**

un·clut·tered /ˌʌnˈklʌtəd; *NAmE* -tərd/ *adj.* (*approving*) not containing too many objects, details or unnecessary items SYN **tidy** OPP **cluttered**

un·coil /ˌʌnˈkɔɪl/ *verb* [I, T] to become or make sth straight after it has been wound or twisted round in a circle: *The snake slowly uncoiled.* ◇ **~ sth/itself** *to uncoil a rope*

un·col·oured (*especially US* **un·col·ored**) /ˌʌnˈkʌləd; *NAmE* -ərd/ *adj.* with no colour; with no colour added

un·combed /ʌnˈkəʊmd; *NAmE* -ˈkoʊmd/ *adj.* (of hair) that has not been brushed or COMBED; very untidy

un·com·fort·able 0‑w /ʌnˈkʌmftəbl; *BrE* also -fət-; *NAmE* also -fərt-/ *adj.*
1 0‑w (of clothes, furniture, etc.) not letting you feel physically comfortable; unpleasant to wear, sit on, etc: *uncomfortable shoes* ◇ *I couldn't sleep because the bed was so uncomfortable.* OPP **comfortable** **2** 0‑w not feeling physically relaxed, warm, etc: *I was sitting in an extremely uncomfortable position.* ◇ *She still finds it uncomfortable to stand without support.* OPP **comfortable** **3** 0‑w anxious, embarrassed or afraid and unable to relax; making you feel like this: *He looked distinctly uncomfortable when the subject was mentioned.* ◇ *There was an uncomfortable silence.* OPP **comfortable** **4** unpleasant or difficult to deal with: *an uncomfortable fact* ◇ *I had the uncomfortable feeling that it was my fault.*

un·com·fort·ably /ʌnˈkʌmftəbli; *BrE* also -fət-; *NAmE* also -fərt-/ *adv.* **1** in a way that makes you feel anxious or embarrassed; in a way that shows you are anxious or embarrassed: *I became uncomfortably aware that no one else was laughing.* ◇ *Her comment was uncomfortably close to the truth.* ◇ *He shifted uncomfortably in his seat when I mentioned money.* **2** in a way that is not physically comfortable: *I was feeling uncomfortably hot.* ◇ *She perched uncomfortably on the edge of the table.*

un·com·mit·ted /ˌʌnkəˈmɪtɪd/ *adj.* **~ (to sb/sth)** not having given or promised support to a particular person, group, belief, action, etc: *The party needs to canvass the uncommitted voters.* ➲ compare COMMITTED

U

un·com·mon /ʌnˈkɒmən; *NAmE* -ˈkɑːm-/ *adj.* **1** not existing in large numbers or in many places SYN **unusual, rare**: *an uncommon occurrence* ◇ *Side effects from the drug are uncommon.* ◇ *It is* **not uncommon** *for college students to live at home.* ◇ *Red squirrels are uncommon in England.* OPP **common** **2** (*formal* or *literary*) unusually large in degree or amount; great SYN **remarkable**: *She showed uncommon pleasure at his arrival.*

un·com·mon·ly /ʌnˈkɒmənli; *NAmE* -ˈkɑːm-/ *adv.* (*formal*) **1** to an unusual degree; extremely: *an uncommonly gifted child* **2** not often; not usually: *Not uncommonly, there is a great deal of rain in August.*

un·com·mu·ni·ca·tive AW /ˌʌnkəˈmjuːnɪkətɪv/ *adj.* (*disapproving*) (of a person) not willing to talk to other people or give opinions SYN **taciturn** OPP **communicative**

un·com·peti·tive /ˌʌnkəmˈpetətɪv/ *adj.* (*business*) not cheaper or better than others and therefore not able to compete equally: *an uncompetitive industry* ◇ *uncompetitive prices* OPP **competitive**

un·com·plain·ing /ˌʌnkəmˈpleɪnɪŋ/ *adj.* (*approving*) not saying that you are unhappy about a difficult or unpleasant situation; not saying that you are in pain ▸ **un·com·plain·ing·ly** *adv.*

un·com·pleted /ˌʌnkəmˈpliːtɪd/ *adj.* that has not been finished: *an uncompleted project*

un·com·pli·cated /ʌnˈkɒmplɪkeɪtɪd; *NAmE* -ˈkɑːm-/ *adj.* simple; without any difficulty or confusion SYN **straightforward**: *an easygoing, uncomplicated young man* ◇ *Why can't I have an uncomplicated life?* OPP **complicated**

un·com·pli·men·tary /ʌnˌkɒmplɪˈmentri; *NAmE* -ˌkɑːm-/ *adj.* rude or insulting: *uncomplimentary remarks* ➲ compare COMPLIMENTARY

un·com·pre·hend·ing /ʌnˌkɒmprɪˈhendɪŋ; *NAmE* -ˌkɑːm-/ *adj.* (*formal*) (of a person) not understanding a situation or what is happening ▸ **un·com·pre·hend·ing·ly** *adv.*: *She looked at him uncomprehendingly.*

un·com·prom·is·ing /ʌnˈkɒmprəmaɪzɪŋ; *NAmE* -ˈkɑːm-/ *adj.* unwilling to change your opinions or behaviour: *an uncompromising attitude* ◇ *He has a reputation for being tough and uncompromising.* ▸ **un·com·prom·is·ing·ly** *adv.*

un·con·cealed /ˌʌnkənˈsiːld/ *adj.* [usually before noun] (of an emotion, etc.) that you do not try to hide SYN **obvious**: *unconcealed curiosity*

un·con·cern /ˌʌnkənˈsɜːn; *NAmE* -ˈsɜːrn/ *noun* [U] (*formal*) a lack of care, interest or worry about sth that other people would care about SYN **indifference**: *She received the news with apparent unconcern.* ➲ compare CONCERN

un·con·cerned /ˌʌnkənˈsɜːnd; *NAmE* -ˈsɜːrnd/ *adj.* **1 ~ (about/by sth)** not worried or anxious about sth because you feel it does not affect you or is not important: *He drove on, apparently unconcerned about the noise the engine was making.* **2 ~ (with sb/sth)** not interested in sth: *Young people are often unconcerned with political issues.* OPP **concerned** ▸ **un·con·cern·ed·ly** /ˌʌnkənˈsɜːnɪdli/ *adv.*

un·con·di·tion·al /ˌʌnkənˈdɪʃənl/ *adj.* without any conditions or limits: *the* ***unconditional surrender*** *of military forces* ◇ *She gave her children* ***unconditional love.*** OPP **conditional** ▸ **un·con·di·tion·al·ly** /-ʃənəli/ *adv.*

un·con·di·tioned /ˌʌnkənˈdɪʃnd/ *adj.* (*psychology*) (of behaviour) not trained or influenced by experience; natural: *an unconditioned response*

un·con·fined AW /ˌʌnkənˈfaɪnd/ *adj.* (*formal*) not limited in space, range or amount: *The animals have unconfined access to pasture.* ◇ *When the news came through joy was unconfined.*

un·con·firmed /ˌʌnkənˈfɜːmd; *NAmE* -ˈfɜːrmd/ *adj.* that has not yet been proved to be true or confirmed: *unconfirmed rumours* ◇ *Unconfirmed reports said that at least six people had been killed.*

un·con·gen·ial /ˌʌnkənˈdʒiːniəl/ *adj.* (*formal*) **1** (of a person) not pleasant or friendly; not like yourself: *uncongenial company* **2 ~ (to sb)** (of a place, job, etc.) not pleasant; not making you feel relaxed; not suitable for your personality: *an uncongenial atmosphere* **3 ~ (to sth)** not suitable for sth; not encouraging sth: *The religious climate at the time was uncongenial to new ideas.* OPP **congenial**

un·con·nect·ed /ˌʌnkəˈnektɪd/ *adj.* not related or connected in any way: *The two crimes are apparently unconnected.* ◇ **~ with/to sth** *My resignation was totally unconnected with recent events.*

un·con·quer·able /ʌnˈkɒŋkərəbl; *NAmE* -ˈkɑːŋ-/ *adj.* too strong to be defeated or changed SYN **invincible**

un·con·scion·able /ʌnˈkɒnʃənəbl; *NAmE* -ˈkɑːn-/ *adj.* [usually before noun] (*formal*) **1** (of an action, etc.) so bad, immoral, etc. that it should make you feel ashamed **2** (often *humorous*) too great, large, long, etc. SYN **excessive**

un·con·scious 0‑w /ʌnˈkɒnʃəs; *NAmE* -ˈkɑːn-/ *adj.*, *noun*

■ ***adj.*** **1** 0‑w in a state like sleep because of an injury or illness, and not able to use your senses: *She was* ***knocked*** *unconscious.* ◇ *They found him lying unconscious on the floor.* **2** 🗝 (of feelings, thoughts, etc.) existing or happening without you realizing or being aware; not deliberate or controlled: *unconscious desires* ◇ *The brochure is full of unconscious humour.* ➲ compare SUBCONSCIOUS **3** 🗝 **~ of sb/sth** not aware of sb/sth; not noticing sth; not conscious **SYN** **oblivious to**: *She is unconscious of the effect she has on people.* ◇ *He was quite unconscious of the danger.* **OPP** **conscious**

▪ ***noun*** **the unconscious** [sing.] (*psychology*) the part of a person's mind with thoughts, feelings, etc. that they are not aware of and cannot control but which can sometimes be understood by studying their behaviour or dreams ➲ compare SUBCONSCIOUS

un·con·scious·ly /ʌnˈkɒnʃəsli; *NAmE* -ˈkɑːn-/ *adv.* without being aware: *Perhaps, unconsciously, I've done something to offend her.* **OPP** **consciously**

un·con·scious·ness /ʌnˈkɒnʃəsnəs; *NAmE* -ˈkɑːn-/ *noun* [U] a state like sleep caused by injury or illness, when you are unable to use your senses: *He had lapsed into unconsciousness.*

un·con·sid·ered /ˌʌnkənˈsɪdəd; *NAmE* -ərd/ *adj.* (*formal*) not thought about, or not thought about with enough care: *I came to regret my unconsidered remarks.*

un·con·sol·able /ˌʌnkənˈsəʊləbl; *NAmE* -ˈsoʊl-/ *adj.* = INCONSOLABLE ▶ **un·con·sol·ably** /-əbli/ *adv.* = INCONSOLABLY

un·con·sti·tu·tion·al **AW** /ˌʌnˌkɒnstɪˈtjuːʃənl; *NAmE* -kɑːnstəˈtuː-/ *adj.* not allowed by the CONSTITUTION of a country, a political system or an organization **OPP** **constitutional** ▶ **un·con·sti·tu·tion·al·ly** /-ʃənəli/ *adv.*

un·con·strained **AW** /ˌʌnkənˈstreɪnd/ *adj.* not restricted or limited: *unconstrained growth* ➲ see also CONSTRAIN

un·con·tam·in·ated /ˌʌnkənˈtæmɪneɪtɪd/ *adj.* not harmed or spoilt by sth (for example, dangerous substances): *uncontaminated water* **OPP** **contaminated**

un·con·ten·tious /ˌʌnkənˈtenʃəs/ *adj.* (*formal*) not likely to cause disagreement between people: *The proposal is relatively uncontentious.* **OPP** **contentious**

un·con·test·ed /ˌʌnkənˈtestɪd/ *adj.* without any opposition or argument: *an uncontested election/divorce* ◇ *These claims have not* ***gone uncontested.***

un·con·trol·lable /ˌʌnkənˈtrəʊləbl; *NAmE* -ˈtroʊ-/ *adj.* that you cannot control or prevent: *an uncontrollable temper* ◇ *uncontrollable bleeding* ◇ *I had an uncontrollable urge to laugh.* ◇ *The ball was uncontrollable.* ◇ *He's an uncontrollable child* (= he behaves very badly and cannot be controlled). ▶ **un·con·trol·lably** /-əbli/ *adv.*: *She began shaking uncontrollably.*

un·con·trolled 🗝 /ˌʌnkənˈtrəʊld; *NAmE* -ˈtroʊld/ *adj.*
1 🗝 (of emotions, behaviour, etc.) that sb cannot control or stop: *uncontrolled anger* ◇ *The thoughts rushed into my mind uncontrolled.* **2** 🗝 that is not limited or managed by law or rules: *the uncontrolled growth of cities* ◇ *uncontrolled dumping of toxic wastes* ➲ compare CONTROLLED

un·con·tro·ver·sial **AW** /ˌʌnˌkɒntrəˈvɜːʃl; *NAmE* ˌʌnkɑːntrəˈvɜːrʃl/ *adj.* not causing, or not likely to cause, any disagreement: *an uncontroversial opinion* ◇ *He chose an uncontroversial topic for his speech.* **OPP** **controversial** ➲ compare NON-CONTROVERSIAL

un·con·ven·tion·al **AW** /ˌʌnkənˈvenʃənl/ *adj.* (often *approving*) not following what is done or considered normal or acceptable by most people; different and interesting **SYN** **unorthodox**: *an unconventional approach to the problem* ◇ *unconventional views* **OPP** **conventional** ▶ **un·con·ven·tion·al·ity** /ˌʌnkənvenʃəˈnæləti/ *noun* [U] **un·con·ven·tion·al·ly** /-ʃənəli/ *adv.*

un·con·vinced **AW** /ˌʌnkənˈvɪnst/ *adj.* not believing or not certain about sth despite what you have been told: **~ (of sth)** *I* ***remain unconvinced*** *of the need for change.* ◇ **~ (by sth)** *She seemed unconvinced by their promises.* ◇ **~ (that…)** *The jury were unconvinced that he was innocent.* **OPP** **convinced**

un·con·vin·cing /ˌʌnkənˈvɪnsɪŋ/ *adj.* not seeming true or real; not making you believe that sth is true: *I find the characters in the book very unconvincing.* ◇ *She managed a weak, unconvincing smile.* **OPP** **convincing** ▶ **un·con·vin·cing·ly** *adv.*

un·cooked /ˌʌnˈkʊkt/ *adj.* not cooked **SYN** **raw**: *Eat plenty of uncooked fruit and vegetables.*

un·cool /ˌʌnˈkuːl/ *adj.* (*informal*) not considered acceptable by fashionable young people **OPP** **cool**

un·co·opera·tive /ˌʌnkəʊˈɒpərətɪv; *NAmE* -koʊˈɑːp-/ *adj.* not willing to be helpful to other people or do what they ask **SYN** **unhelpful** **OPP** **cooperative**

un·co·or·din·ated /ˌʌnkəʊˈɔːdɪneɪtɪd; *NAmE* -koʊˈɔːrd-/ *adj.* **1** if a person is **uncoordinated**, they are not able to control their movements well, and are therefore not very skilful at some sports and physical activities **2** (of movements or parts of the body) not controlled; not moving smoothly or together **3** (of plans, projects, etc.) not well organized; with no thought for how the different parts work together

un·cork /ˌʌnˈkɔːk; *NAmE* -ˈkɔːrk/ *verb* **~ sth** to open a bottle by removing the CORK from the top **OPP** **cork**

un·cor·rob·or·ated /ˌʌnkəˈrɒbəreɪtɪd; *NAmE* -ˈrɑːb-/ *adj.* (of a statement or claim) not supported by any other evidence; not having been CORROBORATED **SYN** **unconfirmed**

un·count·able /ʌnˈkaʊntəbl/ (also **ˌnon-ˈcount**) *adj.* (*grammar*) a noun that is **uncountable** cannot be made plural or used with *a* or *an*, for example *water*, *bread* and *information* **OPP** **countable** ➲ compare COUNTLESS

ˈuncount noun *noun* (*grammar*) an uncountable noun **OPP** **count noun**

un·couple /ˌʌnˈkʌpl/ *verb* **~ sth (from sth)** to remove the connection between two vehicles, two parts of a train, etc.

un·couth /ʌnˈkuːθ/ *adj.* (of a person or their behaviour) rude or socially unacceptable **SYN** **coarse**: *uncouth laughter* ◇ *an uncouth young man*

un·cover /ʌnˈkʌvə(r)/ *verb* **1** **~ sth** to remove sth that is covering sth: *Uncover the pan and let the soup simmer.* **2** **~ sth** to discover sth that was previously hidden or secret: *Police have uncovered a plot to kidnap the President's son.*

un·covered /ʌnˈkʌvəd; *NAmE* -ərd/ *adj.* not covered by anything: *His head was uncovered.*

un·crit·ic·al /ˌʌnˈkrɪtɪkl/ *adj.* (usually *disapproving*) not willing to criticize sb/sth or to judge whether sb/sth is right or wrong: *Her uncritical acceptance of everything I said began to irritate me.* **OPP** **critical** ▶ **un·crit·ic·al·ly** /-ɪkli/ *adv.*

un·crowd·ed /ʌnˈkraʊdɪd/ *adj.* not full of people: *The beach was pleasantly uncrowded.* **OPP** **crowded**

un·crowned /ˌʌnˈkraʊnd/ *adj.* (of a king or queen) not yet CROWNED

IDM **the ˌuncrowned ˈking/ˈqueen (of sth)** the person considered to be the best, most famous or successful in a particular place or area of activity

unc·tion /ˈʌŋkʃn/ *noun* [U] **1** the act of pouring oil on sb's head or another part of their body as part of an important religious ceremony ➲ see also EXTREME UNCTION **2** (*formal, disapproving*) behaviour or speech that is not sincere and that expresses too much praise or admiration of sb

unc·tu·ous /ˈʌŋktjuəs; *NAmE* -tʃuəs/ *adj.* (*formal, disapproving*) friendly or giving praise in a way that is not sincere and which is therefore unpleasant ▶ **unc·tu·ous·ly** *adv.*

un·culti·vated /ʌnˈkʌltɪveɪtɪd/ *adj.* (of land) not used for growing crops **OPP** **cultivated**

un·cul·tured **AW** /ˌʌnˈkʌltʃəd; *NAmE* -tʃərd/ *adj.* (of people) not well educated; not able to understand or enjoy art, literature, etc. **OPP** **cultured**

U

un·curl /ˌʌnˈkɜːl; *NAmE* -ˈkɜːrl/ *verb* [I, T] to become straight, or to make sth become straight, after being in a curled position: *The snake slowly uncurled.* ◇ **~ sth/itself** *The cat uncurled itself and jumped off the wall.* OPP **curl up**

un·cut /ˌʌnˈkʌt/ *adj.* **1** left to grow; not cut short: *The uncut grass came up to her waist.* **2** (of a book, film/movie, etc.) left in its complete form; without any parts removed; not CENSORED: *the original uncut version* **3** (of a PRECIOUS STONE) not shaped by cutting: *uncut diamonds* **4** not cut into separate pieces: *an uncut loaf of bread*

un·dam·aged /ʌnˈdæmɪdʒd/ *adj.* not damaged or spoilt: *There was a slight collision but my car was undamaged.* ◇ *He emerged from the court case with his reputation undamaged.*

un·dated /ˌʌnˈdeɪtɪd/ *adj.* **1** without a date written or printed on it: *an undated letter* **2** of which the date is not known: *undated archaeological remains* ➲ compare DATED

un·daunt·ed /ˌʌnˈdɔːntɪd/ *adj.* [not usually before noun] (*formal*) still enthusiastic and determined, despite difficulties or disappointment SYN **undeterred**: *He seemed undaunted by all the opposition to his idea.*

un·decided /ˌʌndɪˈsaɪdɪd/ *adj.* [not usually before noun] **1** not having made a decision about sb/sth: **~ (about sb/sth)** *I'm still undecided (about) who to vote for.* ◇ **~ (as to sth)** *He was undecided as to what to do next.* **2** not having been decided: *The venue for the World Cup remains undecided.* ➲ compare DECIDED

un·declared /ˌʌndɪˈkleəd; *NAmE* -ˈklerd/ *adj.* not admitted to; not stated in an open way; not having been declared: *No income should remain undeclared.* ◇ *Undeclared goods* (= that the customs are not told about) *may be confiscated.*

un·defeat·ed /ˌʌndɪˈfiːtɪd/ *adj.* (especially in sport) not having lost or been defeated: *They are undefeated in 13 games.* ◇ *the undefeated world champion*

un·defend·ed /ˌʌndɪˈfendɪd/ *adj.* **1** not protected or guarded SYN **unprotected**: *undefended borders* **2** if a case in court is **undefended**, no defence is made against it

un·defined AW /ˌʌndɪˈfaɪnd/ *adj.* not made clear or definite: *The money was lent for an undefined period of time.*

un·de·lete /ˌʌndɪˈliːt/ *verb* [T, I] **~ (sth)** (*computing*) to cancel an action of DELETING a document, a file, text, etc. on a computer, so that it appears again

un·demand·ing /ˌʌndɪˈmɑːndɪŋ/ *adj.* **1** not needing a lot of effort or thought: *an undemanding job* **2** (of a person) not asking for a lot of attention or action from other people OPP **demanding**

un·demo·crat·ic /ˌʌndeməˈkrætɪk/ *adj.* against or not acting according to the principles of DEMOCRACY: *undemocratic decisions* ◇ *an undemocratic regime* OPP **democratic** ▶ **un·demo·crat·ic·al·ly** /-kli/ *adv.*: *an undemocratically elected government* ◇ *He was accused of acting undemocratically.*

un·demon·stra·tive /ˌʌndɪˈmɒnstrətɪv; *NAmE* -ˈmɑːn-/ *adj.* not showing feelings openly, especially feelings of affection OPP **demonstrative**

un·deni·able AW /ˌʌndɪˈnaɪəbl/ *adj.* true or certain; that cannot be denied SYN **indisputable**: *He had undeniable charm.* ◇ *It is an undeniable fact that crime is increasing.* OPP **deniable** ▶ **un·deni·ably** /-əbli/ *adv.*: *undeniably impressive*

under 0-w /ˈʌndə(r)/ *prep., adv., adj.*

■ ***prep.*** **1** 0-w in, to or through a position that is below sth: *Have you looked under the bed?* ◇ *She placed the ladder under* (= just lower than) *the window.* ◇ *The dog squeezed under the gate and ran into the road.* **2** 0-w below the surface of sth; covered by sth: *The boat lay under several feet of water.* **3** 0-w less than; younger than: *an annual income of under £10 000* ◇ *It took us under an hour.* ◇ *Nobody under 18 is allowed to buy alcohol.* **4** 0-w used to say who or what controls, governs or manages sb/sth: *The country is now under martial law.* ◇ *The coinage was reformed under Elizabeth I* (= when she was queen). ◇ *She has a staff of 19 working under her.* ◇ *Under its new conductor, the orchestra has established an international reputation.* **5** 0-w according to an agreement, a law or a system: *Six suspects are being held under the Prevention of Terrorism Act.* ◇ *Under the terms of the lease you had no right to sublet the property.* ◇ *Is the television still under guarantee?* **6** 0-w experiencing a particular process: *The hotel is still under construction.* ◇ *The matter is under investigation.* **7** 0-w affected by sth: *The wall collapsed under the strain.* ◇ *I've been feeling under stress lately.* ◇ *I'm under no illusions about what hard work this will be.* ◇ *You'll be under anaesthetic, so you won't feel a thing.* **8** using a particular name: *She also writes under the pseudonym of Barbara Vine.* **9** found in a particular part of a book, list, etc: *If it's not under 'sports', try looking under 'games'.*

■ ***adv.*** **1** 0-w below sth: *He pulled up the covers and crawled under.* **2** 0-w below the surface of water: *She took a deep breath and stayed under for more than a minute.* ◇ *The boat was going under fast.* **3** 0-w less; younger: *prices of ten dollars and under* ◇ *children aged 12 and under* **4** in or into an unconscious state: *He felt himself going under.*

■ ***adj.*** [only before noun] lower; underneath: *the under layer* ◇ *the under surface of a leaf*

under- /ˈʌndə(r)/ *prefix* **1** (in nouns and adjectives) below; beneath: *undergrowth* ◇ *undercover* **2** (in nouns) lower in age or rank: *the under-fives* ◇ *an undergraduate* **3** (in adjectives and verbs) not enough: *underripe* ◇ *undercooked*

under·achieve /ˌʌndərəˈtʃiːv/ *verb* [I] to do less well than you could do, especially in school work ▶ **under·achieve·ment** *noun* [U] **under·achiever** *noun*

under·age /ˈʌndəreɪdʒ/ *adj.* [only before noun] done by people who are too young by law: *underage drinking* ➲ see also AGE

under·arm /ˈʌndərɑːm; *NAmE* -ɑːrm/ *adj., adv.*

■ ***adj.*** **1** [only before noun] connected with a person's ARMPIT: ***underarm hair/deodorant/sweating*** **2** an **underarm** throw of a ball is done with the hand kept below the level of the shoulder ➲ compare OVERARM

■ ***adv.*** if you throw, etc. **underarm**, you throw keeping your hand below the level of your shoulder ➲ compare OVERARM

under·belly /ˈʌndəbeli; *NAmE* -dərb-/ *noun* [sing.] **1** the weakest part of sth that is most easily attacked: *The trade deficit remains the* ***soft underbelly*** *of the US economy.* **2** the underneath part of an animal: (*figurative*) *He became familiar with the dark underbelly of life in the city* (= the parts that are usually hidden).

under·bid /ˌʌndəˈbɪd; *NAmE* -dərˈb-/ *verb* (**under·bid·ding, under·bid, under·bid**) **~ sb/sth** to make a lower bid than sb else, for example when trying to win a contract

under·brush /ˈʌndəbrʌʃ; *NAmE* -dərb-/ (*NAmE*) (*BrE* **under·growth**) *noun* [U] a mass of bushes and plants that grow close together under trees in woods and forests

under·car·riage /ˈʌndəkærɪdʒ; *NAmE* -dərk-/ (*also* **ˈlanding gear**) *noun* the part of an aircraft, including the wheels, that supports it when it is landing and taking off ➲ VISUAL VOCAB page V43

under·charge /ˌʌndəˈtʃɑːdʒ; *NAmE* ˌʌndərˈtʃɑːrdʒ/ *verb* [I, T] **~ (sb) (for sth)** to charge too little for sth, usually by mistake OPP **overcharge**

under·class /ˈʌndəklɑːs; *NAmE* ˈʌndərklæs/ *noun* [sing.] a social class that is very poor and has no status: *The long-term unemployed are becoming a new underclass.*

under·class·man /ˌʌndəˈklɑːsmən; *NAmE* -dərˈklæs-/, **under·class·woman** /ˌʌndəˈklɑːswʊmən; *NAmE* -dərˈklæs-/ *noun* (*pl.* **-men** /-mən/, **-women** /-wɪmɪn/) (in the US) a student in the first or second year of HIGH SCHOOL or college ➲ compare UPPERCLASSMAN

under·clothes /ˈʌndəkləʊðz; *NAmE* ˈʌndərkloʊðz/ *noun* [pl.] (*also* **under·cloth·ing** /-kləʊðɪŋ; *NAmE* -kloʊ-/ [U]) (*formal*) = UNDERWEAR

under·coat /ˈʌndəkəʊt; *NAmE* ˈʌndərkoʊt/ *noun* [C, U] a layer of paint under the final layer; the paint used for making this ➲ compare TOPCOAT

under·cook /ˌʌndəˈkʊk; *NAmE* -dərˈk-/ *verb* [usually passive] **~ sth** to not cook sth for long enough, with the result that it is not ready to eat

under·cover /ˌʌndəˈkʌvə(r); *NAmE* -dərˈk-/ *adj.* [usually before noun] working or done secretly in order to find out information for the police, a government, etc: *an **undercover agent*** ◇ *an **undercover operation/investigation*** ▶ **under·cover** *adv.*: *The illegal payments were discovered by a journalist **working undercover**.*

under·cur·rent /ˈʌndəkʌrənt; *NAmE* -dərkɜːr-/ *noun* **~ (of sth)** a feeling, especially a negative one, that is hidden but whose effects are felt **SYN** **undertone**: *I detect an undercurrent of resentment towards the new proposals.*

under·cut *verb, noun*

■ ***verb*** /ˌʌndəˈkʌt; *NAmE* ˌʌndərˈkʌt/ (**under·cut·ting**, **under·cut**, **under·cut**) **1 ~ sb/sth** to sell goods or services at a lower price than your COMPETITORS: *to undercut sb's prices* ◇ *We were able to undercut our European rivals by 5%.* **2 ~ sb/sth** to make sb/sth weaker or less likely to be effective **SYN** **undermine**: *Some members of the board were trying to undercut the chairman's authority.*

■ ***noun*** /ˈʌndəkʌt; *NAmE* ˈʌndərkʌt/ a way of cutting sb's hair in which the hair is left quite long on top but the hair on the lower part of the head is cut much shorter ➲ VISUAL VOCAB page V49

under·devel·oped /ˌʌndədɪˈveləpt; *NAmE* -dərdɪ-/ *adj.* (of a country, society, etc.) having few industries and a low standard of living ➲ compare DEVELOPED, DEVELOPING, UNDEVELOPED **HELP** 'A **developing** country' is now the usual expression. ▶ **under·devel·op·ment** *noun* [U]

under·dog /ˈʌndədɒg; *NAmE* ˈʌndərdɔːg; -dɑːg/ *noun* a person, team, country, etc. that is thought to be in a weaker position than others and therefore not likely to be successful, win a competition, etc: *Before the game we were definitely the underdogs.* ◇ *In politics, he was a champion of the underdog* (= always fought for the rights of weaker people). **OPP** **overdog**

under·done /ˌʌndəˈdʌn; *NAmE* -dərˈd-/ *adj.* not completely cooked ➲ compare WELL DONE, OVERDONE

under·employed /ˌʌndərɪmˈplɔɪd/ *adj.* not having enough work to do; not having work that makes full use of your skills and abilities

under·esti·mate **AW** *verb, noun*

■ ***verb*** /ˌʌndərˈestɪmeɪt/ **1 ~ sth** | **~ what, how, etc...** to think or guess that the amount, cost or size of sth is smaller than it really is: *to underestimate the cost of the project* ◇ *We underestimated the time it would take to get there.* **2 ~ sb/sth** to not realize how good, strong, determined, etc. sb really is: *Never underestimate your opponent.* **OPP** **overestimate** ➲ compare UNDERRATE

■ ***noun*** /ˌʌndərˈestɪmət/ (also **under·esti·ma·tion** /ˌʌndərˌestɪˈmeɪʃn/ [C, U]) an estimate about the size, cost, etc. of sth that is too low: *My guess of 400 proved to be a serious underestimate.* **OPP** **overestimate**

under·expose /ˌʌndərɪkˈspəʊz; *NAmE* -ˈspoʊz/ *verb* [usually passive] **~ sth** to allow too little light to reach the film when you take a photograph **OPP** **overexpose**

under·fed /ˌʌndəˈfed; *NAmE* -dərˈf-/ *adj.* having had too little food to eat **SYN** **malnourished** **OPP** **overfed**

under·floor /ˌʌndəˈflɔː(r); *NAmE* -dərˈf-/ *adj.* [only before noun] placed underneath the floor: *underfloor heating*

under·foot /ˌʌndəˈfʊt; *NAmE* -dərˈf-/ *adv.* under your feet; on the ground where you are walking: *The ground was dry and firm underfoot.* ◇ *I was nearly **trampled underfoot** by the crowd of people rushing for the door.*

under·fund·ed /ˌʌndəˈfʌndɪd; *NAmE* -dərˈf-/ *adj.* (of an organization, a project, etc.) not having enough money to spend, with the result that it cannot function well: ***seriously/chronically underfunded***

under·gar·ment /ˈʌndəgɑːmənt; *NAmE* -dərgɑːrm-/ *noun* (*old-fashioned* or *formal*) a piece of underwear

under·go **AW** /ˌʌndəˈgəʊ; *NAmE* ˌʌndərˈgoʊ/ *verb* (**under·goes** /-ˈgəʊz; *NAmE* -ˈgoʊz/, **under·went** /-ˈwent/, **under·gone** /-ˈgɒn; *NAmE* -ˈgɔːn; -ˈgɑːn/) **~ sth** to experience sth, especially a change or sth unpleasant: *to **undergo tests/trials/repairs*** ◇ *My mother **underwent** major **surgery** last year.* ◇ *Some children **undergo a** complete **transformation** when they become teenagers.*

under·gradu·ate /ˌʌndəˈgrædʒuət; *NAmE* -dərˈg-/ *noun* a university or college student who is studying for their first degree: *a first-year undergraduate* ◇ *an **undergraduate course/student/degree*** ➲ note at STUDENT

under·ground 🔑 *adj., adv., noun*

■ ***adj.*** /ˌʌndəˈgraʊnd; *NAmE* -dərˈg-/ [only before noun] **1** 🔑 under the surface of the ground: *underground passages/caves/streams* ◇ *underground cables* ➲ compare OVERGROUND **2** operating secretly and often illegally, especially against a government: *an underground resistance movement*

■ ***adv.*** /ˌʌndəˈgraʊnd; *NAmE* -dərˈg-/ **1** 🔑 under the surface of the ground: *Rescuers found victims trapped several feet underground.* ◇ *toxic waste buried deep underground* **2** in or into a secret place in order to hide from the police, the government, etc: *He **went underground** to avoid arrest.*

■ ***noun*** /ˈʌndəgraʊnd; *NAmE* -dərg-/ **1** (often **the Underground**) (*BrE*) (*NAmE* **sub·way**) [sing.] an underground railway/railroad system in a city: *underground stations* ◇ *the London Underground* ◇ *I always travel by underground.* ➲ VISUAL VOCAB page V47 ➲ compare METRO, TUBE **2 the underground** [sing.+ sing./pl. v.] a secret political organization, usually working against the government of a country

> **British/American**
>
> **underground / subway / metro / tube**
>
> ■ A city's underground railway/railroad system is usually called the **underground** (often **the Underground**) in *BrE* and the **subway** in *NAmE*. Speakers of *BrE* also use **subway** for systems in American cities and **metro** for systems in other European countries. **The Metro** is the name for the systems in Paris and Washington, D.C. London's system is often called **the Tube**.

the ˌunderground eˈconomy (*NAmE*) (*BrE* **the ˌblack eˈconomy**) *noun* [sing.] business activity or work that is done without the knowledge of the government or other officials so that people avoid paying tax on the money they earn

under·growth /ˈʌndəgrəʊθ; *NAmE* ˈʌndərgroʊθ/ (*BrE*) (*NAmE* **under·brush**) *noun* [U] a mass of bushes and plants that grow close together under trees in woods and forests: *They used their knives to clear a path through the dense undergrowth.* ◇ *The murder weapon was found concealed in undergrowth.*

under·hand /ˌʌndəˈhænd; *NAmE* -dərˈh-/ (also *less frequent* **under·hand·ed** /-ˈhændɪd/) *adj.* (*disapproving*) secret and dishonest: *I would never have expected her to behave in such an underhand way.*

under·in·sured /ˌʌndərɪnˈʃʊəd; -ˈʃɔːd; *NAmE* -ˈʃʊrd/ *adj.* not having enough insurance protection

under·lay /ˈʌndəleɪ; *NAmE* ˈʌndərleɪ/ *noun* [U, C] a layer of thick material placed under a carpet to protect it

under·lie **AW** /ˌʌndəˈlaɪ; *NAmE* ˌʌndərˈlaɪ/ *verb* (**under·lying**, **under·lay** /-ˈleɪ/, **under·lain** /-ˈleɪn/) [no passive] **~ sth** (*formal*) to be the basis or cause of sth: *These ideas underlie much of his work.* ◇ *It is a principle that underlies all the party's policies.* ➲ see also UNDERLYING

under·line /ˌʌndəˈlaɪn; *NAmE* -dərˈl-/ (also **under·score** especially in *NAmE*) *verb* **1 ~ sth** to draw a line under a word, sentence, etc. **2** to emphasize or show that sth is important or true: **~ sth** *The report underlines the importance of pre-school education.* ◇ **~ how, what, etc...**

U

Her question underlined how little she understood him. ◇ **~ that...** *The report underlined that the project enjoyed considerable support in both countries.* ◇ **it is underlined that ...** *It should be underlined that these are only preliminary findings.*

under·ling /ˈʌndəlɪŋ; *NAmE* ˈʌndərlɪŋ/ *noun* (*disapproving*) a person with a lower rank or status SYN **minion**

under·lying AW /ˌʌndəˈlaɪɪŋ; *NAmE* -dərˈl-/ *adj.* [only before noun] **1** important in a situation but not always easily noticed or stated clearly: *The underlying assumption is that the amount of money available is limited.* ◇ *Unemployment may be an underlying cause of the rising crime rate.* **2** existing under the surface of sth else: *the underlying rock formation* ➲ see also UNDERLIE

under·manned /ˌʌndəˈmænd; *NAmE* -dərˈm-/ *adj.* (of a hospital, factory, etc.) not having enough people working in order to be able to function well SYN **understaffed** OPP **overmanned**

under·men·tioned /ˌʌndəˈmenʃnd; *NAmE* -dərˈm-/ *adj.* (*BrE, formal*) used in a book or document to refer to sth that is mentioned later

under·mine /ˌʌndəˈmaɪn; *NAmE* -dərˈm-/ *verb* **1 ~ sth** to make sth, especially sb's confidence or authority, gradually weaker or less effective: *Our confidence in the team has been seriously undermined by their recent defeats.* ◇ *This crisis has undermined his position.* **2 ~ sth** to make sth weaker at the base, for example by digging under it

under·neath 🔑 /ˌʌndəˈniːθ; *NAmE* -dərˈn-/ *prep., adv., noun*

■ ***prep., adv.*** **1** 🔑 under or below sth else, especially when it is hidden or covered by the thing on top: *The coin rolled underneath the piano.* ◇ *This jacket's too big, even with a sweater underneath.* **2** 🔑 used to talk about sb's real feelings or character, as opposed to the way they seem to be: *Underneath her cool exterior she was really very frightened.* ◇ *He seems bad-tempered, but he's very soft-hearted underneath.*

■ ***noun*** **the underneath** [sing.] the lower surface or part of sth: *She pulled the drawer out and examined the underneath carefully.*

under·nour·ished /ˌʌndəˈnʌrɪʃt; *NAmE* -dərˈnɜːr-/ *adj.* in bad health because of a lack of food or a lack of the right type of food SYN **malnourished**: *severely undernourished children* ▶ **under·nour·ish·ment** /-ˈnʌrɪʃmənt; *NAmE* -ˈnɜːr-/ *noun* [U]

under·paid /ˌʌndəˈpeɪd; *NAmE* -dərˈp-/ *adj.* not paid enough for the work you do: *Nurses complain of being **overworked and underpaid**.*

under·pants /ˈʌndəpænts; *NAmE* -dərp-/ *noun* [pl.] **1** (also *informal* **pants**) (*BrE*) a piece of men's underwear worn under their trousers/pants **2** (*NAmE*) a piece of underwear worn by men or women under trousers/pants, a skirt, etc.

U

under·pass /ˈʌndəpɑːs; *NAmE* ˈʌndərpæs/ *noun* a road or path that goes under another road or railway/railroad track ➲ compare OVERPASS

under·pay /ˌʌndəˈpeɪ; *NAmE* -dərˈp-/ *verb* (**under·paid**, **under·paid** /-peɪd/) [usually passive] **~ sb** to pay sb too little money, especially for their work OPP **overpay**

under·per·form /ˌʌndəpəˈfɔːm; *NAmE* ˌʌndərpərˈfɔːrm/ *verb* [I] to not be as successful as was expected

under·pin /ˌʌndəˈpɪn; *NAmE* -dərˈp-/ *verb* (**-nn-**) **1 ~ sth** (*formal*) to support or form the basis of an argument, a claim, etc: *The report is underpinned by extensive research.* **2 ~ sth** (*technical*) to support a wall by putting metal, concrete, etc. under it ▶ **under·pin·ning** *noun* [C, U]

under·play /ˌʌndəˈpleɪ; *NAmE* -dərˈp-/ *verb* **~ sth** (*especially BrE*) to make sth seem less important than it really is SYN **play down, downplay** OPP **overplay**

under·pre·pared /ˌʌndəprɪˈpeəd; *NAmE* ˌʌndərprɪˈperd/ *adj.* not having done enough preparation for sth you have to do

under·priced /ˌʌndəˈpraɪst; *NAmE* -dərˈp-/ *adj.* something that is **underpriced** is sold at a price that is too low and less than its real value

under·priv·il·eged /ˌʌndəˈprɪvəlɪdʒd; *NAmE* -dərˈp-/ *adj.* **1** [usually before noun] having less money and fewer opportunities than most people in society SYN **disadvantaged**: *underprivileged sections of the community* ◇ ***educationally/socially underprivileged** groups* ➲ compare PRIVILEGED **2 the underprivileged** *noun* [pl.] people who are underprivileged

under·rate /ˌʌndəˈreɪt/ *verb* **~ sb/sth** to not recognize how good, important, etc. sb/sth really is: *He's seriously underrated as a writer.* ◇ *an underrated movie* ➲ compare OVERRATE, UNDERESTIMATE

ˌunder-reˈhearsed *adj.* (of a play or other performance) that has not been prepared and practised enough

ˌunder-ˌrepreˈsent·ed *adj.* not having as many representatives as would be expected or needed: *Women are under-represented at senior levels in business.*

ˌunder-ˌreˈsourced AW *adj.* not provided with as much money or as many staff, materials, etc. as are needed: *Nurses are overstretched and the hospital is seriously under-resourced.*

under·score *verb, noun*

■ ***verb*** /ˌʌndəˈskɔː(r); *NAmE* -dərˈs-/ (*especially NAmE*) = UNDERLINE

■ ***noun*** /ˈʌndəskɔː(r); *NAmE* -dərs-/ (*computing*) the symbol (_) that is used to draw a line under a letter or word and used in computer commands and in Internet addresses

under·sea /ˈʌndəsiː; *NAmE* ˈʌndərsiː/ *adj.* [only before noun] found, used or happening below the surface of the sea: *undersea cables/earthquakes*

under·sec·re·tary /ˌʌndəˈsekrətri; *NAmE* ˌʌndərˈsekrəteri/ *noun* (*pl.* **-ies**) **1** (in Britain) a senior CIVIL SERVANT in charge of one part of a government department ➲ compare PERMANENT UNDERSECRETARY **2** (in Britain) a junior minister who reports to the minister in charge of a government department **3** (in the US) an official of high rank in a government department, directly below a member of a cabinet

under·sell /ˌʌndəˈsel; *NAmE* ˌʌndərˈsel/ *verb* (**un·der·sold**, **un·der·sold** /-ˈsəʊld; *NAmE* -ˈsoʊld/) **1 ~ sth** to sell goods or services at a lower price than your COMPETITORS **2 ~ sth** to sell sth at a price lower than its real value **3 ~ sb/sth/yourself** to make people think that sb/sth is not as good or as interesting as they really are: *Don't undersell yourself at the interview.*

under·shirt /ˈʌndəʃɜːt; *NAmE* ˈʌndərʃɜːrt/ (*NAmE*) (*BrE* **vest**) *noun* a piece of underwear worn under a shirt, etc. next to the skin ➲ compare SINGLET

under·shoot /ˌʌndəˈʃuːt; *NAmE* -dərˈʃ-/ *verb* (**under·shot**, **under·shot**) [I, T] **~ (sth)** (of an aircraft) to land before reaching the RUNWAY ▶ **under·shoot** *noun*

under·shorts /ˈʌndəʃɔːts; *NAmE* ˈʌndərʃɔːrts/ *noun* [pl.] (*NAmE*) UNDERPANTS that are worn by men

under·side /ˈʌndəsaɪd; *NAmE* -dərs-/ *noun* the side or surface of sth that is underneath SYN **bottom**

the under·signed /ˌʌndəˈsaɪnd; *NAmE* -dərˈs-/ *noun* (*pl.* **the under·signed**) (*formal*) the person who has signed that particular document: *We, the undersigned, agree to...*

under·sized /ˌʌndəˈsaɪzd; *NAmE* -dərˈs-/ *adj.* not as big as normal

under·skirt /ˈʌndəskɜːt; *NAmE* ˈʌndərskɜːrt/ *noun* a skirt that is worn under another skirt as underwear

under·sold *past tense, past part.* of UNDERSELL

under·spend /ˌʌndəˈspend; *NAmE* -dərˈs-/ *verb* (**under·spent**, **under·spent**) [I, T] to not spend enough money on sth: **~ (on sth)** *The inquiry found that the company had seriously underspent on safety equipment.* ◇ **~ sth** *We've underspent our budget this year.* ▶ **under·spend** /ˈʌndəspend; *NAmE* ˈʌndərs-/ *noun* [sing.]: (*BrE*) *a £1 million underspend*

Synonyms

understand

see • get • follow • grasp • comprehend

These words all mean to know or realize sth, for example why sth happens, how sth works or what sth means.

understand to know or realize the meaning of words, a language, what sb says, etc; to know or realize how or why sth happens, how it works or why it is important: *I don't understand the instructions.* ◇ *Doctors still don't understand much about the disease.*

see to understand what is happening, what sb is saying, how sth works or how important sth is: *'It opens like this.' ' Oh, **I see**.'* ◇ *Oh yes, **I see what you mean**.*

get (*informal*) to understand a joke, what sb is trying to tell you, or a situation that they are trying to describe: *She didn't get the joke.* ◇ *I don't get you.*

follow to understand an explanation, a story or the meaning of sth: *Sorry—I don't quite follow.* ◇ *The plot is almost impossible to follow.*

grasp to come to understand a fact, an idea or how to do sth: *They failed to grasp the importance of his words.*

UNDERSTAND OR GRASP?

You can use **understand** or **grasp** for the action of realizing the meaning or importance of sth for the first time: *It's a difficult concept for children to understand/grasp.* Only **understand** can be used to talk about languages, words or writing: ~~*I don't grasp French/the instructions.*~~

comprehend (often used in negative statements) (*formal*) to understand a fact, idea or reason: *The concept of infinity is almost impossible for the human mind to comprehend.*

PATTERNS

- to understand/see/get/follow/grasp/comprehend **what/why/how...**
- to understand/see/grasp/comprehend **that...**
- to understand/see/get/grasp **the point/idea** (of sth)
- to be **easy/difficult/hard** to understand/see/follow/grasp/comprehend
- to **fully** understand/see/grasp/comprehend sth

under·staffed /ˌʌndəˈstɑːft; *NAmE* ˌʌndərˈstæft/ *adj.* [not usually before noun] not having enough people working and therefore not able to function well SYN **undermanned** OPP **overstaffed**

under·stand 0-w /ˌʌndəˈstænd; *NAmE* -dərˈs-/ *verb* (**under·stood**, **under·stood** /-ˈstʊd/) (not used in the progressive tenses)

WORD FAMILY
understand *verb* (≠ misunderstand)
understandable *adj.*
misunderstood *adj.*
understanding *adj.*, *noun* (≠ misunderstanding)

▸ MEANING **1** 0-w [T, I] to know or realize the meaning of words, a language, what sb says, etc: **~ (sth)** *Can you understand French?* ◇ *Do you understand the instructions?* ◇ *She didn't understand the form she was signing.* ◇ *I'm not sure that I understand. Go over it again.* ◇ *I don't want you doing that again. Do you understand?* ◇ **~ what...** *I don't understand what he's saying.*

▸ HOW STH WORKS/HAPPENS **2** 0-w [T, I] to know or realize how or why sth happens, how it works or why it is important: **~ (sth)** *Doctors still don't understand much about the disease.* ◇ *No one is answering the phone—I can't understand it.* ◇ **~ why, what, etc...** *I could never understand why she was fired.* ◇ **~ sb/sth doing sth** *I just can't understand him taking the money.* ◇ (*formal*) *I just can't understand his taking the money.* ◇ **~ that...** *He was the first to understand that we live in a knowledge economy.*

▸ KNOW SB **3** 0-w [T, I] to know sb's character, how they feel and why they behave in the way they do: **~ sb** *Nobody understands me.* ◇ *He doesn't understand women at all.* ◇ **~ what, how, etc...** *They understand what I have been through.* ◇ **~ (that...)** *I quite understand that you need some time alone.* ◇ *If you want to leave early, I'm sure he'll understand.* ◇ **~ sb doing sth** *I quite understand you needing some time alone.*

▸ THINK/BELIEVE **4** [T] (*formal*) to think or believe that sth is true because you have been told that it is: **~ (that)...** *I understand (that) you wish to see the manager.* ◇ *Am I to understand that you refuse?* ◇ **~ sb/sth to be/have sth** *The Prime Minister is understood to have been extremely angry about the report.* ◇ **it is understood that...** *It is understood that the band are working on their next album.*

▸ BE AGREED **5** [T] **it is understood that...** to agree sth with sb without it needing to be said: *I thought it was understood that my expenses would be paid.*

▸ MISSING WORD **6** [T, usually passive] **~ sth** to realize that a word in a phrase or sentence is not expressed and to supply it in your mind: *In the sentence 'I can't drive', the object 'a car' is understood.*

IDM **ˌmake yourself underˈstood** to make your meaning clear, especially in another language: *He doesn't speak much Japanese but he can make himself understood.* ➲ more at GIVE *v.*

under·stand·able /ˌʌndəˈstændəbl; *NAmE* -dərˈs-/ *adj.* **1** (of behaviour, feelings, reactions, etc.) seeming normal and reasonable in a particular situation SYN **natural**: *Their attitude is **perfectly understandable**.* ◇ *It was an understandable mistake to make.* **2** (of language, documents, etc.) easy to understand SYN **comprehensible**: *Warning notices must be readily understandable.*

under·stand·ably /ˌʌndəˈstændəbli; *NAmE* -dərˈs-/ *adv.* in a way that seems normal and reasonable in a particular situation SYN **naturally**: *They were understandably disappointed with the result.*

under·stand·ing 0-w /ˌʌndəˈstændɪŋ; *NAmE* -dərˈs-/ *noun, adj.*

■ ***noun*** **1** 0-w [U, sing.] **~ (of sth)** the knowledge that sb has about a particular subject or situation: *The committee has little or no understanding of the problem.* ◇ *The existence of God is beyond human understanding* (= humans cannot know whether God exists or not). **2** 0-w [C, usually sing.] an informal agreement: *We finally **came to an understanding** about what hours we would work.* ◇ *We have this understanding that nobody talks about work over lunch.* **3** 0-w [U, sing.] the ability to understand why people behave in a particular way and the willingness to forgive them when they do sth wrong: *We must tackle the problem with sympathy and understanding.* ◇ *We are looking for a better understanding between the two nations.* **4** 0-w [U, C] **~ (of sth)** the particular way in which sb understands sth SYN **interpretation**: *My understanding of the situation is ...* ◇ *The statement is open to various understandings.*

IDM **on the understanding that...** (*formal*) used to introduce a condition that must be agreed before sth else can happen: *They agreed to the changes on the understanding that they would be introduced gradually.*

■ ***adj.*** showing sympathy for other people's problems and being willing to forgive them when they do sth wrong SYN **sympathetic**: *She has very understanding parents.* ▸ **under·stand·ing·ly** *adv.*

under·state /ˌʌndəˈsteɪt; *NAmE* -dərˈs-/ *verb* **~ sth** to state that sth is smaller, less important or less serious than it really is: *It would be a mistake to understate the seriousness of the problem.* OPP **overstate**

under·stated /ˌʌndəˈsteɪtɪd; *NAmE* -dərˈs-/ *adj.* (*approving*) if a style, colour, etc. is **understated**, it is pleasing and elegant in a way that is not too obvious SYN **subtle**

under·state·ment /ˈʌndəsteɪtmənt; *NAmE* -dərs-/ *noun* **1** [C] a statement that makes sth seem less important, impressive, serious, etc. than it really is: *To say we were pleased is an understatement* (= we were extremely pleased). ◇ *'These figures are a bit disappointing.' 'That's got to be **the understatement of the year**.'* **2** [U] the practice of making things seem less impressive, important, serious, etc. than they really are: *typical English understatement* ◇ *He always goes for subtlety and understatement in his movies.* OPP **overstatement**

U

under·stood *past tense, past part.* of UNDERSTAND

under·study /ˈʌndəstʌdi; *NAmE* -dərs-/ *noun, verb*
■ *noun* (*pl.* -ies) ~ (**to sb**) an actor who learns the part of another actor in a play so that they can play that part if necessary
■ *verb* (under·stud·ies, under·study·ing, under·stud·ied, under·stud·ied) ~ **sb/sth** to learn a part in a play as an understudy; to act as an understudy to sb

under·take AW /ˌʌndəˈteɪk; *NAmE* -dərˈt-/ *verb* (under·took /-ˈtʊk/, under·taken /-ˈteɪkən/) (*formal*) **1** ~ **sth** to make yourself responsible for sth and start doing it: *to **undertake a task/project** ◇ University professors both teach and **undertake research**. ◇ The company has announced that it will undertake a full investigation into the accident.* **2** ~ **to do sth** | ~ **that...** to agree or promise that you will do sth: *He undertook to finish the job by Friday.*

under·taker /ˈʌndəteɪkə(r); *NAmE* -dərt-/ (also *formal* ˈ**funeral director**) (*NAmE* also **mor·ti·cian**) *noun* a person whose job is to prepare the bodies of dead people to be buried or CREMATED, and to arrange funerals

under·tak·ing AW /ˌʌndəˈteɪkɪŋ; *NAmE* -dərˈt-/ *noun* **1** [C] a task or project, especially one that is important and/or difficult SYN **venture**: *He is interested in buying the club as a commercial undertaking. ◇ In those days, the trip across country was a dangerous undertaking.* **2** [C] (*formal*) an agreement or a promise to do sth: ~ (**to do sth**) *a government undertaking to spend more on education* ◇ ~ (**that...**) *The landlord gave a written undertaking that the repairs would be carried out.* **3** /ˈʌndəteɪkɪŋ; *NAmE* -dərt-/ [U] the business of an undertaker

ˌ**under-the-ˈcounter** *adj.* (*informal*) illegal

under·tone /ˈʌndətəʊn; *NAmE* ˈʌndərtoʊn/ *noun* ~ (**of sth**) a feeling, quality or meaning that is not expressed directly but is still noticeable from what sb says or does SYN **undercurrent**: *His soft words contained an undertone of warning. ◇ The play does not have the political undertones of the novel.* ➲ compare OVERTONE
IDM **in an ˈundertone** | **in ˈundertones** in a quiet voice

under·took AW *past tense* of UNDERTAKE

under·tow /ˈʌndətəʊ; *NAmE* ˈʌndərtoʊ/ *noun* [usually sing.] **1** a current in the sea or ocean that moves in the opposite direction to the water near the surface: *The children were carried out to sea by the strong undertow.* **2** ~ (**of sth**) a feeling or quality that influences people in a particular situation even though they may not really be aware of it

under·trial /ˈʌndətraɪəl; *NAmE* ˈʌndərt-/ *noun* (*IndE*) a person who has been charged with a crime: *The undertrials will appear in court next week.*

under·used /ˌʌndəˈjuːzd; *NAmE* -dərˈj-/ (also *formal* **under·util·ized**) *adj.* not used as much as it could or should be ▶ **under·use** /ˌʌndəˈjuːs; *NAmE* -dərˈj-/ (also *formal* **under·util·iza·tion**) *noun* [U]

under·util·ized (*BrE* also **-ised**) /ˌʌndəˈjuːtəlaɪzd; *NAmE* -dərˈj-/ *adj.* (*formal*) = UNDERUSED ▶ **under·util·iza·tion**, **-isa·tion** /ˌʌndəˌjuːtəlaɪˈzeɪʃn; *NAmE* -dərˌjuːtələˈz-/ *noun* [U] = UNDERUSE

under·value /ˌʌndəˈvæljuː; *NAmE* -dərˈv-/ *verb* [usually passive] ~ **sb/sth** to not recognize how good, valuable or important sb/sth really is: *Education is currently undervalued in this country. ◇ He believes his house has been undervalued.* OPP **overvalue**

under·water 0‑w /ˌʌndəˈwɔːtə(r); *NAmE* -dərˈw-/ *adj.* [only before noun]
found, used or happening below the surface of water: *underwater creatures ◇ an underwater camera* ▶ **under·water** 0‑w *adv.*: *Take a deep breath and see how long you can stay underwater.*

under·way /ˌʌndəˈweɪ; *NAmE* -dərˈw-/ *adj.* [not before noun]
IDM **underway** = UNDER WAY at WAY

under·wear 0‑w /ˈʌndəweə(r); *NAmE* ˈʌndərwer/ *noun* [U] (also *formal* **under·clothes**, **under·cloth·ing**) clothes that you wear under other clothes and next to the skin: *She packed one change of underwear.*

under·weight /ˌʌndəˈweɪt; *NAmE* -dərˈw-/ *adj.* (especially of a person) weighing less than the normal or expected weight: *She is a few pounds underweight for* (= in relation to) *her height.* OPP **overweight** ➲ COLLOCATIONS at DIET

under·went *past tense* of UNDERGO

under·whelmed /ˌʌndəˈwelmd; *NAmE* -dərˈw-/ *adj.* (*informal*, *humorous*) not impressed with or excited about sth at all: *We were distinctly underwhelmed by the director's speech.* ➲ compare OVERWHELMED

under·whelm·ing /ˌʌndəˈwelmɪŋ; *NAmE* -dərˈw-/ *adj.* (*informal*, *humorous*) not impressing or exciting you at all: *the contrast between his overwhelming guitar-playing and his underwhelming singing*

under·wired /ˌʌndəˈwaɪəd; *NAmE* ˌʌndərˈwaɪərd/ (*BrE*) (*NAmE* **under·wire** /ˌʌndəˈwaɪə(r); *NAmE* ˌʌndərˈwaɪər/) *adj.* (of a BRA) having a thin metal strip sewn into the bottom half of each CUP to improve the shape

under·world /ˈʌndəwɜːld; *NAmE* ˈʌndərwɜːrld/ *noun* [sing.] **1** the people and activities involved in crime in a particular place: *the criminal underworld ◇ the Glasgow underworld* **2 the underworld** (in MYTHS and LEGENDS, for example those of ancient Greece) the place under the earth where people are believed to go when they die

under·write /ˌʌndəˈraɪt; *NAmE* -dərˈr-/ *verb* (under·wrote /-ˈrəʊt; *NAmE* -ˈroʊt/, under·writ·ten /-ˈrɪtn/) (*technical*) **1** ~ **sth** to accept financial responsibility for an activity so that you will pay for special costs or for losses it may make **2** ~ **sth** to accept responsibility for an insurance policy so that you will pay money in case loss or damage happens **3** ~ **sth** to agree to buy shares that are not bought by the public when new shares are offered for sale

under·writer /ˈʌndəraɪtə(r)/ *noun* **1** a person or organization that underwrites insurance policies, especially for ships **2** a person whose job is to estimate the risks involved in a particular activity and decide how much sb must pay for insurance

un·des·cend·ed /ˌʌndɪˈsendɪd/ *adj.* (*medical*) (of a TESTICLE) staying inside the body instead of moving down normally into the SCROTUM

un·deserved /ˌʌndɪˈzɜːvd; *NAmE* -ˈzɜːrvd/ *adj.* that sb does not deserve and therefore unfair: *The criticism was totally undeserved. ◇ an undeserved victory* ▶ **un·deserved·ly** /-dɪˈzɜːvɪdli; *NAmE* -ˈzɜːrv-/ *adv.*

un·deserv·ing /ˌʌndɪˈzɜːvɪŋ; *NAmE* -ˈzɜːrv-/ *adj.* ~ (**of sth**) (*formal*) not deserving to have or receive sth: *He was undeserving of her affections.* OPP **deserving**

un·desir·able /ˌʌndɪˈzaɪərəbl/ *adj.*, *noun*
■ *adj.* not wanted or approved of; likely to cause trouble or problems: ***undesirable consequences/effects** ◇ It would be highly undesirable to increase class sizes further. ◇ prostitution and other undesirable practices* OPP **desirable** ▶ **un·desir·ably** /-əbli/ *adv.*
■ *noun* [usually pl.] a person who is not wanted in a particular place, especially because they are considered dangerous or criminal: *He's been mixing with drug addicts and other undesirables.*

un·detect·able /ˌʌndɪˈtektəbl/ *adj.* impossible to see or find: *The sound is virtually undetectable to the human ear.* OPP **detectable**

un·detect·ed /ˌʌndɪˈtektɪd/ *adj.* not noticed by anyone: *How could anyone break into the palace undetected? ◇ The disease often **goes/remains undetected** for many years.*

un·deterred /ˌʌndɪˈtɜːd; *NAmE* -ˈtɜːrd/ *adj.* if sb is **undeterred** by sth, they do not allow it to stop them from doing sth

un·devel·oped /ˌʌndɪˈveləpt/ *adj.* **1** (of land) not used for farming, industry, building, etc. **2** (of a country) not having modern industries, and with a low standard of liv-

U

ing **3** not grown to full size: *undeveloped limbs* ➲ compare UNDERDEVELOPED

un·did *past tense of* UNDO

un·dies /ˈʌndiz/ *noun* [pl.] (*informal*) underwear

un·dif·fer·en·ti·ated /ˌʌndɪfəˈrenʃieɪtɪd/ *adj.* having parts that you cannot distinguish between; not split into different parts or sections: *a view of society as an undifferentiated whole* ◇ *an undifferentiated target audience*

un·dig·ni·fied /ʌnˈdɪɡnɪfaɪd/ *adj.* causing you to look silly and to lose the respect of other people: *There was an undignified scramble for the best seats.* OPP **dignified**

un·diluted /ˌʌndaɪˈluːtɪd; *BrE* also -ˈljuːtɪd/ *adj.* **1** (of a liquid) not made weaker by having water added to it; not having been DILUTED **2** (of a feeling or quality) not mixed or combined with anything and therefore very strong SYN **unadulterated**

un·dimin·ished AW /ˌʌndɪˈmɪnɪʃt/ *adj.* that has not become smaller or weaker: *They continued with undiminished enthusiasm.*

un·dis·charged /ˌʌndɪsˈtʃɑːdʒd; *NAmE* -ˈtʃɑːrdʒd/ *adj.* (*law*) an **undischarged** BANKRUPT is a person who has been officially stated to be bankrupt by a court but who still has to pay his or her debts

un·dis·cip·lined /ʌnˈdɪsəplɪnd/ *adj.* lacking control and organization; behaving badly OPP **disciplined**

un·dis·closed /ˌʌndɪsˈkləʊzd; *NAmE* -ˈkloʊzd/ *adj.* not made known or told to anyone; not having been DISCLOSED: *He was paid an undisclosed sum.*

un·dis·cov·ered /ˌʌndɪsˈkʌvəd; *NAmE* -ərd/ *adj.* that has not been found or noticed; that has not been discovered: *a previously undiscovered talent*

un·dis·guised /ˌʌndɪsˈɡaɪzd/ *adj.* (especially of a feeling) that you do not try to hide from other people; not DISGUISED: *a look of undisguised admiration*

un·dis·mayed /ˌʌndɪsˈmeɪd/ *adj.* [not before noun] (*formal*) not worried or frightened by sth unpleasant or unexpected SYN **undaunted**

un·dis·puted /ˌʌndɪˈspjuːtɪd/ *adj.* **1** that cannot be questioned or proved to be false; that cannot be DISPUTED SYN **irrefutable**: *undisputed facts* **2** that everyone accepts or recognizes: *the undisputed champion of the world*

un·dis·tin·guished /ˌʌndɪˈstɪŋɡwɪʃt/ *adj.* not very interesting, successful or attractive: *an undistinguished career* OPP **distinguished**

un·dis·turbed /ˌʌndɪˈstɜːbd; *NAmE* -ˈstɜːrbd/ *adj.* **1** [not usually before noun] not moved or touched by anyone or anything SYN **untouched**: *The treasure had lain undisturbed for centuries.* **2** not interrupted by anyone SYN **uninterrupted**: *She succeeded in working undisturbed for a few hours.* **3** [not usually before noun] **~ (by sth)** not affected or upset by sth SYN **unconcerned**: *He seemed undisturbed by the news of her death.* ➲ compare DISTURBED

un·div·ided /ˌʌndɪˈvaɪdɪd/ *adj.* **1** not split into smaller parts; not divided: *an undivided Church* **2** [usually before noun] total; complete; not divided: *undivided loyalty* ◇ *You must be prepared to give the job your* ***undivided attention.***

undo 0‑ /ʌnˈduː/ *verb* (**un·does** /ʌnˈdʌz/, **un·did** /ʌnˈdɪd/, **un·done** /ʌnˈdʌn/)
1 0‑ **~ sth** to open sth that is fastened, tied or wrapped: *to* ***undo a button/knot/zip, etc.*** ◇ *to* ***undo a jacket/shirt, etc.*** ◇ *I undid the package and took out the books.* OPP **do up** **2 ~ sth** to cancel the effect of sth: *He undid most of the good work of the previous manager.* ◇ *It's not too late to try and* ***undo*** *some of* ***the damage.*** ◇ *UNDO* (= a command on a computer that cancels the previous action) **3** [usually passive] **~ sb/sth** (*formal*) to make sb/sth fail: *The team was undone by the speed and strength of their opponents.*

un·dock /ʌnˈdɒk; *NAmE* -ˈdɑːk/ *verb* **~ sth** (*computing*) to remove a computer from a DOCKING STATION OPP **dock**

un·docu·ment·ed /ˌʌnˈdɒkjumentɪd; *NAmE* -ˈdɑːk-/ *adj.* **1** not supported by written evidence: *undocumented accusations* **2** not having the necessary documents, especially permission to live and work in a foreign country: *undocumented immigrants*

un·do·ing /ʌnˈduːɪŋ/ *noun* [sing.] the reason why sb fails at sth or is unsuccessful in life SYN **downfall**: *That one mistake was his undoing.*

un·done /ʌnˈdʌn/ *adj.* [not usually before noun] **1** (especially of clothing) not fastened or tied: *Her blouse had* ***come undone.*** **2** (especially of work) not finished: *Most of the work had been left undone.* **3** (*old use*) (of a person) defeated and without any hope for the future

un·doubt·ed /ʌnˈdaʊtɪd/ *adj.* [usually before noun] used to emphasize that sth exists or is definitely true SYN **indubitable**: *She has an undoubted talent as an organizer.* ▸ **un·doubt·ed·ly** *adv.*: *There is undoubtedly a great deal of truth in what he says.*

undreamed-of /ʌnˈdriːmd ɒv; *NAmE* ʌv/ (also **undreamt-of** /ʌnˈdremt ɒv; *NAmE* ʌv/ especially in *BrE*) *adj.* much more or much better than you thought was possible: *undreamed-of success*

un·dress /ʌnˈdres/ *verb, noun*
■ ***verb*** [I, T] to take off your clothes; to remove sb else's clothes: *She undressed and got into bed.* ◇ **~ sb** *to undress a child* ◇ *He* ***got undressed*** *in a small cubicle next to the pool.* OPP **dress**
■ ***noun*** [U] (*formal*) the fact of sb wearing no, or few, clothes: *He appeared at the window in a* ***state of undress.***

un·dressed /ʌnˈdrest/ *adj.* [not usually before noun] not wearing any clothes: *She began to* ***get undressed*** (= remove her clothes). OPP **dressed**

un·drink·able /ʌnˈdrɪŋkəbl/ *adj.* not good or pure enough to drink OPP **drinkable**

undue /ˌʌnˈdjuː; *NAmE* ˌʌnˈduː/ *adj.* [only before noun] (*formal*) more than you think is reasonable or necessary SYN **excessive**: *They are taking undue advantage of the situation.* ◇ *The work should be carried out without undue delay.* ◇ *We did not want to put any undue pressure on them.* ➲ compare DUE *adj.* (6)

un·du·late /ˈʌndjuleɪt; *NAmE* -dʒə-/ *verb* [I] (*formal*) to go or move gently up and down like waves: *The countryside undulates pleasantly.*

un·du·la·tion /ˌʌndjuˈleɪʃn; *NAmE* -dʒə-/ *noun* [C, U] a smooth curving shape or movement like a series of waves

un·duly /ˌʌnˈdjuːli; *NAmE* ˌʌnˈduːli/ *adv.* (*formal*) more than you think is reasonable or necessary SYN **excessively**: *He did not sound unduly worried at the prospect.* ◇ *The levels of pollution in this area are unduly high.* ◇ *The thought did not disturb her unduly.* ➲ compare DULY

un·dying /ʌnˈdaɪɪŋ/ *adj.* [only before noun] lasting for ever SYN **eternal**: *undying love*

un·earned /ˌʌnˈɜːnd; *NAmE* ˌʌnˈɜːrnd/ *adj.* [usually before noun] used to describe money that you receive but do not earn by working: *Declare all* ***unearned income.***

un·earth /ʌnˈɜːθ; *NAmE* ʌnˈɜːrθ/ *verb* **1 ~ sth** to find sth in the ground by digging SYN **dig up**: *to unearth buried treasures* **2 ~ sth** to find or discover sth by chance or after searching for it SYN **dig up**: *I unearthed my old diaries when we moved house.* ◇ *The newspaper has unearthed some disturbing facts.*

un·earth·ly /ʌnˈɜːθli; *NAmE* -ˈɜːrθ-/ *adj.* [usually before noun] very strange; not natural and therefore frightening: *an unearthly cry* ◇ *an unearthly light*
IDM **at an unearthly 'hour** (*informal*) very early, especially when this is annoying: *The job involved getting up at some unearthly hour to catch the first train.*

un·ease /ʌnˈiːz/ (also **un·easi·ness** /ʌnˈiːzinəs/) *noun* [U, sing.] the feeling of being worried or unhappy about sth SYN **anxiety**: *a deep* ***feeling/sense of unease*** ◇ *There was a growing unease about their involvement in the war.* ◇ *He was unable to hide his unease at the way the situation was developing.*

un·easy /ʌnˈiːzi/ *adj.* **1** feeling worried or unhappy about a particular situation, especially because you think that sth bad or unpleasant may happen or because you are not

U

sure that what you are doing is right SYN **anxious**: *an uneasy laugh* ◇ **~ about sth** *He was beginning to feel distinctly uneasy about their visit.* ◇ **~ about doing sth** *She felt uneasy about leaving the children with them.* ➲ SYNONYMS at WORRIED **2** not certain to last; not safe or settled: *an uneasy peace* ◇ *The two sides eventually reached an uneasy compromise.* **3** that does not enable you to relax or feel comfortable: *She woke from an* ***uneasy sleep*** *to find the house empty.* **4** used to describe a mixture of two things, feelings, etc. that do not go well together: *an* ***uneasy mix*** *of humour and violence* ◇ *Old farmhouses and new villas stood together in uneasy proximity.* ▶ **un·eas·ily** /ʌnˈiːzɪli/ *adv.*: *I wondered uneasily what he was thinking.* ◇ *She shifted uneasily in her chair.* ◇ *His socialist views* ***sit uneasily*** *with his huge fortune.*

un·eat·able /ʌnˈiːtəbl/ *adj.* (of food) not good enough to be eaten ➲ see also INEDIBLE

un·eat·en /ʌnˈiːtn/ *adj.* not eaten: *Bill put the uneaten food away.*

un·eco·nom·ic /ˌʌnˌiːkəˈnɒmɪk; ˌʌnˌek-; *NAmE* -ˈnɑːm-/ *adj.* **1** (of a business, factory, etc.) not making a profit SYN **unprofitable**: *uneconomic industries* OPP **economic** **2** = UNECONOMICAL

un·eco·nom·ic·al AW /ˌʌnˌiːkəˈnɒmɪkl; ˌʌnˌek-; *NAmE* -ˈnɑːm-/ (also **un·eco·nom·ic**) *adj.* **~ (to do sth)** using too much time or money, or too many materials, and therefore not likely to make a profit: *It soon proved uneconomical to stay open 24 hours a day.* OPP **economical**

un·edify·ing /ʌnˈedɪfaɪɪŋ/ *adj.* (*formal, especially BrE*) unpleasant in a way that makes you feel disapproval: *the unedifying sight of the two party leaders screeching at each other* ➲ compare EDIFYING

un·edu·cated /ʌnˈedʒukeɪtɪd/ *adj.* having had little or no formal education at a school; showing a lack of education: *an uneducated workforce* ◇ *an uneducated point of view* ➲ compare EDUCATED

un·elect·ed /ˌʌnɪˈlektɪd/ *adj.* not having been chosen by people in an election: *unelected bureaucrats*

un·emo·tion·al /ˌʌnɪˈməʊʃənl; *NAmE* -ˈmoʊ-/ *adj.* not showing your feelings: *an unemotional speech* ◇ *She seemed very cool and unemotional.* OPP **emotional** ▶ **un·emo·tion·al·ly** *adv.*

un·employ·able /ˌʌnɪmˈplɔɪəbl/ *adj.* lacking the skills or qualities that you need to get a job OPP **employable**

un·employed 0-π /ˌʌnɪmˈplɔɪd/ *adj.* without a job although able to work SYN **jobless**: *How long have you been unemployed?* ◇ *an unemployed builder* ➲ COLLOCATIONS at UNEMPLOYMENT ▶ **the un·employed** 0-π *noun* [pl.]: *a programme to get the* ***long-term unemployed*** *back to work* ◇ *I've joined the ranks of the unemployed* (= I've lost my job).

U

un·employ·ment 0-π /ˌʌnɪmˈplɔɪmənt/ *noun* [U] **1** 0-π the fact of a number of people not having a job; the number of people without a job: *an area of* ***high/low unemployment*** ◇ ***rising/falling unemployment*** ◇ *It was a time of* ***mass unemployment.*** ◇ *measures to help* ***reduce/tackle unemployment*** ◇ *the* ***level/rate of unemployment*** ◇ ***unemployment benefit/statistics*** ➲ COLLOCATIONS at ECONOMY **2** 0-π the state of not having a job: *Thousands of young people are facing* ***long-term unemployment.*** ➲ compare EMPLOYMENT **3** (*US*) = UNEMPLOYMENT BENEFIT: *Since losing his job, Mike has been collecting unemployment.*

unem'ployment benefit (*BrE*) (*US* **unem,ployment compen'sation, unemployment**) *noun* [U] (also **unem'ployment benefits** [pl.]) money paid by the government to sb who is unemployed: *people on* (= receiving) *unemployment benefit* ◇ *Applications for unemployment benefits dropped last month.* ➲ see also JOBSEEKER'S ALLOWANCE

un·en·cum·bered /ˌʌnɪnˈkʌmbəd; *NAmE* -bərd/ *adj.* **1** not having or carrying anything heavy or anything that makes you go more slowly **2** (of property) not having any debts left to be paid

Collocations

Unemployment

Losing your job

- **lose** your job
- (*BrE*) **become/be made** redundant
- **be offered/take** voluntary redundancy/early retirement
- **face/be threatened with** dismissal/(*BrE*) the sack/(*BrE*) compulsory redundancy
- **dismiss/fire/**(*especially BrE*) **sack** an employee/a worker/a manager
- **lay off** staff/workers/employees
- (*AustralE, NZE, SAfrE*) **retrench** workers
- **cut/reduce/downsize/slash** the workforce
- (*BrE*) **make** staff/workers/employees redundant

Being unemployed

- **be** unemployed/out of work/out of a job
- **seek/look for** work/employment
- **be on/collect/draw/get/receive** (*both BrE*) unemployment benefit/jobseeker's allowance
- **be/go/live/sign** (*BrE, informal*) on the dole
- **claim/draw/get** (*BrE, informal*) the dole
- **be on/qualify for** (*NAmE*) unemployment (compensation)
- **be/go/live/depend** (*NAmE*) on welfare
- **collect/receive** (*NAmE*) welfare
- **combat/tackle/cut/reduce** unemployment

un·end·ing /ʌnˈendɪŋ/ *adj.* seeming to last for ever: *a seemingly unending supply of money*

un·en·dur·able /ˌʌnɪnˈdjʊərəbl; *NAmE* -ˈdʊr-/ *adj.* (*formal*) too bad, unpleasant, etc. to bear SYN **unbear·able**: *unendurable pain*

un·envi·able /ʌnˈenviəbl/ *adj.* [usually before noun] difficult or unpleasant; that you would not want to have: *She was given the* ***unenviable task*** *of informing the losers.* OPP **enviable**

un·equal /ʌnˈiːkwəl/ *adj.* **1** [usually before noun] in which people are treated in different ways or have different advantages in a way that seems unfair SYN **unfair**: *an unequal distribution of wealth* ◇ *an unequal contest* **2 ~ (in sth)** different in size, amount, etc: *The sleeves are unequal in length.* ◇ *The rooms upstairs are of unequal size.* **3 ~ to sth** (*formal*) not capable of doing sth: *She felt unequal to the task she had set herself.* OPP **equal** ▶ **un·equal·ly** /-kwəli/ *adv.*

un·equalled (*US* **un·equaled**) /ʌnˈiːkwəld/ *adj.* better than all others SYN **unparalleled**: *an unequalled record of success*

un·equivo·cal /ˌʌnɪˈkwɪvəkl/ *adj.* (*formal*) expressing your opinion or intention very clearly and firmly SYN **unambiguous**: *an unequivocal rejection* ◇ *The answer was an unequivocal 'no'.* OPP **equivocal** ➲ SYNONYMS at PLAIN ▶ **un·equivo·cal·ly** /-kəli/ *adv.*

un·err·ing /ʌnˈɜːrɪŋ/ *adj.* always right or accurate SYN **unfailing**: *She had an unerring instinct for a good business deal.* ▶ **un·err·ing·ly** *adv.*

UNESCO /juːˈneskəʊ; *NAmE* -koʊ/ (also **Unesco**) *abbr.* United Nations Educational, Scientific and Cultural Organization

un·eth·ic·al AW /ʌnˈeθɪkl/ *adj.* not morally acceptable: *unethical behaviour* OPP **ethical** ▶ **un·eth·ic·al·ly** /-kli/ *adv.*

un·even /ʌnˈiːvn/ *adj.* **1** not level, smooth or flat: *The floor felt uneven under his feet.* OPP **even** **2** not following a regular pattern; not having a regular size and shape SYN **irregular**: *Her breathing was quick and uneven.* ◇ *uneven teeth* OPP **even** **3** not having the same quality in all parts: *an uneven performance* (= with some good parts and some bad parts) **4** (of a contest or match) in which one group, team or player is much better than the other SYN **unequal** OPP **even** **5** organized in a way that is not regular and/or fair SYN **unequal**: *an uneven distribution of resources* OPP **even** ▸ **un·even·ly** *adv.* **un·even·ness** *noun* [U]

un,even 'bars (*NAmE*) (*BrE* **asym,metric 'bars**) *noun* [pl.] two bars on posts of different heights that are used by women for doing GYMNASTIC exercises on

un·event·ful /ˌʌnɪ'ventfl/ *adj.* in which nothing interesting, unusual or exciting happens: *an uneventful life* OPP **eventful** ▸ **un·event·ful·ly** /-fəli/ *adv.*: *The day passed uneventfully.*

un·ex·cep·tion·able /ˌʌnɪk'sepʃənəbl/ *adj.* **1** (*formal*) not giving any reason for criticism: *a man of unexceptionable character* **2** (*informal*) not very new or exciting

un·ex·cep·tion·al /ˌʌnɪk'sepʃənl/ *adj.* not interesting or unusual SYN **unremarkable** ➲compare EXCEPTIONAL

un·ex·cit·ing /ˌʌnɪk'saɪtɪŋ/ *adj.* not interesting; boring OPP **exciting**

un·ex·pect·ed 0→ /ˌʌnɪk'spektɪd/ *adj.* if sth is **unexpected**, it surprises you because you were not expecting it: *an unexpected result* ◇ *an unexpected visitor* ◇ *The announcement was not **entirely unexpected**.* ▸ **the unexpected** 0→ *noun* [sing.]: *Police officers must be prepared for the unexpected.* **un·ex·pec·ted·ly** 0→ *adv.*: *They had arrived unexpectedly.* ◇ *an unexpectedly large bill* ◇ *The plane was unexpectedly delayed.* ◇ *Not unexpectedly, most local business depends on tourism.* **un·ex·pect·ed·ness** *noun* [U] ➲compare EXPECT, EXPECTED

un·ex·pired /ˌʌnɪk'spaɪəd; *NAmE* -'spaɪərd/ *adj.* [usually before noun] (of an agreement or a period of time) still valid; not yet having come to an end or EXPIRED

un·ex·plained /ˌʌnɪk'spleɪnd/ *adj.* for which the reason or cause is not known; that has not been explained: *an unexplained mystery* ◇ *He died in unexplained circumstances.*

un·ex·ploded /ˌʌnɪk'spləʊdɪd; *NAmE* -'sploʊ-/ *adj.* [only before noun] (of a bomb, etc.) that has not yet exploded

un·ex·plored /ˌʌnɪk'splɔːd; *NAmE* -'splɔːrd/ *adj.* **1** (of a country or an area of land) that nobody has investigated or put on a map; that has not been explored **2** (of an idea, a theory, etc.) that has not yet been examined or discussed thoroughly

un·ex·pressed /ˌʌnɪk'sprest/ *adj.* (of a thought, a feeling or an idea) not shown or made known in words, looks or actions; not expressed

un·ex·pur·gated /ˌʌn'ekspəgeɪtɪd; *NAmE* -pərg-/ *adj.* (of a text) complete and containing all the original material, even if it is offensive: *This is the full unexpurgated version of the diaries.*

un·fail·ing /ʌn'feɪlɪŋ/ *adj.* that you can rely on to always be there and always be the same: *unfailing support* ◇ *She fought the disease with **unfailing good humour**.* ▸ **un·fail·ing·ly** *adv.*: *unfailingly loyal/polite*

un·fair 0→ /ˌʌn'feə(r); *NAmE* -'fer/ *adj.* not right or fair according to a set of rules or principles; not treating people equally SYN **unjust**: *unfair criticism* ◇ **~** (**on/to sb**) *It seems unfair on him to make him pay for everything.* ◇ *It would **be unfair** not to let you have a choice.* ◇ *They had been given an **unfair advantage**.* ◇ ***unfair dismissal*** (= a situation in which sb is illegally dismissed from their job) ◇ *measures to prevent unfair competition between member countries* ◇ *Life seems so unfair sometimes.* ◇ *It's so unfair!* OPP **fair** ▸ **un·fair·ly** 0→ *adv.*: *She claims to have been unfairly dismissed.* ◇ *The tests discriminate unfairly against older people.* **un·fair·ness** *noun* [U]

un·faith·ful /ʌn'feɪθfl/ *adj.* **~** (**to sb**) having sex with sb who is not your husband, wife or usual partner: *Have you ever been unfaithful to him?* OPP **faithful** ▸ **un·faith·ful·ness** *noun* [U]

un·famil·iar /ˌʌnfə'mɪliə(r)/ *adj.* **1** that you do not know or recognize: *She felt uneasy in the unfamiliar surroundings.* ◇ **~ to sb** *Please highlight any terms that are unfamiliar to you.* **2 ~ with sth** not having any knowledge or experience of sth: *an introductory course for students who are unfamiliar with computers* OPP **familiar** ▸ **un·famili·ar·ity** /ˌʌnfəˌmɪli'ærəti/ *noun* [U]

un·fash·ion·able /ʌn'fæʃnəbl/ *adj.* not popular or fashionable at a particular time: *an unfashionable part of London* ◇ *unfashionable ideas* OPP **fashionable** ▸ **un·fash·ion·ably** *adv.*: *a man with unfashionably long hair*

un·fas·ten /ʌn'fɑːsn; *NAmE* ʌn'fæsn/ *verb* **~ sth** to undo sth that is fastened: *to unfasten a belt/button, etc.* OPP **fasten**

un·fath·om·able /ʌn'fæðəməbl/ *adj.* (*formal*) **1** too strange or difficult to be understood: *an unfathomable mystery* **2** if sb has an **unfathomable** expression, it is impossible to know what they are thinking

un·favour·able (*especially US* **un·favor·able**) /ʌn'feɪvərəbl/ *adj.* (*formal*) **1 ~** (**for/to sth**) (of conditions, situations, etc.) not good and likely to cause problems or make sth more difficult: *The conditions were unfavourable for agriculture.* ◇ *an unfavourable exchange rate* **2** showing that you do not approve of or like sb/sth: *an unfavourable comment* ◇ *The documentary presents him in a very **unfavourable light**.* ◇ *an **unfavourable comparison*** (= one that makes one thing seem much worse than another) OPP **favourable** ▸ **un·favour·ably** (*BrE*) (*NAmE* **un·favor·ably**) *adv.*: *In this respect, Britain **compares unfavourably** with other European countries.*

un·fazed /ʌn'feɪzd/ *adj.* (*informal*) not worried or surprised by sth unexpected that happens OPP **fazed**

un·feas·ible /ʌn'fiːzəbl/ *adj.* not possible to do or achieve OPP **feasible**

un·feel·ing /ʌn'fiːlɪŋ/ *adj.* not showing care or sympathy for other people

un·feigned /ʌn'feɪnd/ *adj.* (*formal*) real and sincere SYN **genuine**: *unfeigned admiration*

un·fenced /ʌn'fenst/ *adj.* (of a road or piece of land) without fences beside or around it

un·fet·tered /ʌn'fetəd; *NAmE* -tərd/ *adj.* (*formal*) not controlled or restricted: *an unfettered free market*

un·filled /ʌn'fɪld/ *adj.* **1** if a job or position is **unfilled**, nobody has been chosen for it **2** if a pause in a conversation is **unfilled**, nobody speaks **3** an **unfilled** cake has nothing inside it **4** (*especially NAmE*) if an order for goods is **unfilled**, the goods have not been supplied

un·fin·ished /ʌn'fɪnɪʃt/ *adj.* not complete; not finished: *We have some **unfinished business** to settle.*

unfit /ʌn'fɪt/ *adj.* **1** not of an acceptable standard; not suitable: **~** (**for sth**) *The housing was **unfit for human habitation**.* ◇ *The food on offer was **unfit for human consumption**.* ◇ **~** (**to eat, drink, live in, etc.**) *This water is unfit to drink.* ◇ *Most of the buildings are unfit to live in.* ◇ **~** (**to do sth**) *They described him as unfit to govern.* ◇ (*technical*) *Many of the houses were condemned as unfit.* ◇ (*technical*) *The court claims she is an unfit mother.* **2** not capable of doing sth, for example because of illness: **~ for sth** *He's still unfit for work.* ◇ **~ to do sth** *The company's doctor found that she was unfit to carry out her normal work.* **3** (*especially BrE*) (of a person) not in good physical condition; not fit, because you have not taken exercise: *The captain is still unfit and will miss tonight's game.* OPP **fit** ▸ **un·fit·ness** *noun* [U]

un·fit·ted /ʌn'fɪtɪd/ *adj.* **~ for sth** | **~ to do sth** (*formal*) not suitable for sth: *She felt herself unfitted for marriage.*

un·flag·ging /ˌʌn'flægɪŋ/ *adj.* [usually before noun] remaining strong; not becoming weak or tired SYN **tireless**: *unflagging energy*

un·flap·pable /ˌʌn'flæpəbl/ *adj.* (*informal*) able to stay calm in a difficult situation SYN **imperturbable**

un·flat·ter·ing /ʌn'flætərɪŋ/ *adj.* making sb/sth seem worse or less attractive than they really are: *an unflattering dress* ◇ *unflattering comments* OPP **flattering**

U

un·flinch·ing /ʌnˈflɪntʃɪŋ/ *adj.* remaining strong and determined, even in a difficult or dangerous situation **SYN steadfast**: *unflinching loyalty* ◇ *an unflinching stare* ▸ **un·flinch·ing·ly** *adv.* ➲ see also FLINCH

un·focused (also **un·focussed**) /ʌnˈfəʊkəst; *NAmE* -ˈfoʊ-/ *adj.* **1** (especially of eyes) not looking at a particular thing or person; not having been focused: *an unfocused look* **2** (of plans, work, etc.) not having a clear aim or purpose; not well organized or clear: *The research is too unfocused to have any significant impact.* ◇ *unfocused questions*

un·fold /ʌnˈfəʊld; *NAmE* ʌnˈfoʊld/ *verb* **1** [T, I] **~ (sth)** to spread open or flat sth that has previously been folded; to become open and flat: *to unfold a map* ◇ *She unfolded her arms.* **OPP fold** **2** [I, T] to be gradually made known; to gradually make sth known to other people: *The audience watched as* ***the story unfolded*** *before their eyes.* ◇ **~ sth (to sb)** *She unfolded her tale to us.*

un·forced /ʌnˈfɔːst; *NAmE* ʌnˈfɔːrst/ *adj.* **1** (especially in sports) an **unforced** error is one that you make by playing badly, not because your opponent has caused you to make a mistake by their skilful play **2** natural; done without effort: *unforced humour*

un·fore·see·able /ˌʌnfɔːˈsiːəbl; *NAmE* -fɔːrˈs-/ *adj.* that you cannot predict or FORESEE: *Building a dam here could have* ***unforeseeable consequences*** *for the environment.* **OPP foreseeable**

un·fore·seen /ˌʌnfɔːˈsiːn; *NAmE* -fɔːrˈs-/ *adj.* that you did not expect to happen **SYN unexpected**: ***unforeseen delays/problems*** ◇ *The project was running late owing to* ***unforeseen circumstances.*** ➲ compare FORESEE

un·for·get·table /ˌʌnfəˈgetəbl; *NAmE* -fərˈg-/ *adj.* if sth is **unforgettable**, you cannot forget it, usually because it is so beautiful, interesting, enjoyable, etc. **SYN memorable** ➲ compare FORGETTABLE

un·for·giv·able /ˌʌnfəˈgɪvəbl; *NAmE* -fərˈg-/ *adj.* if sb's behaviour is **unforgivable**, it is so bad or unacceptable that you cannot forgive the person **SYN inexcusable** **OPP forgivable** ▸ **un·for·giv·ably** *adv.*

un·for·giv·ing /ˌʌnfəˈgɪvɪŋ; *NAmE* -fərˈg-/ *adj.* (*formal*) **1** (of a person) unwilling to forgive other people when they have done sth wrong **OPP forgiving** **2** (of a place, situation, etc.) unpleasant and causing difficulties for people

un·formed /ˌʌnˈfɔːmd; *NAmE* ˌʌnˈfɔːrmd/ *adj.* (*formal*) not fully developed: *unformed ideas*

un·forth·com·ing /ˌʌnfɔːθˈkʌmɪŋ; *NAmE* -fɔːrθ-/ *adj.* not wanting to help or give information about sth **SYN reticent**: *He was very unforthcoming about what had happened.* **OPP forthcoming**

un·for·tu·nate 0-w /ʌnˈfɔːtʃənət; *NAmE* -ˈfɔːrtʃ-/ *adj., noun*

U

- ***adj.*** **1** 0-w having bad luck; caused by bad luck **SYN unlucky**: *He was unfortunate to lose in the final round.* ◇ *It was an unfortunate accident.* **OPP fortunate** **2** 0-w (*formal*) if you say that a situation is **unfortunate**, you wish that it had not happened or that it had been different **SYN regrettable**: *She described the decision as 'unfortunate'.* ◇ *It was unfortunate that he couldn't speak English.* ◇ *You're putting me in a* ***most unfortunate*** *position.* ➲ LANGUAGE BANK at IMPERSONAL **3** embarrassing and/or offensive: *It was an unfortunate choice of words.*
- ***noun*** (*literary*) a person who does not have much luck, money, etc: *one of life's unfortunates*

un·for·tu·nate·ly 0-w /ʌnˈfɔːtʃənətli; *NAmE* -ˈfɔːrtʃ-/ *adv.* used to say that a particular situation or fact makes you sad or disappointed, or gets you into a difficult position **SYN regrettably**: *Unfortunately, I won't be able to attend the meeting.* ◇ *I can't make it, unfortunately.* ◇ *Unfortunately for him, the police had been informed and were waiting outside.* ◇ *It won't be finished for a few weeks. Unfortunately!* **OPP fortunately**

un·found·ed AW /ʌnˈfaʊndɪd/ *adj.* not based on reason or fact: ***unfounded allegations/rumours, etc.*** ◇ *Speculation about a divorce* ***proved*** *totally* ***unfounded.***

un·freeze /ˌʌnˈfriːz/ *verb* (**un·froze** /-ˈfrəʊz; *NAmE* -ˈfroʊz/, **un·frozen** /-ˈfrəʊzn; *NAmE* -ˈfroʊzn/) **1** [T, I] **~ (sth)** if you **unfreeze** sth that has been frozen or very cold, or it **unfreezes**, it melts or warms until it reaches a normal temperature ➲ compare DEFROST, DE-ICE, THAW **2** [T] **~ sth** to remove official controls on money or an economy: *The party plans to unfreeze some of the cash held by local government.* **OPP freeze**

un·friend·ly 0-w /ʌnˈfrendli/ *adj.* not kind or pleasant to sb: *an unfriendly atmosphere* ◇ **~ (to/towards sb)** *There's no need to be so unfriendly towards them.* ◇ *the use of* ***environmentally unfriendly*** *products* (= that harm the environment) **OPP friendly** ▸ **un·friend·li·ness** *noun* [U]

un·ful·filled /ˌʌnfʊlˈfɪld/ *adj.* **1** (of a need, wish, etc.) that has not been satisfied or achieved: ***unfulfilled ambitions/hopes/promises, etc.*** **2** if a person feels **unfulfilled**, they feel that they could achieve more in their life or work **OPP fulfilled**

un·ful·fil·ling /ˌʌnfʊlˈfɪlɪŋ/ *adj.* not causing sb to feel satisfied and useful: *an unfulfilling job*

un·funny /ʌnˈfʌni/ *adj.* not funny or amusing, especially when sth is supposed to be funny: *The show was deeply unfunny.*

un·furl /ˌʌnˈfɜːl; *NAmE* ˌʌnˈfɜːrl/ *verb* [I, T] when sth that is curled or rolled tightly **unfurls**, or you **unfurl** it, it opens: *The leaves slowly unfurled.* ◇ **~ sth** *to unfurl a flag*

un·fur·nished /ʌnˈfɜːnɪʃt; *NAmE* -ˈfɜːrn-/ *adj.* without furniture: *We rented an unfurnished apartment.* **OPP furnished**

un·gain·ly /ʌnˈgeɪnli/ *adj.* moving in a way that is not smooth or elegant **SYN awkward**: *He was a tall, ungainly boy of 18.*

un·gentle·man·ly /ʌnˈdʒentlmənli/ *adj.* (of a man's behaviour) not polite or pleasant; not acceptable **OPP gentlemanly**

un·glam·or·ous /ʌnˈglæmərəs/ *adj.* not attractive or exciting; dull: *an unglamorous job* **OPP glamorous**

un·glued /ʌnˈgluːd/ *adj.*
IDM **come unˈglued** (*NAmE, informal*) **1** to become very upset **2** if a plan, etc. **comes unglued**, it does not work successfully

un·god·ly /ʌnˈgɒdli; *NAmE* -ˈgɑːd-/ *adj.* (*old-fashioned*) not showing respect for God; evil **OPP godly**
IDM **at an ungodly ˈhour** very early or very late and therefore annoying

un·gov·ern·able /ʌnˈgʌvənəbl; *NAmE* -ˈgʌvərn-/ *adj.* **1** (of a country, region, etc.) impossible to govern or control **2** (*formal*) (of a person's feelings) impossible to control **SYN uncontrollable**: *ungovernable rage*

un·gra·cious /ʌnˈgreɪʃəs/ *adj.* (*formal*) not polite or friendly, especially towards sb who is being kind to you **OPP gracious** ▸ **un·gra·cious·ly** *adv.*

un·gram·mat·ical /ˌʌngrəˈmætɪkl/ *adj.* not following the rules of grammar **OPP grammatical**

un·grate·ful /ʌnˈgreɪtfl/ *adj.* not showing or expressing thanks for sth that sb has done for you or given to you **OPP grateful** ▸ **un·grate·ful·ly** /-fəli/ *adv.*

un·guard·ed /ʌnˈgɑːdɪd; *NAmE* -ˈgɑːrd-/ *adj.* **1** not protected or watched: *The museum was unguarded at night.* ◇ *an unguarded fire* (= that has nothing to stop people from burning themselves on it) **2** (of a remark, look, etc.) said or done carelessly, at a time when you are not thinking about the effects of your words or are not paying attention: *an unguarded remark* ◇ *It was something I'd let out* ***in an unguarded moment.*** ➲ compare GUARDED

un·guent /ˈʌŋgwənt/ *noun* [C, U] (*formal*) a soft substance that is used for rubbing onto the skin to heal it

un·gu·late /ˈʌŋgjʊlət; -leɪt/ *noun* (*technical*) any animal which has HOOFS, such as a cow or horse

un·hand /ˌʌnˈhænd/ *verb* **~ sb** (*old-fashioned* or *humorous*) to release a person that you are holding

un·hap·pily /ʌnˈhæpɪli/ *adv.* **1** in an unhappy way: *He sighed unhappily.* **2** used to say that a particular situation or fact makes you sad or disappointed **SYN** **unfortunately**: *Unhappily, such good luck is rare.* ◇ *His wife, unhappily, died five years ago.* **OPP** **happily**

un·happy /ʌnˈhæpi/ *adj.* (**un·hap·pier**, **un·happi·est**) **HELP** **more unhappy** and **most unhappy** are also common
1 not happy; sad: *to **be/look/seem/sound unhappy*** ◇ *an unhappy childhood* ◇ *I didn't realize but he was **deeply unhappy** at that time.* **2** **~** (**about/at/with sth**) not pleased or satisfied with sth: *They were unhappy with their accommodation.* ◇ *He was unhappy at being left out of the team.* **3** (*formal*) unfortunate or not suitable: *an unhappy coincidence* ◇ *It was an unhappy choice of words.* ▸ **un·hap·pi·ness** *noun* [U]

un·harmed /ʌnˈhɑːmd; *NAmE* ʌnˈhɑːrmd/ *adj.* not injured or damaged; not harmed

UNHCR /ˌjuː en ˌeɪtʃ siː ˈɑː(r)/ *abbr.* United Nations High Commission for Refugees (an organization whose function is to help and protect REFUGEES)

un·healthy /ʌnˈhelθi/ *adj.* **1** not having good health; showing a lack of good health: *They looked poor and unhealthy.* ◇ *unhealthy skin* ◇ *His eyeballs were an unhealthy yellow.* **2** harmful to your health; likely to make you ill/sick: *unhealthy living conditions* ◇ *an **unhealthy diet/lifestyle*** **3** not normal and likely to be harmful **SYN** **unwholesome**: *He had an unhealthy interest in disease and death.* **OPP** **healthy** ▸ **un·health·ily** /-ɪli/ *adv.*

un·heard /ʌnˈhɜːd; *NAmE* ʌnˈhɜːrd/ *adj.* **1** that nobody pays attention to: *Their protests **went unheard**.* **2** not listened to or heard: *a previously unheard tape of their conversations*

unheard-of /ʌnˈhɜːd ɒv; *NAmE* ʌnˈhɜːrd ʌv/ *adj.* that has never been known or done; very unusual: *He'd dyed his hair, which was almost unheard-of in the 1960s.* ◇ *It is almost unheard-of for a new band to be offered such a deal.*

un·heat·ed /ʌnˈhiːtɪd/ *adj.* having no form of heating: *an unheated bathroom* **OPP** **heated**

un·heed·ed /ʌnˈhiːdɪd/ *adj.* (*formal*) that is heard, seen or noticed but then ignored: *Her warning **went unheeded**.* ➲ compare HEED

un·help·ful /ʌnˈhelpfl/ *adj.* not helpful or useful; not willing to help sb: *an unhelpful response* ◇ *The taxi driver was being very unhelpful.* **OPP** **helpful** ▸ **un·help·ful·ly** /-fəli/ *adv.*

un·her·ald·ed /ʌnˈherəldɪd/ *adj.* (*formal*) not previously mentioned; happening without any warning

un·hesi·tat·ing /ʌnˈhezɪteɪtɪŋ/ *adj.* done or given immediately and confidently: *He gave an unhesitating 'yes' when asked if he would go through the experience again.* ▸ **un·hesi·tat·ing·ly** *adv.*

un·hin·dered /ʌnˈhɪndəd; *NAmE* -dərd/ *adj.* without anything stopping or preventing the progress of sb/sth: *She had unhindered access to the files.* ◇ *He was able to **pass unhindered** through several military checkpoints.* ➲ see also HINDER

un·hinge /ʌnˈhɪndʒ/ *verb* [usually passive] **~ sb** to make sb mentally ill

un·hitch /ʌnˈhɪtʃ/ *verb* **~ sth** to undo sth that is tied to sth else: *to unhitch a trailer* ➲ see also HITCH

un·holy /ʌnˈhəʊli; *NAmE* -ˈhoʊ-/ *adj.* **1** dangerous; likely to be harmful: *an **unholy alliance** between the medical profession and the pharmaceutical industry* **2** not respecting the laws of a religion **OPP** **holy** **3** [only before noun] (*informal*) used to emphasize how bad sth is: *She wondered how she had got into this unholy mess.*

un·hook /ʌnˈhʊk/ *verb* **~ sth** (**from sth**) to remove sth from a hook; to undo the hooks on clothes, etc: *He unhooked his coat from the door.* ◇ *She unhooked her bra.*

un·hur·ried /ʌnˈhʌrid; *NAmE* -ˈhɜːr-/ *adj.* (*formal*) relaxed and calm; not done too quickly **OPP** **hurried** ▸ **un·hur·ried·ly** *adv.*: *Lynn walked unhurriedly into the kitchen.*

un·hurt /ʌnˈhɜːt; *NAmE* ʌnˈhɜːrt/ *adj.* [not before noun] not injured or harmed **SYN** **unharmed**: *He escaped from the crash unhurt.* **OPP** **hurt**

un·hygien·ic /ˌʌnhaɪˈdʒiːnɪk; *NAmE* usually -ˈdʒen-/ *adj.* not clean and therefore likely to cause disease or infection **OPP** **hygienic**

uni /ˈjuːni/ *noun* (*BrE, informal*) university: *friends from uni* ◇ *Where were you **at uni**?*

uni- /ˈjuːni/ *combining form* (in nouns, adjectives and adverbs) one; having one: *uniform* ◇ *unilaterally*

uni·cam·eral /ˌjuːnɪˈkæmərəl/ *adj.* (*technical*) (of a parliament) that has only one main governing body

UNICEF /ˈjuːnɪsef/ *abbr.* United Nations Children's Fund (an organization within the United Nations that helps to take care of the health and education of children all over the world)

uni·cel·lu·lar /ˌjuːnɪˈseljələ(r)/ *adj.* (*biology*) (of a living thing) consisting of only one cell: *unicellular organisms*

uni·corn /ˈjuːnɪkɔːn; *NAmE* -kɔːrn/ *noun* (in stories) an animal like a white horse with a long straight horn on its head

uni·cycle /ˈjuːnɪsaɪkl/ (also **mono·cycle**) *noun* a vehicle that is similar to a bicycle but that has only one wheel ➲ VISUAL VOCAB page V41

un·iden·ti·fi·able **AW** /ˌʌnaɪˈdentɪfaɪəbl/ *adj.* impossible to identify: *He had an unidentifiable accent.* ◇ *Many of the bodies were unidentifiable except by dental records.* **OPP** **identifiable**

un·iden·ti·fied /ˌʌnaɪˈdentɪfaɪd/ *adj.* not recognized or known; not identified: *an unidentified virus* ◇ *The painting was sold to an unidentified American dealer* (= his or her name was not given).

ˌUnifiˈcation Church *noun* a religious and political organization begun in Korea in 1954 by Sun Myung Moon

uni·form **AW** /ˈjuːnɪfɔːm; *NAmE* -fɔːrm/ *noun, adj.*

■ ***noun*** **1** [C, U] the special set of clothes worn by all members of an organization or a group at work, or by children at school: *a **military/police/nurse's uniform*** ◇ *soldiers **in uniform*** ◇ *The hat is part of the **school uniform**.* ◇ *Do you have to **wear uniform**?* **2** [C, usually sing., U] (*NAmE*) (*BrE* **strip**) the clothes worn by the members of a sports team when they are playing: *a striped baseball uniform* ◇ *the team's **away uniform*** (= that they use when playing games away from home) **3** [sing., U] the type of clothes that a person or group usually wears: *my standard teenage uniform of sweatshirt and jeans*

■ ***adj.*** not varying; the same in all parts and at all times: *uniform rates of pay* ◇ *The walls were a uniform grey.* ◇ *Growth has not been uniform across the country.* ◇ *uniform lines of terraced houses* (= they all looked the same) ▸ **uni·form·ity** **AW** /ˌjuːnɪˈfɔːməti/ *noun* [U, sing.]: *They tried to ensure uniformity across the different departments.* ◇ *the drab uniformity of the houses* **uni·form·ly** **AW** *adv.*: *The principles were applied uniformly across all the departments.* ◇ *The quality is uniformly high.* ◇ *Pressure must be uniformly distributed over the whole surface.*

uni·formed /ˈjuːnɪfɔːmd; *NAmE* -fɔːrmd/ *adj.* wearing a uniform: *a uniformed chauffeur*

unify **AW** /ˈjuːnɪfaɪ/ *verb* (**uni·fies**, **uni·fy·ing**, **uni·fied**, **uni·fied**) **~ sth** to join people, things, parts of a country, etc. together so that they form a single unit: *The new leader hopes to unify the country.* ◇ *the task of unifying Europe* ◇ *a unified transport system* ▸ **uni·fi·ca·tion** **AW** /ˌjuːnɪfɪˈkeɪʃn/ *noun* [U]: *the unification of Germany*

uni·lat·eral /ˌjuːnɪˈlætrəl/ *adj.* done by one member of a group or an organization without the agreement of the other members: *a unilateral decision* ◇ *a unilateral declaration of independence* ◇ *They were forced to take unilateral action.* ◇ *They had campaigned vigorously for **unilateral***

U

nuclear disarmament (= when one country gets rid of its nuclear weapons without waiting for other countries to do the same). ➲ compare BILATERAL, MULTILATERAL, TRILATERAL ▶ **uni·lat·eral·ly** /-rəli/ *adv.*

uni·lat·eral·ism /ˌjuːnɪˈlætrəlɪzəm/ *noun* [U] belief in or support of unilateral action, especially the policy of getting rid of nuclear weapons without waiting for other countries to do the same ▶ **uni·lat·eral·ist** *noun*: *the defeat of the unilateralists on nuclear disarmament* **uni·lat·eral·ist** *adj.*: *unilateralist defence policy*

un·imagin·able /ˌʌnɪˈmædʒɪnəbl/ *adj.* (*formal*) impossible to think of or to believe exists; impossible to imagine: *unimaginable wealth* ◇ *This level of success would have been unimaginable just last year.* OPP **imaginable** ▶ **un·imagin·ably** *adv.*

un·imagina·tive /ˌʌnɪˈmædʒɪnətɪv/ *adj.* lacking in original or new ideas SYN **dull**: *an unimaginative solution to a problem* ◇ *a boring unimaginative man* OPP **imaginative**

un·im·paired /ˌʌnɪmˈpeəd; *NAmE* -ˈperd/ *adj.* (*formal*) not damaged or spoiled: *Although he's ninety, his mental faculties remain unimpaired.* OPP **impaired**

un·im·peach·able /ˌʌnɪmˈpiːtʃəbl/ *adj.* (*formal, approving*) that you cannot doubt or question: *evidence from an unimpeachable source*

un·im·peded /ˌʌnɪmˈpiːdɪd/ *adj.* (*formal*) with nothing blocking or stopping sb/sth: *an unimpeded view of the bay* ◇ *free and unimpeded trade*

un·im·port·ant 0‑w /ˌʌnɪmˈpɔːtnt; *NAmE* -ˈpɔːrtnt/ *adj.*
not important: *unimportant details* ◇ ***relatively/comparatively unimportant*** ◇ *They dismissed the problem as unimportant.* ◇ *This consideration was not unimportant.* ◇ *I was just a young girl from a small town and I felt very unimportant.* ▶ **un·im·port·ance** *noun* [U]

un·im·pressed /ˌʌnɪmˈprest/ *adj.* ~ (**by/with sb/sth**) not thinking that sb/sth is particularly good, interesting, etc; not impressed by sb/sth

un·im·pres·sive /ˌʌnɪmˈpresɪv/ *adj.* ordinary; not special in any way: *His academic record was unimpressive.* OPP **impressive**

un·inflect·ed /ˌʌnɪnˈflektɪd/ *adj.* (*linguistics*) (of a word or language) not changing its form to show different functions in grammar

un·in·forma·tive /ˌʌnɪnˈfɔːmətɪv; *NAmE* -ˈfɔːrm-/ *adj.* not giving enough information: *The reports of the explosion were brief and uninformative.* OPP **informative**

un·in·formed /ˌʌnɪnˈfɔːmd; *NAmE* -ˈfɔːrmd/ *adj.* having or showing a lack of knowledge or information about sth: *an* ***uninformed comment/criticism*** ◇ *The public is generally uninformed about these diseases.* OPP **informed**

un·in·hab·it·able /ˌʌnɪnˈhæbɪtəbl/ *adj.* not fit to live in; impossible to live in: *The building was totally uninhabitable.* OPP **habitable**

un·in·hab·it·ed /ˌʌnɪnˈhæbɪtɪd/ *adj.* with no people living there; not INHABITED: *an uninhabited island*

un·in·hib·it·ed /ˌʌnɪnˈhɪbɪtɪd/ *adj.* behaving or expressing yourself freely without worrying about what other people think SYN **unrestrained**: *uninhibited dancing* OPP **inhibited**

the un·initi·ated /ˌʌnɪˈnɪʃieɪtɪd/ *noun* [pl.] people who have no special knowledge or experience of sth: *To the uninitiated the system seems too complicated.* ▶ **un·initi·ated** *adj.*

un·in·jured AW /ʌnˈɪndʒəd; *NAmE* -dʒərd/ *adj.* [not usually before noun] not hurt or injured in any way SYN **unhurt**: *They escaped from the crash uninjured.*

un·in·spired /ˌʌnɪnˈspaɪəd; *NAmE* -ˈspaɪərd/ *adj.* not original or exciting SYN **dull** OPP **inspired**

un·in·spir·ing /ˌʌnɪnˈspaɪərɪŋ/ *adj.* not making people interested or excited: *The view from the window was uninspiring.* OPP **inspiring**

un·in·stall /ˌʌnɪnˈstɔːl/ *verb* ~ **sth** (*computing*) to remove a program from a computer: *Uninstall any programs that you no longer need.*

un·in·sur·able /ˌʌnɪnˈʃʊərəbl; -ˈʃɔːrə-; *NAmE* -ˈʃʊrə-/ *adj.* something that is **uninsurable** cannot be given insurance because it involves too much risk

un·in·sured /ˌʌnɪnˈʃʊəd; -ˈʃɔːd; *NAmE* -ˈʃʊrd/ *adj.* not having insurance; not covered by insurance: *an uninsured driver* ◇ *an uninsured claim*

un·in·tel·li·gent AW /ˌʌnɪnˈtelɪdʒənt/ *adj.* not intelligent: *He was not unintelligent, but he was lazy.*

un·in·tel·li·gible /ˌʌnɪnˈtelɪdʒəbl/ *adj.* impossible to understand SYN **incomprehensible**: *She turned away and muttered something unintelligible.* ◇ ~ **to sb** *A lot of the jargon they use is unintelligible to outsiders.* OPP **intelligible** ▶ **un·in·tel·li·gib·ly** /-əbli/ *adv.*

un·in·tend·ed /ˌʌnɪnˈtendɪd/ *adj.* an **unintended** effect, result or meaning is one that you did not plan or intend to happen

un·in·ten·tion·al /ˌʌnɪnˈtenʃənl/ *adj.* not done deliberately, but happening by accident: *Perhaps I misled you, but it was quite unintentional* (= I did not mean to). OPP **intentional** ▶ **un·in·ten·tion·al·ly** /-ʃənəli/ *adv.*: *They had unintentionally provided wrong information.*

un·inter·est·ed /ʌnˈɪntrəstɪd; -trest-/ *adj.* ~ (**in sb/sth**) not interested; not wanting to know about sb/sth: *He was totally uninterested in sport.* ◇ *She seemed cold and uninterested.* ➲ note at INTERESTED

un·inter·est·ing /ʌnˈɪntrəstɪŋ; -trest-/ *adj.* not attracting your attention or interest; not interesting ➲ note at INTERESTED

un·inter·rupt·ed /ˌʌnˌɪntəˈrʌptɪd/ *adj.* not stopped or blocked by anything; continuous and not interrupted: *We had an uninterrupted view of the stage.* ◇ *eight hours of uninterrupted sleep* ◇ *We managed to eat our meal uninterrupted by phone calls.*

un·in·vited /ˌʌnɪnˈvaɪtɪd/ *adj.* doing sth or going somewhere when you have not been asked or invited to, especially when sb does not want you to: *uninvited guests at a party* ◇ *He turned up uninvited.*

un·in·vit·ing /ˌʌnɪnˈvaɪtɪŋ/ *adj.* not attractive or pleasant: *The water looked cold and uninviting.* OPP **inviting**

un·in·volved AW /ˌʌnɪnˈvɒlvd; *NAmE* -ˈvɑːlvd/ *adj.* ~ (**in /with sth**) not taking part in sth; not connected with sb/sth, especially on an emotional level: *My mum was distant and cold and very uninvolved in my life.* OPP **involved**

union 0‑w /ˈjuːniən/ *noun*
1 0‑w (also ˌ**trade** ˈ**union**) (*BrE* also ˌ**trades** ˈ**union**) (*NAmE* also ˈ**labor union**) [C] an organization of workers, usually in a particular industry, that exists to protect their interests, improve conditions of work, etc: *I've* ***joined the union***. ◇ *a* ***union member*** **2** 0‑w [C] an association or a club for people or organizations with the same interest: *the Scottish Rugby Union* ➲ see also STUDENTS' UNION (2) **3** 0‑w [C] a group of states or countries that have the same central government or that agree to work together: *the former Soviet Union* ◇ *the European Union* **4 Union** [sing.] the US (used especially at the time of the Civil War): *the Union and the Confederacy* ◇ *the State of the Union address by the President* **5** 0‑w [U, sing.] the act of joining two or more things together; the state of being joined together; the act of two people joining together: *a summit to discuss economic and monetary union* ◇ *Northern Ireland's union with Britain* ◇ *sexual union* **6** [C] (*old-fashioned*) a marriage: *Their union was blessed with six children.*

union·ist /ˈjuːniənɪst/ *noun* **1** = TRADE UNIONIST **2 Union·ist** a person who believes that Northern Ireland should stay part of the United Kingdom **3 Union·ist** a supporter of the Union during the Civil War in the US ▶ **union·ism** /ˈjuːniənɪzəm/ *noun* [U]

union·ize (*BrE* also **-ise**) /ˈjuːniənaɪz/ *verb* [T, I] ~ (**sth**) to organize people to become members of a TRADE/LABOR UNION; to become a member of a trade/labor union: *a unionized workforce* ◇ *They were forbidden to unionize.*

▸ **union·iza·tion, -isa·tion** /ˌjuːniənaɪˈzeɪʃn; *NAmE* -nəˈz-/ *noun* [U]

the ˌUnion ˈJack *noun* [sing.] the name for the national flag of the United Kingdom

unique 0‑w AW /juˈniːk/ *adj.*
1 0‑w being the only one of its kind: *Everyone's fingerprints are unique.* HELP You can use **absolutely**, **totally** or **almost** with **unique** in this meaning. **2** 0‑w very special or unusual: *a unique talent* ◇ *The preview offers a unique opportunity to see the show without the crowds.* ◇ *The deal will put the company in a unique position to export goods to Eastern Europe.* HELP You can use **more**, **very**, etc. with **unique** in this meaning. **3** 0‑w ~ (**to sb/sth**) belonging to or connected with one particular person, place or thing: *an atmosphere that is unique to New York* ◇ *The koala is unique to Australia.* ▸ **unique·ly** AW *adv.*: *Her past experience made her uniquely suited to lead the campaign.* ◇ *The UK, uniquely, has not had to face the problem of mass unemployment.* ◇ *He was a uniquely gifted teacher.* **unique·ness** AW *noun* [U]: *The author stresses the uniqueness of the individual.*

uni·sex /ˈjuːnɪseks/ *adj.* intended for or used by both men and women: *a unisex hair salon* ◇ *unisex jeans*

uni·son /ˈjuːnɪsn/ *noun*
IDM **in ˈunison (with sb/sth)** **1** if people do or say sth **in unison**, they all do it at the same time **2** if people or organizations are working **in unison**, they are working together, because they agree with each other **3** (*music*) if singers or musicians sing or play **in unison**, they sing or play notes at the same PITCH or at one or more OCTAVES apart

unit 0‑w /ˈjuːnɪt/ *noun*
▸ SINGLE THING **1** 0‑w a single thing, person or group that is complete by itself but can also form part of sth larger: *The cell is the unit of which all living organisms are composed.* ◇ *The **basic unit** of society is the family.* **2** (*business*) a single item of the type of product that a company sells: *The game's selling price was $15 per unit.* ◇ *What's the **unit cost**?*
▸ GROUP OF PEOPLE **3** 0‑w a group of people who work or live together, especially for a particular purpose: ***army/military/police units*** ◇ *Medical units were operating in the disaster area.*
▸ IN HOSPITAL **4** 0‑w a department, especially in a hospital, that provides a particular type of care or treatment: *the intensive care unit* ◇ *a maternity unit*
▸ FURNITURE **5** 0‑w a piece of furniture, especially a cupboard, that fits with and matches others of the same type: *a fitted kitchen with white units* ◇ ***floor/wall units*** ◇ ***bedroom/kitchen/storage units*** ➲ VISUAL VOCAB page V22
▸ MEASUREMENT **6** ~ (**of sth**) a fixed quantity, etc. that is used as a standard measurement: *a **unit of time/length/weight*** ◇ *a **unit of currency**, such as the euro or the dollar* ◇ *Women are advised not to drink more than fourteen units of alcohol per week.*
▸ SMALL MACHINE **7** a small machine that has a particular purpose or is part of a larger machine: *a waste disposal unit* ◇ *the central processing unit of a computer*
▸ IN TEXTBOOK **8** one of the parts into which a TEXTBOOK or a series of lessons is divided: *The present perfect is covered in Unit 8.*
▸ FLAT/APARTMENT/HOUSE **9** (also **ˈhome unit**) (*AustralE, NZE*) a single flat/apartment or house in a building or group of buildings containing a number of them
▸ NUMBER **10** any whole number from 0 to 9: *a column for the tens and a column for the units*

Uni·tar·ian /ˌjuːnɪˈteəriən; *NAmE* -ˈter-/ *noun* a member of a Christian Church that does not believe in the TRINITY and has no formal teachings ▸ **Uni·tar·ian** *adj.* **Uni·tar·ian·ism** /-ɪzəm/ *noun* [U]

uni·tary /ˈjuːnətri; *NAmE* -teri/ *adj.* **1** (*technical*) (of a country or an organization) consisting of a number of areas or groups that are joined together and are controlled by one government or group: *a single unitary state* ◇ (*BrE*) *a **unitary authority*** (= a type of local council, introduced in some areas from 1995 to replace existing local governments which consisted of county and district councils) **2** (*formal*) single; forming one unit

unite 0‑w /juˈnaɪt/ *verb*
1 0‑w [I] to join together with other people in order to do sth as a group: **~ in sth** *Local resident groups have **united in opposition** to the plan.* ◇ **~ in doing sth** *We will unite in fighting crime.* ◇ **~ (behind/against sb/sth)** *Will they unite behind the new leader?* ◇ *Nationalist parties united to oppose the government's plans.* **2** 0‑w [T, I] to make people or things join together to form a unit; to join together: **~ (sb/sth)** *A special bond unites our two countries.* ◇ *His aim was to unite Italy.* ◇ *The two countries united in 1887.* ◇ **~ (sb/sth) (with sb/sth)** *She unites keen business skills with a charming personality.*

united 0‑w /juˈnaɪtɪd/ *adj.*
1 0‑w (of countries) joined together as a political unit or by shared aims: *the United States of America* ◇ *efforts to build a united Europe* **2** 0‑w (of people or groups) in agreement and working together: *We need to become a more united team.* ◇ *They are united in their opposition to the plan.* ◇ *We should present **a united front*** (= an appearance of being in agreement with each other). **3** used in the names of some teams and companies: *Manchester United* ◇ *United Distillers*

the Uˌnited ˈFree Church *noun* [sing.] a church formed in Scotland in 1900 from the union of the Free Church of Scotland and the United Presbyterian Church

the Uˌnited ˈKingdom *noun* [sing.] (*abbr.* (**the**) **UK**) England, Scotland, Wales and Northern Ireland (considered as a political unit)

the Uˌnited ˈNations *noun* [sing.+ sing./pl. v.] (*abbr.* (**the**) **UN**) an association of many countries which aims to improve economic and social conditions and to solve political problems in the world in a peaceful way

the ˌUnited Nations Seˈcurity Council *noun* = SECURITY COUNCIL

ˌUnited ˌPress Interˈnational *noun* (*abbr.* **UPI**) a US company that collects news and sells it to newspapers and radio and television stations

the Uˌnited ˈStates (of Aˈmerica) *noun* (*abbr.* (**the**) **US**, (**the**) **USA**) a large country in N America consisting of 50 states and the District of Columbia HELP Although **United States** is sometimes found with a plural verb after it, this is quite rare and it is much more common to use a singular verb. ➲ note at AMERICAN

ˌunit ˈtrust (*BrE*) (*NAmE* **ˈmutual fund**) *noun* a company that offers a service to people by investing their money in various different businesses

unity /ˈjuːnəti/ *noun* (*pl.* **-ies**) **1** [U, sing.] the state of being in agreement and working together; the state of being joined together to form one unit: *European unity* ◇ *a plea for unity within the party* ◇ *unity of purpose* OPP **disunity** **2** [U] (in art, etc.) the state of looking or being complete in a natural and pleasing way: *The design lacks unity.* **3** [C] (in literature and theatre) any of the principles of CLASSICAL or NEOCLASSICAL theatre that restrict the action of a play to a single story, day and place: *the unities of action, time and place* **4** [sing.] (*formal*) a single thing that may consist of a number of different parts: *If society is to exist as a unity, its members must have shared values.* **5** [U] (*mathematics*) the number one

Univ. *abbr.* (in writing) University

uni·ver·sal /ˌjuːnɪˈvɜːsl; *NAmE* -ˈvɜːrsl/ *adj.* **1** done by or involving all the people in the world or in a particular group: *Such problems are a universal feature of old age.* ◇ *Agreement on this issue is almost universal.* ◇ ***universal suffrage*** (= the right of all the people in a country to vote) **2** true or right at all times and in all places: *universal facts about human nature* ▸ **uni·ver·sal·ity** /ˌjuːnɪvɜːˈsæləti; *NAmE* -vɜːrˈs-/ *noun*: *the universality of religious experience*

ˌuniˌversal ˈgrammar *noun* [U, C] (*linguistics*) the set of rules that is thought to be able to describe all languages

ˌuniˌversal ˈindicator *noun* (*chemistry*) a substance that changes colour when another substance touches it, indicating whether it is an acid or an ALKALI

U

uni·ver·sal·ly /ˌjuːnɪˈvɜːsəli; *NAmE* -ˈvɜːrs-/ *adv.* **1** by everyone: *to be universally accepted* **2** everywhere or in every situation: *This treatment is not universally available.* ◇ *The theory does not apply universally.*

Uniˈversal Time *noun* [U] = GMT

uni·verse /ˈjuːnɪvɜːs; *NAmE* -vɜːrs/ *noun*
1 **the universe** [sing.] the whole of space and everything in it, including the earth, the planets and the stars: *theories of how the universe began* **2** [C] a system of stars, planets, etc. in space outside our own: *The idea of a parallel universe is hard to grasp.* ◇ *He lives in a little universe of his own.* **3** [sing.] a set of experiences of a particular type: *the moral universe*

uni·ver·sity /ˌjuːnɪˈvɜːsəti; *NAmE* -ˈvɜːrs-/ *noun* [C, U] (*pl.* -ies) (*abbr.* Univ.)
an institution at the highest level of education where you can study for a degree or do research: *Is there a university in this town?* ◇ *Ohio State University* ◇ *the University of York* ◇ *York University* ◇ (*BrE*) *Both their children are* ***at university***. ◇ (*BrE*) *He's hoping to* ***go to university*** *next year.* ◇ *a* ***university course/degree/lecturer*** ⊃ COLLOCATIONS at EDUCATION ⊃ note at COLLEGE ⊃ see also STATE UNIVERSITY
IDM **the university of ˈlife** (*informal*) the experience of life thought of as giving sb an education, instead of the person gaining formal qualifications: *a degree from the university of life*

Unix™ /ˈjuːnɪks/ *noun* [U] (*computing*) an OPERATING SYSTEM which can be used by many people at the same time

un·just /ˌʌnˈdʒʌst/ *adj.* not deserved or fair: *an unjust law* OPP **just** ▸ **un·just·ly** *adv.*: *She felt that she had been unjustly treated.*

un·jus·ti·fi·able /ʌnˈdʒʌstɪfaɪəbl/ *adj.* (of an action) impossible to excuse or accept because there is no good reason for it SYN **indefensible**: *an unjustifiable delay* OPP **justifiable** ▸ **un·jus·ti·fi·ably** /-əbli/ *adv.*

un·jus·ti·fied AW /ʌnˈdʒʌstɪfaɪd/ *adj.* not fair or necessary SYN **unwarranted**: *The criticism was wholly unjustified.* OPP **justified**

un·kempt /ˌʌnˈkempt/ *adj.* (*formal*) (especially of sb's hair or general appearance) not well cared for; not neat or tidy SYN **dishevelled**: *greasy, unkempt hair*

un·kind /ˌʌnˈkaɪnd/ *adj.*
~ (to sb/sth) (to do sth) unpleasant or unfriendly; slightly cruel: *an unkind remark* ◇ *He was never actually unkind to them.* ◇ *It would be unkind to go without him.* OPP **kind** ▸ **un·kind·ly** *adv.*: *'That's your problem,' she remarked unkindly.* **un·kind·ness** *noun* [U]

un·know·able /ʌnˈnəʊəbl; *NAmE* -ˈnoʊ-/ *adj.* (*formal*) that cannot be known: *a distant, unknowable divine power*

un·know·ing /ʌnˈnəʊɪŋ; *NAmE* -ˈnoʊ-/ *adj.* [usually before noun] (*formal*) not aware of what you are doing or what is happening: *He was the unknowing cause of all the misunderstanding.* ⊃ compare KNOWING ▸ **un·know·ing·ly** *adv.*: *She had unknowingly broken the rules.*

un·known /ˌʌnˈnəʊn; *NAmE* -ˈnoʊn/ *adj., noun*
▪ ***adj.*** **1** **~ (to sb)** not known or identified: *a species of insect previously unknown to science* ◇ *He was trying,* ***for some unknown reason***, *to count the stars.* ◇ *The man's identity remains unknown.* **2** (of people) not famous or well known: *an unknown actor* ◇ *The author is virtually unknown outside Poland.* **3** never happening or existing: *The disease is as yet unknown in Europe* (= there have been no cases there). ◇ *It was* ***not unknown for*** *people to have to wait several hours* (= it happened sometimes).
IDM **an ˌunknown ˈquantity** a person or thing whose qualities or abilities are not yet known **unknown to sb** without the person mentioned being aware of it: *Unknown to me, he had already signed the agreement.*
▪ ***noun*** **1** **the unknown** [sing.] places or things that are not known about: *a journey into the unknown* ◇ *a fear of the unknown* **2** [C] a person who is not well known: *A young unknown played the leading role.* **3** [C] a fact or an influence that is not known: *There are so many unknowns in the proposal.* **4** [C] (*mathematics*) a quantity that does not have a known value: *X and Y in the equation are both unknowns.*

the ˌUnknown ˈSoldier *noun* [sing.] a soldier who has been killed in a war, whose body has not been identified, and who is buried in special ceremony. The **Unknown Soldier** is a symbol for all the soldiers killed in a particular war or in wars generally: *the tomb of the Unknown Soldier*

un·lace /ʌnˈleɪs/ *verb* **~ sth** to undo the LACES of shoes, clothes, etc. OPP **lace up**

un·laden /ˌʌnˈleɪdn/ *adj.* (*technical*) (of a vehicle) not loaded: *a vehicle with an unladen weight of 3 000 kg* ⊃ compare LADEN

un·law·ful /ʌnˈlɔːfl/ *adj.* (*formal*) not allowed by the law SYN **illegal** OPP **lawful** ▸ **un·law·ful·ly** /-fəli/ *adv.*

unˌlawful ˈkilling *noun* (*law*) a murder or other killing which is considered a crime, for example when a person dies because sb is careless: *The two police officers were accused of unlawful killing.*

un·lead·ed /ˌʌnˈledɪd/ *adj.* (of petrol/gas) not containing LEAD and therefore less harmful to the environment OPP **leaded** ▸ **un·lead·ed** *noun* [U]: *Unleaded is cheaper than diesel.*

un·learn /ˌʌnˈlɜːn; *NAmE* ˌʌnˈlɜːrn/ *verb* **~ sth** to deliberately forget sth that you have learned, especially sth bad or wrong: *You'll have to unlearn all the bad habits you learned with your last piano teacher.*

un·leash /ʌnˈliːʃ/ *verb* **~ sth (on/upon sb/sth)** to suddenly let a strong force, emotion, etc. be felt or have an effect: *The government's proposals unleashed a storm of protest in the press.*

un·leav·ened /ˌʌnˈlevnd/ *adj.* (of bread) made without any YEAST and therefore flat ⊃ see also LEAVEN

un·less /ənˈles/ *conj.*
1 used to say that sth can only happen or be true in a particular situation: *You won't get paid for time off unless you have a doctor's note.* ◇ *I won't tell them—not unless you say I can.* ◇ *Unless I'm mistaken, she was back at work yesterday.* ◇ *He hasn't got any hobbies—unless you call watching TV a hobby.* **2** used to give the only situation in which sth will not happen or be true: *I sleep with the window open unless it's really cold.* ◇ *Unless something unexpected happens, I'll see you tomorrow.* ◇ *Have a cup of tea—unless you'd prefer a cold drink?* HELP **Unless** is used to talk about a situation that could happen, or something that could be true, in the future. If you know that something has not happened or that sth is not true, use **if... not**: *If you weren't always in such a hurry* (= but you are), *your work would be much better.* ◇ ~~*Your work would be much better unless you were always in such a hurry.*~~

un·let·tered /ˌʌnˈletəd; *NAmE* -tərd/ *adj.* (*formal*) unable to read

un·licensed AW /ʌnˈlaɪsnst/ *adj.* without a licence: *an unlicensed vehicle* OPP **licensed**

un·like /ˌʌnˈlaɪk/ *prep., adj.*
▪ ***prep.*** **1** different from a particular person or thing: *Music is quite unlike any other art form.* ◇ *The sound was* ***not unlike*** *that of birds singing.* **2** used to contrast sb/sth with another person or thing: *Unlike most systems, this one is very easy to install.* ⊃ LANGUAGE BANK at CONTRAST **3** not typical of sb/sth: *It's very unlike him to be so late.* OPP **like**
▪ ***adj.*** [not before noun] (of two people or things) different from each other: *They are both teachers. Otherwise they are quite unlike.* ⊃ compare ALIKE, LIKE

un·like·ly /ʌnˈlaɪkli/ *adj.* (**un·like·lier, un·likeli·est**) HELP **more unlikely** and **most unlikely** are the usual forms
1 not likely to happen; not probable: **~ (to do sth)** *The project seemed unlikely to succeed.* ◇ **~ (that...)** *It's most* (= very) *unlikely that she'll arrive before seven.* ◇ ***In the unlikely event of*** *a problem arising, please contact the hotel manager.* **2** [only before noun] not the person, thing or place

U

that you would normally think of or expect: *He seems a most unlikely candidate for the job.* ◇ *They have built hotels in the most unlikely places.* **3** ⊶ [only before noun] difficult to believe **SYN** **implausible**: *She gave me an unlikely explanation for her behaviour.* **OPP** **likely** ▸ **un·like·li·hood** /ʌnˈlaɪklihʊd/, **un·like·li·ness** /-nəs/ *noun* [U]

un·lim·it·ed /ʌnˈlɪmɪtɪd/ *adj.* as much or as many as is possible; not limited in any way: *The ticket gives you unlimited travel for seven days.* ◇ *The court has the power to impose an unlimited fine for this offence.* ◇ *You will be allowed unlimited access to the files.*

un·lined /ˌʌnˈlaɪnd/ *adj.* **1** not marked with lines: *unlined paper/skin* **2** (of a piece of clothing, etc.) made without an extra layer of cloth on the inside **OPP** **lined**

un·list·ed /ˌʌnˈlɪstɪd/ *adj.* **1** not on a published list, especially of STOCK EXCHANGE prices: *an unlisted company* **2** (of a telephone number) not listed in the public telephone book, at the request of the owner of the telephone. The telephone company will not give unlisted numbers to people who ask for them. ➲ see also EX-DIRECTORY

unlit /ˌʌnˈlɪt/ *adj.* **1** dark because there are no lights or the lights are not switched on: *an unlit passage* **2** not yet burning: *an unlit cigarette* **OPP** **lighted**

un·load ⊶ /ˌʌnˈləʊd; *NAmE* ˌʌnˈloʊd/ *verb* **1** ⊶ [T, I] to remove things from a vehicle or ship after it has taken them somewhere: **~ sth from sth** *Everyone helped to unload the luggage from the car.* ◇ **~ (sth)** *This isn't a suitable place to unload the van.* ◇ *The truck driver was waiting to unload.* **OPP** **load** **2** ⊶ [T] **~ sth** to remove the contents of sth after you have finished using it, especially the bullets from a gun or the film from a camera **OPP** **load** **3** [T] **~ sth/sb (on/onto sb)** (*informal*) to pass the responsibility for sb/sth to sb else: *It's his problem, not something he should unload onto you.* **4** [T] **~ sth (on/onto sb/sth)** (*informal*) to get rid of or sell sth, especially sth illegal or of bad quality: *They want to unload their shares at the right price.*

un·lock /ˌʌnˈlɒk; *NAmE* ˌʌnˈlɑːk/ *verb* **1** **~ sth** to undo the lock of a door, window, etc, using a key: *to unlock the door* **OPP** **lock** **2** **~ sth** to discover sth and let it be known: *The divers hoped to unlock some of the secrets of the seabed.*

un·locked /ˌʌnˈlɒkt; *NAmE* ˌʌnˈlɑːkt/ *adj.* not locked: *Don't leave your desk unlocked.*

unlooked-for /ʌnˈlʊkt fɔː(r)/ *adj.* (*formal*) not expected: *unlooked-for developments*

un·loose /ˌʌnˈluːs/ (also **un·loosen** /ʌnˈluːsn/) *verb* **~ sth** (*old-fashioned* or *formal*) to make sth loose: *He unloosed his tie.*

un·loved /ˌʌnˈlʌvd/ *adj.* (*formal*) not loved by anyone: *unloved children*

un·love·ly /ˌʌnˈlʌvli/ *adj.* (*formal*) not attractive: *an unlovely building*

un·luck·ily /ʌnˈlʌkɪli/ *adv.* unfortunately; as a result of bad luck: *He was injured in the first game and unluckily missed the final.* **OPP** **luckily**

un·lucky ⊶ /ʌnˈlʌki/ *adj.* (**un·luck·ier**, **un·lucki·est**) **HELP** You can also use **more unlucky** and **most unlucky**. **1** ⊶ **~ (to do sth)** having bad luck or happening because of bad luck; not lucky **SYN** **unfortunate**: *He was very unlucky not to win.* ◇ *By some unlucky chance, her name was left off the list.* **2** ⊶ **~ (to do sth)** causing bad luck: *Some people think it's unlucky to walk under a ladder.* ◇ *Thirteen is often considered an unlucky number.* **OPP** **lucky**

un·made /ˌʌnˈmeɪd/ *adj.* **1** an **unmade** bed is not ready for sleeping in because the sheets, etc. have not been arranged neatly **2** (*BrE*) an **unmade** road does not have a hard smooth surface

un·man·age·able /ʌnˈmænɪdʒəbl/ *adj.* difficult or impossible to control or deal with **OPP** **manageable**

un·man·ly /ʌnˈmænli/ *adj.* (*formal*) not having the qualities that are admired or expected in a man **OPP** **manly**

un·manned /ˌʌnˈmænd/ *adj.* if a machine, a vehicle, a place or an activity is **unmanned**, it does not have or need a person to control or operate it: *an unmanned spacecraft* ◇ *an unmanned Mars mission* **OPP** **manned**

un·man·ner·ly /ʌnˈmænəli; *NAmE* -nərli/ *adj.* (*formal*) not having or showing good manners; not polite

un·marked /ʌnˈmɑːkt; *NAmE* ʌnˈmɑːrkt/ *adj.* **1** without a sign or words to show what or where sth is: *an unmarked police car* ◇ *He was buried in an unmarked grave.* ➲ compare MARKED **2** (*especially BrE*) (of a player in a team game, especially football (SOCCER)) with no player from the other team staying close to prevent them from getting the ball: *He headed the ball to the unmarked Gray.* **3** (*linguistics*) (of a word or form of a word) not showing any particular feature or style, such as being formal or informal **OPP** **marked**

un·mar·ried /ˌʌnˈmærid/ *adj.* not married **SYN** **single**: *an unmarried mother*

un·mask /ˌʌnˈmɑːsk; *NAmE* ˌʌnˈmæsk/ *verb* **~ sb/sth** to show the true character of sb, or a hidden truth about sth **SYN** **expose**: *to unmask a spy*

un·matched /ˌʌnˈmætʃt/ *adj.* **~ (by sb/sth)** (*formal*) better than all others: *He had a talent unmatched by any other politician of this century.*

un·mem·or·able /ʌnˈmemərəbl/ *adj.* that cannot be remembered because it was not special **OPP** **memorable**

un·men·tion·able /ʌnˈmenʃənəbl/ *adj.* [usually before noun] too shocking or embarrassing to be mentioned or spoken about: *an unmentionable disease*

unmet /ˌʌnˈmet/ *adj.* (*formal*) (of needs, etc.) not satisfied: *a report on the unmet needs of elderly people*

un·mind·ful /ʌnˈmaɪndfl/ *adj.* **~ of sb/sth** (*formal*) not giving thought or attention to sb/sth **OPP** **mindful**

un·miss·able /ʌnˈmɪsəbl/ *adj.* that you must not miss because it is so good: *an unmissable opportunity*

un·mis·tak·able (also *less frequent* **un·mis·take·able**) /ˌʌnmɪˈsteɪkəbl/ *adj.* that cannot be mistaken for sb/sth else: *Her accent was unmistakable.* ◇ *the unmistakable sound of gunfire* ▸ **un·mis·tak·ably** (also *less frequent* **un·mis·take·ably**) /-əbli/ *adv.*: *His accent was unmistakably British.*

un·miti·gated /ʌnˈmɪtɪgeɪtɪd/ *adj.* [only before noun] used to mean 'complete', usually when describing sth bad **SYN** **absolute**: *The evening was an unmitigated disaster.* ➲ see also MITIGATE

un·modi·fied **AW** /ˌʌnˈmɒdɪfaɪd; *NAmE* ˈmɑːd-/ *adj.* not MODIFIED

un·mol·est·ed /ˌʌnməˈlestɪd/ *adj.* [not usually before noun] (*formal*) not disturbed or attacked by sb; not prevented from doing sth

un·moti·vated **AW** /ˌʌnˈməʊtɪveɪtɪd; *NAmE* -ˈmoʊ-/ *adj.* **1** not having interest in or enthusiasm for sth, especially work or study: *unmotivated students* **2** without a reason or MOTIVE: *an unmotivated attack* **OPP** **motivated**

un·moved /ˌʌnˈmuːvd/ *adj.* **~ (by sth)** not feeling pity or sympathy, especially in a situation where it would be normal to do so: *Alice seemed totally unmoved by the whole experience.* ◇ *She pleaded with him but he remained unmoved.*

un·mov·ing /ˌʌnˈmuːvɪŋ/ *adj.* (*formal*) not moving: *He stood, unmoving, in the shadows.*

un·music·al /ˌʌnˈmjuːzɪkl/ *adj.* **1** (of a sound) unpleasant to listen to: *His voice was harsh and unmusical.* **2** (of a person) unable to play or enjoy music **OPP** **musical**

un·named /ˌʌnˈneɪmd/ *adj.* whose name is not given or not known: *information from an unnamed source* ◇ *Two casualties, as yet unnamed, are still in the local hospital.*

un·nat·ural /ʌnˈnætʃrəl/ *adj.* **1** different from what is normal or expected, or from what is generally accepted as being right: *It seems unnatural for a child to spend so much time alone.* ◇ *There was an unnatural silence and then a scream.* ◇ *unnatural sexual practices* ◇ *He gave an unnatural smile* (= that did not seem genuine). **2** different from anything in nature: *Her leg was bent at an unnatural angle.* ◇ *an unnatural death* (= one not from natural causes) **OPP** **natural** ▸ **un·nat·ur·al·ly** /-rəli/ *adv.*: *She was, not*

U

unnaturally, very surprised at the news. ◇ *His eyes were unnaturally bright.*

un·neces·sary 0‑ᵣ /ʌnˈnesəsəri; *NAmE* -seri/ *adj.* **1** 0‑ᵣ not needed; more than is needed SYN **unjustified**: *unnecessary expense* ◇ *They were found guilty of causing unnecessary suffering to animals.* ◇ *All this fuss is* **totally unnecessary**. OPP **necessary** **2** 0‑ᵣ (of remarks, etc.) not needed in the situation and likely to be offensive SYN **uncalled for**: *That last comment was a little unnecessary, wasn't it?* ▶ **un·neces·sar·ily** /ˌʌnˈnesəsərəli; *NAmE* ˌʌnˌnesəˈserəli/ *adv.*: *There's no point worrying him unnecessarily.* ◇ *unnecessarily complicated instructions*

un·nerve /ˌʌnˈnɜːv; *NAmE* ˌʌnˈnɜːrv/ *verb* **~ sb** to make sb feel nervous or frightened or lose confidence: *His silence unnerved us.* ◇ *She appeared strained and a little unnerved.* ▶ **un·nerv·ing** *adj.* **un·nerv·ing·ly** *adv.*

un·noticed /ˌʌnˈnəʊtɪst; *NAmE* -ˈnoʊ-/ *adj.* [not before noun] not seen or noticed: *His kindness did not* **go unnoticed** *by his staff.*

un·num·bered /ˌʌnˈnʌmbəd; *NAmE* -bərd/ *adj.* not marked with a number; not NUMBERED: *unnumbered seats*

UNO /ˌjuː en ˈəʊ; *NAmE* ˈoʊ, ˈjuːnəʊ; *NAmE* -noʊ/ *abbr.* United Nations Organization ➲ see also UNITED NATIONS

un·ob·jec·tion·able /ˌʌnəbˈdʒekʃənəbl/ *adj.* (*formal*) (of an idea, etc.) that you can accept SYN **acceptable**

un·ob·served /ˌʌnəbˈzɜːvd; *NAmE* -ˈzɜːrvd/ *adj.* without being seen: *It's not easy for somebody to get into the building unobserved.*

un·ob·tain·able AW /ˌʌnəbˈteɪnəbl/ *adj.* [not usually before noun] that cannot be obtained OPP **obtainable**

un·ob·tru·sive /ˌʌnəbˈtruːsɪv/ *adj.* (*formal*, often *approving*) not attracting unnecessary attention: *The service at the hotel is efficient and unobtrusive.* OPP **obtrusive** ▶ **un·ob·tru·sive·ly** *adv.*: *Dora slipped unobtrusively in through the back door.*

un·occu·pied /ˌʌnˈɒkjupaɪd; *NAmE* -ˈɑːk-/ *adj.* **1** empty, with nobody living there or using it: *an unoccupied house* ◇ *I sat down at the nearest unoccupied table.* **2** (of a region or country) not controlled by foreign soldiers: *unoccupied territory* OPP **occupied**

un·offi·cial /ˌʌnəˈfɪʃl/ *adj.* **1** that does not have permission or approval from sb in authority: *an unofficial agreement/strike* ◇ *Unofficial estimates put the figure at over two million.* **2** that is not part of sb's official business: *The former president paid an unofficial visit to China.* OPP **official** ▶ **un·offi·cial·ly** /-ʃəli/ *adv.*

un·opened /ʌnˈəʊpənd; *NAmE* -ˈoʊ-/ *adj.* not opened yet: *The letter was returned unopened.*

un·opposed /ˌʌnəˈpəʊzd; *NAmE* -ˈpoʊzd/ *adj.* [not usually before noun] not opposed or stopped by anyone: *The party leader was re-elected unopposed.*

un·organ·ized (*BrE* also **-ised**) /ʌnˈɔːɡənaɪzd; *NAmE* -ˈɔːrɡ-/ *adj.* **1** (of workers) without a TRADE/LABOR UNION or other organization to represent or support them **2** = DISORGANIZED **3** not having been organized: *unorganized data* ➲ compare ORGANIZED

un·ortho·dox /ʌnˈɔːθədɒks; *NAmE* ʌnˈɔːrθədɑːks/ *adj.* different from what is usual or accepted: *unorthodox methods* OPP **orthodox** ➲ compare HETERODOX

un·pack /ˌʌnˈpæk/ *verb* **1** [T, I] **~ (sth)** to take things out of a suitcase, bag, etc: *I unpacked my bags as soon as I arrived.* ◇ *She unpacked all the clothes she needed and left the rest in the case.* ◇ *She went to her room to unpack.* OPP **pack** **2** [T] **~ sth** to separate sth into parts so that it is easier to understand: *to unpack a theory*

un·paid /ˌʌnˈpeɪd/ *adj.* **1** not yet paid: *unpaid bills* **2** done or taken without payment: *unpaid work* ◇ *unpaid leave* OPP **paid** **3** (of people) not receiving payment for work that they do: *unpaid volunteers* OPP **paid**

un·pal·at·able /ʌnˈpælətəbl/ *adj.* **~ (to sb)** **1** (of facts, ideas, etc.) unpleasant and not easy to accept SYN **distasteful**: *Only then did I learn the unpalatable truth.* **2** not pleasant to taste: *unpalatable food* OPP **palatable**

un·par·al·leled AW /ʌnˈpærəleld/ *adj.* (*formal*) used to emphasize that sth is bigger, better or worse than anything else like it SYN **unequalled**: *It was an unparalleled opportunity to develop her career.* ◇ *The book has enjoyed a success unparalleled in recent publishing history.* ➲ compare PARALLEL *v.*

un·par·don·able /ʌnˈpɑːdnəbl; *NAmE* -ˈpɑːrd-/ *adj.* that cannot be forgiven or excused SYN **unforgivable, inexcusable** OPP **pardonable**

un·par·lia·men·tary /ˌʌnˌpɑːləˈmentri; *NAmE* -ˌpɑːrl-/ *adj.* against the accepted rules of behaviour in a parliament: *unparliamentary language*

un·pat·ri·ot·ic /ˌʌnˌpætriˈɒtɪk; *NAmE* -ˌpeɪtriˈɑːt-/ *adj.* not supporting your own country OPP **patriotic**

un·per·turbed /ˌʌnpəˈtɜːbd; *NAmE* ˌʌnpərˈtɜːrbd/ *adj.* not worried or anxious: *She seemed unperturbed by the news.* OPP **perturbed**

un·pick /ˌʌnˈpɪk/ *verb* **~ sth** to take out STITCHES from a piece of sewing or knitting

un·placed /ˌʌnˈpleɪst/ *adj.* (*BrE*) not one of the first three to finish in a race or competition

un·planned /ˌʌnˈplænd/ *adj.* not planned in advance: *an unplanned pregnancy*

un·play·able /ˌʌnˈpleɪəbl/ *adj.* (*especially BrE*) not able to be played; impossible to play on or with: *The ball was unplayable* (= it was hit so well that it was impossible to hit it back). ➲ compare PLAYABLE

un·pleas·ant 0‑ᵣ /ʌnˈpleznt/ *adj.* **1** 0‑ᵣ not pleasant or comfortable SYN **disagreeable**: *an unpleasant experience* ◇ *The minerals in the water made it unpleasant to drink.* **2** 0‑ᵣ **~ (to sb)** not kind, friendly or polite: *He was very unpleasant to me.* ◇ *She said some very unpleasant things about you.* OPP **pleasant** ▶ **un·pleas·ant·ly** *adv.*: *The drink is very sweet, but not unpleasantly so.* ◇ *He laughed unpleasantly.*

un·pleas·ant·ness /ʌnˈplezntnəs/ *noun* [U] bad feeling or arguments between people

un·plug /ˌʌnˈplʌɡ/ *verb* (**-gg-**) **~ sth** to remove the plug of a piece of electrical equipment from the electricity supply OPP **plug sth in**

Un·plugged™ /ˌʌnˈplʌɡd/ *adj.* (sometimes after noun) (of pop or ROCK music or musicians) performed or performing with ACOUSTIC rather than electric instruments: *an Unplugged concert* ◇ *Bob Dylan Unplugged*

un·pol·luted /ˌʌnpəˈluːtɪd/ *adj.* that has not been POLLUTED (= made dirty by harmful substances)

un·popu·lar /ʌnˈpɒpjələ(r); *NAmE* -ˈpɑːp-/ *adj.* not liked or enjoyed by a person, a group or people in general: *an unpopular choice* ◇ *an unpopular government* ◇ **~ with/among sb** *The proposed increase in income tax proved* **deeply unpopular** *with the electorate.* OPP **popular** ▶ **un·popu·lar·ity** /ˌʌnˌpɒpjuˈlærəti; *NAmE* -ˌpɑːp-/ *noun* [U]: *the growing unpopularity of the military regime*

un·pre·ced·ent·ed AW /ʌnˈpresɪdentɪd/ *adj.* that has never happened, been done or been known before: *The situation is unprecedented in modern times.* ▶ **un·pre·ced·ent·ed·ly** *adv.*: *a period of unprecedentedly high food prices*

un·pre·dict·able AW /ˌʌnprɪˈdɪktəbl/ *adj.* **1** that cannot be predicted because it changes a lot or depends on too many different things: *unpredictable weather* ◇ *The result is entirely unpredictable.* **2** if a person is **unpredictable**, you cannot predict how they will behave in a particular situation OPP **predictable** ▶ **un·pre·dict·abil·ity** AW /ˌʌnprɪˌdɪktəˈbɪləti/ *noun* [U]: *the unpredictability of the English weather* **un·pre·dict·ably** *adv.*

un·pre·ju·diced /ʌnˈpredʒədɪst/ *adj.* not influenced by an unreasonable fear or dislike of sth/sb; willing to consider different ideas and opinions OPP **prejudiced**

U

un·pre·medi·tated /ˌʌnpriːˈmedɪteɪtɪd/ *adj.* (*formal*) (of a crime or bad action) not planned in advance OPP **premeditated**

un·pre·pared /ˌʌnprɪˈpeəd; *NAmE* -ˈperd/ *adj.* **1** ~ (**for sth**) not ready or not expecting sth: *She was totally unprepared for his response.* **2** ~ (**to do sth**) (*formal*) not willing to do sth: *She was unprepared to accept that her marriage was over.* OPP **prepared**

un·pre·pos·sess·ing /ˌʌnˌpriːpəˈzesɪŋ/ *adj.* (*formal*) not attractive; not making a good or strong impression SYN **unattractive** ➲ compare PREPOSSESSING

un·pre·ten·tious /ˌʌnprɪˈtenʃəs/ *adj.* (*approving*) not trying to appear more special, intelligent, important, etc. than you really are OPP **pretentious**

un·prin·cipled AW /ʌnˈprɪnsəpld/ *adj.* (*formal*) without moral principles SYN **dishonest** OPP **principled**

un·print·able /ʌnˈprɪntəbl/ *adj.* (of words or comments) too offensive or shocking to be printed and read by people OPP **printable**

un·prob·lem·at·ic /ˌʌnˌprɒbləˈmætɪk; *NAmE* -ˌprɑːb-/ (also *less frequent* **un·prob·lem·at·ic·al** /-ɪkl/) *adj.* not having or causing problems OPP **problematic** ▸ **un·prob·lem·at·ic·al·ly** /-kli/ *adv.*

un·pro·duct·ive /ˌʌnprəˈdʌktɪv/ *adj.* not producing very much; not producing good results: *unproductive land* ◊ *an unproductive meeting* ◊ *I've had a very unproductive day.* OPP **productive** ▸ **un·pro·duct·ive·ly** *adv.*

un·pro·fes·sion·al /ˌʌnprəˈfeʃənl/ *adj.* not reaching the standard expected in a particular profession: *She was found guilty of unprofessional conduct.* OPP **professional** ➲ compare NON-PROFESSIONAL ▸ **un·pro·fes·sion·al·ly** /-ʃənəli/ *adv.*

un·prof·it·able /ʌnˈprɒfɪtəbl; *NAmE* -ˈprɑːf-/ *adj.* **1** not making enough financial profit: *unprofitable companies* **2** (*formal*) not bringing any advantage OPP **profitable** ▸ **un·prof·it·ably** /-əbli/ *adv.*

un·prom·is·ing /ʌnˈprɒmɪsɪŋ; *NAmE* -ˈprɑːm-/ *adj.* not likely to be successful or show good results OPP **promising**

un·prompt·ed /ʌnˈprɒmptɪd; *NAmE* -ˈprɑːm-/ *adj.* said or done without sb asking you to say or do it: *Quite unprompted, Sam started telling us exactly what had happened that night.* ➲ see also PROMPT

un·pro·nounce·able /ˌʌnprəˈnaʊnsəbl/ *adj.* (of a word, especially a name) too difficult to pronounce OPP **pronounceable**

un·pro·tect·ed /ˌʌnprəˈtektɪd/ *adj.* **1** not protected against being hurt or damaged **2** not covered to prevent it from causing damage or injury: *Machinery was often unprotected and accidents were frequent.* **3** (of sex) done without using a CONDOM

un·proven /ʌnˈpruːvn/ *adj.* not proved or tested: *unproven theories* ➲ compare PROVEN

un·pro·voked /ˌʌnprəˈvəʊkt; *NAmE* -ˈvoʊkt/ *adj.* (especially of an attack) not caused by anything the person being attacked has said or done: *an act of unprovoked aggression* ◊ *Her angry outburst was totally unprovoked.* ➲ see also PROVOKE

un·pub·lished AW /ʌnˈpʌblɪʃt/ *adj.* not published: *an unpublished novel*

un·pun·ished /ʌnˈpʌnɪʃt/ *adj.* not punished: *He promised that the murder would not **go unpunished**.*

un·put·down·able /ˌʌnpʊtˈdaʊnəbl/ *adj.* (*informal*) (of a book) so exciting or interesting that you cannot stop reading it

un·quali·fied /ˌʌnˈkwɒlɪfaɪd; *NAmE* -ˈkwɑːl-/ *adj.* **1** not having the right knowledge, experience or qualifications to do sth: *an unqualified instructor* ◊ ~ **to do sth** *I feel unqualified to comment on the subject.* ◊ ~ **for sth** *He was totally unqualified for his job as a senior manager.* **2** /ʌnˈkwɒlɪfaɪd/ [usually before noun] complete; not limited by any negative qualities: *The event was not an unqualified success.* ◊ *I gave her my unqualified support.* OPP **qualified**

un·quench·able /ʌnˈkwentʃəbl/ *adj.* (*formal*) that cannot be satisfied: *He had an **unquenchable thirst** for life.* ➲ see also QUENCH

un·ques·tion·able /ʌnˈkwestʃənəbl/ *adj.* (*formal*) that cannot be doubted: *a man of unquestionable honesty* OPP **questionable** ▸ **un·ques·tion·ably** /-əbli/ *adv.*: *It was unquestionably a step in the right direction.*

un·ques·tioned /ʌnˈkwestʃənd/ *adj.* (*formal*) **1** so obvious that it cannot be doubted: *His courage remains unquestioned.* **2** accepted as right or true without really being considered: *an unquestioned assumption*

un·ques·tion·ing /ʌnˈkwestʃənɪŋ/ *adj.* (*formal*) done or given without asking questions, expressing doubt, etc: *unquestioning obedience* ▸ **un·ques·tion·ing·ly** *adv.*

un·quiet /ˌʌnˈkwaɪət/ *adj.* [usually before noun] (*literary*) not calm; anxious and RESTLESS

un·quote /ˌʌnˈkwəʊt; *NAmE* ˌʌnˈkwoʊt/ *noun* IDM see QUOTE

un·ravel /ʌnˈrævl/ *verb* (-ll-, *US* -l-) **1** [T, I] ~ (**sth**) if you **unravel** threads that are twisted, WOVEN or knitted, or if they **unravel**, they become separated: *I unravelled the string and wound it into a ball.* **2** [I] (of a system, plan, relationship, etc.) to start to fail or no longer stay together as a whole **3** [T, I] ~ (**sth**) to explain sth that is difficult to understand or is mysterious; to become clearer or easier to understand: *The discovery will help scientists unravel the mystery of the Ice Age.*

un·read /ˌʌnˈred/ *adj.* (of a book, etc.) that has not been read: *a pile of unread newspapers*

un·read·able /ʌnˈriːdəbl/ *adj.* **1** (of a book, etc.) too dull or difficult to be worth reading **2** = ILLEGIBLE **3** if sb's face or expression is **unreadable**, you cannot tell what they are thinking or feeling **4** (*computing*) (of a computer file, disk, etc.) containing information that a computer is not able to read

un·real /ˌʌnˈrɪəl; *NAmE* ˌʌnˈriːəl/ *adj.* **1** so strange that it is more like a dream than reality: *The party began to take on an unreal, almost nightmarish quality.* **2** not related to reality SYN **unrealistic**: *Many people have unreal expectations of what marriage will be like.* **3** (*informal*) used to say that you like sth very much or that sth surprises you: *'That's unreal!' she laughed.* ▸ **un·real·ity** /ˌʌnriˈæləti/ *noun* [U]

un·real·is·tic /ˌʌnrɪəˈlɪstɪk; *NAmE* -riːə-/ *adj.* not showing or accepting things as they are: *unrealistic expectations* ◊ ***It is unrealistic to** expect them to be able to solve the problem immediately.* OPP **realistic** ▸ **un·real·is·tic·al·ly** *adv.*: *These prices are unrealistically high.*

un·real·ized (*BrE* also **-ised**) /ˌʌnˈriːəlaɪzd; *BrE* also -ˈrɪəl-/ *adj.* **1** not achieved or created: *an unrealized ambition* ◊ *Their potential is unrealized.* **2** (*finance*) not sold or changed into the form of money: *unrealized assets*

un·rea·son·able 0‑w /ʌnˈriːznəbl/ *adj.* not fair; expecting too much: *The job was beginning to make unreasonable demands on his free time.* ◊ *The fees they charge are not unreasonable.* ◊ ***It would be unreasonable to** expect somebody to come at such short notice.* ◊ *He was being totally unreasonable about it.* OPP **reasonable** ▸ **un·rea·son·able·ness** *noun* [U] **un·rea·son·ably** /-əbli/ *adv.*

un·rea·son·ing /ʌnˈriːzənɪŋ/ *adj.* [usually before noun] (*formal*) not based on facts or reason SYN **irrational**: *unreasoning fear*

un·rec·og·niz·able (*BrE* also **-is·able**) /ˌʌnrekəgˈnaɪzəbl/ *adj.* (of a person or thing) so changed or damaged that you do not recognize them or it: *He was unrecognizable without his beard.* OPP **recognizable**

un·rec·og·nized (*BrE* also **-ised**) /ʌnˈrekəgnaɪzd/ *adj.* **1** that people are not aware of or do not realize is important: *The problem of ageism in the workplace often **goes unrecognized**.* **2** (of a person) not having received the admiration they deserve for sth that they have done or achieved

U

un·re·con·struct·ed /ˌʌnriːkənˈstrʌktɪd/ *adj.* [only before noun] (*disapproving*) (of people and their beliefs) not having changed, although the situation they are in has changed

un·re·cord·ed /ˌʌnrɪˈkɔːdɪd; *NAmE* -ˈkɔːrd-/ *adj.* not written down or recorded: *Many crimes **go unrecorded**.*

un·re·fined /ˌʌnrɪˈfaɪnd/ *adj.* **1** (of a substance) not separated from the other substances that it is combined with in its natural form: *unrefined sugar* **2** (of a person or their behaviour) not polite or educated **OPP refined**

un·re·gen·er·ate /ˌʌnrɪˈdʒenərət/ *adj.* (*formal*) not trying to change your bad habits or bad behaviour

un·regu·lated **AW** /ˌʌnˈregjuleɪtɪd/ *adj.* not controlled by laws or regulations

un·re·lated /ˌʌnrɪˈleɪtɪd/ *adj.* **1** not connected; not related to sth else **SYN unconnected**: *The two events were totally unrelated.* **2** (of people, animals, etc.) not belonging to the same family **OPP related**

un·re·lent·ing /ˌʌnrɪˈlentɪŋ/ *adj.* (*formal*) **1** (of an unpleasant situation) not stopping or becoming less severe **SYN relentless**: *unrelenting pressure* ◇ *The heat was unrelenting.* **2** if a person is **unrelenting**, they continue with sth without considering the feelings of other people **SYN relentless**: *He was unrelenting in his search for the truth about his father.* ▶ **un·re·lent·ing·ly** *adv.*

un·re·li·able **AW** /ˌʌnrɪˈlaɪəbl/ *adj.* that cannot be trusted or depended on: *The trains are notoriously unreliable.* ◇ *He's totally unreliable as a source of information.* **OPP reliable** ▶ **un·re·li·abil·ity** /ˌʌnrɪˌlaɪəˈbɪləti/ *noun* [U]: *the unreliability of some statistics*

un·re·lieved /ˌʌnrɪˈliːvd/ *adj.* (*formal*) (of an unpleasant situation) continuing without changing

un·re·mark·able /ˌʌnrɪˈmɑːkəbl; *NAmE* -ˈmɑːrk-/ *adj.* ordinary; not special or remarkable in any way: *an unremarkable life*

un·re·marked /ˌʌnrɪˈmɑːkt; *NAmE* -ˈmɑːrkt/ *adj.* (*formal*) not noticed: *His absence **went unremarked**.*

un·re·mit·ting /ˌʌnrɪˈmɪtɪŋ/ *adj.* (*formal*) never stopping: *unremitting hostility* ▶ **un·re·mit·ting·ly** *adv.*: *unremittingly gloomy weather*

un·re·peat·able /ˌʌnrɪˈpiːtəbl/ *adj.* **1** too offensive or shocking to be repeated: *He called me several unrepeatable names.* **2** that cannot be repeated or done again: *an unrepeatable experience* **OPP repeatable**

un·re·pent·ant /ˌʌnrɪˈpentənt/ *adj.* showing no shame about your actions or beliefs **OPP repentant** ▶ **un·re·pent·ant·ly** *adv.*

un·re·port·ed /ˌʌnrɪˈpɔːtɪd; *NAmE* -ˈpɔːrt-/ *adj.* not reported to the police or sb in authority or to the public: *Many cases of bullying **go unreported**.*

U

un·rep·re·sen·ta·tive /ˌʌnˌreprɪˈzentətɪv/ *adj.* **~ (of sb/sth)** not typical of a group of people or things and therefore not useful as a source of information about that group **SYN untypical**: *an unrepresentative sample* **OPP representative**

un·re·quit·ed /ˌʌnrɪˈkwaɪtɪd/ *adj.* (*formal*) (of love) not returned by the person that you love ➲ compare REQUITE

un·re·served /ˌʌnrɪˈzɜːvd; *NAmE* -ˈzɜːrvd/ *adj.* **1** (of seats in a theatre, etc.) not paid for in advance; not kept for the use of a particular person **2** (*formal*) complete and without any doubts: *He offered us his unreserved apologies.*

un·re·served·ly /ˌʌnrɪˈzɜːvɪdli; *NAmE* -ˈzɜːrv-/ *adv.* completely; without hesitating or having any doubts: *We apologize unreservedly for any offence we have caused.*

un·re·solved **AW** /ˌʌnrɪˈzɒlvd; *NAmE* -ˈzɑːlvd; -ˈzɔːlvd/ *adj.* (*formal*) (of a problem or question) not yet solved or answered; not having been resolved

un·re·spon·sive **AW** /ˌʌnrɪˈspɒnsɪv; *NAmE* -ˈspɑːn-/ *adj.* **~ (to sth)** (*formal*) not reacting to sb/sth; not giving the response that you would expect or hope for: *a politician who is unresponsive to the mood of the country* **OPP responsive**

un·rest /ʌnˈrest/ *noun* [U] a political situation in which people are angry and likely to protest or fight: ***industrial/civil/social/political/popular unrest*** ◇ *There is **growing unrest** in the south of the country.* ➲ COLLOCATIONS at WAR

un·re·strained **AW** /ˌʌnrɪˈstreɪnd/ *adj.* (*formal*) not controlled; not having been RESTRAINED: *unrestrained aggression*

un·re·strict·ed **AW** /ˌʌnrɪˈstrɪktɪd/ *adj.* not controlled or limited in any way **SYN unlimited**: *We have unrestricted access to all the facilities.* **OPP restricted**

un·re·ward·ed /ˌʌnrɪˈwɔːdɪd; *NAmE* -ˈwɔːrd-/ *adj.* not receiving the success that you are trying to achieve: *Real talent often **goes unrewarded**.*

un·re·ward·ing /ˌʌnrɪˈwɔːdɪŋ; *NAmE* -ˈwɔːrd-/ *adj.* (of an activity, etc.) not bringing feelings of satisfaction or achievement **OPP rewarding**

un·ripe /ˌʌnˈraɪp/ *adj.* not yet ready to eat: *unripe fruit* **OPP ripe**

un·rivalled (*especially BrE*) (*NAmE* usually **un·rivaled**) /ʌnˈraɪvld/ *adj.* (*formal*) better or greater than any other **SYN unsurpassed**

un·roll /ʌnˈrəʊl; *NAmE* ʌnˈroʊl/ *verb* **1** [T, I] **~ (sth)** if you **unroll** paper, cloth, etc. that was in a roll or if it **unrolls**, it opens and becomes flat: *We unrolled our sleeping bags.* ➲ compare ROLL **2** [I] (of events) to happen one after another in a series: *We watched the events unroll before the cameras.*

un·round·ed /ˌʌnˈraʊndɪd/ *adj.* (*phonetics*) (of a speech sound) pronounced with the lips not forming a narrow round shape **OPP rounded**

un·ruf·fled /ʌnˈrʌfld/ *adj.* (of a person) calm **SYN unperturbed**: *He remained unruffled by their accusations.*

un·ruled /ˌʌnˈruːld/ *adj.* (of paper) not having printed lines on it

un·ruly /ʌnˈruːli/ *adj.* difficult to control or manage **SYN disorderly**: *an unruly class* ◇ *unruly behaviour* ◇ *unruly hair* (= difficult to keep looking neat) ▶ **un·ru·li·ness** *noun* [U]

un·sad·dle /ʌnˈsædl/ *verb* **1** [T, I] **~ (sth)** to take the saddle off a horse **2** [T] **~ sb** to throw a rider off **SYN unseat**

un·safe /ʌnˈseɪf/ *adj.* **1** (of a thing, a place or an activity) not safe; dangerous: *The roof was declared unsafe.* ◇ *It was considered unsafe to release the prisoners.* ◇ *unsafe sex* (= for example, sex without a CONDOM) **2** (of people) in danger of being harmed: *He felt unsafe and alone.* **3** (*BrE, law*) (of a decision in a court of law) based on evidence that may be false or is not good enough: *Their convictions were declared unsafe.* **OPP safe**

un·said /ʌnˈsed/ *adj.* [not before noun] thought but not spoken: *Some things are better **left unsaid**.*

un·sale·able (also **un·sal·able**) /ʌnˈseɪləbl/ *adj.* that cannot be sold, because it is not good enough or because nobody wants to buy it **OPP saleable**

un·salt·ed /ʌnˈsɔːltɪd; *BrE* also -ˈsɒlt-; *NAmE* -ˈsɑːlt-/ *adj.* (especially of food) without added salt: *unsalted butter*

un·sani·tary /ʌnˈsænətri; *NAmE* -teri/ *adj.* (*especially NAmE*) = INSANITARY

un·sat·is·fac·tory /ˌʌnˌsætɪsˈfæktəri/ *adj.* not good enough **SYN inadequate, unacceptable** **OPP satisfactory** ▶ **un·sat·is·fac·tor·ily** /-tərəli/ *adv.*

un·sat·is·fied /ʌnˈsætɪsfaɪd/ *adj.* **1** (of a need, demand, etc.) not dealt with **2** (of a person) not having got what you hoped; not having had enough of sth ➲ compare DISSATISFIED, SATISFIED

un·sat·is·fy·ing /ˌʌnˈsætɪsfaɪɪŋ/ *adj.* not giving you any satisfaction **OPP satisfying**: *a shallow, unsatisfying relationship*

un·sat·ur·ated fat /ʌnˌsætʃəreɪtɪd ˈfæt/ *noun* [U, C] a type of fat found in nuts, seeds and vegetable oils that does not encourage the harmful development of CHOLESTEROL: *Avocados are high in unsaturated fat.* ➲ see also MONOUNSATURATED FAT, POLYUNSATURATED FAT, SATURATED FAT, TRANS-FATTY ACID

un·savoury (*especially US* **un·savory**) /ʌnˈseɪvəri/ *adj.* unpleasant or offensive; not considered morally acceptable: *an unsavoury incident* ◇ *Her friends are all pretty unsavoury characters.*

un·scathed /ʌnˈskeɪðd/ *adj.* [not before noun] not hurt SYN **unharmed**: *The hostages **emerged** from their ordeal **unscathed**.*

un·sched·uled AW /ʌnˈʃedjuːld; *NAmE* ʌnˈskedʒuːld/ *adj.* that was not planned in advance SYN **unplanned**: *an unscheduled stop*

un·sci·en·tif·ic /ˌʌnˌsaɪənˈtɪfɪk/ *adj.* (often *disapproving*) not scientific; not done in a careful, logical way: *an unscientific approach to a problem* ➲ compare NON-SCIENTIFIC

un·scram·ble /ˌʌnˈskræmbl/ *verb* **1** **~ sth** to change a word, message, television signal, etc. that has been sent in a code so that it can be read or understood OPP **scramble** **2** **~ sth** to arrange sth that is confused or in the wrong order in a clear correct way

un·screw /ˌʌnˈskruː/ *verb* **1** [T, I] **~ (sth)** to undo sth by twisting or turning it; to become undone in this way: *I can't unscrew the lid of this jar.* **2** [T] **~ sth** to take the screws out of sth: *You'll have to unscrew the handles to paint the door.*

un·script·ed /ʌnˈskrɪptɪd/ *adj.* (of a speech, broadcast, etc.) not written or prepared in detail in advance OPP **scripted**

un·scru·pu·lous /ʌnˈskruːpjələs/ *adj.* without moral principles; not honest or fair SYN **unprincipled**: *unscrupulous methods* OPP **scrupulous** ▶ **un·scru·pu·lous·ly** *adv.* **un·scru·pu·lous·ness** *noun* [U]

un·sea·son·able /ʌnˈsiːznəbl/ *adj.* unusual for the time of year: *unseasonable weather* OPP **seasonable** ▶ **un·sea·son·ably** /-əbli/ *adv.*: *unseasonably warm*

un·sea·son·al /ʌnˈsiːzənl/ *adj.* not typical of or not suitable for the time of year: *unseasonal weather* OPP **seasonal**

un·seat /ˌʌnˈsiːt/ *verb* **1** **~ sb** to remove sb from a position of power **2** **~ sb** to make sb fall off a horse or bicycle: *The horse unseated its rider at the first fence.*

un·seed·ed /ʌnˈsiːdɪd/ *adj.* not chosen as a SEED in a sports competition, especially in TENNIS: *unseeded players* OPP **seeded**

un·see·ing /ˌʌnˈsiːɪŋ/ *adj.* (*literary*) not noticing or really looking at anything although your eyes are open ▶ **un·see·ing·ly** *adv.*: *They stared unseeingly at the wreckage.*

un·seem·ly /ʌnˈsiːmli/ *adj.* (*old-fashioned* or *formal*) (of behaviour, etc.) not polite or suitable for a particular situation SYN **improper** OPP **seemly**

un·seen /ˌʌnˈsiːn/ *adj.* **1** that cannot be seen: *unseen forces* ◇ *He was killed by a single shot from an unseen soldier.* ◇ *I managed to slip out of the room unseen.* **2** not previously seen: *unseen dangers* ◇ *The exam consists of an essay and an **unseen translation**.* IDM see SIGHT *n.*

un·self·con·scious /ˌʌnselfˈkɒnʃəs; *NAmE* -ˈkɑːn-/ *adj.* not worried about or aware of what other people think of you OPP **self-conscious** ▶ **un·self·con·scious·ly** *adv.*

un·self·ish /ʌnˈselfɪʃ/ *adj.* giving more time or importance to other people's needs, wishes, etc. than to your own SYN **selfless**: *unselfish motives* OPP **selfish** ▶ **un·self·ish·ly** *adv.* **un·self·ish·ness** *noun* [U]

un·sen·ti·men·tal /ˌʌnˌsentɪˈmentl/ *adj.* not having or expressing emotions such as love or pity; not allowing such emotions to influence what you do OPP **sentimental**

un·ser·vice·able /ʌnˈsɜːvɪsəbl; *NAmE* -ˈsɜːrv-/ *adj.* not suitable to be used OPP **serviceable**

un·set·tle /ˌʌnˈsetl/ *verb* **~ sb** to make sb feel upset or worried, especially because a situation has changed: *Changing schools might unsettle the kids.*

un·set·tled /ʌnˈsetld/ *adj.* **1** (of a situation) that may change; making people uncertain about what might happen: *These were difficult and unsettled times.* ◇ *The weather has been very unsettled* (= it has changed a lot). **2** not calm or relaxed: *They all felt restless and unsettled.* **3** (of an argument, etc.) that continues without any agreement being reached SYN **unresolved** **4** (of a bill, etc.) not yet paid

un·set·tling /ʌnˈsetlɪŋ/ *adj.* making you feel upset, nervous or worried

un·shaded /ˌʌnˈʃeɪdɪd/ *adj.* (of a source of light) without a SHADE or other covering: *an unshaded light bulb*

un·shak·able (*BrE* also **un·shake·able**) /ʌnˈʃeɪkəbl/ *adj.* (of a feeling or an attitude) that cannot be changed or destroyed SYN **firm**

un·shaken /ˌʌnˈʃeɪkən/ *adj.* **~ (in sth)** not having changed a particular feeling or attitude: *They remain unshaken in their loyalty.*

un·shaven /ˌʌnˈʃeɪvn/ *adj.* not having shaved or been shaved recently: *He looked pale and unshaven.* ◇ *his unshaven face* ➲ compare SHAVEN

un·sight·ly /ʌnˈsaɪtli/ *adj.* not pleasant to look at SYN **ugly**

un·skilled /ˌʌnˈskɪld/ *adj.* not having or needing special skills or training: *unskilled manual workers* ◇ *unskilled work* OPP **skilled**

un·smil·ing /ʌnˈsmaɪlɪŋ/ *adj.* (*formal*) not smiling; looking unfriendly: *His eyes were hard and unsmiling.* ▶ **un·smil·ing·ly** *adv.*

un·soci·able /ʌnˈsəʊʃəbl; *NAmE* -ˈsoʊ-/ *adj.* **1** not enjoying the company of other people; not friendly OPP **sociable** **2** = UNSOCIAL

un·social /ˌʌnˈsəʊʃl; *NAmE* ˌʌnˈsoʊʃl/ (also *less frequent* **un·soci·able**) (*BrE*) *adj.* outside the normal times of working: *I work long and unsocial hours.*

un·sold /ˌʌnˈsəʊld; *NAmE* ˌʌnˈsoʊld/ *adj.* not bought by anyone: *Many of the houses remain unsold.*

un·soli·cit·ed /ˌʌnsəˈlɪsɪtɪd/ *adj.* not asked for and sometimes not wanted: *unsolicited advice*

un·solved /ˌʌnˈsɒlvd; *NAmE* ˌʌnˈsɑːlvd/ *adj.* not having been solved: *an **unsolved murder/mystery/problem***

un·sophis·ti·cated /ˌʌnsəˈfɪstɪkeɪtɪd/ *adj.* **1** not having or showing much experience of the world and social situations: *unsophisticated tastes* **2** simple and basic; not complicated SYN **crude**: *unsophisticated equipment* OPP **sophisticated**

un·sorted /ˌʌnˈsɔːtɪd; *NAmE* -ˈsɔːrt-/ *adj.* not sorted, or not arranged in any particular order: *a pile of unsorted papers*

un·sound /ˌʌnˈsaʊnd/ *adj.* **1** not acceptable; not holding acceptable views: *ideologically unsound* ◇ *The use of disposable products is considered ecologically unsound.* **2** containing mistakes; that you cannot rely on SYN **unreliable**: *The methods used were unsound.* **3** (of a building, etc.) in poor condition; weak and likely to fall down: *The roof is **structurally unsound**.* OPP **sound** ▶ **un·sound·ness** *noun* [U]
IDM **of ˌunsound ˈmind** (*law*) not responsible for your actions because of a mental illness

un·spar·ing /ʌnˈspeərɪŋ; *NAmE* -ˈsper-/ *adj.* **~ (in sth)** (*formal*) **1** not caring about people's feelings: *She is unsparing in her criticism.* ◇ *an unsparing portrait of life in the slums* **2** giving or given generously: *He won his mother's unsparing approval.* ➲ compare SPARING ▶ **un·spar·ing·ly** *adv.*

un·speak·able /ʌnˈspiːkəbl/ *adj.* (*literary*, usually *disapproving*) that cannot be described in words, usually because it is so bad SYN **indescribable** ▶ **un·speak·ably** /-əbli/ *adv.*

un·speci·fied AW /ˌʌnˈspesɪfaɪd/ *adj.* not stated clearly or definitely; not having been SPECIFIED: *The story takes place at an unspecified date.*

U

un·spec·tacu·lar /ˌʌnspek'tækjələ(r)/ *adj.* not exciting or special: *He had a steady but unspectacular career.*

un·spoiled /ˌʌn'spɔɪld/ (*BrE* also **un·spoilt** /ˌʌn'spɔɪlt/) *adj.* (*approving*) **1** (of a place) beautiful because it has not been changed or built on **2** (of a person) not made unpleasant, bad-tempered, etc. by being praised too much **OPP** **spoilt**

un·spoken /ˌʌn'spəʊkən; *NAmE* -'spoʊ-/ *adj.* (*formal*) not stated; not said in words but understood or agreed between people **SYN** **unstated**: *an unspoken assumption* ◇ *Something unspoken hung in the air between them.*

un·sport·ing /ˌʌn'spɔːtɪŋ; *NAmE* -'spɔːrt-/ *adj.* (*disapproving*) not fair or generous in your behaviour or treatment of others, especially of an opponent in a game **OPP** **sporting**

un·sports·man·like /ˌʌn'spɔːtsmənlaɪk; *NAmE* -'spɔːrts-/ *adj.* (*disapproving*) not behaving in a fair, generous and polite way, especially when playing a sport or game: *unsportsmanlike conduct*

un·stable **AW** /ʌn'steɪbl/ *adj.* **1** likely to change suddenly **SYN** **volatile**: *The political situation remains highly unstable.* **2** if people are **unstable**, their behaviour and emotions change often and suddenly because their minds are upset ⊃ note at MENTALLY ILL **3** likely to move or fall **4** (*technical*) (of a substance) not staying in the same chemical or ATOMIC state: *chemically unstable* **OPP** **stable** ⊃ see also INSTABILITY

un·stated /ʌn'steɪtɪd/ *adj.* (*formal*) not stated; not said in words but understood or agreed between people **SYN** **unspoken**: *Their reasoning was based on a set of unstated assumptions.*

un·steady 0-w /ʌn'stedi/ *adj.*
1 0-w not completely in control of your movements so that you might fall: *She is still a little* ***unsteady on her feet*** *after the operation.* **2** 0-w shaking or moving in a way that is not controlled: *an unsteady hand* **OPP** **steady** ▸ **un·stead·ily** /-ɪli/ *adv.* **un·steadi·ness** *noun* [U]

un·stint·ing /ʌn'stɪntɪŋ/ *adj.* given or giving generously: *unstinting support* ◇ **~ in sth** *They were unstinting in their praise.* ▸ **un·stint·ing·ly** *adv.*

un·stop·pable /ʌn'stɒpəbl; *NAmE* -'stɑːp-/ *adj.* that cannot be stopped or prevented: *an unstoppable rise in prices* ◇ *On form, the team was simply unstoppable.*

un·stressed **AW** /ʌn'strest/ *adj.* (*phonetics*) (of a syllable) pronounced without emphasis **OPP** **stressed**

un·struc·tured **AW** /ʌn'strʌktʃəd; *NAmE* -tʃərd/ *adj.* without structure or organization

un·stuck /ˌʌn'stʌk/ *adj.*
IDM ˌcome unˈstuck **1** to become separated from sth it was stuck or fastened to: *The flap of the envelope had come unstuck.* **2** (*BrE, informal*) (of a person, plan, etc.) to fail completely, with bad results

U

un·sub·scribe /ˌʌnsəb'skraɪb/ *verb* [I, T] **~ (from sth)** | **~ sb/sth** (*computing*) to remove your email address from an Internet MAILING LIST

un·sub·stan·ti·ated /ˌʌnsəb'stænʃieɪtɪd/ *adj.* (*formal*) not proved to be true by evidence **SYN** **unsupported**: *an* ***unsubstantiated claim/rumour, etc.***

un·suc·cess·ful 0-w /ˌʌnsək'sesfl/ *adj.*
not successful; not achieving what you wanted to: *His efforts to get a job proved unsuccessful.* ◇ *They were unsuccessful in meeting their objectives for the year.* ◇ *She made several unsuccessful attempts to see him.* **OPP** **successful** ▸ **un·suc·cess·ful·ly** *adv.*

un·suit·able /ʌn'suːtəbl; *BrE* also -'sjuː-/ *adj.* **~ (for sb/sth)** not right or appropriate for a particular person, purpose or occasion: *He was wearing shoes that were totally unsuitable for climbing.* **OPP** **suitable** ▸ **un·suit·abil·ity** *noun* [U] **un·suit·ably** *adv.*: *They were unsuitably dressed for the occasion.*

un·suit·ed /ʌn'suːtɪd; *BrE* also -'sjuː-/ *adj.* **1 ~ (to/for sth)** | **~ (to do sth)** not having the right or necessary qualities for sth: *He is unsuited to academic work.* ◇ *She was totally unsuited for the job.* **2** if two people are **unsuited** to each other they do not have the same interests, etc. and are therefore not likely to make a good couple **OPP** **suited**

un·sul·lied /ʌn'sʌlid/ *adj.* (*literary*) not spoiled by anything; still pure or in the original state **SYN** **unspoiled**

un·sung /ˌʌn'sʌŋ/ *adj.* [usually before noun] (*formal*) not praised or famous but deserving to be: *the unsung heroes of the war*

un·sup·port·ed /ˌʌnsə'pɔːtɪd; *NAmE* -'pɔːrt-/ *adj.* **1** (of a statement, etc.) not proved to be true by evidence **SYN** **unsubstantiated**: *Their claims are unsupported by research findings.* **2** not helped or paid for by sb/sth else: *She has brought up three children unsupported.* **3** not physically supported: *Sections of the structure have been left unsupported.*

un·sure /ˌʌn'ʃʊə(r); -'ʃɔː(r); *NAmE* -'ʃʊr/ *adj.* [not before noun] **1** not certain of sth; having doubts: **~ about/of sth** *There were a lot of things I was unsure about.* ◇ **~ how, what, etc...** *I was unsure how to reply to this question.* ◇ **~ of/as to how, what, etc...** *He was unsure of what to do next.* ◇ *They were unsure as to what the next move should be.* **2 ~ (of yourself)** lacking confidence in yourself: *Like many women, deep down she was unsure of herself.* **OPP** **sure**

un·sur·passed /ˌʌnsə'pɑːst; *NAmE* ˌʌnsər'pæst/ *adj.* (*formal*) better or greater than any other **SYN** **unrivalled**

un·sur·prised /ˌʌnsə'praɪzd; *NAmE* -sər'p-/ *adj.* [not usually before noun] not surprised: *She appeared totally unsurprised at the news.*

un·sur·pris·ing /ˌʌnsə'praɪzɪŋ; *NAmE* -sər'p-/ *adj.* not causing surprise **OPP** **surprising** ▸ **un·sur·pris·ing·ly** *adv.*: *Unsurprisingly, the plan failed.*

un·sus·pect·ed /ˌʌnsə'spektɪd/ *adj.* not predicted or known; that you were not previously aware of

un·sus·pect·ing /ˌʌnsə'spektɪŋ/ *adj.* [usually before noun] feeling no suspicion; not aware of danger or of sth bad: *He had crept up on his unsuspecting victim from behind.*

un·sus·tain·able **AW** /ˌʌnsə'steɪnəbl/ *adj.* that cannot be continued at the same level, rate, etc: *unsustainable growth* **OPP** **sustainable**

un·sweet·ened /ˌʌn'swiːtnd/ *adj.* (of food or drinks) without sugar or a similar substance having been added

un·swerv·ing /ʌn'swɜːvɪŋ; *NAmE* -'swɜːrv-/ *adj.* (*formal*) strong and not changing or becoming weaker: ***unswerving loyalty/support, etc.***

un·sym·pa·thet·ic /ˌʌnˌsɪmpə'θetɪk/ *adj.* **1 ~ (to/towards sb)** not feeling or showing any sympathy: *I told him about the problem but he was totally unsympathetic.* **2 ~ (to/towards sth)** not in agreement with sth; not supporting an idea, aim, etc: *The government was unsympathetic to public opinion.* **3** (of a person) not easy to like; unpleasant **OPP** **sympathetic** ▸ **un·sym·pa·thet·ic·al·ly** /-kli/ *adv.*: *'You've only got yourself to blame,' she said unsympathetically.*

un·sys·tem·at·ic /ˌʌnˌsɪstə'mætɪk/ *adj.* not organized into a clear system **OPP** **systematic** ▸ **un·sys·tem·at·ic·al·ly** *adv.*

un·taint·ed /ʌn'teɪntɪd/ *adj.* **~ (by sth)** (*formal*) not damaged or spoiled by sth unpleasant; not TAINTED

un·tal·ent·ed /ʌn'tæləntɪd/ *adj.* without a natural ability to do sth well **OPP** **talented**

un·tamed /ˌʌn'teɪmd/ *adj.* allowed to remain in a wild state; not changed, controlled or influenced by anyone; not TAMED

un·tan·gle /ˌʌn'tæŋgl/ *verb* **1 ~ sth (from sth)** to undo string, hair, wire, etc. that has become twisted or has knots in it **2 ~ sth** to make sth that is complicated or confusing easier to deal with or understand

un·tapped /ˌʌn'tæpt/ *adj.* available but not yet used: *untapped reserves of oil*

un·ten·able /ʌn'tenəbl/ *adj.* (*formal*) (of a theory, position, etc.) that cannot be defended against attack or criticism: *His position had become untenable and he was forced to resign.* OPP **tenable**

un·test·ed /ˌʌn'testɪd/ *adj.* not tested; of unknown quality or value

un·think·able /ʌn'θɪŋkəbl/ *adj.* ~ (**for sb**) (**to do sth**) | ~ (**that…**) impossible to imagine or accept SYN **inconceivable**: *It was unthinkable that she could be dead.* OPP **thinkable** ▶ **the un·think·able** *noun* [sing.]: *Suddenly the unthinkable happened and he drew out a gun.* ◇ *The time has come to* ***think the unthinkable*** (= consider possibilities that used to be unacceptable).

un·think·ing /ʌn'θɪŋkɪŋ/ *adj.* (*formal*) not thinking about the effects of what you do or say; not thinking much about serious things SYN **thoughtless** ▶ **un·think·ing·ly** *adv.*

un·tidy 0-π /ʌn'taɪdi/ *adj.* (**un·tidi·er, un·tidi·est**)
1 0-π not neat or well arranged; in a state of confusion: *an untidy desk* ◇ *untidy hair* **2** 0-π (of a person) not keeping things neat or well organized: *Why do you have to be so untidy?* OPP **tidy** ▶ **un·tidi·ly** /-ɪli/ *adv.* **un·tidi·ness** *noun* [U]

untie /ʌn'taɪ/ *verb* ~ **sth** to undo a knot in sth; to undo sth that is tied: *to untie a knot* ◇ *I quickly untied the package and peeped inside.* ◇ *He untied the rope and pushed the boat into the water.*

until 0-π /ən'tɪl/ *conj., prep.* (also *informal* **till, til, 'til**) up to the point in time or the event mentioned: *Let's wait until the rain stops.* ◇ *Until she spoke I hadn't realized she wasn't English.* ◇ *You're not going out until you've finished this.* ◇ *Until now I have always lived alone.* ◇ *They moved here in 2009. Until then they'd always been in the London area.* ◇ *He continued working* ***up until*** *his death.* ◇ *The street is full of traffic* ***from morning till night.*** ◇ *You can stay on the bus until London* (= until you reach London).

un·time·ly /ʌn'taɪmli/ *adj.* (*formal*) **1** happening too soon or sooner than is normal or expected SYN **premature**: *She met a tragic and* ***untimely death*** *at 25.* **2** happening at a time or in a situation that is not suitable SYN **ill-timed**: *His interruption was untimely.* OPP **timely**

un·tir·ing /ʌn'taɪərɪŋ/ *adj.* (*approving*) continuing to do sth for a long period of time with a lot of effort and/or enthusiasm SYN **tireless**

un·titled /ˌʌn'taɪtld/ *adj.* (of a work of art) without a title

unto /'ʌntə; *before vowels* 'ʌntu/ *prep.* (*old use*) **1** to or towards sb/sth: *The angel appeared unto him in a dream.* **2** until a particular time or event: *The knights swore loyalty unto death.*

un·told /ˌʌn'təʊld; *NAmE* ˌʌn'toʊld/ *adj.* **1** [only before noun] used to emphasize how large, great, unpleasant, etc. sth is SYN **immeasurable**: *untold misery/wealth* ◇ *These gases cause* ***untold damage*** *to the environment.* **2** (of a story) not told to anyone

un·touch·able /ʌn'tʌtʃəbl/ *adj., noun*
■ ***adj.*** **1** a person who is **untouchable** is in a position where they are unlikely to be punished or criticized: *Given his political connections, he thought he was untouchable.* **2** that cannot be touched or changed by other people: *The department's budget is untouchable.* **3** (in India in the past) belonging to or connected with the Hindu social class (or CASTE) that was considered by other classes to be the lowest
■ ***noun*** (often **Untouchable**) (in India in the past) a member of a Hindu social class (or CASTE) that was considered by other classes to be the lowest

un·touched /ʌn'tʌtʃt/ *adj.* [not usually before noun] **1** ~ (**by sth**) not affected by sth, especially sth bad or unpleasant; not damaged: *The area has remained relatively untouched by commercial development.* **2** (of food or drink) not eaten or drunk: *She left her meal untouched.* **3** not changed in any way: *The final clause in the contract will be left untouched.*

un·to·ward /ˌʌntə'wɔːd; *NAmE* ʌn'tɔːrd/ *adj.* unusual and unexpected, and usually unpleasant: *That's the plan —unless* ***anything untoward*** *happens.* ◇ *He had noticed* ***nothing untoward.***

un·trained /ˌʌn'treɪnd/ *adj.* ~ (**in sth**) not trained to perform a particular job or skill; without formal training in sth: *untrained in keyboard skills* ◇ *untrained teachers* ◇ ***To the untrained eye,*** *the products look remarkably similar.*

un·tram·melled (*especially US* **un·tram·meled**) /ʌn'træmld/ *adj.* ~ (**by sth**) (*formal*) not restricted or limited by sth ➲ compare TRAMMEL

un·treat·ed /ˌʌn'triːtɪd/ *adj.* **1** not receiving medical treatment: *If untreated, the illness can become severe.* **2** (of substances) not made safe by chemical or other treatment: *untreated sewage* **3** (of wood) not treated with substances to preserve it

un·tried /ˌʌn'traɪd/ *adj.* **1** without experience of doing a particular job: *She chose two untried actors for the leading roles.* **2** not yet tried or tested to discover if it works or is successful SYN **untested**: *This is a new and relatively untried procedure.*

un·true /ʌn'truː/ *adj.* **1** not true; not based on facts: *These accusations are totally untrue.* ◇ *an untrue claim* ◇ *It* ***is untrue to say*** *that something like this could never happen again.* **2** ~ (**to sb/sth**) (*formal*) not loyal to sb/sth SYN **unfaithful**: *If he agreed to their demands, he would have to be untrue to his own principles.* OPP **true**

un·trust·worthy /ʌn'trʌstwɜːði; *NAmE* -wɜːrði/ *adj.* that cannot be trusted OPP **trustworthy**

un·truth /ˌʌn'truːθ/ *noun* (*pl.* **un·truths** /ˌʌn'truːðz; -'truːθs/) **1** [C] (*formal*) a lie. People often say 'untruth' to avoid saying 'lie'. ➲ compare TRUTH **2** [U] the state of being false

un·truth·ful /ʌn'truːθfl/ *adj.* saying things that you know are not true OPP **truthful** ▶ **un·truth·ful·ly** /-fəli/ *adv.*

un·turned /ˌʌn'tɜːnd; *NAmE* ˌʌn'tɜːrnd/ *adj.* IDM see STONE *n.*

un·tutored /ˌʌn'tjuːtəd; *NAmE* ˌʌn'tuːtərd/ *adj.* (*formal*) not having been formally taught about sth

un·typ·ical /ʌn'tɪpɪkl/ *adj.* ~ (**of sb/sth**) not typical: *an untypical example* ◇ *Schools in this area are quite untypical of schools in the rest of the country.* ◇ *All in all, it had been a* ***not untypical*** *day* (= it had been very like other days). OPP **typical** ➲ compare ATYPICAL ▶ **un·typ·ic·al·ly** *adv.*

un·usable /ˌʌn'juːzəbl/ *adj.* in such a bad condition or of such low quality that it cannot be used OPP **usable**

un·used¹ /ˌʌn'juːzd/ *adj.* not being used at the moment; never having been used ➲ compare DISUSED

un·used² /ʌn'juːst/ *adj.* not having much experience of sth and therefore not knowing how to deal with it; not used to sth: ~ **to sth** *This is an easy routine, designed for anyone who is unused to exercise.* ◇ ~ **to doing sth** *She was unused to talking about herself.* OPP **used**

un·usual 0-π /ʌn'juːʒuəl; -ʒəl/ *adj.*
1 0-π different from what is usual or normal SYN **uncommon**: ***It's unusual*** *for the trees to flower so early.* ◇ *She has a very unusual name.* ◇ *It's* ***not unusual*** *for young doctors to work a 70-hour week* (= it happens often). **2** 0-π different from other similar things and therefore interesting and attractive: *an unusual colour*

un·usual·ly 0-π /ʌn'juːʒuəli; -ʒəli/ *adv.*
1 0-π used before adjectives to emphasize that a particular quality is greater than normal: *unusually high levels of radiation* ◇ *an unusually cold winter* **2** 0-π used to say that a particular situation is not normal or expected: *Unusually for him, he wore a tie.*

un·utter·able /ʌn'ʌtərəbl/ *adj.* [only before noun] (*formal*) used to emphasize how great a particular emotion or quality is: *unutterable sadness* ▶ **un·utter·ably** /-əbli/ *adv.*

un·var·nished /ʌn'vɑːnɪʃt; *NAmE* -'vɑːrn-/ *adj.* **1** [only before noun] (*formal*) with nothing added: *It was the plain*

U

unvarnished truth. **2** (of wood, etc.) not covered with VARNISH

un·vary·ing /ʌn'veərɪŋ; *NAmE* -'veri-; -'væri-/ *adj.* (*formal*) never changing: *an unvarying routine*

un·veil /ˌʌn'veɪl/ *verb* **1** **~ sth** to remove a cover or curtain from a painting, statue, etc. so that it can be seen in public for the first time: *The Queen unveiled a plaque to mark the official opening of the hospital.* **2** **~ sth** to show or introduce a new plan, product, etc. to the public for the first time SYN **reveal**: *They will be unveiling their new models at the Motor Show.*

un·voiced /ˌʌn'vɔɪst/ *adj.* **1** thought about but not expressed in words **2** (*phonetics*) (of consonants) produced without moving your VOCAL CORDS; not VOICED SYN **voiceless**: *unvoiced consonants such as 'p' and 't'*

un·waged /ˌʌn'weɪdʒd/ *adj.* (*BrE*) **1** (of a person) not earning money by working OPP **waged** **2** (of work) for which you are not paid SYN **unpaid** **3** **the unwaged** *noun* [pl.] people who are unwaged

un·want·ed /ˌʌn'wɒntɪd; *NAmE* -'wɑːnt-; -'wɔːnt-/ *adj.* that you do not want: *unwanted advice* ◇ *unwanted pregnancies* ◇ *It is very sad when children* ***feel unwanted*** (= feel that other people do not care about them).

un·war·rant·ed /ʌn'wɒrəntɪd; *NAmE* -'wɔːr-; -'wɑːr-/ *adj.* (*formal*) not reasonable or necessary; not appropriate SYN **unjustified**: *Much of the criticism was totally unwarranted.*

un·wary /ʌn'weəri; *NAmE* -'weri/ *adj.* **1** [only before noun] not aware of the possible dangers or problems of a situation and therefore likely to be harmed in some way ⇨ compare WARY **2** **the unwary** *noun* [pl.] people who are unwary: *The stock market is full of traps for the unwary.*

un·washed /ˌʌn'wɒʃt; *NAmE* -'wɔːʃt; -'wɑːʃt/ *adj.* not washed; dirty: *a pile of unwashed dishes* ◇ *Their clothes were dirty and their hair unwashed.*

un·waver·ing /ʌn'weɪvərɪŋ/ *adj.* (*formal*) not changing or becoming weaker in any way: *unwavering support* ▸ **un·waver·ing·ly** *adv.*

un·wel·come /ʌn'welkəm/ *adj.* not wanted: *an unwelcome visitor* ◇ *To avoid attracting unwelcome attention he kept his voice down.* OPP **welcome**

un·wel·com·ing /ʌn'welkəmɪŋ/ *adj.* **1** (of a person) not friendly towards sb who is visiting or arriving **2** (of a place) not attractive; looking uncomfortable to be in OPP **welcoming**

un·well /ʌn'wel/ *adj.* [not before noun] (rather *formal*) ill/sick: *She said she was feeling unwell and went home.* OPP **well**

un·whole·some /ˌʌn'həʊlsəm; *NAmE* -'hoʊl-/ *adj.* **1** harmful to health; not looking healthy **2** that you consider unpleasant or not natural SYN **unhealthy** OPP **wholesome**

U

un·wieldy /ʌn'wiːldi/ *adj.* **1** (of an object) difficult to move or control because of its size, shape or weight SYN **cumbersome** **2** (of a system or group of people) difficult to control or organize because it is very large or complicated

un·will·ing 🔑 /ʌn'wɪlɪŋ/ *adj.* **1** 🔑 [not usually before noun] **~ (to do sth)** not wanting to do sth and refusing to do it: *They are unwilling to invest any more money in the project.* ◇ *She was unable, or unwilling, to give me any further details.* **2** [only before noun] not wanting to do or be sth, but forced to by other people SYN **reluctant**: *an unwilling hero* ◇ *He became the unwilling object of her attention.* OPP **willing** ▸ **un·will·ing·ly** 🔑 *adv.* **un·will·ing·ness** *noun* [U]

un·wind /ˌʌn'waɪnd/ *verb* (**un·wound**, **un·wound** /ˌʌn'waʊnd/) **1** [T, I] **~ (sth) (from sth)** to undo sth that has been wrapped into a ball or around sth: *to unwind a ball of string* ◇ *He unwound his scarf from his neck.* ◇ *The bandage gradually unwound and fell off.* **2** [I] to stop worrying or thinking about problems and start to relax SYN **relax**, **wind down**: *Music helps me unwind after a busy day.*

un·wise /ˌʌn'waɪz/ *adj.* **~ (to do sth)** showing a lack of good judgement SYN **foolish**: *It would be unwise to comment on the situation without knowing all the facts.* ◇ *an unwise investment* OPP **wise** ▸ **un·wise·ly** *adv.*: *Perhaps unwisely, I agreed to help.*

un·wit·ting /ʌn'wɪtɪŋ/ *adj.* [only before noun] not aware of what you are doing or of the situation you are involved in: *He became an unwitting accomplice in the crime.* ◇ *She was the unwitting cause of the argument.*

un·wit·ting·ly /ʌn'wɪtɪŋli/ *adv.* without being aware of what you are doing or the situation that you are involved in: *She had broken the law unwittingly, but still she had broken it.* OPP **wittingly**

un·wont·ed /ʌn'waʊntɪd; *NAmE* -'woʊn-/ *adj.* (*formal*) not usual or expected: *He spoke with unwonted enthusiasm.*

un·work·able /ʌn'wɜːkəbl; *NAmE* -'wɜːrk-/ *adj.* not practical or possible to do successfully: *an unworkable plan* ◇ *The law as it stands is unworkable.* OPP **workable**

un·world·ly /ʌn'wɜːldli; *NAmE* -'wɜːrld-/ *adj.* **1** not interested in money or the things that it buys **2** lacking experience of life SYN **naive** OPP **worldly** **3** having qualities that do not seem to belong to this world: *The landscape had a stark, unworldly beauty.*

un·wor·ried /ʌn'wʌrid; *NAmE* -'wɜːr-/ *adj.* [not usually before noun] (*formal*) not worried; calm; relaxed: *She appeared unworried by criticism.*

un·worthy /ʌn'wɜːði; *NAmE* ʌn'wɜːrði/ *adj.* (*formal*) **1** **~ (of sth)** not having the necessary qualities to deserve sth, especially respect: *He considered himself unworthy of the honour they had bestowed on him.* OPP **worthy** **2** **~ (of sb)** not acceptable from sb, especially sb who has an important job or high social position SYN **unbefitting**: *Such opinions are unworthy of educated people.* ▸ **un·worthi·ness** *noun* [U]: *feelings of unworthiness*

un·wound *past tense, past part.* of UNWIND

un·wrap /ʌn'ræp/ *verb* (-pp-) **~ sth** to take off the paper, etc. that covers or protects sth: *Don't unwrap your present until your birthday.* OPP **wrap up**

un·writ·ten /ˌʌn'rɪtn/ *adj.* **1** **~ law, rule, agreement, etc.** a law, etc. that everyone knows about and accepts even though it has not been made official: *an unwritten understanding that nobody leaves before five o'clock* **2** (of a book, etc.) not yet written: *The photographs were to be included in his as yet unwritten autobiography.*

un·yield·ing /ʌn'jiːldɪŋ/ *adj.* (*formal*) **1** if a person is **unyielding**, they are not easily influenced and they are unlikely to change their mind SYN **inflexible** **2** an **unyielding** substance or object does not bend or break when pressure is put on it

unzip /ˌʌn'zɪp/ *verb* (-pp-) **1** [T, I] **~ (sth)** if you **unzip** a piece of clothing, a bag, etc, or if it **unzips**, you open it by undoing the ZIP that fastens it OPP **zip up** **2** [T] **~ sth** (*computing*) to return a file to its original size after it has been COMPRESSED (= made smaller) SYN **decompress** OPP **zip**

up 🔑 /ʌp/ *adv., prep., adj., verb, noun*

■ ***adv.*** HELP For the special uses of **up** in phrasal verbs, look at the entries for the verbs. For example **break up** is in the phrasal verb section at **break**. **1** 🔑 towards or in a higher position: *He jumped up from his chair.* ◇ *The sun was already up* (= had risen) *when they set off.* ◇ *They live up in the mountains.* ◇ *It didn't take long to put the tent up.* ◇ *I pinned the notice up on the wall.* ◇ *Lay the cards face up* (= facing upwards) *on the table.* ◇ *You look nice with your hair up* (= arranged on top of or at the back of your head). ◇ ***Up you come!*** (= said when lifting a child) **2** 🔑 to or at a higher level: *She turned the volume up.* ◇ *Prices are still going up* (= rising). ◇ *United were 3–1 up at half-time.* ◇ *The wind is getting up* (= blowing more strongly). ◇ *Sales are* ***well up on*** *last year.* ⇨ LANGUAGE BANK at INCREASE **3** 🔑 to the place where sb/sth is: *A car drove up and he got in.* ◇ *She went straight up to the door and knocked loudly.* **4** to or at an important place, especially a large city: *We're going up to New York for the day.* ◇ (*BrE, formal*) *His son's up at Oxford* (= Oxford University). **5** to a place in the north of a country: *They've moved* **up north**. ◇ *We drove up to Inverness to see my father.* **6** into pieces or parts: *She tore the paper up.* ◇ *They've had the road up* (= with the surface broken or removed) *to lay some pipes.* ◇ *How shall we divide up the work?* **7** completely: *We ate all the food up.* ◇ *The stream has dried up.* **8** so as to be formed or brought together: *The government agreed to set up a committee of inquiry.* ◇ *She gathered up her belongings.* **9** so as to be finished or closed: *I have some paperwork to finish up.* ◇ *Do your coat up; it's cold.* **10** (of a period of time) finished; over: *Time's up. Stop writing and hand in your papers.* **11** out of bed: *I stayed up late* (= did not go to bed until late) *last night.* ◇ (*BrE*) *He's* **up and about** *again after his illness.* **12** (*informal*) used to say that sth is happening, especially sth unusual or unpleasant: *I could tell* **something was up** *by the looks on their faces.* ◇ **What's up?** (= What is the matter?) ◇ **What's up with** *him? He looks furious.* ◇ *Is anything up? You can tell me.* HELP In *NAmE* **What's up?** can just mean 'What's new?' or 'What's happening?' There may not be anything wrong.

IDM **be up to sb** to be sb's duty or responsibility; to be for sb to decide: *It's not up to you to tell me how to do my job.* ◇ *Shall we eat out or stay in? It's up to you.* **not be 'up to much** (*BrE*) to be of poor quality; to not be very good: *His work isn't up to much.* **up against sth** (*informal*) facing problems or opposition: *Teachers are up against some major problems these days.* ◇ *She's really* **up against it** (= in a difficult situation). **ˌup and 'down 1** moving upwards and downwards: *The boat bobbed up and down on the water.* **2** in one direction and then in the opposite direction: *She was pacing up and down in front of her desk.* **3** sometimes good and sometimes bad: *My relationship with him was up and down.* **4** (*NAmE, informal*) if you swear **up and down** that sth is true, you say that it is definitely true **ˌup and 'running** (of a system, for example a computer system) working; being used: *By that time the new system should be up and running.* **up before sb/sth** appearing in front of sb in authority for a judgement to be made about sth that you have done: *He came up before the local magistrate for speeding.* **up for sth 1** on offer for sth: *The house is up for sale.* **2** being considered for sth, especially as a candidate: *Two candidates are up for election.* **3** (*informal*) willing to take part in a particular activity: *We're going clubbing tonight. Are you* **up for it?** **'up there** (*informal*) among or almost the best, worst, most important, etc: *It may not have been the worst week of my life but it's up there.* ◇ *OK, it's not my absolute dream, but it's up there.* **up to sth 1** as far as a particular number, level, etc: *I can take up to four people* (= but no more than four) *in my car.* ◇ *The temperature went up to 35°C.* **2** (also **up until sth**) not further or later than sth; until sth: *Read up to page 100.* ◇ *Up to now he's been very quiet.* **3** as high or as good as sth: *Her latest book isn't up to her usual standard.* **4** (also **up to doing sth**) physically or mentally capable of sth: *He's not up to the job.* ◇ *I don't feel up to going to work today.* **5** (*informal*) doing sth, especially sth bad: *What's she up to?* ◇ *What've you been up to?* ◇ *I'm sure he's* **up to no good** (= doing sth bad).

■ ***prep.*** **1** to or in a higher position somewhere: *She climbed up the flight of steps.* ◇ *The village is further up the valley.* **2** along or further along a road or street: *We live just up the road, past the post office.* **3** towards the place where a river starts: *a cruise up the Rhine*

IDM **up and down sth** in one direction and then in the opposite direction along sth: *I looked up and down the corridor.* **ˌup 'yours!** (*taboo, slang*) an offensive way of being rude to sb, for example because they have said sth that makes you angry

■ ***adj.*** **1** [only before noun] directed or moving upwards: *an up stroke* ◇ *the up escalator* **2** [not before noun] (*informal*) cheerful; happy or excited: *The mood here is resolutely up.* **3** [not before noun] (of a computer system) working: *Our system should be up by this afternoon.*

■ ***verb*** (-pp-) **1** [I] **up and...** (*informal* or *humorous*) to suddenly move or do sth unexpected: *He* **upped and left** *without telling anyone.* **2** [T] **~ sth** to increase the price or amount of sth SYN **raise**: *The buyers upped their offer by £1000.*

IDM **ˌup 'sticks** (*BrE*) (*NAmE* **ˌpull up 'stakes**) (*informal*) to suddenly move from your house and go to live somewhere else ➲ more at ANTE

■ ***noun***

IDM **on the 'up** increasing or improving: *Business confidence is on the up.* **on the ˌup and 'up** (*informal*) **1** (*BrE*) becoming more and more successful: *The club has been on the up and up since the beginning of the season.* **2** (*NAmE*) = ON THE LEVEL at LEVEL *n.*: *The offer seems to be on the up and up.* **ˌups and 'downs** the mixture of good and bad things in life or in a particular situation or relationship

up- /ʌp/ *prefix* (in adjectives, verbs and related nouns) higher; upwards; towards the top of sth: *upland* ◇ *upturned* ◇ *upgrade* ◇ *uphill*

ˌup-'anchor *verb* [I] (of a ship or its CREW) to raise the ANCHOR from the water in order to be ready to sail

ˌup-and-'coming *adj.* likely to be successful and popular in the future: *up-and-coming young actors*

up·beat /ˈʌpbiːt/ *adj.* (*informal*) positive and enthusiastic; making you feel that the future will be good SYN **optimistic**: *The tone of the speech was upbeat.* ◇ *The meeting ended on an upbeat note.* OPP **downbeat**

up·braid /ʌpˈbreɪd/ *verb* **~ sb (for sth/for doing sth)** (*formal*) to criticize sb or speak angrily to them because you do not approve of sth that they have said or done SYN **reproach**

up·bring·ing /ˈʌpbrɪŋɪŋ/ *noun* [sing., U] the way in which a child is cared for and taught how to behave while it is growing up: *to have had a sheltered upbringing* ◇ *He was a Catholic by upbringing.*

UPC /ˌjuː piː ˈsiː/ *abbr.* (*NAmE, technical*) Universal Product Code: *The Universal Product Code symbol, also known as the 'barcode', is printed on products for sale and contains information that a computer can read.*

up·chuck /ˈʌptʃʌk/ *verb* [I, T] **~ (sth)** (*NAmE, informal*) to VOMIT

up·com·ing /ˈʌpkʌmɪŋ/ *adj.* [only before noun] (*especially NAmE*) going to happen soon: *the upcoming presidential election* ◇ *a single from the band's upcoming album*

ˌup-'country *adj.* [only before noun] connected with an area of a country that is not near large towns ▶ **ˌup-'country** *adv.*

up·date *verb, noun*

■ ***verb*** /ˌʌpˈdeɪt/ **1 ~ sth** to make sth more modern by adding new parts, etc: *It's about time we updated our software.* **2** to give sb the most recent information about sth; to add the most recent information to sth SYN **bring up to date**: **~ sb (on sth)** *I called the office to update them on the day's developments.* ◇ **~ sth** *Our records are regularly updated.*

■ ***noun*** /ˈʌpdeɪt/ **1 ~ (on sth)** a report or broadcast that gives the most recent information about sth; a new version of sth containing the most recent information: *a news update* **2** (*computing*) the most recent improvements to a computer program that are sent to users of the program

upend /ʌpˈend/ *verb* **~ sb/sth** to turn sb/sth upside down: *The bicycle lay upended in a ditch.*

up·field /ˌʌpˈfiːld/ *adv.* (*sport*) towards your opponent's end of the playing field

up·front /ˌʌpˈfrʌnt/ *adj.* **1 ~ (about sth)** not trying to hide what you think or do SYN **honest, frank**: *He's been upfront about his intentions since the beginning.* **2** [only before noun] paid in advance, before other payments are made: *There will be an upfront fee of 4%.* ➲ see also UP FRONT at FRONT

up·grad·ation /ˌʌpgreɪˈdeɪʃn; ˌʌpgrəˈd-/ *noun* [U] (*IndE*) the fact of UPGRADING sth: *the upgradation of civic facilities in large cities*

up·grade /ˌʌpˈgreɪd/ *verb* [often passive] **1 ~ sth** to make a piece of machinery, computer system, etc. more powerful and efficient **2 ~ sb (to sth)** to give sb a more important

U

job SYN **promote 3** **~ sb** (**to sth**) to give sb a better seat on a plane, room in a hotel, etc. than the one that they have paid for **4** **~ sth** to improve the condition of a building, etc. in order to provide a better service: *to upgrade the town's leisure facilities* ➲ compare DOWNGRADE ▶ **up·grade** /ˈʌpɡreɪd/ *noun*

up·heav·al /ʌpˈhiːvl/ *noun* [C, U] a big change that causes a lot of confusion, worry and problems SYN **disruption**: *the latest upheavals in the education system* ◇ *I can't face the upheaval of moving house again.* ◇ *a period of emotional upheaval*

up·hill /ˌʌpˈhɪl/ *adj., adv.*
- *adj.* **1** sloping upwards: *an* ***uphill climb/slope*** ◇ *The last part of the race is all uphill.* OPP **downhill** **2** **~ battle, struggle, task, etc.** an argument or a struggle that is difficult to win and takes a lot of effort over a long period of time
- *adv.* towards the top of a hill or slope: *We cycled uphill for over an hour.* ◇ *The path slopes steeply uphill.* OPP **downhill**

up·hold /ʌpˈhəʊld; *NAmE* -ˈhoʊld/ *verb* (**up·held**, **up·held** /-ˈheld/) **1** **~ sth** to support sth that you think is right and make sure that it continues to exist: *We have a duty to uphold the law.* **2** **~ sth** (especially of a court of law) to agree that a previous decision was correct or that a request is reasonable: *to* ***uphold a conviction/an appeal/a complaint*** ▶ **up·hold·er** *noun*: *an upholder of traditional values*

up·hol·ster /ʌpˈhəʊlstə(r); *NAmE* -ˈhoʊl-/ *verb* [usually passive] **~ sth** (**in sth**) to cover a chair, etc. with soft material (= PADDING) and cloth

up·hol·ster·er /ʌpˈhəʊlstərə(r); *NAmE* -ˈhoʊl-/ *noun* a person whose job is to upholster furniture

up·hol·stery /ʌpˈhəʊlstəri; *NAmE* -ˈhoʊl-/ *noun* [U] **1** soft covering on furniture such as ARMCHAIRS and SOFAS **2** the process or trade of UPHOLSTERING

UPI /ˌjuː piː ˈaɪ/ *abbr.* UNITED PRESS INTERNATIONAL

up·keep /ˈʌpkiːp/ *noun* [U] **1** **~** (**of sth**) the cost or process of keeping sth in good condition SYN **maintenance**: *Tenants are responsible for the upkeep of rented property.* **2** **~** (**of sb/sth**) the cost or process of giving a child or an animal the things that they need: *He makes payments to his ex-wife for the upkeep of their children.*

up·land /ˈʌplənd/ *noun* [usually pl.] an area of high land that is not near the coast ▶ **up·land** *adj.* [only before noun]: *upland agriculture*

up·lift *noun, verb*
- *noun* /ˈʌplɪft/ [U, sing.] **1** the fact of sth being raised or of sth increasing: *an uplift in sales* ◇ *an uplift bra* (= that raises the breasts) **2** a feeling of hope and happiness: *The news gave them a much needed uplift.* **3** (also **up·thrust**) (*geology*) the process or result of land being moved to a higher level by movements inside the earth
- *verb* /ˌʌpˈlɪft/ **~ sb** (*formal*) to make sb feel happier or give sb more hope

U

up·lift·ed /ˌʌpˈlɪftɪd/ *adj.* **1** [not before noun] feeling happy and full of hope **2** (*literary*) lifted upwards: *a sea of uplifted faces*

up·lift·ing /ˌʌpˈlɪftɪŋ/ *adj.* making you feel happier or giving you more hope: *an uplifting experience/speech*

up·light·er /ˈʌplaɪtə(r)/ (also **up·light** /ˈʌplaɪt/) *noun* a lamp in a room that is designed to send light upwards ➲ compare DOWNLIGHTER

up·link /ˈʌplɪŋk/ *noun* (*technical*) a communications link to a SATELLITE

up·load *verb, noun*
- *verb* /ˌʌpˈləʊd; *NAmE* -ˈloʊd/ **~ sth** (*computing*) to move data to a larger computer system from a smaller one OPP **download** ➲ COLLOCATIONS at EMAIL
- *noun* /ˈʌpləʊd; *NAmE* -loʊd/ (*computing*) data that has been moved to a larger computer system from a smaller one OPP **download**

up·mar·ket /ˌʌpˈmɑːkɪt; *NAmE* -ˈmɑːrk-/ (*BrE*) (*NAmE* **up·scale**) *adj.* [usually before noun] designed for or used by people who belong to a high social class or have a lot of money: *an upmarket restaurant* OPP **downmarket** ▶ ˌ**upˈmarket** (*BrE*) (*NAmE* ˌ**upˈscale**) *adv.*: *The company has been forced to move more upmarket.*

upon 0‑w /əˈpɒn; *NAmE* əˈpɑːn; əˈpɔːn/ *prep.* **1** 0‑w (*formal, especially BrE*) = ON: *The decision was based upon two considerations.* HELP Although the word **upon** has the same meaning as **on**, it is usually used in more formal contexts or in phrases such as: *once upon a time* and: *row upon row of seats.* **2** **...upon...** used to emphasize that there is a large number or amount of sth: *mile upon mile of dusty road* ◇ *thousands upon thousands of letters*

IDM (**almost**) **uˈpon you** if sth in the future is **almost upon you**, it is going to arrive or happen very soon: *The summer season was almost upon them again.* ➲ more at ONCE *adv.*

upper 0‑w /ˈʌpə(r)/ *adj., noun*
- *adj.* [only before noun] **1** 0‑w located above sth else, especially sth of the same type or the other of a pair: *the upper lip* ◇ *the upper deck* **2** 0‑w at or near the top of sth: *the upper arm* ◇ *the upper slopes of the mountain* ◇ *a member of the upper middle class* ◇ *salaries at the upper end of the pay scale* ◇ *There is an upper limit of £20 000 spent on any one project.* **3** (of a place) located away from the coast, on high ground or towards the north of an area: *the upper reaches of the river* OPP **lower**

IDM **gain, get, have, etc. the ˌupper ˈhand** to get an advantage over sb so that you are in control of a particular situation ➲ more at STIFF *adj.*
- *noun* [usually pl.] **1** the top part of a shoe that is attached to the SOLE: *shoes with leather uppers* ➲ VISUAL VOCAB page V52 **2** (*informal*) a drug that makes you feel excited and full of energy ➲ compare DOWNER

IDM **on your ˈuppers** (*BrE, informal*) having very little money

ˌ**upper ˈcase** *noun* [U] capital letters (= the large form of letters, for example A, B, C rather than a, b, c): *Headings should be in upper case.* ➲ compare LOWER CASE ▶ ˌ**upper ˈcase** *adj.*: *upper-case letters*

ˌ**upper ˈchamber** *noun* = UPPER HOUSE

the ˌupper ˈclass *noun* [sing.] (also **the ˌupper ˈclasses** [pl.]) the groups of people that are considered to have the highest social status and that have more money and/or power than other people in society: *a member of the upper class/upper classes* ▶ ˌ**upper ˈclass** *adj.*: *Her family is very upper class.* ◇ *an upper-class accent* ➲ compare LOWER CLASS, MIDDLE CLASS, WORKING CLASS

upper·class·man /ˌʌpəˈklɑːsmən; *NAmE* ˌʌpərˈklæs-/, **upper·class·woman** /ˌʌpəˈklɑːswʊmən; *NAmE* ˌʌpərˈklæs-/ *noun* (*pl.* **-men** /-mən/, **-women** /-wɪmɪn/) (in the US) a student in the last two years of HIGH SCHOOL or college ➲ compare UNDERCLASSMAN

the ˌupper ˈcrust *noun* [sing.+ sing./pl. v.] (*informal*) the people who belong to the highest social class SYN **aristocracy** ▶ ˌ**upper-ˈcrust** *adj.*

upper·cut /ˈʌpəkʌt; *NAmE* ˈʌpərkʌt/ *noun* (in boxing) a way of hitting sb on the chin, in which you bend your arm and move your hand upwards

ˌ**upper ˈhouse** (also ˌ**upper ˈchamber**) (also ˌ**second ˈchamber** especially in *BrE*) *noun* [sing.] one of the parts of a parliament in countries which have a parliament that is divided into two parts. In Britain it is the House of Lords and in the US it is the Senate. ➲ compare LOWER HOUSE

upper·most /ˈʌpəməʊst; *NAmE* ˈʌpərmoʊst/ *adj., adv.*
- *adj.* **1** [usually before noun] (*formal*) higher or nearer the top than other things: *the uppermost branches of the tree* **2** [not usually before noun] more important than other things in a particular situation: *These thoughts were* ***uppermost in my mind.***
- *adv.* (*formal*) in the highest position; facing upwards: *Place the material on a flat surface, shiny side uppermost.*

ˈ**upper school** *noun* (*BrE*) a school, or the classes in a school, for older students, usually between the ages of 14 and 18 ➲ compare LOWER SCHOOL, MIDDLE SCHOOL

up·pity /ˈʌpəti/ *adj.* (*old-fashioned, informal*) behaving as if you are more important than you really are, especially when this means that you refuse to obey orders

up·raised /ˌʌpˈreɪzd/ *adj.* lifted upwards: *She strode towards them, her fist upraised.*

up·right /ˈʌpraɪt/ *adj., adv., noun*
■ ***adj.*** **1** (of a person) not lying down, and with the back straight rather than bent: *an upright posture* ◇ *Gradually raise your body into an upright position.* **2** placed in a vertical position: *Keep the bottle upright.* ◇ *an upright freezer* (= one that is taller than it is wide) ◇ *an upright piano* (= one with vertical strings) **3** (of a person) behaving in a moral and honest way SYN **upstanding**: *an upright citizen*
IDM see BOLT *adv.*
■ ***adv.*** in or into a vertical position: *She sat upright in bed.* ◇ *He managed to pull himself upright.*
■ ***noun*** **1** a long piece of wood, metal or plastic that is placed in a vertical position, especially in order to support sth **2** = UPRIGHT PIANO

up·right·ness /ˈʌpraɪtnəs/ *noun* [U] behaviour or attitudes that are very moral and honest

ˌ**upright piˈano** (also **up·right**) *noun* a piano in which the strings are vertical ➲ VISUAL VOCAB page V31 ➲ compare GRAND PIANO, SPINET

up·ris·ing /ˈʌpraɪzɪŋ/ *noun* ~ (**against sth**) a situation in which a group of people join together in order to fight against the people who are in power SYN **rebellion**, **revolt**: *an armed uprising against the government* ◇ *a* ***popular uprising*** (= by the ordinary people of the country) ◇ *to* ***crush/suppress an uprising***

up·river /ˌʌpˈrɪvə(r)/ *adv.* = UPSTREAM

up·roar /ˈʌprɔː(r)/ *noun* [U, sing.] **1** a situation in which people shout and make a lot of noise because they are angry or upset about sth: *The room was* ***in*** *(****an****)* ***uproar***. ◇ *Her comments provoked (an) uproar from the audience.* **2** a situation in which there is a lot of public criticism and angry argument about sth that sb has said or done SYN **outcry**: *The article caused (an) uproar.*

up·roari·ous /ʌpˈrɔːriəs/ *adj.* [usually before noun] **1** in which there is a lot of noise and people laugh or shout a lot: *an uproarious party* **2** extremely funny: *an uproarious story* ▸ **up·roari·ous·ly** *adv.*: *The audience laughed uproariously.* ◇ *uproariously funny*

up·root /ˌʌpˈruːt/ *verb* **1** [T] ~ **sth** to pull a tree, plant, etc. out of the ground **2** [I, T] to leave a place where you have lived for a long time; to make sb do this: *We decided to uproot and head for Scotland.* ◇ ~ **yourself/sb** *If I accept the job, it will mean uprooting my family and moving to Italy.*

up·rush /ˈʌprʌʃ/ *noun* [sing.] ~ **of sth** (*formal*) a sudden feeling of sth such as joy or fear: *an uprush of joy*

ups-a-daisy /ˈʊpsə deɪzi; ˈʌpsə/ *exclamation* = UPSY-DAISY

up·scale /ˌʌpˈskeɪl/ (*NAmE*) (*BrE* **up·mar·ket**) *adj.* [usually before noun] designed for or used by people who belong to a high social class or have a lot of money OPP **downscale** ▸ ˌ**upˈscale** (*NAmE*) (*BrE* ˌ**upˈmarket**) *adv.*

up·sell /ˈʌpsel/ *verb* (**upsold**, **upsold** /ˈʌpsəʊld; *NAmE* -soʊld/) [I] (*business*) to persuade a customer to buy more products or a more expensive product than they originally intended: *You can usually upsell to about half the customers.* ▸ **up·sell·ing** /ˈʌpselɪŋ/ *noun* [U]: (*business*) *You can make great profits from upselling.*

upset 🔑 *verb, adj., noun*
■ ***verb*** /ʌpˈset/ (**up·set·ting**, **upset**, **upset**) **1** 🔑 to make sb/yourself feel unhappy, anxious or annoyed SYN **distress**: ~ **sb/yourself** *This decision is likely to upset a lot of people.* ◇ *Don't upset yourself about it—let's just forget it ever happened.* ◇ **it upsets sb that...** *It upset him that nobody had bothered to tell him about it.* ◇ **it upsets sb to do sth** *It upsets me to think of her all alone in that big house.* **2** ~ **sth** to make a plan, situation, etc. go wrong: *He arrived an hour late and upset all our arrangements.* **3** ~ **sb's stomach** to make sb feel sick after they have eaten or drunk sth **4** ~ **sth** to make sth fall over by hitting it by accident: *She stood up suddenly, upsetting a glass of wine.*
IDM **upset the ˈapple cart** to cause problems for sb or spoil their plans, arrangements, etc.
■ ***adj.*** /ˌʌpˈset/ **1** 🔑 [not before noun] ~ (**about sth**) | ~ (**that ...**) unhappy or disappointed because of sth unpleasant that has happened: *There's no point getting upset about it.* **2** 🔑 **an** ˌ**upset ˈstomach** an illness in the stomach that makes you feel sick or have DIARRHOEA
■ ***noun*** /ˈʌpset/ **1** [U] a situation in which there are problems or difficulties, especially when these are unexpected: *The company has survived the recent upset in share prices.* ◇ *His health has not been improved by all the upset at home.* **2** [C] (in a competition) a situation in which a person or team beats the person or team that was expected to win **3** [C] an illness in the stomach that makes you feel sick or have DIARRHOEA: *a stomach upset* **4** [U, C] feelings of unhappiness and disappointment caused by sth unpleasant that has happened: *It had been the cause of much emotional upset.*

up·set·ting 🔑 /ʌpˈsetɪŋ/ *adj.* making you feel unhappy, anxious or annoyed: *an upsetting experience*

up·shift /ˈʌpʃɪft/ *verb* [I] (*NAmE*) to change into a higher gear in a vehicle

the up·shot /ˈʌpʃɒt; *NAmE* -ʃɑːt/ *noun* [sing.] the final result of a series of events SYN **outcome**: *The upshot of it all was that he left college and got a job.*

up·side /ˈʌpsaɪd/ *noun* [sing.] the more positive aspect of a situation that is generally bad OPP **downside**

ˌ**upside ˈdown** 🔑 *adv.*
in or into a position in which the top of sth is where the bottom is normally found and the bottom is where the top is normally found: *The canoe floated upside down on the lake.* OPP **right side up** ▸ ˌ**upside ˈdown** 🔑 *adj.* [not usually before noun]: *The painting looks like it's upside down to me.*
IDM **turn sth** ˌ**upside ˈdown 1** to make a place untidy when looking for sth: *The police turned the whole house upside down looking for clues.* **2** to cause large changes and confusion in a person's life: *His sudden death turned her world upside down.*

up·si·lon /ʌpˈsaɪlən; ˈʊpsɪlɒn; *NAmE* ˈʊpsɪlɑːn/ *noun* the 20th letter of the Greek alphabet (Υ, υ)

up·skill /ˈʌpskɪl/ *verb* [T, I] ~ (**sb**) (*business*) to teach sb new skills; to learn new skills: *The company has invested heavily in upskilling its workforce.* ▸ **up·skill·ing** /ˈʌpskɪlɪŋ/ *noun* [U]

up·stage /ˌʌpˈsteɪdʒ/ *adv., adj., verb*
■ ***adv., adj.*** at or towards the back of the stage in a theatre OPP **downstage**
■ ***verb*** ~ **sb** to say or do sth that makes people notice you more than the person that they should be interested in: *She was furious at being upstaged by her younger sister.*

up·stairs 🔑 /ˌʌpˈsteəz; *NAmE* -ˈsterz/ *adv., noun*
■ ***adv.*** 🔑 up the stairs; on or to a floor of a house or other building higher than the one that you are on: *The cat belongs to the people who live upstairs.* ◇ *I carried her bags upstairs.* ◇ *She went upstairs to get dressed.* OPP **downstairs** ▸ **up·stairs** 🔑 *adj.* [only before noun]: *an upstairs room*
IDM see KICK *v.*
■ ***noun*** 🔑 [sing.] the floor or floors in a building that are above the ground floor: *We've converted the upstairs into an office.* OPP **downstairs**

up·stand·ing /ˌʌpˈstændɪŋ/ *adj.* [usually before noun] (*formal*) behaving in a moral and honest way SYN **upright**: *an upstanding member of the community*
IDM **be upˈstanding** (*BrE, formal*) used in a formal situation to tell people to stand up: *Ladies and gentlemen, please be upstanding and join me in a toast to the bride and groom.*

U

up·start /ˈʌpstɑːt; *NAmE* -stɑːrt/ *noun* (*disapproving*) a person who has just started in a new position or job but who behaves as if they are more important than other people, in a way that is annoying

up·state /ˌʌpˈsteɪt/ *adv.* (*US*) in or to a part of a state that is far from its main cities, especially a northern part: *They retired and went to live upstate.* ▶ **up·state** *adj.* [only before noun]: *upstate New York*

up·stream /ˌʌpˈstriːm/ (also *less frequent* **up·river**) *adv.* **~ (of/from sth)** along a river, in the opposite direction to the way in which the water flows: *The nearest town is about ten miles upstream.* ◇ *upstream of/from the bridge* OPP **downstream**

up·surge /ˈʌpsɜːdʒ; *NAmE* -sɜːrdʒ/ *noun* [usually sing.] (*formal*) a sudden large increase in sth: **~ (in sth)** *an upsurge in violent crime* ◇ **~ (of sth)** *a recent upsurge of interest in his movies*

up·swell /ˈʌpswel/ (also **up·swell·ing** /ˈʌpswelɪŋ/) *noun* [sing.] **~ of sth** (*formal*) an increase in sth, especially a feeling: *a huge upswell of emotion*

up·swept /ˈʌpswept/ (also **ˈswept-up**) *adj.* curved or sloping upwards: *an upswept moustache*

up·swing /ˈʌpswɪŋ/ *noun* [usually sing.] **~ (in sth)** a situation in which sth improves or increases over a period of time SYN **upturn**: *an upswing in economic activity* ◇ *an upswing in the team's fortunes*

upsy-daisy /ˈʊpsi deɪzi; ˈʌpsi/ (also **ups-a-daisy**, **oops-a-daisy**) *exclamation* said when you have made a mistake, dropped sth, fallen down, etc. or when sb else has

up·take /ˈʌpteɪk/ *noun* [U, sing.] **1 ~ (of sth)** the use that is made of sth that has become available: *There has been a high uptake of the free training.* **2 ~ (of sth)** (*technical*) the process by which sth is taken into a body or system; the rate at which this happens: *the uptake of oxygen by muscles* IDM **be ˌquick/ˌslow on the ˈuptake** (*informal*) to be quick/slow to understand sth: *Is he always this slow on the uptake?*

up·tempo /ˈʌptempəʊ; *NAmE* -poʊ/ *adj.* (especially of music) fast: *uptempo dance tunes*

up·thrust /ˈʌpθrʌst/ *noun* [U] **1** (*physics*) the force with which a liquid or gas pushes up against an object that is floating in it **2** (*geology*) = UPLIFT

up·tick /ˈʌptɪk/ *noun* (*economics*) (*NAmE*) a small increase in the level or value of sth: *The futures market is showing an uptick.* OPP **downtick**

up·tight /ˌʌpˈtaɪt/ *adj.* **~ (about sth)** (*informal*) **1** anxious and/or angry about sth: *Relax! You're getting too uptight about it.* **2** (*especially NAmE*) nervous about showing your feelings: *an uptight teenager*

up·time /ˈʌptaɪm/ *noun* [U] the time during which a machine, especially a computer, is working OPP **downtime**

U

ˌup to ˈdate *adj.* **1** modern; fashionable: *This technology is bang up to date* (= completely modern). ◇ *up-to-date clothes* ◇ *up-to-date equipment* **2** having or including the most recent information: *We are keeping up to date with the latest developments.* ◇ *up-to-date records* ◇ *She* ***brought him up to date*** *with what had happened.* ➲ see also OUT OF DATE

ˌup-to-the-ˈminute *adj.* [usually before noun] **1** having or including the most recent information: *up-to-the-minute news* **2** modern; fashionable: *up-to-the-minute designs* ➲ see also UP TO THE MINUTE at MINUTE *n.*

up·town /ˌʌpˈtaʊn/ *adv.*, *adj.* (*NAmE*)

▪ ***adv.*** in or to the parts of a town or city that are away from the centre, where people live: *They live in an apartment uptown.* ◇ *We walked uptown a couple of blocks until we found a cab.* ➲ compare DOWNTOWN, MIDTOWN

▪ ***adj.*** **1** [only before noun] in, to or typical of the parts of a town or city that are away from the centre, where people live: *an uptown train* **2** typical of an area of a town or city where people have a lot of money: *uptown prices* ◇ *an uptown girl*

up·trend /ˈʌptrend/ *noun* [sing.] (*NAmE*) a situation in which business activity or performance increases or improves over a period of time OPP **downtrend**

up·turn /ˈʌptɜːn; *NAmE* -tɜːrn/ *noun* [usually sing.] **~ (in sth)** a situation in which sth improves or increases over a period of time SYN **upswing**: *an upturn in the economy* ◇ *The restaurant trade is on the upturn.* OPP **downturn**

up·turned /ˌʌpˈtɜːnd; *NAmE* ˌʌpˈtɜːrnd/ *adj.* [usually before noun] **1** pointing or facing upwards: *an upturned nose* (= that curves upwards at the end) ◇ *She looked down at the sea of upturned faces.* **2** turned upside down: *She sat on an upturned box.*

uPVC /ˌjuː ˌpiː ˌviː ˈsiː/ *noun* [U] the abbreviation for 'unplasticized polyvinyl chloride' (a strong plastic used to make window frames and pipes)

up·ward 0‑ᵂ /ˈʌpwəd; *NAmE* -wərd/ *adj.* [only before noun]
1 0‑ᵂ pointing towards or facing a higher place: *an upward gaze* **2** increasing in amount or price: *an upward movement in property prices* OPP **downward**

ˌupwardly ˈmobile *adj.* moving towards a higher social position, usually in which you become richer: *upwardly mobile immigrant groups* ◇ *an upwardly mobile lifestyle* ▶ **ˌupward moˈbility** *noun* [U]

up·wards 0‑ᵂ /ˈʌpwədz; *NAmE* -wərdz/ (*especially BrE*) (also **up·ward** especially in *NAmE*) *adv.*
1 0‑ᵂ towards a higher place or position: *A flight of steps led upwards to the front door.* ◇ *Place your hands on the table with the palms facing upwards.* OPP **downwards** **2** towards a higher amount or price: *Bad weather forced the price of fruit upwards.* ◇ *The budget has been revised upwards.* OPP **downwards** **3 ~ of sth** more than the amount or number mentioned: *You should expect to pay upwards of £50 for a hotel room.*

up·wind /ˌʌpˈwɪnd/ *adv.* in the opposite direction to the way in which the wind is blowing: *to sail upwind* ◇ *The house was upwind of the factory and its smells* (= the wind did not blow the smells towards the house). OPP **downwind** ▶ **up·wind** *adj.*

ur- /ʊə(r); *NAmE* ʊr/ *prefix* (*formal*) earliest or original

ur·an·ium /juˈreɪniəm/ *noun* [U] (*symb.* U) a chemical element. Uranium is a heavy, silver-white, RADIOACTIVE metal, used mainly in producing nuclear energy.

Ura·nus /ˈjʊərənəs; jʊˈreɪnəs; *NAmE* ˈjʊr-; jʊˈr-/ *noun* the planet in the SOLAR SYSTEM that is 7th in order of distance from the sun

urban 0‑ᵂ /ˈɜːbən; *NAmE* ˈɜːrbən/ *adj.* [usually before noun]
1 0‑ᵂ connected with a town or city: *damage to both urban and rural environments* ◇ *urban areas* ◇ *urban life* ◇ *urban development* (= the process of building towns and cities or making them larger) ◇ ***urban renewal/regeneration*** (= the process of improving the buildings, etc. in the poor parts of a town or city) ◇ *efforts to control* ***urban sprawl*** (= the spread of city buildings into the countryside) ➲ compare RURAL **2** connected with types of music such as RHYTHM AND BLUES and REGGAE that are played by black musicians: *today's urban music scene* ◇ *urban radio shows*

ur·bane /ɜːˈbeɪn; *NAmE* ɜːrˈb-/ *adj.* (especially of a man) good at knowing what to say and how to behave in social situations; appearing relaxed and confident ▶ **ur·bane·ly** *adv.* **ur·ban·ity** /ɜːˈbænəti; *NAmE* ɜːrˈb-/ *noun* [U]

ur·ban·ite /ˈɜːbənaɪt; *NAmE* ˈɜːrb-/ *noun* a person who lives in a town or city

ur·ban·ized (*BrE* also **-ised**) /ˈɜːbənaɪzd; *NAmE* ˈɜːrb-/ *adj.* **1** (of an area, a country, etc.) having a lot of towns, streets, factories, etc. rather than countryside **2** (of people) living and working in towns and cities rather than in the country: *an increasingly urbanized society* ▶ **ur·ban·iza·tion, -isa·tion** /ˌɜːbənaɪˈzeɪʃn; *NAmE* ˌɜːrbənəˈz-/ *noun* [U]

ˌurban ˈmyth (also **ˌurban ˈlegend**) *noun* a story about an amusing or strange event that is supposed to have happened, which is often repeated and which many people believe is true

ur·chin /ˈɜːtʃɪn; *NAmE* ˈɜːrtʃɪn/ *noun* **1** (*old-fashioned*) a young child who is poor and dirty, often one who has no home: *a dirty little street urchin* **2** = SEA URCHIN

Urdu /ˈʊəduː; ˈɜːduː; *NAmE* ˈʊrduː; ˈɜːrduː/ *noun* [U] the official language of Pakistan, also widely used in India

-ure *suffix* (in nouns) the action, process or result of: *closure* ◇ *failure*

urea /jʊˈriːə/ *noun* [U] (*technical*) a clear substance containing NITROGEN that is found especially in URINE

ur·ethra /jʊˈriːθrə/ *noun* (*anatomy*) the tube that carries liquid waste out of the body. In men and male animals SPERM also flows along this tube. ▶ **ur·eth·ral** *adj.* [only before noun]

ur·eth·ritis /ˌjʊərəˈθraɪtɪs; *NAmE* ˌjʊr-/ *noun* [U] (*medical*) infection of the urethra

urge 🔑 /ɜːdʒ; *NAmE* ɜːrdʒ/ *verb, noun*

■ ***verb*** **1** 🔑 to advise or try hard to persuade sb to do sth: **~ sb to do sth** *She urged him to stay.* ◇ **~ that...** *The report urged that all children be taught to swim.* ◇ **~ (sb) + speech** *'Why not give it a try?' she urged (him).* ➲ SYNONYMS at RECOMMEND **2** 🔑 **~ sth (on/upon sb)** to recommend sth strongly: *The situation is dangerous and the UN is urging caution.* **3 ~ sb/sth + adv./prep.** (*formal*) to make a person or an animal move more quickly and/or in a particular direction, especially by pushing or forcing them: *He urged his horse forward.*

PHR V **ˌurge sb↔ˈon** to encourage sb to do sth or support them so that they do it better: *She could hear him urging her on as she ran past.*

■ ***noun*** 🔑 a strong desire to do sth: *sexual urges* ◇ **~ to do sth** *I had a sudden urge to hit him.*

ur·gent 🔑 /ˈɜːdʒənt; *NAmE* ˈɜːrdʒ-/ *adj.*

1 🔑 that needs to be dealt with or happen immediately SYN **pressing**: *an urgent appeal for information* ◇ *a problem that requires urgent attention* ◇ *'Can I see you for a moment?' 'Is it urgent?'* ◇ *Mark the message 'urgent', please.* ◇ *The law is* ***in urgent need of*** *reform.* **2** 🔑 showing that you think that sth needs to be dealt with immediately: *an urgent whisper* ▶ **ur·gen·cy** /-dʒənsi/ *noun* [U, sing.]: *This is a matter of some urgency.* ◇ *The attack added a new urgency to the peace talks.* **ur·gent·ly** *adv.*: *New equipment is urgently needed.* ◇ *I need to speak to her urgently.* ◇ *'We must find him,' she said urgently.*

urgh /ɜx; *NAmE* ərx/ *exclamation* = UGH: *Urgh! There's a dead fly in my coffee!*

ur·inal /jʊəˈraɪnl; ˈjʊərɪnl; *NAmE* ˈjʊrənl/ *noun* a type of toilet for men that is attached to the wall; a room or building containing urinals

urin·ary /ˈjʊərɪnəri; *NAmE* ˈjʊrəneri/ *adj.* [usually before noun] (*medical*) connected with URINE or the parts of the body through which it passes

urin·ate /ˈjʊərɪneɪt; *NAmE* ˈjʊrən-/ *verb* [I] (*formal* or *technical*) to get rid of URINE from the body ▶ **urin·ation** /ˌjʊərɪˈneɪʃn; *NAmE* ˌjʊrəˈn-/ *noun* [U]

urine /ˈjʊərɪn; -raɪn; *NAmE* ˈjʊrən/ (also *informal* **wee** especially in *BrE*) *noun* [U] the waste liquid that collects in the BLADDER and that you pass from your body

URL /ˌjuː ɑːr ˈel/ *abbr.* (*computing*) uniform/universal resource locator (the address of a WORLD WIDE WEB page)

urn /ɜːn; *NAmE* ɜːrn/ *noun* **1** a tall decorated container, especially one used for holding the ASHES of a dead person **2** a large metal container with a tap, used for making and/or serving tea or coffee: *a tea urn*

ur·ology /jʊəˈrɒlədʒi; *NAmE* jʊˈrɑːl-/ *noun* [U] (*medical*) the scientific study of the URINARY system ▶ **uro·logic·al** /ˌjʊərəˈlɒdʒɪkl; *NAmE* ˌjʊrəˈlɑːdʒ-/ *adj.* **ur·olo·gist** /-dʒɪst/ *noun*

Ursa Major /ˌɜːsə ˈmeɪdʒə(r); *NAmE* ˌɜːrsə/ (also **the ˌGreat ˈBear**) *noun* [sing.] (*astronomy*) a large group of stars that can be clearly seen from the northern HEMISPHERE

Ursa Minor /ˌɜːsə ˈmaɪnə(r); *NAmE* ˌɜːrsə/ (also **the ˌLittle ˈBear**) *noun* [sing.] a group of stars that can be clearly seen from the northern HEMISPHERE and that includes the POLE STAR

ur·sine /ˈɜːsaɪn; *NAmE* ˈɜːrs-/ *adj.* [usually before noun] (*technical* or *literary*) connected with BEARS; like a bear

ur·ti·caria /ˌɜːtɪˈkeəriə; *NAmE* ˌɜːrtɪˈkeriə/ (also **nettle-rash, hives**) *noun* [U] (*medical*) red spots on the skin that ITCH (= make you want to scratch), caused by an ALLERGIC reaction, for example to certain foods

US (also **U.S.** especially in *US*) /ˌjuː ˈes/ *abbr.* UNITED STATES (OF AMERICA): *She became a US citizen.* ◇ *the US dollar*

us 🔑 /əs; *strong form* ʌs/ *pron.*

(the object form of *we*) **1** 🔑 used when the speaker or writer and another or others are the object of a verb or preposition, or after the verb *be*: *She gave us a picture as a wedding present.* ◇ *We'll take the dog with us.* ◇ *Hello, it's us back again.* **2** (*BrE, informal*) me: *Give us the newspaper, will you?*

USA (also **U.S.A.** especially in *US*) /ˌjuː es ˈeɪ/ *abbr.* UNITED STATES OF AMERICA: *Do you need a visa for the USA?*

us·able /ˈjuːzəbl/ *adj.* that can be used; in good enough condition to be used: *The bike is rusty but usable.* ◇ *How can we display this data in a usable form?* OPP **unusable**

USAF /ˌjuː es eɪ ˈef/ *abbr.* United States Air Force

usage /ˈjuːsɪdʒ; ˈjuːz-/ *noun* **1** [U, C] the way in which words are used in a language: *current English usage* ◇ *It's not a word* ***in common usage.*** **2** [U] the fact of sth being used; how much sth is used: *land usage* ◇ *Car usage is predicted to increase.*

USB /ˌjuː es ˈbiː/ *abbr.* (*computing*) universal serial bus (the system for connecting other pieces of equipment to a computer): *All new PCs now have USB sockets.* ◇ *a USB port*

USˈB drive (also *informal* **USˈB stick**) *noun* = FLASH DRIVE ➲ VISUAL VOCAB page V54

USCIS /ˌjuː es siː aɪ ˈes/ *abbr.* United States Citizenship and Immigration Services (the US government department that deals with people from other countries who want to visit or live in the US or to become a US citizen, part of the Department of Homeland Security)

use 🔑 *verb, noun*

■ ***verb*** /juːz/ (**used, used** /juːzd/) **1** 🔑 [T] to do sth with a machine, a method, an object, etc. for a particular purpose: **~ sth** *Can I use your phone?* ◇ *Have you ever used this software before?* ◇ *How often do you use* (= travel by) *the bus?* ◇ *They were able to achieve a settlement without using military force.* ◇ *I have some information you may be able to use* (= to get an advantage from). ◇ **~ sth for sth/for doing sth** *The blue files are used for storing old invoices.* ◇ **~ sth to do sth** *Police used tear gas to disperse the crowds.* ◇ **~ sth as sth** *The building is currently being used as a warehouse.* ◇ *You can't keep using your bad back as an excuse.* **2** 🔑 [T] **~ sth** to take a particular amount of a liquid, substance, etc. in order to achieve or make sth: *This type of heater uses a lot of electricity.* ◇ *I hope you haven't used all the milk.* **3** 🔑 [T] **~ sth** to say or write particular words or a particular type of language: *The poem uses simple language.* ◇ *That's a word I never use.* ◇ *You have to use the past tense.* **4** [T] **~ sb** (*disapproving*) to be kind, friendly, etc. to sb with the intention of getting an advantage for yourself from them SYN **exploit**: *Can't you see he's just* ***using you for his own ends?*** ◇ *I felt used.* **5** [T, I] **~ (sth)** to take illegal drugs: *Most of the inmates have used drugs at some point in their lives.* ◇ (*slang*) *She's been using since she was 13.*

IDM **I, you, etc. could use sth** (*informal*) used to say that you would like to have sth very much: *I think we could all use a drink after that!* **use your ˈhead** (*BrE* also **use your ˈloaf**) (*informal*) used to tell sb to think about sth, especially when they have asked for your opinion or said sth stupid: *'Why don't you want to see him again?' 'Oh, use your head!'* ORIGIN From rhyming slang, in which **loaf of bread** stands for 'head'.

PHR V **ˌuse sth↔ˈup** 🔑 to use all of sth so that there is

U

none left: *Making soup is a good way of using up leftover vegetables.*

■ ***noun*** /juːs/ **1** 🗝 [U, sing.] the act of using sth; the state of being used: *A ban was imposed on the use of chemical weapons.* ◇ *The software is designed for use in schools.* ◇ *I'm not sure that this is the most valuable use of my time.* ◇ *The chapel was built in the 12th century and is still* ***in use*** *today.* ◇ *The bar is* ***for the use of*** *members only.* **2** 🗝 [C, U] a purpose for which sth is used; a way in which sth is or can be used: *I'm sure you'll think of a use for it.* ◇ *This chemical has a wide range of industrial uses.* ➲ see also SINGLE-USE **3** [U] **~ (of sth)** the right or opportunity to use sth, for example sth that belongs to sb else: *I have the use of the car this week.* **4** [U] the ability to use your mind or body: *He lost the use of his legs* (= became unable to walk) *in an accident.*

IDM **be no 'use (to sb)** 🗝 (also *formal* **be of no 'use**) to be useless: *You can throw those away—they're no use to anyone.* **be of 'use (to sb)** (*formal*) to be useful: *Can I be of any use* (= can I help)? **come into/go out of, etc. 'use** to start/stop being used: *When did this word come into common use?* **have its/their/your 'uses** (*informal*, often *humorous*) to be useful sometimes: *I know you don't like him, but he has his uses.* **have no 'use for sb** to dislike sb: *I've no use for people who don't make an effort.* **have no 'use for sth** to not need sth **it's no 'use (doing sth) | what's the 'use (of doing sth)?** 🗝 used to say that there is no point in doing sth because it will not be successful or have a good result: *What's the use of worrying about it?* ◇ *It's no use—I can't persuade her.* **make 'use of sth/sb** 🗝 to use sth/sb, especially in order to get an advantage: *We could make better use of our resources.* **put sth to good 'use** to be able to use sth for a purpose, and get an advantage from doing so: *She'll be able to put her languages to good use in her new job.*

used[1] 🗝 /juːst/ *adj.*
familiar with sth because you do it or experience it often: **~ to doing sth** *I'm not used to eating so much at lunchtime.* ◇ **~ to sth** *I found the job tiring at first but I soon* ***got used to*** *it.* ➲ note at USED TO

used[2] 🗝 /juːzd/ *adj.* [usually before noun]
that has belonged to or been used by sb else before **SYN** **second-hand**: *used cars*

used to 🗝 /ˈjuːst tə; *before vowels and finally* ˈjuːst tu/ *modal verb* (*negative* **didn't use to** /-juːs/ (*BrE* also, *old-fashioned* or *formal* **used not to** *short form* **usedn't to** /ˈjuːsnt tə; *before vowels and finally* ˈjuːsnt tu/)
used to say that sth happened continuously or frequently during a period in the past: *I used to live in London.* ◇ *We used to go sailing on the lake in summer.* ◇ *I didn't use to like him much when we were at school.* ◇ *You used to see a lot of her, didn't you?* ➲ note at MODAL

Which Word?

used to / be used to

- Do not confuse **used to do sth** with **be used to sth**.
- You use **used to do sth** to talk about something that happened regularly or was the case in the past, but is not now: *I used to smoke, but I gave up a couple of years ago.*
- You use **be used to sth/to doing sth** to talk about something that you are familiar with so that it no longer seems new or strange to you: *We're used to the noise from the traffic now.* ◇ *I'm used to getting up early.* You can also use **get used to sth**: *Don't worry — you'll soon get used to his sense of humour.* ◇ *I didn't think I could ever get used to living in a big city after living in the country.*

use·ful 🗝 /ˈjuːsfl/ *adj.*
1 🗝 that can help you to do or achieve what you want: *a useful gadget* ◇ **~ (to do sth)** *It can be useful to write a short summary of your argument first.* ◇ **~ (to sb)** *He might be useful to us.* ◇ **~ (for sth/for doing sth)** *These plants are particularly useful for brightening up shady areas.* ◇ *Don't just sit watching television—****make yourself useful!*** ◇ *This information could* ***prove useful.*** ◇ *Your knowledge of German may* ***come in useful*** (= be useful in a particular situation). ◇ *Some products can be recycled at the end of their useful life.* **2** (*BrE, informal*) good; of the right standard **SYN** **competent**: *He's a very useful player.* ▶ **use·ful·ly** /-fəli/ *adv.*: *The money could be more usefully spent on new equipment.*

Grammar Point

used to

- Except in negatives and questions, the correct form is **used to**: *I used to go there every Saturday.* ◇ ~~*I use to go there every Saturday.*~~
- To form questions, use *did*: *Did she use to have long hair?* Note that the correct spelling is **use to**, not 'used to'.
- The negative form is usually **didn't use to**, but in *BrE* this is quite informal and is not usually used in writing.
- The negative form **used not to** (*rather formal*) and the question form **used you to...?** (*old-fashioned and very formal*) are only used in *BrE*, usually in writing.

use·ful·ness /ˈjuːsfəlnəs/ *noun* [U] the fact of being useful or possible to use: *There are doubts about the usefulness of these tests.* ◇ *The building has outlived its usefulness.*

use·less 🗝 /ˈjuːsləs/ *adj.*
1 🗝 not useful; not doing or achieving what is needed or wanted: *This pen is useless.* ◇ **~ (to do sth)** *He knew it was useless to protest.* ◇ **~ (doing sth)** *It's useless worrying about it.* ◇ *She tried to work, but it was useless* (= she wasn't able to). **2 ~ (at sth/at doing sth)** (*informal*) not very good at sth; not able to do things well: *I'm useless at French.* ◇ *Don't ask her to help. She's useless.* ▶ **use·less·ly** *adv.* **use·less·ness** *noun* [U]

Use·net /ˈjuːznet/ *noun* [U] (*computing*) a service on the Internet used by groups of users who email each other because they share a particular interest

user 🗝 /ˈjuːzə(r)/ *noun*
1 🗝 a person or thing that uses sth: *road users* ◇ *computer software users* ◇ *a user manual* ➲ see also END-USER **2** (*slang*) a person who uses illegal drugs

'user fee *noun* (*NAmE*) a tax on a service that is provided for the public

ˌuser-'friend·ly *adj.* easy for people who are not experts to use or understand ▶ **ˌuser-'friendli·ness** *noun* [U]

'user group *noun* a group of people who use a particular thing and who share information about it, especially people who share information about computers on the Internet

user·name /ˈjuːzəneɪm; *NAmE* -zərn-/ *noun* (*computing*) the name you use in order to be able to use a computer program or system: *Please enter your username.*

usher /ˈʌʃə(r)/ *noun, verb*

■ ***noun*** **1** a person who shows people where to sit in a church, public hall, etc. **2** an official who has special responsibilities in court, for example allowing people in and out of the court **3** a friend of the BRIDEGROOM at a wedding, who has special duties

■ ***verb*** **~ sb + adv./prep.** to take or show sb where they should go: *The secretary ushered me into his office.* ➲ SYNONYMS at TAKE

PHR V **ˌusher sth↔'in** (*formal*) to be the beginning of sth new or to make sth new begin: *The change of management ushered in fresh ideas and policies.*

ush·er·ette /ˌʌʃəˈret/ *noun* (*especially BrE*) a woman whose job is to lead people to their seats in a theatre or cinema/movie theater

USN /ˌjuː es ˈen/ *abbr.* United States Navy

USP /ˌjuː es ˈpiː/ *noun* (*business*) the abbreviation for unique selling proposition or unique selling point (a feature of a product or service that makes it different from all the

U

others that are available and is a reason for people to choose it): *You need to come up with a USP.*

USS /ˌjuː es ˈes/ *abbr.* United States Ship (used before the name of a ship in the US navy): *USS Oklahoma*

USSR /ˌjuː es es ˈɑː(r)/ *abbr.* (the former) Union of Soviet Socialist Republics

usual 🔑 /ˈjuːʒuəl; -ʒəl/ *adj.* **1** 🔑 that happens or is done most of the time or in most cases SYN **normal**: *She made all the usual excuses.* ◇ *He came home later than usual.* ◇ *She sat in her usual seat at the back.* ◇ *He didn't sound like his usual happy self.* ◇ **~** (**for sb/sth**) (**to do sth**) ***It is usual to*** *start a speech by thanking everybody for coming.* ➲ compare UNUSUAL **2 the usual** *noun* [sing.] (*informal*) what usually happens; what you usually have, especially the drink that you usually have

IDM **as usual** 🔑 in the same way as what happens most of the time or in most cases: *Steve, as usual, was the last to arrive.* ◇ *As usual at that hour, the place was deserted.* ◇ *Despite her problems, she carried on working as usual.* ➲ more at BUSINESS, PER

usu·al·ly 🔑 /ˈjuːʒuəli; -ʒəli/ *adv.* in the way that is usual or normal; most often: *I'm usually home by 6 o'clock.* ◇ *We usually go by car.* ◇ *How long does the journey usually take?*

us·urer /ˈjuːʒərə(r)/ *noun* (*old-fashioned, disapproving*) a person who lends money to people at unfairly high rates of interest

us·uri·ous /juːˈʒʊəriəs; *NAmE* juːˈʒʊr-/ *adj.* (*formal*) lending money at very high rates of interest

usurp /juːˈzɜːp; *NAmE* -ˈzɜːrp/ *verb* **~ sb/sth** (*formal*) to take sb's position and/or power without having the right to do this ▶ **usurp·ation** /ˌjuːzɜːˈpeɪʃn; *NAmE* -zɜːrˈp-/ *noun* [U, C] **usurp·er** *noun*

usury /ˈjuːʒəri/ *noun* [U] (*old-fashioned, disapproving*) the practice of lending money to people at unfairly high rates of interest

Utd *abbr.* UNITED

Ute /juːt/ *noun* (*pl.* Ute *or* Utes) a member of a Native American people many of whom live in the US states of Colorado and Utah

ute /juːt/ *noun* (*AustralE, NZE, informal*) a vehicle with low sides and no roof at the back used, for example, by farmers SYN **pickup**

uten·sil /juːˈtensl/ *noun* (*formal*) a tool that is used in the house: ***cooking/kitchen utensils*** ➲ VISUAL VOCAB page V23

utero ➲ IN UTERO

uterus /ˈjuːtərəs/ *noun* (*anatomy*) the organ in women and female animals in which babies develop before they are born SYN **womb** ▶ **uter·ine** /ˈjuːtəraɪn/ *adj.* [only before noun] ➲ see also INTRAUTERINE DEVICE

utili·tar·ian /ˌjuːtɪlɪˈteəriən; *NAmE* -ˈter-/ *adj.* **1** (*formal*) designed to be useful and practical rather than attractive **2** (*philosophy*) based on or supporting the ideas of utilitarianism

utili·tar·ian·ism /ˌjuːtɪlɪˈteəriənɪzəm; *NAmE* -ˈter-/ *noun* [U] (*philosophy*) the belief that the right course of action is the one that will produce the greatest happiness of the greatest number of people

util·ity AW /juːˈtɪləti/ *noun, adj.*

■ ***noun*** (*pl.* -ies) **1** [C] (*especially NAmE*) a service provided for the public, for example an electricity, water or gas supply: *the administration of* ***public utilities*** ➲ COLLOCATIONS at HOUSE **2** [U] (*formal*) the quality of being useful SYN **usefulness 3** [C] (*computing*) a piece of computer software that performs a particular task

■ ***adj.*** [only before noun] that can be used for several different purposes: *an all-round utility player* (= one who can play equally well in several different positions in a sport)

uˈtility room *noun* a room, especially in a private house, that contains large pieces of equipment such as a WASHING MACHINE, FREEZER, etc.

uˈtility vehicle (*also* **uˈtility truck**) *noun* a small truck with low sides designed for carrying light loads

util·ize (*BrE also* **-ise**) AW /ˈjuːtəlaɪz/ *verb* **~ sth** (**as sth**) (*formal*) to use sth, especially for a practical purpose SYN **make use of**: *The Romans were the first to utilize concrete as a building material.* ◇ *The resources at our disposal could have been better utilized.* ▶ **util·iza·tion**, **-isa·tion** AW /ˌjuːtəlaɪˈzeɪʃn; *NAmE* -ləˈz-/ *noun* [U]

ut·most /ˈʌtməʊst; *NAmE* -moʊst/ *adj., noun*

■ ***adj.*** (*also less frequent* **ut·ter·most**) [only before noun] greatest; most extreme: *This is a matter of the utmost importance.* ◇ *You should study this document with the utmost care.*

■ ***noun*** [sing.] the greatest amount possible: *Our resources are strained to the utmost.* ◇ *He* ***did his utmost*** (= tried as hard as possible) *to persuade me not to go.*

uto·pia /juːˈtəʊpiə; *NAmE* -ˈtoʊ-/ (*also* **Utopia**) *noun* [C, U] an imaginary place or state in which everything is perfect

ORIGIN From the title of a book by Sir Thomas More, which describes a place like this.

uto·pian /juːˈtəʊpiən; *NAmE* -ˈtoʊ-/ (*also* **Utopian**) *adj.* having a strong belief that everything can be perfect, often in a way that does not seem to be realistic or practical: *utopian ideals* ◇ *a utopian society* ▶ **uto·pian·ism** (*also* **Utopianism**) *noun* [U]

utter /ˈʌtə(r)/ *adj., verb*

■ ***adj.*** [only before noun] used to emphasize how complete sth is: *That's complete and utter nonsense!* ◇ *To my utter amazement she agreed.* ◇ *He felt an utter fool.* ▶ **ut·ter·ly** *adv.*: *We're so utterly different from each other.* ◇ *She utterly failed to convince them.*

■ ***verb*** **~ sth** (*formal*) to make a sound with your voice; to say sth: *to utter a cry* ◇ *She did not* ***utter a word*** *during lunch* (= said nothing).

ut·ter·ance /ˈʌtərəns/ *noun* (*formal*) **1** [U] the act of expressing sth in words: *to give utterance to your thoughts* **2** [C] something that you say: *one of her few recorded public utterances*

ut·ter·most /ˈʌtəməʊst; *NAmE* ˈʌtərmoʊst/ *adj., noun* [sing.] = UTMOST

ˈU-turn *noun* **1** a turn of 180° that a vehicle makes so that it can move forwards in the opposite direction: *to* ***do/make a U-turn*** **2** (*informal*) a complete change in policy or behaviour, usually one that is embarrassing

UUP /ˌjuː juː ˈpiː/ *abbr.* Ulster Unionist Party (a political party in Northern Ireland that wants it to remain part of the United Kingdom)

UV /ˌjuː ˈviː/ *abbr.* ULTRAVIOLET: *UV radiation*

UVA /juː viː ˈeɪ/ *noun* [U] ULTRAVIOLET RAYS that are relatively long: *UVA rays*

UVB /ˌjuː viː ˈbiː/ *noun* [U] ULTRAVIOLET RAYS that are relatively short: *UVB rays*

UVC /ˌjuː viː ˈsiː/ *noun* [U] ULTRAVIOLET RAYS that are very short and do not get through the OZONE LAYER: *UVC radiation*

uvula /ˈjuːvjələ/ *noun* (*pl.* **uvu·lae** /-liː/) (*anatomy*) a small piece of flesh that hangs from the top of the inside of the mouth just above the throat ➲ VISUAL VOCAB page V48

uvu·lar /ˈjuːvjələ(r)/ *adj.* (*phonetics*) (of a consonant) produced by placing the back of the tongue against or near the uvula

ux·or·ial /ʌkˈsɔːriəl/ *adj.* (*formal*) connected with a wife

Uzi™ /ˈuːzi/ *noun* a type of SUB-MACHINE GUN designed in Israel

U

Vv

V /viː/ *noun, abbr., symbol*
■ ***noun*** (also **v**) (*pl.* **Vs, V's, v's** /viːz/) **1** [C, U] the 22nd letter of the English alphabet: *'Violin' begins with (a) V/'V'.* **2** a thing shaped like a V: *Ahead was the deep V of a gorge with water pouring down it.* ➲ see also V-CHIP, V-NECK, V-SIGN
■ ***abbr.*** (in writing) VOLT(S): *a 1.5 V battery*
■ ***symbol*** (also **v**) the number 5 in ROMAN NUMERALS

v *abbr.* **1** (also **vs** especially in *NAmE*) (in sport or in a legal case) VERSUS (= against): *England v West Indies ◇ the State vs Kramer* (= a case in a court of law) **2** (in writing) (*BrE, informal*) very: *I was v pleased to get your letter.* **3** VIDE

vac /væk/ *noun* (*BrE, informal*) a university vacation

va·cancy /ˈveɪkənsi/ *noun* (*pl.* -ies) **1** [C] a job that is available for sb to do: ***job vacancies*** *◇ a temporary vacancy ◇* **~ (for sb/sth)** *vacancies for bar staff ◇ to* ***fill a vacancy*** ➲ SYNONYMS at JOB **2** [C] a room that is available in a hotel, etc: *I'm sorry, we have no vacancies.* **3** [U] lack of interest or ideas SYN **emptiness**: *the vacancy of her expression*

va·cant /ˈveɪkənt/ *adj.* **1** (of a seat, hotel room, house, etc.) empty; not being used SYN **unoccupied**: *vacant properties ◇ The seat next to him was vacant. ◇* (*especially NAmE*) *a* ***vacant lot*** (= a piece of land in a city that is not being used) ➲ compare ENGAGED, OCCUPIED **2** (*formal*) if a job in a company is **vacant**, nobody is doing it and it is available for sb to take: *When the post finally fell* (= became) *vacant, they offered it to Fiona. ◇* (*BrE*) ***Situations Vacant*** (= a section in a newspaper where jobs are advertised) **3** (of a look, an expression, etc.) showing no sign that the person is thinking of anything: *a vacant look* ▶ **va·cant·ly** *adv.*: *to stare vacantly*

ˌvacant posˈsession *noun* [U] (*BrE, technical*) the fact of owning a house that is empty because the people who lived there have moved out

vac·ate /vəˈkeɪt; veɪˈk-; *NAmE* also ˈveɪkeɪt/ *verb* (*formal*) **1 ~ sth** to leave a building, seat, etc, especially so that sb else can use it: *Guests are requested to vacate their rooms by noon on the day of departure.* **2 ~ sth** to leave a job, position of authority, etc. so that it is available for sb else

vac·ation 🔑 /vəˈkeɪʃn; veɪˈk-/ *noun, verb*
■ ***noun*** **1** 🔑 [C] (in Britain) one of the periods of time when universities or courts of law are closed; (in the US) one of the periods of time when schools, colleges, universities or courts of law are closed: *the* ***Christmas/Easter/summer vacation*** *◇* (*BrE*) *the* ***long vacation*** (= the summer vacation) ➲ see also VAC **2** 🔑 (*NAmE*) (*BrE* **holi·day**) [U, C] a period of time spent travelling or resting away from home: *They're* ***on vacation*** *in Hawaii right now. ◇ You look tired—you should* ***take a vacation****. ◇ The job includes two weeks' paid vacation. ◇ a* ***vacation home*** ➲ COLLOCATIONS at TRAVEL ➲ note at HOLIDAY
■ ***verb*** [I] (*NAmE*) (*BrE* **holi·day**) to spend a holiday somewhere: *They are currently vacationing in Florida.*

vac·ation·er /vəˈkeɪʃnə(r); veɪˈk-/ (*NAmE*) (*BrE* **holi·day·maker**) *noun* a person who is visiting a place on holiday/vacation

vac·cin·ate /ˈvæksɪneɪt/ *verb* [often passive] **~ sb (against sth)** to give a person or an animal a vaccine, especially by INJECTING it, in order to protect them against a disease: *I was vaccinated against tetanus.* ➲ COLLOCATIONS at ILL ➲ compare IMMUNIZE, INOCULATE ▶ **vac·cin·ation** /ˌvæksɪˈneɪʃn/ *noun* [C, U]: *Make sure your vaccinations are up to date. ◇ vaccination against typhoid*

vac·cine /ˈvæksiːn; *NAmE* vækˈsiːn/ *noun* [C, U] a substance that is put into the blood and that protects the body from a disease: *a measles vaccine ◇ There is no vaccine against HIV infection.*

vacil·late /ˈvæsəleɪt/ *verb* [I] (*formal*) to keep changing your opinion or thoughts about sth, especially in a way that annoys other people SYN **waver** ▶ **va·cil·la·tion** /ˌvæsəˈleɪʃn/ *noun* [U, C]

vacu·ity /vəˈkjuːəti/ *noun* [U] (*formal*) lack of serious thought or purpose

vacu·ole /ˈvækjuəʊl; *NAmE* -oʊl/ *noun* **1** (*biology*) a small space within a cell, usually filled with liquid **2** (*medical*) a small hole in the TISSUE of the body, usually caused by disease

vacu·ous /ˈvækjuəs/ *adj.* (*formal*) showing no sign of intelligence or sensitive feelings: *a vacuous expression* ▶ **vacu·ous·ly** *adv.* **vacu·ous·ness** *noun* [U]

vac·uum /ˈvækjuəm/ *noun, verb*
■ ***noun*** **1** a space that is completely empty of all substances, including all air or other gas: *a vacuum pump* (= one that creates a vacuum) ◇ ***vacuum-packed*** *foods* (= in a package from which most of the air has been removed) **2** [usually sing.] a situation in which sb/sth is missing or lacking: *His resignation has created a vacuum which cannot easily be filled.* **3** [usually sing.] the act of cleaning sth with a vacuum cleaner: *to give a room a quick vacuum*
IDM **in a ˈvacuum** existing separately from other people, events, etc. when there should be a connection: *This kind of decision cannot ever be made in a vacuum.*
■ ***verb*** [T, I] **~ (sth)** to clean sth using a vacuum cleaner SYN **hoover**: *Have you vacuumed the stairs?*

ˈvacuum cleaner (*BrE* also **Hoover™**) *noun* an electrical machine that cleans floors, carpets, etc. by sucking up dirt and dust ➲ VISUAL VOCAB page V17

ˈvacuum flask (also **flask**) (both *BrE*) (*US* **ˈvacuum bottle**) *noun* a container like a bottle with double walls with a vacuum between them, used for keeping liquids hot or cold ➲ compare THERMOS

vade mecum /ˌvɑːdi ˈmeɪkəm/ *noun* (from *Latin, formal*) a book or written guide which you keep with you all the time, because you find it helpful

vaga·bond /ˈvæɡəbɒnd; *NAmE* -bɑːnd/ *noun* (*old-fashioned, disapproving*) a person who has no home or job and who travels from place to place

va·gar·ies /ˈveɪɡəriz/ *noun* [pl.] (*formal*) changes in sb/sth that are difficult to predict or control

va·gina /vəˈdʒaɪnə/ *noun* the passage in the body of a woman or female animal between the outer sex organs and the WOMB ▶ **va·ginal** /vəˈdʒaɪnl/ *adj.* **va·gi·nal·ly** *adv.*

va·grancy /ˈveɪɡrənsi/ *noun* [U] (*law*) the crime of living on the streets and BEGGING (= asking for money) from people

va·grant /ˈveɪɡrənt/ *noun* (*formal* or *law*) a person who has no home or job, especially one who BEGS (= asks for money) from people ▶ **va·grant** *adj.*

vague /veɪɡ/ *adj.* (**vaguer, vaguest**) **1** not clear in a person's mind: *to have a* ***vague impression/memory/recollection*** *of sth ◇ They had only a* ***vague idea*** *where the place was.* **2 ~ (about sth)** not having or giving enough information or details about sth: *She's a little vague about her plans for next year. ◇ The politicians made vague promises about tax cuts. ◇ He was accused of being deliberately vague. ◇ We had only a vague description of the attacker.* **3** (of a person's behaviour) suggesting a lack of clear thought or attention SYN **absent-minded**: *His vague manner concealed a brilliant mind.* **4** not having a clear shape SYN **indistinct**: *In the darkness they could see the vague outline of a church.* ▶ **vague·ness** *noun* [U]

vague·ly /ˈveɪɡli/ *adv.* **1** in a way that is not detailed or exact: *a vaguely worded statement ◇ I can vaguely remember my first day at school.* **2** slightly: *There was something vaguely familiar about her face. ◇ He was vaguely aware of footsteps behind him.* **3** in a way that shows that you are not paying attention or thinking clearly: *He smiled vaguely, ignoring her questions.*

vain /veɪn/ *adj.* **1** that does not produce the result you want SYN **useless**: *She closed her eyes tightly* ***in a vain attempt*** *to hold back the tears. ◇ I knocked loudly* ***in the vain hope*** *that someone might answer.* **2** (*disapproving*) too proud of your own appearance, abilities or achievements

SYN **conceited**: *She's too vain to wear glasses.* ➲ see also VANITY

IDM **in 'vain** without success: *They tried in vain to persuade her to go.* ◇ *All our efforts were in vain.* ➲ more at NAME *n.*

vain·glori·ous /ˌveɪnˈglɔːriəs/ *adj.* (*literary, disapproving*) too proud of your own abilities or achievements ▸ **vain·glory** /ˌveɪnˈglɔːri/ *noun* [U]

vain·ly /ˈveɪnli/ *adv.* without success: *He shouted after them, vainly trying to attract their attention.*

val·ance /ˈvæləns/ *noun* **1** a narrow piece of cloth like a short curtain that hangs around the frame of a bed, under a shelf, etc. ➲ VISUAL VOCAB page V20 **2** (*especially NAmE*) = PELMET

vale /veɪl/ *noun* (*old use* or *literary*) (also used in modern place names) a valley: *a wooded vale* ◇ *the Vale of the White Horse*

val·edic·tion /ˌvælɪˈdɪkʃn/ *noun* [C, U] (*formal*) the act of saying goodbye, especially in a formal speech

val·edic·tor·ian /ˌvælɪdɪkˈtɔːriən/ *noun* (*NAmE*) the student who has the highest marks/grades in a particular group of students and who gives the valedictory speech at a GRADUATION ceremony

val·edic·tory /ˌvælɪˈdɪktəri/ *adj.* [usually before noun] (*formal*) connected with saying goodbye, especially at a formal occasion: *a valedictory speech*

va·lency /ˈveɪlənsi/ *noun* [C, U] (*pl.* -ies) (also **va·lence** /ˈveɪləns/ especially in *NAmE*) **1** (*chemistry*) a measurement of the power of an atom to combine with others, by the number of HYDROGEN atoms it can combine with or DISPLACE: *Carbon has a valency of 4.* **2** (*linguistics*) the number of GRAMMATICAL elements that a word, especially a verb, combines with in a sentence

val·en·tine /ˈvæləntaɪn/ *noun* **1** (also **'valentine card**) a card that you send to sb that you love on St Valentine's Day (14 February), often without putting your name on it **2** a person that you send a valentine to

'Valentine's Day ➲ ST VALENTINE'S DAY

val·er·ian /vəˈlɪəriən; *NAmE* -ˈlɪr-/ *noun* [U] a drug obtained from the root of a plant with the same name, used to make people feel calmer

valet *noun, verb*

■ ***noun*** /ˈvæleɪ; ˈvælɪt; *NAmE* also væˈleɪ/ **1** a man's personal servant who takes care of his clothes, serves his meals, etc. **2** (*BrE*) a hotel employee whose job is to clean the clothes of hotel guests **3** (*NAmE*) a person who parks your car for you at a hotel or restaurant

■ ***verb*** /ˈvælɪt/ **1** [T] **~ sth** (*BrE*) to clean a person's car thoroughly, especially on the inside: *a car valeting service* **2** [I] to perform the duties of a valet

Val·halla /vælˈhælə/ *noun* [U] (in ancient Scandinavian stories) a palace in which some chosen men who had died in battle went to live with the god Odin for ever

vali·ant /ˈvæliənt/ *adj.* (especially *literary*) very brave or determined **SYN** **courageous**: *valiant warriors* ◇ *She made a* ***valiant attempt*** *not to laugh.* ▸ **vali·ant·ly** *adv.*

valid 🔑 **AW** /ˈvælɪd/ *adj.*
1 🔑 that is legally or officially acceptable: *a valid passport* ◇ *a bus pass valid for 1 month* ◇ *They have a valid claim to compensation.* **2** based on what is logical or true: *She had valid reasons for not supporting the proposals.* ◇ *The point you make is perfectly valid.* **3** (*computing*) that is accepted by the system: *a valid password* **OPP** **invalid** ▸ **val·id·ly** **AW** *adv.*: *The contract had been validly drawn up.*

val·id·ate **AW** /ˈvælɪdeɪt/ *verb* (*formal*) **1 ~ sth** to prove that sth is true: *to validate a theory* **OPP** **invalidate** **2 ~ sth** to make sth legally valid: *to validate a contract* **OPP** **invalidate** **3 ~ sth** to state officially that sth is useful and of an acceptable standard: *Check that their courses have been validated by a reputable organization.* ▸ **val·id·ation** **AW** /ˌvælɪˈdeɪʃn/ *noun* [U, C]

val·id·ity **AW** /vəˈlɪdəti/ *noun* [U] **1** the state of being legally or officially acceptable: *The period of validity of the agreement has expired.* **2** the state of being logical and true: *We had doubts about the validity of their argument.*

val·ise /vəˈliːz; *NAmE* vəˈliːs/ *noun* (*old-fashioned*) a small bag for carrying clothes, used when you are travelling

Val·ium™ /ˈvæliəm/ *noun* [U] a drug used to reduce anxiety

Val·kyrie /ˈvælkɪri; vælˈkɪəri; *NAmE* vælˈkɪri; -ˈkaɪri/ *noun* (in ancient Scandinavian stories) one of the twelve female servants of the god Odin, who selected men who had been killed in battle and took them to VALHALLA

val·ley 🔑 /ˈvæli/ *noun*
an area of low land between hills or mountains, often with a river flowing through it; the land that a river flows through: *a small town set in a valley* ◇ *a wooded valley* ◇ *the valley floor* ◇ *the Shenandoah Valley* ➲ VISUAL VOCAB page V4

'Valley Girl *noun* (*NAmE, informal*) a girl from a rich family who is only interested in things like shopping, thought to be typical of one of those living in the San Fernando Valley of California

val·our (*especially US* **valor**) /ˈvælə(r)/ *noun* [U] (*literary*) great courage, especially in war **SYN** **bravery** ▸ **val·or·ous** /ˈvælərəs/ *adj.* **IDM** see DISCRETION

valu·able 🔑 /ˈvæljuəbl/ *adj.*
1 🔑 **~ (to sb/sth)** very useful or important: *a valuable experience* ◇ *The book provides valuable information on recent trends.* ◇ *This advice was to* ***prove valuable.*** **2** 🔑 worth a lot of money: *valuable antiques* ◇ *Luckily, nothing valuable was stolen.* **OPP** **valueless, worthless** ➲ compare INVALUABLE, PRICELESS

> **Synonyms**
>
> **valuable**
>
> **precious** • **priceless** • **irreplaceable**
>
> These words all describe sth that is worth a lot of money or very important to sb.
>
> **valuable** worth a lot of money: *The thieves took three pieces of valuable jewellery.*
>
> **precious** rare and worth a lot of money; loved or valued very much: *a precious Chinese vase, valued at half a million pounds* ◇ *precious memories of our time together*
>
> **priceless** extremely valuable; loved or valued very much: *a priceless collection of antiques*
>
> **irreplaceable** too valuable or special to be replaced
>
> PATTERNS
> - valuable/precious/priceless/irreplaceable **possessions**
> - valuable/precious/priceless **antiques/jewels/jewellery**

valu·ables /ˈvæljuəblz/ *noun* [pl.] things that are worth a lot of money, especially small personal things such as jewellery, cameras, etc. ➲ SYNONYMS at THING

valu·ation /ˌvæljuˈeɪʃn/ *noun* [C, U] **1** a professional judgement about how much money sth is worth; its estimated value: *Surveyors carried out a valuation of the property.* ◇ *Experts set a high valuation on the painting.* ◇ *land valuation* **2** (*formal*) a judgement about how useful or important sth is; its estimated importance: *She puts a high valuation on trust between colleagues.*

V

value 🔑 /ˈvæljuː/ *noun, verb*

> WORD FAMILY
> **value** *noun, verb*
> **valuable** *adj.*
> **invaluable** *adj.* (≠ valueless)
> **valuables** *noun*

■ ***noun***
▸ HOW MUCH STH IS WORTH **1** 🔑 [U, C] how much sth is worth in money or other goods for which it can be exchanged: *to* ***go up/rise/increase in value*** ◇ *to* ***go down/fall/drop in value*** ◇ *rising property values* ◇ *The winner will receive a prize* ***to the value of*** *£1 000.* ◇ *Sports cars tend to* ***hold their value*** *well.* ➲ SYNONYMS at PRICE ➲ see also MARKET VALUE, STREET VALUE **2** 🔑 [U] (*especially BrE*) how much sth is worth compared with its

price: *to be* ***good/excellent value*** (= worth the money it costs) ◇ *to be* ***bad/poor value*** (= not worth the money it costs) ◇ *Larger sizes give the best* ***value for money.***

▸ BEING USEFUL/IMPORTANT **3** [U] the quality of being useful or important SYN **benefit**: *The value of regular exercise should not be underestimated.* ◇ *The arrival of canals was* ***of great value*** *to many industries.* ◇ *to* ***be of little/no value*** *to sb* ◇ *This ring has great* ***sentimental value*** *for me.* ◇ *I suppose it has a certain* ***novelty value*** (= it's interesting because it's new). ◇ *food with a high nutritional value* ◇ *The story has very little news value.*

▸ BELIEFS **4** **values** [pl.] beliefs about what is right and wrong and what is important in life: *moral values* ◇ *a return to traditional values in education, such as firm discipline* ◇ *The young have a completely different* ***set of values*** *and expectations.*

▸ MATHEMATICS **5** [C] the amount represented by a letter or symbol: *Let y have the value 33.*

■ ***verb***

▸ CONSIDER IMPORTANT **1** (not used in the progressive tenses) to think that sb/sth is important: **~ sb/sth (as sth)** *I really value him as a friend.* ◇ **~ sb/sth (for sth)** *The area is valued for its vineyards.* ◇ *a valued member of staff*

▸ DECIDE WORTH **2** [usually passive] **~ sth (at sth)** to decide that sth is worth a particular amount of money: *The property has been valued at over $2 million.*

ˌvalue ˈadded tax *noun* [U] = VAT

ˌvalue-ˈfree *adj.* not influenced by personal opinions

ˈvalue judgement (also **ˈvalue judgment** especially in *NAmE*) *noun* [C, U] (sometimes *disapproving*) a judgement about how good or important sth is, based on personal opinions rather than facts

ˌvalue-ˈladen *adj.* influenced by personal opinions: *'Freedom fighter' is a value-laden word.*

value·less /ˈvæljuːləs/ *adj.* (*formal*) without value or worth SYN **worthless** OPP **valuable**

valuer /ˈvæljuːə(r)/ *noun* a person whose job is to estimate how much property, land, etc. is worth

valve /vælv/ *noun* **1** a device for controlling the flow of a liquid or gas, letting it move in one direction only ➲ VISUAL VOCAB page V41 **2** a structure in the heart or in a VEIN that lets blood flow in one direction only **3** a device in some BRASS musical instruments for changing the note ➲ VISUAL VOCAB page V30

vam·oose /vəˈmuːs/ *verb* [I] (*old-fashioned, informal*) to leave quickly

vamp /væmp/ *noun* (*old-fashioned, disapproving*) a sexually attractive woman who tries to control men

vam·pire /ˈvæmpaɪə(r)/ *noun* (in stories) a dead person who leaves his or her grave at night to suck the blood of living people

ˈvampire bat *noun* a S American BAT (= an animal like a mouse with wings) that sucks the blood of other animals

vam·pir·ism /ˈvæmpaɪərɪzəm/ *noun* [U] the behaviour or practices of VAMPIRES

van /væn/ *noun*

1 a covered vehicle with no side windows in its back half, usually smaller than a lorry/truck, used for carrying goods or people: *a furniture van* ◇ *a police van* (= for carrying police officers or prisoners) ◇ *a delivery van* ◇ *a van driver* ➲ VISUAL VOCAB page V46 **2** (*NAmE*) a covered vehicle with side windows, usually smaller than a lorry/truck, that can carry about twelve passengers **3** (*BrE*) a closed coach/car on a train for carrying bags, cases, etc. or mail: *a luggage van*

IDM **in the ˈvan** (*BrE, formal*) at the front or in the leading position

van·adium /vəˈneɪdiəm/ *noun* [U] (*symb.* V) a chemical element. Vanadium is a soft poisonous silver-grey metal that is added to some types of steel to make it stronger.

ˈvan conversion *noun* (*US*) = CONVERSION VAN

van·dal /ˈvændl/ *noun* a person who deliberately destroys or damages public property

van·dal·ism /ˈvændəlɪzəm/ *noun* [U] the crime of destroying or damaging sth, especially public property, deliberately and for no good reason: *an act of vandalism* ➲ COLLOCATIONS at CRIME

van·dal·ize (*BrE* also **-ise**) /ˈvændəlaɪz/ *verb* [usually passive] **~ sth** to damage sth, especially public property, deliberately and for no good reason

vane /veɪn/ *noun* a flat blade that is moved by wind or water and is part of the machinery in a WINDMILL, etc. ➲ see also WEATHERVANE

van·guard /ˈvængɑːd; *NAmE* -gɑːrd/ *noun* (usually **the vanguard**) [sing.] **1** the leaders of a movement in society, for example in politics, art, industry, etc: *The company is proud to be* ***in the vanguard of*** *scientific progress.* **2** the part of an army, etc. that is at the front when moving forward to attack the enemy OPP **rearguard**

van·illa /vəˈnɪlə/ *noun, adj.*

■ ***noun*** [U] a substance obtained from the BEANS of a tropical plant, also called vanilla, used to give flavour to sweet foods, for example ice cream: (*BrE*) *vanilla essence* ◇ (*NAmE*) *vanilla extract* ◇ (*BrE*) *a vanilla pod* ◇ (*NAmE*) *a vanilla bean*

■ ***adj.*** **1** flavoured with vanilla: *vanilla ice cream* **2** (*informal, especially NAmE*) ordinary; not special in any way: *The city is pretty much plain vanilla.*

van·il·lin /vəˈnɪlɪn/ *noun* [U] a strong-smelling chemical which gives VANILLA its smell

van·ish /ˈvænɪʃ/ *verb* **1** [I] to disappear suddenly and/or in a way that you cannot explain: *The magician vanished in a puff of smoke.* ◇ *My glasses seem to have vanished.* ◇ *He* ***vanished without trace.*** **2** [I] to stop existing: *the vanishing woodlands of Europe* ◇ *All hopes of a peaceful settlement had now vanished.* IDM see ACT *n.*, FACE *n.*

ˈvanishing point *noun* [usually sing.] (*technical*) the point in the distance at which parallel lines appear to meet

van·ity /ˈvænəti/ *noun* (*pl.* **-ies**) **1** [U] (*disapproving*) too much pride in your own appearance, abilities or achievements: *She had no personal vanity* (= about her appearance). ➲ see also VAIN **2** [U] (*literary*) the quality of being unimportant, especially compared with other things that are important: *the vanity of human ambition in the face of death* **3** **vanities** [pl.] behaviour or attitudes that show people's vanity: *Politics is too often concerned only with the personal vanities of politicians.* **4** (also **ˈvanity table**) [C] (*NAmE*) = DRESSING TABLE

ˈvanity case *noun* a small bag or case with a mirror in it, used for carrying make-up

ˈvanity unit *noun* (*BrE*) a WASHBASIN fixed into a flat surface with cupboards underneath ➲ VISUAL VOCAB page V21

van·quish /ˈvæŋkwɪʃ/ *verb* **~ sb/sth** (*literary*) to defeat sb completely in a competition, war, etc. SYN **conquer**

the van·quished /ˈvæŋkwɪʃt/ *noun* [pl.] (*literary*) people who have been completely defeated in a competition, war, etc.

vant·age point /ˈvɑːntɪdʒ pɔɪnt; *NAmE* ˈvæn-/ (also *formal* **vant·age**) *noun* a position from which you watch sth; a point in time or a situation from which you consider sth, especially the past: *The cafe was a good vantage point for watching the world go by.* ◇ *From the vantage point of the present, the war seems to have achieved nothing.*

vapid /ˈvæpɪd/ *adj.* (*formal*) lacking interest or intelligence SYN **dull** ▸ **vap·id·ity** /vəˈpɪdəti/ *noun* [U]

vapor (*NAmE*) = VAPOUR

va·por·ize (*BrE* also **-ise**) /ˈveɪpəraɪz/ *verb* [I, T] **~ (sth)** (*technical*) to turn into gas; to make sth turn into gas ▸ **va·por·iza·tion, -isa·tion** /ˌveɪpəraɪˈzeɪʃn; *NAmE* -rəˈz-/ *noun* [U]

va·por·ous /ˈveɪpərəs/ *adj.* (*formal*) full of vapour; like vapour: *clouds of vaporous air*

va·pour (*especially US* **vapor**) /ˈveɪpə(r)/ *noun* [C, U] a mass of very small drops of liquid in the air, for example steam: *water vapour*

ˈ**vapour trail** (*especially US* ˈ**va·por trail**) *noun* the white line that is left in the sky by a plane

va·pour·ware (*especially US* **va·por·ware**) /ˈveɪpəweə(r); *NAmE* -pərwer/ *noun* [U] (*computing*) a piece of software or other computer product that has been advertised but is not available to buy yet, either because it is only an idea or because it is still being written or designed

vari·abil·ity AW /ˌveəriəˈbɪləti; *NAmE* ˌver-; ˌvær-/ *noun* [U] the fact of sth being likely to vary: *climatic variability* ◇ *a degree of variability in the exchange rate*

vari·able AW /ˈveəriəbl; *NAmE* ˈver-; ˈvær-/ *adj., noun*
■ *adj.* **1** often changing; likely to change SYN **fluctuating**: *variable temperatures* ◇ *The acting is of variable quality* (= some of it is good and some of it is bad). ➲ compare INVARIABLE **2** able to be changed: *The drill has variable speed control.* ◇ *variable lighting* ▶ **vari·ably** AW /-iəbli/ *adv.*
■ *noun* a situation, number or quantity that can vary or be varied: *With so many variables, it is difficult to calculate the cost.* ◇ *The temperature remained constant while pressure was a variable in the experiment.* OPP **constant**

vari·ance AW /ˈveəriəns; *NAmE* ˈver-; ˈvær-/ *noun* [U, C] (*formal*) the amount by which sth changes or is different from sth else: *variance in temperature* ◇ *a note with subtle variances of pitch*
IDM **at** ˈ**variance** (**with sb/sth**) (*formal*) disagreeing with or opposing sb/sth: *These conclusions are totally at variance with the evidence.*

vari·ant AW /ˈveəriənt; *NAmE* ˈver-; ˈvær-/ *noun* ~ (**of/on sth**) a thing that is a slightly different form or type of sth else: *This game is a variant of baseball.* ▶ **vari·ant** *adj.*: *variant forms of spelling* ◇ *a variant form of oxygen known as ozone*

vari·ation 0‑w AW /ˌveəriˈeɪʃn; *NAmE* ˌver-/ *noun*
1 0‑w [C, U] ~ (**in/of sth**) a change, especially in the amount or level of sth: *The dial records very slight variations in pressure.* ◇ *Currency exchange rates are always subject to variation.* ◇ ***regional/seasonal variation*** (= depending on the region or time of year) **2** 0‑w [C] ~ (**on sth**) a thing that is different from other things in the same general group: *This soup is a spicy variation on a traditional favourite.* **3** [C] ~ (**on sth**) (*music*) any of a set of short pieces of music based on a simple tune repeated in a different and more complicated form: *a set of variations on a theme by Mozart* ◇ (*figurative*) *His numerous complaints are all* ***variations on a theme*** (= all about the same thing).

vari·cose vein /ˌværɪkəʊs ˈveɪn; *NAmE* -koʊs/ *noun* a VEIN, especially one in the leg, which has become swollen and painful

var·ied 0‑w AW /ˈveərid; *NAmE* ˈverid; ˈvær-/ *adj.* (usually *approving*)
1 0‑w of many different types: *varied opinions* ◇ *a wide and varied selection of cheeses* **2** 0‑w not staying the same, but changing often: *He led a full and varied life.*

varie·gated /ˈveəriəgeɪtɪd; ˈveərɪg-; *NAmE* ˈver-/ *adj.* **1** (*technical*) having spots or marks of a different colour: *a plant with variegated leaves* ➲ VISUAL VOCAB page V9 **2** (*formal*) consisting of many different types of thing or person

var·iety 0‑w /vəˈraɪəti/ *noun* (*pl.* -ies)
1 0‑w [sing.] ~ (**of sth**) several different sorts of the same thing: *There is* ***a wide variety of*** *patterns to choose from.* ◇ *He resigned for a variety of reasons.* ◇ *This tool can be used in a variety of ways.* ◇ *I was impressed by the variety of dishes on offer.* **2** 0‑w [U] the quality of not being the same or not doing the same thing all the time SYN **diversity**: *We all need variety in our diet.* ◇ *We want more variety in our work.* **3** 0‑w [C] ~ (**of sth**) a type of a thing, for example a plant or language, that is different from the others in the same general group: *Apples come in a great many varieties.* ◇ *a rare variety of orchid* ◇ *different varieties of English* ◇ *My cooking is of the 'quick and simple' variety.* **4** (*NAmE* also **vaude·ville**) [U] a form of theatre or television entertainment that consists of a series of short performances, such as singing, dancing and funny acts: *a* ***variety show/theatre***

IDM **variety is the spice of** ˈ**life** (*saying*) new and exciting experiences make life more interesting

vaˈ**riety meats** *noun* [pl.] (*NAmE*) = OFFAL

vaˈ**riety store** *noun* (*old-fashioned, NAmE*) a shop/store that sells a wide range of goods at low prices

vari·fo·cals /ˈveərɪfəʊklz; *NAmE* ˈverɪfoʊklz/ *noun* [pl.] a pair of glasses in which each LENS varies in thickness from the upper part to the lower part. The upper part is for looking at things at a distance, and the lower part is for looking at things that are close to you. ➲ compare BIFOCALS ▶ **vari·focal** *adj.* ➲ compare BIFOCAL

vari·ous 0‑w /ˈveəriəs; *NAmE* ˈver-; ˈvær-/ *adj.*
1 0‑w several different SYN **diverse**: *Tents come in various shapes and sizes.* ◇ *She took the job for various reasons.* ◇ *There are various ways of doing this.* **2** (*formal*) having many different features SYN **diverse**: *a large and various country*

vari·ous·ly /ˈveəriəsli; *NAmE* ˈver-; ˈvær-/ *adv.* (*formal*) in several different ways, usually by several different people: *He has been* ***variously described*** *as a hero, a genius and a bully.* ◇ *The cost has been variously estimated at between £10 million and £20 million.*

var·mint /ˈvɑːmɪnt; *NAmE* ˈvɑːrm-/ *noun* (*old-fashioned, informal*) **1** a person, especially a child, who causes trouble **2** a wild animal, especially a FOX, that causes problems

var·nish /ˈvɑːnɪʃ; *NAmE* ˈvɑːrnɪʃ/ *noun, verb*
■ *noun* [U, C] a liquid that is painted onto wood, metal, etc. and that forms a hard shiny transparent surface when it is dry ➲ VISUAL VOCAB page V49 ➲ see also NAIL VARNISH
■ *verb* to put varnish on the surface of sth: ~ **sth** *The doors are then stained and varnished.* ◇ (*BrE*) *Josie was sitting at her desk, varnishing her nails.* ◇ ~ **sth + noun** *Her nails were varnished a brilliant shade of red.*

var·sity /ˈvɑːsəti; *NAmE* ˈvɑːrs-/ *noun, adj.*
■ *noun* [C, U] (*pl.* -ies) **1** (*NAmE*) the main team that represents a college or HIGH SCHOOL, especially in sports competitions **2** (*BrE, old use* or *IndE* or *SAfrE*) university: *She's still at varsity.*
■ *adj.* [only before noun] (*BrE, informal*) used when describing activities connected with the universities of Oxford and Cambridge, especially sports competitions: *the varsity match*

vary 0‑w AW /ˈveəri; *NAmE* ˈveri; ˈværi/ *verb* (**vary·ing, var·ied, var·ied**)
1 0‑w [I] ~ (**in sth**) (of a group of similar things) to be different from each other in size, shape, etc. SYN **differ**: *The students' work varies considerably in quality.* ◇ *The quality of the students' work varies considerably.* ◇ *New techniques were introduced with* ***varying degrees of*** *success.* **2** 0‑w [I] to change or be different according to the situation: ~ **with sth** *The menu varies with the season.* ◇ ~ **according to sth** *Prices vary according to the type of room you require.* ◇ ~ **from sth to sth** | ~ (**between A and B**) *Class numbers vary between 25 and 30.* ◇ *'What time do you start work?' 'It varies.'* **3** 0‑w [T] ~ **sth** to make changes to sth to make it slightly different: *The job enables me to vary the hours I work.*

> **WORD FAMILY**
> **vary** *verb*
> **varied** *adj.*
> **variable** *adj.*
> **variation** *noun*
> **various** *adj.*
> **variety** *noun*

vas·cu·lar /ˈvæskjələ(r)/ *adj.* [usually before noun] (*technical*) of or containing VEINS (= the tubes that carry liquids around the bodies of animals and plants)

vas def·er·ens /ˌvæs ˈdefərenz/ *noun* (*pl.* **vasa def·er·en·tia** /ˌveɪsə defəˈrenʃiə/) (*anatomy*) the tube through which SPERM pass from the TESTIS on their way out of the body

vase /vɑːz; *NAmE* veɪs; veɪz/ *noun* a container made of glass, etc, used for holding cut flowers or as a decorative object: *a vase of flowers* ➲ VISUAL VOCAB page V18

vas·ec·tomy /vəˈsektəmi/ *noun* (*pl.* -ies) (*medical*) a medical operation to remove part of each of the tubes in a

V

man's body that carry SPERM, after which he is not able to make a woman pregnant

Vas·el·ine™ /ˈvæsəliːn/ *noun* [U] a thick soft clear substance that is used on skin to heal or protect it, or as a LUBRICANT to stop surfaces from sticking together

vaso·con·stric·tion /ˌveɪzəʊkənˈstrɪkʃn; *NAmE* -zoʊ-/ *noun* [U] (*biology* or *medical*) a process in which BLOOD VESSELS become narrower, which tends to increase BLOOD PRESSURE

vaso·di·lation /ˌveɪzəʊdaɪˈleɪʃn; *NAmE* -zoʊ-/ *noun* [U] (*biology* or *medical*) a process in which BLOOD VESSELS become wider, which tends to reduce BLOOD PRESSURE

vas·sal /ˈvæsl/ *noun* **1** a man in the Middle Ages who promised to fight for and be loyal to a king or other powerful owner of land, in return for being given land to live on **2** a country that depends on and is controlled by another country

vast 🔑 /vɑːst; *NAmE* væst/ *adj.* extremely large in area, size, amount, etc. SYN **huge**: *a vast area of forest* ◇ *a vast crowd* ◇ *a vast amount of information* ◇ *At dusk bats appear* ***in vast numbers***. ◇ *His business empire was vast.* ◇ *In* ***the vast majority*** *of cases, this should not be a problem.* ▶ **vast·ness** *noun* [U, C]: *the vastness of space*

vast·ly /ˈvɑːstli; *NAmE* ˈvæstli/ *adv.* very much: *I'm a vastly different person now.* ◇ *The quality of the training has vastly improved.*

VAT /ˌviː eɪ ˈtiː; væt/ *noun* [U] (*BrE*) the abbreviation for 'value added tax' (a tax that is added to the price of goods and services): *Prices include VAT.* ◇ *£27.50 + VAT*

vat /væt/ *noun* a large container for holding liquids, especially in industrial processes: *distilling vats* ◇ *a vat of whisky*

Vati·can /ˈvætɪkən/ *noun* **the Vatican** **1** [sing.] the group of buildings in Rome where the POPE lives and works **2** [sing.+ sing./pl. v.] the centre of government of the Roman Catholic Church

vaude·ville /ˈvɔːdəvɪl/ *noun* [U] **1** (*NAmE*) = VARIETY **2** (*BrE* also ˈ**music hall**) a type of entertainment popular in the late 19th and early 20th centuries, including singing, dancing and comedy

ˈ**vaudeville theater** (*NAmE*) (*BrE* ˈ**music hall**) *noun* a theatre used for popular entertainment in the late 19th and early 20th centuries

vault /vɔːlt/ *noun, verb*

■ ***noun*** **1** a room with thick walls and a strong door, especially in a bank, used for keeping valuable things safe **2** a room under a church or in a CEMETERY, used for burying people **3** a roof or ceiling in the form of an ARCH or a series of ARCHES **4** a jump made by vaulting ➲ see also POLE VAULT

■ ***verb*** [I, T] to jump over an object in a single movement, using your hands or a pole to push you: **~ over sth** *She vaulted over the gate and ran up the path.* ◇ **~ sth** *to vault a fence* ➲ see also POLE VAULT

V

vault·ed /ˈvɔːltɪd/ *adj.* (*architecture*) made in the shape of an ARCH or a series of ARCHES; having a ceiling or roof of this shape: *a vaulted ceiling/cellar* ➲ VISUAL VOCAB page V12

vault·ing /ˈvɔːltɪŋ/ *noun* [U] (*architecture*) a pattern of ARCHES in a ceiling or roof

ˈ**vaulting horse** (also **horse**) *noun* a large object with legs, and sometimes handles, that GYMNASTS use to vault over

vaunt·ed /ˈvɔːntɪd/ *adj.* [usually before noun] (*formal*) proudly talked about or praised as being very good, especially when this is not deserved: *Their* ***much vaunted*** *reforms did not materialize.*

va-va-voom /ˌvɑː vɑː ˈvuːm; ˌvæ væ/ *noun* [U] (*informal*) the quality of being exciting or sexually attractive ORIGIN First used in the 1950s in the US to represent the sound of a car engine running.

VC /ˌviː ˈsiː/ *noun* [sing.] the abbreviation for 'Victoria Cross' (a MEDAL for special courage that is given to members of the British and Commonwealth armed forces): *He was awarded the VC.* ◇ *Col James Blunt VC*

ˈ**V-chip** *noun* a computer chip in a television RECEIVER that can be programmed to block material that contains sex and violence

VCR /ˌviː siː ˈɑː(r)/ *noun* (*especially NAmE*) the abbreviation for 'video cassette recorder' (a machine which is used to play videos or to record programmes from a television): *Don't forget to program the VCR.*

VD /ˌviː ˈdiː/ *abbr.* VENEREAL DISEASE

VDU /ˌviː diː ˈjuː/ (*BrE*) (*NAmE* **VDT** /ˌviː diː ˈtiː/) *noun* the abbreviation for 'visual display unit/video display terminal' (a machine with a screen like a television that displays information from a computer)

veal /viːl/ *noun* [U] meat from a CALF (= a young cow)

vec·tor /ˈvektə(r)/ *noun* **1** (*mathematics*) a quantity that has both size and direction: *Acceleration and velocity are both vectors.* ➲ compare SCALAR **2** (*biology*) an insect, etc. that carries a particular disease from one living thing to another **3** (*technical*) a course taken by an aircraft

Veda /ˈveɪdə; ˈviːdə/ *noun* an ancient holy text of Hinduism

Vedic /ˈveɪdɪk; ˈviːd-/ *adj., noun*

■ ***adj.*** relating to the Vedas

■ ***noun*** [U] the language of the Vedas

vee·jay /ˈviː dʒeɪ/ *noun* = VIDEO JOCKEY

veep /viːp/ *noun* (*NAmE, informal*) VICE-PRESIDENT

veer /vɪə(r); *NAmE* vɪr/ *verb* **1** [I] **+ adv./prep.** (especially of a vehicle) to change direction suddenly SYN **swerve**: *The bus veered onto the wrong side of the road.* **2** [I] **+ adv./prep.** (of a conversation or way of behaving or thinking) to change in the way it develops: *The debate veered away from the main topic of discussion.* ◇ *His emotions veered between fear and anger.* **3** [I] **+ adv./prep.** (*technical*) (of the wind) to change direction: *The wind veered to the west.*

veg /vedʒ/ *noun, verb*

■ ***noun*** [U, C] (*pl.* **veg**) (*BrE, informal*) a vegetable or vegetables: *a fruit and veg stall* ◇ *He likes the traditional* ***meat and two veg*** *for his main meal.*

■ ***verb*** (-gg-)

PHR V ˌ**veg ˈout** (*informal*) to relax by doing sth that needs very little effort, for example watching television

vegan /ˈviːɡən/ *noun* a person who does not eat any animal products such as meat, milk or eggs. Some vegans do not use animal products such as silk or leather.

Vege·bur·ger™ /ˈvedʒibɜːɡə(r); *NAmE* -bɜːrɡ-/ *noun* = VEGGIE BURGER

Vege·mite™ /ˈvedʒɪmaɪt/ *noun* [U] (*AustralE, NZE*) a dark substance made from YEAST, spread on bread, etc.

vege·table 🔑 /ˈvedʒtəbl/ *noun* **1** 🔑 (also *informal* **veg·gie** especially in *NAmE*) a plant or part of a plant that is eaten as food. Potatoes, BEANS and onions are all vegetables: ***green vegetables*** (= for example CABBAGE) ◇ ***root vegetables*** (= for example CARROTS) ◇ *a salad of raw vegetables* ◇ *a* ***vegetable garden/patch/plot*** ◇ *vegetable matter* (= plants in general) ➲ VISUAL VOCAB page V27 ➲ compare ANIMAL, FRUIT, MINERAL **2** (*BrE* also **cab·bage**) a person who is physically alive but not capable of much mental or physical activity, for example because of an accident or illness: *Severe brain damage turned him into a vegetable.* **3** a person who has a boring life: *Since losing my job I've been a vegetable.*

vege·tal /ˈvedʒətl/ *adj.* (*formal*) connected with plants

vege·tar·ian /ˌvedʒəˈteəriən; *NAmE* -ˈter-/ (also *BrE informal* **veg·gie**) *noun* a person who does not eat meat or fish: *Is she a vegetarian?* ➲ compare FRUITARIAN, HERBIVORE ▶ **vege·tar·ian** *adj.*: *Are you vegetarian?* ◇ *a vegetarian diet* (= with no meat or fish in it) ◇ *a vegetarian restaurant* (= that serves no meat or fish) **vege·tar·ian·ism** /-ɪzəm/ *noun* [U]

vege·tate /ˈvedʒəteɪt/ *verb* [I] (of a person) to spend time doing very little and feeling bored

vege·tated /ˈvedʒəteɪtɪd/ *adj.* having the amount of plant life mentioned: *a **densely/sparsely vegetated** area*

vege·ta·tion /ˌvedʒəˈteɪʃn/ *noun* [U] plants in general, especially the plants that are found in a particular area or environment: *The hills are covered in lush green vegetation.*

vege·ta·tive /ˈvedʒɪtətɪv; *NAmE* -teɪtɪv/ *adj.* **1** relating to plant life **2** (*medical*) (of a person) alive but showing no sign of brain activity ➲ see also PERSISTENT VEGETATIVE STATE

veg·gie /ˈvedʒi/ *noun* (*informal*) **1** (*BrE*) = VEGETARIAN: *He's turned veggie* (= become a vegetarian). **2** (*especially NAmE*) = VEGETABLE ▶ **veg·gie** *adj.*

ˈ**veggie burger** (also **Vege·bur·ger™**) *noun* a BURGER made with vegetables, especially BEANS, instead of meat

vehe·ment /ˈviːəmənt/ *adj.* showing very strong feelings, especially anger SYN **forceful**: *a **vehement denial/attack/protest, etc.*** ◇ *He had been vehement in his opposition to the idea.* ▶ **vehe·mence** /-məns/ *noun* [U] **vehe·ment·ly** *adv.*: *The charge was vehemently denied.*

ve·hicle 0-w AW /ˈviːəkl; *NAmE* also ˈviːhɪkl/ *noun* **1** 0-w (rather *formal*) a thing that is used for transporting people or goods from one place to another, such as a car or lorry/truck: *motor vehicles* (= cars, buses, lorries/trucks, etc.) ◇ *Are you the driver of this vehicle?* ◇ *rows of parked vehicles* ➲ VISUAL VOCAB pages V46, V47 **2 ~** (**for sth**) something that can be used to express your ideas or feelings or as a way of achieving sth: *Art may be used as a vehicle for propaganda.* ◇ *The play is an ideal vehicle for her talents.*

ve·hicu·lar /vəˈhɪkjələ(r); *NAmE* viːˈh-/ *adj.* (*formal*) intended for vehicles or consisting of vehicles: *vehicular access* ◇ *The road is closed to vehicular traffic.*

veil /veɪl/ *noun, verb*

■ ***noun*** **1** a covering of very thin transparent material worn, especially by women, to protect or hide the face, or as part of a hat, etc: *a bridal veil* **2** a piece of cloth worn by NUNS over the head and shoulders **3** [sing.] (*formal*) something that stops you from learning the truth about a situation: *Their work is carried out behind a veil of secrecy.* ◇ *It would be better to **draw a veil** over what happened next* (= not talk about it). **4** [sing.] (*formal*) a thin layer that stops you from seeing sth: *The mountain tops were hidden beneath a veil of mist.*

IDM **take the ˈveil** (*old-fashioned*) to become a NUN

■ ***verb*** **1 ~ sth/yourself** to cover your face with a veil **2 ~ sth** (*literary*) to cover sth with sth that hides it partly or completely SYN **shroud**: *A fine drizzle began to veil the hills.*

veiled /veɪld/ *adj.* **1** not expressed directly or clearly because you do not want your meaning to be obvious: *a **thinly veiled** threat* ◇ *She made a **veiled reference to** his past mistakes.* **2** wearing a veil: *a mysterious veiled woman*

vein /veɪn/ *noun* **1** [C] any of the tubes that carry blood from all parts of the body towards the heart: *the jugular vein* ➲ compare ARTERY ➲ see also DEEP VEIN THROMBOSIS, VARICOSE VEIN **2** [C] any of the very thin tubes that form the frame of a leaf or an insect's wing **3** [C] a narrow strip of a different colour in some types of stone, wood and cheese **4** [C] a thin layer of minerals or metal contained in rock: *a vein of gold* SYN **seam** **5** [sing.] **~** (**of sth**) an amount of a particular quality or feature in sth: *They had tapped a rich vein of information in his secretary.* **6** [sing., U] a particular style or manner: *A number of other people commented **in a similar vein**.* ◇ *'And that's not all,' he continued in angry vein.*

veined /veɪnd/ *adj.* having or marked with veins or thin lines: *thin blue-veined hands* ◇ *veined marble*

vein·ing /ˈveɪnɪŋ/ *noun* [U] a pattern of veins or thin lines: *the blue veining in Gorgonzola cheese*

vein·ous /ˈveɪnəs/ *adj.* (*technical*) having VEINS that are very noticeable

velar /ˈviːlə(r)/ *noun* (*phonetics*) a speech sound made by placing the back of the tongue against or near the back part of the mouth, for example /k/ or /g/ in the English words *key* and *go* ▶ **velar** *adj.*

Vel·cro™ /ˈvelkrəʊ; *NAmE* -kroʊ/ *noun* [U] a material for fastening clothes, etc. with two different surfaces, one rough and one smooth, that stick to each other when they are pressed together ➲ VISUAL VOCAB page V51

veld /velt/ *noun* [U] (in South Africa) flat open land with grass and no trees ➲ compare PAMPAS, PRAIRIE, SAVANNAH, STEPPE

vel·lum /ˈveləm/ *noun* [U] **1** material made from the skin of a sheep, GOAT or CALF, used for making book covers and, in the past, for writing on **2** smooth cream-coloured paper used for writing on

vel·oci·rap·tor /vəˌlɒsɪˈræptə(r); *NAmE* -ˌlɑːs-/ *noun* a small DINOSAUR that moved fairly quickly

vel·ocity /vəˈlɒsəti; *NAmE* -ˈlɑːs-/ *noun* [U, C] (*pl.* -ies) **1** (*technical*) the speed of sth in a particular direction: *the velocity of light* ◇ *to **gain/lose velocity*** ◇ *a **high-velocity** rifle* **2** (*formal*) high speed: *Jaguars can move with an astonishing velocity.*

velo·drome /ˈvelədrəʊm; *NAmE* -droʊm/ *noun* a track or building used for cycle racing

vel·our /vəˈlʊə(r); *NAmE* vəˈlʊr/ *noun* [U] a type of silk or cotton cloth with a thick soft surface like VELVET

velum /ˈviːləm/ *noun* (*pl.* **vela** /ˈviːlə/) (*anatomy*) a layer of TISSUE that covers sth, especially the soft PALATE inside the mouth

vel·vet /ˈvelvɪt/ *noun* [U] a type of cloth made from silk, cotton or NYLON, with a thick soft surface: *a velvet dress* ◇ *velvet curtains/drapes* IDM see IRON *adj.*

vel·vet·een /ˌvelvəˈtiːn/ *noun* [U] a type of cotton cloth that looks like VELVET but is less expensive

vel·vety /ˈvelvəti/ *adj.* pleasantly smooth and soft: *velvety skin* ◇ *a velvety red wine*

vena cava /ˌviːnə ˈkeɪvə/ *noun* (*pl.* **venae cavae** /ˌviːniː ˈkeɪviː/) (*anatomy*) either of the two VEINS that take blood without OXYGEN in it towards the heart

venal /ˈviːnl/ *adj.* (*formal*) prepared to do dishonest or immoral things in return for money SYN **corrupt**: *venal journalists* ▶ **ve·nal·ity** /viːˈnæləti/ *noun* [U]

vend /vend/ *verb* **~ sth** (*formal*) to sell sth

ven·detta /venˈdetə/ *noun* **1** a long and violent disagreement between two families or groups, in which people are murdered in return for previous murders SYN **feud** **2 ~** (**against sb**) a long argument or disagreement in which one person or group does or says things to harm another: *He has accused the media of pursuing a vendetta against him.* ◇ *She conducted a **personal vendetta** against me.*

vending machine /ˈvendɪŋ məʃiːn/ *noun* a machine from which you can buy cigarettes, drinks, etc. by putting coins into it

vend·or /ˈvendə(r)/ *noun* **1** a person who sells things, for example food or newspapers, usually outside on the street: *street vendors* **2** (*formal*) a company that sells a particular product: *software vendors* **3** (*law*) a person who is selling a house, etc. ➲ compare SELLER

ven·eer /vəˈnɪə(r); *NAmE* vəˈnɪr/ *noun, verb*

■ ***noun*** **1** [C, U] a thin layer of wood or plastic that is glued to the surface of cheaper wood, especially on a piece of furniture **2** [sing.] **~** (**of sth**) (*formal*) an outer appearance of a particular quality that hides the true nature of sb/sth: *Her veneer of politeness began to crack.*

■ ***verb*** **~ sth** (**with/in sth**) to cover the surface of sth with a veneer of wood, etc.

ven·er·able /ˈvenərəbl/ *adj.* **1** (*formal*) **venerable** people or things deserve respect because they are old, important, wise, etc: *a venerable old man* ◇ *a venerable institution* **2 the Venerable...** [only before noun] (in the Anglican Church), a title of respect used when talking about an ARCHDEACON: *the Venerable Martin Roberts* **3 the Venerable...** [only before noun] (in the Roman

V

Catholic Church), a title given to a dead person who is very holy but who has not yet been made a SAINT

ven·er·ate /ˈvenəreɪt/ *verb* **~ sb/sth (as sth)** (*formal*) to have and show a lot of respect for sb/sth, especially sb/sth that is considered to be holy or very important SYN **revere** ▸ **ven·er·ation** /ˌvenəˈreɪʃn/ *noun* [U]: *The relics were objects of veneration.*

ven·ereal /vəˈnɪəriəl; *NAmE* -ˈnɪr-/ *adj.* [only before noun] relating to diseases spread by sexual contact: *a venereal infection*

veˌnereal diˈsease *noun* [C, U] (*abbr.* VD) a disease that is caught by having sex with an infected person

ven·etian blind /vəˌniːʃn ˈblaɪnd/ *noun* a BLIND for a window that has flat horizontal plastic or metal strips going across it that you can turn to let in as much light as you want ➲ VISUAL VOCAB page V18

ven·geance /ˈvendʒəns/ *noun* [U] (*formal*) the act of punishing or harming sb in return for what they have done to you, your family or friends SYN **revenge**: *a desire for vengeance* ◇ **~ on/upon sb** *to take vengeance on sb* ◇ *He swore vengeance on his child's killer.*

IDM **with a ˈvengeance** (*informal*) to a greater degree than is expected or usual: *She set to work with a vengeance.*

venge·ful /ˈvendʒfl/ *adj.* (*formal*) showing a desire to punish sb who has harmed you ▸ **vengeful·ly** /-fəli/ *adv.*

ve·nial /ˈviːniəl/ *adj.* [usually before noun] (*formal*) (of a SIN or mistake) not very serious and therefore able to be forgiven

ven·ison /ˈvenɪsn; -zn/ *noun* [U] meat from a DEER

Venn diagram

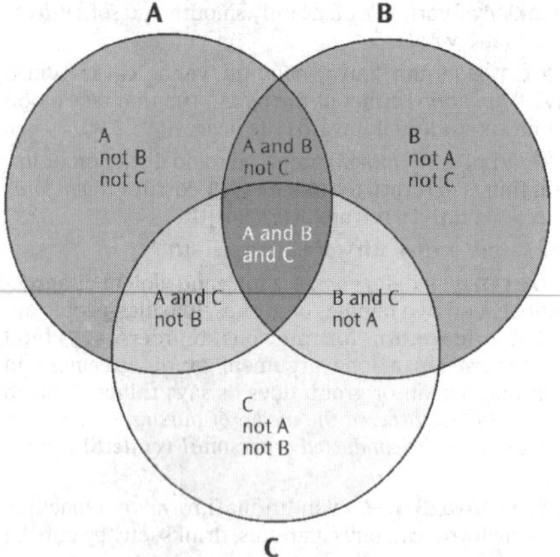

Venn dia·gram /ˈven daɪəɡræm/ *noun* (*mathematics*) a picture showing SETS (= groups of things that have a shared quality) as circles that cross over each other, to show which qualities the different sets have in common

venom /ˈvenəm/ *noun* [U] **1** the poisonous liquid that some snakes, spiders, etc. produce when they bite or sting you **2** (*formal*) strong bitter feeling; hatred and a desire to hurt sb: *a look of pure venom* IDM see SPIT *v.*

ven·om·ous /ˈvenəməs/ *adj.* **1** (of a snake, etc.) producing venom **2** (*formal*) full of bitter feeling or hatred: *a venomous look* ▸ **ven·om·ous·ly** *adv.*

ven·ous /ˈviːnəs/ *adj.* (*technical*) of or contained in VEINS (= the tubes that carry liquids around the bodies of animals and plants): *venous blood*

vent /vent/ *noun, verb*

■ ***noun* 1** an opening that allows air, gas or liquid to pass out of or into a room, building, container, etc: ***air/heating vents*** ➲ VISUAL VOCAB page V42 ➲ compare REGISTER **2** (*technical*) the opening in the body of a bird, fish, REPTILE or other small animal, through which waste matter is passed out **3** a long thin opening at the bottom of the back or side of a coat or jacket

IDM **give (full) vent to sth** (*formal*) to express a feeling, especially anger, strongly: *She gave full vent to her feelings in a violent outburst.*

■ ***verb*** **~ sth (on sb)** (*formal*) to express feelings, especially anger, strongly: *He vented his anger on the referee.*

ven·ti·late /ˈventɪleɪt/ *verb* **1 ~ sth** to allow fresh air to enter and move around a room, building, etc: *a well-ventilated room* ◇ *The bathroom is ventilated by means of an extractor fan.* **2 ~ sth** (*formal*) to express your feelings or opinions publicly SYN **air** ▸ **ven·ti·lation** /ˌventɪˈleɪʃn/ *noun* [U]: *a ventilation shaft* ◇ *Make sure that there is adequate ventilation in the room before using the paint.*

ven·ti·la·tor /ˈventɪleɪtə(r)/ *noun* **1** a device or an opening for letting fresh air come into a room, etc. **2** a piece of equipment with a PUMP that helps sb to breathe by sending air in and out of their lungs: *He was put on a ventilator.*

ven·tral /ˈventrəl/ *adj.* [only before noun] (*biology*) on or connected with the part of a fish or an animal that is underneath (or that in humans faces forward): *a fish's ventral fin* ➲ VISUAL VOCAB page V10

ven·tricle /ˈventrɪkl/ *noun* (*anatomy*) **1** either of the two lower spaces in the heart that PUMP blood to the LUNGS or around the body ➲ compare AURICLE **2** any hollow space in the body, especially one of four main hollow spaces in the brain

ven·trilo·quism /venˈtrɪləkwɪzəm/ *noun* [U] the art of speaking without moving your lips and of making it look as if your voice is coming from another person ▸ **ven·trilo·quist** /venˈtrɪləkwɪst/ *noun*: *Entertainment included a ventriloquist.* ◇ *a ventriloquist's dummy*

ven·ture 0‑ /ˈventʃə(r)/ *noun, verb*

■ ***noun*** a business project or activity, especially one that involves taking risks SYN **undertaking**: *A disastrous business venture lost him thousands of dollars.* ➲ see also JOINT VENTURE

■ ***verb* 1** 0‑ [I] **+ adv./prep.** to go somewhere even though you know that it might be dangerous or unpleasant: *They ventured nervously into the water.* ◇ *He's never ventured abroad in his life.* **2** [T] (*formal*) to say or do sth in a careful way, especially because it might upset or offend sb: **~ sth** *She hardly dared to venture an opinion.* ◇ **~ to do sth** *I ventured to suggest that she might have made a mistake.* ◇ **+ speech** *'And if I say no?' she ventured.* ◇ **~ that...** *He ventured that the data might be flawed.* **3** [T] **~ sth (on sth)** to risk losing sth valuable or important if you are not successful at sth SYN **gamble**: *It was wrong to venture his financial security on such a risky deal.*

IDM **nothing ˈventured, nothing ˈgained** (*saying*) used to say that you have to take risks if you want to achieve things and be successful

PHR V **ˈventure into/on sth** to do sth, even though it involves risks: *This is the first time the company has ventured into movie production.*

ˈventure capital *noun* [U] (*business*) money that is invested in a new company to help it develop, which may involve a lot of risk ➲ compare WORKING CAPITAL

ˈVenture Scout (*BrE*) (*US* **Exˈplorer Scout**) *noun* a member of the senior branch of the SCOUT ASSOCIATION for young people between the ages of 15 or 16 and 20

ven·ture·some /ˈventʃəsəm; *NAmE* -tʃərs-/ *adj.* (*formal* or *literary*) willing to take risks SYN **daring**

venue /ˈvenjuː/ *noun* a place where people meet for an organized event, for example a concert, sporting event or conference: *The band will be playing at 20 different venues on their UK tour.* ◇ *Please note the change of venue for this event.* ➲ SYNONYMS at PLACE

Venus /ˈviːnəs/ *noun* the planet in the SOLAR SYSTEM that is second in order of distance from the sun, between Mercury and the earth

Venus fly·trap /ˌviːnəs ˈflaɪtræp/ *noun* a small CARNIVOROUS (= flesh-eating) plant with leaves that trap insects by closing quickly around them

V

ver·acity /vəˈræsəti/ *noun* [U] (*formal*) the quality of being true; the habit of telling the truth SYN **truth, truthfulness**: *They questioned the veracity of her story.*

ver·anda (also **ver·an·dah**) /vəˈrændə/ *noun* **1** (*especially BrE*) (*NAmE* usually **porch**) a platform with an open front and a roof, built onto the side of a house on the ground floor: *After dinner, we sat talking on the veranda.* **2** (*AustralE, NZE*) a roof over the part of the street where people walk in front of a shop/store SYN **awning**

verb /vɜːb; *NAmE* vɜːrb/ *noun* (*grammar*) a word or group of words that expresses an action (such as *eat*), an event (such as *happen*) or a state (such as *exist*): ***regular/irregular verbs*** ◇ ***transitive/intransitive verbs*** ➲ see also PHRASAL VERB

ver·bal /ˈvɜːbl; *NAmE* ˈvɜːrbl/ *adj.* **1** relating to words: *The job applicant must have good verbal skills.* ◇ *non-verbal communication* (= expressions of the face, GESTURES, etc.) **2** spoken, not written: *a* ***verbal agreement/warning*** ◇ *verbal instructions* ➲ compare ORAL **3** (*grammar*) relating to verbs: *a verbal noun*

ver·bal·ize (*BrE* also **-ise**) /ˈvɜːbəlaɪz; *NAmE* ˈvɜːrb-/ *verb* [T, I] **~ (sth)** (*formal*) to express your feelings or ideas in words SYN **put into words**: *He's a real genius but he has difficulty verbalizing his ideas.*

ver·bal·ly /ˈvɜːbəli; *NAmE* ˈvɜːrb-/ *adv.* in spoken words and not in writing or actions: *The company had received complaints both verbally and in writing.*

ver·ba·tim /vɜːˈbeɪtɪm; *NAmE* vɜːrˈb-/ *adj., adv.* exactly as spoken or written SYN **word for word**: *a verbatim report* ◇ *He reported the speech verbatim.*

ver·bena /vɜːˈbiːnə; *NAmE* vɜːrˈb-/ *noun* [U, C] a garden plant with bright flowers

ver·bi·age /ˈvɜːbiɪdʒ; *NAmE* ˈvɜːrb-/ *noun* [U] (*formal, disapproving*) the use of too many words, or of more difficult words than are needed, to express an idea

ver·bose /vɜːˈbəʊs; *NAmE* vɜːrˈboʊs/ *adj.* (*formal, disapproving*) using or containing more words than are needed SYN **long-winded**: *a verbose speaker/style* ▶ **ver·bos·ity** /vɜːˈbɒsəti; *NAmE* vɜːrˈbɑːs-/ *noun* [U]

ver·dant /ˈvɜːdnt; *NAmE* ˈvɜːrdnt/ *adj.* (*literary*) (of grass, plants, fields, etc.) fresh and green

ver·dict /ˈvɜːdɪkt; *NAmE* ˈvɜːrd-/ *noun* **1** a decision that is made by a JURY in court, stating if sb is considered guilty of a crime or not: *Has the jury* ***reached a verdict****?* ◇ *The jury* ***returned a verdict*** (= gave a verdict) *of guilty.* ➲ COLLOCATIONS at JUSTICE ➲ see also MAJORITY VERDICT, OPEN VERDICT **2 ~ (on sth/sb)** a decision that you make or an opinion that you give about sth, after you have tested it or considered it carefully: *The coroner* ***recorded a verdict*** *of accidental death.* ◇ *The panel will* ***give their verdict*** *on the latest video releases.* ◇ *Well, what's your verdict?*

ver·di·gris /ˈvɜːdɪgriː; -griːs; *NAmE* ˈvɜːrd-/ *noun* [U] the greenish substance which forms, for example on roofs, when COPPER reacts with the air

ver·dure /ˈvɜːdjə(r); *NAmE* ˈvɜːrd-/ *noun* [U] (*literary*) thick green plants growing in a particular place

verge /vɜːdʒ; *NAmE* vɜːrdʒ/ *noun, verb*

■ ***noun*** (*BrE*) a piece of grass at the edge of a path, road, etc: *a grass verge* ➲ compare SOFT SHOULDER

IDM **on/to the verge of sth/of doing sth** very near to the moment when sb does sth or sth happens: *He was on the verge of tears.* ◇ *They are on the verge of signing a new contract.*

■ ***verb***

PHR V **ˈverge on sth** to be very close to an extreme state or condition SYN **border on sth**: *Some of his suggestions verged on the outrageous.*

ver·ger /ˈvɜːdʒə(r); *NAmE* ˈvɜːrdʒ-/ *noun* (*especially BrE*) an official whose job is to take care of the inside of a church and to perform some simple duties during church services

ver·ify /ˈverɪfaɪ/ *verb* (**veri·fies, veri·fy·ing, veri·fied, veri·fied**) (*formal*) **1** to check that sth is true or accurate: **~ sth** *We have no way of verifying his story.* ◇ **~ that...** *Please verify that there is sufficient memory available before loading the program.* ◇ **~ whether, what, etc...** *I'll leave you to verify whether these claims are true.* **2 ~ sth** | **~ that...** to show or say that sth is true or accurate SYN **confirm**: *Her version of events was verified by neighbours.* ▶ **veri·fi·able** /ˈverɪfaɪəbl/ *adj.*: *a verifiable fact* **veri·fi·ca·tion** /ˌverɪfɪˈkeɪʃn/ *noun* [U]: *the verification of hypotheses*

ver·ily /ˈverɪli/ *adv.* (*old use*) really; truly

veri·sim·ili·tude /ˌverɪsɪˈmɪlɪtjuːd; *NAmE* -tuːd/ *noun* [U] (*formal*) the quality of seeming to be true or real SYN **authenticity**: *To add verisimilitude, the stage is covered with sand for the desert scenes.*

ver·it·able /ˈverɪtəbl/ *adj.* [only before noun] (*formal* or *humorous*) a word used to emphasize that sb/sth can be compared to sb/sth else that is more exciting, more impressive, etc. SYN **positive**: *The meal that followed was a veritable banquet.*

ver·ity /ˈverəti/ *noun* (*pl.* -ies) **1** [usually pl.] (*formal*) a belief or principle about life that is accepted as true: *the* ***eternal verities*** *of life* **2** [U] (*old use*) truth

vermi·celli /ˌvɜːmɪˈtʃeli; *NAmE* ˌvɜːrm-/ *noun* [U] **1** PASTA in the shape of very thin sticks, often broken into small pieces and added to soups **2** (*BrE*) small pieces of chocolate in the shape of very thin sticks broken into pieces, used to decorate cakes

ver·mil·ion /vəˈmɪliən; *NAmE* vərˈm-/ *adj.* bright red in colour ▶ **ver·mil·ion** *noun* [U]

ver·min /ˈvɜːmɪn; *NAmE* ˈvɜːrmɪn/ *noun* [pl.] **1** wild animals or birds that destroy plants or food, or attack farm animals and birds: *On farms the fox is considered vermin and treated as such.* **2** insects that live on the bodies of animals and sometimes humans: *The room was crawling with vermin.* **3** (*disapproving*) people who are very unpleasant or dangerous to society

ver·min·ous /ˈvɜːmɪnəs; *NAmE* ˈvɜːrm-/ *adj.* (*formal*) covered with vermin

ver·mouth /ˈvɜːməθ; *NAmE* vərˈmuːθ/ *noun* [U] a strong wine, flavoured with HERBS and spices, often mixed with other drinks as a COCKTAIL

ver·nacu·lar /vəˈnækjələ(r); *NAmE* vərˈn-/ *noun* **1** (usually **the vernacular**) [sing.] the language spoken in a particular area or by a particular group, especially one that is not the official or written language **2** [U] (*technical*) a style of ARCHITECTURE concerned with ordinary houses rather than large public buildings ▶ **ver·nacu·lar** *adj.*

ver·nal /ˈvɜːnl; *NAmE* ˈvɜːrnl/ *adj.* [only before noun] (*formal* or *literary*) connected with the season of spring: *the vernal equinox*

ver·nis·sage /ˌvɜːnɪˈsɑːʒ; *NAmE* ˌvɜːrn-/ *noun* (*pl.* **ver·nis·sages** /ˌvɜːnɪˈsɑːʒ; *NAmE* ˌvɜːrn-/) an occasion when a few invited people can look at paintings before they go on show to the public

ver·ruca /vəˈruːkə/ (*BrE*) (*NAmE* ˈ**plantar wart**) *noun* a small hard lump like a WART on the bottom of the foot, which can be easily spread from person to person

ver·sa·tile /ˈvɜːsətaɪl; *NAmE* ˈvɜːrsətl/ *adj.* (*approving*) **1** (of a person) able to do many different things: *He's a versatile actor who has played a wide variety of parts.* **2** (of food, a building, etc.) having many different uses: *Eggs are easy to cook and are an extremely versatile food.* ▶ **ver·sa·til·ity** /ˌvɜːsəˈtɪləti; *NAmE* ˌvɜːrs-/ *noun* [U]: *She is a designer of extraordinary versatility.*

verse /vɜːs; *NAmE* vɜːrs/ *noun* **1** [U] writing that is arranged in lines, often with a regular rhythm or pattern of RHYME SYN **poetry**: *Most of the play is written in verse, but some of it is in prose.* ➲ see also BLANK VERSE, FREE VERSE **2** [C] a group of lines that form a unit in a poem or song: *a hymn with six verses* **3 verses** [pl.] (*old-fashioned*) poetry: *a book of comic verses* **4** [C] any one of the short NUMBERED divisions of a chapter in the Bible IDM see CHAPTER

versed /vɜːst; *NAmE* vɜːrst/ *adj.* **~ in sth** having a lot of knowledge about sth, or skill at sth SYN **expert in, practised in**: *He was* ***well versed in*** *employment law.*

V

ver·si·fi·ca·tion /ˌvɜːsɪfɪˈkeɪʃn; *NAmE* ˌvɜːrs-/ *noun* [U] (*formal*) the art of writing poetry in a particular pattern; the pattern in which poetry is written

vers·ify /ˈvɜːsɪfaɪ; *NAmE* ˈvɜːrs-/ *verb* (**ver·si·fies, ver·si·fy·ing, ver·si·fied, ver·si·fied**) [I, T] **~ (sth)** (*formal*, sometimes *disapproving*) to write sth in verse ▸ **ver·si·fier** *noun*

ver·sion 0-w AW /ˈvɜːʃn; -ʒn; *NAmE* ˈvɜːrʒn/ *noun* **1** 0-w a form of sth that is slightly different from an earlier form or from other forms of the same thing: *There are two versions of the game, a long one and a short one.* ◇ *the* **latest version** *of the software package* ◇ *the* **de luxe/luxury version** ➲ see also BETA VERSION **2** 0-w a description of an event from the position of a particular person or group of people: *She gave us her version of what had happened that day.* ◇ *Their versions of how the accident happened conflict.* ➲ SYNONYMS at REPORT **3** 0-w a film/movie, play, piece of music, etc. that is based on a particular piece of work but is in a different form, style or language: *the film version of 'War and Peace'* ◇ *The English version of the novel is due for publication next year.* ➲ see also THE AUTHORIZED VERSION, COVER VERSION

verso /ˈvɜːsəʊ; *NAmE* ˈvɜːrsoʊ/ *noun* (*pl.* -os) (*technical*) the page on the left side of an open book OPP **recto**

ver·sus /ˈvɜːsəs; *NAmE* ˈvɜːrsəs/ *prep.* (*abbr.* v, vs) **1** (*sport* or *law*) used to show that two teams or sides are against each other: *It is France versus Brazil in the final.* ◇ *in the case of the State versus Ford* **2** used to compare two different ideas, choices, etc.: *It was the promise of better job opportunities versus the inconvenience of moving away and leaving her friends.*

ver·tebra /ˈvɜːtɪbrə; *NAmE* ˈvɜːrt-/ *noun* (*pl.* **ver·te·brae** /-reɪ; -riː/) any of the small bones that are connected together to form the SPINE ➲ VISUAL VOCAB page V48 ▸ **ver·te·bral** *adj.* [only before noun]

ver·te·brate /ˈvɜːtɪbrət; *NAmE* ˈvɜːrt-/ *noun* (*technical*) any animal with a BACKBONE, including all MAMMALS, birds, fish, REPTILES and AMPHIBIANS ➲ compare INVERTEBRATE ▸ **ver·te·brate** *adj.*

ver·tex /ˈvɜːteks; *NAmE* ˈvɜːrt-/ *noun* (*pl.* **ver·ti·ces** /-tɪsiːz/ or **ver·texes**) **1** (*geometry*) a point where two lines meet to form an angle, especially the point of a triangle or CONE opposite the base ➲ VISUAL VOCAB page V58 **2** (*technical*) the highest point or top of sth

ver·ti·cal 0-w /ˈvɜːtɪkl; *NAmE* ˈvɜːrt-/ *adj.*, *noun*

■ ***adj.*** **1** 0-w (of a line, pole, etc.) going straight up or down from a level surface or from top to bottom in a picture, etc. SYN **perpendicular**: *the vertical axis of the graph* ◇ *The cliff was almost vertical.* ◇ *There was a vertical drop to the ocean.* ➲ compare HORIZONTAL **2** having a structure in which there are top, middle and bottom levels: *a vertical flow of communication* ▸ **ver·ti·cal·ly** /-kli/ *adv.*

■ ***noun*** (usually **the vertical**) a vertical line or position SYN **perpendicular**: *The wall is several degrees off the vertical.*

ver·tigin·ous /vɜːˈtɪdʒɪnəs; *NAmE* vɜːrˈt-/ *adj.* (*formal*) causing a feeling of vertigo SYN **dizzying**: *From the path there was a vertiginous drop to the valley below.*

ver·tigo /ˈvɜːtɪgəʊ; *NAmE* ˈvɜːrtɪgoʊ/ *noun* [U] the feeling of DIZZINESS and fear, and of losing your balance, that is caused in some people when they look down from a very high place

verve /vɜːv; *NAmE* vɜːrv/ *noun* [U, sing.] energy, excitement or enthusiasm SYN **gusto**: *It was a performance of verve and vitality.*

very 0-w /ˈveri/ *adv.*, *adj.*

■ **adv.** (*abbr.* v) **1** 0-w used before adjectives, adverbs and determiners to mean 'in a high degree' or 'extremely': *very small* ◇ *very quickly* ◇ *Very few people know that.* ◇ *Thanks very much.* ◇ *'Do you like it?' 'Yeah, I do.* ***Very much.'*** ◇ *'Is it what you expected?' 'Oh yes,* ***very much so****.'* ◇ *'Are you busy?' 'Not very.'* ◇ *The new building has been very much admired.* ◇ *I'm* **not very** (= not at all) *impressed.* ◇ *I'm* ***very very*** *grateful.* **2** 0-w used to emphasize a superlative adjective or before *own*: *They wanted the* ***very best*** *quality.* ◇ *Be there by six* ***at the very latest****.* ◇ *At last he had his* ***very own*** *car* (= belonging to him and to nobody else). **3 the ~ same** exactly the same: *Mario said the very same thing.*

■ ***adj.*** [only before noun] **1** used to emphasize that you are talking about a particular thing or person and not about another SYN **actual**: *Those were her very words.* ◇ *He might be phoning her* ***at this very moment****.* ◇ *That's* ***the very thing*** *I need.* **2** used to emphasize an extreme place or time: *It happens at the very beginning of the book.* **3** used to emphasize a noun SYN **mere**: *The* ***very thought of*** *drink made him feel sick.* ◇ *'I can't do that!' she gasped, appalled at* ***the very idea****.* IDM see EYE *n.*

Grammar Point

very / very much

- **Very** is used with adjectives, past participles used as adjectives, and adverbs: *I am very hungry.* ◇ *I was very pleased to get your letter.* ◇ *You played very well.* But notice this use: *I'm* ***very much afraid*** *that your son may be involved in the crime.*
- **Very** is not used with past participles that have a passive meaning. **Much**, **very much** or **greatly** (*formal*) are usually used instead: *Your help was very much appreciated.* ◇ *He was much loved by everyone.* ◇ *She was greatly admired.*
- **Very** is used to emphasize superlative adjectives: *my very best work* ◇ *the very youngest children.* However, with comparative adjectives **much**, **very much**, **a lot**, etc. are used: *Your work is very much better.* ◇ *much younger children.*
- **Very** is not used with adjectives and adverbs that already have an extreme meaning. You are more likely to use an adverb such as *absolutely*, *completely*, etc: *She was absolutely furious.* ◇ *I'm completely exhausted.* ◇ *You played really brilliantly.*
- **Very** is not used with verbs. Use **very much** instead: *We enjoyed staying with you very much.*

ˌ**very high** ˈ**frequency** *noun* [U] = VHF

Very light /ˈveri laɪt/ *noun* a bright coloured light that is fired from a gun as a signal from a ship that it needs help

ves·icle /ˈvesɪkl/ *noun* **1** (*biology*) a small bag or hollow structure in the body of a plant or an animal **2** (*medical*) a small swelling filled with liquid under the skin SYN **blister**

ves·pers /ˈvespəz; *NAmE* -pərz/ *noun* [U] the service of evening prayer in some Christian Churches ➲ compare EVENSONG, MATINS

ves·sel /ˈvesl/ *noun* **1** (*formal*) a large ship or boat: *ocean-going vessels* **2** (*old use* or *technical*) a container used for holding liquids, such as a bowl, cup, etc: *a Bronze Age drinking vessel* **3** a tube that carries blood through the body of a person or an animal, or liquid through the parts of a plant ➲ see also BLOOD VESSEL

vest /vest/ *noun*, *verb*

■ ***noun*** **1** (*BrE*) (*NAmE* **under·shirt**) a piece of underwear worn under a shirt, etc. next to the skin: *a cotton vest* ➲ compare SINGLET **2** a special piece of clothing that covers the upper part of the body: *a bullet-proof vest* ◇ *a running vest* **3** (*NAmE*) (*BrE* **waist·coat**) a short piece of clothing with buttons down the front but no sleeves, usually worn over a shirt and under a jacket, often forming part of a man's suit ➲ VISUAL VOCAB page V50

■ ***verb***

PHR V ˈ**vest in sb/sth** (*law*) (of power, property, etc.) to belong to sb/sth legally ˈ**vest sth in sb** | ˈ**vest sb with sth** [often passive] (*formal*) **1** to give sb the legal right or power to do sth: *Overall authority is vested in the Supreme Council.* ◇ *The Supreme Council is vested with overall authority.* **2** to make sb the legal owner of land or property

ˌ**vested** ˈ**interest** *noun* **~ (in sth)** a personal reason for wanting sth to happen, especially because you get some advantage from it: *They have a vested interest in keeping* *the club as exclusive as possible.* ◇ *Vested interests* (= people with a vested interest) *are opposing the plan.*

ves·ti·bule /ˈvestɪbjuːl/ *noun* **1** (*formal*) an entrance hall of a large building, for example where hats and coats can be left **2** (*technical*) a space at the end of a coach/car on a train that connects it with the next coach/car

ves·tige /ˈvestɪdʒ/ *noun* (*formal*) **1** a small part of sth that still exists after the rest of it has stopped existing **SYN** **trace**: *the* ***last vestiges*** *of the old colonial regime* **2** usually used in negative sentences, to say that not even a small amount of sth exists: *There's not a vestige of truth in the rumour.*

ves·tigial /veˈstɪdʒiəl/ *adj.* [usually before noun] (*formal* or *technical*) remaining as the last small part of sth that used to exist: *vestigial traces of an earlier culture* ◇ *It is often possible to see the vestigial remains of rear limbs on some snakes.*

vest·ment /ˈvestmənt/ *noun* [usually pl.] a piece of clothing worn by a priest during church services

ves·try /ˈvestri/ *noun* (*pl.* **-ies**) a room in a church where a priest prepares for a service by putting on special clothes and where various objects used in worship are kept **SYN** **sacristy**

vet /vet/ *noun, verb*

▪ ***noun*** **1** (*especially BrE*) (*NAmE* usually **vet·er·in·ar·ian**) (also *BrE formal* ˈ**veterinary surgeon**) a person who has been trained in the science of animal medicine, whose job is to treat animals who are sick or injured **2** **vet's** (*pl.* **vets**) the place where a vet works: *I've got to take the dog to the vet's tomorrow.* **3** (*NAmE, informal*) = VETERAN: *a Vietnam vet*

▪ ***verb*** (**-tt-**) (*BrE*) **1** **~ sb** to find out about a person's past life and career in order to decide if they are suitable for a particular job **SYN** **screen**: *All candidates are carefully vetted for security reasons.* ➲ see also POSITIVE VETTING **2** **~ sth** to check the contents, quality, etc. of sth carefully **SYN** **screen**: *All reports are vetted before publication.*

vetch /vetʃ/ *noun* [U, C] a plant of the PEA family. There are several types of vetch, one of which is used as food for farm animals.

vet·eran /ˈvetərən/ *noun* **1** a person who has a lot of experience in a particular area or activity: *the veteran American actor, Clint Eastwood* **2** (also *NAmE informal* **vet**) a person who has been a soldier, sailor, etc. in a war: *war veterans* ◇ *a Vietnam vet*

ˌ**veteran** ˈ**car** *noun* (*BrE*) a car made before 1916 ➲ compare VINTAGE

ˈ**Veterans Day** *noun* a holiday in the US on 11 November, in honour of members of the armed forces and others who have died in war ➲ see also MEMORIAL DAY, REMEMBRANCE SUNDAY

vet·er·in·ar·ian /ˌvetərɪˈneəriən; *NAmE* -ˈner-/ *noun* (*NAmE*) = VET

vet·er·in·ary /ˈvetnri; ˈvetrənəri; *NAmE* ˈvetərəneri/ *adj.* [only before noun] connected with caring for the health of animals: ***veterinary medicine/science***

ˈ**veterinary surgeon** *noun* (*BrE, formal*) = VET

veto /ˈviːtəʊ; *NAmE* -toʊ/ *noun, verb*

▪ ***noun*** (*pl.* **-oes**) **1** [C, U] the right to refuse to allow sth to be done, especially the right to stop a law from being passed or a decision from being taken: *The British government used its veto to block the proposal.* ◇ *to have the* ***power/right of veto*** ◇ *the use of the presidential veto* **2** [C] **~ (on sth/on doing sth)** an occasion when sb refuses to allow sth to be done **SYN** **ban**: *For months there was a veto on employing new staff.*

▪ ***verb*** (**ve·toes**, **veto·ing**, **ve·toed**, **ve·toed**) **1** **~ sth** to stop sth from happening or being done by using your official authority (= by using your veto): *Plans for the dam have been vetoed by the Environmental Protection Agency.* ➲ COLLOCATIONS at POLITICS **2** **~ sth** to refuse to accept or do what sb has suggested **SYN** **rule out**: *I wanted to go camping but the others quickly vetoed that idea.*

vex /veks/ *verb* **~ sb** (*old-fashioned* or *formal*) to annoy or worry sb ▶ **vex·ing** *adj.*: *a vexing problem*

vex·ation /vekˈseɪʃn/ *noun* (*old-fashioned* or *formal*) **1** [U] the state of feeling upset or annoyed **2** [C] a thing that upsets or annoys you

vex·atious /vekˈseɪʃəs/ *adj.* (*old-fashioned* or *formal*) making you feel upset or annoyed

vexed /vekst/ *adj.* **1** **~ question/issue** a problem that is difficult to deal with **SYN** **thorny**: *The conference spent days discussing the vexed question of border controls.* **2** **~ (at/with sb/sth)** (*old-fashioned*) upset or annoyed

VHF /ˌviː eɪtʃ ˈef/ *abbr.* very high frequency (a range of radio waves used for high-quality broadcasting)

VHS™ /ˌviː eɪtʃ ˈes/ *abbr.* video home system (a system used by VIDEO RECORDERS and some CAMCORDERS)

via **O‑w** **AW** /ˈvaɪə; ˈviːə/ *prep.*

1 O‑w through a place: *We flew home via Dubai.* **2** by means of a particular person, system, etc: *I heard about the sale via Jane.* ◇ *The news programme came to us via satellite.*

vi·able /ˈvaɪəbl/ *adj.* **1** that can be done; that will be successful **SYN** **feasible**: *a* ***viable option/proposition*** ◇ *There is no* ***viable alternative.*** ◇ *to be* ***commercially/politically/financially/economically viable*** **2** (*biology*) capable of developing and surviving independently: *viable organisms* ▶ **via·bil·ity** /ˌvaɪəˈbɪləti/ *noun* [U]: *commercial viability*

via·duct /ˈvaɪədʌkt/ *noun* a long high bridge, usually with ARCHES, that carries a road or railway/railroad across a river or valley ➲ VISUAL VOCAB page V12

Viagra™ /vaɪˈæɡrə/ *noun* [U] a drug used to treat IMPOTENCE in men

vial /ˈvaɪəl/ *noun* (*especially NAmE*) = PHIAL

vibes /vaɪbz/ *noun* [pl.] **1** (also *formal* **vi·bra·tions**) (also **vibe** [sing.]) (*informal*) a mood or an atmosphere produced by a particular person, thing or place: ***good/bad vibes*** ◇ *The vibes weren't right.* **2** = VIBRAPHONE: *a jazzy vibes backing*

vi·brant /ˈvaɪbrənt/ *adj.* **1** full of life and energy **SYN** **exciting**: *a vibrant city* ◇ *Thailand is at its most vibrant during the New Year celebrations.* **2** (of colours) very bright and strong **SYN** **brilliant**: *The room was decorated in vibrant reds and yellows.* ➲ SYNONYMS at BRIGHT **3** (of music, sounds, etc.) loud and powerful: *vibrant rhythms* ▶ **vi·brancy** /-brənsi/ *noun* [U] **vi·brant·ly** *adv.*

vi·bra·phone /ˈvaɪbrəfəʊn; *NAmE* -foʊn/ *noun* [C] (also *informal* **vibes** [pl.]) a musical instrument used especially in JAZZ, that has two rows of metal bars that you hit, and a motor that makes them vibrate

vi·brate /vaɪˈbreɪt; *NAmE* usually ˈvaɪbreɪt/ *verb* [I, T] to move or make sth move from side to side very quickly and with small movements: **~ (sth)** *Every time a train went past the walls vibrated.* ◇ **~ with sth** *The atmosphere seemed to vibrate with tension.*

vi·bra·tion /vaɪˈbreɪʃn/ *noun* **1** [C, U] a continuous shaking movement or feeling: *We could feel the vibrations from the trucks passing outside.* ◇ *a reduction in the level of vibration in the engine* **2** **vibrations** [pl.] (*formal*) = VIBES

vi·brato /vɪˈbrɑːtəʊ; *NAmE* -toʊ/ *noun* [U, C] (*pl.* **-os**) (*music*) a shaking effect in singing or playing a musical instrument, made by rapid slight changes in PITCH (= how high or low a sound is)

vi·bra·tor /vaɪˈbreɪtə(r)/ *noun* an electrical device that produces a continuous shaking movement, used in MASSAGE or for sexual pleasure

vicar /ˈvɪkə(r)/ *noun* **1** (*especially BrE*) an Anglican priest who is in charge of a church and the area around it (called a PARISH) **2** (*NAmE*) a priest in the US Episcopal Church ➲ compare CURATE, MINISTER, PRIEST, RECTOR

vic·ar·age /ˈvɪkərɪdʒ/ *noun* a vicar's house

vic·ari·ous /vɪˈkeəriəs; *NAmE* vaɪˈker-/ *adj.* [only before noun] felt or experienced by watching or reading about sb else doing sth, rather than by doing it yourself: *He got a vicarious thrill out of watching his son score the winning goal.* ▶ **vic·ari·ous·ly** *adv.*

V

vice /vaɪs/ *noun* **1** [U] criminal activities that involve sex or drugs: *plain-clothes detectives from the vice squad* **2** [U, C] evil or immoral behaviour; an evil or immoral quality in sb's character: *The film ended most satisfactorily: vice punished and virtue rewarded.* ◇ *Greed is a terrible vice.* ◇ (*humorous*) *Cigarettes are my only vice.* **3** (*BrE*) (*NAmE* **vise**) [C] a tool with two metal blocks that can be moved together by turning a screw. The vice is used to hold an object firmly while work is done on it: *He held my arm in a* ***vice-like*** (= very firm) ***grip***. ➲ VISUAL VOCAB page V17

vice- /vaɪs/ *combining form* (in nouns and related adjectives) next in rank to sb and able to represent them or act for them: *vice-captain*

ˌvice ˈadmiral *noun* an officer of very high rank in the navy

ˌvice ˈchancellor *noun* the head of a university in Britain, who is in charge of the work of running the university. (Compare the CHANCELLOR, who is the official head of a university but only has duties at various ceremonies.)

ˌvice-ˈpresident *noun* (*abbr.* VP) **1** the person below the president of a country in rank, who takes control of the country if the president is not able to **2** (*NAmE*) a person in charge of a particular part of a business company: *the vice-president of sales* ▸ **ˌvice-presiˈdential** *adj.* [usually before noun]

vice·roy /ˈvaɪsrɔɪ/ *noun* (often used as a title) a person who is sent by a king or queen to govern a COLONY

vice versa /ˌvaɪs ˈvɜːsə; ˌvaɪsi; *NAmE* ˈvɜːrsə/ *adv.* used to say that the opposite of what you have just said is also true: *You can cruise from Cairo to Aswan or vice versa* (= also from Aswan to Cairo).

the vicin·ity /vəˈsɪnəti/ *noun* [sing.] the area around a particular place: *Crowds gathered* ***in the vicinity of*** *Trafalgar Square.* ◇ *There is no hospital* ***in the immediate vicinity***.

vi·cious /ˈvɪʃəs/ *adj.* **1** violent and cruel SYN **brutal**: *a vicious attack* ◇ *a vicious criminal* ◇ *She has a vicious temper.* **2** (of animals) aggressive and dangerous: *a vicious dog* **3** (of an attack, criticism, etc.) full of hatred and anger: *She wrote me a vicious letter.* **4** (*informal*) very bad or severe: *a vicious headache* ◇ *a vicious spiral of rising prices* ▸ **vi·cious·ly** *adv.* **vi·cious·ness** *noun* [U]: *Police were shocked by the viciousness of the assault.*

ˌvicious ˈcircle *noun* [sing.] a situation in which one problem causes another problem which then makes the first problem worse ➲ compare VIRTUOUS CIRCLE

vi·cis·si·tude /vɪˈsɪsɪtjuːd; *NAmE* -tuːd/ *noun* [usually pl.] (*formal*) one of the many changes and problems in a situation or in your life, that you have to deal with

vic·tim 🔑 /ˈvɪktɪm/ *noun*
1 🔑 a person who has been attacked, injured or killed as the result of a crime, a disease, an accident, etc: ***murder/rape, etc. victims*** ◇ ***accident/earthquake/famine, etc. victims*** ◇ ***AIDS/cancer/stroke, etc. victims*** ◇ *victims of crime* ◇ *She was the* ***innocent victim*** *of an arson attack.* ◇ *Schools are the latest victims of cuts in public spending.* **2** 🔑 a person who has been tricked SYN **target**: *They were the victims of a cruel hoax.* ➲ see also FASHION VICTIM **3** an animal or a person that is killed and offered as a SACRIFICE: *a sacrificial victim*
IDM **fall ˈvictim (to sth)** (*formal*) to be injured, damaged or killed by sth

vic·tim·ize (*BrE* also **-ise**) /ˈvɪktɪmaɪz/ *verb* [often passive] **~ sb** to make sb suffer unfairly because you do not like them, their opinions, or sth that they have done: *For years the family had been victimized by racist neighbours.* ◇ *The union claimed that some of its members had been victimized for taking part in the strike.* ▸ **vic·tim·iza·tion, -isa·tion** /ˌvɪktɪmaɪˈzeɪʃn; *NAmE* -məˈz-/ *noun* [U]

vic·tim·less /ˈvɪktɪmləs/ *adj.* a **victimless** crime is one in which nobody seems to suffer or be harmed

ˌvictim supˈport *noun* [U] a service provided by the police that helps people who are victims of crime

vic·tor /ˈvɪktə(r)/ *noun* (*literary*) the winner of a battle, competition, game, etc.

Vic·toria Cross /vɪkˌtɔːriə ˈkrɒs; *NAmE* ˈkrɔːs/ *noun* (*abbr.* VC) a MEDAL for special courage that is given to members of the British and Commonwealth armed forces

Vic·tor·ian /vɪkˈtɔːriən/ *adj., noun*
■ ***adj.*** **1** connected with the period from 1837 to 1901 when Queen Victoria ruled Britain: *Victorian architecture* ◇ *the Victorian age* **2** having the attitudes that were typical of society during Queen Victoria's REIGN: *Victorian attitudes to sex* (= being easily shocked by sexual matters) ◇ *She advocated a return to Victorian values* (= hard work, pride in your country, etc.).
■ ***noun*** a British person who was alive during the period from 1837 to 1901, when Queen Victoria ruled

Vicˌtoria ˈsponge *noun* [C, U] a type of SPONGE CAKE that is made with fat in the mixture

vic·tori·ous /vɪkˈtɔːriəs/ *adj.* having won a victory; that ends in victory SYN **successful, triumphant**: *the victorious army/team* ◇ **~ in sth** *He* ***emerged victorious*** *in the elections.* ▸ **vic·tori·ous·ly** *adv.*

vic·tory 🔑 /ˈvɪktəri/ *noun* (*pl.* -ies) [C, U] **~ (over/against sb/sth)** success in a game, an election, a war, etc: *the team's 3–2 victory against Poland* ◇ *to* ***win a victory*** ◇ *a* ***decisive/narrow victory*** ◇ *an election victory* ◇ *She is confident of victory in Saturday's final.* ◇ ***victory celebrations/parades*** ➲ see also MORAL VICTORY
IDM **roar, romp, sweep, etc. to victory** to win sth easily: *He swept to victory in the final of the championship.* IDM see SWEEP *v.*

vict·ual·ler /ˈvɪtlə(r)/ (also **ˌlicensed ˈvictualler**) *noun* (*BrE, law*) a person who is legally allowed to sell alcoholic drinks

vict·uals /ˈvɪtlz/ *noun* [pl.] (*old-fashioned*) food and drink

vi·cuña /vɪˈkuːnjə/ *noun* a wild animal with a long neck and very soft wool, which lives in S America. Vicuñas are related to LLAMAS.

vide /ˈviːdeɪ/ *verb* (*abbr.* v) **~ sth** used (meaning 'see') as an instruction in books to tell the reader to look at a particular book, passage, etc. for more information

video 🔑 /ˈvɪdiəʊ; *NAmE* -oʊ/ *noun, verb*
■ ***noun*** (*pl.* -os) **1** 🔑 (also **video·tape**) [U, C] a type of MAGNETIC tape used for recording moving pictures and sound; a box containing this tape, also called a **video cassette**: *The movie will be released* ***on video*** *in June.* ◇ *Do we have a* ***blank video***? **2** 🔑 [U] a system of recording moving pictures and sound, either using VIDEOTAPE or a DIGITAL method of storing data: *A wedding is the perfect subject for video.* ◇ *the use of video in schools* **3** 🔑 [C] a copy of a film/movie, programme, etc. that is recorded on VIDEOTAPE: *a video of 'ET'* ◇ *a* ***home video*** (= not a professional one) ◇ *a* ***video shop/store*** ➲ COLLOCATIONS at CINEMA **4** (also **ˈmusic video**) [C] a short film made by a pop or rock band to be shown with a song when it is played on television **5** (also **ˈvideo clip**) [C] a short film or recording of an event, made using DIGITAL technology and viewed on a computer, especially over the Internet: *The school made a short* ***promotional video***. ◇ *Upload your videos and share them with friends and family online.* **6** [C] (*BrE*) = VIDEO CASSETTE RECORDER: *to* ***programme the video*** *to record the football match*
■ ***verb*** (also *formal* **video·tape**) **~ sth/sb** (*especially BrE*) to record a television programme using a VIDEO CASSETTE RECORDER; to film sb/sth using a video camera: *Did you remember to video that programme?* ◇ *Videoing students can be a useful teaching exercise.*

ˈvideo arcade *noun* a place where you can play video games on machines that you use coins to operate

ˈvideo camera *noun* a special camera for making video films ➲ see also CAMCORDER

ˈvideo card (also **ˈgraphics adapter**) *noun* (*computing*) a device that allows images to be shown on a computer screen

ˌ**video caˈssette recorder** *noun* (*abbr.* VCR) (also **video**, ˌ**video caˈssette player**, ˈ**video recorder**) a piece of equipment that you use to record and play films/movies and TV programmes on video

video·con·fer·en·cing /ˈvɪdiəʊkɒnfərənsɪŋ; *NAmE* ˈvɪdioʊkɑːn-/ *noun* [U] a system that enables people in different parts of the world to have a meeting by watching and listening to each other using video screens

ˈ**video diary** *noun* a series of video recordings made by sb over a period of time, in which they record their experiences, thoughts and feelings

video·disc /ˈvɪdiəʊdɪsk; *NAmE* -oʊ-/ *noun* [U, C] a plastic disc that you can record films/movies and programmes on, for showing on a television screen ➲ see also DVD

ˈ**video game** *noun* a game in which you press buttons to control and move images on a screen

ˈ**video jockey** (also **VJ**, **vee·jay**) *noun* a person who introduces music videos on television

ˌ**video ˈnasty** *noun* (*BrE, informal*) a video film/movie that shows offensive scenes of sex and violence

video·phone /ˈvɪdiəʊfəʊn; *NAmE* -oʊfoʊn/ *noun* a type of telephone with a screen that enables you to see the person you are talking to

video·tape /ˈvɪdiəʊteɪp; *NAmE* -oʊ-/ *noun, verb*
■ ***noun*** [U, C] = VIDEO
■ ***verb* ~ sth** (*formal*) = VIDEO: *a videotaped interview*

video·tex /ˈvɪdiəʊteks; *NAmE* -oʊ-/ *noun* [U] (*US*) = VIEWDATA

vie /vaɪ/ *verb* (**vying** /ˈvaɪɪŋ/, **vied**, **vied**) [I] (*formal*) to compete strongly with sb in order to obtain or achieve sth **SYN compete**: **~ (with sb) (for sth)** *She was surrounded by men all vying for her attention.* ◇ *a row of restaurants vying with each other for business* ◇ **~ (to do sth)** *Screaming fans vied to get closer to their idol.*

view 0➡ /vjuː/ *noun, verb*
■ ***noun***
▸ OPINION **1** 0➡ [C] a personal opinion about sth; an attitude towards sth: *to have* ***different/conflicting/opposing views*** ◇ *to have* ***strong*** *political* ***views*** ◇ **~ (about/on sth)** *His views on the subject were well known.* ◇ *This evidence* ***supports the view*** *that there is too much violence on television.* ◇ *We* ***take the view*** *that it would be wrong to interfere.* ◇ ***In my view*** *it was a waste of time.* ◇ *What is needed is a frank* ***exchange of views***. ➲ see also POINT OF VIEW ➲ LANGUAGE BANK at ACCORDING TO, OPINION
▸ WAY OF UNDERSTANDING **2** 0➡ [sing.] **~ (of sth)** a way of understanding or thinking about sth: *He has an optimistic view of life.* ◇ *the Christian view of the world* ◇ *The traditional view was that marriage was meant to last.* ➲ see also WORLD VIEW
▸ WHAT YOU CAN SEE **3** 0➡ [U, sing.] used when you are talking about whether you can see sth or whether sth can be seen in a particular situation: *The lake soon* ***came into view***. ◇ *The sun disappeared* ***from view***. ◇ *There was nobody* ***in view***. ◇ *Sit down—you're blocking my view.* ◇ *I didn't have a good view of the stage.* ➲ note at SIGHT **4** 0➡ [C] what you can see from a particular place or position, especially beautiful countryside: *There were magnificent views of the surrounding countryside.* ◇ *The view from the top of the tower was spectacular.* ◇ *a* ***sea/mountain view*** ◇ *I'd like a room with a view.*
▸ PHOTOGRAPH/PICTURE **5** [C] a photograph or picture that shows an interesting place or scene: *a book with views of Paris*
▸ CHANCE TO SEE STH **6** (also **view·ing**) [C] a special chance to see or admire sth: *a* ***private view*** (= for example, of an art exhibition)

IDM **have, etc. sth in ˈview** (*formal*) to have a particular aim, plan, etc. in your mind **SYN have sth in mind** **in full ˈview (of sb/sth)** completely visible, directly in front of sb/sth: *He was shot in full view of a large crowd.* **in view of sth** (*formal*) considering sth: *In view of the weather, the event will now be held indoors.* **on ˈview** being shown in a public place so that people can look at it **with a view to sth/to doing sth** (*formal*) with the intention or hope of doing sth: *He's painting the house with a view to selling it.* ➲ more at BIRD, DIM *adj.*, HEAVE *v.*, LONG *adj.*

■ ***verb***
▸ THINK ABOUT STH **1** 0➡ to think about sb/sth in a particular way: **~ (sb/sth as sth)** *When the car was first built, the design was viewed as highly original.* ◇ *How do you view your position within the company?* ◇ **~ sb/sth with sth** *She viewed him with suspicion.* ➲ SYNONYMS AT REGARD
▸ LOOK AT STH **2** 0➡ **~ sth** (*formal*) to look at sth, especially when you look carefully: *People came from all over the world to view her work.* ◇ *A viewing platform gave stunning views over the valley.* ➲ SYNONYMS at LOOK **3 ~ sth** (*formal*) to visit a house, etc. with the intention of buying or renting it: *The property can only be viewed by appointment.*
▸ WATCH TV, FILM/MOVIE **4 ~ sth** (*formal*) to watch television, a film/movie, etc: *The show has a viewing audience of six million* (= six million people watch it). ◇ *an opportunity to view the movie before it goes on general release* ➲ note at LOOK

Synonyms

view

sight • scene • panorama

These are all words for a thing that you can see, especially from a particular place.

view what you can see from a particular place or position, especially beautiful natural scenery: *The cottage had a delightful sea view.*

sight a thing that you see or can see, especially sth that is impressive or unusual: *It's a spectacular sight as the flamingos lift into the air.*

scene a view that you see, especially one with people and/or animals moving about and doing things: *It was a delightful rural scene.*

panorama a view of a wide area of land: *The tower offers a breathtaking panorama of Prague.*

PATTERNS
- a view/panorama **of** sth
- a **beautiful/breathtaking** view/sight/scene/panorama
- a **magnificent/spectacular** view/sight/panorama
- to **take in** the view/sight/scene
- to **admire** the view/sight

view·data /ˈvjuːdeɪtə; *NAmE* also -dætə/ (*US* also **videotex**) *noun* [U] an information system in which computer data is sent along telephone lines and shown on a television screen

view·er /ˈvjuːə(r)/ *noun* **1** a person watching television: *The programme attracted millions of viewers.* ➲ COLLOCATIONS at TELEVISION **2** a person who looks at or considers sth: *Some of her art is intended to shock the viewer.* ◇ *viewers of the current political scene* **3** a device for looking at SLIDES (= photographs on special film), for example a small box with a light in it

viewer·ship /ˈvjuːəʃɪp; *NAmE* ˈvjuːər-/ *noun* [usually sing.] the number or type of people who watch a particular television programme or television channel

view·find·er /ˈvjuːfaɪndə(r)/ *noun* the part of a camera that you look through to see the area that you are photographing

view·point /ˈvjuːpɔɪnt/ *noun* **1 ~ (on sth)** a way of thinking about a subject **SYN point of view**: *Try looking at things from a different viewpoint.* ◇ *She will have her own viewpoint on the matter.* ◇ *From a practical viewpoint, I'd advise you not to go.* **2** a direction or place from which you look at sth **SYN angle**: *The artist has painted the scene from various viewpoints.* ➲ see also POINT OF VIEW

view·port /ˈvjuːpɔːt; *NAmE* -pɔːrt/ *noun* **1** (*computing*) an area inside a frame on a screen, for viewing information **2** a window in a SPACECRAFT

V

vigil /ˈvɪdʒɪl/ *noun* [C, U] a period of time when people stay awake, especially at night, in order to watch a sick person, say prayers, protest, etc: *His parents* ***kept a*** *round-the-clock* ***vigil*** *at his bedside.*

vigi·lant /ˈvɪdʒɪlənt/ *adj.* (*formal*) very careful to notice any signs of danger or trouble SYN **alert, watchful**: *A pilot must remain vigilant at all times.* ▶ **vigi·lance** /-əns/ *noun* [U] SYN **watchfulness**: *She stressed the need for constant vigilance.* **vigi·lant·ly** *adv.*

vigi·lante /ˌvɪdʒɪˈlænti/ *noun* (sometimes *disapproving*) a member of a group of people who try to prevent crime or punish criminals in their community, especially because they think the police are not doing this ▶ **vigi·lant·ism** /ˌvɪdʒɪˈlæntɪzəm/ *noun* [U]

vi·gnette /vɪnˈjet/ *noun* (*formal*) **1** a short piece of writing or acting that clearly shows what a particular person, situation, etc. is like **2** a small picture or drawing, especially on the first page of a book

vig·or·ous /ˈvɪgərəs/ *adj.* **1** very active, determined or full of energy SYN **energetic**: *a vigorous campaign against tax fraud* ◇ *a vigorous opponent of the government* ◇ *Take* ***vigorous exercise*** *for several hours a week.* **2** strong and healthy: *a vigorous young man* ◇ *This plant is a vigorous grower.* ▶ **vig·or·ous·ly** *adv.*

vig·our (*especially US* **vigor**) /ˈvɪgə(r)/ *noun* [U] energy, force or enthusiasm SYN **vitality**: *He worked with renewed vigour and determination.*

Vi·king /ˈvaɪkɪŋ/ *noun* a member of a race of Scandinavian people who attacked and sometimes settled in parts of NW Europe, including Britain, in the 8th to the 11th centuries

vile /vaɪl/ *adj.* (**viler, vil·est**) **1** (*informal*) extremely unpleasant or bad SYN **disgusting**: *a vile smell* ◇ *The weather was really vile most of the time.* ◇ *He was in a vile mood.* ➲ SYNONYMS at TERRIBLE **2** (*formal*) morally bad; completely unacceptable SYN **wicked**: *the vile practice of taking hostages* ▶ **vile·ly** /ˈvaɪlli/ *adv.* **vile·ness** *noun* [U]

vil·ify /ˈvɪlɪfaɪ/ *verb* (**vili·fies, vili·fy·ing, vili·fied, vili·fied**) **~ sb/sth (as sth)** | **~ sb/sth (for sth/for doing sth)** (*formal*) to say or write unpleasant things about sb/sth so that other people will have a low opinion of them SYN **malign, revile** ▶ **vili·fi·ca·tion** /ˌvɪlɪfɪˈkeɪʃn/ *noun* [U]: *the vilification of single parents by right-wing politicians*

villa /ˈvɪlə/ *noun* **1** (*BrE*) a house where people stay on holiday/vacation: *We rented a holiday villa in Spain.* **2** a house in the country with a large garden, especially in southern Europe **3** (*BrE*) a large house in a town: *a Victorian villa in North London* **4** (in Roman times) a country house or farm with land attached to it

vil·lage 0-w /ˈvɪlɪdʒ/ *noun*

1 0-w [C] a very small town located in a country area: *We visited towns and villages all over Spain.* ◇ *a* ***fishing/mountain/seaside village*** ◇ (*especially BrE*) *the village shop* ◇ *Her books are about village life.* ➲ VISUAL VOCAB page V3 HELP Do not use **village** to talk about small towns in the US. In *NAmE* **village** is used for a small place in another country that seems more old-fashioned than a town in the US. **2** 0-w **the village** [sing.] (*especially BrE*) the people who live in a village: *The whole village was invited to the party.*

ˌvillage ˈidiot *noun* a person in a village who is thought to be stupid; a stupid person

vil·la·ger /ˈvɪlɪdʒə(r)/ *noun* a person who lives in a village

vil·lain /ˈvɪlən/ *noun* **1** the main bad character in a story, play, etc: *He often plays the part of the villain.* **2** a person who is morally bad or responsible for causing trouble or harm: *the heroes and villains of the 20th century* ◇ *Industrialized nations are the real environmental villains.* **3** (*BrE, informal*) a criminal

IDM **the ˈvillain of the piece** (especially *humorous*) the person or thing that is responsible for all the trouble in a situation

vil·lain·ous /ˈvɪlənəs/ *adj.* [usually before noun] (*formal*) very evil; very unpleasant

vil·lainy /ˈvɪləni/ *noun* [U] (*formal* or *humorous*) immoral or cruel behaviour

vil·lein /ˈvɪleɪn/ *noun* (in the Middle Ages) a poor man who had to work for a richer man in return for a small piece of land to grow food on

vil·lus /ˈvɪləs/ *noun* (*pl.* **villi** /ˈvɪlaɪ; -liː/) (*biology*) any one of the many small thin parts shaped like fingers that stick out from some surfaces on the inside of the body (for example in the INTESTINE). Villi increase the area of these surfaces so that substances can be absorbed by the body more easily.

vim /vɪm/ *noun* [U] (*old-fashioned, informal*) energy

vin·ai·grette /ˌvɪnɪˈgret/ *noun* [U] a mixture of oil, VINEGAR and various HERBS, etc, used to add flavour to a salad SYN **French dressing**

vin·da·loo /ˌvɪndəˈluː/ *noun* [U, C] (*pl.* **-oos**) a very spicy Indian dish, usually containing meat or fish: *lamb vindaloo*

vin·di·cate /ˈvɪndɪkeɪt/ *verb* (*formal*) **1 ~ sth** to prove that sth is true or that you were right to do sth, especially when other people had a different opinion SYN **justify**: *I have every confidence that this decision will be fully vindicated.* **2 ~ sb** to prove that sb is not guilty when they have been accused of doing sth wrong or illegal: *New evidence emerged, vindicating him completely.* ▶ **vin·di·ca·tion** /ˌvɪndɪˈkeɪʃn/ *noun* [U, sing.]: *Anti-nuclear protesters regarded the Chernobyl accident as a clear vindication of their campaign.*

vin·dic·tive /vɪnˈdɪktɪv/ *adj.* trying to harm or upset sb, or showing that you want to, because you think that they have harmed you SYN **spiteful**: *He accused her of being vindictive.* ◇ *a vindictive comment* ▶ **vin·dic·tive·ly** *adv.* **vin·dic·tive·ness** *noun* [U]

vine /vaɪn/ *noun* **1** a climbing plant that produces GRAPES: *grapes on the vine* ◇ *vine leaves* ➲ see also GRAPEVINE **2** any climbing plant with long thin STEMS; one of these STEMS

vin·egar /ˈvɪnɪgə(r)/ *noun* [U] a liquid with a bitter taste made from MALT (= a type of grain) or wine, used to add flavour to food or to preserve it: *malt/wine vinegar* ◇ *onions pickled in vinegar* ➲ see also BALSAMIC VINEGAR

vin·egary /ˈvɪnɪgəri/ *adj.* having a taste or smell that is typical of vinegar: *a vinegary wine*

vine·yard /ˈvɪnjəd; *NAmE* -jərd/ *noun* a piece of land where GRAPES are grown in order to produce wine; a business that produces wine from the GRAPES it grows in a vineyard ➲ VISUAL VOCAB page V2 ➲ compare WINERY

vino /ˈviːnəʊ; *NAmE* -noʊ/ *noun* [U] (*informal, humorous*) wine

vin·tage /ˈvɪntɪdʒ/ *noun, adj.*

▪ ***noun*** **1** the wine that was produced in a particular year or place; the year in which it was produced: *the 1999 vintage* ◇ *2005 was a particularly fine vintage.* **2** [usually sing.] the period or season of gathering GRAPES for making wine: *The vintage was later than usual.*

▪ ***adj.*** [only before noun] **1 vintage** wine is of very good quality and has been stored for several years **2** (*BrE*) (of a vehicle) made between 1919 and 1930 and admired for its style and interest ➲ compare VETERAN CAR **3** typical of a period in the past and of high quality; the best work of the particular person: *a collection of vintage designs* ◇ *vintage TV drama* ◇ *The opera is vintage Rossini.* **4 ~ year** a particularly good and successful year: *2008 was not a vintage year for the movies.*

vint·ner /ˈvɪntnə(r)/ *noun* (*old-fashioned, formal*) a person whose business is buying and selling wines or a person who grows GRAPES and makes wine

vinyl /ˈvaɪnl/ *noun* [U] **1** a strong plastic that can bend easily, used for making wall, floor and furniture coverings, book covers, and, especially in the past, records **2** records made of vinyl, in contrast to CDs: *My dad had to buy CDs of all the albums he already owned on vinyl.*

viol /ˈvaɪəl/ *noun* an early type of musical instrument with strings, shaped like a VIOLIN

V

viola /vi'əʊlə; *NAmE* -'oʊ-/ *noun* a musical instrument with strings, that you hold under your chin and play with a BOW. A viola is larger than a VIOLIN and plays lower notes: *a viola player* ➲ VISUAL VOCAB page V30

vio·late AW /'vaɪəleɪt/ *verb* **1 ~ sth** (*formal*) to go against or refuse to obey a law, an agreement, etc. SYN **flout**: *to violate international law* **2 ~ sth** (*formal*) to disturb or not respect sb's peace, PRIVACY, etc: *She accused the press photographers of violating her privacy.* **3 ~ sth** to damage or destroy a holy or special place SYN **desecrate**: *to violate a grave* **4 ~ sb** (*literary* or *old-fashioned*) to force sb to have sex SYN **rape** ▶ **vio·la·tion** AW /,vaɪə'leɪʃn/ *noun* [U, C]: *They were in open violation of the treaty.* ◇ *gross violations of human rights* **vio·la·tor** *noun*

vio·lence 🔑 /'vaɪələns/ *noun* [U]
1 🔑 violent behaviour that is intended to hurt or kill sb: ***crimes/acts/threats of violence*** ◇ **~** (**against sb**) *He condemned the protesters'* ***use of violence*** *against the police.* ◇ ***domestic violence*** (= between family members) ◇ *Why do they always have to* ***resort to violence****?* ◇ ***Violence broke out/erupted*** *inside the prison last night.* ◇ *Is there too much sex and violence on TV?* **2** 🔑 physical or emotional force and energy: *The violence of her feelings surprised him.*

vio·lent 🔑 /'vaɪələnt/ *adj.*
1 🔑 involving or caused by physical force that is intended to hurt or kill sb: ***violent crime*** ◇ *Students were involved in violent clashes with the police.* ◇ *He met with a* ***violent death*** (= he was murdered, killed in a fight, etc.). ◇ *Her husband was a violent man.* ◇ *The crowd suddenly* ***turned violent****.* ◇ *Children should not be allowed to watch violent movies* (= that show a lot of violence). **2** 🔑 showing or caused by very strong emotion: *There was a violent reaction from the public.* **3** 🔑 very strong and sudden SYN **intense, severe**: *I took a violent dislike to him.* ◇ *a violent explosion* ◇ *a violent change* ◇ *a violent headache* **4** (of a colour) extremely bright: *Her dress was a violent pink.*

vio·lent·ly 🔑 /'vaɪələntli/ *adv.*
1 🔑 with great energy or strong movement, especially caused by a strong emotion such as fear or hatred: *She shook her head violently.* ◇ *to shiver violently* **2** 🔑 very strongly or severely: *He was violently sick.* ◇ *They are violently opposed to the idea.* **3** 🔑 in a way that involves physical violence: *The crowd reacted violently.*

vio·let /'vaɪələt/ *noun* **1** [C] a small wild or garden plant with purple or white flowers with a sweet smell that appear in spring **2** [U] a bluish-purple colour: *dressed in violet* ▶ **vio·let** *adj.*: *violet eyes* IDM see SHRINK *v.*

vio·lin /,vaɪə'lɪn/ *noun* a musical instrument with strings, that you hold under your chin and play with a BOW: *Brahms' violin concerto* ➲ VISUAL VOCAB page V30 ➲ compare VIOLA ➲ see also FIDDLE

vio·lin·ist /,vaɪə'lɪnɪst/ *noun* a person who plays a violin

vio·list *noun* **1** /vi'əʊlɪst; *NAmE* -'oʊl-/ a person who plays a VIOLA **2** /'vaɪəlɪst/ a person who plays a VIOL

vio·lon·cello /,vaɪələn'tʃeləʊ; *NAmE* -loʊ/ *noun* (*pl.* -os) (*formal*) = CELLO

VIP /,vi: aɪ 'pi:/ *noun* the abbreviation for 'Very Important Person' (a famous or important person who is treated in a special way) SYN **celebrity, dignitary**: *the VIP lounge* ◇ *to get* ***the VIP treatment***

viper /'vaɪpə(r)/ *noun* **1** a small poisonous snake **2** (*formal*) a person who harms other people

vir·ago /vɪ'rɑ:gəʊ; *NAmE* -goʊ/ *noun* (*pl.* -os) (*literary, disapproving*) a woman who is aggressive and tries to tell people what to do

viral /'vaɪrəl/ *adj.* like or caused by a virus: ***a viral infection*** ◇ ***a viral email*** (= that is sent on from one person to others, who then send it on again)

'viral marketing *noun* [U] a way of advertising in which information about a company's products or services is sent by email to people who then send it on by email to other people they know

vir·gin /'vɜ:dʒɪn; *NAmE* 'vɜ:rdʒ-/ *noun, adj.*
■ ***noun*** **1** [C] a person who has never had sex **2 the** (**Blessed**) **Virgin** [sing.] the Virgin Mary, mother of Jesus Christ **3** [C] a person who has no experience of a particular activity: *a political virgin* ◇ *an Internet virgin*
■ ***adj.*** **1** [usually before noun] in its original pure or natural condition and not changed, touched or spoiled: ***virgin forest/land/territory*** ◇ ***virgin snow*** (= fresh and not marked) **2** [only before noun] with no sexual experience: *a virgin bride* ◇ *the* ***virgin birth*** (= the belief that Mary was a virgin before and after giving birth to Jesus)

vir·gin·al /'vɜ:dʒɪnl; *NAmE* 'vɜ:rdʒ-/ *adj.* of or like a virgin; pure and innocent: *She was dressed in virginal white.*

Vir·ginia creep·er /və,dʒɪniə 'kri:pə(r); *NAmE* vər'dʒ-/ *noun* [U, C] a climbing plant, often grown on walls, with large leaves that turn red in the autumn/fall

vir·gin·ity /və'dʒɪnəti; *NAmE* vər'dʒ-/ *noun* [U] the state of being a virgin: *He* ***lost his virginity*** (= had sex for the first time) *when he was 18.*

Virgo /'vɜ:gəʊ; *NAmE* 'vɜ:rgoʊ/ *noun* **1** [U] the 6th sign of the ZODIAC, the VIRGIN **2** [C] (*pl.* -os) a person born when the sun is in this sign, that is between 23 August and 23 September, approximately

vir·id·ian /vɪ'rɪdiən/ *noun* [U] (*technical*) a bluish-green PIGMENT used in art; the colour of this pigment

vir·ile /'vɪraɪl; *NAmE* 'vɪrəl/ *adj.* (usually *approving*) **1** (of men) strong and full of energy, especially sexual energy **2** having or showing the strength and energy that is considered typical of men: *a virile performance* ◇ *virile athleticism*

vir·il·ity /və'rɪləti/ *noun* [U] **1** sexual power in men: *displays of male virility* ◇ *a need to prove his virility* **2** strength or energy: *economic virility*

vir·ology /vaɪ'rɒlədʒi; *NAmE* -'rɑ:l-/ *noun* [U] the scientific study of viruses and the diseases caused by them ▶ **vir·olo·gist** /vaɪ'rɒlədʒɪst; *NAmE* -'rɑ:l-/ *noun*

vir·tual AW /'vɜ:tʃuəl; *NAmE* 'vɜ:rtʃ-/ *adj.* [only before noun] **1** almost or very nearly the thing described, so that any slight difference is not important: *The country was sliding into a state of virtual civil war.* ◇ *The company has a virtual monopoly in this area of trade.* ◇ *He married a virtual stranger.* **2** made to appear to exist by the use of computer software, for example on the Internet: *New technology has enabled development of an online 'virtual library'.*

vir·tu·al·ly 🔑 AW /'vɜ:tʃuəli; *NAmE* 'vɜ:rtʃ-/ *adv.*
1 🔑 almost or very nearly, so that any slight difference is not important: *to be virtually impossible* ◇ ***Virtually all*** *students will be exempt from the tax.* ◇ *He virtually admitted he was guilty.* ◇ *This year's results are virtually the same as last year's.* **2** (*computing*) by the use of computer software that makes sth appear to exist; using VIRTUAL REALITY technology

,virtual 'memory (also **,virtual 'storage**) *noun* [U] (*computing*) extra memory that is automatically created when all the normal memory is being used

,virtual re'ality *noun* [U] images created by a computer that appear to surround the person looking at them and seem almost real

,virtual 'world *noun* images, sounds and text used by a computer to create a world where people can communicate with each other, play games and pretend to live another life

vir·tue /'vɜ:tʃu:; *NAmE* 'vɜ:rtʃu:/ *noun* **1** [U] (*formal*) behaviour or attitudes that show high moral standards: *He led a life of virtue.* ◇ *She was certainly no* ***paragon of virtue****!* **2** [C] a particular good quality or habit: *Patience is not one of her virtues, I'm afraid.* **3** [C, U] an attractive or useful quality SYN **advantage**: *The plan* ***has the virtue of*** *simplicity.* ◇ *He was extolling the virtues of the Internet.* ◇ *They could see* ***no virtue in*** *discussing it further.*
IDM **by/in virtue of sth** (*formal*) by means of or because of sth: *She got the job by virtue of her greater experience.* **make a ,virtue of ne'cessity** to manage to gain an advantage from sth that you have to do and cannot avoid **,virtue is its own re'ward** (*saying*) the reward for acting in a

V

moral or correct way is the knowledge that you have done so, and you should not expect more than this, for example praise from other people or payment ➲ more at EASY *adj.*

vir·tu·os·ity /ˌvɜːtʃuˈɒsəti; *NAmE* ˌvɜːrtʃuˈɑːs-/ *noun* [U] (*formal*) a very high degree of skill in performing or playing: *technical virtuosity* ◇ *a performance of breathtaking virtuosity*

vir·tu·oso /ˌvɜːtʃuˈəʊsəʊ; -ˈəʊzəʊ; *NAmE* ˌvɜːrtʃuˈoʊsoʊ; -ˈoʊzoʊ/ *noun, adj.*
■ ***noun*** (*pl.* **vir·tu·osos** or **vir·tu·osi** /-siː; -ziː/) a person who is extremely skilful at doing sth, especially playing a musical instrument: *a piano virtuoso*
■ ***adj.*** [only before noun] showing extremely great skill: *a virtuoso performance* ◇ *a virtuoso pianist*

vir·tu·ous /ˈvɜːtʃuəs; *NAmE* ˈvɜːrtʃ-/ *adj.* **1** (*formal*) behaving in a very good and moral way SYN **irreproachable**: *a wise and virtuous man* ◇ *She lived an entirely virtuous life.* **2** (*disapproving* or *humorous*) claiming to behave better or have higher moral standards than other people: *He was feeling virtuous because he had finished and they hadn't.* ▸ **vir·tu·ous·ly** *adv.*

ˌvirtuous ˈcircle *noun* (*formal*) a series of events in which each one seems to increase the good effects of the previous one ➲ compare VICIOUS CIRCLE

viru·lent /ˈvɪrələnt; -rjəl-/ *adj.* **1** (of a disease or poison) extremely dangerous or harmful and quick to have an effect **2** (*formal*) showing strong negative and bitter feelings: *virulent criticism* ◇ *virulent nationalism* ▸ **viru·lence** /-ləns/ *noun* [U] **viru·lent·ly** *adv.*

virus 0-w /ˈvaɪrəs/ *noun*
1 0-w a living thing, too small to be seen without a MICROSCOPE, that causes infectious disease in people, animals and plants: *the flu virus* ◇ *a virus infection* ➲ COLLOCATIONS at ILL, LIFE **2** 0-w (*informal*) a disease caused by a virus: *There's a virus going around the office.* **3** 0-w instructions that are hidden within a computer program and are designed to cause faults or destroy data ➲ COLLOCATIONS at EMAIL ➲ see also VIRAL

visa /ˈviːzə/ *noun* a stamp or mark put in your passport by officials of a foreign country that gives you permission to enter, pass through or leave their country: *to* ***apply for a visa*** ◇ *an* ***entry/tourist/transit/exit visa***

vis·age /ˈvɪzɪdʒ/ *noun* (*literary*) a person's face

vis-à-vis /ˌviːz ɑː ˈviː/ *prep.* (from *French*) **1** in relation to: *Britain's role vis-à-vis the United States* **2** in comparison with: *It was felt that the company had an unfair advantage vis-à-vis smaller companies elsewhere.*

vis·cera /ˈvɪsərə/ *noun* [pl.] (*anatomy*) the large organs inside the body, such as the heart, lungs and stomach

vis·ceral /ˈvɪsərəl/ *adj.* **1** (*literary*) resulting from strong feelings rather than careful thought: *She had a visceral dislike of all things foreign.* **2** (*technical*) relating to the viscera

vis·cid /ˈvɪsɪd/ *adj.* (*formal* or *technical*) sticky and SLIMY: *the viscid lining of the intestine*

V

vis·cose /ˈvɪskəʊz; -kəʊs; *NAmE* -koʊs; -koʊz/ *noun* [U] (*especially BrE*) a chemical made from CELLULOSE, used to make FIBRES which can be used to make clothes, etc.

vis·count /ˈvaɪkaʊnt/ *noun* (in Britain) a NOBLEMAN of a rank below an EARL and above a BARON

vis·count·cy /ˈvaɪkaʊntsi/ *noun* the rank or position of a viscount

vis·count·ess /ˈvaɪkaʊntəs/ *noun* **1** a woman who has the rank of a VISCOUNT **2** the wife of a VISCOUNT

vis·cous /ˈvɪskəs/ *adj.* (*technical*) (of a liquid) thick and sticky; not flowing freely ▸ **vis·cos·ity** /vɪˈskɒsəti; *NAmE* -ˈskɑːs-/ *noun* [U]

vise (*NAmE*) (*BrE* **vice**) /vaɪs/ *noun* [C] a tool with two metal blocks that can be moved together by turning a screw. The vise is used to hold an object firmly while work is done on it: *He held my arm in a* ***vise-like*** (= very firm) ***grip.*** ➲ VISUAL VOCAB page V17

visi·bil·ity AW /ˌvɪzəˈbɪləti/ *noun* [U] **1** how far or well you can see, especially as affected by the light or the weather: ***good/poor/bad/zero visibility*** ◇ *Visibility was down to about 100 metres in the fog.* ◇ *The car has excellent* ***all-round visibility*** (= you can see what is around you very easily from it). **2** the fact or state of being easy to see: ***high visibility*** *equipment for cyclists* ◇ *The advertisements were intended to increase the company's visibility in the marketplace* (= to make people more aware of their products and services).

vis·ible 0-w AW /ˈvɪzəbl/ *adj.*
1 0-w that can be seen: *The house is* ***clearly visible*** *from the beach.* ◇ *Most stars are not* ***visible to the naked eye.*** **2** 0-w that is obvious enough to be noticed SYN **obvious**: *visible benefits* ◇ *a visible police presence* ◇ *He showed no visible sign of emotion.* ◇ *She made a visible effort to control her anger.* ➲ compare INVISIBLE

ˌvisible miˈnority *noun* (*CanE*) a group whose members are clearly different in race from those of the majority race in a society

vis·ibly AW /ˈvɪzəbli/ *adv.* in a way that is easily noticeable: *He was visibly shocked.* ◇ *She paled visibly at the news.*

vi·sion 0-w AW /ˈvɪʒn/ *noun*
1 0-w [U] the ability to see; the area that you can see from a particular position: *to have* ***good/perfect/poor/blurred/normal vision*** ◇ ***20–20 vision*** (= the ability to see perfectly) ◇ *Cats have good* ***night vision.*** ◇ *The couple moved outside her* ***field of vision.*** ◇ *He glimpsed something on the edge of his vision.* ➲ note at SIGHT ➲ see also TUNNEL VISION **2** 0-w [C] an idea or a picture in your imagination: *He had a vision of a world in which there would be no wars.* ◇ *I* ***had visions*** *of us getting hopelessly lost.* **3** 0-w [C] a dream or similar experience, especially of a religious kind: *The idea came to her in a vision.* **4** 0-w [U] the ability to think about or plan the future with great imagination and intelligence SYN **foresight**: *a leader of vision* **5** [C] **a ~ (of sth)** (*literary*) a person of great beauty or who shows the quality mentioned: *She was a vision in white lace.* ◇ *a vision of loveliness* **6** [U] the picture on a television or cinema/movie theater screen: *We apologize for the loss of vision.*

vi·sion·ary /ˈvɪʒənri; *NAmE* -ʒəneri/ *adj., noun*
■ ***adj.*** **1** (*approving*) original and showing the ability to think about or plan the future with great imagination and intelligence: *a visionary leader* **2** relating to dreams or strange experiences, especially of a religious kind: *visionary experiences*
■ ***noun*** (*pl.* **-ies**) (*usually approving*) a person who has the ability to think about or plan the future in a way that is intelligent or shows imagination

visit 0-w /ˈvɪzɪt/ *verb, noun*
■ ***verb*** **1** 0-w [T] **~ sb/sth** to go to see a person or a place for a period of time: *She went to visit relatives in Wales.* ◇ *The Prime Minister is visiting Japan at the moment.* ◇ *You should visit your dentist at least twice a year.* **2** 0-w [T] **~ sth** (*computing*) to go to a website on the Internet: *For more information, visit our website.* **3** 0-w [I, T] to stay somewhere for a short time: *We don't live here. We're just visiting.* ◇ **~ sth** *The lake is also visited by seals in the summer.* **4** 0-w [T] **~ sth** to make an official visit to sb, for example to perform checks or give advice: *government inspectors visiting schools*
PHR V **ˈvisit sth on/upon sb/sth** (*old use*) to punish sb/sth: *The sins of the fathers are visited upon the children* (= children are blamed or suffer for what their parents have done). **ˈvisit with sb** (*NAmE*) to spend time with sb, especially talking socially: *Come and visit with me some time.*
■ ***noun*** **1** 0-w **~ (to sb/sth) (from sb)** an occasion or a period of time when sb goes to see a place or person and spends time there: *It's my first visit to New York.* ◇ *They're on an* ***exchange visit*** *to France.* ◇ *If you have time,* ***pay a visit to*** *the local museum.* ◇ *We had a visit from the police last night.* ◇ *Is this a* ***social visit,*** *or is it business?* ◇ *a visit to the doctor* ◇ (*BrE*) *a* ***home visit*** (= when your doctor visits you) ➲ see also FLYING VISIT **2** 0-w (*computing*) an occasion when sb looks at a website on the Internet: *Visits to our website have doubled in a year.* **3** 0-w **~ (with sb)** (*NAmE, informal*) an occasion when two or more people meet to talk in an informal way

vis·it·ation /ˌvɪzɪˈteɪʃn/ *noun* **1** [U] (*NAmE*) the right of a parent who is divorced or separated from his or her partner to visit a child who is living with the partner: *She is seeking more liberal visitation with her daughter.* ◇ *visitation rights* ➲ compare ACCESS *n.* (3) **2** [C, U] **~ (of/from sb/sth)** (*formal*) an official visit, especially to check that rules are being obeyed and everything is as it should be **3** [C] **~ (of/from sb/sth)** (*formal*) an unexpected appearance of sth, for example a GHOST **4** [C] **~ (of sth)** (*formal*) a disaster that is believed to be a punishment from God: *a visitation of plague*

vis·it·ing /ˈvɪzɪtɪŋ/ *adj.* [only before noun] a **visiting** professor or lecturer is one who is teaching for a fixed period at a particular university or college, but who normally teaches at another one

ˈvisiting card (*BrE*) (*NAmE* **ˈcalling card**) (also **card** *BrE, NAmE*) *noun* (especially in the past) a small card with your name on it which you leave with sb after, or instead of, a formal visit ➲ compare BUSINESS CARD

vis·it·or 🔑 /ˈvɪzɪtə(r)/ *noun*
~ (to…) a person who visits a person or place: *We've got visitors coming this weekend.* ◇ *Do you get many visitors?* ◇ *She's a frequent visitor to the US.* ◇ *The theme park attracts 2.5 million visitors a year.* ◇ *How can we attract more visitors to our website?* ➲ see also HEALTH VISITOR

ˈvisitors' book *noun* a book in which visitors write their names, addresses and sometimes comments, for example, at a hotel or place of public interest

visor /ˈvaɪzə(r)/ *noun* **1** a part of a helmet that can be pulled down to protect the eyes and face ➲ VISUAL VOCAB page V53 **2** a curved piece of plastic, etc. worn on the head above the eyes to protect them from the sun **3** a small piece of plastic, etc. inside the front window of a car that can be pulled down to protect the driver's eyes from the sun ➲ VISUAL VOCAB page V42 **4** (*NAmE*) = BILL (9)

vista /ˈvɪstə/ *noun* **1** (*literary*) a beautiful view, for example, of the countryside, a city, etc. SYN **panorama** **2** (*formal*) a range of things that might happen in the future SYN **prospect**: *This new job could open up whole new vistas for her.*

vis·ual AW /ˈvɪʒuəl/ *adj., noun*
■ ***adj.*** of or connected with seeing or sight: *I have a very good visual memory.* ◇ *the visual arts* ◇ *The building makes a tremendous visual impact.* ▶ **visu·al·ly** AW *adv.*: ***visually handicapped/impaired*** ◇ *visually exciting*
■ ***noun*** a picture, map, piece of film, etc. used to make an article or a talk easier to understand or more interesting: *He used striking visuals to get his point across.*

ˌvisual ˈaid *noun* [usually pl.] a picture, video, etc. used in teaching to help people to learn or understand sth ➲ WRITING TUTOR page WT13

ˌvisual diˈsplay unit *noun* (*computing*) = VDU

ˌvisual ˈfield *noun* (*technical*) = FIELD OF VISION

visu·al·ize (*BrE* also **-ise**) AW /ˈvɪʒuəlaɪz/ *verb* to form a picture of sb/sth in your mind SYN **imagine**: **~ sb/sth/yourself (as sth)** *Try to visualize him as an old man.* ◇ **~ what, how, etc…** *I can't visualize what this room looked like before it was decorated.* ◇ **~ sb/sth/yourself doing sth** *It can help to visualize yourself making your speech clearly and confidently.* ◇ **~ doing sth** *She couldn't visualize climbing the mountain.* ▶ **visu·al·iza·tion**, **-isa·tion** AW /ˌvɪʒuəlaɪˈzeɪʃn; *NAmE* -ləˈz-/ *noun* [U, C]

vita /ˈviːtə/ *noun* (*US*) = CURRICULUM VITAE

vital 🔑 /ˈvaɪtl/ *adj.*
1 🔑 necessary or essential in order for sth to succeed or exist: **~ (for sth)** *the vitamins that are vital for health* ◇ **~ (to sth)** *Good financial accounts are vital to the success of any enterprise.* ◇ *Reading is* ***of vital importance*** *in language learning.* ◇ *The police play* ***a vital role*** *in our society.* ◇ **~ that…** ***It is vital that*** *you keep accurate records when you are self-employed.* ◇ **~ to do sth** *It was vital to show that he was not afraid.* ➲ SYNONYMS at ESSENTIAL ➲ LANGUAGE BANK at EMPHASIS, IMPERSONAL **2** [only before noun] connected with or necessary for staying alive: *the* ***vital organs*** (= the brain, heart, lungs, etc.) **3** (of a person) full of energy and enthusiasm SYN **dynamic**

Language Bank

vital

Saying that something is necessary

- **It is vital that** journalists can verify the accuracy of their reports.
- Journalists play a **vital/crucial** role in educating the public.
- Public trust is a **crucial** issue for all news organizations.
- The ability to write well is **essential** for any journalist.
- The Internet has become an **indispensable** tool for reporters.
- In journalism, accuracy is **paramount**. / …is **of paramount importance.**
- **It is imperative that** journalists maintain the highest possible standards of reporting.

➲ Synonyms at ESSENTIAL
➲ Language Banks at EMPHASIS, IMPERSONAL

vi·tal·ity /vaɪˈtæləti/ *noun* [U] energy and enthusiasm SYN **vigour**: *She is bursting with vitality and new ideas.*

vi·tal·ly /ˈvaɪtəli/ *adv.* extremely; in an essential way: *Education is* ***vitally important*** *for the country's future.*

the vi·tals /ˈvaɪtlz/ *noun* [pl.] (*old-fashioned* or *humorous*) the organs of the body that are essential for staying alive, for example the brain, heart, lungs, etc.

ˌvital ˈsign *noun* [usually pl.] (*medical*) a measurement that shows that sb is alive, such as the rate of their breathing, their body temperature or their HEARTBEAT

ˌvital staˈtistics *noun* [pl.] **1** figures that show the number of births and deaths in a country **2** (*BrE, informal*) the measurements of a woman's chest, waist and hips

vita·min /ˈvɪtəmɪn; *NAmE* ˈvaɪt-/ *noun* a natural substance found in food that is an essential part of what humans and animals eat to help them grow and stay healthy. There are many different vitamins: *breakfast cereals enriched with vitamins* ◇ *vitamin deficiency* ◇ *vitamin pills* ➲ COLLOCATIONS at DIET

ˌvitamin ˈC (also **asˌcorbic ˈacid**) *noun* [U] a vitamin found in fruits such as oranges and lemons, and in green vegetables: *Oranges are rich in vitamin C.*

viti·ate /ˈvɪʃieɪt/ *verb* [usually passive] **~ sth** (*formal*) to spoil or reduce the effect of sth

viti·cul·ture /ˈvɪtɪkʌltʃə(r); ˈvaɪt-/ *noun* [U] (*technical*) the science or practice of growing GRAPES

vit·re·ous /ˈvɪtriəs/ *adj.* (*technical*) hard, shiny and transparent like glass: *vitreous enamel*

ˌvitreous ˈhumour (*especially US* **ˌvitreous ˈhumor**) *noun* [U] (*anatomy*) the transparent jelly-like substance inside the eye ➲ compare AQUEOUS HUMOUR

vit·rify /ˈvɪtrɪfaɪ/ *verb* (**vit·ri·fies**, **vit·ri·fy·ing**, **vit·ri·fied**, **vit·ri·fied**) [I, T] **~ (sth)** (*technical*) to change or make sth change into glass, or a substance like glass ▶ **vit·ri·fi·ca·tion** /ˌvɪtrɪfɪˈkeɪʃn/ *noun* [U]

vit·riol /ˈvɪtriəl/ *noun* [U] (*formal*) very cruel and bitter comments or criticism SYN **abuse**

vit·ri·ol·ic /ˌvɪtriˈɒlɪk; *NAmE* -ˈɑːlɪk/ *adj.* (*formal*) (of language or comments) full of anger and hatred SYN **bitter**: *The newspaper launched a vitriolic attack on the president.*

vitro ➲ IN VITRO

vi·tu·per·ation /vɪˌtjuːpəˈreɪʃn; *NAmE* vaɪˌtuː-/ *noun* [U] (*formal*) cruel and angry criticism SYN **abuse** ▶ **vi·tu·pera·tive** /vɪˈtjuːpərətɪv; *NAmE* vaɪˈtuːpəreɪtɪv/ *adj.*: *a vituperative attack*

viva[1] /ˈviːvə/ *exclamation* used for expressing support for sb or sth

V

viva² /ˈvaɪvə/ *noun* (*BrE*) = VIVA VOCE

viv·ace /vɪˈvɑːtʃeɪ/ *noun* (*music*) (from *Italian*) a piece of music to be played in a quick lively way ▶ **viv·ace** *adv., adj.*

viv·acious /vɪˈveɪʃəs; *NAmE* also vaɪˈv-/ *adj.* (*approving*) (especially of a woman) having a lively, attractive personality: *He had three pretty, vivacious daughters.* ▶ **viv·acious·ly** *adv.* **viv·acity** /vɪˈvæsəti; *NAmE* also vaɪˈv-/ *noun* [U]: *He was charmed by her beauty and vivacity.*

viv·ar·ium /vaɪˈveəriəm; vɪˈv-; *NAmE* -ˈver-/ *noun* (*pl.* **viv·ar·ia** /vaɪˈveəriə; vɪˈv-; *NAmE* -ˈver-/) a container for keeping live animals in, especially for scientific study

viva voce /ˌvaɪvə ˈvəʊtʃi; *NAmE* ˈvoʊtʃi/ (*BrE* also **viva**) *noun* (from *Latin*) a spoken exam, especially in a British university

vive la dif·fer·ence /ˌviːv lɑː ˌdɪfəˈrɒns; *NAmE* -ˈrɑːns/ *exclamation* (from *French*, *humorous*) used to show that you think it is good that there is a difference between two people or things, especially a difference between men and women

vivid /ˈvɪvɪd/ *adj.* **1** (of memories, a description, etc.) producing very clear pictures in your mind SYN **graphic**: *vivid memories* ◇ *He gave a vivid account of his life as a fighter pilot.* **2** (of light, colours, etc.) very bright: *vivid blue eyes* ➲ SYNONYMS at BRIGHT **3** (of sb's imagination) able to form pictures of ideas, situations, etc. easily in the mind ▶ **viv·id·ly** *adv.*: *I vividly remember the day we first met.* **viv·id·ness** *noun* [U]: *the vividness of my dream*

viv·ip·ar·ous /vɪˈvɪpərəs/ *adj.* (*biology*) (of an animal) producing live babies from its body rather than eggs ➲ compare OVIPAROUS, OVOVIVIPAROUS

vivi·sec·tion /ˌvɪvɪˈsekʃn/ *noun* [U] the practice of doing experiments on live animals for medical or scientific research

vivo ➲ IN VIVO

vixen /ˈvɪksn/ *noun* **1** a female FOX (= a wild animal of the dog family) **2** (*old-fashioned*) an unpleasant and bad-tempered woman

viz. /vɪz/ *adv.* (*formal, especially BrE*) used to introduce a list of things that explain sth more clearly or are given as examples SYN **namely**: *four major colleges of surgery, viz. London, Glasgow, Edinburgh and Dublin*

viz·ier /vɪˈzɪə(r); *NAmE* vɪˈzɪr/ (also **wazir**) *noun* an important official in some Muslim countries in the past

VJ /ˈviː dʒeɪ/ *abbr.* = VIDEO JOCKEY

VLE /ˌviː el ˈiː/ *noun* (*BrE*) the abbreviation for 'virtual learning environment' (a software system for teaching and learning using the Internet)

ˈV-neck *noun* an opening for the neck in a piece of clothing shaped like the letter V; a piece of clothing with a V-neck: *a V-neck sweater* ◇ *a navy V-neck* ➲ VISUAL VOCAB page V51 ➲ picture at NECK ▶ **ˈV-necked** *adj.*: *a V-necked sweater*

VOA /ˌviː əʊ ˈeɪ; *NAmE* oʊ/ *abbr.* VOICE OF AMERICA

V

vo·cabu·lary O‑ /vəˈkæbjələri; *NAmE* -leri/ *noun* [C, U] (*pl.* **-ies**)
1 O‑ all the words that a person knows or uses: *to have a **wide/limited vocabulary*** ◇ *your **active vocabulary*** (= the words that you use) ◇ *your **passive vocabulary*** (= the words that you understand but don't use) ◇ *Reading will increase your vocabulary.* ◇ *The word 'failure' is not in his vocabulary* (= for him, failure does not exist). ➲ SYNONYMS at LANGUAGE ➲ see also DEFINING VOCABULARY **2** O‑ all the words in a particular language: *When did the word 'bungalow' first enter the vocabulary?* ➲ SYNONYMS at LANGUAGE **3** the words that people use when they are talking about a particular subject: *The word has become part of advertising vocabulary.* ➲ SYNONYMS at LANGUAGE **4** (also *informal* **vocab** /ˈvəʊkæb; *NAmE* ˈvoʊkæb/) a list of words with their meanings, especially in a book for learning a foreign language

vocal /ˈvəʊkl; *NAmE* ˈvoʊkl/ *adj., noun*
■ ***adj.*** **1** [only before noun] connected with the voice: *vocal music* ◇ *the vocal organs* (= the tongue, lips, etc.) ➲ SYNONYMS at SPOKEN **2** telling people your opinions or protesting about sth loudly and with confidence: *He has been very vocal in his criticism of the government's policy.* ◇ *The protesters are a small but vocal minority.*
■ ***noun*** [usually pl.] the part of a piece of music that is sung, rather than played on a musical instrument: *backing vocals* ◇ *In this recording Armstrong himself is **on vocals**.*

ˌvocal ˈcords *noun* [pl.] the thin strips of TISSUE in the throat that are moved by the flow of air to produce the voice

vo·cal·ic /vəʊˈkælɪk; *NAmE* voʊ-/ *adj.* (*phonetics*) relating to or consisting of a vowel or vowels ➲ compare CONSONANTAL

vo·cal·ist /ˈvəʊkəlɪst; *NAmE* ˈvoʊ-/ *noun* a singer, especially in a pop, rock or JAZZ band: *a **lead/guest/backing vocalist*** ➲ compare INSTRUMENTALIST

vo·cal·iza·tion (*BrE* also **-isa·tion**) /ˌvəʊkəlaɪˈzeɪʃn; *NAmE* ˌvoʊkələˈzeɪʃn/ *noun* (*formal*) **1** [C] a word or sound that is produced by the voice: *the vocalizations of animals* **2** [U] the process of producing a word or sound with the voice

vo·cal·ize (*BrE* also **-ise**) /ˈvəʊkəlaɪz; *NAmE* ˈvoʊ-/ *verb* (*formal*) **1** [T] **~ sth** to use words to express sth SYN **articulate, express**: *Showing children pictures sometimes helps them to vocalize their ideas.* **2** [I, T] **~ (sth)** to say or sing sounds or words: *Your baby will begin to vocalize long before she can talk.*

vo·cal·ly /ˈvəʊkəli; *NAmE* ˈvoʊ-/ *adv.* **1** in a way that uses the voice: *to communicate vocally* **2** by speaking in a loud and confident way: *They protested vocally.*

vo·ca·tion /vəʊˈkeɪʃn; *NAmE* voʊ-/ *noun* **1** [C] a type of work or way of life that you believe is especially suitable for you SYN **calling**: *Nursing is not just a job—it's a vocation.* ◇ *She believes that she has found her true vocation in life.* ◇ *You missed your vocation—you should have been an actor.* ➲ COLLOCATIONS at JOB **2** [C, U] **~ (for sth)** a belief that a particular type of work or way of life is especially suitable for you: *He has a vocation for teaching.* ◇ *She is a doctor with a strong sense of vocation.* **3** [C, U] a belief that you have been chosen by God to be a priest or NUN: *a vocation to the priesthood*

vo·ca·tion·al /vəʊˈkeɪʃənl; *NAmE* voʊ-/ *adj.* connected with the skills, knowledge, etc. that you need to have in order to do a particular job: ***vocational education/qualifications/training***

voˈcational school *noun* [C, U] (in the US) a school that teaches skills that are necessary for particular jobs

voca·tive /ˈvɒkətɪv; *NAmE* ˈvɑːk-/ *noun* (*grammar*) (in some languages) the form of a noun, a pronoun or an adjective used when talking to a person or thing ➲ compare ABLATIVE, ACCUSATIVE, DATIVE, GENITIVE, NOMINATIVE ▶ **voca·tive** *adj.*: *the vocative case*

vo·cif·er·ous /vəˈsɪfərəs; *NAmE* voʊˈs-/ *adj.* (*formal*) expressing your opinions or feelings in a loud and confident way SYN **strident**: *vociferous protests* ◇ *a vociferous critic of the president's stance* ▶ **vo·cif·er·ous·ly** *adv.*: *to complain vociferously*

vodka /ˈvɒdkə; *NAmE* ˈvɑːdkə/ *noun* **1** [U] a strong clear alcoholic drink, made from grain, originally from Russia **2** [C] a glass of vodka: *I'll have a vodka and lime.*

vogue /vəʊg; *NAmE* voʊg/ *noun* [C, usually sing., U] **~ (for sth)** a fashion for sth: *the vogue for child-centred education* ◇ *Black is **in vogue** again.* ➲ COLLOCATIONS at FASHION

voice O‑ /vɔɪs/ *noun, verb*
■ ***noun***
▸ SOUND FROM MOUTH **1** O‑ [C, U] the sound or sounds produced through the mouth by a person speaking or singing: *I could hear voices in the next room.* ◇ *to speak **in a deep/soft/loud/quiet, etc. voice*** ◇ *'I promise,' she said in a **small voice*** (= a quiet, shy voice). ◇ *to **raise/lower your voice*** (= to speak louder/more quietly) ◇ ***Keep your voice down*** (= speak quietly). ◇ *Don't take that **tone of voice** with me!* ◇ *Her voice shook with emotion.* ◇ *'There you are,' said a voice behind me.* ◇ *When did his **voice break*** (= become deep like a man's)? ◇ *He was suffering from flu and had **lost his voice***

(= could not speak). ◇ *She has a good singing voice.* ◇ *She was **in good voice** (= singing well) at the concert tonight.*
▸ -VOICED **2** (in adjectives) having a voice of the type mentioned: *low-voiced* ◇ *squeaky-voiced*
▸ OPINION **3** [sing.] **~ (in sth)** the right to express your opinion and influence decisions: *Employees should **have a voice** in the decision-making process.* **4** [C] a particular attitude, opinion or feeling that is expressed; a feeling or an opinion that you become aware of inside yourself: *He pledged that his party would listen to the voice of the people.* ◇ *Very few **dissenting voices** were heard on the right of the party.* ◇ *the **voice of reason/sanity/conscience*** ◇ *'Coward!' a tiny **inner voice** insisted.*
▸ GRAMMAR **5** [sing.] **the active/passive ~** the form of a verb that shows whether the subject of a sentence performs the action (*the active voice*) or is affected by it (*the passive voice*)
▸ PHONETICS **6** [U] sound produced by movement of the VOCAL CORDS used in the pronunciation of vowels and some consonants ➲ see also VOICED, VOICELESS
IDM **give voice to sth** to express your feelings, worries, etc. **make your 'voice heard** to express your feelings, opinions, etc. in a way that makes people notice and consider them **with ˌone 'voice** as a group; with everyone agreeing: *The various opposition parties speak with one voice on this issue.* ➲ more at FIND *v.*, SOUND *n.*, STILL *adj.*, TOP *n.*
■ ***verb***
▸ GIVE OPINION **1 ~ sth** to tell people your feelings or opinions about sth: *to **voice complaints/criticisms/doubts/objections, etc.*** ◇ *A number of parents have **voiced concern** about their children's safety.*
▸ PHONETICS **2 ~ sth** to produce a sound with a movement of your VOCAL CORDS as well as your breath ➲ compare UNVOICED, VOICELESS

'voice box *noun* the area at the top of the throat that contains the VOCAL CORDS SYN **larynx**

voiced /vɔɪst/ *adj.* (*phonetics*) (of consonants) produced by moving your VOCAL CORDS. For example, the consonants /b/, /d/ and /g/ are voiced. OPP **unvoiced**

voice·less /'vɔɪsləs/ *adj.* (*phonetics*) (of consonants) produced without moving your VOCAL CORDS. For example, the consonants /p/, /t/ and /k/ are voiceless. SYN **unvoiced** OPP **voiced**

voice·mail /'vɔɪsmeɪl/ *noun* [U] an electronic system which can store telephone messages, so that sb can listen to them later

the ˌVoice of A'merica *noun* [sing.] (*abbr.* VOA) an official US government service that broadcasts news and other programmes in English and many other languages around the world

'voice-over *noun* information or comments in a film/movie, television programme, etc. that are given by a person who is not seen on the screen: *She earns a lot of money doing voice-overs for TV commercials.*

voice·print /'vɔɪsprɪnt/ *noun* (*technical*) a printed record of a person's speech, showing the different FREQUENCIES and lengths of sounds as a series of waves

'voice recognition *noun* [U] **1** technology that allows a computer to identify a voice **2** = SPEECH RECOGNITION

void /vɔɪd/ *noun, adj., verb*
■ ***noun*** [usually sing.] (*formal* or *literary*) a large empty space: *Below him was nothing but a black void.* ◇ (*figurative*) *The void left by his mother's death was never filled.*
■ ***adj.*** **1 ~ of sth** (*formal*) completely lacking sth SYN **devoid**: *The sky was void of stars.* **2** (*law*) (of a contract, an agreement etc.) not valid or legal: *The agreement was declared void.* **3** (*formal*) empty: *void spaces* IDM see NULL
■ ***verb*** **1 ~ sth** (*law*) to state officially that sth is no longer valid SYN **invalidate, nullify** **2 ~ sth** (*formal*) to empty waste matter from the BLADDER or BOWELS

'void deck *noun* (*SEAsianE*) the ground floor of a block of flats/apartments, which is left empty and is usually for the use of all the people who live in the building

voile /vɔɪl/ *noun* [U] a type of cloth made of cotton, wool or silk that is almost transparent, used for making clothes

VoIP /vɔɪp/ (also **ˌIP te'lephony**) *noun* [U] the abbreviation for 'voice over Internet protocol' (a telephone system that allows users to make and receive calls using the Internet)

vol. AW *abbr.* VOLUME *n.*: *the Complete Works of Byron Vol. 2*

vola·tile /'vɒlətaɪl; *NAmE* 'vɑːlətl/ *adj.* **1** (often *disapproving*) (of a person or their moods) changing easily from one mood to another: *a highly volatile personality* **2** (of a situation) likely to change suddenly; easily becoming dangerous SYN **unstable**: *a highly volatile situation from which riots might develop* ◇ *a volatile exchange rate* **3** (*technical*) (of a substance) that changes easily into a gas: *Petrol is a volatile substance.* ▸ **vola·til·ity** /ˌvɒlə'tɪləti; *NAmE* ˌvɑːl-/ *noun* [U]

vol-au-vent /'vɒl ə vɒ̃; *NAmE* ˌvɔːl oʊ 'vɑ̃ː/ *noun* (*BrE*, from *French*) a small round case of light PASTRY filled with meat, fish, etc. in a cream sauce, often eaten with your fingers at parties

vol·can·ic /vɒl'kænɪk; *NAmE* vɑːl-; vɔːl-/ *adj.* caused or produced by a volcano: *volcanic rocks* ◇ *volcanic eruptions*

vol·cano /vɒl'keɪnəʊ; *NAmE* vɑːl'keɪnoʊ; vɔːl'keɪnoʊ/ *noun* (*pl.* **-oes** or **-os**) a mountain with a large opening at the top through which gases and LAVA (= hot liquid rock) are forced out into the air, or have been in the past: *An active volcano may erupt at any time.* ◇ *a dormant volcano* (= one that is not active at present) ◇ *an extinct volcano* (= one that is no longer active)

vol·can·ology /ˌvɒlkə'nɒlədʒi; *NAmE* ˌvɑːlkə'nɑːl-; ˌvɔːlkə'nɑːl-/ (also **vul·can·ology**) *noun* [U] the scientific study of volcanoes

vole /vəʊl; *NAmE* voʊl/ *noun* a small animal like a mouse or RAT that lives in fields or near rivers ➲ see also WATER VOLE

vol·ition /və'lɪʃn; *NAmE* also voʊ'l-/ *noun* [U] (*formal*) the power to choose sth freely or to make your own decisions SYN **free will**: *They left entirely **of their own volition*** (= because they wanted to).

vol·ley /'vɒli; *NAmE* 'vɑːli/ *noun, verb*
■ ***noun*** **1** (in some sports, for example TENNIS or football (SOCCER)) a hit or kick of the ball before it touches the ground: *She hit a forehand volley into the net.* **2** a lot of bullets, stones, etc. that are fired or thrown at the same time: *A volley of shots rang out.* ◇ *Police fired a volley over the heads of the crowd.* **3** a lot of questions, comments, insults, etc. that are directed at sb quickly one after the other SYN **torrent**: *She faced a volley of angry questions from her mother.*
■ ***verb*** [T, I] **~ (sth)** (in some sports, for example TENNIS or football (SOCCER)) to hit or kick the ball before it touches the ground: *He volleyed the ball into the back of the net.*

vol·ley·ball /'vɒlibɔːl; *NAmE* 'vɑːl-; 'vɔːl-/ *noun* [U] a game in which two teams of six players use their hands to hit a large ball backwards and forwards over a high net while trying not to let the ball touch the ground on their own side ➲ see also BEACH VOLLEYBALL

volt /vəʊlt; vɒlt; *NAmE* voʊlt/ *noun* (*abbr.* V) a unit for measuring the force of an electric current: *a high security fence with 5 000 volts passing through it*

volt·age /'vəʊltɪdʒ; *NAmE* 'voʊlt-/ *noun* [U, C] electrical force measured in volts: ***high/low voltage***

volte-face /ˌvɒlt 'fɑːs; *NAmE* ˌvɔːlt/ *noun* [sing.] (*formal*) a complete change of opinion or plan SYN **about-turn**: *This represents a volte-face in government thinking.*

volt·meter /'vəʊltmiːtə(r); *NAmE* 'voʊlt-/ *noun* an instrument for measuring VOLTAGE

vol·uble /'vɒljʊbl; *NAmE* 'vɑːljə-/ *adj.* (*formal*) **1** talking a lot, and with enthusiasm, about a subject: *Evelyn was very voluble on the subject of women's rights.* **2** expressed in many words and spoken quickly: *voluble protests* ▸ **vol·ubly** /'vɒljʊbli; *NAmE* 'vɑːljə-/ *adv.*

V

vol·ume 0→ AW /ˈvɒljuːm; *NAmE* ˈvɑːl-; -jəm/ *noun* **1** 0→ [U, C] the amount of space that an object or a substance fills; the amount of space that a container has: *How do you measure the volume of a gas?* ◇ *jars of different volumes* **2** 0→ [U, C] the amount of sth: *the* **sheer volume** (= large amount) *of business* ◇ *This work has grown in volume recently.* ◇ *New roads are being built to cope with the increased volume of traffic.* ◇ *Sales volumes fell 0.2% in June.* **3** 0→ [U] the amount of sound that is produced by a television, radio, etc: *to* **turn the volume up/down** **4** 0→ [C] (*abbr.* vol.) a book, that is part of a series of books: *an encyclopedia in 20 volumes* **5** [C] (*formal*) a book: *a library of over 50 000 volumes* ◇ *a slim volume of poetry* **6** [C] (*abbr.* vol.) a series of different issues of the same magazine, especially all the issues for one year: *'New Scientist' volume 142, number 3* IDM see SPEAK

vo·lu·min·ous /vəˈluːmɪnəs/ *adj.* (*formal*) **1** (of clothing) very large; having a lot of cloth SYN **ample**: *a voluminous skirt* **2** (of a piece of writing, a book, etc.) very long and detailed **3** (of a container, piece of furniture, etc.) very large: *I sank down into a voluminous armchair.* ▶ **vo·lu·min·ous·ly** *adv.*

volu·mize (*BrE* also **-ise**) /ˈvɒljʊmaɪz; *NAmE* ˈvɑːl-/ *verb* **~ sth** to make hair look thicker ▶ **volu·mizer** /ˈvɒljʊmaɪzə(r); *NAmE* ˈvɑːl-/ *noun*

vol·un·tar·ily AW /ˈvɒləntrəli; *NAmE* ˌvɑːlənˈterəli/ *adv.* **1** willingly; without being forced: *He was not asked to leave—he went voluntarily.* **2** without payment; free: *The fund is voluntarily administered.*

vol·un·tary AW /ˈvɒləntri; *NAmE* ˈvɑːlənteri/ *adj., noun*
■ ***adj.*** **1** done willingly, not because you are forced: *a voluntary agreement* ◇ *Attendance on the course is purely voluntary.* ◇ *to pay* **voluntary contributions** *into a pension fund* ◇ (*BrE*) *He took* **voluntary redundancy.** OPP **compulsory** **2** [usually before noun] (of work) done by people who choose to do it without being paid: *I do some* **voluntary work** *at the local hospital.* ◇ *She works there on a* **voluntary basis.** ◇ **voluntary services/bodies/agencies/organizations** (= organized, controlled or supported by people who choose to do this and are usually not paid) ◇ **the voluntary sector** (= organizations which are set up to help people and which do not make a profit, for example charities) **3** [only before noun] (of a person) doing a job without wanting to be paid for it: *a voluntary worker* **4** (*technical*) (of movements of the body) that you can control OPP **involuntary**
■ ***noun*** (*pl.* -ies) a piece of music played before, during or after a church service, usually on an organ

ˌVoluntary ˌService Overˈseas *noun* [U] (*abbr.* VSO) a British charity that sends skilled people such as doctors and teachers to work in other countries as volunteers

vol·un·teer AW /ˌvɒlənˈtɪə(r); *NAmE* ˌvɑːlənˈtɪr/ *noun, verb*
■ ***noun*** **1** a person who does a job without being paid for it: *volunteer helpers* ◇ *Schools need volunteers to help children to read.* **2** a person who offers to do sth without being forced to do it: *Are there any volunteers to help clear up?* **3** a person who chooses to join the armed forces without being forced to join ➲ compare CONSCRIPT
■ ***verb*** **1** [I, T] to offer to do sth without being forced to do it or without getting paid for it: **~ to do sth** *Jill volunteered to organize a petition.* ◇ **~ (for/as sth)** *Several staff members volunteered for early retirement.* ◇ **~ sth (for/as sth)** *He volunteered his services as a driver.* **2** [T] **~ sth** | **+ speech** to suggest sth or tell sb sth without being asked: *to volunteer advice* **3** [I] **~ (for sth)** | **~ to do sth** to join the army, etc. without being forced to: *to volunteer for military service* **4** [T] **~ sb (for/as sth)** | **~ sb to do sth** to suggest sb for a job or an activity, even though they may not want to do it: *They volunteered me for the job of interpreter.*

the ˌVolunteer Reˈserve Forces *noun* [pl.] the parts of the British armed forces for people who are volunteers and train in their free time so they can be used in a national emergency

vo·lup·tu·ary /vəˈlʌptʃuəri; *NAmE* -ueri/ *noun* (*pl.* -ies) (*formal*, usually *disapproving*) a person who enjoys physical, especially sexual, pleasures very much

vo·lup·tu·ous /vəˈlʌptʃuəs/ *adj.* **1** (*formal*) (of a woman) attractive in a sexual way with large breasts and hips SYN **buxom**: *a voluptuous woman* ◇ *a voluptuous body* **2** (*literary*) giving you physical pleasure SYN **sensual**: *voluptuous perfume* ▶ **vo·lup·tu·ous·ly** *adv.* **vo·lup·tu·ous·ness** *noun* [U]

vomit /ˈvɒmɪt; *NAmE* ˈvɑːm-/ *verb, noun*
■ ***verb*** (also *informal* ˌ**throw ˈup**) [I, T] to bring food from the stomach back out through the mouth SYN **be sick**: *The smell made her want to vomit.* ◇ **~ sth up** *He had vomited up his supper.* ◇ **~ sth** *The injured man was vomiting blood.* ➲ see also SICK
■ ***noun*** [U] food from the stomach brought back out through the mouth

voo·doo /ˈvuːduː/ *noun* [U] a religion that is practised especially in Haiti and involves magic and WITCHCRAFT

vor·acious /vəˈreɪʃəs/ *adj.* (*formal*) **1** eating or wanting large amounts of food SYN **greedy**: *a voracious eater* ◇ *to have a* **voracious appetite** **2** wanting a lot of new information and knowledge SYN **avid**: *a voracious reader* ◇ *a boy with a voracious and undiscriminating appetite for facts* ▶ **vor·acious·ly** *adv.* **vor·acity** /vəˈræsəti/ *noun* [U]

vor·tex /ˈvɔːteks; *NAmE* ˈvɔːrt-/ *noun* (*pl.* **vor·texes** or **vor·ti·ces** /-tɪsiːz/) **1** (*technical*) a mass of air, water, etc. that spins around very fast and pulls things into its centre SYN **whirlpool, whirlwind** **2** (*literary*) a very powerful feeling or situation that you cannot avoid or escape from: *They were caught up in a whirling vortex of emotion.*

vo·tary /ˈvəʊtəri; *NAmE* ˈvoʊt-/ *noun* (*pl.* -ies) **~ of sb/sth** (*formal*) a person who worships or loves sb/sth: *a votary of John Keats*

vote 0→ /vəʊt; *NAmE* voʊt/ *noun, verb*
■ ***noun*** **1** 0→ [C] **~ (for/against sb/sth)** a formal choice that you make in an election or at a meeting in order to choose sb or decide sth: *There were 21 votes for and 17 against the motion, with 2 abstentions.* ◇ *The motion was passed by 6 votes to 3.* ◇ *The chairperson has the* **casting/deciding vote.** ◇ *The Green candidate won over 3 000 of the 14 000* **votes cast.** **2** 0→ [C] **~ (on sth)** an occasion when a group of people vote on sth: *to* **have/take a vote** *on an issue* ◇ *The issue was* **put to the vote.** ◇ *The vote was unanimous.* ➲ SYNONYMS at ELECTION **3** 0→ **the vote** [sing.] the total number of votes in an election: *She obtained 40% of the vote.* ◇ *The party increased their share of the vote.* **4** 0→ **the vote** [sing.] the vote given by a particular group of people, or for a particular party, etc: *the student vote* ◇ *the Labour vote* **5** 0→ **the vote** [sing.] the right to vote, especially in political elections: *In Britain and the US, people get the vote at 18.* ➲ see also BLOCK VOTE
■ ***verb*** **1** 0→ [I, T] to show formally by marking a paper or raising your hand which person you want to win an election, or which plan or idea you support: **~ (for/against sb/sth)** *Did you vote for or against her?* ◇ *How did you vote at the last election?* ◇ **~ in favour of sth** *Over 60% of members voted in favour of* (= for) *the motion.* ◇ **~ (on sth)** *We'll listen to the arguments on both sides and then vote on it.* ◇ *Only about half of the electorate bothered to vote.* ◇ **~ sth** *We voted Democrat in the last election.* ◇ **~ to do sth** *Parliament voted to set up an independent inquiry into the matter.* ➲ COLLOCATIONS at POLITICS **2** 0→ [T, usually passive] **~ sb/sth + noun** to choose sb/sth for a position or an award by voting: *He was voted most promising new director.* **3** [T, usually passive] **~ sth + noun** to say that sth is good or bad: *The event was voted a great success.* **4** [T] **~ sb/yourself sth** to agree to give sb/yourself sth by voting: *The directors have just voted themselves a huge pay increase.* **5** [T] **~ (that)...** to suggest sth or support a suggestion that sb has made: *I vote (that) we go out to eat.*
IDM ˌ**vote with your ˈfeet** to show what you think about sth by going or not going somewhere: *Shoppers voted with their feet and avoided the store.*
PHR V ˌ**vote sb/sth↔ˈdown** to reject or defeat sb/sth by voting for sb/sth else ˌ**vote sb ˈin** | ˌ**vote sb ˈinto/ˈonto sth** to choose sb for a position by voting: *He was voted in as*

V

treasurer. ◇ *She was voted onto the board of governors.* **ˌvote sb ˈout | ˌvote sb ˈout of/ˈoff sth** to dismiss sb from a position by voting: *He was voted out of office.* **ˌvote sth↔ˈthrough** to bring a plan, etc. into effect by voting for it: *A proposal to merge the two companies was voted through yesterday.*

Collocations

Voting in elections

Running for election

- **conduct/hold** an election/a referendum
- (*especially NAmE*) **run for** office/election/governor/mayor/president/the White House
- (*especially BrE*) **stand for** election/office/Parliament/the Labour Party/a second term
- **hold/call/contest** a general/national election
- **launch/run** a presidential election campaign
- **support/back** a candidate
- **sway/convince/persuade** voters/the electorate
- **appeal to/attract/woo/target** (*NAmE*) swing voters/(*BrE*) floating voters
- **fix/rig/steal** an election/the vote

Voting

- **go to/be turned away from** (*especially BrE*) a polling station/(*NAmE*) a polling place
- **cast** a/your vote/ballot (for sb)
- **vote for** the Conservative candidate/the Democratic party
- **mark/spoil** your ballot paper
- **count** (*BrE*) the postal votes/(*especially NAmE*) the absentee ballots
- **go to/be defeated at** the ballot box
- **get/win/receive/lose** votes
- **get/win** (60% of) the popular/black/Hispanic/Latino/Muslim vote
- **win** the election/(*in the US*) the primaries/a seat in Parliament/a majority/power
- **lose** an election/the vote/your majority/your seat
- **win/come to power in** a landslide (victory) (= with many more votes than any other party)
- **elect/re-elect sb (as)** mayor/president/an MP/senator/congressman/congresswoman

Taking power

- **be sworn** into office/in as president
- **take/administer** (*in the US*) the oath of office
- **swear/take** (*in the UK*) an/the oath of allegiance
- **give/deliver** (*in the US*) the president's inaugural address
- **take/enter/hold/leave** office
- **appoint sb (as)** ambassador/governor/judge/minister
- **form** a government/a cabinet
- **serve** two terms as prime minister/in office

➲ more collocations at ECONOMY, POLITICS

ˌvote of ˈconfidence *noun* [usually sing.] a formal vote to show that people support a leader, a political party, an idea, etc.

ˌvote of ˌno ˈconfidence *noun* [usually sing.] a formal vote to show that people do not support a leader, a political party, an idea, etc.

ˌvote of ˈthanks *noun* [usually sing.] a short formal speech in which you thank sb for sth and ask other people to join you in thanking them

voter /ˈvəʊtə(r); *NAmE* ˈvoʊ-/ *noun* a person who votes or has the right to vote, especially in a political election: *A clear majority of voters were in favour of the motion.* ◇ *Only 60% of eligible voters actually used their vote.* ➲ COLLOCATIONS at VOTE ➲ see also FLOATING VOTER, SWING VOTER

vot·ing /ˈvəʊtɪŋ; *NAmE* ˈvoʊ-/ *noun* [U] the action of choosing sb/sth in an election or at a meeting: *He was eliminated in the first round of voting.* ◇ *Voting will take place on May 1.* ◇ *tactical voting* ◇ *to be of voting age*

ˈvoting booth *noun* (*especially NAmE*) = POLLING BOOTH

ˈvoting machine *noun* a machine in which votes can be recorded automatically, used, for example, in the US

vo·tive /ˈvəʊtɪv; *NAmE* ˈvoʊ-/ *adj.* [usually before noun] (*technical*) presented to a god as a sign of thanks: *votive offerings*

vouch /vaʊtʃ/ *verb*

PHR V **ˈvouch for sb/sth** (*formal*) to say that you believe that sb will behave well and that you will be responsible for their actions: *Are you willing to vouch for him?* ◇ *I can vouch for her ability to work hard.* **ˈvouch for sth** (*formal*) to say that you believe that sth is true or good because you have evidence for it SYN **confirm**: *I was in bed with the flu. My wife can vouch for that.*

vouch·er /ˈvaʊtʃə(r)/ *noun* a printed piece of paper that can be used instead of money to pay for sth, or that allows you to pay less than the usual price of sth: *a voucher for a free meal* ◇ *a travel voucher* ◇ *This discount voucher entitles you to 10% off your next purchase.* ➲ see also LUNCHEON VOUCHER

vouch·safe /ˌvaʊtʃˈseɪf/ *verb* **~ sth (to sb) | ~ sb sth | ~ that... | + speech** (*old-fashioned* or *formal*) to give, offer or tell sth to sb, especially in order to give them a special advantage: *He vouchsafed to me certain family secrets.*

vow /vaʊ/ *noun, verb*

- ***noun*** a formal and serious promise, especially a religious one, to do sth: *to **make/take a vow*** ◇ *to **break/keep a vow*** ◇ *to break your **marriage vows*** ◇ *Nuns take **a vow of** chastity.* ➲ COLLOCATIONS at MARRIAGE
- ***verb*** to make a formal and serious promise to do sth or a formal statement that is true: **~ to do sth** *She vowed never to speak to him again.* ◇ **~ (that)...** *He vowed (that) he had not hurt her.* ◇ **~ sth** *They vowed eternal friendship.* ◇ **+ speech** *'I'll be back,' she vowed.*

vowel /ˈvaʊəl/ *noun* (*phonetics*) **1** a speech sound in which the mouth is open and the tongue is not touching the top of the mouth, the teeth, etc, for example /ɑː, e, ɔː/ : *vowel sounds* ◇ *Each language has a different vowel system.* ➲ see also CARDINAL VOWEL **2** a letter that represents a vowel sound. In English the vowels are a, e, i, o, and u. ➲ compare CONSONANT ➲ see also DIPHTHONG

vox pop /ˌvɒks ˈpɒp; *NAmE* ˌvɑːks ˈpɑːp/ *noun* [C, U] (*BrE, informal*) the opinion of members of the public, especially when it is broadcast or published

voy·age /ˈvɔɪɪdʒ/ *noun, verb*

- ***noun*** a long journey, especially by sea or in space: *an around-the-world voyage* ◇ *a voyage in space* ◇ *The Titanic sank on its **maiden voyage*** (= first journey). ◇ (*figurative*) *Going to college can be a voyage of self-discovery.*
- ***verb*** [I] **+ adv./prep.** (*literary*) to travel, especially in a ship and over a long distance

voy·ager /ˈvɔɪɪdʒə(r)/ *noun* (*old-fashioned* or *literary*) a person who goes on a long journey, especially by ship to unknown parts of the world

voy·eur /vwaɪˈɜː(r); vɔɪˈɜː(r)/ *noun* (*disapproving*) **1** a person who gets pleasure from secretly watching other people have sex **2** a person who enjoys watching the problems and private lives of others ▶ **voy·eur·ism** /vwaɪˈɜːrɪzəm; vɔɪˈɜː-/ *noun* [U] **voy·eur·is·tic** /ˌvwaɪəˈrɪstɪk; ˌvɔɪəˈr-/ *adj.*: *a voyeuristic interest in other people's lives*

VP /ˌviː ˈpiː/ *abbr.* VICE-PRESIDENT

vroom /vruːm/ *noun* [U] used to represent the loud sound made by a vehicle moving very fast: *Vroom! A sports car roared past.*

vs *abbr.* (*especially NAmE*) VERSUS

ˈV-sign *noun* a sign that you make by holding up your hand and making a V-shape with your first and second fingers. When the PALM (= inside part) of your hand is facing away

V

from you, the sign means 'victory'; when the palm is facing towards you the sign is used as a way of being rude to other people. ➲ compare TWO FINGERS

VSO /ˌviː es ˈəʊ; *NAmE* ˈoʊ/ *abbr.* VOLUNTARY SERVICE OVERSEAS

VTOL /ˌviː tiː əʊ ˈel; *NAmE* oʊ/ *abbr.* vertical take-off and landing (used to refer to an aircraft that can take off and land by going straight up or straight down)

vul·can·ized (*BrE* also **-ised**) /ˈvʌlkənaɪzd/ *adj.* (*technical*) (of rubber) treated with SULPHUR at great heat to make it stronger

vul·can·ology /ˌvʌlkəˈnɒlədʒi; *NAmE* -ˈnɑːl-/ *noun* [U] = VOLCANOLOGY

vul·gar /ˈvʌlɡə(r)/ *adj.* **1** not having or showing good taste; not polite, elegant or well behaved SYN **coarse, in bad taste**: *a vulgar man* ◇ *vulgar decorations* ◇ *She found their laughter and noisy games coarse and rather vulgar.* **2** rude and likely to offend SYN **crude**: *vulgar jokes* ▶ **vul·gar·ly** *adv.*: *He eyed her vulgarly.*

ˌvulgar ˈfraction *noun* (*BrE*) a FRACTION (= a number less than one) that is shown as numbers above and below a line: *¾ and ⅝ are vulgar fractions.* ➲ compare DECIMAL FRACTION

vul·gar·ian /vʌlˈɡeəriən; *NAmE* -ˈɡer-/ *noun* (*formal*) a person who does not have polite manners or good taste

vul·gar·ism /ˈvʌlɡərɪzəm/ *noun* (*formal*) a rude word or expression, especially one relating to sex

vul·gar·ity /vʌlˈɡærəti/ *noun* [U, C] the fact of being rude or not having good taste; a rude object, picture, etc: *She was offended by the vulgarity of their jokes.* ◇ *a pornographic magazine full of vulgarities*

vul·gar·ize (*BrE* also **-ise**) /ˈvʌlɡəraɪz/ *verb* **~ sth** (*formal, disapproving*) to spoil sth by changing it so that it is more ordinary than before and not of such a high standard ▶ **vul·gar·iza·tion, -isa·tion** /ˌvʌlɡəraɪˈzeɪʃn; *NAmE* -rəˈz-/ *noun* [U]

ˌvulgar ˈLatin *noun* [U] the spoken form of Latin which was used in the western part of the Roman Empire

the Vul·gate /ˈvʌlɡeɪt; -ɡət/ *noun* [sing.] the main Latin version of the Bible prepared in the late 4th century

vul·ner·able /ˈvʌlnərəbl/ *adj.* **~ (to sb/sth)** weak and easily hurt physically or emotionally: *to be vulnerable to attack* ◇ *She looked very vulnerable standing there on her own.* ◇ *In cases of food poisoning, young children are especially vulnerable.* ◇ *The sudden resignation of the financial director put the company in a very* ***vulnerable position.*** ▶ **vul·ner·abil·ity** /ˌvʌlnərəˈbɪləti/ *noun* [U]: **~ (of sb/sth) (to sth)** *financial vulnerability* ◇ *the vulnerability of newborn babies to disease* **vul·ner·ably** /-əbli/ *adv.*

vul·pine /ˈvʌlpaɪn/ *adj.* (*formal*) of or like a FOX

vul·ture /ˈvʌltʃə(r)/ *noun* **1** a large bird, usually without feathers on its head or neck, that eats the flesh of animals that are already dead: ***vultures circling/wheeling*** *overhead* ➲ VISUAL VOCAB page V10 **2** a person who hopes to gain from the troubles or sufferings of other people

vulva /ˈvʌlvə/ *noun* (*anatomy*) the outer opening of the female sex organs

vuvu·zela /vuːvuːˈzeɪlə/ *adj.* (*SAfrE*) a long plastic instrument in the shape of a TRUMPET, that makes a very loud noise when you blow it and is popular with football fans in South Africa

vying *pres. part.* of VIE

V

W /ˈdʌbljuː/ *noun, abbr.*
■ **noun** (also **w**) [C, U] (*pl.* **Ws, W's, w's** /ˈdʌbljuːz/) the 23rd letter of the English alphabet: *'Water' begins with (a) W/'W'.*
■ **abbr.** **1** west; western **2** WATT: *a 100W light bulb*

W-2 form /ˌdʌbljuː ˈtuː fɔːm; *NAmE* fɔːrm/ *noun* (in the US) an official document that an employer gives to an employee that shows the amount of pay and tax for the year

wack /wæk/ *adj.* (*informal, especially US*) **1** very bad; not of good quality: *That movie was really wack.* **2** very strange

wacko /ˈwækəʊ; *NAmE* -koʊ/ *adj., noun* (*informal*)
■ **adj.** crazy; not sensible: *wacko opinions*
■ **noun** (*pl.* **-os** or **-oes**) (*especially NAmE*) a crazy person

wacky (also **whacky**) /ˈwæki/ *adj.* (**wack·ier, wacki·est**) (*informal*) funny or amusing in a slightly crazy way **SYN** **zany**: *wacky ideas* ◇ *Some of his friends are pretty* ***wild and wacky*** *characters.*

wad /wɒd; *NAmE* wɑːd/ *noun, verb*
■ **noun** **1** a thick pile of pieces of paper, paper money, etc. folded or rolled together: *He pulled a thick wad of £10 notes out of his pocket.* ◇ (*BrE, slang*) *They had a wad/wads of money* (= a large amount). **2** a mass of soft material, used for blocking sth or keeping sth in place: *The nurse used a wad of cotton wool to stop the bleeding.*
■ **verb** (**-dd-**) **1** **~ sth (up)** (*especially NAmE*) to fold or press sth into a tight wad **2** **~ sth** to fill sth with soft material for warmth or protection

wad·ding /ˈwɒdɪŋ; *NAmE* ˈwɑːd-/ *noun* [U] soft material that you wrap around things to protect them

wad·dle /ˈwɒdl; *NAmE* ˈwɑːdl/ *verb* [I] (**+ adv./prep.**) to walk with short steps, swinging from side to side, like a DUCK ▶ **wad·dle** *noun* [sing.]: *She walked with a waddle.*

wade /weɪd/ *verb* **1** [I, T] to walk with an effort through sth, especially water or mud: (**+ adv./prep.**) *He waded into the water to push the boat out.* ◇ *Sometimes they had to wade waist-deep through mud.* ◇ **~ sth** *They waded the river at a shallow point.* **2** (*NAmE*) (*BrE* **pad·dle**) [I] to walk or stand with no shoes or socks in shallow water in the sea, a lake, etc.
PHR V **ˌwade ˈin** | **ˌwade ˈinto sth** (*informal*) to enter a fight, a discussion or an argument in an aggressive or not very sensitive way: *The police waded into the crowd with batons.* ◇ *You shouldn't have waded in with all those unpleasant accusations.* **ˌwade ˈinto sb** (*informal*) to attack sb with words in an angry aggressive way **ˌwade ˈthrough sth** [no passive] to deal with or read sth that is boring and takes a lot of time: *I spent the whole day wading through the paperwork on my desk.*

wader /ˈweɪdə(r)/ *noun* **1** (also **ˈwading bird**) [C] any of several different types of bird with long legs that feed in shallow water **2** **waders** [pl.] long rubber boots that reach up to your THIGH, that you wear for standing in water, especially when fishing: *a pair of waders*

wadi /ˈwɒdi; *NAmE* ˈwɑːdi/ *noun* (in the Middle East and N Africa) a valley or channel that is dry except when it rains

ˈwading pool (*NAmE*) (*BrE* **ˈpaddling pool**) *noun* a shallow swimming pool for children to play in, especially a small plastic one that you fill with water

wafer /ˈweɪfə(r)/ *noun* **1** a thin crisp light biscuit/cookie, often eaten with ice cream **2** a very thin round piece of special bread given by the priest during COMMUNION **3** **~ (of sth)** a very thin piece of sth

ˌwafer-ˈthin *adj.* very thin ➲ compare PAPER-THIN

waf·fle /ˈwɒfl; *NAmE* ˈwɑːfl; ˈwɔːfl/ *noun, verb*
■ **noun** **1** [C] a crisp flat cake with a pattern of squares on both sides, often eaten with sweet sauce, cream, etc. on top: *a waffle iron* (= for making waffles with) **2** [U] (*BrE, informal*) language that uses a lot of words but does not say anything important or interesting: *The report is just full of waffle.*
■ **verb** **1** [I] **~ (on) (about sth)** (*BrE, informal, disapproving*) to talk or write using a lot of words but without saying anything interesting or important: *The principal waffled on about exam results but no one was listening.* **2** [I] **~ (on/over sth)** (*NAmE, informal*) to be unable to decide what to do about sth or what you think about sth: *The senator was accused of waffling on major issues.*

waft /wɒft; *NAmE* wɑːft; wæft/ *verb, noun*
■ **verb** [I, T] to move, or make sth move, gently through the air **SYN** **drift**: **+ adv./prep.** *The sound of their voices wafted across the lake.* ◇ *Delicious smells wafted up from the kitchen.* ◇ **~ sth + adv./prep.** *The scent of the flowers was wafted along by the breeze.*
■ **noun** (*formal*) a smell or a line of smoke carried through the air: *wafts of perfume/smoke*

Wag /wæg/ *noun* (*BrE, informal*) one of a group of 'wives and girlfriends' of famous men, especially members of a sports team: *Wags at the World Cup*

wag /wæg/ *verb, noun*
■ **verb** (**-gg-**) **1** [T, I] **~ (sth)** if a dog **wags** its tail, or its tail **wags**, its tail moves from side to side several times **2** [T] **~ sth** to shake your finger or your head from side to side or up and down, often as a sign of disapproval **3** [T] **~ sth** (*AustralE, NZE*) to stay away from school without permission: *to wag school* **IDM** see TAIL *n.*, TONGUE *n.*
■ **noun** **1** (*old-fashioned, especially BrE*) a person who enjoys making jokes **SYN** **joker** **2** a wagging movement

wage 🔑 /weɪdʒ/ *noun, verb*
■ **noun** 🔑 [sing.] (also **wages** [pl.]) a regular amount of money that you earn, usually every week, for work or services: *wages of £200 a week* ◇ *a* ***weekly wage*** *of £200* ◇ ***wage cuts*** ◇ *a* ***wage increase*** *of 3%* ◇ (*BrE*) *a* ***wage rise*** *of 3%* ◇ ***wage demands/claims/settlements*** ◇ *Wages are paid on Fridays.* ◇ *There are extra benefits for people on* ***low wages.*** ◇ *The staff have agreed to a voluntary* ***wage freeze*** (= a situation in which wages are not increased for a time). ➲ **SYNONYMS** at INCOME ➲ **COLLOCATIONS** at FINANCE ➲ compare SALARY ➲ see also LIVING WAGE, MINIMUM WAGE
■ **verb** to begin and continue a war, a battle, etc: **~ sth** *The rebels have waged a guerrilla war since 2007.* ◇ **~ sth against/on sb/sth** *He alleged that a press campaign was being waged against him.*

waged /weɪdʒd/ *adj.* **1** (of a person) having regular paid work: *waged workers* **2** (of work) for which you are paid: *waged employment* **3** **the waged** *noun* [pl.] people who have regular paid work **OPP** **unwaged**

ˈwage earner *noun* a person who earns money, especially a person who works for wages: *We have two wage earners in the family.*

ˈwage packet *noun* (*BrE*) = PAY PACKET

wager /ˈweɪdʒə(r)/ *noun, verb*
■ **noun** (*old-fashioned* or *formal*) an arrangement to risk money on the result of a particular event **SYN** **bet**
■ **verb** (*old-fashioned* or *formal*) **1** [I, T] to bet money **SYN** **bet**: **~ on sth** *She always wagered on an outsider.* ◇ **~ sth (on sth)** *to wager £50 on a horse* ◇ **~ sth/sb that…** *I had wagered a great deal of money that I would beat him.* **2** [T] **~ (that)…** used to say that you are so confident that sth is true or will happen that you would be willing to bet money on it **SYN** **bet**: *I'll wager that she knows more about it than she's saying.*

wag·gish /ˈwægɪʃ/ *adj.* (*old-fashioned*) funny, clever and not serious: *waggish remarks*

wag·gle /ˈwægl/ *verb* [T, I] **~ (sth)** (*informal*) to make sth move with short movements from side to side or up and down; to move in this way: *Can you waggle your ears?* ▶ **wag·gle** *noun*

Wag·ner·ian /vɑːgˈnɪəriən; *NAmE* -ˈnɪr-/ *adj.* **1** related to the music of the German COMPOSER Richard Wagner; typical of this music **2** (*humorous*) very big or great, or in a style that is too serious or exaggerated: *a hangover of Wagnerian proportions*

wagon /ˈwæɡən/ *noun* **1** (*BrE*) (*NAmE* ˈ**freight car**) a railway/railroad truck for carrying goods **2** (*BrE* also **waggon**) a vehicle with four wheels, pulled by horses or OXEN and used for carrying heavy loads **3** (also **cart**) (both *NAmE*) (*BrE* **trol·ley**) a small table on very small wheels, used for carrying or serving food or drink ➲ see also BANDWAGON, STATION WAGON
IDM **be/go on the ˈwagon** (*informal*) to not drink alcohol, either for a short time or permanently

wag·on·load /ˈwæɡənləʊd; *NAmE* -loʊd/ *noun* an amount of goods carried on a wagon

ˈ**wagon train** *noun* a long line of WAGONS and horses, used by people travelling west in N America in the 19th century

wag·tail /ˈwæɡteɪl/ *noun* a small bird with a long tail that moves up and down when the bird is walking

wah-wah /ˈwɑː wɑː/ *noun* [U] (*music*) a special effect made on electric musical instruments, especially the GUITAR, which varies the quality of the sound

waif /weɪf/ *noun* a small thin person, usually a child, who looks as if they do not have enough to eat: *the* ***waifs and strays*** *of our society* (= people with no home) ▸ ˈ**waif-like** *adj.*: *waif-like young girls*

wail /weɪl/ *verb, noun*
■ ***verb*** **1** [I] to make a long loud high cry because you are sad or in pain: *The little girl was wailing miserably.* ◇ *women wailing and weeping* **2** [T, I] to cry or complain about sth in a loud high voice SYN **moan**: **+ speech** *'It's broken,' she wailed.* ◇ **~ (about sth)** *There's no point wailing about something that happened so long ago.* **3** [I] (of things) to make a long high sound: *Ambulances raced by with sirens wailing.* ▸ **wail·ing** *noun* [sing., U]: *a high-pitched wailing*
■ ***noun*** a long loud high cry expressing pain or sadness; a sound similar to this SYN **moan**: *a wail of despair* ◇ *the distant wail of sirens*

wains·cot /ˈweɪnskət/ *noun* (*old use*) = SKIRTING BOARD

waist 0-w /weɪst/ *noun*
1 0-w the area around the middle of the body between the RIBS and the hips, often narrower than the areas above and below: *He put his arm around her waist.* ◇ *She was paralysed* ***from the waist down*** (= in the area below her waist). ◇ *The workmen were* ***stripped to the waist*** (= wearing no clothes on the top half of their bodies). ➲ COLLOCATIONS at PHYSICAL ➲ VISUAL VOCAB page V48 **2** 0-w the part of a piece of clothing that covers the waist: *a skirt with an elasticated waist* **3** **-waisted** (in adjectives) having the type of waist mentioned: *a high-waisted dress*

waist·band /ˈweɪstbænd/ *noun* the strip of cloth that forms the waist of a piece of clothing, especially at the top of a skirt or trousers/pants: *an elasticated waistband*

waist·coat /ˈweɪskəʊt; *NAmE* usually ˈweskət; *NAmE* also ˈweɪskoʊt/ (*BrE*) (*NAmE* **vest**) *noun* a short piece of clothing with buttons down the front but no sleeves, usually worn over a shirt and under a jacket, often forming part of a man's suit ➲ VISUAL VOCAB page V50

ˌ**waist-ˈdeep** *adj., adv.* up to the waist: *The water was waist-deep.* ◇ *We waded waist-deep into the muddy water.*

W

ˌ**waist-ˈhigh** *adj., adv.* high enough to reach the waist: *waist-high grass* ◇ *The grass had grown waist-high.*

waist·line /ˈweɪstlaɪn/ *noun* **1** the amount that a person measures around the waist, used to talk about how fat or thin they are: *an expanding waistline* **2** the place on a piece of clothing where your waist is SYN **waist**

wait 0-w /weɪt/ *verb, noun*
■ ***verb*** **1** 0-w [I, T] to stay where you are or delay doing sth until sb/sth comes or sth happens: *She rang the bell and waited.* ◇ **+ adv./prep.** *Have you been waiting long?* ◇ *I've been waiting (for) twenty minutes.* ◇ *I'll wait outside until the meeting's over.* ◇ **~ for sb/sth** *Wait for me!* ◇ **~ for sb/sth to do sth** *We're waiting for the rain to stop before we go out.* ◇ **~ to do sth** *Hurry up! We're waiting to go.* ◇ **~ your turn** *You'll just have to wait your turn* (= wait until your turn comes). **2** 0-w [I, T] to hope or watch for sth to happen, especially for a long time: **~ (for sth)** *Leeds United had waited for success for eighteen years.* ◇ *This is just the opportunity I've been waiting for.* ◇ **~ for sb/sth to do sth** *He's waiting for me to make a mistake.* ◇ **~ your chance** *I waited my chance and slipped out when no one was looking.* **3** 0-w **be waiting** [I] (of things) to be ready for sb to have or use: **~ (for sb)** *There's a letter waiting for you at home.* ◇ **~ to do sth** *The hotel had a taxi waiting to collect us.* **4** 0-w [I] to be left to be dealt with at a later time because it is not urgent: *I've got some calls to make but they* ***can wait*** *until tomorrow.*
IDM **an ˌaccident/a diˌsaster waiting to ˈhappen** a thing or person that is very likely to cause danger or a problem in the future because of the condition it is in or the way they behave **I, they, etc. can't ˈwait/can hardly ˈwait** 0-w used when you are emphasizing that sb is very excited about sth or keen to do it: *The children* ***can't wait for*** *Christmas to come.* ◇ *I can hardly wait to see him again.* **keep sb ˈwaiting** to make sb have to wait or be delayed, especially because you arrive late: *I'm sorry to have kept you waiting.* ˌ**wait and ˈsee** used to tell sb that they must be patient and wait to find out about sth later: *We'll just have to wait and see—there's nothing we can do at the moment.* ◇ *a wait-and-see policy* ◇ *'Where are we going?' 'Wait and see!'* **wait at ˈtable** (*formal*) to serve food to people, for example at a formal meal ˈ**wait for it** (*informal, especially BrE*) **1** used to say that you are about to tell sb sth that is surprising or amusing: *They're off on a trip, to—wait for it—the Maldives!* **2** used to tell sb not to start doing sth yet, but to wait until you tell them **wait a minute/moment/second** **1** 0-w to wait for a short time: *Can you wait a second while I make a call?* **2** 0-w used when you have just noticed or remembered sth, or had a sudden idea: *Wait a minute—this isn't the right key.* **wait on sb hand and ˈfoot** (*disapproving*) to take care of sb's needs so well that they do not have to do anything for themselves **wait ˈtables** (*NAmE*) to work serving food to people in a restaurant ˈ**wait till/until…** (*informal*) used to show that you are very excited about telling or showing sth to sb: *Wait till you see what I've found!* **what are we ˈwaiting for?** (*informal*) used to suggest that you should all start doing what you have been discussing **what are you ˈwaiting for?** (*informal*) used to tell sb to do sth now rather than later: *If the car needs cleaning, what are you waiting for?* (**just**) **you ˈwait** used to emphasize a threat, warning or promise: *I'll be famous one day, just you wait!* ➲ more at DUST *n.*, WING *n.*
PHR V ˌ**wait aˈbout/aˈround** to stay in a place, with nothing particular to do, for example because you are expecting sth to happen or sb to arrive ˌ**wait beˈhind** (*especially BrE*) to stay after other people have gone, especially to speak to sb privately ˌ**wait ˈin** (*BrE*) to stay at home because you are expecting sb to come, telephone, etc. ˈ**wait on sb** to act as a servant to sb, especially by serving food to them ˈ**wait on sth/sb** (*informal, especially NAmE*) to wait for sth to happen before you do or decide sth: *She is waiting on the result of a blood test.* ˌ**wait sth↔ˈout** to wait until an unpleasant event has finished: *We sheltered in a doorway to wait out the storm.* ˌ**wait ˈup** (*NAmE*) used to ask sb to stop or go more slowly so that you can join them ˌ**wait ˈup (for sb)** to wait for sb to come home at night before you go to bed
■ ***noun*** [usually sing.] **~ (for sb/sth)** an act of waiting; an amount of time waited: *We had* ***a long wait*** *for the bus.* ◇ *He now faces an agonizing two-month wait for the test results.* IDM see LIE *v.*

wait·er 0-w /ˈweɪtə(r)/ (*feminine* **wait·ress**) *noun* a person whose job is to serve customers at their tables in a restaurant, etc: *I'll ask the waitress for the bill.* ◇ *Waiter, could you bring me some water?* ➲ note at GENDER ➲ see also DUMB WAITER, SERVER

wait·ing /ˈweɪtɪŋ/ *noun* [U] **1** the fact of staying where you are or delaying doing sth until sb/sth comes or sth happens: ***No waiting*** (= on a sign at the side of the road, telling vehicles that they must not stop there). **2** the fact of working as a waiter or waitress ➲ see also WAITRESSING

ˈ**waiting game** *noun* [sing.] a policy of waiting to see how a situation develops before you decide how to act

ˈ**waiting list** *noun* a list of people who are waiting for sth such as a service or medical treatment that is not yet available: *There are no places available right now but I'll* ***put you on a waiting list****.* ◇ *There's a waiting list to join the golf club.* ◇ (*BrE*) *The government has promised to cut hospital waiting lists.*

ˈ**waiting room** *noun* a room where people can sit while they are waiting, for example for a bus or train, or to see a doctor or dentist

ˈ**wait list** *noun* (*NAmE*) = WAITING LIST: *She was on a wait list for a liver transplant.*

ˈ**wait-list** *verb* **~ sb** (*NAmE*) to put sb's name on a WAITING LIST: *He's been wait-listed for a football scholarship to Stanford.*

wait·person /ˈweɪtpɜːsn; *NAmE* -pɜːrsn/ *noun* (*pl.* **-persons**) (*NAmE*) a person whose job is to serve customers at their tables in a restaurant, etc.

wait·ress /ˈweɪtrəs/ *noun* ➲ WAITER

wait·ress·ing /ˈweɪtrəsɪŋ/ *noun* [U] the job of being a waitress: *I did some waitressing when I was a student.*

wait·staff /ˈweɪtstɑːf; *NAmE* -stæf/ *noun* [U] (*NAmE*) the people whose job is to serve customers at their tables in a restaurant, etc.

waive /weɪv/ *verb* **~ sth** to choose not to demand sth in a particular case, even though you have a legal or official right to do so SYN **forgo**

waiver /ˈweɪvə(r)/ *noun* (*law*) a situation in which sb gives up a legal right or claim; an official document stating this

wake 0‑ /weɪk/ *verb, noun*

■ ***verb*** (**woke** /wəʊk/, **woken** /ˈwəʊkən/) **1** 0‑ [I, T] to stop sleeping; to make sb stop sleeping: **~ (up)** *What time do you usually wake up in the morning?* ◇ *I always wake early in the summer.* ◇ *Wake up! It's eight o'clock.* ◇ **~ to sth** (*formal*) *They woke to a clear blue sky.* ◇ **~ from sth** (*formal*) *She had just woken from a deep sleep.* ◇ **~ to do sth** *He woke up to find himself alone in the house.* ◇ **~ sb (up)** *Try not to wake the baby up.* ◇ *I was woken by the sound of someone moving around.* ➲ note at AWAKE **2** [T] **~ sth** (*literary* or *formal*) to make sb remember sth or feel sth again: *The incident woke memories of his past sufferings.*

IDM **wake ˌup and smell the ˈcoffee** (*informal*) (usually in orders) used to tell sb to become aware of what is really happening in a situation, especially when this is sth unpleasant

PHR V **ˌwake ˈup** to become more lively and interested: *Wake up and listen!* ➲ see also WAKE (1) **ˌwake sb↔ˈup** to make sb feel more lively: *A cold shower will soon wake you up.* ◇ *The class needs waking up.* ➲ see also WAKE (1) **ˌwake ˈup to sth** to become aware of sth; to realize sth: *He hasn't yet woken up to the seriousness of the situation.*

■ ***noun*** **1** an occasion before or after a funeral when people gather to remember the dead person, traditionally held the night before the funeral to watch over the body before it is buried **2** the track that a boat or ship leaves behind on the surface of the water ➲ VISUAL VOCAB page V5

IDM **in the wake of sb/sth** coming after or following sb/sth: *There have been demonstrations on the streets in the wake of the recent bomb attack.* ◇ *A group of reporters followed in her wake.* ◇ *The storm left a trail of destruction in its wake.*

wake·board·ing /ˈweɪkbɔːdɪŋ; *NAmE* -bɔːrd-/ *noun* [U] the sport of riding on a short wide board called a **wakeboard** while being pulled along through the water by a fast boat ▶ **wake·board** *verb* [I] ➲ VISUAL VOCAB page V40

wake·ful /ˈweɪkfl/ *adj.* (*formal*) **1** not sleeping; unable to sleep SYN **sleepless**: *He lay wakeful all night.* **2** (of a period at night) spent with little or no sleep SYN **sleepless**: *She had spent many wakeful nights worrying about him.* ▶ **wake·ful·ness** *noun* [U]

waken /ˈweɪkən/ *verb* (*formal*) **1** [I, T] to wake, or make sb wake, from sleep: **~ (up)** *The child had just wakened.* ◇ **~ sb (up)** *I was wakened by a knock at the door.* ➲ note at AWAKE **2** [T] **~ sth** to make sb remember sth or feel sth again: *The dream wakened a forgotten memory.*

ˈ**wake-up call** *noun* **1** a telephone call that you arrange to be made to you at a particular time, for example in a hotel, in order to wake you up: *I asked for a wake-up call at 6.30 a.m.* **2** an event that makes people realize that there is a problem that they need to do sth about: *These riots should be a wake-up call for the government.*

wakey-wakey /ˌweɪki ˈweɪki/ *exclamation* (*BrE, informal, humorous*) used to tell sb to wake up

wak·ing /ˈweɪkɪŋ/ *adj.* [only before noun] used to describe time when you are awake: *She spends all her waking hours caring for her mother.* ▶ **wak·ing** *noun* [U]: *the dreamlike state between waking and sleeping*

Wal·dorf salad /ˌwɔːldɔːf ˈsæləd; *NAmE* -dɔːrf/ *noun* [U, C] a salad made from apples, nuts, CELERY and MAYONNAISE (= sauce made with egg and oil)

walk 0‑ /wɔːk/ *verb, noun*

■ ***verb*** **1** 0‑ [I, T] to move or go somewhere by putting one foot in front of the other on the ground, but without running: *The baby is just learning to walk.* ◇ *'How did you get here?' 'I walked.'* ◇ **+ adv./prep.** *He walked slowly away from her.* ◇ *The door opened and Jo walked in.* ◇ *She missed the bus and had to walk home.* ◇ *The school is* ***within*** *easy* ***walking distance of*** *the train station.* ◇ **~ sth** *Children here walk several miles to school.* **2** 0‑ (also **go walking**) (both *especially BrE*) [I, T] to spend time walking for pleasure: (**+ adv./prep.**) *We're going walking in the mountains this summer.* ◇ *I walked across Scotland with a friend.* ◇ **~ sth** *They love walking the moors.* **3** [T] **~ sb + adv./prep.** to go somewhere with sb on foot, especially in order to make sure they get there safely: *He always walked her home.* **4** [T] **~ sth + adv./prep.** to take an animal for a walk; to make an animal walk somewhere: *They walk their dogs every day.* ➲ SYNONYMS at TAKE **5** [I] (*informal*) to disappear; to be taken away: *Lock up any valuables. Things tend to walk here* (= be stolen). **6** [I] (*literary*) (of a GHOST) to appear

IDM **run before you can ˈwalk** to do things that are difficult, without learning the basic skills first **walk the ˈbeat** (of police officers) to walk around the area that they are responsible for **walk ˈfree** to be allowed to leave court, etc, without receiving any punishment ˈ**walk it** (*informal*) **1** to go somewhere on foot instead of in a vehicle **2** to easily achieve sth that you want: *It's not a difficult exam. You'll walk it!* **walk sb off their ˈfeet** (*informal*) to make sb walk so far or so fast that they are very tired **walk off the ˈjob** (*NAmE*) to stop working in order to go on strike **walk the ˈplank** (in the past) to walk along a board placed over the side of a ship and fall into the sea, as a punishment **walk the ˈstreets** to walk around the streets of a town or city: *Is it safe to walk the streets alone at night?* **walk ˈtall** to feel proud and confident **ˌwalk the ˈwalk** (*informal, approving*) to act in a way that shows people you are really good at what you do, and not just good at talking about it: *You can talk the talk but can you walk the walk?* ➲ more at AIR *n.*, AISLE, LINE *n.*, MEMORY LANE, THIN *adj.*, TIGHTROPE

PHR V **ˌwalk aˈway (from sb/sth)** to leave a difficult situation or relationship, etc. instead of staying and trying to deal with it **ˌwalk aˈway with sth** (*informal*) to win or obtain sth easily: *She walked away with the gold medal.* **ˌwalk ˈin on sb/sth** to enter a room when sb in there is doing sth private and does not expect you **ˌwalk ˈinto sth** (*informal*) **1** to become involved in an unpleasant situation, especially because you were not sensible enough to avoid it: *I realized I'd walked into a trap.* **2** to succeed in getting a job very easily **ˌwalk ˈinto sth/sb** to crash into sth/sb while you are walking, for example because you do not see them **ˌwalk ˈoff** to leave a person or place suddenly because you are angry or upset **ˌwalk sth↔ˈoff** to go for a walk after a meal so that you feel less full: *We walked off a heavy Sunday lunch.* **ˌwalk ˈoff with sth** (*informal*) **1** to win sth easily **2** to take sth that is not yours; to steal sth **ˌwalk ˈout** (*informal*) (of workers) to stop working in order to go on strike ➲ related noun WALKOUT **ˌwalk ˈout (of sth)** 0‑ to leave a meeting, performance, etc. suddenly, especially in order to show your disapproval **ˌwalk ˈout (on sb)** (*informal*) to suddenly leave sb that you are having a relationship with

W

and that you have a responsibility for SYN **desert**: *How could she walk out on her kids?* ˌ**walk ˈout (on sth)** (*informal*) to stop doing sth that you have agreed to do before it is completed: *I never walk out on a job half done.* ˌ**walk (all) ˈover sb** (*informal*) **1** to treat sb badly, without considering them or their needs: *She'll always let him walk all over her.* **2** to defeat sb easily ➲ related noun WALKOVER ˌ**walk sb ˈthrough sth** to help sb learn or become familiar with sth, by showing them each stage of the process in turn: *She walked me through a demonstration of the software.* ➲ related noun WALK-THROUGH ˌ**walk ˈup (to sb/sth)** 🔑 to walk towards sb/sth, especially in a confident way

■ ***noun*** **1** 🔑 [C] a journey on foot, usually for pleasure or exercise: *Let's* ***go for a walk.*** ◇ *I like to have a walk in the evenings.* ◇ *She's* ***taken the dog for a walk.*** ◇ *He set out on the long walk home.* ◇ *The office is ten minutes' walk from here.* ◇ *a ten-minute walk* ◇ *It's only a short walk to the beach.* **2** 🔑 [C] a path or route for walking, usually for pleasure; an organized event when people walk for pleasure: *a circular walk* ◇ *There are some interesting walks in the area.* ◇ *a guided walk around the farm* **3** [sing.] a way or style of walking; the act or speed of walking rather than running: *I recognized him by his walk.* ◇ *The horse slowed to a walk.* **4** [C] (*NAmE*) a SIDEWALK or path

IDM **a ˌwalk in the ˈpark** (*informal*) a thing that is very easy to do or deal with: *The role isn't exactly a walk in the park.* **a walk of ˈlife** a person's job or position in society SYN **background**: *She has friends from all walks of life.*

Vocabulary Building

Ways of walking

- **creep** *He could hear someone creeping around downstairs.*
- **limp** *One player limped off the field with a twisted ankle.*
- **pace** *I found him in the corridor nervously pacing up and down.*
- **pad** *She spent the morning padding about the house in her slippers.*
- **plod** *They wearily plodded home through the rain.*
- **shuffle** *The queue gradually shuffled forward.*
- **stagger** *They staggered out of the pub, completely drunk.*
- **stomp** *She stomped out of the room, slamming the door behind her.*
- **stroll** *Families were strolling around the park.*
- **tiptoe** *They tiptoed upstairs so they wouldn't wake the baby.*
- **trudge** *We trudged up the hill.*

walk·about /ˈwɔːkəbaʊt/ *noun* **1** (*BrE*) an occasion when an important person walks among ordinary people to meet and talk to them **2** (*AustralE*) a journey (originally on foot) that is made by an Australian Aboriginal in order to live in the traditional manner

IDM **go ˈwalkabout 1** (*informal*) to be lost or not where you should be: *My rucksack seems to have gone walkabout.* **2** (of an Australian Aboriginal) to go into the country away from white society in order to live in the traditional manner

walk·er /ˈwɔːkə(r)/ *noun* **1** (*especially BrE*) a person who walks, usually for pleasure or exercise: *The coastal path is a popular route for walkers.* **2 a fast, slow, etc. ~** a person who walks fast, slow, etc. **3** (*NAmE*) (*BrE* **Zim·mer frame™**, *informal* **Zim·mer**) a metal frame that people use to help them to walk, for example people who are old or who have sth wrong with their legs: *He now needs a walker to get around.* ➲ picture at FRAME **4** (*NAmE*) (*BrE* ˈ**baby walker**) a frame with wheels and a HARNESS for a baby who can walk around a room, supported by the frame

walk·ies /ˈwɔːkiz/ *noun* [pl.] (*BrE, informal*) a walk with a dog: *to go for walkies*

walkie-talkie /ˌwɔːki ˈtɔːki/ *noun* (*informal*) a small radio that you can carry with you and use to send or receive messages

ˈ**walk-in** *adj.* [only before noun] **1** large enough to walk into: *a walk-in closet* **2** not arranged in advance; where you do not need to arrange a time in advance: *a walk-in interview* ◇ *a walk-in clinic*

walk·ing 🔑 /ˈwɔːkɪŋ/ *noun, adj.*

■ ***noun*** [U] **1** 🔑 (*especially BrE*) the activity of going for walks in the countryside for exercise or pleasure: *to* ***go walking*** ◇ *walking boots* ◇ *a walking holiday in Scotland* ➲ see also POWER WALKING **2** the sport of walking a long distance as fast as possible without running

■ ***adj.*** [only before noun] (*informal*) used to describe a human or living example of the thing mentioned: *She's a walking dictionary* (= she knows a lot of words).

ˈ**walking bus** *noun* (in Britain) a way for a group of children to walk safely in a group with an adult to and from school, along a route that passes by the children's homes

ˈ**walking papers** *noun* [pl.] (*NAmE, informal*) the letter or notice dismissing sb from a job

ˈ**walking stick** (also **stick** especially in *BrE*) *noun* a stick that you carry and use as a support when you are walking ➲ picture at STICK

the ˌwalking ˈwounded *noun* [pl.] people who have been injured in a battle or an accident but who are still able to walk

Walk·man™ /ˈwɔːkmən/ *noun* (*pl.* **-mans** /-mənz/) a type of PERSONAL STEREO

ˈ**walk-on** *adj.* **~ part/role** used to describe a very small part in a play or film/movie, without any words to say

walk·out /ˈwɔːkaʊt/ *noun* **1** a sudden strike by workers **2** the act of suddenly leaving a meeting as a protest against sth

walk·over /ˈwɔːkəʊvə(r)/ *noun* an easy victory in a game or competition

ˈ**walk-through** *noun* **1** an occasion when you practise a performance, etc. without an audience being present **2** a careful explanation of the details of a process

ˈ**walk-up** *noun* (*NAmE*) a tall building with stairs but no lift/elevator; an office or a flat/apartment in such a building

walk·way /ˈwɔːkweɪ/ *noun* a passage or path for walking along, often outside and raised above the ground

wall 🔑 /wɔːl/ *noun, verb*

■ ***noun*** **1** 🔑 a long vertical solid structure, made of stone, brick or concrete, that surrounds, divides or protects an area of land: *The fields were divided by stone walls.* ◇ *He sat on the wall and watched the others playing.* ➲ VISUAL VOCAB page V15 ➲ see also SEA WALL **2** 🔑 any of the vertical sides of a building or room: *I'm going to paint the walls white and the ceiling pink.* ◇ *Hang the picture* ***on the wall*** *opposite the window.* ◇ *She leaned against the wall.* ➲ COLLOCATIONS at DECORATE **3** something that forms a barrier or stops you from making progress: *The boat struck a solid wall of water.* ◇ *The investigators were confronted by a* ***wall of silence.*** **4** the outer layer of sth hollow such as an organ of the body or a cell of an animal or a plant: *the abdominal wall* ◇ *the wall of an artery*

IDM **go to the ˈwall** (*informal*) (of a company or an organization) to fail because of lack of money **off the ˈwall** (*informal*) unusual and amusing; slightly crazy: *Some of his ideas are really off the wall.* ◇ *off-the-wall ideas* **up the ˈwall** (*informal*) crazy or angry: *That noise is driving me up the wall.* ◇ *I mustn't be late or Dad will go up the wall.* ˌ**walls have ˈears** (*saying*) used to warn people to be careful what they say because other people may be listening ➲ more at BACK *n.*, BOUNCE *v.*, BRICK *n.*, FLY *n.*, HIT *v.*, FOUR, HANDWRITING, HEAD *n.*, WRITING

■ ***verb*** [usually passive] **~ sth** to surround an area, a town, etc. with a wall or walls: *a walled city*

PHR V ˌ**wall sth↔ˈin** [usually passive] to surround sth/sb with a wall or barrier ˌ**wall sth↔ˈoff** [usually passive] to separate one place or area from another with a wall ˌ**wall sb↔'up** [usually passive] to keep sb as a prisoner behind walls ˌ**wall sth↔'up** [usually passive] to fill an opening with a wall, bricks, etc. so that you can no longer use it

wal·laby /'wɒləbi; *NAmE* 'wɑːl-/ *noun* (*pl.* **-ies**) an Australian animal like a small KANGAROO, that moves by jumping on its strong back legs and keeps its young in a POUCH (= a pocket of skin) on the front of the mother's body

wal·lah /'wɒlə; *NAmE* 'wɑːlə/ *noun* (*informal* or *IndE*) a person connected with a particular job: *office wallahs*

'**wall anchor** (*NAmE*) (*BrE* **Rawl·plug™**, '**wall plug**) *noun* a small plastic tube, closed at one end, that you put into a wall to hold a screw

wall·chart /'wɔːltʃɑːt; *NAmE* -tʃɑːrt/ *noun* a large piece of paper on which there is information, fixed to a wall for people to look at

wall·cov·er·ing /'wɔːlkʌvərɪŋ/ *noun* [U, C] WALLPAPER or cloth used to decorate the walls in a room

wal·let 0→ /'wɒlɪt; *NAmE* 'wɑːl-; 'wɔːl-/ *noun* **1** 0→ (*NAmE* also **bill·fold**) a small flat folding case made of leather or plastic used for keeping paper money and credit cards in ➲ VISUAL VOCAB page V52 **2** a flat leather, plastic or cardboard case for carrying documents in: *a document wallet*

wall·flower /'wɔːlflaʊə(r)/ *noun* **1** a garden plant with yellow, orange or red flowers with a sweet smell that appear in late spring **2** (*informal*) a person who does not dance at a party because they do not have sb to dance with or because they are too shy

wall·ing /'wɔːlɪŋ/ *noun* [U] **1** material from which a wall is built: *stone walling* **2** the act or skill of building a wall or walls: *a firm that does paving and walling*

ˌ**wall-'mounted** *adj.* fixed onto a wall: *wall-mounted lights*

wal·lop /'wɒləp; *NAmE* 'wɑːl-/ *noun, verb*
- ***noun*** [sing.] (*informal*) a heavy powerful hit
- ***verb*** (*informal*) **1 ~ sb/sth** to hit sb/sth very hard SYN **thump** **2 ~ sb/sth** to defeat sb completely in a contest, match, etc. SYN **thrash**: *We walloped them 6–0.*

wal·lop·ing /'wɒləpɪŋ; *NAmE* 'wɑːl-/ *noun, adj.* (*informal*)
- ***noun*** [usually sing.] **1** a heavy defeat: *Our team got a real walloping last week.* **2** an act of hitting sb very hard several times, often as a punishment
- ***adj.*** [only before noun] very big: *They had to pay a walloping great fine.*

wal·low /'wɒləʊ; *NAmE* 'wɑːloʊ/ *verb, noun*
- ***verb*** **1** [I] **~ (in sth)** (of large animals or people) to lie and roll about in water or mud, to keep cool or for pleasure: *hippos wallowing in the river* ◇ *He loves to wallow in a hot bath after a game.* **2** [I] **~ in sth** (often *disapproving*) to enjoy sth that causes you pleasure: *She wallowed in the luxury of the hotel.* ◇ *to* ***wallow in despair/self-pity*** (= to think about your unhappy feelings all the time and seem to be enjoying them)
- ***noun*** [sing.] an act of wallowing: *pigs having a wallow in the mud*

'**wall painting** *noun* a picture painted straight onto the surface of a wall

wall·paper /'wɔːlpeɪpə(r)/ *noun, verb*
- ***noun*** [U] **1** thick paper, often with a pattern on it, used for covering the walls and ceiling of a room: *wallpaper paste* ◇ *a roll of wallpaper* ◇ *to hang wallpaper* ➲ COLLOCATIONS at DECORATE **2** (*computing*) the background pattern or picture that you choose to have on the screen of your computer, mobile/cell phone, etc.
- ***verb*** (also **paper**) [T, I] **~ (sth)** to put wallpaper onto the walls of a room

'**wall plug** *noun* = RAWLPLUG

'**Wall Street** *noun* [U] the US financial centre and STOCK EXCHANGE in New York City (used to refer to the business that is done there): *Share prices fell on Wall Street today.* ◇ *Wall Street responded quickly to the news.*

'**wall tent** (*NAmE*) (*BrE* '**frame tent**) *noun* a large tent with a roof and walls that do not slope much ➲ compare DOME TENT, RIDGE TENT

ˌ**wall-to-'wall** *adj.* [only before noun] **1** covering the floor of a room completely: ***wall-to-wall carpets/carpeting*** ➲ VISUAL VOCAB page V20 **2** (*informal*) continuous; happening or existing all the time or everywhere: *wall-to-wall TV sports coverage*

wally /'wɒli; *NAmE* 'wɔːli; 'wɑːli/ *noun* (*pl.* **-ies**) (*BrE, informal*) a stupid person

wal·nut /'wɔːlnʌt/ *noun* **1** [C] the light brown nut of the walnut tree that has a rough surface and a hard round shell in two halves ➲ VISUAL VOCAB page V28 **2** (also '**walnut tree**) [C] the tree on which walnuts grow **3** [U] the brown wood of the walnut tree, used in making furniture

wal·rus /'wɔːlrəs/ *noun* an animal like a large SEAL (= a sea animal with thick fur, that eats fish and lives around coasts), that has two long outer teeth called TUSKS and lives in Arctic regions

ˌ**walrus mou'stache** *noun* (*informal*) a long thick MOUSTACHE that hangs down on each side of the mouth

Walter Mitty /ˌwɔːltə(r) 'mɪti/ *noun* a person who imagines that their life is full of excitement and adventures when it is in fact just ordinary ORIGIN From the name of the main character in James Thurber's story *The Secret Life of Walter Mitty.*

waltz /wɔːls; wɔːlts/ *noun, verb*
- ***noun*** a dance in which two people dance together to a regular rhythm; a piece of music for this dance: *to dance a/the waltz* ◇ *a Strauss waltz*
- ***verb*** **1** [I, T] to dance a waltz: **(+ adv./prep.)** *I watched them waltzing across the floor.* ◇ **~ sb + adv./prep.** *He waltzed her around the room.* **2** [I] **+ adv./prep.** (*informal*) to walk or go somewhere in a very confident way: *I don't like him waltzing into the house as if he owned it.* **3** [I] **~ (through sth)** to complete or achieve sth without any difficulty: *The recruits have waltzed through their training.*

PHR V ˌ**waltz 'off (with sth/sb)** (*informal*) to leave a place or person in a way that is very annoying, often taking sth that is not yours: *He just waltzed off with my car!*

WAN /wæn/ *noun* (*pl.* **WANs**) (*computing*) the abbreviation for 'wide area network' (a system in which computers in different places are connected, usually over a large area) ➲ compare LAN

wan /wɒn; *NAmE* wɑːn/ *adj.* looking pale and weak: *his grey, wan face* ◇ *She gave me a wan smile* (= showing no energy or enthusiasm). ▸ **wanly** *adv.*: *He smiled wanly.*

wan·anchi /ˌwʌnʌ'ɪntʃi/ *noun* [pl.] (*EAfrE*) people; the public

wand /wɒnd; *NAmE* wɑːnd/ *noun* **1** (also ˌ**magic 'wand**) a straight thin stick that is held by sb when performing magic or magic tricks: *The fairy waved her wand and the table disappeared.* ◇ *You can't expect me to just* ***wave a (magic) wand*** *and make everything all right again.* **2** any object in the shape of a straight thin stick: *a mascara wand* ➲ VISUAL VOCAB page V49

wan·der 0→ /'wɒndə(r); *NAmE* 'wɑːn-/ *verb, noun*
- ***verb*** **1** 0→ [I, T] to walk slowly around or to a place, often without any particular sense of purpose or direction: **+ adv./prep.** *She wandered aimlessly around the streets.* ◇ *We wandered back towards the car.* ◇ **~ sth** *The child was found wandering the streets alone.* **2** 0→ [I] to move away from the place where you ought to be or the people you are with SYN **stray**: **~ away/off** *The child wandered off and got lost.* ◇ **~ from/off sth** *They had wandered from the path into the woods.* **3** 0→ [I] (of a person's mind or thoughts) to stop being directed on sth and to move without much control to other ideas, subjects, etc. SYN **drift**: *It's easy to be distracted and* ***let your attention wander.*** ◇ *Try not to* ***let your mind wander.*** ◇ **~ away, back, to, etc. sth** *Her thoughts wandered back to her youth.* **4** [I] (of a person's eyes) to move slowly from looking at one thing to looking at another thing or in other directions: *She* ***let her gaze wander.*** ◇ **+ adv./prep.** *His eyes wandered towards the photographs on the wall.* **5** [I] **(+ adv./prep.)** (of a road or

W

river) to curve instead of following a straight course: *The road wanders along through the hills.*
■ ***noun*** [sing.] a short walk in or around a place, usually with no special purpose: *I went to the park and had a wander around.*

wan·der·er /ˈwɒndərə(r); *NAmE* ˈwɑːn-/ *noun* a person who keeps travelling from place to place with no permanent home

wan·der·ings /ˈwɒndərɪŋz; *NAmE* ˈwɑːn-/ *noun* [pl.] (*literary*) journeys from place to place, usually with no special purpose

wan·der·lust /ˈwɒndəlʌst; *NAmE* ˈwɑːndərl-/ *noun* [U] (from *German*) a strong desire to travel

wane /weɪn/ *verb, noun*
■ ***verb* 1** [I] to become gradually weaker or less important SYN **decrease, fade**: *Her enthusiasm for the whole idea was waning rapidly.* **2** [I] (of the moon) to appear slightly smaller each day after being round and full OPP **wax**
IDM see WAX *v.*
■ ***noun*** [sing.]
IDM **on the ˈwane** becoming smaller, less important or less common SYN **declining**: *Her popularity has been on the wane for some time.*

wan·gle /ˈwæŋgl/ *verb* (*informal*) to get sth that you or another person wants by persuading sb or by a clever plan: **~ sth** *She had wangled an invitation to the opening night.* ◇ *We should be able to* ***wangle it*** *so that you can start tomorrow.* ◇ *He managed to* ***wangle his way*** *onto the course.* ◇ **~ sth from/out of sb** *I'll try to wangle some money out of my parents.* ◇ **~ sb sth** *He had wangled her a seat on the plane.*

wank /wæŋk/ *verb, noun*
■ ***verb*** [I] (*BrE, taboo, slang*) to MASTURBATE
■ ***noun*** [usually sing.] (*BrE, taboo, slang*) an act of MASTURBATION

wank·er /ˈwæŋkə(r)/ *noun* (*BrE, taboo, slang*) an offensive word used to insult sb, especially a man, and to show anger or dislike: *a bunch of wankers*

wanna /ˈwɒnə; *NAmE* ˈwɔːnə; ˈwɑːnə/ (*informal, nonstandard*) the written form of the word some people use to mean 'want to' or 'want a', which is not considered to be correct: *I wanna go.* ◇ *Wanna drink?* (= Do you want...)
HELP You should not write this form, unless you are copying somebody's speech.

wan·nabe /ˈwɒnəbi; *NAmE* ˈwɑːn-; ˈwɔːn-/ *noun* (*informal, disapproving*) a person who behaves, dresses, etc. like sb famous because they want to be like them

want /wɒnt; *NAmE* wɑːnt; wɔːnt/ *verb, noun*
■ ***verb*** [T] (not usually used in the progressive tenses)
▸ WISH **1** to have a desire or a wish for sth: **~ sth** *Do you want some more tea?* ◇ *She's always wanted a large family.* ◇ ***All I want is*** *the truth.* ◇ *Thanks for the present—it's* ***just what I wanted.*** ◇ *I can do whatever I want.* ◇ ***The last thing I wanted was to*** *upset you.* ◇ *The party wants her as leader.* ◇ **~ (to do sth)** *What do you want to do tomorrow?* ◇ *'It's time you did your homework.' 'I don't want to!'* ◇ *There are two points which I wanted to make.* ◇ ***I just wanted*** *to know if everything was all right.* ◇ (*informal*) *You can come too,* ***if you want.*** ◇ **~ sb/sth to do sth** *Do you want me to help?* ◇ *We didn't want this to happen.* ◇ *I want it (to be) done as quickly as possible.* HELP Notice that you cannot say 'want that...': ~~*I want that you do it quickly.*~~ When the infinitive is used after **want**, it must have **to**: ~~*I want study in America.*~~: **~ sb/sth doing sth** *I don't want you coming home so late.* ◇ **~ sb/sth + adj.** *Do you want your coffee black or white?*
▸ NEED **2** (*informal*) to need sth: **~ sth** *We'll want more furniture for the new office.* ◇ *What this house wants is a good clean.* ◇ **~ doing sth** *The plants want watering daily.* ◇ **~ to be/have sth** *The plants want to be watered daily.* **3** [usually passive] **~ sb (+ adv./prep.)** to need sb to be present in the place or for the purpose mentioned: *She's wanted immediately in the director's office.* ◇ *Excuse me, you're wanted on the phone.* ➲ see also WANTED
▸ SHOULD/OUGHT TO **4 ~ to do sth** (*informal*) used to give advice to sb, meaning 'should' or 'ought to': *If possible, you want to avoid alcohol.* ◇ *He wants to be more careful.* ◇ *You don't want to do it like that.*
▸ FEEL SEXUAL DESIRE **5 ~ sb** to feel sexual desire for sb
▸ LACK **6 ~ sth** (*formal*) to lack sth SYN **be short of**: *He doesn't want courage.*
IDM **not want to ˈknow (about sth)** (*informal*) to take no interest in sth because you do not care about it or it is too much trouble: *I've tried to ask her advice, but she doesn't want to know* (= about my problems). ◇ *'How much was it?'* ***'You don't want to know'*** (= it is better if you don't know). **want ˈrid of sb/sth** (*BrE, informal*) to want to be free of sb/sth that has been annoying you or that you do not want: *Are you trying to say you want rid of me?* **what do you ˈwant?** used to ask sb in a rude or angry way why they are there or what they want you to do ➲ more at NONE *pron.*, PART *n.*, TRUCK *n.*, WASTE *v.*, WAY *n.*
PHR V **ˈwant for sth** (especially in negative sentences) (*formal*) to lack sth that you really need: *He's ensured that his children will* ***want for nothing*** (= will have everything they need). **want sth from/out of sth/sb** to hope to get sth from a particular experience or person: *I had to discover what I really wanted out of life.* ◇ *What do you want from me?* **ˌwant ˈin/ˈout** (*informal, especially NAmE*) to want to come in or out of a place: *The dog wants in.* **ˌwant ˈin** | **ˌwant ˈin/ˈinto sth** (*informal*) to want to be involved in sth: *He wants in on the deal.* **ˌwant ˈout** | **ˌwant ˈout of sth** (*informal*) to want to stop being involved in sth: *Jenny was fed up. She wanted out.*
■ ***noun*** (*formal*)
▸ STH YOU NEED **1** [C, usually pl.] something that you need or want: *She spent her life pandering to the wants of her children.*
▸ LACK **2** [U, sing.] **~ of sth** (*formal*) a situation in which there is not enough of sth; a lack of sth: *a want of adequate medical facilities*
▸ BEING POOR **3** [U] (*formal*) the state of being poor, not having food, etc: *Visitors to the slums were clearly shocked to see so many families living* ***in want.***
IDM **for (the) want of sth** because of a lack of sth; because sth is not available: *The project failed for want of financial backing.* ◇ *We call our music 'postmodern' for the want of a better word.* **in want of sth** (*formal*) needing sth: *The present system is in want of a total review.* **not for (the) want of doing sth** used to say that if sth is not successful, it is not because of a lack of effort: *If he doesn't manage to convince them, it won't be for* ***want of trying*** (= he has tried hard).

> **More About**
>
> **offers and invitations**
>
> - **Would you like...?** is the most usual polite question form for offers and invitations, especially in *BrE*: *Would you like a cup of coffee?*
> - **Do you want...?** is less formal and more direct. It is more common in *NAmE* than in *BrE*: *We're going to a club tonight. Do you want to come with us?*
> - **Would you care...?** is very formal and now sounds old-fashioned.

ˈwant ads *noun* [pl.] (*NAmE*) = CLASSIFIED ADVERTISEMENTS

want·ed /ˈwɒntɪd; *NAmE* ˈwɑːn-/ *adj.* being searched for by the police, in connection with a crime: *He is wanted by the police in connection with the deaths of two people.* ◇ *Italy's most wanted man*

want·ing /ˈwɒntɪŋ; *NAmE* ˈwɑːn-; ˈwɔːn-/ *adj.* [not before noun] (*formal*) **1 ~ (in sth)** not having enough of sth SYN **lacking**: *The students were certainly not wanting in enthusiasm.* **2 ~ (in sth)** not good enough: *This explanation is wanting in many respects.* ◇ *The new system was tried and* ***found wanting.***

wan·ton /ˈwɒntən; *NAmE* ˈwɑːn-/ *adj.* (*formal*) **1** [usually before noun] causing harm or damage deliberately and for

W

Collocations

War and peace

Starting a war

- **declare/make/wage** war (on sb/sth)
- **go to** war (against/with sb)
- **cause/spark/provoke/foment/quell** unrest
- **incite/lead/crush/suppress** a revolt/rebellion
- **launch/mount/carry out** a surprise/terrorist attack
- **prevent/halt/represent** an escalation of the conflict
- **be torn apart by/be on the brink of** civil war
- **enter/invade/occupy** sb's territory
- **lead/launch/resist/repel** an invasion

Military operations

- **adopt/develop/implement/pursue** a military strategy
- **carry out/execute/perform** military operations/ manoeuvres/(*especially US*) maneuvers
- **send/deploy/station/pull back/withdraw** troops
- **go on/fly/carry out** a reconnaissance/rescue mission
- **train/equip/deploy** army/military/combat units
- **lead/launch/conduct** a raid/a surprise attack/an (air/ airborne/amphibious) assault (on sb)
- **employ/use** guerrilla tactics
- **conduct/wage** biological/guerrilla warfare
- **fight/crush/defeat** the rebels/the insurgency
- **suffer/inflict** a crushing defeat
- **achieve/win** a decisive victory
- **halt/stop** the British/German/Russian advance
- **order/force** a retreat

Fighting

- **join/serve in** the army/navy/air force
- **be/go/remain/serve** on active duty
- **serve/complete/return from** a tour of duty
- **be sent** to the front (line)
- **attack/strike/engage/defeat/kill/destroy** the enemy
- **see/report/be engaged in** heavy fighting
- **call for/be met with** armed resistance
- **come under** heavy/machine-gun/mortar fire
- **fire** a machine-gun/mortar shells/rockets (at sb/sth)
- **shoot** a rifle/a pistol/bullets/missiles
- **launch/fire** a cruise/ballistic/anti-tank missile
- **use** biological/chemical/nuclear weapons
- **inflict/suffer/sustain** heavy losses/casualties
- **be hit/killed by** enemy/friendly/artillery fire
- **become/be held as** a prisoner of war

Civilians in war

- **harm/kill/target/protect** innocent/unarmed civilians
- **cause/avoid/limit/minimize** civilian casualties/ collateral damage
- **impose/enforce/lift** a curfew
- **engage in/be a victim of** ethnic cleansing
- **be sent to** an internment/a concentration camp
- **accept/house/resettle** refugees fleeing from war
- **fear/threaten** military/violent reprisals
- **commit/be accused of** war crimes/crimes against humanity/genocide

Making peace

- **make/bring/win/achieve/maintain/promote** peace
- **call for/negotiate/broker/declare** a ceasefire/a temporary truce
- **sign** a ceasefire agreement
- **call for/bring/put an end to** hostilities
- **demand/negotiate/accept** the surrender of sb/sth
- **establish/send (in)** a peacekeeping force
- **negotiate/conclude/ratify/sign/accept/reject/break/ violate** a peace treaty

no acceptable reason: *wanton destruction* ◇ *a wanton disregard for human life* **2** (*old-fashioned, disapproving*) (usually of a woman) behaving in a very immoral way; having many sexual partners ▶ **wan·ton·ly** *adv.* **wan·ton·ness** *noun* [U]

WAP /wæp/ *abbr.* wireless application protocol (a technology that links devices such as mobile phones/cell phones to the Internet): *a WAP-enabled phone*

wap·iti /ˈwɒpɪti; *NAmE* ˈwɑːp-/ *noun* (*pl.* **wap·iti**) (*NAmE* also **elk**) a very large N American DEER ➲ picture at ELK

war 🔑 /wɔː(r)/ *noun*
1 🔑 [U, C] a situation in which two or more countries or groups of people fight against each other over a period of time: *the Second World War* ◇ *the threat of (a) nuclear war* ◇ *to* ***win/lose a/the war*** ◇ *the* ***war between*** *England and Scotland* ◇ *England's* ***war with/against*** *Scotland* ◇ *It was the year Britain* ***declared war on*** *Germany.* ◇ *Social and political problems led to* ***the outbreak*** (= the beginning) ***of war.*** ◇ *Where were you living when* ***war broke out?*** ◇ *The government does not want to* ***go to war*** (= start a war) *unless all other alternatives have failed.* ◇ *How long have they been* ***at war?*** ◇ *a* ***war hero*** ◇ (*formal*) *In the Middle Ages England* ***waged war*** *on France.* ◇ *More troops are being despatched to the* ***war zone.*** ◇ (*formal*) *the* ***theatre of war*** (= the area in which fighting takes place) ➲ see also CIVIL WAR, COLD WAR, COUNCIL OF WAR, PHONEY WAR, POST-WAR, PRISONER OF WAR, WARRING, WORLD WAR **2** 🔑 [C, U] a situation in which there is aggressive competition between groups, companies, countries, etc: *the class war* ◇ *a trade war* ➲ see also PRICE WAR **3** 🔑 [U, sing.] **~ (against/on sb/sth)** a fight or an effort over a long period of time to get rid of or stop sth unpleasant: *The government* ***has declared war on*** *drug dealers.* ◇ *We seem to be winning the war against crime.* ➲ SYNONYMS at CAMPAIGN
IDM **have been in the ˈwars** (*informal*) to have been injured in a fight or an accident: *You look like you've been in the wars—who gave you that black eye?* **a ˌwar of ˈnerves** an attempt to defeat your opponents by putting pressure on them so that they lose courage or confidence **a ˌwar of ˈwords** a bitter argument or disagreement over a period of time between two or more people or groups: *the political war of words over tax* ➲ more at FAIR *adj.*

war·ble /ˈwɔːbl; *NAmE* ˈwɔːrbl/ *verb* **1** [T, I] **~ (sth)** | **+ speech** (*humorous*) to sing, especially in a high voice that is not very steady: *He warbled his way through the song.* **2** [I, T] **~ (sth)** (of a bird) to sing with rapidly changing notes ▶ **war·ble** *noun*

warb·ler /ˈwɔːblə(r); *NAmE* ˈwɔːrb-/ *noun* a small bird. There are many types of warbler, some of which have a musical call.

war·chalk·ing /ˈwɔːtʃɔːkɪŋ; *NAmE* ˈwɔːr-/ *noun* [U] (*informal*) the action of drawing a symbol on the wall of a building to show that you can get a free Internet connection near that place

ˈwar chest *noun* an amount of money that a government or an organization has available to spend on a particular plan, project, etc.

ˈwar crime *noun* a cruel act that is committed during a war and is against the international rules of war

ˈwar criminal *noun* a person who has committed war crimes

ˈwar cry *noun* a word or phrase that is shouted by people fighting in a battle in order to give themselves courage and to frighten the enemy

ward /wɔːd; *NAmE* wɔːrd/ *noun, verb*
■ ***noun*** **1** a separate room or area in a hospital for people with the same type of medical condition: *a* ***maternity/surgical/psychiatric/children's, etc. ward*** ◇ *He worked as a nurse* ***on the children's ward.*** **2** (in Britain) one of the areas into which a city is divided and which elects and is represented by a member of the local council **3** (*law*) a person, especially a child, who is under the legal protection of

W

a court or another person (called a GUARDIAN): *The child was made a **ward of court**.*

■ *verb*

PHR V ˌward sb/sth↔ˈoff to protect or defend yourself against danger, illness, attack, etc: *to ward off criticism* ◇ *She put up her hands to ward him off.*

-ward (also *less frequent* **-wards**) *suffix* (in adjectives) in the direction of: *backward* ◇ *eastward* ◇ *homeward* ▸ **-wards** (also **-ward** especially in *NAmE*) (in adverbs): *onwards* ◇ *forwards*

ˈwar dance *noun* a dance that is performed by members of some peoples, for example before battle or to celebrate a victory

war·den /ˈwɔːdn; *NAmE* ˈwɔːrdn/ *noun* **1** a person who is responsible for taking care of a particular place and making sure that the rules are obeyed: *a forest warden* ◇ (*BrE*) *the warden of a youth hostel* ➲ see also CHURCHWARDEN, DOG WARDEN, GAME WARDEN, TRAFFIC WARDEN **2** (*especially NAmE*) the person in charge of a prison **3** (in Britain), a title given to the head of some colleges and institutions: *the Warden of Wadham College, Oxford*

war·der /ˈwɔːdə(r); *NAmE* ˈwɔːrd-/ (*feminine* **ward·ress** /ˈwɔːdrəs; *NAmE* ˈwɔːrd-/) *noun* (*BrE*) a person who guards prisoners in a prison ➲ compare GUARD *n.* (1)

ward·robe /ˈwɔːdrəʊb; *NAmE* ˈwɔːrdroʊb/ *noun* **1** a large cupboard for hanging clothes in which is either a piece of furniture or (in British English) built into the wall: *a fitted wardrobe* ➲ VISUAL VOCAB page V20 ➲ compare CLOSET **2** [usually sing.] the clothes that a person has: *everything you need for your summer wardrobe* ➲ COLLOCATIONS at FASHION **3** [usually sing.] the department in a theatre or television company that takes care of the clothes that actors wear

ˈwardrobe mistress, **ˈwardrobe master** *noun* a person whose job is to take care of the clothes that the actors in a theatre company, etc. wear on stage

ward·room /ˈwɔːdruːm; -rʊm; *NAmE* ˈwɔːrd-/ *noun* a room in a ship, especially a WARSHIP, where the officers live and eat

-wards ➲ -WARD

ward·ship /ˈwɔːdʃɪp; *NAmE* ˈwɔːrd-/ *noun* [U] (*law*) the fact of a child being cared for by a GUARDIAN (= a person who is not his or her parent) or of being protected by a court ➲ see also WARD *n.* (3)

ware /weə(r); *NAmE* wer/ *noun* **1** [U] (in compounds) objects made of the material or in the way or place mentioned: *ceramic ware* ◇ *a collection of local ware* ◇ *basketware* ➲ see also EARTHENWARE, FLATWARE, GLASSWARE, SILVERWARE **2** [U] (in compounds) objects used for the purpose or in the room mentioned: *bathroom ware* ◇ *ornamental ware* ◇ *homeware* ➲ see also KITCHENWARE, TABLEWARE **3 wares** [pl.] (*old-fashioned*) things that sb is selling, especially in the street or at a market: *He travelled from town to town selling his wares.*

ware·house /ˈweəhaʊs; *NAmE* ˈwerh-/ *noun* a building where large quantities of goods are stored, especially before they are sent to shops/stores to be sold ➲ VISUAL VOCAB page V13

W

ware·hous·ing /ˈweəhaʊzɪŋ; *NAmE* ˈwerh-/ *noun* [U] the practice or business of storing things in a warehouse

war·fare /ˈwɔːfeə(r); *NAmE* ˈwɔːrfer/ *noun* [U] **1** the activity of fighting a war, especially using particular weapons or methods: ***air/naval/guerrilla, etc. warfare*** ◇ *countries engaged in warfare* ➲ COLLOCATIONS at WAR ➲ see also BIOLOGICAL WARFARE, CHEMICAL WARFARE, GERM WARFARE **2** the activity of competing in an aggressive way with another group, company, etc: ***class/gang warfare*** ◇ *The debate soon degenerated into open warfare.* ➲ see also PSYCHOLOGICAL WARFARE

war·farin /ˈwɔːfərɪn; *NAmE* ˈwɔːrf-/ *noun* [U] a substance that is used as a poison to kill RATS and also for people as a medicine to make the blood thinner, for example in the treatment of THROMBOSIS

ˈwar game *noun* **1** a practice battle that is used to test military plans and equipment **2** a game or activity in which imaginary battles are fought, for example by moving models of soldiers, ships, etc. around on a table, or on a computer

ˈwar gaming *noun* [U] the activity of playing war games (2)

war·head /ˈwɔːhed; *NAmE* ˈwɔːrhed/ *noun* the EXPLOSIVE part of a MISSILE: *nuclear warheads*

war·horse /ˈwɔːhɔːs; *NAmE* ˈwɔːrhɔːrs/ *noun* **1** (in the past) a large horse used in battle **2** (*informal*) an old soldier or politician who has a lot of experience

wari·ly, wari·ness ➲ WARY

war·like /ˈwɔːlaɪk; *NAmE* ˈwɔːrl-/ *adj.* (*formal*) **1** aggressive and wanting to fight SYN **belligerent**: *a warlike nation* **2** connected with fighting wars SYN **military**: *warlike preparations*

war·lock /ˈwɔːlɒk; *NAmE* ˈwɔːrlɑːk/ *noun* a man who is believed to have magic powers, especially evil ones

war·lord /ˈwɔːlɔːd; *NAmE* ˈwɔːrlɔːrd/ *noun* (*disapproving*) the leader of a military group that is not official and that fights against other groups within a country or an area

warm 0━ /wɔːm; *NAmE* wɔːrm/ *adj., verb, noun, adv.*

■ *adj.* (**warm·er, warm·est**)

▸ AT PLEASANT TEMPERATURE **1** 0━ at a fairly high temperature in a way that is pleasant, rather than being hot or cold: *a warm breeze* ◇ *Wash the blouse in warm soapy water.* ◇ *It's **nice and warm** in here.* ◇ *Are you warm enough?* ◇ *The children jumped up and down to **keep warm**.* ◇ *You'll be as **warm as toast** in here.*

▸ CLOTHES/BUILDINGS **2** 0━ keeping you warm or staying warm in cold weather: *a warm pair of socks* ◇ *This sleeping bag is very warm.* ◇ *a warm house*

▸ FRIENDLY **3** 0━ showing enthusiasm and/or affection; friendly: *His smile was warm and friendly.* ◇ *The speaker was given **a warm welcome/reception**.* ◇ *Please send her my warmest congratulations.*

▸ COLOURS **4** (of colours) containing red, orange or yellow, which creates a pleasant, comfortable and relaxed feeling or atmosphere: *The room was decorated in warm shades of red and orange.*

▸ IN GAME **5** [not before noun] used to say that sb has almost guessed the answer to sth or that they have almost found sb/sth that has been hidden: *Keep guessing—you're getting warmer.*

▸ **warm·ly** *adv.*: *They were warmly dressed in coats and scarves.* ◇ *The play was warmly received by the critics.* ➲ see also WARMTH

■ *verb*

▸ MAKE/BECOME WARM **1** 0━ [T, I] to make sth/sb warm or warmer; to become warm or warmer: **~ sth/sb/yourself (up)** *I'll warm up some milk.* ◇ *Come in and warm yourself by the fire.* ◇ *The alcohol warmed and relaxed him.* ◇ **~ (up)** *As the climate warms (up) the ice caps will melt.*

▸ BECOME FRIENDLY **2** [I, T] **~ (sb)** to become more friendly, loving, etc; to make sb feel or become more friendly, loving, etc. ➲ see also GLOBAL WARMING, HOUSE-WARMING

IDM **warm the ˈcockles (of sb's ˈheart)** (*BrE*) to make sb feel happy or sympathetic ➲ more at DEATH

PHR V ˌ**warm ˈdown** to do gentle exercises to help your body relax after doing a particular sport or activity ➲ related noun WARM-DOWN **ˈwarm to/towards sb** to begin to like sb: *I warmed to her immediately.* **ˈwarm to/towards sth** to become more interested in or enthusiastic about sth: *The speaker was now warming to her theme.* ˌ**warm ˈup 1** 0━ to prepare for physical exercise or a performance by doing gentle exercises or practice ➲ related noun WARM-UP **2** 0━ (of a machine, an engine, etc.) to run for a short time in order to reach the temperature at which it will operate well ˌ**warm ˈup** | ˌ**warm sb/sth↔ˈup** to become more lively or enthusiastic; to make sb/sth more lively or enthusiastic: *The party soon warmed up.* ˌ**warm sth↔ˈup** 0━ to heat previously cooked food again for eating

■ *noun*

▸ PLACE **the warm** [sing.] a place where the temperature is warm: *Come inside into the warm.*

■ ***adv.*** (warm·er, warm·est) (*informal*) in a way that makes you feel warm SYN **warmly**: ***Wrap up warm*** *before you go outside!*

ˌ**warm-ˈblooded** *adj.* (of animals) having a warm blood temperature that does not change if the temperature around them changes ➲ compare COLD-BLOODED, HOT-BLOODED

ˈ**warm-down** *noun* [usually sing.] a series of gentle exercises that you do to help your body relax after doing a particular sport or activity

warm·er /ˈwɔːmə(r); *NAmE* ˈwɔːrm-/ *noun* (especially in compounds) a piece of clothing, a device, etc. that warms sb/sth: *a plate warmer* ➲ see also LEG WARMER

ˌ**warm-ˈhearted** *adj.* (of a person) kind, friendly and sympathetic ➲ compare COLD-HEARTED

warm·ing /ˈwɔːmɪŋ; *NAmE* ˈwɔːrmɪŋ/ *noun* [U] the process of making sth, or of becoming, warm or warmer: *atmospheric warming* ➲ see also GLOBAL WARMING ▸ **warm·ing** *adj.*: *the warming rays of the sun* ◇ *a warming drink*

ˈ**warming pan** *noun* a metal container with a long handle that, in the past, was filled with hot coals and used to warm beds

war·mon·ger /ˈwɔːmʌŋɡə(r); *NAmE* ˈwɔːrm-/ *noun* (*formal, disapproving*) a person, especially a politician or leader, who wants to start a war or encourages people to start a war ▸ **war·mon·ger·ing** *noun* [U] **war·mon·ger·ing** *adj.* [only before noun]

warmth 🔑 /wɔːmθ; *NAmE* wɔːrmθ/ *noun* [U]
1 🔑 the state or quality of being warm, rather than hot or cold: *She felt the warmth of his arms around her.* ◇ *The animals huddled together for warmth.* ◇ *He led the child into the warmth and safety of the house.* **2** 🔑 the state or quality of being enthusiastic and/or friendly: *They were touched by the warmth of the welcome.*

ˈ**warm-up** *noun* [usually sing.] **1** a short practice or a series of gentle exercises that you do to prepare yourself for doing a particular sport or activity: *warm-up exercises* **2** a short performance of music, comedy, etc. that is intended to prepare the audience for the main show: *a warm-up act*

warn 🔑 /wɔːn; *NAmE* wɔːrn/ *verb*
1 🔑 [T, I] to tell sb about sth, especially sth dangerous or unpleasant that is likely to happen, so that they can avoid it: **~ sb** *I tried to warn him, but he wouldn't listen.* ◇ *If you're thinking of getting a dog,* ***be warned****—they take a lot of time and money.* ◇ **~ (sb) about/against sb/sth** *He warned us against pickpockets.* ◇ **~ (sb) of sth** *Police have warned of possible delays.* ◇ **~ (sb) that...** *She was warned that if she did it again she would lose her job.* ◇ **~ sb what, how, etc...** *I had been warned what to expect.* ◇ **~ (sb) + speech** *'Beware of pickpockets,' she warned (him).* **2** 🔑 [I, T] to strongly advise sb to do or not to do sth in order to avoid danger or punishment SYN **advise**: **~ (sb) against/about sth** *The guidebook warns against walking alone at night.* ◇ **~ sb (to do sth)** *He warned Billy to keep away from his daughter.* **3** [T] **~ sb (for sth)** (in sport, etc.) to give sb an official warning after they have broken a rule: *The referee warned him for dangerous play.*
PHR V ˌ**warn sb ˈoff (sth) 1** to tell sb to leave or stay away from a place or person, especially in a threatening way: *The farmer warned us off his land when we tried to camp there.* **2** to advise sb not to do sth or to stop doing sth: **~ doing sth** *We were warned off buying the house.*

warn·ing 🔑 /ˈwɔːnɪŋ; *NAmE* ˈwɔːrn-/ *noun*
1 🔑 [C, U] a statement, an event, etc. telling sb that sth bad or unpleasant may happen in the future so that they can try to avoid it: *Doctors* ***issued a warning against*** *eating any fish caught in the river.* ◇ *to give sb* ***fair/advance/adequate warning*** *of sth* ◇ *The bridge collapsed* ***without (any) warning.*** ◇ *Let me give you* ***a word of warning.*** ◇ *a government* ***health warning*** ➲ see also EARLY WARNING **2** 🔑 [C] a statement telling sb that they will be punished if they continue to behave in a particular way SYN **caution**: *to give sb a* ***verbal/written/final warning*** ▸ **warn·ing** *adj.* [only before noun]: *She had ignored the* ***warning signs*** *of trouble ahead.* ◇ *Police fired a number of* ***warning shots.*** ◇ ***Warning bells began to ring*** (= it was a sign that sth was wrong) *when her letters were returned unopened.*

ˌ**warning ˈtriangle** *noun* a red triangle that a driver puts on the road next to his or her car as a warning to other drivers when the car has stopped because of a fault, an accident, etc.

warp /wɔːp; *NAmE* wɔːrp/ *verb, noun*
■ ***verb* 1** [I, T] **~ (sth)** to become, or make sth become, twisted or bent out of its natural shape, for example because it has become too hot, too damp, etc: *The window frames had begun to warp.* **2** [T] **~ sth** to influence sb so that they begin to behave in an unacceptable or shocking way: *His judgement was warped by prejudice.*
■ ***noun* the warp** [sing.] (*technical*) the threads on a LOOM (= a machine used for making cloth) that other threads are passed over and under in order to make cloth ➲ compare WEFT ➲ see also TIME WARP

war·paint /ˈwɔːpeɪnt; *NAmE* ˈwɔːrp-/ *noun* [U] **1** paint that some peoples, for example Native American peoples, put on their bodies and faces before fighting a battle **2** (*informal, humorous*) make-up, especially when it is thick or bright

war·path /ˈwɔːpɑːθ; *NAmE* ˈwɔːrpæθ/ *noun*
IDM **(be/go) on the ˈwarpath** (*informal*) (to be) angry and wanting to fight or punish sb

warped /wɔːpt; *NAmE* wɔːrpt/ *adj.* **1** (*disapproving*) (of a person) having ideas that most people think are strange or unpleasant: *a warped mind* ◇ *a warped sense of humour* **2** bent or twisted and not in the normal shape

war·plane /ˈwɔːpleɪn; *NAmE* ˈwɔːrp-/ *noun* a military plane that is designed for fighting in the air or dropping bombs

ˈ**warp speed** *noun* [sing.] (*informal, humorous*) a very fast speed ORIGIN From the US television series *Star Trek*, in which a 'warp drive' allowed space travel at speeds faster than the speed of light.

war·rant /ˈwɒrənt; *NAmE* ˈwɔːr-; ˈwɑːr-/ *noun, verb*
■ ***noun* 1** [C] a legal document that is signed by a judge and gives the police authority to do sth: *an arrest warrant* ◇ **~ for sth** *They* ***issued a warrant*** *for her arrest.* ◇ **~ to do sth** *They had a warrant to search the house.* ➲ see also DEATH WARRANT, SEARCH WARRANT **2** [C] **~ (for sth)** a document that gives you the right to receive money, services, etc. **3** [U] **~ (for sth/for doing sth)** (*formal*) (usually in negative sentences) an acceptable reason for doing sth: *There is no warrant for such criticism.*
■ ***verb*** (*formal*) to make sth necessary or appropriate in a particular situation SYN **justify**: **~ sth** *Further investigation is clearly warranted.* ◇ **~ (sb/sth) doing sth** *The situation scarcely warrants their/them being dismissed.* ➲ see also UNWARRANTED
IDM **I/I'll warrant (you)** (*old-fashioned*) used to tell sb that you are sure of sth and that they can be sure of it too

ˈ**warrant officer** *noun* a member of one of the middle ranks in the army, the British AIR FORCE and the US navy: *Warrant Officer Gary Owen*

war·ranty /ˈwɒrənti; *NAmE* ˈwɔːr-; ˈwɑːr-/ *noun* (*pl.* -ies) [C, U] a written agreement in which a company selling sth promises to repair or replace it if there is a problem within a particular period of time SYN **guarantee**: *The television comes with a full two-year warranty.* ◇ *Is the car still* ***under warranty?***

war·ren /ˈwɒrən; *NAmE* ˈwɔːr-; ˈwɑːr-/ *noun* = RABBIT WARREN: (*figurative*) *The offices were a warren of small rooms and passages.*

war·ring /ˈwɔːrɪŋ/ *adj.* [only before noun] involved in a war: *A ceasefire has been agreed by the country's three warring factions.*

war·rior /ˈwɒriə(r); *NAmE* ˈwɔːr-/ *noun* (*formal*) (especially in the past) a person who fights in a battle or war: *a warrior nation* (= whose people are skilled in fighting) ◇ *a Zulu warrior*

W

war·ship /ˈwɔːʃɪp; *NAmE* ˈwɔːrʃɪp/ *noun* a ship used in war

wart /wɔːt; *NAmE* wɔːrt/ *noun* **1** a small hard lump that grows on your skin and that is caused by a virus **2** (*NAmE*) = VERRUCA

IDM ˌ**warts and ˈall** (*informal*) including all the bad or unpleasant features of sb/sth: *She still loves him, warts and all.*

wart·hog /ˈwɔːthɒg; *NAmE* ˈwɔːrthɑːg/ *noun* an African wild pig with two large outer teeth called TUSKS and lumps like warts on its face

war·time /ˈwɔːtaɪm; *NAmE* ˈwɔːrt-/ *noun* [U] the period during which a country is fighting a war: *Different rules applied in wartime.* ▸ **war·time** *adj.* [only before noun]: *Fruit was a luxury in wartime Britain.* ⊃ compare PEACETIME

ˈ**war-torn** *adj.* [only before noun] a **war-torn** country or area is severely affected by the fighting that is taking place there

warty /ˈwɔːti; *NAmE* ˈwɔːrti/ *adj.* covered with WARTS

ˈ**war widow** *noun* a woman whose husband was killed in a war

wary /ˈweəri; *NAmE* ˈweri/ *adj.* (*comparative* **wari·er**, no *superlative*) careful when dealing with sb/sth because you think that there may be a danger or problem SYN **cautious**: **~ (of sb/sth)** *Be wary of strangers who offer you a ride.* ◇ **~ (of doing sth)** *She was wary of getting involved with him.* ◇ *He gave her a wary look.* ◇ *The police will need to* **keep a wary eye on** *this area of town* (= watch it carefully, in case there is trouble). ⊃ compare UNWARY ▸ **wari·ly** /-rəli/ *adv.*: *The cat eyed him warily.* **wari·ness** *noun* [U]: *feelings of wariness* ◇ *There was a wariness in her tone.*

was /wəz; *strong form* wɒz; *NAmE* wʌz/ ⊃ BE

was·abi /wəˈsɑːbi/ *noun* [U] (from *Japanese*) a root vegetable with a strong taste like HORSERADISH, used in Japanese cooking, especially with raw fish

wash 🔑 /wɒʃ; *NAmE* wɑːʃ; wɔːʃ/ *verb, noun*

■ *verb* **1** 🔑 [T] to make sth/sb clean using water and usually soap: **~ sth/sb** *These jeans need washing.* ◇ *to wash the car* ◇ *to wash your hands* ◇ *Wash the fruit thoroughly before eating.* ◇ **~ sth from sth** *She washed the blood from his face.* ◇ **~ sth/sb + adj.** *The beach had been washed clean by the tide.* ⊃ SYNONYMS at CLEAN **2** 🔑 [I, T] (*especially BrE*) to make yourself clean using water and usually soap: *I washed and changed before going out.* ◇ **~ yourself** *She was no longer able to wash herself.* **3** [I] (**+ adv./prep.**) (of clothes, cloth, etc.) to be able to be washed without losing colour or being damaged: *This sweater washes well.* **4** [I, T] (of water) to flow or carry sth/sb in a particular direction: **+ adv./prep.** *Water washed over the deck.* ◇ **~ sth/sb + adv./prep.** *Pieces of the wreckage were* **washed ashore**. ◇ *He was* **washed overboard** *by a huge wave.*

IDM **wash your dirty linen in ˈpublic** (*BrE, disapproving*) to discuss your personal affairs in public, especially sth embarrassing **wash your ˈhands of sb/sth** to refuse to be responsible for or involved with sb/sth: *When her son was arrested again she washed her hands of him.* **sth won't/doesn't ˈwash (with sb)** used to say that sb's explanation, excuse, etc. is not valid or that you/sb else will not accept it: *That excuse simply won't wash with me.*

PHR V ˌ**wash sb/sth↔aˈway** 🔑 (of water) to remove or carry sb/sth away to another place: *Part of the path had been washed away by the sea.* ˌ**wash sth↔ˈdown (with sth)** **1** to clean sth large or a surface with a lot of water: *Wash down the walls before painting them.* **2** to drink sth after, or at the same time as, eating sth: *For lunch we had bread and cheese, washed down with beer.* ˌ**wash ˈoff** 🔑 to be removed from the surface of sth or from clothes by washing: *Those grease stains won't wash off.* ˌ**wash sth↔ˈoff (sth)** 🔑 to remove sth from the surface of sth or from clothes by washing: *Wash that mud off your boots before you come in.* ˌ**wash ˈout** 🔑 (of a dirty mark) to be removed from clothes by washing: *These ink stains won't wash out.* ˌ**wash sth↔ˈout 1** 🔑 to wash the inside of sth to remove dirt, etc: *to wash out empty bottles* **2** to remove a substance from sth by washing: *Wash the dye out with shampoo.* **3** (of rain) to make a game, an event, etc. end early or prevent it from starting: *The game was completely washed out.* ⊃ related noun WASHOUT ˌ**wash ˈover sb 1** (also ˌ**wash ˈthrough sb**) (*literary*) (of a feeling) to suddenly affect sb strongly, so that they are not aware of anything else: *Waves of nausea washed over him.* **2** to happen to or around sb without affecting them: *She manages to let criticism just wash over her.* ˌ**wash ˈup 1** 🔑 (*BrE*) (also **do the dishes** *NAmE, BrE*) to wash plates, glasses, etc. after a meal ⊃ related noun WASHING-UP **2** 🔑 (*NAmE*) to wash your face and hands: *Go and get washed up.* ˌ**wash sth↔ˈup 1** (*BrE*) to wash dishes after a meal: *I didn't wash up the pans.* **2** (of water) to carry sth onto land: *The body was found washed up on a beach.*

■ *noun* **1** [C, usually sing.] (*especially BrE*) an act of cleaning sb/sth using water and usually soap: *These towels are ready for a wash.* ◇ *I'll just* **have a** *quick* **wash** *before dinner.* ◇ *I'm doing a dark wash* (= washing all the dark clothes together). ◇ *Your shirt's* **in the wash** (= being washed or waiting to be washed). ◇ *My sweater shrank in the wash.* ◇ *That blouse shouldn't look like that after only two washes.* ⊃ see also CAR WASH **2 the wash** [sing.] an area of water that has waves and is moving a lot, especially after a boat has moved through it; the sound made by this: *The dinghy was rocked by the wash of a passing ferry.* ◇ *They listened to the wash of waves on the beach.* **3** [C] a thin layer of a liquid, especially paint, that is put on a surface: *The walls were covered with a pale yellow wash.* ⊃ see also WHITEWASH **4** [C, U] a liquid containing soap, used for cleaning your skin: *an antiseptic skin wash* ⊃ see also MOUTHWASH

IDM **it will (all) come out in the ˈwash** (*informal*) **1** used to say that the truth about a situation will be made known at some time in the future **2** used to make sb less anxious by telling them that any problems or difficulties will be solved in the future

wash·able /ˈwɒʃəbl; *NAmE* ˈwɑːʃ-; ˈwɔːʃ-/ *adj.* that can be washed without being damaged: *machine washable* (= that can be washed in a washing machine)

wash·bag /ˈwɒʃbæg; *NAmE* ˈwɔːʃ-; ˈwɑːʃ-/ *noun* (*BrE*) = SPONGE BAG

wash·basin /ˈwɒʃbeɪsn; *NAmE* ˈwɑːʃ-; ˈwɔːʃ-/ (also **basin**) (both *especially BrE*) (also **sink** *NAmE, BrE*) (*NAmE* also **wash·bowl**) *noun* a large bowl that has taps/faucets and is fixed to the wall in a bathroom, used for washing your hands and face in ⊃ VISUAL VOCAB page V21

wash·board /ˈwɒʃbɔːd; *NAmE* ˈwɑːʃbɔːrd; ˈwɔːʃ-/ *noun* a board with a surface with RIDGES on it, used in the past for rubbing clothes on when washing them; a similar board played as a musical instrument

wash·cloth /ˈwɒʃklɒθ; *NAmE* ˈwɑːʃklɔːθ; ˈwɔːʃ-/ (*NAmE*) (*BrE* **flan·nel, face·cloth**) *noun* a small piece of cloth used for washing yourself

wash·day /ˈwɒʃdeɪ; *NAmE* ˈwɑːʃ-; ˈwɔːʃ-/ (also ˈ**washing day**) *noun* the day in sb's house when the clothes, etc. are washed, especially when this happens on the same day each week

ˌ**washed ˈout** *adj.* **1** (of cloth, clothes or colours) no longer brightly coloured, often as a result of frequent washing: *She didn't like jeans that looked too washed out.* ◇ *a pair of washed-out old jeans* ◇ *The walls were a washed-out blue colour.* **2** (of a person) pale and tired SYN **exhausted**: *He always looks washed out at the end of the week.*

ˌ**washed ˈup** *adj.* (*informal*) no longer successful and unlikely to succeed again in the future: *Her singing career was all washed up by the time she was 27.*

wash·er /ˈwɒʃə(r); *NAmE* ˈwɑːʃ-; ˈwɔːʃ-/ *noun* **1** a small flat ring made of rubber, metal or plastic placed between two surfaces, for example under a NUT (2) to make a connection tight ⊃ VISUAL VOCAB page V17 **2** (*informal*) a WASHING MACHINE ⊃ see also DISHWASHER

ˌ**washer-ˈdryer** *noun* an electric machine that washes and dries clothes, etc.

ˌ**washer-ˈup** *noun* (*BrE, informal*) a person who washes dishes

wash·er·wom·an /ˈwɒʃəwʊmən; *NAmE* ˈwɑːʃər-; ˈwɔːʃər-/ *noun* (*pl.* **-women** /-wɪmɪn/) a woman in the past whose job was to wash clothes, etc. for other people

wash·ing 🔑 /ˈwɒʃɪŋ; *NAmE* ˈwɑːʃ-; ˈwɔːʃ-/ *noun* [U] **1** 🔑 the act of cleaning sth using water and usually soap: *a gentle shampoo for frequent washing* ◇ *I* ***do the washing*** (= wash the clothes) *in our house.* ➲ see also BRAINWASHING **2** 🔑 (*BrE*) clothes, sheets, etc. that are waiting to be washed, being washed or have just been washed: *a pile of dirty washing* ◇ *Would you* ***hang the washing out*** (= hang it outside to dry)?

ˈ**washing day** *noun* = WASHDAY

ˈ**washing line** *noun* (*BrE*) = CLOTHES LINE

ˈ**washing machine** *noun* an electric machine for washing clothes

ˈ**washing powder** *noun* [U] (*BrE*) soap or DETERGENT in the form of powder for washing clothes

ˈ**washing soda** *noun* [U] = SODIUM CARBONATE

ˌ**washing-ˈup** (*BrE*) *noun* [U] **1** the act of washing plates, glasses, pans, etc. after a meal: *If you cook, I'll* ***do the washing-up.*** ◇ *a washing-up bowl* **2** the dirty plates, glasses, pans, etc. that have to be washed after a meal: *The sink was still full of last night's washing-up.*

washing-ˈup liquid *noun* [U] (*BrE*) liquid soap for washing dishes, pans, etc.

wash·out /ˈwɒʃaʊt; *NAmE* ˈwɑːʃ-; ˈwɔːʃ-/ *noun* (*informal*) an event, etc. that is a complete failure, especially because of rain

wash·room /ˈwɒʃruːm; -rʊm; *NAmE* ˈwɑːʃ-; ˈwɔːʃ-/ *noun* (*old-fashioned, NAmE*) a toilet/bathroom, especially one that is in a public building

wash·stand /ˈwɒʃstænd; *NAmE* ˈwɑːʃ-; ˈwɔːʃ-/ *noun* (especially in the past) a special table in a bedroom that holds a BASIN for washing yourself in

wash·tub /ˈwɒʃtʌb; *NAmE* ˈwɑːʃ-; ˈwɔːʃ-/ *noun* (in the past) a large metal container for washing clothes, etc. in

wasn't /ˈwɒznt; *NAmE* also ˈwʌznt/ ➲ BE

Wasp /wɒsp; *NAmE* wɑːsp/ (also **WASP**) *noun* (*especially NAmE*, usually *disapproving*) the abbreviation for 'White Anglo-Saxon Protestant' (a white American whose family originally came from northern Europe and is therefore thought to be from the most powerful section of society): *a privileged Wasp background*

wasp /wɒsp; *NAmE* wɑːsp/ *noun* a black and yellow flying insect that can sting: *a wasp sting* ◇ *a wasps' nest* ➲ VISUAL VOCAB page V11

wasp·ish /ˈwɒspɪʃ; *NAmE* ˈwɑːs-/ *adj.* (*formal*) bad-tempered and unpleasant SYN **irritable** ▸ **wasp·ish·ly** *adv.*

was·sail /ˈwɒseɪl; *NAmE* ˈwɑːs-/ *verb* (*old use*) **1** [I] to enjoy yourself by drinking alcohol with others **2** [I] to go from house to house at Christmas time singing CAROLS ▸ **was·sail·er** *noun*

wast·age /ˈweɪstɪdʒ/ *noun* **1** [U, sing.] **~ (of sth)** the fact of losing or destroying sth, especially because it has been used or dealt with carelessly: *It was a new production technique aimed at minimizing wastage.* **2** [U] the amount of sth that is wasted: *There is little wastage from a lean cut of meat.* **3** [U] (*BrE*) the loss of employees because they stop working or move to other jobs; the number of students who do not finish a particular course of study: *Half of the posts will be lost through* ***natural wastage.*** ◇ *student wastage rates*

waste 🔑 /weɪst/ *verb, noun, adj.*

■ ***verb***

▸ NOT USE WELL **1** 🔑 to use more of sth than is necessary or useful: **~ sth** *to waste time/food/energy* ◇ **~ sth on sth** *Why waste money on clothes you don't need?* ◇ **~ sth (in) doing sth** *She* ***wasted no time*** *in rejecting the offer* (= she rejected it immediately). ◇ *You're* ***wasting your time*** *trying to explain it to him* (= because he will not understand). **2 ~ sth (on sb/sth)** to give, say, use, etc. sth good where it is not valued or used in the way that it should be: *Don't waste your sympathy on him—he got what he deserved.* ◇ *Her comments were not wasted on Chris* (= he understood what she meant). **3** 🔑 [usually passive] to not make good or full use of sb/sth: **~ sb/sth** *It was a wasted opportunity.* ◇ **~ sb/sth as sth** *You're wasted as a sales manager—you should have been an actor.*

▸ KILL SB **4 ~ sb** (*informal, especially NAmE*) to get rid of sb, usually by killing them

▸ DEFEAT SB **5 ~ sb** (*NAmE, informal*) to defeat sb very badly in a game or competition

IDM **waste your ˈbreath** to say sth that nobody takes any notice of ˌ**waste not, ˈwant not** (*saying*) if you never waste anything, especially food or money, you will always have it when you need it

PHR V ˌ**waste aˈway** (of a person) to become thin and weak, especially because of illness SYN **become emaciated**

■ ***noun***

▸ NOT GOOD USE **1** 🔑 [U, sing.] **~ (of sth)** the act of using sth in a careless or unnecessary way, causing it to be lost or destroyed: *I hate unnecessary waste.* ◇ *It seems such a waste to throw good food away.* ◇ *I hate to see good food* ***go to waste*** (= be thrown away). ◇ *The report is critical of the department's waste of resources.* ◇ *What a waste of paper!* **2** 🔑 [sing.] a situation in which it is not worth spending time, money, etc. on sth: *These meetings are a complete* ***waste of time.*** ◇ *They believe the statue is a waste of taxpayers' money.*

▸ MATERIALS **3** 🔑 [U] (also **wastes** [pl.]) materials that are no longer needed and are thrown away: ***household/industrial waste*** ◇ *toxic wastes* ◇ ***waste disposal*** (= the process of getting rid of waste) **4** (also ˌ**waste ˈmatter**) [U] material that the body gets rid of as solid or liquid material: *The farmers use both animal and human waste as fertilizer.*

▸ LAND **5 wastes** [pl.] (*formal*) a large area of land where there are very few people, animals or plants: *the frozen wastes of Siberia*

IDM **a waste of ˈspace** (*informal*) a person who is useless or no good at anything

■ ***adj.*** [usually before noun]

▸ LAND **1** 🔑 not suitable for building or growing things on and therefore not used SYN **derelict**: *The car was found on a piece of waste ground.*

▸ MATERIALS **2** 🔑 no longer needed for a particular process and therefore thrown away: *waste plastic*

IDM **lay sth ˈwaste | lay ˈwaste (to) sth** (*formal*) to destroy a place completely

waste·bas·ket /ˈweɪstbɑːskɪt; *NAmE* -bæs-/ (*NAmE*) (*BrE* ˌ**waste-ˈpaper basket**) *noun* a BASKET or other container for waste paper, etc. ➲ picture at BASKET ➲ VISUAL VOCAB pages V18, V56

ˈ**waste bin** *noun* (*BrE*) a container that you put rubbish/garbage in

wasted /ˈweɪstɪd/ *adj.* **1** [only before noun] (of an action) unsuccessful because it does not produce the result you wanted: *We had a wasted trip—they weren't in.* **2** too thin, especially because of illness: *thin wasted legs* **3** (*slang*) strongly affected by alcohol or drugs

ˈ**waste-disposal unit** (also ˈ**waste disposer**) *noun* (*NAmE* usually ˈ**garbage dis·posal, dis·posal**) a machine connected to the waste pipe of a kitchen SINK, for cutting food waste into small pieces

waste·ful /ˈweɪstfl/ *adj.* using more of sth than is necessary; not saving or keeping sth that could be used: *The whole process is wasteful and inefficient.* ◇ **~ of sth** *an engine that is wasteful of fuel* ▸ **waste·ful·ly** /-fəli/ *adv.* **waste·ful·ness** *noun* [U]

waste·land /ˈweɪstlænd/ *noun* [C, U] an area of land that cannot be used or that is no longer used for building or growing things on: *industrial wasteland* ◇ *the desert wastelands of Arizona* ◇ (*figurative*) *The mid 1970s are seen as a cultural wasteland for rock music.*

ˌ**waste ˈpaper** *noun* [U] paper that is not wanted and is thrown away

W

ˌwaste-ˈpaper basket (*BrE*) (*NAmE* **waste·basket**) *noun* a BASKET or other container for waste paper, etc. ➲ picture at BASKET ➲ VISUAL VOCAB pages V18, V56

ˈwaste product *noun* a useless material or substance produced while making sth else

waster /ˈweɪstə(r)/ *noun* **1** (often in compounds) a person or thing that uses too much of sth in an unnecessary way: *He's a time-waster.* **2** (*informal, disapproving*) a person who is useless or no good at anything

waste·water /ˈweɪstwɔːtə(r); *NAmE* also -wɑːt-/ *noun* [U] (*especially NAmE*) used water that contains waste substances from homes, factories and farms: *municipal water and wastewater systems* ◇ *a wastewater treatment plant* ➲ compare SEWAGE

wast·ing /ˈweɪstɪŋ/ *adj.* a **wasting** disease or illness is one that causes sb to gradually become weaker and thinner

wast·rel /ˈweɪstrəl/ *noun* (*literary*) a lazy person who spends their time and/or money in a careless and stupid way

watch 0▬ /wɒtʃ; *NAmE* wɑːtʃ/ *verb, noun*

■ *verb* **1** 0▬ [T, I] to look at sb/sth for a time, paying attention to what happens: **~ sb/sth** *to watch television/a football game* ◇ **~ sth for sth** *He watched the house for signs of activity.* ◇ **~ (for sth)** *He watched for signs of activity in the house.* ◇ *'Would you like to play?' 'No thanks—I'll just watch.'* ◇ *We watched to see what would happen next.* ◇ **~ what, how, etc ...** *Watch what I do, then you try.* ◇ **~ sb/sth doing sth** *She watched the kids playing in the yard.* ◇ **~ sb/sth do sth** *They watched the bus disappear into the distance.* ➲ SYNONYMS at LOOK **2** 0▬ [T] **~ sb/sth (for sb)** to take care of sb/sth for a short time: *Could you watch my bags for me while I buy a paper?* **3** 0▬ (*BrE* also **mind**) [T] (*informal*) to be careful about sth: **~ sth/yourself** *Watch yourself!* (= be careful, because you're in a dangerous situation) ◇ *Watch your bag—there are thieves around.* ◇ *I have to* **watch every penny** (= be careful what I spend). ◇ *Watch your head on the low ceiling.* ◇ **~ where, what, etc...** *Hey, watch where you're going!*

IDM **watch the ˈclock** (*disapproving*) to be careful not to work longer than the required time; to think more about when your work will finish than about the work itself ➲ see also CLOCK-WATCHER **a watched ˌpot never ˈboils** (*saying*) used to say that when you are impatient for sth to happen, time seems to pass very slowly **ˈwatch it** (*informal*) used as a warning to sb to be careful **watch your ˈmouth/ˈtongue** to be careful what you say in order not to offend sb or make them angry **watch the ˈtime** to be sure that you know what the time is, so that you finish sth at the correct time, or are not late for sth: *I'll have to watch the time. I need to leave early today.* **watch this ˈspace** (*informal*) used in orders, to tell sb to wait for more news about sth to be announced: *I can't tell you any more right now, but watch this space.* **watch the ˈworld go by** to relax and watch people in a public place: *We sat outside a cafe, watching the world go by.* ➲ more at LANGUAGE, STEP *n.*

PHR V **ˈwatch for sb/sth** to look and wait for sb/sth to appear or for sth to happen: *The cat was on the wall, watching for birds.* **ˌwatch ˈout** 0▬ (*informal*) used to warn sb about sth dangerous: *Watch out! There's a car coming!* **ˌwatch ˈout for sb/sth 1** 0▬ to make an effort to be aware of what is happening, so that you will notice if anything bad or unusual happens: *The cashiers were asked to watch out for forged banknotes.* **2** to be careful of sth: *Watch out for the stairs—they're steep.* **ˌwatch ˈover sb/sth** (*formal*) to take care of sb/sth; to guard and protect sb/sth

■ *noun* **1** 0▬ [C] a type of small clock that you wear on your wrist, or (in the past) carried in your pocket: *She kept looking anxiously at her watch.* ◇ *My watch is fast/slow.* ➲ picture at CLOCK ➲ see also STOPWATCH, WRISTWATCH **2** [sing., U] the act of watching sb/sth carefully in case of possible danger or problems: *The police have* **mounted a watch** *outside the hotel.* ◇ *I'll* **keep watch** *while you go through his papers* (= watch and warn you if somebody is coming). ◇ *The government is* **keeping a close watch** *on how the situation develops.* ➲ see also NEIGHBOURHOOD WATCH **3** [C, U] a fixed period of time, usually while other people are asleep, during which sb watches for any danger so that they can warn others, for example on a ship; the person or people who do this: *I'm* **on first watch**. ◇ *I go* **on watch** *in an hour.* ➲ see also NIGHT-WATCHMAN

IDM **be on the ˈwatch (for sb/sth)** to be looking carefully for sb/sth that you expect to see, especially in order to avoid possible danger: *Be on the watch for thieves.* ➲ more at CLOSE² *adj.*

watch·able /ˈwɒtʃəbl; *NAmE* ˈwɑːtʃ-/ *adj.* (*informal*) entertaining or pleasant to watch

watch·band /ˈwɒtʃbænd; *NAmE* ˈwɑːtʃ-/ (*NAmE*) (*BrE* **ˈwatch strap**) *noun* a thin strip of leather, etc. for fastening your watch around your wrist

watch·dog /ˈwɒtʃdɒg; *NAmE* ˈwɑːtʃdɔːg/ *noun* a person or group of people whose job is to check that companies are not doing anything illegal or ignoring people's rights: *a consumer watchdog* ➲ compare GUARD DOG

watch·er /ˈwɒtʃə(r); *NAmE* ˈwɑːtʃ-/ *noun* (often in compounds) a person who watches and studies sb/sth regularly: *an industry/a market watcher* ➲ see also BIRD-WATCHER, CLOCK-WATCHER

watch·ful /ˈwɒtʃfl; *NAmE* ˈwɑːtʃ-/ *adj.* paying attention to what is happening in case of danger, accidents, etc: *Her expression was watchful and alert.* ◇ *His mother* **kept a watchful eye on** *him.* ◇ *The children played* **under the watchful eye of** *their teacher.* ▶ **watch·ful·ly** /-fəli/ *adv.* **watch·ful·ness** *noun* [U]

ˌwatching ˈbrief *noun* [sing.] the task of watching a group, especially a political organization, to make sure that it is doing everything it should and nothing wrong or illegal

watch·maker /ˈwɒtʃmeɪkə(r); *NAmE* ˈwɑːtʃ-/ *noun* a person who makes and repairs watches and clocks as a job

watch·man /ˈwɒtʃmən; *NAmE* ˈwɑːtʃ-/ *noun* (*pl.* **-men** /-mən/) (*old-fashioned*) a man whose job is to guard a building, for example a bank, an office building or a factory, especially at night ➲ see also NIGHTWATCHMAN

ˈwatch strap (*BrE*) (*NAmE* **ˈwatch·band**) *noun* a thin strip of leather, etc. for fastening your watch around your wrist

watch·tower /ˈwɒtʃtaʊə(r); *NAmE* ˈwɑːtʃ-/ *noun* a tall tower from which soldiers, etc. watch when they are guarding a place

watch·word /ˈwɒtʃwɜːd; *NAmE* ˈwɑːtʃwɜːrd/ *noun* a word or phrase that expresses sb's beliefs or attitudes, or that explains what sb should do in a particular situation: *Quality is our watchword.*

water 0▬ /ˈwɔːtə(r); *NAmE* also ˈwɑːt-/ *noun, verb*

■ *noun* **1** 0▬ [U] a liquid without colour, smell or taste that falls as rain, is in lakes, rivers and seas, and is used for drinking, washing, etc: *a glass of water* ◇ **drinking water** ◇ *water pollution* ◇ **clean/dirty water** ◇ *water shortages* ◇ *There is hot and cold* **running water** *in all the bedrooms.* ➲ see also BATHWATER **2** 0▬ [U] an area of water, especially a lake, river, sea or ocean: *We walked down to the water's edge.* ◇ *She fell into the water.* ◇ **shallow/deep water** ◇ *In the lagoon the water was calm.* ➲ see also BACKWATER, BREAKWATER **3** 0▬ **waters** [pl.] the water in a particular lake, river, sea or ocean: *the grey waters of the River Clyde* ◇ *This species is found in* **coastal waters** *around the Indian Ocean.* **4** 0▬ [U] the surface of a mass of water: *She dived under the water.* ◇ *The leaves floated on the water.* ➲ see also UNDERWATER **5 waters** [pl.] an area of sea or ocean belonging to a particular country: *We were still in British waters.* ◇ *fishing in international waters* ➲ see also TERRITORIAL WATERS **6 waters** [pl.] **murky, uncharted, stormy, dangerous, etc. ~** used to describe a situation, usually one that is difficult, dangerous or not familiar: *The conversation got into the murky waters of jealousy and relationships.* ◇ *The government has warned of stormy waters ahead.* HELP There are many other compounds ending in **water**. You will find them at their place in the alphabet.

IDM **by water** (*formal*) using a boat or ship **it's (all) water**

W

under the ˈbridge used to say that sth happened in the past and is now forgotten or no longer important **like ˈwater** (*informal*) in large quantities: *He spends money like water.* **not hold ˈwater** (*informal*) if an argument, an excuse, a theory, etc. does not **hold water**, you cannot believe it **sb's ˈwaters break** when a pregnant woman's **waters break**, the liquid in her WOMB passes out of her body just before the baby is born **(like) water off a ˌduck's ˈback** (*informal*) used to say that sth, especially criticism, has no effect on sb/sth: *I can't tell my son what to do; it's water off a duck's back with him.* ➲ more at BLOOD, BLOW *v.*, COLD *adj.*, DEAD *adj.*, DEEP *adj.*, DIP *v.*, DUCK *n.*, FISH *n.*, HEAD *n.*, HELL, HORSE *n.*, HOT *adj.*, PASS *v.*, POUR, STILL *adj.*, TEST *v.*, TREAD *adj.*

▪ *verb* **1** [T] **~ sth** to pour water on plants, etc: *to* ***water the plants/garden*** **2** [I] (of the eyes) to become full of tears: *The smoke made my eyes water.* **3** [I] (of the mouth) to produce SALIVA: *The smells from the kitchen made our mouths water.* **4** [T] **~ sth** to give water to an animal to drink: *to water the horses* ◇ (*humorous*) *After a tour of the grounds, the guests were* ***fed and watered.*** **5** [T, usually passive] **~ sth** (*technical*) (of a river, etc.) to provide an area of land with water: *The valley is watered by a stream.* **6** [T] **~ sth** to add water to an alcoholic drink: *watered wine*

PHR V **ˌwater sth↔ˈdown** **1** to make a liquid weaker by adding water **SYN** **dilute** **2** [usually passive] to change a speech, a piece of writing, etc. in order to make it less strong or offensive **SYN** **dilute**

the ˈWater Bearer *noun* [sing.] = AQUARIUS (1)

water·bed /ˈwɔːtəbed; *NAmE* ˈwɔːtərb-; ˈwɑːt-/ *noun* a bed with a rubber or plastic MATTRESS that is filled with water

water·bird /ˈwɔːtəbɜːd; *NAmE* ˈwɔːtərbɜːrd; ˈwɑːt-/ *noun* a bird that lives near and walks or swims in water, especially rivers or lakes

ˈwater biscuit *noun* (*BrE*) a thin crisp plain biscuit, usually eaten with butter and/or cheese

water·board·ing /ˈwɔːtəbɔːdɪŋ; *NAmE* ˈwɔːtərbɔːrd-; ˈwɑːt-/ *noun* [U] a way of trying to force sb to give you information by pouring water onto their face while making them lie on their back, so that they feel as if they are DROWNING

water·borne /ˈwɔːtəbɔːn; *NAmE* ˈwɔːtərbɔːrn; ˈwɑːt-/ *adj.* spread or carried by water: *cholera and other waterborne diseases* ◇ *waterborne goods* ➲ compare AIRBORNE

ˈwater buffalo *noun* (*pl.* **water buf·falo** or **water buf·faloes**) a large Asian animal of the cow family, used for pulling vehicles and farm equipment in tropical countries

ˈwater butt (*BrE*) (*NAmE* **ˈrain barrel**) *noun* a large BARREL for collecting rain as it flows off a roof ➲ VISUAL VOCAB page V16

ˈwater cannon *noun* a machine that produces a powerful flow of water, used by the police to control crowds of people

the ˈWater Carrier *noun* [sing.] = AQUARIUS (1)

ˈwater chestnut *noun* the thick round white root of a tropical plant that grows in water, often used in Chinese cooking

ˈwater clock *noun* (in the past) a clock that used the flow of water to measure time

ˈwater closet *noun* (*abbr.* WC) (*old-fashioned*) a toilet

water·col·our (*especially US* **water·color**) /ˈwɔːtəkʌlə(r); *NAmE* ˈwɔːtərk-; ˈwɑːt-/ *noun* **1 watercolours** [pl.] paints that you mix with water, not oil, and use for painting pictures ➲ COLLOCATIONS at ART **2** [C] a picture painted with these paints

water·col·our·ist (*especially US* **water·col·or·ist**) /ˈwɔːtəkʌlərɪst; *NAmE* ˈwɔːtər-/ *noun* a person who paints with watercolours

ˈwater-cooled *adj.* (of machines, etc.) cooled using water

ˈwater cooler *noun* **1** a machine, for example in an office, that cools water and supplies it for drinking **2** used when referring to a place where office workers talk in an informal way, for example near the water cooler: *It was a story they'd shared around the water cooler.*

water·course /ˈwɔːtəkɔːs; *NAmE* ˈwɔːtərkɔːrs; ˈwɑːt-/ *noun* (*technical*) a stream or an artificial channel for water

water·cress /ˈwɔːtəkres; *NAmE* ˈwɔːtərk-; ˈwɑːt-/ *noun* [U] a water plant with small round green leaves and thin STEMS. It has a strong taste and is often eaten raw in salads.

ˌwatered ˈsilk *noun* [U] a type of shiny silk cloth with a pattern on it that looks like water in waves

water·fall /ˈwɔːtəfɔːl; *NAmE* ˈwɔːtərf-; ˈwɑːt-/ *noun* a place where a stream or river falls from a high place, for example over a CLIFF or rock ➲ VISUAL VOCAB page V4

ˈwater feature *noun* an artificial area of water, or structure with water flowing through it, which is intended to make a garden more attractive and interesting ➲ VISUAL VOCAB page V16

ˈwater fountain *noun* (*NAmE*) = DRINKING FOUNTAIN

water·fowl /ˈwɔːtəfaʊl; *NAmE* ˈwɔːtərf-; ˈwɑːt-/ *noun* [usually pl.] (*pl.* **water·fowl**) a bird that can swim and lives near water, especially a DUCK or GOOSE

water·front /ˈwɔːtəfrʌnt; *NAmE* ˈwɔːtərf-; ˈwɑːt-/ *noun* [usually sing.] a part of a town or an area that is next to water, for example in a HARBOUR: *a waterfront apartment*

ˈwater gun *noun* (*NAmE*) = WATER PISTOL

water·hole /ˈwɔːtəhəʊl; *NAmE* ˈwɔːtərhoʊl; ˈwɑːt-/ (also **ˈwatering hole**) *noun* a place in a hot country, where animals go to drink

ˈwater ice *noun* [U, C] (*BrE*) = SORBET

ˈwatering can *noun* a metal or plastic container with a handle and a long SPOUT, used for pouring water on plants ➲ VISUAL VOCAB page V16

ˈwatering hole *noun* **1** = WATERHOLE **2** (*informal, humorous*) a bar or place where people go to drink

ˈwatering place *noun* (*old-fashioned*) a town with a natural supply of MINERAL WATER where people go for their health **SYN** **spa**

ˈwater jump *noun* an area of water that horses or runners have to jump over in a race or competition

water·less /ˈwɔːtələs; *NAmE* ˈwɔːtərləs; ˈwɑːt-/ *adj.* with no water: *a waterless barren region*

ˈwater level *noun* [U, C] the height that the surface of a mass of water rises or falls to, or the height it is at

ˈwater lily *noun* a plant that floats on the surface of water, with large round flat leaves and white, yellow or pink flowers

water·line /ˈwɔːtəlaɪn; *NAmE* ˈwɔːtərl-; ˈwɑːt-/ *noun* **the waterline** [sing.] the level that the water reaches along the side of a ship

water·logged /ˈwɔːtəlɒgd; *NAmE* ˈwɔːtərlɔːgd; ˈwɑːt-/ *adj.* **1** (of soil, a field, etc.) so full of water that it cannot hold any more and becomes flooded: *They couldn't play because the pitch was waterlogged.* **2** (of a boat, etc.) so full of water that it can no longer float

Water·loo /ˌwɔːtəˈluː; *NAmE* ˌwɔːtərˈluː; ˈwɑːt-/ *noun* [sing.] **sb's ~** a final defeat for sb: *This was the point at which he was to* ***meet his Waterloo.*** **ORIGIN** From the battle of **Waterloo** in 1815, in which the British (under the Duke of Wellington) and the Prussians finally defeated Napoleon.

ˈwater main *noun* a large underground pipe that supplies water to buildings, etc.

water·mark /ˈwɔːtəmɑːk; *NAmE* ˈwɔːtərmɑːrk; ˈwɑːt-/ *noun* a symbol or design in some types of paper, which can be seen when the paper is held against the light ➲ see also HIGH-WATER MARK, LOW-WATER MARK

ˈwater meadow *noun* [usually pl.] a field near a river that is often flooded

W

water·melon /ˈwɔːtəmelən; *NAmE* ˈwɔːtərm-; ˈwɑːt-/ *noun* [C, U] a type of large MELON with hard, dark green skin, red flesh and black seeds ➲ VISUAL VOCAB page V26

water·mill /ˈwɔːtəmɪl; *NAmE* ˈwɔːtərm-; ˈwɑːt-/ *noun* a MILL next to a river in which the machinery for GRINDING grain into flour is driven by the power of the water turning a wheel

ˈ**water moccasin** *noun* = COTTONMOUTH

ˈ**water pistol** (*NAmE* also ˈ**water gun**, ˈ**squirt gun**) *noun* a toy gun that shoots water

ˈ**water polo** *noun* [U] a game played by two teams of people swimming in a swimming pool. Players try to throw a ball into the other team's goal.

ˈ**water power** *noun* [U] power produced by the movement of water, used to drive machinery or produce electricity

water·proof /ˈwɔːtəpruːf; *NAmE* ˈwɔːtərp-; ˈwɑːt-/ *adj.*, *noun*, *verb*

■ ***adj.*** that does not let water through or that cannot be damaged by water: *waterproof clothing* ◇ *a waterproof camera*

■ ***noun*** [usually pl.] a piece of clothing made from material that does not let water through: *You'll need waterproofs* (= a waterproof jacket and trousers/pants).

■ ***verb* ~ sth** to make sth waterproof

ˈ**water rat** *noun* = WATER VOLE

ˈ**water-repellent** *adj.* a material, etc. that is **water-repellent** is specially treated so that water runs off it rather than going into it: *a water-repellent coating*

ˈ**water-resist·ant** *adj.* that does not let water through easily: *a water-resistant jacket*

water·shed /ˈwɔːtəʃed; *NAmE* ˈwɔːtərʃed; ˈwɑːt-/ *noun* **1** [C] **~ (in sth)** an event or a period of time that marks an important change: *The middle decades of the 19th century marked a watershed in Russia's history.* **2** [C] a line of high land where streams on one side flow into one river, and streams on the other side flow into a different river **3 the watershed** [sing.] (in Britain) the time before which programmes that are not considered suitable for children may not be shown on television: *the 9 o'clock watershed*

water·side /ˈwɔːtəsaɪd; *NAmE* ˈwɔːters-; ˈwɑːt-/ *noun* [sing.] the area at the edge of a river, lake, etc: *They strolled down to the waterside.* ◇ *a waterside cafe*

water·ski /ˈwɔːtəskiː; *NAmE* ˈwɔːtərs-; ˈwɑːt-/ *verb*, *noun*

■ ***verb*** [I] to SKI on water while being pulled by a fast boat ▶ **water·ski·ing** *noun* [U]: *We snorkelled and did some waterskiing.* ➲ VISUAL VOCAB page V40

■ ***noun*** either of the pair of long flat boards on which a person stands in order to waterski

ˈ**water softener** *noun* [U, C] a device or substance that removes particular minerals, especially CHALK, from water

ˈ**water sports** *noun* [pl.] sports that are done on or in water, for example sailing and WATERSKIING

water·spout /ˈwɔːtəspaʊt; *NAmE* ˈwɔːtərs-; ˈwɑːt-/ *noun* a column of water that is pulled up from the sea during a storm by a rapidly spinning column of air

W

ˈ**water strider** (*NAmE*) (*BrE* ˈ**pond skater**) *noun* an insect which moves quickly across the surface of water

ˈ**water supply** *noun* [C, U] the water provided for a town, an area or a building; the act of or system for supplying water to a town, etc: *a* ***clean/contaminated water supply*** ◇ *to improve the water supply to rural villages*

ˈ**water table** *noun* [usually sing.] (*technical*) the level at and below which water is found in the ground

water·tight /ˈwɔːtətaɪt; *NAmE* ˈwɔːtərt-; ˈwɑːt-/ *adj.* **1** that does not allow water to get in or out: *a watertight container* **2** (of an excuse, a plan, an argument, etc.) carefully prepared so that it contains no mistakes, faults or weaknesses: *a watertight alibi* ◇ *The case has to be made watertight.*

ˈ**water tower** *noun* a tall structure with a tank of water at the top from which water is supplied to buildings in the area around it

ˈ**water vole** (also ˈ**water rat**) *noun* an animal like a RAT that swims and lives in a hole beside a river or lake

water·way /ˈwɔːtəweɪ; *NAmE* ˈwɔːtərw-; ˈwɑːt-/ *noun* a river, CANAL, etc. along which boats can travel: *inland waterways* ◇ *a navigable waterway*

water·wheel /ˈwɔːtəwiːl; *NAmE* ˈwɔːtərw-; ˈwɑːt-/ *noun* a wheel turned by the movement of water, used, especially in the past, to drive machinery

ˈ**water wings** *noun* [pl.] (*old-fashioned*) a pair of plastic bags filled with air that children wear on their arms when they learn to swim

water·works /ˈwɔːtəwɜːks; *NAmE* ˈwɔːtərwɜːrks; ˈwɑːt-/ *noun* (*pl.* **water·works**) **1** [C+sing./pl. v.] a building with machinery for supplying water to an area **2** [pl.] (*informal* or *humorous*) the organs of the body through which URINE (= waste water) is passed

IDM ▶ **turn on the ˈwaterworks** (*informal, disapproving*) to start crying, especially in order to get sympathy or attention

watery /ˈwɔːtəri; *NAmE* ˈwɑːt-/ *adj.* **1** of or like water; containing a lot of water: *a watery fluid* ◇ *His eyes were red and watery.* ◇ (*literary*) *She was rescued from a* ***watery grave*** (= saved from DROWNING). **2** weak and/or pale: *a watery sun* ◇ *His eyes were a watery blue.* ◇ *a watery smile* (= weak and without much feeling) **3** (of food, drink, etc.) containing too much water; thin and having no taste: *watery soup*

Wat·ford /ˈwɒtfəd; *NAmE* ˈwɑːtfərd/ *noun* (*BrE*) a town in Hertfordshire, north of London, that is considered to mark the northern limit of the area of London and SE England. The expression **north of Watford** means the parts of Britain outside this area: *civil servants who seem to think the world ends north of Watford*

watt /wɒt; *NAmE* wɑːt/ *noun* (*abbr.* W) a unit for measuring electrical power: *a 60-watt light bulb*

watt·age /ˈwɒtɪdʒ; *NAmE* ˈwɑːt-/ *noun* [U] (*technical*) an amount of electrical power expressed in watts

wat·tle /ˈwɒtl; *NAmE* ˈwɑːtl/ *noun* **1** [U] sticks twisted together as a material for making fences, walls, etc: *walls made of* ***wattle and daub*** **2** [C] a piece of red skin that hangs down from the throat of a bird such as a TURKEY **3** [C, U] (*especially AustralE*) a name for various types of ACACIA tree

wave 0-w /weɪv/ *noun*, *verb*

■ ***noun***

▸ OF WATER **1** 0-w [C] a raised line of water that moves across the surface of the sea, ocean, etc: *Huge* ***waves were breaking*** *on the shore.* ◇ *Surfers flocked to the beach to* ***ride the waves***. ◇ *the gentle sound of* ***waves lapping*** ◇ *Children were playing* ***in the waves***. ◇ *Seagulls bobbed* ***on the waves***. ◇ *The wind made little waves on the pond.* ➲ VISUAL VOCAB page V4 ➲ see also TIDAL WAVE

▸ OF ACTIVITY/FEELING **2** 0-w [C] a sudden increase in a particular activity or feeling: *a* ***wave of opposition/protest/violence, etc.*** ◇ *a* ***crime wave*** ◇ *A wave of fear swept over him.* ◇ *Guilt and horror flooded her* ***in waves***. ◇ *A wave of panic spread through the crowd.* ➲ see also BRAINWAVE, HEATWAVE

▸ LARGE NUMBER **3** 0-w [C] a large number of people or things suddenly moving or appearing somewhere: *Wave after wave of aircraft passed overhead.* ➲ see also NEW WAVE

▸ MOVEMENT OF ARM/HAND/BODY **4** 0-w [C] a movement of your arm and hand from side to side: *She declined the offer with a wave of her hand.* ◇ *He* ***gave us a wave*** *as the bus drove off.* **5 the wave** (*NAmE*) (*BrE* ˌ**Mexican** ˈ**wave**) [sing.] a continuous movement that looks like a wave on the sea, made by a large group of people, especially people watching a sports game, when one person after another stands up, raises their arms, and then sits down again

▸ OF HEAT/SOUND/LIGHT **6** 0-w [C] the form that some types of energy such as heat, sound, light, etc. take as they move: ***radio/sound/ultrasonic waves*** ➲ see also AIRWAVES, LONG WAVE, MEDIUM WAVE, MICROWAVE, SHOCK WAVE, SHORT WAVE, SOUND WAVE

▸ IN HAIR **7** [C] if a person's hair has **a wave** or **waves**, it is not straight but curls slightly ➲ see also PERMANENT WAVE
▸ SEA **8 the waves** [pl.] (*literary*) the sea ➲ see also WAVY
IDM **make 'waves** (*informal*) to be very active in a way that makes people notice you, and that may sometimes cause problems ➲ more at CREST *n.*, RIDE *v.*
■ ***verb***
▸ MOVE HAND/ARM **1** 🔑 [I, T] to move your hand or arm from side to side in the air in order to attract attention, say hello, etc: *The people on the bus waved and we waved back.* ◇ **~ at/to sb** *Why did you wave at him?* ◇ **~ sth** (**about/around**) *A man in the water was shouting and waving his arms around frantically.* ◇ **~ sth at sb** *She waved her hand dismissively at the housekeeper.* ◇ **~ sb sth** *My mother was crying as I* ***waved her goodbye.*** ◇ **~ sth to sb** *My mother was crying as I* ***waved goodbye*** *to her.* **2** 🔑 [I, T] to show where sth is, show sb where to go, etc. by moving your hand in a particular direction: **+ adv./prep.** *She waved vaguely in the direction of the house.* ◇ **~ sth/sb + adv./prep.** *'He's over there,' said Ali,* ***waving a hand*** *towards some trees.* ◇ *I showed my pass to the security guard and he waved me through.* **3** 🔑 [T] to hold sth in your hand and move it from side to side: **~ sth** *Crowds lined the route, waving flags and cheering.* ◇ **~ sth + adv./prep.** *'I'm rich!' she exclaimed, waving the money under his nose.*
▸ MOVE FREELY **4** 🔑 [I] to move freely and gently, for example in the wind, while one end or side is held in position: *The flag waved in the breeze.*
▸ HAIR **5** [I] to curl slightly: *His hair waves naturally.* **6** [T] **~ sth** to make sb's hair curl slightly: *She's had her hair waved.*
IDM **like waving a red flag in front of a 'bull** (*US*) (*BrE* **a red rag to a 'bull**) something that is likely to make sb very angry ➲ more at FLAG *n.*
PHR V **,wave sth↔a'side/a'way** to not accept sth because you do not think it is necessary or important SYN **dismiss**: *My objections to the plan were waved aside.* **,wave sth/sb↔'down** to signal to a vehicle or its driver to stop by waving your hand **,wave sb↔'off** to wave goodbye to sb as they are leaving

wave·band /'weɪvbænd/ *noun* = BAND: *a radio set with medium and short wavebands*

,wave-cut 'platform *noun* (*technical*) an area of land between the CLIFFS and the sea which is covered by water when the sea is at its highest level

wave·form /'weɪvfɔːm; *NAmE* -fɔːrm/ *noun* (*physics*) a curve showing the shape of a wave at a particular time

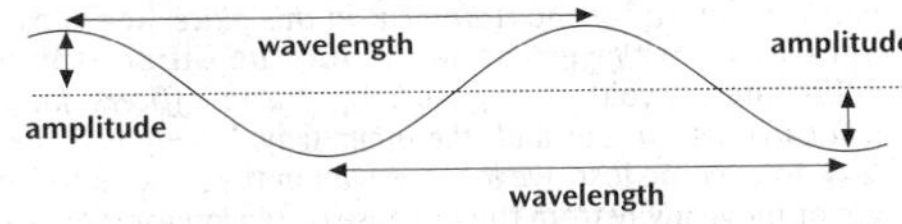

wave·length /'weɪvleŋθ/ *noun* **1** the distance between two similar points on a wave of energy, such as light or sound **2** the size of a radio wave that is used by a particular radio station, etc. for sending signals or broadcasting programmes
IDM **be on the same 'wavelength | be on sb's 'wavelength** (*informal*) to have the same way of thinking or the same ideas or feelings as sb else

wave·let /'weɪvlət/ *noun* (*literary*) a small wave on the surface of a lake, the sea or the ocean

'wave machine *noun* a machine that makes waves in the water in a swimming pool

waver /'weɪvə(r)/ *verb* **1** [I] to be or become weak or unsteady: *His voice wavered with emotion.* ◇ *Her determination never wavered.* ◇ *She never wavered in her determination to succeed.* **2** [I] **~ (between A and B)** | **~ (on/over sth)** to hesitate and be unable to make a decision or choice SYN **hesitate**: *She's wavering between buying a house in the city or moving away.* **3** [I] (especially of light) to move in an unsteady way ▶ **waver·er** /'weɪvərə(r)/ *noun*: *The strength of his argument convinced the waverers.*

wavy /'weɪvi/ *adj.* (**wavi·er**, **wavi·est**) having curves; not straight: *brown wavy hair* ◇ *a pattern of wavy lines* ➲ picture at CURVED

wax /wæks/ *noun, verb*
■ ***noun*** [U] **1** a solid substance that is made from BEESWAX or from various fats and oils and used for making CANDLES, polish, models, etc. It becomes soft when it is heated: *styling wax for the hair* ◇ *floor wax* ◇ *wax crayons* ◇ *wax polish* ➲ see also PARAFFIN WAX, SEALING WAX **2** a soft sticky yellowish substance that is found in your ears
IDM see BALL *n.*
■ ***verb*** **1** [T] **~ sth** to polish sth with wax **2** [T, usually passive] **~ sth** to cover sth with wax: *waxed paper* ◇ *a waxed jacket* **3** [T, often passive] **~ sth** to remove hair from a part of the body using wax: *to wax your legs/to have your legs waxed* **4** [I] (of the moon) to seem to get gradually bigger until its full form is visible OPP **wane** **5** [I] **+ lyrical, eloquent, sentimental, etc.** (*formal*) to become LYRICAL, etc. when speaking or writing: *He waxed lyrical on the food at the new restaurant.*
IDM **,wax and 'wane** (*literary*) to increase then decrease in strength, importance, etc. over a period of time

'wax bean *noun* (*NAmE*) a type of BEAN that is a long thin yellow POD, cooked and eaten whole as a vegetable

'waxed paper (*NAmE* also **'wax paper**) *noun* [U] paper covered with a thin layer of wax, used to wrap food or when cooking

waxen /'wæksn/ *adj.* **1** (*formal*) made of wax: *waxen images* **2** (*literary*) pale and looking ill/sick: *a waxen face*

'wax paper *noun* (*NAmE*) = GREASEPROOF PAPER, WAXED PAPER

wax·work /'wæksw3ːk; *NAmE* -w3ːrk/ *noun* **1** a model of a person that is made of wax **2 wax·works** (*pl.* waxworks) (*especially BrE*) (*NAmE* usually **'wax museum**) a museum where you can see wax models of famous people

waxy /'wæksi/ *adj.* made of wax; looking or feeling like wax

way 🔑 /weɪ/ *noun, adv.*
■ ***noun***
▸ METHOD/STYLE **1** 🔑 [C] a method, style or manner of doing sth: **~ to do sth** *That's not* ***the right way*** *to hold a pair of scissors.* ◇ (*informal, disapproving*) ***That's no way*** *to speak to your mother!* ◇ **~ of doing sth** *I'm not happy with this way of working.* ◇ **~ (that...)** *It's not what you say, it's the way that you say it.* ◇ *I* ***hate the way*** *she always criticizes me.* ◇ *I told you we should have done it* ***my way!*** ◇ *Infectious diseases can be acquired in several ways.* ◇ *I generally get what I want* ***one way or another*** (= by some means). ➲ see also THIRD WAY
▸ BEHAVIOUR **2** 🔑 [C] a particular manner or style of behaviour: *They grinned at her* ***in a friendly way.*** ◇ ***It was not his way*** *to admit that he had made a mistake.* ◇ *Don't worry, if she seems quiet—****it's just her way.*** ◇ *He was showing off,* ***as is the way*** *with adolescent boys.* **3 ways** [pl.] the typical way of behaving and living of a particular group of people: *After ten years I'm used to the strange British ways.*
▸ ROUTE/ROAD **4** 🔑 [C, usually sing.] **~ (from...) (to...)** a route or road that you take in order to reach a place: *the* ***best/quickest/shortest way*** *from A to B* ◇ *Can you* ***tell me the way*** *to Leicester Square?* ◇ *to* ***ask sb the way*** ◇ *We went the* ***long way round.*** **5** 🔑 [C, usually sing.] the route along which sb/sth is moving; the route that sb/sth would take if there was nothing stopping them/it: ***Get out of my way!*** *I'm in a hurry.* ◇ *Riot police with shields were blocking the demonstrators' way.* ◇ *We fought our way through the dense vegetation.* ◇ *Unfortunately they ran into a snowstorm along the way.* ➲ see also RIGHT OF WAY **6** [C] a road, path or street for travelling along: *There's a way across the fields.* ➲ see also FREEWAY, HIGHWAY, MOTORWAY, RAILWAY, WATERWAY **7** 🔑 **Way** used in the names of streets: *106 Headley Way*
▸ DIRECTION **8** 🔑 [C, usually sing.] **which, this, that, etc. ~** a particular direction; in a particular direction: *Which way did they go?* ◇ *We just missed a car coming* ***the other way.*** ◇

W

Look **both ways** (= look left and right) *before crossing the road.* ◇ *Make sure that sign's* **the right way up**. ◇ *Kids were running* **this way and that** (= in all directions). ◇ *They decided to split the money four ways* (= between four different people). ◇ (*figurative*) *Which way* (= for which party) *are you going to vote?* ➲ see also EACH WAY, ONE-WAY, THREE-WAY, TWO-WAY

▸ FOR ENTERING/LEAVING **9** 🗝 [C, usually sing.] a means of going into or leaving a place, such as a door or gate: *the* **way in/out** ◇ *They escaped out the back way.* ➲ see also COMPANIONWAY

▸ DISTANCE/TIME **10** 🗝 [sing.] (also *NAmE informal* **ways**) a distance or period of time between two points: *A little way up on the left is the Museum of Modern Art.* ◇ *September was* **a long way off**. ◇ (*figurative*) *The area's wine industry still has* **a way to go** *to full maturity.* ◇ *You came* **all this way** *to see us?* ◇ (*NAmE, informal*) *We still have* **a ways to go**.

▸ AREA **11** [sing.] (*informal*) an area, a part of a country, etc: *I think he lives somewhere* **over** *London* **way**. ◇ *I'll stop by and see you next time I'm* **down your way**.

▸ ASPECT **12** 🗝 [C] a particular aspect of sth SYN **respect**: *I have changed in every way.* ◇ *It's been quite a day,* **one way and another** (= for several reasons).

▸ CONDITION/STATE **13** [sing.] a particular condition or state: *The economy's* **in a bad way**. ◇ *I don't know how we're going to manage,* **the way things are**.

IDM **across the 'way** (*BrE* also **over the 'way**) on the other side of the street, etc: *Music blared from the open window of the house across the way.* **ˌall the 'way 1** 🗝 (also **the ˌwhole 'way**) during the whole journey/period of time: *She didn't speak a word to me all the way back home.* **2** completely; as much as it takes to achieve what you want: *I'm fighting him all the way.* ◇ *You can feel that the audience is with her all the way.* **(that's/it's) always the 'way** (*informal*) used to say that things often happen in a particular way, especially when it is not convenient **any way you 'slice it** (*NAmE, informal*) however you choose to look at a situation **'be/be 'born/be 'made that way** (of a person) to behave or do things in a particular manner because it is part of your character: *It's not his fault he's so pompous—he was born that way.* **be ˌset in your 'ways** to have habits or opinions that you have had for a long time and that you do not want to change **by the 'way** 🗝 (also **by the 'by/'bye**) (*informal*) used to introduce a comment or question that is not directly related to what you have been talking about: *By the way, I found that book you were looking for.* ◇ *What's the time, by the way?* ◇ *Oh by the way, if you see Jackie, tell her I'll call her this evening.* **by way of sth** by a route that includes the place mentioned SYN **via**: *The artist recently arrived in Paris from Bulgaria by way of Vienna.* ◇ *She came to TV by way of drama school.* **by way of/in the way of sth** as a form of sth; for sth; as a means of sth: *He received £600 by way of compensation from the company.* ◇ *She rolled her eyes by way of an answer and left.* **come your 'way** to happen to you by chance, or when you were not expecting it: *He took whatever came his way.* **cut both/two 'ways** (of an action, argument, etc.) to have two opposite effects or results **either way | one way or the other** used to say that it does not matter which one of two possibilities happens, is chosen or is true: *Was it his fault or not? Either way, an explanation is due.* ◇ *We could meet today or tomorrow—I don't mind one way or the other.* **every 'which way** (*informal*) in all directions: *Her hair tumbled every which way.* **get into/out of the way of (doing) sth** to become used to doing sth/to lose the habit of doing sth: *The women had got into the way of going up on the deck every evening.* **get in the way of** to prevent sb from doing sth; to prevent sth from happening: *He wouldn't allow emotions to get in the way of him doing his job.* **get/have your own 'way** to get or do what you want, especially when sb has tried to stop you: *She always gets her own way in the end.* **give 'way** to break or fall down: *The pillars gave way and a section of the roof collapsed.* ◇ *Her numb leg gave way beneath her and she stumbled clumsily.* **give 'way (to sb/sth) 1** to stop resisting sb/sth; to agree to do sth that you do not want to do: *He refused to give way on any of the points.* **2** (*BrE*) to allow sb/sth to be or go first: *Give way to traffic already on the roundabout.* **give way to sth 1** to allow yourself to be very strongly affected by sth, especially an emotion: *Flinging herself on the bed, she gave way to helpless misery.* **2** to be replaced by sth: *The storm gave way to bright sunshine.* **go all the 'way (with sb)** (*informal*) to have full SEXUAL INTERCOURSE with sb **go a long/some way towards doing sth** to help very much/a little in achieving sth: *The new law goes a long way towards solving the problem.* **go out of your 'way (to do sth)** to make a special effort to do sth: *He would always go out of his way to be friendly towards her.* **go your own 'way** to do as you choose, especially when sb has advised you against it: *It's best to let her go her own way if you don't want a fight.* **go sb's way 1** to travel in the same direction as sb: *I'm going your way—I'll walk with you.* **2** (of events) to go well for you; to be in your favour: *By the third round he knew the fight was going his way.* **go the way of all 'flesh** (*saying*) to die **have it your 'own way!** (*informal*) used to say in an angry way that although you are not happy about sth that sb has said, you are not going to argue: *Oh OK, then. Have it your own way.* **have it/things/everything your 'own way** to have what you want, especially by opposing other people **have a way of doing sth** used to say that sth often happens in a particular way, especially when it is out of your control: *First love affairs have a way of not working out.* **have a way with sb/sth** to be good at dealing with sb/sth: *He has a way with small children.* ◇ *She has a way with words* (= is very good at expressing herself). **have/want it 'both ways** to have or want to have the advantages of two different situations or ways of behaving that are impossible to combine: *You can't have it both ways. If you can afford to go out all the time, you can afford to pay off some of your debts.* **have your (wicked) way with sb** (*old-fashioned, humorous*) to persuade sb to have sex with you **in a big/small way** on a large/small scale: *The new delivery service has taken off in a big way.* ◇ *Many people are investing in a small way in the stock market.* **in ˌmore ways than 'one** used to show that a statement has more than one meaning: *With the first goal he used his head in more ways than one.* **in her, his, its, etc. (own) 'way** in a manner that is appropriate to or typical of a person or thing but that may seem unusual to other people: *I expect she does love you in her own way.* **in a 'way | in 'one way | in 'some ways** to some extent; not completely: *In a way it was one of our biggest mistakes.* **in the/sb's 'way** 🗝 stopping sb from moving or doing sth: *You'll have to move—you're in my way.* ◇ *I left them alone, as I felt I was in the way.* **in the way of sth** used in questions and negative sentences to talk about the types of sth that are available: *There isn't much in the way of entertainment in this place.* **keep/stay out of sb's 'way** 🗝 to avoid sb **look the other 'way** to deliberately avoid seeing sb/sth: *Prison officers know what's going on, but look the other way.* **lose your 'way 1** 🗝 to become lost: *We lost our way in the dark.* **2** to forget or move away from the purpose or reason for sth: *I feel that the project has lost its way.* **make your 'way (to/towards sth)** to move or get somewhere; to make progress: *Will you be able to* **make your own way** *to the airport* (= get there without help, a ride, etc.)? ◇ *Is this your plan for* **making your way in the world**? **make 'way (for sb/sth)** to allow sb/sth to pass; to allow sb/sth to take the place of sb/sth: *Make way for the Lord Mayor!* ◇ *Tropical forest is felled to make way for grassland.* **ˌmy way or the 'highway** (*NAmE, informal*) used to say that sb else has either to agree with your opinion or to leave **(there are) no two ways a'bout it** (*saying*) used to show that you are certain about sth: *It was the wrong decision—there are no two ways about it.* **(there is) ˌno 'way** 🗝 (*informal*) used to say that there is no possibility that you will do sth or that sth will happen: *'Do you want to help?' 'No way!'* ◇ *No way am I going to drive them there.* ◇ *There's no way we could afford that sort of money.* **on your/the/its 'way 1** 🗝 going or coming: *I'd better be on my way* (= I must leave) *soon.* ◇ *The letter should be on its way to you.* **2** 🗝 during the journey: *He stopped for breakfast on the way.* ◇ *She grabbed her camera and bag on her way out.* **3** (of a baby) not yet born: *They've got three kids and one on the way.* **the ˌother way 'round 1** 🗝 in the opposite position, direction or order: *I*

W

think it should go on the other way round. **2** the opposite situation: *I didn't leave you. It was the other way round* (= you left me). **ˌout of the ˈway 1** no longer stopping sb from moving or doing sth: *I moved my legs out of the way so that she could get past.* ◇ *I didn't say anything until Dad was out of the way.* **2** finished; dealt with: *Our region is poised for growth once the election is out of the way.* **3** used in negative sentences to mean 'unusual': *She had obviously noticed nothing out of the way.* ➲ see also OUT-OF-THE-WAY **ˌout of your ˈway** not on the route that you planned to take: *I'd love a ride home—if it's not out of your way.* **see your ˈway (ˈclear) to doing sth/to do sth** to find that it is possible or convenient to do sth: *Small builders cannot see their way clear to take on many trainees.* **see which way the ˈwind is blowing** to get an idea of what is likely to happen before doing sth **(not) stand in sb's ˈway** to (not) prevent sb from doing sth: *If you believe you can make her happy, I won't stand in your way.* **that's the way the cookie ˈcrumbles** (*informal*) that is the situation and we cannot change it, so we must accept it **there's more than ˌone way to skin a ˈcat** (*saying, humorous*) there are many different ways to achieve sth **to ˈmy way of thinking** in my opinion **under ˈway** (also **under·way**) having started: *Preparations are well under way for a week of special events in May.* **a/the/sb's way of ˈlife** the typical pattern of behaviour of a person or group: *the American way of life* **the ˌway of the ˈworld** the way that most people behave; the way that things happen, which you cannot change: *The rich and powerful make the decisions—that's the way of the world.* **ˌways and ˈmeans** the methods and materials available for doing sth: *ways and means of raising money* **a way ˈinto sth** (also **a way ˈin to sth**) something that allows you to join a group of people, an industry, etc. that it is difficult to join, or to understand sth that it is difficult to understand **the way to sb's ˈheart** the way to make sb like or love you: *The way to a man's heart is through his stomach* (= by giving him good food). **way to ˈgo!** (*NAmE, informal*) used to tell sb that you are pleased about sth they have done: *Good work, guys! Way to go!* **ˌwork your ˈway through college, round the world, etc.** to have a job or series of jobs while studying, travelling, etc. in order to pay for your education, etc. **ˌwork your way ˈthrough sth** to do sth from beginning to end, especially when it takes a lot of time or effort: *She worked her way through the pile of documents.* **ˌwork your way ˈup** to move regularly to a more senior position in a company: *He worked his way up from messenger boy to account executive.* ➲ more at CHANGE *v.*, CLAW *v.*, CLEAR *v.*, DOWNHILL, EASY *adj.*, ERROR, FAMILY *n.*, FEEL *v.*, FIND *v.*, HARD *adj.*, HARM *n.*, HEAD *n.*, KNOW *v.*, LAUGH *v.*, LIE *v.*, LONG *adj.*, MEND *v.*, MIDDLE *adj.*, OPEN *v.*, ORDINARY, PARTING *n.*, PAVE, PAY *v.*, PICK *v.*, RUB *v.*, SEPARATE *adj.*, SHAPE *n.*, SHOW *v.*, SMOOTH *v.*, SWEET *adj.*, SWING *v.*, TALK *v.*, WELL *adv.*, WILL *n.*, WRONG *adj.*

■ ***adv.*** **1** (used with a preposition or an adverb) very far; by a large amount: *She finished the race* ***way ahead*** *of the other runners.* ◇ *I must be going home; it's* ***way past*** *my bedtime.* ◇ *The price is* ***way above*** *what we can afford.* ◇ *They live* ***way out*** *in the suburbs.* ◇ *This skirt is way* (= a lot) *too short.* ◇ *I guessed that there would be a hundred people there, but I was* ***way out*** (= wrong by a large amount). **2** (used with an adjective) (*informal, especially NAmE*) very: *Things just got way difficult.* ◇ *I'm way glad to hear that.*

IDM **ˈway back (in...)** a long time ago: *I first met him way back in the 80s.*

way·farer /ˈweɪfeərə(r); *NAmE* -fer-/ *noun* (*old-fashioned* or *literary*) a person who travels from one place to another, usually on foot

way·lay /weɪˈleɪ/ *verb* (**way·laid, way·laid** /-ˈleɪd/) **~ sb** to stop sb who is going somewhere, especially in order to talk to them or attack them: *I got waylaid on my way here.*

way·mark /ˈweɪmɑːk; *NAmE* -mɑːrk/ *noun* (*BrE*) a mark or sign on a route in the countryside to show the way to people who are walking, etc: *Turn right where you see a waymark arrow.* ▶ **way·marked** /-mɑːkt; *NAmE* -mɑːrkt/ *adj.*: *waymarked routes*

ˌway ˈout *noun* **1** (*BrE*) a door used for leaving a building SYN **exit 2** a way of escaping from a difficult situation: *She was in a mess and could see no way out.*

IDM **on the way ˈout 1** as you are leaving **2** going out of fashion

ˌway-ˈout *adj.* (*old-fashioned, informal*) unusual or strange SYN **weird**: *way-out ideas*

way·point /ˈweɪpɔɪnt/ *noun* **1** a place where you stop during a journey **2** (*technical*) the COORDINATES, checked by a computer, of each stage of a flight or journey by sea

-ways *suffix* (in adjectives and adverbs) in the direction of: *lengthways* ◇ *sideways*

the ˌWays and ˈMeans Committee *noun* [sing. + sing./pl. v.] a group of members of the US House of Representatives which makes suggestions about laws concerning tax and trade in order to provide money for the US government

way·side /ˈweɪsaɪd/ *noun* [sing.] the area at the side of a road or path: *a wayside inn* ◇ *wild flowers growing by the wayside*

IDM **fall by the ˈwayside** to fail or be unable to make progress

ˈway station *noun* (*especially NAmE*) a place where people stop to eat or rest during a long journey

way·ward /ˈweɪwəd; *NAmE* -wərd/ *adj.* (*formal*) difficult to control SYN **headstrong**: *a wayward child* ◇ *wayward emotions* ▶ **way·ward·ness** *noun* [U]

wazir /wəˈzɪə(r); *NAmE* -ˈzɪr/ *noun* = VIZIER

wazoo /wæˈzuː/ *noun* (*US, slang*) a person's bottom (the part they sit on) or ANUS

IDM **ˌout/ˌup the waˈzoo** in large numbers or amounts

Wb *abbr.* WEBER

WC /ˌdʌbljuː ˈsiː/ *noun* (*BrE*) (on signs and doors in public places) toilet (the abbreviation for 'water closet')

w/c *abbr.* (used in writing) (*BrE*) week commencing (the week that begins on the date mentioned): *the schedule for w/c 19 November*

we /wi; *strong form* wiː/ *pron.* (used as the subject of a verb) **1** I and another person or other people; I and you: *We've moved to Atlanta.* ◇ *We'd* (= the company would) *like to offer you the job.* ◇ *Why don't we go and see it together?* **2** people in general: *We should take more care of our historic buildings.* ➲ see also THE ROYAL 'WE'

weak /wiːk/ *adj.* (**weaker, weakest**)
▸ NOT PHYSICALLY STRONG **1** not physically strong: *She is still weak after her illness.* ◇ *His legs felt weak.* ◇ *She suffered from a weak heart.*
▸ LIKELY TO BREAK **2** that cannot support a lot of weight; likely to break: *That bridge is too weak for heavy traffic.*
▸ WITHOUT POWER **3** easy to influence; not having much power: *a weak and cowardly man* ◇ ***In a weak moment*** (= when I was easily persuaded) *I said she could borrow the car.* ◇ *a weak leader* ◇ *The unions have always been weak in this industry.*
▸ POOR/SICK PEOPLE **4 the weak** *noun* [pl.] people who are poor, sick or without power
▸ CURRENCY/ECONOMY **5** not FINANCIALLY strong or successful: *a weak currency* ◇ *The economy is very weak.*
▸ NOT GOOD AT STH **6** not good at sth: *a weak team* ◇ **~ in sth** *I was always weak in the science subjects.*
▸ NOT CONVINCING **7** that people are not likely to believe or be persuaded by SYN **unconvincing**: *weak arguments* ◇ *I enjoyed the movie but I thought the ending was very weak.*
▸ HARD TO SEE/HEAR **8** not easily seen or heard: *a weak light/signal/sound*
▸ WITHOUT ENTHUSIASM **9** done without enthusiasm or energy: *a weak smile* ◇ *He made a weak attempt to look cheerful.*
▸ LIQUID **10** a **weak** liquid contains a lot of water: *weak tea*
▸ POINT/SPOT **11 ~ point/spot** the part of a person's

character, an argument, etc. that is easy to attack or criticize: *The team's weak points are in defence.* ◇ *He knew her weak spot where Steve was concerned.*
▸ GRAMMAR **12** a **weak** verb forms the past tense and past participle by adding a regular ending and not by changing a vowel. In English this is done by adding *-d*, *-ed* or *-t* (for example *walk*, *walked*)
▸ PHONETICS **13** (of the pronunciation of some words) used when there is no stress on the word. For example, the weak form of *and* is /ən/ or /n/, as in *bread and butter* /ˌbred n ˈbʌtə(r)/. OPP **strong**
IDM ˌ**weak at the ˈknees** (*informal*) hardly able to stand because of emotion, fear, illness, etc: *His sudden smile made her go weak at the knees.* **the weak link (in the ˈchain)** the point at which a system or an organization is most likely to fail ➲ more at SPIRIT *n.*

weak·en /ˈwiːkən/ *verb* **1** [T, I] ~ **(sb/sth)** to make sb/sth less strong or powerful; to become less strong or powerful: *The team has been weakened by injury.* ◇ *The new evidence weakens the case against her.* ◇ *His authority is steadily weakening.* OPP **strengthen 2** [T, I] ~ **(sth)** to make sth less physically strong; to become less physically strong: *The explosion had weakened the building's foundations.* ◇ *She felt her legs weaken.* **3** [I, T] to become or make sb become less determined or certain about sth: *You must not agree to do it. Don't weaken.* ◇ ~ **sth** *Nothing could weaken his resolve to continue.*

ˈ**weak force** *noun* (*technical*) one of the four FUNDAMENTAL FORCES in the universe, which is produced between PARTICLES in an atom ➲ see also ELECTROMAGNETISM, GRAVITY, STRONG FORCE

ˌ**weak-ˈkneed** *adj.* (*informal*) lacking courage or strength

weak·ling /ˈwiːklɪŋ/ *noun* (*disapproving*) a person who is not physically strong

weak·ly /ˈwiːkli/ *adv.* in a weak way: *She* ***smiled weakly*** *at them.* ◇ *'I'm not sure about it,' he said weakly.*

weak·ness 0‐ /ˈwiːknəs/ *noun*
1 0‐ [U] lack of strength, power or determination: *The sudden weakness in her legs made her stumble.* ◇ *the weakness of the dollar against the pound* ◇ *He thought that crying was a* ***sign of weakness***. OPP **strength 2** 0‐ [C] a weak point in a system, sb's character, etc: *It's important to know your own* ***strengths and weaknesses***. ◇ *Can you spot the weakness in her argument?* OPP **strength 3** [C, usually sing.] ~ **(for sth/sb)** difficulty in resisting sth/sb that you like very much: *He has a weakness for chocolate.*

weal /wiːl/ *noun* a sore red mark on sb's skin where they have been hit

wealth 0‐ /welθ/ *noun*
1 0‐ [U] a large amount of money, property, etc. that a person or country owns: *a person of wealth and influence* ◇ *His personal wealth is estimated at around $100 million.* ◇ *the* ***distribution of wealth*** *in Britain* ➲ COLLOCATIONS at FINANCE **2** 0‐ [U] the state of being rich: *The purpose of industry is to create wealth.* ◇ *Good education often depends on wealth.* **3** [sing.] ~ **of sth** a large amount of sth: *a wealth of information* ◇ *The new manager brings* ***a great wealth of experience*** *to the job.* ➲ compare RICHNESS

W

wealthy /ˈwelθi/ *adj.* (**wealth·ier, wealthi·est**) **1** having a lot of money, possessions, etc. SYN **rich**: *a wealthy nation* ◇ *The couple are said to be fabulously wealthy.* ◇ *They live in a wealthy suburb of Chicago.* ➲ SYNONYMS at RICH **2 the wealthy** *noun* [pl.] people who are rich

wean /wiːn/ *verb* ~ **sb/sth (off/from sth)** to gradually stop feeding a baby or young animal with its mother's milk and start feeding it with solid food
PHR V ˈ**wean sb off/from sth** to make sb gradually stop doing or using sth: *The doctor tried to wean her off sleeping pills.* ˈ**wean sb on sth** [usually passive] to make sb experience sth regularly, especially from an early age: *He was weaned on a diet of rigid discipline and duty.*

weapon 0‐ /ˈwepən/ *noun*
1 0‐ an object such as a knife, gun, bomb, etc. that is used for fighting or attacking sb: *nuclear weapons* ◇ *a* ***lethal/deadly weapon*** ◇ *The police still haven't found the* ***murder weapon***. ◇ *He was charged with carrying an* ***offensive weapon***. ➲ COLLOCATIONS at WAR ➲ see also BIOLOGICAL WEAPON, CHEMICAL WEAPON **2** 0‐ something such as knowledge, words, actions, etc. that can be used to attack or fight against sb/sth: *Education is the only weapon to fight the spread of the disease.* ◇ *Guilt is the* ***secret weapon*** *for the control of children.* IDM see DOUBLE-EDGED

weap·on·ize (*BrE* also **-ise**) /ˈwepənaɪz/ *verb* ~ **sth** to make sth suitable for use as a weapon: *They may have weaponized quantities of anthrax.* ▸ **weap·on·iza·tion, -isa·tion** /ˌwepənaɪˈzeɪʃn; *NAmE* -nəˈz-/ *noun* [U]

ˌ**weapon of ˌmass deˈstruction** *noun* (*abbr.* WMD) a weapon such as a nuclear weapon, a CHEMICAL WEAPON or a BIOLOGICAL WEAPON that can cause a lot of destruction and kill many people

weap·on·ry /ˈwepənri/ *noun* [U] all the weapons of a particular type or belonging to a particular country or group: *high-tech weaponry* ◇ *US weaponry*

wear 0‐ /weə(r); *NAmE* wer/ *verb, noun*
■ **verb** (**wore** /wɔː(r)/, **worn** /wɔːn; *NAmE* wɔːrn/)
▸ CLOTHING/DECORATION **1** 0‐ [T] ~ **sth** to have sth on your body as a piece of clothing, a decoration, etc: *She was wearing a new coat.* ◇ *Do I have to wear a tie?* ◇ *Was she wearing a seat belt?* ◇ *He wore glasses.* ◇ *All delegates must wear a badge.* ◇ *She always wears black* (= black clothes). ➲ COLLOCATIONS at FASHION
▸ HAIR **2** [T] to have your hair in a particular style; to have a beard or MOUSTACHE: ~ **sth + adj.** *She wears her hair long.* ◇ ~ **sth** *to wear a beard*
▸ EXPRESSION ON FACE **3** [T] ~ **sth** to have a particular expression on your face: *He wore a puzzled look on his face.* ◇ *His face wore a puzzled look.*
▸ DAMAGE WITH USE **4** 0‐ [I, T] to become, or make sth become thinner, smoother or weaker through continuous use or rubbing: *The carpets are starting to wear.* ◇ **+ adj.** *The sheets have worn thin.* ◇ ~ **sth + adj.** *The stones have been worn smooth by the constant flow of water.* **5** 0‐ [T] ~ **sth + adv./prep.** to make a hole, path, etc. in sth by continuous use or rubbing: *I've* ***worn holes*** *in all my socks.*
▸ STAY IN GOOD CONDITION **6** [I] ~ **well** to stay in good condition after being used for a long time: *That carpet is wearing well, isn't it?* ◇ (*figurative, humorous*) *You're wearing well—only a few grey hairs!*
▸ ACCEPT/ALLOW **7** [T] (usually used in questions and negative sentences) ~ **sth** (*BrE, informal*) to accept or allow sth, especially sth that you do not approve of
IDM **wear your ˌheart on your ˈsleeve** to allow your feelings to be seen by other people **wear ˈthin** to begin to become weaker or less acceptable: *These excuses are wearing a little thin* (= because we've heard them so many times before). **wear the ˈtrousers** (*BrE*) (*NAmE* **wear the ˈpants**) (often *disapproving*) (especially of a woman) to be the person in a marriage or other relationship who makes most of the decisions ➲ more at CAP *n.*
PHR V ˌ**wear aˈway** | ˌ**wear sth↔aˈway** 0‐ to become, or make sth become, gradually thinner or smoother by continuously using or rubbing it: *The inscription on the coin had worn away.* ◇ *The steps had been worn away by the feet of thousands of pilgrims.* ˌ**wear ˈdown** | ˌ**wear sth↔ˈdown** to become, or make sth become, gradually smaller or smoother by continuously using or rubbing it: *Notice how the tread on this tyre has worn down.* ˌ**wear sb/sth↔ˈdown** to make sb/sth weaker or less determined, especially by continuously attacking or putting pressure on them or it over a period of time: *Her persistence paid off and she eventually wore me down.* ˌ**wear ˈoff** 0‐ to gradually disappear or stop: *The effects of the drug will soon wear off.* ˌ**wear ˈon** (of time) to pass, especially in a way that seems slow: *As the evening wore on, she became more and more nervous.* ˌ**wear ˈout** | ˌ**wear sth↔ˈout** 0‐ to become, or make sth become, thin or no longer able to be used, usually because it has been used too much: *He wore out two pairs of shoes last year.* ˌ**wear yourself/sb ˈout** 0‐ to make yourself/sb feel very tired: *The kids have totally worn me out.* ◇ *You'll wear yourself out if you carry on working so hard.*

■ ***noun*** [U]
▸ CLOTHING **1** (usually in compounds) used especially in shops/stores to describe clothes for a particular purpose or occasion: ***casual/evening, etc. wear*** ◇ ***children's/ladies' wear*** ➲ see also FOOTWEAR, MENSWEAR, SPORTSWEAR, UNDERWEAR **2** the fact of wearing sth: *casual clothes for everyday wear* ◇ *These woollen suits are not designed for wear in hot climates.* ➲ SYNONYMS at CLOTHES
▸ USE **3** the amount or type of use that sth has over a period of time: *You should get years of wear out of that carpet.*
▸ DAMAGE **4** the damage or loss of quality that is caused when sth has been used a lot: *His shoes were beginning to show signs of wear.*
IDM **ˌwear and ˈtear** the damage to objects, furniture, property, etc. that is the result of normal use: *The insurance policy does not cover damage caused by normal wear and tear.* ➲ more at WORSE *n.*

wear·able /ˈweərəbl; *NAmE* ˈwer-/ *adj.* (of clothes, etc.) pleasant and comfortable to wear; suitable to be worn

wear·er /ˈweərə(r); *NAmE* ˈwer-/ *noun* the person who is wearing sth; a person who usually wears the thing mentioned: *The straps can be adjusted to suit the wearer.* ◇ *contact lens wearers*

wear·ing /ˈweərɪŋ; *NAmE* ˈwer-/ *adj.* that makes you feel very tired mentally or physically SYN **exhausting**

weari·some /ˈwɪərisəm; *NAmE* ˈwɪr-/ *adj.* (*formal*) that makes you feel very bored and tired SYN **tedious**

weary /ˈwɪəri; *NAmE* ˈwɪri/ *adj., verb*
■ ***adj.*** (**weari·er, weari·est**) **1** very tired, especially after you have been working hard or doing sth for a long time: *a weary traveller* ◇ *She suddenly felt old and weary.* ◇ *a weary sigh* **2** (*literary*) making you feel tired or bored: *a weary journey* **3 ~ of sth/of doing sth** (*formal*) no longer interested in or enthusiastic about sth: *Students soon grow weary of listening to a parade of historical facts.* ▸ **wear·ily** /ˈwɪərəli; *NAmE* ˈwɪr-/ *adv.*: *He closed his eyes wearily.* **weari·ness** *noun* [U]
■ ***verb*** (**wear·ies, weary·ing, wear·ied, wear·ied**) **1** [T] **~ sb** (*formal*) to make sb feel tired SYN **tire** **2** [I] **~ of sth/of doing sth** to lose your interest in or enthusiasm for sth SYN **tire**: *She soon wearied of his stories.*

weasel /ˈwiːzl/ *noun, verb*
■ ***noun*** a small wild animal with reddish-brown fur, a long thin body and short legs. Weasels eat smaller animals.
■ ***verb*** (-ll-, *NAmE* -l-)
PHR V **ˌweasel ˈout (of sth)** (*informal, disapproving, especially NAmE*) to avoid doing sth that you ought to do or have promised to do: *He's now trying to weasel out of our agreement.*

ˈweasel word *noun* [usually pl.] (*informal, disapproving*) a word that has little meaning, or more than one meaning, that you use when you want to avoid saying sth in a clear or direct way

wea·ther 0‑ /ˈweðə(r)/ *noun, verb*
■ ***noun*** [U] **1** 0‑ the condition of the atmosphere at a particular place and time, such as the temperature, and if there is wind, rain, sun, etc: ***hot/cold/wet/fine/summer/windy, etc. weather*** ◇ *Did you have* ***good weather*** *on your trip?* ◇ *I'm not going out in this weather!* ◇ *There's going to be* ***a change in the weather.*** ◇ ***if the weather holds/breaks*** (= if the good weather continues/changes) ◇ *The weather is very changeable at the moment.* ◇ *'Are you going to the beach tomorrow?' 'It depends on the weather.'* ◇ *We'll have the party outside,* ***weather permitting*** (= if it doesn't rain). ◇ ***a weather map/chart*** ◇ *a weather report* **2** 0‑ **the weather** (*informal*) a report of what the weather will be like, that is on the radio or television, or in the newspapers: *to listen to the weather*
IDM **in ˈall weathers** (*BrE*) in all kinds of weather, good and bad: *She goes out jogging in all weathers.* **keep a ˈweather eye on sb/sth** to watch sb/sth carefully in case you need to take action **under the ˈweather** (*informal*) if you are or feel **under the weather**, you feel slightly ill/sick and not as well as usual ➲ more at BRASS, HEAVY
■ ***verb*** **1** [I, T] to change, or make sth change, colour or shape because of the effect of the sun, rain or wind: *This brick weathers to a warm pinkish-brown colour.* ◇ **~ sth** *Her face was weathered by the sun.* **2** [T] **~ sth** to come safely through a difficult period or experience: *The company just managed to weather the recession.* ◇ *She refuses to resign, intending to* ***weather the storm*** (= wait until the situation improves again).

Collocations

The weather

Good weather

- **be bathed in/bask in/be blessed with/enjoy** bright/brilliant/glorious sunshine
- the sun **shines/warms sth/beats down (on sth)**
- the sunshine **breaks/streams through sth**
- fluffy/wispy clouds **drift across the sky**
- a gentle/light/stiff/cool/warm/sea breeze **blows in/comes in off the sea**
- the snow **crunches beneath/under sb's feet/boots**

Bad weather

- thick/dark/storm clouds **form/gather/roll in/cover the sky/block out the sun**
- the sky **darkens/turns black**
- a fine mist **hangs in the air**
- a dense/heavy/thick fog **rolls in**
- the rain **falls/comes down (in buckets/sheets)/pours down**
- snow **falls/comes down/covers sth**
- the wind **blows/whistles/howls/picks up/whips through sth/sweeps across sth**
- strong/gale-force winds **blow/gust (up to 80 mph)**
- a storm **is approaching/is moving inland/hits/strikes/rages**
- thunder **rolls/rumbles/sounds**
- (forked/sheet) lightning **strikes/hits/flashes**
- a (blinding/snow) blizzard **hits/strikes/blows/rages**
- a tornado **touches down/hits/strikes/destroys sth/rips through sth**
- **forecast/expect/predict** rain/snow/a category-four hurricane
- (*NAmE*) **pour (down)**/(*BrE*) **pour (down) with** rain
- **get caught in/seek shelter from/escape** the rain
- **be covered/shrouded in** mist/a blanket of fog
- **be in for/brave/shelter from** a/the storm
- **hear** rolling/distant thunder
- **be battered/buffeted by** strong winds
- (*BrE*) **be blowing** a gale
- **battle against/brave** the elements

The weather improves

- the sun **breaks through the clouds**
- the sky **clears/brightens (up)/lightens (up)**
- the clouds **part/clear**
- the rain **stops/lets up/holds off**
- the wind **dies down**
- the storm **passes**
- the mist/fog **lifts/clears**

ˈweather balloon *noun* a BALLOON that carries instruments into the atmosphere to measure weather conditions

ˈweather-beaten *adj.* [usually before noun] (especially of a person or their skin) rough and damaged because the person spends a lot of time outside

wea·ther·board /ˈweðəbɔːd; *NAmE* ˈweðərbɔːrd/ (also **clap·board** especially in *NAmE*) *noun* one of a series of long, narrow, horizontal pieces of wood, each with one edge thicker than the other. They are fixed to the outside walls of a house with the bottom of one over the top of the one below, to cover the wall and protect it from rain and

W

wind: *a weatherboard house* ▸ ˈ**wea·ther·boarded** *adj.* ˈ**wea·ther·board·ing** *noun* [U]

ˈ**weather centre** (*BrE*) (*US* ˈ**weather bureau**) *noun* a place where information about the weather is collected and reports are prepared

wea·ther·cock /ˈweðəkɒk; *NAmE* ˈweðərkɑːk/ *noun* a WEATHERVANE in the shape of a male chicken (called a COCK or ROOSTER)

weathercock

ˈ**weather forecast** (also **fore·cast**) *noun* a description, for example on the radio or television, of what the weather will be like tomorrow or for the next few days

wea·ther·ing /ˈweðərɪŋ/ *noun* [U] the action of sun, rain or wind on rocks, making them change shape or colour

wea·ther·ize (*BrE* also **-ise**) /ˈweðəraɪz/ *verb* **~ sth** (*NAmE*) to protect a building against the effects of cold weather, for example by providing INSULATION

wea·ther·man /ˈweðəmæn; *NAmE* -ðərm-/ (*pl.* **-men** /-men/), **wea·ther·girl** /ˈweðəɡɜːl; *NAmE* -ðərɡɜːrl/ *noun* (*informal*) a person on radio or television whose job is describing the weather and telling people what it is going to be like

wea·ther·proof /ˈweðəpruːf; *NAmE* -ðərp-/ *adj.* that is not affected by weather; that protects sb/sth from wind and rain: *The finished roof should be weatherproof for years.* ◇ *a weatherproof jacket*

ˈ**weather station** *noun* a place where weather conditions are studied and recorded

ˈ**weather strip** (*NAmE*) (*BrE* ˈ**draught excluder**) *noun* a piece of material that helps to prevent cold air coming through a door, window, etc.

wea·ther·vane /ˈweðəveɪn; *NAmE* -ðərv-/ *noun* a metal object on the roof of a building that turns easily in the wind and shows which direction the wind is blowing from ➲ see also WEATHERCOCK

weave /wiːv/ *verb, noun*

■ ***verb*** (**wove** /wəʊv; *NAmE* woʊv/, **woven** /ˈwəʊvn; *NAmE* ˈwoʊvn/) **HELP** In sense 4 **weaved** is used for the past tense and past participle. **1** [T, I] to make cloth, a carpet, a BASKET, etc. by crossing threads or strips across, over and under each other by hand or on a machine called a LOOM: **~ A from B** *The baskets are woven from strips of willow.* ◇ **~ B into A** *The strips of willow are woven into baskets.* ◇ **~ sth together** *threads woven together* ◇ **~ (sth)** *Most spiders weave webs that are almost invisible.* ◇ *She is skilled at spinning and weaving.* **2** [T] **~ A (out of/from B) | ~ B (into A)** to make sth by twisting flowers, pieces of wood, etc. together: *She deftly wove the flowers into a garland.* **3** [T] to put facts, events, details, etc. together to make a story or a closely connected whole: **~ (sth into) sth** *to weave a narrative* ◇ **~ sth together** *The biography weaves together the various strands of Einstein's life.* **4** (**weaved, weaved**) [I, T] to move along by running and changing direction continuously to avoid things that are in your way: **+ adv./prep.** *She was weaving in and out of the traffic.* ◇ *The road weaves through a range of hills.* ◇ **~ your way + adv./prep.** *He had to weave his way through the milling crowds.*

IDM **weave your ˈmagic | weave a ˈspell (over sb)** (*especially BrE*) to perform or behave in a way that is attractive or interesting, or that makes sb behave in a particular way: *Will Ronaldo be able to weave his magic against Italy on Wednesday?*

■ ***noun*** the way in which threads are arranged in a piece of cloth that has been woven; the pattern that the threads make

weaver /ˈwiːvə(r)/ *noun* a person whose job is weaving cloth

ˈ**weaver bird** *noun* a tropical bird that builds large nests by weaving sticks and pieces of grass together in a complicated way

web 🔑 /web/ *noun*

1 🔑 [C] = SPIDER'S WEB: *A spider had spun a perfect web outside the window.* ➲ **VISUAL VOCAB** page V11 **2** 🔑 [C] a complicated pattern of things that are closely connected to each other: *a web of streets* ◇ *We were caught in a* ***tangled web*** *of relationships.* **3** 🔑 **the Web** (also **the web**) [sing.] = WORLD WIDE WEB: *I found the information* ***on the Web.*** ➲ **COLLOCATIONS** at EMAIL **4** [C] a piece of skin that joins the toes of some birds and animals that swim, for example DUCKS and FROGS

Web 2.0 /ˌweb tuː pɔɪnt ˈəʊ; *NAmE* ˈoʊ/ *noun* [U] the developments in the way that people use the Internet that allow users free access and give them more control over the information

web·bed /webd/ *adj.* [only before noun] a bird or an animal (such as a DUCK or FROG) that has **webbed feet** has pieces of skin between the toes ➲ **VISUAL VOCAB** page V10

web·bing /ˈwebɪŋ/ *noun* [U] strong strips of cloth that are used to make belts, etc, and to support the seats of chairs, etc.

web·cam (*NAmE* **Web·cam™**) /ˈwebkæm/ *noun* a video camera that is connected to a computer so that what it records can be seen on a website as it happens ➲ **VISUAL VOCAB** page V54

web·cast /ˈwebkɑːst; *NAmE* ˈwebkæst/ *noun* a live broadcast that is sent out on the Internet

ˈ**Web-enabled** *adj.* able to be connected to and used with the Internet: *a Web-enabled interface*

weber /ˈveɪbə(r)/ *noun* (*abbr.* **Wb**) (*physics*) a unit for measuring MAGNETIC FLUX

web·head /ˈwebhed/ *noun* (*informal*) a person who uses the Internet a lot

webli·og·raphy /ˌwebliˈɒɡrəfi; *NAmE* -ˈɑːɡ-/ *noun* (*pl.* **-ies**) a list of websites or electronic works about a particular subject that have been used by a person writing an article, etc: *a Poe webliography* ◇ *a selected webliography on new Irish poetry*

web·log /ˈweblɒɡ; *NAmE* -lɔːɡ; -lɑːɡ/ *noun* = BLOG

web·master /ˈwebmɑːstə(r); *NAmE* -mæs-/ *noun* (*computing*) a person who is responsible for particular pages of information on the World Wide Web

ˈ**web page** *noun* a document that is connected to the World Wide Web and that anyone with an Internet connection can see, usually forming part of a website: *We learned how to create and register a new web page.*

web·site 🔑 /ˈwebsaɪt/ *noun*

a place connected to the Internet, where a company or an organization, or an individual person, puts information: *I found this information* ***on their website.*** ◇ *For current prices please* ***visit our website.*** ➲ **COLLOCATIONS** at EMAIL ➲ **VISUAL VOCAB** page V55

web·zine /ˈwebziːn/ *noun* a magazine published on the Internet, not on paper

wed /wed/ *verb* (**wed·ded, wed·ded** or **wed, wed**) [I, T] (not used in the progressive tenses) (*old-fashioned* or used in newspapers) to marry: *The couple plan to wed next summer.* ◇ **~ sb** *Rock star to wed top model* (= in a newspaper HEADLINE).

we'd /wiːd; wid/ *short form* **1** we had **2** we would

wed·ded /ˈwedɪd/ *adj.* **1 ~ to sth** (*formal*) if you are **wedded** to sth, you like or support it so much that you are not willing to give it up: *She's wedded to her job.* **2** [usually before noun] (*old-fashioned* or *formal*) legally married: *your* ***lawfully wedded*** *husband* ◇ *to live together in* ***wedded bliss*** **3** [not before noun] **~ (to sth)** (*formal* or *literary*) combined or united with sth

wed·ding 🔑 /ˈwedɪŋ/ *noun*

a marriage ceremony, and the meal or party that usually follows it: *a* ***wedding present*** ◇ *a* ***wedding ceremony/re-***

W

ception ◇ *Have you been invited to their wedding?* ◇ *She looked beautiful on her **wedding day**.* ◇ *All her friends could hear **wedding bells*** (= they thought she would soon get married). ➲ COLLOCATIONS at MARRIAGE ➲ see also DIAMOND WEDDING, GOLDEN WEDDING, SHOTGUN WEDDING, SILVER WEDDING, WHITE WEDDING

'wedding anniversary *noun* the celebration every year of the date when two people were married: *Today's our wedding anniversary.*

'wedding band *noun* a wedding ring in the form of a plain band, usually of gold ➲ VISUAL VOCAB page V53

'wedding breakfast *noun* (*BrE, formal*) a special meal after a marriage ceremony

'wedding cake *noun* [C, U] a cake covered with ICING, and usually with several layers, eaten at a wedding party

'wedding dress *noun* a dress that a woman wears at her wedding, especially a long white one

'wedding ring *noun* a ring that is given during a marriage ceremony and worn afterwards to show that you are married ➲ VISUAL VOCAB page V53

'wedding tackle *noun* [U] (*BrE, slang*) a man's sexual organs

wedge /wedʒ/ *noun, verb*

■ ***noun* 1** a piece of wood, rubber, metal, etc. with one thick end and one thin pointed end that you use to keep a door open, to keep two things apart, or to split wood or rock: *He hammered the wedge into the crack in the stone.* ◇ (*figurative*) *I don't want to **drive a wedge** between the two of you* (= to make you start disliking each other). **2** something that is shaped like a wedge or that is used like a wedge: *a wedge of cake* ◇ *shoes with wedge heels* ➲ VISUAL VOCAB page V52 **3** a GOLF CLUB that has the part that you hit the ball with shaped like a wedge IDM see THIN *adj.*

■ ***verb* 1 ~ sth + adv./prep.** to put or squeeze sth tightly into a narrow space, so that it cannot move easily SYN **jam**: *The boat was now wedged between the rocks.* ◇ *She wedged herself into the passenger seat.* **2 ~ sth (+ adj.)** to make sth stay in a particular position, especially open or shut, by placing sth against it: *to wedge the door open*

'wedge issue *noun* (*NAmE*) an important and difficult political issue, used by a political party to draw supporters away from an opposing party

wedgie /'wedʒi/ *noun* (*informal*) an act of lifting sb up by his/her underwear, usually done as a joke

wed·lock /'wedlɒk; *NAmE* -lɑːk/ *noun* [U] (*old-fashioned* or *law*) the state of being married: *children born **in/out of wedlock*** (= whose parents are/are not married)

Wed·nes·day 🔑 /'wenzdeɪ; -di/ *noun* [C, U] (*abbr.* **Wed.**, **Weds.**)
the day of the week after Tuesday and before Thursday HELP To see how **Wednesday** is used, look at the examples at **Monday.** ORIGIN Originally translated from the Latin for 'day of Mercury' *Mercurii dies* and named after the Germanic god *Odin*.

wee /wiː/ *adj., noun, verb*

■ ***adj.*** (*informal*) **1** (*especially ScotE*) very small in size: *a wee girl* **2** small in amount; little: *Just a wee drop of milk for me.* ◇ *I felt **a wee bit** guilty about it.*

IDM **the wee small 'hours** (*ScotE*) (*NAmE* **the wee 'hours**) = THE SMALL/EARLY HOURS at HOUR

■ ***noun*** (also **'wee-wee**) (*informal, especially BrE*) (often used by young children or when you are talking to them) **1** [sing.] an act of passing liquid waste (called URINE) from your body: *to **do/have a wee*** **2** [U] = URINE: *a puddle of wee*

■ ***verb*** (also **'wee-wee**) [I] (*informal, especially BrE*) (often used by young children or when you are talking to them) to pass liquid waste (called URINE) from the body: *Do you need to wee?*

weed /wiːd/ *noun, verb*

■ ***noun* 1** [C] a wild plant growing where it is not wanted, especially among crops or garden plants: *The yard was overgrown with weeds.* **2** [U] any wild plant without flowers that grows in water and forms a green floating mass **3 the weed** [sing.] (*humorous*) TOBACCO or cigarettes: *I wish I could give up the weed* (= stop smoking). **4** [U] (*informal*) the drug CANNABIS **5** [C] (*BrE, informal, disapproving*) a person with a weak character or body

■ ***verb*** [T, I] **~ (sth)** to take out weeds from the ground: *I've been weeding the flower beds.*

PHR V **,weed sth/sb↔'out** to remove or get rid of people or things from a group because they are not wanted or are less good than the rest

weed·kill·er /'wiːdkɪlə(r)/ *noun* [U, C] a substance that is used to destroy weeds

weedy /'wiːdi/ *adj.* (**weed·ier**, **weedi·est**) **1** (*BrE, informal, disapproving*) having a thin weak body: *a weedy little man* **2** full of or covered with weeds

,Wee 'Free *noun* a member of the part of the Free Church of Scotland that did not join with the United Presbyterian Church in 1900 to form the United Free Church

Wee·juns™ /'wiːdʒənz/ *noun* [pl.] (*US*) MOCCASIN style shoes

week 🔑 /wiːk/ *noun*

1 🔑 a period of seven days, either from Monday to Sunday or from Sunday to Saturday: ***last/this/next week*** ◇ *It rained all week.* ◇ *What **day of the week** is it?* ◇ *He comes to see us **once a week**.* **2** 🔑 any period of seven days: *a **two-week** vacation* ◇ *The course lasts five weeks.* ◇ ***a week ago** today* (= seven days ago) ◇ *She'll be back **in a week**.* **3** 🔑 the five days other than Saturday and Sunday: *They live in town **during the week** and go to the country for the weekend.* ◇ (*BrE*) *I never have the time to go out **in the week**.* **4** 🔑 the part of the week when you go to work: *a 35-hour week* ◇ *The firm is introducing a shorter **working week**.*

IDM **today, tomorrow, Monday, etc. 'week** (*BrE*) (also **a ,week (from) to'day, etc.** *NAmE, BrE*) seven days after the day that you mention: *I'll see you Thursday week.* **,week after 'week** 🔑 (*informal*) continuously for many weeks: *Week after week the drought continued.* **,week by 'week** 🔑 as the weeks pass: *Week by week he grew a little stronger.* **week ,in, week 'out** happening every week: *Every Sunday, week in, week out, she goes to her parents for lunch.* **a ,week next/on/this 'Monday, etc.** | **a ,week to'morrow, etc.** 🔑 (*BrE*) (also **a ,week from 'Monday, etc.** *NAmE, BrE*) seven days after the day that you mention: *It's my birthday a week on Tuesday.* **a ,week 'yesterday, last 'Monday, etc.** 🔑 (*especially BrE*) seven days before the day that you mention: *She started work a week yesterday.* ➲ more at OTHER *adj.*

week·day /'wiːkdeɪ/ *noun* any day except Saturday and Sunday: *The centre is open from 9 a.m. to 6 p.m. on weekdays.* ▶ **week·days** *adv.*: *open weekdays from 9 a.m. to 6 p.m.*

week·end 🔑 /,wiːk'end; *NAmE* 'wiːkend/ *noun, verb*

■ ***noun* 1** 🔑 Saturday and Sunday: *Are you doing anything **over the weekend**?* ◇ *Have a good weekend!* ◇ *It happened **on the weekend of** 24 and 25 April.* ◇ (*BrE*) *The office is closed **at the weekend**.* ◇ (*especially NAmE*) *The office is closed **on the weekend**.* ◇ (*BrE, informal*) *I like to go out **on a weekend**.* ◇ *We go skiing most weekends in winter.* ➲ see also DIRTY WEEKEND, LONG WEEKEND **2** 🔑 Saturday and Sunday, or a slightly longer period, as a holiday/vacation: *He won a weekend for two in Rome.* ◇ *a weekend break*

■ ***verb*** [I] **+ adv./prep.** to spend the weekend somewhere: *They're weekending in Paris.*

week·end·er /,wiːk'endə(r)/ *noun* **1** a person who visits or lives in a place only on Saturdays and Sundays **2** (*AustralE, informal*) a house in the country that people go to for weekends and holidays/vacations

,weekend 'warrior *noun* (*NAmE*) a person who works all week, especially in an office or other indoor job, and uses the weekends to go out and do more active and/or dangerous physical activities

'week-long *adj.* lasting for a week: *a week-long visit to Rome* ◇ *week-long courses*

week·ly 🔑 /'wiːkli/ *adj., noun*

■ ***adj.*** happening, done or published once a week or every

W

week: *weekly meetings* ◇ *a weekly magazine* ▸ **week·ly** *adv.*: *Employees are paid weekly.* ◇ *The newspaper is published twice weekly.*
■ ***noun*** (*pl.* -ies) a newspaper or magazine that is published every week

week·night /ˈwiːknaɪt/ *noun* any night of the week except Saturday, Sunday and sometimes Friday night: *I have to stay in on weeknights.*

weenie /ˈwiːni/ *noun* (*NAmE, informal*) **1** (*disapproving*) a person who is not strong, brave or confident SYN **wimp**: *Don't be such a weenie!* **2** = FRANKFURTER **3** (*slang*) a word for a PENIS, used especially by children

weeny /ˈwiːni/ *adj.* (**ween·ier**, **weeni·est**) (*informal*) extremely small SYN **tiny**: *Weren't you just a weeny bit scared?* ➲ see also TEENY

weep /wiːp/ *verb, noun*
■ ***verb*** (**wept**, **wept** /wept/) **1** [I, T] (*formal* or *literary*) to cry, usually because you are sad: *She started to weep uncontrollably.* ◇ ***I could have wept*** *thinking about what I'd missed.* ◇ **~ for/with sth** *He wept for joy.* ◇ **~ at/over sth** *I do not weep over his death.* ◇ **~ sth** *She wept bitter tears of disappointment.* ◇ **~ to do sth** *I wept to see him looking so sick.* ◇ **+ speech** *'I'm so unhappy!' she wept.* **2** [I] (usually used in the progressive tenses) (of a wound) to produce liquid: *His legs were covered with weeping sores* (= sores which had not healed).
■ ***noun*** [sing.] an act of crying: *Sometimes you feel better for a good weep.*

weep·ing /ˈwiːpɪŋ/ *adj.* [only before noun] (of some trees) with branches that hang downwards: *a **weeping willow/fig/birch***

weepy /ˈwiːpi/ *adj., noun*
■ ***adj.*** (*informal*) sad and tending to cry easily: *She was feeling tired and weepy.*
■ ***noun*** (also **weepie**) (*pl.* -ies) (*informal*) a sad film/movie or play that makes you want to cry SYN **tear jerker**

wee·vil /ˈwiːvl/ *noun* a small insect with a hard shell, that eats grain, nuts and other seeds and destroys crops

ˈwee-wee *noun, verb* = WEE

the weft /weft/ (also *less frequent* **the woof**) *noun* [sing.] the threads that are twisted under and over the threads that are held on a LOOM (= a frame or machine for making cloth) ➲ compare WARP

weigh 0‑ /weɪ/ *verb*
1 0‑ *linking verb* (**+ noun**) to have a particular weight: *How much do you weigh* (= how heavy are you)? ◇ *She weighs 60 kilos.* ◇ *These cases **weigh a ton*** (= are very heavy). **2** 0‑ [T] **~ sb/sth/yourself** to measure how heavy sb/sth is, usually by using SCALES: *He weighed himself on the bathroom scales.* ◇ *She weighed the stone in her hand* (= estimated how heavy it was by holding it). **3** [T] to consider sth carefully before making a decision: **~ sth** (**up**) *You must weigh up the pros and cons* (= consider the advantages and disadvantages of sth). ◇ *She weighed up all the evidence.* ◇ **~** (**up**) **sth against sth** *I weighed the benefits of the plan against the risks involved.* **4** [I] **~** (**with sb**) (**against sb/sth**) to have an influence on sb's opinion or the result of sth: *His past record **weighs heavily** against him.* **5** [T] **~ anchor** to lift an ANCHOR out of the water and into a boat before sailing away
IDM **weigh your ˈwords** to choose your words carefully so that you say exactly what you mean
PHR V **ˌweigh sb↔ˈdown** to make sb feel worried or anxious SYN **burden**: *The responsibilities of the job are weighing her down.* ◇ *He is weighed down with guilt.* **ˌweigh sb/sth↔ˈdown** to make sb/sth heavier so that they are not able to move easily: *I was weighed down with baggage.* **ˌweigh ˈin** (**at sth**) to have your weight measured, especially before a contest, race, etc: *Both boxers weighed in at several pounds below the limit.* ➲ related noun WEIGH-IN **ˌweigh ˈin** (**with sth**) (*informal*) to join in a discussion, an argument, an activity, etc. by saying sth important, persuading sb, or doing sth to help: *We all weighed in with our suggestions.* ◇ *Finally the government weighed in with financial aid.* **ˈweigh on sb/sth** to make sb anxious or worried: *The responsibilities **weigh heavily** on him.* ◇ *Something was weighing on her mind.* **ˌweigh sth↔ˈout** to measure an amount of sth by weight: *She weighed out a kilo of flour.* **ˌweigh sb↔ˈup** to form an opinion of sb by watching or talking to them

weigh·bridge /ˈweɪbrɪdʒ/ *noun* a machine for weighing vehicles and their loads, usually with a platform onto which the vehicle is driven

ˈweigh-in *noun* the occasion when the weight of a BOXER, JOCKEY, etc. is checked officially

ˈweighing machine *noun* a machine for weighing large objects or for weighing people in a public place

weight 0‑ /weɪt/ *noun, verb*
■ ***noun***
▸ BEING HEAVY **1** 0‑ [U, C] how heavy sb/sth is, which can be measured in, for example, kilograms or pounds: *It is about 76 kilos **in weight**.* ◇ *Bananas are sold by weight.* ◇ *In the wild, this fish can reach a weight of 5lbs.* ◇ *She is trying to **lose weight*** (= become less heavy and less fat). ◇ *He's **put on/gained weight*** (= become heavier and fatter) *since he gave up smoking.* ◇ *Sam has a weight problem* (= is too fat). ◇ *No more for me. I have to **watch my weight**.* ➲ COLLOCATIONS at DIET ➲ see also OVERWEIGHT, UNDERWEIGHT **2** 0‑ [U] the fact of being heavy: *He staggered a little **under the weight of** his backpack.* ◇ *I just hoped the branch would **take my weight**.* ◇ *The pillars have to support the weight of the roof.* ◇ *Don't put any weight on that ankle for at least a week.* ➲ see also DEADWEIGHT
▸ HEAVY OBJECT **3** 0‑ [C] an object that is heavy: *The doctor said he should not lift heavy weights.* **4** [C] an object used to keep sth in position or as part of a machine: *weights on a fishing line* ➲ see also PAPERWEIGHT
▸ RESPONSIBILITY/WORRY **5** [sing.] **~** (**of sth**) a great responsibility or worry SYN **burden**: *The full weight of responsibility falls on her.* ◇ *The news was certainly a **weight off my mind*** (= I did not have to worry about it any more). ◇ *Finally telling the truth was **a great weight off my shoulders**.*
▸ INFLUENCE/STRENGTH **6** [U] importance, influence or strength: *The many letters of support **added weight** to the campaign.* ◇ *The President has now offered to **lend** his **weight to** the project.* ◇ *Your opinion **carries weight** with the boss.* ◇ *How can you ignore **the sheer weight of** medical opinion?* ◇ *The weight of evidence against her is overwhelming.*
▸ FOR MEASURING/LIFTING **7** [C, U] a unit or system of units by which weight is measured: *tables of weights and measures* ◇ ***imperial/metric weight*** **8** [C] a piece of metal that is known to weigh a particular amount and is used to measure the weight of sth, or lifted by people to improve their strength and as a sport: *a set of weights* ◇ *She lifts weights as part of her training.* ◇ *He does a lot of **weight training**.*
IDM **take the weight off your feet** (*informal*) to sit down and rest, especially when you are tired: *Come and sit down and take the weight off your feet for a while.* **throw your ˈweight about/around** (*informal*) to use your position of authority or power in an aggressive way in order to achieve what you want **throw/put your weight behind sth** to use all your influence and power to support sth **weight of ˈnumbers** the combined power, strength or influence of a group: *They won the argument by sheer weight of numbers.* ➲ more at GROAN *v.*, PULL *v.*, PUNCH *v.*, WORTH *adj.*
■ ***verb***
▸ ATTACH HEAVY OBJECT **1** **~ sth** (**down**) (**with sth**) to attach a weight to sth in order to keep it in the right position or make it heavier: *The fishing nets are weighted with lead.*
▸ GIVE IMPORTANCE **2** [usually passive] **~ sth** to give different values to things to show how important you think each of them is compared with the others: *The results of the survey were weighted to allow for variations in the sample.* ◇ *a **weighted vote*** (= one that is worth more than a single vote) ◇ (*NAmE*) *a **weighted grade*** (= given at school for a course that is more advanced or harder and so has a higher value)

weight·ed /ˈweɪtɪd/ *adj.* [not before noun] arranged in such a way that a particular person or thing has an advantage or a disadvantage SYN **biased**: **~ towards sb/sth** *The proposal is weighted towards smaller businesses.* ◇ **~ against sb/sth** *Everything seemed weighted against them.* ◇ **~ in favour of sb/sth** *The course is heavily weighted in favour of engineering.*

weight·ing /ˈweɪtɪŋ/ *noun* **1** [U] (*BrE*) extra money that you get paid for working in a particular area because it is expensive to live there **2** [C, U] a value that you give to each of a number of things to show how important it is compared with the others: *Each of the factors is given a weighting on a scale of 1 to 10.* ◇ *Each question in the exam has equal weighting.*

weight·less /ˈweɪtləs/ *adj.* having no weight or appearing to have no weight, for example because there is no GRAVITY: *Astronauts work in weightless conditions.* ▸ **weight·less·ness** *noun* [U]

weight·lift·ing /ˈweɪtlɪftɪŋ/ *noun* [U] the sport or activity of lifting heavy weights ▸ **weight·lift·er** *noun*

weighty /ˈweɪti/ *adj.* (**weight·ier**, **weighti·est**) (*formal*) **1** important and serious: *weighty matters* **2** heavy: *a* ***weighty volume/tome*** ▸ **weight·ily** /-ɪli/ *adv.* **weighti·ness** *noun* [U]

weir /wɪə(r); *NAmE* wɪr/ *noun* a low wall or barrier built across a river in order to control the flow of water or change its direction

weird /wɪəd; *NAmE* wɪrd/ *adj., verb*

■ ***adj.*** (**weird·er**, **weird·est**) **1** very strange or unusual and difficult to explain SYN **strange**: *a weird dream* ◇ *She's a really weird girl.* ◇ *He's got some weird ideas.* ◇ *It's really weird seeing yourself on television.* ◇ *the* ***weird and wonderful*** *creatures that live beneath the sea* **2** strange in a mysterious and frightening way SYN **eerie**: *She began to make weird inhuman sounds.* ▸ **weird·ly** *adv.*: *The town was weirdly familiar.* **weird·ness** *noun* [U]

■ ***verb***

PHR V ˌ**weird sb ˈout** (*informal*) to seem strange or worrying to sb and make them feel uncomfortable: *The whole concept really weirds me out.*

weirdo /ˈwɪədəʊ; *NAmE* ˈwɪrdoʊ/ *noun* (*pl.* **-os** /-əʊz/) (*informal, disapproving*) a person who looks strange and/or behaves in a strange way

welch /weltʃ; welʃ/ *verb* = WELSH

wel·come 🔑 /ˈwelkəm/ *verb, adj., noun, exclamation*

■ ***verb*** **1** 🔑 [T, I] to say hello to sb in a friendly way when they arrive somewhere: **~ (sb)** *They were at the door to welcome us.* ◇ *a welcoming smile* ◇ **~ sb to sth** *It is a pleasure to welcome you to our home.* **2** 🔑 [T] **~ sb** to be pleased that sb has come or has joined an organization, activity, etc: *They* ***welcomed*** *the new volunteers* ***with open arms*** (= with enthusiasm). **3** 🔑 [T] **~ sth** to be pleased to receive or accept sth: *I'd welcome any suggestions.* ◇ *I* ***warmly welcome*** *this decision.* ◇ *In general, the changes they had made were to be welcomed.*

■ ***adj.*** **1** 🔑 that you are pleased to have, receive, etc: *a welcome sight* ◇ *Your letter was very welcome.* ◇ *The fine weather* ***made a welcome change.*** **2** 🔑 (of people) accepted or wanted somewhere: *Children are always welcome at the hotel.* ◇ *Our neighbours* ***made us welcome*** *as soon as we arrived.* ◇ *I had the feeling we were not welcome at the meeting.* **3** 🔑 **~ to do sth** (*informal*) used to say that you are happy for sb to do sth if they want to: *They're welcome to stay here as long as they like.* **4 ~ to sth** (*informal*) used to say that you are very happy for sb to have sth because you definitely do not want it: *It's an awful job. If you want it, you're* ***welcome to it!***

IDM **you're ˈwelcome** 🔑 used as a polite reply when sb thanks you for sth: *'Thanks for your help.' 'You're welcome.'*

■ ***noun*** **1** 🔑 [C, U] something that you do or say to sb when they arrive, especially sth that makes them feel you are happy to see them: *Thank you for your* ***warm welcome.*** ◇ *The winners were* ***given an*** *enthusiastic* ***welcome*** *when they arrived home.* ◇ *a* ***speech/smile of welcome*** ◇ *to receive a* ***hero's welcome*** **2** [C] the way that people react to sth, which shows their opinion of it: *This new comedy deserves a* ***warm welcome.*** ◇ *The proposals were* ***given a*** *cautious* ***welcome*** *by the trade unions.*

IDM **outstay/overstay your ˈwelcome** to stay somewhere as a guest longer than you are wanted

■ ***exclamation*** 🔑 used as a GREETING to tell sb that you are pleased that they are there: *Welcome home!* ◇ *Welcome to Oxford!* ◇ *Good evening everybody. Welcome to the show!*

ˈ**welcome mat** *noun*

IDM **lay, put, roll, etc. out the ˈwelcome mat (for sb)** (*especially NAmE*) to make sb feel welcome; to try to attract visitors, etc.

wel·com·ing /ˈwelkəmɪŋ/ *adj.* **1** (of a person) friendly towards sb who is visiting or arriving **2** (of a place) attractive and looking comfortable to be in OPP **unwelcoming**

weld /weld/ *verb, noun*

■ ***verb*** **1** [T, I] to join pieces of metal together by heating their edges and pressing them together: **~ (sth)** *to weld a broken axle* ◇ **~ A (on) (to B)** *The car has had a new wing welded on.* ◇ **~ A and B (together)** *All the parts of the sculpture have to be welded together.* **2** [T] to unite people or things into a strong and effective group: **~ sb/sth into sth** *They had welded a bunch of untrained recruits into an efficient fighting force.* ◇ **~ sth together** *The crisis helped to weld the party together.*

■ ***noun*** a joint made by welding

weld·er /ˈweldə(r)/ *noun* a person whose job is welding metal

wel·fare AW /ˈwelfeə(r); *NAmE* -fer/ *noun* [U] **1** the general health, happiness and safety of a person, an animal or a group SYN **well-being**: *We are concerned about the child's welfare.* **2** practical or financial help that is provided, often by the government, for people or animals that need it: *The state is still the main provider of welfare.* ◇ *child welfare* ◇ *a social welfare programme* ◇ ***welfare provision/services/work*** **3** (*especially NAmE*) (*BrE* also ˌ**social seˈcurity**) money that the government pays regularly to people who are poor, unemployed, sick, etc: *They would rather work than live* ***on welfare.*** ➲ COLLOCATIONS at UNEMPLOYMENT

ˌ**welfare ˈstate** *noun* **1** (often **the Welfare State**) [usually sing.] a system by which the government provides a range of free services to people who need them, for example medical care, money for people without work, care for old people, etc. **2** [C] a country that has such a system

wel·kin /ˈwelkɪn/ *noun* [U] (*literary* or *old use*) the sky or heaven

IDM **let/make the welkin ˈring** to make a very loud noise

well 🔑 /wel/ *adv., adj., exclamation, noun, verb*

■ ***adv.*** (**bet·ter** /ˈbetə(r)/, **best** /best/) **1** 🔑 in a good, right or acceptable way: *The kids all behaved well.* ◇ *The conference was very well organized.* ◇ ***Well done!*** (= expressing admiration for what sb has done) ◇ *His campaign was not* ***going well.*** ◇ *These animals make very good pets if treated well* (= with kindness). ◇ *People* ***spoke well of*** (= spoke with approval of) *him.* ◇ *She* ***took it*** *very* ***well*** (= did not react too badly), *all things considered.* ◇ *They lived well* (= in comfort and spending a lot of money) *and were generous with their money.* ◇ *She was determined to marry well* (= marry sb rich and/or with a high social position). **2** 🔑 thoroughly and completely: *Add the lemon juice and mix well.* ◇ *The surface must be well prepared before you start to paint.* ◇ *How well do you know Carla?* ◇ *He's well able to take care of himself.* ◇ (*BrE, informal*) *I was well annoyed, I can tell you.* **3** 🔑 to a great extent or degree: *He was driving at well over the speed limit.* ◇ *a well-loved tale* ◇ *The castle is* ***well worth*** *a visit.* ◇ *He liked her* ***well enough*** (= to a reasonable degree) *but he wasn't going to make a close friend of her.* **4 can/could well** easily: *She could well afford to pay for it herself.* **5 can/could/may/might well** probably: *You may well be right.* ◇ ***It may well be that*** *the train is delayed.* **6 can/could/may/might well** with good reason: ***I can't very well*** *leave now.* ◇ ***I couldn't very well*** *refuse to help them, could I?* ◇ *'What are we doing here?'* ***'You may well ask*** (= I don't really know either).'

IDM **as well (as sb/sth)** 🔑 in addition to sb/sth; too: *Are they coming as well?* ◇ *They sell books as well as newspapers.*

W

◇ *She is a talented musician as well as being a photographer.* ➲ note at ALSO **be doing 'well** 0-w to be getting healthier after an illness; to be in good health after a birth: *Mother and baby are doing well.* **(you, etc.) may/might as well be hanged/hung for a ˌsheep as (for) a 'lamb** (*saying*) if you are going to be punished for doing sth wrong, whether it is a big or small thing, you may as well do the big thing **be well on the way to sth/doing sth** to have nearly achieved sth and be going to achieve it soon: *She is well on the way to recovery.* ◇ *He is well on the way to establishing himself among the top ten players in the world.* **be ˌwell 'out of sth** (*BrE, informal*) to be lucky that you are not involved in sth **be ˌwell 'up in sth** to know a lot about sth: *He's well up in all the latest developments.* **do 'well** 0-w to be successful: *Jack is doing very well at school.* **do 'well by sb** to treat sb generously **do 'well for yourself** to become successful or rich **do 'well out of sb/sth** to make a profit or get money from sb/sth **do 'well to do sth** to be sensible or wise to do sth: *He* ***would do well to*** *concentrate more on his work.* ◇ *You did well to sell when the price was high.* **leave/let well a'lone** (*BrE*) (*NAmE* **let well enough a'lone**) to not get involved in sth that does not concern you: *When it comes to other people's arguments, it's better to leave well alone.* **may/might (just) as well do sth** to do sth because it seems best in the situation that you are in, although you may not really want to do it: *If no one else wants it, we might as well give it to him.* **ˌwell and 'truly** (*informal*) completely: *By that time we were well and truly lost.* **'well away** (*BrE, informal*) **1** having made good progress: *If we got Terry to do that, we'd be well away.* **2** drunk or fast asleep **ˌwell 'in (with sb)** (*informal*) to be good friends with sb, especially sb important: *She seems to be well in with all the right people.* ➲ more at BLOODY[1], FUCKING, JOLLY *adv.*, KNOW *v.*, MEAN *v.*, PRETTY *adv.*

■ ***adj.*** (**bet·ter** /ˈbetə(r)/, **best** /best/) **1** 0-w [not usually before noun] in good health: *I don't* ***feel*** *very* ***well.*** ◇ *Is she well enough to travel?* ◇ ***Get well soon!*** (= for example, on a card) ◇ *I'm better now, thank you.* ◇ (*informal*) *He's not a well man.* **2** [not before noun] in a good state or position: *It seems that* ***all is not well*** *at home.* ◇ ***All's well that ends well*** (= used when sth has ended happily, even though you thought it might not). **3** [not before noun] **(as) ~ (to do sth)** sensible; a good idea: *It would be* ***just as well*** *to call and say we might be late.* ◇ (*formal*) *It would be well to start early.*

IDM **ˌall very 'well (for sb) (to do sth)** (*informal*) used to criticize or reject a remark that sb has made, especially when they were trying to make you feel happier about sth: *It's all very well for you to say it doesn't matter, but I've put a lot of work into this and I want it to be a success.* **ˌall well and 'good** (*informal*) quite good but not exactly what is wanted: *That's all well and good, but why didn't he call her to say so?*

■ ***exclamation*** **1** 0-w used to express surprise, anger or relief: ***Well, well****—I would never have guessed it!* ◇ ***Well, really!*** *What a thing to say!* ◇ *Well, thank goodness that's over!* **2** 0-w used to show that you accept that sth cannot be changed: *Well, it can't be helped.* ◇ *'We lost.'* ***'Oh, well.*** *Better luck next time.'* **3** 0-w used to agree to sth, rather unwillingly: *Well, I suppose I could fit you in at 3.45.* ◇ *Oh,* ***very well,*** *then, if you insist.* **4** 0-w used when continuing a conversation after a pause: *Well, as I was saying...* **5** 0-w used to say that sth is uncertain: *'Do you want to come?' 'Well, I'm not sure.'* **6** 0-w used to show that you are waiting for sb to say sth: *Well? Are you going to tell us or not?* **7** 0-w used to mark the end of a conversation: *Well, I'd better be going now.* **8** 0-w used when you are pausing to consider your next words: *I think it happened, well, towards the end of last summer.* **9** used when you want to correct or change sth that you have just said: *There were thousands of people there—well, hundreds, anyway.*

IDM **well I 'never ('did)!** (*old-fashioned*) used to express surprise ➲ more at SAY *v.*

■ ***noun*** **1** a deep hole in the ground from which people obtain water. The sides of wells are usually covered with brick or stone and there is usually some covering or a small wall at the top of the well. **2** = OIL WELL **3** a narrow space in a building that drops down from a high to a low level and usually contains stairs or a lift/elevator ➲ see also STAIRWELL **4** (*BrE*) the space in front of the judge in a court, where the lawyers sit

■ ***verb*** **1** [I] **~ (up)** (of a liquid) to rise to the surface of sth and start to flow: *Tears were welling up in her eyes.* **2** [I] **~ (up)** (*literary*) (of an emotion) to become stronger: *Hate welled up inside him as he thought of the two of them together.*

Synonyms

well

all right • OK • fine • healthy • strong • fit

These words all describe sb who is not ill and is in good health.

well [not usually before noun] (*rather informal*) in good health: *I'm not feeling very well.* ◇ *Is he well enough to travel?* NOTE **Well** is used especially to talk about your own health, to ask sb about their health or to make a comment on it.

all right [not before noun] (*rather informal*) not feeling ill; not injured: *Are you feeling all right?*

OK [not before noun] (*informal*) not feeling ill; not injured: *She says she's OK now, and will be back at work tomorrow.*

ALL RIGHT OR OK?

These words are slightly less positive than the other words in this group. They are both used in spoken English to talk about not actually being ill or injured, rather than being positively in good health. Both are rather informal but **OK** is slightly more informal than **all right**.

fine [not before noun] (not used in negative statements) (*rather informal*) completely well: *'How are you?' 'Fine, thanks.'* NOTE **Fine** is used especially to talk about your health, especially when sb asks you how you are. It is also used to talk about sb's health when you are talking to sb else. Unlike **well** it is not often used to ask sb about their health or make a comment on it: *~~Are you keeping fine?~~*

healthy in good health and not likely to become ill: *Keep healthy by exercising regularly.*

strong in good health and not suffering from an illness: *After a few weeks she was feeling stronger.* NOTE **Strong** is often used to talk about becoming healthy again after an illness.

fit (*especially BrE*) in good physical health, especially because you take regular physical exercise: *I go swimming every day in order to keep fit.*

PATTERNS

- all right/OK/fit **for** sth
- all right/OK/fit **to do sth**
- to **feel/look** well/all right/OK/fine/healthy/strong/fit
- to **keep (sb)** well/healthy/fit
- **perfectly** well/all right/OK/fine/healthy/fit
- **physically** well/healthy/strong/fit

Grammar Point

well

- Compound adjectives beginning with **well** are generally written with no hyphen when they are used alone after a verb, but with a hyphen when they come before a noun: *She is well dressed.* ◇ *a well-dressed woman.* The forms without hyphens are given in the entries in the dictionary, but forms with hyphens can be seen in some examples.
- The comparative and superlative forms of these are usually formed with **better** and **best**: *better-known poets* ◇ *the best-dressed person in the room.*

W

we'll /wiːl; wil/ *short form* **1** we will **2** we shall

ˌwell adˈjusted *adj.* (of a person) able to deal with people, problems and life in general in a normal, sensible way ➲ compare MALADJUSTED

ˌwell adˈvised *adj.* [not before noun] ~ (**to do sth**) acting in the most sensible way: *You **would be well advised to** tackle this problem urgently.* ➲ compare ILL-ADVISED

ˌwell apˈpointed *adj.* (*formal*) having all the necessary equipment; having comfortable and attractive furniture, etc.

ˌwell atˈtended *adj.* attended by a lot of people: *a well-attended conference*

ˌwell ˈbalanced *adj.* **1** containing a sensible variety of the sort of things or people that are needed: *a well-balanced diet* ◇ *The team was not well balanced.* **2** (of a person or their behaviour) sensible and emotionally in control: *His response was well balanced.*

ˌwell beˈhaved *adj.* behaving in a way that other people think is polite or correct: *a well-behaved child* ◇ *The audience was surprisingly well behaved.*

ˈwell-being *noun* [U] general health and happiness: ***emotional/physical/psychological well-being*** ◇ *to **have a sense of well-being***

ˌwell ˈborn *adj.* (*formal*) from a rich family or a family of high social class

ˌwell ˈbred *adj.* (*old-fashioned, formal*) having or showing good manners; typical of a high social class: *a well-bred young lady* ◇ *She was too well bred to show her disappointment.* OPP **ill-bred**

ˌwell ˈbuilt *adj.* **1** (of a person) with a solid, strong body **2** (of a building or machine) strongly made

ˌwell conˈnected *adj.* (*formal*) (of a person) having important or rich friends or relatives

ˌwell ˈcut *adj.* (of clothes) made well and therefore probably expensive

ˌwell deˈfined *adj.* easy to see or understand: *well-defined rules* ◇ *These categories are not well defined.* OPP **ill-defined**

ˌwell deˈveloped *adj.* fully developed; fully grown: *He had a well-developed sense of his own superiority.*

ˌwell disˈposed *adj.* ~ (**towards/to sb/sth**) having friendly feelings towards sb or a positive attitude towards sth OPP **ill-disposed**

ˌwell ˈdocumented *adj.* having a lot of written evidence to prove, support or explain it: *The problem is well documented.* ◇ *well-documented facts*

ˌwell ˈdone *adj.* (of food, especially meat) cooked thoroughly or for a long time: *He prefers his steak well done.* ➲ compare RARE, UNDERDONE

ˌwell ˈdressed *adj.* wearing fashionable or expensive clothes: *This is what today's well-dressed man is wearing.*

ˌwell ˈearned *adj.* much deserved: *a well-earned rest*

ˌwell enˈdowed *adj.* **1** (*informal, humorous*) (of a woman) having large breasts **2** (*informal, humorous*) (of a man) having large GENITALS **3** (of an organization) having a lot of money: *well-endowed colleges*

ˌwell eˈstablished *adj.* having a respected position, because of being successful, etc. over a long period: *a well-established firm* ◇ *He is now well established in his career.*

ˌwell ˈfed *adj.* having plenty of good food to eat regularly: *well-fed family pets* ◇ *The animals all looked well fed and cared for.*

ˌwell ˈformed *adj.* (of sentences) written or spoken correctly according to the rules of grammar

ˌwell ˈfounded (also *less frequent* **ˌwell ˈgrounded**) *adj.* having good reasons or evidence to cause or support it: *well-founded suspicions* ◇ *His fear turned out to be well founded.* OPP **ill-founded**

ˌwell ˈgroomed *adj.* (of a person) looking clean, neat and carefully dressed

ˌwell ˈgrounded *adj.* **1** ~ **in sth** having a good training in a subject or skill **2** = WELL FOUNDED

ˌwell ˈheeled *adj.* (*informal*) having a lot of money SYN **rich, wealthy**

ˌwell ˈhung *adj.* **1** (of meat) having been left for several days before being cooked in order to improve the flavour **2** (of a man) (*informal*) having a large PENIS

ˌwell inˈformed *adj.* having or showing knowledge or information about many subjects or about one particular subject: *a well-informed decision* OPP **ill-informed**

wel·ling·ton /ˈwelɪŋtən/ (also **ˌwellington ˈboot**, *informal* **welly**) (all *BrE*) (*NAmE* **ˌrubber ˈboot**) *noun* one of a pair of long rubber boots, usually reaching almost up to the knee, that you wear to stop your feet getting wet: *a pair of wellingtons* ➲ VISUAL VOCAB page V52

ˌwell inˈtentioned *adj.* intending to be helpful or useful but not always succeeding very well SYN **well meaning**

ˌwell ˈkept *adj.* **1** kept neat and in good condition: *well-kept gardens* **2** (of a secret) known only to a few people

ˌwell ˈknown 0-π *adj.*
1 0-π known about by a lot of people SYN **famous**: *a well-known actor* ◇ *His books are not well known.* **2** 0-π (of a fact) generally known and accepted: *It is a well-known fact that caffeine is a stimulant.*

ˌwell ˈmannered *adj.* (*formal*) having good manners SYN **polite** OPP **ill-mannered**

ˌwell ˈmatched *adj.* able to live together, play or fight each other, etc. because they are similar in character, ability, etc: *a well-matched couple* ◇ *The two teams were well matched.*

ˌwell ˈmeaning *adj.* intending to do what is right and helpful but often not succeeding SYN **well intentioned**: *a well-meaning attempt to be helpful* ◇ *He's very well meaning.*

ˌwell ˈmeant *adj.* done, said, etc. in order to be helpful but often not succeeding: *well-meant comments* ◇ *His offer was well meant.*

well·ness /ˈwelnəs/ *noun* [U] (*especially NAmE*) the state of being healthy

ˌwell-ˈnigh *adv.* (*formal*) almost: *Defence was well-nigh impossible against such opponents.*

ˌwell ˈoff *adj.* **1** (*comparative* **better ˈoff**) having a lot of money SYN **rich**: *a well-off family* ◇ *They are much better off than us.* ➲ SYNONYMS at RICH **2** (*comparative* **better ˈoff**, *superlative* **best ˈoff**) in a good situation: *I've got my own room so I'm well off.* ◇ *Some people don't know when they're well off.* OPP **badly off**

IDM **be well ˈoff for sth** (*BrE*) to have enough of sth: *We're well off for jobs around here* (= there are many available).

ˌwell ˈoiled *adj.* operating smoothly and well: *The system ran like a well-oiled machine.*

ˌwell ˈpaid *adj.* earning or providing a lot of money: *well-paid managers* ◇ *The job is very well paid.*

ˌwell preˈserved *adj.* not showing many signs of age; kept in good condition

ˌwell ˈread *adj.* having read many books and therefore having gained a lot of knowledge

ˌwell ˈrounded *adj.* **1** having a variety of experiences and abilities and a fully developed personality: *well-rounded individuals* **2** providing or showing a variety of experience, ability, etc: *a well-rounded education* **3** (of a person's body) pleasantly round in shape

ˌwell ˈrun *adj.* managed smoothly and well: *a well-run hotel*

ˌwell ˈspoken *adj.* having a way of speaking that is considered correct or elegant

well·spring /ˈwelsprɪŋ/ *noun* (*literary*) a supply or source of a particular quality, especially one that never ends

ˌwell ˈthought of *adj.* respected, admired and liked: *Their family has always been well thought of around here.*

ˌwell thought ˈout *adj.* carefully planned

W

ˌwell ˈthumbed *adj.* a **well-thumbed** book has been read many times

ˌwell ˈtimed *adj.* done or happening at the right time or at an appropriate time SYN **timely**: *a well-timed intervention* ◇ *Your remarks were certainly well timed.* OPP **ill-timed**

ˌwell-to-ˈdo *adj.* having a lot of money SYN **rich**, **wealthy**: *a well-to-do family* ◇ *They're very well-to-do.*

ˌwell ˈtravelled (*BrE*) (*NAmE* **ˌwell ˈtraveled**) *adj.* **1** (of a person) having travelled to many different places **2** (of a route) used by a lot of people

ˌwell ˈtried *adj.* used many times before and known to be successful: *a well-tried method*

ˌwell ˈtrodden *adj.* (*formal*) (of a road or path) much used

ˌwell ˈturned *adj.* (*formal*) expressed in an elegant way: *a well-turned phrase*

ˌwell ˈused *adj.* used a lot: *a well-used path*

ˈwell-wisher *noun* a person who wants to show that they support sb and want them to be happy, successful, etc.

ˌwell ˈworn *adj.* **1** worn or used a lot or for a long time: *a well-worn jacket* ◇ *Most British visitors beat a well-worn path to the same tourist areas of the US.* **2** (of a phrase, story, etc.) heard so often that it does not sound interesting any more SYN **hackneyed**

welly /ˈweli/ *noun, verb*
- **noun** (*pl.* -ies) (*BrE, informal*) = WELLINGTON: *a pair of green wellies*

IDM **give it some ˈwelly** (*BrE, informal*) to use a lot of physical effort
- **verb** (**wel·lies, welly·ing, wel·lied, wel·lied**) **~ sth (+ adv./prep.)** (*BrE, informal*) to hit or kick sth very hard: *He wellied the ball over the bar.*

Welsh /welʃ/ *noun, adj.*
- **noun** **1** [U] the Celtic language of Wales: *Do you speak Welsh?* **2** **the Welsh** [pl.] the people of Wales
- **adj.** of or connected with Wales, its people or its language: *Welsh poetry*

welsh /welʃ/ (also **welch**) *verb* [I] **~ (on sb/sth)** (*disapproving, informal*) to not do sth that you have promised to do, for example to not pay money that you owe: *'I'm not in the habit of welshing on deals,' said Don.*

the ˌWelsh Asˈsembly (also **the ˌNational Asˌsembly for ˈWales**) *noun* [sing.] the group of people who are elected as a government for Wales with limited independence from the British Parliament that includes the power to make certain laws

ˌWelsh ˈdresser *noun* (*BrE*) = DRESSER

ˌWelsh ˈrarebit (also **rare·bit**) *noun* [U] (*BrE*) a hot dish of cheese melted on TOAST

welt /welt/ *noun* a raised mark on the skin where sth has hit or rubbed you SYN **weal**

Welt·an·schau·ung /ˈveltænʃaʊʊŋ/ *noun* (*pl.* **Welt·an·schau·ung·en** /-ən/) (from *German, formal*) a particular philosophy or view of life

wel·ter /ˈweltə(r)/ *noun* [sing.] **~ of sth** (*formal*) a large and confusing amount of sth: *a welter of information*

wel·ter·weight /ˈweltəweɪt; *NAmE* -tərw-/ *noun* a BOXER weighing between 61 and 67 kilograms, heavier than a LIGHTWEIGHT: *a welterweight champion*

wench /wentʃ/ *noun* (*old use* or *humorous*) a young woman

wend /wend/ *verb* [T, I] **~ (your way) (+ adv./prep.)** (*old use* or *literary*) to move or travel slowly somewhere: *Leo wended his way home through the wet streets.*

Wendy house /ˈwendi haʊs/ *noun* (*BrE*) = PLAYHOUSE

went *past tense of* GO

wept *past tense, past part.* of WEEP

were /wə(r); *strong form* wɜː(r)/ ➲ BE

we're /wɪə(r); *NAmE* wɪr/ *short form* we are

weren't /wɜːnt/ *short form* were not

were·wolf /ˈweəwʊlf; *NAmE* ˈwerw-/ *noun* (*pl.* -wolves /-wʊlvz/) (in stories) a person who sometimes changes into a WOLF, especially at the time of the full moon

Wer·nicke's area /ˈwɜːnɪkəz eəriə; ˈveənɪkəz; *NAmE* ˈwɜːrnɪkəz eriə; ˈvern-/ *noun* (*anatomy*) an area in the brain concerned with understanding language

west 🔑 /west/ *noun, adj., adv.*
- **noun** [U, sing.] (*abbr.* W) **1** 🔑 (usually **the west**) the direction that you look towards to see the sun go down; one of the four main points of the COMPASS: *Which way is west?* ◇ *Rain is spreading from the west.* ◇ *He lives* **to the west of** (= further west than) *the town.* ➲ picture at COMPASS ➲ compare EAST, NORTH, SOUTH **2** 🔑 **the West** Europe, N America and Canada, contrasted with Eastern countries: *I was born in Japan, but I've lived in the West for some years now.* **3** **the West** (*NAmE*) the western side of the US: *the history of the American West* ➲ see also THE MIDWEST, THE WILD WEST **4** **the West** (in the past) Western Europe and N America, when contrasted with the Communist countries of Eastern Europe: *East-West relations*
- **adj.** [only before noun] (*abbr.* W) **1** 🔑 in or towards the west: *West Africa* ◇ *the west coast of Scotland* **2** 🔑 a **west wind** blows from the west ➲ compare WESTERLY
- **adv.** 🔑 towards the west: *This room faces west.*

west·bound /ˈwestbaʊnd/ *adj.* travelling or leading towards the west: *westbound traffic* ◇ *the westbound carriageway of the motorway*

the ˌWest ˈCoast *noun* [sing.] the states on the west coast of the US, especially California

the ˈWest Country *noun* [sing.] the counties in the south-west of England

the ˌWest ˈEnd *noun* [sing.] the western area of central London where there are many theatres, shops/stores and hotels

west·er·ly /ˈwestəli; *NAmE* -ərli/ *adj., noun*
- **adj.** **1** [only before noun] in or towards the west: *travelling in a westerly direction* **2** [usually before noun] (of winds) blowing from the west: *westerly gales* ➲ compare WEST
- **noun** (*pl.* -ies) a wind that blows from the west: *light westerlies*

west·ern 🔑 /ˈwestən; *NAmE* -ərn/ *adj., noun*
- **adj.** **1** 🔑 [only before noun] (*abbr.* W) (also **Western**) located in the west or facing west: *western Spain* ◇ *Western Europe* ◇ *the western slopes of the mountain* **2** 🔑 (usually **Western**) connected with the west part of the world, especially Europe and N America: *Western art* ➲ see also COUNTRY AND WESTERN
- **noun** a film/movie or book about life in the western US in the 19th century, usually involving COWBOYS

west·ern·er /ˈwestənə(r); *NAmE* -ərn-/ *noun* **1** a person who comes from or lives in the western part of the world, especially western Europe or N America **2** **Westerner** a person who was born in or who lives in western Canada or the US

west·ern·iza·tion (*BrE* also **-isa·tion**) /ˌwestənaɪˈzeɪʃn; *NAmE* -ərnəˈz-/ *noun* [U] the process of becoming westernized

west·ern·ize (*BrE* also **-ise**) /ˈwestənaɪz; *NAmE* -ərn-/ *verb* [usually passive] **~ sth** to bring ideas or ways of life that are typical of western Europe and N America to other countries: *The islands have been westernized by the growth of tourism.* ▸ **west·ern·ized, -ised** *adj.*: *a westernized society*

west·ern·most /ˈwestənməʊst; *NAmE* -ərnmoʊst/ *adj.* located furthest west: *the westernmost tip of the island*

the West Indies /ˌwest ˈɪndiz; -diːz/ *noun* [pl.] several groups of islands between the Caribbean and the Atlantic, that include the Antilles and the Bahamas ▸ **ˌWest ˈIndian** *adj.* **ˌWest ˈIndian** *noun*

West·min·ster /ˈwestmɪnstə(r)/ *noun* [U] the British parliament and government: *The rumours were still circulating at Westminster.* ORIGIN From the name of the part of London with the Houses of Parliament, Downing Street and many government offices.

ˌ**west-north-ˈwest** *noun* [sing.] (*abbr.* WNW) the direction at an equal distance between west and north-west ▶ ˌ**west-north-ˈwest** *adv.*

the ˈWest Side *noun* [sing.] the western part of Manhattan in New York City which includes Broadway and Central Park

ˌ**west-south-ˈwest** *noun* [sing.] (*abbr.* WSW) the direction at an equal distance between west and south-west ▶ ˌ**west-south-ˈwest** *adv.*

west·wards /ˈwestwədz; *NAmE* -wərdz/ (also **westward**) *adv.* towards the west: *to turn westwards* ▶ **westward** *adj.*: *in a westward direction*

Synonyms

wet

moist • damp • soaked • drenched • saturated

These words all describe things covered with or full of liquid, especially water.

wet covered with or full of liquid, especially water: *The car had skidded on the wet road.* ◇ *You'll get wet* (= in the rain) *if you go out now.*

moist slightly wet, often in a way that is pleasant or useful: *a lovely rich moist cake*

damp slightly wet, often in a way that is unpleasant: *The cottage was cold and damp.*

soaked (*rather informal*) very wet: *You're soaked through!* (= completely wet)

drenched very wet: *We were caught in the storm and came home drenched to the skin.*

SOAKED OR DRENCHED?

Both of these words can be used with *with* or *in*: *soaked/drenched with/in sweat/blood.* **Soaked** but not usually **drenched** can also be used before a noun: *their soaked clothes* ◇ ~~*their drenched clothes*~~

saturated very wet: *The ground is completely saturated: it would be pointless to plant anything.*

PATTERNS

- wet/moist/damp/soaked/drenched/saturated **with** sth
- soaked/drenched **in** sth
- sb's **coat/shirt/shoes/clothes/hair** is/are wet/damp/soaked/drenched
- wet/moist/damp/saturated **ground/earth**
- to **get** wet/moist/damp/soaked/drenched/saturated

wet 🔑 /wet/ *adj., verb, noun*

■ ***adj.*** (**wet·ter**, **wet·test**) **1** 🔑 covered with or containing liquid, especially water: *wet clothes* ◇ *wet grass* ◇ *You'll **get wet*** (= in the rain) *if you go out now.* ◇ *Try not to get your shoes wet.* ◇ *His face was wet with tears.* ◇ *We were all **soaking wet*** (= extremely wet). ◇ *Her hair was still **dripping wet**.* ◇ *My shirt was **wet through*** (= completely wet). **2** 🔑 (of weather, etc.) with rain: *a wet day* ◇ *a wet climate* ◇ ***It's wet** outside.* ◇ *It's going to be wet tomorrow.* ◇ *It was the wettest October for many years.* **3** 🔑 (of paint, ink, etc.) not yet dry: *Keep off! Wet paint.* **4** if a child or its NAPPY/DIAPER is **wet**, its nappy/diaper is full of URINE **5** (*BrE*) (of a person) (*informal, disapproving*) lacking a strong character **SYN** **feeble**, **wimpish**: *'Don't be so wet,' she laughed.* ▶ **wetly** *adv.* **wet·ness** *noun* [U]

IDM **all ˈwet** (*NAmE, informal*) completely wrong (**still**) ˌ**wet behind the ˈears** (*informal, disapproving*) young and without much experience **SYN** **naive** ➲ more at FOOT *n.*

■ ***verb*** (**wet·ting**, **wet**, **wet** or **wet·ting**, **wet·ted**, **wet·ted**) **~ sth** to make sth wet: *Wet the brush slightly before putting it in the paint.*

IDM **wet the/your ˈbed** [no passive] to URINATE in your bed by accident: *It is quite common for small children to wet their beds.* ˈ**wet yourself** | **wet your ˈpants/ˈknickers** [no passive] to URINATE in your underwear by accident

■ ***noun*** **1 the wet** [sing.] wet weather; rain: *Come in out of the wet.* **2** [U] liquid, especially water: *The dog shook the wet from its coat.* **3** [C] (*BrE, disapproving*) a conservative politician who supports MODERATE policies rather than extreme ones: *Tory wets* **4** [C] (*BrE, informal, disapproving*) a person who lacks a strong character **SYN** **wimp**

wet·back /ˈwetbæk/ *noun* (*US, taboo, slang*) an offensive word for a Mexican person, especially one who enters the US illegally

ˌ**wet ˈblanket** *noun* (*informal, disapproving*) a person who is not enthusiastic about anything and who stops other people from enjoying themselves

ˈ**wet dock** *noun* a place for ships to stay in order to be repaired, have goods put onto them, etc, in which there is enough water for the ship to float ➲ compare DRY DOCK

ˌ**wet ˈdream** *noun* a sexually exciting dream that a man has that results in an ORGASM

ˈ**wet fish** *noun* [U] (*BrE*) fresh raw fish for sale in a shop, etc.

wet·land /ˈwetlənd/ *noun* [C, U] (also **wetlands** [pl.]) an area of wet land: *The wetlands are home to a large variety of wildlife.* ▶ **wet·land** *adj.* [only before noun]: *wetland birds*

ˈ**wet look** *noun* [sing.] the appearance of hair being shiny and wet, obtained by using hair GEL or by treating it with chemicals ▶ ˈ**wet-look** *adj.*: *wet-look hair gel*

ˈ**wet nurse** *noun* (usually in the past) a woman employed to feed another woman's baby with her own breast milk

ˈ**wet room** *noun* (*BrE*) a bathroom in which the shower is not separated from the rest of the room

wet·suit /ˈwetsuːt; *BrE* also -sjuːt/ *noun* a piece of clothing made of rubber that fits the whole body closely, worn by people swimming underwater or sailing ➲ VISUAL VOCAB page V34

wet·ware /ˈwetweə(r); *NAmE* -wer/ *noun* [U] (*computing*) the human brain, considered as a computer program or system

we've /wiːv; wiv/ *short form* we have

whack /wæk/ *verb, noun*

■ ***verb*** **1 ~ sb/sth** (*informal*) to hit sb/sth very hard: *She whacked him with her handbag.* ◇ *James whacked the ball over the net.* **2 ~ sth + adv./prep.** (*informal*) to put sth somewhere without much care: *Just whack your bags in the corner.* **3 ~ sb** (*NAmE, slang*) to murder sb

■ ***noun*** [usually sing.] (*informal*) **1** the act of hitting sb/sth hard; the sound made by this: *He gave the ball a good whack.* ◇ *I heard the whack of the bullet hitting the wood.* **2** (*BrE*) a share of sth; an amount of sth: *Don't leave all the work to her. Everyone should do their fair whack.* ◇ *You have to pay the full whack. There are no reductions.* ◇ *He charges **top whack*** (= the highest amount possible).

IDM **out of ˈwhack** (*informal, especially NAmE*) **1** no longer correct or working properly: *The system is clearly out of whack.* ◇ *All the traveling had thrown my body out of whack.* **2** not agreeing with or the same as sth else: *Expectations and reality got out of whack.*

whacked /wækt/ (also ˌ**whacked ˈout**) *adj.* [not usually before noun] (*BrE, informal*) very tired: *I'm whacked!*

whack·ing /ˈwækɪŋ/ (also ˈ**whacking great**) *adj.* (*BrE, informal*) used to emphasize how big or how much sth is **SYN** **whopping**: *a whacking great hole in the roof* ◇ *They were fined a whacking £100 000.*

whacko (also **wacko**) /ˈwækəʊ; *NAmE* -koʊ/ *adj.* (*informal*) crazy

whacky = WACKY

whale /weɪl/ *noun* a very large animal that lives in the sea and looks like a very large fish. There are several types of whale, some of which are hunted: *whale meat* ➲ see also BLUE WHALE, KILLER WHALE, PILOT WHALE, SPERM WHALE

IDM **have a ˈwhale of a time** (*informal*) to enjoy yourself very much; to have a very good time

W

whale·bone /ˈweɪlbəʊn; *NAmE* -boʊn/ *noun* [U] a thin hard substance found in the upper JAW of some types of whale, used in the past to make some clothes stiffer

whaler /ˈweɪlə(r)/ *noun* **1** a ship used for hunting whales **2** a person who hunts whales

whal·ing /ˈweɪlɪŋ/ *noun* [U] the activity or business of hunting and killing WHALES

wham /wæm/ *exclamation* (*informal*) **1** used to represent the sound of a sudden, loud hit: *The bombs went down—wham!—right on target.* **2** used to show that sth that is unexpected has suddenly happened: *I saw him yesterday and—wham!—I realized I was still in love with him.*

whammy /ˈwæmi/ *noun* (*pl.* -ies) (*informal*) an unpleasant situation or event that causes problems for sb/sth: *With this government we've had a* ***double whammy*** *of tax increases and benefit cuts.* ORIGIN From the 1950s American cartoon *Li'l Abner*, in which one of the characters could **shoot a whammy** (put a curse on sb) by pointing a finger with one eye open, or a **double whammy** with both eyes open.

wha·nau /ˈfɑːnaʊ/ *noun* (*pl.* **wha·nau**) (*NZE*) a family or community of related families who live together in the same area

wharf /wɔːf; *NAmE* wɔːrf/ *noun* (*pl.* **wharves** /wɔːvz; *NAmE* wɔːrvz/ or **wharfs**) a flat structure built beside the sea or a river where boats can be tied up and goods unloaded

what ⚷ /wɒt; *NAmE* wɑːt; wʌt/ *pron., det.*
1 ⚷ used in questions to ask for particular information about sb/sth: *What is your name?* ◇ *What* (= what job) *does he do?* ◇ *What time is it?* ◇ *What kind of music do you like?* ➲ compare WHICH **2** ⚷ the thing or things that; whatever: *What you need is a good meal.* ◇ *Nobody knows what will happen next.* ◇ *I spent what little time I had with my family.* **3** ⚷ used to say that you think that sth is especially good, bad, etc.: *What awful weather!* ◇ *What a beautiful house!*

IDM **and ˈwhat not | and what ˈhave you** (*informal*) and other things of the same type: *It's full of old toys, books and what not.* **get/give sb what ˈfor** (*BrE, informal*) to be punished/punish sb severely: *I'll give her what for if she does that again.* **or ˈwhat** (*informal*) **1** used to emphasize your opinion: *Is he stupid or what?* **2** used when you are not sure about sth: *I don't know if he's a teacher or what.* ◇ *Are we going now or what?* **what?** (*informal*) **1** ⚷ used when you have not heard or have not understood sth: *What? I can't hear you.* **2** ⚷ used to show that you have heard sb and to ask what they want: *'Mummy!' 'What?' 'I'm thirsty.'* **3** ⚷ used to express surprise or anger: *'It will cost $500.' 'What?'* ◇ *'I asked her to marry me.'* ***'You what?'*** **ˈwhat about...?** (*informal*) **1** ⚷ used to make a suggestion: *What about a trip to France?* **2** ⚷ used to introduce sb/sth into the conversation: *What about you, Joe? Do you like football?* **ˈwhat-d'you-call-him/-her/-it/-them | ˈwhat's-his/-her/-its/-their-name** used instead of a name that you cannot remember: *She's just gone out with old what-d'you-call-him.* **what for?** ⚷ for what purpose or reason?: *What is this tool for?* ◇ *What did you do that for* (= why did you do that)? ◇ *'I need to see a doctor.' 'What for?'* **what if...?** ⚷ what would happen if?: *What if the train is late?* ◇ *What if she forgets to bring it?* **what ˈof it?** (*informal*) used when admitting that sth is true, to ask why it should be considered important: *Yes, I wrote the article. What of it?* **what's ˌup with ˈthat?** (*especially NAmE*) used to suggest that sth you have heard is a stupid idea or does not make sense: *They dropped their best player. What's up with that?* **what's ˈwhat** (*informal*) what things are useful, important, etc: *She certainly knows what's what.* **what's with sb?** (*NAmE, informal*) used to ask why sb is behaving in a strange way: *What's with you? You haven't said a word all morning.* **what's with sth?** (*NAmE, informal*) used to ask the reason for sth: *What's with all this walking? Can't we take a cab?* **what with sth** used to list the various reasons for sth: *What with the cold weather and my bad leg, I haven't been out for weeks.*

whatch·am·acall·it /ˈwɒtʃəməkɔːlɪt; *NAmE* ˈwɑːt-; ˈwʌt-/ *noun* (*informal*) used when you cannot think of the name of sth: *Have you got a whatchamacallit? You know... a screwdriver?*

what·ever ⚷ /wɒtˈevə(r); *NAmE* wət-; wɑːt-/ *det., pron., adv.*
■ ***det., pron.*** **1** ⚷ any or every; anything or everything: *Take whatever action is needed.* ◇ *Do whatever you like.* **2** ⚷ used when you are saying that it does not matter what sb does or what happens, because the result will be the same: *Whatever decision he made I would support it.* ◇ *You have our support, whatever you decide.* **3** (*especially BrE*) used in questions to express surprise or confusion: *Whatever do you mean?* ◇ *Chocolate-flavoured carrots!* ***Whatever next?*** **4** (*informal, ironic*) used as a reply to tell sb that you do not care what happens or that you are not interested in what they are talking about: *'You should try a herbal remedy.' 'Yeah, whatever.'* **5** (*informal*) used to say that you do not mind what you do, have, etc. and that anything is acceptable: *'What would you like to do today?' 'Whatever.'*

IDM **or whatˈever** (*informal*) or sth of a similar type: *It's the same in any situation: in a prison, hospital or whatever.* **whatˈever you do** used to warn sb not to do sth under any circumstances: *Don't tell Paul, whatever you do!*

■ ***adv.*** **1** (also **what·so·ever**) **no, nothing, none, etc. ~** not at all; not of any kind: *They received no help whatever.* ◇ *'Is there any doubt about it?' 'None whatsoever.'* **2** (*informal*) used to say that it does not matter what sb does, or what happens, because the result will be the same: *We told him we'd back him whatever.*

what·not /ˈwɒtnɒt; *NAmE* ˈwɑːtnɑːt/ *noun* [U] **and ~** (*informal*) used when you are referring to sth, but are not being exact and do not mention its name: *It's a new firm. They make toys and whatnot.*

whats·it /ˈwɒtsɪt; *NAmE* ˈwɑːt-; ˈwʌt-/ *noun* (*informal, especially BrE*) used when you cannot think of the word or name you want, or do not want to use a particular word: *I've got to make a whatsit for the party. That's it—a flan.*

wheat /wiːt/ *noun* [U] a plant grown for its grain that is used to produce the flour for bread, cakes, PASTA, etc; the grain of this plant: *wheat flour* ➲ COLLOCATIONS at FARMING ➲ VISUAL VOCAB page V28

IDM **sort out/separate the ˌwheat from the ˈchaff** to distinguish useful or valuable people or things from ones that are not useful or have no value

the ˈWheat Belt *noun* [sing.] the western central region of the US including the Great Plains where wheat is an important crop

wheat·germ /ˈwiːtdʒɜːm; *NAmE* -dʒɜːrm/ *noun* [U] the centre of the wheat grain, which is especially good for your health

wheat·meal /ˈwiːtmiːl/ *noun* [U] a type of flour made from wheat, that uses more of the grain than WHITE FLOUR

whee /wiː/ *exclamation* used to express excitement

whee·dle /ˈwiːdl/ *verb* (*disapproving*) to persuade sb to give you sth or do sth by saying nice things that you do not mean SYN **coax**: **~ sth** (**out of sb**) *The kids can always wheedle money out of their father.* ◇ **~ sb into doing sth** *She wheedled me into lending her my new coat.* ◇ **+ speech** *'Come on, Em,' he wheedled.*

wheel ⚷ /wiːl/ *noun, verb*
■ ***noun***
▸ ON/IN VEHICLES **1** ⚷ [C] one of the round objects under a car, bicycle, bus, etc. that turns when it moves: *He braked suddenly, causing the front wheels to skid.* ◇ *One of the boys was pushing the other along in a little box* ***on wheels.*** **2** ⚷ [C, usually sing.] the round object used to steer a car, etc. or ship: *This is the first time I've sat* ***behind the wheel*** *since the accident.* ◇ *A car swept past with Laura* ***at the wheel.*** ◇ *Do you want to* ***take the wheel*** (= drive) *now?* ➲ see also HELM, STEERING WHEEL **3** **wheels** [pl.] (*informal*) a car: *At last he had his own wheels.*
▸ IN MACHINE **4** ⚷ [C] a flat round part in a machine: *gear wheels* ➲ see also CARTWHEEL, CATHERINE WHEEL, FER-

W

RIS WHEEL, MILL WHEEL, SPINNING WHEEL, WATER-WHEEL

▸ ORGANIZATION/SYSTEM **5 wheels** [pl.] **~ (of sth)** an organization or a system that seems to work like a complicated machine that is difficult to understand: *the **wheels of bureaucracy/commerce/government, etc.*** ◇ *It was Rob's idea. I merely **set the wheels in motion*** (= started the process).

▸ -WHEELED **6** (in adjectives) having the number or type of wheels mentioned: *a sixteen-wheeled lorry*

▸ -WHEELER **7** (in nouns) a car, bicycle, etc. with the number of wheels mentioned: *a three-wheeler*

IDM ˌ**wheels within ˈwheels** a situation which is difficult to understand because it involves complicated or secret processes and decisions: *There are wheels within wheels in this organization—you never really know what is going on.* ➲ more at COG, GREASE *v.*, OIL *v.*, REINVENT, SHOULDER *n.*, SPOKE

■ *verb*

▸ MOVE STH WITH WHEELS **1** [T] **~ sth (+ adv./prep.)** to push or pull sth that has wheels: *She wheeled her bicycle across the road.* **2** [T] **~ sb/sth (+ adv./prep.)** to move sb/sth that is in or on sth that has wheels: *The nurse wheeled him along the corridor.*

▸ MOVE IN CIRCLE **3** [I] **(+ adv./prep.)** to move or fly in a circle: *Birds wheeled above us in the sky.*

▸ TURN QUICKLY **4** [I, T] to turn quickly or suddenly and face the opposite direction; to make sb/sth do this: **(+ adv./prep.)** *She wheeled around and started running.* ◇ **~ sb/sth (+ adv./prep.)** *He wheeled his horse back to the gate.*

IDM ˌ**wheel and ˈdeal** (usually used in the progressive tenses) to do a lot of complicated deals in business or politics, often in a dishonest way

PHR V ˌ**wheel sth↔ˈout** to show or use sth to help you do sth, even when it has often been seen or heard before: *They wheeled out the same old arguments we'd heard so many times before.*

ˈ**wheel arch** *noun* a space in the body of a vehicle over a wheel, shaped like an ARCH

wheel·bar·row /ˈwiːlbærəʊ; *NAmE* -roʊ/ (also **barrow**) *noun* a large open container with a wheel and two handles that you use outside to carry things ➲ VISUAL VOCAB page V16

wheel·base /ˈwiːlbeɪs/ *noun* [sing.] (*technical*) the distance between the front and back wheels of a car or other vehicle

wheel·chair /ˈwiːltʃeə(r); *NAmE* -tʃer/ *noun* a special chair with wheels, used by people who cannot walk because of illness, an accident, etc: *Does the hotel have **wheelchair access**?* ◇ *He's been **confined to a wheelchair** since the accident.* ◇ *wheelchair users*

ˈ**wheel clamp** *noun* (*BrE*) = CLAMP, DENVER BOOT

wheeler-dealer /ˌwiːlə ˈdiːlə(r)/ *noun* (*informal*) a person who does a lot of complicated deals in business or politics, often in a dishonest way

wheel·house /ˈwiːlhaʊs/ *noun* a small CABIN with walls and a roof on a ship where the person steering stands at the wheel

wheelie /ˈwiːli/ *noun* (*informal*) a trick that you can do on a bicycle or motorcycle by balancing on the back wheel, with the front wheel off the ground: *to do a wheelie*

ˈ**wheelie bin** *noun* (*BrE, informal*) a large container with a lid and wheels, that you keep outside your house and use for putting rubbish in

wheel·wright /ˈwiːlraɪt/ *noun* a person whose job is making and repairing wheels, especially wooden ones

wheeze /wiːz/ *verb, noun*

■ *verb* [I, T] to breathe noisily and with difficulty: *He was coughing and wheezing all night.* ◇ **+ speech** *'I have a chest infection,' she wheezed.*

■ *noun* [usually sing.] **1** the high whistling sound that your chest makes when you cannot breathe easily **2** (*old-fashioned, BrE, informal*) a clever trick or plan

wheezy /ˈwiːzi/ *adj.* making the high whistling sound that your chest makes when you cannot breathe easily: *I'm wheezy today.* ◇ *a wheezy cough* ▸ **wheez·ily** /-ɪli/ *adv.* **wheezi·ness** *noun* [U]

whelk /welk/ *noun* a small SHELLFISH that can be eaten

whelp /welp/ *noun, verb*

■ *noun* (*technical*) a young animal of the dog family; a PUPPY or CUB

■ *verb* [I, T] **~ (sth)** (*formal*) (of a female dog) to give birth to a PUPPY or PUPPIES

when 🔑 /wen/ *adv., pron., conj.*

■ *adv.* **1** 🔑 (used in questions) at what time; on what occasion: *When did you last see him?* ◇ *When can I see you?* ◇ *When* (= in what circumstances) *would such a solution be possible?* **2** 🔑 used after an expression of time to mean 'at which' or 'on which': *Sunday is the only day when I can relax.* ◇ *There are times when I wonder why I do this job.* **3** 🔑 at which time; on which occasion: *The last time I went to Scotland was in May, when the weather was beautiful.*

■ *pron.* 🔑 what/which time: *Until when can you stay?* ◇ *'I've got a new job.' 'Since when?'*

■ *conj.* **1** 🔑 at or during the time that: *I loved history when I was at school.* **2** 🔑 after: *Call me when you've finished.* **3** 🔑 at any time that; whenever: *Can you spare five minutes when it's convenient?* **4** 🔑 just after which: *He had just drifted off to sleep when the phone rang.* **5** 🔑 considering that: *How can they expect to learn anything when they never listen?* **6** although: *She claimed to be 18, when I know she's only 16.* IDM see AS *conj.*

whence /wens/ *adv.* (*old use*) from where: *They returned whence they had come.*

when·ever 🔑 /wenˈevə(r)/ *conj., adv.*

■ *conj.* **1** 🔑 at any time that; on any occasion that: *You can ask for help whenever you need it.* **2** 🔑 every time that: *Whenever she comes, she brings a friend.* ◇ *The roof leaks whenever it rains.* ◇ *We try to help **whenever possible**.* **3** used when the time when sth happens is not important: *'When do you need it by?' 'Saturday or Sunday. Whenever.'* ◇ *It's not urgent—we can do it next week or whenever.*

■ *adv.* used in questions to mean 'when', expressing surprise: *Whenever did you find time to do all that cooking?*

where 🔑 /weə(r); *NAmE* wer/ *adv., conj.*

■ *adv.* **1** 🔑 in or to what place or situation: *Where do you live?* ◇ *I wonder where they will take us to.* ◇ *Where* (= at what point) *did I go wrong in my calculations?* ◇ *Where* (= in what book, newspaper, etc.) *did you read that?* ◇ *Just where* (= to what situation or final argument) *is all this leading us?* **2** 🔑 used after words or phrases that refer to a place or situation to mean 'at, in or to which': *It's one of the few countries where people drive on the left.* **3** 🔑 the place or situation in which: *We then moved to Paris, where we lived for six years.*

■ *conj.* (in) the place or situation in which: *This is where I live.* ◇ *Sit where I can see you.* ◇ *Where people were concerned, his threshold of boredom was low.* ◇ *That's where* (= the point in the argument at which) *you're wrong.*

where·abouts *noun, adv.*

■ *noun* /ˈweərəbaʊts; *NAmE* ˈwer-/ [U+sing./pl. v.] the place where sb/sth is: *His whereabouts are/is still unknown.*

■ *adv.* /ˌweərəˈbaʊts; *NAmE* ˌwer-/ used to ask the general area where sb/sth is: *Whereabouts did you find it?*

where·as 🔑 AW /ˌweərˈæz; *NAmE* ˌwer-/ *conj.* **1** 🔑 used to compare or contrast two facts: *Some of the studies show positive results, whereas others do not.* ➲ LANGUAGE BANK at CONTRAST **2** (*law*) used at the beginning of a sentence in an official document to mean 'because of the fact that…'

where·by AW /weəˈbaɪ; *NAmE* wer-/ *adv.* (*formal*) by which; because of which: *They have introduced a new system whereby all employees must undergo regular training.*

where·fore /ˈweəfɔː(r); *NAmE* ˈwerf-/ *noun* IDM see WHY *n.*

where·in /weərˈɪn; *NAmE* wer-/ *adv., conj.* (*formal*) in which place, situation or thing; in what way: *Wherein lies the difference between conservatism and liberalism?*

W

where·of /weər'ɒv; *NAmE* wer'ʌv/ *conj.* (*old use* or *humorous*) of what or which: *I know whereof I speak* (= I know a lot about what I am talking about).

where·upon /ˌweərə'pɒn; *NAmE* ˌwerə'pɑːn/ *conj.* (*formal*) and then; as a result of this: *He told her she was a liar, whereupon she walked out.*

wher·ever 0 /weər'evə(r); *NAmE* wer-/ *conj., adv.*
■ ***conj.*** **1** 0 in any place: *Sit wherever you like.* ◇ *He comes from Boula,* ***wherever that may be*** (= I don't know where it is). **2** 0 in all places that SYN **everywhere**: *Wherever she goes, there are crowds of people waiting to see her.* **3** 0 in all cases that SYN **whenever**: *Use wholegrain breakfast cereals* ***wherever possible.***
IDM **or wher'ever** (*informal*) or any other place: *tourists from Spain, France or wherever*
■ ***adv.*** used in questions to mean 'where', expressing surprise: *Wherever can he have gone to?*

the where·withal /'weəwɪðɔːl; *NAmE* 'werw-/ *noun* [sing.] **~ (to do sth)** the money, things or skill that you need in order to be able to do sth: *They lacked the wherewithal to pay for the repairs.*

whet /wet/ *verb* (-tt-) **~ sth** to increase your desire for or interest in sth: *The book will* ***whet your appetite*** *for more of her work.*

whether 0 /'weðə(r)/ *conj.*
1 0 used to express a doubt or choice between two possibilities: *He seemed undecided* ***whether*** *to go* ***or*** *stay.* ◇ *It remains to be seen* ***whether or not*** *this idea can be put into practice.* ◇ *I asked him* ***whether*** *he had done it all himself* ***or whether*** *someone had helped him.* ◇ *I'll see whether she's at home* (= or not at home). ◇ *It's doubtful whether there'll be any seats left.* ➲ note at IF **2** 0 used to show that sth is true in either of two cases: *You are entitled to a free gift whether you accept our offer of insurance or not.* ◇ *I'm going* ***whether*** *you like it* ***or not.*** ◇ ***Whether or not*** *we're successful, we can be sure that we did our best.*

whet·stone /'wetstəʊn; *NAmE* -stoʊn/ *noun* a stone that is used to make tools, knives and weapons sharp

whew /hwjuː; fjuː/ *exclamation* a sound that people make to show that they are surprised or RELIEVED about sth or that they are very hot or tired: *Whew—and I thought it was serious!* ◇ *Ten grand? Whew!* ➲ compare PHEW

whey /weɪ/ *noun* [U] the thin liquid that is left from sour milk after the solid part (called CURDS) has been removed

which 0 /wɪtʃ/ *pron., det.*
1 0 used in questions to ask sb to be exact about one or more people or things from a limited number: *Which is better exercise—swimming or tennis?* ◇ *Which of the applicants has got the job?* ◇ *Which of the patients have recovered?* ◇ *Which way is the wind blowing?* ➲ compare WHAT **2** 0 used to be exact about the thing or things that you mean: *Houses which overlook the lake cost more.* ◇ *It was a crisis for which she was totally unprepared.* HELP **That** can be used instead of **which** in this meaning, but it is not used immediately after a preposition: *It was a crisis* ***that*** *she was totally unprepared* ***for.*** **3** 0 used to give more information about sth: *His best movie, which won several awards, was about the life of Gandhi.* ◇ *Your claim ought to succeed,* ***in which case*** *the damages will be substantial.* HELP **That** cannot be used instead of **which** in this meaning.
IDM **ˌwhich is 'which** 0 used to talk about distinguishing one person or thing from another: *The twins are so alike I can't tell which is which.*

which·ever /wɪtʃ'evə(r)/ *det., pron.* **1** used to say what feature or quality is important in deciding sth: *Choose whichever brand you prefer.* ◇ *Pensions should be increased annually in line with earnings or prices, whichever is the higher.* ◇ *Whichever of you gets here first will get the prize.* **2** used to say that it does not matter which, as the result will be the same: *It takes three hours, whichever route you take.* ◇ *The situation is an awkward one,* ***whichever way you look at it.*** ◇ *Whichever they choose, we must accept their decision.*

whiff /wɪf/ *noun, verb*
■ ***noun*** [usually sing.] **1 ~ (of sth)** a smell, especially one that you only smell for a short time: *a whiff of cigar smoke* ◇ *He caught a whiff of perfume as he leaned towards her.* **2 ~ (of sth)** a slight sign or feeling of sth: *a whiff of danger* **3** (*NAmE*) (in GOLF or BASEBALL) an unsuccessful attempt to hit the ball
■ ***verb*** **1** [I] (*BrE, informal*) to smell bad **2** [I] (*NAmE*) (in GOLF or BASEBALL) to try without success to hit the ball

whiffy /'wɪfi/ *adj.* (*BrE, informal*) smelling bad

Whig /wɪg/ *noun* in Britain in the past, a member of a party that supported progress and reform and that later became the Liberal Party

while 0 /waɪl/ *conj., noun, verb*
■ ***conj.*** (also *formal* **whilst** /waɪlst/ especially in *BrE*) **1** 0 during the time that sth is happening SYN **when**: *We must have been burgled while we were asleep.* ◇ *Her parents died while she was still at school.* ◇ *While I was waiting at the bus stop, three buses went by in the opposite direction.* **2** 0 at the same time as sth else is happening: *You can go swimming while I'm having lunch.* ◇ *shoes mended while you wait* **3** 0 used to contrast two things: *While Tom's very good at science, his brother is absolutely hopeless.* ➲ LANGUAGE BANK at CONTRAST **4** 0 (used at the beginning of a sentence) although; despite the fact that...: *While I am willing to help, I do not have much time available.* ➲ LANGUAGE BANK at NEVERTHELESS **5** (*NEngE*) until: *I waited while six o'clock.*
IDM **ˌwhile you're/I'm etc. 'at it** used to suggest that sb could do sth while they are doing sth else: *'I'm just going to buy some postcards.' 'Can you get me some stamps while you're at it?'*
■ ***noun*** 0 [sing.] a period of time: *They chatted* ***for a while.*** ◇ *I'll be back in* ***a little while*** (= a short time). ◇ *I haven't seen him for* ***quite a while*** (= a fairly long time). ◇ *They walked back together, talking* ***all the while*** (= all the time).
IDM see ONCE *adv.*, WORTH *adj.*
■ ***verb***
PHR V **ˌwhile sth↔a'way** to spend time in a pleasant lazy way: *We whiled away the time reading and playing cards.*

whim /wɪm/ *noun* [C, U] a sudden wish to do or have sth, especially when it is sth unusual or unnecessary: *He was forced to pander to* ***her every whim.*** ◇ *We bought the house* ***on a whim.*** ◇ *My duties seem to change daily* ***at the whim of*** *the boss.* ◇ *the whims of fashion* ◇ *She hires and fires people* ***at whim.***

whim·per /'wɪmpə(r)/ *verb, noun*
■ ***verb*** [I, T] to make low, weak crying noises; to speak in this way: *The child was lost and began to whimper.* ◇ **+ speech** *'Don't leave me alone,' he whimpered.*
■ ***noun*** a low weak cry that a person or an animal makes when they are hurt, frightened or sad

whim·si·cal /'wɪmzɪkl/ *adj.* unusual and not serious in a way that is either amusing or annoying: *to have a whimsical sense of humour* ◇ *Much of his writing has a whimsical quality.* ▶ **whim·si·cal·ly** /-kli/ *adv.*

whimsy /'wɪmzi/ *noun* [U] a way of thinking or behaving, or a style of doing sth that is unusual and not serious, in a way that is either amusing or annoying

whine /waɪn/ *verb, noun*
■ ***verb*** **1** [I, T] (**+ speech**) | **~ that...** to complain in an annoying, crying voice: *Stop whining!* ◇ *'I want to go home,' whined Toby.* ➲ SYNONYMS at COMPLAIN **2** [I] to make a long high unpleasant sound because you are in pain or unhappy: *The dog whined and scratched at the door.* **3** [I] (of a machine) to make a long high unpleasant sound ▶ **whiny** *adj.*: *a whiny voice/tone* ◇ *a whiny kid/brat*
■ ***noun*** [usually sing.] **1** a long high sound that is usually unpleasant or annoying: *the steady whine of the engine* **2** a long high cry that a child or dog makes when it is hurt or wants sth **3** a high tone of voice that you use when you complain about sth

whinge /wɪndʒ/ *verb* (*pres. part.* **whinge·ing** or **whing·ing**) [I] **~ (about sb/sth)** (*BrE, informal, disapproving*) to com-

W

plain in an annoying way: *She's always whingeing about how unfair everything is.* ▸ **whinge** *noun* **whin·ger** *noun*

whinny /ˈwɪni/ *verb* (**whin·nies, whinny·ing, whin·nied, whin·nied**) [I] (of a horse) to make a quiet NEIGH ▸ **whinny** *noun* (*pl.* -ies)

whip /wɪp/ *noun, verb*

■ ***noun*** **1** [C] a long thin piece of rope or leather, attached to a handle, used for making animals move or punishing people: *He cracked his whip and the horse leapt forward.* **2** [C] an official in a political party who is responsible for making sure that party members attend and vote in important government debates: *the chief whip* **3** [C] a written instruction telling members of a political party how to vote on a particular issue ➲ see also THREE-LINE WHIP **4** [U, C] a sweet dish made from cream, eggs, sugar and fruit mixed together

IDM **have/hold, etc. the ˈwhip hand (over sb/sth)** to be in a position where you have power or control over sb/sth ➲ more at CRACK *v.*, FAIR *adj.*

■ ***verb*** (-pp-) **1** [T] **~ sb/sth** to hit a person or an animal hard with a whip, as a punishment or to make them go faster or work harder **2** [I, T] to move, or make sth move, quickly and suddenly or violently in a particular direction: **+ adv./prep.** *A branch whipped across the car window.* ◇ *Her hair whipped around her face in the wind.* ◇ **~ sth** *The waves were being whipped by 50 mile an hour winds.* **3** [T] **~ sth + adv./prep.** to remove or pull sth quickly and suddenly: *She whipped the mask off her face.* ◇ *The man whipped out a knife.* **4** [T] to stir cream, etc. very quickly until it becomes stiff: **~ sth** *Serve the pie with* ***whipped cream.*** ◇ **~ sth up** *Whip the egg whites up into stiff peaks.* ➲ VISUAL VOCAB page V25 **5** [T] **~ sb/sth** (*NAmE, informal*) to defeat sb very easily in a game: *The team whipped its opponents by 35 points.* ➲ compare THRASH *v.* (3) **6** [T] **~ sth** (*BrE, informal*) to steal sth

PHR V **ˌwhip ˈthrough sth** (*informal*) to do or finish sth very quickly: *We whipped through customs in ten minutes.* **ˌwhip sb/sth↔ˈup 1** to deliberately try and make people excited or feel strongly about sth SYN **rouse**: *The advertisements were designed to whip up public opinion.* ◇ *He was a speaker who could really* ***whip up a crowd.*** **2** to quickly make a meal or sth to eat: *She whipped up a delicious lunch for us in 15 minutes.*

whip·lash /ˈwɪplæʃ/ *noun* **1** [C, usually sing.] a hit with a whip **2** [U] = WHIPLASH INJURY: *He was very bruised and suffering from whiplash.*

ˈwhiplash injury *noun* [C, U] (also **whip·lash**) a neck injury caused when your head moves forward and back suddenly, especially in a car accident

whip·per·snap·per /ˈwɪpəsnæpə(r); *NAmE* ˈwɪpərs-/ *noun* (*old-fashioned, informal*) a young and unimportant person who behaves in a way that others think is too confident and rude

whip·pet /ˈwɪpɪt/ *noun* a small thin dog, similar to a GREYHOUND, that can run very fast and is often used for racing

whip·ping /ˈwɪpɪŋ/ *noun* [usually sing.] an act of hitting sb with a whip, as a punishment

ˈwhipping boy *noun* a person who is often blamed or punished for things other people have done

ˈwhipping cream *noun* [U] cream that becomes thicker when it is stirred quickly (=WHIPPED)

whip·poor·will /ˈwɪpəwɪl; *NAmE* -pərw-/ *noun* a brown N American bird with a cry that sounds like its name

ˈwhip-round *noun* (*BrE, informal*) if a group of people have a **whip-round**, they all give money so they can buy sth for sb

whir (*especially NAmE*) = WHIRR

whirl /wɜːl; *NAmE* wɜːrl/ *verb, noun*

■ ***verb*** **1** [I, T] to move, or make sb/sth move, around quickly in a circle or in a particular direction SYN **spin**: (**+ adv./prep.**) *Leaves whirled in the wind.* ◇ *She whirled around to face him.* ◇ *the whirling blades of the helicopter* ◇ **~ sb/sth (+ adv./prep.)** *Tom whirled her across the dance floor.* **2** [I] if your mind, thoughts, etc. **whirl**, you feel confused and excited and cannot think clearly SYN **reel**: *I couldn't sleep—my mind was whirling from all that had happened.* ◇ *So many thoughts whirled around in her mind.*

■ ***noun*** [sing.] **1** a movement of sth spinning round and round: *a whirl of dust* ◇ (*figurative*) *Her mind was* ***in a whirl*** (= in a state of confusion or excitement). **2** a number of activities or events happening one after the other: *Her life was one long whirl of parties.* ◇ *It's easy to get caught up in the* ***social whirl.***

IDM **give sth a ˈwhirl** (*informal*) to try sth to see if you like it or can do it

whirli·gig /ˈwɜːligɪg; *NAmE* ˈwɜːrl-/ *noun* **1** something that is very active and always changing: *the whirligig of fashion* **2** (*old-fashioned*) a MERRY-GO-ROUND at a FAIRGROUND for children to ride on

whirl·pool /ˈwɜːlpuːl; *NAmE* ˈwɜːrl-/ *noun* **1** a place in a river or the sea where currents of water spin round very fast SYN **eddy**: (*figurative*) *She felt she was being dragged into a whirlpool of emotion.* **2** (also **ˌwhirlpool ˈbath**) a special bath/BATHTUB or swimming pool for relaxing in, in which the water moves in circles ➲ see also JACUZZI

whirl·wind /ˈwɜːlwɪnd; *NAmE* ˈwɜːrl-/ *noun, adj.*

■ ***noun*** **1** a very strong wind that moves very fast in a spinning movement and causes a lot of damage **2** a situation or series of events where a lot of things happen very quickly: *To recover from the divorce, I threw myself into a whirlwind of activities.*

■ ***adj.*** [only before noun] happening very fast: *a whirlwind romance* ◇ *a whirlwind tour of America*

whirr (*especially BrE*) (*NAmE* usually **whir**) /wɜː(r)/ *verb, noun*

■ ***verb*** (-rr-) [I] to make a continuous low sound like the parts of a machine moving: *The clock began to whirr before striking the hour.*

■ ***noun*** (also **whir·ring**) [usually sing.] a continuous low sound, for example the sound made by the regular movement of a machine or the wings of a bird: *the whirr of a motor* ◇ *There was a whirring of machinery.*

whisk /wɪsk/ *verb, noun*

■ ***verb*** **1 ~ sth** to mix liquids, eggs, etc. into a stiff light mass, using a fork or special tool SYN **beat**: *Whisk the egg whites until stiff.* **2 ~ sb/sth + adv./prep.** to take sb/sth somewhere very quickly and suddenly: *Jamie whisked her off to Paris for the weekend.* ◇ *The waiter whisked away the plates before we had finished.*

■ ***noun*** a kitchen UTENSIL (= a tool) for stirring eggs, etc. very fast: *an electric whisk* ➲ VISUAL VOCAB pages V22, V23, V25

whis·ker /ˈwɪskə(r)/ *noun* **1** [C] any of the long stiff hairs that grow near the mouth of a cat, mouse, etc. **2 whis·kers** [pl.] (*old-fashioned* or *humorous*) the hair growing on a man's face, especially on his cheeks and chin ➲ VISUAL VOCAB page V10

IDM **be, come, etc. within a whisker of sth/doing sth** (*BrE*) to almost do sth: *They came within a whisker of being killed.* **by a ˈwhisker** by a very small amount ➲ more at CAT

whis·kered /ˈwɪskəd; *NAmE* -kərd/ (also **whis·kery** /ˈwɪskəri/) *adj.* having whiskers

whisky (*BrE*) (*US, IrishE* **whis·key**) /ˈwɪski/ *noun* (*pl.* **whis·kies, whis·keys**) **1** [U, C] a strong alcoholic drink made from MALTED grain. It is sometimes drunk with water and/or ice: *a bottle of whisky* ◇ *Scotch whisky* ◇ *highland whiskies* ➲ see also BOURBON, SCOTCH **2** [C] a glass of whisky: *a whisky and soda* ◇ *Two whiskies, please.* ➲ see also SCOTCH

whis·per 0→ /ˈwɪspə(r)/ *verb, noun*

■ ***verb*** **1** 0→ [I, T] to speak very quietly to sb so that other people cannot hear what you are saying SYN **murmur**: *Don't you know it's rude to whisper?* ◇ **~ about sth** *What are you two whispering about?* ◇ **+ speech** *'Can you meet me tonight?' he whispered.* ◇ **~ sth (to sb)** *She leaned over and whispered something in his ear.* ◇ **~ (to sb) that...** *He whispered to me that he was afraid.* **2** [T, often passive] **~ that... | it is whispered that...** to say or suggest sth

W

about sb/sth in a private or secret way: *It was whispered that he would soon die and he did.* **3** [I] (+ **adv./prep.**) (*literary*) (of leaves, the wind, etc.) to make a soft, quiet sound
■ ***noun*** **1** a low quiet voice or the sound it makes SYN **murmur**: *They spoke **in whispers**.* ◇ *Her voice dropped to a whisper.* ➲ see also STAGE WHISPER **2** (also **whis·per·ing**) (*literary*) a soft sound SYN **murmur**: *I could hear the whispering of the sea.* **3** a piece of news that is spread by being talked about but may not be true SYN **rumour**: *I've heard whispers that he's leaving.*

'whispering campaign *noun* an attempt to damage sb's reputation by saying unpleasant things about them and passing this information from person to person

whist /wɪst/ *noun* [U] a card game for two pairs of players in which each pair tries to win the most cards

whis·tle /'wɪsl/ *noun, verb*
■ ***noun*** **1** a small metal or plastic tube that you blow to make a loud high sound, used to attract attention or as a signal: *The referee finally **blew the whistle** to stop the game.* ➲ see also TIN WHISTLE **2** the sound made by blowing a whistle: *He scored the winning goal just seconds before the final whistle.* **3** the sound that you make by forcing your breath out when your lips are closed: *a shrill whistle* ➲ see also WOLF WHISTLE **4** the high loud sound produced by air or steam being forced through a small opening, or by sth moving quickly through the air **5** a piece of equipment that makes a high loud sound when air or steam is forced through it: *The train whistle blew as we left the station.* ◇ *a factory whistle* IDM see BLOW *v.*, CLEAN *adj.*
■ ***verb*** **1** [T, I] to make a high sound or a musical tune by forcing your breath out when your lips are closed: **~ (sth)** *to whistle a tune* ◇ *He whistled in amazement.* ◇ *The crowd booed and whistled as the player came onto the field.* ◇ **~ to sb/sth** *She whistled to the dog to come back.* ◇ **~ at sb/sth** *Workmen whistled at her as she walked past.* **2** [I] to make a high sound by blowing into a whistle: *The referee whistled for a foul.* **3** [I] (of a KETTLE or other machine) to make a high sound: *The kettle began to whistle.* ◇ *The microphone was making a strange whistling sound.* **4** [I] **+ adv./prep.** to move quickly, making a high sound: *The wind whistled down the chimney.* ◇ *A bullet whistled past his ear.* **5** [I] (of a bird) to make a high sound
IDM **sb can 'whistle for sth** (*BrE, informal*) used to say that you are not going to give sb sth that they have asked for

'whistle-blower *noun* (used especially in newspapers) a person who informs people in authority or the public that the company they work for is doing sth wrong or illegal

'whistle-stop *adj.* [only before noun] visiting a lot of different places in a very short time: *to go on a **whistle-stop tour** of Europe* ◇ *politicians on a whistle-stop election campaign*

Whit /wɪt/ *adj.* connected with Whitsun: *Whit Monday*

whit /wɪt/ *noun* [sing.] (*old-fashioned*) (usually in negative sentences) a very small amount SYN **jot**
IDM **not a 'whit** | **not one 'whit** not at all; not the smallest amount

white /waɪt/ *adj., noun*
■ ***adj.*** (whiter, whit·est) **1** having the colour of fresh snow or of milk: *a crisp white shirt* ◇ *white bread* ◇ *a set of perfect white teeth* ◇ *His hair was **as white as snow**.* ◇ *The horse was almost **pure white** in colour.* **2** belonging to or connected with a race of people who have pale skin: *white middle-class families* ◇ *She writes about her experiences as a black girl in a predominantly white city.* **3** (of the skin) pale because of emotion or illness: *white with shock* ◇ *She went **white as a sheet** when she heard the news.* **4** (*BrE*) (of tea or coffee) with milk added: *Two white coffees, please.* ◇ *Do you take your coffee black or white?* ➲ compare BLACK ▶ **white·ness** *noun* [U, sing.]
■ ***noun*** **1** [U] the colour of fresh snow or of milk: *the pure white of the newly painted walls* ◇ *She was dressed all in white.* **2** [C, usually pl.] a member of a race or people who have pale skin **3** [U, C] white wine: *Would you like red or white?* ◇ *a very dry white* **4** [C, U] the part of an egg that surrounds the YOLK (= the yellow part): *Use the whites of two eggs.* **5** [C, usually pl.] the white part of the eye: *The whites of her eyes were bloodshot.* ➲ VISUAL VOCAB page V48 **6 whites** [pl.] white clothes, sheets, etc. when they are separated from coloured ones to be washed: (*BrE*) *Don't wash whites and coloureds together.* ◇ (*NAmE*) *Don't wash whites and colors together.* **7 whites** [pl.] white clothes worn for playing some sports: ***cricket/tennis whites*** IDM see BLACK *n.*
IDM **,whiter than 'white** (of a person) completely honest and morally good: *The government must be seen to be whiter than white.*

white·bait /'waɪtbeɪt/ *noun* [pl.] very small young fish of several types that are fried and eaten whole

,white 'blood cell (also **'white cell**) (also *technical* **leuco·cyte**) *noun* (*biology*) any of the clear cells in the blood that help to fight disease

white·board /'waɪtbɔːd; *NAmE* -bɔːrd/ *noun* a large board with a smooth white surface that teachers, etc. write on with special pens ➲ VISUAL VOCAB page V57 ➲ compare BLACKBOARD

,white 'bread *noun* [U] bread made with WHITE FLOUR

'white-bread *adj.* [only before noun] (*NAmE, informal*) ordinary and traditional: *a white-bread town*

white·caps /'waɪtkæps/ (*NAmE*) (*BrE* **,white 'horses**) *noun* [pl.] waves in the sea or ocean with white tops on them

,white 'Christmas *noun* a Christmas during which there is snow on the ground

,white-'collar *adj.* [usually before noun] working in an office, rather than in a factory, etc; connected with work in offices: *white-collar workers* ◇ *a white-collar job* ◇ *white-collar crime* (= in which office workers steal from their company, etc.) ➲ compare BLUE-COLLAR, PINK-COLLAR

,white 'dwarf *noun* (*astronomy*) a small star that is near the end of its life and is very DENSE (= solid and heavy)

,white 'elephant *noun* [usually sing.] a thing that is useless and no longer needed, although it may have cost a lot of money: *The new office block has become an expensive white elephant.* ORIGIN From the story that in Siam (now Thailand) the king would give a white elephant as a present to somebody that he did not like. That person would have to spend all their money on looking after the rare animal.

,white 'fish *noun* [U, C] (*pl.* **white fish**) fish with pale flesh

,white 'flag *noun* [usually sing.] a sign that you accept defeat and wish to stop fighting: *to **raise/show/wave the white flag***

,white 'flight *noun* [U] (*US*) a situation where white people who can afford it go to live outside the cities because they are worried about crime in city centres

,white 'flour *noun* [U] flour made from WHEAT grains, from which most of the BRAN (= outer covering) and WHEATGERM (= centre part) have been removed

'white goods *noun* [pl.] large pieces of electrical equipment in the house, such as WASHING MACHINES, etc. ➲ compare BROWN GOODS

White·hall /'waɪthɔːl/ *noun* **1** [U] a street in London where there are many government offices **2** [sing.+ sing./pl. v.] a way of referring to the British Government: *Whitehall are/is refusing to comment.*

,white 'heat *noun* [U] the very high temperature at which metal looks white

,white 'hope *noun* [sing.] (*informal*) a person who is expected to bring success to a team, an organization, etc: *He was once **the great white hope** of British boxing.*

,white 'horses (*BrE*) (*NAmE* **white·caps**) *noun* [pl.] waves in the sea or ocean with white tops on them

,white-'hot *adj.* **1** (of metal or sth burning) so hot that it looks white **2** very strong and INTENSE

the 'White House *noun* [sing.] **1** the official home of the President of the US in Washington, DC **2** the US President and his or her officials: *The White House has issued a statement.* ◇ *White House aides*

W

ˌwhite ˈknight *noun* a person or an organization that rescues a company from being bought by another company at too low a price

ˌwhite-ˈknuckle ride *noun* a ride at a FAIRGROUND that makes you feel very excited and frightened at the same time

ˌwhite ˈlie *noun* a harmless or small lie, especially one that you tell to avoid hurting sb

ˌwhite ˈlight *noun* [U] ordinary light that has no colour

ˌwhite ˈmeat *noun* [U] **1** meat that is pale in colour when it has been cooked, such as chicken ➲ compare RED MEAT **2** pale meat from the breast of a chicken or other bird that has been cooked

whiten /ˈwaɪtn/ *verb* [I, T] to become white or whiter; to make sth white or whiter: *He gripped the wheel until his knuckles whitened.* ◇ **~ sth** *Snow had whitened the tops of the trees.*

ˌwhite ˈnoise *noun* [U] unpleasant noise, like the noise that comes from a television or radio that is turned on but not TUNED IN

ˈwhite-out *noun* weather conditions in which there is so much snow or cloud that it is impossible to see anything ➲ see also WITEOUT

the ˌwhite ˈpages *noun* [pl.] a telephone book (on white paper), or a section of a book, that lists the names, addresses and telephone numbers of people living in a particular area

ˌWhite ˈPaper *noun* (in Britain) a government report that gives information about sth and explains government plans before a new law is introduced ➲ compare GREEN PAPER

ˌwhite ˈpepper *noun* [U] a greyish-brown powder made from dried BERRIES (called PEPPERCORNS), used to give flavour to food

ˌwhite ˈsauce *noun* [U] a thick sauce made from butter, flour and milk SYN **béchamel**

ˌwhite ˈspirit *noun* [U] (*BrE*) a clear liquid made from petrol/gas, used as a cleaning substance or to make paint thinner

ˌwhite ˈstick *noun* a long thin white stick carried by blind people to help them walk around without knocking things and to show others that they are blind

ˌwhite ˈtie *noun* a man's white BOW TIE, also used to mean very formal evening dress for men: *dressed in white tie and tails*

ˌwhite-ˈtie *adj.* (of social occasions) very formal, when men are expected to wear white BOW TIES and jackets with TAILS: *Is it a white-tie affair?*

ˌwhite-ˈvan man *noun* (*BrE, informal*) used to refer to the sort of man who drives a white van in an aggressive way, thought of as a symbol of the rude and sometimes violent way in which some men behave today

white·wall /ˈwaɪtwɔːl/ *noun* **1** (*BrE* also ˌ**whitewall ˈtyre**) (*NAmE* also **whitewall tire**) a tyre with a white line going round it for decoration **2 whitewalls** [pl.] (*especially US*) the shaved area at the sides of the head when the hair is cut in a very short style

white·wash /ˈwaɪtwɒʃ; *NAmE* -wɑːʃ; -wɔːʃ/ *noun, verb*

■ ***noun*** **1** [U] a mixture of CHALK or LIME and water, used for painting houses and walls white **2** [U, sing.] (*disapproving*) an attempt to hide unpleasant facts about sb/sth SYN **cover-up**: *The opposition claimed the report was a whitewash.* **3** [C, usually sing.] (*informal*) (in sport) a victory in every game in a series: *a 7–0 whitewash* ◇ *a whitewash victory*

■ ***verb*** **1 ~ sth** to cover sth such as a wall with whitewash **2 ~ sb/sth** (*disapproving*) to try to hide unpleasant facts about sb/sth; to try to make sth seem better than it is: *His wife had wanted to whitewash his reputation after he died.* **3 ~ sb/sth** (*especially BrE*) (in sport) to defeat an opponent in every game in a series

ˌwhite ˈwater *noun* [U] **1** a part of a river that looks white because the water is moving very fast over rocks: *a stretch of white water* ◇ *white-water rafting* ➲ VISUAL VOCAB page V40 **2** a part of the sea or ocean that looks white because it is very rough and the waves are high

ˌwhite ˈwedding *noun* a traditional wedding, especially in a church, at which the BRIDE wears a white dress

ˌwhite ˈwine *noun* **1** [U, C] pale yellow wine: *a bottle of dry white wine* ◇ *chilled white wine* **2** [C] a glass of white wine ➲ compare RED WINE, ROSÉ

ˌwhite ˈwitch *noun* a person who does magic that does not harm other people

whitey /ˈwaɪti/ *noun* (*slang*) an offensive word for a white person, used by black people

whither /ˈwɪðə(r)/ *adv., conj.* **1** (*old use*) where; to which: *Whither should they go?* ◇ *They did not know whither they should go.* ◇ *the place whither they were sent* **2** (*formal*) used to ask what is likely to happen to sth in the future: *Whither modern architecture?*

whit·ing /ˈwaɪtɪŋ/ *noun* [C, U] (*pl.* **whit·ing**) a small sea fish with white flesh that is used for food

whit·ish /ˈwaɪtɪʃ/ *adj.* fairly white in colour: *a bird with a whitish throat*

Whit·sun /ˈwɪtsn/ *noun* [U, C] the 7th Sunday after Easter and the days close to it

ˌWhit ˈSunday *noun* [U, C] (*BrE*) = PENTECOST

Whit·sun·tide /ˈwɪtsntaɪd/ *noun* [U] the week or days close to Whit Sunday

whit·tle /ˈwɪtl/ *verb* to form a piece of wood, etc. into a particular shape by cutting small pieces from it: **~ A (from B)** *He whittled a simple toy from the piece of wood.* ◇ **~ B (into A)** *He whittled the piece of wood into a simple toy.*
PHR V ˌ**whittle sth↔aˈway** to make sth gradually decrease in value or amount ˌ**whittle sth↔ˈdown** to reduce the size or number of sth: *I finally managed to whittle down the names on the list to only five.*

whizz (*especially BrE*) (also **whiz** especially in *NAmE*) /wɪz/ *verb, noun*

■ ***verb*** (*informal*) **1** [I] **+ adv./prep.** to move very quickly, making a high continuous sound: *A bullet whizzed past my ear.* ◇ *He whizzed down the road on his motorbike.* **2** [I] **+ adv./prep.** to do sth very quickly: *She whizzed through the work.*

■ ***noun*** (*informal*) a person who is very good at sth: *She's a whizz at crosswords.*

ˈwhizz-kid (*especially BrE*) (*NAmE* usually **ˈwhiz-kid**) *noun* (*informal*) a person who is very good and successful at sth, especially at a young age: *financial whizz-kids*

whizzy /ˈwɪzi/ *adj.* (**whiz·zier, whiz·ziest**) (*informal*) having features that make use of advanced technology: *a whizzy new hand-held computer*

WHO /ˌdʌbljuː eɪtʃ ˈəʊ; *NAmE* ˈoʊ/ *abbr.* World Health Organization (an international organization that aims to fight and control disease)

who 0→ /huː/ *pron.*
1 0→ used in questions to ask about the name, identity or function of one or more people: *Who is that woman?* ◇ *I wonder who that letter was from.* ◇ *Who are you phoning?* ◇ *Who's the money for?* **2** 0→ used to show which person or people you mean: *The people who called yesterday want to buy the house.* ◇ *The people (who) we met in France have sent us a card.* **3** 0→ used to give more information about sb: *Mrs Smith, who has a lot of teaching experience at junior level, will be joining the school in September.* ◇ *And then Mary, who we had been talking about earlier, walked in.* ➲ compare WHOM
IDM **who am ˈI, who are ˈyou, etc. to do sth?** used to ask what right or authority sb has to do sth: *Who are you to tell me I can't park here?* **who's ˈwho** people's names, jobs, status, etc: *You'll soon find out who's who in the office.* ➲ see also WHO'S WHO

whoa /wəʊ; *NAmE* woʊ/ *exclamation* used as a command to a horse, etc. to make it stop or stand still

who'd /huːd/ *short form* **1** who had **2** who would

W

who·dun·nit (*BrE*) (also **who·dun·it** *NAmE, BrE*) /ˌhuːˈdʌnɪt/ *noun* (*informal*) a story, play, etc. about a murder in which you do not know who did the murder until the end

who·ever 0-w /huːˈevə(r)/ *pron.* **1** 0-w the person or people who; any person who: *Whoever says that is a liar.* ◇ *Send it to whoever is in charge of sales.* **2** 0-w used to say that it does not matter who, since the result will be the same: *Come out of there, whoever you are.* ◇ *I don't want to see them, whoever they are.* **3** used in questions to mean 'who', expressing surprise: *Whoever heard of such a thing!*

whole 0-w /həʊl; *NAmE* hoʊl/ *adj., noun, adv.*
■ ***adj.*** **1** 0-w [only before noun] full; complete: *He spent the whole day writing.* ◇ *We drank a whole bottle each.* ◇ *The whole country* (= all the people in it) *mourned her death.* ◇ *Let's forget the **whole thing**.* ◇ *She wasn't telling the **whole truth**.* **2** 0-w [only before noun] used to emphasize how large or important sth is: *We offer a whole variety of weekend breaks.* ◇ *I can't afford it—that's **the whole point**.* **3** 0-w not broken or damaged SYN **in one piece**: *Owls usually swallow their prey whole* (= without chewing it). ➲ note at HALF ▸ **whole·ness** *noun* [U] ➲ see also WHOLLY
IDM Most idioms containing **whole** are at the entries for the nouns and verbs in the idioms, for example **go the whole hog** is at **hog**. **a ˈwhole lot** 0-w (*informal*) very much; a lot: *I'm feeling a whole lot better.* **a ˈwhole lot (of sth)** 0-w (*informal*) a large number or amount: *There were a whole lot of people I didn't know.* ◇ *I lost a whole lot of money.* **the ˌwhole ˈlot** 0-w everything; all of sth: *I've sold the whole lot.*
■ ***noun*** **1** 0-w [C] a thing that is complete in itself: *Four quarters make a whole.* ◇ *The subjects of the curriculum form a coherent whole.* **2** 0-w [sing.] **the ~ of sth** all that there is of sth: *The effects will last for the whole of his life.* ➲ note at HALF
IDM **as a ˈwhole** 0-w as one thing or piece and not as separate parts: *The festival will be great for our city and for the country as a whole.* **on the whole** 0-w considering everything; in general: *On the whole, I'm in favour of the idea.*
■ ***adv.*** **~ new/different/other...** (*informal*) completely new/different: *It's a whole new world out here.* ◇ *That's a whole other story.*

whole·food /ˈhəʊlfuːd; *NAmE* ˈhoʊl-/ *noun* [U] (also **wholefoods** [pl.]) food that is considered healthy because it is in a simple form, has not been REFINED, and does not contain artificial substances

whole·grain /ˈhəʊlɡreɪn; *NAmE* ˈhoʊl-/ *adj.* made with or containing whole grains, for example of WHEAT

whole·heart·ed /ˌhəʊlˈhɑːtɪd; *NAmE* ˌhoʊlˈhɑːrtəd/ *adj.* (*approving*) complete and enthusiastic: *The plan was given wholehearted support.* ▸ **whole·heart·ed·ly** *adv.*: *to agree wholeheartedly*

whole·meal /ˈhəʊlmiːl; *NAmE* ˈhoʊl-/ (*BrE*) (also **whole-wheat** *NAmE, BrE*) *adj.* **wholemeal/wholewheat** bread or flour contains the whole grains of WHEAT, etc. including the HUSK

W

ˈwhole note (*NAmE*) (*BrE* **semi·breve**) *noun* (*music*) a note that lasts as long as four CROTCHETS/QUARTER NOTES ➲ picture at MUSIC

ˌwhole ˈnumber *noun* (*mathematics*) a number that consists of one or more units, with no FRACTIONS (= parts of a number less than one)

whole·sale /ˈhəʊlseɪl; *NAmE* ˈhoʊl-/ *adj.* [only before noun] **1** connected with goods that are bought and sold in large quantities, especially so they can be sold again to make a profit: *wholesale prices* ➲ compare RETAIL **2** (especially of sth bad) happening or done to a very large number of people or things: *the wholesale slaughter of innocent people* ▸ **whole·sale** *adv.*: *We buy the building materials wholesale.* ◇ *These young people die wholesale from heroin overdoses.*

whole·sal·ing /ˈhəʊlseɪlɪŋ; *NAmE* ˈhoʊl-/ *noun* [U] the business of buying and selling goods in large quantities, especially so they can be sold again to make a profit ➲ compare RETAILING ▸ **whole·saler** *noun*: *fruit and vegetable wholesalers*

whole·some /ˈhəʊlsəm; *NAmE* ˈhoʊl-/ *adj.* **1** good for your health: *fresh, wholesome food* **2** morally good; having a good moral influence: *It was clean wholesome fun.* OPP **unwholesome** ▸ **whole·some·ness** *noun* [U]

ˈwhole step (*US*) (*BrE* **tone**) *noun* (*music*) one of the five longer INTERVALS in a musical SCALE, for example the INTERVAL between C and D or between E and F♯

whole·wheat /ˈhəʊlwiːt; *NAmE* ˈhoʊl-/ (*BrE* also **whole-meal**) *adj.* **wholewheat** bread or flour contains the whole grains of WHEAT, etc. including the HUSK

who'll /huːl/ *short form* who will

whol·ly /ˈhəʊlli; *NAmE* ˈhoʊlli/ *adv.* (*formal*) completely SYN **totally**: *wholly inappropriate behaviour* ◇ *The government is not wholly to blame for the recession.*

whom 0-w /huːm/ *pron.* (*formal*) used instead of 'who' as the object of a verb or preposition: *Whom did they invite?* ◇ *To whom should I write?* ◇ *The author whom you criticized in your review has written a reply.* ◇ *Her mother, in whom she confided, said she would support her unconditionally.*

Grammar Point

whom

- **Whom** is not used very often in spoken English. **Who** is usually used as the object pronoun, especially in questions: *Who did you invite to the party?*
- The use of **whom** as the pronoun after prepositions is very formal: *To whom should I address the letter?* ◇ *He asked me with whom I had discussed it.* In spoken English it is much more natural to use **who** and put the preposition at the end of the sentence: *Who should I address the letter to?* ◇ *He asked me who I had discussed it with.*
- In defining relative clauses the object pronoun **whom** is not often used. You can either use **who** or **that**, or leave out the pronoun completely: *The family (who/that/whom) I met at the airport were very kind.*
- In non-defining relative clauses **who** or, more formally, **whom** (but not *that*) is used and the pronoun cannot be left out: *Our doctor, who/whom we all liked very much, retired last week.* This pattern is not used very much in spoken English.

whom·ever /ˌhuːmˈevə(r)/, **whom·so·ever** /ˌhuːmsəʊˈevə(r); *NAmE* -soʊ-/ *pron.* (*literary*) used instead of 'whoever' as the object of a verb or preposition: *He was free to marry whomever he chose.*

whoop /wuːp; huːp/ *noun, verb*
■ ***noun*** a loud cry expressing joy, excitement, etc: *whoops of delight*
■ ***verb*** [I] to shout loudly because you are happy or excited
IDM **ˌwhoop it ˈup** /wuːp; *NAmE* wʊp/ (*informal*) **1** to enjoy yourself very much with a noisy group of people **2** (*NAmE*) to make people excited or enthusiastic about sth

whoo·pee /wʊˈpiː/ *exclamation, noun*
■ ***exclamation*** used to express happiness: *Whoopee, we've won!*
■ ***noun*** [U]
IDM **make ˈwhoopee** (*old-fashioned, informal*) to celebrate in a noisy way

ˈwhoopee cushion *noun* a rubber CUSHION that makes a noise like a FART when sb sits on it, used as a joke

whoop·ing cough /ˈhuːpɪŋ kɒf; *NAmE* kɔːf/ *noun* [U] an infectious disease, especially of children, that makes them cough and have difficulty breathing

whoops /wʊps/ *exclamation* **1** used when sb has almost had an accident, broken sth, etc.: *Whoops! Careful, you almost spilt coffee everywhere.* **2** used when you have done sth embarrassing, said sth rude by accident, told a secret, etc.: *Whoops, you weren't supposed to hear that.*

whoosh /wʊʃ; wuːʃ/ *noun, verb*
■ ***noun*** [usually sing.] (*informal*) the sudden movement and sound of air or water rushing past: *a whoosh of air* ◇ *There was a whoosh as everything went up in flames.*
■ ***verb*** [I] + **adv./prep.** (*informal*) to move very quickly with the sound of air or water rushing

whop·per /ˈwɒpə(r); *NAmE* ˈwɑːp-/ *noun* (*informal*) **1** something that is very big for its type: *Pete has caught a whopper* (= a large fish). **2** a lie: *She's told some whoppers about her past.*

whop·ping /ˈwɒpɪŋ; *NAmE* ˈwɑːp-/ (also ˈ**whopping great**) *adj.* [only before noun] (*informal*) very big: *The company made a whopping 75 million dollar loss.*

whore /hɔː(r)/ *noun* **1** (*old-fashioned*) a female PROSTITUTE **2** (*taboo*) an offensive word used to refer to a woman who has sex with a lot of men

who're /ˈhuːə(r)/ *short form* who are

whore·house /ˈhɔːhaʊs; *NAmE* ˈhɔːrh-/ *noun* (*old-fashioned*) a BROTHEL (= a place where people pay to have sex)

whor·ing /ˈhɔːrɪŋ/ *noun* [U] (*old-fashioned*) the activity of having sex with a PROSTITUTE

whorl /wɜːl; *NAmE* wɜːrl/ *noun* **1** a pattern made by a curved line that forms a rough circle, with smaller circles inside bigger ones: *the whorls on your fingertips* **2** (*technical*) a ring of leaves, flowers, etc. around the STEM of a plant

who's /huːz/ *short form* **1** who is **2** who has

whose 🔑 /huːz/ *det., pron.*
1 🔑 used in questions to ask who sth belongs to: *Whose house is that?* ◇ *I wonder whose this is.* **2** 🔑 used to say which person or thing you mean: *He's a man whose opinion I respect.* ◇ *It's the house whose door is painted red.* **3** 🔑 used to give more information about a person or thing: *Isobel, whose brother he was, had heard the joke before.*

who·so·ever /ˌhuːsəʊˈevə(r); *NAmE* -soʊ-/ *pron.* (*old use*) = WHOEVER

ˌ**who's** ˈ**who** *noun* a list or book of facts about famous people: *The list of delegates attending read like a who's who of the business world.* ORIGIN From the reference book *Who's Who*, which gives information about many well-known people and what they have done.

who've /huːv/ *short form* who have

whup /wʌp/ *verb* (-pp-) **~ sb/sth** (*informal, especially US*) to defeat sb easily in a game, a fight, an election, etc.

why 🔑 /waɪ/ *adv., exclamation, noun*
■ ***adv.*** **1** 🔑 used in questions to ask the reason for or purpose of sth: *Why were you late?* ◇ *Tell me why you did it.* ◇ *'I would like you to go.' '**Why me?**'* ◇ (*informal*) ***Why oh why*** *do people keep leaving the door open?* **2** 🔑 used in questions to suggest that it is not necessary to do sth: *Why get upset just because you got one bad grade?* ◇ *Why bother to write? We'll see him tomorrow.* **3** 🔑 used to give or talk about a reason: *That's why I left so early.* ◇ *I know you did it—I just want to know why.* ◇ ***The reason why*** *the injection needs repeating every year is that the virus changes.*
IDM **why** ˈ**ever** used in questions to mean 'why', expressing surprise: *Why ever didn't you tell us before?* ˌ**why** ˈ**not?** 🔑 used to make or agree to a suggestion: *Why not write to her?* ◇ *'Let's eat out.' '**Why not?**'* ◇ ***Why don't*** *we go together?*
■ ***exclamation*** (*old-fashioned* or *NAmE*) used to express surprise, lack of patience, etc.: *Why Jane, it's you!* ◇ *Why, it's easy—a child could do it!*
■ ***noun***
IDM **the** ˌ**whys and** (**the**) ˈ**wherefores** the reasons for sth: *I had no intention of going into the whys and the wherefores of the situation.*

WI *abbr.* **1** West Indies **2** /ˌdʌbljuː ˈaɪ/ Women's Institute (a British women's organization in which groups of women meet regularly to take part in various activities)

Wicca /ˈwɪkə/ *noun* [U] a modern form of WITCHCRAFT, practised as a religion ▸ **Wic·can** /ˈwɪkən/ *adj.*

wick /wɪk/ *noun, verb*
■ ***noun*** **1** the piece of string in the centre of a CANDLE which you light so that the candle burns ➲ VISUAL VOCAB page V19 **2** the piece of material in an oil lamp which absorbs the oil and which you light so that the lamp burns
IDM **get on sb's** ˈ**wick** (*BrE, informal*) to annoy sb
■ ***verb*** **~ sth** (**away**) (of a material) to take small drops of liquid from an area and move them away: *Wool socks wick away sweat.*

wicked /ˈwɪkɪd/ *adj., noun*
■ ***adj.*** (wick·ed·er, wick·ed·est) HELP You can also use **more wicked** and **most wicked**. **1** morally bad SYN **evil**: *a wicked deed* ◇ *stories about a wicked witch* **2** (*informal*) slightly bad but in a way that is amusing and/or attractive SYN **mischievous**: *a wicked grin* ◇ *Jane has a wicked sense of humour.* **3** dangerous, harmful or powerful: *He has a wicked punch.* ◇ *a wicked-looking knife* **4** (*slang*) very good: *This song's wicked.* ▸ **wick·ed·ly** *adv.*: *Martin grinned wickedly.* ◇ *a wickedly funny comedy* ◇ *a wickedly sharp blade* **wick·ed·ness** *noun* [U]
■ ***noun*** **the wicked** [pl.] people who are wicked
IDM (**there's**) **no peace/rest for the** ˈ**wicked** (usually *humorous*) used when sb is complaining that they have a lot of work to do

wicker /ˈwɪkə(r)/ *noun* [U] thin sticks of wood twisted together to make BASKETS, furniture, etc: *a wicker chair*

wick·er·work /ˈwɪkəwɜːk; *NAmE* ˈwɪkərwɜːrk/ *noun* [U] BASKETS, furniture, etc. made from wicker

wicket /ˈwɪkɪt/ *noun* (in CRICKET) **1** either of the two sets of three vertical sticks (called STUMPS) with pieces of wood (called BAILS) lying across the top. The BOWLER tries to hit the wicket with the ball. ➲ VISUAL VOCAB page V36 **2** the area of ground between the two wickets
IDM **keep** ˈ**wicket** to act as a WICKETKEEPER ➲ more at STICKY *adv.*

ˈ**wicket gate** *noun* a small gate, especially one at the side of a larger one

wicket·keep·er /ˈwɪkɪtkiːpə(r)/ (also *BrE informal* **keep·er**) *noun* (in CRICKET) a player who stands behind the WICKET in order to stop or catch the ball ➲ VISUAL VOCAB page V36

wide 🔑 /waɪd/ *adj., adv., noun*

WORD FAMILY
wide *adj., adv.*
widely *adv.*
widen *verb*
width *noun*

■ ***adj.*** (wider, wid·est)
▸ FROM ONE SIDE TO THE OTHER **1** 🔑 measuring a lot from one side to the other: *a wide river* ◇ *Sam has a wide mouth.* ◇ *a jacket with wide lapels* ◇ *Her face broke into a **wide grin**.* OPP **narrow** ➲ see also WIDTH **2** 🔑 measuring a particular distance from one side to the other: ***How wide** is that stream?* ◇ *It's about 2 metres wide.* ◇ *The road was just wide enough for two vehicles to pass.*
▸ LARGE NUMBER/AMOUNT **3** 🔑 including a large number or variety of different people or things; covering a large area: *a **wide range/choice/variety** of goods* ◇ *Her music appeals to a wide audience.* ◇ *Jenny has a wide circle of friends.* ◇ *a manager with wide experience of industry* ◇ *It's the best job in **the whole wide world**.* ◇ *The incident has received wide coverage in the press.* ◇ *The festival attracts people from a wide area.*
▸ DIFFERENCE/GAP **4** 🔑 very big: *There are wide variations in prices.*
▸ GENERAL **5** (only used in the comparative and superlative) general; not only looking at details: *the wider aims of the project* ◇ *We are talking about education **in its widest sense**.*
▸ EYES **6** fully open: *She stared at him with wide eyes.*
▸ NOT CLOSE **7** **~** (**of sth**) far from the point aimed at: *Her shot was wide* (*of the target*).
▸ -WIDE **8** (in adjectives and adverbs) happening or existing in the whole of a country, etc: *a nationwide search* ◇ *We need to act on a Europe-wide scale.*
IDM **give sb/sth a wide** ˈ**berth** to not go too near sb/sth; to avoid sb/sth: *He gave the dog a wide berth.* **wide of the**

W

'**mark** not accurate: *Their predictions turned out to be wide of the mark.*

■ **adv.** (wider, wid·est) as far or fully as possible: *The door was **wide open**.* ◇ *The championship is still **wide open*** (= anyone could win). ◇ *She had a fear of **wide-open spaces**.* ◇ *He stood with his legs **wide apart**.* ◇ *In a few seconds she was **wide awake**.* ◇ ***Open** your mouth **wide**.* IDM see CAST *v.*, FAR *adv.*

■ ***noun*** (*sport*) a ball that has been BOWLED (= thrown) where the BATSMAN or BATTER cannot reach it

Synonyms

wide / broad

These adjectives are frequently used with the following nouns:

wide ~	broad ~
street	shoulders
river	back
area	smile
range	range
variety	agreement
choice	outline

- **Wide** is the word most commonly used to talk about something that measures a long distance from one side to the other. **Broad** is more often used to talk about parts of the body. (Although **wide** can be used with *mouth*.) It is used in more formal or written language to describe the features of the countryside, etc: *a broad river* ◇ *a broad stretch of meadowland.*
- Both **wide** and **broad** can be used to describe something that includes a large variety of different people or things: *a wide/broad range of products.* **Broad**, but not **wide**, can be used to mean 'general' or 'not detailed': *All of us are in broad agreement on this matter.*

ˌwide-angle ˈlens *noun* a camera LENS that can give a wider view than a normal lens

ˈwide boy *noun* (*BrE, informal, disapproving*) a man who makes money in dishonest ways

ˌwide-ˈeyed *adj.* **1** with your eyes fully open because of fear, surprise, etc: *She stared at him in wide-eyed amazement.* **2** having little experience and therefore very willing to believe, trust or accept sb/sth SYN **naive**

wide·ly 0→ /ˈwaɪdli/ *adv.*
1 0→ by a lot of people; in or to many places: *a widely held belief* ◇ *The idea is now widely accepted.* ◇ *He has travelled widely in Asia.* ◇ *Her books are **widely read*** (= a lot of people read them). ◇ *He's an educated, **widely-read** man* (= he has read a lot of books). **2** 0→ to a large degree; a lot: *Standards vary widely.*

widen /ˈwaɪdn/ *verb* **1** [I, T] to become wider; to make sth wider: *Her eyes widened in surprise.* ◇ **~ into sth** *Here the stream widens into a river.* ◇ **~ sth** *They may have to widen the road to cope with the increase in traffic.* **2** [I, T] to become larger in degree or range; to make sth larger in degree or range: *the widening gap between rich and poor* ◇ **~ sth** *We plan to widen the scope of our existing activities by offering more language courses.* ◇ *The legislation will be widened to include all firearms.*

ˌwide-ˈranging *adj.* including or dealing with a large number of different subjects or areas: *The commission has been given wide-ranging powers.* ◇ *a wide-ranging discussion*

wide·screen /ˈwaɪdskriːn/ *noun* [U] a way of presenting images on television with the width a lot greater than the height SYN **letterbox**: *a widescreen TV*

wide·spread AW /ˈwaɪdspred/ *adj.* existing or happening over a large area or among many people: *widespread damage* ◇ *The plan received widespread support throughout the country.*

widg·eon = WIGEON

widget /ˈwɪdʒɪt/ *noun* **1** (*informal*) used to refer to any small device that you do not know the name of **2** (*business*) a product that does not exist, used as an example of a typical product when making calculations: *Company A produces two million widgets a year.* **3** (*computing*) a small box on a web page that delivers changing information, such as news items or weather reports, while the rest of the page remains the same

widow /ˈwɪdəʊ; *NAmE* ˈwɪdoʊ/ *noun, verb*

■ ***noun*** a woman whose husband has died and who has not married again

■ ***verb* be widowed** if sb **is widowed**, their husband or wife has died: *She was widowed when she was 35.* ▸ **widowed** *adj.*: *his widowed father*

wid·ow·er /ˈwɪdəʊə(r); *NAmE* ˈwɪdoʊ-/ *noun* a man whose wife has died and who has not married again

widow·hood /ˈwɪdəʊhʊd; *NAmE* ˈwɪdoʊ-/ *noun* [U] the state or period of being a widow or widower

ˌwidow's ˈpeak *noun* hair growing in the shape of a V on sb's FOREHEAD ➲ **VISUAL VOCAB** page V49

width 0→ /wɪdθ; wɪtθ/ *noun*
1 0→ [U, C] the measurement from one side of sth to the other; how wide sth is: *It's about 10 metres **in width**.* ◇ *The terrace runs **the full width of** the house.* ◇ *The carpet is available in different widths.* **2** [C] a piece of material of a particular width: *You'll need two widths of fabric for each curtain.* **3** [C] the distance between the two long sides of a swimming pool: *How many widths can you swim?* ➲ compare LENGTH

width·ways /ˈwɪdθweɪz; ˈwɪtθ-/ *adv.* along the width and not the length: *Cut the cake in half widthways.* ➲ compare LENGTHWAYS

wield /wiːld/ *verb* **1 ~ sth** to have and use power, authority, etc: *She wields enormous power within the party.* **2 ~ sth** to hold sth, ready to use it as a weapon or tool SYN **brandish**: *He was wielding a large knife.*

wie·ner /ˈwiːnə(r)/ *noun* (*NAmE*) **1** = FRANKFURTER **2** (*slang*) a word for a PENIS, used especially by children

wife 0→ /waɪf/ *noun* (*pl.* **wives** /waɪvz/) the woman that a man is married to; a married woman: *the doctor's wife* ◇ *She's his second wife.* ◇ *an increase in the number of working wives* ➲ **COLLOCATIONS** at MARRIAGE ➲ see also FISHWIFE, HOUSEWIFE, MIDWIFE, TROPHY WIFE IDM see HUSBAND *n.*, OLD, WORLD

wife·ly /ˈwaɪfli/ *adj.* (*old-fashioned* or *humorous*) typical or expected of a wife: *wifely duties*

ˈwife-swapping *noun* [U] (*informal*) the practice of exchanging sexual partners between a group of married couples

Wi-fi™ /ˈwaɪ faɪ/ *noun* [U] (*computing*) the abbreviation for 'wireless fidelity' (a system for sending data over computer networks using radio waves instead of wires)

wig /wɪg/ *noun, verb*

■ ***noun*** a piece of artificial hair that is worn on the head, for example to hide the fact that a person is BALD, to cover sb's own hair, or by a judge and some other lawyers in some courts of law

■ ***verb*** (-gg-)

PHR V **ˌwig ˈout** (*NAmE, informal*) to become very excited, very anxious or angry about sth; to go crazy

wig·eon (also **widg·eon**) /ˈwɪdʒən/ *noun* (*pl.* **wig·eon**, **widg·eon**) a type of wild DUCK

wig·gle /ˈwɪgl/ *verb, noun*

■ ***verb*** [I, T] (*informal*) **~ sth** to move from side to side or up and down in short quick movements; to make sth move in this way SYN **wriggle**: *He removed his shoes and wiggled his toes.* ◇ *Her bottom wiggled as she walked past.*

■ ***noun*** a small movement from side to side or up and down

ˈwiggle room *noun* [U] (*informal*) the chance to change sth or to understand it in a different way: *The buyer still*

W

has some wiggle room when the deal is under contract. ◇ The amendment leaves no wiggle room for lawmakers.

wig·gly /ˈwɪɡli/ *adj.* (*informal*) (of a line) having many curves in it SYN **wavy**

wight /waɪt/ *noun* (*literary* or *old use*) **1** a GHOST or other spirit **2** (especially following an adjective) a person, considered in a particular way: *a poor wight*

wig·wam /ˈwɪɡwæm; *NAmE* -wɑːm/ *noun* a type of tent, shaped like a DOME or CONE, used by Native Americans in the past ➲ see also TEPEE

wiki /ˈwɪki/ *noun* a website that allows any user to change or add to the information it contains: *There's a wiki page hosted by the conference where you can share ideas and information.*

wilco /ˈwɪlkəʊ; *NAmE* -koʊ/ *exclamation* people say **Wilco!** in communication by radio to show that they agree to do sth

wild 🔑 /waɪld/ *adj., noun*

■ ***adj.*** (wild·er, wild·est)

▸ ANIMALS/PLANTS **1** 🔑 living or growing in natural conditions; not kept in a house or on a farm: ***wild animals/flowers*** ◇ *a wild rabbit* ◇ *wild strawberries* ◇ *The plants* ***grow wild*** *along the banks of rivers.*

▸ SCENERY/LAND **2** 🔑 in its natural state; not changed by people: *wild moorland*

▸ OUT OF CONTROL **3** 🔑 lacking discipline or control: *The boy is wild and completely out of control.* ◇ *He had a wild look in his eyes.*

▸ FEELINGS **4** 🔑 full of very strong feeling: *wild laughter* ◇ *The crowd* ***went wild.*** ◇ *It makes me wild* (= very angry) *to see such waste.*

▸ NOT SENSIBLE **5** 🔑 not carefully planned; not sensible or accurate: *He made a wild guess at the answer.* ◇ *wild accusations*

▸ EXCITING **6** (*informal*) very good, enjoyable or exciting: *We had a wild time in New York.*

▸ ENTHUSIASTIC **7** ~ **about sb/sth** (*informal*) very enthusiastic about sb/sth: *She's totally wild about him.* ◇ *I'm not wild about the idea.*

▸ WEATHER/SEA **8** affected by storms and strong winds SYN **stormy**: *a wild night* ◇ *The sea was wild.*

▸ **wild·ness** *noun* [U] ➲ see also WILDLY

IDM **beyond sb's wildest ˈdreams** far more, better, etc. than you could ever have imagined or hoped for **not/never in sb's wildest ˈdreams** used to say that sth has happened in a way that sb did not expect at all: *Never in my wildest dreams did I think I'd meet him again.* **run ˈwild 1** to grow or develop freely without any control: *The ivy has run wild.* ◇ *Let your* ***imagination run wild*** *and be creative.* **2** if children or animals **run wild**, they behave as they like because nobody is controlling them **wild ˈhorses would not drag, make, etc. sb** (**do sth**) used to say that nothing would prevent sb from doing sth or make them do sth they do not want to do ➲ more at SOW *v.*

■ ***noun* 1 the wild** [sing.] a natural environment that is not controlled by people: *The bird is too tame now to survive* ***in the wild.*** **2 the wilds** [pl.] areas of a country far from towns or cities, where few people live: *the wilds of Alaska* ◇ (*humorous*) *They live on a farm somewhere out* ***in the wilds.***

ˌwild ˈboar *noun* = BOAR

ˈwild card *noun* **1** (in card games) a card that has no value of its own and takes the value of any card that the player chooses **2** (*sport*) an opportunity for sb to play in a competition when they have not qualified in the usual way; a player who enters a competition in this way **3** (*computing*) a symbol that has no meaning of its own and can represent any letter or number **4** a person or thing whose behaviour or effect is difficult to predict

wild·cat /ˈwaɪldkæt/ *adj., verb, noun*

■ ***adj.*** [only before noun] **1** a **wildcat strike** happens suddenly and without the official support of a TRADE/LABOR UNION **2** (of a business or project) that has not been carefully planned and that will probably not be successful; that does not follow normal standards and methods

■ ***verb*** (-tt-) [I] (*NAmE*) to look for oil in a place where nobody has found any yet ▸ **wild·cat·ter** *noun*

■ ***noun*** a type of small wild cat that lives in mountains and forests

wilde·beest /ˈwɪldəbiːst/ *noun* (*pl.* **wilde·beest**) (also **gnu**) a large ANTELOPE with curved horns: *a herd of wildebeest*

wil·der·ness /ˈwɪldənəs; *NAmE* -dərn-/ *noun* [usually sing.] **1** a large area of land that has never been developed or used for growing crops because it is difficult to live there: *The Antarctic is the world's last great wilderness.* ◇ (*NAmE*) *a* ***wilderness area*** (= one where it is not permitted to build houses or roads) ◇ (*figurative*) *the barren wilderness of modern life* **2** a place that people do not take care of or control: *Their garden is a wilderness of grass and weeds.*

IDM **in the ˈwilderness** no longer in an important position, especially in politics

wild·fire /ˈwaɪldfaɪə(r)/ *noun* [U] IDM see SPREAD *v.*

wild·fowl /ˈwaɪldfaʊl/ *noun* [pl.] birds that people hunt for sport or food, especially birds that live near water such as DUCKS and GEESE

ˌwild ˈgoose chase *noun* a search for sth that is impossible for you to find or that does not exist, that makes you waste a lot of time

wild·life /ˈwaɪldlaɪf/ *noun* [U] animals, birds, insects, etc. that are wild and live in a natural environment: *Development of the area would endanger wildlife.* ◇ *a* ***wildlife habitat/sanctuary***

wild·ly 🔑 /ˈwaɪldli/ *adv.*

1 🔑 in a way that is not controlled: *She looked wildly around for an escape.* ◇ *His heart was beating wildly.* **2** 🔑 extremely; very: *The story had been wildly exaggerated.* ◇ *It is not a wildly funny play.*

the ˌWild ˈWest *noun* [sing.] the western states of the US during the years when the first Europeans were settling there, used especially when you are referring to the fact that there was not much respect for the law there

wiles /waɪlz/ *noun* [pl.] clever tricks that sb uses in order to get what they want or to make sb behave in a particular way

wil·ful (*especially BrE*) (*NAmE* usually **will·ful**) /ˈwɪlfl/ *adj.* (*disapproving*) **1** [usually before noun] (*formal, disapproving* or *law*) (of a bad or harmful action) done deliberately, although the person doing it knows that it is wrong: *wilful damage* **2** determined to do what you want; not caring about what other people want SYN **headstrong**: *a wilful child* ▸ **wil·ful·ly** /-fəli/ *adv.* **wil·ful·ness** *noun* [U]

will 🔑 /wɪl/ *modal verb, verb, noun*

■ ***modal verb*** (*short form* **'ll** /l/, *negative* **will not**, *short form* **won't** /wəʊnt; *NAmE* woʊnt/, *pt* **would** /wəd; *strong form* wʊd/, *short form* **'d** /d/, *negative* **would not**, *short form* **wouldn't** /ˈwʊdnt/) **1** 🔑 used for talking about or predicting the future: *You'll be in time if you hurry.* ◇ *How long will you be staying in Paris?* ◇ *Fred said he'd be leaving soon.* ◇ *By next year all the money will have been spent.* **2** 🔑 used for showing that sb is willing to do sth: *I'll check this letter for you, if you want.* ◇ *They won't lend us any more money.* ◇ *He wouldn't come—he said he was too busy.* ◇ *We said we would keep them.* **3** 🔑 used for asking sb to do sth: *Will you send this letter for me, please?* ◇ *You'll water the plants while I'm away, won't you?* ◇ *I asked him if he wouldn't mind calling later.* **4** 🔑 used for ordering sb to do sth: *You'll do it this minute!* ◇ *Will you be quiet!* **5** 🔑 used for stating what you think is probably true: *That'll be the doctor now.* ◇ *You'll have had dinner already, I suppose.* **6** 🔑 used for stating what is generally true: *If it's made of wood it will float.* ◇ *Engines won't run without lubricants.* **7** 🔑 used for stating what is true or possible in a particular case: *This jar will hold a kilo.* ◇ *The door won't open!* **8** 🔑 used for talking about habits: *She'll listen to music, alone in her room, for hours.* ◇ *He would spend hours on the telephone.* HELP If you put extra stress on the word **will** or **would** in this meaning, it shows that the habit annoys you: *He ˈwill comb his hair at the table, even though he knows I don't like it.* ➲ note at MODAL, SHALL

W

■ *verb* (*third person sing. pres. t.* will) [I] (only used in the simple present tense) (*old-fashioned* or *formal*) to want or like: *Call it what you will, it's still a problem.*

■ *verb* **1** to use the power of your mind to do sth or to make sth happen: **~ sth** *As a child he had thought he could fly, if he willed it enough.* ◇ **~ sb/sth to do sth** *She willed her eyes to stay open.* ◇ *He willed himself not to panic.* **2 ~ sth | ~ that...** (*old use*) to intend or want sth to happen: *They thought they had been victorious in battle because God had willed it.* **3** to formally give your property or possessions to sb after you have died, by means of a WILL *n.* (3): **~ sb sth** *Joe had willed them everything he possessed.* ◇ **~ sth (to sb)** *Joe had willed everything he possessed to them.*

■ *noun* **1** [C, U] the ability to control your thoughts and actions in order to achieve what you want to do; a feeling of strong determination to do sth that you want to do: *to have a* ***strong will*** ◇ *to have* ***an iron will/a will of iron*** ◇ *Her decision to continue shows great strength of will.* ◇ *In spite of what happened, he never lost* ***the will to live.*** ◇ *The meeting turned out to be a* ***clash of wills.*** ◇ *She always wants to impose her will on other people* (= to get what she wants). ➲ see also FREE WILL, WILLPOWER **2** [sing.] what sb wants to happen in a particular situation: *I don't want to go against your will.* ◇ (*formal*) *It is God's will.* **3** (also **tes·ta·ment**) [C] a legal document that says what is to happen to sb's money and property after they die: *I ought to* ***make a will.*** ◇ *My father left me the house in his will.* ➲ see also LIVING WILL **4 -willed** (in adjectives) having the type of will mentioned: *a strong-willed young woman* ◇ *weak-willed greedy people*

IDM **against your 'will** when you do not want to: *I was forced to sign the agreement against my will.* **at 'will** whenever or wherever you like: *They were able to come and go at will.* **where there's a ˌwill there's a 'way** (*saying*) if you really want to do sth then you will find a way of doing it **with a 'will** in a willing and enthusiastic way **with the ˌbest will in the 'world** used to say that you cannot do sth, even though you really want to: *With the best will in the world I could not describe him as a good father.*

will·ful (*NAmE*) = WILFUL

wil·lie = WILLY

the wil·lies /'wɪliz/ *noun* [pl.] (*informal*) if sth **gives you the willies**, you are frightened by it or find it unpleasant

will·ing /'wɪlɪŋ/ *adj.*
1 [not usually before noun] **~ (to do sth)** not objecting to doing sth; having no reason for not doing sth: *They keep a list of people (who are) willing to work nights.* ◇ *I'm* ***perfectly willing*** *to discuss the problem.* **2** [usually before noun] ready or pleased to help and not needing to be persuaded; done or given in an enthusiastic way: ***willing helpers/volunteers*** ◇ *willing support* ◇ *She's very willing.* OPP **unwilling** ▶ **will·ing·ly** *adv.*: *People would willingly pay more for better services.* ◇ *'Will you help me?' 'Willingly.'* **will·ing·ness** *noun* [U, sing.] IDM see GOD, SHOW *v.*, SPIRIT

will-o'-the-wisp /ˌwɪl ə ðə 'wɪsp/ *noun* [usually sing.] **1** a thing that is impossible to obtain; a person that you cannot depend on **2** a blue light that is sometimes seen at night on soft wet ground and is caused by natural gases burning

wil·low /'wɪləʊ; *NAmE* 'wɪloʊ/ *noun* **1** [C] a tree with long thin branches and long thin leaves, that often grows near water ➲ VISUAL VOCAB page V8 ➲ see also PUSSY WILLOW **2** [U] the wood of the willow tree, used especially for making CRICKET BATS

wil·lowy /'wɪləʊi; *NAmE* 'wɪloʊi/ *adj.* (*approving*) (of a person, especially a woman) tall, thin and attractive

will·power /'wɪlpaʊə(r)/ *noun* [U] the ability to control your thoughts and actions in order to achieve what you want to do

willy (also **wil·lie**) /'wɪli/ *noun* (*pl.* -ies) (*BrE, informal*) a word for a PENIS, used especially by children or when speaking to children ➲ see also WILLIES

willy-nilly /ˌwɪli 'nɪli/ *adv.* (*informal*) **1** whether you want to or not: *She was forced willy-nilly to accept the company's proposals.* **2** in a careless way without planning: *Don't use your credit card willy-nilly.*

wilt /wɪlt/ *verb* **1** [I, T] **~ (sth)** if a plant or flower **wilts**, or sth **wilts** it, it bends towards the ground because of the heat or a lack of water SYN **droop** **2** [I] (*informal*) to become weak or tired or less confident SYN **flag**: *The spectators were wilting visibly in the hot sun.* ◇ *He was wilting under the pressure of work.* **3 thou wilt** (*old use*) used to mean 'you will', when talking to one person

wilt·ed /'wɪltɪd/ *adj.* **wilted** vegetable leaves, for example LETTUCE leaves, have been cooked for a short time and then used in a salad

wily /'waɪli/ *adj.* (**wili·er, wili·est**) clever at getting what you want, and willing to trick people SYN **cunning**: *The boss is a wily old fox.*

wimp /wɪmp/ *noun, verb*
■ *noun* (*informal, disapproving*) a person who is not strong, brave or confident SYN **weed** ▶ **wimp·ish** (also **wimpy**) *adj.*: *wimpish behaviour*
■ *verb*
PHR V **ˌwimp 'out (of sth)** (*informal, disapproving*) to not do sth that you intended to do because you are too frightened or not confident enough to do it

wim·ple /'wɪmpl/ *noun* a head covering made of cloth folded around the head and neck, worn by women in the Middle Ages and now by some NUNS

win /wɪn/ *verb, noun*
■ *verb* (**win·ning, won, won** /wʌn/) **1** [I, T] to be the most successful in a competition, race, battle, etc: *Which team won?* ◇ **~ at sth** *to* ***win at cards/chess, etc.*** ◇ **~ against sb/sth** *France won by six goals to two against Denmark.* ◇ **~ sth** *to* ***win an election/a game/a war, etc.*** ◇ *She loves to win an argument.* **2** [T] to get sth as the result of a competition, race, election, etc: **~ sth** *Britain won five gold medals.* ◇ *He won £3 000 in the lottery.* ◇ *How many states did the Republicans win?* ◇ **~ sth from sb** *The Conservatives won the seat from Labour in the last election.* ◇ **~ yourself/sb sth** *You've won yourself a trip to New York.* **3** [T] **~ sth** to achieve or get sth that you want, especially by your own efforts: *They are trying to* ***win support for*** *their proposals.* ◇ *The company has won a contract to supply books and materials to schools.* ◇ *She won the admiration of many people in her battle against cancer.* ➲ see also NO-WIN, WINNER, WINNING, WIN-WIN

IDM **you, he, etc. ˌcan't 'win** (*informal*) used to say that there is no acceptable way of dealing with a particular situation **you can't win them 'all | you 'win some, you 'lose some** (*informal*) used to express sympathy for sb who has been disappointed about sth **'you win** (*informal*) used to agree to what sb wants after you have failed to persuade them to do or let you do sth else: *OK, you win, I'll admit I was wrong.* **win (sth) ˌhands 'down** (*informal*) to win sth very easily **win sb's 'heart** to make sb love you **ˌwin or 'lose** whether you succeed or fail: *Win or lose, we'll know we've done our best.* ➲ more at DAY, SPUR *n.*

PHR V **ˌwin sb↔a'round/'over/'round (to sth)** to get sb's support or approval by persuading them that you are right: *She's against the idea but I'm sure I can win her over.* **ˌwin sth/sb↔'back** to get or have again sth/sb that you had before: *The party is struggling to win back voters who have been alienated by recent scandals.* **ˌwin 'out/'through** (*informal*) to be successful despite difficulties: *It won't be easy but we'll win through in the end.*

■ *noun* a victory in a game, contest, etc: *two wins and three defeats* ◇ *They have not had a win so far this season.* ◇ *France swept to a 6–2 win over Denmark.*

wince /wɪns/ *verb* [I] **~ (at sth)** to suddenly make an expression with your face that shows that you are feeling pain or embarrassment: *He winced as a sharp pain shot through his left leg.* ◇ *I still wince when I think about that stupid thing I said.* ▶ **wince** *noun* [usually sing.]: *a wince of pain*

winch /wɪntʃ/ *noun, verb*
■ *noun* a machine for lifting or pulling heavy objects using a rope or chain

W

■ ***verb*** **~ sb/sth + adv./prep.** to lift sb/sth up into the air using a winch

Win·ches·ter /ˈwɪntʃɪstə(r)/ (also ˌ**Winchester ˈrifle**) *noun* a type of long gun that fires several bullets one after the other

wind¹ ⊶ /wɪnd/ *noun, verb* ➲ see also WIND²

■ ***noun*** **1** ⊶ [C, U] (also **the wind**) air that moves quickly as a result of natural forces: ***strong/high winds*** ◇ ***gale-force winds*** ◇ *a* ***light wind*** ◇ *a* ***north/south/east/west wind*** ◇ *a* ***chill/cold/biting wind*** *from the north* ◇ *The wind is blowing from the south.* ◇ *The trees were swaying* ***in the wind.*** ◇ ***A gust of wind*** *blew my hat off.* ◇ *The weather was hot, without a* ***breath of wind.*** ◇ *The wall gives some protection from the* ***prevailing wind.*** ◇ *The wind is getting up* (= starting to blow strongly). ◇ *The wind has dropped* (= stopped blowing strongly). ◇ ***wind speed/direction*** ➲ **COLLOCATIONS** at WEATHER ➲ see also CROSSWIND, DOWNWIND, HEADWIND, TAILWIND, TRADE WIND, WINDY **2** (*BrE*) (*NAmE* **gas**) [U] air that you swallow with food or drink; gas that is produced in your stomach or INTESTINES that makes you feel uncomfortable: *I can't eat beans—they give me wind.* ◇ *Try to bring the baby's wind up.* **3** [U] breath that you need when you do exercise or blow into a musical instrument: *I need time to get my wind back after that run.* ◇ *He kicked Gomez in the stomach, knocking the wind out of him.* ➲ see also SECOND WIND **4** [U+sing./pl. v.] (also **winds** [pl.]) the group of musical instruments in an ORCHESTRA that produce sounds when you blow into them; the musicians who play those instruments: *music for wind and strings* ◇ *The wind section played beautifully.* ➲ compare WOODWIND

IDM **break ˈwind** to release gas from your BOWELS through your ANUS **get ˈwind of sth** (*informal*) to hear about sth secret or private **get/have the ˈwind up (about sth)** (*informal*) to become/be frightened about sth **in the ˈwind** about to happen soon, although you do not know exactly how or when **like the ˈwind** very quickly **put the ˈwind up sb** (*BrE, informal*) to make sb frightened **take the ˈwind out of sb's sails** (*informal*) to make sb suddenly less confident or angry, especially when you do or say sth that they do not expect **a wind/the winds of ˈchange** (used especially by journalists) an event or a series of events that has started to happen and will cause important changes or results: *A wind of change was blowing through the banking world.* ➲ more at CAUTION *n.*, FOLLOWING, ILL *adj.*, SAIL *v.*, STRAW, WAY *n.*

■ ***verb*** **1** [usually passive] **~ sb** to make sb unable to breathe easily for a short time: *He was momentarily winded by the blow to his stomach.* **2 ~ sb** (*BrE*) to gently hit or rub a baby's back to make it BURP (= release gas from its stomach through its mouth) **SYN** **burp** ➲ see also LONG-WINDED

wind² ⊶ /waɪnd/ *verb* ➲ see also WIND¹ (**wound, wound** /waʊnd/)

1 ⊶ [I, T] (of a road, river, etc.) to have many bends and twists: **+ adv./prep.** *The path wound down to the beach.* ◇ **~ its way + adv./prep.** *The river winds its way between two meadows.* ➲ see also WINDING **2** ⊶ [T] **~ sth + adv./prep.** to wrap or twist sth around itself or sth else: *He wound the wool into a ball.* ◇ *Wind the bandage around your finger.* **3** ⊶ [T, I] to make a clock or other piece of machinery work by turning a KNOB, handle, etc. several times; to be able to be made to work in this way: **~ sth (up)** *He had forgotten to wind his watch.* ◇ **~ up** *It was one of those old-fashioned gramophones that winds up.* ➲ see also WIND-UP **4** ⊶ [T, I] to operate a tape, film, etc. so that it moves nearer to its ending or starting position: **~ sth forward/back** *He wound the tape back to the beginning.* ◇ **~ forward/back** *Wind forward to the bit where they discover the body.* **5** [T] **~ sth** to turn a handle several times: *You operate the trapdoor by winding this handle.* **IDM** see LITTLE FINGER ▸ **wind** *noun*: *Give the handle another couple of winds.*

PHR V ˌ**wind ˈdown 1** (of a person) to rest or relax after a period of activity or excitement **SYN** **unwind 2** (of a piece of machinery) to go slowly and then stop ˌ**wind sth↔ˈdown 1** to bring a business, an activity, etc. to an end gradually over a period of time: *The government is winding down its nuclear programme.* **2** to make sth such as the window of a car move downwards by turning a handle, pressing a button, etc: *Can I wind my window down?* ˌ**wind ˈup** (*informal*) (of a person) to find yourself in a particular place or situation: *I always said he would wind up in prison.* ◇ **~ doing sth** *We eventually wound up staying in a little hotel a few miles from town.* ◇ **+ adj.** *If you take risks like that you'll wind up dead.* ˌ**wind ˈup** | ˌ**wind sth↔ˈup** to bring sth such as a speech or meeting to an end: *The speaker was just winding up when the door was flung open.* ◇ *If we all agree, let's wind up the discussion.* ˌ**wind sb↔ˈup** (*BrE, informal*) to deliberately say or do sth in order to annoy sb: *Calm down! Can't you see he's only winding you up?* ◇ *That can't be true! You're winding me up.* ➲ related noun WIND-UP ˌ**wind sth↔ˈup 1** to stop running a company, business, etc. and close it completely **2** to make sth such as the window of a car move upwards by turning a handle, pressing a button, etc.

wind·bag /ˈwɪndbæɡ/ *noun* (*informal, disapproving*) a person who talks too much, and does not say anything important or interesting

wind-blown /ˈwɪnd bləʊn; *NAmE* bloʊn/ *adj.* **1** carried from one place to another by the wind **2** made untidy by the wind: *wind-blown hair*

wind·break /ˈwɪndbreɪk/ *noun* a row of trees, a fence, etc. that provides protection from the wind

wind·cheat·er /ˈwɪndtʃiːtə(r)/ (*old-fashioned, BrE*) (*NAmE* **wind·break·er** /ˈwɪndbreɪkə(r)/) *noun* a jacket designed to protect you from the wind

wind chill /ˈwɪnd tʃɪl/ *noun* [U] the effect of low temperature combined with wind on sb/sth: *Take the* ***wind-chill factor*** *into account.*

wind chimes /ˈwɪnd tʃaɪmz/ *noun* [pl.] a set of hanging pieces of metal, etc. that make a pleasant ringing sound in the wind

wind-down /ˈwaɪnd daʊn/ (also ˌ**winding-ˈdown**) *noun* [sing.] a gradual reduction in activity as sth comes to an end: *The wind-down of the company was handled very efficiently.*

wind·er /ˈwaɪndə(r)/ *noun* a device or piece of machinery that winds sth, for example sth that winds a watch or the film in a camera

wind·fall /ˈwɪndfɔːl/ *noun* **1** an amount of money that sb/sth wins or receives unexpectedly: *The hospital got a sudden windfall of £300 000.* ◇ *windfall profits* ◇ *The government imposed a* ***windfall tax*** (= a tax on profits to be paid once only, not every year) *on some industries.* **2** a fruit, especially an apple, that the wind has blown down from a tree

wind farm /ˈwɪnd fɑːm; *NAmE* fɑːrm/ *noun* an area of land on which there are a lot of WINDMILLS or WIND TURBINES for producing electricity ➲ **COLLOCATIONS** at ENVIRONMENT

wind gauge /ˈwɪnd ɡeɪdʒ/ *noun* = ANEMOMETER

the Win·dies /ˈwɪndɪz; -diːz/ *noun* [pl.] (*informal*) the West Indian CRICKET team

wind·ing /ˈwaɪndɪŋ/ *adj.* having a curving and twisting shape: *a long and winding road*

winding-down /ˌwaɪndɪŋ ˈdaʊn/ *noun* = WIND DOWN

winding sheet /ˈwaɪndɪŋ ʃiːt/ *noun* (especially in the past) a piece of cloth that a dead person's body was wrapped in before it was buried **SYN** **shroud**

wind instrument /ˈwɪnd ɪnstrəmənt/ *noun* any musical instrument that you play by blowing ➲ compare BRASS, WOODWIND

wind·lass /ˈwɪndləs/ *noun* a type of WINCH (= a machine for lifting or pulling heavy objects)

wind·less /ˈwɪndləs/ *adj.* (*formal*) without wind: *a windless day* **OPP** **windy**

wind machine /ˈwɪnd məʃiːn/ *noun* **1** a machine used in the theatre or in films/movies that blows air to give the

W

effect of wind **2** a machine used in ORCHESTRAS to produce the sound of wind

wind·mill /ˈwɪndmɪl/ *noun* **1** a building with machinery for GRINDING grain into flour that is driven by the power of the wind turning long arms (called SAILS) ➲ VISUAL VOCAB page V2 **2** a tall thin structure with parts that turn round, used to change the power of the wind into electricity **3** (*BrE*) (*NAmE* **pin·wheel**) a toy with curved plastic parts that form the shape of a flower which turns round on the end of a stick when you blow on it IDM see TILT *v.*

win·dow 0‑ /ˈwɪndəʊ; *NAmE* ˈwɪndoʊ/ *noun* **1** 0‑ an opening in the wall or roof of a building, car, etc, usually covered with glass, that allows light and air to come in and people to see out; the glass in a window: *She **looked out of the window**. ◇ to **open/close the window** ◇ the **bedroom/car/kitchen, etc. window** ◇ a broken window* ➲ VISUAL VOCAB pages V15, V42 ➲ see also BAY WINDOW, DORMER WINDOW, FRENCH WINDOW, PICTURE WINDOW, ROSE WINDOW, SASH WINDOW **2** 0‑ = SHOP WINDOW: *I saw the dress I wanted **in the window**. ◇ a window display* **3** 0‑ an area within a frame on a computer screen, in which a particular program is operating or in which information of a particular type is shown: *to **create/open a window*** ➲ VISUAL VOCAB page V55 **4** 0‑ a small area of sth that you can see through, for example to talk to sb or read sth on the other side: *There was a long line of people at the box-office window. ◇ The address must be clearly visible through the window of the envelope.* **5** [sing.] **~ on/into sth** a way of seeing and learning about sth: *Television is a sort of **window on the world**. ◇ It gave me an intriguing window into the way people live.* **6** a time when there is an opportunity to do sth, although it may not last long: *We now have a small **window of opportunity** in which to make our views known.*
IDM **fly/go out** (**of**) **the ˈwindow** (*informal*) to stop existing; to disappear completely: *As soon as the kids arrived, order went out of the window.*

ˈwindow box *noun* a long narrow box outside a window, in which plants are grown ➲ VISUAL VOCAB page V15

ˈwindow cleaner *noun* a person whose job is to clean windows

ˈwindow dressing *noun* [U] **1** the art of arranging goods in shop/store windows in an attractive way **2** (*disapproving*) the fact of doing or saying sth in a way that creates a good impression but does not show the real facts: *The reforms are seen as window dressing.*

ˈwindow ledge *noun* = WINDOWSILL

win·dow·less /ˈwɪndəʊləs; *NAmE* -doʊ-/ *adj.* without windows: *a tiny, windowless cell*

win·dow·pane /ˈwɪndəʊpeɪn; *NAmE* -doʊ-/ *noun* a piece of glass in a window ➲ VISUAL VOCAB page V15

ˈwindow shade *noun* (*NAmE*) = BLIND

ˈwindow-shopping *noun* [U] the activity of looking at the goods in shop/store windows, usually without intending to buy anything: *to go window-shopping* ➲ COLLOCATIONS at SHOPPING

win·dow·sill /ˈwɪndəʊsɪl; *NAmE* ˈwɪndoʊ-/ (also **sill**, **ˈwindow ledge**) *noun* a narrow shelf below a window, either inside or outside: *Place the plants on a sunny windowsill.* ➲ VISUAL VOCAB page V15

wind·pipe /ˈwɪndpaɪp/ *noun* the tube in the throat that carries air to the lungs SYN **trachea** ➲ VISUAL VOCAB page V48

wind·screen /ˈwɪndskriːn/ (*BrE*) (*NAmE* **wind·shield**) *noun* the window across the front of a vehicle ➲ COLLOCATIONS at DRIVING ➲ VISUAL VOCAB page V42

ˈwindscreen wiper (*BrE*) (*NAmE* **ˈwindshield wiper**) (also **wiper** *BrE*, *NAmE*) *noun* a blade with a rubber edge that moves across a windscreen to make it clear of rain, snow, etc. ➲ VISUAL VOCAB page V42

wind·shield /ˈwɪndʃiːld/ *noun* **1** (*NAmE*) (*BrE* **windscreen**) the window across the front of a vehicle ➲ VISUAL VOCAB page V42 **2** a glass or plastic screen that provides protection from the wind, for example at the front of a motorcycle

wind·sock /ˈwɪndsɒk; *NAmE* -sɑːk/ *noun* a tube made of soft material, open at both ends, that hangs at the top of a pole, to show the direction of the wind

wind·storm /ˈwɪndstɔːm; *NAmE* -stɔːrm/ *noun* (*NAmE*) a storm where there is very strong wind but little rain or snow

wind·surf·er /ˈwɪndsɜːfə(r); *NAmE* -sɜːrf-/ *noun* **1** (also **sail·board** *BrE*, *NAmE*) a long narrow board with a sail, that you stand on and sail across water on **2** a person on a windsurfer

wind·surf·ing /ˈwɪndsɜːfɪŋ; *NAmE* -sɜːrf-/ (also **board·sail·ing**) *noun* [U] the sport of sailing on water standing on a windsurfer: *to go windsurfing* ➲ VISUAL VOCAB page V40 ▸ **wind·surf** *verb* [I]: *Most visitors come to sail or windsurf.*

wind·swept /ˈwɪndswept/ *adj.* **1** (of a place) having strong winds and little protection from them: *the windswept Atlantic coast* **2** looking as though you have been in a strong wind: *windswept hair*

wind tunnel /ˈwɪnd tʌnl/ *noun* a large tunnel where aircraft, etc. are tested by forcing air past them

wind turbine /ˈwɪnd tɜːbaɪn; *NAmE* tɜːrb-/ *noun* a type of modern WINDMILL used for producing electricity ➲ VISUAL VOCAB page V7

wind-up /ˈwaɪnd ʌp/ *adj.*, *noun*
■ ***adj.*** [only before noun] **1** that you operate by turning a key or handle: *an old-fashioned wind-up gramophone* **2** intended to bring sth to an end: *a wind-up speech*
■ ***noun*** (*BrE*, *informal*) something that sb says or does in order to be deliberately annoying, especially as a joke

wind·ward /ˈwɪndwəd; *NAmE* -wərd/ *adj.*, *noun*
■ ***adj.*** on the side of sth from which the wind is blowing: *the windward side of the boat* OPP **leeward** ➲ see also LEE ▸ **wind·ward** *adv.* OPP **leeward**
■ ***noun*** [U] the side or direction from which the wind is blowing: *to sail to windward* ➲ compare LEEWARD

windy /ˈwɪndi/ *adj.* (**wind·ier**, **windi·est**) **1** (of weather, etc.) with a lot of wind: *a windy day* OPP **windless** **2** (of a place) getting a lot of wind: *windy hills* **3** (*informal*, *disapproving*) (of speech) involving speaking for longer than necessary and in a way that is complicated and not clear

the ˌWindy ˈCity *noun* [sing.] a name for the US city of Chicago

wine 0‑ /waɪn/ *noun*, *verb*
■ ***noun*** **1** 0‑ [U, C] an alcoholic drink made from the juice of GRAPES that has been left to FERMENT. There are many different kinds of wine: *a bottle of wine ◇ a glass of **dry/sweet wine** ◇ **red/rosé/white wine** ◇ **sparkling wine*** ➲ see also TABLE WINE **2** [U, C] an alcoholic drink made from plants or fruits other than GRAPES: *elderberry/rice wine* **3** [U] (also **wine ˈred**) a dark red colour
■ ***verb***
IDM **ˌwine and ˈdine** (**sb**) to go to restaurants, etc. and enjoy good food and drink; to entertain sb by buying them good food and drink: *The firm spent thousands wining and dining potential clients.*

ˈwine bar *noun* a bar or small restaurant where wine is the main drink available

ˈwine cellar (also **cel·lar**) *noun* an underground room where wine is stored; the wine stored in this room

ˌwine ˈcooler *noun* **1** (*NAmE*) a drink made with wine, fruit juice, ice and SODA WATER **2** **ˈwine cooler** a container for putting a bottle of wine in to cool it

ˈwine farm *noun* (*SAfrE*) a VINEYARD (= a place where GRAPES are grown for making wine)

ˈwine glass *noun* a glass for drinking wine from ➲ VISUAL VOCAB page V19

wine·grow·er /ˈwaɪngrəʊə(r); *NAmE* -groʊ-/ *noun* a person who grows GRAPES for wine

ˈwine gum *noun* (*BrE*) a small fruit-flavoured sweet/candy

W

'wine list *noun* a list of wines available in a restaurant ➲ COLLOCATIONS at RESTAURANT

wine·maker /'waɪnmeɪkə(r)/ *noun* a person who produces wine ▶ **wine·mak·ing** /'waɪnmeɪkɪŋ/ *noun* [U]

win·ery /'waɪnəri/ *noun* (*pl.* -ies) (*especially NAmE*) a place where wine is made ➲ compare VINEYARD

,wine 'vinegar *noun* [U] VINEGAR which is made from wine rather than from grain or apples

wing 🔑 /wɪŋ/ *noun, verb*

■ ***noun***

▸ OF BIRD/INSECT **1** 🔑 [C] one of the parts of the body of a bird, insect or BAT that it uses for flying: *The swan* ***flapped its wings*** *noisily.* ◇ *wing feathers* ➲ VISUAL VOCAB pages V10, V11

▸ OF PLANE **2** 🔑 [C] one of the large flat parts that stick out from the side of a plane and help to keep it in the air when it is flying ➲ VISUAL VOCAB page V43

▸ OF BUILDING **3** [C] one of the parts of a large building that sticks out from the main part: *the east wing* ◇ *the new wing of the hospital*

▸ OF CAR **4** (*BrE*) (*NAmE* **fend·er**) [C] a part of a car that is above a wheel: *There was a dent in the nearside wing.* ➲ VISUAL VOCAB page V42

▸ OF ORGANIZATION **5** [C] one section of an organization that has a particular function or whose members share the same opinions SYN **arm**: *the radical wing of the party* ◇ *the political wing of the National Resistance Army* ➲ see also LEFT WING, RIGHT WING

▸ IN FOOTBALL/HOCKEY **6** [C] = WINGER ➲ see also LEFT WING, RIGHT WING **7** [C] the far left or right side of the sports field: *He plays on the wing.*

▸ IN THEATRE **8** **the wings** [pl.] the area at either side of the stage that cannot be seen by the audience

IDM **get your 'wings** to pass the exams that mean you are allowed to fly a plane **(waiting) in the 'wings** ready to take over a particular job or be used in a particular situation when needed **on a ,wing and a 'prayer** with only a very slight chance of success **on the 'wing** (*literary*) (of a bird, insect, etc.) flying **take sb under your 'wing** to take care of and help sb who has less experience of sth than you **take 'wing** (*literary*) (of a bird, insect, etc.) to fly away: (*figurative*) *Her imagination took wing.* ➲ more at CLIP *v.*, SPREAD *v.*

■ ***verb***

▸ FLY **1** [T, I] **~ (its way) + adv./prep.** (*literary*) to fly somewhere: *A solitary seagull winged its way across the bay.*

▸ GO QUICKLY **2** [T] **~ its way + adv./prep.** to be sent somewhere very quickly: *An application form will be winging its way to you soon.*

IDM **'wing it** (*informal*) to do sth without planning or preparing it first SYN **improvise**: *I didn't know I'd have to make a speech—I just had to wing it.*

'wing back *noun* (in football (SOCCER)) a player who plays near the edge of the field and who both attacks and defends

'wing chair *noun* a comfortable chair that has a high back with pieces pointing forwards at the sides

,wing 'collar *noun* a high stiff shirt COLLAR for men, worn with formal clothes

'wing commander *noun* an officer of high rank in the British AIR FORCE: *Wing Commander Brian Moore*

wing·ding /'wɪŋdɪŋ/ *noun* (*old-fashioned, NAmE, informal*) a party

winged /wɪŋd/ *adj.* **1** having wings: *winged insects* OPP **wingless** **2** **-winged** (in adjectives) having the number or type of wings mentioned: *a long-winged bird*

wing·er /'wɪŋə(r)/ *noun* (also **wing**) (*sport*) either of the attacking players who play towards the side of the playing area in sports such as football (SOCCER) or HOCKEY

wing·less /'wɪŋləs/ *adj.* (especially of insects) without wings OPP **winged**

'wing mirror (*BrE*) (*NAmE* **'side-view mirror**) *noun* a mirror that sticks out from the side of a vehicle and allows the driver to see behind the vehicle ➲ VISUAL VOCAB page V42

'wing nut *noun* a NUT (2) for holding things in place, which has parts that stick out at the sides so that you can turn it easily

wing·span /'wɪŋspæn/ *noun* the distance between the end of one wing and the end of the other when the wings are fully stretched: *a bird with a two-foot wingspan*

wing·tips /'wɪŋtɪps/ *noun* [pl.] (*NAmE*) strong leather shoes that fasten with LACES and have an extra piece of leather with small holes in it over the toe

wink /wɪŋk/ *verb, noun*

■ ***verb*** **1** [I] **~ (at sb)** to close one eye and open it again quickly, especially as a private signal to sb, or to show sth is a joke: *He winked at her and she knew he was thinking the same thing that she was.* ➲ compare BLINK **2** [I] to shine with an unsteady light; to flash on and off SYN **blink**: *We could see the lights of the ship winking in the distance.*

PHR V **'wink at sth** to pretend that you have not noticed sth, especially sth bad or illegal

■ ***noun*** an act of winking, especially as a signal to sb: *He gave her a knowing wink.* ➲ see also FORTY WINKS

IDM **not get/have a 'wink of sleep | not sleep a 'wink** to not be able to sleep: *I didn't get a wink of sleep last night.* ◇ *I hardly slept a wink.* ➲ more at NOD *n.*, NUDGE *n.*, TIP *v.*

win·kle /'wɪŋkl/ *noun, verb*

■ ***noun*** (*BrE*) (also **peri·win·kle** *NAmE, BrE*) a small SHELLFISH, like a SNAIL, that can be eaten

■ ***verb*** (*BrE, informal*)

PHR V **,winkle sth/sb↔'out (of sth)** to get sth/sb out of a place or position, especially when this is not easy to do **,winkle sth 'out of sb** to get information from sb, especially with difficulty SYN **extract**: *She always manages to winkle secrets out of people.*

Win·ne·bago™ /,wɪnɪ'beɪgəʊ; *NAmE* -goʊ/ *noun* (*NAmE*) (*pl.* **Win·ne·bago** or **-os**) a large vehicle designed for people to live and sleep in when they are camping; a type of RV

win·ner 🔑 /'wɪnə(r)/ *noun*

1 🔑 a person, a team, an animal, etc. that wins sth: *The winners of the competition will be announced next month.* ◇ *There are no winners in a divorce* (= everyone suffers). **2** [usually sing.] (*informal*) a thing or person that is successful or likely to be successful: *I think your idea is a winner.* ◇ *The design is very good. We could be* **onto a winner** (= we may do or produce sth successful). **3** [sing.] (*sport*) a goal or point that causes a team or a person to win a game: *Rooney scored the winner after 20 minutes* ➲ compare LOSER

IDM see PICK *v.*

win·ning 🔑 /'wɪnɪŋ/ *adj.*

1 🔑 [only before noun] that wins or has won sth, for example a race or competition: *the winning horse* ◇ *the winning goal* **2** [usually before noun] attractive in a way that makes other people like you: *a winning smile* ▶ **win·ning·ly** *adv.* IDM see CARD *n.*

win·ning·est /'wɪnɪŋɪst/ *adj.* (*NAmE, informal*) having won the most games, races or competitions: *the winningest coach in the history of the US national team*

'winning post *noun* (*especially BrE*) a post that shows where the end of a race is: *to be first past the winning post*

win·nings /'wɪnɪŋz/ *noun* [pl.] money that sb wins in a competition or game or by gambling

win·now /'wɪnəʊ; *NAmE* -noʊ/ *verb* **~ sth** to blow air through grain in order to remove its outer covering (called the CHAFF)

PHR V **,winnow sb/sth 'out (of sth)** (*formal*) to remove people or things from a group so that only the best ones are left SYN **sift out**

wino /'waɪnəʊ; *NAmE* -noʊ/ *noun* (*pl.* -os) (*informal*) a person who drinks a lot of cheap alcohol and who has no home

win·some /'wɪnsəm/ *adj.* (*formal*) (of people or their manner) pleasant and attractive SYN **engaging**: *a winsome smile* ▶ **win·some·ly** *adv.*

W

win·ter 0-w /ˈwɪntə(r)/ *noun, verb*
■ ***noun*** 0-w [U, C] the coldest season of the year, between autumn/fall and spring: *a* ***mild/severe/hard winter*** ◇ *Our house can be very cold* ***in*** *(****the****)* ***winter.*** ◇ *They worked on the building all through the winter.* ◇ *We went to New Zealand last winter.* ◇ *the* ***winter months*** ◇ *a* ***winter coat*** IDM see DEAD *n.*
■ ***verb*** [I] (+ **adv./prep.**) to spend the winter somewhere: *Many British birds winter in Africa.* ➲ compare OVERWINTER

ˌwinter ˈsports *noun* [pl.] sports that people do on snow or ice ➲ VISUAL VOCAB page V39

win·ter·time /ˈwɪntətaɪm; *NAmE* -tərt-/ *noun* [U] the period of time when it is winter: *The days are shorter in (the) wintertime.*

win·try /ˈwɪntri/ *adj.* **1** typical of winter; cold: *wintry weather* ◇ *a wintry landscape* ◇ ***wintry showers*** (= of snow) **2** not friendly SYN **frosty**: *a wintry smile*

ˌwin-ˈwin *adj.* [only before noun] (of a situation) in which there is a good result for each person or group involved: *This is a* ***win-win situation*** *all around.*

wipe /waɪp/ *verb, noun*
■ ***verb*** **1** to rub sth against a surface, in order to remove dirt or liquid from it; to rub a surface with a cloth, etc. in order to clean it: **~ sth (on sth)** *Please wipe your feet on the mat.* ◇ *He wiped his hands on a clean towel.* ◇ **~ sth with sth** *She was sniffing and wiping her eyes with a tissue.* ◇ **~ sth + adj.** *He wiped his plate clean with a piece of bread.* **2** to remove dirt, liquid, etc. from sth by using a cloth, your hand, etc: **~ sth (from/off sth)** *He wiped the sweat from his forehead.* ◇ (*figurative*) *Wipe that stupid smile off your face.* ◇ **~ sth away/off/up** *She wiped off her make-up.* ◇ *Use that cloth to wipe up the mess.* **3** to remove information, sound, images, etc. from a computer, tape or video SYN **erase**: **~ sth off (sth)** *You must have wiped off that programme I recorded.* ◇ **~ sth** *Somebody had wiped all the tapes.* **4** to deliberately forget an experience because it was unpleasant or embarrassing SYN **erase**: **~ sth from sth** *I tried to wipe the whole episode from my mind.* ◇ **~ sth out** *You can never wipe out the past.*
IDM **wipe sb/sth off the ˌface of the ˈearth | wipe sth off the ˈmap** to destroy or remove sb/sth completely **wipe the slate ˈclean** to agree to forget about past mistakes or arguments and start again with a relationship ➲ more at FLOOR *n.*
PHR V **ˌwipe sth↔ˈdown** to clean a surface completely, using a wet cloth: *She took a cloth and wiped down the kitchen table.* **wipe sth off sth** to remove sth from sth: *Billions of pounds were wiped off share prices today.* **ˌwipe ˈout** (*informal*) to fall over, especially when you are doing a sport such as SKIING or SURFING **ˌwipe sb↔ˈout** (*informal*) to make sb extremely tired: *All that travelling has wiped her out.* ➲ see also WIPED OUT **ˌwipe sb/sth↔ˈout** [often passive] to destroy or remove sb/sth completely: *Whole villages were wiped out by the earthquake.* ◇ *Last year's profits were virtually wiped out.* ◇ *a campaign to wipe out malaria* ➲ related noun WIPEOUT
■ ***noun*** **1** an act of cleaning sth using a cloth: *Can you give the table a quick wipe?* **2** a special piece of thin cloth or soft paper that has been treated with a liquid and that you use to clean away dirt and bacteria: *Remember to take nappies and* ***baby wipes.***

ˌwiped ˈout *adj.* [not before noun] (*informal*) extremely tired: *You look wiped out.*

wipe·out /ˈwaɪpaʊt/ *noun* (*informal*) **1** [U, C] complete destruction, failure or defeat: *The party faces virtual wipeout in the election.* ◇ *a 5-0 wipeout* **2** [C] a fall from a SURFBOARD

wiper /ˈwaɪpə(r)/ *noun* = WINDSCREEN WIPER

wire 0-w /ˈwaɪə(r)/ *noun, verb*
■ ***noun*** **1** 0-w [U, C] metal in the form of thin thread; a piece of this: *a coil of copper wire* ◇ *a wire basket* ◇ *The box was fastened with a rusty wire.* ➲ picture at CORD ➲ see also BARBED WIRE, HIGH WIRE, TRIPWIRE **2** 0-w [C, U] a piece of wire that is used to carry an electric current or signal: *overhead wires* ◇ *fuse wire* ◇ *The telephone wires had been cut.* ➲ see also HOT-WIRE **3 the wire** [sing.] a wire fence: *Three prisoners escaped by crawling under the wire.* **4** [C] (*informal, especially NAmE*) = TELEGRAM: *We sent a wire asking him to join us.* ➲ see also WIRY
IDM **get your ˈwires crossed** (*informal*) to become confused about what sb has said to you so that you think they meant sth else **go, come, etc. (right) down to the ˈwire** (*informal*) if you say that a situation goes **down to the wire**, you mean that the result will not be decided or known until the very end ➲ more at LIVE², PULL *v.*
■ ***verb*** **1 ~ sth (up)** to connect a building, piece of equipment, etc. to an electricity supply using wires: *Make sure the plug is wired up correctly.* **2 ~ sb/sth up (to sth) | ~ sb/sth to sth** to connect sb/sth to a piece of equipment, especially a TAPE RECORDER or computer system: *He was wired up to a police tape recorder.* **3 ~ sth (for sth)** to put a special device somewhere in order to listen secretly to other people's conversations SYN **bug**: *The room had been wired for sound.* **4** (*especially NAmE*) to send sb a message by TELEGRAM: **~ sth (to sb)** *He wired the news to us.* ◇ **~ sb (sth)** *He wired us the news.* **5** to send money from one bank to another using an electronic system: **~ sth (to sb)** *The bank wired the money to her.* ◇ **~ sb sth** *The bank wired her the money.* **6 ~ sth** to join things together using wire

ˈwire cutters *noun* [pl.] a tool for cutting wire: *a pair of wire cutters* ➲ VISUAL VOCAB page V17

wired /ˈwaɪəd; *NAmE* ˈwaɪərd/ *adj.* **1** connected to a system of computers: *Many colleges now have wired dormitories.* **2** (of glass, material, etc.) containing wires that make it strong or stiff **3** (*informal*) excited or nervous; not relaxed **4** (*informal, especially NAmE*) under the influence of alcohol or an illegal drug

ˈwire fraud *noun* [U, C] FRAUD (= dishonest ways of getting money) using computers and telephones

wire·less /ˈwaɪələs; *NAmE* ˈwaɪərləs/ *noun, adj.*
■ ***noun*** **1** [C] (*old-fashioned, especially BrE*) a radio: *I heard it on the wireless.* **2** [U] a system of sending and receiving signals: *a message sent by wireless*
■ ***adj.*** not using wires: *wireless communications* ▶ **wire·less·ly** *adv.*

ˌwire ˈnetting *noun* [U] wire that is twisted into a net, used especially for fences

wire·pull·er /ˈwaɪəpʊlə(r); *NAmE* ˈwaɪər-/ *noun* (*NAmE*) a person who is able to control or influence events without people realizing it

ˈwire service *noun* (*especially NAmE*) an organization that supplies news to newspapers and to radio and television stations

ˈwire strippers *noun* [pl.] a tool for removing the plastic covering from electric wires

wire·tap·ping /ˈwaɪətæpɪŋ; *NAmE* ˈwaɪərt-/ *noun* [U] the act of secretly listening to other people's telephone conversations by attaching a device to the telephone line ▶ **wire·tap** *verb* (-pp-) **~ sth wire·tap** *noun*: *the use of illegal wiretaps* ➲ see also TAP

ˌwire ˈwool *noun* [U] (*BrE*) = STEEL WOOL

wir·ing /ˈwaɪərɪŋ/ *noun* [U] the system of wires that is used for supplying electricity to a building or machine: *to check the wiring* ◇ *a wiring diagram*

wiry /ˈwaɪəri/ *adj.* (**wiri·er**, **wiri·est**) **1** (of a person) thin but strong SYN **sinewy**: *a wiry little man* **2** (of hair, plants, etc.) stiff and strong; like wire

wis·dom /ˈwɪzdəm/ *noun* [U] **1** the ability to make sensible decisions and give good advice because of the experience and knowledge that you have: *a woman of great wisdom* ◇ *words of wisdom* **2 ~ of sth/of doing sth** how sensible sth is: *I* ***question the wisdom of*** *giving a child so much money.* **3** the knowledge that a society or culture has gained over a long period of time: *the collective wisdom of the Native American people*
IDM **conventional/received ˈwisdom** the view or belief that most people hold: *Conventional wisdom has it that riots only ever happen in cities.* **in his/her/its, etc. (infinite) ˈwisdom** used when you are saying that you do not

W

understand why sb has done sth: *The government in its wisdom has decided to support the ban.* ➲ more at PEARL

'wisdom tooth *noun* any of the four large teeth at the back of the mouth that do not grow until you are an adult

wise 🔑 /waɪz/ *adj., verb*

■ ***adj.*** (wiser, wis·est) **1** 🔑 (of people) able to make sensible decisions and give good advice because of the experience and knowledge that you have: *a wise old man* ◇ *I'm* ***older and wiser*** *after ten years in the business.* **2** 🔑 (of actions and behaviour) sensible; based on good judgement SYN **prudent**: *a wise decision* ◇ ***It was very wise to*** *leave when you did.* ◇ *The wisest course of action is just to say nothing.* ◇ *I was grateful for her wise counsel.* ▶ **wise·ly** *adv.*: *She nodded wisely.* ◇ *He wisely decided to tell the truth.*

IDM **be none the 'wiser | not be any the 'wiser 1** to not understand sth, even after it has been explained to you: *I've read the instructions, but I'm still none the wiser.* **2** to not know or find out about sth bad that sb has done: *If you put the money back, no one will be any the wiser.* **be ˌwise after the e'vent** (often *disapproving*) to understand sth, or realize what you should have done, only after sth has happened **be/get 'wise to sb/sth** (*informal*) to become aware that sb is being dishonest: *He thought he could fool me but I got wise to him.* **put sb 'wise (to sth)** (*informal*) to inform sb about sth

■ ***verb***

PHR V **ˌwise 'up (to sth)** (*informal*) to become aware of the unpleasant truth about a situation

-wise *suffix* (in adjectives and adverbs) **1** in the manner or direction of: *likewise* ◇ *clockwise* **2** (*informal*) concerning: *Things aren't too good businesswise.*

wise·acre /'waɪzeɪkə(r)/ *noun* (*old-fashioned, informal, especially NAmE*) a person who is annoying because they are very confident and think they know a lot

wise·crack /'waɪzkræk/ *noun* (*informal*) a clever remark or joke ▶ **wise·crack** *verb* [I, T]: **(+ speech)** *He plays a wise-cracking detective.*

'wise guy *noun* **1** (*informal, disapproving, especially NAmE*) a person who speaks or behaves as if they know more than other people SYN **know-all 2** (*US, slang*) a member of the Mafia

'wise woman *noun* (*old use*) a woman with knowledge of traditional medicines and magic

wish 🔑 /wɪʃ/ *verb, noun*

■ ***verb* 1** 🔑 [T] (not usually used in the present progressive tense) to want sth to happen or to be true even though it is unlikely or impossible: **~ (that)...** *I wish I were taller.* ◇ (*BrE* also) *I wish I was taller.* ◇ *I wish I hadn't eaten so much.* ◇ *'Where is he now?'* ***'I only wish*** *I knew!'* ◇ *I wish you wouldn't leave your clothes all over the floor.* HELP 'That' is nearly always left out, especially in speech.: **~ sb/sth/yourself + adj.** *He's dead and it's no use wishing him alive again.* ◇ **~ sb/sth/yourself + adv./prep.** *She wished herself a million miles away.* **2** 🔑 [I, T] (*especially BrE, formal*) to want to do sth; to want sth to happen: *You may stay until morning,* ***if you wish.*** ◇ *'I'd rather not talk now.'* ***'(Just) as you wish.'*** ◇ **~ to do sth** *This course is designed for people wishing to update their computer skills.* ◇ *I wish to speak to the manager.* ◇ *I don't wish* (= I don't mean) *to be rude, but could you be a little quieter?* ◇ **~ sb sth** *She could not believe that he wished her harm.* ◇ **~ sb/sth to do sth** *He was not sure whether he wished her to stay or go.* **3** 🔑 [I] **~ (for sth)** to think very hard that you want sth, especially sth that can only be achieved by good luck or magic: *She shut her eyes and wished for him to get better.* ◇ *If you wish really hard, maybe you'll get what you want.* ◇ *It's no use wishing for the impossible.* ◇ *He has everything he could possibly wish for.* **4** 🔑 [T] to say that you hope that sb will be happy, lucky, etc: **~ sb sth** *I wished her a happy birthday.* ◇ *Wish me luck!* ◇ **~ sb well** *We wish them both well in their retirement.*

IDM **I 'wish!** (*informal*) used to say that sth is impossible or very unlikely, although you wish it were possible SYN **if only**: *'You'll have finished by tomorrow.' 'I wish!'*

PHR V **ˌwish sth a'way** to try to get rid of sth by wishing it did not exist **'wish sb/sth on sb** (*informal*) (used in negative sentences) to want sb to have sth unpleasant: *I wouldn't wish something like that on my worst enemy.*

■ ***noun* 1** 🔑 [C] a desire or a feeling that you want to do sth or have sth: **~ (to do sth)** *She expressed a wish to be alone.* ◇ *He* ***had no wish to*** *start a fight.* ◇ *His dearest wish* (= what he wants most of all) *is to see his grandchildren again.* ◇ **~ for sth** *I can understand her wish for secrecy.* ◇ **~ that...** *It was her dying wish that I should have it.* **2** 🔑 [C] a thing that you want to have or to happen: *to carry out sb's wishes* ◇ *I'm sure that you will get your wish.* ◇ *She married* ***against*** *her parents'* ***wishes.*** ➲ see also DEATH WISH **3** 🔑 [C] an attempt to make sth happen by thinking hard about it, especially in stories when it often happens by magic: *Throw some money in the fountain and* ***make a wish.*** ◇ *The genie granted him three wishes.* ◇ *The prince's* ***wish came true.*** **4** 🔑 **wishes** [pl.] **~ (for sth)** used especially in a letter or card to say that you hope that sb will be happy, well or successful: *We all send our* ***best wishes*** *for the future.* ◇ *Give my good wishes to the family.* ◇ ***With best wishes*** (= for example, at the end of a letter)

IDM **if wishes were ˌhorses, beggars would/might 'ride** (*saying*) wishing for sth does not make it happen **your wish is my com'mand** (*humorous*) used to say that you are ready to do whatever sb asks you to do **the wish is father to the 'thought** (*saying*) we believe a thing because we want it to be true

Grammar Point

wish

- After the verb **wish** in sense 1, a past tense is always used in a *that* clause: *Do you wish (that) you* ***had*** *a better job?* In more formal English, especially in *NAmE*, many people use *were* after *I, he, she, it* instead of *was*: *I wish he* ***were*** *here tonight.*

wish·bone /'wɪʃbəʊn; *NAmE* -boʊn/ *noun* a V-shaped bone between the neck and breast of a chicken, DUCK, etc. When the bird is eaten, this bone is sometimes pulled apart by two people, and the person who gets the larger part can make a wish.

ˌwishful 'thinking *noun* [U] the belief that sth that you want to happen is happening or will happen, although this is actually not true or very unlikely: *I've got a feeling that Alex likes me, but that might just be wishful thinking.*

'wishing well *noun* a WELL that people drop a coin into and make a wish

'wish list *noun* (*informal*) all the things that you would like to have, or that you would like to happen

wishy-washy /'wɪʃi wɒʃi; *NAmE* -wɑːʃi; -wɔːʃi/ *adj.* (*informal, disapproving*) **1** not having clear or firm ideas or beliefs: *a wishy-washy liberal* **2** not bright in colour: *a wishy-washy blue*

wisp /wɪsp/ *noun* **~ (of sth) 1** a small, thin piece of hair, grass, etc. **2** a long thin line of smoke or cloud

wispy /'wɪspi/ *adj.* consisting of small, thin pieces; not thick: *wispy hair/clouds* ◇ *a wispy beard*

wis·teria /wɪ'stɪəriə; *NAmE* -'stɪr-/ (also **wis·taria** /wɪ'steəriə; *NAmE* -'ster-/) *noun* [U] a climbing plant with bunches of pale purple or white flowers that hang down

wist·ful /'wɪstfl/ *adj.* thinking sadly about sth that you would like to have, especially sth in the past that you can no longer have: *a wistful smile* ▶ **wist·ful·ly** /-fəli/ *adv.*: *She sighed wistfully.* ◇ *'If only I had known you then,' he said wistfully.* **wist·ful·ness** *noun* [U]

wit /wɪt/ *noun* **1** [U, sing.] the ability to say or write things that are both clever and amusing: *to have a* ***quick/sharp/dry/ready wit*** ◇ *a woman of wit and intelligence* ◇ *a book full of the* ***wit and wisdom*** *of his 30 years in politics* **2** [C] a person who has the ability to say or write things that are both clever and

WORD FAMILY
wit *noun*
witty *adj.*
witticism *noun*
outwit *verb*

W

amusing: *a well-known wit and raconteur* **3 wits** [pl.] your ability to think quickly and clearly and to make good decisions: *He needed all his wits to find his way out.* ◇ *The game was a long* ***battle of wits****.* ◇ *Kate paused and* ***gathered her wits****.* ◇ *a chance to* ***pit your wits against*** (= compete with, using your intelligence) *our quiz champion* **4 -witted** (in adjectives) having the type of intelligence mentioned: *a quick-witted group of students* **5** [U] **~ to do sth** the intelligence or good sense to know what is the right thing to do: *At least you had the wit to ask for help.* ◇ *It should not be* ***beyond the wit of man*** *to resolve this dispute.* ➲ see also WITLESS

IDM **be at your wits' 'end** to be so worried by a problem that you do not know what to do next **be frightened/ scared/terrified out of your 'wits** to be very frightened **have/keep your 'wits about you** to be aware of what is happening around you and ready to think and act quickly **to 'wit** (*old-fashioned, formal*) you use **to wit** when you are about to be more exact about sth that you have just referred to: *Pilot error, to wit failure to follow procedures, was the cause of the accident.* ➲ more at LIVE[1]

witch /wɪtʃ/ *noun* **1** a woman who is believed to have magic powers, especially to do evil things. In stories, she usually wears a black pointed hat and flies on a BROOMSTICK. **2** (*disapproving*) an ugly unpleasant old woman IDM see BREW *n.*

witch·craft /ˈwɪtʃkrɑːft; *NAmE* -kræft/ *noun* [U] the use of magic powers, especially evil ones

ˈwitch doctor *noun* (especially in Africa) a person who is believed to have special magic powers that can be used to heal people ➲ compare MEDICINE MAN

ˈwitch hazel *noun* [U] a liquid that is used for treating injuries on the skin

ˈwitch-hunt *noun* (usually *disapproving*) an attempt to find and punish people who hold opinions that are thought to be unacceptable or dangerous to society

the ˈwitching hour *noun* [sing.] the time, late at night, when it is thought that magic things can happen

Wite·out™ /ˈwaɪtaʊt/ *noun* [U] (*NAmE*) a white liquid that you use to cover mistakes that you make when you are writing or typing, and that you can write on top of; a type of CORRECTION FLUID ➲ see also WHITE-OUT

with 🔑 /wɪð; wɪθ/ *prep.*

HELP For the special uses of **with** in phrasal verbs, look at the entries for the verbs. For example **bear with sb/sth** is in the phrasal verb section at **bear**. **1** 🔑 in the company or presence of sb/sth: *She lives with her parents.* ◇ *I have a client with me right now.* ◇ *a nice steak with a bottle of red wine* **2** 🔑 having or carrying sth: *a girl with* (= who has) *red hair* ◇ *a jacket with a hood* ◇ *He looked at her with a hurt expression.* ◇ *They're both in bed with flu.* ◇ *a man with a suitcase* **3** 🔑 using sth: *Cut it with a knife.* ◇ *It is treated with acid before being analysed.* **4** 🔑 used to say what fills, covers, etc. sth: *The bag was stuffed with dirty clothes.* ◇ *Sprinkle the dish with salt.* **5** 🔑 in opposition to sb/sth; against sb/sth: *to fight with sb* ◇ *to play tennis with sb* ◇ *at war with a neighbouring country* ◇ *I had an argument with my boss.* **6** 🔑 concerning; in the case of: *Be careful with the glasses.* ◇ *Are you pleased with the result?* ◇ *Don't be angry with her.* ◇ *With these students it's pronunciation that's the problem.* **7** 🔑 used when considering one fact in relation to another: *She won't be able to help us with all the family commitments she has.* ◇ *It's much easier compared with last time.* **8** 🔑 including: *The meal with wine came to $20 each.* ◇ *With all the lesson preparation I have to do I work 12 hours a day.* **9** 🔑 used to show the way in which sb does sth: *He behaved with great dignity.* ◇ *She sleeps with the window open.* ◇ *Don't stand with your hands in your pockets.* **10** 🔑 because of; as a result of: *She blushed with embarrassment.* ◇ *His fingers were numb with cold.* **11** 🔑 because of sth and as it happens: *The shadows lengthened with the approach of sunset.* ◇ *Skill comes with practice.* **12** in the same direction as sth: *Marine mammals generally swim with the current.* **13** 🔑 used to show who has possession of or responsibility for sth: *The keys are with reception.* ◇ *Leave it with me.* **14** 🔑 employed by; using the services of: *She acted with a touring company for three years.* ◇ *I bank with HSBC.* **15** showing separation from sth/sb: *I could never part with this ring.* ◇ *Can we dispense with the formalities?* **16** despite sth: *With all her faults I still love her.* **17** used in exclamations: *Off to bed with you!* ◇ *Down with school!*

IDM **be 'with me/you** (*informal*) to be able to understand what sb is talking about: *Are you with me?* ◇ *I'm afraid I'm not quite with you.* **be 'with sb (on sth)** to support sb and agree with what they say: *We're all with you on this one.* **'with it** (*informal*) **1** knowing about current fashions and ideas SYN **trendy**: *Don't you have anything more with it to wear?* **2** understanding what is happening around you SYN **alert**: *You don't seem very with it today.* **with 'that** straight after that; then: *He muttered a few words of apology and with that he left.*

with·draw 🔑 /wɪðˈdrɔː; wɪθˈd-/ *verb* (**with·drew** /-ˈdruː/, **with·drawn** /-ˈdrɔːn/)

1 🔑 [I, T] to move back or away from a place or situation; to make sb/sth do this SYN **pull out**: *Government troops were forced to withdraw.* ◇ **~ (sb/sth) (from sth)** *Both powers withdrew their forces from the region.* ◇ *She withdrew her hand from his.* **2** 🔑 [T] to stop giving or offering sth to sb: **~ sth** *Workers have threatened to withdraw their labour* (= go on strike). ◇ *He withdrew his support for our campaign.* ◇ **~ sth from sth** *The drug was* ***withdrawn from sale*** *after a number of people suffered serious side effects.* **3** 🔑 [I, T] to stop taking part in an activity or being a member of an organization; to stop sb/sth from doing these things: **~ (from sth)** *There have been calls for Britain to withdraw from the EU.* ◇ **~ sb/sth (from sth)** *The horse had been withdrawn from the race.* **4** 🔑 [T] **~ sth (from sth)** to take money out of a bank account: *I'd like to withdraw £250 please.* ➲ COLLOCATIONS at FINANCE **5** 🔑 [T] **~ sth** (*formal*) to say that you no longer believe that sth you previously said is true SYN **retract**: *The newspaper withdrew the allegations the next day.* **6** [I] **~ (from sth) (into sth/ yourself)** to become quieter and spend less time with other people: *She's beginning to withdraw into herself.*

with·draw·al /wɪðˈdrɔːəl; wɪθˈd-/ *noun* **1** [U, C] the act of moving or taking sth away or back: *the withdrawal of support* ◇ *the withdrawal of the UN troops from the region* ◇ *the withdrawal of a product from the market* **2** [U] the act of no longer taking part in sth or being a member of an organization: *his withdrawal from the election* ◇ *a campaign for Britain's withdrawal from the EU* **3** [C] the act of taking an amount of money out of your bank account: *You can* ***make withdrawals*** *of up to $250 a day.* ➲ COLLOCATIONS at FINANCE **4** [U] the period of time when sb is getting used to not taking a drug that they have become ADDICTED to, and the unpleasant effects of doing this: *I got* ***withdrawal symptoms*** *after giving up smoking.* **5** [C, usually sing., U] the act of saying that you no longer believe that sth you have previously said is true SYN **retraction**: *The newspaper published a withdrawal the next day.* **6** [U] (*psychology*) the behaviour of sb who wants to be alone and does not want to communicate with other people

with·drawn /wɪðˈdrɔːn/ *adj.* not wanting to talk to other people; extremely quiet and shy

wither /ˈwɪðə(r)/ *verb* **1** [I, T] **~ (sth)** if a plant **withers** or sth **withers** it, it dries up and dies: *The grass had withered in the warm sun.* **2** [I] **~ (away)** to become less or weaker, especially before disappearing completely: *All our hopes just withered away.*

withered /ˈwɪðəd; *NAmE* -ərd/ *adj.* [usually before noun] **1** (of plants) dried up and dead SYN **shrivelled**: *withered leaves* **2** (of people) looking old because they are thin and weak and have very dry skin **3** (of parts of the body) thin and weak and not fully developed because of disease: *withered limbs*

wither·ing /ˈwɪðərɪŋ/ *adj.* (of a look, remark, etc.) intended to make sb feel silly or ashamed: *withering scorn* ◇ *She gave him a withering look.* ▶ **wither·ing·ly** *adv.*

with·ers /ˈwɪðəz; *NAmE* -ərz/ *noun* [pl.] the highest part of a horse's back, between its shoulders

W

with·hold /wɪð'həʊld; wɪθ'h-; *NAmE* -'hoʊld/ *verb* (**with·held, with·held** /-'held/) **~ sth (from sb/sth)** (*formal*) to refuse to give sth to sb SYN **keep back**: *She was accused of withholding information from the police.*

with'holding tax *noun* [C, U] (in the US) an amount of money that an employer takes out of sb's income as tax and pays directly to the government ➲ compare PAY AS YOU EARN

with·in 0➔ /wɪ'ðɪn/ *prep., adv.*
■ ***prep.* 1** 0➔ before a particular period of time has passed; during a particular period of time: *You should receive a reply within seven days.* ◇ *The ambulance arrived* ***within minutes of*** *the call being made.* ◇ *Two elections were held* ***within the space of*** *a year.* **2** 0➔ not further than a particular distance from sth: *a house within a mile of the station* ◇ *Is it* ***within walking distance?*** **3** 0➔ inside the range or limits of sth: *That question is not within the scope of this talk.* ◇ *We are now within range of enemy fire.* ◇ *He finds it hard to live within his income* (= without spending more than he earns). **4** 0➔ (*formal*) inside sth/sb: *The noise seems to be coming from within the building.* ◇ *There is discontent within the farming industry.*
■ ***adv.*** (*formal*) inside: *Cleaner required. Apply within.* (= on a sign)

with·out 0➔ /wɪ'ðaʊt/ *prep., adv.*
■ ***prep.* 1** 0➔ not having, experiencing or showing sth: *They had gone two days without food.* ◇ *He found the place without difficulty.* ◇ *She spoke without much enthusiasm.* **2** 0➔ not in the company of sb: *Don't go without me.* **3** 0➔ not using or taking sth: *Can you see without your glasses?* ◇ *Don't go out without your coat.* **4** 0➔ not doing the action mentioned: **~ doing sth** *He left without saying goodbye.* ◇ *You can't make an omelette without breaking eggs.* ◇ ***Without wanting to*** *criticize, I think you could have done better.* (= used before you make a critical comment) ◇ **~ sb doing sth** *The party was organized without her knowing anything about it.*
■ ***adv.*** not having or showing sth: *Do you want a room with a bath or one without?* ◇ *If there's none left we'll have to* ***do without.*** ◇ *I'm sure we'll* ***manage without.***

,with-'profit (also **,with-'profits**) *adj.* (*BrE*) used to describe an insurance policy or an investment where the amount paid includes a share in the company's profits

with·stand /wɪð'stænd; wɪθ's-/ *verb* (**with·stood, with·stood** /-'stʊd/) **~ sth** (*formal*) to be strong enough not to be hurt or damaged by extreme conditions, the use of force, etc. SYN **resist, stand up to**: *The materials used have to be able to withstand high temperatures.* ◇ *They had withstood siege, hunger and deprivation.*

wit·less /'wɪtləs/ *adj.* silly or stupid; not sensible SYN **foolish**
IDM **be scared/bored 'witless** (*informal*) to be extremely frightened or bored

wit·ness 0➔ /'wɪtnəs/ *noun, verb*
■ ***noun***
▸ PERSON WHO SEES STH **1** 0➔ (also **eye·wit·ness**) [C] a person who sees sth happen and is able to describe it to other people: *Police have appealed for witnesses to the accident.* ◇ *a witness to the killing* ➲ COLLOCATIONS at CRIME, JUSTICE
▸ IN COURT **2** 0➔ [C] a person who gives evidence in court: *a* ***defence/prosecution witness*** ◇ *to appear as (a)* ***witness for the defence/prosecution***
▸ OF SIGNATURE **3** 0➔ [C] a person who is present when an official document is signed and who also signs it to prove that they saw this happen: *He was one of the witnesses at our wedding.*
▸ OF RELIGIOUS BELIEFS **4** [U] evidence of a person's strong religious beliefs, that they show by what they say and do in public ➲ see also JEHOVAH'S WITNESS
IDM **be (a) 'witness to sth 1** (*formal*) to see sth take place: *He has been witness to a terrible murder.* **2** to show that sth is true; to provide evidence for sth: *His good health is a witness to the success of the treatment.* **bear/give 'witness (to sth)** to provide evidence of the truth of sth
■ ***verb***
▸ SEE STH **1** 0➔ [T] **~ sth** to see sth happen (typically a crime or an accident): *She was shocked by the violent scenes she had witnessed.* ◇ *Police have appealed for anyone who witnessed the incident to contact them.* ◇ *We are now witnessing an unprecedented increase in violent crime.* ➲ SYNONYMS at NOTICE
▸ OF TIME/PLACE **2** [T] **~ sth** to be the place, period, organization, etc. in which particular events take place: *Recent years have witnessed a growing social mobility.* ◇ *The retail trade is witnessing a sharp fall in sales.*
▸ SIGNATURE **3** [T] **~ sth** to be present when an official document is signed and sign it yourself to prove that you saw this happen: *to witness a signature*
▸ BE SIGN/PROOF **4** [T, I, usually passive] to be a sign or proof of sth: **~ sth** *There has been increasing interest in her life and work,* ***as witnessed by*** *the publication of two new biographies.* ◇ **~ to sth** *The huge attendance figures for the exhibition witness to a healthy interest in modern art.* **5** [T] **~ sth** (*formal*) used when giving an example that proves sth you have just said: *Authentic Italian cooking is very healthy—witness the low incidence of heart disease in Italy.*
▸ TO RELIGIOUS BELIEFS **6** [I] **~ (to sth)** (*especially NAmE*) to speak to people about your strong religious beliefs SYN **testify**

Synonyms

witness

observer • onlooker • passer-by • bystander • eyewitness

These are all words for a person who sees sth happen.

witness a person who sees sth happen and is able to describe it to other people; a person who gives evidence in a court of law: *Police have appealed for* ***witnesses to*** *the accident.*

observer a person who sees sth happen: *According to observers, the plane exploded shortly after take-off.*

onlooker a person who watches sth that is happening but is not involved in it: *A crowd of onlookers gathered at the scene of the crash.*

passer-by a person who is going past sb/sth by chance, especially when sth unexpected happens: *Police asked passers-by if they had witnessed the accident.*

bystander a person who is near and can see what is happening when sth such as an accident or fight takes place: *Three* ***innocent bystanders*** *were killed in the crossfire.*

eyewitness a person who has seen a crime or accident and can describe it afterwards.

PATTERNS
- a(n) witness/observer/onlooker/passer-by/bystander/ an eyewitness **sees** sth
- a(n) observer/onlooker/passer-by/bystander **witnesses** sth

'witness box (*BrE*) (*NAmE* **'witness stand**) (also **stand** *BrE, NAmE*) *noun* the place in court where people stand to give evidence ➲ COLLOCATIONS at JUSTICE

wit·ter /'wɪtə(r)/ *verb* [I] **~ (on) (about sth)** (*BrE, informal, usually disapproving*) to talk about sth unimportant and boring for a long time: *What's he wittering on about?*

wit·ti·cism /'wɪtɪsɪzəm/ *noun* a clever and amusing remark

wit·ting·ly /'wɪtɪŋli/ *adv.* (*formal*) in a way that shows that you are aware of what you are doing SYN **intentionally**: *It was clear that, wittingly or unwittingly, he had offended her.* OPP **unwittingly**

witty /'wɪti/ *adj.* (**wit·tier, wit·ti·est**) able to say or write clever, amusing things: *a witty speaker* ◇ *a witty remark* ➲ SYNONYMS at FUNNY ▸ **wit·tily** *adv.* **wit·ti·ness** *noun* [U]

wives *pl.* of WIFE

W

wiz·ard /ˈwɪzəd; *NAmE* -ərd/ *noun* **1** (in stories) a man with magic powers **2** a person who is especially good at sth: *a* ***computer/financial, etc. wizard*** **3** (*computing*) a program that makes it easy to use another program or perform a task by giving you a series of simple choices

wiz·ard·ry /ˈwɪzədri; *NAmE* -ərd-/ *noun* [U] a very impressive and clever achievement; great skill: *electronic wizardry* ◇ *The second goal was sheer wizardry.*

wiz·ened /ˈwɪznd/ *adj.* looking smaller and having many folds and lines in the skin, because of being old **SYN shrivelled**: *a wizened little man* ◇ *wizened apples*

WLTM *abbr.* would like to meet (used in personal advertisements)

WMD /ˌdʌblju: em ˈdi:/ *abbr.* WEAPON OF MASS DESTRUCTION

woad /wəʊd; *NAmE* woʊd/ *noun* [U] a blue substance that people used to paint their bodies and faces with in ancient times

wob·ble /ˈwɒbl; *NAmE* ˈwɑ:bl/ *verb, noun*

■ ***verb*** **1** [I, T] to move from side to side in an unsteady way; to make sth do this: *This chair wobbles.* ◇ (*figurative*) *Her voice wobbled with emotion.* ◇ **~ sth** *Don't wobble the table—I'm trying to write.* **2** [I] **+ adv./prep.** to go in a particular direction while moving from side to side in an unsteady way: *He wobbled off on his bike.* **3** [I] to hesitate or lose confidence about doing sth: *Yesterday the president showed the first signs of wobbling over the issue.*

■ ***noun*** **1** [usually sing.] a slight unsteady movement from side to side: *The handlebars developed a wobble.* **2** a moment when you hesitate or lose confidence about sth: *The team is experiencing a mid-season wobble.*

wobble·board /ˈwɒblbɔ:d; *NAmE* ˈwɑ:blbɔ:rd/ *noun* a musical instrument consisting of a piece of board which is shaken to produce low sounds, originally played by Australian Aborigines

wob·bly /ˈwɒbli; *NAmE* ˈwɑ:bli/ *adj., noun*

■ ***adj.*** (*informal*) **1** moving in an unsteady way from side to side: *a chair with a wobbly leg* ◇ *a wobbly tooth* ◇ *He's still a bit wobbly after the operation* (= not able to stand firmly). **2** not firm or confident **SYN shaky**: *the wobbly singing of the choir* ◇ *The evening got off to a wobbly start.*

■ ***noun***

IDM throw a ˈwobbly (*BrE, informal*) to suddenly become very angry or upset

wodge /wɒdʒ; *NAmE* wɑ:dʒ/ *noun* **~ (of sth)** (*BrE, informal*) a large piece or amount of sth: *a thick wodge of ten-pound notes*

woe /wəʊ; *NAmE* woʊ/ *noun* (*old-fashioned* or *humorous*) **1 woes** [pl.] the troubles and problems that sb has: *financial woes* ◇ *Thanks for listening to my woes.* **2** [U] great unhappiness **SYN misery**: *a tale of woe*

IDM ˌwoe beˈtide sb | ˈwoe to sb (*formal* or *humorous*) a phrase that is used to warn sb that there will be trouble for them if they do sth or do not do sth: *Woe betide anyone who gets in her way!* **ˌwoe is ˈme!** *exclamation* (*old use* or *humorous*) a phrase that is used to say that you are very unhappy

woe·be·gone /ˈwəʊbɪɡɒn; *NAmE* ˈwoʊbɪɡɔ:n; -ɡɑ:n/ *adj.* (*formal*) looking very sad **SYN miserable**: *a woebegone expression*

woe·ful /ˈwəʊfl; *NAmE* ˈwoʊfl/ *adj.* **1** [usually before noun] very bad or serious; that you disapprove of **SYN deplorable**: *She displayed a woeful ignorance of the rules.* **2** (*literary* or *formal*) very sad: *a woeful face* ◇ *woeful tales of broken romances* ▸ **woe·ful·ly** /-fəli/ *adv.*

wog /wɒɡ; *NAmE* wɑ:ɡ/ *noun* **1** (*BrE, taboo, slang*) a very offensive word for a person who does not have white skin **2** (*AustralE, taboo, slang*) an offensive word for a person from southern Europe or whose parents came from southern Europe **3** (*AustralE, informal*) an illness, usually one that is not very serious: *A flu wog struck.*

wok /wɒk; *NAmE* wɑ:k/ *noun* (from *Chinese*) a large pan shaped like a bowl, used for cooking food, especially Chinese food ➲ VISUAL VOCAB page V24

woke *past tense* of WAKE

woken *past part.* of WAKE

wolds /wəʊldz; *NAmE* woʊldz/ *noun* [pl.] used in the names of places in Britain for an area of high open land: *the Yorkshire Wolds*

wolf /wʊlf/ *noun, verb*

■ ***noun*** (*pl.* **wolves** /wʊlvz/) a large wild animal of the dog family, that lives and hunts in groups: *a pack of wolves*

IDM keep the ˈwolf from the door (*informal*) to have enough money to avoid going hungry; to stop sb feeling hungry **throw sb to the ˈwolves** to leave sb to be roughly treated or criticized without trying to help or defend them **a wolf in sheep's ˈclothing** a person who seems to be friendly or harmless but is really an enemy ➲ more at CRY *v.*, LONE

■ ***verb*** **~ sth (down)** (*informal*) to eat food very quickly, especially by putting a lot of it in your mouth at once **SYN gobble**

wolf·hound /ˈwʊlfhaʊnd/ *noun* a very large tall dog with long hair and long legs, originally used for hunting wolves: *an Irish wolfhound*

wolf·ish /ˈwʊlfɪʃ/ *adj.* (*formal*) like a wolf: *wolfish yellow eyes* ◇ (*figurative*) *a wolfish grin* (= showing sexual interest in sb) ▸ **wolf·ish·ly** *adv.*

ˈwolf whistle *noun* a whistle with a short rising note and a long falling note, used by sb, usually a man, to show that they find sb else attractive, especially sb passing in the street: *She was fed up with the builders' wolf whistles each morning.* ▸ **ˈwolf-whistle** *verb* [I, T] **~ (sb)**

wolverine /ˈwʊlvəri:n/ *noun* a wild animal that looks similar to a small bear, with short legs, long brown hair and a long tail. Wolverines live in cold, northern areas of Europe and North America.

wolves *pl.* of WOLF

woman 0→ /ˈwʊmən/ *noun* (*pl.* **women** /ˈwɪmɪn/) **1** 0→ [C] an adult female human: *men, women and children* ◇ *a 24-year-old woman* ◇ *I prefer to see a woman doctor.* **2** [U] female humans in general: (*informal*) *She's all woman!* (= has qualities that are typical of women) **3** [C] (in compounds) a woman who comes from the place mentioned or whose job or interest is connected with the thing mentioned: *an Englishwoman* ◇ *a businesswoman* ◇ *a Congresswoman* ◇ *a horsewoman* ➲ note at GENDER **4** [C] a female worker, especially one who works with her hands: *We used to have a woman to do the cleaning.* **5** [sing.] (*old-fashioned*) a rude way of addressing a female person in an angry or important way: *Be quiet, woman!* **6** [C] (*sometimes disapproving*) a wife or sexual partner: *He's got a new woman in his life.* ➲ see also FALLEN WOMAN, KEPT WOMAN, OTHER WOMAN

IDM be your own ˈman/ˈwoman to act or think independently, not following others or being ordered: *Working for herself meant that she could be her own woman.* ➲ more at HEART, HELL, HONEST, MAN *n.*, PART *n.*, POSSESSED, SUBSTANCE, WORLD

woman·hood /ˈwʊmənhʊd/ *noun* [U] (*formal*) **1** the state of being a woman, rather than a girl: *He watched his daughters grow to womanhood.* **2** women in general: *the womanhood of this country* ➲ compare MANHOOD

woman·ish /ˈwʊmənɪʃ/ *adj.* (*disapproving*) (especially of a man) behaving in a way that is more suitable for a woman; more suitable for women than men: *He has a womanish manner.* ◇ *a womanish novel*

woman·iz·ing (*BrE* also **-is·ing**) /ˈwʊmənaɪzɪŋ/ *noun* [U] (*disapproving*) the fact of having sexual relationships with many different women **SYN philandering** ▸ **woman·izer, -iser** *noun*

woman·kind /ˈwʊmənkaɪnd/ *noun* [U] (*old-fashioned, formal*) women in general ➲ compare MANKIND

woman·ly /ˈwʊmənli/ *adj.* (*approving*) behaving, dressing, etc. in a way that people think is typical of or very suitable for a woman **SYN feminine**: *womanly qualities* ◇ *a soft womanly figure* ▸ **woman·li·ness** *noun* [U]

W

womb /wuːm/ *noun* the organ in women and female animals in which babies develop before they are born **SYN** **uterus**

wom·bat /ˈwɒmbæt; *NAmE* ˈwɑːm-/ *noun* an Australian animal like a small BEAR, that carries its young in a POUCH (= a pocket of skin) on the front of the mother's body

women·folk /ˈwɪmɪnfəʊk; *NAmE* -foʊk/ *noun* [pl.] (*formal* or *humorous*) all the women in a community or family, especially one that is led by men: *The male hunters brought back the food for their womenfolk to cook.* ➲ compare MENFOLK

women's lib·ber /ˌwɪmɪnz ˈlɪbə(r)/ *noun* (*old-fashioned, informal*, often *disapproving*) a person who supports Women's Liberation (2)

ˌ**women's libeˈration** *noun* [U] (*old-fashioned*) **1** (also *informal* **women's lib** /ˌwɪmɪnz ˈlɪb/) the freedom of women to have the same social and economic rights as men **2 Women's Liberation** (also *informal* **Women's Lib**) the movement that aimed to achieve equal social and economic rights for women

ˈ**women's studies** *noun* [U+sing./pl. v.] the study of women and their role in history, literature and society: *to major in women's studies.*

womens·wear /ˈwɪmɪnzweə(r); *NAmE* -wer/ *noun* [U] (used especially in shops/stores) clothes for women

won *past tense, past part.* of WIN

won·der 0‑ᵚ /ˈwʌndə(r)/ *verb, noun*

■ ***verb* 1** 0‑ᵚ [T, I] to think about sth and try to decide what is true, what will happen, what you should do, etc: **~ who, where, etc...** *I wonder who she is.* ◇ *I was just beginning to wonder where you were.* ◇ **~ (about sth)** *'Why do you want to know?' 'No particular reason. I was just wondering.'* ◇ *We were wondering about next April for the wedding.* ◇ **+ speech** *'What should I do now?' she wondered.* **2** 0‑ᵚ [T] **~ if, whether...** used as a polite way of asking a question or asking sb to do sth: *I wonder if you can help me.* ◇ *I was wondering whether you'd like to come to a party.* **3** [I, T] to be very surprised by sth: **~ (at sth)** *She wondered at her own stupidity.* ◇ (*BrE, informal*) *He's gone and left us to do all the work,* ***I shouldn't wonder*** (= I wouldn't be surprised if he had). ◇ **~ (that)...** *I wonder (that) he didn't hurt himself jumping over that wall.* ◇ ***I don't wonder*** *you're tired. You've had a busy day.*

■ ***noun* 1** [U] a feeling of surprise and admiration that you have when you see or experience sth beautiful, unusual or unexpected **SYN** **awe**: *He retained a childlike sense of wonder.* ◇ *She gazed down* ***in wonder*** *at the city spread below her.* **2** [C] something that fills you with surprise and admiration **SYN** **marvel**: *The Grand Canyon is one of the natural wonders of the world.* ◇ *the wonders of modern technology* ◇ *That's the wonder of poetry—you're always discovering something new.* ◇ *the* ***Seven Wonders of the World*** (= the seven most impressive structures of the ancient world) **3** [sing.] (*informal*) a person who is very clever at doing sth; a person or thing that seems very good or effective: *Dita, you're a wonder! I would never have thought of doing that.* ◇ *Have you seen the* ***boy wonder*** *play yet?* ◇ *a new wonder drug*

IDM **do ˈwonders (for sb/sth)** to have a very good effect on sb/sth: *The news has done wonders for our morale.* **(it's) no/little/small ˈwonder (that)...** it is not surprising: *It is little wonder (that) she was so upset.* ◇ (*informal*) *No wonder you're tired, you've been walking for hours.* **it's a ˈwonder (that)...** (*informal*) it is surprising or strange: *It's a wonder (that) more people weren't hurt.* **wonders will never ˈcease** (*informal*, usually *ironic*) a phrase used to express surprise and pleasure at sth: *'I've cleaned my room.' 'Wonders will never cease!'* **work ˈwonders** to achieve very good results: *Her new diet and exercise programme has worked wonders for her.* ➲ more at CHINLESS, NINE

won·der·ful 0‑ᵚ /ˈwʌndəfl; *NAmE* -dərfl/ *adj.*
1 0‑ᵚ very good, pleasant or enjoyable: *a wonderful surprise* ◇ *We had a wonderful time last night.* ◇ *You've all been* ***absolutely wonderful!*** ◇ ***It's wonderful*** *to see you!* **2** 0‑ᵚ making you feel surprise or admiration **SYN** **remarkable**: *It's wonderful what you can do when you have to.*

Synonyms

wonderful

lovely • **delightful**

These words all describe an experience, feeling or sight that gives you great pleasure.

wonderful that you enjoy very much; that gives you great pleasure; extremely good: *We had a wonderful time last night.* ◇ *The weather was absolutely wonderful.*

lovely (*rather informal, especially BrE*) that you enjoy very much; that gives you great pleasure; very attractive: *What a lovely day!* (= the weather is very good) ◇ *It's been lovely having you here.*

delightful that gives you great pleasure; very attractive: *a delightful little fishing village*

WONDERFUL, LOVELY OR DELIGHTFUL?

All these words can describe times, events, places, sights, feelings and the weather. **Wonderful** can also describe a chance or ability. **Lovely** is the most frequent in spoken British English, but in North American English **wonderful** is the most frequent, both spoken and written. **Delightful** is used especially to talk about times, events and places.

PATTERNS

- wonderful/lovely/delightful **weather/views/scenery**
- It's wonderful/lovely **to be/feel/find/have/know/see...**
- **It would be** wonderful/lovely/delightful **if...**
- It's wonderful/lovely **that...**
- That **sounds** wonderful/lovely/delightful.
- **really/quite/absolutely** wonderful/lovely/delightful

won·der·ful·ly /ˈwʌndəfəli; *NAmE* -dərf-/ *adv.* (*formal*) **1** very; very well: *The hotel is wonderfully comfortable.* ◇ *Things have worked out wonderfully (well).* **2** unusually; in a surprising way: *He's wonderfully fit for his age.*

won·der·ing·ly /ˈwʌndrɪŋli/ *adv.* (*formal*) in a way that shows surprise and/or admiration: *She gazed at him wonderingly.*

won·der·land /ˈwʌndəlænd; *NAmE* -dərl-/ *noun* [usually sing.] **1** an imaginary place in children's stories **2** a place that is exciting and full of beautiful and interesting things

won·der·ment /ˈwʌndəmənt; *NAmE* -dərm-/ *noun* [U] (*formal*) a feeling of pleasant surprise or WONDER

won·drous /ˈwʌndrəs/ *adj.* (*literary*) strange, beautiful and impressive **SYN** **wonderful** ▸ **won·drous·ly** *adv.*

wonga /ˈwɒŋɡə; *NAmE* ˈwɑːŋɡə/ *noun* [U] (*BrE, slang*) money

wonk /wɒŋk; *NAmE* wɑːŋk/ *noun* (*especially US, informal, disapproving*) **1** a person who works too hard and is considered boring **2** a person who takes too much interest in the details of political policy: *the President's chief economic policy wonk*

wonky /ˈwɒŋki; *NAmE* ˈwɑːŋki/ *adj.* (*BrE, informal*) not steady; not straight: *a wonky chair*

wont /wəʊnt; *NAmE* wɔːnt/ *adj., noun*

■ ***adj.*** [not before noun] **~ (to do sth)** (*old-fashioned, formal*) in the habit of doing sth **SYN** **accustomed**: *He was wont to fall asleep after supper.*

■ ***noun*** [sing.] (*old-fashioned, formal*) something a person often does **SYN** **habit**: *She got up early, as was her wont.*

won't /wəʊnt; *NAmE* woʊnt/ *short form* will not

won·ton /ˌwɒnˈtɒn; *NAmE* ˈwɑːntɑːn/ *noun* (from *Chinese*) a small piece of food wrapped in DOUGH, often served in Chinese soup or as DIM SUM

woo /wuː/ *verb* **1 ~ sb** to try to get the support of sb: *Voters are being wooed with promises of lower taxes.* **2 ~ sb** (*old-fashioned*) (of a man) to try to persuade a woman to love him and marry him **SYN** **court**

W

wood 0→ /wʊd/ *noun*
1 0→ [U, C] the hard material that the TRUNK and branches of a tree are made of; this material when it is used to build or make things with, or as a fuel: *He chopped some wood for the fire.* ◇ *a plank of wood* ◇ *All the furniture was made **of wood**.* ◇ *a wood floor* ◇ *furniture made of a variety of different woods* ➲ VISUAL VOCAB page V8 ➲ see also DEAD WOOD, HARDWOOD, SOFTWOOD, WOODEN, WOODY **2** 0→ [C] (also **woods** [pl.]) an area of trees, smaller than a forest: *a large wood* ◇ *a walk in the woods* ➲ VISUAL VOCAB page V3 ➲ see also WOODED **3** [C] a heavy wooden ball used in the game of BOWLS **4** [C] a GOLF CLUB with a large head, that was usually made of wood in the past ➲ compare IRON
IDM **not see the ˌwood for the ˈtrees** (*BrE*) (*NAmE* **not see the ˌforest for the ˈtrees**) to not see or understand the main point about sth, because you are paying too much attention to small details **not ˌout of the ˈwoods** (*informal*) not yet free from difficulties or problems ➲ more at KNOCK *v.*, NECK *n.*, TOUCH *v.*

wood·block /ˈwʊdblɒk; *NAmE* -blɑːk/ *noun* **1** each of the small flat pieces of wood that are fitted together to cover a floor: *a woodblock floor* ➲ compare PARQUET **2** a piece of wood with a pattern cut into it, used for printing

wood·carv·ing /ˈwʊdkɑːvɪŋ; *NAmE* -kɑːrv-/ *noun* [U, C] the process of shaping a piece of wood with a sharp tool; a decorative object made in this way ▶ **wood·carver** *noun*

wood·chuck /ˈwʊdtʃʌk/ (also **ground·hog**) *noun* a small N American animal of the SQUIRREL family

wood·cock /ˈwʊdkɒk; *NAmE* -kɑːk/ *noun* (*pl.* **wood·cock** or **wood·cocks**) a brown bird with a long straight beak, short legs and a short tail, hunted for food or sport

wood·cut /ˈwʊdkʌt/ *noun* a print that is made from a pattern cut in a piece of wood

wood·cut·ter /ˈwʊdkʌtə(r)/ *noun* (*old-fashioned*) a person whose job is cutting down trees

wood·ed /ˈwʊdɪd/ *adj.* (of land) covered with trees

wood·en 0→ /ˈwʊdn/ *adj.*
1 0→ [usually before noun] made of wood: *a wooden box* **2** not showing enough natural expression, emotion or movement SYN **stiff**: *The actor playing the father was too wooden.* ▶ **wood·en·ly** *adv.*: *She speaks her lines very woodenly.* **wood·en·ness** *noun* [U]

ˌwooden ˈspoon *noun* a spoon made of wood, used in cooking for stirring and mixing ➲ VISUAL VOCAB page V23
IDM **get, win, take, etc. the ˌwooden ˈspoon** (*BrE, informal*) to come last in a race or competition

wood·land /ˈwʊdlənd/ *noun* [U, C] (also **wood·lands** [pl.]) an area of land that is covered with trees: *ancient woodland* ◇ *The house is fringed by fields and woodlands.* ◇ *woodland walks*

wood·louse /ˈwʊdlaʊs/ *noun* (*pl.* **wood·lice** /ˈwʊdlaɪs/) a small grey creature like an insect, with a hard shell, that lives in decaying wood or damp soil ➲ VISUAL VOCAB page V11

wood·man /ˈwʊdmən/ *noun* (*pl.* **-men** /-mən/) (also **woods·man**) a person who works or lives in a forest, taking care of and sometimes cutting down trees, etc.

wood·peck·er /ˈwʊdpekə(r)/ *noun* a bird with a long beak that it uses to make holes in trees when it is looking for insects to eat

ˈwood pigeon *noun* a bird of the PIGEON family, that lives in woods and fields rather than in cities

wood·pile /ˈwʊdpaɪl/ *noun* a pile of wood that will be used for fuel

ˈwood pulp *noun* [U] wood that has been broken into small pieces and crushed until it is soft. It is used for making paper.

wood·shed /ˈwʊdʃed/ *noun* a small building for storing wood in, especially for fuel

woods·man /ˈwʊdzmən/ *noun* (*pl.* **-men** /-mən/) = WOODMAN

woodsy /ˈwʊdzi/ *adj.* (*informal, especially NAmE*) covered with trees; connected with woods

wood·turn·ing /ˈwʊdtɜːnɪŋ; *NAmE* -tɜːrn-/ *noun* [U] the process of shaping a piece of wood by turning it against a sharp tool on a machine (called a LATHE) ▶ **wood·turn·er** *noun*

wood·wind /ˈwʊdwɪnd/ *noun* [U+sing./pl. v.] (also **wood·winds** [pl.]) (especially in *NAmE*) the group of musical instruments in an ORCHESTRA that are mostly made of wood or metal and are played by blowing. FLUTES, CLARINETS and BASSOONS are all woodwind instruments: *the woodwind section of the orchestra* ➲ VISUAL VOCAB page V30 ➲ compare BRASS, PERCUSSION, STRINGS, WIND *n.* (4), WIND INSTRUMENT

wood·work /ˈwʊdwɜːk; *NAmE* -wɜːrk/ *noun* [U] **1** things made of wood in a building or room, such as doors and stairs: *The woodwork needs painting.* ◇ (*BrE*) *He **hit the woodwork*** (= the wooden frame of the goal in the game of football/SOCCER, etc.) *twice before scoring.* **2** (*BrE*) (also **ˈwood·work·ing** *NAmE, BrE*) the activity or skill of making things from wood
IDM **blend/fade into the ˈwoodwork** to behave in a way that does not attract any attention; to disappear or hide **come/crawl out of the ˈwoodwork** (*informal, disapproving*) if you say that sb **comes/crawls out of the woodwork**, you mean that they have suddenly appeared in order to express an opinion or to take advantage of a situation: *When he won the lottery, all sorts of distant relatives came out of the woodwork.*

wood·worm /ˈwʊdwɜːm; *NAmE* -wɜːrm/ *noun* **1** [C] a small WORM that eats wood, making a lot of small holes in it **2** [U] the damage caused by woodworms: *The beams are riddled with woodworm.*

woody /ˈwʊdi/ *adj.* **1** (of plants) having a thick, hard STEM like wood **2** covered with trees: *a woody valley* **3** having a smell like wood

woof /wʊf/ *exclamation, verb, noun*
■ ***exclamation*** (*informal*) a word used to describe the loud noise that a dog makes: *'Woof! Woof!' he barked.* ▶ **woof** *verb* [I]
■ ***noun*** = WEFT

woof·er /ˈwuːfə(r)/ *noun* a LOUDSPEAKER for reproducing the low notes in a SOUND SYSTEM ➲ compare TWEETER

woo hoo /ˌwuː ˈhuː/ *exclamation* (*informal*) used when you are glad because sth happens that you enjoy: *Woo hoo! The weekend is here.*

wool 0→ /wʊl/ *noun* [U]
1 0→ the soft fine hair that covers the body of sheep, GOATS and some other animals **2** 0→ long thick thread made from animal's wool, used for knitting: *a ball of wool* ➲ VISUAL VOCAB page V35 **3** 0→ cloth made from animal's wool, used for making clothes, etc: *This scarf is 100% wool.* ◇ *pure new wool* ◇ *a wool blanket* ➲ see also COTTON WOOL, DYED IN THE WOOL, LAMBSWOOL, STEEL WOOL, WIRE WOOL IDM see PULL *v.*

wool·len (*BrE*) (*NAmE* **wool·en**) /ˈwʊlən/ *adj.* **1** [usually before noun] made of wool: *a woollen blanket* ◇ *woollen cloth* **2** [only before noun] involved in making cloth from wool: *the woollen industry*

wool·lens (*BrE*) (*NAmE* **wool·ens**) /ˈwʊlənz/ *noun* [pl.] clothes made of wool, especially knitted clothes

wool·ly /ˈwʊli/ *adj., noun*
■ ***adj.*** (*NAmE* also **wooly**) (**wool·lier, wool·li·est**) **1** covered with wool or with hair like wool: *woolly monkeys* **2** (*informal, especially BrE*) made of wool; like wool SYN **woollen**: *a woolly hat* **3** (of people or their ideas, etc.) not thinking clearly; not clearly expressed SYN **confused**: *woolly arguments* ▶ **wool·li·ness** *noun* [U]
■ ***noun*** (*pl.* **-ies**) (*informal*) **1** (*BrE*, becoming *old-fashioned*) a piece of clothing made of wool, especially one that has been knitted **2** (*AustralE, NZE*) a sheep

Woop Woop /ˈwʊp wʊp/ *noun* (*AustralE, informal*) a humorous name for a town or area that is a long way from a big city

woozy /ˈwuːzi/ *adj.* (*informal*) **1** feeling unsteady, confused and unable to think clearly **2** (*especially NAmE*) feeling as though you might VOMIT

wop /wɒp; *NAmE* wɑːp/ *noun* (*taboo, slang*) a very offensive word for a person from southern Europe, especially an Italian

Wor·ces·ter sauce /ˌwʊstə ˈsɔːs; *NAmE* ˌwʊstər/ (also **Wor·ces·ter·shire sauce** /ˌwʊstəʃə; *NAmE* ˌwʊstərʃɪr/) *noun* [U] a dark thin sauce made of VINEGAR, SOY SAUCE and spices

word 🔑 /wɜːd; *NAmE* wɜːrd/ *noun, verb, exclamation*

■ ***noun***

▸ UNIT OF LANGUAGE **1** 🔑 [C] a single unit of language which means sth and can be spoken or written: *Do not write more than 200 words.* ◇ *Do you know the words to this song?* ◇ *What's the Spanish* ***word for*** *'table'?* ◇ *He was a true friend* ***in all senses of the word.*** ◇ *Tell me what happened* ***in your own words.*** ◇ *I could hear every word they were saying.* ◇ *He couldn't* ***find the words*** *to thank her enough.* ◇ ***Words fail me*** (= I cannot express how I feel). ◇ *There are no words to say how sorry we are.* ◇ *I can't remember her exact words.* ◇ *Angry* ***is not the word for it***—*I was furious.* ➲ see also BUZZWORD, FOUR-LETTER WORD, HOUSEHOLD WORD, SWEAR WORD

▸ STH YOU SAY **2** 🔑 [C] a thing that you say; a remark or statement: ***Have a word with*** *Pat and see what she thinks.* ◇ *Could I have a quick word with you* (= speak to you quickly)? ◇ ***A word of warning****: read the instructions very carefully.* ◇ *words of love* ◇ *She left* ***without a word*** (= without saying anything). ◇ *I don't believe a word of his story* (= I don't believe any of it). ◇ *a man* ***of few words*** (= who doesn't talk very much) ◇ *I'd like to say a few words about future plans.* ◇ *Remember—***not a word to** (= don't tell) *Peter about any of this.* ◇ *He* ***never breathed a word*** *of this to me.*

▸ PROMISE **3** 🔑 [sing.] a promise or guarantee that you will do sth or that sth will happen or is true: ***I give you my word*** *that this won't happen again.* ◇ *I give you my* ***word of honour*** (= my sincere promise) ... ◇ *We never doubted her word.* ◇ *We only* ***have his word for it*** *that the cheque is in the post.* ◇ *to* ***keep your word*** (= do what you promised) ◇ *He promised to help and* ***was as good as his word*** (= did what he promised). ◇ *He's a* ***man of his word*** (= he does what he promises). ◇ *I trusted her not to* ***go back on her word*** (= break her promise). ◇ *I can't prove it—you'll have to* ***take my word for it*** (= believe me).

▸ INFORMATION/NEWS **4** [sing.] a piece of information or news: *There's been no word from them since before Christmas.* ◇ *She* ***sent word*** *that she would be late.* ◇ *If* ***word gets out*** *about the affair, he will have to resign.* ◇ ***Word has it that*** *she's leaving.* ◇ ***The word is*** *they've split up.* ◇ *He likes to* ***spread the word*** *about the importance of healthy eating.*

▸ BIBLE **5 the Word** (also **the ˌWord of ˈGod**) [sing.] the Bible and its teachings

IDM **by ˌword of ˈmouth** because people tell each other and not because they read about it: *The news spread by word of mouth.* **(right) from the word ˈgo** (*informal*) from the very beginning **(not) get a word in ˈedgeways** (*BrE*) (*NAmE* **(not) get a word in ˈedgewise**) (not) to be able to say anything because sb else is speaking too much: *When Mary starts talking, no one else can get a word in edgeways.* **have a word in sb's ˈear** (*BrE*) to speak to sb privately about sth **have/exchange ˈwords (with sb) (about sth)** (*especially BrE*) to have an argument with sb: *We've had words.* ◇ *Words were exchanged.* **in ˈother words** 🔑 used to introduce an explanation of sth: *They asked him to leave—in other words he was fired.* ➲ LANGUAGE BANK at I.E. **(not) in so/as many ˈwords** (not) in exactly the same words as sb says were used: *'Did she say she was sorry?' 'Not in so many words.'* ◇ *He didn't approve of the plan and said so in as many words.* **in a ˈword** (*informal*) used for giving a very short, usually negative, answer or comment: *'Would you like to help us?' 'In a word, no.'* **in words of one ˈsyllable** using very simple language: *Could you say that again in words of one syllable?* **the last/final word (on sth)** the last comment or decision about sth: *He always has to* ***have the last word*** *in any argument.* **(upon) my ˈword** (*old-fashioned*) used to show that you are surprised about sth **not have a good word to ˈsay for sb/sth** (*informal*) to never say anything good about sb/sth: *Nobody had a good word to say about him.* **put in a (good) ˈword for sb** to praise sb to sb else in order to help them get a job, etc. **put ˈwords into sb's mouth** to suggest that sb has said sth when in fact they have not **say/give the ˈword** to give an order; to make a request: *Just say the word, and I'll go.* **take sb at their ˈword** to believe exactly what sb says or promises **take the ˈwords right out of sb's mouth** to say what sb else was going to say **too funny, silly, ridiculous, etc. for ˈwords** extremely funny, silly, ridiculous, etc. **ˌword for ˈword** 🔑 in exactly the same words or (when translated) exactly equivalent words: *She repeated their conversation word for word to me.* ◇ *a word-for-word translation* **sb's word is their ˈbond** somebody's promise can be relied on completely **words to that efˈfect** used to show that you are giving the general meaning of what sb has said rather than the exact words: *He told me to leave—or words to that effect.* ➲ more at ACTION *n.*, BANDY *v.*, DIRTY *adj.*, EAT, FAMOUS, HANG *v.*, LAST *det.*, LOST *adj.*, MINCE *v.*, MUM *adj.*, OPERATIVE *adj.*, PLAY *n.*, PRINT *v.*, WAR *n.*, WEIGH, WRITTEN

■ ***verb*** [often passive] **~ sth** to write or say sth using particular words: *How was the letter worded* (= what did it say exactly)? ▸ **word·ed** *adj.*: *a carefully worded speech* ◇ *a strongly worded letter of protest*

■ ***exclamation*** **word!** (*NAmE*) used to show that you accept or agree with what sb has just said

Synonyms

word

term • phrase • expression • idiom

These are all words for a unit of language used to express sth.

word a single unit of language which means sth and can be spoken or written: *Do not write more than 200 words.* ◇ *He uses a lot of long words.*

term (*rather formal*) a word or phrase used as the name of sth, especially one connected with a particular type of language: *technical/legal/scientific terms* ◇ *'Old man' is a slang term for 'father'.*

phrase a group of words which have a particular meaning when used together: *Who coined the phrase 'desktop publishing'?* NOTE In grammar, a **phrase** is a group of words without a finite verb, especially one that forms part of a sentence: 'the green car' and 'on Friday morning' are phrases.

expression a word or phrase: *He tends to use a lot of slang expressions that I've never heard before.*

idiom a group of words whose meaning is different from the meanings of the individual words: *'Let the cat out of the bag' is an idiom meaning to tell a secret by mistake.*

PATTERNS

- a word/term **for** sth
- a **new** word/term/phrase/expression
- a **technical/colloquial** word/term/phrase/expression
- a **slang** word/term/phrase
- an **idiomatic** phrase/expression
- to **use** a(n) word/term/phrase/expression/idiom
- to **coin** a(n) word/term/phrase/expression
- a(n) word/term/phrase/expression/idiom **means** sth

ˈword break (also **ˈword division**) *noun* (*technical*) a point at which a word is split between two lines of text

ˈword class *noun* (*grammar*) one of the classes into which words are divided according to their grammar, such as noun, verb, adjective, etc. SYN **part of speech**

word·ing /ˈwɜːdɪŋ; *NAmE* ˈwɜːrd-/ *noun* [U, C, usually sing.] the words that are used in a piece of writing or speech, especially when they have been carefully chosen: *The*

W

wording was deliberately ambiguous. ➲ SYNONYMS at LANGUAGE

word·less /ˈwɜːdləs; *NAmE* ˈwɜːrd-/ *adj.* (*formal* or *literary*) **1** [usually before noun] without saying any words; silent: *a wordless cry/prayer* **2** (of people) not saying anything ▸ **word·less·ly** *adv.*

ˌword-ˈperfect (*BrE*) (*NAmE* **ˌletter-ˈperfect**) *adj.* able to remember and repeat sth exactly without making any mistakes

word·play /ˈwɜːdpleɪ; *NAmE* ˈwɜːrd-/ *noun* [U] making jokes by using words in a clever or amusing way, especially by using a word that has two meanings, or different words that sound the same ➲ compare PUN

ˈword processing *noun* [U] the use of a computer to create, store and print a piece of text, usually typed in from a keyboard

ˈword processor *noun* a computer that runs a word processing program and is usually used for writing letters, reports, etc.

word·search /ˈwɜːdsɜːtʃ; *NAmE* ˈwɜːrdsɜːrtʃ/ *noun* a game consisting of letters arranged in a square, containing several hidden words that you must find ➲ VISUAL VOCAB page V33

word·smith /ˈwɜːdsmɪθ; *NAmE* ˈwɜːrd-/ *noun* a person who is skilful at using words

wordy /ˈwɜːdi; *NAmE* ˈwɜːrdi/ *adj.* (usually *disapproving*) using too many words, especially formal ones SYN **verbose**: *a wordy and repetitive essay* ▸ **wordi·ness** *noun* [U]

wore *past tense* of WEAR

work 🔑 /wɜːk; *NAmE* wɜːrk/ *verb, noun*

■ ***verb***

▸ DO JOB/TASK **1** 🔑 [I] to do sth that involves physical or mental effort, especially as part of a job: *I can't work if I'm cold.* ◇ **~ at sth** *I've been working at my assignment all day.* ◇ **~ on sth** *He is working on a new novel.* ◇ *She's outside, working on the car.* ◇ **+ noun** *Doctors often work very long hours.* **2** 🔑 [I] to have a job: *Both my parents work.* ◇ **~ for sb/sth** *She works for an engineering company.* ◇ **~ in sth** *I've always worked in education.* ◇ **~ with sb/sth** *Do you enjoy working with children?* ◇ **~ as sth** *My son is working as a teacher.*

▸ MAKE EFFORT **3** [T] **~ yourself/sb + adv./prep.** to make yourself/sb work, especially very hard: *She works herself too hard.* **4** 🔑 [I] to make efforts to achieve sth: **~ for sth** *She dedicated her life to working for peace.* ◇ **~ to do sth** *The committee is working to get the prisoners freed.*

▸ MANAGE **5** [T] **~ sth** to manage or operate sth to gain benefit from it: *to work the land* (= grow crops on it, etc.) ◇ *He works a large area* (= selling a company's goods, etc.). ◇ (*figurative*) *She was a skilful speaker who knew how to **work a crowd*** (= to excite them or make them feel sth strongly).

▸ MACHINE/DEVICE **6** 🔑 [I] to function; to operate: *The phone isn't working.* ◇ *It works by electricity.* ◇ *Are they any closer to understanding how the brain works?* **7** [T] **~ sth** to make a machine, device, etc. operate: *Do you know how to work the coffee machine?* ◇ *The machine is worked by wind power.*

W

▸ HAVE RESULT/EFFECT **8** 🔑 [I] to have the result or effect that you want: *The pills the doctor gave me aren't working.* ◇ *My plan worked, and I got them to agree.* ◇ **~ on sb/sth** *His charm doesn't work on me* (= does not affect or impress me). **9** [I] to have a particular effect: **~ against sb** *Your age can work against you in this job.* ◇ **~ in sb's favour** *Speaking Italian should work in his favour.* **10** [T] **~ sth** to cause or produce sth as a result of effort: *You can work miracles with very little money if you follow our home decoration tips.*

▸ USE MATERIAL **11** [T] to make a material into a particular shape or form by pressing, stretching, hitting it, etc: **~ sth** *to work clay* ◇ *to work gold* ◇ **~ sth into sth** *to work the mixture into a paste* **12** [I] **~ in/with sth** (of an artist, etc.) to use a particular material to produce a picture or other item: *an artist working in oils* ◇ *a craftsman working with wool*

▸ OF PART OF FACE/BODY **13** [I] (*formal*) to move violently: *He stared at me in horror, his mouth working.*

▸ MOVE GRADUALLY **14** [I, T] to move or pass to a particular place or state, usually gradually: **+ adv./prep.** *It will take a while for the drug to work out of your system.* ◇ **~ your way + adv./prep.** (*figurative*) *He worked his way to the top of his profession.* ◇ **~ yourself/sth + adj.** *I was tied up, but managed to work myself free.* ◇ **+ adj.** *The screw had **worked loose**.*

IDM Most idioms containing **work** are at the entries for the nouns and adjectives in the idioms, for example **work your fingers to the bone** is at **finger**. **ˈwork it/things** (*informal*) to arrange sth in a particular way, especially by being clever: *Can you work it so that we get free tickets?*

PHR V **ˌwork aˈround/ˈround to sth/sb** to gradually turn a conversation towards a particular topic, subject, etc: *It was some time before he worked around to what he really wanted to say.* **ˈwork at sth** to make great efforts to achieve sth or do sth well: *He's working at losing weight.* ◇ *Learning to play the piano isn't easy. You have to **work at it**.* **ˌwork sth ˈin | work sth into sth** **1** to try to include sth: *Can't you work a few more jokes into your speech?* **2** to add one substance to another and mix them together: *Gradually work in the butter.* **ˌwork sth↔ˈoff** **1** to get rid of sth, especially a strong feeling, by using physical effort: *She worked off her anger by going for a walk.* **2** to earn money in order to be able to pay a debt: *They had a large bank loan to work off.* **ˈwork on sb** to try to persuade sb to agree to sth or to do sth: *He hasn't said he'll do it yet, but I'm working on him.* **ˈwork on sth** to try hard to improve or achieve sth: *You need to work on your pronunciation a bit more.* ◇ *'Have you sorted out a babysitter yet?' 'No, but **I'm working on it**.'* **ˌwork ˈout** **1** 🔑 to train the body by physical exercise: *I work out regularly to keep fit.* ➲ related noun WORKOUT **2** 🔑 to develop in a successful way: *My first job didn't work out.* ◇ *Things have worked out quite well for us.* **ˌwork ˈout (at sth)** if sth **works out** at sth, you calculate that it will be a particular amount: **+ adj.** *It'll work out cheaper to travel by bus.* **ˌwork sb↔ˈout** (*BrE*) to understand sb's character: *I've never been able to work her out.* **ˌwork sth↔ˈout** **1** 🔑 to calculate sth: *to work out the answer* **2** 🔑 (*especially BrE*) to find the answer to sth SYN **solve**: *to work out a problem* ◇ **~ what, where, etc...** *Can you work out what these squiggles mean?* ◇ *I couldn't work out where the music was coming from.* **3** 🔑 to plan or think of sth: *I've worked out a new way of doing it.* **4** [usually passive] to remove all the coal, minerals, etc. from a mine over a period of time: *a worked-out silver mine* **ˌwork sb↔ˈover** (*slang*) to attack sb and hit them, for example to make them give you information **ˈwork to sth** to follow a plan, schedule, etc: *to work to a budget* ◇ *We're working to a very tight deadline* (= we have little time in which to do the work). **ˈwork towards sth** to try to reach or achieve a goal **ˌwork sth↔ˈup** to develop or improve sth with some effort: *I can't work up any enthusiasm for his idea.* ◇ *She went for a long walk to work up an appetite.* **ˌwork sb/yourself ˈup (into sth)** to make sb/yourself reach a state of great excitement, anger, etc: *Don't work yourself up into a state about it. It isn't worth it.* ◇ *What are you so worked up about?* **ˌwork sth ˈup into sth** to bring sth to a more complete or more acceptable state: *I'm working my notes up into a dissertation.* **ˌwork ˈup to sth** to develop or move gradually towards sth, usually sth more exciting or extreme: *The music worked up to a rousing finale.* ◇ *I began by jogging in the park and worked up to running five miles a day.*

■ ***noun***

▸ JOB/TASK **1** 🔑 [U] the job that a person does especially in order to earn money SYN **employment**: *She had been **out of work*** (= without a job) *for a year.* ◇ (*BrE*) *They are **in work*** (= have a job). ◇ *He **started work** as a security guard.* ◇ *It is difficult to find work in the present economic climate.* ◇ *I'm still looking for work.* ◇ *She's planning to **return to work** once the children start school.* ◇ *What **line of work** are you in* (= what type of work do you do)? ◇ ***before/after work*** (= in the morning/evening each day) ◇ ***full-time/part-time/unpaid/voluntary work*** ➲ COLLOCATIONS at JOB, UNEMPLOYMENT **2** 🔑 [U] the duties that you have and the activities that you do as part of your job: *Police work is mainly routine.* ◇ *The accountant described his work to the sales staff.* ➲ see also PIECEWORK, SOCIAL WORK **3** ⊶ [U] tasks that need to be done: *There is plenty of* ***work to be done*** *in the garden.* ◇ *Taking care of a baby is* ***hard work.*** ◇ *I have some work for you to do.* ◇ *Stop talking and get on with your work.* ➲ see also HOMEWORK, SCHOOLWORK **4** [U] materials needed or used for doing work, especially books, papers, etc: *She often brings work* (= for example, files and documents) *home with her from the office.* ◇ *His work was spread all over the floor.* ➲ see also PAPERWORK

▸ PLACE OF JOB **5** ⊶ [U] (used without *the*) the place where you do your job: *I* ***go to work*** *at 8 o'clock.* ◇ *When do you* ***leave for work****?* ◇ *The new legislation concerns health and safety* ***at work.*** ◇ *I have to* ***leave work*** *early today.* ◇ *Her friends* ***from work*** *came to see her in the hospital.*

▸ EFFORT **6** ⊶ [U] the use of physical strength or mental power in order to do or make sth: *She earned her grades through sheer* ***hard work.*** ◇ *We* ***started work on*** *the project in 2009.* ◇ *Work continues on renovating the hotel.* ◇ *The work of building the bridge took six months.* ◇ *The art collection was his* ***life's work.*** ◇ *She* ***set them to work*** *painting the fence.* ➲ see also DONKEY WORK, FIELDWORK

▸ PRODUCT OF WORK **7** ⊶ [U] a thing or things that are produced as a result of work: *She's an artist whose work I really admire.* ◇ *Is this* ***all your own work*** (= did you do it without help from others)? ◇ *The book is a detailed and thorough* ***piece of work*** *covering all aspects of the subject.*

▸ RESULT OF ACTION **8** [U] the result of an action; what is done by sb: *The damage is clearly the work of vandals.*

▸ BOOK/MUSIC/ART **9** ⊶ [C] a book, piece of music, painting, etc: *the* ***collected/complete works*** *of Tolstoy* ◇ ***works of fiction/literature*** ◇ *Beethoven's piano works* ➲ compare OPUS ➲ see also WORK OF ART

▸ BUILDING/REPAIRING **10 works** [pl.] (often in compounds) activities involving building or repairing sth: *roadworks* ◇ *They expanded the shipyards and started engineering works.* ➲ see also PUBLIC WORKS

▸ FACTORY **11 works** (*pl.* works) [C+sing./pl. v.] (often in compounds) a place where things are made or industrial processes take place: *an engineering works* ◇ *a brickworks* ➲ SYNONYMS at FACTORY

▸ PARTS OF MACHINE **12 the works** [pl.] the moving parts of a machine, etc. SYN **mechanism**

▸ EVERYTHING **13 the works** [pl.] (*informal*) everything: *We went to the chip shop and had the works: fish, chips, gherkins, mushy peas.*

▸ PHYSICS **14** [U] the use of force to produce movement ➲ see also JOULE

IDM **all ˌwork and no ˈplay (makes ˌJack a dull ˈboy)** (*saying*) it is not healthy to spend all your time working; you need to relax too **at ˈwork 1** having an effect on sth: *She suspected that secret influences were at work.* **2** ⊶ **~ (on sth)** busy doing sth: *He is still at work on the painting.* ◇ *Danger—men at work.* **get (down) to/set to ˈwork** ⊶ to begin; to make a start: *We set to work on the outside of the house* (= for example, painting it). **give sb the ˈworks** (*informal*) to give or tell sb everything **ˌgood ˈworks** kind acts to help others **go/set about your ˈwork** to do/start to do your work: *She went cheerfully about her work.* **have your ˈwork cut out** (*informal*) to be likely to have difficulty doing sth: *You'll have your work cut out to get there by nine o'clock.* **in the ˈworks** something that is **in the works** is being discussed, planned or prepared and will happen or exist soon SYN **in the pipeline** **the work of a ˈmoment, ˈsecond, etc.** (*formal*) a thing that takes a very short time to do ➲ more at DAY, DEVIL, DIRTY *adj.*, HAND *n.*, HARD *adj.*, JOB, LIGHT *adj.*, NASTY, NICE, SHOOT *v.*, SHORT *adj.*, SPANNER

work·able /ˈwɜːkəbl; *NAmE* ˈwɜːrk-/ *adj.* **1** (of a system, an idea, etc.) that can be used successfully and effectively SYN **practical**: *a workable plan* **2** that you can shape, spread, dig, etc: *Add more water until the dough is workable.* **3** (of a mine, etc.) that can still be used and will make a profit

work·aday /ˈwɜːkədeɪ; *NAmE* ˈwɜːrk-/ *adj.* [usually before noun] (*formal*) ordinary; not very interesting SYN **everyday**

Synonyms

work

employment • career • profession • occupation • trade

These are all words for the work that sb does in return for payment, especially over a long period of time.

work the job that sb does, especially in order to earn money: *It's very difficult to find work at the moment.*

employment (*rather formal*) work, especially when it is done to earn money; the state of being employed or the situation in which people have work: *Only half the people here are in paid employment.*

career the job or series of jobs that sb has in a particular area of work, usually involving more responsibility as time passes: *He had a very distinguished career in the Foreign Office.*

profession a type of job that needs special training or skill, especially one that needs a high level of education: *He hopes to enter the medical profession.* NOTE **The profession** is all the people who work in a particular profession: *the legal profession.* **The professions** are the traditional jobs that need a high level of education and training, such as being a doctor or lawyer.

occupation (*rather formal*) a job or profession: *Please state your name, age, and occupation.*

trade a job, especially one that involves working with your hands and requires special training and skills: *Carpentry is a highly skilled trade.*

PATTERNS

- **in/out of** work/employment
- (a) **full-time/part-time** work/employment/career/occupation
- **permanent/temporary** work/employment
- (a) **well-paid** work/employment/profession/occupation
- (a) **low-paid** work/employment/occupation
- to **look for/seek/find** work/employment/a career/an occupation
- to **get/obtain/give sb/offer sb/create/generate/provide** work/employment

work·ahol·ic /ˌwɜːkəˈhɒlɪk; *NAmE* ˌwɜːrkəˈhɔːlɪk; -ˈhɑːl-/ *noun* (*informal*, usually *disapproving*) a person who works very hard and finds it difficult to stop working and do other things

work·around /ˈwɜːkəraʊnd; *NAmE* ˈwɜːrk-/ *noun* (*computing*) a way in which you can solve or avoid a problem when the most obvious solution is not possible

ˈwork basket *noun* (*old-fashioned*, *BrE*) a container for the things you need for sewing

work·bench /ˈwɜːkbentʃ; *NAmE* ˈwɜːrk-/ (also **bench**) *noun* a long heavy table used for doing practical jobs, working with tools, etc.

work·book /ˈwɜːkbʊk; *NAmE* ˈwɜːrk-/ (*BrE*) (*NAmE* **ˈexercise book**) *noun* a book with exercises in it, often with spaces for students to write answers in, to help them practise what they have learnt ➲ VISUAL VOCAB page V57

work·day /ˈwɜːkdeɪ; *NAmE* ˈwɜːrk-/ *noun* **1** (*NAmE*) (*BrE* **ˌworking ˈday**) the part of a day during which you work: *an 8-hour workday* **2** = WORKING DAY (2): *workday traffic*

ˌworked ˈup *adj.* [not before noun] **~ (about sth)** (*informal*) very excited or upset about sth: *There's no point in* ***getting worked up*** *about it.*

work·er ⊶ /ˈwɜːkə(r); *NAmE* ˈwɜːrk-/ *noun* **1** ⊶ (often in compounds) a person who works, especially one who does a particular kind of work: *farm/factory/office workers* ◇ *rescue/aid/research workers* ◇ ***temporary/***

W

part-time/casual workers ◇ *manual/skilled/unskilled workers* ➲ COLLOCATIONS at JOB ➲ see also GUEST WORKER, SEX WORKER, SOCIAL WORKER **2** [usually pl.] a person who is employed in a company or industry, especially sb who does physical work rather than organizing things or managing people: *Conflict between employers and workers intensified and the number of strikes rose.* ◇ *talks between workers and management* **3** (usually after an adjective) a person who works in a particular way: *a* ***hard/fast/quick/slow worker*** **4** a female BEE that helps do the work of the group of bees but does not reproduce ➲ compare DRONE, QUEEN BEE IDM see FAST *adj.*

ˈ**work experience** *noun* [U] **1** the work or jobs that you have done in your life so far: *The opportunities available will depend on your previous work experience and qualifications.* **2** (*BrE*) a period of time that a young person, especially a student, spends working in a company as a form of training ➲ compare INTERNSHIP

work·fare /ˈwɜːkfeə(r); *NAmE* ˈwɜːrkfer/ *noun* [U] a system in which unemployed people have to work in order to get money for food, rent, etc. from the government

work·force /ˈwɜːkfɔːs; *NAmE* ˈwɜːrkfɔːrs/ *noun* [C+sing./pl. v.] **1** all the people who work for a particular company, organization, etc. SYN **staff**: *The factory has a 1 000-strong workforce.* ◇ *Two thirds of the workforce is/are women.* ➲ COLLOCATIONS at UNEMPLOYMENT **2** all the people in a country or an area who are available for work: *A quarter of the local workforce is/are unemployed.*

work·horse /ˈwɜːkhɔːs; *NAmE* ˈwɜːrkhɔːrs/ *noun* a person or machine that you can rely on to do hard and/or boring work

work·house /ˈwɜːkhaʊs; *NAmE* ˈwɜːrk-/ (*BrE*) (also **poor·house** *NAmE, BrE*) *noun* (in Britain in the past) a building where very poor people were sent to live and given work to do

work·ing /ˈwɜːkɪŋ; *NAmE* ˈwɜːrk-/ *adj., noun*

■ ***adj.*** [only before noun] **1** having a job for which you are paid SYN **employed**: *the working population* ◇ *a* ***working mother*** ➲ see also HARD-WORKING **2** having a job that involves hard physical work rather than office work, studying, etc: *a* ***working man*** ◇ *a working men's club* **3** connected with your job and the time you spend doing it: *long* ***working hours*** ◇ *poor* ***working conditions*** ◇ *I have a good* ***working relationship*** *with my boss.* ◇ *She spent most of her* ***working life*** *as a teacher.* ◇ *recent changes in* ***working practices*** **4** a **working** breakfast or lunch is one at which you discuss business **5** used as a basis for work, discussion, etc. but likely to be changed or improved in the future: *a working theory* ◇ *Have you decided on a working title for your thesis yet?* **6** if you have a **working** knowledge of sth, you can use it at a basic level **7** the **working** parts of a machine are the parts that move in order to make it function **8** a **working** majority is a small majority that is enough to enable a government to win votes in parliament and make new laws IDM see ORDER *n.*

■ ***noun*** [usually pl.] **1** ~ (**of sth**) the way in which a machine, a system, an organization, etc. works: *an introduction to the workings of Congress* ◇ *the workings of the human mind* ◇ *the machine's inner workings* **2** the parts of a mine or QUARRY where coal, metal, stone, etc. is or has been dug from the ground

W

ˌ**working** ˈ**capital** *noun* [U] (*business*) the money that is needed to run a business rather than the money that is used to buy buildings and equipment when starting the business ➲ compare VENTURE CAPITAL

the ˌ**working** ˈ**class** *noun* [sing.+ sing./pl. v.] (also **the** ˌ**working** ˈ**classes** [pl.]) the social class whose members do not have much money or power and are usually employed to do MANUAL work (= physical work using their hands): *the political party of the working class* ◇ *The working class has/have rejected them in the elections.* ➲ compare MIDDLE CLASS, UPPER CLASS ▶ ˌ**working-**ˈ**class** *adj.*: *a working-class background*

ˌ**working** ˈ**day** *noun* (*BrE*) **1** (*NAmE* **work·day**) the part of a day during which you work: *I spend most of my working day sitting at a desk.* **2** (also *less frequent* **work·day**) a day on which you usually work or on which most people usually work: *Sunday is a normal working day for me.* ◇ *Thousands of working days were lost through strikes last year.* ◇ *Allow two working days* (= not Saturday or Sunday) *for delivery.*

ˈ**working girl** *noun* (*informal*) **1** (becoming *old-fashioned*) a PROSTITUTE. People say 'working girl' to avoid saying 'prostitute'. **2** (sometimes *offensive*) a woman who has a paid job

ˈ**working paper** *noun* **1** [C] a report written by a group of people chosen to study an aspect of law, education, health, etc. **2** **working papers** [pl.] (in the US) an official document that enables sb under 16 years old or born outside the US to have a job

ˈ**working party** (*BrE*) (also ˈ**working group** *NAmE, BrE*) *noun* [C+sing./pl. v.] ~ (**on sth**) a group of people chosen to study a particular problem or situation in order to suggest ways of dealing with it

ˌ**working** ˈ**week** (*BrE*) (*NAmE* **work·week**) *noun* the total amount of time that you spend at work during the week: *a 40-hour working week*

ˌ**work-life** ˈ**balance** *noun* [sing.] the number of hours per week you spend working, compared with the number of hours you spend with your family, relaxing, etc: *Part-time working is often the best way to improve your work-life balance.*

work·load /ˈwɜːkləʊd; *NAmE* ˈwɜːrkloʊd/ *noun* the amount of work that has to be done by a particular person or organization: *a heavy workload* ◇ *We have taken on extra staff to cope with the increased workload.* ➲ COLLOCATIONS at JOB

work·man /ˈwɜːkmən; *NAmE* ˈwɜːrk-/ *noun* (*pl.* **-men** /-mən/) **1** a man who is employed to do physical work **2** (with an adjective) a person who works in the way mentioned: *a good/bad workman*

work·man·like /ˈwɜːkmənlaɪk; *NAmE* ˈwɜːrk-/ *adj.* done, made, etc. in a skilful and thorough way but not usually very original or exciting

work·man·ship /ˈwɜːkmənʃɪp; *NAmE* ˈwɜːrk-/ *noun* [U] the skill with which sb makes sth, especially when this affects the way it looks or works: *Our buyers insist on high standards of workmanship and materials.*

work·mate /ˈwɜːkmeɪt; *NAmE* ˈwɜːrk-/ *noun* (*especially BrE*) a person that you work with, often doing the same job, in an office, a factory, etc. SYN **colleague**

ˌ**work of** ˈ**art** *noun* (*pl.* ˌ**works of** ˈ**art**) **1** a painting, statue, etc: *A number of priceless works of art were stolen from the gallery.* **2** something that is attractive and skilfully made: *The bride's dress was a work of art.*

work·out /ˈwɜːkaʊt; *NAmE* ˈwɜːrk-/ *noun* a period of physical exercise that you do to keep fit: *She does a 20-minute workout every morning.*

ˈ**work permit** *noun* an official document that sb needs in order to work in a particular foreign country

work·place /ˈwɜːkpleɪs; *NAmE* ˈwɜːrk-/ *noun* (often **the workplace**) [sing.] the office, factory, etc. where people work: *the introduction of new technology into the workplace*

ˈ**work placement** *noun* [U, C] (*BrE*) = PLACEMENT (2)

ˈ**work release** *noun* [U] (*US*) a system that allows prisoners to leave prison during the day to go to work

work·room /ˈwɜːkruːm; -rʊm; *NAmE* ˈwɜːrk-/ *noun* a room in which work is done, especially work that involves making things: *The jeweller has a workroom at the back of his shop.*

works *noun* ➲ WORK

ˌ**works** ˈ**council** *noun* (*especially BrE*) a group of employees who represent all the employees at a factory, etc. in discussions with their employers over conditions of work

work·sheet /ˈwɜːkʃiːt; *NAmE* ˈwɜːrk-/ *noun* **1** a piece of paper on which there is a series of questions and exercises to be done by a student **2** a piece of paper on which work that has been done or has to be done is recorded

work·shop /'wɜːkʃɒp; *NAmE* 'wɜːrkʃɑːp/ *noun* **1** a room or building in which things are made or repaired using tools or machinery ➲ SYNONYMS at FACTORY **2** a period of discussion and practical work on a particular subject, in which a group of people share their knowledge and experience: *a drama workshop* ◇ *a poetry workshop* ➲ COLLOCATIONS at EDUCATION

'work-shy *adj.* (*BrE, disapproving*) unwilling to work SYN **lazy**

work·space /'wɜːkspeɪs; *NAmE* 'wɜːrk-/ *noun* **1** [U, C] a space in which to work, especially in an office **2** [C] (*computing*) a place where information that is being used by one person on a computer network is stored

work·sta·tion /'wɜːksteɪʃn; *NAmE* 'wɜːrk-/ *noun* the desk and computer at which a person works; one computer that is part of a computer network ➲ VISUAL VOCAB page V56

work·top /'wɜːktɒp; *NAmE* 'wɜːrktɑːp/ (also **'work surface** both *BrE*) (*NAmE* **counter, counter·top**) *noun* a flat surface in a kitchen for preparing food on ➲ VISUAL VOCAB page V22

ˌwork-to-'rule *noun* [usually sing.] a situation in which workers refuse to do any work that is not in their contracts, in order to protest about sth ➲ compare GO-SLOW

work·week /'wɜːkwiːk; *NAmE* 'wɜːrk-/ (*NAmE*) (*BrE* **ˌworking 'week**) *noun* the total amount of time that you spend at work during the week

world 🗝 /wɜːld; *NAmE* wɜːrld/ *noun*
▸ THE EARTH/ITS PEOPLE **1** 🗝 **the world** [sing.] the earth, with all its countries, peoples and natural features: *to sail* ***around the world*** ◇ *travelling (**all over**) **the world*** ◇ *a map of the world* ◇ *French is spoken in many **parts of the world**.* ◇ *Which is the largest city **in the world**?* ◇ *He's the world's highest paid entertainer.* ◇ *a meeting of world leaders* ◇ *campaigning for world peace* **2** 🗝 [C, usually sing.] a particular part of the earth; a particular group of countries or people; a particular period of history and the people of that period: *the Arab world* ◇ *the English-speaking world* ◇ *the industrialized and developing worlds* ◇ *the ancient/modern world* ➲ see also THE FIRST WORLD, THE NEW WORLD, THE OLD WORLD, THE THIRD WORLD
▸ ANOTHER PLANET **3** [C] a planet like the earth: *There may be other worlds out there.*
▸ TYPE OF LIFE **4** 🗝 [C] the people or things belonging to a particular group or connected with a particular interest, job, etc: *the **animal/plant/insect world*** ◇ *the world of fashion* ◇ *stars from the sporting and artistic worlds* **5** 🗝 [usually sing.] (usually used with an adjective) everything that exists of a particular kind; a particular kind of life or existence: ***the natural world*** (= animals, plants, minerals, etc.) ◇ *They are a couple in **the real world** as well as in the movie.* ◇ *The island is a world of brilliant colours and dramatic sunsets.* ◇ *They had little contact with the **outside world*** (= people and places that were not part of their normal life).
▸ PERSON'S LIFE **6** 🗝 [sing.] a person's environment, experiences, friends and family, etc: *Parents are the most important people in a child's world.* ◇ *When his wife died, his entire world was turned upside down.*
▸ SOCIETY **7** 🗝 [sing.] our society and the way people live and behave; the people in the world: *We live in a rapidly changing world.* ◇ *He's too young to understand the **ways of the world**.* ◇ *The **whole world** was waiting for news of the astronauts.* ◇ *She felt that the world was against her.* ◇ ***The eyes of the world** are on the President.* **8 the world** [sing.] a way of life where possessions and physical pleasures are important, rather than spiritual values: *monks and nuns renouncing the world* ➲ see also OLDE WORLDE, OLD-WORLD
▸ HUMAN EXISTENCE **9** [sing.] the state of human existence: *this world and the next* (= life on earth and existence after death)

IDM **be ˌall the 'world to sb** to be loved by and very important to sb **the best of 'both/'all possible worlds** the benefits of two or more completely different situations that you can enjoy at the same time: *If you enjoy the coast and the country, you'll get the best of both worlds on this walk.* **be 'worlds apart** to be completely different in attitudes, opinions, etc. **come/go 'down/'up in the world** to become less/more important or successful in society **come into the 'world** (*literary*) to be born **do sb/sth the 'world of good** to make sb feel much better; to improve sth: *A change of job would do you the world of good.* **for all the world as if/though... | for all the world like sb/sth** (*formal*) exactly as if...; exactly like sb/sth: *She behaved for all the world as if nothing unusual had happened.* ◇ *He looked for all the world like a schoolboy caught stealing apples.* **have the world at your 'feet** to be very successful and admired **how, why, etc. in the 'world** (*informal*) used to emphasize sth and to show that you are surprised or annoyed: *What in the world did they think they were doing?* **in an ideal/a perfect 'world** used to say that sth is what you would like to happen or what should happen, but you know it cannot: *In an ideal world we would be recycling and reusing everything.* **in the 'world** 🗝 used to emphasize what you are saying: *There's nothing in the world I'd like more than to visit New York.* ◇ *Don't rush—we've got **all the time in the world**.* ◇ *You look as if you haven't got **a care in the world**!* **(be/live) in a world of your 'own** if you are **in a world of your own**, you are so concerned with your own thoughts that you do not notice what is happening around you **a man/woman of the 'world** a person with a lot of experience of life, who is not easily surprised or shocked **not for (all) the 'world** used to say that you would never do sth: *I wouldn't hurt you for the world.* **the... of this world** (*informal*) used to refer to people of a particular type: *We all envy the Bill Gateses of this world* (= the people who are as rich and successful as Bill Gates). **ˌout of this 'world** (*informal*) used to emphasize how good, beautiful, etc. sth is: *The meal was out of this world.* **see the 'world** to travel widely and gain wide experience **set/put the world to 'rights** to talk about how the world could be changed to be a better place: *We stayed up all night, setting the world to rights.* **set the 'world on fire** (*BrE* also **set the 'world alight**) (*informal*) (usually used in negative sentences) to be very successful and gain the admiration of other people: *He's never going to set the world on fire with his paintings.* **what is the world 'coming to?** used to express disapproval, surprise or shock, especially at changes in people's attitudes or behaviour: *When I listen to the news these days, I sometimes wonder what the world is coming to.* **(all) the ˌworld and his 'wife** (*BrE, informal, humorous*) everyone; a large number of people **a 'world away (from sth)** used to emphasize how different two things are: *His new luxury mansion was a world away from the tiny house where he was born.* **the ˌworld is your 'oyster** there is no limit to the opportunities open to you **a/the 'world of difference** (*informal*) used to emphasize how much difference there is between two things: *There's a world of difference between liking someone and loving them.* **the (whole) world 'over** everywhere in the world: *People are basically the same the world over.* ➲ more at BRAVE *adj.*, DEAD *adj.*, END *n.*, LOST, PROMISE *v.*, SMALL *adj.*, TOP *n.*, WATCH *v.*, WAY *n.*, WILL *n.*, WORST *n.*

the ˌWorld 'Bank *noun* [sing.] an international organization that lends money to countries who are members at times when they are in difficulty and need more money

'world-beater *noun* a person or thing that is better than all others ▸ **'world-beating** *adj.*

ˌworld-'class *adj.* as good as the best in the world: *a world-class athlete*

the ˌWorld 'Cup *noun* (in sports) a competition between national teams from all over the world, usually held every few years: *The next Rugby World Cup will take place in three years' time.*

ˌworld 'English *noun* [U] the English language, used throughout the world for international communication, including all of its regional varieties, such as Australian, Indian and South African English

ˌworld-'famous *adj.* known all over the world: *a world-famous scientist* ◇ *His books are world-famous.*

W

ˌWorld ˈHeritage Site *noun* a natural or MAN-MADE place that is recognized as having great international importance and is therefore protected

ˌworld ˈlanguage *noun* a language that is known or spoken in many countries

world·ly /ˈwɜːldli; *NAmE* ˈwɜːrld-/ *adj.* (*literary*) **1** [only before noun] connected with the world in which we live rather than with spiritual things: *worldly success* ◇ *your worldly goods* (= the things that you own) OPP **spiritual** **2** having a lot of experience of life and therefore not easily shocked: *At 15, he was more worldly than his older cousins who lived in the country.* OPP **unworldly** ▸ **world·li·ness** *noun* [U]

ˌworldly-ˈwise *adj.* having a lot of experience of life and therefore not easily shocked

ˈworld music *noun* [U] traditional music from non-Western countries; Western popular music that includes elements of traditional music from non-Western countries

ˌworld ˈpower *noun* a powerful country that has a lot of influence in international politics

the ˌWorld ˈSeries™ *noun* a series of BASEBALL games played every year between the winners of the American League and the National League

ˌworld ˈview *noun* a person's way of thinking about and understanding life, which depends on their beliefs and attitudes: *Your education is bound to shape your world view.*

ˌworld ˈwar *noun* [C, U] a war that involves many countries

ˌWorld ˌWar ˈOne (also **ˌWorld ˌWar ˈI**) *noun* = THE FIRST WORLD WAR

ˌWorld ˌWar ˈTwo (also **ˌWorld ˌWar ˈII**) *noun* = THE SECOND WORLD WAR

ˈworld-weary *adj.* no longer excited by life; showing this SYN **jaded** ▸ **ˈworld-weariness** *noun* [U]

world·wide /ˈwɜːldwaɪd; *NAmE* ˈwɜːrld-/ *adj.* [usually before noun] affecting all parts of the world: *an increase in worldwide sales* ◇ *The story has attracted worldwide attention.* ▸ **ˌworld·ˈwide** *adv.*: *We have 2 000 members worldwide.*

the ˌWorld Wide ˈWeb (also **the Web**) *noun* (*abbr.* WWW) a system for finding information on the Internet, in which documents are connected to other documents using HYPERTEXT links: *to browse a site on the World Wide Web* ➲ VISUAL VOCAB page V55

worm /wɜːm; *NAmE* wɜːrm/ *noun, verb*

■ ***noun*** **1** [C] a long thin creature with no bones or legs, that lives in soil: *birds looking for worms* ➲ see also EARTHWORM, LUGWORM **2 worms** [pl.] long thin creatures that live inside the bodies of humans or animals and can cause illness: *The dog has worms.* ➲ see also HOOKWORM, TAPEWORM **3** [C] the young form of an insect when it looks like a short worm: *This apple is full of worms.* ➲ see also GLOW-WORM, SILKWORM, WOODWORM **4** [C] (*computing*) a computer program that is a type of virus and that spreads across a network by copying itself **5** [C, usually sing.] (*informal, disapproving*) a person you do not like or respect, especially because they have a weak character and do not behave well towards other people

IDM **the ˌworm will ˈturn** (*saying*) a person who is normally quiet and does not complain will protest when the situation becomes too hard to bear ➲ more at CAN² *n.*, EARLY *adj.*

■ ***verb*** **1 ~ your way + adv./prep.** to use a twisting and turning movement, especially to move through a narrow or crowded place: *She wormed her way through the crowd to the reception desk.* **2 ~ sth** to give an animal medicine that makes worms pass out of its body in the FAECES

PHR V **ˌworm your way/yourself ˈinto sth** (*disapproving*) to make sb like you or trust you, in order to gain some advantage for yourself SYN **insinuate yourself**: *He managed to worm his way into her life.* **ˌworm sth ˈout of sb** (*informal*) to make sb tell you sth, by asking them questions in a clever way for a long period of time: *We eventually wormed the secret out of her.*

ˈworm-eaten *adj.* full of holes made by WORMS or WOODWORMS

worm·ery /ˈwɜːməri; *NAmE* ˈwɜːrm-/ *noun* (*pl.* -ies) a container in which WORMS are kept, for example in order to produce COMPOST

worm·hole /ˈwɜːmhəʊl; *NAmE* ˈwɜːrmhoʊl/ *noun* **1** a hole made by a worm or young insect **2** (*physics*) a possible connection between regions of SPACE-TIME that are far apart

worm·wood /ˈwɜːmwʊd; *NAmE* ˈwɜːrm-/ *noun* [U] a plant with a bitter flavour, used in making alcoholic drinks and medicines

wormy /ˈwɜːmi; *NAmE* ˈwɜːrmi/ *adj.* containing WORMS: *a wormy apple*

worn /wɔːn; *NAmE* wɔːrn/ *adj.* **1** [usually before noun] (of a thing) damaged or thinner than normal because it is old and has been used a lot: *an old pair of worn jeans* ◇ *The stone steps were worn and broken.* ➲ see also WELL WORN **2** (of a person) looking very tired SYN **weary**: *She came out of the ordeal looking thin and worn.* ➲ see also WEAR *v.*

ˌworn ˈout *adj.* **1** (of a thing) badly damaged and/or no longer useful because it has been used a lot: *These shoes are worn out.* ◇ *the gradual replacement of worn-out equipment* ◇ *a speech full of worn-out old clichés* **2** [not usually before noun] (of a person) looking or feeling very tired, especially as a result of hard work or physical exercise: *Can we sit down? I'm worn out.* ➲ compare OUTWORN

wor·ried 0-w /ˈwʌrid; *NAmE* ˈwɜːr-/ *adj.* thinking about unpleasant things that have happened or that might happen and therefore feeling unhappy and afraid: *Don't look so worried!* ◇ **~ about sb/sth** *I'm not worried about her—she can take care of herself.* ◇ *Doctors are worried about the possible spread of the disease.* ◇ **~ by sth** *We're not too worried by these results.* ◇ **~ (that…)** *The police are worried that the man may be armed.* ◇ *I was worried you wouldn't come.* ◇ *Where have you been? I've been* **worried sick** (= extremely worried). ◇ *Try not to* **get worried**. ◇ *She gave me a worried look.* ▸ **wor·ried·ly** *adv.*: *He glanced worriedly at his father.*

IDM **you had me ˈworried** (*informal*) used to tell sb that you were worried because you had not understood what they had said correctly: *You had me worried for a moment—I thought you were going to resign!*

wor·rier /ˈwʌriə(r); *NAmE* ˈwɜːr-/ *noun* a person who worries a lot about unpleasant things that have happened or that might happen

wor·ri·some /ˈwʌrisəm; *NAmE* ˈwɜːr-/ *adj.* (*especially NAmE*) that makes you worry

worry 0-w /ˈwʌri; *NAmE* ˈwɜːri/ *verb, noun*

■ ***verb*** (**wor·ries, worry·ing, wor·ried, wor·ried**) **1** 0-w [I] to keep thinking about unpleasant things that might happen or about problems that you have: ***Don't worry.*** *We have plenty of time.* ◇ **~ about sb/sth** *Don't worry about me. I'll be all right.* ◇ *He's always worrying about his weight.* ◇ **~ over sb/sth** *There's no point in worrying over things you can't change.* ◇ **~ (that)…** *I worry that I won't get into college.* **2** 0-w [T] to make sb/yourself anxious about sb/sth: **~ sb/yourself (about sb/sth)** *What worries me is how I am going to get another job.* ◇ **~ sb/yourself + adj. (about sb/sth)** *He's* ***worried himself sick*** (= become extremely anxious) *about his daughter.* ◇ **it worries sb that…** *It worries me that he hasn't come home yet.* ◇ **it worries sb to do sth** *It worried me to think what might happen.* **3** 0-w [T] to annoy or disturb sb: **~ sb** *The noise never seems to worry her.* ◇ **~ sb with sth** *Don't keep worrying him with a lot of silly questions.* **4** [T] **~ sth** (of a dog) to attack animals, especially sheep, by chasing and/or biting them

IDM **ˌnot to ˈworry** (*informal, especially BrE*) it is not important; it does not matter: *Not to worry—I can soon fix it.* ◇ *Not to worry — no harm done.*

PHR V **ˈworry at sth** **1** to bite sth and shake or pull it: *Rebecca worried at her lip.* ◇ *He began to worry at the knot in the cord.* **2** to think about a problem a lot and try and find a solution

W

Synonyms

worried

concerned • nervous • anxious • uneasy

These words all describe feeling unhappy and afraid because you are thinking about unpleasant things that might happen or might have happened.

worried thinking about unpleasant things that might happen or might have happened and therefore feeling unhappy and afraid

concerned worried and feeling concern about sth

WORRIED OR CONCERNED?

Concerned is usually used when you are talking about a problem that affects another person, society, the world, etc, while **worried** can be used for this or for more personal matters.

nervous feeling worried about sth or slightly afraid of sth

anxious feeling worried or nervous about sth

WORRIED, NERVOUS OR ANXIOUS?

Worried is the most frequent word to describe how you feel when you are thinking about a problem or something bad that might happen. **Anxious** can describe a stronger feeling and is more formal. **Nervous** is more often used to describe how you feel before you do something very important such as an exam or an interview, or something unpleasant or difficult. **Nervous** can describe sb's personality: *a very nervous girl* is often or usually nervous; *a worried girl* is worried on a particular occasion or about a particular thing. **Worried** describes her feelings, not her personality. **Anxious** may describe feelings or personality.

uneasy feeling worried or unhappy about a particular situation, especially because you think sth bad may happen or because you are not sure that what you are doing is right

PATTERNS

- worried/concerned/nervous/anxious/uneasy **about (doing)** sth
- worried/concerned/anxious **for** sb/sth
- worried/concerned/nervous/anxious **that...**
- a(n) worried/concerned/nervous/anxious/uneasy **expression/look/smile**
- to **get** worried/nervous/anxious

■ ***noun*** (*pl.* -ies) **1** O➡ [U] the state of worrying about sth **SYN anxiety**: *The threat of losing their jobs is a constant source of worry to them.* ◇ *to be frantic **with worry*** **2** O➡ [C] something that worries you: *family/financial worries* ◇ **~ (about/over sth)** *worries about the future* ◇ **~ (for/to sb)** *Mugging is a real worry for many old people.* ◇ *My only worry is that...*

IDM **ˈno worries!** (*informal*) it's not a problem; it's all right (often used as a reply when sb thanks you for sth)

ˈworry beads *noun* [pl.] small BEADS on a string that you move and turn in order to keep calm

worry·ing O➡ /ˈwʌriɪŋ; *NAmE* ˈwɜːr-/ *adj.* that makes you worry: *a worrying development* ◇ *It must be worrying for you not to know where he is.* ◇ *It is particularly worrying that nobody seems to be in charge.* ◇ *It's been a **worrying time** for us all.* ▶ **worry·ing·ly** *adv.*: *worryingly high levels of radiation* ◇ *Worryingly, the plan contains few details on how spending will be cut.*

worry·wart /ˈwʌriwɔːt; *NAmE* ˈwɜːriwɔːrt/ *noun* (*NAmE, informal*) a person who worries about unimportant things

wors /vɔːs; *NAmE* vɔːrs/ *noun* [U] (*SAfrE*) SAUSAGE

worse O➡ /wɜːs; *NAmE* wɜːrs/ *adj., adv., noun*

■ ***adj.*** (comparative of *bad*) **1** O➡ of poorer quality or lower standard; less good or more unpleasant: *The rooms were awful and the food was worse.* ◇ *The weather **got worse** during the day.* ◇ *I've been to **far worse** places.* ◇ **~ than sth** *The interview was **much worse than** he had expected.* ◇ **~ than doing sth** ***There's nothing worse than** going out in the cold with wet hair.* **2** O➡ **~ (than sth/doing sth)** more serious or severe: *They were trying to prevent an **even worse** tragedy.* ◇ *The crisis was getting **worse and worse**.* ◇ *Don't tell her that—you'll only **make things worse**.* ◇ *Never mind—it **could be worse*** (= although the situation is bad, it is not as bad as it might have been). **3** O➡ [not before noun] more ill/sick or unhappy: *If he gets any worse we'll call the doctor.* ◇ *He told her she'd let them down and she felt **worse than ever**.*

IDM **come off ˈworse** to lose a fight, competition, etc. or suffer more compared with others **go from ˌbad to ˈworse** (of a bad condition, situation, etc.) to get even worse **ˌworse ˈluck!** (*BrE, informal*) used to show that you are disappointed about sth: *I shall have to miss the party, worse luck!* ➲ more at BARK *n.*, FATE *n.*

■ ***adv.*** (comparative of *badly*) **1** O➡ **~ (than sth)** less well: *I didn't do it very well, but, if anything, he did it worse than I did.* **2** O➡ **~ (than sth)** more seriously or severely: *It's raining worse than ever.* **3** O➡ **~ (than sth)** used to introduce a statement about sth that is more serious or unpleasant than things already mentioned: *She'd lost her job. Even worse, she'd lost her house and her children, too.*

IDM **be ˌworse ˈoff (than sb/sth)** O➡ to be poorer, unhappier, etc. than before or than sb else: *The increase in taxes means that we'll be £30 a month worse off than before.* **you can/could do worse than do sth** used to say that you think sth is a good idea: *If you want a safe investment, you could do a lot worse than put your money in a building society.*

■ ***noun*** [U] more problems or bad news: *I'm afraid there is worse to come.*

IDM **be none the ˈworse (for sth)** to not be harmed by sth: *The kids were none the worse for their adventure.* **the ˌworse for ˈwear** (*informal*) **1** in a poor condition because of being used a lot **2** drunk ➲ more at BETTER *n.*, CHANGE *n.*

worsen /ˈwɜːsn; *NAmE* ˈwɜːrsn/ *verb* [I, T] to become or make sth worse than it was before **SYN deteriorate**: *The political situation is steadily worsening.* ◇ *Her health has worsened considerably since we last saw her.* ◇ **~ sth** *Staff shortages were worsened by the flu epidemic.* ▶ **worsen·ing** *noun* [sing.]: *a worsening of the international debt crisis* **worsen·ing** *adj.*: *worsening weather conditions*

wor·ship O➡ /ˈwɜːʃɪp; *NAmE* ˈwɜːrʃɪp/ *noun, verb*

■ ***noun*** **1** O➡ [U] the practice of showing respect for God or a god, by saying prayers, singing with others, etc; a ceremony for this: ***an act/a place of worship*** ◇ *ancestor worship* ◇ *morning worship* (= a church service in the morning) **2** [U] a strong feeling of love and respect for sb/sth **SYN adoration** ➲ see also HERO WORSHIP **3 His, Your, etc. Worship** [C] (*BrE, formal*) a polite way of addressing or referring to a MAGISTRATE or MAYOR

■ ***verb*** (-pp-, *NAmE* also -p-) **1** O➡ [T] **~ sb/sth** to show respect for God or a god, especially by saying prayers, singing, etc. with other people in a religious building ➲ COLLOCATIONS at RELIGION **2** O➡ [I] to go to a service in a religious building: *We worship at St Mary's.* ◇ *He worshipped at the local mosque.* **3** O➡ [T] **~ sb/sth** to love and admire sb very much, especially so much that you cannot see their faults: *She worships her children.* ◇ *He worshipped her from afar* (= he loved her but did not tell her his feelings). ◇ *She **worships the ground he walks on**.*

wor·ship·ful /ˈwɜːʃɪpfl; *NAmE* ˈwɜːrʃ-/ *adj.* [only before noun] **1** (*formal*) showing or feeling respect and admiration for sb/sth **2 Worshipful** used in Britain in the titles of some MAYORS and some groups of CRAFTSMEN: *the Worshipful Company of Goldsmiths*

wor·ship·per (*NAmE* also **wor·ship·er**) /ˈwɜːʃɪpə(r); *NAmE* ˈwɜːrʃ-/ *noun* a person who worships God or a god: *regular worshippers at St Andrew's Church* ◇ (*figurative*) *sun worshippers lying on the beach*

worst O➡ /wɜːst; *NAmE* wɜːrst/ *adj., adv., noun, verb*

■ ***adj.*** O➡ (superlative of *bad*) of the poorest quality or lowest standard; worse than any other person or thing of a similar kind: *It was **by far the worst** speech he had ever made.* ◇

W

What's the worst thing that could happen? ◇ What she said confirmed my **worst fears** (= proved they were right).

IDM **be your ˌown worst ˈenemy** to be the cause of your own problems **come off ˈworst** to lose a fight, competition, etc. or suffer more compared with others

■ ***adv.*** (superlative of *badly*) most badly or seriously: *He was voted the worst dressed celebrity.* ◇ *Manufacturing industry was worst affected by the fuel shortage.* ◇ ***Worst of all***, *I lost the watch my father had given me.*

■ ***noun*** **the worst** [sing.] the most serious or unpleasant thing that could happen; the part, situation, possibility, etc. that is worse than any other: *The worst of the storm was over.* ◇ *When they did not hear from her, they **feared the worst**.* ◇ ***The worst of it** is that I can't even be sure if they received my letter.* ◇ *He was always optimistic, even when things were **at their worst**.*

IDM **at (the) ˈworst** used for saying what is the worst thing that can happen: *At the very worst, he'll have to pay a fine.* **bring out the ˈworst in sb** to make sb show their worst qualities: *Pressure can bring out the worst in people.* **do your ˈworst** (of a person) to do as much damage or be as unpleasant as possible: *Let them do their worst—we'll fight them every inch of the way.* **get the ˈworst of it** to be defeated: *He'd been in a fight and had obviously got the worst of it.* **if the ˌworst comes to the ˈworst** (*NAmE* also **if ˌworst comes to ˈworst**) if the situation becomes too difficult or dangerous: *If the worst comes to the worst, we'll just have to sell the house.* **the worst of ˈall (possible) worlds** all the disadvantages of every situation

■ ***verb*** **~ sb** (*old-fashioned* or *formal*) [usually passive] to defeat sb in a fight, a contest or an argument SYN **get the better of**

ˈworst-case *adj.* [only before noun] involving the worst situation that could happen: *In the **worst-case scenario** more than ten thousand people might be affected.*

worst·ed /ˈwʊstɪd/ *noun* [U] a type of cloth made of wool with a smooth surface, used for making clothes: *a grey worsted suit*

worth /wɜːθ; *NAmE* wɜːrθ/ *adj., noun*

■ ***adj.*** [not before noun] (used like a preposition, followed by a noun, pronoun or number, or by the *-ing* form of a verb) **1** **~ sth** having a value in money, etc: *Our house is worth about £100 000.* ◇ *How much is this painting worth?* ◇ *to be **worth a bomb/packet/fortune*** (= a lot of money) ◇ *It isn't worth much.* ◇ *If you answer this question correctly, it's worth five points.* ➲ SYNONYMS at PRICE **2** used to recommend the action mentioned because you think it may be useful, enjoyable, etc.: **~ sth** *The museum is certainly worth a visit.* ◇ **~ doing sth** *This idea is **well worth** considering.* ◇ *It's worth making an appointment before you go.* **3** **~ sth/doing sth** important, good or enjoyable enough to make sb feel satisfied, especially when difficulty or effort is involved: *Was it worth the effort?* ◇ *The new house really wasn't worth all the expense involved.* ◇ *The job involves a lot of hard work but **it's worth it**.* ◇ *The trip was expensive but it was **worth every penny**.* ➲ see also WORTHWHILE **4** **~ sth** (of a person) having money and possessions of a particular value: *He's worth £10 million.*

IDM **for ˌall sb/it is ˈworth** **1** with great energy, effort and determination: *He was rowing for all he was worth.* **2** in order to get as much as you can from sb/sth: *She is milking her success for all it's worth.* **for ˌwhat it's ˈworth** (*informal*) used to emphasize that what you are saying is only your own opinion or suggestion and may not be very helpful: *I prefer this colour, for what it's worth.* **(the game is) not worth the ˈcandle** (*old-fashioned, saying*) the advantages to be gained from doing sth are not great enough, considering the effort or cost involved **not worth the paper it's ˈwritten/ˈprinted on** (of an agreement or official document) having no value, especially legally, or because one of the people involved has no intention of doing what they said they would **ˌworth your/its ˈsalt** deserving respect, especially because you do your job well: *Any teacher worth her salt knows that.* **ˌworth your/its ˌweight in ˈgold** very useful or valuable: *A good mechanic is worth his weight in gold.* **ˌworth sb's ˈwhile** interesting or useful for sb to do: *It will be worth your while to come to the meeting.* ◇ *He'll do the job if you **make it worth his while*** (= pay him well). ➲ more at BIRD, JOB

■ ***noun*** [U] **1** **ten dollars', £40, etc. ~ of sth** an amount of sth that has the value mentioned: *The winner will receive ten pounds' worth of books.* ◇ *a dollar's worth of change* **2** **a week's, month's, etc. ~ of sth** an amount of sth that lasts a week, etc. **3** the financial, practical or moral value of sb/sth: *Their contribution was of great worth.* ◇ *The activities help children to develop a sense of their own worth.* ◇ *A good interview enables candidates to prove their worth* (= show how good they are). ◇ *a personal net worth of $10 million*

IDM see CENT *n.*, MONEY

worth·less /ˈwɜːθləs; *NAmE* ˈwɜːrθ-/ *adj.* **1** having no practical or financial value: *Critics say his paintings are worthless.* OPP **valuable** **2** (of a person) having no good qualities or useful skills: *a worthless individual* ◇ *Constant rejections made him feel worthless.* ▸ **worth·less·ness** *noun* [U]: *a sense of worthlessness*

worth·while /ˌwɜːθˈwaɪl; *NAmE* ˌwɜːrθ-/ *adj.* important, enjoyable, interesting, etc; worth spending time, money or effort on: *It was in aid of a **worthwhile cause*** (= a charity, etc.) ◇ *The smile on her face made it all worthwhile.* ◇ **~ for sb to do sth** *High prices in the UK **make it worthwhile** for buyers to look abroad.* ◇ **~ to do sth** ***It is worthwhile to** include really high-quality illustrations.* ◇ **~ doing sth** *It didn't seem worthwhile writing it all out again.* HELP This word can be written **worth while**, except when it is used before a noun.

worthy /ˈwɜːði; *NAmE* ˈwɜːrði/ *adj., noun*

■ ***adj.*** (**wor·thier**, **wor·thi·est**) **1** **~ (of sb/sth)** (*formal*) having the qualities that deserve sb/sth: *to be worthy of attention* ◇ *A number of the report's findings are **worthy of note**.* ◇ *No composer was considered worthy of the name until he had written an opera.* ◇ *a worthy champion* (= one who deserved to win) ◇ *He felt he was not worthy of her.* OPP **unworthy** **2** [usually before noun] having qualities that deserve your respect, attention or admiration SYN **deserving**: *The money we raise will be going to a very **worthy cause**.* ◇ *a worthy member of the team* **3** having good qualities but not very interesting or exciting: *her worthy but dull husband* **4** **~ of sb/sth** typical of what a particular person or thing might do, give, etc: *He gave a speech that was worthy of Martin Luther King.* **5** **-worthy** (in compounds) deserving, or suitable for, the thing mentioned: *trustworthy* ◇ *roadworthy* ▸ **wor·thily** /-ɪli/ *adv.* **worthi·ness** *noun* [U]

■ ***noun*** (*pl.* **-ies**) (often *humorous*) an important person: *a meeting attended by local worthies*

wot (*BrE, non-standard*, often *humorous*) a way of writing 'what', used to show that sb is speaking very informal English: *'Wot's going on?' he shouted.*

wotcha /ˈwɒtʃə; *NAmE* ˈwɑːtʃə/ *exclamation* (*BrE, informal*) used as a friendly way of saying hello to a person: *Wotcha Dave—thanks for coming.*

would / *strong form* wʊd; *weak form* wəd; əd/ *modal verb* (*short form* **'d** /d/, *negative* **would not**, *short form* **wouldn't** /ˈwʊdnt/)

1 used as the past form of *will* when reporting what sb has said or thought: *He said he would be here at eight o'clock* (= His words were: 'I will be there at eight o'clock.'). ◇ *She asked if I would help.* ◇ *They told me that they probably wouldn't come.* **2** used for talking about the result of an event that you imagine: *She'd look better with shorter hair.* ◇ *If you went to see him, he would be delighted.* ◇ *Hurry up! It would be a shame to miss the beginning of the play.* ◇ *She'd be a fool to accept it* (= if she accepted). **3** used for describing a possible action or event that did not in fact happen, because sth else did not happen first: *If I had seen the advertisement in time I would have applied for the job.* ◇ *They would never have met if she hadn't gone to Emma's party.* **4** **so that/in order that sb/sth ~** used for saying why sb does sth: *She burned the letters so that her husband would never read them.* **5** **wish (that) sb/sth ~** used for saying what you want to happen: *I wish you'd be quiet for a minute.* **6** used to show that sb/sth was not willing or refused to do sth: *She wouldn't change it, even though she* *knew it was wrong.* ◇ *My car wouldn't start this morning.* **7** 🔑 used to ask sb politely to do sth: ***Would you mind*** *leaving us alone for a few minutes?* ◇ *Would you open the door for me, please?* **8** 🔑 used in polite offers or invitations: ***Would you like*** *a sandwich?* ◇ *Would you have dinner with me on Friday?* **9** 🔑 **~ like, love, hate, prefer, etc. sth/(sb) to do sth | ~ rather do sth/sb did sth** used to say what you like, love, hate, etc.: *I'd love a coffee.* ◇ *I'd be only too glad to help.* ◇ *I'd hate you to think I was criticizing you.* ◇ *I'd rather come with you.* ◇ *I'd rather you came with us.* **10** 🔑 **~ imagine, say, think, etc. (that)...** used to give opinions that you are not certain about: *I would imagine the job will take about two days.* ◇ *I'd say he was about fifty.* **11** 🔑 **I would...** used to give advice: ***I wouldn't*** *have any more to drink,* ***if I were you.*** **12** 🔑 used for talking about things that often happened in the past SYN **used to**: *When my parents were away, my grandmother would take care of me.* ◇ *He'd always be the first to offer to help.* **13** (usually *disapproving*) used for talking about behaviour that you think is typical: *'She said it was your fault.' 'Well,* ***she would say that, wouldn't she?*** *She's never liked me.'* **14 ~ that...** (*literary*) used to express a strong wish: *Would that he had lived to see it.* ➲ note at MODAL, SHOULD

'would-be *adj.* [only before noun] used to describe sb who is hoping to become the type of person mentioned: *a would-be actor* ◇ *advice for would-be parents*

wound[1] 🔑 /wu:nd/ *noun, verb* ➲ see also WOUND[2]

■ ***noun*** **1** 🔑 an injury to part of the body, especially one in which a hole is made in the skin using a weapon: *a* ***leg/head, etc. wound*** ◇ *a* ***bullet/knife/gunshot/stab wound*** ◇ *an old* ***war wound*** ◇ *The nurse* ***cleaned the wound.*** ◇ *The* ***wound healed*** *slowly.* ◇ *He died from the wounds he had received to his chest.* ➲ SYNONYMS at INJURE ➲ COLLOCATIONS at INJURY ➲ see also FLESH WOUND **2** 🔑 mental or emotional pain caused by sth unpleasant that has been said or done to you: *After a serious argument, it can take some time for the wounds to heal.* ◇ *Seeing him again* ***opened up old wounds.*** IDM see LICK *v.*, REOPEN, RUB *v.*

■ ***verb*** [often passive] **1** 🔑 **~ sb/sth** to injure part of the body, especially by making a hole in the skin using a weapon: *He had been wounded in the arm.* **2** 🔑 **~ sb** to hurt sb's feelings: *She felt* ***deeply wounded*** *by his cruel remarks.*

wound[2] /waʊnd/ *past tense, past part.* of WIND ➲ see also WOUND[1]

wound·ed 🔑 /'wu:ndɪd/ *adj.*

1 🔑 injured by a weapon, for example in a war: *wounded soldiers* ◇ ***seriously wounded*** ◇ *There were 79 killed and 230 wounded.* **2** feeling emotional pain because of sth unpleasant that sb has said or done: *wounded pride* **3 the wounded** *noun* [pl.] people who are wounded, for example in a war

wound·ing /'wu:ndɪŋ/ *adj.* that hurts sb's feelings: *He found her remarks deeply wounding.*

wove *past tense* of WEAVE

woven *past part.* of WEAVE

wow /waʊ/ *exclamation, verb, noun*

■ ***exclamation*** (also **wowee** /ˌwaʊ'i:/) (*informal*) used to express great surprise or admiration: *Wow! You look terrific!*

■ ***verb*** **~ sb (with sth)** (*informal*) to impress sb very much, especially with a performance: *He wowed audiences around the country with his new show.*

■ ***noun*** **1** [sing.] (*informal*) a great success: *Don't worry. You'll be a wow.* **2** [U] (*technical*) gradual changes in the PITCH of sound played on a record or tape ➲ compare FLUTTER

'wow factor *noun* [sing.] (*informal*) the quality sth has of being very impressive or surprising to people: *If you want to sell your house quickly, it needs a wow factor.*

wow·ser /'waʊzə(r)/ *noun* (*AustralE, NZE, informal*) **1** a person who criticizes people who are enjoying themselves SYN **killjoy** **2** a person who does not drink alcohol SYN **teetotaller**

WPC /ˌdʌblju: pi: 'si:/ *noun* (*BrE*) the abbreviation for 'woman police constable' (a woman police officer of the lowest rank): *WPC (Linda) Green*

wpm *abbr.* words per minute: *to type at 60 wpm*

WRAC /ræk; ˌdʌblju: ɑ:r eɪ 'si:/ *abbr.* (in Britain) Women's Royal Army Corps

wrack = RACK *v.*

WRAF /ræf; ˌdʌblju: ɑ:r eɪ 'ef/ *abbr.* (in Britain) Women's Royal Air Force

wraith /reɪθ/ *noun* the GHOST of a person that is seen a short time before or after that person dies SYN **spectre**: *a wraith-like figure* (= a very thin, pale person)

wran·gle /'ræŋgl/ *noun, verb*

■ ***noun*** **~ (with sb)(over sth) | ~ (between A and B)** an argument that is complicated and continues over a long period of time: *a legal wrangle between the company and their suppliers* ▸ **wran·gling** *noun* [U, C]

■ ***verb*** [I] **~ (with sb) (over/about sth)** to argue angrily and usually for a long time about sth: *They're still wrangling over the financial details.*

wran·gler /'ræŋglə(r)/ *noun* (*NAmE, informal*) a COWBOY or a COWGIRL, especially one who takes care of horses

wrap 🔑 /ræp/ *verb, noun*

■ ***verb*** (-pp-) **1** 🔑 [T] **~ sth (up) (in sth)** to cover sth completely in paper or other material, for example when you are giving it as a present: *He spent the evening wrapping up the Christmas presents.* ◇ *individually wrapped chocolates* ➲ see also GIFT-WRAP **2** 🔑 [T] to cover sth/sb in material, for example in order to protect it/them: **~ A (up) in B** *Wrap the meat in foil before you cook it.* ◇ *I wrapped the baby (up) in a blanket.* ◇ **~ B round/around A** *I wrapped a blanket around the baby.* ➲ see also SHRINK-WRAPPED **3** 🔑 [T] **~ sth around/round sth/sb** to put sth firmly around sth/sb: *A scarf was wrapped around his neck.* ◇ *His arms were wrapped around her waist.* **4** [T, I] (*computing*) to cause text to be carried over to a new line automatically as you reach the end of the previous line; to be carried over in this way: **~ sth (around/round)** *How can I wrap the text around?* ◇ **~ (around/round)** *The text wraps around if it is too long to fit the screen.* ➲ compare UNWRAP

IDM **be ˌwrapped 'up in sb/sth** to be so involved with sb/sth that you do not pay enough attention to other people or things SYN **absorbed**, **engrossed** ➲ more at LITTLE FINGER

PHR V **ˌwrap 'up | ˌwrap it 'up** (*slang*) usually used as an order to tell sb to stop talking or causing trouble, etc. **ˌwrap 'up | ˌwrap sb/yourself 'up** to put warm clothes on sb/yourself: *She told them to* ***wrap up warm/warmly.*** **ˌwrap sth↔'up** (*informal*) to complete sth such as an agreement or a meeting in an acceptable way: *That just about wraps it up for today.*

■ ***noun*** **1** [C] a piece of cloth that a woman wears around her shoulders for decoration or to keep warm **2** [U] paper, plastic, etc. that is used for wrapping things in: *We stock a wide range of cards and* ***gift wrap.*** ➲ see also PLASTIC WRAP **3** [sing.] used when making a film/movie to say that filming has finished: *Cut! That's a wrap.* **4** [C] a type of SANDWICH made with a cold TORTILLA rolled around meat or vegetables

IDM **under 'wraps** (*informal*) being kept secret until some time in the future: *Next year's collection is still being kept under wraps.*

'wrap-around *adj.* **1** curving or stretching round at the sides: *wrap-around sunglasses* **2** (of a piece of clothing) having one part that is pulled over to cover another part at the front and then loosely fastened: *a wrap-around skirt*

wrap·arounds /'ræpəraʊndz/ *noun* [pl.] a pair of SUNGLASSES that fit closely and curve round the sides of the head

wrapped /ræpt/ *adj.* (*AustralE, informal*) extremely pleased: *The minister declared that he was wrapped.*

wrap·per /'ræpə(r)/ *noun* **1** a piece of paper, plastic, etc. that is wrapped around sth, especially food, when you buy it in order to protect it and keep it clean: (*BrE*) *sweet wrappers* ◇ (*NAmE*) *candy wrappers* **2** (*WAfrE*) a piece of cloth that is worn as an item of clothing around the waist and legs

W

wrap·ping 0-w /'ræpɪŋ/ *noun* [U] (also **wrappings** [pl.]) paper, plastic, etc. used for covering sth in order to protect it: *She tore the cellophane wrapping off the box.* ◇ *shrink wrapping* (= plastic designed to SHRINK around objects so that it fits them tightly) ◇ *The painting was still in its wrappings.*

'wrapping paper *noun* [U] coloured paper used for wrapping presents: *a* ***piece/sheet/roll of wrapping paper***

wrasse /ræs/ *noun* (*pl.* wrasse or wrasses) a sea fish with thick lips and strong teeth

wrath /rɒθ; *NAmE* ræθ/ *noun* [U] (*old-fashioned* or *formal*) extreme anger: *the wrath of God* ▶ **wrath·ful** /-fl/ *adj.* **wrath·ful·ly** *adv.*

wreak /ri:k/ *verb* **~ sth** (**on sb**) (*formal*) to do great damage or harm to sb/sth: *Their policies would* ***wreak havoc*** *on the economy.* ◇ *He swore to* ***wreak vengeance*** *on those who had betrayed him.*

wreath /ri:θ/ *noun* (*pl.* wreaths /ri:ðz/) **1** an arrangement of flowers and leaves, especially in the shape of a circle, placed on graves, etc. as a sign of respect for sb who has died: *The Queen* ***laid a wreath*** *at the war memorial.* **2** an arrangement of flowers and/or leaves in the shape of a circle, traditionally hung on doors as a decoration at Christmas: *a holly wreath* **3** a circle of flowers or leaves worn on the head, and used in the past as a sign of honour: *a laurel wreath* **4** (*literary*) a circle of smoke, cloud, etc.

wreathe /ri:ð/ *verb* (*formal*) **1** [T, usually passive] **~ sth** (**in/with sth**) to surround or cover sth: *The mountain tops were wreathed in mist.* ◇ (*figurative*) *Her face was* ***wreathed in smiles*** (= she was smiling a lot). **2** [I] **+ adv./prep.** to move slowly and lightly, especially in circles SYN **weave**: *smoke wreathing into the sky*

wreck /rek/ *noun, verb*

■ ***noun*** **1** a ship that has sunk or that has been very badly damaged ➲ see also SHIPWRECK **2** a car, plane, etc. that has been very badly damaged in an accident: *Two passengers are still trapped in the wreck.* ➲ SYNONYMS at CRASH **3** [usually sing.] (*informal*) a person who is in a bad physical or mental condition: *Physically, I was a total wreck.* ◇ *The interview reduced him to* ***a nervous wreck.*** **4** (*informal*) a vehicle, building, etc. that is in very bad condition: *The house was a wreck when we bought it.* ◇ (*figurative*) *They still hoped to salvage something from the wreck of their marriage.* **5** (*NAmE*) = CRASH: ***a car/train wreck***

■ ***verb*** **1 ~ sth** to damage or destroy sth: *The building had been wrecked by the explosion.* ◇ *The road was littered with wrecked cars.* **2 ~ sth** (**for sb**) to spoil sth completely: *The weather wrecked all our plans.* ◇ *A serious injury nearly wrecked his career.* **3** [usually passive] **~ sth** to damage a ship so much that it sinks or can no longer sail: *The ship was wrecked off the coast of France.* ➲ see also SHIPWRECK

wreck·age /'rekɪdʒ/ *noun* [U] the parts of a vehicle, building, etc. that remain after it has been badly damaged or destroyed: *A few survivors were pulled from the wreckage.* ◇ *Pieces of wreckage were found ten miles away from the scene of the explosion.* ◇ (*figurative*) *Could nothing be rescued from the wreckage of her dreams?*

wrecked /rekt/ *adj.* **1** [only before noun] having been wrecked: *a wrecked ship/marriage* **2** [not before noun] (*BrE, slang*) very drunk

wreck·er /'rekə(r)/ *noun* **1** a person who ruins another person's plans, relationship, etc. **2** (*NAmE*) a vehicle used for moving other vehicles that have been damaged in an accident

'wrecking ball *noun* a heavy metal ball that swings from a CRANE and is used to hit a building to make it fall down

wren /ren/ *noun* a very small brown bird

wrench /rentʃ/ *verb, noun*

■ ***verb*** **1** [T, I] to pull or twist sth/sb/yourself suddenly and violently SYN **jerk**: **~ (sth/sb/yourself) + adv./prep.** *The bag was wrenched from her grasp.* ◇ *He grabbed Ben, wrenching him away from his mother.* ◇ (*figurative*) *Guy wrenched his mind back to the present.* ◇ **~ (sth/sb/yourself) + adj.** *They wrenched the door open.* ◇ *She managed to wrench herself free.* **2** [T] **~ sth** to twist and injure a part of your body, especially your ankle or shoulder SYN **twist**: *She wrenched her knee when she fell.* **3** [T, I] (*formal*) to make sb feel great pain or unhappiness, especially so that they make a sound or cry: **~ (sth) (from sb)** *His words wrenched a sob from her.* ◇ *a wrenching experience* ◇ **~ at sth** *Her words wrenched at my heart.* ➲ see also GUT-WRENCHING

■ ***noun*** **1** (*especially NAmE*) (*BrE* usually **span·ner**) [C] a metal tool with a specially shaped end for holding and turning things, including one which can be adjusted to fit objects of different sizes, also called a MONKEY WRENCH or an ADJUSTABLE SPANNER ➲ VISUAL VOCAB page V17 **2** [sing.] pain or unhappiness that you feel when you have to leave a person or place that you love: *Leaving home was a terrible wrench for me.* **3** [C, usually sing.] a sudden and violent twist or pull: *She stumbled and gave her ankle a painful wrench.*

IDM **throw a 'wrench in/into sth** (*NAmE, informal*) = THROW A MONKEY WRENCH IN/INTO STH

wrest /rest/ *verb*

PHR V **'wrest sth from sb/sth** (*formal*) **1** to take sth such as power or control from sb/sth with great effort: *They attempted to* ***wrest control*** *of the town from government forces.* **2** to take sth from sb that they do not want to give, suddenly or violently SYN **wrench**: *He wrested the gun from my grasp.*

wres·tle /'resl/ *verb* **1** [I, T] to fight sb by holding them and trying to throw or force them to the ground, sometimes as a sport: *As a boy he had boxed and wrestled.* ◇ **~ with sb** *Armed guards wrestled with the intruder.* ◇ **~ sb (+ adv./prep.)** *Shoppers wrestled the raider to the ground.* **2** [I, T] to struggle to deal with sth that is difficult SYN **battle, grapple**: **~ (with) sth** *She had spent the whole weekend wrestling with the problem.* ◇ *He wrestled with the controls as the plane plunged.* ◇ **~ to do sth** *She has been wrestling to raise the money all year.*

wrest·ler /'reslə(r)/ *noun* a person who takes part in the sport of wrestling

wrest·ling /'reslɪŋ/ *noun* [U] a sport in which two people fight by holding each other and trying to throw or force the other one to the ground

wretch /retʃ/ *noun* **1** a person that you feel sympathy or pity for: *a poor wretch* **2** (often *humorous*) an evil, unpleasant or annoying person

wretch·ed /'retʃɪd/ *adj.* **1** (of a person) feeling ill/sick or unhappy: *You look wretched—what's wrong?* ◇ *I felt wretched about the way things had turned out.* **2** (*formal*) extremely bad or unpleasant SYN **awful**: *She had a wretched time of it at school.* ◇ *The animals are kept in the most wretched conditions.* **3** (*formal*) making you feel sympathy or pity SYN **pitiful**: *She finally agreed to have the wretched animal put down.* **4** [only before noun] (*informal*) used to show that you think that sb/sth is extremely annoying: *Is it that wretched woman again?* ▶ **wretch·ed·ly** *adv.* **wretch·ed·ness** *noun* [U]

wrig·gle /'rɪgl/ *verb, noun*

■ ***verb*** **1** [I, T] to twist and turn your body or part of it with quick short movements SYN **wiggle**: **~ (about/around)** *The baby was wriggling around on my lap.* ◇ **~ sth** *She wriggled her toes.* **2** [I, T] to move somewhere by twisting and turning your body or part of it SYN **squirm**: **(+ adv./prep.)** *The fish wriggled out of my fingers.* ◇ **+ adj.** *She managed to wriggle free.* ◇ **~ your way/yourself + adv./prep.** *They wriggled their way through the tunnel.*

PHR V **,wriggle 'out of sth/out of doing sth** (*informal, disapproving*) to avoid doing sth that you should do, especially by thinking of clever excuses: *He tried desperately to wriggle out of giving a clear answer.*

■ ***noun*** [usually sing.] an act of wriggling

wring /rɪŋ/ *verb* (wrung, wrung /rʌŋ/) **1 ~ sth (out)** to twist and squeeze clothes, etc. in order to get the water out of them ➲ picture at SQUEEZE **2 ~ sth** if you **wring** a bird's neck, you twist it in order to kill the bird

IDM **,wring sb's 'hand** to squeeze sb's hand very tightly

when you shake hands ˌ**wring your ˈhands** to hold your hands together, and twist and squeeze them in a way that shows you are anxious or upset, especially when you cannot change the situation ˌ**wring sb's ˈneck** (*informal*) when you say that you will **wring sb's neck**, you mean that you are very angry or annoyed with them

PHR V ˈ**wring sth from/out of sb** to obtain sth from sb with difficulty, especially by putting pressure on them SYN **extract**

wring·er /ˈrɪŋə(r)/ *noun* = MANGLE

IDM **go through the ˈwringer** (*informal*) to have a difficult or unpleasant experience, or a series of them

ˌ**wringing ˈwet** *adj.* (especially of clothes) very wet

wrin·kle /ˈrɪŋkl/ *noun, verb*

■ ***noun* 1** a line or small fold in your skin, especially on your face, that forms as you get older: *There were fine wrinkles around her eyes.* ➲ COLLOCATIONS at PHYSICAL **2** [usually pl.] a small fold that you do not want in a piece of cloth or paper SYN **crease**

■ ***verb* 1** [T, I] to make the skin on your face form into lines or folds; to form lines or folds in this way: **~ sth (up)** *She wrinkled up her nose in distaste.* ◇ *He wrinkled his brow in concentration.* ◇ **~ (up)** *His face wrinkled in a grin.* **2** [I, T] **~ (sth)** to form raised folds or lines in an untidy way; to make sth do this: *Her stockings were wrinkling at the knees.*

wrin·kled /ˈrɪŋkld/ *adj.* (of skin, clothing, etc.) having wrinkles

wrink·ling /ˈrɪŋklɪŋ/ *noun* [U] the process by which WRINKLES form in the skin

wrin·kly /ˈrɪŋkli/ *adj., noun*

■ ***adj.*** (*informal*) (of skin, clothing, etc.) having WRINKLES

■ ***noun*** (*pl.* **-ies**) (*BrE, informal*) an offensive word for an old person, used by younger people

wrist 0-w /rɪst/ *noun*

the joint between the hand and the arm: *She's broken her wrist.* ◇ *He wore a copper bracelet* ***on his wrist.*** ➲ VISUAL VOCAB page V48 IDM see SLAP *n.*

wrist·band /ˈrɪstbænd/ *noun* a strip of material worn around the wrist, as a decoration, to absorb sweat during exercise, or to show support for sth: *He was wearing an anti-racism wristband.*

wrist·watch /ˈrɪstwɒtʃ; *NAmE* -wɑːtʃ/ *noun* a watch that you wear on your wrist

writ /rɪt/ *noun, verb*

■ ***noun* ~ (for sth) (against sb)** a legal document from a court telling sb to do or not to do sth: *The company has been* ***served with a writ*** *for breach of contract.* ◇ *We fully intend to* ***issue a writ*** *against the newspaper.* ➲ see also HOLY WRIT

■ ***verb*** (*old use*) *past part.* of WRITE

IDM ˌ**writ ˈlarge** (*literary*) **1** easy to see or understand: *Mistrust was writ large on her face.* **2** (used after a noun) being a large or obvious example of the thing mentioned: *This is deception writ large.*

write 0-w /raɪt/ *verb* (**wrote** /rəʊt; *NAmE* roʊt/, **writ·ten** /ˈrɪtn/)

▸ LETTERS/NUMBERS **1** 0-w [I, T] to make letters or numbers on a surface, especially using a pen or a pencil: *In some countries children don't start learning to* ***read and write*** *until they are six.* ◇ **~ in/on/with sth** *Please write in pen on both sides of the paper.* ◇ *I haven't got anything to write with.* ◇ **~ sth** *Write your name at the top of the paper.* ◇ *The teacher wrote the answers on the board.* ◇ *The 'b' had been wrongly written as a 'd'.*

▸ BOOK/MUSIC/PROGRAM **2** 0-w [T, I] to produce sth in written form so that people can read, perform or use it, etc: **~ sth** *to write a novel/a song/an essay/a computer program, etc.* ◇ *Who was 'The Grapes of Wrath' written by?* ◇ *Which opera did Verdi write first?* ◇ **~ sth about/on sth** *He hopes to write a book about his experiences one day.* ◇ *She had to write a report on the project.* ◇ **~ (about sth)** *I wanted to travel and then write about it.* ◇ *He writes for the 'New Yorker'* (= works as a writer). ◇ *No decision has been made* ***at the time of writing.*** ◇ **~ sb sth** *She wrote him several poems.*

▸ A LETTER **3** 0-w [I, T] to put information, a message of good wishes, etc. in a letter and send it to sb: *Bye! Don't forget to write.* ◇ *Can you write and confirm your booking?* ◇ *I'm writing to enquire about language courses.* ◇ **~ to sb** *She wrote to him in France.* ◇ **~ sth (to sb)** *I wrote a letter to the Publicity Department.* ◇ **~ sb sth** *I wrote the Publicity Department a letter.* ◇ **~ that...** *She wrote that they were all fine.* ◇ **~ sb** (*NAmE*) *Write me while you're away.* ◇ **~ sb that...** (*NAmE*) *He wrote me that he would be arriving Monday.* ◇ **~ doing sth** *They wrote thanking us for the present.*

▸ STATE IN WRITING **4** 0-w [T, I] to state the information or the words mentioned: **~ that...** *In his latest book he writes that the theory has since been disproved.* ◇ **~ of sth** *Ancient historians wrote of a lost continent beneath the ocean.* ◇ **+ speech** *'Of all my books,' wrote Dickens, 'I like this the best.'*

▸ CHEQUE/FORM **5** 0-w [T] to put information in the appropriate places on a cheque or other form: **~ sth (out)** *to write out a cheque* ◇ **~ sb (out) sth** *I'll write you a receipt.*

▸ COMPUTING **6** [T, I] **~ (sth) to/onto sth** to record data in the memory of a computer: *An error was reported when he tried to write data to the file for the first time.*

▸ OF PEN/PENCIL **7** [I] to work correctly or in the way mentioned: *This pen won't write.*

IDM **be written all over sb's ˈface** (of a feeling) to be very obvious to other people from the expression on sb's face: *Guilt was written all over his face.* **have sth/sb written all ˈover it/sb** (*informal*) to show clearly the quality mentioned or the influence of the person mentioned: *It was a performance with star quality written all over it.* ◇ *This essay has got Mike written all over it.* **nothing (much) to write ˈhome about** (*informal*) not especially good; ordinary **that's all she ˈwrote** (*NAmE, informal*) used when you are stating that there is nothing more that can be said about sth or that sth is completely finished ➲ more at WORTH *adj.*

PHR V ˌ**write aˈway** = WRITE OFF/AWAY ˌ**write ˈback (to sb)** 0-w to write sb a letter replying to their letter SYN **reply**: *I'm afraid I never wrote back.* ◇ *She wrote back saying that she couldn't come.* ˌ**write sth↔ˈdown 1** 0-w to write sth on paper, especially in order to remember or record it: *Write down the address before you forget it.* **2** (*business*) to reduce the value of ASSETS when stating it in a company's accounts ➲ related noun WRITE-DOWN ˌ**write ˈin (to sb/sth) (for sth)** to write a letter to an organization or a company, for example to ask about sth or to express an opinion: *I'll write in for more information.* ˌ**write sb/sth↔ˈin** (*NAmE, politics*) to add an extra name to your voting paper in an election in order to be able to vote for them ➲ related noun WRITE-IN ˌ**write sth ˈinto sth** to include a rule or condition in a contract or an agreement when it is made ˌ**write ˈoff/aˈway (to sb/sth) (for sth)** to write to an organization or a company, usually in order to ask them to send you sth SYN **send off**: *I've written off for the catalogue.* ˌ**write sth↔ˈoff 1** (*business*) to cancel a debt; to recognize that sth is a failure, has no value, etc: *to write off a debt/an investment* **2** (*BrE*) to damage sth, especially a vehicle, so badly that it cannot be repaired ➲ related noun WRITE-OFF ➲ see also TOTAL ˌ**write sb/sth↔ˈoff (as sth)** to decide that sb/sth is a failure or not worth paying any attention to SYN **dismiss** ˌ**write sth↔ˈout** to write sth on paper, including all the details, especially a piece of work or an account of sth ➲ see also WRITE (5) ˌ**write sb↔ˈout (of sth)** to remove a character from a regular series on television or radio ˌ**write sth↔ˈup** to record sth in writing in a full and complete form, often using notes that you made earlier: *to write up your notes/the minutes of a meeting* ➲ related noun WRITE-UP

ˈ**write-back** *noun* [C, U] (*business*) a situation where an ASSET gets a value which it was thought to have lost; an amount of money entered in the financial records because of this

ˈ**write-down** *noun* (*business*) a reduction in the value of ASSETS, etc.

ˈ**write-in** *noun* (*US*) a vote for sb who is not an official candidate in an election, in which you write their name on your BALLOT PAPER

W

ˈwrite-off *noun* **1** (*BrE*) a vehicle that has been so badly damaged in an accident that it is not worth spending money to repair it **2** [sing.] (*informal*) a period of time during which you do not achieve anything: *With meetings and phone calls, yesterday was a complete write-off.* **3 ~ (of sth)** (*business*) an act of cancelling a debt and accepting that it will never be paid

ˌwrite-proˈtect *verb* **~ sth** (*computing*) to protect the information on a computer disk from being changed or DELETED (= destroyed)

writer 0-ᴡ /ˈraɪtə(r)/ *noun*
1 0-ᴡ a person whose job is writing books, stories, articles, etc: *writers of poetry* ◇ *a* ***travel/cookery, etc. writer*** **2** 0-ᴡ a person who has written a particular thing: *the writer of this letter* **3** 0-ᴡ (with an adjective) a person who forms letters in a particular way when they are writing: *a messy writer*

ˌwriter's ˈblock *noun* [U] a problem that writers sometimes have when they cannot think of what to write and have no new ideas

ˌwriter's ˈcramp *noun* [U] a pain or stiff feeling in the hand caused by writing for a long time

ˈwrite-up *noun* an article in a newspaper or magazine in which sb writes what they think about a new book, play, product, etc.

writhe /raɪð/ *verb* [I] **~ (about/around) (in/with sth)** to twist or move your body without stopping, often because you are in great pain: *She was writhing around on the floor in agony.* ◇ *The snake writhed and hissed.* ◇ (*figurative*) *He was writhing* (= suffering a lot) *with embarrassment.*

writ·ing 0-ᴡ /ˈraɪtɪŋ/ *noun*
1 0-ᴡ [U] the activity of writing, in contrast to reading, speaking, etc: *Our son's having problems with his* ***reading and writing*** (= at school) ◇ *a* ***writing case*** (= containing paper, pens, etc.) **2** 0-ᴡ [U] the activity of writing books, articles, etc, especially as a job: *Only later did she discover a talent for writing.* ◇ *He is leaving the band to concentrate on his writing.* ◇ ***creative writing*** ◇ ***feminist/travel, etc. writing*** ➲ see also SONGWRITING **3** 0-ᴡ [U] books, articles, etc. in general: *The review is a brilliant piece of writing.* **4** 0-ᴡ **writings** [pl.] a group of pieces of writing, especially by a particular person or on a particular subject: *His experiences in India influenced his later writings.* ◇ *the writings of Hegel* **5** 0-ᴡ [U] words that have been written or painted on sth: *There was writing all over the desk.* **6** 0-ᴡ [U] the particular way in which sb forms letters when they write SYN **handwriting**: *Who's this from? I don't recognize the writing.*
IDM **in ˈwriting** 0-ᴡ in the form of a letter, document, etc. (that gives proof of sth): *All telephone reservations must be confirmed in writing.* ◇ *Could you* ***put*** *your complaint* ***in writing?*** ◇ *You must* ***get it in writing.*** **the ˌwriting is on the ˈwall | see the ˌwriting on the ˈwall** (*NAmE* also **the ˌhandwriting on the ˈwall**) (*saying*) used when you are describing a situation in which there are signs that sth is going to have problems or that it is going to be a failure: *It is amazing that not one of them saw the writing on the wall.* ORIGIN From the Bible story in which strange writing appeared on a wall during a feast given by King Belshazzar, predicting Belshazzar's death and the fall of his city.

ˈwriting paper *noun* [U] = NOTEPAPER

writ·ten 0-ᴡ /ˈrɪtn/ *adj.*
1 0-ᴡ [usually before noun] expressed in writing rather than in speech: *written instructions* **2** 0-ᴡ [usually before noun] (of an exam, a piece of work, etc.) involving writing rather than speaking or practical skills: *a written test* ◇ *written communication skills* **3** 0-ᴡ [only before noun] in the form of a letter, document, etc. and therefore official: *a written apology* ◇ *a written contract* ➲ see also WRITE *v.*
IDM **the ˌwritten ˈword** language expressed in writing rather than in speech: *the permanence of the written word*

W

Synonyms

wrong

false • mistaken • incorrect • inaccurate • misguided • untrue

These words all describe sth that is not right or correct, or sb who is not right about sth.

wrong not right or correct; (of a person) not right about sb/sth: *I got all the answers wrong.* ◇ *We were wrong to assume she'd agree.*

false not true or correct; wrong because it is based on sth that is not true or correct: *A whale is a fish.* ***True or false?*** ◇ *She gave false information to the insurance company.*

mistaken wrong in your opinion or judgement; based on a wrong opinion or bad judgement: *You're completely mistaken about Jane.*

incorrect (*rather formal*) wrong according to the facts; containing mistakes: *Many of the figures were incorrect.*

inaccurate wrong according to the facts; containing mistakes: *The report was badly researched and quite inaccurate.*

INCORRECT OR INACCURATE?

A fact, figure or spelling that is wrong is **incorrect**; information, a belief or a description based on incorrect facts can be **incorrect** or **inaccurate**; something that is produced, such as a film, report or map, that contains incorrect facts is **inaccurate**.

misguided wrong because you have understood or judged a situation badly: *In her misguided attempts to help, she only made the situation worse.*

untrue not based on facts, but invented or guessed: *These accusations are totally untrue.*

PATTERNS

- to be wrong/mistaken **about** sth
- wrong/false/mistaken/incorrect/inaccurate/untrue **information**
- a(n) false/mistaken/incorrect/inaccurate/misguided **belief**
- a(n) wrong/incorrect **answer**

wrong 0-ᴡ /rɒŋ; *NAmE* rɔːŋ/ *adj., adv., noun, verb*
▪ ***adj.***
▸ NOT CORRECT **1** 0-ᴡ not right or correct: *I got all the answers wrong.* ◇ *He was driving on the wrong side of the road.* ◇ *Sorry, I must have dialled the wrong number.* ◇ *You're holding the camera* ***the wrong way up!*** ◇ *That picture is* ***the wrong way round.*** OPP **right 2** 0-ᴡ [not before noun] (of a person) not right about sth/sb SYN **mistaken**: *I think she lives at number 44, but I could be wrong.* ◇ **~ (about sth/sb)** *You were wrong about Tom; he's not married after all.* ◇ **~ (to do sth)** *We were wrong to assume that she'd agree.* ◇ *She would* ***prove him wrong*** (= prove that he was wrong) *whatever happened.* ◇ (*informal*) *You think you've beaten me but* ***that's where you're wrong.*** ◇ (*informal*) ***Correct me if I'm wrong*** (= I may be wrong) *but didn't you say you two knew each other?*
▸ CAUSING PROBLEMS **3** 0-ᴡ [not before noun] causing problems or difficulties; not as it should be: *Is* ***anything wrong?*** *You look worried.* ◇ ***'What's wrong?'*** *'Oh, nothing.'* ◇ **~ with sb/sth** *There's* ***something wrong*** *with the printer.* ◇ *The doctor could find* ***nothing wrong*** *with him.* ◇ *I* ***have something wrong with*** *my foot.*
▸ NOT SUITABLE **4** 0-ᴡ [usually before noun] not suitable, right or what you need: **~ (sth) (for sth)** *He's the wrong person for the job.* ◇ **~ (sth to do)** *I realized that it was the wrong thing to say.* ◇ *We don't want this document* ***falling into the wrong hands.*** ◇ *It was his bad luck to be* ***in the wrong place at the wrong time*** (= so that he got involved in trouble without intending to).
▸ NOT MORALLY RIGHT **5** 0-ᴡ [not usually before noun] not morally right or honest: *This man has* ***done nothing wrong.*** ◇ **~ (of/for sb) (to do sth)** *It is wrong to tell lies.* ◇ *It was wrong*

of me to get so angry. ◇ **~ with sth/with doing sth** *What's wrong with eating meat?* ◇ **~ that...** *It is wrong that he should not be punished for what he did.*
▶ **wrong·ness** *noun* [U] (*formal*)
IDM **from/on the ˌwrong side of the ˈtracks** from or living in a poor area or part of town **get (hold of) the ˌwrong end of the ˈstick** (*BrE, informal*) to understand sth in the wrong way **on the ˌwrong side of the ˈlaw** in trouble with the police **take sth the wrong ˈway** to be offended by a remark that was not intended to be offensive ➲ more at BACK *v.*, BARK *v.*, BED *n.*, FAR *adv.*, FOOT *n.*, NOTE *n.*, RUB *v.*, SIDE *n.*, TRACK *n.*
■ ***adv.*** 🔑 (used after verbs) in a way that produces a result that is not correct or that you do not want: *My name is spelt wrong.* ◇ *The program won't load. What am I* ***doing wrong?*** ◇ *I was trying to apologize but it* ***came out wrong*** (= what I said sounded wrong). ◇ *'I thought you were going out.' 'Well you must have* ***thought wrong****, then!'* OPP **right**
IDM **get sb ˈwrong** (*informal*) to not understand correctly what sb means: ***Don't get me wrong*** (= do not be offended by what I am going to say), *I think he's doing a good job, but ...* **get sth ˈwrong** (*informal*) **1** 🔑 to not understand a situation correctly: *No, you've got it all wrong. She's his wife.* **2** 🔑 to make a mistake with sth: *I must have got the figures wrong.* **go ˈwrong 1** 🔑 to make a mistake: *If you do what she tells you, you won't go far wrong.* ◇ *Where did we go wrong with those kids* (= what mistakes did we make for them to behave so badly)? **2** 🔑 (of a machine) to stop working correctly: *My watch keeps going wrong.* **3** 🔑 to experience problems or difficulties: *The relationship started to go wrong when they moved abroad.* ◇ *What else can go wrong* (= what other problems are we going to have)? **you can't go ˈwrong (with sth)** (*informal*) used to say that sth will always be acceptable in a particular situation: *For a quick lunch you can't go wrong with pasta.* ➲ more at FOOT *n.*
■ ***noun* 1** [U] behaviour that is not honest or morally acceptable: *Children must be taught the difference between right and wrong.* ◇ *Her son can* **do no wrong** *in her eyes.* **2** [C] (*formal*) an act that is not legal, honest or morally acceptable: *It is time to forgive past wrongs if progress is to be made.* OPP **right**
IDM **in the ˈwrong** responsible for an accident, a mistake, an argument, etc: *The motorcyclist was clearly in the wrong.* **two ˌwrongs don't make a ˈright** (*saying*) used to say that if sb does sth bad to you, the situation will not be improved by doing sth bad to them ➲ more at RIGHT *v.*
■ ***verb*** [usually passive] **~ sb** (*formal*) to treat sb badly or in an unfair way: *He felt deeply wronged by the allegations.*

Which Word?

wrong / wrongly / wrongfully

- In informal language **wrong** can be used as an adverb instead of **wrongly**, when it means 'incorrectly' and comes after a verb or its object: *My name was spelled wrong.* ◇ *I'm afraid you guessed wrong.* **Wrongly** is used before a past participle or a *that* clause: *My name was wrongly spelt.* ◇ *She guessed wrongly that he was a teacher.*
- **Wrongfully** is usually used in a formal legal situation with words like *convicted, dismissed and imprisoned.*

wrong·doer /ˈrɒŋduːə(r); *NAmE* ˈrɔːŋ-; ˈrɑːŋ-/ *noun* (*formal*) a person who does sth dishonest or illegal SYN **criminal, offender**

wrong·doing /ˈrɒŋduːɪŋ; *NAmE* ˈrɔːŋ-/ *noun* [U, C] (*formal*) illegal or dishonest behaviour SYN **crime, offence**

ˌwrong-ˈfoot *verb* **~ sb** (*BrE*) to put sb in a difficult or embarrassing situation by doing sth that they do not expect: *It was an attempt to wrong-foot the opposition.*

wrong·ful /ˈrɒŋfl; *NAmE* ˈrɔːŋ-/ *adj.* [usually before noun] (*law*) not fair, morally right or legal: *She decided to sue her employer for wrongful dismissal.* ▶ **wrong·ful·ly** /-fəli/ *adv.*: *to be wrongfully convicted/dismissed* ➲ note at WRONG

ˌwrong-ˈheaded *adj.* having or showing bad judgement: *wrong-headed beliefs*

wrong·ly 🔑 /ˈrɒŋli; *NAmE* ˈrɔːŋ-/ *adv.* in a way that is unfair, immoral or not correct: *She was wrongly accused of stealing.* ◇ *He assumed, wrongly, that she did not care.* ◇ *The sentence had been wrongly translated.* ◇ *They knew they had acted wrongly.* ◇ ***Rightly or wrongly****, they felt they should have been better informed* (= I do not know whether they were right to feel this way). ➲ note at WRONG

wrote *past tense* of WRITE

wrought /rɔːt/ *verb* **~ sth** (*formal* or *literary*) (used only in the past tense) caused sth to happen, especially a change: *This century wrought major changes in our society.* ◇ *The storm wrought havoc in the south.* HELP **Wrought** is an old form of the past tense of **work**.

ˌwrought ˈiron *noun* [U] a form of iron used to make decorative fences, gates, etc: *The gates were made of wrought iron.* ◇ *wrought-iron gates* ➲ compare CAST IRON

wrung *past tense, past part.* of WRING

wry /raɪ/ *adj.* [usually before noun] **1** showing that you are both amused and disappointed or annoyed: *'At least we got one vote,' she said with a wry smile.* ◇ *He pulled a wry face when I asked him how it had gone.* **2** amusing in a way that shows IRONY: *a wry comedy about family life* ◇ *a wry comment* ◇ *wry humour* ▶ **wryly** *adv.*: *to smile wryly* **wry·ness** *noun* [U]

WTO /ˌdʌbljuː tiː ˈəʊ; *NAmE* ˈoʊ/ *abbr.* World Trade Organization (an international organization that encourages international trade and economic development, especially by reducing restrictions on trade)

Wu /wuː/ *noun* [U] a form of Chinese spoken in Jiangsu, Zhejiang and Shanghai

wun·der·kind /ˈwʊndəkɪnd; *NAmE* -dərk-/ *noun* (*pl.* **wunder·kind·er** /ˈwʊndəkɪndə(r); *NAmE* -dərk-/) (from *German*, sometimes *disapproving*) a person who is very successful at a young age

Wur·litz·er™ /ˈwɜːlɪtsə(r); *NAmE* ˈwɜːrl-/ *noun* a large musical organ, especially one used in the cinemas/movie theaters of the 1930s

wuss /wʊs/ *noun* (*slang*) a person who is not strong or brave: *Don't be such a wuss!*

WWW /ˌdʌbljuː dʌbljuː ˈdʌbljuː/ *abbr.* = WORLD WIDE WEB: *several useful WWW addresses*

WYSIWYG /ˈwɪziwɪg/ *abbr.* (*computing*) what you see is what you get (what you see on the computer screen is exactly the same as will be printed)

W

X /eks/ (also **x**) *noun, symbol*

■ ***noun*** (*pl.* Xs, X's, x's /ˈeksɪz/) **1** [C, U] the 24th letter of the English alphabet: *'Xylophone' begins with (an) X/'X'.* **2** [U] (*mathematics*) used to represent a number whose value is not mentioned: *The equation is impossible for any value of x greater than 2.* **3** [U] a person, a number, an influence, etc. that is not known or not named: *Let's suppose X knows what Y is doing.* ➲ see also X CHROMOSOME, X-RATED, X-RAY

■ ***symbol*** **1** the number 10 in ROMAN NUMERALS **2** used to represent a kiss at the end of a letter, etc.: *Love from Kathy XXX.* **3** used to show a vote for sb in an election: *Write X beside the candidate of your choice.* **4** used to show that a written answer is wrong ➲ compare TICK *n.* (1) **5** used to show position, for example on a map: *X marks the spot.*

ˈX chromosome *noun* (*biology*) a SEX CHROMOSOME. Two X chromosomes exist in the cells of human females. In human males each cell has one X chromosome and one Y chromosome.

xenon /ˈzenɒn; ˈziː-; *NAmE* -nɑːn/ *noun* [U] (*symb.* Xe) a chemical element. Xenon is a gas that is found in very small quantities in the air and is used in some special electric lamps.

xeno·pho·bia /ˌzenəˈfəʊbiə; *NAmE* -ˈfoʊ-/ *noun* [U] (*disapproving*) a strong feeling of dislike or fear of people from other countries: *a campaign against racism and xenophobia* ▸ **xeno·pho·bic** /-ˈfəʊbɪk; *NAmE* -ˈfoʊ-/ *adj.*

xeno·trans·plan·ta·tion /ˌziːnəʊˌtrænsplɑːnˈteɪʃn; -ˌtrænz-; *NAmE* ˌziːnoʊ-; -plænˈt-/ *noun* [U] (*medical*) the process of taking organs from animals and putting them into humans for medical purposes

Xerox™ /ˈzɪərɒks; *NAmE* ˈzɪrɑːks/ *noun* a process for producing copies of letters, documents, etc. using a special machine; a copy made using this process: *a Xerox machine*

xerox /ˈzɪərɒks; *NAmE* ˈzɪrɑːks/ *verb* **~ sth** to make a copy of a letter, document, etc. by using Xerox or a similar process **SYN** **photocopy**: *Could you xerox this letter, please?*

X factor /ˈeks fæktə(r)/ *noun* [sing.] a special quality, especially one that is essential for success and is difficult to describe: *She certainly has the X factor that all great singers have.*

Xhosa /ˈkɔːsə; ˈkəʊ-; *NAmE* ˈkoʊ-/ *noun* [U] a language spoken by the Xhosa people in South Africa

xi /saɪ; zaɪ; ksaɪ; gzaɪ/ *noun* the 14th letter of the Greek alphabet (Ξ, ξ)

Xiang (also **Hsiang**) /ʃiːˈæŋ/ *noun* [U] a form of Chinese spoken mainly in Hunan

-xion ➲ -ION

XL /ˌeks ˈel/ *abbr.* extra large (used for sizes of things, especially clothes): *an XL T-shirt*

Xmas /ˈkrɪsməs; ˈeksməs/ *noun* [C, U] (*informal*) used as a short form of 'Christmas', usually in writing: *A merry Xmas to all our readers!*

XML /ˌeks em ˈel/ *abbr.* (*computing*) Extensible Mark-up Language (a system used for marking the structure of text on a computer, for example when creating website pages)

ˈX-rated *adj.* (especially of a film/movie) that people under 18 are not allowed to see because it contains sex and/or violence

X-ray /ˈeks reɪ/ *noun, verb*

■ ***noun*** **1** [usually pl.] a type of RADIATION that can pass through objects that are not transparent and make it possible to see inside them: *an X-ray machine* (= one that produces X-rays) **2** a photograph made by X-rays, especially one showing bones or organs in the body: *a chest X-ray* ◇ *The doctor studied the X-rays of her lungs.* ◇ *to take an X-ray* **3** a medical examination using X-rays: *I had to go for an X-ray.*

■ ***verb*** **~ sth** to photograph and examine bones and organs inside the body, using X-rays: *He had to have his chest X-rayed.*

xylem /ˈzaɪləm/ *noun* [U] (*biology*) the material in plants that carries water and minerals upwards from the root ➲ compare PHLOEM

xylo·phone /ˈzaɪləfəʊn; *NAmE* -foʊn/ *noun* a musical instrument made of two rows of wooden bars of different lengths that you hit with two small sticks ➲ compare GLOCKENSPIEL ➲ **VISUAL VOCAB** page V30

Y /waɪ/ *noun, abbr.*

■ ***noun*** (also **y**) (*pl.* **Ys**, **Y's**, **y's** /waɪz/) **1** [C, U] the 25th letter of the English alphabet: *'Year' begins with (a) Y/'Y'.* **2** [U] (*mathematics*) used to represent a number whose value is not mentioned: *Can the value of y be predicted from the value of x?* **3** [U] a person, a number, an influence, etc. that is not known or not named: *Let's suppose X knows what Y is doing.* ➲ see also Y CHROMOSOME, Y-FRONTS

■ ***abbr.*** **the Y** (*NAmE, informal*) YMCA, YWCA

■ ***symbol*** the symbol for the chemical element YTTRIUM

-y *suffix* **1** (also **-ey**) (in adjectives) full of; having the quality of: *dusty* ◇ *clayey* **2** (in adjectives) tending to: *runny* ◇ *sticky* **3** (in nouns) the action or process of: *inquiry* **4** (also **-ie**) (in nouns, showing affection): *doggy* ◇ *daddy*

ya /jə/ *pron., det.* (*informal, non-standard*) used in writing as a way of showing the way people sometimes pronounce the word 'you' or 'your': *He said, 'I got something for ya.'*

yaar /jɑː; *NAmE* jɑːr/ *noun* (*IndE, informal*) (used as a friendly way of addressing sb) a friend: *Let's go for a drink, yaar!*

yacht /jɒt; *NAmE* jɑːt/ (*NAmE* also **sail·boat**) *noun* a large sailing boat, often also with an engine and a place to sleep on board, used for pleasure trips and racing: *a **yacht club/race*** ◇ *a motor yacht* ◇ *a luxury yacht* ➲ VISUAL VOCAB page V45 ➲ compare DINGHY

yacht·ing /ˈjɒtɪŋ; *NAmE* ˈjɑːt-/ *noun* [U] the sport or activity of sailing or racing yachts

yachts·man /ˈjɒtsmən; *NAmE* ˈjɑːt-/, **yachts·woman** /ˈjɒtswʊmən; *NAmE* ˈjɑːt-/ *noun* (*pl.* **-men** /-mən/, **-women** /-wɪmɪn/) a person who sails a yacht for pleasure or as a sport: *a round-the-world yachtsman*

yack *verb* = YAK

yada yada yada (also **yadda yadda yadda**) /ˌjædə jædə ˈjædə/ *exclamation* (*NAmE, informal*) used when you are talking about sth to show that some of the details are not worth saying because they are not important or are boring or obvious: *His new girlfriend is attractive, funny, smart, yada yada yada.*

yah /jɑː/ *exclamation* **1** a way of writing 'yes' to show that the speaker has an upper-class accent **2** used to show that you have a low opinion of sb/sth: *Yah, you missed!*

yahoo /ˈjɑːhuː; jəˈhuː/ *noun, exclamation*

■ ***noun*** (*pl.* **-oos**) (*disapproving*) a rude, noisy or violent person

■ ***exclamation*** /jɑːˈhuː; jæˈhuː/ (*informal*) used to show that you are very happy: *Yahoo, we did it!*

Yah·weh /ˈjɑːweɪ/ *noun* = JEHOVAH

yak /jæk/ *noun, verb*

■ ***noun*** an animal of the cow family, with long horns and long hair, that lives in central Asia

■ ***verb*** (**-kk-**) (also **yack**) [I] (*informal*, often *disapproving*) to talk continuously about things that are not very serious or important: *She just kept yakking on.*

yakka /ˈjækə/ *noun* [U] (*AustralE, NZE, informal*) work, especially of a hard physical kind: *hard yakka*

Yale lock™ /ˈjeɪl lɒk; *NAmE* lɑːk/ *noun* (*BrE*) a type of lock that is often fitted in the front door of a house and which opens by using a flat key with a series of pointed edges

y'all /jɔːl/ *pron.* = YOU-ALL

yam /jæm/ *noun* [C, U] the large root of a tropical plant that is cooked as a vegetable ➲ VISUAL VOCAB page V27

yang /jæŋ/ *noun* [U] (from *Chinese*) (in Chinese philosophy) the bright active male principle of the universe ➲ compare YIN

Yank /jæŋk/ (also **Yan·kee**) *noun* (*BrE, informal*, often *disapproving*) a slightly offensive word for a person from the US; an American

yank /jæŋk/ *verb* [T, I] (*informal*) to pull sth/sb hard, quickly and suddenly: **~ sth/sb (+ adv./prep.)** *He yanked her to her feet.* ◇ **~ sth/sb + adj.** *I yanked the door open.* ◇ **(+ adv./prep.)** *Liz yanked at my arm.* ▸ **yank** *noun*: *She gave the rope a yank.*

Yan·kee /ˈjæŋki/ *noun* **1** (*NAmE*) a person who comes from or lives in any of the northern states of the US, especially New England **2** a soldier who fought for the Union (= the northern states) in the American Civil War **3** (*BrE, informal*) = YANK

yap /jæp/ *verb* (**-pp-**) **1** [I] **~ (at sb/sth)** (especially of small dogs) to BARK a lot, making a high, sharp and usually irritating sound: *The dogs yapped at his heels.* ◇ *yapping dogs* **2** [I] (*informal*) to talk in a silly, noisy and usually irritating way ▸ **yap** *noun*

yard 0┳ /jɑːd; *NAmE* jɑːrd/ *noun*
1 0┳ (*BrE*) an area outside a building, usually with a hard surface and a surrounding wall: *the prison yard* ◇ *The children were playing in the yard at the front of the school.* ➲ see also BACKYARD **2** 0┳ (*NAmE*) (*BrE* **gar·den**) a piece of land next to or around your house where you can grow flowers, fruit, vegetables, etc, usually with a LAWN (= an area of grass) ➲ VISUAL VOCAB page V36 ➲ see also BACKYARD **3** 0┳ (usually in compounds) an area of land used for a special purpose or business: *a boat yard* HELP You will find other compounds ending in **yard** at their place in the alphabet. ➲ SYNONYMS at FACTORY **4** 0┳ (*abbr.* **yd**) a unit for measuring length, equal to 3 feet (36 inches) or 0.9144 of a metre **5** (*technical*) a long piece of wood fastened to a MAST that supports a sail on a boat or ship IDM see INCH *n.*, NINE

yard·age /ˈjɑːdɪdʒ; *NAmE* ˈjɑːrd-/ *noun* [C, U] (*technical*) **1** size measured in yards or square yards **2** (in AMERICAN FOOTBALL) the number of yards that a team or player has moved forward

yard·arm /ˈjɑːdɑːm; *NAmE* ˈjɑːrdɑːrm/ *noun* (*technical*) either end of the long piece of wood fastened to a ship's MAST that supports a sail

Yardie /ˈjɑːdi; *NAmE* ˈjɑːrdi/ *noun* (*BrE, informal*) (in the UK) a member of a group of criminals from Jamaica or the West Indies

ˈyard sale *noun* (*NAmE*) a sale of things from sb's house, held in their yard ➲ see also GARAGE SALE

yard·stick /ˈjɑːdstɪk; *NAmE* ˈjɑːrd-/ *noun* **1** (*especially NAmE*) a ruler for measuring one yard **2** a standard used for judging how good or successful sth is: *a yardstick by which to measure sth* ◇ *Exam results are not the only yardstick of a school's performance.*

yar·mulke (also **yar·mulka**) /ˈjɑːmʊlkə; *NAmE* ˈjɑːrm-/ (also **kippa**) *noun* a small round cap worn on top of the head by Jewish men; a type of SKULLCAP

yarn /jɑːn; *NAmE* jɑːrn/ *noun* **1** [U, C] thread that has been spun, used for knitting, making cloth, etc. ➲ VISUAL VOCAB page V35 **2** [C] (*informal*) a long story, especially one that is exaggerated or invented: *He used to **spin yarns** (= tell stories) about his time in the Army.* IDM see PITCH *v.*

yar·row /ˈjærəʊ; *NAmE* -roʊ/ *noun* [U, C] a plant with flat groups of many small white or pinkish flowers that have a strong smell

yash·mak /ˈjæʃmæk/ *noun* a piece of cloth covering most of the face, worn by some Muslim women

yaw /jɔː/ *verb* [I] (*technical*) (of a ship or plane) to turn to one side, away from a straight course, in an unsteady way ▸ **yaw** *noun* [C, U]

yawl /jɔːl/ *noun* **1** a type of boat with sails **2** a ROWING BOAT carried on a ship

yawn 0┳ /jɔːn/ *verb, noun*

■ ***verb*** **1** 0┳ [I] to open your mouth wide and breathe in deeply through it, usually because you are tired or bored: *He stood up, stretched and yawned.* **2** [I] (of a large hole or an empty space) to be very wide and often frightening and difficult to get across SYN **gape**: *A crevasse yawned at their feet.* ◇ (*figurative*) *There's a **yawning gap** between rich and poor.*

■ ***noun* 1** 🗝 an act of yawning: *She stifled another yawn and tried hard to look interested.* **2** [usually sing.] (*informal*) a boring event, idea, etc: *The meeting was one big yawn from start to finish.*

yaws /jɔːz/ *noun* [U] a tropical skin disease that causes large red swellings

yay /jeɪ/ *exclamation, adv.* (*informal, especially NAmE*)
■ ***exclamation*** used to show that you are very pleased about sth: *I won! Yay!*
■ ***adv.* 1** to this degree SYN **so**: *The fish I caught was yay big.* **2** to a high degree SYN **extremely**: *Yay good movie!*

'Y chromosome *noun* (*biology*) a SEX CHROMOSOME. In human males each cell has one X chromosome and one Y chromosome. In human females there is never a Y chromosome.

yd *abbr.* (*pl.* **yds**) YARD: *12 yds of silk*

ye *pron., det.*
■ ***pron.*** /jiː; *weak form* ji/ (*old use* or *dialect*) a word meaning 'you', used when talking to more than one person: *Gather ye rosebuds while ye may.*
■ ***det.*** /jiː/ a word meaning 'the', used in the names of pubs, shops, etc. to make them seem old: *Ye Olde Starre Inn*

yea /jeɪ/ *adv., noun* (*old use*) yes ➲ compare NAY

yeah 🗝 /jeə/ *exclamation* (*informal*) yes

IDM **,oh 'yeah?** used when you are commenting on what sb has just said: *'We're off to France soon.' 'Oh yeah? When's that?'* ◇ *'I'm going to be rich one day.' 'Oh yeah?'* (= I don't believe you.) **,yeah, 'right** used to say that you do not believe what sb has just said, disagree with it, or are not interested in it: *'You'll be fine.' 'Yeah, right.'*

year 🗝 /jɪə(r); jɜː(r); *NAmE* jɪr/ *noun* (*abbr.* **yr**)
1 🗝 (also **,calendar 'year**) [C] the period from 1 January to 31 December, that is 365 or 366 days, divided into 12 months: *in the year 1865* ◇ *I lost my job earlier this year.* ◇ *Elections take place every year.* ◇ *The museum is open* ***all (the) year round*** (= during the whole year). ➲ see also LEAP YEAR, NEW YEAR **2** 🗝 [C] a period of 12 months, measured from any particular time: *It's exactly a year since I started working here.* ◇ *She gave up teaching three years ago.* ◇ *in the first year of their marriage* ◇ *the pre-war/war/post-war years* (= the period before/during/after the war) ◇ *I have happy memories of my years in Poland* (= the time I spent there). ➲ see also GAP YEAR, LIGHT YEAR, OFF YEAR **3** 🗝 [C] a period of 12 months connected with a particular activity: *the* ***academic/school year*** ◇ *the* ***tax year*** ➲ see also FINANCIAL YEAR **4** [C] (*especially BrE*) (at a school, etc.) a level that you stay in for one year; a student at a particular level: *We started German in year seven.* ◇ *a year-seven pupil* ◇ *The first years do French.* ◇ *She was in my year at school.* **5** 🗝 [C, usually pl.] age; time of life: *He was 14* ***years old*** *when it happened.* ◇ *She looks young for her years.* ◇ *They were both only 20* ***years of age.*** ◇ *a twenty-year-old man* ◇ *He died in his sixtieth year.* ◇ *She's* ***getting on in years*** (= is no longer young). **6** 🗝 **years** [pl.] (*informal*) a long time: *It's years since we last met.* ◇ *They haven't seen each other* ***for years.*** ◇ *That's the best movie I've seen* ***in years.*** ◇ *We've had a lot of fun* ***over the years.***

IDM **man, woman, car, etc. of the 'year** a person or thing that people decide is the best in a particular field in a particular year **not/never in a hundred, etc. 'years** (*informal*) used to emphasize that you will/would never do sth: *I'd never have thought of that in a million years.* **put 'years on sb** to make sb feel or look older **take 'years off sb** to make sb feel or look younger **,year after 'year** every year for many years **,year by 'year** as the years pass; each year: *Year by year their affection for each other grew stronger.* **the year 'dot** (*BrE*) (*NAmE* **the year 'one**) (*informal*) a very long time ago: *I've been going there every summer since the year dot.* **year 'in, year 'out** every year **,year of 'grace | ,year of our 'Lord** (*formal*) any particular year after the birth of Christ **,year on 'year** (used especially when talking about figures, prices, etc.) each year, compared with the last year: *Spending has increased year on year.* ◇ *a year-on-year increase in spending* ➲ more at ADVANCED, DECLINE *v.*, DONKEY, SEVEN, TURN *n.*

Y

year·book /ˈjɪəbʊk; *NAmE* ˈjɪrbʊk/ *noun* **1** a book published once a year, giving details of events, etc. of the previous year, especially those connected with a particular area of activity **2** (*especially NAmE*) a book that is produced by the senior class in a school or college, containing photographs of students and details of school activities

year·ling /ˈjɪəlɪŋ; *NAmE* ˈjɪrlɪŋ/ *noun* an animal, especially a horse, between one and two years old

,year-'long *adj.* [only before noun] continuing for a whole year: *a year-long dispute*

year·ly /ˈjɪəli; ˈjɜːli; *NAmE* ˈjɪrli/ *adj.* **1** happening once a year or every year: *Pay is reviewed on a yearly basis.* **2** paid, valid or calculated for one year: ***yearly income/interest*** ▸ **year·ly** *adv.*: *The magazine is issued twice yearly* (= twice every year).

yearn /jɜːn; *NAmE* jɜːrn/ *verb* [I] (*literary*) to want sth very much, especially when it is very difficult to get SYN **long**: **~ (for sth/sb)** *The people yearned for peace.* ◇ *There was a yearning look in his eyes.* ◇ **~ to do sth** *She yearned to escape from her office job.*

yearn·ing /ˈjɜːnɪŋ; *NAmE* ˈjɜːrnɪŋ/ *noun* [C, U] (*formal*) a strong and emotional desire SYN **longing**: **~ (for sb/sth)** *a yearning for a quiet life* ◇ **~ (to do sth)** *She had no great yearning to go back.* ▸ **yearn·ing·ly** *adv.*

,year-'round *adj.* all through the year: *an island with year-round sunshine*

yeast /jiːst/ *noun* [U, C] a FUNGUS used in making beer and wine, or to make bread rise ▸ **yeasty** *adj.*: *a yeasty smell*

'yeast extract *noun* [U] a black substance made from yeast, spread on bread, etc. ➲ see also MARMITE

'yeast infection (*NAmE*) (*BrE* **thrush**) *noun* an infectious disease that affects the VAGINA

yebo /ˈjebɒ; *NAmE* -bɔː/ *exclamation* (*SAfrE, informal*) **1** yes **2** hello: *Yebo Craig. Thanks for the email.*

yell /jel/ *verb, noun*
■ ***verb*** [I, T] to shout loudly, for example because you are angry, excited, frightened or in pain: **~ (at sb/sth)** *He yelled at the other driver.* ◇ **~ at sb to do sth** *She yelled at the child to get down from the wall.* ◇ **~ with sth** *They yelled with excitement.* ◇ **~ out (in sth)** *She yelled out in pain.* ◇ **+ speech** *'Be careful!' he yelled.* ◇ **~ sth (at sb/sth)** *The crowd yelled encouragement at the players.* ◇ **~ out sth** *He yelled out her name.* ➲ SYNONYMS at SHOUT
■ ***noun* 1** a loud cry of pain, excitement, etc: *to* ***let out/give a yell*** ◇ *a yell of delight* **2** (*NAmE*) an organized shout of support for a team at a sports event

yel·low 🗝 /ˈjeləʊ; *NAmE* ˈjeloʊ/ *adj., noun, verb*
■ ***adj.*** (**yel·lower, yel·lowest**) **1** 🗝 having the colour of lemons or butter: *pale yellow flowers* ◇ *a bright yellow waterproof jacket* **2** (*taboo*) an offensive word used to describe the light brown skin of people from some E Asian countries **3** (*informal, disapproving*) easily frightened SYN **cowardly** ▸ **yel·low·ness** *noun* [U, sing.]
■ ***noun*** 🗝 [U, C] the colour of lemons or butter: *She was dressed in yellow.* ◇ *the reds and yellows of the trees*
■ ***verb*** [I, T] **~ (sth)** to become yellow; to make sth become yellow

'yellow-belly *noun* (*old-fashioned, informal, disapproving*) a COWARD (= sb who is not brave) ▸ **'yellow-bellied** *adj.* [usually before noun]

,yellow 'card *noun* (in football (SOCCER)) a card shown by the REFEREE to a player as a warning about bad behaviour ➲ compare RED CARD

,yellow 'fever *noun* [U] an infectious tropical disease that makes the skin turn yellow and often causes death

,yellow 'flag *noun* **1** a type of yellow IRIS (= a flower) that grows near water **2** a yellow flag on a ship showing that sb has or may have an infectious disease

yel·low·ham·mer /ˈjeləʊhæmə(r); *NAmE* -loʊ-/ *noun* a small bird, the male of which has a yellow head, neck and breast

yel·low·ish /ˈjeləʊɪʃ; *NAmE* -loʊ-/ (also *less frequent* **yel·lowy** /ˈjeləʊi; *NAmE* -loʊ-/) *adj.* fairly yellow in colour: *The paper had a yellowish tinge because it was so old.*

ˌyellow ˈjournalism *noun* [U] (*US*) newspaper reports that are exaggerated and written to shock readers ORIGIN From a comic strip *The Yellow Kid* that was printed in yellow ink to attract readers' attention.

ˌyellow ˈline *noun* (in Britain) a yellow line painted at the side of a road to show that you can only park your car there at particular times or for a short time: ***double yellow lines*** (= two lines that mean you cannot park there at all)

ˌYellow ˈPages™ (*BrE*) (*NAmE* **ˌyellow ˈpages**) *noun* [pl.] a book with yellow pages that gives a list of companies and organizations and their telephone numbers, arranged according to the type of services they offer

ˌyellow ˈribbon *noun* (in the US) a piece of yellow material that sb ties around a tree as a sign that they are thinking about sb who has gone away, especially a soldier fighting in a war, or sb taken as a HOSTAGE or prisoner, and that they hope that the person will soon return safely

yelp /jelp/ *verb* [I, T] (+ **speech**) to give a sudden short cry, usually of pain ▶ **yelp** *noun*

yen /jen/ *noun* **1** (*pl.* **yen**) [C] the unit of money in Japan **2 the yen** [sing.] (*finance*) the value of the yen compared with the value of the money of other countries **3** [C, usually sing.] **~** (**for sth/to do sth**) a strong desire SYN **longing**: *I've always had a yen to travel around the world.*

yeo·man /ˈjəʊmən; *NAmE* ˈjoʊ-/ *noun* (*pl.* **-men** /-mən/) **1** (in Britain in the past) a farmer who owned and worked on his land **2** an officer in the US Navy who does mainly office work

yeo·man·ry /ˈjəʊmənri; *NAmE* ˈjoʊ-/ *noun* [sing.+ sing./pl. v.] **1** (in Britain in the past) the social class of farmers who owned their land **2** (in Britain in the past) farmers who became soldiers and provided their own horses

yeow /jiːˈaʊ/ *exclamation* (*informal*) used to express sudden pain

yep /jep/ *exclamation* (*informal*) used to say 'yes': *'Are you ready?' 'Yep.'*

yer /jə(r)/ *pron., det.* (*informal, non-standard*) used in writing as a way of showing the way people sometimes pronounce the word 'you' or 'your': *See yer when I get back.* ◇ *What's yer name?*

yes 🔑 /jes/ *exclamation, noun*

■ ***exclamation*** **1** 🔑 used to answer a question and say that sth is correct or true: *'Is this your car?' 'Yes, it is.'* ◇ *'Are you coming? Yes or no?'* **2** 🔑 used to show that you agree with what has been said: *'I enjoyed her latest novel.' 'Yes, me too.'* ◇ *'It's an excellent hotel.'* ***'Yes, but*** (= I don't completely agree) *it's too expensive.'* **3** 🔑 used to disagree with sth negative that sb has just said: *'I've never met her before.' 'Yes, you have.'* **4** 🔑 used to agree to a request or to give permission: *'Dad, can I borrow the car?' 'Yes, but be careful.'* ◇ *We're hoping that they will* ***say yes to*** *our proposals.* **5** 🔑 used to accept an offer or invitation: *'Would you like a drink?'* ***'Yes, please/thanks.'*** **6** 🔑 used for asking sb what they want: *Yes? How can I help you?* **7** 🔑 used for replying politely when sb calls you: *'Waiter!' 'Yes, sir?'* **8** 🔑 used to show that you have just remembered sth: *Where did I put the keys? Oh, yes—in my pocket!* **9** 🔑 used to encourage sb to continue speaking: *'I'm going to Paris this weekend.' 'Yes…'* **10** 🔑 used to show that you do not believe what sb has said: *'Sorry I'm late—the bus didn't come.' 'Oh yes?'* **11** 🔑 used to emphasize what you have just said: *Mrs Smith has just won £2 million—yes!—£2 million!* **12** 🔑 used to show that you are excited or extremely pleased about sth that you have done or sth that has happened: *'They've scored another goal.' 'Yes!!'* **13 yes, yes** used to show that you are impatient or irritated about sth: *'Hurry up—it's late.' 'Yes, yes—I'm coming.'*

IDM **ˌyes and ˈno** used when you cannot give a clear answer to a question: *'Are you enjoying it?' 'Yes and no.'*

■ ***noun*** 🔑 (*pl.* **yes·ses** or **yeses** /ˈjesɪz/) an answer that shows that you agree with an idea, a statement, etc; a person who says 'yes': *I need a simple yes or no to my questions.* ◇ *There will be two ballot boxes—one for yesses and one for noes.* ◇ *I'll put you down as a yes.*

yesh·iva /jəˈʃiːvə/ *noun* a college or school for Orthodox Jews

ˈyes-man *noun* (*pl.* **-men** /-men/) (*disapproving*) a person who always agrees with people in authority in order to gain their approval

yes·sir /ˈjesə(r); ˈjessɜː(r)/ *exclamation* (*informal, especially NAmE*) used to emphasize your opinion or say that you agree very strongly: *Yessir, she was beautiful.*

yes·ter·day 🔑 /ˈjestədeɪ; ˈjestədi; *NAmE* -tərd-/ *adv., noun, adj.*

■ ***adv.*** on the day before today: *They arrived yesterday.* ◇ *I can remember our wedding as if it were yesterday.* ◇ *Where were you yesterday morning?* ◇ *To think I was lying on a beach only* ***the day before yesterday.*** IDM see BORN *v.*

■ ***noun*** [U] **1** 🔑 the day before today: *Yesterday was Sunday.* ◇ *What happened at yesterday's meeting?* **2** 🔑 (also **yes·ter·days** [pl.]) the recent past: *Yesterday's students are today's employees.* ◇ *All her yesterdays had vanished without a trace.*

■ ***adj.*** [not before noun] (*informal*, often *humorous*) no longer fashionable or new: *Email—that's* ***so yesterday!***

yes·ter·year /ˈjestəjɪə(r); *NAmE* ˈjestərjɪr/ *noun* [U] (*old-fashioned* or *literary*) the past, especially a time when attitudes and ideas were different

yet 🔑 /jet/ *adv., conj.*

■ ***adv.*** **1** 🔑 used in negative sentences and questions to talk about sth that has not happened but that you expect to happen: (*BrE*) *I haven't received a letter from him yet.* ◇ (*NAmE*) *I didn't receive a letter from him yet.* ◇ *'Are you ready?' 'No, not yet.'* ◇ *We* ***have yet to*** *decide what action to take* (= We have not decided what action to take). ➲ note at ALREADY **2** 🔑 (used in negative sentences) now; as soon as this: *Don't go yet.* ◇ *We don't need to start yet.* **3** 🔑 from now until the period of time mentioned has passed: *He'll be busy for ages yet.* ◇ *They won't arrive for at least two hours yet.* **4 could, might, may, etc. do sth ~** used to say that sth could, might, etc. happen in the future, even though it seems unlikely: *We may win yet.* ◇ (*formal*) *She could yet surprise us all.* **5** 🔑 **the best, longest, etc. sth ~** (**done**) the best, longest, etc. thing of its kind made, produced, written, etc. until now/then: *the most comprehensive study yet of his music* ◇ *It was the highest building yet constructed.* **6** 🔑 **~ another/more | ~ again** used to emphasize an increase in number or amount or the number of times sth happens: *snow, snow and yet more snow* ◇ *yet another diet book* ◇ *Prices were cut* ***yet again*** (= once more, after many other times). **7 ~ worse, more importantly, etc.** used to emphasize an increase in the degree of sth (= how bad, important, etc. it is) SYN **even, still**: *a recent and yet more improbable theory*

IDM **as ˈyet** 🔑 until now or until a particular time in the past: *an as yet unpublished report* ◇ *As yet little was known of the causes of the disease.*

■ ***conj.*** 🔑 despite what has just been said SYN **nevertheless**: *It's a small car, yet it's surprisingly spacious.* ◇ *He has a good job, and yet he never seems to have any money.*

yeti /ˈjeti/ (also **Aˌbominable ˈSnowman**) *noun* a large creature like a BEAR or a man covered with hair, that some people believe lives in the Himalayan mountains

yew /juː/ *noun* **1** [C, U] (also **ˈyew tree**) a small tree with dark green leaves and small red BERRIES ➲ VISUAL VOCAB page V8 **2** [U] the wood of the yew tree

ˈY-Fronts™ *noun* [pl.] (*BrE*) men's UNDERPANTS, with an opening in the front sewn in the shape of a Y upside-down: *a pair of Y-Fronts*

YHA /ˌwaɪ eɪtʃ ˈeɪ/ *abbr.* Youth Hostels Association (an organization that exists in many countries and provides cheap simple accommodation)

yid /jɪd/ *noun* (*taboo, slang*) a very offensive word for a Jewish person

Y

Yid·dish /ˈjɪdɪʃ/ *noun* [U] a Jewish language, originally used in central and eastern Europe, based on a form of German with words from Hebrew and several modern languages ▸ **Yid·dish** *adj.*

yield /jiːld/ *verb, noun*
■ ***verb*** **1** [T] **~ sth** to produce or provide sth, for example a profit, result or crop: *Higher-rate deposit accounts yield good returns.* ◇ *The research has yielded useful information.* ◇ *trees that no longer yield fruit* **2** [I] (*formal*) to stop resisting sth/sb; to agree to do sth that you do not want to do **SYN** **give way**: *After a long siege, the town was forced to yield.* ◇ **~ to sth/sb** *He reluctantly yielded to their demands.* ◇ *I yielded to temptation and had a chocolate bar.* **3** [T] **~ sth/sb (up) (to sb)** (*formal*) to allow sb to win, have or take control of sth that has been yours until now **SYN** **surrender**: *He refused to yield up his gun.* ◇ (*figurative*) *The universe is slowly yielding up its secrets.* **4** [I] to move, bend or break because of pressure: *Despite our attempts to break it, the lock would not yield.* **5** [I] **~ (to sb/sth)** (*NAmE, IrishE*) to allow vehicles on a bigger road to go first **SYN** **give way**: *Yield to oncoming traffic.* ◇ *a yield sign*
PHR V ˈ**yield to sth** (*formal*) to be replaced by sth: *Barges yielded to road vehicles for transporting goods.*
■ ***noun*** [C, U] the total amount of crops, profits, etc. that are produced: *a high crop yield* ◇ *a reduction in milk yield* ◇ *This will give a yield of 10% on your investment.*

yield·ing /ˈjiːldɪŋ/ *adj.* (*formal*) **1** (of a substance) soft and easy to bend or move when you press it **2** (of a person) willing to do what other people want **3** (used with an adverb) giving the amount of crops, profits, etc. mentioned: ***high/low yielding*** *crops*

yikes /jaɪks/ *exclamation* (*informal*) used to show that you are surprised or suddenly afraid

yin /jɪn/ *noun* [U] (from *Chinese*) (in Chinese philosophy) the dark, not active, female principle of the universe ➲ compare YANG

yip·pee /jɪˈpiː; *NAmE* ˈjɪpi/ *exclamation* (*old-fashioned, informal*) used to show you are pleased or excited

ylang-ylang (also **ilang-ilang**) /ˌiːlæŋ ˈiːlæŋ/ *noun* **1** [U] an oil from the flowers of a tropical tree, used in PERFUMES and AROMATHERAPY **2** [U, C] a tree with yellow flowers from which this oil is obtained

YMCA /ˌwaɪ em siː ˈeɪ/ (also *NAmE informal* **the Y**) *abbr.* Young Men's Christian Association (an organization that exists in many countries and provides accommodation and social and sports activities): *We stayed at the YMCA.*

yo /jəʊ; *NAmE* joʊ/ *exclamation* (*slang*) used by young people to say hello

yob /jɒb; *NAmE* jɑːb/ (also **yobbo** /ˈjɒbəʊ; *NAmE* ˈjɑːboʊ/ *pl.* -os) *noun* (*BrE, informal*) a rude, noisy and sometimes aggressive and violent boy or young man **SYN** **lout** ▸ **yob·bish** *adj.* [usually before noun]

yodel /ˈjəʊdl; *NAmE* ˈjoʊdl/ *verb, noun*
■ ***verb*** (-ll-, *especially US* -l-) [I, T] **~ (sth)** to sing or call in the traditional Swiss way, changing your voice frequently between its normal level and a very high level
■ ***noun*** a song or musical call in which sb yodels

yoga /ˈjəʊgə; *NAmE* ˈjoʊgə/ *noun* [U] **1** a Hindu philosophy that teaches you how to control your body and mind in the belief that you can become united with the spirit of the universe in this way **2** a system of exercises for your body and for controlling your breathing, used by people who want to become fitter or to relax ➲ VISUAL VOCAB page V35 ▸ **yogic** /ˈjəʊgɪk; *NAmE* ˈjoʊ-/ *adj.*: *yogic techniques*

yogi /ˈjəʊgi; *NAmE* ˈjoʊgi/ *noun* (*pl.* yogis) an expert in, or teacher of, the philosophy of yoga

yog·urt (also **yog·hurt, yog·hourt**) /ˈjɒgət; *NAmE* ˈjoʊgərt/ *noun* [U, C] a thick white liquid food, made by adding bacteria to milk, served cold and often flavoured with fruit; an amount of this sold in a small pot: *natural yogurt* ◇ *There's a yogurt left if you're still hungry.* ◇ *a lemon yogurt*

yoke /jəʊk; *NAmE* joʊk/ *noun, verb*
■ ***noun*** **1** [C] a long piece of wood that is fastened across the necks of two animals, especially OXEN, so that they can pull heavy loads **2** [sing.] (*literary* or *formal*) rough treatment or sth that restricts your freedom and makes your life very difficult to bear: *the yoke of imperialism* **3** [C] a piece of wood that is shaped to fit across a person's shoulders so that they can carry two equal loads **4** [C] a part of a dress, skirt, etc. that fits around the shoulders or hips and from which the rest of the cloth hangs
■ ***verb*** **1** to join two animals together with a yoke; to attach an animal to sth with a yoke: **~ A and B together** *A pair of oxen, yoked together, was used.* ◇ **~ sth to sth** *an ox yoked to a plough* **2** [usually passive] **~ A and B together** | **~ sth to sth** (*formal*) to bring two people, countries, ideas, etc. together so that they are forced into a close relationship: *The Hong Kong dollar was yoked to the American dollar for many years.*

yokel /ˈjəʊkl; *NAmE* ˈjoʊkl/ *noun* (often *humorous*) if you call a person a **yokel**, you are saying that they do not have much education or understanding of modern life, because they come from the countryside

yolk /jəʊk; *NAmE* joʊk/ *noun* [C, U] the round yellow part in the middle of an egg: *Separate the whites from the yolks.*

Yom Kip·pur /ˌjɒm ˈkɪpə(r); kɪˈpʊə(r); *NAmE* ˌjɑːm kɪˈpʊr; ˌjɔːm/ *noun* [U] a Jewish religious holiday in September or October when people eat nothing all day and say prayers of PENITENCE in the SYNAGOGUE, also known as the Day of Atonement

yomp /jɒmp; *NAmE* jɑːmp/ *verb* [I] **+ adv./prep.** (*BrE, informal*) (of a soldier) to march with heavy equipment over rough ground ▸ **yomp** *noun*: *a 30-mile yomp*

yon /jɒn; *NAmE* jɑːn/ *det., adv.*
■ ***det.*** (*old use* or *dialect*) that: *There's an old farm over yon hill.*
■ ***adv.*** **IDM** see HITHER

yon·der /ˈjɒndə(r); *NAmE* ˈjɑːn-/ *det.* (*old use* or *dialect*) that is over there; that you can see over there: *Let's rest under yonder tree.* ▸ **yon·der** *adv.*: *Whose is that farm over yonder?*

yonks /jɒŋks; *NAmE* jɑːŋks/ *noun* [U] (*BrE, informal,* becoming *old-fashioned*) a long time: *I haven't seen you for yonks!*

yoof /juːf/ *noun* [U] (*BrE, informal, humorous*) a non-standard spelling of 'youth', used to refer to young people as a group, especially as the group that particular types of entertainment, magazines, etc. are designed for ▸ **yoof** *adj.* [only before noun]

yoo-hoo /ˈjuː huː/ *exclamation* (*informal,* becoming *old-fashioned*) used to attract sb's attention, especially when they are some distance away

yore /jɔː(r)/ *noun*
IDM **of ˈyore** (*old use* or *literary*) long ago: *in days of yore*

York·shire pud·ding /ˌjɔːkʃə ˈpʊdɪŋ; *NAmE* ˌjɔːrkʃər/ *noun* [U, C] a type of British food made from BATTER that is baked until it rises, traditionally eaten with ROAST beef

Yorkshire terrier /ˌjɔːkʃə ˈteriə(r); *NAmE* ˌjɔːrkʃər/ *noun* a very small dog with long brown and grey hair

Yor·uba /ˈjɒrʊbə; *NAmE* ˈjɔːrəbə/ *noun* [U] a language spoken by the Yoruba people of W Africa, especially in SW Nigeria

you 🔑 /ju; *NAmE* jə *strong form* juː/ *pron.*
1 🔑 used as the subject or object of a verb or after a preposition to refer to the person or people being spoken or written to: *You said you knew the way.* ◇ *I thought she told you.* ◇ *Can I sit next to you?* ◇ *I don't think that hairstyle is you* (= it doesn't suit your appearance or personality). **2** 🔑 used with nouns and adjectives to speak to sb directly: *You girls, stop talking!* ◇ *You stupid idiot!* **3** 🔑 used for referring to people in general: *You learn a language better if you visit the country where it is spoken.* ◇ *It's a friendly place—people come up to you in the street and start talking.*

you-all /ˈjuː ɔːl/ (also **y'all**) *pron.* (*informal*) used especially in the southern US to mean *you* when talking to more than one person: *Have you-all brought swimsuits?*

Y

you'd /juːd/ *short form* **1** you had **2** you would

you'll /juːl/ *short form* you will

young 0‑ /jʌŋ/ *adj., noun*

■ **adj.** (young·er /ˈjʌŋɡə(r)/, young·est /ˈjʌŋɡɪst/) **1** 0‑ having lived or existed for only a short time; not fully developed: *young babies* ◇ *a young country* ◇ *Caterpillars eat the young leaves of this plant.* ◇ *a young wine* ◇ *The night is* ***still young*** (= it has only just started). OPP **old 2** 0‑ not yet old; not as old as others: *young people* ◇ *talented young football players* ◇ *I am the youngest of four sisters.* ◇ ***In his younger days*** *he played rugby for Wales.* ◇ *I met the young Michelle Obama at Princeton.* ◇ *Her grandchildren keep her young.* ◇ *My son's thirteen but he's* ***young for his age*** (= not as developed as other boys of the same age). ◇ *They* ***married young*** (= at an early age). ◇ *My mother* ***died young.*** OPP **old 3** 0‑ consisting of young people or young children; with a low average age: *They have a young family.* ◇ *a young audience* **4** suitable or appropriate for young people SYN **youthful**: *young fashion* ◇ *The clothes she wears are much too young for her.* **5 ~ man/lady/woman** used to show that you are angry or annoyed with a particular young person: *I think you owe me an apology, young lady!* **6 the younger** used before or after a person's name to distinguish them from an older relative: *the younger Kennedy* ◇ (*BrE, formal*) *William Pitt the younger* ➲ compare THE ELDER at ELDER *adj.*, JUNIOR *adj.* (3)

IDM **be getting ˈyounger** (*informal*) used to say that people seem to be doing sth at a younger age than they used to, or that they seem younger because you are now older: *The band's fans are getting younger.* ◇ *Why do police officers seem to be getting younger?* **not be getting any ˈyounger** (*informal*) used when you are commenting that time is passing and that you are growing older **ˌyoung at ˈheart** thinking and behaving like a young person even when you are old ➲ more at OLD, ONLY *adv.*

■ **noun** [pl.] **1** 0‑ **the young** young people considered as a group: *It's a movie that will appeal to the young.* ◇ *It's a book for* ***young and old alike.*** **2** 0‑ young animals of a particular type or that belong to a particular mother: *a mother bird feeding her young*

young·ish /ˈjʌŋɪʃ/ *adj.* fairly young: *a youngish president*

ˌyoung ofˈfender *noun* (*BrE*) a criminal who, according to the law, is not yet an adult but no longer a child: *a young offender institution*

ˌyoung ˈperson *noun* (*BrE, law*) a person between the ages of 14 and 17

young·ster /ˈjʌŋstə(r)/ *noun* (*informal*) a young person or a child: *The camp is for youngsters aged 8 to 14.*

ˌyoung ˈthing *noun* (*informal*) a young adult: *bright young things working in the computer business*

ˌyoung ˈTurk *noun* (*old-fashioned*) a young person who wants great changes to take place in the established political system

your 0‑ /jɔː(r); *NAmE* jʊr *weak form* jə(r)/ *det.* (the possessive form of *you*) **1** 0‑ of or belonging to the person or people being spoken or written to: *I like your dress.* ◇ *Excuse me, is this your seat?* ◇ *The bank is on your right.* **2** 0‑ of or belonging to people in general: *Dentists advise you to have your teeth checked every six months.* ◇ *In Japan you are taught great respect for your elders.* **3** (*informal*) used to show that sb/sth is well known or often talked about: *This is your typical English pub.* ◇ (*ironic, disapproving*) ***You and your*** *bright ideas!* **4 Your** used in some titles, especially those of royal people: *Your Majesty* ◇ *Your Excellency*

you're /jʊə(r); jɔː(r); *NAmE* jʊr; *NAmE weak form* jər/ *short form* you are

yours 0‑ /jɔːz; *NAmE* jərz; jɔːrz; jʊrz/ *pron.*

1 0‑ of or belonging to you: *Is that book yours?* ◇ *Is she a friend of yours?* ◇ *My hair is very fine. Yours is much thicker.* **2** 0‑ (usually **Yours**) used at the end of a letter before signing your name: (*BrE*) ***Yours sincerely/faithfully*** ◇ (*NAmE*) ***Sincerely Yours*** ◇ (*NAmE*) ***Yours Truly*** **3** (*BrE, informal*) your home: *Let's go back to yours after the show.*

your·self 0‑ /jɔːˈself; *weak form* jə-; *NAmE* jər-; jɔːr-; jʊr-/ (*pl.* **your·selves** /-ˈselvz/) *pron.*

1 0‑ (the reflexive form of *you*) used when the person or people being spoken to both cause and are affected by an action: *Have you hurt yourself?* ◇ *You don't seem quite yourself today* (= you do not seem well or do not seem as happy as usual). ◇ *Enjoy yourselves!* **2** 0‑ used to emphasize the fact that the person who is being spoken to is doing sth: *Do it yourself—I don't have time.* ◇ *You can try it out for yourselves.* ◇ *You yourself are one of the chief offenders.* **3** you: *We sell a lot of these to people like yourself.* ◇ *'And yourself,' he replied, 'How are you?'*

IDM **(all) by yourˈself/yourˈselves 1** alone; without anyone else: *How long were you by yourself in the house?* **2** without help: *Are you sure you did this exercise by yourself?* **(all) to yourˈself/yourˈselves** for only you to have, use, etc: *I'm going to be away next week so you'll have the office to yourself.* **be yourˈself** to act naturally: *Don't act sophisticated—just be yourself.*

youse (also **yous**) /juːz/ *pron.* (*non-standard, dialect*) a word meaning 'you', used when talking to more than one person

youth 0‑ /juːθ/ *noun* (*pl.* **youths** /juːðz/)

1 0‑ [U] the time of life when a person is young, especially the time before a child becomes an adult: *He had been a talented musician in his youth.* **2** 0‑ [U] the quality or state of being young: *She brings to the job a rare combination of youth and experience.* **3** 0‑ [C] (often *disapproving*) a young man: *The fight was started by a gang of youths.* **4** 0‑ (also **the youth**) [pl.] young people considered as a group: *the nation's youth* ◇ *the youth of today* ◇ *youth culture* ◇ *youth unemployment*

ˈyouth club *noun* (in Britain) a club where young people can meet each other and take part in various activities

ˌyouth ˈcustody *noun* [U] (*BrE*) a period of time when a young criminal is kept in a type of prison as a punishment: *He was sentenced to two years' youth custody.* ◇ *a youth custody centre*

youth·ful /ˈjuːθfl/ *adj.* **1** typical of young people: *youthful enthusiasm/energy/inexperience* **2** young or seeming younger than you are: *She's a very youthful 65.* ▸ **youth·ful·ly** /-fəli/ *adv.* **youth·ful·ness** *noun* [U]

ˈyouth hostel *noun* a building that provides cheap and simple accommodation and meals, especially to young people who are travelling ➲ COLLOCATIONS at TRAVEL

ˈyouth hostelling *noun* [U] (*BrE*) the activity of staying in different youth hostels and walking, etc. between them: *to go youth hostelling*

YouTube™ /ˈjuːtjuːb; *NAmE* ˈjuːtuːb/ *noun* [U] a website where people can watch and share short videos

you've /juːv/ *short form* you have

yowl /jaʊl/ *verb* [I] to make a long loud cry that sounds unhappy SYN **wail** ▸ **yowl** *noun*

ˈyo-yo *noun, verb, adj.*

■ **noun** (also **Yo Yo™**) (*pl.* **yo-yos, Yo Yos**) a toy that consists of two round pieces of plastic or wood joined together, with a piece of string wound between them. You put one end of the string around your finger and make the yo-yo go up and down: *He kept bouncing up and down* ***like a yo-yo.***

■ **verb** [I] (+ **adv./prep.**) to change repeatedly in size, amount, quality, etc. from one extreme to another: *When I was young my weight yo-yoed between 140 and 190 pounds.*

■ **adj.** [only before noun] changing repeatedly in size, amount, quality, etc. from one extreme to another: *She worries about her pattern of yo-yo dieting.*

yr (also **yr.** especially in *NAmE*) *abbr.* **1** (*pl.* **yrs**) YEAR(S): *children aged 4–11 yrs* **2** YOUR

yt·ter·bium /ɪˈtɜːbiəm; *NAmE* ɪˈtɜːrb-/ *noun* [U] (*symb.* Yb) a chemical element. Ytterbium is a silver-white metal used to make steel stronger and in some X-RAY machines.

yt·trium /ˈɪtriəm/ *noun* [U] (*symb.* Y) a chemical element. Yttrium is a grey-white metal used in MAGNETS.

Y

yuan /ju'ɑːn/ *noun* (*pl.* **yuan**) the unit of money in China ➲ see also RENMINBI

yucca /'jʌkə/ *noun* a tropical plant with long stiff pointed leaves on a thick straight STEM, often grown indoors

yuck (*BrE* also **yuk**) /jʌk/ *exclamation* (*informal*) used to show that you think sth is disgusting or unpleasant: *It's filthy! Yuck!*

yucky (*BrE* also **yukky**) /'jʌki/ *adj.* (*informal*) disgusting or very unpleasant: *yucky food*

Yue /jə'weɪ; jʊ'eɪ/ *noun* = CANTONESE

Yule /juːl/ *noun* [C, U] (*old use* or *literary*) the festival of Christmas

'yule log *noun* **1** a large LOG of wood traditionally burnt on Christmas Eve **2** a chocolate cake in the shape of a LOG, traditionally eaten at Christmas

Yule·tide /'juːltaɪd/ *noun* [U, C] (*old use* or *literary*) the period around Christmas Day: *Yuletide food and drink*

yum /jʌm/ (also **,yum-'yum**) *exclamation* (*informal*) used to show that you think sth tastes or smells very nice

yummy /'jʌmi/ *adj.* (*informal*) very good to eat **SYN** **delicious**: *a yummy cake*

'yummy mummy *noun* (*pl.* **-ies**) (*BrE*, *informal*) an attractive young woman who is the mother of a young child or children: *celebrity yummy mummies*

yup·pie (also **yuppy**) /'jʌpi/ *noun* (*pl.* **-ies**) (*informal*, often *disapproving*) a young professional person who lives in a city and earns a lot of money that they spend on expensive and fashionable things **ORIGIN** Formed from the first letters of the words 'young urban professional'.

yup·pify /'jʌpɪfaɪ/ *verb* (**yup·pi·fies**, **yup·pi·fy·ing**, **yup·pi·fied**, **yup·pi·fied**) [often passive] **~ sth** (*informal*, *disapproving*) to make sth such as an area of a city more expensive and fashionable, and attractive to yuppies: *a yuppified area of London* ▸ **yup·pi·fi·ca·tion** /ˌjʌpɪfɪ'keɪʃn/ *noun* [U]

yurt /jɜːt; *NAmE* jɜːrt/ *noun* a type of traditional tent used in Mongolia and Siberia

YWCA /ˌwaɪ dʌbljuː siː 'eɪ/ (also *NAmE informal* **the Y**) *abbr.* Young Women's Christian Association (an organization that exists in many countries and provides accommodation and social and sports activities): *members of the YWCA*

Zz

Z (also **z**) /zed; *US* ziː/ *noun* (*pl.* **Zs**, **Z's**, **z's** /zedz; *US* ziːz/) **1** [C, U] the 26th and last letter of the English alphabet: *'Zebra' begins with (a) Z/'Z'.* **2** **Z's** [pl.] (*NAmE, informal, humorous*) sleep: *I need to* ***catch some Z's.*** IDM see A *n.*

'Z angles *noun* = ALTERNATE ANGLES

zany /'zeɪni/ *adj.* (**zani·er**, **zani·est**) (*informal*) strange or unusual in an amusing way SYN **wacky**: *zany humour*

zap /zæp/ *verb* (**-pp-**) (*informal*) **1** [T] to destroy, kill or hit sb/sth suddenly and with force: **~ sb/sth** *The monster* ***got zapped*** *by a flying saucer* (= in a computer game). ◇ *It's vital to zap stress fast.* ◇ **~ sb/sth with sth** *He jumped like a man who'd been zapped with 1 000 volts.* **2** [I] **+ adv./prep.** to do sth very fast: *I'm zapping through* (= reading very fast) *some modern novels at the moment.* **3** [I, T] **~ (sth)** to use the REMOTE CONTROL to change television channels quickly **4** [I, T] **~ (sb/sth) + adv./prep.** to move, or make sb/sth move, very fast in the direction mentioned SYN **zip**: *The racing cars zapped past us.*

zap·per /'zæpə(r)/ *noun* (*informal*) **1** = REMOTE CONTROL **2** a device or weapon that attacks or destroys sth quickly: *a bug zapper*

ZAR *abbr.* the written abbreviation for the South African RAND (= the national money of South Africa).

zeal /ziːl/ *noun* [U, C] **~ (for/in sth)** (*formal*) great energy or enthusiasm connected with sth that you feel strongly about: *her* ***missionary/reforming/religious/political zeal***

zealot /'zelət/ *noun* (often *disapproving*) a person who is extremely enthusiastic about sth, especially religion or politics SYN **fanatic**

zeal·ot·ry /'zelətri/ *noun* [U] (often *disapproving*) the attitude or behaviour of a zealot: *religious zealotry*

zeal·ous /'zeləs/ *adj.* (*formal*) showing great energy and enthusiasm for sth, especially because you feel strongly about it: *a zealous reformer* ▸ **zeal·ous·ly** *adv.*

zebra /'zebrə; 'ziːbrə/ *noun* (*pl.* **zebra** or **zebras**) an African wild animal like a horse with black and white lines (=STRIPES) on its body

ˌzebra 'crossing *noun* (*BrE*) an area of road marked with broad black and white lines where vehicles must stop for people to walk across ➲ see also PEDESTRIAN CROSSING.

zebu /'ziːbuː/ *noun* (*pl.* **zebus** or **zebu**) an animal of the cow family with long horns and a HUMP (= high part) on its back, kept on farms especially in hot climates.

zeit·geist /'zaɪtgaɪst/ *noun* [sing.] (from *German, formal*) the general mood or quality of a particular period of history, as shown by the ideas, beliefs, etc. common at the time SYN **spirit of the times**

Zen /zen/ *noun* [U] a Japanese form of Buddhism

zen·ith /'zenɪθ/ *noun* **1** the highest point that the sun or moon reaches in the sky, directly above you **2** (*formal*) the time when sth is strongest and most successful SYN **peak** OPP **nadir**

zephyr /'zefə(r)/ *noun* (*old-fashioned* or *literary*) a soft gentle wind

Zep·pelin /'zepəlɪn/ *noun* a type of large AIRSHIP

zero /'zɪərəʊ; *NAmE* 'zɪroʊ; 'ziː-/ *number, verb*

■ ***number*** **1** (*pl.* **-os**) (*BrE* also **nought**) 0: *Five, four, three, two, one, zero... We have lift-off.* **2** a temperature, pressure, etc. that is equal to zero on a scale: *It was ten degrees below zero last night* (= −10°C). ◇ *The thermometer had fallen to zero.* **3** the lowest possible amount or level; nothing at all: *I rated my chances as zero.* ◇ *zero inflation*

■ ***verb*** (**zer·oes**, **zero·ing**, **zer·oed**, **zer·oed**) **~ sth** to turn an instrument, control, etc. to zero

PHR V **ˌzero 'in on sb/sth** **1** to fix all your attention on the person or thing mentioned: *They zeroed in on the key issues.* **2** to aim guns, etc. at the person or thing mentioned

ˌzero-'carbon *adj.* in which the amount of CARBON DIOXIDE produced has been reduced to nothing or is balanced by actions that protect the environment SYN **carbon neutral**: *a zero-carbon house*

ˌzero 'gravity *noun* [U] (*abbr.* ˌzero 'G) a state in which there is no GRAVITY, or where gravity has no effect, for example in space

ˌzero 'grazing *noun* [U] a farming method that involves keeping cows inside and bringing them cut grass, rather than letting them feed in the fields

'zero hour *noun* [U] the time when an important event, an attack, etc. is planned to start

ˌzero-'rated *adj.* (*BrE, technical*) (of goods, services, etc.) that you do not need to pay VAT (= value added tax) on

ˌzero-'sum game *noun* a situation in which what is gained by one person or group is lost by another person or group

ˌzero 'tolerance *noun* [U] the policy of applying laws very strictly so that people are punished even for offences that are not very serious

zest /zest/ *noun* **1** [sing., U] **~ (for sth)** enjoyment and enthusiasm SYN **appetite**: *He had a great* ***zest for life.*** **2** [U, sing.] the quality of being exciting, interesting and enjoyable: *The slight risk added zest to the experience.* **3** [U] the outer skin of an orange, a lemon, etc, when it is used to give flavour in cooking ➲ compare PEEL, RIND, SKIN ▸ **zest·ful** /-fl/ *adj.* **zesty** /'zesti/ *adj.*

zeta /'ziːtə/ *noun* the 6th letter of the Greek alphabet (Z, ζ)

zeug·ma /'zjuːgmə; *NAmE* 'zuːg-/ *noun* [C, U] (*technical*) the use of a word which must be understood in two different ways at the same time in order to make sense, for example 'The bread was baking, and so was I'.

zig·gurat /'zɪgəræt/ *noun* in ancient Mesopotamia, a tower with steps going up the sides, sometimes with a TEMPLE at the top

zig·zag /'zɪgzæg/ *noun, verb*

■ ***noun*** a line or pattern that looks like a series of letter W's as it bends to the left and then to the right again: *The path descended the hill in a series of zigzags.* ▸ **zig·zag** *adj.* [only before noun]: *a zigzag line/path/pattern*

■ ***verb*** (**-gg-**) [I] (**+ adv./prep.**) to move forward by making sharp sudden turns first to the left and then to the right: *The narrow path zigzags up the cliff.*

zilch /zɪltʃ/ *noun* [U] (*informal*) nothing: *I arrived in this country with zilch.*

zilla (also **zillah**) /'zɪlə/ *noun* (in S Asia) a district that has its own local government

zil·lion /'zɪljən/ *noun* (*informal, especially NAmE*) a very large number: *There were zillions of people there.*

Zim·mer frame™ /'zɪmə freɪm; *NAmE* 'zɪmər/ (also *informal* **Zim·mer** /'zɪmə(r)/) (both *BrE*) (*NAmE* **walk·er**) *noun* a metal frame that people use to help them to walk, for example people who are old or who have sth wrong with their legs ➲ picture at FRAME

zinc /zɪŋk/ *noun* **1** [U] (*symb.* **Zn**) a chemical element. Zinc is a bluish-white metal that is mixed with COPPER to produce BRASS and is often used to cover other metals to prevent them from RUSTING. **2** [C] (*informal*) (in some places in Africa) a sheet of CORRUGATED IRON that is used to make a roof, shelter, etc: *They built a temporary home out of zincs.*

ˌzinc 'oxide *noun* [U] (*symb.* **ZnO**) a substance used in creams as a treatment for certain skin conditions

'zine (also **zine**) /ziːn/ *noun* (*informal*) a magazine, especially a FANZINE

zing /zɪŋ/ *verb, noun*

■ ***verb*** (*informal*) **1** [I, T] **~ (sth) + adv./prep.** to move or to make sth move very quickly, often with a high whistling sound: *electrical pulses zinging down a wire* **2** [T] **~ sb/sth (for/on sth)** (*NAmE*) to criticize sb strongly

■ ***noun*** [U] (*informal*) interest or excitement ▸ **zingy** *adj.*

zing·er /'zɪŋə(r)/ *noun* (*informal, especially NAmE*) a clever or amusing remark: *She opened the speech with a real zinger.*

Zion·ism /'zaɪənɪzəm/ *noun* [U] a political movement that was originally concerned with establishing an independent state for Jewish people, and is now concerned with developing the state of Israel ▶ **Zion·ist** /'zaɪənɪst/ *noun, adj.*

zip /zɪp/ *noun, verb*

■ ***noun*** **1** (also **'zip fastener**) (both *BrE*) (also **zip·per** *NAmE, BrE*) [C] a thing that you use to fasten clothes, bags, etc. It consists of two rows of metal or plastic teeth that you can pull together to close sth or pull apart to open it: *to **do up/undo/open/close a zip** ◇ My zip's stuck.* ➲ VISUAL VOCAB page V51 **2** [U] (*informal*) energy or speed **3** [sing.] (*informal, especially NAmE*) nothing.

■ ***verb*** (-pp-) **1** [T] to fasten clothes, bags, etc. with a zip/zipper: **~ sth** *I zipped and buttoned my jacket.* ◇ **~ sb/yourself into sth** *The children were safely zipped into their sleeping bags.* ◇ **~ sth + adj.** *He zipped his case shut.* ➲ compare UNZIP **2** [I] **~ (up/together)** to be fastened with a zip/zipper: *The sleeping bags can zip together.* **3** [I, T] **~ (sth) + adv./prep.** (*informal*) to move very quickly or to make sth move very quickly in the direction mentioned: *A sports car zipped past us.* **4** [T] **~ sth** (*computing*) to COMPRESS a file (= make it smaller) OPP **unzip**

PHR V **,zip 'up** | **,zip sb/sth 'up** to be fastened with a zip/zipper; to fasten sth with a zip/zipper: *This jacket zips up right to the neck.* ◇ *Shall I zip you up* (= fasten your dress, etc.)*?* ➲ compare UNZIP

'zip code (also **ZIP code**) (*US*) (*BrE, CanE* **post·code**) *noun* a group of letters and/or numbers that are used as part of an address so that post/mail can be separated into groups and delivered more quickly

Ziploc bag™ /'zɪplɒk bæg; *NAmE* -lɑːk/ *noun* (*NAmE*) a small plastic bag for storing food, that has edges that seal when you press them together in order to keep the air out

zip·per /'zɪpə(r)/ (*especially NAmE*) (*BrE* also **zip**, **'zip fastener**) *noun* a thing that you use to fasten clothes, bags, etc. It consists of two rows of metal or plastic teeth that you can pull together to close sth or pull apart to open it.

zippy /'zɪpi/ *adj.* (**zip·pier**, **zip·pi·est**) (*informal*) **1** able to move very quickly: *a zippy little car* **2** lively and exciting, especially in flavour: *a wine with a zippy tang*

'zip-up *adj.* [only before noun] (*especially BrE*) (of clothing, a bag, etc.) fastened with a zip/zipper: *a zip-up top*

zir·co·nium /zɜː'kəʊniəm; *NAmE* zɜːr'koʊ-/ *noun* [U] (*symb.* Zr) a chemical element. Zirconium is a hard silver-grey metal that does not CORRODE very easily.

zit /zɪt/ *noun* (*informal, especially NAmE*) a spot on the skin, especially on the face SYN **pimple** ➲ compare SPOT

zith·er /'zɪðə(r)/ *noun* a musical instrument with a lot of metal strings stretched over a flat wooden box, that you play with your fingers or a PLECTRUM

zo·diac /'zəʊdiæk; *NAmE* 'zoʊ-/ *noun* **1 the zodiac** [sing.] the imaginary area in the sky in which the sun, moon and planets appear to lie, and which has been divided into twelve equal parts each with a special name and symbol: *the **signs of the zodiac*** **2** [C] a diagram of these twelve parts, and signs that some people believe can be used to predict how the planets will influence our lives ▶ **zo·di·ac·al** /zəʊ'daɪəkl; *NAmE* zoʊ-/ *adj.*

zom·bie /'zɒmbi; *NAmE* 'zɑːmbi/ *noun* **1** (*informal*) a person who seems only partly alive, without any feeling or interest in what is happening **2** (in some African and Caribbean religions and in horror stories) a dead body that has been made alive again by magic

zonal /'zəʊnl; *NAmE* 'zoʊnl/ *adj.* (*technical*) connected with zones; arranged in zones

zone 🔑 /zəʊn; *NAmE* zoʊn/ *noun, verb*

■ ***noun*** **1** 🔑 an area or a region with a particular feature or use: *a **war/security/demilitarized, etc. zone** ◇ an **earthquake/danger, etc. zone** ◇ a **pedestrian zone*** (= where vehicles may not go) ➲ see also NO-FLY ZONE, TIME ZONE, TWILIGHT **2** 🔑 one of the areas that a larger area is divided into for the purpose of organization: *postal charges to countries in zone 2* **3** an area or a part of an object, especially one that is different from its surroundings: *When the needle enters the red zone the engine is too hot.* ◇ *the erogenous zones of the body* ➲ see also CRUMPLE ZONE **4** one of the parts that the earth's surface is divided into by imaginary lines that are parallel to the EQUATOR: *the northern/southern temperate zone*

IDM **in the 'zone** (*NAmE, informal*) in a state in which you feel confident and are performing at your best: *When I'm in the zone, writing is the most satisfying thing in the world.*

■ ***verb*** [usually passive] **1 ~ sth (for sth)** to keep an area of land to be used for a particular purpose: *The town centre was zoned for office development.* **2 ~ sth** to divide an area of land into smaller areas ▶ **zon·ing** *noun* [U]

PHR V **,zone 'out** (*especially NAmE, informal*) to fall asleep, become unconscious or stop paying attention: *I just zoned out for a moment.*

zoned /zəʊnd; *NAmE* zoʊnd/ *adj.* **1** divided into areas designed for a particular use: *zoned housing land* **2** (also **,zoned 'out**) (both *NAmE, informal*) not behaving or thinking normally because of the effects of a drug

zonked /zɒŋkt; *NAmE* zɑːŋkt; zɔːŋkt/ *adj.* [not before noun] **~ (out)** (*slang*) extremely tired or suffering from the effects of alcohol or drugs

zoo /zuː/ *noun* (*pl.* **zoos**) (also *formal* **,zoological 'garden**) a place where many kinds of wild animals are kept for the public to see and where they are studied, bred and protected

zoo·keep·er /'zuːkiːpə(r)/ *noun* a person who works in a zoo, taking care of the animals

zoo·logic·al /,zəʊə'lɒdʒɪkl; ,zuːə'l-; *NAmE* ,zoʊə'lɑːdʒ-/ *adj.* connected with the science of ZOOLOGY

,zoological 'garden *noun* (also **,zoological 'gardens** [pl.]) (*formal*) = ZOO

zo·olo·gist /zəʊ'ɒlədʒɪst; zu'ɒl-; *NAmE* zoʊ'ɑːl-/ *noun* a scientist who studies zoology

zo·ology /zəʊ'ɒlədʒi; zu'ɒl-; *NAmE* zoʊ'ɑːl-/ *noun* [U] the scientific study of animals and their behaviour

zoom /zuːm/ *verb, noun*

■ ***verb*** **1** [I] **+ adv./prep.** (*informal*) to move or go somewhere very fast SYN **rush, whizz**: *Traffic zoomed past us.* ◇ *For five weeks they zoomed around Europe.* **2** [I] **~ (up) (to…)** (*informal*) (of prices, costs, etc.) to increase a lot quickly and suddenly: *House prices have zoomed up this year.*

PHR V **,zoom 'in/'out** (of a camera) to show the object that is being photographed from closer/further away, with the use of a ZOOM LENS: *The camera zoomed in on her face.*

■ ***noun*** **1** [C] = ZOOM LENS: *a zoom shot* **2** [sing.] the sound of a vehicle moving very fast

'zoom lens (also **zoom**) *noun* a camera LENS that you use to make the thing that you are photographing appear nearer to you or further away from you than it really is ➲ VISUAL VOCAB page V35

zoot suit /'zuːt suːt; *BrE* also sjuːt/ *noun* a man's suit with wide trousers/pants and a long loose jacket with wide shoulders that was popular in the 1940s

zorb·ing /'zɔːbɪŋ; *NAmE* 'zɔːrb-/ *noun* [U] a sport in which sb is put inside a large transparent plastic ball which is then rolled along the ground or down hills

Zoro·ast·rian·ism /,zɒrəʊ'æstriənɪzəm; *NAmE* ,zɔːroʊ-/ *noun* [U] a religion started in ancient Persia by Zoroaster, that teaches that there is one God and a continuing struggle in the world between forces of light and dark ▶ **Zoro·ast·rian** *noun, adj.* ➲ see also PARSEE

zuc·chini /zu'kiːni/ *noun* (*pl.* **zuc·chini** or **zuc·chi·nis**) (*NAmE*) (*BrE* **cour·gette**) a long vegetable with dark green skin and white flesh ➲ VISUAL VOCAB page V27

Zulu /'zuːluː/ *noun* **1** [C] a member of a race of black people who live in South Africa **2** [U] the language spoken by Zulus and many other black South Africans ▶ **Zulu** *adj.*

Zuni /'zuːni/ *noun* (*pl.* **Zuni** or **Zunis**) a member of a Native American people many of whom live in western New Mexico

zwie·back /'zwiːbæk/ *noun* [U] (*NAmE*, from *German*) slices of sweet bread that are cooked again until they are dry and hard

zy·deco /'zaɪdɪkəʊ; *NAmE* -koʊ/ *noun* [U] a type of dance music, originally played by black Americans in Louisiana

zy·gote /'zaɪgəʊt; *NAmE* -goʊt/ *noun* (*biology*) a single cell that develops into a person or animal, formed by the joining together of a male and a female GAMETE (= a cell that is provided by each parent)

Z

Oxford Writing Tutor

Using the Oxford Advanced Learner's Dictionary to improve your writing

Whether you are writing a business email or a long research essay, your dictionary can be a powerful tool to assist you in becoming a better writer in English.

1. Using the main part of the dictionary

You can use the main A–Z of the dictionary to help you:

- **Choose your words carefully.** Many words in English have similar or related meanings, but are used in different contexts or situations.

Look carefully at the example sentences provided in the entries for words you want to use. Also look at any **synonym notes**, **vocabulary notes** and **topic notes** to help you choose the most appropriate word. If you need academic vocabulary, look for the AW symbol.

- **Combine words naturally and effectively.** In English, certain pairs of words go together and sound natural to native speakers (for example, *heavy rain*)—and others do not (~~*strong rain*~~). This is called **collocation.** Information on which words collocate with one another can be found in the example sentences in the dictionary entries.

Look up the key nouns you have used in your writing to check which verbs or adjectives are usually used with them.

- **Become more flexible.** Rather than repeating the same word or phrase many times in your work, try to find other ways to express your ideas.

Look for the SYN symbol to find synonyms and also study the **synonyms notes**. Look for **word families** and try using words in the same family that are different parts of speech (e.g. *different*, adjective and *differ*, verb). For example, you could write: *French **is different from** English in this respect*. You could also express this: *French **differs from** English in this respect*.

- **Edit and check your work.** You can use your dictionary to check any problem areas such as spelling, parts of speech, irregular forms, grammar, phrasal verbs and prepositions.

2. Using the Writing Tutor

In the following pages you will find examples of essays and practical types of writing that you can use as models for your own work. You will also find advice about planning, organizing and writing each type of text.

- **Examples of written texts.** Look carefully at:
  - the structure and organization of the text
  - the way ideas and paragraphs are linked
  - the language and style
  - the notes on particular points
- **Tips** These are quick reminders and advice to help when you are writing.
- **Language banks** give you some useful phrases that you can use in each type of writing.

Check that you are familiar with these phrases and know how to use them correctly.

You can add other phrases when you meet them in your reading. In the main part of the dictionary there are more notes like this which give you further phrases and examples to show you how to use them. (*For example, look at the note at 'however'*)

Contents

The writing process.	
What makes writing formal?	WT2
Answering the question	WT4
Writing a comparison essay	WT6
Writing an argument essay	WT8
Writing a longer essay or dissertation	WT10
Oral presentations	WT12
Writing a summary	WT14
Reporting on data	WT16
Writing a report	WT18
Writing a book or film/movie review	WT20
Discussing pictures and cartoons	WT22
Writing a formal letter	WT24
Writing emails (business and academic)	WT26
Writing a CV/résumé and covering letter	WT30

The Writing Process

Each individual writer has their own aims and needs and their own way of approaching various parts of the writing process. However, whether you are writing a short essay, an article, a report or a research paper, the overall process is generally the same.

1 Preliminary Phase

Ask yourself some planning questions that will help guide the rest of the process.

What is the purpose of this piece of writing?

For example:

- To answer a specific essay, examination or research question
- To convince others of your point of view
- To communicate your knowledge or understanding to others, such as a teacher or an examiner

Who is my audience?

For example:

- A teacher or professor
- Fellow students or colleagues
- An employer
- The general public

The answers (you may have more than one purpose or type of audience) will help you to choose the appropriate level of formality. They will also help you make decisions about the amount of research required, as well as the kinds of examples and supporting evidence you will use.

2 Pre-Writing Phase

Explore

Brainstorm for ideas using whatever method suits you best:

- Mind maps
- Lists of interesting concepts, facts, questions, etc.
- Conversations with colleagues

Research

Next, research your topic and gather information from a variety of sources:

- Books and journals
- The media
- Websites
- Interviews or questionnaires
- Scientific studies

When you read sources, take detailed notes and keep an accurate record of each source. (*Look at page WT10.*)

Organize

After carrying out your research, you can draft a thesis (your main argument, statement or idea) to guide you.

Then, using your notes, make a detailed outline of the logical plan of your essay, article or report to support this thesis, giving a structure to your writing before you begin to write.

- Decide roughly how many words you will give to each part of your essay/report.
- Collect or prepare any visual aids such as charts or diagrams that you might need.

3 Writing Phase

In this phase, you will draft and revise several times until you have what you consider to be a final draft.

Draft

Write your draft in formal sentences and paragraphs.

- Remain focused on your thesis or main idea. If you do change this, go back and adapt your original plan to ensure that your essay/report continues to support the new thesis.
- Follow your outline, modifying it if necessary.
- In early drafts, concentrate on structure rather than spelling and punctuation.

Review/Edit

In this step, you read your writing with a critical eye.

In early drafts, ask yourself:

- Have you answered the question or achieved your original purpose?
- Have you introduced your subject, developed it logically and come to a conclusion?
- Is your supporting evidence appropriate and complete? Do you need more examples, statistics or quotes?
- Have you used headings to help the reader, if appropriate?
- Are the relationships between ideas clear and clearly signalled to the reader?
- Is each part the right length for the demands of the topic – with no part too long?

In later drafts, ask yourself:

- Have you used paragraph breaks well?
- Is the level of formality appropriate for your readers?
- Have you chosen your words carefully, using correct collocations?
- Have you avoided repeating the same words or phrases too often (except technical terms)?
- Have you met any word count requirements?

If possible, ask someone else to read your text.

After each review, return to the drafting step, revising and editing your writing as necessary.

Using sources in essays

Ask yourself:
Have you quoted or mentioned sources to support your points?
Have you used the citation style recommended by your teachers or institution?
Have you listed your references in the style recommended?

(Look also at page WT11.)

4 Presentation Phase

Proofread

When you have a final draft of your writing, you will need to read it once more to find and correct surface errors.

Tip

- Try to leave some time between your final draft and proofreading as you will find it easier to see your mistakes.

Check for

- Spelling
- Punctuation
- Grammatical mistakes.

You may find it helpful to ask someone else to proofread your final draft as a last step.

Format

Check with your teacher or tutor how you should present your work in terms of:

- Font size • Margins • Line spacing
- Paper size

Examinations

In an exam, you will not have time for all these stages, but your answers will be more successful if you:

- brainstorm ideas
- organize and plan
- re-read, check and edit

What makes writing formal?

Whatever type of text you are writing, your aim should always be to express your ideas clearly and in a way that your readers can easily understand.

When you read, notice the kind of language that is used in the type of writing you need to do.

To make your writing more formal, consider:

1. **Word choice.**
   - It is usually best to use standard English words and phrases, that is, those with no label in the dictionary.
   - Only use words and phrases marked *formal* if you are sure they are appropriate.
   - Avoid anything marked *informal*, *slang*, *offensive*, etc.
   - Use suitable synonyms for common words such as *do*, *put*, *get*, *make*. e.g. *Several operations* ***were carried out/performed*** (not *done*).
   - Words that are frequently used in academic writing are marked **AW** in the dictionary.
2. **Short forms**
   - Avoid contracted forms (e.g. *haven't*, *I'm*) and abbreviations (e.g. *ad – advertisement*)
3. **Sentence structure**
   - In formal writing you are likely to be expressing complex ideas. To do this you will need to write sentences using relative pronouns (e.g. *which*, *that*), subordinating conjunctions (e.g. *although*, *because*, *if*) and coordinating conjunctions (e.g. *and*, *but*, *or*).
   - Very long sentences with many clauses can be difficult to understand. Aim for **clarity**.

Academic writing

This tends to be **impersonal** in style in order to be objective. This makes it sound formal. When you read in your subject, notice how the writers express themselves. The following points may help you in your writing:

- Limit the use of the **first person pronouns** (*I* and *we*). Rather than *In this study I aim to…*, write: *This study aims to…* or *The aim of this study is to…* Look at how *I* and *we* are used in your subject area. Avoid using *you*.
- **Passive forms** are often used as they focus attention on the verb, not the person e.g. *A study was conducted to see…*; *It can be argued that…*
- Patterns with **it and an adjective** are often used: *It is clear that…*; *It is necessary to…*
- **Nouns** are often used as subjects of active verbs: *The results show that…*
- **Complex noun phrases** with prepositions are very common: *The advantages of X are…*; *the use of light treatment in 95 patients with…*

Answering the question

At all times, you must ensure that you really understand an examination question or assignment title and address all the required parts.

Questions can be considered in terms of three main components:

- **Topic**
- **Scope and focus**
- **Question type**

Topic

The topic(s) of the question will usually be clear from the question itself. For example: *Explain the process of photosynthesis.*
When you write your answer think about why the examiner has chosen to ask about this topic.

Scope and focus

Often, the wording of the question will include a word or phrase that either limits or expands the topic in a very specific way. These phrases show you the focus of the question. Try to avoid common mistakes, such as:

- **Covering too broad an area.** For example, if the question asks about textile mills in the American South in the 1930s, think very carefully about including information about the 1920s or 1940s, or about textile mills in other parts of the country.
- **Writing with too narrow a focus.** For example, if you are asked about the impact of climate change on South America, you should not write about its impact only on Brazil.
- **Including irrelevant information.** For example, if you are asked about using nuclear power as an energy source, you should not write about wind or solar power.
- **Only answering half of the question.** For example, if the question asks *What other effects will a reduction in air travel have and will the advantages outweigh the disadvantages?* you need to discuss both questions.

Question types

The depth and type of information that you provide in your answer depends on the kind of question being asked. The table on the next page shows the key words that might appear in different types of questions.

1. Knowledge Questions
These ask you to recall important facts and are the simplest question.

2. Comprehension Questions
These ask you to demonstrate your understanding of concepts. You must clearly show that you understand the ideas and theories that underlie the facts.

3. Application Questions
Here you use your knowledge of facts and concepts to address a specific problem. These questions require you to move beyond simple recollection.

4. Analysis Questions
These examine relationships between/among various facts and concepts.

5. Synthesis Questions
These ask you to create a new product or structure in written form.

6. Evaluation Questions
These ask you to make value judgments and present your own opinions. This kind of question is very common in academic work. It is important to support your opinions by citing the work and views of experts in the field, if possible.

IELTS Academic Writing

- Task 1: This is usually a combination of comprehension and analysis questions: *Summarize the information… and make comparisons where relevant.*
- Task 2: This is usually an evaluation question: *At what age should young people be considered adults? Explain your position.*

Question Types

Level of Difficulty

4. Analysis Questions

Key verbs

- analyze
- compare
- contrast
- distinguish
- differentiate
- subdivide
- classify
- categorize
- select
- infer
- prioritize

Example:
Compare the merits of 'renting' and 'squatting' as solutions to housing problems for the poor in cities in the developing world.

5. Synthesis Questions

Key verbs

- design
- plan
- construct
- create
- compose
- produce
- develop
- invent
- combine

Example:
Design an experiment to investigate whether listening to music improves students' performance in their studies.

6. Evaluation Questions

Key verbs

- discuss
- evaluate
- compare
- consider
- examine
- explore
- comment (on)
- justify
- appraise
- weigh
- support
- recommend

Example:
Discuss the argument that the use of force in self-defence is justifiable.

3. Application Questions

Key verbs

- apply
- show
- solve
- choose
- organize
- generalize
- prepare
- relate (X to Y)

Example:
Show how a national minimum wage will affect levels of unemployment and total output.

2. Comprehension Questions

Key verbs

- explain
- summarize
- illustrate
- restate
- paraphrase
- give examples
- express
- distinguish (between)
- trace
- match

Example:
Give three examples of human activities that have major effects on our climate.

1. Knowledge Questions

Key verbs

- outline
- define
- describe
- give
- state
- summarize
- label
- identify
- name
- list

Example:
Define the term 'muscle tone' and describe how it can help good posture.

Writing a comparison essay

You may often need to **compare** and **contrast** things in exams, academic essays, work and everyday life. Here is an example of a comparison essay.

Are private schools better than state schools? Discuss.

Paragraph 1—Introduction

[1]Sentences 1 and 2 catch the reader's interest.
[2]The next sentence gives a definition of the two types of school. (Note: a definition is optional)
[3]The 4th sentence indicates the scope of the essay and leads to the next paragraph.

For parents, few things are more important than their child's education. In many countries, parents of school-age children can choose to send their child to a private school rather than to a state school.[1] In this essay, state schools are defined as those that do not charge tuition fees because they are funded and run by local or central government; private schools, on the other hand, are funded almost entirely by the fees that they charge.[2] Before deciding where to educate their child, parents need to examine the differences between the two types of school, particularly as regards the curriculum, the quality of tuition and student achievement.[3]

Paragraph 2—Similarities
Aims, teaching and assessment

The writer notes 2 similarities here before emphasizing 5 differences in paragraphs 3–5.

Private and state schools are comparable in some respects. Like state schools, private schools aim to develop the knowledge, skills and character of students, in order to prepare them for their future lives. Both types of school are also very similar in the way they organize their teaching and assessment, using terms or semesters with assessments at the end of the academic year.

Paragraph 3—Difference 1
The curriculum

Despite these similarities indicates that the writer is now going to list the differences.

Despite these similarities, there are a number of marked differences in the way that state and private schools operate. The range of subjects taught at state schools is largely limited by the demands of the national curriculum. In contrast, private schools can offer a greater choice of subjects, because they generally have more money to spend on equipment, technology and staff than state schools do.

Paragraph 4—Difference 2
Quality of teachers

Teachers working within the state system must have recognized teaching qualifications and are paid according to a national scale. Private schools, however, are in a position to offer higher salaries and may therefore be able to attract subject specialists who have considerable expertise in their field.

Paragraph 5—Differences 3-5 Class size, discipline and academic standards

In general, it is true to say that while state schools have a high student-teacher ratio, private schools tend to offer smaller classes. This may lead to better discipline in private schools with the result that students may achieve somewhat higher academic standards.

Paragraph 6—Conclusion

[1]The first sentence summarizes the findings in paragraphs 2–5.
[2]The second sentence gives the writer's personal opinion.

It is clear, therefore, that there are significant differences between private and state schools, and that private schools may offer advantages.[1] The benefits of private schooling must, however , be balanced against the cost involved and each family's budget priorities.[2]

Key

Blue shows ways of introducing similarities

Yellow shows ways of introducing contrasts

Collocations: adjectives + nouns

To find interesting and appropriate adjectives to use with nouns, look up the nouns in the dictionary: e.g. *difference*; *expertise*; *ratio*; *standard*

Collocations: prepositions

To find the correct preposition to use after a verb or noun, look up the word in the dictionary: e.g. *difference; balance*

Preparing to write

- **Brainstorm ideas** about similarities and differences. For example, arrange points in a table:

Characteristics	State Schools	Private Schools	Similar or different?
Funding	*Government*	*Fees*	*Different*
Class size	*Usually large*	*Usually smaller*	*Different*

- **Highlight the similarities and the differences** and decide which are more important. For this essay the differences are more important.
- **Choose which points to include** in the essay and which to leave out.
- Decide how to **define** the two things you are comparing. Here *funding* formed the basis of the definition.
- Choose the **organization structure** (*see below*). Here **Type A1** was used.

Shorter essays **Type A1**: to emphasize the **differences** Introduction **Similarities** of X and Y **Differences** between X and Y Conclusion OR **Type A2**: To emphasize the **similarities**, reverse the second and third sections.	OR **Type B1**: Introduction Characteristics of X Characteristics of Y Show how Y is **similar** to or **different** from X Conclusion
Longer essays **Type C1** Introduction Aspect 1: compare X and Y Aspect 2: compare X and Y (and so on) Conclusion	OR **Type A1** or **A2** above.

Language bank

Similarities *X… Similarly, Y…* *Both X and Y…* *X… Y also…* Both + plural noun…e.g. *Both types of school…* Like X, Y… e.g. *Like state schools, private schools…* *X and Y are similar in that they both…* *X is similar to Y in terms of / with regard to…* *X resembles Y in that they both…* *X is the same as Y.*	**Differences** *X… On the other hand, Y… / Y, on the other hand,…* *Unlike X, Y…* *X… In contrast, Y… / While X …, Y…* *X…, while Y…* *X… However, Y… / X… Y, however,…* *X differs from Y in terms of / with regard to…* (e.g. *their sources of funding.*) *X is different from / contrasts with Y in that…* *X…, whereas Y… / Whereas X…, Y…*

Being more precise:
Similarities
X is almost / nearly / virtually / just / exactly / precisely *the same as Y.*
X and Y are very / rather / quite *similar.*
Differences
X is slightly / a little / somewhat *smaller than Y.*
X is much / considerably smaller *than Y.*
X and Y are completely / totally / entirely / quite *different.*
X and Y are not quite / exactly / entirely *the same.*

Writing an argument essay

Many essays that you have to write, whether during your school or college course or in an examination, will require you to present a reasoned argument on a particular issue. This will often be based on your research into the topic, but some questions may ask you to give your opinion. In both cases your argument must be clearly organized and supported with information, evidence and reasons. The language tends to be formal and impersonal.

'Manned space missions should now be replaced with unmanned missions.' Discuss.

Paragraph 1—Introduction

[1] Introduces the topic.
[2] States the focus of the essay.

It is clear that the study of space and the planets is by nature expensive. Scientists and politicians must constantly attempt to balance costs with potential research benefits.[1] A major question to be considered is whether the benefits of manned space flight are worth the costs.[2]

Paragraph 2—Introduces the argument

The first point (manned missions are not cost effective) with a quote from an expert to give authority.

[1] This is a useful way to introduce a quotation.

For Nobel Prize-winning physicist Steven Weinberg the answer is clear. As he noted in 2007[1] in a lecture at the Space Telescope Science Institute in Baltimore. 'Human beings don't serve any useful function in space. They radiate heat, they're very expensive to keep alive, and unlike robotic missions, they have a natural desire to come back, so that anything involving human beings is enormously expensive.'

Paragraph 3—Development

Reasons and data are given to support the writer's point of view.

Unmanned missions are much less expensive than manned, having no requirement for airtight compartments, food or life support systems. They are also lighter and therefore require less fuel and launch equipment. According to NASA, the 1992 manned Space Shuttle Endeavor cost $1.7 billion to build and requires approximately $450 million for each launch. In contrast, the entire unmanned Voyager mission from 1972 until 1989, when it observed Neptune, cost only $865 million.

Paragraph 4—Development

Introduces the second point (unmanned projects are more scientifically productive).

In addition to their relative cost effectiveness, unmanned projects generally yield a much greater volume of data. While manned flights have yet to extend beyond the orbit of Earth's moon, unmanned missions have explored almost our entire solar system, and have recently observed an Earth-like planet in a nearby solar system. Manned missions would neither be able to travel so far, be away so long, nor collect so much data while at the same time guaranteeing the astronauts' safe return.

Paragraph 5—Counterargument

[1] Presents the argument: *Some may argue* suggests that the writer will go on to argue against this position.
[2] Refutes it. *However* introduces the argument against [1].

Some may argue that only manned space flight possesses the ability to inspire and engage the general population, providing much-needed momentum for continued governmental funding and educational interest in mathematics and the sciences.[1] However, media coverage of recent projects such as the Mars Rover, the Titan moon lander, and the Hubble telescope's photographs of extrasolar planets demonstrates that unmanned missions clearly have the ability to attract and hold public interest.[2]

Paragraph 6—Conclusion

Summarizes the writer's points and states his/her conclusion on the title.
[1] *Thus* introduces the conclusion.
[2] *I would argue that* clearly shows the writer's position.

Thus,[1] taking into account the lower cost, the greater quantity of data and widepsread popular support, I would argue that[2] for now, at least, unmanned space missions undoubtedly yield the most value in terms of public spending.

Linking words and phrases guide the reader through the argument and show the writer's opinion.

Adverbs can be used to show your opinion.

These phrases make the argument less personal and more objective.

Experts are quoted to support the argument.

Preparing to write

- Brainstorm your ideas on the question, read and research the topic (unless in an examination). Which do you think are the strongest arguments? Decide what your viewpoint will be.
- Select 2 or 3 strong ideas on each side, with supporting examples, ideas or evidence. For some questions you can use evidence from your personal experience.
- Decide how to organize your essay to persuade readers of your case.
- Note down some useful vocabulary on the topic.

Structure 1 (used in the model essay)	**Structure 2**
Introduction Arguments **for** your case + supporting evidence, examples or reasons Arguments **against** + evidence Evaluation of arguments Summary and conclusion *It is possible to reverse arguments for and against.*	Introduction Argument 1:+ supporting evidence, examples or reasons Counterargument Argument 2: + supporting evidence, examples or reasons Counterargument (and so on) Evaluation of arguments Summary and conclusion

Tips

- Look carefully at the **title or question** and make sure you really answer it.
- Use **general statements** to convey the main ideas, and then provide **evidence**, **examples**, **details** and **reasons** to support these statements.
- Use **paragraph divisions** and **connecting words and phrases** to make the structure of your essay clear to your readers.
- For **language** to help you structure your argument, look at the notes at 'addition', 'first'.

Showing your position

When you write an argument essay, you can show what your opinion is on the issue or question without using personal phrases such as *I think*... or *In my opinion*,.... You can do this by choosing words carefully as you write. Some examples are given below. Look out for more in your reading.

Language bank

<table>
<tr>
<td>
Adjectives
important, major, serious, significant
e.g. An important point to consider is...; This was a highly significant discovery.

Patterns with It + adjective
clear, likely, possible, surprising, evident
e.g. It is clear that the study of space is expensive.
important, difficult, necessary, possible, interesting
e.g. It is important to consider the practical effects of these measures.
</td>
<td rowspan="2">
Verbs
These help show how certain you are about a point or an argument.
Modal verbs: can, could; may, might; will, would (the first of each pair is most certain)
Compare: I argue that... (very certain). / I would argue that... (not so certain)
It + verb: It appears that, It seems that...
It + passive verb: It can be seen that...; It should/must be noted/emphasized that...
Showing verbs: show, indicate, demonstrate, suggest, imply (These have a non-human subject)
Arguing verbs: argue, suggest, consider, conclude (These can have a human subject e.g. I)
</td>
</tr>
<tr>
<td rowspan="2">
Adverbs and phrases
clearly, indeed, in fact, of course
generally, usually, mainly, widely
perhaps, probably, certainly, possibly
rarely, sometimes, often
e.g. Clearly, this is a serious issue that deserves further study.
This book is generally held to be her greatest novel.
</td>
</tr>
<tr>
<td>
Linking words and phrases
Firstly (= I have several points to make)
Furthermore...; In addition,... Moreover,...
(= I have another important point)
However,... (to introduce a counterargument)
Thus,... Therefore,... (to introduce a conclusion)
</td>
</tr>
</table>

Writing a longer essay or dissertation

When you have a longer essay or dissertation to write, you will go through the same process of preparing and writing as for shorter essays. (*Look at page WT2.*) However, there are additional things to bear in mind.

The title

If your title or a question has been given to you, check that you understand exactly what it means. (*Pages WT4–5*). If you are writing the title yourself, choose a clear title with definite boundaries.

Ask yourself:
- How can I define my subject so that it is not too wide in scope?

e.g. **Not** *How does Dickens reflect Victorian society in his novels?* **but** *How does Little Dorrit reflect Dickens's view of Victorian society?*

Reading and research: evaluate your sources

The quality of your research will play a vital part in the success of your writing. Keep the question or title in mind when you look for source material in books, journals or websites.

Ask yourself:
- Is the content relevant?
- Is it reliable? Is it written by someone who is an expert in the field?
- Is it biased in any way?
- Is there evidence to support information on anonymous websites?

If you are using surveys, questionnaires, market research or other studies, look carefully at the statistics and consider if the results are valid and the conclusions justified.

Making notes

When you are reading, make clear, accurate notes which summarize the key points and main information. Keep a note of the full reference for your source (title, author, date, publisher and page numbers).

Ask yourself:
- Have I summarized the information accurately?
- Is this part particularly useful? If so, have I written down the exact words used and the page number, so that I can quote it?

Planning and organizing

A long text is usually divided into sections with subheadings and it has a list of references or a bibliography at the end.

When you plan your work, ask yourself:
- How long should my text and each part be?
- Have I organized my notes, grouping together writers who have made similar points?
- Do I agree with their opinions?
- What is the point I want to make to my readers?
- What do I want my readers to know by the end?
- Have I planned what to write in the introduction, body and conclusion?

Using other people's ideas

When you have finished writing, look carefully at how you have used other people's words and ideas.

Ask yourself:
- Have I considered and discussed other people's ideas adequately?
- Have I paraphrased their ideas accurately?
- Have I made it clear which words/ideas are mine and whose words/ideas I have quoted?
- Have I included in my list of references all the works I have used and referred to?

Dissertations

A dissertation may differ from a long essay in the way in which it is organized. Check with your tutor. A dissertation will usually have all or some of the following chapters or parts:

- Title
- Contents
- Abstract (*a short text summarizing your dissertation*)
- Introductory chapter (broad to narrow focus: *to give the background, justify your research, explain your approach, give major arguments and current ideas on your topic and show the structure of your dissertation*)
- Review of the literature
- Methodology (*how you carried out any empirical research*)
- Results/findings
- Discussion
- Conclusion (narrow to broad focus: a *summary of your arguments and an evaluation of your work; further research needed*)
- Bibliography or list of references

Quoting and writing a bibliography

If you use the words or ideas of another person, you must always say where these have come from. If you do not, you might be accused of **plagiarism** (= copying another person's ideas or words and pretending that they are yours).

1. Author-date (Harvard) system

Used especially in social and physical sciences.

In the essay or dissertation

In your text, give the family name of the author or editor of the book or article you are referring to and the year of publication in brackets after your quotation or statement. For example:

> Dialects are not inferior. Most linguists agree that 'a standard language is not linguistically better .' (Swan, 2005:52).
>
> Mason (1995) describes the procedure for a teacher to evaluate each student quickly during an oral presentation.

Give both authors if there are two, but if there are more, cite the first author and add 'et al.' (= and others):
(Mason and Wood 2008) or (Mason *et al.*, 2008).

Give the full reference in your bibliography.

The bibliography

In this system, it is often called **References** and is a list of the works that you have mentioned in your text. Give the full reference.

> Swan, Michael. (2005) *Grammar*. Oxford: Oxford University Press.

You need to write:
- The surname of the author or editor, followed by the initials or first name
- The year of publication in brackets
- The title of the book, in *italics* or <u>underlined</u>

Mention the author briefly in the essay and then at the end write a full reference in your **bibliography** or list of references. Different institutions have different styles for this, so check to see the method and punctuation to use, and be consistent.

- The edition number if it is not the first edition
- The place of publication (sometimes omitted)
- The publisher

2. Footnote/endnote system

This is a common style to use in writing on arts subjects. One version is described here.

In the essay or dissertation

Give details of the source in a numbered **footnote** at the bottom of the page, or at the end of the essay in an **endnote.** Put the same number in your text after the reference:

> Phillips suggests that "parts of the city have remained untouched by the influences of modern life"[1]. He goes on to say that "it is unlike any city in the world"[2].

Footnote

> [1] Patrick Phillips, *A Brief Guide to Rome* (London: Spire Press, 2001) p.36.

If your next quote is from the same source you can just write **ibid.** and the page number:

> [2] ibid. p.38

Later references can be shorter:

> [23]Phillips , *Guide to Rome*, pp.56–60

The bibliography

Give a full list of references at the end of your text, in alphabetical order by the authors' names. Use this order:

> Phillips, Patrick, *A Brief Guide to Rome*. London: Spire Press, 2001

Other examples

These apply to both systems, but in the author-date system, the year will go after the author's name.

Books
If the book is **edited**:
Wehmeier, S. ed. *Oxford Advanced Learner's Dictionary*. 7th ed. Oxford: Oxford University Press, 2005

For an **article** in an edited book or journal:
Johns, A.M., and T. Dudley-Evans, 'English for Specific Purposes: International in Scope, Specific in Purpose', *TESOL Quarterly* 25 (2), 1991, 297–314.

Newspaper articles
Fennell, E. 'How is the recession hitting lawyers?' *The Times*, 31 July 2008, p.54.

Electronic resources
Include as much detail as you can find.
In your **text**, cite by author if known, otherwise by title or URL, and the year if possible: (Directgov, 2008).
In your **bibliography** give the author, the title, volume/page, type of medium, date and publishing organization. Provide the URL and the date you last accessed the page:
Directgov. 2008.< http://www.direct.gov.uk/en/index.htm> accessed 27 October 2009.

Oral presentations

You may have to give an oral presentation or talk as part of your academic course, for an examination or at work. In many ways, preparing a talk is similar to preparing an essay. The guidelines below apply to most types of talk.

Preparing an oral presentation

Good preparation is the most important factor for a successful presentation.

1. First steps

- Check the **time** allowed for your talk and any **guidelines** you have been given.
- Think about the **purpose** of your talk: is it to inform, to entertain or to persuade your audience?
- Think about the **audience**. Who are they? How much do they already know? How much do you need to tell them? What will interest them?
- Decide on the **topic** if you do not know this already. If you do, decide on the specific area that you will present. Be realistic about how much you can cover in the time allowed.
- **Collect** your ideas and gather more information if you need to.

2. Writing your talk

- Make notes on what you want to include. Think about what you *must* tell the audience, what you *should* tell them and what you *would like* to tell them if you have time.
- Produce an outline or a plan of your talk.

Tips
- **Structure** your talk as you would an essay: have an introduction, a middle and a conclusion.
- Use **headings** to show the different sections of your talk.

- Some people prefer to write out the whole talk like an essay. If you do this, it is better not to read this when you give your talk, but make notes as below and talk from those.

3. Producing notes

- Make notes in English on cards that you can refer to while you are speaking.
- **Open** with an introduction to the title and an overview of what you want to say:

The benefits of learning a foreign language 1

Show OHT/Slide 1

Intro:
Good morning. My talk today examines the benefits of learning a foreign language.

Overview:
I intend to outline 3 imp. benefits of learning another lang.

The benefits of learning a foreign language 2

Show OHT/Slide 2

The first benefit I shall describe is practical – communicate with other nationalities

A further benefit is increased cultural understanding – breaks down barriers / bridges gap between cultures.

The final benefit that I shall describe is improved cognitive skills – research shows → brain power

Number note card.

Note the **number** of the visual you will show.

Write out and **highlight** key words and phrases to **guide** your audience through your talk.

- Try to get the attention of your audience at the beginning with e.g. a story, joke or surprising fact.
- **Close** with a summary and an invitation for people to ask questions.
- Some people find it helpful to write out the whole introduction and conclusion.

4. Preparing visual aids

Visual aids help you to communicate your talk to the audience, if they are prepared carefully and used well.

Tips

- If you use PowerPoint™ or OHTs (overhead transparencies), writing and diagrams must be large and clear.
- Do not put too much information on each slide.
- If you use posters or pictures, check that the people at the back of the room will be able to see/read them.
- Avoid writing/drawing things on a whiteboard during your talk.

Examples of OHTs

The benefits of learning a foreign language 2

Three main benefits:

- Practical uses
- Increased cultural understanding
- Improved cognitive skills

Leave lots of white space.

Use headings and bullets to show the relationship between ideas.

Use notes, not sentences.

The benefits of learning a foreign language 3

1. **Practical uses for:**
   - Travel
   - Work
   - Study

5. Practising your talk

The more you practise, the more confident you will feel and the better your talk will be.

- First, practise your talk alone several times until you can speak fluently and confidently from your notes and keep to the time allowed.
- Then practise with one or more friends listening. Is the talk clear? Is your voice loud and clear? Are you looking at the audience?
- If you can, practise at least once with the equipment you will use.
- Use your dictionary or dictionary CD-ROM to check pronunciation, vocabulary and grammar.

6. Preparing for questions

- Try to predict some of the questions your audience may ask you and practise your answers.

Language bank

Introduction

Good morning. My talk today examines…
The subject/title of my talk/paper is…
Hello. Today I'm going to talk about/discuss…

Explaining structure

In this talk I intend to outline…
In my talk I will discuss the main features of….
I am going to examine three benefits/advantages of…

Introducing each point

The first/second/next/last point/area…I would like to discuss is…
I want to begin by looking at…
I'd now like to look at another/the second benefit of…

Clarifying

In other words,…
That is to say…

Changing the subject

So, I have discussed…
Now I'd like to turn to…
Moving on to the next/second/last benefit…

Concluding

So, I have talked about…
To sum up/summarize: in my talk I have…
In conclusion, I believe it is clear that…
To conclude: the benefits I have described in my talk are important and therefore I consider that…

Answering difficult questions

"I'm sorry, I don't quite understand your question. Could you repeat it?"
"Well, I'm not sure about that, but I think…"

Writing a summary

A summary is a shortened version of a text containing only the key information. The aim is to present readers with a short, clear account of the ideas in the text. Summary writing is an important skill in both academic and business contexts. Follow the steps in order to write a successful summary.

Preparing to write

Select the key information:

- Read the text carefully, looking up words you don't know. It is important to understand the whole sequence of the argument. Ask yourself what the text is about. Think about the purpose of your summary and what your readers need to know.
- Highlight the **key information** (the main ideas). Omit details such as examples, quotations, information in brackets, repetitions, figures of speech and most figures and statistics.
- Underline any information which you are not sure about. Only include it in your summary if you have space.
- Make notes on the key information in your own words.

Are we living in a surveillance society?

The number of CCTV (or closed-circuit television) cameras in Britain has grown enormously in recent years. There are now more than 4 million, which makes an astonishing one camera for every 14 people.

CCTV has been used for many years for the surveillance of public areas associated with an obvious security risk, such as military installations, airports, casinos and banks. However, since the 1990s, there has been a huge increase in the surveillance of everyday locations such as city and town centres, car parks, shops and traffic. Added to this, more and more individuals are buying their own consumer CCTV systems for personal or commercial use. The most common function of these systems is to survey the area in front of a house or business and record any antisocial or criminal behaviour. People who buy these systems range from wealthy individuals who are afraid of being targeted by burglars, to people who are not wealthy at all but who live in high-crime areas, such as inner cities, and are trying to protect themselves.

For some people, the huge increase in public surveillance is a threat to the individual's civil liberties and is a sign that society is becoming increasingly authoritarian. They argue that the individual's right to privacy and right to live anonymously is an important aspect of being British. They also fear that present or future governments might abuse the information gathered by surveillance in order to manipulate, control or persecute the population, as happens in George Orwell's novel *1984*.

Individuals and groups in favour of CCTV, including the police, believe that it is a valuable weapon against crime. In fact, there is no strong evidence that CCTV reduces crime overall. It may act as a deterrent in certain locations, but the crime is displaced to another location. It is not even always a good deterrent. Many criminals aren't afraid of CCTV because they know that the cameras may not be running, or that no one is likely to be watching the screens. Few crimes are solved through CCTV. Sometimes CCTV footage is analysed retrospectively to identify criminals after a crime has taken place, but even this process is enormously time-consuming and expensive. One promising new development is the computer monitoring of CCTV, where computers are programmed to notice unusual movements, such as those of a car thief in a supermarket car park, and sound an alarm. Meanwhile we can expect the argument about the rights and wrongs of CCTV to continue.

Writing the summary

Write a first draft of your summary using the information you have selected.

- **Organize** the ideas in your notes into a logical order. This need not be the same order as in the original text, but must show the same argument.
- **Condense** the information where possible.
- **Express the ideas in your own words.** This will usually be shorter than the original. Rewrite phrases in the text, but keep any **key terms** from the subject area.
- Do not give your own opinion on the topic.

Your own words: try using synonyms or rephrasing words and expressions such as adjective + noun phrases. Use the dictionary to help you.

- *everyday* → ***ordinary***
- *their own consumer CCTV systems for personal ... use* → ***private systems***
- *no strong evidence* → ***no clear proof***
- *promising* → ***that may be effective***

Introduce **new terms** and concepts to condense and clarify the argument. For example, **opponents** and **supporters** can be used to refer to those against, and those in favour of, CCTV.

Britain has a very high number of CCTV cameras. **Originally** used for locations with an obvious security risk, CCTV surveillance has **now** spread to ordinary public areas, **while** individuals are **also** buying private systems to protect themselves from crime.

Opponents of the growth in CCTV surveillance base their arguments on the threat to civil liberties and the danger of government misuse of the data acquired by surveillance.

Supporters of CCTV argue that it reduces crime, although there is no clear proof of this. If it acts as a deterrent, crime probably moves to another area. Often it is not a deterrent and it does not solve many crimes. However, the technology is developing in ways that may be effective.

Combine sentences in new ways to condense the argument, e.g. by linking the key ideas with different conjunctions and adverbs from those in the original text.

Rephrase information to shorten it: try changing the verb form or the part of speech. Examples and word families in the dictionary can help.
e.g. **passive** → **active verb**: *Few crimes **are solved** through CCTV* → ***it does not solve many crimes***
noun → **verb**: *One promising new **development** is ...* → ***the technology is developing***

Working on the draft

Ask yourself these questions:

- **Is it the right length?**
  If there is a word limit, try to stay as close to it as possible. If your summary is too long, you can usually reduce it further by:
  – cutting adjectives, e.g. *locations with an obvious security risk* → *locations with a security risk; no clear proof* → *no proof*
  – replacing phrases with shorter versions, e.g. *a lot of/not a lot of* → *many/few*
  If it is still too long, go back and reduce your key information.
- **Does it contain all the important points from the text?**
- **Does it read well?**
- **Are the grammar and spelling correct?**

Reporting on data

The most common types of graphs and charts are **line graphs** (showing developments over a period of time), **bar charts** (comparing the proportions or amounts of different things) and **pie charts** (comparing percentages of parts of a whole piece of data).

Preparing to write

Interpreting a line graph

It is essential that you understand the information presented in the diagram before you begin writing.

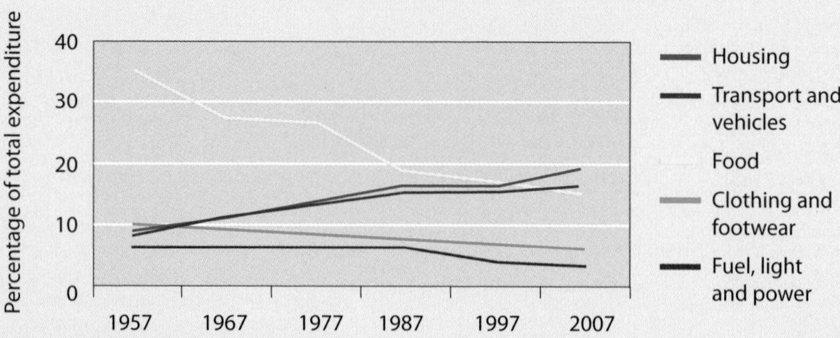

(Statistics from Office for National Statistics)

You should ask yourself these questions:

What is the information about?	*the proportion of their money that UK households spent on certain things, on average, over a period of 50 years*
What do the numbers on each axis represent?	*horizontal axis: years; vertical axis: percentages*
What changes do the lines show?	*Two show an increase and three show a decrease.*
How do the lines stand in relation to each other?	*Two almost always remain below the rest; expenditure is always lower.*
Which feature of the lines stands out most?	*Expenditure on food shows a huge decrease.*
What conclusions can be drawn from the graph?	*Patterns of household expenditure have changed over 50 years; expenditure on food has changed the most.*

Writing the report

- **Language**: **accuracy** and **clarity** are the essential features of a good report. The language you use should be plain and simple, but academic in style.
- **Vocabulary**: the range of language you need for describing data is small. (*See the Language Bank*)
- **Organization**: organize the information so that you highlight the **main trends** or features. There is usually more than one suitable way of doing this. For example, for the graph above, you could focus on the relationship between the various spending categories, **or** you could focus on the different directions each has taken over 50 years. (*Look at the structure of the report on the next page*)

Summarize the information in the graph by selecting and reporting the main features and make comparisons where relevant.

The graph shows what proportion of their total expenditure households in the UK spent, over a fifty year period, in five different categories: housing; transport and vehicles; food; clothing and footwear; and fuel, light and power.

Paragraph 1 —Introduction
Describes the subject of the data.

Between 1957 and 2007 expenditure in all five categories changed to some extent, but the most marked change was in the food category.[1] At the beginning of the period the proportion of expenditure on food was more than three times as high as that in all the other categories, representing more than thirty per cent of total household expenditure.[2] However, by 2007 this figure had more than halved to around fifteen per cent, and was slightly less than expenditure on both housing and transport.[3]

Paragraph 2—Trends
[1] a general comment on the trends shown in the graph + main trend.
[2–3] provide supporting detail on the main trend.

The two other areas where proportions of expenditure fell over the period are clothing and footwear, and fuel, light and power.[1] However, the changes here were much less dramatic.[2] Expenditure on the former dropped steadily from ten per cent to five per cent, and on the latter from six per cent to three per cent.[3] For most of the fifty-year period, these categories used up a significantly smaller proportion of the household budget than the others.[4]

Paragraph 3—Trends
More detail on other trends where expenditure has fallen.
[1, 2] a general comment, explained in detail in [3].
[4] compares these trends with other expenditure.

In two categories, housing and transport, the proportions of expenditure almost doubled, rising from nine and eight per cent to nineteen and sixteen per cent respectively.[1] Thus, by the end of the period, the highest proportion of household expenditure went on housing, and the lowest on fuel, light and power.[2]

Paragraph 4—Trends
[1] more detail on trends where spending rose.
[2] summarizes the main contrast in the trends.

In conclusion, the graph shows that the patterns of spending in UK households changed to some extent over the period 1957 to 2007, the part of the budget spent on food showing the most marked change.

Paragraph 5—Conclusion
This summarizes the report with a general conclusion.

Core language for describing graphs

Language bank

General	**Pie charts: describing proportions of a whole**
The graph/chart shows/represents/indicates… *The figures show/indicate (that)…* draw conclusions from e.g.: *The following conclusions can be drawn from the data.*	*More/Less than* half *of the total…* *Only* a third/a quarter… *Just/well under/over* 50%… *The biggest/smallest proportion/sector…* *The vast majority of…* *As many (people were learning French) as (Spanish).*
Bar charts: describing differences between amounts	**Graphs: describing developments over time**
There were almost *twice/three times/half as many …as* Far/slightly/20% *fewer X… than Y…* Many/far/a few/20% *more X…than Y…* *A greater proportion of… than of…* *20% of women…, while only 10% of men…* *80% of (adults send emails), compared to 34% (who prefer texts).*	*a* small/slight/gradual *increase/decrease* *a* significant/marked/dramatic *increase/decrease* *a* small/slight *rise/fall/dip* *steady growth* *to rise/increase/fall/decrease/decline/drop* *to rise/fall* steadily/dramatically/sharply/rapidly *Customer numbers have fluctuated.* *(Online sales) reached an all-time high/low.* *The graph shows a marked change in…*

Writing a report

A report describes a study, an investigation, or a project. Its purpose is to provide recommendations or updates, and sometimes to persuade the readers to accept an idea. It is written by a single person or a group who has investigated the issue. It is read by people who require the information.

Tip

- Reports can vary in length but a good rule to remember is that they should be as long as necessary and as short as possible.

Think about the reader

You need to make the objective of the report clear so that the people who are reading the report know why they are reading. Thinking about the readers and what they need to know will help improve your report.

- Is the purpose of the report clear throughout?
- Can the readers find the information they need?
- Will diagrams or tables make the information clearer?
- Should I just present the facts or include recommendations as well?

Organizing your report

A typical report should follow the structure outlined below. Shorter reports might not need all the sections but they should at least include the highlighted sections.

1 Title

Your title should tell the reader exactly what the report is about.

2 Contents List

If your report has a number of sections it is important to include a table of contents so that the readers can find the information they want. A good way to structure a report is to use numbered headings:

2.0 Research
2.1 Focus groups
2.2 Technology for accessing the Internet

3 Summary

This section is often called an **Executive Summary**. It tells the reader what the objectives of the report are as well as the main findings, conclusions and any recommendations.

4 Introduction

This should give the reader the background to the report: why you are writing it. You should also include what the report will cover (and what it won't) and how you got the information you have based the report on.

5 Body of the report

The main body of the report will follow the structure in the Contents List. It will give precise information about the research you have carried out and what you have discovered from it. The information here should be mainly factual and not based on opinion. Tables, charts and bulleted lists can make the information clearer. Some of the more detailed information can go into Appendices and the Bibliography.

6 Conclusions

This is where you give your opinions on the facts that you have discovered.

7 Recommendations

If you have been asked to give recommendations, they should be based on your conclusions. You should also let the reader know what you predict will happen if your recommendations are followed.

8 Appendices

In a long report, you should put very detailed information in the Appendices with cross-references to them in the body of the report.

9 Bibliography

If your report refers to a number of other publications, you should list these in a Bibliography.

Executive summary

The summary below gives some useful language in context. In the Language bank are some other phrases that you can use in reports. Notice that the language used should be **clear**, **accurate** and **formal**. *We* and *I* are often used in internal reports, for example for describing research.

Web Page Design

The purpose of this report is to compare two different web designs. The reason for this is to decide what kind of web page is most likely to attract new customers and to encourage existing customers to buy more products from us.

We asked two developers to produce alternative web pages for our company. We asked Developer A to produce a simple, easy-to-use design and we asked Developer B to produce a more sophisticated design with lots of eye-catching graphics. We conducted our research by asking a group of twenty existing customers and twenty non-customers to use the web page over a month. The group was made up of people with a range of ages, professions, incomes, and computer expertise. We divided the group in two and asked one sub-group to use Design A and the other to use Design B. We asked each sub-group to log on once a day and to use the web page to perform certain tasks, including: buying products, getting information, returning damaged products, and tracking deliveries. We also asked the sub-groups to assess how attractive they found their designs and whether they would be encouraged to return to the web page.

In addition, we researched the technology that people had available for accessing the Internet, including the devices people used and the connection speeds available.

We found that, on the whole, people preferred to be able to purchase products quickly and easily. In conclusion, users do not visit a site such as ours for entertainment. While they initially enjoyed some of the aspects of Design B these could take a long time to load and users eventually became bored.

We recommend that we adopt Design A with two or three of the more practical features from Design B.

Language bank

Stating objectives

The purpose/aim/objective of this report is to…
This report aims to…
This reports presents/gives information on…

Outlining research

We asked (two developers) to…
We conducted our research by… (e.g. *asking a group of…*)
We examined/looked at/researched… (e.g. *the problem/the cost/several companies*)
We surveyed… (e.g. *a total of 250 employees*)
We compared A and B.
The group was made up of…

Presenting findings

We found that, on the whole,…
According to the majority of respondents…
Overall people preferred…
50% of those surveyed said (that)…

Giving Conclusions

In conclusion…
The research shows/demonstrates (that)…
The research shows/demonstrates + noun (e.g. *the effect of…*)
From the research/the evidence we conclude that…

Giving recommendations

We recommend that…
It is recommended that…
The best solution is/would be to… (e.g. *to adopt design A*)
The best solution is/would be + noun (e.g. *a reduction in office hours*)
If we do A, we will see B.
This will have an impact on + noun (e.g. *costs/productivity/the business*)

Writing a review of a book or film/movie

The main purpose of a book review is to give information to a potential reader so that they can decide whether or not they want to read the book. A review of a film/movie has the same purpose. You can approach it in the same way as a book review.

Asking a question is one way to engage the reader. Or you could start with a personal opinion.

This is one of many **synonyms** of 'interesting'. Look at the note at the dictionary entry 'interesting'.

It is usual to use the present tense to describe the story.

Most **nouns** can be enhanced with an **adjective** – but make sure it is a natural collocation.

Linking words aid organization and can also give your opinion.

***Wuthering Heights* by Emily Bronte**

Is it a darkly passionate tale of love? Or should we call it a highly original gothic story? The classic novel *Wuthering Heights* by Emily Brontë is, in my opinion, a unique and gripping blend of these genres. Written in 1847, it is an epic family saga full of desire, hate, revenge and regret, focusing on the main characters of Heathcliff and Catherine. The atmospheric setting of the wild Yorkshire moors cleverly mirrors these violent emotions.

When Catherine's father adopts the starving orphan boy Heathcliff, Catherine's brother Hindley feels deeply hurt and resentful. She, on the other hand, develops an immensely strong bond with Heathcliff, which becomes an all-consuming love. Upon her father's death, Hindley becomes the head of the family and forces Heathcliff to assume the position of a servant. Despite loving Heathcliff, Catherine chooses to marry Edgar Linton, who is closer to her class and position in society. It is this decision which leads to heartbreak and tragedy, not only for them but for many others.

Heathcliff could be described as an anti-hero with his rough manners and lack of control. Likewise, Catherine displays many flaws, but the reader can still empathize with these characters. In fact, this is the main reason why I believe this novel is so brilliant. It rings with truth. The reader may be horrified at the way that Heathcliff and Catherine behave, and yet, at the same time, the writer ensures that we never hate them because the reasons for their actions are crystal clear.

The main part of the book relies on a narrator, Ellen Dean, who is a servant at Wuthering Heights and I think that this is a useful device which holds the complex plot together. However, *Wuthering Heights* is not what I would call an 'easy read'. There is dense description and some of the dialogue is written in dialect, which can be difficult to follow.

Nevertheless, I persevered and, all in all, I can highly recommend *Wuthering Heights*. I challenge you to remain unmoved after reading this exceptional book.

The **title** and **author's name** should appear in the introductory paragraph.

Information about the **setting** and **era** can be useful.

Collocations of adverb + adjective show your vocabulary knowledge. Look up **hurt** adjective.

Including information on the **style of writing** can be helpful.

Conclusion. Restate your opinion of the book as a recommendation to read it or not to read it.

Writing your review

1. Read or re-read the book and make notes

Your notes should try to answer the questions a reader might have:

- What kind of book is it?
- What happens in the story?
- Who are the main characters?
- What is the main theme of the book?
- Is it well written?
- Would you recommend this book?

2. Organize your notes

You can use the same plan as the model review (see below). A successful review will contain these elements, but the order can be changed.

Paragraph 1— Introduction General comments about the book.
Paragraph 2—Plot A brief summary of what happens.
Paragraph 3—Characters Briefly describe and comment on the main characters.
Paragraph 4—Other information Anything else important that you want to say about the book.
Paragraph 5—Conclusion Include your personal recommendation here.

3. Write your review

Remember not to include too many details and don't give away the ending of the book. The reviewer recommends this book but the review also contains some criticisms. It is a good idea to try to write about both positive and negative aspects of the book.

Tips

- Remember at all times that the person who reads your review has NOT read the book!
- Use your dictionary to help you find synonyms of words such as **book** or **story**.
- Find a range of adjectives to use to describe the book, plot and characters.

Reviews of non-fiction books

The purpose of a non-fiction book review is basically the same as fiction but the potential reader will have different questions:

- What is the author's reason for writing the book?
- Is it well organized? Can you follow the argument easily and find the important information?
- Does the author support his/her findings well?
- How does it compare to other books on the same subject?

Language bank

Beginnings *It is a fascinating tale of*… (e.g. *rural life*) *This moving account of*… (e.g. *a young man's experiences*) *I found this story far-fetched and unconvincing.*	**Giving your opinion** *The writer excels at*… (e.g. *describing*…) *I was impressed by*… *One aspect I found a little disappointing was*… *One possible flaw is that*…
Details/plot *Written in…, the story begins with*… *The events unfold in*… *The tale is set in*…	**Conclusions** *I would highly recommend this rewarding book.* *I thoroughly enjoyed this book. In fact I couldn't put it down!* *By the end of this book, you feel*… *I was left unmoved by this story.* *I would strongly advise against reading this book.*
Characters *The writer introduces us to*… *The principal characters are*… *My favourite character is undoubtedly*… *The story focuses on*… *We experience all this through the eyes of*…	

Discussing pictures and cartoons

This task may occur in written or spoken examinations. Describing photographs or pictures can be similar to interpreting cartoons. There may not be a caption or any speech, but the photo can still have a message. You can also discuss the effect it has on you.

Look at the cartoon and the interpretation below.

"It is good to see people doing their bit for the environment!"

The cartoon shows a bird's-eye view of part of a European city or town. There is a large factory, several rows of houses, two vehicles and some people.[1] In the foreground, there is a rubbish collection truck, with two men collecting household waste for recycling. On the left of the cartoon, a man is putting a bottle in a street recycling bin. Watching him are two other men who are obviously managers in the local factory.[2] The caption reads "It is so good to see people doing their bit for the environment!"[3]

The caption is clearly the words that one of the factory managers is saying to his colleague, because the focus of attention is on them and also on the man with the bottle: all three of them are drawn in detail[1] and they also stand out because of the black clothing they are wearing.[2]

Another important element in the cartoon is the factory and the pollution from its chimneys. The cartoonist has exaggerated the size of the factory in relation to the surrounding houses and has also exaggerated the pollution by blackening a wide expanse of sky.[3] These aspects of the picture show the way that the pollution from the factory dominates the town and causes a serious environmental impact.

The factory itself is a symbol representing industry in general.[4] It seems that the man who is dropping off his one empty bottle in the recycling bin has driven there in his car, so he has probably damaged the environment more than if he had just thrown the bottle away. He represents ordinary people.[4]

The cartoon is about our attitude to the environment. It is clear that the cartoonist is suggesting that while people focus on small-scale activities, such as recycling household waste, they are ignoring much more serious environmental problems such as the pollution from industries and from cars.[1] He/she uses irony to show that we are becoming complacent about saving the environment. This is done by contrasting what the factory managers are saying with what is really happening all around them: serious pollution that they themselves are responsible for.

Personally, I believe that the cartoonist is right. Many people are now very good about recycling their household waste. But, because we do this, we have become complacent about pollution and feel we are doing enough to protect the environment. We need also to address other more important sources of environmental damage.

Paragraph 1—Description
[1] General description
[2] Detailed description
[3] Caption or speech bubble

Paragraphs 2–4 — Artistic techniques
[1] Technique 1–detail
[2] Technique 2–emphasis
[3] Technique 3–exaggeration
[4] Technique 4–symbolism

Paragraph 5—Message
[1] Use of irony

Paragraph 6—Personal reaction

Key

shows the key language in each section.

focuses on prepositions and phrasal verbs.

Writing a description and interpretation

Follow these steps when you prepare for this task. Think about the questions and make notes; then, when you write, use some of the phrases in the Language banks and take note of the tips.

Stage 1—Description

The scene:

- What is the scene in the cartoon/picture?
- Where is it?
- What are the major features?

Details:

- Who/What is in the picture?
- What are they doing?
- What is happening?

Language bank

The scene is of... (e.g. *a café in which two people...*)
The cartoon shows/depicts...
There is/are... (e.g. *two people who look angry.*)
In the centre of the cartoon is/are..., (who/which...)
At the top/bottom of the cartoon is/are...
On the left/right...
In the foreground/background...
The central feature of the cartoon is...
You can use prepositions e.g. ***behind** the houses*
Avoid using: ~~I/You can see~~... ; ~~In the picture~~...

Tips

- Only describe the details that are important for the message.
- Try to avoid using short simple sentences such as: ~~*In the centre is a man. He is shouting.*~~ **Relative sentences** are particularly useful: *In the centre is a man who is shouting.*

The caption or speech bubble:

- What is written in the caption or in any speech bubbles?
- Who is talking and to whom?

Language bank

The caption reads "..."
One man is saying to the other "..."
The woman is asking whether...
He/She is commenting that...
He/She is wondering whether... (to go/he/she should go...)

Stage 2—Interpretation

Tip

- Start a new paragraph for this section. Give evidence and reasons for your interpretation.

Artistic techniques:

How does the artist draw attention to important parts of the cartoon/picture? Does he/she use:

- detail? Where?
- emphasis? What is emphasized? How?
- exaggeration? What is exaggerated?
- symbolism? Which objects or people are symbols? What do they mean?

Language bank

The focus of attention is on...
X is/are drawn in detail, (which shows/to show...)
X stand(s) out because of the...
The most important element in the cartoon is...
This aspect of the cartoon indicates...
The X symbolize(s)/represent(s)...
The cartoonist has exaggerated X (in order to.../ because...)
The reason for this is that...
Use your dictionary to find synonyms so that you use a wide range of vocabulary, e.g. *clearly/obviously; indicate/show*

Message:

- What is the cartoon/picture really about?
- What is the artist trying to say?
- How does he/she try to persuade you? Does he/she use **irony** (contrasting the way the cartoon shows things with the way they really are) or **analogy** (using a simple situation to make a more complex situation clear)?

Language bank

The cartoon is about/refers to/deals with...
The cartoon has to do with...
The cartoonist is obviously trying to show...
What the cartoon is saying is that...
I take/understand the cartoon to mean that...

Stage 3—Personal reaction:

- Do you agree or disagree with the message?
- Why?

Tip

- Start a new paragraph for this section.

Language bank

Personally, I believe that the cartoonist is right.
I only partly/partially agree with the artist's message because...
In my opinion/view, the artist is wrong, because...
Use phrases such as *I think...*; *In my opinion...*; or *It seems to me that...*
Do not use ~~According to me/my opinion...~~

Writing a formal letter

Writing a letter of complaint

The important things to remember about writing formal letters are the layout, which follows particular conventions, and the language, which must be formal or semi-formal and polite, even when you are complaining.

6 Fore Street
Kensington
London W8 9NW

Customer Services Manager
FlyHigh Airways
PO Box 589
London W3 5NJ

1 August 2009

Dear Sir/Madam

Booking reference: Porter POR 1359AZ

My wife and I and our two children, aged 2 and 4, were passengers on flight LZ238 from London to Orlando, USA on July 23rd 2009. I am writing to complain about a number of aspects of the service we received.

Paragraph 1
Explain clearly why you are writing.

Firstly, when the flight was delayed, the staff at the airline's information desk were very unhelpful. We were not even given a voucher for a drink or meal, when it was clear the delay would be at least seven hours. This meant that we had to spend a considerable amount of money in the restaurant.

Paragraph 2
Explain the problem and how you were affected.

Then, when we were finally able to board, families were not allowed to board first, although we had paid for this. As a result we were not able to sit together, making our children, already very tired, extremely distressed.

Paragraph 3
Explain any further problem and the consequences.

It is a legal requirement for airline operators to provide suitable refreshments in the event of a long delay. I would therefore expect some compensation for your failure both to comply with this regulation and to provide us with the priority boarding for which we had paid.

Paragraph 4
State clearly what action you wish the company to take.

I enclose our boarding passes and look forward to hearing from you shortly.

Yours faithfully

S R Porter (Dr)

Ending
General comment. Say you would like a quick reply.

Writing the letter

Layout

Look carefully at the layout of the model letter and note:

- Your address, but not your name, goes at the top on the right.
- The name and address of the person you are writing to goes on the left.
- If you do not know a name, use a position e.g. 'Customer Services Manager'.
- The date goes under either address.
- Give some kind of reference or use a heading (e.g. **Poor service levels**)

Key Yellow = key language

Tips

- **Tone**: be polite and formal, but keep your language simple and clear.
- Use short sentences rather than long ones.
- Try not to be emotional; avoid *you/you didn't* if possible.

If you are writing in **American English**, remember:

- Use American spelling and punctuation e.g. Mrs., Dr., etc.
- End your letter **Sincerely**, **Sincerely yours**, or **Yours truly**,.

Language bank

Openings and closings	What do you want?
Dear Sir/Madam..........Yours faithfully *Dear Ms Walker..........Yours sincerely*	Definite: *a full/partial refund, a replacement, an apology* More flexible: *compensation, reimbursement, recompense*
Introducing the topic *I am writing to complain about/to express my dissatisfaction with...* *The purpose of this letter is to express my disappointment with...*	**Endings** *I look forward to your swift reply.* *I look forward to hearing from you at your earliest convenience.* *I look forward to hearing from you without delay.* *I very much hope to hear from you shortly.* *I await your prompt reply.*
Describing the problem Strong adjectives: *appalled, distressed, disgusted, shocked* Less strong: *disappointed, dismayed, dissatisfied.*	

Writing a letter to a newspaper

This should still be a formal letter, but because it is for the public, it should show your opinion clearly or tell people something interesting or new. It can be direct and feel quite personal – you can use *I*, *we* and *you*.

A title attracts the readers' attention

Give information about you if relevant.

Use strong adjectives

Exclamation marks are acceptable to show how you feel.

A challenge to readers can be effective.

Ending: No finishing phrase is needed.

Sir

The craze for reality TV

As a student in my early twenties I am part of a key audience for TV channels. Why then, do I find so little to interest or entertain me? One trend I find particularly appalling is the increase in 'reality' TV programmes such as Survivor, Big Brother and Fear Factor, to name but a few.

'Reality' TV shows involve 'real' people performing ridiculous and often dangerous acts and generally behaving horribly towards each other. These shows appeal to that part of us which takes pleasure in watching the humiliation of others and I believe that programme-makers are being irresponsible by promoting this. It is demeaning to both the participants and the viewers.

Even worse, these programmes are having a negative effect on society, particularly on young people, who no longer feel any shame at watching or taking part in this kind of disgraceful behaviour. A national survey recently stated that one in seven British teenagers hopes to become famous by going on a show like this! The average British adult watches 26 hours of television per week. Reality TV is not only a waste of time, but it is dangerous. I believe it can and will affect our society, dragging it down into the gutter.

It is time we made a stand against reality TV, in favour of quality TV. How can we do it? Start by changing the channel.

Maria Fedora
Madrid

Paragraph 1
Clear introduction of the topic and the writer's opinion.

Paragraph 2
Main point, with reasons.

Paragraph 3
Further point to support main one, with reasons and/or examples.

Paragraph 4
Repeats the writer's opinion and offers a challenge.

Writing emails

- Emails **vary in formality** depending on how well you know the reader and what your status is in relation to them.
- All emails should be polite, but they **vary in level of politeness** depending on who you are writing to and what you are asking them.
- Writers use level of formality and politeness to achieve an appropriate **tone**.
- Emails between colleagues of a similar status can be informal and personal, but should still be polite and friendly.

Email etiquette

- Always use a short, informative **subject line**, not single general words e.g. *Urgent* or *Enquiry*.
- Mention **attachments** and say what they contain. Don't leave the body of the email empty.
- **Acknowledge** email attachments you receive. *Thanks* + your name is often enough.
- **Re-read** your email before you send it to make sure it is understandable and not offensive.

Writing business emails

Formal – An enquiry to a company – *formal, polite*

Tips

Formal business emails are shorter and less formal than letters.

- You should **not** use very informal language, incomplete sentences, exclamation marks or emoticons.
- You **can** use contracted verb forms, except where first impressions are important.
- You can become **less formal** as you establish a working relationship with somebody.

Greeting: full name as this is the first contact with this company.

Abbreviations: ***promo*** is acceptable in formal emails, as are ***asap*** *(as soon as possible)*, ***ad*** *(advertisement)*, ***re***: *(regarding)*

Language: formal vocabulary: ***purchase*** *= buy*, ***require*** *= need*.

Modal verbs (***could***, ***would***) make the request more formal and polite.

Ending: formal and friendly

To: office@trainersrus.com
Cc: Andrea.penn@fgt.com
Subject: Query about training DVDs

Dear Mr Baxter

I am the HR assistant at FeelGood Training plc. I am contacting you to say that we have received the promo material about your sales training DVDs and are interested in purchasing some.

Could you please send us some more information regarding their content as we are not sure which would be the most useful for our staff.

We would also require a price list and payment terms.

Looking forward to your reply

Regards
Renata Klein

Renata Klein, HR assistant
FeelGood Training plc
484 London Road,Uxbridge,UX3 6HO
www.fgt.com

Clear **subject line**

Opening: introduce yourself (use your position, not your name) and explain why you are writing.

We rather than *I* makes the message less personal and more formal

Close: Most writers use one before their name. Give your full name in the first email. The reader can use *Renata* or *Ms Klein* in a reply.

Signature: give your position and contact details.

A reply – *Less formal (semi-formal), polite*

Greeting and close: Jim chooses to use first names – correspondence will now tend to be less formal.

Language sets a polite, semi-formal, friendly tone:

- ***We're happy to...*** OR ***We're pleased to...*** NOT: ~~*We're delighted to*~~... – too formal for emails
- ***Please feel free to...*** NOT: ~~*Please don't hesitate to*~~... – too formal
- ***Should you need help***: more formal than '***If you*** ...'

To: Renata.klein@fgt.com
Subject: Re: Query about training DVDs

Dear Renata

Thank you for your interest in our training material. We're happy to provide you with more detailed information regarding the contents of the DVDs. Attached you'll find a PDF containing a brochure plus purchasing agreement where you'll find terms and conditions are clearly explained.

Should you need help choosing a product to suit your company's needs, please feel free to contact us again. Either email me or alternatively you can speak to one of our customer service team by calling 05 471 375 31.

Best regards

Jim

Jim Baxter, Marketing Manager
Trainers-R-Us
j.baxter@trainersrus.com

Opening: a formal, polite opening sentence is appropriate for the first reply.

Say what's in the **attachment**.

Contracted forms can be used as the language is less formal now.

Language bank

Greetings

Formal	Semi-formal	Informal
Dear Ms Klein/Dear Professor Smith/Dear Chris White (if you don't know the gender). Do **not** use title and first name: ~~*Dear Ms Mary.*~~	*Dear Renata*	*Hi/Hi Renata/Hello/ Hello Renata*
Dear All (to a group)	*Dear All*	*Hi everyone/Hello all*
FAO/For the attention of the Sales Manager	—	—

Closes

Best wishes/Best regards/Regards + your full name. Add position and contact details.	*All the best/Best/Yours/ Many thanks* + your first name or your full name. (or formal closes)	*Thanks/Cheers/Speak to you soon* + your first name.

Requesting action

Very polite	Polite	Informal request
Would it be possible (for you) to send me…?/ *I would be grateful if you could send me…*	*Could you (please) send me…?*	*Can you send me…?/ Pls can you let me have…?*
I was wondering if you have had a chance to do it yet?	*Have you had a chance to [do it yet?]…?*	*Have you [done it yet]?*
Would it be possible for me to come…?	*Could I come…?*	*Can I come…?*
I would really appreciate your help./I would be very grateful (indeed) for your help.	*Thank you./Many thanks*	*Thanks*

Writing academic emails

- Academic emails are usually **personal**, not official. You are writing to a specific, named individual, not to somebody in their official role.
- The level of **politeness** you need will vary. If you are asking a favour of an academic outside your university, you need to express a higher level of politeness than if you are asking your own teacher for a meeting. Emails between colleagues can be very **informal**.
- Remember to use a level of formality and politeness to achieve an appropriate **tone**.

Formal – A request from a student to an academic from a different department

Low status writer to high status reader whom he does not know.

Tone: *Personal, very formal, very polite*

```
Subject: Request for statistical help

Dear Dr Barr

I am a first year PhD student in the
department of linguistics and my
research topic is a quantitative
study of verb forms in academic writing.
As I need to use advanced statistical
tools for processing the data, my
supervisor, Dr John Pugh, suggested
I contact you to ask for advice.
Would it be possible for me to come
and see you to discuss what I need?
I attach a copy of my draft research
proposal to give you an idea of the
scope of my study.

I would be very grateful indeed for
your help.

Best wishes

David Samuels
```

Clear **subject** line

Greeting: use ***Dear*** + academic title and family name, or Mr, Ms, etc. and family name

Introduce yourself by giving your position in the university.

Say **why you are writing**. Mention any academic contact.

Be specific about what you want the reader to do.

Give **supporting details.**

Would it be possible… Very polite. OR *Could I possibly…* (**Not** ~~*I kindly request*~~ – too official)

Ending: very polite OR: *I would really appreciate your help.* (**Not:** ~~*Thank you for your time*~~ – official. **Not:** ~~*Thank you for your attention*~~ – very formal spoken)

Close: OR *Best regards, Regards*. Give your full name. Add position and contact details if necessary.

Less formal – request from a student to their own supervisor

Lower status writer to higher status reader whom she knows very well.

Tone: *Personal, polite, less formal*

```
Subject: Meeting this week?

Dear Ruth

I was wondering if you've had a
chance to look at my paper yet. If so,
could we have a meeting some time this
week? The best day for me would be
Tues. I start my fieldwork at the end
of the week and it would be very useful
to have some feedback before then.

Many thanks

Nicole
```

Subject: use ? to show a request

Greeting: first names can be used as they know each other well.

A polite indirect question. Use it to remind somebody of higher status about something.

Could, would: Less abrupt/direct forms. Use them to make a suggestion/request to somebody of higher status.

Abbreviations can be used as style is less formal.

Close: informal – Nicole has the right to ask for a meeting

Using American style in emails

- If you are writing emails in an American English environment, the points about formality, politeness and tone on pages WT26–27 still apply. The language you use will be very similar. However, there are one or two things that you should be aware of, as shown below.

Formality

The main difference between American and British style in emails is that US emails do not use the very formal language that British emails often do and can be more direct. Look at these examples:

British (formal)	**American**
I would be grateful If you could send your payment to…	*Please send your payment to…*
A list of fees can be found on our website.	*You can find a list of fees on our website.*
Please don't hesitate to contact me…	*Please feel free to contact me.*

Business emails

Notice how the date is written. (BrE: 19/8/2009)

Notice the use of full stops and commas in these emails. Use full stops after abbreviations.

Use US spellings (e.g. customize, flavor, center, etc.) consistently.

Direct but polite questions using "you" are fine when writing to Americans.

Close: *Sincerely yours*, or *Sincerely*, are good ways to close a business email.

```
To:        kmiller@charitytrainers.org
From:      risai@newgreenspaces.jp
Date:      08/19/2009
Subject:   Request for customized training

Dear Ms. Miller,

I am writing to ask about the possibility of
organizing a customized training program for
a group of five of our mid-level managers. We
would be interested in having them learn more
about staff recruitment, project management, and
fundraising practices in the American charity
and nonprofit sector. Could you please let me
know what scheduling and pricing options are
available for a week-long course fulfilling these
requirements?

Sincerely yours,
Risa Inyaka
New Green Spaces, Japan
```

Academic emails

Short, clear subject line

Attachments should be no larger than 2MB, if possible

Use full stops after short titles

Close: courteous and fairly formal

```
To:            jacobi@bussch.clemson.edu
From:          rwagner@stud.clemson.edu
Date:          8/23/2009
Subject:       Proposed meeting this week
Attachments:   mif.doc

Dear Dr. Jacobi,

I'm planning to submit the attached paper to
'Markets in Focus' next week. I wonder if it might
be possible for us to meet to discuss it before I
send it off? I'd be very grateful for your comments
and advice. I'm available every day after 3p.m., or
in the mornings on either Tuesday or Thursday.

Many thanks,
Ross Wagner
```

Writing a CV or résumé

A well-written, well-produced, appropriate CV (*British English*) or résumé (*American English*) is vital for getting you to the interview stage for a job. Use the examples and advice here to help you. On page WT32 you will find an example of a good covering (cover) letter.

Tips

- Adapt your CV/résumé so that it is appropriate for the job you are applying for.
- Keep your CV short - no more than 2 pages if possible.
- Present yourself positively and accurately.
- Make your CV attractive and easy to read: use capitals, bold type, spacing and underlining.
- Choose a typeface such as Times New Roman, Arial or Verdana. Use at least 10 pt.

British style CV (curriculum vitae) – *new graduate*

Name Pamela Janet Mason
Address 29 Greenlands Avenue, London, SW3 6RF
Telephone 01924 786512 **Mobile** 0779 9238182
e-mail pam_mason@scapenet.com

Objective To find a role in a film or TV production company that will enable me to acquire and develop the skills required for a career in film or television.

Profile An outgoing and articulate graduate with work experience in both television and teaching

Education and qualifications
2009 - MA in Media Studies. Bristol University. Expected 2010
2005–2009 BA in Media Studies with French (2:1) Bristol University
1997–2004 Beacon School, London
3 A levels: Drama (A); French (A); German (B)
5 AS levels 9 GCSEs

Work experience
October 2007–June 2008: Language assistant in secondary school in France. Taught English to large classes and small groups. Ran a film club and a holiday dance and drama club. Assisted with school drama productions.
September 2004–August 2005: Production assistant at Oordman and Associates Filmmakers, London N16. Performed office and on-set duties.
June–September 2004: Tutor for Jacaranda Drama Workshops. Led groups of teenagers of different backgrounds in dance and drama activities.
July–August 2003: Host at Adventure Camping holiday campsite in France. Led the children's club for 4-10 year olds and performed various practical duties on the campsite.

Skills
Languages: French – near native-speaker fluency (CEF C1); German (B2).
Good keyboard skills. Familiarity with Word, Excel and film editing packages.
Clean driving licence.

Interests
Drama, both acting and directing; singing (was member of university choral society). Regular volunteer at a local centre for the homeless.

References – attached

Personal information. You can omit the labels. There is no need to mention your age, gender, nationality, race, religion or marital status. Don't send a photo unless you are asked to.

Profile and objective. Some people do not include these, but they do give an employer an idea of who you are.

Education. Put the most recent first. Add prizes and awards. Omit primary school. Try to give British equivalents of your qualifications.

Work experience. Put this in reverse order. Experienced candidates: put this before Education and write more about your most recent post.

Skills. Your practical abilities. Include exams passed. Write more here if you are experienced.

Interests. Keep this short. Include a sport, a creative and a community activity, if you can. Avoid vague subjects such as *reading* or *travel*.

References. Give the names, titles, and addresses when you send your CV, either here or on a separate page.

American style résumé – *new graduate*

These are similar to British style CVs. But notice:

- For new graduates your résumé should be only one page.
- Describe your work experience in terms of self-motivation, teamwork, organization, problem-solving, and enthusiasm.

Tip

- The standard US paper size is not A4 (210 x 297mm) but 216 x 279mm.

Provide your college or temporary **address** if you have one.

Objective. To summarize your goals and customize your résumé for specific positions. State a realistic short-term goal and/or a job for which you are currently qualified.

Use **bold** to highlight key information.

Use US **spelling** and **punctuation**.

Jane Q. Student
jqstudent@mba.nau.edu

Present Address:	Permanent Address:
508 Blackbird's Roost	50, rue de Vaugirard
Flagstaff, AZ, USA 86011	Saint-Sulpice, France 75006
Tel +1 929 555 1212	Tel +33 1234 567 890

OBJECTIVE To obtain an entry-level management position within an international hospitality organization.

EDUCATION **Masters in Business Administration** (M.B.A.), 2006-2008
Northern Arizona University, Flagstaff, Arizona, USA
B.A. in International Hospitality, 2002-2006
Université de Savoie, Chambéry, France

EXPERIENCE **Travel Agent**, Sep. 2006-Present
Kokopelli Extreme Tours, Sedona, Arizona, USA
Organized adventure package tours for large student groups, trained and supervized new staff members, and maintained partner relationships.
Camp Counselor, Jun 2002-Aug 2006
Voyageurs Summer Camp, Voglans, France
Group leader for children aged 10-15. Developed curriculum for campers and led overnight hiking trips.

HONORS Agent of the Month, Kokopelli Extreme Tours, March 2008
Voted 'Most Popular Counselor,' Voyageurs, 2005 & 2006

SKILLS & INTERESTS Fluent in French and English; conversational Spanish
Enjoy web design in HTML and Flash

Language bank

Action verbs

Use action verbs to describe your achievements and make them look more dynamic.
Examples: *achieved, administered, analyzed, advised, arranged, compiled, conducted, coordinated, created, designed, developed, devised, distributed, evaluated, examined. executed, implemented, increased, introduced, instructed, liaised, managed, mentored, monitored, negotiated, organized, oversaw, prepared, recommended, reduced, researched, represented, solved, supervised, trained.*

Positive adjectives

Use positive adjectives to describe yourself.
Examples: *active, adaptable, committed, competent, dynamic, effective, efficient, enthusiastic, experienced, flexible, (highly) motivated, organized, professional, proficient, qualified, successful.*

Other useful phrases

Skills

Native French speaker
Near-native command of English
Good spoken and written German
Computer literate *Familiar with HTML*
Experienced trainer and facilitator

Education and experience

Baccalauréat, série C (equivalent of A levels in Maths and Physics)
The qualifications described below do not have exact equivalents in the British/American system.
Four weeks' work experience at…
Summer internship at a marketing firm.

Personal qualities

Work well as part of a team
Work well under pressure
Able to meet deadlines
Welcome new challenges *Can-do attitude*

Writing a covering letter

A covering letter (*NAmE* cover letter) accompanies a CV/résumé or an application form. In Britain and North America they are usually typed on a single page. A good letter uses formal language and presents some key arguments for why your application should be taken seriously.

Flat 3
19 Strangelands Road
London
NE23 6ZB
Tel: 0207 337 34589
20 January 2010

Mrs F Hunter
Human Resources Manager
Timson Office Supplies
Unit 5 Males Industrial Estate
Cambridge CB7 9HD

Dear Mrs Hunter

Senior Accounts Clerk

I am writing to apply for the post of senior accounts clerk advertised in the Cambridge Evening News of 17 January.

As you will see from my enclosed CV I am currently an accounts clerk in a medium-sized printing firm. In addition to my normal bookkeeping duties, I am responsible for invoicing and chasing up late payments. I also deal with credit checks on potential customers.

I am committed to pursuing a career in management accounting and am currently studying for further professional qualifications by distance learning. I am particularly interested in your post as it would enable me to gain experience of working in a larger company with the opportunities for professional training and development that this brings. In addition to my skills and experience as an accounts clerk, I would bring to the post a proven ability to deal successfully and tactfully with customers and clients.

I am available for interview for the next three weeks.

I look forward to hearing from you.

Yours sincerely

Dilip Patel
Dilip Patel
Enc. CV

For advice on layout see Formal letters pages

The date could also be January 20, 2010, 20/1/10 (*BrE*), or (*NAmE*) 1/20/10

In a cover letter use the words **post**, **position** or **vacancy**, not *job*.

Avoid contracted forms such as *I'm*.

Use **Yours faithfully** here if you have begun Dear Sir or Madam.

Sign your name and print it in full underneath.

Enc. or **encl.** shows you have enclosed something.

Key phrases

Paragraph 1 states your purpose for writing. Say which job you are applying for and how/where you heard about it.

Paragraph 2 outlines your current job and responsibilities. Make it relevant to the post you are applying for.

Paragraph 3 says why you want the job and what you can bring to the company. It is very important to say what *you* can do for *them*.

Paragraph 4 gives other relevant information and when you are available for interview.

Language bank

Since graduating from…, I have…
I have considerable/extensive experience in (the field of…)
I consider/feel that my qualifications and work experience could/might be of interest to the company.
If called for (an) interview, I would be available at any time convenient for you.
Please find attached a copy of my curriculum vitae/résumé for your consideration.
I look forward to hearing from you in due course.

Visual Vocabulary Builder Contents

V2 City and countryside
V4 Mountains and coast
V6 The environment
V8 Trees, plants and flowers
V10 The animal kingdom
V12 Architecture
V13 Buildings
V14 Homes
V15 House
V16 Garden / Yard
V17 DIY and cleaning
V18 Living room
V19 Dining room
V20 Bedroom
V21 Bathroom
V22 Kitchen
V24 Cooking
V26 Fruit and vegetables
V28 Herbs, spices, nuts and cereals
V29 Packaging
V30 Musical instruments
V32 Toys and games
V34 Hobbies
V36 Sports
V40 Extreme sports
V41 Cycles
V42 Cars
V43 Aircraft
V44 Boats and ships
V46 Vehicles
V48 The body
V49 Hair and make-up
V50 Clothes
V52 Accessories
V54 Computing
V56 Office
V57 Classroom
V58 Shapes, solids and angles
V59 The earth and the solar system
V60 The British Isles
V62 Canada and the United States of America
V64 Australia and New Zealand

City and countryside

City

1 skyscraper
2 crane
3 office block (*BrE*) / office building (*NAmE*)
4 dome
5 museum
6 clock tower
7 hoarding (*BrE*) (*also* billboard *especially NAmE*)
8 cinema (*BrE*) / movie theater (*NAmE*)
9 banner
10 flag
11 flagpole (*also* flagstaff)
12 alley (*also* alleyway)
13 awning
14 fountain
15 statue
16 shopping centre (*BrE*) shopping center (*NAmE*)
17 arcade
18 street light (*BrE also* street lamp)
19 lamp post (*especially BrE*)
20 market
21 market stall
22 road sign
23 theatre (*BrE*) / theater (*especially US*)
24 shop (*BrE*) store (*NAmE*)
25 cafe (*also* café)
26 postbox / letter box (*both BrE*) mailbox (*NAmE*)
27 busker
28 traffic lights (*NAmE also* stoplights)
29 bollard
30 litter bin (*BrE*) trash can (*NAmE*)
31 pedestrian precinct (*BrE*) / pedestrian mall (*NAmE*)
32 taxi rank (*BrE*) (*also* taxi stand *especially NAmE*)
33 railings
34 pavement (*BrE*) sidewalk (*NAmE*)
35 kerb (*BrE*) curb (*NAmE*)
36 parking meter (*also* meter)
37 pedestrian crossing (*BrE*) crosswalk (*NAmE*)
38 cycle lane (*BrE*) bicycle lane (*NAmE*)
39 bus stop
40 high street (*BrE*) main street (*NAmE*)

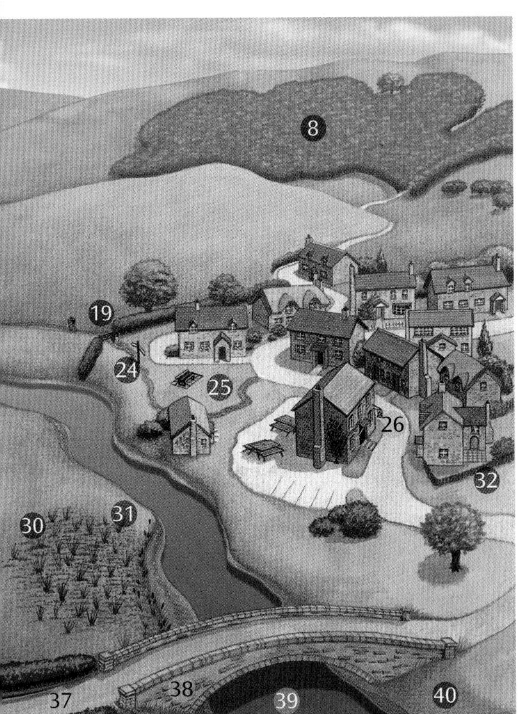

Countryside

1 windmill
2 hill
3 hay
4 haystack
5 vineyard
6 copse (*also* coppice)
7 stream
8 wood (*also* woods)
9 furrow
10 polytunnel
11 pasture
12 crops
13 tractor
14 field
15 farmyard
16 orchard
17 footpath
18 footbridge
19 stile
20 silo
21 farmhouse
22 stable
23 hedge
24 signpost
25 village green (*BrE*)
26 village
27 duck pond
28 farm
29 meadow
30 marsh
31 reeds
32 fence
33 barn
34 hedgerow
35 ditch
36 livestock
37 lane
38 bridge
39 river
40 riverbank

Mountains and coast

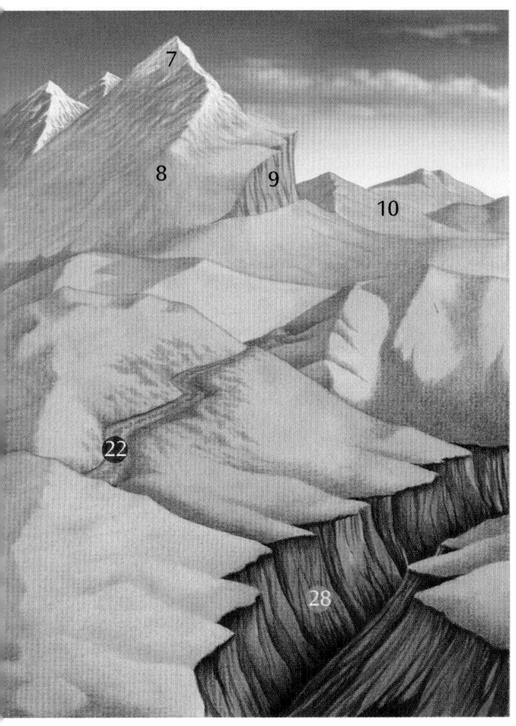

Mountains

1 summit
2 ridge
3 glacier
4 snow
5 mountain range
6 plateau
7 peak
8 mountain
9 precipice
10 foothills
11 snowline
12 ice
13 source
14 waterfall
15 forest
16 lake
17 conifers
18 glade (*also* clearing)
19 tributary
20 river
21 meander
22 pass
23 slope
24 scree
25 track
26 boulder
27 valley
28 gorge (*also* canyon)

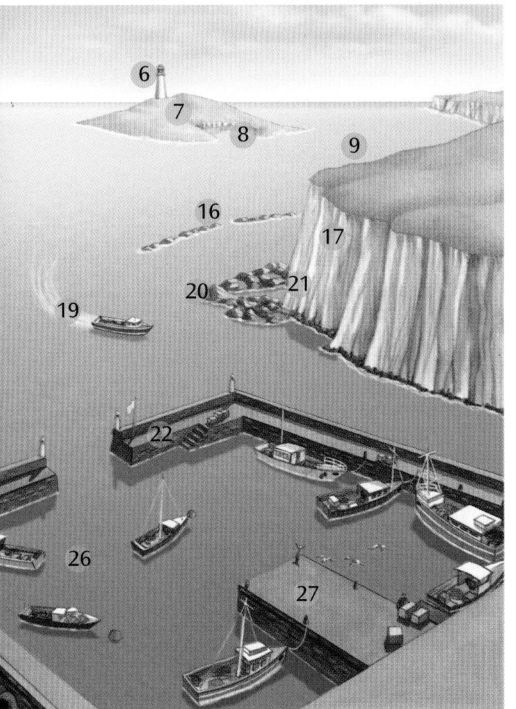

Coast

1 coastal path
2 cave
3 headland (*also* promontory)
4 horizon
5 sea (*BrE*) ocean (*NAmE*)
6 lighthouse
7 island
8 cove
9 clifftop
10 dune (*also* sand dune)
11 estuary
12 wave
13 spit
14 crest
15 foam
16 reef
17 cliff
18 sandbank
19 wake
20 rock
21 rock pool (*BrE*) tide pool (*NAmE*)
22 quay
23 beach
24 bay
25 shingle
26 harbour (*BrE*) harbor (*NAmE*)
27 jetty (*NAmE also* dock)
28 sand
29 seashore

The environment

Causes of the greenhouse effect

- **Carbon dioxide** is produced by **vehicle exhaust fumes** (1) and by **burning fossil fuels** (2) from power plants (*BrE also* power stations), factories and homes. This causes temperatures to rise. Trees, which absorb carbon dioxide, are felled by logging, causing **deforestation** (3).
- **Nitrogen oxide** comes from vehicles and power plants, and from agricultural fertilizers and pesticides used in **intensive farming** (4).
- Many **household products**, such as **refrigerators** and **aerosols**, emit **CFCs** (**chlorofluorocarbons**) which damage the ozone layer.
- **Methane gas** is released from household and industrial waste in **landfill sites** (5), and also from **cattle** (6).
- Sunlight causes these **greenhouse gases** to undergo **chemical change** and react with **water vapour** (*BrE*) (*NAmE* **vapor**), creating **acid rain**.

Acid rain

- **Acid rain** (7) falls on leaves and bark, damaging trees and plants in **forests**. **Nutrients** are **leached out** of the soil, and plants die.
- **Acid levels** build up in **lakes** and **rivers** (8), poisoning and killing fish.
- **Acid corrosion** attacks buildings, eating away at metal, stone and wood.
- **Pollution** from **smog** (9) causes **respiratory diseases** such as **asthma** and **bronchitis**.

Global warming

- **Global warming** can cause **climate change** and **environmental disaster**. Long-term changes in **temperature**, **wind**, **pressure**, **precipitation** (rain and snow) and **humidity** present challenges to our survival.
- **Environmental degradation**, such as **desertification** and **desiccation**, creates problems in many parts of the world.
- **Rising temperatures** cause **ice caps** to **melt**. **Rising sea levels** lead to coastal and river **flooding** and **erosion**.
- **Extreme events** occur, such as **storms**, **drought**, **forest fires**, **soil erosion**, **landslides**, **avalanches**, **tsunamis** and the sudden appearance of **pests** and **diseases**.

Solutions and sustainability

- **Wind turbines** (1), **solar power** and **hydroelectric power** (2) provide **alternative sources of energy** that are **renewable** and do not pollute the air.
- In the home, **solar panels** (3), **insulation**, **energy efficient light bulbs** and **biodegradable products** are **environmentally friendly**. Rubbish can be sorted for **recycling** in **bins** (4) and **bottle banks** (5), and **biodegradable waste** becomes **compost** (6).
- Using a **bicycle** (7), an **electric car** (8) or **public transport** (9) helps to **reduce carbon emissions**. Avoiding long-distance travel and buying local, seasonal food with **low food miles** reduces your **carbon footprint.**
- **Reforestation** (10) and **organic farming** (11) help to restore the earth's balance. Trees give off **oxygen**, absorb **carbon dioxide** and provide **habitats for wildlife. Organic farming** is **chemical free.**

SOME RECYCLABLE MATERIALS

- batteries
- cans
- cardboard
- engine oil
- fluorescent tubes
- glass
- organic garden waste
- paper
- plastic bottles
- scrap metal
- textiles
- timber

Trees, plants and flowers

Trees

foliage
blossom
bud
twig
branch
limb
trunk
leaf
twig
roots
tree
rings
wood
bark
log

Evergreen trees

berry
palm
yew
needles
cone (*BrE* *also* fir cone)
fir

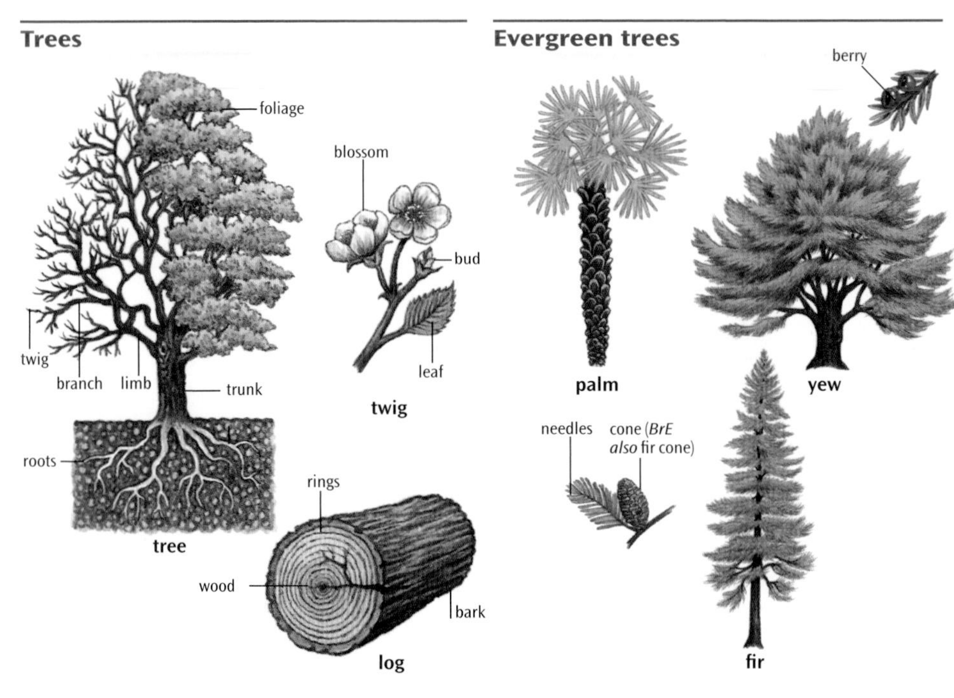

Deciduous trees

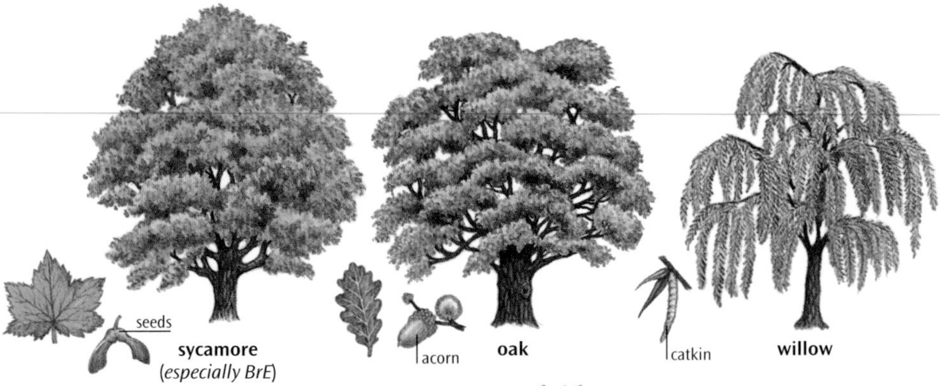

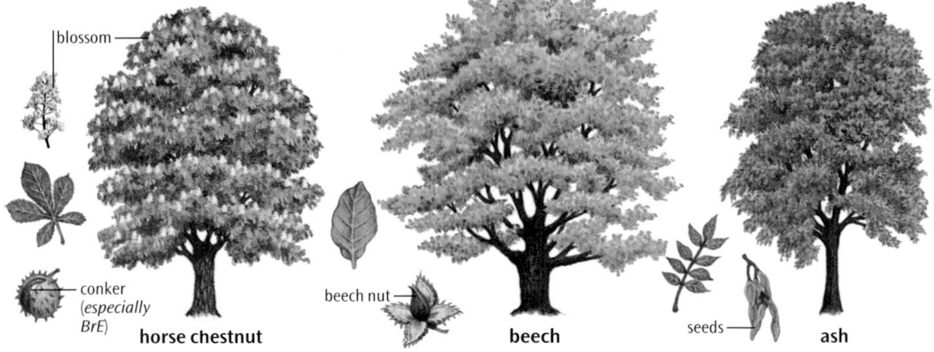

seeds
sycamore (*especially BrE*)
acorn
oak
catkin
willow

blossom
conker (*especially BrE*)
horse chestnut
beech nut
beech
seeds
ash

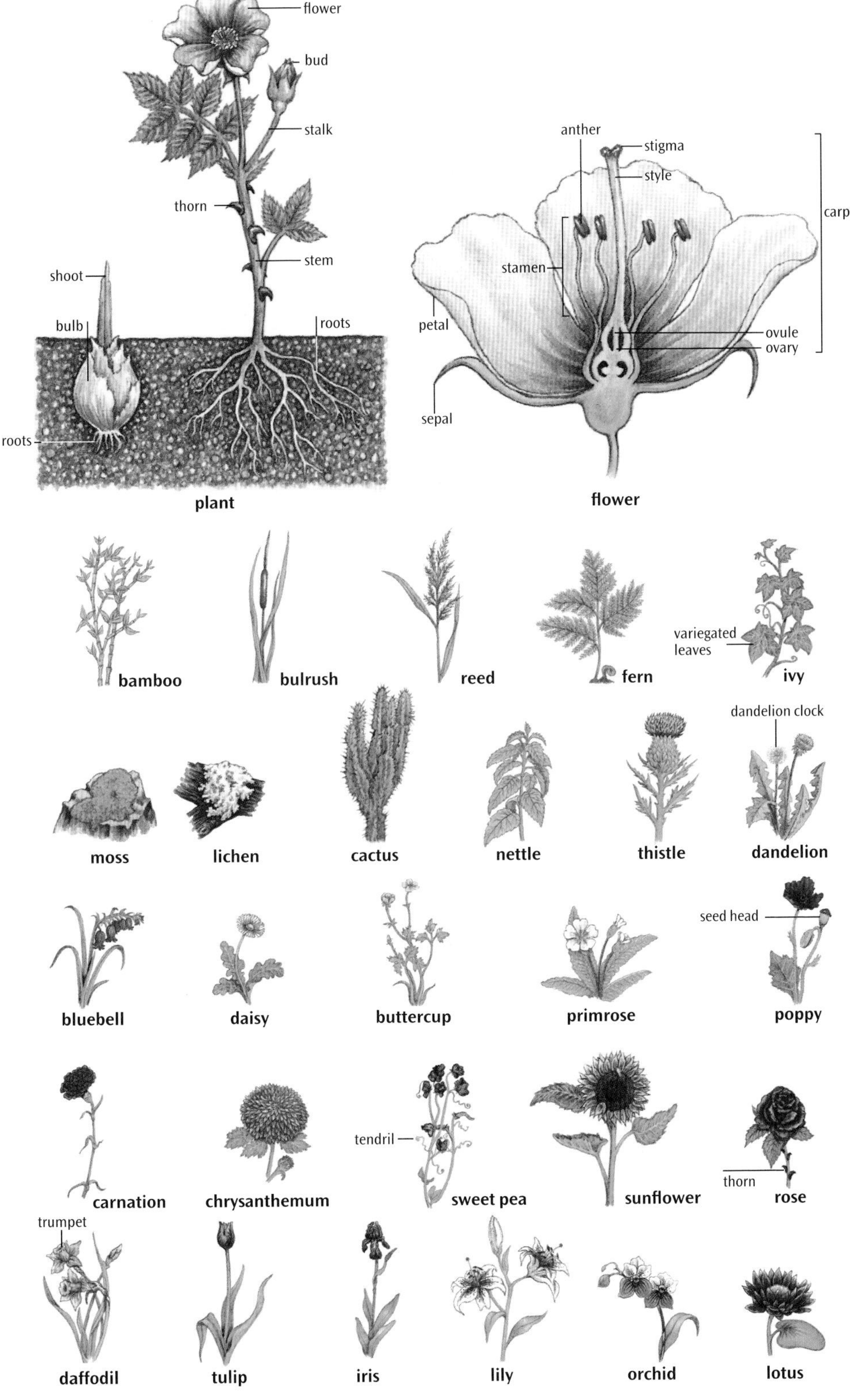

plant

flower

bamboo

bulrush

reed

fern

ivy

moss

lichen

cactus

nettle

thistle

dandelion

bluebell

daisy

buttercup

primrose

poppy

carnation

chrysanthemum

sweet pea

sunflower

rose

daffodil

tulip

iris

lily

orchid

lotus

The animal kingdom

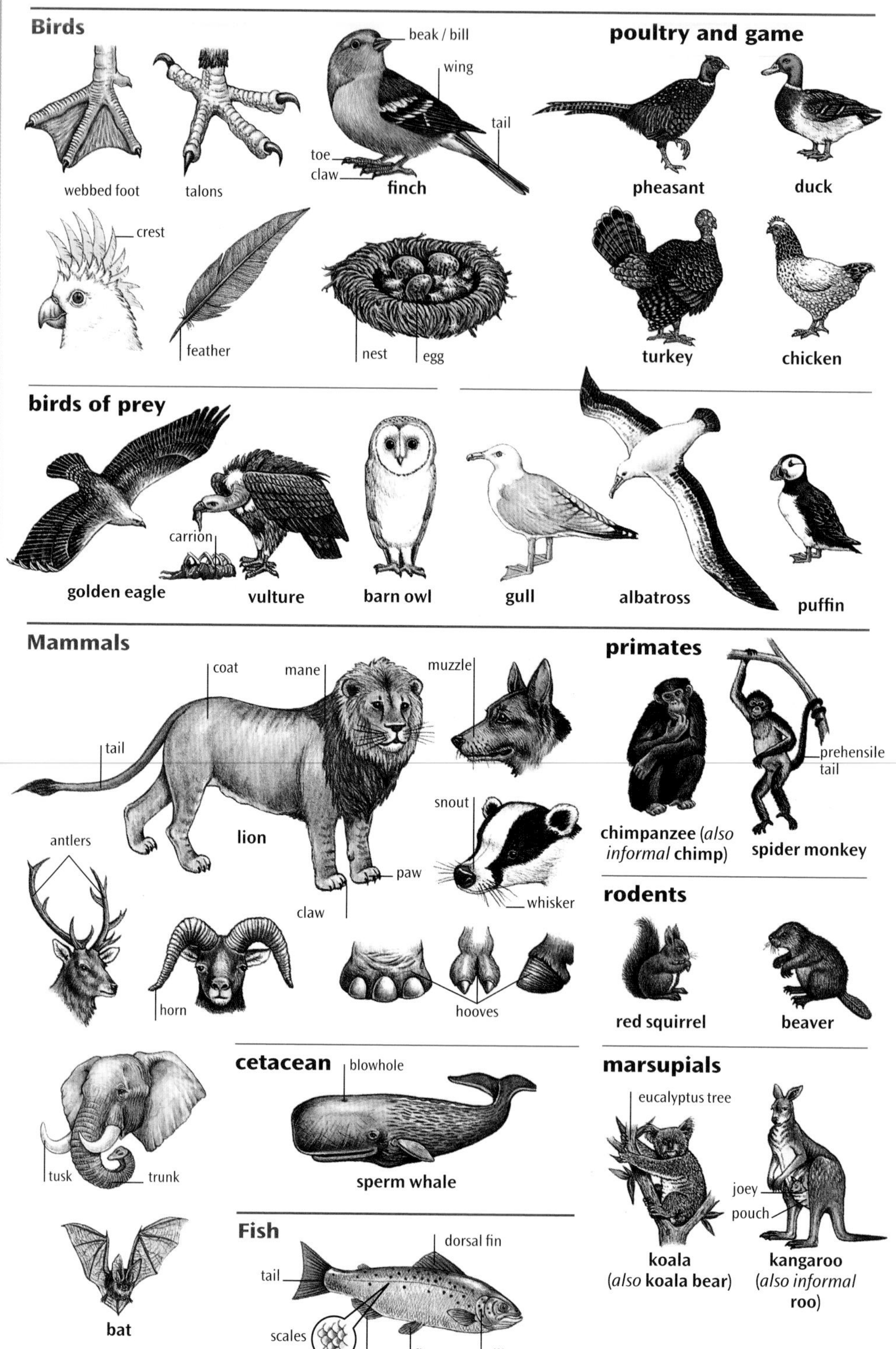
Birds
webbed foot
talons
beak / bill
wing
tail
toe
claw
finch
poultry and game
pheasant
duck
crest
feather
nest
egg
turkey
chicken
birds of prey
golden eagle
carrion
vulture
barn owl
gull
albatross
puffin
Mammals
coat
mane
muzzle
tail
lion
snout
paw
claw
whisker
antlers
horn
hooves
primates
chimpanzee (also informal chimp)
prehensile tail
spider monkey
rodents
red squirrel
beaver
tusk
trunk
cetacean
blowhole
sperm whale
marsupials
eucalyptus tree
joey
pouch
koala (also koala bear)
kangaroo (also informal roo)
bat
Fish
tail
dorsal fin
scales
fin
gill
ventral fin
trout

Amphibians

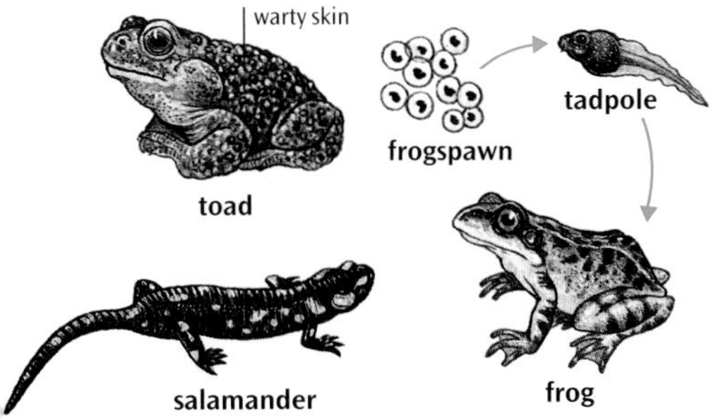

warty skin
toad
frogspawn
tadpole
salamander
frog

Reptiles

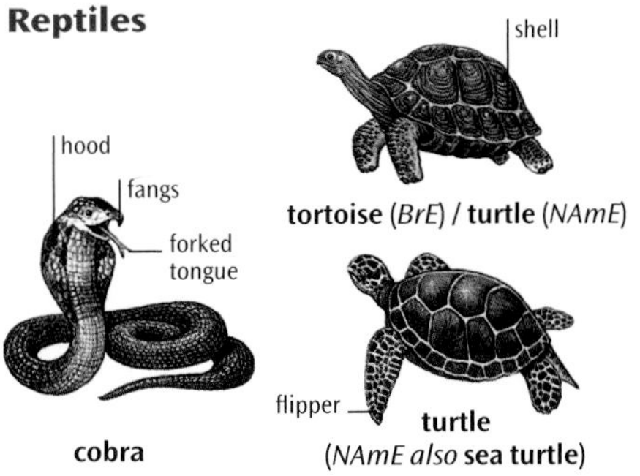

hood
fangs
forked tongue
cobra
shell
tortoise (*BrE*) / turtle (*NAmE*)
flipper
turtle
(*NAmE also* sea turtle)

Insects

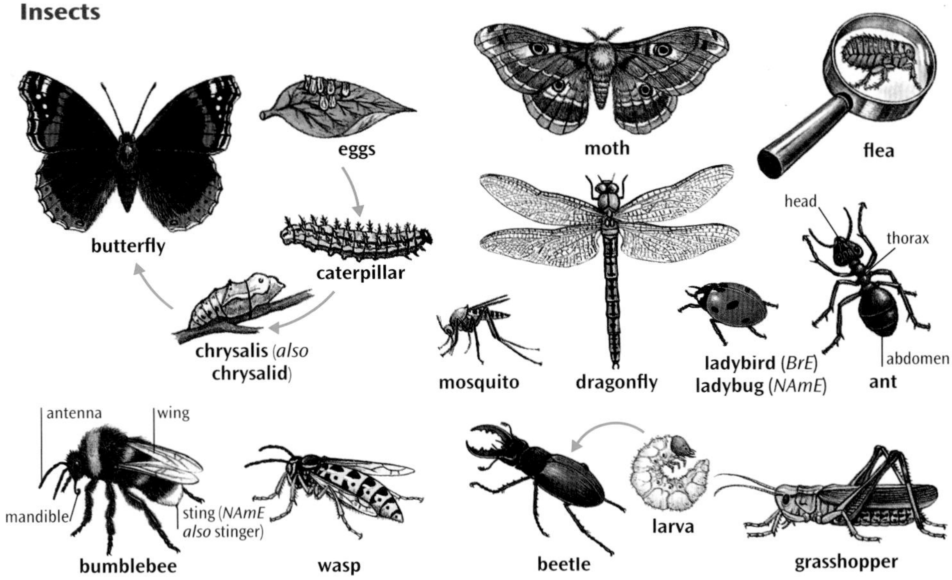

butterfly
eggs
caterpillar
chrysalis (*also* chrysalid)
moth
flea
mosquito
dragonfly
ladybird (*BrE*)
ladybug (*NAmE*)
head
thorax
abdomen
ant
antenna
wing
mandible
sting (*NAmE also* stinger)
bumblebee
wasp
beetle
larva
grasshopper

Crustaceans

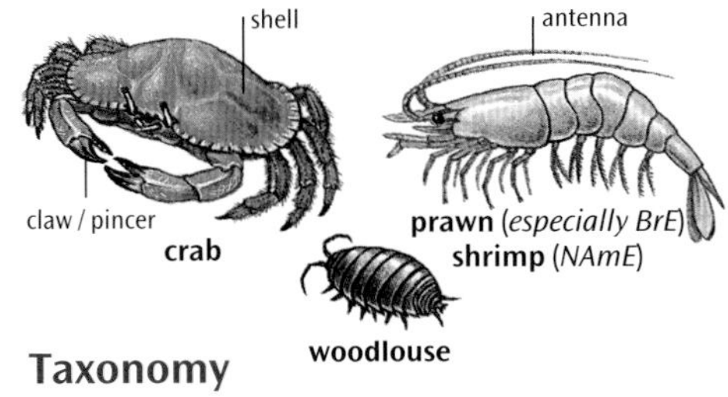

shell
claw / pincer
crab
antenna
prawn (*especially BrE*)
shrimp (*NAmE*)
woodlouse

Arachnids

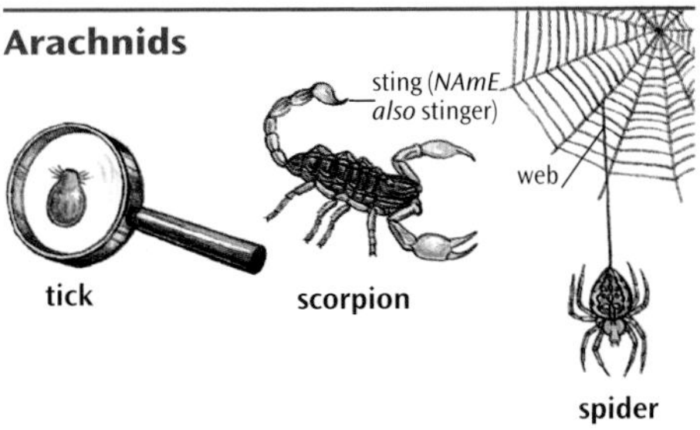

tick
sting (*NAmE also* stinger)
scorpion
web
spider

Taxonomy

Living things are grouped on the basis of their similarities and differences into smaller and smaller groups. This scientific process of classification is called **taxonomy**. The main groups, from the largest to the smallest, are:

- **kingdom** (animal or plant)
- **phylum** (*plural* **phyla**) (e.g. mollusc, arthropod)
- **class** (e.g. mammal, gastropod, insect)
- **order** (e.g. primate, marsupial)
- **family**
- **genus** (*plural* **genera**)
- **species**

Gastropods

shell
snail
slug

Cephalopod

tentacle
sucker
octopus

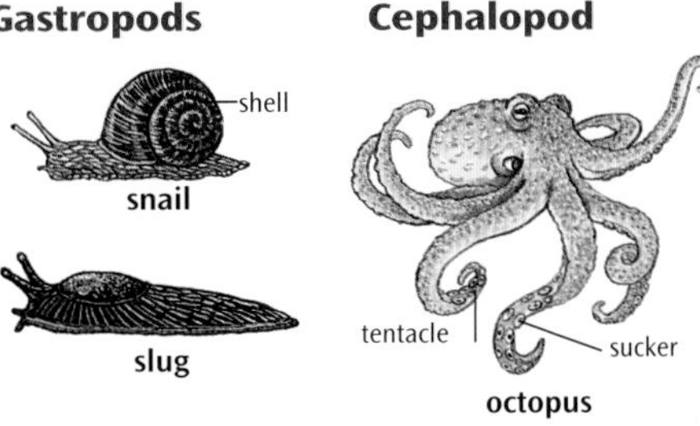

Architecture

geodesic dome

gargoyle

obelisk pedestal

dome

rotunda

arch

vaulted ceiling

colonnade

cloister plinth column

portico

Bridges

humpback bridge (*BrE*)

suspension bridge

cantilever bridge

viaduct

aqueduct

Buildings

amphitheatre

fort

palace

castle

stately home

glasshouse

pyramid

log cabin

pub (*BrE*)

warehouse

lighthouse

oil rig
oil platform

hut

barn

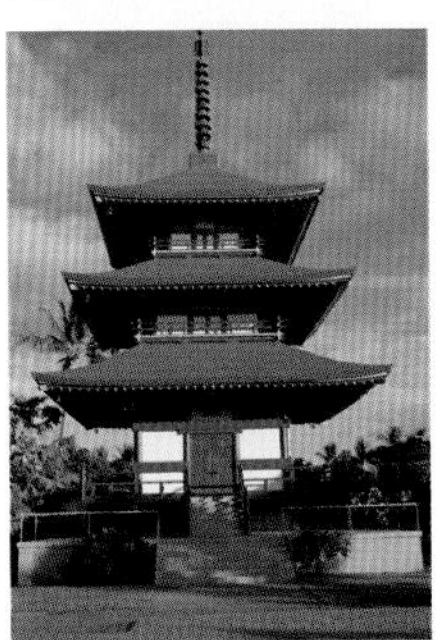
pagoda

Work connected with building

	person	**work** – all [U]
building houses and other buildings:	**builder**	**building**
designing buildings:	**architect**	**architecture**
designing roads and bridges, etc.:	**civil engineer**	**civil engineering**
building walls, etc. with bricks:	**bricklayer**	**bricklaying**
repairing or building roofs:	**roofer**	**roofing**
making doors and window frames from wood:	**joiner**	**joinery**
making and repairing wooden objects and structures:	**carpenter**	**carpentry**
fitting glass into the frames of windows, etc.:	**glazier**	**glazing**
putting plaster on walls:	**plasterer**	**plastering**
fitting and repairing water pipes, toilets, etc.:	**plumber**	**plumbing**
connecting, repairing, etc. electrical equipment:	**electrician**	**wiring**

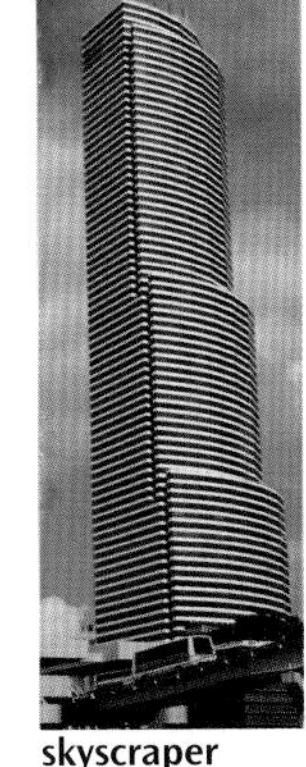
skyscraper

Homes

semi-detached house (*BrE*)

duplex (*especially NAmE*)

town house (*BrE*)

row house (*NAmE*)

terraced house (*BrE*)

block of flats (*BrE*)

apartment building (*NAmE*)

bungalow (*BrE*)

thatched cottage

mobile home (*especially NAmE*)

houseboat

Other types of home

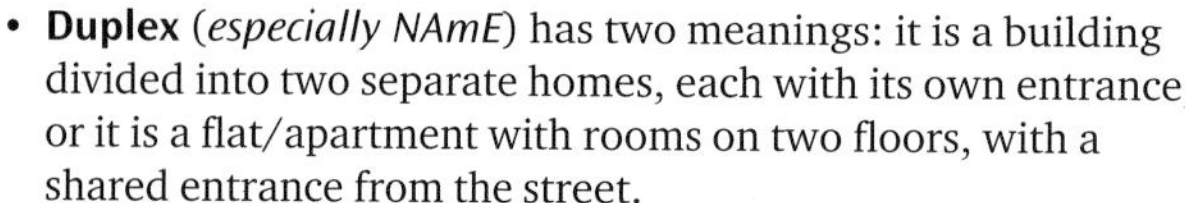
- **Duplex** (*especially NAmE*) has two meanings: it is a building divided into two separate homes, each with its own entrance, or it is a flat/apartment with rooms on two floors, with a shared entrance from the street.

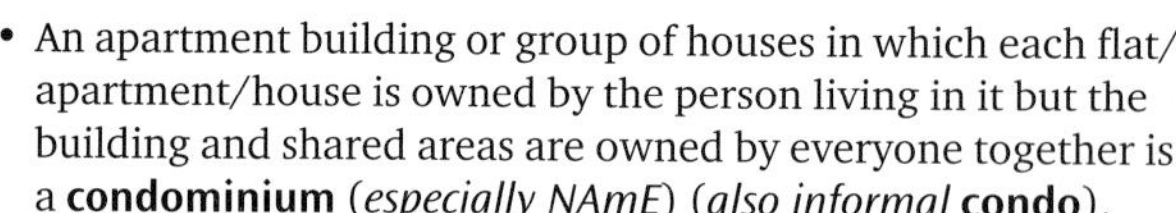
- An apartment building or group of houses in which each flat/apartment/house is owned by the person living in it but the building and shared areas are owned by everyone together is a **condominium** (*especially NAmE*) (*also informal* **condo**).

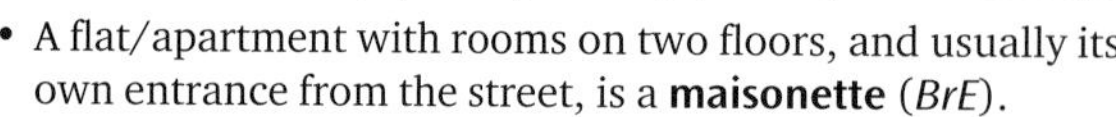
- A flat/apartment with rooms on two floors, and usually its own entrance from the street, is a **maisonette** (*BrE*).

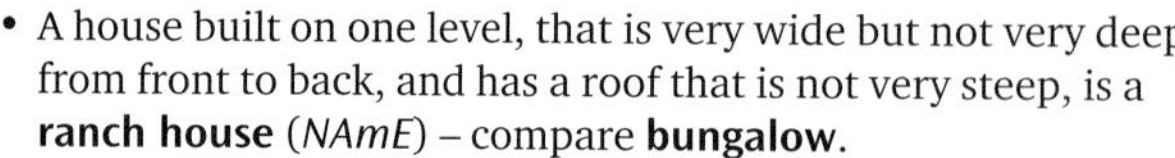
- A house built on one level, that is very wide but not very deep from front to back, and has a roof that is not very steep, is a **ranch house** (*NAmE*) – compare **bungalow**.

- A very large house is a **mansion**.

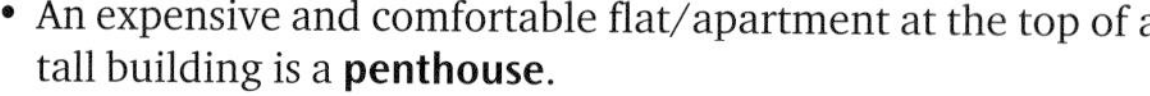
- An expensive and comfortable flat/apartment at the top of a tall building is a **penthouse**.

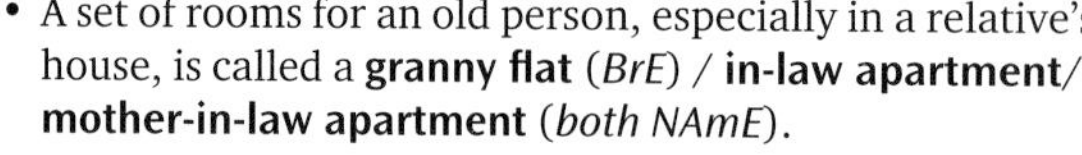
- A set of rooms for an old person, especially in a relative's house, is called a **granny flat** (*BrE*) / **in-law apartment/ mother-in-law apartment** (*both NAmE*).

House

1 chimney pot
2 chimney
3 aerial (*BrE*) antenna (*NAmE, BrE*)
4 ridge
5 gable
6 roof
7 skylight
8 dormer window
9 eaves
10 burglar alarm
11 gutter
12 drainpipe (*NAmE also* downspout)
13 shutter
14 windowpane
15 sash window
16 casement window
17 balcony
18 window box
19 windowsill
20 porch
21 tile
22 hanging basket
23 door knocker
24 French window (*BrE*) French door (*NAmE*)
25 bay window
26 letter box (*BrE*) mail slot (*NAmE*)
27 front door
28 wall
29 garage
30 brick
31 doorstep
32 basement
33 step
34 drive (*also* driveway)

Where you live

- The area surrounding a house is the **neighbourhood** (*BrE*) / **neighborhood** (*NAmE*).
- A person who lives next or near to you is your **neighbour** (*BrE*) / **neighbor** (*NAmE*).

  The next house, room or building is **next door:**
  ▸ *our next-door neighbours*
- An area where people live that is outside the main part of a city or town is called a **suburb**, or **the suburbs.** The adjective is **suburban:**
  ▸ *suburban houses/streets*
- An area where a large number of houses are planned and built as a group is called an **estate** or a **development:**
  ▸ *a new housing estate/development*
- If you go and live in another house, you **move**, or **move house**. You **move in/move into** a new house, then **move out/move out of** it when you stop living there.

Buying or renting a house

- A house that is available to buy is **for sale** or **on the market**:
  ▸ *This property has been on the market for about six weeks.*
- A person whose job is to buy and sell houses and land for other people is an **estate agent** (*BrE*) / **real estate agent** (*NAmE*).
- When you borrow money from a bank or building society in order to buy a house, you **take out a mortgage**.
- If you pay money for the use of a room, house, etc., you **rent** it (**from** sb). The money that you pay, probably each month, is **rent**. The person who rents a room, house, etc. is a **tenant** and the person who owns the property is a **landlord** (or **landlady** if it is a woman):
  ▸ *The landlord has put the rent up again.*

Garden (*BrE*) / Yard (*NAmE*)

1 greenhouse
2 shed
3 hedge
4 bird table (*BrE*) bird feeder (*NAmE*)
5 parasol / sunshade
6 conservatory (*BrE*)
7 pergola
8 climber
9 gate
10 fence
11 sunlounger (*BrE*) (*also* lounger, *BrE, NAmE*)
12 deckchair
13 barbecue (*also* BBQ)
14 water butt (*BrE*) rain barrel (*NAmE*)
15 bench
16 trellis
17 stake
18 deck
19 flowerpot
20 patio
21 planter
22 flower bed
23 compost bin
24 border
25 lawn
26 cane
27 water feature
28 pond
29 cold frame (*also* frame)
30 seedling
31 cloche
32 vegetable patch / vegetable plot

DIY and cleaning

Tools

Cleaning

Decorating

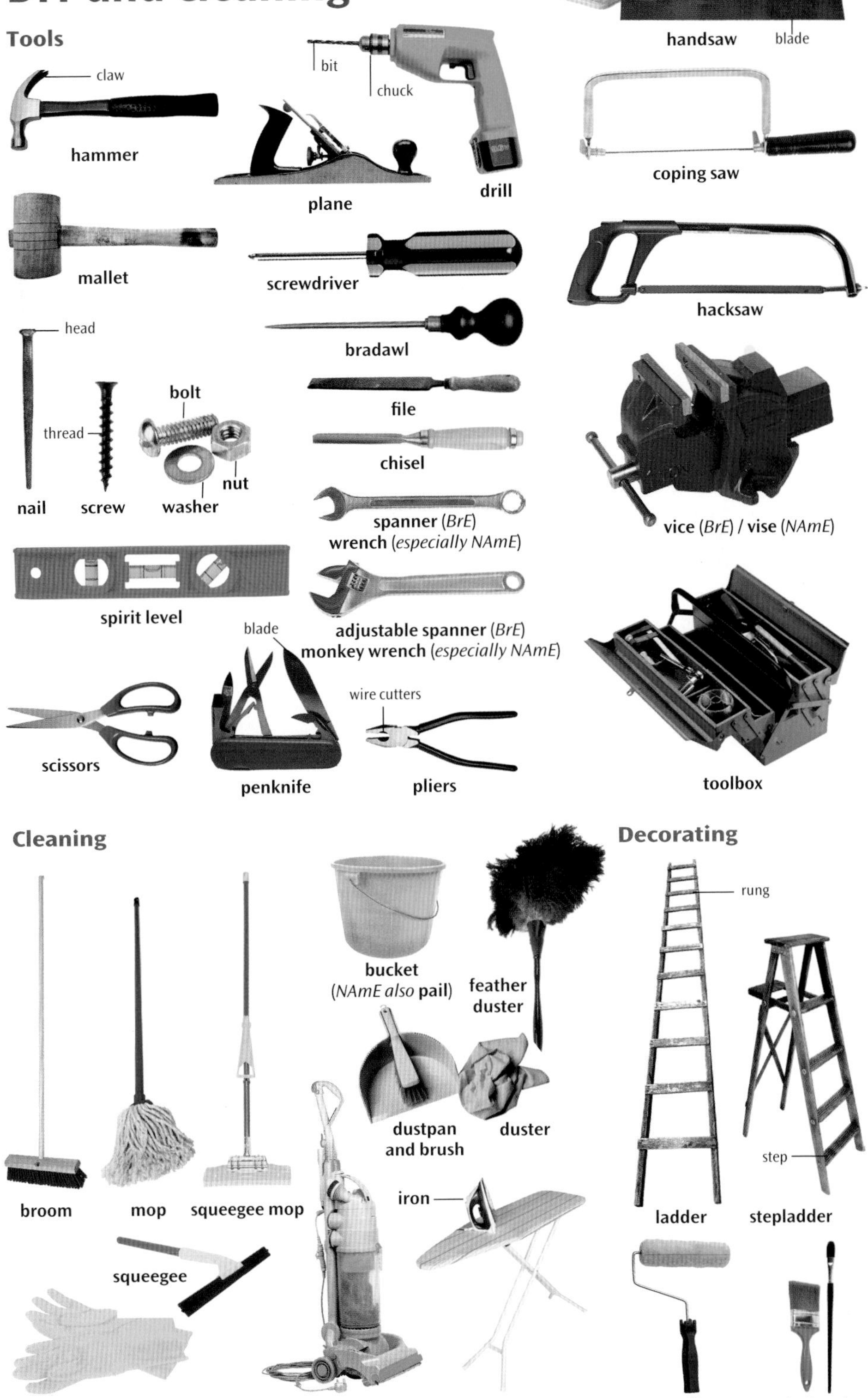
claw
hammer
bit
chuck
drill
plane
handsaw
blade
coping saw
mallet
screwdriver
hacksaw
bradawl
head
thread
bolt
nut
washer
nail
screw
file
chisel
vice (BrE) / vise (NAmE)
spanner (BrE)
wrench (especially NAmE)
spirit level
blade
adjustable spanner (BrE)
monkey wrench (especially NAmE)
wire cutters
scissors
penknife
pliers
toolbox
bucket
(NAmE also pail)
feather duster
rung
dustpan and brush
duster
broom
mop
squeegee mop
iron
ladder
stepladder
step
squeegee
rubber gloves
vacuum cleaner
(BrE also Hoover™)
ironing board
roller
paintbrushes

Living room

1 hi-fi system
2 speakers
3 waste-paper basket (*BrE*) / wastebasket (*NAmE*)
4 mantelpiece (*also* mantel *especially NAmE*)
5 coal scuttle
6 fire surround
7 fireplace
8 grate
9 hearth
10 poker
11 house plant (*BrE also* pot plant)
12 plant pot
13 armchair
14 rug
15 bookcase
16 ornament (*especially BrE*)
17 bookend
18 flat-screen TV
19 vase
20 coaster
21 footstool
22 coffee table
23 remote control
24 radiator
25 magazine rack
26 recliner
27 scatter cushion (*BrE*) throw pillow (*NAmE*)
28 throw
29 sofa / couch
30 occasional table
31 floorboards

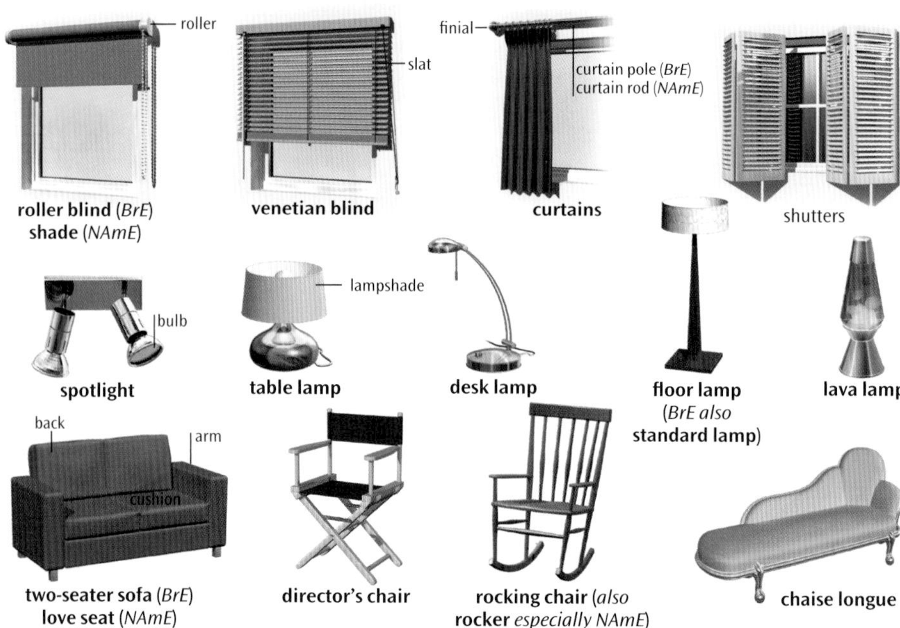

roller blind (*BrE*) **shade** (*NAmE*)

venetian blind

curtains

spotlight

table lamp

desk lamp

floor lamp (*BrE also* **standard lamp**)

lava lamp

two-seater sofa (*BrE*) **love seat** (*NAmE*)

director's chair

rocking chair (*also* **rocker** *especially NAmE*)

chaise longue

Dining room

1 fruit bowl
2 cheeseboard
3 cheese knife
4 sideboard
5 drawer
6 cutlery (*especially BrE*) flatware (*NAmE*)
7 napkin
8 bowl
9 plate
10 place mat (*BrE also* table mat)
11 side plate
12 glass
13 pepper pot (*especially BrE*) pepper shaker (*NAmE*)
14 salt cellar (*BrE*) salt shaker (*NAmE*)
15 butter knife
16 butter dish
17 serving dish
18 lid
19 gravy boat
20 candlestick
21 candle
22 wick
23 carafe
24 dining chair
25 high chair
26 dining table
27 tablecloth

Bedroom

1 bedside table (*especially BrE*) (*NAmE usually* nightstand, night table)
2 clock radio
3 headboard
4 pillow
5 pillowcase
6 bottom sheet
7 double bed
8 duvet
9 en suite (*BrE, from French*)
10 built-in/fitted wardrobe (*BrE*) / closet (*especially NAmE*)
11 rail
12 hanger
13 chest of drawers (*NAmE also* bureau, dresser)
14 drawer
15 full-length mirror
16 mirror
17 dressing table (*NAmE also* vanity, vanity table)
18 stool
19 fitted carpet (*BrE*) wall-to-wall carpet (*NAmE*)
20 rug

11
9
12
10
13
14
15
3
16
4
5
6
8
1
2
7
17
18
20
19

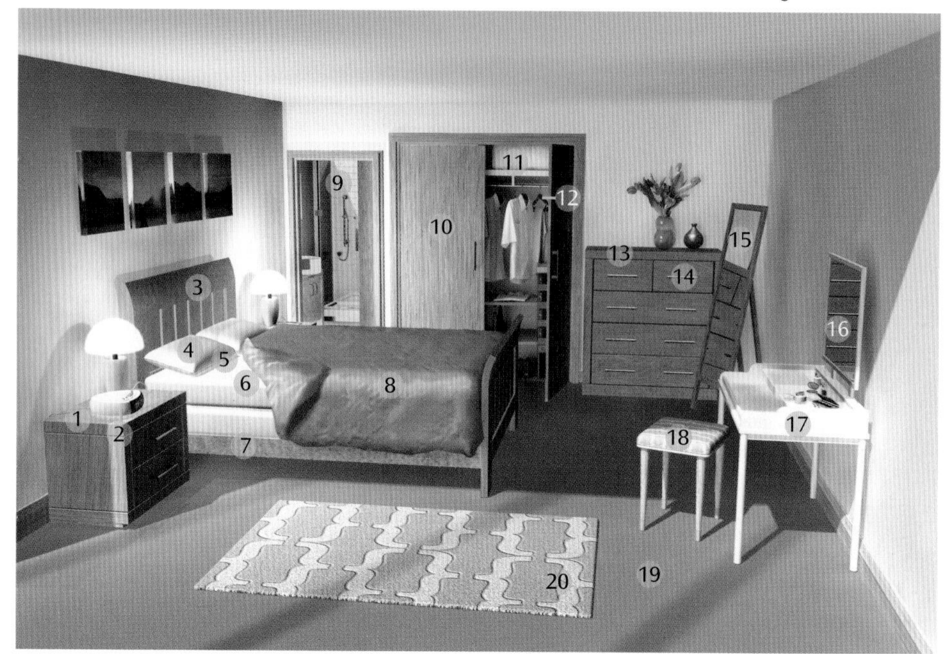

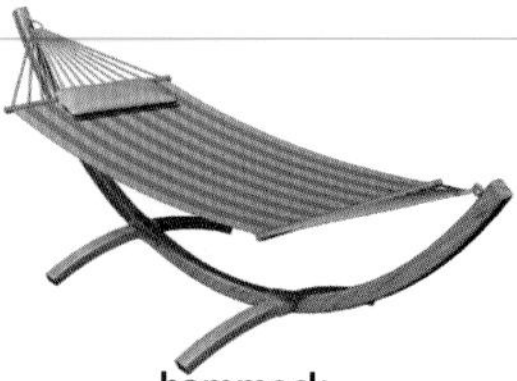

hammock

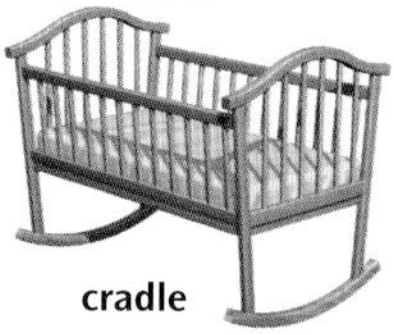

cradle

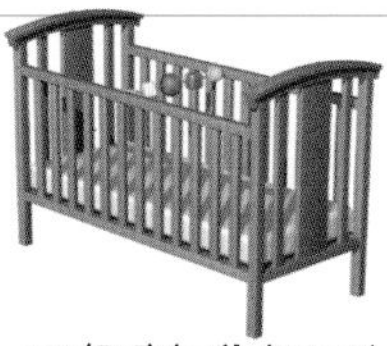

cot (*BrE*) / **crib** (*NAmE*)

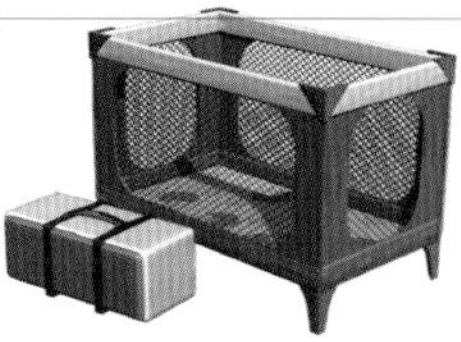

travel cot

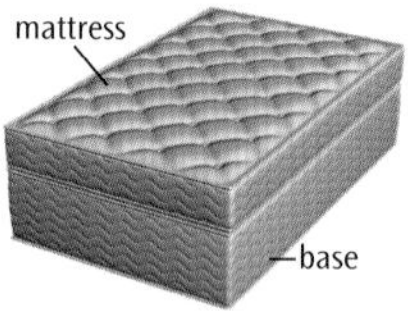

mattress
base

divan (*BrE*)

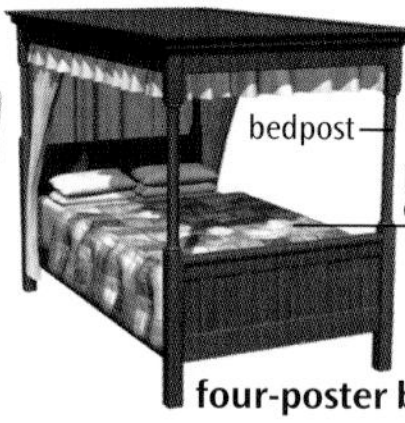

canopy
bedpost
patchwork quilt

four-poster bed

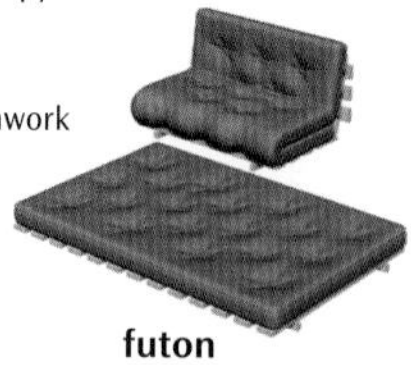

futon

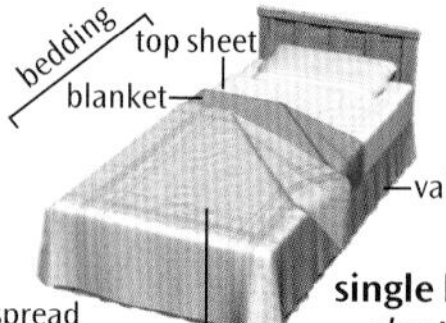

bedding
top sheet
blanket
valance
bedspread (*BrE also* bedcover) (*NAmE also* spread)

single bed (*NAmE also* **twin bed**)

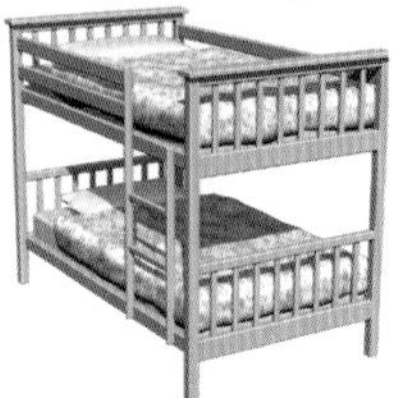

bunk beds

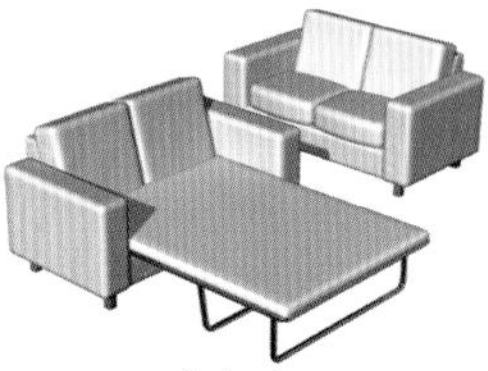

sofa bed

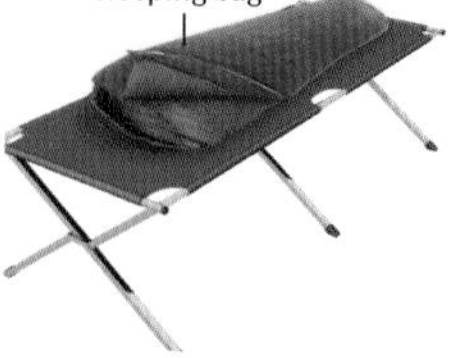

sleeping bag

camp bed (*BrE*) **cot** (*NAmE*)

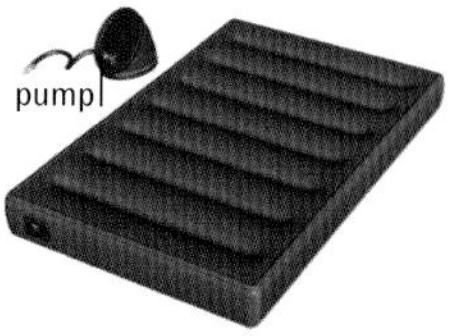

pump

air bed (*BrE*) / **air mattress** (*especially NAmE*)

Bathroom

1 bathroom cabinet
2 toothbrush holder
3 beaker
4 mixer tap
5 washbasin
6 soap dispenser
7 flannel (*BrE*) washcloth (*NAmE*)
8 vanity unit (*BrE*)
9 shower cubicle
10 shower head
11 soap dish
12 shower tray
13 plughole (*BrE*) drain (*US*)
14 towel rail (*BrE*) towel rack (*NAmE*)
15 hand towel
16 bath towel
17 bathroom scales
18 bath (*BrE*) / bathtub (*especially NAmE*)
19 bath mat
20 tiling
21 bath panel
22 tap (*especially BrE*) faucet (*NAmE*)
23 bathrobe (*also* robe)
24 bidet
25 toilet
26 cistern (*BrE*)
27 toilet paper
28 toilet brush

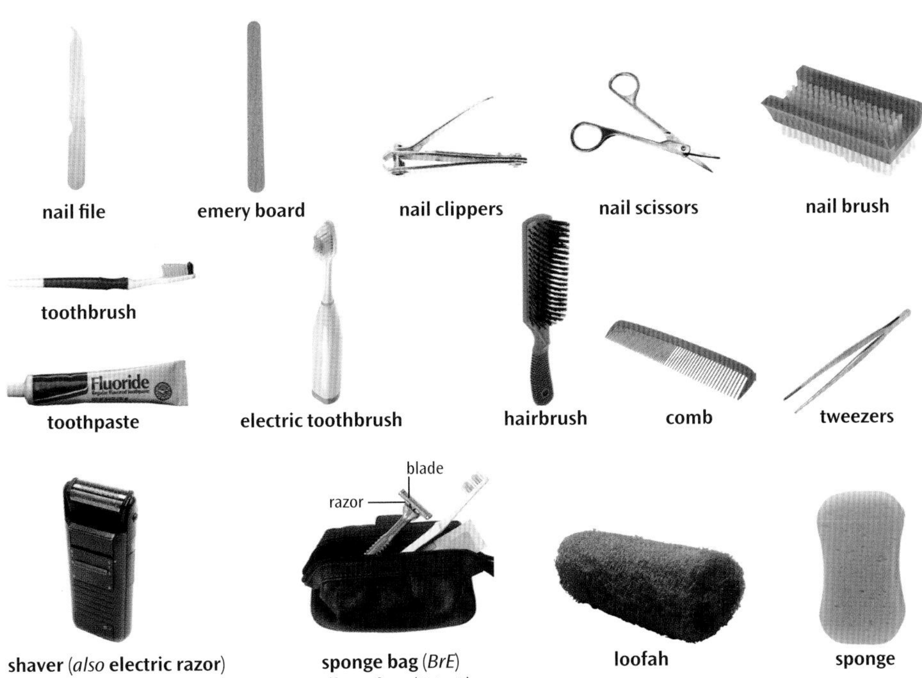

Kitchen

1 microwave
2 worktop (*BrE*) counter (*NAmE*)
3 knife block
4 kitchen units
5 cooker hood
6 splashback
7 gas ring (*especially BrE*) / burner (*NAmE*)
8 hob (*BrE*) / stovetop (*NAmE*)
9 drawer
10 oven glove (*also* oven mitt)
11 grill (*BrE*)
12 oven
13 fridge (*BrE*) refrigerator (*NAmE*)
14 breakfast bar
15 stool
16 toaster
17 door
18 shelf
19 kitchen roll holder
20 kitchen paper (*BrE*) paper towel (*NAmE*)
21 draining board (*BrE*) drainboard (*NAmE*)
22 dishcloth (*NAmE usually* dishrag)
23 sink
24 tap (*especially BrE*) faucet (*NAmE*)
25 dishwasher
26 tea towel (*BrE*) dishtowel (*NAmE*)

Appliances

blender (*BrE also* **liquidizer**)

hand-held blender

food processor

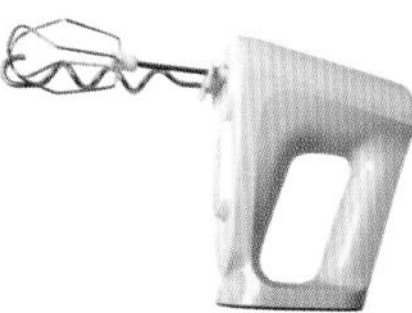
electric whisk

Coffee and tea

electric kettle

espresso maker

cafetière (*BrE*)
French press (*NAmE*)

coffee maker
(*also* **coffee machine**)

teapot

Kitchen utensils

Cutting
bread knife
serrated blade
handle
carving knife
edge
point
steel
cleaver
peeler
palette knife
chopping board (*BrE*)
cutting board (*NAmE*)
paring knife
kitchen scissors
Measuring
measuring spoons
measuring cups
OUNCES
METRIC mL
measuring jug
timer
Opening
corkscrew
bottle opener
tin opener (*BrE*)
can opener (*NAmE*)
Crushing, grating, squeezing
potato masher
grater
zester
lemon-squeezer (*BrE*)
juicer (*NAmE*)
garlic press
(*also* garlic crusher)
nutcracker
pestle
mortar
pestle and mortar
pepper mill
Other utensils
colander
sieve (*BrE*)
sifter (*NAmE*)
ladle
wooden spoon
whisk
basting brush
spatula
fish slice (*BrE*)
spatula (*NAmE*)
ramekin
tongs
ice-cream scoop
cake slice
rolling pin

Cooking

flambé

stir-fry

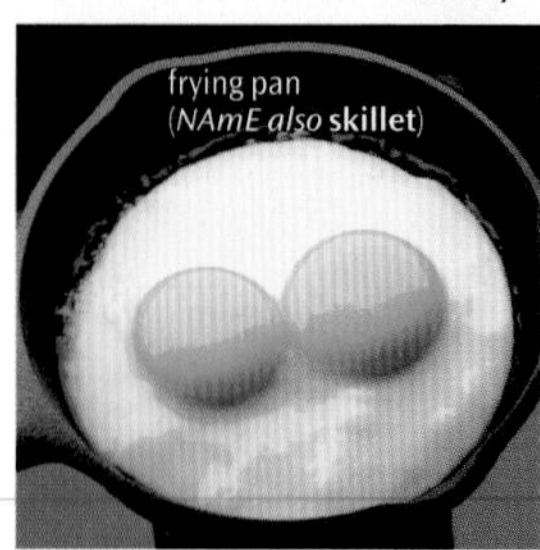

fry

tongs

barbecue

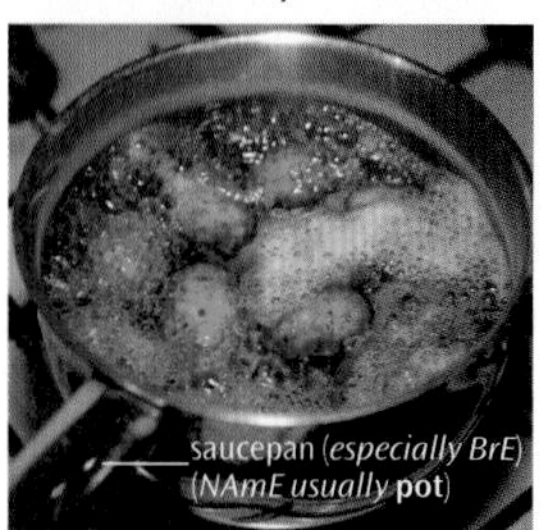

boil

steam

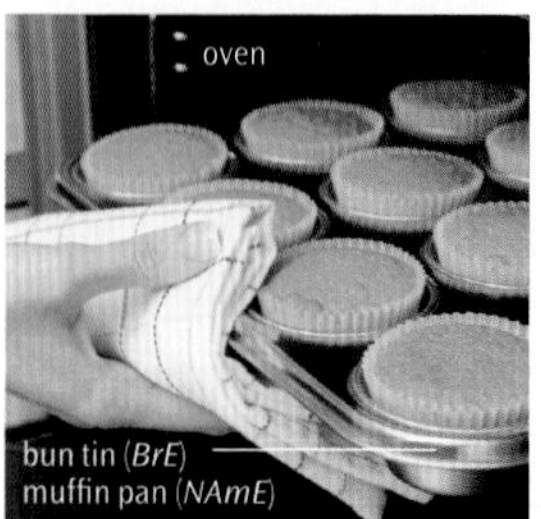

bake

casserole

Cook

- When talking generally about preparing meals, use the verb **to cook**:
  ▸ *When you're cooking for your family, make an extra serving.*

You can **cook** food or a meal:
  ▸ *Lucas is cooking dinner.*
  ▸ *Cook the onion gently until soft.*

... or the food or the meal can **cook**:
  ▸ *Add the meat and let it cook for ten minutes.*

There are different verbs for particular ways of cooking: with water or oil, or in dry heat.

Fry

- You can **fry** meat, fish, eggs, etc. in a shallow pan of hot oil, or the meat, fish, eggs, etc. can **fry**:
  ▸ *Fry the onion and garlic for five minutes.*
  ▸ *The smell of frying bacon made her mouth water.*
- Chips (*BrE*) / French fries (*NAmE*), etc. can be completely covered in very hot oil and **deep-fried**.
- You can **sauté** food by frying it quickly in a little hot fat:
  ▸ *new potatoes sautéed in butter and thyme*

Boil

- You can **boil** vegetables, eggs, rice, etc. by covering them with water and heating to **boiling point** (=100°C):
  ▸ *Boil the potatoes until tender, then drain.*
- You can also just **boil** the water:
  ▸ *I'm boiling the water for the pasta now.*

... or the container the water is in:
  ▸ *Boil a large pan of salted water.*

- The vegetables, the water, or (in British English) the container, can **boil**:
  ▸ *The potatoes were boiling away merrily.*
  ▸ *The kettle's boiled! Do you want some tea?* (*BrE*)
- If you **bring something to the boil** (*BrE*) / **a boil** (*NAmE*) you heat it until it boils; you can then **simmer** it or let it **simmer** by letting it boil gently for a period of time:
  ▸ *Simmer the carrots in a large pan of water.*
  ▸ *Bring to the boil and let it simmer for five minutes.*
- You can **poach** food by cooking it gently in a small amount of liquid:
  ▸ *Gently poach the salmon fillets for eight minutes.*

Preparation

chop

dice

slice

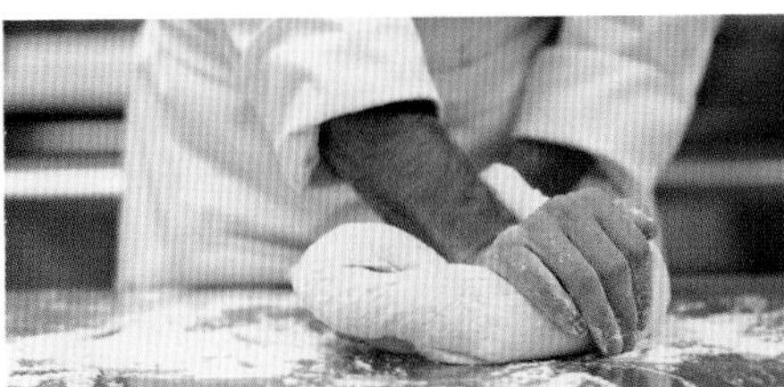
knead

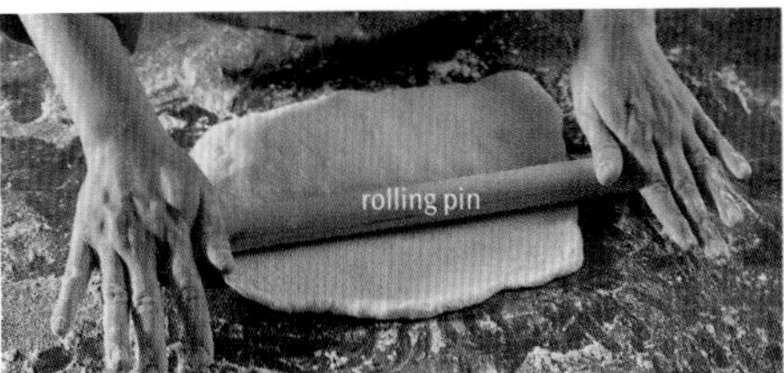

roll out

mash

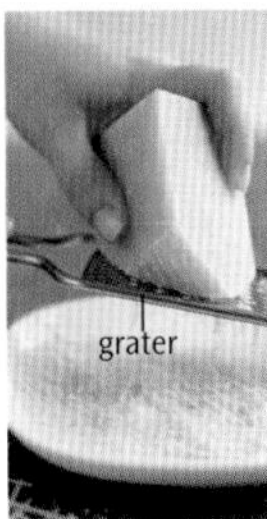

grate

whip

Steam

- You can **steam** fish, vegetables, etc. by placing the food above boiling water in a covered container with holes in the bottom so the steam reaches it:
  - ▸ *Chinese rice is always white and usually prepared by steaming.*

Roast

- You can **roast** large pieces of meat, potatoes, etc. by covering the surface of the food with oil in the heat of an oven.

Grill

- You can **grill** (*BrE*) / **broil** (*NAmE*) food under direct heat on a **grill pan** (*BrE*) / **broiler pan** (*NAmE*).

Bake

- You can **bake** bread, cakes, potatoes, etc. in the dry heat of an oven or a fire:
  - ▸ *He baked a cake for her birthday.*

... or the bread, cakes, etc. can **bake**:
  - ▸ *While the cake is baking, avoid opening the oven door.*

- **Baking** can be used for things that are baked, or for the activity of baking them:
  - ▸ *A nice smell of baking came from the kitchen.*
  - ▸ *My grandmother always used to bake/do the baking on Saturdays.*

GRAMMAR POINT

- The past participle (**-ed** form) of most cooking verbs can be used as an adjective before an item of food, meaning 'that has been cooked in this way':
  - ▸ *a cooked breakfast* (*BrE*) *a warm breakfast* (*NAmE*)
  - ▸ *a boiled egg*
  - ▸ *sautéed potatoes* (*also sauté potatoes*)
  - ▸ *BUT roast chicken*
- The gerund (**-ing** form) of some cooking verbs can be used as an adjective before an item of food, meaning 'suitable to be cooked in this way':
  - ▸ *cooking apples* (= that must be cooked before they are eaten)
  - ▸ *stewing steak*

... or before a piece of equipment, meaning 'suitable to be used when cooking in this way':
  - ▸ *a frying pan*
  - ▸ *a baking tray* (*BrE*) / *baking sheet* (*NAmE*)

Fruit and vegetables

- Some fruit and vegetables are always countable:
  ▸ *Do you like bananas?*

  Some are always uncountable:
  ▸ *Celery is usually eaten raw.*
- Some may be countable or uncountable, depending on whether you are thinking of them as plants or as food and on how they are prepared as food. If you are thinking of a fruit or vegetable as a plant you are usually talking about the whole fruit or vegetable, so it will be countable:
  ▸ *Plant the cabbages in rows.*
- Larger fruit or vegetables, that you do not eat whole, are uncountable as food:
  ▸ *duck with spring cabbage*

  Others may be eaten whole (countable)...
  ▸ *baked apples*
  ▸ *baby carrots*

  ... or prepared in such a way that they are not eaten whole (uncountable in British English but still countable in American English):
  ▸ *stewed apple* (*BrE*) / *stewed apples* (*NAmE*)
  ▸ *grated raw carrot* (*BrE*) / *grated raw carrots* (*NAmE*)

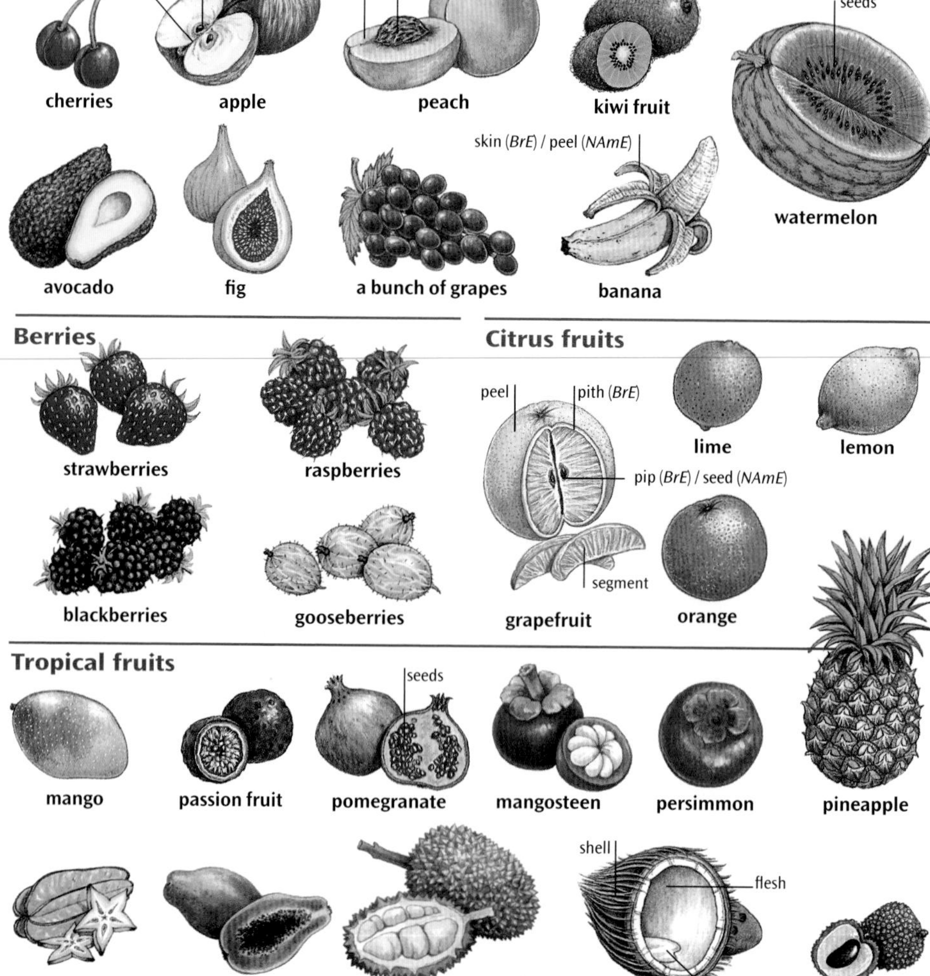

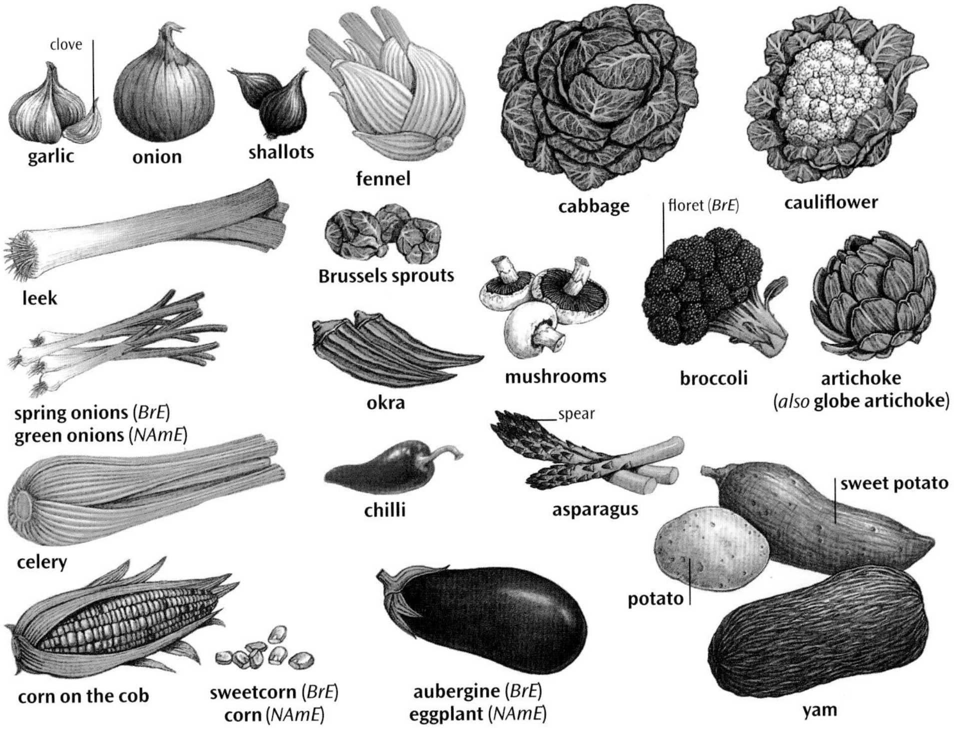

clove
garlic
onion
shallots
fennel
cabbage
cauliflower
floret (*BrE*)
leek
Brussels sprouts
mushrooms
broccoli
artichoke
(*also* globe artichoke)
spring onions (*BrE*)
green onions (*NAmE*)
okra
spear
celery
chilli
asparagus
sweet potato
potato
corn on the cob
sweetcorn (*BrE*)
corn (*NAmE*)
aubergine (*BrE*)
eggplant (*NAmE*)
yam

Squash

marrow (*BrE*)
pumpkin
courgette (*BrE*)
zucchini (*NAmE*)

Peas and beans

pod
green beans
peas
kidney beans
chickpeas
(*especially BrE*)
garbanzos (*NAmE*)
bean sprouts

Root vegetables

carrot
parsnip
moolis / daikons
beetroot (*BrE*)
beet (*NAmE*)
swede (*BrE*)
rutabaga (*NAmE*)
turnip

Salad vegetables

radishes
lettuce
tomato
peppers (*BrE*)
bell peppers (*NAmE*)
cucumber

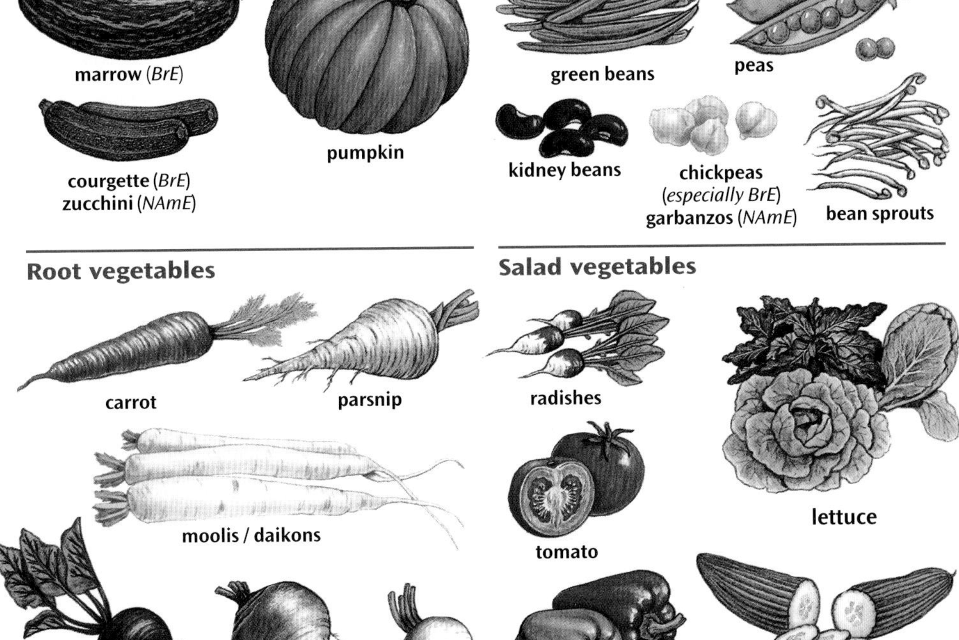

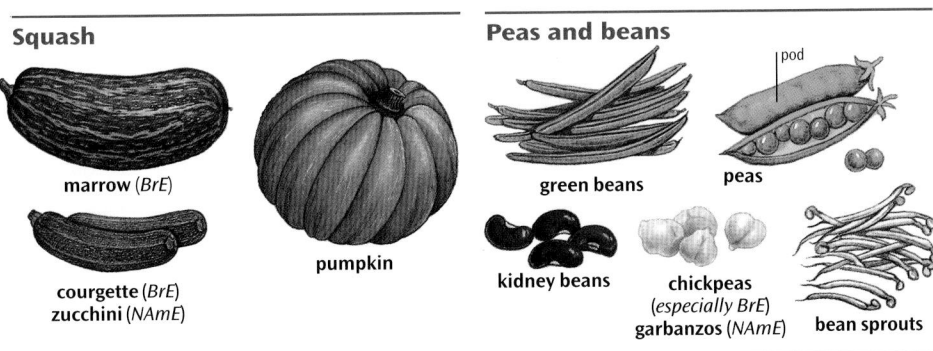

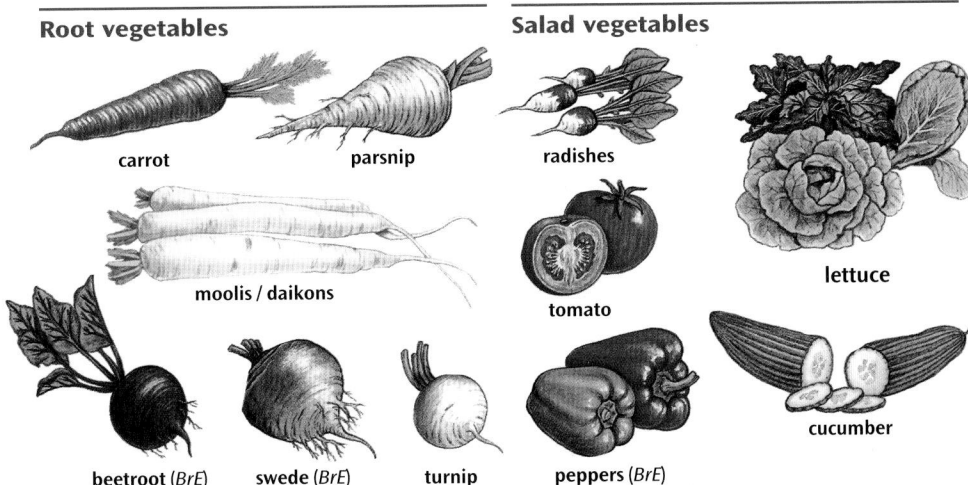

Herbs, spices, nuts and cereals

Herbs

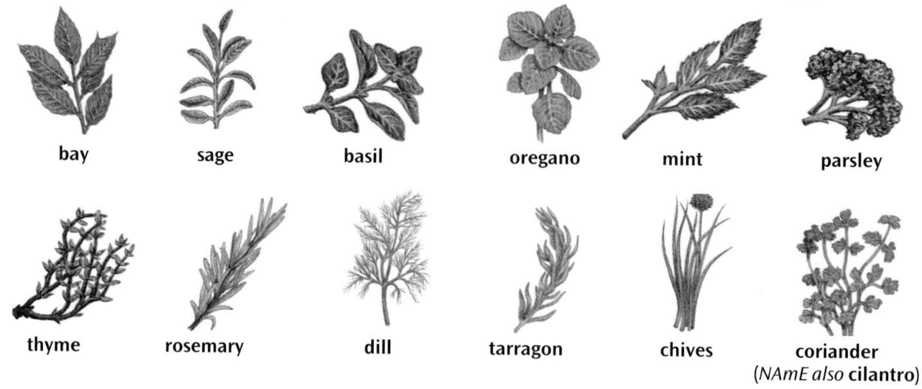

bay | sage | basil | oregano | mint | parsley

thyme | rosemary | dill | tarragon | chives | coriander (*NAmE also* **cilantro**)

Spices

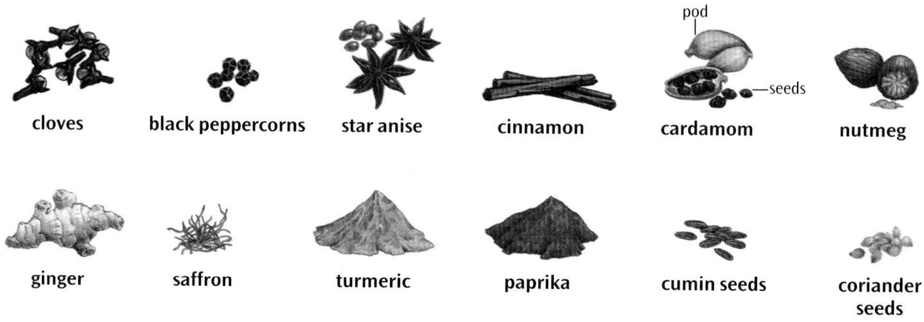

cloves | black peppercorns | star anise | cinnamon | cardamom (pod, seeds) | nutmeg

ginger | saffron | turmeric | paprika | cumin seeds | coriander seeds

Nuts

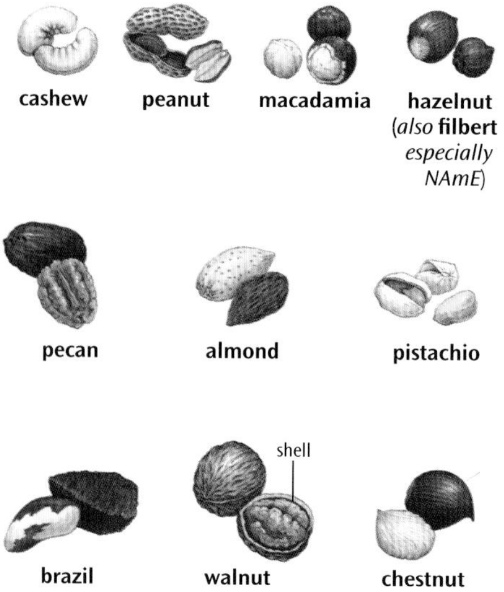

cashew

peanut

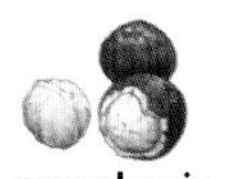
macadamia

hazelnut (*also* **filbert** *especially NAmE*)

pecan

almond

pistachio

brazil

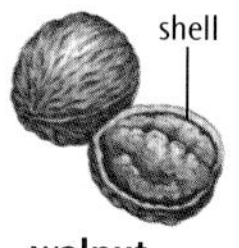

walnut

chestnut

Cereals

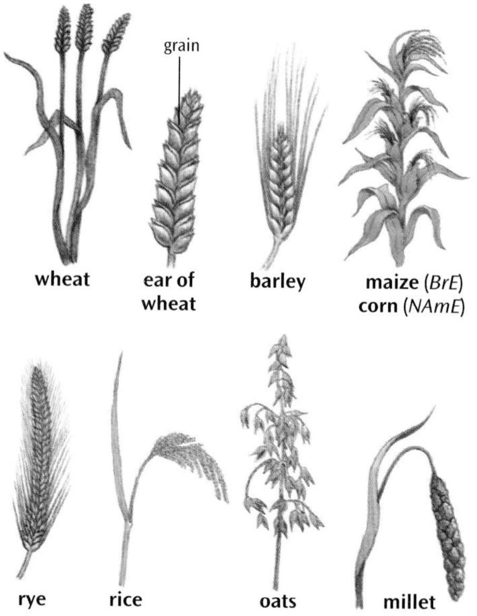

wheat

ear of wheat

barley

maize (*BrE*) corn (*NAmE*)

rye

rice

oats

millet

Packaging

multipack
blister pack
box
box (*BrE also* packet)
matchbox
stick
packet (*BrE*) stick (*NAmE*)
packet (*BrE*) pack (*NAmE*)
packet (*BrE*) package (*NAmE*)
packet (*BrE*) roll (*NAmE*)
cap / top
top
tube
sachet (*BrE*) packet (*NAmE*)
roll
straw
carton (*BrE*) juice box (*NAmE*)
carton
carton (*BrE also* pot)
tub
nozzle
top
aerosol can
can
cork
screw-top
bottle
lid
tin
ring pull (*BrE*) pull tab (*NAmE*)
lid
tin / can (*both BrE*) / can (*NAmE*)
punnet (*BrE*)
tray
label
jar
bag (*BrE also* packet)
bag
shopping bag
carrier bag (*BrE*)
shopping basket
shopping trolley (*BrE*) shopping cart (*NAmE*)

Musical instruments

Playing an instrument

- When talking generally about playing musical instruments, **the** is usually used before the name of the instrument:
  - ▸ *He played* ***the*** *trumpet in a jazz band.*
  - ▸ *She decided to take up* (= start learning to play) ***the*** *flute.*
- **The** is not usually used when two or more instruments are mentioned:
  - ▸ *She teaches violin, cello and piano.*
- The preposition **on** is used to say who is playing which instrument:
  - ▸ *The CD features James Galway* ***on*** *the flute.*
  - ▸ *She sang and he accompanied her* ***on*** *the piano.*
- **The** is not usually used when you are talking about pop or jazz musicians:
  - ▸ *John Squire on guitar*
  - ▸ *Miles Davis played trumpet.*

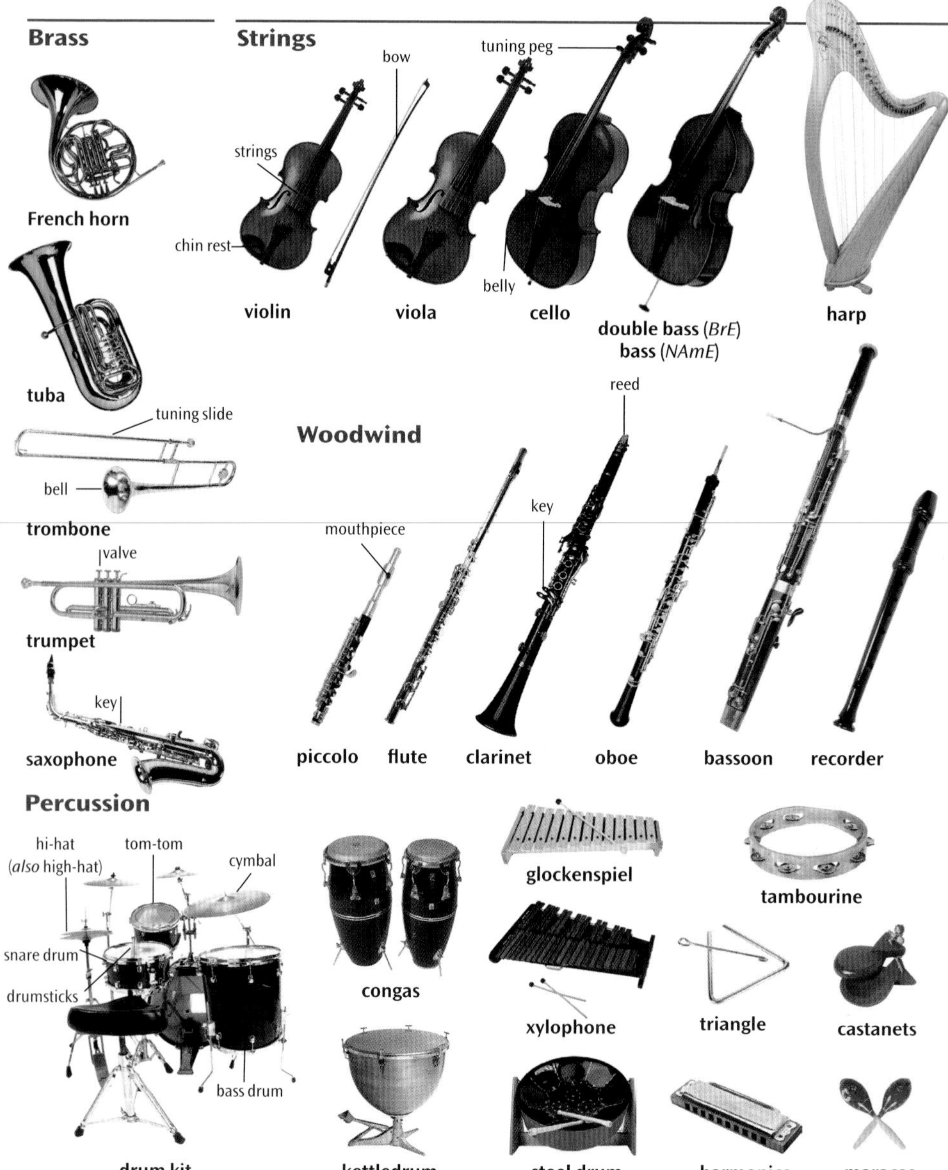

Describing instruments

- There are four **sections** of instruments in an **orchestra**: **strings**, **woodwind**, **brass** and **percussion**.
- Different bands or **ensembles** can be formed when instruments from the different sections play separately:
  - ▶ *a brass band*
  - ▶ *a wind band*
  - ▶ *a string quartet*
  - ▶ *a jazz trio*
- Particular adjectives are used before the names of musical instruments to describe the type of instrument it is:
  - ▶ *a tenor saxophone*
  - ▶ *a classical guitar*
  - ▶ *a bass drum*

GRAMMAR POINT

- The names of instruments can be used like adjectives before other nouns:
  - ▶ *a clarinet lesson*
  - ▶ *Chopin's Piano Concerto No. 1*
  - ▶ *She's going to do her cello practice.*

People who play instruments

- Some musical instruments have a special name, ending in **–ist** or **–er** for the people who play them:
  - ▶ *The violinist lifted his bow.*
  - ▶ *The South African drummer, Louis Moholo*
- Check near the entry for each instrument to find the correct word. If there is no special word, you use **player** after the name of the instrument:
  - ▶ *the quartet's viola player*
- When talking about pop or jazz, people often use **player** even when there is a word for the person like **saxophonist** or **bassist**:
  - ▶ *A brilliant young sax player*
  - ▶ *We're looking for a new bass player.*

- In an orchestra playing classical music, **principal**, **deputy principal** (*BrE*), **associate principal** (*NAmE*) and **assistant principal** (*NAmE*) are used with the names of instruments to describe a player's position or importance:
  - ▶ *He became principal cellist within a few years.*
- A person who directs (or **conducts**) an orchestra is a **conductor**. The principal violinist (who **leads** the orchestra) is the **leader** (*BrE*) or the **concertmaster** (*NAmE*).

Music for instruments

- Music is **composed** or **written** for an instrument. In a piece of music written for a group of instruments, each has a different **part** to play:
  - ▶ *There are parts for oboe and bassoon.*
- If there is more than one part for the same type of instrument, the terms **first** and **second**, and sometimes **third** and **fourth**, are used:
  - ▶ *She's a second violin* (= plays the second violin part).
  - ▶ *the deep low notes of the third horn*
- A **solo** is a part for one instrument playing alone. A **soloist** plays it:
  - ▶ *She performs regularly as a soloist and in chamber music.*
  - ▶ *I love the saxophone solo in this song.*

More illustrations at ACCORDION and MUSIC.

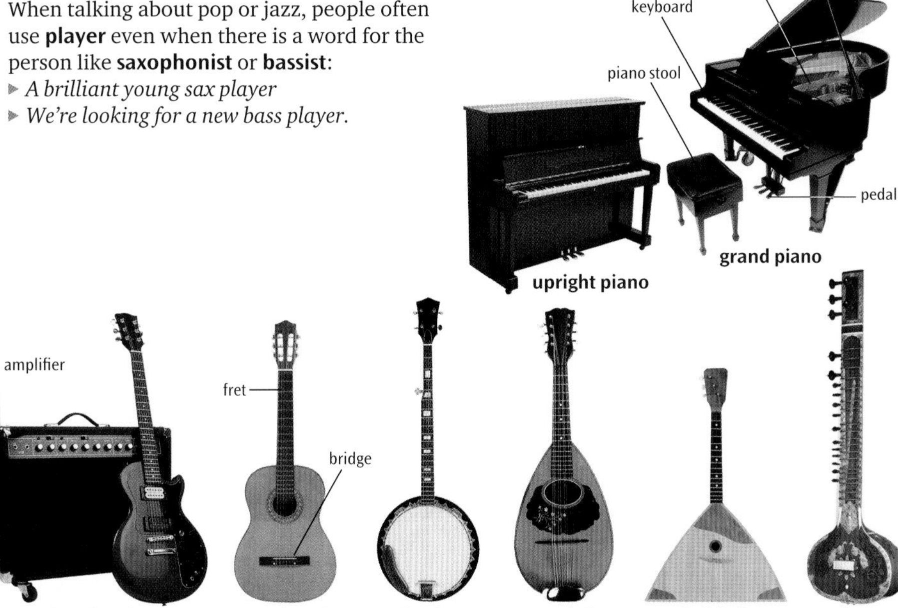

Toys and games

Frisbee™

kite

skipping rope (*BrE*) / **jump rope** (*NAmE*)

sandpit (*BrE*) **sandbox** (*NAmE*)

swing

slide

trampoline

climbing frame (*BrE*) **jungle gym** (*NAmE*)

teddy bear (*BrE also* **teddy**)

soft toy (*BrE*) / **stuffed animal** (*especially NAmE*)

rag doll

glove puppet (*BrE*) **hand puppet** (*NAmE*)

rocking horse

building blocks

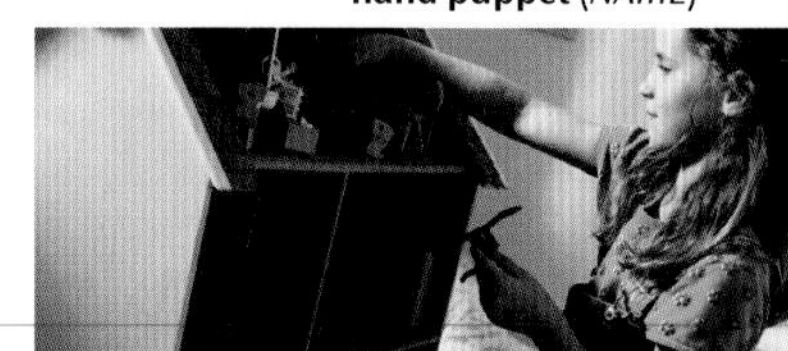
doll's house (*BrE*) / **dollhouse** (*NAmE*)

playing cards / cards

pack of cards (*BrE*) **deck of cards** (*especially NAmE*)

suits

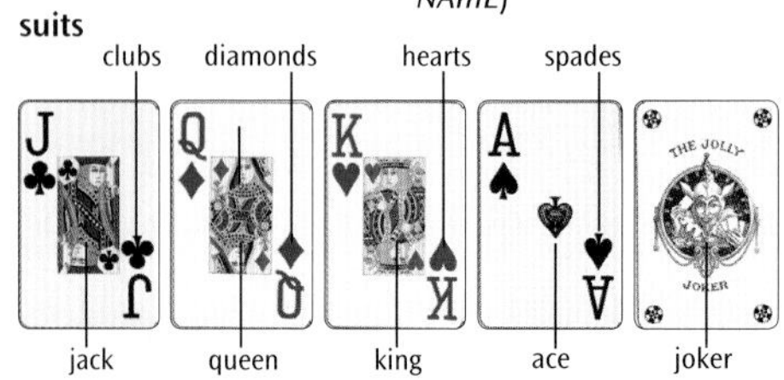

court cards (*BrE*) **face cards** (*especially NAmE*)

Cards

- To mix the playing cards is to **shuffle** them:
  - ▸ *Shuffle the cards well.*
  - ▸ *Shall I shuffle?*
- To give cards to each individual person who is playing the game is to **deal** them (**out**). The person who does this is called the **dealer**:
  - ▸ *Whose turn is it to deal?*
  - ▸ *Deal the cards.*
- To divide the pack of cards into two or three parts is to **cut** them:
  - ▸ *Cut the cards to see who starts.*
- A card which is on the table showing the picture side is **face up**. A card which is on the table so that you cannot see the picture side is **face down**.
- The cards that you have in your hand when you play cards is a **hand**.
  - ▸ *I knew I'd win – I had a really good hand* (=I had good cards).

dominoes

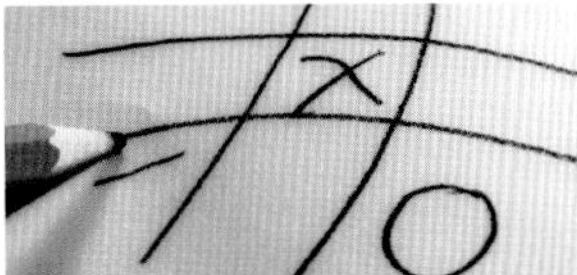

noughts and crosses (*BrE*) / **tic-tac-toe** (*NAmE*)

Chinese chequers (*BrE*) / **Chinese checkers** (*NAmE*)

snakes and ladders (*BrE*)

chess

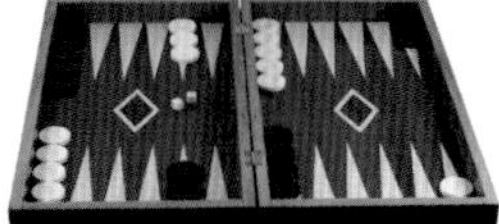

backgammon

Puzzles

- A game that tests your knowledge or intelligence is a **puzzle**:
  - ▸ *to do a puzzle*
  - ▸ *a mathematical puzzle*
- A picture on cardboard or wood that is cut into small pieces which you have to join together is a **jigsaw** (**puzzle**).
- A word game with black and white squares where you write the word in the white squares is a **crossword** (**puzzle**). To find the right word, you have to **solve a clue**:
  - ▸ *I can't do this crossword, the clues are too difficult.*
  - ▸ *to solve a crossword puzzle*

Playing games

- The official statements that tell you what you can or cannot do in a game are the **rules**; something which is not allowed in a game is **against the rules**.
- To play a game in a dishonest or unfair way: **cheat**; *noun* [U]: **cheating**; a person who cheats is **a cheat**:
  - ▸ *You can't do that, it's cheating.*
  - ▸ *He's such a cheat.*

Board games

- A game played on a flat hard piece of wood or cardboard is a **board game**.
- A small cube with a different number of spots on each side, used in certain games, is called a **dice** (*also* **die** *especially NAmE*) (*plural* **dice**).
- A small round flat object that is used in some games to show where a player is on the board is a **counter**.
- To take a piece or a counter and move it to another place on the board: **move** (something):
  - ▸ *You can only move your counter one square in any direction.*
- The time in a game when one person must do something (for example move a piece) is called a **move**, **turn**, **go** (*plural* **goes**):
  - ▸ *It's your move/turn/go.*
  - ▸ *You've just had two goes.*

Chess

- A stage in the game of chess when a player's king could be taken by the other person is called **check** *noun* [U]. When you are in this position, you are **in check**.
- When one player cannot move his king out of check and the game ends is called **checkmate** *noun* [U].
- The end of a game of chess when neither player can win is **stalemate** *noun* [U].

sudoku

wordsearch

crossword (*also* **crossword puzzle**)

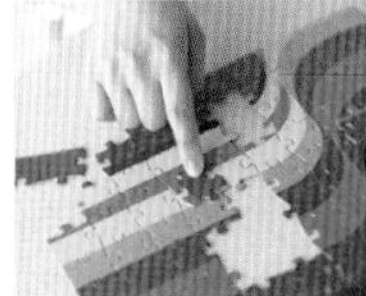

jigsaw (**puzzle**) (*BrE*) (*also* **puzzle** *especially NAmE*)

Hobbies

orienteering

caving (*BrE*) / **spelunking** (*NAmE*)

archery

ice skating

scuba-diving

snorkelling (*also* **snorkeling** *especially US*)

in-line skating

skateboarding

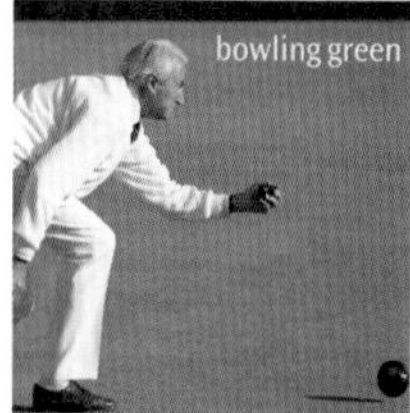

bowls

tenpin bowling

darts

pool

golf

Golf

- A game of golf is called a **round of golf** (nine or eighteen **holes**).
- At the start of each hole a player **tees off** by hitting the ball from the **tee** (= an area of flat ground).
- The act of hitting the ball is called a **shot**. The swinging movement players make with their arms and body when they hit the ball is called their **swing**:
  ▸ *My golf swing is in need of improvement.*
- Players attempt to hit their ball down the **fairway** (= a long strip of short grass), avoiding the **bunker** (*NAmE also* **sand trap, trap**) and **the rough** (= the part of the golf course with long grass making it difficult to hit the ball), to the **green**.
- The **green** is an area of short grass on which you **putt** your ball (= hit the ball gently so that it rolls across the ground a short distance into or towards the **hole**).

Snooker, pool and billiards

- **Snooker** is a game for two people, played on a long table covered with green cloth (**baize**). Players use **cues** to hit the **cue ball** (white) against the other balls (fifteen red, and six of other colours) in order to **pot** the coloured balls (= hit them into **pockets** at the edge of the table), in a particular order.
- Snooker also refers to a position in the game of snooker in which one player has made it very difficult for the opponent to play a shot within the rules.
- A game of snooker is called a **frame**:
  ▸ *He won the frame easily.*
- **Pool** is similar to snooker, but is played with a cue ball (white), a black ball, and two sets of coloured balls (seven solid colours and seven striped balls).
- **Billiards** is played with three balls (one white, one white with a spot, and one red). Each player uses one of the white balls as the cue ball. Points are scored by pocketing a ball after contact with another ball, or by striking your cue ball against the other two balls.

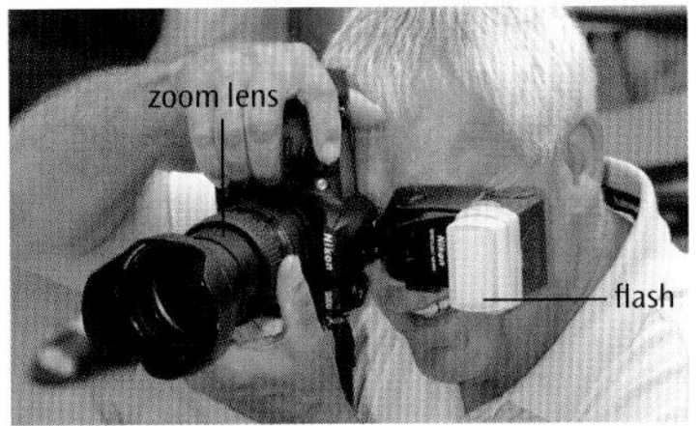

photography

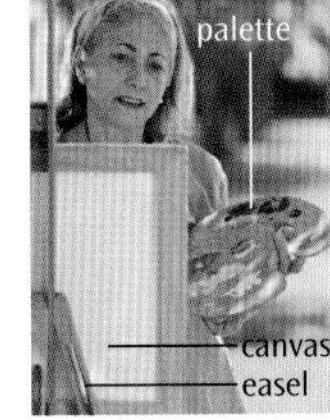

painting

pottery

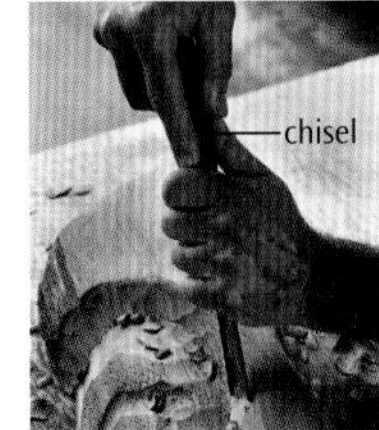

woodcarving

model making

stamp collecting

gardening

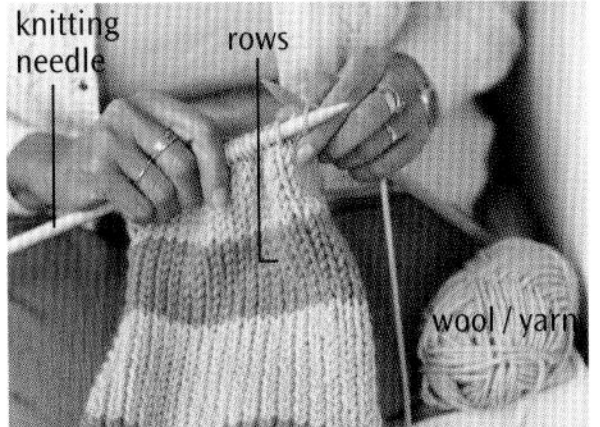

knitting

crochet

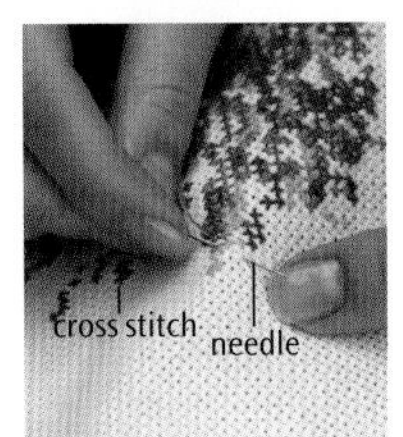

embroidery

sewing

reel of cotton (*especially BrE*)
spool of thread (*especially NAmE*)

Keeping fit

press-up (*BrE*)
push-up (*especially NAmE*)

sit-up

jogging

yoga

exercise bike

barbell

dumb-bell

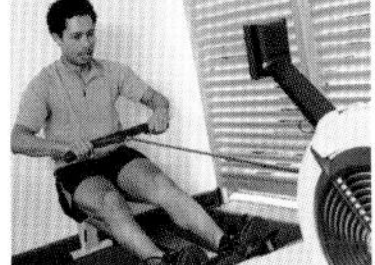
rowing machine

treadmill

Staying healthy

- If you are **fit** (*BrE*), **physically fit**, or **in shape** (*especially NAmE*), you are healthy and strong, especially as a result of diet and exercise:
  - *Top athletes have to be very fit.* (*BrE*)
  - *The doctor said I should **get** more **exercise** (BrE also ...**take** more **exercise**).*
  - *No cream for me – I'm **on a diet**.*
  - *She cycles up to 90 miles a day to **keep fit**.* (*BrE*)
  - *I still run every day to **stay in shape**.* (*especially NAmE*)

Aerobics, step, and circuit training

- **Aerobics** involves physical exercises to make the heart and lungs stronger, often done in classes and to music:
  - *do an aerobics class*
- **Step** is a type of aerobics that you do by stepping on and off a raised piece of equipment called a **step**.
- **Circuit training** is a type of training in which different exercises are each done for a short time.

Sports

Talking about a particular sport

- You can **play** a specific sport:
  - ▸ *Do you play tennis?*
- This is used particularly for competitive sports in which one team or person **plays** or **plays against** another:
  - ▸ *We played them in last year's final.*
  - ▸ *Who are you playing against this afternoon?*
- Members of a sports team **play for** their team:
  - ▸ *He used to play for the Dallas Cowboys.*
- If the name of a sport or an activity ends in **–ing** we often use it with the verb **to go**:
  - ▸ *I go swimming twice a week.*
  - ▸ *Have you ever been rock climbing?*
- Typical sports and activities with this pattern include: **go skiing**; **go sailing**; **go riding** (*BrE*) or **go horseback riding** (*NAmE*); and **go dancing.** Check at the entry for each sport to see if it can be used in this way.

Other sports and activities can take the verbs to do or to go to:

- *I do aerobics once or twice a week.*
- *I go to judo* (= to my judo class) *on Mondays.*

Team Sports

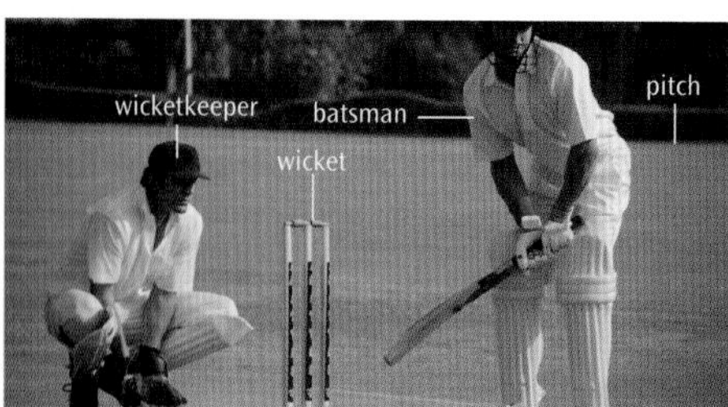

cricket

basketball

baseball

rugby

soccer (*BrE also* **football**)

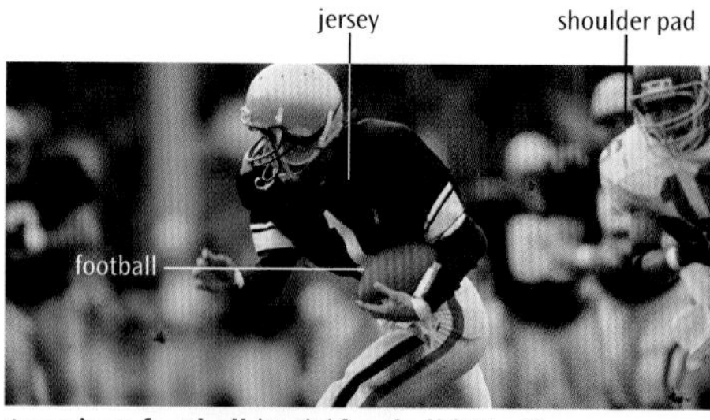

American football (*BrE*) / **football** (*NAmE*)

hockey (*BrE*) / **field hockey** (*NAmE*)

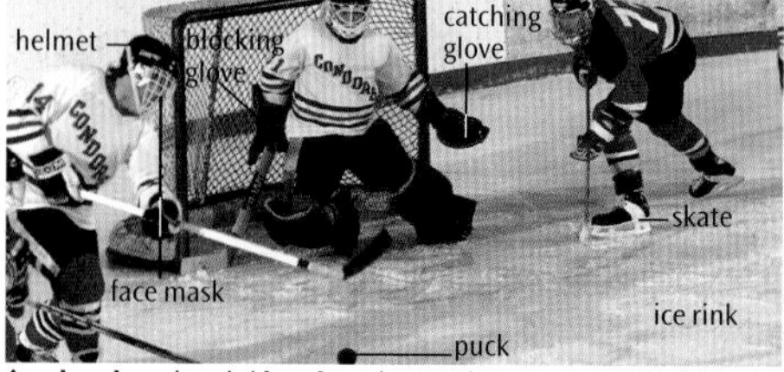

ice hockey (*BrE*) / **hockey** (*NAmE*)

Where sports are played

- The area that is specially marked for playing a sports game is often called a **pitch** (*BrE*), **field** or **court**, depending on the sport being played:
  - ▶ *a cricket/ football/rugby/hockey pitch* (*BrE*)
  - ▶ *a soccer/baseball field* (*especially NAmE*)
  - ▶ *a tennis/badminton/squash/basketball court*
- A large sports ground surrounded by rows of seats for **spectators** is called a **stadium** (*plural* **stadiums** or **stadia**):
  - ▶ *an all-seater stadium*

GRAMMAR POINT

- Names of American sports teams always start with 'the'; names of British sports teams almost never do. Names of sports teams may look either singular or plural but always take a plural verb:
  - ▶ *The Jazz are playing the Chicago Bulls.*
  - ▶ *Aston Villa have started the season well.*
- Teams are often referred to just by the name of the place they come from. In American English this means a singular verb is used, but in British English the verb is still plural.
  - ▶ *Cincinnati is having a great season.*
  - ▶ *Norwich were disappointed with the score.*

Swimming

crawl

butterfly

backstroke

breaststroke

Racket sports

tennis

badminton

squash

table tennis (*BrE*) / **Ping-Pong™** (*NAmE*)

People who take part in sports

- A person who **plays** a particular sport is usually called a football/tennis/basketball **player**:
  - ▸ *Welsh rugby players could get £2000 each from a new sponsorship deal.*
- Some sports have a special name for the players or people who do them. Some of these names end in **-er** but others do not follow a particular pattern. Check near the entry for each sport to find the correct word.
  - ▸ *talented young footballers* (*BrE only*)
  - ▸ *an Olympic boxer*
  - ▸ *top athletes from around the world*
  - ▸ *cyclists competing in the Tour de France*

Track events

hurdling

sprinting

Track events
- ***run*** *the 100 metres*
- ***run*** *the relay*

Field events

the high jump

the discus

the pole vault

the hammer

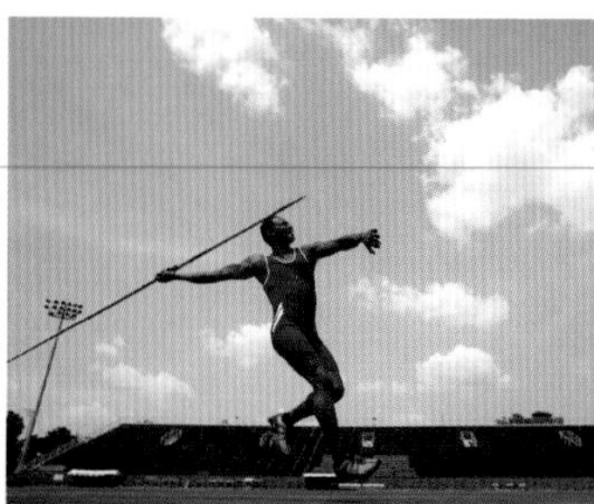
the javelin

Field events
- ***do*** *the long jump*
- ***do*** *the high jump*
- ***do*** *the pole vault*
- ***do*** *the triple jump*
- ***throw*** *the javelin*
- ***throw*** *the discus*
- ***throw*** *the hammer*
- ***put*** *the shot*

Equestrian sports

horse racing

showjumping

polo

Talking about sports in general

- You can **do sport** (*BrE*):
  ▸ *Do you do a lot of sport?*

  ...or you can **play sports** (*especially NAmE*):
  ▸ *We played sports together when we were kids.*

  ...but these verbs are not used very often. It is more usual to talk about liking sport/sports or **being good at** sport/sports:
  ▸ *Are you good at sport?* (*BrE*)
  ▸ *Are you good at sports?* (*NAmE*)
  ▸ *What sports do you like best?*
- Do **not** say that you 'practise' sport or a sport if you just mean that you do or play it. Say:
  ▸ *I love sport.* (*BrE*)
  ▸ *I love sports.* (*NAmE*)
  (No other verb is necessary.)
  NOT ~~I love practising sport.~~
- Say which sports you play:
  ▸ *Every Sunday I play volleyball or badminton with my friends.*
  NOT ~~Every Sunday I practise sport with my friends~~.
- However, you can use the verb 'practise', especially in American English (where it is spelt 'practice'), if it means 'to train':
  ▸ *The team is practicing for its big game.* (*NAmE*)
  ▸ *The team are in training for their big match.* (*BrE*)

GRAMMAR POINT

- The names of sports can be used like adjectives before other nouns:
  ▸ *a tennis match*
  ▸ *cycling shorts*
  ▸ *a football team*
- The words sports and sporting (but not 'sport') can be used in the same way:
  ▸ *a sports club*
  ▸ *sports shoes*
  ▸ *a sporting event*
  ▸ *sporting goods*

cycling

gymnastics

boxing

fencing

Winter sports

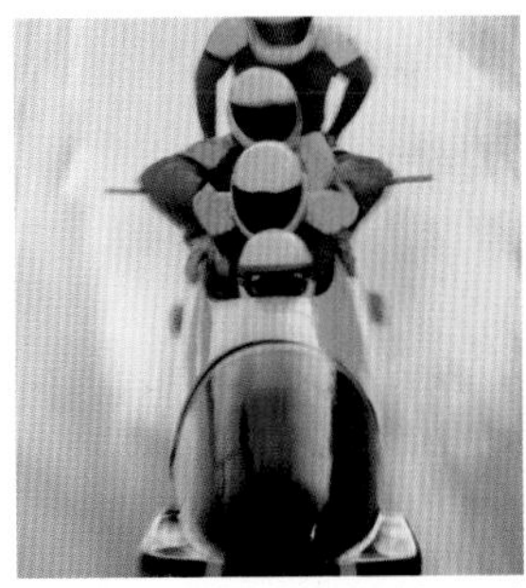
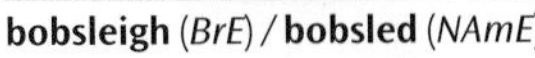
bobsleigh (*BrE*) / **bobsled** (*NAmE*)

the luge

downhill skiing

cross-country skiing

Extreme sports

paragliding

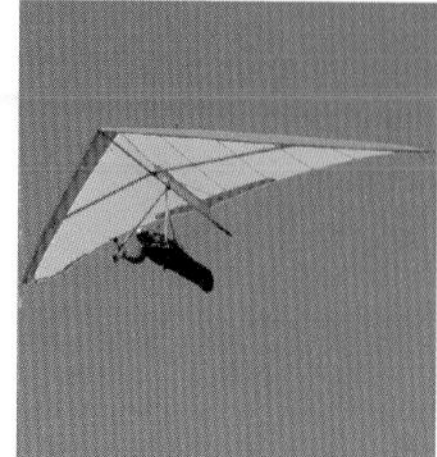
hang-gliding

skydiving

snowboarding

abseiling (*BrE*)
rappelling (*NAmE*)

bungee jumping

waterskiing

wakeboarding

- Activities that involve danger or speed or both are often called **extreme sports**. Many extreme sports are done on or in water.
- **Surfing** and **bodyboarding** are similar, but a surfer stands on a surfboard to ride on the waves while a bodyboarder lies on their stomach on a bodyboard. **Kitesurfing** involves riding on a type of surfboard and being pulled along by a kite.
- **Waterskiing** and **wakeboarding** both involve being pulled through the water by a fast boat: a waterskier wears one or two waterskis, while a wakeboarder stands sideways on a wakeboard.
- Other extreme sports involve jumping from great heights. **Skydivers** jump from a plane and fall for as long as they safely can before opening their **parachutes**. You can jump from the side of a mountain, wearing a kind of parachute in **paragliding**, or a frame like a very large kite in **hang-gliding**. **Parasailing** and **base jumping** are both also done wearing parachutes. In parasailing you are pulled behind a fast boat and rise into the air. A base jumper jumps from the top of a tall building or bridge (BASE stands for building, antenna, span, earth).
- In **rock climbing**, a rope is attached to the climber and the rock for safety– this is called **belaying**. The climber wears a **harness** to which the rope is attached with a metal ring called a **karabiner**.
- **Skateboarders** and **snowboarders** may ride on a **half-pipe**: a U-shaped structure or a U-shaped channel cut into the snow. They do jumps and tricks, for example a **fakie**, an **ollie**, or a **kick-turn**.

windsurfing

surfing

jet-skiing

bodyboarding

white-water rafting

kitesurfing / kiteboarding

parkour

Cycles

Other types of bicycle and motorcycle

- An early type of bicycle with a very large front wheel and a very small back wheel is a **penny-farthing**.
- A stationary bicycle that is used indoors to exercise is an **exercise bike**.
- A motorcycle with a small engine and pedals is a **moped**.

Cars

1 rear-view mirror
2 visor
3 windscreen (*BrE*) windshield (*NAmE*)
4 windscreen wiper (*BrE*) windshield wiper (*NAmE*)
5 wing mirror (*BrE*) side-view mirror (*NAmE*)
6 door handle
7 air vent
8 glove compartment glove box
9 satnav (*also* sat nav)
10 dashboard
11 milometer (*BrE*) odometer (*NAmE*)
12 speedometer
13 rev counter
14 fuel gauge
15 steering wheel
16 ignition
17 horn
18 gear lever (*BrE*) gear shift (*NAmE*)
19 clutch
20 brake
21 accelerator (*BrE*) / gas pedal (*especially NAmE*)
22 handbrake (*especially BrE*) / emergency brake (*NAmE*)
23 headrest
24 passenger seat
25 driver's seat
26 seat belt

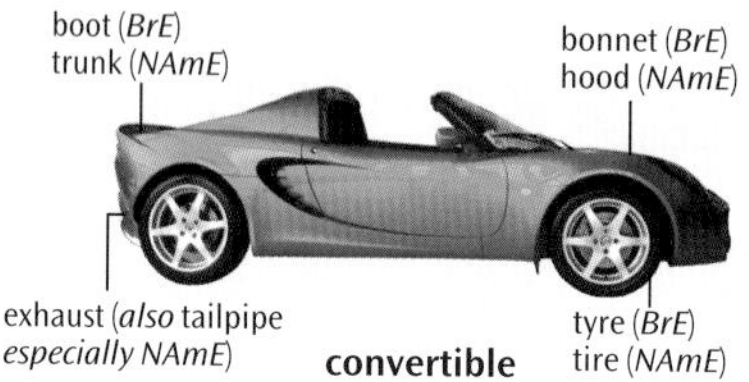

convertible

saloon (*BrE*)
sedan (*NAmE*)

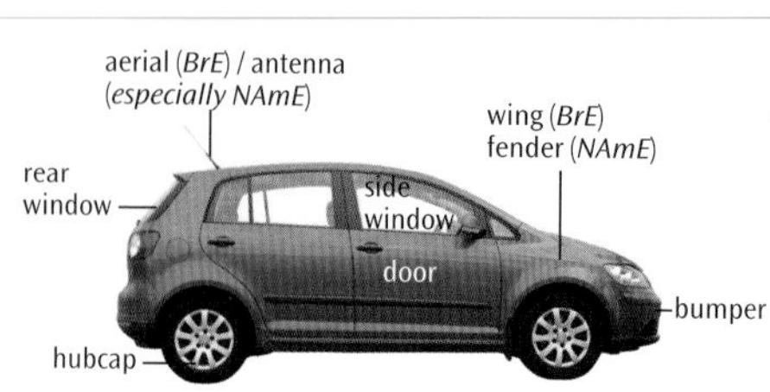

hatchback

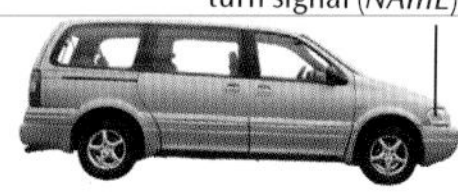

people carrier (*BrE*)
minivan (*especially NAmE*)

four-wheel drive

sports car
(*US also* **sport car**)

estate car (*BrE*)
station wagon (*NAmE*)

Verbs to talk about driving

- to control the direction in which the car is going: **steer**
- to change direction suddenly: **swerve**
- to signal that your car is going to turn: **indicate**
- to make a car go faster: **speed up**, **accelerate**, **put your foot down**
- to make a car go more slowly: **slow down**, **brake**, **put the brake on**
- to put the engine into a higher/lower gear as you get faster/slower: **change up/down**
- to allow another vehicle to go before you: **give way** (*BrE*) / **yield** (*NAmE*)
- to pass another vehicle because you are moving faster: **overtake**
- to turn round and go back along the same road: **do/make a U-turn**
- to stop and leave the car: **park**

Aircraft

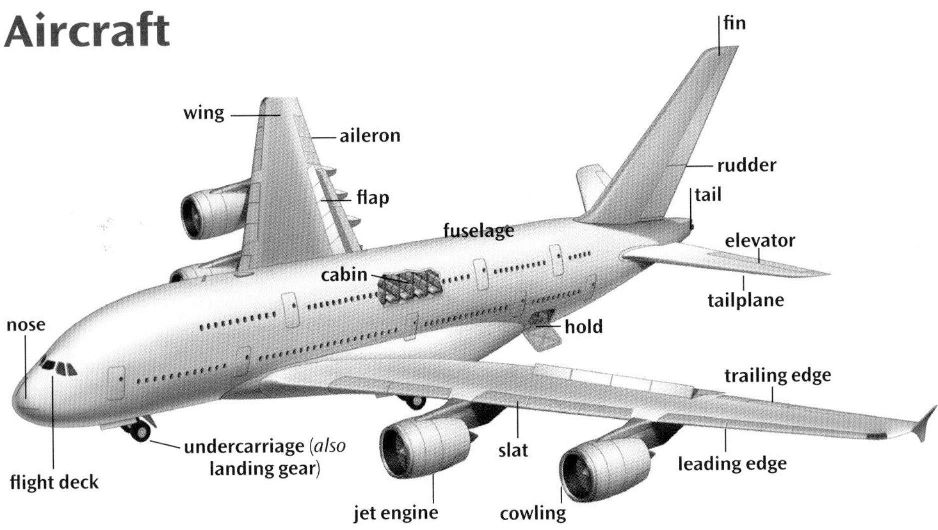

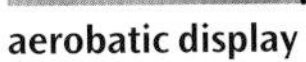
aerobatic display

light aircraft

helicopter

ski-plane

glider

microlight (*BrE*)

seaplane

fighter

biplane

At the airport

- An airport building where journeys begin and end is a **terminal**. You go to the **check-in desk** and say you have arrived (**check in**).
- You check in the **baggage** (*especially NAmE*) that will go into the **hold** (= the part of the plane where goods are stored) but you carry your **hand luggage** (especially *BrE*) / **carry-on baggage** (*especially NAmE*) with you onto the plane. If your bags are heavier than the weight limit you have to **pay excess baggage**.
- You wait in the **departure lounge** and when your flight **is boarding** (= is ready for passengers to get on) you leave the terminal from a **gate**.
- When you arrive at your destination in a different country you **disembark** and go through **immigration**. Collect your **luggage** (*especially BrE*) from **baggage reclaim** (*BrE*) / **baggage claim** (*NAmE*) and exit through **customs**.

airship

hot-air balloon

Boats and ships

container ship

lifeboat

ferry

hovercraft

hydrofoil

catamaran

liner

canal boat / narrowboat

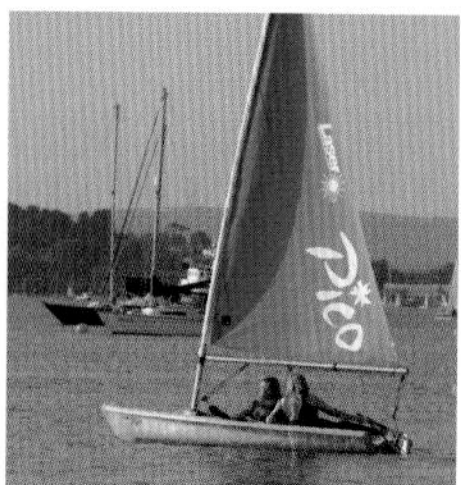
sailing dinghy (*NAmE also* **sailboat**)

More kinds of boat

- Any large boat that is used for carrying passengers or goods by sea is a **ship**, or (formal) a **vessel**:
  ▸ *In which country was this vessel registered?*
- A ship that carries goods from one place to another is a **freighter** or **cargo ship**, and one that is used for carrying large amounts of petrol, oil, etc. is an (**oil**) **tanker**.
- A boat that is used for catching fish is a **fishing boat**, and a special type of fishing boat which pulls a long net through the sea to catch fish is a **trawler**.
- **Lifeboat** has two meanings: it is a special boat that is used to rescue people who are in danger at sea, or it is a small boat that is kept on a ship and used by people to escape if the ship is going to sink.
- **Raft** also has two meanings: it is a small boat made of rubber or plastic that is filled with air, or it is a flat structure made of pieces of wood tied together and used as a boat.

Groups of boats

- A group of boats that sail and work together is a **fleet**:
  ▸ *a fishing fleet*
- A group of boats travelling together is a **flotilla** or a **convoy**:
  ▸ *The boats travelled **in convoy**.*
  ▸ *We were travelling in a flotilla of boats.*

paddle steamer (*BrE*) / paddleboat (*NAmE*)

cruiser / cabin cruiser

speedboat

rowing boat (*BrE*) / rowboat (*NAmE*)

kayak (*BrE also* **canoe**)

canoe

punt

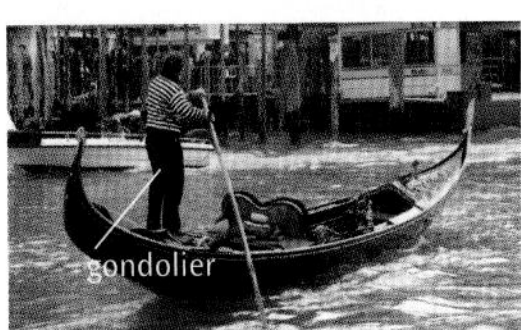

gondola

Travelling by boat

- You **sail** a sailing boat or yacht, **row** a rowing boat, and **paddle** a canoe or kayak:
  - ▶ *My brother's planning to sail (his yacht) to Bermuda.*
  - ▶ *They rowed (the boat) back to shore.*
- You **go sailing**, **go yachting**, **go rowing** and **go canoeing**.
- When you get on a ship you **board** (it), or (*formal*) **embark**:
  - ▶ *We boarded the ship at midday.*
  - ▶ *One passenger had embarked at Alexandria.*
- When you get off a ship you **go ashore**, or (*formal*) **disembark**.
- To begin a journey by sea is to **set sail** (**from**/**to**/**for** a place):
  - ▶ *Twenty competitors set sail from Rio on the round-the-world race.*
- When you are on a ship you are **on board** or **aboard**:
  - ▶ *There were a thousand passengers on board.*
  - ▶ *All aboard please!*
- When you are sailing on the sea in a ship, you are **at sea**.
- A holiday where you travel by boat and visit a number of places is a **cruise**:
  - ▶ *They're going on a cruise.*
- A long journey by sea is a **voyage**:
  - ▶ *Captain Cook made his first voyage to the South Pacific in 1768.*
- If a boat moves backwards and forwards it **pitches**; if it moves from side to side it **rolls**:
  - ▶ *The trawler was pitching and rolling violently in the storm.*
- To be carried along by wind or water in no particular direction is to **drift**:
  - ▶ *The boat drifted out to sea.*

Parts of boats

- The side of a boat that is on the left when you are facing the front: **port**
- The side of a boat that is on the right when you are facing the front: **starboard**
- The top outside floor of a boat is called the **deck**:
  - ▶ *Let's go and sit **on deck**.*
- The other floors are also called **decks**:
  - ▶ *the lower deck of a ship*
- A small room in a boat where you can sleep is a **cabin**, and a kind of bed in a cabin is a **bunk** or a **berth**:
  - ▶ *a cabin with four berths*
- The kitchen on a boat is the **galley** and a round window is called a **porthole**.

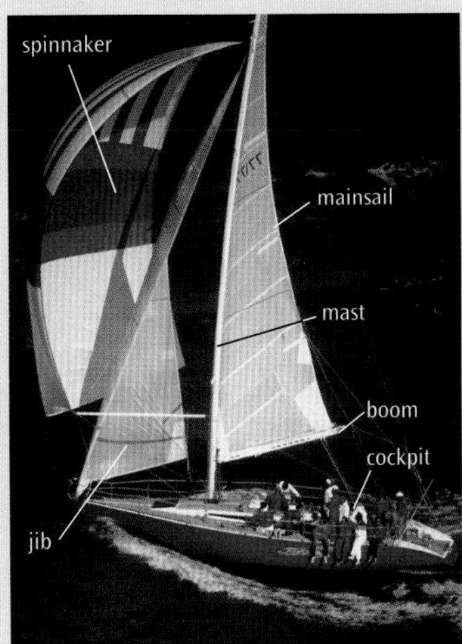

yacht (*NAmE also* **sailboat**)

Steering a boat

- A piece of wood or metal in the water at the back of a boat that is used for controlling its direction is a **rudder**.
- A bar that is used to turn the rudder of a small boat in order to steer it is a **tiller**.
- A handle or wheel used for steering a larger boat or ship is called the **helm**.
- The part of a ship where the captain and other officers stand when they are controlling the ship is **the bridge**.

Vehicles

Buses

double-decker

single-decker

minibus

school bus

bus (*BrE also* **coach**)

Trucks, etc.

articulated lorry (*BrE*) / **tractor-trailer** (*NAmE*)

lorry (*BrE*) / **truck** (*especially NAmE*)

transporter

tanker

van

forklift truck

breakdown truck (*BrE*)
tow truck (*especially NAmE*)

pickup (*also* **pickup truck**)

Jeep™

Transporting goods

- Items that are carried by lorries, trains, aeroplanes and ships are called **freight** [U]:
  ▶ *a freight train*
- Items that are carried by road or rail are also called **goods** (*BrE*) (*pl.*):
  ▶ *a goods vehicle*
- Items that are carried by air and sea are also called **cargo** [C, U]:
  ▶ *a cargo plane*
- Something that is being carried, usually in large amounts, is a **load**:
  ▶ *A lorry shed its load* (= accidentally dropped its load) *on the motorway.*
- A load of goods that is sent from one place to another is a **shipment**.
- A large metal box in which goods are transported by sea, rail or road is a **container**.

caravan (*BrE*) / **camper** (*NAmE*)

camper (*BrE*) / **recreational vehicle** (**RV**) (*NAmE*)

tractor

taxi (*also* **cab, taxicab**)

Trains, etc.

high-speed train

freight train (*BrE also* **goods train**)

passenger train

underground (*BrE*) / **subway** (*NAmE*)

steam train

funicular

cable car

tram (*BrE*) / **streetcar** (*US*)

Construction vehicles

excavator

bulldozer

cement mixer

dumper truck (*NAmE also* **dump truck**)

The body

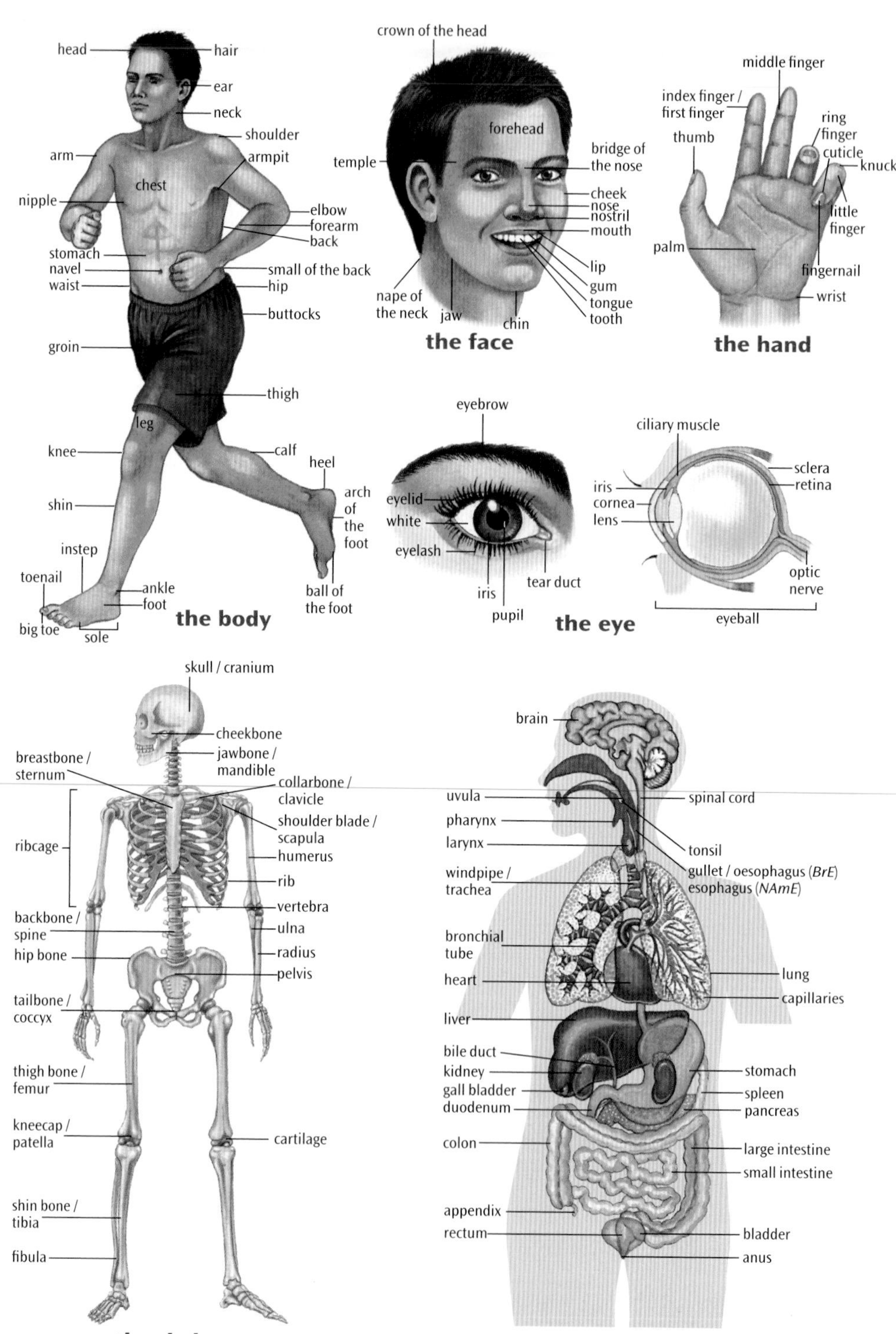

head
hair
ear
neck
shoulder
arm
armpit
chest
nipple
elbow
forearm
back
stomach
navel
waist
small of the back
hip
buttocks
groin
thigh
leg
knee
calf
heel
shin
arch of the foot
instep
toenail
ankle
foot
big toe
sole
ball of the foot
the body
crown of the head
forehead
temple
bridge of the nose
cheek
nose
nostril
mouth
lip
gum
tongue
tooth
nape of the neck
jaw
chin
the face
middle finger
index finger / first finger
ring finger
thumb
cuticle
knuckle
little finger
palm
fingernail
wrist
the hand
eyebrow
eyelid
white
eyelash
iris
pupil
tear duct
the eye
ciliary muscle
sclera
retina
iris
cornea
lens
optic nerve
eyeball
skull / cranium
cheekbone
jawbone / mandible
breastbone / sternum
collarbone / clavicle
shoulder blade / scapula
ribcage
humerus
rib
vertebra
backbone / spine
ulna
radius
hip bone
pelvis
tailbone / coccyx
thigh bone / femur
kneecap / patella
cartilage
shin bone / tibia
fibula
the skeleton
brain
uvula
spinal cord
pharynx
larynx
tonsil
gullet / oesophagus (BrE) esophagus (NAmE)
windpipe / trachea
bronchial tube
heart
lung
capillaries
liver
bile duct
kidney
stomach
gall bladder
spleen
duodenum
pancreas
colon
large intestine
small intestine
appendix
rectum
bladder
anus
the internal organs

Hair

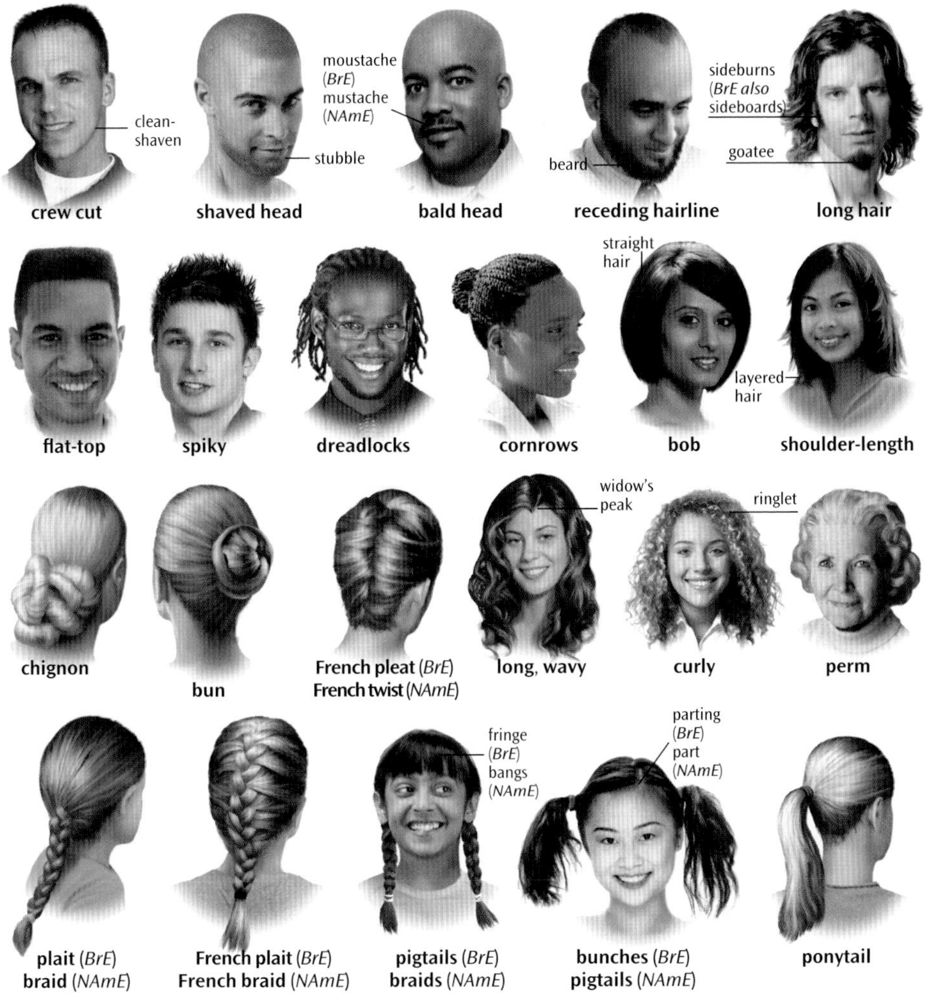

clean-shaven
crew cut
stubble
shaved head
moustache (BrE) mustache (NAmE)
bald head
beard
receding hairline
sideburns (BrE also sideboards)
goatee
long hair
flat-top
spiky
dreadlocks
cornrows
straight hair
bob
layered hair
shoulder-length
chignon
bun
French pleat (BrE) French twist (NAmE)
widow's peak
long, wavy
ringlet
curly
perm
plait (BrE) braid (NAmE)
French plait (BrE) French braid (NAmE)
fringe (BrE) bangs (NAmE)
pigtails (BrE) braids (NAmE)
parting (BrE) part (NAmE)
bunches (BrE) pigtails (NAmE)
ponytail

Make-up

sponge
foundation
concealer
brush
blusher (NAmE also blush)
compact
mirror
powder
eyeliner (also liner)
eyeshadow
applicator
lip gloss
lip liner
lipstick
wand
mascara
nail polish (BrE also nail varnish)

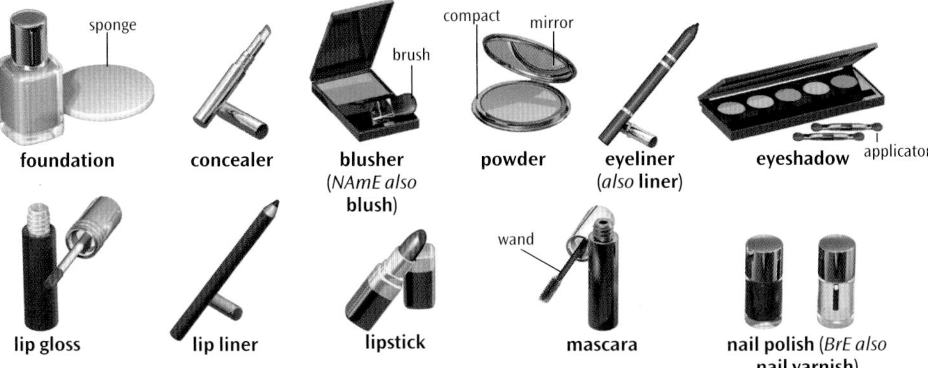

Clothes

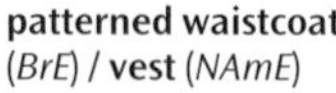

patterned waistcoat (*BrE*) / **vest** (*NAmE*)

striped

polka dots

tartan / plaid

bow ties

suit

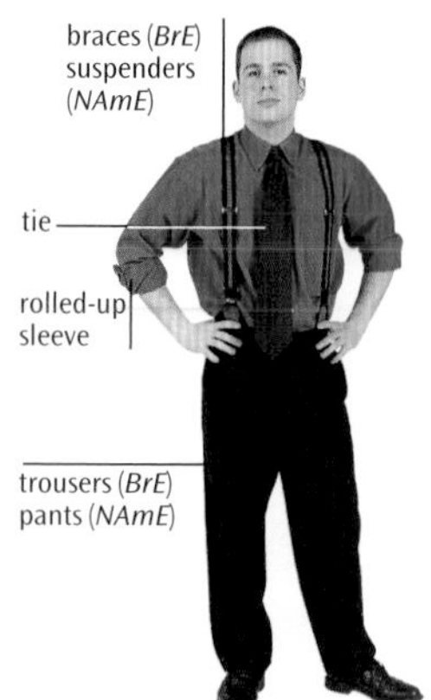

- The general word for what you wear is **clothes** (*plural*) or **clothing** [U] (*formal*):
  ▶ *She always wears such lovely clothes.*
  ▶ *a piece of clothing*
- A set of clothes that you wear together, especially for a particular occasion or purpose, is an **outfit**.
- Any piece of clothing worn on the top part of the body, especially by women, can be called a **top**.
- The clothes which some children wear at school, or which some people wear at work, are called a **uniform** [C, U].
- When police officers wear ordinary clothes instead of uniforms, they are in **plain clothes**:
  ▶ *a plain clothes police sergeant*

coats and jackets

overcoat

raincoat

body warmer

denim jacket

leather jacket

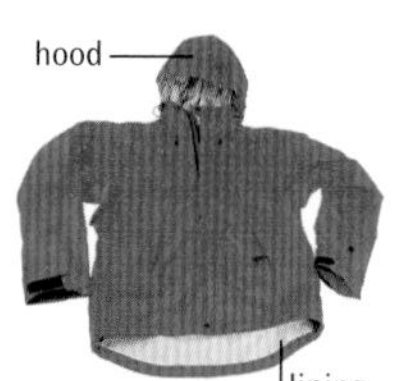

anorak

Describing clothes and the way people look

Clothes can be:

- attractive and designed well: **elegant**
- untidy and dirty: **scruffy**
- clean, tidy and rather formal: **smart** (*especially BrE*)
- not formal: **casual**
- fashionable and attractive: **stylish**
- very fashionable: **trendy** (*informal*)
- fitting closely to your body: **tight, close-fitting, skintight**
- not fitting closely: **loose, baggy**
- if a piece of clothing is not too big and not too small, it **fits** you:
  ▶ *These jeans don't fit me any more.*
- If a piece of clothing looks good on you, it **suits** you:
  ▶ *It's a nice coat, but it doesn't really suit you.*

sleeveless dress

skirt

British and American differences

- a short piece of clothing with buttons down the front but no sleeves, usually worn over a shirt and under a jacket:
  British English **waistcoat**
  American English **vest**
- a piece of underwear worn under a shirt, etc. next to the skin:
  British English **vest**
  American English **undershirt**
- a piece of clothing that covers the body from the waist down, and is divided into two parts to cover each leg separately:
  British English **trousers**
  American English **pants**
- a piece of men's underwear worn under their trousers/pants:
  British English **pants** (*or* **underpants**)
  American English **underpants**
- a loose dress with no sleeves, usually worn over a shirt or blouse:
  British English **pinafore**
  American English **jumper**
- a knitted woollen or cotton piece of clothing for the upper part of the body with long sleeves and no buttons:
  British English **jumper**
  American English **sweater**
- straps for holding trousers/pants up:
  British English **braces**
  American English **suspenders**
- short elastic fastenings for holding up socks or stockings:
  British English **suspenders**
  American English **garters**

Fastening clothes

- To talk about fastening a piece of clothing in general, use **do** sth **up**, **fasten** sth; *opposite*: **undo** sth:
  - ▶ *Do your coat up.*
  - ▶ *Your shirt is undone.*
- There are some special verbs for particular types of fastener:
  - ▶ buttons: **button** sth (**up**); *opposite:* **unbutton** sth
  - ▶ a zip: **zip** sth **up**; *opposite:* **unzip** sth

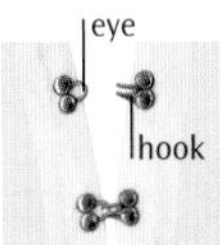

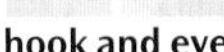

hook and eye

press stud / popper (*both BrE*)
snap (*NAmE*)

sweaters
(*BrE also* **jumpers**)

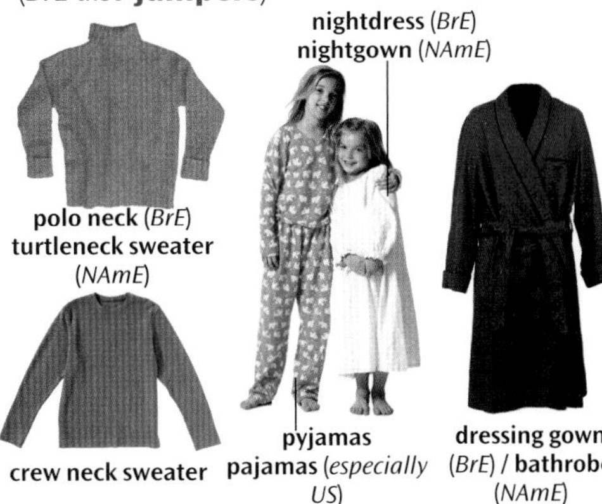

polo neck (*BrE*)
turtleneck sweater (*NAmE*)

crew neck sweater

pyjamas
pajamas (*especially US*)

dressing gown (*BrE*) / **bathrobe** (*NAmE*)

fasteners

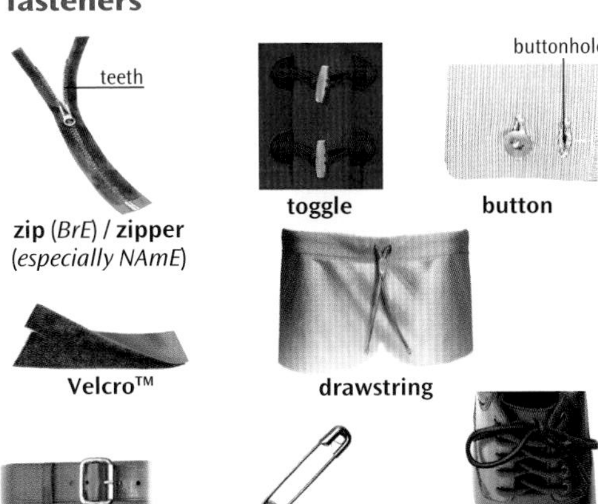

zip (*BrE*) / **zipper** (*especially NAmE*)

toggle

button

Velcro™

drawstring

buckle

safety pin

lace

Accessories

Shoes

slingback

mule

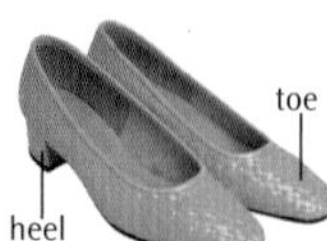

court shoes (*BrE*)
pumps (*NAmE*)

flats
(*BrE also* **pumps**)

clogs

stiletto

wedge

platform

kitten heels

slippers

sandal

jelly shoe

flip-flops
(*NAmE also* **thongs**)

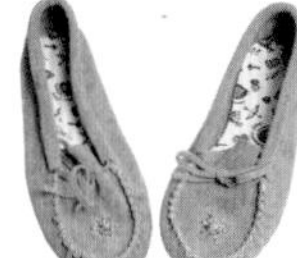
moccasins

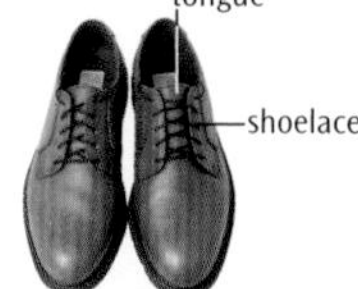

lace-ups (*especially BrE*) / **oxfords** (*especially NAmE*)

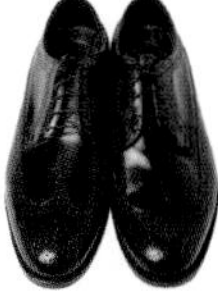
brogues

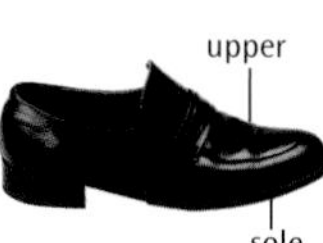

loafer

trainers (*BrE*)
sneakers (*NAmE*)

baseball boots

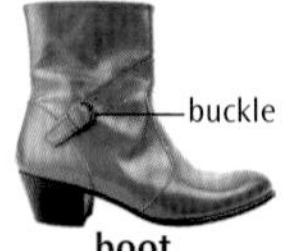

boot

cowboy boot

hiking boots
(*also* **walking boots**)

wellingtons (*BrE*)
rubber boots (*NAmE*)

Bags

handbag (*NAmE also* **purse**)

shoulder bag

clutch bag

bumbag (*BrE*)
fanny pack (*NAmE*)

backpack (*BrE also* **rucksack**)

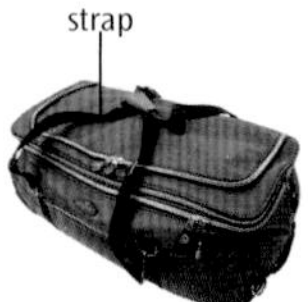

holdall (*BrE*)
duffel bag (*NAmE*)

purse (*especially BrE*) / **change purse** (*NAmE*)

wallet (*NAmE also* **billfold**)

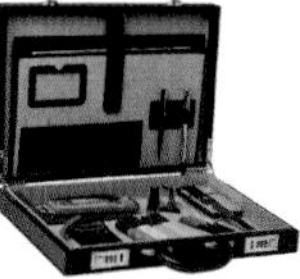
attaché case
(*also* **briefcase**)

briefcase

suitcase

trunk

Hats

brim

band

panama | boater | trilby | cowboy hat | bowler (*BrE*) derby (*NAmE*)

peak (*BrE*) bill (*NAmE*)

top hat | mortar board | cap | cloth cap / flat cap (*both BrE*) | baseball cap

visor

pom pom (*BrE also* bobble)

beret | hard hat | crash helmet | beanie | bobble hat

sou'wester | hood | sun hats | sombrero

Gloves

Scarves

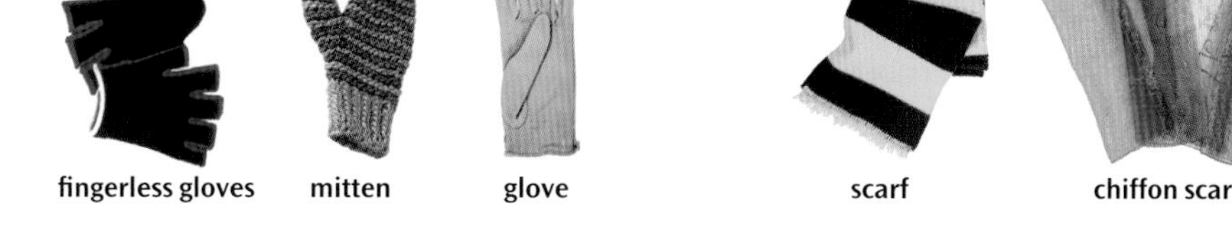

fingerless gloves | mitten | glove | scarf | chiffon scarf

Jewellery

stud | clip-on earring | pendant | medallion | locket | chain

hoop earring | dangly earrings | string of beads

signet ring | wedding ring wedding band | cufflinks

bangle | charm bracelet | brooch (*BrE*) pin (*NAmE*) | badge (*also* button *especially NAmE*) | pearl necklace

Computing

flatbed scanner

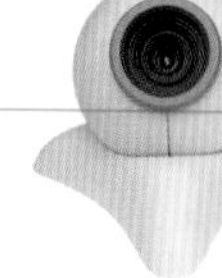
webcam (*NAmE also* Webcam™)

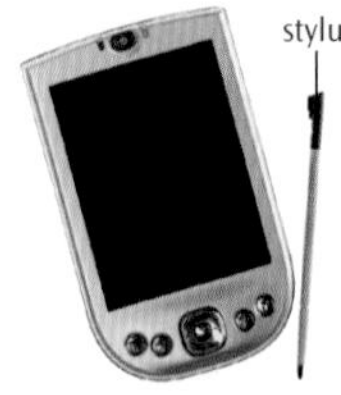

PDA

digital camera

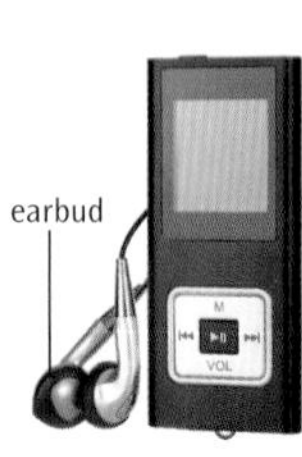

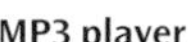
MP3 player

headset

Equipment

- This computer has a **processor speed** of 3 GHz (= gigahertz), 2 Gb (= gigabytes) of **RAM** (=**random access memory**) and a **hard disk capacity** of 500 Gb.
- It comes with a 56K **modem** and a **speech recognition** system.
- The **multimedia** system includes a **sound card** with 4D stereo sound and a **graphics card** with 128 Mb of **video RAM** for a **high resolution** colour **display**.
- With **DVD** (= **digital versatile disc** or **digital videodisc**) you can watch films/movies.
- You pay extra for the **laser printer**, **scanner** and other **peripherals**.
- The new **operating system** should be compatible with existing **hardware**.
- You can **download** the pictures from your **digital camera** and **burn** them to a **CD**.
- **Wi-fi**™ (= **wireless fidelity**) broadband connections are not only in computer stores but in coffee shops, public libraries and bookstores – you can log into the Internet without physically plugging into anything.

Getting started

- **PC users** should **log on** to the **network** by **entering** their **username** and **password**.
- **Load** the **program** into the computer.
- **Save** your **files** onto your **hard disk** and **back** them **up** onto **CDs** or **DVDs**.
- Important **data** is **archived** on the central **file server**.

When things go wrong

- I can't **log in** – the **server** is **down**.
- The **system** keeps **crashing** – I've lost all my files.
- You'll have to switch off and **reboot**.
- **Error**. Username contains **invalid characters**.
- My computer can't **read** this disk.
- The **virus** in the **software** was **programmed** to **corrupt** the hard disk.
- A **firewall** provides essential security for your computer network.
- Download and install this **patch** to fix the fault.

Window

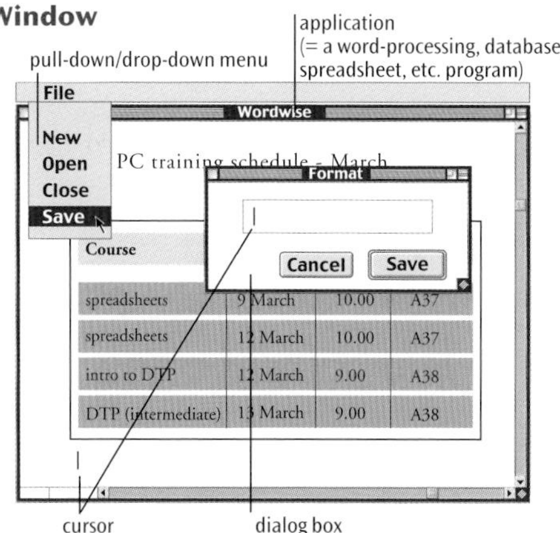

User interface

- **Click on** the **window** to make it **active**.
- You can **run** several **applications** at the same time.
- To **create** a new **document**, **select** New from the File **menu**.
- **Insert** the **cursor** at the beginning of the line.
- Use the **mouse** to **drag** the **icon** to the **desktop**.
- **Scroll up** or **down** the text by clicking on the **scroll bar**.
- Search and replace **options** are **activated** from the command **prompt**.
- **Interactive** computer **terminals** allow visitors to take an 'electronic walk' through a **virtual** Pompeii.

Screen

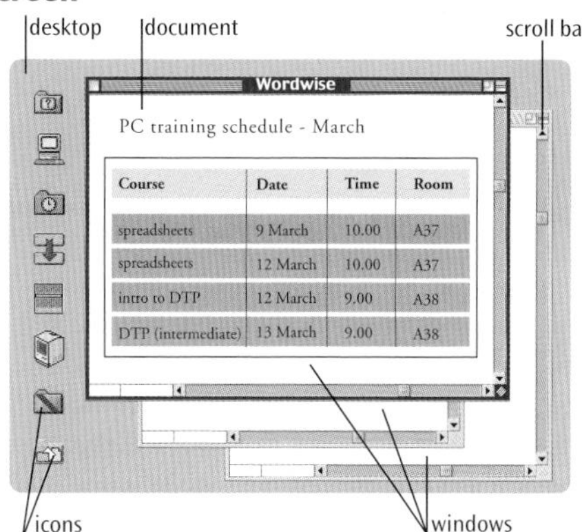

The Internet

- There is a wide range range of **ISPs** (= **Internet Service Providers**).
- My free time is spent **surfing** the **net** in **Internet cafes**.
- It's a **software package** that helps you **browse the Web**.
- This **search engine** indexes over a million **websites.**
- **Do a search on** language schools in the UK.
- Brief summaries are **hyperlinked** to the complete texts.
- The site's **webmaster** says it has over 100,000 **hits** a day.
- This **chat room** is a forum for debating civil liberties issues **online**.
- My **email address** is 'joanna_smith@oup.com' (said 'joanna underscore smith at o-u-p dot com).
- The **web address** / **URL** (= **uniform/universal resource locator**) is 'www.oup.com/elt' (said 'double-U, double-U, double-U dot o-u-p dot com slash e-l-t).
- The website lets you **upload** photos, then edit and share them.
- You can **download** images to your PC much more quickly with **broadband** than with a **dial-up** connection.
- **Bookmarking** a page stores the information which enables you to revisit a favourite website instantly.
- **Cookies** are files used by some websites to gain information about their visitors, or to simplify the login process by saving usernames and passwords.
- He maintains a personal **weblog** in which he writes (= **blogs**) extensively about film and his own film-making.
- Most **spam** mails disguise the sender's identity.
- **VoIP** allows you to use your computer as a telephone, or use the Internet to transmit your call over ordinary phone lines.

Home page

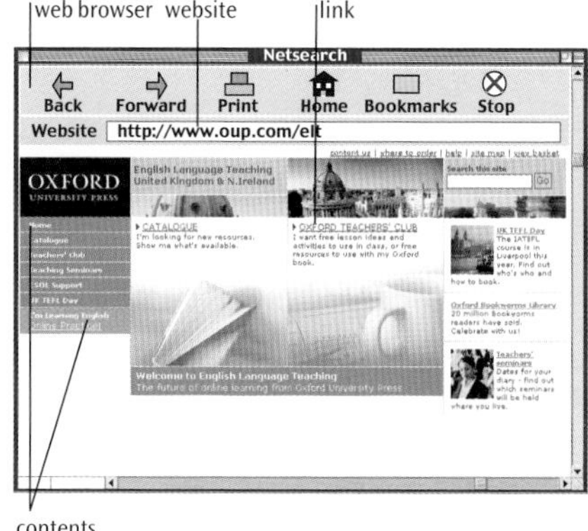

Office

1 wall planner
2 noticeboard (*BrE*) bulletin board (*NAmE*)
3 flip chart
4 data projector
5 laptop
6 meeting/conference room
7 water cooler
8 desk lamp
9 workstation / PC
10 partition
11 in tray (*NAmE also* in box)
12 out tray (*BrE*) out box (*US*)
13 calendar
14 pen holder
15 mouse mat (*BrE*) mouse pad (*especially NAmE*)
16 flatbed scanner
17 calculator
18 desk diary (*BrE*) datebook (*NAmE*)
19 desk
20 stationery tray
21 waste-paper basket (*BrE*) / wastebasket (*NAmE*)
22 swivel chair
23 arm
24 printer
25 hard copy / printout
26 castor
27 filing cabinet (*BrE*) file cabinet (*NAmE*)
28 suspension file
29 photocopier

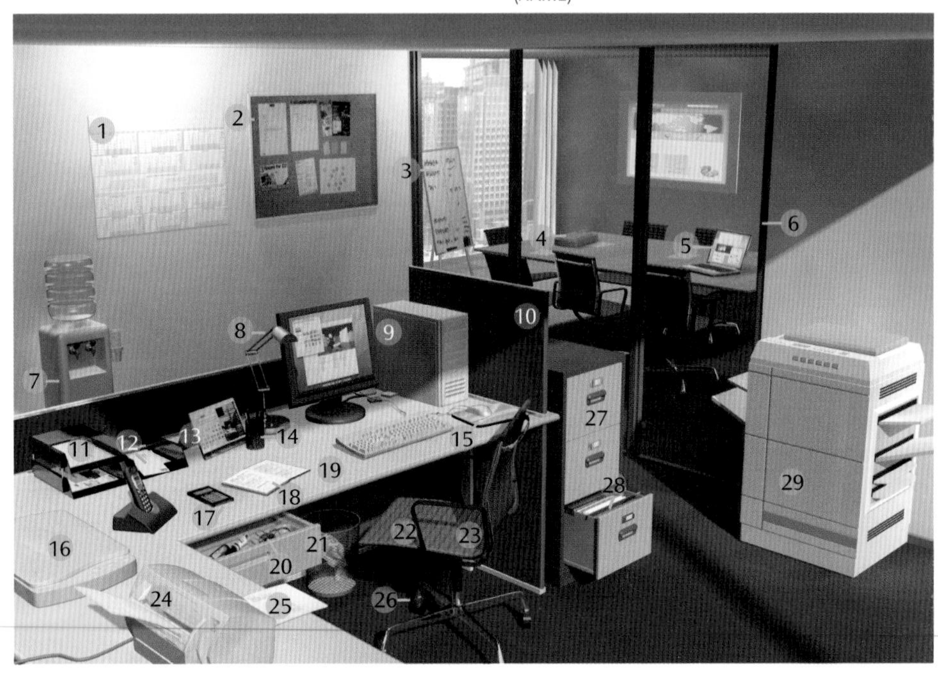

Stationery and office supplies

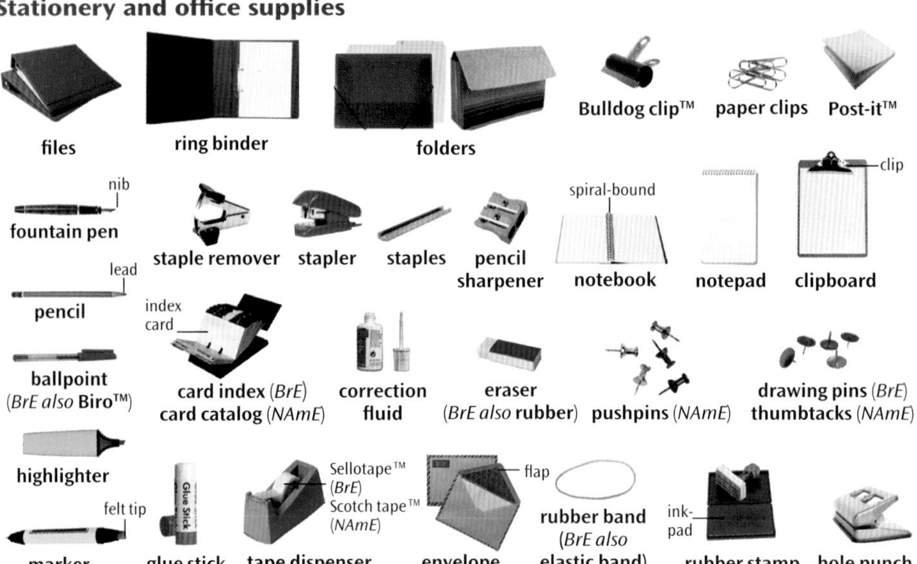

Classroom

1 projector
2 corridor (*NAmE also* hallway)
3 poster
4 locker
5 interactive whiteboard
6 whiteboard
7 board pen
8 sports field
9 desk
10 school bag
11 backpack (*BrE also* rucksack)
12 textbook (*NAmE also* text)
13 workbook (*BrE*) exercise book (*NAmE*)
14 exercise book (*BrE*) notebook (*NAmE*)
15 pencil case
16 satchel
17 protractor
18 ruler
19 set square (*BrE*) triangle (*NAmE*)

Laboratory equipment

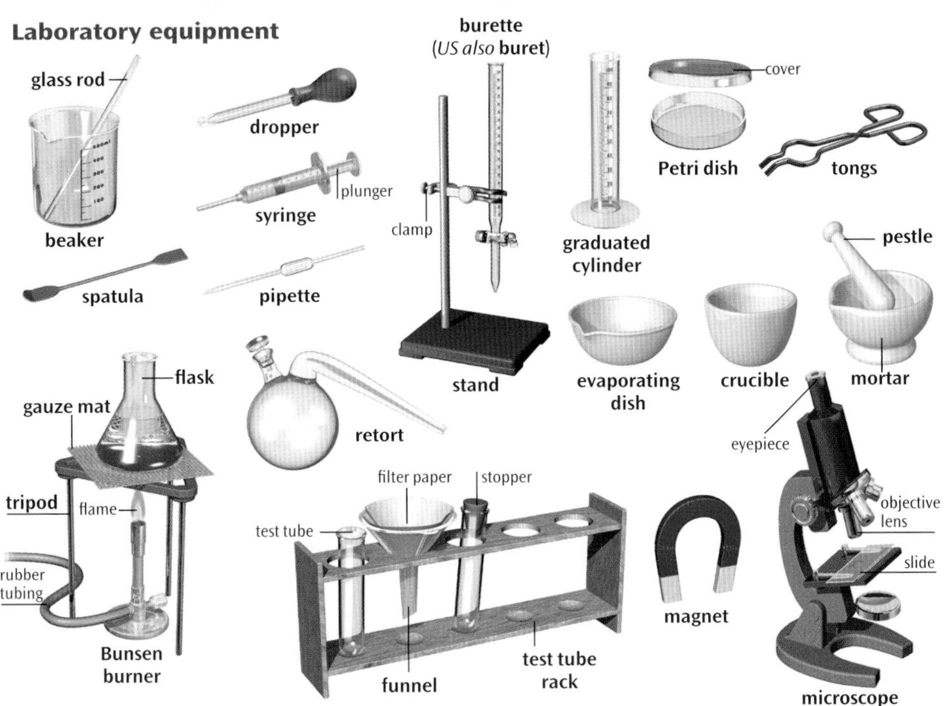

Shapes, solids and angles

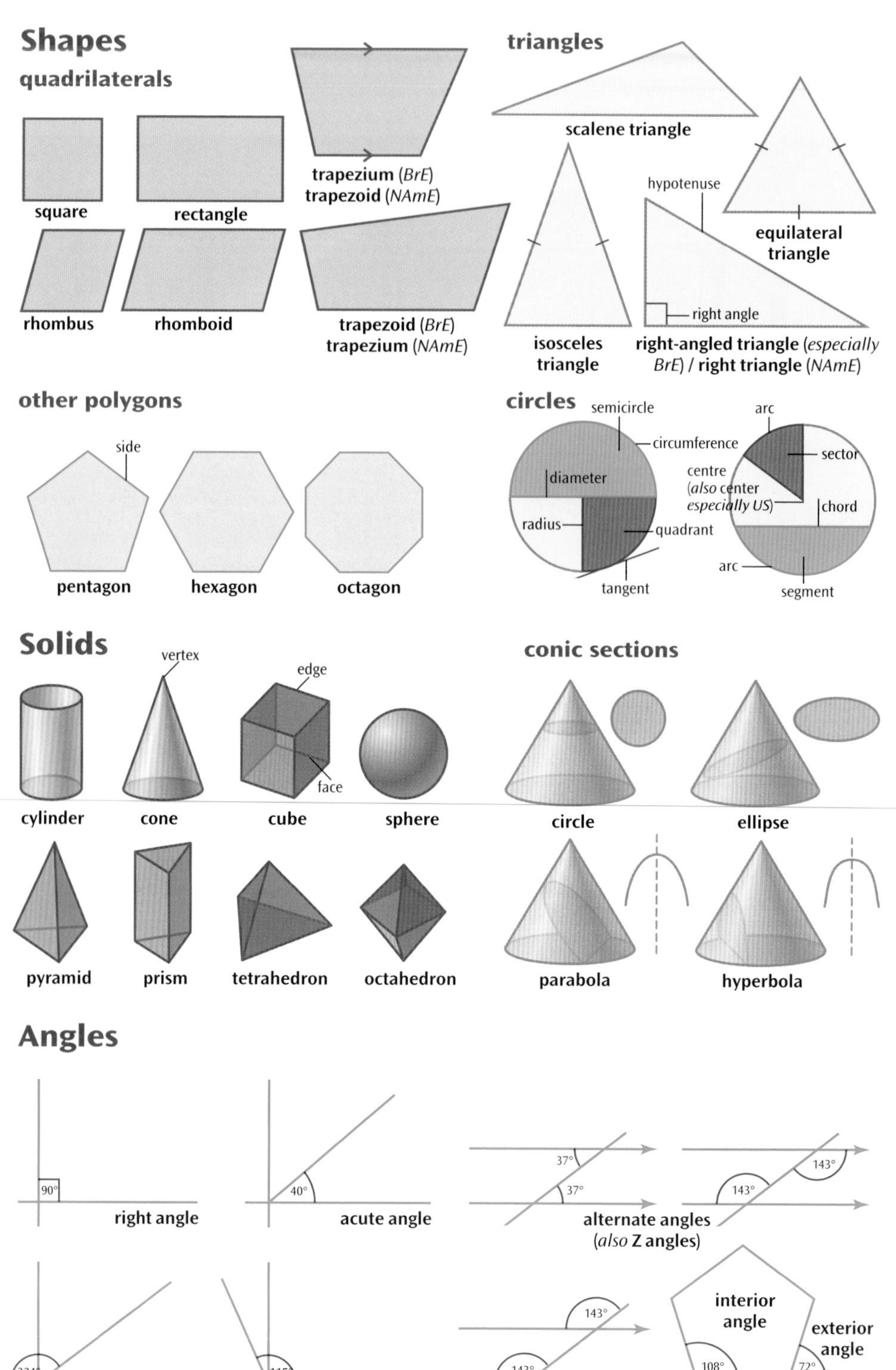

The earth and the solar system

The earth

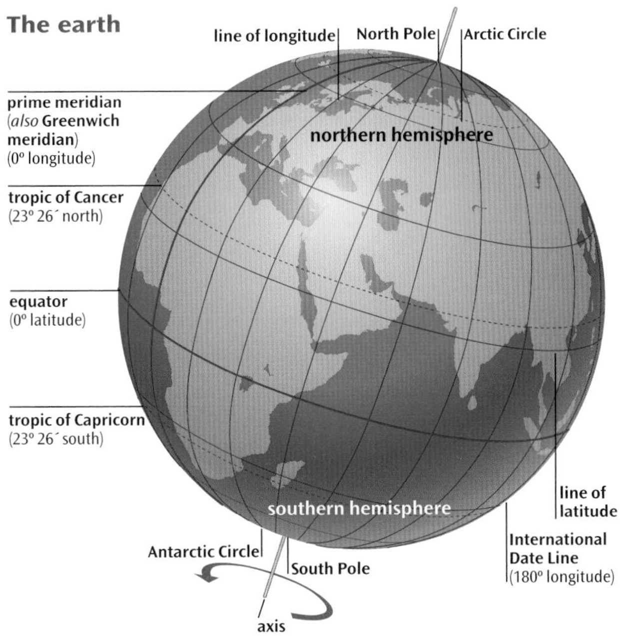

The seasons

earth's orbit around the sun 149 597 910km

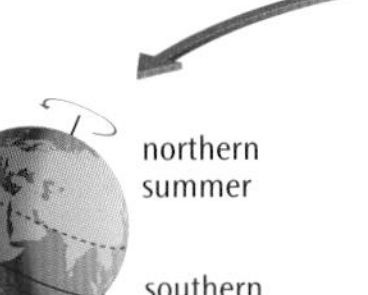

northern winter
southern summer
22 December solstice

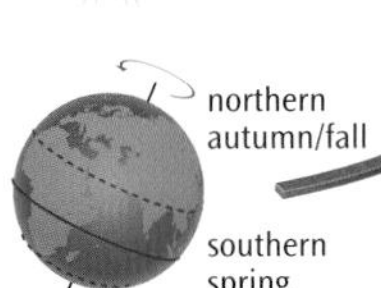

The solar system

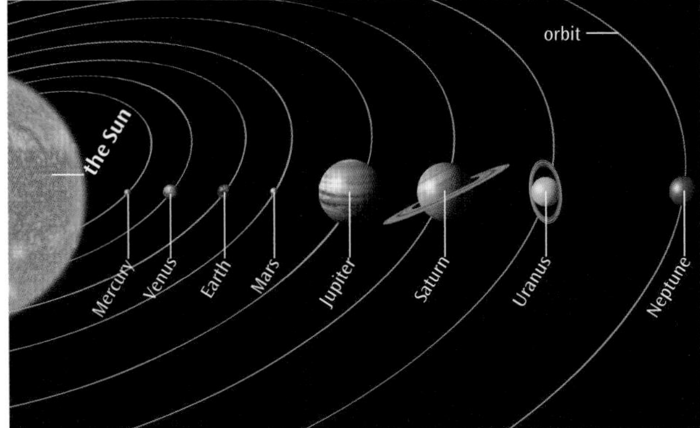

The world

- A **map** is a drawing or plan of the world or a part of the world.
- An **atlas** is a book of maps and a **globe** is a model of the earth in the shape of a ball.
- The planet where we live, and its surface: **earth**, **the earth** (*also* **the Earth**).
- The earth, including all the countries, people, etc.: **world** (*often* **the world**).
- The study of the world, including its natural and man-made features (seas, mountains, countries, cities, etc.), is **geography** [U]; *adjective*: **geographical**; *person*: **geographer**.
- The study of the rocks, etc. which form the surface of the earth is **geology** [U]; *adjective*: **geological**; *person*: **geologist**.

Seasons

- When talking about the seasons we normally do not use **the**, but we may do if we want to talk about a particular winter, summer, etc.:
  - ▶ *I love spring – it's my favourite season.*
  - ▶ *That was the summer we went to Australia.*

The stars and planets

- The planets in the solar system **orbit** (= go round) the sun.
- Everything that exists, including the earth, the planets, the stars, etc. is called **the universe**.
- A group of stars with a name is a **constellation** and a very large group of stars is a **galaxy**.
- A piece of rock moving through space is a **meteor** and a meteor that has landed on earth is a **meteorite**.
- The scientific study of the stars, planets, etc. is **astronomy** [U]; *adjective*: **astronomical**; *person*: **astronomer**.
- The belief that the positions and movements of the stars and planets influence what people do and what happens to them is **astrology** [U]; *adjective*: **astrological**; *person*: **astrologer**.

See also GEOGRAPHICAL NAMES

The British Isles

Britain or **Great Britain** (**GB**) is a geographical area consisting of **England**, **Scotland** and **Wales** (but not **Ireland**).

The name **Britain** is also incorrectly used to refer to the political state, officially called the **United Kingdom of Great Britain and Northern Ireland**. This is abbreviated to the **United Kingdom** or the **UK**.

The British Isles is a group of islands that includes Britain and Ireland, and a number of smaller islands. The **Republic of Ireland** (also the **Irish Republic**; formerly **Eire**) is an independent state occupying the southern part of the island of Ireland.

To refer to the nationality of the people of Britain or the United Kingdom, you use the adjective **British**. **English** describes people from England, and should not be used to describe people from **Ireland**, **Scotland** or **Wales**, who are **Irish**, **Scottish** and **Welsh**. There is further information in the notes at the entries for **British** and **Scottish**.

There are special adjectives and nouns to describe people from some cities, for example a person from London is a **Londoner**, from Dublin a **Dubliner**, from Glasgow a **Glaswegian**, from Aberdeen an **Aberdonian**, from Manchester a **Mancunian** and from Liverpool a **Liverpudlian**. A Londoner who speaks with the local accent is also called a **Cockney**. There are also informal names for people from some cities: **Brummie** (from Birmingham); **Scouse** or **Scouser** (from Liverpool); and **Geordie** (from Tyneside, which stretches from Newcastle to the coast).

UNITED KINGDOM
ENGLAND
WALES
ISLE OF MAN
REPUBLIC OF IRELAND
Irish Sea
English Channel
St. George's Channel
Bristol Channel
Strait of Dover
Donegal Bay
Donegal Mountains
Foyle
Londonderry
Lough Neagh
Belfast
Lisburn
Erne
Newry
Mourne Mountains
852m Slieve Donard
Lough Conn
Lough Mask
Lough Corrib
Lough Ree
Galway
Galway Bay
Shannon
Boyne
Liffey
Dublin
Lough Derg
Barrow
Wicklow Mountains
Limerick
Suir
Waterford
Blackwater
Dingle Bay
1041m Carrauntoohill
Cork
Douglas
Dumfries
Carlisle
Solway Firth
Eden
Lake District
978m Scafell Pike
Pennines
Tyne
upon Tyne
Sunderland
Durham
Hartlepool
Middlesbrough
Tees
Swale
North York Moors
The North-West
The North-East
York
Kingston upon Hull
Blackpool
Preston
Leeds
Bradford
Blackburn
Ouse
Aire
Huddersfield
Humber
Bolton
Liverpool
Mersey
Manchester
Peak District
Sheffield
Anglesey
Holyhead
Colwyn Bay
Chester
Stoke-on-Trent
Trent
Lincoln
Caernarfon
1085m Snowdon
Dee
Snowdonia
Derby
Nottingham
The Wash
The Midlands
East Midlands
The Fens
Wensum
Norwich
Great Yarmouth
Shrewsbury
Leicester
Peterborough
East Anglia
Wolverhampton
Birmingham
Cambrian Mountains
Cardigan Bay
Aberystwyth
Severn
Coventry
Great Ouse
Worcester
Avon
Warwick
Northampton
Cambridge
Ipswich
Stratford-upon-Avon
Hereford
Wye
Milton Keynes
Stansted
Stour
Colchester
Luton
Gloucester
Cotswold Hills
Oxford
Chiltern Hills
The Home Counties
Thames Estuary
Milford Haven
Brecon Beacons
Usk
Thames
Watford
London
Southend-on-Sea
Margate
Newport
Swindon
Slough
Heathrow
Swansea
Cardiff
Bristol
Salisbury Plain
Reading
North Downs
Canterbury
Bath
Dover
Gatwick
Exmoor
Salisbury
Taunton
Southampton
South Downs
Brighton
Hastings
Exe
Bournemouth
Portsmouth
Eastbourne
The West Country
Exeter
Poole
Isle of Wight
Dartmoor
Plymouth
Truro
Land's End
Isles of Scilly
St. Peter Port
Guernsey
Jersey
Channel Islands
St. Helier

Canada and the United States of America

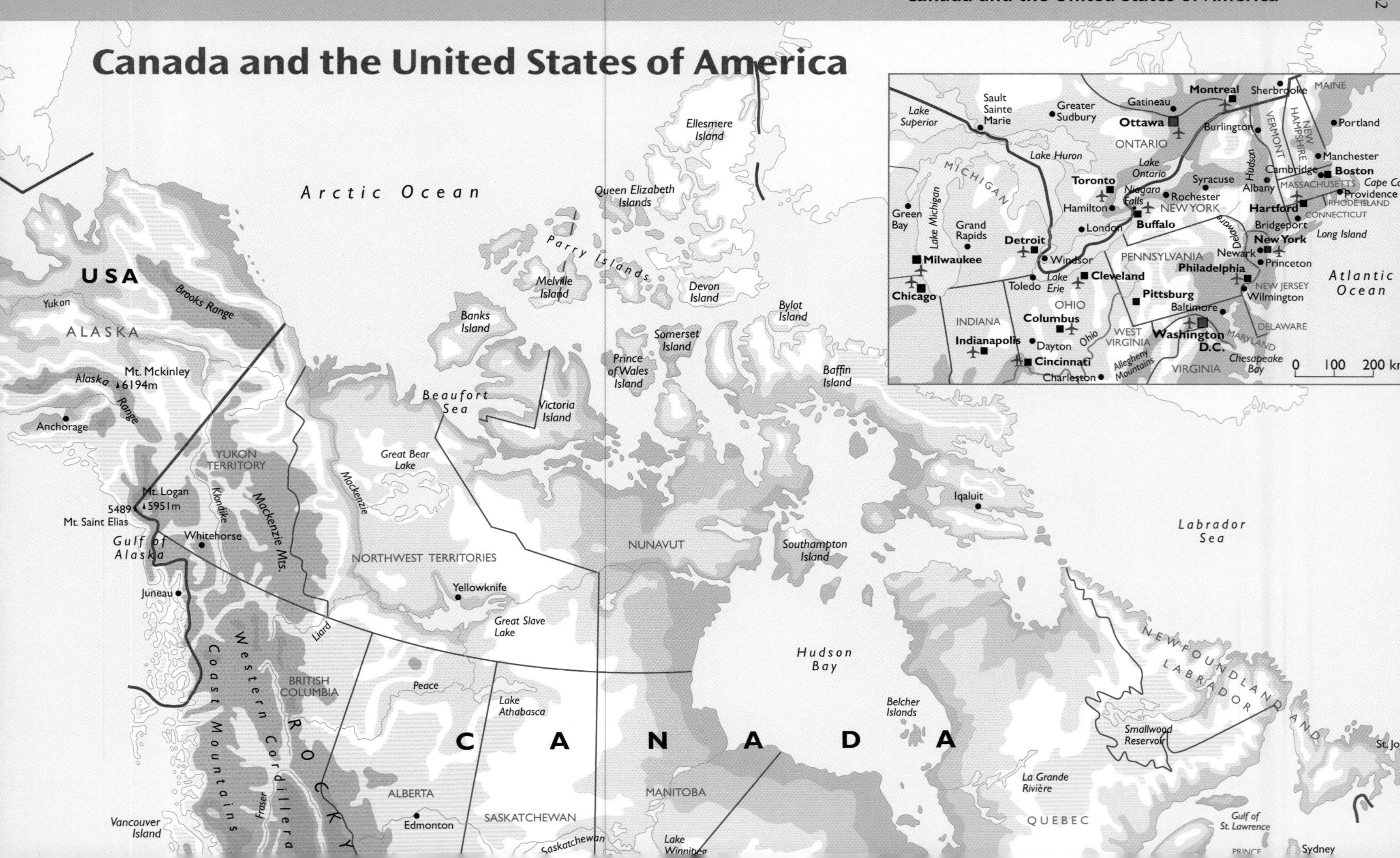

UNITED STATES OF AMERICA
MOUNTAINS
Great Plains
Pacific Ocean
Atlantic Ocean
Gulf of Mexico
WASHINGTON
OREGON
IDAHO
MONTANA
WYOMING
NORTH DAKOTA
SOUTH DAKOTA
NEBRASKA
NEVADA
CALIFORNIA
UTAH
COLORADO
ARIZONA
NEW MEXICO
KANSAS
OKLAHOMA
TEXAS
MINNESOTA
IOWA
MISSOURI
ARKANSAS
LOUISIANA
WISCONSIN
ILLINOIS
MICHIGAN
INDIANA
OHIO
KENTUCKY
TENNESSEE
MISSISSIPPI
ALABAMA
GEORGIA
FLORIDA
SOUTH CAROLINA
NORTH CAROLINA
VIRGINIA
WEST VIRGINIA
PENNSYLVANIA
NEW YORK
NEW JERSEY
MARYLAND
DELAWARE
VERMONT
NEW HAMPSHIRE
MASSACHUSETTS
RHODE ISLAND
CONNECTICUT
MAINE
NOVA SCOTIA
BRUNSWICK
HAWAII
Kauai
Oahu
Honolulu
Maui
Hawaii
Victoria
Kelowna
Calgary
Saskatoon
Regina
Winnipeg
Thunder Bay
Seattle
Spokane
Portland
Salem
Eugene
Columbia
Great Falls
Billings
Boise
Idaho Falls
Snake
Missouri
Bismarck
Fargo
Duluth
St. Paul
Minneapolis
Rapid City
Sioux Falls
Sierra Nevada
Reno
Great Salt Lake
Salt Lake City
Provo
Cheyenne
Fort Collins
Mt. Elbert 4399m
Denver
Colorado Springs
Colorado
Sacramento
San Francisco
Berkeley
San José
Fresno
4418m Mt. Whitney
Death Valley
Las Vegas
Bakersfield
Hollywood
Los Angeles
San Diego
Grand Canyon
Phoenix
Mesa
Tucson
Santa Fe
Albuquerque
El Paso
Amarillo
Lubbock
Omaha
Lincoln
Topeka
Kansas City
Wichita
Oklahoma City
Tulsa
Arkansas
Fort Worth
Dallas
Austin
San Antonio
Houston
Rio Grande
Corpus Christi
Cedar Rapids
Des Moines
Madison
Milwaukee
Chicago
Mississippi
Springfield
St. Louis
Lake Superior
Great Lakes
Lake Michigan
Lake Huron
Lake Erie
Lake Ontario
Detroit
Indianapolis
Louisville
Lexington
Memphis
Little Rock
Jackson
Nashville
Knoxville
Tennessee
Birmingham
Montgomery
Mobile
Baton Rouge
New Orleans
Atlanta
Augusta
Columbia
Charleston
Savannah
Jacksonville
Tallahassee
Orlando
Tampa
The Everglades
Fort Lauderdale
Miami
Key West
Florida Keys
Charlotte
Raleigh
Appalachian Mountains
Richmond
Norfolk
Virginia Beach
Chesapeake Bay
Washington D.C.
Ohio
Cleveland
Pittsburgh
Philadelphia
Delaware
New York
Hudson
Buffalo
Toronto
Ottawa
Montreal
St. Lawrence
Saguenay
Quebec City
Fredericton
Moncton
Saint John
Halifax
international boundary
internal boundary
capital city
over 1 million inhabitants
town or city
major airport
river
lake
metres
5000
3000
2000
1000
500
300
200
100
0
sea level
peak or highest point
0
250
500 km

Australia and New Zealand

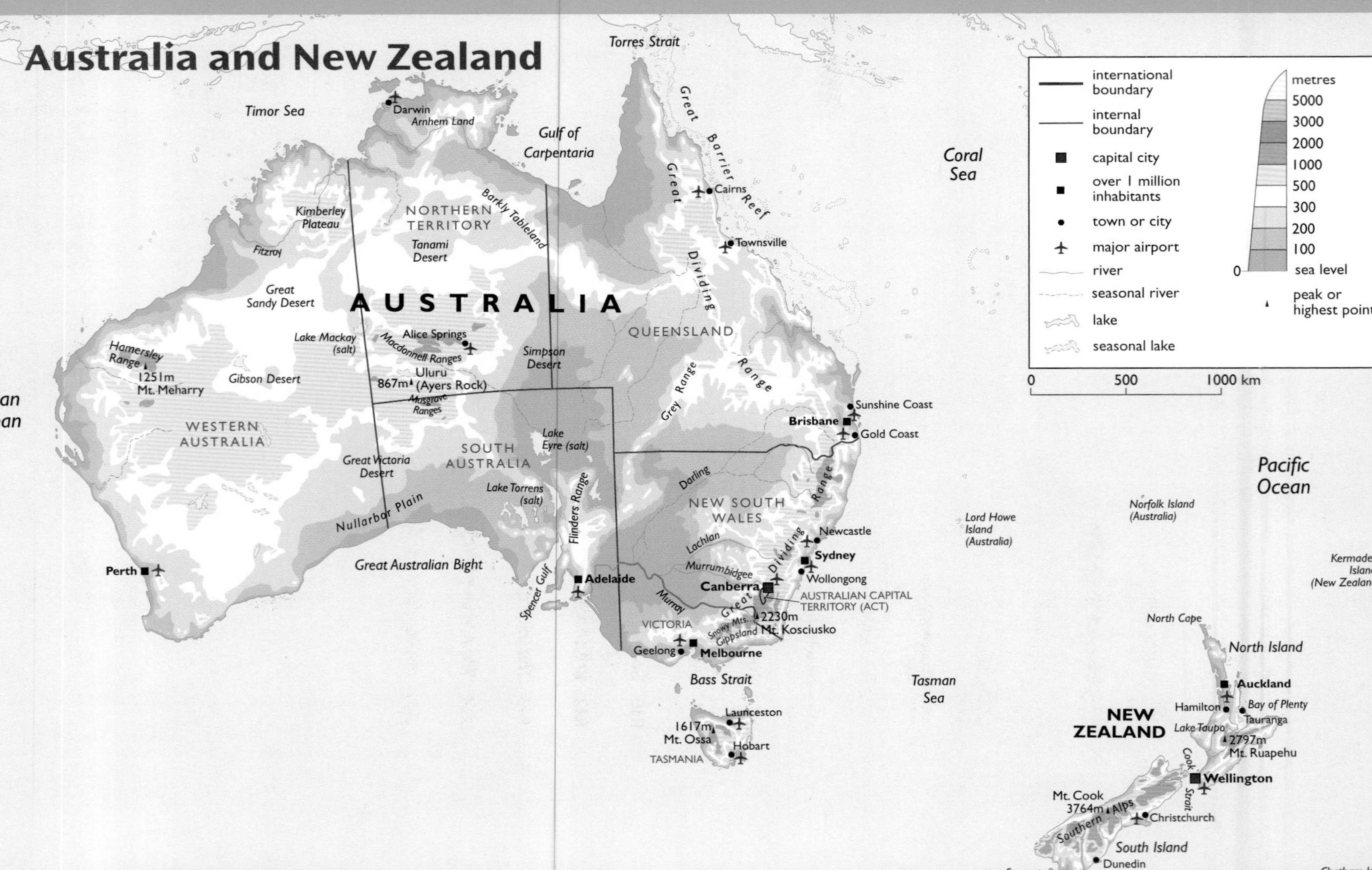
Timor Sea
Darwin
Arnhem Land
Gulf of Carpentaria
Torres Strait
Great Barrier Reef
Great Dividing Range
Cairns
Townsville
Coral Sea
Kimberley Plateau
Fitzroy
NORTHERN TERRITORY
Barkly Tableland
Tanami Desert
Great Sandy Desert
AUSTRALIA
QUEENSLAND
Hamersley Range
1251m
Mt. Meharry
Gibson Desert
Lake Mackay (salt)
Alice Springs
Macdonnell Ranges
Uluru
867m (Ayers Rock)
Musgrave Ranges
Simpson Desert
Grey Range
Indian Ocean
WESTERN AUSTRALIA
SOUTH AUSTRALIA
Great Victoria Desert
Lake Eyre (salt)
Lake Torrens (salt)
Flinders Range
Nullarbor Plain
Great Australian Bight
Perth
Spencer Gulf
Adelaide
Sunshine Coast
Brisbane
Gold Coast
Darling
NEW SOUTH WALES
Lachlan
Murrumbidgee
Murray
Newcastle
Sydney
Wollongong
Canberra
AUSTRALIAN CAPITAL TERRITORY (ACT)
Snowy Mts.
2230m
Mt. Kosciusko
Gippsland
VICTORIA
Geelong
Melbourne
Bass Strait
Launceston
1617m
Mt. Ossa
Hobart
TASMANIA
Tasman Sea
Lord Howe Island (Australia)
Norfolk Island (Australia)
Pacific Ocean
Kermadec Islands (New Zealand)
North Cape
North Island
Auckland
Hamilton
Bay of Plenty
Tauranga
Lake Taupo
2797m
Mt. Ruapehu
NEW ZEALAND
Cook Strait
Wellington
Mt. Cook
3764m
Southern Alps
Christchurch
South Island
Dunedin
Stewart
Chatham Islands
international boundary
internal boundary
capital city
over 1 million inhabitants
town or city
major airport
river
seasonal river
lake
seasonal lake
metres
5000
3000
2000
1000
500
300
200
100
0
sea level
peak or highest point
0
500
1000 km

Reference section contents

R2 Irregular verbs

R5 Verbs

R9 Phrasal verbs

R11 Nouns and adjectives

R13 Collocation

R14 Idioms

R15 Notes on usage

R20 The language of literary criticism

R22 Punctuation

R25 Numbers

R31 Common first names

R36 Geographical names

R42 British and American English

R43 The Oxford 3000™

R44 The Academic Word List

R45 Pronunciation and phonetic symbols in the dictionary

Irregular verbs

This appendix lists all the verbs with irregular forms that are included in the dictionary, except for those formed with a hyphenated prefix and the modal verbs (e.g. can, must). Irregular forms that are only used in certain senses are marked with an asterisk (e.g. *abode). Full information on usage, pronunciation, etc. is given at the entry.

Infinitive	Past tense	Past participle
abide	abided, *abode	abided, *abode
arise	arose	arisen
awake	awoke	awoken
babysit	babysat	babysat
bear	bore	borne
beat	beat	beaten
become	became	become
befall	befell	befallen
beget	begot, *begat	begot, *begotten
begin	began	begun
behold	beheld	beheld
bend	bent	bent
beseech	beseeched, besought	beseeched, besought
beset	beset	beset
bespeak	bespoke	bespoken
bet	bet	bet
betake	betook	betaken
bid[1]	bid	bid
bid[2]	bade, bid	bidden, bid
bind	bound	bound
bite	bit	bitten
bleed	bled	bled
blow	blew	blown, *blowed
break	broke	broken
breastfeed	breastfed	breastfed
breed	bred	bred
bring	brought	brought
broadcast	broadcast	broadcast
browbeat	browbeat	browbeaten
build	built	built
burn	burnt, burned	burnt, burned
burst	burst	burst
bust	bust, busted	bust, busted
buy	bought	bought
cast	cast	cast
catch	caught	caught
choose	chose	chosen
cleave	cleaved, *cleft, *clove	cleaved, *cleft, *cloven
cling	clung	clung
come	came	come
cost	cost, *costed	cost, *costed
creep	crept	crept
cut	cut	cut
deal	dealt	dealt
dig	dug	dug
dive	dived; (*NAmE also* dove)	dived
draw	drew	drawn
dream	dreamt, dreamed	dreamt, dreamed
drink	drank	drunk
drip-feed	drip-fed	drip-fed
drive	drove	driven
dwell	dwelt, dwelled	dwelt, dwelled
eat	ate	eaten
fall	fell	fallen
feed	fed	fed
feel	felt	felt
fight	fought	fought
find	found	found
fit	fitted; (*NAmE usually* fit)	fitted; (*NAmE usually* fit)
flee	fled	fled
fling	flung	flung
floodlight	floodlit	floodlit
fly	flew, *flied	flown, *flied
forbear	forbore	forborne
forbid	forbade	forbidden
forecast	forecast, forecasted	forecast, forecasted
foresee	foresaw	foreseen
foretell	foretold	foretold
forget	forgot	forgotten
forgive	forgave	forgiven
forgo	forwent	forgone
forsake	forsook	forsaken
forswear	forswore	forsworn
freeze	froze	frozen
gainsay	gainsaid	gainsaid
get	got	got; (*NAmE, spoken*) gotten
give	gave	given
go	went	gone, *been
grind	ground	ground
grow	grew	grown
hamstring	hamstrung	hamstrung
hang	hung, *hanged	hung, *hanged
hear	heard	heard
heave	heaved, *hove	heaved, *hove
hew	hewed	hewed, hewn
hide	hid	hidden
hit	hit	hit
hold	held	held
hurt	hurt	hurt
inlay	inlaid	inlaid
input	input, inputted	input, inputted
inset	inset	inset
intercut	intercut	intercut
interweave	interwove	interwoven
keep	kept	kept
kneel	knelt; (*NAmE also* kneeled)	knelt; (*NAmE also* kneeled)
knit	knitted, *knit	knitted, *knit
know	knew	known
lay	laid	laid
lead	led	led
lean	leaned; (*BrE also* leant)	leaned; (*BrE also* leant)
leap	leapt, leaped	leapt, leaped
learn	learnt, learned	learnt, learned
leave	left	left
lend	lent	lent
let	let	let
lie[1]	lay	lain
light	lit, *lighted	lit, *lighted
lose	lost	lost
make	made	made
mean	meant	meant

Infinitive	Past tense	Past participle
meet	met	met
miscast	miscast	miscast
mishear	misheard	misheard
mishit	mishit	mishit
mislay	mislaid	mislaid
mislead /ˌmɪsˈliːd/	misled /ˌmɪsˈled/	misled /ˌmɪsˈled/
misread /ˌmɪsˈriːd/	misread /ˌmɪsˈred/	misread /ˌmɪsˈred/
misspell	misspelled, misspelt	misspelled, misspelt
misspend	misspent	misspent
mistake	mistook	mistaken
misunderstand	misunderstood	misunderstood
mow	mowed	mown, mowed
offset	offset	offset
outbid	outbid	outbid
outdo	outdid	outdone
outgrow	outgrew	outgrown
output	output	output
outrun	outran	outrun
outsell	outsold	outsold
outshine	outshone	outshone
overcome	overcame	overcome
overdo	overdid	overdone
overdraw	overdrew	overdrawn
overeat	overate	overeaten
overfeed	overfed	overfed
overfly	overflew	overflown
overhang	overhung	overhung
overhear	overheard	overheard
overlay	overlaid	overlaid
overlie	overlay	overlain
overpay	overpaid	overpaid
override	overrode	overridden
overrun	overran	overrun
oversee	oversaw	overseen
oversell	oversold	oversold
overshoot	overshot	overshot
oversleep	overslept	overslept
overspend	overspent	overspent
overtake	overtook	overtaken
overthrow	overthrew	overthrown
overwrite	overwrote	overwritten
partake	partook	partaken
pay	paid	paid
plead	pleaded; (*NAmE also* pled)	pleaded; (*NAmE also* pled)
preset	preset	preset
proofread /ˈpruːfriːd/	proofread /ˈpruːfred/	proofread /ˈpruːfred/
prove	proved	proved; (*also* proven *especially in NAmE*)
put	put	put
quit	quit; (*BrE also* quitted)	quit; (*BrE also* quitted)
read /riːd/	read /red/	read /red/
rebuild	rebuilt	rebuilt
recast	recast	recast
redo	redid	redone
redraw	redrew	redrawn
rehear	reheard	reheard
remake	remade	remade
rend	rent	rent
rerun	reran	rerun
resell	resold	resold
reset	reset	reset
resit	resat	resat
restring	restrung	restrung
retake	retook	retaken
retell	retold	retold
rethink	rethought	rethought
rewind	rewound	rewound

Infinitive	Past tense	Past participle
rewrite	rewrote	rewritten
rid	rid	rid
ride	rode	ridden
ring[2]	rang	rung
rise	rose	risen
run	ran	run
saw	sawed	sawn; (*NAmE also* sawed)
say	said	said
see	saw	seen
seek	sought	sought
sell	sold	sold
send	sent	sent
set	set	set
sew	sewed	sewn, sewed
shake	shook	shaken
shear	sheared	shorn, sheared
shed	shed	shed
shine	shone, *shined	shone, *shined
shit	shit, shat; (*BrE also* shitted)	shit, shat; (*BrE also* shitted)
shoe	shod	shod
shoot	shot	shot
show	showed	shown, *showed
shrink	shrank, shrunk	shrunk
shut	shut	shut
simulcast	simulcast	simulcast
sing	sang	sung
sink	sank, *sunk	sunk
sit	sat	sat
slay	slew	slain
sleep	slept	slept
slide	slid	slid
sling	slung	slung
slink	slunk	slunk
slit	slit	slit
smell	smelled; (*BrE also* smelt)	smelled; (*BrE also* smelt)
smite	smote	smitten
sow	sowed	sown, sowed
speak	spoke	spoken
speed	speeded, *sped	speeded, *sped
spell	spelt, spelled	spelt, spelled
spend	spent	spent
spill	spilled; (*BrE also* spilt)	spilled; (*BrE also* spilt)
spin	spun	spun
spit	spat; (*also* spit *especially in NAmE*)	spat; (*also* spit *especially in NAmE*)
split	split	split
spoil	spoiled; (*BrE also* spoilt)	spoiled; (*BrE also* spoilt)
spotlight	spotlit, *spotlighted	spotlit, *spotlighted
spread	spread	spread
spring	sprang; (*NAmE also* sprung)	sprung
stand	stood	stood
stave	staved, *stove	staved, *stove
steal	stole	stolen
stick	stuck	stuck
sting	stung	stung
stink	stank, stunk	stunk
strew	strewed	strewed, strewn
stride	strode	—
strike	struck	struck; (*NAmE also* stricken)
string	strung	strung
strive	strove, *strived	striven, *strived
sublet	sublet	sublet
swear	swore	sworn
sweep	swept	swept
swell	swelled	swollen, swelled

Infinitive	Past tense	Past participle
swim	swam	swum
swing	swung	swung
take	took	taken
teach	taught	taught
tear	tore	torn
telecast	telecast	telecast
tell	told	told
think	thought	thought
throw	threw	thrown
thrust	thrust	thrust
tread	trod	trodden, trod
typecast	typecast	typecast
typeset	typeset	typeset
unbend	unbent	unbent
underbid	underbid	underbid
undercut	undercut	undercut
undergo	underwent	undergone
underlie	underlay	underlain
underpay	underpaid	underpaid
undersell	undersold	undersold
understand	understood	understood
undertake	undertook	undertaken
underwrite	underwrote	underwritten
undo	undid	undone
unfreeze	unfroze	unfrozen
unwind	unwound	unwound
uphold	upheld	upheld
upset	upset	upset
wake	woke	woken
waylay	waylaid	waylaid
wear	wore	worn
weave	wove, *weaved	woven, *weaved
wed	wedded, wed	wedded, wed
weep	wept	wept
wet	wet, wetted	wet, wetted
win	won	won
wind[2] /waɪnd/	wound /waʊnd/	wound /waʊnd/
withdraw	withdrew	withdrawn
withhold	withheld	withheld
withstand	withstood	withstood
wring	wrung	wrung
write	wrote	written

Full forms	Short forms	Negative short forms
***be* present tense**		
I am	I'm	I'm not
you are	you're	you aren't/you're not
he is	he's	he isn't/he's not
she is	she's	she isn't/she's not
it is	it's	it isn't/it's not
we are	we're	we aren't/we're not
you are	you're	you aren't/you're not
they are	they're	they aren't/they're not
***be* past tense**		
I was	—	I wasn't
you were	—	you weren't
he was	—	he wasn't
she was	—	she wasn't
it was	—	it wasn't
we were	—	we weren't
you were	—	you weren't
they were	—	they weren't
***have* present tense**		
I have	I've	I haven't/I've not
you have	you've	you haven't/you've not
he has	he's	he hasn't/he's not
she has	she's	she hasn't/she's not
it has	it's	it hasn't/it's not
we have	we've	we haven't/we've not
you have	you've	you haven't/you've not
they have	they've	they haven't/they've not
***have* past tense** (all persons)		
had	I'd you'd etc.	hadn't
***do* present tense**		
I do	—	I don't
you do	—	you don't
he does	—	he doesn't
she does	—	she doesn't
it does	—	it doesn't
we do	—	we don't
you do	—	you don't
they do	—	they don't
***do* past tense** (all persons)		
did	—	didn't

	be	*do*	*have*
present participle	being	doing	having
past participle	been	done	had

be, do, have

- The negative full forms are formed by adding **not**.
- Questions in the present and past are formed by placing the verb before the subject:
  ▸ *am I?* *isn't he?* *was I?* *weren't we?* *do I?* *don't you?* *did I?* *didn't I?* *have I?* *hadn't they?* etc.
- Questions using the negative full form are more formal:
  ▸ *has he not?* *do you not?* etc.
- The short negative question form for **I am** is **aren't**:
  ▸ *aren't I?*
- When **do** or **have** is used as a main verb, questions and negative statements can be formed with **do/does/doesn't** and **did/didn't**:
  ▸ *How did you do it?*
  ▸ *I don't do any teaching now.*
  ▸ *Do you have any money on you?*
  ▸ *We didn't have much time.*
- The short forms *'ve*, *'s* and *'d* are not usually used when **have** is a main verb:
  ▸ *I have a shower every morning.*
  NOT ~~*I've a shower every morning.*~~
- The short form *'s* can be added to other subjects:
  ▸ *Sally's ill.* *The car's been damaged.*
- The **other tenses** of **be**, **do** and **have** are formed in the same way as those of other verbs:
  ▸ *will be* *would be* *has been*
  will do *would do* *has done*
  will have *would have* *have had*; etc.
- The **pronunciation** of each form of **be**, **do** and **have** is given at its entry in the dictionary.

Verbs

Transitive and intransitive

- ▸ *He sighed.*
  ▸ *She cut her hand.*
  ▸ *The soup tastes salty.*

Each of these sentences has a subject (**he**, **she**, **the soup**) and a verb (**sigh**, **cut**, **taste**).

In the first sentence, **sigh** stands alone. Verbs like this are called INTRANSITIVE.

In the second sentence, **cut** is TRANSITIVE because it is used with an object (**her hand**).

In the third sentence, **taste** has no object but it cannot be used alone without an adjective. An adjective like **salty** that gives more information about the subject of a verb is called a COMPLEMENT. Verbs that take complements are called LINKING VERBS.

Verb codes

- In the dictionary, grammatical codes at the start of each meaning show you whether a verb is always transitive or always intransitive, or whether it can be sometimes transitive and sometimes intransitive.

The code [I] shows you that in this meaning **change** is always intransitive.

change /tʃeɪndʒ/ *verb, noun*
▪ *verb*
▸ BECOME/MAKE DIFFERENT **1** [I] to become different: *Rick hasn't changed. He looks exactly the same as he did at school.* ◇ *changing attitudes towards education* ◇ *Her life changed completely when she won the lottery.* **2** [T] **~ sb/sth** to make sb/sth different: *Fame hasn't really changed him.* ◇ *Computers have changed the way people work.* **3** [I, T] to pass or make sb/sth pass from one state or form into another: *Wait for the traffic lights to change.* ◇ **~ (from A) to/into B** *The lights changed from red to green.* ◇ *Caterpillars change into butterflies.* ◇ **~ sb/sth (from A) to/into B** *With a wave of her magic wand, she changed the frog into a handsome prince.*

The code [T] shows you that in this meaning **change** is always transitive.

The code [I, T] shows you that in this meaning **change** is sometimes intransitive and sometimes transitive.

Transitive verbs are the most common type of verb. A verb that is always transitive in all its meanings is just marked *verb*, and no other verb code is given.

Verb frames

- Transitive verbs can take different types of object – a noun, phrase or clause. Both transitive and intransitive verbs can combine with different prepositions or adverbs. Different linking verbs can take either adjectives or nouns as complements.

pro·vide /prəˈvaɪd/ *verb*
1 to give sth to sb or make it available for them to use SYN **supply**: **~ sth** *The hospital has a commitment to provide the best possible medical care.* ◇ *The report was not expected to provide any answers.* ◇ *Please answer questions in the space provided.* ◇ **~ sth for sb** *We are here to provide a service for the public.* ◇ **~ sb with sth** *We are here to provide the public with a service.* **2 ~ that...** (*formal*) (of a law or rule) to state that sth will or must happen SYN **stipulate**: *The final section provides that any work produced for the company is thereafter owned by the company.* ➔ see also PROVISION

In the dictionary, the different patterns (or 'verb frames') in which a verb can be used are shown in **bold type**, usually just before an example showing that pattern in context.

If a particular verb, or one particular meaning of a verb, is always used in the same pattern, this pattern is shown in **bold type** before the definition.

Intransitive verbs [I]

- Intransitive verbs do not take an object. When they are used alone after a subject, there is no verb frame.

The example showing this use will usually appear first, before any other patterns and examples.

shiver /ˈʃɪvə(r)/ *verb, noun*
▪ *verb* [I] (of a person) to shake slightly because you are cold, frightened, excited, etc: *Don't stand outside shivering—come inside and get warm!* ◇ *He shivered at the thought of the cold, dark sea.* ◇ **~ with sth** *to shiver with cold/excitement/pleasure, etc.*

Some intransitive verbs are often used with a particular preposition or adverb. This pattern will be shown in bold type, usually before an example.

- Some intransitive verbs are always or usually used with a preposition or adverb, but not always the same one. These are often verbs showing movement in a particular direction:
  ▸ *A runaway car came **hurtling towards** us.*
  ▸ *A group of swans **floated by**.*

In the dictionary this use will be shown by the frame + **adv./prep.** If a preposition or adverb is often used, but not always, there will be brackets round the frame: (+ **adv./prep.**)

hur·tle /ˈhɜːtl; *NAmE* ˈhɜːrtl/ *verb* [I] + **adv./prep.** to move very fast in a particular direction: *A runaway car **came hurtling** towards us.*

Transitive verbs [T]

- Transitive verbs must have an object. The object can be a noun or a pronoun, a noun phrase or a clause.

  For information on verbs that take a clause as the object, see page R7.

  The frames used to show a transitive verb with a noun, pronoun or noun phrase as object are ~ **sb**, ~ **sth** and ~ **sb/sth**.

ac·com·mo·date AW /əˈkɒmədeɪt; *NAmE* əˈkɑːm-/ *verb* **1** [T] **~ sb** to provide sb with a room or place to sleep, live or sit: *The hotel can accommodate up to 500 guests.* **2** [T] **~ sb/sth** to provide enough space for sb/sth: *Over 70 minutes of music can be accommodated on one CD.* **3** [T] **~ sth** (*formal*) to consider sth, such as sb's opinion or a fact, and be influenced by it when you are deciding what to do or explaining sth: *Our proposal tries to accommodate the special needs of minority groups.*

~ **sb** is used when the object is a person.

~ **sth** is used when the object is a thing.

~ **sb/sth** is used when the object can be a person or a thing.

As with intransitive verbs, some transitive verbs are often used with a preposition or an adverb.

If there is a wide range of possible prepositions or adverbs a frame such as **sb/sth** + **adv./prep.** is used.

hack /hæk/ *verb, noun*
▪ *verb* **1** [T, I] to cut sb/sth with rough, heavy blows: **~ sb/sth + adv./prep.** *I hacked the dead branches off.* ◇ *They were hacked to death as they tried to escape.* ◇ *We had to* ***hack our way*** *through the jungle.* ◇ **+ adv./prep.** *We hacked away at the bushes.* **2** [T] **~ sb/sth + adv./prep.** to kick sth roughly or without control: *He hacked the ball away.* **3** (*computing*) [I, T] to secretly find a way of looking at and/or changing information on sb else's computer system without permission: **~ into sth** *He hacked into the bank's computer.* ◇ **~ sth** *They had hacked secret data.*

If a particular preposition or adverb is used, then it is given in the frame.

Transitive verbs with two objects

- Some verbs, like **sell** and **buy**, can be used with two objects. This is shown by the frame ~ **sb sth**:
  - ▸ *I sold Jim a car.*
  - ▸ *I bought Mary a book.*

  You can often express the same idea by using the verb as an ordinary transitive verb and adding a prepositional phrase starting with **to** or **for**:
  - ▸ *I* ***sold*** *a car* ***to*** *Jim.*
  - ▸ *I* ***bought*** *a book* ***for*** *Mary.*

  These will be shown by the frames ~ **to sb** and ~ **for sb**.

bake 0-ᴡ /beɪk/ *verb*
1 0-ᴡ [T, I] to cook food in an oven without extra fat or liquid; to be cooked in this way: **~ (sth)** *baked apples* ◇ *the delicious smell of baking bread* ◇ **~ sth for sb** *I'm baking a birthday cake for Alex.* ◇ **~ sb sth** *I'm baking Alex a cake.*
⊃ COLLOCATIONS at COOKING ⊃ VISUAL VOCAB page V24

A pair of examples, with different frames, shows the same idea expressed in two different ways.

Linking verbs

- ▸ *His voice sounds hoarse.*
  ▸ *Elena became a doctor.*

  In these sentences the linking verb (**sound**, **become**) is followed by a complement, an adjective (**hoarse**) or a noun phrase (**a doctor**) that tells you more about the subject.

  Verbs that have an adjective as the complement have the frame + **adj.**, and verbs with a noun phrase as the complement have the frame + **noun**. Verbs that can take either an adjective or a noun phrase as the complement may have the frame + **adj./noun**, or the two frames may be shown separately with an example for each.

be·come 0-ᴡ /bɪˈkʌm/ *verb* (be·came /bɪˈkeɪm/, be·come)
1 0-ᴡ *linking verb* to start to be sth: **+ adj.** *It was becoming more and more difficult to live on his salary.* ◇ *It soon became apparent that no one was going to come.* ◇ *She was becoming confused.* ◇ **+ noun** *She became queen in 1952.* ◇ *The bill will become law next year.*

The linking verb **become** can be used with either an adjective or a noun phrase.

There are also verbs that take both an object and a complement:
- ▸ *She considered herself lucky.*
- ▸ *They elected him president.*

The complement (**lucky**, **president**) tells you more about the object (**herself**, **him**) of the verb. The frames for these verbs are ~ **sb/sth + adj.**, **sb/sth + noun** or **sb/sth + adj./noun**.

Verbs used with 'that clauses'

- The frame ~ **that...** shows that a verb is followed by a clause beginning with **that**:
  - ▸ *She* ***replied that*** *she would prefer to walk.*

  However, it is not always necessary to use the word **that** itself:
  - ▸ *I* ***said that*** *he would come.*
  - ▸ *I* ***said*** *he would come.*

  These two sentences mean the same. In the dictionary they are shown by the frame

~ (that)... and a single example is given, using brackets:

▸ ***I said (that)*** *he would come.*

Some verbs can be used with both a noun phrase and a 'that clause'. The frame for verbs used like this is **~ sb that...** or **~ sb (that)...**:

▸ *Can you* ***remind me that*** *I need to buy some milk?*

▸ *I* ***told her (that)*** *I would be late.*

Verbs used with 'wh- clauses'

■ A 'wh-clause' (or phrase) is a clause or phrase beginning with one of the following words: **wh**ich, **wh**at, **wh**ose, **wh**y, **wh**ere, **wh**en, **wh**o, **wh**om, how, if, **wh**ether:

▸ *I* ***wonder what*** *the new job will be like.*

▸ *He doesn't* ***care how*** *he looks.*

▸ *Did you* ***see which*** *way they went?*

In the dictionary, verbs used like this have a frame such as **~ how, what, etc. ...** or **~ why, where, etc. ...**

The particular 'wh-words' given in each frame will be words that are typical for that verb, but the 'etc.' shows that other 'wh- clauses' are possible.

won·der 0-π /ˈwʌndə(r)/ *verb, noun*
■ ***verb* 1** 0-π [T, I] to think about sth and try to decide what is true, what will happen, what you should do, etc: **~ who, where, etc...** *I wonder who she is.* ◇ *I was just beginning to wonder where you were.* ◇ **~ (about sth)** *'Why do you want to know?' 'No particular reason. I was just wondering.'* ◇ *We were wondering about next April for the wedding.* ◇ **+ speech** *'What should I do now?' she wondered.* **2** 0-π [T] **~ if, whether...** used as a polite way of asking a question or asking sb to do sth: *I wonder if you can help me.* ◇ *I was wondering whether you'd like to come to a party.*

If there is no 'etc.' in the frame, then this verb or meaning can only take the particular 'wh-words' that are listed.

Some verbs can be used with both a noun phrase and a 'wh-clause'. Verbs used like this have a frame such as **~ sb where, when, etc. ...**

▸ *I* ***asked him where*** *the library was.*

▸ *I* ***told her when*** *the baby was due.*

▸ *He* ***teaches his students how*** *to research a subject thoroughly.*

Verbs with infinitive phrases

■ **Eat** and **to eat** are both the infinitive form of the verb. **Eat** is called a BARE INFINITIVE and **to eat** is called a TO-INFINITIVE. Most verbs that take an infinitive are used with the to-infinitive. The frame for these verbs is **~ to do sth**:

▸ *The goldfish* ***need to be fed.***

▸ *She never* ***learned to read.***

Some verbs can be used with both a noun phrase and a to-infinitive. The frame for these is **~ sb to do sth**, **~ sth to do sth** or **~ sb/sth to do sth**. The noun phrase can be the object of the main verb:

▸ *Can you persuade* ***Sheila*** *to chair the meeting?*

or the noun phrase and the infinitive phrase together can be the object:

▸ *I expected* ***her to pass*** *her driving test first time.*

▸ *We'd love* ***you to come*** *and visit us.*

Only two groups of verbs are used with a bare infinitive (without **to**). One is the group of MODAL VERBS (or MODAL AUXILIARIES). These are the special verbs like **can**, **must** and **will** that go before a main verb and show that an action is possible, necessary, etc. These verbs have special treatment in the dictionary and are labelled *modal verb*.

A small group of ordinary verbs, for example **see** and **hear**, can be used with a noun phrase and a bare infinitive. The frame for these is **~ sb do sth**, **~ sth do sth** or **~ sb/sth do sth**:

▸ *She* ***watched him eat*** *his lunch.*

▸ *Did you* ***hear the phone ring*** *just then?*

Verbs with '*-ing* phrases'

■ An '*-ing* phrase' is a phrase containing a PRESENT PARTICIPLE (or GERUND). The present participle is the form of the verb that ends in *-ing*, for example **doing**, **eating** or **catching**. Sometimes the '*-ing* phrase' consists of a present participle on its own. The frame for a verb that takes an '*-ing* phrase' is **~ doing sth**:

▸ *She never stops talking!*

▸ *I started looking for a job two years ago.*

Some verbs can be used with both a noun phrase and an '*-ing* phrase'. The frame for this is **~ sb doing sth**, **~ sth doing sth** or **~ sb/sth doing sth**. The noun phrase can be the object of the main verb:

▸ *His comments set* ***me*** *thinking.*

▸ *I can smell* ***something*** *nice cooking.*

or the noun phrase and the '*-ing* phrase' together can be the object:

▸ *I hate* ***him joking*** (= the fact that he jokes) *about serious things.*

In this pattern, you can replace **him** with the possessive pronoun **his**:

▸ *I hate* ***his joking*** *about serious things.*

However, sentences with a possessive pronoun sound very formal and the object pronoun is more common, especially in American English. In cases where the verb itself is formal and the possessive pronoun may well be used, this is shown in the dictionary entry.

Verbs with direct speech

- Verbs like **say**, **answer** and **demand** can be used either to report what somebody has said using a 'that clause' or to give their exact words in DIRECT SPEECH, using quotation marks (''). Verbs that can be used with direct speech have the frame + **speech**. Compare these two sentences:
  - + **speech** *'It's snowing,' she said.*
  - ~ **(that)…** *She said (that) it was snowing.*

  Some verbs can be used with both direct speech and a noun phrase, to show who is being spoken to. The frame for this is ~ **sb** + **speech**:
  - *'Tom's coming to lunch,' she **told him**.*

Verbs in the passive

- Most transitive verbs can be used in the passive:
  - *Jill's behaviour **annoyed me**.*
  - ***I was annoyed by** Jill's behaviour.*

If a verb can be active or passive, the same verb frame is used. If the verb is often passive, there will be an example in the passive.

con·firm 0‑ᴡ AW /kən'fɜːm; *NAmE* -'fɜːrm/ *verb*
1 0‑ᴡ to state or show that sth is definitely true or correct, especially by providing evidence: **~ sth** *Rumours of job losses were later confirmed* ◇ *His guilty expression confirmed my suspicions.* ◇ *Please write to confirm your reservation* (= say that it is definite). ◇ **~ (that)…** *Has everyone confirmed (that) they're coming?* ◇ **~ what/when, etc…** *Can you confirm what happened?* ◇ **it is confirmed that…** *It has been confirmed that the meeting will take place next week.* **2** 0‑ᴡ **~ sth** | **~ sb (in sth)** to make sb feel or believe sth even more strongly: *The walk in the mountains confirmed his fear of heights.* **3** 0‑ᴡ to make a position, an agreement, etc. more definite or official; to establish sb/sth firmly: **~ sth** *After a*

If a pattern is *only* used in the passive, then the frame is put in the passive. This happens especially with verbs that take 'it' and a 'that clause'.

If a transitive verb cannot be used in the passive, the label [no passive] appears before the definition.

Verbs in different patterns

- Many verbs, for example **watch**, can be used in a number of different ways:
  - **~ sb/sth do sth** *I watched him eat.*
  - **~ sb/sth doing sth** *I watched him eating.*
  - **~ sb/sth** *I watched the pianist's left hand.*
  - **~ what, how, etc. …** *I watched how the pianist used her left hand.*

  The dictionary entry for each verb shows the different ways in which it can be used by giving a range of example sentences. The frame before each example shows what type of grammatical pattern is being used. When an example follows another one illustrating the same pattern, the frame is not repeated.

  Sometimes patterns can combine with each other to form a longer pattern. This happens especially with patterns involving particular prepositions or adverbs; and sometimes there is a choice of two or three different prepositions or adverbs:
  - **~ sth** *We shared the pizza.*
  - **~ sth out** *We shared out the pizza.*
  - **~ sth among sb** *We shared the pizza among the four of us.*
  - **~ sth between sb** *We shared the pizza between the four of us.*
  - **~ sth out among sb** *We shared the pizza out among the four of us.*
  - **~ sth out between sb** *We shared the pizza out between the four of us.*

  In cases like this the dictionary does not always give a separate frame and example for each different combination. It may use brackets to show where part of a long frame can be left out, and slashes to show where there is a choice between two or three different words in the frame:

▸ DIVIDE BETWEEN PEOPLE **2** 0‑ᴡ [T] **~ sth** (**out**) (**among/between sb**) to divide sth between two or more people: *We shared the pizza between the four of us.* ➲ see also JOB-SHARING, POWER-SHARING

The frame ~ **(sb)**, ~ **(sth)** or ~ **(sb/sth)** may also be used, where a verb can be used without an object (that is, it can be intransitive), but is more commonly used with a noun phrase as object. In these cases the more common, transitive, use, is given in the first example(s), and any intransitive examples are placed after that:

broad·cast 0‑ᴡ /'brɔːdkɑːst; *NAmE* -kæst/ *verb, noun*
■ *verb* (**broad·cast, broad·cast** or **broad·cast, broad·casted**)
1 0‑ᴡ [T, I] **~ (sth)** to send out programmes on television or radio: *The concert will be **broadcast live*** (= at the same time as it takes place) *tomorrow evening.* ◇ *They began broadcasting in 1922.* ➲ COLLOCATIONS at TELEVISION

Sb and **sth** may also appear within brackets within longer frames, for example to show a verb that can take a preposition, adverb or 'that clause' either with or without a noun phrase as another object:

warn 0‑ᴡ /wɔːn; *NAmE* wɔːrn/ *verb*
1 0‑ᴡ [T, I] to tell sb about sth, especially sth dangerous or unpleasant that is likely to happen, so that they can avoid it: **~ sb** *I tried to warn him, but he wouldn't listen.* ◇ *If you're thinking of getting a dog, **be warned**—they take a lot of time and money.* ◇ **~ (sb) about/against sb/sth** *He warned us against pickpockets.* ◇ **~ (sb) of sth** *Police have warned of possible delays.* ◇ **~ (sb) that…** *She was warned that if she did it again she would lose her job.* ◇ **~ sb what, how, etc…** *I had been warned what to expect.* ◇ **~ (sb) + speech** *'Beware of pickpockets,' she warned (him).*

Phrasal verbs

What are phrasal verbs?

- ▸ *Jan **turned down** the chance to work abroad.*
  ▸ *Buying that new car has really **eaten into** my savings.*
  ▸ *I don't think I can **put up with** his behaviour much longer.*

  PHRASAL VERBS (sometimes called MULTI-WORD VERBS) are verbs that consist of two, or sometimes three, words. The first word is a verb and it is followed by an adverb (turn **down**) or a preposition (eat **into**) or both (put **up with**). These adverbs or prepositions are sometimes called PARTICLES.

- In this dictionary, phrasal verbs are listed at the end of the entry for the main verb in a section marked PHR V. They are listed in alphabetical order of the particles following them:

PHR V ˌ**fight ˈback (against sb/sth)** to resist strongly or attack sb who has attacked you: *Don't let them bully you. Fight back!* ◇ *It is time to fight back against street crime.* ˌ**fight sth↔ˈback/ˈdown** to try hard not to do or show sth, especially not to show your feelings: *I was fighting back the tears.* ◇ *He fought down his disgust.* ˌ**fight sb/sth↔ˈoff** to resist sb/sth by fighting against them/it: *The jeweller was stabbed as he tried to fight the robbers off.* ˌ**fight ˈout sth** | ˌ**fight it ˈout** to fight or argue until an argument has been settled: *The conflict is still being fought out.* ◇ *They hadn't reached any agreement so we left them to fight it out.*

Meaning of phrasal verbs

- ▸ *He **sat down** on the bed.*

  The meaning of some phrasal verbs, such as **sit down**, is easy to guess because the verb and the particle keep their usual meaning. However, many phrasal verbs have idiomatic meanings that you need to learn. The separate meanings of **put**, **up** and **with**, for example, do not add up to the meaning of **put up with** (= tolerate).

- Some particles have particular meanings that are the same when they are used with a number of different verbs:
  ▸ *I didn't see the point of **hanging around** waiting for him, so I went home.*
  ▸ *I wish you wouldn't leave all those books **lying around**.*

  Around adds the meaning of 'with no particular purpose or aim' and is also used in a similar way with many other verbs, such as **play**, **sit** and **wait**.

- The meaning of a phrasal verb can sometimes be explained with a one-word verb. However, phrasal verbs are frequently used in spoken English and, if there is a one-word equivalent, it is usually more formal in style:
  ▸ *I wish my ears didn't **stick out** so much.*
  ▸ *The garage **projects** five metres beyond the front of the house.*

  Both **stick out** and **project** have the same meaning – 'to extend beyond a surface' – but they are very different in style. **Stick out** is used in informal contexts, and **project** in formal or technical contexts.

Grammar of phrasal verbs

- Phrasal verbs can be TRANSITIVE (they take an object) or INTRANSITIVE (they have no object). Some phrasal verbs can be used in both ways:
  ▸ *For heaven's sake **shut** her **up**. (transitive)*
  ▸ *He told me to **shut up**. (intransitive)*

- INTRANSITIVE phrasal verbs are written in the dictionary without **sb** (somebody) or **sth** (something) after them. This shows that they do not have an object:

ˌ**eat ˈout** to have a meal in a restaurant, etc. rather than at home: *Do you feel like eating out tonight?*

  Eat out is intransitive, and the two parts of the verb cannot be separated by any other word. You can say:
  ▸ *Shall we eat out tonight?*
  BUT NOT ~~*Shall we eat tonight out?*~~

- In order to use TRANSITIVE phrasal verbs correctly, you need to know where to put the object. With some phrasal verbs (often called SEPARABLE verbs), the object can go either between the verb and the particle or after the particle:
  ▸ *She **tore** the letter **up**.*
  ▸ *She **tore up** the letter.*

- When the object is a long phrase, it usually comes after the particle:
  ▸ *She **tore up** all the letters he had sent her.*

- When the object is a pronoun (for example **it** standing for 'the letter'), it must always go between the verb and the particle:
  ▸ *She read the letter and then **tore** it **up**.*

- In the dictionary, verbs that are separable are written like this:
  tear sth ↔ up

- The double arrow between the object and the particle shows that the object may come either before or after the particle:

ˌcall sth↔ˈoff 🔑 to cancel sth; to decide that sth will not happen: *to call off a deal/trip/strike* ◇ *They have called off their engagement* (= decided not to get married). ◇ *The game was called off because of bad weather.*

You can say:
▸ *They **called** the deal **off**.*
AND *They **called off** the deal.*

- With other phrasal verbs (sometimes called INSEPARABLE verbs), the two parts of the verb cannot be separated by an object:
▸ *I didn't really **take to** her husband.*
NOT ~~*I didn't really take her husband to.*~~
▸ *I didn't really **take to** him.*
NOT ~~*I didn't really take him to.*~~

In the dictionary, verbs that are inseparable are written like this:
take to sb

When you see **sb** or **sth** after the two parts of a phrasal verb, and there is no double arrow, you know that they cannot be separated by an object:

ˌrun ˈinto sb (*informal*) to meet sb by chance: *Guess who I ran into today!*

You can say:
▸ *I **ran into** Joe yesterday.*
BUT NOT ~~*I ran Joe into.*~~

- There are a few phrasal verbs in which the two parts of the verb must be separated by the object. You can say:
▸ *They changed the plans and **messed** everyone **around**.*
BUT NOT ~~*They changed the plans and messed around everyone.*~~

- In the dictionary, these verbs are written like this:
mess sb around
When you see **sb** or **sth** between the two parts of a phrasal verb and there is no double arrow, you know that they must be separated by the object.

- Some transitive phrasal verbs can be made passive:
▸ *The deal **has been called off**.*
When this is common, you will find an example at the dictionary entry.

Phrasal verbs used with phrases and clauses

Like other verbs, some phrasal verbs can be used with another phrase or clause. The different types of clause and phrase are explained on pages R7–8. When a phrasal verb can be used with a particular type of clause or phrase, an example is given in the dictionary entry, labelled with a special frame:

~ that	*We **found out** later **that** we had been at the same school.*
~ how, what, etc ...	*I can't **figure out how** to do this.*
~ to do sth	*It didn't **occur to** her **to ask** for help.*
~ doing sth	*I didn't **bargain on finding** Matthew there as well.*
+ speech	***'Help!'** he **cried out**.*

Related nouns

A particular phrasal verb may have a noun related to it. This noun will be mentioned at the verb entry:

ˌbreak ˈin 🔑 to enter a building by force: *Burglars had broken in while we were away.* ➲ related noun BREAK-IN
ˌbreak sb/sth ˈin 1 to train sb/sth in sth new that they must do: *to break in new recruits* ◇ *The young horse was not yet broken in* (= trained to carry a rider). **2** to wear sth, especially new shoes, until they become comfortable
ˌbreak ˈin (on sth) to interrupt or disturb sth: *She longed to break in on their conversation but didn't want to appear rude.* ◇ **+ speech** *'I didn't do it!' she broke in.*
ˌbreak ˈinto sth 1 🔑 to enter a building by force; to open a car, etc. by force: *We had our car broken into last week.* ➲ related noun BREAK-IN **2** to begin laughing, singing, etc. suddenly: *As the President's car drew up, the crowd broke into loud applause.*

ˌbreak ˈout 🔑 (of war, fighting or other unpleasant events) to start suddenly: *They had escaped to America shortly before war broke out in 1939.* ◇ *Fighting had broken out between rival groups of fans.* ◇ *Fire broke out during the night.* ➲ related noun OUTBREAK **ˌbreak ˈout (of sth)** to escape from a place or situation: *Several prisoners broke out of the jail.* ◇ *She needed to break out of her daily routine and do something exciting.* ➲ related noun BREAKOUT

A noun is often related in meaning to only one or two of the phrasal verbs using a particle. **Break-in** is related to **break in** and the first meaning of **break into sth**, but not to **break sb/sth in** or **break in (on sth)**. **Breakout** is related to **break out (of sth)**, whereas the noun **outbreak** relates to **break out**.

Nouns and adjectives

Nouns
Countable and uncountable

The two biggest groups of nouns are COUNTABLE nouns (or COUNT nouns) and UNCOUNTABLE nouns (also called UNCOUNT nouns or MASS nouns). Most countable nouns are words for separate things that can be counted, like **apples**, **books** or **teachers**. Uncountable nouns are usually words for things that are thought of as a quantity or mass, like **water** or **time**.

However, there are some nouns in English that you might expect to be countable but which are not. For example, **furniture**, **information** and **equipment** are all uncountable nouns in English, although they are countable in some other languages.

Countable nouns [C]

A countable noun has a singular form and a plural form. When it is singular, it must always have a DETERMINER (a word such as **a**, **the**, **both**, **each**) in front of it. In the plural it can be used with or without a determiner:

▸ *I'm having **a** driving **lesson** this afternoon.*
▸ *I've had **several lessons** already.*
▸ ***Lessons** cost £20 an hour.*

Countable nouns are the most common type of noun. If they have only one meaning, or if all the meanings are countable, they are just marked *noun*. For nouns that have a number of meanings, some of which are not countable, each meaning that is countable is marked [C].

Uncountable nouns [U]

An uncountable noun has only one form, not a separate singular and plural. It can be used with or without a determiner:

▸ *Can we make **space** for an extra chair?*
▸ *There isn't **much space** in this room.*

If an uncountable noun is the subject of a verb, the verb is singular:

▸ *Extra money **has been found** for this project.*

With nouns such as **furniture**, **information** and **equipment**, as with many other uncountable nouns, you can talk about amounts of the thing or separate parts of the thing by using phrases like **a piece of**, **three items of**, **some bits of**. Nouns like **piece**, **item** and **bit** are called PARTITIVES when used in this way:

▸ *I picked up **some information** that might interest you.*
▸ *I picked up **two pieces of information** that might interest you.*

Plural nouns [pl.]

Some nouns are always plural and have no singular form. Nouns that refer to things that have two parts joined together, for example **glasses**, **jeans** and **scissors**, are often plural nouns. You can usually also talk about **a pair of jeans**, **a pair of scissors**, etc.

▸ *I'm going to buy **some** new **jeans**.*
▸ *I'm going to buy **a** new **pair of jeans**.*

An example is given in the entry for the noun to show that it can be used in this way.

Some plural nouns, such as **police** and **cattle**, look as if they are singular. Nouns like this usually refer to a group of people or animals of a particular type, when they are considered together as one unit. They also take a plural verb:

▸ ***Police are searching** for a man who escaped from Pentonville prison today.*
▸ *The **cattle are fed** on barley and grass.*

Singular nouns [sing.]

Some nouns are always singular and have no plural form. Many nouns like this can be used in only a limited number of ways. For example, some singular nouns must be or are often used with a particular determiner in front of them or with a particular preposition after them. The correct determiner or preposition is shown before the definition. In the case of **fillip** the pattern given is **a ~ (to/for sth)**:

> **fil·lip** /ˈfɪlɪp/ *noun* [sing.] **a ~ (to/for sth)** (*formal*) a thing or person that causes sth to improve suddenly SYN **boost**: *A drop in interest rates gave a welcome fillip to the housing market.*

Nouns with singular or plural verbs
[sing.+sing./pl. v.] [C+sing./pl. v.] [U+sing./pl. v.]

In British English some singular nouns (or countable nouns in their singular form) can be used with a plural verb as well as a singular one. Nouns like this usually refer to a group of people, an organization, or a place, and can be thought of either as the organization, place or group (singular) or as many individual people (plural). In the dictionary an example is usually given to show agreement with a singular and a plural verb:

▸ *The **Vatican has/have** issued a further statement this morning.*

▸ *The **committee has/have** decided to dismiss him.*

These nouns are marked [sing.+sing./pl. v.] if they are always singular in form, and [C+sing./pl. v.] if they also have a plural form. The plural form always agrees with a plural verb.

NOTE In American English the singular form of these nouns must take a singular verb:

▸ *The government **says it is** committed to tax reform.*

Some uncountable nouns can be used with a plural verb as well as a singular one. These include some nouns that end in **-s** and therefore look as though they are plural:

▸ *His **whereabouts are/is** still unknown.*

and some nouns that refer to a group of people or things and can be thought of either as a group (singular) or as many individual people or things (plural):

▸ ***Personnel is/are** currently reviewing pay scales.*

Patterns with nouns

- Many nouns are followed by a particular preposition, adverb or other pattern:
  ▸ *My comments were taken as an allegation of negligence.*

The correct pattern to use is shown in **bold type**, either before the definition or before an individual example. Where any part of a pattern is optional, it is given in brackets.

al·le·ga·tion /ˌæləˈɡeɪʃn/ *noun* a public statement that is made without giving proof, accusing sb of doing sth that is wrong or illegal **SYN accusation**: *to **investigate/deny/withdraw an allegation*** ◇ **~ of sth** *Several newspapers **made allegations** of corruption in the city's police department.* ◇ **~ (of sth) against sb** *allegations of dishonesty against him* ◇ **~ about sb/sth** *The committee has made serious allegations about interference in its work.* ◇ **~ that...** *an allegation that he had been dishonest* ➲ SYNONYMS at CLAIM

The example sentences show the patterns in use.

Adjectives

- Many adjectives can be used both before a noun:
  ▸ *a serious expression*
  ▸ *grey hair*

  and after a LINKING VERB:
  ▸ *She looked serious.*
  ▸ *His hair had turned grey.*

- However, some adjectives, or particular meanings of adjectives, are always used before a noun, and cannot be used after a linking verb. They are called ATTRIBUTIVE adjectives:
  ▸ *the chief reason*

- Others are only used after a linking verb. They are called PREDICATIVE adjectives:
  ▸ *The baby is awake.*

→ For more information about LINKING VERBS, look at page R6.

[only before noun] [usually before noun]

Attributive adjectives are labelled [only before noun]. The label [usually before noun] is used when it is rare but possible to use the adjective after a verb.

Senses **1** and **3** can only be used before a noun.

con·tin·en·tal /ˌkɒntɪˈnentl; *NAmE* ˌkɑːn-/ *adj., noun* ■ ***adj.*** **1** (also **Continental**) [only before noun] (*BrE*) of or in the continent of Europe, not including Britain and Ireland: *a popular continental holiday resort* ◇ *Britain's continental neighbours* **2** (*BrE*) following the customs of countries in western and southern Europe: *a continental lifestyle* ◇ *The shutters and the balconies make the street look almost continental.* **3** [only before noun] connected with the main part of the N American continent: *Prices are often higher in Hawaii than in the continental United States.*

Sense **2** has no grammar label because it can be used both before a noun and after a linking verb.

[not before noun] [not usually before noun]

Predicative adjectives, labelled [not before noun], are used only after a linking verb, never before a noun. The label [not usually before noun] is used when it is rare but possible to use the adjective before a noun.

The grammar label straight after the *adj.* label shows that both meanings must be used after a linking verb.

rife /raɪf/ *adj.* [not before noun] **1** if sth bad or unpleasant is **rife** in a place, it is very common there **SYN widespread**: *It is a country where corruption is rife.* ◇ *Rumours are rife that he is going to resign.* **2 ~ (with sth)** full of sth bad or unpleasant: *Los Angeles is rife with gossip about the stars' private lives.*

[after noun]

A few adjectives always follow the noun they describe. This is shown in the dictionary by the label [after noun]:

gal·ore /ɡəˈlɔː(r)/ *adj.* [after noun] (*informal*) in large quantities: *There will be games and prizes galore.*

Collocation

What is collocation?

COLLOCATION is the way in which particular words tend to occur or belong together. For example, you can say:

▶ *Meals will be served outside on the terrace, **weather permitting**.*
BUT NOT ~~*Meals will be served outside on the terrace, weather allowing.*~~

Both these sentences seem to mean the same thing: **allow** and **permit** have very similar meanings. But in this combination only **permitting** is correct. It COLLOCATES with **weather** and **allowing** does not.

Types of collocation

In order to write and speak natural and correct English, you need to know, for example:

- which adjectives are used with a particular noun
- which nouns a particular adjective is used with
- which verbs are used with a particular noun
- which adverbs are used to intensify a particular adjective

Collocation in this dictionary

To find out which adjectives to use with a particular noun, look at the examples at the entry for the noun. Typical adjectives used with the noun are separated by a slash (/):

Can you say '**pink** wine'?

> **wine** 0‑╥ /waɪn/ *noun, verb*
> ■ ***noun* 1** 0‑╥ [U, C] an alcoholic drink made from the juice of GRAPES that has been left to FERMENT. There are many different kinds of wine: *a bottle of wine* ◇ *a glass of **dry/sweet wine*** ◇ ***red/rosé/white wine*** ◇ ***sparkling wine***
> ➲ see also TABLE WINE

(No, **rosé**)

If you look up an adjective you will see what nouns are commonly used with it:

Which words can be used with the adjective **heady**?

> **heady** /ˈhedi/ *adj.* (**head·ier, headi·est**) **1** [usually before noun] having a strong effect on your senses; making you feel excited and confident SYN **intoxicating**: *the heady days of youth* ◇ *the heady scent of hot spices* ◇ *a heady mixture of desire and fear* ➲ SYNONYMS at EXCITING

(**days, scent, mixture**)

Look at the examples in a noun entry to find out what verbs can be used with it:

Which verbs are used with **mortgage**?

> **mort·gage** /ˈmɔːɡɪdʒ; *NAmE* ˈmɔːrɡ-/ *noun, verb*
> ■ ***noun*** (also *informal* ˌ**home ˈloan**) a legal agreement by which a bank or similar organization lends you money to buy a house, etc., and you pay the money back over a particular number of years; the sum of money that you borrow: *to **apply for/take out/pay off a mortgage*** ◇ *mortgage rates* (= of interest) ◇ *a mortgage on the house* ◇ *a mortgage of £60 000* ◇ *monthly mortgage payments*

(**apply for, take out, pay off**)

If you look up an adjective, you will see which adverbs you can use to intensify it:

Strongly or **bitterly** disappointed?

> **dis·ap·point·ed** 0‑╥ /ˌdɪsəˈpɔɪntɪd/ *adj.*
> upset because sth you hoped for has not happened or been as good, successful, etc. as you expected: **~ (at/by sth)** *They were **bitterly disappointed** at the result of the game.* ◇ *I was disappointed by the quality of the wine.* ◇ **~ (in/with sb/sth)** *I'm disappointed in you—I really thought I could trust you!* ◇ *I was very disappointed with myself.* ◇ **~ (to see, hear, etc.)** *He was disappointed to see she wasn't at the party.* ◇ **~ (that...)** *I'm disappointed (that) it was sold out.* ◇ **~ (not) to be...** *She was disappointed not to be chosen.*

(**bitterly**)

Important collocations are printed in bold type within the examples. If the meaning of the collocation is not obvious there is a short explanation after it in brackets.

having unexpected luck

hoping you will be lucky

> **luck** 0‑╥ /lʌk/ *noun, verb*
> ■ ***noun*** [U] **1** 0‑╥ good things that happen to you by chance, not because of your own efforts or abilities: ***With (any) luck**, we'll be home before dark.* ◇ (*BrE*) ***With a bit of luck**, we'll finish on time.* ◇ *So far I have had no luck with finding a job.* ◇ *I **could hardly believe my luck** when he said yes.* ◇ *It was **a stroke of luck** that we found you.* ◇ ***By sheer luck** nobody was hurt in the explosion.* ◇ *We **wish her luck** in her new career.* ◇ *You're **in luck*** (= lucky) *—there's one ticket left.* ◇ *You're **out of luck**. She's not here.* ◇ *What a piece of luck!* ➲ see also BEGINNER'S LUCK **2** 0‑╥ chance; the

being lucky

hoping someone else will be lucky

not being lucky

Idioms

What are idioms?

An idiom is a phrase whose meaning is difficult or sometimes impossible to guess by looking at the meanings of the individual words it contains. For example, the phrase **be in the same boat** has a literal meaning that is easy to understand, but it also has a common idiomatic meaning:

▸ *I found the job difficult at first. But we were all in the same boat; we were all learning.*

Here, **be in the same boat** means 'to be in the same difficult or unfortunate situation'.

Some idioms are imaginative expressions such as proverbs and sayings:

▸ *Too many cooks spoil the broth.* (= If too many people are involved in something, it will not be well done.)

If the expression is well known, part of it may be left out:

▸ *Well, I knew everything would go wrong – it's the usual story of too many cooks!*

Other idioms are short expressions that are used for a particular purpose:

▸ *Hang in there!* (used to encourage somebody in a difficult situation)

▸ *Get lost!* (a rude way of saying 'go away')

Many idioms, however, are not vivid in this way. They are considered as idioms because their form is fixed:

▸ *for certain*

▸ *in any case*

Idioms in the dictionary

Idioms are defined at the entry for the first 'full' word (a noun, a verb, an adjective or an adverb) that they contain. This means ignoring any grammatical words such as articles and prepositions. Idioms follow the main senses of a word, in a section marked IDM:

> IDM **in the blink of an 'eye** very quickly; in a short time **on the 'blink** (*informal*) (of a machine) no longer working correctly

The words **in**, **the** and **on** in these idioms do not count as 'full' words, and so the idioms are not listed at the entries for these words.

Deciding where idioms start and stop is not always easy. If you hear the expression:

▸ *They decided to bury the hatchet and try to be friends again.*

you might think that **hatchet** is the only word you do not know and look that up. In fact, **bury the hatchet** is an idiomatic expression and it is defined at **bury**. At **hatchet** you will find a cross-reference directing you to **bury**:

> **hatchet** /ˈhætʃɪt/ *noun* a small AXE (= a tool with a heavy blade for chopping things) with a short handle ➲ picture at AXE IDM see BURY

Sometimes one 'full' word of an idiom can be replaced by another. For example, in the idiom **be a bag of nerves**, **bag** can be replaced by **bundle**. This is shown as **be a bag/bundle of nerves** and the idiom is defined at the first full fixed word, **nerve**. If you try to look the phrase up at either **bag** or **bundle** you will find a cross-reference to **nerve** at the end of the idioms section.

> IDM **not go a bundle on sb/sth** (*BrE, informal*) to not like sb/sth very much ➲ more at DROP *v.*, NERVE *n.*

A few very common verbs and the adjectives **bad** and **good** have so many idioms that they cannot all be listed in the entry. Instead, there is a note telling you to look at the entry for the next noun, verb, adjective, etc. in the idiom:

> IDM Most idioms containing **go** are at the entries for the nouns and adjectives in the idioms, for example **go it alone** is at **alone**.

In some idioms, many alternatives are possible. In the expression **disappear into thin air**, you could replace **disappear** with **vanish**, **melt** or **evaporate**. In the dictionary this is shown as **disappear, vanish, etc. into thin air**, showing that you can use other words with a similar meaning to disappear in the idiom. Since the first 'full' word of the idiom is not fixed, the expression is defined at **thin** with a cross-reference only at **air**.

If you cannot find an idiom in the dictionary, look it up at the entry for one of the other main words in the expression.

Some idioms only contain grammatical words such as **one**, **it**, or **in**. These idioms are defined at the first word that appears in them. For example, the idiom **one up on sb** is defined at the entry for **one**.

Idioms are given in alphabetical order within the idioms sections. Grammatical words such as **a/an** or **the**, **sb/sth** and the possessive forms **your**, **sb's**, **his**, **her**, etc., as well as words in brackets ( ) or after a slash (/), are ignored.

Notes on usage

In the dictionary you will find many notes on various aspects of usage in English. These notes are listed below according to the type of note.

Which Word?

These notes show the differences between words that are often confused. The word in **bold** shows you the entry where you can find the note.

above / over
actual / current / present
affect / effect
agenda / diary / schedule / timetable
alone / lonely / lone
also / as well / too
although / even though / though
altogether / all together
answer / reply
around / round / about
as / like
ashamed / embarrassed
awake / awaken / wake up / waken
back – at the back / at the rear / behind
baggage / luggage
bath / bathe / swim / sunbathe
begin / start
beside / besides
besides / apart from / except
blind / blindly
borrow / lend
calm / calmness
can / may
care – take care of / look after / care for
cautious / careful
close / shut
compliment / complement
country / state
court / law court / court of law
deep / deeply
disabled / handicapped
distrust / mistrust
economic / economical
especially / specially
farther / further / farthest / furthest
firstly / first of all / at first
front – in front of / in the front of
good / goodness
hard / hardly
hate / hatred
high / tall
historic / historical
infer / imply
interested / interesting / uninterested / disinterested / uninteresting
last / take
lastly / at last
light / lighting
long – (for) long / (for) a long time
loud / loudly / aloud
near / close
next / nearest
noise / sound
old – older / elder
partly / partially
peace / peacefulness
persuade / convince
quick / quickly / fast
quite / fairly / rather / pretty
regretfully / regrettably
right / rightly
rise / raise
say / tell
sensible / sensitive
shade / shadow
slow / slowly
storey / floor
surely / certainly
tight / tightly
used to / be used to
wrong / wrongly / wrongfully

Vocabulary Building

These notes help you to choose more interesting and varied words to use and so increase your vocabulary. The word in **bold** gives you the general area of meaning of the note and shows you where to find it.

approximately – ways of saying approximately
bad and very bad
a **bar** of chocolate
body – actions expressing emotions
break – verbs that mean 'break'
cry – verbs for ways of crying
do – household jobs: do or make?
face – expressions on your face
fat – saying that somebody is fat
good and very good
hand – verbs for ways of using your hands
laugh – verbs for different ways of laughing
learn – verbs for learning
nice and very nice
object – nouns for objects you can use
piece – words for pieces of things
rain and storms
smell – adjectives and nouns
teach and teachers – verbs and nouns
thin – saying that somebody is thin
thing – other words for thing
walk – verbs for ways of walking

Grammar Point

These notes help make clear points of grammar that often cause problems. The word in **bold** shows you the entry where you can find the note.

avenge / revenge
can / could / be able to / manage
dare
depend on
each / every
enjoy
half / whole / quarter
hardly / scarcely / barely / no sooner
if / whether
kind / sort
late / lately
likely
many / a lot of / lots of
modal verbs
much / a lot of / lots of
must / have (got) to / must not / don't have to
need
neither / either
none of
one / ones
per cent – expressing percentages
proportion
school
shall / will
should / ought / had better
should / would
sit
staff
used to
very / very much
well
whom
wish

British/American

These notes explain differences between British and American usage. The word in **bold** shows you the entry where you can find the note.

already / just / yet
bit – a bit / a little
college / university
course / program
different from / to / than
floor
have – have you got? / do you have?
holiday / vacation
hospital
inclusive / through
phone / call / ring
platform / track
post / mail
presently
rent / hire / let
rubbish / garbage / trash / refuse
school – at/in school
sea / ocean
toilet / bathroom
underground / subway / metro / tube

More About

These notes give you more information about an aspect of life or language in Britain and America and show you the correct words to use. The word in **bold** shows you the topic of the note and the entry where you can find it.

American
British – describing people from Britain
course – ways of saying 'of course'
exam – words for exams and tests
gender – ways of talking about men and women
hello – greetings
lawyer – words for different kinds of lawyer
meal
name – names and titles
road
Scottish – describing things from Scotland
student – words for students at different levels
want – offers and invitations

Synonyms

These notes show the differences between groups of words with similar meanings. The words in each group are given order of frequency – from the most common to the least common. The word in **bold** shows you the entry where you can find the note.

action / measure / step / act / move
admit / acknowledge / recognize / concede / confess
advertisement / publicity / ad / commercial / promotion / trailer
afraid / frightened / scared / terrified / alarmed / paranoid
agree / accept / approve / go along with sb/sth / consent
almost / nearly / practically
angry / mad / indignant / cross / irate
artificial / synthetic / false / man-made / fake / imitation
ask / enquire / demand
basis / foundation / base
beat / batter / pound / lash / hammer
beautiful / pretty / handsome / attractive / lovely / good-looking / gorgeous
become / get / go / turn
big / large / great
bill / account / invoice / check
bitter / pungent / sour / acrid / sharp / acid
border / boundary / frontier
boring / dull / tedious
bottom / base / foundation / foot
bright / brilliant / vivid / vibrant
build / construct / assemble / erect / put sth up
building / property / premises / complex / structure / block
burn / char / scald / scorch / singe
call / cry out / exclaim / blurt / burst out
campaign / battle / struggle / drive / war / fight
care / caution / prudence
certain / bound / sure / definite / guaranteed
cheap / competitive / budget / affordable / reasonable / inexpensive
cheat / fool / deceive / betray / take in / trick / con
check / examine / inspect / go over sth

choice / favourite / preference / selection / pick
choose / select / pick / decide / opt / go for
claim / allegation / assertion
classic / classical
clean / wash / rinse / cleanse / dry-clean
clear / obvious / apparent / evident / plain
clothes / clothing / garment / dress / wear / gear
coast / beach / seaside / coastline / sand / seashore
cold / cool / freezing / chilly / lukewarm / tepid
collect / gather / accumulate / amass
colour / shade / hue / tint / tinge
comment / note / remark / observe
complain / protest / object / grumble / moan / whine
condition / state
consist of sb/sth / comprise / make up sth / constitute / be composed of sb/sth
continuous / continual
costs / spending / expenditure / expenses / overheads / outlay
country / landscape / countryside / terrain / land / scenery
crash / slam / collide / smash / wreck
cut / slash / cut sth back / scale sth back / rationalize / downsize
damage / hurt / harm / impair
declare / state / indicate / announce
demand / require / expect / insist / ask
difficult / hard / challenging / demanding / taxing
dirty / dusty / filthy / muddy / soiled / grubby / stained
discussion / conversation / dialogue / talk / debate / consultation / chat / gossip
disease / illness / disorder / infection / condition / ailment / bug
disgusting / foul / revolting / repulsive / offensive / gross
double / dual
economic / financial / commercial / monetary / budgetary
election / vote / poll / referendum / ballot
electric / electrical
entertainment / fun / recreation / relaxation / play / pleasure / amusement
environment / setting / surroundings / background
equipment / material / gear / kit / apparatus
essential / vital / crucial / critical / decisive / indispensable
examine / analyse / review / study / discuss
example / case / instance / specimen / illustration
excellent / outstanding / perfect / superb
excited / ecstatic / elated / euphoric / rapturous / exhilarated
exciting / dramatic / heady / thrilling / exhilarating
expensive / costly / overpriced / pricey
explode / blow up / go off / burst / erupt / detonate
fabric / cloth / material / textile
factory / plant / mill / works / yard / workshop / foundry
fast / quick / rapid
fear / terror / panic / alarm / fright
fight / clash / brawl / struggle / scuffle
floor / ground / land / earth
frighten / scare / alarm / terrify
fun / pleasure / (a) good time / enjoyment / (a) great time
funny / amusing / entertaining / witty / humorous / comic / hilarious
glad / happy / pleased / delighted / proud / relieved / thrilled
great / cool / fantastic / fabulous / terrific / brilliant / awesome
happy / satisfied / content / contented / joyful / blissful
hate / dislike / can't stand / despise / can't bear / loathe / detest
hide / conceal / cover / disguise / mask / camouflage
hit / knock / bang / strike / bump / bash
hold / hold on / cling / clutch / grip / grasp / clasp / hang on
honest / frank / direct / open / outspoken / straight / blunt
hurt / ache / burn / sting / tingle / itch / throb
identify / know / recognize / name / make sb/sth out
illness / sickness / ill health / trouble
imagine / think / see / envisage / envision
income / wage / wages / pay / salary / earnings
injure / wound / hurt / bruise / sprain / pull / strain
intelligent / smart / clever / brilliant / bright
interest / hobby / game / pastime
interesting / fascinating / compelling / stimulating / gripping / absorbing
interview / interrogation / audience / consultation
job / position / post / vacancy / appointment
label / tag / sticker
land / lot / ground / space / plot
language / vocabulary / terms / wording / terminology
lid / top / cork / cap / plug
like / love / be fond of / be keen on sth / adore
limit / restriction / control / constraint / restraint / limitation
look / watch / see / view / observe
look / glance / gaze / stare / glimpse / glare
love / like / be fond of sb / adore / be devoted to sb / care for sb / dote on sb
luck / chance / coincidence / accident / fate / destiny
mad / crazy / nuts / batty / out of your mind / (not) in your right mind
main / major / key / central / principal / chief / prime
make / do / create / develop / produce / generate / form
mark / stain / fingerprint / streak / speck / blot / smear / spot
mentally ill / insane / neurotic / psychotic / disturbed / unstable
mention / refer to sb/sth / speak / cite / quote
mistake / error / inaccuracy / slip / howler / misprint
mix / stir / mingle / blend
money / cash / change
naked / bare
narrow / thin
nervous / neurotic / on edge / jittery
notice / note / detect / observe / witness
old / elderly / aged / long-lived / mature
option / choice / alternative / possibility
order / tell / instruct / direct / command

painful / sore / raw / inflamed / excruciating / burning / itchy
patch / dot / mark / spot
payment / premium / contribution / subscription / repayment / deposit / instalment
photograph / picture / photo / shot / snapshot / snap / print
picture / painting / drawing / portrait / print / sketch
place / site / area / position / point / location / scene / spot / venue
plain / simple / stark / bare / unequivocal
pleasure / delight / joy / privilege / treat / honour
poor / disadvantaged / needy / impoverished / deprived / penniless / hard up
pressure / stress / tension / strain
price / cost / value / expense / worth
product / goods / commodity / merchandise / produce
pull / drag / draw / haul / tow / tug
purpose / aim / intention / plan / point / idea
rate / charge / fee / rent / fine / fare / toll / rental
reason / explanation / grounds / basis / excuse / motive / justification / pretext
recommend / advise / advocate / urge
regard / call / find / consider / see / view
report / story / account / version
rest / break / respite / time out / breathing space
result / consequence / outcome / repercussion
return / come back / go back / get back / turn back
rich / wealthy / prosperous / affluent / well off / comfortable
right / correct
rude / cheeky / insolent / disrespectful / impolite / impertinent / discourteous
satisfaction / happiness / pride / contentment / fulfilment
satisfying / rewarding / pleasing / gratifying / fulfilling
save / budget / economize / tighten your belt
save / rescue / bail out / redeem
see / spot / catch / glimpse
serious / grave / earnest / solemn
shine / gleam / glow / sparkle / glisten / shimmer / glitter / twinkle / glint
shock / appal / horrify / disgust / sicken / repel
shout / yell / cry / scream / cheer / bellow / raise your voice
sight / view / vision
sign / indication / symptom / symbol / indicator / signal
sit / sit down / be seated / take a seat / perch
situation / circumstances / position / conditions / things / the case / state of affairs
sleep / doze / nap / snooze
soil / mud / dust / clay / land / earth / dirt / ground
speaker / communicator / gossip / talker
speech / lecture / address / talk / sermon
spoken / oral / vocal
stand / get up / stand up / rise / get to your feet / be on your feet
stare / gaze / peer / glare
start / begin / start off / kick off / commence / open
statement / comment / announcement / remark / declaration / observation
stress / emphasize
structure / framework / form / composition / construction / fabric
student / pupil / schoolboy /schoolchild /schoolgirl
successful / profitable / commercial / lucrative / economic
sure / confident / convinced / certain / positive / clear
surprise / startle / amaze / stun / astonish / take sb aback / astound
take / lead / escort / drive / show / walk / guide / usher / direct
talk / discuss / speak / communicate / debate / consult
target / objective / goal / object / end
task / duties / mission / job / chore
tax / duty / customs / tariff / rates
terrible / awful / horrible / dreadful / vile / horrendous
thing / stuff / property / possessions / junk / belongings / goods / valuables
think / believe / feel / reckon / be under the impression
throw / toss / hurl / fling / chuck / lob / bowl / pitch
trip / journey / tour / expedition / excursion / outing / day out
true / right / correct
trust / depend on sb/sth / rely on sb/sth / count on sb/sth / believe in sb
understand / see / get / follow / grasp / comprehend
valuable / precious / priceless / irreplaceable
view / sight / scene / panorama
well / all right / OK / fine / healthy / strong / fit
wet / moist / damp / soaked / drenched / saturated
wide / broad
witness / observer / onlooker / passer-by / bystander / eyewitness
wonderful / lovely / delightful
word / term / phrase / expression / idiom
work / employment / career / profession / occupation / trade
worried / concerned / nervous / anxious / uneasy
wrong / false / mistaken / incorrect / inaccurate / misguided / untrue

Collocations

These notes show useful words and phrases connected with particular topics, and a selection of verbs to use with those words and phrases. The word in **bold** shows you the entry where you can find the note.

age – The ages of life
art – Fine arts
biotechnology – Biotechnology
business – Business
child – Children
cinema – Cinema/the movies
cooking – Cooking
crime – Crime
decorate – Decorating and home improvement
diet – Diet and exercise
driving – Driving
economy – The economy
education – Education
email – Email and the Internet

environment – The environment
farming – Farming
fashion – Clothes and fashion
finance – Finance
house – Moving house
ill – Illnesses
injury – Injuries
international – International relations
job – Jobs
justice – Criminal justice
life – The living world
literature – Literature
marriage – Marriage and divorce
music – Music
phone – Phones
physical – Physical appearance
politics – Politics
race – Race and immigration
religion – Religion
restaurant – Restaurants
scientific – Scientific research
shopping – Shopping
television – Television
town – Town and country
travel – Travel and tourism
unemployment – Unemployment
vote – Voting in elections
war – War and peace
weather – The weather

Language Bank

These notes show you how to express similar ideas in a variety of ways, particularly in writing. The word in **bold** shows you the entry where you can find the note.

about – Saying what a text is about
according to – Reporting someone's opinion
addition – Adding another item
argue – Verbs for reporting an opinion
because – Explaining reasons
cause – X causes Y
conclusion – Summing up an argument
consequently – Describing the effect of something
contrast – Highlighting differences
define – Defining terms
e.g. – Giving examples
emphasis – Highlighting an important point
evidence – Giving proof
except – Making an exception
expect – Discussing predictions
fall – Describing a decrease
first – Ordering your points
generally – Ways of saying 'in general'
however – Ways of saying 'but'
i.e. – Explaining what you mean
illustrate – Referring to a chart, graph or table
impersonal – Giving opinions using impersonal language
increase – Describing an increase
nevertheless – Conceding a point and making a counter-argument
opinion – Giving your personal opinion
perhaps – Making an opinion sound less definite
process – Describing a process
proportion – Describing fractions and proportions
similarly – Making comparisons
surprising – Highlighting interesting data
therefore – Ways of saying 'For this reason...'
vital – Saying that something is necessary

The language of literary criticism

Figurative language

Imagery is language that produces pictures in the mind. The term can be used to discuss the various stylistic devices listed below, especially **figures of speech** (= ways of using language to convey or suggest a meaning beyond the literal meaning of the words).

Metaphor is the imaginative use of a word or phrase to describe something else, to show that the two have the same qualities:

▸ *All the world's a stage*
And all the men and women merely players.
— William Shakespeare, *As You Like It*

In **simile** the comparison between the two things is made explicit by the use of the words 'as' or 'like':

▸ *I wandered lonely **as** a cloud*
— William Wordsworth, *Daffodils*

▸ ***Like as** the waves make towards the pebbled shore,*
***So** do our minutes hasten to their end.*
— Shakespeare, Sonnet 60

Metonymy is the fact of referring to something by the name of something else closely connected with it, used especially as a form of shorthand for something familiar or obvious, as in 'I've been reading Shakespeare' instead of 'I've been reading the plays of Shakespeare'.

Allegory is a style of writing in which each character or event is a symbol representing a particular quality. In John Bunyan's *Pilgrim's Progress* Christian escapes from the City of Destruction, travels through the Slough of Despond, visits Vanity Fair and finally arrives at the Celestial City. He meets characters such as the Giant Despair and Mr Worldly Wiseman and is accompanied by Faithful and Hopeful.

Personification is the act of representing objects or qualities as human beings:

▸ *Love bade me welcome: yet my soul drew back,*
Guilty of dust and sin.
— George Herbert, *Love*

Pathetic fallacy is the effect produced when animals and things are shown as having human feelings. For example, in John Milton's poem, *Lycidas*, the flowers are shown as weeping for the dead shepherd, Lycidas.

Patterns of sound

Alliteration is the use of the same letter or sound at the beginning of words that are close together. It was used systematically in Old English poetry but in modern English poetry is generally only used for a particular effect:

▸ *On the **b**ald street **b**reaks the **b**lank day.*
— Alfred, Lord Tennyson, *In Memoriam*

Assonance is the effect created when two syllables in words that are close together have the same vowel sound but different consonants, or the same consonants but different vowels:

▸ *It seemed that out of battle I **escaped***
*Down some profound dull tunnel long since **scooped**...*
— Wilfred Owen, *Strange Meeting*

Onomatopoeia is the effect produced when the words used contain similar sounds to the noises they describe:

▸ *murmuring of innumerable bees*
— Tennyson, *The Princess*

Other stylistic effects

Irony is the use of words that say the opposite of what you really mean, often in order to make a critical comment.

Hyperbole is the use of exaggeration:

▸ *An hundred years should go to praise*
Thine eyes and on thy forehead gaze
— Andrew Marvell, *To His Coy Mistress*

An **oxymoron** is a phrase that combines two words that seem to be the opposite of each other:

▸ *Parting is such **sweet sorrow***
— Shakespeare, *Romeo and Juliet*

A **paradox** is a statement that contains two opposite ideas or seems to be impossible:

▸ *The Child is father of the Man.*
— Wordsworth, 'My heart leaps up ...'

Poetry

Lyric poetry is usually fairly short and expresses thoughts and feelings. Examples are Wordsworth's *Daffodils* and Dylan Thomas's *Fern Hill*.

Epic poetry can be much longer and deals with the actions of great men and women or the history of nations. Examples are Homer's *Iliad* and Virgil's *Aeneid*.

Narrative poetry tells a story, like Chaucer's *Canterbury Tales*, or Coleridge's *Rime of the Ancient Mariner*.

Dramatic poetry takes the form of a play, and includes the plays of Shakespeare (which also contain scenes in **prose**).

A **ballad** is a traditional type of narrative poem with short **verses** or **stanzas** and a simple **rhyme scheme** (= pattern of rhymes).

An **elegy** is a type of lyric poem that expresses sadness for someone who has died. Thomas Gray's *Elegy Written in a Country Churchyard* mourns all who lived and died quietly and never had the chance to be great.

An **ode** is a lyric poem that addresses a person or thing or celebrates an event. John Keats wrote five great odes, including *Ode to a Nightingale*, *Ode on a Grecian Urn* and *To Autumn*.

Metre is the rhythm of poetry determined by the arrangement of stressed and unstressed, or long and short, syllables in each line of the poem.

Prosody is the theory and study of metre.

Iambic pentameter is the most common metre in English poetry. Each line consists of five **feet** (pentameter), each containing an unstressed syllable followed by a stressed syllable (iambic):

▸ *The curféw tólls the knéll of párting dáy*
— Gray's *Elegy*

Most lines of iambic pentameter, however, are not absolutely regular in their pattern of stresses:

▸ *Sháll I compáre thee tó a súmmer's day?*
— Shakespeare, Sonnet 18

A **couplet** is a pair of lines of poetry with the same metre, especially ones that rhyme:

▸ *For never was a story of more woe*
Than this of Juliet and her Romeo.
— Shakespeare, *Romeo and Juliet*

A **sonnet** is a poem of 14 lines, in English written in iambic pentameter, and with a fixed pattern of rhyme, often ending with a rhyming couplet.

Blank verse is poetry written in iambic pentameters that do not rhyme. A lot of Shakespeare's dramatic verse is in blank verse, as is Milton's epic *Paradise Lost*.

Free verse is poetry without a regular metre or rhyme scheme. Much twentieth century poetry is written in free verse, for example T. S. Eliot's *The Waste Land*.

Drama

The different **genres** of drama include **comedy**, **tragedy** and **farce**.

Catharsis is the process of releasing and providing relief from strong emotions such as pity and fear by watching the same emotions being played out on stage.

A **deus ex machina** is an unexpected power or event that suddenly appears to resolve a situation that seems hopeless. It is often used to talk about a character in a play or story who only appears at the end.

Dramatic irony is when a character's words carry an extra meaning, especially because of what is going to happen that the character does not know about. For example, King Duncan in Shakespeare's *Macbeth* is pleased to accept Macbeth's hospitality, not knowing that Macbeth is going to murder him that night.

Hubris is too much pride or self-confidence, especially when shown by a tragic hero or heroine who tries to defy the gods or fate.

Nemesis is what happens when the hero or heroine's past mistakes or sins finally cause his or her downfall and death.

A **soliloquy** is a speech in a play for one character who is alone on the stage and speaks his or her thoughts aloud. The most famous soliloquy in English drama is Hamlet's beginning 'To be or not to be…'

Narrative

A **novel** is a **narrative** (= a story) long enough to fill a complete book. The story may be told by a **first-person narrator**, who is a character in the story and relates what happens to himself or herself, or there may be an **omniscient narrator** who relates what happens to all the characters in the third person.

A **short story** is a story that is short enough to be read from beginning to end without stopping.

The **denouement** is the end of a book or play in which everything is explained or settled. It is often used to talk about mystery or detective stories.

Stream of consciousness is a style of writing used in novels that shows the continuous flow of a character's thoughts and feelings without using the usual methods of description or conversation. It was used particularly in the twentieth century by writers such as James Joyce and Virginia Woolf.

Punctuation

. full stop (*BrE*) period (*NAmE*)

- at the end of a sentence that is not a question or an exclamation:
  - ▶ *I knocked at the door. There was no reply.*
  - ▶ *I knocked again.*
- sometimes in abbreviations:
  - ▶ *Jan. e.g. a.m. etc.*
- in internet and email addresses (said 'dot')
  - ▶ *http://www.oup.com*

, comma

- to separate words in a list, though they are often omitted before *and*:
  - ▶ *a bouquet of red, pink and white roses*
  - ▶ *tea, coffee, milk or hot chocolate*
- to separate phrases or clauses:
  - ▶ *If you keep calm, take your time, concentrate and think ahead, then you're likely to pass your test.*
  - ▶ *Worn out after all the excitement of the party, the children soon fell asleep.*
- before and after a clause or phrase that gives additional, but not essential, information about the noun it follows:
  - ▶ *The Pennine Hills, which are very popular with walkers, are situated between Lancashire and Yorkshire.*

  (do not use commas before and after a clause that **defines** the noun it follows)
  - ▶ *The hills that separate Lancashire from Yorkshire are called the Pennines.*
- to separate main clauses, especially long ones, linked by a conjunction such as *and, as, but, for, or*:
  - ▶ *We had been looking forward to our holiday all year, but unfortunately it rained every day.*
- to separate an introductory word or phrase, or an adverb or adverbial phrase that applies to the whole sentence, from the rest of the sentence:
  - ▶ *Oh, so that's where it was.*
  - ▶ *As it happens, however, I never saw her again.*
  - ▶ *By the way, did you hear about Sue's car?*
- to separate a tag question from the rest of the sentence:
  - ▶ *It's quite expensive, isn't it?*
  - ▶ *You live in Bristol, right?*
- before or after 'he said', etc. when writing down conversation:
  - ▶ *'Come back soon,' she said.*
- before a short quotation:
  - ▶ *Disraeli said, 'Little things affect little minds'.*

: colon

- to introduce a list of items:
  - ▶ *These are our options: we go by train and leave before the end of the show; or we take the car and see it all.*
- in formal writing, before a clause or phrase that gives more information about the main clause. (You can use a semicolon or a full stop, but not a comma, instead of a colon here.)
  - ▶ *The garden had been neglected for a long time: it was overgrown and full of weeds.*
- to introduce a quotation, which may be indented:
  - ▶ *As Kenneth Morgan writes:*

    The truth was, perhaps, that Britain in the years from 1914 to 1983 had not changed all that fundamentally.

    Others, however, have challenged this view...

; semicolon

- instead of a comma to separate parts of a sentence that already contain commas:
  - ▶ *She was determined to succeed whatever the cost; she would achieve her aim, whoever might suffer on the way.*
- in formal writing, to separate two main clauses, especially those not joined by a conjunction:
  - ▶ *The sun was already low in the sky; it would soon be dark.*

? question mark

- at the end of a direct question:
  - ▶ *Where's the car?*
  - ▶ *You're leaving already?*

  Do not use a question mark at the end of an indirect question:
  - ▶ *He asked if I was leaving.*
- especially with a date, to express doubt:
  - ▶ *John Marston (?1575–1634)*

! exclamation mark (*BrE*) exclamation point (*NAmE*)

- at the end of a sentence expressing surprise, joy, anger, shock or another strong emotion:
  - ▸ *That's marvellous!*
  - ▸ *'Never!' she cried.*
- in informal written English, you can use more than one exclamation mark, or an exclamation mark and a question mark:
  - ▸ *'Your wife's just given birth to triplets.' 'Triplets!?'*

' apostrophe

- with *s* to indicate that a thing or person belongs to somebody:
  - ▸ *my friend's brother*
  - ▸ *the waitress's apron*
  - ▸ *King James's crown / King James' crown*
  - ▸ *the students' books*
  - ▸ *the women's coats*
- in short forms, to indicate that letters or figures have been omitted:
  - ▸ *I'm (I am)*
  - ▸ *they'd (they had/they would)*
  - ▸ *the summer of '89 (1989)*
- sometimes, with s to form the plural of a letter, a figure or an abbreviation:
  - ▸ *roll your r's*
  - ▸ *during the 1990's*

- hyphen

- to form a compound from two or more other words:
  - ▸ *hard-hearted*
  - ▸ *fork-lift truck*
  - ▸ *mother-to-be*
- to form a compound from a prefix and a proper name:
  - ▸ *pre-Raphaelite*
  - ▸ *pro-European*
- when writing compound numbers between 21 and 99 in words:
  - ▸ *seventy-three*
  - ▸ *thirty-one*
- sometimes, in British English, to separate a prefix ending in a vowel from a word beginning with the same vowel:
  - ▸ *co-operate*
  - ▸ *pre-eminent*
- after the first section of a word that is divided between one line and the next:
  - ▸ *decide what to do in order to avoid mis-takes of this kind in the future*

— dash

- in informal English, instead of a colon or semicolon, to indicate that what follows is a summary or conclusion of what has gone before:
  - ▸ *Men were shouting, women were screaming, children were crying—it was chaos.*
  - ▸ *You've admitted that you lied to me—how can I trust you again?*
- singly or in pairs to separate a comment or an afterthought from the rest of the sentence:
  - ▸ *He knew nothing at all about it—or so he said.*

... dots / ellipsis

- to indicate that words have been omitted, especially from a quotation or at the end of a conversation:
  - ▸ *...challenging the view that Britain... had not changed all that fundamentally.*

/ slash / oblique

- to separate alternative words or phrases:
  - ▸ *have a pudding and/or cheese*
  - ▸ *single/married/widowed/divorced*
- in internet and email addresses to separate the different elements (often said 'forward slash')
  - ▸ *http://www.oup.com/elt/*

' ' " " quotation marks

- to enclose words and punctuation in direct speech:
  - ▸ *'Why on earth did you do that?' he asked.*
  - ▸ *'I'll fetch it,' she replied.*
- to draw attention to a word that is unusual for the context, for example a slang expression, or to a word that is being used for special effect, such as irony:
  - ▸ *He told me in no uncertain terms to 'get lost'.*
  - ▸ *Thousands were imprisoned in the name of 'national security'.*
- around the titles of articles, books, poems, plays, etc:
  - ▸ *Keats's 'Ode to Autumn'*
  - ▸ *I was watching 'Match of the Day'.*
- around short quotations or sayings:
  - ▸ *Do you know the origin of the saying: 'A little learning is a dangerous thing'?*
- in American English, double quotation marks are used:
  - ▸ *"Help! I'm drowning!"*

( ) brackets (*BrE*) parentheses (*NAmE or formal*)

- to separate extra information or a comment from the rest of a sentence:
  - ▸ *Mount Robson (12 972 feet) is the highest mountain in the Canadian Rockies.*
  - ▸ *He thinks that modern music (i.e. anything written after 1900) is rubbish.*
- to enclose cross-references:
  - ▸ *This moral ambiguity is a feature of Shakespeare's later works (see Chapter Eight).*
- around numbers or letters in text:
  - ▸ *Our objectives are (1) to increase output, (2) to improve quality and (3) to maximize profits.*

[ ] square brackets (*BrE*) brackets (*NAmE*)

- around words inserted to make a quotation grammatically correct:
  - ▸ *Britain in [these] years was without…*

italics

- to show emphasis:
  - ▸ I'm not going to do it – *you* are.
  - ▸ ... proposals which we cannot accept *under any circumstances*
- to indicate the titles of books, plays, etc:
  - ▸ Joyce's *Ulysses*
  - ▸ the title role in Puccini's *Tosca*
  - ▸ a letter in *The Times*
- for foreign words or phrases:
  - ▸ the English oak (*Quercus robur*)
  - ▸ I had to renew my *permesso di soggiorno* (residence permit).

Quoting conversation

When you write down a conversation, you normally begin a new paragraph for each new speaker.

Quotation marks enclose the words spoken:

▸ *'You're sure of this?' I asked.*
He nodded grimly.
'I'm certain.'

Verbs used to indicate direct speech, for example *he said, she complained*, are separated by commas from the words spoken, unless a question mark or an exclamation mark is used:

- ▸ *'That's all I know,' said Nick.*
- ▸ *Nick said, 'That's all I know.'*
- ▸ *'Why?' asked Nick.*

When *he said* or *said Nick* follows the words spoken, the comma is placed inside the quotation marks, as in the first example above. If, however, the writer puts the words *said Nick* within the actual words Nick speaks, the comma is outside the quotation marks:

- ▸ *'That', said Nick, 'is all I know.'*

Double quotation marks are used to indicate direct speech being quoted by somebody else within direct speech:

- ▸ *'But you said you loved me! "I'll never leave you, Sue, as long as I live." That's what you said, isn't it?'*

Numbers

Writing and saying numbers

Numbers over 20

- are written with a hyphen:
  35 *thirty-five*
  67 *sixty-seven*
- When writing a cheque we often use words for the pounds or dollars and figures for the pence or cents:
  £22.45 *twenty-two pounds (and) 45 pence*
  $79.30 *seventy-nine dollars (and) 30/100*

Numbers over 100

329 *three hundred and twenty nine*

- The **and** is pronounced /n/ and the stress is on the final number.
- In American English the **and** is sometimes left out.

Numbers over 1000

1100 *one thousand one hundred*
(also informal) eleven hundred
2500 *two thousand five hundred*
(also informal, especially in NAmE) twenty-five hundred

- These informal forms are most common for whole hundreds between 1100 and 1900.
- A comma or (in *BrE*) a space is often used to divide large numbers into groups of 3 figures:
  - ▸ *33,423* or *33 423 (thirty three thousand four hundred and twenty three)*
  - ▸ *2,768,941* or *2 768 941 (two million seven hundred and sixty-eight thousand nine hundred and forty-one)*

A or one?

130 *a / one hundred and thirty*
1000000 *a / one million*

- **one** is more formal and more precise and can be used for emphasis:
  - ▸ *The total cost was one hundred and sixty three pounds exactly.*
  - ▸ *It cost about a hundred and fifty quid.*
- **a** can only be used at the beginning of a number:
  1000 *a/one thousand*
  2100 *two thousand one hundred*
  ~~*two thousand a hundred*~~
- **a** is not usually used between 1100 and 1999:
  1099 *a/one thousand and ninety-nine*
  1100 *one thousand one hundred*
  1340 *one thousand three hundred and forty*
  ~~*a thousand three hundred and forty*~~

Ordinal numbers

1st	*first*	5th	*fifth*
2nd	*second*	9th	*ninth*
3rd	*third*	12th	*twelfth*
4th	*fourth*	21st	*twenty-first*
			etc.

Fractions

½ *a/one half*
⅓ *a/one third*
¼ *a/one quarter (NAmE also a/one fourth)*
(for emphasis use **one** instead of **a**)
1/12 *one twelfth*
1/16 *one sixteenth*
⅔ *two thirds*
¾ *three quarters (NAmE also three fourths)*
9/10 *nine tenths*

More complex fractions

- use **over**:
  19/56 *nineteen **over** fifty-six*
  31/144 *thirty-one **over** one four four*

Whole numbers and fractions

- link with **and**:
  2½ *two **and** a half*
  5⅔ *five **and** two thirds*
- **one** plus a fraction is followed by a plural noun:
  1½pts *one and a half **pints***

Fractions / percentages and noun phrases

- use **of**:
  - ▸ ***a** fifth **of** the women questioned*
  - ▸ *three quarters **of** the population*
  - ▸ *75% **of** the population*
- with **half** do not use **a**, and **of** can sometimes be omitted:
  - ▸ *Half (of) the work is already finished.*
- do not use **of** in expressions of measurement or quantity:
  - ▸ *How much is half a pint of milk?*
  - ▸ *It takes me half an hour by bus.*
- use **of** before pronouns:
  - ▸ *We can't start – only half **of** us are here.*

Fractions / percentages and verbs

- If a fraction/percentage is used with an uncountable or a singular noun the verb is generally singular:
  - ▸ *Fifty per cent of the land is cultivated.*
  - ▸ *Half (of) the land is cultivated.*

- If the noun is singular but represents a group of people, the verb is singular in American English but in British English it may be singular or plural:
  - ▸ *Three quarters/75% of the workforce is/are against the strike.*
- If the noun is plural, the verb is plural:
  - ▸ *Two thirds/65% of children play computer games.*

Decimals

- write and say with a point (.) (not a comma)
- say each figure after the point separately:

79.3	*seventy-nine point three*
3.142	*three point one four two*
0.67	(*zero*) *point six seven*
	(*BrE also*) *nought point six seven*

Mathematical expressions

+	plus
−	minus
×	times/multiplied by
÷	divided by
=	equals/is
%	per cent (*NAmE* usually percent)
3^2	three squared
5^3	five cubed
6^{10}	six to the power of ten
√	square root of

The figure '0'

The figure 0 has several different names in English, although in American English *zero* is commonly used in all cases:

Zero

- used in precise scientific, medical and economic contexts and to talk about temperature:
  - ▸ *It was ten degrees below zero last night.*
  - ▸ *zero inflation/growth/profit*

Nought

- used in British English to talk about a number, age, etc.:
  - ▸ *A million is written with six noughts.*
  - ▸ *The car goes from nought to sixty in ten seconds.*
  - ▸ *clothes for children aged nought to six*

'o' /əʊ/ *NAmE* /oʊ/

- used when saying a bank account number, telephone number, etc.

Nil

- used to talk about the score in a team game, for example in football:
  - ▸ *The final score was one nil.* (1–0)
- used to mean 'nothing at all':
  - ▸ *The doctors rated her chances as nil.*

Telephone numbers

- All numbers are said separately. 0 is pronounced /əʊ/ (*BrE*) or /oʊ/ (*NAmE*):
  - ▸ (01865) 556767
    o one eight six five, five five six seven six seven (or *double five six seven six seven*)

Temperature

- The Celsius or Centigrade (°C) scale is officially used in Britain and for scientific purposes in the US:
  - ▸ *a high of thirty-five degrees Celsius*
  - ▸ *The normal temperature of the human body is 37°C.*
- The Fahrenheit (°F) scale is used in all other contexts in the US and is also still commonly used in Britain. The words 'degrees Fahrenheit/Centigrade/Celsius' are often omitted:
  - ▸ *Temperatures soared to over a hundred. (100°F)*
  - ▸ *She's ill in bed with a temperature of a hundred and two. (102°F)*

Money

In Britain

- ▸ *100 pence/p = 1 British pound (£1)*
- ▸ *It costs 90p/90 pence return on the bus.*
- when talking about an individual coin: *a twenty pence piece/a twenty p piece*
- when talking about pounds and pence people often only say the numbers: *It only cost five ninety nine. (£5.99)*
- in informal British English:

£1	*a quid*
£5	*five quid* or *a fiver*
£10	*ten quid* or *a tenner*

In the US

1c	one cent	a penny
5c	five cents	a nickel
10c	ten cents	a dime
25c	twenty-five cents	a quarter
$1.00	one dollar	a dollar bill

- in informal American English dollars are called **bucks**:
  - ▸ *This shirt cost fifty bucks.*

Writing and saying dates

British English

- *14 October 1998* or *14th October 1998 (14/10/98)*
- *Her birthday is on **the** ninth **of** December.*
- *Her birthday is on December **the** ninth.*

American English

- *October 14, 1998 (10/14/98)*
- *Her birthday is December 9th.*

Years

1999 *nineteen ninety-nine*
1608 *sixteen o eight* (or, less commonly, *nineteen hundred and ninety-nine* and *sixteen hundred and eight*)
1700 *seventeen hundred*
2000 *(the year) two thousand*
2002 *two thousand and two*
2015 *twenty fifteen*

AD 76 / A.D. 76 *AD seventy-six*
76 CE / 76 C.E. *seventy-six* CE

(Both these expressions mean '76 years after the beginning of the Christian calendar'.)

1000 BC / 1000 B.C. *one thousand BC*
1000 BCE / 1000 B.C.E *one thousand BCE*

(Both these expressions mean '1000 years before the beginning of the Christian calendar'.)

Age

- when saying a person's age use only numbers:
  - *Sue is ten and Tom is six.*
  - *She left home at sixteen.*
- a man/woman/boy/girl, etc. of ...
  - *They've got a girl of three and a boy of five.*
  - *a young woman of nineteen*
- in writing, in descriptions or to emphasize sb's age use **... years old**:
  - *She was thirty-one years old and a barrister by profession.*
  - *He is described as white, 5ft 10 ins tall and about 50 years old.*
  - *You're forty years old – stop behaving like a teenager!*
- **... years old** is also used for things:
  - *The monument is 120 years old.*
- You can also say **a ... year-old/month-old/week-old**, etc.:
  - *Youth training is available to all sixteen-year-olds.*
  - *a ten week-old baby*
  - *a remarkable 1000 year-old tomb*
- Use **... years of age** in formal or written contexts:
  - *Not applicable to persons under eighteen years of age*
- Use **the ... age group** to talk about people between certain ages:
  - *He took first prize in the 10–16 age group.*
- To give the approximate age of a person:
  13–19 *in his/her teens*
  21–29 *in his/her twenties*
  31–33 *in his/her early thirties*
  34–36 *in his/her mid thirties*
  37–39 *in his/her late thirties*
- To refer to a particular event you can use **at/by/before, etc. the age of ...**
  - *Most smokers start smoking cigarettes before the age of sixteen.*

Numbers in time

There is often more than one way of telling the time:

Half hours

6:30 *six thirty*
half past six (*BrE*)
half six (*BrE informal*)

Other times

5:45	*five forty-five*	*(a) quarter to six* (*BrE*) *(a) quarter to/of six* (*NAmE*)
2:15	*two fifteen*	*(a) quarter past two* (*BrE*) *(a) quarter after two*(*NAmE*)
1:10	*one ten*	*ten past one* (*BrE*) *ten after one* (*NAmE*)
3:05	*three o five*	*five past three* (*BrE*) *five after three* (*NAmE*)
1:55	*one fifty-five*	*five to two* (*BrE*) *five to/of two* (*NAmE*)

- with 5, 10, 20 and 25 the word **minutes** is not necessary, but it is used with other numbers:
  10.25 *twenty-five past/after ten*
  10.17 *seventeen **minutes** past/after ten*
- use **o'clock** only for whole hours:
  - *It's three o'clock.*
- If it is necessary to specify the time of day use **in the morning, in the afternoon, in the evening** or **at night.**
- in more formal contexts use:
  a.m. = in the morning or after midnight
  p.m. = in the afternoon, in the evening or before midnight
  - *He gets up at 4 a.m. to deliver the mail.*

  Do not use **o'clock** with **a.m.** or **p.m.**:
  - *~~He gets up at 4 o'clock a.m.~~*
  - *He gets up at 4 o'clock in the morning.*
  - *~~I'll see you at 6 o'clock p.m.~~*
  - *I'll see you at 6 o'clock this evening.*

Twenty-four hour clock

- used for military purposes and in some other particular contexts, for example on train timetables in Britain:
  13:52 *thirteen fifty-two* (1:52 p.m.)
  22:30 *twenty-two thirty* (10:30 p.m.)
- for military purposes whole hours are said as **hundred hours:**
  0400 *(o) four hundred hours* (4 a.m.)
  2400 *twenty four hundred hours* (midnight)

Expressing time

When referring to days, weeks, etc. in the past, present and future the following expressions are used, speaking from a point of view in the present:

	past	**present**	**future**
morning	yesterday morning	this morning	tomorrow morning
afternoon	yesterday afternoon	this afternoon	tomorrow afternoon
evening	yesterday evening	this evening	tomorrow evening
night	last night	tonight	tomorrow night
day	yesterday	today	tomorrow
week	last week	this week	next week
month	last month	this month	next month
year	last year	this year	next year

To talk about a time further back in the past or further forward in the future use:

past	**future**
the day before yesterday	the day after tomorrow
the week/month/year before last	the week/month/year after next
two days/weeks, etc. ago	in two days/weeks, etc. time

To talk about sth that happens regularly use expressions with **'every'**

▸ *He has to work **every third** weekend.*

▸ *I wash my hair **every other** day* (= every second day).

In British English a period of two weeks is a **fortnight**.

▸ *I've got a **fortnight's** holiday in Spain.*

Prepositions of time

in (the)

parts of the day (not night)	*in the morning(s), in the evening(s), etc.*
months	*in February*
seasons	*in (the) summer*
years	*in 1995*
decades	*in the 1920s*
centuries	*in the 20th century*

at (the)

clock time	*at 5 o'clock* *at 7.45 p.m.*
night	*at night*
holiday periods	*at Christmas* *at the weekend (BrE)*

on (the)

day of the week	*on Saturdays*
dates	*on (the) 20th (of) May* *(NAmE also on May 20th)*
particular days	*on Good Friday* *on New Year's Day* *on my birthday* *on the following day*

Numbers in measurement in Britain and America

item being measured	unit of measurement	examples
length of time	hours (hrs) minutes (mins) seconds (secs)	*Cover the pan and simmer gently for one hour.* *He took just two minutes to knock out his opponent.* *The fastest time was 12 mins 26 secs.*
person's height	feet and inches metres and centimetres (UK)	*She's 1.63 metres tall.* *He's only five feet four (inches).* *He's only five foot four.*
distance by road	miles	*It is 42 miles to Liverpool.* *The signpost said: 'Liverpool 42'.*
speed	miles per hour (mph) kilometres per hour (kph) kilometres per second, etc. miles an hour (*informal*)	*She was driving at 75 miles per hour.* *a speed limit of 50kph* *Light travels at 299 792 kilometres per second.* *a hundred-mile-an-hour police chase*
distance in sport	metres yards / miles (US)	*the women's 800 metres freestyle* *a six-mile run*
area of land (for example farmland)	acres / hectares	*a house with 10 acres of grounds* *a 2 000-hectare farm*
regions or areas of a country	square miles square kilometres (UK)	*Dartmoor covers an area of more than 350 square miles.* *Population density is only 24 people per square kilometre.*
area of a room/ garden, etc.	square yards / feet square metres (UK) ... by... (...×...)	*5 000 square feet of office space* *15 square metres of carpet (5m × 3m)* *a carpet fifteen metres square (15m × 15m)* *a room sixteen feet by twelve (16ft × 12ft)*
weight of food	pounds and ounces kilograms and grams (UK) cups (US, in cooking)	*Fold in 6 ounces of flour.* *250 grams of Brie please* *Add half a cup of sugar.*
weight of a person	stones and pounds (UK) pounds only (US)	*She weighs 8st 10lb.* *My brother weighs 183 pounds.*
weight of a baby	pounds and ounces kilograms (UK)	*The baby weighed 6lb 4oz at birth.*
heavy items/ large amounts	tons / tonnes pounds kilograms (UK)	*The price of copper fell by £11 a tonne* *a car packed with 140 pounds of explosive* *a 40kg sack of gravel* *Our baggage allowance is only 20 kilos.*
milk	pints / half pints (UK) pints / quarts / gallons (US)	*a one-pint carton of milk* *a quart of milk*
beer	pints / half pints (UK)	*a half of lager please* (= half a pint) *(informal)*
wine, bottled drinks	litres / centilitres	*a litre of juice*
other liquids	litres (UK) fluid ounces / gallons (US) millilitres (scientific context)	*half a litre of cooking oil* *5 litres of paint; 2 gallons of paint* *100 ml sulphuric acid*
liquid in cooking	fluid ounces millilitres (UK)	*Add 8 fl oz milk and beat thoroughly.*
petrol (*BrE*) (*NAmE* gasoline)/diesel	gallons (US) litres (UK)	*My new car does over 50 miles to the gallon.*

As the table shows, both metric and non-metric systems of measurement can be used in many cases, especially in the UK. Often the choice depends on the speaker or the situation. In the UK the metric system must now be used on packaging and for displaying prices by weight or measurement in shops. The metric system is always used in a scientific context. In the US the metric system is much less widely used.

Metric measures

(with approximate non-metric equivalents)

	Metric			Non-metric
Length	10 millimetres (mm)	=	1 centimetre (cm)	= 0.394 inch
	100 centimetres	=	1 metre (m)	= 39.4 inches/1.094 yards
	1000 metres	=	1 kilometre (km)	= 0.6214 mile
Area	100 square metres (m^2)	=	1 are (a)	= 0.025 acre
	100 ares	=	1 hectare (ha)	= 2.471 acres
	100 hectares	=	1 square kilometre (km^2)	= 0.386 square mile
Weight	1000 milligrams (mg)	=	1 gram (g)	= 15.43 grains
	1000 grams	=	1 kilogram (kg)	= 2.205 pounds
	1000 kilograms	=	1 tonne	= 19.688 hundredweight
Capacity	10 millilitres (ml)	=	1 centilitre	= 0.018 pint (0.021 US pint)
	100 centilitres (cl)	=	1 litre (l)	= 1.76 pints (2.1 US pints)
	10 litres	=	1 decalitre (dal)	= 2.2 gallons (2.63 US gallons)

Non-metric measures

(with approximate metric equivalents)

	Non-metric			Metric
Length	1 inch (in)	—		= 25.4 millimetres
	12 inches	=	1 foot (ft)	= 30.48 centimetres
	3 feet	=	1 yard (yd)	= 0.914 metre
	220 yards	=	1 furlong	= 201.17 metres
	8 furlongs	=	1 mile	= 1.609 kilometres
	1760 yards	=	1 mile	= 1.609 kilometres
Area	1 square (sq) inch	—		= 6.452 sq centimetres (cm^2)
	144 sq inches	=	1 sq foot	= 929.03 sq centimetres
	9 sq feet	=	1 sq yard	= 0.836 sq metre
	4840 sq yards	=	1 acre	= 0.405 hectare
	640 acres	=	1 sq mile	= 259 hectares/ 2.59 sq kilometres
Weight	437 grains	=	1 ounce (oz)	= 28.35 grams
	16 ounces	=	1 pound (lb)	= 0.454 kilogram
	14 pounds	=	1 stone (st)	= 6.356 kilograms
	8 stone	=	1 hundredweight (cwt)	= 50.8 kilograms
	20 hundredweight	=	1 ton	= 1016.04 kilograms
British capacity	20 fluid ounces (fl oz)	=	1 pint (pt)	= 0.568 litre
	2 pints	=	1 quart (qt)	= 1.136 litres
	8 pints	=	1 gallon (gal.)	= 4.546 litres
American capacity	16 US fluid ounces	=	1 US pint	= 0.473 litre
	2 US pints	=	1 US quart	= 0.946 litre
	4 US quarts	=	1 US gallon	= 3.785 litres

Common first names

Variant spellings and forms are given.
Short forms and pet names follow the name from which they are formed.

Female names

Abigail /ˈæbɪɡeɪl/ **Abbie** /ˈæbi/
Aimee /ˈeɪmi/
Aisling /ˈæʃlɪŋ/ *(IrishE)*
Alexandra /ˌælɪɡˈzɑːndrə; *NAmE* -ˈzændrə/ **Alex** /ˈælɪks/, **Sandy** /ˈsændi/
Alexis /æˈleksɪs/ *(NAmE)*
Alice /ˈælɪs/
Alison, *(NAmE)* **Allison** /ˈælɪsn/
Alyssa /æˈlɪsə/ *(NAmE)*
Amanda /əˈmændə/ **Mandy** /ˈmændi/
Amber /ˈæmbə(r)/
Amelia /əˈmiːliə/
Amy /ˈeɪmi/
Angela /ˈændʒələ/
Anita /əˈniːtə/
Ann, Anne /æn/, **Anna** /ˈænə/
Annabel, Annabelle /ˈænəbel/
Annette /æˈnet/
Antonia /ænˈtəʊniə; *NAmE* -ˈtoʊ-/
Aoife /ˈiːfə/ *(IrishE)*
Ashley /ˈæʃli/
Audrey /ˈɔːdri/
Ava /ˈeɪvə/
Barbara, Barbra /ˈbɑːbrə; *NAmE* ˈbɑːrbrə/
Beatrice /ˈbɪətrɪs; *NAmE* ˈbɪr-/
Becky see REBECCA
Belinda /bəˈlɪndə/
Bernadette /ˌbɜːnəˈdet; *NAmE* ˌbɜːrn-/
Beryl /ˈberəl/
Beth, Betsy, Betty see ELIZABETH
Bethany /ˈbeθəni/
Brenda /ˈbrendə/
Brianna /ˌbraɪˈænə; ˌbriˈænə/ *(NAmE)*
Bridget, Bridgit, Brigid /ˈbrɪdʒɪt/
Brooke /brʊk/
Caitlin, Kaitlin, Kaitlyn /ˈkeɪtlɪn/
Carol, Carole /ˈkærəl/
Caroline /ˈkærəlaɪn/, **Carolyn** /ˈkærəlɪn/ **Carrie** /ˈkæri/
Catherine, Katherine, Katharine, Kathryn /ˈkæθrɪn/ **Cathy, Kathy** /ˈkæθi/, **Kate** /keɪt/, **Katie, Katy** /ˈkeɪti/
Cecily /ˈsesɪli/
Charlotte /ˈʃɑːlət; *NAmE* ˈʃɑːrlət/
Cheryl /ˈʃerəl; ˈtʃe-/
Chloe /ˈkləʊi; *NAmE* ˈkloʊi/
Christina /krɪˈstiːnə/ **Chrissie** /ˈkrɪsi/, **Tina** /ˈtiːnə/
Christine /ˈkrɪstiːn/ **Chris** /krɪs/
Ciara /ˈkɪərə; *NAmE* ˈkɪrə/ *(IrishE)*
Cindy /ˈsɪndi/
Clare, Claire /kleə(r); *NAmE* kler/
Claudia /ˈklɔːdiə; ˈklaʊdiə/
Cleo, Clio /ˈkliːəʊ; *NAmE* ˈkliːoʊ/
Constance /ˈkɒnstəns; *NAmE* ˈkɑːn-/ **Connie** /ˈkɒni; *NAmE* ˈkɑːni/
Cynthia /ˈsɪnθiə/
Daisy /ˈdeɪzi/
Daphne /ˈdæfni/
Dawn /dɔːn/
Deborah /ˈdebrə/ **Debbie** /ˈdebi/, **Deb** /deb/
Delia /ˈdiːliə/
Denise /dəˈniːz; -niːs/
Diana /daɪˈænə/, **Diane** /daɪˈæn/ **Di** /daɪ/
Doris /ˈdɒrɪs; *NAmE* ˈdɔːr-/
Dorothy /ˈdɒrəθi; *NAmE* ˈdɔːr-/
Edith /ˈiːdɪθ/
Edna /ˈednə/
Eileen /ˈaɪliːn/
Elaine /ɪˈleɪn/
Eleanor /ˈelənə(r)/ **Ellie** /ˈeli/
Eliza /ɪˈlaɪzə/ **Liza** /ˈlaɪzə; ˈliːzə/
Elizabeth, Elisabeth /ɪˈlɪzəbəθ/ **Beth** /beθ/, **Betsy** /ˈbetsi/, **Betty** /ˈbeti/, **Liz** /lɪz/, **Lizzie** /ˈlɪzi/
Ella /ˈelə/
Ellen /ˈelən/
Ellie see ELEANOR
Elspeth /ˈelspəθ/
Emily /ˈeməli/
Emma /ˈemə/
Erin /ˈerɪn/
Ethel /ˈeθəl/
Eunice /ˈjuːnɪs/
Eve /iːv/
Evelyn /ˈiːvlɪn/
Fay /feɪ/
Felicity /fəˈlɪsəti/
Fiona /fiˈəʊnə; *NAmE* -ˈoʊ-/
Florence /ˈflɒrəns; *NAmE* ˈflɔːr-/
Frances /ˈfrɑːnsɪs; -sɪz; *NAmE* ˈfræn-/ **Fran** /fræn/
Freda /ˈfriːdə/
Freya /ˈfreɪə/
Georgia /ˈdʒɔːdʒə; *NAmE* ˈdʒɔːrdʒə/
Georgina /ˌdʒɔːˈdʒiːnə; *NAmE* ˌdʒɔːrˈdʒ-/ **Georgie** /ˈdʒɔːdʒi; *NAmE* ˈdʒɔːrdʒi/
Geraldine /ˈdʒerəldiːn/
Germaine /ˌdʒɜːˈmeɪn; *NAmE* ˌdʒɜːrˈm-/
Gertrude /ˈɡɜːtruːd; *NAmE* ˈɡɜːrt-/
Gillian /ˈdʒɪliən/ **Jill, Gill** /dʒɪl/, **Jilly** /ˈdʒɪli/
Gladys /ˈɡlædɪs/

Glenda /ˈglendə/
Grace /greɪs/
Gwendoline /ˈgwendəlɪn/ **Gwen** /gwen/
Hailey /ˈheɪli/
Hannah /ˈhænə/
Harriet /ˈhæriət/
Hazel /ˈheɪzl/
Heather /ˈheðə(r)/
Helen /ˈhelən/
Hilary /ˈhɪləri/
Hilda /ˈhɪldə/
Holly /ˈhɒli; *NAmE* ˈhɑːli/
Imogen /ˈɪmədʒən/
Ingrid /ˈɪŋgrɪd/
Irene /aɪˈriːni; ˈaɪriːn; aɪˈriːn/
Iris /ˈaɪrɪs/
Isabel, Isabelle, (*especially ScotE*) **Isobel** /ˈɪzəbel/, **Isabella** /ˌɪzəˈbelə/
Jacqueline /ˈdʒækəlɪn/ **Jackie** /ˈdʒæki/
Jade /dʒeɪd/
Jane /dʒeɪn/
Janet /ˈdʒænɪt/ **Jan** /dʒæn/
Janice, Janis /ˈdʒænɪs/ **Jan** /dʒæn/
Jasmine /ˈdʒæzmɪn/
Jean /dʒiːn/
Jeanette /dʒəˈnet/
Jennifer /ˈdʒenɪfə(r)/ **Jenny** /ˈdʒeni/, **Jen** /dʒen/
Jessica /ˈdʒesɪkə/ **Jess** /dʒes/
Jill, Jilly see GILLIAN
Jo see JOANNA, JOSEPHINE
Joanna /dʒəʊˈænə; *NAmE* dʒoʊ-/, **Joanne** /dʒəʊˈæn; *NAmE* dʒoʊ-/ **Jo** /dʒəʊ; *NAmE* dʒoʊ/
Jocelyn /ˈdʒɒsəlɪn; *NAmE* ˈdʒɑːs-/
Jodie /ˈdʒəʊdi; *NAmE* ˈdʒoʊ-/
Josephine /ˈdʒəʊzəfiːn; *NAmE* ˈdʒoʊ-/ **Jo** /dʒəʊ; *NAmE* dʒoʊ/, **Josie** /ˈdʒəʊzi; *NAmE* ˈdʒoʊ-/
Joyce /dʒɔɪs/
Judith /ˈdʒuːdɪθ/ **Judy** /ˈdʒuːdi/
Julia /ˈdʒuːliə/, **Julie** /ˈdʒuːli/
June /dʒuːn/
Kaitlin, Kaitlyn (*NAmE*) see CAITLIN
Karen, Karin /ˈkærən; ˈkɑːrən/
Katherine, Katharine, Kathryn, Kathy, Kate, Katie, Katy see CATHERINE
Kay /keɪ/
Kayla /ˈkeɪlə/
Kaylee /ˈkeɪli/ (*NAmE*)
Kim /kɪm/
Kirsten /ˈkɜːstən; *NAmE* ˈkɜːrs-/ **Kirsty** /ˈkɜːsti; *NAmE* ˈkɜːrs-/
Laura /ˈlɔːrə/
Lauren /ˈlɒrən; *NAmE* ˈlɔːr-/
Leah /ˈliːə/
Lesley /ˈlezli/
Lily /ˈlɪli/
Linda /ˈlɪndə/
Lisa /ˈliːzə; -sə/
Liza see ELIZA
Liz, Lizzie see ELIZABETH
Lois /ˈləʊɪs; *NAmE* ˈloʊ-/
Lorna /ˈlɔːnə; *NAmE* ˈlɔːrnə/
Louise /luˈiːz/
Lucinda /luːˈsɪndə/
Lucy /ˈluːsi/
Lydia /ˈlɪdiə/
Lyn /lɪn/
Madeleine, (*NAmE*) **Madeline** /ˈmædlɪn/
Madison /ˈmædɪsn/ (*NAmE*)
Maeve /meɪv/ (*IrishE*)
Maggie see MARGARET
Maisie /ˈmeɪzi/
Mandy see AMANDA
Margaret /ˈmɑːgrət; *NAmE* ˈmɑːrg-/ **Maggie** /ˈmægi/
Margery, Marjorie /ˈmɑːdʒəri; *NAmE* ˈmɑːrdʒ-/
Maria /məˈriːə/
Marian, Marion /ˈmæriən/
Marie /məˈriː/
Marilyn /ˈmærəlɪn/
Marion see MARIAN
Martha /ˈmɑːθə; *NAmE* ˈmɑːrθə/
Martina /mɑːˈtiːnə; *NAmE* mɑːrˈt-/
Mary /ˈmeəri; *NAmE* ˈmeri/
Maud /mɔːd/
Mavis /ˈmeɪvɪs/
Megan /ˈmegən/
Melanie /ˈmeləni/
Melinda /məˈlɪndə/
Melissa /məˈlɪsə/
Meryl /ˈmerəl/
Mia /ˈmiːə/
Michelle /mɪˈʃel/
Millie /ˈmɪli/
Miranda /mɪˈrændə/
Miriam /ˈmɪriəm/
Moira /ˈmɔɪrə/
Molly /ˈmɒli; *NAmE* ˈmɑːli/
Monica /ˈmɒnɪkə; *NAmE* ˈmɑːn-/
Morgan /ˈmɔːgən; *NAmE* ˈmɔːrg-/
Muriel /ˈmjʊəriəl; *NAmE* ˈmjʊr-/
Nadia /ˈnædiə; ˈnɑːdiə/
Nancy /ˈnænsi/
Naomi /ˈneɪəmi; neɪˈəʊmi; *NAmE* -ˈoʊ-/
Natalie /ˈnætəli/
Natasha /nəˈtæʃə/
Niamh /niːv/ (*IrishE*)
Nicola /ˈnɪkələ/ **Nicky** /ˈnɪki/
Nicole /nɪˈkəʊl; -ˈkɒl; *NAmE* nɪˈkoʊl/
Nora /ˈnɔːrə/
Norma /ˈnɔːmə; *NAmE* ˈnɔːrmə/
Olive /ˈɒlɪv; *NAmE* ˈɑːlɪv/
Olivia /əˈlɪviə/
Paige /peɪdʒ/
Pamela /ˈpæmələ/ **Pam** /pæm/
Patricia /pəˈtrɪʃə/ **Pat** /pæt/, **Patty** /ˈpæti/
Paula /ˈpɔːlə/
Pauline /ˈpɔːliːn/
Penelope /pəˈneləpi/ **Penny** /ˈpeni/

Philippa /ˈfɪlɪpə/ **Pippa** /ˈpɪpə/
Phoebe /ˈfiːbi/
Phyllis /ˈfɪlɪs/
Polly /ˈpɒli; *NAmE* ˈpɑːli/
Poppy /ˈpɒpi; *NAmE* ˈpɑːpi/
Priscilla /prɪˈsɪlə/
Prudence /ˈpruːdəns/
Rachel /ˈreɪtʃəl/
Rebecca /rɪˈbekə/ **Becky** /ˈbeki/
Robin /ˈrɒbɪn; *NAmE* ˈrɑːbɪn/
Roisin /rəʊˈʃiːn; *NAmE* roʊ-/ *(IrishE)*
Rosalind /ˈrɒzəlɪnd; *NAmE* ˈrɑːz-/,
Rosalyn /ˈrɒzəlɪn; *NAmE* ˈrɑːz-/
Ros /rɒz; *NAmE* rɑːz/
Rose /rəʊz; *NAmE* roʊz/
Rosie /ˈrəʊzi; *NAmE* ˈroʊzi/
Rosemary /ˈrəʊzməri; *NAmE* ˈroʊzmeri/
Rosie /ˈrəʊzi; *NAmE* ˈroʊzi/
Ruby /ˈruːbi/
Ruth /ruːθ/
Sally /ˈsæli/
Samantha /səˈmænθə/ **Sam** /sæm/
Sandra /ˈsɑːndrə; *NAmE* ˈsæn-/ **Sandy** /ˈsændi/
Sandy see ALEXANDRA, SANDRA
Sarah /ˈseərə; *NAmE* ˈserə/,
Sara /ˈseərə; ˈsɑːrə; *NAmE also* ˈserə/
Shannon /ˈʃænən/
Sharon /ˈʃærən/
Sheila, Shelagh /ˈʃiːlə/
Shirley /ˈʃɜːli; *NAmE* ˈʃɜːrli/
Sian /ʃɑːn/ *(WelshE)*
Sibyl see SYBIL
Silvia, Sylvia /ˈsɪlviə/
Sinead /ʃɪˈneɪd/ *(IrishE)*
Siobhan /ʃɪˈvɔːn/ *(IrishE)*
Sophia /səˈfiːə; -ˈfaɪə/,
Sophie, Sophy /ˈsəʊfi; *NAmE* ˈsoʊfi/
Stella /ˈstelə/
Stephanie /ˈstefəni/
Susan /ˈsuːzən/ **Sue** /suː/, **Susie, Suzy** /ˈsuːzi/
Susanna(h) /suːˈzænə/, **Suzanne** /suːˈzæn/
Susie, Suzy /ˈsuːzi/
Sybil, Sibyl /ˈsɪbl/
Sylvia, Silvia /ˈsɪlviə/
Taylor /ˈteɪlə(r)/
Teresa, Theresa /təˈriːzə; -ˈreɪzə/
Tessa /ˈtesə/, **Tess** /tes/
Thelma /ˈθelmə/
Tina see CHRISTINA
Toni /ˈtəʊni; *NAmE* ˈtoʊni/ *(NAmE)*
Tracy, Tracey /ˈtreɪsi/
Ursula /ˈɜːsjələ; *NAmE* ˈɜːrs-/
Valerie /ˈvæləri/ **Val** /væl/
Vanessa /vəˈnesə/
Vera /ˈvɪərə; *NAmE* ˈvɪrə/
Veronica /vəˈrɒnɪkə; *NAmE* -ˈrɑːn-/
Victoria /vɪkˈtɔːriə/
Vicki, Vickie, Vicky, Vikki /ˈvɪki/
Violet /ˈvaɪələt/
Virginia /vəˈdʒɪniə; *NAmE* vərˈdʒɪnjə/
Vivien, Vivienne /ˈvɪviən/
Wendy /ˈwendi/
Winifred /ˈwɪnɪfrɪd/ **Winnie** /ˈwɪni/
Yvonne /ɪˈvɒn; iːˈvɒn; *NAmE* -ˈvɑːn/
Zoe /ˈzəʊi; *NAmE* ˈzoʊi/

Male names

Aaron /ˈeərən; *NAmE* ˈerən/
Abraham /ˈeɪbrəhæm/
Adam /ˈædəm/
Adrian /ˈeɪdriən/
Aidan /ˈeɪdn/
Alan, Allan, Allen /ˈælən/
Albert /ˈælbət; *NAmE* -bərt/
Al /æl/, **Bert** /bɜːt; *NAmE* bɜːrt/
Alexander /ˌælɪɡˈzɑːndə(r); *NAmE* -ˈzæn-/
Alex /ˈælɪks/, **Sandy** /ˈsændi/
Alfred /ˈælfrɪd/ **Alfie** /ˈælfi/
Alistair, Alisdair, Alasdair /ˈælɪsteə(r); *NAmE* -ter/
Allan, Allen see ALAN
Andrew /ˈændruː/ **Andy** /ˈændi/
Angus /ˈæŋɡəs/ *(ScotE)*
Anthony, Antony /ˈæntəni/
Tony /ˈtəʊni; *NAmE* ˈtoʊni/
Archibald /ˈɑːtʃɪbɔːld; *NAmE* ˈɑːrtʃ-/
Archie /ˈɑːtʃi; *NAmE* ˈɑːrtʃi/
Arnold /ˈɑːnəld; *NAmE* ˈɑːrn-/
Arthur /ˈɑːθə(r); *NAmE* ˈɑːrθ-/
Austin /ˈɒstɪn; *NAmE* ˈɑːs-/
Barry /ˈbæri/
Basil /ˈbæzl/
Benjamin /ˈbendʒəmɪn/ **Ben** /ben/
Bernard /ˈbɜːnəd; *NAmE* ˈbɜːrnərd/
Bernie /ˈbɜːni; *NAmE* ˈbɜːrni/
Bert see ALBERT, HERBERT
Bill, Billy see WILLIAM
Bob, Bobby see ROBERT
Bradford /ˈbrædfəd; *NAmE* -fərd/
Brad /bræd/ *(especially NAmE)*
Bradley /ˈbrædli/
Brandon /ˈbrændən/
Brendan /ˈbrendən/ *(IrishE)*
Brian, Bryan /ˈbraɪən/
Bruce /bruːs/
Bud /bʌd/ *(NAmE)*
Caleb /ˈkeɪləb/
Callum /ˈkæləm/
Cameron /ˈkæmərən/
Carl /kɑːl; *NAmE* kɑːrl/
Cecil /ˈsesl/

Charles /tʃɑːlz; *NAmE* tʃɑːrlz/
Charlie /ˈtʃɑːli; *NAmE* ˈtʃɑːrli/, **Chuck** /tʃʌk/
Christopher /ˈkrɪstəfə(r)/ **Chris** /krɪs/
Chuck see CHARLES
Cian /ʃɑːn/ *(IrishE)*
Ciaran /ˈkɪərən; *NAmE* ˈkɪr-/ *(IrishE)*
Clark /klɑːk; *NAmE* klɑːrk/
Clifford /ˈklɪfəd; *NAmE* -fərd/ **Cliff**
Clint /klɪnt/
Clive /klaɪv/
Colin /ˈkɒlɪn; *NAmE* ˈkɑːl-; ˈkoʊl-/
Conor, *(NAmE)* **Connor** /ˈkɒnə(r); *NAmE* ˈkɑːn-/
Craig /kreɪg/
Cyril /ˈsɪrɪl/
Dale /deɪl/
Daniel /ˈdænjəl/ **Dan** /dæn/, **Danny** /ˈdæni/
Darrell /ˈdærəl/
Darren /ˈdærən/
David /ˈdeɪvɪd/ **Dave** /deɪv/
Dean /diːn/
Dennis, Denis /ˈdenɪs/
Derek /ˈderɪk/
Dermot /ˈdɜːmət; *NAmE* ˈdɜːrm-/ *(IrishE)*
Desmond /ˈdezmənd/
Dick see RICHARD
Dirk /dɜːk; *NAmE* dɜːrk/
Dominic /ˈdɒmɪnɪk; *NAmE* ˈdɑːm-/
Donald /ˈdɒnəld; *NAmE* ˈdɑːn-/
Douglas /ˈdʌgləs/ **Doug** /dʌg/
Duane, Dwane /dweɪn/ *(especially NAmE)*
Duncan /ˈdʌŋkən/
Dwight /dwaɪt/ *(especially NAmE)*
Dylan /ˈdɪlən/
Eamonn, Eamon /ˈeɪmən/ *(IrishE)*
Ed, Eddie, Eddy see EDWARD
Edmond, Edmund /ˈedmənd/
Edward /ˈedwəd; *NAmE* -wərd/
Ed /ed/, **Eddie**, **Eddy** /ˈedi/, **Ted** /ted/
Edwin /ˈedwɪn/
Elijah /ɪˈlaɪdʒə/
Elmer /ˈelmə(r)/ *(NAmE)*
Elroy /ˈelrɔɪ/ *(NAmE)*
Emlyn /ˈemlɪn/ *(WelshE)*
Eric /ˈerɪk/
Ernest /ˈɜːnɪst; *NAmE* ˈɜːrn-/
Ethan /ˈiːθən/
Eugene /juːˈdʒiːn; ˈjuː-/ **Gene** /dʒiːn/ *(NAmE)*
Evan /ˈevən/
Fergus /ˈfɜːgəs; *NAmE* ˈfɜːrg-/ *(IrishE, ScotE)*
Francis /ˈfrɑːnsɪs; -sɪz; *NAmE* ˈfræn-/
Frank /fræŋk/
Frederick /ˈfredərɪk/
Fred /fred/, **Freddie, Freddy** /ˈfredi/
Gabriel /ˈgeɪbrɪəl/
Gareth /ˈgærəθ/
Gary /ˈgæri/
Gavin /ˈgævɪn/
Gene see EUGENE
Geoffrey, Jeffrey /ˈdʒefri/ **Geoff, Jeff** /dʒef/

George /dʒɔːdʒ; *NAmE* dʒɔːrdʒ/
Geraint /ˈgeraɪnt/ *(WelshE)*
Gerald /ˈdʒerəld/ **Gerry, Jerry** /ˈdʒeri/
Gerard /ˈdʒerɑːd; -rəd; *NAmE* ˈdʒerɑːrd/
Gilbert /ˈgɪlbət; *NAmE* -bərt/
Glen /glen/
Godfrey /ˈgɒdfri; *NAmE* ˈgɑːd-/
Gordon /ˈgɔːdn; *NAmE* ˈgɔːrdn/
Graham, Grahame, Graeme /ˈgreɪəm/
Gregory /ˈgregəri/ **Greg** /greg/
Guy /gaɪ/
Harold /ˈhærəld/
Harrison /ˈhærɪsən/
Harvey /ˈhɑːvi; *NAmE* ˈhɑːrvi/
Henry /ˈhenri/ **Hank** /hæŋk/, **Harry** /ˈhæri/
Herbert /ˈhɜːbət; *NAmE* ˈhɜːrbərt/
Bert /bɜːt; *NAmE* bɜːrt/, **Herb** /hɜːb; *NAmE* hɜːrb/
Horace /ˈhɒrɪs; *NAmE* ˈhɑːr-/
Howard /ˈhaʊəd; *NAmE* -ərd/
Hubert /ˈhjuːbət; *NAmE* -bərt/
Hugh /hjuː/
Hugo /ˈhjuːgəʊ; *NAmE* -goʊ/
Ian /ˈiːən/
Isaac /ˈaɪzək/
Isaiah /aɪˈzaɪə; *NAmE* aɪˈzeɪə/
Ivan /ˈaɪvn/
Ivor /ˈaɪvə(r)/
Jack /dʒæk/
Jacob /ˈdʒeɪkəb/ **Jake** /dʒeɪk/
James /dʒeɪmz/
Jim /dʒɪm/, **Jimmy** /ˈdʒɪmi/, **Jamie** /ˈdʒeɪmi/
Jason /ˈdʒeɪsn/
Jasper /ˈdʒæspə(r)/
Jayden /ˈdʒeɪdn/ *(NAmE)*
Jed /dʒed/
Jeff, Jeffrey see GEOFFREY
Jeremy /ˈdʒerəmi/ **Jerry** /ˈdʒeri/
Jerome /dʒəˈrəʊm; *NAmE* -ˈroʊm/
Jerry see GERALD, JEREMY
Jesse /ˈdʒesi/ *(especially NAmE)*
Jim, Jimmy see JAMES
Joe see JOSEPH
John /dʒɒn; *NAmE* dʒɑːn/
Johnny /ˈdʒɒni; *NAmE* ˈdʒɑːni/
Jonathan /ˈdʒɒnəθən; *NAmE* ˈdʒɑːn-/
Jon /dʒɒn; *NAmE* dʒɑːn/
Jordan /ˈdʒɔːdn; *NAmE* ˈdʒɔːrdn/
Joseph /ˈdʒəʊzɪf; -sɪf/ **Joe** /dʒəʊ; *NAmE* dʒoʊ/
Joshua /ˈdʒɒʃuə; *NAmE* ˈdʒɑːʃ-/
Julian /ˈdʒuːliən/
Justin /ˈdʒʌstɪn/
Keith /kiːθ/
Kenneth /ˈkenɪθ/ **Ken** /ken/, **Kenny** /ˈkeni/
Kevin /ˈkevɪn/
Kieran /ˈkɪərən; *NAmE* ˈkɪr-/
Kirk /kɜːk; *NAmE* kɜːrk/
Kit see CHRISTOPHER
Kyle /kaɪl/
Lance /lɑːns; *NAmE* læns/

Laurence, Lawrence /ˈlɒrəns; *NAmE* ˈlɔːr-/
Larry /ˈlæri/, **Laurie** /ˈlɒri; *NAmE* ˈlɔːri/

Len, Lenny see LEONARD

Leo /ˈliːəʊ; *NAmE* -oʊ/

Leonard /ˈlenəd; *NAmE* -ərd/
Len /len/, **Lenny** /ˈleni/

Leslie /ˈlezli/ **Les** /lez/

Lester /ˈlestə(r)/

Lewis /ˈluːɪs/ **Lew** /luː/

Liam /ˈliːəm/

Logan /ˈləʊgən; *NAmE* ˈloʊ-/ *(NAmE)*

Louis /ˈluːi; ˈluːɪs/ **Lou** /luː/ *(especially NAmE)*

Luke /luːk/

Malcolm /ˈmælkəm/

Mark /mɑːk; *NAmE* mɑːrk/

Martin /ˈmɑːtɪn; *NAmE* ˈmɑːrt-/

Matthew /ˈmæθjuː/ **Matt** /mæt/

Maurice, Morris /ˈmɒrɪs; *NAmE* ˈmɔːr-/

Max /mæks/

Michael /ˈmaɪkəl/
Mike /maɪk/, **Mick** /mɪk/, **Micky, Mickey** /ˈmɪki/

Miles, Myles /maɪlz/

Morris see MAURICE

Mort /mɔːt; *NAmE* mɔːrt/ *(NAmE)*

Murray /ˈmʌri/ *(ScotE)*

Myles see MILES

Nathan /ˈneɪθən/ **Nat** /næt/

Nathaniel /nəˈθænjəl/ **Nat** /næt/

Neil, Neal /niːəl/

Nicholas /ˈnɪkələs/ **Nick** /nɪk/, **Nicky** /nɪki/

Nigel /ˈnaɪdʒəl/

Noah /ˈnəʊə; *NAmE* ˈnoʊə/

Noel /ˈnəʊəl; *NAmE* ˈnoʊ-/

Norman /ˈnɔːmən; *NAmE* ˈnɔːrm-/

Oliver /ˈɒlɪvə(r); *NAmE* ˈɑːl-/
Ollie /ˈɒli; *NAmE* ˈɑːli/

Oscar /ˈɒskə(r); *NAmE* ˈɑːs-/

Owen /ˈəʊɪn; *NAmE* ˈoʊɪn/ *(WelshE)*

Patrick /ˈpætrɪk/ **Pat** /pæt/, **Paddy** /ˈpædi/

Paul /pɔːl/

Peter /ˈpiːtə(r)/ **Pete** /piːt/

Philip /ˈfɪlɪp/ **Phil** /fɪl/

Ralph /rælf; reɪf/

Randolph, Randolf /ˈrændɒlf; *NAmE* -dɑːlf/
Randy /ˈrændi/ *(especially NAmE)*

Raymond /ˈreɪmənd/ **Ray** /reɪ/

Reece /riːs/

Rex /reks/

Richard /ˈrɪtʃəd; *NAmE* -ərd/
Rick /rɪk/, **Ricky** /ˈrɪki/, **Ritchie** /ˈrɪtʃi/, **Dick** /dɪk/

Robert /ˈrɒbət; *NAmE* ˈrɑːbərt/
Rob /rɒb; *NAmE* rɑːb/, **Robbie** /ˈrɒbi; *NAmE* ˈrɑːbi/,
Bob /bɒb; *NAmE* bɑːb/, **Bobby** /ˈbɒbi; *NAmE* ˈbɑːbi/

Robin /ˈrɒbɪn; *NAmE* ˈrɑːb-/

Roderick /ˈrɒdərɪk; *NAmE* ˈrɑːd-/

Rodney /ˈrɒdni; *NAmE* ˈrɑːd-/
Rod /rɒd; *NAmE* rɑːd/

Roger /ˈrɒdʒə(r); *NAmE* ˈrɑːdʒ-/

Ronald /ˈrɒnəld; *NAmE* ˈrɑːn-/
Ron /rɒn; *NAmE* rɑːn/, **Ronnie** /ˈrɒni; *NAmE* ˈrɑːni/

Rory /ˈrɔːri/

Ross /rɒs; *NAmE* rɑːs/

Roy /rɔɪ/

Russell /ˈrʌsl/

Ryan /ˈraɪən/

Samuel /ˈsæmjuəl; *NAmE* -jəl/
Sam /sæm/, **Sammy** /ˈsæmi/

Sandy see ALEXANDER

Scott /skɒt; *NAmE* skɑːt/

Seamas, Seamus /ˈʃeɪməs/ *(IrishE)*

Sean /ʃɔːn/

Sebastian /səˈbæstiən; *NAmE* -tjən/ **Seb** /seb/

Sidney, Sydney /ˈsɪdni/**Sid** /sɪd/

Simon /ˈsaɪmən/

Stanley /ˈstænli/ **Stan** /stæn/

Stephen, Steven /ˈstiːvən/ **Steve** /stiːv/

Stewart, Stuart /ˈstjuːət; *NAmE* ˈstuːərt/

Ted see EDWARD

Terence /ˈterəns/ **Terry** /ˈteri/

Theodore /ˈθiːədɔː(r)/ **Theo** /ˈθiːəʊ; *NAmE* -oʊ/

Thomas /ˈtɒməs; *NAmE* ˈtɑːm-/
Tom /tɒm; *NAmE* tɑːm/, **Tommy** /ˈtɒmi; *NAmE* ˈtɑːmi/

Timothy /ˈtɪməθi/ **Tim** /tɪm/

Toby /ˈtəʊbi; *NAmE* ˈtoʊ-/

Tom, Tommy see THOMAS

Tony see ANTHONY

Trevor /ˈtrevə(r)/

Tyler /ˈtaɪlə(r)/

Victor /ˈvɪktə(r)/ **Vic** /vɪk/

Vincent /ˈvɪnsnt/ **Vince** /vɪns/

Walter /ˈwɔːltə(r)/

Warren /ˈwɒrən; *NAmE* ˈwɔːr-/

Wayne /weɪn/ *(NAmE)*

Wilbur /ˈwɪlbə(r)/

William /ˈwɪljəm/
Bill /bɪl/, **Billy** /ˈbɪli/, **Will** /wɪl/, **Willy** /ˈwɪli/

Zachary /ˈzækəri/

Geographical names

These lists show the spelling and pronunciation of geographical names.

If a country has different words for the country, adjective and person, all are given, (eg **Denmark**; **Danish**, **a Dane**). To make the plural of a word for a person from a particular country, add **–s**, except for **Swiss** and for words ending in **-ese** (eg **Japanese**), which stay the same, and for words that end in **-man** or **-woman**, which change to **-men** or **-women**.

(Inclusion in this list does not imply status as a sovereign state.)

Afghanistan /æf'gænɪstæn; -stɑːn/ **Afghan** /'æfgæn/
Africa /'æfrɪkə/ **African** /'æfrɪkən/
Albania /æl'beɪniə/ **Albanian** /æl'beɪniən/
Algeria /æl'dʒɪəriə; *NAmE* -'dʒɪr-/
Algerian /æl'dʒɪəriən; *NAmE* -'dʒɪr-/
America /ə'merɪkə/ **American** /ə'merɪkən/
Andorra /æn'dɔːrə/ **Andorran** /æn'dɔːrən/
Angola /æŋ'gəʊlə; *NAmE* -'goʊ-/
Angolan /æŋ'gəʊlən; *NAmE* -'goʊ-/
Antarctica /æn'tɑːktɪkə; *NAmE* -'tɑːrk-/
Antarctic /æn'tɑːktɪk; *NAmE* -'tɑːrk-/
Antigua and Barbuda /æn,tiːgə ən bɑː'bjuːdə; *NAmE* bɑːr'b-/
Antiguan /æn'tiːgən/
Barbudan /bɑː'bjuːdən; *NAmE* bɑːr'b-/
(the) Arctic Ocean /,ɑːktɪk 'əʊʃn; *NAmE* ,ɑːrktɪk 'oʊʃn/
Arctic /'ɑːktɪk; *NAmE* 'ɑːrk-/
Argentina /,ɑːdʒən'tiːnə; *NAmE* ,ɑːrdʒ-/
Argentinian /,ɑːdʒən'tɪniən; *NAmE* ,ɑːrdʒ-/
Argentine /'ɑːdʒəntaɪn; *NAmE* 'ɑːrdʒ-/
Armenia /ɑː'miːniə; *NAmE* ɑːr'm-/
Armenian /ɑː'miːniən; *NAmE* ɑːr'm-/
Asia /'eɪʒə; 'eɪʃə/ **Asian** /'eɪʒn; 'eɪʃn/
(the) Atlantic Ocean /ət,læntɪk 'əʊʃn; *NAmE* 'oʊʃn/
Australasia /,ɒstrə'leɪʒə; -'leɪʃə; *NAmE* ,ɔːstrə'leɪʒə; -'leɪʃə/
Australasian /,ɒstrə'leɪʒn; -'leɪʃn; *NAmE* ,ɔːstrə'leɪʒn; -'leɪʃn/
Australia /ɒ'streɪliə; *NAmE* ɔː's-/
Australian /ɒ'streɪliən; *NAmE* ɔː's-/
Austria /'ɒstriə; *NAmE* 'ɔːs-/ **Austrian** /'ɒstriən; *NAmE* 'ɔːs-/
Azerbaijan /,æzəbaɪ'dʒɑːn; *NAmE* -zərb-/
Azerbaijani /,æzəbaɪ'dʒɑːni; *NAmE* -zərb-/
Azeri /ə'zeəri; *NAmE* ə'zeri/
(the) Bahamas /bə'hɑːməz/ **Bahamian** /bə'heɪmiən/
Bahrain /bɑː'reɪn/ **Bahraini** /bɑː'reɪni/
Bangladesh /,bæŋglə'deʃ/ **Bangladeshi** /,bæŋglə'deʃi/
Barbados /bɑː'beɪdɒs; *NAmE* bɑːr'beɪdoʊs/
Barbadian /bɑː'beɪdiən; *NAmE* bɑːr'b-/
Belarus /,belə'ruːs/ **Belarusian** /,belə'ruːsiən/
Belorussian /,belə'rʌʃn/
Belgium /'beldʒəm/ **Belgian** /'beldʒən/
Belize /bə'liːz; be'l-/ **Belizean** /bə'liːziən; be'l-/
Benin /be'niːn/ **Beninese** /,benɪ'niːz/
Bhutan /buː'tɑːn/ **Bhutani** /buː'tɑːni/
Bhutanese /,buːtə'niːz/
Bolivia /bə'lɪviə/ **Bolivian** /bə'lɪviən/
Bosnia and Herzegovina /,bɒzniə ən ,hɜːtsəgə'viːnə; *NAmE* ,bɑːzniə ən ,hɜːrts-; ,bɔːz-/
Bosnian /'bɒzniən; *NAmE* 'bɑːz-; 'bɔːz-/
Herzegovinian /,hɜːtsəgə'vɪniən; *NAmE* ,hɜːrts-/
Botswana /bɒt'swɑːnə; *NAmE* bɑːt-/
Botswanan /bɒt'swɑːnən; *NAmE* bɑːt-/
person **a Motswana** /mɒt'swɑːnə; *NAmE* mɑːt-/
people **Batswana** /bæt'swɑːnə/
Brazil /brə'zɪl/ **Brazilian** /brə'zɪliən/
Brunei /bruː'naɪ/ **Bruneian** /bruː'naɪən/
Bulgaria /bʌl'geəriə; *NAmE* -'ger-/
Bulgarian /bʌl'geəriən; *NAmE* -'ger-/
Burkina /bɜː'kiːnə; *NAmE* bɜːr'k-/
Burkinan /,bɜː'kiːnən; *NAmE* ,bɜːr'k-/
Burkinabe /bɜː,kiːnə'beɪ; *NAmE* bɜːr,k-/
Burma /'bɜːmə; *NAmE* 'bɜːrmə/
Burmese /bɜː'miːz; *NAmE* bɜːr'm-/
➲ see also **Myanmar**
Burundi /bʊ'rʊndi/ **Burundian** /bʊ'rʊndiən/
Cambodia /kæm'bəʊdiə; *NAmE* -'boʊ-/
Cambodian /kæm'bəʊdiən; *NAmE* -'boʊ-/
Cameroon /,kæmə'ruːn/ **Cameroonian** /,kæmə'ruːniən/
Canada /'kænədə/ **Canadian** /kə'neɪdiən/
Cape Verde /,keɪp 'vɜːd; *NAmE* 'vɜːrd/
Cape Verdean /,keɪp 'vɜːdiən; *NAmE* 'vɜːrd-/
(the) Caribbean Sea /,kærəbiːən 'siː; kə'rɪbiən/
Caribbean /,kærə'biːən; kə'rɪbiən/
Central African Republic /,sentrəl ,æfrɪkən rɪ'pʌblɪk/
Central African /,sentrəl 'æfrɪkən/
Chad /tʃæd/ **Chadian** /'tʃædiən/
Chile /'tʃɪli/ **Chilean** /'tʃɪliən/
China /'tʃaɪnə/ **Chinese** /tʃaɪ'niːz/
Colombia /kə'lɒmbiə; -'lʌm-; *NAmE* -'loʊm-/
Colombian /kə'lɒmbiən; -'lʌm-; *NAmE* -'loʊm-/
Comoros /'kɒmərəʊz; *NAmE* 'kɑːməroʊz/
Comoran /kə'mɔːrən/
Congo /'kɒŋgəʊ; *NAmE* 'kɑːŋgoʊ/
Congolese /,kɒŋgə'liːz; *NAmE* ,kɑːŋ-/
(the) Democratic Republic of the Congo (DR Congo) /,demə,krætɪk rɪ,pʌblɪk əv ðə 'kɒŋgəʊ; *NAmE* 'kɑːŋgoʊ/ **Congolese** /,kɒŋgə'liːz; *NAmE* ,kɑːŋ-/
Costa Rica /,kɒstə 'riːkə; *NAmE* ,kɑːstə; ,koʊstə/
Costa Rican /,kɒstə 'riːkən; *NAmE* ,kɑːstə; ,koʊstə/
Côte d'Ivoire /,kəʊt diː'vwɑː; *NAmE* ,koʊt diː'vwɑːr/
Ivorian /aɪ'vɔːriən/ ➲ see also **Ivory Coast**
Croatia /krəʊ'eɪʃə; *NAmE* kroʊ-/
Croatian /krəʊ'eɪʃn; *NAmE* kroʊ-/
Cuba /'kjuːbə/ **Cuban** /'kjuːbən/
Cyprus /'saɪprəs/ **Cypriot** /'sɪpriət/
(the) Czech Republic /,tʃek rɪ'pʌblɪk/ **Czech** /tʃek/
Denmark /'denmɑːk; *NAmE* -mɑːrk/
Danish /'deɪnɪʃ/ **a Dane** /deɪn/
Djibouti /dʒɪ'buːti/ **Djiboutian** /dʒɪ'buːtiən/
Dominica /,dɒmɪ'niːkə; *NAmE* ,dɑːmə'n-/
Dominican /,dɒmɪ'niːkən; *NAmE* ,dɑːmə'n-/
(the) Dominican Republic /də,mɪnɪkən rɪ'pʌblɪk/
Dominican /də'mɪnɪkən/
East Timor /,iːst 'tiːmɔː(r)/ **East Timorese** /,iːst tɪmə'riːz/
Ecuador /'ekwədɔː(r)/
Ecuadorian, Ecuadorean /,ekwə'dɔːriən/
Egypt /'iːdʒɪpt/ **Egyptian** /i'dʒɪpʃn/
El Salvador /,el 'sælvədɔː(r)/ **Salvadorean** /,sælvə'dɔːriən/
Equatorial Guinea /,ekwətɔːriəl 'gɪni/
Equatorial Guinean /,ekwətɔːriəl 'gɪniən/
Eritrea /,erɪ'treɪə; *NAmE* -'triːə/
Eritrean /,erɪ'treɪən; *NAmE* -'triːən/

Estonia /e'stəʊniə; *NAmE* e'stoʊ-/
Estonian /e'stəʊniən; *NAmE* e'stoʊ-/

Ethiopia /ˌi:θi'əʊpiə; *NAmE* -'oʊ-/
Ethiopian /ˌi:θi'əʊpiən; *NAmE* -'oʊ-/

Europe /'jʊərəp; *NAmE* 'jʊrəp/
European /ˌjʊərə'pi:ən; *NAmE* ˌjʊrə-/

Fiji /'fi:dʒi:/ **Fijian** /fi:'dʒi:ən; *NAmE also* 'fi:dʒi:ən/

Finland /'fɪnlənd/ **Finnish** /'fɪnɪʃ/ **a Finn** /fɪn/

France /frɑ:ns; *NAmE* fræns/ **French** /frentʃ/ **a Frenchman** /'frentʃmən/ **a Frenchwoman** /'frentʃwʊmən/

FYROM /'faɪrɒm; *NAmE* -rɑ:m/ ➲ see also **Former Yugoslav Republic of Macedonia**

Gabon /gæ'bɒn; *NAmE* gæ'boʊn/ **Gabonese** /ˌgæbə'ni:z/

(the) Gambia /'gæmbiə/ **Gambian** /'gæmbiən/

Georgia /'dʒɔ:dʒə; *NAmE* 'dʒɔ:rdʒə/
Georgian /'dʒɔ:dʒən; *NAmE* 'dʒɔ:rdʒən/

Germany /'dʒɜ:məni; *NAmE* 'dʒɜ:rm-/
German /'dʒɜ:mən; *NAmE* 'dʒɜ:rm-/

Ghana /'gɑ:nə/ **Ghanaian** /gɑ:'neɪən/

Greece /gri:s/ **Greek** /gri:k/

Grenada /grə'neɪdə/ **Grenadian** /grə'neɪdiən/

Guatemala /ˌgwɑ:tə'mɑ:lə; *BrE also* ˌgwæt-/
Guatemalan /ˌgwɑ:tə'mɑ:lən; *BrE also* ˌgwæt-/

Guinea /'gɪni/ **Guinean** /'gɪniən/

Guinea-Bissau /ˌgɪni bɪ'saʊ/ **Guinean** /'gɪniən/

Guyana /gaɪ'ænə/ **Guyanese** /ˌgaɪə'ni:z/

Haiti /'heɪti/ **Haitian** /'heɪʃn/

Honduras /hɒn'djʊərəs; *NAmE* hɑ:n'dʊrəs/
Honduran /hɒn'djʊərən; *NAmE* hɑ:n'dʊrən/

Hungary /'hʌŋgəri/ **Hungarian** /hʌŋ'geəriən; *NAmE* -'ger-/

Iceland /'aɪslənd/ **Icelandic** /aɪs'lændɪk/
an Icelander /'aɪsləndə(r)/

India /'ɪndiə/ **Indian** /'ɪndiən/

(the) Indian Ocean /ˌɪndiən 'əʊʃn; *NAmE* 'oʊʃn/

Indonesia /ˌɪndə'ni:ʒə; *BrE also* -'ni:ziə/
Indonesian /ˌɪndə'ni:ʒn; *BrE also* -'ni:ziən/

Iran /ɪ'rɑ:n; ɪ'ræn/ **Iranian** /ɪ'reɪniən/

Iraq /ɪ'rɑ:k; ɪ'ræk/ **Iraqi** /ɪ'rɑ:ki; ɪ'ræki/

Israel /'ɪzreɪl/ **Israeli** /ɪz'reɪli/

Italy /'ɪtəli/ **Italian** /ɪ'tæliən/

(the) Ivory Coast /ˌaɪvəri 'kəʊst; *NAmE* 'koʊst/
Ivorian /aɪ'vɔ:riən/ ➲ see also **Côte d'Ivoire**

Jamaica /dʒə'meɪkə/ **Jamaican** /dʒə'meɪkən/

Japan /dʒə'pæn/ **Japanese** /ˌdʒæpə'ni:z/

Jordan /'dʒɔ:dn; *NAmE* 'dʒɔ:rdn/
Jordanian /dʒɔ:'deɪniən; *NAmE* dʒɔ:r'd-/

Kazakhstan /ˌkæzək'stæn; -'stɑ:n/
Kazakh /kə'zæk; 'kæzæk/

Kenya /'kenjə; *NAmE also* 'ki:njə/
Kenyan /'kenjən; *NAmE also* 'ki:njən/

Kiribati /ˌkɪrɪ'bɑ:ti; -'bæs; *NAmE* 'kɪrəbæs/ **Kiribati**

Korea /kə'riə/ **Korean** /kə'riən/
➲ see also **North Korea, South Korea**

Kuwait /kʊ'weɪt/ **Kuwaiti** /kʊ'weɪti/

Kyrgyzstan /ˌkɜ:gɪ'stæn; ˌkɪəgɪ's-; -'stɑ:n; *NAmE* ˌkɪrg-/
Kyrgyz /'kɜ:gɪz; 'kɪəgɪz; *NAmE* 'kɪrg-/

Laos /laʊs/ **Laotian** /'laʊʃn; *NAmE also* leɪ'oʊʃn/ **Lao** /laʊ/

Latvia /'lætviə/ **Latvian** /'lætviən/

Lebanon /'lebənən; *NAmE also* -nɑ:n/ **Lebanese** /ˌlebə'ni:z/

Lesotho /lə'su:tu:/ person **a Mosotho** /mə'su:tu:/ people **Basotho** /bə'su:tu:/

Liberia /laɪ'bɪəriə; *NAmE* -'bɪr-/
Liberian /laɪ'bɪəriən; *NAmE* -'bɪr-/

Libya /'lɪbiə/ **Libyan** /'lɪbiən/

Liechtenstein /'lɪktənstaɪn; 'lɪxt-/
Liechtenstein /'lɪktənstaɪn; 'lɪxt-/
a Liechtensteiner /'lɪktənstaɪnə(r); 'lɪxt-/

Lithuania /ˌlɪθju'eɪniə; *NAmE* ˌlɪθu-/
Lithuanian /ˌlɪθju'eɪniən; *NAmE* ˌlɪθu-/

Luxembourg /'lʌksəmbɜ:g; *NAmE* -bɜ:rg/
Luxembourg /'lʌksəmbɜ:g; *NAmE* -bɜ:rg/
a Luxembourger /'lʌksəmbɜ:gə(r); *NAmE* -bɜ:rgər/

(the) Former Yugoslav Republic of Macedonia /ˌfɔ:mə ˌju:gəslɑ:v rɪˌpʌblɪk əv ˌmæsə'dəʊniə; *NAmE* ˌfɔ:rmər ˌju:gəslɑ:v rɪˌpʌblɪk əv ˌmæsə'doʊniə; *NAmE also* -goʊ-/
Macedonian /ˌmæsə'dəʊniən; *NAmE* -'doʊ-/

Madagascar /ˌmædə'gæskə(r)/ **Madagascan** /ˌmædə'gæskən/ **Malagasy** /ˌmælə'gæsi/

Malawi /mə'lɑ:wi/ **Malawian** /mə'lɑ:wiən/

Malaysia /mə'leɪʒə; *BrE also* -'leɪziə/
Malaysian /mə'leɪʒn; *BrE also* -'leɪziən/

(the) Maldives /'mɔ:ldi:vz/ **Maldivian** /mɔ:l'dɪviən/

Mali /'mɑ:li/ **Malian** /'mɑ:liən/

Malta /'mɔ:ltə/ **Maltese** /mɔ:l'ti:z/

(the) Marshall Islands /'mɑ:ʃl aɪləndz; *NAmE* 'mɑ:rʃl/
Marshallese /ˌmɑ:ʃə'li:z; *NAmE* ˌmɑ:rʃ-/

Mauritania /ˌmɒrɪ'teɪniə; *NAmE* ˌmɔ:r-/
Mauritanian /ˌmɒrɪ'teɪniən; *NAmE* ˌmɔ:r-/

Mauritius /mə'rɪʃəs; *NAmE* mɔ:'r-/
Mauritian /mə'rɪʃn; *NAmE* mɔ:'r-/

Mexico /'meksɪkəʊ; *NAmE* -koʊ/ **Mexican** /'meksɪkən/

Micronesia /ˌmaɪkrə'ni:ziə; *NAmE* -'ni:ʒə/
Micronesian /ˌmaɪkrə'ni:ziən; *NAmE* -'ni:ʒn/

Moldova /mɒl'dəʊvə; *NAmE* mɑ:l'doʊvə; mɔ:l-/
Moldovan /mɒl'dəʊvn; *NAmE* mɑ:l'doʊvn; mɔ:l-/

Monaco /'mɒnəkəʊ; *NAmE* 'mɑ:nəkoʊ/
Monégasque /ˌmɒni'gæsk; ˌmɒneɪ'g-; *NAmE* ˌmɑ:n-/

Mongolia /mɒŋ'gəʊliə; *NAmE* mɑ:ŋ'goʊ-/
Mongolian /mɒŋ'gəʊliən; *NAmE* mɑ:ŋ'goʊ-/
Mongol /'mɒŋgl; *NAmE* 'mɑ:ŋ-/

Montenegro /ˌmɒntɪ'ni:grəʊ; *NAmE* ˌmɑ:ntə'neɪgroʊ; -'neg-/
Montenegrin /ˌmɒntɪ'ni:grɪn; *NAmE* ˌmɑ:ntə'neɪgrɪn; -'neg-/

Morocco /mə'rɒkəʊ; *NAmE* mə'rɑ:koʊ/
Moroccan /mə'rɒkən; *NAmE* -'rɑ:k-/

Mozambique /ˌməʊzæm'bi:k; *NAmE* ˌmoʊ-/
Mozambican /ˌməʊzæm'bi:kən; *NAmE* ˌmoʊ-/

Myanmar /miˌæn'mɑ:(r)/ ➲ see also **Burma**

Namibia /nə'mɪbiə/ **Namibian** /nə'mɪbiən/

Nauru /'naʊru:/ **Nauruan** /naʊ'ru:ən/

Nepal /nə'pɔ:l/ **Nepalese** /ˌnepə'li:z/

(the) Netherlands /'neðələndz; *NAmE* -ðərl-/ **Dutch** /dʌtʃ/ **a Dutchman** /'dʌtʃmən/ **a Dutchwoman** /'dʌtʃwʊmən/

New Zealand (NZ) /ˌnju: 'zi:lənd; *NAmE* ˌnu:/
New Zealand, a New Zealander /ˌnju: 'zi:ləndə(r); *NAmE* ˌnu:/

Nicaragua /ˌnɪkə'rægjuə; *NAmE* -gwə/
Nicaraguan /ˌnɪkə'rægjuən; *NAmE* -gwən/

Niger /ni:'ʒeə(r)/ **Nigerien** /ni:'ʒeəriən/

Nigeria /naɪ'dʒɪəriə; *NAmE* -'dʒɪr-/
Nigerian /naɪ'dʒɪəriən; *NAmE* -'dʒɪr-/

North Korea /ˌnɔ:θ kə'riə; *NAmE* ˌnɔ:rθ/
North Korean /ˌnɔ:θ kə'riən; *NAmE* ˌnɔ:rθ/

Norway /'nɔ:weɪ; *NAmE* 'nɔ:rweɪ/
Norwegian /nɔ:'wi:dʒən; *NAmE* nɔ:r'w-/

Oman /əʊ'mɑ:n; *BrE also* -'mæn; *NAmE* oʊ'mɑ:n/
Omani /əʊ'mɑ:ni; *BrE also* -'mæni; *NAmE* oʊ'mɑ:ni/

(the) Pacific Ocean /pəˌsɪfɪk 'əʊʃn; *NAmE* 'oʊʃn/

Pakistan /ˌpækɪ'stæn; ˌpɑ:kɪ-; -'stɑ:n/
Pakistani /ˌpækɪ'stæni; ˌpɑ:kɪ-; -'stɑ:ni/

Palau /pə'laʊ/ **Palauan** /pə'laʊən/

Panama /'pænəmɑ:/ **Panamanian** /ˌpænə'meɪniən/

Papua New Guinea (PNG) /ˌpæpjuə ˌnju: 'gɪni; *BrE also* ˌpæpuə; *NAmE* ˌpæpuə ˌnu: 'gɪni/
Papua New Guinean /ˌpæpjuə ˌnju: 'gɪniən; *BrE also* ˌpæpuə; *NAmE* ˌpæpuə ˌnu: 'gɪniən/

Paraguay /'pærəgwaɪ/ **Paraguayan** /ˌpærə'gwaɪən/

Peru /pəˈruː/ **Peruvian** /pəˈruːviən/
(the) Philippines /ˈfɪlɪpiːnz/ **Philippine** /ˈfɪlɪpiːn/
a Filipino /ˌfɪlɪˈpiːnəʊ; *NAmE* -noʊ/ **a Filipina** /ˌfɪlɪˈpiːnə/
Poland /ˈpəʊlənd; *NAmE* ˈpoʊ-/
Polish /ˈpəʊlɪʃ; *NAmE* ˈpoʊ-/ **a Pole** /pəʊl; *NAmE* poʊl/
Portugal /ˈpɔːtʃʊgl; *NAmE* ˈpɔːrtʃ-/
Portuguese /ˌpɔːtʃʊˈgiːz; *NAmE* ˌpɔːrtʃ-/
Qatar /ˈkʌtɑː(r); ˈkæt-; *NAmE* ˈkɑːtɑːr; kəˈtɑːr/
Qatari /kʌˈtɑːri; kæˈt-; *NAmE* ˈkɑːtɑːri; kəˈtɑːri/
Romania /ruˈmeɪniə/ **Romanian** /ruˈmeɪniən/
Russia /ˈrʌʃə/ **Russian** /ˈrʌʃn/
Rwanda /ruˈændə/ **Rwandan** /ruˈændən/
Samoa /səˈməʊə; *NAmE* səˈmoʊə/
Samoan /səˈməʊən; *NAmE* səˈmoʊən/
San Marino /ˌsæn məˈriːnəʊ; *NAmE* -noʊ/
São Tomé and Principe /ˌsaʊ təˌmeɪ ən ˈprɪnsɪpeɪ/
Saudi Arabia /ˌsaʊdi əˈreɪbiə/
Saudi /ˈsaʊdi/ **Saudi Arabian** /ˌsaʊdi əˈreɪbiən/
Senegal /ˌsenɪˈgɔːl/ **Senegalese** /ˌsenɪgəˈliːz/
Serbia /ˈsɜːbiə; *NAmE* ˈsɜːrb-/
Serbian /ˈsɜːbiən; *NAmE* ˈsɜːrb-/ **Serb** /sɜːb; *NAmE* sɜːrb/
(the) Seychelles /seɪˈʃelz/ **Seychellois** /ˌseɪʃelˈwɑː/
Sierra Leone /siˌerə liˈəʊn; *NAmE* liˈoʊn/
Sierra Leonean /siˌerə liˈəʊniən; *NAmE* liˈoʊniən/
Singapore /ˌsɪŋəˈpɔː(r)/ **Singaporean** /ˌsɪŋəˈpɔːriən/
Slovakia /sləˈvækiə; *NAmE* sloʊˈv-/ **Slovak** /ˈsləʊvæk; *NAmE* ˈsloʊ-/ **Slovakian** /sləˈvækiən; *NAmE* sloʊˈv-/
Slovenia /sləˈviːniə; *NAmE* sloʊˈv-/ **Slovene** /ˈsləʊviːn; *NAmE* ˈsloʊ-/ **Slovenian** /sləˈviːniən; *NAmE* sloʊˈv-/
(the) Solomon Islands /ˈsɒləmən aɪləndz; *NAmE* ˈsɑːl-/
a Solomon Islander /ˈsɒləmən aɪləndə(r); *NAmE* ˈsɑːl-/
Somalia /səˈmɑːliə/ **Somali** /səˈmɑːli/
South Africa /ˌsaʊθ ˈæfrɪkə/
South African /ˌsaʊθ ˈæfrɪkən/
South Korea /ˌsaʊθ kəˈriə/ **South Korean** /ˌsaʊθ kəˈriən/
Spain /speɪn/
Spanish /ˈspænɪʃ/ **a Spaniard** /ˈspænɪəd; *NAmE* -njərd/
Sri Lanka /ˌsri ˈlæŋkə; *NAmE also* ˈlɑːŋkə/
Sri Lankan /ˌsri ˈlæŋkən; *NAmE also* ˈlɑːŋ-/
St Kitts and Nevis /snt ˌkɪts ən ˈniːvɪs; *NAmE also* seɪnt/
Kittitian /kɪˈtɪʃn/ **Nevisian** /niːˈvɪsiən; *NAmE* nəˈvɪʒn/
St Lucia /ˌsnt ˈluːʃə; *NAmE also* ˌseɪnt/
St Lucian /ˌsnt ˈluːʃən; *NAmE also* ˌseɪnt/
St Vincent and the Grenadines /snt ˌvɪnsnt ən ðə ˈgrenədiːnz; *NAmE also* seɪnt/
Vincentian /vɪnˈsenʃn/

Sudan /suˈdɑːn; -ˈdæn/ **Sudanese** /ˌsuːdəˈniːz/
Suriname /ˌsʊərɪˈnɑːm; -ˈnæm; *NAmE* ˌsʊr-/
Surinamese /ˌsʊərɪnəˈmiːz; *NAmE* ˌsʊr-/
Swaziland /ˈswɑːzilænd/ **Swazi** /ˈswɑːzi/
Sweden /ˈswiːdn/ **Swedish** /ˈswiːdɪʃ/ **a Swede** /swiːd/
Switzerland /ˈswɪtsələnd; *NAmE* -ərl-/ **Swiss** /swɪs/
Syria /ˈsɪriə/ **Syrian** /ˈsɪriən/
Tajikistan /tæˌdʒiːkɪˈstæn; -ˈstɑːn/ **Tajik** /tæˈdʒiːk/
Tanzania /ˌtænzəˈniːə/ **Tanzanian** /ˌtænzəˈniːən/
Thailand /ˈtaɪlænd/ **Thai** /taɪ/
Togo /ˈtəʊgəʊ; *NAmE* ˈtoʊgoʊ/
Togolese /ˌtəʊgəˈliːz; *NAmE* ˌtoʊ-/
Tonga /ˈtɒŋə; ˈtɒŋgə; *NAmE* ˈtɑːŋgə/
Tongan /ˈtɒŋən; ˈtɒŋgən; *NAmE* ˈtɑːŋgən/
Trinidad and Tobago /ˌtrɪnɪdæd ən təˈbeɪgəʊ; *NAmE* -goʊ/
Trinidadian /ˌtrɪnɪˈdædiən/ **Tobagan** /təˈbeɪgən/
Tobagonian /ˌtəʊbəˈgəʊniən; *NAmE* ˌtoʊbəˈgoʊ-/
Tunisia /tjuˈnɪziə; *NAmE usually* tuˈniːʒə/
Tunisian /tjuˈnɪziən; *NAmE usually* tuˈniːʒən/
Turkey /ˈtɜːki; *NAmE* ˈtɜːrki/
Turkish /ˈtɜːkɪʃ; *NAmE* ˈtɜːrkɪʃ/ **a Turk** /tɜːk; *NAmE* tɜːrk/
Turkmenistan /tɜːkˌmenɪˈstæn; -ˈstɑːn; *NAmE* tɜːrk-/
Turkmen /ˈtɜːkmen; *NAmE* ˈtɜːrk-/
Tuvalu /tuːˈvɑːluː/ **Tuvaluan** /ˌtuːvɑːˈluːən/
Uganda /juːˈgændə/ **Ugandan** /juːˈgændən/
Ukraine /juːˈkreɪn/ **Ukrainian** /juːˈkreɪniən/
(the) United Arab Emirates (UAE) /juˌnaɪtɪd ˌærəb ˈemɪrəts/
Emirati /emɪˈrɑːti/
(the) United States of America (USA) /juˌnaɪtɪd ˌsteɪts əv əˈmerɪkə/ **American** /əˈmerɪkən/
Uruguay /ˈjʊərəgwaɪ; *NAmE* ˈjʊr-/
Uruguayan /ˌjʊərəˈgwaɪən; *NAmE* ˌjʊr-/
Uzbekistan /ʊzˌbekɪˈstæn; -ˈstɑːn/ **Uzbek** /ˈʊzbek/
Vanuatu /ˌvænuːˈɑːtuː; ˌvænwɑːˈtuː/
Vanuatuan /ˌvænwɑːˈtuːən/
(the) Vatican City /ˌvætɪkən ˈsɪti/
Venezuela /ˌvenəˈzweɪlə/ **Venezuelan** /ˌvenəˈzweɪlən/
Vietnam /ˌvjetˈnæm; ˌviːet-; -ˈnɑːm/
Vietnamese /ˌvjetnəˈmiːz; viːˌetnə-/
Yemen /ˈjemən/ **Yemeni** /ˈjeməni/
Zambia /ˈzæmbiə/ **Zambian** /ˈzæmbiən/
Zimbabwe /zɪmˈbɑːbwi; -ˈbɑːbweɪ/
Zimbabwean /zɪmˈbɑːbwiən/

The British Isles /ðə ˌbrɪtɪʃ ˈaɪlz/

(the) United Kingdom (UK) /juˌnaɪtɪd ˈkɪŋdəm/
Great Britain /ˌgreɪt ˈbrɪtn/
England /ˈɪŋglənd/
Scotland /ˈskɒtlənd; *NAmE* ˈskɑːt-/
Wales /weɪlz/
Northern Ireland /ˌnɔːðən ˈaɪələnd; *NAmE* ˌnɔːrðərn ˈaɪərlənd/
(the) Republic of Ireland (ROI) /rɪˌpʌblɪk əv ˈaɪələnd; *NAmE* ˈaɪərlənd/

Towns and cities in the British Isles

Aberdeen /ˌæbəˈdiːn; *NAmE* ˌæbərˈdiːn/
Aberystwyth /ˌæbəˈrɪstwɪθ/
Ayr /eə(r); *NAmE* er/
Bath /bɑːθ; *NAmE* bæθ/
Belfast /ˈbelfɑːst; ˌbelˈfɑːst; *NAmE* ˈbelfæst/
Berwick-upon-Tweed /ˌberɪk əpɒn ˈtwiːd; *NAmE* əpɑːn/
Birmingham /ˈbɜːmɪŋəm; *NAmE* ˈbɜːrmɪŋhæm/
Blackburn /ˈblækbɜːn; *NAmE* ˈblækbɜːrn/
Blackpool /ˈblækpuːl/
Bolton /ˈbəʊltən; *NAmE* ˈboʊ-/
Bournemouth /ˈbɔːnməθ; *NAmE* ˈbɔːrn-/
Bradford /ˈbrædfəd; *NAmE* -fərd/
Brighton /ˈbraɪtn/
Bristol /ˈbrɪstl/
Caernarfon /kəˈnɑːvn; *NAmE* kɑːrˈnɑːrvn; kə(r)-/
Cambridge /ˈkeɪmbrɪdʒ/
Canterbury /ˈkæntəbəri; *NAmE also* -tərberi/
Cardiff /ˈkɑːdɪf; *NAmE* ˈkɑːrdɪf/
Carlisle /kɑːˈlaɪl; *NAmE* ˈkɑːrlaɪl/
Chester /ˈtʃestə(r)/

Colchester /ˈkəʊltʃɪstə(r); *NAmE* ˈkoʊltʃestər/
Colwyn Bay /ˌkɒlwɪn ˈbeɪ; *NAmE* ˌkɑːl-; ˌkoʊl-/
Cork /kɔːk; *NAmE* kɔːrk/
Coventry /ˈkɒvəntri; *NAmE* ˈkɑːv-/
Derby /ˈdɑːbi; *NAmE* ˈdɑːrbi/
Douglas /ˈdʌɡləs/
Dover /ˈdəʊvə(r); *NAmE* ˈdoʊ-/
Dublin /ˈdʌblɪn/
Dumfries /dʌmˈfriːs/
Dundee /dʌnˈdiː/
Durham /ˈdʌrəm; *NAmE also* ˈdɜːr-/
Eastbourne /ˈiːstbɔːn; *NAmE* -bɔːrn/
East Kilbride /ˌiːst kɪlˈbraɪd/
Edinburgh /ˈedɪnbrə; -bərə/
Exeter /ˈeksɪtə(r)/
Fort William /ˌfɔːt ˈwɪljəm; *NAmE* ˌfɔːrt/
Galway /ˈɡɔːlweɪ/
Glasgow /ˈɡlɑːzɡəʊ; *NAmE* ˈɡlæzɡoʊ/
Gloucester /ˈɡlɒstə(r); *NAmE* ˈɡlɑːs-; ˈɡlɔːs-/
Great Yarmouth /ˌɡreɪt ˈjɑːməθ; *NAmE* ˈjɑːrm-/
Hartlepool /ˈhɑːtlipuːl; *NAmE* ˈhɑːrt-/
Hastings /ˈheɪstɪŋz/
Hereford /ˈherɪfəd; *NAmE* -fərd/
Holyhead /ˈhɒlihed; *NAmE* ˈhɑːl-/
Huddersfield /ˈhʌdəzfiːld; *NAmE* -dərz-/
Inverness /ˌɪnvəˈnes; *NAmE* -vərˈn-/
Ipswich /ˈɪpswɪtʃ/
John o'Groats /ˌdʒɒn ə ˈɡrəʊts; *NAmE* ˌdʒɑːn ə ˈɡroʊts/
Kilmarnock /kɪlˈmɑːnək; *NAmE* -ˈmɑːrn-/
Kingston upon Hull /ˌkɪŋstən əpɒn ˈhʌl; *NAmE* əpɑːn/
Leeds /liːdz/
Leicester /ˈlestə(r)/
Limerick /ˈlɪmərɪk/
Lincoln /ˈlɪŋkən/
Lisburn /ˈlɪzbɜːn; *NAmE* -bɜːrn/
Liverpool /ˈlɪvəpuːl; *NAmE* -vərp-/
London /ˈlʌndən/
Londonderry /ˈlʌndənderi/
Luton /ˈluːtn/
Manchester /ˈmæntʃɪstə(r)/
Margate /ˈmɑːɡeɪt; *NAmE* ˈmɑːrɡ-/
Middlesbrough /ˈmɪdlzbrə/
Milford Haven /ˌmɪlfəd ˈheɪvn; *NAmE* -fərd/
Milton Keynes /ˌmɪltn ˈkiːnz; ˌmɪltən/
Newcastle upon Tyne /ˌnjuːkɑːsl əpɒn ˈtaɪn; *NAmE* ˌnuːkæsl əpɑːn/
Newport /ˈnjuːpɔːt; *NAmE* ˈnuːpɔːrt/
Newry /ˈnjuːri; *NAmE* ˈnuː-/
Northampton /nɔːθˈhæmptən; *NAmE* nɔːrθ-/
Norwich /ˈnɒrɪdʒ; *NAmE* ˈnɑːr-/
Nottingham /ˈnɒtɪŋəm; *NAmE* ˈnɑːtɪŋəm; -hæm/
Oxford /ˈɒksfəd; *NAmE* ˈɑːksfərd/
Perth /pɜːθ; *NAmE* pɜːrθ/
Peterborough /ˈpiːtəbʌrə; *NAmE* -bəroʊ/
Plymouth /ˈplɪməθ/
Poole /puːl/
Portsmouth /ˈpɔːtsməθ; *NAmE* ˈpɔːrts-/
Preston /ˈprestən/
Reading /ˈredɪŋ/
Salisbury /ˈsɔːlzbəri; *NAmE also* -beri/
Sheffield /ˈʃefiːld/
Shrewsbury /ˈʃrəʊzbəri; *NAmE* ˈʃroʊz-; *NAmE also* -beri/
Slough /slaʊ/
Southampton /saʊˈθæmptən/
Southend-on-Sea /ˌsaʊθend ɒn ˈsiː; *NAmE* ɑːn/
St Andrews /ˌsnt ˈændruːz; *NAmE also* ˌseɪnt/
St Helier /ˌsnt ˈheliə(r); *NAmE also* ˌseɪnt/
Stirling /ˈstɜːlɪŋ; *NAmE* ˈstɜːrlɪŋ/
Stoke-on-Trent /ˌstəʊk ɒn ˈtrent; *NAmE* ˌstoʊk ɑːn/
Stornoway /ˈstɔːnəweɪ; *NAmE* ˈstɔːrn-/
St Peter Port /snt ˈpiːtə pɔːt; *NAmE* snt ˈpiːtər pɔːrt; *NAmE also* seɪnt/
Stratford-upon-Avon /ˌstrætfəd əpɒn ˈeɪvn; *NAmE* -fərd əpɑːn/
Sunderland /ˈsʌndələnd; *NAmE* -dərl-/
Swansea /ˈswɒnzi; *NAmE* ˈswɑːnzi/
Swindon /ˈswɪndən/
Taunton /ˈtɔːntən/
Truro /ˈtrʊərəʊ; *NAmE* ˈtrʊroʊ/
Warwick /ˈwɒrɪk; *NAmE* ˈwɑːrɪk; ˈwɔːr-/
Waterford /ˈwɔːtəfəd; *NAmE* ˈwɔːtərfərd; ˈwɑːt-/
Watford /ˈwɒtfəd; *NAmE* ˈwɑːtfərd/
Wolverhampton /ˌwʊlvəˈhæmptən; *NAmE* -vərˈh-/
Worcester /ˈwʊstə(r)/
York /jɔːk; *NAmE* jɔːrk/

The United States of America and Canada

The states of the United States of America

Alabama /ˌæləˈbæmə/
Alaska /əˈlæskə/
Arizona /ˌærɪˈzəʊnə; *NAmE* -ˈzoʊ-/
Arkansas /ˈɑːkənsɔː; *NAmE* ˈɑːrk-/
California /ˌkæləˈfɔːniə; *NAmE* -ˈfɔːrn-/
Colorado /ˌkɒləˈrɑːdəʊ; *NAmE* ˌkɑːləˈrædoʊ/
Connecticut /kəˈnetɪkət/
Delaware /ˈdeləweə(r); *NAmE* -wer/
Florida /ˈflɒrɪdə; *NAmE* ˈflɔːr-/
Georgia /ˈdʒɔːdʒə; *NAmE* ˈdʒɔːrdʒə/
Hawaii /həˈwaɪi/
Idaho /ˈaɪdəhəʊ; *NAmE* -hoʊ/
Illinois /ˌɪləˈnɔɪ/
Indiana /ˌɪndiˈænə/
Iowa /ˈaɪəwə/
Kansas /ˈkænzəs/
Kentucky /kenˈtʌki/
Louisiana /luˌiːziˈænə/
Maine /meɪn/
Maryland /ˈmeərilənd; *NAmE* ˈmerəl-/
Massachusetts /ˌmæsəˈtʃuːsɪts/
Michigan /ˈmɪʃɪɡən/
Minnesota /ˌmɪnɪˈsəʊtə; *NAmE* -ˈsoʊtə/
Mississippi /ˌmɪsɪˈsɪpi/
Missouri /mɪˈzʊəri; *NAmE* məˈzʊri/
Montana /mɒnˈtænə; *NAmE* mɑːn-/
Nebraska /nəˈbræskə/
Nevada /nəˈvɑːdə; *NAmE* nəˈvædə/
New Hampshire /ˌnjuː ˈhæmpʃə(r); *NAmE* ˌnuː/
New Jersey /ˌnjuː ˈdʒɜːzi; *NAmE* ˌnuː ˈdʒɜːrzi/
New Mexico /ˌnjuː ˈmeksɪkəʊ; *NAmE* ˌnuː ˈmeksɪkoʊ/
New York /ˌnjuː ˈjɔːk; *NAmE* ˌnuː ˈjɔːrk/
North Carolina /ˌnɔːθ kærəˈlaɪnə; *NAmE* ˌnɔːrθ/
North Dakota /ˌnɔːθ dəˈkəʊtə; *NAmE* ˌnɔːrθ dəˈkoʊtə/
Ohio /əʊˈhaɪəʊ; *NAmE* oʊˈhaɪoʊ/
Oklahoma /ˌəʊkləˈhəʊmə; *NAmE* ˌoʊkləˈhoʊmə/

Oregon /ˈɒrɪgən; *NAmE* ˈɔːrəgən; ˈɑːr-/
Pennsylvania /ˌpensl'veɪniə/
Rhode Island /ˌrəʊd ˈaɪlənd; *NAmE* ˌroʊd/
South Carolina /ˌsaʊθ kærəˈlaɪnə/
South Dakota /ˌsaʊθ dəˈkəʊtə; *NAmE* dəˈkoʊtə/
Tennessee /ˌtenəˈsiː/
Texas /ˈteksəs/
Utah /ˈjuːtɑː/
Vermont /vəˈmɒnt; *NAmE* vərˈmɑːnt/
Virginia /vəˈdʒɪniə; *NAmE* vərˈdʒ-/
Washington /ˈwɒʃɪŋtən; *NAmE* ˈwɑːʃ-; ˈwɔːʃ-/
West Virginia /ˌwest vəˈdʒɪniə; *NAmE* vərˈdʒ-/
Wisconsin /wɪsˈkɒnsɪn; *NAmE* -ˈkɑːn-/
Wyoming /waɪˈəʊmɪŋ; *NAmE* -ˈoʊmɪŋ/

Towns and cities in the United States

Albany /ˈɔːlbəni/
Albuquerque /ˈælbəkɜːki; *NAmE* -kɜːrki/
Amarillo /ˌæməˈrɪləʊ; *NAmE* -loʊ/
Anchorage /ˈæŋkərɪdʒ/
Atlanta /ətˈlæntə; *NAmE* æt-/
Augusta /ɔːˈgʌstə/
Austin /ˈɒstɪn; *NAmE* ˈɔːstɪn/
Bakersfield /ˈbeɪkəzfiːld; *NAmE* -ərz-/
Baltimore /ˈbɔːltɪmɔː(r)/
Baton Rouge /ˌbætn ˈruːʒ/
Berkeley /ˈbɜːkli; *NAmE* ˈbɜːrkli/
Billings /ˈbɪlɪŋz/
Birmingham /ˈbɜːmɪŋəm; *NAmE* ˈbɜːrmɪŋhæm/
Bismarck /ˈbɪzmɑːk; *NAmE* -mɑːrk/
Boise /ˈbɔɪsi/
Boston /ˈbɒstən; *NAmE* ˈbɔːs-/
Bridgeport /ˈbrɪdʒpɔːt; *NAmE* -pɔːrt/
Buffalo /ˈbʌfələʊ; *NAmE* -loʊ/
Burlington /ˈbɜːlɪŋtən; *NAmE* ˈbɜːrl-/
Cambridge /ˈkeɪmbrɪdʒ/
Cedar Rapids /ˌsiːdə ˈræpɪdz; *NAmE* ˌsiːdər/
Charleston /ˈtʃɑːlstən; *NAmE* ˈtʃɑːrl-/
Charlotte /ˈʃɑːlət; *NAmE* ˈʃɑːrlət/
Cheyenne /ʃaɪˈæn/
Chicago /ʃɪˈkɑːgəʊ; *NAmE* -goʊ/
Cincinnati /ˌsɪnsɪˈnæti/
Cleveland /ˈkliːvlənd/
Colorado Springs /ˌkɒləraːdəʊ ˈsprɪŋz; *NAmE* ˌkɑːlərædoʊ/
Columbus /kəˈlʌmbəs/
Corpus Christi /ˌkɔːpəs ˈkrɪsti; *NAmE* ˌkɔːrpəs/
Dallas /ˈdæləs/
Dayton /ˈdeɪtn/
Denver /ˈdenvə(r)/
Des Moines /dɪ ˈmɔɪn/
Detroit /dɪˈtrɔɪt/
Duluth /dəˈluːθ/
El Paso /el ˈpæsəʊ; *NAmE* -soʊ/
Eugene /juːˈdʒiːn/
Fargo /ˈfɑːgəʊ; *NAmE* ˈfɑːrgoʊ/
Fort Collins /ˌfɔːt ˈkɒlɪnz; *NAmE* ˌfɔːrt ˈkɑːlɪnz/
Fort Lauderdale /ˌfɔːt ˈlɔːdədeɪl; *NAmE* ˌfɔːrt ˈlɔːdərdeɪl/
Fort Worth /ˌfɔːt ˈwɜːθ; *NAmE* ˌfɔːrt ˈwɜːrθ/
Fresno /ˈfreznəʊ; *NAmE* ˈfreznoʊ/
Grand Rapids /ˌgrænd ˈræpɪdz/
Great Falls /ˌgreɪt ˈfɔːlz/
Green Bay /ˌgriːn ˈbeɪ/
Hartford /ˈhɑːtfəd; *NAmE* ˈhɑːrtfərd/
Honolulu /ˌhɒnəˈluːluː; *NAmE* ˌhɑːnə-/
Houston /ˈhjuːstən/
Idaho Falls /ˌaɪdəhəʊ ˈfɔːlz; *NAmE* -hoʊ/
Indianapolis /ˌɪndiəˈnæpəlɪs/
Jackson /ˈdʒæksən/
Jacksonville /ˈdʒæksənvɪl/
Juneau /ˈdʒuːnəʊ; *NAmE* -noʊ/
Kansas City /ˌkænzəs ˈsɪti/
Key West /ˌkiː ˈwest/
Knoxville /ˈnɒksvɪl; *NAmE* ˈnɑːks-/
Las Vegas /ˌlæs ˈveɪgəs/
Lexington /ˈleksɪŋtən/
Lincoln /ˈlɪŋkən/
Little Rock /ˈlɪtl rɒk; *NAmE* rɑːk/
Los Angeles /ˌlɒs ˈændʒəliːz; *NAmE* ˌlɔːs ˈændʒələs/
Louisville /ˈluːivɪl/
Lubbock /ˈlʌbək/
Madison /ˈmædɪsən/
Manchester /ˈmæntʃestə(r)/
Memphis /ˈmemfɪs/
Mesa /ˈmeɪsə/
Miami /maɪˈæmi/
Milwaukee /mɪlˈwɔːki/
Minneapolis /ˌmɪniˈæpəlɪs/
Mobile /məʊˈbiːl; *NAmE* moʊ-/
Montgomery /mɒntˈgɒməri; *NAmE* mɑntˈgɑːm-/
Nashville /ˈnæʃvɪl/
New Orleans /ˌnjuː ɔːˈliːənz; *NAmE* ˌnuː ˈɔːrlənz/
New York /ˌnjuː ˈjɔːk; *NAmE* ˌnuː ˈjɔːrk/
Newark /ˈnjuːək; *NAmE* ˈnuːərk/
Norfolk /ˈnɔːfək; *NAmE* ˈnɔːrfək/
Oklahoma City /ˌəʊkləhəʊmə ˈsɪti; *NAmE* ˌoʊkləhoʊmə/
Omaha /ˈəʊməhɑː; *NAmE* ˈoʊ-/
Orlando /ɔːˈlændəʊ; *NAmE* ɔːrˈlændoʊ/
Philadelphia /ˌfɪləˈdelfiə/
Phoenix /ˈfiːnɪks/
Pittsburgh /ˈpɪtsbɜːg; *NAmE* -bɜːrg/
Portland /ˈpɔːtlənd; *NAmE* ˈpɔːrt-/
Princeton /ˈprɪnstən/
Providence /ˈprɒvɪdəns; *NAmE* ˈprɑːv-/
Provo /ˈprəʊvəʊ; *NAmE* ˈproʊvoʊ/
Raleigh /ˈrɑːli; *NAmE* ˈrɔːli/
Rapid City /ˌræpɪd ˈsɪti/
Reno /ˈriːnəʊ; *NAmE* ˈriːnoʊ/
Richmond /ˈrɪtʃmənd/
Rochester /ˈrɒtʃɪstə(r); *NAmE* ˈrɑːtʃəs-/
Sacramento /ˌsækrəˈmentəʊ; *NAmE* -toʊ/
Salem /ˈseɪləm/
Salt Lake City /ˌsɔːlt leɪk ˈsɪti/
San Antonio /ˌsæn ænˈtəʊniəʊ; *NAmE* ænˈtoʊnioʊ/
San Diego /ˌsæn diˈeɪgəʊ; *NAmE* -goʊ/
San Francisco /ˌsæn frənˈsɪskəʊ; *NAmE* -koʊ/
San Jose /ˌsæn həʊˈzeɪ; *NAmE* hoʊ-/
Santa Fe /ˌsæntə ˈfeɪ/
Savannah /səˈvænə/
Seattle /siˈætl/
Sioux Falls /ˌsuː ˈfɔːlz/
Spokane /spəʊˈkæn; *NAmE* spoʊ-/
Springfield /ˈsprɪŋfiːld/
St Paul /ˌsnt ˈpɔːl; *NAmE also* ˌseɪnt/
St Louis /ˌsnt ˈluːɪs; *NAmE also* ˌseɪnt/
Syracuse /ˈsɪrəkjuːs/
Tallahassee /ˌtæləˈhæsi/
Tampa /ˈtæmpə/

Toledo /təˈliːdəʊ; *NAmE* -doʊ/
Topeka /təˈpiːkə/
Tucson /ˈtuːsɒn; *NAmE* -sɑːn/
Tulsa /ˈtʌlsə/
Virginia Beach /vəˌdʒɪniə ˈbiːtʃ; *NAmE* vərˌdʒ-/
Washington D.C. /ˌwɒʃɪŋtən diː ˈsiː; *NAmE* ˌwɑːʃ-; ˌwɔːʃ-/
Wichita /ˈwɪtʃɪtɔː/
Wilmington /ˈwɪlmɪŋtən/

The provinces and territories of Canada

Alberta /ælˈbɜːtə; *NAmE* ælˈbɜːrtə/
British Columbia /ˌbrɪtɪʃ kəˈlʌmbiə/
Manitoba /ˌmænɪˈtəʊbə; *NAmE* -ˈtoʊ-/
New Brunswick /ˌnjuː ˈbrʌnzwɪk; *NAmE* ˌnuː/
Newfoundland and Labrador /ˌnjuːfəndlənd ən ˈlæbrədɔː(r); *NAmE* ˌnuː-/
Northwest Territories /ˌnɔːθwest ˈterətriz; *NAmE* ˌnɔːrθwest ˈterətɔːriz/
Nova Scotia /ˌnəʊvə ˈskəʊʃə; *NAmE* ˌnoʊvə ˈskoʊʃə/
Nunavut /ˈnʊnəvʊt/
Ontario /ɒnˈteəriəʊ; *NAmE* ɑːnˈterioʊ/
Prince Edward Island /ˌprɪns ˈedwəd aɪlənd; *NAmE* ˈedwərd/
Quebec /kwɪˈbek/
Saskatchewan /səˈskætʃəwən/
Yukon Territory /ˈjuːkɒn terətri; *NAmE* ˈjuːkɑːn terətɔːri/

Towns and cities in Canada

Calgary /ˈkælɡəri/
Edmonton /ˈedməntən/
Fredericton /ˈfredrɪktən/
Gatineau /ˌɡætɪˈnəʊ; *NAmE* ˌɡætəˈnoʊ/
Greater Sudbury /ˌɡreɪtə ˈsʌdbəri; *NAmE* ˌɡreɪtər ˈsʌdberi/
Halifax /ˈhælɪfæks/
Hamilton /ˈhæmɪltən/
Iqaluit /ɪˈkæluːɪt/
Kelowna /keˈləʊnə; *NAmE* -ˈloʊ-/
London /ˈlʌndən/
Moncton /ˈmʌŋktən/
Montreal /ˌmɒntriˈɔːl; *NAmE* ˌmɑːn-/
Niagara Falls /naɪˌæɡrə ˈfɔːlz/
Ottawa /ˈɒtəwə; *NAmE* ˈɑːt-/
Quebec City /kwɪˌbek ˈsɪti/
Regina /rɪˈdʒaɪnə/
Saguenay /ˈsæɡɪneɪ/
Saint John /ˌseɪnt ˈdʒɒn; *NAmE* ˈdʒɑːn/
Saskatoon /ˌsæskəˈtuːn/
Sault Sainte Marie /ˌsuː seɪnt məˈriː/
Sherbrooke /ˈʃɜːbrʊk; *NAmE* ˈʃɜːrb-/
St John's /ˌsnt ˈdʒɒnz; *NAmE* ˌsnt ˈdʒɑːnz; *NAmE also* ˌseɪnt/
Sydney /ˈsɪdni/
Thunder Bay /ˌθʌndə ˈbeɪ; *NAmE* -dər/
Toronto /təˈrɒntəʊ; *NAmE* təˈrɑːntoʊ/
Vancouver /vænˈkuːvə(r)/
Victoria /vɪkˈtɔːriə/
Whitehorse /ˈwaɪthɔːs; *NAmE* -hɔːrs/
Windsor /ˈwɪnzə(r)/
Winnipeg /ˈwɪnɪpeɡ/
Yellowknife /ˈjeləʊnaɪf; *NAmE* -loʊ-/

Australia and New Zealand

The states of Australia

Australian Capital Territory (ACT) /ɒˌstreɪliən kæpɪtl ˈterətri; *NAmE* ɔːˌstreɪliən; ˈterətɔːri/
New South Wales /ˌnjuː saʊθ ˈweɪlz; *NAmE* ˌnuː/
Northern Territory /ˌnɔːðən ˈterətri; *NAmE* ˌnɔːrðərn ˈterətɔːri/
Queensland /ˈkwiːnzlənd/
South Australia /ˌsaʊθ ɒˈstreɪliə; *NAmE* ɔːˈstreɪliə/
Tasmania /tæzˈmeɪniə/
Victoria /vɪkˈtɔːriə/
Western Australia /ˌwestən ɒˈstreɪliə; *NAmE* ˌwestərn ɔːˈstreɪliə/

Towns and cities in Australia and New Zealand

Adelaide /ˈædəleɪd/
Alice Springs /ˌælɪs ˈsprɪŋz/
Auckland /ˈɔːklənd/
Brisbane /ˈbrɪzbən/
Cairns /keənz; *NAmE* kernz/
Canberra /ˈkænbərə; *NAmE also* -berə/
Christchurch /ˈkraɪstʃɜːtʃ; *NAmE* -tʃɜːrtʃ/
Darwin /ˈdɑːwɪn; *NAmE* ˈdɑːrwɪn/
Dunedin /dʌˈniːdɪn/
Geelong /dʒɪˈlɒŋ; *NAmE* dʒəˈlɔːŋ/
Gold Coast /ˈɡəʊld kəʊst; *NAmE* ˈɡoʊld koʊst/
Hamilton /ˈhæmɪltən/
Hobart /ˈhəʊbɑːt; *NAmE* ˈhoʊbɑːrt/
Launceston /ˈlɒnsəstən; *NAmE* ˈlɑːn-/
Melbourne /ˈmelbən; *NAmE* -bərn/
Newcastle /ˈnjuːkɑːsl; *NAmE* ˈnuːkæsl/
Perth /pɜːθ; *NAmE* pɜːrθ/
Sunshine Coast /ˈsʌnʃaɪn kəʊst; *NAmE* koʊst/
Sydney /ˈsɪdni/
Tauranga /taʊˈræŋə; təʊˈrɒŋə; *NAmE* taʊˈrɑːŋə; toʊ-/
Townsville /ˈtaʊnsvɪl/
Wellington /ˈwelɪŋtən/
Wollongong /ˈwʊləŋɡɒŋ; *NAmE* ˈwʊləŋɡɔːŋ; -ɡɑːŋ/

British and American English

American English differs from British English not only in pronunciation but also in vocabulary, spelling and grammar.

Pronunciation

- When the American pronunciation is different from the British pronunciation it is given after the British pronunciation in the dictionary: **tomato** /tə'mɑːtəʊ; (*NAmE*) tə'meɪtoʊ/.
- Some important differences: Stressed vowels are usually longer in American English. In **packet**, for example, the /æ/ is longer.
- In British English the consonant /r/ is pronounced only before a vowel (for example in **red** and **bedroom**). In all other cases the /r/ is silent (for example in **car**, **learn**, **over**). In American English the /r/ is always pronounced.
- In American English the t between vowels is pronounced as a soft d /d/, so that **writer** and **rider** sound similar. British English speakers usually pronounce the t as /t/.

Vocabulary

The dictionary tells you which words are used only in American English or have different meanings in British and American English, for example **cookie**, **elevator**, **trunk**.

Spelling

- The dictionary shows different spellings in British and American English. The following differences are particularly common:
- In verbs which end in *l* and are not stressed on the final syllable, the *l* is not doubled in the *-ing* form and the past participle: **cancelling**; (*NAmE*) **canceling**.
- Words which end in *-tre* are spelt *-ter* in American English: **centre**; (*NAmE*) **center**.
- Words which end in *-our* are usually spelt *-or* in American English: **colour**; (*NAmE*) **color**.
- Words which end in *-ogue* are usually spelt *-og* in American English: **dialogue**; (*NAmE*) **dialog**.
- In British English many verbs can be spelt with either *-ize* or *-ise*. In American English only the spelling with *-ize* is possible: **realize, -ise**; (*NAmE*) **realize**.

Grammar

Present perfect/Simple past

In American English the simple past can be used with **already**, **just** and **yet**. In British English the present perfect is used:

▸ *I have already given her the present.* (*BrE*)
▸ *I already gave her the present.* (*NAmE*)
▸ *I've just seen her.* (*BrE*)
▸ *I just saw her.* (*NAmE*)
▸ *Have you heard the news yet?* (*BrE*)
▸ *Did you hear the news yet?* (*NAmE*)

Have/have got

In British English it is possible to use **have got** or **have** to express the idea of possession. In American English only **have** can be used in questions and negative sentences:

▸ *They have/have got two computers.* (*BrE* and *NAmE*)
▸ *Have you got a computer? Yes, I have.* (*BrE*)
▸ *Do you have a computer? Yes, I do.* (*BrE* and *NAmE*)

Get/gotten

In American English the past participle of **get** is **gotten**:

▸ *Your English has got better.* (*BrE*)
▸ *Your English has gotten better.* (*NAmE*)

Prepositions and adverbs

Some prepositions and adverbs are used differently in British and American English, for example **stay at home** (*BrE*); **stay home** (*NAmE*).

Form of the adverb

In informal American English the adverb form ending in *-ly* is often not used:

▸ *He looked at me really strangely.* (*BrE*)
▸ *He looked at me really strange.* (*NAmE*)

Shall

Shall is not used instead of **will** in American English for the first person singular of the future:

▸ *I shall/will be here tomorrow.* (*BrE*)
▸ *I will be here tomorrow.* (*NAmE*)

Nor is it used in polite offers:

▸ *Shall I open the window?* (*BrE*)
▸ *Should I open the window?* (*NAmE*)

Irregular verbs

In British English the past simple and past participle of many verbs can be formed with *-ed* or *-t*, for example **burned/burnt**. In American English only the forms ending in *-ed* are used:

▸ *They burned/burnt the documents.* (*BrE*)
▸ *They burned the documents.* (*NAmE*)

When the past participle is used as an adjective, British English prefers the *-t* form, whereas in American English the *-ed* form is preferred, with the exception of **burnt**:

▸ *a spoilt child* (*BrE*)
▸ *a spoiled child* (*NAmE*)
▸ *burnt toast* (*BrE* and *NAmE*)

Go/Come and...

In these expressions **and** is often omitted:

▸ *Go and take a look outside.* (*BrE*)
▸ *Go take a look outside.* (*NAmE*)

On the telephone

▸ *Hello, is that David?* (*BrE*)
▸ *Hello, is this David?* (*NAmE*)

The Oxford 3000™

The keywords of the **Oxford 3000** have been carefully selected by a group of language experts and experienced teachers as the words which should receive priority in vocabulary study because of their importance and usefulness. The selection is based on three criteria.

The words which occur most **frequently** in English are included, based on the information in the British National Corpus and the Oxford Corpus Collection. (A corpus is an electronically held collection of written or spoken texts, often consisting of hundreds of millions of words – for more information, visit the OALD website.) However, being frequent in the corpus alone is not enough for a word to qualify as a keyword: it may be that the word is used very frequently, but only in a narrowly defined area, such as newspapers or scientific articles. In order to avoid including these restricted words, we include as keywords only those words which are frequent across a **range** of different types of text. In other words, keywords are both frequent and used in a variety of contexts. In addition, the list includes some very important words which happen not to be used frequently, even though they are very **familiar** to most users of English. These include, for example, words for parts of the body, words used in travel, and words which are useful for explaining what you mean when you do not know the exact word for something. These words were identified by consulting a panel of over seventy experts in the fields of teaching and language study.

The words of the **Oxford 3000** are shown in the main section of the dictionary in larger print, and with a key symbol 🔑 immediately following. The most useful parts of the entries (particular parts of speech, meanings, phrasal verbs and idioms) are marked with a small key symbol. The entries for keywords often have extra information in the form of more examples of use, special notes explaining synonyms or related words, or helpful illustrations. This means that the keywords make an excellent starting point for expanding your vocabulary. With most keywords, there is far more to learn about them than the first meaning in the entry: often these words have many meanings, have a large family of words derived from them, or are used in a variety of patterns.

The list covers British and American English. Some basic phrases are also included. Proper names (names of people, places, etc. beginning with a capital letter) are not included in the list.

In order to make the definitions in this dictionary easy to understand, we have written them using the keywords of the **Oxford 3000**. All words used in normal definition text are keywords, or are on the list of language study terms, shown below. Numbers and proper names are also used in definitions. When it has been necessary to use a specialist term which is not in the **Oxford 3000**, the word is shown in SMALL CAPITALS. If you do not know the meaning of this word, look it up in the dictionary: it will help you to understand the definition that you are interested in, and will probably be a useful word to learn because it will be related to the original word you looked up.

For more information on the **Oxford 3000**, and to download a copy of the list, visit the OALD website at **http://www.oup.com/elt/oald**

Language study terms

Knowing these words will be useful in your study of English and will also help you to use the **Oxford Advanced Learner's Dictionary** more effectively. It includes words to do with grammar, pronunciation and punctuation.

abbreviation *n.*
active *adj., n.*
adjective *n.*
adverb *n.*
apostrophe *n.*
article *n.*
auxiliary (*also* auxiliary verb) *n.*
bracket *n.*
clause *n.*
colon *n.*
comma *n.*
comparative *adj., n.*
compound *n., adj.*
conditional *adj., n.*
conjunction *n.*
consonant *n.*
contraction *n.*
countable *adj.*
continuous
➲progressive
derivative *n.*
determiner *n.*
dialect *n.*
entry *n.*
exclamation *n.*
exclamation mark (*especially BrE*) (*NAmE usually* exclamation point) *n.*
figurative *adj.*
full stop *n.* (*BrE*)
gerund *n.*
hyphen *n.*
idiom *n.*
imperative *adj., n.*
indirect speech
➲reported speech
infinitive *n.*
inverted commas
➲quotation marks
ironic *adj.*
irregular *adj.*
literal *adj.*

literary *adj.*
modal *n.*
noun *n.*
object *n.*
ordinal *n.*
paragraph *n.*
parenthesis *n.*
part of speech (*also* word class) *n.*
participle *n.*
particle *n.*
passive *adj.*, *n.*
perfect *adj.*
period *n.* (*NAmE*)
phrasal verb *n.*
plural *n.*, *adj.*
possessive *adj.*, *n.*
prefix *n.*
preposition *n.*
progressive (*also* continuous) *adj.*
pronoun *n.*
punctuation *n.*
question mark *n.*
question tag (*also* tag question) *n.*
quotation marks (*BrE also* inverted commas) *n.*
reflexive *adj.*
register *n.*
regular *adj.*
relative *adj.*
reported speech (*also* indirect speech) *n.*
saying *n.*
semicolon *n.*
simple *adj.*
singular *n.*, *adj.*
slang *n.*
slash *n.*
subject *n.*
suffix *n.*
superlative *adj.*, *n.*
syllable *n.*
taboo *adj.*
tag question ➲question tag
tense *n.*
uncountable *adj.*
verb *n.*
vowel *n.*
word class ➲part of speech

The Academic Word List:

A tool for vocabulary learning

Averil Coxhead
Victoria University of Wellington New Zealand

You are holding a dictionary which contains many thousands of words. As a learner of English as a second or even third language, how can you decide which words you need to spend your valuable time on? One way you can do this is by looking at the frequency of words. That is, how often these words occur in your reading and listening material in English. What you read and listen to might depend on your purposes for learning English. If, for example, you want to study in an English-medium university, it will be important to focus on words that you will meet often at university.

How can this dictionary help you decide which words to learn for your studies? This dictionary includes words from the Academic Word List (AWL). The list was developed by analysing a corpus or body of academic written texts to find out which words occurred across a range of 28 subject areas (such as Biology, History, Marketing, and International Law) in four academic disciplines (Arts, Commerce, Law, and Science). These words were selected because of their range and frequency of occurrence. They are outside the first 2000 words of English. The AWL contains 570 word families and covers roughly 10% of a written academic text, which means that ten words in every 100 can be found in the list.

In this dictionary, you will find that words from the AWL are labelled **AW**. Words in the Oxford 3000 word list of general English are also highlighted. The AWL and the Oxford 3000 lists have some words in common because the AWL excludes the first 2000 words while the Oxford 3000 includes the first 2000 words and 1000 words more. Examples of some words that are shared include *abandon* and *academic*.

What are some other challenges for learners when it comes to academic vocabulary? First and foremost, it is important to know the meaning of a word and to recognise its meaning when the word is presented in context. Some words, such as 'require', carry roughly the same meaning in most contexts. Other words have developed very specific meanings depending on an area of study. An example is the word 'significant' which carries a particular meaning in statistical studies. You can use this dictionary to help you find out more about the meanings of words in context.

Another challenge is using tools such as this dictionary to enhance your understanding. The dictionary includes words that commonly occur with a target word, its pronunciation, and examples or sentences with the target word in it. All of this information can help you develop a fuller understanding of a word.

There is a saying which goes, 'If you don't use it, you'll lose it'. Make sure you try to use words, from the AWL for example, in your writing and speaking. That way you can get feedback and further develop your knowledge of these words. You also need useful strategies to cement your learning. If you find yourself looking up the same word more than once or you find specialised words for your studies, you may need to develop word cards or design a vocabulary notebook to help you learn.

If we think of language as a toolbox for life, this dictionary contains many useful tools for your learning. The AWL is a vocabulary tool that might help you prepare for your future studies.

You can find out more about the AWL on this website: **http://www.victoria.ac.nz/lals/staff/averil-coxhead.aspx.**

Pronunciation and phonetic symbols

The British pronunciations given are those of younger speakers of General British. This includes RP (Received Pronunciation) and a range of similar accents which are not strongly regional. The American pronunciations chosen are also as far as possible the most general (not associated with any particular region). If there is a difference between British and American pronunciations of a word, the British one is given first, with *NAmE* before the American pronunciation.

Consonants

p	pen	/pen/	s	see	/siː/
b	bad	/bæd/	z	zoo	/zuː/
t	tea	/tiː/	ʃ	shoe	/ʃuː/
d	did	/dɪd/	ʒ	vision	/ˈvɪʒn/
k	cat	/kæt/	h	hat	/hæt/
g	get	/get/	m	man	/mæn/
tʃ	chain	/tʃeɪn/	n	now	/naʊ/
dʒ	jam	/dʒæm/	ŋ	sing	/sɪŋ/
f	fall	/fɔːl/	l	leg	/leg/
v	van	/væn/	r	red	/red/
θ	thin	/θɪn/	j	yes	/jes/
ð	this	/ðɪs/	w	wet	/wet/

The symbol (r) indicates that British pronunciation will have /r/ only if a vowel sound follows directly at the beginning of the next word, as in **far away**; otherwise the /r/ is omitted. For American English, all the /r/ sounds should be pronounced.

/x/ represents a fricative sound as in /lɒx/ for Scottish **loch**, Irish **lough**.

Vowels and diphthongs

iː	see	/siː/	
i	happy	/ˈhæpi/	
ɪ	sit	/sɪt/	
e	ten	/ten/	
æ	cat	/kæt/	
ɑː	father	/ˈfɑːðə(r)/	
ɒ	got	/gɒt/	*(British English)*
ɔː	saw	/sɔː/	
ʊ	put	/pʊt/	
u	actual	/ˈæktʃuəl/	
uː	too	/tuː/	
ʌ	cup	/kʌp/	
ɜː	fur	/fɜː(r)/	
ə	about	/əˈbaʊt/	
eɪ	say	/seɪ/	
əʊ	go	/gəʊ/	*(British English)*
oʊ	go	/goʊ/	*(American English)*
aɪ	my	/maɪ/	
ɔɪ	boy	/bɔɪ/	
aʊ	now	/naʊ/	
ɪə	near	/nɪə(r)/	*(British English)*
eə	hair	/heə(r)/	*(British English)*
ʊə	pure	/pjʊə(r)/	*(British English)*

Many British speakers use /ɔː/ instead of the diphthong /ʊə/, especially in common words, so that **sure** becomes /ʃɔː(r)/, etc.

The sound /ɒ/ does not occur in American English, and words which have this vowel in British pronunciation will instead have /ɑː/ or /ɔː/ in American English. For instance, **got** is /gɒt/ in British English, but /gɑːt/ in American English, while **dog** is British /dɒg/, American /dɔːg/.

The three diphthongs /ɪə eə ʊə/ are found only in British English. In corresponding places, American English has a simple vowel followed by /r/, so **near** is /nɪr/, **hair** is /her/, and **pure** is /pjʊr/.

Nasalized vowels, marked with /˜/, may be retained in certain words taken from French, as in **penchant** /ˈpɒ̃ʃɒ̃/, **coq au vin** /ˌkɒk əʊ ˈvæ̃/.

Syllabic consonants

The sounds /l/ and /n/ can often be 'syllabic' – that is, they can form a syllable by themselves without a vowel. There is a syllabic /l/ in the usual pronunciation of **middle** /ˈmɪdl/, and a syllabic /n/ in **sudden** /ˈsʌdn/.

Weak vowels /i/ and /u/

The sounds represented by /iː/ and /ɪ/ must always be made different, as in **heat** /hiːt/ compared with **hit** /hɪt/. The symbol /i/ represents a vowel that can be sounded as either /iː/ or /ɪ/, or as a sound which is a compromise between them. In a word such as **happy** /ˈhæpi/, younger speakers use a quality more like /iː/, but short in duration. When /i/ is followed by /ə/ the sequence can also be pronounced /jə/. So the word **dubious** can be /ˈdjuːbiəs/ or /ˈdjuːbjəs/.

In the same way, the two vowels represented /uː/ and /ʊ/ must be kept distinct but /u/ represents a weak vowel that varies between them. If /u/ is followed directly by a consonant sound, it can also be pronounced as /ə/. So **stimulate** can be /ˈstɪmjuleɪt/ or /ˈstɪmjəleɪt/.

Weak forms and strong forms

Certain very common words, for example **at**, **and**, **for**, **can**, have two pronunciations. We give the usual (weak) pronunciation first. The second pronunciation (strong) must be used if the word is stressed, and also generally when the word is at the end of a sentence. For example:

▸ *Can* /kən/ *you help?*
▸ *I'll help if I can* /kæn/.

Stress

The mark /ˈ/ shows the main stress in a word. Compare **able** /ˈeɪbl/, stressed on the first syllable, with **ability** /əˈbɪləti/, stressed on the second. A stressed syllable is relatively loud, long in duration, said clearly and distinctly, and made noticeable by the pitch of the voice.

Longer words may have one or more secondary stresses coming before the main stress. These are marked with /ˌ/ as in **abbreviation** /əˌbriːviˈeɪʃn/, **agricultural** /ˌæɡrɪˈkʌltʃərəl/. They feel like beats in a rhythm leading up to the main stress.

Weak stresses coming after the main stress in a word can sometimes be heard, but they are not marked in this dictionary.

When two words are put together in a phrase, the main stress in the first word may shift to the place of the secondary stress to avoid a clash between two stressed syllables next to each other. For instance, **ˌafterˈnoon** has the main stress on **noon**, but in the phrase **ˌafternoon ˈtea** the stress on **noon** is missing. **ˌWell ˈknown** has the main stress on **known**, but in the phrase **ˌwell-known ˈactor** the stress on **known** is missing.

Stress in phrasal verbs

One type of phrasal verb has a single strong stress on the first word. Examples are **ˈcome to sth**, **ˈgo for sb**, **ˈlook at sth**. This stress pattern is kept in all situations, and the second word is never stressed. If the second word is one which normally appears in a weak form, remember that the strong form must be used at the end of a phrase.

Another type of phrasal verb is shown with two stresses. The pattern shown in the dictionary, with the main stress on the second word, is the one which is used when the verb is said on its own, or when the verb as a whole is the last important word in a phrase:

▸ *What time are you ˌcoming ˈback?*
▸ *He ˌmade it ˈup.*
▸ *ˌFill them ˈin.*

But the speaker will put a strong stress on any other important word if it comes later than the verb. The stress on the second word of the verb is then weakened or lost, especially if it would otherwise be next to the other strong stress. This happens whether the important word which receives the strong stress is between the two parts of the phrasal verb, or after both of them.

▸ *We ˌcame back ˈearly.*
▸ *I ˌfilled in a ˈform.*
▸ *ˌFill this ˈform in.*

If more than one stress pattern is possible, or the stress depends on the context, no stress is shown.

Stress in idioms

Idioms are shown in the dictionary with at least one main stress unless more than one stress pattern is possible or the stress depends on the context. The learner should not change the position of this stress when speaking or the special meaning of the idiom may be lost.

Tapping of /t/

In American English, if a /t/ sound is between two vowels, and the second vowel is not stressed, the /t/ can be pronounced very quickly, and made voiced so that it is like a brief /d/ or the r-sound of certain languages.Technically, the sound is a 'tap', and can be symbolised by /t̬/. So Americans can pronounce **potato** as /pəˈteɪt̬oʊ/, tapping the second /t/ in the word (but not the first, because of the stress). British speakers don't generally do this.

The conditions for tapping also arise very frequently when words are put together, as in **not only**, **what I**, etc. In this case it doesn't matter whether the following vowel is stressed or not, and even British speakers can use taps in this situation, though they sound rather casual.

The glottal stop

In both British and American varieties of English, a /t/ which comes at the end of a word or syllable can often be pronounced as a glottal stop /ʔ/ (a silent gap produced by holding one's breath briefly) instead of a /t/. For this to happen, the next sound must not be a vowel or a syllabic /l/. So **football** can be /ˈfʊʔbɔːl/ instead of /ˈfʊtbɔːl/, and **button** can be /ˈbʌʔn/ instead of /ˈbʌtn/. But a glottal stop would not be used for the /t/ sounds in **bottle** or **better** because of the sounds which come afterwards.

mop, Stockdisc/Stockbyte/Getty Images, Inc./mop), V19 (R McVay/PhotoDisc/Getty Images, Inc./fish knife and fork), V21 (J Atlas/Brand X Pictures/Jupiterimages (UK) Ltd./loofah, image100/Corbis Corporation/nail file, L Manning/Corbis Corporation/toothpaste, Stockbyte/ Getty Images, Inc./sponge), V22 (Lynx/ICONOTEC/ espresso maker), V23 (L Manning/Corbis Corporation/ measuring spoons, T Northcut/PhotoDisc/Getty Images, Inc./measuring jug, Photolibrary RF/ramekin), V24 (Glow Images RF/Glow Images Inc./fry, Image Source Ltd./bake, barbecue, Jetta Productions/Dana Neely/Tetra Images LLC/flambé), V25 (J Baigrie/Digital Vision/Getty Images, Inc./grate, Ben Fink Photo Inc./Brand X Pictures/ Jupiterimages (UK) Ltd./roll out, Creativ Studio Heinemann/Westend61 GmbH/mash, Fancy/Veer Incorporated/whip, image100/Corbis Corporation/dice, Image Source Ltd./chop, Jetta Productions/Dana Neely/ Tetra Images LLC/knead, J Silva/Digital Vision/Getty Images, Inc./slice), V30 (C Squared Studios/PhotoDisc Getty Images, Inc./bassoon, double bass, kettledrum, oboe, piccolo, trumpet, xylophone, Stockbyte/Getty Images, Inc./tuba), V31 (C Squared Studios/PhotoDisc/ Getty Images, Inc./sitar, Stockbyte/Getty Images, Inc./ upright piano), V32 (Buccina Studios/PhotoDisc/Getty Images, Inc./doll's house, Comstock Images/ Jupiterimages (UK) Ltd./building blocks, Dex Image/ sandpit, G Doyle/Stockbyte/Getty Images, Inc./kite, O Drew/National Geographic/climbing frame, Dynamic Graphics/Creatas Images/Jupiterimages (UK) Ltd./playing cards, D Laurens/PhotoAlto/swing, L Manning/Corbis Corporation/soft toy, PhotoDisc/Getty Images, Inc./ trampoline, RubberBall Productions/skipping rope), V33 (Image Source Ltd./wordsearch, Medioimages/Getty Images, Inc./noughts and crosses), V34 (Digital Vision/ Getty Images, Inc./bowls, Duomo TIPS RF/ Tips Italia RF/ skateboarding, Image Source Ltd./in-line skating, snorkelling, P Lee Harvey/ Cultura Limited/orienteering, PhotoLink/PhotoDisc/Getty Images, Inc./darts, PNC/ Brand X Pictures/ Jupiterimages (UK) Ltd./golf, Polka Dot Images/Jupiterimages (UK) Ltd./pool), V35 (Henry Arden/ Image Source Ltd./press-up, S Baccon/Digital Vision/ Getty Images, Inc./sewing, BananaStock/Jupiterimages (UK) Ltd./gardening, T Grill/ Corbis Corporation/ painting, Richard Gross/Corbis Corporation/pottery, woodcarving, J Henley/Blend Images, LLC/stamp collecting, Image Source Ltd./rowing machine, JGI/Blend Images, LLC/treadmill, R Lewine/Image Source Ltd./ barbell, dumb-bell, yoga, D Madison/Digital Vision/Getty Images, Inc./jogging, S Mason/PhotoDisc/Getty Images, Inc./crochet, Moodboard/Mike Watson Images Limited/ exercise bike, Photolibrary RF/sit-up, Polka Dot Images/ Jupiterimages (UK) Ltd./knitting), V36 (Duomo TIPS RF/ Tips Italia RF/ice hockey, D Hammond/Design Pics Inc./ baseball, rugby, Moodboard/Mike Watson Images Limited/soccer, PhotoLink/PhotoDisc/Getty Images, Inc./ American football, A Somvanshi/India Picture RF/ cricket), V37 (Glow Images RF/Glowimages Inc./ backstroke, Goodshoot/Jupiterimages (UK) Ltd./ badminton, image100/Corbis Corporation/butterfly, Image Source Ltd./squash, R Michael/Corbis Corporation/ crawl), V38 (B Blankenburg/Corbis Corporation/ showjumping, E Calderoni/Score Royalty Free Images/ Aflo Foto Agency Inc./hammer, M Colomb/Digital Vision/ Getty Images, Inc./horse racing, CS Productions/Brand X Pictures/Jupiterimages (UK) Ltd./javelin, pole vault, T Levine/zefa/Corbis Corporation/discus, D Madison/ Photographer's Choice/Getty Images, Inc./high jump, J Oliver/Digital Vision/Getty Images, Inc./sprinting, PhotoLink/PhotoDisc/Getty Images, Inc./hurdling), V39 (K Aoki/Score Royalty Free Images/Aflo Foto Agency Inc./ downhill skiing, Digital Vision/Getty Images, Inc./luge, Image Source Ltd./fencing, D Madison/Digital Vision/ Getty Images, Inc./bobsleigh, cross-country skiing, R McVay/Digital Vision/Getty Images, Inc./cycling, R Michael/Corbis Corporation/gymnastics), V40 (B Blankenburg/Corbis Corporation/jet-skiing, windsurfing, Brand X Pictures/Jupiterimages (UK) Ltd./ bodyboarding, Buzz Pictures/Purestock/Superstock, Inc./ surfing, Digital Vision/Getty Images, Inc./skydiving, DLILLC/Corbis Corporation/bungee jumping, Image Source Ltd./abseiling, parkour, D Leniuk/Radius Images/ Masterfile Corporation/kitesurfing, D Madison/Corbis Corporation/white-water rafting, Thinkstock Images/ Jupiterimages (UK) Ltd./snowboarding, K Weatherly/ PhotoDisc/Getty Images, Inc./waterskiing), V41 (C Squared Studios/PhotoDisc/Getty Images, Inc./bicycle, child's bicycle, tandem, tricycle, Glow Images RF/ Glowimages Inc./dirt bike, Moodboard/Mike Watson Images Limited/quad bike, J Nazz/Corbis Corporation/ racing bike, unicycle, K Weatherly/PhotoDisc/Getty Images, Inc./mountain bike), V43 (Creatas Images/ Jupiterimages (UK) Ltd./seaplane, P Mastrovito/Image Source Ltd./hot-air balloon, L Mayer/Creatas Images/ Jupiterimages (UK) Ltd./ski-plane, Photolibrary RF/ helicopter, StockTrek/Purestock/Superstock, Inc./fighter, P Tom/ICONOTEC/microlight), V44 (CAMP/RelaXimages/ rowing boat), V45 (Creatas Images/Jupiterimages (UK) Ltd./canoe, Medioimages/PhotoDisc/Getty Images, Inc./ yacht, L Riß/Westend61 GmbH/gondola, K Weatherly/ PhotoDisc/Getty Images, Inc./kayak), V46 (A Berg/Digital Vision/Getty Images, Inc./forklift truck, Thinkstock Images/Jupiterimages (UK) Ltd./breakdown truck), V47 (Thinkstock Images/Jupiterimages (UK) Ltd./black cab), V51 (M Andersen/RubberBall Productions/nightwear, T Northcut/PhotoDisc/Getty Images, Inc./crew-neck sweater), V52 (Stockbyte/Getty Images, Inc./handbag, shoulder bag), V53 (S Cole/ PhotoDisc Getty Images, Inc./ sombrero), V54 (Y Arcurs/Tetra Images LLC/laptop, Brand X Pictures/Jupiterimages (UK) Ltd./headset, G Doyle & C Griffin/Stockbyte/ Getty Images, Inc./router, webcam, Tetra Images LLC/PC), V56 (C Squared Studios/PhotoDisc/ Getty Images, Inc./envelopes, Stockbyte/Getty Images, Inc./Post-it™)

V17, V24–25, V32–34, V42–46, V50–51 text adapted from Oxford Learner's Wordfinder Dictionary © Oxford University Press 1997

Maps © Oxford University Press

Design by Peter Burgess

Cover design by Ruth Bateson, Liza Whitney

Text capture, processing and typesetting by Oxford University Press

Typesetting by Data Standards Limited

Printed in China

ACKNOWLEDGEMENTS

Illustrations by: Julian Baker & Janet Baker (JB Illustrations) basket, dreamcatcher, gazebo, oxbow, stile, pp V2–7, V15–16, V42–43, V48, V55, V59 (earth, seasons); M Dunn chart; Hardlines optical illusion; K Hiscock pp V8–11, V26–28; M Jones matchstick figure; KJA-artists.com ball-and-socket joint, ball bearing, barbed wire, bevelled, blade, block and tackle, bolt, chip, cogwheel, cord, dovetail joint, elk, knot, label, money, piston, plug, rabbit, ratchet, sprocket wheel, staircase, pp V29, V51; Oxford University Press concentric, convex, ideogram, musical notation, rebus, Venn diagram, wavelength; P Schramm/ Meiklejohn Illustration bar, bow 1, bow 2, bridge, catapult, cat's cradle, curved, froth, hook, neck, ring, shade, spring, squeeze, pp V18–22, V49, V56–57; Q2AMedia ankh, broken, corrugated, edge, filter, frame, handle, hieroglyphics, key, möbius strip, peg, pipe, pushchair, rack, roundabout, scale, pp V58, V59 (solar system); G White helix

The Publishers would like to thank the following for their kind permission to reproduce photographs and other copyright material: Alamy Ltd. pp V12 (V Abbey/gargoyle, B Boston/ aqueduct, curved-light/viaduct, David R Frazier Photolibrary, Inc./humpback bridge, graficart.net/ portico, J Kase/cantilever bridge, H Sadura/geodesic dome), V14 (P Evans/thatched cottage, Eye Candy Images 4/houseboat, M Frost/Adams Picture Library/block of flats, KAKIMAGE/apartment building, J Kase/terraced house, philipus/duplex, M Richardson/bungalow, mobile home), V17 (D Hurst/ironing board, Image Farm Inc./ bradawl), V21 (D Hurst/electric toothbrush, stockpix/nail scissors), V22 (ilian studio/electric kettle), V23 (D Amado/ paring knife, D Hurst/measuring cups, J F T L IMAGES/ kitchen scissors, Stockbyte/Getty Images, Inc./cake slice), V24 (discpicture/steam, A Shalamov/stir-fry, Studio EYE/ Photo Agency EYE/casserole, E Westmacott/boil), V32 (J Helgason/teddy bear, InspireStock Inc./Frisbee™, Stockbyte/Getty Images, Inc./rocking horse, THINGX/ slide), V33 (W Heidasch/dominoes, Ilanphoto/ PhotoStock-Israel/Chinese chequers, G Kollidas/ backgammon, S May/sudoku, reppans/crossword, L Ryder/snakes and ladders), V34 (C Hochachka/Design Pics Inc./caving, T Kraus/tenpin bowling, TongRo Image Stock/archery, J Warrington/scuba-diving), V35 (Images-USA/photography, VStock/Tetra Images LLC/model making, I Zhorov/embroidery), V36 (A Muttitt/hockey), V40 (M-E Keith/hang-gliding, PHOVOIR/ FCM Graphic/ paragliding), V41 (S Sloan/scooter), V42 (Best View Stock/ four-wheel drive, ilian car/convertible, sportscar, Luminis/estate car, hatchback, people carrier, I Montero/ saloon), V43 (P Brogden/light aircraft, E Clendennen/ aerobatic display, Thierry GRUN-Aero/biplane, A Scott/ airship), V44 (Dacorum Gold/container ship, David R. Frazier Photolibrary, Inc./liner, C George/canal boat, Greece/hydrofoil, Images-USA/speedboat, J Kase/ catamaran, I MacDonald/paddle steamer, R Naude/ hovercraft, D Newham/ferry, I Patrick/lifeboat, A Stiop/ cruiser, J Sullivan/sailing dinghy), V46 (M Dalton/single-decker bus, J Kase/articulated lorry, lorry, minibus, tanker, transporter, van, E Nguyen/US school bus, philipus/pickup, Pixoi Ltd./double-decker bus, A Schein/ bus, A Stone/Jeep™), V47 (M Anderson/high-speed train, L Ashley/cab, A Bell/freight train, passenger train, I Blair/ funicular, H Ibrahim/Photov.com/underground, J Kase/ caravan, I MacDonald/bulldozer, Photolink Ltd./cable car, R Rayworth/steam train, M Richardson/tractor, RMT/ cement mixer, Steppenwolf/tram, C Young/dumper truck), V50 (P Hakimata/suit, S Lihodeev/dress), V52 (T Large/baseball boots, T Payne/jelly shoe, P Springett/ platform, SugarStock Ltd./clutch bag, H Threlfall/wedge, E Westmacott/flats), V53 (D Templeton/sou'wester), V54 (A Buckin/flash drive, CreativeAct-Technology series/ digital camera, MP3 player, O Leedham/scanner, D Tolokonov/PDA), V56 (I Genkin/notepad, something else/glue stick); Corbis Corporation pp V33 (BLOOMimage/jigsaw), V37 (Floresco Productions/table tennis, Moodboard/Mike Watson Images Limited/ breaststroke, tennis), V38 (Moodboard/Mike Watson Images Limited/polo), V40 (Moodboard/Mike Watson Images Limited/wakeboarding), V43 (Ben Blankenburg/ glider), V47 (A Levenson/excavator, Moodboard/Mike Watson Images Limited/camper); Corel pp V12 (cloister), V13 (amphitheatre, castle, glasshouse, hut, lighthouse, log cabin, oil rig, pub, pyramid, skyscraper, stately home, warehouse), V39 (boxing), V45 (punt); Hemera Technologies Inc. all A–Z photographs, pp V13 (barn), V16 (all except sprinkler, strimmer), V17 (all except bradawl, ironing board, mop, squeegee mop, toolbox), V19 (all except cake slice, fish knife and fork), V21 (comb, emery board, hairbrush, nail brush, nail clippers, shaver, sponge bag, toothbrush, tweezers), V22 (all except electric kettle, espresso maker), V23 (all except cake slice, fish slice, garlic press, measuring cups, measuring jug, measuring spoons, paring knife, potato masher, ramekin), V30 (castanets, cello, clarinet, congas, drum kit, French horn, flute, glockenspiel, harmonica, harp, maracas, recorder, saxophone, steel drum, tambourine, triangle, trombone, viola, violin), V31 (all except sitar, upright piano), V32 (glove puppet, pack of cards, suits), V33 (chess), V41 (D-lock, helmet, light, motorcycle pump), V50 (all except dress, suit), V51 (all except crew neck, nightwear, polo neck), V52 (all except baseball boots, clutch bag, flats, handbag, jelly shoe, platform, shoulder bag, wedge) V53 (all except charm bracelet, locket, sombrero, sou'wester), V56 (all except correction fluid, envelopes, glue stick, highlighter, notepad, Post-it™); Oxford University Press pp V14 (semi-detached house, PictureNet/Corbis Corporation/row house), V23 (fish slice, garlic press, potato masher), V32 (M Mason/rag doll), V34 (J Kase/Alamy Ltd./ice skating), V36 (M Karrass/Corbis Corporation/basketball), V51 (polo neck), V53 (charm bracelet, locket), V56 (correction fluid, drawing pins, highlighter), V60–61, V62–63, V64; Photolibrary Group Ltd. pp cover (R Chapple Stock/ Photolibrary RF/dictionary, J Cundy/Image Source Ltd./ Oxford, H Huber/Westend61 GmbH/fern, Glow Images RF/Glowimages Inc./book, Ingram Publishing Limited/ steps, Y Kushima/Amana Images Inc./parasol, M Roessler/Corbis/sky, J Woodhouse/Radius Images/ Masterfile Corporation/bicycle), V12 (Alanie/Life File/ PhotoDisc/Getty Images, Inc./rotunda, R Chapple Stock/ Photolibrary RF/vaulted ceiling, FOTOG/Tetra Images LLC/suspension bridge, D Fox/Purestock/Superstock, Inc./colonnade, Ingram Publishing RF/Ingram Publishing Limited/arch, M Milbradt/Brand X Pictures/Jupiterimages (UK) Ltd./obelisk, S Nicolas/ICONOTEC/dome), V13 (M Fife/PhotoDisc/Getty Images, Inc./fort, hinkstock Images/Jupiterimages (UK) Ltd./pagoda, R Kaestner/ Corbis Corporation/palace), V14 (A Jones/Image Source Ltd./town house), V16 (Comstock Images/Jupiterimages (UK) Ltd./strimmer, Tetra Images LLC/sprinkler), V17 (Lynx/ICONOTEC/toolbox, Photolibrary RF/squeegee